DICTIONARY OF AMERICAN BIOGRAPHY
AMERICAN
COUNCIL
OF
LEARNED
SOCIETIES
CSS

DICTIONARY
OF AMERICAN BIOGRAPHY

PUBLISHED UNDER THE AUSPICES OF
THE AMERICAN COUNCIL OF LEARNED SOCIETIES

The American Council of Learned Societies, organized in 1919 for the purpose of advancing the study of the humanities and of the humanistic aspects of the social sciences, is a nonprofit federation comprising forty-six national scholarly groups. The Council represents the humanities in the United States in the International Union of Academies, provides fellowships and grants-in-aid, supports research-and-planning conferences and symposia, and sponsors special projects and scholarly publications.

CONSTITUENT SOCIETIES

AMERICAN PHILOSOPHICAL SOCIETY, 1743
AMERICAN ACADEMY OF ARTS AND SCIENCES, 1780
AMERICAN ANTIQUARIAN SOCIETY, 1812
AMERICAN ORIENTAL SOCIETY, 1842
AMERICAN NUMISMATIC SOCIETY, 1858
AMERICAN PHILOLOGICAL ASSOCIATION, 1869
ARCHAEOLOGICAL INSTITUTE OF AMERICA, 1879
SOCIETY OF BIBLICAL LITERATURE, 1880
MODERN LANGUAGE ASSOCIATION OF AMERICA, 1883
AMERICAN HISTORICAL ASSOCIATION, 1884
AMERICAN ECONOMIC ASSOCIATION, 1885
AMERICAN FOLKLORE SOCIETY, 1888
AMERICAN DIALECT SOCIETY, 1889
AMERICAN PSYCHOLOGICAL ASSOCIATION, 1892
ASSOCIATION OF AMERICAN LAW SCHOOLS, 1900
AMERICAN PHILOSOPHICAL ASSOCIATION, 1901
AMERICAN ANTHROPOLOGICAL ASSOCIATION, 1902
AMERICAN POLITICAL SCIENCE ASSOCIATION, 1903
BIBLIOGRAPHICAL SOCIETY OF AMERICA, 1904
ASSOCIATION OF AMERICAN GEOGRAPHERS, 1904
HISPANIC SOCIETY OF AMERICA, 1904
AMERICAN SOCIOLOGICAL ASSOCIATION, 1905
AMERICAN SOCIETY OF INTERNATIONAL LAW, 1906
ORGANIZATION OF AMERICAN HISTORIANS, 1907
AMERICAN ACADEMY OF RELIGION, 1909
COLLEGE FORUM, NCTE, 1911
COLLEGE ART ASSOCIATION OF AMERICA, 1912
HISTORY OF SCIENCE SOCIETY, 1924
LINGUISTIC SOCIETY OF AMERICA, 1924
MEDIEVAL ACADEMY OF AMERICA, 1925
AMERICAN MUSICOLOGICAL SOCIETY, 1934
SOCIETY OF ARCHITECTURAL HISTORIANS, 1940
ECONOMIC HISTORY ASSOCIATION, 1940
ASSOCIATION FOR ASIAN STUDIES, 1941
AMERICAN SOCIETY FOR AESTHETICS, 1942
AMERICAN ASSOCIATION FOR THE ADVANCEMENT OF SLAVIC STUDIES, 1948
METAPHYSICAL SOCIETY OF AMERICA, 1950
AMERICAN STUDIES ASSOCIATION, 1950
AMERICAN SOCIETY OF COMPARATIVE LAW, 1951
RENAISSANCE SOCIETY OF AMERICA, 1954
SOCIETY FOR ETHNOMUSICOLOGY, 1955
AMERICAN SOCIETY FOR LEGAL HISTORY, 1956
AMERICAN SOCIETY FOR THEATRE RESEARCH, 1956
SOCIETY FOR FRENCH HISTORICAL STUDIES, 1956
AFRICAN STUDIES ASSOCIATION, 1957
SOCIETY FOR THE HISTORY OF TECHNOLOGY, 1958
SOCIETY FOR CINEMA STUDIES, 1959
AMERICAN COMPARATIVE LITERATURE ASSOCIATION, 1960
LATIN AMERICAN STUDIES ASSOCIATION, 1966
MIDDLE EAST STUDIES ASSOCIATION, 1966
ASSOCIATION FOR THE ADVANCEMENT OF BALTIC STUDIES, 1968
AMERICAN SOCIETY FOR EIGHTEENTH-CENTURY STUDIES, 1969
ASSOCIATION FOR JEWISH STUDIES, 1969
SIXTEENTH CENTURY STUDIES CONFERENCE, 1970
DICTIONARY SOCIETY OF NORTH AMERICA, 1975
GERMAN STUDIES ASSOCIATION, 1976
SOCIETY FOR DANCE HISTORY SCHOLARS, 1979
SONNECK SOCIETY FOR AMERICAN MUSIC, 1983

DICTIONARY
OF
American Biography

Comprehensive Index

COMPLETE THROUGH SUPPLEMENT TEN

CHARLES SCRIBNER'S SONS

Macmillan Library Reference USA
Simon & Schuster Macmillan
New York

Simon & Schuster and Prentice Hall International
London Mexico City New Delhi Singapore Sydney Toronto

The preparation of the original twenty volumes of the Dictionary was made possible by the public-spirited action of the New York Times Company and its president, the late Adolph S. Ochs, in furnishing a large subvention. The original twenty volumes and Supplements 1 through 8 were prepared by the American Council of Learned Societies and Supplements 9 and 10 and the Index were prepared by the Publisher under agreement with the American Council of Learned Societies. Entire responsibility for the contents of the Dictionary and its first eight Supplements rests with the American Council of Learned Societies. Responsibility for the contents of Supplements Nine and Ten rests with the Publisher.

Charles Scribner's Sons
An imprint of Simon & Schuster Macmillan
1633 Broadway
New York, New York 10019

Library of Congress Cataloging-in-Publication Data

Dictionary of American biography.
Comprehensive index: complete through supplement ten.
p. cm.
ISBN 0-684-80482-4 (alk. paper)
1. Dictionary of American Biography—Indexes.
2. United States—Biography—Dictionaries—Indexes.
E176.D563 Index 4 920.073—dc20 96-30813

1 3 5 7 9 11 13 15 17 19 20 18 16 14 12 10 8 6 4 2

Printed in the United States of America

The paper used in this publication meets the requirements of ANSI/NISO Z39.48-1992 (Permanence of Paper).

EDITORIAL AND PRODUCTION STAFF

Managing Editor
STEPHEN WAGLEY

Indexers
WILLIAM BURGESS, MODOC PRESS
CYNTHIA CRIPPEN, AEIOU, INC.

Production Manager
DABNEY SMITH

Publisher
KAREN DAY

President, Macmillan Reference USA
GORDON MACOMBER

CONTENTS

Introduction ix

Subjects of Biographies 1

Contributors with Subjects 247

Birthplaces 361

Schools and Colleges 457

Occupations. 553

Topics 723

INTRODUCTION

The *Dictionary of American Biography* was published originally in twenty volumes between 1928 and 1936. Ten supplementary volumes were added between 1944 and 1995. In 1946, the twenty base volumes were reissued in ten double volumes. In the current format, Volume 1 (Abbe-Brazer) contains Volumes I and II of the original edition, but these are now denominated "Part 1" and "Part 2" of the Volume. Volumes 2 through 10 are arranged similarly, the Second Part in each instance representing a volume of the original series, with the original pagination maintained.

This index references the ten-volume edition and Supplements 1–10. Owners of the base set in twenty volumes may consult the following table for easy transposition from volume references in this index.

Current, 10-Volume Edition of A–Z Base Set	Original, 20-Volume Edition of A–Z Base Set
Volume 1, Part 1	Volume I
Volume 1, Part 2	Volume II
Volume 2, Part 1	Volume III
Volume 2, Part 2	Volume IV
Volume 3, Part 1	Volume V
Volume 3, Part 2	Volume VI
Volume 4, Part 1	Volume VII
Volume 4, Part 2	Volume VIII
Volume 5, Part 1	Volume IX
Volume 5, Part 2	Volume X
Volume 6, Part 1	Volume XI
Volume 6, Part 2	Volume XII
Volume 7, Part 1	Volume XIII
Volume 7, Part 2	Volume XIV
Volume 8, Part 1	Volume XV
Volume 8, Part 2	Volume XVI
Volume 9, Part 1	Volume XVII
Volume 9, Part 2	Volume XVIII
Volume 10, Part 1	Volume XIX
Volume 10, Part 2	Volume XX

For example: You wish to locate Benjamin Franklin. Turning to *Franklin, Benjamin* in the "Subjects of Biographies" division of the Index, you find

Franklin, Benjamin, Jan. 17, 1706–Apr. 17, 1790
Vol. 3, Part 2–585

By reference to the table above, Volume 3, Part 2 is seen to be Volume VI of the twenty-volume edition. There, on page 585, you will find your reference.

MAIN DIVISIONS OF THE INDEX VOLUME

1. *Subjects:* Alphabetical list of the persons about whom articles have been written, with the dates of birth and death and the volume, part, and page of the article.
2. *Contributors:* The names of all contributors arranged alphabetically, followed by the names of the persons whose biographies they wrote.
3. *Birthplaces:* The name of each state or foreign country in which the subject of an article was born, followed by lists of those persons born within that state or country.
4. *Schools and Colleges:* The educational institutions attended by the subjects of the biographies, followed in each case by an alphabetical list of those persons in the *Dictionary* who attended the institution.
5. *Occupation:* The persons in the *Dictionary* grouped according to occupation, using in most instances the occupation or occupations given at the beginning of the article.
6. *Topics.* An index of all the topics of importance discussed substantively in the *Dictionary.* Certain specific topics have been collected in groups, for example, homesteads and plantations, ships, nicknames, etc.

HOW TO USE THE INDEX

1. To find the name of the subject of an article included in the *Dictionary,* the reader should turn to the first main division (pp. 1–245) to find out if the name is in the *Dictionary.*
2. To find the name of the contributor of a particular article in the A-Z base volumes, the reader should first find the initials at the end of the article and then refer to the list of contributors at the beginning of the particular volume. In the supplements, the full name of each contributor is given at the end of each article.

3. To find the names of other articles by the same contributor, the reader should consult the second main division of the Index (pp. 247–359).

4. To find the name of a state or foreign country in which one of the subjects was born, the reader should consult the particular article.

5. To find what subjects were born in any state or country, the reader should refer to the third main division of the Index (pp. 361–454).

6. To find the school or college attended by the subjects of the biographies, the reader should refer to the specific articles.

7. To find all the names of subjects who have attended any school or college, the reader should refer to the fourth main division of the Index (pp. 457–547). In a number of instances the person attended one or more institutions. In all cases the name of the subject is given under the name of the institution from which he received a degree. In many instances the name will also be found under the name of the institution with which he was closely associated for a period of time.

8. To find the occupation or occupations of any subject of a biography, the reader should refer to the beginning of the particular biography.

9. To find all the names of subjects who practiced a particular occupation, the reader should refer to the fifth main division of the Index (pp. 553–721).

THE PUBLISHERS

SUBJECTS OF BIOGRAPHIES

Aandahl, Fred George, Apr. 9, 1897–Apr. 7, 1966.
Supp. 8–1
Abbe, Cleveland, Dec. 3, 1838–Oct. 28, 1916.
Vol. 1, Pt. 1–1
Abbett, Leon, Oct. 8, 1836–Dec. 4, 1894.
Vol. 1, Pt. 1–2
Abbey, Edwin Austin, Apr. 1, 1852–Aug. 1, 1911.
Vol. 1, Pt. 1–3
Abbey, Henry, July 11, 1842–June 7, 1911.
Vol. 1, Pt. 1–8
Abbey, Henry Eugene, June 27, 1846–Oct. 17, 1896.
Vol. 1, Pt. 1–8
Abbot, Benjamin, Sept. 17, 1762–Oct. 25, 1849.
Vol. 1, Pt. 1–9
Abbot, Ezra, Apr. 28, 1819–Mar. 21, 1884.
Vol. 1, Pt. 1–10
Abbot, Francis Ellingwood, Nov. 6, 1836–Oct. 23, 1903.
Vol. 1, Pt. 1–11
Abbot, Gorham Dummer, Sept. 3, 1807–Aug. 3, 1874.
Vol. 1, Pt. 1–12
Abbot, Henry Larcom, Aug. 13, 1831–Oct. 1, 1927.
Vol. 1, Pt. 1–13
Abbot, Joel, Jan. 18, 1793–Dec. 14, 1855.
Vol. 1, Pt. 1–14
Abbot, Willis John, Mar. 16, 1863–May 19, 1934.
Supp. 1–1
Abbott, Austin, Dec. 18, 1831–Apr. 19, 1896.
Vol. 1, Pt. 1–15
Abbott, Benjamin, 1732–Aug. 14, 1796.
Vol. 1, Pt. 1–16
Abbott, Benjamin Vaughan, June 4, 1830–Feb. 17, 1890.
Vol. 1, Pt. 1–16
Abbott, Charles Conrad, June 4, 1843–July 27, 1919.
Vol. 1, Pt. 1–17
Abbott, Edith, Sept. 26, 1876–July 28, 1957.
Supp. 6–1
Abbott, Edward, July 15, 1841–Apr. 5, 1908.
Vol. 1, Pt. 1–18
Abbott, Eleanor Hallowell, Sept. 22, 1872–June 2, 1958.
Supp. 6–2
Abbott, Emma, Dec. 9, 1850–Jan. 5, 1891.
Vol. 1, Pt. 1–18
Abbott, Frank, Sept. 5, 1836–Apr. 20, 1897.
Vol. 1, Pt. 1–19
Abbott, Frank Frost, Mar. 27, 1860–July 23, 1924.
Vol. 1, Pt. 1–20
Abbott, Grace, Nov. 17, 1878–June 19, 1939.
Supp. 2–1
Abbott, Horace, July 29, 1806–Aug. 8, 1887.
Vol. 1, Pt. 1–21
Abbott, Jacob, Nov. 14, 1803–Oct. 31, 1879.
Vol. 1, Pt. 1–21
Abbott, John Stevens Cabot, Sept. 18, 1805–June 17, 1877.
Vol. 1, Pt. 1–22
Abbott, Joseph Carter, July 15, 1825–Oct. 8, 1881.
Vol. 1, Pt. 1–23
Abbott, Lyman, Dec. 18, 1835–Oct. 22, 1922.
Vol. 1, Pt. 1–24
Abbott, Robert Sengstacke, Nov. 28, 1868–Feb. 29, 1940.
Supp. 2–2
Abbott, Samuel Warren, June 12, 1837–Oct. 22, 1904.
Vol. 1, Pt. 1–25
Abbott, William A. ("Bud"), Oct. 2, 1896–Apr. 25, 1974.
Supp. 9–1
Abbott, William Hawkins, Oct. 27, 1819–Jan. 8, 1901.
Vol. 1, Pt. 1–26
Abeel, David, June 12, 1804–Sept. 4, 1846.
Vol. 1, Pt. 1–26
Abel, John Jacob, May 19, 1857–May 26, 1938.
Supp. 2–4
Abel, Rudolf Ivanovich, 1903–Nov. 15, 1971.
Supp. 9–2
Abel-Henderson, Annie Heloise, Feb. 18, 1873–Mar. 14, 1947.
Supp. 4–1
Abell, Arunah Shepherdson, Aug. 10, 1806–Apr. 19, 1888.
Vol. 1, Pt. 1–27
Abercromby, James, 1706–Apr. 23, 1781.
Vol. 1, Pt. 1–28
Abernethy, George, Oct. 7, 1807–May 2, 1877.
Vol. 1, Pt. 1–29
Abernethy, Roy, Sept. 29, 1906–Feb. 28, 1977.
Supp. 10–1
Abert, John James, Sept. 17, 1788–Jan. 27, 1863.
Supp. 1–2
Aborn, Milton, May 18, 1864–Nov. 12, 1933.
Supp. 1–3
Abrams, Albert, Dec. 8, 1863–Jan. 13, 1924.
Vol. 1, Pt. 1–30
Abrams, Creighton Williams, Jr., Sept. 15, 1914–Sept. 4, 1974.
Supp. 9–4
Abt, Isaac Arthur, Dec. 18, 1867–Nov. 22, 1955.
Supp. 5–1
Accau (Accault) Michel. [*See* Aco, Michel, fl. 1680–1702.]
Ace, Jane, Oct. 12, 1905–Nov. 11, 1974.
Supp. 9–5
Acheson, Dean Gooderham, Apr. 11, 1893–Oct. 12, 1971.
Supp. 9–7
Acheson, Edward Goodrich, Mar. 9, 1856–July 6, 1931.
Supp. 1–4
Acker, Charles Ernest, Mar. 19, 1868–Oct. 18, 1920.
Vol. 1, Pt. 1–31
Aco, Michel, fl. 1680–1702.
Vol. 1, Pt. 1–31
Acosta, Bertram Blanchard ("Bert"), Jan. 1, 1895–Sept. 1, 1954.
Supp. 5–2
Acrelius, Israel, Dec. 4, 1714–Apr. 25, 1800.
Vol. 1, Pt. 1–32
Adair, James, *c.* 1709–*c.* 1783.
Vol. 1, Pt. 1–33
Adair, John, Jan. 9, 1757–May 19, 1840.
Vol. 1, Pt. 1–34
Adamic, Louis, Mar. 23, 1899–Sept. 4, 1951.
Supp. 5–3
Adams, Abigail, Nov. 11, 1744–Oct. 28, 1818.
Vol. 1, Pt. 1–35
Adams, Abijah, *c.* 1754–May 18, 1816.
Vol. 1, Pt. 1–35
Adams, Alva, May 14, 1850–Nov. 1, 1922.
Vol. 1, Pt. 1–36
Adams, Alvin, June 16, 1804–Sept. 1, 1877.
Vol. 1, Pt. 1–37
Adams, Andrew, Dec. 11, 1736–Nov. 27, 1797.
Vol. 1, Pt. 1–37
Adams, Andy, May 3, 1859–Sept. 26, 1935.
Supp. 1–5
Adams, Annette Abbott, Mar. 12, 1877–Oct. 26, 1956.
Supp. 6–3
Adams, Brooks, June 24, 1848–Feb. 13, 1927.
Vol. 1, Pt. 1–38
Adams, Charles, Dec. 19, 1845?-Aug. 19, 1895.
Vol. 1, Pt. 1–39
Adams, Charles Baker, Jan. 11, 1814–Jan. 18, 1853.
Vol. 1, Pt. 1–39
Adams, Charles Follen, Apr. 21, 1842–Mar. 8, 1918.
Vol. 1, Pt. 1–40
Adams, Charles Francis, Aug. 2, 1866–June 11, 1954.
Supp. 5–5
Adams, Charles Francis, Aug. 18, 1807–Nov. 21, 1886.
Vol. 1, Pt. 1–40
Adams, Charles Francis, May 27, 1835–Mar. 20, 1915.
Vol. 1, Pt. 1–48
Adams, Charles Kendall, Jan. 24, 1835–July 26, 1902.
Vol. 1, Pt. 1–52
Adams, Charles R., Feb. 9, 1834–July 4, 1900.
Vol. 1, Pt. 1–54
Adams, Cyrus Cornelius, Jan. 7, 1849–May 4, 1928.
Supp. 1–6

Adams, Daniel, Sept. 29, 1773–June 8, 1864.
Vol. 1, Pt. 1–54
Adams, Daniel Weissiger, 1820–June 13, 1872.
Vol. 1, Pt. 1–55
Adams, Dudley W., Nov. 30, 1831–Feb. 13, 1897.
Vol. 1, Pt. 1–56
Adams, Ebenezer, Oct. 22, 1765–Aug. 15, 1841.
Vol. 1, Pt. 1–56
Adams, Edward Dean, Apr. 9, 1846–May 20, 1931.
Supp. 1–7
Adams, Edwin, Feb. 3, 1834–Oct. 28, 1877.
Vol. 1, Pt. 1–57
Adams, Eliphalet, Mar. 26, 1677–Oct. 4, 1753.
Vol. 1, Pt. 1–58
Adams, Ephraim Douglass, Dec. 18, 1865–Sept. 1, 1930.
Supp. 1–8
Adams, Franklin Pierce, Nov. 15, 1881–Mar. 23, 1960.
Supp. 6–4
Adams, Frank Ramsay, July 7, 1883–Oct. 8, 1963.
Supp. 7–1
Adams, Frederick Upham, Dec. 10, 1859–Aug. 28, 1921.
Vol. 1, Pt. 1–58
Adams, George Burton, June 3, 1851–May 26, 1925.
Vol. 1, Pt. 1–59
Adams, Hannah, Oct. 2, 1755–Dec. 15, 1831.
Vol. 1, Pt. 1–60
Adams, Henry Brooks, Feb. 16, 1838–Mar. 27, 1918.
Vol. 1, Pt. 1–61
Adams, Henry Carter, Dec. 31, 1851–Aug. 11, 1921.
Vol. 1, Pt. 1–67
Adams, Henry Cullen, Nov. 28, 1850–July 9, 1906.
Vol. 1, Pt. 1–69
Adams, Herbert Baxter, Apr. 16, 1850–July 30, 1901.
Vol. 1, Pt. 1–69
Adams, Herbert Samuel, Jan. 28, 1858–May 21, 1945.
Supp. 3–1
Adams, Isaac, Aug. 16, 1802–July 19, 1883.
Vol. 1, Pt. 1–71
Adams, James Hopkins, Mar. 15, 1812–July 13, 1861.
Vol. 1, Pt. 1–71
Adams, James Truslow, Oct. 18, 1878–May 18, 1949.
Supp. 4–2
Adams, Jasper, Aug. 27, 1793–Oct. 25, 1841.
Vol. 1, Pt. 1–72
Adams, John, July 1, 1825–Nov. 30, 1864.
Vol. 1, Pt. 1–82
Adams, John, Oct. 19, 1735–July 4, 1826.
Vol. 1, Pt. 1–72
Adams, John, Sept. 18, 1772–Apr. 24, 1863.
Vol. 1, Pt. 1–82
Adams, John Coleman, Oct. 25, 1849–June 22, 1922.
Vol. 1, Pt. 1–83
Adams, John Quincy, July 11, 1767–Feb. 23, 1848.
Vol. 1, Pt. 1–84
Adams, Joseph Alexander, 1803–Sept. 11, 1880.
Vol. 1, Pt. 1–93
Adams, Joseph Quincy, Mar. 23, 1881–Nov. 10, 1946.
Supp. 4–4
Adams, Maude, Nov. 11, 1872–July 17, 1953.
Supp. 5–7
Adams, Nehemiah, Feb. 19, 1806–Oct 6, 1878.
Vol. 1, Pt. 1–93
Adams, Randolph Greenfield, Nov. 7, 1892–Jan. 4, 1951.
Supp. 5–8
Adams, Robert, Feb. 26, 1846–June 1, 1906.
Vol. 1, Pt. 1–94
Adams, Samuel, Sept. 27, 1722–Oct. 2, 1803.
Vol. 1, Pt. 1–95
Adams, Samuel Hopkins, Jan. 26, 1871–Nov. 15, 1958.
Supp. 6–6
Adams, Thomas Sewall, Dec. 29, 1873–Feb. 8, 1933.
Supp. 1–9
Adams, Walter Sydney, Dec. 20, 1876–May 11, 1956.
Supp. 6–7
Adams, William, Jan. 25, 1807–Aug. 31, 1880.
Vol. 1, Pt. 1–101
Adams, William Lysander, Feb. 5, 1821–Apr. 26, 1906.
Vol. 1, Pt. 1–101
Adams, William Taylor, July 30, 1822–Mar. 27, 1897.
Vol. 1, Pt. 1–102
Adams, William Wirt, Mar. 22, 1819–May 1, 1888.
Vol. 1, Pt. 1–103
Addams, Jane, Sept. 6, 1860–May 21, 1935.
Supp. 1–100
Adderley, Julian Edwin ("Cannonball"), Sept. 15, 1928–Aug. 8, 1975.
Supp. 9–10
Addicks, John Edward O'Sullivan, Nov. 21, 1841–Aug. 7, 1919.
Vol. 1, Pt. 1–104
Ade, George, Feb. 9, 1866–May 16, 1944.
Supp. 3–2
Adee, Alvey Augustus, Nov. 27, 1842–July 5, 1924.
Vol. 1, Pt. 1–105
Adgate, Andrew, d. 1793.
Vol. 1, Pt. 1–107
Adie, David Craig, Sept. 3, 1888–Feb. 23, 1943.
Supp. 3–4
Adkins, Homer Burton, Jan. 16, 1892–Aug. 10, 1949.
Supp. 4–5
Adler, Cyrus, Sept. 13, 1863–Apr. 7, 1940.
Supp. 2–5
Adler, Elmer, July 22, 1884–Jan. 11, 1962.
Supp. 7–2
Adler, Felix, Aug. 13, 1851–Apr. 24, 1933.
Supp. 1–13
Adler, Felix, June 17, 1897–Feb. 1, 1960.
Supp. 6–8
Adler, George J., 1821–Aug. 24, 1868.
Vol. 1, Pt. 1–107
Adler, Polly, Apr. 16, 1900–June 9, 1962.
Supp. 7–3
Adler, Samuel, Dec. 3, 1809–June 9, 1891.
Vol. 1, Pt. 1–108
Adler, Sara, 1858–Apr. 28, 1953.
Supp. 5–10
Adlum, John, Apr. 29, 1759–Mar. 1, 1836.
Vol. 1, Pt. 1–109
Adonis, Joe, Nov. 22, 1902–Nov. 26, 1971.
Supp. 9–11
Adrain, Robert, Sept. 30, 1775–Aug. 10, 1843.
Vol. 1, Pt. 1–109
Adrian, Gilbert, Mar. 3, 1903–Sept. 13, 1959.
Supp. 6–9
Affleck, Thomas, July 13, 1812–Dec. 30, 1868.
Vol. 1, Pt. 1–110
Agassiz, Alexander, Dec. 17, 1835–Mar. 27, 1910.
Vol. 1, Pt. 1–111
Agassiz, Elizabeth Cabot Cary, Dec. 5, 1822–June 27, 1907.
Vol. 1, Pt. 1–114
Agassizi Jean Louis Rodolphe, May 28, 1807–Dec. 14, 1873.
Vol. 1, Pt. 1–114
Agate, Alfred T., Feb. 14, 1812–Jan. 5, 1846.
Vol. 1, Pt. 1–122
Agate, Frederick Styles, Jan. 29, 1803–May 1, 1844.
Vol. 1, Pt. 1–123
Agee, James Rufus, Nov. 27, 1909–May 16, 1955.
Supp. 5–11
Aggrey, James Emman Kwegyir, Oct. 18, 1875–July 30, 1927.
Supp. 1–14
Agnew, Cornelius Rea, Aug. 8, 1830–Apr. 18, 1888.
Vol. 1, Pt. 1–123
Agnew, David Hayes, Nov. 24, 1818–Mar. 22, 1892.
Vol. 1, Pt. 1–124
Agnew, Eliza, Feb. 2, 1807–June 14, 1883.
Vol. 1, Pt. 1–125
Agnus, Felix, May 5, 1839–Oct. 31, 1925.
Vol. 1, Pt. 1–125
Agramonte y Simoni, Aristides, June 3, 1868–Aug. 17, 1931.
Supp. 1–14
Aiken, Charles Augustus, Oct. 20, 1827–Jan. 14, 1892.
Vol. 1, Pt. 1–126
Aiken, Conrad Potter, Aug. 5, 1889–Aug. 17, 1973.
Supp. 9–13
Aiken, David Wyatt, Mar. 17, 1828–Apr. 6, 1887.
Vol. 1, Pt. 1–127
Aiken, George L., Dec. 19, 1830–Apr. 27, 1876.
Vol. 1, Pt. 1–127
Aiken, William, Jan. 28, 1806–Sept. 6, 1887.
Vol. 1, Pt. 1–128
Aikens, Andrew Jackson, Oct. 31, 1830–Jan. 22, 1909.
Vol. 1, Pt. 1–129
Aime, Valcour, 1798–Dec. 31, 1867.
Vol. 1, Pt. 1–130

Ainslie, Hew, Apr. 5, 1792–Mar. 11, 1878.
Vol. 1, Pt. 1–130
Ainslie, Peter, Jun 3, 1867–Feb. 23, 1934.
Supp. 1–15
Ainsworth, Frederick Crayton, Sept. 11, 1852–June 5, 1934.
Supp. 1–16
Aitken, Robert, 1734–July 15, 1802.
Vol. 1, Pt. 1–131
Aitken, Robert Grant, Dec. 31, 1864–Oct. 29, 1951.
Supp. 5–13
Akeley, Carl Ethan, May 19, 1864–Nov. 17, 1926.
Vol. 1, Pt. 1–132
Akeley, Mary Leonore, Jan. 29, 1878–July 19, 1966.
Supp. 8–2
Akerman, Amos Tappan, Feb. 23, 1821–Dec. 21, 1880.
Vol. 1, Pt. 1–133
Akers, Benjamin Paul, July 10, 1825–May 21, 1861.
Vol. 1, Pt. 1–134
Akers, Elizabeth Chase, Oct. 9, 1832–Aug. 7, 1911.
Vol. 1, Pt. 1–134
Akins, Zoë, Oct. 30, 1886–Oct. 29, 1958.
Supp. 6–10
Ako, Michel. [*See* Aco, Michel, fl. 1680–1702.]
Alarcón, Hernando de, fl. 1540.
Vol. 1, Pt. 1–135
Albee, Edward Franklin, Oct. 8, 1857–Mar. 11, 1930.
Supp. 1–17
Albee, Ernest, Aug. 8, 1865–May 25, 1927.
Vol. 1, Pt. 1–136
Albers, Josef, Mar. 19, 1888–Mar. 25, 1976.
Supp. 10–2
Albright, Jacob, May 1, 1759–May 18, 1808.
Vol. 1, Pt. 1–136
Albright, William Foxwell, May 24, 1891–Sept. 19, 1971.
Supp. 9–15
Albro, Lewis Colt, Feb. 6, 1876–Mar. 1, 1924.
Vol. 1, Pt. 1–137
Alcorn, James Lusk, Nov. 4, 1816–Dec. 20, 1894.
Vol. 1, Pt. 1–137
Alcott, Amos Bronson, Nov. 29, 1799–Mar. 4, 1888.
Vol. 1, Pt. 1–139
Alcott, Louisa May, Nov. 29, 1832–Mar. 6, 1888.
Vol. 1, Pt. 1–141
Alcott, William Andrus, Aug. 6, 1798–Mar. 29, 1859.
Vol. 1, Pt. 2–142
Alden, Cynthia May Westover, May 31, 1862–Jan. 8, 1931
Supp. 1–18
Alden, Ebenezer, Mar. 17, 1788–Jan. 26, 1881.
Vol. 1, Pt. 1–143
Alden, Henry Mills, Nov. 11, 1836–Oct. 7, 1919.
Vol. 1 Pt. 1–144
Alden, Ichabod, Aug. 11, 1739–Nov. 11, 1778.
Vol. 1, Pt. 1–145
Alden, Isabella Macdonald, Nov. 3, 1841–Aug. 5, 1930.
Supp. 1–19
Alden, James, Mar. 31, 1810–Feb. 6, 1877.
Vol. 1, Pt. 1–145
Alden, John, *c.* 1599–Sept. 12, 1687.
Vol. 1, Pt. 1–146
Alden, John Ferris, Mar. 19, 1852–Feb. 27, 1917.
Vol. 1, Pt. 1–147
Alden, Joseph, Jan. 4, 1807–Aug. 30, 1885.
Vol. 1, Pt. 1–147
Alden, Raymond MacDonald, Mar. 30, 1873–Sept. 27, 1924
Vol. 1, Pt. 1–148
Alden, Timothy, Aug. 28, 1771–July 5, 1839.
Vol. 1, Pt. 1–149
Alden, William Livingston, Oct. 9, 1837–Jan. 14, 1908.
Vol. 1, Pt. 1–150
Alderman, Edwin Anderson, May 15, 1861–Apr. 29, 1931.
Supp. 1–21
Aldrich, Bess Genevra Streeter, Feb. 17, 1881–Aug. 3, 1954
Supp. 5–14
Aldrich, Charles Anderson, Mar. 4, 1888–Oct. 6, 1949.
Supp. 4–7
Aldrich, Chester Holmes, June 4, 1871–Dec. 26, 1940.
Supp. 2–7
Aldrich, Edgar, Feb. 5, 1848–Sept. 15, 1921.
Vol. 1, Pt. 1–150
Aldrich, Louis, Oct. 1, 1843–June 17, 1901.
Vol. 1, Pt. 1–151
Aldrich, Nelson Wilmarth, Nov. 6, 1841–Apr. 16, 1915.
Vol. 1, Pt. 1–151
Aldrich, Richard, July 31, 1863–June 2, 1937.
Supp. 2–8
Aldrich, Thomas Bailey, Nov. 11, 1836–Mar. 19, 1907.
Vol. 1, Pt. 1–158
Aldrich, Winthrop William, Nov. 2, 1885–Feb. 25, 1974.
Supp. 9–16
Aldridge, Ira Fredrick, *c.* 1805–Aug. 10, 1867.
Vol. 1, Pt. 1–160
Alemany, José Sadoc, July 13, 1814–Apr. 14, 1888.
Vol. 1, Pt. 1–161
Alexander, Abraham, 1717–Apr. 23, 1786.
Vol. 1, Pt. 1–162
Alexander, Archibald, Apr. 17, 1772–Oct. 22, 1851.
Vol. 1, Pt. 1–162
Alexander, Barton Stone, Sept. 4, 1819–Dec. 15, 1878.
Vol. 1, Pt. 1–163
Alexander, de Alva Stanwood, July 17, 1845–Jan. 30, 1925.
Vol. 1, Pt. 1–164
Alexander, Edward Porter, May 26, 1835–Apr. 28, 1910.
Vol. 1, Pt. 1–164
Alexander, Francis, Feb. 3, 1800–*c.* 1881.
Vol. 1, Pt. 1–166
Alexander, Franz Gabriel, Jan. 22, 1891–Mar. 8, 1964.
Supp. 7–5
Alexander, Gross, June 1, 1852–Sept. 6, 1915.
Vol. 1, Pt. 1–167
Alexander, Grover Cleveland, Feb. 26, 1887–Nov. 4, 1950.
Supp. 4–9
Alexander, Hartley Burr, Apr. 9, 1873–July 27, 1939.
Supp. 2–8
Alexander, James, 1691–Apr. 2, 1756.
Vol. 1, Pt. 1–167
Alexander, John Henry, June 26, 1812–Mar. 2, 1867.
Vol. 1, Pt. 1–168
Alexander, John White, Oct. 7, 1856–May 31, 1915.
Vol. 1, Pt. 1–169
Alexander, Joseph Addison, Apr. 24, 1809–Jan. 28, 1860.
Vol. 1, Pt. 1–173
Alexander, Samuel Davies, May 3, 1819–Oct. 26, 1894.
Vol. 1, Pt. 1–173
Alexander, Stephen, Sept. 1, 1806–June 25, 1883.
Vol. 1, Pt. 1–174
Alexander, William, 1726–Jan. 15, 1783.
Vol. 1, Pt. 1–175
Alexander, William De Witt, Apr. 2, 1833–Feb. 22, 1913.
Vol. 1, Pt. 1–176
Alexander, Will Winton, July 15, 1884–Jan. 13, 1956.
Supp. 6–11
Alfonce (Alfonse), Jean. [*See* Allefonsce, Jean, *c.* 1485–1557.]
Alford, Leon Pratt, Jan. 3, 1877–Jan. 2, 1942.
Supp. 35
Alger, Cyrus, Nov. 11, 1781–Feb. 4, 1856.
Vol. 1, Pt. 1–177
Alger, Horatio, Jan. 13, 1834–July 18, 1899.
Vol. 1, Pt. 1–178
Alger, Russell Alexander, Feb. 27, 1836–Jan. 24, 1907.
Vol. 1, Pt. 1–179
Alger, William Rounseville, Dec. 28, 1822–Feb. 7, 1905.
Vol. 1, Pt. 1–180
Alinsky, Saul David, Jan. 30, 1909–June 12, 1972.
Supp. 9–18
Alison, Francis, 1705–Nov. 28, 1779.
Vol. 1, Pt. 1–181
Allaire, James Peter, 1785–May 20, 1858.
Vol. 1, Pt. 1–182
Allan, John, Jan. 3/14, 1746/7–Feb. 7, 1805.
Vol. 1, Pt. 1–182
Allefonsce, Jean, *c.* 1482–*c.* 1557.
Vol. 1, Pt. 1–183
Allen, Alexander Viets Griswold, May 4, 1841–July 1, 1908.
Vol. 1, Pt. 1–184
Allen, Andrew, June 1740–Mar. 7, 1825.
Vol. 1, Pt. 1–184
Allen, Anthony Benezet, June 24, 1802–Jan. 12, 1892.
Vol. 1, Pt. 1–185
Allen, Arthur Augustus, Dec. 28, 1885–Jan. 17, 1964.
Supp. 7–7
Allen, Charles, Apr. 17, 1827–Jan. 13, 1913.
Vol. 1, Pt. 1–186

Allen, David Oliver, Sept. 14, 1799–July 19, 1863.
Vol. 1, Pt. 1–186
Allen, Edgar, May 2, 1892–Mar. 3, 1943.
Supp. 3–6
Allen, Edward Ellis, Aug. 1, 1861–Apr. 14, 1950.
Supp. 4–10
Allen, Edward Tyson, Dec–26, 1875–May 27, 1942.
Supp. 3–7
Allen, Elisha Hunt, Jan. 28, 1804–Jan. 1, 1883.
Vol. 1, Pt. 1–187
Allen, Elizabeth Chase Akers. [*See* Akers, Elizabeth Chase 1832–1911.]
Allen, Ethan, Jan. 10, 1737/8–Feb. 12, 1789.
Vol. 1, Pt. 1–188
Allen, Florence Ellinwood, Mar. 23, 1884–Sept. 12, 1966.
Supp. 8–4
Allen, Forrest Clare ("Phog"), Nov. 18, 1885–Sept. 16, 1974.
Supp. 9–20
Allen, Fred, May 31, 1894–Mar. 17, 1956.
Supp. 6–12
Allen, Frederic de Forest, May 25, 1844–Aug. 4, 1897.
Vol. 1, Pt. 1–189
Allen, Frederick Lewis, July 5, 1890–Feb. 13, 1954.
Supp. 5–16
Allen, George, Dec. 17, 1808–May 28, 1876.
Vol. 1, Pt. 1–190
Allen, George Edward, Feb. 29, 1896–Apr. 23, 1973.
Supp. 9–21
Allen, George Venable, Nov. 3, 1903–July 11, 1970.
Supp. 8–5
Allen, Glover Morrill, Feb. 8, 1879–Feb. 15, 1942.
Supp. 3–8
Allen, Gracie, July 26, 1905–Aug. 27, 1964.
Supp. 7–8
Allen, Harrison, Apr. 17, 1841–Nov. 14, 1897.
Vol. 1, Pt. 1–191
Allen, Henry Justin, Sept. 11, 1868–Jan. 17, 1950.
Supp. 4–11
Allen, Henry Tureman, Apr. 13, 1859–Aug. 30, 1930.
Supp. 1–22
Allen, Henry Watkins, Apr. 29, 1820–Apr. 22, 1866.
Vol. 1, Pt. 1–191
Allen, Hervey, Dec. 8, 1889–Dec. 28, 1949.
Supp. 4–13
Allen, Horatio, May 10, 1802–Jan. 1, 1890.
Vol. 1, Pt. 1–193
Allen, Ira, May 1, 1751–Jan. 15, 1814.
Vol. 1, Pt. 1–194
Allen, James Browning, Dec. 28, 1912–June 1, 1978.
Supp. 10–4
Allen, James Edward, Jr., Apr. 25, 1911–Oct. 16, 1971.
Supp. 9–24
Allen, James Lane, Dec. 21, 1849–Feb. 18, 1925.
Vol. 1, Pt. 1–195
Allen, Jeremiah Mervin, May 18, 1833–Dec. 29, 1903.
Vol. 1, Pt. 1–197
Allen, Joel Asaph, July 19, 1838–Aug. 29, 1921.
Vol. 1, Pt. 1–197
Allen, John, Nov. 4, 1810–Mar. 8, 1892.
Vol. 1, Pt. 1–198
Allen, John F., 1829–Oct. 2, 1900.
Vol. 1, Pt. 1–199
Allen, John James, Sept. 25, 1797–Sept. 18, 1871.
Vol. 1, Pt. 1–199
Allen, Joseph Henry, Aug. 21, 1820–Mar. 20, 1898.
Vol. 1, Pt. 1–200
Allen, Kelcey, Nov. 11, 1875–July 23, 1951.
Supp. 5–17
Allen, Lewis Falley, Jan. 1, 1800–May 2, 1890.
Vol. 1, Pt. 1–201
Allen, Nathan, Apr. 25, 1813–Jan. 1, 1889.
Vol. 1, Pt. 1–201
Allen, Nathan H., Apr. 14, 1848–May 9, 1925.
Vol. 1, Pt. 1–202
Allen, Paul, Feb. 15, 1775–Aug. 18, 1826.
Vol. 1. Pt. 1–202
Allen, Philip, Sept. 1, 1785–Dec. 16, 1865.
Vol. 1, Pt. 1–203
Allen, Richard, Feb. 14, 1760–Mar. 26, 1831.
Vol. 1, Pt. 1–204
Allen, Richard Lamb, Oct. 20, 1803–Sept. 22, 1869.
Vol. 1, Pt. 1–205
Allen, Robert, July 1812–Aug. 5, 1886.
Vol. 1, Pt. 1–206
Allen, Thomas, Aug. 29, 1813–Apr. 8, 1882.
Vol. 1, Pt. 1–206
Allen, Thomas M., Oct. 21, 1797–Oct. 10, 1871.
Vol. 1, Pt. 1–207
Allen, Timothy Field, Apr. 24, 1837–Dec. 5, 1902.
Vol. 1, Pt. 1–207
Allen, Viola Emily, Oct. 27, 1867–May 9, 1948.
Supp. 4–14
Allen, WIlliam, Aug. 5, 1704–Sept. 6, 1780.
Vol. 1, Pt. 1–208
Allen, William, Jan. 2, 1784–July 16, 1868.
Vol. 1, Pt. 1–209
Allen, William, Dec. 18, 1803–July 11, 1879.
Vol. 1, Pt. 1–210
Allen, William Francis, Sept. 5, 1830–Dec. 9, 1889.
Vol. 1, Pt. 1–211
Allen, William Frederick, Oct. 9, 1846–Nov. 9, 1915.
Vol. 1, Pt. 1–211
Allen, William Henry, Oct. 21, 1784–Aug. 18, 1813.
Vol. 1, Pt. 1–212
Allen, William Henry, Mar. 27, 1808–Aug. 29, 1882.
Vol. 1, Pt. 1–213
Allen, William Joshua, June 9, 1829–Jan. 26, 1901.
Vol. 1, Pt. 1–213
Allen, William Vincent, Jan. 28, 1847–Jan. 12, 1924.
Vol. 1, Pt. 1–214
Allen, Young John, Jan. 3, 1836–May 30, 1907.
Vol. 1, Pt. 1–215
Allen, Zachariah, Sept. 15, 1795–Mar. 17, 1882.
Vol. 1, Pt. 1–215
Allerton, Isaac, *c.* 1586–Feb. 1658/9.
Vol. 1, Pt. 1–216
Allerton, Samuel Waters, May 26, 1828–Feb. 22, 1914.
Vol. 1, Pt. 1–217
Allibone, Samuel Austin, Apr. 17, 1816–Sept. 2, 1889.
Vol. 1, Pt. 1–218
Alline, Henry, June 14, 1748–Feb. 2, 1784.
Vol. 1, Pt. 1–218
Allinson, Anne Crosby Emery, Jan. 1, 1871–Aug. 16, 1932.
Supp. 1–23
Allinson, Francis Greenleaf, Dec. 16, 1856–June 23, 1931.
Supp. 1–24
Allis, Edward Phelps, May 12, 1824–Apr. 1, 1889.
Vol. 1, Pt. 1–219
Allison, Nathaniel, May 22, 1876–Aug. 30, 1932.
Supp. 1–25
Allison, Richard, 1757–Mar. 22, 1816.
Supp. 1–26
Allison, Samuel King, Nov. 13, 1900–Sept. 15, 1965.
Supp. 7–10
Allison, William Boyd, Mar. 2, 1829–Aug. 4, 1908.
Vol. 1, Pt. 1–220
Alloez (Alloues), Claude Jean. [*See* Allouez, Claude Jean, 1622–1689.]
Allouez, Claude Jean, June 6, 1622–Aug. 27, 1689.
Vol. 1, Pt. 1–222
Allport, Gordon Willard, Nov. 11, 1897–Oct. 9, 1967.
Supp. 8–7
Allston, Robert Francis Withers, Apr. 21, 1801–Apr. 7, 1864.
Vol. 1, Pt. 1–223
Allston, Washington, Nov. 5, 1779–July 9, 1843.
Vol. 1, Pt. 1–224
Allyn, Robert, Jan. 25, 1817–Jan. 7, 1894.
Vol. 1, Pt. 1–225
Almy, John Jay, Apr. 24, 1815–May 16, 1895.
Vol. 1, Pt. 1–226
Aloes (Aloues) Claude Jean. [*See* Allouez, Claude Jean, 1622–1689.]
Alphonce (Alphonse), Jean. [*See* Allefonsce, Jean, *c.* 1482–*c.* 1557.]
Alphonsa, Mother, May 20, 1851–July 9, 1926.
Vol. 1, Pt. 1–227
Alsop, George, b. 1638.
Vol. 1, Pt. 1–227
Alsop, Mary O'Hara, July 10, 1885–Oct. 14, 1980.
Supp. 10–5

Alsop, Richard, Jan. 23, 1761–Aug. 20, 1815.
Vol. 1, Pt. 1–228
Alsop, Stewart Johonnot Oliver, May 17, 1914–May 26, 1974.
Supp. 9–26
Alston, Joseph, *c.* 1779–Sept. 10, 1816.
Vol. 1, Pt. 1–229
Alston, Theodosia (Burr). [*See* Burr, Theodosia, 1783–1813.]
Alter, David, Dec. 3, 1807–Sept. 18, 1881.
Vol. 1, Pt. 1–230
Altgeld, John Peter, Dec. 30, 1847–Mar. 12, 1902.
Vol. 1, Pt. 1–231
Altham, John, 1589–Nov. 5, 1640.
Vol. 1, Pt. 1–231
Altman, Benjamin, July 12, 1840–Oct. 7, 1913.
Vol. 1, Pt. 1–232
Altmeyer, Arthur Joseph, May 8, 1891–Oct. 16, 1972.
Supp. 9–27
Altsheler, Joseph Alexander, Apr. 29, 1862–June 5, 1919.
Vol. 1, Pt. 1–233
Alvarado, Juan Bautista, Feb. 14, 1809–July 13, 1882.
Vol. 1, Pt. 1–233
Alvey, Richard Henry, Mar. 6, 1826–Sept. 14, 1906.
Vol. 1, Pt. 1–234
Alvord, Benjamin, Aug. 18, 1813–Oct. 16, 1884.
Vol. 1, Pt. 1–235
Alvord, Clarence Walworth, May 21, 1868–Jan. 24, 1928.
Vol. 1, Pt. 1–236
Alvord, Corydon Alexis, May 12, 1813–Nov. 28, 1874.
Vol. 1, Pt. 1–237
Alvord, Henry Elijah, Mar. 11, 1844–Oct. 1, 1904.
Vol. 1, Pt. 1–238
Amadas, Philip, fl. 1584–85.
Vol. 1, Pt. 1–239
Amateis, Louis, Dec. 13, 1855–Mar. 16, 1913.
Vol. 1, Pt. 1–239
Ambler, James Markham Marshall, Dec. 30, 1848–Oct. 30, 1881.
Vol. 1, Pt. 1–240
Ament, William Scott, Sept. 14, 1851–Jan. 6, 1909.
Vol. 1, Pt. 1–241
Ameringer, Oscar, Aug. 4, 1870–Nov. 5, 1943.
Supp. 3–9
Ames, Adelbert, Oct. 31, 1835–Apr. 13, 1933.
Supp. 1–27
Ames, Charles Gordon, Oct. 3, 1828–Apr. 15, 1912.
Vol. 1, Pt. 1–241
Ames, Edward Raymond, May 20, 1806–Apr. 25, 1879.
Vol. 1, Pt. 1–242
Ames, Edward Scribner, Apr. 21, 1870–June 29, 1958.
Supp. 6–13
Ames, Ezra, May 5, 1768–Feb. 23, 1836.
Vol. 1, Pt. 1–243
Ames, Fisher, Apr. 9, 1758–July 4, 1808.
Vol. 1, Pt. 1–244
Ames, Frederick Lothrop, June 8, 1835–Sept. 13, 1893
Vol. 1, Pt. 1–246
Ames, Herman Vandenburg, Aug. 7, 1865–Feb. 7, 1935.
Supp. 1–28
Ames, James Barr, June 22, 1846–Jan. 8, 1910.
Vol. 1, Pt. 1–247
Ames, James Tyler, May 13, 1810–Feb. 16, 1883.
Vol. 1, Pt. 1–248
Ames, Joseph Alexander, 1816–Oct. 30, 1872.
Vol. 1, Pt. 1–249
Ames, Joseph Sweetman, July 3, 1864–June 24, 1943.
Supp. 3–11
Ames, Mary Clemmer. [*See* Clemmer, Mary, 1831–1884.]
Ames, Nathaniel, July 22, 1708–July 11, 1764.
Vol. 1, Pt. 1–250
Ames, Nathan Peabody, Sept. 1, 1803–Apr. 3, 1847.
Vol. 1, Pt. 1–249
Ames, Oakes, Jan. 10, 1804–May 8, 1873.
Vol. 1, Pt. 1–251
Ames, Oakes, Sept. 26, 1874–Apr. 28, 1950.
Supp. 4–16
Ames, Oliver, Apr. 11, 1779–Sept. 11, 1863.
Vol. 1, Pt. 1–253
Ames, Oliver, Nov. 5, 1807–Mar. 9, 1877.
Vol. 1, Pt. 1–253
Ames, Oliver, Feb. 4, 1831–Oct. 22, 1895.
Vol. 1, Pt. 1–254
Ames, Samuel, Sept. 6, 1806–Dec. 20, 1865.
Vol. 1, Pt. 1–256
Ames, Winthrop, Nov. 25, 1870–Nov. 3, 1937.
Supp. 2–10
Amherst, Jeffery, Jan. 29, 1717–Aug. 3, 1797.
Vol. 1, Pt. 1–256
Amidon, Charles Fremont, Aug. 17, 1856–Dec. 26, 1937.
Supp. 2–11
Amlie, Thomas Ryum, Apr. 17, 1897–Aug. 22, 1973.
Supp. 9–29
Ammann, Othmar Hermann, Mar. 26, 1879–Sept. 22, 1965.
Supp. 7–11
Ammen, Daniel, May 16, 1819–July 11, 1898.
Vol. 1, Pt. 1–258
Ammen, Jacob, Jan. 7, 1807–Feb. 6, 1894,.
Vol. 1, Pt. 1–259
Ammons, Elias Milton, July 28, 1860–May 20, 1925.
Vol. 1, Pt. 1–259
Amory, Thomas, May 1682–June 20, 1728.
Vol. 1, Pt. 1–260
Anagnos, Michael, Nov. 7, 1837–June 29, 1906.
Vol. 1, Pt. 1–261
Anderson, Alexander, Apr. 21, 1775–Jan. 17, 1870.
Vol. 1, Pt. 1–262
Anderson, Benjamin McAlester, May 1, 1886–Jan. 19, 1949.
Supp. 4–17
Anderson, Clinton Presba, Oct. 23, 1895–Nov. 11, 1975.
Supp. 9–30
Anderson, David Lawrence, Feb. 4, 1850–Feb. 16, 1911.
Vol. 1, Pt. 1–262
Anderson, Edward ("Eddie"), Sept. 18, 1906–Feb. 28, 1977.
Supp. 10–7
Anderson, Edwin Hatfield, Sept. 27, 1861–Apr. 29, 1947.
Supp. 4–18
Anderson, Elizabeth Milbank, Dec. 20, 1850–Feb. 22, 1921.
Vol. 1, Pt. 1–263
Anderson, Galusha, Mar. 7, 1832–July 20, 1918.
Vol. 1, Pt. 1–264
Anderson, George Thomas, Mar. 3, 1824–Apr. 4, 1901.
Vol. 1, Pt. 1–265
Anderson, Henry Tompkins, Jan. 27, 1812–Sept. 19, 1872.
Vol. 1, Pt. 1–265
Anderson, James Patton, Feb. 12, 1822–Sept. 1, 1872.
Vol. 1, Pt. 1–266
Anderson, John Alexander, June 26, 1834–May 18, 1892.
Vol. 1, Pt. 1–267
Anderson, Joseph, Nov. 5, 1757–Apr. 17, 1837.
Vol. 1, Pt. 1–267
Anderson, Joseph Reid, Feb. 6, 1813–Sept. 7, 1892.
Vol. 1, Pt. 1–268
Anderson, Margaret Carolyn, Nov. 24, 1886–Oct. 18, 1973.
Supp. 9–32
Anderson, Martin Brewer, Feb. 12, 1815–Feb. 22, 1890.
Vol. 1, Pt. 1–269
Anderson, Mary, July 28, 1859–May 29, 1940.
Supp. 2–12
Anderson, Mary, Aug. 27, 1872–Jan. 29, 1964.
Supp. 7–12
Anderson, Maxwell, Dec. 15, 1888–Feb. 28, 1959.
Supp. 6–14
Anderson, Paul Y., Aug. 29, 1893–Dec. 6, 1938.
Supp. 2–13
Anderson, Richard Clough, Jan. 12, 1750–Oct. 16, 1826.
Vol. 1, Pt. 1–270
Anderson, Richard Clough, Aug. 4, 1788–July 24, 1826.
Vol. 1, Pt. 1–271
Anderson, Richard Heron, Oct. 7, 1821–June 26, 1879.
Vol. 1, Pt. 1–271
Anderson, Robert, June 14, 1805–Oct. 26, 1871.
Vol. 1, Pt. 1–274
Anderson, Sherwood, Sept. 13, 1876–Mar. 8, 1941.
Supp. 3–12
Anderson, Victor Vance, Dec. 26, 1879–July 26, 1960.
Supp. 6–16
Anderson, William, Dec. 1762–Dec. 1829.
Vol. 1, Pt. 1–275
André, Louis, May 28, 1631 or 1623–Sept. 19, 1715.
Vol. 1, Pt. 1–276
Andreis, Andrew James Felix Bartholomew de, Dec. 12, 1778–Oct. 15, 1820.
Vol. 1, Pt. 1–276

Andrew, Abram Piatt, Feb. 12, 1873–June 3, 1936.
Supp. 2–15
Andrew, James Osgood, May 3, 1794–Mar. 2, 1871.
Vol. 1, Pt. 1–277
Andrew, John Albion, May 31, 1818–Oct. 30, 1867.
Vol. 1, Pt. 1–279
Andrew, Samuel, Jan. 29, 1656–Jan. 24, 1738.
Vol. 1, Pt. 1–281
Andrews, Alexander Boyd, July 23, 1841–Apr. 17, 1915.
Vol. 1, Pt. 1–282
Andrews, Bert, June 2, 1901–Aug. 21, 1953.
Supp. 5–18
Andrews, Charles, May 27, 1827–Oct. 22, 1918.
Vol. 1, Pt. 1–282
Andrews, Charles Bartlett, Nov. 4, 1836–Sept. 12, 1902.
Vol. 1, Pt. 1–283
Andrews, Charles McLean, Feb. 22, 1863–Sept. 9, 1943.
Supp. 3–15
Andrews, Chauncey Hummason, Dec. 2, 1823–Dec. 25, 1893.
Vol. 1, Pt. 1–283
Andrews, Christopher Columbus, Oct. 27, 1829–Sept. 21, 1922.
Vol. 1, Pt. 1–284
Andrews, Edward Gayer, Aug. 7, 1825–Dec. 31, 1907.
Vol. 1, Pt. 1–285
Andrews, Elisha Benjamin, Jan. 10, 1844–Oct. 30, 1917.
Vol. 1, Pt. 1–286
Andrews, Frank Maxwell, Feb. 3, 1884–May 3, 1943.
Supp. 3–16
Andrews, Garnett, May 15, 1837–May 6, 1903.
Vol. 1, Pt. 1–291
Andrews, George Leonard, Aug. 31, 1828–Apr. 4, 1899.
Vol. 1, Pt. 1–291
Andrews, George Pierce, Sept. 29, 1835–May 24, 1902.
Vol. 1, Pt. 1–292
Andrews, Israel DeWolf, d. Feb. 17, 1871.
Supp. 1–29
Andrews, Israel Ward, Jan. 3, 1815–Apr. 18, 1888.
Vol. 1, Pt. 1–293
Andrews, John, Apr. 4, 1746–Mar. 29, 1813.
Vol. 1, Pt. 1–293
Andrews, John Bertram, Aug. 2, 1880–Jan. 4, 1943.
Supp. 3–18
Andrews, Joseph, *c.* 1805–May 7, 1873.
Vol. 1, Pt. 1–294
Andrews, Lorin, Apr. 1, 1819–Sept. 18, 1861.
Vol. 1, Pt. 1–295
Andrews, Lorrin, Apr. 29, 1795–Sept. 29, 1868.
Vol. 1, Pt. 1–295
Andrews, Roy Chapman, Jan. 26, 1884–Mar. 11, 1960.
Supp. 6–17
Andrews, Samuel James, July 31, 1817–Oct. 11, 1906.
Vol. 1, Pt. 1–296
Andrews, Sherlock James, Nov. 17, 1801–Feb. 11, 1880.
Vol. 1, Pt. 1–297
Andrews, Sidney, Oct. 7, 1835–Apr. 10, 1880.
Vol. 1, Pt. 1–297
Andrews, Stephen Pearl, Mar. 22, 1812–May 21, 1886.
Vol. 1, Pt. 1–298
Andrews, William Loring, Sept. 9, 1837–Mar. 19, 1920.
Vol. 1, Pt. 1–299
Andrews, William Watson, Feb. 26, 1810–Oct. 17, 1897.
Vol. 1, Pt. 1–299
Andros, Sir Edmund, Dec. 6, 1637–Feb. 1714.
Vol. 1, Pt. 1–300
Andrus, Ethel Percy, Sept. 21, 1884–July 13, 1967.
Supp. 8–9
Angel, Benjamin Franklin, Nov. 28, 1815–Sept. 11, 1894.
Vol. 1, Pt. 1–302
Angela, Mother, Feb. 21, 1824–Mar. 4, 1887.
Vol. 1, Pt. 1–302
Angeli, Pier, June 19, 1932–Sept. 10, 1971.
Supp. 9–34
Angell, Ernest, June 1, 1889–Jan. 11, 1973.
Supp. 9–35
Angell, George Thorndike, June 5, 1823–Mar. 16, 1909.
Vol. 1, Pt. 1–303
Angell, Israel, Aug. 24, 1740–May 4, 1832.
Vol. 1, Pt. 1–304
Angell, James Burrill, Jan. 7, 1829–Apr. 1, 1916.
Vol. 1, Pt. 1–304
Angell, James Rowland, May 8, 1869–Mar. 4, 1949.
Supp. 4–19
Angell, Joseph Kinnicutt, Apr. 30, 1794–May 1, 1857.
Vol. 1, Pt. 1–309
Angell, William Gorham, Nov. 21, 1811–May 13, 1870.
Vol. 1, Pt. 1–310
Angle, Paul McClelland, Dec. 25, 1900–May 11, 1975.
Supp. 9–37
Anglin, Margaret Mary, Apr. 3, 1876–Jan. 7, 1958.
Supp. 6–19
Annenberg, Moses Louis, Feb. 11, 1878–July 20, 1942.
Supp. 3–19
Anshutz, Thomas Pollock, Oct. 5, 1851–June 16, 1912.
Vol. 1, Pt. 1–310
Anson, Adrian Constantine, Apr. 17, 1852–Apr. 14, 1922.
Vol. 1, Pt. 1–311
Antes, Henry, 1701–July 20, 1755.
Vol. 1, Pt. 1–312
Anthon, Charles, Nov. 19, 1797–July 29, 1867.
Vol. 1, Pt. 1–313
Anthon, Charles Edward, 1823–June 7, 1883.
Vol. 1, Pt. 1–314
Anthon, John, May 14, 1784–Mar. 5, 1863.
Vol. 1, Pt. 1–314
Anthony, Andrew Varick Stout, Dec. 4, 1835–July 2, 1906.
Vol. 1, Pt. 1–315
Anthony, George Tobey, June 9, 1824–Aug. 5, 1896.
Vol. 1, Pt. 1–315
Anthony, Henry Bowen, Apr. 1, 1815–Sept. 2, 1884.
Vol. 1, Pt. 1–316
Anthony, John Gould, May 17, 1804–Oct. 16, 1877.
Vol. 1, Pt. 1–317
Anthony, John J., Sept. 1, 1898–July 16, 1970.
Supp. 8–10
Anthony, Katharine Susan, Nov. 27, 1877–Nov. 20, 1965.
Supp. 7–13
Anthony, Sister, 1814–Dec. 8, 1897.
Vol. 1, Pt. 1–318
Anthony, Susan Brownell, Feb. 15, 1820–Mar. 13, 1906.
Vol. 1, Pt. 1–318
Anthony, William Arnold, Nov. 17, 1835–May 29, 1908.
Supp. 1–30
Antin, Mary, June 13, 1881–May 17, 1949.
Supp. 4–23
Antoine, Père, Nov. 18, 1748–Jan. 19, 1829.
Vol. 1, Pt. 1–321
Anza, Juan Bautista de, b. 1735.
Vol. 1, Pt. 1–322
Apes, William, b. Jan. 31, 1798.
Vol. 1, Pt. 1–323
Apgar, Virginia, June 7, 1909–Aug. 7, 1974.
Supp. 9–39
Appenzeller, Henry Gerhard, Feb. 6, 1858–June 11, 1902.
Vol. 1, Pt. 1–323
Apple, Thomas Gilmore, Nov. 14, 1829–Sept. 17, 1898.
Vol. 1, Pt. 1–324
Appleby, John Francis, May 23, 1840–Nov. 8, 1917.
Vol. 1, Pt. 1–325
Applegate, Jesse, July 5, 1811–Apr. 22, 1888.
Vol. 1, Pt. 1–325
Appleton, Daniel, Dec. 10, 1785–Mar. 27, 1849.
Vol. 1, Pt. 1–326
Appleton, James, Feb. 14, 1785–Aug. 25, 1862.
Vol. 1, Pt. 1–327
Appleton, Jesse, Nov. 17, 1772–Nov. 12, 1819.
Vol. 1, Pt. 1–328
Appleton, John, July 12, 1804–Feb. 7, 1891.
Vol. 1, Pt. 1–328
Appleton, John, Feb. 11, 1815–Aug. 22, 1864.
Vol. 1, Pt. 1–329
Appleton, Nathan, Oct. 6, 1779–July 14, 1861.
Vol. 1, Pt. 1–330
Appleton, Nathaniel Walker, June 14, 1755–Apr. 15, 1795
Vol. 1, Pt. 1–332
Appleton, Samuel, June 22, 1766–July 12, 1853.
Vol. 1, Pt. 1–332
Appleton, Thomas Gold, Mar. 31, 1812–Apr. 17, 1884.
Vol. 1, Pt. 1–333
Appleton, William Henry, Jan. 27, 1814–Oct. 19, 1899.
Vol. 1, Pt. 1–334
Appleton, William Sumner, May 20, 1874–Nov. 24, 1947.
Supp. 4–24
Appleton, William Worthen, Nov. 29, 1845–Jan. 27, 1924.
Vol. 1, Pt. 1–334

Apthorp, William Foster, Oct. 24, 1848–Feb. 19, 1913.
Vol. 1, Pt. 1–335
Arbuckle, John, 1839–Mar. 27, 1912.
Vol. 1, Pt. 1–336
Archbold, John Dustin, July 26, 1848–Dec. 5, 1916.
Vol. 1, Pt. 1–337
Archdale, John, *c.* May 5, 1642–*c.* July 4, 1717.
Vol. 1, Pt. 1–337
Archer, Branch Tanner, 1790–Sept. 22, 1856.
Vol. 1, Pt. 1–338
Archer, Frederic, June 16, 1838–Oct. 22, 1901.
Vol. 1, Pt. 1–339
Archer, James J., Dec. 19, 1817–Oct. 24, 1864.
Vol. 1, Pt. 1–340
Archer, John, May 5, 1741–Sept. 28, 1810.
Vol. 1, Pt. 1–340
Archer, Samuel, 1771–Apr. 14, 1839.
Vol. 1, Pt. 1–341
Archer, Stevenson, Oct. 11, 1786–June 26, 1848.
Vol. 1 Pt. 1–342
Archer, William Segar, Mar. 5, 1789–Mar. 28, 1855.
Vol. 1, Pt. 1–342
Archipenko, Alexander, May 30, 1887–Feb. 25, 1964.
Supp. 7–14
Arden, Edwin Hunter Pendleton, Feb. 4, 1864–Oct. 2, 1918.
Vol. 1, Pt. 1–343
Arden, Elizabeth, Dec. 31, 1878–Oct. 18, 1966.
Supp. 8–12
Arendt, Hannah, Oct. 14, 1906–Dec. 4, 1975.
Supp. 9–40
Arensberg, Walter Conrad, Apr. 4, 1878–Jan 29, 1954.
Supp. 5–19
Arents, Albert, Mar. 14, 1840–May 15, 1914. 1–343
Argall, Philip, Aug. 27, 1854–Mar. 19, 1922.
Vol. 1, Pt. 1–344
Argall, Sir Samuel, fl. 1609–1624.
Vol. 1, Pt. 1–345
Arlen, Michael, Nov. 16, 1895–June 23, 1956.
Supp. 6–20
Arliss, George, Apr. 10, 1868–Feb. 5, 1946.
Supp. 4–25
Armistead, George, Apr. 10, 1780–Apr. 25, 1818.
Vol. 1, Pt. 1–346
Armistead, Lewis Addison, Feb. 18, 1817–July 3, 1863.
Vol. 1, Pt. 1–347
Armour, Philip Danforth, May 16, 1832–Jan. 6, 1901.
Vol. 1, Pt. 1–347
Armour, Thomas Dickson ("Tommy"), Sept. 24, 1895–Sept. 11, 1968.
Supp. 8–14
Armsby, Henry Prentiss, Sept. 21, 1853–Oct. 19, 1921.
Vol. 1, Pt. 1–349
Armstrong, David Maitland, Apr. 15, 1836–May 26, 1918.
Vol. 1, Pt. 1–350
Armstrong, Edward Cooke, Aug. 24, 1871–Mar. 5, 1944.
Supp. 3–21
Armstrong, Edwin Howard, Dec. 18, 1890–Jan. 31, 1954.
Supp. 5–21
Armstrong, Frank C., Nov. 22, 1835–Sept. 8, 1909.
Vol. 1, Pt. 1–351
Armstrong, George Buchanan, Oct. 27, 1822–May 5, 1871.
Vol. 1, Pt. 1–351
Armstrong, George Dod, Sept. 15, 1813–May 11, 1899.
Vol. 1, Pt. 1–352
Armstrong, George Washington, Aug. 11, 1836–June 30, 1901.
Vol. 1, Pt. 1–353
Armstrong, Hamilton Fish, Apr. 7, 1893–Apr. 24, 1973.
Supp. 9–43
Armstrong, Henry Worthington ("Harry"), July 22, 1879–Feb. 28, 1951.
Supp. 5–23
Armstrong, John, Oct. 13, 1717–Mar. 9, 1795.
Vol. 1, Pt. 1–353
Armstrong, John, Apr. 20, 1755–Feb. 4, 1816.
Vol. 1, Pt. 1–354
Armstrong, John, Nov. 25, 1758–Apr. 1, 1843.
Vol. 1, Pt. 1–355
Armstrong, Louis ("Satchmo"), Aug. 4, 1901–July 6, 1971.
Supp. 9–45
Armstrong, Paul, Apr. 25, 1869–Aug. 30, 1915.
Vol. 1, Pt. 1–358
Armstrong, Robert, Sept. 28, 1792–Feb. 23, 1854.
Vol. 1, Pt. 1–359
Armstrong, Samuel Chapman, Jan. 30, 1839–May 11, 1893.
Vol. 1, Pt. 1–359
Armstrong, Samuel Turell, Apr. 29, 1784–Mar. 26, 1850.
Vol. 1, Pt. 1–360
Arno, Peter, Jan. 8, 1904–Feb. 22, 1968.
Supp. 8–15
Arnold, Aza, Oct. 4, 1788–1865.
Vol. 1, Pt. 1–361
Arnold, Benedict, Jan. 14, 1741–June 14, 1801.
Vol. 1, Pt. 1–362
Arnold, Edward, Feb. 18, 1890–Apr. 26, 1956.
Supp. 6–21
Arnold, George, June 24, 1834–Nov. 9, 1865.
Vol. 1, Pt. 1–367
Arnold, Harold DeForest, Sept. 3, 1883–July 10, 1933.
Supp. 1–31
Arnold, Henry Harley, June 25, 1886–Jan. 15, 1950.
Supp. 4–27
Arnold, Isaac Newton, Nov. 30, 1815–Apr. 24, 1884.
Vol. 1, Pt. 1–368
Arnold, Jonathan, Dec. 3, 1741–Feb. 1, 1793.
Vol. 1, Pt. 1–369
Arnold, Lauren Briggs, Aug. 14, 1814–Mar. 7, 1888.
Vol. 1, Pt. 1–369
Arnold, Leslie Philip, Aug. 28, 1893–Mar. 21, 1961.
Supp. 7–16
Arnold, Lewis Golding, Jan. 15, 1817–Sept. 22, 1871.
Vol. 1, Pt. 1–370
Arnold, Richard, Apr. 12, 1828–Nov. 8, 1882.
Vol. 1, Pt. 1–371
Arnold, Richard Dennis, Aug. 19, 1808–July 10, 1876.
Vol. 1, Pt. 1–371
Arnold, Samuel Greene, Apr. 12, 1821–Feb. 13, 1880.
Vol. 1, Pt. 1–372
Arnold, Thurman Wesley, June 2, 1891–Nov. 7, 1969.
Supp. 8–16
Aronson, Boris Solomon, Oct. 15, 1900–Nov. 16, 1980.
Supp. 10–8
Arquette, Clifford, Dec. 28, 1905–Sept. 23, 1974.
Supp. 9–47
Arrington, Alfred W., Sept. 17, 1810–Dec. 31, 1867.
Vol. 1, Pt. 1–373
Arthur, Chester Alan, Oct. 5, 1830–Nov. 18, 1886.
Vol. 1, Pt. 1–373
Arthur, Joseph Charles, Jan. 11, 1850–Apr. 30, 1942.
Supp. 3–22
Arthur, Peter M., 1831–July 17, 1903.
Vol. 1, Pt. 1–376
Arthur, Timothy Shay, June 6, 1809–Mar. 6, 1885.
Vol. 1, Pt. 1–377
Arthur, William, Dec. 5, 1797–Oct. 27, 1875,.
Vol. 1, Pt. 1–379
Artzybasheff, Boris, May 25, 1899–July 16, 1965.
Supp. 7–17
Arvey, Jacob M., Nov. 3, 1895–Aug. 25, 1977.
Supp. 10–9
Arvin, Newton, Aug. 23, 1900–Mar. 21, 1963.
Supp. 7–18
Arzner, Dorothy Emma, Jan. 3, 1897–Oct. 1, 1979.
Supp. 10–11
Asboth, Alexander Sandor, Dec. 18, 1811–Jan. 21, 1868.
Vol. 1, Pt. 1–379
Asbury, Francis, Aug. 20/21, 1745–Mar. 31, 1816.
Vol. 1, Pt. 1–379
Asbury, Herbert, Sept. 1, 1891–Feb. 24, 1963.
Supp. 7–19
Asch, Morris Joseph, July 4, 1833–Oct. 5, 1902.
Vol. 1, Pt. 1–383
Ascoli, Max, June 25, 1898–Jan. 1, 1978.
Supp. 10–13
Ashburner, Charles Albert, Feb. 9, 1854–Dec. 24, 1889.
Vol. 1, Pt. 1–383
Ashby, Turner, Oct. 23, 1828–June 6, 1862.
Vol. 1, Pt. 1–384
Ashe, John, *c.* 1720–Oct. 1781.
Vol. 1, Pt. 1–385

Ashe, John Baptista, 1748–Nov. 27, 1802.
Vol. 1, Pt. 1–386
Ashe, Samuel, 1725–Feb. 3, 1813.
Vol. 1, Pt. 1–386
Ashe, Thomas Samuel, July 19, 1812–Feb. 4, 1887.
Vol. 1, Pt. 1–387
Ashe, William Shepperd, Sept. 14, 1814–Sept. 1862.
Vol. 1, Pt. 1–387
Asher, Joseph Mayor, Sept. 23, 1872–Nov. 9, 1909.
Vol. 1, Pt. 1–388
Ashford, Bailey Kelly, Sept. 18, 1873–Nov 1, 1934.
Supp. 1–32
Ashford, Emmett Littleton, Nov. 23, 1914–Mar. 1, 1980.
Supp. 10–14
Ashhurst, John, Aug. 23, 1839–July 7, 1900.
Vol. 1, Pt. 1–389
Ashley, James Mitchell, Nov. 14, 1824–Sept. 16, 1896.
Vol. 1, Pt. 1–389
Ashley, William Henry, *c.* 1778–Mar. 26, 1838.
Vol. 1, Pt. 1–391
Ashmead, Isaac, Dec. 22, 1790–Mar. 1, 1870.
Vol. 1, Pt. 1–392
Ashmead, William Harris, Sept. 19, 1855–Oct. 17, 1908.
Vol. 1, Pt. 1–392
Ashmore, William, Dec. 25, 1824–Apr. 21, 1909.
Vol. 1, Pt. 1–393
Ashmun, George, Dec. 25, 1804–July 17, 1870.
Vol. 1, Pt. 1–393
Ashmun, Jehudi, Apr. 21, 1794–Aug. 25, 1828.
Vol. 1, Pt. 1–394
Ashurst, Henry Fountain, Sept. 13, 1874–May 31, 1962.
Supp. 7–20
Aspinwall, William, May 23, 1743–Apr. 16, 1823.
Vol. 1, Pt. 1–395
Aspinwall, William Henry, Dec. 16, 1807–Jan. 18, 1875.
Vol. 1, Pt. 1–396
Astor, John Jacob, July 17, 1763–Mar. 29, 1848.
Vol. 1, Pt. 1–397
Astor, John Jacob, June 10, 1822–Feb. 22, 1890.
Vol. 1, Pt. 1–399
Astor, John Jacob, July 13, 1864–Apr. 15, 1912.
Vol. 1, Pt. 1–400
Astor, William Backhouse, Sept. 19, 1792–Nov. 24, 1875.
Vol. 1, Pt. 1–401
Astor, William Vincent, Nov. 15, 1891–Feb. 3, 1959.
Supp. 6–23
Astor, William Waldorf, Mar. 31, 1848–Oct. 18, 1919.
Vol. 1, Pt. 1–402
Atchison, David Rice, Aug. 11, 1807–Jan. 26, 1886.
Vol. 1, Pt. 1–402
Athenagoras I, Mar. 25, 1886–July 6, 1972.
Supp. 9–49
Atherton, Charles Gordon, July 4, 1804–Nov. 15, 1853.
Vol. 1, Pt. 1–404
Atherton, George Washington, June 20, 1837–July 24, 1906.
Vol. 1, Pt. 1–404
Atherton, Gertrude Franklin (Horn), Oct. 30, 1857–June 14, 1948.
Supp. 4–30
Atherton, Joshua, June 20, 1737–Apr. 3, 1809.
Vol. 1, Pt. 1–404
Atkins, Jearum, fl. 1840–1880.
Vol. 1, Pt. 1–405
Atkinson, Edward, Feb. 10, 1827–Dec. 11, 1905.
Vol. 1, Pt. 1–406
Atkinson, George Francis, Jan. 26, 1854–Nov. 15, 1918.
Vol. 1, Pt. 1–407
Atkinson, George Henry, May 10, 1819–Feb. 25, 1889.
Vol. 1, Pt. 1–408
Atkinson, George Wesley, June 29, 1845–Apr. 14, 1925.
Vol. 1, Pt. 1–409
Atkinson, Henry, 1782–June 14, 1842.
Vol. 1, Pt. 1–410
Atkinson, Henry Avery, Aug. 26, 1877–Jan. 24, 1960.
Supp. 6–24
Atkinson, John, Dec. 6, 1835–Dec. 8, 1897.
Vol. 1, Pt. 1–410
Atkinson, Thomas, Aug. 6, 1807–Jan. 4, 1881.
Vol. 1, Pt. 1–411
Atkinson, William Biddle, June 21, 1832–Nov. 23, 1909.
Vol. 1, Pt. 1–411
Atkinson, William Yates, Nov. 11, 1854–Aug. 8, 1899.
Vol. 1, Pt. 1–412
Atkinson, Wilmer, June 13, 1840–May 10, 1920.
Vol. 1, Pt. 1–412
Atlas, Charles S., 1893–Dec. 23, 1972.
Supp. 9–51
Atlee, John Light, Nov. 2, 1799–Oct. 1, 1885.
Vol. 1, Pt. 1–413
Atlee, Washington Lemuel, Feb. 22, 1808–Sept. 6, 1878.
Vol. 1, Pt. 1–414
Atterbury, Grosvenor, July 7, 1869–Oct. 18, 1956.
Supp. 6–25
Atterbury, Wilham Wallace, Jan. 31, 1866–Sept. 20, 1935.
Supp. 1–33
Attucks, Crispus, *c.* 1723–Mar. 5, 1770.
Vol. 1, Pt. 1–415
Atwater, Caleb, Dec. 25, 1778–Mar. 13, 1867.
Vol. 1, Pt. 1–415
Atwater, Lyman Hotchkiss, Feb. 3, 1813–Feb. 17, 1883.
Vol. 1, Pt. 1–416
Atwater, Wilbur Olin, May 3, 1844–Sept. 22, 1907.
Vol. 1, Pt. 1–417
Atwood, Charles B., May 18, 1849–Dec. 19, 1895.
Vol. 1, Pt. 1–418
Atwood, David, Dec. 15, 1815–Dec. 11, 1889.
Vol. 1, Pt. 1–419
Atwood, Lewis John, Apr. 8, 1827–Feb. 23, 1909.
Vol. 1, Pt. 1–419
Atwood, Wallace Walter, Oct. 1, 1872–July 24, 1949.
Supp. 4–31
Atzerodt, George A., *c.* 1832–1865. [*See* Booth, John Wilkes.]
Auchincloss, Hugh Dudley, Jr., Aug. 15, 1897–Nov. 20, 1976.
Supp. 10–16
Auchmuty, Richard Tylden, July 15, 1831–July 18, 1893.
Vol. 1, Pt. 1–420
Auchmuty, Robert, d. 1750.
Vol. 1, Pt. 1–421
Auchmuty, Robert, d. November 1788.
Vol. 1, Pt. 1–421
Auchmuty, Samuel, Jan. 26, 1722–Mar. 4, 1777.
Vol. 1, Pt. 1–422
Auden, Wystan Hugh, Feb. 21, 1907–Sept. 28, 1973.
Supp. 9–53
Audsley, George Ashdown, Sept. 6, 1838–June 21, 1925.
Vol. 1, Pt. 1–422
Audubon, John James, Apr. 26, 1785–Jan. 27, 1851.
Vol. 1, Pt. 1–423
Auer, John, Mar. 30, 1875–Apr. 30, 1948.
Supp. 4–34
Augur, Christopher Columbus, July 10, 1821–Jan. 16, 1898.
Vol. 1, Pt. 1–427
Augur, Hezekiah, Feb. 21, 1791–Jan. 10, 1858.
Vol. 1, Pt. 1–428
Augustus, John, 1785–June 21, 1859.
Vol. 1, Pt. 1–429
Austell, Alfred, Jan. 14, 1814–Dec. 7, 1881.
Vol. 1, Pt. 1–429
Austen, (Elizabeth) Alice, Mar. 17, 1866–June 9, 1952.
Supp. 5–24
Austen, Peter Townsend, Sept. 10, 1852–Dec. 30, 1907.
Vol. 1, Pt. 1–430
Austin, Benjamin, Nov. 18, 1752–May 4, 1820.
Vol. 1, Pt. 1–431
Austin, David, Mar. 19, 1759–Feb. 5, 1831.
Vol. 1, Pt. 1–432
Austin, Henry, Dec. 4, 1804–Dec. 17, 1891.
Vol. 1, Pt. 1–432
Austin, James Trecothick, Jan. 10, 1784–May 8, 1870.
Vol. 1, Pt. 1–433
Austin, Jane Goodwin, Feb. 25, 1831–Mar. 30, 1894.
Vol. 1, Pt. 1–434
Austin, Jonathan Loring, Jan. 2, 1748–May 10, 1826.
Vol. 1, Pt. 1–435
Austin, Mary, Sept. 9, 1868–Aug. 13, 1934.
Supp. 1–34
Austin, Moses, Oct. 4, 1761–June 10, 1821.
Vol. 1, Pt. 1–435
Austin, Samuel, Oct. 7, 1760–Dec. 4, 1830.
Vol. 1, Pt. 1–436
Austin, Stephen Fuller, Nov. 3, 1793–Dec. 27, 1836.
Vol. 1, Pt. 1437

Austin, Warren Robinson, Nov. 12, 1877–Dec. 25, 1962.
Supp. 7–22
Austin, William, Mar. 2, 1778–June 27, 1841.
Vol. 1, Pt. 1–440
Averell, William Woods, Nov. 5, 1832–Feb. 3, 1900.
Vol. 1, Pt. 1–441
Avery, Benjamin Parke, Nov. 11, 1828–Nov. 8, 1875.
Vol. 1, Pt. 1–443
Avery, Isaac Wheeler, May 2, 1837–Sept. 8, 1897.
Vol. 1, Pt. 1–444
Avery, John, Sept. 18, 1837–Sept. 1, 1887.
Vol. 1, Pt. 1–444
Avery, Milton Clark, Mar. 7, 1893–Jan. 3, 1965.
Supp. 7–24
Avery, Oswald Theodore, Oct. 21, 1877–Feb. 20, 1955.
Supp. 5–25
Avery, Samuel Putnam, Mar. 17, 1822–Aug. 11, 1904.
Vol. 1, Pt. 1–445
Avery, Sewell Lee, Nov. 4, 1874–Oct. 31, 1960.
Supp. 6–27
Avery, William Waigstill, May 25, 1816–July 3, 1864.
Vol. 1, Pt. 1–445
Awl, William Maclay, May 24, 1799–Nov. 19, 1876.
Vol. 1, Pt. 1–446
Axtell, Samuel Beach, Oct. 14, 1819–Aug. 6 or 7, 1891.
Vol. 1, Pt. 1–446
Ayala, Juan Manuel de, fl. 1775.
Vol. 1, Pt. 1–447
Aycock, Charles Brantley, Nov. 1, 1859–Apr. 4, 1912.
Vol. 1, Pt. 1–447
Aydelotte, Frank, Oct. 16, 1880–Dec. 17, 1956.
Supp. 6–29
Ayer, Edward Everett, Nov. 16, 1841–May 3, 1927.
Vol. 1, Pt. 1–448
Ayer, Francis Wayland, Feb. 4, 1848–Mar. 5, 1923.
Vol. 1, Pt. 1–449
Ayer, James Cook, May 5, 1818–July 3, 1878.
Vol. 1, Pt. 1–450
Ayllon, Lucas Vasquez de, *c.* 1475–Oct. 18, 1526.
Vol. 1, Pt. 1–451
Aylwin, John Cushing, *c.* 1780–Jan. 28, 1813.
Vol. 1, Pt. 1–452
Ayres, Anne, Jan. 3, 1816–Feb. 9, 1896.
Vol. 1, Pt. 1–452
Ayres, Brown, May 25, 1856–Jan. 28, 1919.
Vol. 1, Pt. 1–453
Ayres, Leonard Porter, Sept. 15, 1879–Oct. 29, 1946.
Supp. 4–35
Ayres, Romeyn Beck, Dec. 20, 1825–Dec. 4, 1888.
Vol. 1, Pt. 1–453
Ayres, William Augustus, Apr. 19, 1867–Feb. 17, 1952.
Supp. 5–26
Azarias, Brother, June 29, 1847–Aug. 20, 1893.
Vol. 1, Pt. 1–454

Baade, Wilhelm Heinrich Walter, Mar. 24, 1893–June 25, 1960.
Supp. 6–30
Babbitt, Benjamin Talbot, 1809–Oct. 20, 1889.
Vol. 1, Pt. 1–455
Babbitt, Irving, Aug. 2, 1865–July 15, 1933.
Supp. 1–36
Babbitt, Isaac, July 26, 1799–May 26, 1862.
Vol. 1, Pt. 1–456
Babcock, George Herman, June 17, 1832–Dec. 16, 1893.
Vol. 1, Pt. 1–456
Babcock, Howard Edward, Feb. 23, 1889–July 12, 1950.
Supp. 4–36
Babcock, James Francis, Feb. 23, 1844–July 19, 1897.
Vol. 1, Pt. 1–457
Babcock, James Woods, Aug. 11, 1856–Mar. 3, 1922.
Vol. 1, Pt. 1–458
Babcock, Joseph Weeks, Mar. 6, 1850–Apr. 27, 1909.
Vol. 1, Pt. 1–458
Babcock, Maltbie Davenport, Aug. 3, 1858–May 18, 1901.
Vol. 1, Pt. 1–459
Babcock, Orville E., Dec. 25, 1835–June 2, 1884.
Vol. 1, Pt. 1–460
Babcock, Stephen Moulton, Oct. 22, 1843–July 2, 1931.
Supp. 1–37
Babcock, Washington Irving, Sept. 26, 1858–Aug. 7, 1917.
Vol. 1, Pt. 1–461
Babson, Roger Ward, July 6, 1875–Mar. 5, 1967.
Supp. 8–18
Baccaloni, Salvatore, Apr. 14, 1900–Dec. 31, 1969.
Supp. 8–19
Bache, Alexander Dallas, July 19, 1806–Feb. 17, 1867.
Vol. 1, Pt. 1–461
Bache, Benjamin Franklin, Aug. 12, 1769–Sept. 10, 1798.
Vol. 1, Pt. 1–462
Bache, Franklin, Oct. 25, 1792–Mar. 19, 1864.
Vol. 1, Pt. 1–463
Bache, Jules Semon, Nov. 9, 1861–Mar. 24, 1944.
Supp. 3–24
Bache, Richard, 1737–July 29, 1811.
Vol. 1, Pt. 1–464
Bache, Theophylact, Jan. 17, 1734/35–Oct. 30, 1807.
Vol. 1, Pt. 1–464
Bachelder, John, Mar. 7, 1817–July 1, 1906.
Vol. 1, Pt. 1–465
Bacheller, Irving, Sept. 26, 1859–Feb. 24, 1950.
Supp. 4–38
Bacher, Otto Henry, Mar. 31, 1856–Aug. 16, 1909.
Vol. 1, Pt. 1–465
Bachman, John, Feb. 4, 1790–Feb. 24, 1874.
Vol. 1, Pt. 1–466
Bachmann, Werner Emmanuel, Nov. 13, 1901–Mar. 22, 1951.
Supp. 5–28
Bachrach, Louis Fabian, July 16, 1881–July 24, 1963.
Supp. 7–25
Backus, Azel, Oct. 13, 1765–Dec. 9, 1817.
Vol. 1, Pt. 1–467
Backus, Isaac, Jan. 9, 1724–Nov. 20, 1806.
Vol. 1, Pt. 1–468
Backus, Truman Jay, Feb. 11, 1842–Mar. 25, 1908.
Vol. 1, Pt. 1–472
Bacon, Alice Mabel, Feb. 6, 1858–May 1, 1918.
Vol. 1, Pt. 1–473
Bacon, Augustus Octavius, Oct. 20, 1839–Feb. 14, 1914.
Vol. 1, Pt. 1–473
Bacon, Benjamin Wisner, Jan. 15, 1860–Feb. 1, 1932.
Supp. 1–38
Bacon, David, Sept. 4, 1771–Aug. 27, 1817.
Vol. 1, Pt. 1–474
Bacon, Delia Salter, Feb. 2, 1811–Sept. 2, 1859.
Vol. 1, Pt. 1–475
Bacon, Edward Payson, May 16, 1834–Feb. 16, 1916.
Vol. 1, Pt. 1–476
Bacon, Edwin Munroe, Oct. 20, 1844–Feb. 24, 1916.
Vol. 1, Pt. 1–476
Bacon, Frank, Jan. 16, 1864–Nov. 19, 1922. 1–477
Bacon, Henry, Nov. 28, 1866–Feb. 16, 1924.
Vol. 1, Pt. 1–477
Bacon, John, Apr. 9, 1738–Oct. 25, 1820.
Vol. 1, Pt. 1–478
Bacon, Leonard, May 26, 1887–Jan. 1, 1954.
Supp. 5–29
Bacon, Leonard, Feb. 19, 1802–Dec. 24, 1881.
Vol. 1, Pt. 1–479
Bacon, Leonard Woolsey, Jan. 1, 1830–May 12, 1907.
Vol. 1, Pt. 1–481
Bacon, Nathaniel, Jan. 2, 1647–Oct. 1676.
Vol. 1, Pt. 1–482
Bacon, Robert, July 5, 1860–May 29, 1919.
Vol. 1, Pt. 1–483
Bacon, Thomas, *c.* 1700–May 24, 1768.
Vol. 1, Pt. 1–484
Badè, William Frederic, Jan. 22, 1871–Mar. 4, 1936.
Supp. 2–16
Badeau, Adam, Dec. 29, 1831–Mar. 19, 1895.
Vol. 1, Pt. 1–485
Badger, Charles Johnston, Aug. 6, 1853–Sept. 7, 1932.
Supp. 1–39
Badger, George Edmund, Apr. 17, 1795–May 11, 1866.
Vol. 1, Pt. 1–485
Badger, Joseph, Mar. 14, 1708–1765.
Vol. 1, Pt. 1–486
Badger, Joseph, Feb. 28, 1757–Apr. 5, 1846.
Vol. 1, Pt. 1–487
Badger, Oscar Charles, Aug. 12, 1823–June 20, 1899.
Vol. 1, Pt. 1–488

Badin, Stephen Theodore, July 17, 1768–Apr. 19, 1853.
Vol. 1, Pt. 1–488
Baekeland, Leo Hendrik, Nov. 14, 1863–Feb. 23, 1944.
Supp. 3–25
Baer, George Frederick, Sept. 26, 1842–Apr. 26, 1914.
Vol. 1, Pt. 1–489
Baer, William Stevenson, Nov. 25, 1872–Apr. 7, 1931.
Supp. 1–40
Baermann, Carl, July 9, 1839–Jan. 17, 1913.
Vol. 1, Pt. 1–491
Baetjer, Frederick Henry, Aug. 7, 1874–July 17, 1933.
Supp. 1–41
Bagby, Arthur Pendleton, 1794–Sept. 21, 1858.
Vol. 1, Pt. 1–491
Bagby, George William, Aug. 13, 1828–Nov. 29, 1883.
Vol. 1, Pt. 1–492
Bagley, William Chandler, Mar. 15, 1874–July 1, 1946.
Supp. 4–39
Bailey, Ann, 1742–Nov. 22, 1825.
Vol. 1, Pt. 1–493
Bailey, Anna Warner, Oct. 1758–Jan. 10, 1851.
Vol. 1, Pt. 1–493
Bailey, Bill, 1912–Dec. 12, 1978.
Supp. 10–19
Bailey, Ebenezer, June 25, 1795–Aug. 5, 1839.
Vol. 1, Pt. 1–494
Bailey, Florence Augusta Merriam, Aug. 8, 1863–Sept. 22, 1948.
Supp. 4–41
Bailey, Francis, *c.* 1735–1815.
Vol. 1, Pt. 1–494
Bailey, Frank Harvey, June 29, 1851–Apr. 9, 1921.
Vol. 1, Pt. 1–495
Bailey, Gamaliel, Dec. 3, 1807–June 5, 1859.
Vol. 1, Pt. 1–496
Bailey, (Irene) Temple, 188?-July 6, 1953.
Supp. 5–33
Bailey, Jacob, 1731–Mar. 22, 1818.
Vol. 1, Pt. 1–497
Bailey, Jacob Whitman, Apr. 29, 1811–Feb. 27, 1857.
Vol. 1, Pt. 1–498
Bailey, James Anthony, 1847–Apr. 11, 1906.
Vol. 1, Pt. 1–498
Bailey, James Montgomery, Sept. 25, 1841–Mar. 4, 1894.
Vol. 1, Pt. 1–499
Bailey, John Moran, Nov. 23, 1904–Apr. 10, 1975.
Supp. 9–57
Bailey, Joseph, May 6, 1825–Mar. 21, 1867.
Vol. 1, Pt. 1–500
Bailey, Joseph Weldon, Oct. 6, 1863–Apr. 13, 1929.
Supp. 1–42
Bailey, Josiah William, Sept. 14, 1873–Dec. 15, 1946.
Supp. 4–42
Bailey, Llberty Hyde, Mar. 15, 1858–Dec. 25, 1954.
Supp. 5–30
Bailey, Lydia R., Feb. 1, 1779–Feb. 21, 1869.
Vol. 1, Pt. 1–500
Bailey, Mildred, Feb. 27, 1907–Dec. 12, 1951.
Supp. 5–32
Bailey, Rufus William, Apr. 13, 1793–Apr. 25, 1863.
Vol. 1, Pt. 1–501
Bailey, Solon Irving, Dec. 29, 1854–June 5, 1931.
Supp. 1–43
Bailey, Theodorus, Apr. 12, 1805–Feb. 10, 1877.
Vol. 1, Pt. 1–501
Bailly, Joseph Alexis, Jan. 21, 1825–June 15, 1883.
Vol. 1, Pt. 1–502
Bain, George Luke Scobie, May 5, 1836–Oct. 22, 1891.
Vol. 1, Pt. 1–503
Bainbridge, William, May 7, 1774–July 27, 1833.
Vol. 1, Pt. 1–504
Baird, Absalom, Aug. 20, 1824–June 14, 1905.
Vol. 1, Pt. 1–507
Baird, Charles Washington, Aug. 28, 1828–Feb. 10, 1887.
Vol. 1, Pt. 1–508
Baird, Henry Carey, Sept. 10, 1825–Dec. 30, 1912.
Vol. 1, Pt. 1–509
Baird, Henry Martyn, Jan. 17, 1832–Nov. 11, 1906.
Vol. 1, Pt. 1–510
Baird, Matthew, 1817–May 19, 1877.
Vol. 1, Pt. 1–511
Baird, Robert, Oct. 6, 1798–Mar. 15, 1863.
Vol. 1, Pt. 1–511
Baird, Samuel John, Sept. 17, 1817–Apr. 10, 1893.
Vol. 1, Pt. 1–512
Baird, Spencer Fullerton, Feb. 3, 1823–Aug. 19, 1888.
Vol. 1, Pt. 1–513
Baker, Benjamin A., Apr. 4, 1818–Sept. 6, 1890.
Vol. 1, Pt. 1–515
Baker, Benjamin Franklin, July 10, 1811–Mar. 11, 1889.
Vol. 1, Pt. 1–516
Baker, Carl Lotus, Sept. 7, 1873–Apr. 10, 1945.
Supp. 3–46
Baker, Daniel, Aug. 17, 1791–Dec. 10, 1857.
Vol. 1, Pt. 1–517
Baker, Dorothy Dodds, Apr. 21, 1907–June 17, 1968.
Supp. 8–20
Baker, Edward Dickinson, Feb. 24, 1811–Oct. 22, 1861.
Vol. 1, Pt. 1–517
Baker, Frank, Aug. 22, 1841–Sept. 30, 1918.
Vol. 1, Pt. 1–519
Baker, George Augustus, Mar. 1821–Apr. 2, 1880.
Vol. 1, Pt. 1–519
Baker, George Fisher, Mar. 27, 1840–May 2, 1931.
Supp. 1–44
Baker, George Pierce, Apr. 4, 1866–Jan. 6, 1935.
Supp. 1–45
Baker, Harvey Humphrey, Apr. 11, 1869–Apr. 10, 1915.
Vol. 1, Pt. 1–520
Baker, Hugh Potter, Jan. 20, 1878–May 24, 1950.
Supp. 4–43
Baker, James, Dec. 19, 1818–May 15, 1898.
Vol. 1, Pt. 1–520
Baker, James Heaton, May 6, 1829–May 25, 1913.
Vol. 1, Pt. 1–521
Baker, James Hutchins, Oct. 13, 1848–Sept. 10, 1925.
Vol. 1, Pt. 1–522
Baker, Jehu, Nov. 4, 1822–Mar. 1, 1903.
Supp. 1–46
Baker, John Franklin, Mar. 13, 1886–June 28, 1963.
Supp. 7–27
Baker, Josephine, June 3, 1906–Apr. 12, 1975.
Supp. 9–59
Baker, La Fayette Curry, Oct. 13, 1826–July 3, 1868.
Vol. 1, Pt. 1–523
Baker, Laurence Simmons, May 15, 1830–Apr. 10, 1907.
Vol. 1, Pt. 1–523
Baker, Lorenzo Dow, Mar. 15, 1840–June 21, 1908.
Vol. 1, Pt. 1–524
Baker, Marcus, Sept. 23, 1849–Dec. 12, 1903.
Vol. 1, Pt. 1–525
Baker, Newton Diehl, Dec. 3, 1871–Dec. 25, 1937.
Supp. 2–17
Baker, Oliver Edwin, Sept. 10, 1883–Dec. 2, 1949.
Supp. 4–44
Baker, Osmon Cleander, July 30, 1812–Dec. 20, 1871.
Vol. 1, Pt. 1–525
Baker, Peter Carpenter, Mar. 22, 1822–May 19, 1889.
Vol. 1, Pt. 1–525
Baker, Ray Stannard, Apr. 17, 1870–July 12, 1946.
Supp. 4–46
Baker, Remember, June 1737–Aug. 1775.
Vol. 1, Pt. 1–526
Baker, Sara Josephine, Nov. 15, 1873–Feb. 21, 1945.
Supp. 3–27
Baker, Walter Ransom Gail, Nov. 30, 1892–Oct. 30, 1960.
Supp. 6–32
Baker, William Mumford, June 5, 1825–Aug. 20, 1883.
Vol. 1, Pt. 1–527
Balaban, Barney, June 8, 1887–Mar. 7, 1971.
Supp. 9–61
Balbach, Edward, July 4, 1839–Dec. 30, 1910.
Vol. 1, Pt. 1–527
Balch, Emily Greene, Jan. 8, 1867–Jan. 9, 1961.
Supp. 7–28
Balch, George Beall, Jan. 3, 1821–Apr. 16, 1908.
Vol. 1, Pt. 1–528
Balch, Thomas Willing, June 13, 1866–June 7, 1927.
Vol. 1, Pt. 1–529
Balchen, Bernt, Oct. 23, 1889–Oct. 17, 1973.
Supp. 9–63

Baldwin, Abraham, Nov. 22, 1754–Mar. 4, 1807.
Vol. 1, Pt. 1–530
Baldwin, Edward Robinson, Sept. 8, 1864–May 6, 1947.
Supp. 4–48
Baldwin, Elihu Whittlesey, Dec. 25, 1789–Oct. 15, 1840.
Vol. 1, Pt. 1–532
Baldwin, Evelyn Briggs, July 22, 1862–Oct. 25, 1933.
Supp. 1–47
Baldwin, Faith, Oct. 1, 1893–Mar. 19, 1978.
Supp. 10–20
Baldwin, Frank Stephen, Apr. 10, 1838–Apr. 8, 1925.
Vol. 1, Pt. 1–533
Baldwin, Henry, Jan. 14, 1780–Apr. 21, 1844.
Vol. 1, Pt. 1–533
Baldwin, Henry Perrine, Aug. 29, 1842–July 8, 1911.
Supp. 1–48
Baldwin, Henry Porter, Feb. 22, 1814–Dec. 31, 1892.
Vol. 1, Pt. 1–534
Baldwin, James Mark, Jan. 12, 1861–Nov. 8, 1934.
Supp. 1–49
Baldwin, John, Oct. 13, 1799–Dec. 28, 1884.
Vol. 1, Pt. 1–535
Baldwin, John Brown, Jan. 11, 1820–Sept. 30, 1873.
Vol. 1, Pt. 1–536
Baldwin, John Denison, Sept. 28, 1809–July 8, 1883.
Vol. 1, Pt. 1–537
Baldwin, Joseph, Oct. 31, 1827–Jan. 13, 1899.
Vol. 1, Pt. 1–537
Baldwin, Joseph Glover, Jan. 1815–Sept. 30, 1864.
Vol. 1, Pt. 1–538
Baldwin, Loammi, Jan. 21, 1744–Oct. 20, 1807.
Vol. 1, Pt. 1–539
Baldwin, Loammi, May 16, 1780–June 30, 1838.
Vol. 1, Pt. 1–540
Baldwin, Matthias William, Nov. 10, 1795–Sept. 7, 1866.
Vol. 1, Pt. 1–541
Baldwin, Roger Sherman, Jan. 4, 1793–Feb. 19, 1863.
Vol. 1, Pt. 1–542
Baldwin, Simeon, Dec. 14, 1761–May 26, 1851.
Vol. 1, Pt. 1–543
Baldwin, Simeon Eben, Feb. 5, 1840–Jan. 30, 1927.
Vol. 1, Pt. 1–544
Baldwin, Theron, July 21, 1801–Apr. 10, 1870.
Vol. 1, Pt. 1–547
Baldwin, William, Mar. 29, 1779–Aug. 31, 1819.
Vol. 1, Pt. 1–547
Baldwin, William Henry, Feb. 5, 1863–Jan. 3, 1905.
Vol. 1, Pt. 1–548
Balestier, Charles Wolcott, Dec. 13, 1861–Dec. 6, 1891.
Vol. 1, Pt. 1–549
Ball, Albert, May 7, 1835–Feb. 7, 1927.
Vol. 1, Pt. 1–550
Ball, Ephraim, Aug. 12, 1812–Jan. 1, 1872.
Vol. 1, Pt. 1–551
Ball, Frank Clayton, Nov. 24, 1857–Mar. 19, 1943.
Supp. 3–29
Ball, George Alexander, Nov. 5, 1862–Oct. 22, 1955.
Supp. 5–34
Ball, Thomas, June 3, 1819–Dec. 11, 1911.
Vol. 1, Pt. 1–552
Ballantine, Arthur Atwood, Aug. 3, 1883–Oct. zo, 1960.
Supp. 6–33
Ballard, Bland Williams, Oct. 16, 1759–Sept. 5, 1853.
Vol. 1, Pt. 1–554
Ballinger, Richard Achilles, July 9, 1858–June 6, 1922.
Vol. 1, Pt. 1–555
Ballou, Adin, Apr. 23, 1803–Aug. 5, 1890.
Vol. 1, Pt. 1–556
Ballou, Hosea, Apr. 30, 1771–June 7, 1852.
Vol. 1, Pt. 1–557
Ballou, Hosea, Oct. 18, 1796–May 27, 1861.
Vol. 1, Pt. 1–559
Ballou, Maturin Murray, Apr. 14, 1820–Mar. 27, 1895.
Vol. 1, Pt. 1–560
Baltimore, Charles Calvert, Third Lord. [*See* Calvert, Charles, 1637–1715.]
Baltimore, George Calvert, First Lord. [*See* Calvert, George, *c.* 1580–1632.]
Bamberger, Louis, May 15, 1851–Mar. 11, 1944.
Supp. 3–30
Bancroft, Aaron, Nov. 10, 1711–Aug. 19, 1839.
Vol. 1, Pt. 1–560
Bancroft, Cecil Franklin Patch, Nov. 25, 1839–Oct. 4, 1901.
Vol. 1, Pt. 1–561
Bancroft, Edgar Addison, Nov. 20, 1857–July 28, 1925.
Vol. 1, Pt. 1–562
Bancroft, Edward, Jan. 9, 1744–Sept. 8, 1821.
Vol. 1, Pt. 1–563
Bancroft, Frederic, Oct. 30, 1860–Feb. 22, 1945.
Supp. 3–31
Bancroft, George, Oct. 3, 1800–Jan. 17, 1891.
Vol. 1, Pt. 1–564
Bancroft, Hubert Howe, May 5, 1832–Mar. 2, 1918.
Vol. 1, Pt. 1–570
Bancroft, Wilder Dwight, Oct. 1, 1867–Feb. 7, 1953.
Supp. 5–35
Bandelier, Adolph Francis Alphonse, Aug. 6, 1840–Mar. 18, 1914.
Vol. 1, Pt. 1–571
Bangs, Francis Nehemiah, Feb. 23, 1828–Nov. 30, 1885.
Vol. 1, Pt. 1–572
Bangs, Frank C., Oct. 13, 1833–June 12, 1908.
Vol. 1, Pt. 1–573
Bangs, John Kendrick, May 27, 1862–Jan. 21, 1922.
Vol. 1, Pt. 1–573
Bangs, Nathan, May 2, 1778–May 3, 1862.
Vol. 1, Pt. 1–574
Banister, John, 1650–May 1692.
Vol. 1, Pt. 1–575
Banister, John, Dec. 26, 1734–Sept. 30, 1788.
Vol. 1, Pt. 1–576
Banister, Zilpah Polly Grant, May 30, 1794–Dec. 3, 1874.
Vol. 1, Pt. 1–576
Bankhead, John Hollis, Sept. 13, 1842–Mar. 1, 1920.
Vol. 1, Pt. 1–577
Bankhead, John Hollis, July 8, 1872–June 12, 1946.
Supp. 4–49
Bankhead, Tallulah, Jan. 31, 1902–Dec. 12, 1968.
Supp. 8–21
Bankhead, William Brockman, Apr. 12, 1874–Sept. 15, 1940.
Supp. 2–19
Banks, Charles Edward, July 6, 1854–Oct. 21, 1931.
Supp. 1–50
Banks, Nathaniel Prentiss, Jan. 30, 1816–Sept. 1, 1894.
Vol. 1, Pt. 1–577
Banner, Peter, fl. 1794–1828.
Vol. 1, Pt. 1–580
Bannister, Nathaniel Harrington, Jan. 13, 1813–Nov. 2, 1847.
Vol. 1, Pt. 1–581
Banvard, John, Nov. 15, 1815–May 16, 1891.
Vol. 1, Pt. 1–582
Banvard, Joseph, May 9, 1810–Sept. 28, 1887.
Vol. 1, Pt. 1–583
Bapst, John, Dec. 17, 1815–Nov. 2, 1887.
Vol. 1, Pt. 1–583
Bara, Theda, July 20, probably 1885–Apr. 7, 1955.
Supp. 5–37
Baraga, Frederic, June 29, 1797–Jan. 19, 1868.
Vol. 1, Pt. 1–584
Baranov, Alexander Andreevich, 1746–Apr. 16/28, 1819.
Vol. 1, Pt. 1–585
Barber, Amzi Lorenzo, June 22, 1843–Apr. 17, 1909.
Vol. 1, Pt. 1–586
Barber, Donn, Oct. 19, 1871–May 29, 1925.
Vol. 1, Pt. 1–587
Barber, Edwin Atlee, Aug. 13, 1851–Dec. 12, 1916.
Vol. 1, Pt. 1–588
Barber, Francis, 1751–Feb. 11, 1783.
Vol. 1, Pt. 1–588
Barber, John Warner, Feb. 2, 1798–June 22, 1885.
Vol. 1, Pt. 1–589
Barber, Ohio Columbus, Apr. 20, 1841–Feb. 4, 1920.
Vol. 1, Pt. 1–589
Barbey, Daniel Edward, Dec. 23, 1889–Apr. 11, 1969.
Supp. 8–22
Barbour, Clarence Augustus, Apr. 21, 1867–Jan. 16, 1937.
Supp. 2–20
Barbour, Henry Gray, Mar. 28, 1886–Sept. 23, 1943.
Supp. 3–32
Barbour, James, June 10, 1775–June 7, 1842.
Vol. 1, Pt. 1–590

Barbour, John Strode, Jr., Dec. 29, 1820–May 14, 1892.
Vol. 1, Pt. 1–592
Barbour, Oliver Lorenzo, July 12, 1811–Dec. 17, 1889.
Vol. 1, Pt. 1–599
Barbour, Philip Pendleton, May 25, 1783–Feb. 25, 1841.
Vol. 1, Pt. 1–594
Barbour, Thomas, Aug. 19, 1884–Jan. 8, 1946.
Supp. 4–51
Barclay, Thomas, Oct. 12, 1753–Apr. 21, 1830.
Vol. 1, Pt. 1–596
Bard, John, Feb. 1, 1716–Mar. 30, 1799.
Vol. 1, Pt. 1–597
Bard, Samuel, Apr. 1, 1742–May 24, 1821.
Vol. 1, Pt. 1–598
Bard, William, Apr. 4, 1778–Oct. 17, 1853.
Vol. 1, Pt. 1–599
Bardeen, Charles William, Aug. 28, 1847–Aug. 24, 1924.
Vol. 1, Pt. 1–600
Barden, Graham Arthur, Sept. 25, 1896–Jan. 29, 1967.
Supp. 8–24
Barker, Albert Smith, Mar. 31, 1843–Jan. 29, 1916.
Vol. 1, Pt. 1–600
Barker, Alexander Crichlow ("Lex"), May 8, 1919–May 11, 1973.
Supp. 9–64
Barker, Benjamin Fordyce, May 2, 1818–May 30, 1891.
Vol. 1, Pt. 1–601
Barker, George Frederick, July 14, 1835–May 24, 1910.
Vol. 1, Pt. 1–601
Barker, Jacob, Dec. 17, 1779–Dec. 26, 1871.
Vol. 1, Pt. 1–602
Barker, James Nelson, June 17, 1784–Mar. 9, 1858.
Vol. 1, Pt. 1–603
Barker, James William, Dec. 5, 1815–June 26, 1869.
Vol. 1, Pt. 1–605
Barker, Jeremiah, Mar. 31, 1752–Oct. 4, 1835.
Vol. 1, Pt. 1–605
Barker, Josiah, Nov. 16, 1763–Sept. 23, 1847.
Vol. 1, Pt. 1–606
Barker, Wharton, May 1, 1846–Apr. 8, 1921.
Vol. 1, Pt. 1–606
Barkley, Alben William, Nov. 24, 1877–Apr. 30, 1956.
Supp. 6–34
Barksdale, William, Aug. 21, 1821–July 3, 1863.
Vol. 1, Pt. 1–607
Barlow, Francis Channing, Oct. 19, 1834–Jan. 11, 1896.
Vol. 1, Pt. 1–608
Barlow, Joel, Mar. 24, 1754–Dec. 24, 1812.
Vol. 1, Pt. 1–609
Barlow, John Whitney, June 26, 1838–Feb. 27, 1914.
Vol. 1, Pt. 1–613
Barlow, Samuel Latham Mitchill, June 5, 1826–July 10, 1889.
Vol. 1, Pt. 1–613
Barlowe, Arthur. [*See* Amadas, Philip, fl. 1584–85.]
Barnabee, Henry Clay, Nov. 14, 1833–Dec. 16, 1917.
Vol. 1, Pt. 1–615
Barnard, Charles, Feb. 13, 1838–Apr. 11, 1920.
Vol. 1, Pt. 1–615
Barnard, Charles Francis, Apr. 17, 1808–Nov. 8, 1884.
Vol. 1, Pt. 1–616
Barnard, Chester Irving, Nov. 7, 1886–June 7, 1961.
Supp. 7–29
Barnard, Daniel Dewey, Sept. 11, 1796–Apr. 24, 1861.
Vol. 1, Pt. 1–617
Barnard, Edward Emerson, Dec. 16, 1857–Feb. 6, 1923.
Vol. 1, Pt. 1–617
Barnard, Frederick Augustus Porter, May 5, 1809–Apr 27, 1889.
Vol. 1, Pt. 1–619
Barnard, George Grey, May 24, 1863–Apr. 24, 1938.
Supp. 2–21
Barnard, Henry, Jan. 24, 1811–July 5, 1900.
Vol. 1, Pt. 1–621
Barnard, John, Nov. 6, 1681–Jan. 24, 1770.
Vol. 1, Pt. 1–625
Barnard, John Gross, May 19, 1815–May 14, 1882.
Vol. 1, Pt. 1–626
Barnes, Albert, Dec. 1, 1798–Dec. 24, 1870.
Vol. 1, Pt. 1–627
Barnes, Albert Coombs, Jan. 2, 1872–July 24, 1951.
Supp. 5–38
Barnes, Charles Reid, Sept. 7, 1858–Feb. 24, 1910.
Vol. 1, Pt. 1–629
Barnes, Charlotte Mary Sanford, 1818–Apr. 14, 1863.
Vol. 1, Pt. 1–629
Barnes, James, Dec. 28, 1801–Feb. 12, 1869.
Vol. 1, Pt. 1–630
Barnes, Joseph K., July 21, 1817–Apr. 5, 1883.
Vol. 1, Pt. 1–631
Barnes, Julius Howland, Feb. 2, 1873–Apr. 17, 1959.
Supp. 6–36
Barnes, Mary Downing Sheldon, Sept. 15, 1850–Aug. 27, 1898.
Vol. 1, Pt. 1–632
Barnett, George Ernest, Feb. 19, 1873–June 17, 1938.
Supp. 2–23
Barney, Joshua, July 6, 1759–Dec. 1, 1818.
Vol. 1, Pt. 1–632
Barnum, Frances Courtenay Baylor. [*See* Baylor, Frances Courtenay, 1848–1920.]
Barnum, Henry A., Sept. 24, 1833–Jan. 29, 1892.
Vol. 1, Pt. 1–635
Barnum, Phineas Taylor, July 5, 1810–Apr. 7, 1891.
Vol. 1, Pt. 1–636
Barnum, Zenus, Dec. 9, 1810–Apr. 5, 1865.
Vol. 1, Pt. 1–639
Barnwell, John, *c.* 1671–June 1724.
Vol. 1, Pt. 1–639
Barnwell, Robert Woodward, Aug. 10, 1801–Nov. 5, 1882.
Vol. 1, Pt. 1–640
Baroody, William Joseph, Jan. 29, 1916–July 28, 1980.
Supp. 10–21
Barr, Amelia Edith Huddleston, Mar. 29, 1831–Mar. 10, 1919.
Vol. 1, Pt. 1–641
Barr, Charles, July 11, 1864–Jan. 24, 1911.
Vol. 1, Pt. 1–641
Barradall, Edward, 1704–June 19, 1743.
Vol. 1, Pt. 1–642
Barrell, Joseph, Dec. 15, 1869–May 4, 1919.
Vol. 1, Pt. 1–642
Barrère, Georges, Oct. 31, 1876–June 14, 1944.
Supp. 3–33
Barrett, Albert Moore, July 15, 1871–Apr. 2, 1936.
Supp. 2–24
Barrett, Benjamin Fiske, June 24, 1808–Aug. 6, 1892.
Vol. 1, Pt. 1–644
Barrett, Charles Simon, Jan. 28, 1866–Apr. 4, 1935.
Supp. 1–51
Barrett, Frank Aloysius, Nov. 10, 1892–May 30, 1962.
Supp. 7–30
Barrett, George Horton, June 9, 1794–Sept. 5, 1860.
Vol. 1, Pt. 1–645
Barrett, Janie Porter, Aug. 9, 1865–Aug. 27, 1948.
Supp. 4–53
Barrett, John, Nov. 28, 1866–Oct. 17, 1938.
Barrett, Kate Waller, Jan. 24, 1858–Feb. 23, 1925.
Vol. 1, Pt. 1–645
Barrett, Lawrence, Apr. 4, 1838–Mar. 20, 1891.
Vol. 1, Pt. 1–646
Barrie, Wendy, Apr. 18, 1912–Feb. 2, 1978
Supp. 10–23
Barringer, Daniel Moreau, July 30, 1806–Sept. 1, 1873.
Vol. 1, Pt. 1–648
Barringer, Rufus, Dec. 2, 1821–Feb. 3, 1895.
Vol. 1, Pt. 1–649
Barron, Clarence Walker, July 2, 1855–Oct. 2, 1928.
Supp. 1–52
Barron, James, 1769–Apr. 21, 1851.
Vol. 1, Pt. 1–649
Barron, Samuel, Nov. 28, 1809–Feb. 26, 1888.
Vol. 1, Pt. 1–650
Barrow, Edward Grant, May 10, 1868–Dec. 15, 1953.
Supp. 5–40
Barrow, Washington, Oct. 5, 1817–Oct. 19, 1866.
Vol. 1, Pt. 1–651
Barrows, Alice Prentice, Nov. 15, 1877–Oct. 2, 1954.
Supp. 5–41
Barrows, David Prescott, June 27, 1873–Sept. 5, 1954.
Supp. 5–42
Barrows, John Henry, July 11, 1847–June 3, 1902.
Vol. 1, Pt. 1–651

Barrows, Samuel June, May 26, 1845–Apr. 21, 1909.
Vol. 1, Pt. 1–652
Barry, John, 1745–Sept. 13, 1803.
Vol. 1, Pt. 1–654
Barry, John Stewart, Jan. 29, 1802–Jan. 14, 1870.
Vol. 1, Pt. 1–654
Barry, Patrick, May 24, 1816–June 23, 1890.
Vol. 1, Pt. 1–655
Barry, Philip James Quinn, June 18, 1896–Dec. 3, 1949.
Supp. 4–54
Barry, William Farquhar, Aug. 18, 1818–July 18, 1879.
Vol. 1, Pt. 1–655
Barry, William Taylor, Feb. 5, 1785–Aug. 30, 1835.
Vol. 1, Pt. 1–656
Barry, William Taylor Sullivan, Dec. 10, 1821–Jan. 29, 1868.
Vol. 1, Pt. 1–658
Barrymore, Ethel, Aug. 15, 1879–June 18, 1959.
Supp. 6–38
Barrymore, Georgiana Emma Drew, 1856–July 2, 1893.
Vol. 1, Pt. 1–659
Barrymore, John, Feb. 15, 1882–May 29, 1942.
Supp. 3–34
Barrymore, Lionel, Apr. 28, 1878–Nov. 15, 1954.
Supp. 5–44
Barrymore, Maurice, 1847–Mar. 26, 1905.
Vol. 1, Pt. 1–659
Barsotti, Charles, Jan. 4, 1850–Mar. 30, 1927.
Vol. 1, Pt. 2–l
Barstow, William Augustus, Sept. 13, 1813–Dec. 13, 1865.
Vol. 1, Pt. 2–l
Barth, Alan, Oct. 21, 1906–Nov. 20, 1970.
Supp. 10–24
Barth, Carl Georg Lange, Feb. 28, 1860–Oct. 28, 1939.
Supp. 2–26
Barthelmess, Richard, May 9, 1895–Aug. 17, 1963.
Supp. 7–32
Bartholdt, Richard, Nov. 2, 1855–Mar. 19, 1932.
Supp. 1–53
Bartholomew, Edward Sheffield, July 8, 1822–May 1858.
Vol. 1, Pt. 2–2
Bartholow, Roberts, Nov. 28, 1831–May 10, 1904.
Vol. 1, Pt. 2–2
Bartlet, William, Jan. 31, 1748 N.S.-Feb. 8, 1841.
Vol. 1, Pt. 2–3
Bartlett, Dewey Follett, Mar. 28, 1919–Mar. 1, 1979.
Supp. 10–26
Bartlett, Edward Lewis ("Bob"), Apr. 20, 1904–Dec. 11, 1968.
Supp. 8–25
Bartlett, Elisha, Oct. 6, 1804–July 19, 1855.
Vol. 1, Pt. 2–3
Bartlett, Francis Alonzo, Nov. 13, 1882–Nov. 21, 1963.
Supp. 7–32
Bartlett, Homer Newton, Dec. 28, 1845–Apr. 3, 1920.
Vol. 1, Pt. 2–5
Bartlett, Ichabod, July 24, 1786–Oct. 19, 1853.
Vol. 1, Pt. 2–5
Bartlett, John, June 14, 1820–Dec. 3, 1905.
Vol. 1, Pt. 2–6
Bartlett, John Russell, Oct. 23, 1805–May 28, 1886.
Vol. 1, Pt. 2–7
Bartlett, John Sherren, 1790–Aug. 23, 1863.
Vol. 1, Pt. 2–8
Bartlett, Joseph, June 10, 1762–Oct. 20, 1827.
Vol. 1, Pt. 2–8
Bartlett, Josiah, Nov. 21, 1729–May 19, 1795.
Vol. 1, Pt. 2–9
Bartlett, Paul Wayland, Jan. 24, 1865–Sept. 20, 1925.
Vol. 1, Pt. 2–11
Bartlett, Samuel Colcord, Nov. 25, 1817–Nov. 16, 1898.
Vol. 1, Pt. 2–15
Bartlett, William Holmes Chambers, Sept. 4, 1804–Feb. 11, 1893.
Supp. 1–54
Bartley, Mordecai, Dec. 16, 1783–Oct. 10, 1870.
Vol. 1, Pt. 2–16
Bartol, Cyrus Augustus, Apr. 30, 1813–Dec. 16, 1900.
Vol. 1, Pt. 2–17
Barton, Benjamin Smith, Feb. 10, 1766–Dec. 19, 1815.
Vol. 1, Pt. 2–17
Barton, Bruce Fairchild, Aug. 5, 1886–July 5, 1967.
Supp. 8–26
Barton, Clara, Dec. 25, 1821–Apr. 12, 1912.
Vol. 1, Pt. 2–18
Barton, David, Dec. 14, 1783–Sept. 28, 1837.
Supp. 1–55
Barton, George Aaron, Nov. 12, 1859–June 28, 1942.
Supp. 3–36
Barton, James Edward, Nov. 1, 1890–Feb. 19, 1962.
Supp. 7–33
Barton, James Levi, Sept. 23, 1855–July 21, 1936.
Supp. 2–27
Barton, John Rhea, Apr. 1794–Jan. 1, 1871.
Vol. 1, Pt. 2–21
Barton, Robert Thomas, Nov. 24, 1842–Jan. 17, 1917.
Vol. 1, Pt. 2–22
Barton, Seth Maxwell, Sept. 8, 1829–Apr. 11, 1900.
Vol. 1, Pt. 2–23
Barton, Thomas Pennant, 1803–Apr. 5, 1869.
Vol. 1, Pt. 2–23
Barton, William, May 26, 1748–Oct. 22, 1831.
Vol. 1, Pt. 2–24
Barton, William Eleazar, June 28, 1861–Dec. 7, 1930.
Supp. 1–56
Barton, William Paul Crillon, Nov. 17, 1786–Feb. 29, 1856.
Vol. 1, Pt. 2–25
Bartram, John, Mar. 23, 1699–Sept. 22, 1777.
Vol. 1, Pt. 2–26
Bartram, William, Feb. 9, 1739–July 22, 1823.
Vol. 1, Pt. 2–28
Baruch, Bernard Mannes, Aug. 19, 1870–June 20, 1965.
Supp. 7–34
Baruch, Simon, July 29, 1840–June 3, 1921.
Vol. 1, Pt. 2–29
Barus, Carl, Feb. 19, 1856–Sept. 20, 1935.
Supp. 1–57
Barzynski, Vincent, Sept. 20, 1838–May 2, 1899.
Vol. 1, Pt. 2–30
Bascom, Florence, July 14, 1862–June 18, 1945.
Supp. 3–37
Bascom, Henry Bidleman, May 27, 1796–Sept. 8, 1850.
Vol. 1, Pt. 2–30
Bascom, John, May 1, 1827–Oct. 2, 1911.
Vol. 1, Pt. 2–32
Bashford, Coles, Jan. 24, 1816–Apr. 25, 1878.
Vol. 1, Pt. 2–33
Bashford, James Whitford, May 29, 1849–Mar. 18, 1919.
Vol. 1, Pt. 2–33
Baskerville, Charles, June 18, 1870–Jan. 28, 1922.
Vol. 1, Pt. 2–34
Bass, Edward, Nov. 23, 1726–Sept. 10, 1803.
Vol. 1, Pt. 2–34
Bass, Sam, July 21, 1851–July 21, 1878.
Vol. 1, Pt. 2–35
Bass, William Capers, Jan. 13, 1831–Nov. 15, 1894.
Vol. 1, Pt. 2–36
Basse, Jeremiah, d. 1725.
Vol. 1, Pt. 2–36
Bassett, Edward Murray, Feb. 7, 1863–Oct. 27, 1948.
Supp. 4–55
Bassett, James, Jan. 31, 1834–Mar. 10, 1906.
Vol. 1, Pt. 2–37
Bassett, John Spencer, Sept. 10, 1867–Jan. 27, 1928.
Vol. 1, Pt. 2–38
Bassett, Richard, Apr. 2, 1745–Sept. 15, 1815.
Vol. 1, Pt. 2–39
Bassett, William Hastings, Mar. 7, 1868–July 21, 1934.
Supp. 1–58
Basso, (Joseph) Hamilton, Sept. 5, 1904–May 13, 1964.
Supp. 7–37
Batchelder, John Putnam, Aug. 6, 1784–Apr. 8, 1868.
Vol. 1, Pt. 2–40
Batchelder, Samuel, June 8, 1784–Feb. 5, 1879.
Vol. 1, Pt. 2–40
Batcheller, George Sherman, July 25, 1837–July 2, 1908.
Vol. 1, Pt. 2–41
Batchelor, George, July 3, 1836–June 21, 1923.
Vol. 1 Pt. 2–41
Bate, William Brimage, Oct. 7, 1826–Mar. 9, 1905.
Vol. 1, Pt. 2–42
Bateman, Harry, May 29, 1882–Jan. 21, 1946.
Supp. 4–57

Bateman, Kate Josephine, Oct. 7, 1843–Apr. 8, 1917.
Vol. 1, Pt. 2–43
Bateman, Newton, July 27, 1822–Oct. 21, 1897.
Vol. 1, Pt. 2–44
Bateman, Sidney Frances Cowell, Mar. 29, 1823–Jan. 13, 1881.
Vol. 1, Pt. 2–45
Bates, Arlo, Dec. 16, 1850–Aug. 24, 1918.
Vol. 1, Pt. 2–45
Bates, Barnabas, 1785–Oct. 11, 1853.
Vol. 1, Pt. 2–46
Bates, Blanche, Aug. 5, 1873–Dec. 25, 1941.
Supp. 3–39
Bates, Daniel Moore, Jan. 28, 1821–Mar. 28, 1879.
Vol. 1, Pt. 2–47
Bates, Edward, Sept. 4, 1793–Mar. 25, 1869.
Vol. 1, Pt. 2–48
Bates, Frederick, June 23, 1777–Aug. 4, 1825.
Vol. 1, Pt. 2–49
Bates, George Handy, Nov. 19, 1845–Oct. 31, 1916.
Vol. 1, Pt. 2–50
Bates, James, Sept. 24, 1789–Feb. 25, 1882.
Vol. 1, Pt. 2–51
Bates, John Coalter, Aug. 26, 1842–Feb. 4, 1919.
Vol. 1, Pt. 2–51
Bates, Joshua, Oct. 10, 1788–Sept. 24, 1864.
Vol. 1, Pt. 2–52
Bates, Katharine Lee, Aug. 29, 1859–Mar. 28, 1929.
Supp. 1–59
Bates, Onward, Feb. 24, 1850–Apr. 4, 1936.
Supp. 2–28
Bates, Samuel Penniman, Jan. 29, 1827–July 14, 1902.
Vol. 1, Pt. 2–53
Bates, Theodore Lewis ("Ted"), Sept. 11, 1901–May 30, 1972.
Supp. 9–66
Bates, Walter, Mar. 14, 1760–Feb. 11, 1842.
Vol. 1, Pt. 2–53
Bateson, Gregory, May 9, 1904–July 4, 1980.
Supp. 10–27
Batterson, James Goodwin, Feb. 23, 1823–Sept. 18, 1901.
Vol. 1, Pt. 2–54
Battey, Robert, Nov. 26, 1828–Nov. 8, 1895.
Vol. 1, Pt. 2–55
Battle, Burrell Bunn, July 24, 1838–Dec. 21, 1917.
Vol. 1, Pt. 2–56
Battle, Cullen Andrews, June 1, 1829–Apr. 8, 1905.
Vol. 1, Pt. 2–56
Battle, John Stewart, July 11, 1890–Apr. 9, 1972.
Supp. 9–67
Battle, Kemp Plummer, Dec. 19, 1831–Feb. 4, 1919.
Vol. 1, Pt. 2–57
Battle, William Horn, Oct. 17, 1802–Mar. 14, 1879.
Vol. 1, Pt. 2–58
Batts, Robert Lynn, Nov. 1, 1864–May 19, 1935.
Supp. 1–60
Bauer, Harold Victor, Apr. 28, 1873–Mar. 12, 1951.
Supp. 5–45
Bauer, Louis Agricola, Jan. 26, 1865–Apr. 12, 1932.
Supp. 1–40
Baugher, Henry Louis, July 18, 1804–Apr. 14, 1868.
Vol. 1, Pt. 2–58
Baum, Hedwig ("Vicki"), Jan. 24, 1888–Aug. 29, 1960.
Supp. 6–39
Baum, Lyman Frank, May 15, 1856–May 6, 1919.
Vol. 1, Pt. 2–59
Bausch, Edward, Sept. 26, 1854–July 30, 1944.
Supp. 3–40
Bausman, Benjamin, Jan. 28, 1824–May 8, 1909.
Vol. 1, Pt. 2–60
Baxley, Henry Willis, June 1803–Mar. 13, 1876.
Vol. 1, Pt. 2–60
Baxter, Elisha, Sept. 1, 1827–May 31, 1899.
Vol. 1 Pt. 2–61
Baxter, Henry, Sept. 8, 1821–Dec. 30, 1873.
Vol. 1, Pt. 2–62
Baxter, John, Mar. 5, 1819–Apr. 2, 1886.
Vol. 1, Pt. 2–63
Baxter, William, July 6, 1820–Feb. 11, 1880.
Vol. 1, Pt. 2–63
Bayard, James Ash(e)ton, July 28, 1767–Aug. 6, 1815.
Vol. 1, Pt. 2–64
Bayard, James Asheton, Nov. 15, 1799–June 13, 1880.
Vol. 1, Pt. 2–66
Bayard, John Bubenheim, Aug. 11, 1738–Jan. 7, 1807.
Vol. 1, Pt. 2–47
Bayard, Nicholas, 1644–1707.
Vol. 1, Pt. 2–68
Bayard, Richard Henry, Sept. 26, 1796–Mar. 4, 1868.
Vol. 1, Pt. 2–69
Bayard, Samuel, Jan. 11, 1767–May 11, 1840.
Vol. 1, Pt. 2–69
Bayard, Thomas Francis, Oct. 29, 1828–Sept. 28, 1898.
Vol. 1, Pt. 2–70
Bayard, William, 1761–Sept. 18, 1826.
Vol. 1, Pt. 2–72
Bayh, Marvella Belle Hern, Feb. 14, 1933–Apr. 24, 1979.
Supp. 10–29
Bayles, James Copper, July 3, 1845–May 7, 1913.
Vol. 1, Pt. 2–73
Bayley, James Roosevelt, Aug. 23, 1814–Oct. 3, 1877.
Vol. 1, Pt. 2–73
Bayley, Richard, 1745–Aug. 17, 1801.
Vol. 1, Pt. 2–74
Baylies, Francis, Oct. 16, 1783–Oct. 28, 1852.
Vol. 1, Pt. 2–75
Baylor, Frances Courtenay, Jan. 20, 1848–Oct. 19, 1920.
Vol. 1, Pt. 2–76
Baylor, George, Jan. 12, 1752–March 1784.
Vol. 1, Pt. 2–76
Baylor, Robert Emmet Bledsoe, May 10, 1793?-Dec. 30, 1873.
Vol. 1, Pt. 2–77
Bayly, Thomas Henry, Dec. 11, 1810–June 22, 1856.
Vol. 1, Pt. 2–78
Bayma, Joseph, Nov. 9, 1816–Feb. 7, 1892.
Vol. 1, Pt. 2–79
Baynham, William, Dec. 7, 1749–Dec. 8, 1814.
Vol. 1, Pt. 2–80
Bazett, Henry Cuthbert, June 25, 1885–July 12, 1950.
Supp. 4–58
Baziotes, William, June 11, 1912–June 5, 1963.
Supp. 7–39
Beach, Alfred Ely, Sept. 1, 1826–Jan. 1, 1896.
Vol. 1, Pt. 2–80
Beach, Amy Marcy Cheney, Sept. 5, 1867–Dec. 27, 1944.
Supp. 3–41
Beach, Frederick Converse, Mar. 27, 1848–June 18, 1918.
Vol. 1, Pt. 2–81
Beach, Harlan Page, Apr. 4, 1854–Mar. 4, 1933.
Supp. 1–62
Beach, Moses Sperry, Oct. 5, 1822–July 25, 1892.
Vol. 1, Pt. 2–81
Beach, Moses Yale, Jan. 15, 1800–July 19, 1868.
Vol. 1, Pt. 2–82
Beach, Mrs. H. H. A. [*See* Beach, Amy Marcy Cheney.]
Beach, Rex, Sept. 1, 1877–Dec. 7, 1949.
Supp 4–59
Beach, Sylvia Woodbridge, Mar. 14, 1887–Oct. 4 or 5, 1962.
Supp. 7–40
Beach, William Augustus, Dec. 9, 1809–June 21, 1884.
Vol. 1, Pt. 2–84
Beach, Wooster, 1794–Jan. 28, 1868.
Vol. 1 Pt. 2–85
Beadle, Erastus Flavel, Sept. 11, 1821–Dec. 18, 1894.
Supp. 1–63
Beadle, William Henry Harrison, Jan. 1, 1838–Nov. 13, 1915.
Vol. 1, Pt. 2–86
Beal, William James, Mar. 11, 1833–May 12, 1924.
Vol. 1, Pt. 2–87
Beale, Edward Fitzgerald, Feb. 4, 1822–Apr. 22, 1893.
Vol. 1, Pt. 2–88
Beale, Joseph Henry, Oct. 12, 1861–Jan. 20, 1943.
Beale, Richard Lee Turberville, May 22, 1819–Apr. 21, 1893.
Vol. 1, Pt. 2–89
Beall, James Glenn, June 5, 1894–Jan. 14, 1971.
Supp. 9–68
Beall, John Yates, Jan. 1, 1835–Feb. 24, 1865.
Vol. 1, Pt. 2–89
Beall, Samuel Wootton, Sept. 26, 1807–Sept. 26, 1868.
Vol. 1, Pt. 2–90
Beals, Ralph Albert, Mar. 29, 1899–Oct. 14, 1954.
Supp. 5–46
Beaman, Charles Cotesworth, May 7, 1840–Dec. 15, 1900.
Vol. 1, Pt. 2–91

Bean, Leon Lenwood, Nov. 13, 1872–Feb. 5, 1967.
Supp. 8–28
Bean, Tarleton Hoffman, Oct. 8, 1846–Dec. 28, 1916.
Vol. 1, Pt. 2–92
Beard, Charles Austin, Nov. 27, 1874–Sept. 1, 1948.
Supp. 4–61
Beard, Daniel Carter, June 21, 1850–June 11, 1941.
Supp. 3–44
Beard, George Miller, May 8, 1839–Jan. 23, 1883.
Vol. 1, Pt. 2–92
Beard, James Carter, June 6, 1837–Nov. 15, 1913.
Vol. 1, Pt. 2–93
Beard, James Henry, May 20, 1812–Apr. 4, 1893.
Vol. 1, Pt. 2–94
Beard, Mary, Nov. 14, 1876–Dec. 4, 1946.
Supp. 4–64
Beard, Mary Ritter, Aug. 5, 1876–Aug. 14, 1958.
Supp. 6–40
Beard, Richard, Nov. 27, 1799–Dec. 2, 1880.
Vol. 1, Pt. 2–94
Beard, Thomas Francis, Feb. 6, 1842–Sept. 28, 1905.
Vol. 1, Pt. 2–95
Beard, William Holbrook, Apr. 13, 1824–Feb. 20, 1900.
Vol. 1, Pt. 2–95
Beardshear, William Miller, Nov. 7, 1850–Aug. 5, 1902.
Vol. 1, Pt. 2–96
Beardsley, Eben Edwards, Jan. 8, 1808–Dec. 21, 1891.
Vol. 1, Pt. 2–96
Beardsley, Samuel, Feb. 6, 1790–May 6, 1860.
Vol. 1, Pt. 2–97
Beary, Donald Bradford, Dec. 4, 1888–Mar. 7, 1966.
Supp. 8–29
Beasley, Frederick, 1777–Nov. 1, 1845.
Vol. 1, Pt. 2–98
Beasley, Mercer, Mar. 27, 1815–Feb. 19, 1897.
Vol. 1, Pt. 2–98
Beattie, Francis Robert, Mar. 31, 1848–Sept. 3, 1906.
Vol. 1, Pt. 2–99
Beatty, Adam, May 10, 1777–June 9, 1858.
Vol. 1 Pt. 2–99
Beatty, Charles Clinton, *c.* 1715–Aug. 13, 1772.
Vol. 1, Pt. 2–109
Beatty, Clyde Raymond, June 10, 1903–July 19, 1965.
Supp. 7–41
Beatty, John, Dec. 19, 1749–Apr. 30, 1826.
Vol. 1, Pt. 2–100
Beatty, John, Dec. 16, 1828–Dec. 21, 1914.
Vol. 1, Pt. 2–101
Beatty, Willard Walcott, Sept. 17, 1891–Sept. 29, 1961.
Supp. 7–42
Beatty, William Henry, Feb. 18, 1838–Aug. 4, 1914.
Vol. 1, Pt. 2–102
Beaty, Amos Leonidas, Sept. 1, 1870–Apr. 29, 1939.
Supp. 2–29
Beauchamp, William, Apr. 26, 1772–Oct. 7, 1824.
Vol. 1, Pt. 2–102
Beauchamp, William Martin, Mar. 25, 1830–Dec. 13, 1925.
Vol. 1, Pt. 2–103
Beaumont, John Colt, Aug. 27, 1821–Aug. 2, 1882.
Vol. 1, Pt. 2–104
Beaumont, William, Nov. 21, 1785–Apr. 25, 1853.
Vol. 1, Pt. 2–104
Beaupré, Arthur Matthias, July 29, 1853–Sept. 13, 1919.
Vol. 1, Pt. 2–110
Beauregard, Pierre Gustave Toutant, May 28, 1818–Feb. 20, 1893.
Vol. 1, Pt. 2–111
Beaux, Cecilia, May 1, 1855–Sept. 17, 1942.
Supp. 3–45
Beaver, James Addams, Oct. 21, 1837–Jan. 31, 1914.
Vol. 1, Pt. 2–112
Beavers, Louise, Mar. 8, 1902–Oct. 26, 1962.
Supp. 7–43
Bechet, Sidney, May 14, 1897–May 14, 1959.
Supp. 6–42
Beck, Carl, Apr. 4, 1856–June 9, 1911.
Vol. 1, Pt. 2–113
Beck, Charies, Aug. 19, 1798–Mar. 19, 1866.
Vol. 1, Pt. 2–113
Beck, James Montgomery, July 9, 1861–Apr. 12, 1936.
Supp. 2–30
Beck, Johann Heinrich, Sept. 12, 1856–May 25, 1924.
Vol. 1, Pt. 2–114
Beck, John Brodhead, Sept. 18, 1794–Apr. 9, 1851.
Vol. 1, Pt. 2–115
Beck, Lewis Caleb, Oct. 4, 1798–Apr. 20, 1853.
Vol. 1, Pt. 2–116
Beck, Martin, July 30, 1867–Nov. 16, 1940.
Supp. 2–32
Beck, Theodric Romeyn, Aug. 11, 1791–Nov. 19, 1855.
Vol. 1, Pt. 2–116
Becker, George Ferdinand, Jan. 5, 1847–Apr. 20, 1919.
Vol. 1, Pt. 2–117
Becket, Frederick Mark, Jan. 11, 1875–Dec. 1, 1942.
Supp. 3–48
Becknell, William, *c.* 1790–*c.* 1832.
Vol. 1, Pt. 2–119
Beckwith, Clarence Augustine, July 21, 1849–Apr. 2, 1931.
Supp. 164
Beckwith, James Carroll, Sept. 23, 1852–Oct. 24, 1917.
Vol. 1, Pt. 2–120
Beckwourth, James P., Apr. 26, 1798–*c.* 1867.
Vol. 1, Pt. 2–122
Bedaux, Charles Eugene, Oct. 11, 1886–Feb. 18, 1944.
Supp. 3–49
Bedford, Gunning, Apr. 7, 1742–September 1797.
Vol. 1, Pt. 2–122
Bedford, Gunning, 1747–Mar. 30, 1812.
Vol. 1, Pt. 2–123
Bedinger, George Michael, Dec. 10, 1756–Dec. 8, 1843.
Vol. 1, Pt. 2–124
Bee, Barnard Elliott, Feb. or Mar. 1824–July 22, 1861.
Vol. 1, Pt. 2–124
Bee, Hamilton Prioleau, July 22, 1822–Oct. 2, 1897.
Vol. 1, Pt. 2–125
Beebe, (Charles) William, July 29, 1877–June 4, 1962.
Supp. 7–45
Beecher, Catharine Esther, Sept. 6, 1800–May 12, 1878.
Vol. 1, Pt. 2–125
Beecher, Charles, Oct. 7, 1815–Apr. 21, 1900.
Vol. 1, Pt. 2–126
Beecher, Charles Emerson, Oct. 9, 1856–Feb. 14, 1904.
Vol. 1, Pt. 2–127
Beecher, Edward, Aug. 27, 1803–July 28, 1895.
Vol. 1, Pt. 2–128
Beecher, Henry Ward, June 24, 1813–Mar. 8, 1887.
Vol. 1, Pt. 2–129
Beecher, Lyman, Oct. 12, 1775–Jan. 10, 1863.
Vol. 1, Pt. 2–135
Beecher, Thomas Kinnicut, Feb. 10, 1824–Mar. 14, 1900.
Vol. 1, Pt. 2–136
Beer, George Louis, July 26, 1872–Mar. 15, 1920.
Vol. 1, Pt. 2–137
Beer, Thomas, Nov. 22, 1889–Apr. 18, 1940.
Supp. 2–33
Beer, William, May 1, 1849–Feb. 1, 1927.
Vol. 1, Pt. 2–138
Beers, Clifford Whittingham, Mar. 30, 1876–July 9, 1943.
Supp. 3–50
Beers, Ethel Lynn, Jan. 13, 1827–Oct. 11, 1879.
Vol. 1, Pt. 2–139
Beers, Henry Augustin, Jan. 2, 1847–Sept. 7, 1926.
Vol. 1, Pt. 2–139
Beery, Wallace Fitzgerald, Apr. 1, 1885–Apr. 15, 1949.
Supp. 4–66
Beeson, Charles Henry, Oct. 2, 1870–Dec. 26, 1949.
Supp. 4–67
Begley, Edward James ("Ed"), Mar. 25, 1901–Apr. 28, 1970
Supp. 8–31
Behan, William James, Sept. 25, 1840–May 4, 1928.
Vol. 1, Pt. 2–140
Behn, Sosthenes, Jan. 30, 1882–June 6, 1957.
Supp. 6–43
Behrend, Bernard Arthur, May 9, 1875–Mar. 25, 1932.
Supp. 1–65
Behrends, Adolphus Julius Frederick, Dec. 18, 1839–May 22 1900.
Vol. 1, Pt. 2–141
Behrendt, Walter Curt, Dec. 16, 1884–Apr. 26, 1945.
Supp. 3–52
Behrens, Henry, Dec. 10, 1815–Oct. 17, 1895.
Vol. 1, Pt. 2–141

Behrman, Samuel Nathaniel, ("S. N."), 1893–Sept. 9, 1973.
Supp. 9–70
Beissel, Johann Conrad, April 1690–July 6, 1768.
Vol. 1, Pt. 2–142
Békésy, Georg von, June 3, 1899–June 13, 1972.
Supp. 9–71
Belasco, David, July 25, 1853–May 14, 1931.
Supp. 1–66
Belcher, Jonathan, Jan. 8, 1681/2–Aug. 31, 1757.
Vol. 1, Pt. 2–143
Belcourt, George Antoine, Apr. 22, 1803–May 31, 1874.
Vol. 1, Pt. 2–145
Belden, Josiah, May 4, 1815–Apr. 23, 1892.
Vol. 1, Pt. 2–145
Belkin, Samuel, Dec. 12, 1911–Apr. 18, 1976.
Supp. 10–30
Belknap, George Eugene, Jan. 22, 1832–Apr. 7, 1903.
Vol. 1, Pt. 2–146
Belknap, Jeremy, June 4, 1744–June 20, 1798.
Vol. 1, Pt. 2–147
Belknap, William Worth, Sept. 22, 1829–Oct. 13, 1890.
Vol. 1, Pt. 2–147
Bell, Alexander Graham, Mar. 3, 1847–Aug. 2, 1922.
Vol. 1, Pt. 2–148
Bell, Alexander Melville, Mar. 1, 1819–Aug. 7, 1905.
Vol. 1, Pt. 2–152
Bell, Bernard Iddings, Oct. 13, 1886–Sept. 5, 1958.
Supp. 6–45
Bell, Charles Henry, Nov. 18, 1823–Nov. 11, 1893.
Vol. 1, Pt. 2–153
Bell, Clark, Mar. 12, 1832–Feb. 22, 1918.
Vol. 1, Pt. 2–153
Bell, De Benneville ("Bert"), Feb. 25, 1894–Oct. 11, 1959.
Supp. 6–47
Bell, Eric Temple, Feb. 7, 1883–Dec. 21, 1960.
Supp. 6–48
Bell, Frederic Somers, Mar. 19, 1859–Mar. 13, 1938.
Supp. 2–34
Bell, Henry Haywood, Apr. 13, 1808–Jan. 11, 1868.
Vol. 1, Pt. 2–154
Bell, Isaac, Nov. 6, 1846–Jan. 20, 1889.
Vol. 1, Pt. 2–155
Bell, Jacob, Dec. 17, 1792–July 21, 1852.
Vol. 1, Pt. 2–155
Bell, James Ford, Aug. 16, 1879–May 7, 1961.
Supp. 7–46
Bell, James Franklin, Jan. 9, 1856–Jan. 8, 1919.
Supp. 1–67
Bell, James Madison, Apr. 3, 1826–1902.
Vol. 1, Pt. 2–156
Bell, James Stroud, June 30, 1847–Apr. 5, 1915.
Vol. 1, Pt. 2–156
Bell, John, Feb. 15, 1797–Sept. 10, 1869.
Vol. 1, Pt. 2–157
Bell, Lawrence Dale, Apr. 5, 1894–Oct. 20, 1956.
Supp. 6–49
Bell, Louis, Dec. 5, 1864–June 14, 1923.
Vol. 1, Pt. 2–159
Bell, Luther Vose, Dec. 20, 1806–Feb, 11, 1862.
Vol. 1, Pt. 2–160
Bell, Peter Hansborough, Mar. 11, 1808–Mar. 8, 1898.
Vol. 1, Pt. 2–160
Bell, Robert, *c.* 1732–Sept. 23, 1784.
Vol. 1, Pt. 2–161
Bell, Samuel, Feb. 8, 1770–Dec. 23, 1850.
Vol. 1, Pt. 2–162
Bellamy, Edward, Mar. 26, 1850–May 22, 1898.
Vol. 1, Pt. 2–163
Bellamy, Elizabeth Whitfield Croom, Apr. 17, 1837–Apr. 13, 1900.
Vol. 1, Pt. 2–164
Bellamy, Joseph, Feb. 20, 1719–Mar. 6, 1790.
Vol. 1, Pt. 2–165
Bellanca, Dorothy Jacobs, Aug. 10, 1894–Aug. 16, 1946.
Supp. 4–69
Bellanca, Giuseppe Mario, Mar. 19, 1886–Dec. 26, 1960.
Supp. 6–51
Bellew, Frank Henry Temple, Apr. 18, 1828–June 29, 1888.
Vol. 1, Pt. 2–165
Bellingham, Richard, *c.* 1592–Dec. 7, 1672.
Vol. 1, Pt. 2–166
Bellomont, Earl of. [*See* Coote, Richard, 1636–1701.]
Bellows, Albert Fitch, Nov. 29, 1829–Nov. 24, 1883.
Vol. 1, Pt. 2–167
Bellows, George Wesley, Aug. 12, 1882–Jan. 8, 1925.
Vol. 1, Pt. 2–167
Bellows, Henry Whitney, June 11, 1814–Jan. 30, 1882.
Vol. 1, Pt. 2–169
Belmont, Alva Ertskin Smith Vanderbilt, Jan. 17, 1853–Jan. 26, 1933.
Supp. 1–68
Belmont, August, Dec. 2, 1816–Nov. 24, 1890.
Vol. 1, Pt. 2–169
Belo, Alfred Horatio, May 27, 1839–Apr. 19, 1901.
Vol. 1, Pt. 2–170
Beman, Nathan Sidney Smith, Nov. 26, 1785–Aug. 6, 1871.
Vol. 1, Pt. 2–171
Bemelmans, Ludwig, Apr. 27, 1898–Oct. 1, 1962.
Supp. 7–47
Bement, Caleb N., 1790–Dec. 22, 1868.
Vol. 1, Pt. 2–172
Bement, Clarence Sweet, Apr. 11, 1843–Jan. 27, 1923.
Vol. 1, Pt. 2–173
Bemis, George, Oct. 13, 1816–Jan. 5, 1878.
Vol. 1, Pt. 2–173
Bemis, Harold Edward, June 3, 1883–Apr. 4, 1931.
Supp. 1–69
Bemis, Samuel Flagg, Oct. 20, 1891–Sept. 26, 1973.
Supp. 9–72
Benavides, Alonzo de, fl. 1600–1664.
Vol. 1, Pt. 2–174
Benbridge, Henry, May 20, 1774–February 1812.
Vol. 1, Pt. 2–175
Benchley, Robert Charles, Sept. 15, 1889–Nov. 21, 1945.
Supp. 3–53
Bender, Charles Albert ("Chief"), May 5, 1883–May 22, 1954.
Supp. 5–47
Bender, George Harrison, Sept. 29, 1896–June 17 or 18, 1961.
Supp. 7–49
Bendix, Vincent, Aug. 12, 1881–Mar. 27, 1945.
Supp. 3–54
Benedict, David, Oct. 10, 1779–Dec. 5, 1874.
Vol. 1, Pt. 2–176
Benedict, Erastus Cornelius, Mar. 19, 1800–Oct. 22, 1880.
Vol. 1, Pt. 2–176
Benedict, Ruth Fulton, June 5, 1887–Sept. 17, 1948.
Supp. 4–70
Benedict, Stanley Rossiter, Mar. 17, 1884–Dec. 21, 1936.
Supp. 2–35
Benét, Stephen Vincent, July 22, 1898–Mar. 13, 1943.
Supp. 3–56
Benét, William Rose, Feb. 2, 1886–May 4, 1950.
Supp. 4–73
Benezet, Anthony, Jan. 31, 1713–May 3, 1784.
Vol. 1, Pt. 2–177
Benham, Henry Washington, Apr. 8, 1813–June 1, 1884.
Vol. 1, Pt. 2–178
Benjamin, Asher, June 15, 1773–July 26, 1845.
Vol. 1, Pt. 2–179
Benjamin, George Hillard, Dec. 25, 1852–Nov. 10, 1927.
Vol. 1, Pt. 2–180
Benjamin, Judah Philip, Aug. 6, 1811–May 6, 1884.
Vol. 1, Pt. 2–181
Benjamin, Nathan, Dec. 14, 1811–Jan. 27, 1855.
Vol. 1, Pt. 2–186
Benjamin, Park, Aug. 14, 1809–Sept. 12, 1864.
Vol. 1, Pt. 2–187
Benjamin, Park, May 11, 1849–Aug. 21, 1922.
Vol. 1, Pt. 2–188
Benjamin, Samuel Greene Wheeler, Feb. 13, 1837–July 19, 1914.
Vol. 1, Pt. 2–189
Benner, Philip, May 19, 1762–July 27, 1832.
Vol. 1, Pt. 2–189
Bennet, Sanford Fillmore, June 21, 1836–June 11, 1898.
Vol. 1, Pt. 2–190
Bennett, Caleb Prew, Nov. 11, 1758–May 9, 1836.
Vol. 1, Pt. 2–190
Bennett, Charles Edwin, Apr. 6, 1858–May 2, 1921.
Vol. 1, Pt. 2–191
Bennett, Constance Campbell, Oct. 22, 1904–July 25, 1965.
Supp. 7–50

Bennett, de Robigne Mortimer, Dec. 23, 1818–Dec. 6, 1882.
Vol. 1, Pt. 2–192
Bennett, Earl W., Jan. 18, 1880–Sept. 18, 1973.
Supp. 9–74
Bennett, Edmund Hatch, Apr. 6, 1824–Jan. 2, 1898.
Vol. 1, Pt. 2–193
Bennett, Emerson, Mar. 16, 1822–May 11, 1905.
Vol. 1, Pt. 2–193
Bennett, Floyd, Oct. 25, 1890–Apr. 25, 1928.
Vol. 1, Pt. 2–194
Bennett, Henry Garland, Dec. 14, 1886–Dec. 22, 1951.
Supp. 5–48
Bennett, Hugh Hammond, Apr. 15, 1881–July 7, 1960.
Supp. 6–52
Bennett, James Gordon, 1795–June 1, 1872.
Vol. 1, Pt. 2–195
Bennett, James Gordon, May 10, 1841–May 14, 1918.
Vol. 1, Pt. 2–199
Bennett, Nathaniel, June 27, 1818–Apr. 20, 1886.
Vol. 1, Pt. 2–202
Bennett, Richard, May 21, 1870–Oct. 22, 1944.
Supp. 3–58
Benning, Henry Lewis, Apr. 2, 1814–July 10, 1875.
Vol. 1, Pt. 2–202
Benny, Jack, Feb. 14, 1894–Dec. 26, 1974.
Supp. 9–75
Bensley, Robert Russell, Nov. 13, 1867–June 11, 1956.
Supp. 6–53
Benson, Egbert, June 21, 1746–Aug. 24, 1833.
Vol. 1, Pt. 2–204
Benson, Eugene, Nov. 1, 1839–Feb. 28, 1908.
Vol. 1, Pt. 2–204
Benson, Frank Weston, Mar. 24, 1862–Nov. 14, 1951.
Supp. 5–49
Benson, Oscar Herman, July 8, 1875–Aug. 15, 1951.
Supp. 5–50
Benson, Sally, Sept. 3, 1900–July 19, 1972.
Supp. 9–77
Benson, William Shepherd, Sept. 25, 1855–May 20, 1932.
Supp. 1–70
Bent, Charles, Nov. 11, 1799–Jan. 19, 1847.
Vol. 1, Pt. 2–205
Bent, Josiah, Apr. 26, 1771–Apr. 26, 1836.
Vol. 1 Pt. 2–205
Bent, Silas, Oct. 10, 1820–Aug. 26, 1887.
Vol. 1, Pt. 2–206
Bent, Silas, May 9, 1882–July 30, 1945.
Supp. 3–59
Bent, William, May 23, 1809–May 19, 1869.
Vol. 1, Pt. 2–206
Bentley, Arthur Fisher, Oct. 16, 1870–May 21, 1957.
Supp. 6–54
Bentley, Elizabeth Terrill, Jan. 1, 1908–Dec. 3, 1963.
Supp. 7–51
Bentley, William, June 22, 1759–Dec. 29, 1819.
Vol. 1, Pt. 2–207
Bentley, Wilson Alwyn, Feb. 9, 1865–Dec. 23, 1931.
Supp. 1–71
Benton, Allen Richardson, Oct. 1, 1822–Jan. 1, 1914.
Vol. 1, Pt. 2–208
Benton, James Gilchrist, Sept. 15, 1820–Aug. 23, 1881.
Vol. 1, Pt. 2–208
Benton, Joel, May 29, 1832–Sept. 15, 1911.
Vol. 1, Pt. 2–209
Benton, Josiah Henry, Aug. 4, 1843–Feb. 6, 1917.
Vol. 1, Pt. 2–210
Benton, Thomas Hart, Mar. 14, 1782–Apr. 10, 1858.
Vol. 1, Pt. 2–210
Benton, Thomas Hart, Sept. 5, 1816–Apr. 10, 1879.
Vol. 1, Pt. 2–213
Benton, Thomas Hart, Apr. 15, 1889–Jan. 19, 1975.
Supp. 9–78
Benton, William Burnett, Apr. 1, 1900–Mar. 18, 1973.
Supp. 9–80
Berenson, Bernard, June 26, 1865–Oct. 6, 1959.
Supp. 6–55
Berenson, Senda, Mar. 19, 1868–Feb. 16, 1954.
Supp. 5–51
Berg, Gertrude Edelstein, Oct. 3, 1899–Sept. 14, 1966.
Supp. 8–32
Berg, Joseph Frederic, June 3, 1812–July 20, 1871.
Vol. 1, Pt. 2–213
Berg, Morris ("Moe"), Mar. 2, 1902–May 30, 1972.
Supp. 9–81
Bergen, Edgar, Feb. 16, 1903–Oct. 1, 1978.
Supp. 10–32
Berger, Daniel, Feb. 14, 1832–Sept. 12, 1920.
Vol. 1, Pt. 2–214
Berger, Meyer, Sept. 1, 1898–Feb. 8, 1959.
Supp. 6–57
Berger, Victor Louis, Feb. 28, 1860–Aug. 7, 1929.
Supp. 1–72
Bergh, Christian, Apr. 30, 1763–June 24, 1843.
Vol. 1, Pt. 2–214
Bergh, Henry, Aug. 29, 1811–Mar. 12, 1888.
Vol. 1, Pt. 2–215
Bergmann, Carl, Apr. 11, 1821–Aug. 10, 1876.
Vol. 1, Pt. 2–216
Bergmann, Max, Feb. 12, 1886–Nov. 7, 1944.
Supp. 3–60
Berkeley, Busby, Nov. 29, 1895–Mar. 14, 1976.
Supp. 10–33
Berkeley, John, d. Mar. 22, 1622.
Vol. 1, Pt. 2–217
Berkeley, Norborne. [*See* Botetourt, Norborne Berkeley, Baron de, *c.* 1718–1770.]
Berkeley, Sir William, 1606–July 9, 1677.
Vol. 1, Pt. 2–217
Berkenmeyer, Wilhelm Christoph, 1686–1751.
Vol. 1, Pt. 2–218
Berkman, Alexander, Nov. 21, 1870–June 28, 1936.
Supp. 2–36
Berkowitz, Henry, Mar. 18, 1857–Feb. 7, 1924.
Vol. 1, Pt. 2–219
Berle, Adolf Augustus, Jr., Jan. 29, 1895–Feb. 17, 1971.
Supp. 9–83
Berliner, Emile, May 20, 1851–Aug. 3, 1929.
Supp. 1–75
Bermudez, Edouard Edmond, Jan. 19, 1832–Aug. 22, 1892.
Vol. 1, Pt. 2–220
Bernard, Bayle. [*See* Bernard, William Bayle, 1807–1875.]
Bernard, Sir Francis, July ?, 1712–June 16, 1779.
Vol. 1, Pt. 2–221
Bernard, John, 1756–Nov. 29, 1828.
Vol. 1, Pt. 2–222
Bernard, Simon, Apr. 22, 1779–Nov. 5, 1839.
Vol. 1, Pt. 2–223
Bernard, William Bayle, Nov. 27, 1807–Aug. 5, 1875.
Vol. 1, Pt. 2–223
Bernays, Augustus Charles, Oct. 13, 1854–May 22, 1907.
Vol. 1, Pt. 2–224
Bernet, John Joseph, Feb. 9, 1868–July 5, 1935.
Supp. 1–76
Bernstein, Aline, Dec. 22, 1882–Sept. 7, 1955.
Supp. 5–52
Bernstein, Herman, Sept. 21, 1876–Aug. 31, 1935.
Supp. 1–77
Bernstein, Theodore Menline, Nov. 17, 1904–June 27, 1979.
Supp. 10–35
Berrien, John Macpherson, Aug. 23, 1781–Jan. 1, 1856.
Vol. 1, Pt. 2–225
Berry, Edward Wilber, Feb. 10, 1875–Sept. 20, 1945.
Supp. 3–61
Berry, George Leonard, Sept. 12, 1882–Dec. 4, 1948.
Supp. 4–74
Berry, Hiram Gregory, Aug. 27, 1824–May 3, 1863.
Vol. 1, Pt. 2–226
Berry, James Henderson, May 15, 1841–Jan. 30, 1913.
Vol. 1, Pt. 2–226
Berry, Martha McChesney, Oct. 7, 1866–Feb. 27, 1942.
Supp. 3–62
Berry, Nathaniel Springer, Sept. 1, 1796–Apr. 27, 1894.
Vol. 1, Pt. 2–227
Berryman, Clifford Kennedy, Apr. 2, 1869–Dec. 11, 1949.
Supp. 4–75
Berryman, John, Oct. 25, 1914–Jan. 7, 1972.
Supp. 9–85
Bertram, John, Feb. 11, 1796–Mar. 22, 1882.
Vol. 1, Pt. 2–228
Berwind, Edward Julius, June 17, 1848–Aug. 18, 1936.
Supp. 2–37

Besse, Arthur Lyman, Apr. 13, 1887–Nov. 24, 1951.
Supp. 5–54
Bessey, Charles Edwin, May 21, 1845–Feb. 25, 1915.
Vol. 1, Pt. 2–229
Bestor, Arthur Eugene, May 19, 1879–Feb. 3, 1944.
Supp. 3–64
Bethune, George Washington, Mar. 18, 1805–Apr. 28, 1862.
Vol. 1, Pt. 2–229
Bethune, Mary McLeod, July 10, 1875–May 18, 1955.
Supp. 5–55
Bettendorf, William Peter, July 1, 1857–June 3, 1910.
Vol. 1, Pt. 2–230
Bettman, Alfred, Aug. 26, 1873–Jan. 21, 1945.
Supp. 3–65
Betts, Samuel Rossiter, June 8, 1786–Nov. 3, 1868.
Vol. 1, Pt. 2–231
Bevan, Arthur Dean, Aug. 9, 1861–June 10, 1943.
Supp. 3–67
Beveridge, Albert Jeremiah, Oct. 6, 1862–Apr. 27, 1927.
Vol. 1, Pt. 2–231
Beverley, Robert, *c.* 1673–1722.
Vol. 1, Pt. 2–233
Bevier, Isabel, Nov. 14, 1860–Mar. 17, 1942.
Supp. 3–67
Bewley, Anthony, May 22, 1804–Sept. 13, 1860.
Vol. 1, Pt. 2–233
Biard, Pierre, *c.* 1567–Nov. 17, 1622.
Vol. 1, Pt. 2–234
Bibb, George Mortlmer, Oct. 30, 1776–Apr. 14, 1859.
Vol. 1, Pt. 2–235
Bibb, William Wyatt, Oct. 2, 1781–July 10, 1820.
Vol. 1, Pt. 2–235
Bible, Dana Xenophon, Oct. 8, 1891–Jan. 19, 1980.
Supp. 10–37
Bickel, Alexander Mordecai, Dec. 17, 1924–Nov. 7, 1974.
Supp. 9–87
Bickel, Karl August, Jan. 20, 1882–Dec. 11, 1972.
Supp. 9–89
Bickel, Luke Washington, Sept. 21, 1866–May 11, 1917.
Vol. 1, Pt. 2–236
Bickerdyke, Mary Ann Ball, July 19, 1817–Nov. 8, 1901.
Vol. 1, Pt. 2–237
Bickett, Thomas Walter, Feb. 28, 1869–Dec. 28, 1921.
Vol. 1, Pt. 2–238
Bickmore, Albert Smith, Mar. 1, 1839–Aug. 12, 1914.
Vol. 1, Pt. 2–238
Bidaga. [*See* Son of Many Beads, 1866–1954.]
Biddle, Anthony Joseph Drexel, Jr., Dec. 17, 1896–Nov. 13, 1961.
Supp. 7–52
Biddle, Clement, May 10, 1740–July 14, 1814.
Vol. 1, Pt. 2–239
Biddle, Francis Beverley, May 9, 1886–Oct. 4, 1968.
Supp. 8–34
Biddle, George, Jan. 24, 1885–Nov. 6, 1973.
Supp. 9–91
Biddle, Horace P., Mar. 24, 1811–May 13, 1900.
Vol. 1, Pt. 2–240
Biddle, James, Feb. 18, 1783–Oct. 1, 1848.
Vol. 1, Pt. 2–240
Biddle, Nicholas, Sept. 10, 1750–Mar. 7, 1778.
Vol. 1, Pt. 2–241
Biddle, Nicholas, Jan. 8, 1786–Feb. 27, 1844.
Vol. 1, Pt. 2–243
Bidlack, Benjamin Alden, Sept. 8, 1804–Feb. 6, 1849.
Vol. 1, Pt. 2–245
Bidwell, Barnabas, Aug. 23, 1763–July 27, 1833.
Vol. 1, Pt. 2–246
Bidwell, John, Aug. 5, 1819–Apr. 4, 1900.
Vol. 1, Pt. 2–247
Bidwell, Marshall Spring, Feb. 16, 1799–Oct. 24, 1872.
Vol. 1, Pt. 2–248
Bidwell, Walter Hilliard, June 21, 1798–Sept. 11, 1881.
Vol. 1, Pt. 2–249
Bieber, Margarete, July 31, 1879–Feb. 25, 1978.
Supp. 10–38
Bien, Julius, Sept. 27, 1826–Dec. 21, 1909.
Vol. 1, Pt. 2–249
Bienville, Jean Baptiste Le Moyne, Sieur de, Feb. 23, 1680–Mar. 7, 1768.
Vol. 1, Pt. 2–250
Bierce, Ambrose Gwinett, June 24, 1842–1914?
Vol. 1, Pt. 2–252
Bierman, Bernard William ("Bernie"), Mar. 11, 1894–Mar. 8, 1977.
Supp. 10–40
Bierstadt, Albert, Jan. 7, 1830–Feb. 18, 1902.
Vol. 1, Pt. 2–253
Bierwirth, John Edward, Apr. 21, 1895–Apr. 3, 1978.
Supp. 10–41
Biffle, Leslie 1, Oct. 9, 1889–Apr. 6, 1966.
Supp. 8–35
Bigelow, Erastus Brigham, Apr. 2, 1814–Dec. 6, 1879.
Vol. 1, Pt. 2–254
Bigelow, Frank Hagar, Aug. 28, 1851–Mar. 2, 1924.
Vol. 1, Pt. 2–255
Bigelow, Harry Augustus, Sept. 22, 1874–Jan. 8, 1950.
Supp. 4–77
Bigelow, Henry Bryant, Oct. 3, 1879–Dec. 11, 1967.
Supp. 8–37
Bigelow, Henry Jacob, Mar. 11, 1818–Oct. 30, 1890.
Vol. 1, Pt. 2–256
Bigelow, Jacob, Feb. 27, 1786–Jan. 10, 1879.
Vol. 1, Pt. 2–257
Bigelow, John, Nov. 25, 1817–Dec. 19, 1911.
Vol. 1, Pt. 2–258
Bigelow, Melville Madison, Aug. 2, 1846–May 4, 1921.
Vol. 1, Pt. 2–260
Bigelow, William Sturgis, Apr. 4, 1850–Oct. 6, 1926.
Vol. 1, Pt. 2–261
Biggers, Earl Derr, Aug. 26, 1884–Apr. 5, 1933.
Supp. 1–79
Biggers, John David, Dec. 19, 1888–Dec. 31, 1973.
Supp. 9–92
Biggs, Asa, Feb. 4, 1811–Mar. 6, 1878.
Vol. 1, Pt. 2–262
Biggs, Edward George Power, Mar. 29, 1906–Mar. 10, 1977.
Supp. 10–42
Biggs, Hermann Michael, Sept. 29, 1859–June 28, 1923.
Vol. 1, Pt. 2–262
Bigler, John, Jan. 8, 1805–Nov. 29, 1871.
Vol. 1, Pt. 2–263
Bigler, William, Jan. 1, 1814–Aug. 9, 1880.
Vol. 1, Pt. 2–264
Bilbo, Theodore Gilmore, Oct. 13, 1877–Aug. 21, 1947.
Supp. 4–78
Billikopf, Jacob, June 1, 1883–Dec. 31, 1950.
Supp. 4–79
Billings, Asa White Kenney, Feb. 8, 1876–Nov. 3, 1949.
Supp. 4–80
Billings, Charles Ethan, Dec. 5, 1835–June 5, 1920.
Vol. 1, Pt. 2–264
Billings, Frank, Apr. 2, 1854–Sept. 20, 1932.
Supp. 1–80
Billings, Frederick, Sept. 27, 1823–Sept. 30, 1890.
Vol. 1, Pt. 2–265
Billings, John Shaw, Apr. 12, 1838–Mar. 11, 1913.
Vol. 1, Pt. 2–266
Billings, Josh. [*See* Shaw, Henry Wheeler, 1818–1885.]
Billings, William, Oct. 7, 1746–Sept. 26, 1800.
Vol. 1, Pt. 2–269
Billingsley, John Sherman, Mar. 10, 1900–Oct. 4, 1966.
Supp. 8–38
Billy the Kid, Nov. 23, 1859–July 15, 1881.
Vol. 1, Pt. 2–271
Bimeler, Joseph Michael, *c.* 1778–Aug. 27, 1853.
Vol. 1, Pt. 2–271
Binford, Jessie Florence, Jan. 20, 1876–July 9, 1966.
Supp. 8–39
Binga, Jesse, Apr. 10, 1865–June 13, 1950.
Supp. 4–82
Bingay, Malcolm Wallace, Dec. 16, 1884–Aug. 21, 1953.
Supp. 5–57
Bingham, Amelia, Mar. 20, 1869–Sept. 1, 1927.
Vol. 1, Pt. 2–272
Bingham, Anne Willing, Aug. 1, 1764–May 11, 1801.
Vol. 1, Pt. 2–273
Bingham, Caleb, Apr. 15, 1757–Apr. 6, 1817.
Vol. 1, Pt. 2–273
Bingham, George Caleb, Mar. 20, 1811–July 7, 1879.
Vol. 1, Pt. 2–274

Bingham, Harry, Mar. 30, 1821–Sept. 12, 1900.
Vol. 1, Pt. 2–275
Bingham, Hiram, Oct. 30, 1789–Nov. 11, 1869.
Vol. 1, Pt. 2–276
Bingham, Hiram, Aug. 16, 1831–Oct. 25, 1908.
Vol. 1, Pt. 2–276
Bingham, Hiram, Nov. 19, 1875–June 6, 1956.
Supp. 6–58
Bingham, John Armor, Jan. 21, 1815–Mar. 19, 1900.
Vol. 1, Pt. 2–277
Bingham, Robert Worth, Nov. 8, 1871–Dec. 18, 1937.
Supp. 2–38
Bingham, Walter Van Dyke, Oct. 20, 1880–July 7, 1952.
Supp. 5–58
Bingham, William, Apr. 8, 1752–Feb. 6, 1804.
Vol. 1, Pt. 2–278
Bingham, William, July 7, 1835–Feb. 18, 1873.
Vol. 1, Pt. 2–279
Binkley, Robert Cedric, Dec. 10, 1897–Apr. 11, 1940.
Supp. 2–40
Binkley, Wilfred Ellsworth, July 29, 1883–Dec. 8, 1965.
Supp. 7–53
Binney, Amos, Oct. 18, 1803–Feb. 18, 1847.
Vol. 1, Pt. 2–279
Binney, Horace, Jan. 4, 1780–Aug. 12, 1875.
Vol. 1, Pt. 2–280
Binns, John, Dec. 22, 1772–June 16, 1860.
Vol. 1, Pt. 2–282
Binns, John Alexander, *c.* 1761–1813.
Vol. 1, Pt. 2–283
Birch, Reginald Bathurst, May 2, 1856–June 17, 1943.
Supp. 3–69
Birch, Thomas, July 26, 1779–Jan. 14, 1851.
Vol. 1, Pt. 2–283
Birch, William Russell, Apr. 9, 1755–Aug. 7, 1834.
Vol. 1, Pt. 2–284
Birchall, Frederick Thomas, 1868–Mar. 7, 1955.
Supp. 5–60
Bird, Arthur, July 23, 1856–Dec. 22, 1923.
Vol. 1, Pt. 2–285
Bird, Frederic Mayer, June 28, 1838–Apr. 2, 1908.
Vol. 1, Pt. 2–285
Bird, Robert Montgomery, Feb. 5, 1806–Jan. 23, 1854.
Vol. 1, Pt. 2–286
Birdseye, Clarence, Dec. 9, 1886–Oct. 7, 1956.
Supp. 6–60
Bird Woman. [*See* Sacagawea, *c.* 1787–1812.]
Birge, Edward Asahel, Sept. 7, 1851–June 9, 1950.
Supp. 4–84
Birge, Henry Warner, Aug. 25, 1825–June 1, 1888.
Vol. 1, Pt. 2–288
Birkbeck, Morris, Jan. 23, 1764–June 4, 1825.
Vol. 1, Pt. 2–289
Birkhoff, George David, Mar. 21, 1884–Nov. 12, 1944.
Supp. 3–70
Birney, David Bell, May 29, 1825–Oct. 18, 1864.
Vol. 1, Pt. 2–290
Birney, James, June 7, 1817–May 8, 1888.
Vol. 1, Pt. 2–291
Birney, James Gillespie, Feb. 4, 1792–Nov. 25, 1857.
Vol. 1, Pt. 2–291
Birney, William, May 28, 1819–Aug. 14, 1907.
Vol. 1, Pt. 2–294
Bishop, Abraham, Feb. 5, 1763–Apr. 28, 1844.
Vol. 1, Pt. 2–294
Bishop, Charles Reed, Jan. 25, 1822–June 7, 1915.
Supp. 1–82
Bishop, Elizabeth, Feb. 8, 1911–Oct. 6, 1979.
Supp. 10–44
Bishop, Joel Prentiss, Mar. 10, 1814–Nov. 4, 1901.
Vol. 1, Pt. 2–295
Bishop, John Peale, May 21, 1892–Apr. 4, 1944.
Supp. 3–71
Bishop, Nathan, Aug. 12, 1808–Aug. 7, 1880
Vol. 1, Pt. 2–296
Bishop, Robert Hamilton, July 26, 1777–Apr. 29, 1855.
Supp. 1–83
Bishop, Robert Roberts, Mar. 30, 1834–Oct. 7, 1909.
Vol. 1, Pt. 2–297
Bishop, Seth Scott, Feb. 7, 1852–Sept. 6, 1923.
Vol. 1, Pt. 2–298
Bishop, William Darius, Sept. 14, 1827–Feb. 4, 1904.
Vol. 1, Pt. 2–298
Bispham, David Scull, Jan. 5, 1857–Oct. 2, 1921.
Vol. 1, Pt. 2–299
Bissell, Edwin Cone, Mar. 2, 1832–Apr. 10, 1894.
Vol. 1, Pt. 2–300
Bissell, George Edwin, Feb. 16, 1839–Aug. 30, 1920.
Vol. 1, Pt. 2–300
Bissell, George Henry, Nov. 8, 1821–Nov. 19, 1884.
Vol. 1, Pt. 2–301
Bissell, William Henry, Apr. 25, 1811–Mar. 18, 1860.
Vol. 1, Pt. 2–302
Bissell, Wilson Shannon, Dec. 31, 1847–Oct 6, 1903.
Vol. 1, Pt. 2–302
Bitter, Karl Theodore Francis, Dec. 6, 1867–Apr. 10, 1915.
Vol. 1, Pt. 2–303
Bitzer, George William, Apr. 21, 1872–Apr. 29, 1944.
Supp. 3–73
Bixby, Horace Ezra, May 8, 1826–Aug. 1, 1912.
Vol. 1, Pt. 2–305
Bixby, James Thompson, July 30, 1843–Dec. 26, 1921.
Vol. 1, Pt. 2–306
Bjerregaard, Carl Henrik Andreas, May 24, 1845–Jan. 28, 1922.
Vol. 1, Pt. 2–307
Black, Douglas MacRae, July 24, 1895–May 15, 1977.
Supp. 10–46
Black, Eli, 1922–Feb. 3, 1975.
Supp. 9–93
Black, Eugene Robert, Jan. 7, 1873–Dec. 19, 1934.
Supp. 1–84
Black, Frank Sweet, Mar. 8, 1853–Mar. 22, 1913.
Vol. 1, Pt. 2–308
Black, Greene Vardiman, Aug. 3, 1836–Aug. 31, 1915.
Vol. 1, Pt. 2–308
Black, Hugo Lafayette, Feb. 27, 1886–Sept. 25, 1971.
Supp. 9–94
Black, James, Sept. 23, 1823–Dec. 16, 1893.
Vol. 1, Pt. 2–310
Black, Jeremiah Sullivan, Jan. 10, 1810–Aug. 19, 1883.
Vol. 1, Pt. 2–310
Black, John Charles, Jan. 27, 1839–Aug. 17, 1915.
Vol. 1, Pt. 2–313
Black, William Murray, Dec. 8, 1855–Sept. 24, 1933.
Supp. 1–85
Blackburn, Gideon, Aug. 27, 1772–Aug. 23, 1838.
Vol. 1, Pt. 2–314
Blackburn, Joseph, fl. 1753–63.
Vol. 1, Pt. 2–315
Blackburn, Joseph Clay Styles, Oct. 1, 1838–Sept. 12, 1918.
Vol. 1, Pt. 2–316
Blackburn, Luke Pryor, June 16, 1816–Sept. 14, 1887.
Vol. 1, Pt. 2–317
Blackburn, William Maxwell, Dec. 30, 1828–Dec. 29, 1898.
Vol. 1, Pt. 2–317
Blackfan, Kenneth Daniel, Sept. 9, 1883–Nov. 29, 1941.
Supp. 3–74
Blackford, Charles Minor, Oct. 17, 1833–Mar. 10, 1903.
Vol. 1, Pt. 2–318
Black Hawk, 1767–Oct. 3, 1838.
Vol. 1, Pt. 2–313
Blackmer, Sydney Alderman, July 13, 1895–Oct. 5, 1973.
Supp. 9–97
Blackmur, Richard Palmer, Jan. 21, 1904–Feb. 2, 1965.
Supp. 7–54
Blackstone, Harry, Sept. 27, 1885–Nov. 16, 1965.
Supp. 7–56
Blackstone, William, 1595–May 26? o.s., 1675.
Vol. 1, Pt. 2–319
Blackton, James Stuart, Jan. 5, 1875–Aug. 13, 1941.
Supp. 3–75
Blackwell, Alice Stone, Sept. 14, 1857–Mar. 15, 1950.
Supp. 4–85
Blackwelf, Antoinette Louisa Brown, May 20, 1825–Nov. 5, 1921.
Vol. 1, Pt. 2–319
Blackwell, Elizabeth, Feb. 3, 1821–May 31, 1910.
Vol. 1, Pt. 2–320
Blackwell, Henry Brown, May 4, 1825–Sept. 7, 1909.
Vol. 1, Pt. 2–321
Blackwell, Lucy Stone. [*See* Stone, Lucy, 1818–1893.]

Bladen, William, Feb. 27, 1673–August 1718.
Vol. 1, Pt. 2–321
Blaikie, William, May 24, 1843–Dec. 6, 1904.
Vol. 1, Pt. 2–322
Blaine, Anita (Eugenie) McCormick, July 4, 1866–Feb. 12, 1954.
Supp. 5–60
Blaine, James Gillespie, Jan. 31, 1830–Jan. 27, 1893.
Vol. 1, Pt. 2–322
Blaine, John James, May 4, 1875–Apr. 16, 1934.
Supp. 1–86
Blair, Austin, Feb. 8, 1818–Aug. 6, 1894.
Vol. 1, Pt. 2–329
Blair, Emily Newell, Jan. 9, 1877–Aug. 3, 1951.
Supp. 5–61
Blair, Francis Preston, Apr. 12, 1791–Oct. 18, 1876.
Vol. 1, Pt. 2–330
Blair, Francis Preston, Feb. 19, 1821–July 9, 1875.
Vol. 1, Pt. 2–332
Blair, Henry William, Dec. 6, 1834–Mar. 14, 1920.
Vol. 1, Pt. 2–334
Blair, James, 1655–Apr. 18, 1743.
Vol. 1, Pt. 2–335
Blair, John, 1687–1771.
Vol. 1, Pt. 2–337
Blair, John, 1732–Aug. 31, 1800.
Vol. 1, Pt. 2–337
Blair, John Insley, Aug. 22, 1802–Dec. 2, 1899.
Vol. 1, Pt. 2–338
Blair, Montgomery, May 10, 1813–July 27, 1883.
Vol. 1, Pt. 2–339
Blair, Samuel, June 14, 1712–July 5, 1751.
Vol. 1, Pt. 2–340
Blair, William Richards, Nov. 7, 1874–Sept. 2, 1962.
Supp. 7–58
Blake, Eli Whitney, Jan. 27, 1795–Aug. 18, 1886.
Vol. 1, Pt. 2–341
Blake, Francis, Dec. 25, 1850–Jan. 19, 1913.
Vol. 1, Pt. 2–342
Blake, Francis Gilman, Feb. 22, 1887–Feb. 1, 1952.
Supp. 5–63
Blake, Homer Crane, Feb. 1, 1822–Jan. 21, 1880.
Vol. 1, Pt. 2–342
Blake, John Lauris, Dec. 21, 1788–July 6, 1857.
Vol. 1, Pt. 2–343
Blake, Lillie Devereux, Aug. 12, 1835–Dec. 30, 1913.
Vol. 1, Pt. 2–343
Blake, Lyman Reed, Aug. 24, 1835–Oct. 5, 1883.
Vol. 1, Pt. 2–344
Blake, Mary Elizabeth McGrath, Sept. 1, 1840–Feb. 26, 1907.
Vol. 1, Pt. 2–345
Blake, William Phipps, June 21, 1825–May 22, 1910.
Vol. 1, Pt. 2–345
Blake, William Rufus, 1805–Apr. 22, 1863.
Vol. 1, Pt. 2–346
Blakeley, George Henry, Apr. 19, 1865–Dec. 25, 1942.
Supp. 3–77
Blakelock, Ralph Albert, Oct. 15, 1847–Aug. 9, 1919.
Vol. 1, Pt. 2–347
Blakely, Johnston, October 1781–October 1814.
Vol. 1, Pt. 2–348
Blakeslee, Erastus, Sept. 2, 1838–July 12, 1908.
Vol. 1, Pt. 2–348
Blakeslee, Howard Walter, Mar. 21, 1880–May 2, 1952.
Supp. 5–64
Blalock, Alfred, Apr. 5, 1899–Sept. 15, 1964.
Supp. 7–59
Blalock, Nelson Gales, Feb. 17, 1836–Mar. 14, 1913.
Vol. 1, Pt. 2–349
Blanc, Antoine, Oct. 11, 1792–June 20, 1860.
Vol. 1, Pt. 2–350
Blanchard, Jonathan, Jan. 19, 1811–May 14, 1892.
Vol. 1, Pt. 2–350
Blanchard, Newton Crain, Jan. 29, 1849–June 22, 1922.
Vol. 1, Pt. 2–351
Blanchard, Thomas, June 24, 1788–Apr. 16, 1864.
Vol. 1, Pt. 2–351
Blanchet, François Norbert, Sept. 3, 1795–June 18, 1883.
Vol. 1, Pt. 2–352
Blanchfield, Florence Aby, Apr. 1, 1882–May 12, 1971.
Supp. 9–99
Bland, Richard, May 6, 1710–Oct. 26, 1776.
Vol. 1, Pt. 2–354
Bland, Richard Parks, Aug. 19, 1835–June 15, 1899.
Vol. 1, Pt. 2–355
Bland, Theodorick, Mar. 21, 1742–June 1, 1790.
Vol. 1, Pt. 2–356
Bland, Thomas, Oct. 4, 1809–Aug. 20, 1885.
Vol. 1, Pt. 2–357
Blandy, William Henry Purnell, June 28, 1890–Jan. 12, 1954.
Supp. 5–65
Blankenburg, Rudolph, Feb. 16, 1843–Apr. 12, 1918.
Vol. 1, Pt. 2–357
Blanshard, Paul, Aug. 27, 1892–Jan. 27, 1980.
Supp. 10–47
Blasdel, Henry Goode, Jan. 20, 1825–July 26, 1900.
Vol. 1, Pt. 2–358
Blashfield, Edwin Howland, Dec. 15, 1848–Oct. 12, 1936.
Supp. 2–41
Blatch, Harriot Eaton Stanton, Jan. 20, 1856–Nov. 20, 1940.
Supp. 2–43
Blatchford, Richard Milford, Apr. 23, 1798–Sept. 4, 1875.
Vol. 1, Pt. 2–359
Blatchford, Samuel, Mar. 9, 1820–July 7, 1893.
Vol. 1, Pt. 2–359
Blaustein, David, May 5, 1866–Aug. 26, 1912.
Vol. 1, Pt. 2–360
Blavatsky, Helena Petrovna Hahn, July 30, 1831–May 8, 1891.
Vol. 1, Pt. 2–361
Blease, Coleman Livingston, Oct. 8, 1868–Jan. 19, 1942.
Supp. 3–77
Bleckley, Logan Edwin, July 3, 1827–Mar. 6, 1907.
Vol. 1 Pt. 2–363
Bledsoe, Albert Taylor, Nov. 9, 1809–Dec. 8, 1877.
Vol. 1, Pt. 2–364
Bleecker, Ann Eliza, October 1752–Nov. 23, 1783.
Vol. 1, Pt. 2–365
Blenk, James Hubert, July 28, 1856–Apr. 20, 1917.
Vol. 1, Pt. 2–366
Blennerhassett, Harman, Oct. 8, 1765–Feb. 2, 1831.
Vol. 1, Pt. 2–367
Bleyer, Wiliard Grosvenor, Aug. 27, 1873–Oct. 31, 1935.
Supp. 1–87
Blichfeldt, Hans Frederik, Jan. 9, 1873–Nov. 16, 1945.
Supp. 3–79
Blinn, Holbrook, Jan. 23, 1872–June 24, 1928.
Vol. 1, Pt. 2–368
Bliss, Aaron Thomas, May 22, 1837–Sept. 16, 1906.
Vol. 1, Pt. 2–368
Bliss, Cornelius Newton, Jan. 26, 1833–Oct. 9, 1911.
Vol. 1, Pt. 2–369
Bliss, Cornelius Newton, Apr. 13, 1874–Apr. 5, 1949.
Supp. 4–87
Bliss, Daniel, Aug. 17, 1823–July 27, 1916.
Vol. 1, Pt. 2–369
Bliss, Edwin Elisha, Apr. 12, 1817–Dec. 20, 1892.
Vol. 1, Pt. 2–370
Bliss, Edwin Munsell, Sept. 12, 1848–Aug. 6, 1919.
Vol. 1, Pt. 2–371
Bliss, Eliphalet Williams, Apr. 12, 1836–July 21, 1903.
Vol. 1, Pt. 2–371
Bliss, Frederick Jones, Jan. 22, 1859–June 3, 1937.
Supp. 2–44
Bliss, George, Apr. 21, 1816–Feb. 2, 1896.
Vol. 1, Pt. 2–372
Bliss, George, May 3, 1830–Sept. 2, 1897.
Vol. 1, Pt. 2–373
Bliss, George William, July 21, 1918–Sept. 11, 1978.
Supp. 10–49
Bliss, Gilbert Ames, May 9, 1876–May 8, 1951.
Supp. 5–67
Bliss, Howard Sweetser, Dec. 6, 1860–May 2, 1920.
Vol. 1, Pt. 2–374
Bliss, Jonathan, Oct. 1, 1742–Oct. 1, 1822.
Vol. 1, Pt. 2–374
Bliss, Philemon, July 28, 1813–Aug. 24, 1889.
Vol. 1, Pt. 2–375
Bliss, Philip Paul, July 9, 1838–Dec. 29, 1876.
Vol. 1, Pt. 2–376
Bliss, Porter Cornelius, Dec. 28, 1838–Feb. 2, 1885.
Vol. 1, Pt. 2–376

Bliss, Robert Woods, Aug. 5, 1875–Apr. 19, 1962.
Supp. 7–60
Bliss, Tasker Howard, Dec–31, 1853–Nov. 9, 1930.
Supp. 1–88
Bliss, William Dwight Porter, Aug. 20, 1856–Oct. 8, 1926.
Vol. 1, Pt. 2–377
Blitz, Antonio, June 21, 1810–Jan. 28, 1877.
Vol. 1, Pt. 2–378
Blitzstein, Marc, Mar. 2, 1905–Jan. 22, 1964.
Supp. 7–60
Bliven, Bruce Ormsby, July 27, 1889–May 27, 1977.
Supp. 10–50
Bloch, Claude Charles, July 12, 1878–Oct. 6, 1967.
Supp. 8–41
Bloch, Ernest, July 24, 1880–July 15, 1959.
Supp. 6–62
Block, Adriaen, fl. 1610–1624.
Vol. 1, Pt. 2–378
Block, Paul, Nov. 2, 1877–June 22, 1941.
Supp. 3–80
Blocker, Dan, Dec. 10, 1928–May 13, 1972.
Supp. 9–101
Blodget, Lorin, May 25, 1823–Mar. 24, 1901.
Vol. 1, Pt. 2–379
Blodget, Samuel, Apr. 1, 1724–Sept. 1, 1807.
Vol. 1, Pt. 2–379
Blodget, Samuel, Aug. 28, 1757–Apr. 11, 1814.
Vol. 1, Pt. 2–380
Blodgett, Benjamin Colman, Mar. 12, 1838–Sept. 22, 1925.
Vol. 1, Pt. 2–381
Blodgett, Henry Williams, July 21, 1821–Feb. 9, 1905.
Vol. 1, Pt. 2–382
Blodgett, John Wood, July 26, 1860–Nov. 21, 1951.
Supp. 5–68
Blodgett, Katharine Burr, Jan. 10, 1898–Oct. 12, 1979.
Supp. 10–51
Bloede, Gertrude, Aug. 10, 1845–Aug. 14, 1905.
Vol. 1, Pt. 2–383
Blondell, Joan, Aug. 30, 1912–Dec. 25, 1979.
Supp. 10–53
Blood, Benjamin Paul, Nov. 21, 1832–Jan. 15, 1919.
Vol. 1, Pt. 2–383
Bloodgood, Joseph Colt, Nov. 1, 1867–Oct. 22, 1935.
Supp. 1–90
Bloodworth, Timothy, 1736–Aug. 24, 1814.
Vol. 1, Pt. 2–384
Bloom, Sol, Mar. 9, 1870–Mar. 7, 1949.
Supp. 4–87
Bloomer, Amelia Jenks, May 27, 1818–Dec. 30, 1894.
Vol. 1, Pt. 2–385
Bloomfield, Joseph, Oct. 18, 1753–Oct. 3, 1823.
Vol. 1, Pt. 2–385
Bloomfield, Leonard, Apr. 1, 1887–Apr. 18, 1949.
Supp. 4–89
Bloomfield, Maurice, Feb. 23, 1855–June 13, 1928.
Vol. 1, Pt. 2–386
Bloomfield, Meyer, Feb. 11, 1878–Mar. 12, 1938.
Supp. 2–45
Bloomfield-Zeisler, Fannie. [*See* Zeisler, Fannie Bloomfield, 1863–1927.]
Bloomgarden, Kermit, Dec. 15, 1904–Sept. 20, 1976.
Supp. 10–54
Bloomgarden, Solomon, March 1870–Jan. 10, 1927.
Vol. 1, Pt. 2–388
Bloor, Ella Reeve, July 8, 1862–Aug. 10, 1951.
Supp. 5–69
Blount, James Henderson, Sept. 12, 1837–Mar. 8, 1903.
Vol. 1, Pt. 2–388
Blount, Thomas, May 10, 1759–Feb. 7, 1812.
Vol. 1, Pt. 2–389
Blount, William, Mar. 26, 1749–Mar. 21, 1800.
Vol. 1, Pt. 2–390
Blount, Willie, Apr. 18, 1768–Sept. 10, 1835.
Vol. 1, Pt. 2–391
Blow, Henry Taylor, July 15, 1817–Sept. 11, 1875.
Vol. 1, Pt. 2–391
Blow, Susan Elizabeth, June 7, 1843–Mar. 26, 1916.
Vol. 1, Pt. 2–392
Blowers, Sampson Salter, Mar. 10, 1742–Oct. 25, 1842.
Vol. 1, Pt. 2–393
Bloxham, William Dunnington, July 9, 1835–Mar. 15, 1911.
Vol. 1, Pt. 2–394
Blue, Ben, Sept. 12, 1901–May 7, 1975.
Supp. 9–102
Blue, Gerald Montgomery ("Monte"), Jan. 11, 1887?–Feb. 18, 1963.
Supp. 7–62
Blue, Victor, Dec. 6, 1865–Jan. 22, 1928.
Vol. 1, Pt. 2–395
Bluemner, Oscar Florians, June 21, 1867–Jan. 12, 1938.
Supp. 2–46
Blum, Robert Frederick, July 9, 1857–June 8, 1903.
Vol. 1, Pt. 2–395
Blunt, Edmund March, June 20, 1770–Jan. 4, 1862.
Vol. 1, Pt. 2–397
Blunt, George William, Mar. 11, 1802–Apr. 19, 1878.
Vol. 1, Pt. 2–398
Blunt, James Gillpatrick, July 21, 1826–July 25, 1881.
Vol. 1, Pt. 2–399
Blythe, Herbert. [*See* Barrymore, Maurice, 1847–1905.]
Boardman, Mabel Thorp, Oct. 12, 1860–Mar. 17, 1946.
Supp. 4–91
Boardman, Thomas Danforth, Jan. 21, 1784–Sept. 10, 1873.
Vol. 1, Pt. 2–400
Boas, Emil Leopold, Nov. 15, 1854–May 3, 1912.
Vol. 1, Pt. 2–400
Boas, Franz, July 9, 1858–Dec. 21, 1942.
Supp. 3–81
Bôcher, Maxime, Aug. 28, 1867–Sept. 12, 1918.
Vol. 1, Pt. 2–401
Bocock, Thomas Stanley, May 18, 1815–Aug. 5, 1891.
Vol. 1, Pt. 2–402
Bodanzky, Artur, Dec. 16, 1877–Nov. 23, 1939.
Supp. 2–47
Bode, Boyd Henry, Oct. 4, 1873–Mar. 29, 1953.
Supp. 5–71
Bodenheim, Maxwell, May 26, 1892–Feb. 7, 1954.
Supp. 5–72
Boehler, Peter, Dec. 31, 1712–Apr. 27, 1775.
Vol. 1, Pt. 2–402
Boehm, Henry, June 8, 1775–Dec. 28, 1875.
Vol. 1, Pt. 2–403
Boehm, John Philip, 1683–Apr. 29, 1749.
Vol. 1, Pt. 2–404
Boehm, Martin, Nov. 30, 1725–Mar. 23, 1812.
Vol. 1, Pt. 2–405
Boeing, William Edward, Oct. 1, 1881–Sept. 28, 1956.
Supp. 6–63
Boelen, Jacob, *c.* 1654–1729.
Vol. 1, Pt. 2–406
Bogan, Louise Marie, Aug. 11, 1897–Feb. 4, 1970.
Supp. 8–42
Bogardus, Everardus, 1607–Sept. 27, 1647.
Vol. 1, Pt. 2–406
Bogardus, James, Mar. 14, 1800–Apr. 13, 1874.
Vol. 1, Pt. 2–407
Bogart, Humphrey DeForest, Dec. 25, 1899–Jan. 14, 1957.
Supp. 6–64
Bogart, John, Feb. 8, 1836–Apr. 25, 1920.
Vol. 1, Pt. 2–408
Boggs, Charles Stuart, Jan. 28, 1811–Apr. 22, 1888.
Vol. 1, Pt. 2–408
Boggs, Lillburn W., Dec. 14, 1792–Mar. 14, 1860.
Vol. 1, Pt. 2–409
Boggs, Thomas Hale, Feb. 15, 1914–Oct. 16, 1972?.
Supp. 9–103
Bogue, Virgil Gay, July 20, 1846–Oct. 14, 1916.
Vol. 1, Pt. 2–410
Bogy, Lewis Vital, Apr. 9, 1813–Sept. 20, 1877.
Vol. 1, Pt. 2–410
Bohlen, Charles Eustis ("Chip"), Aug. 30, 1904–Jan. 1, 1974.
Supp. 9–105
Bohm, Max, Jan. 21, 1861–Sept. 19, 1923.
Vol. 1, Pt. 2–411
Bohune, Lawrence, d. Mar. 19, 1621.
Vol. 1, Pt. 2–412
Boies, Henry Martyn, Aug. 18, 1837–Dec. 12, 1903.
Vol. 1, Pt. 2–412
Boies, Horace, Dec. 7, 1827–Apr. 4, 1923.
Vol. 1, Pt. 2–413

Boise, Reuben Patrick, June 9, 1819–Apr. 10, 1907.
Vol. 1, Pt. 2–414
Boisen, Anton Theophilus, Oct. 29, 1876–Oct. 1, 1965.
Supp. 7–63
Boissevain, Inez Milholland, Aug. 6, 1886–Nov. 25, 1916.
Vol. 1, Pt. 2–415
Bok, Edward William, Oct. 9, 1863–Jan. 9, 1930.
Supp. 1–91
Boker, George Henry, Oct. 6, 1823–Jan. 2, 1890.
Vol. 1, Pt. 2–415
Boldt, George C., Apr. 25, 1851–Dec. 5, 1916.
Vol. 1, Pt. 2–418
Boll, Jacob, May 29, 1828–Sept. 29, 1880.
Vol. 1, Pt. 2–419
Boller, Alfred Pancoast, Feb. 23, 1840–Dec. 9, 1912.
Vol. 1, Pt. 2–420
Bolles, Frank, Oct. 31, 1856–Jan. 10, 1894.
Vol. 1, Pt. 2–421
Bollman, Justus Erich, 1769–Dec. 9, 1821.
Vol. 1, Pt. 2–421
Bollman, William, *c.* 1710–*c.* 1776.
Vol. 1, Pt. 2–420
Bolm, Adolph Rudolphovitch, Sept. 25, 1884–Apr. 16, 1951.
Supp. 5–74
Bolton, Frances Payne Bingham, Mar. 29, 1885–Mar. 9, 1977.
Supp. 10–56
Bolton, Henry Carrington, Jan. 28, 1843–Nov. 19, 1903.
Vol. 1, Pt. 2–422
Bolton, Herbert Eugene, July 20, 1870–Jan. 30, 1953.
Supp. 5–76
Bolton, Sarah Knowles, Sept. 15, 1841–Feb. 21, 1916.
Vol. 1, Pt. 2–423
Bolton, Sarah Tittle Barrett, Dec. 18, 1814–Aug. 4, 1893.
Vol. 1, Pt. 2–424
Boltwood, Bertram Borden, July 27, 1870–Aug. 15, 1927.
Vol. 1, Pt. 2–424
Boltzius, Johann Martin, Dec. 15, 1703–Nov. 19, 1765.
Vol. 1, Pt. 2–425
Bolza, Oskar, May 12, 1857–July 5, 1942.
Supp. 3–86
Bomberger, John Henry Augustus, Jan. 13, 1817–Aug. 1890.
Vol. 1, Pt. 2–426
Bomford, George, 1782–Mar. 25, 1848.
Vol. 1, Pt. 2–427
Bonaparte, Charles Joseph, June 9, 1851–June 28, 1921.
Vol. 1, Pt. 2–427
Bonaparte, Elizabeth Patterson, Feb. 6, 1785–Apr. 4, 1879.
Vol. 1, Pt. 2–428
Bonaparte, Jerome Napoleon, Nov. 5, 1830–Sept. 3, 1893.
Vol. 1, Pt. 2–429
Bonard, Louis, 1809–Feb. 21, 1871.
Vol. 1, Pt. 2–429
Bond, Carrie Jacobs, Aug. 11, 1862–Dec. 28, 1946.
Supp. 4–93
Bond, Elizabeth Powell, Jan. 25, 1841–Mar. 29, 1926.
Vol. 1, Pt. 2–430
Bond, George Phillips, May 20, 1825–Feb. 17, 1865.
Vol. 1, Pt. 2–430
Bond, Hugh Lennox, Dec. 16, 1828–Oct. 24, 1893.
Vol. 1, Pt. 2–431
Bond, Shadrach, *c.* 1773–Apr. 13, 1832.
Vol. 1, Pt. 2–432
Bond, Thomas, 1712–Mar. 26, 1784.
Vol. 1, Pt. 2–433
Bond, William Cranch, Sept. 9, 1789–Jan. 29, 1859.
Vol. 1, Pt. 2–434
Boner, John Henry, Jan. 31, 1845–Mar. 6, 1903.
Vol. 1, Pt. 2–435
Bonfils, Frederick Gilmer, Dec. 31, 1860–Feb. 2, 1933.
Supp. 1–93
Bonham, Milledge Luke, Dec. 25, 1813–Aug. 27, 1890.
Vol. 1, Pt. 2–436
Bonner, John, *c.* 1643–Jan. 30, 1725/6.
Vol. 1, Pt. 2–436
Bonner, Robert, Apr. 28, 1824–July 6, 1899.
Vol. 1, Pt. 2–437
Bonneville, Benjamin Louis Eulalie de, Apr. 14, 1796–June 12, 1878.
Vol. 1, Pt. 2–438
Bonney, Charles Carroll, Sept. 4, 1831–Aug. 23, 1903.
Vol. 1, Pt. 2–439
Bonney, William H., 1859–1881. [*See* Billy the Kid, 1859–1881.]
Bonsal, Stephen, Mar. 29, 1865–June 8, 1951.
Supp. 5–78
Bonstelle, Jessie, 1872–Oct. 14, 1932.
Supp. 1–96
Bontemps, Arna Wendell, Oct. 13, 1902–June 4, 1973.
Supp. 9–107
Bonwill, William Gibson Arlington, Oct. 4, 1833–Sept. 24, 1899.
Vol. 1, Pt. 2–440
Bonzano, Adolphus, Dec. 5, 1830–May 5, 1913.
Vol. 1, Pt. 2–441
Boole, Ella Alexander, July 26, 1858–Mar. 13, 1952.
Supp. 5–79
Boone, Daniel, Nov. 2, N.S., 1734–Sept. 26, 1820.
Vol. 1, Pt. 2–441
Boorman, James, 1783–Jan. 24, 1866.
Vol. 1, Pt. 2–443
Booth, Agnes, Oct. 4, 1846–Jan. 2, 1910.
Vol. 1, Pt. 2–444
Booth, Albert James, Jr. ("Albie"), Feb. 1, 1908–Mar. 1, 1959.
Supp. 6–66
Booth, Ballington, July 28, 1857–Oct. 5, 1940.
Supp. 2–48
Booth, Edwin Thomas, Nov. 13, 1833–June 7, 1893.
Vol. 1, Pt. 2–444
Booth, Evangeline Cory, Dec. 25, 1865–July 17, 1950.
Supp. 4–95
Booth, James Curtis, July 28, 1810–Mar. 21, 1888.
Vol. 1, Pt. 2–447
Booth, John Wilkes, 1838–Apr. 26, 1865.
Vol. 1, Pt. 2–448
Booth, Junius Brutus, May 1, 1796–Nov. 30, 1852.
Vol. 1, Pt. 2–452
Booth, Mary Louise, Apr. 19, 1831–Mar. 5, 1889.
Vol. 1, Pt. 2–454
Booth, Newton, Dec. 30, 1825–July 14, 1892.
Vol. 1, Pt. 2–455
Booth-Tucker, Emma Moss, Jan. 8, 1860–Oct. 28, 1903.
Vol. 1, Pt. 2–456
Boott, Kirk, Oct. 20, 1790–Apr. 11, 1837.
Vol. 1, Pt. 2–456
Borah, William Edgar, June 29, 1865–Jan. 19, 1940.
Supp. 2–49
Borchard, Edwin Montefiore, Oct. 17, 1884–July 22, 1951.
Supp. 5–81
Borden, Gail, Nov. 9, 1801–Jan. 11, 1874.
Vol. 1, Pt. 2–457
Borden, Lizzie Andrew, July 19, 1860–June 1, 1927.
Supp. 1–97
Borden, Richard, Apr. 12, 1795–Feb. 25, 1874.
Vol. 1, Pt. 2–458
Borden, Simeon, Jan. 29, 1798–Oct. 28, 1856.
Vol. 1, Pt. 2–459
Bordlex, John Beale, Feb. 11, 1727–Jan. 26, 1804.
Vol. 1, Pt. 2–460
Boré, Jean Étienne, Dec. 27, 1741–Feb. 2, 1820.
Vol. 1, Pt. 2–461
Boreman, Arthur Ingram, July 24, 1823–Apr. 19, 1896.
Vol. 1, Pt. 2–461
Borg, George William, Oct. 24, 1887–Feb. 21, 1960.
Supp. 6–67
Borglum, John Gutzon de la Mothe, Mar. 25, 1867–Mar. 6, 1941.
Supp. 3–87
Borglum, Solon Hannibal, Dec. 22, 1868–Jan. 31, 1922.
Vol. 1, Pt. 2–462
Bori, Lucrezia, Dec. 24, 1887–May 14, 1960.
Supp. 6–68
Borie, Adolphe, Jan. 5, 1877–May 14, 1934.
Supp. 1–97
Borie, Adolph Edward, Nov. 25, 1809–Feb. 5, 1880.
Vol. 1, Pt. 2–464
Boring, Edwin Garrigues, Oct. 23, 1886–July 1, 1968.
Supp. 8–43
Boring, William Alciphron, Sept. 9, 1859–May 5, 1937.
Supp. 2–53
Borland, Solon, Sept. 21, 1808–Jan. 1 or 31, 1864.
Vol. 1, Pt. 2–464
Borzage, Frank, Apr. 23, 1893–June 19, 1962.
Supp. 7–65
Boss, Lewis, Oct. 26, 1846–Oct. 5, 1912.
Vol. 1, Pt. 2–465

Boston, Charles Anderson, Aug. 31, 1863–Mar. 8, 1935.
Supp. 1–98
Boswell, Connie (Connee), Dec. 3, 1907–Oct. 11, 1976.
Supp. 10–58
Bostwick, Arthur Elmore, Mar. 8, 1860–Feb. 13, 1942.
Supp. 3–90
Bosworth, Edward Increase, Jan. 10, 1861–July 1, 1927.
Vol. 1, Pt. 2–466
Bosworth, Francke Huntington, Jan. 25, 1843–Oct. 17, 1925.
Vol. 1, Pt. 2–466
Boteler, Alexander Robinson, May 16, 1815–May 8, 1892.
Vol. 1, Pt. 2–467
Botetourt, Norborne Berkeley, Baron de, *c.* 1718–Oct. 15, 1770.
Vol. 1, Pt. 2–468
Botsford, George Willis, May 9, 1862–Dec. 13, 1917.
Vol. 1, Pt. 2–468
Botta, Anne Charlotte Lynch, Nov. 11, 1815–Mar. 23, 1891.
Vol. 1, Pt. 2–469
Botta, Vincenzo, Nov. 11, 1818–Oct. 5, 1894.
Vol. 1, Pt. 2–470
Bottineau, Pierre, *c.* 1817–July 26, 1895.
Vol. 1, Pt. 2–470
Bottome, Margaret McDonald, Dec. 29, 1827–Nov. 4, 1906.
Vol. 1, Pt. 2–471
Botts, Charles Tyler, 1809–1884.
Vol. 1, Pt. 2–472
Botts, John Minor, Sept. 16, 1802–Jan. 7, 1869.
Vol. 1, Pt. 2–472
Bouché, René Robert, Sept. 20, 1905–July 3, 1963.
Supp. 7–66
Boucher, Horace Edward, Apr. 24, 1873–Apr. 27, 1935.
Supp. 1–99
Boucher. Jonathan, Mar. 12, 1737/8–Apr. 27, 1804.
Vol. 1, Pt. 2–473
Boucicault, Dion, Dec. 26, 1820–Sept. 18, 1890.
Vol. 1, Pt. 2–475
Bouck, William C., Jan. 7, 1786–Apr. 19, 1859.
Vol. 1, Pt. 2–476
Boudin, Louis Boudinoff, Feb. 15, 1874–May 29, 1952.
Supp. 5–82
Boudinot, Elias, May 2, 1740–Oct. 24, 1821.
Vol. 1, Pt. 2–477
Boudinot, Elias, *c.* 1803–June 22, 1839.
Vol. 1, Pt. 2–478
Boudinot, Elias Cornelius, Aug. 1, 1835–Sept. 27, 1890.
Vol. 1, Pt. 2–479
Bouligny, Dominique, *c.* 1771–Mar. 5, 1833.
Vol. 1, Pt. 2–479
Bounetheau, Henry Brintnell, Dec. 14, 1797–Jan. 31, 1877.
Vol. 1, Pt. 2–479
Bouquet, Henry, 1719–Sept. 2, 1765.
Vol. 1, Pt. 2–480
Bouquillon, Thomas Joseph, May 16, 1840–Nov. 5, 1902.
Vol. 1, Pt. 2–481
Bourgmont, Étienne Venyard, Sieur de, *c.* 1680–*c.* 1730
Vol. 1, Pt. 2–482
Bourke, John Gregory, June 23, 1846–June 8, 1896.
Vol. 1, Pt. 2–483
Bourke-White, Margaret, June 14, 1904–Aug. 27, 1971.
Supp. 9–110
Bourne, Benjamin, Dec. 9, 1755–Sept. 17, 1808.
Vol. 1, Pt. 2–483
Bourne, Edward Gaylord, June 24, 1860–Feb. 24, 1908.
Vol. 1, Pt. 2–484
Bourne, George, June 13, 1780–Nov. 20, 1845.
Vol. 1, Pt. 2–485
Bourne, Jonathan, Feb. 23, 1855–Sept. 1, 1940.
Supp. 2–54
Bourne, Nehemiah, *c.* 1611–1691.
Vol. 1, Pt. 2–485
Bourne, Randolph Silliman, May 30, 1886–Dec. 22, 1918.
Vol. 1, Pt. 2–486
Boutell, Henry Sherman, Mar. 14, 1856–Mar. 11, 1926.
Vol. 1, Pt. 2–486
Boutelle, Charles Addison, Feb. 9, 1839–May 21, 1901.
Vol. 1, Pt. 2–487
Bouton, John Bell, Mar. 15, 1830–Nov. 18, 1902.
Vol. 1, Pt. 2–488
Bouton, Nathaniel, June 29, 1799–June 6, 1878.
Vol. 1, Pt. 2–488
Boutwell, George Sewall, Jan. 28, 1818–Feb. 27, 1905.
Vol. 1, Pt. 2–489
Bouvet, Marie Marguerite, Feb. 14, 1865–May 27, 1915.
Vol. 1, Pt. 2–490
Bouvier, John, 1787–Nov. 18, 1851.
Vol. 1, Pt. 2–490
Bovard, Oliver Kirby, May 27, 1872–Nov. 3, 1945.
Supp. 3–91
Bovie, William T., Sept. 11, 1882–Jan. 1, 1958.
Supp. 6–69
Bow, Clara Gordon, July 29, 1905–Sept. 26, 1965.
Supp. 7–67
Bowden, John, Jan. 7, 1751–July 31, 1817.
Vol. 1, Pt. 2–491
Bowditch, Charles Pickering, Sept. 30, 1842–June 1, 1921.
Vol. 1, Pt. 2–492
Bowditch, Henry Ingersoll, Aug. 9, 1808–Jan. 14, 1892.
Vol. 1, Pt. 2–492
Bowditch, Henry Pickering, Apr. 4, 1840–Mar. 13, 1911.
Vol. 1, Pt. 2–494
Bowditch, Nathaniel, Mar. 26, 1773–Mar. 17, 1838.
Vol. 1, Pt. 2–496
Bowdoin, James, Aug. 7, 1726–Nov. 6, 1790.
Vol. 1, Pt. 2–498
Bowdoin, James, Sept. 22, 1752–Oct. 11, 1811.
Vol. 1, Pt. 2–501
Bowen, Abel, Dec. 3, 1790–Mar. 11, 1850.
Vol. 1, Pt. 2–502
Bowen, Catherine Drinker, Jan. 1, 1897–Nov. 1, 1973
Supp. 9–112
Bowen, Francis, Sept. 8, 1811–Jan. 21, 1890.
Vol. 1, Pt. 2–503
Bowen, George, Apr. 30, 1816–Feb. 5, 1888.
Vol. 1, Pt. 2–504
Bowen, Henry Chandler, Sept. 11, 1813–Feb. 24, 1896.
Vol. 1, Pt. 2–505
Bowen, Herbert Wolcott, Feb. 29, 1856–May 29, 1927.
Vol. 1, Pt. 2–505
Bowen, Ira Sprague, Dec. 21, 1898–Feb. 6, 1973.
Supp. 9–113
Bowen, Louise De Koven, Feb. 26, 1859–Nov. 9, 1953.
Supp. 5–84
Bowen, Norman Levi, June 21, 1887–Sept. 11, 1956.
Supp. 6–70
Bowen, Thomas Meade, Oct. 26, 1835–Dec. 30, 1906.
Vol. 1, Pt. 2–506
Bowers, Claude Gernade, Nov. 20, 1878–Jan. 21, 1958.
Supp. 6–72
Bowers, Elizabeth Crocker, Mar. 12, 1830–Nov. 6, 1895.
Vol. 1, Pt. 2–507
Bowers, Lloyd Wheaton, Mar. 9, 1859–Sept. 9, 1910.
Vol. 1, Pt. 2–508
Bowers, Theodore Shelton, Oct. 10, 1832–Mar. 6, 1866.
Vol. 1, Pt. 2–508
Bowes, Edward J., June 14, 1874–June 13, 1946.
Supp. 4–96
Bowie, James, 1799–Mar. 6, 1836.
Vol. 1, Pt. 2–509
Bowie, Oden, Nov. 10, 1826–Dec. 4, 1894.
Vol. 1, Pt. 2–510
Bowie, Richard Johns, June 23, 1807–Mar. 12, 1881.
Vol. 1, Pt. 2–511
Bowie, Robert, March 1750–Jan. 8, 1818.
Vol. 1, Pt. 2–511
Bowie, William, May 6, 1872–Aug. 28, 1940.
Supp. 2–55
Bowker, Richard Rogers, Sept. 4, 1848–Nov. 12, 1933.
Supp. 1–100
Bowler, Metcalf, 1726–Sept. 24, 1789.
Vol. 1, Pt. 2–512
Bowles, Jane Auer, Feb. 22, 1917–May 4, 1973.
Supp. 9–115
Bowles, Samuel, June 8, 1797–Sept. 8, 1851.
Vol. 1, Pt. 2–513
Bowles, Samuel, Feb. 9, 1826–Jan. 16, 1878.
Vol. 1, Pt. 2–514
Bowles, Samuel, Oct. 15, 1851–Mar. 14, 1915.
Vol. 1, Pt. 2–518
Bowles, William Augustus, Oct. 22, 1763–Dec. 23, 1805.
Vol. 1, Pt. 2–519

Bowman, Isaiah, Dec. 26, 1878–Jan. 6, 1950.
Supp. 4–98
Bowman, John Bryan, Oct. 16, 1824–Sept. 29, 1891.
Vol. 1, Pt. 2–520
Bowman, Thomas, July 15, 1817–Mar. 3, 1914.
Vol. 1, Pt. 2–521
Bowne, Borden Parker, Jan. 14, 1847–Apr. 1, 1910.
Vol. 1, Pt. 2–522
Bowne, John, *c.* Mar. 1, 1627/28–Oct. 10, 1695.
Vol. 1, Pt. 2–523
Boyce, James Petigru, Jan. 11, 1827–Dec. 28, 1888.
Vol. 1, Pt. 2–523
Boyd, Belle, May 9, 1843–June 11, 1900.
Vol. 1, Pt. 2–524
Boyd, David French, Oct. 5, 1834–May 27, 1899.
Vol. 1, Pt. 2–525
Boyd, Harriet Ann. [*See* Hawes, Harriet Ann Boyd, 1871–1945.]
Boyd, James, July 2, 1888–Feb. 25, 1944.
Supp. 3–92
Boyd, John Parker, Dec. 21, 1764–Oct. 4, 1830.
Vol. 1, Pt. 2–526
Boyd, Julian Parks, Nov. 3, 1903–May 28, 1980.
Supp 10–60
Boyd, Louise Arner, Sept. 16, 1887–Sept. 14, 1972.
Supp. 9–117
Boyd, Lynn, Nov. 22, 1800–Dec. 17, 1859.
Vol. 1, Pt. 2–527
Boyd, Richard Henry, Mar. 15, 1843–Aug. 23, 1922.
Vol. 1, Pt. 2–528
Boyd, Thomas Alexander, July 3, 1898–Jan. 27, 1935.
Supp. 1–102
Boyd, Thomas Duckett, Jan. 20, 1854–Nov. 2, 1932.
Supp. 1–103
Boyd, William, June 5, 1898–Sept. 12, 1972.
Supp. 9–118
Boyd, William Kenneth, Jan. 10, 1879–Jan. 19, 1938.
Supp. 2–56
Boyden, Roland William, Oct. 18, 1863–Oct. 25, 1931.
Supp. 1–104
Boyden, Seth, Nov. 17, 1788–Mar. 31, 1870.
Vol. 1, Pt. 2–528
Boyden, Uriah Atherton, Feb. 17, 1804–Oct. 17, 1879.
Vol. 1, Pt. 2–529
Boyé, Martin Hans, Dec. 6, 1812–Mar. 5, 1909.
Vol. 1, Pt. 2–530
Boyer, Charles, Aug. 28, 1899–Aug. 26, 1978.
Supp. 10–61
Boyesen, Hjalmar Hjorth, Sept. 23, 1849–Oct. 4, 1895.
Vol. 1, Pt. 2–530
Boyle, Harold Vincent ("Hal"), Feb. 21, 1911–Apr. 1, 1974.
Supp. 9–119
Boyle, Jeremiah Tilford, May 22, 1818–July 28, 1871.
Vol. 1, Pt. 2–532
Boyle, John, Oct. 28, 1774–Jan. 28, 1835.
Vol. 1, Pt. 2–532
Boyle, John J., Jan. 12, 1851–Feb. 10, 1917.
Vol. 1, Pt. 2–533
Boyle, Michael J., June 11, 1879–May 17, 1958.
Supp. 6–73
Boyle, Thomas, June 29, 1776?-Oct. 12, 1825?.
Vol. 1, Pt. 2–534
Boylston, Zabdiel, Mar. 9, 1679–Mar. 1, 1766.
Vol. 1, Pt. 2–535
Boynton, Charles Brandon, June 12, 1806–Apr. 27, 1883.
Vol. 1, Pt. 2–536
Boynton, Edward Carlisle, Feb. 1, 1824–May 13, 1893.
Vol. 1, Pt. 2–537
Bozeman, John M., 1835–Apr. 20, 1867.
Vol. 1, Pt. 2–537
Bozeman, Nathan, Mar. 25, 1825–Dec. 16, 1905.
Vol. 1, Pt. 2–538
Bozman, John Leeds, Aug. 25, 1757–Apr. 20, 1823.
Vol. 1, Pt. 2–539
Brace, Charles Loring, June 19, 1826–Aug. 11, 1890.
Vol. 1, Pt. 2–539
Brace, Charles Loring, June 2, 1855–May 24, 1938.
Supp. 2–57
Brace, Dewitt Bristol, Jan. 5, 1859–Oct. 2, 1905.
Vol. 1, Pt. 2–540
Brace, Donald Clifford, Dec. 27, 1881–Sept. 20, 1955.
Supp. 5–85
Brace, John Pierce, Feb. 10, 1793–Oct. 18, 1872.
Vol. 1, Pt. 2–541
Brachvogel, Udo, Sept. 26, 1835–Jan. 30, 1913.
Vol. 1, Pt. 2–541
Brackenridge, Henry Marie, May 11, 1786–Jan. 18, 1871.
Vol. 1, Pt. 2–543
Brackenridge, Hugh Henry, 1748–June 25, 1816.
Vol. 1, Pt. 2–544
Brackenridge, William D., June 10, 1810–Feb. 3, 1893.
Vol. 1, Pt. 2–545
Brackett, Anna Callender, May 21, 1836–Mar. 9, 1911.
Vol. 1, Pt. 2–546
Brackett, Charles William, Nov. 26, 1892–Mar. 9, 1969.
Supp. 8–45
Brackett, Edward Augustus, Oct. 1, 1818–Mar. 15, 1908.
Vol. 1, Pt. 2–547
Brackett, Jeffrey Richardson, Oct. 20, 1860–Dec. 4, 1949.
Supp. 4–100
Bradbury, James Ware, June 10, 1802–Jan. 6, 1901.
Vol. 1, Pt. 2–547
Bradbury, Theophilus, Nov. 13, 1739–Sept. 6, 1803.
Vol. 1, Pt. 2–548
Bradbury, William Batchelder, Oct. 6, 1816–Jan. 7, 1868.
Vol. 1, Pt. 2–549
Braddock, Edward, 1695–July 13, 1755.
Vol. 1, Pt. 2–550
Braddock, James J., Dec. 6, 1905–Nov. 29, 1974.
Supp. 9–121
Braden, Spruille, Mar. 13, 1894–Jan. 10, 1978.
Supp. 10–64
Bradford, Alden, Nov. 19, 1765–Oct. 26, 1843.
Vol. 1, Pt. 2–551
Bradford, Alexander Warfield, Feb. 23, 1815–Nov. 5, 1867.
Vol. 1, Pt. 2–551
Bradford, Amory Howe, Apr. 14, 1846–Feb. 18, 19 11.
Vol. 1, Pt. 2–552
Bradford, Andrew, 1686–Nov. 24, 1742.
Vol. 1, Pt. 2–552
Bradford, Augustus Williamson, Jan. 9, 1806–Mar. 1, 1881.
Vol. 1, Pt. 2–553
Bradford, Edward Green, July 17, 1819–Jan. 16, 1884.
Vol. 1, Pt. 2–555
Bradford, Edward Hickling, June 9, 1848–May 7, 1926.
Vol. 1, Pt. 2–555
Bradford, Gamaliel, Jan. 15, 1831–Aug. 20, 1911.
Vol. 1, Pt. 2–556
Bradford, Gamaliel, Oct. 9, 1863–Apr. 11, 1932.
Supp. 1–105
Bradford, John, June 6, 1749–Mar. 20, 1830.
Vol. 1, Pt. 2–557
Bradford, Joseph, Oct. 24, 1843–Apr. 13, 1886.
Vol. 1, Pt. 2–558
Bradford, Roark Whitney Wickliffe, Aug. 21, 1896–Nov. 13, 1948.
Supp. 4–101
Bradford, Thomas, May 4, 1745–May 7, 1838.
Vol. 1, Pt. 2–558
Bradford, William, 1589/90–May 9/19, 1657.
Vol. 1, Pt. 2–559
Bradford, William, May 20, 1663–May 23, 1752.
Vol. 1, Pt. 2–563
Bradford, William, Jan. 19, 1721/22–Sept. 25, 1791.
Vol. 1, Pt. 2–564
Bradford, William, Sept 14, 1755–Aug. 23, 1795.
Vol. 1, Pt. 2–566
Bradford, William, Apr. 30, 1823–Apr. 25, 1892.
Vol. 1, Pt. 2–566
Bradish, Luther, Sept. 15, 1783–Aug. 30, 1863.
Vol. 1, Pt. 2–567
Bradley, Charles Henry, Feb. 13, 1860–Jan. 30, 1922.
Vol. 1, Pt. 2–568
Bradley, Charles William, June 27, 1807–Mar. 8, 1865.
Vol. 1, Pt. 2–568
Bradley, Denis Mary, Feb. 25, 1846–Dec. 13, 1903.
Vol. 1, Pt. 2–569
Bradley, Frank Howe, Sept. 20, 1838–Mar. 27, 1879.
Vol. 1, Pt. 2–570
Bradley, Frederick Worthen, Feb. 21, 1863–July 6, 1933.
Supp. 1–107
Bradley, John Edwin, Aug. 8, 1839–Oct. 7, 1912.
Vol. 1, Pt. 2–570

Bradley, Joseph P., Mar. 14, 1813–Jan. 22, 1892.
Vol. 1, Pt. 2–571
Bradley, Lydia Moss, July 31, 1816–Jan. 16, 1908.
Vol. 1, Pt. 2–573
Bradley, Milton, Nov. 8, 1836–May 30, 1911.
Vol. 1, Pt. 2–574
Bradley, Stephen Row, Feb. 20, 1754–Dec. 9, 1830.
Vol. 1, Pt. 2–575
Bradley, William Czar, Mar. 23, 1782–Mar. 3, 1867.
Vol. 1, Pt. 2–576
Bradley, William O'Connell, Mar. 18, 1847–May 23, 1914.
Vol. 1, Pt. 2–576
Bradstreet, Anne, *c.* 1612–Sept. 16, 1672.
Vol. 1, Pt. 2–577
Bradstreet, John, *c.* 1711–Sept. 25, 1774.
Vol. 1, Pt. 2–578
Bradstreet, Simon, March 1603–March 1697.
Vol. 1, Pt. 2–579
Bradwell, James Bolesworth, Apr. 16, 1828–Nov. 29, 1907
Vol. 1, Pt. 2–580
Bradwell, Myra, Feb. 12, 1831–Feb. 14, 1894.
Vol. 1, Pt. 2–581
Brady, Alice, Nov. 2, 1892–Oct. 28, 1939.
Supp. 2–58
Brady, Anthony Nicholas, Aug. 22, 1843–July 22, 1913.
Vol. 1, Pt. 2–581
Brady, Cyrus Townsend, Dec. 20, 1861–Jan. 24, 1920.
Vol. 1, Pt. 2–582
Brady, James Topham, Apr. 9, 1815–Feb. 9, 1869.
Vol. 1, Pt. 2–583
Brady, John Green, May 25, 1848–Dec. 17, 1918.
Supp. 1–108
Brady, Mathew B., *c.* 1823–Jan. 15, 1896.
Vol. 1, Pt. 2–584
Brady, Mildred Alice Edie, June 3, 1906–July 27, 1965.
Supp. 7–68
Brady, William Aloysius, June 19, 1863–Jan. 6, 1950.
Supp. 4–103
Bragdon, Claude Fayette, Aug. 1, 1866–Sept. 17, 1946.
Supp. 4–105
Bragg, Braxton, Mar. 22, 1817–Sept. 27, 1876.
Vol. 1, Pt. 2–585
Bragg, Edward Stuyvesant, Feb. 20, 1827–June 20, 1912.
Vol. 1, Pt. 2–587
Bragg, Thomas, Nov. 9, 1810–Jan. 21, 1872.
Vol. 1, Pt. 2–588
Brainard, Daniel, May 15, 1812–Oct. 10, 1866.
Vol. 1, Pt. 2–589
Brainard, John Gardiner Calkins, Oct. 21, 1796–Sept. 26 1828.
Vol. 1, Pt. 2–590
Brainerd, David, Apr. 20, 1718–Oct. 9, 1747.
Vol. 1, Pt. 2–591
Brainerd, Erastus, Feb. 25, 1855–Dec. 25, 1922.
Vol. 1, Pt. 2–592
Brainerd, Ezra, Dec. 17, 1844–Dec. 8, 1924.
Vol. 1, Pt. 2–593
Brainerd, John, Feb. 28, 1720–Mar. 18, 1781.
Vol. 1, Pt. 2–593
Brainerd, Lawrence, Mar. 16, 1794–May 9, 1870.
Vol. 1, Pt. 2–594
Brainerd, Thomas, June 17, 1804–Aug. 21, 1866.
Vol. 1, Pt. 2–594
Bramlette, Thomas E., Jan. 3, 1817–Jan. 12, 1875.
Vol. 1, Pt. 2–595
Branch, John, Nov. 4, 1782–Jan. 4, 1863.
Vol. 1, Pt. 2–596
Branch, Lawrence O'Bryan, Nov. 28, 1820–Sept. 17, 1862.
Vol. 1, Pt. 2–597
Brand, Max. [*See* Faust, Frederick Shiller, 1892–1944.]
Brandegee, Frank Bosworth, July 8, 1864–Oct. 14, 1924.
Vol. 1, Pt. 2–598
Brandegee, Townshend Stith, Feb. 16, 1843–Apr. 7, 1925.
Vol. 1, Pt. 2–599
Brandeis, Louis Dembitz, Nov. 13, 1856–Oct. 5, 1941.
Supp. 3–93
Brandon, Gerard Chittocque, Sept. 15, 1788–Mar. 28, 1850.
Vol. 1, Pt. 2–600
Braniff, Thomas Elmer, Dec. 6, 1883–Jan. 10, 1954.
Supp. 5–85
Brann, William Cowper, Jan. 4, 1855–Apr. 2, 1898.
Supp. 1–108
Brannan, John Milton, July 1, 1819–Dec. 16, 1892.
Vol. 1, Pt. 2–600
Brannan, Samuel, Mar. 2, 1819–May 5, 1889.
Vol. 1, Pt. 2–601
Branner, John Casper, July 4, 1850–Mar. 1, 1922.
Vol. 1, Pt. 2–602
Brannon, Henry, Nov. 26, 1837–Nov. 24, 1914.
Vol. 1, Pt. 2–603
Brant, Joseph, 1742–Nov. 24, 1807.
Vol. 1, Pt. 2–604
Brantley, Theodore, Feb. 12, 1851–Sept. 16, 1922.
Vol. 1, Pt. 2–605
Brashear, John Alfred, Nov. 24, 1840–Apr. 8, 1920.
Vol. 1, Pt. 2–605
Braslau, Sophie, Aug. 16, 1892–Dec. 22, 1935.
Supp. 1–109
Brattle, Thomas, June 20, 1658–May 18, 1713.
Vol. 1, Pt. 2–606
Brattle, William, Nov. 22, 1662–Feb. 15, 1716/17.
Vol. 1, Pt. 2–607
Bratton, John, Mar. 7, 1831–Jan. 12, 1898.
Vol. 1, Pt. 2–608
Braun, Wernher von, Mar. 23, 1912–June 16, 1977.
Supp. 10–65
Brawley, William Hiram, May 13, 1841–Nov. 15, 1916.
Vol. 1, Pt. 2–609
Braxton, Carter, Sept. 10, 1736–Oct. 10, 1797.
Vol. 1, Pt. 2–609
Bray, Thomas, 1656–Feb. 15, 1729/30.
Vol. 1, Pt. 2–610
Brayman, Mason, May 23, 1813–Feb. 27, 1895.
Vol. 1, Pt. 2–611
Brayton, Charles Ray, Aug. 16, 1840–Sept. 23, 1910.
Vol. 1, Pt. 2–612
Brazer, John, Sept. 21, 1789–Feb. 25, 1846.
Vol. 1, Pt. 2–612
Brearly, David, June 11, 1745–Aug. 16, 1790.
Vol. 2, Pt. 1–1
Breasted, James Henry, Aug. 27, 1865–Dec. 2, 1935.
Supp. 1–110
Breaux, Joseph Arsenne, Feb. 18, 1838–July 23, 1926.
Vol. 2, Pt. 1–2
Breck, George William, Sept. 1, 1863–Nov. 22, 1920.
Vol. 2, Pt. 1–2
Breck, James Lloyd, June 27, 1818–Mar. 30, 1876.
Vol. 2, Pt. 1–3
Breck, Samuel, July 17, 1771–Aug, 31, 1862.
Vol. 2, Pt. 1–4
Breckenridge, James, Mar. 7, 1763–May 13, 1833.
Vol. 2, Pt. 1–5
Breckenridge, Sophonisba Preston, Apr. 1, 1866–July 30, 1948.
Supp. 4–106
Breckinridge, Aida de Acosta, July 28, 1884–May 27, 1962.
Supp. 7–69
Breckinridge, Desha, Aug. 5, 1867–Feb. 18, 1935.
Supp. 1–113
Breckinridge, Henry Skillman, May 25, 1886–May 2, 1960.
Supp. 6–75
Breckinridge, John, Dec. 2, 1760–Dec. 14, 1806.
Vol. 2, Pt. 1–6
Breckinridge, John, July 4, 1797–Aug. 4, 1841.
Vol. 2, Pt. 1–6
Breckinridge, John Cabell, Jan. 15, 1821–May 17, 1875.
Vol. 2, Pt. 1–7
Breckinridge, Robert Jefferson, Mar. 8, 1800–Nov. 27, 1871.
Vol. 2, Pt. 1–10
Breckinridge, William Campbell Preston, Aug. 28, 1837–Nov. 19, 1904.
Vol. 2, Pt. 1–11
Breed, Ebenezer, May 12, 1766–Dec. 23, 1839.
Vol. 2, Pt. 1–12
Breen, Joseph Ignatius, Oct. 14, 1890–Dec. 7, 1965.
Supp. 7–70
Breen, Patrick, d. Dec. 21, 1868.
Vol. 2, Pt. 1–13
Breese, Kidder Randolph, Apr. 14, 1831–Sept. 13, 1881.
Vol. 2, Pt. 1–13

Breese, Sidney, July 15, 1800–June 27, 1878.
Vol. 2, Pt. 1–14
Brennan, Alfred Laurens, Feb. 14, 1853–June 14, 1921.
Vol. 2, Pt. 1–16
Brennan, Francis James, May 7, 1894–July 2, 1968.
Supp. 8–46
Brennan, Walter, July 25, 1894–Sept. 21, 1974.
Supp. 9–122
Brennemann, Joseph, Sept. 25, 1872–July 2, 1944.
Supp. 3–100
Brenner, Victor David, June 12, 1871–Apr. 5, 1924.
Vol. 2, Pt. 1–17
Brenon, Herbert, Jan. 13, 1880–June 21, 1958.
Supp. 6–76
Brent, Charles Henry, Apr. 9, 1862–Mar. 27, 1929.
Supp. 1–115
Brent, George, Mar. 15, 1904–May 26, 1979.
Supp. 10–68
Brent, Margaret, 1600–1670/71.
Vol. 2, Pt. 1–18
Brentano, Lorenz, Nov. 4, 1813–Sept. 17, 1891.
Vol. 2, Pt. 1–19
Brereton, John. [*See* Brierton, John, fl. 1572–1619.]
Brereton, Lewis Hyde, June 21, 1890–July 19, 1967.
Supp. 8–47
Brett, George Platt, Dec. 8, 1858–Sept. 19, 1936.
Supp. 2–59
Brett, William Howard, July 1, 1846–Aug. 24, 1918.
Vol. 2, Pt. 1–20
Brevoort, James Renwick, July 20, 1832–Dec. 15, 1918.
Vol. 2, Pt. 1–21
Brewer, Charles, Mar. 27, 1804–Oct. 11, 1885.
Vol. 2, Pt. 1–21
Brewer, David Josiah, June 20, 1837–Mar. 28, 1910.
Vol. 2, Pt. 1–22
Brewer, Mark Spencer, Oct. 22, 1837–Mar. 18, 1901.
Vol. 2, Pt. 1–24
Brewer, Thomas Mayo, Nov. 21, 1814–Jan. 23, 1880.
Vol. 2, Pt. 1–24
Brewer, William Henry, Sept. 14, 1828–Nov. 2, 1910.
Vol. 2, Pt. 1–25
Brewster, Benjamin Harris, Oct. 13, 1816–Apr. 4, 1888.
Vol. 2, Pt. 1–26
Brewster, Frederick Carroll, May 15, 1825–Dec. 30, 1898.
Vol. 2, Pt. 1–27
Brewster, James, Aug. 6, 1788–Nov. 22, 1866.
Vol. 2, Pt. 1–27
Brewster, Osmyn, Aug. 2, 1797–July 15, 1889.
Vol. 2, Pt. 1–28
Brewster, Ralph Owen, Feb. 22, 1888–Dec. 25, 1961.
Supp. 7–72
Brewster, William, 1567–Apr. 10, 1644.
Vol. 2, Pt. 1–29
Brewster, William, July 5, 1851–July 11, 1919.
Vol. 2, Pt. 1–30
Brice, Calvin Stewart, Sept. 17, 1845–Dec. 15, 1898.
Vol. 2, Pt. 1–31
Brice, Fanny, Oct. 29, 1891–May 29, 1951.
Supp. 5–87
Brickell, Henry Herschel, Sept. 13, 1889–May 29, 1952.
Supp. 5–88
Brickell, Robert Coman, Apr. 4, 1824–Nov. 20, 1900.
Vol. 2, Pt. 1–32
Bridger, James, Mar. 17, 1804–July 17, 1881.
Vol. 2, Pt. 1–33
Bridgers, Robert Rufus, Nov. 28, 1819–Dec. 10, 1888.
Vol. 2, Pt. 1–33
Bridges, Calvin Blackman, Jan. 11, 1889–Dec. 27, 1938.
Supp. 2–60
Bridges, (Henry) Styles, Sept. 9, 1898–Nov. 26, 1961.
Supp. 7–73
Bridges, Robert, d. 1656.
Vol. 2, Pt. 1–34
Bridges, Robert, Mar. 5, 1806–Feb. 20, 1882.
Vol. 2, Pt. 1–35
Bridges, Thomas Jefferson Davis ("Tommy"), Dec. 28, 1906–Apr. 19, 1968.
Supp. 8–49
Bridgman, Elijah Coleman, Apr. 22, 1801–Nov. 2, 1861.
Vol. 2, Pt. 1–36
Bridgman, Frederic Arthur, Nov. 10, 1847–Jan. 13, 1927.
Vol. 2, Pt. 1–36
Bridgman, Herbert Lawrence, May 30, 1844–Sept. 24, 1924.
Vol. 2, Pt. 1–37
Bridgman, Laura Dewey, Dec. 21, 1829–May 24, 1889.
Vol. 2, Pt. 1–38
Bridgman, Percy Williams, Apr. 21, 1882–Aug. 20, 1961.
Supp. 7–74
Brierton, John, fl. 1572–1619.
Vol. 2, Pt. 1–39
Briggs, Charles Augustus, Jan. 15, 1841–June 8, 1913.
Vol. 2, Pt. 1–40
Briggs, Charles Frederick, Dec. 30, 1804–June 20, 1877.
Vol. 2, Pt. 1–41
Briggs, Clare A., Aug. 5, 1875–Jan. 3, 1930.
Supp. 1–117
Briggs, George Nixon, Apr. 12, 1796–Sept. 12. 1861.
Vol. 2, Pt. 1–41
Briggs, LeBaron Russell, Dec 11, 1855–Apr. 24, 1934.
Supp. 1–118
Briggs, Lloyd Vernon, Aug. 13, 1863–Feb. 28, 1941.
Supp. 3–101
Briggs, Lyman James, May 7, 1874–Mar. 25, 1963.
Supp. 7–76
Brigham, Albert Perry, June 12, 1855–Mar. 31, 1932.
Supp. 1–119
Brigham, Amariah, Dec. 26, 1798–Sept. 8, 1849.
Vol. 2, Pt. 1–42
Brigham, Joseph Henry, Dec. 12, 1838–June 29, 1904.
Vol. 2, Pt. 1–43
Brigham, Mary Ann, Dec. 6, 1829–June 29, 1889.
Vol. 2, Pt. 1–44
Bright, Edward, Oct. 6, 1808–May 17, 1894.
Vol. 2, Pt. 1–44
Bright, James Wilson, Oct. 2, 1852–Nov. 29, 1926.
Vol. 2, Pt. 1–45
Bright, Jesse David, Dec. 18, 1812–May 20, 1875.
Vol. 2, Pt. 1–45
Bright Eyes, 1854–May 26, 1903.
Vol. 2, Pt. 1–46
Brightly, Frederick Charles, Aug. 26, 1812–Jan. 24, 1888.
Vol. 2, Pt. 1–47
Brightman, Edgar Sheffield, Sept. 20, 1884–Feb. 25, 1953.
Supp. 5–90
Brill, Abraham Arden, Oct. 12, 1874–Mar. 2, 1948.
Supp. 4–107
Brill, Nathan Edwin, Jan. 13, 1859–Dec. 13, 1925.
Vol. 2, Pt. 1–47
Brincklé, William Draper, Feb. 9, 1798–Dec. 16, 1862.
Vol. 2, Pt. 1–48
Brinkerhoff, Jacob, Aug. 31, 1810–July 19, 1880.
Vol. 2, Pt. 1–49
Brinkerhoff, Roeliff, June 28, 1828–June 4, 1911.
Vol. 2, Pt. 1–49
Brinkley, John Richard, July 8, 1885–May 26, 1942.
Supp. 3–103
Brinton, Clarence Crane, Feb. 2, 1898–Sept. 7, 1968.
Supp. 8–50
Brinton, Daniel Garrison, May 13, 1837–July 31, 1899.
Vol. 2, Pt. 1–50
Brinton, John Hill, May 21, 1832–Mar. 18, 1907.
Vol. 2, Pt. 1–51
Brisbane, Albert, Aug. 22, 1809–May 1, 1890.
Vol. 2, Pt. 1–52
Brisbane, Arthur, Dec. 12, 1864–Dec. 25, 1936.
Supp. 2–62
Bristed, Charles Astor, Oct. 6, 1820–Jan. 14, 1874.
Vol. 2, Pt. 1–53
Bristed, John, Oct. 17, 1778–Feb. 23, 1855.
Vol. 2, Pt. 1–54
Bristol, John Bunyan, Mar. 14, 1826–Aug. 31, 1909.
Vol. 2, Pt. 1–54
Bristol, Mark Lambert, Apr. 17, 1868–May 13, 1939.
Supp. 2–65
Bristol, William Henry, July 5, 1859–June 18, 1930.
Supp. 1–120
Bristow, Benjamin Helm, June 20, 1832–June 22, 1896.
Vol. 2, Pt. 1–55
Bristow, George Frederick, Dec. 19, 1825–Dec. 13, 1898.
Vol. 2, Pt. 1–56

Bristow, Joseph Little, July 22, 1861–July 14, 1944. Supp. 3–105
Britton, Barbara, Sept. 26, 1920–Jan. 17, 1980. Supp. 10–69
Britton, Nathaniel Lord, Jan. 15, 1859–June 25, 1934. Supp. 1–121
Broadhead, Garland Carr, Oct. 30, 1827–Dec. 12, 1912. Vol. 2, Pt. 1–57
Broadhead, James Overton, May 29, 1819–Aug. 7, 1898. Vol. 2, Pt. 1–58
Broadus, John Albert, Jan. 24, 1827–Mar. 16, 1895. Vol. 2, Pt. 1–59
Brockett, Linus Pierpont, Oct. 16, 1820–Jan. 13, 1893. Vol. 2, Pt. 1–60
Brockmeyer, Henry C. [*See* Brokmeyer, Henry C., 1828–1906.]
Brockway, Zebulon Reed, Apr. 28, 1827–Oct. 21, 1920. Vol. 2, Pt. 1–60
Broderick, David Colbreth, Feb. 4, 1820–Sept. 16, 1859. Vol. 2, Pt. 1–61
Brodhead, Daniel, Sept. 17, 1736–Nov. 15, 1809. Vol. 2, Pt. 1–62
Brodhead, John Romeyn, Jan. 2, 1814–May 6, 1873. Vol. 2, Pt. 1–63
Bröel, Max, June 8, 1870–Oct. 26, 1941. Supp. 3–106
Brokenshire, Norman Ernest, June 10, 1898–May 4, 1965. Supp. 7–77
Brokmeyer, Henry C., Aug. 12, 1828–July 26, 1906. Vol. 2, Pt. 1–64
Bromfield, John, Apr. 11, 1779–Dec. 9, 1849. Vol. 2, Pt. 1–65
Bromfield, Louis, Dec. 27, 1896–Mar. 18, 1956. Supp. 6–77
Bromley, Isaac Hill, Mar. 6, 1833–Aug. 11, 1898. Vol. 2, Pt. 1–66
Brondel, John Baptist, Feb. 23, 1842–Nov. 3, 1903. Vol. 2, Pt. 1–67
Bronk, Detlev Wulf, Aug. 13, 1897–Nov. 17, 1975. Supp. 9–124
Bronson, Henry, Jan. 30, 1804–Nov. 26, 1893. Vol. 2, Pt. 1–68
Bronson, Walter Cochrane, Aug. 17, 1862–June 2, 1928. Vol. 2, Pt. 1–68
Brooke, Charles Frederick Tucker, June 4, 1883–June 22, 1946 Supp. 4–109
Brooke, Francis Taliaferro, Aug. 27, 1763–Mar. 3, 1851. Vol. 2, Pt. 1–69
Brooke, John Mercer, Dec. 18, 1826–Dec. 14, 1906. Vol. 2, Pt. 1–69
Brooke, John Rutter, July 21, 1838–Sept. 5, 1926. Vol. 2, Pt. 1–70
Brooker, Charles Frederick, Mar. 4, 1847–Dec. 20, 1926. Vol. 2, Pt. 1–71
Brookhart, Smith Wildman, Feb. 2, 1869–Nov. 15, 1944. Supp. 3–107
Brookings, Robert Somers, Jan. 22, 1850–Nov. 15, 1932. Supp. 1–122
Brooks, Alfred Hulse, July 18, 1871–Nov. 22, 1924. Vol. 2, Pt. 1–72
Brooks, Byron Alden, Dec. 12, 1845–Sept. 28, 1911. Vol. 2, Pt. 1–74
Brooks, Charles, Oct. 30, 1795–July 7, 1872. Vol. 2, Pt. 1–74
Brooks, Charles Timothy, June 20, 1813–June 14, 1883. Vol. 2, Pt. 1–75
Brooks, Elbridge Streeter, Apr. 14, 1846–Jan. 7, 1902. Vol. 2, Pt. 1–75
Brooks, Erastus, Jan. 31, 1815–Nov. 25, 1886. Vol. 2, Pt. 1–76
Brooks, George Washington, Mar. 16, 1821–Jan. 6, 1882,. Vol. 2, Pt. 1–77
Brooks, James, Nov. 10, 1810–Apr. 30, 1873. Vol. 2, Pt. 1–77
Brooks, James Gordon, Sept. 3, 1801–Feb. 20, 1841. Vol. 2, Pt. 1–79
Brooks, John, 1752–Mar. 1, 1825. Vol. 2, Pt. 1–79
Brooks, John Graham, July 19, 1846–Feb. 8, 1938. Supp. 2–66
Brooks, Maria Gowen, *c.* 1794–Nov. 11, 1845. Vol. 2, Pt. 1–81
Brooks, Mary Elizabeth Aiken. [*See* Brooks, James Gordon, 1801–1841.]
Brooks, Noah, Oct. 24, 1830–Aug. 16, 1903. Vol. 2, Pt. 1–82
Brooks, Overton, Dec. 21, 1897–Sept. 16, 1961. Supp. 7–78
Brooks, Peter Chardon, Jan. 11, 1767–Jan. 1, 1849. Vol. 2, Pt. 1–83
Brooks, Phillips, Dec. 13, 1835–Jan. 23, 1893. Vol. 2, Pt. 1–83
Brooks, Preston Smith, Aug. 6, 1819–Jan. 27, 1857. Vol. 2, Pt. 1–88
Brooks, Richard Edwin, Oct. 28, 1865–May 2, 1919. Vol. 2, Pt. 1–88
Brooks, Thomas Benton, June 19, 1836–Nov. 22, 1900. Vol. 2, Pt. 1–89
Brooks, Van Wyck, Feb. 16, 1886–May 2, 1963. Supp. 7–79
Brooks, William Thomas Harbaugh, Jan. 28, 1821–July 19, 1870. Vol. 2, Pt. 1–92
Brooks, William Keith, Mar. 25, 1848–Nov. 12, 1908. Vol. 2, Pt. 1–90
Brooks, William Robert, June 11, 1844–May 3, 1921. Vol. 2, Pt. 1–91
Brophy, John, Nov. 6, 1883–Feb. 19, 1963. Supp. 7–81
Brophy, Thomas D'Arcy, Oct. 18, 1893–July 29, 1967. Supp. 8–52
Brophy, Truman William, Apr. 12, 1848–Feb. 4, 1928. Vol. 2, Pt. 1–93
Bross, William, Nov. 4, 1813–Jan. 27, 1890. Vol. 2, Pt. 1–93
Brough, Charles Hillman, July 9, 1876–Dec. 26, 193. Supp. 1–123
Brough, John, Sept. 17, 1811–Aug. 29, 1865. Vol. 2, Pt. 1–94
Brougham, John, May 9, 1810–June 7, 1880. Vol. 2, Pt. 1–95
Broun, Heywood Campbell, Dec. 7, 1888–Dec. 18, 1939. Supp. 2–67
Broward, Napoleon Bonaparte, Apr. 19, 1857–Oct. 1, 1910. Vol. 2, Pt. 1–96
Browder, Earl Russell, May 20, 1891–June 27, 1973. Supp. 9–126
Brower, Jacob Vradenberg, Jan 21, 1844–June 1, 1905. Vol. 2, Pt. 1–97
Browere, John Henri Isaac, Nov. 18, 1792–Sept. 10, 1834. Vol. 2, Pt. 1–97
Brown, Aaron Venable, Aug. 15, 1795–Mar. 8, 1859. Vol. 2, Pt. 1–98
Brown, Addison, Feb. 21, 1830–Apr. 9, 1913. Vol. 2, Pt. 1–99
Brown, Albert Gallatin, May 31, 1813–June 12, 1880. Vol. 2, Pt. 1–100
Brown, Alexander, Nov. 17, 1764–Apr. 3, 1834. Vol. 2, Pt. 1–101
Brown, Alexander, Sept. 5, 1843–Aug. 25, 1906. Vol. 2, Pt. 1–103
Brown, Alexander Ephraim, May 14, 1852–Apr. 26, 1911. Vol. 2, Pt. 1–103
Brown, Antoinette. [*See* Blackwell, Antoinette Louisa Brown, 1825–1921.]
Brown, Bedford, 1792–Dec. 6, 1870. Vol. 2, Pt. 1–104
Brown, Benjamin Gratz, May 28, 1826–Dec. 13, 1885. Vol. 2, Pt. 1–105
Brown, Carleton, July 15, 1869–June 25, 1941. Supp. 3–108
Brown, Charles Brockden, Jan. 17, 1771–Feb. 22, 1810. Vol. 2, Pt. 1–107
Brown, Charles Reynolds, Oct. 1, 1862–Nov. 28, 1950. Supp. 4–110
Brown, Charles Rufus, Feb. 22, 1849–Feb. 1, 1914. Vol. 2, Pt. 1–110
Brown, Charlotte Emerson, Apr. 21, 1838–Feb. 5, 1895. Vol. 2, Pt. 1–110
Brown, Charlotte Hawkins, June 11, 1883–Jan. 11, 1961. Supp. 7–82

Brown, Clarence James, July 14, 1893–Aug. 23, 1965.
Supp. 7–84
Brown, David Paul, Sept. 28, 1795–July 11, 1872.
Vol. 2, Pt. 1–111
Brown, Ebenezer, 1795–Jan. 3, 1889.
Vol. 2, Pt. 1–112
Brown, Elmer Ellsworth, Aug. 28, 1861–Nov. 3, 1934.
Supp. 1–124
Brown, Ernest William, Nov. 29, 1866–July 22, 1938.
Supp. 2–69
Brown, Ethan Allen, July 4, 1766–Feb. 24, 1852.
Vol. 2, Pt. 1–113
Brown, Fayette, Dec. 17, 1823–Jan. 20, 1910.
Vol. 2, Pt. 1–113
Brown, Francis, Jan. 11, 1784–July 27, 1820.
Vol. 2, Pt. 1–114
Brown, Francis, Dec. 26, 1849–Oct. 15, 1916.
Vol. 2, Pt. 1–115
Brown, Frederic Tilden, Oct. 7, 1853–May 7, 1910.
Vol. 2, Pt. 1–116
Brown, George, Apr. 17, 1787–Aug. 26, 1859.
Vol. 2, Pt. 1–116
Brown, George, Oct. 11, 1823–May 6, 1892.
Vol. 2, Pt. 1–117
Brown, George Pliny, Nov. 10, 1836–Feb. 1, 1910.
Vol. 2, Pt. 1–118
Brown, George Scratchley, Aug. 17, 1918–Dec. 5, 1978.
Supp. 10–71
Brown, George William, Oct. 13, 1812–Sept. 5, 1890.
Vol. 2, Pt. 1–118
Brown, Gertrude Foster, July 29, 1867–Mar. 1, 1956.
Supp. 6–79
Brown, Goold, Mar. 7, 1791–Mar. 31, 1857.
Vol. 2, Pt. 1–119
Brown, Henry Billings, Mar. 2, 1836–Sept. 4, 1913.
Vol. 2, Pt. 1–120
Brown, Henry Cordis, Nov. 18, 1820–Mar. 6, 1906.
Vol. 2, Pt. 1–121
Brown, Henry Kirke, Feb. 24, 1814–July 10, 1886.
Vol. 2, Pt. 1–121
Brown, Isaac Van Arsdale, Nov. 4, 1784–Apr. 19, 1861.
Vol. 2, Pt. 1–124
Brown, Jacob Jennings, May 9, 1775–Feb. 24, 1828.
Vol. 2, Pt. 1–124
Brown, James, Sept. 11, 1766–Apr. 7, 1835.
Vol. 2, Pt. 1–126
Brown, James, Feb. 4, 1791–Nov. 1, 1877.
Vol. 2, Pt. 1–126
Brown, James, May 19, 1800–Mar. 10, 1855.
Vol. 2, Pt. 1–127
Brown, James Salisbury, Dec. 23, 1802–Dec. 29, 1879.
Vol. 2, Pt. 1–127
Brown, John, Jan. 27, 1736–Sept. 20, 1803.
Vol. 2, Pt. 1–128
Brown, John, Oct. 19, 1744–Oct. 19, 1780.
Vol. 2, Pt. 1–129
Brown, John, Sept. 12, 1757–Aug. 28, 1837.
Vol. 2, Pt. 1–130
Brown, John, May 9, 1800–Dec. 2, 1859.
Vol. 2, Pt. 1–131
Brown, John A., May 21, 1788–Dec. 31, 1872.
Vol. 2, Pt. 1–134
Brown, John Appleton, July 12, 1844–Jan. 18, 1902.
Vol. 2, Pt. 1–135
Brown, John Calvin, Jan. 6, 1827–Aug. 17, 1889.
Vol. 2, Pt. 1–135
Brown, John Carter, Aug. 28, 1797–June 10, 1874.
Vol. 2, Pt. 1–136
Brown, John George, Nov. 11, 1831–Feb. 8, 1913.
Vol. 2, Pt. 1–137
Brown, John Mason, Jr., July 3, 1900–Mar. 16, 1969.
Supp. 8–53
Brown, John Mifflin, Sept. 8, 1817–Mar. 16, 1893.
Vol. 2, Pt. 1–138
Brown, John Newton, June 29, 1803–May 14, 1868.
Vol. 2, Pt. 1–139
Brown, John Porter, Aug. 17, 1814–Apr. 28, 1872.
Vol. 2, Pt. 1–139
Brown, John Young, June 28, 1835–Jan. 11, 1904.
Vol. 2, Pt. 1–140
Brown, Johnny Mack, Sept. 1, 1904–Nov. 14, 1974.
Supp. 9–127
Brown, Joseph, Dec. 3/14, 1733–Dec. 3, 1785.
Vol. 2, Pt. 1–141
Brown, Joseph Emerson, Apr. 15, 1821–Nov. 30, 1894.
Vol. 2, Pt. 1–141
Brown, Joseph Rogers, Jan. 26, 1810–July 23, 1876.
Vol. 2, Pt. 1–143
Brown, Lawrason, Sept. 29, 1871–Dec. 26, 1937.
Supp. 2–70
Brown, Margaret Wise, May 23, 1910–Nov. 13, 1952.
Supp. 5–92
Brown, Mather, Oct. 7, 1761–May 25, 1831.
Vol. 2, Pt. 1–144
Brown, Morris, Feb. 12, 1770–May 9, 1849.
Vol. 2, Pt. 1–145
Brown, Moses, Sept. 12/23, 1738–Sept. 7, 1836.
Vol. 2, Pt. 1–146
Brown, Moses, Oct. 2, 1742–Feb. 9, 1827.
Vol. 2, Pt. 1–147
Brown, Neill Smith, Apr. 18, 1810–Jan. 30, 1886.
Vol. 2, Pt. 1–147
Brown, Nicholas, July 28, 1729 o.s.-May 29, 1791.
Vol. 2, Pt. 1–148
Brown, Nicholas, Apr. 4, 1769–Sept. 27, 1841.
Vol. 2, Pt. 1–149
Brown, Obadiah, July 15, 1771–Oct. 15, 1822.
Vol. 2, Pt. 1–150
Brown, Olympia, Jan. 5, 1835–Oct. 23, 1926.
Vol. 2, Pt. 1–151
Brown, Percy, Nov. 24, 1875–Oct. 8, 1950.
Supp. 4–111
Brown, Phoebe Hinsdale, May 1, 1783–Aug. 10, 1861.
Vol. 2, Pt. 1–151
Brown, Prentiss Marsh, June 18, 1889–Dec. 19, 1973.
Supp. 9–129
Brown, Ralph Hall, Jan. 12, 1898–Feb. 23, 1948.
Supp. 4–112
Brown, Samuel, Jan. 30, 1769–Jan. 12, 1830.
Vol. 2, Pt. 1–152
Brown, Samuel Gilman, Jan. 4, 1813–Nov. 4, 1885.
Vol. 2, Pt. 1–153
Brown, Samuel Robbins, June 16, 1810–June 20, 1880.
Vol. 2, Pt. 1–153
Brown, Simon, Nov. 29, 1802–Feb. 26, 1873.
Vol. 2, Pt. 1–154
Brown, Solyman, Nov. 17, 1790–Feb. 13, 1876.
Vol. 2, Pt. 1–155
Brown, Sylvanus, May 24, 1747 o.s.-July 30, 1824.
Vol. 2, Pt. 1–156
Brown, Walter Folger, May 31, 1869–Jan. 26, 1961.
Supp. 7–85
Brown, William, 1752–Jan. 11, 1792.
Vol. 2, Pt. 1–157
Brown, William Adams, Dec. 29, 1865–Dec. 15, 1943.
Supp. 3–110
Brown, William Carlos, July 29, 1853–Dec. 6, 1924.
Vol. 2, Pt. 1–157
Brown, William Garrott, Apr. 24, 1868–Oct. 19, 1913.
Vol. 2, Pt. 1–158
Brown, William Henry, Feb. 29, 1836–June 25, 1910.
Vol. 2, Pt. 1–159
Brown, William Hill, 1765–Sept. 2, 1793.
Supp. 1–25
Brown, William Hughey, Jan. 15, 1815–Oct. 12, 1875.
Vol. 2, Pt. 1–160
Brown, William Wells, *c.* 1816–Nov. 6, 1884.
Vol. 2, Pt. 1–161
Browne, Benjamin Frederick, July 14, 1793–Nov. 23, 1873.
Vol. 2, Pt. 1–161
Browne, Charles Albert, Aug. 12, 1870–Feb. 3, 1947.
Supp. 4–113
Browne, Charles Farrar, Apr. 26, 1834–Mar. 6, 1867.
Vol. 2, Pt. 1–162
Browne, Daniel Jay, b. Dec. 4, 1804.
Vol. 2, Pt. 1–164
Browne, Francis Fisher, Dec. 1, 1843–May 11, 1913.
Vol. 2, Pt. 1–165
Browne, Herbert Wheildon Cotton, Nov. 22, 1860–Apr. 1946.
Supp. 4–115

Browne, Irving, Sept. 14, 1835 Feb. 6, 1899.
Vol. 2, Pt. 1–165
Browne, John, d. Apr. 10, 1662.
Vol. 2, Pt. 1–166
Browne, John Ross, Feb. 11, 1821–Dec. 8, 1875.
Vol. 2, Pt. 1–167
Browne, Junius Henri, Oct. 14, 1833–Apr. 2, 1902.
Vol. 2, Pt. 1–168
Browne, Thomas, d. Aug. 3, 1825.
Vol. 2, Pt. 1–168
Browne, William, Mar. 5, 1737–Feb. 13, 1802.
Vol. 2, Pt. 1–169
Browne, William Hand, Dec. 31, 1828–Dec. 13, 1912.
Vol. 2, Pt. 1–170
Brownell, Henry Howard, Feb. 6, 1820–Oct. 31, 1872.
Vol. 2, Pt. 1–171
Brownell, Thomas Church, Oct. 19, 1779–Jan. 13, 1865.
Vol. 2, Pt. 1–171
Brownell, William Crary, Aug. 30, 1851–July 22, 1928.
Vol. 2, Pt. 1–172
Browning, John Moses, Jan. 21, 1855–Nov. 26, 1926.
Vol. 2, Pt. 1–174
Browning, Orville Hickman, Feb. 10, 1806–Aug. 10, 1881.
Vol. 2, Pt. 1–175
Browning, Tod, July 12, 1880–Oct. 6, 1962.
Supp. 7–86
Brownlee, James Forbis, July 29, 1891–Oct. 12, 1960.
Supp. 6–80
Brownlee, William Craig, 1784–Feb. 10, 1860.
Vol. 2, Pt. 1–176
Brownlow, William Gannaway, Aug. 29, 1805–Apr. 29, 1877.
Vol. 2, Pt. 1–177
Brownson, Orestes Augustus, Sept. 16, 1803–Apr. 17, 1876.
Vol. 2, Pt. 1–178
Brownson, Willard Herbert, July 8, 1845–Mar. 16, 1935.
Supp. 1–126
Bruce, Andrew Alexander, Apr. 15, 1866–Dec. 6, 1934.
Supp. 1–128
Bruce, Archibald, Feb. 1777–Feb. 22, 1818.
Vol. 2, Pt. 1–179
Bruce, Blanche K., Mar. 1, 1841–Mar. 17, 1898.
Vol. 2, Pt. 1–180
Bruce, David Kirkpatrick Este, Feb. 12, 1898–Dec. 5, 1977.
Supp. 10–73
Bruce, Edward Bright, Apr. 13, 1879–Jan. 26, 1943.
Supp. 3–111
Bruce, George, June 26, 1781–July 5, 1866.
Vol. 2, Pt. 1–181
Bruce, Lenny, Oct. 13, 1925–Aug. 3, 1966.
Supp. 8–55
Bruce, Philip Alexander, Mar. 7, 1856–Aug. 16, 1933.
Supp. 1–129
Bruce, Robert, Feb. 20, 1778–June 14, 1846.
Vol. 2, Pt. 1–181
Bruce, William Cabell, Mar. 12, 1860–May 9, 1946.
Supp. 4–116
Brucker, Wilber Marion, June 23, 1894–Oct. 28, 1968.
Supp. 8–56
Brühl, Gustav, May 31, 1826–Feb. 16, 1903.
Vol. 2, Pt. 1–182
Brulé, Étienne, *c.* 1592–1632.
Vol. 2, Pt. 1–183
Brumby, Richard Trapier, Aug. 4, 1804–Oct. 6, 1875.
Vol. 2, Pt. 1–184
Brumidi, Constantino, July 26, 1805–Feb. 19, 1880.
Vol. 2, Pt. 1–184
Brundage, Avery, Sept. 28, 1887–May 8, 1975.
Supp. 9–130
Brunner, Arnold William, Sept. 25, 1857–Feb. 12, 1925.
Vol. 2, Pt. 1–185
Bruno, Angelo, 1911–Mar. 21, 1980.
Supp. 10–75
Brunswick, Ruth Mack, Feb. 17, 1897–Jan. 24, 1946.
Supp. 4–117
Brunton, David William, June 11, 1849–Dec. 20, 1927.
Vol. 2, Pt. 1–186
Brush, Charles Francis, Mar. 17, 1849–June 15, 1929.
Supp. 1–129
Brush, Edward Nathaniel, Apr. 23, 1852–Jan. 10, 1933.
Supp. 1–130
Brush, George de Forest, Sept. 28, 1855–Apr. 24, 1941.
Supp. 3–112
Brush, George Jarvis, Dec. 15, 1831–Feb. 6, 1912.
Vol. 2, Pt. 1–187
Bruté de Rémur, Simon William Gabriel, Mar. 20, 1779–June 26, 1839.
Vol. 2, Pt. 1–188
Bryan, Charles Wayland, Feb. 10, 1867–Mar. 4, 1945.
Supp. 3–114
Bryan, George, Aug. 11, 1731–Jan. 27, 1791.
Vol. 2, Pt. 1–189
Bryan, John Stewart, Oct. 23, 1871–Oct. 16, 1944.
Supp. 3–115
Bryan, Kirk, July 22, 1888–Aug. 22, 1950.
Supp. 4–118
Bryan, Mary Edwards, May 17, 1842–June 15, 1913.
Vol. 2, Pt. 1–190
Bryan, Thomas Barbour, Dec. 22, 1828–Jan. 25, 1906.
Vol. 2, Pt. 1–190
Bryan, William Jennings, Mar. 19, 1860–July 26, 1925.
Vol. 2, Pt. 1–191
Bryant, Gridley, Aug. 26, 1789–June 13, 1867.
Vol. 2, Pt. 1–197
Bryant, John Howard, July 22, 1807–Jan. 14, 1902.
Vol. 2, Pt. 1–198
Bryant, Joseph Decatur, Mar. 12, 1845–Apr. 7, 1914.
Vol. 2, Pt. 1–199
Bryant, Louise Frances Stevens, Sept. 19, 1885–Aug. 29, 1959.
Supp. 6–80
Bryant, Ralph Clement, Jan. 22, 1877–Feb. 1, 1939.
Supp. 2–72
Bryant, William Cullen, Nov. 3, 1794–June 12, 1878.
Vol. 2, Pt. 1–200
Bryce, Lloyd Stephens, Sept. 20, 1851–Apr. 2, 1917.
Vol. 2, Pt. 1–205
Bryson, Lyman Lloyd, July 12, 1888–Nov. 24, 1959.
Supp. 6–82
Buchanan, Edgar, Mar. 20, 1903–Apr. 4, 1979.
Supp. 10–76
Buchanan, Franklin, Sept. 17, 1800–May 11, 1874.
Vol. 2, Pt. 1–206
Buchanan, James, Apr. 23, 1791–June 1, 1868.
Vol. 2, Pt. 1–207
Buchanan, John, 1772–Nov. 6, 1844.
Vol. 2, Pt. 1–214
Buchanan, Joseph, Aug. 24, 1785–Sept. 29, 1829.
Vol. 2, Pt. 1–215
Buchanan, Joseph Ray, Dec. 6, 1851–Sept. 13, 1924.
Vol. 2, Pt. 1–215
Buchanan, Joseph Rodes, Dec. 11, 1814–Dec. 26, 1899.
Vol. 2, Pt. 1–216
Buchanan, Robert Christie, Mar. 1, 1811–Nov. 29, 1878.
Vol. 2, Pt. 1–217
Buchanan, Scott Milross, Mar. 17, 1895–Mar. 25, 1968.
Supp. 8–58
Buchanan, Thomas, Dec. 24, 1744–Nov. 10, 1815.
Vol. 2, Pt. 1–218
Buchanan, William Insco, Sept. 10, 1852–Oct. 16, 1909.
Vol. 2, Pt. 1–219
Bucher, John Conrad, June 10, 1730–Aug. 15, 1780.
Vol. 2, Pt. 1–220
Buchman, Frank Nathan Daniel, June 4, 1878–Aug. 7, 1961.
Supp. 7–88
Buchtel, John Richards, Jan. 18, 1820–May 23, 1892.
Vol. 2, Pt. 1–221
Buck, Albert Henry, Oct. 20, 1842–Nov. 16, 1922.
Vol. 2, Pt. 1–221
Buck, Daniel, Nov. 9, 1753–Aug. 16, 1816.
Vol. 2, Pt. 1–222
Buck, Dudley, Mar. 10, 1839–Oct. 6, 1909.
Vol. 2, Pt. 1–222
Buck, Franklyn Howard, Mar. 17, 1884–Mar. 25, 1950.
Supp. 4–119
Buck, Gurdon, May 4, 1807–Mar. 6, 1877.
Vol. 2, Pt. 1–223
Buck, Leffert Lefferts, Feb. 5, 1837–July 17, 1909.
Vol. 2, Pt. 1–224
Buck, Pearl Comfort Sydenstricker, June 26, 1892–Mar. 6, 1973.
Supp. 9–132.

Buck, Philo Melvin, May 15, 1846–Sept. 8, 1924.
Vol. 2, Pt. 1–225

Buckalew, Charles Rollin, Dec. 28, 1821–May 19, 1899.
Vol. 2, Pt. 1–225

Buckhout, Isaac Craig, Nov. 7, 1830–Sept. 27, 1874.
Vol. 2, Pt. 1–226

Buckingham, Joseph Tinker, Dec. 21, 1779–Apr. 11, 1861.
Vol. 2, Pt. 1–227

Buckingham, William Alfred, May 28, 1804–Feb. 5, 1875.
Vol. 2, Pt. 1–228

Buckland, Cyrus, Aug. 10, 1799–Feb. 26, 1891.
Vol. 2, Pt. 1–229

Buckland, Ralph Pomeroy, Jan. 20, 1812–May 27, 1892.
Vol. 2, Pt. 1–230

Buckler, Thomas Hepburn, Jan. 4, 1812–Apr. 20, 1901.
Vol. 2, Pt. 1–230

Buckley, James Monroe, Dec. 16, 1836–Feb. 8, 1920.
Vol. 2, Pt. 1–231

Buckley, Oliver Ellsworth, Aug. 8, 1887–Dec. 14, 1959.
Supp. 6–84

Buckley, Samuel Botsford, May 9, 1809–Feb. 18, 1883.
Vol. 2, Pt. 1–232

Buckminster, Joseph Stevens, May 26, 1784–June 9, 1812.
Vol. 2, Pt. 1–233

Bucknell, William, Apr. 1, 1811–Mar. 5, 1890.
Vol. 2, Pt. 1–234

Buckner, Emory Roy, Aug. 7, 1877–Mar. 11, 1941.
Supp. 3–116

Buckner, Simon Bolivar, Apr. 1, 1823–Jan. 8, 1914.
Vol. 2, Pt. 1–234

Buckner, Simon Bolivar, July 18, 1886–June 18, 1945.
Supp. 3–117

Budd, Edward Gowen, Dec. 28, 1870–Nov. 30, 1946.
Supp. 4–120

Budd, Joseph Lancaster, July 3, 1835–Dec. 20, 1904.
Vol. 2, Pt. 1–236

Budd, Ralph, Aug. 20, 1879–Feb. 2, 1962.
Supp. 7–89

Budenz, Louis Francis, July 17, 1891–Apr. 27, 1972.
Supp. 9–134

Buehler, Huber Gray, Dec. 3, 1864–June 20, 1924.
Vol. 2, Pt. 1–237

Buel, Jesse, Jan. 4, 1778–Oct. 6, 1839.
Vol. 2, Pt. 1–238

Buell, Abel, Feb. 1, 1741/42–Mar. 10, 1822.
Vol. 2, Pt. 1–239

Buell, Don Carlos, Mar. 23, 1818–Nov. 19, 1898.
Vol. 2, Pt. 1–240

Buffalo Bill. [*See* Cody, William Frederick, 1846–1917.]

Buffum, Arnold, Dec. 13, 1782–Mar. 13, 1859.
Vol. 2, Pt. 1–241

Buford, Abraham, July 31, 1749–June 30, 1833.
Vol. 2, Pt. 1–242

Buford, Abraham, Jan. 18, 1820–June 9, 1884.
Vol. 2, Pt. 1–242

Buford, John, Mar. 4, 1826–Dec. 16, 1863.
Vol. 2, Pt. 1–243

Buford, Napoleon Bonaparte, Jan. 13, 1807–Mar. 28, 1883.
Vol. 2, Pt. 1–244

Buley, Roscoe Carlyle, July 8, 1893–Apr. 25, 1968.
Supp. 8–59

Bulfinch, Charles, Aug. 8, 1763–Apr. 4, 1844.
Vol. 2, Pt. 1–245

Bulfinch, Thomas, July 15, 1796–May 27, 1867.
Vol. 2, Pt. 1–247

Bulkeley, Morgan Gardner, Dec. 26, 1837–Nov. 6, 1922.
Vol. 2, Pt. 1–248

Bulkeley, Peter, Jan. 31, 1582/3–Mar. 9, 1658/9.
Vol. 2, Pt. 1–249

Bulkley, John Williams, Nov. 3, 1802–June 19, 1888.
Vol. 2, Pt. 1–250

Bulkley, Lucius Duncan, Jan. 12, 1845–July 20, 1928.
Vol. 2, Pt. 1–250

Bull, Ephraim Wales, Mar. 4, 1806–Sept. 26, 1895.
Vol. 2, Pt. 1–251

Bull, William, 1683–Mar. 21, 1755.
Vol. 2, Pt. 1–252

Bull, William, Sept. 24, 1710–July 4, 1791.
Vol. 2, Pt. 1–252

Bull, William Tillinghast, May 18, 1849–Feb. 22, 1909.
Vol. 2, Pt. 1–253

Bullard, Henry Adams, Sept. 9, 1788–Apr. 17, 1851.
Vol. 2, Pt. 1–254

Bullard, Robert Lee, Jan. 15, 1861–Sept. 11, 1947.
Supp. 4–122

Bullard, William Hannum Grubb, Dec. 6, 1866–Nov. 24, 1927.
Vol. 2, Pt. 1–255,

Bullitt, Alexander Scott, 1762–Apr. 13, 1816.
Vol. 2, Pt. 1–255

Bullitt, Henry Massie, Feb. 28, 1817–Feb. 5, 1880.
Vol. 2, Pt. 1–256

Bullitt, William Christian, Jan. 25, 1891–Feb. 15, 1967.
Supp. 8–60

Bulloch, Archibald, 1729/30–Feb. 1777.
Vol. 2, Pt. 1–257

Bulloch, James Dunwody, June 25, 1823–Jan. 7, 1901.
Vol. 2, Pt. 1–257

Bullock, Rufus Brown, Mar. 28, 1834–Apr. 27, 1907.
Vol. 2, Pt. 1–258

Bullock, William A., 1813–Apr. 12, 1867.
Vol. 2, Pt. 1–259

Bumstead, Freeman Josiah, Apr. 21, 1826–Nov. 28, 1879.
Vol. 2, Pt. 1–260

Bumstead, Henry Andrews, Mar. 12, 1870–Dec. 31, 1920.
Vol. 2, Pt. 1–260

Bumstead, Horace, Sept. 29, 1841–Oct. 14, 1919.
Vol. 2, Pt. 1–261

Bunce, Oliver Bell, Feb. 8, 1828–May 15, 1890.
Vol. 2, Pt. 1–262

Bunce, William Gedney, Sept. 19, 1840–Nov. 5, 1916.
Vol. 2, Pt. 1–263

Bunche, Ralph Johnson, Aug. 7, 1904–Dec. 9, 1971.
Supp. 9–136

Bundy, Harvey Hollister, Mar. 30, 1888–Oct. 7, 1963.
Supp. 7–90

Bundy, Jonas Mills, Apr. 17, 1835–Sept. 8, 1891.
Vol. 2, Pt. 1–263

Bunker, Arthur Hugh, July 29, 1895–May 19, 1964.
Supp. 7–91

Bunner, Henry Cuyler, Aug. 3, 1855–May 11, 1896.
Vol. 2, Pt. 1–264

Burbank, Luther, Mar. 7, 1849–Apr. 11, 1926.
Vol. 2, Pt. 1–265

Burbridge, Stephen Gano, Aug. 19, 1831–Dec. 2, 1894.
Vol. 2, Pt. 1–270

Burchard, Samuel Dickinson, Sept. 6, 1812–Sept. 25, 1891.
Vol. 2, Pt. 1–271

Burchfield, Charles Ephraim, Apr. 9, 1893–Jan. 10, 1967.
Supp. 8–62

Burdeck, Francis Marion, Aug. 1, 1845–June 3, 1920.
Vol. 2, Pt. 1–273

Burden, Henry, Apr. 22, 1791–Jan. 19, 1871.
Vol. 2, Pt. 1–272

Burdette, Robert Jones, July 30, 1844–Nov. 19, 1914.
Vol. 2, Pt. 1–272

Burdick, Eugene Leonard, Dec. 12, 1918–July 26, 1965.
Supp. 7–93

Burdick, Usher Lloyd, Feb. 21, 1879–Aug. 19, 1960.
Supp. 6–85

Burgess, Alexander, Oct. 31, 1819–Oct. 8, 1901.
Vol. 2, Pt. 1–274

Burgess, Edward, June 30, 1848–July 12, 1891.
Vol. 2, Pt. 1–275

Burgess, Frank Gelett, Jan. 30, 1866–Sept. 18, 1951.
Supp. 5–93

Burgess, George, Oct. 31, 1809–Apr. 23, 1866.
Vol. 2, Pt. 1–276

Burgess, George Kimball, Jan. 4, 1874–July 2, 1932.
Supp. 1–131

Burgess, John William, Aug. 26, 1844–Jan. 13, 1933.
Supp. 1–132

Burgess, Neil, June 29, 1851?–Feb. 19, 1910.
Vol. 2, Pt. 1–276

Burgess, Thornton Waldo, Jan. 14, 1874–June 5, 1965.
Supp. 7–94

Burgess, W(illiam) Starling, Dec. 25, 1878–Mar. 19, 1947.
Supp. 4–123

Burgevine, Henry Andrea, 1836–June 26, 1865.
Vol. 2, Pt. 1–277

Burgis, William, fl. 1718–1731.
Vol. 2, Pt. 1–278

Burk, Frederic Lister, Sept. 1, 1862–June 12, 1924.
Vol. 2, Pt. 1–278
Burk, John Daly, *c.* 1775–Apr. 11, 1808.
Vol. 2, Pt. 1–279
Burke, AEdanus, 1743–Mar. 30, 1802.
Vol. 2, Pt. 1–280
Burke, Billie, Aug. 7, 1886–May 14, 1970.
Supp. 8–64
Burke, Charles St. Thomas, Mar. 27, 1822–Nov. 10, 1854.
Vol. 2, Pt. 1–280
Burke, John G. [*See* Bourke, John Gregory, 1846–1896.]
Burke, John Joseph, June 6, 1875–Oct. 30, 1936.
Supp. 2–72
Burke, Stevenson, Nov. 26, 1826–Apr. 24, 1904.
Vol. 2, Pt. 1–281
Burke, Thomas, *c.* 1747–Dec. 2, 1783.
Vol. 2, Pt. 1–282
Burke, Thomas, Dec. 22, 1849–Dec. 4, 1925.
Vol. 2, Pt. 1–283
Burleigh, Charles Calistus, Nov. 3, 1810–June 13, 1878.
Vol. 2, Pt. 1–284
Burleigh, George Shepard, Mar. 26, 1821–July 20, 1903.
Vol. 2, Pt. 1–285
Burleigh, Henry Thacker, Dec. 2, 1866–Sept. 12, 1949.
Supp. 4–125
Burleigh, William Henry, Feb. 2, 1812–Mar. 18, 1871.
Vol. 2, Pt. 1–286
Burleson, Albert Sidney, June 7, 1863–Nov. 24, 1937.
Supp. 2–74
Burleson, Edward, Dec. 15, 1798–Dec. 26, 1851.
Vol. 2. Pt. 1–286
Burleson, Hugh Latimer, Apr. 25, 1865–Aug 1, 1933.
Supp. 1–134
Burleson, Rufus Clarence, Aug. 7, 1823–May 14, 1901.
Vol. 2, Pt. 1–287
Burlin, Natalie Curtis, Apr. 26, 1875–Oct. 23, 1921.
Vol. 2, Pt. 1–288
Burlingame, Anson, Nov. 14, 1820–Feb. 23, 1870.
Vol. 2, Pt. 1–289
Burlingame, Edward Livermore, May 30, 1848–Nov. 15, 1922.
Vol. 2, Pt. 1–290
Burlingham, Charles Culp, Aug. 31, 1858–June 6, 1959.
Supp. 6–87
Burnam, John Miller, Apr. 9, 1864–Nov. 21, 1921.
Vol. 2, Pt. 1–291
Burnap, George Washington, Nov. 30, 1802–Sept. 8, 1859.
Vol. 2, Pt. 1–292
Burnet, David Gouverneur, Apr. 4, 1788–Dec. 5, 1870.
Vol. 2, Pt. 1–292
Burnet, Jacob, Feb. 22, 1770–May 10, 1853.
Vol. 2, Pt. 1–294
Burnet, William, Dec. 2, 1730 o.s.–Oct. 7, 1791.
Vol. 2, Pt. 1–296
Burnet, William, March 1688–Sept. 7, 1729.
Vol. 2, Pt. 1–295
Burnett, Charles Henry, May 28, 1842–Jan. 30, 1902.
Vol. 2, Pt. 1–296
Burnett, Chester Arthur ("Howlin' Wolf"), June 19, 1910–Jan. 10, 1976.
Supp. 10–77
Burnett, Frances Eliza Hodgson, Nov. 24, 1849–Oct. 29, 1924.
Vol. 2, Pt. 1–297
Burnett, Henry Lawrence, Dec. 26, 1838–Jan. 4, 1916.
Vol. 2, Pt. 1–298
Burnett, Joseph, Nov. 11, 1820–Aug. 11, 1894.
Vol. 2, Pt. 1–299
Burnett, Leo, Oct. 21, 1891–June 7, 1971.
Supp. 9–139
Burnett, Peter Hardeman, Nov. 15, 1807–May 17, 1895.
Vol. 2, Pt. 1–300
Burnett, Swan Moses, Mar. 16, 1847–Jan. 18, 1906.
Vol. 2, Pt. 1–301
Burnham, Clara Louise Root, May 26, 1854–June 20, 1927.
Vol. 2, Pt. 1–301
Burnham, Daniel Hudson, Sept. 4, 1846–June 1, 1912.
Vol. 2, Pt. 1–302
Burnham, Frederick Russell, May 11, 1861–Sept. 1, 1947.
Supp. 4–126
Burnham, Sherburne Wesley, Dec. 12, 1838–Mar. 11, 1921.
Vol. 2, Pt. 1–307
Burnham, William Henry, Dec. 3, 1855–June 25, 1941.
Supp. 3–119
Burns, Anthony, May 31, 1834–July 27, 1862.
Vol. 2, Pt. 1–308
Burns, Bob, Aug. 2, 1890–Feb. 2, 1956.
Supp. 6–88
Burns, Otway, 1775?-Oct. 25, 1850.
Vol. 2, Pt. 1–308
Burns, Raymond Joseph, Mar. 25, 1886–July 7, 1977.
Supp. 10–79
Burns, William John, Oct. 19, 1861–Apr. 14, 1932.
Supp. 1–134
Burnside, Ambrose Everett, May 23, 1824–Sept. 13, 1881.
Vol. 2, Pt. 1–309
Burpee, David, Apr. 5, 1893–June 24, 1980.
Supp. 10–80
Burr, Aaron, Feb. 6, 1756–Sept. 14, 1836.
Vol. 2, Pt. 1–314
Burr, Aaron, Jan. 4, 1715/16–Sept. 24, 1757.
Vol. 2, Pt. 1–313
Burr, Alfred Edmund, Mar. 27, 1815–Jan. 8, 1900.
Vol. 2, Pt. 1–321
Burr, Enoch Fitch, Oct. 21, 1818–May 8, 1907.
Vol. 2, Pt. 1–321
Burr, George Lincoln, Jan. 30, 1857–June 27, 1938.
Supp. 2–75
Burr, Theodosia, June 21, 1783–Jan. 1813.
Vol. 2, Pt. 1–322
Burr, William Hubert, July 14, 1851–Dec. 13, 1934.
Supp. 1–135
Burrage, Henry Sweetser, Jan. 7, 1837–Mar. 9, 1926.
Vol. 2, Pt. 1–323
Burrage, Walter Lincoln, Oct. 26, 1860–Jan. 26, 1935.
Supp. 1–136
Burrall, William Porter, Sept. 18, 1806–Mar. 3, 1874.
Vol. 2, Pt. 1–324
Burrell, David James, Aug. 1, 1844–Dec. 5, 1926.
Vol. 2, Pt. 1–324
Burrill, Alexander Mansfield, June 19, 1807–Feb. 7, 1869.
Vol. 2, Pt. 1–325
Burrill, James, Apr. 25, 1772–Dec. 25, 1820.
Vol. 2, Pt. 1–325
Burrill, Thomas Jonathan, Apr. 25, 1839–Apr. 14, 1916.
Vol. 2, Pt. 1–326
Burrington, George, *c.* 1680–Feb. 1759.
Vol. 2, Pt. 1–327
Burritt, Elihu, Dec. 8, 1810–Mar. 6, 1879.
Vol. 2, Pt. 1–328
Burroughs, Bryson, Sept. 8, 1869–Nov. 16, 1934.
Supp. 1–137
Burroughs, Edgar Rice, Sept. 1, 1875–Mar. 19, 1950.
Supp. 4–128
Burroughs, John, Apr. 3, 1837–Mar. 29, 1921.
Vol. 2, Pt. 1–330
Burroughs, John Curtis, Dec. 2, 1817–Apr. 21, 1892.
Vol. 2, Pt. 1–334
Burroughs, William Seward, Jan. 28, 1855–Sept. 15, 1898.
Supp. 1–138
Burrow, Trigant, Sept. 7, 1875–May 24, 1950.
Supp. 4–130
Burrowes, Edward Thomas, July 25, 1852–Mar. 19, 1918.
Vol. 2, Pt. 1–334
Burrowes, Thomas Henry, Nov. 16, 1805–Feb. 25, 1871.
Vol. 2, Pt. 1–335
Burrows, Julius Caesar, Jan. 9, 1837–Nov. 16, 1915.
Vol. 2, Pt. 1–336
Burrows, William, Oct. 6, 1785–Sept. 5, 1813.
Vol. 2, Pt. 1–337
Burson, William Worth, Sept. 22, 1832–Apr. 10, 1913.
Vol. 2, Pt. 1–337
Burt, John, Apr. 18, 1814–Aug. 16, 1886.
Vol. 2, Pt. 1–338
Burt, Mary Elizabeth, June 11, 1850–Oct. 17, 1918.
Vol. 2, Pt. 1–339
Burt, William Austin, June 13, 1792–Aug. 18, 1858.
Vol. 2, Pt. 1–339
Burton, Asa, Aug. 25, 1752–May 1, 1836.
Vol. 2, Pt. 1–340
Burton, Clarence Monroe, Nov. 18, 1853–Oct. 23, 1932.
Supp. 1–139

Burton, Ernest De Witt, Feb. 4, 1856–May 26, 1925.
Vol. 2, Pt. 1–341
Burton, Frederick Russell, Feb. 23, 1861–Sept. 30, 1909.
Vol. 2, Pt. 1–342
Burton, Harold Hitz, June 22, 1888–Oct. 28, 1964.
Supp. 7–95
Burton, Hutchins Gordon, *c.* 1774–Apr. 21, 1836.
Vol. 2, Pt. 1–34
Burton, Marion Le Roy, Aug. 30, 1874–Feb. 18, 1925.
Vol. 2, Pt. 1–343
Burton, Nathaniel Judson, Dec. 17, 1824–Oct. 13, 1887.
Vol. 2, Pt. 1–344
Burton, Richard Eugene, Mar. 14, 1861–Apr. 8, 1940.
Supp. 2–76
Burton, Theodore Elijah, Dec. 20, 1851–Oct. 28, 1929.
Supp. 1–141
Burton, Warren, Nov. 23, 1800–June 6, 1866.
Vol. 2, Pt. 1–344
Burton, William, Oct. 16, 1789–Aug. 5, 1866.
Vol. 2, Pt. 1–345
Burton, William Evans, Sept. 24, 1804–Feb. 10, 1860.
Vol. 2, Pt. 1–346
Busch, Adolphus, July 10, 1839–Oct. 10, 1913.
Supp. 1–141
Busch, Hermann, June 24, 1897–June 3, 1975.
Supp. 9–140
Bush, George, June 12, 1796–Sept. 19, 1859.
Vol. 2, Pt. 1–347
Bush, Lincoln, Dec. 14, 1860–Dec. 10, 1940.
Supp. 2–77
Bush, Prescott Sheldon, May 15, 1895–Oct. 8, 1972.
Supp. 9–141
Bush, Vannevar ("Van"), Mar. 11, 1890–June 28, 1974.
Supp. 9–143
Bush-Brown, Henry Kirke, Apr. 21, 1857–Mar. 1, 1935.
Supp. 1–143
Bushman, Francis Xavier, Jan. 10, 1883–Aug. 23, 1966.
Supp. 8–65
Bushnell, Asa Smith, Sept. 16, 1834–Jan. 15, 1904.
Vol. 2, Pt. 1–347
Bushnell, David, *c.* 1742–1824.
Vol. 2, Pt. 1–348
Bushnell, George Ensign, Sept. 10, 1853–July 19, 1924.
Vol. 2, Pt. 1–349
Bushnell, Horace, Apr. 14, 1802–Feb. 17, 1876.
Vol. 2, Pt. 1–350
Bussey, Cyrus, Oct. 5, 1833–Mar. 2, 1915.
Vol. 2, Pt. 1–354
Butler, Andrew Pickens, Nov. 18, 1796–May 25, 1857.
Vol. 2, Pt. 1–355
Butler, Benjamin Franklin, Dec. 14, 1795–Nov. 8, 1858.
Vol. 2, Pt. 1–356
Butler, Benjamin Franklin, Nov. 5, 1818–Jan. 11, 1893.
Vol. 2, Pt. 1–357
Butler, Burridge Davenal, Feb. 5, 1868–Mar. 30, 1948.
Supp. 4–131
Butler, Charles, Jan. 15, 1802–Dec. 13, 1897.
Vol. 2, Pt. 1–359
Butler, Ezra, Sept. 24, 1763–July 12, 1838.
Vol. 2, Pt. 1–360
Butler, Howard Crosby, Mar. 7, 1872–Aug. 13?, 1922.
Vol. 2, Pt. 1–361
Butler, John, 1728–May 1796.
Vol. 2, Pt. 1–361
Butler, John Wesley, Oct. 13, 1851–Mar. 17, 1918.
Vol. 2, Pt. 1–362
Butler, Marion, May 20, 1863–June 3, 1938.
Supp. 2–78
Butler, Matthew Calbraith, Mar. 8, 1836–Apr. 14, 1909.
Vol. 2, Pt. 1–363
Butler, Nicholas Murray, Apr. 2, 1862–Dec. 7, 1947.
Supp. 4–133
Butler, Pierce, July 11, 1744–Feb. 15, 1822.
Vol. 2, Pt. 1–364
Butler, Pierce, Mar. 17, 1866–Nov. 16, 1939.
Supp. 2–79
Butler, Pierce Mason, Apr. 11, 1798–Aug. 20, 1847.
Vol. 2, Pt. 1–365
Butler, Richard, Apr. 1, 1743–Nov. 4, 1791.
Vol. 2, Pt. 1–366
Butler, Simeon, Mar. 25, 1770?–Nov. 7, 1847.
Vol. 2, Pt. 1–366
Butler, Smedley Darlington, July 30, 1881–June 21, 1940.
Supp. 2–80
Butler, Thomas Belden, Aug. 22, 1806–June 8, 1873.
Vol. 2, Pt. 1–367
Butler, Walter N., d. Oct. 30, 1781.
Vol. 2, Pt. 1–367
Butler, William, Dec. 17, 1759–Sept. 23, 1821.
Vol. 2, Pt. 1–368
Butler, William, Jan. 30, 1818–Aug. 18, 1899.
Vol. 2, Pt. 1–369
Butler, William Allen, Feb. 20, 1825–Sept. 9, 1902.
Vol. 2, Pt. 1–369
Butler, William Orlando, Apr. 19, 1791–Aug. 6, 1880.
Vol. 2, Pt. 1–371
Butler, Zebulon, Jan. 23, 1731–July 28, 1795.
Vol. 2, Pt. 1–372
Butterfield, Daniel, Oct. 31, 1831–July 17, 1901.
Vol. 2, Pt. 1–372
Butterfield, John, Nov. 18, 1801–Nov. 14, 1869.
Vol. 2, Pt. 1–374
Butterfield, Kenyon Leech, June 11, 1868–Nov. 26, 1935.
Supp. 1–144
Butterick, Ebenezer, May 29, 1826–Mar. 31, 1903.
Vol. 2, Pt. 1–375
Butterworth, Benjamin, Oct. 22, 1837–Jan. 16, 1898.
Vol. 2, Pt. 1–376
Butterworth, Hezekiah, Dec. 22, 1839–Sept. 5, 1905.
Vol. 2, Pt. 1–376
Butterworth, William Walton ("Walt"), Sept. 7, 1903–Mar. 31, 1975.
Supp. 9–145
Buttrick, George Arthur, Mar. 23, 1892–Jan. 23, 1980.
Supp. 10–82
Buttrick, Wallace, Oct. 23, 1853–May 27, 1926.
Vol. 2, Pt. 1–377
Butts, Isaac, Jan. 11, 1816–Nov. 20, 1874.
Vol. 2, Pt. 1–378
Butts, James Wallace ("Wally"), Feb. 7, 1905–Dec. 17, 1973.
Supp. 9–147
Buttz, Henry Anson, Apr. 18, 1835–Oct. 6, 1920.
Vol. 2, Pt. 1–379
Byerly, William Elwood, Dec. 13, 1849–Dec. 20, 1935.
Supp. 1–145
Byford, William Heath, Mar. 20, 1817–May 21, 1890.
Vol. 2, Pt. 1–379
Byington, Cyrus, Mar. 11, 1793–Dec. 31, 1868.
Vol. 2, Pt. 1–380
Byington, Spring, Oct. 17, 1893–Sept. 7, 1971.
Supp. 9–148
Byles, Mather, Mar. 15, 1706/7–July 5, 1788.
Vol. 2, Pt. 1–381
Bynum, William Preston, June 16, 1820–Dec. 30, 1909.
Vol. 2, Pt. 1–382
Byoir, Carl Robert, June 24, 1888–Feb. 3, 1957.
Supp. 6–89
Byrd, Harry Flood, June 10, 1887–Oct. 20, 1966.
Supp. 8–67
Byrd, Richard Evelyn, Oct. 25, 1888–Mar. 11, 1957.
Supp. 6–91
Byrd, William, 1652–Dec. 4, 1704.
Vol. 2, Pt. 1–382
Byrd, William, Mar. 28, 1674–Aug. 26, 1744.
Vol. 2, Pt. 1–383
Byrne, Andrew, Dec. 5, 1802–June 10, 1862.
Vol. 2, Pt. 1–384
Byrne, Donn. [*See* Donn-Byrne, Brian Oswald, 1889–1928.]
Byrne, John, Oct. 13, 1825–Oct. 1, 1902.
Vol. 2, Pt. 1–385
Byrnes, James Francis, May 2, 1879–Apr. 9, 1972.
Supp. 9–149
Byrnes, Thomas F., 1842–May 7, 1910.
Vol. 2, Pt. 1–386
Byrns, Joseph Wellington, July 20, 1869–June 4, 1936.
Supp. 2–82

Cabell, James Branch, Apr. 14, 1879–May 5, 1958.
Supp. 6–94
Cabell, James Lawrence, Aug. 26, 1813–Aug. 13, 1889.
Vol. 2, Pt. 1–386

Cabell, Joseph Carrington, Dec. 28, 1778–Feb. 5, 1856.
Vol. 2, Pt. 1–387
Cabell, Nathaniel Francis, July 23, 1807–Sept. 1, 1891.
Vol. 2, Pt. 1–388
Cabell, Samuel Jordan, Dec. 15, 1756–Aug. 4, 1818.
Vol. 2, Pt. 1–388
Cabell, William, Mar. 13, 1729/30–Mar. 23, 1798.
Vol. 2, Pt. 1–389
Cabell, William H., Dec. 16, 1772–Jan. 12, 1853.
Vol. 2, Pt. 1–390
Cabell, William Lewis, Jan. 1, 1827–Feb. 22, 1911.
Vol. 2, Pt. 1–390
Cabet, Étienne, Jan. 1, 1788–Nov. 8, 1856.
Vol. 2, Pt. 1–391
Cable, Frank Taylor, June 19, 1863–May 21, 1945.
Supp. 3–120
Cable, George Washington, Oct. 12, 1844–Jan. 31, 1925.
Vol. 2, Pt. 1–392
Cabot, Arthur Tracy, Jan. 25, 1852–Nov. 4, 1912.
Vol. 2, Pt. 1–393
Cabot, Charles Sebastian Thomas, July 6, 1918–Aug. 23, 1977.
Supp. 10–85
Cabot, Edward Clarke, Apr. 17, 1818–Jan. 5, 1901.
Vol. 2, Pt. 1–394
Cabot, George, Jan. 16, 1752–Apr. 18, 1823.
Vol. 2, Pt. 1–395
Cabot, Godfrey Lowell, Feb. 26, 1861–Nov. 2, 1962.
Supp. 7–97
Cabot, Hugh, Aug. 11, 1872–Aug. 14, 1945.
Supp. 3–121
Cabot, Richard Clarke, May 21, 1868–May 7, 1939.
Supp. 2–83
Cabrillo, Juan Rodriguez, d. Jan.3, 1543.
Vol. 2, Pt. 1–396
Cabrini, Francis Xavier, July 15, 1850–Dec. 22, 1917.
Supp. 1–146
Cadillac, Antoine de la Mothe Sieur, *c.* 1656–Oct. 18, 1730.
Vol. 2, Pt. 1–397
Cadman, Charles Wakefield, Dec. 24, 1881–Dec. 30, 1946.
Supp. 4–138
Cadman, Samuel Parkes, Dec. 18, 1864–July 12, 1936.
Supp. 2–85
Cadwalader, John, Jan. 1742–Feb. 10, 1786.
Vol. 2, Pt. 1–398
Cadwalader, John, Apr. 1, 1805–Jan. 26, 1879.
Vol. 2, Pt. 1–398
Cadwalader, Lambert, 1743–Sept. 13, 1823.
Vol. 2, Pt. 1–399
Cadwalader, Thomas, 1707/8–Nov. 14, 1799.
Vol. 2, Pt. 1–400
Cady, Daniel, Apr. 29, 1773–Oct. 31, 1859.
Vol. 2, Pt. 1–401
Cady, Sarah Louise Ensign, Sept. 13, 1829–Nov. 8, 1912.
Vol. 2, Pt. 1–402
Caffery, Donelson, Sept. 10, 1835–Dec. 30, 1906.
Vol. 2, Pt. 1–402
Caffery, Jefferson, Dec. 1, 1886–Apr. 13, 1974.
Supp. 9–153
Caffin, Charles Henry, June 4, 1854–Jan. 14, 1918.
Vol. 2, Pt. 1–403
Cahan, Abraham, July 7, 1860–Aug. 31, 1951.
Supp. 5–95
Cahill, Holger, Jan. 13, 1887–July 8, 1960.
Supp. 6–95
Cahn, Edmond Nathaniel, Jan. 17, 1906–Aug. 9, 1964.
Supp. 7–99
Cain, Harry Pulliam, Jan. 10, 1906–Mar. 3, 1979.
Supp. 10–86
Cain, James Mallahan, July 1, 1892–Oct. 27, 1977.
Supp. 10–88
Cain, Richard Harvey, Apr. 12, 1825–Jan. 18, 1887.
Vol. 2, Pt. 1–403
Cain, William, May 14, 1847–Dec. 7, 1930.
Supp. 1–148
Caines, George, 1771–July 10, 1825.
Vol. 2, Pt. 1–404
Cajori, Florian, Feb. 28, 1859–Aug. 14, 1930.
Supp. 1–148
Calder, Alexander, July 22, 1898–Nov. 11, 1976.
Supp. 10–89
Calder, Alexander Stirling, Jan. 11, 1870–Jan. 7, 1945.
Supp. 3–123
Caldwell, Alexander, Mar. 1, 1830–May 19, 1917.
Vol. 2, Pt. 1–405
Caldwell, Charles, May 14, 1772–July 9, 1853.
Vol. 2, Pt. 1–406
Caldwell, Charles Henry Bromedge, June 11, 1823–Nov. 30, 1877.
Vol. 2, Pt. 1–406
Caldwell, David, Mar. 22, 1725–Aug. 25, 1824.
Vol. 2, Pt. 1–407
Caldwell, Eugene Wilson, Dec. 3, 1870–June 20, 1918.
Vol. 2, Pt. 1–407
Caldwell, Henry Clay, Sept. 4, 1832–Feb. 15, 1915.
Vol. 2, Pt. 1–408
Caldwell, James, Apr. 1734–Nov. 24, 1781.
Vol. 2, Pt. 1–408
Caldwell, Joseph, Apr. 21, 1773–Jan. 27, 1835.
Vol. 2, Pt. 1–409
Caldwell, Otis William, Dec. 18, 1869–July 5, 1947.
Supp. 4–139
Calef, Robert, 1648–Apr. 13, 1719.
Vol. 2, Pt. 1–410
Calhoun, John, Oct. 14, 1806–Oct. 13, 1859.
Vol. 2, Pt. 1–410
Calhoun, John Caldwell, Mar. 18, 1782–Mar. 31, 1850.
Vol. 2, Pt. 1–411
Calhoun, Patrick, Mar. 21, 1856–June 16, 1943.
Supp. 3–125
Calhoun, William Barron, Dec. 29, 1795–Nov. 8, 1865.
Vol. 2, Pt. 1–419
Calhoun, William James, Oct. 5, 1848–Sept. 19, 1916.
Vol. 2, Pt. 1–420
California Joe, May 8, 1829–Oct. 29, 1876.
Vol. 2, Pt. 1–421
Calkins, Earnest Elmo, Mar. 25, 1868–Oct. 4, 1964.
Supp. 7–100
Calkins, Gary Nathan, Jan. 18, 1869–Jan. 4, 1943.
Supp. 3–126
Calkins, Mary Whiton, Mar. 30, 1863–Feb. 26, 1930.
Supp. 1–149
Calkins, Norman Allison, Sept. 9, 1822–Dec. 22, 1895.
Vol. 2, Pt. 1–421
Calkins, Phineas Wolcott, June 10, 1831–Dec. 31, 1924.
Vol. 2, Pt. 1–422
Calkins, Wolcott. [*See* Calkins, Phineas Wolcott, 1831–1924.]
Call, Richard Keith, 1791–Sept. 14, 1862.
Vol. 2, Pt. 1–422
Callahan, Patrick Henry, Oct. 15, 1865–Feb. 4, 1940.
Supp. 2–86
Callas, Maria, Dec. 2, 1923–Sept. 16, 1977.
Supp. 10–92
Callaway, Morgan, Nov. 3, 1862–Apr. 3, 1936.
Supp. 2–88
Callaway, Samuel Rodger, Dec. 24, 1850–June 1, 1904.
Vol. 2, Pt. 1–423
Callender, Guy Stevens, Nov. 9, 1865–Aug. 8, 1915.
Vol. 2, Pt. 1–424
Callender, James Thomson, 1758–July 17, 1803.
Vol. 2, Pt. 1–425
Callender, John, 1706–Jan. 26, 1748.
Vol. 2, Pt. 1–426
Callimachos, Panos Demetrios, Dec. 4, 1879–Oct. 13, 1963.
Supp. 7–102
Calverley, Charles, Nov. 1, 1833–Feb. 25, 1914.
Vol. 2, Pt. 1–426
Calvert, Charles, Aug. 27, 1637–Feb. 21, 1715.
Vol. 2, Pt. 1–427
Calvert, Charles Benedict, Aug. 23, 1808–May 12, 1864.
Vol. 2, Pt. 1–427
Calvert, George, *c.* 1580–Apr. 15, 1632.
Vol. 2, Pt. 1–428
Calvert, George Henry, June 2, 1803–May 24, 1889.
Vol. 2, Pt. 1–429
Calvert, Leonard, 1606–June 9, 1647.
Vol. 2, Pt. 1–430
Calverton, Victor Francis, June 25, 1900–Nov. 20, 1940.
Supp. 2–89
Calvin, Samuel, Feb. 2, 1840–Apr. 17, 1911.
Vol. 2, Pt. 1–431
Cambreleng, Churchill Caldom, 1786–Apr. 30, 1862.
Vol. 2, Pt. 1–432

Cambridge, Godfrey MacArthur, Feb. 26, 1933–Nov. 29,1976.
Supp. 10–94
Camden, Johnson Newlon, Mar. 6, 1828–Apr. 25, 1908.
Vol. 2, Pt. 1–433
Cameron, Andrew Carr, Sept. 28, 1834–May 28, 1890.
Vol. 2, Pt. 1–433
Cameron, Archibald, *c.* 1771–Dec. 4, 1836.
Vol. 2, Pt. 1–434
Cameron, James Donald, May 14, 1833–Aug. 30, 1918.
Vol. 2, Pt. 1–435
Cameron, Robert Alexander, Feb. 22, 1828–Mar. 15, 1894.
Vol. 2, Pt. 1–436
Cameron, Simon, Mar. 8, 1799–June 26, 1889.
Vol. 2, Pt. 1–437
Cameron, William Evelyn, Nov. 29, 1842–Jan. 25, 1927.
Vol. 2, Pt. 1–439
Camm, John, 1718–1778.
Vol. 2, Pt. 1–440
Cammerhoff, John Christopher Frederick, July 28, 1721–Apr. 28, 1751.
Vol. 2, Pt. 1–441
Camp, David Nelson, Oct. 13, 1820–Oct. 19, 1916.
Vol. 2, Pt. 1–441
Camp, Hiram, Apr. 9, 1811–July 8, 1893.
Vol. 2, Pt. 1–442
Camp, John Lafayette, Feb. 20, 1828–July 16, 1891
Vol. 2, Pt. 1–443
Camp, John Lafayette, Sept. 23, 1855–Aug. 10, 1918,
Vol. 2, Pt. 1–443
Camp, Walter Chauncey, Apr. 7, 1859–Mar. 14, 1925.
Vol. 2, Pt. 1–444
Campanius, John, Aug. 15, 1601–Sept. 17, 1683.
Vol. 2, Pt. 1–445
Campau, Joseph, Feb. 25, 1769–July 23, 1863.
Vol. 2, Pt. 1–446
Campbell, Alexander, Sept. 12, 1778–Mar. 4, 1866.
Vol. 2, Pt. 1–446
Campbell, Allen, Oct. 11, 1815–Mar. 18, 1894.
Vol. 2, Pt. 1–448
Campbell, Andrew, June 14, 1821–Apr. 13, 1890.
Vol. 2, Pt. 1–449
Campbell, Bartley, Aug. 12, 1843–July 30, 1888.
Vol. 2, Pt. 1–450
Campbell, Charles, May 1, 1807–July 11, 1876.
Vol. 2, Pt. 1–451
Campbell, Charles Macfie, Sept. 8, 1876–Aug. 7, 1943.
Supp. 3–127
Campbell, Douglas Houghton, Dec. 16, 1859–Feb. 24, 1953.
Supp. 5–97
Campbell, Francis Joseph, Oct. 9, 1832–June 30, 1914.
Vol. 2, Pt. 1–451
Campbell, George Washington, Feb. 8, 1769–Feb. 17, 1848.
Vol. 2, Pt. 1–452
Campbell, George Washington, Jan. 12, 1817–July 15, 1898.
Vol. 2, Pt. 1–452
Campbell, Henry Fraser, Feb. 10, 1824–Dec. 15, 1891.
Vol. 2, Pt. 1–453
Campbell, James, Sept. 1, 1812–Jan. 27, 1893.
Vol. 2, Pt. 1–454
Campbell, James Hepburn, Feb. 8, 1820–Apr. 12, 1895.
Vol. 2 Pt. 1–455
Campbell, James Valentine, Feb. 25, 1823–Mar. 26, 1890.
Vol. 2, Pt. 1–455
Campbell, John. [*See* Loudoun, John Campbell, Fourth Earl of, 1705–1782.]
Campbell, John, 1653–Mar. 4, 1727/28.
Vol. 2, Pt. 1–456
Campbell, John Archibald, June 24, 1811–Mar. 12, 1889.
Vol. 2 Pt. 1–456
Campbell, John Wilson, Feb. 23, 1782–Sept. 24, 1833.
Vol. 2, Pt. 1–459
Campbell, John Wood, Jr., June 8, 1910–July 11, 1971.
Supp. 9–155
Campbell, Josiah A. Patterson, Mar. 2, 1830–Jan. 10, 1917.
Vol. 2, Pt. 1–460
Campbell, Lewis Davis, Aug. 9, 1811–Nov. 26, 1882.
Vol. 2, Pt. 1–461
Campbell, Marius Robinson, Sept. 30, 1858–Dec. 7, 1940.
Supp. 2–90
Campbell, Prince Lucien, Oct. 6, 1861–Aug. 14, 1925.
Vol. 2, Pt. 1–462
Campbell, Robert, Mar. 1804–Oct. 16, 1879.
Vol. 2, Pt. 1–462
Campbell, Thomas, Feb. 1, 1763–Jan. 4, 1854.
Vol. 2, Pt. 1–463
Campbell, Thomas Joseph, Apr. 29, 1848–Dec. 14, 1925.
Vol. 2, Pt. 1–463
Campbell, Lord William, d. Sept. 5, 1778.
Vol. 2, Pt. 1–464
Campbell, William, 1745–Aug. 22, 1781.
Vol. 2, Pt. 1–465
Campbell, William, June 24, 1876–Dec. 16, 1936.
Supp. 2–91
Campbell, William Bowen, Feb. 1, 1807–Aug. 19, 1867.
Vol. 2, Pt. 1–466
Campbell, William Edward March, Sept. 18, 1893–May 15, 1954.
Supp. 5–99
Campbell, William Henry, Sept. 14, 1808–Dec. 7, 1890.
Vol. 2, Pt. 1–466
Campbell, William W., June 10, 1806–Sept. 7, 1881.
Vol. 2, Pt. 1–467
Campbell, William Wallace, Apr. 11, 1862–June 14, 1938.
Supp. 2–91
Canaga, Alfred Bruce, Nov. 2, 1850–Dec. 24, 1906.
Vol. 2, Pt. 1–468
Canby, Edward Richard Sprigg, Aug. 1817–Apr. 11, 1873.
Vol. 2, Pt. 1–468
Canby, Henry Seidel, Sept. 6, 1878–Apr. 5, 1961.
Supp. 7–103
Candee, Leverett, June 1, 1795–Nov. 27, 1863.
Vol. 2, Pt. 1–469
Candler, Allen Daniel, Nov. 4, 1834–Oct. 26, 1910.
Vol. 2, Pt. 1–470
Candler, Asa Griggs, Dec. 30, 1851–Mar. 12, 1929.
Vol. 2, Pt. 1–470
Candler, Warren Akin, Aug. 23, 1857–Sept. 25, 1941.
Supp. 3–128
Canfield, James Hulme, Mar. 18, 1847–Mar. 29, 1909.
Vol. 2, Pt. 1–472
Canfield, Richard A., June 17, 1855–Dec. 11, 1914.
Vol. 2, Pt. 1–472
Cannon, Annie Jump, Dec. 11, 1863–Apr. 13, 1941.
Supp. 3–130
Cannon, Charles James, Nov. 4, 1800–Nov. 9, 1860.
Vol. 2, Pt. 1–473
Cannon, Clarence, Apr. 11, 1879–May 12, 1964.
Supp. 7–104
Cannon, George Quayle, Jan. 11, 1827–Apr. 12, 1901.
Vol. 2, Pt. 1–474
Cannon, Harriet Starr, May 7, 1823–Apr. 5, 1896.
Vol. 2, Pt. 1–475
Cannon, Ida Maud, June 29, 1877–July 8, 1960.
Supp. 6–97
Cannon, James, Nov. 13, 1864–Sept. 6, 1944.
Supp. 3–131
Cannon, James Graham, July 26, 1858–July 5, 1916.
Vol. 2, Pt. 1–475
Cannon, James Thomas, Apr. 10, 1910–Dec. 5, 1973.
Supp. 9–156
Cannon, Joseph Gurney, May 7, 1836–Nov. 12, 1926.
Vol. 2, Pt. 1–476
Cannon, Newton, May 22, 1781–Sept. 16, 1841.
Vol. 2, Pt. 1–477
Cannon, Walter Bradford, Oct. 19, 1871–Oct. 1, 1945.
Supp. 3–133
Cannon, William, Mar. 15, 1809–Mar. 1, 1865.
Vol. 2, Pt. 1–478
Canonchet, d. Apr. 1676.
Vol. 2, Pt. 1–479
Canonge, Louis Placide, June 29, 1822–Jan. 22, 1893.
Vol. 2, Pt. 1–479
Canonicus, *c.* 1565–1647.
Vol. 2, Pt. 1–480
Cantor, Eddie, Jan. 31, 1892–Oct. 10, 1964.
Supp. 7–105
Cantril, Albert Hadley, June 16, 1906–May 28, 1969.
Supp. 8–69
Capehart, Homer Earl, June 6, 1897–Sept. 3, 1979.
Supp. 10–96
Capen, Elmer Hewitt, Apr. 5, 1838–Mar. 22, 1905.
Vol. 2, Pt. 1–481

Capen, Nahum, Apr. 1, 1804–Jan. 8, 1886.
Vol. 2, Pt. 1–481
Capen, Samuel Billings, Dec. 12, 1842–Jan. 29, 1914.
Vol. 2, Pt. 1–482
Capen, Samuel Paul, Mar. 21, 1878–June 22, 1956.
Supp. 6–98
Capers, Ellison, Oct. 14, 1837–Apr. 22, 1908.
Vol. 2, Pt. 1–483
Capers, William, Jan. 26, 1790–Jan. 29, 1855.
Vol. 2, Pt. 1–483
Capone, Alphonse, Jan. 17, 1899–Jan. 25, 1947.
Supp. 4–140
Capp, Al, Sept. 28, 1909–Nov. 5, 1979.
Supp. 10–97
Capper, Arthur, July 14, 1865–Dec. 19, 1951.
Supp. 5–100
Capps, Edward, Dec. 21, 1866–Aug. 21, 1950.
Supp. 4–142
Capps, Washington Lee, Jan. 31, 1864–May 31, 1935.
Supp. 1–150
Capron, Horace, Aug. 31, 1804–Feb. 22, 1885.
Vol. 2, Pt. 1–484
Captain Jack, 1837?–Oct. 3, 1873.
Vol. 2, Pt. 1–485
Caraway, Hattie Ophelia Wyatt, Feb. 1, 1878–Dec. 21, 1950.
Supp. 4–144
Caraway, Thaddeus Horatius, Oct. 17, 1871–Nov. 6, 1931.
Supp. 1–151
Carbutt, John, Dec. 2, 1832–July 26, 1905.
Vol. 2, Pt. 1–485
Cárdenas, Garcia Lópéz de, fl. 1540.
Vol. 2, Pt. 1–486
Cardozo, Benjamin Nathan, May 24, 1870–July 9, 1938.
Supp. 2–93
Cardozo, Jacob Newton, June 17, 1786–Aug. 30, 1873.
Vol. 2, Pt. 1–486
Carey, Henry Charles, Dec. 15, 1793–Oct. 13, 1879.
Vol. 2, Pt. 1–487
Carey, Joseph Maull, Jan. 19, 1845–Feb. 5, 1924.
Vol. 2, Pt. 1–487
Carey, Mathew, Jan. 28, 1760–Sept. 16, 1839.
Vol. 2, Pt. 1–489
Carey, Max George ("Scoops"), Jan. 11, 1890–May 30, 1976.
Supp. 10–99
Carleton, Henry, *c.* 1785–Mar. 28, 1863.
Vol. 2, Pt. 1–491
Carleton, Henry Guy, June 21, 1856–Dec. 10, 1910.
Vol. 2, Pt. 1–492
Carleton, Will, Oct. 21, 1845–Dec. 18, 1912.
Vol. 2, Pt. 1–492
Carlile, John Snyder, Dec. 16, 1817–Oct. 24, 1878.
Vol. 2, Pt. 1–493
Carlisle, Floyd Leslie, Mar. 5, 1881–Nov. 9, 1942.
Supp. 3–137
Carlisle, James Mandeville, May 22, 1814–May 19, 1877.
Vol. 2, Pt. 1–494
Carlisle, John Griflfin, Sept. 5, 1835–July 31, 1910.
Vol. 2, Pt. 1–494
Carll, John Franklin, May 7, 1828–Mar. 13, 1904.
Vol. 2, Pt. 1–496
Carlson, Anton Julius, Jan. 29, 1875–Sept. 2, 1956.
Supp. 6–99
Carlson, Chester Floyd, Feb. 8, 1890–Sept. 19, 1968.
Supp. 8–70
Carlson, Evans Fordyce, Feb. 26, 1896–May 27, 1947.
Supp. 4–145
Carlson, Richard Dutoit, Apr. 29, 1912–Nov. 25, 1977.
Supp. 10–100
Carmack, Edward Ward, Nov. 5, 1858–Nov. 9, 1908.
Vol. 2, Pt. 1–496
Carmichael, Oliver Cromwell, Oct. 3, 1891–Sept. 25,1966.
Supp. 8–72
Carmichael, William, d. Feb. 9, 1795.
Vol. 2, Pt. 1–497
Carnahan, James, Nov. 15, 1775–Mar. 3, 1859.
Vol. 2, Pt. 1–498
Carnap, Rudolf, May 18, 1891–Sept. 14, 1970.
Supp. 8–74
Carnegie, Andrew, Nov. 25, 1835–Aug. 11, 1919.
Vol. 2, Pt. 1–499
Carnegie, Dale, Nov. 24, 1888–Nov. 1, 1955.
Supp. 5–101
Carnegle, Hattie, Mar. 14, 1886–Feb. 22, 1956.
Supp. 6–100
Carnegie, Mary Crowninshield Endicott Chamberlain, Mar. 15, 1864–May 17, 1957.
Supp. 6–101
Carney, Thomas, Aug. 20, 1824–July 28, 1888.
Vol. 2, Pt. 1–506
Carnochan, John Murray, July 4, 1817–Oct. 28, 1887.
Vol. 2, Pt. 1–506
Carondelet, Francisco Luis Hector, Baron de, *c.* 1748–Aug. 10, 1807.
Vol. 2, Pt. 1–507
Carothers, Wallace Hume, Apr. 27, 1896–Apr. 29, 1937.
Supp. 2–96
Carpenter, Cyrus Clay, Nov. 24, 1829–May 29, 1898.
Vol. 2, Pt. 1–508
Carpenter, Edmund Janes, Oct. 16, 1845–Feb. 21, 1924.
Vol. 2, Pt. 1–509
Carpenter, Francis Bicknell, Aug. 6, 1830–May 23, 1900.
Vol. 2, Pt. 1–510
Carpenter, Frank George, May 8, 1855–June 18, 1924.
Vol. 2, Pt. 1–510
Carpenter, Franklin Reuben, Nov. 5, 1848–Apr. 1, 1910.
Vol. 2, Pt. 1–511
Carpenter, George Rice, Oct. 25, 1863–Apr. 8, 1909.
Vol. 2, Pt. 1–511
Carpenter, John Alden, Feb. 28, 1876–Apr. 26, 1951.
Supp. 5–103
Carpenter, Matthew Hale, Dec. 22, 1824–Feb. 24, 1881.
Vol. 2, Pt. 1–512
Carpenter, Stephen Cullen, died *c.* 1820.
Vol. 2, Pt. 1–513
Carpenter, Stephen Haskins, Aug. 7, 1831–Dec. 7, 1878.
Vol. 2, Pt. 1–513
Carpenter, Walter Samuel, Jr., Jan. 8, 1888–Feb. 2, 1976.
Supp. 10–101
Carr, Benjamin, 1769–May 24, 1831.
Vol. 2, Pt. 1–514
Carr, Charlotte Elizabeth, May 3, 1890–July 12, 1956.
Supp. 6–102
Carr, Dabney, Apr. 27, 1773–Jan. 8, 1837.
Vol. 2, Pt. 1–515
Carr, Dabney Smith, Mar. 5, 1802–Mar. 24, 1854.
Vol. 2, Pt. 1–515
Carr, Elias, Feb. 25, 1839–July 22, 1900.
Vol. 2, Pt. 1–516
Carr, Eugene Asa, Mar. 20, 1830–Dec. 2, 1910.
Vol. 2, Pt. 1–516
Carr, John Dickson, Nov. 30, 1906–Feb. 27, 1977.
Supp. 10–103
Carr, Joseph Bradford, Aug. 16, 1828–Feb. 24, 1895.
Vol. 2, Pt. 1–517
Carr, Matthew. [*See* Carr, Thomas Matthew, 1750–1820.]
Carr, Thomas Matthew, 1750–Sept. 29, 1820.
Vol. 2, Pt. 1–518
Carr, Wilbur John, Oct. 31, 1870–June 26, 1942.
Supp. 3–138
Carrel, Alexis, June 28, 1873–Nov. 5, 1944.
Supp. 3–139
Carrère, John Merven, Nov. 9, 1858–Mar. 1, 1911.
Vol. 2, Pt. 1–518
Carrick, Samuel, July 17, 1760–Aug. 17, 1809.
Vol. 2, Pt. 1–520
Carrier, Willis Haviland, Nov. 26, 1876–Oct. 7, 1950.
Supp. 4–148
Carrington, Elaine Stern, June 14, 1891–May 4, 1958.
Supp. 6–103
Carrington, Henry Beebee, Mar. 2, 1824–Oct. 26, 1912.
Vol. 2, Pt. 1–520
Carrington, Paul, Mar. 16, 1733–June 23, 1818.
Vol. 2, Pt. 1–522
Carroll, Charles, Sept. 19, 1737–Nov. 14, 1832.
Vol. 2, Pt. 1–522
Carroll, Daniel, July 22, 1730–May 7, 1796.
Vol. 2, Pt. 1–523
Carroll, Earl, Sept. 16, 1893–June 17, 1948.
Supp. 4–149
Carroll, Howard, Sept. 17, 1854–Dec. 30, 1916.
Vol. 2, Pt. 1–524

Carroll, James, June 5, 1854–Sept. 16, 1907.
Vol. 2, Pt. 1–525
Carroll, John, Jan. 8, 1735–Dec. 3, 1815.
Vol. 2, Pt. 1–526
Carroll, John Lee, Sept. 30, 1830–Feb. 27, 1911.
Vol. 2, Pt. 1–528
Carroll, Leo Grattan, Oct. 25, 1886–Oct. 16, 1972.
Supp. 9–157
Carroll, Samuel Sprigg, Sept. 21, 1832–Jan. 28, 1893.
Vol. 2, Pt. 1–528
Carroll, William, Mar. 3, 1788–Mar. 22, 1844.
Vol. 2, Pt. 1–529
Carrora, Joseph. [*See* Dundee, Johnny, 1893–1965.]
Carruth, Fred Hayden, Oct. 31, 1862–Jan. 3, 1932.
Supp. 1–152
Carryl, Guy Wetmore, Mar. 4, 1873–Apr. 1, 1904.
Vol. 2, Pt. 1–530
Carson, Christopher, Dec. 24, 1809–May 23, 1868.
Vol. 2, Pt. 1–530
Carson, Hampton Lawrence, Feb. 21, 1852–July 18, 1929.
Supp. 1–153
Carson, Jack, Oct. 27, 1910–Jan. 2, 1963.
Supp. 7–107
Carson, John Renshaw, June 28, 1886–Oct. 31, 1940.
Supp. 2–97
Carson, Joseph, Apr. 19, 1808–Dec. 30, 1876.
Vol. 2, Pt. 1–532
Carson, Rachel Louise, May 27, 1907–Apr. 14, 1964.
Supp. 7–108
Carson, Simeon Lewis, Jan. 16, 1882–Sept. 8, 1954.
Supp. 5–104
Carter, Boake, Sept. 28, 1898–Nov. 16, 1944.
Supp. 3–142
Carter, Caroline Louise Dudley, June 10, 1862–Nov. 13, 1937.
Supp. 2–98
Carter, Elias, May 30, 1781–Mar. 23, 1864.
Vol. 2, Pt. 1–533
Carter, Franklin, Sept. 30, 1837–Nov. 22, 1919.
Vol. 2, Pt. 1–533
Carter, Henry Alpheus Peirce, Aug. 7, 1837–Nov. 1, 1891.
Vol. 2, Pt. 1–534
Carter, Henry Rose, Aug. 25, 1852–Sept. 14, 1925.
Vol. 2, Pt. 1–535
Carter, James Coolidge, Oct. 14, 1827–Feb. 14, 1905.
Vol. 2, Pt. 1–536
Carter, James Gordon, Sept 7, 1795–July 21, 1849.
Vol. 2, Pt. 1–538
Carter, Jesse Benedict, June 16, 1872–July 20, 1917.
Vol. 2, Pt. 1–539
Carter, John, 1737–1781.
Vol. 2, Pt. 1–539
Carter, John, July 21, 1745–Aug. 19, 1814.
Vol. 2, Pt. 1–540
Carter, Landon, Jan. 29, 1760–June 5, 1800.
Vol. 2, Pt. 1–541
Carter, Mrs. Leslie. [*See* Carter, Caroline Louise Dudley, 1862–1937.]
Carter, Maybelle Addington, May 10, 1909–Oct. 23, 1978.
Supp. 10–104
Carter, Robert, 1663–Aug. 4, 1732.
Vol. 2, Pt. 1–541
Carter, Robert, Feb. 5, 1819–Feb. 15, 1879.
Vol. 2, Pt. 1–542
Carter, Samuel Powhatan, Aug. 6, 1819–May 26, 1891.
Vol. 2, Pt. 1–543
Carter, Thomas Henry, Oct. 30, 1854–Sept. 17, 1911.
Vol. 2, Pt. 1–544
Carter, William Hodding, Jr., Feb. 3, 1907–Apr. 4, 1972.
Supp. 9–159
Carter, William Samuel, Aug. 11, 1859–Mar. 15, 1923.
Vol. 2, Pt. 1–545
Carteret, Philip, 1639–1682.
Vol. 2, Pt. 1–546
Cartwright, Peter, Sept. 1, 1785–Sept. 25, 1872.
Vol. 2, Pt. 1–546
Carty, John Joseph, Apr. 14, 1861–Dec. 27, 1932.
Supp. 1–155
Carus, Paul, July 18, 1852–Feb. 11, 1919.
Vol. 2, Pt. 1–548
Caruso, Enrico, Feb. 25, 1873–Aug. 2, 1921.
Vol. 2, Pt. 1–549
Caruthers, William Alexander, *c.* 1800–Aug. 29, 1846.
Vol. 2, Pt. 1–551
Carvalho, Solomon Solis, Jan. 16, 1856–Apr. 12, 1942.
Supp. 3–143
Carver, George Washington, *c.* 1861–Jan. 5, 1943.
Supp. 3–145
Carver, John, *c.* 1576–Apr. 5, 1621.
Vol. 2, Pt. 1–551
Carver, Jonathan, Apr. 13, 1710–Jan. 31, 1780.
Vol. 2, Pt. 1–552
Cary, Alice, Apr. 26, 1820–Feb. 12, 1871.
Vol. 2, Pt. 1–552
Cary, Annie Louise, Oct. 22, 1842–Apr. 3, 1921.
Vol. 2, Pt. 1–553
Cary, Archibald, 1721–1787.
Vol. 2, Pt. 1–554
Cary, Edward, June 5, 1840–May 23, 1917.
Vol. 2, Pt. 1–554
Cary, Elisabeth Luther, May 18, 1867–July 13, 1936.
Supp. 2–99
Cary, Lott, 1780?–Nov. 10, 1828.
Vol. 2, Pt. 1–555
Cary, Phoebe, Sept. 4, 1824–July 31, 1871.
Vol. 2, Pt. 1–555
Casadesus, Robert Marcel, Apr. 7, 1899–Sept. 19, 1972.
Supp. 9–161
Casals, Pablo, Dec. 29, 1876–Oct. 22, 1973.
Supp. 9–163
Casanowicz, Immanuel Moses, July 25, 1853–Sept. 26, 1927.
Vol. 2, Pt. 1–556
Case, Francis Higbee, Dec. 9, 1896–June 22, 1962.
Supp. 7–110
Case, Jerome Increase, Dec. 11, 1818–Dec. 22, 1891.
Vol. 2, Pt. 1–556
Case, Leonard, July 29, 1786–Dec. 7, 1864.
Vol. 2, Pt. 1–557
Case, Leonard, June 27, 1820–Jan. 6, 1880.
Vol. 2, Pt. 1–558
Case, Shirley Jackson, Sept. 28, 1872–Dec. 5, 1947.
Supp. 4–151
Case, William Scoville, June 27, 1863–Feb. 28, 1921.
Vol. 2, Pt. 1–558
Casey, Joseph, Dec. 17, 1814–Feb. 10, 1879.
Vol. 2, Pt. 1–559
Casey, Silas, July 12, 1807–Jan. 22, 1882.
Vol. 2, Pt. 1–560
Casey, Thomas Lincoln, May 10, 1831–Mar. 25, 1896.
Supp. 1–156
Cash, Wilbur Joseph, May 2, 1900–July 1, 1941.
Supp. 2–147
Casilear, John William, June 25, 1811–Aug. 17, 1893.
Vol. 2, Pt. 1–560
Cass, George Washington, Mar. 12, 1810–Mar. 21, 1888.
Vol. 2, Pt. 1–561
Cass, Lewis, Oct. 9, 1782–June 17, 1866.
Vol. 2, Pt. 1–562
Cassatt, Alexander Johnston, Dec. 8, 1839–Dec. 28, 1906.
Vol. 2, Pt. 1–564
Cassatt, Mary, May 22, 1845–June 14, 1926.
Vol. 2, Pt. 1–567
Cassidy, Jack, Mar. 5, 1927–Dec. 12, 1976.
Supp. 10–105
Cassidy, Marshall Whiting, Feb. 21, 1892–Oct. 23, 1968.
Supp. 8–75
Cassidy, William, Aug. 12, 1815–Jan. 23, 1873.
Vol. 2, Pt. 1–568
Cassin, John, Sept. 6, 1813–Jan. 10, 1869.
Vol. 2, Pt. 1–568
Cassoday, John Bolivar, July 7, 1830–Dec. 30, 1907.
Supp. 1–157
Castle, Irene Foote, Apr. 7, 1893–Jan. 25, 1969.
Supp. 8–76
Castle, Vernon Blythe, May 2, 1887–Feb. 15, 1918.
Vol. 2, Pt. 1–569
Castle, William Richards, Jr., June 19, 1878–Oct. 13, 1963.
Supp. 7–112
Caswell, Alexis, Jan. 29, 1799–Jan. 8, 1877.
Vol. 2, Pt. 1–570
Caswell, Richard, Aug. 3, 1729–Nov. 1789.
Vol. 2, Pt. 1–571

Cataldo, Joseph Maria, Mar. 17, 1837–Apr. 9, 1928.
Supp. 1–158
Catchings, Waddill, Sept. 6, 1879–Dec. 31, 1967.
Supp. 8–78
Catesby, Mark, *c.* 1679–Dec. 23, 1749.
Vol. 2, Pt. 1–571
Cathcart, James Leander, June 1, 1767–Oct. 6, 1843.
Vol. 2, Pt. 1–572
Cathcart, William, Nov. 8, 1826–July 8, 1908.
Vol. 2, Pt. 1–573
Cather, Willa, Dec. 7, 1873–Apr. 24, 1947.
Supp. 4–153
Catherwood, Mary Hartwell, Dec. 16, 1847–Dec. 26, 1902.
Vol. 2, Pt. 1–573
Catlett, Sidney, Jan. 17, 1910–Mar. 25, 1951.
Supp. 5–105
Catlin, George, July 26, 1796–Dec. 23, 1872.
Vol. 2, Pt. 1–574
Caton, John Dean, Mar. 19, 1812–July 30, 1895.
Vol. 2, Pt. 1–575
Catron, John, *c.* 1786–May 30, 1865.
Vol. 2, Pt. 1–576
Catt, Carrie Clinton Lane Chapman, Jan. 9, 1859–Mar. 9, 1947.
Supp. 4–155
Cattell, Alexander Gilmore, Feb. 12, 1816–Apr. 8, 1894.
Vol. 2, Pt. 1–577
Cattell, James McKeen, May 25, 1860–Jan. 20, 1944.
Supp. 3–148
Cattell, William Cassaday, Aug. 30, 1827–Feb. 11, 1898.
Vol. 2, Pt. 1–578
Catton, Charles Bruce, Oct. 9, 1899–Aug. 28, 1978.
Supp. 10–107
Cavanagh, Jerome Patrick ("Jerry"), June 16, 1928–Nov. 27, 1979.
Supp. 10–108
Cavert, Samuel McCrea, Sept. 9, 1888–Dec. 21, 1976.
Supp. 10–110
Cawein, Madison Julius, Mar. 23, 1865–Dec. 8, 1914.
Vol. 2, Pt. 1–578
Cayton, Horace Roscoe, Apr. 12, 1903–Jan. 22, 1970.
Supp. 8–79
Cayvan, Georgia, 1858–Nov. 19, 1906.
Vol. 2, Pt. 1–580
Cazenove, Théophile, Oct. 13, 1740–Mar. 6, 1811.
Vol. 2, Pt. 1–580
Celestin, Oscar ("Papa"), Jan. 1, 1884–Dec. 15, 1954.
Supp. 5–106
Céloron de Blainville, Pierre Joseph de, Dec. 29, 1693–Apr. 12, 1759.
Vol. 2, Pt. 1–581
Cerf, Bennett Alfred, May 25, 1898–Aug. 27, 1971.
Supp. 9–164
Cermak, Anton Joseph, May 9, 1873–Mar. 6, 1933.
Supp. 1–159
Cerré, Jean Gabriel, Aug. 12, 1734–Apr. 4, 1805.
Vol. 2, Pt. 1–582
Cesare, Oscar Edward, Oct. 7, 1883–July 24, 1948.
Supp. 4–159
Cesnola, Luigi Palma di, June 29, 1832–Nov. 20, 1904.
Vol. 2, Pt. 1–583
Chace, Elizabeth Buffum, Dec. 9, 1806–Dec. 12, 1899.
Vol. 2, Pt. 1–584
Chadbourne, Paul Ansel, Oct. 21, 1823–Feb. 23, 1883.
Vol. 2, Pt. 1–585
Chadwick, French Ensor, Feb. 29, 1844–Jan. 27, 1919.
Vol. 2, Pt. 1–586
Chadwick, George Whitefield, Nov. 13, 1854–Apr. 4, 1931.
Supp. 1–160
Chadwick, Henry, Oct. 5, 1824–Apr. 20, 1908.
Vol. 2, Pt. 1–587
Chadwick, James Read, Nov. 2, 1844–Sept. 23, 1905.
Vol. 2, Pt. 1–588
Chadwick, John White, Oct. 19, 1840–Dec. 11, 1904.
Vol. 2, Pt. 1–588
Chafee, Zechariah, Jr., Dec. 7, 1885–Feb. 8, 1957.
Supp. 6–104
Chaffee, Adna Romanza, Apr. 14, 1842–Nov. 1, 1914.
Vol. 2, Pt. 1–589
Chaffee, Adna Romanza, Sept. 23, 1884–Aug. 22, 1941.
Supp. 3–151
Chaffee, Jerome Bonaparte, Apr. 17, 1825–Mar. 9, 1886.
Vol. 2, Pt. 1–590
Chaffee, Roger Bruce, Feb. 15, 1935–Jan. 27, 1967.
Supp. 8–81
Chafin, Eugene Wilder, Nov. 1, 1852–Nov. 30, 1920.
Vol. 2, Pt. 1–590
Chaillé-Long, Charles, July 2, 1842–Mar. 24, 1917.
Vol. 2, Pt. 1–591
Chaliapin, Boris Fyodorovich, Oct. 5, 1904–May 18, 1979.
Supp. 10–112
Chalkley, Thomas, May 3, 1675–Nov. 4, 1741.
Vol. 2, Pt. 1–592
Chalmers, James Ronald, Jan. 11, 1831–Apr. 9, 1898.
Vol. 2, Pt. 1–593
Chalmers, William James, July 10, 1852–Dec. 10, 1938.
Supp. 2–100
Chamberlain, Alexander Francis, Jan. 12, 1865–Apr. 8, 1914.
Vol. 2, Pt. 1–594
Chamberlain, Charles Joseph, Feb. 23, 1863–Jan. 5, 1943.
Supp. 3–153
Chamberlain, Daniel Henry, June 23, 1835–Apr. 13, 1907.
Vol. 2, Pt. 1–595
Chamberlain, George Earle, Jan. 1, 1854–July 9, 1928.
Vol. 2, Pt. 1–595
Chamberlain, Henry Richardson, Aug. 25, 1859–Feb. 15, 1911.
Vol. 2, Pt. 1–596
Chamberlain, Jacob, Apr. 13, 1835–Mar. 2, 1908.
Vol. 2, Pt. 1–597
Chamberlain, Joseph Perkins, Oct. 1, 1873–May 21, 1951.
Supp. 5–107
Chamberlain, Joshua Lawrence, Sept. 8, 1828–Feb. 24, 1914.
Vol. 2, Pt. 1–597
Chamberlain, Mellen, June 4, 1821–June 25, 1900.
Vol. 2, Pt. 1–598
Chamberlain, Nathan Henry, Dec. 28, 1828?–Apr. 1, 1901.
Vol. 2, Pt. 1–599
Chamberlain, William Isaac, Feb. 11, 1837–June 30, 1920.
Vol. 2, Pt. 1–600
Chamberlin, Edward Hastings, May 18, 1899–July 16, 1967.
Supp. 8–82
Chamberlin, Thomas Chrowder, Sept. 25, 1843–Nov. 15, 1928.
Vol. 2, Pt. 1–600
Chambers, Charles Julius. [*See* Chambers, James Julius, 1850–1920.]
Chambers, Ezekiel Forman, Feb. 28, 1788–Jan. 30, 1867.
Vol. 2, Pt. 1–602
Chambers, George, Feb. 24, 1786–Mar. 25, 1866.
Vol. 2, Pt. 1–602
Chambers, James Julius, Nov. 21, 1850–Feb. 12, 1920.
Vol. 2, Pt. 1–603
Chambers, John, Oct. 6, 1780–Sept. 21, 1852.
Vol. 2, Pt. 1–603
Chambers, Julius. [*See* Chambers, James Julius, 1850–1920.]
Chambers, Robert William, May 26, 1865–Dec. 16, 1933.
Supp. 1–162
Chambers, Talbott Wilson, Feb. 25, 1819–Feb. 3, 1896.
Vol. 2, Pt. 1–604
Chambers, Whittaker, Apr. I, 1901–July 9, 1961.
Supp. 7–113
Champion, Gower, June 22, 1919–Aug. 25, 1980.
Supp. 10–113
Champlain, Samuel de, *c.* 1567–Dec. 25, 1635.
Vol. 2, Pt. 1–605
Champlin, John Denison, Jan. 29, 1834–Jan. 8, 1915.
Vol. 2, Pt. 1–607
Champlin, John Wayne, Feb. 7, 1831–July 24, 1901.
Vol. 2, Pt. 1–608
Champlin, Stephen, Nov. 17, 1789–Feb. 20, 1870.
Vol. 2, Pt. 1–609
Champney, Benjamin, Nov. 17, 1817–Dec. 11, 1907.
Vol. 2, Pt. 1–609
Champney, James Wells, July 16, 1843–May 1, 1903.
Vol. 2, Pt. 1–610
Chanche, John Mary Joseph, Oct. 4, 1795–July 22, 1852.
Vol. 2, Pt. 1–610
Chandler, Charles Frederick, Dec. 6, 1836–Aug. 25, 1925.
Vol. 2, Pt. 1–611
Chandler, Elizabeth Margaret, Dec. 24, 1807–Nov. 2, 1834.
Vol. 2, Pt. 1–613

Chandler, Harry, May 17, 1864–Sept. 23, 1944.
Supp. 3–154
Chandler, John, Feb. 1, 1762–Sept. 25, 1841.
Vol. 2, Pt. 1–613
Chandler, John Scudder, Apr. 12, 1849–June 19, 1934.
Supp. 1–163
Chandler, Joseph Ripley, Aug. 25, 1792–July 10, 1880.
Vol. 2, Pt. 1–614
Chandler, Julian Alvin Carroll, Oct. 29, 1872–May 31, 1934.
Supp. 1–164
Chandler, Norman, Sept. 14, 1899–Oct. 20, 1973.
Supp. 9–167
Chandler, Peleg Whitman, Apr. 12, 1816–May 28, 1889.
Vol. 2, Pt. 1–615
Chandler, Raymond Thornton, July 23, 1888–Mar. 26, 1959.
Supp. 6–106
Chandler, Seth Carlo, Sept. 17, 1846–Dec. 31, 1913.
Vol. 2, Pt. 1–615
Chandler, Thomas Bradbury, Apr. 26, 1726–June 17, 1790.
Vol. 2, Pt. 1–616
Chandler, William Eaton, Dec. 28, 1835–Nov. 30, 1917.
Vol. 2, Pt. 1–616
Chandler, Zachariah, Dec. 10, 1813–Nov. 1, 1879.
Vol. 2, Pt. 1–618
Chaney, Lon, Apr. 1, 1883–Aug. 26, 1930.
Supp. 1–165
Chaney, Lon, Jr., Feb. 10, 1906–July 13, 1973.
Supp. 9–168
Chanfrau, Francis S., Feb. 22, 1824–Oct. 2, 1884.
Vol. 2, Pt. 2–1
Chanfrau, Henrietta Baker, 1837–Sept. 21, 1909.
Vol. 2, Pt. 2–2
Chang and Eng, May 1811–Jan. 17, 1874.
Vol. 2, Pt. 2–2
Channing, Edward, June 15, 1856–Jan. 7, 1931.
Supp. 1–166
Channing, Edward Tyrrell, Dec. 12, 1790–Feb. 8, 1856.
Vol. 2, Pt. 2–3
Channing, Walter, Apr. 15, 1786–July 27, 1876.
Vol. 2, Pt. 2–3
Channing, William Ellery, Apr. 7, 1780–Oct. 2, 1842.
Vol. 2, Pt. 2–4
Channing, William Ellery, Nov. 29, 1818–Dec. 23, 1901.
Vol. 2, Pt. 2–7
Channing, William Francis, Feb. 22, 1820–Mar. 19, 1901.
Vol. 2, Pt. 2–8
Channing, William Henry, May 25, 1810–Dec. 23, 1884.
Vol. 2, Pt. 2–9
Chanute, Octave, Feb. 18, 1832–Nov. 23, 1910.
Vol. 2, Pt. 2–10
Chapelle, Dickey, Mar. 14, 1918–Nov. 4, 1965.
Supp. 7–115
Chapelle, Placide Louis, Aug. 28, 1842–Aug. 9, 1905.
Vol. 2, Pt. 2–11
Chapin, Aaron Lucius, Feb. 6, 1817–July 22, 1892.
Vol. 2, Pt. 2–12
Chapin, Alonzo Bowen, Mar. 10, 1808–July 9, 1858.
Vol. 2, Pt. 2–13
Chapin, Calvin, July 22, 1763–Mar. 16, 1851.
Vol. 2, Pt. 2–13
Chapin, Charles Value, Jan. 17, 1856–Jan. 31, 1941.
Supp. 3–157
Chapin, Chester William, Dec. 16, 1798–June 10, 1883.
Vol. 2, Pt. 2–14
Chapin, Edwin Hubbell, Dec. 29, 1814–Dec. 26, 1880.
Vol. 2, Pt. 2–15
Chapin, Henry Dwight, Feb. 4, 1857–June 27, 1942.
Supp. 3–159
Chapin, James Paul, July 9, 1889–Apr. 5, 1964.
Supp. 7–116
Chapin, Roy Dikeman, Feb. 23, 1880–Feb. 16, 1936.
Supp. 2–101
Chaplin, Charles Spencer ("Charlie"), Apr. 16, 1889–Dec. 25, 1977.
Supp. 10–114
Chaplin, Jeremiah, Jan. 2, 1776–May 7, 1841.
Vol. 2, Pt. 2–15
Chaplin, Ralph Hosea, Aug. 30, 1887–Mar. 23, 1961.
Supp. 7–118
Chapman, Alvan Wentworth, Sept. 28, 1809–Apr. 6, 1899.
Vol. 2, Pt. 2–16
Chapman, Frank Michler, June 12, 1864–Nov. 15, 1945.
Supp. 3–161
Chapman, Henry Cadwalader, Aug. 17, 1845–Sept. 7, 1909.
Vol. 2, Pt. 2–17
Chapman, John, *c.* 1775–Mar. 11, 1847.
Vol. 2, Pt. 2–17
Chapman, John Arthur, June 25, 1900–Jan. 19, 1972.
Supp. 9–170
Chapman, John Gadsby, Dec. 8, 1808–Nov. 28, 1889.
Vol. 2, Pt. 2–18
Chapman, John Jay, Mar. 2, 1862–Nov. 4, 1933.
Supp. 1–168
Chapman, John Wilbur, June 17, 1859–Dec. 25, 1918
Vol. 2, Pt. 2–19
Chapman, Maria Weston, July 25, 1806–July 12, 1885.
Vol. 2, Pt. 2–19
Chapman, Nathaniel, May 28, 1780–July 1, 1853.
Vol. 2, Pt. 2–19
Chapman, Oscar Littleton, Oct. 22, 1896–Feb. 7, 1978.
Supp. 10–118
Chapman, Reuben, July 15, 1802–May 17, 1882
Vol. 2, Pt. 2–20
Chapman, Victor Emmanuel, Apr. 17, 1890–June 23, 1916.
Vol. 2, Pt. 2–21
Chappell, Absalom Harris, Dec. 18, 1801–Dec. 11, 1878.
Vol. 2, Pt. 2–21
Charles, Ezzard Mack, July 7, 1921–May 28, 1975.
Supp. 9–171
Charles, William, 1776–Aug. 29, 1820.
Vol. 2, Pt. 2–22
Charless, Joseph, July 16, 1772–July 28, 1834.
Vol. 2, Pt. 2–23
Charlevoix, Pierre Francois Xavier de, Oct. 24, 1682–Feb. 1, 1761.
Vol. 2, Pt. 2–23
Charlton, Thomas Usher Pulaski, Nov. 1779–Dec. 14, 1835.
Vol. 2, Pt. 2–24
Chase, Edna Woolman, Mar. 14, 1877–Mar. 20, 1957.
Supp. 6–107
Chase, George, Dec. 29, 1849–Jan. 8, 1924.
Vol. 2, Pt. 2–25
Chase, Harry Woodburn, Apr. 11, 1883–Apr. 20, 1955.
Supp. 5–108
Chase, Ilka, Apr. 8, 1905–Feb. 15, 1978.
Supp. 10–120
Chase, Irah, Oct. 5, 1793–Nov. 1, 1864.
Vol. 2, Pt. 2–25
Chase, (Mary) Agnes Merrill, Apr. 20, 1869–Sept. 24, 1963.
Supp. 7–119
Chase, Mary Ellen, Feb. 24, 1887–July 28, 1973.
Supp. 9–172
Chase, Philander, Dec. 14, 1775–Sept. 20, 1852.
Vol. 2, Pt. 2–26
Chase, Pliny Earle, Aug. 18, 1820–Dec. 17, 1886.
Vol. 2, Pt. 2–27
Chase, Salmon Portland, Jan. 13, 1808–May 7, 1873.
Vol. 2, Pt. 2–27
Chase, Samuel, Apr. 17, 1741–June 19, 1811.
Vol. 2, Pt. 2–34
Chase, Thomas, June 16, 1827–Oct. 5, 1892.
Vol. 2, Pt. 2–37
Chase, William Merritt, Nov. 1, 1849–Oct. 25, 1916.
Vol. 2, Pt. 2–38
Chatard, Francis Silas, Dec. 13, 1834–Sept. 7, 1918.
Vol. 2, Pt. 2–39
Chatterton, Ruth, Dec. 24, 1893–Nov. 24, 1961.
Supp. 7–120
Chaumonot, Pierre Joseph Marie, Mar. 9, 1611–Feb. 21, 1693.
Vol. 2, Pt. 2–40
Chauncey, Isaac, Feb. 20, 1772–Jan. 27, 1840.
Vol. 2, Pt. 2–40
Chauncy, Charles, 1592–Feb. 19, 1671/2.
Vol. 2, Pt. 2–41
Chauncy, Charles, Jan. 1, 1705–Feb. 10, 1787.
Vol. 2, Pt. 2–42
Chauvenet, William, May 24, 1820–Dec. 13, 1870.
Vol. 2, Pt. 2–43
Chavez, Dennis, Apr. 8, 1888–Nov. 18, 1962.
Supp. 7–121
Chavis, John, *c.* 1763–1838.
Vol. 2, Pt. 2–44

Cheatham, Benjamin Franklin, Oct. 20, 1820–Sept. 4, 1886.
Vol. 2, Pt. 2–45
Checkley, John, 1680–Feb. 15, 1754.
Vol. 2, Pt. 2–46
Cheesman, Forman, Dec. 11, 1763–Oct. 10, 1821.
Vol. 2, Pt. 2–46
Cheetham, James, 1772–Sept. 19, 1810.
Vol. 2, Pt. 2–47
Cheever, Ezekiel, Jan. 25, 1614/15–Aug. 21, 1708.
Vol. 2, Pt. 2–47
Cheever, George Barrell, Apr. 17, 1807–Oct. 1, 1890.
Vol. 2, Pt. 2–48
Cheever, Henry Theodore, Feb. 6, 1814–Feb. 13, 1897.
Vol. 2, Pt. 2–49
Cheney, Benjamin Pierce, Aug. 12, 1815–July 23, 1895.
Vol. 2, Pt. 2–50
Cheney, Charles Edward, Feb. 12, 1836–Nov. 15, 1916.
Vol. 2, Pt. 2–51
Cheney, Ednah Dow Littlehale, June 27, 1824–Nov. 19, 1904.
Vol. 2, Pt. 2–51
Cheney, John, Oct. 20, 1801–Aug. 20, 1885.
Vol. 2, Pt. 2–52
Cheney, John Vance, Dec. 29, 1848–May 1, 1922.
Vol. 2, Pt. 2–53
Cheney, Oren Burbank, Dec. 10, 1816–Dec. 22, 1903.
Vol. 2, Pt. 2–53
Cheney, Person Cobby, Feb. 25, 1828–June 19, 1901.
Vol. 2, Pt. 2–54
Cheney, Seth Wells, Nov. 26, 1810–Sept. 10, 1856.
Vol. 2, Pt. 2–55
Cheney, Ward, Feb. 23, 1813–Mar. 22, 1876.
Vol. 2, Pt. 2–56
Chennault, Claire Lee, Sept. 6, 1893–July 27, 1958.
Supp. 6–108
Cherrington, Ernest Hurst, Nov. 24, 1877–Mar. 13, 1950.
Supp. 4–160
Chesebrough, Caroline, Mar. 30, 1825–Feb. 16, 1873.
Vol. 2, Pt. 2–56
Cheshire, Joseph Blount, Mar. 27, 1850–Dec. 27, 1932.
Supp. 1–169
Chesnut, James, Jan. 18, 1815–Feb. 1, 1885.
Vol. 2, Pt. 2–57
Chessman, Caryl Whittier, May 27, 1921–May 2, 1960.
Supp. 6–110
Chester, Colby Mitchell, Feb. 29, 1844–May 4, 1932.
Supp. 1–170
Chester, Colby Mitchell, July 23, 1877–Sept. 26, 1965.
Supp. 7–122
Chester, George Randolph, 1869–Feb. 26, 1924.
Vol. 2, Pt. 2–58
Chester, Joseph Lemuel, Apr. 30, 1821–May 26, 1882.
Vol. 2, Pt. 2–58
Chetlain, Augustus Louis, Dec. 26, 1824–Mar. 15, 1914.
Vol. 2, Pt. 2–60
Chever, James W., Apr. 20, 1791–May 2, 1857.
Vol. 2, Pt. 2–60
Cheverus, John Louis Ann Magdalen Lefebre de, Jan. 28, 1768–July 19, 1836.
Vol. 2, Pt. 2–61
Cheves, Langdon, Sept. 17, 1776–June 26, 1857.
Vol. 2, Pt. 2–62
Chew, Benjamin, Nov. 29, 1722–Jan. 20, 1810.
Vol. 2, Pt. 2–64
Cheyney, Edward Potts, Jan. 17, 1861–Feb. 1, 1947.
Supp. 4–162
Chickering, Jonas, Apr. 5, 1798–Dec. 8, 1853.
Vol. 2, Pt. 2–65
Chiera, Edward, Aug. 5, 1885–June 20, 1933.
Supp. 1–171
Child, Charles Manning, Feb. 2, 1869–Dec. 19, 1954.
Supp. 5–109
Child, David Lee, July 8, 1794–Sept. 18, 1874.
Vol. 2, Pt. 2–65
Child, Francis James, Feb. 1, 1825–Sept. 11, 1896.
Vol. 2, Pt. 2–66
Child, Frank Samuel, Mar. 20, 1854–May 4, 1922.
Vol. 2, Pt. 2–67
Child, Lydia Maria Francis, Feb. 11, 1802–Oct. 20, 1880.
Vol. 2, Pt. 2–67
Child, Richard Washburn, Aug. 5, 1881–Jan. 31, 1935.
Supp. 1–172
Child, Robert, *c.* 1613–1654.
Supp. 1–174
Childe, John, Aug. 30, 1802–Feb. 2, 1858.
Vol. 2, Pt. 2–69
Childs, Cephas Grier, Sept. 8, 1793–July 7, 1871.
Vol. 2, Pt. 2–69
Childs, George William, May 12, 1829–Feb. 3, 1894.
Vol. 2, Pt. 2–70
Childs, Richard Spencer, May 24, 1882–Sept. 26, 1978.
Supp. 10–121
Childs, Thomas, 1796–Oct. 8, 1853.
Vol. 2, Pt. 2–71
Chilton, William Paris, Aug. 10, 1810–Jan. 20, 1871.
Vol. 2, Pt. 2–71
Chini, Eusebio Francisco. [*See* Kino, Eusebio Francisco, 1645–1711.]
Chipman, Daniel, Oct. 22, 1765–Apr. 23, 1850.
Vol. 2, Pt. 2–72
Chipman, Nathaniel, Nov. 15, 1752–Feb. 15, 1843.
Vol. 2, Pt. 2–73
Chipman, Ward, July 30, 1754–Feb. 9, 1824.
Vol. 2, Pt. 2–74
Chisholm, Hugh Joseph, May 2, 1847–July 8, 1912.
Vol. 2, Pt. 2–74
Chisolm, Alexander Robert, Nov. 19, 1834–Mar. 10, 1910.
Vol. 2, Pt. 2–75
Chisolm, John Julian, Apr. 16, 1830–Nov. 2, 1903.
Vol. 2, Pt. 2–76
Chisum, John Simpson, Aug. 15, 1824–Dec. 23, 1884.
Vol. 2, Pt. 2–77
Chittenden, Hiram Martin, Oct. 25, 1858–Oct. 9, 1917.
Vol. 2, Pt. 2–77
Chittenden, Martin, Mar. 12, 1763–Sept. 5, 1840.
Vol. 2, Pt. 2–78
Chittenden, Russell Henry, Feb. 18, 1856–Dec. 26, 1943.
Supp. 3–162
Chittenden, Simeon Baldwin, Mar. 29, 1814–Apr. 14, 1889.
Vol. 2, Pt. 2–79
Chittenden, Thomas, Jan. 6, 1730–Aug. 25, 1797.
Vol. 2, Pt. 2–80
Chivers, Thomas Holley, Oct. 18, 1809–Dec. 18, 1858.
Vol. 2, Pt. 2–81
Choate, Anne Hyde Clarke, Oct. 27, 1886–May 17, 1967.
Supp. 8–83
Choate, Joseph Hodges, Jan. 24, 1832–May 14, 1917.
Vol. 2, Pt. 2–83
Choate, Rufus, Oct. 1, 1799–July 13, 1859.
Vol. 2, Pt. 2–86
Chopin, Kate O'Flaherty, Feb. 8, 1851–Aug. 22, 1904.
Vol. 2, Pt. 2–90
Chorpenning, George, June 1, 1820–Apr. 3, 1894.
Vol. 2, Pt. 2–91
Chotzinoff, Samuel, July 4, 1889–Feb. 9, 1964.
Supp. 7–123
Chouart, Medart, [*See* Grosseilliers, Medart Chouart, Sieur de, 1621?–1698?.]
Chouteau, Auguste. [*See* Chouteau, René Auguste, 1750–1829.]
Chouteau, Auguste Pierre, May 9, 1786–Dec. 25, 1838.
Vol. 2, Pt. 1–292
Chouteau, Jean Pierre, Oct. 10, 1758–July 10, 1849.
Vol. 2, Pt. 2–93
Chouteau, Pierre, Jan. 19, 1789–Sept. 6, 1865.
Vol. 2, Pt. 2–93
Chouteau, Pierre. [*See* Chouteau, Jean Pierre, 1758–1849.]
Chouteau, René Auguste, Sept. 1749–Feb. 24, 1829.
Vol. 2, Pt. 2–94
Chovet, Abraham, May 25, 1704–Mar. 24, 1790.
Vol. 2, Pt. 2–95
Christian, Henry Asbury, Feb. 17, 1876–Aug. 24, 1951.
Supp. 5–111
Christian, William, *c.* 1743–Apr. 9, 1786.
Vol. 2, Pt. 2–96
Christiancy, Isaac Peckham, Mar. 12, 1812–Sept. 8, 1890.
Vol. 2, Pt. 2–96
Christie, John Walter, May 6, 1865–Jan. 11, 1944.
Supp. 3–165
Christy, David, b. 1802.
Vol. 2, Pt. 2–97
Christy, Edwin P., 1815–May 21, 1862.
Vol. 2, Pt. 2–98

Christy, Howard Chandler, Jan. 10, 1873–Mar. 4, 1952.
Supp. 5–112
Chrysler, Walter Percy, Apr. 2, 1875–Aug. 18, 1940.
Supp. 2–103
Church, Alonzo, Apr. 9, 1793–May 18, 1862.
Vol. 2, Pt. 2–98
Church, Benjamin, 1639–Jan. 17, 1718.
Vol. 2, Pt. 2–99
Church, Benjamin, Aug. 24, 1734–1776.
Vol. 2, Pt. 2–100
Church, Frederick Edwin, May 4, 1826–Apr. 7, 1900.
Vol. 2, Pt. 2–101
Church, Frederick Stuart, Dec. 1, 1842–Feb. 18, 1924.
Vol. 2, Pt. 2–101
Church, George Earl, Dec. 7, 1835–Jan. 5, 1910.
Vol. 2, Pt. 2–102
Church, Irving Porter, July 22, 1851–May 8, 1931.
Supp. 1–175
Church, John Adams, Apr. 5, 1843–Feb. 12, 1917.
Vol. 2, Pt. 2–103
Church, Pharcellus, Sept. 11, 1801–June 5, 1886.
Vol. 2, Pt. 2–104
Church, Thomas Dolliver, Apr. 27, 1902–Aug. 30, 1978.
Supp. 10–123
Church, William Conant, Aug. 11, 1836–May 23, 1917.
Vol. 2, Pt. 2–104
Churchill, Thomas James, Mar. 10, 1824–Mar. 10, 1905.
Vol. 2, Pt. 2–105
Churchill, William, Oct. 5, 1859–June 9, 1920.
Vol. 2, Pt. 2–106
Churchill, Winston, Nov. 10, 1871–March 12, 1947.
Supp. 4–163
Churchman, William Henry, Nov. 23, 1818–May 18, 1882.
Vol. 2, Pt. 2–106
Cicotte, Edward Victor, June 19, 1884–May 5, 1969.
Supp. 8–85
Cilley, Joseph, 1734–Aug. 25, 1799.
Vol. 2, Pt. 2–107
Cist, Charles, Aug. 15, 1738–Dec. 1, 1805.
Vol. 2, Pt. 2–108
Cist, Charles, Apr. 24, 1792–Sept. 5, 1868.
Vol. 2, Pt. 2–108
Cist, Henry Martyn, Feb. 20, 1839–Dec. 17, 1902.
Vol. 2, Pt. 2–109
Cist, Jacob, Mar. 13, 1782–Dec. 30, 1825.
Vol. 2, Pt. 2–109
Claflin, Horace Brigham, Dec. 18, 1811–Nov. 14, 1885.
Vol. 2, Pt. 2–110
Claflin, John, July 24, 1850–June 11, 1938.
Supp. 2–104
Claflin, Tennessee, 1845–1923. [*See* Woodhull, Victoria Claflin, 1838–1927.]
Claflin, William, Mar. 6, 1818–Jan. 5, 1905.
Vol. 2, Pt. 2–110
Clagett, Wyseman, August 1721–Dec. 4, 1784.
Vol. 2, Pt. 2–111
Claghorn, George, July 6, 1748–Feb. 3, 1824.
Vol. 2, Pt. 2–112
Claiborne, John Francis Hamtramck, Apr. 24, 1807–May 17, 1884.
Vol. 2, Pt. 2–112
Claiborne, Nathaniel Herbert, Nov. 14, 1777–Aug. 15, 1859.
Vol. 2, Pt. 2–113
Claiborne, William, *c.* 1587–*c.* 1677.
Vol. 2, Pt. 2–114
Claiborne, William Charles Coles, 1775–Nov. 23, 1817.
Vol. 2, Pt. 2–115
Clap, Thomas, June 26, 1703–Jan. 7, 1767.
Vol. 2, Pt. 2–116
Clapp, Asa, Mar. 15, 1762–Apr. 17, 1848.
Vol. 2, Pt. 2–117
Clapp, Charles Horace, June 5, 1883–May 9, 1935.
Supp. 1–175
Clapp, George Alfred. [*See* Dockstader, Lew, 1856–1924.]
Clapp, Margaret Antoinette, Apr. 11, 1910–May 3, 1974.
Supp. 9–174
Clapp, William Warland, Apr. 11, 1826–Dec. 8, 1891.
Vol. 2, Pt. 2–118
Clapper, Raymond Lewis, May 30, 1892–Feb. 1, 1944.
Supp. 3–166
Clark, Abraham, Feb. 15, 1726–Sept. 15, 1794.
Vol. 2, Pt. 2–118
Clark, Alvan, Mar. 8, 1804–Aug. 19, 1887.
Vol. 2, Pt. 2–119
Clark, Alvan Graham, July 10, 1832–June 9, 1897.
Vol. 2, Pt. 2–120
Clark, Arthur Hamilton, Dec. 27, 1841–July 5, 1922.
Vol. 2, Pt. 2–120
Clark, Bennett Champ, Jan. 8, 1890–July 13, 1954.
Supp. 5–113
Clark, Bobby, June 16, 1888–Feb. 12, 1960.
Supp. 6–112
Clark, Champ, Mar. 7, 1850–Mar. 2, 1921.
Vol. 2, Pt. 2–121
Clark, Charles, 1810–Dec. 18, 1877.
Vol. 2, Pt. 2–122
Clark, Charles Edgar, Aug. 10, 1843–Oct. 2, 1922.
Vol. 2, Pt. 2–122
Clark, Charles Heber, July 11, 1847–Aug. 10, 1915.
Vol. 2, Pt. 2–123
Clark, Charles Hopkins, Apr. 1, 1848–Sept. 5, 1926.
Vol. 2, Pt. 2–124
Clark, Daniel, 1766–Aug. 16, 1813.
Vol. 2, Pt. 2–125
Clark, Daniel, Oct. 24, 1809–Jan. 2, 1891
Vol. 2, Pt. 2–125
Clark, Felton Grandison, Oct. 13, 1903–July 5, 1970.
Supp. 8–86
Clark, Francis Edward, Sept. 12, 1851–May 26, 1927.
Vol. 2, Pt. 2–126
Clark, George Rogers, Nov. 19, 1752–Feb. 13, 1818.
Vol. 2, Pt. 2–127
Clark, George Whitefield, Feb. 15, 1831–Nov. 10, 1911.
Vol. 2, Pt. 2–130
Clark, Greenleaf, Aug. 23, 1835–Dec. 4, 1904.
Vol. 2, Pt. 2–131
Clark, Grenville, Nov. 5, 1882–Jan. 13, 1967.
Supp. 8–87
Clark, Henry James, June 22, 1826–July 1, 1873.
Vol. 2, Pt. 2–131
Clark, Horace Francis, Nov. 29, 1815–June 19, 1873.
Vol. 2, Pt. 2–132
Clark, James, Jan. 16, 1779–Sept. 27, 1839.
Vol. 2, Pt. 2–133
Clark, John, Feb. 28, 1766–Oct. 12, 1832.
Vol. 2, Pt. 2–134
Clark, John Bates, Jan. 26, 1847–Mar. 21, 1938.
Supp. 2–105
Clark, John Maurice, Nov. 30, 1884–June 27, 1963
Supp. 7–124
Clark, Jonas, Dec. 14, 1730 o.s.–Nov. 15, 1805.
Vol. 2, Pt. 2–135
Clark, Jonas Gilman, Feb. 1, 1815–May 23, 1900.
Vol. 2, Pt. 2–135
Clark, Joseph James ("Jocko"), Nov. 12, 1893–July 13, 1971.
Supp. 9–175
Clark, Joseph Sylvester, Dec. 19, 1800–Aug. 17, 1861.
Vol. 2, Pt. 2–136
Clark, Joshua Reuben, Jr., Sept. 1, 1871–Oct. 6, 1961.
Supp. 7–125
Clark, Lewis Gaylord, Oct. 5, 1808–Nov. 3, 1873.
Vol. 2, Pt. 2–137
Clark, Myron Holley, Oct. 23, 1806–Aug. 23, 1892.
Vol. 2, Pt. 2–138
Clark, Sheldon, Jan. 31, 1785–Apr. 10, 1840.
Vol. 2, Pt. 2–138
Clark, Thomas March, July 4, 1812–Sept. 7, 1903.
Vol. 2, Pt. 2–139
Clark, Tom Campbell, Sept. 23, 1899–June 13, 1977.
Supp. 10–125
Clark, Walter, Aug. 19, 1846–May 19, 1924.
Vol. 2, Pt. 2–140
Clark, Walter Leighton, Jan. 9, 1859–Dec. 18, 1935.
Supp. 1–176
Clark, Walter Van Tilburg, Aug. 3, 1909–Nov. 10, 1971.
Supp. 9–177
Clark, William, Aug. 1, 1770–Sept. 1, 1838.
Vol. 2, Pt. 2–141
Clark, William Andrews, Jan. 8, 1839–Mar. 2, 1925.
Vol. 2, Pt. 2–144
Clark, William Bullock, Dec. 15, 1860–July 27, 1917.
Vol. 2, Pt. 2–146

Clark, William Smith, July 31, 1826–Mar. 9, 1886.
Vol. 2, Pt. 2–146
Clark, William Thomas, June 29, 1831–Oct. 12, 1905.
Vol. 2, Pt. 2–147
Clark, Willis Gaylord, Oct. 5, 1808–June 12, 1841.
Vol. 2, Pt. 2–148
Clarke, Sir Caspar Purdon, Dec. 21, 1846–Mar. 29, 1911.
Vol. 2, Pt. 2–149
Clarke, Elijah, 1733–Jan. 15, 1799.
Vol. 2, Pt. 2–150
Clarke, Francis Devereux, Jan. 31, 1849–Sept. 7, 1913.
Vol. 2, Pt. 2–150
Clarke, Frank Wigglesworth, Mar. 19, 1847–May 23, 1931.
Supp. 1–177
Clarke, George, 1676–Jan. 12, 1760.
Vol. 2, Pt. 2–151
Clarke, Helen Archibald, Nov. 13, 1860–Feb. 8, 1926.
Vol. 2, Pt. 2–152
Clarke, James Freeman, Apr. 4, 1810–June 8, 1888.
Vol. 2, Pt. 2–153
Clarke, James Paul, Aug. 18, 1854–Oct. 1, 1916.
Vol. 2, Pt. 2–154
Clarke, John, Oct. 8, 1609–Apr. 28, 1676.
Vol. 2, Pt. 2–154
Clarke, John Hessin, Sept. 18, 1857–Mar. 22, 1945.
Supp. 3–167
Clarke, John Mason, Apr. 15, 1857–May 29, 1925.
Vol. 2, Pt. 2–156
Clarke, John Sleeper, Sept. 3, 1833–Sept. 24, 1899.
Vol. 2, Pt. 2–156
Clarke, Jonas. [*See* Clark, Jonas, 1730–1805.]
Clarke, Joseph Ignatius Constantine, July 31, 1846–Feb. 27, 1925.
Vol. 2, Pt. 2–157
Clarke, McDonald, June 18, 1798–Mar. 5, 1842.
Vol. 2, Pt. 2–160
Clarke, Mary Bayard Devereux, May 13, 1827–Mar. 30, 1886.
Vol. 2, Pt. 2–158
Clarke, Mary Francis, Mar. 2, 1803–Dec. 4, 1887.
Vol. 2, Pt. 2–159
Clarke, Rebecca Sophia, Feb. 22, 1833–Aug. 16, 1906.
Vol. 2, Pt. 2–160
Clarke, Richard, May 1, 1711–Feb. 27, 1795.
Vol. 2, Pt. 2–161
Clarke, Robert, May 1, 1829–Aug. 26, 1899.
Vol. 2, Pt. 2–162
Clarke, Thomas Benedict, Dec. 11, 1848–Jan. 18, 1931.
Supp. 1–178
Clarke, Thomas Shields, Apr. 25, 1860–Nov. 15, 1920.
Vol. 2, Pt. 2–162
Clarke, Walter, *c.* 1638–May 23, 1714.
Vol. 2, Pt. 2–163
Clarke, William Newton, Dec. 2, 1841–Jan. 14, 1912.
Vol. 2, Pt. 2–164
Clarkson, Coker Fifield, Jan. 21, 1811–May 7, 1890.
Vol. 2, Pt. 2–164
Clarkson, John Gibson, July 1, 1861–Feb. 4, 1909.
Vol. 2, Pt. 2–165
Clarkson, Matthew, Oct. 17, 1758–Apr. 25, 1825.
Vol. 2 Pt. 2–166
Clausen, Claus Lauritz, Nov. 3, 1820–Feb. 20, 1892.
Vol. 2, Pt. 2–166
Claxton, Kate, 1848–May 5, 1924.
Vol. 2, Pt. 2–167
Clay, Albert Tobias, Dec. 4, 1866–Sept. 14, 1925.
Vol. 2, Pt. 2–168
Clay, Cassius Marcellus, Oct. 19, 1810–July 22, 1903.
Vol. 2, Pt. 2–169
Clay, Clement Claiborne, Dec. 13, 1816–Jan. 3, 1882.
Vol. 2, Pt. 2–170
Clay, Clement Comer, Dec. 17, 1789–Sept. 7, 1866.
Vol. 2, Pt. 2–171
Clay, Edward Williams, Apr. 19, 1799–Dec. 31, 1857.
Vol. 2, Pt. 2–172
Clay, Green, Aug. 14, 1757–Oct. 31, 1826.
Vol. 2, Pt. 2–172
Clay, Henry, Apr. 12, 1777–June 29, 1852.
Vol. 2, Pt. 2–173
Clay, Joseph, Oct. 16, 1741–Nov. 15, 1804.
Vol. 2, Pt. 2–179
Clay, Joseph, Aug. 16, 1764–Jan. 11, 1811.
Vol. 2, Pt. 2–180
Clay, Lucius DuBignon, Apr. 23, 1897–Apr. 16, 1978.
Supp. 10–127
Clay, Matthew, Mar. 25, 1754–May 27, 1815.
Vol. 2, Pt. 2–181
Claypole, Edward Waller, June 1, 1835–Aug. 17, 1901.
Vol. 2, Pt. 2–181
Clayton, Augustin Smith, Nov. 27, 1783–June 21, 1839.
Vol. 2, Pt. 2–182
Clayton, Henry De Lamar, Feb. 10, 1857–Dec. 21, 1929.
Supp. 1–179
Clayton, John, *c.* 1685–Dec. 15, 1773.
Vol. 2, Pt. 2–184
Clayton, John Middleton, July 24, 1796–Nov. 9, 1856.
Vol. 2, Pt. 2–185
Clayton, Joshua, Dec. 20, 1744–Aug. 11, 1798.
Vol. 2, Pt. 2–186
Clayton, Powell, Aug. 7, 1833–Aug. 25, 1914.
Vol. 2, Pt. 2–187
Clayton, Thomas, July 1777–Aug. 21, 1854.
Vol. 2, Pt. 2–188
Clayton, William Lockhart, Feb. 7, 1880–Feb. 8, 1966.
Supp. 8–88
Cleaveland, Moses, Jan. 29, 1754–Nov. 16, 1806.
Vol. 2, Pt. 2–188
Cleaveland, Parker, Jan. 15, 1780–Oct. 15, 1858.
Vol. 2, Pt. 2–189
Cleburne, Patrick Ronayne, Mar. 17, 1828–Nov. 30, 1864.
Vol. 2, Pt. 2–190
Cleghorn, Sarah Norcliffe, Feb. 4, 1876–Apr. 4, 1959.
Supp. 6–113
Clemens, Jeremiah, Dec. 28, 1814–May 21, 1865.
Vol. 2, Pt. 2–191
Clemens, Samuel Langhorne, Nov. 30, 1835–Apr. 21, 1910.
Vol. 2, Pt. 2–192
Clement, Edward Henry, Apr. 19, 1843–Feb. 7, 1920.
Vol. 2, Pt. 2–198
Clement, Frank Goad, June 2, 1920–Nov. 4, 1969.
Supp. 8–90
Clement, Martin Withington, Dec. 5, 1881–Aug. 30, 1966.
Supp. 8–92
Clement, Rufus Early, June 26, 1900–Nov. 7, 1967.
Supp. 8–94
Clemente, Roberto, Aug. 18, 1934–Dec. 31, 1972.
Supp. 9–178.
Clements, Frederic Edward, Sept. 16, 1874–July 26, 1945.
Supp. 3–168
Clements, Judson Claudius, Feb. 12, 1846–June 18, 1917.
Vol. 2, Pt. 2–199
Clements, William Lawrence, Apr. 1, 1861–Nov. 6, 1934.
Supp. 1–179
Clemmer, Mary, May 6, 1839–Aug. 18, 1884.
Vol. 2, Pt. 2–199
Clemson, Thomas Green, July 1, 1807–Apr. 6, 1888.
Vol. 2, Pt. 2–200
Clerc, Laurent, Dec. 26, 1785–July 18, 1869.
Vol. 2, Pt. 2–201
Cleveland, Aaron, Oct. 29, 1715–Aug. 11, 1757.
Vol. 2, Pt. 2–202
Cleveland, Benjamin, May 26, 1738–Oct. 1806.
Vol. 2, Pt. 2–202
Cleveland, Chauncey Fitch, Feb. 16, 1799–June 6, 1887.
Vol. 2, Pt. 2–203
Cleveland, Grover. [*See* Cleveland, Stephen Grover, 1837–1908.]
Cleveland, Horace William Shaler, Dec. 16, 1814–Dec. 5, 1900.
Vol. 2, Pt. 2–203
Cleveland, Richard Jeffry, Dec. 19, 1773–Nov. 23, 1860.
Vol. 2, Pt. 2–204
Cleveland, Stephen Grover, Mar. 18, 1837–June 24, 1908.
Vol. 2, Pt. 2–205
Clevenger, Shobal Vail, Oct. 22, 1812–Sept. 1843.
Vol. 2, Pt. 2–212
Clevenger, Shobal Vail, Mar. 24, 1843–Mar. 24, 1920.
Vol. 2, Pt. 2–213
Clewell, John Henry, Sept. 19, 1855–Feb. 20, 1922.
Vol. 2, Pt. 2–214
Clews, Henry, Aug. 14, 1834–Jan. 31, 1923.
Vol. 2, Pt. 2–215
Clifford, John Henry, Jan. 16, 1809–Jan. 2, 1876.
Vol. 2, Pt. 2–215

Clifford, Nathan, Aug. 18, 1803–July 25, 1881.
Vol. 2, Pt. 2–216
Cliffton, William, 1772–Dec. 1799.
Vol. 2, Pt. 2–218
Clift, Edward Montgomery, Oct. 17, 1920–July 23, 1966.
Supp. 8–95
Clifton, Josephine, 1813–Nov. 21, 1847.
Vol. 2, Pt. 2–219
Clinch, Charles Powell, Oct. 20, 1797–Dec. 16, 1880.
Vol. 2, Pt. 2–219
Cline, Genevieve Rose, July 2, 1879–Oct. 25, 1959.
Supp. 6–114
Clingman, Thomas Lanier, July 27, 1812–Nov. 3, 1897.
Vol. 2, Pt. 2–220
Clinton, De Witt, Mar. 2, 1769–Feb. 11, 1828.
Vol. 2, Pt. 2–221
Clinton, George, *c.* 1686–July 10, 1761.
Vol. 2, Pt. 2–225
Clinton, George, July 26, 1739–Apr. 20, 1812.
Vol. 2, Pt. 2–226
Clinton, George Wylie, Mar. 28, 1859–May 12, 1921.
Vol. 2, Pt. 2–228
Clinton, James, Aug. 9, 1733–Dec. 22, 1812.
Vol. 2, Pt. 2–229
Clopton, David, Sept. 29, 1820–Feb. 5, 1892.
Vol. 2, Pt. 2–230
Clopton, John, Feb. 7, 1756–Sept. 11, 1816.
Vol. 2, Pt. 2–230
Closson, William Baxter, Oct. 13, 1848–May 31, 1926.
Vol. 2, Pt. 2–231
Clothier, William Jackson, Sept. 27, 1881–Sept. 4, 1962.
Supp. 7–127
Cloud, Henry Roe, December 28, 1886–Feb. 9, 1950.
Supp. 4–165
Cloud, Noah Bartlett, Jan. 26, 1809–Nov. 5, 1875.
Vol. 2, Pt. 2–232
Clough, John Everett, July 16, 1836–Nov. 24, 1910.
Vol. 2, Pt. 2–232
Clough, William Pitt, Mar. 20, 1845–Aug. 17, 1916.
Vol. 2, Pt. 2–233
Cluett, Sanford Lockwood, June 6, 1874–May 18, 1968.
Supp. 8–97
Clurman, Harold Edgar, Sept. 18, 1901–Sept. 9, 1980.
Supp. 10–129
Clyde, George Dewey, July 21, 1898–Apr. 2, 1972.
Supp. 9–180
Clyman, James, Feb. 1, 1792–Dec. 27, 1881.
Vol. 2, Pt. 2–234
Clymer, George, Mar. 16, 1739–Jan. 24, 1813.
Vol. 2, Pt. 2–234
Clymer, George E., 1754–Aug. 27, 1834.
Vol. 2, Pt. 2–235
Coakley, Cornelius Godfrey, Aug. 14, 1862–Nov. 22, 1934.
Supp. 1–181
Coalter, John. [*See* Colter, John, *c.* 1775–1813.]
Coan, Titus, Feb. 1, 1801–Dec. 1, 1882.
Vol. 2, Pt. 2–236
Coates, Florence Earle, July 1, 1850–Apr. 6, 1927.
Vol. 2, Pt. 2–237
Coates, George Henry, June 23, 1849–Oct. 18, 1921.
Vol. 2, Pt. 2–238
Coates, Samuel, Aug. 24, 1748–June 4, 1830.
Vol. 2, Pt. 2–238
Cobb, Andrew Jackson, Apr. 12, 1857–Mar. 27, 1925.
Vol. 2, Pt. 2–239
Cobb, David, Sept. 14, 1748–Apr. 17, 1830.
Vol. 2, Pt. 2–239
Cobb, Elijah, July 4, 1768–Nov. 2, 1848.
Vol. 2, Pt. 2–240
Cobb, Frank Irving, Aug. 6, 1869–Dec. 21, 1923.
Vol. 2, Pt. 2–241
Cobb, Howell, Sept. 7, 1815–Oct. 9, 1868.
Vol. 2, Pt. 2–241
Cobb, Irvin Shrewsbury, June 23, 1876–Mar. 10, 1944.
Supp. 3–170
Cobb, Jonathan Holmes, July 8, 1799–Mar. 12, 1882.
Vol. 2, Pt. 2–244
Cobb, Lee J., Dec. 9, 1911–Feb. 11, 1976.
Supp. 10–131
Cobb, Lyman, Sept. 18, 1800–Oct. 26?, 1864.
Vol. 2, Pt. 2–244
Cobb, Nathan Augustus, June 30, 1859–June 4, 1932.
Supp. 1–182
Cobb, Sylvanus, July 17, 1798–Oct. 31, 1866.
Vol. 2, Pt. 2–245
Cobb, Sylvanus, June 5, 1823–July 20, 1887.
Vol. 2, Pt. 2–246
Cobb, Thomas Reade Rootes, Apr. 10, 1823–Dec. 13, 1862.
Vol. 2, Pt. 2–246
Cobb, Tyrus Raymond ("Ty"), Dec. 18, 1886–July 17, 1961.
Supp. 7–127
Cobb, William Henry, Apr. 2, 1846–May 1, 1923.
Vol. 2, Pt. 2–247
Cobbett, William, Mar. 9, 1763–June 18, 1835.
Vol. 2, Pt. 2–248
Cobo, Albert Eugene, Oct. 2, 1893–Sept. 12, 1957.
Supp. 6–114
Coburn, Abner, Mar. 22, 1803–Jan. 4, 1885.
Vol. 2, Pt. 2–249
Coburn, Foster Dwight, May 7, 1846–May 11, 1924.
Vol. 2, Pt. 2–250
Cochran, Alexander Smith, Feb. 28, 1874–June 20, 1929.
Vol. 2, Pt. 2–250
Cochran, Jacqueline, May 11, 1910?–Aug. 9, 1980.
Supp. 10–132
Cochran, John, Sept. 1, 1730–Apr. 6, 1807.
Vol. 2, Pt. 2–251
Cochrane, Elizabeth. [*See* Seaman, Elizabeth Cochrane, 1867–1922.]
Cochrane, Gordon Stanley ("Mickey"), Apr. 6, 1903–June 28, 1962.
Supp. 7–129
Cochrane, Henry Clay, Nov. 7, 1842–Apr. 27, 1913.
Vol. 2, Pt. 2–252
Cochrane, John, Aug. 27, 1813–Feb. 7, 1898.
Vol. 2, Pt. 2–252
Cocke, John Hartwell, Sept. 19, 1780–July 1, 1866.
Vol. 2, Pt. 2–253
Cocke, Philip St. George, Apr. 17, 1809–Dec. 26, 1861.
Vol. 2, Pt. 2–254
Cocke, William, 1748–Aug. 22, 1828.
Vol. 2, Pt. 2–255
Cockerell, Theodore Dru Alison, Aug. 22, 1866–Jan. 26, 1948.
Supp. 4–166
Cockerill, John Albert, Dec. 4, 1845–Apr. 10, 1896.
Vol. 2, Pt. 2–256
Cockran, William Bourke, Feb. 28, 1854–Mar. 1, 1923.
Vol. 2, Pt. 2–256
Cockrell, Francis Marion, Oct. 1, 1834–Dec. 13, 1915.
Vol. 2, Pt. 2–257
Coddington, William, 1601–Nov. 1, 1678.
Vol. 2, Pt. 2–258
Codman, John, Oct. 16, 1814–Apr. 6, 1900.
Vol. 2, Pt. 2–259
Cody, William Frederick, Feb. 26, 1846–Jan. 10, 1917.
Vol. 2, Pt. 2–260
Coe, George Albert, Mar. 26, 1862–Nov. 9, 1951.
Supp. 5–115
Coe, George Simmons, Mar. 27, 1817–May 3, 1896.
Vol. 2, Pt. 2–261
Coe, Israel, Dec. 14, 1794–Dec. 18, 1891.
Vol. 2, Pt. 2–261
Coe, Virginius ("Frank"), 1907–June 2, 1980.
Supp. 10–133
Coerne, Louis Adolphe, Feb. 27, 1870–Sept. 11, 1922.
Vol. 2, Pt. 2–262
Cofer, Martin Hardin, Apr. 1, 1832–Mar. 22, 1881.
Vol. 2, Pt. 2–263
Coffey, James Vincent, Dec. 14, 1846–Jan. 15, 1919.
Vol. 2, Pt. 2–264
Coffin, Charles Albert, Dec. 30, 1844–July 14, 1926.
Vol. 2, Pt. 2–264
Coffin, Charles Carleton, July 26, 1823–Mar. 2, 1896.
Vol. 2, Pt. 2–265
Coffin, Charles Fisher, Apr. 3, 1823–Sept. 9, 1916.
Vol. 2, Pt. 2–266
Coffin, Henry Sloane, Jan. 5, 1877–Nov. 25, 1954.
Supp. 5–116
Coffin, Howard Earle, Sept. 6, 1873–Nov. 21, 1937.
Supp. 2–108
Coffin, Sir Isaac, May 16, 1759–July 23, 1839.
Vol. 2, Pt. 2–266

Coffin, James Henry, Sept. 6, 1806–Feb. 6, 1873.
Vol. 2, Pt. 2–267
Coffin, John, 1756–June 12, 1838.
Vol. 2, Pt. 2–268
Coffin, Levi, Oct. 28, 1789–Sept. 16, 1877.
Vol. 2, Pt. 2–268
Coffin, Lorenzo S., Apr. 9, 1823–Jan. 17, 1915.
Vol. 2, Pt. 2–269
Coffin, Robert Peter Tristram, Mar. 18, 1892–Jan. 20, 1955.
Supp. 5–117
Coffin, William Anderson, Jan. 31, 1855–Oct. 26, 1925.
Vol. 2, Pt. 2–270
Coffman, Lotus Delta, Jan. 7, 1875–Sept. 22, 1938.
Supp. 2–109
Cogdell, John Stevens, Sept. 19, 1778–Feb. 25, 1847.
Vol. 2, Pt. 2–270
Coggeshall, George, Nov. 2, 1784–Aug. 6, 1861.
Vol. 2, Pt. 2–271
Coggeshall, William Turner, Sept. 6, 1824–Aug. 2, 1867.
Vol. 2, Pt. 2–272
Coghill, George Ellett, Mar. 17, 1872–July 23, 1941.
Supp. 3–171
Coghlan, Rose, Mar. 18, 1851–Apr. 2, 1932.
Supp. 1–183
Cogswell, Joseph Green, Sept. 27, 1786–Nov. 26, 1871.
Vol. 2, Pt. 2–273
Cogswell, William Browne, Sept. 22, 1834–June 7, 1921.
Vol. 2, Pt. 2–274
Cohan, George Michael, July 3, 1878–Nov. 5, 1942.
Supp. 3–173
Cohen, Felix Solomon, July 3, 1907–Oct. 19, 1953.
Supp. 5–119
Cohen, Jacob Da Silva Solis, Feb. 28, 1838–Dec. 22, 1927.
Vol. 2, Pt. 2–275
Cohen, John Sanford, Feb. 26, 1870–May 13, 1935.
Supp. 1–183
Cohen, Mendes, May 4, 1831–Aug. 13, 1915.
Vol. 2, Pt. 2–275
Cohen, Meyer Harris ("Mickey"), 1914–July 29, 1976.
Supp. 10–134
Cohen, Morris Raphael, July 25, 1880–Jan. 28, 1947.
Supp. 4–168
Cohen, Octavus Roy, June 26, 1891–Jan. 6, 1959.
Supp. 6–116
Cohn, Alfred A., Mar. 26, 1880–Feb. 3, 1951.
Supp. 5–120
Cohn, Alfred Einstein, Apr. 16, 1879–July 20, 1957.
Supp. 6–117
Cohn, Edwin Joseph, Dec. 17, 1892–Oct. 1, 1953.
Supp. 5–121
Cohn, Harry, July 23, 1891–Feb. 27, 1958.
Supp. 6–118
Coit, Henry Augustus, Jan. 20, 1830–Feb. 5, 1895.
Vol. 2, Pt. 2–276
Coit, Henry Leber, Mar. 16, 1854–Mar. 12, 1917.
Vol. 2, Pt. 2–277
Coit, Stanton, Aug. 11, 1857–Feb. 15, 1944.
Supp. 3–175
Coit, Thomas Winthrop, June 28, 1803–June 21, 1885.
Vol. 2, Pt. 2–278
Coke, Richard, Mar. 13, 1829–May 14, 1897.
Vol. 2, Pt. 2–278
Coke, Thomas, Sept. 9, 1747–May 3, 1814.
Vol. 2, Pt. 2–279
Coker, David Robert, Nov. 20, 1870–Nov. 28, 1938.
Supp. 2–110
Coker, James Lide, Jan. 3, 1837–June 25, 1918.
Vol. 2, Pt. 2–280
Colburn, Dana Pond, Sept. 29, 1823–Dec. 15, 1859.
Vol. 2, Pt. 2–281
Colburn, Irving Wightman, May 16, 1861–Sept. 4, 1917.
Vol. 2, Pt. 2–282
Colburn, Warren, Mar. 1, 1793–Sept. 13, 1833.
Vol. 2, Pt. 2–282
Colburn, Zerah, Sept. 1, 1804–Mar. 2, 1839.
Vol. 2, Pt. 2–283
Colby, Bainbridge, Dec. 22, 1869–Apr. 11, 1950.
Supp. 4–170
Colby, Frank Moore, Feb. 10, 1865–Mar. 3, 1925.
Vol. 2, Pt. 2–284
Colby, Gardner, Sept. 3, 1810–Apr. 2, 1879.
Vol. 2, Pt. 2–284
Colby, Luther, Oct. 12, 1814–Oct. 7, 1894.
Vol. 2, Pt. 2–285
Colcord, Lincoln Ross, Aug. 14, 1883–Nov. 16, 1947.
Supp. 4–171
Colden, Cadwallader, Feb. 7, 1688 N.S.-Sept. 28, 1776.
Vol. 2, Pt. 2–286
Colden, Cadwallader David, Apr. 4, 1769–Feb. 7, 1834.
Vol. 2, Pt. 2–287
Colden, Jane, Mar. 27, 1724–Mar. 10, 1766.
Vol. 2, Pt. 2–288
Cole, Arthur Charles, Apr. 22, 1886–Feb. 26, 1976.
Supp. 10–136
Cole, Charles Woolsey, Feb. 8, 1906–Feb. 6, 1978.
Supp. 10–137
Cole, Chester Cicero, June 4, 1824–Oct. 4, 1913.
Vol. 2, Pt. 2–289
Cole, Frank Nelson, Sept. 20, 1861–May 26, 1926.
Vol. 2, Pt. 2–290
Cole, George Watson, Sept. 6, 1850–Oct. 10, 1939.
Supp. 2–111
Cole, Joseph Foxcroft, Nov. 9, 1837–May 2, 1892.
Vol. 2, Pt. 2–290
Cole, Nat ("King"), Mar. 17, 1919–Feb. 15, 1965.
Supp. 7–131
Cole, Thomas, Feb. 1, 1801–Feb. 11, 1848.
Vol. 2, Pt. 2–291
Cole, Timothy, Apr. 6, 1852–May 17, 1931.
Supp. 1–185
Coleman, Charles Caryl, Apr. 25, 1840–Dec. 4, 1928.
Vol. 2, Pt. 2–292
Coleman, John Aloysius, Dec. 24, 1901–Feb. 24, 1977.
Supp. 10–138
Coleman, Leighton, May 3, 1837–Dec. 14, 1907.
Vol. 2, Pt. 2–293
Coleman, Lyman, June 14, 1796–Mar. 16, 1882.
Vol. 2, Pt. 2–293
Coleman, William, Feb. 14, 1766–July 14, 1829.
Vol. 2, Pt. 2–294
Coleman, William Tell, Feb. 29, 1824–Nov. 22, 1893.
Vol. 2, Pt. 2–295
Coles, Edward, Dec. 15, 1786–July 7, 1868.
Vol. 2, Pt. 2–296
Colfax, Schuyler, Mar. 23, 1823–Jan. 13, 1885.
Vol. 2, Pt. 2–297
Colgate, James Boorman, Mar. 4, 1818–Feb. 7, 1904.
Vol. 2, Pt. 2–298
Colgate, William, Jan. 25, 1783–Mar. 25, 1857.
Vol. 2, Pt. 2–299
Collamer, Jacob, Jan. 8, 1791–Nov. 9, 1865.
Vol. 2, Pt. 2–300
Collens, Thomas Wharton, June 23, 1812–Nov 3, 1879.
Vol. 2, Pt. 2–300
Colles, Christopher, 1738–Oct. 4, 1816.
Vol. 2, Pt. 2–301
Collier, Barron Gift, Mar. 23, 1873–Mar. 13, 1939.
Supp. 2–112
Collier, Constance, Jan. 22, 1878–Apr. 25, 1955.
Supp. 5–123
Collier, Henry Walkins, Jan. 17, 1801–Aug. 28, 1855.
Vol. 2, Pt. 2–302
Collier, Hiram Price, May 25, 1860–Nov. 3, 1913.
Vol. 2, Pt. 2–303
Collier, John, May 4, 1884–May 8, 1968.
Supp. 8–98
Collier, Peter, Aug. 17, 1835–June 29, 1896.
Vol. 2, Pt. 2–304
Collier, Peter Fenelon, Dec. 12, 1849–Apr. 24, 1909.
Vol. 2, Pt. 2–304
Collier, Price. [*See* Collier, Hiram Price, 1860–1913.]
Collins, Edward Knight, Aug. 5, 1802–Jan. 22, 1878.
Vol. 2, Pt. 2–305
Collins, Edward Trowbridge, May 2, 1887–Mar. 25, 1951.
Supp. 5–124
Collins, Frank Shipley, Feb. 6, 1848–May 25, 1920.
Vol. 2, Pt. 2–306
Collins, Guy N., Aug. 9, 1872–Aug. 14, 1938.
Supp. 2–113
Collins, John, Nov. 1, 1717–Mar. 4, 1795.
Vol. 2, Pt. 2–307

Collins, John Anderson, fl. 1810–1879.
Vol. 2, Pt. 2–307
Collins, Napoleon, Mar. 4, 1814–Aug. 9, 1875
Vol. 2, Pt. 2–308
Collins, Patrick Andrew, Mar. 12, 1844–Sept. 14, 1905.
Vol. 2, Pt. 2–309
Collyer, Robert, Dec. 8, 1823–Nov. 30, 1912.
Vol. 2, Pt. 2–310
Colman, Benjamin, Oct. 19, 1673–Aug. 29, 1747.
Vol. 2, Pt. 2–311
Colman, Henry, Sept. 12, 1785–Aug. 17, 1849.
Vol. 2, Pt. 2–312
Colman, John, Jan. 3, 1670–*c.* 1753.
Vol. 2, Pt. 2–312
Colman, Lucy Newhall, July 26, 1817–Jan. 18, 1906.
Vol. 2, Pt. 2–313
Colman, Norman Jay, May 16, 1827–Nov. 3, 1911.
Vol. 2, Pt. 2–314
Colman, Ronald Charles, Feb. 9, 1891–May 19, 1958.
Supp. 6–119
Colman, Samuel, Mar. 4, 1832–Mar. 26, 1920.
Vol. 2, Pt. 2–314
Colombo, Joseph Anthony, June 16, 1923–May 22, 1978.
Supp. 10–140
Colpitts, Edwin Henry, Jan. 9, 1872–Mar. 6, 1949.
Supp. 4–173
Colquitt, Alfred Holt, Apr. 20, 1824–Mar. 26, 1894.
Vol. 2, Pt. 2–315
Colquitt, Walter Terry, Dec. 27, 1799–May 7, 1855.
Vol. 2, Pt. 2–316
Colston, Raleigh Edward, Oct. 31, 1825–July 29, 1896.
Vol. 2, Pt. 2–317
Colt, LeBaron Bradford, June 25, 1846–Aug. 18, 1924.
Vol. 2, Pt. 2–317
Colt, Samuel, July 19, 1814–Jan. 10, 1862.
Vol. 2, Pt. 2–318
Colter, John, *c.* 1775–November 1813.
Vol. 2, Pt. 2–319
Colton, Calvin, Sept. 14, 1789–Mar. 13, 1857.
Vol. 2, Pt. 2–320
Colton, Elizabeth Avery, Dec. 30, 1872–Aug. 26, 1924.
Vol. 2, Pt. 2–321
Colton, Gardner Quincy, Feb. 7, 1814–Aug. 9, 1898.
Vol. 2, Pt. 2–321
Colton, George Radcliffe, Apr. 10, 1865–Apr. 6, 1916.
Vol. 2, Pt. 2–322
Colton, Walter, May 9, 1797–Jan. 22, 1851.
Vol. 2, Pt. 2–323
Coltrane, John William, Sept. 23, 1926–July 17, 1967.
Supp. 8–99
Colum, Padraic, Dec. 8, 1881–Jan. 11, 1972.
Supp. 9–181
Colver, Nathaniel, May 10, 1794–Sept. 25, 1870.
Vol. 2, Pt. 2–324
Colver, William Byron, Sept. 26, 1870–May 28, 1926.
Vol. 2, Pt. 2–325
Colvin, Stephen Sheldon, Mar. 29, 1869–July 15, 1923.
Vol. 2, Pt. 2–325
Colvocoresses, George Musalas, Oct. 22, 1816–June 3, 1872.
Vol. 2, Pt. 2–326
Colwell, Stephen, Mar. 25, 1800–Jan. 15, 1871.
Vol. 2, Pt. 2–327
Coman, Charlotte Buell, 1833–Nov. 11, 1924.
Vol. 2, Pt. 2–327
Combs, Earle Bryan, May 14, 1899–July 21, 1976.
Supp. 10–141
Combs, Leslie, Nov. 29, 1793–Aug. 22, 1881.
Vol. 2, Pt. 2–328
Combs, Moses Newell, 1753–Apr. 12, 1834.
Vol. 2, Pt. 2–328
Comer, Braxton Bragg, Nov. 7, 1848–Aug. 15, 1927.
Vol. 2, Pt. 2–329
Comfort, Will Levington, Jan. 17, 1878–Nov. 2, 1932.
Supp. 1–186
Comiskey, Grace Elizabeth Reidy, May 15, 1893–Dec. 10, 1956.
Supp. 6–120
Commons, John Rogers, Oct. 13, 1862–May 11, 1945.
Supp. 3–176
Compton, Arthur Holly, Sept. 10, 1892–Mar. 15, 1962.
Supp. 7–132
Compton, Karl Taylor, Sept. 14, 1887–June 22, 1954.
Supp. 5–125
Comstock, Anthony, Mar. 7, 1844–Sept. 21, 1915.
Vol. 2, Pt. 2–330
Comstock, Elizabeth L., Oct. 30, 1815–Aug. 3, 1891.
Vol. 2, Pt. 2–331
Comstock, George Cary, Feb. 12, 1855–May 11, 1934.
Supp. 1–186
Comstock, George Franklin, Aug. 24, 1811–Sept. 27, 1892.
Vol. 2, Pt. 2–332
Comstock, Henry Tompkins Paige, 1820–Sept. 27, 1870.
Vol. 2, Pt. 2–333
Comstock, John Henry, Feb. 24, 1849–Mar. 20, 1931.
Supp. 1–187
Conant, Alban Jasper, Sept. 24, 1821–Feb. 3, 1915.
Vol. 2, Pt. 2–333
Conant, Charles Arthur, July 2, 1861–July 5, 1915.
Vol. 2, Pt. 2–334
Conant, Hannah O'Brien Chaplin, Sept. 5, 1809–Feb. 18, 1865.
Vol. 2, Pt. 2–335
Conant, Hezekiah, July 28, 1827–Jan. 22, 1902.
Vol. 2, Pt. 2–335
Conant, James Bryant, Mar. 26, 1893–Feb. 11, 1978.
Supp. 10–142
Conant, Roger, *c.* 1592–Nov. 19, 1679.
Vol. 2, Pt. 2–336
Conant, Thomas Jefferson, Dec. 13, 1802–Apr. 30, 1891.
Vol. 2, Pt. 2–337
Conaty, Thomas James, Aug. 1, 1847–Sept. 18, 1915.
Vol. 2, Pt. 2–337
Conboy, Martin, Aug. 28, 1878–Mar. 5, 1944.
Supp. 3–180
Conboy, Sara Agnes McLaughlin, Apr. 3, 1870–Jan. 7, 1928.
Vol. 2, Pt. 2–338
Condit, John, July 8, 1755–May 4, 1834.
Vol. 2, Pt. 2–338
Condon, Albert Edwin ("Eddie"), Nov. 16, 1905–Aug. 4, 1973.
Supp. 9–182
Condon, Edward Uhler, Mar. 2, 1902–Mar. 26, 1974.
Supp. 9–184
Condon, Thomas, Mar. 3, 1822–Feb. 11, 1907.
Vol. 2, Pt. 2–339
Cone, Claribel, Nov. 14, 1864–Sept. 20, 1929.
Supp. 4–174
Cone, Etta, Nov. 30, 1870–Aug. 31, 1949.
Supp. 4–174
Cone, Fairfax Mastick, Feb. 21, 1903–June 20, 1977.
Supp. 10–145
Cone, Hutchinson Ingham, Apr. 26, 1871–Feb. 12, 1941.
Supp. 3–181
Cone, Moses Herman, June 29, 1857–Dec. 8, 1908.
Vol. 2, Pt. 2–340
Cone, Orello, Nov. 16, 1835–June 23, 1905.
Vol. 2, Pt. 2–341
Cone, Russell Glenn, Mar. 22, 1896–Jan. 21, 1961.
Supp. 7–135
Cone, Spencer Houghton, Apr. 30, 1785–Aug. 28, 1855.
Vol. 2, Pt. 2–342
Coney, Jabez, Oct. 21, 1804–Jan. 23, 1872.
Vol. 2, Pt. 2–342
Coney, John, Jan. 5, 1655–Aug. 20, 1722.
Vol. 2, Pt. 2–343
Congdon, Charles Taber, Apr. 7, 1821–Jan. 18, 1891.
Vol. 2, Pt. 2–343
Conger, Edwin Hurd, Mar. 7, 1843–May 18, 1907.
Vol. 2, Pt. 2–344
Conklin, Edwin Grant, Nov. 24, 1863–Nov. 21, 1952.
Supp. 5–127
Conklin, Jennie Maria Drinkwater. [*See* Drinkwater, Jennie Maria, 1841–1900.]
Conkling, Alfred, Oct. 12, 1789–Feb. 5, 1874.
Vol. 2, Pt. 2–345
Conkling, Roscoe, Oct. 30, 1829–Apr. 18, 1888.
Vol. 2, Pt. 2–346
Connally, Thomas Terry ("Tom"), Aug. 19, 1877–Oct. 28, 1963.
Supp. 7–136
Connelly, Cornelia, Jan. 15, 1809–Apr. 18, 1879.
Vol. 2, Pt. 2–347

Connelly, Henry, 1800–July 1866.
Vol. 2, Pt. 2–348
Connelly, Marcus Cook ("Marc"), Dec. 13, 1890–Dec. 21, 1980.
Supp. 10–146
Connelly, Pierce Francis, b. Mar. 29, 1841.
Vol. 2, Pt. 2–348
Conner, Charlotte Mary Sanford Barnes. [*See* Barnes, Charlotte Mary Sanford, 1818–1863.]
Conner, David, 1792–Mar. 20, 1856.
Vol. 2, Pt. 2–349
Conner, James, Sept. 1, 1829–June 26, 1883.
Vol. 2, Pt. 2–350
Conney, John. [*See* Coney, John, 1655–1722.]
Connick, Charles Jay, Sept. 27, 1875–Dec. 28, 1945.
Supp. 3–183
Connolly, John, *c.* 1743–Jan. 30, 1813.
Supp. 1–188
Connolly, John, 1750–Feb. 6, 1825.
Vol. 2, Pt. 2–351
Connolly, Maureen Catherine, Sept. 17, 1934–June 21, 1969.
Supp. 8–101
Connolly, Thomas H., Dec. 31, 1870–Apr. 28, 1961.
Supp. 7–139
Connor, Henry Groves, July 3, 1852–Nov. 23, 1924.
Vol. 2, Pt. 2–352
Connor, Patrick Edward, Mar. 17, 1820–Dec. 17, 1891.
Vol. 2, Pt. 2–352
Connor, Robert Digges Wimberly, Sept. 26, 1878–Feb. 25, 1950.
Supp. 4–175
Connor, Theophilus ("Bull") Eugene, July 11, 1897–Mar. 10, 1973.
Supp. 9–185
Conover, Harry Sayles, Aug. 29, 1911–July 21, 1965.
Supp. 7–140
Conover, Obadiah Milton, Oct. 8, 1825–Apr. 29, 1884.
Vol. 2, Pt. 2–353
Conrad, Charles Magill, Dec. 24, 1804–Feb. 11, 1878.
Vol. 2, Pt. 2–354
Conrad, Frank, May 4, 1874–Dec. 11, 1941.
Supp. 3–184
Conrad, Holmes, Jan. 31, 1840–Sept. 4, 1916.
Vol. 2, Pt. 2–354
Conrad, Maximilian Arthur, Jr., Mar. 6, 1903–Apr. 3, 1979.
Supp. 10–148
Conrad, Robert Taylor, June 10, 1810–June 27, 1858.
Vol. 2, Pt. 2–355
Conried, Heinrich, Sept. 13, 1855–Apr. 27, 1909.
Vol. 2, Pt. 2–356
Considérant, Victor Prosper, Oct. 12, 1808–Dec. 27, 1893.
Vol. 2, Pt. 2–357
Considine, Robert ("Bob") Bernard, Nov. 4, 1906–Sept. 25, 1975.
Supp. 9–187
Conte, Richard, Mar. 24, 1916–Apr. 15, 1975.
Supp. 9–188
Converse, Charles Crozat, Oct. 7, 1832–Oct. 18, 1918.
Vol. 2, Pt. 2–358
Converse, Edmund Cogswell, Nov. 7, 1849–Apr. 4, 1921.
Vol. 2, Pt. 2–359
Converse, Frederick Shepherd, Jan. 5, 1871–June 8, 1940.
Supp. 2–114
Converse, James Booth, Apr. 8, 1844–Oct. 31, 1914.
Vol. 2, Pt. 2–360
Converse, John Heman, Dec. 2, 1840–May 31, 1910.
Vol. 2, Pt. 2–360
Conway, Elias Nelson, May 17, 1812–Feb. 28, 1892.
Vol. 2, Pt. 2–361
Conway, Frederick Bartlett, Feb. 10, 1819–Sept. 7, 1874.
Vol. 2, Pt. 2–362
Conway, James Sevier, Dec. 9, 1798–Mar. 3, 1855.
Vol. 2, Pt. 2–363
Conway, Martin Franklin, Nov. 19, 1827–Feb. 15, 1882.
Vol. 2, Pt. 2–363
Conway, Moncure Daniel, Mar. 17, 1832–Nov. 15, 1907.
Vol. 2, Pt. 2–364
Conway, Thomas, Feb. 27, 1735–*c.* 1800.
Vol. 2, Pt. 2–365
Conwell, Henry, *c.* 1745–Apr. 22, 1842.
Vol. 2, Pt. 2–366
Conwell, Russell Herman, Feb. 15, 1843–Dec. 6, 1925.
Vol. 2, Pt. 2–367
Conyngham, Gustavus, *c.* 1744–Nov. 27, 1819.
Vol. 2, Pt. 2–368
Coode, John, d. 1709.
Vol. 2, Pt. 2–369
Cook, Albert Stanburrough, Mar. 6, 1853–Sept. 1, 1927.
Vol. 2, Pt. 2–370
Cook, Clarence Chatham, Sept. 8, 1828–June 2, 1900.
Vol. 2, Pt. 2–371
Cook, Flavius Josephus, Jan. 26, 1838–June 24, 1901.
Vol. 2, Pt. 2–371
Cook, Frederick Albert, June 10, 1865–Aug. 5, 1940.
Supp. 2–115
Cook, George Cram, Oct. 7, 1873–Jan. 14, 1924.
Vol. 2, Pt. 2–372
Cook, George Hammell, Jan. 5, 1818–Sept. 22, 1889.
Vol. 2, Pt. 2–373
Cook, Isaac, July 4, 1810–June 23, 1886.
Vol. 2, Pt. 2–374
Cook, James Merrill, Nov. 19, 1807–Apr. 12, 1868.
Vol. 2, Pt. 2–375
Cook, John Williston, Apr. 20, 1844–July 16, 1922.
Vol. 2, Pt. 2–374
Cook, Joseph. [*See* Cook, Flavius Josephus, 1838–1901.]
Cook, Martha Elizabeth Duncan Walker, July 23, 1806–Sept. 15, 1874.
Vol. 2, Pt. 2–376
Cook, Philip, July 30, 1817–May 20, 1894.
Vol. 2, Pt. 2–377
Cook, Robert Johnson, Mar. 21, 1849–Dec. 3, 1922.
Vol. 2, Pt. 2–377
Cook, Russell S., Mar. 6, 1811–Sept. 4, 1864.
Vol. 2, Pt. 2–378
Cook, Tennessee Céleste Claflin, Lady, 1845–1923. [*See* Woodhull, Victoria, 1838–1927.]
Cook, Walter, July 23, 1846–Mar. 25, 1916.
Vol. 2, Pt. 2–379
Cook, Walter Wheeler, June 4, 1873–Nov. 7, 1943.
Supp. 3–185
Cook, Will Marion, Jan. 27, 1869–July 19, 1944.
Supp. 3–187
Cook, Zebedee, Jan. 11, 1786–Jan. 24, 1858.
Vol. 2, Pt. 2–380
Cooke, Ebenezer, *c.* 1670–*c.* 1732.
Supp. 1–189
Cooke, Elisha, Sept. 16, 1637–Oct. 31, 1715.
Vol. 2, Pt. 2–380
Cooke, Elisha, Dec. 20, 1678–Aug. 24, 1737.
Vol. 2, Pt. 2–381
Cooke, George Willis, Apr. 23, 1848–Apr. 30, 1923.
Vol. 2, Pt. 2–382
Cooke, Henry David, Nov. 23, 1825–Feb. 24, 1881.
Vol. 2, Pt. 2–382
Cooke, Jay, Aug. 10, 1821–Feb. 16, 1905.
Vol. 2, Pt. 2–383
Cooke, John Esten, Mar. 2, 1783–Oct. 19, 1853.
Vol. 2, Pt. 2–384
Cooke, John Esten, Nov. 3, 1830–Sept. 27, 1886.
Vol. 2, Pt. 2–385
Cooke, John Rogers, 1788–Dec. 15, 1854.
Vol. 2, Pt. 2–386
Cooke, Josiah Parsons, Oct. 12, 1827–Sept. 3, 1894.
Vol. 2, Pt. 2–387
Cooke, Morris Llewellyn, May, 11, 1872–Mar. 5, 1960.
Supp. 6–121
Cooke, Philip Pendleton, Oct. 26, 1816–Jan. 20, 1850.
Vol. 2, Pt. 2–388
Cooke, Philip St. George, June 13, 1809–Mar. 20, 1895.
Vol. 2, Pt. 2–389
Cooke, Robert Anderson, Aug. 17, 1880–May 7, 1960.
Supp. 6–123
Cooke, Rose Terry, Feb. 17, 1827–July 18, 1892.
Vol. 2, Pt. 2–390
Cooke, Samuel, Dec. 19, 1898–May 22, 1965.
Supp. 7–141
Coolbrith, Ina Donna, Mar. 10, 1842–Feb. 29, 1928.
Vol. 2, Pt. 2–390
Cooley, Edwin Gilbert, Mar. 12, 1857–Sept. 28, 1923.
Supp. 1–190

Cooley, Harold Dunbar, July 26, 1897–Jan. 15, 1974.
Supp. 9–190
Cooley, Lyman Edgar, Dec. 5, 1850–Feb. 3, 1917.
Vol. 2, Pt. 2–391
Cooley, Mortimer Elwyn, Mar. 28, 1855–Aug. 25, 1944.
Supp. 3–188
Cooley, Thomas Benton, June 23, 1871–Oct. 13, 1945.
Supp. 3–189
Cooley, Thomas McIntyre, Jan. 6, 1824–Sept. 12, 1898.
Vol. 2, Pt. 2–392
Coolidge, Archibald Cary, Mar. 6, 1866–Jan. 14, 1928.
Vol. 2, Pt. 2–393
Coolidge, Calvin, July 4, 1872–Jan. 5, 1933.
Supp. 1–191
Coolidge, Charles Allerton, Nov. 30, 1858–Apr. 1, 1936.
Supp. 2–117
Coolidge, Elizabeth Penn Sprague, Oct. 30, 1864–Nov. 4, 1953.
Supp. 5–128
Coolidge, Julian Lowell, Sept. 28, 1873–Mar. 5, 1954.
Supp. 5–129
Coolidge, Thomas Jefferson, Aug. 26, 1831–Nov. 17, 1920.
Vol. 2, Pt. 2–395
Coolidge, Thomas Jefferson, Sept. 17, 1893–Aug. 6, 1959.
Supp. 6–124
Coomaraswamy, Ananda Kentish, Aug. 22, 1877–Sept. 9, 1947.
Supp. 4–176
Coombe, Thomas, Oct. 21, 1747–Aug. 15, 1822.
Vol. 2, Pt. 2–395
Coontz, Robert Edward, June 11, 1864–Jan. 26, 1935.
Supp. 1–199
Cooper, Edward, Oct. 26, 1824–Feb. 25, 1905.
Vol. 2, Pt. 2–396
Cooper, Elias Samuel, Nov. 25, 1820–Oct. 13, 1862.
Vol. 2, Pt. 2–397
Cooper, Ezekiel, Feb. 22, 1763–Feb. 21, 1847.
Vol. 2, Pt. 2–397
Cooper, Gary, May 7, 1901–May 13, 1961.
Supp. 7–142
Cooper, Henry Ernest, Aug. 28, 1857–May 14, 1929.
Vol. 2, Pt. 2–398
Cooper, Hugh Lincoln, Apr. 28, 1865–June 24, 1937.
Supp. 2–118
Cooper, Jacob, Dec. 7, 1830–Jan. 31, 1904.
Vol. 2, Pt. 2–399
Cooper, James, May 8, 1810–Mar. 28, 1863.
Vol. 2, Pt. 2–400
Cooper, James Fenimore, Sept. 15, 1789–Sept. 14, 1851.
Vol. 2, Pt. 2–400
Cooper, James Graham, June 19, 1830–July 19, 1902.
Vol. 2, Pt. 2–406
Cooper, John Montgomery, Oct. 28, 1881–May 22, 1949.
Supp. 4–178
Cooper, Joseph Alexander, Nov. 25, 1823–May 20, 1910.
Vol. 2, Pt. 2–407
Cooper, Kent, Mar. 22, 1880–Jan. 31, 1965.
Supp. 7–144
Cooper, (Leon) Jere, July 20, 1893–Dec. 18, 1957.
Supp. 6–125
Cooper, Mark Anthony, Apr. 20, 1800–Mar. 17, 1885.
Vol. 2, Pt. 2–407
Cooper, Myles, Feb. 1737–May 20, 1785.
Vol. 2, Pt. 2–408
Cooper, Oswald Bruce, Apr. 13, 1879–Dec. 17, 1940.
Supp. 2–119
Cooper, Peter, Feb. 12, 1791–Apr. 4, 1883.
Vol. 2, Pt. 2–409
Cooper, Samuel, Mar. 28, 1725–Dec. 23, 1783.
Vol. 2, Pt. 2–410
Cooper, Samuel, June 12, 1798–Dec. 3, 1876.
Vol. 2, Pt. 2–411
Cooper, Sarah Brown Ingersoll, Dec. 12, 1836–Dec. 11, 1896.
Vol. 2, Pt. 2–412
Cooper, Susan Fenimore, Apr. 17, 1813–Dec. 31, 1894.
Vol. 2, Pt. 2–412
Cooper, Theodore, Jan. 13, 1839–Aug. 24, 1919.
Vol. 2, Pt. 2–413
Cooper, Thomas, Oct. 22, 1759–May 11, 1839.
Vol. 2, Pt. 2–414
Cooper, Thomas Abthorpe, Dec. 16, 1776–Apr. 21, 1849.
Vol. 2, Pt. 2–416
Cooper, William, Dec. 2, 1754–Dec. 22, 1809.
Vol. 2, Pt. 2–417
Cooper, William John, Nov. 24, 1882–Sept. 19, 1935.
Supp. 1–199
Cooper-Poucher, Matilda S., Feb. 2, 1839–Apr. 5, 1900.
Vol. 2, Pt. 2–418
Coote, Richard, 1636–Mar. 5, 1701.
Vol. 2, Pt. 2–418
Cope, Arthur Clay, June 27, 1909–June 4, 1966.
Supp. 8–102
Cope, Caleb, July 18, 1797–May 12, 1888.
Vol. 2, Pt. 2–420
Cope, Edward Drinker, July 28, 1840–Apr. 12, 1897.
Vol. 2, Pt. 2–420
Cope, Thomas Pym, Aug. 26, 1768–Nov. 22, 1854.
Vol. 2, Pt. 2–421
Cope, Walter, Oct. 20, 1860–Nov. 1, 1902.
Vol. 2, Pt. 2–422
Copeland, Charles Townsend, Apr. 27, 1860–July 24, 1952.
Supp. 5–131
Copeland, Charles W., 1815–Feb. 5, 1895.
Vol. 2, Pt. 2–423
Copeland, Royal Samuel, Nov. 7, 1868–June 17, 1938.
Supp. 2–120
Copley, Ira Clifton, Oct. 25, 1864–Nov. 2, 1947.
Supp. 4–180
Copley, John Singleton, 1738–Sept. 9, 1815.
Vol. 2, Pt. 2–423
Copley, Lionel, d. Sept. 9, 1693.
Vol. 2, Pt. 2–430
Copley, Thomas, 1595–*c.* 1652.
Vol. 2, Pt. 2–430
Coppée, Henry, Oct. 13, 1821–Mar. 21, 1895.
Vol. 2, Pt. 2–431
Coppens, Charles, May 24, 1835–Dec. 14, 1920.
Vol. 2, Pt. 2–432
Coppet, Edward J. de. [*See* De Coppet, Edward J., 1855–1916.]
Copway, George, 1818–*c.* 1863.
Vol. 2, Pt. 2–433
Coquillett, Daniel William, Jan. 23, 1856–July 8, 1911.
Vol. 2, Pt. 2–433
Coram, Thomas, 1668–Mar. 29, 1751.
Vol. 2, Pt. 2–434
Corbett, Harvey Wiley, Jan. 8, 1873–Apr. 21, 1954.
Supp. 5–133
Corbett, Henry Winslow, Feb. 18, 1827–Mar. 31, 1903.
Vol. 2, Pt. 2–435
Corbett, James John, Sept. 1, 1866–Feb. 18, 1933.
Supp. 1–200
Corbin, Austin, July 11, 1827–June 4, 1896.
Vol. 2, Pt. 2–436
Corbin, Daniel Chase, Oct. 1, 1832–June 29, 1918.
Vol. 2, Pt. 2–437
Corbin, Henry Clark, Sept. 15, 1842–Sept. 8, 1909.
Supp. 1–201
Corbin, Margaret, Nov. 12, 1751–Jan. 16, 1800.
Vol. 2, Pt. 2–438
Corby, William, Oct. 2, 1833–Dec. 28, 1897.
Vol. 2, Pt. 2–438
Corcoran, James Andrew, Mar. 30, 1820–July 16, 1889.
Vol. 2, Pt. 2–439
Corcoran, William Wilson, Dec. 27, 1798–Feb. 24, 1888.
Vol. 2, Pt. 2–440
Cordier, Andrew Wellington, Mar. 3, 1901–July 11, 1975.
Supp. 9–191
Cordiner, Ralph Jarron, Mar. 20, 1900–Dec. 5, 1973.
Supp. 9–193
Cordon, Guy, Apr. 24, 1890–June 6, 1969.
Supp. 8–103
Corey, Lewis, Oct. 13, 1892–Sept. 17, 1953.
Supp. 5–134
Corey, William Ellis, May 4, 1866–May 11, 1934.
Supp. 1–202
Cori, Gerty Theresa Radnitz, Aug. 15, 1896–Oct. 26, 1957.
Supp. 6–126
Coriat, Isador Henry, Dec. 10, 1875–May 26, 1943.
Supp. 3–190
Corliss, George Henry, June 2, 1817–Feb. 21, 1888.
Vol. 2, Pt. 2–441

Cornbury, Edward Hyde, Viscount, 1661–Apr. 1, 1723.
Vol. 2, Pt. 2–441
Cornell, Alonzo B., Jan. 22, 1832–Oct. 15, 1904.
Vol. 2, Pt. 2–442
Cornell, Ezekiel, Mar. 27, 1733–Apr. 25, 1800.
Vol. 2, Pt. 2–444
Cornell, Ezra, Jan. 11, 1807–Dec. 9, 1874.
Vol. 2, Pt. 2–444
Cornell, Katharine, Feb. 16, 1893–June 12, 1974.
Supp. 9–194
Corning, Erastus, Dec. 14, 1794–Apr. 9, 1872.
Vol. 2, Pt. 2–446
Cornoyer, Paul, Aug. 15, 1864–June 17, 1923.
Vol. 2, Pt. 2–447
Cornstalk, *c.* 1720–1777.
Vol. 2, Pt. 2–447
Cornwallis, Kinahan, Dec. 24, 1839–Aug. 15, 1917.
Vol. 2, Pt. 2–448
Coronado, Francisco Vázquez, 1510–1554.
Vol. 2, Pt. 2–449
Correll, Charles James, Feb. 2, 1890–Sept. 26, 1972.
Supp. 9–196
Corrigan, Michael Augustine, Aug. 13, 1839–May 5, 1902.
Vol. 2, Pt. 2–450
Corrothers, James David, July 2, 1869–Feb. 12, 1917.
Vol. 2, Pt. 2–452
Corse, John Murray, Apr. 27, 1835–Apr. 27, 1893.
Vol. 2, Pt. 2–452
Corson, Hiram, Nov. 6, 1828–June 15, 1911.
Vol. 2, Pt. 2–453
Corson, Juliet, Feb. 14, 1842–June 18, 1897.
Vol. 2, Pt. 2–454
Corson, Robert Rodgers, May 3, 1831–Feb. 19, 1904.
Vol. 2, Pt. 2–455
Cort, Edwin Charles, Mar. 14, 1879–Jan. 10, 1950.
Supp. 4–181
Cort, Stewart Shaw, May 9, 1911–May 25, 1980.
Supp. 10–149
Cortambert, Louis Richard, 1808–Mar. 28, 1881.
Vol. 2, Pt. 2–455
Cortelyou, George Bruce, July 26, 1862–Oct. 23, 1940.
Supp. 2–122
Corthell, Elmer Lawrence, Sept. 30, 1840–May 16, 1916.
Vol. 2, Pt. 2–456
Cortissoz, Royal, Feb. 10, 1869–Oct. 17, 1948.
Supp. 4–182
Corwin, Edward Samuel, Jan. 19, 1878–Apr. 29, 1963.
Supp. 7–146
Corwin, Edward Tanjore, July 12, 1834–June 22, 1914.
Vol. 2, Pt. 2–457
Corwin, Thomas, July 29, 1794–Dec. 18, 1865.
Vol. 2, Pt. 2–457
Cory, Charles Barney, Jan. 31, 1857–July 29, 1921.
Vol. 2, Pt. 2–458
Cosby, William, *c.* 1690–Mar. 10, 1735/6.
Vol. 2, Pt. 2–459
Costain, Thomas Bertram, May 8, 1885–Oct. 8, 1965.
Supp. 7–147
Costansó, Miguel, fl. 1769–1811.
Vol. 2, Pt. 2–460
Costello, Frank, Jan. 26, 1891–Feb. 18, 1973.
Supp. 9–197
Costello, Lou, Mar. 6, 1906–Mar. 3, 1959.
Supp. 6–127
Coster, F. Donald. [*See* Musica, Philip Mariano Fausto, 1884–1938.]
Costigan, Edward Prentiss, July 1, 1874–Jan. 17, 1939.
Supp. 2–123
Costigan, George Purcell, July 19, 1870–Nov. 18, 1934.
Supp. 1–203
Cotton, John, Dec. 4, 1584–Dec. 23, 1652.
Vol. 2, Pt. 2–460
Cotton, Joseph Potter, July 22, 1875–Mar. 10, 1931.
Supp. 1–204
Cottrell, Calvert Byron, Aug. 10, 1821–June 12, 1893.
Vol. 2, Pt. 2–462
Cottrell, Frederick Gardner, Jan. 10, 1877–Nov. 16, 1948.
Supp. 4–183
Couch, Darius Nash, July 23, 1822–Feb. 12, 1897.
Vol. 2, Pt. 2–463
Couch, Harvey Crowley, Aug. 21, 1877–July 30, 1941.
Supp. 3–191
Coudert, Frederic René, Mar. 1, 1832–Dec. 20, 1903.
Vol. 2, Pt. 2–464
Coudert, Frederic René, Feb. 11, 1871–Apr. 1, 1955.
Supp. 5–136
Coudert, Frederic René, Jr., May 7, 1898–May 21, 1972.
Supp. 9–199
Coues, Elliott, Sept. 9, 1842–Dec. 25, 1899.
Vol. 2, Pt. 2–465
Coughlin, Charles Edward, Oct. 25, 1891–Oct. 27, 1979.
Supp. 10–150
Couldock, Charles Walter, Apr. 26, 1815–Nov. 27, 1898.
Vol. 2, Pt. 2–466
Coulter, Ernest Kent, Nov. 14, 1871–May 1, 1952.
Supp. 5–137
Coulter, John Merle, Nov. 20, 1851–Dec. 23, 1928.
Vol. 2, Pt. 2–467
Councilman, William Thomas, Jan. 1, 1854–May 26, 1933.
Supp. 1–205
Couper, James Hamilton, Mar. 4, 1794–June 3, 1866.
Vol. 2, Pt. 2–468
Courant, Richard, Jan. 8, 1888–Jan. 27, 1972.
Supp. 9–200
Courtney, Charles Edward, Nov. 13, 1849–July 17, 1920.
Vol. 2, Pt. 2–469
Coutard, Henri, Apr. 27, 1876–Mar. 16, 1950.
Supp. 4–185
Couzens, James, Aug. 26, 1872–Oct. 22, 1936.
Supp. 2–125
Covici, Pascal ("Pat"), Nov. 4, 1885–Oct. 14, 1964.
Supp. 7–148
Covode, John, Mar. 18, 1808–Jan. 11, 1871.
Vol. 2, Pt. 2–470
Cowan, Edgar, Sept. 19, 1815–Aug. 31, 1885.
Vol. 2, Pt. 2–470
Cowell, Sidney Frances. [*See* Bateman, Sidney Frances Cowell, 1823–81.]
Cowen, John Kissig, Oct. 28, 1844–Apr. 26, 1904.
Vol. 2, Pt. 2–471
Cowen, Joshua Lionel, Aug. 25, 1880–Sept. 8, 1965.
Supp. 7–149
Cowl, Jane, Dec. 14, 1883–June 22, 1950.
Supp. 4–186
Cowles, Edwin, Sept. 19, 1825–Mar. 4, 1890.
Vol. 2, Pt. 2–472
Cowles, Gardner, Feb. 28, 1861–Feb. 28, 1946.
Supp. 4–188
Cowles, Henry Chandler, Feb. 27, 1869–Sept. 12, 1939.
Supp. 2–127
Cowley, Charles, Jan. 9, 1832–Feb. 6, 1908.
Vol. 2, Pt. 2–472
Cox, Edward Eugene, Apr. 3, 1880–Dec. 24, 1952.
Supp. 5–138
Cox, George Barnsdale, Apr. 29, 1853–May 20, 1916.
Vol. 2, Pt. 2–473
Cox, Hannah Peirce, Nov. 12, 1797–Apr. 15, 1876.
Vol. 2, Pt. 2–474
Cox, Henry Hamilton, *c.* 1769–*c.* 1821.
Vol. 2, Pt. 2–475
Cox, Jacob Dolson, Oct. 27, 1828–Aug. 8, 1900.
Vol. 2, Pt. 2–476
Cox, James Middleton, Mar. 31, 1870–July 15, 1957.
Supp. 6–128
Cox, James Middleton, Jr., June 27, 1903–Oct. 27, 1974.
Supp. 9–202
Cox, Kenyon, Oct. 27, 1856–Mar. 17, 1919.
Vol. 2, Pt. 2–478
Cox, Lemuel, 1736–Feb. 18, 1806.
Vol. 2, Pt. 2–479
Cox, Palmer, Apr. 28, 1840–July 24, 1924.
Vol. 2, Pt. 2–480
Cox, Rowland, July 9, 1842–May 13, 1900.
Vol. 2, Pt. 2–480
Cox, Samuel Hanson, Aug. 25, 1793–Oct. 2, 1880.
Vol. 2, Pt. 2–481
Cox, Samuel Sullivan, Sept. 30, 1824–Sept. 10, 1889.
Vol. 2, Pt. 2–482
Cox, Wallace Maynard ("Wally"), Dec. 6, 1924–Feb. 15, 1973.
Supp. 9–203
Cox, William Ruffin, Mar. 11, 1832–Dec. 26, 1919.
Vol. 2, Pt. 2–483
Coxe, Arthur Cleveland, May 10, 1818–July 20, 1896.
Vol. 2, Pt. 2–484

Coxe, Daniel, August 1673–Apr. 25, 1739.
Vol. 2, Pt. 2–484
Coxe, Eckley Brinton, June 4, 1839–May 13, 1895.
Vol. 2, Pt. 2–485
Coxe, John Redman, Sept. 16, 1773–Mar. 22, 1864.
Vol. 2, Pt. 2–486
Coxe, Richard Smith, January 1792–Apr. 28, 1865.
Vol. 2, Pt. 2–487
Coxe, Tench, May 22, 1755–July 16, 1824.
Vol. 2, Pt. 2–488
Coxe, William, May 3, 1762–Feb. 25, 1831.
Vol. 2, Pt. 2–489
Coxetter, Louis Mitchell, Dec. 10, 1818–July 10, 1873.
Vol. 2, Pt. 2–490
Coxey, Jacob Sechler, Apr. 16, 1854–May 18, 1951.
Supp. 5–139
Coyle, Grace Longwell, Mar. 22, 1892–Mar. 8, 1962.
Supp. 7–151
Cozzens, Frederick Swartwout, Mar. 11, 1818–Dec. 23, 1869.
Vol. 2, Pt. 2–490
Cozzens, James Gould, Aug. 19, 1903–Aug. 9, 1978.
Supp. 10–152
Crabtree, Lotta, Nov. 7, 1847–Sept. 25, 1924.
Vol. 2, Pt. 2–491
Craddock, Charles Egbert. [*See* Murfree, Mary Noailles, 1850–1922.]
Crafts, James Mason, Mar. 8, 1839–June 20, 1917.
Vol. 2, Pt. 2–492
Crafts, William, Jan. 24, 1787–Sept. 23, 1826.
Vol. 2, Pt. 2–493
Craig, Austin, July 14, 1824–Aug. 27, 1881.
Vol. 2, Pt. 2–494
Craig, Cleo Frank, Apr. 6, 1893–Apr. 21, 1978.
Supp. 10–154
Craig, Daniel H., *c.* 1814–Jan. 5, 1895.
Vol. 2, Pt. 2–495
Craig, Malin, Aug. 5, 1875–July 25, 1945.
Supp. 3–193
Craig, Thomas, Dec. 20, 1855–May 8, 1900.
Vol. 2, Pt. 2–496
Craig, Winchell McKendree, Apr. 27, 1892–Feb. 12, 1960.
Supp. 6–130
Craighead, Edwin Boone, Mar. 3, 1861–Oct. 22, 1920.
Vol. 2, Pt. 2–496
Craigie, Andrew, June 7, 1743–Sept. 19, 1819.
Vol. 2, Pt. 2–497
Craik, James, 1730–Feb. 6, 1814.
Vol. 2, Pt. 2–498
Cram, Ralph Adams, Dec. 16, 1863–Sept. 22, 1942.
Supp. 3–194
Cramer, Michael John, Feb. 6, 1835–Jan. 23, 1898.
Vol. 2, Pt. 2–499
Cramp, Charles Henry, May 9, 1828–June 6, 1913.
Vol. 2, Pt. 2–499
Cramp, William, Sept. 22, 1807–July 6, 1879.
Vol. 2, Pt. 2–500
Cranch, Christopher Pearse, Mar. 8, 1813–Jan. 20, 1892.
Vol. 2, Pt. 2–501
Cranch, William, July 17, 1769–Sept. 1, 1855.
Vol. 2, Pt. 2–502
Crandall, Charles Henry, June 19, 1858–Mar. 23, 1923.
Vol. 2, Pt. 2–503
Crandall, Prudence, Sept. 3, 1803–Jan. 28, 1889.
Vol. 2, Pt. 2–503
Crane, Anne Moncure, Jan. 7, 1838–Dec. 10, 1872.
Vol. 2, Pt. 2–504
Crane, Bob Edward, July 13, 1928–June 29, 1978.
Supp. 10–155
Crane, Charles Richard, Aug. 7, 1858–Feb. 15, 1939.
Supp. 2–128
Crane, Frank, May 12, 1861–Nov. 5, 1928.
Vol. 2, Pt. 2–504
Crane, Frederick Evan, Mar. 2, 1869–Nov. 21, 1947.
Supp. 4–190
Crane, Harold Hart, July 21, 1899–Apr. 27, 1932.
Supp. 1–206
Crane, John, Dec. 7, 1744–Aug. 21, 1805.
Vol. 2, Pt. 2–505
Crane, Jonathan Townley, June 18, 1819–Feb. 16, 1880.
Vol. 2, Pt. 2–506
Crane, Stephen, Nov. 1, 1871–June 5, 1900.
Vol. 2, Pt. 2–506
Crane, Thomas Frederick, July 12, 1844–Dec. 9, 1927.
Vol. 2, Pt. 2–508
Crane, William Henry, Apr. 30, 1845–Mar. 7, 1928.
Vol. 2, Pt. 2–509
Crane, William Montgomery, Feb. 1, 1784–Mar. 18, 1846.
Vol. 2, Pt. 2–510
Crane, Winthrop Murray, Apr. 23, 1853–Oct. 2, 1920.
Vol. 2, Pt. 2–510
Cranston, Earl, June 27, 1840–Aug. 18, 1932.
Supp. 1–208
Cranston, John, 1625–Mar. 12, 1680.
Vol. 2, Pt. 2–511
Cranston, Samuel, August 1659–Apr. 26, 1727.
Vol. 2, Pt. 2–512
Crapsey, Adelaide, Sept. 9, 1878–Oct. 8, 1914.
Vol. 2, Pt. 2–513
Crapsey, Algernon Sidney, June 28, 1847–Dec. 31, 1927.
Vol. 2, Pt. 2–513
Crary, Isaac Edwin, Oct. 2, 1804–May 8, 1854.
Vol. 2, Pt. 2–514
Cratty, Mabel, June 30, 1868–Feb. 27, 1928.
Vol. 2, Pt. 2–515
Cravath, Erastus Milo, July 1, 1833–Sept. 4, 1900.
Vol. 2, Pt. 2–516
Cravath, Paul Drennan, July 14, 1861–July 1, 1940.
Supp. 2–130
Craven, Braxton, Aug. 22, 1822–Nov. 7, 1882.
Vol. 2, Pt. 2–516
Craven, Frank, Aug. 24, 1875?–Sept. 1, 1945.
Supp. 3–197
Craven, John Joseph, Sept. 8, 1822–Feb. 14, 1893.
Vol. 2, Pt. 2–517
Craven, Thomas Tingey, Dec. 20, 1808–Aug. 23, 1887.
Vol. 2, Pt. 2–517
Craven, Tunis Augustus MacDonough, Jan. 11, 1813–Aug. 5, 1864.
Vol. 2, Pt. 2–518
Crawford, Francis Marion, Aug. 2, 1854–Apr. 9, 1909.
Vol. 2, Pt. 2–519
Crawford, George Walker, Dec. 22, 1798–July 22, 1872.
Vol. 2, Pt. 2–520
Crawford, James Pyle Wickersham, Feb. 19, 1882–Sept. 22, 1939.
Supp. 2–131
Crawford, Joan, May 23, 1906–May 10, 1977.
Supp. 10–157
Crawford, John, May 3, 1746–May 9, 1813.
Vol. 2, Pt. 2–521
Crawford, John Martin, Oct 18, 1845–Aug. 11, 1916.
Vol. 2, Pt. 2–522
Crawford, John Wallace (Captain Jack), Mar. 4, 1847–Feb. 28, 1917.
Vol. 2, Pt. 2–522
Crawford, Martin Jenkins, Mar. 17, 1820–July 23, 1883.
Vol. 2, Pt. 2–523
Crawford, Samuel Earl, Apr. 18, 1880–June 15, 1968.
Supp. 8–105
Crawford, Samuel Johnson, Apr. 15, 1835–Oct. 21, 1913.
Vol. 2, Pt. 2–523
Crawford, Thomas, Mar. 22, 1813?–Oct. 10, 1857.
Vol. 2, Pt. 2–524
Crawford, William, 1732–June 11, 1782.
Vol. 2, Pt. 2–527
Crawford, William Harris, Feb. 24, 1772–Sept. 15, 1834.
Vol. 2, Pt. 2–527
Crazy Horse, *c.* 1849–Sept. 5, 1877.
Vol. 2, Pt. 2–530
Creamer, David, Nov. 20, 1812–Apr. 8, 1887.
Vol. 2, Pt. 2–531
Creath, Jacob, Feb. 22, 1777–Mar. 13, 1854.
Vol. 2, Pt. 2–531
Creath, Jacob, Jan. 17, 1799–Jan. 8, 1886.
Vol. 2, Pt. 2–532
Creel, George, Dec. 1, 1876–Oct. 2, 1953.
Supp. 5–141
Creelman, James, Nov. 12, 1859–Feb. 12, 1915.
Vol. 2, Pt. 2–533
Creesy, Josiah Perkins, Mar. 23, 1814–June 5, 1871.
Vol. 2, Pt. 2–533

Creighton, Edward, Aug. 31, 1820–Nov. 5, 1874.
Vol. 2, Pt. 2–534
Creighton, James Edwin, Apr. 8, 1861–Oct. 8, 1924.
Vol. 2, Pt. 2–535
Creighton, John Andrew, Oct. 15, 1831–Feb. 7, 1907.
Vol. 2, Pt. 2–535
Creighton, William, Oct. 29, 1778–Oct. 1, 1851.
Vol. 2, Pt. 2–536
Crerar, John, Mar. 8, 1827–Oct. 19, 1889.
Vol. 2, Pt. 2–537
Cresap, Michael, June 29, 1742–Oct. 18, 1775.
Vol. 2, Pt. 2–538
Cresap, Thomas, *c.* 1702–*c.* 1790.
Vol. 2, Pt. 2–538
Crespi, Juan, 1721–Jan. 1, 1782.
Vol. 2, Pt. 2–539
Cresson, Elliott, Mar. 2, 1796–Feb. 20, 1854.
Vol. 2, Pt. 2–540
Cresson, Ezra Townsend, June 18, 1838–Apr. 19, 1926.
Vol. 2, Pt. 2–540
Creswell, John Angel James, Nov. 18, 1828–Dec. 23, 1891.
Vol. 2, Pt. 2–541
Cret, Paul Philippe, Oct. 23, 1876–Sept. 8, 1945.
Supp. 3–199
Crétin, Joseph, Dec. 19, 1799–Feb. 22, 1857.
Vol. 2, Pt. 2–542
Crèvecoeur, J. Hector St. John. [*See* Crèvecoeur, Michel Guillaume, Jean de, 1735–1813.]
Crèvecoeur, Michel-Guillaume Jean de, Jan. 31, 1735–Nov. 12, 1813.
Vol. 2, Pt. 2–542
Crile, George Washington, Nov. 11, 1864–Jan. 7, 1943.
Supp. 3–200
Crimmins, John Daniel, May 18, 1844–Nov. 9, 1917.
Vol. 2, Pt. 2–544
Crisp, Charles Frederick, Jan. 29, 1845–Oct. 23, 1896.
Vol. 2, Pt. 2–544
Crisp, Donald, July 27, 1880–May 25, 1974.
Supp. 9–205
Crissinger, Daniel Richard, Dec. 10, 1860–July 12, 1942.
Supp. 3–203
Crittenden, George Bibb, Mar. 20, 1812–Nov. 27, 1880.
Vol. 2, Pt. 2–545
Crittenden, John Jordan, Sept. 10, 1787–July 26, 1863.
Vol. 2, Pt. 2–546
Crittenden, Thomas Leonidas, May 15, 1819–Oct. 23, 1893.
Vol. 2, Pt. 2–549
Crittenden, Thomas Theodore, Jan. 1, 1832–May 29, 1909.
Vol. 2, Pt. 2–550
Crittenton, Charles Nelson, Feb. 20, 1833–Nov. 16, 1909.
Vol. 2, Pt. 2–550
Crocker, Alvah, Oct. 14, 1801–Dec. 26, 1874.
Vol. 2, Pt. 2–551
Crocker, Charles, Sept. 16, 1822–Aug. 14, 1888.
Vol. 2, Pt. 2–552
Crocker, Francis Bacon, July 4, 1861–July 9, 1921.
Vol. 2, Pt. 2–553
Crocker, Hannah Mather, June 27, 1752–July 11, 1829.
Vol. 2, Pt. 2–553
Crocker, Uriel, Sept. 13, 1796–July 19, 1887.
Vol. 2, Pt. 2–554
Crocker, William, Jan. 27, 1874–Feb. 11, 1950.
Supp. 4–191
Crockett, David, Aug. 17, 1786–Mar. 6, 1836.
Vol. 2, Pt. 2–555
Croghan, George, d. Aug. 31, 1782.
Vol. 2, Pt. 2–556
Croghan, George, Nov. 15, 1791–Jan. 8, 1849.
Vol. 2, Pt. 2–557
Croix, Teodoro De, June 30, 1730–1792.
Vol. 2, Pt. 2–557
Croker, Richard, Nov. 23, 1841–Apr. 29, 1922.
Vol. 2, Pt. 2–558
Croly, David Goodman, Nov. 3, 1829–Apr. 29, 1889.
Vol. 2, Pt. 2–560
Croly, Herbert David, Jan. 23, 1869–May 17, 1930.
Supp. 1–209
Croly, Jane Cunningham, Dec. 19, 1829–Dec. 23, 1891.
Vol. 2, Pt. 2–560
Crompton, George, Mar. 23, 1829–Dec. 29, 1886.
Vol. 2, Pt. 2–561
Crompton, William, Sept. 10, 1806–May 1, 1891.
Vol. 2, Pt. 2–561
Cromwell, Dean Bartlett, Sept. 20, 1879–Aug. 3, 1962.
Supp. 7–152
Cromwell, Gladys Louise Husted, Nov. 28, 1885–Jan. 24, 1919.
Vol. 2, Pt. 2–562
Cromwell, William Nelson, Jan. 17, 1854–July 19, 1948.
Supp. 4–192
Crook, George, Sept. 23, 1829–Mar. 21, 1890.
Vol. 2, Pt. 2–563
Crooks, George Richard, Feb. 3, 1822–Feb. 20, 1897.
Vol. 2, Pt. 2–564
Crooks, Ramsay, Jan. 2, 1787–June 6, 1859.
Vol. 2, Pt. 2–565
Cropsey, Jaspar Francis, Feb. 18, 1823–June 22, 1900.
Vol. 2, Pt. 2–565
Crosby, Ernest Howard, Nov. 4, 1856–Jan. 3, 1907.
Vol. 2, Pt. 2–566
Crosby, Fanny, Mar. 24, 1820–Feb. 12, 1915.
Vol. 2, Pt. 2–567
Crosby, Harry Lillis ("Bing"), May 2, 1903–Oct. 14, 1977.
Supp. 10–158
Crosby, Howard, Feb. 27, 1826–Mar. 29, 1891.
Vol. 2, Pt. 2–567
Crosby, John Schuyler, Sept. 19, 1839–Aug. 8, 1914.
Vol. 2, Pt. 2–568
Crosby, Peirce, Jan. 16, 1824–June 15, 1899.
Vol. 2, Pt. 2–569
Crosby, Percy Lee, Dec. 8, 1891–Dec. 8, 1964.
Supp. 7–153
Crosby, William Otis, Jan. 14, 1850–Dec. 31, 1925.
Vol. 2, Pt. 2–569
Crosley, Powel, Jr., Sept. 18, 1886–Mar. 28, 1961.
Supp. 7–154
Cross, Arthur Lyon, Nov. 14, 1873–June 21, 1940.
Supp. 2–132
Cross, Charles Whitman, Sept. 1, 1854–Apr. 20, 1949.
Supp. 4–194
Cross, Edward, Nov. 11, 1798–Apr. 6, 1887.
Vol. 2, Pt. 2–570
Cross, Milton John, Apr. 16, 1897–Jan. 3, 1975.
Supp. 9–206
Cross, Samuel Hazzard, July 1, 1891–Oct. 14, 1946.
Supp. 4–195
Cross, Wilbur Lucius, Apr. 10, 1862–Oct. 5, 1948.
Supp. 4–196
Crosser, Robert, June 7, 1874–June 3, 1957.
Supp. 6–131
Crosswaith, Frank Rudolph, July 16, 1892–June 17, 1965.
Supp. 7–155
Croswell, Edwin, May 29, 1797–June 13, 1871.
Vol. 2, Pt. 2–571
Croswell, Harry, June 16, 1778–Mar. 13, 1858.
Vol. 2, Pt. 2–571
Crothers, Rachel, Dec. 12, 1878–July 5, 1958.
Supp. 6–133
Crothers, Samuel McChord, June 7, 1857–Nov. 9, 1927.
Vol. 2, Pt. 2–572
Crounse, Lorenzo, Jan. 27, 1834–May 13, 1909.
Vol. 2, Pt. 2–573
Crouse, Russel McKinley, Feb. 20, 1893–Apr. 3, 1966.
Supp. 8–107
Crouter, Albert Louis Edgerton, Sept. 15, 1846–June 26, 1925.
Vol. 2, Pt. 2–574
Crowder, Enoch Herbert, Apr. 11, 1859–May 7, 1932.
Supp. 1–210
Crowe, Francis Trenholm, Oct. 12, 1882–Feb. 26, 1946.
Supp. 4–198
Crowell, Luther Childs, Sept. 7, 1840–Sept. 16, 1903.
Vol. 2, Pt. 2–575
Crowley, Leo Thomas, Aug. 15, 1889–Apr. 15, 1972.
Supp. 9–208
Crowne, John, 1640–April 1712.
Vol. 2, Pt. 2–576
Crowne, William, *c.* 1617–1683.
Vol. 2, Pt. 2–576
Crowninshield, Benjamin Williams, Dec. 27, 1772–Feb. 3, 1851.
Vol. 2, Pt. 2–577
Crowninshield, Francis Welch, June 24, 1872–Dec. 28, 1947.
Supp. 4–199

Crowninshield, Frederic, Nov. 27, 1845–Sept. 13, 1918.
Vol. 2, Pt. 2–578
Crowninshield, George, May 27, 1766–Nov. 26, 1817.
Vol. 2, Pt. 2–578
Crowninshield, Jacob, May 31, 1770–Apr. 15, 1808.
Vol. 2, Pt. 2–579
Croy, Homer, Mar. 11, 1883–May 24, 1965.
Supp. 7–156
Crozer, John Price, Jan. 13, 1793–Mar. 11, 1866.
Vol. 2, Pt. 2–579
Crozet, Claude, Jan. 1, 1790–Jan. 29, 1864.
Vol. 2, Pt. 2–580
Crozier, William, Feb. 19, 1855–Nov. 10, 1942.
Supp. 3–204
Cruger, Henry, Nov. 22, 1739–Apr. 24, 1827.
Vol. 2, Pt. 2–581
Cruger, John, July 18, 1710–Dec. 27, 1791.
Vol. 2, Pt. 2–582
Crumbine, Samuel Jay, Sept. 17, 1862–July 12, 1954.
Supp. 5–143
Crump, Edward Hull, Oct. 2, 1874–Oct. 16, 1954.
Supp. 5–144
Crump, William Wood, Nov. 25, 1819–Feb. 27, 1897.
Vol. 2, Pt. 2–582
Crunden, Frederick Morgan, Sept. 1, 1847–Oct. 28, 1911.
Vol. 2, Pt. 2–583
Cubberley, Ellwood Patterson, June 6, 1868–Sept. 14, 1941.
Supp. 3–205
Cubero, Pedro Rodriguez, 1645–1704.
Vol. 2, Pt. 2–584
Cudahy, Edward Aloysius, Jr., Aug. 22, 1885–Jan. 8, 1966.
Supp. 8–109
Cudahy, Michael, Dec. 7, 1841–Nov. 27, 1910.
Vol. 2, Pt. 2–584
Cuffe, Paul, Jan. 17, 1759–Sept. 9, 1817.
Vol. 2, Pt. 2–585
Culberson, Charles Allen, June 10, 1855–March 19, 1925.
Vol. 2, Pt. 2–585
Culberson, David Browning, Sept. 29, 1830–May 7, 1900.
Vol. 2, Pt. 2–586
Culbertson, Ely, July 22, 1891–Dec. 27, 1955.
Supp. 5–145
Culbertson, Josephine Murphy, 1899–Mar. 23, 1956.
Supp. 6–134
Cullen, Countée Porter, May 30, 1903–Jan. 9, 1946.
Supp. 4–200
Cullen, Hugh Roy, July 3, 1881–July 4, 1957.
Supp. 6–135
Cullen, Thomas Stephen, Nov. 20, 1868–Mar. 4, 1953.
Supp. 5–146
Cullinan, Joseph Stephen, Dec. 31, 1860–Mar. 11, 1937.
Supp. 2–133
Cullis, Charles, Mar. 7, 1833–June 18, 1892.
Vol. 2, Pt. 2–587
Cullom, Shelby Moore, Nov. 22, 1829–Jan. 28, 1914.
Vol. 2, Pt. 2–588
Cullum, George Washington, Feb. 25, 1809–Feb. 28, 1892.
Vol. 2, Pt. 2–589
Culpeper, Thomas Lord, 1635–Jan. 27, 1689.
Vol. 2, Pt. 2–590
Cuming, Sir Alexander, *c.* 1690–Aug. 1775.
Vol. 2, Pt. 2–591
Cuming, Fortescue, Feb. 26, 1762–1828.
Vol. 2, Pt. 2–592
Cumming, Alfred, Sept. 4, 1802–Oct. 9, 1873.
Vol. 2, Pt. 2–592
Cummings, Amos Jay, May 15, 1841–May 2, 1902.
Vol. 2, Pt. 2–593
Cummings, Charles Amos, June 26, 1833–Aug. 11, 1905.
Vol. 2, Pt. 2–594
Cummings, Edward, Apr. 20, 1861–Nov. 2, 1926.
Vol. 2, Pt. 2–594
Cummings, E. E., Oct. 14, 1894–Sept. 3, 1962.
Supp. 7–157
Cummings, Homer Stillé, Apr. 30, 1870–Sept. 10, 1956.
Supp. 6–136
Cummings, John, Feb. 12, 1785–June 8, 1867.
Vol. 2, Pt. 2–595
Cummings, Joseph, Mar. 3, 1817–May 7, 1890.
Vol. 2, Pt. 2–596
Cummings, Thomas Seir, Aug. 26, 1804–Sept. 24, 1894.
Vol. 2, Pt. 2–596
Cummings, Walter Joseph, June 24, 1879–Aug. 20, 1967.
Supp. 8–111
Cummins, Albert Baird, Feb. 15, 1850–July 30, 1926.
Vol. 2, Pt. 2–597
Cummins, George David, Dec. 11, 1822–June 26, 1876.
Vol. 2, Pt. 2–599
Cummins, Maria Susanna, Apr. 9, 1827–Oct. 1, 1866.
Vol. 2, Pt. 2–600
Cunliffe-Owen, Philip Frederick, Jan. 30, 1855–June 30, 1926.
Vol. 2, Pt. 2–600
Cunningham, Ann Pamela, Aug. 15, 1816–May 1, 1875.
Vol. 2, Pt. 2–601
Cunningham, Imogen, Apr. 12, 1883–June 24, 1976.
Supp. 10–161
Cunningham, Kate (Richards) O'Hare. [*See* O'Hare, Kate Richards Cunningham, 1877–1948.]
Cuppia, Jerome Chester, Sept. 29, 1890–Sept. 20, 1966.
Supp. 8–112
Cupples, Samuel, Sept. 13, 1831–Jan. 6, 1912.
Vol. 2, Pt. 2–602
Cuppy, William Jacob (Will), Aug. 23, 1884–Sept. 19, 1949.
Supp. 4–201
Curley, James Michael, Nov. 20, 1874–Nov. 12, 1958.
Supp. 6–138
Curme, George Oliver, Jan. 14, 1860–Apr 29, 1948.
Supp. 4–203
Curran, John Joseph, June 20, 1859–Nov. 7, 1936.
Supp. 2–134
Curran, Thomas Jerome, Nov. 28, 1898–July 29, 1958.
Supp. 6–141
Currier, Charles Warren, Mar. 22, 1857–Sept. 23, 1918.
Vol. 2, Pt. 2–602
Currier, Moody, Apr. 22, 1806–Aug. 23, 1898.
Vol. 2, Pt. 2–603
Currier, Nathaniel, Mar. 27, 1813–Nov. 20, 1888.
Vol. 2, Pt. 2–604
Curry, George Law, July 2, 1820–July 28, 1878.
Vol. 2, Pt. 2–604
Curry, Jabez Lamar Monroe, June 5, 1825–Feb. 12, 1903.
Vol. 2, Pt. 2–605
Curry, John Steuart, Nov. 14, 1897–Aug. 29, 1946.
Supp. 4–204
Curtin, Andrew Gregg, Apr. 23, 1815?–Oct. 7, 1894.
Vol. 2, Pt. 2–606
Curtin, Jeremiah, Sept. 6, 1840?–Dec. 14, 1906.
Vol. 2, Pt. 2–608
Curtis, Alfred Allen, July 4, 1831–July 11, 1908.
Vol. 2, Pt. 2–608
Curtis, Benjamin Robbins, Nov. 4, 1809–Sept. 15, 1874.
Vol. 2, Pt. 2–609
Curtis, Charles, Jan. 25, 1860–Feb. 8, 1936.
Supp. 2–136
Curtis, Charles Pelham, May 8, 1891–Dec. 23, 1959.
Supp. 6–142
Curtis, Cyrus Hermann Kotzschmar, June 18, 1850–June 7, 1933.
Supp. 1–212
Curtis, Edward Lewis, Oct. 13, 1853–Aug. 26, 1911.
Vol. 2, Pt. 2–611
Curtis, Edward Sheriff, Feb. 19, 1868–Oct. 19, 1952.
Supp. 5–148
Curtis, Edwin Upton, Mar. 26, 1861–Mar. 28, 1922.
Vol. 2, Pt. 2–612
Curtis, George, Feb. 23, 1796–Jan. 9, 1856.
Vol. 2, Pt. 2–612
Curtis, George Ticknor, Nov. 28, 1812–Mar. 28, 1894.
Vol. 2, Pt. 2–613
Curtis, George William, Feb. 24, 1824–Aug. 31, 1892.
Vol. 2, Pt. 2–614
Curtis, Heber Doust, June 27, 1872–Jan. 9, 1942.
Supp. 3–207
Curtis, John Green, Oct. 29, 1844–Sept. 20, 1913.
Vol. 2, Pt. 2–616
Curtis, Moses Ashley, May 11, 1808–Apr. 10, 1872.
Vol. 2, Pt. 2–617
Curtis, Newton Martm, May 21, 1835–Jan. 8, 1910.
Vol. 2, Pt. 2–618
Curtis, Olin Alfred, Dec. 10, 1850–Jan. 8, 1918.
Vol. 2, Pt. 2–619

Curtis, Samuel Ryan, Feb. 3, 1805–Dec. 26, 1866.
Vol. 2, Pt. 2–619
Curtis, William Eleroy, Nov. 5, 1850–Oct. 5, 1911.
Vol. 2, Pt. 2–620
Curtiss, Glenn Hammond, May 21, 1878–July 23, 1930.
Supp. 1–213
Curtiss, Samuel Ives, Feb. 5, 1844–Sept. 22, 1904.
Vol. 2, Pt. 2–621
Curtiz, Michael, Dec. 24, 1888–Apr. 11, 1962.
Supp. 7–159
Curwen, Samuel, Dec. 17, 1715–Apr. 9, 1802.
Vol. 2, Pt. 2–622
Curwood, James Oliver, June 12, 1878–Aug. 13, 1927.
Vol. 2, Pt. 2–622
Cushing, Caleb, Jan. 17, 1800–Jan. 2, 1879.
Vol. 2, Pt. 2–623
Cushing, Frank Hamilton, July 22, 1857–Apr. 10, 1900.
Vol. 2, Pt. 2–630
Cushing, Harvey Williams, Apr. 9, 1869–Oct. 7, 1939.
Supp. 2–137
Cushing, John Perkins, Apr. 22, 1787–Apr. 12, 1862.
Vol. 2, Pt. 2–630
Cushing, Josiah Nelson, May 4, 1840–May 17, 1905.
Vol. 2, Pt. 2–631
Cushing, Luther Stearns, June 22, 1803–June 22, 1856.
Vol. 2, Pt. 2–632
Cushing, Richard James, Aug. 24, 1895–Nov. 2, 1970.
Supp. 8–114
Cushing, Thomas, Mar. 24, 1725–Feb. 28, 1788.
Vol. 2, Pt. 2–632
Cushing, William, Mar. 1, 1732–Sept. 13, 1810.
Vol. 2, Pt. 2–633
Cushing, William Barker, Nov. 4, 1842–Dec. 17, 1874.
Vol. 2, Pt. 2–635
Cushman, Austin Thomas ("Joe"), Dec. 18, 1901–June 12, 1978.
Supp. 10–163
Cushman, Charlotte Saunders, July 23, 1816–Feb 17, 1876.
Vol. 3, Pt. 1–1
Cushman, George Hewitt, June 5, 1814–Aug. 3, 1876.
Vol. 3, Pt. 1–3
Cushman, Joseph Augustine, Jan. 31, 1881–Apr. 16, 1949.
Supp. 4–205
Cushman, Joshua, Apr. 11, 1761–Jan. 27, 1834.
Vol. 3, Pt. 1–3
Cushman, Pauline, June 10, 1835–Dec. 2, 1893.
Vol. 3, Pt. 1–4
Cushman, Robert, *c.* 1579–1625.
Vol. 3, Pt. 1–5
Cushman, Susan Webb, Mar. 17, 1822–May 10, 1859.
Vol. 3, Pt. 1–5
Cushman, Vera Charlotte Scott, Sept. 19, 1876–Feb. 1, 1946.
Supp. 4–207
Cushny, Arthur Robertson, Mar. 6, 1866–Feb. 25, 1926.
Vol. 3, Pt. 1–6
Custer, George Armstrong, Dec. 5, 1839–June 25, 1876.
Vol. 3, Pt. 1–7
Custis, George Washington Parke, Apr. 30, 1781–Oct. 10 1857.
Vol. 3, Pt. 1–9
Cutbush, James, 1788–Dec. 15, 1823.
Vol. 3, Pt. 1–10
Cutler, Carroll, Jan. 31, 1829–Jan. 24, 1894.
Vol. 3, Pt. 1–10
Cutler, Elliott Carr, July 30, 1888–Aug. 16, 1947.
Supp. 4–208
Cutler, James Goold, Apr. 24, 1848–Apr. 21, 1927.
Vol. 3, Pt. 1–11
Cutler, Lizzie Petit, 1831–Jan. 16, 1902.
Vol. 3, Pt. 1–12
Cutler, Manasseh, May 13, 1742–July 28, 1823.
Vol. 3, Pt. 1–12
Cutler, Robert, June 12, 1895–May 8, 1974.
Supp. 9–209
Cutler, Timothy, May 31, 1684–Aug. 17, 1765.
Vol. 3, Pt. 1–14
Cutter, Charles Ammi, Mar. 14, 1837–Sept. 6, 1903.
Vol. 3, Pt. 1–15
Cutter, Ephraim, Sept. 1, 1832–Apr. 25, 1917.
Vol. 3, Pt. 1–16
Cutter, George Washington, 1801–Dec. 25, 1865.
Vol. 3, Pt. 1–17
Cutting, Bronson Murray, June 23, 1883–May 6, 1935.
Supp. 1–215
Cutting, James Ambrose, 1814–Aug. 6, 1867.
Vol. 3, Pt. 1–17
Cutting, Robert Fulton, June 24, 1852–Sept. 21, 1934.
Supp. 1–216
Cuyler, Theodore, Sept. 14, 1819–Apr. 5, 1876.
Vol. 3, Pt. 1–18
Cuyler, Theodore Ledyard, Jan. 10, 1822–Feb. 26, 1909.
Vol. 3, Pt. 1–18

Dablon, Claude, Jan. 21, 1619, or Feb. 1618–May 3 or Sept. 20, 1697.
Vol. 3, Pt. 1–19
Dabney, Charles William, June 19, 1855–June 15, 1945.
Supp. 3–208
Dabney, Richard, 1787–Nov. 25, 1825.
Vol. 3, Pt. 1–20
Dabney, Robert Lewis, Mar. 5, 1820–Jan. 3, 1898.
Vol. 3, Pt. 1–20
Dabney, Thomas Smith Gregory, Jan. 4, 1798–Feb. 28, 1885.
Vol. 3, Pt. 1–21
Dabney, Virginius, Feb. 15, 1835–June 2, 1894.
Vol. 3, Pt. 1–22
Daboll, Nathan, Apr. 24, 1750–Mar. 9, 1818.
Vol. 3, Pt. 1–23
Dabrowski, Joseph, Jan. 19, 1842–Feb. 15, 1903.
Vol. 3, Pt. 1–23
Da Costa, Jacob Mendez, Feb. 7, 1833–Sept. 11, 1900.
Vol. 3, Pt. 1–24
Da Costa, John Chalmers, Nov. 15, 1863–May 16, 1933.
Supp. 1–217
Daeger, Albert Thomas, Mar. 5, 1872–Dec. 2, 1932.
Supp. 1–218
Daft, Leo, Nov. 13, 1843–Mar. 28, 1922.
Vol. 3, Pt. 1–25
Dagg, John Leadley, Feb. 13, 1794–June 11, 1884.
Vol. 3, Pt. 1–26
Daggett, David, Dec. 31, 1764–Apr. 12, 1851.
Vol. 3, Pt. 1–26
Daggett, Ellsworth, May 24, 1845–Jan. 5, 1923.
Vol. 3, Pt. 1–27
Daggett Naphtali, Sept. 8, 1727–Nov. 25, 1780.
Vol. 3, Pt. 1–28
Dahl, Theodor Halvorson, Apr. 2, 1845–Jan. 18, 1923.
Vol. 3, Pt. 1–28
Dahlgren, John Adolphus Bernard, Nov. 13, 1809–July 12, 1870.
Vol. 3, Pt. 1–29
Dahlgren, Sarah Madeleine Vinton, July 13, 1825–May 28, 1898.
Vol. 3, Pt. 1–31
Dailey, Dan, Jr., Dec. 14, 1915–Oct. 16, 1978.
Supp. 10–165
Dakin, Henry Drysdale, Mar. 12, 1880–Feb. 10, 1952.
Supp. 5–149
Dakin, James Harrison, Aug. 24, 1806–May 10, 1852.
Supp. 1–219
Dalcho, Frederick, 1770–Nov. 24, 1836.
Vol. 3, Pt. 1–32
Dale, Charles Marks, Sept. 6, 1881–Nov. 16, 1971.
Supp. 9–213
Dale, Chester, May 3, 1883–Dec. 16, 1962.
Supp. 7–161
Dale, Maud Murray Thompson, June 25, 1875–Aug. 5, 1953.
Supp. 5–150
Dale, Richard, Nov. 6, 1756–Feb. 26, 1826.
Vol. 3, Pt. 1–32
Dale, Samuel, 1772–May 24, 1841.
Vol. 3, Pt. 1–33
Dale, Sir Thomas, d. Aug. 9, 1619.
Vol. 3, Pt. 1–34
Daley, Arthur John, July 31, 1904–Jan. 3, 1974.
Supp. 9–214
Daley, Cass, July 17, 1915–Mar. 22, 1975.
Supp. 9–215
Daley, Richard Joseph, May 15, 1902–Dec. 20, 1976.
Supp. 10–166

Dall, Caroline Wells Healey, June 22, 1822–Dec. 17, 1912.
Vol. 3, Pt. 1–35
Dall, William Healey, Aug. 21, 1845–Mar. 27, 1927.
Vol. 3, Pt. 1–35
Dallas, Alexander James, June 21, 1759–Jan. 16, 1817.
Vol. 3, Pt. 1–36
Dallas, George Mifflin, July 10, 1792–Dec. 31, 1864.
Vol. 3, Pt. 1–38
Dallin, Cyrus Edwin, Nov. 22, 1861–Nov. 14, 1944.
Supp. 3–210
D'Aloes, Claude Jean. [*See* Allouez, Claude Jean, 1622–1689.]
Dalton, John Call, Feb. 2, 1825–Feb. 12, 1889.
Vol. 3, Pt. 1–40
Dalton, Robert, 1867–Oct. 5, 1892.
Vol. 3, Pt. 1–40
Daly, Arnold. [*See* Daly, Peter Christopher Arnold, 1875–1927.]
Daly, Augustin. [*See* Daly, John Augustin, 1838–1899.]
Daly, Charles Patrick, Oct. 31, 1816–Sept. 19, 1899.
Vol. 3, Pt. 1–41
Daly, John Augustin, July 20, 1838–June 7, 1899.
Vol. 3, Pt. 1–42
Daly, Marcus, Dec. 5, 1841–Nov. 12, 1900.
Vol. 3, Pt. 1–45
Daly, Peter Christopher Arnold, Oct. 22, 1875–Jan. 13, 1927.
Vol. 3, Pt. 1–46
Daly, Reginald Aldworth, May 19, 1871–Sept. 19, 1957.
Supp. 6–143
Dalzell, John, Apr. 19, 1845–Oct. 2, 1927.
Vol. 3, Pt. 1–47
Dalzell, Robert M., 1793–Jan. 19, 1873.
Vol. 3, Pt. 1–48
Damon, Ralph Shepard, July 6, 1897–Jan. 4, 1956.
Supp. 6–145
Damrosch, Frank Heino, June 22, 1859–Oct. 22, 1937.
Supp. 2–140
Damrosch, Leopold, Oct. 22, 1832–Feb. 15, 1885.
Vol. 3, Pt. 1–48
Damrosch, Walter Johannes, Jan. 30, 1862–Dec. 22, 1950.
Supp. 4–210
Dana, Charles Anderson, Aug. 8, 1819–Oct. 17, 1897.
Vol. 3, Pt. 1–49
Dana, Charles Anderson, Apr. 25, 1881–Nov. 27, 1975.
Supp. 9–216
Dana, Charles Loomis, Mar. 25, 1852–Dec. 12, 1935.
Supp. 1–220
Dana, Edward Salisbury, Nov. 16, 1849–June 16, 1935.
Supp. 1–221
Dana, Francis, June 13, 1743–Apr. 25, 1811.
Vol. 3, Pt. 1–52
Dana, James, 1735–Aug. 18, 1812.
Vol. 3, Pt. 1–54
Dana, James Dwight, Feb. 12, 1813–Apr. 14, 1895.
Vol. 3, Pt. 1–55
Dana, James Freeman, Sept. 23, 1793–Apr. 14, 1827.
Vol. 3, Pt. 1–56
Dana, John Cotton, Aug. 19, 1856–July 21, 1929.
Vol. 3, Pt. 1–56
Dana, Napoleon Jackson Tecumseh, Apr. 15, 1822–July 15, 1905.
Vol. 3, Pt. 1–58
Dana, Richard, June 26, 1700–May 17, 1772.
Vol. 3, Pt. 1–58
Dana, Richard Henry, Nov. 15, 1787–Feb. 2, 1879.
Vol. 3, Pt. 1–59
Dana, Richard Henry, Aug. 1, 1815–Jan. 6, 1882.
Vol. 3, Pt. 1–60
Dana, Samuel Luther, July 11, 1795–Mar. 11, 1868.
Vol. 3, Pt. 1–61
Dana, Samuel Whittelsey, Feb. 13, 1760–July 21, 1830.
Vol. 3, Pt. 1–61
Dancel, Christian, Feb. 14, 1847–Oct. 13, 1898.
Vol. 3, Pt. 1–62
Dandridge, Dorothy Jean, Nov. 9, 1922–Sept. 8, 1965.
Supp. 7–162
Dandy, Walter Edward, Apr. 6, 1886–Apr. 19, 1946.
Supp. 4–213
Dane, Nathan, Dec. 29, 1752–Feb. 15, 1835.
Vol. 3, Pt. 1–63
Danenhower, John Wilson, Sept. 30, 1849–Apr. 20, 1887.
Vol. 3, Pt. 1–64
Danforth, Charles, Aug. 30, 1797–Mar. 22, 1876.
Vol. 3, Pt. 1–65
Danforth, Moseley Isaac, Dec. 11, 1800–Jan. 19, 1862.
Vol. 3, Pt. 1–66
Danforth, Thomas, November 1623–Nov. 5, 1699.
Vol. 3, Pt. 1–66
Danforth, Thomas, May 22, 1703–*c.* 1786.
Vol. 3, Pt. 1–67
Daniel, John Moncure, Oct. 24, 1825–Mar. 30, 1865.
Vol. 3, Pt. 1–67
Daniel, John Warwick, Sept. 5, 1842–June 29, 1910.
Vol. 3, Pt. 1–68
Daniel, Peter Vivian, Apr. 24, 1784–May 31, 1860.
Vol. 3, Pt. 1–69
Daniels, Farrington, Mar. 8, 1889–June 23, 1972.
Supp. 9–217
Daniels, Frank Albert, Aug. 15, 1856–Jan. 12, 1935.
Supp. 1–222
Daniels, Fred Harris, June 16, 1853–Aug. 30, 1913.
Vol. 3, Pt. 1–69
Daniels, Josephus, May 18, 1862–Jan. 15, 1948.
Supp. 4–215
Daniels, Winthrop More, Sept. 30, 1867–Jan. 2, 1944.
Supp. 3–211
Dannreuther, Gustav, July 21, 1853–Dec. 19, 1923.
Vol. 3, Pt. 1–70
Da Ponte, Lorenzo, Mar. 10, 1749–Aug. 17, 1838.
Vol. 3, Pt. 1–71
Darby, John, Sept. 27, 1804–Sept. 1, 1877.
Vol. 3, Pt. 1–72
Darby, William, Aug. 14, 1775–Oct. 9, 1854.
Vol. 3, Pt. 1–73
Dare, Virginia, b. Aug. 18, 1587.
Vol. 3, Pt. 1–73
Dargan, Edmund Strother, Apr. 15, 1805–Nov. 24, 1879.
Vol. 3, Pt. 1–74
Dargan, Edwin Preston, Sept. 7, 1879–Dec. 13, 1940.
Supp. 2–141
Darin, Bobby, May 14, 1936–Dec. 20, 1973.
Supp. 9–219
Darke, William, May 6, 1736–Nov. 26, 1801.
Vol. 3, Pt. 1–74
Darley, Felix Octavius Carr, June 23, 1822–Mar. 27, 1888.
Vol. 3, Pt. 1–75
Darling, Flora Adams, July 25, 1840–Jan. 6, 1910.
Vol. 3, Pt. 1–76
Darling, Henry, Dec. 27, 1823–Apr. 20, 1891.
Vol. 3, Pt. 1–77
Darling, Jay Norwood ("Ding"), Oct. 21, 1876–Feb. 12, 1962.
Supp. 7–163
Darling, Samuel Taylor, Apr. 6, 1872–May 20, 1925.
Vol. 3, Pt. 1–77
Darlington, William, Apr. 28, 1782–Apr. 23, 1863.
Vol. 3, Pt. 1–78
Darrow, Clarence Seward, Apr. 18, 1857–Mar. 13, 1938.
Supp. 2–141
Dart, Henry Paluché, Feb. 5, 1858–Sept. 27, 1934.
Supp. 1–223
Darton, Nelson Horatio, Dec. 17, 1865–Feb. 28, 1948.
Supp. 4–218
Darwell, Jane, Oct. 15, 1880–Aug. 14, 1967.
Supp. 8–116
Daugherty, Harry Micajah, Jan. 26, 1860–Oct. 12, 1941.
Supp. 3–214
Daveis, Charles Stewart, May 10, 1788–Mar. 29, 1865.
Vol. 3, Pt. 1–79
Daveiss, Joseph Hamilton, Mar. 4, 1774–Nov. 8, 1811.
Vol. 3, Pt. 1–80
Davenport, Charles Benedict, June 1, 1866–Feb. 8, 1944.
Supp. 3–214
Davenport, Edward Loomis, Nov. 15, 1815–Sept. 1, 1877.
Vol. 3, Pt. 1–80
Davenport, Eugene, June 20, 1856–Mar. 31, 1941.
Supp. 3–216
Davenport, Fanny Lily Gypsy, Apr. 10, 1850–Sept. 26, 1898.
Vol. 3, Pt. 1–82
Davenport, George, 1783–July 4, 1845.
Vol. 3, Pt. 1–82
Davenport, Herbert Joseph, Aug. 10, 1861–June 16, 1931.
Supp. 1–224

Davenport, Homer Calvin, Mar. 8, 1867–May 2, 1912.
Vol. 3, Pt. 1–83
Davenport, Ira Erastus, Sept. 17, 1839–July 8, 1911.
Vol. 3, Pt. 1–84
Davenport, James, 1716–1757.
Vol. 3, Pt. 1–84
Davenport, John, 1597–Mar. 1669/70.
Vol. 3, Pt. 1–85
Davenport, Russell Wheeler, July 12, 1899–Apr. 19, 1954.
Supp. 5–152
Davenport, Thomas, July 9, 1802–July 6, 1851.
Vol. 3, Pt. 1–87
Davenport, William H., 1841–1877. [*See* Davenport, Ira Erastus, 1839–1911.]
Davey, John, June 6, 1846–Nov. 8, 1923.
Vol. 3, Pt. 1–88
D'Avezac, Auguste Geneviève Valentin, May 1780–Feb. 15, 1851.
Vol. 3, Pt. 1–89
David, John Baptist Mary, June 4, 1761–July 12, 1841.
Vol. 3, Pt. 1–89
Davidge, John Beale, 1768–Aug. 23, 1829.
Vol. 3, Pt. 1–91
Davidge, William Pleater, Apr. 17, 1814–Aug. 7, 1888.
Vol. 3, Pt. 1–91
Davidoff, Leo Max, Jan. 16, 1898–Dec. 24, 1975.
Supp. 9–220
Davidson, George, May 9, 1825–Dec. 2, 1911.
Vol. 3, Pt. 1–92
Davidson, Israel, May 27, 1870–June 27, 1939.
Supp. 2–144
Davidson, James Wood, Mar. 9, 1829–*c.* June 15, 1905.
Vol. 3, Pt. 1–93
Davidson, Jo, Mar. 30, 1883–Jan. 2, 1952.
Supp. 5–153
Davidson, John Wynn, Aug. 18, 1823–June 26, 1881.
Vol. 3, Pt. 1–93
Davidson, Lucretia Maria, Sept. 27, 1808–Aug. 27, 1825.
Vol. 3, Pt. 1–94
Davidson, Margaret Miller, Mar. 26, 1823–Nov. 25, 1838.
Vol. 3, Pt. 1–94
Davidson, Robert, 1750–Dec. 13, 1812.
Vol. 3, Pt. 1–95
Davidson, Thomas, Oct. 25, 1840–Sept. 14, 1900.
Vol. 3, Pt. 1–95
Davidson, William Lee, 1746–Feb. 1, 1781.
Vol. 3, Pt. 1–97
Davie, William Richardson, June 20, 1756–Nov. 29, 1820.
Vol. 3, Pt. 1–98
Davies, Arthur Bowen, Sept. 26, 1862–Oct. 24, 1928.
Vol. 3, Pt. 1–99
Davies, Henry Eugene, July 2, 1836–Sept. 6, 1894.
Vol. 3, Pt. 1–101
Davies, John Vipond, Oct. 13, 1862–Oct. 4, 1939.
Supp. 2–145
Davies, Joseph Edward, Nov. 29, 1876–May 9, 1958.
Supp. 6–146
Davies, Marion Cecilia, Jan. 3, 1897–Sept. 22, 1961.
Supp. 7–165
Davies, Samuel, Nov. 3, 1723–Feb. 4, 1761.
Vol. 3, Pt. 1–102
Daviess, Joseph Hamilton. [*See* Daveiss, Joseph Hamilton, 1774–1811.]
Daviess, Maria Thompson, Nov. 25, 1872–Sept. 3, 1924.
Vol. 3, Pt. 1–103
Davis, Abraham Lincoln, Jr., Nov. 2, 1914–June 24, 1978.
Supp. 10–170
Davis, Adelle, Feb. 25, 1904–May 31, 1974.
Supp. 9–221
Davis, Alexander Jackson, July 24, 1803–Jan. 14, 1892.
Vol. 3, Pt. 1–103
Davis, Andrew Jackson, Aug. 11, 1826–Jan. 13, 1910.
Vol. 3, Pt. 1–105
Davis, Andrew McFarland, Dec. 30, 1833–Mar. 29, 1920.
Vol. 3, Pt. 1–105
Davis, Arthur Powell, Feb. 9, 1861–Aug. 7, 1933.
Supp. 1–224
Davis, Arthur Vining, May 30, 1867–Nov. 17, 1962.
Supp. 7–166
Davis, Benjamin Oliver, Sr., July 1, 1877–Nov. 26, 1970.
Supp. 8–118
Davis, Bernard George, Dec. 11, 1906–Aug. 27, 1972.
Supp. 9–222
Davis, Charles Harold, Jan. 7, 1856–Aug. 5, 1933.
Supp. 1–226
Davis, Charles Henry, Jan. 16, 1807–Feb. 18, 1877.
Vol. 3, Pt. 1–106
Davis, Charles Henry, Aug. 28, 1845–Dec. 27, 1921.
Vol. 3, Pt. 1–107
Davis, Charles Henry Stanley, Mar. 2, 1840–Nov. 7, 1917.
Vol. 3, Pt. 1–108
Davis, Cushman Kellogg, June 16, 1838–Nov. 27, 1900.
Vol. 3, Pt. 1–109
Davis, David, Mar. 9, 1815–June 26, 1886.
Vol. 3, Pt. 1–110
Davis, Dwight Filley, July 5, 1879–Nov. 28, 1945.
Supp. 3–217
Davis, Edmund Jackson, Oct. 2, 1827–Feb. 7, 1883.
Vol. 3, Pt. 1–112
Davis, Edwin Hamilton, Jan. 22, 1811–May 15, 1888.
Vol. 3, Pt. 1–113
Davis, Elmer Holmes, Jan. 13, 1890–May 18, 1958.
Supp. 6–148
Davis, Ernest R. ("Ernie"), Dec. 14, 1939–May 18, 1963.
Supp. 7–167
Davis, Francis Breese, Jr., Sept. 16, 1883–Dec. 22, 1962.
Supp. 7–169
Davis, Garret, Sept. 10, 1801–Sept. 22, 1872.
Vol. 3, Pt. 1–113
Davis, George, Mar. 1, 1820–Feb. 23, 1896.
Vol. 3, Pt. 1–114
Davis, George Breckenridge, Feb. 13, 1847–Dec. 15, 1914.
Vol. 3, Pt. 1–115
Davis, George Whitefield, July 26, 1839–July 12, 1918.
Vol. 3, Pt. 1–115
Davis, Harvey Nathaniel, June 6, 1881–Dec. 3, 1952.
Supp. 5–154
Davis, Henry, Sept. 15, 1771–Mar. 8, 1852.
Vol. 3, Pt. 1–116
Davis, Henry Gassaway, Nov. 16, 1823–Mar. 11, 1916.
Vol. 3, Pt. 1–117
Davis, Henry Gassett, Nov. 4, 1807–Nov. 18, 1896.
Vol. 3, Pt. 1–118
Davis, Henry Winter, Aug. 16, 1817–Dec. 30, 1865.
Vol. 3, Pt. 1–119
Davis, Horace, Mar. 16, 1831–July 12, 1916.
Vol. 3, Pt. 1–121
Davis, James John, Oct. 27, 1873–Nov. 22, 1947.
Supp. 4–219
Davis, Jeff, May 6, 1862–Jan. 3, 1913.
Vol. 3, Pt. 1–122
Davis, Jefferson, June 3, 1808–Dec. 6, 1889.
Vol. 3, Pt. 1–123
Davis, Jefferson Columbus, Mar. 2, 1828–Nov. 30, 1879.
Vol. 3, Pt. 1–131
Davis, Jerome Dean, Jan. 17, 1838–Nov. 4, 1910.
Vol. 3, Pt. 1–131
Davis, John, Jan. 25, 1761–Jan. 14, 1847.
Vol. 3, Pt. 1–132
Davis, John, *c.* 1780–*c.* 1838.
Vol. 3, Pt. 1–133
Davis, John, Jan. 13, 1787–Apr. 19, 1854.
Vol. 3, Pt. 1–133
Davis, John Chandler Bancroft, Dec. 29, 1822–Dec. 27, 1907
Vol. 3, Pt. 1–134
Davis, John Lee, Sept. 3, 1825–Mar. 12, 1889.
Vol. 3, Pt. 1–136
Davis, John Staige, Jan. 15, 1872–Dec. 23, 1946.
Supp. 4–220
Davis, John Warren, Feb. 11, 1888–July 12, 1980.
Supp. 10–171
Davis, John Wesley, Apr. 16, 1799–Aug. 22, 1859.
Vol. 3, Pt. 1–136
Davis, John William, Apr. 13, 1873–Mar. 24, 1955.
Supp. 5–155
Davis, Joseph Robert, Jan. 12, 1825–Sept. 15, 1896.
Vol. 3, Pt. 1–137
Davis, Katharine Bement, Jan. 15, 1860–Dec. 10, 1935.
Supp. 1–227
Davis, Mary Evelyn Moore, Apr. 12, 1852–Jan. 1, 1909.
Vol. 3, Pt. 1–137

Davis, Matthew Livmgston, Oct. 28, 1773–June 21, 1850.
Vol. 3, Pt. 1–138
Davis, Meyer, Jan. 10, 1885–Apr. 5, 1976.
Supp. 10–173
Davis, Nathan Smith, Jan. 9, 1817–June 16, 1904.
Vol. 3, Pt. 1–139
Davis, Noah, Sept. 10, 1818–Mar. 20, 1902.
Vol. 3, Pt. 1–140
Davis, Noah Knowles, May 15, 1830–May 3, 1910.
Vol. 3, Pt. 1–140
Davis, Norman Hezekiah, Aug. 9, 1878–July 2, 1944.
Supp. 3–218
Davis, Oscar King, Jan. 13, 1866–June 3, 1932.
Supp. 1–228
Davis, Owen Gould, Jan. 28, 1874–Oct. 14, 1956.
Supp. 6–149
Davis, Paulina Kellogg Wright, Aug. 7, 1813–Aug. 24, 1876.
Vol. 3, Pt. 1–141
Davis, Pauline Morton Sabin, 1887–Dec. 27, 1955.
Supp. 5–156
Davis, Phineas, 1800–Sept. 27, 1835.
Vol. 3, Pt. 1–142
Davis, Raymond Cazallis, June 23, 1836–June 10, 1919.
Vol. 3, Pt. 1–142
Davis, Rebecca Blaine Harding, June 24, 1831–Sept. 29, 1910.
Vol. 3, Pt. 1–143
Davis, Reuben, Jan. 18, 1813–Oct. 14, 1890.
Vol. 3, Pt. 1–144
Davis, Richard Harding, Apr. 18, 1864–Apr. 11, 1916.
Vol. 3, Pt. 1–144
Davis, Stuart, Dec. 7, 1894–June 24, 1964.
Supp. 7–170
Davis, Varina Anne Jefferson, June 27, 1864–Sept. 18, 1898.
Vol. 3, Pt. 1–145
Davis, Varina Howel, May 7, 1826–Oct. 16, 1906.
Vol. 3, Pt. 1–146
Davis, Watson, Apr. 29, 1896–June 27, 1967.
Supp. 8–119
Davis, William Augustine, Sept. 21, 1809–Jan. 15, 1875.
Vol. 3, Pt. 1–146
Davis, William Hammatt, Aug. 29, 1879–Aug. 13, 1964.
Supp. 7–171
Davis, William Morris, Feb. 12, 1850–Feb. 5, 1934.
Supp. 1–229
Davis, William Thomas, Mar. 3, 1822–Dec. 3, 1907.
Vol. 3, Pt. 1–147
Davis, Winnie. [*See* Davis, Varina Anne Jefferson, 1864–1898.]
Davison, George Willets, Mar. 25, 1872–June 16, 1953.
Supp. 5–157
Davison, Gregory Caldwell, Aug. 12, 1871–May 7, 1935.
Supp. 1–231
Davison, Henry Pomeroy, June 13, 1867–May 6, 1922.
Vol. 3, Pt. 1–148
Davisson, Clinton Joseph, Oct. 22, 1881–Feb. 1, 1958.
Supp. 6–150
Dawes, Charles Gates, Aug. 27, 1865–Apr. 23, 1951.
Supp. 5–159
Dawes, Henry Laurens, Oct. 30, 1816–Feb. 5, 1903.
Vol. 3, Pt. 1–149
Dawes, Rufus Cutler, July 30, 1867–Jan. 8, 1940.
Supp. 2–146
Dawes, William, Apr. 6, 1745–Feb. 25, 1799.
Vol. 3, Pt. 1–150
Dawkins, Henry, fl. 1753–1780.
Vol. 3, Pt. 1–150
Dawley, Almena, 1890–Dec. 12, 1956.
Supp. 6–152
Dawson, Francis Warrington, May 17, 1840–Mar. 12, 1889.
Vol. 3, Pt. 1–151
Dawson, Henry Barton, June 8, 1821–May 23, 1889.
Vol. 3, Pt. 1–152
Dawson, John, 1762–Mar. 30, 1814.
Vol. 3, Pt. 1–152
Dawson, Thomas Cleland, July 30, 1865–May 1, 1912.
Vol. 3, Pt. 1–53
Dawson, William Crosby, Jan. 4, 1798–May 5, 1856.
Vol. 3, Pt. 1–154
Dawson, William Levi, Apr. 26, 1886–Nov. 9, 1970.
Supp. 8–120
Day, Arthur Louis, Oct. 30, 1869–Mar. 2, 1960.
Supp. 6–152
Day, Benjamin Henry, Apr. 10, 1810–Dec. 21, 1889.
Vol. 3, Pt. 1–155
Day, Clarence Shepard, Nov. 18, 1874–Dec. 28, 1935.
Supp. 1–232
Day, David Alexander, Feb. 17, 1851–Dec. 17, 1897.
Vol. 3, Pt. 1–156
Day, David Talbot, Sept. 10, 1859–Apr. 15, 1925.
Vol. 3, Pt. 1–156
Day, Dorothy, Nov. 8, 1897–Nov. 29, 1980.
Supp. 10–175
Day, Edmund Ezra, Dec. 7, 1883–Mar. 23, 1951.
Supp. 5–160
Day, Frank Miles, Apr. 5, 1861–June 15, 1918.
Vol. 3, Pt. 1–157
Day, George Parmly, Sept. 4, 1876–Oct. 24, 1959.
Supp. 6–154
Day, Henry Noble, Aug. 4, 1808–Jan. 12, 1890.
Vol. 3, Pt. 1–158
Day, Holman Francis, Nov. 6, 1865–Feb. 19, 1935.
Supp. 1–234
Day, Horace H., July 10, 1813–Aug. 23, 1878.
Vol. 3, Pt. 1–159
Day, James Gamble, June 28, 1832–May 1, 1898.
Vol. 3, Pt. 1–159
Day, James Roscoe, Oct. 17, 1845–Mar. 13, 1923.
Vol. 3, Pt. 1–160
Day, Jeremiah, Aug. 3, 1773–Aug. 22, 1867.
Vol. 3, Pt. 1–161
Day, Luther, July 9, 1813–Mar. 8, 1885.
Vol. 3, Pt. 1–162
Day, Stephen, *c.* 1594–Dec. 22, 1668.
Vol. 3, Pt. 1–163
Day, William Rufus, Apr. 17, 1849–July 9, 1923.
Vol. 3, Pt. 1–163
Dayton, Elias, May 1, 1737–Oct. 22, 1807.
Vol. 3, Pt. 1–165
Dayton, Jonathan, Oct. 16, 1760–Oct. 9, 1824.
Vol. 3, Pt. 1–166
Dayton, William Lewis, Feb. 17, 1807–Dec. 1, 1864.
Vol. 3, Pt. 1–166
Deady, Matthew Paul, May 12, 1824–Mar. 24, 1893.
Vol. 3, Pt. 1–167
Dealey, George Bannerman, Sept. 18, 1859–Feb. 26, 1946.
Supp. 4–221
Dean, Amos, Jan. 16, 1803–Jan. 26, 1868.
Vol. 3, Pt. 1–168
Dean, Bashford, Oct. 28, 1867–Dec. 6, 1928.
Vol. 3, Pt. 1–169
Dean, Gordon Evans, Dec. 28, 1905–Aug. 15, 1958.
Supp. 6–155
Dean, James Byron, Feb. 8, 1931–Sept. 30, 1955.
Supp. 5–162
Dean, Jay Hanna ("Dizzy"), Jan. 16, 1911–July 17, 1974.
Supp. 9–223
Dean, Julia, July 22, 1830–Mar. 6, 1868.
Vol. 3, Pt. 1–170
Dean "Man Mountain." [*See* Leavitt, Frank Simmons, 1889–1953.]
Dean Sidney, Nov. 16, 1818–Oct. 29, 1901.
Vol. 3, Pt. 1–171
Dean, William Henry, Jr., July 6, 1910–Jan. 9, 1952.
Supp. 5–163
Deane, Charles, Nov. 10, 1813–Nov. 13, 1889.
Vol. 3, Pt. 1–171
Deane, Samuel, July 10, 1733–Nov. 12, 1814.
Vol. 3, Pt. 1–172
Deane, Silas, Dec. 24, 1737–Sept. 23, 1789.
Vol. 3, Pt. 1–173
De Angelis, Thomas Jefferson, Nov. 30, 1859–Mar. 20, 1933.
Supp. 1–234
Dearborn, Henry, Feb. 23, 1751–June 6, 1829.
Vol. 3, Pt. 1–174
Dearborn, Henry Alexander Scammwell, Mar. 3, 1783–July 29, 1851.
Vol. 3, Pt. 1–176
Dearing, John Lincoln, Dec. 10, 1858–Dec. 20, 1916.
Vol. 3, Pt. 1–177
Dearth, Henry Golden, Apr. 22, 1864–Mar. 27, 1918.
Vol. 3, Pt. 1–177
Deas, Zachariah Cantey, Oct. 25, 1819–Mar. 6, 1882.
Vol. 3, Pt. 1–178

Deaver, John Blair, July 25, 1855–Sept. 25, 1931.
Supp. 1–235
De Bardeleben, Henry Fairchild, July 22, 1840–Dec. 6, 1910.
Vol. 3, Pt. 1–179
De Barenne, Joannes Gregorius Dusser. [*See* Dusser de Barenne, Joannes Gregorius, 1885–1940.]
De Berdt, Dennys, *c.* 1694–Apr. 11, 1770.
Vol. 3, Pt. 1–180
De Bow, James Dunwoody Brownson, July 10, 1820–Feb. 27, 1867.
Vol. 3, Pt. 1–130
De Brahm, William Gerard, 1717–*c.* 1799.
Vol. 3, Pt. 1–182
Debs, Eugene Victor, Nov. 5, 1855–Oct. 20, 1926.
Vol. 3, Pt. 1–183
Debye, Peter Joseph William, Mar. 24, 1884–Nov. 2, 1966.
Supp. 8–121
De Camp, Joseph Rodefer, Nov. 5, 1858–Feb. 11, 1923.
Vol. 3, Pt. 1–185
Decatur, Stephen, 1752–Nov. 14, 1808.
Vol. 3, Pt. 1–186
Decatur, Stephen, Jan. 5, 1779–Mar. 22, 1820.
Vol. 3, Pt. 1–187
De Coppet, Edward J., May 28, 1855–Apr. 30, 1916.
Vol. 3, Pt. 1–190
De Costa, Benjamin Franklin, July 10, 1831–Nov. 4, 1904.
Vol. 3, Pt. 1–190
De Cuevas, Marquis, May 26, 1885–Feb. 22, 1961.
Supp. 7–173
Deemer, Horace Emerson, Sept. 24, 1858–Feb. 26, 1917.
Vol. 3, Pt. 1–191
Deems, Charles Force, Dec. 4, 1820–Nov. 18, 1893.
Vol. 3, Pt. 1–192
Deere, John, Feb. 7, 1804–May 17, 1886.
Vol. 3, Pt. 1–193
"Deerfoot," 1828–Jan. 18, 1897.
Vol. 3, Pt. 1–194
Deering, Nathaniel, June 25, 1791–Mar. 25, 1881.
Vol. 3, Pt. 1–194
Deering, William, Apr. 25, 1826–Dec. 9, 1913.
Vol. 3, Pt. 1–195
De Fontaine, Felix Gregory, 1834–Dec. 11, 1896.
Vol. 3, Pt. 1–196
De Forest, Alfred Victor, Apr. 7, 1888–Apr. 5, 1945.
Supp. 3–219
De Forest, David Curtis, Jan. 10, 1774–Feb. 22, 1825.
Vol. 3, Pt. 1–196
De Forest, Erastus Lyman, June 27, 1834–June 6, 1888.
Vol. 3, Pt. 1–197
De Forest, John Kinne Hyde, June 25, 1844–May 8, 1911.
Vol. 3, Pt. 1–198
De Forest, John William, May 31, 1826–July 17, 1906.
Vol. 3, Pt. 1–199
De Forest, Lee, Aug. 26, 1873–June 30, 1961.
Supp. 7–174
De Forest, Robert Weeks, Apr. 25, 1848–May 6, 1931.
Supp. 1–236
De Graffenried, Christopher. [*See* Graffenried, Christopher Baron de, 1661–1743.]
De Kruif, Paul Henry, Mar. 2, 1890–Feb. 28, 1971.
Supp. 9–225
De Haas, Jacob. [*See* Haas, Jacob Judah Aaron de, 1872–1937.]
De Haas, John Philip, *c.* 1735–June 3, 1786.
Vol. 3, Pt. 1–199
De Haven, Edwin Jesse, May 7, 1816–May 1, 1865.
Vol. 3, Pt. 1–200
Deindörfer, Johannes, July 28, 1828–May 14, 1907.
Vol. 3, Pt. 1–201
Deitzler, George Washington, Nov. 30, 1826–Apr. 10, 1884.
Vol. 3, Pt. 1–201
De Kay, George Colman, Mar. 5, 1802–Jan. 31, 1849.
Vol. 3, Pt. 1–202
De Kay, James Ellsworth, Oct. 12, 1792–Nov. 21, 1851.
Vol. 3, Pt. 1–203
De Koven, Henry Louis Reginald, Apr. 3, 1859–Jan. 16, 1920.
Vol. 3, Pt. 1–204
De Koven, James, Sept. 19, 1831–Mar. 19, 1879.
Vol. 3, Pt. 1–205
De Lacy, Walter Washington, Feb. 22, 1819–May 13, 1892.
Vol. 3, Pt. 1–206
Delafield, Edward, May 7, 1794–Feb. 13, 1875.
Vol. 3, Pt. 1–207
Delafield, Francis, Aug. 3, 1841–July 17, 1915.
Vol. 3, Pt. 1–208
Delafield, John, Mar. 16, 1748–July 3, 1824.
Vol. 3, Pt. 1–208
Delafield, John, Jan. 22, 1786–Oct. 22, 1853.
Vol. 3, Pt. 1–209
Delafield, Richard, Sept. 1, 1798–Nov. 5, 1873.
Vol. 3, Pt. 1–210
De Lamar, Joseph Raphael, Sept. 2, 1843–Dec. 1, 1918.
Vol. 3, Pt. 1–210
Delamater, Cornelius Henry, Aug. 30, 1821–Feb. 7, 1889.
Vol. 3, Pt. 1–211
De Lancey, James, Nov. 27, 1703–July 30, 1760.
Vol. 3, Pt. 1–212
De Lancey, James, 1732–1800.
Vol. 3, Pt. 1–213
De Lancey, James, 1746–May 2, 1804.
Vol. 3, Pt. 1–214
De Lancey, Oliver, Sept. 16, 1718–Oct. 27, 1785.
Vol. 3, Pt. 1–214
De Lancey, William Heathcote, Oct. 8, 1797–Apr. 5, 1865.
Vol. 3, Pt. 1–215
Deland, Margaret, Feb. 23, 1857–Jan. 13, 1945.
Supp. 3–221
De Langlade, Charles Michel, May 1729–*c.* 1801.
Vol. 3, Pt. 1–216
Delano, Amassa, Feb. 21, 1763–Apr. 21, 1823.
Vol. 3, Pt. 1–217
Delano, Columbus, June 5, 1809–Oct. 23, 1896.
Vol. 3, Pt. 1–217
Delano, Jane Arminda, Mar. 12, 1862–Apr. 15, 1919.
Vol. 3, Pt. 1–218
Delano, William Adams, Jan. 21, 1874–Jan. 12, 1960.
Supp. 6–157
Delany, Martin Robinson, May 6, 1812–Jan. 24, 1885.
Vol. 3, Pt. 1–219
Delany, Patrick Bernard, Jan. 28, 1845–Oct. 19, 1924.
Vol. 3, Pt. 1–220
Delavan, Edward Cornelius, 1793–Jan. 15, 1871.
Vol. 3, Pt. 1–221
De La Warr, Thomas West, Baron, July 9, 1577–June 7, 1618.
Vol. 3, Pt. 1–221
DeLee, Joseph Bolivar, Oct. 28, 1869–Apr. 2, 1942.
Supp. 3–222
De Leeuw, Adolph Lodewyk, May 6, 1861–Dec. 5, 1942.
Supp. 3–223
De Leon, Daniel, Dec. 14, 1852–May 11, 1914.
Vol. 3, Pt. 1–222
De Leon, Thomas Cooper, May 21, 1839–Mar. 19, 1914.
Vol. 3, Pt. 1–224
Deléry, François Charles, Jan. 28, 1815–June 12, 1880.
Vol. 3, Pt. 1–224
Dell, Floyd James, June 28, 1887–July 23, 1969.
Supp. 8–124
Dellenbaugh, Frederick Samuel, Sept. 13, 1853–Jan. 29, 1935.
Supp. 1–237
Del Mar, Alexander, Aug. 6, 1836–July 1, 1926.
Vol. 3, Pt. 1–225
Delmas, Delphin Michael, Apr. 14, 1844–Aug. 1, 1928.
Vol. 3, Pt. 1–226
Delmonico, Lorenzo, Mar. 13, 1813–Sept. 3, 1881.
Vol. 3, Pt. 1–226
De Long, George Washington, Aug. 22, 1844–Oct. 30, 1881.
Vol. 3, Pt. 1–227
Del Ruth, Roy, Oct. 18, 1895–Apr. 27, 1961.
Supp. 7–177
De Luca, Giuseppe, Dec. 25, 1876–Aug. 26, 1950.
Supp. 4–223
De Mézières y Clugny, Athanase, *c.* 1715–Nov. 2, 1779.
Vol. 3, Pt. 1–228
DeMille, Cecil Blount, Aug. 12, 1881–Jan. 21, 1959.
Supp. 6–158
De Mille, Henry Churchill, Sept. 17, 1853–Feb. 10, 1893.
Vol. 3, Pt. 1–229
Deming, Henry Champion, May 23, 1815–Oct. 9, 1872.
Vol. 3, Pt. 1–230
Deming, Philander, Feb. 6, 1829–Feb. 9, 1915.
Vol. 3, Pt. 1–231

Deming, William. [*See* Denning, William, 1736–1830.]
Demme, Charles Rudolph, Apr. 10, 1795–Sept. 1, 1863.
Vol. 3, Pt. 1–232
Dempster, John, Jan. 2, 1794–Nov. 28, 1863.
Vol. 3, Pt. 1–233
Demuth, Charles, 1883–Oct. 23, 1935.
Supp. 1–238
Denby, Charles, June 16, 1830–Jan. 13, 1904.
Vol. 3, Pt. 1–233
Denby, Edwin, Feb. 18, 1870–Feb. 8, 1929.
Vol. 3, Pt. 1–234
Denfeld, Louis Emil, Apr. 13, 1891–Mar. 28, 1972.
Supp. 9–226
Dennett, Tyler (Wilbur), June 13, 1883–Dec. 29, 1949.
Supp. 4–223
Dennie, Joseph, Aug. 30, 1768–Jan. 7, 1812.
Vol. 3, Pt. 1–235
Denning, William, 1736–Dec. 19, 1830.
Vol. 3, Pt. 1–237
Dennis, Alfred Lewis Pinneo, May 21, 1874–Nov. 14, 1930.
Supp. 1–239
Dennis, Eugene, Aug. 10, 1905–Jan. 31, 1961.
Supp. 7–179
Dennis, Frederic Shepard, Apr. 17, 1850–Mar. 8, 1934.
Supp. 1–239
Dennis, Graham Barclay, June 1, 1855–Aug. 18, 1923.
Vol. 3, Pt. 1–237
Dennis, James Shepard, Dec. 15, 1842–Mar. 21, 1914.
Vol. 3, Pt. 1–238
Dennis, Patrick. [*See* Tanner, Edward Everett, III, 1921–1976.]
Dennison, Aaron Lufkin, Mar. 6, 1812–Jan. 9, 1895.
Vol. 3, Pt. 1–239
Dennison, Henry Sturgis, Mar. 4, 1877–Feb. 29, 1952.
Supp. 5–164
Dennison, Walter, Aug. 9, 1869–Mar. 18, 1917.
Vol. 3, Pt. 1–240
Dennison, William, Nov. 23, 1815–June 15, 1882.
Vol. 3, Pt. 1–241
Denny, George Vernon, Jr., Aug. 29, 1899–Nov. 11, 1959.
Supp. 6–160
Densmore, Frances, May 21, 1867–June 5, 1957.
Supp. 6–161
Dent, Frederick Tracy, Dec. 17, 1821–Dec. 24, 1892.
Vol. 3, Pt. 1–242
Denver, James William, Oct. 23, 1817–Aug. 9, 1892.
Vol. 3, Pt. 1–242
De Palma, Ralph, 1883–Mar. 31, 1956.
Supp. 6–163
De Paolis, Alessio, Mar. 5, 1893–Mar. 9, 1964.
Supp. 7–178
De Pauw, Washington Charles, Jan. 4, 1822–May 5, 1887.
Vol. 3, Pt. 1–244
Depew, Chauncey Mitchell, Apr. 23, 1834–Apr. 5, 1928.
Vol. 3, Pt. 1–244
De Peyster, Abraham, July 8, 1657–Aug. 2, 1728.
Vol. 3, Pt. 1–247
De Peyster, John Watts, Mar. 9, 1821–May 4, 1907.
Vol. 3, Pt. 1–247
De Priest, Oscar Stanton, Mar. 9, 1871–May 12, 1951.
Supp. 5–165
De Quille, Dan. [*See* Wright, William, 1829–1898.]
Derbigny, Pierre Auguste Charles Bourguignon, 1767–Oct. 6, 1829.
Vol. 3, Pt. 1–248
Derby, Elias Hasket, Aug. 16, 1739–Sept. 8, 1799.
Vol. 3, Pt. 1–249
Derby, Elias Hasket, Jan. 10, 1766–Sept. 16, 1826.
Vol. 3, Pt. 1–250
Derby, Elias Hasket, Sept. 24, 1803–Mar. 31, 1880.
Vol. 3, Pt. 1–251
Derby, George Horatio, Apr. 3, 1823–May 15, 1861.
Vol. 3, Pt. 1–251
Derby, Richard, Sept. 16, 1712–Nov. 9, 1783.
Vol. 3, Pt. 1–252
Dercum, Francis Xavier, Aug. 10, 1856–Apr. 23, 1931.
Supp. 1–240
Dern, George Henry, Sept. 8, 1872–Aug. 27, 1936.
Supp. 2–147
De Rose, Peter, Mar. 10, 1900–Apr. 23, 1953.
Supp. 5–167
De Rosset, Moses John, July 4, 1838–May 1, 1881.
Vol. 3, Pt. 1–253
De Saussure, Henry William, Aug. 16, 1763–Mar. 29, 1839.
Vol. 3, Pt. 1–253
De Schweinitz, Edmund Alexander. [*See* Schweinitz, Edmund Alexander de, 1825–1887.]
De Schweinitz, George Edmund. [*See* Schweintz, George Edmund de, 1858–1938.]
De Seversky, Alexander Procofieff, June 7, 1894–Aug. 24, 1974
Supp. 9–228
Desha, Joseph, Dec. 9, 1768–Oct. 12, 1842.
Vol. 3, Pt. 1–254
De Smet, Pierre-Jean, Jan. 30, 1801–May 23, 1873.
Vol. 3, Pt. 1–255
De Soto, Hernando, *c.* 1500–May 21, 1542.
Vol. 3, Pt. 1–256
De Sylva, George Gard ("Buddy"), Jan. 27, 1896–July 11, 1950.
Supp. 4–225
Detmold, Christian Edward, Feb. 2, 1810–July 2, 1887.
Vol. 3, Pt. 1–258
De Trobriand, Régis Denis De Keredern, June 4, 1816–July 15, 1897.
Vol. 3, Pt. 1–258
Dett, Robert Nathaniel, Oct. 11, 1882–Oct. 2, 1943.
Supp. 3–224
Deutsch, Gotthard, Jan. 31, 1859–Oct. 14, 1921.
Vol. 3, Pt. 1–259
Devaney, John Patrick, June 30, 1883–Sept. 21, 1941.
Supp. 3–226
De Vargas Zapata y Lujan Ponce De Leon, Diego, *c.* 1650–Apr. 4, 1704.
Vol. 3, Pt. 1–260
Devens, Charles, Apr. 4, 1820–Jan. 7, 1891.
Vol. 3, Pt. 1–260
De Vere, Maximilian Schele. [*See* Schele, De Vere, Maximilian, 1820–1898.]
Devereux, John Henry, Apr. 5, 1832–Mar. 17, 1886.
Vol. 3, Pt. 1–262
Devers, Jacob Loucks, Sept. 8, 1887–Oct. 15, 1979.
Supp. 10–176
Devin, Thomas Casimer, Dec. 10, 1822–Apr. 4, 1878.
Vol. 3, Pt. 1–263
Devine, Andrew ("Andy"), Oct. 7, 1905–Feb. 18, 1977.
Supp. 10–178
Devine, Edward Thomas, May 6, 1867–Feb. 27, 1948.
Supp. 4–226
De Vinne, Theodore Low, Dec. 25, 1828–Feb. 16, 1914.
Vol. 3, Pt. 1–263
DeVoto, Bernard Augustine, Jan. 11, 1897–Nov. 13, 1955.
Supp. 5–168
Devoy, John, Sept. 3, 1842–Sept. 29, 1928.
Vol. 3, Pt. 1–264
De Vries, David Pietersen, fl. 1618–1655.
Vol. 3, Pt. 1–265
Dew, Thomas Roderick, Dec. 5, 1802–Aug. 6, 1846.
Vol. 3, Pt. 1–266
Dewees, William Potts, May 5, 1768–May 20, 1841.
Vol. 3, Pt. 1–267
Dewey, Chester, Oct. 25, 1784–Dec. 15, 1867.
Vol. 3, Pt. 1–267
Dewey, George, Dec. 26, 1837–Jan. 16, 1917.
Vol. 3, Pt. 1–268
Dewey, John, Oct. 20, 1859–June 1, 1952.
Supp. 5–169
Dewey, Melvil, Dec. 10, 1851–Dec. 26, 1931.
Supp. 1–241
Dewey, Orville, Mar. 28, 1794–Mar. 21, 1882.
Vol. 3, Pt. 1–272
Dewey, Richard Smith, Dec. 6, 1845–Aug. 4, 1933.
Supp. 1–243
Dewey, Thomas Edmund, Mar. 24, 1902–Mar. 16, 1971.
Supp. 9–229
De Wilde, Brandon, Apr. 9, 1942–July 6, 1972.
Supp. 9–231
Dewing, Francis, fl. 1716–1722.
Vol. 3, Pt. 1–272
Dewing, Maria Richards Oakey, Oct. 27, 1845–Dec. 13, 1927.
Vol. 3, Pt. 1–273
Dewing, Thomas Wilmer, May 4, 1851–Nov. 5, 1938.
Supp. 2–149

De Witt, Simeon, Dec. 25, 1756–Dec. 3, 1834.
Vol. 3, Pt. 1–274
De Wolf, James, Mar. 18, 1764–Dec. 21, 1837.
Vol. 3, Pt. 1–275
De Wolfe, Elsie, Dec. 20, 1865–July 12, 1950.
Supp. 4–228
Dexter, Franklin, Nov. 5, 1793–Aug. 14, 1857.
Vol. 3, Pt. 1–275
Dexter, Franklin Bowditch, Sept. 11, 1842–Aug. 13, 1920.
Vol. 3, Pt. 1–276
Dexter, Henry, Oct. 11, 1806–June 23, 1876.
Vol. 3, Pt. 1–277
Dexter, Henry, Mar. 14, 1813–July 11, 1910.
Vol. 3, Pt. 1–278
Dexter, Henry Martyn, Aug. 13, 1821–Nov. 13, 1890.
Vol. 3, Pt. 1–279
Dexter, Samuel, Mar. 16, 1726–June 10, 1810.
Vol. 3, Pt. 1–280
Dexter, Samuel, May 14, 1761–May 4, 1816.
Vol. 3, Pt. 1–280
Dexter, Timothy, Jan. 22, 1747–Oct. 23, 1806.
Vol. 3, Pt. 1–281
Dexter, Wirt, Oct. 25, 1832–May 17, 1890.
Vol. 3, Pt. 1–282
De Young, Michel Harry, Sept. 30, 1849–Feb. 15, 1925.
Vol. 3, Pt. 1–283
D'Harnoncourt, René, May 17, 1901–Aug. 13, 1968.
Supp. 8–125
Diat, Louis Felix, May 5, 1885–Aug. 29, 1957.
Supp. 6–164
Diaz, Abby Morton, 1821–Apr. 1, 1904.
Vol. 3, Pt. 1–284
Dibble, Roy Floyd, Mar. 12, 1887–Dec. 3, 1929.
Vol. 3, Pt. 1–285
Dibrell, George Gibbs, Apr. 12, 1822–May 6, 1888.
Vol. 3, Pt. 1–286
Dick, Elisha Cullen, Mar. 15, 1762–Sept. 22, 1825.
Vol. 3, Pt. 1–286
Dick, Robert Paine, Oct. 5, 1823–Sept. 12, 1898.
Vol. 3, Pt. 1–287
Dickerson, Edward Nicoll, Feb. 11, 1824–Dec. 12, 1889.
Vol. 3, Pt. 1–288
Dickerson, Mahlon, Apr. 17, 1770–Oct. 5, 1853.
Vol. 3, Pt. 1–289
Dickerson, Philemon, June 26, 1788–Dec. 10, 1862.
Vol. 3, Pt. 1–290
Dickey, Theophilus Lyle, Oct. 2, 1811–July 22, 1885.
Vol. 3, Pt. 1–290
Dickie, George William, July 17, 1844–Aug. 17, 1918.
Vol. 3, Pt. 1–291
Dickins, John, *c.* Aug. 24, 1747–Sept. 27, 1798.
Vol. 3, Pt. 1–292
Dickinson, Anna Elizabeth, Oct. 28, 1842–Oct. 22, 1932.
Supp. 1–244
Dickinson, Anson, Apr. 19, 1779–Mar. 9, 1852.
Vol. 3, Pt. 1–293
Dickinson, Charles Monroe, Nov. 15, 1842–July 3, 1924.
Vol. 3, Pt. 1–294
Dickinson, Daniel Stevens, Sept. 11, 1800–Apr. 12, 1866.
Vol. 3, Pt. 1–294
Dickinson, Donald McDonald, Jan. 17, 1846–Oct. 15, 1917.
Vol. 3, Pt. 1–295
Dickinson, Edwin De Witt, May 19, 1887–Mar. 26, 1961.
Supp. 7–181
Dickinson, Emily Elizabeth, Dec. 10, 1830–May 15, 1886.
Vol. 3, Pt. 1–297
Dickinson, Jacob McGavock, Jan. 30, 1851–Dec. 13, 1928.
Vol. 3, Pt. 1–298
Dickinson, John, Nov. 8, 1732–Feb. 14, 1808.
Vol. 3, Pt. 1–299
Dickinson, John, Feb. 24, 1894–Apr. 9, 1952.
Supp. 5–173
Dickinson, John Woodbridge, Oct. 12, 1825–Feb. 16, 1901.
Vol. 3, Pt. 1–301
Dickinson, Jonathan, Apr. 22, 1688–Oct. 7, 1747.
Vol. 3, Pt. 1–301
Dickinson, Philemon, Apr. 5, 1739–Feb. 4, 1809.
Vol. 3, Pt. 1–302
Dickinson, Preston, Sept. 9, 1889–Nov. 30, 1930.
Supp. 1–245
Dickinson, Robert Latou, Feb. 21, 1861–Nov. 29, 1950.
Supp. 4–230
Dickman, Joseph Theodore, Oct. 6, 1857–Oct. 23, 1927.
Vol. 3, Pt. 1–303
Dickson, David, July 6, 1809–Feb. 18, 1885.
Vol. 3, Pt. 1–304
Dickson, Earle Ensign, Oct. 10, 1892–Sept. 21, 1961.
Supp. 7–182
Dickson, Leonard Eugene, Jan. 22, 1874–Jan. 17, 1954.
Supp. 5–174
Dickson, Robert, *c.* 1765–June 20, 1823.
Vol. 3, Pt. 1–305
Dickson, Samuel Henry, Sept. 20, 1798–Mar. 31, 1872.
Vol. 3, Pt. 1–305
Dickson, Thomas, Mar. 26, 1824–July 31, 1884.
Vol. 3, Pt. 1–306
Didier, Eugene Lemoine, Dec. 22, 1838–Sept. 8, 1913.
Vol. 3, Pt. 1–307
Dielman, Frederick, Dec. 25, 1847–Aug. 25, 1935.
Supp. 1–246
Dies, Martin, Nov. 5, 1900–Nov. 14, 1972.
Supp. 9–233
Dietrichson, Johannes Wilhelm Christian, Apr. 4 or Aug. 23, 1815–Nov. 14, 1883.
Vol. 3, Pt. 1–307
Dietz, Peter Ernest, July 10, 1878–Oct. 11, 1947.
Supp. 4–232
Digges, Dudley, June 9, 1880–Oct. 24, 1947.
Supp. 4–233
Dike, Samuel Warren, Feb. 13, 1839–Dec. 3, 1913.
Vol. 3, Pt. 1–308
Dill, Clarence Cleveland, Sept. 21, 1884–Jan. 14, 1978.
Supp. 10–179
Dill, James Brooks, July 25, 1854–Dec. 2, 1910.
Vol. 3, Pt. 1–309
Dillard, James Hardy, Oct. 24, 1856–Aug. 2, 1940.
Supp. 2–150
Dille, John Flint, Apr. 27, 1884–Sept. 10, 1957.
Supp. 6–165
Diller, Burgoyne, Jan. 13, 1906–Jan. 30, 1965.
Supp. 7–183
Diller, Joseph Silas, Aug. 27, 1850–Nov. 13, 1928.
Supp. 1–247
Dillinger, John, June 28, 1902–July 22, 1934.
Supp. 1–248
Dillingham, Charles Bancroft, May 30, 1868–Aug. 30, 1934.
Supp. 1–249
Dillingham, Walter Francis, Apr. 5, 1875–Oct. 22, 1963.
Supp. 7–184
Dillingham, William Paul, Dec. 12, 1843–July 12, 1923.
Vol. 3, Pt. 1–310
Dillon, John Forrest, Dec. 25, 1831–May 6, 1914.
Vol. 3, Pt. 1–311
Dillon, Sidney, May 7, 1812–June 9, 1892.
Vol. 3, Pt. 1–312
Dilworth, Richardson, Aug. 29, 1898–Jan. 23, 1974.
Supp. 9–234
Diman, Jeremiah Lewis, May 1, 1831–Feb. 3, 1881.
Vol. 3, Pt. 1–312
Dimitry, Alexander, Feb. 7, 1805–Jan. 30, 1883.
Vol. 3, Pt. 1–313
Dimitry, Charles Patton, July 31, 1837–Nov. 10, 1910.
Vol. 3, Pt. 1–314
Dingley, Nelson, Feb. 15, 1832–Jan. 13, 1899.
Vol. 3, Pt. 1–314
Dingman, Mary Agnes, Apr. 9, 1864–Mar. 21, 1961.
Supp. 7–185
Dinsmoor, Robert, Oct. 7, 1757–Mar. 16, 1836.
Vol. 3, Pt. 1–315
Dinwiddie, Albert Bledsoe, Apr. 3, 1871–Nov. 21, 1935.
Supp. 1–250
Dinwiddie, Courtenay, Oct. 9, 1882–Sept. 13, 1943.
Supp. 3–227
Dinwiddie, Edwin Courtland, Sept. 29, 1867–May 5, 1935.
Supp. 1–251
Dinwiddie, Robert, 1693–July 27, 1770.
Vol. 3, Pt. 1–316
Dirksen, Everett McKinley, Jan. 4, 1896–Sept. 7, 1969.
Supp. 8–127
Disbrow, William Stephen, Mar. 18, 1861–Dec. 26, 1922.
Vol. 3, Pt. 1–317

Disney, Roy Oliver, June 24, 1893–Dec. 20, 1971.
Supp. 9–236
Disney, Walter Elias ("Walt"), Dec. 5, 1901–Dec. 15, 1966.
Supp. 8–129
Disston, Henry, May 23, 1819–Mar. 16, 1878.
Vol. 3, Pt. 1–318
Disturnell, John, Oct. 6, 1801–Oct. 1, 1877.
Vol. 3, Pt. 1–319
Ditmars, Raymond Lee, June 20, 1876–May 12, 1942.
Supp. 3–228
Ditrichstein, Leo, Jan. 6, 1865–June 28, 1928.
Vol. 3, Pt. 1–319
Ditson, George Leighton, Aug. 5, 1812–Jan. 29, 1895.
Vol. 3, Pt. 1–320
Ditson, Oliver, Oct. 20, 1811–Dec. 21, 1888.
Vol. 3, Pt. 1–321
Dittemore, John Valentine, Sept. 20, 1876–May 10, 1937.
Supp. 2–151
Diven, Alexander Samuel, Feb. 10, 1809–June 11, 1896.
Vol. 3, Pt. 1–322
Divine, Father, *c.* 1878/1880–Sept. 10, 1965.
Supp. 7–186
Dix, Dorothea Lynde, Apr. 4, 1802–July 17, 1887.
Vol. 3, Pt 1–323
Dix, Dorothy. [*See* Gilmer, Elizabeth Meriwether, 1870–1951.]
Dix, John Adams, July 24, 1798–Apr. 21, 1879.
Vol. 3, Pt. 1–325
Dix, John Homer, Sept. 30, 1811–Aug. 25, 1884.
Vol. 3, Pt. 1–327
Dix, Morgan, Nov. 1, 1827–Apr. 29, 1908.
Vol. 3, Pt. 1–327
Dixon, James, Aug. 5, 1814–Mar. 27, 1873.
Vol. 3, Pt. 1–328
Dixon, Joseph, Jan. 18, 1799–June 15, 1869.
Vol. 3, Pt. 1–329
Dixon, Luther Swift, June 17, 1825–Dec. 6, 1891.
Vol. 3, Pt. 1–330
Dixon, Roland Burrage, Nov. 6, 1875–Dec. 19, 1934.
Supp. 1–252
Dixon, Thomas, Jan. 11, 1864–Apr. 3, 1946.
Supp. 4–234
Dixon, William, Sept. 25, 1850–Mar. 9, 1913.
Vol. 3, Pt. 1–331
Dixwell, John, *c.* 1607–Mar. 18, 1688/9.
Vol. 3, Pt. 1–331
Doak, Samuel, August 1749–Dec. 12, 1830.
Vol. 3, Pt. 1–332
Doane, George Washington, May 27, 1799–Apr. 27, 1859.
Vol. 3, Pt. 1–333
Doane, Thomas, Sept. 20, 1821–Oct. 22, 1897.
Vol. 3, Pt. 1–334
Doane, William Croswell, Mar. 2, 1832–May 17, 1913.
Vol. 3, Pt. 1–334
Dobbin, James Cochran, Jan. 17, 1814–Aug. 4, 1857.
Vol. 3, Pt. 1–335
Dobbs, Arthur, Apr. 2, 1689–Mar. 28, 1765.
Vol. 3, Pt. 1–336
Dobie, Gilmour, Jan. 31, 1878–Dec. 23, 1948.
Supp. 4–236
Dobie, J(ames) Frank, Sept. 26, 1888–Sept. 18, 1964.
Supp. 7–188
Dobzhansky, Theodosius Grigorievich, Jan. 25, 1900–Dec. 18, 1975.
Supp. 9–238
Dock, Christopher, *c.* 1698–1771.
Vol. 3, Pt. 1–337
Dock, Lavinia Lloyd, Feb. 26, 1858–Apr. 17, 1956.
Supp. 6–166
Dockstader, Lew, Aug. 7, 1856–Oct. 26, 1924.
Vol. 3, Pt. 1–338
Dod, Albert Baldwin, Mar. 24, 1805–Nov. 19, 1845.
Vol. 3, Pt. 1–338
Dod, Daniel, Sept. 8, 1778–May 9, 1823.
Vol. 3, Pt. 1–339
Dod, Thaddeus, Mar. 7, 1740 o.s.–May 20, 1793.
Vol. 3, Pt. 1–340
Dodd, Bella Visono, Oct. 1904–Apr. 29, 1969.
Supp. 8–132
Dodd, Frank Howard, Apr. 12, 1844–Jan. 10, 1916.
Vol. 3, Pt. 1–340
Dodd, Lee Wilson, July 11, 1879–May 16, 1933.
Supp. 1–253
Dodd, Monroe Elmon, Sept. 8, 1878–Aug. 6, 1952.
Supp. 5–175
Dodd, Samuel Calvin Tate, Feb. 20, 1836–Jan. 30, 1907.
Vol. 3, Pt. 1–341
Dodd, Thomas Joseph, May 15, 1907–May 24, 1971.
Supp. 9–240
Dodd, William Edward, Oct. 21, 1869–Feb. 9, 1940.
Supp. 2–152
Doddridge, Joseph, Oct. 14, 1769–Nov. 9, 1826.
Vol. 3, Pt. 1–342
Doddridge, Philip, May 17, 1773–Nov. 19, 1832.
Vol. 3, Pt. 1–343
Dodge, Augustus Caesar, Jan. 2, 1812–Nov. 20, 1883.
Vol. 3, Pt. 1–344
Dodge, David Low, June 14, 1774–Apr. 23, 1852.
Vol. 3, Pt. 1–344
Dodge, Ebenezer, Apr. 21, 1819–Jan. 5, 1890.
Vol. 3, Pt. 1–345
Dodge, Grace Hoadley, May 21, 1856–Dec. 27, 1914.
Vol. 3, Pt. 1–346
Dodge, Grenville Mellen, Apr. 12, 1831–Jan. 3, 1916.
Vol. 3, Pt. 1–347
Dodge, Henry, Oct. 12, 1782–June 19, 1867.
Vol. 3, Pt. 1–348
Dodge, Henry Chee, 1860–Jan. 7, 1947.
Supp. 4–237
Dodge, Jacob Richards, Sept. 28, 1823–Oct. 1, 1902.
Vol. 3, Pt. 1–349
Dodge, Joseph Morrell, Nov. 18, 1890–Dec. 2, 1964.
Supp. 7–189
Dodge, Mary Abigail, Mar. 31, 1833–Aug. 17, 1896.
Vol. 3, Pt. 1–350
Dodge, Mary Elizabeth Mapes, Jan. 26, 1831–Aug. 21, 1905.
Vol. 3, Pt. 1–351
Dodge, Raymond, Feb. 20, 1871–Apr. 8, 1942.
Supp. 3–229
Dodge, Theodore Ayrault, May 28, 1842–Oct. 25, 1909.
Vol. 3, Pt. 1–351
Dodge, William De Leftwich, Mar. 9, 1867–Mar. 25, 1935.
Supp. 1–254
Dodge, William Earl, Sept. 4, 1805–Feb. 9, 1883.
Vol. 3, Pt. 1–352
Dods, John Bovee, 1795–Mar. 21, 1872.
Vol. 3, Pt. 1–353
Doe, Charles, Apr. 11, 1830–Mar. 9, 1896.
Vol. 3, Pt. 1–354
Doheny, Edward Laurence, Aug. 10, 1856–Sept. 8, 1935.
Supp. 1–254
Doherty, Henry Latham, May 15, 1870–Dec. 26, 1939.
Supp. 2–154
Dolan, Thomas, Oct. 27, 1834–June 12, 1914.
Vol. 3, Pt. 1–355
Dold, Jacob, June 25, 1825–Oct. 25, 1909.
Vol. 3, Pt. 1–356
Dole, Charles Fletcher, May 17, 1845–Nov. 27, 1927.
Vol. 3, Pt. 1–357
Dole, James Drummond, Sept. 27, 1877–May 14, 1958.
Supp. 6–168
Dole, Nathan Haskell, Aug. 31, 1852–May 9, 1935.
Supp. 1–255
Dole, Sanford Ballard, Apr. 23, 1844–June 9, 1926.
Vol. 3, Pt. 1–358
D'Olier, Franklin, Apr. 28, 1877–Dec. 10, 1953.
Supp. 5–177
Dollar, Robert, Mar. 20, 1844–May 16, 1932.
Supp. 1–256
Dolliver, Jonathan Prentiss, Feb. 6, 1858–Oct. 15, 1910.
Vol. 3, Pt. 1–359
Dolph, Joseph Norton, Oct. 19, 1835–Mar. 10, 1897.
Vol. 3, Pt. 1–360
Dombrowski, Joseph. [*See* Dabrowski, Joseph, 1842–1903.]
Dominguez, Francisco Atanasio. [*See* Escalante, Silvestre Velez De, fl. 1768–1779.]
Donahoe, Patrick, Mar. 17, 1811–Mar. 18, 1901.
Vol. 3, Pt. 1–361
Donahue, Peter, Jan. 11, 1822–Nov. 26, 1885.
Vol. 3, Pt. 1–362
Donaldson, Henry Herbert, May 12, 1857–Jan. 23, 1938.
Supp. 2–156

Donaldson, Jesse Monroe, Aug. 17, 1885–Mar. 25, 1970.
Supp. 8–133
Donck, Adriaen Van Der. [*See* Van Der Donck, Adrian, 1620–1655.]
Donelson, Andrew Jackson, Aug. 25, 1799–June 26, 1871.
Vol. 3, Pt. 1–363
Dongan, Thomas, 1634–Dec. 14, 1715.
Vol. 3, Pt. 1–364
Doniphan, Alexander William, July 9, 1808–Aug. 8, 1887.
Vol. 3, Pt. 1–365
Donlevy, Brian, Feb. 9, 1901–Apr. 5, 1972.
Supp. 9–241
Donlevy, Harriet Farley. [*See* Farley, Harriet, 1817–1907.]
Donn-Byrne, Brian Oswald, Nov. 20, 1889–June 18, 1928.
Vol. 3, Pt. 1–366
Donnell, Forrest C., Aug. 20, 1884–Mar. 3, 1980.
Supp. 10–180
Donnell, James C., Apr. 20, 1854–Jan. 10, 1927.
Vol. 3, Pt. 1–366
Donnell, Robert, April 1784–May 24, 1855.
Vol. 3, Pt. 1–367
Donnelly, Charles Francis, Oct. 14, 1836–Jan. 31, 1909.
Vol. 3, Pt. 1–368
Donnelly, Eleanor Cecilia, Sept. 6, 1838–Apr. 30, 1917.
Vol. 3, Pt. 1–369
Donnelly, Ignatius, Nov. 3, 1831–Jan. 1, 1901.
Vol. 3, Pt. 1–369
Donoghue, John, 1853–July 1, 1903.
Vol. 3, Pt. 1–371
Donovan, James Britt, Feb. 29, 1916–Jan. 19, 1970.
Supp. 8–134
Donovan, John Joseph, Sept. 8, 1858–Jan. 9, 1937.
Supp. 2–157
Donovan, William Joseph, Jan. 1, 1883–Feb. 8, 1959.
Supp. 6–169
D'Ooge, Martin Luther, July 17, 1839–Sept. 12, 1915.
Vol. 3, Pt. 1–372
Dooley, Thomas Anthony, III, Jan. 17, 1927–Jan. 18, 1961.
Supp. 7–190
Doolittle, Amos, May 18, 1754–Jan. 30, 1832.
Vol. 3, Pt. 1–372
Doolittle, Charles Leander, Nov. 12, 1843–Mar. 3, 1919.
Vol. 3, Pt. 1373
Doolittle, Eric, July 26, 1869–Sept. 21, 1920.
Vol. 3, Pt. 1–374
Doolittle, James Rood, Jan. 3, 1815–July 27, 1897.
Vol. 3, Pt. 1–374
Doran, George Henry, Dec. 19, 1869–Jan. 7, 1956.
Supp. 6–171
Dorchester, Daniel, Mar. 11, 1827–Mar. 13, 1907.
Vol. 3, Pt. 1–375
Doremus, Robert Ogden, Jan. 11, 1824–Mar. 22, 1906.
Vol. 3, Pt. 1–376
Doremus, Sarah Platt Haines, Aug. 3, 1802–Jan. 29, 1877.
Vol. 3, Pt. 1–377
Dorgan, Thomas Aloysius, Apr. 29, 1877–May 2, 1929.
Vol. 3, Pt. 1–378
Dorion, Marie, *c.* 1791–Sept. 3, 1850.
Vol. 3, Pt. 1–379
Dorn, Harold Fred, July 30, 1906–May 9, 1963.
Supp. 7–191
Dornin, Thomas Aloysius, May 1, 1800–Apr. 22, 1874.
Vol. 3, Pt. 1–380
Dorr, Julia Caroline Ripley, Feb. 13, 1825–Jan. 18, 1913.
Vol. 3, Pt. 1–381
Dorr, Thomas Wilson, Nov. 5, 1805–Dec. 27, 1854.
Vol. 3, Pt. 1–381
Dorrell, William, Mar. 15, 1752–Aug. 28, 1846.
Vol. 3, Pt. 1–382
Dorsch, Eduard, Jan. 10, 1822–Jan. 10, 1887.
Vol. 3, Pt. 1–383
Dorset, Marion, Dec. 14, 1872–July 14, 1935.
Supp. 1–258
Dorsey, Anna Hanson McKenney, Dec. 12, 1815–Dec. 25, 1896.
Vol. 3, Pt. 1–384
Dorsey, George Amos, Feb. 6, 1868–Mar. 29, 1931.
Supp. 1–258
Dorsey, James Owen, Oct. 31, 1848–Feb. 4, 1895.
Vol. 3, Pt. 1–384
Dorsey, John Syng, Dec. 23, 1783–Nov. 12, 1818.
Vol. 3, Pt. 1–385
Dorsey, Sarah Anne Ellis, Feb. 16, 1829–July 4, 1879.
Vol. 3, Pt. 1–386
Dorsey, Stephen Wallace, Feb. 28, 1842–Mar. 20, 1916.
Vol. 3, Pt. 1–387
Dorsey, Thomas Francis ("Tommy"), Nov. 19, 1905–Nov. 26, 1956.
Supp. 6–172
Dorsheimer, William Edward, Feb. 5, 1832–Mar. 26, 1888.
Vol. 3, Pt. 1–387
Dos Passos, John Randolph, July 31, 1844–Jan. 27, 1917.
Vol. 3, Pt. 1–388
Dos Passos, John Roderigo, Jan. 14, 1896–Sept. 28, 1970.
Supp. 8–135
Doty, Elihu, Sept. 20, 1809–Nov. 30, 1864.
Vol. 3, Pt. 1–389
Doty, James Duane, Nov. 5, 1799–June 13, 1865.
Vol. 3, Pt. 1–390
Doubleday, Abner, June 26, 1819–Jan. 26, 1893.
Vol. 3, Pt. 1–391
Doubleday, Frank Nelson, Jan. 8, 1862–Jan. 30, 1934.
Supp. 1–259
Doubleday, Nelson, June 16, 1889–Jan. 11, 1949.
Supp. 4–239
Doubleday, Neltje de Graff, Oct. 23, 1865–Feb. 21, 1918.
Vol. 3, Pt. 1–392
Dougherty, Dennis Joseph, Aug. 16, 1865–May 31, 1951.
Supp. 5–178
Dougherty, Raymond Philip, Aug. 5, 1877–July 13, 1933.
Supp. 1–260
Doughton, Robert Lee, Nov. 7, 1863–Oct. 2, 1954.
Supp. 5–180
Doughty, Thomas, July 19, 1793–July 22, 1856.
Vol. 3, Pt. 1–392
Doughty, William Henry, Feb. 5, 1836–Mar. 27, 1905.
Vol. 3, Pt. 1–393
Douglas, Aaron, May 26, 1899–Feb. 2, 1979.
Supp. 10–182
Douglas, Amanda Minnie, July 14, 1831–July 18, 1916.
Vol. 3, Pt. 1–394
Douglas, Benjamin, Apr. 3, 1816–June 26, 1894.
Vol. 3, Pt. 1–394
Douglas, Helen Gahagan, Nov. 25, 1908–June 28, 1980.
Supp. 10–182
Douglas, Henry Kyd, Sept. 29, 1838–Dec. 18, 1903.
Vol. 3, Pt. 1–395
Douglas, James, Nov. 4, 1837–June 25 1918.
Vol. 3, Pt. 1–396
Douglas, Lewis Williams, July 2, 1894–Mar. 7, 1974.
Supp. 9–242
Douglas, Lloyd Cassel, Aug. 27, 1877–Feb. 13, 1951.
Supp. 5–181
Douglas, Paul Howard, Mar. 26, 1892–Sept. 24, 1976.
Supp. 10–185
Douglas, Stephen Arnold, Apr. 23, 1813–June 3, 1861.
Vol. 3, Pt. 1–397
Douglas, William, Jan. 27, 1742/3–May 28, 1777.
Vol. 3, Pt. 1–403
Douglas, William Lewis, Aug. 22, 1845–Sept. 17, 1924.
Vol. 3, Pt. 1–404
Douglas, William Orville, Oct. 16, 1898–Jan. 19, 1980.
Supp. 10–187
Douglass, Andrew Ellicott, July 5, 1867–Mar. 20, 1962.
Supp. 7–193
Douglass, David Bates, Mar. 21, 1790–Oct. 21, 1849.
Vol. 3, Pt. 1–405
Douglass, Frederick, February 1817?–Feb. 20, 1895.
Vol. 3, Pt. 1–406
Douglass, William, *c.* 1691–Oct. 21, 1752.
Vol. 3, Pt. 1–407
Doull, James Angus, Sept. 8, 1889–Apr. 6, 1963.
Supp. 7–194
Dove, Arthur Garfield, Aug. 2, 1880–Nov. 23, 1946.
Supp. 4–240
Dove, David James, *c.* 1696–April 1769.
Vol. 3, Pt. 1–408
Dow, Alex, Apr. 12, 1862–Mar. 22, 1942.
Supp. 3–230
Dow, Henry, 1634–May 6, 1707.
Vol. 3, Pt. 1–409

Dow, Herbert Henry, Feb. 26, 1866–Oct. 15, 1930.
Supp. 1–261
Dow, Lorenzo, Oct. 16, 1777–Feb. 2, 1834.
Vol. 3, Pt. 1–410
Dow, Lorenzo, July 10, 1825–Oct. 12, 1899.
Vol. 3, Pt. 1–410
Dow, Neal, Mar. 20, 1804–Oct. 2, 1897.
Vol. 3, Pt. 1–411
Dowell, Greensville, Sept. 1, 1822–June 9, 1881.
Vol. 3, Pt. 1–412
Dowie, John Alexander, May 25, 1847–Mar. 9, 1907.
Vol. 3, Pt. 1–413
Dowling, Austin, Apr. 6, 1868–Nov. 29, 1930.
Supp. 1–262
Dowling, Noel Thomas, Aug. 14, 1885–Feb. 11, 1969.
Supp. 8–138
Downer, Eliphalet, Apr. 4, 1744–Apr. 3, 1806.
Vol. 3, Pt. 1–414
Downer, Samuel, Mar. 8, 1807–Sept. 20, 1881.
Vol. 3, Pt. 1–415
Downes, John, Dec. 23, 1784–Aug. 11, 1854.
Vol. 3, Pt. 1–415
Downes (Edwin) Olin, Jan. 27, 1886–Aug. 22, 1955.
Supp. 5–183
Downey, John, *c.* 1765–July 21, 1826.
Vol. 3, Pt. 1–416
Downey, June Etta, July 13, 1875–Oct. 11, 1932.
Supp. 1–263
Downey, Sheridan, Mar. 9, 1884–Oct. 25, 1961.
Supp. 7–195
Downing, Andrew Jackson, Oct. 30, 1815–July 28, 1852.
Vol. 3, Pt. 1–417
Downing, Charles, July 9, 1802–Jan. 18, 1885.
Vol. 3, Pt. 1–418
Downing, George, Aug. 1623–July 1684.
Vol. 3, Pt. 1–419
Dowse, Thomas, Dec. 28, 1772–Nov. 4, 1856.
Vol. 3, Pt. 1–419
Doyle, Alexander, Jan. 28, 1857–Dec. 21, 1922.
Vol. 3, Pt. 1–420
Doyle, Alexander Patrick, Feb. 28, 1857–Aug. 9, 1912.
Vol. 3, Pt. 1–421
Doyle, John Thomas, Nov. 26, 1819–Dec. 23, 1906.
Vol. 3, Pt. 1–421
Doyle, Sarah Elizabeth, Mar. 23, 1830–Dec. 21, 1922.
Vol. 3, Pt. 1–423
Drake, Alexander Wilson, 1843–Feb. 4, 1916.
Vol. 3, Pt. 1–423
Drake, Benjamin, 1795–Apr. 1, 1841.
Vol. 3, Pt. 1–424
Drake, Charles Daniel, Apr. 11, 1811–Apr. 1, 1892.
Vol. 3, Pt. 1–425
Drake, Daniel, Oct. 20, 1785–Nov. 6, 1852.
Vol. 3, Pt. 1–426
Drake, Edwin Laurentine, Mar. 29, 1819–Nov. 8, 1880.
Vol. 3, Pt. 1–427
Drake, Frances Ann Denny, Nov. 6, 1797–Sept. 1, 1875.
Vol. 3, Pt. 1–428
Drake, Francis Marion, Dec. 30, 1830–Nov. 20, 1903.
Vol. 3, Pt. 1–429
Drake, Francis Samuel, Feb. 22, 1828–Feb. 22, 1885.
Vol. 3, Pt. 1–430
Drake, John Burroughs, Jan. 17, 1826–Nov. 12, 1895.
Vol. 3, Pt. 1–430
Drake, Joseph Rodman, Aug. 7, 1795–Sept. 21, 1820.
Vol. 3, Pt. 1–431
Drake, Samuel, Nov. 15, 1768–Oct. 16, 1854.
Vol. 3, Pt. 1–432
Drake, Samuel Adams, Dec. 19, 1833–Dec. 4, 1905.
Vol. 3, Pt. 1–432
Drake, Samuel Gardner, Oct. 11, 1798–June 14, 1875.
Vol. 3, Pt. 1–433
Draper, Andrew Sloan, June 21, 1848–Apr. 27, 1913.
Vol. 3, Pt. 1–434
Draper, Dorothy, Nov. 22, 1889–Mar. 10, 1969.
Supp. 8–140
Draper, Eben Sumner, June 17, 1858–Apr. 9, 1914.
Vol. 3, Pt. 1–435
Draper, Henry, Mar. 7, 1837–Nov. 20, 1882.
Vol. 3, Pt. 1–435
Draper, Ira, Dec. 24, 1764–Jan. 22, 1848.
Vol. 3, Pt. 1–437
Draper, John, Oct. 29, 1702–Nov. 29, 1762.
Vol. 3, Pt. 1–437
Draper, John William, May 5, 1811–Jan. 4, 1882.
Vol. 3, Pt. 1–438
Draper, Lyman Copeland, Sept. 4, 1815–Aug. 26, 1891.
Vol. 3, Pt. 1–441
Draper, Margaret Green, fl. 1750–1807.
Vol. 3, Pt. 1–442
Draper, Richard, Feb. 24, 1726/7–June 5, 1774.
Vol. 3, Pt. 1–443
Draper, Ruth, Dec. 2, 1884–Dec. 30, 1956.
Supp. 6–173
Draper, William Franklin, Apr. 9, 1842–Jan. 28, 1910.
Vol. 3, Pt. 1–443
Drayton, John, June 22, 1766–Nov. 27, 1822.
Vol. 3, Pt. 1–444
Drayton, Percival, Aug. 25, 1812–Aug. 4, 1865.
Vol. 3, Pt. 1–445
Drayton, Thomas Fenwick, Aug. 24, 1808–Feb. 18, 1891.
Vol. 3, Pt. 1–446
Drayton, William, Mar. 21, 1732–May 18, 1790.
Vol. 3, Pt. 1–447
Drayton, William, Dec. 30, 1776–May 24, 1846.
Vol. 3, Pt. 1–448
Drayton, William Henry, September 1742–Sept. 3, 1779.
Vol. 3, Pt. 1–448
Dreier, Katherine Sophie, 1877–Mar. 29, 1952.
Supp. 5–184
Dreier, Margaret. [*See* Robins, Margaret Dreier, 1868–1945.]
Dreier, Mary Elisabeth, Sept. 26, 1875–Aug. 15, 1963.
Supp. 7–196
Dreiser, Theodore, Aug. 27, 1871–Dec. 28, 1945.
Supp. 3–232
Dresel, Otto, *c.* 1826–July 26, 1890.
Vol. 3, Pt. 1–449
Dressen, Charles Walter, Sept. 20, 1898–Aug. 10, 1966.
Supp. 8–141
Dresser, Louise Kerlin, Oct. 5, 1882–Apr. 24, 1965.
Supp. 7–197
Dressler, Marie, Nov. 9, 1871–July 28, 1934.
Supp. 1–264
Drew, Charles Richard, June 3, 1904–Apr. 1, 1950.
Supp. 4–242
Drew, Daniel, July 29, 1797–Sept. 18, 1879.
Vol. 3, Pt. 1–450
Drew, Georgiana Emma. [*See* Barrymore, Georgiana Emma Drew, 1856–1893.]
Drew, John, Nov. 13, 1853–July 9, 1927.
Vol. 3, Pt. 1–452
Drew, John, Sept. 3, 1827–May 21, 1862.
Vol. 3, Pt. 1–451
Drew, Louisa Lane, Jan. 10, 1820–Aug. 31, 1897.
Vol. 3, Pt. 1–454
Drexel, Anthony Joseph, Sept. 13, 1826–June 30, 1893.
Vol. 3, Pt. 1–455
Drexel, Francis Martin, Apr. 7, 1792–June 5, 1863.
Vol. 3, Pt. 1–456
Drexel, Joseph William, Jan. 24, 1833–Mar. 25, 1888.
Vol. 3, Pt. 1457
Drexel, Katharine Mary, Nov. 26, 1858–Mar. 3, 1955.
Supp. 5–185
Dreyfus, Max, Apr. 1, 1874–May 12, 1964.
Supp. 7–198
Drinker, Catharine Ann. [*See* Janvier, Catharine Ann, 1841–1922.]
Drinker, Cecil Kent, Mar. 17, 1887–Apr. 14, 1956.
Supp. 6–174
Drinkwater, Jennie Maria, Apr. 12, 1841–Apr. 28, 1900.
Vol. 3, Pt. 1–457
Dripps, Isaac L., April 14, 1810–Dec. 28, 1892.
Vol. 3, Pt. 1–458
Driscoll, Alfred Eastlack, Oct. 25, 1902–March 9, 1975.
Supp. 9–244
Drisler, Henry, Dec. 27, 1818–Nov. 30, 1897.
Vol. 3, Pt. 1–458
Dromgoole, William Allen, Oct. 25, 1860–Sept. 1, 1934.
Supp. 1–265
Dropsie, Moses Aaron, Mar. 9, 1821–July 8, 1905.
Vol. 3, Pt. 1–459

Drown, Thomas Messinger, Mar. 19, 1842–Nov. 16, 1904.
Vol. 3, Pt. 1–460
Druillettes, Gabriel, Sept. 29, 1610–Apr. 8, 1681.
Vol. 3, Pt. 1–462
Drum, Hugh Aloysius, Sept. 19, 1879–Oct. 3, 1951.
Supp. 5–186
Drumgoole, John Christopher, Aug. 15, 1816–Mar. 28, 1888.
Vol. 3, Pt. 1–462
Drury, John Benjamin, Aug. 15, 1838–Mar. 21, 1909.
Vol. 3, Pt. 1–463
Drury, Newton Bishop, Apr. 9, 1889–Dec. 14, 1978.
Supp. 10–190
Dryden, John Fairfield, Aug. 7, 1839–Nov. 24, 1911.
Vol. 3, Pt. 1–463
Dryfoos, Orvil E., Nov. 8, 1912–May 25, 1963.
Supp. 7–199
Duane, Alexander, Sept. 1, 1858–June 10, 1926.
Vol. 3, Pt. 1–464
Duane, James, Feb. 6, 1733–Feb. 1, 1797.
Vol. 3, Pt. 1–465
Duane, James Chatham, June 30, 1824–Nov. 8, 1897.
Vol. 3 Pt. 1–466
Duane, Wiliiam, May 17, 1760–Nov. 24, 1835.
Vol. 3, Pt. 1–467
Duane, William, Feb. 17, 1872–Mar. 7, 1935.
Supp. 1–266
Duane, William John, May 9, 1780–Sept. 26, 1865.
Vol. 3, Pt. 1–468
Dubbs, Joseph Henry, Oct. 5, 1838–Apr. 1, 1910.
Vol. 3, Pt. 1–469
Dubois, Augustus Jay, Apr. 25, 1849–Oct. 19, 1915.
Vol. 3, Pt. 1–470
Dubois, John, Aug. 24, 1764–Dec. 20, 1842.
Vol. 3, Pt. 1–470
Du Bois, Shirley Lola Graham, Nov. 11, 1904–Mar. 27, 1977.
Supp. 10–192
Du Bois, William Edward Burghardt, Feb. 23, 1868–Aug. 27, 1963.
Supp. 7–200
Du Bois, William Ewing, Dec. 15, 1810–July 14, 1881.
Vol. 3, Pt. 1–472
Du Bose, William Porcher, Apr. 11, 1836–Aug. 18, 1918.
Vol. 3, Pt. 1–472
Du Bourg, Louis Guillaume Valentin, Feb. 13, 1766–Dec. 12, 1833.
Vol. 3, Pt. 1–473
Dubuque, Julien, Jan. 10, 1762–Mar. 24, 1810.
Vol. 3, Pt. 1–475
Du Chaillu, Paul Belloni, July 31, 1835–Apr. 30, 1903.
Vol. 3, Pt. 1475
Duché, Jacob, Jan. 31, 1737/38–Jan. 3, 1798.
Vol. 3, Pt. 1–476
Duchesne, Rose Philippine, Aug. 29, 1769–Nov. 18, 1852.
Vol. 3, Pt. 1–477
Duchin, Edward Frank ("Eddy"), Apr. 1, 1909–Feb. 9, 1951.
Supp. 5–187
Dudley, Benjamin Winslow, Apr. 12, 1785–Jan. 20, 1870.
Vol. 3, Pt. 1–478
Dudley, Charles Benjamin, July 14, 1842–Dec. 21, 1909.
Vol. 3, Pt. 1–479
Dudley, Charles Edward, May 23, 1780–Jan. 23, 1841.
Vol. 3, Pt. 1–480
Dudley, Edward Bishop, Dec. 15, 1789–Oct. 30, 1855.
Vol. 3, Pt. 1–480
Dudley, Joseph, Sept. 23, 1647–Apr. 2, 1720.
Vol. 3, Pt. 1–481
Dudley, Paul, Sept. 3, 1675–Jan. 25, 1751.
Vol. 3, Pt. 1–483
Dudley, Thomas, 1576–July 31, 1653.
Vol. 3, Pt. 1–484
Dudley, William Russel, Mar. 1, 1849–June 4, 1911.
Vol. 3, Pt. 1–485
Duer, John, Oct. 7, 1782–Aug. 8, 1858.
Vol. 3, Pt. 1–485
Duer, William, Mar. 18, 1747–May 7, 1799.
Vol. 3, Pt. 1–486
Duer, William Alexander, Sept. 8, 1780–May 30, 1858.
Vol. 3, Pt. 1–488
Duff, James Henderson, Jan. 21, 1883–Dec. 20, 1969.
Supp. 8–143
Duff, Mary Ann Dyke, 1794–Sept. 5, 1857.
Vol. 3, Pt. 1–488
Duffield, George, Oct. 7, 1732–Feb. 2, 1790.
Vol. 3, Pt. 1–489
Duffield, George, July 4, 1794–June 26, 1868.
Vol. 3, Pt. 1–490
Duffield, Samuel Augustus Willoughby, Sept. 24, 1843–May 12, 1887.
Vol. 3, Pt. 1–491
Duffy, Edmund, Mar. 1, 1899–Sept. 13, 1962.
Supp. 7–205
Duffy, Francis Patrick, May 2, 1871–June 26, 1932.
Supp. 1–267
Duffy, Francis Ryan, June 23, 1888–Aug. 16, 1979.
Supp. 10–193
Duffy, Hugh, Nov. 26, 1866–Oct. 19, 1954.
Supp. 5–188
Dufour, John James, *c.* 1763–Feb. 9, 1827.
Vol. 3, Pt. 1–491
Duganne, Augustine Joseph Hickey, 1823–Oct. 20, 1884.
Vol. 3, Pt. 1–492
Dugdale, Richard Louis, 1841–July 23, 1883.
Vol. 3, Pt. 1–493
Duggar, Benjamin Minge, Sept. 1, 1872–Sept. 10, 1956.
Supp. 6–175
Dugué, Charles Oscar, May 1, 1821–Aug. 29, 1872.
Vol. 3, Pt. 1–493
Duhring, Louis Adolphus, Dec. 23, 1845–May 8, 1913.
Vol. 3, Pt. 1–494
Duke, Basil Wilson, May 28, 1838–Sept. 16, 1916.
Vol. 3, Pt. 1–495
Duke, Benjamin Newton, Apr. 27, 1855–Jan. 8, 1929.
Vol. 3, Pt. 1–496
Duke, James Buchanan, Dec. 23, 1856–Oct. 10, 1925.
Vol. 3, Pt. 1–497
Duke, Vernon, Oct. 10, 1903–Jan. 16, 1969.
Supp. 8–144
Dulany, Daniel, 1685–Dec. 5, 1753.
Vol. 3, Pt. 1–498
Dulany, Daniel, June 28, 1722–Mar. 17, 1797.
Vol. 3, Pt. 1–499
Dulles, Allen Welsh, Apr. 7, 1893–Jan. 29, 1969.
Supp. 8–146
Dulles, John Foster, Feb. 25, 1888–May 24, 1959.
Supp. 6–177
Duluth, Daniel Greysolon, Sieur, 1636–Feb. 25, 1710.
Vol. 3, Pt. 1–500
Dumaine, Frederic Christopher, Mar. 6, 1866–May 27, 1951.
Supp. 5–190
Dummer, Jeremiah, Sept. 14, 1645–May 25, 1718.
Vol. 3, Pt. 1–501
Dummer, Jeremiah, *c.* 1679–May 19, 1739.
Vol. 3, Pt. 1–502
Dumont, Allen Balcom, Jan. 29, 1901–Nov. 15, 1965.
Supp. 7–206
Dumont, Margaret, Oct. 20, 1889–Mar. 6, 1965.
Supp. 7–207
Dun, Robert Graham, Aug. 7, 1826–Nov. 10, 1900.
Vol. 3, Pt. 1–503
Dunbar, Charles Franklin, July 28, 1830–Jan. 29, 1900.
Vol. 3, Pt. 1–503
Dunbar, (Helen) Flanders, May 14, 1902–Aug. 21, 1959.
Supp. 6–180
Dunbar, Moses, June 14, 1746–Mar. 19, 1777.
Vol. 3, Pt. 1–504
Dunbar, Paul Laurence, June 27, 1872–Feb. 9, 1906.
Vol. 3, Pt. 1–505
Dunbar, Robert, Dec. 13, 1812–Sept. 18, 1890.
Vol. 3, Pt. 1–506
Dunbar, William, 1749–October 1810.
Vol. 3, Pt. 1–507
Duncan, Donald Franklin, June 6, 1891–May 15, 1971.
Supp. 9–245
Duncan, Isadora, May 27, 1878–Sept. 14, 1927.
Vol. 3, Pt. 1–508
Duncan, James, May 5, 1857–Sept. 14, 1928.
Supp. 1–269
Duncan, James, May 5, 1857–Sept. 14, 1928.
Vol. 3, Pt. 1–510
Duncan, Joseph, Feb. 22, 1794–Jan. 15, 1844.
Vol. 3, Pt. 1–510

Duncan, Robert Kennedy, Nov. 1, 1868–Feb. 18, 1914.
Vol. 3, Pt. 1–511
Dundee, Johnny, Nov. 22, 1893–Apr. 22, 1965.
Supp. 7–209
Dunglison, Robley, Jan. 4, 1798–April 1, 1869.
Vol. 3, Pt. 1–512
Dunham, Henry Morton, July 27, 1853–May 4, 1929.
Vol. 3, Pt. 1–513
Duniway, Abigail Jane Scott, Oct. 22, 1834–Oct. 11, 1915.
Vol. 3, Pt. 1–513
Dunlap, John, 1747–Nov. 27, 1812.
Vol. 3, Pt. 1–514
Dunlap, Robert Pinckney, Aug. 17, 1794–Oct. 20, 1859.
Vol. 3, Pt. 1–515
Dunlap, William, Feb. 19, 1766–Sept. 28, 1839.
Vol. 3, Pt. 1–516
Dunlop, James, 1795–April 9, 1856.
Vol. 3, Pt. 1–518
Dunmore, John Murray, Earl of, 1732–Mar. 5, 1809.
Vol. 3, Pt. 1–519
Dunn, Charles, Dec. 28, 1799–Apr. 7, 1872.
Vol. 3, Pt. 1–520
Dunn, Michael, Oct. 20, 1934–Aug. 29, 1973.
Supp. 9–246
Dunn, William McKee, Dec. 12, 1814–July 24, 1887.
Vol. 3, Pt. 1–521
Dunn, Williamson, Dec. 25, 1781–Nov. 11, 1854.
Vol. 3, Pt. 1–522
Dunne, Finley Peter, July 10, 1867–Apr. 24, 1936.
Supp. 2–158
Dunning, Albert Elijah, Jan. 5, 1844–Nov. 14, 1923.
Vol. 3, Pt. 1–522
Dunning, John Ray, Sept. 24, 1907–Aug. 25, 1975.
Supp. 9–248
Dunning, William Archibald, May 12, 1857–Aug. 25, 1922.
Vol. 3, Pt. 1–523
Dunster, Henry, 1609–Feb. 27, 1658/59?.
Vol. 3, Pt. 1–524
Dunwoody, William Hood, Mar. 14, 1841–Feb. 8, 1914.
Vol. 3, Pt. 1–524
Du Ponceau, Pierre Étienne, June 3, 1760–April 1, 1844.
Vol. 3, Pt. 1–525
Du Pont, Alfred Irénée, May 12. 1864–Apr. 29, 1935.
Supp. 1–270
Du Pont, Eleuthère Irénée, June 24, 1771–Oct. 31, 1834.
Vol. 3, Pt. 1–526
Du Pont, Francis Irénée, Dec. 3, 1873–Mar. 16, 1942.
Supp. 3–238
Du Pont, Henry, Aug. 8, 1812–Aug. 8, 1889.
Vol. 3, Pt. 1–528
Du Pont, Henry Algernon, July 30, 1838–Dec. 31, 1926.
Vol. 3, Pt. 1–528
Du Pont, Irénée, Dec. 21, 1876–Dec. 19, 1963.
Supp. 7–209
Du Pont, Lammot, Oct. 12, 1880–July 24, 1954.
Supp. 5–191
Du Pont, Pierre Samuel, Jan. 15, 1870–Apr. 5, 1954.
Supp. 5–192
Du Pont, Samuel Francis, Sept. 27, 1803–June 23, 1865.
Vol. 3, Pt. 1–529
Du Pont, Thomas Coleman, Dec. 11, 1863–Nov. 11, 1930.
Supp. 1–271
Du Pont, Victor Marie, Oct. 1, 1767–Jan. 30, 1827.
Vol. 3, Pt. 1–533
Dupratz, Antoine Simon Le Page, fl. 1718–1758.
Vol. 3, Pt. 1–534
Dupuy, Eliza Ann, 1814–Jan. 15, 1881.
Vol. 3, Pt. 1–534
Durand, Asher Brown, Aug. 21, 1796–Sept. 17, 1886.
Vol. 3, Pt. 1–535
Durand, Cyrus, Feb. 27, 1787–Sept. 18, 1868.
Vol. 3, Pt. 1–538
Durand, Élie Magloire, Jan. 25, 1794–Aug. 14, 1873.
Vol. 3, Pt. 1–538
Durand, William Frederick, Mar. 5, 1859–Aug. 9, 1958.
Supp. 6–181
Durant, Charles Ferson, Sept. 19, 1805–March 2, 1873.
Vol. 3, Pt. 1–540
Durant, Henry, June 18, 1802–Jan. 22, 1875.
Vol. 3, Pt. 1–540
Durant, Henry Fowle, Feb. 20, 1822–Oct. 3, 1881.
Vol. 3, Pt. 1–541
Durant, Thomas Clark, Feb. 6, 1820–Oct. 5, 1885.
Vol. 3, Pt. 1–542
Durant, Thomas Jefferson, Aug. 8, 1817–Feb. 3, 1882.
Vol. 3, Pt. 1–543
Durant, William Crapo, Dec. 8, 1861–Mar. 18, 1947.
Supp. 4–243
Durante, James Francis ("Jimmy"), Feb. 10, 1893–Jan. 29, 1980.
Supp. 10–195
Duranty, Walter, May 25, 1884–Oct. 3, 1957.
Supp. 6–183
Durbin, John Price, Oct. 10, 1800–Oct. 19, 1876.
Vol. 3, Pt. 1–544
Durell, Edward Henry, July 14, 1810–March 29, 1887.
Vol. 3, Pt. 1–545
Durfee, Job, Sept. 20, 1790–July 26, 1847.
Vol. 3, Pt. 1–546
Durfee, Thomas, Feb. 6, 1826–June 6, 1901.
Vol. 3, Pt. 1–546
Durfee, William Franklin, Nov. 15, 1833–Nov. 14, 1899.
Vol. 3, Pt. 1–547
Durfee, Zoheth Sherman, April 22, 1831–June 8, 1880.
Vol. 3, Pt. 1–548
Durham, Caleb Wheeler, Feb. 6, 1848–March 28, 1910.
Vol. 3, Pt. 1–549
Durivage, Francis Alexander, 1814–Feb. 1, 1881.
Vol. 3, Pt. 1–549
Durkee, John, Dec. 11, 1728–May 29, 1782.
Vol. 3, Pt. 1–550
Durkin, Martin Patrick, Mar. 18, 1894–Nov. 13, 1955.
Supp. 5–194
Durrett, Reuben Thomas, Jan. 22, 1824–Sept. 16, 1913.
Vol. 3, Pt. 1–550
Durrie, Daniel Steele, Jan. 2, 1819–Aug. 31, 1892.
Vol. 3, Pt. 1–451
Durstine, Roy Sarles, Dec. 13, 1886–Nov. 28, 1962.
Supp. 7–211
Duryea, Charles Edgar, Dec. 15, 1861–Sept. 28, 1938.
Supp. 2–160
Duryea, Hermanes Barkulo, Dec. 13, 1863–Jan. 25, 1916.
Vol. 3, Pt. 1–552
Duryea, James Frank, Oct. 8, 1869–Feb. 15, 1967.
Supp. 8–148
Duryée, Abram, April 29, 1815–Sept. 27, 1890.
Vol. 3, Pt. 1–553
Du Simitièrre, Pierre Eugène, *c.* 1736–Oct. 1784.
Vol. 3, Pt. 1–553
Dusser de Barenne, Joannes Gregorius, June 6, 1885–June 9, 1940.
Supp. 2–161
Dustin, Hannah, b. Dec. 23, 1657.
Vol. 3, Pt. 1–554
Dutton, Clarence Edward, May 15, 1841–Jan. 4, 1912.
Vol. 3, Pt. 1–555
Dutton, Henry, Feb. 12, 1796–Apr. 12, 1869.
Vol. 3, Pt. 1–555
Dutton, Samuel Train, Oct. 16, 1849–Mar. 28, 1919.
Vol. 3, Pt. 1–556
Duval, William Pope, 1784–Mar. 19, 1854.
Vol. 3, Pt. 1–557
Duvall, Gabriel, Dec. 6, 1752–Mar. 6, 1844.
Supp. 1–272
Duveneck, Frank, Oct. 9, 1848–Jan. 3, 1919.
Vol. 3, Pt. 1–558
Du Vigneaud, Vincent, May 18, 1901–Dec. 11, 1978.
Supp. 10–196
Duyckinck, Evert Augustus, Nov. 23, 1816–Aug. 13, 1878.
Vol. 3, Pt. 1–561
Duyckinck, George Long, Oct. 17, 1823–Mar. 30, 1863.
Vol. 3, Pt. 1–562
Dwenger, Joseph, Sept. 7, 1837–Jan. 22, 1893.
Vol. 3, Pt. 1–562
Dwiggins, William Addison, June 19, 1880–Dec. 25, 1956.
Supp. 6–185
Dwight, Arthur Smith, Mar. 18, 1864–Apr. 1, 1946.
Supp. 4–245
Dwight, Benjamin Woodbridge, Apr. s, 1816–Sept. 18, 1889.
Vol. 3, Pt. 1–563

Dwight, Edmund, Nov. 28, 1780–Apr. 1, 1849.
Vol. 3, Pt. 1–563
Dwight, Francis, Mar. 14, 1808–Dec. 15, 1845.
Vol. 3, Pt. 1–564
Dwight, Harrison Gray Otis, Nov. 22, 1803–Jan. 25, 1862.
Vol. 3, Pt. 1–565
Dwight, Henry Otis, June 3, 1843–June 20, 1917.
Vol. 3, Pt. 1–566
Dwight, John Sullivan, May 13, 1813–Sept. 5, 1893.
Vol. 3, Pt. 1–567
Dwight, Nathaniel, Jan. 31, 1770–June 11, 1831.
Vol. 3, Pt. 1–568
Dwight, Sereno Edwards, May 18, 1786–Nov. 30, 1850.
Vol.3, Pt. 1–569
Dwight, Theodore, Mar. 3, 1796–Oct. 16, 1866.
Vol. 3 Pt. 1–570
Dwight, Theodore. Dec. 15, 1764–June 12, 1846.
Vol. 3, Pt. 1–569
Dwight, Theodore William, July 18, 1822–June 29, 1892.
Vol. 3, Pt. 1–571
Dwight, Thomas, Oct. 13, 1843–Sept. 9, 1911.
Vol. 3, Pt. 1–573
Dwight, Timothy, May 14, 1752–Jan. 11, 1817.
Vol. 3, Pt. 1–573
Dwight, Timothy, Nov. 16, 1828–May 26, 1916.
Vol. 3, Pt. 1–577
Dwight, William, July 14, 1831–Apr. 21, 1888.
Vol. 3, Pt. 1–578
Dworshak, Henry Clarence, Aug. 29, 1894–July 23, 1962.
Supp. 7–212
Dyar, Harrison Gray, Feb. 14, 1866–Jan. 21, 1929.
Vol. 3, Pt. 1–578
Dye, William McEntyre, Feb. 1831–Nov. 13, 1899.
Vol. 3, Pt. 1–579
Dyer, Alexander Brydie, Jan. 10, 1815–May 20, 1874.
Vol. 3, Pt. 1–580
Dyer, Eliphalet, Sept. 14, 1721–May 13, 1807.
Vol. 3, Pt. 1–581
Dyer, Isadore, Nov. 2, 1865–Oct. 12, 1920.
Vol. 3, Pt. 1–582
Dyer, Louis, Sept. 30, 1851–July 20, 1908.
Vol. 3, Pt. 1–582
Dyer, Mary, d. June 1, 1660.
Vol. 3, Pt. 1–584
Dyer, Nehemiah Mayo, Feb. 19, 1839–Jan. 27, 1910.
Vol. 3, Pt. 1–584
Dyer, Rolla Eugene, Nov. 4, 1886–June 2, 1971.
Supp. 9–249
Dyett, Thomas Ben, 1886–Nov. 2, 1971.
Supp. 9–250
Dykstra, Clarence Addison, Feb. 25, 1883–May 6, 1950.
Supp. 4–246
Dykstra, John, Apr. 6, 1898–Mar. 2, 1972.
Supp. 9–251
Dylander, John, *c.* 1709–Nov. 2, 1741.
Vol. 3, Pt. 1–585
Dymond, John, May 3, 1836–Mar. 5, 1922.
Vol. 3, Pt. 1–585
Dyott, Thomas W., 1771–Jan. 17, 1861.
Vol. 3, Pt. 1–586

Eads, James Buchanan, May 23, 1820–Mar. 8, 1887.
Vol. 3, Pt. 1–587
Eagels, Jeanne, June 26, 1894(1890?)-Oct. 3, 1929.
Vol. 3, Pt. 1–589
Eakins, Thomas, July 25, 1844–June 25, 1916.
Vol. 3, Pt. 1–590
Eames, Charles, Mar. 20, 1812–Mar. 16, 1867.
Vol. 3, Pt. 1–592
Eames, Charles Ormand, Jr., June 17, 1907–Aug. 21, 1978.
Supp. 10–199
Eames, Wilberforce, Oct. 12, 1855–Dec. 6, 1937.
Supp. 2–162
Earhart, Amelia Mary, July 24, 1897–July 2?, 1937.
Supp. 2–163
Earle, Alice Morse, Apr. 27, 1853–Feb. 16, 1911.
Vol. 3, Pt. 1–593
Earle, Edward Mead, May 20, 1894–June 24, 1954.
Supp. 5–195
Earle, George Howard, III, Dec. 5, 1890–Dec. 30, 1974.
Supp. 9–253
Earle, James, May 1, 1761–Aug. 18, 1796.
Vol. 3, Pt. 1–594
Earle, Mortimer Lamson, Oct. 14, 1864–Sept. 26, 1905.
Vol. 3, Pt. 1–594
Earle, Pliny, Dec. 17, 1762–Nov. 29, 1832.
Vol. 3, Pt. 1–595
Earle, Pliny (son of Pliny), Dec. 31, 1809–May 17, 1892.
Vol. 3, Pt. 1–595
Earle, Ralph, May 11, 1751–Aug. 16, 1801.
Vol. 3, Pt. 1–596
Earle, Ralph, May 3, 1874–Feb. 13, 1939.
Supp. 2–165
Earle, Thomas, Apr. 21, 1796–July 14, 1849.
Vol. 3, Pt. 1–597
Early, John, Jan. 1, 1786–Nov. 5, 1873.
Vol. 3, Pt. 1–597
Early, Jubal Anderson, Nov. 3, 1816–Mar. 2, 1894.
Vol. 3, Pt. 1–598
Early, Peter, June 20, 1773–Aug. 15, 1817.
Vol. 3, Pt. 1–599
Early, Stephen Tyree, Aug. 27, 1889–Aug. 11, 1951.
Supp. 1–196
Easley, Ralph Montgomery, Feb. 25, 1856–Sept. 7, 1939.
Supp. 2–166
East, Edward Murray, Oct. 4, 1879–Nov. 9, 1938.
Supp. 2–167
Easter, Luscious Luke, Aug. 4, 1915–Mar. 29, 1979.
Supp. 10–201
Eastman, Arthur MacArthur, June 8, 1810–Sept. 3, 1877.
Vol. 3, Pt. 1–600
Eastman, Charles Gamage, June 1, 1816–Sept. 16, 1860.
Vol. 3, Pt. 1–600
Eastman, Enoch Worthen, Apr. 15, 1810–Jan. 9, 1885.
Vol. 3, Pt. 1–601
Eastman, George, July 12, 1854–Mar. 14, 1932.
Supp. 1–274
Eastman, Harvey Gridley, Oct. 16, 1832–July 13, 1878.
Vol. 3, Pt. 1–602
Eastman, John Robie, July 29, 1836–Sept. 26, 1913.
Vol. 3, Pt. 1–602
Eastman, Joseph Bartlett, June 26, 1882–Mar. 15, 1944.
Supp. 3–240
Eastman, Max Forrester, Jan. 4, 1883–Mar. 25, 1969.
Supp. 8–149
Eastman, Timothy Corser, May 30, 1821–Oct. 11, 1893.
Vol. 3, Pt. 1–603
Eastman, William Reed, Oct. 19, 1835–Mar. 25, 1925.
Vol. 3, Pt. 1–604
Easton, John, *c.* 1625–Dec. 12, 1705.
Vol. 3, Pt. 1–604
Easton, Nichoias, 1593–Aug. 15, 1675.
Vol. 3, Pt. 1–605
Eaton, Amos, May 17, 1776–May 10, 1842.
Vol. 3, Pt. 1–605
Eaton, Benjamin Harrison, Dec. 15, 1833–Oct. 29, 1904.
Vol. 3, Pt. 1–606
Eaton, Charles Aubrey, Mar. 29, 1868–Jan. 23, 1953.
Supp. 5–197
Eaton, Cyrus Stephen, Dec. 27, 1883–May 9, 1979.
Supp. 10–203
Eaton, Daniel Cady, Sept. 12, 1834–June 29, 1895.
Vol. 3, Pt. 1–606
Eaton, Dorman Bridgman, June 27, 1823–Dec. 23, 1899.
Vol. 3, Pt. 1–607
Eaton, Homer, Nov. 16, 1834–Feb. 9, 1913.
Vol. 3, Pt. 1–608
Eaton, John, Dec. 5, 1829–Feb. 9, 1906.
Vol. 3, Pt. 1–608
Eaton, John Henry, June 18, 1790–Nov. 17, 1856.
Vol. 3, Pt. 1–609
Eaton, Joseph Oriel, Feb 8, 1829–Feb. 7, 1875.
Vol. 3, Pt. 1–610
Eaton, Margaret L. O'Neill. [*See* O'Neale, Margaret, 1796–1879.]
Eaton, Nathaniel, *c.* 1609–1674.
Vol. 3, Pt. 1–611
Eaton, Samuel, 1596?–Jan. 9, 1665.
Vol. 3, Pt. 1–611
Eaton, Theophilus, 1590–Jan. 7, 1658.
Vol. 3, Pt. 1–612

Eaton, William, Feb. 23, 1764–June 1, 1811.
Vol. 3 Pt. 1–613
Eaton, Wyatt, May 6, 1849–June 7, 1896.
Vol. 3, Pt. 1–613
Eberle, Edward Walter, Aug. 17, 1864–July 6, 1929.
Vol. 3, Pt. 1–614
Eberle, John, Dec. 10, 1787–Feb. 2, 1838.
Vol. 3, Pt. 1–615
Eccles, Marriner Stoddard, Sept. 9, 1890–Dec. 18, 1977.
Supp. 10–204
Echols, John, Mar. 20, 1823–May 24, 1896.
Vol. 3 Pt. 2–1
Eckart, Wiliiam Roberts, June 17, 1841–Dec. 8, 1914.
Vol. 3, Pt. 2–2
Eckels, James Herron, Nov. 22, 1858–Apr. 14, 1907.
Vol. 3, Pt. 2–3
Eckert, Thomas Thompson, Apr. 23, 1825–Oct. 20, 1910.
Vol. 3, Pt. 2–3
Eckford, Henry, Mar. 12, 1775–Nov. 12, 1832.
Vol. 3, Pt. 2–4
Eckstein, John, *c.* 1750–*c.* 1817.
Vol. 3, Pt. 2–5
Eckstorm, Fannie Hardy, June 18, 1865–Dec. 31, 1946.
Supp. 4–248
Eddis, William, fl. 1769–1777.
Vol. 3, Pt. 2–5
Eddy, Clarence, June 23, 1851–Jan. 10, 1937.
Supp. 2–168
Eddy, Daniel Clarke, May 21, 1823–July 26, 1896.
Vol. 3, Pt. 2–6
Eddy, Harrison Prescott, Apr. 29, 1870–June 15, 1937.
Supp. 2–169
Eddy, Henry Turner, June 9, 1844–Dec. 11, 1921.
Vol. 3, Pt. 2–7
Eddy, Manton Sprague, May 16, 1892–Apr. 10, 1962.
Supp. 7–213
Eddy, Mary Morse Baker, July 16, 1821–Dec. 3, 1910.
Vol. 3, Pt. 2–7
Eddy, Nelson, June 29, 1901–Mar. 6, 1967.
Supp. 8–150
Eddy, Thomas, Sept. 5, 1758–Sept. 16, 1827.
Vol. 3, Pt. 2–15
Edebohls, George Michael, May 8, 1853–Aug. 8, 1908.
Vol. 3, Pt. 2–15
Eden, Charles, 1673–Mar. 26, 1722.
Vol. 3, Pt. 2–16
Eden, Robert, Sept. 14, 1741–Sept. 2, 1784.
Vol. 3, Pt. 2–16
Edes, Benjamin, Oct. 14, 1732–Dec. 11, 1803.
Vol. 3, Pt. 2–17
Edes, Robert Thaxter, Sept. 23, 1838–Jan. 12, 1923.
Vol. 3, Pt. 2–18
Edeson, Robert, June 3, 1868–Mar. 24, 1931.
Supp. 1–277
Edgar, Charles, Apr. 9, 1862–Feb. 15, 1922.
Vol. 3, Pt. 2–18
Edge, Walter Evans, Nov. 20, 1873–Oct. 29, 1956.
Supp. 6–186
Edgerton, Alfred Peck, Jan. 11, 1813–May 14, 1897.
Vol. 3, Pt. 2–19
Edgerton, Sidney, Aug. 17, 1818–July 19, 1900.
Vol. 3, Pt. 2–20
Edgrene, August Hjalmar, Oct. 18, 1840–Dec. 9, 1903.
Vol. 3, Pt. 2–20
Edison, Charles, Aug. 3, 1890–July 31, 1969.
Supp. 8–151
Edison, Thomas Alva, Feb. 11, 1847–Oct. 18, 1931.
Supp. 1–277
Edman, Irwin, Nov. 28, 1896–Sept. 4, 1954.
Supp. 5–198
Edmands, John, Feb. 1, 1820–Oct. 17, 1915.
Vol. 3, Pt. 2–21
Edmonds, Francis William, Nov. 22, 1806–Feb. 7, 1863.
Vol. 3, Pt. 2–22
Edmonds, John Worth, Mar. 13, 1799–Apr. 5, 1874.
Vol. 3, Pt. 2–23
Edmondson, William, 1882?–Feb. 7, 1951.
Supp. 5–199
Edmunds, Charles Wallis, Feb. 22, 1873–Mar. 1, 1941.
Supp. 3–242
Edmunds, George Franklin, Feb. 1, 1828–Feb. 27, 1919.
Vol. 3, Pt. 2–24
Edsall, David Linn, July 6, 1869–Aug. 12, 1945.
Supp. 3–243
Edwards, Bela Bates, July 4, 1802–Apr. 20, 1852.
Vol. 3, Pt. 2–27
Edwards, Charles, Mar. 17, 1797–May 30, 1868.
Vol. 3, Pt. 2–27
Edwards, Clarence Ransom, Jan. 1, 1860–Feb. 14, 1931.
Supp. 1–281
Edwards, Everett Eugene, Feb. 12, 1900–May 1, 1952.
Supp. 5–201
Edwards, Henry Waggaman, Oct. 1779–July 22, 1847.
Vol. 3, Pt. 2–28
Edwards, John, *c.* 1671–Apr. 8, 1746.
Vol. 3, Pt. 2–29
Edwards, John, 1748–1837.
Vol. 3, Pt. 2–29
Edwards, Jonathan, May 26, 1745–Aug. 1, 1801.
Vol. 3, Pt. 2–37
Edwards, Jonathan, Oct. 5, 1703–Mar. 22, 1758.
Vol. 3, Pt. 2–30
Edwards, Julian, Dec. 11, 1855–Sept. 5, 1910.
Vol. 3, Pt. 2–39
Edwards, Justin, Apr. 25, 1787–July 23, 1853.
Vol. 3, Pt. 2–39
Edwards, Morgan, May 9, 1722 o.s.–Jan. 28, 1795.
Vol. 3, Pt. 2–40
Edwards, Ninian, Mar. 17, 1775–July 20, 1833.
Vol. 3, Pt. 2–41
Edwards, Ninian Wirt, Apr. 15, 1809–Sept. 2, 1889.
Vol. 3, Pt. 2–42
Edwards, Oliver, Jan. 30, 1835–Apr. 28, 1904.
Vol. 3, Pt. 2–43
Edwards, Pierpont, Apr. 8, 1750–Apr. 5, 1826.
Vol. 3, Pt. 2–43
Edwards, Richard Stanislaus, Feb. 18, 1885–June 2, 1956.
Supp. 6–188
Edwards, Talmadge, 1747–June 4, 1821.
Vol. 3, Pt. 2–44
Edwards, Weldon Nathaniel, Jan. 25, 1788–Dec. 18, 1873.
Vol. 3, Pt. 2–45
Edwards, William, Nov. 11, 1770–Dec. 29, 1851.
Vol. 3, Pt. 2–46
Edwards, William Henry, Mar. 15, 1822–Apr. 4, 1909.
Vol. 3, Pt. 2–46
Edwin, David, Dec. 1776–Feb. 22, 1841.
Vol. 3, Pt. 2–47
Eells, Dan Parmelee. Apr. 16, 1825–Aug. 23, 1903.
Vol. 3, Pt. 2–48
Egan, Maurice Francis, May 24, 1852–Jan. 15, 1924.
Vol. 3, Pt. 2–49
Egan, Michael, 1761–July 22, 1814.
Vol. 3, Pt. 2–50
Egan, Patrick, Aug. 13, 1841–Sept. 30, 1919.
Vol. 3, Pt. 2–51
Eggleston, Edward, Dec. 10, 1837–Sept. 2, 1902.
Vol. 3, Pt. 2–52
Eggleston, George Cary, Nov. 26, 1839–Apr. 14, 1911.
Vol. 3, Pt. 254
Egle, William Henry, Sept. 17, 1830–Feb. 19, 1901.
Vol. 3, Pt. 2–55
Egleston, Thomas, Dec. 9, 1832–Jan. 15, 1900.
Vol. 3, Pt. 2–56
Eglevsky, André Yevgenyevich, Dec. 21, 1917–Dec. 4, 1977.
Supp. 10–206
Egtvedt, Clairmont ("Claire") Leroy, Oct. 18, 1892–Oct. 19, 1975.
Supp. 9–255
Ehninger, John Whetten, July 22, 1827–Jan. 22, 1889.
Vol. 3, Pt. 2–56
Ehrlich, Arnold Bogumil, Jan. 15, 1848–Nov. 5, 1919.
Vol. 3, Pt. 257
Eichberg, Julius, June 13, 1824–Jan. 18, 1893.
Vol. 3, Pt. 2–57
Eichelberger, Clark Mell, July 29, 1896–Jan. 26, 1980.
Supp. 10–208
Eichelberger, Robert Lawrence, Mar. 9, 1886–Sept. 26, 1961.
Supp. 7–214
Eichholtz, Jacob, Nov. 2, 1776–May 11, 1842.
Vol. 3, Pt. 2–58

Eickemeyer, Rudolf, Oct. 31, 1831–Jan. 23, 1895.
Vol. 3, Pt. 2–59
Eidlitz, Cyrus Lazelle Warner, July 27, 1853–Oct. 5, 1921.
Vol. 3, Pt. 2–60
Eidlitz, Leopold, Mar. 29, 1823–Mar. 22, 1908.
Vol. 3, Pt. 2–61
Eielsen, Elling, Sept. 19, 1804–Jan. 10, 1883.
Vol. 3, Pt. 2–61
Eigenmann, Carl H., Mar. 9, 1863–Apr. 24, 1927.
Vol. 3, Pt. 2–62
Eilers, Frederic Anton, Jan. 14, 1839–Apr. 22, 1917.
Vol. 3, Pt. 2–63
Eilshemius, Louis Michel, Feb. 4, 1864–Dec. 29, 1941.
Supp. 3–244
Eimbeck, William, Jan. 29, 1841–Mar. 27, 1909.
Vol. 3, Pt. 2–64
Einhorn, David, Nov. 10, 1809–Nov. 2, 1879.
Vol. 3, Pt. 2–65
Einstein, Albert, Mar. 14, 1879–Apr. 18, 1955.
Supp. 5–202
Eiseley, Loren Corey, Sept. 3, 1907–July 9, 1977.
Supp. 10–209
Eisenhart, Luther Pfahler, Jan. 13, 1876–Oct. 28, 1965.
Supp. 7–216
Eisenhower, Dwight David, Oct. 14, 1890–Mar. 28, 1969.
Supp. 8–153
Eisenhower, Mamie Geneva Doud, Nov. 14, 1896–Nov. 1, 1979.
Supp. 10–210
Eisler, Gerhart, Feb. 20, 1897–Mar. 21, 1968.
Supp. 8–161
Eklund, Carl Robert, Jan. 27, 1909–Nov. 4, 1962.
Supp. 7–216
Elbert, Samuel, 1740–Nov. 1, 1788.
Vol. 3, Pt. 2–65
Elder, Ruth, Sept. 12, 1904–Oct. 9, 1977.
Supp. 10–213
Elder, Samuel James, Jan. 4, 1850–Jan. 22, 1918.
Vol. 3, Pt. 2–66
Elder, Susan Blanchard, Apr. 19, 1835–Nov. 3, 1923.
Vol. 3, Pt. 2–67
Elder, William, July 23, 1806–Apr. 5, 1885.
Vol. 3, Pt. 2–68
Elder, William Henry, Mar. 22, 1819–Oct. 31, 1904.
Vol. 3, Pt. 2–69
Eldridge, Shalor Winchell, Aug. 29, 1816–Jan. 16, 1899.
Vol. 3, Pt. 2–69
Eliot, Charles, Nov. 1, 1859–Mar. 25, 1897.
Vol. 3, Pt. 2–70
Eliot, Charies William, Mar. 20, 1834–Aug. 22, 1926.
Vol. 3, Pt. 2–71
Eliot, Jared, Nov. 7, 1685–Apr. 22, 1763.
Vol. 3, Pt. 2–78
Eliot, John, 1604–May 21, 1690.
Vol. 3, Pt. 2–79
Eliot, Samuel, Dec. 22, 1821–Sept. 14, 1898.
Vol. 3, Pt. 2–80
Eliot, Samuel Atkins, Mar. 5, 1798–Jan. 29, 1862.
Vol. 3, Pt. 2–81
Eliot, T(homas) S(tearns), Sept. 26, 1888–Jan. 4, 1965.
Supp. 7–217
Eliot, William Greenleaf, Aug. 5, 1811–Jan. 23, 1887.
Vol. 3, Pt. 2–82
Elkin, William Lewis, Apr. 29, 1855–May 30, 1933.
Supp. 1–282
Elkins, Stephen Benton, Sept. 26, 1841–Jan. 4, 1911.
Vol. 3, Pt. 2–83
Elkins, William Lukens, May 2, 1832–Nov. 7, 1903.
Vol. 3, Pt. 2–84
Ellender, Allen Joseph, Sept. 24, 1890–July 27, 1972.
Supp. 9–256.
Ellery, Frank, July 23, 1794–Mar. 24, 1871.
Vol. 3, Pt. 2–85
Ellery, William, Dec. 22, 1727–Feb. 15, 1820.
Vol. 3, Pt. 2–86
Ellet, Charles, Jan. 1, 1810–June 21, 1862.
Vol. 3, Pt. 2–87
Ellet, Elizabeth Fries Lummis, Oct. 1818–June 3, 1877.
Vol. 3, Pt. 2–88
Ellicott, Andrew, Jan. 24, 1754–Aug. 28, 1820.
Vol. 3, Pt. 2–89
Ellicott, Joseph, Nov. 1, 1760–Aug. 19, 1826.
Vol. 3, Pt. 2–90
Ellington, Earl Buford, June 27, 1907–Apr. 3, 1972.
Supp. 9–257
Ellington, Edward Kennedy ("Duke"), Apr. 29, 1899–May 24, 1974.
Supp. 9–259
Elliot, Cass ("Mama"), Sept. 19, 1941–July 29, 1974.
Supp. 9–261
Elliot, Daniel Giraud, Mar. 7, 1835–Dec. 22, 1915.
Vol. 3, Pt. 2–91
Elliot, James, Aug. 18, 1775–Nov. 10, 1839.
Vol. 3, Pt. 2–92
Elliot, Jonathan, 1784–Mar. 12, 1846.
Vol. 3, Pt. 2–92
Elliott, Aaron Marshall, Jan. 24, 1844–Nov. 9, 1910.
Vol. 3, Pt. 2–93
Elliott, Benjamin, Mar. 1787–Sept. 1836.
Vol. 3, Pt. 2–94
Elliott, Charles, May 16, 1792–Jan. 8, 1869.
Vol. 3, Pt. 2–95
Elliott, Charles Burke, Jan. 6, 1861–Sept. 18, 1935.
Supp. 1–283
Elliott, Charles Loring, Oct. 12, 1812–Aug. 25, 1868.
Vol. 3, Pt. 2–95
Elliott, Jesse Duncan, July 14, 1782–Dec. 10, 1845.
Vol. 3 Pt. 2–96
Elliott, John, Apr. 22, 1858–May 26, 1925.
Vol. 3, Pt. 2–97
Elliott, John Lovejoy, Dec. 2, 1868–Apr. 12, 1942.
Supp. 3–246
Elliott, Maxine, Feb. 5, 1871–Mar. 5, 1940.
Supp. 2–170
Elliott, Sarah Barnwell, 1848–Aug. 30, 1928.
Vol. 3, Pt. 2–98
Elliott, Stephen, Nov. 11, 1771–Mar. 28, 1830.
Vol. 3, Pt. 2–99
Elliott, Walter Hackett Robert, Jan. 6, 1842–Apr. 18, 1928.
Vol. 3, Pt. 2–99
Elliott, Washington Lafayette, Mar. 31, 1825–June 29, 1888.
Vol. 3, Pt. 2–100
Elliott, William, Apr. 27, 1788–Feb. 3, 1863.
Vol. 3, Pt. 2–101
Elliott, William Yandell, III, May 13, 1896–Jan. 9, 1979.
Supp. 10–214
Ellis, Calvin, Aug. 15, 1826–Dec. 14, 1883.
Vol. 3, Pt. 2–101
Ellis, Carleton, Sept. 20, 1876–Jan. 13, 1941.
Supp. 3–247
Ellis, Clyde Taylor, Dec. 21, 1908–Feb. 9, 1980.
Supp. 10–218
Ellis, Edward Sylvester, Apr. 11, 1840–June 20, 1916.
Vol. 3, Pt. 2–102
Ellis, George Edward, Aug. 8, 1814–Dec. 20, 1894.
Vol. 3, Pt. 2–103
Ellis, George Washington, May 4, 1875–Nov. 26, 1919.
Vol. 3, Pt. 2–104
Ellis, Henry, Aug. 29, 1721–Jan. 21, 1806.
Vol. 3, Pt. 2–104
Ellis, Job Bicknell, Jan. 21, 1829–Dec. 30, 1905.
Vol. 3, Pt. 2–105
Ellis, John Washington, July 15, 1817–Dec. 28, 1910.
Vol. 3, Pt. 2–106
Ellis, John Willis, Nov. 23, 1820–July 7, 1861.
Vol. 3, Pt. 2–106
Ellis, Powhatan, Jan. 17, 1790–Mar. 18, 1863.
Vol. 3, Pt. 2–108
Ellis, Seth Hockett, Jan. 3, 1830–June 23, 1904.
Vol. 3, Pt. 2–108
Ellmaker, (Emmett) Lee, Aug. 7, 1896–Mar. 27, 1951.
Supp. 5–204
Ellsworth, Elmer Ephraim, Apr. 11, 1837–May 24, 1861.
Vol. 3, Pt. 2–109
Ellsworth, Henry Leavitt, Nov. 10, 1791–Dec. 27, 1858.
Vol. 3, Pt. 2–110
Ellsworth, Henry William, Apr. 7, 1814–Aug. 14, 1864.
Vol. 3, Pt. 2–111
Ellsworth, Lincoln, May 12, 1880–May 26, 1951.
Supp. 5–205
Ellsworth, Oliver, Apr. 29, 1745–Nov. 26, 1807.
Vol. 3, Pt. 2–111

Ellsworth, William Wolcott, Nov. 10, 1791–Jan. 15, 1868.
Vol. 3, Pt. 2–115
Elman, Harry ("Ziggy"), May 26, 1914–June 26, 1968.
Supp. 8–162
Elman, Mischa, Jan. 20, 1891–Apr. 5, 1967.
Supp. 8–164
Elman, Robert, Nov. 9, 1897–Dec. 23, 1956.
Supp. 6–189
Elmer, Ebenezer, Aug. 23, 1752–Oct. 18, 1843.
Vol. 3, Pt. 2–116
Elmer, Jonathan, Nov. 29, 1745–Sept. 3, 1817.
Vol. 3, Pt. 2–116
Elmer, Lucius Quintius Cincinnatus, Feb. 3, 1793–Mar. 11, 1883.
Vol. 3, Pt. 2–117
Elmore, Franklin Harper, Oct. 15, 1799–May 29, 1850.
Vol. 3, Pt. 2–118
Elmslie, George Grant, Feb. 20, 1871–Apr. 23, 1952.
Supp. 5–207
Elsberg, Charles Albert, Aug. 24, 1871–March 18, 1948.
Supp. 4–249
Elsberg, Louis, Apr. 2, 1836–Feb. 19, 1885.
Vol. 3, Pt. 2–119
Elson, Louis Charles, Apr. 17, 1848–Feb. 14, 1920.
Vol. 3, Pt. 2–119
Elvehjem, Conrad Arnold, May 27, 1901–July 27, 1962.
Supp. 7–223
Elwell, Frank Edwin, June 15, 1858–Jan. 23, 1922.
Vol. 3, Pt. 2–120
Elwell, John Johnson, June 22, 1820–Mar. 13, 1900.
Vol. 3, Pt. 2–122
Elwyn, Alfred Langdon, July 9, 1804–Mar. 15, 1884.
Vol. 3, Pt. 2–122
Ely, Hanson Edward, Nov. 23, 1867–Apr. 28, 1958.
Supp. 6–190
Ely, Richard Theodore, Apr. 13, 1854–Oct. 4, 1943.
Supp. 3–248
Elzey, Arnold, Dec. 18, 1816–Feb. 21, 1871.
Vol. 3, Pt. 2–123
Embree, Edwin Rogers, July 31, 1883–Feb. 21, 1950.
Supp. 4–250
Embree, Elihu, Nov. 11, 1782–Dec. 4, 1820.
Vol. 3, Pt. 2–124
Embury, Emma Catherine, *c.* 1806–Feb. 10, 1863.
Vol. 3, Pt. 2–124
Embury, Philip, 1728–1773.
Vol. 3, Pt. 2–125
Emerson, Benjamin Kendall, Dec. 20, 1843–Apr. 7, 1932.
Supp. 1–284
Emerson, Edward Waldo, July 10, 1844–Jan. 27, 1930.
Vol. 3, Pt. 2–126
Emerson, Ellen Russell, Jan. 16, 1837–June 12, 1907.
Vol. 3, Pt. 2–126
Emerson, George Barrell, Sept. 12, 1797–Mar. 4, 1881.
Vol. 3, Pt. 2–127
Emerson, Gouverneur, Aug. 4, 1795–July 2, 1874.
Vol. 3, Pt. 2–128
Emerson, Haven, Oct. 19, 1874–May 21, 1957.
Supp. 6–192
Emerson, James Ezekiel, Nov. 2, 1823–Feb. 17, 1900.
Vol. 3, Pt. 2–129
Emerson, Joseph, Oct. 13, 1777–May 14, 1833.
Vol. 3, Pt. 2–129
Emerson, Mary Moody, Aug. 25, 1774–May 1, 1863.
Vol. 3, Pt. 2–130
Emerson, Oliver Farrar, May 24, 1860–Mar. 13, 1927.
Vol. 3, Pt. 2–131
Emerson, Ralph, May 8, 1831–Aug. 19, 1914.
Vol. 3, Pt. 2–131
Emerson, Ralph Waldo, May 25, 1803–Apr. 27, 1882.
Vol. 3, Pt. 2–132
Emerson, Rollins Adams, May 5, 1873–Dec. 8, 1947.
Supp. 4–252
Emerson, William, May 6, 1769–May 12, 1811.
Vol. 3, Pt. 2–141
Emerton, Ephraim, Feb. 18, 1851–Mar. 3, 1935.
Supp. 1–285
Emerton, James Henry, Mar. 31, 1847–Dec. 5, 1930.
Supp. 1–286
Emery, Albert Hamilton, June 21, 1834–Dec. 2, 1926.
Vol. 3, Pt. 2–142
Emery, Charles Edward, Mar. 29, 1838–June 1, 1898.
Vol. 3, Pt. 2–142
Emery, Henry Crosby, Dec. 21, 1872–Feb. 6, 1924.
Vol. 3, Pt. 2–143
Emery, Lucilius Alonzo, July 27, 1840–Aug. 26, 1920.
Vol. 3, Pt. 2–144
Emery, Stephen Albert, Oct. 4, 1841–Apr. 15, 1891.
Vol. 3, Pt. 2–145
Emmet, Thomas Addis, Apr. 24, 1764–Nov. 14, 1827.
Vol. 3, Pt. 2–145
Emmet, Thomas Addis, May 29, 1828–Mar. 1, 1919.
Vol. 3, Pt. 2–147
Emmet, William Le Roy, July 10, 1859–Sept. 26, 1941.
Supp. 3–251
Emmett, Burton, Nov. 11, 1871–May 6, 1935.
Supp. 1–287
Emmett, Daniel Decatur, Oct. 29, 1815–June 28, 1904.
Vol. 3, Pt. 2–148
Emmons, Ebenezer, May 16, 1799–Oct. 1, 1863.
Vol. 3, Pt. 2–149
Emmons, George Foster, Aug. 23, 1811–July 23, 1884.
Vol. 3, Pt. 2–149
Emmons, Nathanael, Apr. 20, 1745 o.s.–Sept. 23, 1840.
Vol. 3, Pt. 2–150
Emmons, Samuel Franklin, Mar. 29, 1841–Mar. 28, 1911.
Vol. 3, Pt. 2–151
Emory, John, Apr. 11, 1789–Dec. 16, 1835.
Vol. 3, Pt. 2–152
Emory, William Hemsley, Sept. 7, 1811–Dec. 1, 1887.
Vol. 3, Pt. 2–153
Emott, James, Mar. 14, 1771–Apr. 7, 1850.
Vol. 3, Pt. 2–154
Emott, James, Apr. 23, 1823–Sept. 11, 1884.
Vol. 3, Pt. 2–154
Endecott, John, *c.* 1589–Mar. 15, 1665.
Vol. 3, Pt. 2–155
Endicott, Charles Moses, Dec. 6, 1793–Dec. 14, 1863.
Vol. 3, Pt. 2–157
Endicott, John. [*See* Endecott, John, *c.* 1589–1665.]
Endicott, Mordecai Thomas, Nov. 26, 1844–Mar. 5, 1926.
Vol. 3, Pt. 2–157
Endicott, William Crowninshield, Nov. 19, 1826–May 6, 1900.
Vol. 3, Pt. 2–158
Enelow, Hyman Gerson, Oct. 26, 1877–Feb. 5, 1934.
Supp. 1–288
Engel, Carl, July 21, 1883–May 6, 1944.
Supp. 3–252
Engelhard, Charles William, Feb. 15, 1917–Mar. 2, 1971.
Supp. 9–262
Engelhardt, Zephyrin, Nov. 13, 1851–Apr. 27, 1934.
Supp. 1–289
Engelmann, George, Feb. 2, 1809–Feb. 4, 1884.
Vol. 3, Pt. 2–159
Engelmann, George Julius, July 2, 1847–Nov. 16, 1903.
Vol. 3, Pt. 2–160
England, John, Sept. 23, 1786–Apr. 11, 1842.
Vol. 3, Pt. 2–161
Engle, Clair William Walter, Sept. 21, 1911–July 30, 1964.
Supp. 7–224
Englis, John, Nov. 27, 1808–Oct. 25, 1888.
Vol. 3, Pt. 2–163
English, Elbert Hartwell, Mar. 6, 1816–Sept. 1, 1884.
Vol. 3, Pt. 2–164
English, George Bethune, Mar. 7, 1787–Sept. 20, 1828.
Vol. 3, Pt. 2–165
English, James Edward, Mar. 13, 1812–Mar. 2, 1890.
Vol. 3, Pt. 2–165
English, Thomas Dunn, June 29, 1819–Apr. 1, 1902.
Vol. 3, Pt. 2–166
English, William Hayden, Aug. 27, 1822–Feb. 7, 1896.
Vol. 3, Pt. 2–167
Enneking, John Joseph, Oct. 4, 1841–Nov. 17, 1916.
Vol. 3, Pt. 2–168
Eno, William Phelps, June 3, 1858–Dec. 3, 1945.
Supp. 3–253
Ensley, Enoch, Nov. 8, 1836–Nov. 18, 1891.
Vol. 3, Pt. 2–169
Entwistle, James, July 8, 1837–Mar. 23, 1910.
Vol. 3, Pt. 2–170
Eppes, John Wayles, Apr. 7, 1773–Sept. 15, 1823.
Vol. 3, Pt. 2–170

Epstein, Abraham, Apr. 20, 1892–May 2, 1942.
Supp. 3–254
Epstein, Jacob, Nov. 10, 1880–Aug. 19, 1959.
Supp. 6–193
Epstein, Philip G., Aug. 22, 1909–Feb. 7, 1952.
Supp. 5–209
Erdman, Charles Rosenbury, July 20, 1866–May 9, 1960.
Supp. 6–195
Ericsson, John, July 31, 1803–Mar. 8, 1889.
Vol. 3, Pt. 2–171
Erlanger, Abraham Lincoln, May 4, 1860–Mar. 7, 1930.
Vol. 3, Pt. 2–176
Erlanger, Joseph, Jan. 5, 1874–Dec. 5, 1965.
Supp. 7–225
Ernst, Harold Clarence, July 31, 1856–Sept. 7, 1922.
Vol. 3, Pt. 2–177
Ernst, Max, Apr. 2, 1891–Apr. 1, 1976.
Supp. 10–219
Ernst, Morris Leopold, Aug. 23, 1888–May 21, 1976.
Supp. 10–220
Ernst, Oswald Herbert, June 27, 1842–Mar. 21, 1926.
Vol. 3, Pt. 2–178
Erpf, Armand Grover, Dec. 8, 1897–Feb. 2, 1971.
Supp. 9–264
Errett, Isaac, Jan. 2, 1820–Dec. 19, 1888.
Vol. 3, Pt. 2–179
Errol, Leon, July 3, 1881–Oct. 12, 1951.
Supp. 5–210
Erskine, John, Sept. 13, 1813–Jan. 27, 1895.
Vol. 3, Pt. 2–180
Erskine, John, Oct. 5, 1879–June 2, 1951.
Supp. 5–211
Erskine, Robert, Sept. 7, 1735–Oct. 2, 1780.
Vol. 3, Pt. 2–180
Erving, George William, July 15, 1769–July 22, 1850.
Vol. 3, Pt. 2–181
Esbjörn, Lars Paul, Oct. 16, 1808–July 2, 1870.
Vol. 3, Pt. 2–182
Escalante, Silvestre Velez De, fl. 1768–1779.
Vol. 3, Pt. 2–183
Esch, John Jacob, Mar. 20, 1861–Apr. 27, 1941.
Supp. 3–256
Esher, John Jacob, Dec. 11, 1823–Apr. 16, 1901.
Vol. 3, Pt. 2–184
Espejo, Antonio De, fl. 1581–1583.
Vol. 3, Pt. 2–184
Espy, James Pollard, May 9, 1785–Jan. 24, 1860.
Vol. 3, Pt. 2–185
Estabrook, Joseph, Dec. 7, 1793–May 18, 1855.
Vol. 3, Pt. 2–186
Estaugh, Elizabeth Haddon, *c.* 1680–Mar. 30, 1762.
Vol. 3, Pt. 2–186
Esterbrook, Richard, Feb. 21, 1813–Oct. 11, 1895.
Vol. 3, Pt. 2–187
Esterly, George, Oct. 17, 1809–June 7, 1893
Vol. 3, Pt. 2–188
Estes, Dana, Mar. 4, 1840–June 16, 1909.
Vol. 3, Pt. 2–188
Estey, Jacob, Sept. 30, 1814–Apr. 15, 1890.
Vol. 3, Pt. 2–189
Etting, Ruth, Nov. 23, 1896–Sept. 24, 1978.
Supp. 10–222
Ettwein, John, June 29, 1721–Jan. 2, 1802.
Vol. 3, Pt. 2–190
Eustis, Dorothy Leib Harrison Wood, May 30, 1886–Sept. 8, 1946.
Supp. 4–253
Eustis, George, Oct. 20, 1796–Dec. 22, 1858.
Vol. 3, Pt. 2–191
Eustis, George, Sept. 29, 1828–Mar. 15, 1872.
Vol. 3, Pt. 2–191
Eustis, Henry Lawrence, Feb. 1, 1819–Jan. 11, 1885.
Vol. 3, Pt. 2–192
Eustis, James Biddle, Aug. 21, 1834–Sept. 9, 1899.
Vol. 3, Pt. 2–193
Eustis, William, June 10, 1753–Feb. 6, 1825.
Vol. 3, Pt. 2–193
Evans, Anthony Walton Whyte, Oct. 31, 1817–Nov. 28, 1886.
Vol. 3, Pt. 2–195
Evans, Augusta Jane, May 8, 1835–May 9, 1909.
Vol. 3, Pt. 2–195
Evans, Bergen Baldwin, Sept. 19, 1904–Feb. 4, 1978.
Supp. 10–223
Evans, Charles, Nov. 13, 1850–Feb. 8, 1935.
Supp. 1–290
Evans, Clement Anselm, Feb. 25, 1833–July 2, 1911.
Vol. 3, Pt. 2–196
Evans, Edward Payson, Dec. 8, 1831–Mar. 6, 1917.
Vol. 3, Pt. 2–197
Evans, Evan, 1671–1721.
Vol. 3, Pt. 2–198
Evans, Frederick William, June 9, 1808–Mar. 6, 1893.
Vol. 3, Pt. 2–198
Evans, George, Jan. 12, 1797–Apr. 6, 1867.
Vol. 3, Pt. 2–199
Evans, George Alfred, Oct. 1, 1850–July 14, 1925.
Vol. 3, Pt. 2–200
Evans, George Henry, Mar. 25, 1805–Feb. 2, 1856.
Vol. 3, Pt. 2–201
Evans, Henry Clay, June 18, 1843–Dec. 12, 1921.
Vol. 3, Pt. 2–202
Evans, Herbert McLean, Sept. 23, 1882–Mar. 6, 1971.
Supp. 9–265
Evans, Hugh Davey, Apr. 26, 1792–July 16, 1868.
Vol. 3, Pt. 2–203
Evans, John, fl. 1703–1731.
Vol. 3, Pt. 2–204.
Evans, John, Mar. 9, 1814–July 3, 1897.
Vol. 3, Pt. 2–204
Evans, Lawrence Boyd, Feb. 3, 1870–Oct. 30, 1928.
Vol. 3, Pt. 2–205
Evans, Lewis, *c.* 1700–June 12, 1756.
Vol. 3, Pt. 2–206
Evans, Nathan George, Feb. 6, 1824–Nov. 30, 1868.
Vol. 3, Pt. 2–207
Evans, Nathaniel, June 8, 1742–Oct. 29, 1767.
Vol. 3, Pt. 2–208
Evans, Oliver, 1755–Apr. 15, 1819.
Vol. 3, Pt. 2–208
Evans, Robley Dunglison, Aug. 18, 1846–Jan. 3, 1912.
Vol. 3, Pt. 2–210
Evans, Thomas, Feb. 23, 1798–May 25, 1868.
Vol. 3, Pt. 2–210
Evans, Thomas Wiltberger, Dec. 23, 1823–Nov. 14, 1897.
Vol. 3, Pt. 2–211
Evans, Walker, Nov. 3, 1903–Apr. 10, 1975.
Supp. 9–267.
Evans, Walter, Sept. 18, 1842–Dec. 30, 1923.
Vol. 3, Pt. 2–212
Evans, Warren Felt, Dec. 23, 1817–Sept. 4, 1889.
Vol. 3, Pt. 2–213
Evans, William John ("Bill"), Aug. 16, 1929–Sept. 15, 1980.
Supp. 10–225
Evans, William Thomas, Nov. 13, 1843–Nov. 25, 1918.
Vol. 3, Pt. 2–214
Evarts, Jeremiah, Feb. 3, 1781–May 10, 1831.
Vol. 3, Pt. 2–215
Evarts, William Maxwell, Feb. 6, 1818–Feb. 28, 1901.
Vol. 3, Pt. 2–215
Eve, Joseph, May 24, 1760–Nov. 14, 1835.
Vol. 3, Pt. 2–218
Eve, Paul Fitzsimons, June 27, 1806–Nov. 3, 1877.
Vol. 3, Pt. 2–219
Everendon, Walter, d. 1725.
Vol. 3, Pt. 2–220
Everett, Alexander Hill, Mar. 19, 1790–June 29, 1847.
Vol. 3, Pt. 2–220
Everett, Charles Carroll, June 19, 1829–Oct. 16, 1900.
Vol. 3, Pt. 2–221
Everett, David, Mar. 29, 1770–Dec. 21, 1813.
Vol. 3, Pt. 2–222
Everett, Edward, Apr. 11, 1794–Jan. 15, 1865.
Vol. 3, Pt. 2–223
Everett, Robert, Jan. 2, 1791–Feb. 25, 1875.
Vol. 3, Pt. 2–226
Everleigh, Ada, Feb. 15, 1876–Jan. 3, 1960.
Supp. 4–255
Everleigh, Minna, July 5, 1878–Sept. 16, 1948.
Supp. 4–255
Evermann, Barton Warren, Oct. 24, 1853–Sept. 27, 1932.
Supp. 1–291

Evers, Medgar Wiley, July 2, 1925–June 12, 1963.
Supp. 7–227
Evola, Natale ("Joe Diamond"), Feb. 22, 1907–Aug. 27, 1973.
Supp. 9–269.
Ewbank, Thomas, Mar. 11, 1792–Sept. 16, 1870.
Vol. 3, Pt. 2–227
Ewell, Benjamin Stoddert, June 10, 1810–June 19, 1894.
Vol. 3, Pt. 2–228
Ewell, James, Feb. 16, 1773–Nov. 2, 1832.
Vol. 3, Pt. 2–229
Ewell, Richard Stoddert, Feb. 8, 1817–Jan. 25, 1872.
Vol. 3, Pt. 2–229
Ewell, Thomas, May 22, 1785–May 1, 1826.
Vol. 3, Pt. 2–230
Ewer, Ferdinand Cartwright, May 22, 1826–Oct. 10, 1883.
Vol. 3, Pt. 2–231
Ewing, Charles, June 8, 1780–Aug. 5, 1832.
Vol. 3, Pt. 2–232
Ewing, Finis, July 10, 1773–July 4, 1841.
Vol. 3, Pt. 2–233
Ewing, Hugh Boyle, Oct. 31, 1826–June 30, 1905.
Vol. 3, Pt. 2–234
Ewing, James, Aug. 3, 1736–Mar. 1, 1806.
Vol. 3, Pt. 2–234
Ewing, James, Dec. 25, 1866–May 16, 1943.
Supp. 3–257
Ewing, James Caruthers Rhea, June 23, 1854–Aug. 20, 1925.
Vol. 3, Pt. 2–235
Ewing, John, July 22, 1732–Sept. 8, 1802.
Vol. 3, Pt. 2–236
Ewing, Oscar Ross, Mar. 8, 1889–Jan. 8, 1980.
Supp. 10–226
Ewing, Thomas, Dec. 28, 1789–Oct. 26, 1871.
Vol. 3, Pt. 2–237
Ewing, Thomas, Aug. 7, 1829–Jan. 21, 1896.
Vol. 3, Pt. 2–238
Ewing, William Maurice, May 12, 1906–May 4, 1974.
Supp. 9–270
Eytinge, Rose, Nov. 21, 1835–Dec. 20, 1911.
Vol. 3, Pt. 2–239
Ezekiel, Moses Jacob, Oct. 28, 1844–Mar. 27, 1917.
Vol. 3, Pt. 2–240

Faber, John Eberhard, Dec. 6, 1822–Mar. 2, 1879.
Vol. 3, Pt. 2–241
Faccioli, Giuseppe, Apr. 7, 1877–Jan. 13, 1934.
Supp. 1–292
Fackler, David Parks, Apr. 4, 1841–Oct. 30, 1924.
Vol. 3, Pt. 2–242
Faesch, John Jacob, 1729–May 26, 1799.
Vol. 3, Pt. 2–243
Fagan, James Fleming, Mar. 1, 1828–Sept. 1, 1893.
Vol. 3, Pt. 2–243
Fagan, Mark Matthew, Sept. 29, 1869–July 16, 1955.
Supp. 5–212
Fages, Pedro, fl. 1767–1796.
Vol. 3, Pt. 2–244
Faget, Jean Charles, June 26, 1818–Dec. 7, 1884.
Vol. 3, Pt. 2–244
Fahnestock, Harris Charles, Feb. 27, 1835–June 4, 1914.
Vol. 3, Pt. 2–245
Fahy, Charles, Aug. 27, 1892–Sept. 17, 1979.
Supp. 10–229
Fair, James Graham, Dec. 3, 1831–Dec. 28, 1894.
Vol. 3, Pt. 2–246
Fairbank, Calvin, Nov. 3, 1816–Oct. 12, 1898.
Vol. 3, Pt. 2–247
Fairbanks, Charles Warren, May 11, 1852–June 4, 1918.
Vol. 3, Pt. 2–248
Fairbanks, Douglas, May 23, 1883–Dec. 12, 1939.
Supp. 2–172
Fairbanks, Erastus, Oct. 28, 1792–Nov. 20, 1864.
Vol. 3, Pt. 2–249
Fairbanks, Henry, May 6, 1830–July 7, 1918.
Vol. 3, Pt. 2–250
Fairbanks, Thaddeus, Jan. 17, 1796–Apr. 12, 1886.
Vol. 3, Pt. 2–251
Fairburn, William Armstrong, Oct. 12, 1876–Oct. 1, 1947.
Supp. 4–256
Fairchild, Blair, June 23, 1877–Apr. 23, 1933.
Supp. 1–293
Fairchild, Charles Stebbins, Apr. 30, 1842–Nov. 24, 1924.
Vol. 3, Pt. 2–251
Fairchild, David Grandison, Apr. 7, 1869–Aug. 6, 1954.
Supp. 5–213
Fairchild, Fred Rogers, Aug. 5, 1877–Apr. 13, 1966.
Supp. 8–165
Fairchild, George Thompson, Oct. 6, 1838–Mar. 16, 1901.
Vol. 3, Pt. 2–252
Fairchild, James Harris, Nov. 25, 1817–Mar. 19, 1902.
Vol. 3, Pt. 2–253
Fairchild, Lucius, Dec. 27, 1831–May 23, 1896.
Vol. 3, Pt. 2–253
Fairchild, Mary Salome Cutler, June 21, 1855–Dec. 20, 1921.
Vol. 3, Pt. 2–254
Fairchild, Muir Stephen, Sept. 2, 1894–Mar. 17, 1950.
Supp. 4–258
Fairchild, Sherman Mills, Apr. 7, 1896–Mar. 28, 1971.
Supp. 9–273
Fairfax, Beatrice. [*See* Manning, Marie, 1873–1945.]
Fairfax, Donald McNeill, Mar. 10, 1821–Jan. 10, 1894.
Vol. 3, Pt. 2–255
Fairfax, Thomas, Oct. 22, 1693–Dec. 9, 1781.
Vol. 3, Pt. 2–255
Fairfield, Edmund Burke, Aug. 7, 1821–Nov. 17, 1904.
Vol. 3, Pt. 2–257
Fairfield, John, Jan. 20, 1797–Dec. 24, 1847.
Vol. 3, Pt. 2–257
Fairfield, Sumner Lmcoln, June 25, 1803–Mar. 6, 1844.
Vol. 3, Pt. 2–258
Fairlamb, James Remington, Jan. 23, 1838–Apr. 16, 1908.
Vol. 3, Pt. 2–259
Fairless, Benjamin F., May 3, 1890–Jan. 1, 1962.
Supp. 7–228
Fairlie, John Archibald, Oct. 30, 1872–Jan. 23, 1947.
Supp. 4–259
Faith, Percy, Apr. 7, 1908–Feb. 9, 1976.
Supp. 10–230.
Falckner, Daniel, Nov. 25, 1666–*c.* 1741.
Vol. 3, Pt. 2–259
Falckner, Justus, Nov. 22, 1672–1723.
Vol. 3, Pt. 2–260
Falk, Maurice, Dec. 15, 1866–Mar. 18, 1946.
Supp. 4–261
Falk, Otto Herbert, June 18, 1865–May 21, 1940.
Supp. 2–173
Falkner, Roland Post, Apr. 14, 1866–Nov. 27, 1940.
Supp. 2–174
Fall, Albert Bacon, Nov. 26, 1861–Nov. 30, 1944.
Supp. 3–258
Fall, Bernard B., Nov. 11, 1926–Feb. 21, 1967.
Supp. 8–167
Fallows, Samuel, Dec. 13, 1835–Sept. 5, 1922.
Vol. 3, Pt. 2–261
Faneuil, Peter, June 20, 1700–Mar. 3, 1743.
Vol. 3, Pt. 2–262
Fannin, James Walker, *c.* Jan. 1, 1804–Mar. 27, 1836.
Vol. 3, Pt. 2–263
Fanning, Alexander Campbell Wilder, 1788–Aug. 18, 1846.
Vol. 3, Pt. 2–264
Fanning, David, *c.* 1755–Mar. 14, 1825.
Vol. 3, Pt. 2–264
Fanning, Edmund, Apr. 24, 1739–Feb. 28, 1818.
Vol. 3, Pt. 2–266
Fanning, Edmund, July 16, 1769–Apr. 23, 1841.
Vol. 3, Pt. 2–265
Fanning, John Thomas, Dec. 31, 1837–Feb. 6, 1911.
Vol. 3, Pt. 2–267
Fanning, Nathaniel, May 31, 1755–Sept. 30, 1805.
Vol. 3, Pt. 2–267
Fanning, Tolbert, May 10, 1810–May 3, 1874.
Vol. 3, Pt. 2–268
Farabee, William Curtis, Feb. 2, 1865–June 24, 1925.
Vol. 3, Pt. 2–269
Farago, Ladislas, Sept. 21, 1906–Oct. 15, 1980.
Supp. 10–231
Faran, James John, Dec. 29, 1808–Dec. 12, 1892.
Vol. 3, Pt. 2–270
Fargo, William George, May 20, 1818–Aug. 3, 1881.
Vol. 3, Pt. 2–271

Faribault, Jean Baptiste, Oct. 29, 1775–Aug. 20, 1860.
Vol. 3, Pt. 2–272
Farish, William Stamps, Feb. 23, 1881–Nov. 29, 1942.
Supp. 3–260
Farley, Harriet, Feb. 18, 1817–Nov. 12, 1907.
Vol. 3 Pt. 2–272
Farley, James Aloysius, May 30, 1888–June 9, 1976.
Supp. 10–232
Farley, John Murphy, Apr. 20, 1842–Sept. 17, 1918.
Vol. 3, Pt. 2–273
Farlow, William Gilson, Dec. 17, 1844–June 3, 1919.
Vol. 3, Pt. 2–274
Farman, Elbert Eli, Apr. 23, 1831–Dec. 30, 1911.
Vol. 3, Pt. 2–275
Farmer, Fannie Merritt, Mar. 23, 1857–Jan. 15, 1915.
Vol. 3, Pt. 2–276
Farmer, Ferdinand, Oct. 13, 1720–Aug. 17, 1786.
Vol. 3, Pt. 2–276
Farmer, Hannah Tobey Shapleigh, Mar. 20, 1823–June 27, 1891.
Vol. 3, Pt. 2–277
Farmer, John, June 12, 1789–Aug. 13, 1838.
Vol. 3, Pt. 2–278
Farmer, John, Feb. 9, 1798–Mar. 24, 1859.
Vol. 3, Pt. 2–278
Farmer, Moses Gerrish, Feb. 9, 1820–May 25, 1893.
Vol. 3, Pt. 2–279
Farnam, Henry, Nov. 9, 1803–Oct. 4, 1883.
Vol. 3, Pt. 2–281
Farnam, Henry Walcott, Nov. 6, 1853–Sept. 5, 1933.
Supp. 1–293
Farnham, Eliza Woodson Burhans, Nov. 17, 1815–Dec. 15, 1864.
Vol. 3, Pt. 2–282
Farnham, Russel, 1784–Oct. 23, 1832.
Vol. 3, Pt. 1–282
Farnham, Thomas Jefferson, 1804–Sept. 13, 1848.
Vol. 3, Pt. 2–283
Farnsworth, Elon John, July 30, 1837–July 3, 1863.
Vol. 3, Pt. 2–284
Farnsworth, John Franklin, Mar. 27, 1820–July 14, 1897.
Vol. 3, Pt. 2–284
Farnsworth, Philo Taylor, Aug. 19, 1906–Mar. 11, 1971.
Supp. 9–274
Farnum, Dustin Lancy, May 27, 1874–July 3, 1929.
Vol. 3, Pt. 2–285
Farnum, Franklyn, June 5, 1878?–July 4, 1961.
Supp. 7–229
Farquhar, Percival, Oct. 19, 1864–Aug. 4, 1953.
Supp. 5–214
Farragut, David Glasgow, July 5, 1801–Aug. 14, 1870.
Vol. 3, Pt. 2–286
Farragut, George, Sept. 29, 1755–June 4, 1817.
Vol. 3, Pt. 2–291
Farrand, Beatrix Cadwalader Jones, June 19, 1872–Feb. 7, 1959.
Supp. 6–196
Farrand, Livingston, June 14, 1867–Nov. 8, 1939.
Supp. 2–176
Farrand, Max, Mar. 29, 1869–June 17, 1945.
Supp. 3–261
Farrar, Edgar Howard, June 20, 1849–Jan. 6, 1922.
Vol. 3, Pt. 2–291
Farrar, Geraldine, Feb. 28, 1882–Mar. 11, 1967.
Supp. 8–168
Farrar, John, July 1, 1779–May 8, 1853.
Vol. 3, Pt. 2–292
Farrar, John Chipman, Feb. 25, 1896–Nov. 5, 1974.
Supp. 9–276
Farrar, Timothy, Mar. 17, 1788–Oct. 27, 1874.
Vol. 3, Pt. 2–293
Farrell, James Augustine, Feb. 15, 1862–Mar. 28, 1943.
Supp. 3–262
Farrell, James Thomas, Feb. 27, 1904–Aug. 22, 1979.
Supp. 10–234
Farrer, Henry, Mar. 23, 1843–Feb. 24, 1903.
Vol. 3, Pt. 2–293
Farrington, Joseph Rider, Oct. 15, 1897–June 19, 1954.
Supp. 5–216
Farrington, Wallace Rider, May 3, 1871–Oct. 6, 1933.
Supp. 1–295
Farson, Negley, May 14, 1890–Dec. 12, 1960.
Supp. 6–197
Farwell, Arthur, Apr. 23, 1872–Jan. 20, 1952.
Sup. 5–217
Farwell,Charles Benjamin, July 1, 1823–Sept. 23, 1903.
Vol. 3, Pt. 2–294
Farwell, John Villiers, July 29, 1825–Aug. 20, 1908.
Vol. 3, Pt. 2–295
Fassett, Cornelia Adèle Strong, Nov. 9, 1831–Jan. 4, 1898.
Vol. 3, Pt. 2–296
Fassett, Jacob Sloat, Nov. 13, 1853–Apr. 21, 1924.
Vol. 3, Pt. 2–296
Father Divine. [*See* Divine, Father.]
Faulk, Andrew Jackson, Nov. 26, 1814–Sept. 4, 1898.
Vol. 3, Pt. 2–297
Faulkner, Charles James, July 6, 1806–Nov. 1, 1884.
Vol. 3, Pt. 2–298
Faulkner, Charles James, Sept. 21, 1847–Jan. 13, 1929.
Vol. 3, Pt. 2–299
Faulkner (Falkner), William Cuthbert, Sept. 25, 1897–July 6, 1962.
Supp. 7–230
Faunce, William Herbert Perry, Jan. 15, 1859–Jan. 31, 1930.
Vol. 3, Pt. 2–299
Fauquier, Francis, 1704?–Mar. 3, 1768.
Vol. 3, Pt. 2–301
Fauset, Jessie Redmon, Apr. 27, 1882?–Apr. 30, 1961.
Supp. 7–236
Faust, Frederick Shiller, May 29, 1892–May 12, 1944.
Supp. 3–264
Faversham, William Alfred, Feb. 12, 1868–Apr. 7, 1940.
Supp. 2–178
Favill, Henry Baird, Aug. 14, 1860–Feb. 20, 1916.
Vol. 3, Pt. 2–301
Fawcett, Edgar, May 26, 1847–May 2, 1904.
Vol. 3, Pt. 2–302
Fay, Edward Allen, Nov. 22, 1843–July 14, 1923.
Vol. 3, Pt. 2–303
Fay, Edwin Whitfield, Jan. 1, 1865–Feb. 17, 1920.
Vol. 3, Pt. 2–304
Fay, Francis Anthony ("Frank"), Nov. 17, 1897–Sept. 25, 1961.
Supp. 7–237
Fay, Jonas, Jan. 28, 1737 N.S.–Mar. 6, 1818.
Vol. 3, Pt. 2–304
Fay, Sidney Bradshaw, Apr. 13, 1876–Aug. 29, 1967.
Supp. 8–168
Fay, Theodore Sedgwick, Feb. 10, 1807–Nov. 24, 1898.
Vol. 3, Pt. 2–305
Fayerweather, Daniel Burton, Mar. 12, 1822–Nov. 15, 1890.
Vol. 3, Pt. 2–306
Favssoux, Peter, 1745–Feb. 1, 1795.
Vol. 3, Pt. 2–307
Fazenda, Louise Marie, June 17, 1896–Apr. 17, 1962.
Supp. 7–238
Fearing, Kenneth Flexner, July 28, 1902–June 26, 1961.
Supp. 7–239
Fearn, John Walker, Jan. 13, 1832–Apr. 7, 1809.
Vol. 3, Pt. 2–307
Featherston, Winfield Scott, Aug. 8, 1819–May 28, 1891.
Vol. 3, Pt. 2–308
Febiger, Christian, 1746–Sept. 20, 1796.
Vol. 3, Pt. 2–309
Fechter, Charles Albert, Oct. 23, 1824–Aug. 5, 1879.
Vol. 3, Pt. 2–309
Fee, John Gregg, Sept. 9, 1816–Jan. 11, 1901.
Vol. 3, Pt. 2–310
Feehan, Patrick Augustine, Aug. 28, 1829–July 12, 1902.
Vol. 3, Pt. 2–311
Feininger, Lyonel (Charles Léonell Adrian), July 17, 1871–Jan. 13, 1956.
Supp. 6–198
Feis, Herbert, June 7, 1893–Mar. 2, 1972.
Supp. 9–277
Fejos, Paul, Jan. 24, 1897–Apr. 23, 1963.
Supp. 7–240
Feke, Robert, *c.* 1705–*c.* 1750.
Vol. 3, Pt. 2–312
Felch, Alpheus, Sept. 28, 1804–June 13, 1896.
Vol. 3, Pt. 2–313
Fell, John, Feb. 5, 1721–May 15, 1798.
Vol. 3, Pt. 2–314

Fels, Joseph, Dec. 16, 1854–Feb. 22, 1914.
Vol. 3, Pt. 2–314
Fels, Samuel Simeon, Feb. 16, 1860–June 23, 1950.
Supp. 4–262
Felsenthal, Bernhard, Jan. 2, 1822–Jan. 12, 1908.
Vol. 3, Pt. 2–315
Felt, Joseph Barlow, Dec. 22, 1789–Sept. 8, 1869.
Vol. 3, Pt. 2–316
Felton, Cornelius Conway, Nov. 6, 1807–Feb. 26, 1862.
Vol. 3, Pt. 2–317
Felton, Rebecca Latimer, June 10, 1835–Jan. 24, 1930.
Vol. 3, Pt. 2–318
Felton, Samuel Morse, July 17, 1809–Jan. 24, 1889.
Vol. 3, Pt. 2–318
Felton, William Harrell, June 19, 1823–Sept. 24, 1909.
Vol. 3, Pt. 2–319
Fendall, Josias, *c.* 1620–*c.* 1687.
Vol. 3, Pt. 2–320
Fenger, Christian, Nov. 3, 1840–Mar. 7, 1902.
Vol. 3, Pt. 2–320
Fenichel, Otto, Dec. 2, 1897–Jan. 22, 1946.
Supp. 4–263
Fenn, William Wallace, Feb. 12, 1862–Mar. 6, 1932.
Supp. 1–296
Fennell, James, Dec. 11, 1766–June 13, 1816.
Vol. 3, Pt. 2–321
Fenneman, Nevin Melancthon, Dec. 26, 1865–July 4, 1945.
Supp. 3–265
Fenner, Arthur, Dec. 10, 1745–Oct. 15, 1805.
Vol. 3, Pt. 2–322
Fenner, Burt Leslie, Sept. 1, 1869–Jan. 24, 1926.
Vol. 3, Pt. 2–323
Fenner, Charles Erasmus, Feb. 14, 1834–Oct. 24, 1911.
Vol. 3, Pt. 2–323
Fenner, James, Jan. 22, 1771–Apr. 17, 1846.
Vol. 3, Pt. 2–324
Fenno, John, Aug. 12, 1751 o.s.–Sept. 14, 1798.
Vol. 3, Pt. 2–325
Fenollosa, Ernest Francisco, Feb. 18, 1853–Sept. 21, 1908.
Vol. 3, Pt. 2–325
Fenton, Reuben Eaton, July 4, 1819–Aug. 25, 1885.
Vol. 3, Pt. 2–326
Fenwick, Benedict Joseph, Sept. 3, 1782–Aug. 11, 1846.
Vol. 3, Pt. 2–327
Fenwick, Edward Dominic, Aug. 19, 1768–Sept. 26, 1832.
Vol. 3, Pt. 2–328
Fenwick, George, 1603–Mar. 15, 1656/7.
Vol. 3, Pt. 2–329
Fenwick, John, 1618–Dec. 1683.
Vol. 3, Pt. 2–330
Fenwicke, John. [*See* Fenwick, John, 1618–1683.]
Ferber, Edna Jessica, Aug. 15, 1885–Apr. 16, 1968.
Supp. 8–170
Ferguson, Alexander Hugh, Feb. 27, 1853–Oct. 20, 1911.
Vol. 3, Pt. 2–331
Ferguson, Elizabeth Graeme, Feb. 3, 1737–Feb. 23, 1801.
Vol. 3, Pt. 2–331
Ferguson, James Edward, Aug. 31, 1871–Sept. 21, 1944.
Supp. 3–266
Ferguson, John Calvin, Mar. 1, 1866–Aug. 3, 1945.
Supp. 3–267
Ferguson, Miriam Amanda Wallace, June 13, 1875–June 25, 1961.
Supp. 7–241
Ferguson, Samuel, Nov. 18, 1874–Feb. 10, 1950.
Supp. 4–264
Ferguson, Thomas Barker, Aug. 8, 1841–Aug. 11, 1922.
Vol. 3, Pt. 2–332
Ferguson, William Porter Frisbee, Dec. 13, 1861–June 23, 1929.
Vol. 3, Pt. 2–334
Ferguson, William Jason, June 8, 1844–May 4, 1930.
Vol. 3, Pt. 2–333
Fermi, Enrico, Sept. 29, 1901–Nov. 28, 1954.
Supp. 5–219
Fernald, Charles Henry, Mar. 16, 1838–Feb. 22, 1921.
Vol. 3, Pt. 2–334
Fernald, James Champlin, Aug. 18, 1838–Nov. 10, 1918.
Vol. 3, Pt. 2–335,
Fernald, Merritt Lyndon, Oct. 5, 1873–Sept. 22, 1950.
Supp. 4–266
Fernós Isern, Antonio, May 10, 1895–Jan. 19, 1974.
Supp. 9–278
Fernow, Bernhard Eduard, Jan. 7, 1851–Feb. 6, 1923.
Vol. 3, Pt. 2–336
Fernow, Berthold, Nov. 28, 1837–Mar. 3, 1908.
Vol. 3, Pt. 2–337
Ferree, Clarence Errol, Mar. 11, 1877–July 26, 1942.
Supp. 3–269
Ferrel, William, Jan. 29, 1817–Sept. 18, 1891.
Vol. 3, Pt. 2–338
Ferrero, Edward, Jan. 18, 1831–Dec. 11, 1899.
Vol. 3, Pt. 2–338
Ferris, George Washington Gale, Feb. 14, 1859–Nov. 22, 1896.
Vol. 3, Pt. 2–339
Ferris, Isaac, Oct. 9, 1798–June 16, 1873.
Vol. 3, Pt. 2–340
Ferris, Jean Léon Gérôme, Aug. 8, 1863–Mar. 18, 1930.
Vol. 3, Pt. 2–340
Ferris, Woodbridge Nathan, Jan. 6, 1853–Mar. 23, 1928.
Vol. 3, Pt. 2–341.
Ferry, Elisha Peyre, Aug. 9, 1825–Oct. 14, 1895.
Vol. 3, Pt. 2–342
Ferry, Orris Sanford, Aug. 15, 1823–Nov. 21, 1875.
Vol. 3, Pt. 2–342
Ferry, Thomas White, June 1, 1827–Oct. 14, 1896.
Vol. 3, Pt. 2–343
Fersen, Hans Axel, Count Von, Sept. 4, 1755–June 20, 1810.
Vol. 3, Pt. 2–344
Fess, Simeon Davidson, Dec. 11, 1861–Dec. 23, 1936.
Supp. 2–180
Fessenden, Francis, Mar. 18, 1839–Jan. 2, 1906.
Vol. 3, Pt. 2–345
Fessenden, James Deering, Sept. 28, 1833–Nov. 18, 1882.
Vol. 3, Pt. 2–345
Fessenden, Reginald Aubrey, Oct. 6, 1866–July 22, 1932.
Supp. 1–296
Fessenden, Samuel, July 16, 1784–Mar. 19, 1869.
Vol. 3, Pt. 2–346
Fessenden, Thomas Green, Apr. 22, 1771–Nov. 11, 1837.
Vol. 3, Pt. 2–347
Fessenden, William Pitt, Oct. 16, 1806–Sept. 8, 1869.
Vol. 3, Pt. 2–348
Fetter, Frank Albert, Mar. 8, 1863–Mar. 21, 1949.
Supp. 4–267
Fetterman, William Judd, 1833?–Dec. 21, 1866.
Vol. 3, Pt. 2–350
Feuchtwanger, Lion, July 7, 1884–Dec. 21, 1958.
Supp. 6–200
Few, Ignatius Alphonso, Apr. 11, 1789–Nov. 28, 1845.
Vol. 3, Pt. 2–351
Few, William, June 8, 1748–July 16, 1828.
Vol. 3, Pt. 2–352
Few, William Preston, Dec. 29, 1867–Oct. 16, 1940.
Supp. 2–181
Fewkes, Jesse Walter, Nov. 14, 1850–May 31, 1930.
Vol. 3, Pt. 2–352
Ffoulke, Charles Mather, July 25, 1841–Apr. 14, 1909.
Vol. 3, Pt. 2–354
Ffrench, Charles Dominic, 1775–Jan. 5, 1851.
Vol. 3, Pt. 2–355
Fiedler, Arthur, Dec. 17, 1894–July 10, 1979.
Supp. 10–236
Field, Benjamin Hazard, May 2, 1814–Mar. 17, 1893.
Vol. 3, Pt. 2–356
Field, Charles William, Apr. 6, 1828–Apr. 9, 1892.
Vol. 3, Pt. 2–356
Field, Cyrus West, Nov. 30, 1819–July 12, 1892.
Vol. 3, Pt. 2–357
Field, David Dudley, May 20, 1781–Apr. 15, 1867.
Vol. 3, Pt. 2–359
Field, David Dudley, Feb. 13, 1805–Apr. 13, 1894.
Vol. 3, Pt. 2–360
Field, Eugene, Sept. 2?, 1850–Nov. 4, 1895.
Vol. 3, Pt. 2–362
Field, Fred Tarbell, Dec. 24, 1876–July 23, 1950.
Supp. 4–268
Field, Henry Martyn, Apr. 3, 1822–Jan. 26, 1907.
Vol. 3, Pt. 2–364
Field, Herbert Haviland, Apr. 25, 1868–Apr. 5, 1921.
Vol. 3, Pt. 2–365

Field, Joseph M., 1810–Jan. 28, 1856.
Vol. 3, Pt. 2–366
Field, Kate. [*See* Field, Mary Katherine Keemle, 1838–1896.]
Field, Marshall, Aug. 18, 1834–Jan. 16, 1906.
Vol. 3, Pt. 2–366
Field, Marshall, III, Sept. 28, 1893–Nov. 8, 1956.
Supp. 6–201
Field, Marshall, IV, June 15, 1916–Sept. 18, 1965.
Supp. 7–243
Field, Mary Katherine Keemle, Oct. 1, 1838–May 19, 1896.
Vol. 3, Pt. 2–368
Field, Maunsell Bradhurst, Mar. 26, 1822–Jan. 21, 1875.
Vol. 3, Pt. 2–368
Field, Richard Stockton, Dec. 31, 1803–May 25, 1870.
Vol. 3, Pt. 2–369
Field, Robert, *c.* 1769–Aug. 9, 1819.
Vol. 3, Pt. 2–370
Field, Roswell Martin, Sept. 1, 1851–Jan. 10, 1919.
Vol. 3, Pt. 2–371
Field, Stephen Dudley, Jan. 31, 1846–May 18, 1913.
Vol. 3, Pt. 2–371
Field, Stephen Johnson, Nov. 4, 1816–Apr. 9, 1899.
Vol. 3, Pt. 2–372
Field, Thomas Warren, 1821–Nov. 25, 1881.
Vol. 3, Pt. 2–376
Field, Walbridge Abner, Apr. 26, 1833–July 15, 1899.
Vol. 3, Pt. 2–376
Fielding, Jerry, June 17, 1922–Feb. 17, 1980.
Supp. 10–238
Fields, Annie Adams, June 6, 1834–Jan. 5, 1915.
Vol. 3, Pt. 2–377
Fields, Dorothy, July 15, 1905–Mar. 28, 1974.
Supp. 9–280
Fields, James Thomas, Dec. 31, 1817–Apr. 24, 1881.
Vol. 3, Pt. 2–378
Fields, Lewis Maurice. [*See* Weber, Joseph Morris, 1867–1942.]
Fields, Lewis Maurice, Jan. 1, 1867–July 20, 1941.
Supp. 3–803
Fields, William Claude, Jan. 29, 1880–Dec. 25, 1946.
Supp. 4–269
Fieser, Louis Frederick, Apr. 7, 1899–July 25, 1977.
Supp. 10–240
Fifer, Joseph Wilson, Oct. 28, 1840–Aug. 6, 1938.
Supp. 2–182
Filene, Edward Albert, Sept. 3, 1860–Sept. 26, 1937.
Supp. 2–183
Fillebrown, Thomas, Jan. 13, 1836–Jan. 22, 1908.
Vol. 3, Pt. 2–379
Fillmore, Charles, Aug. 22, 1854–July 5, 1948.
Supp. 4–270
Fillmore, John Comfort, Feb. 4, 1843–Aug. 14, 1898.
Vol. 3, Pt. 2–379
Fillmore, Millard, Jan. 7, 1800–Mar. 8, 1874.
Vol. 3, Pt. 2–380
Filson, John, *c.* 1747–October 1788.
Vol. 3, Pt. 2–382
Finch, Francis Miles, June 9, 1827–July 31, 1907.
Vol. 3, Pt. 2–383
Finck, Henry Theophilus, Sept. 22, 1854–Oct. 1, 1926.
Vol. 3, Pt. 2–383
Findlay, James, Oct. 12, 1770–Dec. 28, 1835.
Vol. 3, Pt. 2–384
Findley, William, 1741–Apr. 5, 1821.
Vol. 3, Pt. 2–385
Fine, Henry Burchard, Sept. 14, 1858–Dec. 22, 1928.
Vol. 3, Pt. 2–386
Fine, John Sydney, Apr. 10, 1893–May 21, 1978.
Supp. 10–241
Fine, Larry, Oct. 5, 1902–Jan. 24, 1975.
Supp. 9–281
Fink, Albert, Oct. 27, 1827–Apr. 3, 1897.
Vol. 3, Pt. 2–387
Finlay, Carlos Juan, Dec. 3, 1833–Aug. 20, 1915.
Vol. 3, Pt. 2–388
Finlay, Hugh, *c.* 1731–Dec. 26, 1801.
Vol. 3, Pt. 2–389
Finletter, Thomas Knight, Nov. 11, 1893–Apr. 24, 1980.
Supp. 10–242
Finley, James Bradley, July 1, 1781–Sept. 6, 1856.
Vol. 3, Pt. 2–389
Finley, John Huston, Oct. 19, 1863–Mar. 7, 1940.
Supp. 2–185
Finley, Martha Farquharson, Apr. 26, 1828–Jan. 30, 1909.
Vol. 3, Pt. 2–390
Finley, Robert, Feb. 15, 1772–Oct. 3, 1817.
Vol. 3, Pt. 2–391
Finley, Samuel, 1715–July 17, 1766.
Vol. 3, Pt. 2–391
Finn, Francis James, Oct. 4, 1859–Nov. 2, 1928.
Vol. 3, Pt. 2–392
Finn, Henry James William, June 17, 1787–Jan. 13, 1840.
Vol. 3, Pt. 2–393
Finney, Charles Grandison, Aug. 29, 1792–Aug. 16, 1875.
Vol. 3, Pt. 2–394
Finney, John Miller Turpin, June 20, 1863–May 30, 1942.
Supp. 3–270
Finotti, Joseph Maria, Sept. 21, 1817–Jan. 10, 1879.
Vol. 3, Pt. 2–396
Firestone, Harvey Samuel, Dec. 20, 1868–Feb. 7, 1938.
Supp. 2–187
Firestone, Harvey Samuel, Jr., Apr. 20, 1898–June 1, 1973.
Supp. 9–283
Fischer. Emil Friedrich August, June 13, 1838–Aug. 11, 1914.
Vol. 3, Pt. 2–396
Fischer, Louis, Feb. 29, 1896–Jan. 15, 1970.
Supp. 8–171
Fischer, Ruth, 1895–Mar. 15, 1961.
Supp. 7–244
Fischetti, John, Sept. 27, 1916–Nov. 18, 1980.
Supp. 10–244
Fish, Carl Russell, Oct. 17, 1876–July 10, 1932.
Supp. 1–297
Fish, Hamilton, Aug. 3, 1808–Sept. 6, 1893.
Vol. 3, Pt. 2–397
Fish, Nicholas, Aug. 28, 1758–June 20, 1833.
Vol. 3, Pt. 2–400
Fish, Preserved, July 3, 1766–July 23, 1846.
Vol. 3, Pt. 2–401
Fish, Stuyvesant, June 24, 1851–Apr. 10, 1923.
Vol. 3, Pt. 2–402
Fishback, William Meade, Nov. 5, 1831–Feb. 9, 1903.
Vol. 3, Pt. 2–403
Fisher, Alfred J., 1892–Oct. 9, 1963.
Supp. 7–245
Fisher, Alvan, Aug. 9, 1792–Feb. 13, 1863.
Vol. 3, Pt. 2–403
Fisher, "Bud." [*See* Fisher, Henry Conroy, 1884–1954.]
Fisher, Charles T., Feb. 16, 1880–Aug. 8, 1963.
Supp. 7–245
Fisher, Clara, July 14, 1811–Nov. 12, 1898.
Vol. 3, Pt. 2–404
Fisher, Clarence Stanley, Aug. 17, 1876–July 20, 1941.
Supp. 3–271
Fisher, Clark, May 27, 1837–Dec. 31, 1903.
Vol. 3, Pt. 2–405
Fisher, Daniel Webster, Jan. 17, 1838–Jan. 28, 1913.
Vol. 3, Pt. 2–405
Fisher, Dorothea Frances Canfield, Feb. 17, 1879–Nov. 9, 1958.
Supp. 6–202
Fisher, Ebenezer, Feb. 6, 1815–Feb. 21, 1879.
Vol. 3, Pt. 2–406
Fisher, Frederic John, Jan. 2, 1878–July 14, 1941.
Supp. 3–273
Fisher, Frederick Bohn, Feb. 14, 1882–Apr. 15, 1938.
Supp. 2–188
Fisher, George Jackson, Nov. 27, 1825–Feb. 3, 1893.
Vol. 3, Pt. 2–406
Fisher, George Park, Aug. 10, 1827–Dec. 20, 1909.
Vol. 3, Pt. 2–407
Fisher, George Purnell, Oct. 13, 1817–Feb. 10, 1899.
Vol. 3, Pt. 2–408
Fisher, Hammond Edward, 1901?–Dec. 27, 1955.
Supp. 5–221
Fisher, Harrison, July 27, 1875–Jan. 19, 1934.
Supp. 1–298
Fisher, Henry Conroy ("Bud"), Apr. 3, 1884–Sept. 7, 1954.
Supp. 5–223
Fisher, Irving, Feb. 27, 1867–Apr. 29, 1947.
Supp. 4–272

Fisher, John Dix, Mar. 27, 1797–Mar. 3, 1850.
Vol. 3, Pt. 2–409
Fisher, Joshua Francis, Feb. 17, 1807–Jan. 21, 1873.
Vol. 3, Pt. 2–409
Fisher, Philip. [*See* Copley, Thomas, 1595–*c.* 1652.]
Fisher, Sidney George, Mar. 2, 1809–July 25, 1871.
Vol. 3, Pt. 2–410
Fisher, Sydney George, Sept. 11, 1856–Feb. 22, 1927.
Vol. 3, Pt. 2–411
Fisher, Theodore Willis, May 29, 1837–Oct. 10, 1914.
Vol. 3, Pt. 2–412
Fisher, Walter Lowrie, July 4, 1862–Nov. 9, 1935.
Supp. 1–299
Fisher, William Arms, Apr. 27, 1861–Dec. 18, 1948.
Supp. 4–276
Fisk, Clinton Bowen, Dec. 8, 1828–July 9, 1890.
Vol. 3, Pt. 2–413
Fisk, James, Oct. 4, 1763–Nov. 17, 1844.
Vol. 3, Pt. 2–414
Fisk, James, Apr. 1, 1834–Jan. 7, 1872.
Vol. 3, Pt. 2–414
Fisk, Wilbur, Aug. 31, 1792–Feb. 22, 1839.
Vol. 3, Pt. 2–415
Fiske, Amos Kidder, May 12, 1842–Sept. 18, 1921.
Vol. 3, Pt. 2–416
Fiske, Bradley Allen, June 13, 1854–Apr. 6, 1942.
Supp. 3–274
Fiske, Daniel Willard, Nov. 11, 1831–Sept. 17, 1904.
Vol. 3, Pt. 2–417
Fiske, Fidelia, May 1, 1816–July 26, 1864.
Vol. 3, Pt. 2–417
Fiske, George Converse, Feb. 28, 1872–Jan. 8, 1927.
Vol. 3, Pt. 2–418
Fiske, Haley, Mar. 18, 1852–Mar. 3, 1929.
Vol. 3, Pt. 2–419
Fiske, Harrison Grey, July 30, 1861–Sept. 2, 1942.
Supp. 3–276
Fiske, John, Apr. 11, 1744–Sept. 28, 1797.
Vol. 3, Pt. 2–420
Fiske, John, Mar. 30, 1842–July 4, 1901.
Vol. 3, Pt. 2–420
Fiske, Minnie Maddern, Dec. 19, 1865–Feb. 15, 1932.
Supp. 1–300
Fiske, Stephen Ryder, Nov. 22, 1840–Apr. 27, 1916.
Vol. 3, Pt. 2–423
Fitch, Asa, Feb. 24, 1809–Apr. 8, 1879.
Vol. 3, Pt. 2–424
Fitch, Clyde. [*See* Fitch, William Clyde, 1865–1909.]
Fitch, John, Jan. 21, 1743–July 2, 1798.
Vol. 3, Pt. 2–425
Fitch, Samuel, Jan. 16, 1724–Oct. 4, 1799.
Vol. 3, Pt. 2–426
Fitch, Thomas, *c.* 1700–July 18, 1774.
Vol. 3, Pt. 2–427
Fitch, William Clyde, May 2, 1865–Sept. 4, 1909.
Vol. 3, Pt. 2–428
Fite, Warner, Mar. 5, 1867–June 23, 1955.
Supp. 5–224
Fitler, Edwin Henry, Dec. 2, 1825–May 31, 1896.
Vol. 3, Pt. 2–431
Fitton, James, Apr. 10, 1805–Sept. 15, 1881.
Vol. 3, Pt. 2–432
Fitz, Henry, Dec. 31, 1808–Nov. 6, 1863.
Vol. 3, Pt. 2–433
Fitz, Reginald Heber, May 5, 1843–Sept. 30, 1913.
Vol. 3, Pt. 2–433
Fitzgerald, Alice Louise Florence, Mar. 13, 1875–Nov. 10, 1962.
Supp. 7–247
Fitzgerald, Desmond, May 20, 1846–Sept. 22, 1926.
Vol. 3, Pt. 2–434
Fitzgerald, Edward, Oct. 26, 1833–Feb. 21, 1907.
Vol. 3, Pt. 2–435
Fitzgerald, Edwin. [*See* Foy, Eddie, 1856–1928.]
Fitzgerald, Francis Scott Key, Sept. 24, 1896–Dec. 21, 1940.
Supp. 2–189
Fitzgerald, John Francis, Feb. 11, 1863–Oct. 2, 1950.
Supp. 4–277
Fitzgerald, Oscar Penn, Aug. 24, 1829–Aug. 5, 1911.
Vol. 3, Pt. 2–436
Fitzgerald, Thomas, Dec. 22, 1819–June 25, 1891.
Vol. 3, Pt. 2–437
Fitzgibbon, Catherine. [*See* Irene, Sister, 1823–1896.]
Fitzhugh, George, Nov. 4, 1806–July 30, 1881.
Vol. 3, Pt. 2–437
Fitzhugh, William, 1651–October 1701.
Vol. 3, Pt. 2–438
Fitzpatrick, Benjamin, June 30, 1802–Nov. 21, 1869.
Vol. 3, Pt. 2–439
Fitzpatrick, Daniel Robert, Mar. 5, 1891–May 18, 1969.
Supp. 8–173
Fitzpatrick, John, Apr. 21, 1870–Sept. 27, 1946.
Supp. 4–279
Fitzpatrick, John Bernard, Nov. 15, 1812–Feb. 13, 1866.
Vol. 3, Pt. 2–440
Fitzpatrick, John Clement, Aug. 10, 1876–Feb. 10, 1940.
Supp. 2–191
Fitzpatrick, Morgan Cassius, Oct. 29, 1868–June 25, 1908.
Vol. 3, Pt. 2–441
Fitzpatrick, Thomas, *c.* 1799–Feb. 7, 1854.
Vol. 3, Pt. 2–442
Fitzsimmons, James Edward ("Sunny Jim"), July 23, 1874–Mar. 11, 1966.
Supp. 8–174
Fitzsimmons, Robert Prometheus, June 4, 1862–Oct. 22, 1917.
Vol. 3, Pt. 2–443
Fitzsimmons or Fitzsimins, Thomas, 1741–Aug. 26, 1811.
Vol. 3, Pt. 2–444
Flad, Henry, July 30, 1824–June 20, 1898.
Vol. 3, Pt. 2–445
Flaget, Benedict Joseph, Nov. 7, 1763–Feb. 11, 1850.
Vol. 3, Pt. 2–445
Flagg, Azariah Cutting, Nov. 28, 1790–Nov. 24, 1873.
Vol. 3, Pt. 2–447
Flagg, Edmund, Nov. 24, 1815–Nov. 1, 1890.
Vol. 3, Pt. 2–447
Flagg, Ernest, Feb. 6, 1857–Apr. 10, 1947.
Supp. 4–280
Flagg, George Whiting, June 26, 1816–Jan. 5, 1897.
Vol. 3, Pt. 2–448
Flagg, James Montgomery, June 18, 1877–May 27, 1960.
Supp. 6–203
Flagg, Jared Bradley, June 16, 1820–Sept. 25, 1899.
Vol. 3, Pt. 2–449
Flagg, Josiah, May 28, 1737–*c.* 1795.
Vol. 3, Pt. 2–449
Flagg, Josiah Foster, Jan. 10, 1788–Dec. 20, 1853.
Vol. 3, Pt. 2–450
Flagg, Thomas Wilson, Nov. 5, 1805–May 6, 1884.
Vol. 3, Pt. 2–450
Flagler, Henry Morrison, Jan. 2, 1830–May 20, 1913.
Vol. 3, Pt. 2–451
Flagler, John Haldane, Sept. 3, 1836–Sept. 8, 1922.
Vol. 3, Pt. 2–452
Flaherty, Robert Joseph, Feb. 16, 1884–July 23, 1951.
Supp. 5–225
Flanagan, Edward Joseph, July 13, 1886–May 15, 1948.
Supp. 4–282
Flanagan, Hallie, Aug. 27, 1890–July 23, 1969.
Supp. 8–176
Flanagan, Webster, Jan. 9, 1832–May 5, 1924.
Vol. 3, Pt. 2–453
Flanagin, Harris, Nov. 3, 1817–Oct. 23, 1874.
Vol. 3, Pt. 2–454
Flanders, Henry, Feb. 13, 1824–Apr. 3, 1911.
Vol. 3, Pt. 2–454
Flanders, Ralph Edward, Sept. 28, 1880–Feb. 19, 1970.
Supp. 8–177
Flandrau, Charles Eugene, July 15, 1828–Sept. 9, 1903.
Vol. 3, Pt. 2–455
Flandrau, Charles Macomb, Dec. 9, 1871–Mar. 28, 1938.
Supp. 2–192
Flannagan, John Bernard, Apr. 7, 1895–Jan. 6, 1942.
Supp. 3–277
Flanner, Janet, Mar. 13, 1892–Nov. 7, 1978.
Supp. 10–245
Flannery, John, Nov. 24, 1835–May 9, 1910.
Vol. 3, Pt. 2–456
Flather, John Joseph, June 9, 1862–May 14, 1926.
Vol. 3, Pt. 2–456
Fleeming, John. [*See* Fleming, John, fl. 1764–1800.]

Fleet, Thomas, Sept. 8, 1685–July 21, 1758.
Vol. 3, Pt. 2–457
Flegenheimer, Arthur, Aug. 6, 1902–Oct. 24, 1935.
Supp. 1–302
Fleischer, Nathaniel Stanley ("Nat"), Nov. 3, 1887–June 25, 1972.
Supp. 9–284
Fleischmann, Charles Louis, Nov. 3, 1834–Dec. 10, 1897.
Vol. 3, Pt. 2–458
Fleisher, Benjamin Wilfrid, Jan. 6, 1870–Aprl 29, 1946.
Supp. 4–284
Fleming, Aretas Brooks, Oct. 15, 1839–Oct. 13, 1923.
Vol. 3, Pt. 2–459
Fleming, Arthur Henry, Apr. 3, 1856–Aug. 11, 1940.
Supp. 2–193
Fleming, John, fl. 1764–1800.
Vol. 3, Pt. 2–459
Fleming, John, Apr. 17, 1807–Oct. 27, 1894.
Vol. 3, Pt. 2–460
Fleming, John Adam, Jan. 28, 1877–July 29, 1956.
Supp. 6–204
Fleming, Walter Lynwood, Apr. 8, 1874–Aug. 3, 1932.
Supp. 1–302
Fleming, William, Feb. 18, 1729–Aug. 5, 1795.
Vol. 3, Pt. 2–461
Fleming, Williamina Paton Stevens, May 15, 1857–May 21, 1911.
Vol. 3, Pt. 2–462
Fleming, William Maybury, Sept. 29, 1817–May 7, 1866.
Vol. 3, Pt. 2–461
Fletcher, Alice Cunningham, Mar. 15, 1838–Apr. 6, 1923.
Vol. 3, Pt. 2–463
Fletcher, Benjamin, d. May 28, 1703.
Supp. 1–303
Fletcher, Calvm, Feb. 4, 1798–May 26, 1866.
Vol. 3, Pt. 2–464
Fletcher, Duncan Upshaw, Jan. 6, 1859–June 17, 1936.
Supp. 2–194
Fletcher, Henry Prather, Apr. 10, 1873–July 10, 1959.
Supp. 6–206
Fletcher, Horace, Aug. 10, 1849–Jan. 13, 1919.
Vol. 3, Pt. 2–464
Fletcher, James Cooley, Apr. 15, 1823–Apr. 23, 1901.
Vol. 3, Pt. 2–465
Fletcher, John Gould, Jan. 3, 1886–May 10, 1950.
Supp. 4–285
Fletcher, Richard, Jan. 8, 1788–June 21, 1869.
Vol. 3, Pt. 2–466
Fletcher, Robert, Mar. 6, 1823–Nov. 8, 1912.
Vol. 3, Pt. 2–467
Fletcher, Robert, Aug. 23, 1847–Jan. 7, 1936.
Supp. 2–195
Fletcher, Thomas Clement, Jan. 22, 1827–Mar. 25, 1899.
Vol. 3, Pt. 2–468
Fletcher, William Asa, June 26, 1788–Sept. 19, 1852.
Vol. 3, Pt. 2–468
Fletcher, William Baldwin, Aug. 18, 1837–Apr. 25, 1907.
Vol. 3, Pt. 2–469
Flexner, Abraham, Nov. 13, 1866–Sept. 21, 1959.
Supp. 6–207
Flexner, Bernard, Feb. 24, 1865–May 3, 1945.
Supp. 3–279
Flexner, Jennie Maas, Nov. 6, 1882–Nov. 17, 1944.
Supp. 3–280
Flexner, Simon, Mar. 25, 1863–May 2, 1946.
Supp. 4–286
Flick, Lawrence Francis, Aug. 10, 1856–July 7, 1938.
Supp. 2–196
Flickinger, Daniel Kumler, May 25, 1824–Aug. 29, 1911.
Vol. 3, Pt. 2–470
Flint, Albert Stowell, Sept. 12, 1853–Feb. 22, 1923.
Vol. 3, Pt. 2–470
Flint, Austin, Oct. 20, 1812–Mar. 13, 1886.
Vol. 3, Pt. 2–471
Flint, Austin, Mar. 28, 1836–Sept. 22, 1915.
Vol. 3, Pt. 2–472
Flint, Charles Louis, Mar. 8, 1824–Feb. 26, 1889.
Vol. 3, Pt. 2–473
Flint, Charles Ranlett, Jan. 24, 1850–Feb. 12, 1934.
Supp. 1–305
Flint, Tlmothy, July 11, 1780–Aug. 16, 1840.
Vol. 3, Pt. 2–474
Flint, Weston, July 4, 1835–Apr. 6, 1906.
Vol. 3, Pt. 2–475
Florence, Thomas Birch, Jan. 26, 1812–July 3, 1875.
Vol. 3, Pt. 2–476
Florence, William Jermyn, July 26, 1831–Nov. 19, 1891.
Vol. 3, Pt. 2–476
Flower, Benjamin Orange, Oct. 19, 1858–Dec. 24, 1918.
Vol. 3, Pt. 2–477
Flower, George, 1788–Jan. 15, 1862.
Vol. 3, Pt. 2–478
Flower, Lucy Louisa Coues, May 10, 1837–Apr. 27, 1921.
Vol. 3, Pt. 2–478
Flower, Richard, 1761–Sept. 2, 1829.
Vol. 3, Pt. 2–479
Flower, Roswell Pettibone, Aug. 7, 1835–May 12, 1899.
Vol. 3, Pt. 2–479
Floy, James, Aug. 20, 1806–Oct. 14, 1863.
Vol. 3, Pt. 2–480
Floyd, John, Apr. 24, 1783–Aug. 16, 1837.
Vol. 3, Pt. 2–481
Floyd, John Buchanan, June 1, 1806–Aug. 26, 1863.
Vol. 3, Pt. 2–482
Floyd, William, Dec. 17, 1734–Aug. 4, 1821.
Vol. 3, Pt. 2–484
Flügel, Ewald, Aug. 4, 1863–Nov. 14, 1914.
Vol. 3, Pt. 2–484
Fly, James Lawrence, Feb. 22, 1898–Jan. 6, 1966.
Supp. 8–178
Flynn, Edward Joseph, Sept. 22, 1891–Aug. 18, 1953.
Supp. 5–227
Flynn, Ehzabeth Gurley, Aug. 7, 1890–Sept. 5, 1964.
Supp. 7–248
Flynn, Errol Leslie, June 20, 1909–Oct. 14, 1959.
Supp. 6–209
Flynn, John Thomas, Oct. 25, 1882–Apr. 13, 1964.
Supp. 7–249
Flynt, Josiah. [*See* Willard, Josiah Flint, 1869–1907.]
Fogarty, Anne Whitney, Feb. 2, 1919–Jan. 15, 1980.
Supp. 10–247
Fogg, George Gilman, May 26, 1813–Oct. 5, 1881.
Vol. 3, Pt. 2–485
Fokine, Michel, Apr. 25, 1880–Aug. 22, 1942
Supp. 3–281
Folger, Charles James, Apr. 16, 1818–Sept. 4, 1884.
Vol. 3, Pt. 2–486
Folger, Henry Clay, June 18, 1857–June 11, 1930.
Vol. 3, Pt. 2–487
Folger, Peter, 1617–1690.
Vol. 3, Pt. 2–488
Folger, Walter, June 12, 1765–Sept. 8, 1849.
Vol. 3, Pt. 2–489
Folin, Otto Knut Olof, Apr. 4, 1867–Oct. 25, 1934.
Supp. 1–306
Folk, Joseph Wingate, Oct. 28, 1869–May 28, 1923.
Vol. 3, Pt. 2–489
Folks, Homer, Feb. 18, 1867–Feb. 13, 1963.
Supp. 7–250
Follen, Charles, Sept. 4, 1796–Jan. 13, 1840.
Vol. 3, Pt. 2–491
Follen, Eliza Lee Cabot, Aug. 15, 1787–Jan. 26, 1860.
Vol. 3, Pt. 2–492
Follen, Karl Theodor Christian. [*See* Follen, Charles, 1796–1840.]
Follett, Mary Parker, Sept. 3, 1868–Dec. 18, 1933.
Supp. 1–308
Folsom, Charles, Dec. 24, 1794–Nov. 8, 1872.
Vol. 3, Pt. 2–493
Folsom, George, May 23, 1802–Mar. 27, 1869.
Vol. 3, Pt. 2–494
Folsom, Marion Bayard, Nov. 23, 1893–Sept. 28, 1976.
Supp. 10–249
Folsom, Nathaniel, Sept. 18, 1726–May 26, 1790.
Vol. 3, Pt. 2–494
Folwell, Samuel, *c.* 1768–Nov. 26, 1813.
Vol. 3, Pt. 2–495
Folwell, William Watts, Feb. 14, 1833–Sept. 18, 1929.
Vol. 3, Pt. 2–495
Fonda, John H., *c.* 1797–*c.* 1868.
Vol. 3, Pt. 2–496

Font, Pedro, d. Sept. 6, 1781.
Vol. 3, Pt. 2–497
Foot, Samuel Augustus, Nov. 8, 1780–Sept. 15, 1846.
Vol. 3, Pt. 2–498
Foot, Solomon, Nov. 19, 1802–Mar. 28, 1866.
Vol. 3, Pt. 2–498
Foote, Andrew Hull, Sept. 12, 1806–June 26, 1863.
Vol. 3, Pt. 2–499
Foote, Arthur William, Mar. 5, 1853–Apr. 8, 1937.
Supp. 2–197
Foote, Henry Stuart, Feb. 28, 1804–May 20, 1880.
Vol. 3, Pt. 2–500
Foote, John Ambrose, June 9, 1874–Apr. 12, 1931.
Supp. 1–309
Foote, Lucius Harwood, Apr. 10, 1826–June 4, 1913.
Vol. 3, Pt. 2–501
Foote, Samuel Augustus. [*See* Foot, Samuel Augustus, 1780–1846.]
Foote, William Henry, Dec. 20, 1794–Nov. 22, 1869.
Supp. 1–310
Foraker, Joseph Benson, July 5, 1846–May 10, 1917.
Vol. 3, Pt. 2–502
Forbes, Edwin, 1839–Mar. 6, 1895.
Vol. 3, Pt. 2–504
Forbes, Esther, June 28, 1891–Aug. 12, 1967.
Supp. 8–180
Forbes, John, 1710–Mar. 11, 1759.
Vol. 3, Pt. 2–504
Forbes, John, d. Sept. 17, 1783.
Vol. 3, Pt. 2–505
Forbes, John, 1769–May 13, 1823.
Vol. 3, Pt. 2–506
Forbes, John Murray, Aug. 13, 1771–June 14, 1831.
Vol. 3, Pt. 2–506
Forbes, John Murray, Feb. 23, 1813–Oct. 12, 1898.
Vol. 3, Pt. 2–507
Forbes, Robert Bennet, Sept. 18, 1804–Nov. 23, 1889.
Vol. 3, Pt. 2–508
Forbes, Stephen Alfred, May 29, 1844–Mar. 13, 1930.
Vol. 3, Pt. 2–509
Forbes, William Cameron, May 21, 1870–Dec. 24, 1959.
Supp. 6–210
Forbush, Edward Howe, Apr. 24, 1858–Mar. 8, 1929.
Vol. 3, Pt. 2–510
Force, Juliana Rieser, Dec. 25, 1876–Aug. 28, 1948.
Supp. 4–289
Force, Manning Ferguson, Dec. 17, 1824–May 8, 1899.
Vol. 3, Pt. 2–511
Force, Peter, Nov. 26, 1790–Jan. 23, 1868.
Vol. 3, Pt. 2–512
Ford, Daniel Sharp, Apr. 5, 1822–Dec. 24, 1899.
Vol. 3, Pt. 2–513
Ford, Edsel Bryant, Nov. 6, 1893–May 26, 1943.
Supp. 3–283
Ford, George Burdett, June 24, 1879–Aug. 13, 1930.
Supp. 1–311
Ford, Gordon Lester, Dec. 16, 1823–Nov. 14, 1891.
Vol. 3, Pt. 2–514
Ford, Guy Stanton, May 9, 1873–Dec. 29, 1962.
Supp. 7–252
Ford, Hannibal Choate, May 8, 1877–Mar. 13, 1955.
Supp. 5–228
Ford, Henry, July 30, 1863–Apr. 7, 1947.
Supp. 4–291
Ford, Henry Jones, Aug. 25, 1851–Aug. 29, 1925.
Vol. 3, Pt. 2–515
Ford, Jacob, Feb. 10, 1738–Jan 11, 1777.
Vol. 3, Pt. 2–516
Ford, John, Feb. 1, 1894–Aug. 31, 1973.
Supp. 9–286
Ford, John Baptiste, Nov. 17, 1811–May 1, 1903.
Vol. 3, Pt. 2–516
Ford, John Thomson, Apr. 16, 1829–Mar. 14, 1894.
Vol. 3, Pt. 2–517
Ford, Mary, July 7, 1924–Sept. 30, 1977.
Supp. 10–251
Ford, Patrick, Apr. 12, 1835–Sept. 23, 1913.
Vol. 3, Pt. 2–518
Ford, Paul Leicester, Mar. 23, 1865–May 8, 1902.
Vol. 3, Pt. 2–518
Ford, Thomas, Dec. 5, 1800–Nov. 3, 1850.
Vol. 3, Pt. 2–520
Ford, Worthington Chauncey, Feb. 16, 1858–Mar. 7, 1941.
Supp. 3–285
Fordney, Joseph Warren, Nov. 5, 1853–Jan. 8, 1932.
Supp. 1–312
Fordyce, John Addison, Feb. 16, 1858–June 4, 1925.
Vol. 3, Pt. 2–521
Forepaugh, Adam, 1831–Jan. 22, 1890.
Vol. 3, Pt. 2–522
Forester, Cecil Scott, Aug. 27, 1899–Apr. 2, 1966.
Supp. 8–181
Forester, Frank. [*See* Herbert, Henry William, 1807–1858.]
Foresti, Eleutario Felice, 1793–Sept. 14, 1858.
Vol. 3, Pt. 2–522
Forgan, James Berwick, Apr. 11, 1852–Oct. 28, 1924.
Vol. 3, Pt. 2–523
Forman, Celia Adler, Dec. 7, 1889–Jan. 31, 1979.
Supp. 10–252
Forman, David, Nov. 3, 1745–Sept. 12, 1797.
Vol. 3, Pt. 2–524
Forman, Joshua, Sept. 6, 1777–Aug. 4, 1848.
Vol. 3, Pt. 2–525
Forman, Justus Miles, Nov. 1, 1875–May 7, 1915.
Vol. 3, Pt. 2–526
Forney, John Wien, Sept. 30, 1817–Dec. 9, 1881.
Vol. 3, Pt. 2–526
Forney, Matthias Nace, Mar. 28, 1835–Jan. 14, 1908.
Vol. 3, Pt. 2–527
Forney, William Henry, Nov. 9, 1823–Jan. 16, 1894.
Vol. 3, Pt. 2–528
Forrest, Edwin, Mar. 9, 1806–Dec. 12, 1872.
Vol. 3, Pt. 2–529
Forrest, French, Oct. 4, 1796–Nov. 22, 1866.
Vol. 3, Pt. 2–531
Forrest, Nathan Bedford, July 13, 1821–Oct. 29, 1877.
Vol. 3, Pt. 2–532
Forrestal, James Vincent, Feb. 15, 1892–May 22, 1949.
Supp. 4–304
Forsyth, John, Oct. 22, 1780–Oct. 21, 1841.
Vol. 3, Pt. 2–533
Forsyth, John, Dec. 31, 1810–Oct. 17, 1886.
Vol. 3, Pt. 2–535
Forsyth, Thomas, Dec. 5, 1771–Oct. 29, 1833.
Vol. 3, Pt. 2–536
Forten, James, Sept. 2, 1766–Mar. 4, 1842.
Vol. 3, Pt. 2–536
Fortescue, Charles LeGeyt, Nov. 7, 1876–Dec. 4, 1936.
Supp. 2–198
Fortier, Alcée, June 5, 1856–Feb. 14, 1914.
Vol. 3, Pt. 2–537
Forward, Walter, Jan. 24, 1786–Nov. 24, 1852.
Vol. 3, Pt. 2–537
Forwood, William Henry, Sept. 7, 1838–May 12, 1915.
Vol. 9, Pt. 2–538
Fosdick, Charles Austin, Sept. 16, 1842–Aug. 22, 1915.
Vol. 3, Pt. 2–539
Fosdick, Harry Emerson, May 24, 1878–Oct. 5, 1969.
Supp. 8–182
Fosdick, Raymond Blaine, June 9, 1883–July 18, 1972.
Supp. 9–287
Fosdick, William Whiteman, Jan. 28, 1825–Mar. 8, 1862.
Vol. 3, Pt. 2–540
Foshag, William Frederick, Mar. 17, 1894–May 21, 1956.
Supp. 6–212
Foss, Cyrus David, Jan. 17, 1834–Jan. 29, 1910.
Vol. 3, Pt. 2–540
Foss, Sam Walter, June 19, 1858–Feb. 26, 1911.
Vol. 3, Pt. 2–541
Foster, Abiel, Aug. 8, 1735–Feb. 6, 1806.
Vol. 3, Pt. 2–542
Foster, Abigail Kelley, Jan. 15, 1810–Jan. 14, 1887.
Vol. 3, Pt. 2–542
Foster, Benjamin, July 31, 1852–Jan. 28, 1926.
Vol. 3, Pt. 2–543
Foster, Charles, Apr. 12, 1828–Jan. 9, 1904.
Vol. 3, Pt. 2–544
Foster, Charles James, Nov. 24, 1820–Sept. 12, 1883.
Vol. 3, Pt. 2–545
Foster, David Skaats, Jan. 23, 1852–June 23, 1920.
Vol. 3, Pt. 2–545

Foster, Ephraim Hubbard, Sept. 17, 1794–Sept. 6, 1854.
Vol. 3, Pt. 2–546
Foster, Frank Hugh, June 18, 1851–Oct. 20, 1935.
Supp. 1–313
Foster, Frank Pierce, Nov. 26, 1841–Aug. 13, 1911.
Vol. 3, Pt. 2–546
Foster, George Burman, Apr. 2, 1858–Dec. 22, 1918.
Vol. 3, Pt. 2–547
Foster, Hannah Webster, 1759–Apr. 17, 1840.
Vol. 3, Pt. 2–548
Foster, John, 1648–Sept. 9, 1681.
Vol. 3, Pt. 2–549
Foster, John Gray, May 27, 1823–Sept. 2, 1874.
Vol. 3, Pt. 2–549
Foster, John Pierrepont Codrington, Mar. 2, 1847–Apr. 1, 1910.
Vol. 3, Pt. 2–550
Foster, John Watson, Mar. 2, 1836–Nov. 15, 1917.
Vol. 3, Pt. 2–551
Foster, Judith Ellen Horton, Nov. 3, 1840–Aug. 11, 1910.
Vol. 3, Pt. 2–552
Foster, Lafayette Sabine, Nov. 22, 1806–Sept. 19, 1880.
Vol. 3, Pt. 2–553
Foster, Murphy James, Jan. 12, 1849–June 12, 1921.
Vol. 3, Pt. 2–554
Foster, Randolph Sinks, Feb. 22, 1820–May 1, 1903.
Vol. 3, Pt. 2–554
Foster, Robert Sanford, Jan. 27, 1834–Mar. 3, 1903.
Vol. 3, Pt. 2–555
Foster, Roger Sherman Baldwin, Apr. 21, 1857–Feb. 22, 1924.
Vol. 3, Pt. 2–556
Foster, Stephen Collins, July 4, 1826–Jan. 13, 1864.
Vol. 3, Pt. 2–557
Foster, Stephen Symonds, Nov. 17, 1809–Sept. 8, 1881.
Vol. 3, Pt. 2–558
Foster, Theodore, Apr. 29, 1752–Jan. 13, 1828.
Vol. 3, Pt. 2–559
Foster, Thomas Jefferson, Jan. 1, 1843–Oct. 14, 1936.
Supp. 2–199
Foster, William Trufant, Jan. 18, 1879–Oct. 8, 1950.
Supp. 4–306
Foster, William Z., Feb. 25, 1881–Sept. 1, 1961.
Supp. 7–254
Foulk, George Clayton, Oct. 30, 1856–Aug. 6, 1893.
Vol. 3, Pt. 2–559
Foulke, William Dudley, Nov. 20, 1848–May 30, 1935.
Supp. 1–314
Foulois, Benjamin Delahauf, Dec. 9, 1879–Apr. 25, 1967.
Supp. 8–184
Fowke, Gerard, June 25, 1855–Mar. 5, 1933.
Supp. 1–315
Fowle, Daniel, October 1715–June 8, 1787.
Vol. 3, Pt. 2–560
Fowle, William Bentley, Oct. 17, 1795–Feb. 6, 1865.
Vol. 3, Pt. 2–561
Fowler, Charles Henry, Aug. 11, 1837–Mar. 20, 1908.
Vol. 3, Pt. 2–562
Fowler, Frank, July 12, 1852–Aug. 18, 1910.
Vol. 3, Pt. 2–562
Fowler, Gene, Mar. 8, 1890–July 2, 1960.
Supp. 6–213
Fowler, George Ryerson, Dec. 25, 1848–Feb. 6, 1906.
Vol. 3, Pt. 2–563
Fowler, Joseph Smith, Aug. 31, 1820–Apr. 1, 1902.
Vol. 3, Pt. 2–564
Fowler, Orin, July 29, 1791–Sept. 3, 1852.
Vol. 3, Pt. 2–565
Fowler, Orson Squire, Oct. 11, 1809–Aug. 18, 1887.
Vol. 3, Pt. 2–565
Fowler, Russell Story, May 1, 1874–Jan. 5, 1959.
Supp. 6–214
Fox, Charles Kemble, Aug. 15, 1833–Jan. 17, 1875.
Vol. 3, Pt. 2–566
Fox, Dixon Ryan, Dec. 7, 1887–Jan. 30, 1945.
Supp. 3–286
Fox, Fontaine Talbot, Jr., June 4, 1884–Aug. 9, 1964.
Supp. 7–257
Fox, George Washington Lafayette, July 3, 1825–Oct. 24, 1877.
Vol. 3, Pt. 2–567
Fox, Gilbert, 1776–1807?.
Vol. 3, Pt. 2–567
Fox, Gustavus Vasa, June 13, 1821–Oct. 29, 1883.
Vol. 3, Pt. 2–568
Fox, Harry, Sept. 29, 1826–Sept. 4, 1883.
Vol. 3, Pt. 2–569
Fox, Jacob Nelson ("Nellie"), Dec. 25, 1927–Dec. 1, 1975.
Supp. 9–288
Fox, John William, Dec. 16, 1863–July 8, 1919.
Vol. 3, Pt. 2–570
Fox, Margaret, Oct. 7, 1833–Mar. 8, 1893.
Vol. 3, Pt. 2–570
Fox, Richard Kyle, Aug. 12, 1846–Nov. 14, 1922.
Vol. 3, Pt. 2–571
Fox, Virgil Keel, May 3, 1912–Oct. 25, 1980.
Supp. 10–254
Fox, William, Jan. 1, 1879–May 8, 1952.
Supp. 5–229
Fox, Williams Carlton, May 20, 1855–Jan. 20, 1924.
Vol. 3, Pt. 2–572
Foxall, Henry, May 24, 1758–Dec. 11, 1823.
Vol. 3, Pt. 2–573
Foxx, James Emory, Oct. 22, 1907–July 21, 1967.
Supp. 8–186
Foy, Eddie, Mar. 9, 1856–Feb. 16, 1928.
Vol. 3, Pt. 2–573
Fraina, Louis C. [*See* Corey, Lewis, 1892–1953.]
Fraley, Frederick, May 28, 1804–Sept. 23, 1901.
Vol. 3, Pt. 2–574
Frame, Alice Seymour Browne, Oct. 29, 1878–Aug. 16, 1941.
Supp. 3–287
Franchère, Gabriel, Nov. 3, 1786–Apr. 12, 1863.
Vol. 3, Pt. 2–575
Francis, Charles Spencer, June 17, 1853–Dec. 1, 1911.
Vol. 3, Pt. 2–576
Francis, Charles Stephen, Jan. 9, 1805–Dec. 1, 1887.
Vol. 3, Pt. 2–576
Francis, David Rowland, Oct. 1, 1850–Jan. 15, 1927.
Vol. 3, Pt. 2–577
Francis, James Bicheno, May 18, 1815–Sept. 18, 1892.
Vol. 3, Pt. 2–578
Francis, John Brown, May 31, 1791–Aug. 9, 1864.
Vol. 3, Pt. 2–579
Francis, John Morgan, Mar. 6, 1823–June 18, 1897.
Vol. 3, Pt. 2–580
Francis, John Wakefield, Nov. 17, 1789–Feb. 8, 1861.
Vol. 3, Pt. 2–581
Francis, Joseph, Mar. 12, 1801–May 10, 1893.
Vol. 3, Pt. 2–582
Francis, Kay, Jan. 13, 1905–Aug. 26, 1968.
Supp. 8–187
Francis, Paul James, Jan. 16, 1863–Feb. 8, 1940.
Supp. 2–201
Francis, Samuel Ward, Dec. 26, 1835–Mar. 25, 1886.
Vol. 3, Pt. 2–583
Francis, Tench, d. Aug. 16, 1758.
Vol. 3, Pt. 2–583
Francis Convers, Nov. 9, 1795–Apr. 7, 1863.
Vol. 3, Pt. 2–577
Franck, James, Aug. 26, 1882–May 21, 1964.
Supp. 7–258
Francke, Kuno, Sept. 27, 1855–June 25, 1930.
Vol. 3, Pt. 2–584
Frank, Glenn, Oct. 1, 1887–Sept. 15, 1940.
Supp. 2–202
Frank, Jerome, Sept. 10, 1889–Jan. 13, 1957.
Supp. 6–215
Frank, Lawrence Kelso, Dec. 6, 1890–Sept. 23, 1968.
Supp. 8–188
Frank, Philipp G., Mar. 20, 1884–July 21, 1966.
Supp. 8–189
Frank, Tenney, May 19, 1876–Apr. 3, 1939.
Supp. 2–203
Frank, Waldo David, Aug. 25, 1889–Jan. 9, 1967.
Supp. 8–191
Frankfurter, Alfred Moritz, Oct. 4, 1906–May 12,
Supp. 7–259
Frankfurter, Felix, Nov. 15, 1882–Feb. 22, 1965.
Supp. 7–260
Frankland, Lady Agnes Surriage, 1726–Apr. 23, 1783.
Vol. 3, Pt. 2–585

Franklin, Benjamin, Jan. 17, 1706–Apr. 17, 1790.
Vol. 3, Pt. 2–585
Franklin, Benjamin, Feb. 1, 1812–Oct. 22, 1878.
Vol. 3, Pt. 2–598
Franklin, Edward Curtis, Mar. 1, 1862–Feb. 13, 1937.
Supp. 2–205
Franklin, Fabian, Jan. 18, 1853–Jan. 9, 1939.
Supp. 2–206
Franklin, James, Feb. 4, 1696/7–February 1735.
Vol. 3, Pt. 2–599
Franklin, Jesse, Mar. 24, 1760–Aug. 31, 1823.
Vol. 3, Pt. 2–600
Franklin, Philip Albright Small, Feb. 1, 1871–Aug. 14, 1939.
Supp. 2–207
Franklin, William, 1731–Nov. 16, 1813.
Vol. 3, Pt. 2–600
Franklin, William Buel, Feb. 27, 1823–Mar. 8, 1903.
Vol. 3, Pt. 2–601
Franz, Shepherd Ivory, May 27, 1874–Oct. 14, 1933.
Supp. 1–316
Franzblau, Rose Nadler, Jan. 1, 1905–Sept. 2, 1979.
Supp. 10–255
Frary, Francis Cowles, July 9, 1884–Feb. 4, 1970.
Supp. 8–193
Frasch, Herman, Dec. 25, 1851?–May 1, 1914.
Vol. 3, Pt. 2–602
Fraser, Charles, Aug. 20, 1782–Oct. 5, 1860.
Vol. 3, Pt. 2–603
Fraser, James Earle, Nov. 4, 1876–Oct. 11, 1953.
Supp. 5–231
Fraser, Leon, Nov. 27, 1889–Apr. 8, 1945.
Supp. 3–289
Fraunces, Samuel, *c.* 1722–Oct. 10, 1795.
Vol. 4, Pt. 1–1
Frayne, Hugh, Nov. 8. 1869–July 13, 1934.
Supp. 1–317
Frazee, John, July 18, 1790–Feb. 24, 1852.
Vol. 4, Pt. 1–1
Frazer, John Fries, July 8, 1812–Oct. 12, 1872.
Vol. 4, Pt. 1–3
Frazer, Joseph Washington, Mar. 4, 1892–Aug. 7, 1971.
Supp. 9–289
Frazer, Oliver, Feb. 4, 1808–Feb. 9, 1864.
Vol. 4, Pt. 1–3
Frazer, Persifor, Aug. 9, 1736–Apr. 24, 1792.
Vol. 4, Pt. 1–4
Frazer, Persifor, July 24, 1844–Apr. 9, 1909.
Vol. 4, Pt. 1–4
Frazier, Charles Harrison, Apr. 19, 1870–July 26, 1936.
Supp. 2–208
Frazier, Edward Franklin, Sept. 24, 1894–May 17, 1962.
Supp. 7–265
Frazier, Lynn Joseph, Dec. 21, 1874–Jan. 11, 1947.
Supp. 4–308
Frear, William, Mar. 24, 1860–Jan. 7, 1922.
Vol. 4, Pt. 1–5
Freas, Thomas Bruce, Nov. 2, 1868–Mar. 15, 1928.
Vol. 4, Pt. 1–6
Frederic, Harold, Aug. 19, 1856–Oct. 19, 1898.
Vol. 4, Pt. 1–7
Freed, Alan J., Dec. 15, 1921–Jan. 20, 1965.
Supp. 7–266
Freed, Arthur, Sept. 9, 1894–Apr. 12, 1973.
Supp. 9–291
Freedman, Andrew, Sept. 1, 1860–Dec. 4, 1915.
Vol. 4, Pt. 1–8
Freeman, Allen Weir, Jan. 7, 1881–July 3, 1954.
Supp. 5–232
Freeman, Bernardus, d. 1741.
Vol. 4, Pt. 1–8
Freeman, Douglas Southall, May 16, 1886–June 13, 1953.
Supp. 5–233
Freeman, Frederick Kemper, June 15, 1841–Sept. 9, 1928.
Vol. 4, Pt. 1–9
Freeman, James, Apr. 22, 1759–Nov. 14, 1835.
Vol. 4, Pt. 1–10
Freeman, James Edwards, 1808–Nov. 21, 1884.
Vol. 4, Pt. 1–11
Freeman, John Ripley, July 27, 1855–Oct. 6, 1932.
Supp. 1–318
Freeman, Joseph, Oct. 7, 1897–Aug. 9, 1965.
Supp. 7–268
Freeman, Mary Eleanor Wilkins, Oct. 31, 1852–Mar. 13, 1910.
Vol. 4, Pt. 1–11
Freeman, Nathaniel, Mar. 28, 1741–Sept. 20, 1827.
Vol. 4, Pt. 1–12
Freeman, Thomas, d. Nov. 8, 1821.
Vol. 4, Pt. 1–13
Freer, Charles Lang, Feb. 25, 1856–Sept. 25, 1919.
Vol. 4, Pt. 1–14
Frelinghuysen, Frederick Theodore, Aug. 4, 1817–May 20, 1885.
Vol. 4, Pt. 1–15
Frelinghuysen, Frederick, Apr. 13, 1753–Apr. 13, 1804.
Vol. 4, Pt. 1–15
Frelinghuysen, Theodore, Mar. 28, 1787–Apr. 12, 1862.
Vol. 4, Pt. 1–16
Frelinghuysen, Theodorus Jacobus, 1691–*c.* 1748.
Vol. 4, Pt. 1–17
Frémont, Jessie Benton, May 31, 1824–Dec. 27, 1902.
Vol. 4, Pt. 1–18
Frémont, John Charles, Jan. 21, 1813–July 13, 1890.
Vol. 4, Pt. 1–19
French, Aaron, Mar. 23, 1823–Mar. 24, 1902.
Vol. 4, Pt. 1–23
French, Alice, Mar. 18, 1850–Jan. 9, 1934.
Supp. 1–320
French, Daniel Chester, Apr. 20, 1850–Oct. 7, 1931.
Supp. 1–320
French, Edwin Davis, Jan. 19, 1851–Dec. 8, 1906.
Vol. 4, Pt. 1–24
French, Lucy Virginia Smith, Mar. 16, 1825–Mar. 31, 1881.
Vol. 4, Pt. 1–25
French, Paul Comly, Mar. 19, 1903–June 3, 1960.
Supp. 6–217
French, William Merchant Richardson, Oct. 1, 1843–June 3, 1914.
Vol. 4, Pt. 1–26
French, William Henry, Jan. 13, 1815–May 20, 1881.
Vol. 4, Pt. 1–25
Freneau, Philip Morin, Jan. 2, 1752–Dec. 19, 1832.
Vol. 4, Pt. 1–27
Freund, Ernst, Jan. 30, 1864–Oct. 20, 1932.
Supp. 1–323
Frey, John Philip, Feb. 24, 1871–Nov. 29, 1957.
Supp. 6–218
Frey, Joseph Samuel Christian Frederick, Sept. 21, 1771–June 5, 1850.
Vol. 4, Pt. 1–28
Frick, Ford Christopher, Dec. 19, 1894–Apr. 8, 1978.
Supp. 10–256
Frick, Henry Clay, Dec. 19, 1849–Dec. 2, 1919.
Vol. 4, Pt. 1–29
Friday, *c.* 1822–May 13, 1881.
Vol. 4, Pt. 1–31
Friedenwald, Aaron, Dec. 20, 1836–Aug. 26, 1902.
Vol. 4, Pt. 1–31
Friedlaender, Israel, Sept. 8, 1876–July 5, 1920.
Vol. 4, Pt. 1–32
Friedlaender, Walter Ferdinand, Mar. 10, 1873–Sept. 6, 1966.
Supp. 8–194
Friedman, William Frederick, Sept. 24, 1891–Nov. 2, 1969.
Supp. 8–195
Fries, Francis, Oct. 17, 1812–Aug. 1, 1863.
Vol. 4, Pt. 1–33
Fries, John, *c.* 1750–February 1818.
Vol. 4, Pt. 1–34
Frieseke, Frederick Carl, Apr. 7, 1874–Aug. 24, 1939.
Supp. 2–209
Frieze, Henry Simmons, Sept. 15, 1817–Dec. 7, 1889.
Vol. 4, Pt. 1–34
Friml, Charles Rudolf, Dec. 7, 1879–Nov. 12, 1972.
Supp. 9–292
Frisbie, Levi, Sept. 15, 1783–July 9, 1822.
Vol. 4, Pt. 1–35
Frisch, Frank Francis ("The Fordham Flash"), Sept. 9, 1898–Mar. 12, 1973.
Supp. 9–293
Frissell, Hollis Burke, July 14, 1851–Aug. 5, 1917.
Vol. 4, Pt. 1–36

Fritschel, Conrad Sigmund, Dec. 2, 1833–Apr. 26, 1900.
Vol. 4, Pt. 1–37
Fritschel, Gottfried Leonhard Wilhelm, Dec. 19, 1836–July 13, 1889.
Vol. 4, Pt. 1–37
Fritz, John, Aug. 21, 1822–Feb. 13, 1913.
Vol. 4, Pt. 1–38
Frizell, Joseph Palmer, Mar. 13, 1832–May 4, 1910.
Vol. 4, Pt. 1–39
Frohman, Charles, June 17, 1860–May 7, 1915.
Vol. 4, Pt. 1–40
Frohman, Daniel, Aug. 22, 1851–Dec. 26, 1940.
Supp. 2–210
Froman, Ellen Jane, Nov. 10, 1907–Apr. 22, 1980.
Supp. 10–257
Fromm, Erich, Mar. 23, 1900–Mar. 18, 1980.
Supp. 10–259
Fromm-Reichmann, Frieda, Oct. 23, 1889–Apr. 28, 1957.
Supp. 6–219
Frost, Arthur Burdett, Jan. 17, 1851–June 22, 1928.
Vol. 4, Pt. 1–41
Frost, Edwin Brant, July 14, 1866–May 14, 1935.
Supp. 1–324
Frost, Holloway Halstead, Apr. 11, 1889–Jan. 26, 1935.
Supp. 1–325
Frost, Robert Lee, Mar. 26, 1874–Jan. 29, 1963.
Supp. 7–270
Frost, Wade Hampton, Mar. 3, 1880–Apr. 30, 1938.
Supp. 2–211
Frothingham, Arthur Lincoln, June 21, 1859–July 28, 1923.
Vol. 4, Pt. 1–42
Frothingham, Nathaniel Langdon, July 23, 1793–Apr. 4, 1870.
Vol. 4, Pt. 1–43
Frothingham, Octavius Brooks, Nov. 26, 1822–Nov. 27, 1895.
Vol. 4, Pt. 1–44
Frothingham, Paul Revere, July 6, 1864–Nov. 27, 1926.
Vol. 4, Pt. 1–44
Frothingham, Richard, Jan. 31, 1812–Jan. 29, 1880.
Vol. 4, Pt. 1–45
Fry, Birkett Davenport, June 24, 1822–Jan. 21, 1891.
Vol. 4, Pt. 1–46
Fry, James Barnet, Feb. 22, 1827–July 11, 1894.
Vol. 4, Pt. 1–47
Fry, Joshua, *c.* 1700–May 31, 1754.
Vol. 4, Pt. 1–48
Fry, Richard, fl. 1731–1741.
Vol. 4, Pt. 1–49
Fry, William Henry, Aug. 10, 1815–Dec. 21, 1864.
Vol. 4, Pt. 1–49
Frye, Joseph, Mar. 8/19, 1711/12–July 25, 1794.
Vol. 4 Pt. 1–50
Frye, William John ("Jack"), Mar. 18, 1904–Feb. 3, 1959.
Supp. 6–220
Frye, William Pierce, Sept. 2, 1831–Aug. 8, 1911.
Vol. 4, Pt. 1–51
Fryer, Douglas Henry, Nov. 7, 1891–Dec. 24, 1960.
Supp. 6–222
Fuertes, Estevan Antonio, May 10, 1838–Jan. 16, 1903.
Vol. 4, Pt. 1–52
Fuertes, Louis Agassiz, Feb. 7, 1874–Aug. 22, 1927.
Vol. 4, Pt. 1–53
Fullam, Frank L., Jan. 6, 1870–July 31, 1951.
Supp. 5–235
Fuller, Andrew S., Aug. 3, 1828–May 4, 1896.
Vol. 4, Pt. 1–53
Fuller, George, Jan. 17, 1822–Mar. 21, 1884.
Vol. 4, Pt. 1–54
Fuller, George Warren, Dec. 21, 1868–June 15, 1934.
Supp. 1–325
Fuller, Henry Blake, Jan. 9, 1857–July 28, 1929.
Vol. 4, Pt. 1–56
Fuller, Hiram, Sept. 6, 1814–Nov. 19, 1880.
Vol. 4, Pt. 1–57
Fuller, John Wallace, July 28, 1827–Mar. 12, 1891.
Vol. 4, Pt. 1–58
Fuller, Joseph Vincent, Sept. 27, 1890–Apr. 1, 1932.
Supp. 1–327
Fuller, Levi Knight, Feb. 24, 1841–Oct. 10, 1896.
Vol. 4, Pt. 1–59
Fuller, Loie, Jan. 15, 1862–Jan. 1, 1928.
Vol. 4, Pt. 1–59
Fuller, Margaret. [*See* Fuller, Sarah Margaret, 1810–1850.]
Fuller, Melville Weston, Feb. 11, 1833–July 4, 1910.
Vol. 4, Pt. 1–60
Fuller, Richard, Apr. 22, 1804–Oct. 20, 1876.
Vol. 4, Pt. 1–62
Fuller, Robert Mason, Oct. 27, 1845–Dec. 28, 1919.
Vol. 4, Pt. 1–63
Fuller, Sarah Margaret, May 23, 1810–July 19, 1850.
Vol. 4, Pt. 1–63
Fuller, Thomas Charles, Feb. 27, 1832–Oct. 20, 1901.
Vol. 4, Pt. 1–66
Fullerton, George Stuart, Aug. 18, 1859–Mar. 23, 1925.
Vol. 4, Pt. 1–66
Fulton, John Farquhar, Nov. 1, 1899–May 29, 1960.
Supp. 6–222
Fulton, Justin Dewey, Mar. 1, 1828–Apr. 16, 1901.
Vol. 4, Pt. 1–68
Fulton, Robert, Nov. 14, 1765–Feb. 24, 1815.
Vol. 4, Pt. 1–68
Fulton, Robert Burwell, Apr. 8, 1849–May 29, 1919.
Vol. 4, Pt. 1–72
Funk, Casimir, Feb. 23, 1884–Nov. 20, 1967.
Supp. 8–197
Funk, Isaac Kauffman, Sept. 10, 1839–Apr. 4, 1912.
Vol. 4, Pt. 1–72
Funk, Wilfred John, Mar. 20, 1883–June 1, 1965.
Supp. 7–274
Funston, Frederick, Nov. 9, 1865–Feb. 19, 1917.
Vol. 4, Pt. 1–73
Furlow, Floyd Charles, Apr. 9, 1877–Apr. 26, 1923.
Vol. 4, Pt. 1–75
Furman, James Clement, Dec. 5, 1809–Mar. 3, 1891.
Vol. 4, Pt. 1–75
Furman, Richard, Oct. 9, 1755–Aug. 25, 1825.
Vol. 4, Pt. 1–76
Furnas, Robert Wilkinson, May 5, 1824–June 1, 1905.
Vol. 4, Pt. 1–77
Furness, Horace Howard, Nov. 2, 1833–Aug. 13, 1912.
Vol. 4, Pt. 1–78
Furness, Horace Howard, Jan. 24, 1865–Apr. 15, 1930.
Vol. 4, Pt. 1–79
Furness, William Henry, Apr. 20, 1802–Jan. 30, 1896.
Vol. 4, Pt. 1–80
Furst, Clyde Bowman, Aug. 29, 1873–Mar. 6, 1931.
Supp. 1–327
Furuseth, Andrew, Mar. 12, 1854–Jan. 22, 1938.
Supp. 2–212
Fussell, Bartholomew, Jan. 9, 1794–Feb. 15, 1871.
Vol. 4, Pt. 1–80

Gabb, William More, Jan. 20, 1839–May 30, 1878.
Vol. 4, Pt. 1–81
Gable, (William) Clark, Feb. 1, 1901–Nov. 16, 1960.
Supp. 6–224
Gabo, Naum, Aug. 5, 1890–Aug. 23, 1977.
Supp. 10–263
Gabrielson, Ira Noel, Sept. 27, 1889–Sept. 7, 1977.
Supp. 10–264
Gabrilowitsch, Ossip, Feb. 7, 1878–Sept. 14, 1936.
Supp. 2–213
Gadsden, Christopher, Feb. 16, 1724–Aug. 28, 1805.
Vol. 4, Pt. 1–82
Gadsden, James, May 15, 1788–Dec. 26, 1858.
Vol. 4, Pt. 1–83
Gaffney, Margaret. [*See* Haughery, Margaret Gaffney, *c.* 1814–1882.]
Gág, Wanda (Hazel), Mar. 11, 1893–June 27, 1946.
Supp. 4–309
Gage, Frances Dana Barker, Oct. 12, 1808–Nov. 10, 1884.
Vol. 4, Pt. 1–84
Gage, Lyman Judson, June 28, 1836–Jan. 26, 1927.
Vol. 4 Pt. 1–85
Gage, Matiida Joslyn, Mar. 24, 1826–Mar. 18, 1898.
Vol. 4, Pt. 1–86
Gage, Thomas, 1721–Apr. 2, 1787.
Vol. 4, Pt. 1–87
Gaillard, David Du Bose, Sept. 4, 1859–Dec. 5, 1913.
Vol. 4, Pt. 1–88
Gaillard, Edwin Samuel, Jan. 16, 1827–Feb. 2, 1885.
Vol. 4, Pt. 1–90

Gaillard, John, Sept. 5, 1765–Feb. 26, 1826.
Vol. 4, Pt. 1–90
Gaillardet, Théodore Frédéric, Apr. 7, 1808–Aug. 13, 1882.
Vol. 4, Pt. 1–91
Gailor, Thomas Frank, Sept. 17, 1856–Oct. 3, 1935.
Supp. 1–329
Gaine, Hugh, 1726/27–Apr. 25, 1807.
Vol. 4, Pt. 1–91
Gaines, Edmund Pendleton, Mar. 20, 1777–June 6, 1849.
Vol. 4, Pt. 1–92
Gaines, George Strother, *c.* 1784–Jan. 21, 1873.
Vol. 4, Pt. 1–93
Gaines, John Pollard, Sept. 22, 1795–Dec. 9, 1857.
Vol. 4, Pt. 1–94
Gaines, Reuben Reid, Oct. 30, 1836–Oct. 13, 1914.
Vol. 4, Pt. 1–95
Gaines, Wesley John, Oct. 4, 1840–Jan. 12, 1912.
Vol. 4, Pt. 1–96
Gaisman, Henry Jaques, Dec. 5, 1869–Aug. 6, 1974.
Supp. 9–297
Gaither, Horace Rowan, Jr., Nov. 23, 1909–Apr. 7, 1961.
Supp. 7–275
Galante, Carmine, Feb. 21, 1910–July 12, 1979.
Supp. 10–266
Galberry, Thomas, 1833–Oct. 10, 1878.
Vol. 4, Pt. 1–97
Galbreath, Charles Burleigh, Feb. 25, 1858–Feb. 23, 1934.
Supp. 1–329
Gale, Benjamin, Dec. 14, 1715–May 6, 1790.
Vol. 4, Pt. 1–97
Gale, Elbridge, Dec. 25, 1824–Nov. 7, 1907.
Vol. 4, Pt. 1–98
Gale, George Washington, Dec. 3, 1789–Sept. 13, 1861.
Vol. 4, Pt. 1–99
Gale, Henry Gordon, Sept. 12, 1874–Nov. 16, 1942.
Supp. 3–290
Gale, Zona, Aug. 26, 1874–Dec. 27, 1938.
Supp. 2–215
Gales, Joseph, Feb. 4, 1761–Aug. 24, 1841.
Vol. 4, Pt. 1–99
Gales, Joseph, Apr. 10, 1786–July 21, 1860.
Vol. 4, Pt. 1–100
Gall, *c.* 1840–Dec. 5, 1894.
Vol. 4, Pt. 1–101
Gallagher, Hugh Patrick, Mar. 26, 1815–Mar. 10, 1882.
Vol. 4, Pt. 1–102
Gallagher, Ralph W., May 27, 1881–July 31, 1952.
Supp. 5–235
Gallagher, William Davis, Aug. 21, 1808–June 27, 1894.
Vol. 4, Pt. 1–102
Gallatin, Abraham Alfonse Albert, Jan. 29, 1761–Aug. 12, 1849.
Vol. 4, Pt. 1–103
Gallaudet, Edward Miner, Feb. 5, 1837–Sept. 26, 1917.
Vol. 4, Pt. 1–110
Gallaudet, Thomas, June 3, 1822–Aug. 27, 1902.
Vol. 4, Pt. 1–110
Gallaudet, Thomas Hopkins, Dec. 10, 1787–Sept. 10, 1851.
Vol. 4, Pt. 1–111
Gallico, Paul William, July 26, 1897–July 15, 1976.
Supp. 10–267
Galli-Curci, Amelita, Nov. 18, 1882–Nov. 26, 1963.
Supp. 7–277
Gallier, James, July 24, 1798–May 16, 1868.
Supp. 1–330
Gallinger, Jacob Harold, Mar. 28, 1837–Aug. 17, 1918.
Vol. 4, Pt. 1–112
Gallitzin, Demetrius Augustine, Dec. 22, 1770–May 6, 1840.
Vol. 4, Pt. 1–113
Galloway, Beverly Thomas, Oct. 16, 1863–June 13, 1938.
Supp. 2–217
Galloway, Charles Betts, Sept. 1, 1849–May 12, 1909.
Vol. 4, Pt. 1–115
Galloway, Joseph, *c.* 1731–Aug. 29, 1803.
Vol. 4, Pt. 1–116
Galloway, Samuel, Mar. 22, 1811–Apr. 5, 1872.
Vol. 4, Pt. 1–117
Gallup, Joseph Adams, Mar. 30, 1769–Oct. 12, 1849.
Vol. 4, Pt. 1–118
Gally, Merritt, Aug. 15, 1838–Mar. 7, 1916.
Vol. 4, Pt. 1–118
Galpin, Charles Josiah, Mar. 16, 1864–June 1, 1947.
Supp. 4–311
Gálvez, Bernardo de, July 23, 1746–Nov. 30, 1786.
Vol. 4, Pt. 1–119
Gambino, Carlo, Aug. 24, 1900–Oct. 15, 1976.
Supp. 10–268
Gamble, Hamilton Rowan, Nov. 29, 1798–Jan. 31, 1864.
Vol. 4, Pt. 1–120
Gambrell, James Bruton, Aug. 21, 1841–June 10, 1921.
Vol. 4, Pt. 1–121
Gambrell, Mary Latimer, Jan. 14, 1898–Aug. 19, 1974.
Supp. 9–298
Gammon, Elijah Hedding, Dec. 23, 1819–July 3, 1891.
Vol. 4, Pt. 1–122
Gamow, George, Mar. 4, 1904–Aug. 20, 1968.
Supp. 8–198
Gannett, Ezra Stiles, May 4, 1801–Aug. 26, 1871.
Vol. 4, Pt. 1–122
Gannett, Frank Ernest, Sept. 15, 1876–Dec. 3, 1957.
Supp. 6–226
Gannett, Henry, Aug. 24, 1846–Nov. 5, 1914.
Vol. 4, Pt. 1–123
Gannett, William Channing, Mar. 13, 1840–Dec. 15, 1923.
Vol. 4, Pt. 1–124
Gano, John, July 22, 1727–Aug. 10, 1804.
Vol. 4, Pt. 1–125
Gano, Stephen, Dec. 25, 1762–Aug. 18, 1828.
Vol. 4, Pt. 1–126
Gansevoort, Leonard, July 1751–Aug. 26, 1810.
Vol. 4, Pt. 1–126
Gansevoort, Peter, July, 1749–July 2, 1812.
Vol. 4, Pt. 1–127
Ganso, Emil, Apr. 14, 1895–Apr. 18, 1941.
Supp. 3–291
Ganss, Henry George, Feb. 22, 1855–Dec. 25, 1912.
Vol. 4, Pt. 1–128
Gantt, Henry Laurence, May 20, 1861–Nov. 23, 1919.
Vol. 4, Pt. 1–129
Ganz, Rudolph, Feb. 24, 1877–Aug. 2, 1972.
Supp. 9–299
Garakonthie, Daniel, *c.* 1600–1676.
Vol. 4, Pt. 1–130
Garcelon, Alonzo, May 6, 1813–Dec. 8, 1906.
Vol. 4, Pt. 1–121
Garcés, Francisco Tomás Hermenegildo, Apr. 12, 1738–July 18, 1781.
Vol. 4, Pt. 1–132
Garden, Alexander, *c.* 1730–Apr. 15, 1791.
Vol. 4, Pt. 1–132
Garden, Alexander, Dec. 4, 1757–Feb. 24, 1829.
Vol. 4, Pt. 1–133
Garden, Mary, Feb. 20, 1874–Jan. 3, 1967.
Supp. 8–200
Gardener, Helen Hamilton, Jan. 21, 1853–July 26, 1925.
Vol. 4, Pt. 1–134
Gardiner, Sir Christopher, fl. 1630–1632.
Vol. 4, Pt. 1–135
Gardiner, Harry Norman, Nov. 6, 1855–Dec. 29, 1927.
Supp. 1–331
Gardiner, James Terry, May 6, 1842–Sept. 10, 1912.
Vol. 4, Pt. 1–136
Gardiner, John, Dec. 4, 1737–Oct. 15, 1793.
Vol. 4, Pt. 1–136
Gardiner, John Sylvester John, June 1765–July 29, 1830.
Vol. 4, Pt. 1–137
Gardiner, Lion, 1599–1663.
Vol. 4, Pt. 1–138
Gardiner, Robert Hallowell, Feb. 10, 1782–Mar. 22, 1864.
Vol. 4, Pt. 1–139
Gardiner, Silvester, June 29, 1708–Aug. 8, 1786.
Vol. 4, Pt. 1–139
Gardner, Caleb, Jan. 24, 1739–Dec. 24, 1806.
Vol. 4, Pt. 1–140
Gardner, Charles Kitchel, June 24, 1787–Nov. 1, 1869.
Vol. 4, Pt. 1–141
Gardner, Erle Stanley, July 17, 1889–Mar. 11, 1970.
Supp. 8–202
Gardner, Gilson, Mar. 16, 1869–Aug. 16, 1935.
Supp. 1–333
Gardner, Helen, Mar. 17, 1878–June 4, 1946.
Supp. 4–312

Gardner, Henry Joseph, June 14, 1818–July 21, 1892.
Vol. 4, Pt. 1–142
Gardner, Isabella Stewart, Apr. 14, 1840–July 17, 1924.
Vol. 4, Pt. 1–142
Gardner, John Lane, Aug. 1, 1793–Feb. 19, 1869.
Vol. 4, Pt. 1–144
Gardner, Leroy Upson, Dec. 9, 1888–Oct. 24, 1946.
Supp. 4–313
Gardner, Oliver Maxwell, Mar. 22, 1882–Feb. 6, 1947.
Supp. 4–315
Garey, Thomas Andrew, July 7, 1830–Aug. 20, 1909.
Vol. 4, Pt. 1–144
Garfield, Harry Augustus, Oct. 11, 1863–Dec. 12, 1942.
Supp. 3–292
Garfield, James Abram, Nov. 19, 1831–Sept. 19, 1881.
Vol. 4, Pt. 1–145
Garfield, James Rudolph, Oct. 17, 1865–Mar. 24, 1950.
Supp. 4–316
Garfield, John, Mar. 4, 1913–May 19, 1952.
Supp. 5–237
Garis, Howard Roger, Apr. 25, 1873–Nov. 5, 1962.
Supp. 7–278
Garland, Augustus Hill, June 11, 1832–Jan. 26, 1899.
Vol. 4, Pt. 1–150
Garland, Hamlin, Sept. 14, 1860–Mar. 4, 1940.
Supp. 2–218
Garland, Judy, June 10, 1922–June 22, 1969.
Supp. 8–203
Garland, Landon Cabell, Mar. 21, 1810–Feb. 12, 1895.
Vol. 4, Pt. 1–151
Garlick, Theodatus, Mar. 30, 1805–Dec. 9, 1884.
Vol. 4, Pt. 1–152
Garman, Charles Edward, Dec. 18, 1850–Feb. 9, 1907.
Vol. 4, Pt. 1–153
Garman, Samuel, June 5, 1843–Sept. 30, 1927.
Vol. 4, Pt. 1–154
Garner, Erroll Louis, June 15, 1921–Jan. 2, 1977.
Supp. 10–270
Garner, James Wilford, Nov. 22, 1871–Dec. 9, 1938.
Supp. 2–220
Garner, John Nance, Nov. 22, 1868–Nov. 7, 1967.
Supp. 8–205
Garnet, Henry Highland, 1815–Feb. 13, 1882.
Vol. 4, Pt. 1–154
Garnett, Alexander Yelverton Peyton, Sept. 19, 1819–July 11, 1888.
Vol. 4, Pt. 1–155
Garnett, James Mercer, June 8, 1770–Apr. 23, 1843.
Vol. 4, Pt. 1–156
Garnett, James Mercer, Apr. 24, 1840–Feb. 18, 1916.
Vol. 4, Pt. 1–157
Garnett, Muscoe Russell Hunter, July 25, 1821–Feb. 14, 1864.
Vol. 4, Pt. 1–158
Garnett, Robert Selden, Dec. 16, 1819–July 13, 1861.
Vol. 4, Pt. 1–158
Garrard, James, Jan. 14, 1749–Jan. 19, 1822.
Vol. 4, Pt. 1–159
Garrard, Kenner, *c.* Sept. 1, 1828–May 15, 1879.
Vol. 4, Pt. 1–16
Garreau, Armand, Sept. 13, 1817–Mar. 28, 1865.
Vol. 4, Pt. 1–160
Garret, William Robertson, Apr. 12, 1839–Feb. 12, 1904.
Vol. 4, Pt. 1–165
Garretson, Austin Bruce, Sept. 14, 1856–Feb. 27, 1931.
Supp. 1–333
Garretson, James Edmund, Oct. 18, 1828–Oct. 26, 1895.
Vol. 4, Pt. 1–161
Garrett, Edmund Henry, Oct. 19, 1853–Apr. 2, 1929.
Vol. 4, Pt. 1–162
Garrett, Finis James, Aug. 26, 1875–May 25, 1956.
Supp. 6–227
Garrett, John Work, July 31, 1820–Sept. 26, 1884.
Vol. 4, Pt. 1–163
Garrett, Robert, May 2, 1783–Feb. 4, 1857.
Vol. 4, Pt. 1–164
Garrett, Thomas, Aug. 21, 1789–Jan. 25, 1871.
Vol. 4, Pt. 1–164
Garrettson, Freeborn, Aug. 15, 1752–Sept. 26, 1827.
Vol. 4, Pt. 1–166
Garrigan, Philip Joseph, Sept. 8, 1840–Oct. 14, 1919.
Vol. 4, Pt. 1–167
Garrison, Cornelius Kingsland, Mar. 1, 1809–May 1, 1885.
Vol. 4, Pt. 1–167
Garrison, Fielding Hudson, Nov. 5, 1870–Apr. 18, 1935.
Supp. 1–334
Garrison, Lindley Miller, Nov. 28, 1864–Oct. 19, 1932.
Supp. 1–335
Garrison, William Re Tallack, June 18, 1834–July 1, 1882.
Vol. 4, Pt. 1–172
Garrison, William Lloyd, Dec. 10, 1805–May 24, 1879.
Vol. 4, Pt. 1–168
Garry, Spokane, 1811–Jan. 13, 1892.
Vol. 4, Pt. 1–173
Garst, Roswell ("Bob"), June 17. 1898–Nov. 5, 1977.
Supp. 10–271
Gartrell, Lucius Jeremiah, Jan. 7, 1821–Apr. 7, 1891.
Vol. 4, Pt. 1–173
Garvey, Marcus Moziah, Aug. 17, 1887–June 10, 1940.
Supp. 2–221
Garvin, Lucius Fayette Clark, Nov. 13, 1841–Oct. 2, 1922.
Vol. 4, Pt. 1–174
Gary, Elbert Henry, Oct. 8, 1846–Aug. 15, 1927.
Vol. 4, Pt. 1–175
Gary, James Albert, Oct. 22, 1833–Oct. 31, 1920.
Vol. 4, Pt. 1–176
Gary, Martin Witherspoon, Mar. 25, 1831–Apr. 9, 1881.
Vol. 4, Pt. 1–177
Gaskill, Harvey Freeman, Jan. 19, 1845–Apr. 1, 1889.
Vol. 4, Pt. 1–177
Gass, Patrick, June 12, 1771–Apr. 30, 1870.
Vol. 4, Pt. 1–178
Gasser, Herbert Spencer, July 5, 1888–May 11, 1963.
Supp. 7–279
Gasson, Thomas Ignatius, Sept. 23, 1859–Feb. 27, 1930.
Vol. 4, Pt. 1–179
Gaston, Herbert Earle, Aug. 20, 1881–Dec. 7, 1956.
Supp. 6–228
Gaston, James McFadden, Dec. 27, 1824–Nov. 15, 1903.
Vol. 4, Pt. 1–179
Gaston, William, Oct. 3, 1820–Jan. 19, 1894.
Vol. 4, Pt. 1–181
Gaston, William, Sept. 19, 1778–Jan. 23, 1844.
Vol. 4, Pt. 1–180
Gates, Caleb Frank, Oct. 18, 1857–Apr. 9, 1946.
Supp. 4–318
Gates, Frederick Taylor, July 2, 1853–Feb. 6, 1929.
Vol. 4, Pt. 1–182
Gates, George Augustus, Jan. 24, 1851–Nov. 20, 1912.
Vol. 4, Pt. 1–183
Gates, Horatio, *c.* 1728/29–Apr. 10, 1806.
Vol. 4, Pt. 1–184
Gates, John Warne, May 8, 1855–Aug. 9, 1911.
Vol. 4, Pt. 1–188
Gates, Sir Thomas, d. 1621.
Vol. 4, Pt. 1–190
Gates, Thomas Sovereign, Mar. 21, 1873–Apr. 8, 1948.
Supp. 4–320
Gatling, Richard Jordan, Sept. 12, 1818–Feb. 26, 1903.
Vol. 4, Pt. 1–191
Gatschet, Albert Samuel, Oct. 3, 1832–Mar. 16, 1907.
Vol. 4, Pt. 1–192
Gatti-Casazza, Giulio, Feb. 3, 1869–Sept. 2, 1940.
Supp. 2–222
Gaul, William Gilbert, Mar 31, 1855–Dec. 21, 1919.
Vol. 4, Pt. 1–193
Gauss, Christian Frederick, Feb. 2, 1878–Nov. 1, 1951.
Supp. 5–238
Gauss, Clarence Edward, Jan. 12, 1887–Apr. 8, 1960.
Supp. 6–229
Gaut, John McReynolds, Oct. 1, 1841–Dec. 19, 1918.
Vol. 4, Pt. 1–193
Gauvreau, Emile Henry, Feb. 4, 1891–Oct. 15, 1956.
Supp. 6–231
Gavin, Frank Stanton Burns, Oct. 31, 1890–Mar. 20, 1938.
Supp. 2–223
Gaxton, William, Dec. 2, 1893–Feb. 2, 1963.
Supp. 7–281
Gay, Ebenezer, Aug. 15, 1696–Mar. 18, 1787.
Vol. 4, Pt. 1–194
Gav, Edwin Francis, Oct. 27, 1867–Feb. 8, 1946.
Supp. 4–321

Gay, Frederick Parker, July 22, 1874–July 14, 1939.
Supp. 2–224
Gay, Sydney Howard, May 22, 1814–June 25, 1888.
Vol. 4, Pt. 1–195
Gay, Winckworth Allan, Aug. 18, 1821–Feb. 23, 1910.
Vol. 4, Pt. 1–195
Gayarré, Charles Étienne Arthur, Jan. 9, 1805–Feb. 11, 1895.
Vol. 4, Pt. 1–196
Gayle, John, Sept. 11, 1792–July 21, 1859.
Vol. 4, Pt. 1–197
Gayler, Charles, Apr. 1, 1820–May 28, 1892.
Vol. 4, Pt. 1–198
Gayley, James, Oct. 11, 1855–Feb. 25, 1920.
Vol. 4, Pt. 1–198
Gaylord, Edward King, Mar. 5, 1873–May 31, 1974.
Supp. 9–301
Gaylord, Willis, 1792–Mar. 27, 1844.
Vol. 4, Pt. 1–199
Gaynor, William Jay, Feb. 23, 1849–Sept. 10, 1913.
Vol. 4, Pt. 1–200
Gayoso de Lemos, Manuel, *c.* 1752–July 18, 1799.
Vol. 4, Pt. 1–20
Gear, John Henry, Apr. 7, 1825–July 14, 1900.
Vol. 4, Pt. 1–202
Geary, John White, Dec. 30, 1819–Feb. 8, 1873.
Vol. 4, Pt. 1–203
Geddes, James, July 22, 1763–Aug. 19, 1838.
Vol. 4, Pt. 1–204
Geddes, James Loraine, Mar. 19, 1827–Feb. 21, 1887.
Vol. 4, Pt. 1–205
Geddes, Norman Bel, Apr. 27, 1893–May 8, 1958.
Supp. 6–232
Geer, William Aughe ("Will"), Mar. 9, 1902–Apr. 22, 1978.
Supp. 10–272
Geers, Edward Franklin, Jan. 25, 1851–Sept. 3, 1924.
Vol. 4, Pt. 1–206
Gehrig, Henry Louis, June 19, 1903–June 2, 1941.
Supp. 3–294
Geiger, Roy Stanley, Jan. 25, 1885–Jan. 23, 1947.
Supp. 4–322
Geismar, Maxwell David, Aug. 1, 1909–July 24, 1979.
Supp. 10–273
Gellatly, John, 1853–Nov. 8, 1931.
Supp. 1–337
Gemünder, August Martin Ludwig, Mar. 22, 1814–Sept. 7, 1895.
Vol. 4, Pt. 1–207
Gemünder, George, Apr. 13, 1816–Jan. 15, 1899. [*See* Gemünder, August M. L.]
Genet, Edmond Charles, Jan. 8, 1763–July 15, 1834.
Vol. 4, Pt. 1–207
Genin, John Nicholas, Oct. 19, 1819–Apr. 30, 1878.
Vol. 4, Pt. 1–209
Genovese, Vito, Nov. 31?, 1897–Feb. 14, 1969.
Supp. 8–207
Genth, Frederick Augustus, May 17, 1820–Feb. 2, 1893.
Vol. 4, Pt. 1–209
Genthe, Arnold, Jan. 8, 1869, Aug. 9, 1942.
Supp. 3–295
Genung, John Franklin, Jan. 27, 1850–Oct. 1, 1919.
Vol. 4, Pt. 1–210
George, Gladys, Sept. 13, 1904–Dec. 8, 1954.
Supp. 5–240
George, Grace, Dec. 25, 1879–May 19, 1961.
Supp. 7–282
George, Henry, Nov. 3, 1862–Nov. 14, 1916.
Vol. 4, Pt. 1–215
George, Henry, Sept. 2, 1839–Oct. 29, 1897.
Vol. 4. Pt. 1–211
George, James Zachariah, Oct. 20, 1826–Aug. 14, 1897.
Vol. 4, Pt. 1–216
George, Walter Franklin, Jan. 29, 1878–Aug. 4, 1957.
Supp. 6–234
George, William Reuben, June 4, 1866–Apr. 25, 1936.
Supp. 2–226
Gerard, James Watson, 1794–Feb. 7, 1874.
Vol. 4, Pt. 1–217
Gerard, James Watson, Aug. 25, 1867–Sept. 6, 1951.
Supp. 5–241
Gerber, (Daniel) Frank, Jan. 12, 1873–Oct. 7, 1952.
Supp. 5–242
Gerber, Daniel (Frank), May 6, 1898–Mar. 16, 1974.
Supp. 9–302 (*see also* Supp. 5–242)
Gerhard, William Wood, July 23, 1809–Apr. 28, 1872.
Vol. 4, Pt. 1–218
Gerhart, Emanuel Vogel, June 13, 1817–May 6, 1904.
Vol. 4, Pt. 1–219
Gericke, Wilhelm, Apr. 18, 1845–Oct. 27, 1925.
Vol. 4, Pt. 1–219
Germer, Lester Halbert, Oct. 10, 1896–Oct. 3, 1971.
Supp. 9–303
Gernsback, Hugo, Aug. 16, 1884–Aug. 19, 1967.
Supp. 8–209
Geronimo, June 1829–Feb. 17, 1909.
Vol. 4, Pt. 1–220
Gerrish, Frederic Henry, Mar. 21, 1845–Sept. 8, 1920.
Vol. 4, Pt. 1–221
Gerry, Elbridge, July 17, 1744–Nov. 23, 1814.
Vol. 4, Pt. 1–222
Gerry, Elbridge Thomas, Dec. 25, 1837–Feb. 18, 1927.
Vol. 4, Pt. 1–227
Gershwin, George, Sept. 26, 1898–July 11, 1937.
Supp. 2–227
Gerster, Arpad Geyza Charles, Dec. 22, 1848–Mar. 11, 1923.
Vol. 4, Pt. 1–228
Gerstle, Lewis, Dec. 17, 1824–Nov. 19, 1902.
Vol. 4, Pt. 1–229
Gesell, Arnold Lucius, June 21, 1880–May 29, 1961.
Supp. 7–283
Gest, Morris, Jan. 17, 1881–May 16, 1942.
Supp. 3–296
Getty, George Franklin, II, July 9, 1924–June 6, 1973.
Supp. 9–305
Getty, George Washington, Oct. 2, 1819–Oct. 1, 1901.
Vol. 4, Pt. 1–230
Getty, Jean Paul, Dec. 15, 1892–June 6, 1976.
Supp. 10–275
Geyer, Henry Sheffie, Dec. 9, 1790–Mar. 5, 1859.
Vol. 4, Pt. 1–231
Ghent, William James, Apr. 29, 1866–July 10, 1942.
Supp. 3–297
Gherardi, Bancroft, Nov. 10, 1832–Dec. 10, 1903.
Vol. 4, Pt. 1–232
Gherardi, Bancroft, Apr. 6, 1873–Aug. 14, 1941.
Supp. 3–298
Gholson, Samuel Jameson, May 19, 1808–Oct. 16, 1883.
Vol. 4, Pt. 1–232
Gholson, Thomas Saunders, Dec. 9, 1808–Dec. 12, 1868.
Vol. 4, Pt. 1–233
Gholson, William Yates, Dec. 25, 1807–Sept. 21, 1870.
Vol. 4, Pt. 1–234
Giancana, Sam ("Mooney"), May 24, 1908–June 19, 1975.
Supp. 9–306
Giannini, Amadeo Peter, May 6, 1870–June 3, 1949.
Supp. 4–324
Gibault, Pierre, Apr. 1737–1804.
Vol. 4, Pt. 1–234
Gibbes, Robert Wilson, July 8, 1809–Oct. 15, 1866.
Vol. 4, Pt. 1–235
Gibbes, William Hasell, Mar. 16, 1754–Feb. 13, 1834.
Vol. 4, Pt. 1–236
Gibbon, John, Apr. 20, 1827–Feb. 6, 1896.
Vol. 4, Pt. 1–236
Gibbons, Abigail Hopper, Dec. 7, 1801–Jan. 16, 1893.
Vol. 4, Pt. 1–237
Gibbons, Euell, Sept. 8, 1911–Dec. 29, 1975.
Supp. 9–307
Gibbons, Floyd, July 16, 1887–Sept. 24, 1939.
Supp. 2–230
Gibbons, Herbert Adams, Apr. 9, 1880–Aug. 7, 1934.
Supp. 1–337
Gibbons, James, July 23, 1834–Mar. 24, 1921.
Vol. 4, Pt. 1–238
Gibbons, James Sloan, July 1, 1810–Oct. 17, 1892.
Vol. 4, Pt. 1–242
Gibbons, Thomas, Dec. 15, 1757–May 16, 1826.
Vol. 4, Pt. 1–242
Gibbons, William, Apr. 8, 1726–Sept. 27, 1800.
Vol. 4, Pt. 1–243
Gibbons, William, Aug. 10, 1781–July 25, 1845.
Vol. 4, Pt. 1–244

Gibbs, Arthur Hamilton, Mar. 9, 1888–May 24, 1964.
Supp. 7–285
Gibbs, George, Jan. 7, 1776–Aug. 5, 1833.
Vol. 4, Pt. 1–244
Gibbs, George, July 17, 1815–Apr. 9, 1873.
Vol. 4, Pt. 1–245
Gibbs, George, Apr. 19, 1861–May 19, 1940.
Supp. 2–231
Gibbs, James Ethan Allen, Aug. 1, 1829–Nov. 25, 1902.
Vol. 4, Pt. 1–246
Gibbs, Josiah Willard, Apr. 30, 1790–Mar. 25, 1861.
Vol. 4, Pt. 1–247
Gibbs, Josiah Willard, Feb. 11, 1839–Apr. 28, 1903.
Vol. 4, Pt. 1–248
Gibbs, Oliver Wolcott, Feb. 21, 1822–Dec. 9, 1908.
Vol. 4, Pt 1–251
Gibbs, (Oliver) Wolcott, Mar. 15, 1902–Aug. 16, 1958.
Supp. 6–236
Gibbs, Wolcott. [*See* Gibbs, Oliver Wolcott, 1822–1908.]
Gibson, Charles Dana, Sept. 14, 1867–Dec. 23, 1944.
Supp. 3–300
Gibson, Edmund Richard ("Hoot"), Aug. 6, 1892–Aug. 23, 1962.
Supp. 7–286
Gibson, George, Oct. 1747–Dec. 14, 1791.
Vol. 4, Pt. 1–252
Gibson, John, May 23, 1740–Apr. 16, 1822.
Vol. 4, Pt. 1–253
Gibson, John Bannister, Nov. 8, 1780–May 3, 1853.
Vol. 4, Pt. 1–254
Gibson, Joshua, Dec. 21, 1911–Jan. 20, 1947.
Supp. 4–327
Gibson, Paris, July 1, 1830–Dec. 16, 1920.
Vol. 4, Pt. 1–256
Gibson, Randall Lee, Sept. 10, 1832–Dec. 15, 1892.
Vol. 4, Pt. 1–256
Gibson, Walter Murray, 1823–Jan. 21, 1888.
Vol. 4, Pt. 1–257
Gibson, William, Mar. 14, 1788–Mar. 2, 1868.
Vol. 4, Pt. 1–258
Gibson, William Hamilton, Oct. 5, 1850–July 16, 1896.
Vol. 4, Pt. 1–259
Giddings, Franklin Henry, Mar. 23, 1885–June 11, 1931.
Supp. 1–339
Giddings, Joshua Reed, Oct. 6, 1795–May 27, 1864.
Vol. 4, Pt. 1–260
Gideon, Peter Miller, Feb. 9, 1820–Oct. 27, 1899.
Vol. 4, Pt. 1–261
Gidley, James Williams, Jan. 7, 1866–Sept. 26, 1931.
Supp. 1–340
Giesler-Anneke, Mathilde Franziska, Apr. 3, 1817–Nov. 25, 1884.
Vol. 4, Pt. 1–262
Gifford, Robert Swain, Dec. 23, 1840–Jan. 15, 1905.
Vol. 4, Pt. 1–263
Gifford, Sanford Robinson, July 10, 1823–Aug. 29, 1880.
Vol. 4, Pt. 1–264
Gifford, Sanford Robinson, Jan. 8, 1892–Feb. 25, 1944.
Supp. 3–301
Gifford, Walter Sherman, Jan. 10, 1885–May 7, 1966.
Supp. 8–210
Gihon, Albert Leary, Sept. 28, 1833–Nov. 17, 1901.
Vol. 4, Pt. 1–265
Gilbert, Alfred Carlton, Feb. 15, 1884–Jan. 24, 1961.
Supp. 7–287
Gilbert, Anne Hartley, Oct. 21, 1821–Dec. 2, 1904.
Vol. 4, Pt. 1–266
Gilbert, Cass, Nov. 24, 1859–May 17, 1934.
Supp. 1–341
Gilbert, Charles Henry, Dec. 5, 1859–Apr. 20, 1928.
Vol. 4, Pt. 1–267
Gilbert, Eliphalet Wheeler, Dec. 19, 1793–July 31, 1853.
Vol. 4, Pt. 1–267
Gilbert, Grove Karl, May 6, 1843–May 1, 1918.
Vol. 4, Pt. 1–268
Gilbert, Henry Franklin Belknap, Sept. 26, 1868–May 19, 1928.
Vol. 4, Pt. 1–269
Gilbert, John, July 10, 1897–Jan. 9, 1936.
Supp. 2–232
Gilbert, John Gibbs, Feb. 27, 1810–June 17, 1889.
Vol. 4, Pt. 1–270
Gilbert, Linda, May 13, 1847–Oct. 24, 1895.
Vol. 4, Pt. 1–271
Gilbert, Rufus Henry, Jan. 26, 1832–July 10, 1885.
Vol. 4, Pt 1–271
Gilbert, Seymour Parker, Oct. 13, 1892–Feb. 23, 1938.
Supp. 2–234
Gilbert, William Lewis, Dec. 30, 1806–June 29, 1890.
Vol. 4, Pt. 1–272
Gilbreth, Lillian Evelyn Moller, May 24, 1878–Jan. 2, 1972.
Supp. 9–309
Gilchrist, Robert, Aug. 21, 1825–July 6, 1888.
Vol. 4, Pt. 1–273
Gilchrist, William Wallace, Jan. 8, 1846–Dec. 20, 1916.
Vol. 4, Pt. 1–274
Gilder, Jeannette Leonard, Oct. 3, 1849–Jan. 17, 1916.
Vol. 4, Pt. 1–274
Gilder, Richard Watson, Feb. 8, 1844–Nov. 18, 1909.
Vol. 4, Pt. 1–275
Gilder, William Henry, Aug. 16, 1838–Feb. 5, 1900.
Vol. 4, Pt. 1–278
Gildersleeve, Basil Lanneau, Oct. 23, 1831–Jan. 9, 1924.
Vol. 4, Pt. 1–278
Gildersleeve, Virginia Crocheron, Oct. 3, 1877–July 7, 1965.
Supp. 7–288
Giles, Chauncey, May 11, 1813–Nov. 6, 1893.
Vol. 4, Pt. 1–282
Giles, Warren Crandall, May 28, 1896–Feb. 7, 1979.
Supp. 10–277
Giles, William Branch, Aug. 12, 1762–Dec. 4, 1830.
Vol. 4, Pt. 1–283
Gill, John, May 17, 1732–Aug. 25, 1785.
Vol. 4, Pt. 1–284
Gill, Laura Drake, Aug. 24, 1860–Feb. 3, 1926.
Vol. 4, Pt. 1–284
Gill, Theodore Nicholas, Mar. 21, 1837–Sept. 25, 1914.
Vol. 4, Pt. 1–285
Gillam, Bernhard, Apr. 28, 1856–Jan. 19, 1896.
Vol. 4, Pt. 1–286
Gillem, Alvan Cullem, July 29, 1830–Dec. 2, 1875.
Vol. 4, Pt. 1–287
Gillespie, Eliza Maria. [*See* Angela, Mother, 1824–1887.]
Gillespie, Mabel, Mar. 4, 1867–Sept. 24, 1923.
Vol. 4, Pt. 1–288
Gillespie, William Mitchell, 1816–Jan. 1, 1868.
Vol. 4, Pt. 1–288
Gillet, Ransom Hooker, Jan. 27, 1800–Oct. 24, 1876.
Vol. 4, Pt. 1–289
Gillett, Ezra Hall, July 15, 1823–Sept. 2, 1875.
Vol. 4, Pt. 1–290
Gillett, Frederick Huntington, Oct. 16, 1851–July 31, 1935.
Supp. 1–343
Gillett, Horace Wadsworth, Dec. 12, 1883–Mar. 2, 1950.
Supp. 4–328
Gillette, Francis, Dec. 14, 1807–Sept. 30, 1879.
Vol. 4, Pt. 1–290
Gillette, Guy Mark, Feb. 3, 1879–Mar. 3, 1973.
Supp. 9–310
Gillette, King Camp, Jan. 5, 1855–July 9, 1932.
Supp. 1–345
Gillette, William Hooker, July 24, 1853–Apr. 29, 1937.
Supp. 2–235
Gilliam, David Tod, Apr. 3, 1844–Oct. 2, 1923.
Vol. 4, Pt. 1–291
Gilliam, James William ("Junior"), Oct. 17, 1928–Oct. 8, 1978.
Supp. 10–278
Gillis, James Martin, Nov. 12, 1876–Mar. 14, 1957.
Supp. 6–237
Gilliss, James Melville, Sept. 6, 1811–Feb. 9, 1865.
Vol. 4 Pt. 1–292
Gilliss, Walter, May 17, 1855–Sept. 24, 1925.
Vol. 4, Pt. 1–293
Gillman, Henry, Nov. 16, 1833–July 30, 1915.
Vol. 4, Pt. 1–294
Gillmore, Quincy Adams, Feb. 28, 1825–Apr. 7, 1888.
Vol. 4, Pt. 1–295
Gillon, Alexander, Aug. 13, 1741–Oct. 6, 1794.
Vol. 4, Pt. 1–296

Gilman, Arthur, June 22, 1837–Dec. 27, 1909.
Vol. 4, Pt. 1–297
Gilman, Arthur Delevan, Nov. 5, 1821–July 11, 1882.
Vol. 4, Pt. 1–297
Gilman, Caroline Howard, Oct. 8, 1794–Sept. 15, 1888.
Vol. 4, Pt. 1–298
Gilman, Charlotte Perkins Stetson, July 3, 1860–Aug. 17, 1935
Supp. 1–346
Gilman, Daniel Coit, July 6, 1831–Oct. 13, 1908.
Vol. 4, Pt. 1–299
Gilman, John Taylor, Dec. 19, 1753–Aug. 31, 1828.
Vol. 4, Pt. 1–303
Gilman, Lawrence, July 5, 1878–Sept. 8, 1939.
Supp. 2–237
Gilman, Nicholas, Aug. 3, 1755–May 2, 1814.
Vol. 4, Pt. 1–304
Gilman, Samuel, Feb. 16, 1791–Feb. 9, 1858.
Vol. 4, Pt. 1–305
Gilmer, Elizabeth Meriwether ("Dorothy Dix"), Nov. 18, 1870–Dec. 16, 1951.
Supp. 5–243
Gilmer, Francis Walker, Oct. 9, 1790–Feb. 25, 1826.
Vol. 4, Pt. 1–306
Gilmer, George Rockingham, Apr. 11, 1790–Nov. 16, 1859.
Vol. 4, Pt. 1–306
Gilmer, John Adams, Nov. 4, 1805–May 14, 1868.
Vol. 4, Pt. 1–307
Gilmer, Thomas Walker, Apr. 6, 1802–Feb. 28, 1844.
Vol. 4, Pt. 1–308
Gilmor, Harry, Jan. 24, 1838–Mar. 4, 1883.
Vol. 4, Pt. 1–309
Gilmore, James Roberts, Sept. 10, 1822–Nov. 16, 1903.
Vol. 4, Pt. 1–309
Gilmore, Joseph Albree, June 10, 1811–Apr. 17, 1867.
Vol. 4, Pt. 1–311
Gilmore, Joseph Henry, Apr. 29, 1834–July 23, 1918.
Vol. 4, Pt. 1–311
Gilmore, Patrick Sarsfield, Dec. 25, 1829–Sept. 24, 1892.
Vol. 4, Pt. 1–312
Gilmour, Richard, Sept. 28, 1824–Apr. 13, 1891.
Vol. 4, Pt. 1–313
Gilpin, Charles Sidney, Nov. 20, 1878–May 6, 1930.
Vol. 4, Pt. 1–314
Gilpin, Edward Woodward, July 13, 1803–Apr. 29, 1876.
Vol. 4, Pt. 1–314
Gilpin, Henry Dilworth, Apr. 14, 1801–Jan. 29, 1860.
Vol. 4, Pt. 1–315
Gilpin, William, Oct. 4, 1813–Jan. 20, 1894.
Vol. 4, Pt. 1–316
Gimbel, Bernard Feustman, Apr. 10, 1885–Sept. 29, 1966.
Supp. 8–212
Ginn, Edwin, Feb. 14, 1838–Jan. 21, 1914.
Vol. 4, Pt. 1–317
Ginter, Lewis, Apr. 4, 1824–Oct. 2, 1897.
Vol. 4, Pt. 1–317
Giovannitti, Arturo, Jan. 7, 1884–Dec. 31, 1959
Supp. 6–238
Gipson, Frederick Benjamin, Feb. 7, 1908–Aug. 14, 1973.
Supp. 9–312
Gipson, Lawrence Henry, Dec. 7, 1880–Sept. 26, 1971.
Supp. 9–314
Girard, Charles Frédéric, Mar. 9, 1822–Jan. 29, 1895.
Vol. 4, Pt. 1–319
Girard, Stephen, May 20, 1750–Dec. 26, 1831.
Vol. 4, Pt. 1–319
Girardeau, John Lafayette, Nov. 14, 1825–June 23, 1898.
Vol. 4, Pt. 1–322
Girdler, Tom Mercer, May 19, 1877–Feb. 4, 1965.
Supp. 7–289
Girsch, Frederick, Mar. 31, 1821–Dec. 18, 1895.
Vol. 4, Pt. 1–322
Girty, Simon, 1741–Feb. 18, 1818.
Vol. 4, Pt. 1–323
Gish, Dorothy, Mar. 11, 1898–June 4, 1968.
Supp. 8–213
Gist, Christopher, *c.* 1706–1759.
Vol. 4, Pt. 1–323
Gist, Mordecai, Feb. 22, 1742/43–Aug. 2, 1792.
Vol. 4, Pt 1–324
Gist, William Henry, Aug. 22, 1807–Sept. 30, 1874.
Vol. 4, Pt. 1–325
Gitlow, Benjamin, Dec. 22, 1891–July 19, 1965.
Supp. 7–290
Gitt, Josiah Williams ("Jess"), Mar. 28, 1884–Oct. 7, 1973.
Supp. 9–315
Glackens, William James, Mar. 13, 1870–May 22, 1938.
Supp. 2–238
Gladden, Washington, Feb. 11, 1836–July 2, 1918.
Vol. 4, Pt. 1–325
Gladwin, Henry, Nov. 19, 1729–June 22, 1791.
Vol. 4, Pt. 1–327
Glasgow, Ellen Anderson Gholson, Apr. 22, 1873–Nov. 21, 1945.
Supp. 3–302
Glaspell, Susan Keating, July 1, 1876–July 27, 1948.
Supp. 4–329
Glass, Carter, Jan. 4, 1858–May 28, 1946.
Supp. 4–330
Glass, Franklin Potts, June 7, 1858–Jan. 10, 1934.
Supp. 1–346
Glass, Hugh, fl. 1823–1833.
Vol. 4, Pt. 1–327
Glass, Montague Marsden, July 23, 1877–Feb. 3, 1934.
Supp. 1–347
Glassford, Pelham Davis, Aug. 8, 1883–Aug. 9, 1959.
Supp. 6–239
Gleason, Frederic Grant, Dec. 18, 1848–Dec. 6, 1903.
Vol. 4, Pt. 1–328
Gleason, Kate, Nov. 25, 1865–Jan. 9, 1933.
Supp. 1–348
Gleason, Ralph Joseph, Mar. 1, 1917–June 3, 1975.
Supp. 9–316
Gleaves, Albert, Jan. 1, 1858–Jan. 6, 1937.
Supp. 2–239
Glenn, Hugh, Jan. 7, 1788–May 28, 1833.
Vol. 4, Pt. 1–329
Glenn, John Mark, Oct. 28, 1858–Apr. 20, 1950.
Supp. 4–332
Glennon, John Joseph, June 14, 1862–Mar. 9, 1946.
Supp. 4–334
Glidden, Charles Jasper, Aug. 29, 1857–Sept. 11, 1927.
Vol. 4, Pt. 1–329
Glidden, Joseph Farwell, Jan. 18, 1813–Oct. 9, 1906.
Vol. 4, Pt. 1–330
Glover, John, Nov. 5, 1732–Jan. 30, 1797.
Vol. 4, Pt. 1–331
Glover, Samuel Taylor, Mar. 9, 1813–Jan. 22, 1884.
Vol. 4, Pt 1–332
Glover, Townend, Feb. 20, 1813–Sept. 7, 1883.
Vol. 4, Pt. 1–333
Gluck, Alma, May 11, 1884–Oct. 27, 1938.
Supp. 2–240
Glueck, Eleanor Touroff, Apr. 12, 1898–Sept. 25, 1972.
Supp. 9–317
Glueck, Nelson, June 4, 1900–Feb. 12, 1971.
Supp. 9–319
Glueck, Sheldon ("Sol"), Aug. 15, 1896–Mar. 10, 1980.
Supp. 10–279
Glynn, James, June 28, 1801–May 13, 1871.
Vol. 4, Pt. 1–334
Glynn, Martin Henry, Sept. 27, 1871–Dec. 14, 1924.
Vol. 4, Pt. 1–334
Gmeiner, John, Dec. 5, 1847–Nov. 11, 1913.
Vol. 4, Pt. 1–335
Gobrecht, Christian, Dec. 23, 1785–July 23, 1844.
Vol. 4, Pt. 1–336
Godbe, William Samuel, June 26, 1833–Aug. 1, 1902.
Vol. 4, Pt. 1–337
Goddard, Calvin Hooker, Oct. 30, 1891–Feb. 22, 1955.
Supp. 5–244
Goddard, Calvin Luther, Jan. 22, 1822–Mar. 29, 1895.
Vol. 4, Pt. 1–338
Goddard, Henry Herbert, Aug. 14, 1866–June 19, 1957.
Supp. 6–240
Goddard, John, Jan. 20, 1723/4–July 1785.
Vol. 4, Pt. 1–338
Goddard, Luther Marcellus, Oct. 27, 1840–May 20, 1917.
Vol. 4, Pt. 1–339
Goddard, Morrill, Oct. 7, 1865–July 1, 1937.
Supp. 2–241
Goddard, Paul Beck, Jan. 26, 1811–July 3, 1866.
Vol. 4, Pt. 1–340

Goddard, Pliny Earle, Nov. 24, 1869–July 12, 1928.
Vol. 4, Pt. 1–340
Goddard, Robert Hutchings, Oct. 5, 1882–Aug. 10, 1945.
Supp. 3–305
Goddard, William, 1740–Dec. 23, 1817.
Vol. 4, Pt. 1–341
Goddu, Louis, Oct. 1, 1837–June 18, 1919.
Vol. 4, Pt. 1–342
Godefroy, Maximilian, fl. 1806–1824.
Vol. 4, Pt. 1–343
Gödel, Kurt Friedrich, Apr. 28, 1906–Jan. 14, 1978.
Supp. 10–281
Godey, Louis Antoine, June 6, 1804–Nov. 29, 1878.
Vol. 4, Pt. 1–343
Godfrey, Benjamin, Dec. 4, 1794–Apr. 13, 1862.
Vol. 4, Pt. 1–344
Godfrey, Thomas, 1704–Dec. 1749.
Vol. 4, Pt. 1–345
Godfrey, Thomas, Dec. 4, 1736–Aug. 3, 1763.
Vol. 4, Pt. 1–346
Godkin, Edwin Lawrence, Oct. 2, 1831–May 21, 1902.
Vol. 4, Pt. 1–347
Godman, John Davidson, Dec. 20, 1794–Apr. 17, 1830.
Vol. 4, Pt. 1–350
Godowsky, Leopold, Feb. 13, 1870–Nov. 21, 1938.
Supp. 2–243
Godwin, Parke, Feb. 25, 1816–Jan. 7, 1904.
Vol. 4, Pt. 1–351
Goebel, William, Jan. 4, 1856–Feb. 3, 1900.
Vol. 4, Pt. 1–352
Goerz, David, June 2, 1849–May 7, 1914.
Vol. 4, Pt. 1–353
Goessmann, Charles Anthony, June 13, 1827–Sept. 1, 1910.
Vol. 4, Pt. 1–354
Goethals, George Washington, June 29, 1858–Jan. 21, 1928.
Vol. 4, Pt. 1–355
Goetschius, John Henry, Mar. 8, 1718–Nov. 14, 1774.
Vol. 4, Pt. 1–357
Goetschius, Percy, Aug. 30, 1853–Oct. 29, 1943.
Supp. 3–308
Goetz, George. [*See* Calverton, Victor Francis, 1900–1940.]
Goetz, George Washington, Feb. 17, 1856–Jan. 15, 1897.
Vol. 4, Pt. 1–358
Goff, Emmet Stull, Sept. 3, 1852–June 6, 1902.
Vol. 4, Pt. 1–359
Goff, John William, Jan. 1, 1848–Nov. 9, 1924.
Vol. 4, Pt. 1–359
Goffe, William, d. 1679?.
Vol. 4, Pt. 1–360
Goforth, William, 1766–May 12, 1817.
Vol. 4, Pt. 1–361
Going, Jonathan, Mar. 7, 1786–Nov. 9, 1844.
Vol. 4, Pt. 1–362
Gold, Harry ("Raymond"), Dec. 11, 1911–Aug. 28, 1972.
Supp. 9–320
Gold, Michael, Apr. 12, 1893–May 14, 1967.
Supp. 8–215
Goldbeck, Robert, Apr. 19, 1839–May 16, 1908.
Vol. 4, Pt. 1–362
Goldberg, Reuben Lucius ("Rube"), July 4, 1883–Dec. 7, 1970.
Supp. 8–217
Goldberger, Joseph, July 16, 1874–Jan. 17, 1929.
Vol. 4, Pt. 1–363
Golden, John, June 27, 1874–June 17, 1955.
Supp. 5–245
Goldenweiser, Alexander Alexandrovich, Jan. 29, 1880–Jul. 6, 1940.
Supp. 2–244
Goldenweiser, Emanuel Alexander, July 31, 1883–Mar. 31, 1953.
Supp. 5–247
Golder, Frank Alfred, Aug. 11, 1877–Jan. 7, 1929.
Vol. 4, Pt. 1–364
Goldfine, Bernard, *c.* Oct. 1889–Sept. 21, 1967.
Supp. 8–218
Goldin, Horace, Dec. 17, 1873–Aug. 22, 1939.
Supp. 2–245
Goldman, Edwin Franko, Jan. 1, 1878–Feb. 21, 1956.
Supp. 6–241
Goldman, Emma, June 27, 1869–May 14, 1940.
Supp. 2–246
Goldman, Mayer C., Sept. 2, 1874–Nov. 24, 1939.
Supp. 2–248
Goldmark, Henry, June 15, 1857–Jan. 15, 1941.
Supp. 3–310
Goldmark, Peter Carl, Dec. 2, 1906–Dec. 7, 1977.
Supp. 10–283
Goldmark, Rubin, Aug. 15, 1872–Mar. 6, 1936.
Supp. 2–249
Goldsborough, Charles, July 15, 1765–Dec. 13, 1834.
Vol. 4, Pt. 1–365
Goldsborough, Louis Malesherbes, Feb. 18, 1805–Feb. 20, 1877.
Vol. 4, Pt. 1–365
Goldsborough, Robert, Dec. 3, 1733–Dec. 22, 1788. (W. C. Mallalieu).
Vol. 4, Pt. 1–366
Goldsborough, Thomas Alan, Sept. 16, 1877–June 16, 1951.
Supp. 5–248
Goldschmidt, Jakob, Dec. 31, 1882–Sept. 23, 1955.
Supp. 5–249
Goldsmith, Middleton, Aug. 5, 1818–Nov. 26, 1887.
Vol. 4, Pt. 1–367
Goldstein, Max Aaron, Apr. 19, 1870–July 27, 1941.
Supp. 3–311
Goldthwaite, George, Dec. 10, 1809–Mar. 16, 1879.
Vol. 4, Pt. 1–368
Goldthwaite, Henry Barnes, Apr. to, 1802–Oct. 19, 1847.
Vol. 4, Pt. 1–369
Goldwater, Sigismund Schulz, Feb. 7, 1873–Oct. 22, 1942.
Supp. 3–312
Goldwyn, Samuel, July 1879–Jan. 31, 1974.
Supp. 9–322
Gomberg, Moses, Feb. 8, 1866–Feb. 12, 1947.
Supp. 4–335
Gompers, Samuel, Jan. 27, 1850–Dec. 13, 1924.
Vol. 4, Pt. 1–369
Gonzales, Ambrose Elliott, May 29, 1857–July 11, 1926.
Vol. 4, Pt. 1–373
Gooch, Sir William, Oct. 21, 1681–Dec. 17, 1751.
Vol. 4, Pt. 1–373
Good, Adolphus Clemens, Dec. 19, 1856–Dec. 13, 1894.
Vol. 4, Pt. 1–375
Good, James Isaac, Dec. 31, 1850–Jan. 22, 1924.
Vol. 4, Pt. 1–375
Good, Jeremiah Haak, Nov. 22, 1822–Jan. 25, 1888.
Vol. 4, Pt. 1–376
Good, John, Dec. 20, 1841–Mar. 23, 1908.
Vol. 4, Pt. 1–377
Goodale, George Lincoln, Aug. 3, 1839–Apr. 12, 1923.
Vol. 4, Pt. 1–378
Goodale, Stephen Lincoln, Aug. 14, 1815–Nov. 5, 1897.
Vol. 4, Pt. 1–379
Goodall, Harvey L., May 28, 1836–Mar. 28, 1900.
Vol. 4, Pt. 1–379
Goodall, Thomas, Sept. 1, 1823–May 10, 1910.
Vol. 4, Pt. 1–380
Goode, George Brown, Feb. 13, 1851–Sept. 6, 1896.
Vol. 4, Pt. 1–381
Goode, John, May 27, 1829–July 14, 1909.
Vol. 4, Pt. 1–382
Goode, John Paul, Nov. 21, 1862–Aug. 5, 1932.
Supp. 1–349
Goodell, Henry Hill, May 20, 1839–Apr. 23, 1905.
Vol. 4, Pt. 1–383
Goodell, William, Feb. 14, 1792–Feb. 18, 1867.
Vol. 4, Pt. 1–383
Goodell, William, Oct. 25, 1792–Feb. 14, 1878.
Vol. 4, Pt. 1–384
Goodenow, John Milton, 1782–July, 1838.
Vol. 4, Pt. 1–385
Goodhue, Benjamin, Sept. 20, 1748–July 28, 1814.
Vol. 4, Pt. 1–386
Goodhue, Bertram Grosvenor, Apr. 28, 1869–Apr. 23, 1924.
Vol. 4, Pt. 1–386
Goodhue, James Madison, Mar. 31, 1810–Aug. 27, 1852.
Vol. 4, Pt. 1–389
Goodloe, Daniel Reaves, May 28, 1814–Jan. 18, 1902.
Vol. 4, Pt. 1–390
Goodloe, William Cassius, June 27, 1841–Nov. 10, 1889.
Vol. 4, Pt. 1–391
Goodman, Charles, 1796–Feb. 11, 1835.
Vol. 4, Pt. 1–392

Goodman, Kenneth Sawyer, Sep. 19, 1883–Nov. 29, 1918.
Vol. 4, Pt. 1–392
Goodman, Louis Earl, Jan. 2, 1892–Sept. 15, 1961.
Supp. 7–292
Goodman, Paul, Sept. 9, 1911–Aug. 2, 1972.
Supp. 9–325
Goodnight, Charles, Mar. 5, 1836–Dec. 12, 1929.
Vol. 4, Pt. 1–393
Goodnough, Xanthus Henry, Oct. 23, 1860–Aug. 10, 1935.
Supp. 1–350
Goodnow, Frank Johnson, Jan. 18, 1859–Nov. 15, 1939.
Supp. 2–250
Goodnow, Isaac Tichenor, Jan. 17, 1814–Mar. 20, 1894.
Vol. 4, Pt. 1–394
Goodrich, Alfred John, May 8, 1847–Apr. 25, 1920.
Vol. 4, Pt. 1–395
Goodrich, Annie Warburton, Feb. 6, 1866–Dec. 31, 1954.
Supp. 5–251
Goodrich, Benjamin Franklin, Nov. 4, 1841–Aug. 3, 1888.
Vol. 4, Pt. 1–396
Goodrich, Charles Augustus, Aug. 19, 1790–June 4, 1862.
Vol. 4, Pt. 1–397
Goodrich, Chauncey, Oct. 20, 1759–Aug. 18, 1815.
Vol. 4, Pt. 1–397
Goodrich, Chauncey, Sept. 10, 1798–Sept. 11, 1858.
Vol. 4, Pt. 1–398
Goodrich, Chauncey, June 4, 1836–Sept. 28, 1925.
Vol. 4, Pt. 1–399
Goodrich, Chauncey Allen, Oct. 23, 1790–Feb. 25, 1860.
Vol. 4, Pt. 1–399
Goodrich, Elizur, Oct. 26, 1734–Nov. 22, 1797.
Vol. 4, Pt. 1–400
Goodrich, Elizur, Mar. 24, 1761–Nov. 1, 1849.
Vol. 4, Pt. 1–401
Goodrich, Frank Boott, Dec. 14, 1826–Mar. 15, 1894.
Vol. 4, Pt. 1–401
Goodrich, Samuel Griswold, Aug. 19, 1793–May 9, 1860.
Vol. 4, Pt. 1–402
Goodrich, Sarah. [*See* Goodridge, Sarah, 1788–1853.]
Goodrich, William Marcellus, July 21, 1777–Sept. 15, 1833.
Vol. 4, Pt. 1–403
Goodridge, Sarah, Feb. 5, 1788–Dec. 28, 1853.
Vol. 4, Pt. 1–404
Goodridge, William Marcellus. [*See* Goodrich, William Marcellus, 1777–1833.]
Goodsell, Daniel Ayres, Nov. 5, 1840–Dec. 5, 1909.
Vol. 4, Pt. 1–405
Goodspeed, Thomas Wakefield, Sept. 4, 1842–Dec. 16, 1927.
Vol. 4, Pt. 1–405
Goodwin, Daniel Raynes, Apr. 12, 1811–Mar. 15, 1890.
Vol. 4, Pt. 1–406
Goodwin, Elijah, Jan. 16, 1807–Sept. 4, 1879.
Vol. 4, Pt. 1–407
Goodwin, Hannibal Williston, Apr. 30, 1822–Dec. 31, 1900.
Vol. 4, Pt. 1–408
Goodwin, Ichabod, Oct. 8, 1794–July 4, 1882.
Vol. 4, Pt. 1–408
Goodwin, John Noble, Oct. 18, 1824–Apr. 29, 1887.
Vol. 4, Pt. 1–409
Goodwin, Nathaniel Carll, July 25, 1857–Jan. 31, 1919.
Vol. 4, Pt. 1–410
Goodwin, William Watson, May 9, 1831–June 15, 1912.
Vol. 4, Pt. 1–411
Goodyear, Anson Conger, June 20, 1877–Apr. 23, 1964.
Supp. 7–293
Goodyear, Charles, Dec. 29, 1800–July 1, 1860.
Vol. 4, Pt. 1–413
Goodyear, Charles, Jan. 1, 1833–May 22, 1896.
Vol. 4, Pt. 1–415
Goodyear, William Henry, Apr. 21, 1846–Feb. 19, 1923.
Vol. 4, Pt. 1–416
Gookin, Daniel, 1612–Mar. 19, 1686/7.
Vol. 4 Pt. 1–417
Goold, Wiliiam A., Nov. 5, 1830–Dec. 19, 1912.
Vol. 4, Pt. 1–418
Gorcey, Leo, June 3, 1917–June 2, 1969.
Supp. 8–220
Gordin, Jacob, May 1, 1853–June 11, 1909.
Vol. 4, Pt. 1–418
Gordon, Andrew, Sept. 17, 1828–Aug. 13, 1887.
Vol. 4, Pt. 1–419
Gordon, George Angier, Jan. 2, 1853–Oct. 25, 1929.
Vol. 4, Pt. 1–419
Gordon, George Byron, Aug. 4, 1870–Jan. 30, 1927.
Vol. 4, Pt. 1–421
Gordon, George Henry, July 19, 1823–Aug. 30, 1886.
Vol. 4, Pt. 1–421
Gordon, George Phineas, Apr. 21, 1810–Jan. 27, 1878.
Vol. 4, Pt. 1–422
Gordon, George Washington, Oct. 5, 1836–Aug. 9, 1911.
Vol. 4, Pt. 1–423
Gordon, James, Dec. 6, 1833–Nov. 28, 1912.
Vol. 4, Pt. 1–423
Gordon, John Brown, Feb. 6, 1832–Jan. 9, 1904.
Vol. 4, Pt. 1–424
Gordon, John Franklin, May 15, 1900–Jan. 6, 1978.
Supp. 10–285
Gordon, Kermit, July 3, 1916–June 22, 1976.
Supp. 10–286
Gordon, Laura De Force, Aug. 17, 1838–Apr. 6, 1907.
Vol. 4, Pt. 1–425
Gordon, Waxey. [*See* Wexler, Irving, 1888–1952.]
Gordon, William, 1728–Oct. 19, 1807.
Vol. 4, Pt. 1–426
Gordon, William Fitzhugh, Jan. 13, 1787–Aug. 28, 1858.
Vol. 4, Pt. 1–426
Gordon, William Washington, Jan. 17, 1796–Mar. 20, 1842.
Vol. 4, Pt. 1–427
Gordy, John Pancoast, Dec. 21, 1851–Dec. 31, 1908.
Vol. 4, Pt. 1–428
Gore, Thomas Pryor, Dec. 10, 1870–Mar. 16, 1949.
Supp. 4–337
Gore, Robert Hayes, May 24, 1886–Dec. 26, 1972.
Supp. 9–326
Gorgas, Josiah, July 1, 1818–May 15, 1883.
Vol. 4, Pt. 1–428
Goreas, William Crawford, Oct. 3, 1854–July 3, 1920.
Vol. 4, Pt. 1–430
Gorham, Jabez, Feb. 18, 1792–Mar. 24, 1869.
Vol. 4, Pt. 1–432
Gorham, John, Feb. 24, 1783–Mar. 27, 1829.
Vol. 4, Pt. 1–433
Gorham, Nathaniel, May 1738–June 11, 1796.
Vol. 4, Pt. 1–433
Gorky, Arshile, 1904 or 1905–July 1, 1948.
Supp. 4–339
Gorman, Arthur Pue, Mar. 11, 1839–June 4, 1906.
Vol. 4, Pt. 1–434
Gorman, Willis Arnold, Jan. 12, 1816–May 20, 1876.
Vol. 4, Pt. 1–435
Gorrell, Edgar Staley, Feb. 3, 1891–Mar. 5, 1945.
Supp. 3–313
Gorrie, John, Oct. 3, 1803–June 16, 1855.
Vol. 4, Pt. 1–436
Gorringe, Henry Honeychurch, Aug. 11, 1841–July 6, 1885.
Vol. 4, Pt. 1–437
Gortner, Ross Aiken, Mar. 20, 1885–Sept. 30, 1942.
Supp. 3–314
Gorton, Samuel, *c.* 1592–1677.
Vol. 4, Pt. 1–438
Goslin, Leon Allen ("Goose"), Oct. 16, 1900–May 15, 1971.
Supp. 9–328
Gosnold, Bartholomew, fl. 1572–1607.
Vol. 4, Pt. 1–439
Goss, Albert Simon, Oct. 14, 1882–Oct. 25, 1950.
Supp. 4–340
Goss, James Walker, Dec. 29, 1812–Nov. 26, 1870.
Vol. 4, Pt. 1–440
Gossett, Benjamin Brown, Aug. 18, 1884–Nov. 13, 1951.
Supp. 5–252
Gostelowe, Jonathan, 1744–Feb. 3, 1795.
Vol. 4, Pt. 1–440
Gotshall, William Charles, May 9, 1870–Aug. 20, 1935.
Supp. 1–351
Gottheil, Gustav, May 28, 1827–Apr. 15, 1903.
Vol. 4, Pt. 1–441
Gottheil, Richard James Horatio, Oct. 13, 1862–May 22, 1936.
Supp. 2–251
Gottschalk, Louis Moreau, May 8, 1829–Dec. 18, 1869.
Vol. 4, Pt. 1–441
Gottschalk, Louis Reichenthal, Feb. 21, 1899–June 23, 1975.
Supp. 9–329

Goucher, John Franklin, June 7, 1845–July 19, 1922.
Vol. 4, Pt. 1–442
Goudsmit, Samuel Abraham, July 11, 1902–Dec. 4, 1978.
Supp. 10–288
Goudy, Frederic William, Mar. 8, 1865–May 11, 1947.
Supp. 4–341
Goudy, William Charles, May 15, 1824–Apr. 27, 1893.
Vol. 4, Pt. 1–443
Gouge, WIlliam M., Nov. 10, 1796–July 14, 1863.
Vol. 4, Pt. 1–444
Gough, John Bartholomew, Aug. 22, 1817–Feb. 18, 1886.
Vol. 4, Pt. 1–445
Gould, Augustus Addison, Apr. 23, 1805–Sept. 15, 1866.
Vol. 4, Pt. 1–446
Gould, Benjamin Apthorp, June 15, 1787–Oct. 24, 1859.
Vol. 4, Pt. 1–447
Gould, Benjamin Apthorp, Sept. 27, 1824–Nov. 26, 1896.
Vol. 4, Pt. 1–447
Gould, Edward Sherman, May 11, 1805–Feb. 21, 1885.
Vol. 4, Pt. 1–449
Gould, Elgin Ralston Lovell, Aug. 15, 1860–Aug. 18, 1915.
Vol. 4, Pt. 1–449
Gould, George Jay, Feb. 6, 1864–May 16, 1923.
Vol. 4, Pt. 1–450
Gould, George Milbry, Nov. 8, 1848–Aug. 8, 1922.
Vol. 4, Pt. 1–451
Gould, Hannah Flagg, Sept. 3, 1789–Sept. 5, 1865.
Vol. 4, Pt. 1–452
Gould, James, Dec. 5, 1770–May 11, 1838.
Vol. 4, Pt. 1–453
Gould, Jay, May 27, 1836–Dec. 2, 1892.
Vol. 4, Pt. 1–454
Gould, Nathaniel Duren, Nov. 26, 1781–May 28, 1864.
Vol. 4, Pt. 1–455
Gould, Robert Simonton, Dec. 16, 1826–June 30, 1904.
Vol. 4, Pt. 1–455
Gould, Thomas Ridgeway, Nov. 5, 1818–Nov. 26, 1881.
Vol. 4, Pt. 1–456
Goulding, Francis Robert, Sept. 28, 1810–Aug. 22, 1881.
Vol. 4, Pt. 1–457
Goupil, Rene, *c.* 1607–Sept. 29, 1642.
Vol. 4, Pt. 1–458
Govan, Daniel Chevilette, July 4, 1829–Mar. 12, 1911.
Vol. 4, Pt. 1–458
Gove, Aaron Estellus, Sept. 26, 1839–Aug. 1, 1919.
Vol. 4, Pt. 1–459
Gowans, William, Mar. 29, 1803–Nov. 27, 1870.
Vol. 4, Pt. 1–459
Gowen, Franklin Benjamin, Feb. 9, 1836–Dec. 14, 1889.
Vol. 4, Pt. 1–460
Grabau, Amadeus William, Jan. 9, 1870–Mar. 20, 1946.
Supp. 4–343
Grabau, Johannes Andreas August, Mar. 18, 1804–June 2, 1879.
Vol. 4, Pt. 1–461
Grable, Betty, Dec. 18, 1916–July 2, 1973.
Supp. 9–331
Gräbner, August Lawrence, July 10, 1849–Dec. 7, 1904.
Vol. 4, Pt. 1–462
Grace, Eugene Gifford, Aug. 27, 1876–July 25, 1960.
Supp. 6–243
Grace, William Russell, May 10, 1832–Mar. 21, 1904.
Vol. 4, Pt. 1–463
Gracie, Archibald, Dec. 1, 1832–Dec. 2, 1864.
Vol. 4, Pt. 1–463
Gradle, Henry, Aug. 17, 1855–Apr. 4, 1911.
Vol. 4, Pt. 1–464
Grady, Henry Francis, Feb. 12, 1882–Sept. 14, 1957.
Supp. 6–244
Grady, Henry Woodfin, May 24, 1850–Dec. 23, 1889.
Vol. 4, Pt. 1–465
Graebner, August Lawrence. [*See* Gräbner, August Lawrence, 1849–1904.]
Graessl, Lawrence, Aug. 18, 1753–*c.* Oct. 12, 1793.
Vol. 4, Pt. 1–466
Graff, Everett Dwight, Aug. 7, 1885–Mar. 11, 1964.
Supp. 7–294
Graff, Frederic, May 23, 1817–Mar. 30, 1890.
Vol. 4, Pt. 1–466
Graff, Frederick, Aug. 27, 1774–Apr. 13, 1847.
Vol. 4, Pt. 1–467
Graffenried, Christopher, Baron de, 1661–1743.
Vol. 4, Pt. 1–468
Grafly, Charles, Dec. 3, 1862–May 5, 1929.
Vol. 4, Pt. 1–468
Grafton, Charles Chapman, Apr. 12, 1830–Aug. 30, 1912.
Vol. 4, Pt. 1–470
Graham, Charles Kinnaird, June 3, 1824–Apr. 15, 1889.
Vol. 4, Pt. 1–471
Graham, David, Feb. 8, 1808–May 27, 1852.
Vol. 4, Pt. 1–471
Graham, Edward Kidder, Oct. 11, 1876–Oct. 26, 1918.
Vol. 4, Pt. 1–472
Graham, Ernest Robert, Aug. 22, 1866–Nov. 22, 1936.
Supp. 2–252
Graham, Evarts Ambrose, Mar. 19, 1883–Mar. 4, 1957.
Supp. 6–245
Graham, Frank Porter, Oct. 14, 1886–Feb. 16, 1972.
Supp. 9–333
Graham, George Rex, Jan. 18, 1813–July 13, 1894.
Vol. 4, Pt. 1–473
Graham, Isabella Marshall, July 29, 1742–July 27, 1814.
Vol. 4, Pt. 1–474
Graham, James, d. Jan. 1700/01.
Vol. 4, Pt. 1–475
Graham, James Duncan, Apr. 4, 1799–Dec. 28, 1865.
Vol. 4, Pt. 1–476
Graham, John, *c.* 1718–Nov. 1795.
Vol. 4, Pt. 1–476
Graham, John, 1774–Aug. 6, 1820.
Vol. 4, Pt. 1–477
Graham, John Andrew, June 10, 1764–Aug. 29, 1841.
Vol. 4, Pt. 1–478
Graham, Joseph, Oct. 13, 1759–Nov. 12, 1836.
Vol. 4, Pt. 1–479
Graham, Philip Leslie, July 18, 1915–Aug. 3, 1963.
Supp. 7–295
Graham, Sylvester, July 5, 1794–Sept. 11, 1851.
Vol. 4, Pt. 1–479
Graham, William Alexander, Sept. 5, 1804–Aug. 11, 1875.
Vol. 4, Pt. 1–480
Graham, William Montrose, Sept. 28, 1834–Jan. 16, 1916.
Vol. 4, Pt. 1–481
Grainger, George Percy, July 8, 1882–Feb. 20, 1961.
Supp. 7–297
Grandgent, Charles Hall, Nov. 14, 1862–Sept. 11, 1939.
Supp. 2–254
Granger, Alfred Hoyt, May 31, 1867–Dec. 3, 1939.
Supp. 2–255
Granger, Francis, Dec. 1, 1792–Aug. 28, 1868.
Vol. 4, Pt. 1–482
Granger, Gideon, July 19, 1767–Dec. 31, 1822.
Vol. 4, Pt. 1–483
Granger, Gordon, Nov. 6, 1822–Jan. 10, 1876.
Vol. 4, Pt. 1–484
Granger, Walter, Nov. 7, 1872–Sept. 6, 1941.
Supp. 3–316
Grant, Albert Weston, Apr. 14, 1856–Sept. 30, 1930.
Vol. 4, Pt. 1–485
Grant, Asahel, Aug. 17, 1807–Apr. 24, 1844.
Vol. 4, Pt. 1–485
Grant, Claudius Buchanan, Oct. 25, 1835–Feb. 28, 1921.
Vol. 4, Pt. 1–486
Grant, Frederick Dent, May 30, 1850–Apr. 11, 1912.
Vol. 4, Pt. 1–487
Grant, George Barnard, Dec. 21, 1849–Aug. 16, 1917.
Vol. 4, Pt. 1–487
Grant, Harry Johnston, Sept. 15, 1881–July 12, 1963.
Supp. 7–298
Grant, James Benton, Jan. 2, 1848–Nov. 1, 1911.
Vol. 4, Pt. 1–488
Grant, Jane Cole, May 29, 1892–Mar. 16, 1972.
Supp. 9–335.
Grant, John Thomas, Dec. 13, 1813–Jan. 18, 1887.
Vol. 4, Pt. 1–489
Grant, Lewis Addison, Jan. 17, 1829–Mar. 20, 1918.
Vol. 4, Pt. 1–490
Grant, Madison, Nov. 19, 1865–May 30, 1937.
Supp. 2–256
Grant, Percy Stickney, May 13, 1860–Feb. 13, 1927.
Vol. 4, Pt. 1–490
Grant, Robert, Jan. 24, 1852–May 19, 1940.
Supp. 2–257

Grant, Ulysses Simpson, Apr. 27, 1822–July 23, 1885.
Vol. 4, Pt. 1–492
Grant, William Thomas, Jr., June 27, 1876–Aug. 6, 1972.
Supp. 9–336
Grant, Zilpah Polly. [*See* Banister, Zilpah Polly Grant, 1794–1874.]
Grass, John, 1837–May 10, 1918.
Vol. 4, Pt. 1–501
Grasselli, Caesar Augustin, Nov. 7, 1850–July 28, 1927.
Vol. 4, Pt. 1–502
Grasty, Charles Henry, Mar. 3, 1863–Jan. 19, 1924.
Vol. 4, Pt. 1–503
Gratiot, Charles, 1752–Apr. 20, 1817.
Vol. 4, Pt. 1–503
Gratz, Barnard, 1738–Apr. 20, 1801.
Vol. 4, Pt. 1–504
Gratz, Michael, 1740–Sept. 8, 1811.
Vol. 4, Pt. 1–504
Gratz, Rebecca, Mar. 4, 1781–Aug. 29, 1869.
Vol. 4, Pt. 1–505
Grau, Maurice, 1849–Mar. 14, 1907.
Vol. 4, Pt. 1–506
Grauer, Benjamin Franklin ("Ben"), June 2, 1908–May 31, 1977.
Supp. 10–290
Graupner, Johann Christian Gottlieb, Oct. 6, 1767–Apr. 16, 1836.
Vol. 4, Pt. 1–506
Gravenor, John. [*See* Altham, John, 1589–1640.]
Graves, Alvin Cushman, Nov. 4, 1909–July 29, 1965.
Supp. 7–299
Graves, David Bibb, Apr. 1, 1873–Mar. 14, 1942.
Supp. 3–317
Graves, Frederick Rogers, Oct. 24, 1858–May 17, 1940.
Supp. 2–258
Graves, James Robinson, Apr. 10, 1820–June 26, 1893.
Vol. 4, Pt. 1–507
Graves, John Temple, Nov. 9, 1856–Aug. 8, 1925.
Vol. 4, Pt. 1–508
Graves, Rosewell Hobart, May 29, 1833–June 3, 1912.
Vol. 4, Pt. 1–509
Graves, William Phillips, Jan. 29, 1870–Jan. 25, 1933.
Supp. 1–352
Graves, William Sidney, Mar. 27, 1865–Feb. 27, 1940.
Supp. 2–259
Graves, Zuinglius Calvin, Apr. 15, 1816–May 18, 1902.
Vol. 4, Pt. 1–510
Gravier, Jacques, May 17, 1651–Apr. 23, 1708.
Vol. 4, Pt. 1–510
Gray, Asa, Nov. 18, 1810–Jan. 30, 1888.
Vol. 4, Pt. 1–511
Gray, Carl Raymond, Sept. 28, 1867–May 9, 1939.
Supp. 2–260
Gray, Elisha, Aug. 2, 1835–Jan. 21, 1901.
Vol. 4, Pt. 1–514
Gray, Francis Calley, Sept. 19, 1790–Dec. 29, 1856.
Vol. 4, Pt. 1–514
Gray, George, May 4, 1840–Aug. 7, 1925.
Vol. 4, Pt. 1–515
Gray, George Alexander, Sept. 28, 1851–Feb. 8, 1912.
Vol. 4, Pt. 1–516
Gray, Gilda, Oct. 24, 1899–Dec. 22, 1959.
Supp. 6–247
Gray, Glen ("Spike"), June 7, 1900–Aug. 23, 1963.
Supp. 7–300
Gray, Harold Edwin, Apr. 15, 1906–Dec. 23, 1972.
Supp. 9–337
Gray, Harold Lincoln, Jan. 20, 1894–May 9, 1968.
Supp. 8–221
Gray, Henry Peters, June 23, 1819–Nov. 12, 1877.
Vol. 4, Pt. 1–517
Gray, Horace, Mar. 24, 1828–Sept. 15, 1902.
Vol. 4, Pt. 1–518
Gray, Isaac Pusey, Oct. 18, 1828–Feb. 14, 1895.
Vol. 4, Pt. 1–519
Gray, John Chipman, July 14, 1839–Feb. 25, 1915.
Vol. 4, Pt. 1–520
Gray, John Purdue, Aug. 6, 1825–Nov. 29, 1886.
Vol. 4, Pt. 1–521
Gray, Joseph W., Aug. 5, 1813–May 26, 1862.
Vol. 4, Pt. 1–522
Gray, Robert, May 10, 1755–1806.
Vol. 4, Pt. 1–522
Gray, William, June 27, 1750, o.s.-Nov. 3, 1825
Vol. 4, Pt. 1–523
Gray, William Scott, Jr., June 5, 1885–Sept. 8, 1960.
Supp. 6–248
Graydon, Alexander, Apr. 10, 1752–May 2, 1818.
Vol. 4, Pt. 1–524
Grayson, William, 1736?–Mar. 12, 1790.
Vol. 4, Pt. 1–525
Greathouse, Clarence Ridgeby, *c.* 1845–Oct. 21, 1899.
Vol. 4, Pt. 1–526
Greaton, John, Mar. 10, 1741–Dec. 16, 1783.
Vol. 4, Pt. 1–526
Greaton, Joseph, Feb. 12, 1679–Aug. 19, 1753.
Vol. 4, Pt. 1–527
Greeley, Horace, Feb. 3, 1811–Nov. 29, 1872.
Vol. 4, Pt. 1–528
Greely, Adolphus Washington, Mar. 27, 1844–Oct. 20, 1935.
Supp. 1–352
Green, Alexander Little Page, June 26, 1806–July 15, 1874.
Vol. 4, Pt. 1–534
Green, Andrew Haswell, Oct. 6, 1820–Nov. 13, 1903.
Vol. 4, Pt. 1–535
Green, Anna Katharine. [*See* Rohlfs, Anna Katharine Green, 1846–1935]
Green, Asa, Feb. 11, 1789–*c.* 1837.
Vol. 4, Pt. 1–536
Green, Ashbel, July 6, 1762–May 19, 1848.
Vol. 4, Pt. 1–536
Green, Bartholomew, Oct. 12, 1666–Dec. 28, 1732.
Vol. 4, Pt. 1–537
Green, Benjamin Edwards, Feb. 5, 1822–May 12, 1907.
Vol. 4, Pt. 1–538
Green, Beriah, Mar. 24, 1795–May 4, 1874.
Vol. 4, Pt. 1–539
Green, Constance McLaughlin, Aug. 21, 1897–Dec. 5, 1975.
Supp. 9–338
Green, Duff, Aug. 15, 1791–June 10, 1875.
Vol. 4, Pt. 1–540
Green, Frances Harriet Whipple, Sept. 1805–June 10, 1878.
Vol. 4, Pt. 1–542
Green, Francis, Aug. 21, 1742 o.s.-Apr. 21, 1809.
Vol. 4, Pt. 1–542
Green, Francis Mathews, Feb. 23, 1835–Dec. 19, 1902.
Vol. 4, Pt. 1–543
Green, Gabriel Marcus, Oct. 19, 1891–Jan. 24, 1919.
Vol. 4, Pt. 1–544
Green, Henrietta Howland Robinson, Nov. 21, 1834–July 3, 1916.
Vol. 4, Pt. 1–545
Green, Henry Woodhull, Sept. 20, 1804–Dec. 19, 1876.
Vol. 4, Pt. 1–546
Green, Horace, Dec. 24, 1802–Nov. 29, 1866.
Vol. 4, Pt. 1–547
Green, Jacob, Feb. 2, 1722–May 24, 1790.
Vol. 4, Pt. 1–548
Green, Jacob, July 26, 1790–Feb. 1, 1841.
Vol. 4, Pt. 1–548
Green, James Stephens, Feb. 28, 1817–Jan. 19, 1870.
Vol. 4, Pt. 1–549
Green, John, Apr. 2, 1835–Dec. 7, 1913.
Vol. 4, Pt. 1–550
Green, John Cleve, Apr. 4, 1800–Apr. 29, 1875.
Vol. 4, Pt. 1–551
Green, Jonas, 1712–Apr. 11, 1767.
Vol. 4, Pt. 1–552
Green, Joseph, 1706–Dec. 11, 1780.
Vol. 4, Pt. 1–553
Green, Lewis Warner, Jan. 28, 1806–May 26, 1863.
Vol. 4, Pt. 1–553
Green, Nathan, 1787?–1825.
Vol. 4, Pt. 1–554
Green, Norvin, Apr. 17, 1818–Feb. 12, 1893.
Vol. 4, Pt. 1–555
Green, Samuel, 1615–Jan. 1, 1701/02.
Vol. 4, Pt. 1–555
Green, Samuel Abbott, Mar. 16, 1830–Dec. 5, 1918.
Vol. 4, Pt. 1–556
Green, Samuel Bowdlear, Sept. 15, 1859–July 11, 1910.
Vol. 4, Pt. 1–556

Green, Samuel Swett, Feb. 20, 1837–Dec. 8, 1918.
Vol. 4, Pt. 1–557
Green, Seth, Mar. 19, 1817–Aug. 20, 1888.
Vol. 4, Pt. 1–558
Green, Theodore Francis, Oct. 2, 1867–May 19, 1966.
Supp. 8–222
Green, Thomas, Aug. 25, 1735–May 1812.
Vol. 4, Pt. 1–558
Green, William, Nov. 10, 1806–July 29, 1880.
Vol. 4, Pt. 1–559
Green, William, Mar. 3, 1870–Nov. 21, 1952.
Supp. 5–253
Green, Wilham Henry, Jan. 27, 1825–Feb. 10, 1900.
Vol. 4, Pt. 1–560
Green, William Joseph, Jr., Mar. 5, 1910–Dec. 21, 1963.
Supp. 7–301
Greenbaum, Edward Samuel, Apr. 13, 1890–June 12, 1970.
Supp. 8–224
Greene, Albert Gorton, Feb. 10, 1802–Jan. 3, 1868.
Vol. 4, Pt. 1–561
Greene, Belle Da Costa, Dec. 13, 1883–May 10, 1950.
Supp. 4–344
Greene, Charles Ezra, Feb. 12, 1842–Oct. 16, 1903.
Vol. 4, Pt. 1–562
Greene, Charles Sumner, Oct. 12, 1868–June 11, 1957.
Supp. 5–255
Greene, Christopher, May 12, 1737–May 14, 1781.
Vol. 4 Pt. 1–563
Greene, Daniel Crosby, Feb. 11, 1843–Sept. 15, 1913.
Vol. 4, Pt. 1–563
Greene, Edward Lee, Aug. 20, 1843–Nov. 10, 1915.
Vol. 4, Pt. 1–564
Greene, Frances Harriet Whipple. [*See* Green, Frances Harriet Whipple, 1805–1878.]
Greene, Francis Vinton, June 27, 1850–May 15, 1921.
Vol. 4, Pt. 1–565
Greene, George Sears, May 6, 1801–Jan. 28, 1899.
Vol. 4, Pt. 1–566
Greene, George Sears, Nov. 26, 1837–Dec. 23, 1922.
Vol. 4, Pt. 1–567
Greene, George Washington, Apr. 8, 1811–Feb. 2, 1883.
Vol. 4, Pt. 1–568
Greene, Henry Mather, Jan. 23, 1870–Oct. 2, 1954.
Supp. 5–255
Greene, Jerome Davis, Oct. 12, 1874–Mar. 29, 1959.
Supp. 6–249
Greene, Nathanael, July 27/Aug. 7, 1742–June 19, 1786.
Vol. 4, Pt. 1–569
Greene, Nathaniel, May 20, 1797–Nov. 29, 1877.
Vol. 4, Pt. 1–573
Greene, Roger Sherman, May 29, 1881–Mar. 27, 1947.
Supp. 4–346
Greene, Samuel Dana, Feb. 11, 1840–Dec. 11, 1884.
Vol. 4, Pt. 1–573
Greene, Samuel Stillman, May 3, 1810–Jan. 24, 1883.
Vol. 4, Pt. 1–574
Greene, William, Mar. 16, 1695/96–Feb. 1758.
Vol. 4, Pt. 1–575
Greene, William, Aug. 16, 1731–Nov. 29, 1809.
Vol. 4, Pt. 1–576
Greene, William Cornell, 1851–Aug. 5, 1911.
Vol. 4, Pt. 1–577
Greener, Richard Theodore, Jan. 30, 1844–May 2, 1922.
Vol. 4, Pt. 1–578
Greenhalge, Frederic Thomas, July 19, 1842–Mar. 5, 1896.
Vol. 4, Pt. 1–579
Greenhow, Robert, 1800–Mar. 27, 1854.
Vol. 4, Pt. 1–580
Greenlaw, Edwin Almiron, Apr. 6, 1874–Sept. 10, 1931.
Supp. 1–355
Greenleaf, Benjamin, Sept. 25, 1786–Oct. 29, 1864.
Vol. 4, Pt. 1–581
Greenleaf, Halbert Stevens, Apr. 12, 1827–Aug. 25, 1906.
Vol. 4, Pt. 1–581
Greenleaf, Moses, Oct. 17, 1777–Mar. 20, 1834.
Vol. 4, Pt. 1–582
Greenleaf, Simon, Dec. 5, 1783–Oct. 6, 1853.
Vol. 4, Pt. 1–583
Greenleaf, Thomas, 1755–Sept. 14, 1798.
Vol. 4, Pt. 1–584
Greenough, Henry, Oct. 5, 1807–Oct. 31, 1883.
Vol. 4, Pt. 1–585
Greenough, Horatio, Sept. 6, 1805–Dec. 18, 1852.
Vol. 4, Pt. 1–586
Greenough, James Bradstreet, May 4, 1833–Oct. 11, 1901.
Vol. 4, Pt. 1–588
Greenough, Richard Saltonstall, Apr. 27, 1819–Apr. 23, 1904.
Vol. 4, Pt. 1–589
Greenslet, Ferris, June 30, 1875–Nov. 19, 1959.
Supp. 6–250
Greenstreet, Sydney Hughes, Dec. 27, 1879–Jan. 18, 1954.
Supp. 5–257
Greenup, Christopher, *c.* 1750–Apr. 27, 1818.
Vol. 4, Pt. 1–589
Greenwald, Emanuel, Jan. 13, 1811–Dec. 21, 1885.
Vol. 4, Pt. 1–590
Greenway, John Campbell, July 6, 1872–Jan. 19, 1926.
Supp. 1–357
Greenwood, Grace. [*See* Lippincott, Sarah Jane Clarke, 1823–1904.]
Greenwood, Isaac, May 11, 1702–Oct. 12, 1745.
Vol. 4, Pt. 1–591
Greenwood, John, May 17, 1760–Nov. 16, 1819.
Vol. 4, Pt. 1–592
Greenwood, Miles, Mar. 19, 1807–Nov. 5, 1885.
Vol. 4, Pt. 1–592
Greer, David Hummell, Mar. 20, 1844–May 19, 1919.
Vol. 4, Pt. 1–593
Greer, James Augustin, Feb. 28, 1833–June 17, 1904.
Vol. 4, Pt. 1–594
Gregg, Alan, July 11, 1890–June 19, 1957.
Supp. 6–252
Gregg, Andrew, June 10, 1755–May 20, 1835.
Vol. 4, Pt. 1–595
Gregg, David McMurtrie, Apr. 10, 1833–Aug. 7, 1916.
Vol. 4, Pt. 1–596
Gregg, John, Sept. 28, 1828–Oct. 7, 1864.
Vol. 4, Pt. 1–597
Gregg, John Andrew, Feb. 18, 1877–Feb. 17, 1953.
Supp. 5–258
Gregg, John Robert, June 17, 1867–Feb. 23, 1948.
Supp. 4–347
Gregg, Josiah, July 19, 1806–Feb. 25, 1850.
Vol. 4, Pt. 1–597
Gregg, Maxcy, 1814–Dec. 14, 1862.
Vol. 4, Pt. 1–598
Gregg, William, Feb. 2, 1800–Sept. 13, 1867.
Vol. 4, Pt. 1–599
Gregg, Willis Ray, Jan. 4, 1880–Sept. 14, 1938.
Supp. 2–261
Gregory, Caspar René, Nov. 6, 1846–Apr 9, 1917.
Vol. 4, Pt. 1–601
Gregory, Charles Noble, Aug. 27, 1851–July 10, 1932.
Supp. 1–358
Gregory, Clifford Verne, Oct. 20, 1883–Nov. 18, 1941.
Supp. 3–318
Gregory, Daniel Seelye, Aug. 21, 1832–Apr. 14, 1915.
Vol. 4, Pt. 1–602
Gregory, Eliot, Oct. 13, 1854?–June 1, 1915.
Vol. 4, Pt. 1–602
Gregory, John Milton, July 6, 1822–Oct. 19, 1898.
Vol. 4, Pt. 1–603
Gregory, Menas Sarkas Boulgourjian, July 14, 1872–Nov. 2, 1941.
Supp. 3–319
Gregory, Samuel, Apr. 19, 1813–Mar. 23, 1872.
Vol. 4, Pt. 1–604
Gregory, Stephen Strong, Nov. 16, 1849–Oct. 24, 1920.
Vol. 4, Pt. 1–605
Gregory, Thomas Barger, Oct. 15, 1860–July 11, 1951.
Supp. 5–259
Gregory, Thomas Watt, Nov. 6, 1861–Feb. 26, 1933.
Supp. 1–358
Greist, John Milton, May 9, 1850–Feb. 23, 1906.
Vol. 4, Pt. 1–605
Grellet, Stephen, Nov. 2, 1773–Nov. 16, 1855.
Vol. 4, Pt. 1–606
Gresham, Walter Quintin, Mar. 17, 1832–May 28, 1895.
Vol. 4, Pt. 1–607
Grew, Joseph Clark, May 27, 1880–May 25, 1965.
Supp. 7–302

Grew, Theophilus, d. 1759.
Vol. 4, Pt. 1–609
Grey, Zane, Jan. 31, 1872–Oct. 23, 1939.
Supp. 2–262
Gridley, Charles Vernon, Nov. 24, 1844–June 5, 1898.
Vol. 4, Pt. 1–610
Gridley, Jeremiah, Mar. 10, 1701/02–Sept. 10, 1767.
Vol. 4, Pt. 1–611
Gridley, Richard, Jan. 3, 1710/11–June 21, 1796.
Vol. 4, Pt. 1–611
Grier, Robert Cooper, Mar. 5, 1794–Sept. 25, 1870.
Vol. 4, Pt. 1–612
Grierson, Benjamin Henry, July 8, 1826–Sept. 1, 1911.
Vol. 4, Pt. 1–613
Grierson, Francis, Sept. 18, 1848–May 29, 1927.
Vol. 4, Pt. 1–614
Grieve, Miller, Jan. 11, 1801–*c.* 1878.
Vol. 4, Pt. 1–615
Griffes, Charles Tomlinson, Sept. 17, 1884–Apr. 8, 1920.
Vol. 4, Pt. 1–616
Griffin, Appleton Prentiss Clark, July 24, 1852–Apr. 16, 1926.
Vol. 4, Pt. 1–617
Griffin, Charles, Dec. 18, 1825–Sept. 15, 1867.
Vol. 4, Pt. 1–617
Griffin, Cyrus, July 16, 1748–Dec. 14, 1810.
Vol. 4, Pt. 1–618
Griffin, Edward Dorr, Jan. 6, 1770–Nov. 8, 1837.
Vol. 4, Pt. 1–619
Griffin, Eugene, Oct. 13, 1855–Apr. 11, 1907.
Vol. 4, Pt. 1–620
Griffin, John Howard, June 16, 1920–Sept. 9, 1980.
Supp. 10–291.
Griffin, Martin Ignatius Joseph, Oct. 23, 1842–Nov. 10, 1911.
Supp. 1–360
Griffin, Robert Stanislaus, Sept. 27, 1857–Feb. 21, 1933.
Supp. 1–361
Griffin, Simon Goodell, Aug. 9, 1824–Jan. 14, 1902.
Vol. 4, Pt. 1–621
Griffin, Solomon Bulkley, Aug. 13, 1852–Dec. 11, 1925.
Vol. 4, Pt. 1–622
Griffing, Josephine Sophie White, Dec. 18, 1814–Feb. 18, 1872.
Vol. 4, Pt. 1–622
Griffis, William Elliot, Sept. 17, 1843–Feb. 5, 1928.
Vol. 4, Pt. 1–623
Griffith, Benjamin, Oct. 16, 1688–*c.* Oct. 5, 1768.
Vol. 4, Pt. 1–624
Griffith, Clark Calvin, Nov. 20, 1869–Oct. 27, 1955.
Supp. 5–260
Griffith, David Wark, Jan. 22, 1875–July 23, 1948.
Supp. 4–348
Griffith, Goldsborough Sappington, Nov. 4, 1814–Feb. 24, 1904.
Vol. 4, Pt. 1–624
Griffith, William, 1766–June 7, 1826.
Vol. 4, Pt. 1–625
Griffiths, John Willis, Oct. 6, 1809?–Mar. 30, 1882.
Vol. 4, Pt. 1–626
Griggs, Everett Gallup, Dec. 27, 1868–Mar. 6, 1938.
Supp. 2–263
Griggs, John William, July 10, 1849–Nov. 28, 1927.
Vol. 4, Pt. 1–627
Grigsby, Hugh Blair, Nov. 22, 1806–Apr. 28, 1881.
Vol. 4, Pt. 1–628
Grim, David, Aug. 25, 1737–Mar. 26, 1826.
Vol. 4, Pt. 1–629
Grimes, Absalom Carlisle, Aug. 22, 1834–Mar. 27, 1911.
Vol. 4, Pt. 1–629
Grimes, James Stanley, May 10, 1807–Sept. 27, 1903.
Vol. 4, Pt. 1–630
Grimes, James Wilson, Oct. 20, 1816–Feb. 7, 1872.
Vol. 4, Pt. 1–631
Grimké, Angelina Emily, 1805–1879. [*See* Grimké, Sarah Moore, 1792–1873.]
Grimké Archibald Henry, Aug. 17, 1849–Feb. 25, 1930.
Vol. 4, Pt. 1–632
Grimké, John Faucheraud, Dec. 16, 1752–Aug. 9, 1819.
Vol. 4, Pt. 1–633
Grimké, Sarah Moore, Nov. 26, 1792–Dec. 23, 1873.
Vol. 4, Pt. 1–634
Grimké, Thomas Smith, Sept. 26, 1786–Oct. 12, 1834.
Vol. 4, Pt. 1–635
Grinnell, Frederick, Aug. 14, 1836–Oct. 21, 1905.
Vol. 4, Pt. 2–1
Grinnell, George Bird, Sept. 20, 1849–Apr. 11, 1938.
Supp. 2–264
Grinnell, Henry, Feb. 13, 1799–June 30, 1874.
Vol. 4, Pt. 2–2
Grinnell, Henry Walton, Nov. 19, 1843–Sept. 2, 1920.
Vol. 4, Pt. 2–2
Grinnell, Joseph, Nov. 17, 1788–Feb. 7, 1885.
Vol. 4, Pt. 2–3
Grinnell, Josiah Bushnell, Dec. 22, 1821–Mar. 31, 1891.
Vol. 4, Pt. 2–4
Grinnell, Moses Hicks, Mar. 3, 1803–Nov. 24, 1877.
Vol. 4, Pt. 2–5
Griscom, Clement Acton, Mar. 15, 1841–Nov. 10, 1912.
Vol. 4, Pt. 2–6
Griscom, John, Sept. 27, 1774–Feb. 26, 1852.
Vol. 4, Pt. 2–7
Griscom, Lloyd Carpenter, Nov. 4, 1872–Feb. 8, 1959.
Supp. 6–253
Griscom, Ludlow, June 17, 1890–May 28, 1959.
Supp. 6–254
Grissom, Virgil Ivan ("Gus"), Apr. 3, 1926–Jan. 27, 1967.
Supp. 8–225
Griswold, Alexander Viets, Apr. 22, 1766–Feb. 15, 1843.
Vol. 4, Pt. 2–7
Griswold, Alfred Whitney, Oct. 27, 1906–Apr. 19, 1963.
Supp. 7–303
Griswold, John Augustus, Nov. 11, 1818–Oct. 31, 1872.
Vol. 4, Pt. 2–4
Griswold, Matthew, Mar. 25, 1714–Apr. 28, 1799.
Vol. 4, Pt. 2–9
Griswold, Roger, May 21, 1762–Oct. 25, 1812.
Vol. 4, Pt. 2–10
Griswold, Rufus Wilmot, Feb. 15, 1815–Aug. 27, 1857.
Vol. 4, Pt. 2–10
Griswold, Stanley, Nov. 14, 1763–Aug. 21, 1815.
Vol. 4, Pt. 2–12
Griswold, William McCrillis, Oct. 9, 1853–Aug. 3, 1899.
Vol. 4, Pt. 2–13
Groesbeck, William Slocum, July 24, 1815–July 7, 1897.
Vol. 4, Pt. 2–13
Grofé, Ferde, Mar. 27, 1892–Apr. 3, 1972.
Supp. 9–339
Gronlund, Laurence, July 13, 1846–Oct. 15, 1899.
Vol. 4, Pt. 2–14
Gropius, Walter Adolf Georg, May 18, 1883–July 5, 1969.
Supp. 8–226
Gropper, William, Dec. 3, 1897–Jan. 7, 1977.
Supp. 10–292
Gros, John Daniel, 1738–May 25, 1812.
Vol. 4, Pt. 2–15
Grose, William, Dec. 16, 1812–July 30, 1900.
Vol. 4, Pt. 2–16
Groseilliers, Médart Chouart, Sieur de, fl. 1625–1684.
Vol. 4, Pt. 2–17
Gross, Charles, Feb. 10, 1857–Dec. 3, 1909.
Vol. 4, Pt. 2–18
Gross, Milt, Mar. 4, 1895–Nov. 28, 1953.
Supp. 5–261
Gross, Samuel David, July 8, 1805–May 6, 1884.
Vol. 4, Pt. 2–18
Gross, Samuel Weissell, Feb. 4, 1837–Apr. 16, 1889.
Vol. 4, Pt. 2–20
Grosscup, Peter Stenger, Feb. 15, 1852–Oct. 1, 1921.
Vol. 4, Pt. 2–21
Grosset, Alexander, Jan. 17, 1870–Oct. 27, 1934.
Supp. 1–361
Grossinger, Jennie, June 16, 1892–Nov. 20, 1972.
Supp. 9–341
Grossmann, Georg Martin, Oct. 18, 1823–Aug. 24, 1897.
Vol. 4, Pt. 2–22
Grossmann, Louis, Feb. 24, 1863–Sept. 21, 1926.
Vol. 4, Pt. 2–23
Grosvenor, Charles Henry, Sept. 20, 1833–Oct. 30, 1917.
Vol. 4, Pt. 2–24
Grosvenor, Edwin Prescott, Oct. 25, 1875–Feb. 28, 1930.
Vol. 4, Pt. 2–24

Grosvenor, Gilbert Hovey, Oct. 28, 1875–Feb. 4, 1966. Supp. 8–227

Grosvenor, John. [*See* Altham, John, 1589–1640.]

Grosvenor, William Mason, Apr. 24, 1835–July 20, 1900. Vol. 4, Pt. 2–26

Grosz, George, July 26, 1893–July 6, 1959. Supp. 6–256

Grote, Augustus Radcliffe, Feb. 7, 1841–Sep. 12, 1903. Vol. 4, Pt. 2–27

Grouard, Frank, Sept. 20, 1850–Aug. 15, 1905. Vol. 4, Pt. 2–27

Grove, Robert Moses ("Lefty"), Mar. 6, 1900–May 22, 1975. Supp. 9–344

Grover, Cuvier, July 29, 1828–June 6, 1885. Vol. 4, Pt. 2–28

Grover, La Fayette, Nov. 29, 1823–May 10, 1911. Vol. 4, Pt. 2–29

Groves, Leslie Richard, Jr., Aug. 17, 1896–July 13, 1970. Supp. 8–229

Grow, Galusha Aaron, Aug. 31, 1822–Mar. 31, 1907. Vol. 4, Pt. 2–30

Grube, Bernhard Adam, June 24, 1715–Mar. 20, 1808. Vol. 4, Pt. 2–31

Gruening, Emil, Oct. 2, 1842–May 30, 1914. Vol. 4, Pt. 2–32

Gruening, Ernest, Feb. 6, 1887–June 26, 1974. Supp. 9–345

Grund, Francis Joseph, 1798–Sept. 29, 1863. Supp. 1–362

Grundy, Felix, Sept. 11, 1777–Dec. 19, 1840. Vol. 4, Pt. 2–32

Grundy, Joseph Ridgway, Jan. 13, 1863–Mar. 3, 1961. Supp. 7–304

Gue, Benjamin T., Dec. 25, 1828–June 1, 1904. Vol. 4, Pt. 2–33

Guérin, Anne-Thérèse, Oct. 2, 1798–May 14, 1856. Vol. 4, Pt. 2–34

Guernsey, Egbert, July 8, 1823–Sept. 19, 1903. Vol. 4, Pt. 2–35

Guess, George. [*See* Sequoyah, 1770?–1843.]

Guest, Edgar Albert, Aug. 20, 1881–Aug. 5, 1959. Supp. 6–258

Guffey, James McClurg, Jan. 19, 1839–Mar. 20, 1930. Vol. 4, Pt. 2–35

Guffey, Joseph F., Dec. 29, 1870–Mar. 6, 1959. Supp. 6–259

Guggenheim, Daniel, July 9, 1856–Sept. 28, 1930. Vol. 4, Pt. 2–36

Guggenheim, Harry Frank, Aug. 23, 1890–Jan. 22, 1971. Supp. 9–347

Guggenheim, Marguerite ("Peggy"), Aug, 26, 1898–Dec. 23, 1979. Supp. 10–294

Guggenheim, Meyer, Feb. 1, 1828–Mar. 15, 1905. Vol. 4, Pt. 2–38

Guggenheim, Simon, Dec. 30, 1867–Nov. 2, 1941. Supp. 3–321

Guggenheim, Solomon Robert, Feb. 2, 1861–Nov. 3, 1949. Supp. 4–351

Guignas, Louis Ignace. [*See* Guignas, Michel, 1681–1752.]

Guignas, Michel, Jan. 22, 1681–Feb. 6, 1752. Vol. 4, Pt. 2–40

Guild, Curtis, Feb. 2, 1860–Apr. 6, 1915. Vol. 4, Pt. 2–41

Guild, Curtis, Jan. 13, 1827–Mar. 12, 1911. Vol. 4, Pt. 2–40

Guild, La Fayette, Nov. 23, 1825–July 4, 1870. Supp. 1–364

Guild, Reuben Aldridge, May 4, 1822–May 13, 1899. Vol. 4, Pt. 2–42

Guilday, Peter Keenan, Mar. 25, 1884–July 31, 1947. Supp. 4–352

Guilford, Nathan, July 19, 1786–Dec. 18, 1854. Vol. 4, Pt. 2–43

Guiney, Louise Imogen, Jan. 7, 1861–Nov. 2, 1920. Vol. 4, Pt. 2–43

Guinzburg, Harold Kleinert, Dec. 13, 1899–Oct. 18, 1961. Supp. 7–306

Guiteras, Juan, Jan. 4, 1852–Oct. 28, 1925. Vol. 4, Pt. 2–44

Gulick, John Thomas, Mar. 13, 1832–Apr. 14, 1923. Vol. 4, Pt. 2–45

Gulick, Luther Halsey, June 10, 1828–Apr. 8, 1891. Vol. 4, Pt. 2–46

Gulick, Luther Halsey, Dec. 4, 1865–Aug. 13, 1918. Vol. 4, Pt. 2–47

Gulick, Sidney Lewis, Apr. 10, 1860–Dec. 20, 1945. Supp. 3–322

Gummere, Francis Barton, Mar. 6, 1855–May 30, 1919. Vol. 4, Pt. 2–48

Gummere, John, 1784–May 31, 1845. Vol. 4, Pt. 2–49

Gummere, Samuel James, Apr. 28, 1811–Oct. 23, 1874. Vol. 4, Pt. 2–49

Gummere, Samuel René, Feb. 19, 1849–May 28, 1920. Vol. 4, Pt. 2–50

Gummere, William Stryker, June 24, 1850–Jan. 26, 1933. Supp. 1–365

Gunn, Frederick William, Oct. 4, 1816–Aug. 16, 1881. Vol. 4, Pt. 2–50

Gunn, James Newton, 1867–Nov. 26, 1927. Vol. 4, Pt. 2–51

Gunn, Ross, May 12, 1897–Oct. 15, 1966. Supp. 8–231

Gunn, Selskar Michael, May 25, 1883–Aug. 2, 1944. Supp. 3–323

Gunnison, Foster, June 9, 1896–Oct. 19, 1961. Supp. 7–307

Gunnison, John Williams, Nov. 11, 1812–Oct. 26, 1853. Vol. 4, Pt. 2–52

Gunsaulus, Frank Wakeley, Jan. 1, 1856–Mar. 17, 1921. Vol. 4, Pt. 2–52

Gunter, Archibald Clavering, Oct. 25. 1847–Feb. 24. 1907. Vol. 4. Pt. 2–54

Gunther, Charles Frederick, Mar. 6, 1837–Feb. 10, 1920. Vol. 4, Pt. 2–54

Gunther, John, Aug. 30, 1901–May 29, 1970. Supp. 8–232

Gunton, George, Sept. 8, 1845–Sept. 11, 1919. Vol. 4, Pt. 2–55

Gurley, Ralph Randolph, May 26, 1797–July 30, 1872. Vol. 4, Pt. 2–56

Gurney, Ephraim Whitman, Feb. 18, 1829–Sept. 12, 1886. Vol. 4, Pt. 2–57

Gurowski, Adam, Sept. 10, 1805–May 4, 1866. Supp. 1–366

Guthe, Karl Eugen, Mar. 5, 1866–Sept. 10, 1915. Vol. 4, Pt. 2–58

Gutherz, Carl, Jan. 28, 1844–Feb. 7, 1907. Vol. 4, Pt. 2–58

Guthrie, Alfred, Apr. 1, 1805–Aug. 17, 1882. Vol. 4, Pt. 2–59

Guthrie, Edwin Ray, Jr., Jan. 9, 1886–Apr. 23, 1959. Supp. 6–261

Guthrie, George Wilkins, Sept. 5, 1848–Mar. 8, 1917. Vol. 4, Pt. 2–60

Guthrie, James, Dec. 5, 1792–Mar. 13, 1869. Vol. 4, Pt. 2–60

Guthrie, Ramon, Jan. 14, 1896–Nov. 22, 1973. Supp. 9–348

Guthrie, Samuel, 1782–Oct. 19, 1848. Vol. 4, Pt. 2–62

Guthrie, Tyrone, July 2, 1900–May 15, 1971. Supp. 9–350

Guthrie, William Dameron, Feb. 3, 1859–Dec. 8, 1935. Supp. 1–367

Guthrie, Woody, July 14, 1912–Oct. 3, 1967. Supp. 8–234

Guttmacher, Alan Frank, May 19, 1898–Mar. 18, 1974. Supp. 9–351

Guy, Seymour Joseph, Jan. 16, 1824–Dec. 10, 1910. Vol. 4, Pt. 2–62

Guyot, Arnold Henry, Sept. 28, 1807–Feb. 8, 1884. Vol. 4, Pt. 2–63

Guzik, Jack, 1886/1888–Feb. 21, 1956. Supp. 6–263

Gwin, William McKendree, Oct. 9, 1805–Sept. 3, 1885. Vol. 4, Pt. 2–64

Gwinnett, Button, *c.* 1735–May 16, 1777. Vol. 4, Pt. 2–65

Haagen-Smit, Arie Jan, Dec. 22, 1900–Mar. 17, 1977. Supp. 10–297

Haan, William George, Oct. 4, 1863–Oct. 26, 1924.
Vol. 4, Pt. 2–66
Haarstick, Henry Christian, July 26, 1836–Jan. 26, 1919.
Vol. 4, Pt. 2–67
Haas, Francis Joseph, Mar. 18, 1889–Aug. 29, 1953.
Supp. 5–263
Haas, Jacob Judah Aaron de, Aug. 13, 1872–Mar. 21, 1937.
Supp. 2–265
Habberton, John, Feb. 24, 1842–Feb. 24, 1921.
Vol. 4, Pt. 2–67
Habersham, Alexander Wylly, Mar. 24, 1826–Mar. 26, 1883.
Vol. 4, Pt. 2–68
Habersham, James, January 1712 o.s.–Aug. 28, 1775.
Vol. 4, Pt. 2–68
Habersham, Joseph, July 28, 1751–Nov. 17, 1815.
Vol. 4, Pt. 2–70
Hack, George, *c.* 1623–*c.* 1665.
Vol. 4, Pt. 2–70
Hackett, Francis, Jan. 21, 1883–Apr. 24, 1962.
Supp. 7–309
Hackett, Frank Warren, Apr. 11, 1841–Aug. 10, 1926.
Vol. 4, Pt. 2–71
Hackett, Horatio Balch, Dec. 27, 1808–Nov. 2, 1875.
Vol. 4, Pt. 2–72
Hackett, James Henry, Mar. 15, 1800–Dec. 28, 1871.
Vol. 4, Pt. 2–72
Hackett, James Keteltas, Sept. 6, 1869–Nov. 8, 1926.
Vol. 4, Pt. 2–74
Hackett, Robert Leo ("Bobby"), Jan. 31, 1915–June 7, 1976.
Supp. 10–298
Hackley, Charles Henry, Jan. 3, 1837–Feb. 10, 1905.
Vol. 4, Pt. 2–75
Hadas, Moses, June 25, 1900–Aug. 17, 1966.
Supp. 8–235
Haddock, Charles Brickett, June 20, 1796–Jan. 15, 1861.
Vol. 4, Pt. 2–76
Haddon, Elizabeth. [*See* Estaugh, Elizabeth Haddon, *c.* 1680–1762.]
Hadfield, George, *c.* 1764–Feb. 5, 1826.
Vol. 4, Pt. 2–76
Hadley, Arthur Twining, Apr. 23, 1856–Mar. 6, 1930.
Vol. 4, Pt. 2–77
Hadley, Henry Kimball, Dec. 20, 1871–Sept. 6, 1937.
Supp. 2–267
Hadley, Herbert Spencer, Feb. 20, 1872–Dec. 1, 1927.
Vol. 4, Pt. 2–80
Hadley, James, Mar. 30, 1821–Nov. 14, 1872.
Vol. 4, Pt. 2–81
Ha-Ga-Sa-Do-Ni. [*See* "Deerfoot," 1828–1897.]
Hagedorn, Hermann Ludwig Gebhard, July 18, 1882–July 27, 1964.
Supp. 7–310
Hagen, Hermann August, May 30, 1817–Nov. 9, 1893.
Vol. 4, Pt. 2–82
Hagen, Walter Charles, Dec. 21, 1892–Oct. 5, 1969.
Supp. 8–237
Hager, John Sharpenstein, Mar. 12, 1818–Mar. 19, 1890.
Vol. 4, Pt. 2–82
Haggerty, Melvin Everett, Jan. 17, 1875–Oct. 6, 1937.
Supp. 2–268
Haggin, James Ben Ali, Dec. 9, 1827–Sept. 12, 1914.
Vol. 4, Pt. 2–83
Hagner, Peter, Oct. 1, 1772–July 16, 1850.
Vol. 4, Pt. 2–84
Hagood, Johnson, Feb. 21, 1829–Jan. 4, 1898.
Vol. 4, Pt. 2–85
Hague, Arnold, Dec. 3, 1840–May 14, 1917.
Vol. 4, Pt. 2–85
Hague, Frank, Jan. 17, 1876–Jan. 1, 1956.
Supp. 6–265
Hague, James Duncan, Feb. 24, 1836–Aug. 3, 1908.
Vol. 4, Pt. 2–87
Hague, Robert Lincoln, Mar. 2, 1880–Mar. 8, 1939.
Supp. 2–269
Hahn, Georg Michael Decker, Nov. 24, 1830–Mar. 15, 1886.
Vol. 4, Pt. 2–87
Haid, Leo, July 15, 1849–July 24, 1924.
Vol. 4, Pt. 2–88
Haight, Charles Coolidge, Mar. 17, 1841–Feb. 8, 1917.
Vol. 4, Pt. 2–89
Haight, Henry Huntly, May 20, 1825–Sept. 2, 1878.
Vol. 4, Pt. 2–90
Hailmann, William Nicholas, Oct. 20, 1836–May 13, 1920.
Vol. 4, Pt. 2–90
Haines, Charles Glidden, Jan. 24, 1792–July 3, 1825.
Vol. 4, Pt. 2–91
Haines, Daniel, Jan. 6, 1801–Jan. 26, 1877.
Vol. 4, Pt. 2–92
Haines, Lynn, Apr. 12, 1876–Oct. 9, 1929.
Vol. 4, Pt. 2–93
Haish, Jacob, Mar. 9, 1826–Feb. 19, 1926.
Vol. 4, Pt. 2–93
Haldeman, Samuel Steman, Aug. 12, 1812–Sept. 10, 1880.
Vol. 4, Pt. 2–94
Haldeman-Julius, Emanuel, July 30, 1889–July 31, 1951.
Supp. 5–264
Halderman, John A., Apr. 15, 1833–Sept. 21, 1908.
Vol. 4, Pt. 2–95
Hale, Benjamin, Nov. 23, 1797–July 15, 1863.
Vol. 4, Pt. 2–96
Hale, Charles, June 7, 1831–Mar. 1, 1882.
Vol. 4 Pt. 2–96
Hale, Charies Reuben, Mar. 14, 1837–Dec. 25, 1900.
Vol. 4, Pt. 2–97
Hale, David, Apr. 25, 1791–Jan. 20, 1849.
Vol. 4, Pt. 2–98
Hale, Edward Everett, Apr. 3, 1822–June 10, 1909.
Vol. 4, Pt. 2–99
Hale, Edward Joseph, Dec. 25, 1839–Feb. 15, 1922.
Vol. 4, Pt. 2–100
Hale, Edwin Moses, Feb. 2, 1829–Jan. 15, 1899.
Vol. 4, Pt. 2–101
Hale, Enoch, Jan. 19, 1790–Nov. 12, 1848.
Vol. 4, Pt. 2–102
Hale, Eugene, June 9, 1836–Oct. 27, 1918.
Vol. 4, Pt. 2–102
Hale, Frederick, Oct. 7, 1874–Sept. 28, 1963.
Supp. 7–312
Hale, George Ellery, June 29, 1868–Feb. 21, 1938.
Supp. 2–270
Hale, Horatio Emmons, May 3, 1817–Dec. 28, 1896.
Vol. 4, Pt. 2–104
Hale, John Parker, Mar. 31, 1806–Nov. 19, 1873.
Vol. 4, Pt. 2–105
Hale, Louise Closser, Oct. 13, 1872–July 26, 1933.
Supp. 1–368
Hale, Lucretia Peabody, Sept. 2, 1820–June 12, 1900.
Vol. 4, Pt. 2–107
Hale, Nathan, Aug. 16, 1784–Feb. 8, 1863.
Vol. 4, Pt. 2–109
Hale, Nathan, June 6, 1755–Sept. 22, 1776.
Vol. 4, Pt. 2–107
Hale, Philip, Mar. 5, 1854–Nov. 13, 1934.
Supp. 1–369
Hale, Philip Leslie, May 21, 1865–Feb. 2, 1931.
Vol. 4, Pt. 2–110
Hale, Robert Safford, Sept. 24, 1822–Dec. 14, 1881.
Vol. 4, Pt. 2–110
Hale, Sarah Josepha Buell, Oct. 24, 1788–Apr. 30, 1879.
Vol. 4, Pt. 2–111
Hale, William Bayard, Apr. 6, 1869–Apr. 10, 1924.
Vol. 4, Pt. 2–112
Hale, William Gardner, Feb. 9, 1849–June 23, 1928.
Vol. 4, Pt. 2–113
Haley, Jack, Aug. 10, 1899–June 6, 1979.
Supp. 10–300
Hall, Abraham Oakey, July 26, 1826–Oct. 7, 1898.
Vol. 4, Pt. 2–114
Hall, Arethusa, Oct. 13, 1802–May 24, 1891.
Vol. 4, Pt. 2–116
Hall, Arthur Crawshay Alliston, Apr. 12, 1847–Feb. 26, 1930.
Vol. 4, Pt. 2–116
Hall, Asaph, Oct. 15, 1829–Nov. 22, 1907.
Vol. 4, Pt. 2–117
Hall, Baynard Rush, Jan. 28, 1798–Jan. 23, 1863.
Vol. 4, Pt. 2–118
Hall, Bolton, Aug. 5, 1854–Dec. 10, 1938.
Supp. 2–271
Hall, Charles Cuthbert, Sept. 3, 1852–Mar. 25, 1908.
Vol. 4, Pt. 2–119

Hall, Charles Francis, 1821–Nov. 8, 1871.
Vol. 4, Pt. 2–120
Hall, Charles Henry, Nov. 7, 1820–Sept. 12, 1895.
Vol. 4, Pt. 2–121
Hall, Charles Martin, Dec. 6, 1863–Dec. 27, 1914.
Vol. 4, Pt. 2–122
Hall, David, 1714–Dec. 24, 1772.
Vol. 4, Pt. 2–123
Hall, Dommick Augustin, *c.* 1765–Dec. 19, 1820.
Vol. 4, Pt. 2–123
Hall, Edwin Herbert, Nov. 7, 1855–Nov. 20, 1938.
Supp. 2–275
Hall, Fitzedward, Mar. 21, 1825–Feb. 1, 1901.
Vol. 4, Pt. 2–124
Hall, Florence Marion Howe, Aug. 25, 1845–Apr. 10, 1922.
Vol. 4, Pt. 2–126
Hall, George Henry, Sept. 21, 1825–Feb. 17, 1913.
Vol. 4, Pt. 2–126
Hall, Granville Stanley, Feb. 1, 1844–Apr. 24, 1924.
Vol. 4, Pt. 2–127
Hall, Hazel, Feb. 7, 1886–May 11, 1924.
Vol. 4, Pt. 2–130
Hall, Henry Bryan, Mar. 11, 1808–Apr. 25, 1884.
Vol. 4, Pt. 2–131
Hall, Hiland, July 20, 1795–Dec. 18, 1885.
Vol. 4, Pt. 2–131
Hall, Isaac Hollister, Dec. 12, 1837–July 2, 1896.
Vol. 4, Pt. 2–132
Hall, James, Aug. 22, 1744–July 25, 1826.
Vol. 4, Pt. 2–133
Hall, James, Aug. 19, 1793–July 5, 1868.
Vol. 4, Pt. 2–134
Hall, James, Sept. 12, 1811–Aug. 7, 1898.
Vol. 4, Pt. 2–135
Hall, James Norman, Apr. 22, 1887–July 6, 1951.
Supp. 5–266
Hall, John, July 31, 1829–Sept. 17, 1898.
Vol. 4, Pt. 2–137
Hall, John Elihu, Dec. 27, 1783–June 12, 1829.
Vol. 4, Pt. 2–138
Hall, Juanita Armethea, Nov. 6, 1901–Feb. 28, 1968.
Supp. 8–238
Hall, Leonard Wood, Oct. 2, 1900–June 2, 1979.
Supp. 10–302
Hall, Luther Egbert, Aug. 30, 1869–Nov. 6, 1921.
Vol. 4, Pt. 2–139
Hall, Lyman, Apr. 12, 1724–Oct. 19, 1790.
Vol. 4, Pt. 2–139
Hall, Nathan Kelsey, Mar. 28, 1810–Mar. 2, 1874.
Vol. 4, Pt. 2–140
Hall, Paul, Aug. 20, 1914–June 22, 1980.
Supp. 10–303
Hall, Samuel, Nov. 2, 1740–Oct. 30, 1807.
Vol. 4, Pt. 2–141
Hall, Samuel, Apr. 23, 1800–Nov. 13, 1870.
Vol. 4, Pt. 2–142
Hall, Samuel Read, Oct. 27, 1795–June 24, 1877.
Vol. 4, Pt. 2–142
Hall, Sarah Ewing, Oct. 30, 1761–Apr. 8, 1830.
Vol. 4, Pt. 2–143
Hall, Sherman, Apr. 30, 1800–Sept. 1, 1879.
Vol. 4, Pt. 2–144
Hall, Thomas, Feb. 4, 1834–Nov. 19, 1911.
Vol. 4, Pt. 2–144
Hall, Thomas Seavey, Apr. 1, 1827–Dec. 1, 1880.
Vol. 4, Pt. 2–145
Hall, Willard, Dec. 24, 1780–May 10, 1875.
Vol. 4, Pt. 2–146
Hall, Willard Preble, May 9, 1820–Nov. 3, 1882.
Vol. 4, Pt. 2–146
Hall, William Whitty, Oct. 15, 1810–May 10, 1876.
Vol. 4, Pt. 2–147
Hallam, Lewis, *c.* 1740–Nov. 1, 1808.
Vol. 4, Pt. 2–148
Halleck, Fitz-Greene, July 8, 1790–Nov. 19, 1867.
Vol. 4, Pt. 2–149
Halleck, Henry Wager, Jan. 16, 1815–Jan. 9, 1872.
Vol. 4, Pt. 2–150
Hallet, Étienne Sulpice, fl. 1789–1796.
Vol. 4, Pt. 2–152
Hallet, Stephen. [*See* Hallet, Étienne Sulpice, fl. 1789–1796]
Hallett, Benjamin, Jan. 18, 1760–Dec. 31, 1849.
Vol. 4, Pt. 2–154
Hallett, Benjamin Franklin, Dec. 2, 1797–Sept. 30, 1862.
Vol. 4, Pt. 2–154
Hallett, Moses, July 16, 1834–Apr. 25, 1913.
Vol. 4, Pt. 2–155
Hallidie, Andrew Smith, Mar. 16, 1836–Apr. 24, 1900.
Vol. 4, Pt. 2–156
Hallock, Charles, Mar. 13, 1834–Dec. 2, 1917.
Vol. 4, Pt. 2–156
Hallock, Gerard, Mar. 18, 1800–Jan. 4, 1866.
Vol. 4, Pt. 2–157
Hallock, William Allen, June 2, 1794–Oct. 2, 1880.
Vol. 4, Pt. 2–158
Hallowell, Benjamin, Aug. 17, 1799–Sept. 7, 1877.
Vol. 4, Pt. 2–159
Hallowell, Richard Price, Dec. 16, 1835–Jan. 5, 1904.
Vol. 4, Pt. 2–160
Halpert, Edith Gregor, Apr. 25, 1900–Oct. 6, 1970.
Supp. 8–239
Halpine, Charles Graham, Nov. 20, 1829–Aug. 3, 1868.
Vol. 4, Pt. 2–160
Halsey, Frederick Arthur, July 12, 1856–Oct. 20, 1935.
Supp. 1–370
Halsey, John, Mar. 1, 1670–1716.
Vol. 4, Pt. 2–161
Halsey, Thomas Lloyd, *c.* 1776–Feb. 2, 1855.
Vol. 4, Pt. 2–162
Halsey, William Frederick, Jr., Oct. 30, 1882–Aug. 16, 1959.
Supp. 6–266
Halsman, Philippe, May 2, 1906–June 25, 1979.
Supp. 10–305
Halstead, Murat, Sept. 2, 1829–July 2, 1908.
Vol. 4, Pt. 2–163
Halsted, George Bruce, Nov. 25, 1853–Mar. 16, 1922.
Vol. 4, Pt. 2–163
Halsted, William Stewart, Sept. 23, 1852–Sept. 7, 1922.
Vol. 4, Pt. 2–164
Hambidge, Jay, Jan. 13, 1867–June 20, 1924.
Vol. 4, Pt. 2–165
Hambleton, Thomas Edward, May 17, 1829–Sept. 21, 1906.
Vol. 4, Pt. 2–167
Hamblin, Joseph Eldridge, Jan. 13, 1828–July 3, 1870.
Vol. 4, Pt. 2–167
Hamblin, Thomas Sowerby, May 14, 1800–Jan. 8, 1853.
Vol. 4, Pt. 2–168
Hamer, Fannie Lou, Oct. 6, 1917–Mar. 14, 1977.
Supp. 10–306
Hamer, Thomas Lyon, July 1800–Dec. 2, 1846.
Vol. 4, Pt. 2–169
Hamilton, Alexander, Jan 11, 1757–July 12, 1804.
Vol. 4, Pt. 2–171
Hamilton, Alexander, 1712–May 11, 1756.
Vol. 4, Pt. 2–170
Hamilton, Alice, Feb. 27, 1869–Sept. 22, 1970.
Supp. 8–241
Hamilton, Allan McLane, Oct. 6, 1848–Nov. 23, 1919.
Vol. 4, Pt. 2–179
Hamilton, Andrew, d. Apr. 26, 1703.
Vol. 4, Pt. 2–180
Hamilton, Andrew, d. Aug. 4, 1741.
Vol. 4, Pt. 2–181
Hamilton, Andrew Jackson, Jan. 28, 1815–Apr. 11, 1875.
Vol. 4, Pt. 2–182
Hamilton, Charles Smith, Nov. 16, 1822–Apr. 17, 1891.
Vol. 4, Pt. 2–183
Hamilton, Clayton, Nov. 14, 1881–Sept. 17, 1946.
Supp. 4–354
Hamilton, Edith, Aug. 12, 1867–May 31, 1963.
Supp. 7–313
Hamilton, Edward John, Nov. 29, 1834–Nov. 21, 1918.
Vol. 4, Pt. 2–184
Hamilton, Frank Hastings, Sept. 10, 1813–Aug. 11, 1886.
Vol. 4, Pt. 2–185
Hamilton, Gail. [*See* Dodge, Mary Abigail, 1833–1896.]
Hamilton, James, *c.* 1710–Aug. 14, 1783.
Vol. 4, Pt. 2–186
Hamilton, James, May 8, 1786–Nov. 15, 1857.
Vol. 4, Pt. 2–187

Hamilton, James Alexander, Apr. 14, 1788–Sept. 24, 1878.
Vol. 4, Pt. 2–188
Hamilton, John Daniel Miller, II, Mar. 2, 1892–Sept. 24, 1973.
Supp. 9–355
Hamilton, John William, Mar. 18, 1845–July 24, 1934.
Supp. 1–371
Harnilton, Maxwell McGaughey, Dec. 20, 1896–Nov. 12, 1957.
Supp. 6–269
Hamilton, Paul, Oct. 16, 1762–June 30, 1816.
Vol. 4, Pt. 2–189
Hamilton, Peter, Nov. 7, 1817–Nov. 22, 1888.
Vol. 4, Pt. 2–190
Hamilton, Schuyler, July 25, 1822–Mar. 18, 1903.
Vol. 4, Pt. 2–191
Hamilton, Walton Hale, Oct. 30, 1881–Oct. 27, 1958.
Supp. 6–271
Hamilton, William Thomas, Dec. 6, 1822–May 24, 1908.
Vol. 4, Pt. 2–192
Hamilton, William Thomas, Sept. 8, 1820–Oct. 26, 1888.
Vol. 4, Pt. 2–191
Hamlin, Alfred Dwight Foster, Sept. 5, 1855–Mar. 21, 1926.
Vol. 4, Pt. 2–193
Hamlin, Charles, Sept. 13, 1837–May 15, 1911.
Vol. 4, Pt. 2–194
Hamlin, Charles Sumner, Aug. 30, 1861–Apr. 24, 1938.
Supp. 2–273
Hamlin, Cyrus, Jan. 5, 1811–Aug. 8, 1900.
Vol. 4, Pt. 2–195
Hamlin, Emmons, Nov. 16, 1821–Apr. 8, 1885.
Vol. 4, Pt. 2–196
Hamlin, Hannibal, Aug. 27, 1809–July 4, 1891.
Vol. 4, Pt. 2–196
Hamlin, Talbot Faulkner, June 16, 1889–Oct. 7, 1956.
Supp. 6–272
Hamlin, William, Oct. 15, 1772–Nov. 22, 1869.
Vol. 4, Pt. 2–198
Hamline, Leonidas Lent, May 10, 1797–Mar. 23, 1865.
Vol. 4, Pt. 2–198
Hammer, William Joseph, Feb. 26, 1858–Mar. 24, 1934.
Supp. 1–373
Hammerstein, Oscar, *c.* 1847–Aug. 1, 1919.
Vol. 4, Pt. 2–199
Hammerstein, Oscar, II, July 12, 1895–Aug. 23, 1960.
Supp. 6–273
Hammett, Henry Pinckney, Dec. 31, 1822–May 8, 1891.
Vol. 4, Pt. 2–200
Hammett, Samuel Adams, Feb. 4, 1816–Dec. 24, 1865.
Vol. 4, Pt. 2–201
Hammett, Samuel Dashiell, May 27, 1894–Jan. 10, 1961.
Supp. 7–314
Hammon, Jupiter, *c.* 1720–*c.* 1800.
Vol. 4, Pt. 2–201
Hammond, Bray, Nov. 20, 1886–July 20, 1968.
Supp. 8–242
Hammond, Charles, Sept. 19, 1779–Apr. 3, 1840.
Vol. 4, Pt. 2–202
Hammond, Edward Payson, Sept. 1, 1831–Aug. 14, 1910.
Vol. 4, Pt. 2–203
Hammond, Edwin, May 20, 1801–Dec. 31, 1870.
Vol. 4, Pt. 2–203
Hammond, George Henry, May 5, 1838–Dec. 29, 1886.
Vol. 4, Pt. 2–204
Hammond, Jabez Delano, Aug. 2, 1778–Aug. 18, 1885.
Vol. 4, Pt. 2–205
Hammond, James Bartlett, Apr. 23, 1839–Jan. 27, 1913
Vol. 4, Pt. 2–206
Hammond, James Henry, Nov. 15, 1807–Nov. 13, 1864.
Vol. 4, Pt. 2–207
Hammond, John Hays, Mar. 31, 1855–June 8, 1936.
Supp. 2–275
Hammond, Laurens, Nov. 11, 1895–July 1, 1973.
Supp. 9–357
Hammond, Nathaniel Job, Dec. 26, 1833–Apr. 20, 1899.
Vol. 4, Pt. 2–208
Hammond, Percy Hunter, Mar. 7, 1873–Apr. 25, 1936.
Supp. 2–277
Hammond, Samuel, Sept. 21, 1757–Sept. 11, 1842.
Vol. 4, Pt. 2–209
Hammond, William Alexander, Aug. 28, 1828–Jan. 5, 1900.
Vol. 4, Pt. 2–210
Hammond, William Gardiner, May 3, 1829–Apr. 12, 1894.
Vol. 4, Pt. 2–211
Hampden, Walter, June 30, 1879–June 11, 1955.
Supp. 5–267
Hampton, Wade, 1751 or 1752–Feb. 4, 1835.
Vol. 4, Pt. 2–212
Hampton, Wade, Mar. 28, 1818–Apr. 11, 1902.
Vol. 4, Pt. 2–213
Hamtranck, John Francis, Apr. 19, 1798–Apr. 21, 1858.
Vol. 4, Pt. 2–215
Hanaford, Phoebe Ann Coffin, May 6, 1829–June 2, 1921
Vol. 4, Pt. 2–216
Hanby, Benjamin Russel, July 22, 1833–Mar. 16, 1867.
Vol. 4, Pt. 2–217
Hanchett, Henry Granger, Aug. 29, 1853–Aug. 19, 1918.
Vol. 4, Pt. 2–217
Hancock, John, Jan. 12, 1736/7–Oct. 8, 1793.
Vol. 4, Pt. 2–218
Hancock, John, Oct. 24, 1824–July 19, 1893.
Vol. 4, Pt. 2–220
Hancock, Thomas, July 13, 1703–Aug. 1, 1764.
Vol. 4, Pt. 2–220
Hancock, Winfield Scott, Feb. 14, 1824–Feb. 9, 1886.
Vol. 4, Pt. 2–221
Hand, Augustus Noble, July 26, 1869–Oct. 28, 1954.
Supp. 5–269
Hand, Daniel, July 16, 1801–Dec. 17, 1891.
Vol. 4, Pt. 2–222
Hand, Edward, Dec. 31, 1744–Sept. 3, 1802.
Vol. 4, Pt. 2–223
Hand, Learned, Jan. 27, 1872–Aug. 18, 1961.
Supp. 7–315
Handerson, Henry Ebenezer, Mar. 21, 1837–Apr. 23, 1918.
Vol. 4, Pt. 2–224
Handley, Harold Willis, Nov. 27, 1909–Aug. 30, 1972.
Supp. 9–359
Handy, Alexander Hamilton, Dec. 25, 1809–Sept. 12, 1883.
Vol. 4, Pt. 2–225
Handy, Wiliiam Christopher, Nov. 16, 1873–Mar. 28, 1958.
Supp. 6–274
Hanna, Edward Joseph, July 21, 1860–July 10, 1944.
Supp. 3–325
Hanna, Marcus Alonzo, Sept. 24, 1837–Feb. 15, 1904.
Vol. 4, Pt. 2–225
Hannagan, Stephen Jerome, Apr. 4, 1899–Feb. 5, 1953.
Supp. 5–270
Hannegan, Edward Allen, June 25, 1807–Feb. 25, 1859.
Vol. 4, Pt. 2–228
Hannegan, Robert Emmet, June 30, 1903–Oct. 6, 1949.
Supp. 4–355
Hansberry, Lorraine Vivian, May 19, 1930–Jan. 12, 1965.
Supp. 7–318
Hansburg, George Bernard, Oct. 1887–Dec. 3, 1975.
Supp. 9–360
Hansen, Alvin Harvey, Aug. 23, 1887–June 6, 1975.
Supp. 9–362
Hansen, George, Apr. 15, 1863–Mar. 31, 1908.
Vol. 4, Pt. 2–229
Hansen, Marcus Lee, Dec. 8, 1892–May 11, 1938.
Supp. 2–278
Hansen, Niels Ebbesen, Jan. 4, 1866–Oct. 5, 1950.
Supp. 4–357
Hansen, William Webster, May 27, 1909–May 23, 1949.
Supp. 4–357
Hanson, Alexander Contee, Oct. 22, 1749–Jan 16 1806.
Vol. 4, Pt. 2–230
Hanson, Alexander Contee, Feb. 27, 1786–Apr. 23, 1819.
Vol. 4, Pt. 2–231
Hanson, James Christian Meinich, Mar. 13, 1864–Nov. 8, 1943.
Supp. 3–326
Hanson, John, Apr. 13, 1721–Nov. 22, 1783.
Vol. 4, Pt. 2–231
Hanson, Ole, Jan. 6, 1874–July 6, 1940.
Supp. 2–279
Hanson, Roger Weightman, Aug. 27, 1827–Jan. 4, 1863.
Vol. 4, Pt. 2–232
Hanus, Paul Henry, Mar. 14, 1855–Dec. 14, 1941.
Supp. 3–327
Hapgood, Hutchins, May 21, 1869–Nov. 18, 1944.
Supp. 3–329

Hapgood, Isabel Florence, Nov. 21, 1850–June 26, 1928.
Vol. 4, Pt. 2–233
Hapgood, Norman, Mar. 28, 1868–Apr. 29, 1937.
Supp. 2–280
Happer, Andrew Patton, Oct. 20, 1818–Oct. 27, 1894.
Vol. 4, Pt. 2–234
Haraden, Jonathan, Nov. 11, 1744–Nov. 23, 1803.
Vol. 4, Pt. 2–234
Harahan, James Theodore, Jan. 12, 1841–Jan. 9
Vol. 4, Pt. 2–235
Harahan, William Johnson, Dec. 22, 1867–Dec.
Supp. 2–282
Haraszthy De Mokcsa, Agoston, *c.* 1812–July 6, 1869.
Vol. 4, Pt. 2–236
Harbaugh, Henry, Oct. 28, 1817–Dec. 28, 1867.
Vol. 4, Pt. 2–237
Harben, William Nathaniel, July 5, 1858–Aug. 7, 1919.
Vol. 4, Pt. 2–238
Harbord, James Guthrie, Mar. 21, 1866–Aug. 20, 1947.
Supp. 4–359
Harby, Isaac, Nov. 9, 1788–Dec. 14, 1828.
Vol. 4, Pt. 2–239
Harcourt, Alfred, Jan. 31, 1881–June 21, 1954.
Supp. 5–271
Hard, William, Sept. 15, 1878–Jan. 30. 1962.
Supp. 7–320
Hardee, William Joseph, Oct. 12, 1815–Nov. 6, 1873.
Vol. 4, Pt. 2–239
Hardenbergh, Henry Janeway, Feb. 6, 1847–Mar. 13, 1918.
Vol. 4, Pt. 2–240
Hardenbergh, Jacob Rutsen, 1736–Nov. 2, 1790.
Vol. 4, Pt. 2–241
Hardey, Mother Mary Aloysia, Dec. 8, 1809–June 17, 1886.
Vol. 4, Pt. 2–242
Hardie, James Allen, May 5, 1823–Dec. 14, 1876.
Vol. 4, Pt. 2–242
Hardin, Ben, Feb. 29, 1784–Sept. 24, 1852.
Vol. 4, Pt. 2–243
Hardin, Charles Henry, July 15, 1820–July 29, 1892.
Vol. 4, Pt. 2–244
Hardin, John, Oct. 1, 1753–May 1792.
Vol. 4, Pt. 2–245
Hardin, John J., Jan. 6, 1810–Feb. 23, 1847.
Vol. 4, Pt. 2–246
Hardin, Martin D., June 21, 1780–Oct. 8, 1823.
Vol. 4, Pt. 2–246
Harding, Abner Clark, Feb. 10, 1807–July 19, 1874.
Vol. 4, Pt. 2–247
Harding, Chester, Sept. 1, 1792–Apr. 1, 1866.
Vol. 4, Pt. 2–248
Harding, George, Oct. 26, 1827–Nov. 17, 1902.
Vol. 4, Pt. 2–249
Harding, Jesper, Nov. 5, 1799–Aug. 21, 1865.
Vol. 4, Pt. 2–250
Harding, Robert, Oct. 6, 1701–Sept. 1, 1772.
Vol. 4, Pt. 2–250
Harding, Seth, Apr. 17, 1734–Nov. 20, 1814.
Vol. 4, Pt. 2–251
Harding, Warren Gamaliel, Nov. 2, 1865–Aug. 2, 1923.
Vol. 4, Pt. 2–252
Harding, William Procter Gould, May 5, 1864–Apr. 7, 1930.
Vol. 4, Pt. 2–257
Harding, William White, Nov. 1, 1830–May 15, 1889.
Vol. 4, Pt. 2–259
Hardwick, Thomas William, Dec. 9, 1872–Jan. 31, 1944.
Supp. 3–330
Hardwicke, Cedric Webster, Feb. 19, 1893–Aug. 6, 1964.
Supp. 7–321
Hardy, Arthur Sherburne, Aug. 13, 1847–Mar. 13, 1930.
Vol. 4, Pt. 2–259
Hardy, Oliver Norvell, Jan. 18, 1892–Aug. 7, 1957.
Supp. 6–276
Hardy, Samuel, *c.* 1758–Oct. 17, 1785.
Vol. 4 Pt. 2–260
Hardy, William Harris, Feb. 12, 1837–Feb. 18, 1917.
Vol. 4, Pt. 2–261
Hare, George Emlen, Sept. 4, 1808–Feb. 15, 1892.
Vol. 4, Pt. 2–261
Hare, James H., Oct. 3, 1856–June 24, 1946.
Supp. 4–360
Hare, John Innes Clark, Oct. 17, 1816–Dec. 29, 1905.
Vol. 4, Pt. 2–262
Hare, Robert, Jan. 17, 1781–May 15, 1858.
Vol. 4, Pt. 2–263
Hare, William Hobart, May 17, 1838–Oct. 23, 1909.
Vol. 4. Pt. 2–264
Hargrove, Robert Kennon, Sept. 17, 1829–Aug. 3, 1905.
Vol. 4, Pt. 2–265
Haring, Clarence, Feb. 9, 1885–Sept. 4, 1960.
Supp. 6–277
Harkins, William Draper, Dec. 28, 1873–Mar. 7, 1951.
Supp. 5–273
Harkness, Albert, Oct. 6, 1822–May 27, 1907.
Vol. 4, Pt. 2–265
Harkness, Edward Stephen, Jan. 22, 1874–Jan. 29, 1940.
Supp. 2–283
Harkness, William, Dec. 17, 1837–Feb. 28, 1903.
Vol. 4, Pt. 2–266
Harlan, James, June 22, 1800–Feb. 18, 1863.
Vol. 4, Pt. 2–267
Harlan, James, Aug. 26, 1820–Oct. 5, 1899.
Vol. 4, Pt. 2–268
Harlan, John Marshall, June 1, 1833–Oct. 14, 1911.
Vol. 4, Pt. 2–269
Harlan, John Marshall, May 20, 1899–Dec. 29, 1971.
Supp. 9–363
Harlan, Josiah, June 12, 1799–October 1871.
Vol. 4, Pt. 2–272
Harlan, Richard, Sept. 19, 1796–Sept. 30, 1843.
Vol. 4, Pt. 2–273
Harland, Henry, Mar. 1, 1861–Dec. 20, 1905.
Vol. 4, Pt. 2–274
Harland, Marion. [*See* Terhune, Mary Virginia Hawes, 1830–1922.]
Harland, Thomas, 1735–Mar. 31, 1807.
Vol. 4, Pt. 2–275
Harlow, Jean, Mar. 3, 1911–June 7, 1937.
Supp. 2–285
Harlow, Ralph Volney, May 4, 1884–Oct. 3, 1956.
Supp. 6–278
Harmar, Josiah, Nov. 10, 1753–Aug. 20, 1813.
Vol. 4, Pt. 2–275
Harmon, Daniel Williams, Feb. 19, 1778–Mar. 26, 1845.
Vol. 4, Pt. 2–276
Harmon, Judson, Feb. 3, 1846–Feb. 22, 1927.
Vol. 4, Pt. 2–276
Harnden, William Frederick, Aug. 23, 1812–Jan. 14, 1845.
Vol. 4, Pt. 2–278
Harnett, Cornelius, Apr. 20, 1723?–Apr. 28, 1781.
Vol. 4, Pt. 2–279
Harney, Benjamin Robertson, Mar. 6, 1871–Mar. 1, 1938.
Supp. 2–286
Harney, William Selby, Aug. 22, 1800–May 9, 1889.
Vol. 4, Pt. 2–280
Harper, Fletcher, Jan. 31, 1806–May 29, 1877.
Vol. 4, Pt. 2–281
Harper, Ida Husted, Feb. 18, 1851–Mar. 14, 1931.
Vol. 4, Pt. 2–281
Harper, James, Apr. 13, 1795–Mar. 27, 1869.
Vol. 4, Pt. 2–282
Harper, John, 1797–1875. [*See* Harper, James, 1795–1869.]
Harper, John Lyell, Sept. 21, 1873–Nov. 28, 1924.
Vol. 4, Pt. 2–283
Harper, Joseph Wesley, 1801–1870. [*See* Harper, James, 1795–1869.]
Harper, Robert Francis, Oct. 18, 1864–Aug. 5, 1914.
Vol. 4, Pt. 2–284
Harper, Robert Goodloe, January 1765–Jan. 14, 1825.
Vol. 4, Pt. 2–285
Harper, William, Jan. 17, 1790–Oct. 10, 1847.
Vol. 4, Pt. 2–286
Harper, William Rainey, July 24, 1856–Jan. 10, 1906.
Vol. 4, Pt. 2–287
Harpster, John Henry, Apr. 27, 1844–Feb. 1, 1911.
Vol. 4, Pt. 2–292
Harpur, Robert, Jan. 25, 1731?–Apr. 15, 1825.
Vol. 4, Pt. 2–293
Harrah, Charles Jefferson, Jan. 1, 1817–Feb. 18, 1890.
Vol. 4, Pt. 2–294
Harrah, William Fisk ("Bill"), Sept. 2, 1911–June 30, 1978.
Supp. 10–308

Harrell, John, Oct. 21, 1806–Dec. 8, 1876.
Vol. 4, Pt. 2–294
Harridge, William ("Will"), Oct. 16, 1885–Apr. 9, 1971.
Supp. 9–365
Harrigan, Edward, Oct. 26, 1845–June 6, 1911.
Vol. 4, Pt. 2–295
Harriman, Edward Henry, Feb. 20, 1848–Sept. 9, 1909.
Vol. 4, Pt. 2–296
Harriman, Edward Roland Noel, Dec. 24, 1895–Feb. 16, 1978.
Supp. 10–309
Harriman, Florence Jaffray Hurst, July 21, 1870–Aug. 30, 1967.
Supp. 8–243
Harriman, Walter, Apr. 8, 1817–July 25, 1884.
Vol. 4, Pt. 2–300
Harrington, Charles, July 29, 1856–Sept. 11, 1908.
Vol. 4, Pt. 2–301
Harrington, John Lyle, Dec. 7, 1868–May 20, 1942.
Supp. 3–331
Harrington, Mark Walrod, Aug. 18, 1848–Oct. 9, 1926.
Vol. 4, Pt. 2–301
Harrington, Samuel Maxwell, Feb. 5, 1803–Nov. 28, 1865.
Vol. 4, Pt. 2–302
Harrington, Thomas Francis, June 10, 1866–Jan. 19, 1919.
Vol. 4, Pt. 2–303
Harris, Benjamin, fl. 1673–1716.
Vol. 4, Pt. 2–303
Harris, Caleb Fiske, Mar. 9, 1818–Oct. 2, 1881.
Vol. 4, Pt. 2–305
Harris, Chapin Aaron, May 6, 1806–Sept. 29, 1860.
Vol. 4, Pt. 2–305
Harris, Charles Kassell, May 1, 1865–Dec. 22, 1930.
Vol. 4, Pt. 2–306
Harris, Daniel Lester, Feb. 6, 1818–July 11, 1879.
Vol. 4, Pt. 2–307
Harris, Elisha, Mar. 5, 1824–Jan. 31, 1884.
Vol. 4, Pt. 2–307
Harris, George Washington, Mar. 20, 1814–Dec. 11, 1869.
Vol. 4, Pt. 2–309
Harris, George, Apr. 1, 1844–Mar. 1, 1922.
Vol. 4, Pt. 2–308
Harris, Ira, May 31, 1802–Dec. 2, 1875.
Vol. 4, Pt. 2–310
Harris, Isham Green, Feb. 10, 1818–July 8, 1897.
Vol. 4, Pt. 2–310
Harris, James Arthur, Sept. 29, 1880–Apr. 24, 1930.
Vol. 4, Pt. 2–311
Harris, Jed, Feb. 25, 1900–Nov. 15, 1979.
Supp. 10–311
Harris, Joel Chandler, Dec. 9, 1848–July 3, 1908.
Vol. 4, Pt. 2–312
Harris, John, 1726–July 29, 1791.
Vol. 4, Pt. 2–314
Harris, John Woods, 1810–Apr. 1, 1887.
Vol. 4, Pt. 2–314
Harris, Joseph, June 29, 1828–Nov. 18, 1892.
Vol. 4, Pt. 2–315
Harris, Julian La Rose, June 21, 1874–Feb. 9, 1963.
Supp. 7–323
Harris, Leroy Ellsworth ("Roy"), Feb. 12, 1898–Oct. 1, 1979.
Supp. 10–312
Harris, Maurice Henry, Nov. 9, 1859–June 23, 1930.
Vol. 4, Pt. 2–316
Harris, Merriman Colbert, July 9, 1846–May 8, 1921.
Vol. 4, Pt. 2–316
Harris, Miriam Coles, July 7, 1834–Jan. 23, 1925.
Vol. 4, Pt. 2–317
Harris, Nathaniel Harrison, Aug. 22, 1834–Aug. 23, 1900.
Vol. 4, Pt. 2–318
Harris, Paul Percy, Apr. 19, 1868–Jan. 27, 1947.
Supp. 4–361
Harris, Rollin Arthur, Apr. 18, 1863–Jan. 20, 1918.
Vol. 4, Pt. 2–318
Harris, Sam Henry, Feb. 3, 1872–July 3, 1941.
Supp. 3–332
Harris, Samuel, June 14, 1814–June 25, 1899.
Vol. 4, Pt. 2–319
Harris, Seymour Edwin, Sept. 8, 1897–Oct. 27, 1974.
Supp. 9–366
Harris, Stanley Raymond ("Bucky"), Nov. 8, 1896–Nov. 8, 1977.
Supp. 10–313
Harris, Thaddeus Mason, July 7, 1768–Apr. 3, 1842.
Vol. 4, Pt. 2–320
Harris, Thaddeus William, Nov. 12, 1795–Jan. 16, 1856.
Vol. 4, Pt. 2–321
Harris, Thomas Lake, May 15, 1823–Mar. 23, 1906.
Vol. 4, Pt. 2–322
Harris, Townsend, Oct. 3, 1804–Feb. 25, 1878.
Vol. 4, Pt. 2–324
Harris, Wiley Pope, Nov. 9, 1818–Dec. 3, 1891.
Vol. 4, Pt. 2–325
Harris, William, Apr. 29, 1765–Oct. 18, 1829.
Vol. 4, Pt. 2–325
Harris, William Alexander, Oct. 29, 1841–Dec. 20, 1909.
Vol. 4, Pt. 2–326
Harris, William Littleton, July 6, 1807–Nov. 26, 1868.
Vol. 4, Pt. 2–327
Harris, William Logan, Nov. 14, 1817–Sept. 2, 1887.
Vol. 4, Pt. 2–327
Harris, William Torrey, Sept. 10, 1835–Nov. 5, 1909.
Vol. 4, Pt. 2–328
Harrison, Alexander. [*See* Harrison, Thomas Alexander, 1853–1930.]
Harrison, Benjamin, 1726?–Apr. 24, 1791.
Vol. 4, Pt. 2–330
Harrison, Benjamin, Aug. 20, 1833–Mar. 13, 1901.
Vol. 4, Pt. 2–331
Harrison, Birge. [*See* Harrison, Lovell Birge, 1854–1929.]
Harrison, Byron Patton, Aug. 29, 1881–June 22, 1941.
Supp. 3–334
Harrison, Carter Henry, Feb. 15, 1825–Oct 28, 1893.
Vol. 4, Pt. 2–335
Harrison, Carter Henry, Jr., Apr. 23, 1860–Dec. 25, 1953.
Supp. 5–274
Harrison, Charles Custis, May 3, 1844–Feb. 12, 1929.
Vol. 4, Pt. 2–336
Harrison, Constance Cary, Apr. 25, 1843–Nov. 21, 1920.
Vol. 4, Pt. 2–337
Harrison, Elizabeth, Sept. 1, 1849–Oct. 31, 1927.
Vol. 4, Pt. 2–338
Harrison, Fairfax, Mar. 13, 1869–Feb. 2, 1938.
Supp. 2–286
Harrison, Francis Burton, Dec. 18, 1873–Nov. 21, 1957.
Supp. 6–279
Harrison, Gabriel, Mar. 25, 1818–Dec. 15, 1902.
Vol. 4, Pt. 2–339
Harrison, George Paul, Mar. 19, 1841–July 17, 1922.
Vol. 4, Pt. 2–340
Harrison, Gessner, June 26, 1807–Apr. 7, 1862.
Vol. 4, Pt. 2–340
Harrison, Henry Baldwin, Sept. 11, 1821–Oct. 29, 1901.
Vol. 4, Pt. 2–341
Harrison, Henry Sydnor, Feb. 12, 1880–July 14, 1930.
Vol. 4, Pt. 2–342
Harrison, James, Oct. 10, 1803–Aug. 3, 1870.
Vol. 4, Pt. 2–343
Harrison, James Albert, Aug. 21, 1848–Jan. 31, 1911.
Vol. 4, Pt. 2–343
Harrison, John, Dec. 17, 1773–July 19, 1833.
Vol. 4, Pt. 2–344
Harrison, Joseph, Sept. 20, 1810–Mar. 27, 1874.
Vol. 4, Pt. 2–345
Harrison, Lovell Birge, Oct. 28, 1854–May 11, 1929.
Vol. 4, Pt. 2–346
Harrison, Pat. [*See* Harrison, Byron Patton, 1881–1941.]
Harrison, Peter, June 14, 1716–Apr. 30, 1775.
Vol. 4, Pt. 2–347
Harrison, Richard Berry, Sept. 28, 1864–Mar. 14, 1935.
Supp. 1–374
Harrison, Ross Granville, Jan. 13, 1870–Sept. 30, 1959.
Supp. 6–281
Harrison, Thomas Alexander, Jan. 17, 1853–Oct. 13, 1930.
Vol. 4, Pt. 2–347
Harrison, William Henry, Feb. 9, 1773–Apr. 4, 1841.
Vol. 4, Pt. 2–348
Harrison, William Pope, Sept. 3, 1830–Feb. 7, 1895.
Vol. 4, Pt. 2–352
Harrisse, Henry, Mar. 24, 1829–May 13, 1910.
Supp. 1–374

Harrod, Benjamin Morgan, Feb. 19, 1837–Sept. 7, 1912.
Vol. 4, Pt. 2–353
Harrod, James, 1742–July 1793.
Vol. 4, Pt. 2–353
Harshberger, John William, Jan. 1, 1869–Apr. 27, 1929.
Vol. 4, Pt. 2–354
Harshe, Robert Bartholow, May 26, 1879–Jan. 11, 1938.
Supp. 2–287
Hart, Abraham, Dec. 15, 1810–July 23, 1885.
Vol. 4, Pt. 2–355
Hart, Albert Bushnell, July 1, 1854–June 16, 1943.
Supp. 3–335
Hart, Charles Henry, Feb. 4, 1847–July 29, 1918.
Vol. 4, Pt. 2–355
Hart, Edmund Hall, Dec. 26, 1839–Apr. 22, 1898.
Vol. 4, Pt. 2–356
Hart, Edward, Nov. 18, 1854–June 6, 1931.
Supp. 1–376
Hart, Edwin Bret, Dec. 25, 1874–Mar. 12, 1953.
Supp. 5–275
Hart, George Overbury, May 10, 1868–Sept. 9, 1933.
Supp. 1–376
Hart, Hastings Hornell, Dec. 14, 1851–May 9, 1932.
Supp. 1–377
Hart, James MacDougal, May 10, 1828–Oct. 24, 1901.
Vol. 4, Pt. 2–356
Hart, James Morgan, Nov. 2, 1839–Apr. 18, 1916.
Vol. 4, Pt. 2–357
Hart, Joel Tanner, Feb. 10, 1810–Mar. 2, 1877.
Vol. 4, Pt. 2–358
Hart, John, 1711?–May 11, 1779.
Vol. 4, Pt. 2–359
Hart, John Seely, Jan. 28, 1810–Mar. 26, 1877.
Vol. 4, Pt. 2–359
Hart, Lorenz Milton, May 2, 1895–Nov. 22, 1943.
Supp. 3–338
Hart, Moss, Oct. 24, 1904–Dec. 20, 1961.
Supp. 7–324
Hart, Philip Aloysius, Dec. 10, 1912–Dec. 26, 1976.
Supp. 10–315
Hart, Samuel, June 4, 1845–Feb. 25, 1917.
Vol. 4, Pt. 2–360
Hart, Virgil Chittenden, Jan. 2, 1840–Feb. 24, 1904.
Vol. 4, Pt. 2–361
Hart, William, Mar. 31, 1823–June 17, 1894.
Vol. 4, Pt. 2–361
Hart, William Surrey, Dec. 6, 1862?–June 23, 1946.
Supp. 4–362
Harte, Francis Brett, Aug. 25, 1836–May 5, 1902.
Vol. 4, Pt. 2–362
Hartford, George Huntington, Sept. 5, 1833–Aug. 29, 1917.
Supp. 5–276
Hartford, George Ludlum, Nov. 7, 1864–Sept. 23, 1957.
Supp. 5–276
Hartford, John Augustine, Feb. 10, 1872–Sept. 20, 1951.
Supp. 5–276
Hartley, Frank, June 10, 1856–June 19, 1913.
Vol. 4, Pt. 2–365
Hartley, Fred Allen, Jr., Feb. 22, 1903–May 11, 1969.
Supp. 8–245
Hartley, Jonathan Scott, Sept. 23, 1845–Dec. 6, 1912.
Vol. 4, Pt. 2–365
Hartley, Marsden, Jan. 4, 1877–Sept. 2, 1943.
Supp. 3–339
Hartley, Thomas, Sept. 7, 1748–Dec. 21, 1800.
Vol. 4, Pt. 2–366
Hartmann, Carl Sadakichi, Nov. 8, 1867?–Nov. 21, 1944.
Supp. 3–341
Hartness, James, Sept. 3, 1861–Feb. 2, 1934.
Supp. 1–378
Hartnett, Charles Leo ("Gabby"), Dec. 20, 1900–Dec. 20, 1972.
Supp. 9–368
Hartranft, Chester David, Oct. 15, 1839–Dec. 30, 1914.
Vol. 4, Pt. 2–367
Hartranft, John Frederick, Dec. 16, 1830–Oct. 17, 1889.
Vol. 4, Pt. 2–368
Hartsfield, William Berry, Mar. 1, 1890–Feb. 22, 1971.
Supp. 9–369
Hartshorne, Henry, Mar. 16, 1823–Feb. 10, 1897.
Vol. 4, Pt. 2–368
Hartsuff, George Lucas, May 28, 1830–May 16, 1874.
Vol. 4, Pt. 2–369
Hartwig, Johann Christoph, Jan. 6, 1714–July 17, 1796.
Vol. 4, Pt. 2–370
Hartzell, Joseph Crane, June 1, 1842–Sept. 6, 1928.
Vol. 4, Pt. 2–370
Harvard, John, November 1607–Sept. 14, 1638.
Vol. 4, Pt. 2–371
Harvey, "Coin." [*See* Harvey, William Hope, 1851–1936.]
Harvey, George Brinton McClellan, Feb. 16, 1864–Aug. 20, 1928.
Vol. 4, Pt. 2–372
Harvey, Hayward Augustus, Jan. 17, 1824–Aug. 28, 1893.
Vol. 4, Pt. 2–373
Harvey, Louis Powelt, July 22, 1820–Apr. 19, 1862.
Vol. 4, Pt. 2–374
Harvey, Sir John, d. 1646.
Supp. 1–379
Harvey, William Hope, Aug. 16, 1851–Feb. 11, 1936.
Supp. 2–288
Harvie, John, 1742–Feb. 6, 1807.
Vol. 4, Pt. 2–375
Hasbrouck, Abraham Bruyn, Nov. 29, 1791–Feb. 23, 1879.
Vol. 4, Pt. 2–375
Hasbrouck, Lydia Sayer, Dec. 20, 1827–Aug. 24, 1910.
Vol. 4, Pt. 2–376
Hascall, Miio Smith, Aug. 5, 1829–Aug. 30, 1904.
Vol. 4, Pt. 2–377
Haseltine, James Henry, Nov. 2, 1833–Nov. 9, 1907.
Vol. 4, Pt. 2–377
Haselton, Seneca, Feb. 26, 1848–July 21, 1921.
Vol. 4, Pt. 2–378
Hasenclever, Peter, Nov. 24, 1716–June 13, 1793.
Vol. 4, Pt. 2–379
Haskell, Charles Nathaniel, Mar. 13, 1860–July 5, 1933.
Supp. 1–380
Haskell, Dudley Chase, Mar. 23, 1842–Dec. 16, 1883.
Vol. 4, Pt. 2–380
Haskell, Ella Louise Knowles, July 31, 1860–Jan. 27, 1911.
Vol. 4, Pt. 2–380
Haskell, Ernest, July 30, 1876–Nov. 2, 1925.
Vol. 4, Pt. 2–381
Haskell, Henry Joseph, Mar. 8, 1874–Aug. 20, 1952.
Supp. 5–278
Hasket, Elias, Apr. 25, 1670–Mar. 9, 1739?.
Vol. 4, Pt. 2–382
Haskins, Charles Homer, Dec. 21, 1870–May 14, 1937.
Supp. 2–289
Hassam, Frederick Childe, Oct. 17, 1859–Aug. 27, 1935.
Supp. 1–381
Hassard, John Rose Greene, Sept. 4, 1836–Apr. 18, 1888.
Vol. 4, Pt. 2–382
Hassaurek, Friedrich, Oct. 8, 1831–Oct. 3, 1885.
Vol. 4, Pt. 2–383
Hasselquist, Tuve Nilsson, Mar. 2, 1816–Feb. 4, 1891.
Vol. 4, Pt. 2–384
Hassler, Ferdinand Rudolph, Oct. 7, 1770–Nov. 20, 1843.
Vol. 4, Pt. 2–385
Hastings, Charles Sheldon, Nov. 27, 1848–Jan. 31, 1932.
Supp. 1–383
Hastings, Danier Oren, Mar. 5, 1874–May 9, 1966.
Supp. 8–246
Hastings, Samuel Dexter, July 24, 1816–Mar. 26, 1903.
Vol. 4, Pt. 2–386
Hastings, Serranus Clinton, Nov. 22, 1814–Feb. 18, 1893.
Vol. 4, Pt. 2–387
Hastings, Thomas, Oct. 15, 1784–May 15, 1872.
Vol. 4, Pt. 2–387
Hastings, Thomas, Mar. 11, 1860–Oct. 22, 1929.
Vol. 4, Pt. 2–388
Hastings, William Wirt, Dec. 31, 1866–Apr. 8, 1938.
Supp. 2–291
Haswell, Anthony, Apr. 6, 1756–May 22, 1816.
Vol. 4, Pt. 2–390
Haswell, Charles Haynes, May 22, 1809–May 12, 1907.
Vol. 4, Pt. 2–391
Hatch, Carl A., Nov. 27, 1889–Sept. 15, 1963.
Supp. 7–326
Hatch, Edward, Dec. 23, 1832–Apr. 11, 1889.
Vol. 4, Pt. 2–392

Hatch, John Porter, Jan. 9, 1822–Apr. 12, 1901.
Vol. 4, Pt. 2–392
Hatch, Rufus, Jun. 24, 1832–Feb. 23, 1893.
Vol. 4, Pt. 2–393
Hatch, William Henry, Sept. 11, 1833–Dec. 23, 1896.
Vol. 4, Pt. 2–394
Hatcher, Orie Latham, Dec. 10, 1868–Apr. 1, 1946.
Supp. 4–364
Hatcher, Robert Anthony, Feb. 6, 1868–Apr. 1, 1944.
Supp. 3–342
Hatcher, William Eldridge, July 25, 1834–Aug. 24, 1912.
Vol. 4, Pt. 2–395
Hatfield, Edwin Francis, Jan. 9, 1807–Sept. 22, 1883.
Vol. 4, Pt. 2–395
Hathaway, Donny, Oct. 1, 1945–Jan. 13, 1979.
Supp. 10–316
Hathorne, William, *c.* 1607–1681.
Vol. 4, Pt. 2–396
Hatlo, Jimmy, Sept. 1, 1898–Dec. 1, 1963.
Supp. 7–327
Hatton, Frank, Apr. 28, 1846–Apr. 30, 1894.
Vol. 4, Pt. 2–397
Haugen, Gilbert Nelson, Apr. 21, 1859–July 18, 1933.
Supp. 1–384
Haugen, Nils Pederson, Mar. 9, 1849–Apr. 23, 1931.
Supp. 1–385
Haughery, Margaret Gaffney, *c.* 1814–Feb. 9, 1882.
Vol. 4, Pt. 2–398
Haughton, Percy Duncan, July 11, 1876–Oct. 27, 1924.
Vol. 4, Pt. 2–398
Hauk, Minnie, Nov. 16, 1852?–Feb. 6, 1929.
Vol. 4, Pt. 2–399
Haupt, Alma Cecelia, Mar. 19, 1893–Mar. 15, 1956.
Supp. 6–283
Haupt, Herman, Mar. 26, 1817–Dec. 14, 1905.
Vol. 4, Pt. 2–400
Haupt, Paul, Nov. 25, 1858–Dec. 15, 1926.
Vol. 4, Pt. 2–401
Hauser, Samuel Thomas, Jan. 10, 1833–Nov. 10, 1914.
Vol. 4, Pt. 2–402
Havell, Robert, Nov. 25, 1793–Nov. 11, 1878.
Vol. 4, Pt. 2–403
Havemeyer, Henry Osborne, Oct. 18, 1847–Dec. 4, 1907.
Vol. 4, Pt. 2–404
Havemeyer, William Frederick, Feb. 12, 1804–Nov. 30, 1874.
Vol. 4, Pt. 2–405
Haven, Alice B. [*See* Haven, Emily Bradley Neal, 1827–1863.]
Haven, Emily Bradley Neal, Sept. 13, 1827–Aug. 23, 1863.
Vol. 4, Pt. 2–406
Haven, Erastus Otis, Nov. 1, 1820–Aug. 2, 1881.
Vol. 4, Pt. 2–406
Haven, Gilbert, Sept. 19, 1821–Jan. 3, 1880.
Vol. 4, Pt. 2–407
Haven, Henry Philemon, Feb. 11, 1815–Apr. 30, 1876.
Vol. 4, Pt. 2–408
Haven, Joseph, Jan. 4, 1816–May 23, 1874.
Vol. 4, Pt. 2–409
Havens, James Smith, May 28, 1859–Feb. 27, 1927.
Vol. 4, Pt. 2–410
Haverly, Christopher, June 30, 1837–Sept. 28, 1901.
Vol. 4, Pt. 2–410
Haverly, Jack H. [*See* Haverly, Christopher, 1837–1901.]
Haviland, Clarence Floyd, Aug. 15, 1875–Jan. 1, 1930.
Vol. 4, Pt. 2–411
Haviland, John, Dec. 15, 1792–Mar. 28, 1852.
Vol. 4, Pt. 2–412
Hawes, Charles Boardman, Jan. 24, 1889–July 15, 1923.
Vol. 4, Pt. 2–413
Hawes, Harriet Ann Boyd, Oct. 11, 1871–Mar. 31, 1945.
Supp. 3–343
Hawkins, Benjamin, Aug. 15, 1754–June 6, 1818.
Vol. 4, Pt. 2–413
Hawkins, Dexter Arnold, June 24, 1825–July 24, 1886.
Vol. 4, Pt. 2–414
Hawkins, Rush Christopher, Sept. 14, 1831–Oct. 25, 1920.
Vol. 4, Pt. 2–415
Hawks, Francis Lister, June 10, 1798–Sept. 27, 1866.
Vol. 4, Pt. 2–416
Hawks, Howard Winchester, May 30, 1896–Dec. 26, 1977.
Supp. 10–318
Hawks, John, 1731–Feb. 16, 1790.
Vol. 4, Pt. 2–417
Hawley, Gideon, Nov. 5, 1727–Oct. 3, 1807.
Vol. 4, Pt. 2–418
Hawley, Gideon, Sept. 26, 1785–July 17, 1870.
Vol. 4, Pt. 2–418
Hawley, James Henry, Jan. 17, 1847–Aug. 3, 1929.
Vol. 4, Pt. 2–419
Hawley, Joseph, Oct. 8, 1723–Mar. 10, 1788.
Vol. 4, Pt. 2–420
Hawley, Joseph Roswell, Oct. 31, 1826–Mar. 18, 1905.
Vol. 4, Pt. 2–421
Hawley, Paul Ramsey, Jan. 31, 1891–Nov. 24, 1965.
Supp. 7–328
Hawley, Willis Chatman, May 5, 1864–July 24, 1941.
Supp. 3–345
Haworth, Joseph, Apr. 7, 1855?–Aug. 28, 1903.
Vol. 4, Pt. 2–422
Haworth, Leland John, July 11, 1904–Mar. 5, 1979.
Supp. 10–319
Hawthorne, Charles Webster, Jan. 8, 1872–Nov. 29, 1930.
Vol. 4, Pt. 2–423
Hawthorne, Julian, June 22, 1846–July 14, 1934.
Supp. 1–386
Hawthorne, Nathaniel, July 4, 1804–May 18 or 19, 1864.
Vol. 4, Pt. 2–424
Hawthorne, Rose. [*See* Alphonsa, Mother, 1851–1926.]
Hay, Charles Augustus, Feb. 11, 1821–June 26, 1893.
Vol. 4, Pt. 2–429
Hay, George, Dec. 15, 1765–Sept. 21, 1830.
Vol. 4, Pt. 2–429
Hay, John Milton, Oct. 8, 1838–July 1, 1905.
Vol. 4, Pt. 2–430
Hay, Mary Garrett, Aug. 29, 1857–Aug. 29, 1928.
Vol. 4, Pt. 2–436
Hay, Oliver Perry, May 22, 1846–Nov. 2, 1930.
Vol. 4, Pt. 2–436
Hayakawa, Sessue, June 10, 1890–Nov. 23, 1973.
Supp. 9–371
Hayden, Amos Sutton, Sept. 17, 1813–Sept. 10, 1880.
Vol. 4, Pt. 2–437
Hayden, Carl Trumbull, Oct. 2, 1877–Jan. 25, 1972.
Supp. 9–372.
Hayden, Charles, July 9, 1870–Jan. 8, 1937.
Supp. 2–292
Hayden, Charles Henry, Aug. 4, 1856–Aug. 4, 1901.
Vol. 4, Pt. 2–438
Hayden, Edward Everett, Apr. 14, 1858–Nov. 17, 1932.
Supp. 1–387
Hayden, Ferdinand Vandiveer, Sept. 7, 1829–Dec. 22, 1887.
Vol. 4, Pt. 2–438
Hayden, Hiram Washington, Feb. 10, 1820–July 18, 1904.
Vol. 4, Pt. 2–440
Hayden, Horace H., Oct. 13, 1769–Jan. 26, 1844.
Vol. 4, Pt. 2–440
Hayden, Joseph Shepard, July 31, 1802–Feb. 17, 1877.
Vol. 4, Pt. 2–442
Hayden, Robert Earl, Aug. 4, 1913–Feb. 25, 1980.
Supp. 10–321
Hayden, William, June 30, 1799–Apr. 7, 1863.
Vol. 4, Pt. 2–442
Hayes, Augustus Allen, Feb. 28, 1806–June 21, 1882.
Vol. 4, Pt. 2–443
Hayes, Carlton Joseph Huntley, May 16, 1882–Sept. 3, 1964.
Supp. 7–329
Hayes, Charles Willard, Oct. 8, 1858–Feb. 8, 1916.
Vol. 4, Pt. 2–444
Hayes, Edward Carey, Feb. 10, 1868–Aug. 7, 1928.
Supp. 1–388
Hayes, Gabby, May 7, 1885–Feb. 9, 1969.
Supp. 8–248
Hayes, Isaac Israel, Mar. 5, 1832–Dec. 17, 1881.
Vol. 4, Pt. 2–445
Hayes, John Lord, Apr. 13, 1812–Apr. 18, 1887.
Vol. 4, Pt. 2–446
Hayes, John William, Dec. 26, 1854–Nov. 25, 1942.
Supp. 3–345
Hayes, Max Sebastian, May 25, 1866–Oct. 11, 1945.
Supp. 3–346
Hayes, Patrick Joseph, Nov. 20, 1867–Sept. 4, 1938.
Supp. 2–293

Hayes, Rutherford Birchard, Oct. 4, 1822–Jan. 17, 1893.
Vol. 4, Pt. 2–446
Hayes, William Henry, 1829–March 1877.
Vol. 4, Pt. 2–451
Hayford, John Fillmore, May 19, 1868–Mar. 10, 1925.
Vol. 4, Pt. 2–452
Haygood, Atticus Green, Nov. 19, 1839–Jan. 19, 1896.
Vol. 4, Pt. 2–452
Haygood, Laura Askew, Oct. 14, 1845–Apr. 29, 1900.
Vol. 4, Pt. 2–453
Haymes, Richard Benjamin ("Dick"), Sept. 13, 1918–Mar. 28, 1980.
Supp. 10–322
Hayne, Isaac, Sept. 23, 1745–Aug. 4, 1781.
Vol. 4, Pt. 2–454
Hayne, Paul Hamilton, Jan. 1, 1830–July 6, 1886.
Vol. 4, Pt. 2–455
Hayne, Robert Young, Nov. 10, 1791–Sept. 24, 1839.
Vol. 4, Pt. 2–456
Haynes, George Edmund, May 11, 1880–Jan. 8, 1960.
Supp. 6–284
Haynes, Henry Doyle ("Homer"), July 29, 1920–Aug. 7, 1971.
Supp. 9–373
Haynes, John, 1594?–Jan. 1653/54.
Vol. 4, Pt. 2–459
Haynes, John Henry, June 27, 1849–June 29, 1910.
Vol. 4, Pt. 2–460
Haynes, Williams, July 29, 1886–Nov. 16, 1970.
Supp. 8–249
Hays, Alexander, July 8, 1819–May 5, 1864.
Vol. 4, Pt. 2–460
Hays, Arthur Garfield, Dec. 12, 1881–Dec. 14, 1954.
Supp. 5–279
Hays, Harry Thompson, Apr. 14, 1820–Aug. 21, 1876.
Vol. 4, Pt. 2–461
Hays, Isaac, July 5, 1796–Apr. 13, 1879.
Vol. 4, Pt. 2–462
Hays, John Coffee, Jan. 28, 1817–Apr. 28, 1883.
Vol. 4, Pt. 2–463
Hays, Paul R., Apr. 2, 1903–Feb. 13, 1980.
Supp. 10–323
Hays, Will H., Nov. 5, 1879–Mar. 7, 1954.
Supp. 5–280
Hays, William Jacob, Aug. 8, 1830–Mar. 13, 1875.
Vol. 4, Pt. 2–463
Hays, William Shakespeare, July 19, 1837–July 23, 1907.
Vol. 4, Pt. 2–464
Hayward, George, Mar. 9, 1791–Oct. 7, 1863.
Vol. 4, Pt. 2–464
Hayward, Leland, Sept. 13, 1902–Mar. 18, 1971.
Supp. 9–375
Hayward, Nathaniel Manley, Jan. 19, 1808–July 18, 1865.
Vol. 4, Pt. 2–465
Hayward, Susan, June 30, 1919–Mar. 14, 1975.
Supp. 9–376
Haywood, Allan Shaw, Oct. 9, 1888–Feb. 21, 1953.
Supp. 5–282
Haywood, John, Mar. 16, 1762–Dec. 22, 1826.
Vol. 4, Pt. 2–466
Haywood, William Dudley, Feb. 4, 1869–May 18, 1928.
Vol. 4, Pt. 2–467
Hazard, Augustus George, Apr. 28, 1802–May 7, 1868.
Vol. 4, Pt. 2–469
Hazard, Jonathan J., 1744?–after 1824.
Vol. 4, Pt. 2–470
Hazard, Rowland Gibson, Oct. 9, 1801–June 24, 1888.
Vol. 4, Pt. 2–471
Hazard, Samuel, May 26, 1784–May 22, 1870.
Vol. 4, Pt. 2–472
Hazard, Thomas, Sept. 15, 1720–Aug. 26, 1798.
Vol. 4, Pt. 2–472
Hazard, Thomas Robinson, Jan. 3, 1797–Mar. 26, 1886.
Vol. 4, Pt. 2–473
Hazard Ebenezer, Jan. 15, 1744–June 13, 1817.
Vol. 4, Pt. 2–469
Hazelius, Ernest Lewis, Sept. 6, 1777–Feb. 20, 1853.
Vol. 4, Pt. 2–474
Hazeltine, Mayo Williamson, Apr. 24, 1841–Sept. 14, 1909.
Vol. 4, Pt. 2–475
Hazelton, George Cochrane, Jan. 20, 1868–June 24, 1921.
Vol. 4, Pt. 2–475
Hazelwood, John, *c.* 1726–Mar. 1, 1800.
Vol. 4, Pt. 2–476
Hazen, Allen, Aug. 28, 1869–July 26, 1930.
Supp. 1–389
Hazen, Henry Allen, Jan. 12, 1849–Jan. 23, 1900.
Vol. 4, Pt. 2–477
Hazen, Moses, June 1, 1733–Feb. 3, 1803.
Vol. 4, Pt. 2–477
Hazen, William Babcock, Sept. 27, 1830–Jan. 16, 1887.
Vol. 4, Pt. 2–478
Headley, Joel Tyler, Dec. 30, 1813–Jan. 16, 1897.
Vol. 4, Pt. 2–479
Headley, Phineas Camp, June 24, 1819–Jan. 5, 1903.
Vol. 4, Pt. 2–480
Heald, Henry Townley, Nov. 8, 1904–Nov. 23, 1975.
Supp. 9–377
Healy, George Peter Alexander, July 15, 1813–June 24, 1894.
Vol. 4, Pt. 2–480
Heap, Samuel Davies, Oct. 8, 1781–Oct. 2, 1853.
Vol. 4, Pt. 2–481
Heard, Augustine, Mar. 30, 1785–Sept. 14, 1868.
Vol. 4, Pt. 2–482
Heard, Dwight Bancroft, May 1, 1869–Mar. 14, 1929.
Vol. 4, Pt. 2–483
Heard, Franklin Fiske, Jan. 17, 1825–Sept. 29, 1889.
Vol. 4, Pt. 2–483
Hearn, Lafcadio, June 27, 1850–Sept. 26, 1904.
Vol. 4, Pt. 2–484
Hearst, George, Sept. 3, 1820–Feb. 28, 1891.
Vol. 4, Pt. 2–487
Hearst, Phoebe Apperson, Dec. 3, 1842–Apr. 13, 1919.
Vol. 4, Pt. 2–488
Hearst, William Randolph, Apr. 20, 1863–Aug. 14, 1951.
Supp. 5–283
Heath, James Ewell, July 8, 1792–June 28, 1862.
Vol. 4, Pt. 2–489
Heath, Perry Sanford, Aug. 31, 1857–Mar. 30, 1927.
Vol. 4, Pt. 2–489
Heath, Thomas Kurton. [*See* McIntyre, James, 1857–1937.]
Heath, Thomas Kurton, Aug. 11, 1853–Aug. 18, 1938.
Supp. 2–412
Heath, William, Mar. 2, 1737–Jan. 24, 1814.
Vol. 4, Pt. 2–490
Heathcote, Caleb, Mar. 6, 1665/66–Mar. 1, 1720/21.
Vol. 4, Pt. 2–491
Heaton, John Langdon, Jan. 29, 1860–Feb. 21, 1935.
Supp. 1–390
Heatter, Gabriel, Sept. 17, 1890–Mar. 30, 1972.
Supp. 9–379
Hébert, Felix Edward ("Eddie"), Oct. 12, 1901–Dec. 29, 1979.
Supp. 10–325
Hébert, Louis, Mar. 13, 1820–Jan. 7, 1901.
Vol. 4, Pt. 2–492
Hébert, Paul Octave, Dec. 12, 1818–Aug. 29, 1880.
Vol. 4, Pt. 2–492
Hecht, Ben, Feb. 28, 1894–Apr. 18, 1964.
Supp. 7–331
Hecht, Selig, Feb. 8, 1892–Sept. 18, 1947.
Supp. 4–366
Heck, Barbara, 1734–Aug. 17, 1804.
Vol. 4, Pt. 2–493
Hecker, Friedrich Karl Franz, Sept. 28, 1811–Mar. 24, 1881.
Vol. 4, Pt. 2–493
Hecker, Isaac Thomas, Dec. 18, 1819–Dec. 22, 1888.
Vol. 4, Pt. 2–495
Heckewelder, John Gottlieb Ernestus, Mar. 12, 1743–Jan. 31, 1823.
Vol. 4, Pt. 2–495
Heckscher, August, Aug. 26, 1848–Apr. 26, 1941.
Supp. 3–348
Hector, Francisco Luis. [*See* Carondelet, Hector, Baron de, *c.* 1748–1807.]
Hedding, Elijah, June 7, 1780–Apr. 9, 1852.
Vol. 4, Pt. 2–497
Hedge, Frederic Henry, Dec. 12, 1805–Aug. 21, 1890.
Vol. 4, Pt. 2–498
Hedge, Levi, Apr. 19, 1766–Jan. 3, 1844.
Vol. 4, Pt. 2–499
Heenan John Carmel, May 2, 1835,–Oct. 25, 1873.
Vol. 4, Pt. 2–499

Heezen, Bruce Charles, Apr. 11, 1924–June 21, 1977.
Supp. 10–326.
Heffelfinger, William Walter "Pudge," Dec. 20, 1867–Apr. 2, 1954.
Supp. 5–288
Heflin, James Thomas, Apr. 9, 1869–Apr. 22, 1951.
Supp. 5–290
Heflin, Van, Dec. 13, 1910–July 23, 1971.
Supp. 9–380
Hegeman, John Rogers, Apr. 18, 1844–Apr. 6, 1919.
Vol. 4, Pt. 2–500
Heilmann, Harry, Aug. 3, 1894–July 9, 1951.
Supp. 5–291
Heilprin, Angelo, Mar. 31, 1853–July 17, 1907.
Vol. 4, Pt. 2–501
Heilprin, Michael, 1823–May 10, 1888.
Vol. 4, Pt. 2–502
Heineman, Daniel Webster ("Dannie"), Nov. 23, 1872–Jan. 31, 1962.
Supp. 7–332
Heinemann, Ernst, Feb. 19, 1848–May 11, 1912.
Vol. 4, Pt. 2–503
Heinrich, Antony Philip, Mar. 11, 1781–May 3, 1861.
Vol. 4, Pt. 2–504
Heinrich, Max, June 14, 1853–Aug. 9, 1916.
Vol. 4, Pt. 2–505
Heintzelman, Samuel Peter, Sept. 30, 1805–May 1, 1880.
Vol. 4, Pt. 2–505
Heintzelman, Stuart, Nov. 19, 1876–July 6, 1935.
Supp. 1–391
Heinz, Henry John, Oct. 11, 1844–May 14, 1919.
Vol. 4, Pt. 2–506
Heinze, Frederick Augustus, Dec. 5, 1869–Nov. 4, 1914.
Vol. 4, Pt. 2–507
Heinzen, Karl Peter, Feb. 22, 1809–Nov. 12, 1880.
Vol. 4, Pt. 2–508
Heiss, Michael, Apr. 12, 1818–Mar. 26, 1890.
Vol. 4, Pt. 2–509
Helbron, Peter, 1739–Apr. 24, 1816.
Vol. 4, Pt. 2–510
Helburn, Milton, Apr. 17, 1902–Apr. 22, 1977.
Supp. 10–328
Helburn, Theresa, Jan. 12, 1887–Aug. 18, 1959.
Supp. 6–285
Held, John, Jr., Jan. 10, 1889–Mar. 2, 1958.
Supp. 6–287
Helffenstein, John Albert Conrad, Feb. 16, 1748–May 17, 1790.
Vol. 4, Pt. 2–511
Heller, Maximilian, Jan. 31, 1860–Mar. 30, 1929.
Vol. 4, Pt. 2–511
Heller, Robert. [*See* Palmer, William Henry, 1828–1878.]
Helm, Charles John, June 21, 1817–February 1868.
Vol. 4, Pt. 2–512
Helm, John Larue, July 4, 1802–Sept. 8, 1867.
Vol. 4, Pt. 2–513
Helmer, Bessie Bradwell, Oct. 20, 1858–Jan. 10, 1927.
Vol. 4, Pt. 2–514
Helmpraecht, Joseph, Jan. 14, 1820–Dec. 15, 1884.
Vol. 4, Pt. 2–515
Helmuth, Justus Henry Christian, May 16, 1745–Feb. 5, 1825.
Vol. 4, Pt. 2–515
Helmuth, William Tod, Oct. 30, 1833–May 15, 1902.
Vol. 4, Pt. 2–516
Helper, Hinton Rowan, Dec. 27, 1829–Mar. 8, 1909.
Vol. 4, Pt. 2–517
Helpern, Milton, Apr. 17, 1902–Apr. 22, 1977.
Supp. 10–328
Hemenway, Mary Porter Tileston, Dec. 20, 1820–Mar. 6, 1894.
Vol. 4, Pt. 2–518
Hemingway, Ernest Miller, July 21, 1899–July 2, 1961.
Supp. 7–333
Hemmeter, John Conrad, Apr. 26, 1863–Feb. 25, 1931.
Vol. 4, Pt. 2–519
Hempel, Charles Julius, Sept. 5, 1811–Sept. 24, 1879.
Vol. 4, Pt. 2–520
Hemphill, John, Dec. 18, 1803–Jan. 4, 1862.
Vol. 4, Pt. 2–520
Hemphill, Joseph, Jan. 7, 1770–May 29, 1842.
Vol. 4, Pt. 2–521
Hempl, George, June 6, 1859–Aug. 14, 1921.
Vol. 4, Pt. 2–521
Hench, Philip Showalter, Feb. 28, 1896–Mar. 30, 1965.
Supp. 7–340
Henchman, Daniel, Jan. 21, 1689–Feb. 25, 1761.
Supp. 1–392
Henck, John Benjamin, Oct. 20, 1815–Jan. 3, 1903.
Vol. 4, Pt. 2–522
Hendel, John William, Nov. 20, 1740–Sept. 29, 1798.
Vol. 4, Pt. 2–523
Henderson, Archibald, Aug. 7, 1768–Oct. 21, 1822.
Vol. 4, Pt. 2–523
Henderson, Charles Richmond, Dec. 17, 1848–Mar. 29, 1915.
Vol. 4, Pt. 2–524
Henderson, Daniel McIntyre, July 10, 1851–Sept. 8, 1906.
Vol. 4, Pt. 2–525
Henderson, David Bremner, Mar. 14, 1840–Feb. 25, 1906.
Vol. 4, Pt. 2–525
Henderson, Fletcher Hamilton, Dec. 18, 1897–Dec. 29, 1952.
Supp. 5–292
Henderson, James Pinckney, Mar. 31, 1808–June 4, 1858.
Vol. 4, Pt. 2–526
Henderson, John, Feb. 28, 1795–Sept. 16, 1857.
Vol. 4, Pt. 2–527
Henderson, John Brooks, Nov. 16, 1826–Apr. 12, 1913.
Vol. 4, Pt. 2–527
Henderson, Lawrence Joseph, June 3, 1878–Feb. 10, 1942.
Supp. 3–349
Henderson, Leonard, Oct. 6, 1772–Aug. 13, 1833.
Vol. 4, Pt. 2–529
Henderson, Paul, Mar. 13, 1884–Dec. 19, 1951.
Supp. 5–294
Henderson, Peter, June 9, 1822–Jan. 17, 1890.
Vol. 4, Pt. 2–530
Henderson, Ray, Dec. 1, 1896–Dec. 31, 1970.
Supp. 8–250
Henderson, Richard, Apr. 20, 1735–Jan. 30, 1785.
Vol. 4, Pt. 2–530
Henderson, Thomas, Aug. 15, 1743–Dec. 15, 1824.
Vol. 4, Pt. 2–532
Henderson William James, Dec. 4, 1855–June 5, 1937.
Supp. 2–295
Henderson, Yandell, Apr. 23, 1873–Feb. 18, 1944.
Supp. 3–352
Hendrick, *c.* 1680–Sept. 8, 1755.
Vol. 4, Pt. 2–532
Hendrick, Burton Jesse, Dec. 8, 1870–Mar. 23, 1949.
Supp. 4–367
Hendrick, Ellwood, Dec. 19, 1861–Oct. 29, 1930.
Vol. 4, Pt. 2–533
Hendricks, Thomas Andrews, Sept. 7, 1819–Nov. 25, 1885.
Vol. 4, Pt. 2–534
Hendricks, William, Nov. 12, 1782–May 16, 1850.
Vol. 4, Pt. 2–535
Hendrix, Eugene Russell, May 17, 1847–Nov. 11, 1927.
Vol. 4, Pt. 2–536
Hendrix, Jimi, Nov. 27, 1942–Sept. 18, 1970.
Supp. 8–252
Hendrix, Joseph Clifford, May 25, 1853–Nov. 9, 1904.
Vol. 4, Pt. 2–536
Heney, Francis Joseph, Mar. 17, 1859–Oct. 31, 1937.
Supp. 2–296
Henie, Sonja, Apr. 8, 1912–Oct. 12, 1969.
Supp. 8–253
Hening, William Waller, 1767/8–Apr. 1, 1828.
Vol. 4, Pt. 2–537
Henkel, Paul, Dec. 15, 1754–Nov. 27, 1825.
Vol. 4, Pt. 2–538
Henley, Robert, Jan. 5, 1783–Oct. 6, 1828.
Vol. 4, Pt. 2–539
Hennepin, Louis, Apr. 7, 1640–1701 or later.
Vol. 4, Pt. 2–540
Hennessy, John, Aug. 20, 1825–Mar. 4, 1900.
Vol. 4, Pt. 2–541
Hennessy, William John, July 11, 1839–Dec. 26, 1917.
Vol. 4, Pt. 2–541
Henni, John Martin, June 15, 1805–Sept. 7, 1881.
Vol. 4, Pt. 2–542
Henningsen, Charles Frederick, Feb. 21, 1815–June 14, 1877.
Vol. 4, Pt. 2–543
Henny, David Christiaan, Nov. 15, 1860–July 14, 1935.
Supp. 1–393
Henri, Robert, June 25, 1865–July 12, 1929.
Vol. 4, Pt. 2–544

Henrici, Arthur Trautwein, Mar. 31, 1889–Apr. 23, 1943.
Supp. 3–354
Henrotin, Charles, Apr. 15, 1843–July 25, 1914.
Vol. 4, Pt. 2–545
Henrotin, Fernand, Sept. 28, 1847–Dec. 9, 1906.
Vol. 4, Pt. 2–545
Henry, Alexander, Aug. 1739–Apr. 4, 1824.
Supp. 1–393
Henry, Alice, Mar. 21, 1857–Feb. 14, 1943.
Supp. 3–355
Henry, Andrew, *c.* 1775–June 10, 1833.
Vol. 4, Pt. 2–546
Henry, Caleb Sprague, Aug. 2, 1804–Mar. 9, 1884.
Vol. 4, Pt. 2–547
Henry, Edward Lamson, Jan. 12, 1841–May 9, 1919.
Vol. 4, Pt. 2–547
Henry, John, 1746–Oct. 1794.
Vol. 4, Pt. 2–548
Henry, John, Nov. 1750–Dec. 16, 1798.
Vol. 4, Pt. 2–549
Henry, John, fl. 1807–1820.
Vol. 4, Pt. 2–549
Henry, Joseph, Dec. 17, 1797–May 13, 1878.
Vol. 4, Pt. 2–550
Henry, Morris Henry, July 26, 1835–May 19, 1895.
Vol. 4, Pt. 2–553
Henry, O. [*See* Porter, William Sydney, 1862–1910.]
Henry, Patrick, May 29, 1736–June 6, 1799.
Vol. 4, Pt. 2–554
Henry, Robert, Dec. 6, 1792–Feb. 6, 1856.
Vol. 4, Pt. 2–559
Henry, William, May 19, 1729–Dec. 15, 1786.
Vol. 4, Pt. 2–560
Henry, William Arnon, June 16, 1850–Nov. 24, 1932.
Supp. 1–394
Henry, William Wirt, Feb. 14, 1831–Dec. 5, 1900.
Vol. 4, Pt. 2–561
Henshall, James Alexander, Feb. 29, 1836–Apr. 4, 1925.
Vol. 4, Pt. 2–562
Henshaw, David, Apr. 2, 1791–Nov. 11, 1852.
Vol. 4, Pt. 2–562
Henshaw, Henry Wetherbee, Mar. 3, 1850–Aug. 1, 1930.
Vol. 4, Pt. 2–564
Henson, Josiah, June 15, 1789–May 5, 1883.
Vol. 4, Pt. 2–564
Henson, Matthew Alexander, Aug. 8, 1866–Mar. 9, 1955.
Supp. 5–295
Hentz, Caroline Lee Whiting, June 1, 1800–Feb. 11, 1856.
Vol. 4, Pt. 2–565
Hepburn, Alonzo Barton, July 24, 1846–Jan. 25, 1922.
Vol. 4, Pt. 2–566
Hepburn, James Curtis, Mar. 13, 1815–Sept. 21, 1911.
Vol. 4, Pt. 2–567
Hepburn, Katharine Houghton, Feb. 2, 1878–Mar. 17, 1951.
Supp. 5–296
Hepburn, William Peters, Nov. 4, 1833–Feb. 7, 1916.
Vol. 4, Pt. 2–568
Hepworth, George Hughes, Feb. 4, 1833–June 7, 1902.
Vol. 4, Pt. 2–569
Herberg, Will, June 30, 1901–Mar. 27, 1977.
Supp. 10–329
Herbermann, Charles George, Dec. 8, 1840–Aug. 24, 1916.
Vol. 4, Pt. 2–570
Herbert, Frederick Hugh, May 29, 1897–May 17, 1958.
Supp. 6–288
Herbert, Henry William, Apr. 7, 1807–May 17, 1858.
Vol. 4, Pt. 2–570
Herbert, Hilary Abner, Mar. 12, 1834–Mar. 6, 1919.
Vol. 4, Pt. 2–572
Herbert, Victor, Feb. 1, 1859–May 26, 1924.
Vol. 4, Pt. 2–573
Herbst, Josephine Frey, Mar. 5, 1892–Jan. 28, 1969.
Supp. 8–255
Herdic, Peter, Dec. 14, 1824–Mar. 2, 1888.
Vol. 4, Pt. 2–574
Herford, Oliver Brooke, Dec. 1, 1863–July 5, 1935.
Supp. 1–395
Hergesheimer, Joseph, Feb. 15, 1880–Apr. 25, 1954.
Supp. 5–297
Hering, Carl, Mar. 29, 1860–May 10, 1926.
Vol. 4, Pt. 2–574
Hering, Constantine, Jan. 1, 1800–July 23, 1880.
Vol. 4, Pt. 2–575
Hering, Rudolph, Feb. 26, 1847–May 30, 1923.
Vol. 4, Pt. 2–576
Herkimer, Nicholas, 1728–Aug. 16, 1777.
Vol. 4, Pt. 2–577
Herman, Lebrecht Frederick, Oct. 2, 1761–Jan. 30, 1848.
Vol. 4, Pt. 2–578
Herndon, William Henry, Dec. 25, 1818–Mar. 18, 1891.
Vol. 4, Pt. 2–579
Herndon, William Lewis, Oct. 25, 1813–Sept. 12, 1857.
Vol. 4, Pt. 2–579
Herne, Chrystal Katharine, June 17, 1882–Sept. 19, 1950.
Supp. 4–368
Herne, James A., Feb. 1, 1839–June 2, 1901.
Vol. 4, Pt. 2–580
Herold, David E. [*See* Booth, John Wilkes, 1838–1865.]
Heron, Matilda Agnes, Dec. 1, 1830–Mar. 7, 1877.
Vol. 4, Pt. 2–582
Heron, William, 1742–Jan. 8, 1819.
Vol. 4, Pt. 2–583
Herr, Herbert Thacker, Mar. 19, 1876–Dec. 19, 1933.
Supp. 1–396
Herr, John, Sept. 18, 1781–May 3, 1850.
Vol. 4, Pt. 2–584
Herreshoff, James Brown, Mar. 18, 1834–Dec. 5, 1930.
Vol. 4, Pt. 2–584
Herreshoff, John Brown, Apr. 24, 1841–July 20, 1915.
Vol. 4, Pt. 2–585
Herreshoff, Nathanael Greene, Mar. 18, 1848–June 2, 1938.
Supp. 2–298
Herrick, Edward Claudius, Feb. 24, 1811–June 11, 1862.
Vol. 4, Pt. 2–586
Herrick, Myron Timothy, Oct. 9, 1854–Mar. 31, 1929.
Vol. 4, Pt. 2–587
Herrick, Robert Welch, Apr. 26, 1868–Dec. 23, 1938.
Supp. 2–299
Herrick, Sophia McIlvaine Bledsoe, Mar. 26, 1837–Oct. 9, 1919.
Vol. 4, Pt. 2–589
Herriman, George Joseph, Aug. 22, 1880–Apr. 25, 1944.
Supp. 3–356
Herring, Augustus Moore, Aug. 3, 1867–July 17, 1926.
Vol. 4, Pt. 2–590
Herring, James, Jan. 12, 1794–Oct. 8, 1867
Vol. 4, Pt. 2–590
Herring, Silas Clark, 1803–June 23, 1881.
Vol. 4, Pt. 2–591
Herrman, Augustine, *c.* 1605–1686.
Vol. 4, Pt. 2–592
Herrmann, Alexander, Feb. 10, 1844–Dec. 17, 1896.
Vol. 4, Pt. 2–593
Herrmann, Bernard, June 29, 1911–Dec. 24, 1975
Supp. 9–381
Herron, Francis Jay, Feb. 17, 1837–Jan. 8, 1902.
Vol. 4, Pt. 2–593
Herron, George Davis, Jan. 21, 1862–Oct. 9, 1925.
Vol. 4, Pt. 2–594
Herschel, Clemens, Mar. 23, 1842–Mar. 1, 1930.
Vol. 4, Pt. 2–595
Hersey, Evelyn Weeks, Dec. 9, 1897–Nov. 3, 1963.
Supp. 7–341
Hershey, Lewis Blaine, Sept. 12, 1893–May 20, 1977.
Supp. 10–331
Hershey, Milton Snavely, Sept. 13, 1857–Oct. 13, 1945.
Supp. 3–357
Herter, Christian, Jan. 8, 1840–Nov. 2, 1883.
Vol. 4, Pt. 2–596
Herter, Christian Archibald, Sept. 3, 1865–Dec. 5, 1910.
Vol. 4, Pt. 2–597
Herter, Christian Archibald, Mar. 28, 1895–Dec. 30, 1966.
Supp. 8–256
Herty, Charles Holmes, Dec. 4, 1867–July 27, 1938.
Supp. 2–300
Hertz, Alfred, July 15, 1872–Apr. 17, 1942.
Supp. 3–359
Hertz, John Daniel, Apr. 10, 1879–Oct. 8, 1961.
Supp. 7–342
Heschel, Abraham Joshua, Jan. 11, 1907–Dec. 23, 1972.
Supp. 9–383
Hess, Alfred Fabian, Oct. 19, 1875–Dec. 5, 1933.
Supp. 1–397

Hess, Victor Franz, June 24, 1883–Dec. 17, 1964.
Supp. 7–343
Hesselius, Gustavus, 1682–May 25, 1755.
Vol. 4, Pt. 2–598
Hesselius, John, 1728–Apr. 9, 1778.
Vol. 4, Pt. 2–598
Hessoun, Joseph, Aug. 8, 1830–July 4, 1906.
Vol. 4, Pt. 2–599
Heth, Henry, Dec. 16, 1825–Sept. 27, 1899.
Vol. 4, Pt. 2–600
Hewat, Alexander, *c.* 1745–*c.* 1829.
Vol. 4, Pt. 2–601
Hewes, Joseph, Jan. 23, 1730–Nov. 10, 1779.
Vol. 4, Pt. 2–601
Hewes, Robert, 1751–July 1830.
Vol. 4, Pt. 2–602
Hewett, Waterman Thomas, Jan. 10, 1846–Sept. 13, 1921.
Vol. 4, Pt. 2–603
Hewit, Augustine Francis, Nov. 27, 1820–July 3, 1897.
Vol. 4, Pt. 2–604
Hewit, Nathaniel Augustus. [*See* Hewit, Augustine Francis, 1820–1897.]
Hewitt, Abram Stevens, July 31, 1822–Jan. 18, 1903.
Vol. 4, Pt. 2–604
Hewitt, Henry Kent, Feb. 11, 1887–Sept. 15, 1972.
Supp. 9–385
Hewitt, James, June 4, 1770–1827.
Vol. 4, Pt. 2–606
Hewitt, John Hill, July 11, 1801–Oct. 7, 1890.
Vol. 4, Pt. 2–606
Hewitt, Peter Cooper, May 5, 1861–Aug. 25, 1921.
Vol. 4, Pt. 2–607
Heydt, Hans Jöst. [*See* Hite, Jost, d. 1760.]
Heye, George Gustav, Sept. 16, 1874–Jan. 20, 1957.
Supp. 6–289
Heyer, John Christian Frederick, July 10, 1793–Nov. 7, 1873.
Vol. 4, Pt. 2–608
Heyward, Du Bose, Aug. 31, 1885–June 16, 1940.
Supp. 2–302
Heyward, Thomas, July 28, 1746–Mar. 6, 1809.
Vol. 4, Pt. 2–609
Heywood, Ezra Hervey, Sept. 29, 1829–May 22, 1893.
Vol. 4, Pt. 2–609
Heywood, Levi, Dec. 10, 1800–July 21, 1882.
Vol. 4, Pt. 2–611
Hiacoomes, *c.* 1610–1690.
Vol. 4, Pt. 2–611
Hibbard, Freeborn Garrettson, Feb. 22, 1811–Jan. 27, 1895.
Vol. 4, Pt. 2–612
Hibben, John Grier, Apr. 19, 1861–May 16, 1933.
Supp. 1–398
Hibben, Paxton Pattison, Dec. 5, 1880–Dec. 5, 1928.
Vol. 5, Pt. 1–1
Hibbins, Ann, d. June 19, 1656.
Vol. 5, Pt. 1–2
Hichborn, Philip, Mar. 4, 1839–May 1, 1910.
Vol. 5, Pt. 1–2
Hickenlooper, Andrew, Aug. 10, 1837–May 12, 1904.
Vol. 5, Pt. 1–3
Hickenlooper, Bourke Blakemore, July 21, 1896–Sept. 4, 1971.
Supp. 9–387
Hickok, James Butler, May 27, 1837–Aug. 2, 1876.
Vol. 5, Pt. 1–4
Hickok, Laurens Perseus, Dec. 29, 1798–May 6, 1888.
Vol. 5, Pt. 1–5
Hickok, Wild Bill. [*See* Hickok, James Butler, 1837–1876.]
Hicks, Elias, Mar. 19, 1748–Feb. 27, 1830.
Vol. 5, Pt. 1–6
Hicks, John, Oct. 18, 1823–Oct. 8, 1890.
Vol. 5, Pt. 1–7
Hicks, John, Apr. 12, 1847–Dec. 20, 1917.
Vol. 5, Pt. 1–7
Hicks, Thomas Holliday, Sept. 2, 1798–Feb. 13, 1865.
Vol. 5, Pt. 1–8
Hiester, Daniel, June 25, 1747–Mar. 7, 1804.
Vol. 5, Pt. 1–9
Hiester, Joseph, Nov. 18, 1752–June 10, 1832.
Vol. 5, Pt. 1–10
Higgins, Andrew Jackson, Aug. 28, 1886–Aug. 1, 1952.
Supp. 5–299
Higgins, Daniel Paul, Sept. 12, 1886–Dec. 26, 1953.
Supp. 5–300
Higgins, Frank Wayland, Aug. 18, 1856–Feb. 12, 1907.
Vol. 5, Pt. 1–10
Higgins, Marguerite, Sept. 3, 1920–Jan. 3, 1966.
Supp. 8–259
Higginson, Francis, 1586–Aug. 6, 1630.
Vol. 5, Pt. 1–11
Higginson, Henry Lee, Nov. 18, 1834–Nov. 14, 1919.
Vol. 5, Pt. 1–12
Higginson, John, Aug. 6, 1616–Dec. 9, 1708.
Vol. 5, Pt. 1–13
Higginson, Nathaniel, Oct. 11, 1652–Oct. 31, 1708.
Vol. 5, Pt. 1–14
Higginson, Stephen, Nov. 28, 1743–Nov. 22, 1828.
Vol. 5, Pt. 1–15
Higginson, Thomas Wentworth, Dec. 22, 1823–May 9, 1911.
Vol. 5, Pt. 1–16
High, Stanley Hoflund, Dec. 30, 1895–Feb. 3, 1961.
Supp. 7–344
Highet, Gilbert, June 22, 1906–Jan. 20, 1978.
Supp. 10–333
Higinbotham, Harlow Niles, Oct. 10, 1838–Apr. 18, 1919.
Vol. 5, Pt. 1–18
Hildreth, Richard, June 28, 1807–July 11, 1865.
Vol. 5, Pt. 1–19
Hildreth, Samuel Clay, May 16, 1866–Sept. 24, 1929.
Vol. 5, Pt. 1–20
Hildreth, Samuel Prescott, Sept. 30, 1783–July 24, 1863.
Vol. 5, Pt. 1–21
Hilgard, Eugene Woldemar, Jan. 5, 1833–Jan. 8, 1916.
Vol. 5, Pt. 1–22
Hilgard, Julius Erasmus, Jan. 7, 1825–May 8, 1891.
Vol. 5, Pt. 1–23
Hilgard, Theodor Erasmus, July 7, 1790–Jan. 29, 1873.
Vol. 5, Pt. 1–23
Hill, Ambrose Powell, Nov. 9, 1825–Apr. 2, 1865.
Vol. 5, Pt. 1–24
Hill, Arthur Middleton, Mar. 23, 1892–Sept. 5, 1972.
Supp. 9–388
Hill, Benjamin Harvey, Sept. 14, 1823–Aug. 16, 1882.
Vol. 5, Pt. 1–25
Hill, Daniel Harvey, July 12, 1821–Sept. 24, 1889.
Vol. 5, Pt. 1–27
Hill, David Bennett, Aug. 29, 1843–Oct. 20, 1910.
Vol. 5, Pt. 1–28
Hill, David Jayne, June 10, 1850–Mar. 2, 1932.
Supp. 1–401
Hill, Edwin Conger, Apr. 23, 1884–Feb. 12, 1957.
Supp. 6–290
Hill, Ernest Rowland, Jan. 29, 1872–Aug. 25, 1948.
Supp. 4–369
Hill, Frank Alpine, Oct. 12, 1841–Sept. 12, 1903.
Vol. 5, Pt. 1–29
Hill, Frederick Trevor, May 5, 1866–Mar. 17, 1930.
Vol. 5, Pt. 1–30
Hill, Frederic Stanhope, 1805–Apr. 7, 1851.
Vol. 5, Pt. 1–30
Hill, George Handel, Oct. 8, 1809–Sept. 27, 1849.
Vol. 5, Pt. 1–31
Hill, George Washington, Oct. 22, 1884–Sept. 13, 1946.
Supp. 4–370
Hill, George William, Mar. 3, 1838–Apr. 16, 1914.
Vol. 5, Pt. 1–32
Hill, Grace Livingston, Apr. 16, 1865–Feb. 23, 1947.
Supp. 4–372
Hill, Henry Barker, Apr. 27, 1849–Apr. 6, 1903.
Vol. 5, Pt. 1–33
Hill, Isaac, Apr. 6, 1789–Mar. 22, 1851.
Vol. 5, Pt. 1–34
Hill, James, Dec. 20, 1734–Aug. 22, 1811.
Vol. 5, Pt. 1–35
Hill, James Jerome, Sept. 16, 1838–May 29, 1916.
Vol. 5, Pt. 1–36
Hill, John, 1770–1850.
Vol. 5, Pt. 1–41
Hill, John Henry, Sept. 11, 1791–July 1, 1882.
Vol. 5, Pt. 1–41
Hill, John Wiley, Nov. 26, 1890–Mar. 17, 1977.
Supp. 10–334

Hill, Joseph Adna, May 5, 1860–Dec. 12, 1938.
Supp. 2–303
Hill, Joshua, Jan. 10, 1812–Mar. 6, 1891.
Vol. 5, Pt. 1–42
Hill, Louis Clarence, Feb. 22, 1865–Nov. 5, 1938.
Supp. 2–304
Hill, Nathaniel Peter, Feb. 18, 1832–May 22, 1900.
Vol. 5, Pt. 1–43
Hill, Patty Smith, Mar. 27, 1868–May 25, 1946.
Supp. 4–373
Hill, Richard, *c.* 1673–September 1729.
Vol. 5, Pt. 1–44
Hill, Robert Andrews, Mar. 25, 1811–July 2, 1900.
Vol. 5, Pt. 1–44
Hill, Thomas, Jan. 7, 1818–Nov. 21, 1891.
Vol. 5, Pt. 1–45
Hill, Thomas, Sept. 11, 1829–June 30, 1908.
Vol. 5, Pt. 1–46
Hill, Ureli Corelli, *c.* 1802–Sept. 2, 1875.
Vol. 5, Pt. 1–47
Hill, Walter Barnard, Sept. 9, 1851–Dec. 28, 1905.
Vol. 5, Pt. 1–47
Hill, William, 1741–Dec. 1, 1816.
Vol. 5, Pt. 1–48
Hillard, George Stillman, Sept. 22, 1808–Jan. 21, 1879.
Vol. 5, Pt. 1–49
Hillebrand, William Francis, Dec. 12, 1853–Feb. 7, 1925.
Vol. 5, Pt. 1–50
Hillegas, Michael, Apr. 22, 1729–Sept. 29, 1804.
Vol. 5, Pt. 1–51
Hillhouse, James, Oct. 20, 1754–Dec. 29, 1832.
Vol. 5, Pt. 1–52
Hillhouse, James Abraham, Sept. 26, 1789–Jan. 4, 1841.
Vol. 5, Pt. 1–52
Hilliard, Francis, Nov. 1, 1806–Oct. 9, 1878.
Vol. 5, Pt. 1–53
Hilliard, Henry Washington, Aug. 4, 1808–Dec. 17, 1892.
Vol. 5, Pt. 1–54
Hillis, David, November 1788–July 8, 1845.
Vol. 5, Pt. 1–50
Hillis, Newell Dwight, Sept. 2, 1858–Feb. 25, 1929.
Vol. 5, Pt. 1–56
Hillman, Sidney, Mar. 23, 1887–July 10, 1946.
Supp. 4–374
Hillman, Thomas Tennessee, Feb. 2, 1844–Aug. 4, 1905.
Vol. 5, Pt. 1–57
Hillquit, Morris, Aug. 1, 1869–Oct. 7, 1933.
Supp. 1–402
Hills, Elijah Clarence, July 2, 1867–Apr. 21, 1932.
Supp. 1–405
Hillyer, Junius, Apr. 23, 1807–June 21, 1886.
Vol. 5, Pt. 1–57
Hillyer, Robert Silliman, June 3, 1895–Dec. 24, 1961.
Supp. 7–346
Hilprecht, Herman Volrath, July 28, 1859–Mar. 19, 1925.
Vol. 5, Pt. 1–58
Hilton, Conrad Nicholson, Dec. 25, 1887–Jan. 3, 1979.
Supp. 10–335
Himes, Charles Francis, June 2, 1838–Dec. 6, 1918.
Vol. 5, Pt. 1–59
Himes, Joshua Vaughan, May 19, 1805–July 27, 1895.
Vol. 5, Pt. 1–60
Hindman, Thomas Carmichael, Jan. 28, 1828–Sept. 28, 1868.
Vol. 5, Pt. 1–61
Hindman, William, Apr. 1, 1743–Jan. 19, 1822.
Vol. 5, Pt. 1–62
Hinds, Asher Crosby, Feb. 6, 1863–May 1, 1919.
Vol. 5, Pt. 1–62
Hindus, Maurice Gerschon, Feb. 27, 1891–July 8, 1969.
Supp. 8–260
Hine, Charles De Lano, Mar. 15, 1867–Feb. 13, 1927.
Vol. 5, Pt. 1–63
Hine, Lewis Wickes, Sept. 26, 1874–Nov. 3, 1940.
Supp. 2–305
Hines, Duncan, Mar. 26, 1880–Mar. 15, 1959.
Supp. 6–291
Hines, Frank Thomas, Apr. 11, 1879–Apr. 3, 1960.
Supp. 6–293
Hines, James J., Dec. 18, 1876–Mar. 26, 1957.
Supp. 6–294
Hines, John Leonard ("Birdie"), May 21, 1868–Oct. 13, 1968.
Supp. 8–261
Hines, Walker Downer, Feb. 2, 1870–Jan. 14, 1934.
Supp. 1–406
Hinkle, Beatrice Moses, Oct. 10, 1874–Feb. 28, 1953.
Supp. 5–301
Hinman, Ehsha, Mar. 9, 1734–Aug. 29, 1805.
Vol. 5, Pt. 1–64
Hinman, George Wheeler, Nov. 19, 1864–Mar. 31, 1927.
Vol. 5, Pt. 1–65
Hinman, Joel, Jan. 27, 1802–Feb. 21, 1870.
Vol. 5, Pt. 1–65
Hinsdale, Burke Aaron, Mar. 31, 1837–Nov. 29, 1900.
Vol. 5, Pt. 1–66
Hinshaw, David Schull, Nov. 4, 1882–Nov. 5, 1953.
Supp. 5–303
Hires, Charles Elmer, Aug. 19, 1851–July 31, 1937.
Supp. 2–306
Hires, Charles Elmer, Jr., Apr. 27, 1891–Mar. 19, 1980.
Supp. 10–338
Hirsch, Emil Gustav, May 22, 1851–Jan. 7, 1923.
Vol. 5, Pt. 1–67
Hirsch, Isaac Seth, Dec. 3, 1880–Mar. 24, 1942.
Supp. 3–360
Hirsch, Maximilian Justice, July 30, 1880–Apr. 3, 1969.
Supp. 8–263
Hirschbein, Peretz, Nov. 7, 1880–Aug. 16, 1948.
Supp. 4–377
Hirschensohn, Chaim, Aug. 31, 1857–Sept 15 1935.
Supp. 1–407
Hirst, Barton Cooke, July 20, 1861–Sept. 2, 1935.
Supp. 1–408
Hirst, Henry Beck, Aug. 23, 1817–Mar. 30, 1874.
Vol. 5, Pt. 1–68
Hirth, William Andrew, Mar. 28, 1875–Oct. 24, 1940.
Supp. 2–307
Hiscock, Frank Harris, Apr. 16, 1856–July 2, 1946.
Supp. 4–379
Hitchcock, Alfred Joseph, Aug. 13, 1899–Apr. 28, 1980.
Supp. 10–339
Hitchcock, Charles Henry, Aug. 23, 1836–Nov. 5, 1910.
Vol. 5, Pt. 1–69
Hitchcock, Edward, May 23, 1828–Feb. 15, 1911.
Vol. 5, Pt. 1–71
Hitchcock, Edward, May 24, 1793–Feb. 27, 1864.
Vol. 5, Pt. 1–70
Hitchcock, Enos, Mar. 7, 1744–Feb. 26, 1803.
Vol. 5, Pt. 1–72
Hitchcock, Ethan Allen, May 18, 1798–Aug. 5, 1870.
Vol. 5, Pt. 1–73
Hitchcock, Ethan Allen, Sept. 19, 1835–Apr. 9, 1909.
Vol. 5, Pt. 1–74
Hitchcock, Frank. [*See* Murdoch, Frank Hitchcock, 1843–1872.]
Hitchcock, Frank Harris, Oct. 5, 1867–Aug. 5, 1935.
Supp. 1–409
Hitchcock, Gilbert Monell, Sept. 18, 1859–Feb. 3, 1934.
Supp. 1–410
Hitchcock, Henry, July 3, 1829–Mar. 18, 1902.
Vol. 5, Pt. 1–75
Hitchcock, James Ripley Wellman, July 3, 1857–May 4, 1918.
Vol. 5, Pt. 1–76
Hitchcock, Peter, Oct. 19, 1781–Mar. 4, 1853.
Vol. 5, Pt. 1–77
Hitchcock, Phineas Warrener, Nov. 30, 1831–July 10, 1881.
Vol. 5, Pt. 1–78
Hitchcock, Raymond, Oct. 22, 1865–Nov. 25, 1929.
Vol. 5, Pt. 1–78
Hitchcock, Ripley. [*See* Hitchcock, James Ripley Wellman, 1857–1918.]
Hitchcock, Roswell Dwight, Aug. 15, 1817–June 16, 1887.
Vol. 5, Pt. 1–79
Hitchcock, Thomas, Feb. 11, 1900–Apr. 19, 1944.
Supp. 3–360
Hite, Jost, d. 1760.
Vol. 5, Pt. 1–80
Hitt, Robert Roberts, Jan. 16, 1834–Sept. 20, 1906.
Vol. 5, Pt. 1–80
Hittell, John Shertzer, Dec. 25, 1825–Mar. 8, 1901.
Vol. 5, Pt. 1–81
Hittell, Theodore Henry, Apr. 5, 1830–Feb. 23, 1917.
Vol. 5, Pt. 1–82

Hoadley, David, Apr. 29, 1774–July 1839.
Vol. 5, Pt. 1–82
Hoadley, John Chipman, Dec. 10, 1818–Oct. 21, 1886.
Vol. 5, Pt. 1–83
Hoadly, George, July 31, 1826–Aug. 26, 1902.
Vol. 5, Pt. 1–84
Hoag, Joseph, Apr. 22, 1762–Nov. 21, 1846.
Vol. 5, Pt. 1–85
Hoagland, Charles Lee, June 6, 1907–Aug. 2, 1946.
Supp. 4–380
Hoagland, Dennis Robert, Apr. 2, 1884–Sept. 5, 1949.
Supp. 4–381
Hoan, Daniel Webster, Mar. 12, 1881–June 11, 1961.
Supp. 7–348
Hoar, Ebenezer Rockwood, Feb. 21, 1816–Jan. 31, 1895.
Vol. 5, Pt. 1–86
Hoar, George Frisbie, Aug. 29, 1826–Sept. 30, 1904.
Vol. 5, Pt. 1–87
Hoar, Leonard, *c.* 1630–Nov. 28, 1675.
Vol. 5, Pt. 1–88
Hoar, Samuel, May 18, 1778–Nov. 2, 1856.
Vol. 5, Pt. 1–89
Hoard, William Dempster, Oct. 10, 1836–Nov. 22, 1918.
Vol. 5, Pt. 1–90
Hoban, James, *c.* 1762–Dec. 8, 1831.
Vol. 5, Pt. 1–91
Hobart, Alice Nourse Tisdale, Jan. 28, 1882–Mar. 14, 1967.
Supp. 8–264
Hobart, Garret Augustus, June 3, 1844–Nov. 21, 1899.
Vol. 5, Pt. 1–92
Hobart, John Henry, Sept. 14, 1775–Sept. 12, 1830.
Vol. 5, Pt. 1–93
Hobart, John Sloss, May 6, 1738–Feb. 4, 1805.
Vol. 5, Pt. 1–94
Hobbs, Alfred Charles, Oct. 7, 1812–Nov. 5, 1891.
Vol. 5, Pt. 1–95
Hobby, William Pettus, Mar. 26, 1878–June 7, 1964.
Supp. 7–349
Hobson, Edward Henry, July 11, 1825–Sept. 14, 1901.
Vol. 5, Pt. 1–96
Hobson, Julius Wilson, May 29, 1919–Mar. 23, 1977.
Supp. 10–341
Hobson, Richmond Pearson, Aug. 17, 1870–Mar. 16, 1937.
Supp. 2–308
Hoch, August, Apr. 20, 1868–Sept. 23, 1919.
Vol. 5, Pt. 1–97
Hocking, William Ernest, Aug. 10, 1873–June 12, 1966.
Supp. 8–265
Hodes, Henry Irving, Mar. 19, 1899–Feb. 14, 1962.
Supp. 7–350
Hodge, Albert Elmer ("Al"), Apr. 18, 1912–Mar. 19, 1979.
Supp. 10–343
Hodge, Archibald Alexander, July 18, 1823–Nov. 11, 1886.
Vol. 5, Pt. 1–97
Hodge, Charles, Dec. 27, 1797–June 19, 1878.
Vol. 5, Pt. 1–98
Hodge, Hugh Lenox, June 27, 1796–Feb. 26, 1873.
Vol. 5, Pt. 1–99
Hodge, John Reed, June 12, 1893–Nov. 12, 1963.
Supp. 7–351
Hodge, William Thomas, Nov. 1, 1874–Jan. 30, 1932.
Supp. 1–411
Hodgen, John Thompson, Jan. 29, 1826–Apr. 28, 1882.
Vol. 5, Pt. 1–100
Hodges, Courtney Hicks, Jan. 5, 1887–Jan. 16, 1966.
Supp. 8–266
Hodges, George, Oct. 6, 1856–May 27, 1919.
Vol. 5, Pt. 1–100
Hodges, Gilbert Ray, Apr. 4, 1924–Apr. 2, 1972.
Supp. 9–389
Hodges, Harry Foote, Feb. 25, 1860–Sept. 24, 1929.
Vol. 5, Pt. 1–101
Hodges, Luther Hartwell, Mar. 9, 1898–Oct. 6, 1974.
Supp. 9–391
Hodgins, Eric Francis, Mar. 2, 1899–Jan. 7, 1971.
Supp. 9–393
Hodgkinson, Francis, June 16, 1867–Nov. 4, 1949.
Supp. 4–383
Hodgkinson, John, *c.* 1767–Sept. 12, 1805.
Vol. 5, Pt. 1–102
Hodgson, William Brown, Sept. 1, 1801–June 26, 1871.
Supp. 1–412
Hodson, William, Apr. 25, 1891–Jan. 15, 1943.
Supp. 3–361
Hodur, Francis, Apr. 2, 1866–Feb. 16, 1953.
Supp. 5–304
Hoe, Richard March, Sept. 12, 1812–June 7, 1886.
Vol. 5, Pt. 1–104
Hoe, Robert, Oct. 29, 1784–Jan. 4, 1833.
Vol. 5, Pt. 1–105
Hoe, Robert, Mar. 10, 1839–Sept. 22, 1909.
Vol. 5, Pt. 1–105
Hoecken, Christian, Feb. 28, 1808–June 19, 1851.
Vol. 5, Pt. 1–106
Hoen, August, Dec. 28, 1817–Sept. 20, 1886.
Vol. 5, Pt. 1–107
Hoenecke, Gustav Adolf Felix Theodor, Feb. 25, 1835–Jan. 3, 1908.
Vol. 5, Pt. 1–108
Hoerr, Normand Louis, May 3, 1902–Dec. 14, 1958.
Supp. 6–295
Hoey, Clyde Roark, Dec. 11, 1877–May 12, 1954.
Supp. 5–306
Hoff, John Van Rensselaer, Apr. 11, 1848–Jan. 14, 1920.
Vol. 5, Pt. 1–109
Hoffa, James Riddle ("Jimmy"), Feb. 14, 1913–1975?.
Supp. 9–395
Hoffman, Charles Fenno, Feb. 7, 1806–June 7, 1884.
Vol. 5, Pt. 1–110
Hoffman, Clare Eugene, Sept. 10, 1875–Nov. 3, 1967.
Supp. 8–268
Hoffman, David, Dec. 24, 1784–Nov. 11, 1854.
Vol. 5, Pt. 1–111
Hoffman, David Murray, Sept. 29, 1791–May 7, 1878.
Vol. 2, Pt. 2–112
Hoffman, Eugene Augustus, Mar. 21, 1829–June 17, 1902.
Vol. 5, Pt. 1–112
Hoffman, Frederick Ludwig, May 2, 1865–Feb. 23, 1946.
Supp. 4–384
Hoffman, John Thompson, Jan. 10, 1828–Mar. 24, 1888.
Vol. 5, Pt. 1–113
Hoffman, Josiah Ogden, Apr. 14, 1766–Jan. 24, 1837.
Vol. 5, Pt. 1–114
Hoffman, Ogden, May 3, 1793–May 1, 1856.
Vol. 5, Pt. 1–115
Hoffman, Paul Gray, Apr. 26, 1891–Oct. 8, 1974.
Supp. 9–397
Hoffman, Richard, Mar. 24, 1831–Aug. 17, 1909.
Vol. 5, Pt. 1–117
Hoffman, Wickham, Apr. 2, 1821–May 21, 1900.
Vol. 5, Pt. 1–117
Hoffmann, Francis Arnold, June 5, 1822–Jan. 23, 1903.
Vol. 5, Pt. 1–118
Hoffman, Paul Gray, Apr. 26, 1891–Oct. 8, 1974.
Supp. 9–397
Hofman, Heinrich Oscar, Aug. 13, 1852–Apr 28, 1924.
Vol. 5, Pt. 1–119
Hofmann, Hans, Mar. 21, 1880–Feb. 17, 1966.
Supp. 8–270
Hofmann, Josef Casimir, Jan. 20, 1876–Feb. 16, 1957.
Supp. 6–297
Hofstadter, Richard, Aug. 6, 1916–Oct. 24, 1970.
Supp. 8–271
Hogan, Frank Smithwick, Jan. 17, 1902–Apr. 2, 1974.
Supp. 9–399
Hogan, John, Jan. 2, 1805–Feb. 5, 1892.
Vol. 5, Pt. 1–119
Hogan, John Vincent Lawless, Feb. 14, 1890–Dec. 29, 1960.
Supp. 6–298
Hoge, Moses, Feb. 15, 1752–July 5, 1820.
Vol. 5, Pt. 1–120
Hoge, Moses Drury, Sept. 17, 1819–Jan. 6, 1899.
Vol. 5, Pt. 1–121
Hogg, George, June 22, 1784–Dec. 5, 1849.
Vol. 5, Pt. 1–122
Hogg, James Stephen, Mar. 24, 1851–Mar. 3, 1906.
Vol. 5, Pt. 1–122
Hogue, Wilson Thomas, Mar. 6, 1852–Feb. 13, 1920.
Vol. 5, Pt. 1–123
Hogun, James, d. Jan. 4, 1781.
Vol. 5, Pt. 1–123
Hohfeld, Wesley Newcomb, Aug. 8, 1879–Oct. 21, 1918.
Vol. 5, Pt. 1–124

Hoisington, Henry Richard, Aug. 23, 1801–May 16, 1858.
Vol. 5, Pt. 1–125
Hoke, Robert Frederick, May 27, 1837–July 3, 1912.
Vol. 5, Pt. 1–126
Hokinson, Helen Elna, June 29, 1893–Nov. 1, 1949.
Supp. 4–385
Holabird, William, Sept. 11, 1854–July 19, 1923.
Vol. 5, Pt. 1–127
Holbrook, Alfred, Feb. 17, 1816–Apr. 16, 1909.
Vol. 5, Pt. 1–128
Holbrook, Frederick, Feb. 15, 1813–Apr. 28, 1909.
Vol. 5, Pt. 1–128
Holbrook, John Edwards, Dec. 30, 1794–Sept. 8, 1871.
Vol. 5, Pt. 1–129
Holbrook, Josiah, 1788–June 17, 1854.
Vol. 5, Pt. 1–130
Holbrook, Stewart Hall, Aug. 22, 1893–Sept. 3, 1964.
Supp. 7–353
Holcomb, Amasa, June 18, 1787–Feb. 27, 1875.
Vol. 5, Pt. 1–131
Holcomb, Silas Alexander, Aug. 25, 1858–Apr. 25, 1920.
Vol. 5, Pt. 1–132
Holcombe, Chester, Oct. 16, 1844–Apr. 25, 1912.
Vol. 5, Pt. 1–132
Holcombe, Henry, Sept. 22, 1762–May 22, 1824.
Vol. 5, Pt. 1–133
Holcombe, James Philemon, Sept. 20, 1820–Aug. 22, 1873.
Vol. 5, Pt. 1–134
Holcombe, William Henry, May 29, 1825–Nov. 28, 1893.
Vol. 5, Pt. 1–135
Holden, Edward Singleton, Nov. 5, 1846–Mar. 16, 1914.
Vol. 5, Pt. 1–136
Holden, Hale, Aug. 11, 1869–Sept. 23, 1940.
Supp. 2–309
Holden, Liberty Emery, June 20, 1833–Aug. 26, 1913.
Vol. 5, Pt. 1–137
Holden, Oliver, Sept. 18, 1765–Sept. 4, 1844.
Vol. 5, Pt. 1–138
Holden, William Woods, Nov. 24, 1818–Mar. 1, 1892.
Vol. 5, Pt. 1–138
Holder, Charles Frederick, Aug. 5, 1851–Oct. 10, 1915.
Vol. 5, Pt. 1–140
Holder, Joseph Bassett, Oct. 26, 1824–Feb. 27, 1888.
Vol. 5, Pt. 1–140
Holdrege, George Ward, Mar. 26, 1847–Sept. 14, 1926.
Supp. 1–413
Holiday, Billie, Apr. 7, 1915–July 17, 1959.
Supp. 6–299
Holladay, Ben, Oct. 1819–July 8, 1887.
Vol. 5, Pt. 1–141
Holland, Clifford Milburn, Mar. 13, 1883–Oct. 27, 1924.
Vol. 5, Pt. 1–142
Holland, Edmund Milton, Sept. 7, 1848–Nov. 24, 1913.
Vol. 5, Pt. 1–143
Holland, Edwin Clifford, *c.* 1794–Sept. 11, 1824.
Vol. 5, Pt. 1–143
Holland, George, Dec. 6, 1791–Dec. 20, 1870.
Vol. 5, Pt. 1–144
Holland, John Philip, Feb. 29, 1840–Aug. 12, 1914.
Vol. 5, Pt. 1–144
Holland, Joseph Jefferson, Dec. 20, 1860–Sept. 25, 1926.
Vol. 5, Pt. 1–146
Holland, Josiah Gilbert, July 24, 1819–Oct 12, 1881.
Vol. 5, Pt. 1–146
Holland, Spessard Lindsey, July 10, 1892–Nov. 6, 1971.
Supp. 9–400
Holland, William Jacob, Aug. 16, 1848–Dec. 13, 1932.
Supp. 1–414
Hollander, Jacob Harry, July 23, 1871–July 9, 1940.
Supp. 2–310
Hollerith, Herman, Feb. 29, 1860–Nov. 17, 1929.
Supp. 1–415
Holley, Alexander Lyman, July 20, 1832–Jan. 29, 1882.
Vol. 5, Pt. 1–148
Holley, Horace, Feb. 13, 1781–July 31, 1827.
Vol. 5, Pt. 1–149
Holley, Marietta, July 16, 1836–Mar. 1, 1926.
Vol. 5, Pt. 1–150
Holley, Myron, Apr. 29, 1779–Mar. 4, 1841.
Vol. 5, Pt. 1–150
Hollick, Charles Arthur, Feb. 6, 1857–Mar. 11, 1933.
Supp. 1–416
Holliday, Cyrus Kurtz, Apr. 3, 1826–Mar. 29, 1900.
Vol. 5, Pt. 1–151
Holliday, Judy, June 21, 1921–June 7, 1965.
Supp. 7–354
Hollingworth, Leta Stetter, May 25, 1886–Nov. 27, 1939.
Supp. 2–312
Hollins, George Nichols, Sept. 20, 1799–Jan. 18, 1878.
Vol. 5, Pt. 1–152
Hollis, Ira Nelson, Mar. 7, 1856–Aug. 14, 1930.
Vol. 5, Pt. 1–152
Hollister, Gideon Hiram, Dec. 14, 1817–Mar. 24, 1881.
Vol. 5, Pt. 1–153
Holloway, John, *c.* 1666–Dec. 14, 1734.
Vol. 5, Pt. 1–154
Holloway, Joseph Flavius, Jan. 18, 1825–Sept. 1, 1896.
Vol. 5, Pt. 1–155
Holls, Frederick William. [*See* Holls, George Frederick William, 1857–1903.]
Holls, George Frederick William, July 1, 1857–July 23, 1903.
Vol. 5, Pt. 1–155
Holly, Charles Hardin ("Buddy"), Sept. 7, 1936–Feb. 3, 1959.
Supp. 6–300
Holly, James Theodore, Oct. 3, 1829–Mar. 13, 1911.
Vol. 5, Pt. 1–156
Hollyer, Samuel, Feb. 24, 1826–Dec. 29, 1919.
Vol. 5, Pt. 1–157
Holman, Jesse Lynch, Oct. 24, 1784–Mar. 28, 1842.
Vol. 5, Pt. 1–158
Holman, William Steele, Sept. 6, 1822–Apr. 22, 1897.
Vol. 5, Pt. 1–158
Holme, Thomas, 1624–1695.
Vol. 5, Pt. 1–159
Holmes, Abiel, Dec. 24, 1763–June 4, 1837.
Vol. 5, Pt. 1–160
Holmes, Bayard Taylor, July 29, 1852–Apr. 3, 1924.
Vol. 5, Pt. 1–161
Holmes, Daniel Henry, July 16, 1851–Dec. 15, 1908.
Vol. 5, Pt. 1–161
Holmes, David, Mar. 10, 1770–Aug. 20, 1832.
Vol. 5, Pt. 1–162
Holmes, Elias Burton, Jan. 8, 1870–July 22, 1958.
Supp. 6–302
Holmes, Ezekiel, Aug. 24, 1801–Feb. 9, 1865.
Vol. 5, Pt. 1–163
Holmes, George Frederick, Aug. 2, 1820–Nov. 4, 1897.
Vol. 5, Pt. 1–164
Holmes, Isaac Edward, Apr. 6, 1796–Feb. 24, 1867.
Vol. 5, Pt. 1–165
Holmes, Israel, Dec. 19, 1800–July 15, 1874.
Vol. 5, Pt. 1–165
Holmes, John, Mar. 28, 1773–July 7, 1843.
Vol. 5, Pt. 1–166
Holmes, John Haynes, Nov. 29, 1879–Apr. 3, 1964.
Supp. 7–355
Holmes, Joseph Austin, Nov. 23, 1859–July 12, 1915.
Vol. 5, Pt. 1–167
Holmes, Julius Cecil, Apr. 24, 1899–July 14, 1968.
Supp. 8–274
Holmes, Mary Jane Hawes, Apr. 5, 1825–Oct. 6, 1907.
Vol. 5, Pt. 1–168
Holmes, Nathaniel, Jan. 2, 1815–Feb. 26, 1901.
Vol. 5, Pt. 1–168
Holmes, Oliver Wendell, Aug. 29, 1809–Oct. 7, 1894.
Vol. 5, Pt. 1–169
Holmes, Oliver Wendell, Mar. 8, 1841–Mar. 6, 1935.
Supp. 1–417
Holmes, Theophilus Hunter, Nov. 13, 1804–June 21, 1880.
Vol. 5, Pt. 1–176
Holmes, William Henry, Dec. 1, 1846–Apr. 20, 1933.
Supp. 1–427
Holsey, Lucius Henry, *c.* 1842–Aug. 3, 1920.
Vol. 5, Pt. 1–176
Holst, Hermann Eduard von, June 19, 1841–Jan. 20, 1904.
Vol. 5, Pt. 1–177
Holt, Arthur Erastus, Nov. 23, 1876–Jan. 13, 1942.
Supp. 3–362
Holt, Edwin Bissell, Aug. 21, 1873–Jan. 25, 1946.
Supp. 4–387

Holt, Edwin Michael, Jan. 14, 1807–May 15, 1884.
Vol. 5, Pt. 1–179
Holt, Hamilton Bowen, Aug. 19, 1872–Apr. 26, 1951.
Supp. 5–307
Holt, Henry, Jan. 3, 1840–Feb. 13, 1926.
Vol. 5, Pt. 1–179
Holt, John, 1721–Jan. 30, 1784.
Vol. 5, Pt. 1–180
Holt, Joseph, Jan. 6, 1807–Aug. 1, 1894.
Vol. 5, Pt. 1–181
Holt, Luther Emmett, Mar. 4, 1855–Jan. 14, 1924.
Vol. 5, Pt. 1–183
Holt, William Franklin, Jan. 18, 1864–Nov. 22, 1951.
Supp. 5–309
Holt, Winifred, Nov. 17, 1870–June 14, 1945.
Supp. 3–364
Holten, Samuel, June 9, 1738–Jan. 2, 1816.
Vol. 5, Pt. 1–184
Holyoke, Edward Augustus, Aug. 1, 1728–Mar. 31, 1829.
Vol. 5, Pt. 1–185
Holyoke, Samuel, Oct. 15, 1762–Feb. 21, 1820.
Vol. 5, Pt. 1–186
Homer, Arthur Bartlett, Apr. 14, 1896–June 18, 1972.
Supp. 9–401
Homer, Louise Dilworth Beatty, Apr. 30, 1871–May 6, 1947.
Supp. 4–388
Homer, Winslow, Feb. 24, 1836–Sept. 29, 1910.
Vol. 5, Pt. 1–186
Homes, Henry Augustus, Mar. 10, 1812–Nov. 3, 1887.
Vol. 5, Pt. 1–191
Hone, Philip, Oct. 25, 1780–May 5, 1851.
Vol. 5, Pt. 1–192
Hontan, Louis-Armand De Lom D'Arce, Baron de la. [*See* Lahontan, Louis Armand de Lom d'Arce, 1666–*c.* 1713]
Hood, Clifford Firoved, Feb. 8, 1894–Nov. 9, 1978.
Supp. 10–344
Hood, James Walker, May 30, 1831–Oct. 30, 1918.
Vol. 5, Pt. 1–192
Hood, John Bell, June 1, 1831–Aug. 30, 1879.
Vol. 5, Pt. 1–193
Hood, Raymond Mathewson, Mar. 29, 1881–Aug. 14, 1934.
Supp. 1–428
Hood, Washington, Feb. 2, 1808–July 17, 1840.
Vol. 5, Pt. 1–194
Hooker, Donald Russell, Sept. 7, 1876–Aug. 1, 1946.
Supp. 4–390
Hooker, Elon Huntington, Nov. 23, 1869–May 10, 1938.
Supp. 2–313
Hooker, Isabella Beecher, Feb. 22, 1822–Jan. 25, 1907.
Vol. 5, Pt. 1–195
Hooker, Joseph, Nov. 13, 1814–Oct. 31, 1879.
Vol. 5, Pt. 1–196
Hooker, Philip, Oct. 28, 1766–Jan. 31, 1836.
Vol. 5, Pt. 1–198
Hooker, Samuel Cox, Apr. 19, 1864–Oct. 12, 1935.
Supp. 1–431
Hooker, Thomas, 1586?–July 7, 1647.
Vol. 5, Pt. 1–199
Hooker, William, fl. 1804–1846.
Vol. 5, Pt. 1–200
Hooker, Worthington, Mar. 3, 1806–Nov. 6, 1867.
Vol. 5, Pt. 1–201
Hooper, Claude Ernest, May 31, 1898–Dec. 15, 1954.
Supp. 5–310
Hooper, Harry Bartholomew, Aug. 24, 1887–Dec. 18, 1974.
Supp. 9–403
Hooper, Jessie Annette Jack, Nov. 8, 1865–May 8, 1935.
Supp. 1–432
Hooper, Johnson Jones, June 9, 1815–June 7, 1862.
Vol. 5, Pt. 1–202
Hooper, Lucy Hamilton, Jan. 20, 1835–Aug. 3, 1893.
Vol. 5, Pt. 1–202
Hooper, Samuel, Feb. 3, 1808–Feb. 14, 1875.
Vol. 5, Pt. 1–203
Hooper, William, June 17, 1742–Oct. 14, 1790.
Vol. 5, Pt. 1–204
Hooton, Earnest Albert, Nov. 20, 1887–May 3, 1954.
Supp. 5–312
Hoover, Charles Franklin, Aug. 2, 1865–June 15, 1927.
Vol. 5, Pt. 1–205
Hoover, Herbert Clark, Aug. 10, 1874–Oct. 20, 1964.
Supp. 7–357
Hoover, Herbert Clark, Jr., Aug. 4, 1903–July 9, 1969.
Supp. 8–275
Hoover, Herbert William, Oct. 30, 1877–Sept. 16, 1954.
Supp. 5–313
Hoover, James Matthews, Aug. 26, 1872–Feb. 11, 1935.
Supp. 1–433
Hoover, John Edgar, Jan. 1, 1895–May 2, 1972.
Supp. 9–404
Hope, Clifford Ragsdale, June 9, 1893–May 16, 1970.
Supp. 8–277
Hope, James Barron, Mar. 23, 1829–Sept. 15, 1887.
Vol. 5, Pt. 1–205
Hope, John, June 2, 1868–Feb. 20, 1936.
Supp. 2–314
Hopkins, Arthur Francis, Oct. 18, 1794–Nov. 10, 1865.
Vol. 5, Pt. 1–206
Hopkins, Cyril George, July 22, 1866–Oct. 6, 1919.
Vol. 5, Pt. 1–207
Hopkins, Edward, 1600–Mar. 1657.
Vol. 5, Pt. 1–207
Hopkins, Edward Augustus, Nov. 29, 1822–June 10, 1891.
Vol. 5, Pt. 1–208
Hopkins, Edward Washburn, Sept. 8, 1857–July 16, 1932.
Supp. 1–433
Hopkins, Esek, Apr. 26, 1718–Feb. 26, 1802.
Vol. 5, Pt. 1–209
Hopkins, Harry Lloyd, Aug. 17, 1890–Jan. 29, 1946.
Supp. 4–391
Hopkins, Isaac Stiles, June 20, 1841–Feb. 3, 1914.
Vol. 5, Pt. 1–210
Hopkins, James Campbell, Apr. 27, 1819–Sept. 3, 1877.
Vol. 5, Pt. 1–211
Hopkins, John Burroughs, Aug. 25, 1742–Dec. 5, 1796.
Vol. 5, Pt. 1–211
Hopkins, John Henry, Jan. 30, 1792–Jan. 9, 1868.
Vol. 5, Pt. 1–212
Hopkins, Johns, May 19, 1795–Dec. 24, 1873.
Vol. 5, Pt. 1–213
Hopkins, Juliet Ann Opie, May 7, 1818–Mar. 9, 1890.
Vol. 5, Pt. 1–214
Hopkins, Lemuel, June 19, 1750–Apr. 14, 1801.
Vol. 5, Pt. 1–215
Hopkins, Mark, Feb. 4, 1802–June 17, 1887.
Vol. 5, Pt. 1–215
Hopkins, Miriam, Oct. 18, 1902–Oct. 9, 1972.
Supp. 9–408
Hopkins, Samuel, Sept. 17, 1721–Dec. 20, 1803.
Vol. 5, Pt. 1–217
Hopkins, Samuel, Apr. 9, 1753–Sept. 16, 1819.
Vol. 5, Pt. 1–218
Hopkins, Stephen, Mar. 7, 1707–July 13, 1785.
Vol. 5, Pt. 1–219
Hopkinson, Francis, Oct. 2, 1737–May 9, 1791.
Vol. 5, Pt. 1–220
Hopkinson, Joseph, Nov. 12, 1770–Jan. 15, 1842.
Vol. 5, Pt. 1–223
Hoppe, William Frederick ("Willie"), Oct. 11, 1887–Feb. 1, 1959.
Supp. 6–303
Hopper, DeWolf, Mar. 30, 1858–Sept. 23, 1935.
Supp. 1–434
Hopper, Edna Wallace, Jan. 17, 1864?–Dec. 14, 1959.
Supp. 6–305
Hopper, Edward, July 22, 1882–May 15, 1967.
Supp. 8–278
Hopper, Hedda, May 2, 1885–Feb. 1, 1966.
Supp. 8–281
Hopper, Isaac Tatem, Dec. 3, 1771–May 7, 1852.
Vol. 5, Pt. 1–224
Hoppin, Augustus, July 13, 1828–Apr. 1, 1896.
Vol. 5, Pt. 1–225
Hoppin, James Mason, Jan. 17, 1820–Nov. 15, 1906.
Vol. 5, Pt. 1–225
Hoppin, Joseph Clark, May 23, 1870–Jan. 30, 1925.
Vol. 5, Pt. 1–226
Hoppin, William Warner, Sept. 1, 1807–Apr. 19, 1890.
Vol. 5, Pt. 1–227
Hopson, Howard Colwell, May 8, 1882–Dec. 22, 1949.
Supp. 4–394

Hopwood, Avery, May 28, 1882–July 1, 1928.
Vol. 5, Pt. 1–228
Horlick, William, Feb. 23, 1846–Sept. 25, 1936.
Supp. 2–316
Hormel, George Albert, Dec. 4, 1860–June 5, 1946.
Supp. 4–395
Hormel, Jay Catherwood, Sept. 11, 1892–Aug. 30, 1954.
Supp. 5–314
Horn, Edward Traill, June 10, 1850–Mar. 4, 1915.
Vol. 5, Pt. 1–228
Horn, George Henry, Apr. 7, 1840–Nov. 24, 1897.
Vol. 5, Pt. 1–229
Horn, Tom, Nov. 21, 1860–Nov. 20, 1903.
Vol. 5, Pt. 1–230
Hornaday, William Temple, Dec. 1, 1854–Mar. 6, 1937.
Supp. 2–316
Hornblower, Joseph Coerten, May 6, 1777–June 11, 1864.
Vol. 5, Pt. 1–230
Hornblower, Josiah, Feb. 23, 1729 N.S.–Jan. 21, 1809.
Vol. 5, Pt. 1–231
Hornblower, William Butler, May 13, 1851–June 16, 1914.
Vol. 5, Pt. 1–232
Horner, Henry, Nov. 30, 1878–Oct. 6, 1940.
Supp. 2–318
Horner, William Edmonds, June 3, 1793–Mar. 13, 1853.
Vol. 5, Pt. 1–233
Horney, Karen Danielssen, Sept. 16, 1885–Dec. 4, 1952.
Supp. 5–315
Hornsby, Rogers, Apr. 27, 1896–Jan. 5, 1963.
Supp. 7–364
Horr, George Edwin, Jan. 19, 1856–Jan. 22, 1927.
Vol. 5, Pt. 1–234
Horrocks, James, *c.* 1734–Mar. 20, 1772.
Vol. 5, Pt. 1–235
Horsfield, Thomas, May 12, 1773–July 24, 1859
Vol. 5, Pt. 1–236
Horsford, Eben Norton, July 27, 1818–Jan. 1, 1893.
Vol. 5, Pt. 1–236
Horsmanden, Daniel, June 4, 1694–Sept. 23, 1778.
Vol. 5, Pt. 1–237
Horst, Louis, Jan. 12, 1884–Jan. 23, 1964.
Supp. 7–366
Horton, Edward Everett, Jr., Mar. 18, 1886–Sept. 29, 1970.
Supp. 8–283
Horton, Samuel Dana, Jan. 16, 1844–Feb. 23, 1895.
Vol. 5, Pt. 1–238
Horton, Valentine Baxter, Jan. 29, 1802–Jan. 14, 1888.
Vol. 5, Pt. 1–238
Hosack, Alexander Eddy, Apr. 6, 1805–Mar. 2, 1871.
Vol. 5, Pt. 1–239
Hosack, David, Aug. 31, 1769–Dec. 22, 1835.
Vol. 5, Pt. 1–239
Hoshour, Samuel Klinefelter, Dec. 9, 1803–Nov. 29, 1883.
Vol. 5, Pt. 1–240
Hosmer, Frederick Lucian, Oct. 16, 1840–June 7, 1929.
Vol. 5, Pt. 1–241
Hosmer, Harriet Goodhue, Oct. 9, 1830–Feb. 21, 1908.
Vol. 5, Pt. 1–242
Hosmer, Hezekiah Lord, Dec. 10, 1814–Oct. 31, 1893.
Vol. 5, Pt. 1–243
Hosmer, James Kendall, Jan. 29, 1834–May 11, 1927.
Vol. 5, Pt. 1–244
Hosmer, Titus, 1737–Aug. 4, 1780.
Vol. 5, Pt. 1–245
Hosmer, William Howe Cuyler, May 25, 1814–May 23, 1877.
Vol. 5, Pt. 1–245
Hotchkiss, Benjamin Berkeley, Oct. 1, 1826–Feb. 14, 1885.
Vol. 5, Pt. 1–246
Hotchkiss, Horace Leslie, Mar. 27, 1842–May 10, 1929.
Vol. 5, Pt. 1–247
Hotz, Ferdinand Carl, July 12, 1843–Mar. 21, 1909.
Vol. 5, Pt. 1–247
Houdini, Harry, Apr. 6, 1874–Oct. 31, 1926.
Vol. 5, Pt. 1–248
Houdry, Eugene Jules, Apr. 18, 1892–July 18, 1962.
Supp. 7–367
Hough, Charles Merrill, May 18, 1858–Apr. 22, 1927.
Vol. 5, Pt. 1–249
Hough, Emerson, June 28, 1857–Apr. 30, 1923.
Vol. 5, Pt. 1–250
Hough, Franklin Benjamin, July 22, 1822–June 11, 1885.
Vol. 5, Pt. 1–250
Hough, George Washington, Oct. 24, 1836–Jan. 1, 1909.
Vol. 5, Pt. 1–252
Hough, Theodore, June 19, 1865–Nov. 30, 1924.
Vol. 5, Pt. 1–252
Hough, Walter, Apr. 23, 1859–Sept. 20, 1935.
Supp. 1–435
Hough, Warwick, Jan. 26, 1836–Oct. 28, 1915.
Vol. 5, Pt. 1–253
Houghton, Alanson Bigelow. Oct. 10, 1863–Sept. 16, 1941.
Supp. 3–365
Houghton, Douglass, Sept. 21, 1809–Oct. 13, 1845.
Vol. 5, Pt. 1–254
Houghton, George Hendric, Feb. 1, 1820–Nov. 17, 1897.
Vol. 5, Pt. 1–255
Houghton, Henry Oscar, Apr. 30, 1823–Aug. 25, 1895.
Vol. 5, Pt. 1–255
Houk, Leonidas Campbell, June 8, 1836–May 25, 1891.
Vol. 5, Pt. 1–256
Hourwich, Isaac Aaronovich, Apr. 26, 1860–July 9, 1924.
Vol. 5, Pt. 1–257
House, Edward Howard, Sept. 5, 1836–Dec. 17, 1901.
Vol. 5, Pt. 1–257
House, Edward Mandell, July 26, 1858–Mar. 28, 1938.
Supp. 2–319
House, Henry Alonzo, Apr. 23, 1840–Dec. 18, 1930.
Vol. 5, Pt. 1–258
House, Royal Earl, Sept. 9, 1814–Feb. 25, 1895.
Vol. 5, Pt. 1–259
House, Samuel Reynolds, Oct. 16, 1817–Aug. 13, 1899.
Vol. 5, Pt. 1–260
Houston, Charles Hamilton, Sept. 3, 1895–Apr. 22, 1950.
Supp. 4–396
Houston, David Franklin, Feb. 17, 1866–Sept. 2, 1940.
Supp. 2–321
Houston, Edwin James, July 9, 1847–Mar. 1, 1914.
Vol. 5, Pt. 1–261
Houston, George Smith, Jan. 17, 1811–Dec. 31, 1879.
Vol. 5, Pt. 1–261
Houston, Henry Howard, Oct. 3, 1820–June 21, 1895.
Vol. 5, Pt. 1–262
Houston, Samuel, Mar. 2, 1793–July 26, 1863.
Vol. 5, Pt. 1–263
Houston, William Churchill, *c.* 1746–Aug. 12, 1788.
Vol. 5, Pt. 1–267
Houstoun, John, Aug. 31, 1744–July 20, 1796.
Vol. 5, Pt. 1–268
Hove, Elling, Mar. 25, 1863–Dec. 17, 1927.
Vol. 5, Pt. 1–268
Hovenden, Thomas, Dec. 23, 1840–Aug. 14, 1895.
Vol. 5, Pt. 1–269
Hovey, Alvah, Mar. 5, 1820–Sept. 6, 1903.
Vol. 5, Pt. 1–270
Hovey, Alvin Peterson, Sept. 6, 1821–Nov. 23, 1891.
Vol. 5, Pt. 1–270
Hovey, Charles Edward, Apr. 26, 1827–Nov. 17, 1897.
Vol. 5, Pt. 1–271
Hovey, Charles Mason, Oct. 26, 1810–Sept. 2, 1887.
Vol. 5, Pt. 1–272
Hovey, Otis Ellis, Apr. 9, 1864–Apr. 15, 1941.
Supp. 3–366
Hovey, Richard, May 4, 1864–Feb. 24, 1900.
Vol. 5, Pt. 1–273
Hovgaard, William, Nov. 28, 1857–Jan. 5, 1950.
Supp. 4–398
Howard, Ada Lydia, Dec. 19, 1829–Mar. 3, 1907.
Vol. 5, Pt. 1–274
Howard, Benjamin, 1760–Sept. 18, 1814.
Vol. 5, Pt. 1–274
Howard, Benjamin Chew, Nov. 5, 1791–Mar. 6, 1872.
Vol. 5, Pt. 1–275
Howard, Blanche Willis, July 21, 1847–Oct. 7, 1898.
Vol. 5, Pt. 1–275
Howard, Bronson Crocker, Oct. 7, 1842–Aug. 4, 1908.
Vol. 5, Pt. 1–276
Howard, Charles Perry, Sept. 14, 1879–July 21, 1938.
Supp. 2–322
Howard, Edgar, Sept. 16, 1858–July 19, 1951.
Supp. 5–318
Howard, Elston Gene ("Ellie"), Feb. 23, 1929–Dec. 14, 1980.
Supp. 10–346

Howard, George Elliott, Oct. 1, 1849–June 9, 1928.
Vol. 5, Pt. 1–277
Howard, Henry, July 5, 1868–Aug. 26, 1951.
Supp. 5–319
Howard, Jacob Merritt, July 10, 1805–Apr. 2, 1871.
Vol. 5, Pt. 1–278
Howard, John Eager, June 4, 1752–Oct. 12, 1827.
Vol. 5, Pt. 1–279
Howard, Joseph Kinsey, Feb. 28, 1906–Aug. 25, 1951.
Supp. 5–320
Howard, Leland Ossian, June 11, 1857–May 1, 1950.
Supp. 4–399
Howard, Leslie, Apr. 3, 1893–June 1, 1943.
Supp. 3–367
Howard, Moe, June 19, 1897–May 4, 1975.
Supp. 9–409
Howard, Oliver Otis, Nov. 8, 1830–Oct. 26, 1909.
Vol. 5, Pt. 1–279
Howard, Roy Wilson, Jan. 1, 1883–Nov. 20, 1964.
Supp. 7–369
Howard, Sidney Coe, June 26, 1891–Aug. 23, 1939.
Supp. 2–324
Howard, Timothy Edward, Jan. 27, 1837–July 9, 1916.
Vol. 5, Pt. 1–281
Howard, Volney Erskine, Oct. 22, 1809–May 14, 1889.
Vol. 5, Pt. 1–282
Howard, William Alanson, Apr. 8, 1813–Apr. 10, 1880.
Vol. 5, Pt. 1–282
Howard, William Travis, Jan. 12, 1821–July 31, 1907.
Supp. 1–436
Howard, Willie, Apr. 13, 1886–Jan. 12, 1949.
Supp. 4–400
Howe, Albion Parris, Mar. 25, 1818–Jan. 25, 1897.
Vol. 5, Pt. 1–283
Howe, Andrew Jackson, Apr. 14, 1825–Jan. 16, 1892.
Vol. 5, Pt. 1–283
Howe, Edgar Watson, May 3, 1853–Oct. 3, 1937.
Supp. 2–325
Howe, Elias, July 9, 1819–Oct. 3, 1867.
Vol. 5, Pt. 1–284
Howe, Frederic Clemson, Nov. 21, 1867–Aug. 3, 1940.
Supp. 2–326
Howe, Frederick Webster, Aug. 28, 1822–Apr. 25, 1891.
Vol. 5, Pt. 1–286
Howe, George, Nov. 6, 1802–Apr. 15, 1883.
Vol. 5, Pt. 1–286
Howe, George Augustus, *c.* 1724–July 6, 1758.
Vol. 5, Pt. 1–287
Howe, Henry, Oct. 11, 1816–Oct. 14, 1893.
Vol. 5, Pt. 1–288
Howe, Henry Marion, Mar. 2, 1848–May 14, 1922.
Vol. 5, Pt. 1–289
Howe, Herbert Alonzo, Nov. 22, 1858–Nov. 2, 1926.
Vol. 5, Pt. 1–289
Howe, James Wong, Aug. 28, 1899–July 12, 1976.
Supp. 10–347
Howe, John Ireland, July 20, 1793–Sept. 10, 1876.
Vol. 5, Pt. 1–290
Howe, Julia Ward, May 27, 1819–Oct. 17, 1910.
Vol. 5, Pt. 1–291
Howe, Louis McHenry, Jan. 14, 1871–Apr. 18, 1936.
Supp. 2–328
Howe, Lucien, Sept. 18, 1848–Dec. 27, 1928.
Vol. 5, Pt. 1–293
Howe, Mark Anthony De Wolfe, Apr. 5, 1808–July 31, 1895.
Vol. 5, Pt. 1–293
Howe, Mark Antony De Wolfe, Aug. 23, 1864–Dec. 6, 1960.
Supp. 6–306
Howe, Mark De Wolfe, May 22, 1906–Feb. 28, 1967.
Supp. 8–284
Howe, Percy Rogers, Sept. 20, 1864–Feb. 28, 1950.
Supp. 4–401
Howe, Quincy, Aug. 17, 1900–Feb. 17, 1977.
Supp. 10–348
Howe, Robert, 1732–Dec. 14, 1786.
Vol. 5, Pt. 1–294
Howe, Samuel, June 20, 1785–Jan. 20, 1828
Vol. 5, Pt. 1–295
Howe, Samuel Gridley, Nov. 10, 1801–Jan. 9, 1876.
Vol. 5, Pt. 1–296
Howe, Timothy Otis, Feb. 24, 1816–Mar. 25, 1883.
Vol. 5, Pt. 1–297
Howe, William, May 12, 1803–Sept. 19, 1852.
Vol. 5, Pt. 1–298
Howe, William F., July 7, 1828–Sept. 1, 1902.
Vol. 5, Pt. 1–299
Howe, William Henry, Nov. 22, 1846–Mar. 16, 1929.
Vol. 5, Pt. 1–299
Howe, William Wirt, Nov. 24, 1833–Mar. 17, 1909.
Vol. 5, Pt. 1–300
Howell, Albert Summers, Apr. 17, 1879–Jan. 3, 1951.
Supp. 5–321
Howell, Clark, Sept. 21, 1863–Nov. 14, 1936.
Supp. 2–329
Howell, David, Jan. 1, 1747–July 30, 1824.
Vol. 5, Pt. 1–301
Howell, Evan Park, Dec. 10, 1839–Aug. 6, 1905.
Vol. 5, Pt. 1–301
Howell, James Bruen, July 4, 1816–June 17, 1880.
Vol. 5, Pt. 1–302
Howell, John Adams, Mar. 16, 1840–Jan. 10, 1918.
Vol. 5, Pt. 1–303
Howell, Richard, Oct. 25, 1754–Apr. 28, 1802.
Vol. 5, Pt. 1–304
Howell, Robert Boyté Crawford, Mar. 10, 1801–Apr. 5, 1868.
Vol. 5, Pt. 1–304
Howell, Thomas Jefferson, Oct. 9, 1842–Dec. 3, 1912.
Vol. 5, Pt. 1–305
Howell, William Henry, Feb. 20, 1860–Feb. 6, 1945.
Supp. 3–369
Howells, William Dean, Mar. 1, 1837–May 11, 1920.
Vol. 5, Pt. 1–306
Howey, Walter Crawford, Jan. 16, 1882–Mar. 21, 1954.
Supp. 5–323
Howison, George Holmes, Nov. 29, 1834–Dec. 31, 1916.
Vol. 5, Pt. 1–311
Howland, Alfred Cornelius, Feb. 12, 1838–Mar. 17, 1909
Vol. 5, Pt. 1–311
Howland, Emily, Nov. 20, 1827–June 29, 1929.
Vol. 5, Pt. 1–312
Howland, Gardiner Greene, Sept. 4, 1787–Nov. 9, 1851.
Vol. 5, Pt. 1–312
Howland, John, Feb. 3, 1873–June 20, 1926.
Vol. 5, Pt. 1–313
Howley, Richard, 1740–1784.
Vol. 5, Pt. 1–314
Howry, Charles Bowen, May 14, 1844–July 20, 1928.
Vol. 5, Pt. 1–315
Howze, Robert Lee, Aug. 22, 1864–Sept. 19, 1926.
Vol. 5, Pt. 1–315
Hoxie, Robert Franklin, Apr. 29, 1868–June 22, 1916.
Vol. 5, Pt. 1–316
Hoxie, Vinnie Ream, Sept. 25, 1847–Nov. 20, 1914.
Vol. 5, Pt. 1–317
Hoxie, William Dixie, July 1, 1866–Jan. 12, 1925.
Vol. 5, Pt. 1–318
Hoyme, Gjermund, Oct. 8, 1847–June 9, 1902.
Vol. 5, Pt. 1–319
Hoyt, Albert Harrison, Dec. 6, 1826–June 10, 1915.
Vol. 5, Pt. 1–319
Hoyt, Charles Hale, July 26, 1860–Nov. 20, 1900.
Vol. 5, Pt. 1–320
Hoyt, Henry Martyn, June 8, 1830–Dec. 1, 1892.
Vol. 5, Pt. 1–321
Hoyt, John Sherman. July 6, 1869–Mar. 30, 1954.
Supp. 5–324
Hoyt, John Wesley, Oct. 13, 1831–May 23, 1912.
Vol. 5, Pt. 1–321
Hrdlicka, Ales, Mar. 29, 1869–Sept. 5, 1943.
Supp. 3–371
Hubbard, Bernard Rosecrans, Nov. 24, 1888–May 28, 1962.
Supp. 7–370
Hubbard, David, *c.* 1792–Jan. 20, 1874.
Vol. 5, Pt. 1–322
Hubbard, Elbert, June 19, 1856–May 7, 1915.
Vol. 5, Pt. 1–323
Hubbard, Frank McKinney, Sept. 1, 1868–Dec. 26, 1930.
Vol. 5, Pt. 1–324
Hubbard, Gardiner Greene, Aug. 25, 1822–Dec. 11, 1897.
Vol. 5, Pt. 1–324

Hubbard, Gurdon Saltonstall, Aug. 22, 1802–Sept. 14, 1886.
Vol. 5, Pt. 1–326
Hubbard, Henry Griswold, Oct. 8, 1814–July 29, 1891.
Vol. 5, Pt. 1–327
Hubbard, Henry Guernsey, May 6, 1850–Jan. 18, 1899.
Vol. 5, Pt. 1–327
Hubbard, John, Mar. 22, 1794–Feb. 6, 1869.
Vol. 5, Pt. 1–328
Hubbard, Joseph Stillman, Sept. 7, 1823–Aug. 16, 1863.
Vol. 5, Pt. 1–329
Hubbard, Kin. [*See* Hubbard, Frank McKinney, 1868–1930.]
Hubbard, Lucius Frederick, Jan. 26, 1836–Feb. 5, 1913.
Vol. 5, Pt. 1–330
Hubbard, Richard Bennett, Nov. 1, 1832–July 12, 1901.
Vol. 5, Pt. 1–331
Hubbard, Richard William, Oct. 15, 1816–Dec. 21, 1888.
Vol. 5, Pt. 1–331
Hubbard, Robert C. ("Cal"), Oct. 31, 1900–Oct. 17, 1977.
Supp. 10–350
Hubbard, Thomas Hamlin, Dec. 20, 1838–May 19, 1915.
Vol. 5, Pt. 1–332
Hubbard, William, *c.* 1621–Sept. 14, 1704.
Vol. 5, Pt. 1–333
Hubbard, Wynant Davis, Aug. 28, 1900–Dec. 9, 1961.
Supp. 7–371
Hubbell, John Lorenzo, Nov. 27, 1853–Nov. 12, 1930.
Supp. 1–437
Hubble, Edwin, Nov. 20, 1899–Sept. 28, 1953.
Supp. 5–325
Hubbs, Rebecca, Dec. 3, 1772–Sept. 29, 1852.
Vol. 5, Pt. 1–334
Huber, Gotthelf Carl, Aug. 30, 1865–Dec. 26, 1934.
Supp. 1–438
Hubert, Conrad, 1855–Mar. 14, 1928.
Vol. 5, Pt. 1–334
Hubley, John, May 21, 1914–Feb. 21, 1977.
Supp. 10–351
Hubner, Charles William, Jan. 16, 1835–Jan. 3, 1929.
Vol. 5, Pt. 1–335
Hudde, Andries, 1608–Nov. 4, 1663.
Vol. 5, Pt. 1–335
Hudson, Charles, Nov. 14, 1795–May 4, 1881.
Vol. 5, Pt. 1–336
Hudson, Claude Silbert, Jan. 26, 1881–Dec. 27, 1952.
Supp. 5–327
Hudson, Daniel Eldred, Dec. 18, 1849–Jan. 12, 1934.
Supp. 1–440
Hudson, Edward, October 1772–Jan. 3, 1833.
Vol. 5, Pt. 1–337
Hudson, Frederic, Apr. 25, 1819–Oct 21, 1875.
Supp. 1–441
Hudson, Henry, d. after June 23, 1611.
Vol. 5, Pt. 1–338
Hudson, Henry Norman, Jan. 28, 1814–Jan. 16, 1886.
Vol. 5, Pt. 1–340
Hudson, Manley Ottmer, May 19, 1886–Apr. 13, 1960.
Supp. 6–307
Hudson, Mary Clemmer Ames. [*See* Clemmer, Mary, 1839–1884.]
Hudson, Thomson Jay, Feb. 22, 1834–May 26, 1903.
Vol. 5, Pt. 1–341
Hudson, William Smith, Mar. 13, 1810–July 20, 1881.
Vol. 5, Pt. 1–342
Huebner, Solomon Stephen, Mar. 6, 1882–July 17, 1964.
Supp. 7–373
Huebsch, Benjamin W., Mar. 21, 1876–Aug. 7, 1964.
Supp. 7–373
Huger, Benjamin, Nov. 22, 1805–Dec. 7, 1877.
Vol. 5, Pt. 1–343
Huger, Daniel Elliott, June 28, 1779–Aug. 21, 1854.
Vol. 5, Pt. 1–343
Huger, Francis Kinloch, Sept. 17, 1773–Feb. 14, 1855.
Vol. 5, Pt. 1–344
Huger, Isaac, Mar. 19, 1742/43–Oct. 17, 1797
Vol. 5, Pt. 1–344
Huger, John, June 5, 1744–Jan. 22, 1804.
Vol. 5, Pt. 1–345
Huggins, Miller James, Apr. 19, 1879–Sept 25, 1929.
Vol. 5, Pt. 1–345
Hughes, Albert William, Jan. 21, 1891–Mar. 22, 1979.
Supp. 10–353
Hughes, Charles Evans, Apr. 11, 1862–Aug. 27, 1948.
Supp. 4–403
Hughes, Charles Frederick, Oct. 14, 1866–May 28, 1934.
Supp. 1–441
Hughes, Christopher, 1786–Sept. 18, 1849.
Vol. 5, Pt. 1–346
Hughes, David Edward, May 16, 1831–Jan. 22, 1900.
Vol. 5, Pt. 1–347
Hughes, Dudley Mays, Oct. 10, 1848–Jan. 20, 1927.
Vol. 5, Pt. 1–348
Hughes, Edwin Holt, Dec. 7, 1866–Feb. 12, 1950.
Supp. 4–408
Hughes, George Wurtz, Sept. 30, 1806–Dec. 3, 1870.
Vol. 5, Pt. 1–348
Hughes, Hector James, Oct. 23, 1871–Mar. 1, 1930.
Vol. 5, Pt. 1–349
Hughes, Henry, d. Oct. 3, 1862.
Vol. 5, Pt. 1–350
Hughes, Howard Robard, Sept. 9, 1869–Jan. 14, 1924.
Vol. 5, Pt. 1–351
Hughes, Howard Robard, Jr., Sept. 24, 1905–Apr. 5, 1976.
Supp. 10–355
Hughes, James, Nov. 24, 1823–Oct. 21, 1873.
Vol. 5, Pt. 1–351
Hughes, James Langston, Feb. 1, 1902–May 22, 1967.
Supp. 8–285
Hughes, John Joseph, June 24, 1797–Jan. 3, 1864.
Vol. 5, Pt. 1–352
Hughes, Price, d. 1715.
Vol. 5, Pt. 1–355
Hughes, Robert Ball, Jan. 19, 1806–Mar. 5, 1868.
Vol. 5, Pt. 1–356
Hughes, Robert William, Jan. 16, 1821–Dec. 10, 1901.
Vol. 5, Pt. 1–357
Hughes, Rupert, Jan. 31, 1872–Sept. 9, 1956.
Supp. 6–308
Huidekoper, Frederic, Apr. 7, 1817–May 16, 1892.
Vol. 5, Pt. 1–358
Huidekoper, Harm Jan, Apr. 3, 1776–May 22, 1854.
Vol. 5, Pt. 1–359
Hulbert, Archer Butler, Jan. 26, 1873–Dec. 24, 1933.
Supp. 1–442
Hulbert, Edwin James, Apr. 30, 1829–Oct. 20, 1910.
Vol. 5, Pt. 1–360
Hull, Clark Leonard, May 24, 1884–May 10, 1952.
Supp. 5–328
Hull, Cordell, Oct. 2, 1871–July 23, 1955.
Supp. 5–331
Hull, Isaac, Mar. 9, 1773–Feb. 13, 1843.
Vol. 5, Pt. 1–360
Hull, John, Dec. 18, 1624–Oct. 1, 1683.
Vol. 5, Pt. 1–362
Hull, Josephine, Jan. 3, 1886¿-Mar. 12, 1957.
Supp. 6–310
Hull, William, June 24, 1753–Nov. 29, 1825.
Vol. 5, Pt. 1–363
Hullihen, Simon P., Dec. 10, 1810–Mar. 27, 1857.
Vol. 5, Pt. 1–364
Humbert, Jean Joseph Amable, Nov. 25, 1755–Jan. 2, 1823.
Vol. 5, Pt. 1–365
Hume, Edgar Erskine, Dec. 26, 1889–Jan. 24, 1952.
Supp. 5–335
Hume, Robert Allen, Mar. 18, 1847–June 24, 1929.
Vol. 5, Pt. 1–365
Hume, William, Nov. 19, 1830–June 25, 1902.
Vol. 5, Pt. 1–366
Humes, Thomas William, Apr. 22, 1815–Jan. 16, 1892.
Vol. 5, Pt. 1–367
Humiston, William Henry, Apr. 27, 1869–Dec. 5, 1923.
Vol. 5, Pt. 1–367
Hummel, Abraham Henry, July 27, 1850–Jan. 22, 1926.
Vol. 5, Pt. 1–368
Humphrey, Doris, Oct. 17, 1895–Dec. 29, 1958.
Supp. 6–312
Humphrey, George Magoffin, Mar. 8, 1890–Jan. 20, 1970.
Supp. 8–289
Humphrey, Heman, Mar. 26, 1779–Apr. 3, 1861.
Vol. 5, Pt. 1–369
Humphrey, Hubert Horatio, Jr., May 27, 1911–Jan. 13, 1978.
Supp. 10–359

Humphreys, Alexander Crombie, Mar. 30, 1851–Aug. 14, 1927
Vol. 5, Pt. 1–370
Humphreys, Andrew Atkinson, Nov. 2, 1810–Dec. 27, 1883.
Vol. 5, Pt. 1–371
Humphreys, Benjamin Grubb, Aug. 24 or 26, 1808–Dec. 20, 1882.
Vol. 5, Pt. 1–372
Humphreys, David, July 10, 1752–Feb. 21, 1818.
Vol. 5, Pt. 1–373
Humphreys, James, Jan. 15, 1748–Feb. 2, 1810.
Vol. 5, Pt. 1–375
Humphreys, Joshua, June 17, 1751–Jan. 12, 1838.
Vol. 5, Pt. 1–376
Humphreys, Milton Wylie, Sept. 15, 1844–Nov. 20, 1928.
Vol. 5, Pt. 1–377
Humphreys, West Hughes, Aug. 26, 1806–Oct. 16, 1882.
Vol. 5, Pt. 1–378
Humphreys, William Jackson, Feb. 3, 1862–Nov. 10, 1949.
Supp, 4–409
Humphries, George Rolfe, Nov. 20, 1894–Apr. 22, 1969.
Supp. 8–290
Huneker, James Gibbons, Jan. 31, 1860–Feb. 9, 1921.
Vol. 5, Pt. 1–379
Hunnewelt, Horatio Hollis, July 27, 1810–Mar. 20, 1902.
Vol. 5, Pt. 1–380
Hunnewell, James, Feb. 10, 1794–May 2, 1869.
Vol. 5, Pt. 1–381
Hunt, Alfred Ephraim, Mar. 31, 1855–Apr. 26, 1899.
Vol. 5, Pt. 1–381
Hunt, Benjamin Weeks, May 18, 1847–June 26, 1934.
Supp. 1–443
Hunt, Carleton, Jan. 1, 1836–Aug. 14, 1921.
Vol. 5, Pt. 1–382
Hunt, Charles Wallace, Oct. 13, 1841–Mar. 27, 1911.
Vol. 5, Pt. 1–383
Hunt, Freeman, Mar. 21, 1804–Mar. 2, 1858.
Vol. 5, Pt. 1–384
Hunt, Gaillard, Sept. 8, 1862–Mar. 20, 1924.
Vol. 5, Pt. 1–385
Hunt, George Wylie Paul, Nov. 1, 1859–Dec. 24, 1934.
Supp. 1–444
Hunt, Haroldson Lafayette, Feb. 17, 1889–Nov. 29, 1974.
Supp. 9–410
Hunt, Harriot Kezia, Nov. 9, 1805–Jan. 2, 1875.
Vol. 5, Pt. 1–385
Hunt, Henry Jackson, Sept. 14, 1819–Feb. 11, 1889.
Vol. 5, Pt. 1–386
Hunt, Isaac, *c.* 1742–1809.
Vol. 5, Pt. 1–387
Hunt, Lester Callaway, July 8, 1892–June 19, 1954.
Supp. 5–336
Hunt, Mary Hannah Hanchett, June 4, 1830–Apr. 24, 1906.
Vol. 5, Pt. 1–388
Hunt, Nathan, Oct. 26, 1758–Aug. 8, 1853.
Vol. 5, Pt. 1–389
Hunt, Reid, Apr. 20, 1870–Mar. 10, 1948.
Supp. 4–410
Hunt, Richard Morris, Oct. 31, 1827–July 31, 1895.
Vol. 5, Pt. 1–389
Hunt, Robert, *c.* 1568–1608.
Vol. 5, Pt. 1–391
Hunt, Robert Woolston, Dec. 9, 1838–July 11, 1923.
Vol. 5, Pt. 1–392
Hunt, Theodore Whitefield, Feb. 19, 1844–Apr. 12, 1930.
Vol. 5, Pt. 1–393
Hunt, Thomas Sterry, Sept. 5, 1826–Feb. 12, 1892.
Vol. 5, Pt. 1–393
Hunt, Ward, June 14, 1810–Mar. 24, 1886.
Vol. 5, Pt. 1–394
Hunt, Washington, Aug. 5, 1811–Feb. 2, 1867.
Vol. 5, Pt. 1–395
Hunt, William Gibbes, Feb. 21, 1791–Aug. 13, 1833.
Vol. 5, Pt. 1–396
Hunt, William Henry, June 12, 1823–Feb. 27, 1884.
Vol. 5, Pt. 1–396
Hunt, William Morris, Mar. 31, 1824–Sept. 8, 1879.
Vol. 5, Pt. 1–397
Hunt, Wilson Price, 1782?–Apr. 1842.
Vol. 5, Pt. 1–398
Hunter, Andrew, 1751–Feb. 24, 1823.
Vol. 5, Pt. 1–399
Hunter, Croil, Feb. 18, 1893–July 21, 1970.
Supp. 8–291
Hunter, David, July 21, 1802–Feb. 2, 1886.
Vol. 5, Pt. 1–400
Hunter, Ivory Joe, Oct. 10, 1911–Nov. 8, 1974.
Supp. 9–413
Hunter, Robert, d. March 1734.
Vol. 5, Pt. 1–401
Hunter, Robert, Apr. 10, 1874–May 15, 1942.
Supp. 3–372
Hunter, Robert Mercer Taliaferro, Apr. 21, 1809–July 18, 1887.
Vol. 5, Pt. 1–403
Hunter, Thomas, Oct. 19, 1831–Oct. 14, 1915.
Vol. 5, Pt. 1–405
Hunter, Walter David, Dec. 14, 1875–Oct. 13, 1925.
Vol. 5, Pt. 1–406
Hunter, Whiteside Godfrey, Dec. 25, 1841–Nov. 2, 1917.
Vol. 5, Pt. 1–406
Hunter, William, Nov. 26, 1774–Dec. 3, 1849.
Vol. 5, Pt. 1–407
Hunter, William C., 1812–June 25, 1891.
Vol. 5, Pt. 1–408
Huntington, Collis Potter, Oct. 22, 1821–Aug. 13, 1900.
Vol. 5, Pt. 1–408
Huntington, Daniel, Oct. 14, 1816–Apr. 18, 1906.
Vol. 5, Pt. 1–412
Huntington, Edward Vermilye, Apr. 26, 1874–Nov. 25, 1952.
Supp. 5–338
Huntington, Ehsha, Apr. 9, 1796–Dec. 13, 1865.
Vol. 5, Pt. 1–413
Huntington, Ellsworth, Sept. 16, 1876–Oct. 17, 1947.
Supp. 4–412
Huntington, Frederic Dan, May 28, 1819–July 11, 1904.
Vol. 5, Pt. 1–413
Huntington, Henry Edwards, Feb. 27, 1850–May 23, 1927.
Vol. 5, Pt. 1–414
Huntington, Jabez, Aug. 7, 1719–Oct. 5, 1786.
Vol. 5, Pt. 1–416
Huntington, Jedediah, Aug. 4, 1743–Sept. 25, 1818.
Vol. 5, Pt. 1–416
Huntington, Jedediah Vincent, Jan. 20, 1815–Mar. 10, 1862.
Vol. 5, Pt. 1–417
Huntington, Margaret Jane Evans, Jan. 9, 1842–Mar. 17, 1926.
Vol. 5, Pt. 1–418
Huntington, Samuel, July 3, 1731–Jan. 5, 1796.
Vol. 5, Pt. 1–418
Huntington, Samuel, Oct. 4, 1765–June 8, 1817.
Vol. 5, Pt. 1–419
Huntington, William Edwards, July 30, 1844–Dec. 6, 1930.
Vol. 5, Pt. 1–420
Huntington. William Reed, Sept. 20, 1838–July 26, 1909.
Vol. 5, Pt. 1–420
Huntley, Chester ("Chet") Robert, Dec. 10, 1911–Mar. 20, 1974.
Supp. 9–414
Hunton, Eppa, Sept. 22, 1822–Oct. 11, 1908.
Vol. 5, Pt. 1–421
Hunton, George Kenneth, Mar. 24, 1888–Nov. 11, 1967.
Supp. 8–293
Hunton, William Lee, Feb. 16, 1864–Oct. 12, 1930.
Vol. 5, Pt. 1–422
Hupp, Louis Gorham, Nov. 13, 1872–Dec. 10, 1961.
Supp. 7–375
Hurd, John Codman, Nov. 11, 1816–June 25, 1892
Vol. 5, Pt. 1–423
Hurd, Nathaniel, Feb. 13, 1730–Dec. 17, 1777.
Vol. 5, Pt. 1–423
Hurlbert, William Henry, July 3, 1827–Sept. 4, 1895.
Vol. 5, Pt. 1–424
Hurlbut, Jesse Lyman, Feb. 15, 1843–Aug. 2, 1930.
Vol. 5, Pt. 1–424
Hurlbut, Stephen Augustus, Nov. 29, 1815–Mar. 27, 1882.
Vol. 5, Pt. 1–425
Hurley, Edward Nash, July 31, 1864–Nov. 14, 1933.
Supp. 1–446
Hurley, Joseph Patrick, Jan. 21, 1894–Oct. 30, 1967.
Supp. 8–294

Hurley, Patrick Jay, Jan. 8, 1883–July 30, 1963.
Supp. 7–376
Hurley, Roy T., June 3, 1896–Oct. 31, 1971.
Supp. 9–416
Hurok, Solomon Isaievitch, Apr. 9, 1888–Mar. 5, 1974.
Supp. 9–417
Hurst, Fannie, Oct. 19, 1889–Feb. 23, 1968.
Supp. 8–296
Hurst, John Fletcher, Aug. 17, 1834–May 4, 1903.
Vol. 5, Pt. 1–426
Hurston, Zora Neale, Jan. 3, 1901–Jan. 28, 1960.
Supp. 6–313
Husbands, Hermon, Oct. 3, 1724–1795.
Vol. 2, Pt. 2–427
Huse, Caleb, Feb. 11, 1831–Mar. 11, 1905.
Vol. 5, Pt. 1–428
Husing, Edward Britt ("Ted"), Nov. 27, 1901–Aug. 10, 1962.
Supp. 7–377
Husk, Charles Ellsworth, Dec. 19, 1872–Mar. 20, 1916.
Vol. 5, Pt. 1–429
Husmann, George, Nov. 4, 1827–Nov. 5, 1902.
Vol. 5, Pt. 1–430
Hussey, Curtis Grubb, Aug. 11, 1802–Apr. 25, 1893.
Vol. 5, Pt. 1–430
Hussey, Obed, 1792–Aug. 4, 1860.
Vol. 5, Pt. 1–431
Hussey, William Joseph, Aug. 10, 1862–Oct. 28, 1926.
Vol. 5, Pt. 1–432
Husting, Paul Oscar, Apr. 25, 1866–Oct. 21, 1917.
Vol. 5, Pt. 1–433
Huston, Charles, July 23, 1822–Jan. 5, 1897.
Vol. 5, Pt. 1–433
Huston, Walter, Apr. 6, 1884–Apr. 7, 1950.
Supp. 4–414
Hutcheson, William Levi, Feb. 7, 1874–Oct. 20, 1953.
Supp. 5–339
Hutchins, Harry Burns, Apr. 8, 1847–Jan. 25, 1930.
Vol. 5, Pt. 1–434
Hutchins, Robert Maynard, Jan. 17, 1899–May 15, 1977.
Supp. 10–363
Hutchins, Thomas, 1730–Apr. 28, 1789.
Vol. 5, Pt. 1–435
Hutchinson, Anne, 1591–1643.
Vol. 5, Pt. 1–436
Hutchinson, Benjamin Peters, July 24, 1829–Mar. 16, 1899.
Vol. 5, Pt. 437
Hutchinson, Charles Lawrence, Mar. 7, 1854–Oct. 7, 1924.
Vol. 5, Pt. 1–438
Hutchinson, James, Jan. 29, 1752–Sept. 5, 1793.
Vol. 5, Pt. 1–438
Hutchinson, Paul, Aug. 10, 1890–Apr. 15, 1956.
Supp. 6–315
Hutchinson, Thomas, Sept. 9, 1711–June 3, 1780.
Vol. 5, Pt. 1–439
Hutchinson, Woods, Jan. 3, 1862–Apr. 26, 1930.
Vol. 5, Pt. 1–443
Hutson, Richard, July 9, 1748–Apr. 12, 1795.
Vol. 5, Pt. 1–443
Hutton, Barbara Woolworth, Nov. 14, 1812–May 11, 1979.
Supp. 10–366
Hutton, Edward Francis, Sept. 7, 1875–July 11, 1962.
Supp. 7–379
Hutton, Frederick Remsen, May 28, 1853–May 14, 1918.
Vol. 5, Pt. 1–444
Hutton, Laurence, Aug. 8, 1843–June 10, 1904.
Vol. 5, Pt. 1–445
Hutton, Levi William, Oct. 22, 1860–Nov. 3, 1928.
Vol. 5, Pt. 1–445
Huxley, Aldous Leonard, July 26, 1894–Nov. 22, 1963.
Supp. 7–380
Hyatt, Alpheus, Apr. 5, 1838–Jan. 15, 1902.
Vol. 5, Pt. 1–446
Hyatt, John Wesley, Nov. 28, 1837–May 10, 1920.
Vol. 5, Pt. 1–447
Hyde, Arthur Mastick, July 12, 1877–Oct. 17, 1947.
Supp. 4–415
Hyde, Charles Cheney, May 22, 1873–Feb. 13, 1952.
Supp. 5–340
Hyde, Edward, *c.* 1650–Sept. 8, 1712.
Vol. 5, Pt. 1–449
Hyde, Edward. [*See* Cornbury, Edward Hyde, Viscount, 1661–1723.]
Hyde, Helen, Apr. 6, 1868–May 13, 1919.
Vol. 5, Pt. 1–449
Hyde, Henry Baldwin, Feb. 15, 1834–May 2, 1899.
Vol. 5, Pt. 1–450
Hyde, James Nevins, June 21, 1840–Sept. 6, 1910
Vol. 5, Pt. 1–451
Hyde, William DeWitt, Sept. 23, 1858–June 29, 1917.
Vol. 5, Pt. 1–452
Hyer, Robert Stewart, Oct. 18, 1860–May 29, 1929.
Vol. 5, Pt. 1–453
Hylan, John Francis, Apr. 20, 1868–Jan. 12, 1936.
Supp. 2–330
Hyrne, Edmund Massingberd, Jan. 14, 1748–Dec. 1783.
Vol. 5, Pt. 1–454
Hyslop, James Hervey, Aug. 18, 1854–June 17, 1920.
Vol. 5, Pt. 1–454
Hyvernat, Henri, June 30, 1858–May 29, 1941.
Supp. 3–374

Iberville, Pierre Le Moyne, Sieur d', July 1661–July 9, 1706.
Vol. 5, Pt. 1–455
Ickes, Harold Le Clair, Mar. 15, 1874–Feb. 3, 1952.
Supp. 5–341
Iddings, Joseph Paxon, Jan. 21, 1857–Sept. 8, 1920.
Vol. 5, Pt. 1–457
Ide, Henry Clay, Sept. 18, 1844–June 13, 1921.
Vol. 5, Pt. 1–458
Ide, John Jay, June 26, 1892–Jan. 12, 1962.
Supp. 7–381
Iglesias, Santiago, Feb. 22, 1872–Dec. 5, 1939.
Supp. 2–331
Ik Marvel. [*See* Mitchell, Donald Grant, 1822–1908.]
Illington, Margaret, July 23, 1879–Mar. 11, 1934.
Supp. 1–447
Ilpendam, Jan Jansen Van. [*See* Van Ilpendam, Jan Jansen, *c.* 1595–1647.]
Imber, Naphtali Herz, Dec. 27, 1856–Oct. 8, 1909.
Vol. 5, Pt. 1–459
Imbert, Antoine, d. *c.* 1835.
Vol. 5, Pt. 1–460
Imboden, John Daniel, Feb. 16, 1823–Aug. 15, 1895.
Vol. 5, Pt. 1–460
Imlay, Gilbert, *c.* 1754–Nov. 20, 1828?.
Vol. 5, Pt. 1–461
Ingalls, John James, Dec. 29, 1833–Aug. 16, 1900.
Vol. 5, Pt. 1–462
Ingalls, Marilla Baker, Nov. 25, 1828–Dec. 17, 1902.
Vol. 5, Pt. 1–463
Ingalls, Melville Ezra, Sept. 6, 1842–July 11, 1914.
Vol. 5, Pt. 1–464
Ingals, Ephraim Fletcher, Sept. 29, 1848–Apr. 30, 1918.
Vol. 5, Pt. 1–464
Inge, William Motter, May 3, 1913–June 10, 1973.
Supp. 9–421
Ingelfinger, Franz Joseph, Aug. 20, 1910–Mar. 26, 1980.
Supp. 10–369
Ingersoll, Charles Jared, Oct. 3, 1782–May 14, 1862.
Vol. 5, Pt. 1–465
Ingersoll, Edward, Apr. 2, 1817–Feb. 19, 1893.
Vol. 5, Pt. 1–467
Ingersoll, Jared, 1722–Aug. 25, 1781.
Vol. 5, Pt. 1–467
Ingersoll, Jared, Oct. 27, 1749–Oct. 31, 1822.
Vol. 5, Pt. 1–468
Ingersoll, Robert Green, Aug. 11, 1833–July 21, 1899.
Vol. 5, Pt. 1–469
Ingersoll, Robert Hawley, Dec. 26, 1859–Sept. 4, 1928.
Vol. 5, Pt. 1–470
Ingersoll, Royal Eason, June 20, 1883–May 20, 1976.
Supp. 10–370
Ingersoll, Royal Rodney, Dec. 4, 1847–Apr. 21, 1931.
Vol. 5, Pt. 1–471
Ingersoll, Simon, Mar. 3, 1818–July 24, 1894.
Vol. 5, Pt. 1–472
Ingham, Charles Cromwell, 1796–Dec. 10, 1863.
Vol. 5, Pt. 1–473
Ingham, Samuel Delucenna, Sept. 16, 1779–June 5, 1860.
Vol. 5, Pt. 1–473

Ingle, Richard, 1609–c. 1653.
Vol. 5, Pt. 1–474
Inglis, Alexander James, Nov. 24, 1879–Apr. 12, 1924.
Vol. 5, Pt. 1–475
Inglis, Charles, 1734–Feb. 24, 1816.
Vol. 5, Pt. 1–476
Ingraham, Duncan Nathaniel, Dec. 6, 1802–Oct. 16, 1891.
Vol. 5, Pt. 1–476
Ingraham, Edward Duffield, Feb. 12, 1793–Nov. 5, 1854.
Vol. 5, Pt. 1–477
Ingraham, Joseph, 1762–1800.
Vol. 5. Pt. 1–478
Ingraham, Joseph Holt, Jan. 25 or 26, 1809–Dec. 18, 1860.
Vol. 5, Pt. 1–479
Ingraham, Prentiss, Dec. 22, 1843–Aug. 16, 1904.
Vol. 5, Pt. 1–480
Ingram, Jonas Howard, Oct. 15, 1886–Sept. 10, 1952.
Supp. 5–344
Inman, George, Dec. 3, 1755–c. February 1789.
Vol. 5, Pt. 1–480
Inman, Henry, July 30, 1837–Nov. 13, 1899.
Vol. 5, Pt. 1–482
Inman, Henry, Oct. 28, 1801–Jan. 17, 1846.
Vol. 5, Pt. 1–481
Inman, John, 1805–Mar. 30, 1850.
Vol. 5, Pt. 1–483
Inman, John Hamilton, Oct. 6, 1844–Nov. 5, 1896.
Vol. 5, Pt. 1–484
Inman, Samuel Martin, Feb. 19, 1843–Jan. 12, 1915.
Vol. 5, Pt. 1–485
Innes, Harry, Jan. 4, 1752 o.s.-Sept. 20, 1816.
Vol. 5, Pt. 1–485
Innes, James, 1754–Aug. 2, 1798.
Vol. 5, Pt. 1–486
Inness, George, May 1, 1825–Aug. 3, 1894.
Vol. 5, Pt. 1–487
Innokentiĭ, Aug. 26, 1797–Mar. 31, 1879.
Vol. 5, Pt. 1–489
Inshtatheamba. [See Bright Eyes, 1854–1903]
Inskip, John Swanel, Aug. 10, 1816–Mar. 7, 1884.
Vol. 5, Pt. 1–490
Insull, Samuel, Nov. 11, 1859–July 16, 1938.
Supp. 2–333
Ïoasaf, Jan. 22/Feb. 4, 1761–November 1799.
Vol. 5 Pt. 1–491
Ioor, William, fl. 1780–1830.
Vol. 5, Pt. 1–491
Iredell, James, Oct. 5, 1751–Oct. 20, 1799.
Vol. 5, Pt. 1–492
Ireland, Charles Thomas, Jr. ("Chick"), Apr. 14, 1921–June 7, 1972.
Supp. 9–422
Ireland, John, Jan. 1, 1827–Mar. 15, 1896.
Vol. 5, Pt. 1–493
Ireland, John, Sept. 11, 1838–Sept. 25, 1918.
Vol. 5, Pt. 1–494
Ireland, Joseph Norton, Apr. 24, 1817–Dec. 29, 1898.
Vol. 5, Pt. 1–497
Irene, Sister, May 12, 1823–Aug. 14, 1896.
Vol. 5, Pt. 1–498
Ironside, Henry Allan, Oct. 14, 1876–Jan. 15, 1951.
Supp. 5–345
Irvine, James, Aug. 4, 1735–Apr. 28, 1819.
Vol. 5, Pt. 1–499
Irvine, William, Nov. 3, 1741–July 29, 1804.
Vol. 5, Pt. 1–500
Irvine, William Mann, Oct. 13, 1865–June 11, 1928.
Vol. 5, Pt. 1–501
Irving, John Beaufain, Nov. 26, 1825–Apr. 20, 1877.
Vol. 5, Pt. 1–501
Irving, John Duer, Aug. 18, 1874–July 20, 1918.
Vol. 5, Pt. 1–502
Irving, John Treat, Dec. 2, 1812–Feb. 27, 1906.
Vol. 5, Pt. 1–503
Irving, Peter, Oct. 30, 1771–June 27, 1838.
Vol. 5, Pt. 1–503
Irving, Pierre Munro, 1803–1876.
Vol. 5, Pt. 1–504
Irving, Roland Duer, Apr. 29, 1847–May 27, 1888.
Vol. 5, Pt. 1–505
Irving, Washington, Apr. 3, 1783–Nov. 28, 1859.
Vol. 5, Pt. 1–505
Irving, William, Aug. 15, 1766–Nov. 9, 1821.
Vol. 5, Pt. 1–511
Irwin, Elisabeth Antoinette, Aug. 29, 1880–Oct. 16, 1942.
Supp. 3–375
Irwin, George Le Roy, Apr. 26, 1868–Feb. 19, 1931.
Vol. 5, Pt. 1–512
Irwin, May, June 27, 1862–Oct. 22, 1938.
Supp. 2–335
Irwin, Robert Benjamin, June 2, 1883–Dec. 12, 1951.
Supp. 5–347
Irwin, William Henry, Sept. 14, 1873–Feb. 24, 1948.
Supp. 4–417
Isaacs, Abram Samuel, Aug. 30, 1851–Dec. 22, 1920.
Vol. 5, Pt. 1–513
Isaacs, Samuel Myer, Jan. 4, 1804–May 19, 1878.
Vol. 5, Pt. 1–513
Isbrandtsen, Hans Jeppesen, Sept. 7, 1891–May 13, 1953.
Supp. 5–348
Isham, Ralph Heyward, July 2, 1890–June 13, 1955.
Supp. 5–349
Isham, Samuel, May 12, 1855–June 12, 1914.
Vol. 5, Pt. 1–514
Isherwood, Benjamin Franklin, Oct. 6, 1822–June 19, 1915.
Vol. 5, Pt. 1–515
Isom, Mary Frances, Feb. 27, 1865–Apr. 15, 1920.
Vol. 5, Pt. 1–516
Iturbi, José, Nov. 28, 1895–June 28, 1980.
Supp. 10–372
Iverson, Alfred, Dec. 3, 1798–Mar. 4, 1873.
Vol. 5, Pt. 1–517
Ives, Charles Edward, Oct. 20, 1874–May 19, 1954.
Supp. 5–351
Ives, Chauncey Bradley, Dec. 14, 1810–Aug. 2, 1894.
Vol. 5, Pt. 1–518
Ives, Eli, Feb. 7, 1778–Oct. 8, 1861.
Vol. 5, Pt. 1–518
Ives, Frederic Eugene, Feb. 17, 1856–May 27, 1937.
Supp. 2–337
Ives, Halsey Cooley, Oct. 27, 1847–May 5, 1911.
Vol. 5, Pt. 1–519
Ives, Irving McNell, Jan. 24, 1896–Feb. 24, 1962.
Supp. 7–382
Ives, James Merritt, Mar. 5, 1824–Jan. 3, 1895.
Vol. 5, Pt. 1–520
Ives, Joseph Christmas, 1828–Nov. 12, 1868.
Vol. 5, Pt. 1–520
Ives, Levi Silliman, Sept. 16, 1797–Oct. 13, 1867.
Vol. 5, Pt. 1–521
Ivins, Anthony Woodward, Sept. 16, 1852–Sept. 23, 1934.
Supp. 1–448
Ivins, William Mills, Apr. 22, 1851–July 23, 1915.
Vol. 5, Pt. 1–522
Izard, George, Oct. 21, 1776–Nov. 22, 1828.
Vol. 5, Pt. 1–523
Izard, Ralph, Jan. 23, 1741/2–May 30, 1804.
Vol. 5, Pt. 1–524

Jack, Captain. [See Captain Jack, 1837?–1873.]
Jackling, Daniel Cowan, Aug. 14, 1869–Mar. 13, 1956.
Supp. 6–316
Jackman, Wilbur Samuel, Jan. 12, 1855–Jan. 28, 1907.
Vol. 5, Pt. 1–525
Jackson, Abraham Reeves, June 17, 1827–Nov. 12, 1892.
Vol. 5, Pt. 1–525
Jackson, Abraham Valentine Williams, Feb. 9, 1862–Aug. 8, 1937
Supp. 2–338
Jackson, Andrew, Mar. 15, 1767–June 8, 1845.
Vol. 5, Pt. 1–526
Jackson, Charles, May 31, 1775–Dec. 13, 1855.
Vol. 5, Pt. 1–534
Jackson, Charles Douglas, Mar. 16, 1902–Sept. 18, 1964.
Supp. 7–383
Jackson, Charles Reginald, Apr. 6, 1903–Sept. 21, 1968.
Supp. 8–297
Jackson, Charles Samuel, Sept. 15, 1860–Dec. 27, 1924.
Vol. 5, Pt. 1–535
Jackson, Charles Thomas, June 21, 1805–Aug. 28, 1880.
Vol. 5, Pt. 1–536

Jackson, Chevalier, Nov. 4, 1865–Aug. 16, 1958.
Supp. 6–317
Jackson, Claiborne Fox, Apr. 4, 1806–Dec. 6, 1862.
Vol. 5, Pt. 1–538
Jackson, Clarence Martin, Apr. 12, 1875–Jan. 17, 1947.
Supp. 4–419
Jackson, David, 1747?–Sept. 17, 1801.
Vol. 5, Pt. 1–538
Jackson, Dugald Caleb, Feb. 13, 1865–July 1, 1951.
Supp. 5–354
Jackson, Dunham, July 24, 1888–Nov. 6, 1946.
Supp. 4–420
Jackson, Edward, Mar. 30, 1856–Oct. 29, 1942.
Supp. 3–377
Jackson, Edward Payson, Mar. 15, 1840–Oct. 12, 1905.
Vol. 5, Pt. 1–539
Jackson, George K., 1758–Nov. 18, 1822.
Vol. 5, Pt. 1–539
Jackson, George Thomas, Dec. 19, 1852–Jan. 3, 1916.
Vol. 5, Pt. 1–540
Jackson, Hall, Nov. 11, 1739–Sept. 28, 1797.
Vol. 5, Pt. 1–541
Jackson, Helen Maria Fiske Hunt, Oct. 15, 1830–Aug. 1885.
Vol. 5, Pt. 1–541
Jackson, Henry Rootes, June 24, 1820–May 23, 1898.
Vol. 5, Pt. 1–543
Jackson, Howell Edmunds, Apr. 8, 1832–Aug. 8, 1895.
Vol. 5, Pt. 1–544
Jackson, James, Sept. 21, 1757–Mar. 19, 1806.
Vol. 5, Pt. 1–544
Jackson, James, Oct. 3, 1777–Aug. 27, 1867.
Vol. 5, Pt. 1–545
Jackson, James, Oct. 18, 1819–Jan. 13, 1887.
Vol. 5, Pt. 1–546
Jackson, James Caleb, Mar. 28, 1811–July 11, 1895.
Vol. 5, Pt. 1–547
Jackson, John Adams, Nov. 5, 1825–*c.* Aug. 30, 1879.
Vol. 5, Pt. 1–547
Jackson, John Brinckerhoff, Aug. 19, 1862–Dec. 20, 1920.
Vol. 5, Pt. 1–548
Jackson, John Davies, Dec. 12, 1834–Dec. 8, 1875.
Vol. 5, Pt. 1–549
Jackson, John George, Sept. 22, 1777–Mar. 28, 1825.
Vol. 5, Pt. 1–550
Jackson, Joseph Henry, July 21, 1894–July 15, 1955.
Supp. 5–355
Jackson, Mahalia, Oct. 26, 1911–Jan. 27, 1972.
Supp. 9–423
Jackson, Mercy Ruggles Bisbe, Sept. 17, 1802–Dec. 13, 1877.
Vol. 5, Pt. 1–550
Jackson, Mortimer Melville, Mar. 5, 1809–Oct. 13, 1889.
Vol. 5, Pt. 1–551
Jackson, Patrick Tracy, Aug. 14, 1780–Sept. 12, 1847.
Vol. 5, Pt. 1–552
Jackson, Robert Houghwout, Feb. 13, 1892–Oct. 9, 1954.
Supp. 5–356
Jackson, Robert R., Sept. 1, 1870–June 12, 1942.
Supp. 3–378
Jackson, Samuel, Mar. 22, 1787–Apr. 5, 1872.
Vol. 5, Pt. 1–553
Jackson, Samuel Macauley, June 19, 1851–Aug. 2, 1912.
Vol. 5, Pt. 1–553
Jackson, Sheldon, May 18, 1834–May 2, 1909.
Vol. 5, Pt. 1–555
Jackson, Shirley Hardie, Dec. 14, 1919–Aug. 8, 1965.
Supp. 7–385
Jackson, Thomas Jonathan, Jan. 21, 1824–May 10, 1863.
Vol. 5, Pt. 1–556
Jackson, William, Mar. 9, 1759–Dec. 18, 1828.
Vol. 5, Pt. 1–559
Jackson, William, Sept. 2, 1783–Feb. 27, 1855.
Vol. 5, Pt. 1–561
Jackson, William Alexander, July 25, 1905–Oct. 18, 1964.
Supp. 7–386
Jackson, William Henry, Apr. 4, 1843–June 30, 1942.
Supp. 3–379
Jackson, William Hicks, Oct. 1, 1835–Mar. 30, 1903.
Vol. 5, Pt. 1–561
Jaclede, Pierre, *c.* 1724–June 20, 1778.
Vol. 5, Pt. 2–520
Jacob, Richard Taylor, Mar. 13, 1825–Sept. 13, 1903.
Vol. 5, Pt. 1–562
Jacob, William Plumer, Mar. 15, 1842–Sept. 19, 1917.
Vol. 5, Pt. 1–568
Jacobi, Abraham, May 6, 1830–July 10, 1919.
Vol. 5, Pt. 1–563
Jacobi, Mary Corinna Putnam, Aug. 31, 1842–June 10, 1906.
Vol. 5, Pt. 1–564
Jacobs, Henry Eyster, Nov. 10, 1844–July 7, 1932.
Supp. 1–449
Jacobs, Hirsch, Apr. 8, 1904–Feb. 13, 1970.
Supp. 8–298
Jacobs, Joseph, Aug. 29, 1854–Jan. 30, 1916.
Vol. 5, Pt. 1–566
Jacobs, Joseph, Aug. 5, 1859–Sept. 7, 1929.
Vol. 5, Pt. 1–567
Jacobs, Michael, Jan. 18, 1808–July 22, 1871.
Vol. 5, Pt. 1–567
Jacobs, Michael Strauss, Mar. 10, 1880–Jan. 24, 1953.
Supp. 5–359
Jacobs, Paul, Aug. 24, 1918–Jan. 3, 1978.
Supp. 10–375
Jacobson, John Christian, Apr. 8, 1795–Nov. 24, 1870.
Vol. 5, Pt. 1–569
Jacoby, Ludwig Sigmund, Oct. 21, 1813–June 20, 1874.
Vol. 5, Pt. 1–569
Jacoby, Neil Herman, Sept. 19, 1909–May 31, 1979.
Supp. 10–376
Jadwin, Edgar, Aug. 7, 1865–Mar. 2, 1931.
Vol. 5, Pt. 1–570
Jaeger, Werner Wilhelm, July 30, 1888–Oct. 19, 1961.
Supp. 7–387
Jaggar, Thomas Augustus, Jr., Jan. 24, 1871–Jan. 17, 1953.
Supp. 5–361
James, Arthur Curtiss, June 1, 1867–June 4, 1941.
Supp. 3–381
James, Arthur Horace, July 14, 1883–Apr. 27, 1973.
Supp. 9–425
James, Charles Tillinghast, Sept. 15, 1805–Oct. 17, 1862.
Vol. 5, Pt. 1–572
James, Charles, Apr. 27, 1880–Dec. 10, 1928.
Vol. 5, Pt. 1–571
James, Daniel, Jr. ("Chappie"), Feb. 11, 1920–Feb. 25, 1978.
Supp. 10–377
James, Daniel Willis, Apr. 15, 1832–Sept. 13, 1907.
Vol. 5, Pt. 1–573
James, Edmund Janes, May 21, 1855–June 17, 1925.
Vol. 5, Pt. 1–574
James, Edward Christopher, May 1, 1841–Mar. 24, 1901.
Vol. 5, Pt. 1–575
James, Edwin, Aug. 27, 1797–Oct. 28, 1861.
Vol. 5, Pt. 1–576
James, Edwin Leland, June 25, 1890–Dec. 3, 1951.
Supp. 5–362
James, George Wharton, Sept. 27, 1858–Nov. 8, 1923.
Vol. 5, Pt. 1–577
James, Henry, June 3, 1811–Dec. 18, 1882.
Vol. 5, Pt. 1–577
James, Henry, Apr. 15, 1843–Feb. 28, 1916.
Vol. 5, Pt. 1–579
James, Jesse Woodson, Sept. 5, 1847–Apr. 3, 1882.
Vol. 5, Pt. 1–585
James, Louis, Oct. 3, 1842–Mar. 5, 1910.
Vol. 5, Pt. 1–586
James, Marquis, Aug. 29, 1891–Nov. 19, 1955.
Supp. 5–363
James, Ollie Murray, July 27, 1871–Aug. 28, 1918.
Vol. 5, Pt. 1–586
James, Thomas, 1782–Dec. 1847.
Vol. 5, Pt. 1–587
James, Thomas Chalkley, Aug. 31, 1766–July 5, 1835.
Vol. 5, Pt. 1–588
James, Thomas Lemuel, Mar. 29, 1831–Sept. 11, 1916.
Vol. 5, Pt. 1–589
James, Thomas Potts, Sept. 1, 1803–Feb. 22, 1882.
Vol. 5, Pt. 1–589
James, William, Jan. 11, 1842–Aug. 26, 1910.
Vol. 5, Pt. 1–590
James, Will Roderick, June 6, 1892–Sept. 3, 1942.
Supp. 3–382
Jameson, Horatio Gates, 1778–Aug. 26, 1855.
Vol. 5, Pt. 1–601

Jameson, John Alexander, Jan. 25, 1824–June 16, 1890.
Vol. 5, Pt. 1–601
Jameson, John Franklin, Sept. 19, 1859–Sept. 28, 1937.
Supp. 2–339
Jamison, Cecilia Viets Dakin Hamilton, 1837–Apr. 11, 1909.
Vol. 5, Pt. 1–602
Jamison, David, 1660–July 26, 1739.
Vol. 5, Pt. 1–603
Jamison, David Flavel, Dec. 14, 1810–Sept. 14, 1864.
Vol. 5, Pt. 1–604
Janauschek, Franziska Magdalena Romance, July 20, 1830–Nov. 28, 1904.
Vol. 5, Pt. 1–605
Janes, Lewis George, Feb. 19, 1844–Sept. 4, 1901.
Vol. 5, Pt. 1–606
Janeway, Edward Gamaliel, Aug. 31, 1841–Feb. 10, 1911.
Vol. 5, Pt. 1–607
Janeway, Theodore Caldwell, Nov. 2, 1872–Dec. 27, 1917.
Vol. 5, Pt. 1–608
Janin, Louis, Nov. 7, 1897–Mar. 6, 1914.
Vol. 5, Pt. 1–608
Janis, Elsie, Mar. 16, 1889–Feb. 26, 1956.
Supp. 6–318
Janney, Eli Hamilton, Nov. 12, 1831–June 16, 1912.
Vol. 5, Pt. 1–609
Janney, Oriver Edward, Mar. 8, 1856–Nov. 17, 1930.
Vol. 5, Pt. 1–610
Janney, Russell Dixon, Apr. 14, 1885–July 14, 1963.
Supp. 7–389
Janney, Samuel McPherson, Jan. 11, 1801–Apr. 30, 1880.
Vol. 5, Pt. 1–611
Jansen, Reinier, d. Mar. 6, 1706 N.S.
Vol. 5, Pt. 1–611
Jansky, Karl Guthe, Oct. 22, 1905–Feb. 14, 1950.
Supp. 4–422
Janson, Kristofer Nagel, May 5, 1841–Nov. 17, 1917.
Vol. 5, Pt. 1–612
Janssen, David, Mar. 27, 1930–Feb. 13, 1980.
Supp. 10–379
Janssens, Francis, Oct. 17, 1843–June 10, 1897.
Vol. 5, Pt. 1–613
Janvier, Catharine Ann, May 1, 1841–July 19, 1922.
Vol. 5, Pt. 1–613
Janvier, Margaret Thomson, Feb. 1844–Feb. 1913.
Vol. 5, Pt. 1–614
Janvier, Thomas Allibone, July 16, 1849–June 18, 1913.
Vol. 5, Pt. 1–615
Jaquess, James Frazier, Nov. 18, 1819–June 17, 1898.
Vol. 5, Pt. 1–615
Jardine, William Marion, Jan. 16, 1879–Jan. 17, 1955.
Supp. 5–364
Jarman, Walton Maxey, May 10, 1904–Sept. 9, 1980.
Supp.10–380.
Jarratt, Devereux, Jan. 17, 1733–Jan. 29, 1801.
Vol. 5, Pt. 1–616
Jarrell, Randall, May 6, 1914–Oct. 14, 1965.
Supp. 7–390
Jarves, Deming, 1790–Apr. 15, 1869.
Vol. 5, Pt. 1–617
Jarves, James Jackson, Aug. 20, 1818–June 28, 1888.
Vol. 5, Pt. 1–618
Jarvis, Abraham, May 5, 1739 o.s.-May 3, 1813.
Vol. 5, Pt. 1–620
Jarvis, Charles H., Dec. 20, 1837–Feb. 25, 1895.
Vol. 5, Pt. 1–621
Jarvis, Edward, Jan. 9, 1803–Oct. 31, 1884.
Vol. 5, Pt. 1–621
Jarvis, John Wesley, 1781–Jan. 14, 1839.
Vol. 5, Pt. 1–622
Jarvis, Thomas Jordan, Jan. 18, 1836–June 17, 1915.
Vol. 5, Pt. 1–623
Jarvis, William, Feb. 2, 1770–Oct. 21, 1859.
Vol. 5, Pt. 1–624
Jarvis, William Chapman, May 13, 1855–July 30, 1895.
Vol. 5, Pt. 1–625
Jasper, William, *c.* 1750–Oct. 9, 1779.
Vol. 5, Pt. 2–1
Jastrow, Joseph, Jan. 30, 1863–Jan. 8, 1944.
Supp. 3–383
Jastrow, Marcus, June 5, 1829–Oct. 13, 1903.
Vol. 5, Pt. 2–l
Jastrow, Morris, Aug. 13, 1861–June 22, 1921.
Vol. 5, Pt. 2–3
Jay, Allen, Oct. 11, 1831–May 8, 1910.
Vol. 5, Pt. 2–3
Jay, Sir James, Oct. 27, 1732–Oct. 12 or 20, 1815.
Vol. 5, Pt. 2–4
Jay, John, Dec. 12, 1745–May 17, 1829.
Vol. 5, Pt. 2–5
Jay, John, June 23, 1817–May 5, 1894.
Vol. 5, Pt. 2–10
Jay, Peter Augustus, Jan. 24, 1776–Feb. 20, 1843.
Vol. 5, Pt. 2–11
Jay, William, June 16, 1789–Oct. 14, 1858.
Vol. 5, Pt. 2–11
Jayne, Horace Fort, Mar. 17, 1859–July 8, 1913.
Vol. 5, Pt. 2–12
Jeanes, Anna, T., Apr. 7, 1822–Sept. 24, 1907.
Vol. 5, Pt. 2–13
Jeffers, John Robinson, Jan. 10, 1887–Jan. 20, 1962.
Supp. 7–391
Jeffers, William Martin, Jan. 2, 1876–Mar. 6, 1953.
Supp. 5–365
Jeffers, William Nicholson, Oct. 16, 1824–July 23, 1883.
Vol. 5, Pt. 2–14
Jefferson, Charles Edward, Aug. 29, 1860–Sept. 12, 1937.
Supp. 2–344
Jefferson, Joseph, 1774–Aug. 4, 1832.
Vol. 5, Pt. 2–14
Jefferson, Joseph, Feb. 20, 1829–Apr. 23, 1905.
Vol. 5, Pt. 2–15
Jefferson, Mark Sylvester William, Mar. 1, 1863–Aug. 8, 1949.
Supp. 4–423
Jefferson, Thomas, Apr. 2/13, 1743–July 4, 1826.
Vol. 5, Pt. 2–17
Jeffery, Edward Turner, Apr. 6, 1843–Sept. 24, 1927.
Vol. 5, Pt. 2–35
Jeffrey, Edward Charles, May 21, 1866–Apr. 19, 1952.
Supp. 5–366
Jeffrey, Joseph Andrew, Jan. 17, 1836–Aug. 27, 1928.
Vol. 5, Pt. 2–36
Jeffrey, Rosa Griffith Vertner Johnson, 1828–Oct. 6, 1894.
Vol. 5, Pt. 2–37
Jeffries, Benjamin Joy, Mar. 26, 1833–Nov. 21, 1915.
Vol. 5, Pt. 2–37
Jeffries, James Jackson, Apr. 15, 1875–Mar. 3, 1953.
Supp. 5–368
Jeffries, John, Feb. 5, 1744/5–Sept. 16, 1819.
Vol. 5, Pt. 2–38
Jelliffe, Smith Ely, Oct. 27, 1866–Sept. 25, 1945.
Supp. 3–384
Jemison, Alice Mae Lee, Oct. 9, 1901–Mar. 6, 1964.
Supp. 7–392
Jemison, Mary, 1743–Sept. 19, 1833.
Vol. 5, Pt. 2–39
Jenckes, Joseph, 1632–Jan. 4, 1717.
Vol. 5, Pt. 2–40
Jenckes, Joseph, 1656–June 15, 1740.
Vol. 5, Pt. 2–40
Jenckes Joseph. [*See* Jenks, Joseph, 1602–1683.]
Jenckes Thomas Allen, Nov. 2, 1818–Nov. 4, 1875.
Vol. 5, Pt. 2–41
Jenifer, Daniel of St. Thomas, 1723–Nov. 16, 1790.
Vol. 5, Pt. 2–42
Jenkins, Albert Gallatin, Nov. 10, 1830–May 21, 1864.
Vol. 5, Pt. 2–43
Jenkins, Charles Jones, Jan. 6, 1805–June 14, 1883.
Vol. 5, Pt. 2–44
Jenkins, Edward Hopkins, May 31, 1850–Nov. 6, 1931.
Vol. 5, Pt. 2–44
Jenkins, Howard Malcolm, Mar. 30, 1842–Oct. 11, 1902.
Vol. 5, Pt. 2–45
Jenkins, James Graham, July 18, 1834–Aug. 6, 1921.
Vol. 5, Pt. 2–46
Jenkins, John, Feb. 15, 1728–November 1785.
Vol. 5, Pt. 2–47
Jenkins, John, Nov. 27, 1751 o.s.-Mar. 19, 1827.
Vol. 5, Pt. 2–47
Jenkins, John Stilwell, Feb. 15, 1818–Sept. 20, 1852.
Vol. 5, Pt. 2–48
Jenkins, Micah, Dec. 1, 1835–May 6, 1864.
Vol. 5, Pt. 2–49

Jenkins, Nathaniel, June 7, 1812–May 20, 1872.
Vol. 5, Pt. 2–49
Jenkins, Thornton Alexander, Dec. 11, 1811–Aug. 9, 1893.
Vol. 5, Pt. 2–50
Jenks, George Charles, Apr. 13, 1850–Sept. 12, 1929.
Vol. 5, Pt. 2–51
Jenks, Jeremiah Whipple, Sept. 2, 1856–Aug. 24, 1929.
Vol. 5, Pt. 2–52
Jenks, Joseph, 1602–March 1683 N.S.
Vol. 5, Pt. 2–53
Jenks, Tudor Storrs, May 7, 1857–Feb. 11, 1922.
Vol. 5, Pt. 2–53
Jenks, William, Nov. 25, 1778–Nov. 13, 1866.
Vol. 5, Pt. 2–54
Jenney, William Le Baron, Sept. 25, 1832–June 15, 1907.
Vol. 5, Pt. 2–55
Jennings, Hennen. [*See* Jennings, James Hennen, 1854–1920.]
Jennings, Herbert Spencer, Apr. 8, 1868–Apr. 14, 1947.
Supp. 4–424
Jennings, James Hennen, May 6, 1854–Mar. 5, 1920.
Vol. 5, Pt. 2–55
Jennings, John, *c.* 1738–Jan. 14, 1802.
Vol. 5, Pt. 2–56
Jennings, Jonathan, 1784–July 26, 1834.
Vol. 5, Pt. 2–57
Jensen, Benton Franklin ("Ben"), Dec. 16, 1892–Feb. 5, 1970.
Supp. 8–299
Jensen, Jens, Sept. 13, 1860–Oct. 1, 1951.
Supp. 5–369
Jensen, Peter Laurits, May 16, 1886–Oct. 25, 1961.
Supp. 7–394
Jepson, Willis Linn, Aug. 19, 1867–Nov. 7, 1946.
Supp. 4–428
Jerome, Chauncey, June 10, 1793–Apr. 20, 1868.
Vol. 5, Pt. 2–58
Jerome, William Travers, Apr. 18, 1859–Feb. 13, 1934.
Supp. 1–450
Jervis, John Bloomfield, Dec. 14, 1795–Jan. 12, 1885.
Vol. 5, Pt. 2–59
Jesse, Richard Henry, Mar. 1, 1853–Jan. 22, 1921.
Vol. 5, Pt. 2–60
Jessup, Henry Harris, Apr. 19, 1832–Apr. 28, 1910.
Vol. 5, Pt. 2–61
Jessup, Walter Albert, Aug. 12, 1877–July 5, 1944.
Supp. 3–386
Jesup, Morris Ketchum, June 21, 1830–Jan. 22, 1908.
Vol. 5, Pt. 2–61
Jesup, Thomas Sidney, Dec. 16, 1788–June 10, 1860.
Vol. 5, Pt. 2–62
Jeter, Jeremiah Bell, July 18, 1802–Feb. 18, 1880.
Vol. 5, Pt. 2–63
Jewell, Harvey, May 26, 1820–Dec. 8, 1881.
Vol. 5, Pt. 2–64
Jewell, Marshall, Oct. 20, 1825–Feb. 10, 1883.
Vol. 5, Pt. 2–65
Jewett, Charles Coffin, Aug. 12, 1816–Jan. 9, 1868.
Vol. 5, Pt. 2–65
Jewett, Clarence Frederick, Sept. 1, 1852–May 3, 1909.
Vol. 5, Pt. 2–66
Jewett, David, June 17, 1772–July 26, 1842.
Vol. 5, Pt. 2–67
Jewett, Frank Baldwin, Sept. 5, 1879–Nov. 18, 1949.
Supp. 4–429
Jewett, Hugh Judge, July 1, 1817–Mar. 6, 1898.
Vol. 5, Pt. 2–68
Jewett, John Punchard, Aug. 16, 1814–May 14, 1884.
Vol. 5, Pt. 2–69
Jewett, Milo Parker, Apr. 27, 1808–June 9, 1882.
Vol. 5, Pt. 2–69
Jewett, Sarah Orne, Sept. 3, 1849–June 24, 1909.
Vol. 5, Pt. 2–70
Jewett, William, Jan. 14, 1792–Mar. 24, 1874.
Vol. 5, Pt. 2–72
Jewett, William Cornell, Feb. 19, 1823–Oct. 27, 1893.
Vol. 5, Pt. 2–73
Jocelyn, Nathaniel, Jan. 31, 1796–Jan. 13, 1881.
Vol. 5, Pt. 2–73
Jogues, Isaac, Jan. 10, 1607–Oct. 18, 1646.
Vol. 5, Pt. 2–74
Johns, Clayton, Nov. 24, 1857–Mar. 5, 1932.
Supp. 1–451
Johns, John July 10, 1796–Apr. 4, 1876.
Vol. 5, Pt. 2–75
Johns, Kensey, June 14, 1759–Dec. 20, 1848.
Vol. 5, Pt. 2–76
Johns, Kensey, Dec. 10, 1791–Mar. 28, 1857.
Vol. 5, Pt. 2–76
Johnsen, Erik Kristian, Sept. 20, 1863–Jan. 21, 1923.
Vol. 5, Pt. 2–77
Johnson. [*See also* Johnston.]
Johnson, Albert, Mar. 5, 1869–Jan. 17, 1957.
Supp. 6–319
Johnson, Alexander, Jan. 2, 1847–May 17, 1941.
Supp. 3–388
Johnson, Alexander Bryan, May 29, 1786–Sept. 9, 1867.
Vol. 5, Pt. 2–78
Johnson, Alexander Smith, July 30, 1817–Jan. 26, 1878.
Vol. 1, Pt. 2–79
Johnson, Allen, Jan. 29, 1870–Jan. 18, 1931.
Vol. 5, Pt. 2–79
Johnson, Alvin Saunders, Dec. 18, 1874–June 9, 1971.
Supp. 9–427
Johnson, Andrew, Dec. 29, 1808–July 31, 1875.
Vol. 5, Pt. 2–81
Johnson, Benjamin Pierce, Nov. 30, 1793–Apr. 12, 1869.
Vol. 5, Pt. 2–90
Johnson, Bradley Tyler, Sept. 29, 1829–Oct. 5, 1903.
Vol. 5, Pt. 2–90
Johnson, Bushrod Rust, Oct. 7, 1817–Sept. 12, 1880.
Vol. 5, Pt. 2–91
Johnson, Byron Bancroft, Jan. 6, 1864–Mar. 28, 1931.
Vol. 5, Pt. 2–92
Johnson, Cave, Jan. 11, 1793–Nov. 23, 1866.
Vol. 5, Pt. 2–93
Johnson, Chapman, Mar. 12, 1779–July 12, 1849.
Vol. 5, Pt. 2–93
Johnson, Charles Spurgeon, July 24, 1893–Oct. 27, 1956.
Supp. 6–321
Johnson, David Bancroft, Jan. 10, 1856–Dec. 26, 1928.
Vol. 5, Pt. 2–94
Johnson, Douglas Wilson, Nov. 30, 1878–Feb. 24, 1944.
Supp. 3–389
Johnson, Eastman. [*See* Johnson, Jonathan Eastman, 1824–1906.]
Johnson, Edward, Sept. 1598–Apr. 23, 1672.
Vol. 5, Pt. 2–95
Johnson, Edward, Apr. 16, 1816–Mar. 2, 1873.
Vol. 5, Pt. 2–95
Johnson, Edward, Aug. 22, 1878–Apr. 20, 1959.
Supp. 6–322
Johnson, Edward Austin, Nov. 23, 1860–July 24, 1944.
Supp. 3–390
Johnson, Edwin Carl, Jan. 1, 1884–May 30, 1970.
Supp. 8–300
Johnson, Edwin Ferry, May 23, 1803–Apr. 12, 1872.
Vol. 5, Pt. 2–96
Johnson, Eldridge Reeves, Feb. 6, 1867–Nov. 14, 1945.
Supp. 3–391
Johnson, Elias Henry, Oct. 15, 1841–Mar. 10, 1906.
Vol. 5, Pt. 2–97
Johnson, Elijah, *c.* 1780–Mar. 23, 1849.
Vol. 5, Pt. 2–97
Johnson, Eilen Cheney, Dec. 20, 1829–June 28, 1899.
Vol. 5, Pt. 2–98
Johnson, Franklin, Nov. 2, 1836–Oct. 9, 1916.
Vol. 5, Pt. 2–99
Johnson, George, Feb. 22, 1889–June 5, 1944.
Supp. 3–393
Johnson, George Francis, Oct. 14, 1857–Nov. 28, 1948.
Supp. 4–431
Johnson, Guy, *c.* 1740–Mar. 5, 1788.
Vol. 5, Pt. 2–100
Johnson, Harold Ogden ("Chic"), Mar. 5, 1891–Feb. 26, 1962.
Supp. 7–588
[*See also* Olsen, John Sigvard ("Ole") 1892–1963.]
Johnson, Harry Gordon, May 26, 1923–May 8, 1977.
Supp. 10–382
Johnson, Helen Louise Kendrick, Jan. 4, 1844–Jan. 3, 1917.
Vol. 5, Pt. 2–100

Johnson, Henry, June 25, 1855–Feb. 7, 1918.
Vol. 5, Pt. 2–101
Johnson, Herschel Vespasian, Sept. 18, 1812–Aug. 16, 1880.
Vol. 5, Pt. 2–102
Johnson, Hiram Warren, Sept. 2, 1866–Aug. 6, 1945.
Supp. 3–393
Johnson, Howard Deering, 1896–June 20, 1972.
Supp. 9–429
Johnson, Hugh Samuel, Aug. 5, 1882–Apr. 15, 1942.
Supp. 3–398
Johnson, Jack, Mar. 31, 1878–June 10, 1946.
Supp. 4–432
Johnson, James, Jan. 1, 1774–Aug. 13, 1826.
Vol. 5, Pt. 2–103
Johnson, James Weldon, June 17, 1871–June 26, 1938.
Supp. 2–345
Johnson, Sir John, Nov. 5, 1742–Jan. 4, 1830.
Vol. 5, Pt. 2–103
Johnson, John Albert, July 28, 1861–Sept. 21, 1909.
Vol. 5, Pt. 2–104
Johnson, John Butler, June 11, 1850–June 23, 1902.
Vol. 5, Pt. 2–105
Johnson, John Graver, Apr. 4, 1841–Apr. 14, 1917.
Vol. 5, Pt. 2–106
Johnson, Jonathan Eastman, July 29, 1824–Apr. 5, 1906.
Vol. 5, Pt. 2–107
Johnson, Joseph, June 15, 1776–Oct. 6, 1862.
Vol. 5, Pt. 2–108
Johnson, Joseph French, Aug. 24, 1853–Jan. 22, 1925.
Vol. 5, Pt. 2–109
Johnson, Levi, Apr. 25, 1786–Dec. 19, 1871.
Vol. 5, Pt. 2–109
Johnson, Louis Arthur, Jan. 10, 1891–Apr. 24, 1966.
Supp. 8–302
Johnson, Lyndon Baines, Aug. 27, 1908–Jan. 22, 1973.
Supp. 9–430
Johnson, Magnus, Sept. 19, 1871–Sept. 13, 1936.
Supp. 2–347
Johnson, Malcolm Malone, Sept. 27, 1904–June 17, 1976.
Supp. 10–383
Johnson, Marmaduke, d. Dec. 25, 1674.
Vol. 5, Pt. 2–110
Johnson, Mordecai Wyatt, Jan. 12, 1890–Sept. 10, 1976.
Supp. 10–385
Johnson, Sir Nathaniel, *c.* 1645–1713.
Vol. 5, Pt. 2–111
Johnson, Nunnally Hunter, Dec. 5, 1897–Mar. 25, 1977.
Supp. 10–387
Johnson, Oliver, Dec. 27, 1809–Dec. 10, 1889.
Vol. 5, Pt. 2–112
Johnson, Osa, Mar. 14, 1894–Jan. 7, 1953.
Supp. 5–370
Johnson, Owen McMahon, Aug. 27, 1878–Jan. 27, 1952.
Supp. 5–371
Johnson, Reverdy, May 21, 1796–Feb. 10, 1876.
Vol. 5, Pt. 2–112
Johnson, Richard Mentor, 1780–Nov. 19, 1850.
Vol. 5, Pt. 2–114
Johnson, Richard W., Feb. 7, 1827–Apr. 21, 1897.
Vol. 5, Pt. 2–116
Johnson, Robert, *c.* 1676–May 3, 1735.
Vol. 5, Pt. 2–116
Johnson, Robert Underwood, Jan. 12, 1853–Oct. 14, 1937.
Supp. 2–348
Johnson, Robert Ward, July 22, 1814–July 26, 1879.
Vol. 5, Pt. 2–117
Johnson, Samuel, Oct. 14, 1696–Jan. 6, 1772.
Vol. 5, Pt. 2–118
Johnson, Samuel, Oct. 10, 1822–Feb. 19, 1882.
Vol. 5, Pt. 2–119
Johnson, Samuel William, July 3, 1830–July 21, 1909.
Vol. 5, Pt. 2–120
Johnson, Seth Whitmore, May 3, 1811–Feb. 13, 1907.
Vol. 5, Pt. 2–121
Johnson, Thomas, Nov. 4, 1732–Oct. 26, 1819.
Vol. 5, Pt. 2–121
Johnson, Tom Loftin, July 18, 1854–Apr. 10, 1911.
Vol. 5, Pt. 2–122
Johnson, Treat Baldwin, Mar. 29, 1875–July 28, 1947.
Supp. 4–434
Johnson, Virginia Wales, Dec. 28, 1849–Jan. 16, 1916.
Vol. 5, Pt. 2–124
Johnson, Walter Perry, Nov. 6, 1887–Dec. 10, 1946.
Supp. 4–435
Johnson, Wendell Andrew Leroy, Apr. 16, 1906–Aug. 1965.
Supp. 7–395
Johnson, Sir William, 1715–July 11, 1774.
Vol. 5, Pt. 2–124
Johnson, William, Dec. 17, 1769–June 25, 1848.
Vol. 5, Pt. 2–128
Johnson, William, Dec. 27, 1771–Aug. 4, 1834.
Vol. 5, Pt. 2–128
Johnson, William Bullein, June 13, 1782–Oct. 2, 1862.
Vol. 5, Pt. 2–129
Johnson, William Ransom, 1782–Feb. 10, 1849.
Vol. 5, Pt. 2–130
Johnson, William Samuel, Oct. 7, 1727–Nov. 14, 1819.
Vol. 5, Pt. 2–131
Johnson, William Woolsey, June 23, 1841–May 14, 1927.
Vol. 5, Pt. 2–134
Johnson, Willis Fletcher, Oct. 7, 1857–Mar. 28, 1931.
Vol. 5, Pt. 2–134
Johnston, Albert Sidney, Feb. 2, 1803–Apr. 6, 1862.
Vol. 5, Pt. 2–135
Johnston, Alexander, Apr. 29, 1849–July 20, 1889.
Vol. 5, Pt. 2–136
Johnston, Annie Fellows, May 15, 1863–Oct. 5, 1931.
Vol. 5, Pt. 2–137
Johnston, Augustus, *c.* 1730–*c.* 1790.
Vol. 5, Pt. 2–138
Johnston, David Claypoole, March 1799–Nov. 8, 1865.
Vol. 5, Pt. 2–139
Johnston, Eric Allen, Dec. 21, 1896–Aug. 22, 1963.
Supp. 7–396
Johnston, Frances Benjamin, Jan. 15, 1864–May 16, 1952.
Supp. 5–373
Johnston, Gabriel, 1699–July 17, 1752.
Vol. 5, Pt. 2–140
Johnston, George Ben, July 25, 1853–Dec. 20, 1916.
Vol. 5, Pt. 2–140
Johnston, Henrietta, d. March 1728/9.
Vol. 5, Pt. 2–141
Johnston, Henry Phelps, Apr. 19, 1842–Feb. 28, 1923.
Vol. 5, Pt. 2–142
Johnston, John, Apr. 11, 1791–Nov. 24, 1880.
Vol. 5, Pt. 2–142
Johnston, John, Oct. 13, 1881–Sept. 12, 1950.
Supp. 4–437
Johnston, John Taylor, Apr. 8, 1820–Mar. 24, 1893.
Vol. 5, Pt. 2–143
Johnston, Joseph Eggleston, Feb. 3, 1807–Mar. 21, 1891.
Vol. 5, Pt. 2–144
Johnston, Joseph Forney, Mar. 23, 1843–Aug. 8, 1913.
Vol. 5, Pt. 2–146
Johnston, Josiah Stoddard, Nov. 24, 1784–May 19, 1833.
Vol. 5, Pt. 2–147
Johnston, Mary, Nov. 21, 1870–May 9, 1936
Supp. 2–349
Johnston, Olin DeWitt Talmadge, Nov. 18, 1896–Apr. 18, 1965.
Supp. 7–398
Johnston, Peter, Jan. 6, 1763–Dec. 8, 1831.
Vol. 5, Pt. 2–147
Johnston, Richard Malcolm, Mar. 8, 1822–Sept. 23, 1898
Vol. 5, Pt. 2–148
Johnston, Robert Matteson, Apr. 11, 1867–Jan. 28, 1920.
Vol. 5, Pt. 2–149
Johnston, Samuel, Dec. 15, 1733–Aug. 17, 1816.
Vol. 5, Pt. 2–150
Johnston, Samuel, Feb. 9, 1835–Apr. 15, 1911.
Vol. 5, Pt. 2–151
Johnston, Thomas, *c.* 1708–May 8, 1767.
Vol. 5, Pt. 2–152
Johnston, William Andrew, Jan. 26, 1871–Feb. 16, 1929.
Vol. 5, Pt. 2–152
Johnston, William Hartshorne, Oct. 19, 1861–Feb. 20, 1933.
Supp. 1–452
Johnston, William Hugh, Dec. 30, 1874–Mar. 26, 1937.
Supp. 2–350
Johnston, William Preston, Jan. 5, 1831–July 16, 1899.
Vol. 5, Pt. 2–153

Johnston, Zachariah, 1742–Jan. 1800.
Vol. 5, Pt. 2–154
Johnstone, Edward Ransom, Dec. 27, 1870–Dec. 29, 1946.
Supp. 4–438
Johnstone, Job, June 7, 1793–Apr. 8, 1862.
Vol. 5, Pt. 2–155
Joline, Adrian Hoffman, June 30, 1850–Oct. 15, 1912.
Vol. 5, Pt. 2–155
Jolliet, Louis, Sept. 1645–1700.
Vol. 5, Pt. 2–156
Jolson, Al, May 26, 1886–Oct. 23, 1950.
Supp. 4–439
Jones, Abner, Apr. 28, 1772–May 29, 1841.
Vol. 5, Pt. 2–157
Jones, Alexander, *c.* 1802–Aug. 22, 1863.
Vol. 5, Pt. 2–158
Jones, Alfred, Apr. 7, 1819–Apr. 28, 1900.
Vol. 5, Pt. 2–158
Jones, Allen, Dec. 24, 1739–Nov. 14, 1807.
Vol. 5, Pt. 2–159
Jones, Amanda Theodosia, Oct. 19, 1835–Mar. 31, 1914.
Vol. 5, Pt. 2–160
Jones, Anson, Jan. 20, 1798–Jan. 9, 1858.
Vol. 5, Pt. 2–161
Jones, Benjamin Allyn, Dec. 31, 1882–June 13, 1961.
Supp. 7–399
Jones Benjamin Franklin, Aug. 8, 1824–May 19, 1903.
Vol. 5, Pt. 2–162
Jones, Calvin, Apr. 2, 1775–Sept. 20, 1846.
Vol. 5, Pt. 2–163
Jones, Catesby A. P. Roger, Apr. 15, 1821–June 20, 1877.
Vol. 5, Pt. 2–164
Jones, Charles Colcock, Oct. 28, 1831–July 19, 1893.
Vol. 5, Pt. 2–165
Jones, David, May 12, 1736–Feb. 5, 1820.
Vol. 5, Pt. 2–165
Jones, David Rumph, Apr. 5, 1825–Jan. 15, 1863.
Vol. 5, Pt. 2–166
Jones, Ernest Lester, Apr. 14, 1876–Apr. 9, 1929.
Vol. 5, Pt. 2–167
Jones, Evan William, 1852–Dec. 30, 1908.
Vol. 5, Pt. 2–168
Jones, Frank, Sept. 15, 1832–Oct. 2, 1902.
Vol. 5, Pt. 2–168
Jones, Gabriel, May 17, 1724–Oct 6, 1806.
Vol. 5, Pt. 2–169
Jones, George, July 30, 1800–Jan. 22, 1870.
Vol. 5, Pt. 2–170
Jones, George, Aug. 16, 1811–Aug. 12, 1891.
Vol. 5, Pt. 2–171
Jones, George Heber, Aug. 14, 1867–May 11, 1919.
Vol. 5, Pt. 2–171
Jones, George Wallace, Apr. 12, 1804–July 22, 1896.
Vol. 5, Pt. 2–172
Jones, Harry Clary, Nov. 11, 1865–Apr. 9, 1916.
Vol. 5, Pt. 2–173
Jones, Herschel Vespasian, Aug. 30, 1861–May 24, 1928.
Vol. 5, Pt. 2–174
Jones, Hilary Pollard, Nov. 14, 1863–Jan. 1, 1938.
Supp. 2–351
Jones, Howard Mumford, Apr. 16, 1892–May 11, 1980.
Supp. 10–388
Jones, Hugh, *c.* I670–Sept. 8, 1760.
Vol. 5, Pt. 2–175
Jones, Hugh Bolton, Oct. 20, 1848–Sept. 24, 1927.
Vol. 5, Pt. 2–175
Jones, Jacob, March 1768–Aug. 3, 1850.
Vol. 5, Pt. 2–176
Jones, James Chamberlayne, June 7, 1809–Oct. 29, 1859.
Vol. 5, Pt. 2–177
Jones, James Kimbrough, Sept. 29, 1829–June 1, 1908.
Vol. 5, Pt. 2–177
Jones, James Ramon, Nov. 6, 1921–May 9, 1977.
Supp. 10–390
Jones, Jehu Glancy, Oct. 7, 1811–Mar. 24, 1878.
Vol. 5, Pt. 2–178
Jones, Jenkin Lloyd, Nov. 14, 1843–Sept. 12, 1918.
Vol. 5, Pt. 2–179
Jones, Jesse Holman, Apr. 5, 1874–June 1, 1956.
Supp. 6–324
Jones, Jim, May 13, 1931–Nov. 18, 1978.
Supp. 10–391
Jones, Joel, Oct. 25, 1795–Feb. 3, 1860.
Vol. 5, Pt. 2–180
Jones, John, 1729–June 23, 1791.
Vol. 5, Pt. 2–181
Jones, John B., Dec. 22, 1834–July 19, 1881.
Vol. 5, Pt. 2–182
Jones, John Beauchamp, Mar. 6, 1810–Feb. 4, 1866.
Vol. 5, Pt. 2–182
Jones, John Marvin, Feb. 26, 1882–Mar. 4, 1976.
Supp. 10–393
Jones, John Paul, July 6, 1747–July 18, 1792.
Vol. 5, Pt. 2–183
Jones, John Percival, Jan. 27, 1829–Nov. 27, 1912.
Vol. 5, Pt. 2–188
Jones, John Peter, Sept. 4, 1847–Oct. 3, 1916.
Vol. 5, Pt. 2–189
Jones, John Price, Aug. 12, 1877–Dec. 23, 1964.
Supp. 7–401
Jones, John Taylor, July 16, 1802–Sept. 13, 1851.
Vol. 5, Pt. 2–190
Jones, John William, Sept. 25, 1836–Mar. 17, 1909.
Vol. 5, Pt. 2–190
Jones, John Winston, Nov. 22, 1791–Jan. 29, 1848.
Vol. 5, Pt. 2–191
Jones, Joseph, 1727–Oct. 26, 1805.
Vol. 5, Pt. 2–192
Jones, Joseph, Sept. 6, 1833–Feb. 17, 1896.
Vol. 5, Pt. 2–193
Jones, Joseph Stevens, Sept. 28, 1809–Dec. 29, 1877.
Vol. 5, Pt. 2–193
Jones, Leonard Augustus, Jan. 13, 1832–Dec. 9, 1909.
Vol. 5, Pt. 2–194
Jones, Lewis Ralph, Dec. 5, 1864–Apr. 1, 1945.
Supp. 3–400
Jones, Lindley Armstrong ("Spike"), Dec. 14, 1911–May 1, 1965.
Supp. 7–403
Jones, Lynds, Jan. 5, 1865–Feb. 11, 1951.
Supp. 5–373
Jones, Mary Harris, May 1, 1830–Nov. 30, 1930.
Vol. 5, Pt. 2–195
Jones, Noble Wymberley, *c.* 1724–Jan. 9, 1805.
Vol. 5, Pt. 2–196
Jones, Richard Foster, July 7, 1886–Sept. 12, 1965.
Supp. 7–402
Jones, Robert Edmond, Dec. 12, 1887–Nov. 26, 1954.
Supp. 5–375
Jones, Robert Reynolds ("Bob"), Oct. 30, 1883–Jan. 16, 1968.
Supp. 8–303
Jones, Robert Tyre, Jr., Mar. 17, 1902–Dec. 18, 1971.
Supp. 9–438
Jones, Rufus Matthew, Jan. 25, 1863–June 16, 1948.
Supp. 4–441
Jones, Samuel, July 26, 1734–Nov. 25, 1819.
Vol. 5, Pt. 2–197
Jones, Samuel, May 26, 1770–Aug. 9, 1853.
Vol. 5, Pt. 2–198
Jones, Samuel Milton, Aug. 8, 1846–July 12, 1904.
Supp. 1–453
Jones, Samuel Porter, Oct. 16, 1847–Oct. 15, 1906.
Vol. 5, Pt. 2–199
Jones, Sybil, Feb. 28, 1808–Dec. 4, 1873.
Vol. 5, Pt. 2–199
Jones, Thomas, Apr. 30, 1731–July 25, 1792.
Vol. 5, Pt. 2–200
Jones, Thomas Ap Catesby, Apr. 24, 1790–May 30, 1858
Vol. 5, Pt. 2–201
Jones, Thomas Goode, Nov. 26, 1844–Apr. 28, 1914.
Vol. 5, Pt. 2–202
Jones, Thomas P., 1774–Mar. 11, 1848.
Vol. 5, Pt. 2–202
Jones, Walter, Oct. 7, 1776–Oct. 14, 1861.
Vol. 5, Pt. 2–203
Jones, Wesley Livsey, Oct. 9, 1863–Nov. 19, 1932.
Supp. 1–454
Jones, William, Oct. 8, 1753–Apr. 9, 1822.
Vol. 5, Pt. 2–204
Jones, William, 1760–Sept. 6, 1831.
Vol. 5, Pt. 2–205

Jones, William, Mar. 28, 1871–Mar. 29, 1909.
Vol. 5, Pt. 2–205
Jones, William Alfred, June 26, 1817–May 6, 1900.
Vol. 5, Pt. 2–206
Jones, William Palmer, Oct. 17, 1819–Sept. 25, 1897.
Vol. 5, Pt. 2–207
Jones, William Patterson, Apr. 23, 1831–Aug. 3, 1886.
Vol. 5, Pt. 2–207
Jones, William Richard, Feb. 23, 1839–Sept. 28, 1889.
Vol. 5, Pt. 2–208
Jones, Willie, *c.* 1741–June 18, 1801.
Vol. 5, Pt. 2–210
Joplin, Janis Lyn, Jan. 19, 1943–Oct. 4, 1970.
Supp. 8–305
Jordan, Benjamin Everett, Sept. 8, 1896–Mar. 15, 1974.
Supp. 9–439
Jordan, David Starr, Jan. 19, 1851–Sept. 19, 1931.
Vol. 5, Pt. 2–211
Jordan, Eben Dyer, Nov. 7, 1857–Aug. 1, 1916.
Vol. 5, Pt. 2–214
Jordan, Edwin Oakes, July 28, 1866–Sept. 2, 1936.
Supp. 2–352
Jordan, John Woolf, Sept. 14, 1840–June 11, 1921.
Vol. 5, Pt. 2–215
Jordan, Kate, Dec. 23, 1862–June 20, 1926.
Vol. 5, Pt. 2–215
Jordan, Louis, July 8, 1908–Feb. 4, 1975.
Supp. 9–441
Jordan, Thomas, Sept. 30, 1819–Nov. 27, 1895.
Vol. 5, Pt. 2–216
Jordan, Virgil Justin, June 3, 1892–Apr. 28, 1965.
Supp. 7–404
Jordan, William George, Mar. 6, 1864–Apr. 20, 1928.
Vol. 5, Pt. 2–217
Joseffy, Rafael, July 3, 1852–June 25, 1915.
Vol. 5, Pt. 2–217
Joseph, *c.* 1840–Sept. 21, 1904.
Vol. 5, Pt. 2–218
Josephson, Matthew, Feb. 15, 1899–Mar. 13, 1978.
Supp. 10–394
Josselyn, John, fl. 1638–1675.
Vol. 5, Pt. 2–219
Joubert de la Muraille, James Hector Marie Nicholas, Sept. 6, 1777–Nov. 5, 1843.
Vol. 5, Pt. 2–220
Jouett, James Edward, Feb. 7, 1826–Sept. 30, 1902.
Vol. 5, Pt. 2–221
Jouett, John, Dec. 7, 1754–Mar. 1, 1822.
Vol. 5, Pt. 2–221
Jouett, Matthew Harris, Apr. 22, 1787–Aug. 10, 1827.
Vol. 5, Pt. 2–222
Joutel, Henri, *c.* 1645–after 1723.
Vol. 5, Pt. 2–223
Joy, Agnes Eliza. [*See* Salm Salm, Agnes Elisabeth Winona Leclerq Joy, Princess, 1840–1912.]
Joy, Charles Turner, Feb. 17, 1895–June 6, 1956.
Supp. 6–326
Joy, Henry Bourne, Nov. 23, 1864–Nov. 6, 1936.
Supp. 2–354
Joy, James Frederick, Dec. 2, 1810–Sept. 24, 1896.
Vol. 5, Pt. 2–224
Joy, Thomas, *c.* 1610–Oct. 21, 1678.
Vol. 5, Pt. 2–225
Joyce, Isaac Wilson, Oct. 11, 1836–July 28, 1905.
Vol. 5, Pt. 2–226
Joynes, Edward Southey, Mar. 2, 1834–June 18, 1917.
Vol. 5, Pt. 2–226
Judah, Samuel, July 10, 1798–Apr. 24, 1869.
Vol. 5, Pt. 2–227
Judah, Samuel Benjamin Helbert, *c.* 1799–July 21, 1876.
Vol. 5, Pt. 2–228
Judah, Theodore Dehone, Mar. 4, 1826–Nov. 2, 1863.
Vol. 5, Pt. 2–229
Juday, Chancey, May 5, 1871–Mar. 29, 1944.
Supp. 3–401
Judd, Charles Hubbard, Feb. 20, 1873–July 18, 1946.
Supp. 4–443
Judd, Edward Starr, July 11, 1878–Nov. 30, 1935.
Supp. 1–455
Judd, Gerrit Parmele, Apr. 23, 1803–July 12, 1873.
Vol. 5, Pt. 2–229
Judd, Norman Buel, Jan. 10, 1815–Nov. 11, 1878.
Vol. 5, Pt. 2–230
Judd, Orange, July 26, 1822–Dec. 27, 1892.
Vol. 5, Pt. 2–231
Judd, Sylvester, July 23, 1813–Jan. 26, 1853.
Vol. 5, Pt. 2–232
Judge, Thomas Augustine, Aug. 23, 1868–Nov. 23, 1933.
Supp. 1–456
Judge, William Quan, Apr. 13, 1851–Mar. 21, 1896.
Vol. 5, Pt. 2–233
Judson, Adoniram, Aug. 9, 1788–Apr. 12, 1850.
Vol. 5, Pt. 2–234
Judson, Adoniram Brown, Apr. 7, 1837–Sept. 20, 1916.
Vol. 5, Pt. 2–235
Judson, Ann Hasseltine, Dec. 22, 1789–Oct. 24, 1826.
Vol. 5, Pt. 2–236
Judson, Edward, Dec. 27, 1844–Oct. 23, 1914.
Vol. 5, Pt. 2–236
Judson, Edward Zane Carroll, Mar. 20, 1823–July 16, 1886.
Vol. 5, Pt. 2–237
Judson, Egbert Putnam, Aug. 9, 1812–Jan. 9, 1893.
Vol. 5, Pt. 2–239
Judson, Emily Chubbuck, Aug. 22, 1817–June 1, 1854.
Vol. 5, Pt. 2–239
Judson, Frederick Newton, Oct. 7, 1845–Oct. 18, 1919.
Vol. 5, Pt. 2–240
Judson, Harry Pratt, Dec. 20, 1849–Mar. 4, 1927.
Vol. 5, Pt. 2–241
Judson, Sarah Hall Boardman, Nov. 4, 1803–Sept. 1, 1845.
Vol. 5, Pt. 2–242
Juengling, Frederick, Oct. 18, 1846–Dec. 31, 1889.
Vol. 5, Pt. 2–243
Juilliard, Augustus D., Apr. 19, 1836–Apr. 25, 1919.
Vol. 5, Pt. 2–244
Julia, Sister, Feb. 13, 1827–Nov. 12, 1901.
Vol. 5, Pt. 2–244
Julian, George Washington, May 5, 1817–July 7, 1899.
Vol. 5, Pt. 2–245
Julian, Percy Lavon, Apr. 11, 1899–Apr. 19, 1975.
Supp. 9–443
Jumel, Stephen, *c.* 1754–May 22, 1832.
Vol. 5, Pt. 2–246
June, Jennie. [*See* Croly, Jane Cunningham, 1829–1901.]
Juneau, Solomon Laurent, Aug. 9, 1793–Nov. 14, 1856.
Vol. 5, Pt. 2–247
Jungman, John George, Apr. 19, 1720–July 17, 1808.
Vol. 5, Pt. 2–248
Junkin, George, Nov. 1, 1790–May 20, 1868.
Vol. 5, Pt. 2–248
Just, Ernest Everett, Aug. 14, 1883–Oct. 27, 1941.
Supp. 3–402

Kaempffert, Waldemar Bernhard, Sept. 23, 1877–Nov. 27, 1956.
Supp. 6–327
Kafer, John Christian, Dec. 27, 1842–Mar. 30, 1906.
Vol. 5, Pt. 2–249
Kagan, Henry Enoch, Nov. 28, 1906–Aug. 16, 1969.
Supp. 8–306
Kah-Ge-Ga-Gah-Bowh. [*See* Copway, George, 1818–*c.* 1863.]
Kahn, Albert, Mar. 21, 1869–Dec. 8, 1942.
Supp. 3–403
Kahn, Florence Prag, Nov. 9, 1866–Nov. 16, 1948.
Supp. 4–446
Kahn, Gustav Gerson, Nov. 6, 1886–Oct. 8, 1941.
Supp. 3–406
Kahn, Julius, Feb. 28, 1861–Dec. 18, 1924.
Vol. 5, Pt. 2–250
Kahn, Louis I., Feb. 20, 1901–Mar. 17, 1974.
Supp. 9–445
Kahn, Otto Herman, Feb. 21, 1867–Mar. 29, 1934.
Supp. 1–457
Kaiser, Alois, Nov. 10, 1840–Jan. 5, 1908.
Vol. 5, Pt. 2–251
Kaiser, Henry John, May 9, 1882–Aug. 24, 1967.
Supp. 8–307
Kalanianaole, Jonah Kuhio, Mar. 26, 1871–Jan. 7, 1922.
Vol. 5, Pt. 2–252
Kalb, Johann, June 29, 1721–Aug. 19, 1780.
Vol. 5, Pt. 2–253

Kalisch, Isidor, Nov. 15, 1816–May 11, 1886.
Vol. 5, Pt. 2–254
Kalisch, Samuel, Apr. 18, 1851–Apr. 29, 1930.
Vol. 5, Pt. 2–254
Kallen, Horace Meyer, Aug. 11, 1882–Feb. 16, 1974.
Supp. 9–447
Kalmus, Herbert Thomas, Nov. 9, 1881–July 11, 1963.
Supp. 7–405
Kalmus, Natalie Mabelle Dunfee, 1883–Nov. 15, 1965.
Supp. 7–405
Kaltenborn, Hans Von, July 9, 1878–June 14, 1965.
Supp. 7–408
Kamaikan, *c.* 1800–*c.* 1880.
Vol. 5, Pt. 2–255
Kanaga, Consuelo Delesseps, May 25, 1894–Feb. 28, 1978.
Supp. 10–397
Kane, Elisha Kent, Feb. 3, 1820–Feb. 16, 1857.
Vol. 5, Pt. 2–256
Kane, Helen, Aug. 4, 1904–Sept. 25, 1966.
Supp. 1–310
Kane, John, Aug. 19, 1860–Aug. 10, 1934.
Supp. 1–458
Kane, John Kintzing, May 16, 1795–Feb. 21, 1858.
Vol. 5, Pt. 2–257
Kane, Thomas Leiper, Jan. 27, 1882–Dec. 26, 1883.
Vol. 5, Pt. 2–258
Kantor, MacKinlay, Feb. 4, 1904–Oct. 11, 1977.
Supp. 10–399
Kapp, Friedrich, Apr. 13, 1824–Oct. 27, 1884.
Vol. 5, Pt. 2–259
Karfiol, Bernard, May 6, 1886–Aug. 16, 1952.
Supp. 5–376
Karloff, Boris, Nov. 23, 1887–Feb. 2, 1969.
Supp. 8–311
Kármán, Theodore (Todor) Von, May 11, 1881–May 7, 1963.
Supp. 7–410
Kasson, John Adam, Jan. 11, 1822–May 18, 1910.
Vol. 5, Pt. 2–260
Katchen, Julius, Aug. 15, 1926–Apr. 29, 1969.
Supp. 8–312
Katte, Walter, Nov. 14, 1830–Mar. 4, 1917.
Vol. 5, Pt. 2–261
Katzer, Frederic Xavier, Feb. 7, 1844–July 20, 1903.
Vol. 5, Pt. 2–261
Kauffman, Calvin Henry, Mar. 10, 1869–June 14, 1931.
Vol. 5, Pt. 2–262
Kaufman, George S, Nov. 16, 1889–June 2, 1961.
Supp. 7–412
Kaufmann, Walter Arnold, July 1, 1921–Sept. 4, 1980.
Supp. 10–401
Kautz, August Valentine, Jan. 5, 1828–Sept. 4, 1895.
Vol. 5, Pt. 2–263
Kavanagh, Edward, Apr. 27, 1795–Jan. 21, 1844.
Vol. 5, Pt. 2–264
Kay, Edgar Boyd, Jan. 15, 1860–Apr. 20, 1931.
Vol. 5, Pt. 2–265
Kaye, Frederick Benjamin, Apr. 20, 1892–Feb. 28, 1930.
Vol. 5, Pt. 2–265
Keagy, John Miller, Aug. 31, 1792–Jan. 13, 1837.
Vol. 5, Pt. 2–266
Kean, Jefferson Randolph, June 27, 1860–Sept. 4, 1950.
Supp. 4–447
Keane, James John, Aug. 26, 1857–Aug. 2, 1929.
Vol. 5, Pt. 2–267
Keane, John Joseph, Sept. 12, 1839–June 22, 1918.
Vol. 5, Pt. 2–267
Kearney, Denis, Feb. 1, 1847–Apr. 24, 1907.
Vol. 5, Pt. 2–268
Kearns, Jack, Aug. 17, 1882–July 7, 1963.
Supp. 7–414
Kearny, Francis, July 23, 1785–Sept. 1, 1837.
Vol. 5, Pt. 2–269
Kearny, Lawrence, Nov. 30, 1789–Nov. 29, 1868.
Vol. 5, Pt. 2–270
Kearny, Philip, June 1, 1814–Sept. 1, 1862.
Vol. 5, Pt. 2–271
Kearny, Stephen Watts, Aug. 30, 1794–Oct. 31, 1848.
Vol. 5, Pt. 2–272
Kearsley, John, June 4, 1684–Jan. 11, 1772.
Vol. 5, Pt. 2–274
Keating, John McLeod, June 12, 1830–Aug. 15, 1906.
Vol. 5, Pt. 2–274
Keating, John Marie, Apr. 30, 1852–Nov. 17, 1893.
Vol. 5, Pt. 2–275
Keating, Kenneth Barnard, May 18, 1900–May 5, 1975.
Supp. 9–449
Keating, William Hypolitus, Aug. 11, 1799–May 17, 1840.
Vol. 5, Pt. 2–276
Keaton, Joseph Francis ("Buster"), V, Oct. 4, 189s-Feb. 1, 1966.
Supp. 8–313
Kedzie, Robert Clark, Jan. 28, 1823–Nov. 7, 1902.
Vol. 5, Pt. 2–277
Keefe, Daniel Joseph, Sept. 27, 1852–Jan. 2, 1929.
Vol. 5, Pt. 2–277
Keeler, James Edward, Sept. 10, 1857–Aug. 12, 1900.
Vol. 5, Pt. 2–278
Keeler, Ralph Olmstead, Aug. 29, 1840–Dec. 17, 1873.
Vol. 5, Pt. 2–279
Keeley, Leslie E., 1832–Feb. 21, 1900.
Vol. 5, Pt. 2–280
Keely, John Ernst Worrell, Sept. 3, 1827–Nov. 18, 1898.
Vol. 5, Pt. 2–280
Keen, Morris Longstreth, May 24, 1820–Nov. 2, 1883.
Vol. 5, Pt. 2–281
Keen, William Williams, Jan. 19, 1837–June 7, 1932.
Supp. 1–459
Keenan, James Francis, Apr. 8, 1858–Feb. 24, 1929.
Vol. 5, Pt. 2–282
Keene, James Robert, 1838–Jan. 3, 1913.
Vol. 5, Pt. 2–283
Keene, Laura, *c.* 1826–Nov. 4, 1873.
Vol. 5, Pt. 2–283
Keene, Thomas Wallace, Oct. 26, 1840–June 1, 1898.
Vol. 5, Pt. 2–284
Keener, William Albert, Mar. 10, 1856–Apr. 22, 1913.
Vol. 5, Pt. 2–285
Keeney, Barnaby Conrad, Oct. 17, 1914–June 18, 1980.
Supp. 10–402
Keep, Henry, June 22, 1818–July 30, 1869.
Vol. 5, Pt. 2–286
Keep, Robert Porter, Apr. 26, 1844–June 3, 1904.
Vol. 5, Pt. 2–286
Kefauver, (Carey) Estes, July 26, 1903–Aug. 10, 1963.
Supp. 7–415
Kefauver, Grayson Neikirk, Aug. 31, 1900–Jan. 4, 1946.
Supp. 4–449
Kehew, Mary Morton Kimball, Sept. 8, 1859–Feb. 13, 1918.
Vol. 5, Pt. 2–287
Keifer, Joseph Warren, Jan. 30, 1836–Apr. 22, 1932.
Supp. 1–460
Keimer, Samuel, Feb. 11, 1688–*c.* 1739.
Vol. 5, Pt. 2–288
Keith, Arthur, Sept. 30, 1864–Feb. 7, 1944.
Supp. 3–407
Keith, Benjamin Franklin, Jan. 26, 1846–Mar. 26, 1914.
Vol. 5, Pt. 2–289
Keith, George, *c.* 1638–Mar. 27, 1716.
Vol. 5, Pt. 2–289
Keith, James, Sept. 7, 1839–Jan. 2, 1918.
Vol. 5, Pt. 2–290
Keith, Minor Cooper, Jan. 19, 1848–June 14, 1929.
Vol. 5, Pt. 2–291
Keith, Sir William, 1680–Nov. 18, 1749.
Vol. 5, Pt. 2–292
Keith, William, Nov. 21, 1839–Apr. 13, 1911.
Vol. 5, Pt. 2–293
Keitt, Lawrence Massillon, Oct. 4, 1824–June 2, 1864.
Vol. 5, Pt. 2–294
Kelland, Clarence Budington, July 11, 1881–Feb. 18, 1964.
Supp. 7–416
Keller, Arthur Ignatius, July 4, 1867–Dec. 2, 1924.
Vol. 5, Pt. 2–294
Keller, Helen Adams, June 27, 1880–June 1, 1968.
Supp. 8–316
Keller, James Gregory, June 27, 1900–Feb. 7, 1977.
Supp. 10–404
Keller, Kaufman Thuma, Nov. 27, 1885–Jan. 21, 1966.
Supp. 8–318
Keller, Mathias, Mar. 20, 1813–Oct. 12, 1875.
Vol. 5, Pt. 2–295

Kellerman, Karl Frederic, Dec. 9, 1879–Aug. 30, 1934.
Supp. 1–461
Kellett, William Wallace, Dec. 20, 1891–July 22, 1951.
Supp. 5–377
Kelley, Alfred, Nov. 7, 1789–Dec. 2, 1859.
Vol. 5, Pt. 2–296
Kelley, Edgar Stillman, Apr. 14, 1857–Nov. 12, 1944.
Supp. 3–408
Kelley, Edith Summers, Apr. 28, 1884–June 9, 1956.
Supp. 6–328
Kelley, Florence, Sept. 12, 1859–Feb. 17, 1932.
Supp. 1–462
Kelley, Hall Jackson, Feb. 24, 1790–Jan. 20, 1874.
Vol. 5, Pt. 2–297
Kelley, James Douglas Jerrold, Dec. 25, 1847–Apr. 30, 1922.
Vol. 5, Pt. 2–298
Kelley, Oliver Hudson, Jan. 7, 1826–Jan. 20, 1913.
Vol. 5, Pt. 2–298
Kelley, William Darrah, Apr. 12, 1814–Jan. 9, 1890.
Vol. 5, Pt. 2–299
Kellogg, Albert, Dec. 6, 1813–Mar. 31, 1887.
Vol. 5, Pt. 2–300
Kellogg, Clara Louise, July 12, 1842–May 13, 1916.
Vol. 5, Pt. 2–301
Kellogg, Edward, Oct. 18, 1790–Apr. 29, 1858.
Vol. 5, Pt. 2–302
Kellogg, Elijah, May 20, 1813–Mar. 17, 1901.
Vol. 5, Pt. 2–302
Kellogg, Frank Billings, Dec. 22, 1856–Dec. 21, 1937
Supp. 2–355
Kellogg, John Harvey, Feb. 26, 1852–Dec. 14, 1943.
Supp. 3–409
Kellogg, Martin, Mar. 15, 1828–Aug. 26, 1903.
Vol. 5, Pt. 2–303
Kellogg, Paul Underwood, Sept. 30, 1879–Nov. 1, 1958.
Supp. 6–329
Kellogg, Samuel Henry, Sept. 6, 1839–May 3, 1899.
Vol. 5, Pt. 2–304
Kellogg, William Pitt, Dec. 8, 1830–Aug. 10, 1918.
Vol. 5, Pt. 2–305
Kellogg, Will Keith, Apr. 7, 1860–Oct. 6, 1951.
Supp. 5–378
Kellor, Frances (Alice), Oct. 20, 1873–Jan. 4, 1952.
Supp. 5–380
Kelly, Aloysius Oliver Joseph, June 13, 1870–Feb. 23, 1911.
Vol. 5, Pt. 2–306
Kelly, Edmond, Mar. 28, 1851–Oct. 4, 1909.
Vol. 5, Pt. 2–307
Kelly, Edward Joseph, May 1, 1876–Oct. 20, 1950.
Supp. 4–450
Kelly, Emmett Leo, Dec. 9, 1898–Mar. 28, 1979.
Supp. 10–406
Kelly, Eugene, Nov. 25, 1808–Dec. 19, 1894.
Vol. 5, Pt. 2–307
Kelly, George Edward, Jan. 16, 1887–June 18, 1974.
Supp. 9–450
Kelly, Howard Atwood, Feb. 20, 1858–Jan. 12, 1943.
Supp. 3–411
Kelly, John, Apr. 20, 1822–June 1, 1886.
Vol. 5, Pt. 2–308
Kelly, John Brendan, Oct. 4, 1889–June 20, 1960.
Supp. 6–330
Kelly, Luther Sage, July 27, 1849–Dec. 17, 1928.
Vol. 5, Pt. 2–309
Kelly, Machine Gun (George Kelly Barnes, Jr.), July 17, 1895–July 17, 1954.
Supp. 5–381
Kelly, Michael J., Dec. 31, 1857–Nov. 8, 1894.
Vol. 5, Pt. 2–309
Kelly, Myra, Aug. 26, 1875–Mar. 30, 1910.
Vol. 5, Pt. 2–310
Kelly, Walter ("Walt") Crawford, Jr., Aug. 25, 1913–Oct. 18, 1973
Supp. 9–452
Kelly, William, Aug. 21, 1811–Feb. 11, 1888.
Vol. 5, Pt. 2–311
Kelpius, Johann, 1673–1708.
Vol. 5, Pt. 2–312
Kelser, Raymond Alexander, Dec. 2, 1892–Apr. 16, 1952.
Supp. 5–382
Kelsey, Francis Willey, May 23, 1858–May 14, 1927.
Vol. 5, Pt. 2–313
Kelsey, Rayner Wickersham, Jan. 29, 1879–Oct. 29, 1934.
Supp. 1–463
Kelton, John Cunningham, June 24, 1828–July 15, 1893.
Vol. 5, Pt. 2–314
Kemble, Frances Anne, Nov. 27, 1809–Jan. 15, 1893.
Vol. 5, Pt. 2–315
Kemble, Gouverneur, Jan. 25, 1786–Sept. 16, 1875.
Vol. 5, Pt. 2–316
Kemeys, Edward, Jan. 31, 1843–May 11, 1907.
Vol. 5, Pt. 2–317
Kemmerer, Edwin Walter, June 29, 1875–Dec. 16, 1945.
Supp. 3–413
Kemp, James, May 20, 1764–Oct. 28, 1827.
Vol. 5, Pt. 2–318
Kemp, James Furman, Aug. 14, 1859–Nov. 17, 1926.
Vol. 5, Pt. 2–319
Kemp, John, Apr. 10, 1763–Nov. 15, 1812.
Vol. 5, Pt. 2–319
Kemp, Robert H., June 6, 1820–May 15, 1897.
Vol. 5, Pt. 2–320
Kemper, Jackson, Dec. 24, 1789–May 24, 1870.
Vol. 5, Pt. 2–321
Kemper, James Lawson, June 11, 1823–Apr. 7, 1895.
Vol. 5, Pt. 2–322
Kemper, Reuben, d. Jan. 28, 1827.
Vol. 5, Pt. 2–323
Kempff, Louis, Oct. 11, 1841–July 29, 1920.
Vol. 5, Pt. 2–323
Kempster, Walter, May 25, 1841–Aug. 22, 1918.
Vol. 5, Pt. 2–324
Kendall, Amos, Aug. 16, 1789–Nov. 12, 1869.
Vol. 5, Pt. 2–324
Kendall, Edward Calvin, Mar. 8, 1886–May 4, 1972.
Supp. 9–453
Kendall, George Wilkins, Aug. 22, 1809–Oct. 21, 1867.
Vol. 5, Pt. 2–327
Kendrick, Asahel Clark, Dec. 7, 1809–Oct. 21, 1895.
Vol. 5, Pt. 2–328
Kendrick, John, *c.* 1740–Dec. 12, 1794.
Vol. 5, Pt. 2–329
Kendrick, John Benjamin, Sept. 6, 1857–Nov. 3, 1933.
Supp. 1–464
Kenedy, Patrick John, Sept. 4, 1843–Jan. 4, 1906.
Vol. 5, Pt. 2–329
Kenna, John Edward, Apr. 10, 1848–Jan. 11, 1893.
Vol. 5, Pt. 2–330
Kennan, George, Feb. 16, 1845–May 10, 1924.
Vol. 5, Pt. 2–331
Kennedy, Archibald, 1685–June 14, 1763.
Vol. 5, Pt. 2–332
Kennedy, George Clayton, Sept. 22, 1919–Mar. 18, 1980.
Supp. 10–407
Kennedy, John Doby, Jan. 5, 1840–Apr. 14, 1896.
Vol. 5, Pt. 2–332
Kennedy, John Fitzgerald, May 29, 1917–Nov. 22, 1963.
Supp. 7–418
Kennedy, John Pendleton, Oct. 25, 1795–Aug. 18, 1870.
Vol. 5, Pt. 2–333
Kennedy, John Stewart, Jan. 4, 1830–Oct. 31, 1909.
Vol. 5, Pt. 2–334
Kennedy, Joseph Camp Griffith, Apr. 1, 1813–July 13, 1887.
Vol. 5, Pt. 2–335
Kennedy, Joseph Patrick, Sept. 6, 1888–Nov. 18, 1969.
Supp. 8–320
Kennedy, Robert Foster, Feb. 7, 1884–Jan. 7, 1952.
Supp. 5–383
Kennedy, Robert Francis, Nov. 20, 1925–June 6, 1968.
Supp. 8–321
Kennedy, Robert Patterson, Jan. 23, 1840–May 6, 1918.
Vol. 5, Pt. 2–336
Kennedy, William Sloane, Sept. 26, 1850–Aug. 4, 1929.
Vol. 5, Pt. 2–336
Kennelly, Arthur Edwin, Dec. 17, 1861–June 18, 1939.
Supp. 2–357
Kenner, Duncan Farrar, Feb. 11, 1813–July 3, 1887.
Vol. 5, Pt. 2–337
Kenney, Mary. [*See* O'Sullivan, Mary Kenney, 1864–1943.]
Kennicott, Robert, Nov. 13, 1835–May 13, 1866.
Vol. 5, Pt. 2–338
Kenny, John V., Apr. 6, 1893–June 2, 1975.
Supp. 9–455

Kenrick, Francis Patrick, Dec. 3, 1796–July 8, 1863.
Vol. 5, Pt. 2–339
Kenrick, Peter Richard, Aug. 17, 1806–Mar. 4, 1896.
Vol. 5, Pt. 2–340
Kenrick, William, Dec. 24, 1789–Feb. 14, 1872.
Vol. 5, Pt. 2–341
Kensett, John Frederick, Mar. 22, 1816–Dec. 14, 1872.
Vol. 5, Pt. 2–342
Kent, Arthur Atwater, Dec. 3, 1873–Mar. 4, 1949.
Supp. 4–451
Kent, Charles Foster, Aug. 13, 1867–May 2, 1925.
Vol. 5, Pt. 2–343
Kent, Edward, Jan. 8, 1802–May 19, 1877.
Vol. 5, Pt. 2–343
Kent, James, July 31, 1763–Dec. 12, 1847.
Vol. 5, Pt. 2–344
Kent, Joseph, Jan. 14, 1779–Nov. 24, 1837.
Vol. 5, Pt. 2–347
Kent, Rockwell, June 21, 1882–Mar. 13, 1971.
Supp. 9–456
Kent, William, Mar. 5, 1851–Sept. 18, 1918.
Vol. 5, Pt. 2–348
Kenton, Simon, Apr. 3, 1755–Apr. 29, 1836.
Vol. 5, Pt. 2–349
Kenton, Stanley Newcomb, Dec. 15, 1911–Aug. 25, 1979.
Supp. 10–408
Kenyon, Josephine Hemenway, May 10, 1880–Jan. 10, 1965.
Supp. 7–427
Kenyon, William Squire, June 10, 1869–Sept. 9, 1933.
Supp. 1–465
Keokuk, fl. 1790–1848.
Vol. 5, Pt. 2–350
Kephart, Ezekiel Boring, Nov. 6, 1834–Jan. 24, 1906.
Vol. 5, Pt. 2–350
Kephart, Isaiah Lafayette, Dec. 10, 1832–Oct. 28, 1908.
Vol. 5, Pt. 2–351
Kephart, John William, Nov. 12, 1872–Aug. 6, 1944.
Supp. 3–414
Keppel, Frederick, Mar. 22, 1845–Mar. 7, 1912.
Vol. 5, Pt. 2–351
Keppel, Frederick Paul, July 2, 1875–Feb. 8, 1943.
Supp. 3–415
Keppler, Joseph, Feb. 1, 1838–Feb. 19, 1894.
Vol. 5, Pt. 2–352
Kerby, William Joseph, Feb. 20, 1870–July 27, 1936.
Supp. 2–359
Kerens, Richard C., Nov. 12, 1842–Sept. 4, 1916.
Vol. 5, Pt. 2–353
Kerfoot, John Barrett, Mar. 1, 1816–July 10, 1881.
Vol. 5, Pt. 2–354
Kerlin, Isaac Newton, May 27, 1834–Oct. 25, 1893.
Vol. 5, Pt. 2–354
Kern, Jerome David, Jan. 27, 1885–Nov. 11, 1945.
Supp. 3–417
Kern, John Worth, Dec. 20, 1849–Aug. 17, 1917.
Vol. 5, Pt. 2–355
Kernan, Francis, Jan. 14, 1816–Sept. 7, 1892.
Vol. 5, Pt. 2–356
Kerner, Otto, Jr., Aug. 15, 1908–May 9, 1976.
Supp. 10–410
Kerney, James, Apr. 29, 1873–Apr. 8, 1934.
Supp. 1–466
Kerouac, Jack, Mar. 12, 1922–Oct. 21, 1969.
Supp. 8–325
Kerr, John Glasgow, Nov. 30, 1824–Aug. 10, 1901.
Vol. 5, Pt. 2–357
Kerr, Robert Samuel, Sept. 11, 1896–Jan. 1, 1963.
Supp. 7–428
Kerr, Sophie, Aug. 23, 1880–Feb. 6, 1965.
Supp. 7–429
Kerr, Walter Craig, Nov. 8, 1858–May 8, 1910.
Vol. 5, Pt. 2–357
Kerr, Washington Caruthers, May 24, 1827–Aug. 9, 1885.
Vol. 5, Pt. 2–358
Kershaw, Joseph Brevard, Jan. 5, 1822–Apr. 13, 1894.
Vol. 5, Pt. 2–359
Kester, Paul, Nov. 2, 1870–June 20, 1933.
Supp. 1–467
Kester, Vaughan, Sept. 12, 1869–July 4, 1911.
Vol. 5, Pt. 2–360
Kettell, Samuel, Aug. 5, 1800–Dec. 3, 1855.
Vol. 5, Pt. 2–360
Kettering, Charles Franklin, Aug. 29, 1876–Nov. 25, 1958.
Supp. 6–332
Key, David McKendree, Jan. 27, 1824–Feb. 3, 1900.
Vol. 5, Pt. 2–361
Key, Francis Scott, Aug. 1, 1779–Jan. 11, 1843.
Vol. 5, Pt. 2–362
Key, Philip Barton, Apr. 12, 1757–July 28, 1815.
Vol. 5, Pt. 2–363
Key, Valdimer Orlando, Jr., Mar. 13, 1908–Oct. 4, 1963.
Supp. 7–430
Keyes, Edward Lawrence, Aug. 28, 1843–Jan. 24, 1924.
Vol. 5, Pt. 2–364
Keyes, Elisha Williams, Jan. 23, 1828–Nov. 29, 1910.
Vol. 5, Pt. 2–365
Keyes, Erasmus Darwin, May 29, 1810–Oct. 14, 1895.
Vol. 5, Pt. 2–365
Keyes, Frances Parkinson, July 21, 1885–July 3, 1970.
Supp. 8–327
Keys, Clement Melville, Apr. 7, 1876–Jan. 12, 1952.
Supp. 5–384
Keyt, Alonzo Thrasher, Jan. 10, 1827–Nov. 9, 1885.
Vol. 5, Pt. 2–366
Kharasch, Morris Selig, Aug. 24, 1895–Oct. 9, 1957.
Supp. 6–333
Kiam, Omar, 1894–Mar. 28, 1954.
Supp. 5–385
Kicking Bird, d. May 3, 1875.
Vol. 5, Pt. 2–367
Kidd, William, *c.* 1645–May 23, 1701.
Vol. 5, Pt. 2–367
Kidder, Alfred Vincent, Oct. 29, 1885–June 11, 1963.
Supp. 7–431
Kidder, Daniel Parish, Oct. 18, 1815–July 29, 1891.
Vol. 5, Pt. 2–369
Kidder, Frederic, Apr. 16, 1804–Dec. 19, 1885.
Vol. 5, Pt. 2–370
Kieft, Willem, Sept. 1597–Sept. 27, 1647.
Vol. 5, Pt. 2–370
Kientpoos. [*See* Captain Jack, 1837?–1873.]
Kier, Samuel M., 1813–Oct. 6, 1874.
Vol. 5, Pt. 2–371
Kiewit, Peter, Sept. 12, 1900–Nov. 2, 1979.
Supp. 10–413
Kilbourne, James, Oct. 19, 1770–Apr. 9, 1850.
Vol. 5, Pt. 2–372
Kilby, Christopher, May 25, 1705–Oct. ¿, 1771.
Supp. 1–467
Kildahl, Johan Nathan, Jan. 4, 1857–Sept. 25, 1920.
Vol. 5, Pt. 2–373
Kilgallen, Dorothy Mae, July 3, 1913–Nov. 8, 1965.
Supp. 7–433
Kilgore, Harley Martin, Jan. 11, 1893–Feb. 28, 1956.
Supp. 6–335
Kilmer, Alfred Joyce, Dec. 6, 1886–July 30, 1918.
Vol. 5, Pt. 2–373
Kilpatrick, Hugh Judson, Jan. 14, 1836–Dec. 2, 1881.
Vol. 5, Pt. 2–374
Kilpatrick, John Reed, June 15, 1889–May 7, 1960.
Supp. 6–936
Kilpatrick, William Heard, Nov. 20, 1871–Feb. 13, 1965.
Supp. 7–434
Kilty, William, 1757–Oct. 10, 1821.
Vol. 5, Pt. 2–375
Kimball, Dan Able, Mar. 1, 1896–July 30, 1970.
Supp. 8–329
Kimball, Dexter Simpson, Oct. 21, 1865–Nov. 1, 1952.
Supp. 5–386
Kimball, Gilman, Dec. 8, 1804–July 27, 1892.
Vol. 5, Pt. 2–376
Kimball, Heber Chase, June 14, 1801–June 22, 1868.
Vol. 5, Pt. 2–377
Kimball, Nathan, Nov. 22, 1823?–Jan. 21, 1898.
Vol. 5, Pt. 2–378
Kimball, Richard Burleigh, Oct. 11, 1816–Dec. 28, 1892.
Vol. 5, Pt. 2–378
Kimball, (Sidney) Fiske, Dec. 8, 1888–Aug. 14, 1955.
Supp. 5–387
Kimball, Sumner Increase, Sept. 2, 1834–June 21, 1923.
Vol. 5, Pt. 2–379
Kimball, William Wirt, Jan 9, 1848–Jan. 26, 1930.
Vol. 5, Pt. 2–380

Kimmel, Husband Edward, Feb. 26, 1882–May 14, 1968.
Supp. 8–330
King, Albert Freeman Africanus, Jan. 18, 1841–Dec. 13, 1914.
Vol. 5, Pt. 2–381
King, Alexander, Nov. 13, 1900–Nov. 17, 1965.
Supp. 7–436
King, Austin Augustus, Sept. 21, 1802–Apr. 22, 1870.
Vol. 5, Pt. 2–382
King, Basil. [*See* King, William Benjamin Basil, 1859–1928.]
King, Carol Weiss, Aug. 24, 1895–Jan. 22, 1952.
Supp. 5–389
King, Charles, Mar. 16, 1789–Sept. 27, 1867.
Vol. 5, Pt. 2–382
King, Charles William, *c.* 1809–Sept. 27, 1845.
Vol. 5, Pt. 2–383
King, Clarence, Jan. 6, 1842–Dec. 24, 1901.
Vol. 5, Pt. 2–384
King, Dan, Jan. 27, 1791–Nov. 13, 1864.
Vol. 5, Pt. 2–386
King, Edward Leonard, Dec. 5, 1873–Dec. 27, 1933.
Supp. 1–468
King, Edward Skinner, May 31, 1861–Sept. 10, 1931.
Vol. 5, Pt. 2–387
King, Edward Smith, Sept. 8, 1848–Mar. 27, 1896.
Vol. 5, Pt. 2–387
King, Ernest Joseph, Nov. 23, 1878–June 25, 1956.
Supp. 6–338
King, Franklin Hiram, June 8, 1848–Aug. 4, 1911.
Vol. 5, Pt. 2–388
King, Grace Elizabeth, Nov. 29, 1851–Jan. 14, 1932.
Vol. 5, Pt. 2–389
King, Henry, May 11, 1842–Mar. 15, 1915.
Vol. 5, Pt. 2–390
King, Henry Churchill, Sept. 18, 1858–Feb. 27, 1934.
Supp. 1–469
King, Henry Melville, Sept. 3, 1838–June 16, 1919.
Vol. 5, Pt. 2–391
King, Horatio, June 21, 1811–May 20, 1897.
Vol. 5, Pt. 2–391
King, James Gore, May 8, 1791–Oct. 3, 1853.
Vol. 5, Pt. 2–392
King, John, Jan. 1, 1813–June 19, 1893.
Vol. 5, Pt. 2–393
King, John Alsop, Jan. 3, 1788–July 7, 1867.
Vol. 5, Pt. 2–394
King, John Pendleton, Apr. 3, 1799–Mar. 19, 1888.
Vol. 5, Pt. 2–395
King, Jonas, July 29, 1792–May 22, 1869.
Vol. 5, Pt. 2–395
King, Martin Luther, Jr., Jan. 15, 1929–Apr. 4, 1968.
Supp. 8–332
King, Preston, Oct. 14, 1806–Nov. 13, 1865.
Vol. 5, Pt. 2–396
King, Richard, July 10, 1825–Apr. 14, 1885.
Vol. 5, Pt. 2–397
King, Richard, Jr., Dec. 17, 1884–May 4, 1974.
Supp. 9–459
King, Rufus, Mar. 24, 1755–Apr. 29, 1827.
Vol. 5, Pt. 2–398
King, Rufus, Jan. 26, 1814–Oct. 13, 1876.
Vol. 5, Pt. 2–400
King, Samuel, Jan. 24, 1748–Dec. 30, 1819.
Vol. 5, Pt. 2–401
King, Samuel Archer, Apr. 9, 1828–Nov. 3, 1914.
Vol. 5, Pt. 2–401
King, Samuel Ward, May 23, 1786–Jan. 21, 1851.
Vol. 5, Pt. 2–402
King, Stanley, May 11, 1883–Apr. 28, 1951.
Supp. 5–390
King, Thomas Butler, Aug. 27, 1800–May 10, 1864.
Vol. 5, Pt. 2–403
King, Thomas Starr, Dec. 17, 1824–Mar. 4, 1864.
Vol. 5, Pt. 2–403
King, William, Feb. 9, 1768–June 17, 1852.
Vol. 5, Pt. 2–405
King, William Benjamin Basil, Feb. 26, 1859–June 22, 1928.
Vol. 5, Pt. 2–406
King, William Rufus Devane, Apr. 7, 1786–Apr. 18, 1853.
Vol. 5, Pt. 2–406
King of William, James, Jan. 28, 1822–May 20, 1856.
Vol. 5, Pt. 2–407
Kingsbury, Albert, Dec. 23, 1862–July 28, 1943.
Supp. 3–418
Kingsbury, John, May 26, 1801–Dec. 21, 1874.
Vol. 5, Pt. 2–408
Kingsford, Thomas, Sept. 29, 1799–Nov. 28, 1869.
Vol. 5, Pt. 2–409
Kingsley, Calvin, Sept. 8, 1812–Apr. 6, 1870.
Vol. 5, Pt. 2–410
Kingsley, Darwin Pearl, May 5, 1857–Oct. 6, 1932.
Supp. 1–470
Kingsley, Elbridge, Sept. 17, 1842–Aug. 28, 1918.
Vol. 5, Pt. 2–411
Kingsley, Elizabeth Seelman, Oct. 9, 1871–June 7, 1957.
Supp. 6–341
Kingsley, James Luce, Aug. 28, 1778–Aug. 31, 1852.
Vol. 5, Pt. 2–411
Kingsley, Norman William, Oct. 26, 1829–Feb. 20, 1913.
Vol. 5, Pt. 2–412
Kinkaid, Thomas Cassin, Apr. 3, 1888–Nov. 17, 1972.
Supp. 9–460
Kinkead, Edgar Benton, Mar. 14, 1863–Apr. 9, 1930.
Vol. 5, Pt. 2–413
Kinloch, Cleland, 1760–Sept. 12, 1823.
Vol. 5, Pt. 2–414
Kinloch, Robert Alexander, Feb. 20, 1826–Dec. 23, 1891.
Vol. 5, Pt. 2–414
Kinne, La Vega George, Nov. 5, 1846–Mar. 16, 1906.
Vol. 5, Pt. 2–415
Kinnersley, Ebenezer, Nov. 30, 1711–July 4, 1778.
Vol. 5, Pt. 2–416
Kinney, Elizabeth Clementine Dodge Stedman, Dec. 1810–Nov. 19, 1889.
Vol. 5, Pt. 2–417
Kinney, William Burnet, Sept. 4, 1799–Oct. 21, 1880.
Vol. 5, Pt. 2–417
Kinnicutt, Leonard Parker, May 22, 1854–Feb. 6, 1911.
Vol. 5, Pt. 2–418
Kino, Eusebio Francisco, *c.* 1645–Mar. 15, 1711.
Vol. 5, Pt. 2–419
Kinsella, Thomas, Dec. 31, 1832–Feb. 11, 1884.
Vol. 5, Pt. 2–420
Kinsey, Alfred Charles, June 23, 1894–Aug. 25, 1956.
Supp. 6–342
Kinsey, John, 1693–May 11, 1750 o.s.
Vol. 5, Pt. 2–421
Kintner, Robert Edmonds, Sept. 12, 1909–Dec. 20, 1980.
Supp. 10–414
Kintpuash. [*See* Captain Jack, 1837?–1873.]
Kinzie, John, Dec. 3, 1763–Jan. 6, 1828.
Vol. 5, Pt. 2–422
Kip, William Ingraham, Oct. 3, 1811–Apr. 7, 1893.
Vol. 5, Pt. 2–422
Kiphuth, Robert John Herman, Nov. 17, 1890–Jan. 7, 1967.
Supp. 8–336
Kiplinger, Willard Monroe, Jan. 8, 1891–Aug. 6, 1967.
Supp. 8–337
Kirby, Allan Price, July 31, 1892–May 2, 1973.
Supp. 9–462
Kirby, Ephraim, Feb. 23, 1757–Oct. 20, 1804.
Vol. 5, Pt. 2–423
Kirby, George Hughes, Feb 9, 1875–Aug. 11, 1935.
Supp. 1–471
Kirby, J. Hudson, Apr. 3, 1819–1848.
Vol. 5, Pt. 2–424
Kirby, Rollin, Sept. 4, 1875–May 9, 1952.
Supp. 5–391
Kirby-Smith, Edmund, May 16, 1824–Mar. 28, 1893.
Vol. 5, Pt. 2–424
Kirchhoff, Charles William Henry, Mar. 28, 1853–July 22, 1916.
Vol. 5, Pt. 2–426
Kirchmayer, John, *c.* 1860–Nov. 29, 1930.
Vol. 5, Pt. 2–426
Kirchwey, Freda, Sept. 26, 1893–Jan. 3, 1976.
Supp. 10–416
Kirchwey, George Washington, July 3, 1855–Mar. 3, 1942.
Supp. 3–420
Kirk, Alan Goodrich, Oct. 30, 1888–Oct. 15, 1963.
Supp. 7–437
Kirk, Edward Norris, Aug. 14, 1802–Mar. 27, 1874.
Vol. 5, Pt. 2–427

Kirk, John Foster, Mar. 22, 1824–Sept. 21, 1904.
Vol. 5, Pt. 2–428
Kirk, Norman Thomas, Jan. 3, 1888–Aug. 13, 1960.
Supp. 6–344
Kirkbride, Thomas Story, July 31, 1809–Dec. 16 1883.
Vol. 5, Pt. 2–429
Kirkland, Caroline Matilda Stansbury, Jan. 12, 1801–Apr. 6, 1864.
Vol. 5, Pt. 2–430
Kirkland, James Hampton, Sept. 9, 1859–Aug. 5, 1939.
Supp. 2–360
Kirkland, John Thornton, Aug. 17, 1770–Apr. 26, 1840.
Vol. 5, Pt. 2–431
Kirkland, Joseph, Jan. 7, 1830–Apr. 29, 1894.
Vol. 5, Pt. 2–431
Kirkland, Samuel, Nov. 20, 1741–Feb. 28, 1808.
Vol. 5, Pt. 2–432
Kirkman, Marshall Monroe, July 10, 1842–Apr. 18, 1921.
Vol. 5, Pt. 2–434
Kirkpatrick, Andrew, Feb. 17, 1756–Jan. 6, 1831.
Vol. 5, Pt. 2–435
Kirkus, Virginia, Dec. 7, 1893–Sept. 10, 1980.
Supp. 10–417.
Kirkwood, Daniel, Sept. 27, 1814–June 11, 1895.
Vol. 5, Pt. 2–436
Kirkwood, John Gamble, May 30, 1907–Aug. 9, 1959.
Supp. 6–345
Kirkwood, Samuel Jordan, Dec. 20, 1813–Sept. 1, 1894.
Vol. 5, Pt. 2–436
Kirlin, Joseph Louis Jerome, Mar. 20, 1868–Nov. 26, 1926.
Vol. 5, Pt. 2–437
Kirstein, Louis Edward, July 9, 1867–Dec. 10, 1942.
Supp. 3–421
Kirtland, Jared Potter, Nov. 10, 1793–Dec. 10, 1877.
Vol. 5, Pt. 2–438
Kiss, Max, Nov. 9, 1882–June 22, 1967.
Supp. 8–338
Kitchin, Claude, Mar. 24, 1869–May 31, 1923.
Vol. 5, Pt. 2–439
Kitchin, William Walton, Oct. 9, 1866–Nov. 9, 1924.
Vol. 5, Pt. 2–440
Kittredge, George Lyman, Feb. 28, 1860–July 23, 1941.
Supp. 3–422
Kittson, Norman Wolfred, Mar. 5, 1814–May 10, 1888.
Vol. 5, Pt. 2–441
Klauder, Charles Zeller, Feb. 9, 1872–Oct. 30, 1938.
Supp. 2–362
Klaw, Marc, May 29, 1858–June 14, 1936.
Supp. 2–363
Kleberg, Robert Justus, Jr., Mar. 29, 1896–Oct. 13, 1974.
Supp. 9–463
Klein, Anne, Aug. 3, 1923–Mar. 19, 1974.
Supp. 9–464
Klein, August Clarence, Apr. 1, 1887–Feb. 3, 1948.
Supp. 4–453
Klein, Bruno Oscar, June 6, 1858–June 22, 1911.
Vol. 5, Pt. 2–442
Klein, Charles, Jan. 7, 1867–May 7, 1915.
Vol. 5, Pt. 2–442
Klein, Charles Herbert ("Chuck"), Oct. 7, 1904–Mar. 28, 1956.
Supp. 6–346
Klein, Joseph Frederic, Oct. 10, 1849–Feb. 11, 1918.
Vol. 5, Pt. 2–443
Klem, William J. (Bill), Feb. 22, 1874–Sept. 16, 1951.
Supp. 5–393
Kline, Franz Josef, May 23, 1910–Mary 13, 1962.
Supp. 7–438
Kline, George, *c.* 1757–Nov. 12, 1820.
Vol. 5, Pt. 2–444
Klingelsmith, Margaret Center, Nov. 27, 1859–Jan. 19, 1931.
Vol. 5, Pt. 2–444
Klippart, John Hancock, July 26, 1823–Oct. 24, 1878.
Vol. 5, Pt. 2–445
Klipstein, Louis Frederick, Jan. 2, 1813–Aug. 20, 1878.
Vol. 5, Pt. 2–446
Klopsch, Louis, Mar. 26, 1852–Mar. 7, 1910.
Vol. 5, Pt. 2–447
Knab, Frederick, Sept. 22, 1865–Nov. 2, 1918.
Vol. 5, Pt. 2–448
Knabe, Valentine Wilhelm Ludwig, June 3, 1803–May 21, 1864.
Vol. 5, Pt. 2–448
Knapp, Bradford, Dec. 24, 1870–June 11, 1938.
Supp. 2–364
Knapp, George, Sept. 25, 1814–Sept. 18, 1883.
Vol. 5, Pt. 2–448
Knapp, Herman, Mar. 17, 1832–Apr. 30, 1911.
Vol. 5, Pt. 2–449
Knapp, Joseph Palmer, May 14, 1864–Jan. 30, 1951.
Supp. 5–394
Knapp, Martin Augustine, Nov. 6, 1843–Feb. 10, 1923.
Vol. 5, Pt. 2–450
Knapp, Philip Coombs, June 3, 1858–Feb. 23, 1920.
Vol. 5, Pt. 2–451
Knapp, Samuel Lorenzo, Jan. 19, 1783–July 8, 1838.
Vol. 3, Pt. 1–452
Knapp, Seaman Asahel, Dec. 16, 1833–Apr. 1, 1911.
Vol. 5, Pt. 2–452
Knapp, William Ireland, Mar. 10, 1835–Dec. 6, 1908.
Vol. 5, Pt. 2–453
Knappen, Theodore Temple, Nov. 21, 1900–Mar. 20, 1951.
Supp. 5–395
Knauth, Oswald Whitman, June 3, 1887–July 13, 1962.
Supp. 7–440
Kneass, Samuel Honeyman, Nov. 5, 1806–Feb. 15, 1858.
Vol. 5, Pt. 2–454
Kneass, Strickland, July 29, 1821–Jan. 14, 1884.
Vol. 5, Pt. 2–455
Kneass, William, Sept. 25, 1780–Aug. 27, 1840.
Vol. 5, Pt. 2–456
Kneeland, Abner, Apr. 7, 1774–Aug. 27, 1844.
Vol. 5, Pt. 2–457
Kneeland, Samuel, Jan. 31, 1697–Dec. 14, 1769.
Vol. 5, Pt. 2–458
Kneeland, Samuel, Aug. 1, 1821–Sept. 27, 1888.
Vol. 5, Pt. 2–459
Kneeland, Stillman Foster, May 17, 1845–Aug. 30, 1926.
Vol. 5, Pt. 2–459
Kneisel, Franz, Jan. 26, 1865–Mar. 26, 1926.
Vol. 5, Pt. 2–460
Knickerbocker, Herman, July 27, 1779–Jan. 30, 1855.
Vol. 5, Pt. 2–461
Knight, Austin Melvin, Dec. 16, 1854–Feb 26, 1927.
Vol. 5, Pt. 2–462
Knight, Daniel Ridgway, Mar. 15, 1840–Mar. 9, 1924.
Vol. 5, Pt. 2–463
Knight, Edward Collings, Dec. 8, 1813–July 21, 1892.
Vol. 5, Pt. 2–463
Knight, Edward Henry, June 1, 1824–Jan. 22, 1883.
Vol. 5, Pt. 2–464
Knight, Frank Hyneman, Nov. 7, 1885–Apr. 15, 1972.
Supp. 9–466
Knight, Frederick Irving, May 18, 1841–Feb. 20, 1909.
Vol. 5, Pt. 2–465
Knight, Goodwin Jess ("Goodie"), Dec. 9, 1896–May 1970.
Supp. 8–339
Knight, Henry Cogswell, Jan. 29, 1789–Jan. 10, 1835.
Vol. 5, Pt. 2–466
Knight, Jonathan, Nov. 22, 1787–Nov. 22, 1858.
Vol. 5, Pt. 2–467
Knight, Jonathan, Sept. 4, 1789–Aug. 25, 1864.
Vol. 5, Pt. 2–467
Knight, Lucian Lamar, Feb. 9, 1868–Nov. 19, 1933.
Supp. 1–471
Knight, Ridgway. [*See* Knight, Daniel Ridgway, 1840–1924.]
Knight, Sarah Kemble, Apr. 19, 1666–Sept. 25, 1727.
Vol. 5, Pt. 2–468
Knopf, Blanche Wolf, July 30, 1893–June 4, 1966.
Supp. 8–341
Knott, Aioysius Leo, May 12, 1829–Apr. 18, 1918.
Vol. 5, Pt. 2–469
Knott, James Proctor, Aug. 29, 1830–June 18, 1911.
Vol. 5, Pt. 2–470
Knowland, William Fife, June 26, 1908–Feb. 23, 1974.
Supp. 9–467
Knowles, John Hilton, May 23, 1926–Mar. 6, 1979.
Supp. 10–419
Knowles, Lucius James, July 2, 1819–Feb. 25, 1884.
Vol. 5, Pt. 2–470
Knowlton, Charles, May 10, 1800–Feb. 20, 1850.
Vol. 5, Pt. 2–471
Knowlton, Frank Hall, Sept. 2, 1860–Nov. 22, 1926.
Vol. 5, Pt. 2–472

Knowlton, Marcus Perrin, Feb. 3, 1839–May 7, 1918.
Vol. 5, Pt. 2–473
Knowlton, Thomas, Nov. 1740–Sept. 16, 1776.
Vol. 5, Pt. 2–474
Knox, Dudley Wright, June 21, 1877–June 11, 1960.
Supp. 6–348
Knox, Frank, Jan. 1, 1874–Apr. 28, 1944.
Supp. 3–424
Knox, George William, Aug. 11, 1853–Apr. 25, 1912.
Vol. 5, Pt. 2–475
Knox, Henry, July 25, 1750–Oct. 25, 1806.
Vol. 5, Pt. 2–475
Knox, John Jay, Mar. 19, 1828–Feb. 9, 1892.
Vol. 5, Pt. 2–477
Knox, Philander Chase, May 6, 1853–Oct. 12, 1921.
Vol. 5, Pt. 2–478
Knox, Rose Markward, Nov. 18, 1857–Sept. 27, 1950.
Supp. 4–454
Knox, Samuel, 1756–Aug. 31, 1832.
Vol. 5, Pt. 2–480
Knox, Thomas Wallace, June 26, 1835–Jan. 6, 1896.
Vol. 5, Pt. 2–481
Knudsen, William S., Mar. 25, 1879–Apr. 27, 1948.
Supp. 4–456
Knutson, Harold, Oct. 20, 1880–Aug. 21, 1953.
Supp. 5–396
Kobbé, Gustav, Mar. 4, 1857–July 27, 1918.
Vol. 5, Pt. 2–482
Kober, George Martin, Mar. 28, 1850–Apr. 24, 1931.
Vol. 5, Pt. 2–483
Koch, Fred Conrad, May 16, 1876–Jan. 26, 1948.
Supp. 4–459
Koch Frederick Henry, Sept. 12, 1877–Aug 16 1944.
Supp. 3–426
Koch, Vivienne, 1911–Nov. 29, 1961.
Supp. 7–441
Kocherthal, Josua von, 1669–Dec. 27, 1719.
Vol. 5, Pt. 2–484
Koehler, Robert, Nov. 28, 1850–Apr. 23, 1917.
Vol. 5, Pt. 2–484
Koehler, Sylvester Rosa, Feb. 11, 1837–Sept. 15, 1900.
Vol. 5, Pt. 2–485
Koemmenich, Louis, Oct. 4, 1866–Aug. 14, 1922.
Vol. 5, Pt. 2–486
Koenig, George Augustus, May 12, 1844–Jan. 14, 1913.
Vol. 5, Pt. 2–486
Koenigsberg, Moses, Apr. 16, 1878–Sept. 21, 1945.
Supp. 3–427
Koerner, Gustave Philip. [*See* Körner, Gustav Philipp, 1809–1896.]
Koffka, Kurt, Mar. 18, 1886–Nov. 22, 1941.
Supp. 3–428
Kofoid, Charles Atwood, Oct. 11, 1865–May 30, 1947.
Supp. 4–461
Kohlberg, Alfred, Jan. 27, 1887–Apr. 7, 1960.
Supp. 6–349
Kohler, Elmer Peter, Nov. 6, 1865–May 24, 1938.
Supp. 2–365
Kohler, Kaufmann, May 10, 1843–Jan. 28, 1926.
Vol. 5, Pt. 2–487
Kohler, Max James, May 22, 1871–July 24, 1934.
Supp. 1–472
Kohler, Walter Jodok, Mar. 3, 1875–Apr. 21, 1940.
Supp. 2–366
Kohler, Walter Jodok, Jr., Apr. 4, 1904–Mar. 21, 1976.
Supp. 10–420
Köhler, Wolfgang, Jan. 21, 1887–June 11, 1967.
Supp. 8–343
Kohlmann, Anthony, July 13, 1771–Apr. 10, 1836.
Vol. 5, Pt. 2–488
Kohlsaat, Herman Henry, Mar. 22, 1853–Oct. 17, 1924.
Vol. 5, Pt. 2–489
Kohut, Alexander, Apr. 22, 1842–May 25, 1894.
Vol. 5, Pt. 2–490
Kohut, George Alexander, Feb. 11, 1874–Dec. 31, 1933.
Supp. 1–473
Kolb, Dielman, Nov. 10, 1691–Dec. 28, 1756.
Vol. 5, Pt. 2–491
Kolb, Lawrence, Feb. 20, 1881–Nov. 17, 1972.
Supp. 9–469
Kolb, Reuben Francis, Apr. 15, 1839–Mar. 23, 1918.
Vol. 5, Pt. 2–492
Kolle, Frederick Strange, Nov. 22, 1872–May 10, 1929.
Vol. 5, Pt. 2–492
Koller, Carl, Dec. 3, 1857–Mar. 21, 1944.
Supp. 3–430
Kollock, Shepard, Sept. 1750–July 28, 1839.
Vol. 5, Pt. 2–493
Koopman, Augustus, Jan. 2, 1869–Jan. 31, 1914.
Vol. 5, Pt. 2–494
Kooweskowe. [*See* Ross, John, *c.* 1790–1866.]
Koren, John, Mar. 3, 1861–Nov. 9, 1923.
Vol. 5, Pt. 2–494
Koren, Ulrik Vilhelm, Dec. 22, 1826–Dec. 20, 1910.
Vol. 5, Pt. 2–495
Körner, Gustav Philipp, Nov. 20, 1809–Apr. 9, 1896.
Vol. 5, Pt. 2–496
Korngold, Erich Wolfgang, May 29, 1897–Nov. 29, 1957.
Supp. 6–351
Kosciuszko, Tadeusz Andrzej Bonawentura, Feb. 12, 1746–Oct. 15, 1817.
Vol. 5, Pt. 2–497
Kostelanetz, André, Dec. 22, 1901–Jan. 13, 1980.
Supp. 10–421
Koussevitzky, Olga Naumoff, July 15, 1901–Jan. 5, 1978.
Supp. 10–422
Koussevitzky, Serge Alexandrovich, July 26, 1874–June 4, 1951.
Supp. 5–397
Kovacs, Ernie, Jan. 23, 1919–Jan. 13, 1962.
Supp. 7–442
Koyl, Charles Herschel, Aug. 14, 1855–Dec. 18, 1931.
Vol. 5, Pt. 2–498
Kracauer, Siegfried, Feb. 8, 1889–Nov. 26, 1966.
Supp. 8–346
Kraemer, Henry, July 22, 1868–Sept. 9, 1924.
Vol. 5, Pt. 2–499
Kraft, James Lewis, Nov. 11, 1874–Feb. 16, 1953.
Supp. 5–399
Krantz, Philip. [See Rombro, Jacob, 1858–1922.]
Krapp, George Philip, Sept. 1, 1872–Apr. 21, 1934.
Supp. 1–474
Kraus, John, Feb. 2, 1815–Mar. 4, 1896.
Vol. 5, Pt. 2–499
Kraus-Boelté, Maria, Nov. 8, 1836–Nov. 1, 1918.
Vol. 5, Pt. 2–500
Krause, Allen Kramer, Feb. 13, 1881–May 12, 1941.
Supp. 3–431
Krauskopf, Joseph, Jan. 21, 1858–June 12, 1923.
Vol. 5, Pt. 2–500
Krauth, Charles Philip, May 7, 1797–May 30, 1867.
Vol. 5, Pt. 2–501
Krauth, Charles Porterfield, Mar. 17, 1823–Jan. 2, 1883.
Vol. 5, Pt. 2–502
Krehbiel, Christian, Oct. 18, 1832–Apr. 30, 1909.
Vol. 5, Pt. 2–503
Krehbiel, Henry Edward, Mar. 10, 1854–Mar. 20, 1923.
Vol. 5, Pt. 2–504
Kreisler, Fritz, Feb. 2, 1875–Jan. 29, 1962.
Supp. 7–443
Kremers, Edward, Feb. 23, 1865–July 9, 1941.
Supp. 3–432
Kresge, Sebastian Spering, July 31, 1867–Oct. 18, 1966.
Supp. 8–347
Kress, Samuel Henry, July 23, 1863–Sept. 22, 1955.
Supp. 5–400
Kreymborg, Alfred Francis, Dec. 10, 1883–Aug. 14, 1966.
Supp. 8–349
Krez, Konrad, Apr. 27, 1828–Mar. 9, 1897.
Vol. 5, Pt. 2–505
Krimmel, John Lewis, 1789–July 15, 1821.
Vol. 5, Pt. 2–506
Krock, Arthur, Nov. 16, 1886–Apr. 12, 1974.
Supp. 9–471
Kroeber, Alfred Louis, June 11, 1876–Oct. 5, 1960.
Supp. 6–352
Kroeger, Adorph Ernst, Dec. 28, 1837–Mar. 8, 1882.
Vol. 5, Pt. 2–507
Kroeger, Ernest Richard, Aug. 10, 1862–Apr. 7, 1934.
Supp. 1–475
Kroger, Bernhard Henry, Jan. 24, 1860–July 21, 1938.
Supp. 2–367

Krol, Bastiaen Jansen, 1595–1674.
Vol. 5, Pt. 2–508
Kronenberger, Louis, Jr., Dec. 9, 1904–Apr. 30, 1980.
Supp. 10–424
Krueger, Walter, Jan. 26, 1881–Aug. 20, 1967.
Supp. 8–351
Kruell, Gustav, Oct. 31, 1843–Jan. 2, 1907.
Vol. 5, Pt. 2–508
Kruesi, John, May 15, 1843–Feb. 22, 1899.
Vol. 5, Pt. 2–509
Krug, Julius Albert, Nov. 23, 1907–Mar. 26, 1970.
Supp. 8–352
Krüsi, Hermann. [*See* Krüsi, Johann Heinrich Hermann, 1817–1903.]
Krüsi, Johann Heinrich Hermann, June 24, 1817–Jan. 28, 1903.
Vol. 5, Pt. 2–510
Kruger, Otto, Sept. 6, 1886–Sept. 6, 1974.
Supp. 9–472
Krupa, Eugene Bertram ("Gene"), Jan. 15, 1909–Oct. 16, 1973.
Supp. 9–473
Krutch, Joseph Wood, Nov. 25, 1893–May 22, 1970.
Supp. 8–343
Kugelman, Frederick Benjamin. [*See* Kaye, Frederick Benjamin, 1892–1930.]
Kuhn, Adam, Nov. 17, 1741–July 5, 1817.
Vol. 5, Pt. 2–510
Kuhn, Joseph Ernst, June 14, 1864–Nov. 12, 1935.
Supp. 1–476
Kuhn, Walt, Oct. 27, 1877–July 13, 1949.
Supp. 4–462
Kuhlman, Kathryn, May 9, 1907–Feb. 20, 1976.
Supp. 10–425
Kuiper, Gerard Peter, Dec. 7, 1905–Dec. 24, 1973.
Supp. 9–475
Kumler, Henry, Jan. 3, 1775–Jan. 8, 1854.
Vol. 5, Pt. 2–511
Kunitz, Moses, Dec. 19, 1887–Apr. 20, 1978.
Supp. 10–426
Kuniyoshi, Yasuo, Sept. 1, 1893–May 14, 1953.
Supp. 5–402
Kunz, George Frederick, Sept. 29, 1856–June 29, 1932.
Supp. 1–476
Kunze, John Christopher, Aug. 5, 1744–July 24, 1807.
Vol. 5, Pt. 2–512
Kunze, Richard Ernest, Apr. 7, 1838–Feb. 7, 1919.
Vol. 5, Pt. 2–513
Kurtz, Benjamin, Feb. 28, 1795–Dec. 29, 1865.
Vol. 5, Pt. 2–514
Kuskov, Ivan Aleksandrovich, 1765–October 1823.
Vol. 5, Pt. 2–514
Kuykendall, Ralph Simpson, Apr. 12, 1885–May 9, 1963.
Supp. 7–445
Kyes, Roger Martin, Mar. 6, 1906–Feb. 13, 1971.
Supp. 9–476
Kyle, David Braden, Oct. 11, 1863–Oct. 23, 1916.
Vol. 5, Pt. 2–515
Kyle, James Henderson, Feb. 24, 1854–July 1, 1901.
Vol. 5, Pt. 2–515
Kyne, Peter Bernard, Oct. 12, 1880–Nov. 25, 1957.
Supp. 6–353
Kynett, Alpha Jefferson, Aug. 12, 1829–Feb. 23, 1899.
Vol. 5, Pt. 2–516

Labaree, Leonard Woods, Aug. 26, 1897–May 5, 1980.
Supp. 10–429
La Barge, Joseph, Oct. 1, 1815–Apr. 3, 1899.
Vol. 5, Pt. 2–517
La Borde, Maximilian, June 5, 1804–Nov. 6, 1873.
Vol. 5, Pt. 2–518
Lacey, John, Feb. 4, 1755–Feb. 17, 1814.
Vol. 5, Pt. 2–519
Lacey, John Fletcher, May 30, 1841–Sept. 29, 1913.
Vol. 5, Pt. 2–519
Lachaise, Gaston, Mar. 19, 1882–Oct. 18, 1935.
Supp. 1–477
Lackaye, Wilton, Sept. 30, 1862–Aug. 22, 1932.
Supp. 1–479
Laclede, Pierre, *c.* 1724–June 20, 1778.
Vol. 5, Pt. 2–520
Lacock, Abner, July 9, 1770–Apr. 12, 1837.
Vol. 5, Pt. 2–521
Lacy, Drury, Oct. 5, 1758–Dec. 6, 1815.
Vol. 5, Pt. 2–522
Lacy, Ernest, Sept. 19, 1863–June 17, 1916.
Vol. 5, Pt. 2–522
Ladd, Alan Walbridge, Sept. 3, 1913–Jan. 29, 1964.
Supp. 7–446
Ladd, Carl Edwin, Feb. 25, 1888–July 23, 1943.
Supp. 3–433
Ladd, Catherine, Oct. 28, 1808–Jan. 30, 1899.
Vol. 5, Pt. 2–524
Ladd, Edwin Fremont, Dec. 13, 1859–June 22, 1925.
Vol. 5, Pt. 2–524
Ladd, George Trumbull, Jan. 19, 1842–Aug. 8, 1921.
Vol. 5, Pt. 2–525
Ladd, Joseph Brown, July 7, 1764–Nov. 2, 1786.
Vol. 5, Pt. 2–526
Ladd, Kate Macy, Apr. 6, 1863–Aug. 27, 1945.
Supp. 3–434
Ladd, William, May 10, 1778–Apr. 9, 1841.
Vol. 5, Pt. 2–527
Ladd, William Sargent, Oct. 10, 1826–Jan. 6, 1893.
Vol. 5, Pt. 2–528
Ladd-Franklin, Christine, Dec. 1, 1847–Mar. 5, 1930.
Vol. 5, Pt. 2–528
Laemmle, Carl, Jan. 17, 1867–Sept. 24, 1939.
Supp. 2–368
La Farge, Christopher Grant, Jan. 5, 1862–Oct. 11, 1938.
Supp. 2–369
La Farge, Christopher Grant, Dec. 10, 1897–Jan. 5, 1956.
Supp. 6–355
La Farge, Grant. [*See* La Farge, Christopher Grant, 1862–1938.]
La Farge, John, Mar. 31, 1835–Nov. 14, 1910.
Vol. 5, Pt. 2–530
LaFarge, John, Feb. 13, 1880–Nov. 24, 1963.
Supp. 7–447
La Farge, Oliver Hazard Perry, Dec. 19, 1901–Aug. 2, 1963.
Supp. 7–448
Lafayette, Marie Joseph Paul Yves Roch Gilbert du Motier, Marquis de, Sept 6, 1757–May 20, 1834.
Vol. 5, Pt. 1–535
Lafever, Minard, Aug. 10, 1798–Sept. 26, 1854.
Supp. 1–479
Laffan, William Mackay, Jan. 22, 1848–Nov. 19, 1909.
Vol. 5, Pt. 2–539
Laffite, Jean, fl. 1809–1821.
Vol. 5, Pt. 2–540
Lafitte, Jean. [*See* Laffite, Jean, fl. 1809–1821.]
La Flesche, Susette. [*See* Bright Eyes, 1854–1903.]
La Follette, Philip Fox, May 8, 1897–Aug. 18, 1965.
Supp. 7–450
La Follette, Robert Marion, June 14, 1855–June 18, 1925.
Vol. 5, Pt. 2–541
La Follette, Robert Marion, Jr., Feb. 6, 1895–Feb. 24, 1953.
Supp. 5–403
Lafon, Thomy, Dec. 28, 1810–Dec. 22, 1893.
Vol. 5, Pt. 2–546
La Guardia, Fiorello Henry, Dec. 11, 1882–Sept. 20, 1947.
Supp. 4–464
Laguna, Theodore de Leo de, July 22, 1876–Sept. 22, 1930.
Vol. 5, Pt. 2–547
Lahey, Frank Howard, June 1, 1880–June 27, 1953.
Supp. 5–404
Lahontan, Louis-Armand de Lom d'Arce, Baron de, June 9, 1666–*c.* 1713.
Vol. 5, Pt. 2–548
Lahr, Bert, Aug. 13, 189s-Dec. 4, 1967.
Supp. 8–354
Laimbeer, Nathalie Schenck, Dec. 4, 1882–Oct. 25, 1929.
Vol. 5, Pt. 2–549
Lait, Jacquin Leonard (Jack), Mar. 13, 1883–Apr. 1, 1954.
Supp. 5–406
Lajoie, Napoleon ("Larry"), Sept. 5, 1875–Feb. 7, 1959.
Supp. 6–356
Lake, Klrsopp, Apr. 7, 1872–Nov. 10, 1946.
Supp. 4–467
Lake, Slmon, Sept. 4, 1866–June 23, 1945.
Supp. 3–435
Lake, Veronica, Nov. 14, 1922–July 7, 1973.
Supp. 9–479

Lalor, Alice. [*See* Teresa, Mother, 1766–1846.]
Lamar, Gazaway Bugg, Oct. 2, 1798–Oct. 5, 1874.
Vol. 5, Pt. 2–549
Lamar, Joseph Rucker, Oct. 14, 1857–Jan. 2, 1916.
Vol. 5, Pt. 2–550
Lamar, Lucius Quintus Cincinnatus, Sept. 17, 1825–Jan. 23, 1893.
Vol. 5, Pt. 2–551
Lamar, Mirabeau Buonaparte, Aug. 16, 1798–Dec. 19, 1859.
Vol. 5, Pt. 2–553
Lamb, Arthur Becket, Feb. 25, 1880–May 15, 1952.
Supp. 5–406
Lamb, Isaac Wixom, Jan. 8, 1840–July 14, 1906.
Vol. 5, Pt. 2–554
Lamb, John, Jan. 1, 1735–May 31, 1800.
Vol. 5, Pt. 2–555
Lamb, Martha Joanna Reade Nash, Aug. 13, 1829–Jan. 2, 1893.
Vol. 5, Pt. 2–556
Lamb, William Frederick, Nov. 21, 1883–Sept. 8, 1952.
Supp. 5–408
Lambdin, James Reid, May 10, 1807–Jan. 31, 1889.
Vol. 5, Pt. 2–557
Lambeau, Earl Louis ("Curly"), Apr. 9, 1898–June 1, 1965.
Supp. 7–451
Lambert, Louis Aloisius, Apr. 13, 1835–Sept. 25, 1910.
Vol. 5, Pt. 2–557
Lamberton, Benjamin Peffer, Feb. 25, 1844–June 9, 1912.
Vol. 5, Pt. 2–558
Lambing, Andrew Arnold, Feb. 1, 1842–Dec. 24, 1918.
Vol. 5, Pt. 2–559
Lambuth, James William, Mar. 2, 1830–Apr. 28, 1892.
Vol. 5, Pt. 2–560
Lambuth, Walter Russell, Nov. 10, 1854–Sept. 26, 1921.
Vol. 5, Pt. 2–560
Lamme, Benjamin Garver, Jan. 12, 1864–July 8, 1924.
Vol. 5, Pt. 2–561
Lamon, Ward Hill, Jan. 6, 1828–May 7, 1893.
Vol. 5, Pt. 2–562
Lamont, Daniel Scott, Feb. 9, 1851–July 23, 1905.
Vol. 5, Pt. 2–563
Lamont, Hammond, Jan. 19, 1864–May 6, 1909.
Vol. 5, Pt. 2–564
Lamont, Thomas William, Sept. 30, 1870–Feb. 2, 1948.
Supp. 4–469
La Mountain, John, 1830–Feb. 14, 1870.
Vol. 5, Pt. 2–564
Lamoureux, Andrew Jackson, Mar. 20, 1850–Feb. 25, 1928.
Vol. 5. Pt. 2–565
Lampson, Sir Curtis Miranda, Sept. 21, 1806–Mar. 12, 1885.
Vol. 5, Pt. 2–566
Lamy, John Baptist, Oct. 11, 1814–Feb. 13, 1888.
Vol. 5, Pt. 2–566
Lancaster, Henry Carrington, Nov. 10, 1882–Jan. 29, 1954.
Supp. 5–409
Landais, Pierre, *c.* 1731–Sept. 17, 1820.
Vol. 5, Pt. 2–567
Lander, Edward, Aug. 11, 1816–Feb. 2, 1907.
Vol. 5, Pt. 2–568
Lander, Frederick West, Dec. 17, 1821–Mar. 2, 1862.
Vol. 5, Pt. 2–569
Lander, Jean Margaret Davenport, May 3, 1829–Aug. 3, 1903.
Vol. 5, Pt. 2–570
Landis, Henry Robert Murray, Feb. 3, 1872–Sept. 14, 1937.
Supp. 2–370
Landis, James McCauley, Sept. 25, 1899–July 30, 1964.
Supp. 7–453
Landis, Jessie Royce, Nov. 25, 1904–Feb. 2, 1972.
Supp. 9–480
Landis, Kenesaw Mountain, Nov. 20, 1866–Nov. 25, 1944.
Supp. 3–437
Landis, Walter Savage, July 5, 1881–Sept. 15, 1944.
Supp. 3–439
Landon, Melville de Lancy, Sept. 7, 1839–Dec. 16, 1910.
Vol. 5, Pt. 2–570
Landowska, Wanda Aleksandra, July 5, 1879–Aug. 16, 1959.
Supp. 6–357
Landreth, David, Sept. 15, 1802–Feb. 22, 1880.
Vol. 5, Pt. 2–571
Landsteiner, Karl, June 14, 1868–June 26, 1943.
Supp. 3–440
Lane, Arthur Bliss, June 16, 1894–Aug. 12, 1956.
Supp. 6–359
Lane, Franklin Knight, July 15, 1864–May 18, 1921.
Vol. 5, Pt. 2–572
Lane, George Martin, Dec. 24, 1823–June 30, 1897.
Vol. 5, Pt. 2–573
Lane, Gertrude Battles, Dec. 21, 1874–Sept. 25, 1941.
Supp. 3–442
Lane, Henry Smith, Feb. 24, 1811–June 18, 1881.
Vol. 5, Pt. 2–574
Lane, Horace M., July 29, 1837–Oct. 27, 1912.
Vol. 5, Pt. 2–575
Lane, James Henry, June 22, 1814–July 11, 1866.
Vol. 5, Pt. 2–576
Lane, James Henry, July 28, 1833–Sept. 21, 1907.
Vol. 5, Pt. 2–578
Lane, John, Apr. 8, 1789–Oct. 10, 1855.
Vol. 5, Pt. 2–578
Lane, Joseph, Dec. 14, 1801–Apr. 19, 1881.
Vol. 5, Pt. 2–579
Lane, Levi Cooper, May 9, 1830–Feb. 18, 1902.
Vol. 5, Pt. 2–580
Lane, Sir Ralph, *c.* 1530–October 1603.
Vol. 5, Pt. 2–581
Lane, Tidence, Aug. 31, 1724–Jan. 30, 1806.
Vol. 5, Pt. 2–582
Lane, Walter Paye, Feb. 18, 1817–Jan. 28, 1892.
Vol. 5, Pt. 2–582
Lane, William Carr, Dec. 1, 1789–Jan. 6, 1863.
Vol. 5, Pt. 2–583
Lang, Benjamin Johnson, Dec. 28, 1837–Apr. 4, 1909.
Vol. 5, Pt. 2–584
Lang, Fritz, Dec. 5, 1890–Aug. 2, 1976.
Supp. 10–430
Lang, Henry Roseman, Sept. 22, 1853–July 25, 1934.
Supp. 1–481
Lang, Lucy Fox Robins, 1884–Jan. 26, 1962.
Supp. 7–454
Langdeel, Christopher Columbus, May 22, 1826–July 6, 1906.
Vol. 5, Pt. 2–585
Langdon, Courtney, Jan. 18, 1861–Nov. 19, 1924.
Vol. 5, Pt. 2–586
Langdon, Harry Philmore, June 15, 1884–Dec. 22, 1944.
Supp. 3–443
Langdon, John, June 26, 1741–Sept. 18, 1819.
Vol. 5, Pt. 2–587
Langdon, Samuel, Jan. 12, 1723–Nov. 29, 1797.
Vol. 5, Pt. 2–588
Langdon, William Chauncy, Aug. 19, 1831–Oct. 29, 1895.
Vol. 5, Pt. 2–589
Langdon, Woodbury, 1738 or 1739–Jan. 13, 1805.
Vol. 5, Pt. 2–590
Lange, Alexis Frederick, Apr. 23, 1862–Aug. 28, 1924.
Vol. 5, Pt. 2–591
Lange, Dorothea, May 25, 1895–Oct. 11, 1965.
Supp. 7–455
Lange, Louis, Sept. 29, 1829–Sept. 25, 1893.
Vol. 5, Pt. 2–591
Langer, William, Sept. 30, 1886–Nov. 8, 1959.
Supp. 6–360
Langer, William Leonard, Mar. 16, 1896–Dec. 26, 1977.
Supp. 10–432
Langford, Nathaniel Pitt, Aug. 9, 1832–Oct. 18, 1911.
Vol. 5, Pt. 2–592
Langford, Samuel, Mar. 4, 1883–Jan. 12, 1956.
Supp. 6–362
Langlade, Charles Michel de. [*See* De Langlade, Charles Michel, 1729–1801.]
Langley, John Williams, Oct. 21, 1841–May 10, 1918.
Vol. 5, Pt. 2–593
Langley, Samuel Pierpont, Aug. 22, 1834–Feb. 27, 1906.
Vol. 5, Pt. 2–594
Langlie, Arthur Bernard, July 25, 1900–July 24, 1966.
Supp. 8–356
Langmuir, Irving, Jan. 13, 1881–Aug. 16, 1957.
Supp. 6–363
Langner, Lawrence, May 30, 1890–Dec. 26, 1962.
Supp. 7–457
Langston, John Mercer, Dec. 14, 1829–Nov. 15, 1897.
Vol. 5, Pt 2–597.
Langstroth, Lorenzo Lorraine, Dec. 25, 1810–Oct. 6, 1895.
Vol. 5, Pt. 2–598

Langworthy, Edward c. 1738–Nov. 1, 1802.
Vol. 5, Pt. 2–599
Langworthy, James Lyon, Jan. 20, 1800–Mar. 14, 1865.
Vol. 5, Pt. 599
Lanham, Frederick Garland ("Fritz"), Jan. 3, 1880–July 31, 1965.
Supp. 7–459
Lanier, James Franklin Doughty, Nov. 22, 1800–Aug. 27, 1881.
Vol. 5, Pt. 2–600
Lanier, Sidney, Feb. 3, 1842–Sept. 7, 1881.
Vol. 5, Pt. 2–601
Lanigan, George Thomas, Dec. 10, 1845–Feb. 5, 1886.
Vol. 5, Pt. 2–605
Lanman, Charles, June 14, 1819–Mar. 4, 1895.
Vol. 5, Pt. 2–606
Lanman, Charles Rockwell, July 8, 1850–Feb. 20, 1941.
Supp. 3–444
Lanman, Joseph, July 11, 1811–Mar. 13, 1874.
Vol. 5, Pt. 2–607
Lansing, Gulian, Feb. 1, 1825–Sept. 12, 1892.
Vol. 5, Pt. 2–607
Lansing, John, b. Jan. 30, 1754.
Vol. 5, Pt. 2–408
Lansing, Robert, Oct. 17, 1864–Oct. 30, 1928.
Vol. 5, Pt. 2–609
Lanston, Tolbert, Feb. 3, 1844–Feb. 18, 1913.
Vol. 5, Pt. 2–611
Lapchick, Joseph Bohomiel, Apr. 12, 1900–Aug. 10, 1970.
Supp. 8–358
Lapham, Increase Allen, Mar. 7, 1811–Sept. 14, 1875.
Vol. 5, Pt. 2–611
Lapham, William Berry, Aug. 21, 1828–Feb. 22, 1894.
Vol. 5, Pt. 2–612
Laramie, Jacques, d. 1821.
Vol. 5, Pt. 2–613
Larcom, Lucy, Mar. 5, 1824–Apr. 17, 1893.
Vol. 5, Pt. 2–614
Lard, Moses E., Oct. 29, 1818–June 17, 1880.
Vol. 5, Pt. 2–614
Lardner, James Lawrence, Nov. 20, 1802–Apr. 12, 1881.
Vol. 5, Pt. 2–615
Lardner, John Abbott, May 4, 1912–Mar. 24, 1960.
Supp. 6–365
Lardner, Ringgold Wilmer, Mar. 6, 1885–Sept. 25, 1933.
Supp. 1–482
Larkin, John, Feb. 2, 1801–Dec. 11, 1858.
Vol. 5, Pt. 2–616
Larkin, Thomas Oliver, Sept. 16, 1802–Oct. 27, 1858.
Vol. 5, Pt. 2–617
Larned, Joseph Gay Eaton, Apr. 29, 1819–June 3, 1870.
Vol. 6, Pt. 1–1
Larned, Josephus Nelson, May 11, 1836–Aug. 15, 1913.
Vol. 6, Pt. 1–2
Larned, William Augustus, Dec. 30, 1872–Dec. 16, 1926.
Vol. 6, Pt. 1–2
LaRoche, René, Sept. 23, 1795–Dec. 9, 1872.
Vol. 6, Pt. 1–3
La Ronde, Louis Denis, Sieur de, 1675–March 1741.
Vol. 6, Pt. 1–4
Larpenteur, Charles, May 8, 1807–Nov. 15, 1872.
Vol. 6, Pt. 1–4
Larrabee, Charles Hathaway, Nov. 9, 1820–Jan. 20, 1883.
Vol. 6, Pt. 1–5
Larrabee, William, Jan. 20, 1832–Nov. 16, 1912.
Vol. 6, Pt. 1–6
Larrabee, William Clark, Dec. 23, 1802–May 5, 1859.
Vol. 6, Pt. 1–7
Larrazolo, Octaviano Ambrosio, Dec. 7, 1859–Apr. 7, 1930.
Vol. 6, Pt. 1–7
Larrínaga, Tulio, Jan. 15, 1847–Apr. 28, 1917.
Vol. 6, Pt. 1–8
Larsen, Peter Laurentius, Aug. 10, 1833–Mar. 1, 1915.
Vol. 6, Pt. 1–9
Larson, Laurence Marcellus, Sept. 23, 1868–Mar. 9, 1938.
Supp. 2–371
La Salle, Robert Cavelier, Sieur de, Nov. 1643–Mar. 19, 1687.
Vol. 6, Pt. 1–10
Lasater, Edward Cunningham, Nov. 5, 1860–Mar. 20, 1930.
Vol. 6, Pt. 1–12
Lashley, Karl Spencer, June 7, 1890–Aug. 7, 1958.
Supp. 6–367
Lasker, Albert Davis, May 1, 1880–May 30, 1952.
Supp. 5–410
Lasky, Jesse Louis, Sept. 13, 1880–Jan. 13, 1958.
Supp. 6–368
Lasser, Jacob Kay, Oct. 7, 1896–May 11, 1954.
Supp. 5–412
Lasswell, Harold Dwight, Feb. 13, 1902–Dec. 18, 1978.
Supp. 10–433
Latané, John Holladay, Apr. 1, 1869–Jan. 1, 1932.
Supp. 1–483
Latham, Milton Slocum, May 23, 1827–Mar. 4, 1882.
Vol. 6, Pt. 1–13
Lathbury, Mary Artemisia, Aug. 10, 1841–Oct. 20, 1913.
Vol. 6, Pt. 1–13
Lathrop, Francis Augustus, June 22, 1849–Oct. 18, 1909.
Vol. 6, Pt. 1–14
Lathrop, George Parsons, Aug. 25, 1851–Apr. 19, 1898.
Vol. 6, Pt. 1–15
Lathrop, John, Jan. 13, 1772–Jan. 30, 1820.
Vol. 6, Pt. 1–16
Lathrop, John Hiram, Jan. 22, 1799–Aug. 2, 1866.
Vol. 6, Pt. 1–16
Lathrop, Julia Clifford, June 29, 1858–Apr. 15, 1932.
Supp. 1–484
Lathrop, Rose Hawthorne. [*See* Alphonsa, Mother, 1851–1926.]
Latil, Alexandre, Oct. 6, 1816–March 1851.
Vol. 6, Pt. 1–17
Latimer, Mary Elizabeth Wormeley, July 26, 1822–Jan. 4, 1904.
Vol. 6, Pt. 1–18
Latimer, Wendell Mitchell, Apr. 22, 1893–July 6, 1955.
Supp. 5–413
La Tour, Le Blond de, d. Oct. 14, 1723.
Vol. 6, Pt. 1–19
Latourette, Kenneth Scott, Aug. 9, 1884–Dec. 26, 1968.
Supp. 8–359
Latrobe, Benjamin Henry, May 1, 1764–Sept. 3, 1820.
Vol. 6, Pt. 1–20
Latrobe, Benjamin Henry, Dec. 19, 1806–Oct. 19, 1878.
Vol. 6, Pt. 1–25
Latrobe, Charles Hazlehurst, Dec. 25, 1834–Sept. 19, 1902.
Vol. 6, Pt. 1–26
Latrobe, John Hazlehurst Boneval, May 4, 1803–Sept. 11, 1891.
Vol. 6, Pt. 1–27
Latta, Alexander Bonner, June 11, 1821–Apr. 28, 1865.
Vol. 6, Pt. 1–28
Lattimore, William, Feb. 9, 1774–Apr. 3, 1843.
Vol. 6, Pt. 1–29
Laudonnière, René Goulaine de, fl. 1562–1582.
Vol. 6, Pt. 1–30
Laufer, Berthold, Oct. 11, 1874–Sept. 13, 1934.
Supp. 1–486.
Laughlin, Harry Hamilton, Mar. 11, 1880–Jan. 6, 1943.
Supp. 3–445
Laughlin, James Laurence, Apr. 2, 1850–Nov. 28, 1933.
Supp. 1–487
Laughton, Charles, July 1, 1899–Dec. 15, 1962.
Supp. 7–460
Launitz, Robert Eberhard Schmidt Von Der, Nov. 4, 1806–Dec. 13, 1870.
Vol. 6, Pt. 1–31
Laurance, John, 1750–Nov. 11, 1810.
Vol. 6, Pt. 1–31
Laurel, Stan, June 16, 1890–Feb. 23, 1965.
Supp. 7–462
Laurence, William Leonard, Mar. 7, 1888–Mar. 19, 1977.
Supp. 10–434
Laurens, Henry, Mar. 6, 1724–Dec. 8, 1792.
Vol. 6, Pt. 1–32
Laurens, John, Oct. 28, 1754–Aug. 27, 1782.
Vol. 6, Pt. 1–35
Laurie, James, May 9, 1811–Mar. 16, 1875.
Vol. 6, Pt. 1–36
La Vérendrye, Pierre Gaultier de Varennes, Sieur de, Nov. 17, 1685–Dec. 6, 1749.
Vol. 6, Pt. 1–37
Law, Andrew, March 1748/49–July 13, 1821.
Vol. 6, Pt. 1–38

Law, Evander McIvor, Aug. 7, 1836–Oct. 31, 1920.
Vol. 6, Pt. 1–38
Law, George, Oct. 25, 1806–Nov. 18, 1881.
Vol. 6, Pt. 1–39
Law, John, Oct. 28, 1796–Oct. 7, 1873.
Vol. 6, Pt. 1–40
Law, Jonathan, Aug. 6, 1674–Nov. 6, 1750.
Vol. 6, Pt. 1–41
Law, Richard, Mar. 7, 1733–Jan. 26, 1806.
Vol. 6, Pt. 1–41
Law, Sallie Chapman Gordon, Aug. 27, 1805–June 28, 1894.
Vol. 6, Pt. 1–42
Lawes, Lewis Edward, Sept. 13, 1883–Apr. 23, 1947.
Supp. 4–471
Lawley, George Frederick, Dec. 8, 1848–Mar. 20, 1928.
Vol. 6, Pt. 1–43
Lawrance, Charles Lanier, Sept. 30, 1882–June 24, 1950.
Supp. 4–473
Lawrance, John. [*See* Laurance, John, 1750–1810.]
Lawrance, Marion. [*See* Lawrance, Uriah Marion, 1850–1924.]
Lawrance, Uriah Marion, Oct. 2, 1850–May 1, 1924.
Vol. 6, Pt. 1–43
Lawrence, Abbott, Dec. 16, 1792–Aug. 18, 1855.
Vol. 6, Pt. 1–44
Lawrence, Amos, Apr. 22, 1786–Dec. 31, 1852.
Vol. 6, Pt. 1–46
Lawrence, Amos Adams, July 31, 1814–Aug. 22, 1886.
Vol. 6, Pt. 1–47
Lawrence, David, Dec. 25, 1888–Feb. 11, 1973.
Supp. 9–481
Lawrence, David Leo, June 18, 1889–Nov. 21, 1966.
Supp. 8–360
Lawrence, Ernest Orlando, Aug. 8, 1901–Aug. 27, 1958.
Supp. 6–369
Lawrence, George Newbold, Oct. 20, 1806–Jan. 17, 1895.
Vol. 6, Pt. 1–49
Lawrence, Gertrude, July 4, 1898–Sept. 6, 1952.
Supp. 5–414
Lawrence, James, Oct. 1, 1781–June 4, 1813.
Vol. 6, Pt. 1–49
Lawrence, Richard Smith, Nov. 22, 1817–Mar. 10, 1892.
Vol. 6, Pt. 1–51
Lawrence, William, Sept. 7, 1783–Oct. 14, 1848.
Vol. 6, Pt. 1–51
Lawrence, William, June 26, 1819–May 8, 1899.
Vol. 6, Pt. 1–52
Lawrence, William, May 30, 1850–Nov. 6, 1941.
Supp. 3–446
Lawrence, William Beach, Oct. 23, 1800–Mar. 26, 1881.
Vol. 6, Pt. 1–53
Lawrie, Alexander, Feb. 25, 1828–Feb. 15, 1917.
Vol. 6, Pt. 1–54
Laws, Samuel Spahr, Mar. 23, 1824–Jan. 9, 1921.
Vol. 6, Pt. 1–54
Lawson, Alexander, Dec. 19, 1773–Aug. 22, 1846.
Vol. 6, Pt. 1–56
Lawson, Andrew Cowper, July 25, 1861–June 16, 1952.
Supp. 5–415
Lawson, Ernest, Mar. 22, 1873–Dec. 18, 1939.
Supp. 2–372
Lawson, James, Nov. 9, 1799–Mar. 24, 1880.
Vol. 6, Pt. 1–56
Lawson, John, d. 1711.
Vol. 6, Pt. 1–57
Lawson, John Howard, Sept. 25, 1894–Aug. 11, 1977.
Supp. 10–435
Lawson, Leonidas Merion, Sept. 10, 1812–Jan. 21, 1864.
Vol. 6, Pt. 1–58
Lawson, Robert Ripley, Oct. 4, 1892–May 26, 1957.
Supp. 6–372
Lawson, Thomas, *c.* 1781 or 1785–May 15, 1861.
Vol. 6, Pt. 1–58
Lawson, Thomas William, Feb. 26, 1857–Feb. 8, 1925.
Vol. 6, Pt. 1–59
Lawson, Victor Freemont, Sept. 9, 1850–Aug. 19, 1925.
Vol. 6, Pt. 1–60
Lawton, Alexander Robert, Nov. 4, 1818–July 2, 1896.
Vol. 6, Pt. 1–61
Lawton, Henry Ware, Mar. 17, 1843–Dec. 19, 1899.
Vol. 6, Pt. 1–62
Lay, Benjamin, 1677–Feb. 3, 1759.
Vol. 6, Pt. 1–63
Lay, Henry Champlin, Dec. 6, 1823–Sept. 17, 1885.
Vol. 6, Pt. 1–64
Lay, John Louis, Jan. 14, 1832–Apr. 17, 1899.
Vol. 6, Pt. 1–64
Lazarsfeld, Paul Felix, Feb. 13, 1901–Aug. 30, 1976.
Supp. 10–437
Lazarus, Emma, July 22, 1849–Nov. 19, 1887.
Vol. 6, Pt. 1–65
Lazarus, Fred, Jr., Oct. 29, 1884–May 27, 1973.
Supp. 9–483
Lazear, Jesse William, May 2, 1866–Sept. 25, 1900.
Vol. 6, Pt. 1–66
Lea, Henry Charles, Sept. 19, 1825–Oct. 24, 1909.
Vol. 6, Pt. 1–67
Lea, Homer, Nov. 17, 1876–Nov. 1, 1912.
Vol. 6, Pt. 1–69
Lea, Isaac, Mar. 4, 1792–Dec. 8, 1886.
Vol. 6, Pt. 1–70
Lea, Luke, Apr. 12, 1879–Nov. 18, 1945.
Supp. 3–448
Lea, Mathew Carey, Aug. 18, 1823–Mar. 15, 1897.
Vol. 6, Pt. 1–71
Leach, Abby, May 28, 1855–Dec. 29, 1918.
Vol. 6, Pt. 1–72
Leach, Daniel Dyer, June 12, 1806–May 16, 1891.
Vol. 6, Pt. 1–72
Leach, Shepherd, Apr. 30, 1778–Sept. 19, 1832.
Vol. 6, Pt. 1–73
Leaf, Wilbur Munro, Dec. 4, 1905–Dec. 21, 1976.
Supp. 10–440
Leahy, Francis William ("Frank"), Aug. 27, 1908–June 21, 1973.
Supp. 9–484
Leahy, William Daniel, May 6, 1875–July 20, 1959.
Supp. 6–373
Leaming, Jacob Spicer, Apr. 2, 1815–May 12, 1885.
Vol. 6, Pt. 1–74
Leaming, Jeremiah, 1717–Sept. 15, 1804.
Vol. 6, Pt. 1–74
Leaming, Thomas, Sept. 1, 1748–Oct. 29, 1797.
Vol. 6, Pt. 1–75
Lear, Ben, May 12, 1879–Nov. 1, 1966.
Supp. 8–362
Lear, Tobias, Sept. 19, 1762–Oct. 11, 1816.
Vol. 6, Pt. 1–76
Lear, William Powell, June 26, 1902–May 14, 1978.
Supp. 10–442
Learned, Ebenezer, Apr. 18, 1728–Apr. 1, 1801.
Vol. 6, Pt. 1–77
Learned, Marion Dexter, July 10, 1857–Aug. 1, 1917.
Vol. 6, Pt. 1–78
Leary, John, Nov. 1, 1837–Feb. 8, 1905.
Vol. 6, Pt. 1–79
Lease, Mary Elizabeth Clyens, Sept. 11, 1853–Oct. 29, 1933.
Supp. 1–488
Leathers, Waller Smith, Dec. 4, 1874–Jan. 26, 1946.
Supp. 4–474
Leavenworth, Francis Preserved, Sept. 3, 1858–Nov. 12, 1928.
Vol. 6, Pt. 1–79
Leavenworth, Henry, Dec. 10, 1783–July 21, 1834.
Vol. 6, Pt. 1–80
Leavitt, Dudley, May 23, 1772–Sept. 15, 1851.
Vol. 6, Pt. 1–80
Leavitt, Erasmus Darwin, Oct. 27, 1836–Mar. 11, 1916.
Vol. 6, Pt. 1–81
Leavitt, Frank McDowell, Mar. 3, 1856–Aug. 6, 1928.
Vol. 6, Pt. 1–82
Leavitt, Frank Simmons (Man Mountain Dean), July 30, 1889–May 29, 1953.
Supp. 5–417
Leavitt, Henrietta Swan, July 4, 1868–Dec. 12, 1921.
Vol. 6, Pt. 1–83
Leavitt, Humphrey Howe, June 18, 1796–Mar. 15, 1873.
Vol. 6, Pt. 1–83
Leavitt, Joshua, Sept. 8, 1794–Jan. 16, 1873.
Vol. 6, Pt. 1–84
Leavitt, Mary Greenleaf Clement, Sept. 22, 1830–Feb. 5, 1912.
Vol. 6, Pt. 1–85

Lebrun, Federico ("Rico"), Dec. 10, 1900–May 9, 1964.
Supp. 7–464
Le Brun, Napoléon Eugène Henry Charles, Jan. 2, 1821–July 9, 1901.
Vol. 6, Pt. 1–86
Lechford, Thomas, fl. 1629–1642.
Vol. 6, Pt. 1–87
Le Clear, Thomas, Mar. 11, 1818–Nov. 26, 1882.
Vol. 6, Pt. 1–87
Le Conte, John, Dec. 4, 1818–Apr. 29, 1891.
Vol. 6, Pt. 1–88
Le Conte, John Lawrence, May 13, 1825–Nov. 15, 1883.
Vol. 6, Pt. 1–89
Le Conte, Joseph, Feb. 26, 1823–July 6, 1901.
Vol. 6, Pt. 1–90
Ledbetter, Huddie ("Leadbelly"), Jan. 21, 1885–Dec. 6, 1949.
Supp. 4–475
Lederer, John, fl. 1669–1670.
Vol. 6, Pt. 1–91
Le Duc, William Gates, Mar. 29, 1823–Oct. 30, 1917.
Vol. 6, Pt. 1–92
Ledyard, John, 1751–Jan. 10, 1789.
Vol. 6, Pt. 1–93
Ledyard, William, Dec. 6, 1738–Sept. 6, 1781.
Vol. 6, Pt. 1–94
Lee, Alfred, Sept. 9, 1807–Apr. 12, 1887.
Vol. 6, Pt. 1–94
Lee, Ann, Feb. 29, 1736–Sept. 8, 1784.
Vol. 6, Pt. 1–95
Lee, Arthur, Dec. 21, 1740–Dec. 12, 1792.
Vol. 6, Pt. 1–96
Lee, Bruce, Nov. 27, 1940–July 20, 1973.
Supp. 9–486
Lee, Canada, May 3, 1907–May 9, 1952.
Supp. 5–418
Lee, Charles, 1731–Oct. 2, 1782.
Vol. 6, Pt. 1–98
Lee, Charles, 1758–June 24, 1815.
Vol. 6, Pt. 1–101
Lee, Charles Alfred, Mar. 3, 1801–Feb. 14, 1872.
Vol. 6, Pt. 1–102
Lee, Eliza Buckminister, *c.* 1788–June 22, 1864.
Vol. 6, Pt. 1–103
Lee, Fitzhugh, Nov. 19, 1835–Apr. 28, 1905.
Vol. 6, Pt. 1–103
Lee, Francis Lightfoot, Oct. 14, 1734–Jan. 11, 1797.
Vol. 6, Pt. 1–105
Lee, Frederic Schiller, June 16, 1859–Dec. 14, 1939.
Supp. 2–373
Lee, George Washington Custis, Sept. 16, 1832–Feb. 18, 1913.
Vol. 6, Pt. 1–105
Lee, Gypsy Rose, Jan. 9, 1914?–Apr. 26, 1970.
Supp. 8–363
Lee, Hannah Farnham Sawyer, 1780–Dec. 27, 1865.
Vol. 6, Pt. 1–106
Lee, Henry, Jan. 29, 1756–Mar. 25, 1818.
Vol. 6, Pt. 1–107
Lee, Henry, Feb. 4, 1782–Feb. 6, 1867.
Vol. 6, Pt. 1–108
Lee, Henry, May 28, 1787–Jan. 30, 1837.
Vol. 6, Pt. 1–109
Lee, Ivy Ledbetter, July 16, 1877–Nov. 9, 1934.
Supp. 1–489
Lee, James Melvin, May 16, 1878–Nov. 17, 1929.
Vol. 6, Pt. 1–110
Lee, James Wideman, Nov. 28, 1849–Oct. 4, 1919.
Vol. 6, Pt. 1–111
Lee, Jason, June 28, 1803–Mar. 12, 1845.
Vol. 6, Pt. 1–111
Lee, Jesse, Mar. 12, 1758–Sept. 12, 1816.
Vol. 6 Pt. 1–112
Lee, John Clifford Hodges, Aug. 1, 1887–Aug. 30, 1958.
Supp. 6–375
Lee, John Doyle, Sept. 6, 1812–Mar. 23, 1877.
Vol. 6, Pt. 1–114
Lee, Joseph, Mar. 8, 1862–July 28, 1937.
Supp. 2–374
Lee, Luther, Nov. 30, 1800–Dec. 13, 1889.
Vol. 6, Pt. 1–115
Lee, Manfred B., Oct. 20, 1905–Apr. 3, 1971.
Supp. 9–487
Lee, Porter Raymond, Dec. 21, 1879–Mar. 8, 1939.
Supp. 2–376
Lee, Richard, d. 1664.
Vol. 6, Pt. 1–116
Lee, Richard Bland, Jan. 20, 1761–Mar. 12, 1827.
Vol. 6, Pt. 1–117
Lee, Richard Henry, Jan. 20, 1732–June 19, 1794.
Vol. 6, Pt. 1–117
Lee, Robert Edward, Jan. 19, 1807–Oct. 12, 1870.
Vol. 6, Pt. 1–120
Lee, Samuel Phillips, Feb. 13, 1812–June 5, 1897.
Vol. 6, Pt. 1–129
Lee, Stephen Dill, Sept. 22, 1833–May 28, 1908.
Vol. 6, Pt. 1–130
Lee, Thomas, Dec. 1, 1769–Oct. 24, 1839.
Vol. 6, Pt. 1–131
Lee, Thomas Sim, Oct. 29, 1745–Nov. 9, 1819.
Vol. 6, Pt. 1–132
Lee, William, Aug. 31, 1739–June 27, 1795.
Vol. 6, Pt. 1–132
Lee, William Granville, Nov. 29, 1859–Nov. 2, 1929.
Vol. 6, Pt. 1–133
Lee, William Henry Fitzhugh, May 31, 1837–Oct. 15, 1891.
Vol. 6, Pt. 1–134
Lee, William Little, Feb. 8, 1821–May 28, 1857.
Vol. 6, Pt. 1–135
Lee, Willis Augustus, May 11, 1888–Aug. 25, 1945.
Supp. 3–450
Leedom, Boyd Stewart, Sept. 28, 1906–Aug. 11, 1969.
Supp. 8–365
Leeds, Daniel, 1652–Sept. 28, 1720.
Vol. 6, Pt. 1–135
Leeds, John, May 18, 1705–March 1790.
Vol. 6, Pt. 1–136
Leemans, Alphonse E. ("Tuffy"), Nov. 12, 1912–Jan. 19, 1979.
Supp. 10–444
Lees, Ann. [*See* Lee, Ann, 1736–1784.]
Leeser, Isaac, Dec. 12, 1806–Feb. 1, 1868.
Vol. 6, Pt. 1–137
Leete, William, *c.* 1613–Apr. 16, 1683.
Vol. 6, Pt. 1–138
Lefevere, Peter Paul, Apr. 30, 1804–Mar. 4, 1869.
Vol. 6, Pt. 1–138
Leffel, James, Apr. 19, 1806–June 11, 1866.
Vol. 6, Pt. 1–139
Lefferts, George Morewood, Feb. 24, 1846–Sept. 21, 1920.
Vol. 6, Pt. 1–140
Lefferts, Marshall, Jan. 15, 1821–July 3, 1876.
Vol. 6, Pt. 1–140
Leffingwell, Russell Cornell, Sept. 10, 1878–Oct. 2, 1960.
Supp. 6–376
Leffler, Isaac, Nov. 25, 1788–Mar. 8, 1866.
Vol. 6, Pt. 1–141
Leffler, Shepherd, Apr. 24, 1811–Sept. 7, 1879.
Vol. 6, Pt. 1–142
Leffmann, Henry, Sept. 9, 1847–Dec. 25, 1930.
Vol. 6, Pt. 1–142
Leflore, Greenwood, June 3, 1800–Aug. 31, 1865.
Vol. 6, Pt. 1–143
Legaré, Hugh Swinton, Jan. 2, 1797–June 20, 1843.
Vol. 6, Pt. 1–144
LeGendre, Charles William, Aug. 26, 1830–Sept. 1, 1899.
Vol. 6, Pt. 1–145
Legge, Alexander, July 13, 1866–Dec. 3, 1933.
Supp. 1–490
Leggett, Mortimer Dormer, Apr. 19, 1821–Jan. 6, 1896.
Vol. 6, Pt. 1–146
Leggett, William, Apr. 30, 1801–May 29, 1839.
Vol. 6 Pt. 1–147
Legler, Henry Eduard, June 22, 1861–Sept. 13, 1917.
Vol. 6, Pt. 1–148
Lehman, Adele Lewisohn, May 17, 1882–Aug. 11, 1965.
Supp. 7–465
Lehman, Arthur, June 1, 1873–May 16, 1936.
Supp. 2–376
Lehman, Herbert Henry, Mar. 28, 1878–Dec. 5, 1963.
Supp. 7–466

Lehman, Irving, Jan. 28, 1876–Sept. 22, 1945.
Supp. 3–451
Lehman, Robert, Sept. 29, 1891–Aug. 9, 1969.
Supp. 8–367
Lehmann, Frederick William, Feb. 28, 1853–Sept. 12, 1931.
Vol. 6, Pt. 1–149
Lehmann, Lotte, Feb. 27, 1888–Aug. 26, 1976.
Supp. 10–445
Leib, Michael, Jan. 8, 1760–Dec. 28, 1822.
Vol. 6, Pt. 1–149
Leiber, Fritz, Jan. 31, 1882–Oct. 14, 1949.
Supp. 4–477
Leibowitz, Samuel Simon, Aug. 14, 1893–Jan. 11, 1978.
Supp. 10–446
Leidy, Joseph, Sept. 9, 1823–Apr. 29, 1891.
Vol. 6, Pt. 1–150
Leigh, Benjamin Watkins, June 18, 1781–Feb. 2, 1849.
Vol. 6, Pt. 1–152
Leigh, Vivien, Nov. 5, 1913–July 7, 1967.
Supp. 8–368
Leigh, William Robinson, Sept. 23, 1866–Mar. 11, 1955.
Supp. 5–420
Leighton, William, fl. 1825–1868.
Vol. 6, Pt. 1–153
Leiper, Thomas, Dec. 15, 1745–July 6, 1825.
Vol. 6, Pt. 1–154
Leipzig, Nate, May 13, 1873–Oct. 13, 1939.
Supp. 2–377
Leipziger, Henry Marcus, Dec. 29, 1854–Dec. 1, 1917.
Vol. 6, Pt. 1–154
Leiserson, William Morris, Apr. 15, 1883–Feb. 12, 1957.
Supp. 6–378
Leishman, John G. A., Mar. 28, 1857–Mar. 27, 1924.
Vol. 6, Pt. 1–155
Leisler, Jacob, 1640–May 16, 1691.
Vol. 6, Pt. 1–156
Leiter, Joseph, Dec. 4, 1868–Apr. 11, 1932.
Supp. 1–491
Leiter, Levi Zeigler, Nov. 2, 1834–June 9, 1904.
Vol. 6, Pt. 1–157
Le Jau, Francis, 1665–Sept. 15, 1717.
Vol. 6, Pt. 1–158
Lejeune, John Archer, Jan. 10, 1867–Nov. 20, 1942.
Supp. 3–452
Leland, Charles Godfrey, Aug. 15, 1824–Mar. 20, 1903.
Vol. 6, Pt. 1–158
Leland, George Adams, Sept. 7, 1850–Mar. 17, 1924.
Vol. 6, Pt. 1–160
Leland, John, May 14, 1754–Jan. 14, 1841.
Vol. 6, Pt. 1–160
Leland, Waldo Gifford, July 17, 1879–Oct. 19, 1966.
Supp. 8–369
Lemke, Peter Henry, July 27, 1796–Nov. 29, 1882.
Vol. 6, Pt. 1–161
Lemke, William Frederick, Aug. 13, 1878–May 30, 1950.
Supp. 4–479
Lemmon, John Gill, Jan. 2, 1832–Nov. 24, 1908.
Vol. 6, Pt. 1–162
LeMoyne, Francis Julius, Sept. 4, 1798–Oct. 14, 1879.
Vol. 6, Pt. 1–163
Le Moyne, Jean Baptiste. [*See* Bienville, Jean Baptiste Le Moyne, Sieur de, 1680–1768.]
Le Moyne, Pierre. [*See* Iberville, Pierre Le Moyne, Sieur d', 1661–1706.]
Le Moyne, William J., Apr. 29, 1831–Nov. 6, 1905.
Vol. 6, Pt. 1–164
Leney, William Satchwell, Jan. 16, 1769–Nov. 26, 1831.
Vol. 6, Pt. 1–165
L'Enfant, Pierre Charles, Aug. 2, 1754–June 14, 1825.
Vol. 6, Pt. 1–165
Lenker, John Nicholas, Nov. 28, 1858–May 16, 1929.
Vol. 6, Pt. 1–169
Lennon, John Brown, Oct. 12, 1850–Jan. 17, 1923.
Vol. 6, Pt. 1–170
Lennon, John Winston Ono, Oct. 9, 1940–Dec. 8, 1980.
Supp. 10–448
Lennox, Charlotte Ramsay, 1720–Jan. 4, 1804.
Vol. 6, Pt. 1–171
Lenox, James, Aug. 19, 1800–Feb. 17, 1880.
Vol. 6, Pt. 1–172
Lenroot, Irvine Luther, Jan. 31, 1869–Jan. 26, 1949.
Supp. 4–481
Lenthall, John, Sept. 16, 1807–Apr. 11, 1882.
Vol. 6, Pt. 1–173
Lenz, Sidney Samuel, July 12, 1873–Apr. 12, 1960.
Supp. 6–379
Leonard, Charles Lester, Dec. 29, 1861–Sept. 22, 1913.
Vol. 6, Pt. 1–173
Leonard, Daniel, May 18, 1740–June 27, 1829.
Vol. 6, Pt. 1–174
Leonard, George, Nov. 23, 1742–Apr. 1, 1826.
Vol. 6, Pt. 1–175
Leonard, Harry Ward, Feb. 8, 1861–Feb. 18, 1915.
Vol. 6, Pt. 1–176
Leonard, Helen Louise. [*See* Russell, Lillian, 1861–1922.]
Leonard, Jack E., Apr. 24, 1911–May 11, 1973.
Supp. 9–489
Leonard, Levi Washburn, June 1, 1790–Dec. 12, 1864.
Vol. 6, Pt. 1–177
Leonard, Robert Josselyn, Feb. 5, 1885–Feb. 9, 1929.
Vol. 6, Pt. 1–177
Leonard, Sterling Andrus, Apr. 23, 1888–May 15, 1931.
Vol. 6, Pt. 1–178
Leonard, William Andrew, July 15, 1848–Sept. 21, 1930.
Vol. 6, Pt. 1–179
Leonard, William Ellery, Jan. 25, 1876–May 2, 1944.
Supp. 3–453
Leonard, Zenas, Mar. 19, 1809–July 14, 1857.
Vol. 6, Pt. 1–180
Leonty, Metropolitan, Aug. 8, 1876–May 14, 1965.
Supp. 7–468
Leopold, Nathan Freudenthal, Jr., Nov. 19, 1904–Aug. 29, 1971.
Supp. 9–490
Leopold, (Rand) Aldo, Jan. 11, 1886–Apr. 21, 1948.
Supp. 4–482
Le Page Du Pratz, Antoine Simon. [*See* Dupratz, Antoine Simon Le Page, fl. 1718–1758.]
Le Roux, Bartholomew, *c.* 1665–July 1713.
Vol. 6, Pt. 1–180
Le Roux, Charles, December 1689–Mar. 22, 1745.
Vol. 6, Pt. 1–181
Léry, Joseph Gaspard Chaussegros de, July 20, 1721–Dec. 11, 1797.
Vol. 6, Pt. 1–182
Leschi, d. Feb. 19, 1858.
Vol. 6, Pt. 1–182
Lesley, J. Peter. [*See* Lesley, Peter, 1819–1903.]
Lesley, Peter, Sept. 17, 1819–June 1, 1903.
Vol. 6, Pt. 1–183
Leslie, Charles Robert, Oct. 19, 1794–May 5, 1859.
Vol. 6, Pt. 1–184
Leslie, Eliza, Nov. 15, 1787–Jan. 1, 1858.
Vol. 6, Pt. 1–185
Leslie, Frank, Mar. 29, 1821–Jan. 10, 1880.
Vol. 6, Pt. 1–186
Leslie, Miriam Florence Folline, *c.* 1836–Sept. 18, 1914.
Vol. 6, Pt. 1–187
Lesquereux, Leo, Nov. 18, 1806–Oct. 25, 1889.
Vol. 6, Pt. 1–188
Lester, Charles Edwards, July 15, 1815–Jan. 29, 1890.
Vol. 6, Pt. 1–189
Lesueur, Charles Alexandre, Jan. 1, 1778–Dec. 12, 1846.
Vol. 6, Pt. 1–190
Le Sueur, Pierre, *c.* 1657–*c.* 1705.
Vol. 6, Pt. 1–191
Letcher, John, Mar. 29, 1813–Jan. 26, 1884.
Vol. 6, Pt. 1–192
Letcher, Robert Perkins, Feb. 10, 1788–Jan. 24, 1861.
Vol. 6, Pt. 1–193
Letchworth, William Pryor, May 26, 1823–Dec. 1, 1910.
Vol. 6, Pt. 1–193
Letterman, Jonathan, Dec. 11, 1824–Mar. 15, 1872.
Vol. 6, Pt. 1–194
Leupp, Francis Ellington, Jan. 2, 1849–Nov. 19, 1918.
Vol. 6, Pt. 1–195
Leutze, Emanuel, May 24, 1816–July 18, 1868.
Vol. 6, Pt. 1–195
Levant, Oscar, Dec. 27, 1906–Aug. 14, 1972.
Supp. 9–491

Levene, Phoebus Aaron Theodore, Feb. 25, 1869–Sept. 6, 1940.
Supp. 2–378
Levenson, Samuel ("Sam"), Dec. 28, 1911–Aug. 27, 1980.
Supp. 10–451
Lever, Asbury Francis, Jan. 5, 1875–Apr. 28, 1940.
Supp. 2–379
Leverett, Frank, Mar. 10, 1859–Nov. 15, 1943.
Supp. 3–455
Leverett, John, 1616–Mar. 16, 1679.
Vol. 6, Pt. 1–196
Leverett, John, Aug. 25, 1662–May 3, 1724.
Vol. 6, Pt. 1–197
Levering, Joseph Mortimer, Feb. 20, 1849–Apr. 4, 1908.
Vol. 6, Pt. 1–198
Levermore, Charles Herbert, Oct. 15, 1856–Oct. 20, 1927.
Vol. 6, Pt. 1–199
Levin, Lewis Charles, Nov. 10, 1808–Mar. 14, 1860.
Vol. 6, Pt. 1–200
Levins, Thomas C., Mar. 14, 1789–May 5, 1843.
Vol. 6, Pt. 1–201
Levinson, Salmon Oliver, Dec. 29, 1865–Feb. 2, 1941.
Supp. 3–456
Levitt, Abraham, July 1, 1880–Aug. 20, 1962.
Supp. 7–469
Levitt, Arthur, June 28, 1900–May 6, 1980.
Supp. 10–452
Levy, Gustave Lehmann, May 23, 1910–Nov. 3, 1976.
Supp. 10–453
Levy, Joseph Leonard, Nov. 24, 1865–Apr. 26, 1917.
Vol. 6, Pt. 1–201
Levy, Louis Edward, Oct. 12, 1846–Feb. 16, 1919.
Vol. 6, Pt. 1–202
Levy, Max, Mar. 9, 1857–July 31, 1926.
Vol. 6, Pt. 1–203
Levy, Uriah Phillips, Apr. 22, 1792–Mar. 22, 1862.
Vol. 6, Pt. 1–203
Lewelling, Henderson. [*See* Luelling, Henderson, 1809–1878.]
Lewelling, Lorenzo Dow, Dec. 21, 1846–Sept. 3, 1900.
Vol. 6, Pt. 1–204
Lewin, Kurt, Sept. 9, 1890–Feb. 12, 1947.
Supp. 4–484
Lewis, Alfred Henry, *c.* 1858–Dec. 23, 1914.
Vol. 6, Pt. 1–205
Lewis, Andrew, 1720–Sept. 26, 1781.
Vol. 6, Pt. 1–206
Lewis, Arthur, Aug. 19, 1846–June 13, 1930.
Vol. 6, Pt. 1–206
Lewis, Charles Bertrand, Feb. 15, 1842–Aug. 21, 1924.
Vol. 6, Pt. 1–207
Lewis, Charlton Thomas, Feb. 25, 1834–May 26, 1904.
Vol. 6, Pt. 1–208
Lewis, Clarence Irving, Apr. 12, 1883–Feb. 3, 1964.
Supp. 7–471
Lewis, Dean De Witt, Aug. 11, 1874–Oct. 9, 1941.
Supp. 3–457
Lewis, Dioclesian, Mar. 3, 1823–May 21, 1886.
Vol. 6, Pt. 1–209
Lewis, Dixon Hall, Aug. 10, 1802–Oct. 25, 1848.
Vol. 6, Pt. 1–209
Lewis, Edmund Darch, Oct. 17, 1835–Aug. 12, 1910.
Vol. 6, Pt. 1–210
Lewis, Ed ("Strangler"), 1890?–Aug. 7, 1966.
Supp. 8–371
Lewis, Ellis, May 16, 1798–Mar. 19, 1871.
Vol. 6, Pt. 1–211
Lewis, Enoch, Jan. 29, 1776–July 14, 1856.
Vol. 6, Pt. 1–211
Lewis, Estelle Anna Blanche Robinson, Apr. 1824–Nov. 24, 1880.
Vol. 6, Pt. 1–212
Lewis, Exum Percival, Sept. 15, 1863–Nov. 17, 1926.
Vol. 6, Pt. 1–213
Lewis, Fielding, July 7, 1725–*c.* Jan. 1, 1782.
Vol. 6, Pt. 1–214
Lewis, Francis, Mar. 21, 1713–Dec. 31, 1802.
Vol. 6, Pt. 1–214
Lewis, Francis Park, May 19, 1855–Sept. 10, 1940.
Supp. 2–380
Lewis, Fulton, Jr., Apr. 30, 1903–Aug. 20, 1966.
Supp. 8–372
Lewis, George William, Mar. 10, 1882–July 12, 1948.
Supp. 4–486
Lewis, Gilbert Newton, Oct. 23, 1875–Mar. 23, 1946.
Supp. 4–487
Lewis, Harry Sinclair, Feb. 7, 1885–Jan. 10, 1951.
Supp. 5–421
Lewis, Isaac Newton, Oct. 12, 1858–Nov. 9, 1931.
Vol. 6, Pt. 1–215
Lewis, James, Oct. 5, 1837–Sept. 10, 1896.
Vol. 6, Pt. 1–216
Lewis, James Hamilton, May 18, 1863–Apr. 9, 1939.
Supp. 2–381
Lewis, John Francis, Mar. 1, 1818–Sept. 2, 1895.
Vol. 6, Pt. 1–217
Lewis, John Henry, May 1, 1914–Apr. 18, 1974.
Supp.9–493
Lewis, John Llewellyn, Feb. 12, 1880–June 11, 1969.
Supp. 8–374
Lewis, Joseph Horace, Oct. 29, 1824–July 6, 1904.
Vol. 6, Pt. 1–218
Lewis, Lawrence, June 20, 1856–Sept. 2, 1890.
Vol. 6, Pt. 1–219
Lewis, Lloyd Downs, May 2, 1891–Apr. 21, 1949.
Supp. 4–489
Lewis, Meriwether, Aug. 18, 1774–Oct. 11, 1809.
Vol. 6, Pt. 1–219
Lewis, Morgan, Oct. 16, 1754–Apr. 7, 1844.
Vol. 6, Pt. 1–222
Lewis, Orlando Faulkland, Sept. 5, 1873–Feb. 24, 1922.
Vol. 6, Pt. 1–223
Lewis, Oscar, Dec. 25, 1914–Dec. 16, 1970.
Supp. 8–377
Lewis, Samuel, Mar. 17, 1799–July 28, 1854.
Vol. 6, Pt. 1–223
Lewis, Sinclair. [*See* Lewis, Harry Sinclair, 1885–1951.]
Lewis, Tayler, Mar. 27, 1802–May 11, 1877.
Vol. 6, Pt. 1–224
Lewis, Wilfred, Oct. 16, 1854–Dec. 19, 1929.
Supp. 1–492
Lewis, William, Feb. 2, 1751 o.s.-Aug. 16, 1819.
Vol. 6, Pt. 1–225
Lewis, William Berkeley, 1784–Nov. 12, 1866.
Vol. 6, Pt. 1–226
Lewis, William David, Sept. 22, 1792–Apr. 1, 1881.
Vol. 6, Pt. 1–226
Lewis, William Draper, Apr. 27, 1867–Sept. 2, 1949.
Supp. 4–490
Lewis, William Gaston, Sept. 3, 1835–Jan. 7, 1901.
Vol. 6, Pt. 1–227
Lewis, William Henry, Nov. 28, 1868–Jan. 1, 1949.
Supp. 4–492
Lewis, Winslow, May 11, 1770–May 19, 1850.
Vol. 6, Pt. 1–228
Lewisohn, Adolph, May 27, 1849–Aug. 17, 1938.
Supp. 2–383
Lewisohn, Ludwig, May 30, 1882–Dec. 31, 1955.
Supp. 5–424
Lewisohn, Sam Adolph, Mar. 21, 1884–Mar. 13, 1951.
Supp. 5–426
Lexow, Clarence, Sept. 16, 1852–Dec. 30, 1910.
Vol. 6, Pt. 1–229
Ley, Willy, Oct. 2, 1906–June 24, 1969.
Supp. 8–379
Leyendecker, Joseph Christian, Mar. 23, 1874–July 25, 1951.
Supp. 5–428
Leyner, John George, Aug. 26. 1860–Aug. 5. 1920.
Vol. 6, Pt. 1–229
Leypoldt, Frederick, Nov. 17, 1835–Mar. 31, 1884.
Vol. 6, Pt. 1–230
L'Halle, Constantin de, d. June 6, 1706.
Vol. 6, Pt. 1–231
L'Halle, Nicolas Benoit Constantin de. [*See* L'Halle, Constantin de, d. 1706.]
Lhévinne, Josef, Dec. 14, 1874–Dec. 2, 1944.
Supp. 3–458
Lhévinne, Rosina, Mar. 29, 1880–Nov. 9, 1976.
Supp. 10–455
L'Hommedieu, Ezra, Aug. 30, 1734–Sept. 27, 1811.
Vol. 6, Pt. 1–232
Libbey, Edward Drummond, Apr. 17, 1854–Nov. 13, 1925.
Vol. 6, Pt. 1–233

Libby, Orin Grant, June 9, 1864–Mar. 29, 1952.
Supp. 5–429
Libby, Willard Frank, Dec. 17, 1908–Sept. 8, 1980.
Supp. 10–456
Libman, Emanuel, Aug. 22, 1872–June 28, 1946.
Supp. 4–494
Lick, James, Aug. 21, 1796–Oct. 1, 1876.
Vol. 6, Pt. 1–234
Lie, Jonas, Apr. 29, 1880–Jan. 10, 1940.
Supp. 2–384
Lieb, John William, Feb. 12, 1860–Nov. 1, 1929.
Vol. 6, Pt. 1–234
Lieber, Francis, Mar. 18, 1800–Oct. 2, 1872.
Vol. 6, Pt. 1–236
Liebling, Abbott Joseph, Oct. 18, 1904–Dec. 28, 1963.
Supp. 7–472
Liebling, Emil, Apr. 12, 1851–Jan. 20, 1914.
Vol. 6, Pt. 1–238
Liebling, Estelle, Apr. 21, 1880–Sept. 25, 1970.
Supp. 8–380
Liebman, Joshua Loth, Apr. 7, 1907–June 9, 1948.
Supp. 4–495
Lienau, Detlef, Feb. 17, 1818–Aug. 29, 1887.
Supp. 1–493
Liggett, Hunter, Mar. 21, 1857–Dec. 30, 1935.
Supp. 1–494
Liggett, Louis Kroh, Apr. 4, 1875–June 5, 1946.
Supp. 4–496
Liggett, Walter William, Feb. 14, 1886–Dec. 9, 1935.
Supp. 1–495
Lightburn, Joseph Andrew Jackson, Sept. 21, 1824–May 17, 1901.
Vol. 6, Pt. 1–239
Ligon, Thomas Watkins, May 1, 1810–Jan. 12, 1881.
Vol. 6, Pt. 1–239
Lile, William Minor, Mar. 28, 1859–Dec. 13, 1935.
Supp. 1–497
Lilienthal, Max, Oct. 16, 1815–Apr. 5, 1882.
Vol. 6, Pt. 1–240
Lillie, Frank Rattray, June 27, 1870–Nov. 5, 1947.
Supp. 4–497
Lillie, Gordon William, Feb. 14, 1860–Feb. 3, 1942.
Supp. 3–459
Lilly, Eli, Apr. 1, 1885–Jan. 24, 1977.
Supp. 10–458
Lilly, Josiah Kirby, Nov. 18, 1861–Feb. 8, 1948.
Supp. 4–499
Limón, José Arcadio, Jan. 12, 1908–Dec. 2, 1972.
Supp. 9–494
Lincecum, Gideon, Apr. 22, 1793–Nov. 28, 1874.
Vol. 6, Pt. 1–241
Lincoln, Abraham, Feb. 12, 1809–Apr. 15, 1865.
Vol. 6, Pt. 1–242
Lincoln, Benjamin, Jan. 24, 1733–May 9, 1810.
Vol. 6, Pt. 1–259
Lincoln, Enoch, Dec. 28, 1788–Oct. 8, 1829.
Vol. 6, Pt. 1–261
Lincoln, John Larkin, Feb. 23, 1817–Oct. 17, 1891.
Vol. 6, Pt. 1–262
Lincoln, Joseph Crosby, Feb. 13, 1870–Mar. 10, 1944.
Supp. 3–460
Lincoln, Levi, May 15, 1749–Apr. 14, 1820.
Vol. 6, Pt. 1–262
Lincoln, Levi, Oct. 25, 1782–May 29, 1868.
Vol. 6, Pt. 1–264
Lincoln, Mary Johnson Bailey, July 8, 1844–Dec. 2, 1921.
Vol. 6, Pt. 1–265
Lincoln, Mary Todd, Dec. 13, 1818–July 16, 1882.
Vol. 6, Pt. 1–265
Lincoln, Robert Todd, Aug. 1, 1843–July 26, 1926.
Vol. 6, Pt. 1–266
Lincoln, Rufus Pratt, Apr. 27, 1840–Nov. 27, 1900.
Vol. 6, Pt. 1–267
Lind, John, Mar. 25, 1854–Sept. 18, 1930.
Vol. 5, Pt. 1–268
Lindabury, Richard Vliet, Oct. 13, 1850–July 15, 1925.
Vol. 6, Pt. 1–269
Lindberg, Conrad Emil, June 9, 1852–Aug. 2, 1930.
Vol. 6, Pt. 1–270
Lindbergh, Charles Augustus, Jan. 20, 1859–May 24, 1924.
Vol. 6, Pt. 1–271
Lindbergh, Charles Augustus, Jr., Feb. 4, 1902–Aug. 26, 1974.
Supp. 9–495
Linde, Christian, Feb. 19, 1817–Nov. 24, 1887.
Vol. 6, Pt. 1–271
Lindeman, Eduard Christian, May 9, 1885–Apr. 13, 1953.
Supp. 5–430
Lindenkohl, Adolph, Mar. 6, 1833–June 22, 1904.
Vol. 6, Pt. 1–272
Lindenthal, Gustav, May 21, 1850–July 31, 1935.
Supp. 1–498
Linderman, Henry Richard, Dec. 26, 1825–Jan. 27, 1879.
Vol. 6, Pt. 1–273
Lindgren, Waldemar, Feb. 14, 1860–Nov. 3, 1939.
Supp. 2–385
Lindheimer, Ferdinand Jacob, May 21, 1801–Dec. 2, 1879.
Vol. 6, Pt. 1–273
Lindley, Curtis Holbrook, Dec. 14, 1850–Nov. 20, 1920.
Vol. 6, Pt. 1–274
Lindley, Daniel, Aug. 24, 1801–Sept. 3, 1880.
Supp. 1–499
Lindley, Jacob, June 13, 1774–Jan. 29, 1857.
Vol. 6, Pt. 1–275
Lindsay, Howard, Mar. 29, 1889–Feb. 11, 1968.
Supp. 8–382
Lindsay, Nicholas Vachel, Nov. 10, 1879–Dec. 5, 1931.
Vol. 6, Pt. 1–276
Lindsay, Vachel. [*See* Lindsay, Nicholas Vachel, 1879–1931.]
Lindsay, William, Sept. 4, 1835–Oct. 15, 1909.
Vol. 6, Pt. 1–277
Lindsey, Benjamin Barr, Nov. 25, 1869–Mar. 26, 1943.
Supp. 3–461
Lindsey, William, Aug. 12, 1858–Nov. 25, 1922.
Vol. 6, Pt. 1–278
Lindsley, John Berrien, Oct. 24, 1822–Dec. 7, 1897.
Vol. 6, Pt. 1–278
Lindsley, Philip, Dec. 21, 1786–May 25, 1855.
Vol. 6, Pt. 1–279
Lingelbach, Anna Lane, Oct. 10, 1873–July 14, 1954.
Supp. 5–432
Lining, John, 1708–Sept. 21, 1760.
Vol. 6, Pt. 1–280
Link, Henry Charles, Aug. 27, 1889–Jan. 9, 1952.
Supp. 5–433
Link, Theodore Carl, Sept. 22, 1904–Feb. 14, 1974.
Supp. 9–499
Linn, John Blair, Mar. 14, 1777–Aug. 30, 1804.
Vol. 6, Pt. 1–281
Linn, Lewis Fields, Nov. 5, 1795–Oct. 3, 1843.
Vol. 6, Pt. 1–282
Linn, William Alexander, Sept. 4, 1846–Feb. 23, 1917.
Vol. 6, Pt. 1–283
Lintner, Joseph Albert, Feb. 8, 1822–May 5, 1898.
Vol. 6, Pt. 1–283
Linton, Ralph, Feb. 27, 1893–Dec. 24, 1953.
Supp. 5–434
Linton, William James, Dec. 7, 1812–Dec. 29, 1897.
Vol. 6, Pt. 1–284
Lipchitz, Jacques, Aug. 22, 1981–May 26, 1973.
Supp. 9–500
Lipman, Jacob Goodale, Nov. 18, 1874–Apr. 19, 1939.
Supp. 2–387
Lippard, George, Apr. 10, 1822–Feb. 9, 1854.
Vol. 6, Pt. 1–285
Lippincott, James Starr, Apr. 12, 1819–Mar. 17, 1885.
Vol. 6, Pt. 1–286
Lippincott, Joseph Wharton, Feb. 28, 1887–Oct. 22, 1976.
Supp. 10–459
Lippincott, Joshua Ballinger, Mar. 18, 1813–Jan. 5, 1886.
Vol. 6, Pt. 1–287
Lippincott, Sara Jane Clarke, Sept. 23, 1823–Apr. 20, 1904.
Vol. 6, Pt. 1–288
Lippitt, Henry, Oct. 9, 1818–June 5, 1891.
Vol. 6, Pt. 1–289
Lippmann, Walter, Sept. 23, 1889–Dec. 14, 1974.
Supp. 9–503
Lipscomb, Abner Smith, Feb. 10, 1789–Dec. 8, 1856.
Vol. 6, Pt. 1–289
Lipscomb, Andrew Adgate, Sept. 16, 1816–Nov. 23, 1890.
Vol. 6, Pt. 1–290
Lisa, Manuel, Sept. 8, 1772–Aug. 12, 1820.
Vol. 6, Pt. 1–291

Lisagor, Peter Irvin, Aug. 5, 1915–Dec. 10, 1976.
Supp. 10–461
List, Georg Friedrich, Aug. 6, 1789–Nov. 30, 1846.
Vol. 6, Pt. 1–291
Listemann, Bernhard, Aug. 28, 1841–Feb. 11, 1917.
Vol. 6, Pt. 1–293
Liston, Charles ("Sonny"), May 8, 1932–Jan. 5, 1971.
Supp. 9–506
Litchfield, Electus Backus, Feb. 15, 1813–May 12, 1889.
Vol. 6, Pt. 1–294
Litchfield, Paul Weeks, July 26, 1875–Mar. 18, 1959.
Supp. 6–380
Littauer, Lucius Nathan, Jan. 20, 1859–Mar. 2, 1944.
Supp. 3–463
Littell, Eliakim, Jan. 2, 1797–May 17, 1870.
Vol. 6, Pt. 1–295
Littell, Squier, Dec. 9, 1803–July 4, 1886.
Vol. 6, Pt. 1–295
Littell, William, 1768–Sept. 26, 1824.
Vol. 6, Pt. 1–296
Little, Arthur Dehon, Dec. 15, 1863–Aug. 1, 1935.
Supp. 1–500
Little, Charles Coffin, July 25, 1799–Aug. 9, 1869.
Vol. 6, Pt. 1–297
Little, Charles Joseph, Sept. 21, 1840–Mar. 11, 1911.
Vol. 6, Pt. 1–298
Little, Charles Sherman, Feb. 12, 1869–June 6, 1936.
Supp. 2–388
Little, George, Apr. 15, 1754–July 22, 1809.
Vol. 6, Pt. 1–298
Little, William Lawson, Jr., June 23, 1910–Feb. 1, 1968.
Supp. 8–383
Little Crow V, *c.* 1803–July 3, 1863.
Vol. 6, Pt. 1–299
Littledale, Clara Savage, Jan. 31, 1891–Jan. 9, 1956.
Supp. 6–382
Littlefield, George Washington, June 21, 1842–Nov. 10, 1920.
Vol. 6, Pt. 1–300
Littlejohn, Abram Newkirk, Dec. 13, 1824–Aug. 3, 1901.
Vol. 6, Pt. 1–301
Littlepage, Lewis, Dec. 19, 1762–July 19, 1802.
Vol. 6, Pt. 1–302
Littleton, Martin Wiley, Jan. 12, 1872–Dec. 19, 1934.
Supp. 1–501
Little Turtle, *c.* 1752–July 14, 1812.
Vol. 6, Pt. 1–300
Liveright, Horace Brisbin, Dec. 10, 1886–Sept. 24, 1933.
Supp. 1–502
Livermore, Abiel Abbot, Oct. 30, 1811–Nov. 28, 1892.
Vol. 6, Pt. 1–303
Livermore, Arthur, July 29, 1766–July 1, 1853.
Vol. 6, Pt. 1–304
Livermore, Edward St. Loe, Apr. 5, 1762–Sept. 15, 1832.
Vol. 6, Pt. 1–304
Livermore, George, July 10, 1809–Aug. 30, 1865.
Vol. 6, Pt. 1–305
Livermore, Mary Ashton Rice, Dec. 19, 1820–May 23, 1905.
Vol. 6, Pt. 1–306
Livermore, Samuel, May 25, 1732–May 18, 1803.
Vol. 6, Pt. 1–307
Livermore, Samuel, Aug. 26, 1786–July 11, 1833.
Vol. 6, Pt. 1–308
Livingston, Burton Edward, Feb. 9, 1875–Feb. 8, 1948.
Supp. 4–500
Livingston, Edward, May 28, 1764–May 23, 1836.
Vol. 6, Pt. 1–309
Livingston, Henry Brockholst, Nov. 25, 1757–Mar. 18, 1823.
Vol. 6, Pt. 1–312
Livingston, James, Mar. 27, 1747–Nov. 29, 1832.
Vol. 6, Pt. 1–313
Livingston, John Henry, May 30, 1746–Jan. 20, 1825.
Vol. 6, Pt. 1–314
Livingston, John William, May 22, 1804–Sept 10, 1885.
Vol. 6, Pt. 1–315
Livingston, Peter Van Brugh, October 1710–Dec. 28, 1792.
Vol. 6, Pt. 1–315
Livingston, Philip, Jan. 15, 1716–June 12, 1778.
Vol. 6, Pt. 1–316
Livingston, Robert, Dec. 13, 1654–Oct. 1, 1728.
Vol. 6, Pt. 1–318
Livingston, Robert R., Aug. 1718–Dec. 9, 1775.
Vol. 6, Pt. 1–319
Livingston, Robert R., Nov. 27, 1746–Feb. 26, 1813.
Vol. 6, Pt. 1–320
Livingston, William, Nov. 1723–July 25, 1790.
Vol. 6, Pt. 1–325
Livingstone, Belle, Jan. 20, 1875?–Feb. 7, 1957.
Supp. 6–383
Livingstone, William, Jan. 21, 1844–Oct. 17, 1925.
Vol. 6, Pt. 1–327
Llewellyn, Karl Nickerson, May 22, 1893–Feb. 13, 1962.
Supp. 7–474
Lloyd, Alfred Henry, Jan. 3, 1864–May 11, 1927.
Vol. 6, Pt. 1–328
Lloyd, David, *c.* 1656–Apr. 6, 1731 o.s.
Vol. 6, Pt. 1–329
Lloyd, Edward, Nov. 15, 1744–July 8, 1796.
Vol. 6, Pt. 1–330
Lloyd, Edward, July 22, 1779–June 2, 1834.
Vol. 6, Pt. 1–221
Lloyd, Harold Clayton, Apr. 20, 1893–Mar. 8, 1971.
Supp. 9–507
Lloyd, Henry Demarest, May 1, 1847–Sept. 28, 1903.
Vol. 6, Pt. 1–331
Lloyd, James, Mar. 24, 1728–Mar. 14, 1810.
Vol. 6, Pt. 1–333
Lloyd, John Uri, Apr. 19, 1849–Apr. 9, 1936.
Supp. 2–389
Lloyd, Marshall Burns, Mar. 10, 1858–Aug. 10, 1927.
Vol. 6, Pt. 1–333
Lloyd, Thomas, Apr. 17, 1640 o.s.–Sept. 10, 1694. o.s.
Vol. 6, Pt. 1–334
Lochman, John George, Dec. 2, 1773–July 10, 1826.
Vol. 6, Pt. 1–335
Locke, Alain Leroy, Sept. 13, 1886–June 9, 1954.
Supp. 5–436
Locke, Bessie, Aug. 7, 1865–Apr. 9, 1952.
Supp. 5–437
Locke, David Ross, Sept. 20, 1833–Feb. 15, 1888.
Vol. 6, Pt. 1–336
Locke, John, Feb. 19, 1792–July 10, 1856.
Vol. 6, Pt. 1–337
Locke, Matthew, 1730–Sept. 7, 1801.
Vol. 6, Pt. 1–338
Locke, Richard Adams, Sept. 22, 1800–Feb. 16, 1871.
Vol. 6, Pt. 1–238
Lockhart, Charles, Aug. 2, 1818–Jan. 26, 1905.
Vol. 6, Pt. 1–339
Lockheed, Allan Haines, Jan. 20, 1889–May 26, 1969.
Supp. 8–384
Lockheed, Malcolm, 1887?–Aug. 13, 1958.
Supp. 6–385
Lockrey, Sarah Hunt, Apr. 21, 1863–Nov. 8, 1929.
Vol. 6, Pt. 1–340
Lockwood, Belva Ann Bennett, Oct. 24, 1830–May 19, 1917.
Vol. 6, Pt. 1–341
Lockwood, James Booth, Oct. 9, 1852–Apr. 9, 1884.
Vol. 6, Pt. 1–341
Lockwood, Ralph Ingersoll, July 8, 1798–Apr. 12, 1858?.
Vol. 6, Pt. 1–342
Lockwood, Robert Wilton, Sept. 12, 1861–Mar. 20, 1914.
Vol. 6, Pt. 1–343
Lockwood, Samuel Drake, Aug. 2, 1789–Apr. 23, 1874.
Vol. 6, Pt. 1–344
Lockwood, Wilton [*See* Lockwood, Robert Wilton, 1861–1914.]
Locy, William Albert, Sept. 14, 1857–Oct. 9, 1924.
Vol. 6, Pt. 1–345
Lodge, George Cabot, Oct. 10, 1873–Aug. 21, 1909.
Vol. 6, Pt. 1–345
Lodge, Henry Cabot, May 12, 1850–Nov. 9, 1924.
Vol. 6, Pt. 1–346
Lodge, John Ellerton, Aug. 1, 1876–Dec. 29, 1942.
Supp. 3–464
Loeb, Jacques, Apr. 7, 1859–Feb. 11, 1924.
Vol. 6, Pt. 1–349
Loeb, James, Aug. 6, 1867–May 29, 1933.
Supp. 1–503
Loeb, Leo, Sept. 21, 1869–Dec. 28, 1959.
Supp. 6–385
Loeb, Louis, Nov. 7, 1866–July 12, 1909.
Vol. 6, Pt. 1–352

Loeb, Milton B., Jan. 28, 1887–Jan. 27–1972.
Supp. 9–510
Loeb, Morris, May 23, 1863–Oct. 8, 1912.
Vol. 6, Pt. 1–353
Loeb, Sophie Irene Simon, July 4, 1876–Jan. 18, 1929.
Vol. 6, Pt. 1–354
Loeffler, Charles Martin, Jan. 30, 1861–May 19, 1935.
Supp. 1–504
Loesser, Frank, June 29, 1910–July 28, 1969.
Supp. 8–385
Loew, Marcus, May 7, 1870–Sept. 5, 1927.
Vol. 6, Pt. 1–355
Loewenthal, Isidor, *c.* 1827–Apr. 27, 1864.
Vol. 6, Pt. 1–356
Loewi, Otto, June 3, 1873–Dec. 25, 1961.
Supp. 7–475
Logan, Benjamin, *c.* 1743–Dec. 11, 1802.
Vol. 6, Pt. 1–356
Logan, Cornelius Ambrose, Aug. 24, 1832–Jan. 30, 1899.
Vol. 6, Pt. 1–357
Logan, Cornelius Ambrosius, May 4, 1806–Feb. 22, 1853.
Vol. 6, Pt. 1–358
Logan, Deborah Norris, Oct. 19, 1761–Feb. 2, 1839.
Vol. 6, Pt. 1–359
Logan, George, Sept. 9, 1753–Apr. 9, 1821.
Vol. 6, Pt. 1–359
Logan, James, Oct. 20, 1674–Oct. 31, 1751.
Vol. 6, Pt. 1–360
Logan, James, *c.* 1725–1780.
Vol. 6, Pt. 1–362
Logan, James Harvey, Dec. 8, 1841–July 16, 1928.
Vol. 6, Pt. 1–363
Logan, John Alexander, Feb. 9, 1826–Dec. 26, 1886.
Vol. 6, Pt. 1–363
Logan, Olive, Apr. 22, 1839–Apr. 27, 1909.
Vol. 6, Pt. 1–365
Logan, Stephen Trigg, Feb. 24, 1800–July 17, 1880.
Vol. 6, Pt. 1–365
Logan, Thomas Muldrup, July 31, 1808–Feb. 13, 1876.
Vol. 6, Pt. 1–366
Logan, Thomas Muldrup, Nov. 3, 1840–Aug. 11, 1914.
Vol. 6, Pt. 1–367
Loguen, Jermain Wesley, *c.* 1813–Sept. 30, 1872.
Vol. 6, Pt. 1–368
Lomax, John Avery, Sept. 23, 1867–Jan. 26, 1948.
Supp. 4–501
Lomax, John Tayloe, Jan. 19, 1781–Oct. 1, 1862.
Vol. 6, Pt. 1–369
Lomax, Louis Emanuel, Aug. 16, 1922–July 30, 1970.
Supp. 8–387
Lomax, Lunsford Lindsay, Nov. 4, 1835–May 28, 1913.
Vol. 6, Pt. 1–369
Lombard, Carole, Oct. 6, 1908–Jan. 16, 1942.
Supp. 3–465
Lombard, Warren Plimpton, May 29, 1855–July 13, 1939.
Supp. 2–390
Lombardi, Vincent Thomas, June 11, 1913–Sept. 3, 1970.
Supp. 8–389
Lombardo, Gaetano Albert ("Guy"), June 19, 1902–Nov. 5, 1977.
Supp. 10–463
London, Jack, Jan. 12, 1876–Nov. 22, 1916.
Vol. 6, Pt. 1–370
London, Meyer, Dec. 29, 1871–June 6, 1926.
Vol. 6, Pt. 1–372
Lonesome Charley. [*See* Reynolds, Charles Alexander, *c.* 1842–1876.]
Long, Armistead Lindsay, Sept. 3, 1825–Apr. 29, 1891.
Vol. 6, Pt. 1–374
Long, Breckinridge, May 16, 1881–Sept. 26, 1958.
Supp. 6–387
Long, Charles Chaillé. [*See* Chaillé-Long, Charles, 1842–1917.]
Long, Crawford Williamson, Nov. 1, 1815–June 16, 1878
Vol. 6, Pt. 1–374
Long, Earl Kemp, Aug. 26, 1895–Sept. 5, 1960.
Supp. 6–390
Long, Edward Vaughn, July 18, 1908–Nov. 6, 1972.
Supp. 9–511
Long, Huey Pierce, Aug. 30, 1893–Sept. 10, 1935.
Supp. 1–506
Long, James, *c.* 1793–Apr. 8, 1822.
Vol. 6, Pt. 1–376
Long, John Davis, Oct. 27, 1838–Aug. 28, 1915.
Vol. 6, Pt. 1–377
Long, John Harper, Dec. 26, 1856–June 14, 1918.
Vol. 6, Pt. 1–378
Long, John Luther, Jan. 1, 1861–Oct. 31, 1927.
Vol. 6, Pt. 1–379
Long, Joseph Ragland, Dec. 15, 1870–Mar. 15, 1932.
Supp. 1–508
Long, Perrin Hamilton, Apr. 7, 1899–Dec. 17, 1965.
Supp. 7–477
Long, Stephen Harriman, Dec. 30, 1784–Sept. 4, 1864.
Vol. 6, Pt. 1–380
Longacre, James Barton, Aug. 11, 1794–Jan. 1, 1869.
Vol. 6, Pt. 1–380
Longcope, Warfield Theobald, Mar. 29, 1877–Apr. 25, 1953.
Supp. 5–438
Longfellow, Ernest Wadsworth, Nov. 23, 1845–Nov. 24, 1921.
Vol. 6, Pt. 1–381
Longfellow, Henry Wadsworth, Feb. 27, 1807–Mar. 24, 1882.
Vol. 6, Pt. 1–382
Longfellow, Samuel, June 18, 1819–Oct. 3, 1892.
Vol. 6, Pt. 1–387
Longfellow, Stephen, Mar. 23, 1776–Aug. 3, 1849.
Vol. 6, Pt. 1–388
Longfellow, William Pitt Preble, Oct. 25, 1836–Aug. 3, 1913.
Vol. 6, Pt. 1–388
Longley, Aleander, Mar. 31, 1832–Apr. 17, 1918.
Vol. 6, Pt. 1–389
Longstreet, Augustus Baldwin, Sept. 22, 1790–July 9, 1870.
Vol. 6, Pt. 1–390
Longstreet, James, Jan. 8, 1821–Jan. 2, 1904.
Vol. 6, Pt. 1–391
Longstreet, William, Oct. 6, 1759–Sept. 1, 1814.
Vol. 6, Pt. 1–393
Longworth, Alice Lee Roosevelt, Feb. 12, 1884–Feb. 21, 1980.
Supp. 10–464
Longworth, Nicholas, Jan. 16, 1782–Feb. 10, 1863.
Vol. 6, Pt. 1–393
Longworth, Nicholas, Nov. 5, 1869–Apr. 9, 1931.
Vol. 6, Pt. 1–394
Longyear, John Munroe, Apr. 15, 1850–May 28, 1922.
Vol. 6, Pt. 1–395
Loomis, Arphaxed, Apr. 9, 1798–Sept. 15, 1885.
Vol. 6, Pt. 1–396
Loomis, Charles Battell, Sept. 16, 1861–Sept. 23, 1911.
Vol. 6, Pt. 1–397
Loomis, Dwight, July 27, 1821–Sept. 17, 1903.
Vol. 6, Pt. 1–397
Loomis, Elias, Aug. 7, 1811–Aug. 15, 1889.
Vol. 6, Pt. 1–398
Loomis, Elmer Howard, May 24, 1861–Jan. 22, 1931.
Vol. 6, Pt. 1–399
Loomis, Mahlon, July 21, 1826–Oct. 13, 1886.
Vol. 6, Pt. 1–399
Loop, Henry Augustus, Sept. 9, 1831–Oct. 20, 1895.
Vol. 6, Pt. 1–400
Loos, Charles Louis, Dec. 23, 1823–Feb. 27, 1912.
Vol. 6, Pt. 1–401
Lopez, Aaron, 1731–May 28, 1782.
Vol. 6, Pt. 1–402
Lopez, Vincent Joseph, Dec. 30, 1895–Sept. 20, 1975.
Supp. 9–512
Loras, Jean Mathias Pierre, Aug. 30, 1792–Feb. 19, 1858.
Vol. 6, Pt. 1–403
Lord, Asa Dearborn, June 17, 1816–Mar. 7, 1875.
Vol. 6, Pt. 1–403
Lord, Chester Sanders, Mar. 18, 1850–Aug. 1, 1933.
Supp. 1–509
Lord, Daniel, Sept. 23, 1795–Mar. 4, 1868.
Vol. 6, Pt. 1–404
Lord, David Nevins, Mar. 4, 1792–July 14, 1880.
Vol. 6, Pt. 1–405
Lord, Eleazar, Sept. 9, 1788–June 3, 1871.
Vol. 6, Pt. 1–405
Lord, Henry Curwen, Apr. 17, 1866–Sept. 15, 1925.
Vol. 6, Pt. 1–406
Lord, Herbert Mayhew, Dec. 6, 1859–June 2, 1930.
Vol 6, Pt. 1–407
Lord, Jeremy. [*See* Redman, Ben Ray.]

Lord, John, Dec. 27, 1810–Dec. 15, 1894.
Vol. 6, Pt. 1–408
Lord, Nathan, Nov. 28, 1792–Sept. 9, 1870.
Vol. 6, Pt. 1–409
Lord, Otis Phillips, July 11, 1812–Mar. 13, 1884.
Vol. 6, Pt. 1–409
Lord, Pauline, Aug. 8, 1890–Oct. 11, 1950.
Supp. 4–503
Lord, William Paine, July 1, 1839–Feb. 17, 1911.
Vol. 6, Pt. 1–410
Lord, William Wilberforce, Oct. 28, 1819–Apr. 22, 1907.
Vol. 6, Pt. 1–411
Loree, Leonor Fresnel, Apr. 23, 1858–Sept. 6, 1940.
Supp. 2–391
Lorillard, Pierre, Oct. 13, 1833–July 7, 1901.
Vol. 6, Pt. 1–411
Lorimer, George Claude, June 4, 1838–Sept. 7, 1904.
Vol. 6, Pt. 1–412
Lorimer, George Horace, Oct. 6, 1867–Oct. 22, 1937.
Supp. 2–393
Lorimer, William, Apr. 27, 1861–Sept. 13, 1934.
Supp. 1–511
Lorimier, Pierre Louis, March 1748–June 26, 1812.
Vol. 6, Pt. 1–413
Loring, Charles Harding, Dec. 26, 1828–Feb. 5, 1907.
Vol. 6, Pt. 1–413
Loring, Charles Morgridge, Nov. 13, 1832–Mar. 18, 1922.
Vol. 6, Pt. 1–414
Loring, Edward Greely, Sept. 28, 1837–Apr. 23, 1888.
Vol. 6, Pt. 1–415
Loring, Ellis Gray, Apr. 14, 1803–May 24, 1858.
Vol. 6, Pt. 1–416
Loring, Frederick Wadsworth, Dec. 12, 1848–Nov. 5, 1871.
Vol. 6, Pt. 1–417
Loring, George Bailey, Nov. 8, 1817–Sept. 14, 1891.
Vol. 6, Pt. 1–417
Loring, Joshua, Aug. 3, 1716–October 1781.
Vol. 6, Pt. 1–418
Loring, Joshua, Nov. 1, 1744–August 1789.
Vol. 6 Pt. 1–419
Loring, William Wing, Dec. 4, 1818–Dec. 30, 1886.
Vol. 6, Pt. 1–420
Lorre, Peter, June 26, 1904–Mar. 23, 1964.
Supp. 7–478
Loskiel, George Henry, Nov. 7, 1740–Feb. 23, 1814.
Vol. 6, Pt. 1–421
Lossing, Benson John, Feb. 12, 1813–June 3, 1891.
Vol. 6, Pt. 1–421
Lothrop, Alice Louise Higgins, May 28, 1870–Sept. 2, 1920.
Vol. 6, Pt. 1–422
Lothrop, Amy. [*See* Warner, Anna Bartlett, 1827–1915.]
Lothrop, Daniel, Aug. 11, 1831–Mar. 18, 1892.
Vol. 6, Pt. 1–423
Lothrop, George Van Ness, Aug. 8, 1817–July 12, 1897.
Vol. 6, Pt. 1–424
Lothrop, Harriett Mulford Stone, June 22, 1844–Aug. 2, 1924.
Vol. 6, Pt. 1–424
Lothropp, John, 1584–Nov. 8, 1653.
Vol. 6, Pt. 1–425
Lotka, Alfred James, Mar. 2, 1880–Dec. 5, 1949.
Supp. 4–505
Lotta. [*See* Crabtree, Lotta, 1847–1924.]
Loucks, Henry Langford, May 24, 1846–Dec. 29, 1928.
Vol. 6, Pt. 1–426
Loudon, Samuel, *c.* 1727–Feb. 24, 1813.
Vol. 6, Pt. 1–427
Loudoun, John Campbell, Fourth Earl of, May 5, 1705–Apr. 27, 1782.
Vol. 6, Pt. 1–428
Loughridge, Robert McGill, Dec. 24, 1809–July 8, 1900.
Vol. 6, Pt. 1–428
Louis, Morris, Nov. 28, 1912–Sept. 7, 1962.
Supp. 7–479
Lounsbury, Thomas Raynesford, Jan. 1, 1838–Apr. 9, 1915.
Vol. 6, Pt. 1–429
Love, Alfred Henry, Sept. 7, 1830–June 29, 1913.
Vol. 6, Pt. 1–431
Love, Emanuel King, July 27, 1850–Apr. 24, 1900.
Vol. 6, Pt. 1–432
Love, Robertus Donnell, Jan. 6, 1867–May 7, 1930.
Vol. 6, Pt. 1–432
Lovejoy, Arthur Oncken, Oct. 10, 1873–Dec. 30, 1962.
Supp. 7–480
Lovejoy, Asa Lawrence, Mar. 14, 1808–Sept. 10, 1882.
Vol. 6, Pt. 1–433
Lovejoy, Elijah Parish, Nov. 9, 1802–Nov. 7, 1837.
Vol. 6, Pt. 1–434
Lovejoy, Owen, Jan. 6, 1811–Mar. 25, 1864.
Vol. 6, Pt. 1–435
Lovejoy, Owen Reed, Sept. 9, 1866–June 29, 1961.
Supp. 7–483
Lovelace, Francis, *c.* 1621–1675.
Vol. 6, Pt. 1–436
Loveland, William Austin Hamilton, May 30, 1826–Dec. 17 1894.
Vol. 6, Pt. 1–437
Lovell, James, Oct. 31, 1737–July 14, 1814.
Vol. 6, Pt. 1–438
Lovell, John, Apr. 1, 1710–1778.
Vol. 6, Pt. 1–439
Lovell, John Epy, Apr. 23, 1795–May 3, 1892.
Vol. 6, Pt. 1–440
Lovell, Joseph, Dec. 22, 1788–Oct. 17, 1836.
Vol. 6, Pt. 1–440
Lovell, Mansfield, Oct. 20, 1822–June 1, 1884.
Vol. 6, Pt. 1–441
Loveman, Amy, May 16, 1881–Dec. 11, 1955.
Supp. 5–439
Lovering, Joseph, Dec. 25, 1813–Jan. 18, 1892.
Vol. 6, Pt. 1–442
Lovett, Robert Morss, Dec. 25, 1870–Feb. 8, 1956.
Supp. 6–391
Lovett, Robert Scott, June 22, 1860–June 19, 1932.
Supp. 1–513
Lovett, Robert Williamson, Nov. 18, 1859–July 2, 1924.
Vol. 6, Pt. 1–443
Lovewell, John, Oct. 14, 1691–May 8, 1725
Vol. 6, Pt. 1–444
Low, Abiel Abbot, Feb. 7, 1811–Jan. 7, 1893.
Vol. 6, Pt. 1–444
Low, Frederick Ferdinand, June 30, 1828–July 21, 1894.
Vol. 6, Pt. 1–445
Low, Isaac, Apr. 13, 1735–July 25, 1791.
Vol. 6, Pt. 1–446
Low, John Gardner, Jan. 10, 1835–Nov. 10, 1907.
Vol. 6, Pt. 1–447
Low, Juliette Gordon, Oct. 31, 1860–Jan. 17, 1927.
Vol. 6, Pt. 1–447
Low, Nicholas, Mar. 30, 1739–Nov. 15, 1826.
Vol. 6, Pt. 1–448
Low, Seth, Jan. 18, 1850–Sept. 17, 1916.
Vol. 6, Pt. 1–449
Low, Will Hicok, May 31, 1853–Nov. 27, 1932.
Supp. 1–513
Lowden, Frank Orren, Jan. 26, 1861–Mar. 20, 1943.
Supp. 3–467
Lowe, Charles, Nov. 18, 1828–June 20, 1874.
Vol. 6, Pt. 1–450
Lowe, Ralph Phillips, Nov. 27, 1805–Dec. 22, 1883.
Vol. 6, Pt. 1–451
Lowe, Thaddeus Sobieski Coulincourt, Aug. 20, 1832–Jan. 16, 1913.
Vol. 6, Pt. 1–452
Lowell, Abbott Lawrence, Dec. 13, 1856–Jan. 6, 1943.
Supp. 3–468
Lowell, Amy, Feb. 9, 1874–May 12, 1925.
Vol. 6, Pt. 1–453
Lowell, Edward Jackson, Oct. 18, 1845–May 11, 1894.
Vol. 6, Pt. 1–455
Lowell, Francis Cabot, Apr. 7, 1775–Aug. 10, 1817.
Vol. 6, Pt. 1–456
Lowell, Guy, Aug. 6, 1870–Feb. 4, 1927.
Vol. 6, Pt. 1–457
Lowell, James Russell, Feb. 22, 1819–Aug. 12, 1891.
Vol. 6, Pt. 1–458
Lowell, John, June 17, 1743–May 6, 1802.
Vol. 6, Pt. 1–464
Lowell, John, Oct. 6, 1769–Mar. 12, 1840.
Vol. 6, Pt. 1–465
Lowell, John, May 11, 1799–Mar. 4, 1836.
Vol. 6, Pt. 1–466

Lowell, John, Oct. 18, 1824–May 14, 1897.
Vol. 6, Pt. 1–466
Lowell, Josephine Shaw, Dec. 16, 1843–Oct. 12, 1905.
Vol. 6, Pt. 1–467
Lowell, Percival, Mar. 13, 1855–Nov. 12, 1916.
Vol. 6, Pt. 1–468
Lowell, Ralph, July 23, 1890–May 16, 1978.
Supp. 10–466
Lowell, Robert Traill Spence, Oct. 8, 1816–Sept. 12, 1891.
Vol. 6, Pt. 1–470
Lowell, Robert Traill Spence, Jr., Mar. 1, 1917–Sept. 12, 1977.
Supp. 10–467
Lowenstein, Allard Kenneth, Jan. 16, 1929–Mar. 14, 1980.
Supp. 10–470
Lower, William Edgar, May 6, 1867–June 17, 1948.
Supp. 4–507
Lowery, Woodbury, Feb. 17, 1853–Apr. 11, 1906.
Vol. 6, Pt. 1–470
Lowes, John Livingston, Dec. 20, 1867–Aug. 15, 1945.
Supp. 3–474
Lowie, Robert Harry, June 12, 1883–Sept. 21, 1957.
Supp. 6–392
Lowndes, Lloyd, Feb. 21, 1845–Jan. 8, 1905.
Vol. 6, Pt. 1–471
Lowndes, Rawlins, Jan. 1721–Aug. 24, 1800.
Vol. 6, Pt. 1–472
Lowndes, William, Feb. 11, 1782–Oct. 27, 1822.
Vol. 6, Pt. 1–473
Lowrey, Mark Perrin, Dec. 30, 1828–Feb. 27, 1885.
Vol. 6, Pt. 1–474
Lowrie, James Walter, Sept. 16, 1856–Jan. 26, 1930.
Vol. 6 Pt. 1–475
Lowrie, Walter, Dec. 10, 1784–Dec. 14, 1868.
Vol. 6, Pt. 1–476
Lowry, Hiram Harrison, May 29, 1843–Jan. 13, 1924.
Vol. 6, Pt. 1–476
Lowry, Robert, Mar. 10, 1830–Jan. 19, 1910.
Vol. 6, Pt. 1–477
Lowry, Thomas, Feb. 27, 1843–Feb. 4, 1909.
Vol. 6, Pt. 1–477
Loy, Matthias, Mar. 17, 1828–Jan. 26, 1915.
Vol. 6, Pt. 1–478
Loyd, Samuel, Jan. 31, 1841–Apr. 10, 1911.
Vol. 6, Pt. 1–479
Lozier, Clemence Sophia Harned, Dec. 11, 1813–Apr. 26, 1888.
Vol. 6, Pt. 1–480
Lubbock, Francis Richard, Oct. 16, 1815–June 22, 1905.
Vol. 6, Pt. 1–480
Lubin, David, June 10, 1849–Jan. 1, 1919.
Vol. 6, Pt. 1–481
Lubin, Isador, June 9, 1896–July 6, 1978.
Supp. 10–471
Lubitsch, Ernst, Jan. 29, 1892–Nov. 30, 1947.
Supp. 4–508
Lucas, Anthony Francis, Sept. 9, 1855–Sept. 2, 1921.
Vol. 6, Pt. 1–482
Lucas, Daniel Bedinger, Mar. 16, 1836–July 28, 1909.
Vol. 6, Pt. 1–483
Lucas, Eliza. [*See* Pinckney, Elizabeth Lucas, 1722–1793.]
Lucas, Frederic Augustus, Mar. 25, 1852–Feb. 9, 1929.
Vol. 6, Pt. 1–484
Lucas, James H., Nov. 12, 1800–Nov. 9, 1873.
Vol. 6, Pt. 1–484
Lucas, John Baptiste Charles, Aug. 14, 1758–Aug. 29, 1842.
Vol. 6, Pt. 1–485
Lucas, Jonathan, 1754–Apr. 1, 1821.
Vol. 6, Pt. 1–486
Lucas, Jonathan, 1775–Dec. 29, 1832.
Vol. 6, Pt. 1–487
Lucas, Robert, Apr. 1, 1781–Feb. 7, 1853.
Vol. 6, Pt. 1–487
Lucas, Scott Wike, Feb. 19, 1892–Feb. 22, 1968.
Supp. 8–391
Luce, Henry Robinson, Apr. 3, 1898–Feb. 28, 1967.
Supp. 8–392
Luce, Henry Winters, Sept. 24, 1868–Dec. 8, 1941.
Supp. 3–476
Luce, Stephen Bleecker, Mar. 25, 1827–July 28, 1917.
Vol. 6, Pt. 1–488
Luchese, Thomas, 1899?–July 13, 1967.
Supp. 8–396
Luciano, Charles ("Lucky"), Nov. 11, 1897?–Jan. 26, 1962.
Supp. 7–484
Luckenbach, J(ohn) Lewis, Nov. 19, 1883–July 4, 1951.
Supp. 5–440
Ludeling, John Theodore, Jan. 27, 1827–Jan. 21, 1891.
Vol. 6, Pt. 1–489
Ludlow, Daniel, Aug. 2, 1750–Sept. 26, 1814.
Vol. 6, Pt. 1–490
Ludlow, Fitz Hugh, Sept. 11, 1836–Sept. 12, 1870.
Vol. 6, Pt. 1–491
Ludlow, Gabriel George, Apr. 16, 1736–Feb. 12, 1808.
Vol. 6, Pt. 1–491
Ludlow, George Duncan, 1734–Nov. 13, 1808.
Vol. 6, Pt. 1–492
Ludlow, Noah Miller, July 3, 1795–Jan. 9, 1886.
Vol. 6, Pt. 1–493
Ludlow, Roger, fl. 1590–1664.
Vol. 6, Pt. 1–493
Ludlow, Thomas William, June 14, 1795–July 17, 1878.
Vol. 6, Pt. 1–494
Ludlow, William, Nov. 27, 1843–Aug. 30, 1901.
Vol. 6, Pt. 1–495
Ludlowe, Roger. [*See* Ludlow, Roger, fl. 1590–1664.]
Ludwell, Philip, fl. 1660–1704.
Vol. 6, Pt. 1–496
Ludwick, Christopher, Oct. 17, 1720–June 17, 1801.
Vol. 6, Pt. 1–497
Luelling, Henderson, Apr. 23, 1809–Dec. 28, 1878.
Vol. 6, Pt. 1–498
Lufbery, Raoul Gervais Victor, Mar. 21, 1885–May 19, 1918.
Vol. 6, Pt. 1–499
Lugosi, Bela, Oct. 30, 1882–Aug. 16, 1956.
Supp. 6–394
Luhan, Mabel Dodge, Feb. 26, 1879–Aug. 13, 1962.
Supp. 7–485
Lukeman, Henry Augustus, Jan. 28, 1871–Apr. 3, 1935.
Supp. 1–515
Lukens, Rebecca Webb Pennock, Jan. 6, 1794–Dec. 10, 1854.
Vol. 6, Pt. 1–499
Luks, George Benjamin, Aug. 13, 1867–Oct. 29, 1933.
Supp. 1–516
Lull, Edward Phelps, Feb. 20, 1836–Mar. 5, 1887.
Vol. 6, Pt. 1–500
Lumbrozo, Jacob, fl. 1656–1665.
Vol. 6, Pt. 1–501
Lummis, Charles Fletcher, Mar. 1, 1859–Nov. 25, 1928.
Vol. 6, Pt. 1–501
Lumpkin, Joseph Henry, Dec. 23, 1799–June 4, 1867.
Vol. 6, Pt. 1–502
Lumpkin, Wilson, Jan. 14, 1783–Dec. 28, 1870.
Vol. 6, Pt. 1–503
Luna y Arellano, Tristan de, fl. 1530–1561.
Vol. 6, Pt. 1–504
Lunceford, James Melvin ("Jimmie"), June 6, 1902–July 12, 1947.
Supp. 4–509
Lundeberg, Harry, Mar. 25, 1901–Jan. 28, 1957.
Supp. 6–396
Lundeen, Ernest, Aug. 4, 1878–Aug. 31, 1940.
Supp. 2–394
Lundie, John, Dec. 14, 1857–Feb. 9, 1931.
Vol. 6, Pt. 1–505
Lundin, Carl Axel Robert, Jan. 13, 1851–Nov. 28, 1915.
Vol. 6, Pt. 1–505
Lundy, Benjamin, Jan. 4, 1789–Aug. 22, 1839.
Vol. 6, Pt. 1–506
Lunn, George Richard, June 23, 1873–Nov. 27, 1948.
Supp. 4–511
Lunt, Alfred David, Jr., Aug. 12, 1892–Aug. 3, 1977.
Supp. 10–472
Lunt, George, Dec. 31, 1803–May 16, 1885.
Vol. 6, Pt. 1–507
Lunt, Orrington, Dec. 24, 1815–Apr. 5, 1897.
Vol. 6, Pt. 1–508
Lurton, Horace Harmon, Feb. 26, 1844–July 12, 1914.
Vol. 6, Pt. 1–509
Lusk, Graham, Feb. 15, 1866–July 18, 1932.
Supp. 1–517

Lusk, William Thompson, May 23, 1838–June 12, 1897.
Vol. 6, Pt. 1–510
Luther, Seth, fl. 1817–1846.
Vol. 6, Pt. 1–511
Lutkin, Peter Christian, Mar. 27, 1858–Dec. 27, 1931.
Vol. 6, Pt. 1–511
Lutz, Frank Eugene, Sept. 15, 1879–Nov. 27, 1943.
Supp. 3–477
Lybrand, William Mitchell, Aug. 14, 1867–Nov. 19, 1960.
Supp. 6–397
Lydenberg, Harry Miller, Nov. 18, 1874–Apr. 16, 1960.
Supp. 6–398
Lydston, George Frank, Mar. 3, 1857–Mar. 14, 1923.
Vol. 6, Pt. 1–513
Lyman, Albert Josiah, Dec. 24, 1845–Aug. 22, 1915.
Vol. 6, Pt. 1–514
Lyman, Benjamin Smith, Dec. 11, 1835–Aug. 30, 1920.
Vol. 6, Pt. 1–514
Lyman, Chester Smith, Jan. 13, 1814–Jan. 29, 1890.
Vol. 6, Pt. 1–515
Lyman, Eugene William, Apr. 4, 1872–Mar. 15, 1948.
Supp. 4–512
Lyman, Joseph Bardwell, Oct. 6, 1829–Jan. 28, 1872.
Vol. 6, Pt. 1–516
Lyman, Phineas, 1715–Sept. 10, 1774.
Vol. 6, Pt. 1–517
Lyman, Theodore, Feb. 20, 1792–July 18, 1849.
Vol. 6, Pt. 1–518
Lyman, Theodore, Aug. 23, 1833–Sept. 9, 1897.
Vol. 6, Pt. 1–519
Lyman, Theodore, Nov. 23, 1874–Oct. 11, 1954.
Supp. 5–441
Lynch, Anne Charlotte. [*See* Botta, Anne Charlotte Lynch, 1815–1891.]
Lynch, Charles, 1736–Oct. 29, 1796.
Vol. 6, Pt. 1–519
Lynch, James Daniel, Jan. 6, 1836–July 19, 1903.
Vol. 6, Pt. 1–520
Lynch, James Mathew, Jan. 11, 1867–July 16, 1930.
Vol. 6, Pt. 1–521
Lynch, John Roy, Sept. 10, 1847–Nov. 2, 1939.
Supp. 2–395
Lynch, Patrick Neeson, Mar. 10, 1817–Feb. 26, 1882.
Vol. 6, Pt. 1–521
Lynch, Robert Clyde, Sept. 8, 1880–May 12, 1931.
Vol. 6, Pt. 1–522
Lynch, Thomas, 1727–Dec. 1776.
Vol. 6, Pt. 1–523
Lynch, Thomas, Aug. 5, 1749–1779.
Vol. 6, Pt. 1–523
Lynch, William Francis, Apr. 1, 1801–Oct. 17, 1865.
Vol. 6, Pt. 1–524
Lynd, Robert Staughton, Sept. 26, 1892–Nov. 1, 1970.
Supp. 8–398
Lynde, Benjamm, Oct. 5, 1700–Oct. 5, 1781.
Vol. 6. Pt. 1–525
Lynde, Francis, Nov. 12, 1856–May 16, 1930.
Vol. 6, Pt. 1–526
Lynds, Elam, 1784–Jan. 8, 1855.
Vol. 6, Pt. 1–527
Lynn, Diana ("Dolly"), Oct. 7, 1926–Dec. 18, 1971.
Supp. 9–514
Lyon, Caleb, Dec. 8, 1821–Sept 7, 1875.
Vol. 6, Pt. 1–527
Lyon, David Gordon, May 24, 1852–Dec. 4, 1935.
Supp. 1–518
Lyon, David Willard, May 13, 1870–Mar. 16, 1949.
Supp. 4–514
Lyon, Francis Strother, Feb. 25, 1800–Dec. 31, 1882.
Vol. 6, Pt. 1–528
Lyon, Harris Merton, Dec. 22, 1883–June 2, 1916.
Vol. 6, Pt. 1–529
Lyon, James, July 1, 1735–Oct. 12, 1794.
Vol. 6, Pt. 1–530
Lyon, James Benjamin, Apr. 21, 1821–Apr. 16, 1909.
Vol. 6, Pt. 1–530
Lyon, Mary, Feb. 28, 1797–Mar. 5, 1849.
Vol. 6, Pt. 1–531
Lyon, Matthew, July 14, 1750–Aug. 1, 1822.
Vol. 6, Pt. 1–532
Lyon, Nathaniel, July 14, 1818–Aug. 10, 1861.
Vol. 6, Pt. 1–534
Lyon, Theodatus Timothy, Jan. 23, 1813–Feb. 6, 1900.
Vol. 6, Pt. 1–535
Lvon, William Penn, Oct. 28, 1822–Apr. 4, 1913.
Vol. 6, Pt. 1–536
Lyons, Leonard, Sept. 10, 1906–Oct. 7, 1976.
Supp. 10–475
Lyons, Peter, 1734/35–July 30, 1809.
Vol. 6, Pt. 1–536
Lyster, Henry Francis Le Hunte, Nov. 8, 1837–Oct. 3, 1894.
Vol. 6, Pt. 1–537
Lytle, William Haines, Nov. 2, 1826–Sept. 20, 1863.
Vol. 6, Pt. 1–538
Lyttelton, William Henry, Dec. 24, 1724–Sept. 14, 1808.
Vol. 6, Pt. 1–538

Maas, Anthony J., Aug. 23, 1858–Feb. 20, 1927.
Vol. 6, Pt. 1–539
Mabery, Charles Frederic, Jan. 13, 1850–June 26, 1927.
Vol. 6, Pt. 1–540
Mabie, Hamilton Wright, Dec 13, 1845–Dec. 31, 1916.
Vol. 6, Pt. 1–540
Mabley, Jackie ("Moms"), *c.* 1894–May 23, 1975.
Supp. 9–517
McAdams, Clark, Jan. 29, 1874–Nov. 29, 1935.
Supp. 1–519
McAdie, Alexander George, Aug. 4, 1863–Nov. 1, 1943.
Supp. 3–478
McAdoo, William Gibbs, Oct. 31, 1863–Feb. 1, 1941.
Supp. 3–479
McAfee, John Armstrong, Dec. 12, 1831–June 12, 1890.
Vol. 6, Pt. 1–541
McAfee, Robert Breckinridge, Feb. 18, 1784–Mar. 12, 1849.
Vol. 6, Pt. 1–542
Macalester, Charles, Apr. 5, 1765–Aug. 29, 1832.
Vol. 6, Pt. 1–543
Macalester, Charles, Feb. 17, 1798–Dec. 9, 1873.
Vol. 6, Pt. 1–543
McAlexander, Ulysses Grant, Aug. 30, 1864–Sept. 18, 1936.
Supp. 2–396
MacAlister, James, Apr. 26, 1840–Dec. 11, 1913.
Vol. 6, Pt. 1–544
McAllister, Charles Albert, May 29, 1867–Jan. 6, 1932.
Vol. 6, Pt. 1–545
McAllister, Hall, Feb. 9, 1826–Dec. 1, 1888.
Vol. 6, Pt. 1–545
McAllister, Matthew Hall, Nov. 26, 1800–Dec. 19, 1865.
Vol. 6, Pt. 1–546
McAllister, Samuel Ward, Dec. 1827–Jan. 31, 1895.
Vol. 6, Pt. 1–547
McAlpine, William Jarvis, Apr. 30, 1812–Feb. 16, 1890.
Vol. 6, Pt. 1–548
McAnally, David Rice, Feb. 17, 1810–July 11, 1895.
Vol. 6, Pt. 1–549
McAndrew, William, Aug. 20, 1863–June 27, 1937.
Supp. 2–398
MacArthur, Arthur, June 2, 1845–Sept. 5, 1912.
Supp. 1–521
MacArthur, Charles Gordon, Nov. 5, 1895–Apr. 21, 1956.
Supp. 6–400
MacArthur, Douglas, Jan. 26, 1880–Apr. 5, 1964.
Supp. 7–487
McArthur, Duncan, Jan. 14, 1772–Apr. 28, 1839.
Vol. 6, Pt. 1–549
McArthur, John, May 13, 1823–Jan. 8, 1890.
Vol. 6, Pt. 1–550
McArthur, John, Nov. 17, 1826–May 15, 1906.
Vol. 6, Pt. 1–551
MacArthur, John Donald, Mar. 6, 1897–Jan. 6, 1978.
Supp. 10–477
MacArthur, Robert Stuart, July 31, 1841–Feb. 23, 1923.
Vol. 6, Pt. 1–552
McArthur, William Pope, Apr. 2, 1814–Dec. 23, 1850.
Vol. 6, Pt. 1–552
Macauley, Edward Yorke. [*See* McCauley, Edward Yorke, 1827–1894.]
McAuley, Jeremiah, *c.* 1839–Sept. 18, 1884.
Vol. 6, Pt. 1–553
McAuley, Thomas, Apr. 21, 1778–May 11, 1862.
Vol. 6, Pt. 1–554

McAuliffe, Anthony Clement, July 2, 1898–Aug. 11, 1975.
Supp. 9–518
McBain, Howard Lee, July 20, 1880–May 7, 1936.
Supp. 2–399
McBride, F(rancis) Scott, July 29, 1872–Apr. 23, 1955.
Supp. 5–442
McBride, Henry, July 25, 1867–Mar. 31, 1962.
Supp. 7–493
McBride, Mary Margaret, Nov. 16, 1899–Apr. 7, 1976.
Supp. 10–478
McBryde, John McLaren, Jan. 1, 1841–Mar. 20, 1923.
Vol. 6, Pt. 1–554
McBurney, Charles, Feb. 17, 1845–Nov. 7, 1913.
Vol. 6, Pt. 1–555
McBurney, Robert Ross, Mar. 31, 1837–Dec. 27, 1898.
Vol. 6, Pt. 1–556
McCabe, Charles Cardwell, Oct. 11, 1836–Dec. 19, 1906.
Vol. 6, Pt. 1–557
McCabe, John Collins, Nov. 12, 1810–Feb. 26, 1875.
Vol. 6, Pt. 1–558
McCabe, William Gordon, Aug. 4, 1841–June 1, 1920.
Vol. 6, Pt. 1–558
McCaffrey, John, Sept. 6, 1806–Sept. 26, 1881.
Vol. 6, Pt. 1–559
McCaine, Alexander, *c.* 1768–June 1, 1856.
Vol. 6, Pt. 1–560
McCaleb, Theodore Howard, Feb. 10, 1810–Apr. 29, 1864.
Vol. 6, Pt. 1–560
McCall, Edward Rutledge, Aug. 6, 1790–July 31, 1853.
Vol. 6, Pt. 1–561
McCall, John Augustine, Mar. 2, 1849–Feb. 18, 1906.
Vol. 6, Pt. 1–562
McCall, Samuel Walker, Feb. 28, 1851–Nov. 4, 1923.
Vol. 6, Pt. 1–562
McCalla, Bowman Hendry, June 19, 1844–May 6, 1910.
Vol. 6, Pt. 1–564
McCalla, William Latta, Nov. 25, 1788–Oct. 12, 1859.
Vol. 6, Pt. 1–564
McCallum, Daniel Craig, Jan. 21, 1815–Dec. 27, 1878.
Vol. 6, Pt. 1–565
MacCallum, William George, Apr. 18, 1874–Feb. 3, 1944.
Supp. 3–482
MacCameron, Robert, Jan. 14, 1866–Dec. 29, 1912.
Vol. 6, Pt. 1–566
McCann, Alfred Watterson, Jan. 9, 1879–Jan. 19, 1931.
Vol. 6, Pt. 1–567
McCann, William Penn, May 4, 1830–Jan. 15, 1906.
Vol. 6, Pt. 1–567
McCardell, Claire, May 24, 1905–Mar. 22, 1958.
Supp. 6–401
McCarran, Patrick Anthony, Aug. 8, 1876–Sept. 28, 1954.
Supp. 5–443
McCarren, Patrick Henry, June 18, 1847–Oct. 23, 1909.
Vol. 6, Pt. 1–568
McCarroll, James, Aug. 3, 1814–Apr. 10, 1892.
Vol. 6, Pt. 1–569
McCartee, Divie Bethune, Jan. 13, 1820–July 17, 1900.
Vol. 6, Pt. 1–569
McCarthy, Charles, June 29, 1873–Mar. 26, 1921.
Vol. 6, Pt. 1–570
McCarthy, Charles Louis (Clem), Sept. 9, 1882–June 4, 1962.
Supp. 7–494
McCarthy, Daniel Joseph, June 22, 1874–Oct. 9, 1958.
Supp. 6–402
McCarthy, Joseph Raymond, Nov. 14, 1908–May 2, 1957.
Supp. 6–404
McCarthy, Joseph Vincent ("Joe"), Apr. 21, 1887–Jan. 13, 1978.
Supp. 10–480
McCartney, Washington, Aug. 24, 1812–July 15, 1856.
Vol. 6, Pt. 1–571
McCauley, Charles Stewart, Feb. 3, 1793–May 21, 1869.
Vol. 6, Pt. 1–572
MacCauley, Clay, May 8, 1843–Nov. 15, 1925.
Vol. 6, Pt. 1–572
McCauley, Edward Yorke, Nov. 2, 1827–Sept. 14, 1894.
Vol. 6, Pt. 1–573
McCauley, Mary Ludwig Hays, Oct. 13, 1754–Jan. 22, 1832.
Vol. 6, Pt. 1–574
McCausland, John, Sept. 13, 1836–Jan. 22, 1927.
Vol. 6, Pt. 1–575
McCaw, James Brown, July 12, 1823–Aug. 13, 1906.
Vol. 6, Pt. 1–575
McCawley, Charles Grymes, Jan. 29, 1827–Oct. 13, 1891.
Vol. 6, Pt. 1–576
McCawley, Charles Laurie, Aug. 24, 1865–Apr. 29, 1935.
Supp. 1–522
McCay, Charles Francis, Mar. 8, 1810–Mar. 13, 1889.
Vol. 6, Pt. 1–577
McCay, Henry Kent, Jan. 8, 1820–July 30, 1886.
Vol. 6, Pt. 1–578
McClain, Emlin, Nov. 26, 1851–May 25, 1915.
Vol. 6, Pt. 1–578
McClatchy, Charles Kenny, Nov. 1, 1858–Apr. 27, 1936.
Supp. 2–400
McClellan, George, Dec. 23, 1796–May 9, 1847.
Vol. 6, Pt. 1–579
McClellan, George, Oct. 29, 1849–Mar. 29, 1913.
Vol. 6, Pt. 1–580
McClellan, George Brinton, Dec. 3, 1826–Oct. 29, 1885.
Vol. 6, Pt. 1–581
McClellan, George Brinton, Nov. 23, 1865–Nov. 30, 1940.
Supp. 2–401
McClellan, Henry Brainerd, Oct. 17, 1840–Oct. 1, 1904.
Vol. 6, Pt. 1–585
McClellan, John Little, Feb. 25, 1896–Nov. 27, 1977.
Supp. 10–481
McClellan, Robert, 1770–Nov. 22, 1815.
Vol. 6, Pt. 1–586
McClelland, Robert, Aug. 1, 1807–Aug. 30, 1880.
Vol. 6, Pt. 1–586
McClenahan, Howard, Oct. 19, 1872–Dec. 17, 1935.
Supp. 1–522
McClernand, John Alexander, May 30, 1812–Sept. 20, 1900.
Vol. 6, Pt. 1–587
McClintic, Guthrie, Aug. 6, 1893–Oct. 29, 1961.
Supp. 7–495
McClintock, Emory, Sept. 19, 1840–July 10, 1916.
Vol. 6, Pt. 1–588
McClintock, James Harvey, Feb. 23, 1864–May 10, 1934.
Supp. 1–523
M'Clintock, John, Oct. 27, 1814–Mar. 4, 1870.
Vol. 6, Pt. 1–589
McClintock, Oliver, Oct. 20, 1839–Oct 10, 1922.
Vol. 6, Pt. 1–590
McCloskey, John, Mar. 10, 1810–Oct. 10, 1885.
Vol. 6, Pt. 1–591
McCloskey, William George, Nov. 10, 1823–Sept. 17, 1909.
Vol. 6, Pt. 1–592
McClung, Clarence Erwin, Apr. 5, 1870–Jan. 17, 1946.
Supp. 4–515
McClure, Alexander Kelly, Jan. 9, 1828–June 6, 1909.
Vol. 6, Pt. 1–593
McClure, Alexander Wilson, May 8, 1808–Sept. 1865.
Vol. 6, Pt. 1–594
McClure, George, *c.* 1770–Aug. 16, 1851.
Vol. 6, Pt. 1–594
McClure, Robert Alexis, Mar. 4, 1897–Jan. 1, 1957.
Supp. 6–406
McClure, Samuel Sidney, Feb. 17, 1857–Mar. 21, 1949.
Supp. 4–516
McClurg, Alexander Caldwell, Sept. 9, 1832–Apr. 15, 1901.
Vol. 6, Pt. 1–595
McClurg, James, *c.* 1746–July 9, 1823.
Vol. 6, Pt. 1–596
McClurg, Joseph Washington, Feb. 22, 1818–Dec. 2, 1900.
Vol. 6, Pt. 1–597
McComas, Louis Emory, Oct. 28, 1846–Nov. 10, 1907.
Vol. 6, Pt. 1–598
McComb, John, Oct. 17, 1763–May 25, 1853.
Vol. 6, Pt. 1–599
McConnel, John Ludlum, Nov. 11, 1826–Jan. 17, 1862.
Vol. 6, Pt. 1–600
McConnell, Francis John, Aug. 18, 1871–Aug. 18, 1953.
Supp. 5–445
McConnell, Ira Welch, Oct. 17, 1871–Jan. 7, 1933.
Supp. 1–524
McCook, Alexander McDowell, April 22, 1831–June 12, 1903.
Vol. 6, Pt. 1–600
McCook, Anson George, Oct. 10, 1835–Dec. 30, 1917.
Vol. 6, Pt. 1–601

McCook, Edward Moody, June 15, 1833–Sept. 9, 1909.
Vol. 6, Pt. 1–602
McCook, Henry Christopher, July 3, 1837–Oct. 31, 1911.
Vol. 6, Pt. 1–603
McCook, John James, Feb. 2, 1843–Jan. 9, 1927.
Vol. 6, Pt. 1–603
McCord, David James, Jan. 1797–May 12, 1855.
Vol. 6, Pt. 1–604
McCord, James Bennett, Apr. 5, 1870–Oct. 5, 1950.
Supp. 4–519
McCord, Louisa Susanna Cheves, Dec. 3, 1810–Nov. 23, 1879.
Vol. 6, Pt. 1–605
McCormack, Buren Herbert ("Mac"), Mar. 4, 1909–Feb. 28, 1972.
Supp. 9–520
McCormack, John Francis, June 14, 1884–Sept. 16, 1945.
Supp. 3–483
McCormack, John William, Dec. 21, 1891–Nov. 22, 1980.
Supp. 10–483
McCormack, Joseph Nathaniel, Nov. 9, 1847–May 4, 1922.
Vol. 6, Pt. 1–606
McCormick, Anne Elizabeth O'Hare, May 16, 1882–May 29, 1954.
Supp. 5–446
McCormick, Cyrus Hall, Feb. 15, 1809–May 13, 1884.
Vol. 6, Pt. 1–607
McCormick, Cyrus Hall, May 16, 1859–June 2, 1936.
Supp. 2–402
McCormlck, Joseph Medill, May 16, 1877–Feb. 25, 1925.
Vol. 6, Pt. 1–609
McCormick, Leander James, Feb. 8, 1819–Feb. 20, 1900.
Vol. 6, Pt. 1–610
McCormick, Lynde Dupuy, Aug. 12, 1895–Aug. 16, 1956.
Supp. 6–407
McCormick, Medill. [*See* McCormick, Joseph Medill, 1877–1925.]
McCormick, Richard Cunningham, May 23, 1832–June 2, 1901.
Vol. 6, Pt. 1–610
McCormick, Robert Sanderson, July 26, 1849–Apr. 16, 1919.
Vol. 6, Pt. 1–612
McCormick, Robert, June 8, 1780–July 4, 1846.
Vol. 6, Pt. 1–611
McCormick, Robert Rutherford, July 30, 1880–Apr. 1, 1955.
Supp. 5–448
McCormick, Ruth Hanna. [*See* Simms, Ruth Hanna McCormick 1880–1944.]
McCormick, Samuel Black, May 6, 1858–Apr. 18, 1928.
Vol. 6, Pt. 1–613
McCormick, Stephen, Aug. 26, 1784–Aug. 28, 1875.
Vol. 6, Pt. 1–614
McCosh, Andrew James, Mar. 15, 1858–Dec. 2, 1908.
Vol. 6, Pt. 1–614
McCosh, James, Apr. 1, 1811–Nov. 16, 1894.
Vol. 6, Pt. 1–615
McCoy, George Braidwood, Jan. 14, 1904–Dec. 22, 1976.
Supp. 10–487
McCoy, Isaac, June 13, 1784–June 21, 1846.
Vol. 6, Pt. 1–617
McCoy, Joseph Geating, Dec. 21, 1837–Oct–19, 1915.
Vol. 6, Pt. 1–618
McCoy, Tim, Apr. 10, 1891–Jan. 29, 1978.
Supp. 10–488
MacCracken, Henry Mitchell, Sept. 28, 1840–Dec. 24, 1918.
Vol. 6, Pt. 1–619
McCracken, Joan, Dec. 31, 1922–Nov. 1, 1961.
Supp. 7–496
McCrady, Edward, Apr. 8, 1833–Nov. 1, 1903.
Vol. 6, Pt. 2–1
McCrae, Thomas, Dec. 16, 1870–June 30, 1935.
Supp. 1–525
McCrary, George Washington, Aug. 29, 1835–June 23, 1890.
Vol. 6, Pt. 2–2
McCreary, Conn, June 17, 1921–June 28, 1979.
Supp. 10–490
McCreary, James Bennett, July 8, 1838–Oct. 8, 1918.
Vol. 6, Pt. 2–3
McCreery, Charles, June 13, 1785–Aug. 27, 1826.
Vol. 6, Pt. 2–3
McCreery, James Work, July 13, 1849–Feb. 20, 1923.
Vol. 6, Pt. 2–4
McCullagh, Joseph Burbridge, Nov. 1842–Dec. 31, 1896,
Vol. 6, Pt. 2–5
McCullers, Carson, Feb. 19, 1917–Sept. 29, 1967.
Supp. 8–399
McCulloch, Ben, Nov. 11, 1811–Mar. 7, 1862.
Vol. 6, Pt. 2–5
McCulloch, Hugh, Dec. 7, 1808–May 24, 1895.
Vol. 6, Pt. 2–6
McCulloch, Oscar Carleton, July 2, 1843–Dec. 10, 1891.
Vol. 6, Pt. 2–8
McCulloch, Robert Paxton, May 9, 1911–Feb. 25, 1977.
Supp. 10–491
McCullough, Ernest, May 22, 1867–Oct. 1, 1931.
Vol. 6, Pt. 2–8
McCullough, John, Nov. 14, 1832–Nov. 8, 1885.
Vol. 6, Pt. 2–9
McCullough, John Griffith, Sept. 16, 1835–May 29, 1915.
Vol. 6, Pt. 2–10
McCumber, Porter James, Feb. 3, 1858–May 18, 1933.
Supp. 1–525
MacCurdy, George Grant, Apr. 17, 1863–Nov. 15, 1947.
Supp. 4–520
McCurdy, Richard Aldrich, Jan. 29, 1835–Mar. 6, 1916.
Vol. 6, Pt. 2–11
McCutcheon, George Barr, July 26, 1866–Oct. 23 1928.
Vol. 6, Pt. 2–12
McDaniel, Hattie, June 10, 1898–Oct. 26, 1952.
Supp. 5–451
McDaniel, Henry Dickerson, Sept. 4, 1836–July 25, 1926.
Vol. 6, Pt. 2–13
McDill, James Wilson, Mar. 4, 1834–Feb. 28, 1894.
Vol. 6, Pt. 2–14
MacDonald, Betty, Mar. 26, 1908–Feb. 7, 1958.
Supp. 6–408
Macdonald, Charles Blair, Nov. 14, 1856–Apr. 21, 1939.
Supp. 2–404
McDonald, Charles James, July 9, 1793–Dec 16, 1860.
Vol. 6, Pt. 2–15
McDonald, David John, Nov. 22, 1902–Aug. 8, 1979.
Supp. 10–493
McDonald, James Grover, Nov. 29, 1886–Sept. 26, 1964.
Supp. 7–497
MacDonald, James Wilson Alexander, Aug. 25, 1824–Aug. 14, 1908.
Vol. 6, Pt. 2–16
MacDonald, Jeanette Anna, June 18, 1907–Jan. 14, 1965.
Supp. 7–499
McDonald, John Bartholomew, Nov. 7, 1844–Mar. 17, 1911.
Vol. 6, Pt. 2–16
McDonald, Joseph Ewing, Aug. 29, 1819–June 21, 1891.
Vol. 6, Pt. 2–17
MacDonald, Ranald, Feb. 3, 1824–Aug. 26, 1894.
Vol. 6, Pt. 2–18
McDonnell, James Smith, Jr., Apr. 9, 1899–Aug. 22, 1980.
Supp. 10–494
McDonogh, John, Dec. 29, 1779–Oct. 26, 1850.
Vol. 6, Pt. 2–19
MacDonough, Thomas, Dec. 31, 1783–Nov. 10, 1825.
Vol. 6, Pt. 2–19
McDougal, David Stockton, Sept. 27, 1809–Aug. 7, 1882.
Vol. 6, Pt. 2–21
McDougall, Alexander, July or Aug. 1732–June 9, 1786.
Vol. 6, Pt. 2–21
McDougall, Alexander, Mar. 16, 1845–May 23, 1923.
Vol. 6, Pt. 2–22
McDougall, Frances Harriet. [*See* Green, Frances Harriet Whipple, 1805–1878.]
McDougall, William, June 22, 1871–Nov. 28, 1938.
Supp. 2–405
McDowell, Charles, *c.* 1743–Mar. 31, 1815.
Vol. 6, Pt. 2–23
MacDowell, Edward Alexander, Dec. 18, 1861–Jan 23 1908.
Vol. 6, Pt. 2–24
McDowell, Ephraim, Nov. 11, 1771–June 25 1830.
Vol. 6, Pt. 2–27
McDowell, Irvin, Oct. 15, 1818–May 4, 1885.
Vol. 6, Pt. 2–29
McDowell, James, Oct. 13, 1795–Aug. 24, 1851.
Vol. 6, Pt. 2–30
McDowell, John, Feb. 11, 1751–Dec. 22, 1820.
Vol. 6, Pt. 2–31

McDowell, John, Sept. 10, 1780–Feb. 13, 1863.
Vol. 6, Pt. 2–32
McDowell, Joseph, Feb. 15, 1756–Aug 11, 1801.
Vol. 6, Pt. 2–33
MacDowell, Katherine Sherwood Bonner, Feb. 26, 1849–July 22, 1883.
Vol. 6, Pt. 2–33
McDowell, Mary Eliza, Nov. 30, 1854–Oct. 14, 1936.
Supp. 2–407
McDowell, William Fraser, Feb. 4, 1858–Apr. 26, 1937.
Supp. 2–409
McDuffie, George, Aug. 10, 1790–Mar. 11, 1851.
Vol. 6, Pt. 2–34
McElrath, Thomas, May 1, 1807–June 6, 1888.
Vol. 6, Pt. 2–36
McElroy, John, May 14, 1782–Sept 12, 1877.
Vol. 6, Pt. 2–36
McElroy, John, Aug. 25, 1846–Oct 12, 1929.
Vol. 6, Pt. 2–37
McElroy, Neil Hosler, Oct. 30, 1904–Nov. 30, 1972.
Supp. 9–521
McElroy, Robert McNutt, Dec. 28, 1872–Jan. 16, 1959.
Supp. 6–409
McElwaine, William Howe, Feb. 11, 1867–Jan. 10, 1908.
Vol. 6, Pt. 2–38
McEnery, Samuel Douglas, May 28, 1837–June 28, 1910.
Vol. 6, Pt. 2–39
McEntee, James Joseph, Sept. 9, 1884–Oct. 13, 1957.
Supp. 6–411
McEntee, Jervis, July 14, 1828–Jan. 27, 1891.
Vol. 6, Pt. 2–39
Macfadden, Bernarr, Aug. 16, 1868–Oct. 12, 1955.
Supp. 5–452
McFadden, Louis Thomas, July 25, 1876–Oct. 1, 1936.
Supp. 2–410
McFarland, George Bradley, Dec. 1, 1866–May 3, 1942.
Supp. 3–485
McFarland, John Horace, Sept. 24, 1859–Oct. 2, 1948.
Supp. 4–521
McFarland, John Thomas, Jan. 2, 1851–Dec. 22, 1913.
Vol. 6, Pt. 2–40
McFarland, Samuel Gamble, Dec. 11, 1830–Apr 25, 1897
Vol. 6, Pt. 2–41
McFarland, Thomas Bard, Apr. 19, 1828–Sept. 16, 1908.
Vol. 6, Pt. 2–42
Macfarlane, Charles William, Nov. 5, 1850–May 15, 1931.
Vol. 6, Pt. 2–42
Macfarlane, Robert, Apr. 23, 1815–Dec 20, 1883.
Vol. 6, Pt. 2–43
McFaul, James Augustine, June 6, 1850–June 16, 1917.
Vol. 6, Pt. 2–44
McFee, William, June 15, 1881–July 2, 1966.
Supp. 8–402
McFerrin, John Berry, June 15, 1807–May 10, 1887.
Vol. 6, Pt. 2–44
MacGahan, Januarius Aloysius, June 12, 1844–June 9, 1878.
Vol. 6, Pt. 2–45
McGarrah, Gates White, July 20, 1863–Nov. 5, 1940.
Supp. 2–410
McGarvey, John William, Mar. 1, 1829–Oct. 6, 1911.
Vol. 6, Pt. 2–46
McGee, William John, Apr. 17, 1853–Sept 4, 1912.
Vol. 6, Pt. 2–47
McGeehan, William O'Connell, Nov. 22, 1879–Nov. 29, 1933.
Supp. 1–526
McGhee, Charles McClung, Jan. 23, 1828–May 5, 1907.
Vol. 6, Pt. 2–48
McGiffert, Arthur Cushman, Mar. 4, 1851–Feb. 25, 1933.
Supp. 1–527
McGiffin, Philo Norton, Dec. 13, 1860–Feb. 11, 1897.
Vol. 6, Pt. 2–48
McGill, John, Nov. 4, 1809–Jan. 14, 1872.
Vol. 6, Pt. 2–49
McGill, Ralph Emerson, Feb. 5, 1898–Feb. 3, 1969.
Supp. 8–403
McGillivray, Alexander, *c.* 1759–Feb. 17, 1793.
Vol. 6, Pt. 2–50
McGilvary, Daniel, May 16, 1828–Aug. 22, 1911.
Vol. 6, Pt. 2–51
McGinley, Phyllis, Mar. 21, 1905–Feb. 22, 1978.
Supp. 10–496
McGivney, Michael Joseph, Aug. 12, 1852–Aug. 14, 1890.
Vol. 6, Pt. 2–52
McGlothlin, William Joseph, Nov. 29, 1867–May 28, 1933.
Supp. 1–529
McGlynn, Edward, Sept. 27, 1837–Jan. 7, 1900.
Vol. 6, Pt. 2–53
McGovern, John, Feb. 18, 1850–Dec. 17, 1917.
Vol. 6, Pt. 2–54
McGowan, Samuel, Oct. 9, 1819–Aug. 9, 1897.
Vol. 6, Pt. 2–55
McGranery, James Patrick, July 8, 1895–Dec. 23, 1962.
Supp. 7–500
McGrath, James, June 26, 1835–Jan. 12, 1898.
Vol. 6, Pt. 2–55
McGrath, James Howard, Nov. 28, 1903–Sept. 2, 1966.
Supp. 8–405
McGrath, Matthew J., Dec. 20, 1876–Jan. 29, 1941.
Supp. 3–486
McGraw, Donald Cushing, May 21, 1897–Feb. 7, 1974.
Supp. 9–522
McGraw, James Herbert, Dec. 17, 1860–Feb. 21, 1948.
Supp. 4–523
McGraw, John Harte, Oct. 4, 1850–June 23, 1910.
Vol. 6, Pt. 2–56
McGraw, John Joseph, Apr. 7, 1873–Feb. 25, 1934.
Supp. 1–529
McGready, James, *c.* 1758–Feb. 1817.
Vol. 6, Pt. 2–56
McGroarty, Susan. [*See* Julia, Sister, 1827–1901.]
McGuffey, William Holmes, Sept. 23, 1800–May 4, 1873.
Vol. 6, Pt. 2–57
McGuire, Charles Bonaventure, Dec. 16, 1768–July 17, 1833.
Vol. 6, Pt. 2–58
McGuire, Hunter Holmes, Oct. 11, 1835–Sept. 19, 1900.
Vol. 6, Pt. 2–59
McGuire, Joseph Deakins, Nov. 26, 1842–Sept. 6, 1916.
Vol. 6, Pt. 2–60
McHale, Kathryn, July 22, 1889–Oct. 8, 1956.
Supp. 6–412
Machebeuf, Joseph Projectus, Aug. 11, 1812–July 10, 1889.
Vol. 6, Pt. 2–61
Machen, John Gresham, July 28, 1881–Jan. 1, 1937.
Supp. 2–411
McHenry, James, Nov. 16, 1753–May 3, 1816.
Vol. 6, Pt. 2–62
McHenry, James, Dec. 20, 1785–July 21, 1845.
Vol. 6, Pt. 2–63
McHugh, Keith Stratton, Feb. 22, 1895–June 7, 1975.
Supp. 9–524
McHugh, Rose John, July 11, 1881–Dec. 12, 1952.
Supp. 5–454
McIlvaine, Charles Pettit, Jan. 18, 1799–Mar. 13, 1873.
Vol. 6, Pt. 2–64
McIlwaine, Richard, May 28, 1834–Aug. 10, 1913.
Vol. 6, Pt. 2–65
McIntire, Ross, Aug. 11, 1889–Dec. 8, 1959.
Supp. 6–413
McIntire, Samuel, January 1757–Feb. 6, 1811.
Vol. 6, Pt. 2–65
Macintosh, Douglas Clyde, Feb. 18, 1877–July 6, 1948.
Supp. 4–524
McIntosh, John Baillie, June 6, 1829–June 29, 1888.
Vol. 6, Pt. 2–69
McIntosh, Lachlan, Mar. 17, 1725–Feb. 20, 1806.
Vol. 6, Pt. 2–69
McIntosh, William, *c.* 1775–May 1, 1825.
Vol. 6, Pt. 2–70
McIntyre, Alfred Robert, Aug. 22, 1886–Nov. 28, 1948.
Supp. 4–526
McIntyre, James, Aug. 8, 1857–Aug. 18, 1937.
Supp. 2–412
McIntyre, James Francis Aloysius, June 25, 1886–July 16, 1979.
Supp. 10–497
McIntyre, Oscar Odd, Feb. 18, 1884–Feb. 14, 1938.
Supp. 2–414
McIver, Charles Duncan, Sept. 27, 1860–Sept. 17, 1906.
Vol. 6, Pt. 2–71
MacIver, Robert Morrison, Apr. 17, 1882–June 15, 1970.
Supp. 8–406
Mack, Connie, Dec. 22, 1862–Feb. 8, 1956.
Supp. 6–414

Mack, Julian William, July 19, 1866–Sept. 5, 1943.
Supp. 3–487
Mackay, Clarence Hungerford, Apr. 17, 1874–Nov. 12, 1938.
Supp. 2–415
McKay, Claude, Sept. 15, 1889–May 22, 1948.
Supp. 4–527
McKay, David Oman, Sept. 8, 1873–Jan. 18, 1970.
Supp. 8–408
McKay, Donald, Sept. 4, 1810–Sept. 20, 1880.
Vol. 6, Pt. 2–72
McKay, Gordon, May 4, 1821–Oct. 19, 1903.
Vol. 6, Pt. 2–73
Mackay, James, 1759?–Mar. 16, 1822.
Vol. 6, Pt. 2–74
McKay, (James) Douglas, June 24, 1893–July 22, 1959
Supp. 6–416
McKay, James Iver, July 17, 1792–Sept. 14, 1853.
Vol. 6, Pt. 2–75
Mackay, John William, Nov. 28, 1831–July 20, 1902.
Vol. 6, Pt. 2–75
MacKaye, Benton, Mar. 6, 1879–Dec. 11, 1975.
Supp. 9–525
MacKaye, James Morrison Steele, June 6, 1842–Feb. 25, 1894.
Vol. 6, Pt. 2–76
MacKaye, Percy Wallace, Mar. 16, 1875–Aug. 31, 1956.
Supp. 6–417
MacKaye, Steele. [*See* MacKaye, James Morrison Steele, 1842–1894.]
McKean, James William, Mar. 10, 1860–Feb. 9, 1949.
Supp. 4–529
McKean, Joseph Borden, July 28, 1764–Sept. 3, 1826.
Vol. 6, Pt. 2–77
McKean, Samuel, Apr. 7, 1787–Dec. 14, 1841.
Vol. 6, Pt. 2–78
McKean, Thomas, Mar. 19, 1734–June 24, 1817.
Vol. 6, Pt. 2–79
McKean, William Wister, Sept. 19, 1800–Apr. 22, 1865.
Vol. 6, Pt. 2–81
McKechnie, William Boyd, Aug. 7, 1886–Oct. 29, 1965.
Supp. 7–501
McKee, John, 1771–Aug. 12, 1832.
Vol. 6, Pt. 2–82
McKeen, Joseph, Oct. 15, 1757–July 15, 1807.
Vol. 6, Pt. 2–83
McKeldin, Theodore Roosevelt, Nov. 20, 1900–Aug. 10, 1974.
Supp. 9–527
McKellar, Kenneth Douglas, Jan. 29, 1869–Oct. 25, 1957.
Supp. 6–418
Mackellar, Patrick, 1717–Oct. 22, 1778.
Vol. 6, Pt. 2–83
MacKellar, Thomas, Aug. 12, 1812–Dec. 29, 1899.
Vol. 6, Pt. 2–84
McKelway, St. Clair, Mar. 15, 1845–July 16, 1915.
Vol. 6, Pt. 2–85
McKendree, William, July 6, 1757–Mar. 5, 1835.
Vol. 6, Pt. 2–85
McKenna, Charles Hyacinth, May 8, 1835–Feb. 21, 1917.
Vol. 6, Pt. 2–87
McKenna, Joseph, Aug. 10, 1843–Nov. 21, 1926.
Vol. 6, Pt. 2–87
McKennan, Thomas McKean Thompson, Mar. 31, 1794–July 9, 1852.
Vol. 6, Pt. 2–88
McKenney, Thomas Loraine, Mar. 21, 1785–Feb. 20, 1859.
Vol. 6, Pt. 2–89
McKenzie, Alexander, Dec. 14, 1830–Aug. 6, 1914.
Vol. 6, Pt. 2–90
Mackenzie, Alexander Slidell, Apr. 6, 1803–Sept. 13, 1848.
Vol. 6, Pt. 2–90
Mackenzie, Donald, June 15, 1783–Jan. 20, 1851.
Vol. 6, Pt. 2–91
Mackenzie, George Henry, Nov. 24, 1837–Apr. 14, 1891.
Vol. 6, Pt. 2–92
Mackenzie, James Cameron, Aug. 15, 1852–May 10, 1931.
Vol. 6, Pt. 2–93
Mackenzie, John Noland, Oct. 20, 1853–May 21, 1925.
Vol. 6, Pt. 2–93
Mackenzie, Kenneth, Apr. 15, 1797–Apr. 26, 1861.
Vol. 6, Pt. 2–94
Mackenzie, Murdo, Apr. 24, 1850–May 30, 1939.
Supp. 2–416
Mackenzie, Ranald Slidell, July 27, 1840–Jan. 19, 1889.
Vol. 6, Pt. 2–95
Mackenzie, Robert Shelton, June 22, 1809–Nov. 21, 1881.
Vol. 6, Pt. 2–96
McKenzie, Robert Tait, May 26, 1867–Apr. 28, 1938.
Supp. 2–417
Mackenzie, William, July 30, 1758–July 23, 1828.
Vol. 6, Pt. 2–97
Mackey, Albert Gallatin, Mar. 12, 1807–June 20, 1881.
Vol. 6, Pt. 2–98
McKim, Charles Follen, Aug. 24, 1847–Sept. 14, 1909.
Vol. 6, Pt. 2–99
McKim, Isaac, July 21, 1775–Apr. 1, 1838.
Vol. 6, Pt. 2–102
McKim, James Miller, Nov. 14, 1810–June 13, 1874.
Vol. 6, Pt. 2–103
McKinley, Albert Edward, Sept. 11, 1870–Feb. 26, 1936.
Supp. 2–418
McKinley, Carlyle, Nov. 22, 1847–Aug. 24, 1904.
Vol. 6, Pt. 2–104
McKinley, John, May 1, 1780–July 19, 1852.
Vol. 6, Pt. 2–104
McKinley, William, Jan. 29, 1843–Sept. 14, 1901.
Vol. 6, Pt. 2–105
McKinley, William Brown, Sept. 5, 1856–Dec. 7, 1926.
Supp. 1–530
McKinly, John, Feb. 24, 1721–Aug. 31, 1796.
Vol. 6, Pt. 2–109
MacKinney, Frank Edward, Sr., June 16, 1904–Jan 9, 1974.
Supp. 9–529
McKinstry, Alexander, Mar. 7, 1822–Oct. 9, 1879.
Vol. 6, Pt. 2–110
McKinstry, Elisha Williams, Apr. 11, 1825–Nov. I, 1901.
Vol. 6, Pt. 2–110
McKnight, Robert, *c.* 1789–March 1846.
Vol. 6, Pt. 2–111
Mackubin, Florence, May 19, 1861–Feb. 2, 1918.
Vol. 6, Pt. 2–112
McLaglen, Victor, Dec. 11, 1886–Nov. 6, 1959.
Supp. 6–420
McLane, Allan, Aug. 8, 1746–May 22, 1829.
Vol. 6, Pt. 2–112
McLane, Louis, May 28, 1786–Oct. 7, 1857.
Vol. 6, Pt. 2–113
McLane, Robert Milligan, June 23, 1815–Apr. 16, 1898.
Vol. 6, Pt. 2–115
McLaren, John, Dec. 20, 1846–Jan. 12, 1943.
Supp. 3–490
McLaren, William Edward, Dec. 13, 1831–Feb. 19, 1905.
Vol. 6, Pt. 2–116
McLaughlin, Andrew Cunningham, Feb. 14, 1861–Sept. 24, 1947.
Supp. 4–530
McLaughlin, Hugh, Apr. 2, 1826?–Dec. 7, 1904.
Vol. 6, Pt. 2–117
McLaughlin, James, Feb. 12, 1842–July 28, 1923.
Vol. 6, Pt. 2–117
McLaurin, Anselm Joseph, Mar. 26, 1848–Dec. 22 1909.
Vol. 6, Pt. 2–118
Maclaurin, Richard Cockburn, June 5, 1870–Jan. 15, 1920.
Vol. 6, Pt. 2–119
McLaws, Lafayette, Jan. 15, 1821–July 24, 1897.
Vol. 6, Pt. 2–120
Maclay, Edgar Stanton, Apr. 18, 1863–Nov. 2, 1919.
Vol. 6, Pt. 2–121
Maclay, Samuel, June 17, 1741–Oct. 5, 1811.
Vol. 6, Pt. 2–122
Maclay, William, July 27, 1734–Apr. 16, 1804.
Vol. 6, Pt. 2–123
Maclay, William Brown, Mar. 20, 1812–Feb. 19, 1882.
Vol. 6, Pt. 2–124
McLean, Angus Wilton, Apr. 20, 1870–June 21, 1935.
Supp. 1–532
McLean, Archibald, Sept. 6, 1849–Dec. 15, 1920.
Vol. 6, Pt. 2–125
McLean, Edward Beale, Jan. 31, 1886–July 27, 1941.
Supp. 3–491
MacLean, George Edwin, Aug. 31, 1850–May 3, 1938.
Supp. 2–419
Maclean, John, Mar. 1, 1771–Feb. 17, 1814.
Vol. 6, Pt. 2–126

McLean, John, Mar. 11, 1785–Apr. 4, 1861.
Vol. 6, Pt. 2–127
Maclean, John, Mar. 3, 1800–Aug. 10, 1886.
Vol. 6, Pt. 2–128
McLean, Robert, Oct. 1, 1891–Dec. 5, 1980.
Supp. 10–498
McLean, Walter, July 30, 1855–Mar. 20, 1930.
Vol. 6, Pt. 2–129
McLean, William Lippard, May 4, 1852–July 30, 1931.
Vol. 6, Pt. 2–130
McLellan, Isaac, May 21, 1806–Aug. 20, 1899.
Vol. 6, Pt. 2–130
McLeod, Alexander, June 12, 1774–Feb. 1, 1833.
Vol. 6, Pt. 2–131
MacLeod, Colin Munro, Jan. 28, 1909–Feb. 11, 1972.
Supp. 9–530
McLeod, Hugh, Aug. 1, 1814–Jan. 2, 1862.
Vol. 6, Pt. 2–132
McLeod, Martin, Aug. 30, 1813–Nov. 20, 1860.
Vol. 6, Pt. 2–133
McLevy, Jasper, Mar. 27, 1878–Nov. 19, 1962.
Supp. 7–502
McLoughlin, John, Oct. 19, 1784–Sept. 3, 1857.
Vol. 6, Pt. 2–134
McLoughlin, Maurice Evans, Jan. 7, 1890–Dec. 10, 1957.
Supp. 6–421
Maclure, William, Oct. 27, 1763–Mar 23 1840.
Vol. 6, Pt. 2–135
McMahon, Bernard, d. Sept. 18, 1816.
Vol. 6, Pt. 2–137
McMahon, Brien, Oct. 6, 1903–July 28, 1952.
Supp. 5–455
McMahon, John Van Lear, Oct. 18, 1800–June 15, 1871.
Vol. 6, Pt. 2–137
McManes, James, Apr. 13, 1822–Nov. 23, 1899.
Vol. 6, Pt. 2–138
McManus, George, Jan. 23, 1884?–Oct. 22, 1954.
Supp. 5–456
McMaster, Guy Humphreys, Jan. 31, 1829–Sept. 13, 1887.
Vol. 6, Pt. 2–139
McMaster, James Alphonsus, Apr. 1, 1820–Dec. 29, 1886.
Vol. 6, Pt. 2–140
McMaster, John Bach, June 29, 1852–May 24, 1932.
Vol. 6, Pt. 2–140
McMath, Robert Emmet, Apr. 28, 1833–May 31, 1918.
Vol. 6, Pt. 2–142
McMichael, Morton, Oct. 20, 1807–Jan. 6, 1879.
Vol. 6, Pt. 2–142
McMillan, James, May 12, 1838–Aug. 10, 1902.
Vol. 6, Pt. 2–143
McMillan, James Winning, Apr. 28, 1825–Mar. 9, 1903.
Vol. 6, Pt. 2–145
McMillin, Alvin Nugent ("Bo"), Jan. 12, 1895–Mar. 31, 1952.
Supp. 5–457
McMillin, Benton, Sept. 11, 1845–Jan. 8, 1933.
Supp. 1–533
McMinn, Joseph, June 22, 1758–Nov. 17, 1824.
Vol. 6, Pt. 2–145
MacMonnies, Frederick William, Sept. 28, 1863–Mar. 22, 1937.
Supp. 2–420
McMurrich, James Playfair, Oct. 16, 1859–Feb. 9, 1939.
Supp. 2–422
McMurry, Frank Morton, July 2, 1862–Aug. 1, 1936.
Supp. 2–423
McMurtrie, Douglas Crawford, July 20, 1888–Sept. 29, 1944.
Supp. 3–492
McMurtrie, WIlliam, Mar. 10, 1851–May 24, 1913.
Vol. 6, Pt. 2–146
McNair, Alexander, May 5, 1775–Mar. 18, 1826.
Vol. 6, Pt. 2–147
McNair, Frederick Vallette, Jan. 13, 1839–Nov 28, 1900.
Vol. 6, Pt. 2–148
McNair, Fred Walter, Dec. 3, 1862–June 30, 1924.
Vol. 6, Pt. 2–148
MacNair, Harley Farnsworth, July 22, 1891–June 22, 1947.
Supp. 4–532
McNair, Lesley James, May 25, 1883–July 25, 1944.
Supp. 3–493
McNamee, Graham, July 10, 1888–May 9, 1942.
Supp. 3–495
McNary, Charles Linza, June 12, 1874–Feb. 25, 1944.
Supp. 3–496
MacNaughtan, Myra Kelly. [*See* Kelly, Myra, 1875–1910.]
MacNeil, Hermon Atkins, Feb. 27, 1866–Oct. 4, 1947.
Supp. 4–533
McNeill, Daniel, Apr. 5, 1748–1833.
Vol. 6, Pt. 2–149
McNeill, George Edwin, Aug. 4, 1837–May 19, 1906.
Vol. 6, Pt. 2–150
McNeill, Hector, Oct. 10, 1728–Dec. 25, 1785.
Vol. 6, Pt. 2–151
McNeill, John Hanson, June 12, 1815–Nov. 10, 1864.
Vol. 6, Pt. 2–151
McNeill, William Gibbs, Oct. 3, 1801–Feb. 16, 1853.
Vol. 6, Pt. 2–152
MacNeven, William James, Mar. 21, 1763–July 12, 1841.
Vol. 6, Pt. 2–153
McNicholas, John Timothy, Dec. 15, 1877–Apr. 22, 1950.
Supp. 4–534
MacNider, Hanford, Oct. 2, 1889–Feb. 17, 1968.
Supp. 8–409
McNulty, Frank Joseph, Aug. 10, 1872–May 26, 1926.
Vol. 6, Pt. 2–154
McNulty, John Augustine, Nov. 1, 1895–July 29, 1956.
Supp. 6–422
McNutt, Alexander, *c.* 1725–*c.* 1811.
Vol. 6, Pt. 2–155
McNutt, Paul Vories, July 19, 1891–Mar. 24, 1955.
Supp. 5–459
Macomb, Alexander, Apr. 3, 1782–June 25, 1841.
Vol. 6, Pt. 2–155
Macomber, Mary Lizzie, Aug. 21, 1861–Feb. 4, 1916.
Vol. 6, Pt. 2–157
Macon, Nathaniel, Dec. 17, 1758–June 29, 1837.
Vol. 6, Pt. 2–157
MacPhail, Leland Stanford ("Larry"), Feb. 3, 1890–Oct. 1, 1975.
Supp. 9–531
McPherson, Aimee Semple, Oct. 9, 1890–Sept. 27, 1944.
Supp. 3–497
McPherson, Edward, July 31, 1830–Dec. 14, 1895.
Vol. 6, Pt. 2–159
McPherson, James Birdseye, Nov. 14, 1828–July 22, 1864.
Vol. 6, Pt. 2–160
McPherson, Logan Grant, Aug. 11, 1863–Mar. 23, 1925.
Vol. 6, Pt. 2–161
McPherson, Smith, Feb. 14, 1848–Jan. 17, 1915.
Vol. 6, Pt. 2–162
McQuaid, Bernard John, Dec. 15, 1823–Jan. 18, 1909.
Vol. 6, Pt. 2–163
McQueen, Terence Stephen ("Steve"), Mar. 24, 1930–Nov. 7, 1980.
Supp. 10–500
McQuillen, John Hugh, Feb. 12, 1826–Mar. 3, 1879.
Vol. 6, Pt. 2–164
McRae, Duncan Kirkland, Aug. 16, 1820–Feb. 12, 1888.
Vol. 6, Pt. 2–164
Macrae, John, Aug. 25, 1866–Feb. 18, 1944.
Supp. 3–499
McRae, Milton Alexander, June 13, 1858–Oct. 11, 1930.
Vol. 6, Pt. 2–165
McRae, Thomas Chipman, Dec. 21, 1851–June 2, 1929.
Vol. 6, Pt. 2–166
McReynolds, James Clark, Feb. 3, 1862–Aug. 24, 1946.
Supp. 4–536
McReynolds, Samuel Davis, Apr. 16, 1872–July 11, 1939.
Supp. 2–424
MacSparran, James, Sept. 10, 1693–Dec. 1, 1757.
Vol. 6, Pt. 2–167
McTammany, John, June 26, 1845–Mar. 26, 1915.
Vol. 6, Pt. 2–168
McTyeire, Holland Nimmons, July 28, 1824–Feb. 15, 1889.
Vol. 6, Pt. 2–169
Macune, Charles William, May 20, 1851–Nov. 3, 1940.
Supp. 2–425
MacVeagh, Charles, June 6, 1860–Dec. 4, 1931.
Supp. 1–534
MacVeagh, Franklin, Nov. 22, 1837–July 6, 1934.
Supp. 1–535
MacVeagh, Isaac Wayne, Apr. 19, 1833–Jan. 11, 1917.
Vol. 6, Pt. 2–170
McVey, Frank Lerond, Nov. 10, 1869–Jan. 4, 1953.
Supp. 5–461

MacVicar, Malcolm, Sept. 30, 1829–May 18, 1904.
Vol. 6, Pt. 2–171
McVickar, John, Aug. 10, 1787–Oct. 29, 1868.
Vol. 6, Pt. 2–172
McVickar, William Neilson, Oct. 19, 1843–June 28, 1910.
Vol. 6, Pt. 2–173
McVicker, James Hubert, Feb. 14, 1822–Mar. 7, 1896.
Vol. 6, Pt. 2–174
MacWhorter, Alexander, July 15, 1734 o.s.–July 20, 1807.
Vol. 6, Pt. 2–175
McWilliams, Carey, Dec. 13, 1905–June 27, 1980.
Supp. 10–501
Macy, Jesse, June 21, 1842–Nov. 3, 1919.
Vol. 6, Pt. 2–176
Macy, John Albert, Apr. 10, 1877–Aug. 26, 1932.
Vol. 6, Pt. 2–177
Macy, Josiah, Feb. 25, 1785–May 15, 1872.
Vol. 6, Pt. 2–178
Macy, Valentine Everit, Mar. 23, 1871–Mar. 21, 1930.
Vol. 6, Pt. 2–179
Madden, John Edward, Dec. 28, 1856–Nov. 3, 1929.
Vol. 6, Pt. 2–180
Madden, Martin Barnaby, Mar. 20, 1855–Apr. 27, 1928.
Vol. 6, Pt. 2–180
Madden, Owen Victor ("Owney"), June 1892–Apr. 24, 1965.
Supp. 7–504
Madigan, Laverne, Sept. 13, 1912–Aug. 21, 1962.
Supp. 7–505
Madison, Dolly Payne, May 20, 1768–July 12, 1849.
Vol. 6, Pt. 2–181
Madison, James, Aug. 27, 1749–Mar. 6, 1812.
Vol. 6, Pt. 2–182
Madison, James, Mar. 5/16, 1750/51–June 28, 1836.
Vol. 6, Pt. 2–184
Maeder, Clara Fisher. [*See* Fisher, Clara, 1811–1898.]
Maes, Camillus Paul, Mar. 13, 1846–May 11, 1915.
Vol. 6, Pt. 2–193
Maestri, Robert Sidney, Dec. 11, 1889–May 6, 1974.
Supp. 9–533
Maffitt, David, d. May 1, 1838.
Vol. 6, Pt. 2–194
Maffitt, John Newland, Feb. 22, 1819–May 15, 1886.
Vol. 6, Pt. 2–195
Magee, Christoher Lyman, Apr. 14, 1848–Mar. 8, 1901.
Vol. 6, Pt. 2–196
Magie, William Jay, Dec. 9, 1832–Jan. 15, 1917.
Vol. 6, Pt. 2–197
Magill, Edward Hicks, Sept. 24, 1825–Dec. 10, 1907.
Vol. 6, Pt. 2–198
Maginnis, Charles Donagh, Jan. 7, 1867–Feb. 16, 1955.
Supp. 5–462
Maginnis, Martin, Oct. 27, 1841–Mar. 27, 1919.
Vol. 6, Pt. 2–199
Magnes, Judah Leon, July 5, 1877–Oct. 27, 1948.
Supp. 4–538
Magoffin, Beriah, Apr. 18, 1815–Feb. 28, 1885.
Vol. 6, Pt. 2–199
Magoffin, James Wiley, 1799–Sept. 27, 1868.
Vol. 6, Pt. 2–200
Magonigle, Harold Van Buren, Oct. 17, 1867–Aug. 29, 1935.
Supp. 1–536
Magoon, Charles Edward, Dec. 5, 1861–Jan. 14, 1920.
Vol. 6, Pt. 2–201
Magoun, George Frederic, Mar. 29, 1821–Jan. 30, 1896.
Vol. 6, Pt. 2–202
Magrath, Andrew Gordon, Feb. 8, 1813–Apr. 9, 1893.
Vol. 6, Pt. 2–203
Magruder, George Lloyd, Nov. 1, 1848–Jan. 28, 1914.
Vol. 6, Pt. 2–204
Magruder, John Bankhead, Aug. 15, 1810–Feb. 18, 1871.
Vol. 6, Pt. 2–204
Magruder, Julia, Sept. 14, 1854–June 9, 1907.
Vol. 6, Pt. 2–206
Maguire, Charles Bonaventure. [*See* McGuire, Charles Bonaventure, 1768–1833.]
Mahan, Alfred Thayer, Sept. 27, 1840–Dec. 1, 1914.
Vol. 6, Pt. 2–206
Mahan, Asa, Nov. 9, 1799–Apr. 4, 1889.
Vol. 6, Pt. 2–208
Mahan, Dennis Hart, Apr. 2, 1802–Sept. 16, 1871.
Vol. 6, Pt. 2–209
Mahan, Milo, May 24, 1819–Sept. 3, 1870.
Vol. 6, Pt. 2–210
Mahler, Herbert, Nov. 6, 1890–Aug. 17, 1961.
Supp. 7–506
Mahone, William, Dec. 1, 1826–Oct. 8, 1895.
Vol. 6, Pt. 2–211
Mahoney, John Friend, Aug. 1, 1889–Feb. 23, 1957.
Supp. 6–423
Maier, Walter Arthur, Oct. 4, 1893–Jan. 11, 1950.
Supp. 4–540
Mailly, William, Nov. 22, 1871–Sept. 4, 1912.
Vol. 6, Pt. 2–212
Main, Charles Thomas, Feb. 16, 1856–Mar. 6, 1943.
Supp. 3–500
Main, John Hanson Thomas, Apr. 2, 1859–Apr. 1, 1931.
Supp. 1–537
Main, Marjorie, Feb. 24, 1890–Apr. 10, 1975.
Supp. 9–535
Maisch, John Michael, Jan. 30, 1831–Sept. 10, 1893.
Vol. 6, Pt. 2–213
Major, Charles, July 25, 1856–Feb. 13, 1913.
Vol. 6, Pt. 2–214
Majors, Alexander, Oct. 4, 1814–Jan. 12, 1900.
Vol. 6, Pt. 2–214
Ma-Ka-Tai-Me-She-Kia-Kiak. [*See* Black Hawk, 1767–1838.]
Makemie, Francis, *c.* 1658–1708.
Vol. 6, Pt. 2–215
Malbone, Edward Greene, August 1777–May 7, 1807.
Vol. 6, Pt. 2–216
Malcolm, Daniel, Nov. 29, 1725–Oct. 23, 1769.
Vol. 6, Pt. 2–218
Malcolm, James Peller, August 1767–Apr. 5, 1815.
Vol. 6, Pt. 2–219
Malcolm X, May 19, 1925–Feb. 21, 1965.
Supp. 7–507
Malcom, Daniel. [*See* Malcolm, Daniel, 1725–1769.]
Malcom, Howard, Jan. 19, 1799–Mar. 25, 1879.
Vol. 6, Pt. 2–220
Malcom, James Peller. [*See* Malcolm, James Peller, 1767–1815.]
Malin, Patrick Murphy, May 8, 1903–Dec. 13, 1964.
Supp. 7–510
Mall, Franklin Paine, Sept. 28, 1862–Nov. 17, 1917.
Vol. 6, Pt. 2–220
Mallary, Rollin Carolas, May 27, 1784–Apr. 15, 1831.
Vol. 6, Pt. 2–221
Mallery, Garrick, Apr. 23, 1831–Oct. 24, 1894.
Vol. 6, Pt. 2–222
Mallet, John William, Oct. 10, 1832–Nov. 7, 1912.
Vol. 6, Pt. 2–223
Mallinckrodt, Edward, Jan. 21, 1845–Feb. 1, 1928.
Vol. 6, Pt. 2–224
Mallinckrodt, Edward, Jr., Nov. 17, 1878–Jan. 19, 1967.
Supp. 8–411
Mallory, Anna Margrethe ("Molla") Bjurstedt, 1892–Nov. 22, 1959.
Supp. 6–424
Mallory, Clifford Day, May 26, 1881–Apr. 7, 1941.
Supp. 3–501
Mallory, Frank Burr, Nov. 12, 1862–Sept. 27, 1941.
Supp. 3–502
Mallory, Stephen Russell, *c.* 1813–Nov. 9, 1873.
Vol. 6, Pt. 2–224
Malone, Dudley Field, June 3, 1882–Oct. 5, 1950.
Supp. 4–541
Malone, Sylvester, May 8, 1821–Dec. 29, 1899.
Vol. 6, Pt. 2–226
Malone, Walter, Feb. 10, 1866–May 18, 1915.
Vol. 6, Pt. 2–227
Maloney, Martin, Dec. 11, 1847–May 8, 1929.
Vol. 6, Pt. 2–227
Malter, Henry, Mar. 23, 1864–Apr. 4, 1925.
Vol. 6, Pt. 2–228
Man Ray, Aug. 27, 1890–Nov. 18, 1976.
Supp. 10–503
Manatt, James Irving, Feb. 17, 1845–Feb. 13, 1915.
Vol. 6, Pt. 2–229
Manderson, Charles Frederick, Feb. 9, 1837–Sept. 28, 1911.
Vol. 6, Pt. 2–230
Maney, George Earl, Aug. 24, 1826–Feb. 9, 1901.
Vol. 6, Pt. 2–231

Mangin, Joseph François, fl. 1794–1818.
Vol. 6, Pt. 2–231
Mangrum, Lloyd Eugene, Aug. 1, 1914–Nov. 17, 1973.
Supp. 9–536
Mangum, Willie Person, May 10, 1792–Sept. 7, 1861.
Vol. 6, Pt. 2–232
Manigault, Arthur Middleton, Oct. 26, 1824–Aug. 16, 1886.
Vol. 6, Pt. 2–233
Manigault, Gabriel, Apr. 21, 1704–June 5, 1781.
Vol. 6, Pt. 2–234
Manigault, Peter, Oct. 10, 1731–Nov. 12, 1773.
Vol. 6, Pt. 2–234
Manigault, Pierre, d. Dec. 1729.
Vol. 6, Pt. 2–235
Mankiewicz, Herman Jacob, Nov. 4, 1897–Mar. 5, 1953.
Supp. 5–463
Manley, John, *c.* 1734–Feb. 12, 1793.
Vol. 6, Pt. 2–236
Manley, Joseph Homan, Oct. 13, 1842–Feb. 7, 1905.
Vol. 6, Pt. 2–236
Manly, Basil, Jan. 29, 1798–Dec. 21, 1868.
Vol. 6, Pt. 2–237
Manly, Basil, Dec. 19, 1825–Jan. 31, 1892.
Vol. 6, Pt. 2–238
Manly, Basil Maxwell, Mar. 14, 1886–May 11, 1950.
Supp. 4–543
Manly, Charles Matthews, Apr. 24, 1876–Oct. 15, 1927.
Vol. 6, Pt. 2–239
Manly, John Matthews, Sept. 2, 1865–Apr. 2, 1940.
Supp. 2–427
Mann, Ambrose Dudley, Apr. 26, 1801–Nov. 1889.
Vol. 6, Pt. 2–239
Mann, Horace, May 4, 1796–Aug. 2, 1859.
Vol. 6, Pt. 2–240
Mann, James, July 22, 1759–Nov. 7, 1832.
Vol. 6, Pt. 2–243
Mann, James Robert, Oct. 20, 1856–Nov. 30, 1922.
Vol. 6, Pt. 2–244
Mann, Louis, Apr. 20, 1865–Feb. 15, 1931.
Vol. 6, Pt. 2–244
Mann, Mary Tyler Peabody, Nov. 16, 1806–Feb. 11, 1887.
Vol. 6, Pt. 2–245
Mann, Newton, Jan. 16, 1836–July 25, 1926.
Vol. 6, Pt. 2–246
Mann, William Julius, May 29, 1819–June 20, 1892.
Vol. 6, Pt. 2–247
Manners, John Hartley, Aug. 10, 1870–Dec. 19, 1928.
Vol. 6, Pt. 2–248
Mannes, Clara Damrosch, Dec. 12, 1869–Mar. 16, 1948.
Supp. 4–544
Mannes, David, Feb. 16, 1866–Apr. 25, 1959.
Supp. 6–426
Mannes, Leopold Damrosch, Dec. 26, 1899–Aug. 11, 1964.
Supp. 7–511
Manning, Damel, May 16, 1831–Dec. 24, 1887.
Vol. 6, Pt. 2–248
Manning, James, Oct. 22, 1738–July 29, 1791.
Vol. 6, Pt. 2–249
Manning, Marie, Jan. 22, 1873?–Nov. 28, 1945.
Supp. 3–503
Manning, Richard Irvine, May 1, 1789–May 1, 1836.
Vol. 6, Pt. 2–251
Manning, Richard Irvine, Aug. 15, 1859–Sept. 11, 1931.
Vol. 6, Pt. 2–251
Manning, Robert, July 18, 1784–Oct. 10, 1842.
Vol. 6, Pt. 2–252
Manning, Thomas Courtland, Sept. 14, 1825–Oct. 11, 1887.
Vol. 6, Pt. 2–253
Manning, Vannoy Hartrog, Dec. 15, 1861–July 13, 1932.
Vol. 6, Pt. 2–253
Manning, William Thomas, May 12, 1866–Nov. 18, 1949.
Supp. 4–546
Mansell, William Albert, Mar. 30, 1864–Mar. 4, 1913.
Vol. 6, Pt. 2–254
Mansfield, Edward Deering, Aug. 17, 1801–Oct. 27, 1880.
Vol. 6, Pt. 2–255
Mansfield, Jared, May 23, 1759–Feb. 3, 1830.
Vol. 6, Pt. 2–256
Mansfield, Jayne, Apr. 19, 1933–June 29, 1967.
Supp. 8–412
Mansfield, Joseph King Fenno, Dec. 22, 1803–Sept. 18, 1862.
Vol. 6, Pt. 2–257
Mansfield, Richard, Oct. 1, 1723–Apr. 12, 1820.
Vol. 6, Pt. 2–258
Mansfield, Richard, May 24, 1854–Aug. 30, 1907.
Vol. 6, Pt. 2–258
Manship, Paul Howard, Dec. 24, 1885–Jan. 31, 1966.
Supp. 8–413
Manson, Otis Frederick, Oct. 10, 1822–Jan. 25, 1888.
Vol. 6, Pt. 2–261
Mantell, Robert Bruce, Feb. 7, 1854–June 27, 1928.
Vol. 6, Pt. 2–262
Mantle, (Robert) Burns, Dec. 23, 1873–Feb. 9, 1948.
Supp. 4–548
Manville, Thomas Franklyn ("Tommy"), Jr., Apr. 9, 1894–Oct. 8, 1967.
Supp. 8–415
Mapes, Charles Victor, July 4, 1836–Jan. 23, 1916.
Vol. 6, Pt. 2–263
Mapes, James Jay, May 29, 1806–Jan. 10, 1866.
Vol. 6, Pt. 2–264
Mappa, Adam Gerard, Nov. 25, 1754–Apr. 15, 1828.
Vol. 6, Pt. 2–265
Maranville, Walter James Vincent ("Rabbit"), Nov. 11, 1891–Jan. 5, 1954.
Supp. 5–465
Marble, Albert Prescott, May 21, 1836–Mar. 25, 1906.
Vol. 6, Pt. 2–265
Marble, Danforth, Apr. 27, 1810–May 13, 1849.
Vol. 6, Pt. 2–266
Marble, Manton Malone, Nov. 15, 1835–July 24, 1917.
Vol. 6, Pt. 2–267
Marburg, Theodore, July 10, 1862–Mar. 3, 1946.
Supp. 4–550
Marbury, Elisabeth, June 19, 1856–Jan. 22, 1933.
Supp. 1–538
Marbut, Curtis Fletcher, July 19, 1863–Aug. 25, 1935.
Supp. 1–539
Marcantonio, Vito Anthony, Dec. 10, 1902–Aug. 9, 1954.
Supp. 5–466
March, Alden, Sept. 20, 1795–June 17, 1869.
Vol. 6, Pt. 2–268
March, Francis Andrew, Oct. 25, 1825–Sept. 9, 1911.
Vol. 6, Pt. 2–268
March, Francis Andrew, Mar. 2, 1863–Feb. 28, 1928.
Vol. 6, Pt. 2–270
March, Frederic, Aug. 31, 1897–Apr. 14, 1975.
Supp. 9–537
March, Peyton Conway, Dec. 27, 1864–Apr. 13, 1955.
Supp. 5–467
March, William Edward. [*See* Campbell, William Edward, March, 1893–1954.]
Marchand, John Bonnett, Aug. 27, 1808–Apr. 13, 1875.
Vol. 6, Pt. 2–270
Marchant, Henry, April 1741–Aug. 30, 1796.
Vol. 6, Pt. 2–271
Marciano, Rocky, Sept. 1, 1923–Aug. 31, 1969.
Supp. 8–417
Marcosson, Isaac Frederick, Sept. 13, 1876–Mar. 14, 1961.
Supp. 7–512
Marcou, Jules, Apr. 20, 1824–Apr. 17, 1898.
Vol. 6, Pt. 2–272
Marcus, Bernard Kent, 1890?–July 16, 1954.
Supp. 5–469
Marcuse, Herbert, July 19, 1898–July 29, 1979.
Supp. 10–506
Marcy, Henry Orlando, June 23, 1837–Jan. 1, 1924.
Vol. 6, Pt. 2–273
Marcy, Randolph Barnes, Apr. 9, 1812–Nov. 22, 1887.
Vol. 6, Pt. 2–273
Marcy, William Learned, Dec. 12, 1786–July 4, 1857.
Vol. 6, Pt. 2–274
Marden, Charles Carroll, Dec. 21, 1867–May 11, 1932.
Vol. 6, Pt. 2–277
Marden, Orison Swett, 1850–Mar. 10, 1924.
Vol. 6, Pt. 2–278
Maréchal, Ambrose, Aug. 28, 1764–Jan. 29, 1828.
Vol. 6, Pt. 2–279
Marest, Pierre Gabriel, Oct. 14, 1662–Sept. 15, 1714.
Vol. 6, Pt. 2–280
Maretzek, Max, June 28, 1821–May 14, 1897.
Vol. 6, Pt. 2–281
Margolis, Max Leopold, Oct. 15, 1866–Apr. 2, 1932.
Vol. 6, Pt. 2–281

Marigny, Bernard, Oct. 28, 1785–Feb. 3, 1868.
Vol. 6, Pt. 2–282
Marin, John (Cheri), Dec. 23, 1870–Oct. 1, 1951.
Supp. 5–470
Marion, Francis, *c.* 1732–Feb. 26, 1795.
Vol. 6, Pt. 2–283
Markham, Charles Henry, May 22, 1861–Nov. 24, 1930.
Vol. 6, Pt. 2–284
Markham, Edwin, Apr. 23, 1852–Mar. 7, 1940.
Supp. 2–428
Markham, William, *c.* 1635–June 12, 1704 o.s.
Vol. 6, Pt. 2–285
Markoe, Abraham, July 2, 1727–Aug. 28, 1806.
Vol. 6, Pt. 2–286
Markoe, Peter, *c.* 1752–Jan. 30, 1792.
Vol. 6, Pt. 2–287
Marks, Amasa Abraham, Apr. 3, 1825–July 19, 1905.
Vol. 6, Pt. 2–288
Marks, Elias, Dec. 2, 1790–June 22, 1886.
Vol. 6, Pt. 2–289
Marland, Ernest Whitworth, May 8, 1874–Oct. 3, 1941.
Supp. 3–504
Marlatt, Abby Lillian, Mar. 7, 1869–June 23, 1943.
Supp. 3–506
Marling, Alfred Erskine, Oct. 5, 1858–May 29, 1935.
Supp. 1–540
Marling, John Leake, Dec. 22, 1825–Oct. 16, 1856.
Vol. 6, Pt. 2–289
Marlowe, Julia, Aug. 17, 1866–Nov. 12, 1950.
Supp. 4–541
Marmaduke, John Sappington, Mar. 14, 1833–Dec. 28, 1887.
Vol. 6, Pt. 2–290
Marquand, Allan, Dec. 10, 1853–Sept. 24, 1924.
Vol. 6, Pt. 2–291
Marquand, Henry Gurdon, Apr. 11, 1819–Feb. 26, 1902.
Vol. 6, Pt. 2–292
Marquand, John Phillips, Nov. 10, 1893–July 16, 1960.
Supp. 6–427
Marquard, Richard William ("Rube"), Oct. 9, 1889–June 1, 1980.
Supp. 10–508
Marquett, Turner Mastin, July 9, 1829–Dec. 22, 1894.
Vol. 6, Pt. 2–293
Marquette, Jacques, June 1, 1637–May 18, 1675.
Vol. 6, Pt. 2–294
Marquis, Albert Nelson, Jan. 20, 1855–Dec. 21, 1943.
Supp. 3–507
Marquis, Donald Robert Perry, July 29, 1878–Dec. 29, 1937.
Supp. 2–430
Marquis, John Abner, Dec. 27, 1861–July 5, 1931.
Vol. 6, Pt. 2–295
Marquis De Cuevas. [*See* De Cuevas, Marquis, 1885–1961.]
Marriott, Williams McKim, Mar. 5, 1885–Nov. 11, 1936.
Supp. 2–432
Marsh, Charles Wesley, Mar. 22, 1834–Nov. 9, 1918.
Vol. 6, Pt. 2–296
Marsh, Frank Burr, Mar. 4, 1880–May 31, 1940.
Supp. 2–433
Marsh, George Perkins, Mar. 15, 1801–July 23, 1882.
Vol. 6, Pt. 2–297
Marsh, Grant Prince, May 11, 1834–Jan. 2, 1916.
Vol. 6, Pt. 2–298
Marsh, James, July 19, 1794–July 3, 1842.
Vol. 6, Pt. 2–299
Marsh, John, Apr. 2, 1788–Aug. 4, 1868.
Vol. 6, Pt. 2–300
Marsh, John, June 5, 1799–Sept. 24, 1856.
Vol. 6, Pt. 2–301
Marsh, Othniel Charles, Oct. 29, 1831–Mar. 18, 1899.
Vol. 6, Pt. 2–302
Marsh, Reginald, Mar. 14, 1898–July 3, 1954.
Supp. 5–472
Marsh, Sylvester, Sept. 30, 1803–Dec. 30, 1884.
Vol. 6, Pt. 2–303
Marsh, William Wallace, Apr. 15, 1836–May 2, 1918.
Vol. 6, Pt. 2–304
Marshall, Benjamin, 1782–Dec. 2, 1858.
Vol. 6, Pt. 2–304
Marshall, Charles Henry, Apr. 8, 1792–Sept. 23, 1865.
Vol. 6, Pt. 2–305
Marshall, Christopher, Nov. 6, 1709–May 4, 1797.
Vol. 6, Pt. 2–306
Marshall, Clara, *c.* 1848–Mar. 13, 1931.
Vol. 6, Pt. 2–307
Marshall, Daniel, 1706–Nov. 2, 1784.
Vol. 6, Pt. 2–308
Marshall, Frank James, Aug. 10, 1877–Nov. 9, 1944.
Supp. 3–508
Marshall, George Catlett, Jr., Dec. 31, 1880–Oct. 16, 1959.
Supp. 6–428
Marshall, Henry Rutgers, July 22, 1852–May 3, 1927.
Vol. 6, Pt. 2–308
Marshall, Humphrey, 1760–June 26, 1841.
Vol. 6, Pt. 2–309
Marshall, Humphrey, Jan. 13, 1812–Mar. 28, 1872.
Vol. 6, Pt. 2–310
Marshall, Humphry, Oct. 10, 1722 o.s.–Nov. 5, 1801.
Vol. 6, Pt. 2–311
Marshall, James Fowle Baldwin, Aug. 8, 1818–May 6, 1891.
Vol. 6, Pt. 2–312
Marshall, James Markham, Mar. 12, 1764–Apr. 26, 1848.
Vol. 6, Pt. 2–313
Marshall, James Wilson, Oct. 8, 1810–Aug. 10, 1885.
Vol. 6, Pt. 2–314
Marshall, John, Sept. 24, 1755–July 6, 1835.
Vol. 6, Pt. 2–315
Marshall, Louis, Oct. 7, 1773–Apr. 1866.
Vol. 6, Pt. 2–325
Marshall, Louis, Dec. 14, 1856–Sept. 11, 1929.
Vol. 6, Pt. 2–326
Marshall, Samuel Lyman Atwood ("Slam"), July 18, 1900–Dec. 17, 1977.
Supp. 10–509
Marshall, Thomas, Apr. 2, 1730–June 22, 1802.
Vol. 6, Pt. 2–328
Marshall, Thomas Alexander, Jan. 15, 1794–Apr. 17, 1871.
Vol. 6, Pt. 2–329
Marshall, Thomas Riley, Mar. 14, 1854–June 1, 1925.
Vol. 6, Pt. 2–330
Marshall, William Edgar, June 30, 1837–Aug. 29, 1906.
Vol. 6, Pt. 2–331
Marshall, William Louis, June 11, 1846–July 2, 1920.
Vol. 6, Pt. 2–332
Marshall, William Rainey, Oct. 17, 1825–Jan. 8, 1896.
Vol. 6, Pt. 2–333
Martel, Charles, Mar. 5, 1860–May 15, 1945.
Supp. 3–509
Martin, Alexander, 1740–Nov. 2, 1807.
Vol. 6, Pt. 2–333
Martin, Anne Henrietta, Sept. 30, 1875–April 15, 1951.
Supp. 5–473
Martin, Artemas, Aug. 3, 1835–Nov. 7, 1918.
Vol. 6, Pt. 2–334
Martin, Edward Sandford, Jan. 2, 1856–June 13, 1939.
Supp. 2–434
Martin, Elizabeth Price, Dec. 14, 1864–Apr. 5, 1932.
Supp. 1–541
Martin, Everett Dean, July 5, 1880–May 10, 1941.
Supp. 3–511
Martin, François-Xavier, Mar. 17, 1762–Dec. 10, 1846.
Vol. 6, Pt. 2–335
Martin, Franklin Henry, July 13, 1857–Mar. 7, 1935.
Supp. 1–542
Martin, Frederick Townsend, Dec. 6, 1849–Mar. 8, 1914.
Vol. 6, Pt. 2–336
Martin, Glenn Luther ("Cy"), Jan. 17, 1886–Dec. 4, 1955.
Supp. 5–475
Martin, Henry Austin, July 23, 1824–Dec. 7, 1884.
Vol. 6, Pt. 2–337
Martin, Henry Newell, July 1, 1848–Oct. 27, 1896.
Vol. 6, Pt. 2–337
Martin, Homer Dodge, Oct. 28, 1836–Feb. 12, 1897.
Vol. 6, Pt. 2–338
Martin, James Green, Feb. 14, 1819–Oct. 4, 1878.
Vol. 6, Pt. 2–340
Martin, John Alexander, Mar. 10, 1839–Oct. 2, 1889.
Vol. 6, Pt. 2–341
Martin, John Hill, Jan. 13, 1823–Apr. 7, 1906.
Vol. 6, Pt. 2–342
Martin, Johnny Leonard Roosevelt ("Pepper"), Feb. 29, 1904–Mar. 5, 1965.
Supp. 7–513

Martin, Joseph William, Jr., Nov. 3, 1884–Mar. 7, 1968.
Supp. 8–420
Martin, Josiah, 1737–1786.
Vol. 6, Pt. 2–343
Martin, Luther, *c.* 1748–July 10, 1826.
Vol. 6, Pt. 2–343
Martin, Thomas Commerford, July 22, 1856–May 17, 1924.
Vol. 6, Pt. 2–345
Martin, Thomas Staples, July 29, 1847–Nov. 12, 1919.
Vol. 6, Pt. 2–346
Martin, Victoria Claflin Woodhull. [*See* Woodhull, Victoria Claflin, 1838–1927.]
Martin, Warren Homer, Aug. 15, 1901–Jan. 22, 1968.
Supp. 8–418
Martin, William Alexander Parsons, Apr. 10, 1827–Dec. 17, 1916.
Vol. 6, Pt. 2–347
Martin, William Thompson, Mar. 25, 1823–Mar. 16, 1910.
Vol. 6, Pt. 2–348
Martindale, John Henry, Mar. 20, 1815–Dec. 13, 1881.
Vol. 6, Pt. 2–349
Martinelli, Giovanni, Oct. 22, 1885–Feb. 2, 1969.
Supp. 8–422
Martinez, Maria, 1887?–July 20, 1980.
Supp. 10–511
Martiny, Philip, May 19, 1858–June 25, 1927.
Vol. 6, Pt. 2–350
Marty, Martin, Jan. 12, 1834–Sept. 19, 1896.
Vol. 6, Pt. 2–352
Martyn, Sarah Towne Smith, Aug. 15, 1805–Nov. 22, 1879.
Vol. 6, Pt. 2–352
Marvel, Ik. [*See* Mitchell, Donald Grant, 1822–1908.]
Marvin, Charles Frederick, Oct. 7, 1858–June 5, 1943.
Supp. 3–511
Marvin, Dudley, May 29, 1786–June 25, 1852.
Vol. 6, Pt. 2–353
Marvin, Enoch Mather, June 12, 1823–Nov. 26, 1877.
Vol. 6, Pt. 2–354
Marwedel, Emma Jacobina Christiana, Feb. 27, 1818–Nov. 17, 1893.
Vol. 6, Pt. 2–354
Marx, Adolf Arthur ("Harpo"), Nov. 23, 1893–Sept. 28, 1964.
Supp. 7–514
Marx, Herbert ("Zeppo"), Feb. 26, 1901–Nov. 30, 1979.
Supp. 10–512
Marx, Julius Henry ("Groucho"), Oct. 2, 1890–Aug. 19, 1977.
Supp. 10–514
Marx, Leonard ("Chico"), Mar. 22, 1891–Oct. 11, 1961.
Supp. 7–514
Marx, Milton ("Gummo"), May 21, 1893–Apr. 21, 1977.
Supp. 10–517
Marzo, Eduardo, Nov. 29, 1852–June 7, 1929.
Vol. 6, Pt. 2–356
Maschke, Heinrich, Oct. 24, 1853–Mar. 1, 1908.
Vol. 6, Pt. 2–356
Masliansky, Zvi Hirsch, May 16, 1856–Jan. 11, 1943.
Supp. 3–512
Maslow, Abraham H., Apr. 1, 1908–June 8, 1970.
Supp. 8–423
Mason, Arthur John, June 1, 1857–June 28, 1933.
Supp. 1–543
Mason, Charles, Oct. 24, 1804–Feb. 25, 1882.
Vol. 6, Pt. 2–357
Mason, Claibourne Rice, Nov. 28, 1800–Jan. 12, 1885.
Vol. 6, Pt. 2–358
Mason, Daniel Gregory, Nov. 20, 1873–Dec. 4, 1953.
Supp. 5–476
Mason, Francis, Apr. 2, 1799–Mar. 3, 1874.
Vol. 6, Pt. 2–358
Mason, Francis Van Wyck, Nov. 11, 1901–Aug. 28, 1978.
Supp. 10–518
Mason, Frank Stuart, Oct. 21, 1883–Oct. 25, 1929.
Vol. 6, Pt. 2–359
Mason, George, *c.* 1629–*c.* 1686.
Vol. 6, Pt. 2–360
Mason, George, 1725–Oct. 7, 1792.
Vol. 6, Pt. 2–361
Mason, Henry, Oct. 10, 1831–May 15, 1890.
Vol. 6, Pt. 2–364
Mason, James Murray, Nov. 3, 1798–Apr. 28, 1871.
Vol. 6, Pt. 2–364
Mason, Jeremiah, Apr. 27, 1768–Oct. 14, 1848.
Vol. 6, Pt. 2–365
Mason, John, *c.* 1600–Jan. 30, 1672.
Vol. 6, Pt. 2–367
Mason, John, Oct. 28, 1858–Jan. 12, 1919.
Vol. 6, Pt. 2–367
Mason, John Mitchell, Mar. 19, 1770–Dec. 26, 1829.
Vol. 6, Pt. 2–368
Mason, John Young, Apr. 18, 1799–Oct. 3, 1859.
Vol. 6, Pt. 2–369
Mason, Jonathan, Sept. 12, 1756–Nov. 1, 1831.
Vol. 6, Pt. 2–370
Mason, Lowell, Jan. 8, 1792–Aug. 11, 1872.
Vol. 6, Pt. 2–371
Mason, Lucy Randolph, July 26, 1882–May 6, 1959.
Supp. 6–433
Mason, Luther Whiting, Apr. 3, 1828–July 14, 1896.
Vol. 6, Pt. 2–372
Mason, Max, Oct. 26, 1877–Mar. 23, 1961.
Supp. 7–516
Mason, Otis Tufton, Apr. 10, 1838–Nov. 5, 1908.
Vol. 6, Pt. 2–372
Mason, Richard Barnes, Jan. 16, 1797–July 25, 1850.
Vol. 6, Pt. 2–373
Mason, Samuel, *c.* 1750–July 1803.
Vol. 6, Pt. 2–374
Mason, Stevens Thomson, Dec. 29, 1760–May 10, 1803.
Vol. 6, Pt. 2–374
Mason, Stevens Thomson, Oct. 27, 1811–Jan. 4, 1843.
Vol. 6, Pt. 2–375
Mason, Thomson, 1733–Feb. 26, 1785.
Vol. 6, Pt. 2–376
Mason, Walt, May 4, 1862–June 22, 1939.
Supp. 2–435
Mason, William, Sept. 2, 1808–May 21, 1883.
Vol. 6, Pt. 2–377
Mason, William, Jan. 24, 1829–July 14, 1908.
Vol. 6, Pt. 2–378
Mason, William Ernest, July 7, 1850–June 16, 1921.
Vol. 6, Pt. 2–379
Masquerier, Lewis, b. Mar. 14, 1802.
Vol. 6, Pt. 2–379
Massassoit, d. 1661.
Vol. 6, Pt. 2–380
Massey, George Betton, Nov. 15, 1856–Mar. 29, 1927.
Vol. 6, Pt. 2–381
Massey, John Edward, Apr. 2, 1819–Apr. 24, 1901.
Vol. 6, Pt. 2–382
Masson, Thomas Lansing, July 21, 1866–June 18, 1934.
Supp. 1–544
Mast, Phineas Price, Jan. 3, 1825–Nov. 20, 1898.
Vol. 6, Pt. 2–382
Masters, Edgar Lee, Aug. 23, 1869–Mar. 5, 1950.
Supp. 4–554
Masterson, William Barclay, Nov. 24, 1853–Oct. 25, 1921.
Vol. 6, Pt. 2–383
Mastin, Claudius Henry, June 4, 1826–Oct. 3, 1898.
Vol. 6, Pt. 2–384
Masury, John Wesley, Jan. 1, 1820–May 14, 1895.
Vol. 6, Pt. 2–384
Matas, Rudolph, Sept. 12, 1860–Sept. 23, 1957.
Supp. 6–434
Mateer, Calvin Wilson, Jan. 9, 1836–Sept. 28, 1908.
Vol. 6, Pt. 2–385
Mather, Cotton, Feb. 12, 1662/63–Feb. 13, 1727/28.
Vol. 6, Pt. 2–386
Mather, Frank Jewett, Jr., July 6, 1868–Nov. 11, 1953.
Supp. 5–478
Mather, Fred, Aug. 2, 1833–Feb. 14, 1900.
Vol. 6, Pt. 2–389
Mather, Increase, June 21, 1639–Aug. 23, 1723.
Vol. 6, Pt. 2–390
Mather, Richard, 1596–Apr. 22, 1669.
Vol. 6, Pt. 2–394
Mather, Samuel, Oct. 30, 1706–June 27, 1785.
Vol. 6, Pt. 2–395
Mather, Samuel, July 13, 1851–Oct. 18, 1931.
Vol. 6, Pt. 2–396

Mather, Samuel Holmes, Mar. 20, 1813–Jan. 14, 1894.
Vol. 6, Pt. 2–397
Mather, Samuel Livingston, July 1, 1817–Oct. 8, 1890.
Vol. 6, Pt. 2–398
Mather, Stephen Tyng, July 4, 1867–Jan. 22, 1930.
Vol. 6, Pt. 2–398
Mather, William Williams, May 24, 1804–Feb. 26, 1859.
Vol. 6, Pt. 2–399
Mather, Winifred Holt. [*See* Holt, Winifred, 1870–1945.]
Matheson, William John, Sept. 15, 1856–May 15, 1930.
Vol. 6, Pt. 2–400
Mathews, Albert, Sept. 8, 1820–Sept. 9, 1903.
Vol. 6, Pt. 2–401
Mathews, Cornelius, Oct. 28, 1817–Mar. 25, 1889.
Vol. 6, Pt. 2–402
Mathews, George, Aug. 30, 1739–Aug. 30, 1812.
Vol. 6, Pt. 2–403
Mathews, Henry Mason, Mar. 29, 1834–Apr. 28, 1884.
Vol. 6, Pt. 2–404
Mathews, John, 1744–Oct. 26, 1802.
Vol. 6, Pt. 2–404
Mathews, John Alexander, May 20, 1872–Jan. 11, 1935.
Supp. 1–545
Mathews, Samuel, *c.* 1600–Jan. 1660.
Vol. 6, Pt. 2–405
Mathews, Shailer, May 26, 1863–Oct. 23, 1941.
Supp. 3–514
Mathews, William, July 28, 1818–Feb. 14, 1909.
Vol. 6, Pt. 2–406
Mathews, William Smythe Babcock, May 8, 1837–Apr. 1, 1912.
Vol. 6, Pt. 2–407
Mathewson, Christopher, Aug. 12, 1880–Oct. 7, 1925.
Vol. 6, Pt. 2–407
Mathewson, Edward Payson, Oct. 16, 1864–July 13, 1948.
Supp. 4–556
Matignon, Francis Anthony, Nov. 10, 1753–Sept. 19, 1818.
Vol. 6, Pt. 2–408
Matlack, Timothy, d. Apr. 14, 1829.
Vol. 6, Pt. 2–409
Matteson, Joel Aldrich, Aug. 2, 1808–Jan. 31, 1873.
Vol. 6, Pt. 2–410
Matteson, Tompkins Harrison, May 9, 1813–Feb. 2, 1884.
Vol. 6, Pt. 2–411
Matthes, François Emile, Mar. 16, 1874–June 21, 1948.
Supp. 4–557
Matthes, Gerard Hendrik, Mar. 16, 1874–Apr. 8, 1959.
Supp. 6–435
Matthew, William Diller, Feb. 19, 1871–Sept. 24, 1930.
Vol. 6, Pt. 2–411
Matthews, Brander. [*See* Matthews, James Brander, 1852–1929]
Matthews, Claude, Dec. 14, 1845–Aug. 28, 1898.
Vol. 6, Pt. 2–412
Matthews, Francis Patrick, Mar. 15, 1887–Oct. 18, 1952.
Supp. 5–479
Matthews, Franklin, May 14, 1858–Nov. 26, 1917.
Vol. 6, Pt. 2–413
Matthews, James Brander, Feb. 21, 1852–Mar. 31, 1929.
Vol. 6, Pt. 2–414
Matthews, John, 1808–Jan. 12, 1870.
Vol. 6, Pt. 2–416
Matthews, Joseph Brown, June 28, 1894–July 16, 1966.
Supp. 8–424
Matthews, Joseph Merritt, June 9, 1874–Oct. 11, 1931.
Vol. 6, Pt. 2–417
Matthews, Nathan, Mar. 28, 1854–Dec. 11, 1927.
Vol. 6, Pt. 2–417
Matthews, Stanley, July 21, 1824–Mar. 22, 1889.
Vol. 6, Pt. 2–418
Matthews, Washington, July 17, 1843–Apr. 29, 1905.
Vol. 6, Pt. 2–420
Matthews, William, Mar. 29, 1822–Apr. 15, 1896.
Vol. 6, Pt. 2–420
Matthiessen, Francis Otto, Feb. 19, 1902–Apr. 1, 1950.
Supp. 4–559
Matthiessen, Frederick William, Mar. 5, 1835–Feb. 11, 1918.
Vol. 6, Pt. 2–421
Mattice, Asa Martines, Aug. 1, 1853–Apr. 19, 1925.
Vol. 6, Pt. 2–422
Mattingly, Garrett, May 6, 1900–Dec. 18, 1962.
Supp. 7–517
Mattison, Hiram, Feb. 8, 1811–Nov. 24, 1868.
Vol. 6, Pt. 2–423
Mattocks, John, Mar. 4, 1777–Aug. 14, 1847.
Vol. 6, Pt. 2–423
Mattoon, Stephen, May 5, 1816–Aug. 15, 1889.
Vol. 6, Pt. 2–424
Mattson, Hans, Dec. 23, 1832–Mar. 5, 1893.
Vol. 6, Pt. 2–425
Matzeliger, Jan Ernst, 1852–1889.
Vol. 6, Pt. 2–426
Mauchly, John William, Aug. 30, 1907–Jan. 8, 1980.
Supp. 10–519
Mauran, John Lawrence, Nov. 19, 1866–Sept. 23, 1933.
Supp. 1–546
Maurer, James Hudson, Apr. 15, 1864–Mar. 16, 1944.
Supp. 3–516
Maurin, Peter Aristide, May 9, 1877–May 15, 1949.
Supp. 4–561
Maury, Dabney Herndon, May 21, 1822–Jan. 11, 1900.
Vol. 6, Pt. 2–427
Maury, Francis Fontaine, Aug. 9, 1840–June 4, 1879.
Vol. 6, Pt. 2–428
Maury, Matthew Fontaine, Jan. 14, 1806–Feb. 1, 1873.
Vol. 6, Pt. 2–428
Maus, Marion Perry, Aug. 25, 1850–Feb. 9, 1930.
Vol. 6, Pt. 2–431
Maverick, (Fontaine) Maury, Oct. 23, 1895–June 7, 1954.
Supp. 5–480
Maverick, Peter, Oct. 22, 1780–June 7, 1831.
Vol. 6, Pt. 2–432
Maverick, Samuel, *c.* 1602–*c.* 1676.
Vol. 6, Pt. 2–432
Maxcy, Jonathan, Sept. 2, 1768–June 4, 1820.
Vol. 6, Pt. 2–433
Maxcy, Virgil, May 5, 1785–Feb. 28, 1844.
Vol. 6, Pt. 2–434
Maxey, Samuel Bell, Mar. 30, 1825–Aug. 16, 1895.
Vol. 6, Pt. 2–435
Maxim, Hiram Percy, Sept. 2, 1869–Feb. 17, 1936.
Supp. 2–436
Maxim, Hiram Stevens, Feb. 5, 1840–Nov. 24, 1916.
Vol. 6, Pt. 2–436
Maxim, Hudson, Feb. 3, 1853–May 6, 1927.
Vol. 6, Pt. 2–437
Maxwell, Augustus Emmett, Sept. 21, 1820–May 5, 1903.
Vol. 6, Pt. 2–438
Maxwell, David Hervey, Sept. 17, 1786–May 24, 1854.
Vol. 6, Pt. 2–439
Maxwell, Elsa, May 24, 1883–Nov. 1, 1963.
Supp. 7–518
Maxwell, George Hebard, June 3, 1860–Dec. 1, 1946.
Supp. 4–563
Maxwell, George Troup, Aug. 6, 1827–Sept. 2, 1897.
Vol. 6, Pt. 2–440
Maxwell, Hugh, 1787–Mar. 31, 1873.
Vol. 6, Pt. 2–441
Maxwell, Lucien Bonaparte, Sept. 14, 1818–July 25, 1875.
Vol. 6, Pt. 2–441
Maxwell, Marvel Marilyn, Aug. 3, 1920–Mar. 20, 1972.
Supp. 9–540
Maxwell, Samuel, May 20, 1825–Feb. 11, 1901.
Vol. 6, Pt. 2–442
Maxwell, William, *c.* 1733–Nov. 4, 1796.
Vol. 6, Pt. 2–443
Maxwell, William, *c.* 1755–1809.
Vol. 6, Pt. 2–444
Maxwell, William, Feb. 27, 1784–Jan. 10, 1857.
Vol. 6, Pt. 2–444
Maxwell, William Henry, Mar. 5, 1852–May 3, 1920.
Vol. 6, Pt. 2–445
May, Andrew Jackson, June 24, 1875–Sept. 6, 1959.
Supp. 6–436
May, Edward Harrison, 1824–May 17, 1887.
Vol. 6, Pt. 2–446
May, Morton Jay, July 13, 1881–May 17, 1968.
Supp. 8–427
May, Samuel Joseph, Sept. 12, 1797–July 1, 1871.
Vol. 6, Pt. 2–447
May, Sophie. [*See* Clarke, Rebecca Sophia, 1833–1906.]
Maybank, Burnet Rhett, Mar. 7, 1899–Sept. 1, 1954.
Supp. 5–481

Maybeck, Bernard Ralph, Feb. 7, 1862–Oct. 3, 1957.
Supp. 6–438
Mayer, Alfred Goldsborough. [*See* Mayor, Alfred Goldsborough, 1868–1922.]
Mayer, Alfred Marshall, Nov. 13, 1836–July 13, 1897.
Vol. 6, Pt. 2–448
Mayer, Brantz, Sept. 27, 1809–Feb. 23, 1879.
Vol. 6, Pt. 2–449
Mayer, Constant, Oct. 3, 1829–May 12, 1911.
Vol. 6, Pt. 2–449
Mayer, Emil, May 23, 1854–Oct. 20, 1931.
Vol. 6, Pt. 2–450
Mayer, Lewis, Mar. 26, 1783–Aug. 25, 1849.
Vol. 6, Pt. 2–451
Mayer, Louis Burt, 1885?–Oct. 29, 1957.
Supp. 6–439
Mayer, Maria Goeppert, June 28, 1906–Feb. 20, 1972.
Supp. 9–541
Mayer, Oscar Gottfried, Mar. 10, 1888–Mar. 5, 1965.
Supp. 7–519
Mayer, Philip Frederick, Apr. 1, 1781–Apr. 16, 1858.
Vol. 6, Pt. 2–452
Mayes, Edward, Dec. 15, 1846–Aug. 9, 1917.
Vol. 6, Pt. 2–452
Mayes, Joel Bryan, Oct. 2, 1833–Dec. 14, 1891.
Vol. 6, Pt. 2–453
Mayhew, Experience, Feb. 5, 1673 N.S.-Nov. 29, 1758.
Vol. 6, Pt. 2–453
Mayhew, Jonathan, Oct. 8, 1720–July 9, 1766.
Vol. 6, Pt. 2–454
Mayhew, Thomas, 1593–Mar. 25, 1682.
Vol. 6, Pt. 2–455
Mayhew, Thomas, *c.* 1621–1657.
Vol. 6, Pt. 2–456
Maynard, Charles Johnson, May 6, 1845–Oct. 15, 1929.
Vol. 6, Pt. 2–457
Maynard, Edward, Apr. 26, 1813–May 4, 1891.
Vol. 6, Pt. 2–457
Maynard, George William, June 12, 1839–Feb. 12, 1913.
Vol. 6, Pt. 2–458
Maynard, George Willoughby, Mar. 5, 1843–Apr. 5, 1923.
Vol. 6, Pt. 2–459
Maynard, Horace, Aug. 30, 1814–May 3, 1882.
Vol. 6, Pt. 2–460
Mayo, Amory Dwight, Jan. 31, 1823–Apr. 8, 1907.
Vol. 6, Pt. 2–461
Mayo, Charles Horace, July 19, 1865–May 26, 1939.
Supp. 2–438
Mayo, Frank, Apr. 18, 1839–June 8, 1896.
Vol. 6, Pt. 2–462
Mayo, George Elton, Dec. 26, 1880–Sept. 1, 1949.
Supp. 4–564
Mayo, Henry Thomas, Dec. 8, 1856–Feb. 23, 1937.
Supp. 2–437
Mayo, Mary Anne Bryant, May 24, 1845–Apr. 21, 1903.
Vol. 6, Pt. 2–462
Mayo, Sarah Carter Edgarton, Mar. 17, 1819–July 9, 1848.
Vol. 6, Pt. 2–463
Mayo, William, *c.* 1684–1744.
Vol. 6, Pt. 2–464
Mayo, William James, June 29, 1861–July 28, 1939.
Supp. 2–438
Mayo, William Kennon, May 29, 1829–Apr. 9, 1900.
Vol. 6, Pt. 2–464
Mayo, William Starbuck, Apr. 15, 1811–Nov. 22, 1895.
Vol. 6, Pt. 2–465
Mayo, William Worrell, May 31, 1819–Mar. 6, 1911.
Vol. 6, Pt. 2–466
Mayor, Alfred Goldsborough, Apr. 16, 1868–June 24, 1922.
Vol. 6, Pt. 2–468
Mayo-Smith, Richmond, Feb. 9, 1854–Nov. 11, 1901.
Vol. 6, Pt. 2–467
Maytag, Frederick Louis, July 14, 1857–Mar. 26, 1937.
Supp. 2–441
Mazureau, Étienne, 1777–May 25, 1849.
Vol. 6, Pt. 2–469
Mazzei, Philip, Dec. 25, 1730–Mar. 19, 1816.
Vol. 6, Pt. 2–469
Mazzuchelli, Samuel Charles, Nov. 4, 1806–Feb. 23, 1864.
Vol. 6, Pt. 2–470
Mead, Charles Marsh, Jan. 28, 1836–Feb. 15, 1911.
Vol. 6, Pt. 2–471
Mead, Edwin Doak, Sept. 29, 1849–Aug. 17, 1937.
Supp. 2–442
Mead, Elwood, Jan. 16, 1858–Jan. 26, 1936.
Supp. 2–443
Mead, George Herbert, Feb. 27, 1863–Apr. 26, 1931.
Supp. 1–547
Mead, James Michael, Dec. 27, 1885–Mar. 15, 1964.
Supp. 7–521
Mead, Larkin Goldsmith, Jan. 3, 1835–Oct. 15, 1910.
Vol. 6, Pt. 2–472
Mead, Margaret, Dec. 16, 1901–Nov. 15, 1978.
Supp. 10–521
Mead, William Rutherford, Aug. 20, 1846–June 20, 1928.
Vol. 6, Pt. 2–473
Meade, George, Feb. 27, 1741–Nov. 9, 1808.
Vol. 6, Pt. 2–473
Meade, George Gordon, Dec. 31, 1815–Nov. 6, 1872.
Vol. 6, Pt. 2–474
Meade, Richard Kidder, July 14, 1746–Feb. 9, 1805.
Vol. 6, Pt. 2–476
Meade, Richard Worsam, June 23, 1778–June 25, 1828.
Vol. 6, Pt. 2–477
Meade, Richard Worsam, Mar. 21, 1807–Apr. 16, 1870.
Vol. 6, Pt. 2–478
Meade, Richard Worsam, Oct. 9, 1837–May 4, 1897.
Vol. 6, Pt. 2–478
Meade, Robert Leamy, Dec. 26, 1841–Feb. 11, 1910.
Vol. 6, Pt. 2–479
Meade, William, Nov. 11, 1789–Mar. 14, 1862.
Vol. 6, Pt. 2–480
Meagher, Thomas Francis, Aug. 23, 1823–July 1, 1867.
Vol. 6, Pt. 2–481
Means, Gaston Bullock, July 11, 1879–Dec. 12, 1938.
Supp. 2–444
Meany, Edmond Stephen, Dec. 28, 1862–Apr. 22, 1935.
Supp. 1–548
Meany, William George, Aug. 16, 1894–Jan. 10, 1980.
Supp. 10–523
Mearns, Edgar Alexander, Sept. 11, 1856–Nov. 1, 1916.
Vol. 6, Pt. 2–482
Mears, David Otis, Feb. 22, 1842–Apr. 29, 1915.
Vol. 6, Pt. 2–483
Mears, Helen Farnsworth, Dec. 21, 1876–Feb. 17, 1916.
Vol. 6, Pt. 2–483
Mears, John William, Aug. 10, 1825–Nov. 10, 1881.
Vol. 6, Pt. 2–484
Mears, Otto, May 3, 1840–June 24, 1931.
Vol. 6, Pt. 2–485
Mease, James, Aug. 11, 1771–May 14, 1846.
Vol. 6, Pt. 2–486
Meason, Isaac, 1742–Jan. 23, 1818.
Vol. 6, Pt. 2–487
Mechem, Floyd Russell, May 9, 1858–Dec. 11, 1928.
Vol. 6, Pt. 2–487
Mecom, Benjamin, b. Dec. 29, 1732.
Vol. 6, Pt. 2–488
Medary, Milton Bennett, Feb. 6, 1874–Aug. 7, 1929.
Vol. 6, Pt. 2–489
Medary, Samuel, Feb. 25, 1801–Nov. 7, 1864.
Vol. 6, Pt. 2–490
Medill, Joseph, Apr. 6, 1823–Mar. 16, 1899.
Vol. 6, Pt. 2–491
Medwick, Joseph ("Ducky") Michael, Nov. 24, 1911–Mar. 21, 1975.
Supp. 9–542
Meehan, Thomas, Mar. 21, 1826–Nov. 19, 1901.
Vol. 6, Pt. 2–492
Meek, Alexander Beaufort, July 17, 1814–Nov. 1, 1865.
Vol. 6, Pt. 2–493
Meek, Fielding Bradford, Dec. 10, 1817–Dec. 21, 1876.
Vol. 6, Pt. 2–493
Meek, Joseph L., 1810–June 20, 1875.
Vol. 6, Pt. 2–494
Meeker, Ezra, Dec. 29, 1830–Dec. 3, 1928.
Vol. 6, Pt. 2–495
Meeker, Jotham, Nov. 8, 1804–Jan. 12, 1855.
Vol. 6, Pt. 2–496
Meeker, Moses, June 17, 1790–July 7, 1865.
Vol. 6, Pt. 2–496

Meeker, Nathan Cook, July 12, 1817–Sept. 29, 1879.
Vol. 6, Pt. 2–497
Meerschaert, Théophile, Aug. 24, 1847–Feb. 21, 1924.
Vol. 6, Pt. 2–498
Mees, Arthur, Feb. 13, 1850–Apr. 26, 1923.
Vol. 6, Pt. 2–499
Mees, Charles Edward Kenneth, May 26, 1882–Aug. 15, 1960.
Supp. 6–441
Megapolensis, Johannes, 1603–1670.
Vol. 6, Pt. 2–499
Megrue, Roi Cooper, June 12, 1883–Feb. 27, 1927.
Vol. 6, Pt. 2–500
Meière, Marie Hildreth, Sept. 3, 1892–May 2, 1961.
Supp. 7–522
Meiggs, Henry, July 7, 1811–Sept. 29, 1877.
Vol. 6, Pt. 2–501
Meigs, Arthur Vincent, Nov. 1, 1850–Jan. 1, 1912.
Vol. 6, Pt. 2–503
Meigs, Charles Delucena, Feb. 19, 1792–June 22, 1869.
Vol. 6, Pt. 2–503
Meigs, James Aitken, July 31, 1829–Nov. 9, 1879.
Vol. 6, Pt. 2–504
Meigs, John, Aug. 31, 1852–Nov. 6, 1911.
Vol. 6, Pt. 2–504
Meigs, John Forsyth, Oct. 3, 1818–Dec. 16, 1882.
Vol. 6, Pt. 2–505
Meigs, Josiah, Aug. 21, 1757–Sept. 4, 1822.
Vol. 6, Pt. 2–506
Meigs, Montgomery Cunningham, May 3, 1816–Jan. 2, 1892.
Vol. 6, Pt. 2–507
Meigs, Return Jonathan, Dec. 17, 1740–Jan. 28, 1823.
Vol. 6, Pt. 2–508
Meigs, Return Jonathan, Nov. 17, 1764–Mar. 29, 1824.
Vol. 6, Pt. 2–509
Meigs, Return Jonathan, Apr. 14, 1801–Oct. 19, 1891.
Vol. 6, Pt. 2–510
Meigs, William Montgomery, Aug. 12, 1852–Dec. 30, 1929.
Vol. 6, Pt. 2–511
Meiklejohn Alexander, Feb. 3, 1872–Dec. 16, 1964.
Supp. 7–523
Meinzer, Oscar Edward, Nov. 28, 1876–June 14, 1948.
Supp. 4–567
Melcher, Frederic Gershom, Apr. 12, 1879–Mar. 9, 1963.
Supp. 7–524
Melchers, Gari, Aug. 11, 1860–Nov. 30, 1932.
Vol. 6, Pt. 2–512
Melchior, Lauritz Lebrecht Hommel, Mar. 20, 1890–Mar. 18, 1973.
Supp. 9–544
Melish, John, June 13, 1771–Dec. 30, 1822.
Vol. 6, Pt. 2–513
Mell, Patrick Hues, July 19, 1814–Jan. 26, 1888.
Vol. 6, Pt. 2–514
Mell, Patrick Hues, May 24, 1850–Oct. 12, 1918.
Vol. 6, Pt. 2–515
Mellen, Charles Sanger, Aug. 16, 1851–Nov. 17, 1927
Vol. 6, Pt. 2–515
Mellen, Grenville, June 19, 1799–Sept. 5, 1841.
Vol. 6, Pt. 2–516
Mellen, Prentiss, Oct. 11, 1764–Dec. 31, 1840.
Vol. 6, Pt. 2–517
Mellette, Arthur Calvin, June 23, 1842–May 25, 1896.
Vol. 6, Pt. 2–518
Mellon, Andrew William, Mar. 24, 1855–Aug. 26, 1937.
Supp. 2–446
Mellon, William Larimer, June 1, 1868–Oct. 8, 1949.
Supp. 4–568
Melsheimer, Friedrich Valentin, Sept. 25, 1749–June 30, 1814.
Vol. 6, Pt. 2–518
Melton, James, Jan. 2, 1904–Apr. 21, 1961.
Supp. 7–525
Meltzer, Samuel James, Mar. 22, 1851–Nov. 7, 1920.
Vol. 6, Pt. 2–519
Melville, David, Mar. 21, 1773–Sept. 3, 1856.
Vol. 6, Pt. 2–520
Melville, George Wallace, Jan. 10, 1841–Mar. 17, 1912.
Vol. 6, Pt. 2–521
Melville, Herman, Aug. 1, 1819–Sept. 28, 1891.
Vol. 6, Pt. 2–522
Membré, Zenobius, 1645–1687?.
Vol. 6, Pt. 2–526
Memminger, Christopher Gustavus, Jan. 9, 1803–Mar. 7, 1888.
Vol. 6, Pt. 2–527
Menard, Michel Branamour, Dec. 5, 1805–Sept. 2, 1856.
Vol. 6, Pt. 2–528
Menard, Pierre, Oct. 7, 1766–June 13, 1844.
Vol. 6, Pt. 2–529
Ménard, René, Sept. 7, 1605–Aug. 1661.
Vol. 6, Pt. 2–530
Mencken, Henry Louis, Sept. 12, 1880–Jan. 29, 1956.
Supp. 6–443
Mendel, Lafayette Benedict, Feb. 5, 1872–Dec. 9, 1935.
Supp. 1–549
Mendelsohn, Erich (*or* Eric), Mar. 21, 1887–Sept. 15, 1953.
Supp. 5–482
Mendelsohn, Samuel, Mar. 3, 1895–Feb. 3, 1966.
Supp. 8–428
Mendenhall, Charles Elwood, Aug. 1, 1872–Aug. 18, 1935.
Supp. 1–550
Mendenhall, Thomas Corwin, Oct. 4, 1841–Mar. 22, 1924.
Vol. 6, Pt. 2–530
Mendes, Frederic De Sola, July 8, 1850–Oct. 26, 1927.
Vol. 6, Pt. 2–532
Mendes, Henry Pereira, Apr. 13, 1852–Oct. 20, 1937,
Supp. 2–452
Meneely, Andrew, May 19, 1802–Oct. 14, 1851.
Vol. 6, Pt. 2–532
Menéndez De Avilés, Pedro, Feb. 15, 1519–Sept. 17, 1574.
Vol. 6, Pt. 2–533
Menetrey, Joseph, Nov. 28, 1812–Apr. 27, 1891.
Vol. 6, Pt. 2–534
Menewa, fl. 1814–1835.
Vol. 6, Pt. 2–535
Mengarini, Gregory, July 21, 1811–Sept. 23, 1886.
Vol. 6, Pt. 2–535
Menjou, Adolphe Jean, Feb. 18, 1890–Oct. 29, 1963.
Supp. 7–526
Menken, Adah Isaacs, June 15, 1835?–Aug. 10, 1868.
Vol. 6, Pt. 2–536
Menninger, Charles Frederick, July 11, 1862–Nov. 28, 1953.
Supp. 5–483
Menninger, William Claire, Oct. 15, 1899–Sept. 6, 1966.
Supp. 8–428
Menocal, Aniceto Garcia, Sept. 1, 1836–July 20, 1908.
Vol. 6, Pt. 2–537
Menoher, Charles Thomas, Mar. 20, 1862–Aug. 11, 1930.
Vol. 6, Pt. 2–538
Mercer, Charles Fenton, June 16, 1778–May 4, 1858.
Vol. 6, Pt. 2–539
Mercer, Henry Chapman, June 24, 1856–Mar. 9, 1930.
Vol. 6, Pt. 2–539
Mercer, Hugh, *c.* 1725–Jan. 12, 1777.
Vol. 6, Pt. 2–541
Mercer, James, Feb. 26, 1736–Oct. 31, 1793.
Vol. 6, Pt. 2–542
Mercer, Jesse, Dec. 16, 1769–Sept. 6, 1841.
Vol. 6, Pt. 2–542
Mercer, John Francis, May 17, 1759–Aug. 30, 1821.
Vol. 6, Pt. 2–543
Mercer, John Herndon ("Johnny"), Nov. 18, 1909–June 25, 1976.
Supp. 10–526
Mercer, Lewis Pyle, June 27, 1847–July 6, 1906.
Vol. 6, Pt. 2–544
Mercer, Margaret, July 1, 1791–Sept. 17, 1846.
Vol. 6, Pt. 2–545
Merchant, Livingston Tallmadge, Nov. 23, 1903–May 15, 1976.
Supp. 10–528
Mercier, Charles Alfred, June 3, 1816–May 12, 1894.
Vol. 6, Pt. 2–546
Merck, George Wilhelm, Mar. 29, 1894–Nov. 9, 1957.
Supp. 6–447
Mercur, Ulysses, Aug. 12, 1818–June 6, 1887.
Vol. 6, Pt. 2–547
Meredith, Edna C. Elliott, Apr 25, 1879–Jan. 1, 1961
Supp. 7–527
Meredith, Edwin Thomas, Dec. 23, 1876–June 17, 1928.
Vol. 6, Pt. 2–547
Meredith, Samuel, 1741–Feb. 10, 1817
Vol. 6, Pt. 2–548

Meredith, William Morris, June 8, 1799–Aug. 17, 1873.
Vol. 6, Pt. 2–548
Mergenthaler, Ottmar, May 1, 1854–Oct. 28, 1899.
Vol. 6, Pt. 2–549
Mergler, Marie Josepha, May 18, 1851–May 17, 1901.
Vol. 6, Pt. 2–550
Merriam, Augustus Chapman, May 30, 1843–Jan. 19, 1895.
Vol. 6, Pt. 2–551
Merriam, Charles, Nov. 31, 1806–July 9, 1887.
Vol. 6, Pt. 2–552
Merriam, Charles Edward, Jr., Nov. 15, 1874–Jan. 8, 1953.
Supp. 5–484
Merriam, Clinton Hart, Dec. 5, 1855–Mar. 19, 1942.
Supp. 3–517
Merriam, Henry Clay, Nov. 13, 1837–Nov. 18, 1912.
Vol. 6, Pt. 2–553
Merriam, John Campbell, Oct. 20, 1869–Oct. 30, 1945.
Supp. 3–519
Merriam, William Rush, July 26, 1849–Feb. 18, 1931.
Vol. 6, Pt. 2–554
Merrick, Edwin Thomas, July 9, 1808–Jan. 12, 1897.
Vol. 6, Pt. 2–555
Merrick, Frederick, Jan. 29, 1810–Mar. 5, 1894.
Vol. 6, Pt. 2–555
Merrick, Pliny, Aug. 2, 1794–Jan. 31, 1867.
Vol. 6, Pt. 2–556
Merrick, Samuel Vaughan, May 4, 1801–Aug. 18, 1870.
Vol. 6, Pt. 2–557
Merrill, Charles Edward, Oct. 19, 1885–Oct. 6, 1956.
Supp. 6–448
Merrill, Daniel, Mar. 18, 1765–June 3, 1833.
Vol. 6, Pt. 2–558
Merrill, Elmer Drew, Oct. 15, 1876–Feb. 25, 1956.
Supp. 6–449
Merrill, Elmer Truesdell, Jan. 1, 1860–Apr. 19, 1936.
Supp. 2–453
Merrill, Frank Dow, Dec. 4, 1903–Dec. 11, 1955.
Supp. 5–486
Merrill, George Edmands, Dec. 19, 1846–June 11. 1908.
Vol. 6, Pt. 2–559
Merrill, George Perkins, May 31, 1854–Aug. 15, 1929.
Vol. 6, Pt. 2–559
Merrill, Gretchen Van Zandt, Nov. 2, 1925–Apr. 15, 1965.
Supp. 7–528
Merrill, James Cushing, Mar. 26, 1853–Oct. 27, 1902.
Vol. 6, Pt. 2–560
Merrill, James Griswold, Aug. 20, 1840–Dec. 22, 1920.
Vol. 6, Pt. 2–561
Merrill, Joshua, Oct. 6, 1820–Jan. 15, 1904.
Vol. 6, Pt. 2–562
Merrill, Samuel, Oct. 29, 1792–Aug. 24, 1855.
Vol. 6, Pt. 2–563
Merrill, Selah, May 2, 1837–Jan. 22, 1909.
Vol. 6, Pt. 2–564
Merrill, Stephen Mason, Sept. 16, 1825–Nov. 12, 1905.
Vol. 6, Pt. 2–565
Merrill, Stuart Fitzrandolph, Aug. 1, 1863–Dec. 1, 1915.
Vol. 6, Pt. 2–566
Merrill, William Bradford, Feb. 27, 1861–Nov. 26, 1928.
Vol. 6, Pt. 2–568
Merrill, Wiiliam Emery, Oct. 11, 1837–Dec. 14, 1891.
Vol. 6, Pt. 2–568
Merrimon, Augustus Summerfield, Sept. 15, 1830–Nov. 14, 1892.
Vol. 6, Pt. 2–569
Merritt, Anna Lea, Sept. 13, 1844–Apr. 7, 1930.
Vol. 6, Pt. 2–570
Merritt, Israel John, Aug. 23, 1829–Dec. 13, 1911.
Vol. 6, Pt. 2–571
Merritt, Leonidas, Feb. 20, 1844–May 9, 1926.
Vol. 6, Pt. 2–571
Merritt, Wesley, June 16, 1834–Dec. 3, 1910.
Vol. 6, Pt. 2–572
Merry, Ann Brunton, May 30, 1769–June 28, 1808.
Vol. 6, Pt. 2–574
Merry, William Lawrence, Dec. 27, 1842–Dec. 14, 1911.
Vol. 6, Pt. 2–574
Merton, Thomas, Jan. 31, 1915–Dec. 10, 1968.
Supp. 8–430
Mervine, William, Mar. 14, 1791–Sept. 15, 1868.
Vol. 6, Pt. 2–575
Merz, Karl, Sept. 19, 1836–Jan. 30, 1890.
Vol. 6, Pt. 2–576
Meserve, Frederick Hill, Nov. 1, 1865–June 25, 1962.
Supp. 7–529
Meserve, Nathaniel, *c.* 1705–June 28, 1758.
Vol. 6, Pt. 2–577
Messer, Asa, May 31, 1769–Oct. 11, 1836.
Vol. 6, Pt. 2–578
Messersmith, George Strausser, Oct. 3, 1883–Jan. 29, 1960.
Supp. 6–450
Messler, Thomas Doremus, May 9, 1833–Aug. 11, 1893.
Vol. 6, Pt. 2–578
Messmer, Sebastian Gebhard, Aug. 29, 1847–Aug. 4, 1930.
Vol. 6, Pt. 2–579
Mesta, Perle Reid Skirvin, Oct. 12, 1889–Mar. 16, 1975.
Supp. 9–546
Metcalf, Lee Warren, Jan. 28, 1911–Jan. 12, 1978.
Supp. 10–529
Metcalf, Ralph Harold, May 30, 1910–Oct. 10, 1978.
Supp. 10–531
Mestrovic, Ivan, Aug. 15, 1883–Jan. 16, 1962.
Supp. 7–530
Metalious, Grace, Sept. 8, 1924–Feb. 25, 1964.
Supp. 7–531
Metcalf, Henry Harrison, Apr. 7, 1841–Feb. 5, 1932
Vol. 6, Pt. 2–580
Metcalf, Joel Hastings, Jan. 4, 1866–Feb. 21, 1925.
Vol. 6, Pt. 2–581
Metcalf, Lee Warren, Jan. 28, 1911–Jan. 12, 1978.
Supp. 10–529
Metcalf, Theron, Oct. 16, 1784–Nov. 13, 1875.
Vol. 6, Pt. 2–582
Metcalf, Willard Leroy, July 1, 1858–Mar. 9, 1925.
Vol. 6, Pt. 2–582
Metcalf, William, Sept. 3, 1838–Dec. 5, 1909.
Vol. 6, Pt. 2–583
Metcalfe, Ralph Harold, May 30, 1910–Oct. 10, 1978.
Supp. 10–531
Metcalfe, Samuel Lytler, Sept. 21, 1798–July 17, 1856.
Vol. 6, Pt. 2–584
Metcalfe, Thomas, Mar. 20, 1780–Aug. 18, 1855.
Vol. 6, Pt. 2–584
Mettauer, John Peter, 1787–Nov. 22, 1875.
Vol. 6, Pt. 2–585
Metz, Christian, Dec. 30, 1794–July 27, 1867.
Vol. 6, Pt. 2–586
Meusel, Robert William, July 19, 1896–Nov. 28, 1977.
Supp. 10–532
Meyer, Adolf, Sept. 13, 1866–Mar. 17, 1950.
Supp. 4–569
Meyer, Agnes Elizabeth Ernst, Jan. 2, 1887–Sept. 1, 1970.
Supp. 8–432
Meyer, Albert Gregory, Mar. 9, 1903–Apr. 9, 1965.
Supp. 7–532
Meyer, Annie Nathan, Feb. 19, 1867–Sept. 23, 1951.
Supp. 5–487
Meyer, André Benoit Mathieu, Sept. 3, 1898–Sept. 9, 1979.
Supp. 10–533
Meyer, Eugene Isaac, Oct. 31, 1875–July 17, 1959.
Supp. 6–452
Meyer, Frank Straus, May 9, 1909–Apr. 1, 1972.
Supp. 9–548
Meyer, George von Lengerke, June 24, 1858–Mar. 9, 1918.
Vol. 6, Pt. 2–587
Meyer, Henry Coddington, Apr. 14, 1844–Mar. 27, 1935.
Supp. 1–552
Meyer, Martin Abraham, Jan. 15, 1879–June 27, 1923.
Vol. 6, Pt. 2–588
Meyerhof, Otto, Apr. 12, 1884–Oct. 6, 1951.
Supp. 5–488
Mezes, Sldney Edward, Sept. 23, 1863–Sept. 10, 1931.
Vol. 6, Pt. 2–588
Miantonomo, d. 1643.
Vol. 6, Pt. 2–589
Mich, Daniel Danforth, Jan. 8, 1905–Nov. 22, 1965.
Supp. 7–535
Michael, Arthur, Aug. 7, 1853–Feb. 8, 1942.
Supp. 3–520
Michaelis, Leonor, Jan. 16, 1875–Oct. 8. 1949.
Supp. 4–572
Michaëlius, Jonas, b. 1584.
Vol. 6, Pt. 2–590

Michaux, André, Mar. 7, 1746–Nov. 1802.
Vol. 6, Pt. 2–591
Michaux, François André, Aug. 16, 1770–Oct. 23, 1855.
Vol. 6, Pt. 2–592
Michaux, Lightfoot Solomon, 1885?–Oct. 20, 1968.
Supp. 8–434
Micheaux, Oscar, Jan. 2?, 1884–Mar. 26, 1951.
Supp. 5–490
Michel, Virgil George, June 26, 1890–Nov. 26, 1938.
Supp. 2–454
Michel, William Middleton, Jan. 22, 1822–June 4, 1894.
Vol. 6, Pt. 2–593
Michelson, Albert Abraham, Dec. 19, 1852–May 9, 1931.
Vol. 6, Pt. 2–593
Michelson, Charles, Apr. 18, 1868–Jan. 8, 1948.
Supp. 4–574
Michener, Ezra, Nov. 24, 1794–June 24, 1887.
Vol. 6, Pt. 2–596
Michie, Peter Smith, Mar. 24, 1839–Feb. 16, 1901.
Vol. 6, Pt. 2–597
Michikinikwa. [*See* Little Turtle, *c.* 1752–1812.]
Michler, Nathaniel, Sept. 13, 1827–Jury 17, 1881.
Supp. 1–552
Middleton, Arthur, 1681–Sept. 7, 1737.
Vol. 6, Pt. 2–598
Middleton, Arthur, June 26, 1742–Jan. 1, 1787.
Vol. 6, Pt. 2–599
Middleton, Henry, 1717–June 13, 1784.
Vol. 6, Pt. 2–600
Middleton, Henry, Sept. 28, 1770–June 14, 1846.
Vol. 6, Pt. 2–600
Middleton, John Izard, Aug. 13, 1785–Oct. 5, 1849.
Vol. 6, Pt. 2–601
Middleton, Nathaniel Russell, Apr. 1, 1810–Sept. 6, 1890.
Vol. 6, Pt. 2–602
Middleton, Peter, d. Jan. 9, 1781.
Vol. 6, Pt. 2–602
Middleton, Thomas Cooke, Mar. 30, 1842–Nov. 19, 1923.
Vol. 6, Pt. 2–603
Midgley, Thomas, May 18, 1889–Nov. 2, 1944.
Supp. 3–521
Mielatz, Charles Frederick William, May 24, 1860–June 2, 1919.
Vol. 6, Pt. 2–604
Mielziner, Jo, Mar. 19, 1901–Mar. 15, 1976.
Supp. 10–534
Mielziner, Moses, Aug. 12, 1828–Feb. 18, 1903.
Vol. 6, Pt. 2–605
Mies Van Der Rohe, Ludwig, Mar. 27, 1886–Aug. 17, 1969.
Supp. 8–435
Mifflin, Lloyd, Sept. 15, 1846–July 16, 1921.
Vol. 6, Pt. 2–605
Mifflin, Thomas, Jan. 10, 1744–Jan. 20, 1800.
Vol. 6, Pt. 2–606
Mifflin, Warner, Oct. 21, 1745–Oct. 16, 1798.
Vol. 6, Pt. 2–608
Mignot, Louis Remy, 1831–Sept. 22, 1870.
Vol. 6, Pt. 2–609
Milburn, William Henry, Sept. 26, 1823–Apr. 10, 1903.
Vol. 6, Pt. 2–610
Miles, Edward, Oct. 14, 1752–Mar. 7, 1828.
Vol. 6, Pt. 2–611
Miles, George Henry, July 31, 1824–July 24, 1871.
Vol. 6, Pt. 2–611
Miles, Henry Adolphus, May 30, 1809–May 31, 1895.
Vol. 6, Pt. 2–612
Miles, Manly, July 20, 1826–Feb. 15, 1898.
Vol. 6, Pt. 2–613
Miles, Nelson Appleton, Aug. 8, 1839–May 15, 1925.
Vol. 6. Pt. 2–614
Miles, Richard Pius, May 17, 1791–Feb. 21, 1860.
Vol. 6, Pt. 2–616
Miles, William Porcher, July 4, 1822–May 11, 1899.
Vol. 6, Pt. 2–616
Milholland, Inez. [*See* Boissevain, Inez Milholland, 1886–1916.]
Milk, Harvey Bernard, May 22, 1930–Nov. 27, 1978.
Supp. 10–536
Millay, Edna St. Vincent, Feb. 22, 1892–Oct. 19, 1950.
Supp. 4–575
Milledge, John, 1757–Feb. 9, 1818.
Vol. 6, Pt. 2–617
Milledoler, Philip, Sept. 22, 1775–Sept. 22, 1852.
Vol. 6, Pt. 2–618
Miller, Charles Henry, Mar. 20, 1842–Jan. 21, 1922.
Vol. 6, Pt. 2–619
Miller, Charles Ransom, Jan. 17, 1849–July 18, 1922.
Vol. 6, Pt. 2–620
Miller, Cincinnatus Hiner, Mar. 10, 1839–Feb. 17, 1913.
Vol. 6, Pt. 2–621
Miller, David Hunter, Jan. 2, 1875–July 21, 1961.
Supp. 7–536
Miller, Dayton Clarence, Mar. 13, 1866–Feb. 23, 1941.
Supp. 3–523
Miller, Edward, May 9, 1760–Mar. 17, 1812.
Vol. 6, Pt. 2–622
Miller, Emily Clark Huntington, Oct. 22, 1833–Nov. 2, 1913.
Vol. 6, Pt. 2–623
Miller, Ezra, May 12, 1812–July 9, 1885.
Vol. 6, Pt. 2–624
Miller, George, Feb. 16, 1774–Apr. 5, 1816.
Vol. 6, Pt. 2–625
Miller, George Abram, July 31, 1863–Feb. 10, 1951.
Supp. 5–491
Miller, Gerrit Smith, Jr., Dec. 6, 1869–Feb. 24, 1956.
Supp. 6–453
Miller, Gilbert Heron, July 3, 1884–Jan. 2, 1969.
Supp. 8–437
Miller, Glenn, Mar. 1, 1904–Dec. 15?, 1944.
Supp. 3–524
Miller, Harriet Mann, June 25, 1831–Dec. 25, 1918.
Vol. 6, Pt. 2–625
Miller, Heinrich. [*See* Miller, John Henry, 1702–1782.]
Miller, Henry, Nov. 1, 1800–Feb. 8, 1874.
Vol. 6, Pt. 2–626
Miller, Henry, Feb. 1, 1860–Apr. 9, 1926.
Vol. 6, Pt. 2–626
Miller, Henry Valentine, Dec. 26, 1891–June 7, 1980.
Supp. 10–538
Miller, James Alexander, Mar. 27, 1874–July 29, 1948.
Supp. 4–577
Miller, James Russell, Mar. 20, 1840–July 2, 1912.
Vol. 6, Pt. 2–627
Miller, Joaquin. [*See* Miller, Cincinnatus Hiner, 1839–1913.]
Miller, John, Nov. 25, 1781–Mar. 18, 1846.
Vol. 6, Pt. 2–628
Miller, John, Apr. 6, 1819–Apr. 14, 1895.
Vol. 6, Pt. 2–629
Miller, John Franklin, Nov. 21, 1831–Mar. 8, 1886.
Vol. 6, Pt. 2–630
Miller, John Henry, Mar. 12, 1702–Mar. 31, 1782.
Vol. 6, Pt. 2–631
Miller, John Peter, Dec. 25, 1709–Sept. 25, 1796.
Vol. 6, Pt. 2–632
Miller, Jonathan Peckham, Feb. 24, 1796–Feb. 17, 1874.
Vol. 6, Pt. 2–632
Miller, Kelly, July 23, 1863–Dec. 29, 1939.
Supp. 2–456
Miller, Kempster Blanchard, Aug. 14, 1870–Nov. 22, 1933.
Supp. 1–553
Miller, Kenneth Hayes, Mar. 11, 1876–Jan. 1, 1952.
Supp. 5–492
Miller, Leslie William, Aug. 5, 1848–Mar. 7, 1931.
Vol. 6, Pt. 2–633
Miller, Lewis, July 24, 1829–Feb. 17, 1899.
Vol. 6, Pt. 2–634
Miller, Nathan Lewis, Oct. 10, 1868–June 26, 1953.
Supp. 5–493
Miller, Oliver, Apr. 15, 1824–Oct. 18, 1892.
Vol. 6, Pt. 2–635
Miller, Olive Thorne. [*See* Miller, Harriet Mann, 1831–1918.]
Miller, Perry Gilbert Eddy, Feb. 25, 1905–Dec. 9, 1963.
Supp. 7–537
Miller, Peter. [*See* Miller, John Peter, 1709–1796.]
Miller, Samuel, Oct. 31, 1769–Jan. 7, 1850.
Vol. 6, Pt. 2–636
Miller, Samuel, Oct. 4, 1820–Oct. 24, 1901.
Vol. 6, Pt. 2–637
Miller, Samuel Freeman, Apr. 5, 1816–Oct. 13, 1890.
Vol. 6, Pt. 2–637
Miller, Stephen Decatur, May 8, 1787–Mar. 8, 1838.
Vol. 6, Pt. 2–640

Miller, Warner, Aug. 12, 1838–Mar. 21, 1918.
Vol. 6, Pt. 2–641
Miller, Webb, Feb. 10, 1892–May 7, 1940.
Supp. 2–457
Miller, William Henry Harrison, Sept. 6, 1840–May 25, 1917.
Vol. 6, Pt. 2–643
Miller, William, Feb. 15, 1782–Dec. 20, 1849.
Vol. 6, Pt. 2–641
Miller, William Snow, Mar. 29, 1858–Dec. 26, 1939.
Supp. 2–457
Miller, Willoughby Dayton, Aug. 1, 1853–July 27, 1907.
Vol. 6, Pt. 2–643
Millet, Francis Davis, Nov. 3, 1846–Apr. 15, 1912.
Vol. 6, Pt. 2–644
Millett, Fred Benjamin, Feb. 19, 1890–Jan. 1, 1976.
Supp. 10–541
Milligan, Robert, July 25, 1814–Mar. 20, 1875.
Vol. 6, Pt. 2–646
Milligan, Robert Wiley Apr. 8, 1843–Oct. 14, 1909.
Vol. 6 Pt. 2–646
Millikan, Clark Blanchard, Aug. 23, 1903–Jan. 2, 1966.
Supp. 8–439
Millikan, Robert Andrews, Mar. 22, 1868–Dec. 19, 1953.
Supp. 5–494
Millikin, Eugene Donald, Feb. 12, 1891–July 26, 1958.
Supp. 6–454
Millington, John, May 11, 1779–July 10, 1868.
Vol. 6, Pt. 2–647
Millis, Harry Alvin, May 14, 1873–June 25, 1948.
Supp. 4–579
Millis, Walter, Mar. 16, 1899–Mar. 17, 1968.
Supp. 8–440
Millmore, Martin, Sept. 14, 1844–July 21, 1883.
Vol. 7, Pt. 1–18
Mills, Anson, Aug. 31, 1834–Nov. 5, 1924.
Vol. 7, Pt. 1–1
Mills, Benjamin, Jan. 12, 1779–Dec. 6, 1831.
Vol. 7, Pt. 1–2
Mills, Benjamin Fay, June 4, 1857–May 1, 1916.
Vol. 7, Pt. 1–2
Mills, Charles Karsner, Dec. 4, 1845–May 28, 1931.
Vol. 7, Pt. 1–3
Mills, Charles Wright, Aug. 28, 1916–Mar. 20, 1962.
Supp. 7–538
Mills, Clark, Dec. 13, 1810–Jan. 12, 1883.
Vol. 7, Pt. 1–4
Mills, Cyrus Taggart, May 4, 1819–Apr. 20, 1884.
Vol. 7, Pt. 1–5
Mills, Darius Ogden, Sept. 5, 1825–Jan. 4, 1910.
Vol. 7, Pt. 1–6
Mills, Elijah Hunt, Dec. 1, 1776–May 5, 1829.
Vol. 7, Pt. 1–7
Mills, Enos Abijah, Apr. 22, 1870–Sept. 21, 1922.
Supp. 1–554
Mills, Hiram Francis, Nov. 1, 1836–Oct. 4, 1921.
Vol. 7, Pt. 1–8
Mills, Lawrence Heyworth, 1837–Jan. 29, 1918.
Vol. 7, Pt. 1–9
Mills, Ogden Livingston, Aug. 23, 1884–Oct. 11, 1937.
Supp. 2–459
Mills, Robert, Aug. 12, 1781–Mar. 3, 1855.
Vol. 7, Pt. 1–9
Mills, Robert, Mar. 9, 1809–Apr. 13, 1888.
Vol. 7, Pt. 1–13
Mills, Roger Quarles, Mar. 30, 1832–Sept. 2, 1911.
Vol. 7, Pt. 1–14
Mills, Samuel John, Apr. 21, 1783–June 16, 1818.
Vol. 7, Pt. 1–15
Mills, Susan Lincoln Tolman, Nov. 18, 1826–Dec. 12, 1912.
Vol. 7, Pt. 1–16
Millspaugh, Charles Frederick, June 20, 1854–Sept. 15, 1923.
Vol. 7, Pt. 1–17
Milner, John Turner, Sept. 29, 1826–Aug. 18, 1898.
Vol. 7, Pt. 1–19
Milner, Moses Embree. [*See* California Joe, 1829–1876.]
Milner, Thomas Picton. [*See* Picton, Thomas, 1822–1891.]
Milroy, Robert Huston, June 11, 1816–Mar. 29, 1890.
Vol. 7, Pt. 1–20
Milton, George Fort, Nov. 19, 1894–Nov. 12, 1955.
Supp. 5–497
Milton, John, Apr. 20, 1807–Apr. 1, 1865.
Vol. 7, Pt. 1–21
Miner, Alonzo Ames, Aug. 17, 1814–June 14, 1895.
Vol. 7, Pt. 1–21
Miner, Charles, Feb. 1, 1780–Oct. 26, 1865.
Vol. 7, Pt. 1–22
Miner, Myrtilla, Mar. 4, 1815–Dec. 17, 1864.
Vol. 7, Pt. 1–23
Ming, John Joseph, Sept. 20, 1838–June 17, 1910.
Vol. 7, Pt. 1–24
Mingus, Charles, Jr., Apr. 22, 1922–Jan. 5, 1979.
Supp. 10–543
Minnigerode, Lucy, Feb. 8, 1871–Mar. 24, 1935.
Supp. 1–555
Minor, Benjamin Blake, Oct. 21, 1818–Aug. 1, 1905.
Vol. 7, Pt. 1–25
Minor, John Barbee, June 2, 1813–July 29, 1895.
Vol. 7, Pt. 1–26
Minor, Lucian, Apr. 24, 1802–July 8, 1858.
Vol. 7, Pt. 1–27
Minor, Raleigh Colston, Jan. 24, 1869–June 14, 1923.
Vol. 7, Pt. 1–27
Minor, Robert, July 15, 1884–Nov. 26, 1952.
Supp. 5–498
Minor, Robert Crannell, Apr. 30, 1839–Aug. 3 1904.
Vol. 7, Pt. 1–28
Minor, Virginia Louisa, Mar. 27, 1824–Aug. 14, 1894.
Vol. 7, Pt. 1–29
Minot, Charles Sedgwick, Dec. 23, 1852–Nov. 19, 1914.
Vol. 7, Pt. 1–30
Minot, George Richards, Dec. 22, 1758–Jan. 2, 1802.
Vol. 7, Pt. 1–31
Minot, George Richards, Dec. 2, 1885–Feb. 25, 1950.
Supp. 4–580
Minto, Walter, Dec. 5, 1753–Oct. 21, 1796.
Vol. 7, Pt. 1–32
Minton, Sherman, Oct. 20, 1890–Apr. 9, 1965.
Supp. 7–540
Minturn, Robert Bowne, Nov. 16, 1805–Jan. 9, 1866.
Vol. 7, Pt. 1–32
Minty, Robert Horatio George, Dec. 4, 1831–Aug. 24, 1906.
Vol. 7, Pt. 1–33
Minuit, Peter, 1580–1638.
Vol. 7, Pt. 1–33
Miranda, Carmen, Feb. 9, 1909–Aug. 5, 1955.
Supp. 5–500
Miró, Esteban Rodriguez, 1744–1795.
Vol. 7, Pt. 1–35
Mirsky, Alfred Ezra, Oct. 17, 1900–June 19, 1974.
Supp. 9–549
Mitchel, John, Nov. 3, 1815–Mar. 20, 1875.
Vol. 7, Pt. 1–35
Mitchel, John Purroy, July 19, 1879–July 6, 1918.
Vol. 7, Pt. 1–37
Mitchel, Ormsby MacKnight, July 28, 1809–Oct. 30, 1862.
Vol. 7, Pt. 1–38
Mitchell, Aibert Graeme, Feb. 21, 1889–June 1, 1941.
Supp. 3–525
Mitchell, Alexander, Oct. 18, 1817–Apr. 19, 1887.
Vol. 7, Pt. 1–39
Mitchell, David Brydie, Oct. 22, 1766–Apr. 22, 1837.
Vol. 7, Pt. 1, 1–40
Mitchell, David Dawson, July 31, 1806–May 23, 1861.
Vol. 7, Pt. 1, 1–41.
Mitchell, Donald Grant, Apr. 12, 1822–Dec. 15, 1908.
Vol. 7, Pt. 1–41
Mitchell, Edward Cushing, Sept. 20, 1829–Feb. 27, 1900.
Vol. 7, Pt. 1–42
Mitchell, Edward Page, Mar. 24, 1852–Jan. 22, 1927.
Vol. 7, Pt. 1–43
Mitchell, Edwin Knox, Dec. 23, 1853–Oct. 5, 1934.
Supp. 1–556
Mitchell, Elisha, Aug. 19, 1793–June 27, 1857.
Vol. 7, Pt. 1–45
Mitchell, George Edward, Mar. 3, 1781–June 28, 1832.
Vol. 7, Pt. 1–46
Mitchell, Henry, Sept. 16, 1830–Dec. 1, 1902.
Vol. 7, Pt. 1–47
Mitchell, Hinckley Gilbert Thomas, Feb. 22, 1846–May 19, 1920.
Vol. 7, Pt. 1–47
Mitchell, Isaac, *c.* 1759–Nov. 26, 1812.
Vol. 7, Pt. 1–48

Mitchell, James Paul, Nov. 12, 1900–Oct. 19, 1964.
Supp. 7–542
Mitchell, James Tyndale, Nov. 9, 1834–July 4, 1915.
Vol. 7, Pt. 1–49
Mitchell, John, d. 1768.
Vol. 7, Pt. 1–50
Mitchell, John, Feb. 4, 1870–Sept. 9, 1919.
Vol. 7, Pt. 1–51
Mitchell, John Ames, Jan. 17, 1845–June 29, 1918.
Vol. 7, Pt. 1–52
Mitchell, John Hipple, June 22, 1835–Dec. 8, 1905.
Vol. 7, Pt. 1–53
Mitchell, John Kearsley, May 12, 1793–Apr. 4, 1858.
Vol. 7, Pt. 1–54
Mitchell, Jonathan, 1624–July 9, 1668.
Vol. 7, Pt. 1–55
Mitchell, Langdon Elwyn, Feb. 17, 1862–Oct. 21, 1935.
Supp. 1–557
Mitchell, Lucy Myers Wright, Mar. 20, 1845–Mar. 10, 1888.
Vol. 7, Pt. 1–56
Mitchell, Lucy Sprague, July 2, 1878–Oct. 15, 1967.
Supp. 8–442
Mitchell, Margaret Julia, June 14, 1837–Mar. 22, 1918.
Vol. 7, Pt. 1–56
Mitchell, Margaret Munnerlyn, Nov. 8, 1900–Aug. 16, 1949.
Supp. 4–583
Mitchell, Maria, Aug. 1, 1818–June 28, 1889.
Vol. 7, Pt. 1–57
Mitchell, Martha Elizabeth Beall, Sept. 2, 1918–May 31, 1976.
Supp. 10–544
Mitchell, Nahum, Feb. 12, 1769–Aug. 1, 1853.
Vol. 7, Pt. 1–58
Mitchell, Nathaniel, 1753–Feb. 21, 1814.
Vol. 7, Pt. 1–59
Mitchell, Robert Byington, Apr. 4, 1823–Jan. 26, 1882.
Vol. 7, Pt. 1–60
Mitchell, Samuel Augustus, Mar. 20, 1792–Dec. 18, 1868.
Vol. 7, Pt. 1–61
Mitchell, Sidney Zollicoffer, Mar. 17, 1862–Feb. 17, 1944.
Supp. 3–526
Mitchell, Silas Weir, Feb. 15, 1829–Jan. 4, 1914.
Vol. 7, Pt. 1–62
Mitchell, Stephen Arnold, Mar. 3, 1903–Apr. 23, 1974.
Supp. 9–551
Mitchell, Stephen Mix, Dec. 9, 1743–Sept. 30, 1835.
Vol. 7, Pt. 1–65
Mitchell, Thomas Duché, 1791–May 13, 1865.
Vol. 7, Pt. 1–66
Mitchell, Thomas Gregory, July 11, 1892–Dec. 17, 1962.
Supp. 7–544
Mitchell, Wesley Clair, Aug. 5, 1874–Oct. 29, 1948.
Supp. 4–584
Mitchell, William, Dec. 20, 1791–Apr. 1, 1869.
Vol. 7, Pt. 1–66
Mitchell, William, 1798–May 11, 1856.
Vol. 7, Pt. 1–67
Mitchell, William, Feb. 24, 1801–Oct. 6, 1886.
Vol. 7, Pt. 1–68
Mitchell, William, Nov. 19, 1832–Aug. 21, 1900.
Vol. 7, Pt. 1–68
Mitchell, William, Dec. 29, 1879–Feb. 19, 1936.
Supp. 2–460
Mitchell, William DeWitt, Sept. 9, 1874–Aug. 24, 1955.
Supp. 5–501
Mitchill, Samuel Latham, Aug. 20, 1764–Sept. 7, 1831.
Vol. 7, Pt. 1–69
Mitropoulos, Dimitri, Mar. 1, 1896–Nov. 2, 1960.
Supp. 6–456
Mitscher, Marc Andrew, Jan. 26, 1887–Feb. 3, 1947.
Supp. 4–588
Mitten, Thomas Eugene, Mar. 31, 1864–Oct. 1, 1929.
Vol. 7, Pt. 1–71
Mix, Tom, Jan. 6, 1880–Oct. 12, 1940.
Supp. 2–462
Mixter, Samuel Jason, May 10, 1855–Jan. 19, 1926.
Vol. 7, Pt. 1–72
Mizner, Addison, 1872–Feb. 5, 1933.
Supp. 1–558
Modjeska, Helena, Oct. 12, 1840–Apr. 8, 1909.
Vol. 7, Pt. 1–73
Modjeski, Ralph, Jan. 27, 1861–June 26, 1940.
Supp. 2–463
Moeller, Henry, Dec. 11, 1849–Jan. 5, 1925.
Vol. 7, Pt. 1–74
Moffat, David Halliday, July 22, 1839–Mar. 18, 1911.
Vol. 7, Pt. 1–75
Moffat, James Clement, May 30, 1811–June 7, 1890.
Vol. 7, Pt. 1–75
Moffat, Jay Pierrepont, July 18, 1896–Jan. 24, 1943.
Supp. 3–528
Moffatt, James, July 4, 1870–June 27, 1944.
Supp. 3–529
Moffett, Cleveland Langston, Apr. 27, 1863–Oct. 14, 1926.
Vol. 7, Pt. 1–76
Moffett, William Adger, Oct. 31, 1869–Apr. 4, 1933.
Supp. 1–560
Moholy-Nagy, László, July 20, 1895–Nov. 24, 1946.
Supp. 4–590
Mohr, Charles Theodore, Dec. 28, 1824–July 17, 1901.
Vol. 7, Pt. 1–77
Möise, Penina, Apr. 23, 1797–Sept. 13, 1880.
Vol. 7, Pt. 1–78
Moisseiff, Leon Solomon, Nov. 10, 1872–Sept. 3, 1943.
Supp. 3–530
Moldehnke, Edward Frederick, Aug. 10, 1836–June 25, 1904.
Vol. 7, Pt. 1–78
Moldenke, Richard George Gottlob, Nov. 1, 1864–Nov. 17, 1930.
Vol. 7, Pt. 1–79
Moley, Raymond Charles, Sept. 27, 1886–Feb. 18, 1975.
Supp. 9–552
Mollenhauer, Emil, Aug. 4, 1855–Dec. 10, 1927.
Vol. 7, Pt. 1–80
Mollhausen, Heinrich Baldwin, Jan. 27, 1825–May 28, 1905.
Vol. 7, Pt. 1–80
Molyneux, Robert, July 24, 1738–Dec. 9, 1808.
Vol. 7, Pt. 1–81
Mombert, Jacob Isidor, Nov. 6, 1829–Oct. 7, 1913.
Vol. 7, Pt. 1–82
Monckton, Robert, June 24, 1726–May 21, 1782.
Vol. 7, Pt. 1–83
Moncure, Richard Cassius Lee, Dec. 11, 1805–Aug. 24, 1882.
Vol. 7, Pt. 1–84
Mondell, Frank Wheeler, Nov. 6, 1860–Aug. 6, 1939.
Supp. 2–464
Monette, John Wesley, Apr. 5, 1803–Mar. 1, 1851.
Vol. 7, Pt. 1–85
Money, Hernando De Soto, Aug. 26, 1839–Sept. 18, 1912.
Vol. 7, Pt. 1–85
Monis, Judah, Feb. 4, 1683–Apr. 25, 1764.
Vol. 7, Pt. 1–86
Monroe, Harriet, Dec. 23, 1860–Sept. 26, 1936.
Supp. 2–466
Monroe, James, Apr. 28, 1758–July 4, 1831.
Vol. 7, Pt. 1–87
Monroe, Marilyn, June 1, 1926–Aug. 5, 1962.
Supp. 7–545
Monroe, Paul, June 7, 1869–Dec. 6, 1947.
Supp. 4–591
Monroe, Vaughn Wilton, Oct. 7, 1911–May 21, 1973.
Supp. 9–554
Monroney, Almer Stillwell ("Mike"), Mar. 2, 1902–Feb. 13, 1980.
Supp. 10–547
Monsky, Henry, Feb. 4, 1890–May 2, 1947.
Supp. 4–593
Montague, Andrew Jackson, Oct. 3, 1862–Jan. 24, 1937.
Supp. 2–467
Montague, Gilbert Holland, May 27, 1880–Feb. 4, 1961.
Supp. 7–547
Montague, Henry James, Jan. 20, 1843–Aug. 11, 1878.
Vol. 7, Pt. 1–93
Montague, William Pepperell, Nov. 11, 1873–Aug. 1, 1953.
Supp. 5–503
Montefiore, Joshua, Aug. 7, 1762–June 26, 1843.
Vol. 7, Pt. 1–93
Monteux, Pierre Benjamin, Apr. 4, 1875–July 1, 1964.
Supp. 7–548
Montgomery, David Henry, Apr. 7, 1837–May 28, 1928.
Vol. 7, Pt. 1–94
Montgomery, Edmund Duncan, Mar. 19, 1835–Apr. 17, 1911.
Vol. 7, Pt. 1–95

Montgomery, George Washington, 1804–June 5, 1841.
Vol. 7, Pt. 1–96
Montgomery, James, Dec. 22, 1814–Dec. 6, 1871.
Vol. 7, Pt. 1–97
Montgomery, James Alan, June 13, 1866–Feb. 6, 1949.
Supp. 4–594
Montgomery, John Berrien, Nov. 17, 1794–Mar. 25, 1873.
Vol. 7, Pt. 1–97
Montgomery, Richard, Dec. 2, 1738–Dec. 31, 1775.
Vol. 7, Pt. 1–98
Montgomery, Thomas Harrison, Mar. 5, 1873–Mar. 19, 1912.
Vol. 7, Pt. 1–99
Montgomery, William Bell, Aug. 21, 1829–Sept. 25, 1904.
Vol. 7, Pt. 1–100
Montoya, Joseph Manuel, Sept. 24, 1915–June 5, 1978.
Supp. 10–548
Montrésor, James Gabriel, Nov. 19, 1702–Jan. 6, 1776.
Vol. 7, Pt. 1–100
Montrésor, John, Apr. 6, 1736–June 26, 1799.
Vol. 7, Pt. 1–101
Mood, Francis Asbury, June 23, 1830–Nov. 12, 1884.
Vol. 7, Pt. 1–102
Moody, (Arthur Edson) Blair, Feb. 13, 1902–July 20, 1954.
Supp. 5–504
Moody, Dwight Lyman, Feb. 5, 1837–Dec. 22, 1899.
Vol. 7, Pt. 1–103
Moody, James, 1744–Apr. 6, 1809.
Vol. 7, Pt. 1–106
Moody, John, May 2, 1868–Feb. 16, 1958.
Supp. 6–457
Moody, Paul, May 21, 1779–July 8, 1831.
Vol. 7, Pt. 1–106
Moody, William Henry, Dec. 23, 1853–July 2, 1917.
Vol. 7, Pt. 1–107
Moody, William Vaughan, July 8, 1869–Oct. 17, 1910.
Vol. 7, Pt. 1–108
Moon, Parker Thomas, Junes, 1892–June 11, 1936.
Supp. 2–468
Mooney, James, Feb. 10, 1861–Dec. 22, 1921.
Vol. 7, Pt. 1–110
Mooney, Thomas Joseph, Dec. 8, 1882–Mar. 6, 1942.
Supp. 3–531
Mooney, William, 1756–Nov. 27, 1831.
Vol. 7, Pt. 1–111
Moore, Addison Webster, July 10, 1866–Aug. 25, 1930.
Vol. 7, Pt. 1–111
Moore, Alfred, May 21, 1755–Oct. 15, 1810.
Vol. 7, Pt. 1–112
Moore, Andrew, 1752–May 24, 1821.
Vol. 7, Pt. 1–113
Moore, Anne Carroll, July 12, 1871–Jan. 20, 1961.
Supp. 7–550
Moore, Annie Aubertine Woodward, Sept. 27, 1841–Sept. 22, 1929.
Vol. 7, Pt. 1–114
Moore, (Austin) Merrill, Sept. 11, 1903–Sept. 20, 1957.
Supp. 6–461
Moore, Bartholomew Figures, Jan. 29, 1801–Nov. 27, 1878.
Vol. 7, Pt. 1–114
Moore, Benjamin, Oct. 5, 1748–Feb. 27, 1816.
Vol. 7, Pt. 1–115
Moore, Charles, Oct. 20, 1855–Sept. 25, 1942.
Supp. 3–533
Moore, Charles Herbert, Apr 10, 1840–Feb 15, 1930.
Vol. 7, Pt. 1–116
Moore, Clarence Lemuel Elisha, May 12, 1876–Dec. 5, 1931.
Vol. 7, Pt. 1–117
Moore, Clement Clarke, July 15, 1779–July 10, 1863.
Vol. 7, Pt. 1–118
Moore, Clifford Herschel, Mar. 11, 1866–Aug. 31, 1931.
Vol. 7, Pt. 1–119
Moore, Edward Mott, July 15, 1814–Mar. 3, 1902.
Vol. 7, Pt. 1–119
Moore, Edwin Ward, June 1810–Oct. 5, 1865.
Vol. 7, Pt. 1–120
Moore, Eliakim Hastings, Jan. 26, 1862–Dec. 30, 1932.
Supp. 1–561
Moore, Ely, July 4, 1798–Jan. 27, 1860.
Vol. 7, Pt. 1–121
Moore, Frank, Dec. 17, 1828–Aug. 10, 1904.
Vol. 7, Pt. 1–122
Moore, Frederick Randolph, June 16, 1857–Mar. 1, 1943.
Supp. 3–534
Moore, Gabriel 1785?–June 9, 1845?.
Vol. 7, Pt. 1–122
Moore, George Fleming, July 17, 1822–Aug. 30, 1883.
Vol. 7, Pt. 1–123
Moore, George Foot, Oct. 15, 1851–May 16, 1931.
Vol. 7, Pt. 1–124
Moore, George Henry, Apr. 20, 1823–May 5, 1892.
Vol. 7, Pt. 1–125
Moore, Grace, Dec. 5, 1901–Jan. 26, 1947.
Supp. 4–596
Moore, Sir Henry, Feb. 7, 1713–Sept. 11, 1769.
Vol. 7, Pt. 1–126
Moore, Henry Ludwell, Nov. 21, 1869–Apr. 28, 1958.
Supp. 6–458
Moore, Hugh Everett, Apr. 27, 1887–Nov. 25, 1972.
Supp. 9–556
Moore, Jacob Bailey, Oct. 31, 1797–Sept. 1, 1853.
Vol. 7, Pt. 1–127
Moore, James, d. 1706.
Vol. 7, Pt. 1–127
Moore, James, 1737–April 1777.
Vol. 7, Pt. 1–128
Moore, James, 1764–June 22, 1814.
Vol. 7, Pt. 1–129
Moore, James Edward, Mar. 2, 1852–Nov. 2, 1918.
Vol. 7, Pt. 1–129
Moore, John, *c.* 1659–Dec. 2, 1732.
Vol. 7, Pt. 1–130
Moore, John, June 24, 1834–July 30, 1901.
Vol. 7, Pt. 1–131
Moore, John Bassett, Dec. 3, 1860–Nov. 12, 1947.
Supp. 4–597
Moore, John Trotwood, Aug. 26, 1858–May 10, 1929.
Vol. 7, Pt. 1–132
Moore, John Weeks, Apr. 11, 1807–Mar. 23, 1889.
Vol. 7, Pt. 1–133
Moore, Joseph Earle, July 9, 1892–Dec. 6, 1957.
Supp. 6–460
Moore, Joseph Haines, Sept. 7, 1878–Mar. 15, 1949.
Supp. 4–600
Moore, Marianne Craig, Nov. 15, 1887–Feb. 5, 1972.
Supp. 9–557
Moore, Maurice, 1735–1777.
Vol. 7, Pt. 1–133
Moore, Nathaniel Fish, Dec. 25, 1782–Apr. 27, 1872.
Vol. 7, Pt. 1–134
Moore, Nicholas. [*See* More, Nicholas, d. 1689.]
Moore, Philip North, July 8, 1849–Jan. 19, 1930.
Vol. 7, Pt. 1–135
Moore, Richard Bishop, May 6, 1871–Jan. 20, 1931.
Vol. 7, Pt. 1–136
Moore, Richard Channing, Aug. 21, 1762–Nov. 11, 1841.
Vol. 7, Pt. 1–136
Moore, Samuel Preston, 1813–May 31, 1889.
Vol. 7, Pt. 1–137
Moore, Thomas Overton, Apr. 10, 1804–June 25, 1876.
Vol. 7, Pt. 1–138
Moore, Thomas Patrick, 1796?–July 21, 1853.
Vol. 7, Pt. 1–139
Moore, Veranus Alva, Apr. 13, 1859–Feb. 11, 1931.
Vol. 7, Pt. 1–140
Moore, Victor Frederick, Feb. 24, 1876–July 23, 1962.
Supp. 7–551
Moore, William, May 6, 1699–May 30, 1783.
Vol. 7, Pt. 1–141
Moore, William, *c.* 1735–July 24, 1793.
Vol. 7, Pt. 1–142
Moore, William Henry, Oct. 25, 1848–Jan. 11, 1923.
Vol. 7, Pt. 1–142
Moore, William Thomas, Aug. 27, 1832–Sept. 7, 1926.
Vol. 7, Pt. 1–145
Moore, Zephaniah Swift, Nov. 20, 1770–June 30, 1823.
Vol. 7, Pt. 1–146
Moorehead, Agnes, Dec. 6, 1906–Apr. 30, 1974.
Supp. 9–559
Moorehead, William Gallogly, Mar. 19, 1836–Mar. 1, 1914.
Vol. 7, Pt. 1–147
Moorhead, James Kennedy, Sept. 7, 1806–Mar. 6, 1884.
Vol. 7, Pt. 1–147

Moosmüller, Oswald William, Feb. 26, 1832–Jan. 10, 1901.
Vol. 7, Pt. 1–148
Morais, Sabato, Apr. 13, 1823–Nov. 11, 1897.
Vol. 7, Pt. 1–149
Moran, Benjamin, Aug. 1, 1820–June 20, 1886.
Vol. 7, Pt. 1–150
Moran, Daniel Edward, Apr. 12, 1864–July 3, 1937.
Supp. 2–469
Moran, Edward, Aug. 19, 1829–June 9, 1901.
Vol. 7, Pt. 1–151
Moran, Eugene Francis, Mar. 24, 1872–Apr. 13, 1961.
Supp. 7–552
Moran, Peter, Mar. 4, 1841–Nov. 9, 1914.
Vol. 7, Pt. 1–152
Moran, Thomas, Jan. 12, 1837–Aug. 26, 1926.
Vol. 7, Pt. 1–152
Morawetz, Victor, Apr. 3, 1859–May 18, 1938.
Supp. 2–470
Mordecai, Alfred, Jan. 3, 1804–Oct. 23, 1887.
Vol. 7, Pt. 1–153
Mordecai, Moses Cohen, Feb. 19, 1804–Dec. 30, 1888.
Vol. 7, Pt. 1–154
More, Nicholas, d. 1689.
Vol. 7, Pt. 1–155
More, Paul Elmer, Dec. 12, 1864–Mar. 9, 1937.
Supp. 2–471
Moreau de Saint-Méry, Médéric-Louis-Élie, Jan. 13, 1750–Jan 28, 1819.
Vol. 7, Pt. 1–156
Moreau-Lislet, Louis Casimir Elisabeth, 1767–Dec. 3, 1832.
Vol. 7, Pt. 1–157
Moreell, Ben, Sept. 4, 1892–July 30, 1978.
Supp. 10–549
Morehead, Charles Slaughter, July 7, 1802–Dec. 21, 1868.
Vol. 7, Pt. 1–157
Morehead, James Turner, May 24, 1797–Dec. 28, 1854.
Vol. 7, Pt. 1–158
Morehead, John Motley, Nov. 3, 1870–Jan. 7, 1965.
Supp. 7–553
Morehead, John Motley, July 4, 1796–Aug. 27, 1866.
Vol. 7, Pt. 1–159
Morehouse, Henry Lyman, Oct. 2, 1834–May 5, 1917.
Vol. 7, Pt. 1–159
Morehouse, Ward, Nov. 24, 1899–Dec. 8, 1966.
Supp. 8–443
Morell, George Webb, Jan. 8, 1815–Feb. 11, 1883.
Vol. 7, Pt. 1–160
Morey, Samuel, Oct. 23, 1762–Apr. 17, 1843.
Vol. 7, Pt. 1–161
Morfit, Campbell, Nov. 19, 1820–Dec. 8, 1897.
Vol. 7, Pt. 1–162
Morford, Henry, Mar. 10, 1823–Aug. 4, 1881.
Vol. 7, Pt. 1–162
Morgan, Abel, 1673–Dec. 16, 1722.
Vol. 7, Pt. 1–163
Morgan, Anne, July 25, 1873–Jan. 29, 1952.
Supp. 5–505
Morgan, Arthur Ernest, June 20, 1878–Nov. 16, 1975.
Supp. 9–560
Morgan, Charles, Apr. 21, 1795–May 8, 1878.
Vol. 7, Pt. 1–164
Morgan, Charles Hill, Jan. 8, 1831–Jan. 10, 1911.
Vol. 7, Pt. 1–165
Morgan, Daniel, 1736–July 6, 1802.
Vol. 7, Pt. 1–166
Morgan, Edwin Barber, May 2, 1806–Oct. 13, 1881.
Vol. 7, Pt. 1–167
Morgan, Edwin Denison, Feb. 8, 1811–Feb. 14, 1883.
Vol. 7, Pt. 1–168
Morgan, Edwin Vernon, Feb. 22, 1865–Apr. 16, 1934.
Supp. 1–563
Morgan, George Washington, Sept. 20, 1820–July 26, 1893.
Vol. 7, Pt. 1–170
Morgan, George, Feb. 14, 1743–Mar. 10, 1810.
Vol. 7, Pt. 1–169
Morgan, Helen, Aug. 2, 1900–Oct. 8, 1941.
Supp. 3–535
Morgan, James Dada, Aug. 1, 1810–Sept. 12, 1896.
Vol. 7, Pt. 1–171
Morgan, James Morris, Mar. 10, 1845–Apr. 21, 1928.
Vol. 7, Pt 1–172
Morgan, John, June 10, 1735–Oct. 15, 1789.
Vol. 7, Pt. 1–172
Morgan, John Harcourt Alexander, Aug. 31, 1867–Aug. 25, 1950.
Supp. 4–601
Morgan, John Hunt, June 1, 1825–Sept. 4, 1864.
Vol. 7, Pt. 1–174
Morgan, John Pierpont, Apr. 17, 1837–Mar. 31, 1913.
Vol. 7, Pt. 1–175
Morgan, John Pierpont, Sept. 7, 1867–Mar. 13, 1943.
Supp. 3–537
Morgan, John Tyler, June 20, 1824–June 11, 1907.
Vol. 7, Pt. 1–180
Morgan, Julia, Jan. 26, 1872–Feb. 2, 1957.
Supp. 6–462
Morgan, Junius Spencer, Apr. 14, 1813–Apr. 8, 1890.
Vol. 7, Pt. 1–181
Morgan, Justin, 1747–Mar. 22, 1798.
Vol. 7, Pt. 1–182
Morgan, Lewis Henry, Nov. 21, 1818–Dec. 17, 1881.
Vol. 7, Pt. 1–183
Morgan, Matthew Somerville, Apr. 27, 1839–June 2, 1890.
Vol. 7, Pt. 1–185
Morgan, Morris Hicky, Feb. 8, 1859–Mar. 16, 1910.
Vol. 7, Pt. 1–186
Morgan, Philip Hicky, Nov. 9, 1825–Aug. 12, 1900.
Vol. 7, Pt. 1–187
Morgan, Thomas Hunt, Sept. 25, 1866–Dec. 4, 1945.
Supp. 3–538
Morgan, Thomas Jefferson, Aug. 17, 1839–July 13, 1902.
Vol. 7, Pt. 1–187
Morgan, William, Aug. 7, 1774?–1826?.
Vol. 7, Pt. 1–188
Morgenthau, Hans Joachim, Feb. 17, 1904–July 19, 1980.
Supp. 10–551
Morgenthau, Henry, Apr. 26, 1856–Nov. 25, 1946.
Supp. 4–602
Morgenthau, Henry, Jr., May 11, 1891–Feb. 6, 1967.
Supp. 8–445
Moriarity, Patrick Eugene, July 4, 1804–July 10, 1875.
Vol. 7, Pt. 1–189
Morini, Austin John, Mar. 4, 1826–July 29, 1909.
Vol. 7, Pt. 1–190
Morison, George Shattuck, Dec. 19, 1842–July 1, 1903.
Vol. 7, Pt. 1–191
Morison, Samuel Eliot, July 9, 1887–May 15, 1976.
Supp. 10–553
Morley, Christopher Darlington, May 5, 1890–Mar. 28, 1957.
Supp. 6–464
Morley, Edward Williams, Jan. 29, 1838–Feb. 24, 1923.
Vol. 7, Pt. 1–192
Morley, Frank, Sept. 9, 1860–Oct. 17, 1937.
Supp. 2–473
Morley, Margaret Warner, Feb. 17, 1858–Dec. 12, 1923.
Vol. 7, Pt. 1–193
Morley, Sylvanus Griswold, June 7, 1883–Sept. 2, 1948.
Supp. 4–605
Morón, Alonzo Graseano, Apr. 12, 1909–Oct. 31, 1971.
Supp. 9–562
Morphy, Paul Charles, June 22, 1837–July 10, 1884.
Vol. 7, Pt. 1–193
Morrell, Benjamin, July 5, 1795–1839.
Vol. 7, Pt. 1–195
Morril, David Lawrence, June 10, 1772–Jan. 28, 1849.
Vol. 7, Pt. 1–195
Morrill, Anson Peaslee, June 10, 1803–July 4, 1887.
Vol. 6, Pt. 2–196
Morrill, Edmund Needham, Feb. 12, 1834–Mar. 14, 1909.
Vol. 7, Pt. 1–197
Morrill, Justin Smith, Apr. 14, 1810–Dec. 28, 1898.
Vol. 7, Pt. 1–198
Morrill, Lot Myrick, May 3, 1812–Jan. 10, 1883.
Vol. 7, Pt. 1–199
Morris, Anthony, Aug. 23, 1654–Oct. 23, 1721.
Vol. 7, Pt. 1–200
Morris, Anthony, Feb. 10, 1766–Nov. 3, 1860.
Vol. 7, Pt. 1–201
Morris, Cadwalader, Apr. 19, 1741 o.s.-Jan. 25, 1795.
Vol. 7, Pt. 1–201
Morris, Caspar, May 2, 1805–Mar. 17, 1884.
Vol. 7, Pt. 1–202

Morris, Charles, July 26, 1784–Jan. 27, 1856.
Vol. 7, Pt. 1–202
Morris, Clara, Mar. 17, 1848–Nov. 20, 1925.
Vol. 7, Pt. 1–203
Morris, Edmund, Aug. 28, 1804–May 4, 1874.
Vol. 7, Pt. 1–204
Morris, Edward Dafydd, Oct. 31, 1825–Nov. 21, 1915.
Vol. 7, Pt. 1–205
Morris, Edward Joy, July 16, 1815–Dec. 31, 1881.
Vol. 7, Pt. 1–206
Morris, Elizabeth, *c.* 1753–Apr. 17, 1826.
Vol. 7, Pt. 1–206
Morris, George Pope, Oct. 10, 1802–July 6, 1864.
Vol. 7, Pt. 1–207
Morris, George Sylvester, Nov. 15, 1840–Mar. 23, 1889.
Vol. 7, Pt. 1–208
Morris, Gouverneur, Jan. 31, 1752–Nov. 6, 1816.
Vol. 7, Pt. 1–209
Morris, John Gottlieb, Nov. 14, 1803–Oct. 10, 1895.
Vol. 7, Pt. 1–212
Morris, Lewis, Oct. 15, 1671–May 21, 1746.
Vol. 7, Pt. 1–213
Morris, Lewis, Apr. 8, 1726–Jan. 22, 1798.
Vol. 7, Pt. 1–214
Morris, Lewis Richard, Nov. 2, 1760–Dec. 29, 1825.
Vol. 7, Pt. 1–215
Morris, Luzon Burritt, Apr. 16, 1827–Aug. 22, 1895.
Vol. 7, Pt. 1–216
Morris, Mary Philipse, 1730–1825. [*See* Morris, Roger, 1727–1794]
Morris, Nelson, Jan. 21, 1838–Aug. 27, 1907.
Vol. 7, Pt. 1–217
Morris, Mrs. Owen. [*See* Morris, Elizabeth, *c.* 1753–1826.]
Morris, Richard, Aug. 15, 1730–Apr. 11, 1810.
Vol. 7, Pt. 1–218
Morris, Richard Valentine, Mar. 8, 1768–May 13, 1815.
Vol. 7, Pt. 1–219
Morris, Robert, Jan. 31, 1734–May 8, 1806.
Vol. 7, Pt. 1–219
Morris, Robert, *c.* 1745–June 2, 1815.
Vol. 7, Pt. 1–223
Morris, Robert, Aug. 31, 1818–July 31, 1888.
Vol. 7, Pt. 1–224
Morris, Robert Hunter, *c.* 1700–Jan. 27, 1764.
Vol. 7, Pt. 1–225
Morris, Roger, Jan. 28, 1727–Sept. 13, 1794.
Vol. 7, Pt. 1–226
Morris, Thomas, Jan. 3, 1776–Dec. 7, 1844.
Vol. 7, Pt. 1–226
Morris, Thomas Armstrong, Dec. 26, 1811–Mar. 22, 1904.
Vol. 7, Pt. 1–227
Morris, William Hopkins, Apr. 22, 1827–Aug. 26, 1900.
Vol. 7, Pt. 1–228
Morrison, Delesseps Story, Jan. 18, 1912–May 22, 1964.
Supp. 7–555
Morrison, Frank, Nov. 23, 1859–Mar. 12, 1949.
Supp. 4–606
Morrison, Jim, Dec. 8, 1943–July 3, 1971.
Supp. 9–563
Morrison, John Irwin, July 25, 1806–July 17, 1882.
Vol. 7, Pt. 1–229
Morrison, Nathan Jackson, Nov. 25, 1828–Apr. 12, 1907.
Vol. 7, Pt. 1–230
Morrison, William McCutchan, Nov. 10, 1867–Mar. 14, 1918.
Vol. 7, Pt. 1–231
Morrison, William Ralls, Sept. 14, 1824?–Sept. 29, 1909.
Vol. 7, Pt. 1–232
Morrison, William, Mar. 14, 1763–Apr. 19, 1837.
Vol. 7, Pt. 1–290
Morrissey, John, Feb. 12, 1831–May 1, 1878.
Vol. 7, Pt. 1–293
Morrow, Dwight Whitney, Jan. 11, 1873–Oct. 5, 1931.
Vol. 7, Pt. 1–234
Morrow, Edwin Porch, Nov. 30, 1877–June 15, 1935.
Supp. 1–564
Morrow, Jeremiah, Oct. 6, 1771–Mar. 22, 1852.
Vol. 7, Pt. 1–235
Morrow, Prince Albert, Dec. 19, 1846–Mar. 17, 1913.
Vol. 7, Pt. 1–236
Morrow, Thomas Vaughan, Apr. 14, 1804–July 16, 1850.
Vol. 7, Pt. 1–237
Morrow, William W., July 15, 1843–July 24, 1929.
Vol. 7, Pt. 1–238
Morse, Anson Daniel, Aug. 13, 1846–Mar. 13, 1916.
Vol. 7, Pt. 1–239
Morse, Charles Wyman, Oct. 21, 1856–Jan. 12, 1933.
Vol. 7, Pt. 1–239
Morse, Edward Sylvester, June 18, 1838–Dec. 20, 1925.
Vol. 7, Pt. 1–242
Morse, Freeman Harlow, Feb. 18, 1807–Feb. 6, 1891.
Vol. 7, Pt. 1–243
Morse, Harmon Northrop, Oct. 15, 1848–Sept. 8, 1920.
Vol. 7, Pt. 1–243
Morse, Henry Dutton, Apr. 20, 1826–Jan. 2, 1888.
Vol. 7 Pt. 1–244
Morse, Jedidiah, Aug. 23, 1761–June 9, 1826.
Vol. 7, Pt. 1–245
Morse, John Lovett, Apr. 21, 1865–Apr. 3, 1940.
Supp. 2–474
Morse, John Torrey, Jan. 9, 1840–Mar. 27, 1937.
Supp. 2–475
Morse, Samuel Finley Breese, Apr. 27, 1791–Apr. 2, 1872.
Vol. 7, Pt. 1–247
Morse, Sidney Edwards, Feb. 7, 1794–Dec. 23, 1871.
Vol. 7, Pt. 1–251
Morse, Wayne Lyman, Oct. 20, 1900–July 22, 1974.
Supp. 9–565
Mortimer, Charles Greenough, July 26, 1900–Dec. 25, 1978.
Supp. 10–554
Mortimer, Mary, Dec. 2, 1816–July 14, 1877.
Vol. 7, Pt. 1–252
Morton, Charles, *c.* 1627–Apr. 11, 1698.
Vol. 7, Pt. 1–253
Morton, Charles Gould, Jan. 15, 1861–July 18, 1933.
Supp. 1–564
Morton, Charles Walter, Feb. 10, 1899–Sept. 23, 1967.
Supp. 8–447
Morton, Ferdinand Joseph ("Jelly Roll"), Sept. 20, 1885?–July 10, 1941.
Supp. 3–541
Morton, Ferdinand Quintin, Sept. 9, 1881–Nov. 8, 1949.
Supp. 4–607
Morton, George, 1585–June 1624.
Vol. 7, Pt. 1–254
Morton, Henry, Dec. 11, 1836–May 9, 1902.
Vol. 7, Pt. 1–254
Morton, James St. Clair, Sept. 24, 1829–June 17, 1864.
Vol. 7, Pt. 1–255
Morton, Jelly Roll. [*See* Morton, Ferdinand Joseph, 1885?–1941.]
Morton, John, *c.* 1724–April 1777.
Vol. 7, Pt. 1–256
Morton, Julius Sterling, Apr. 22, 1832–Apr. 27, 1902.
Vol. 7, Pt. 1–257
Morton, Levi Parsons, May 16, 1824–May 16, 1920.
Vol. 7, Pt. 1–258
Morton, Marcus, Feb. 19, 1784–Feb. 6, 1864.
Vol. 7, Pt. 1–259
Morton, Marcus, Apr. 8, 1819–Feb. 10, 1891.
Vol. 7, Pt. 1–260
Morton, Nathaniel, 1613–June 29, 1685 o.s.
Vol. 7, Pt. 1–261
Morton, Oliver Perry, Aug. 4, 1823–Nov. 1, 1877.
Vol. 7, Pt. 1–262
Morton, Paul, May 22, 1857–Jan. 19, 1911.
Vol. 7, Pt. 1–264
Morton, Robert Russa, Aug. 26, 1867–May 31, 1940.
Supp. 2–476
Morton, Rogers Clark Ballard, Sept. 19, 1914–Apr. 19, 1979.
Supp. 10–556
Morton, Samuel George, Jan. 26, 1799–May 15, 1851.
Vol. 7, Pt. 1–265
Morton, Sarah Wentworth Apthorp, 1759–May 14, 1846.
Vol. 7, Pt. 1–266
Morton, Thomas, fl. 1622–1647.
Vol. 7, Pt. 1–267
Morton, William Thomas Green, Aug. 9, 1819–July 15, 1868.
Vol. 7, Pt. 1–268
Morton, William James, July 3, 1845–Mar. 26, 1920.
Vol. 7, Pt. 1–267
Morwitz, Edward, June 11, 1815–Dec. 13, 1893.
Vol. 7, Pt. 1–271

Mosby, John Singleton, Dec. 6, 1833–May 30, 1916.
Vol. 7, Pt. 1–272
Moscone, George Richard, Nov. 24, 1929–Nov. 27, 1978.
Supp. 10–558
Moscoso de Alvarado, Luis de, fl. 1530–1543.
Vol. 7, Pt. 1–273
Moseley, Edward Augustus, Mar. 23, 1846–Apr. 18, 1911.
Vol. 7, Pt. 1–274
Mosely, Philip Edward, Sept. 21, 1905–Jan. 13, 1972.
Supp. 9–567
Moser, Christopher Otto, May 29, 1885–July 11, 1935.
Supp. 1–565
Moses, Anna Mary Robertson ("Grandma"), Sept. 7, 1860–Dec. 13, 1961.
Supp. 7–556
Moses, Bernard, Aug. 27, 1846–Mar. 4, 1930.
Vol. 7, Pt. 1–274
Moses, Franklin J., 1838–Dec. 11, 1906.
Vol. 7, Pt. 1–275
Moses, George Higgins, Feb. 9, 1869–Dec. 20, 1944.
Supp. 3–542
Moses, Montrose Jonas, Sept. 2, 1878–Mar. 29, 1934.
Supp. 1–566
Mosessohn, David Nehemiah, Jan. 1, 1883–Dec. 16, 1930.
Vol. 7, Pt. 1–276
Mosher, Eliza Maria, Oct. 2, 1846–Oct. 16, 1928.
Vol. 7, Pt. 1–277
Mosher, Thomas Bird, Sept. 11, 1852–Aug. 31, 1923.
Vol. 7, Pt. 1–278
Moskowitz, Belle Lindner Israels, Oct. 5, 1877–Jan. 2, 1933.
Supp. 1–567
Mosler, Henry, June 6, 1841–Apr. 21, 1920.
Vol. 7, Pt. 1–279
Moss, Frank, Mar. 16, 1860–June 5, 1920.
Vol. 7, Pt. 1–279
Moss, John Calvin, Jan. 5, 1838–Apr. 8, 1892.
Vol. 7, Pt. 1–280
Moss, Lemuel, Dec. 27, 1829–July 12, 1904.
Vol. 7, Pt. 1–281
Moss, Sanford Alexander, Aug. 23, 1872–Nov. 10, 1946.
Supp. 4–608
Most, Johann Joseph, Feb. 5, 1846–Mar. 17, 1906.
Vol. 7, Pt. 1–282
Mostel, Samuel Joel ("Zero"), Feb. 28, 1915–Sept. 8, 1977.
Supp. 10–559
Motley, John Lothrop, Apr. 15, 1814–May 29, 1877.
Vol. 7, Pt. 1–282
Motley, Willard Francis, July 14, 1909–Mar. 4, 1965.
Supp. 7–557
Mott, Charles Stewart, June 2, 1875–Feb. 2, 1973.
Supp. 9–567
Mott, Frank Luther, Apr. 4, 1886–Oct. 23, 1964.
Supp. 7–559
Mott, Gershom, Apr. 7, 1822–Nov. 29, 1884.
Vol. 7, Pt. 1–287
Mott, James, June 20, 1788–Jan. 26, 1868.
Vol. 7, Pt. 1–288
Mott, John R., May 25, 1865–Jan. 31, 1955.
Supp. 5–506
Mott, Lucretia Coffin, Jan. 3, 1793–Nov. 11, 1880.
Vol. 7, Pt. 1–288
Mott, Valentine, Aug. 20, 1785–Apr. 26, 1865.
Vol. 7, Pt. 1–290
Moulton, Ellen Louise Chandler, Apr. 10, 1835–Aug. 10, 1908.
Vol. 7, Pt. 1–291
Moulton, Forest Ray, Apr. 29, 1872–Dec. 7, 1952.
Supp. 5–508
Moulton, Richard Green, May 5, 1849–Aug. 15, 1924.
Vol. 7, Pt. 1–291
Moultrie, John, Jan. 18, 1729–Mar. 19, 1798.
Vol. 7, Pt. 1–292
Moultrie, William, Nov. 23/Dec. 4, 1730–Sept. 27, 1805.
Vol. 7, Pt. 1–293
Mount, William Sidney, Nov. 26, 1807–Nov. 19, 1868.
Vol. 7, Pt. 1–294
Mourt, George. [*See* Morton, George, 1585–1624.]
Mouton, Alexander, Nov. 19, 1804–Feb. 12, 1885.
Vol. 7, Pt. 1–295
Mowatt, Anna Cora Ogden, Mar. 5, 1819–July 21, 1870.
Vol. 7, Pt. 1–295
Mowbray, George Mordey, May 5, 1814–June 21, 1891.
Vol. 7, Pt. 1–297
Mowbray, Henry Siddons, Aug. 5, 1858–Jan. 13, 1928.
Vol. 7, Pt. 1–298
Mower, Joseph Anthony, Aug. 22, 1827–Jan. 6, 1870.
Vol. 7, Pt. 1–299
Mowrer, Edgar Ansel, Mar. 8, 1892–Mar. 2, 1977.
Supp. 10–562
Mowry, William Augustus, Aug. 13, 1829–May 22, 1917.
Vol. 7, Pt. 1–300
Moxham, Arthur James, Sept. 19, 1854–May 16, 1931.
Vol. 7, Pt. 1–301
Moxom, Philip Stafford, Aug. 10, 1848–Aug. 13, 1923.
Vol. 7, Pt. 1–301
Moylan, Stephen, 1737–Apr. 13, 1811.
Vol. 7, Pt. 1–302
Mozier, Joseph, Aug. 22, 1812–Oct. 3, 1870.
Vol. 7, Pt. 1–303
Mudd, Samuel A. [*See* Booth, John Wilkes, 1838–1865.]
Mudge, Enoch, June 28, 1776–Apr. 2, 1850.
Vol. 7, Pt. 1–304
Mudge, James, Apr. 5, 1844–May 7, 1918.
Vol. 7, Pt. 1–305
Muhammad, Elijah, Oct. 7, 1897–Feb. 25, 1975.
Supp. 9–569
Muhlenberg, Frederick Augustus, Aug. 25, 1818–Mar. 21, 1901.
Vol. 7, Pt. 1–306
Muhlenberg, Frederick Augustus Conrad, Jan. 1, 1750–June 4, 1801.
Vol. 7, Pt. 1–307
Muhlenberg, Gotthilf Henry Ernest, Nov. 17, 1753–May 23, 1815.
Vol. 7, Pt. 1–308
Mühlenberg, Henry Augustus Philip, May 13, 1782–Aug. 11, 1844.
Vol. 7, Pt. 1–309
Muhlenberg, Henry Melchior, Sept. 6, 1711–Oct. 7, 1787.
Vol. 7, Pt. 1–310
Muhlenberg, John Peter Gabriel, Oct. 1, 1746–Oct. 1, 1807.
Vol. 7, Pt. 1–311
Mühlenberg, William Augustus, Sept. 16, 1796–Apr. 8, 1877.
Vol. 7, Pt. 1–313
Muir, Charles Henry, July 18, 1860–Dec. 8. 1933.
Supp. 1–568
Muir, John, Apr. 21, 1838–Dec. 24, 1914.
Vol. 7, Pt. 1–314
Muldoon, William, May 25, 1852–June 3, 1933.
Supp. 1–569
Mulford, Clarence Edward, Feb. 3, 1883–May 10, 1956.
Supp. 6–466
Mulford, Elisha, Nov. 19, 1833–Dec. 9, 1885.
Vol. 7, Pt. 1–317
Mulford, Prentice, Apr. 5, 1834–*c.* May 27, 1891.
Vol. 7, Pt. 1–317
Mulholland, St. Clair Augustin, Apr. 1, 1839–Feb. 17, 1910.
Vol. 7, Pt. 1–318
Mulholland, William, Sept. 11, 1855–July 22, 1935.
Supp. 1–569
Mullan, John, July 31, 1830–Dec. 28, 1909.
Vol. 7, Pt. 1–319
Mullany, James Robert Madison, Oct. 26, 1818–Sept. 17, 1887.
Vol. 7, Pt. 1–320
Mullany, Patrick Francis. [*See* Azarias, Brother, 1847–1893.]
Müller, Hermann Joseph, Dec. 21, 1890–Apr. 5, 1967.
Supp. 8–448
Muller, Wilhelm Max, May 15, 1862–July 12, 1919.
Vol. 7, Pt. 1–320
Mulligan, Charles J., Sept. 28, 1866–Mar. 25, 1916.
Vol. 7, Pt. 1–321
Mulliken, Samuel Parsons, Dec. 19, 1864–Oct. 24, 1934.
Supp. 1–570
Mullin, Willard Harlan, Sept. 14, 1902–Dec. 21, 1978.
Supp. 10–563
Mullins, Edgar Young, Jan. 5, 1860–Nov. 23, 1928.
Vol. 7, Pt. 1–322
Mulry, Thomas Maurice, Feb. 13, 1855–Mar. 10, 1916.
Vol. 7, Pt. 1–323
Mumford, James Gregory, Dec. 2, 1863–Oct. 18, 1914.
Vol. 7, Pt. 1–324

Munch, Charles, Sept. 26, 1891–Nov. 6, 1968.
Supp. 8–450
Mundé, Paul Fortunatus, Sept. 7, 1846–Feb. 7, 1902.
Vol. 7, Pt. 1–325
Mundelein, George William, July 2, 1872–Oct. 2, 1939.
Supp. 2–477
Mundt, Karl Earl, June 3, 1900–Aug. 16, 1974.
Supp. 9–571
Munford, Robert, d. 1784.
Vol. 7, Pt. 1–325
Munford, William, Aug. 15, 1775–June 21, 1825.
Vol. 7, Pt. 1–326
Munger, Robert Sylvester, July 24, 1854–Apr. 20, 1923.
Vol. 7, Pt. 1–327
Munger, Theodore Thornton, Mar. 5, 1830–Jan. 11, 1910.
Vol. 7, Pt. 1–327
Muni, Paul, Sept. 22, 1895–Aug. 25, 1967.
Supp. 8–452
Munn, Orson Desaix, June 11, 1824–Feb. 28, 1907.
Vol. 7, Pt. 1–328
Muñoz Marín, Luis, Feb. 18, 1898–Apr. 30, 1980.
Supp. 10–564
Muñoz-Rivera, Luis, July 17, 1859–Nov. 15, 1916.
Vol. 7, Pt. 1–329
Munro, Dana Carleton, June 7, 1866–Jan. 13, 1933.
Vol. 7, Pt. 1–330
Munro, George, Nov. 12, 1825–Apr. 23, 1896.
Vol. 7, Pt. 1–331
Munro, Henry, 1730–May 30, 1801.
Vol. 7, Pt. 1–332
Munro, William Bennett, Jan. 5, 1875–Sept. 4, 1957.
Supp. 6–467
Munroe, Charles Edward, May 24, 1849–Dec. 7, 1938.
Supp. 2–479
Munsell, Joel, Apr. 14, 1808–Jan. 15, 1880.
Vol. 7, Pt. 1–333
Munsey, Frank Andrew, Aug. 21, 1854–Dec. 22, 1925.
Vol. 7, Pt. 1–334
Munson, Thomas Volney, Sept. 26, 1843–Jan. 21, 1913.
Vol. 7, Pt. 1–335
Munson, Thurman Lee, June 7, 1947–Aug. 2, 1979.
Supp. 10–566
Munson, Walter Davld, Feb. 18, 1843–Apr. 24, 1908.
Vol. 7, Pt. 1–336
Münsterberg, Hugo, June 1, 1863–Dec. 16, 1916.
Vol. 7, Pt. 1–337
Murat, Achille, Jan. 21, 1801–Apr. 15, 1847.
Vol. 7, Pt. 1–339
Murchison, Clinton Williams, Oct. 17, 1895–June 20, 1969.
Supp. 8–454
Murchison, John Dabney, Sept. 5, 1921–June 14, 1979.
Supp. 10–568
Murdoch, Frank Hitchcock, Mar. 11, 1843–Nov. 13, 1872.
Vol. 7, Pt. 1–340
Murdock, James, Feb. 16, 1776–Aug. 10, 1856.
Vol. 7, Pt. 1–342
Murdock, James Edward, Jan. 25, 1811–May 19, 1893.
Vol. 7, Pt. 1–341
Murdock, Joseph Ballard, Feb. 13, 1851–Mar. 20, 1931.
Vol. 7, Pt. 1–342
Murdock, Victor, Mar. 18, 1871–July 8, 1945.
Supp. 3–544
Murel, John A. [*See* Murrell, John A., fl. 1804–1844.]
Murfee, James Thomas, Sept. 13, 1833–Apr. 23. 1912.
Vol. 7, Pt. 1–343.
Murfree, Mary Noailles, Jan. 24, 1850–July 31, 1922.
Vol. 7, Pt. 1–344
Murietta (Murieta), Joaquin. [*See* Murrieta, Joaquin, *c.* 1832–1853.]
Murphey, Archibald De Bow, 1777?–Feb. 1, 1832.
Vol. 7, Pt. 1–345
Murphy, Audie Leon, June 20, 1924–May 28, 1971.
Supp. 9–574
Murphy, Charles Francis, June 20, 1858–Apr. 25, 1924.
Vol. 7, Pt. 1–346
Murphy, Dominic Ignatius, May 31, 1847–Apr. 13, 1930.
Vol. 7, Pt. 1–347
Murphy, Edgar Gardner, Aug. 31, 1869–June 23, 1913.
Vol. 7, Pt. 1–348
Murphy, Francis, Apr. 24, 1836–June 30, 1907.
Vol. 7, Pt. 1–349
Murphy, Frank, Apr. 13, 1890–July 19, 1949.
Supp. 4–610
Murphy, Franklin, Jan. 3, 1846–Feb. 24, 1920.
Vol. 7, Pt. 1–350
Murphy, Frederick E., Dec. 5, 1872–Feb. 14, 1940.
Supp. 2–480
Murphy, Gardner, July 8, 1895–Mar. 18, 1979.
Supp. 10–569
Murphy, Gerald Clery, Mar. 25, 1888–Oct. 17, 1964.
Supp. 7–560
Murphy, Henry Cruse, July 5, 1810–Dec. 1, 1882.
Vol. 7, Pt. 1–350
Murphy, Isaac, Oct. 16, 1802–Sept. 8, 1882.
Vol. 7, Pt. 1–352
Murphy, James Bumgardner, Aug. 4, 1884–Aug. 24, 1950.
Supp. 4–615
Murphy, John, Mar. 12, 1812–May 27, 1880.
Vol. 7, Pt. 1–352
Murphy, John Benjamin, Dec. 21, 1857–Aug. 11, 1916.
Vol. 7, Pt. 1–353
Murphy, John Francis, Dec. 11, 1853–Jan. 30, 1921.
Vol. 7, Pt. 1–354
Murphy, John W., Jan. 20, 1828–Sept. 27, 1874.
Vol. 7, Pt. 1–355
Murphy, Michael Charles, Feb. 28, 1861–June 4, 1913.
Vol. 7, Pt. 1–355
Murphy, Robert Daniel, Oct. 28, 1894–Jan. 9, 1978.
Supp. 10–571
Murphy, William Sumter, 1796?–July 13, 1844.
Vol. 7, Pt. 1–356
Murphy, William Walton, Apr. 3, 1816–June 8, 1886.
Vol. 7, Pt. 1–357
Murray, Alexander, July 12, 1754 or 1755–Oct. 6, 1821.
Vol. 7, Pt. 1–357
Murray, David, Oct. 15, 1830–Mar. 6, 1905.
Vol. 7, Pt. 1–358
Murray, James Edward, May 3, 1876–Mar. 23, 1961.
Supp. 7–561
Murray, James Ormsbee, Nov. 27, 1827–Mar. 27, 1899.
Vol. 7, Pt. 1–359
Murray, John, 1737–Oct. 11, 1808.
Vol. 7, Pt. 1–359
Murray, John, Dec. 10, 1741–Sept. 3, 1815.
Vol. 7, Pt. 1–360
Murray, John Gardner, Aug. 31, 1857–Oct. 3, 1929.
Vol. 7, Pt. 1–362
Murray, Joseph, *c.* 1694–Apr. 28, 1757.
Vol. 7, Pt. 1–363
Murray, Judith Sargent Stevens, May 1, 1751–July 6, 1820.
Vol. 7, Pt. 1–364
Murray, Lindley, June 7, 1745–Jan. 16, 1826.
Vol. 7, Pt. 1–365
Murray, Louise Shipman Welles, Jan. 2, 1854–Apr. 22, 1931.
Vol. 7, Pt. 1–366
Murray, Mae, May 10, 1889–Mar. 23, 1965.
Supp. 7–563
Murray, Philip, May 25, 1886–Nov. 9, 1952.
Supp. 5–509
Murray, Robert, 1721–July 22, 1786.
Vol. 7, Pt. 1–367
Murray, Thomas Edward, Oct. 21, 1860–July 21, 1929.
Vol. 7, Pt. 1–367
Murray, Thomas Edward, June 20, 1891–May 26, 1961.
Supp. 7–564
Murray, William Henry David, Nov. 21, 1869–Oct. 15, 1956.
Supp. 6–468
Murray, William Vans, Feb. 9, 1760–Dec. 11, 1803.
Vol. 7, Pt. 1–368
Murrell, John A., fl. 1804–1844.
Vol. 7, Pt. 1–369
Murrieta, Joaquin, *c.* 1832–July 25, 1853.
Vol. 7, Pt. 1–370
Murrow, Edward (Egbert) Roscoe, Apr. 25, 1908–Apr. 27, 1965.
Supp. 7–565
Murrow, Joseph Samuel, June 7, 1835–Sept. 8, 1929.
Vol. 7, Pt. 1–370
Murtaugh, Daniel Edward ("Danny"), Oct. 8, 1917–Dec. 2, 1976.
Supp. 10–573

Muse, Clarence, Oct. 7, 1889–Oct. 13, 1979.
Supp. 10–575
Musica, Philip Mariano Fausto, May 12, 1884–Dec. 16, 1938.
Supp. 2–480
Musin, Ovide, Sept. 22, 1854–Nov. 24, 1929.
Vol. 7, Pt. 1–371
Musmanno, Michael Angelo, Apr. 7, 1897–Oct. 12, 1968.
Supp. 8–455
Mussey, Ellen Spencer, May 13, 1850–Apr. 21, 1936.
Supp. 2–482
Mussey, Reuben Dimond, June 23, 1780–June 21, 1866.
Vol. 7, Pt. 1–372
Muste, Abraham Johannes, Jan. 8, 1885–Feb. 11, 1967.
Supp. 8–457
Muybridge, Eadweard, Apr. 9, 1830–May 8, 1904.
Vol. 7, Pt. 1–373
Muzzey, David Saville, Oct. 9, 1870–Apr. 14, 1965.
Supp. 7–567
Myer, Albert James, Sept. 20, 1829–Aug. 24, 1880.
Vol. 7, Pt. 1–374
Myers, Abraham Charles, May ?, 1811–June 20, 1889.
Vol. 7, Pt. 1–375
Myers, Gustavus, Mar. 20, 1872–Dec. 7, 1942.
Supp. 3–545
Myers, Jerome, Mar. 20, 1867–June 19, 1940.
Supp. 2–483
Myerson, Abraham, Nov. 23, 1881–Sept. 3, 1948.
Supp. 4–617
Myles, John, *c.* 1621–Feb. 3, 1683.
Vol. 7, Pt. 1–376
Myrick, Herbert, Aug. 20, 1860–July 6, 1927.
Vol. 7, Pt. 1–376

Nabokov, Nicolas, Apr. 17, 1903–Apr. 6, 1978.
Supp. 10–579
Nabokov, Vladimir Vladimirovich, Apr. 23, 1899–July 2, 1977.
Supp. 10–580
Nack, James M., Jan. 4, 1809–Sept. 23, 1879.
Vol. 7, Pt. 1–377
Nadal, Ehrman Syme, Feb. 13, 1843–July 26, 1922.
Vol. 7, Pt. 1–378
Nadelman, Elie, Feb. 20, 1882–Dec. 28, 1946.
Supp. 4–618
Nagel, Conrad, Mar. 16, 1897–Feb. 24, 1970.
Supp. 8–459
Nairne, Thomas, d. April 1715.
Vol. 7, Pt. 1–379
Naish, Joseph Carrol, Jan. 21, 1897–Jan. 24, 1973.
Supp. 9–577
Naismith, James, Nov. 6, 1861–Nov. 28, 1939.
Supp. 2–484
Nancrède, Charles Beylard Guérard de, Dec. 10, 1847–Apr. 12, 1921.
Vol. 7, Pt. 1–379
Nancrède, Paul Joseph Guérard de, Mar. 16, 1761–Dec. 15, 1841.
Vol. 7, Pt. 1–380
Nanuntenoo. [*See* Canonchet, d. 1676.]
Napton, William Barclay, Mar. 23, 1808–Jan. 8, 1883.
Vol. 7, Pt. 1–381
Narváez, Panfilo de, *c.* 1478–1528.
Vol. 7, Pt. 1–382
Nasby, Petroleum V. [*See* Locke, David Ross, 1833–1888]
Nash, Abner, *c.* 1740–Dec. 2, 1786.
Vol. 7, Pt. 1–383
Nash, Arthur, June 26, 1870–Oct. 30, 1927.
Vol. 7, Pt. 1–384
Nash, Charles Sumner, Feb. 18, 1856–Nov. 22, 1926.
Vol. 7, Pt. 1–385
Nash, Charles Williams, Jan. 28, 1864–June 6, 1948.
Supp. 4–620
Nash, Daniel, May 28, 1763–June 4, 1836.
Vol. 7, Pt. 1–386
Nash, Francis, *c.* 1742–Oct. 7, 1777.
Vol. 7, Pt. 1–386
Nash, Frederick, Feb. 19, 1781–Dec. 4, 1858.
Vol. 7, Pt. 1–387
Nash, Frederick Ogden, Aug. 19, 1902–May 19, 1971.
Supp. 9–578
Nash, Henry Sylvester, Dec. 23, 1854–Nov. 6, 1912.
Vol. 7, Pt. 1–388
Nash, John Henry, Mar. 12, 1871–May 24, 1947.
Supp. 4–621
Nash, Simeon, Sept. 21, 1804–Jan. 18, 1879.
Vol. 7, Pt. 1–388
Nason, Elias, Apr. 21, 1811–June 17, 1887.
Vol. 7, Pt. 1–389
Nason, Henry Bradford, June 22, 1831–Jan. 18, 1895.
Vol. 7, Pt. 1–390
Nassau, Robert Hamill, Oct. 11, 1835–May 6, 1921.
Vol. 7, Pt. 1–390
Nast, Condé Montrose, Mar. 26, 1873–Sept. 19, 1942.
Supp. 3–546
Nast, Thomas, Sept. 27, 1840–Dec. 7, 1902.
Vol. 7, Pt. 1–391
Nast, Willlam, June 15, 1807–May 16, 1899.
Vol. 7, Pt. 1–393
Nathan, George Jean, Feb. 14, 1882–Apr. 8, 1958.
Supp. 6–470
Nathan, Maud, Oct. 20, 1862–Dec. 15, 1946.
Supp. 4–622
Nation, Carry Amelia Moore, Nov. 25, 1846–June 9, 1911.
Vol. 7, Pt. 1–394
Navarre, Pierre, Mar. 28, 1790?–Mar. 20, 1874.
Vol. 7, Pt. 1–395
Nazimova, Alla, June 4, 1878–July 13, 1945.
Supp. 3–547
Neagle, John, Nov. 4, 1796–Sept. 17, 1865.
Vol. 7, Pt. 1–396
Neal, Alice Bradley. [*See* Haven, Emily Bradley Neal, 1827–1863.]
Neal, David Dalhoff, Oct. 20, 1838–May 2, 1915.
Vol. 7, Pt. 1–397
Neal, John, Aug. 25, 1793–June 20, 1876.
Vol. 7, Pt. 1–398
Neal, Joseph Clay, Feb. 3, 1807–July 17, 1847.
Vol. 7, Pt. 1–399
Neal, Josephine Bicknell, Oct. 10, 1880–Mar. 19, 1955.
Supp. 5–511
Neale, Leonard, Oct. 15, 1746–June 18, 1817.
Vol. 7, Pt. 1–400
Needham, James, d. Sept. 1673.
Vol. 7, Pt. 1–401
Neef, Francis Joseph Nicholas, Dec. 6, 1770–Apr. 6, 1854.
Vol. 7, Pt. 1–402
Neely, Matthew Mansfield, Nov. 9, 1874–Jan. 18, 1958.
Supp. 6–472
Neely, Thomas Benjamin, June 12, 1841–Sept. 4, 1925.
Vol. 7, Pt. 1–402
Nef, John Ulric, June 14, 1862–Aug. 13, 1915.
Vol. 7, Pt. 1–403
Negley, James Scott, Dec. 22, 1826–Aug. 7, 1901.
Vol. 7, Pt. 1–404
Nehrling, Henry, May 9, 1853–Nov. 22, 1929.
Vol. 7, Pt. 1–405
Neidhard, Charles, Apr. 19, 1809–Apr. 17, 1895.
Vol. 7, Pt. 1–406
Neighbors, Robert Simpson, Nov. 3, 1815–Sept. 14, 1859.
Vol. 7, Pt. 1–407
Neill, Edward Duffield, Aug. 9, 1823–Sept. 26, 1893.
Vol. 7, Pt. 1–408
Neill, John, July 9, 1819–Feb. 11, 1880.
Vol. 7, Pt. 1–409
Neill, Thomas Hewson, Apr. 9, 1826–Mar. 12, 1885.
Vol. 7, Pt. 1–409
Neill, William, d. Aug. 8, 1860.
Vol. 7, Pt. 1–410
Neilson, John, Mar. 11, 1745–Mar. 3, 1833.
Vol. 7, Pt. 1–411
Neilson, William Allan, Mar. 28, 1869–Feb. 13, 1946.
Supp. 4–624
Neilson, William George, Aug. 12, 1842–Dec. 29, 1906.
Vol. 7, Pt. 1–412
Nell, William Cooper, Dec. 20, 1816–May 25, 1874.
Vol. 7, Pt. 1–413
Nelson, Charles Alexander, Apr. 14, 1839–Jan. 13,
Vol. 7, Pt. 1–413
Nelson, David, Sept. 24, 1793–Oct. 17, 1844.
Vol. 7, Pt. 1–414
Nelson, Donald Marr, Nov. 17, 1888–Sept. 29, 1959.
Supp. 6–473
Nelson, Edward William, May 8, 1855–May 19, 1934.
Supp. 1–571

Nelson, Henry Loomis, Jan. 5, 1846–Feb. 29, 1908.
Vol. 7, Pt. 1–415
Nelson, Hugh, Sept. 30, 1768–Mar. 18, 1836.
Vol. 7, Pt. 1–416
Nelson, John, 1654–Nov. 15, 1734.
Vol. 7, Pt. 1–417
Nelson, Julius, Mar. 6, 1858–Feb. 15, 1916.
Vol. 7, Pt. 1–418
Nelson, Knute, Feb. 2, 1843–Apr. 28, 1923.
Vol. 7, Pt. 1–418
Nelson, Marjorie Maxine, Dec. 24, 1909–Nov. 28, 1962.
Supp. 7–568
Nelson, Nels Christian, Apr. 9, 1875–March 5, 1964.
Supp. 7–569
Nelson, Nelson Olsen, Sept. 11, 1844–Oct. 5, 1922.
Vol. 7, Pt 1–419
Nelson, Oswald George ("Ozzie"), Mar. 20, 1906–June 3, 1975.
Supp. 9–580
Nelson, Rensselaer Russell, May 12, 1826–Oct. 15, 1904.
Vol. 7, Pt. 1–420
Nelson, Reuben, Dec. 16, 1818–Feb. 20, 1879.
Vol. 7, Pt. 1–421
Nelson, Roger, 1759–June 7, 1815.
Vol. 7, Pt. 1–421
Nelson, Samuel, Nov. 10, 1792–Dec. 13, 1873
Vol. 7, Pt. 1–422
Nelson, Thomas, Dec. 26, 1738–Jan. 4, 1789.
Vol. 7, Pt. 1–424
Nelson, Thomas Henry, *c.* 1823–Mar. 14, 1896.
Vol. 7, Pt. 1–424
Nelson, William, 1711–Nov. 19, 1772.
Vol. 7, Pt. 1–425
Nelson, William, Sept. 27, 1824–Sept. 29, 1862.
Vol. 7, Pt. 1–426
Nelson, William, Feb. 10, 1847–Aug. 10, 1914.
Vol. 7, Pt. 1–427
Nelson, William Rockhill, Mar. 7, 1841–Apr. 13, 1915.
Vol. 7, Pt. 1–427
Nerinckx, Charles, Oct. 2, 1761–Aug. 12, 1824.
Vol. 7, Pt. 1–428
Nesbit, Evelyn Florence, Dec. 25, 1884–Jan. 17, 1967.
Supp. 8–460
Nesbitt, John Maxwell, *c.* 1730–Jan. 22, 1802.
Vol. 7, Pt. 1–429
Nesmith, James Willis, July 23, 1820–June 17, 1885.
Vol. 7, Pt. 1–430
Nesmith, John, Aug. 3, 1793–Oct. 15, 1869.
Vol. 7, Pt. 1–431
Nessler, Karl Ludwig, May 2, 1872–Jan. 22, 1951.
Supp. 5–512
Nestle, Charles. [*See* Nessler, Karl Ludwig, 1872–1951.]
Nestor, Agnes, June 24, 1880–Dec. 28, 1948.
Supp. 4–625
Nettleton, Alvred Bayard, Nov. 14, 1838–Aug. 10, 1911.
Vol. 7, Pt. 1–431
Nettleton, Asahel, Apr. 21, 1783–May 16, 1844.
Vol. 7, Pt. 1–432
Nettleton, Edwin S., Oct. 22, 1831–Apr. 22, 1901.
Vol. 7, Pt. 1–433
Neuberger, Richard Lewis, Dec. 26, 1912–Mar. 9, 1960.
Supp. 6–474
Neuendorff, Adolph Heinrich Anton Magnus, June 13, 1843–Dec. 4, 1897.
Vol. 7, Pt. 1–434
Neumann, Franz Leopold, May 23, 1900–Sept. 2, 1954.
Supp. 5–513
Neumann, John Nepomucene, Mar. 28, 1811–Jan.5, 1860.
Vol. 7, Pt. 1–435
Neumann, John Von. [*See* Von Neumann, John, 1903–1957.]
Neumark, David, Aug. 3, 1866–Dec. 15, 1924.
Vol. 7, Pt. 1–436
Neutra, Richard Joseph, Apr. 8, 1892–Apr. 15, 1970.
Supp. 8–462
Nevada, Emma, Feb. 7, 1859–June 20, 1940.
Supp. 2–485
Nevers, Ernest Alonzo ("Ernie"), June 11, 1903–May 3, 1976.
Supp. 10–584
Neville, John, July 26, 1731–July 29, 1803.
Vol. 7, Pt. 1–437
Neville, Wendell Cushing, May 12, 1870–July 8, 1930.
Vol. 7, Pt. 1–438
Nevin, Alfred, Mar. 14, 1816–Sept. 2, 1890.
Vol. 7, Pt. 1–438
Nevin, Edwin Henry, May 9, 1814–June 2, 1889.
Vol. 7, Pt. 1–439
Nevin, Ethelbert Woodbridge, Nov. 25, 1862–Feb.17, 1901.
Vol. 7, Pt. 1–440
Nevin, George Balch, Mar. 15, 1859–Apr. 17, 1933.
Vol. 7, Pt. 1–441
Nevin, John Williamson, Feb. 20, 1803–June 6, 1886.
Vol. 7, Pt. 1–442
Nevin, Robert Peebles, July 31, 1820–June 28, 1908.
Vol. 7, Pt. 1–443
Nevins, Joseph Allan, May 20, 1890–Mar. 5, 1971.
Supp. 9–581
Nevius, John Livingston, Mar. 4, 1829–Oct. 19, 1893.
Vol. 7, Pt. 1–444
New, Harry Stewart, Dec. 31, 1858–May 9, 1937.
Supp. 2–486
Newberry, John Stoughton, Nov. 18, 1826–Jan. 2, 1887.
Vol. 7, Pt. 1–444
Newberry, John Strong, Dec. 22, 1822–Dec. 7, 1892.
Vol. 7, Pt. 1–445
Newberry, Oliver, Nov. 17, 1789–July 30, 1860.
Vol. 7, Pt. 1–446
Newberry, Truman Handy, Nov. 5, 1864–Oct. 3, 1945.
Supp. 3–549
Newberry, Walter Loomis, Sept. 18, 1804–Nov. 6, 1868.
Vol. 7, Pt. 1–447
Newbold, William Romaine, Nov. 20, 1865–Sept. 26, 1926.
Vol. 7, Pt. 1–448
Newbrough, John Ballou, June 5, 1828–Apr. 22, 1891.
Vol. 7, Pt. 1–449
Newcomb, Charles Leonard, Aug. 7, 1854–Mar. 13, 1930.
Vol. 7, Pt. 1–449
Newcomb, Harvey, Sept. 2, 1803–Aug. 30, 1863.
Vol. 7, Pt. 1–450
Newcomb, Josephine Louise LeMonnier, Oct. 31, 1816–Apr. 7, 1901.
Vol. 7, Pt. 1–451
Newcomb, Simon, Mar. 12, 1835–July 11, 1909.
Vol. 7, Pt. 1–452
Newcomer, Christian, Jan 21, 1749 o.s.–Mar. 12, 1830.
Vol. 7, Pt. 1–455
Newel, Stanford, June 7, 1839–Apr. 6, 1907.
Vol. 7, Pt. 1–456
Newell, Edward Theodore, Jan. 15, 1886–Feb. 18, 1941.
Supp. 3–551
Newell, Frederick Haynes, Mar. 5, 1862–July 5, 1932.
Vol. 7, Pt. 1–456
Newell, Peter Sheaf Hersey, Mar. 5, 1862–Jan. 15, 1924.
Vol. 7, Pt. 1–457
Newell, Robert, Mar. 30, 1807–November 1869.
Vol. 7, Pt. 1–458
Newell, Robert Henry, Dec. 13, 1836–July 1901.
Vol. 7, Pt. 1–458
Newell, William Augustus, Sept. 5, 1817–Aug. 8, 1901.
Vol. 7, Pt. 1–459
Newell, William Wells, Jan. 24, 1839–Jan. 21, 1907.
Vol. 7, Pt. 1–460
Newhouse, Samuel, Oct. 14, 1853–Sept. 22, 1930.
Vol. 7, Pt. 1–461
Newhouse, Samuel Irving, May 24, 1895–Aug. 29, 1979.
Supp. 10–585
Newlands, Francis Griffith, Aug. 28, 1848–Dec. 24, 1917.
Vol. 7, Pt. 1–462
Newlon, Jesse Homer, July 16, 1882–Sept. 1, 1941.
Supp. 3–552
Newman, Albert Henry, Aug. 25, 1852–June 4, 1933.
Supp. 1–572
Newman, Alfred, Mar. 17, 1900–Feb. 17, 1970.
Supp. 8–464
Newman, Barnett, Jan. 29, 1905–July 4, 1970.
Supp. 8–466
Newman, Henry, Nov. 20, 1670–June 26, 1743.
Vol. 7, Pt. 1–463
Newman, Henry Roderick, *c.* 1843–1918.
Vol. 7, Pt. 1–464
Newman, John Philip, Sept. 1, 1826–July 5, 1899.
Vol. 7, Pt. 1–464

Newman, Robert Loftin, Nov. 10, 1827–Mar. 31, 1912.
Vol. 7, Pt. 1–465
Newman, Samuel Phillips, June 6, 1797–Feb. 10, 1842.
Vol. 7, Pt. 1–466
Newman, William H., Sept. 6, 1847–Aug. 10, 1918.
Supp. 1–573
Newman, Wilham Truslow, June 23, 1843–Feb. 14, 1920.
Vol. 7, Pt. 1–467
Newport, Christopher, d. Aug. 1617.
Vol. 7, Pt. 1–467
Newsam, Albert, May 20, 1809–Nov. 20, 1864.
Vol. 7, Pt. 1–469
Newsom, Herschel David, May 1, 1905–July 2, 1970.
Supp. 8–468
Newton, Henry Jotham, Feb. 9, 1823–Dec. 23, 1895.
Vol. 7, Pt. 1–469
Newton, Hubert Anson, Mar. 19, 1830–Aug. 12, 1896.
Vol. 7, Pt. 1–470
Newton, Isaac, Jan. 10, 1794–Nov. 23, 1858.
Vol. 7, Pt. 1–471
Newton, Isaac, Mar. 31, 1800–June 19, 1867.
Vol. 7, Pt. 1–472
Newton, John, Aug. 24, 1823–May 1, 1895.
Vol. 7, Pt. 1–473
Newton, Joseph Fort, July 21, 1876–Jan. 24, 1950.
Supp. 4–627
Newton, Richard, July 26, 1812–May 25, 1887.
Vol. 7, Pt. 1–474
Newton, Richard Heber, Oct. 31, 1840–Dec. 19, 1914.
Vol. 7, Pt. 1–474
Newton, Robert Safford, Dec. 12, 1818–Oct. 9, 1881.
Vol. 7, Pt. 1–475
Newton, Thomas, June 10, 1660–May 28, 1721.
Vol. 7, Pt. 1–476
Newton, Thomas, Nov. 21, 1768–1847.
Vol. 7, Pt. 1–477
Newton, William Wilberforce, Nov. 4, 1843–June 25, 1914.
Vol. 7, Pt. 1–478
Ney, Elisabet, Jan. 26, 1833–June 29, 1907.
Vol. 7, Pt. 1–478
Neyland, Robert Reese, Jr., Feb. 17, 1892–Mar. 28, 1962.
Supp. 7–571
Ng Poon Chew, Apr. 28, 1866–Mar. 13, 1931.
Vol. 7, Pt. 1–479
Niblack, Albert Parker, July 25, 1859–Aug. 20, 1929.
Vol. 7, Pt. 1–480
Niblack, William Ellis, May 19, 1822–May 7, 1893.
Vol. 7, Pt. 1–481
Niblo, William, 1789–Aug. 21, 1878.
Vol. 7, Pt. 1–482
Nicholas, George, 1754?–June 1799.
Vol. 7, Pt. 1–482
Nicholas, John, 1756?–Dec. 31, 1819.
Vol. 7, Pt. 1–483
Nicholas, Philip Norborne, 1775?–Aug. 18, 1849.
Vol. 7, Pt. 1–484
Nicholas, Robert Carter, Jan. 28, 1728–Sept. 8, 1780.
Vol. 7, Pt. 1–485
Nicholas, Wilson Cary, Jan. 31, 1761–Oct. 10, 1820.
Vol. 7, Pt. 1–486
Nicholls, Francis Redding Tillou, Aug. 20, 1834–Jan 4, 1912.
Vol. 7, Pt. 1–487
Nicholls, Rhoda Holmes, Mar. 28, 1854–Sept. 7, 1930.
Vol. 7, Pt. 1–488
Nichols, Charles Henry, Oct. 19, 1820–Dec. 16, 1889.
Vol. 7, Pt. 1–489
Nichols, Charles Lemuel, May 29, 1851–Feb. 19, 1929.
Vol. 7, Pt. 1–490
Nichols, Clarina Irene Howard, Jan. 25, 1810–Jan. 11, 1885.
Vol. 7, Pt. 1–490
Nichols, Dudley, Apr. 6, 1895–Jan. 5, 1960.
Supp. 6–475
Nichols, Edward Leamington, Sept. 14, 1854–Nov. 10, 1937.
Supp. 2–487
Nichols, Ernest Fox, June 1, 1869–Apr. 29, 1924.
Vol. 7, Pt. 1–491
Nichols, George Ward, June 21, 1831–Sept. 15, 1885.
Vol. 7, Pt. 1–494
Nichols, James Robinson, July 18, 1819–Jan. 2, 1888.
Vol. 7, Pt. 1–494
Nichols, Mary Sargeant Neal Gove, Aug. 10, 1810–May 30, 1884.
Vol. 7, Pt. 1–495
Nichols, Roy Franklin, Mar. 3, 1896–Jan. 11, 1973.
Supp. 9–583
Nichols, Ruth Rowland, Feb. 23, 1901–Sept. 25, 1960.
Supp. 6–477
Nichols, Thomas Low, 1815–1901.
Vol. 7, Pt. 1–496
Nichols, William Ford, June 9, 1849–June 5, 1924.
Vol. 7, Pt. 1–497
Nicholson, Alfred Osborne Pope, Aug. 31, 1808–Mar. 23, 1876.
Vol. 7, Pt. 1–498
Nicholson, Eliza Jane Poitevent Holbrook, Mar. 11, 1849–Feb. 15, 1896.
Vol. 7, Pt. 1–499
Nicholson, Francis, Nov. 12, 1655–Mar. 5, 1728.
Vol. 7, Pt. 1–499
Nicholson, James, *c.* 1736–Sept. 2, 1804.
Vol. 7, Pt. 1–502
Nicholson, James Bartram, Jan. 28, 1820–Mar. 4, 1901.
Vol. 7, Pt. 1–503
Nicholson, James William Augustus, Mar. 10, 1821–Oct. 28, 1887.
Vol. 7, Pt. 1–503
Nicholson, John, d. Dec. 5, 1800.
Vol. 7, Pt. 1–504
Nicholson, Joseph Hopper, May 15, 1770–Mar. 4, 1817.
Vol. 7, Pt. 1–505
Nicholson, Meredith, Dec. 9, 1866–Dec. 21, 1947.
Supp. 4–629
Nicholson, Samuel, 1743–Dec. 29, 1811.
Vol. 7, Pt. 1–506
Nicholson, Samuel Danford, Feb. 22, 1859–Mar. 24, 1923.
Vol. 7, Pt. 1–507
Nicholson, Seth Barnes, Nov. 12, 1891–July 2, 1963.
Supp. 7–572
Nicholson, Timothy, Nov. 2, 1828–Sept. 15, 1924.
Vol. 7, Pt. 1–507
Nicholson, William Thomas, Mar. 22, 1834–Oct. 17, 1893.
Vol. 7, Pt. 1–509
Nicholson, William Jones, Jan. 16, 1856–Dec. 20, 1931.
Vol. 7, Pt. 1–508
Nicola, Lewis, 1717–Aug. 9, 1807.
Vol. 7, Pt. 1–509
Nicolay, John George, Feb. 26, 1832–Sept. 26, 1901.
Vol. 7, Pt. 1–510
Nicolet, Jean, 1598–Nov. 1, 1642.
Vol. 7, Pt. 1–511
Nicoll. [*See also* Nicolls.]
Nicoll, De Lancey, June 24, 1854–Mar. 31, 1931.
Vol. 7, Pt. 1–512
Nicoll, James Craig, Nov. 22, 1847–July 25, 1918.
Vol. 7, Pt. 1–513
Nicollet, Joseph Nicolas, July 24, 1786–Sept. 11, 1843.
Vol. 7, Pt. 1–514
Nicolls, Matthias, Mar. 29, 1626–Dec. 22, 1687?.
Vol. 7, Pt. 1–514
Nicolls, Rlchard, 1624–May 28, 1672.
Vol. 7, Pt. 1–515
Nicolls, William, 1657–May 1723.
Vol. 7, Pt. 1–516
Niebuhr, Helmut Richard, Sept. 3, 1894–July 5, 1962.
Supp. 7–573
Niebuhr, Karl Paul Reinhold ("Reinie"), June 21, 1892–June 1, 1971.
Supp. 9–584
Niedringhaus, Frederick Gottlieb, Oct. 21, 1837–Nov. 25, 1922.
Vol. 7, Pt. 1–517
Niehaus, Charles Henry, Jan. 24, 1855–June 19, 1935.
Supp. 1–574
Nielsen, Alice, June 7, 1870?–Mar. 8, 1943.
Supp. 3–553
Nielsen, Arthur Charles, Sept. 5, 1897–June 1, 1980.
Supp. 10–587
Nieman, Lucius William, Dec. 13, 1857–Oct 1, 1935.
Supp. 1–576
Niemeyer, John Henry, June 25, 1839–Dec. 7, 1932.
Vol. 7, Pt. 1–518

Nies, James Buchanan, Nov. 22, 1856–June 18, 1922.
Vol. 7, Pt. 1–519
Nies, Konrad, Oct. 17, 1861–Aug. 10, 1921.
Vol. 7, Pt. 1–519
Nieuwland, Julius Arthur, Feb. 14, 1878–June 11, 1936.
Supp. 2–488
Niles, David K., Nov. 23, 1892–Sept. 28, 1952.
Supp. 5–514
Niles, Hezekiah, Oct. 10, 1777–Apr. 2, 1839.
Vol. 7, Pt. 1–521
Niles, John Jacob, Apr. 28, 1892–Mar. 1, 1980.
Supp. 10–589
Niles, John Milton, Aug. 20, 1787–May 31, 1856.
Vol. 7, Pt. 1–522
Niles, Nathaniel, Apr. 3, 1741–Oct. 31, 1828.
Vol. 7, Pt. 1–523
Niles, Nathaniel, Dec. 27, 1791–Nov. 16, 1869.
Vol. 7, Pt. 1–524
Niles, Samuel, May 1, 1674–May 1, 1762.
Vol. 7, Pt. 1–524
Nimitz, Chester William, Feb. 24, 1885–Feb. 20, 1966.
Supp. 8–469
Nin, Anaïs, Feb. 21, 1903–Jan. 14, 1977.
Supp. 10–590
Nipher, Francis Eugene, Dec. 10, 1847–Oct. 6, 1926.
Vol. 7, Pt. 1–525
Nisbet, Charles, Jan. 21, 1736–Jan. 18, 1804.
Vol. 7, Pt. 1–526
Nisbet, Eugenius Aristides, Dec. 7, 1803–Mar. 18, 1871.
Vol. 7, Pt. 1–527
Nitchie, Edward Bartlett, Nov. 18, 1876–Oct. 5, 1917.
Vol. 7, Pt. 1–528
Nitschmann, David, Dec. 27, 1696–Oct. 8, 1772.
Vol. 7, Pt. 1–529
Nixon, John, Mar. 1, 1727–Mar. 24, 1815.
Vol. 7, Pt. 1–530
Nixon, John, 1733–Dec. 31, 1808.
Vol. 7, Pt. 1–530
Nixon, John Thompson, Aug. 31, 1820–Sept. 28, 1889.
Vol. 7, Pt. 1–531
Nixon, William Penn, Mar. 19, 1833–Feb. 20, 1912.
Vol. 7, Pt. 1–532
Niza, Marcos de, d. Mar. 25, 1558.
Vol. 7, Pt. 1–533
Nizza, Marcos de. [*See* Niza, Marcos de, d. 1558.]
Noah, Mordecai Manuel, July 19, 1785–Mar. 22, 1851.
Vol. 7, Pt. 1–534
Noailles, Louis Marie, Vicomte de, Apr. 17, 1756–Jan. 5, 1804.
Vol. 7, Pt. 1–535
Nobili, John, Apr. 8, 1812–Mar. 1, 1856.
Vol. 7, Pt. 1–536
Noble, Alfred, Aug. 7, 1844–Apr. 19, 1914.
Vol. 7, Pt. 1–536
Noble, Frederick Alphonso, Mar. 17, 1832–Dec. 31, 1917.
Vol. 7, Pt. 1–537
Noble, Gladwyn Kingsley, Sept. 20, 1894–Dec. 9, 1940.
Supp. 2–489
Noble, James, Dec. 16, 1783–Feb. 26, 1831.
Vol. 7, Pt. 1–538
Noble, John Willock, Oct. 26, 1831–Mar. 22, 1912.
Vol. 7, Pt. 1–539
Noble, Samuel, Nov. 22, 1834–Aug. 14, 1888.
Vol. 7, Pt. 1–540
Nock, Albert Jay, Oct. 13, 1870–Aug. 19, 1945.
Supp. 3–554
Noeggerath, Emil Oscar Jacob Bruno, Oct. 5, 1827–May 3, 1895.
Vol. 7, Pt. 1–541
Noguchi, Hideyo, Nov. 24, 1876–May 21, 1928.
Vol. 7, Pt. 1–542
Nolan, Bob, Apr. 1, 1908–June 15, 1980.
Supp. 10–592
Nolan, Philip, *c.* 1771–Mar. 21, 1801.
Vol. 7, Pt. 1–543
Nolen, John, June 14, 1869–Feb. 18, 1937.
Supp. 2–490
Noll, John Francis, Jan. 25, 1875–July 31, 1956.
Supp. 6–478
Noonan, James Patrick, Dec. 15, 1878–Dec. 4, 1929.
Vol. 7, Pt. 1–544
Norbeck, Peter, Aug. 27, 1870–Dec. 20, 1936.
Supp. 2–491
Norcross, Orlando Whitney, Oct. 25, 1839–Feb. 27, 1920.
Vol. 7, Pt. 1–545
Nordberg, Bruno Victor, Apr. 11, 1857–Oct. 30, 1924.
Vol. 7, Pt. 1–546
Norden, Carl Lukas, Apr. 23, 1880–June 15, 1965.
Supp. 7–576
Nordheimer, Isaac, 1809–Nov. 3, 1842.
Vol. 7, Pt. 1–547
Nordhoff, Charles, Aug. 31, 1830–July 14, 1901.
Vol. 7, Pt. 1–548
Nordhoff, Charles Bernard, Feb. 1, 1887–Apr. 10, 1947.
Supp. 5–266
Nordica, Lillian, May 12, 1859–May 10, 1914.
Vol. 7, Pt. 1–548
Norelius, Eric, Oct. 26, 1833–Mar. 15, 1916.
Vol. 7, Pt. 1–549
Norell, Norman, Apr. 20, 1900–Oct. 25, 1972.
Supp. 9–586
Norman, John, *c.* 1748–June 8, 1817.
Vol. 7, Pt. 1–550
Norris, Benjamin Franklin, Mar. 5, 1870–Oct. 25, 1902.
Vol. 7, Pt. 1–551
Norris, Charles Gilman Smith, Apr. 23, 1881–July 25, 1945.
Supp. 3–555
Norris, Edward, d. Dec. 23, 1659.
Vol. 7, Pt. 1–552
Norris, Frank. [*See* Norris, Benjamin Franklin, 1870–1902.]
Norris, George Washington, Nov. 6, 1808–Mar. 4, 1875.
Vol. 7, Pt. 1–553
Norris, George William, July 11, 1861–Sept. 2, 1944.
Supp. 3–557
Norris, Isaac, July 26, 1671–June 4, 1735.
Vol. 7, Pt. 1–553
Norris, Isaac, Oct. 23, 1701–July 13, 1766.
Vol. 7, Pt. 1–554
Norris, James Flack, Jan. 20, 1871–Aug. 4, 1940.
Supp. 2–492
Norris, John Franklyn, Sept. 18, 1877–Aug. 20, 1952.
Supp. 5–516
Norris, Kathleen Thompson, July 16, 1880–Jan. 18, 1966.
Supp. 8–471
Norris, Mary Harriott, Mar. 16, 1848–Sept. 14, 1919.
Vol. 7, Pt. 1–555
Norris, William, July 2, 1802–Jan. 5, 1867.
Vol. 7, Pt. 1–555
Norris, William Fisher, Jan. 6, 1839–Nov. 18, 1901.
Vol. 7, Pt. 1–556
Norsworthy, Naomi, Sept. 29, 1877–Dec. 25, 1916.
Vol. 7, Pt. 1–557
North, Edward, Mar. 9, 1820–Sept. 13, 1903.
Vol. 7, Pt. 1–558
North, Elisha, Jan. 8, 1771–Dec. 29, 1843.
Vol. 7, Pt. 1–559
North, Frank Joshua, Mar. 10, 1840–Mar. 14, 1885.
Vol. 7, Pt. 1–559
North, Frank Mason, Dec. 3, 1850–Dec. 17, 1935.
Supp. 1–577
North, Simeon, July 13, 1765–Aug. 25 1852.
Vol. 7, Pt. 1–561
North, Simeon, Sept. 7, 1802–Feb. 9, 1884.
Vol. 7, Pt. 1–561
North, Simon Newton Dexter, Nov. 29, 1848–Aug. 3, 1924.
Vol. 7, Pt. 1–562
North, William, 1755–Jan. 3, 1836.
Vol. 7, Pt. 1–563
Northen, William Jonathan, July 9, 1835–Mar. 25, 1913.
Vol. 7, Pt. 1–564
Northend, Charles, Apr. 2, 1814–Aug. 7, 1895.
Vol. 7, Pt. 1–564
Northrop, Birdsey Grant, July 18, 1817–Apr. 27, 1898.
Vol. 7, Pt. 1–565
Northrop, Cyrus, Sept. 30, 1834–Apr. 3, 1922.
Vol. 7, Pt. 1–566
Northrop, Lucius Bellinger, Sept. 8, 1811–Feb. 9, 1894.
Vol. 7, Pt. 1–567
Norton, Alice Peloubet. [*See* Norton, Mary Alice Peloubet, 1860–1928].
Norton, Andrews, Dec. 31, 1786–Sept. 18, 1853.
Vol. 7, Pt. 1–568
Norton, Charles Eliot, Nov. 16, 1827–Oct. 21, 1908.
Vol. 7, Pt. 1–569

Norton, Charles Hotchkiss, Nov. 23, 1851–Oct. 27, 1942.
Supp. 3–561
Norton, Elijah Hise, Nov. 21, 1821–Aug. 5, 1914.
Vol. 7, Pt. 1–572
Norton, John, May 6, 1606–Apr. 5, 1663.
Vol. 7, Pt. 1–572
Norton, John Nicholas, 1820–Jan. 18, 1881.
Vol. 7, Pt. 1–574
Norton, John Pitkin, July 19, 1822–Sept. 5, 1852.
Vol. 7, Pt. 1–574
Norton, Mary Alice Peloubet, Feb. 25, 1860–Feb. 23, 1928.
Vol. 7, Pt. 1–575
Norton, Mary Teresa Hopkins, Mar. 7, 1875–Aug. 2, 1959.
Supp. 6–479
Norton, William Edward, June 28, 1843–Feb. 28, 1916.
Vol. 7, Pt. 1–576
Norton, William Warder, Sept. 17, 1891–Nov. 7, 1945.
Supp. 3–563
Norwood, Robert Winkworth, Mar. 27, 1874–Sept. 28, 1932.
Vol. 7, Pt. 1–577
Noss, Theodore Bland, May 10, 1852–Feb. 28, 1909.
Vol. 7, Pt. 1–578
Notestein, Wallace, Dec. 16, 1878–Feb. 2, 1969.
Supp. 8–472
Nott, Abraham, Feb. 5, 1768–Jun 19, 1830.
Vol. 7, Pt. 1–578
Nott, Charles Cooper, Sept. 16, 1827–Mar. 6, 1916.
Vol. 7, Pt. 1–579
Nott, Eliphalet, Jun 25, 1773–Jan. 29, 1866.
Vol. 7, Pt. 1–580
Nott, Henry Junius, Nov. 4, 1797–Oct. 9, 1837.
Vol. 7, Pt. 1–581
Nott, Josiah Clark, Mar. 31, 1804–Mar. 31, 1873.
Vol. 7, Pt. 1–582
Nott, Samuel, Jan. 23, 1754–May 26, 1852.
Vol. 7, Pt. 1–583
Notz, Frederick William Augustus, Feb. 2, 1841–Dec. 16, 1921.
Vol. 7, Pt. 1–583
Nourse, Edwin Griswold, May 20, 1883–Apr. 7, 1974.
Supp. 9–588.
Novarro, Ramon, Feb. 6, 1899–Oct. 31, 1968.
Supp. 8–473
Novy, Frederick George, Dec. 9, 1864–Aug. 8, 1957.
Supp. 6–481
Noyan, Gilles-Augustin Payen de, 1697–Feb. 26, 1751.
Vol. 7, Pt. 1–584
Noyan, Pierre-Jacques Payen de, Nov. 3, 1695–*c.* 1763.
Vol. 7, Pt. 1–585
Noyes, Alexander Dana, Dec. 14, 1862–Apr. 22, 1945.
Supp. 3–564
Noyes, Arthur Amos, Sept. 13, 1866–June 3, 1936.
Supp. 2–493
Noyes, Clara Dutton, Oct. 3, 1869–June 3, 1936.
Supp. 2–494
Noyes, Crosby Stuart, Feb. 16, 1825–Feb. 21, 1908.
Vol. 7, Pt. 1–586
Noyes, Edward Follansbee, Oct. 3, 1832–Sept. 4, 1890.
Vol. 7, Pt. 1–587
Noyes, Frank Brett, July 7, 1863–Dec. 1, 1948.
Supp. 4–630
Noyes, George Rapall, Mar. 6, 1798–June 3, 1868.
Vol. 7, Pt. 1–587
Noyes, Henry Drury, Mar. 24, 1832–Nov. 12, 1900.
Vol. 7, Pt. 1–588
Noyes, John Humphrey, Sept. 3, 1811–Apr. 13, 1886.
Vol. 7, Pt. 1–589
Noyes, La Verne, Jan. 7, 1849–July 24, 1919.
Vol. 7, Pt. 1–590
Noyes, Walter Chadwick, Aug. 8, 1865–June 12, 1926.
Vol. 7, Pt. 1–591
Noyes, William Albert, Nov. 6, 1857–Oct. 24, 1941.
Supp. 3–565
Noyes, William Albert, Jr., Apr. 18, 1898–Nov. 25, 1980.
Supp. 10–594
Noyes, William Curtis, Aug. 19, 1805–Dec. 25, 1864.
Vol. 7, Pt. 1–592
Nugent, John Frost, June 28, 1868–Sept. 18, 1931.
Vol. 7, Pt. 1–592
Núñez, Cabeza de Vaca, Alvar, *c.* 1490–*c.* 1557.
Vol. 7, Pt. 1–593
Nunó, Jaime, Sept. 8, 1824–July 17, 1908.
Vol. 7, Pt. 1–594
Nurse, Rebecca, 1621–July 19, 1692.
Vol. 7, Pt. 1–595
Nuthead, William, *c.* 1654–1695.
Vol. 7, Pt. 1–596
Nuttall, Thomas, Jan. 5, 1786–Sept. 10, 1859.
Vol. 7, Pt. 1–596
Nutting, Charles Cleveland, May 25, 1858–Jan. 23, 1927.
Vol. 7, Pt. 1–597
Nutting, Mary Adelalde, Nov. 1, 1858–Oct. 3, 1948.
Supp. 4–631
Nutting, Wallace, Nov. 17, 1861–July 18, 1941.
Supp. 3–566
Nye, Edgar Wilson, Aug. 25, 1850–Feb. 22, 1896.
Vol. 7, Pt. 1–598
Nye, Gerald Prentice, Dec. 18, 1892–July 18, 1971.
Supp. 9–590
Nye, James Warren, June 10, 1814–Dec. 25, 1876.
Vol. 7, Pt. 1–600

Oakes, George Washington Ochs, Oct. 27, 1861–Oct. 26, 1931.
Vol. 7, Pt. 1–600
Oakes, Thomas Fletcher, July 15, 1843–Mar. 14, 1919.
Vol. 7, Pt. 1–602
Oakes, Urian, *c.* 1631–July 25, 1681.
Vol. 7, Pt. 1–602
Oakie, Jack, Nov. 12, 1903–Jan. 23, 1978.
Supp. 10–597
Oakley, Annie, Aug. 13, 1860–Nov. 3, 1926.
Vol. 7, Pt. 1–603
Oakley, Thomas Jackson, Nov. 10, 1783–May 11, 1857.
Vol. 7, Pt. 1–604
Oates, William Calvin, Nov. 30, 1835–Sept. 9, 1910.
Vol. 7, Pt. 1–605
Oatman, Johnson, Apr. 21, 1856–Sept. 25, 1922.
Vol. 7, Pt. 1–605
Ober, Frederick Albion, Feb. 13, 1849–May 31, 1913.
Vol. 7, Pt. 1–606
Oberhoffer, Emil Johann, Aug. 10, 1867–May 22, 1933.
Supp. 1–578
Oberholser, Harry Church, June 25, 1870–Dec. 25, 1963.
Supp. 7–578
Oberholtzer, Ellis Paxson, Oct. 5, 1868–Dec. 8, 1936.
Supp. 2–495
Oberholtzer, Sara Louisa Vickers, May 20, 1841–Feb. 2, 1930.
Vol. 7, Pt. 1–607
Oberndorf, Clarence Paul, Feb. 16, 1882–May 30, 1954.
Supp. 5–517
Oberon, Merle, Feb. 19, 1911–Nov. 23, 1979.
Supp. 10–598
O'Brian, John Lord, Oct. 14, 1874–Apr. 10, 1973.
Supp. 9–593
O'Brien, Edward Charles, Apr. 20, 1860–June 21, 1927.
Vol. 7, Pt. 1–607
O'Brien, Fitz-James, *c.* 1828–Apr. 6, 1862.
Vol. 7, Pt. 1–608
O'Brien, Frederick, June 16, 1869–Jan. 9, 1932.
Vol. 7, Pt. 1–609
O'Brien, Jeremiah, 1744–Sept. 5, 1818.
Vol. 7, Pt. 1–610
O'Brien, Justin, Nov. 26, 1906–Dec. 7, 1968.
Supp. 8–475
O'Brien, Matthew Anthony, May 1804–Jan. 15, 1871.
Vol. 7, Pt. 1–610
O'Brien, Morgan Joseph, Apr. 28, 1852–June 16, 1937.
Supp. 2–496
O'Brien, Richard, *c.* 1758–Feb. 14, 1824.
Vol. 7, Pt. 1–611
O'Brien, Robert David ("Davey"), Dec. 11, 1917–Nov. 18, 1977.
Supp. 10–600
O'Brien, Robert Lincoln, Sept. 14, 1865–Nov. 23, 1955.
Supp. 5–518
O'Brien, Thomas James, July 30, 1842–May 19, 1933.
Supp. 1–578
O'Brien, William Shoney, *c.* 1826–May 2, 1878.
Vol. 7, Pt. 1–612
O'Brien, Willis Harold, Mar. 2, 1886–Nov. 8, 1962.
Supp. 7–579

O'Callaghan, Edmund Bailey, Feb. 28, 1797–May 29, 1880.
Vol. 7, Pt. 1–613
O'Callaghan, Jeremiah, 1780–Feb. 23, 1861.
Vol. 7, Pt. 1–613
O'Callahan, Joseph Timothy, May 14, 1905–Mar. 18, 1964.
Supp. 7–580
Occidente, Maria del. [*See* Brooks, Maria Gowen, *c.* 1794–1845.]
Occom, Samson, 1723–July 14, 1792.
Vol. 7, Pt. 1–614
Occonostota. [*See* Oconostota, d. 1785.]
Ochs, Adolph Simon, 1858–1935. [*See* Vol. I, Prefatory Material, pages xvii–xxi.]
Ochs, Julius, June 29, 1826–Oct. 26, 1888.
Vol. 7, Pt. 1–615
Ochs, Phil, Dec. 19, 1940–Apr. 9, 1976.
Supp. 10–601
Ochsner, Albert John, Apr. 3, 1858–July 25, 1925.
Vol. 7, Pt. 1–616
Ockerson, John Augustus, Mar. 4, 1848–Mar. 22, 1924.
Vol. 7, Pt. 1–617
O'Connell, William Henry, Dec. 8, 1859–Apr. 22, 1944.
Supp. 3–568
O'Connor, Edwin Greene, July 29, 1918–Mar. 23, 1968.
Supp. 8–476
O'Connor, James, Sept. 10, 1823–May 27, 1890.
Vol. 7 Pt 1–618
O'Connor, Mary Flannery, Mar. 25, 1925–Aug. 3, 1964.
Supp. 7–581
O'Connor, Michael, Sept. 27, 1810–Oct. 18, 1872.
Vol. 7, Pt. 1–618
O'Connor, William Douglas, Jan. 2, 1832–May 9, 1889.
Vol. 7, Pt. 1–619
O'Conor, Charles, Jan. 22, 1804–May 12, 1884.
Vol. 7, Pt. 1–620
Oconostota, d. 1785.
Vol. 7, Pt. 1–621
O'Daniel, Wilbert Lee ("Pappy"), Mar. 11, 1890–May 11, 1969.
Supp. 8–477
Odell, Benjamin Barker, Jan 14, 1854–May 9, 1926.
Vol. 7, Pt. 1–622
Odell, George Clinton Densmore, Mar. 19, 1866–Oct. 17, 1949.
Supp. 4–633
Odell, Jonathan, Sept. 25, 1737–Nov. 25, 1818.
Vol. 7, Pt. 1–623
Odenbach, Frederick Louis, Oct. 21, 1857–Mar. 15, 1933.
Supp. 1–579
Odenheimer, William Henry, Aug. 11, 1817–Aug. 14, 1879.
Vol. 7, Pt. 1–624
Odets, Clifford, July 18, 1906–Aug. 14, 1963.
Supp. 7–583
Odin, John Mary, Feb. 25, 1801–May 25, 1870.
Vol. 7, Pt. 1–625
O'Donnell, Emmett, Jr. ("Rosy"), Sept. 15, 1906–Dec. 26, 1971.
Supp. 9–595
O'Donnell, Kenneth Patrick, Mar. 4, 1924–Sept. 9, 1977.
Supp. 10–603
O'Donnell, Thomas Jefferson, June 2, 1856–June 11, 1925.
Vol. 7, Pt. 1–626
O'Donovan, William Rudolf, Mar. 28, 1844–Apr. 20, 1920.
Vol. 7, Pt. 1–627
O'Doul, Francis Joseph ("Lefty"), Mar. 4, 1897–Dec. 7, 1969.
Supp. 8–478
Odum, Howard Washington, May 24, 1884–Nov. 8, 1954.
Supp. 5–519
O'Dwyer, Joseph, Oct. 12, 1841–Jan. 7, 1898.
Vol. 7, Pt. 1–627
O'Dwyer, William, July 11, 1890–Nov. 24, 1964.
Supp. 7–584
Oehmler, Leo Carl Martin, Aug. 15, 1867–Nov. 3, 1930.
Vol. 7, Pt. 1–628
Oemler, Arminius, Sept. 12, 1827–Aug. 8, 1897.
Vol. 7, Pt. 1–629
Oertel, Johannes Adam Simon, Nov 3, 1823–Dec. 9, 1909.
Vol. 7, Pt. 1–630
O'Fallon, Benjamin, Sept. 20, 1793–Dec. 17, 1842.
Vol. 7, Pt. 1–631
O'Fallon, James, Mar. 11, 1749–1794?.
Vol. 7, Pt. 1–632
O'Fallon, John, Nov. 17, 1791–Dec. 17, 1865.
Vol. 7, Pt. 1–632
O'Ferrall, Charles Triplett, Oct. 21, 1840–Sept. 22, 1905.
Vol. 7, Pt. 1–633
Offley, David, d. Oct. 4, 1838.
Vol. 7, Pt. 1–634
Oftedal, Sven, Mar. 22, 1844–Mar. 30, 1911.
Vol. 7, Pt. 1–635
Ogburn, William Fielding, June 29, 1886–Apr. 27, 1959.
Supp. 6–482
Ogden, Aaron, Dec. 3, 1756–Apr. 19, 1839.
Vol. 7, Pt. 1–636
Ogden, David, 1707–1798.
Vol. 7, Pt. 1–637
Ogden, David Bayard, Oct. 31, 1775–July 16, 1849.
Vol. 7, Pt. 1–638
Ogden, Francis Barber, Mar. 3, 1783–July 4, 1857.
Vol. 7, Pt. 1–639
Ogden, Herbert Gouverneur, Apr. 4, 1846–Feb. 25, 1906.
Vol. 7, Pt. 1–640
Ogden, Peter Skene, 1794–Sept. 1854.
Vol. 7, Pt. 1–640
Ogden, Robert Curtis, June 20, 1836–Aug. 6, 1913.
Vol. 7, Pt. 1–641
Ogden, Rollo, Jan. 19, 1856–Feb. 22, 1937.
Supp. 2–498
Ogden, Samuel, Dec. 9, 1746–Dec. 1, 1810.
Vol. 7, Pt. 1–642
Ogden, Thomas Ludlow, Dec. 12, 1773–Dec. 17, 1844.
Vol. 7, Pt. 1–643
Ogden, Uzal, 1744–Nov. 4, 1822.
Vol. 7, Pt. 1–643
Ogden, William Butler, June 15, 1805–Aug. 3, 1877.
Vol. 7, Pt. 1–644
Ogg, Frederic Austin, Feb. 8, 1878–Oct. 23, 1951.
Supp. 5–521
Ogilvie, James, d. Sept. 18, 1820.
Vol. 7, Pt. 1–645
Ogilvie, John, 1724–Nov. 26, 1774.
Vol. 7, Pt. 1–646
Ogle, Samuel, *c.* 1702–May 3, 1752.
Vol. 7, Pt. 1–647
Oglesby, Richard James, July 25, 1824–Apr. 24, 1899.
Vol. 7, Pt. 1–648
Oglethorpe, James Edward, Dec. 22, 1696–June 30, 1785.
Vol. 7, Pt. 2–1
O'Gorman, Thomas, May 1, 1843–Sept. 18, 1921.
Vol. 7, Pt. 2–3
O'Hara, James, 1752–Dec. 16, 1819.
Vol. 7, Pt. 2–3
O'Hara, John Henry, Jan. 31, 1905–Apr. 11, 1970.
Supp. 8–480
O'Hara, Theodore, Feb. 11, 1820–June 6, 1867.
Vol. 7, Pt. 2–4
O'Hare, Kate (Richards) Cunningham, Mar. 26, 1877–Jan. 10, 1948.
Supp. 4–635
O'Higgins, Harvey Jerrold, Nov. 14, 1876–Feb. 28, 1929.
Vol. 7, Pt. 2–5
Ohlmacher, Albert Philip, Aug. 19, 1865–Nov. 9, 1916.
Vol. 7, Pt. 2–6
Ohrbach, Nathan M. ("N. M."), Aug. 31, 1885–Nov. 19, 1972.
Supp. 9–597
O'Kelly, James, *c.* 1735–Oct. 16, 1826.
Vol. 7, Pt. 2–7
Okey, John Waterman, Jan. 3, 1827–July 25, 1885.
Vol. 7, Pt. 2–8
O'Laughlin, Michael, *c.* 1838–Sept. 23, 1867. [*See* Booth, John Wilkes, 1838–1865]
Olcott, Chancellor John. [*See* Olcott, Chauncey, 1860–1932.]
Olcott, Chauncey, July 21, 1860–Mar. 18, 1932.
Vol. 7, Pt. 2–8
Olcott, Eben Erskine, Mar. 11, 1854–June 5, 1929.
Vol. 7, Pt. 2–9
Olcott, Henry Steel, Aug. 2, 1832–Feb. 17, 1907.
Vol. 7, Pt. 2–10
Olden, Charles Smith, Feb. 19, 1799–Apr. 7, 1876.
Vol. 7, Pt. 2–ll

Older, Fremont, Aug. 30, 1856–Mar. 3, 1935.
Supp. 1–580
Oldfather, William Abbott, Oct. 23, 1880–May 27, 1945.
Supp. 3–571
Oldfield, ("Barney") Berna Eli, Jan. 29, 1878–Oct. 4, 1946.
Supp. 4–636
Oldham, John, *c.* 1600–July 1636.
Vol. 7, Pt. 2–12
Oldham, William Fitzjames, Dec. 15, 1854–Mar. 27, 1937.
Supp. 2–499
Oldham, Williamson Simpson, June 19, 1813–May 8, 1868.
Vol. 7, Pt. 2–12
Olds, Irving Sands, Jan. 22, 1887–Mar. 4, 1963.
Supp. 7–586
Olds, Leland, Dec. 31, 1890–Aug. 3, 1960.
Supp. 6–483
Olds, Ransom Eli, June 3, 1864–Aug. 26, 1950.
Supp. 4–637
Olds, Robert Edwin, Oct. 22, 1875–Nov. 24, 1932.
Supp. 1–582
Oldschool, Oliver. [*See* Sargent, Nathan, 1794–1875.]
O'Leary, Daniel, June 29, 1846?–May 29, 1933.
Supp. 1–583
Olin, Stephen, Mar. 2, 1797–Aug. 16, 1851.
Vol. 7, Pt. 2–13
Oliphant, Herman, Aug. 31, 1884–Jan. 11, 1939.
Supp. 2–500
Oliver, Andrew, Mar. 28, 1706–Mar. 3, 1774.
Vol. 7, Pt. 2–14
Oliver, Andrew, Nov. 13, 1731–Dec. 6, 1799.
Vol. 7, Pt. 2–15
Oliver, Charles Augustus, Dec. 14, 1853–Apr. 8, 1911.
Vol. 7, Pt. 2–16
Oliver, Fitch Edward, Nov. 25, 1819–Dec. 8, 1892.
Vol. 7, Pt. 2–17
Oliver, George Tener, Jan. 26, 1848–Jan. 22, 1919.
Vol. 7, Pt. 2–18
Oliver, Henry Kemble, Nov. 24, 1800–Aug. 12, 1885.
Vol. 7, Pt. 2–18
Oliver, Henry William, Feb. 25, 1840–Feb. 8, 1904
Vol. 7, Pt. 2–19
Oliver, James, Aug. 28, 1823–Mar. 2, 1908.
Vol. 7, Pt. 2–20
Oliver, Joseph, *c.* 1885–Apr. 8, 1938.
Supp. 2–501
Oliver, "King." [*See* Oliver, Joseph, *c.* 1885–1938.]
Oliver, Paul Ambrose, July 18, 1830–May 17, 1912.
Vol. 7, Pt. 2–21
Oliver, Peter, Mar. 26, 1713–October 1791.
Vol. 7, Pt. 2–22
Olmstead, Albert Ten Eyck, Mar. 23, 1880–Apr. 11, 1945.
Supp. 3–572
Olmstead, Gideon. [*See* Olmsted, Gideon, 1749–1845.]
Olmsted, Denison, June 18, 1791–May 13, 1859.
Vol. 7, Pt. 2–23
Olmsted, Frederick Law, July 24, 1870–Dec. 25, 1957.
Supp. 6–485
Olmsted, Frederick Law, Apr. 26, 1822–Aug. 28, 1903.
Vol. 7, Pt. 2–24
Olmsted, Gideon, Feb. 12, 1749–Feb. 8, 1845.
Vol. 7, Pt. 2–28
Olmsted, John Charles, Sept. 14, 1852–Feb. 24, 1920.
Vol. 7, Pt. 2–29
Olmsted, Marlin Edgar, May 21, 1847–July 19, 1913.
Vol. 7, Pt. 2–30
Olney, Jesse, Oct. 12, 1798–July 30, 1872.
Vol. 7, Pt. 2–31
Olney, Richard, Sept. 15, 1835–Apr. 8, 1917.
Vol. 7, Pt. 2–32
Olsen, John Sigvard ("Ole"), Nov. 6, 1892–Jan. 26, 1963.
Supp. 7–588
Olson, Floyd Bjerstjerne, Nov. 13, 1891–Aug. 22, 1936.
Supp. 2–503
Olyphant, David Washington Cincinnatus, Mar. 7, 1789–June 10, 1851.
Vol. 7, Pt. 2–34
Olyphant, Robert Morrison, Sept. 9, 1824–May 3, 1918.
Vol. 7, Pt. 2–34
O'Mahoney, Joseph Christopher, Nov. 5, 1884–Dec. 1, 1962.
Supp. 7–589
O'Mahony, John, 1816–Feb. 6, 1877.
Vol. 7, Pt. 2–35
O'Malley, Frank Ward, Nov. 30, 1875–Oct. 19, 1932.
Vol. 7, Pt. 2–36
O'Malley, Walter Francis, Oct. 9, 1903–Aug. 9, 1979.
Supp. 10–605
Oñate, Juan de, *c.* 1549–*c.* 1624.
Vol. 7, Pt. 2–37
Onderdonk, Benjamin Tredwell, July 15, 1791–Apr. 30, 1861.
Vol. 7, Pt. 2–38
Onderdonk, Henry, June 11, 1804–June 22, 1886.
Vol. 7, Pt. 2–39
Onderdonk, Henry Ustick, Mar. 16, 1789–Dec. 6, 1858.
Vol. 7, Pt. 2–40
O'Neal, Edward Asbury, Sept. 20, 1818–Nov. 7, 1890.
Vol. 7, Pt. 2–41
O'Neal, Edward Asbury, III, Oct. 26, 1875–Feb. 26, 1958.
Supp. 6–487
O'Neale, Margaret, 1796–Nov. 8, 1879.
Vol. 7, Pt. 2–41
O'Neall, John Belton, Apr. 10, 1793–Dec. 27, 1863.
Vol. 7, Pt. 2–42
O'Neill, C. William ("Bill"), Feb. 14, 1916–Aug. 20, 1978.
Supp. 10–607
O'Neill, Eugene, Oct. 16, 1888–Nov. 27, 1953.
Supp. 5–522
O'Neill, James, Nov. 15, 1849–Aug. 10, 1920.
Vol. 7, Pt. 2–43
O'Neill, John, Mar. 8, 1834–Jan. 7, 1878.
Vol. 7, Pt. 2–44
O'Neill, Margaret L. [*See* O'Neale, Margaret, 1796–1879.]
O'Neill, Rose Cecil, June 25, 1874–Apr. 6, 1944.
Supp. 3–573
Onsager, Lars, Nov. 27, 1903–Oct. 5, 1976.
Supp. 10–608
Opdyke, George, Dec. 7, 1805–June 12, 1880.
Vol. 7, Pt. 2–45
Oppenheim, James, May 24, 1882–Aug. 4, 1932.
Vol. 7, Pt. 2–46
Oppenheimer, Julius Robert, Apr. 22, 1904–Feb. 18, 1967.
Supp. 8–482
Opper, Frederick Burr, Jan. 2, 1857–Aug. 27, 1937.
Supp. 2–504
Optic, Oliver. [*See* Adams, William Taylor, 1822–1897.]
Orcutt, Hiram, Feb. 3, 1815–Apr. 17, 1899.
Vol. 7, Pt. 2–47
Ord, Edward Otho Cresap, Oct. 18, 1818–July 22, 1883.
Vol. 7, Pt. 2–48
Ord, George, Mar. 4, 1781–Jan. 24, 1866.
Vol. 7, Pt. 2–49
Ordronaux, John, Aug. 3, 1830–Jan. 20, 1908.
Vol. 7, Pt. 2–50
Ordway, John, *c.* 1775–*c.* 1817.
Vol. 7, Pt. 2–51
O'Reilly, Alexander, 1722–Mar. 23, 1794.
Vol. 7, Pt. 2–51
O'Reilly, Henry, Feb. 6, 1806–Aug. 17, 1886.
Vol. 7, Pt. 2–52
O'Reilly, John Boyle, June 28, 1844–Aug. 10, 1890.
Vol. 7, Pt. 2–53
O'Reilly, Robert Maitland, Jan. 14, 1845–Nov. 3, 1912.
Vol. 7, Pt. 2–54
O'Rielly, Henry. [*See* O'Reilly, Henry, 1806–1886.]
Ormsby, Waterman Lilly, 1809–Nov. 1, 1883.
Vol. 7, Pt. 2–55
Orne, John, Apr. 29, 1834–Nov. 29, 1911.
Vol. 7, Pt. 2–55
Orr, Alexander Ector, Mar. 2, 1831–June 3, 1914.
Vol. 7, Pt. 2–56
Orr, Gustavus John, Aug. 9, 1819–Dec. 11, 1887.
Vol. 7, Pt. 2–57
Orr, Hugh, Jan. 2, 1715–Dec. 6, 1798.
Vol. 7, Pt. 2–57
Orr, James Lawrence, May 12, 1822–May 5, 1873.
Vol. 7, Pt. 2–59
Orr, Jehu Amaziah, Apr. 10, 1828–Mar. 9, 1921.
Vol. 7, Pt. 2–60
Orry-Kelly, Dec. 31, 1897–Feb. 26, 1964.
Supp. 7–591
Orth, Godlove Stein, Apr. 22, 1817–Dec. 16, 1882.
Vol. 6, Pt. 2–60
Orthwein, Charles F., Jan. 28, 1839–Dec. 28, 1898.
Vol. 7, Pt. 2–61

Orton, Edward Francis Baxter, Mar. 9, 1829–Oct. 16, 1899.
Vol. 7, Pt. 2–62
Orton, Harlow South, Nov. 23, 1817–July 4, 1895.
Vol. 7, Pt. 2–63
Orton, Helen Fuller, Nov. 1, 1872–Feb. 16, 1955.
Supp. 5–526
Orton, James, Apr. 21, 1830–Sept. 25, 1877.
Vol. 7, Pt. 2–64
Orton, William, June 14, 1826–Apr. 22, 1878.
Vol. 7, Pt. 2–65
Ortynsky, Stephen Soter, Jan. 29, 1866–Mar. 24, 1916.
Vol. 7, Pt. 2–66
Ory, Edward ("Kid"), Dec. 1886–Jan. 23, 1973.
Supp. 9–598
Osborn, Charles, Aug. 21, 1775–Dec. 29, 1850.
Vol. 7, Pt. 2–66
Osborn, Chase Salmon, Jan. 22, 1860–Apr. 11, 1949.
Supp. 4–639
Osborn, Henry Fairfield, Aug. 8, 1857–Nov. 6, 1935.
Supp. 1–584
Osborn, Henry Fairfield, Jan. 15, 1887–Sept. 16, 1969.
Supp. 8–485
Osborn, Henry Stafford, Aug. 17, 1823–Feb. 2, 1894.
Vol. 7, Pt. 2–67
Osborn, Laughton, *c.* 1809–Dec. 13, 1878.
Vol. 7, Pt. 2–68
Osborn, Norris Galpin, Apr. 17, 1858–May 6, 1932.
Vol. 7, Pt. 2–69
Osborn, Selleck, *c.* 1782–*c.* October 1826.
Vol. 7, Pt. 2–69
Osborn, Thomas Andrew, Oct. 26, 1836–Feb. 4, 1898.
Vol. 7, Pt. 2–70
Osborn, Thomas Ogden, Aug. 11, 1832–Mar. 27, 1904.
Vol. 7, Pt. 2–71
Osborn, William Henry, Dec. 21, 1820–Mar. 2, 1894.
Vol. 7, Pt. 2–72
Osborne, James Walker, Jan. 5, 1859–Sept. 7, 1919.
Vol. 7, Pt. 2–73
Osborne, Thomas Burr, Aug. 5, 1859–Jan. 29, 1929.
Vol. 7, Pt. 2–74
Osborne, Thomas Mott, Sept. 23, 1859–Oct. 20, 1926.
Vol. 7, Pt. 2–75
Osceola, *c.* 1800–Jan. 30, 1838.
Vol. 7, Pt. 2–76
Osgood, Frances Sargent Locke, June 18, 1811–May 12, 1850.
Vol. 7, Pt. 2–77
Osgood, George Laurie, Apr. 3, 1844–Dec. 12, 1922.
Vol. 7, Pt. 2–78
Osgood, Herbert Levi, Apr. 9, 1855–Sept. 11, 1918.
Vol. 7, Pt. 2–78
Osgood, Howard, Jan. 4, 1831–Nov. 28, 1911.
Vol. 7, Pt. 2–79
Osgood, Jacob, Mar. 16, 1777–Nov. 29, 1844.
Vol. 7, Pt. 2–80
Osgood, Samuel, Feb. 3, 1747/48–Aug. 12, 1813.
Vol. 7, Pt. 2–81
Osgood, William Fogg, Mar. 10, 1864–July 22, 1943.
Supp. 3–574
O'Shaughnessy, Michael Maurice, May 28, 1864–Oct. 12, 1934.
Supp. 1–587
O'Shaughnessy, Nelson Jarvis Waterbury, Feb. 12, 1876–July 25, 1932.
Supp. 1–589
O'Shea, Michael Vincent, Sept. 17, 1866–Jan. 14, 1932.
Vol. 7, Pt. 2–82
Osler, William, July 12, 1849–Dec. 29, 1919.
Vol. 7, Pt. 2–83
Ossoli, Margaret Fuller. [*See* Fuller, Sarah Margaret, 1810–1850.]
Ostenaco. [*See* Outacity, fl. 1756–1777.]
Osten Sacken, Carl Robert Romanovich von der, Aug 21, 1828–May 20, 1906.
Vol. 7, Pt. 2–87
Osterhaus, Peter Joseph, Jan. 4, 1823–Jan. 2, 1917.
Vol. 7, Pt. 2–88
Osterhout, Winthrop John Vanleuven, Aug. 2, 1871–Apr. 9, 1964.
Supp. 7–592
Ostromislensky, Iwan Iwanowich, Sept. 8, 1880–Jan. 16, 1939.
Supp. 2–505
O'Sullivan, John Louis, November 1813–Feb. 24, 1895.
Vol. 7, Pt. 2–89
O'Sullivan, Mary Kenney, Jan. 8, 1864–Jan. 18, 1943.
Supp. 3–575
Oswald, Lee Harvey, Oct. 18, 1939–Nov. 24, 1963.
Supp. 7–593
Otacite, [*See* Outacity, fl. 1756–1777.]
Otermín, Antonio de, fl. 1678–1683.
Vol. 7, Pt. 2–89
Otey, James Hervey, Jan. 27, 1800–Apr. 23, 1863.
Vol. 7, Pt. 2–90
Otis, Arthur Sinton, July 28, 1886–Jan. 1, 1964.
Supp. 7–594
Otis, Bass, July 17, 1784–Nov. 3, 1861.
Vol. 7, Pt. 2–91
Otis, Charles Eugene, May 11, 1846–Nov. 8, 1917.
Vol. 7, Pt. 2–92
Otis, Charles Rollin, Apr. 29, 1835–May 24, 1927.
Vol. 7, Pt. 2–93
Otis, Elisha Graves, Aug. 3, 1811–Apr. 8, 1861.
Vol. 7, Pt. 2–93
Otis, Elwell Stephen, Mar. 25, 1838–Oct. 21, 1909.
Vol. 7, Pt. 2–94
Otis, Fessenden Nott, Mar. 6, 1825–May 24, 1900.
Vol. 7, Pt. 2–95
Otis, George Alexander, Nov. 12, 1830–Feb. 23, 1881.
Vol. 7, Pt. 2–96
Otis, Harrison Gray, Oct. 8, 1765–Oct. 28, 1848.
Vol. 7, Pt. 2–98
Otis, Harrison Gray, Feb. 10, 1837–July 30, 1917.
Vol. 7, Pt. 2–100
Otis, James, Feb. 5, 1725–May 23, 1783.
Vol. 7, Pt. 2–101
Ott, Isaac, Nov. 30, 1847–Jan. 1, 1916.
Vol. 7, Pt. 2–105
Ott, Melvin Thomas ("Mel"), Mar. 2, 1909–Nov. 21, 1958.
Supp. 6–488
Ottassite. [*See* Outacity, fl. 1756–1777.]
Ottendorfer, Anna Behr Uhl, Feb. 13, 1815–Apr. 1, 1884.
Vol. 7, Pt. 2–106
Ottendorfer, Oswald, Feb. 26, 1826–Dec. 15, 1900.
Vol. 7, Pt. 2–107
Otterbein, Philip William, June 3, 1726–Nov. 17, 1813.
Vol. 7, Pt. 2–107
Ottley, Roi, Aug. 2, 19O6–Oct. 1, 1960.
Supp. 6–489
Otto, Bodo, 1711–June 12, 1787.
Vol. 7, Pt. 2–108
Otto, John Conrad, Mar. 15, 1774–June 26, 1844.
Vol. 7, Pt. 2–109
Otto, William Tod, Jan. 19, 1816–Nov. 7, 1905.
Vol. 7, Pt. 2–110
Ouconnastote. [*See* Oconostota, d. 1785.]
Ouimet, Francis Desales, May 8, 1893–Sept. 2, 1967.
Supp. 8–486
Ouray, *c.* 1833–Aug. 24, 1880.
Vol. 7, Pt. 2–110
Oursler, (Charles) Fulton, Jan. 22, 1893–May 24, 1952.
Supp. 5–527
Outacity, fl. 1756–1777.
Vol. 7, Pt. 2–111
Outcault, Richard Felton, Jan. 14, 1863–Sept. 25, 1928.
Vol. 7, Pt. 2–112
Outerbridge, Alexander Ewing, July 31, 1850–Jan. 15, 1928.
Vol. 7, Pt. 2–112.
Outerbridge, Eugenius Harvey, Mar. 8, 1860–Nov. 10, 1932.
Supp. 1–589
Overman, Frederick, *c.* 1803–Jan. 7, 1852.
Vol. 7, Pt. 2–113
Overman, Lee Slater, Jan. 3, 1854–Dec. 12, 1930.
Vol. 7, Pt. 2–114
Overstreet, Harry Allen, Oct. 25, 1875–Aug. 17, 1970.
Supp. 8–487
Overton, John, Apr. 9, 1766–Apr. 12, 1833.
Vol. 7, Pt. 2–115
Owen, David Dale, June 24, 1807–Nov. 13, 1860.
Vol. 7, Pt. 2–116
Owen, Edward Thomas, Mar. 4, 1850–Nov. 9, 1931.
Vol. 7, Pt. 2–117
Owen, Griffith, *c.* 1647–Aug. 19, 1717.
Vol. 7, Pt. 2–118

Owen, Robert Dale, Nov. 9, 1801–June 24, 1877.
Vol. 7, Pt. 2–118
Owen, Robert Latham, Feb. 2, 1856–July 19, 1947.
Supp. 4–640
Owen, Stephen Joseph, Apr. 21, 1898–May 17, 1964.
Supp. 7–595
Owen, Thomas McAdory, Dec. 15, 1866–Mar. 25, 1920.
Supp. 1–590
Owen, William Florence, 1844–May 4, 1906.
Vol. 7, Pt. 2–120
Owens, James Cleveland ("Jesse"), Sept. 12, 1913–Mar. 31, 1980.
Supp. 10–610
Owens, John Edmond, Apr. 2, 1823–Dec. 7, 1886.
Vol. 7, Pt. 2–121
Owens, Michael Joseph, Jan. 1, 1859–Dec. 27, 1923.
Vol. 7, Pt. 2–122
Owre, Alfred, Dec. 16, 1870–Jan. 2, 1935.
Supp. 1–591
Owsley, Frank Lawrence, Jan. 20, 1890–Oct. 21, 1956.
Supp. 6–491
Owsley, William, 1782–Dec. 9, 1862.
Vol. 7, Pt. 2–122
Oxnam, Garfield Bromley, Aug. 14, 1891–Mar. 12, 1963.
Supp. 7–596

Paca, William, Oct. 31, 1740–Oct. 13, 1799.
Vol. 7, Pt. 2–123
Pace, Edward Aloysius, July 3, 1861–Apr. 26, 1938.
Supp. 2–506
Pacheco, Romualdo, Oct. 31, 1831–Jan. 23, 1899.
Vol. 7, Pt. 2–124
Pack, Charles Lathrop, May 7, 1857–June 14, 1937.
Supp. 2–507
Packard, Alpheus Spring, Dec. 23, 1798–July 13, 1884.
Vol. 7, Pt. 2–125
Packard, Alpheus Spring, Feb. 19, 1839–Feb. 14, 1905.
Vol. 7, Pt. 2–126
Packard, Frederick Adolphus, Sept. 26, 1794–Nov. 11, 1867.
Vol. 7, Pt. 2–127
Packard, James Ward, Nov. 5, 1863–Mar. 20, 1928.
Vol. 7, Pt. 2–128
Packard, John Hooker, Aug. 15, 1832–May 21, 1907.
Vol. 7, Pt. 2–129
Packard, Joseph, Dec. 23, 1812–May 3, 1902.
Vol. 7, Pt. 2–130
Packard, Silas Sadler, Apr. 28, 1826–Oct. 27, 1898.
Vol. 7, Pt. 2–130
Packer, Asa, Dec. 29, 1805–May 17, 1879.
Vol. 7, Pt. 2–131
Packer, William Fisher, Apr. 2, 1807–Sept. 27, 1870.
Vol. 7, Pt. 2–132
Paddock, Algernon Sidney, Nov. 9, 1830–Oct. 17, 1897.
Vol. 7, Pt. 2–133
Paddock, Benjamin Henry, Feb. 29, 1828–Mar. 9, 1891.
Vol. 7, Pt. 2–133
Paddock, John Adams, Jan. 19, 1825–Mar. 4, 1894.
Vol. 7, Pt. 2–134
Padilla, Juan de, *c.* 1500–*c.* 1544.
Vol. 7, Pt. 2–135
Page, Charles Grafton, Jan. 25, 1812–May 5, 1868.
Vol. 7, Pt. 2–135
Page, David Perkins, July 4, 1810–Jan. 1, 1848.
Vol. 7, Pt. 2–136
Page, John, Apr. 17, 1743 o.s.-Oct. 11, 1808.
Vol. 7, Pt. 2–137
Page, Joseph Francis ("Joe"), Oct. 28, 1917–Apr. 21, 1980.
Supp. 10–613
Page, Leigh, Oct. 13, 1884–Sept. 14, 1952.
Supp. 5–528
Page, Mann, 1691–Jan. 24, 1730.
Vol. 7, Pt. 2–138
Page, Oran Thaddeus ("Lips"), Jan. 27, 1908–Nov. 5, 1954.
Supp. 5–529
Page, Richard Lucian, Dec. 20, 1807–Aug. 9, 1901.
Vol. 7, Pt. 2–139
Page, Thomas Jefferson, Jan. 4, 1808–Oct. 26, 1899.
Vol. 7, Pt. 2–140
Page, Thomas Nelson, Apr. 23, 1853–Nov. 1, 1922.
Vol. 7, Pt. 2–141
Page, Thomas Walker, Dec. 4, 1866–Jan. 13, 1937.
Supp. 2–508
Page, Walter Hines, Aug. 15, 1855–Dec. 21, 1918.
Vol. 7, Pt. 2–142
Page, William, Jan. 1811–Sept. 30, 1885.
Vol. 7, Pt. 2–144
Paine, Albert Bigelow, July 10, 1861–Apr. 9, 1937.
Supp. 2–509
Paine, Byron, Oct. 10, 1827–Jan. 13, 1871.
Vol. 7, Pt. 2–145
Paine, Charles, Apr. 15, 1799–July 6, 1853.
Vol. 7, Pt. 2–146
Paine, Charles Jackson, Aug. 26, 1833–Aug. 12, 1916.
Vol. 7, Pt. 2–147
Paine, Elijah, Jan. 21, 1757–Apr. 28, 1842.
Vol. 7, Pt. 2–148
Paine, Halbert Eleazer, Feb. 4, 1826–Apr. 14, 1905.
Vol. 7, Pt. 2–148
Paine, Henry Warren, Aug. 30, 1810–Dec. 26, 1893.
Vol. 7, Pt. 2–149
Paine, John Alsop, Jan. 14, 1840–July 24, 1912.
Vol. 7, Pt. 2–150
Paine, John Knowles, Jan. 9, 1839–Apr. 25, 1906.
Vol. 7, Pt. 2–151
Paine, Martyn, July 8, 1794–Nov. 10, 1877.
Vol. 7, Pt. 2–153
Paine, Ralph Delahaye, Aug. 28, 1871–Apr. 29, 1925.
Vol. 7, Pt. 2–154
Paine, Robert, Nov. 12, 1799–Oct. 19, 1882.
Vol. 7, Pt. 2–155
Paine, Robert Treat, Mar. 11, 1731–May 11, 1814.
Vol. 7, Pt. 2–156
Paine, Robert Treat, Dec. 9, 1773–Nov. 13, 1811.
Vol. 7, Pt. 2–157
Paine, Robert Treat, Oct. 28, 1835–Aug. 11, 1910.
Vol. 7, Pt. 2–158
Paine, Thomas, Jan. 29, 1737–June 8, 1809.
Vol. 7, Pt. 2–159
Painter, Gamaliel, May 22, 1743–May 21, 1819.
Vol. 7, Pt. 2–166
Painter, William, Nov. 20, 1838–July 15, 1906.
Vol. 7, Pt. 2–167
Pal, George, Feb. 1, 1908–May 2, 1980.
Supp. 10–614
Paley, Barbara Cushing ("Babe"), July 5, 1915–July 6, 1978.
Supp. 10–616
Paley, John, Feb. 6, 1871–Dec. 23, 1907.
Vol. 7, Pt. 2–168
Palfrey, John Carver, Dec. 25, 1833–Jan. 29, 1906.
Vol. 7, Pt. 2–168
Palfrey, John Gorham, May 2, 1796–Apr. 26, 1881.
Vol. 7, Pt. 2–169
Palladino, Lawrence Benedict, Aug. 15, 1837–Aug. 19, 1927.
Vol. 7, Pt. 2–170
Pallen, Condé Benoist, Dec. 5, 1858–May 26, 1929.
Vol. 7, Pt. 2–171
Palmer, Albert Marshman, July 27, 1838–Mar. 7, 1905.
Vol. 7, Pt. 2–172
Palmer, Alexander Mitchell, May 4, 1872–May 11, 1936.
Supp. 2–510
Palmer, Alice Elvira Freeman, Feb. 21, 1855–Dec. 6, 1902.
Vol. 7, Pt. 2–173
Palmer, Alonzo Benjamin, Oct. 6, 1815–Dec. 23, 1887.
Vol. 7, Pt. 2–175
Palmer, Benjamin Morgan, Jan. 25, 1818–May 28, 1902.
Vol. 7, Pt. 2–175
Palmer, Bertha Honoré, May 22, 1849–May 5, 1918.
Vol. 7, Pt. 2–176
Palmer, Daniel David, Mar. 7, 1845–Oct. 20, 1913.
Vol. 7, Pt. 2–177
Palmer, Elihu, Aug. 7, 1764–Apr. 7, 1806.
Vol. 7, Pt. 2–177
Palmer, Erastus Dow, Apr. 2, 1817–Mar. 9, 1904.
Vol. 7, Pt. 2–179
Palmer, George Herbert, Mar. 19, 1842–May 7, 1933.
Vol. 7, Pt. 2–180
Palmer, Henry Wilbur, July 10, 1839–Feb. 15, 1913.
Vol. 7, Pt. 2–183
Palmer, Horatio Richmond, Apr. 26, 1834–Nov. 15, 1907.
Vol. 7, Pt. 2–183

Palmer, Innis Newton, Mar. 30, 1824–Sept. 9, 1900.
Vol. 7, Pt. 2–184
Palmer, James Croxall, June 29, 1811–Apr. 24, 1883.
Vol. 7, Pt. 2–185
Palmer, James Shedden, Oct. 13, 1810–Dec. 7, 1867.
Vol. 7, Pt. 2–185
Palmer, Joel, Oct. 4, 1810–June 9, 1881.
Vol. 7, Pt. 2–186
Palmer, John McAuley, Sept. 13, 1817–Sept. 25, 1900.
Vol. 7, Pt. 2–187
Palmer, John McAuley, Apr. 23, 1870–Oct. 26, 1955.
Supp. 5–530
Palmer, John Williamson, Apr. 4, 1825–Feb. 26, 1906.
Vol. 7, Pt. 2–188
Palmer, Joseph, Mar. 31, 1716–Dec. 25, 1788.
Vol. 7, Pt. 2–189
Palmer, Nathaniel Brown, Aug. 8, 1799–June 21, 1877.
Vol. 7, Pt. 2–189
Palmer, Potter, May 20, 1826–May 4, 1902.
Vol. 7, Pt. 2–190
Palmer, Mrs. Potter. [*See* Palmer, Bertha Honore, 1849–1918.]
Palmer, Ray, Nov. 12, 1808–Mar. 29, 1887.
Vol. 7, Pt. 2–191
Palmer, Thomas Witherell, Jan. 25, 1830–June 1, 1913.
Vol. 7, Pt. 2–192
Palmer, Walter Launt, Aug. 1, 1854–Apr. 16, 1932.
Vol. 7, Pt. 2–193
Palmer, Walter Walker, Feb. 27, 1882–Oct. 28, 1950.
Supp. 4–642
Palmer, William Adams, Sept. 12, 1781–Dec. 3, 1860.
Vol. 7, Pt. 2–193
Palmer, William Henry, *c.* 1830–Nov. 28, 1878.
Vol. 7, Pt. 2–194
Palmer, William Jackson, Sept. 18, 1836–Mar. 13, 1909.
Vol. 7, Pt. 2–195
Palmore, William Beverly, Feb. 24, 1844–July 5, 1914.
Vol. 7, Pt. 2–196
Palóu, Francisco, *c.* 1722–*c.* 1789.
Vol. 7, Pt. 2–196
Pammel, Louis Hermann, Apr. 19, 1862–Mar. 23, 1931.
Vol. 7, Pt. 2–197
Pancoast, Henry Khunrath, Feb. 26, 1875–May 20, 1939.
Supp. 2–512
Pancoast, Joseph, Nov. 23, 1805–Mar. 7, 1882.
Vol. 7, Pt. 2–198
Pancoast, Seth, July 28, 1823–Dec. 16, 1889.
Vol. 7, Pt. 2–199
Pangborn, Clyde Edward, Oct. 28, 1894–Mar. 29, 1958.
Supp. 6–492
Panofsky, Erwin, Mar. 30, 1892–Mar. 14, 1968.
Supp. 8–489
Pansy. [*See* Alden, Isabella Macdonald, 1841–1930.]
Panton, William, 1742?–Feb. 26, 1801.
Vol. 7, Pt. 2–199
Papanicolaou, George Nicholas, May 13, 1883–Feb. 19, 1962.
Supp. 7–598
Pardee, Ario, Nov. 19, 1810–Mar. 26, 1892.
Vol. 7, Pt. 2–200
Pardee, Don Albert, Mar. 29, 1837–Sept. 26, 1919.
Vol. 7, Pt. 2–201
Pardow, William O'Brien, June 13, 1847–Jan. 23, 1909.
Vol. 7, Pt. 2–202
Paris, Walter, Feb. 28, 1842–Nov. 26, 1906.
Vol. 7, Pt. 2–203
Parish, Elijah, Nov. 7, 1762–Oct 15 1825.
Vol. 7, Pt. 2–203
Park, Edwards Amasa, Dec. 29, 1808–June 4, 1900.
Vol. 7, Pt. 2–204
Park, James, Jan. 11, 1820–Apr. 21, 1883.
Vol. 7, Pt. 2–205
Park, Maud Wood, Jan. 25, 1871–May 8, 1955.
Supp. 5–531
Park, Robert Ezra, Feb. 14, 1864–Feb. 7, 1944.
Supp. 3–577
Park, Roswell, Oct. 1, 1807–July 16, 1869.
Vol. 7, Pt. 2–207
Park, Roswell, May 4, 1852–Feb. 15, 1914.
Vol. 7, Pt. 2–207
Park, Trenor William, Dec. 8, 1823–Dec. 13, 1882.
Vol. 7, Pt. 2–208
Park, William Hallock, Dec. 30, 1863–Apr. 6, 1939.
Supp. 2–513
Parke, Benjamin, Sept. 2, 1777–July 12, 1835.
Vol. 7, Pt. 2–209
Parke, John, Apr. 7, 1754–Dec. 11, 1789.
Vol. 7, Pt. 2–210
Parke, John Grubb, Sept. 22, 1827–Dec. 16, 1900.
Vol. 7, Pt. 2–211
Parker, Alton Brooks, May 14, 1852–May 10, 1926.
Vol. 7, Pt. 2–212
Parker, Alvin Pierson, Aug. 7, 1850–Sept. 10, 1924.
Vol. 7, Pt. 2–214
Parker, Amasa Junius, June 2, 1807–May 13, 1890.
Vol. 7, Pt. 2–214
Parker, Arthur Caswell, Apr. 5, 1881–Jan. 1, 1955.
Supp. 5–533
Parker, Carleton Hubbell, Mar. 31, 1878–Mar. 17, 1918.
Vol. 7, Pt. 2–215
Parker, Charlie ("Bird"), Aug. 29, 1920–Mar. 12, 1955.
Supp. 5–534
Parker, Cortlandt. [*See* Parker, John Cortlandt, 1818–1907.]
Parker, Dorothy Rothschild, Aug. 22, 1893–June 7, 1967.
Supp. 8–491
Parker, Edward Pickering, Nov. 4, 1912–Jan. 1, 1974.
Supp. 9–601
Parker, Edwin Brewington, Sept. 7, 1868–Oct. 30, 1929.
Vol. 7, Pt. 2–216
Parker, Edwin Pond, Jan. 13, 1836–May 28, 1920.
Vol. 7, Pt. 2–217
Parker, Edwin Wallace, Jan. 21, 1833–June 4, 1901.
Vol. 7, Pt. 2–218
Parker, Ely Samuel, 1828–Aug. 31, 1895.
Vol. 7, Pt. 2–219
Parker, Foxhall Alexander, Aug. 5, 1821–June 10, 1879.
Vol. 7, Pt. 2–220
Parker, Francis Wayland, Oct. 9, 1837–Mar. 2, 1902.
Vol. 7, Pt. 2–221
Parker, George Howard, Dec. 23, 1864–Mar. 26, 1955.
Supp. 5–535
Parker, Henry Taylor, Apr. 29, 1867–Mar. 30, 1934.
Supp. 1–592
Parker, Horatio William, Sept. 15, 1863–Dec. 18, 1919.
Vol. 7, Pt. 2–221
Parker, Isaac, June 17, 1768–July 25, 1830.
Vol. 7, Pt. 2–224
Parker, Isaac Charles, Oct. 15, 1838–Nov. 17, 1896.
Vol. 7, Pt. 2–225
Parker, James, *c.* 1714–July 2, 1770.
Vol. 7, Pt. 2–226
Parker, James, Mar. 3, 1776–Apr. 1, 1868.
Vol. 7, Pt. 2–227
Parker, James Cutler Dunn, June 2, 1828–Nov. 27, 1916.
Vol. 7, Pt. 2–228
Parker, Jane Marsh, June 16, 1836–Mar. 13, 1913.
Vol. 7, Pt. 2–229
Parker, Joel, Jan. 25, 1795–Aug. 17, 1875.
Vol. 7, Pt. 2–230
Parker, Joel, Aug. 27, 1799–May 2, 1873.
Vol. 7, Pt. 2–231
Parker, Joel, Nov. 24, 1816–Jan. 2, 1888.
Vol. 7, Pt. 2–232
Parker, John, July 13, 1729–Sept. 17, 1775.
Vol. 7, Pt. 2–232
Parker, John Cortlandt, June 27, 1818–July 29, 1907.
Vol. 7, Pt. 2–233
Parker, John Johnston, Nov. 20, 1885–Mar. 17, 1958.
Supp. 6–493
Parker, John Milliken, Mar. 16, 1863–May 20, 1939.
Supp. 2–514
Parker, Josiah, May 11, 1751–Mar. 14, 1810.
Vol. 7, Pt. 2–234
Parker, Peter, June 18, 1804–Jan. 10, 1888.
Vol. 7, Pt. 2–234
Parker, Quanah. [*See* Quanah, *c.* 1845–1911.]
Parker, Richard Elliot, Dec. 27, 1783–Sept. 10, 1840.
Vol. 7, Pt. 2–235
Parker, Richard Green, Dec. 25, 1798–Sept. 25, 1869.
Vol. 7, Pt. 2–236
Parker, Samuel, Apr. 23, 1779–Mar. 21, 1866.
Vol. 7, Pt. 2–237

Parker, Samuel Chester, May 31, 1880–July 21, 1924.
Vol. 7, Pt. 2–238
Parker, Theodore, Aug. 24, 1810–May 10, 1860.
Vol. 7, Pt. 2–238
Parker, Theodore Bissell, Aug. 20, 1889–Apr. 27, 1944.
Supp. 3–580
Parker, Thomas, June 8, 1595–Apr. 24, 1677.
Vol. 7, Pt. 2–241
Parker, Willard, Sept. 2, 1800–Apr. 25, 1884.
Vol. 7, Pt. 2–242
Parker, William Harwar, Oct. 8, 1826–Dec. 30, 1896.
Vol. 7, Pt. 2–243
Parkhurst, Charles, Oct. 29, 1845–Feb. 27, 1921.
Vol. 7, Pt. 2–244
Parkhurst, Charles Henry, Apr. 17, 1842–Sept. 8, 1933.
Vol. 7, Pt. 2–244
Parkhurst, John Adelbert, Sept. 24, 1861–Mar. 1, 1925.
Vol. 7, Pt. 2–246
Parkinson, Thomas Ignatius, Nov. 27, 1881–June 17, 1959.
Supp. 6–496
Parkman, Francis, Sept. 16, 1823–Nov. 8, 1893.
Vol. 7, Pt. 2–247
Parks, Larry, Dec. 13, 1914–Apr. 13, 1975.
Supp. 9–602
Parks, William, *c.* 1698–Apr. 1, 1750.
Vol. 7, Pt. 2–250
Parley, Peter. [*See* Goodrich, Samuel Griswold, 1793–1860.]
Parmentier, Andrew, July 3, 1780–Nov. 26, 1830.
Supp. 1–593
Parmly, Eleazar, Mar. 13, 1797–Dec. 13, 1874.
Vol. 7, Pt. 2–251
Parr, Samuel Wilson, Jan. 21, 1857–May 16, 1931.
Vol. 7, Pt. 2–252
Parrington, Vernon Louis, Aug. 3, 1871–June 16, 1929.
Vol. 7, Pt. 2–253
Parris, Albion Keith, Jan. 19, 1788–Feb. 11, 1857.
Vol. 7, Pt. 2–254
Parris, Alexander, Nov. 24, 1780–June 16, 1852.
Vol. 7, Pt. 2–254
Parris, Samuel, 1653–Feb. 27, 1719/20.
Vol. 7, Pt. 2–255
Parrish, Anne, Oct. 17, 1760–Dec. 26, 1800.
Vol. 7, Pt. 2–256
Parrish, Celestia Susannah, Sept. 12, 1853–Sept. 7, 1918.
Vol. 7, Pt. 2–257
Parrish, Charles, Aug. 27, 1826–Dec. 27, 1896.
Vol. 7, Pt. 2–257
Parrish, Edward, May 31, 1822–Sept. 9, 1872.
Vol. 7, Pt. 2–258
Parrish, Joseph, Sept. 2, 1779–Mar. 18, 1840.
Vol. 7, Pt. 2–259
Parrish, Maxfield, July 25, 1870–Mar. 30, 1966.
Supp. 8–493
Parrott, Enoch Greenleafe, Nov. 27, 1815–May 10, 1879.
Vol. 7, Pt. 2–260
Parrott, Robert Parker, Oct. 5, 1804–Dec. 24, 1877.
Vol. 7, Pt. 2–260
Parry, Charles Christopher, Aug. 28, 1823–Feb. 20, 1890.
Vol. 7, Pt. 2–261
Parry, Charles Thomas, Sept. 15, 1821–July 18, 1887.
Vol. 7, Pt. 2–262
Parry, John Stubbs, Jan. 4, 1843–Mar. 11, 1876.
Vol. 7, Pt. 2–263
Parsons, Albert Richard, June 24, 1848–Nov. 11, 1887.
Vol. 7, Pt. 2–264
Parsons, Albert Ross, Sept. 16, 1847–June 14, 1933.
Vol. 7, Pt. 2–265
Parsons, Elsie Worthington Clews, Nov. 27, 1875–Dec. 19, 1941.
Supp. 3–581
Parsons, Frank, Nov. 14, 1854–Sept. 26, 1908.
Vol. 7, Pt. 2–266
Parsons, John Edward, Oct. 24, 1829–Jan. 16, 1915.
Vol. 7, Pt. 2–267
Parsons, Lewis Baldwin, Apr. 5, 1818–Mar. 16, 1907.
Vol. 7, Pt. 2–267
Parsons, Lewis Eliphalet, Apr. 28, 1817–June 8, 1895.
Vol. 7, Pt. 2–268
Parsons, Louella Rose Oettinger, Aug. 6, 1881–Dec. 9, 1972.
Supp. 9–603
Parsons, Samuel Bowne, Feb. 14, 1819–Jan. 4, 1906.
Vol. 7, Pt. 2–269
Parsons, Samuel Holden, May 14, 1737–Nov. 17, 1789.
Vol. 7, Pt. 2–270
Parsons, Talcott, Dec. 13, 1902–May 8, 1979.
Supp. 10–617
Parsons, Theophilus, Feb. 24, 1750–Oct. 30, 1813.
Vol. 7, Pt. 2–271
Parsons, Theophilus, May 17, 1797–Jan. 26, 1882.
Vol. 7, Pt. 2–273
Parsons, Thomas William, Aug. 18, 1819–Sept. 3, 1892.
Vol. 7, Pt. 2–274
Parsons, Usher, Aug. 18, 1788–Dec. 19, 1868.
Vol. 7, Pt. 2–275
Parsons, William Barclay, Apr. 15, 1859–May 9, 1932.
Vol. 7, Pt. 2–276
Partington, Mrs. [*See* Shillaber, Benjamin Penhallow, 1814–1890.]
Parton, Arthur, Mar. 26, 1842–Mar. 7, 1914.
Vol. 7, Pt. 2–278
Parton, James, Feb. 9, 1822–Oct. 17, 1891.
Vol. 7, Pt. 2–279
Parton, Sara Payson Willis, July 9, 1811–Oct. 10, 1872.
Vol. 7, Pt. 2–280
Partridge, Alden, Feb. 12, 1785–Jan. 17, 1854.
Vol. 7, Pt. 2–281
Partridge, James Rudolph, *c.* 1823–Feb. 24, 1884.
Vol. 7, Pt. 2–282
Partridge, Richard, Dec. 9, 1681–Mar. 6, 1759.
Vol. 7, Pt. 2–283
Partridge, William Ordway, Apr. 11, 1861–May 22, 1930.
Vol. 7, Pt. 2–284
Parvin, Theodore Sutton, Jan. 15, 1817–June 28, 1901.
Vol. 7, Pt. 2–285
Parvin, Theophilus, Jan. 9, 1829–Jan. 29, 1898.
Vol. 7, Pt. 2–286
Pascalis-Ouvrière, Felix, *c.* 1750–July 29, 1833.
Vol. 7, Pt. 2–286
Paschal, George Washington, Nov. 23, 1812–Feb. 16, 1878.
Vol. 7, Pt. 2–287.
Pasco, Samuel, June 28, 1834–Mar. 13, 1917.
Vol. 7, Pt. 2–288
Pasquin, Anthony. [*See* Williams, John, 1761–1818.]
Passavant, William Alfred, Oct. 9, 1821–June 3, 1894.
Vol. 7, Pt. 2–289
Pastor, Antonio, May 28, 1837–Aug. 26, 1908.
Vol. 7, Pt. 2–290
Pastorius, Francis Daniel, Sept. 26, 1651–*c.* Jan. 1, 1720.
Vol. 7, Pt. 2–290
Pasvolsky, Leo, Apr. 22, 1893–May 5, 1953.
Supp. 5–537
Patch, Alexander McCarrell, Nov. 23, 1889–Nov. 212, 1945.
Supp. 3–582
Patch, Sam, *c.* 1807–Nov. 13, 1829.
Vol. 7, Pt. 2–291
Patchen, Kenneth, Dec. 13, 1911–Jan. 8, 1972.
Supp. 9–604
Pate, Maurice, Oct. 14, 1894–Jan. 19, 1965.
Supp. 7–599
Paterson, John, 1744–July 19, 1808.
Vol. 7, Pt. 2–292
Paterson, William, Dec. 24, 1745–Sept. 9, 1806.
Vol. 7, Pt. 2–293
Patillo, Henry, 1726–1801.
Vol. 7, Pt. 2–295
Patman, John William Wright, Aug. 6, 1893–Mar. 7, 1976.
Supp. 10–618
Paton, Lewis Bayles, June 27, 1864–Jan. 24, 1932.
Vol. 7, Pt. 2–295
Patri, Angelo, Nov. 27, 1876–Sept. 13, 1965.
Supp. 7–600
Patrick, Edwin Hill ("Ted"), Sept. 3, 1901–Mar. 11, 1964.
Supp. 7–601
Patrick, Hugh Talbot, May 11, 1860–Jan. 5, 1939.
Supp. 2–515
Patrick, Marsena Rudolph, Mar. 11, 1811–July 27, 1888.
Vol. 7, Pt. 2–296
Patrick, Mary Mills, Mar. 10, 1850–Feb. 25, 1940.
Supp. 2–516
Patrick, Mason Mathews, Dec. 13, 1863–Jan. 29, 1942.
Supp. 3–584

Patten, Gilbert, Oct. 25, 1866–Jan. 16, 1945.
Supp. 3–585
Patten, James A., May 8, 1852–Dec. 8, 1928.
Vol. 7, Pt. 2–297
Patten, Simon Nelson, May 1, 1852–July 24, 1922.
Vol. 7, Pt. 2–298
Patten, William, Mar. 15, 1861–Oct. 27, 1932.
Vol. 7, Pt. 2–300
Patterson, Alicia, Oct. 15, 1906–July 2, 1963.
Supp. 7–603
Patterson, Daniel Todd, Mar. 6, 1786–Aug. 25, 1839.
Vol. 7, Pt. 2–301
Patterson, Eleanor Medill, Nov. 7, 1881–July 24, 1948.
Supp. 4–643
Patterson, James Kennedy, Mar. 26, 1833–Aug. 15, 1922.
Vol. 7, Pt. 2–302
Patterson, James Willis, July 2, 1823–May 4, 1893.
Vol. 7, Pt. 2–303
Patterson, John Henry, Dec. 13, 1844–May 7, 1922.
Vol. 7, Pt. 2–304
Patterson, Joseph Medill, Jan. 6, 1879–May 25, 1946.
Supp. 4–645
Patterson, Morris, Oct. 26, 1809–Oct. 23, 1878.
Vol. 7, Pt. 2–305
Patterson, Richard Cunningham, Jr., Jan. 31, 1886–Sept. 30, 1966.
Supp. 8–494
Patterson, Robert, May 30, 1743–July 22, 1824.
Vol. 7, Pt. 2–305
Patterson, Robert, Jan. 12, 1792–Aug. 7, 1881.
Vol. 7, Pt. 2–306
Patterson, Robert Mayne, July 17, 1832–Apr. 5, 1911.
Vol. 7, Pt. 2–307
Patterson, Robert Porter, Feb. 12, 1891–Jan. 22, 1952.
Supp. 5–538
Patterson, Rufus Lenoir, June 11, 1872–Apr. 11, 1943.
Supp. 3–587
Patterson, Thomas MacDonald, Nov. 4, 1839–July 23, 1916.
Vol. 7, Pt. 2–308
Patterson, Thomas Harman, May 10, 1820–Apr. 9, 1889.
Vol. 7, Pt. 2–307
Patterson, William, Nov. 1, 1752–July 7, 1835.
Vol. 7, Pt. 2–309
Patterson, William Allan ("Pat"), Oct. 1, 1899–June 13, 1980.
Supp. 10–620
Pattie, James Ohio, 1804–1850?.
Vol. 7, Pt. 2–310
Pattison, Granville Sharp, *c.* 1791–Nov. 12, 1851.
Vol. 7, Pt. 2–311
Pattison, James William, July 14, 1844–May 29, 1915.
Vol. 7, Pt. 2–311
Pattison, John M., June 13, 1847–June 18, 1906.
Vol. 7, Pt. 2–312
Pattison, Robert Emory, Dec 8, 1850–Aug. 1, 1904.
Vol. 7, Pt. 2–313
Pattison, Thomas, Feb. 8, 1822–Dec. 17, 1891.
Vol. 7, Pt. 2–314
Patton, Francis Landey, Jan. 22, 1843–Nov. 25, 1932.
Vol. 7, Pt. 2–315
Patton, George Smith, Nov. 11, 1885–Dec. 21, 1945.
Supp. 3–588
Patton, John Mercer, Aug. 10, 1797–Oct. 29, 1858.
Vol. 7, Pt. 2–316
Patton, WIlliam, Aug. 23, 1798–Sept. 9, 1879.
Vol. 7, Pt. 2–317
Pauger, Adrien de, d. June 9, 1726.
Vol. 7, Pt. 2–318
Paul, Alice, Jan. 11, 1885–July 9, 1977.
Supp. 10–622
Paul, Elliot Harold, Feb. 13, 1891–Apr. 7, 1958.
Supp. 6–497
Paul, Father. [*See* Francis, Paul James, 1863–1940.]
Paul, Henry Martyn, June 25, 1851–Mar. 15, 1931.
Vol. 7, Pt. 2–319
Paul, John. [*See* Webb, Charles Henry, 1834–1905.]
Paul, Josephine Bay, Aug. 10, 1900–Aug. 6, 1962.
Supp. 7–604
Paul, William Darwin ("Shorty"), Jan. 31, 1900–Dec. 13, 1977.
Supp. 10–623
Paulding, Hiram, Dec. 11, 1797–Oct. 20, 1878.
Vol. 7, Pt. 2–320
Paulding, James Kirke, Aug. 22, 1778–Apr. 6, 1860.
Vol. 7, Pt. 2–321
Pavy, Octave, June 22, 1844–June 6, 1884.
Vol. 7, Pt. 2–324
Pawnee Bill. [*See* Lillie, Gordon William, 1860–1942.]
Payne, Bruce Ryburn, Feb. 18, 1874–Apr. 21, 1937.
Supp. 2–517
Payne, Christopher Harrison, Sept. 7, 1848–Dec. 4, 1925.
Vol. 7, Pt. 2–323
Payne, Daniel Alexander, Feb. 24, 1811–Nov. 29, 1893.
Vol. 7, Pt. 2–324
Payne, Henry B., Nov. 30, 1810–Sept. 9, 1896.
Vol. 7, Pt. 2–325
Payne, Henry Clay, Nov. 23, 1843–Oct–4, 1904.
Vol. 7, Pt. 2–326
Payne, John Barton, Jan. 26, 1855–Jan. 24, 1935.
Supp. 1–594
Payne, John Howard, June 9, 1791–Apr. 9, 1852.
Vol. 7, Pt. 2–327
Payne, Lewis Thornton Powell, 1845–1865. [*See* Booth, John Wilkes, 1838–1865.]
Payne, Oliver Hazard, July 21, 1839–June 27, 1917.
Vol. 7, Pt. 2–329
Payne, Sereno Elisha, June 26, 1843–Dec. 10, 1914.
Vol. 7, Pt. 2–330
Payne, William Harold, May 12, 1836–June 18, 1907.
Vol. 7, Pt. 2–331
Payne, William Morton, Feb. 14, 1858–July 11, 1919.
Vol. 7, Pt. 2–332
Payne-Gaposchkin, Cecilia Helena, May 10, 1900–Dec. 7, 1979.
Supp. 10–625
Payson, Edward, July 25, 1783–Oct. 22, 1827.
Vol. 7, Pt. 2–333
Payson, Seth, Sept. 30, 1758–Feb. 26, 1820.
Vol. 7, Pt. 2–334
Peabody, Andrew Preston, Mar. 19, 1811–Mar. 10, 1893.
Vol. 7, Pt. 2–334
Peabody, Cecil Hobart, Aug 9, 1855–May 4, 1934.
Supp. 1–595
Peabody, Elizabeth Palmer, May 16, 1804–Jan. 3, 1894.
Vol. 7, Pt. 2–335
Peabody, Endicott, May 30, 1857–Nov. 17, 1944.
Supp. 3–591
Peabody, Francis Greenwood, Dec. 4, 1847–Dec. 28, 1936.
Supp. 2–518
Peabody, George, Feb. 18, 1795–Nov. 4, 1869.
Vol. 7, Pt. 2–336
Peabody, George Foster, July 27, 1852–Mar. 4, 1938.
Supp. 2–520
Peabody, Joseph, Dec. 12, 1757–Jan. 5, 1844.
Vol. 7, Pt. 2–338
Peabody, Josephine Preston, May 30, 1874–Dec. 4, 1922.
Vol. 7, Pt. 2–339
Peabody, Lucy Whitehead, Mar. 2, 1861–Feb. 26, 1949.
Supp. 4–646
Peabody, Nathaniel, Mar. 1, 1741–June 27, 1823.
Vol. 7, Pt. 2–340
Peabody, Oliver William Bourn, July 9, 1799–July 5, 1848.
Vol. 7, Pt. 2–340
Peabody, Robert Swain, Feb. 22, 1845–Sept. 23, 1917.
Vol. 7, Pt. 2–341
Peabody, Selim Hobart, Aug. 20, 1829–May 26, 1903.
Vol. 7, Pt. 2–342
Peabody, William Bourn Oliver, July 9, 1799–May 28, 1847.
Vol. 7, Pt. 2–343
Peale, Anna Claypoole, Mar. 6, 1791–Dec. 25, 1878.
Vol. 7, Pt. 2–344
Peale, Charles Willson, Apr. 15, 1741–Feb. 22, 1827.
Vol. 7, Pt. 2–344
Peale, James, 1749–May 24, 1831.
Vol. 7, Pt. 2–347
Peale, Raphael, Feb. 17, 1774–Mar. 4, 1825.
Vol. 7, Pt. 2–348
Peale, Rembrandt, Feb. 22, 1778–Oct. 3, 1860.
Vol. 7, Pt. 2–348
Peale, Sarah Miriam, May 9, 1800–Feb. 4, 1885.
Vol. 7, Pt. 2–350

Peale, Titian Ramsay, Nov. 17, 1799–Mar. 13, 1885.
Vol. 7, Pt. 2–351
Pearce, Charles Sprague, Oct. 13, 1851–May 18, 1914.
Vol. 7, Pt. 2–352
Pearce, James Alfred, Dec. 14, 1805–Dec. 20, 1862.
Vol. 7, Pt. 2–352
Pearce, Richard, June 29, 1837–May 18, 1927.
Vol. 7, Pt. 2–353
Pearce, Richard Mills, Mar. 3, 1874–Feb. 16, 1930.
Vol. 7, Pt. 2–354
Pearce, Stephen Austen, Nov. 7, 1836–Apr. 8, 1900.
Vol. 7, Pt. 2–355
Pearl, Raymond, June 3, 1879–Nov. 17, 1940.
Supp. 2–521
Pearse, John Barnard Sweet, Apr. 19, 1842–Aug. 24, 1914.
Vol. 7, Pt. 2–356
Pearson, Drew, Dec. 13, 1897–Sept. 1, 1969.
Supp. 8–496
Pearson, Edmund Lester, Feb. 11, 1880–Aug. 8, 1937.
Supp. 2–522
Pearson, Edward Jones, Oct. 4, 1863–Dec. 7, 1928.
Vol. 7, Pt. 2–357
Pearson, Eliphalet, June 11, 1752–Sept. 12, 1826.
Vol. 7, Pt. 2–358
Pearson, Fred Stark, July 3, 1861–May 7, 1915.
Vol. 7, Pt. 2–358
Pearson, Leonard, Aug. 17, 1868–Sept. 20, 1909.
Vol. 7, Pt. 2–359
Pearson, Raymond Allen, Apr. 9, 1873–Feb. 13, 1939.
Supp. 2–523
Pearson, Richmond Mumford, June 28, 1805–Jan. 5, 1878.
Vol. 7, Pt. 2–360
Pearson, Thomas Gilbert, Nov. 10, 1873–Sept. 3, 1943.
Supp. 3–592
Pearsons, Daniel Kimball, Apr. 14, 1820–Apr 27, 1912.
Vol. 7, Pt. 2–361
Peary, Josephine Diebitsch, May 22, 1863–Dec. 19, 1955.
Supp. 5–539
Peary, Robert Edwin, May 6, 1856–Feb. 20, 1920.
Vol. 7, Pt. 2–362
Pease, Alfred Humphreys, May 6, 1838–July 13, 1882.
Vol. 7, Pt. 2–367
Pease, Calvin, Sept. 9, 1776–Sept. 17, 1839.
Vol. 7, Pt. 2–368
Pease, Elisha Marshall, Jan. 3, 1812–Aug. 26, 1883.
Vol. 7, Pt. 2–368
Pease, Joseph Ives, Aug. 9, 1809–July 2, 1883.
Vol. 7, Pt. 2–369
Peaslee, Edmund Randolph, Jan. 22, 1814–Jan. 21, 1878.
Vol. 7, Pt. 2–370
Peattie, Donald Culross, June 21, 1898–Nov. 16, 1964.
Supp. 7–605
Peavey, Frank Hutchinson, Jan. 18, 1850–Dec. 30, 1901.
Vol. 7, Pt. 2–371
Peay, Austin, June 1, 1876–Oct. 2, 1927.
Vol. 7, Pt. 2–371
Peck, Charles Horton, Mar. 30, 1833–July 11, 1917.
Vol. 7, Pt. 2–372
Peck, Charles Howard, June 18, 1870–Mar. 28, 1927.
Vol. 7, Pt. 2–373
Peck, George, Aug. 8, 1797–May 20, 1876.
Vol. 7, Pt. 2–374
Peck, George Record, May 15, 1843–Feb. 22, 1923.
Vol. 7, Pt. 2–375
Peck, George Washington, Dec. 4, 1817–June 6, 1859.
Vol. 7, Pt. 2–375
Peck, George Wilbur, Sept. 28, 1840–Apr. 16, 1916.
Vol. 7, Pt. 2–376
Peck, Harry Thurston, Nov. 24, 1856–Mar. 23, 1914.
Vol. 7, Pt. 2–377
Peck, James Hawkins, *c.* 1790–Apr. 29, 1836.
Vol. 7, Pt. 2–379
Peck, Jesse Truesdell, Apr. 4, 1811–May 17, 1883.
Vol. 7, Pt. 2–379
Peck, John James, Jan. 4, 1821–Apr. 21, 1878.
Vol. 7, Pt. 2–380
Peck, John Mason, Oct. 31, 1789–Mar. 14, 1858.
Vol. 7, Pt. 2–381
Peck, Lillie, Dec. 28, 1888–Feb. 21, 1957.
Supp. 6–499
Peck, Thomas Ephraim, Jan. 29, 1822–Oct. 2, 1893.
Vol. 7, Pt. 2–382
Peck, Tracy, May 24, 1838–Nov. 24, 1921.
Vol. 7, Pt. 2–382
Peck, Wilham Dandridge, May 8, 1763–Oct. 3, 1822.
Vol. 7, Pt. 2–383
Peckham, George Williams, Mar. 23, 1845–Jan. 10, 1914.
Vol. 7, Pt. 2–384
Peckham, Rufus Wheeler, Nov. 8, 1838–Oct. 24, 1909.
Vol. 7, Pt. 2–385
Peckham, Stephen Farnum, Mar. 26, 1839–July 11, 1918.
Vol. 7, Pt. 2–386
Peckham, Wheeler Hazard, Jan. 1, 1833–Sept. 27, 1905.
Vol. 7, Pt. 2–387
Pecora, Ferdinand, Jan. 6, 1882–Dec. 7, 1971.
Supp. 9–606
Pedder, James, July 29, 1775–Aug. 27, 1859.
Vol. 7, Pt. 2–387
Peek, Frank William, Aug. 20, 1881–July 26, 1933.
Vol. 7, Pt. 2–388
Peek, George Nelson, Nov. 19, 1873–Dec. 17, 1943.
Supp. 3–593
Peers, Benjamin Orrs, Apr. 20, 1800–Aug. 20, 1842.
Vol. 7, Pt. 2–389
Peerson, Cleng, 1783–Dec. 16, 1865.
Vol. 7, Pt. 2–390
Peet, Harvey Prindle, Nov. 19, 1794–Jan. 1, 1873.
Vol. 7, Pt. 2–390
Peet, Isaac Lewis, Dec. 4, 1824–Dec. 27, 1898.
Vol. 7, Pt. 2–391
Peet, Stephen Denison, Dec. 2, 1831–May 24, 1914.
Vol. 7, Pt. 2–392
Peffer, William Alfred, Sept. 10, 1831–Oct. 6, 1912.
Vol. 7, Pt. 2–393
Pegler, Westbrook, Aug. 2, 1894–June 24, 1969.
Supp. 8–497
Pegram, George Braxton, Oct. 24, 1876–Aug. 12, 1958.
Supp. 6–500
Pei, Mario Andrew, Feb. 16, 1901–Mar. 2, 1978.
Supp. 10–626
Peirce, Benjamin, Apr. 4, 1809–Oct. 6, 1880.
Vol. 7, Pt. 2–393
Peirce, Benjamin Osgood, Feb. 11, 1854–Jan. 14, 1914.
Vol. 7, Pt. 2–397
Peirce, Bradford Kinney, Feb. 3, 1819–Apr. 19, 1889.
Vol. 7, Pt. 2–398
Peirce, Charles Sanders, Sept. 10, 1839–Apr. 19, 1914.
Vol. 7, Pt. 2–398
Peirce, Cyrus, Aug. 15, 1790–Apr. 5, 1860.
Vol. 7, Pt. 2–403
Peirce, Henry Augustus, Dec. 15, 1808–July 29, 1885.
Vol. 7, Pt. 2–404
Peirce, James Mills, May 1, 1834–Mar. 21, 1906.
Vol. 7, Pt. 2–405
Peirce, William, *c.* 1590–1641.
Vol. 7, Pt. 2–406
Peixotto, Benjamin Franklin, Nov. 13, 1834–Sept. 18, 1890.
Vol. 7, Pt. 2–406
Pelham, Henry, Feb. 14, 1748/49–1806.
Vol. 7, Pt. 2–407
Pelham, John, Sept. 14, 1838–Mar. 17, 1863.
Vol. 7, Pt. 2–408
Pelham, Peter, *c.* 1695–Dec. 1751.
Vol. 7, Pt. 2–409
Pelham, Robert A., Jan. 4, 1859–June 12, 1943.
Supp. 3–595
Pellew, Henry Edward, Apr. 26, 1828–Feb. 4, 1923.
Vol. 7, Pt. 2–409
Peloubet, Francis Nathan, Dec. 2, 1931–Mar. 27, 1920.
Vol. 7, Pt. 2–410
Pelz, Paul Johannes, Nov. 18, 1841–Mar. 30, 1918.
Vol. 7, Pt. 2–411
Pemberton, Brock, Dec. 14, 1885–Mar. 11, 1950.
Supp. 4–648
Pemberton, Israel, May 10, 1715–Apr. 22, 1779.
Vol. 7, Pt. 2–412
Pemberton, James, Aug. 26, 1723–Feb. 9, 1809.
Vol. 7, Pt. 2–413
Pemberton, John, Nov. 27, 1727–Jan. 31, 1795.
Vol. 7, Pt. 2–413

Pemberton, John Clifford, Aug. 10, 1814–July 13, 1881.
Vol. 7, Pt. 2–414
Peñalosa Briceño, Diego Dioniso de, *c.* 1622–*c.* 1687.
Vol. 7, Pt. 2–415
Pender, William Dorsey, Feb. 6, 1834–July 18, 1863.
Vol. 7, Pt. 2–416
Pendergast, Thomas Joseph, July 22, 1872–Jan. 26, 1945.
Supp. 3–596
Pendleton, Edmund, Sept. 9, 1721–Oct. 26, 1803.
Vol. 7, Pt. 2–417
Pendleton, Edmund Monroe, Mar. 19, 1815–Jan. 26, 1884.
Vol. 7, Pt. 2–419
Pendleton, Ellen Fitz, Aug. 7, 1864–July 26, 1936.
Supp. 2–524
Pendleton, George Hunt, July 29, 1825–Nov. 24, 1889.
Vol. 7, Pt. 2–419
Pendleton, James Madison, Nov. 20, 1811–Mar. 4, 1891.
Vol. 7, Pt. 2–420
Pendleton, John B., 1798–Mar. 10, 1866.
Vol. 7, Pt. 2–421
Pendleton, John Strother, Mar. 1, 1802–Nov. 19, 1868.
Vol. 7, Pt. 2–422
Pendleton, William Kimbrough, Sept. 8, 1817–Sept. 1, 1899.
Vol. 7, Pt. 2–422
Pendleton, William Nelson, Dec. 26, 1809–Jan. 15, 1883.
Vol. 7, Pt. 2–423
Penfield, Edward, June 2, 1866–Feb. 8, 1925.
Vol. 7, Pt. 2–424
Penfield, Frederic Courtland, Apr. 23, 1855–June 19, 1922.
Vol. 7, Pt. 2–425
Penfield, William Lawrence, Apr. 2, 1846–May 9, 1909.
Vol. 7, Pt. 2–426
Penfold, Joseph Weller, Nov. 18, 1907–May 25, 1973.
Supp. 9–607
Penhallow, Samuel, July 2, 1665–Dec. 2, 1726.
Vol. 7, Pt. 2–427
Penick, Charles Clifton, Dec. 9, 1843–Apr. 13, 1914.
Vol. 7, Pt. 2–428
Penington, Edward, Sept. 3, 1667–Nov. 11, 1701.
Vol. 7, Pt. 2–428
Penington, Edward, Dec. 4, 1726–Sept. 30, 1796.
Vol. 7, Pt. 2–429
Penn, John, July 14, 1729–Feb. 9, 1795.
Vol. 7, Pt. 2–430
Penn, John, May 6, 1740–Sept. 14, 1788.
Vol. 7, Pt 2–431
Penn, Richard, 1735–May 27, 1811.
Vol. 7, Pt. 2–431
Penn, Thomas, Mar. 9, 1702–Mar. 21, 1775.
Vol. 7, Pt. 2–432
Penn, William, Oct. 14, 1644–July 30, 1718.
Vol. 7, Pt. 2–433
Pennell, Joseph, July 4, 1857–Apr. 23, 1926.
Vol. 7, Pt. 2–437
Penney, James Cash ("J. C."), Sept. 16, 1875–Feb. 12, 1971.
Supp. 9–609
Penniman, James Hosmer, Nov. 8, 1860–Apr. 6, 1931.
Vol. 7, Pt. 2–441
Pennington, James W. c., 1809–October 1870.
Vol. 7, Pt. 2–441
Pennington, William, May 4, 1796–Feb. 16, 1862.
Vol. 7, Pt. 2–442
Pennington, William Sandford, 1757–Sept. 17, 1826.
Vol. 7, Pt. 2–443
Pennock, Alexander Mosely, Oct. 1, 1814–Sept. 20, 1876.
Vol. 7, Pt. 2–444
Pennoyer, Sylvester, July 6, 1831–May 31, 1902.
Vol. 7, Pt. 2–445
Pennypacker, Elijah Funk, Nov. 29, 1804–Jan. 4, 1888.
Vol. 7, Pt. 2–446
Pennypacker, Galusha, June 1, 1844–Oct. 1, 1916.
Vol. 7, Pt. 2–446
Pennypacker, Samuel Whitaker, Apr. 9, 1843–Sept. 2, 1916.
Vol. 7, Pt. 2–447
Penrose, Boies, Nov. 1, 1860–Dec. 31, 1921.
Vol. 7, Pt. 2–448
Penrose, Charles Bingham, Oct. 6, 1798–Apr. 6, 1857.
Vol. 7, Pt. 2–449
Penrose, Richard Alexander Fullerton, Dec. 17, 1863–July 31, 1931.
Vol. 7, Pt. 2–450
Penrose, Spencer, Nov. 2, 1865–Dec. 7, 1939.
Supp. 2–525
Pentecost, George Frederick, Sept. 23, 1842–Aug. 7, 1920.
Vol. 7, Pt. 2–451
Pepper, George Seckel, June 11, 1808–May 2, 1890.
Vol. 7, Pt. 2–452
Pepper, George Wharton, Mar. 16, 1867–May 24, 1961.
Supp. 7–606
Pepper, William, Jan. 21, 1810–Oct. 15, 1864.
Vol. 7, Pt. 2–452
Pepper, William, Aug. 21, 1843–July 28, 1898.
Vol. 7, Pt. 2–453
Pepper, William, III, May 1, 1874–Dec. 3, 1947.
Supp. 4–650
Pepperrell, Sir William, June 27, 1696–July 6, 1759.
Vol. 7, Pt. 2–456
Perabo, Johann Ernst, Nov. 14, 1845–Oct. 29, 1920.
Vol. 7, Pt. 2–457
Peralta, Pedro de, *c.* 1584–1666.
Vol. 7, Pt. 2–458
Perché, Napoleon Joseph, Jan. 10, 1805–Dec. 27, 1883.
Vol. 7, Pt. 2–459
Percival, James Gates, Sept. 15, 1795–May 2, 1856.
Vol. 7, Pt. 2–460
Percival, John, Apr. 5, 1779–Sept. 17, 1862.
Vol. 7, Pt. 2–461
Percy, George, Sept. 4, 1580–*c.* Mar. 1632.
Vol. 7, Pt. 2–462
Percy, William Alexander, May 14, 1885–Jan. 21, 1942.
Supp. 3–597
Perdue, Arthur William, Aug. 8, 1885–June 27, 1977.
Supp. 10–628
Perelman, Sidney Joseph, Feb. 1, 1904–Oct. 16, 1979.
Supp. 10–630
Perez, Leander Henry, July 16, 1891–Mar. 19, 1969.
Supp. 8–499
Perham, Josiah, Jan. 31, 1803–Oct. 4, 1868.
Vol. 7, Pt. 2–462
Periam, Jonathan, Feb. 17, 1823–Dec. 9, 1911.
Vol. 7, Pt. 2–463
Perin, Charles Page, Aug. 23, 1861–Feb. 16, 1937.
Supp. 2–526
Perkins, Charles Callahan, Mar. 1, 1823–Aug. 25, 1886.
Vol. 7, Pt. 2–464
Perkins, Charles Elliott, Nov. 24, 1840–Nov. 8, 1907.
Vol. 7, Pt. 2–465
Perkins, Dwight Heald, Mar. 26, 1867–Nov. 2, 1941.
Supp. 3–598
Perkins, Eli. [*See* Landon, Melville de Lancey, 1839–1910.]
Perkins, Elisha, Jan. 16, 1741–Sept. 6, 1799.
Vol. 7, Pt. 2–466
Perkins, Frances, Apr. 10, 1880–May 14, 1965.
Supp. 7–607
Perkins, Frederic Beecher, Sept. 27, 1828–Jan. 27, 1899.
Vol. 7, Pt. 2–467
Perkins, George Clement, Aug. 23, 1839–Feb. 26, 1923.
Vol. 7, Pt. 2–468
Perkins, George Douglas, Feb. 29, 1840–Feb. 3, 1914.
Vol. 7, Pt. 2–469
Perkins, George Hamilton, Oct. 20, 1836–Oct. 28, 1899.
Vol. 7, Pt. 2–469
Perkins, George Henry, Sept. 25, 1844–Sept. 12, 1933.
Vol. 7, Pt. 2–470
Perkins, George Walbridge, Jan. 31, 1862–June 18, 1920.
Vol. 7, Pt. 2–471
Perkins, Jacob, July 9, 1766–July 30, 1849.
Vol. 7, Pt. 2–472
Perkins, James Breck, Nov. 4, 1847–Mar. 11, 1910.
Vol. 7, Pt. 2–473
Perkins, James Handasyd, July 31, 1810–Dec. 14, 1849.
Vol. 7, Pt. 2–474
Perkins, James Handasyd, Jan. 11, 1876–July 12, 1940.
Supp. 2–527
Perkins, Justin, Mar. 5, 1805–Dec. 31, 1869.
Vol. 7, Pt. 2–475
Perkins, Marion, 1908–Dec. 17, 1961.
Supp. 7–610
Perkins, Maxwell Evarts, Sept. 20, 1884–June 17, 1947.
Supp. 4–651
Perkins, Samuel Elliott, Dec. 6, 1811–Dec. 17, 1879.
Vol. 7, Pt. 2–476

Perkins, Thomas Handasyd, Dec. 15, 1764–Jan. 11, 1854.
Vol. 7, Pt. 2–477
Perkins, Thomas Nelson, May 6, 1870–Oct. 7, 1937.
Supp. 2–528
Perley, Ira, Nov. 9, 1799–Feb. 26, 1874.
Vol. 7, Pt. 2–478
Perlman, Philip Benjamin, Mar. 5, 1890–July 31, 1960.
Supp. 6–502
Perlman, Selig, Dec. 9, 1888–Aug. 14, 1959.
Supp. 6–503
Perrin, Bernadotte, Sept. 15, 1847–Aug. 31, 1920.
Vol. 7, Pt. 2–478
Perrine, Charles Dillon, July 28, 1867–June 21, 1951.
Supp. 5–540
Perrine, Frederic Auten Combs, Aug. 25, 1862–Oct. 21, 1908.
Vol. 7, Pt. 2–479
Perrine, Henry, Apr. 5, 1797–Aug. 7, 1840.
Vol. 7, Pt. 2–480
Perrot, Nicolas, 1644–*c.* 1718.
Vol. 7, Pt. 2–481
Perry, Antoinette, June 27, 1888–June 28, 1946.
Supp. 4–652
Perry, Arthur Latham, Feb. 27, 1830–July 9, 1905.
Vol. 7, Pt. 2–482
Perry, Benjamin Franklin, Nov. 20, 1805–Dec. 3, 1886.
Vol. 7, Pt. 2–483
Perry, Bliss, Nov. 25, 1860–Feb. 13, 1954.
Supp. 5–541
Perry, Christopher Raymond, Dec 4, 1761–June 1, 1818.
Vol. 7, Pt. 2–484
Perry, Clarence Arthur, Mar. 4, 1872–Sept. 5, 1944.
Supp. 3–600
Perry, Edward Aylesworth, Mar. 15, 1831–Oct. 15, 1889.
Vol. 7, Pt. 2–484
Perry, Edward Baxter, Feb. 14, 1855–June 13, 1924.
Vol. 7, Pt. 2–485
Perry, Enoch Wood, July 31, 1831–Dec. 14, 1915.
Vol. 7, Pt. 2–485
Perry, Matthew Calbraith, Apr. 10, 1794–Mar. 4, 1858.
Vol. 7, Pt. 2–486
Perry, Nora, 1831–May 13, 1896.
Vol. 7, Pt. 2–489
Perry, Oliver Hazard, Aug. 20, 1785–Aug. 23, 1819.
Vol. 7, Pt. 2–490
Perry, Pettis, Jan. 4, 1897–July 24, 1965.
Supp. 7–611
Perry, Ralph Barton, July 3, 1876–Jan. 22, 1957.
Supp. 6–504
Perry, Rufus Lewis, Mar. 11, 1834–June 18, 1895.
Vol. 7, Pt. 2–492
Perry, Stuart, Nov. 2, 1814–Feb. 9, 1890.
Vol. 7, Pt. 2–492
Perry, Thomas Sergeant, Jan. 23, 1845–May 7, 1928.
Vol. 7, Pt. 2–493
Perry, Walter Scott, Dec. 26, 1855–Aug. 22, 1934.
Supp. 1–596
Perry, William, Dec. 20, 1788–Jan. 11, 1887.
Vol. 7, Pt. 2–494
Perry, William Flake, 1823–Dec. 18, 1901.
Vol. 7, Pt. 2–494
Perry, William Stevens, Jan. 22, 1832–May 13, 1898.
Vol. 7, Pt. 2–495
Pershing, John Joseph, Sept. 13, 1860–July 15, 1948.
Supp. 4–653
Person, Thomas, Jan. 19, 1733–Nov. 16, 1800.
Vol. 7, Pt. 2–496
Persons, Warren Milton, Mar. 12, 1878–Oct. 11, 1937.
Supp. 2–529
Peter, Hugh, 1598–Oct. 16, 1660.
Vol. 7, Pt. 2–496
Peter, John Frederick, May 19, 1746–July 19, 1813.
Vol. 7, Pt. 2–498
Peter, Robert, Jan. 21, 1805–Apr. 26, 1894.
Vol. 7, Pt. 2–499
Peter, Sarah Worthington King, May 10, 1800–Feb. 6, 1877.
Vol. 7, Pt. 2–500
Peterkin, George William, Mar. 21, 1841–Sept. 22, 1916.
Vol. 7, Pt. 2–501
Peterkin, Julia Mood, Oct. 31, 1880–Aug. 10, 1961.
Supp. 7–612
Peters, Absalom, Sept. 19, 1793–May 18, 1869.
Vol. 7, Pt. 2–502
Peters, Christian Henry Frederick, Sept. 19, 1813–July 19, 1890.
Vol. 7, Pt. 2–502
Peters, Edward Dyer, June 1, 1849–Feb. 17, 1917.
Vol. 7, Pt. 2–504
Peters, John Andrew, Oct. 9, 1822–Apr. 2, 1904.
Vol. 7, Pt. 2–504
Peters, John Charles, July 6, 1819–Oct. 21, 1893.
Vol. 7, Pt. 2–505
Peters, John Punnett, Dec. 16, 1852–Nov. 10, 1921.
Vol. 7, Pt. 2–506
Peters, Madison Clinton, Nov. 6, 1859–Oct. 12, 1918.
Vol. 7, Pt. 2–507
Peters, Phillis Wheatley. [*See* Wheatley, Phillis, *c.* 1754–1784.]
Peters, Richard, *c.* 1704–July 10, 1776.
Vol. 7, Pt. 2–508
Peters, Richard, June 22, 1744–Aug. 22, 1828.
Vol. 7, Pt. 2–509
Peters, Richard, Nov. 10, 1810–Feb. 6, 1889.
Vol. 7, Pt. 2–510
Peters, Samuel Andrew, Nov. 20, 1735–Apr. 19, 1826.
Vol. 7, Pt. 2–511
Peters, William Cumming, Mar. 10, 1805–Apr. 20, 1866.
Vol. 7, Pt. 2–512
Peterson, Charles Jacobs, July 20, 1819–Mar. 4, 1887.
Vol. 7, Pt. 2–512
Peterson, Henry, Dec. 7, 1818–Oct. 10, 1891.
Vol. 7, Pt. 2–513
Petigru, James Louis, May 10, 1789–Mar. 9, 1863.
Vol. 7, Pt. 2–514
Petri, Angelo, Sept. 5, 1883–Oct. 4, 1961.
Supp. 7–613
Pettengill, Samuel Barrett, Jan. 19, 1886–Mar. 20, 1974.
Supp. 9–610
Pettigrew, Charles, Mar. 20, 1743–Apr. 7, 1807.
Vol. 7, Pt. 2–515
Pettigrew, James Johnston, July 4, 1828–July 17, 1863.
Vol. 7, Pt. 2–516
Pettigrew, Richard Franklin, July 23, 1848–Oct. 5, 1926.
Vol. 7, Pt. 2–516
Pettit, Charles, 1736–Sept. 3, 1806.
Vol. 7, Pt. 2–517
Pettit, Thomas McKean, Dec. 26, 1797–May 30, 1853.
Vol. 7, Pt. 2–518
Pettus, Edmund Winston, July 6, 1821–July 27, 1907.
Vol. 7, Pt. 2–519
Pew, John Howard, Jan. 27, 1882–Nov. 27, 1971.
Supp. 9–611
Pew, Joseph Newton, Jr., Nov. 12, 1886–Apr. 9, 1963.
Supp. 7–615
Peyton, John Lewis, Sept. 15, 1824–May 21, 1896.
Vol. 7, Pt. 2–520
Pfahler, George Edward, Jan. 29, 1874–Jan. 29, 1957.
Supp. 6–505
Pfister, Alfred, Sept. 3, 1880–Apr. 3, 1964.
Supp. 7–616
Pfund, August Herman, Dec. 28, 1879–Jan. 4, 1949.
Supp. 4–658
Phelan, David Samuel, July 16, 1841–Sept. 21, 1915.
Vol. 7, Pt. 2–520
Phelan, James, Apr. 23, 1824–Dec. 23, 1892.
Vol. 7, Pt. 2–521
Phelan, James, Dec. 7, 1856–Jan. 30, 1891.
Vol. 7, Pt. 2–522
Phelan, James Duval, Apr. 20, 1861–Aug. 7, 1930.
Vol. 7, Pt. 2–523
Phelps, Almira Hart Lincoln, July 15, 1793–July 15, 1884.
Vol. 7, Pt. 2–524
Phelps, Anson Greene, Mar. 24, 1781–Nov. 30, 1853.
Vol. 7, Pt. 2–525
Phelps, Austin, Jan. 7, 1820–Oct. 13, 1890.
Vol. 7, Pt. 2–526
Phelps, Charles Edward, May 1, 1833–Dec. 27, 1908.
Vol. 7, Pt. 2–527
Phelps, Edward John, July 11, 1822–Mar. 9, 1900.
Vol. 7, Pt. 2–528
Phelps, Elizabeth Stuart, 1815–1852, and Phelps, Elizabeth Stuart, 1844–1911. [*See* Ward, Elizabeth Stuart Phelps, 1844–1911.]

Phelps, Guy Rowland, Apr. 1, 1802–Mar. 18, 1869.
Vol. 7, Pt. 2–529
Phelps, John Smith, Dec. 22, 1814–Nov. 20, 1886.
Vol. 7, Pt. 2–530
Phelps, Oliver, Oct. 21, 1749–Feb. 21, 1809.
Vol. 7, Pt. 2–530
Phelps, Thomas Stowell, Nov. 2, 1822–Jan. 10, 1901.
Vol. 7, Pt. 2–531
Phelps, Wllliam Franklin, Feb. 15, 1822–Aug. 15, 1907.
Vol. 7, Pt. 2–532
Phelps, William Lyon, Jan. 2, 1865–Aug. 21, 1943.
Supp. 3–601
Phelps, William Walter, Aug. 24, 1839–June 17, 1894.
Vol. 7, Pt. 2–533
Philip, d. Aug. 12, 1676.
Vol. 7, Pt. 2–534
Philip, John Woodward, Aug. 26, 1840–June 30, 1900.
Vol. 7, Pt. 2–534
Philipp, Emanuel Lorenz, Mar. 25, 1861–June 15, 1925.
Vol. 7, Pt. 2–535
Philips, John Finis, Dec. 31, 1834–Mar. 13, 1919.
Vol. 7, Pt. 2–536
Philips, Martin Wilson, June 17, 1806–Feb. 26, 1889.
Vol. 7, Pt. 2–537
Philipse, Frederick, Nov. 6, 1626–1702.
Vol. 7, Pt. 2–538
Philipson, David, Aug. 9, 1862–June 29, 1949.
Supp. 4–659
Phillips, David Graham, Oct. 31, 1867–Jan. 24, 1911.
Vol. 7, Pt. 2–538
Phillips, Francis Clifford, Apr. 2, 1850–Feb. 16, 1920.
Vol. 7, Pt. 2–539
Phillips, Frank, Nov. 28, 1873–Aug. 23, 1950.
Supp. 4–660
Phillips, George, 1593–July 1, 1644.
Vol. 7, Pt. 2–540
Phillips, Harry Irving, Nov. 26, 1889–Mar. 15, 1965.
Supp. 7–617
Phillips, Henry, Sept. 6, 1838–June 6, 1895.
Vol. 7, Pt. 2–541
Phillips, John, Dec. 27, 1719–Apr. 21, 1795.
Vol. 7, Pt. 2–542
Phillips, John Sanburn, July 2, 1861–Feb. 28, 1949.
Supp. 4–661
Phillips, Lena Madesin, Oct. 15, 1881–May 22, 1955.
Supp. 5–542
Phillips, Philip, Aug. 13, 1834–June 25, 1895.
Vol. 7, Pt. 2–542
Phillips, Samuel, Feb. 5, 1752–Feb. 10, 1802.
Vol. 7, Pt. 2–543
Phillips, Thomas Wharton, Feb. 23, 1835–July 21, 1912.
Vol. 7, Pt. 2–544
Phillips, Ulrich Bonnell, Nov. 4, 1877–Jan. 21, 1934.
Supp. 1–597
Phillips, Walter Polk, June 14, 1846–Jan. 31, 1920.
Vol. 7, Pt. 2–545
Phillips, Wendell, Nov. 29, 1811–Feb. 2, 1884.
Vol. 7, Pt. 2–546
Phillips, Willard, Dec. 19, 1784–Sept. 9, 1873.
Vol. 7, Pt. 2–547
Phillips, William, Mar. 30, 1750 o.s.-May 26, 1827.
Vol. 7, Pt. 2–548
Phillips, William, May 30, 1878–Feb. 23, 1968.
Supp. 8–500
Phillips, William Addison, Jan. 14, 1824–Nov. 30, 1893.
Vol. 7, Pt. 2–548
Phinizy, Ferdinand, Jan. 20, 1819–Oct. 20, 1889.
Vol. 7, Pt. 2–549
Phipps, Henry, Sept. 27, 1839–Sept. 22, 1930.
Vol. 7, Pt. 2–550
Phipps, Lawrence Cowle, Aug. 30, 1862–Mar. 1, 1958.
Supp. 6–506
Phips, Sir William, Feb. 2, 1650/51–Feb. 18, 1694/95.
Vol. 7, Pt. 2–551
Phisterer, Frederick, Oct. 11, 1836–July 13, 1909.
Vol. 7, Pt. 2–552
Phoenix, John. [*See* Derby, George Horatio, 1823–1861.]
Phyfe, Duncan, 1768–Aug. 16, 1854.
Vol. 7, Pt. 2–553
Physick, Philip Syng, July 7, 1768–Dec. 15, 1837.
Vol. 7, Pt. 2–554
Piatigorsky, Gregor, Apr. 17, 1903–Aug. 6, 1976.
Supp. 10–632
Piatt, Donn, June 29, 1819–Nov. 12, 1891.
Vol. 7, Pt. 2–555
Piatt, John James, Mar. 1, 1835–Feb. 16, 1917.
Vol. 7, Pt. 2–556
Piatt, Sarah Morgan Bryan, Aug. 11, 1836–Dec. 22, 1919.
Vol. 7, Pt. 2–557
Piccard, Jean Felix, Jan. 28, 1884–Jan. 28, 1963.
Supp. 7–618
Pick, Lewis Andrew, Nov. 18, 1890–Dec. 2, 1956.
Supp. 6–507
Pickard, Samuel Thomas, Mar. 1, 1828–Feb. 12, 1915.
Vol. 7, Pt. 2–558
Pickens, Andrew, Sept. 19, 1739–Aug. 11, 1817.
Vol. 7, Pt. 2–558
Pickens, Francis Wilkinson, Apr. 7, 1805–Jan. 25, 1869.
Vol. 7, Pt. 2–559
Pickens, Israel, Jan. 30, 1780–Apr. 23, 1827.
Vol. 7, Pt. 2–561
Pickens, William, Jan. 15, 1881–Apr. 6, 1954.
Supp. 5–543
Pickering, Charles, Nov. 10, 1805–Mar. 17, 1878.
Vol. 7, Pt. 2–562
Pickering, Edward Charles, July 19, 1846–Feb. 3, 1919.
Vol. 7, Pt. 2–562
Pickering, John, *c.* 1738–Apr. 11, 1805.
Vol. 7, Pt. 2–563
Pickering, John, Feb. 7, 1777–May 5, 1846.
Vol. 7, Pt. 2–564
Pickering, Timothy, July 17, 1745–Jan. 29, 1829.
Vol. 7, Pt. 2–565
Picket, Albert, Apr. 15, 1771–Aug. 3, 1850.
Vol. 7, Pt. 2–568
Pickett, Albert James, Aug. 13, 1810–Oct. 28, 1858.
Vol. 7, Pt. 2–569
Pickett, George Edward, Jan. 25, 1825–July 30, 1875.
Vol. 7, Pt. 2–570
Pickett, James Chamberlayne, Feb. 6, 1793–July 10, 1872.
Vol. 7, Pt. 2–571
Pickford, Mary, Apr. 8, 1892–May 29, 1979.
Supp. 10–634
Picknell, William Lamb, Oct. 23, 1853–Aug. 8, 1897.
Vol. 7, Pt. 2–572
Picton, Thomas, May 16, 1822–Feb. 20, 1891.
Vol. 7, Pt. 2–572
Pidgin, Charles Felton, Nov. 11, 1844–June 3, 1923.
Vol. 7, Pt. 2–573
Pieper, Franz August Otto, June 27, 1852–June 3, 1931.
Vol. 7, Pt. 2–574
Pierce, Benjamin, Dec. 25, 1757–Apr. 1, 1839.
Vol. 7, Pt. 2–575
Pierce, Edward Allen, Aug. 31, 1874–Dec. 16, 1974.
Supp. 9–613
Pierce, Edward Lillie, Mar. 29, 1829–Sept. 5, 1897.
Vol. 7, Pt. 2–575
Pierce, Franklin, Nov. 23, 1804–Oct. 8, 1869.
Vol. 7, Pt. 2–576
Pierce, George Foster, Feb. 3, 1811–Sept. 3, 1884.
Vol. 7, Pt. 2–580
Pierce, Gilbert Ashville, Jan. 11, 1839–Feb. 15, 1901.
Vol. 7, Pt. 2–581
Pierce, Henry Lillie, Aug. 23, 1825–Dec. 17, 1896.
Vol. 7, Pt. 2–582
Pierce, John Davis, Feb. 18, 1797–Apr. 5, 1882.
Vol. 7, Pt. 2–583
Pierce, Robert Willard, Oct. 8, 1914–Sept. 6, 1978.
Supp. 10–636
Pierce, William Leigh, *c.* 1740–Dec. 10, 1789.
Vol. 7, Pt. 2–583
Pierpont, Francis Harrison, Jan. 25, 1814–Mar. 24, 1899.
Vol. 7, Pt. 2–584
Pierpont, James, Jan. 4, 1659/60–Nov. 22, 1714.
Vol. 7, Pt. 2–585
Pierpont, John, Apr. 6, 1785–Aug. 27, 1866.
Vol. 7, Pt. 2–586
Pierrepont, Edwards, Mar. 4, 1817–Mar. 6, 1892.
Vol. 7, Pt. 2–587
Pierson, Abraham, 1609–Aug. 9, 1678.
Vol. 7, Pt. 2–587

Pierson, Abraham, *c.* 1645–Mar. 5, 1707.
Vol. 7, Pt. 2–588
Pierson, Arthur Tappan, Mar. 6, 1837–June 3, 1911.
Vol. 7, Pt. 2–589
Pierson, Hamilton Wilcox, Sept. 22, 1817–Sept. 7, 1888.
Vol. 7, Pt. 2–591
Pierz, Franz, Nov. 20, 1785–Jan. 22, 1880.
Vol. 7, Pt. 2–591
Piez, Charles, Sept. 24, 1866–Oct. 2, 1933.
Supp. 1–598
Piggot, Robert, May 20, 1795–July 23, 1887.
Vol. 7, Pt. 2–592
Piggott, James, *c.* 1739–Feb. 20, 1799.
Vol. 7, Pt. 2–592
Pike, Albert, Dec. 29, 1809–Apr. 2, 1891.
Vol. 7, Pt. 2–593
Pike, James Shepherd, Sept. 8, 1811–Nov. 29, 1882.
Vol. 7, Pt. 2–595
Pike, Mary Hayden Green, Nov. 30, 1824–Jan. 15, 1908.
Vol. 7, Pt. 2–597
Pike, Nicolas, Oct. 6, 1743–Dec. 9, 1819.
Vol. 7, Pt. 2–597
Pike, Robert, *c.* 1616–Dec. 12, 1708.
Vol. 7, Pt. 2–598
Pike, Zebulon Montgomery, Jan. 5, 1779–Apr. 27, 1813.
Vol. 7, Pt. 2–599
Pilat, Ignaz Anton, June 27, 1820–Sept. 17, 1870.
Vol. 7, Pt. 2–600
Pilcher, Joshua, Mar. 15, 1790–June 5, 1843.
Vol. 7, Pt. 2–601
Pilcher, Lewis Stephen, July 28, 1845–Dec. 24, 1934.
Supp. 1–599
Pilcher, Paul Monroe, Apr. 11, 1876–Jan. 4, 1917.
Vol. 7, Pt. 2–601
Pilkington, James, Jan. 4, 1851–Apr. 25, 1929.
Vol. 7, Pt. 2–602
Pilling, James Constantine, Nov. 16, 1846–July 26, 1895.
Vol. 7, Pt. 2–603
Pillow, Gideon Johnson, June 8, 1806–Oct. 8, 1878.
Vol. 7, Pt. 2–603
Pillsbury, Charles Alfred, Dec. 3, 1842–Sept. 17, 1899.
Vol. 7, Pt. 2–604
Pillsbury, Harry Nelson, Dec. 5, 1872–June 17, 1906.
Vol. 7, Pt. 2–606
Pillsbury, John Elliott, Dec. 15, 1846–Dec. 30, 1919.
Vol. 7, Pt. 2–606
Pillsbury, John Sargent, July 29, 1828–Oct. 18, 1901.
Vol. 7, Pt. 2–607
Pillsbury, Parker, Sept. 22, 1809–July 7, 1898.
Vol. 7, Pt. 2–608
Pilmore, Joseph, Oct. 31, 1739–July 24, 1825.
Vol. 7, Pt. 2–609
Pilsbury, Amos, Feb. 8, 1805–July 14, 1873.
Vol. 7, Pt. 2–610
Pinchback, Pinckney Benton Stewart, May 10, 1837–Dec. 21, 1921.
Vol. 7, Pt. 2–611
Pinchot, Amos Richards Eno, Dec. 6, 1873–Feb. 18, 1944.
Supp. 3–603
Pinchot, Cornelia Elizabeth Bryce, Aug. 26, 1881–Sept. 9, 1960.
Supp. 6–509
Pinchot, Gifford, Aug. 11, 1865–Oct. 4, 1946.
Supp. 4–663
Pinckney, Charles, Oct. 26, 1757–Oct. 29, 1824.
Vol. 7, Pt. 2–611
Pinckney, Charles Cotesworth, Feb. 25, 1746–Aug. 16, 1825.
Vol. 7, Pt. 2–614
Pinckney, Elizabeth Lucas, *c.* 1722–May 26, 1793.
Vol. 7, Pt. 2–616
Pinckney, Henry Laurens, Sept. 24, 1794–Feb. 3, 1863.
Vol. 7, Pt. 2–617
Pinckney, Thomas, Oct. 23, 1750–Nov. 2, 1828.
Vol. 7, Pt. 2–617
Pincus, Gregory Goodwin ("Goody"), Apr. 9, 1903–Aug. 22, 1967.
Supp. 8–502
Pine, Robert Edge, 1730–Nov. 19, 1788.
Vol. 7, Pt. 2–620
Piñero Jiménez, Jesús Toribio, Apr. 16, 1897–Nov. 19, 1952.
Supp. 5–545
Pingree, Hazen Stuart, Aug. 30, 1840–June 18, 1901.
Vol. 7, Pt. 2–621
Pinkerton, Allan, Aug. 25, 1819–July 1, 1884.
Vol. 7, Pt. 2–622
Pinkerton, Lewis Letig, Jan. 28, 1812–Jan. 28, 1875.
Vol. 7, Pt. 2–623
Pinkham, Lydia Estes, Feb. 9, 1819–May 17, 1883.
Vol. 7, Pt. 2–624
Pinkney, Edward Coote, Oct. 1, 1802–Apr. 11, 1828.
Vol. 7, Pt. 2–625
Pinkney, Ninian, June 7, 1811–Dec. 15, 1877.
Vol. 7, Pt. 2–625
Pinkney, William, Mar. 17, 1764–Feb. 25, 1822.
Vol. 7, Pt. 2–626
Pinney, Norman, Oct. 21, 1804–Oct. 1, 1862.
Vol. 7, Pt. 2–629
Pino, José. [*See* Son of Many Beads, *c.* 1866–1954.]
Pintard, John, May 18, 1759–June 21, 1844.
Vol. 7, Pt. 2–629
Pintard, Lewis, Oct. 1, 1732–Mar. 25, 1818.
Vol. 7, Pt. 2–630
Pinto, Isaac, June 12, 1720–Jan. 17, 1791.
Vol. 7, Pt. 2–631
Pinza, Ezio, May 18, 1892–May 9, 1957.
Supp. 6–510
Piper, Charles Vancouver, June 16, 1867–Feb. 11, 1926.
Vol. 7, Pt. 2–632
Piper, William Thomas, Jan. 8, 1881–Jan. 15, 1970.
Supp. 8–503
Pippin, Horace, Feb. 22, 1888–July 6, 1946.
Supp. 4–666
Pirsson, Louis Valentine, Nov. 3, 1860–Dec. 8, 1919.
Vol. 6, Pt. 2–633
Pise, Charles Constantine, Nov. 22, 1801–May 26, 1866.
Vol. 7, Pt. 2–634
Piston, Walter Hamor, Jan. 20, 1894–Nov. 12, 1976.
Supp. 10–637
Pitcairn, John, 1722–June 1775.
Vol. 7, Pt. 2–635
Pitcairn, John, Jan. 10, 1841–July 22, 1916.
Vol. 7, Pt. 2–635
Pitcher, Molly. [*See* McCauley, Mary Ludwig Hays, 1754–1832.]
Pitcher, Zina, Apr. 12, 1797–Apr. 5, 1872.
Vol. 7, Pt. 2–636
Pitchlynn, Peter Perkins, Jan. 30, 1806–Jan. 17, 1881.
Vol. 7, Pt. 2–637
Pitkin, Frederick Walker, Aug. 31, 1837–Dec. 18, 1886.
Vol. 7, Pt. 2–638
Pitkin, Timothy, Jan. 21, 1766–Dec. 18, 1847.
Vol. 7, Pt. 2–639
Pitkin, Walter Boughton, Feb. 6, 1878–Jan. 25, 1953.
Supp. 5–546
Pitkin, William, 1635–Dec. 15, 1694.
Vol. 7, Pt. 2–639
Pitkin, William, Apr. 30, 1694–Oct. 1, 1769.
Vol. 7, Pt. 2–640
Pitkin, William, 1725–Dec. 12, 1789.
Vol. 7, Pt. 2–641
Pitman, Benn, July 24, 1822–Dec. 28, 1910.
Vol. 7, Pt. 2–641
Pitney, Mahlon, Feb. 5, 1858–Dec. 9, 1924.
Vol. 7, Pt. 2–642
Pittman, Key, Sept. 19, 1872–Nov. 10, 1940.
Supp. 2–530
Pittock, Henry Lewis, Mar. 1, 1836–Jan. 28, 1919.
Vol. 7, Pt. 2–643
Pitts, Hiram Avery, *c.* 1800–Sept. 19, 1860.
Vol. 7, Pt. 2–644
Pitts, Zasu, Jan. 3, 1898–June 7, 1963.
Supp. 7–620
Placide, Henry, Sept. 8, 1799–Jan. 23, 1870.
Vol. 7, Pt. 2–644
Plaisted, Harris Merrill, Nov. 2, 1828–Jan. 31, 1898.
Vol. 7, Pt. 2–645
Plant, Henry Bradley, Oct. 27, 1819–June 23, 1899.
Vol. 7, Pt. 2–646
Plater, George, Nov. 8, 1735–Feb. 10, 1792.
Vol. 7, Pt. 2–647
Plath, Sylvia, Oct. 27, 1932–Feb. 11, 1963.
Supp. 7–621

Platner, Samuel Ball, Dec. 4, 1863–Aug. 20, 1921.
Vol. 7, Pt. 2–648
Platt, Charles Adams, Oct. 16, 1861–Sept. 12, 1933.
Vol. 8, Pt. 1–1
Platt, Orville Hitchcock, July 19, 1827–Apr. 21, 1905.
Vol. 8, Pt. 1–2
Platt, Thomas Collier, July 15, 1833–Mar. 6, 1910.
Vol. 8, Pt. 1–4
Pleasants, James, Oct. 24, 1769–Nov. 9, 1836.
Vol. 8, Pt. 1–6
Pleasants, John Hampden, Jan. 4, 1797–Feb. 27, 1846.
Vol. 8, Pt. 1–7
Pleasonton, Alfred, June 7, 1824–Feb. 17, 1897.
Vol. 8, Pt. 1–8
Plimpton, George Arthur, July 13, 1855–July 1, 1936.
Supp. 2–532
Plotz, Harry, Apr. 17, 1890–Jan. 6, 1947.
Supp. 4–667
Plowman, George Taylor, Oct. 19, 1869–Mar. 26, 1932.
Vol. 8, Pt. 1–9
Plumb, Glenn Edward, Sept. 30, 1866–Aug. 1, 1922.
Vol. 8, Pt. 1–9
Plumb, Preston B., Oct. 12, 1837–Dec. 20, 1891.
Vol. 8, Pt. 1–10
Plumbe, John, July 1809–July 1857.
Vol. 8, Pt. 1–11
Plumer, William, June 25, 1759–Dec. 22, 1850.
Vol. 8, Pt. 1–12
Plumer, William Swan, July 26, 1802–Oct. 22, 1880.
Vol. 8, Pt. 1–13
Plumley, Frank, Dec. 17, 1844–Apr. 30, 1924.
Vol. 8, Pt. 1–14
Plummer, Henry, d. Jan. 10, 1864.
Vol. 8, Pt. 1–15
Plummer, Henry Stanley, Mar. 3, 1874–Dec. 31, 1936.
Supp. 2–533
Plummer, Jonathan, July 13, 1761–Sept. 13, 1819.
Vol. 8, Pt. 1–16
Plummer, Mary Wright, Mar. 8, 1856–Sept. 21, 1916.
Vol. 8, Pt. 1–17
Plunkett, Charles Peshall, Feb. 15. 1864–Mar. 24, 1931.
Vol. 8, Pt. 1–17
Pocahontas, *c.* 1595–Mar. 1617.
Vol. 8, Pt. 1–18
Poe, Edgar Allan, Jan. 19, 1809–Oct. 7, 1849.
Vol. 8, Pt. 1–19
Poe, Orlando Metcalfe, Mar. 7, 1832–Oct. 2, 1895.
Vol. 8, Pt. 1–28
Poindexter, George, 1779–Sept. 5, 1853.
Vol. 8, Pt. 1–29
Poindexter, Miles, Apr. 22, 1868–Sept. 21, 1946.
Supp. 4–669
Poinsett, Joel Roberts, Mar. 2, 1779–Dec. 12, 1851.
Vol. 8, Pt. 1–30
Polak, John Osborn, Mar. 12, 1870–June 29, 1931.
Vol. 8, Pt. 1–32
Poland, Luke Potter, Nov. 1, 1815–July 2, 1887.
Vol. 8, Pt. 1–33
Poling, Daniel Alfred, Nov. 30, 1884–Feb. 7, 1968.
Supp. 8–505
Polk, Frank Lyon, Sept. 13, 1871–Feb. 7, 1943.
Supp. 3–605
Polk, James Knox, Nov. 2, 1795–June 15, 1849.
Vol. 8, Pt. 1–34
Polk, Leonidas, Apr. 10, 1806–June 14, 1864.
Vol. 8, Pt. 1–39
Polk, Leonidas Lafayette, Apr. 24, 1837–June 11, 1892.
Vol. 8, Pt. 1–40
Polk, Lucius Eugene, July 10, 1833–Dec. 1, 1892.
Vol. 8, Pt. 1–41
Polk, Thomas, *c.* 1732–Jan. 26, 1794.
Vol. 8, Pt. 1–42
Polk, Trusten, May 29, 1811–Apr. 16, 1876.
Vol. 8, Pt. 1–43
Polk, William, July 9, 1758–Jan. 14, 1834.
Vol. 8, Pt. 1–43
Polk, William Mecklenburg, Aug. 15, 1844–June 23, 1918.
Vol. 8, Pt. 1–44
Polk, Willis Jefferson, Oct. 3, 1867–Sept. 10, 1924.
Vol. 8, Pt. 1–45
Pollak, Gustav, May 4, 1849–Nov. 1, 1919.
Vol. 8, Pt. 1–46
Pollak, Walter Heilprin, June 4, 1887–Oct. 2, 1940.
Supp. 2–534
Pollard, Edward Alfred, Feb. 27, 1831–Dec. 16, 1872.
Vol. 8, Pt. 1–47
Pollard, Joseph Percival, Jan. 29, 1869–Dec. 17, 1911.
Vol. 8, Pt. 1–48
Pollock, Channing, Mar. 4, 1880–Aug. 17, 1946.
Supp. 4–670
Pollock, James, Sept. 11, 1810–Apr. 19, 1890.
Vol. 8, Pt. 1–49
Pollock, Oliver, *c.* 1737–Dec. 17, 1823.
Vol. 8, Pt. 1–50
Pollock, (Paul) Jackson, Jan. 28, 1912–Aug. 11, 1956.
Supp. 6–511
Polock, Moses, May 14, 1817–Aug. 16, 1903.
Vol. 8, Pt. 1–51
Pomerene, Atlee, Dec. 6, 1863–Nov. 12, 1937.
Supp. 2–535
Pomeroy, John Norton, Apr. 12, 1828–Feb. 15, 1885.
Vol. 8, Pt. 1–52
Pomeroy, Marcus Mills, Dec. 25, 1833–May 30, 1896.
Vol. 8, Pt. 1–53
Pomeroy, Samuel Clarke, Jan. 3, 1816–Aug. 27, 1891.
Vol. 8, Pt. 1–54
Pomeroy, Seth, May 20, 1706–Feb. 19, 1777.
Vol. 8, Pt. 1–55
Ponce de León, Juan, *c.* 1460–1521.
Vol. 8, Pt. 1–56
Pond, Allen Bartlit, Nov. 21, 1858–Mar. 17, 1929.
Vol. 8, Pt. 1–57
Pond, Enoch, July 29, 1791–Jan. 21, 1882.
Vol. 8, Pt. 1–58
Pond, Frederick Eugene, Apr. 8, 1856–Nov. 1, 1925.
Vol. 8, Pt. 1–58
Pond, George Edward, Mar. 11, 1837–Sept. 22, 1899.
Vol. 8, Pt. 1–59
Pond, Irving Kane, May 1, 1857–Sept. 29, 1939.
Supp. 2–536
Pond, James Burton, June 11, 1838–June 21, 1903.
Vol. 8, Pt. 1–60
Pond, Peter, Jan. 18, 1740–1807.
Vol. 8, Pt. 1–61
Pond, Samuel William, Apr. 10, 1808–Dec. 12, 1891.
Vol. 8, Pt. 1–61
Pons, Lily, Apr. 12, 1898–Feb. 13, 1976.
Supp. 10–639
Pontiac, d. 1769.
Vol. 8, Pt. 1–62
Pool, Joe Richard, Feb. 18, 1911–July 14, 1968.
Supp. 8–506
Pool, John, June 16, 1826–Aug. 16, 1884.
Vol. 8, Pt. 1–64
Pool, Maria Louise, Aug. 20, 1841–May 19, 1898.
Vol. 8, Pt. 1–65
Poole, Ernest Cook, Jan. 23, 1880–Jan. 10, 1950.
Supp. 4–671
Poole, Fitch, June 13, 1803–Aug. 19, 1873.
Vol. 8, Pt. 1–65
Poole, William Frederick, Dec. 24, 1821–Mar. 1, 1894.
Vol. 8, Pt. 1–66
Poor, Charles Henry, June 9, 1808–Nov. 5, 1882.
Vol. 8, Pt. 1–67
Poor, Daniel, June 27, 1789–Feb. 3, 1855.
Vol. 8, Pt. 1–68
Poor, Enoch, June 21, 1736–Sept. 8, 1780.
Vol. 8, Pt. 1–69
Poor, Henry Varnum, Dec. 8, 1812–Jan. 4, 1905.
Vol. 8, Pt. 1–70
Poor, John, July 8, 1752–Dec. 5, 1829.
Vol. 8, Pt. 1–71
Poor, John Alfred, Jan. 8, 1808–Sept. 5, 1871.
Vol. 8, Pt. 1–71
Poore, Benjamin Perley, Nov. 2, 1820–May 29, 1887.
Vol. 8, Pt. 1–73
Pope, Albert Augustus, May 20, 1843–Aug. 10, 1909.
Vol. 8, Pt. 1–74
Pope, Franklin Leonard, Dec. 2, 1840–Oct. 13, 1895.
Vol. 8, Pt. 1–75

Pope, James Pinckney, Mar. 31, 1884–Jan. 23, 1966.
Supp. 8–507
Pope, John, Mar. 16, 1822–Sept. 23, 1892.
Vol. 8, Pt. 1–76
Pope, John Russell, Apr. 24, 1874–Aug. 27, 1937.
Supp. 2–538
Pope, Nathaniel, Jan. 5, 1784–Jan. 22, 1850.
Vol. 8, Pt. 1–77
Popham, George, d. Feb. 5, 1608.
Vol. 8, Pt. 1–78
Porcher, Francis Peyre, Dec. 14, 1825–Nov. 19, 1895.
Vol. 8, Pt. 1–79
Pormort, Philemon, *c.* 1595–*c.* 1656.
Vol. 8, Pt. 1–80
Porter, Albert Gallatin, Apr. 20, 1824–May 3, 1897.
Vol. 8, Pt. 1–80
Porter, Alexander, June 24, 1785–Jan. 13, 1844.
Vol. 8, Pt. 1–81
Porter, Andrew, Sept. 24, 1743–Nov. 16, 1813.
Vol. 8, Pt. 1–82
Porter, Arthur Kingsley, Feb. 6, 1883–July 8, 1933.
Supp. 1–601
Porter, Benjamin Curtis, Aug. 29, 1845–Apr. 2, 1908.
Vol. 8, Pt. 1–83
Porter, Cole, June 9, 1891–Oct. 15, 1964.
Supp. 7–622
Porter, David, Feb. 1, 1780–Mar. 3, 1843.
Vol. 8, Pt. 1–83
Porter, David Dixon, June 8, 1813–Feb. 13, 1891.
Vol. 8, Pt. 1–85
Porter, David Rittenhouse, Oct. 31, 1788–Aug. 6, 1867.
Vol. 8, Pt. 1–89
Porter, Ebenezer, Oct. 5, 1772–April 8, 1834.
Vol. 8, Pt. 1–89
Porter, Edwin Stanton, Apr. 21, 1870–Apr. 30, 1941.
Supp. 3–606
Porter, Fitz-John, Aug. 31, 1822–May 21, 1901.
Vol. 8, Pt. 1–90
Porter, Gene Stratton, Aug. 17, 1863–Dec. 6, 1924.
Supp. 1–601
Porter, Holbrook Fitz-John, Feb. 28, 1858–Jan. 25, 1933.
Vol. 8, Pt. 1–91
Porter, Horace, Apr. 15, 1837–May 29, 1921.
Vol. 8, Pt. 1–92
Porter, James Davis, Dec. 17, 1828–May 18, 1912.
Vol. 8, Pt. 1–93
Porter, James Madison, Jan. 6, 1793–Nov. 11, 1862.
Vol. 8, Pt. 1–94
Porter, Jermain Gildersleeve, Jan. 8, 1852–Apr. 14, 1933.
Vol. 8, Pt. 1–95
Porter, John Addison, Mar. 15, 1822–Aug. 25, 1866.
Vol. 8, Pt. 1–96
Porter, John Luke, Sept. 19, 1813–Dec. 14, 1893.
Vol. 8, Pt. 1–97
Porter, Katherine Anne, May 15, 1890–Sept. 18, 1980.
Supp. 10–641
Porter, Noah, Dec. 14, 1811–Mar. 4, 1892.
Vol. 8, Pt. 1–97
Porter, Peter Buell, Aug. 14, 1773–Mar. 20, 1844.
Vol. 8, Pt. 1–99
Porter, Robert Percival, June 30, 1852–Feb. 28, 1917.
Vol. 8, Pt. 1–100
Porter, Rufus, May 1, 1792–Aug. 13, 1884.
Vol. 8, Pt. 1–101
Porter, Russell Williams, Dec. 13, 1871–Feb. 22, 1949.
Supp. 4–674
Porter, Samuel, Jan. 12, 1810–Sept. 3, 1901.
Vol. 8, Pt. 1–102
Porter, Sarah, Aug. 16, 1813–Feb. 17, 1900.
Vol. 8, Pt. 1–103
Porter, Stephen Geyer, May 18, 1869–June 27, 1930.
Vol. 8, Pt. 1–103
Porter, Thomas Conrad, Jan. 22, 1822–Apr. 27, 1901.
Vol. 8, Pt. 1–104
Porter, William Sydney, Sept. 11, 1862–June 5, 1910.
Vol. 8, Pt. 1–105
Porter, William Townsend, Sept. 24, 1862–Feb. 16, 1949.
Supp. 4–675
Porter, William Trotter, Dec. 24, 1809–July 19, 1858.
Vol. 8, Pt. 1–107
Portier, Michael, Sept. 7, 1795–May 14, 1859.
Vol. 8, Pt. 1–108
Portolá, Gaspar de, fl. 1734–1784.
Vol. 8. Pt. 1–109
Pory, John, 1572–Sept. 1635.
Vol. 8, Pt. 1–110
Posey, Alexander Lawrence, Aug. 3, 1873–May 27, 1908.
Vol. 8, Pt. 1–111
Posey, Thomas, July 9, 1750–Mar. 19, 1818.
Vol. 8, Pt. 1–111
Post, Augustus, Dec. 8, 1873–Oct. 4, 1952.
Supp. 5–547
Post, Charles William, Oct. 26, 1854–May 9, 1914.
Vol. 8, Pt. 1–112
Post, Christian Frederick, *c.* 1710–May 1, 1785.
Vol. 8, Pt. 1–113
Post, Emily Price, Oct. 3, 1873–Sept. 25, 1960.
Supp. 6–514
Post, George Adams, Sept. 1, 1854–Oct. 31, 1925.
Vol. 8, Pt. 1–114
Post, George Browne, Dec. 15, 1837–Nov. 28, 1913.
Vol. 8, Pt. 1–115
Post, George Edward, Dec. 17, 1838–Sept. 29, 1909.
Vol. 8, Pt. 1–116
Post, Isaac, Feb. 26, 1798–May 9, 1872.
Vol. 8, Pt. 1–117
Post, Louis Freeland, Nov. 15, 1849–Jan. 10, 1928.
Vol. 8, Pt. 2–118
Post, Marjorie Merriweather, Mar. 25, 1887–Sept. 12, 1973.
Supp. 9–614
Post, Melville Davisson, Apr. 19, 1871–June 23, 1930.
Vol. 8, Pt. 1–119
Post, Truman Marcellus, June 3, 1810–Dec. 31, 1886.
Vol. 8, Pt. 1–120
Post, Wiley, Nov. 22, 1899–Aug. 15, 1935.
Supp. 1–609
Post, Wright, Feb. 19, 1766–June 14, 1828.
Vol. 8, Pt. 1–121
Postl, Carl. [*See* Sealsfield, Charles, 1793–1864.]
Poston, Charles Debrill, Apr. 20, 1825–June 24, 1902.
Vol. 8, Pt. 1–121
Potamian, Brother, Sept. 29, 1847–Jan. 20, 1917.
Vol. 8, Pt. 1–122
Potofsky, Jacob Samuel, Nov. 16, 1894–Aug. 5, 1979.
Supp. 10–642
Pott, Francis Lister Hawks, Feb. 22, 1864–Mar. 7, 1949.
Supp. 4–677
Pott, John, ?–*c.* 1642.
Vol. 8, Pt. 1–123
Potter, Alonzo, July 6, 1800–July 4, 1865.
Vol. 8, Pt. 1–124
Potter, Charles Edward, Oct. 30, 1916–Nov. 23, 1979.
Supp. 10–644
Potter, Charles Francis, Oct. 28, 1885–Oct. 4, 1962.
Supp. 7–623
Potter, Edward Clark, Nov. 26, 1857–June 21, 1923.
Vol. 8, Pt. 1–125
Potter, Eliphalet Nott, Sept. 20, 1836–Feb. 6, 1901.
Vol. 8, Pt. 1–126
Potter, Elisha Reynolds, June 20, 1811–Apr. 10, 1882.
Vol. 8, Pt. 1–126
Potter, Ellen Culver, Aug. 5, 1871–Feb. 9, 1958.
Supp. 6–515
Potter, Henry Codman, May 25, 1835–July 21 1908.
Vol. 8, Pt. 1–127
Potter, Horatio, Feb. 9, 1802–Jan. 2, 1887.
Vol. 8, Pt. 1–129
Potter, James, 1729–Nov. 1789.
Vol. 8, Pt. 1–129
Potter, Louis McClellan, Nov. 14, 1873–Aug. 29, 1912.
Vol. 8, Pt. 1–130
Potter, Nathaniel, 1770–Jan. 2, 1843.
Vol. 8, Pt. 1–131
Potter, Paul Meredith, June 3, 1853–Mar. 7, 1921.
Vol. 8, Pt. 1–132
Potter, Platt, Apr. 6, 1800–Aug. 11, 1891.
Vol. 8, Pt. 1–132
Potter, Robert, *c.* 1800–Mar. 2, 1842.
Vol. 8, Pt. 1–133
Potter, Robert Brown, July 16, 1829–Feb. 19, 1887.
Vol. 8, Pt. 1–134

Potter, William Bancroft, Feb. 19, 1863–Jan. 15, 1934.
Supp. 1–604
Potter, William James, Feb. 1, 1829–Dec. 21, 1893.
Vol. 8, Pt. 1–135
Potts, Benjamin Franklin, Jan. 29, 1836–June 17, 1887.
Vol. 8, Pt. 1–135
Potts, Charles Sower, Jan. 30, 1864–Feb. 16, 1930.
Vol. 8, Pt. 1–136
Potts, Jonathan, Apr. 11, 1745–Oct. 1781.
Vol. 8, Pt. 1–137
Potts, Richard, July 19, 1753–Nov. 25, 1808.
Vol. 8, Pt. 1–138
Pou, Edward William, Sept. 9, 1863–Apr. 1, 1934.
Supp. 1–605
Poulson, Niels, Feb. 27, 1843–May 3, 1911.
Vol. 8, Pt. 1–138
Poulson, Zachariah, Sept. 5, 1761–July 31, 1844.
Vol. 8, Pt. 1–139
Pound, Cuthbert Winfred, June 20, 1864–Feb. 3, 1935.
Supp. 1–606
Pound, Ezra Loomis, Oct. 30, 1885–Oct. 30, 1972.
Supp. 9–616
Pound, (Nathan) Roscoe, Oct. 27, 1890–July 1, 1964.
Supp. 7–624
Pound, Thomas, *c.* 1650–1703.
Vol. 8, Pt. 1–140
Pourtalès, Louis François de, Mar. 4, 1823–July 18, 1880.
Vol. 8, Pt. 1–141
Powderly, Terence Vincent, Jan. 22, 1849–June 24, 1924.
Vol. 8, Pt. 1–142
Powdermaker, Hortense, Dec. 24, 1896–June 15, 1970.
Supp. 8–509
Powel, John Hare, Apr. 22, 1786–June 14, 1856.
Vol. 8, Pt. 1–143
Powell. [*See* Osceola, *c.* 1800–1838.]
Powell, Adam Clayton, Sr., May 5, 1865–June 12, 1953.
Supp. 5–547
Powell, Adam Clayton, Jr., Nov. 29, 1908–Apr. 4, 1972.
Supp. 9–619
Powell, Alma Webster, Nov. 20, 1874–Mar. 11, 1930.
Vol. 8, Pt. 1–144
Powell, Edward Payson, May 9, 1833–May 14, 1915.
Vol. 8, Pt. 1–144
Powell, George Harold, Feb. 8, 1872–Feb. 18, 1922.
Vol. 8, Pt. 1–145
Powell, John Benjamin, Apr. 18, 1886–Feb. 28, 1947.
Supp. 4–678
Powell, John Wesley, Mar. 24, 1834–Sept. 23, 1902.
Vol. 8, Pt. 1–146
Powell, Lazarus Whitehead, Oct. 6, 1812–July 3, 1867.
Vol. 8, Pt. 1–148
Powell, Lucien Whiting, Dec. 13, 1846–Sept. 27, 1930.
Vol. 8, Pt. 1–149
Powell, Maud, Aug. 22, 1868–Jan. 8, 1920.
Vol. 8, Pt. 1–149
Powell, Richard Ewing ("Dick"), Nov. 14, 1904–Jan. 2, 1963.
Supp. 7–628
Powell, Snelling, 1758–Apr. 8, 1821.
Vol. 8, Pt. 1–150
Powell, Thomas, Sept. 3, 1809–Jan. 14, 1887.
Vol. 8, Pt. 1–151
Powell, Thomas Reed, Apr. 29, 1880–Aug. 16, 1955.
Supp. 5–549
Powell, Wilham Bramwell, Dec. 22, 1836–Feb. 6, 1904.
Vol. 8, Pt. 1–152
Powell, William Byrd, Jan. 8, 1799–May 13, 1866.
Vol. 8 Pt. 1–152
Powell, William Henry, Feb. 14, 1823–Oct. 6, 1879.
Vol. 8, Pt. 1–153
Power, Frederick Belding, Mar. 4, 1853–Mar. 26, 1927.
Vol. 8, Pt. 1–154
Power, Frederick Dunglison, Jan. 23, 1851–June 14, 1911.
Vol. 8, Pt. 1–155
Power, Frederick Tyrone, May 2, 1869–Dec. 30, 1931.
Vol. 8, Pt. 1–156
Power, John, June 19, 1792–Apr. 14, 1849.
Vol. 8, Pt. 1–156
Power, Tyrone, May 5, 1914–Nov. 15, 1958.
Supp. 6–516
Power, Tyrone. [*See* Power, Frederick Tyrone, 1869–1931.]
Powers, Daniel William, June 14, 1818–Dec. 11, 1897.
Vol. 8, Pt. 1–157
Powers, Francis Gary, Aug. 17, 1929–Aug. 1, 1977.
Supp. 10–646
Powers, Hiram, July 29, 1805–June 27, 1873.
Vol. 8, Pt. 1–158
Powhatan, d. 1618.
Vol. 8, Pt. 1–160
Pownall, Thomas, 1722–Feb. 25, 1805.
Vol. 8, Pt. 1–161
Poydras, Julien de Lalande, Apr. 3, 1746–June 23, 1824.
Vol. 8, Pt. 1–163
Poznanski, Gustavus, 1804–Jan. 7, 1879.
Vol. 8, Pt. 1–164
Prall, David Wight, Oct. 5, 1886–Oct. 21, 1940.
Supp. 2–540
Prang, Louis, Mar. 12, 1824–June 14, 1909.
Vol. 8, Pt. 1–165
Prang, Mary Amelia Dana Hicks, Oct. 7, 1836–Nov. 7, 1927.
Vol. 8, Pt. 1–166
Pratt, Bela Lyon, Dec. 11, 1867–May 18, 1917.
Vol. 8, Pt. 1–166
Pratt, Charles, Oct. 2, 1830–May 4, 1891.
Vol. 8, Pt. 1–168
Pratt, Daniel, July 20, 1799–May 13, 1873.
Vol. 8, Pt. 1–170
Pratt, Daniel, Apr. 11, 1809–June 20, 1887.
Vol. 8, Pt. 1–170
Pratt, Eliza Anna Farman, Nov. 1, 1837–May 22, 1907.
Vol. 8, Pt. 1–171
Pratt, Enoch, Sept. 10, 1808–Sept. 17, 1896.
Vol. 8, Pt. 1–171
Pratt, Francis Ashbury, Feb. 15, 1827–Feb. 10, 1902.
Vol. 8, Pt. 1–172
Pratt, James Bissett, June 22, 1875–Jan. 15, 1944.
Supp. 3–608
Pratt, John, Apr. 14, 1831–*c.* 1900.
Vol. 8, Pt. 1–173
Pratt, John Lee, Oct. 22, 1879–Dec. 20, 1975.
Supp. 9–621
Pratt, Matthew, Sept. 23, 1734–Jan. 9, 1805.
Vol. 8, Pt. 1–174
Pratt, Orson, Sept. 19, 1811–Oct. 3, 1881.
Supp. 1–607
Pratt, Parley Parker, Apr. 12, 1807–May 13, 1857.
Vol. 8, Pt. 1–175
Pratt, Richard Henry, Dec. 6, 1840–Mar. 15, 1924.
Vol. 8, Pt. 1–175
Pratt, Sereno Stansbury, Mar. 12, 1858–Sept. 14, 1915.
Vol. 8, Pt. 1–176
Pratt, Silas Gamaliel, Aug. 4, 1846–Oct. 30, 1916.
Vol. 8, Pt. 1–177
Pratt, Thomas George, Feb. 18, 1804–Nov. 9, 1869.
Vol. 8, Pt. 1–178
Pratt, Thomas Willis, July 4, 1812–July 10, 1875.
Vol. 8, Pt. 1–179
Pratt, Waldo Selden, Nov. 10, 1857–July 29, 1939.
Supp. 2–541
Pratt, William Veazie, Feb. 28, 1869–Nov. 25, 1957.
Supp. 6–518
Pratt, Zadock, Oct. 30, 1790–Apr. 6, 1871.
Vol. 8, Pt. 1–179
Pratte, Bernard, June 11, 1771–Apr. 1, 1836.
Vol. 8, Pt. 1–180
Pray, Isaac Clark, May 15, 1813–Nov. 28, 1869.
Vol. 8, Pt. 1–181
Preber, Christian. [*See* Priber, Christian, fl. 1734–1744.]
Preble, Edward, Aug. 15, 1761–Aug. 25, 1807.
Vol. 8, Pt. 1–182
Preble, George Henry, Feb. 25, 1816–Mar. 1, 1885.
Vol. 8 Pt. 1–183
Preble, Wiliiam Pitt, Nov. 27, 1783–Oct. 11, 1857.
Vol. 8, Pt. 1–184
Preetorius, Emil, Mar. 15, 1827–Nov. 19, 1905.
Vol. 8, Pt. 1–185
Prefontaine, Steve Roland ("Pre"), Jan. 25, 1951–May 30, 1975.
Supp. 9–623
Prendergast, Maurice Brazil, Oct. 27, 1861–Feb. 1, 1924.
Vol. 8, Pt. 1–186

Prentice, George Dennison, Dec. 18, 1802–Jan. 22, 1870.
Vol. 8, Pt. 1–186
Prentice, Samuel Oscar, Aug. 8, 1850–Nov. 2, 1924.
Vol. 8, Pt. 1–187
Prentis, Henning Webb, Jr., July 11, 1884–Oct. 29, 1959.
Supp. 6–519
Prentiss, Benjamin Mayberry, Nov. 23, 1819–Feb. 8, 1901.
Vol. 8, Pt. 1–188
Prentiss, Elizabeth Payson, Oct. 26, 1818–Aug. 13, 1878.
Vol. 8, Pt. 1–188
Prentiss, George Lewis, May 12, 1816–Mar. 18, 1903.
Vol. 8, Pt. 1–189
Prentiss, Samuel, Mar. 31, 1782–Jan. 15, 1857.
Vol. 8, Pt. 1–190
Prentiss, Seargent Smith, Sept. 30, 1808–July 1, 1850.
Vol. 8, Pt. 1–191
Presbrey, Eugene Wiley, Mar. 13, 1853–Sept. 9, 1931.
Vol. 8 Pt. 1–192
Prescott, Albert Benjamin, Dec. 12, 1832–Feb. 25, 1905.
Vol. 8, Pt. 1–192
Prescott, George Bartlett, Sept. 16, 1830–Jan. 18, 1894.
Vol. 8, Pt. 1–193
Prescott, Oliver, Apr. 27, 1731–Nov. 17, 1804.
Vol. 8, Pt. 1–194
Prescott, Samuel, Aug. 19, 1751–*c.* 1777.
Vol. 8, Pt. 1–195
Prescott, Samuel Cate, Apr. 5, 1872–Mar. 20, 1962.
Supp. 7–629
Prescott, WIlliam, Feb. 20, 1726–Oct. 13, 1795.
Vol. 8, Pt. 1–195
Prescott, William Hickling, May 14, 1796–Jan. 28, 1859.
Vol. 8, Pt. 1–196
Presley, Elvis Aron, Jan. 8, 1935–Aug. 16, 1977.
Supp. 10–648
Presser, Theodore, July 3, 1848–Oct. 28, 1925.
Vol. 8, Pt. 1–200
Pressman, Lee, July 1, 1906–Nov. 19, 1969.
Supp. 8–510
Preston, Ann, Dec. 1, 1813–Apr. 18, 1872.
Vol. 8, Pt. 1–201
Preston, Harriet Waters, Aug. 6, 1836–May 14, 1911.
Vol. 8, Pt. 1–202
Preston, John Smith, Apr. 20, 1809–May 1, 1881.
Vol. 8, Pt. 1–202
Preston, Jonas, Jan. 25, 1764–Apr. 4, 1836.
Vol. 8, Pt. 1–203
Preston, Margaret Junkin, May 19, 1820–Mar. 28, 1897.
Vol. 8, Pt. 1–204
Preston, Thomas Scott, July 23, 1824–Nov. 4, 1891.
Vol. 8, Pt. 1–205
Preston, William, Oct. 16, 1816–Sept. 21, 1887.
Vol. 8, Pt. 1–205
Preston, William Ballard, Nov. 29, 1805–Nov. 16, 1862.
Vol. 8, Pt. 1–206
Preston, William Campbell, Dec. 27, 1794–May 22, 1860.
Vol. 8, Pt. 1–207
Preus, Christian Keyser, Oct. 13, 1852–May 28, 1921.
Vol. 8, Pt. 1–208
Prevost, François Maire, *c.* 1764–May 18, 1842.
Vol. 8, Pt. 1–209
Priber, Christian, fl. 1734–1744.
Vol. 8, Pt. 1–210
Price, Bruce, Dec. 12, 1845–May 29, 1903.
Vol. 8, Pt. 1–210
Price, Eli Kirk, July 20, 1797–Nov. 15, 1884.
Vol. 8, Pt. 1–211
Price, Eli Kirk, May 10, 1860–Jan. 24, 1933.
Supp. 1–608
Price, George Edward McCready, Aug. 26, 1870–Jan. 24, 1963.
Supp. 7–631
Price, George Moses, May 21, 1864–July 30, 1942.
Supp. 3–609
Price, Hiram, Jan. 10, 1814–May 30, 1901.
Vol. 8, Pt. 1–212
Price, Joseph, Jan. 1, 1853–June 6, 1911.
Vol. 8, Pt. 1–213
Price, Rodman McCamley, May 5, 1816–June 7, 1894.
Vol. 8, Pt. 1–214
Price, Stephen, Sept. 25, 1782–Jan. 20, 1840.
Vol. 8, Pt. 1–215
Price, Sterling, Sept. 20, 1809–Sept. 29, 1867.
Vol. 8, Pt. 1–216
Price, Theodore Hazeltine, Feb. 9, 1861–May 4, 1935.
Supp. 1–609
Price, Thomas Frederick, Aug. 19, 1860–Sept. 12, 1919.
Vol. 8, Pt. 1–217
Price, Thomas Lawson, Jan. 19, 1809–July 16, 1870.
Vol. 8, Pt. 1–218
Price, Thomas Randolph, Mar. 18, 1839–May 7, 1903.
Vol. 8, Pt. 1–219
Price, William Cecil, Apr. 1, 1818–Aug. 6, 1907.
Vol. 8, Pt. 1–220
Price, William Thompson, Dec. 17, 1846–May 3, 1920.
Vol. 8, Pt. 1–221
Priest, Edward Dwight, Nov. 9, 1861–Mar. 26, 1931.
Vol. 8, Pt. 1–221
Priest, Ivy Maude Baker, Sept. 7, 1905–June 23, 1975.
Supp. 9–624
Priestley, James, d. Feb. 6, 1821.
Vol. 8, Pt. 1–222
Priestley, Joseph, Mar. 13, 1733–Feb. 6, 1804.
Vol. 8, Pt. 1–223
Prima, Luigi ("Louis"), Dec. 7, 1911–Aug. 24, 1978.
Supp. 10–650
Prime, Benjamin Youngs, Dec. 9, 1733 o.s.–Oct. 31, 1791.
Vol. 8, Pt. 1–226
Prime, Edward Dorr Griffin, Nov. 2, 1814–Apr. 7, 1891.
Vol. 8, Pt. 1–227
Prime, Samuel Irenaeus, Nov. 4, 1812–July 18, 1885.
Vol. 8, Pt. 1–228
Prime, William Cowper, Oct. 31, 1825–Feb. 13, 1905.
Vol. 8, Pt. 1–228
Prince, Frederick Henry, Nov. 24, 1859–Feb. 2, 1953.
Supp. 5–550
Prince, Le Baron Bradford, July 3, 1840–Dec 8, 1922.
Vol. 8, Pt. 1–229
Prince, Morton, Dec. 21, 1854–Aug. 31, 1929.
Vol. 8, Pt. 1–230
Prince, Thomas, May 15, 1687–Oct. 22, 1758.
Vol. 8, Pt. 1–232
Prince, William, *c.* 1725–1802.
Vol. 8, Pt. 1–233
Prince, William, Nov. 10, 1766–Apr. 9, 1842.
Vol. 8 Pt. 1–233
Prince, William Robert, Nov. 6, 1795–Mar. 28, 1869.
Vol. 8, Pt. 1–234
Pring, Martin, *c.* 1580–1626.
Vol. 8, Pt. 1–235
Pringle, Cyrus Guernsey, May 6, 1838–May 25, 1911.
Vol. 8, Pt. 1–236
Pringle, Henry Fowles, Aug. 23, 1897–Apr. 7, 1958.
Supp. 6–520
Pringle, Joel Roberts Poinsett, Feb. 4, 1873–Sept. 25, 1932.
Vol. 8, Pt. 1–237
Pringle, John Julius, July 22, 1753–Mar. 17, 1843.
Vol. 8, Pt. 1–237
Printz, Johan Björnsson, July 20, 1592–May 3, 1663.
Vol. 8, Pt. 1–238
Prinze, Freddie, June 22, 1954–Jan. 29, 1977.
Supp. 10–651
Pritchard, Frederick John, Dec. 24, 1874–Jan. 13, 1931.
Vol. 8, Pt. 1–239
Pritchard, Jeter Connelly, July 12, 1857–Apr. 10, 1921.
Vol. 8, Pt. 1–240
Pritchett, Henry Smith, Apr. 16, 1857–Aug. 28, 1939.
Supp. 2–541
Procter, John Robert, Mar. 16, 1844–Dec. 12, 1903.
Vol. 8, Pt. 1–241
Procter, William, May 3, 1817–Feb. 9, 1874.
Vol. 8, Pt. 1–242
Proctor, Frederick Francis, *c.* 1851–Sept. 4, 1929.
Vol. 8, Pt. 1–242
Proctor, Henry Hugh, Dec. 8, 1868–May 12, 1933.
Vol. 8, Pt. 1–243
Proctor, Joseph, May 7, 1816–Oct. 2, 1897.
Vol. 8, Pt. 1–244
Proctor, Lucien Brock, Mar. 6, 1823–Apr. 1, 1900.
Vol. 8. Pt. 1–245
Proctor, Redfield, June 1, 1831–Mar. 4, 1908.
Vol. 8, Pt. 1–245

Proctor, William Cooper, Aug. 25, 1862–May 2, 1934.
Supp. 1–610
Profaci, Joseph, Oct. 2, 1897–June 7, 1962.
Supp. 7–632
Prokosch, Eduard, May 15, 1876–Aug. 11, 1938.
Supp. 2–543
Prophet. [*See* Tenskwatawa, 1768?–1834?]
Prosser, Charles Smith, Mar. 24, 1860–Sept. 11, 1916.
Vol. 8, Pt. 1–247
Proud, Robert, May 10, 1728–July 5, 1813.
Vol. 8, Pt. 1–247
Prouty, Charles Azro, Oct. 9, 1853–July 8, 1921.
Vol. 8, Pt. 1–248
Prouty, Charles Tyler, May 30, 1909–May 10, 1974.
Supp. 9–626
Prouty, Olive Higgins, 1882?–Mar. 24, 1974.
Supp. 9–627
Provoost, Samuel, Feb. 26, 1742 o.s.–Sept. 6, 1815.
Vol. 8, Pt. 1–249
Provost, Etienne, *c.* 1782–July 3, 1850.
Vol. 8, Pt. 1–250
Provosty, Olivier Otis, Aug. 3, 1852–Aug. 3, 1924.
Vol. 8, Pt. 1–251
Prudden, Theophil Mitchell, July 7, 1849–Apr. 10, 1924.
Vol. 8, Pt. 1–252
Prud'homme, John Francis Eugene, Oct. 4, 1800–June 27, 1892.
Vol. 8, Pt. 1–253
Pruyn, John Van Shaick Lansing, June 22, 1811–Nov. 21, 1877.
Vol. 8, Pt. 1–253
Pruyn, Robert Hewson, Feb. 14, 1815–Feb. 26, 1882.
Vol. 8, Pt. 1–254
Pryber, Christian. [*See* Priber, Christian, fl. 1734–1744.]
Pryor, Arthur W., Sept. 22, 1870–June 18, 1942.
Supp. 3–610
Pryor, Nathaniel, *c.* 1775–June 10, 1831.
Vol. 8, Pt. 1–255
Pryor, Roger Atkinson, July 19, 1828–Mar. 14, 1919.
Vol. 8, Pt. 1–255
Puget, Peter Richings. [*See* Richings, Peter, 1797–1871.]
Pugh, Ellis, June 1656–Oct. 3, 1718.
Vol. 8, Pt. 1–257
Pugh, Evan, Feb. 29, 1828–Apr. 29, 1864.
Vol. 8, Pt. 1–257
Pugh, George Ellis, Nov. 28, 1822–July 19, 1876.
Vol. 8, Pt. 1–258
Pujo, Arsène Paulin, Dec. 16, 1861–Dec. 31, 1939.
Supp. 2–544
Pulaski, Casimir, *c.* 1748–Oct. 1779.
Vol. 8, Pt. 1–259
Pulitzer, Joseph, Apr. 10, 1847–Oct. 29, 1911.
Vol. 8, Pt. 1–260
Pulitzer, Joseph, Jr., Mar. 21, 1885–Mar. 30, 1955.
Supp. 5–551
Pulitzer, Margaret Leech, Nov. 7, 1893–Feb. 24, 1974.
Supp. 9–628
Pulitzer, Ralph, June 11, 1879–June 14, 1939.
Supp. 2–545
Puller, Lewis Burwell ("Chesty"), June 26, 1898–Oct. 11, 1971.
Supp. 9–629
Pullman, George Mortimer, Mar. 3, 1831–Oct. 19, 1897.
Vol. 8, Pt. 1–263
Pulte, Joseph Hippolyt, Oct. 6, 1811–Feb. 25, 1884.
Vol. 8, Pt. 1–264
Pumpelly, Raphael, Sept. 8, 1837–Aug. 10, 1923.
Vol. 8, Pt. 1–264
Pupin, Michael Idvorsky, Oct. 4, 1858–Mar. 12, 1935.
Supp. 1–611
Purcell, John Baptist, Feb. 26, 1800–July 4, 1883.
Vol. 8, Pt. 1–266
Purdue, John, Oct. 31, 1802–Sept. 12, 1876.
Vol. 8, Pt. 1–268
Purdy, Corydon Tyler, May 17, 1859–Dec. 26, 1944.
Supp. 3–611
Purdy, Lawson, Sept. 13, 1863–Aug. 30, 1959.
Supp. 6–521
Purnell, Benjamin, Mar. 27, 1861–Dec. 16, 1927.
Supp. 1–615
Purnell, William Henry, Feb. 3, 1826–Mar. 30, 1902.
Vol. 8, Pt. 1–268
Purple, Samuel Smith, June 24, 1822–Sept. 29, 1900.
Vol. 8, Pt. 1–269
Purry, Jean Pierre, 1675–*c.* July 1736.
Vol. 8, Pt. 1–270
Pursh, Frederick, Feb. 4, 1774–July 11, 1820.
Vol. 8, Pt. 1–271
Purtell, William Arthur, May 6, 1897–May 31, 1978.
Supp. 10–652
Purviance, David, Nov. 14, 1766–Aug. 19, 1847.
Vol. 8, Pt. 1–271
Puryear, Bennet, July 23, 1826–Mar. 30, 1914.
Vol. 8, Pt. 1–272
Pusey, Caleb, *c.* 1650–Feb. 25, 1727 o.s.
Vol. 8, Pt. 1–273
Pusey, William Allen, Dec. 1, 1865–Aug. 29, 1940.
Supp. 2–546
Pushmataha, *c.* 1765–Dec. 24, 1824.
Vol. 8, Pt. 1–274
Putnam, Arthur, Sept. 6, 1873–May 27, 1930.
Vol. 8, Pt. 1–274
Putnam, Charles Pickering, Sept. 15, 1844–Apr. 22, 1914.
Vol. 8, Pt. 1–275
Putnam, Eben, Oct. 10, 1868–Jan. 22, 1933.
Vol. 8, Pt. 1–276
Putnam, Frederic Ward, Apr. 16, 1839–Aug. 14, 1915.
Vol. 8, Pt. 1–276
Putnam, George Haven, Apr. 2, 1844–Feb. 27, 1930.
Vol. 8, Pt. 1–278
Putnam, (George) Herbert, Sept. 20, 1861–Aug. 14, 1955.
Supp. 5–554
Putnam, George Palmer, Feb. 7, 1814–Dec. 20, 1872.
Vol. 8, Pt. 1–279
Putnam, Gideon, Apr. 17, 1763–Dec. 1, 1812.
Vol. 8, Pt. 1–280
Putnam, Helen Cordelia, Sept. 14, 1857–Feb. 3, 1951.
Supp. 5–552
Putnam, Israel, Jan. 7, 1718–May 29, 1790.
Vol. 8, Pt. 1–281
Putnam, James Jackson, Oct. 3, 1846–Nov. 4, 1918.
Vol. 8, Pt. 1–282
Putnam, James Osborne, July 4, 1818–Apr. 24, 1903.
Vol. 8, Pt. 1–283
Putnam, Nina Wilcox, Nov. 28, 1885–Mar. 8, 1962.
Supp. 7–633
Putnam, Rufus, April 9, 1738–May 4, 1824.
Vol. 8, Pt. 1–284
Putnam, Ruth, July 18, 1856–Feb. 12, 1931.
Vol. 8, Pt. 1–285
Putnam, William Le Baron, May 26, 1835–Feb. 5, 1918.
Vol. 8, Pt. 1–285
Pye, Watts Orson, Oct. 20, 1878–Jan. 9, 1926.
Vol. 8, Pt. 1–286
Pyle, Ernest Taylor, Aug. 3, 1900–Apr. 18, 1945.
Supp. 3–612
Pyle, Howard, Mar. 5, 1853–Nov. 9, 1911.
Vol. 8, Pt. 1–287
Pyle, Robert, Mar. 7, 1877–Sept. 28, 1951.
Supp. 5–555
Pyle, Walter Lytle, Dec. 20, 1871–Oct. 8, 1921.
Vol. 8, Pt. 1–290
Pynchon, John, *c.* 1626–Jan. 17, 1702/03.
Vol. 8, Pt. 1–290
Pynchon, Thomas Ruggles, Jan. 19, 1823–Oct. 6, 1904.
Vol. 8, Pt. 1–291
Pynchon, William, *c.* 1590–Oct. 29, 1662.
Vol. 8, Pt. 1–292

Quackenbush, Stephen Platt, Jan. 23, 1823–Feb. 4, 1890.
Vol. 8, Pt. 1–293
Quanah, *c.* 1845–Feb. 23, 1911.
Vol. 8, Pt. 1–294
Quantrill, William Clarke, July 31, 1837–June 6, 1865.
Vol. 8, Pt. 1–294
Quarter, William, Jan. 21, 1806–Apr. 10, 1848.
Vol. 8, Pt. 1–295
Quartley, Arthur, May 24, 1839–May 19, 1886.
Vol. 8, Pt. 1–296
Quay, Matthew Stanley, Sept. 30, 1833–May 28, 1904.
Vol. 8, Pt. 1–296
Quayle, William Alfred, June 25, 1860–Mar. 9, 1925.
Vol. 8, Pt. 1–298

Queen, Walter W., Oct. 6, 1824–Oct. 24, 1893.
Vol. 8, Pt. 1–298
Quelch, John, *c.* 1665–June 30, 1704.
Vol. 8, Pt. 1–299
Quesnay, Alexandre-Marie, Nov. 23, 1755–Feb. 8, 1820.
Vol. 8, Pt. 1–300
Quezon, Manuel Luis, Aug. 19, 1878–Aug. 1, 1944.
Supp. 3–613
Quick, John Herbert, Oct. 23, 1861–May 10, 1925.
Vol. 8, Pt. 1–301
Quidor, John, Jan. 26, 1801–Dec. 13, 1881.
Vol. 8, Pt. 1–302
Quigg, Lemuel Ely, Feb. 12, 1863–July 1, 1919.
Vol. 8, Pt. 1–302
Quigley, James Edward, Oct. 15, 1854–July 10, 1915.
Vol. 8, Pt. 1–303
Quill, Michael Joseph, Sept. 18, 1905–Jan. 28, 1966.
Supp. 8–512
Quimby, Phineas Parkhurst, Feb. 16, 1802–Jan. 16, 1866.
Vol. 8, Pt. 1–304
Quinan, John Russell, Aug. 7, 1822–Nov. 11, 1890.
Vol. 8, Pt. 1–305
Quinby, Isaac Ferdinand, Jan. 29, 1821–Sept. 18, 1891.
Vol. 8, Pt. 1–306
Quincy, Edmund, Feb. 1, 1808–May 17, 1877.
Vol. 8, Pt. 1–306
Quincy, Josiah, Feb. 23, 1744–Apr. 26, 1775.
Vol. 8, Pt. 1–307
Quincy, Josiah, Feb. 4, 1772–July 1, 1864.
Vol. 8, Pt. 1–308
Quincy, Josiah Phillips, Nov. 28, 1829–Oct. 31, 1910.
Vol. 8, Pt. 1–311
Quine, William Edward, Feb. 9, 1847–Dec. 7, 1922.
Supp. 1–616
Quinn, Arthur Hobson, Feb. 9, 1875–Oct. 16, 1960.
Supp. 6–523
Quinn, Edmond Thomas, Dec. 20, 1868–Sept. 9, 1929.
Vol. 8, Pt. 1–312
Quintard, Charles Todd, Dec. 22, 1824–Feb. 15, 1898.
Vol. 8, Pt. 1–313
Quintard, George William, Apr. 22, 1822–Apr. 2, 1913.
Vol. 8, Pt. 1–314
Quitman, John Anthony, Sept. 1, 1798–July 17, 1858.
Vol. 8, Pt. 1–315

Raby, James Joseph, Sept. 17, 1874–Jan. 15, 1934.
Vol. 8, Pt. 1–316
Rachford, Benjamm Knox, Nov. 28, 1857–May 5, 1929.
Vol. 8, Pt. 1–317
Rachmaninoff, Sergei Vasilyevich, Apr. 2, 1873–Mar. 28, 1943.
Supp. 3–615
Radcliff, Jacob, Apr. 20, 1764–May 6, 1844.
Vol. 8, Pt. 1–318
Radcliffe, George Lovic Pierce, Aug. 22, 1877–July 19, 1974.
Supp. 9–633
Rademacher, Hans, Apr. 3, 1892–Feb. 7, 1969.
Supp. 8–513
Radford, Arthur William, Feb. 27, 1896–Aug. 17, 1973.
Supp. 9–635
Radford, William, Sept. 9, 1809–Jan. 8, 1890.
Vol. 8, Pt. 1–319
Radin, Max, Mar. 29, 1880–June 22, 1950.
Supp. 4–680
Radin, Paul, Apr. 2, 1883–Feb. 21, 1959.
Supp. 6–524
Radisson, Pierce Esprit, 1636–*c.* 1710.
Vol. 8, Pt. 1–320
Rae, John, June 1, 1796–July 14, 1872.
Vol. 8, Pt. 1–321
Raffeiner, John Stephen, Dec. 26, 1785–July 16 1861.
Vol. 8, Pt. 1–322
Rafinesque, Constantine Samuel, Oct. 22, 1783–Sept. 18, 1840.
Vol. 8, Pt. 1–322
Raft, George, Sept. 26, 1895–Nov. 24, 1980.
Supp. 10–655
Rafter, George W., Dec. 9, 1851–Dec. 29, 1907.
Vol. 8, Pt. 1–324
Raguet, Condy, Jan. 28, 1784–Mar. 21, 1842.
Vol. 8, Pt. 1–325
Raht, August Wilhelm, Feb. 25, 1843–Dec. 25, 1916.
Vol. 8, Pt. 1–326
Rahv, Philip, Mar. 10. 1908–Dec. 22, 1973.
Supp. 9–636
Raines, John, May 6, 1840–Dec. 16, 1909.
Vol. 8, Pt. 1–326
Rainey, Gertrude Malissa Nix Pridgett, Apr. 26, 1886–Dec. 22, 1939.
Supp. 2–547
Rainey, Henry Thomas, Aug. 20, 1860–Aug. 19, 1934.
Supp. 1–617
Rainey, Joseph Hayne, June 21, 1832–Aug. 1, 1887.
Vol. 8, Pt. 1–327
Rainey, "Ma." [*See* Rainey, Gertrude Malissa Nix Pridgett, 1886–1939.]
Rains, Claude, Nov. 10, 1889–May 30, 1967.
Supp. 8–515
Rains, Gabriel James, June 4, 1803–Aug. 6, 1881.
Vol. 8, Pt. 1–328
Rains, George Washington, 1817–Mar. 21, 1898.
Vol. 8, Pt. 1–329
Rainsford, William Stephen, Oct. 30, 1850–Dec. 17, 1933.
Supp. 1–618
Râle, Sébastien, d. Aug. 23, 1724.
Vol. 8, Pt. 1–330
Ralph, James, *c.* 1695–Jan. 24, 1762.
Vol. 8, Pt. 1–331
Ralph, Julian, May 27, 1853–Jan. 20, 1903.
Vol. 8, Pt. 1–332
Ralston, Samuel Moffett, Dec. 1, 1857–Oct. 14, 1925.
Vol. 8, Pt. 1–333
Ralston, William Chapman, June 12, 1826–Aug. 27, 1875.
Vol. 8, Pt. 1–333
Ramage, John, *c.* 1748–Oct. 24, 1802.
Vol. 8, Pt. 1–334
Rambaut, Mary Lucinda Bonney, June 8, 1816–July 24, 1900.
Vol. 8, Pt. 1–335
Ramée, Joseph Jacques, Apr. 18, 1764–May 18, 1842.
Vol. 8, Pt. 1–336
Ramsay, Alexander, 1754?–Nov. 24, 1824.
Vol. 8, Pt. 1–337
Ramsay, David, Apr. 2, 1749–May 8, 1815.
Vol. 8, Pt. 1–338
Ramsay, Erskine, Sept. 24, 1864–Aug. 17, 1953.
Supp. 5–556
Ramsay, Francis Munroe, Apr. 5, 1835–July 19, 1914.
Vol. 8, Pt. 1–339
Ramsay, George Douglas, Feb. 21, 1802–May 23, 1882.
Vol. 8, Pt. 1–340
Ramsay, Nathaniel, May 1, 1741–Oct. 24, 1817.
Vol. 8, Pt. 1–340
Ramseur, Stephen Dodson, May 31, 1837–Oct. 20, 1864.
Vol. 8, Pt. 1–341
Ramsey, Alexander, Sept. 8, 1815–Apr. 22, 1903.
Vol. 8, Pt. 1–341
Ramsey, James Gettys McGready, March 25, 1797–Apr. 11, 1884.
Vol. 8, Pt. 1–342
Ramspeck, Robert C. Word ("Bob"), Sept. 5, 1890–Sept. 10, 1972.
Supp. 9–638
Rand, Addison Crittenden, Sept. 17, 1841–Mar. 9, 1900.
Vol. 8, Pt. 1–343
Rand, Benjamin, July 17, 1856–Nov. 9, 1934.
Supp. 1–619
Rand, Edward Kennard, Dec. 20, 1871–Oct. 28, 1945.
Supp. 3–617
Rand, Edward Sprague, June 23, 1782–Oct. 22, 1863.
Vol. 8, Pt. 1–344
Rand, James Henry, May 29, 1859–Sept. 15, 1944.
Supp. 3–618
Rand, Sally, Feb. 2, 1904–Aug. 31, 1979.
Supp. 10–656
Randall, Alexander Williams, Oct. 31, 1819–July 26, 1872.
Vol. 8, Pt. 1–344
Randall, Benjamin, Feb. 7, 1749–Oct. 22, 1808.
Vol. 8, Pt. 1–345
Randall, Burton Alexander, Sept. 21, 1858–Jan. 4, 1932.
Vol. 8, Pt. 1–346
Randall, Clarence Belden, Mar. 5, 1891–Aug. 4, 1967.
Supp. 8–517

Randall, Henry Stephens, May 3, 1811–Aug. 14, 1876.
Vol. 8, Pt. 1–347
Randall, James Garfield, June 24, 1881–Feb. 20, 1953.
Supp. 5–556
Randall, James Ryder, Jan. 1, 1839–Jan. 14, 1908.
Vol. 8, Pt. 1–348
Randall, Robert Richard, c. 1750–June 1801.
Vol. 8, Pt. 1–348
Randall, Samuel, Feb. 10, 1778–Mar. 5, 1864.
Vol. 8, Pt. 1–349
Randall, Samuel Jackson, Oct. 10, 1828–Apr. 13, 1890.
Vol. 8, Pt. 1–350
Randall, Samuel Sidwell, May 27, 1809–June 3, 1881.
Vol. 8, Pt. 1–351
Randall, Wyatt William, Jan. 10, 1867–July 22, 1930.
Vol. 8, Pt. 1–352
Randolph, Alfred Magill, Aug. 31, 1836–Apr. 6, 1918.
Vol. 8, Pt. 1–352
Randolph, Asa Philip, Apr. 15, 1889–May 16, 1979.
Supp. 10–658
Randolph, Edmund, Aug. 10, 1753–Sept. 12, 1813.
Vol. 8, Pt. 1–353
Randolph, Edmund, June 9, 1819–Sept. 8, 1861.
Vol. 8, Pt. 1–355
Randolph, Edward, c. July 9, 1632–April 1703.
Vol. 8, Pt. 1–356
Randolph, Epes, Aug. 16, 1856–Aug. 22, 1921.
Vol. 8, Pt. 1–357
Randolph, George Wythe, Mar. 10, 1818–Apr. 3, 1867.
Vol. 8, Pt. 1–358
Randolph, Isham, Mar. 25, 1848–Aug. 2, 1920.
Vol. 8, Pt. 1–359
Randolph, Jacob, Nov. 25, 1796–Feb. 29, 1848.
Vol. 8, Pt. 1–360
Randolph, Sir John, c. 1693–March 2, 1736/37.
Vol. 8, Pt. 1–361
Randolph, John, 1727 or 1728–Jan. 31, 1784.
Vol. 8, Pt. 1–362
Randolph, John, June 2, 1773–May 24, 1833.
Vol. 8, Pt. 1–363
Randolph, Lillian, Dec. 6, 1914–Sept. 12, 1980.
Supp. 10–661
Randolph, Peyton, c. 1721–Oct. 22, 1775.
Vol. 8, Pt. 1–367
Randolph, Sarah Nicholas, Oct. 12, 1839–Apr. 25, 1892.
Vol. 8, Pt. 1–368
Randolph, Theodore Fitz, June 24, 1826–Nov. 7, 1883.
Vol. 8, Pt. 1–369
Randolph, Thomas Jefferson, Sept. 11, 1792–Oct. 7, 1875.
Vol. 8, Pt. 1–369
Randolph, Thomas Mann, Oct. 1, 1768–June 20, 1828.
Vol. 8, Pt. 1–370
Randolph, William, c. 1651–Apr. 11, 1711.
Vol. 8, Pt. 1–371
Raney, George Pettus, Oct. 11, 1845–Jan. 8, 1911.
Vol. 8, Pt. 1–372
Ranger, Henry Ward, Jan. 29, 1858–Nov. 7, 1916.
Vol. 8, Pt. 1–373
Rankin, Jeannette Pickering, June 11, 1880–May 18, 1973.
Supp. 9–640
Rankin, Jeremiah Eames, Jan. 2, 1828–Nov. 28, 1904.
Vol. 8, Pt. 1–374
Rankin, John Elliott, Mar. 29, 1882–Nov. 26, 1960.
Supp. 6–525
Rankin, McKee, Feb. 6, 1844–Apr. 17, 1914.
Vol. 8, Pt. 1–374
Rankine, William Birch, Jan. 4, 1858–Sept. 30, 1905.
Vol. 8, Pt. 1–375
Ranney, Ambrose Loomis, June 10, 1848–Dec. 1, 1905.
Vol. 8, Pt. 1–376
Ranney, Rufus Percival, Oct. 30, 1813–Dec. 6, 1891.
Vol. 8, Pt. 1–376
Ranney, William Tylee, May 9, 1813–Nov. 18, 1857.
Vol. 8, Pt. 1–377
Ransohoff, Joseph, May 26, 1853–Mar. 10, 1921.
Vol. 8, Pt. 1–378
Ransom, John Crowe, Apr. 30, 1888–July 3, 1974.
Supp. 9–641
Ransom, Matt Whitaker, Oct. 8, 1826–Oct. 8, 1904.
Vol. 8, Pt. 1–379
Ransom, Thomas Edward Greenfield, Nov. 29, 1834–Oct. 29, 1864.
Vol. 8, Pt. 1–379
Ransome, Frederick Leslie, Dec. 2, 1868–Oct. 6, 1935.
Supp. 1–620
Ranson, Stephen Walter, Aug. 28, 1880–Aug. 30, 1942.
Supp. 3–619
Rantoul, Robert, Nov. 23, 1778–Oct. 24, 1858.
Vol. 8, Pt. 1–380
Rantoul, Robert, Aug. 13, 1805–Aug. 7, 1852.
Vol. 8, Pt. 1–381
Rapaport, David, Sept. 30, 1911–Dec. 14, 1960.
Supp. 6–526
Raphall, Morris Jacob, Oct. 3, 1798–June 23, 1868.
Vol. 8, Pt. 1–382
Rapp, George, Nov. 1, 1757–Aug. 7, 1847.
Vol. 8, Pt. 1–383
Rapp, Wilhelm, July 14, 1828–Mar. 1, 1907.
Vol. 8, Pt. 1–384
Rarey, John Solomon, Dec. 6, 1827–Oct. 4, 1866.
Vol. 8, Pt. 1–385
Raskob, John Jakob, Mar. 19, 1879–Oct. 15, 1950.
Supp. 4–681
Rasle, Sébastien. [*See* Râle, Sébastien, d. 1724.]
Rathbone, Basil, June 13, 1892–July 21, 1967.
Supp. 8–518
Rathbone, Justus Henry, Oct. 29, 1839–Dec. 9, 1889.
Vol. 8, Pt. 1–385
Rathbone, Monroe Jackson ("Jack"), Mar. 1, 1900–Aug. 2, 1976.
Supp. 10–663
Rathbun, Richard, Jan. 25, 1852–July 16, 1918.
Vol. 8, Pt. 1–386
Rattermann, Heinrich Armin, Oct. 14, 1832–Jan. 6, 1923.
Vol. 8, Pt. 1–387
Rau, Charles, 1826–July 25, 1887.
Vol. 8, Pt. 1–388
Rauch, Frederick Augustus, July 27, 1806–Mar. 2, 1841.
Vol. 8, Pt. 1–389
Rauch, John Henry, Sept. 4, 1828–Mar. 24, 1894.
Vol. 8, Pt. 1–390
Raue, Charles Gottlieb, May 11, 1820–Aug. 21, 1896.
Vol. 8, Pt. 1–391
Raulston, John Tate, Sept. 22, 1868–July 11, 1956.
Supp. 6–528
Raum, Green Berry, Dec. 3, 1829–Dec. 18, 1909.
Vol. 8, Pt. 1–391
Rauschenbusch, Walter, Oct. 4, 1861–July 25, 1918.
Vol. 8, Pt. 1–392
Rautenstrauch, Walter, Sept. 7, 1880–Jan. 3, 1951.
Supp. 5–558
Ravalli, Antonio, May 16, 1811–Oct. 2, 1884.
Vol. 8, Pt. 1–393
Ravenel, Edmund, Dec. 8, 1797–July 27, 1871.
Vol. 8, Pt. 1–394
Ravenel, Harriott Horry Rutledge, Aug. 12, 1832–July 2, 1912.
Vol. 8, Pt. 1–395
Ravenel, Henry William, May 19, 1814–July 17, 1887.
Vol. 8, Pt. 1–396
Ravenel, Mazyck Porcher, June 16, 1861–Jan. 14, 1946.
Supp. 4–683
Ravenel, St. Julien, Dec. 19, 1819–Mar. 17, 1882.
Vol. 8, Pt. 1–397
Ravenscroft, John Stark, May 17, 1772–Mar. 5, 1830.
Vol. 8, Pt. 1–397
Ravoux, Augustin, Jan. 11, 1815–Jan. 17, 1906.
Vol. 8, Pt. 1–398
Rawle, Francis, c. 1662–Mar. 5, 1726/27.
Vol. 8, Pt. 1–399
Rawle, Francis, Aug. 7, 1846–Jan. 28, 1930.
Vol. 8, Pt. 1–400
Rawle, William, Apr. 28, 1759–Apr. 12, 1836.
Vol. 8, Pt. 1–400
Rawle, William Henry, Aug. 31, 1823–Apr. 19, 1889.
Vol. 8, Pt. 1–401
Rawlings, Marjorie Kinnan, Aug. 8, 1896–Dec. 14, 1953.
Supp. 5–559
Rawlins, John Aaron, Feb. 13, 1831–Sept. 6, 1869.
Vol. 8, Pt. 1–402
Rawlinson, Frank Joseph, Jan. 9, 1871–Aug. 14, 1937.
Supp. 2–548

Ray, Charles Bennett, Dec. 25, 1807–Aug. 15, 1886. Vol. 8, Pt. 1–403
Ray, Isaac, Jan. 16, 1807–Mar. 31, 1881. Vol. 8, Pt. 1–404
Ray, Man. [*See* Man Ray, 1890–1976.]
Rayburn, Samuel Taliaferro ("Sam"), Jan. 6, 1882–Nov. 16, 1961. Supp. 7–634
Raymond, Alexander Gillespie, Oct. 2, 1909–Sept. 6, 1956. Supp. 6–529
Raymond, Benjamin Wright, Oct. 23, 1801–Apr. 5, 1883. Vol. 8, Pt. 1–405
Raymond, Charles Walker, Jan. 14, 1842–May 3, 1913. Vol. 8, Pt. 1–406
Raymond, Daniel, 1786–1849?. Vol. 8, Pt. 1–406
Raymond, George Lansing, Sept. 3, 1839–July 11, 1929. Vol. 8, Pt. 1–407
Raymond, Harry Howard, Dec. 16, 1864–Dec. 27, 1935. Supp. 1–621
Raymond, Henry Jarvis, Jan. 24, 1820–June 18, 1869. Vol. 8, Pt. 1–408
Raymond, John Howard, Mar. 7, 1814–Aug. 14, 1878. Vol. 8, Pt. 1–412
Raymond, John T., Apr. 5, 1836–Apr. 10, 1887. Vol. 8, Pt. 1–413
Raymond, Miner, Aug. 29, 1811–Nov. 25, 1897. Vol. 8, Pt. 1–413
Raymond, Rossiter Worthington, Apr. 27, 1840–Dec. 31, 1918. Vol. 8, Pt. 1–414
Rayner, Isidor, Apr. 11, 1850–Nov. 25, 1912. Vol. 8, Pt. 1–415
Rayner, Kenneth, *c.* 1810–Mar. 5, 1884. Vol. 8, Pt. 1–416
Razaf, Andy, Dec. 16, 1895–Feb. 3, 1973. Supp. 9–644
Rea, Samuel, Sept. 21, 1855–Mar. 24, 1929. Vol. 8, Pt. 1–417
Reach, Alfred James, May 25, 1840–Jan. 14, 1928. Vol. 8, Pt. 1–418
Read, Charles, *c.* 1713–Dec. 27, 1774. Vol. 8, Pt. 1–419
Read, Charles William, May 12, 1840–Jan. 25, 1890. Vol. 8, Pt. 1–420
Read, Conyers, Apr. 25, 1881–Dec. 23, 1959. Supp. 6–531
Read, Daniel, Nov. 16, 1757–Dec. 4, 1836. Vol. 8, Pt. 1–420
Read, Daniel, June 24, 1805–Oct. 3, 1878. Vol. 8, Pt. 1–421
Read, George, Sept. 18, 1733–Sept. 21, 1798. Vol. 8, Pt. 1–422
Read, George Campbell, 1787–Aug. 22, 1862. Vol. 8, Pt. 1–424
Read, George Windle, Nov. 19, 1860–Nov. 6, 1934. Supp. 1–622
Read, Jacob, 1752–July 16, 1816. Vol. 8, Pt. 1–425
Read, John, Jan. 29, 1679/80–Feb. 7, 1749. Vol. 8, Pt. 1–425
Read, John, July 17, 1769–July 13, 1854. Vol. 8, Pt. 1–427
Read, John Meredith, July 21, 1797–Nov. 29, 1874. Vol. 8, Pt. 1–427
Read, John Meredith, Feb. 21, 1837–Dec. 27, 1896. Vol. 8, Pt. 1–428
Read, Nathan, July 2, 1759–Jan. 20, 1849. Vol 8. Pt. 1–429
Read, Opie Pope, Dec. 22, 1852–Nov. 2, 1939. Supp. 2–549
Read, Thomas, 1740?–Oct. 26, 1788. Vol. 8, Pt. 1–430
Read, Thomas Buchanan, Mar. 12, 1822–May 11, 1872. Vol. 8, Pt. 1–431
Reade, Edwin Godwin, Nov. 13, 1812–Oct. 18, 1894. Vol. 8, Pt. 1–432
Reagan, John Henninger, Oct. 8, 1818–Mar. 6, 1905. Vol. 8, Pt. 1–432
Realf, Richard, June 14, 1834–Oct. 28, 1878. Vol. 8, Pt. 1–434
Ream, Norman Bruce, Nov. 5, 1844–Feb. 9, 1915. Vol. 8, Pt. 1–435
Record, Samuel James, Mar. 10, 1881–Feb. 3, 1945. Supp. 3–620
Rector, Henry Massey, May 1, 1816–Aug. 12, 1899. Vol. 8, Pt. 1–436
Red Cloud, 1822–Dec. 10, 1909. Vol. 8, Pt. 1–437
Red Eagle. [*See* Weatherford, William, *c.* 1780–1824.]
Redfield, Amasa Angell, May 19, 1837–Oct. 19, 1902. Vol. 8, Pt. 1–439
Redfield, Isaac Fletcher, Apr. 10, 1804–Mar. 23, 1876. Vol. 8, Pt. 1–439
Redfield, Justus Starr, Jan. 2, 1810–Mar. 24, 1888. Vol. 8, Pt. 1–440
Redfield, Robert, Dec. 4, 1897–Oct. 16, 1958. Supp 6–532
Redfield, William c., Mar. 26, 1789–Feb. 12, 1857. Vol. 8, Pt. 1–441
Redfield, William Cox, June 18, 1858–June 13, 1932. Vol. 8, Pt. 1–442
Red Jacket, *c.* 1758–Jan. 20, 1830. Vol. 8, Pt. 1–437
Redman, Ben Ray, Feb. 21, 1896–Aug. 1, 1961. Supp. 7–637
Redman, John, Feb. 27, 1722–Mar. 19, 1808. Vol. 8, Pt. 1–443
Redpath, James, 1833–Feb. 10, 1891. Vol. 8, Pt. 1–443
Red Wing, *c.* 1750–*c.* 1825. Vol. 8, Pt. 1–438
Redwood, Abraham, Apr. 15, 1709–Mar. 8, 1788. Vol. 8, Pt. 1–444
Reece, Brazilla Carroll, Dec. 22, 1889–Mar. 19, 1961. Supp. 7–638
Reed, Daniel Alden, Sept. 15, 1875–Feb. 19, 1959. Supp. 6–534
Reed, David, Feb. 6, 1790–June 7, 1870. Vol. 8, Pt. 1–445
Reed, David Aiken, Dec. 21, 1880–Feb. 10, 1953. Supp. 5–560
Reed, Earl Howell, July 5, 1863–July 9, 1931. Vol. 8, Pt. 1–446
Reed, Elizabeth Armstrong, May 16, 1842–June 16, 1915. Vol. 8, Pt. 1–446
Reed, Henry Hope, July 11, 1808–Sept. 27, 1854. Vol. 8, Pt. 1–447
Reed, James, Jan. 8, 1722 o.s.–Feb. 13, 1807. Vol. 8, Pt. 1–448
Reed, James, Dec. 8, 1834–May 21, 1921. Vol. 8, Pt. 1–448
Reed, James Alexander, Nov. 9, 1861–Sept. 8, 1944. Supp. 3–621
Reed, James Hay, Sept. 10, 1853–June 17, 1927. Vol. 8, Pt. 1–449
Reed, John, Jan. 6, 1757–May 28, 1845. Vol. 8, Pt. 1–450
Reed, John, Oct. 22, 1887–Oct. 19, 1920. Vol. 8, Pt. 1–450
Reed, Joseph, Aug. 27, 1741–Mar. 5, 1785. Vol. 8, Pt. 1–451
Reed, Luman, June 4, 1787–June 7, 1836. Vol. 8, Pt. 1–453
Reed, Mary, Dec. 4, 1854–Apr. 8, 1943. Supp. 3–623
Reed, Myrtle, Sept. 27, 1874–Aug. 17, 1911. Vol. 8, Pt. 1–453
Reed, Richard Clark, Jan. 24, 1851–July 9, 1925. Vol. 8, Pt. 1–454
Reed, Sampson, June 10, 1800–July 8, 1880. Vol. 8, Pt. 1–455
Reed, Simeon Gannett, Apr. 23, 1830–Nov. 7, 1895. Vol. 8, Pt. 1–456
Reed, Stanley Forman, Dec. 31, 1884–Apr. 2, 1980. Supp. 10–664
Reed, Thomas Brackett, Oct. 18, 1839–Dec. 7, 1902. Vol. 8, Pt. 1–456
Reed, Walter, Sept. 13, 1851–Nov. 22, 1902. Vol. 8, Pt. 1–459
Reed, William Bradford, June 30, 1806–Feb. 18, 1876. Vol. 8, Pt. 1–461

Reeder, Andrew Horatio, July 12, 1807–July 5, 1864.
Vol. 8, Pt. 1–462
Reedy, William Marion, Dec. 11, 1862–July 28, 1920.
Vol. 8, Pt. 1–463
Rees, James, Dec. 25, 1821–Sept. 12, 1889.
Vol. 8, Pt. 1–464
Rees, John Krom, Oct. 27, 1851–Mar. 9, 1907.
Vol. 8, Pt. 1–465
Reese, Abram, Apr. 21, 1829–Apr. 25, 1908.
Vol. 8, Pt. 1–465
Reese, Charles Lee, Nov. 4, 1862–Apr. 12, 1940.
Supp. 2–550
Reese, Heloise Bowles, May 4, 1919–Dec. 28, 1977.
Supp. 10–665
Reese, Isaac, Apr. 29, 1821–Jan. 1, 1908.
Vol. 8, Pt. 1–466
Reese, Jacob, July 14, 1825–Mar. 25, 1907.
Vol. 8, Pt. 1–467
Reese, John James, June 16, 1818–Sept. 4, 1892.
Vol. 8, Pt. 1–468
Reese, Lizette Woodworth, Jan. 9, 1856–Dec. 17, 1935.
Supp. 1–623
Reeve, Tapping, Oct. 1744–Dec. 13, 1823.
Vol. 8, Pt. 1–468
Reeves, Arthur Middleton, Oct. 7, 1856–Feb. 25, 1891.
Vol. 8, Pt. 1–470
Reeves, Daniel F., June 30, 1912–Apr. 15, 1971.
Supp. 9–645
Reeves, Joseph Mason, Nov. 20, 1872–Mar. 25, 1948.
Supp. 4–685
Regan, Agnes Gertrude, Mar. 26, 1869–Sept. 30, 1943.
Supp. 3–624
Rehan, Ada, Apr. 22, 1860–Jan. 8, 1916.
Vol. 8, Pt. 1–470
Rehn, Frank Knox Morton, Apr. 12, 1848–July 6, 1914.
Vol. 8, Pt. 1–472
Reichel, Charles Gotthold, July 14, 1751–Apr. 18, 1825.
Vol. 8, Pt. 1–473
Reichel, William Cornelius, May 9, 1824–Oct. 25, 1876.
Vol. 8, Pt. 1–474
Reichenbach, Hans, Sept. 26, 1891–Apr. 9, 1953.
Supp. 5–562
Reick, William Charles, Sept. 29, 1864–Dec. 7, 1924.
Vol. 8, Pt. 1–474
Reid, Christian. [*See* Tiernan, Frances Christine Fisher, 1846–1920.]
Reid, David Boswell, June 1805–Apr. 5, 1863.
Vol. 8, Pt. 1–475
Reid, David Settle, Apr. 19, 1813–June 19, 1891.
Vol. 8, Pt. 1–476
Reid, Gilbert, Nov. 29, 1857–Sept. 30 1927.
Vol. 8, Pt. 1–476
Reid, Helen Miles Rogers, Nov. 23, 1882–July 27, 1970.
Supp. 8–519
Reid, Ira De Augustine, July 2, 1901–Aug. 15, 1968.
Supp. 8–521
Reid, James L., Dec. 26, 1844–June 1, 1910.
Vol. 8, Pt. 1–477
Reid, John Morrison, May 30, 1820–May 16, 1896.
Vol. 8, Pt. 1–478
Reid, Mayne. [*See* Reid, Thomas Mayne, 1818–1883.]
Reid, Mont Rogers, Apr. 7, 1889–May 11, 1943.
Supp. 3–625
Reid, Ogden Mills, May 16, 1882–Jan. 3, 1947.
Supp. 4–686
Reid, Robert, July 29, 1862–Dec. 2, 1929.
Vol. 8, Pt. 1–479
Reid, Rose Marie, Sept. 12, 1906–Dec. 18, 1978.
Supp. 10–667
Reid, Samuel Chester, Aug. 25. 1783–Jan. 28, 1861.
Vol. 8, Pt. 1–480
Reid, Thomas Mayne, Apr. 4, 1818–Oct. 22, 1883.
Vol. 8, Pt. 1–481
Reid, Whitelaw, Oct. 27, 1837–Dec. 15, 1912.
Vol. 8, Pt. 1–482
Reid, William Shields, Apr. 21, 1778–June 23, 1853.
Vol. 8, Pt. 1–486
Reid, William Wharry, 1799–Dec. 9, 1866.
Vol. 8, Pt. 1–486
Reiersen, Johan Reinert, Apr. 17, 1810–Sept. 6, 1864.
Vol. 8, Pt. 1–487
Reik, Theodor, May 12, 1888–Dec. 31, 1969.
Supp. 8–523
Reilly, Marion, July 16, 1879–Jan. 27, 1928.
Vol. 8, Pt. 1–488
Reinagle, Alexander, 1756–Sept. 21, 1809.
Vol. 8, Pt. 1–489
Reiner, Fritz, Dec. 19, 1888–Nov. 15, 1963.
Supp. 7–639
Reinhardt, Ad, Dec. 24, 1913–Aug. 30, 1967.
Supp. 8–524
Reinhardt, Aurelia Isabel Henry, Apr. 1, 1877–Jan. 28, 1948.
Supp. 4–687
Reinhart, Benjamin Franklin, Aug. 29, 1829–May 3, 1885.
Vol. 8, Pt. 1–490
Reinhart, Charles Stanley, May 16, 1844–Aug. 30, 1896.
Vol. 8, Pt. 1–490
Reinsch, Paul Samuel, June 10, 1869–Jan. 24, 1923.
Vol. 8, Pt. 1–491
Reisinger, Hugo, Jan. 29, 1856–Sept. 27, 1914.
Vol. 8, Pt. 1–492
Reisner, George Andrew, Nov. 5, 1867–June 6, 1942.
Supp. 3–626
Reitzel, Robert, Jan. 27, 1849–Mar. 31, 1898.
Vol. 8, Pt. 1–493
Rellstab, John, Sept. 19, 1858–Sept. 22, 1930.
Vol. 8, Pt. 1–494
Remey, George Collier, Aug. 10, 1841–Feb. 10, 1928.
Vol. 8, Pt. 1–495
Remington, Eliphalet, Oct. 27, 1793–Aug. 12, 1861.
Vol. 8, Pt. 1–495
Remington, Frederic, Oct. 4, 1861–Dec. 26, 1909.
Vol. 8, Pt. 1–496
Remington, Joseph Price, Mar. 26, 1847–Jan. 1, 1918.
Vol. 8, Pt. 1–497
Remington, Philo, Oct. 31, 1816–Apr. 4, 1889.
Vol. 8, Pt. 1–498
Remington, William Walter, Oct. 25, 1917–Nov. 24, 1954.
Supp. 5–563
Remond, Charles Lenox, Feb. 1, 1810–Dec. 22, 1873.
Vol. 8, Pt. 1–499
Remsen, Ira, Feb. 10, 1846–Mar. 4, 1927.
Vol. 8, Pt. 1–500
Rémy, Henri, *c.* 1811–Feb. 21, 1867.
Vol. 8, Pt. 1–502
Renaldo, Duncan, Apr. 23, 1904–Sept. 3, 1980.
Supp. 10–668
Renick, Felix, Nov. 5, 1770–Jan. 27, 1848.
Vol. 8, Pt. 1–503
Rennie, Michael, Aug. 25, 1909–June 10, 1971.
Supp. 9–647
Reno, Jesse Lee, June 20, 1823–Sept. 14, 1862.
Vol. 8 Pt. 1–504
Reno, Milo, Jan. 5, 1866–May 5, 1936.
Supp. 2–551
Renwick, Edward Sabine, Jan. 3, 1823–Mar. 19, 1912.
Vol. 8, Pt. 1–504
Renwick, Henry Brevoort, Sept. 4, 1817–Jan. 27, 1895.
Vol. 8, Pt. 1–505
Renwick, James, May 30, 1792–Jan. 12, 1863.
Vol. 8 Pt. 1–506
Renwick, James, Nov. 1, 1818–June 23, 1895.
Vol. 8, Pt. 1–507
Repplier, Agnes, Apr. 1, 1855–Dec. 15, 1950.
Supp. 4–688
Requa, Mark Lawrence, Dec. 25, 1865–Mar. 6, 1937.
Supp. 2–552
Requier, Augustus Julian, May 27, 1825–Mar. 19, 1887.
Vol. 8, Pt. 1–509
Rese, Frederick, Feb. 6, 1791–Dec. 30, 1871.
Vol. 8, Pt. 1–509
Resor, Stanley Burnet, Apr. 30, 1879–Oct. 29, 1962.
Supp. 7–641
Restarick, Henry Bond, Dec. 26, 1854–Dec. 8, 1933.
Supp. 1–624
Reuling, George, Nov. 11, 1839–Nov. 25, 1915.
Vol. 8, Pt. 1–510
Reuter, Dominic, Dec. 5, 1856–May 4, 1933.
Vol. 8, Pt. 1–511
Reuterdahl, Henry, Aug. 12, 1871–Dec. 22, 1925.
Vol. 8, Pt. 1–511

Reuther, Walter Philip, Sept. 1, 1907–May 9, 1970.
Supp. 8–525
Revel, Bernard, Sept. 17, 1885–Dec. 2, 1940.
Supp. 2–553
Revell, Fleming Hewitt, Dec. 11, 1849–Oct. 11, 1931.
Vol. 8, Pt. 1–512
Revell, Nellie MacAleney, 1872–Aug. 12, 1958.
Supp. 6–536
Revels, Hiram Rhoades, Sept. 1822–Jan. 16, 1901.
Vol. 8, Pt. 1–513
Revere, Joseph Warren, May 17, 1812–Apr. 20, 1880.
Vol. 8, Pt. 1–513
Revere, Paul, Jan. 1, 1735–May 10, 1818.
Vol. 8, Pt. 1–514
Revson, Charles Haskell, Oct. 11, 1906–Aug. 24, 1975.
Supp. 9–648
Reynolds, Alexander Welch, Aug. 1817–May 26, 1876.
Vol. 8, Pt. 1–516
Reynolds, Charles Alexander, Mar. 20, 1842?–June 25, 1876.
Vol. 8, Pt. 1–516
Reynolds, Edwin, Mar. 23, 1831–Feb. 19, 1909.
Vol. 8, Pt. 1–517
Reynolds, George McClelland, Jan. 15, 1865–Feb. 26, 1940.
Supp. 2–554
Reynolds, John, 1713–Feb. 3, 1788.
Vol. 8, Pt. 1–518
Reynolds, John, Feb. 26, 1788–May 8, 1865.
Vol. 8, Pt. 1–519
Reynolds, John Fulton, Sept. 20, 1820–July 1, 1863.
Vol. 8, Pt. 1–520
Reynolds, Joseph Jones, Jan. 4, 1822–Feb. 25, 1899.
Vol. 8, Pt. 1–521
Reynolds, Julian Sargeant, June 30, 1936–June 13, 1971.
Supp. 9–649
Reynolds, Milton, 1892–Jan. 23, 1976.
Supp. 10–669
Reynolds, Quentin James, Apr. 11, 1902–Mar. 17, 1965.
Supp. 7–642
Reynolds, Richard Samuel, Sr., Aug. 15, 1881–July 29, 1955.
Supp. 5–565
Reynolds, Robert Rice, June 18, 1884–Feb. 13, 1963.
Supp. 7–643
Reynolds, Samuel Godfrey, Mar. 9, 1801–Mar. 1, 1881.
Vol. 8, Pt. 1–522
Reynolds, William, Dec. 18, 1815–Nov. 5, 1879.
Vol. 8, Pt. 1–522
Reynolds, William Neal, Mar. 22, 1863–Sept. 10, 1951.
Supp. 5–566
Rezanov, Nikolai Petrovich, Apr. 8, 1764–Mar. 13, 1807.
Vol. 8, Pt. 1–523
Rhea, John, 1753–May 27, 1832.
Vol. 8, Pt. 1–524
Rhees, Morgan John, Dec. 8, 1760–Sept. 17, 1804.
Supp. 1–624
Rhees, Rush, Feb. 8, 1860–Jan. 5, 1939.
Supp. 2–555
Rhees, William Jones, Mar. 13, 1830–Mar. 18, 1907.
Vol. 8, Pt. 1–525
Rhett, Robert Barnwell, Dec. 21, 1800–Sept. 14, 1876.
Vol. 8, Pt. 1–526
Rhind, Alexander Colden, Oct. 31, 1821–Nov. 8, 1897.
Vol. 8, Pt. 1–528
Rhind, Charles, fl. 1810–1845.
Vol. 8, Pt. 1–529
Rhine, Joseph Banks, Sept. 29, 1895–Feb. 20, 1980.
Supp. 10–671
Rhoads, Cornelius Packard, June 20, 1898–Aug. 13, 1959.
Supp. 6–537
Rhoads, James E., Jan. 21, 1828–Jan. 2, 1895.
Vol. 8, Pt. 1–530
Rhodes, Eugene Manlove, Jan. 19, 1869–June 27, 1934.
Supp. 1–625
Rhodes, James Ford, May 1, 1848–Jan. 22, 1927.
Vol. 8, Pt. 1–531
Ribaut, Jean, *c.* 1520–Oct. 12, 1565.
Vol. 8, Pt. 1–533
Ricca, Paul, July 10, 1898–Oct. 11, 1972.
Supp. 9–651
Rice, Alexander Hamilton, Aug. 30, 1818–July 22, 1895.
Vol. 8, Pt. 1–534
Rice, Alice Caldwell Hegan, Jan. 11, 1870–Feb. 10, 1942.
Supp. 3–628
Rice, Calvin Winsor, Nov. 4, 1868–Oct. 2, 1934.
Supp. 1–626
Rice, Charles, Oct. 4, 1841–May 13, 1901.
Vol. 8, Pt. 1–535
Rice, Charles Allen Thorndike, June 18, 1851–May 16, 1889.
Vol. 8, Pt. 1–535
Rice, Dan, Jan. 25, 1823–Feb. 22, 1900.
Vol. 8, Pt. 1–536
Rice, David, Dec. 29, 1733–June 18, 1816.
Vol. 8, Pt. 1–537
Rice, Edgar Charles ("Sam"), Feb. 20, 1890–Oct. 13, 1974.
Supp. 9–652
Rice, Edmund, Feb. 14, 1819–July 11, 1889.
Vol. 8, Pt. 1–538
Rice. Edwin Wilbur, July 24, 1831–Dec. 3, 1929.
Vol. 8, Pt. 1–538
Rice, Edwin Wilbur, May 6, 1862–Nov. 25, 1935.
Supp. 1–627
Rice, Elmer, Sept. 28, 1892–May 8, 1967.
Supp. 8–528
Rice, Fenelon Bird, Jan. 2, 1841–Oct. 26, 1901.
Vol. 8, Pt. 1–539
Rice, George Samuel, Sept. 8, 1866–Jan. 4, 1950.
Supp. 4–690
Rice, (Henry) Grantland, Nov. 1, 1880–July 13, 1954.
Supp. 5–568
Rice, Henry Mower, Nov. 29, 1816–Jan. 15, 1894.
Vol. 8, Pt. 1–540
Rice, Isaac Leopold, Feb. 22, 1850–Nov. 2, 1915.
Vol. 8, Pt. 1–541
Rice, John Andrew, Feb. 1, 1888–Nov. 17, 1968.
Supp. 8–530
Rice, John Holt, Nov. 28, 1777–Sept. 3, 1831.
Vol. 8, Pt. 1–541
Rice, Luther, Mar. 25, 1783–Sept. 25, 1836.
Vol. 8, Pt. 1–542
Rice, Nathan Lewis, Dec. 29, 1807–June 11, 1877.
Vol. 8, Pt. 1–543
Rice, Richard Henry, Jan. 9, 1863–Feb. 10, 1922.
Vol. 8, Pt. 1–544
Rice, Thomas Dartmouth, May 20, 1808–Sept. 19, 1860.
Vol. 8, Pt. 1–545
Rice, Victor Moreau, Apr. 5, 1818–Oct. 18, 1869.
Vol. 8, Pt. 1–546
Rice, William Marsh, Mar. 14, 1816–Sept. 23, 1900.
Vol. 8, Pt. 1–546
Rice, William North, Nov. 21, 1845–Nov. 13, 1928.
Vol. 8, Pt. 1–547
Rich, Isaac, Oct. 24, 1801–Jan. 13, 1872.
Vol. 8, Pt. 1–548
Rich, Obadiah, 1783–Jan. 20, 1850.
Vol. 8, Pt. 1–549
Rich, Robert, June 23, 1883–Apr. 28, 1968.
Supp. 8–531
Richard, Gabriel, Oct. 15, 1767–Sept. 13, 1832.
Vol. 8, Pt. 1–549
Richard, James William, Feb. 14, 1843–Mar. 7, 1909.
Vol. 8, Pt. 1–551
Richards, Charles Brinckerhoff, Dec. 23, 1833–Apr. 20, 1919.
Vol. 8, Pt. 1–551
Richards, Charles Herbert, Mar. 18, 1839–Feb. 16, 1925.
Vol. 8, Pt. 1–552
Richards, Dickinson Woodruff, Oct. 30, 1895–Feb. 23, 1973.
Supp. 9–654
Richards, Ellen Henrietta Swallow, Dec. 3, 1842–Mar. 30, 1911.
Vol. 8, Pt. 1–553
Richards, John Kelvey, Mar. 15, 1856–Mar. 1, 1909.
Vol. 8, Pt. 1–554
Richards, Joseph William, July 28, 1864–Oct. 12, 1921.
Vol. 8, Pt. 1–555
Richards, Laura Elizabeth Howe, Feb. 27, 1850–Jan. 14, 1943.
Supp. 3–629
Richards, Robert Hallowell, Aug. 26, 1844–Mar. 27, 1945.
Supp. 1–630
Richards, Theodore William, Jan. 31, 1868–Apr. 2, 1928.
Vol. 8, Pt. 1–556
Richards, Thomas Addison, Dec. 3, 1820–June 28, 1900.
Vol. 8, Pt. 1–559

Richards, Vincent, Mar. 20, 1903–Sept. 28, 1959. Supp. 6–538
Richards, Wilham, Aug. 22, 1793–Nov. 7, 1847. Vol. 8, Pt. 1–560
Richards, William Trost, Nov. 14, 1833–Nov. 8, 1905. Vol. 8, Pt. 1–561
Richards, Zalmon, Aug. 11, 1811–Nov. 1, 1899. Vol. 8, Pt. 1–561
Richardson, Albert Deane, Oct. 6, 1833–Dec. 2, 1869. Vol. 8, Pt. 1–562
Richardson, Anna Euretta, Sept. 5, 1883–Feb. 3, 1931. Vol. 8, Pt. 1–563
Richardson, Charles Williamson, Aug. 22, 1861–Aug. 25, 1929. Vol. 8, Pt. 1–564
Richardson, Charles Francis, May 29, 1851–Oct. 8, 1913. Vol. 8, Pt. 1–564
Richardson, Edmund, June 28, 1818–Jan. 11, 1886. Vol. 8, Pt. 1–565
Richardson, Henry Hobson, Sept. 29, 1838–Apr. 27, 1886. Vol. 8, Pt. 1–566
Richardson, Israel Bush, Dec. 26, 1815–Nov. 3, 1862. Vol. 8, Pt. 1–570
Richardson, James Daniel, Mar. 10, 1843–July 24, 1914. Vol. 8, Pt. 1–570
Richardson, Joseph, Sept. 17, 1711–Dec. 3, 1784. Vol. 8, Pt. 1–571
Richardson, Maurice Howe, Dec. 31, 1851–July 30, 1912. Vol. 8, Pt. 1–572
Richardson, Robert, Sept. 25, 1806–Oct. 22, 1876. Vol. 8, Pt. 1–572
Richardson, Rufus Byam, Apr. 18, 1845–Mar. 10, 1914. Vol. 8, Pt. 1–574
Richardson, Sid Williams, Apr. 25, 1891–Sept. 30, 1959. Supp. 6–539
Richardson, Tobias Gibson, Jan. 3, 1827–May 26, 1892. Vol. 8, Pt. 1–575
Richardson, Wilds Preston, Mar. 20, 1861–May 20, 1929. Vol. 8, Pt. 1–576
Richardson, Willard, June 24, 1802–July 26, 1875. Vol. 8, Pt. 1–576
Richardson, William Adams, Nov. 2, 1821–Oct. 19, 1896. Vol. 8, Pt. 1–577
Richardson, William Lambert, Sept. 6, 1842–Oct. 20, 1932. Vol. 8, Pt. 1–578
Richardson, William Merchant, Jan. 4, 1774–Mar. 23, 1838. Vol. 8, Pt. 1–579
Richberg, Donald Randall, July 10, 1881–Nov. 27, 1960. Supp. 6–541
Richings, Peter, May 19, 1798–Jan. 18, 1871. Vol. 8, Pt. 1–580
Richmond, Charles Wallace, Dec. 31, 1868–May 19, 1932. Vol. 8, Pt. 1–581
Richmond, Dean, Mar. 31, 1804–Aug. 27, 1866. Vol. 8, Pt. 1–582
Richmond, John Lambert, Apr. 5, 1785–Oct. 12, 1855. Vol. 8, Pt. 1–583
Richmond, John Wilkes, Sept. 25, 1775–Mar. 4, 1857. Vol. 8, Pt. 1–583
Richmond, Mary Ellen, Aug. 5, 1861–Sept. 12, 1928. Vol. 8, Pt. 1–584
Richter, Conrad Michael, Oct. 13, 1890–Oct. 30, 1968. Supp. 8–532
Richtmyer, Floyd Karker, Oct. 12, 1881–Nov. 7, 1939. Supp. 2–556
Rickard, Clinton, May 19, 1882–June 14, 1971. Supp. 9–655
Rickard, George Lewis, Jan. 2, 1871–Jan. 6, 1929. Vol. 8, Pt. 1–585
Rickenbacker, Edward Vernon ("Eddie"), Oct. 8, 1890–July 23, 1973. Supp. 9–657
Rickert, Martha Edith, July 11, 1871–May 23, 1938. Supp. 2–557
Ricketson, Daniel, July 30, 1813–July 16, 1898. Vol. 8, Pt. 1–586
Ricketts, Claude Vernon, Feb. 23, 1906–July 6, 1964. Supp. 7–644
Ricketts, Howard Taylor, Feb. 9, 1871–May 3, 1910. Supp. 1–628
Ricketts, James Brewerton, June 21, 1817–Sept. 22, 1887. Vol. 8, Pt. 1–587
Ricketts, Palmer Chamberlaine, Jan. 17, 1856–Dec. 10, 1934. Supp. 1–629
Rickey, Wesley Branch, Dec. 20, 1881–Dec. 9, 1965. Supp. 7–645
Ricord, Frederick William, Oct. 7, 1819–Aug. 12, 1897. Vol. 8, Pt. 1–587
Ricord, Philippe, Dec. 10, 1800–Oct. 22, 1889. Vol. 8, Pt. 1–588
Riddell, John Leonard, Feb. 20, 1807–Oct. 7, 1865. Vol. 8, Pt. 1–589
Ridder, Bernard Herman, Mar. 20, 1883–May 5, 1975. Supp. 9–659
Ridder, Herman, Mar. 5, 1851–Nov. 1, 1915. Vol. 8, Pt. 1–590
Riddle, Albert Gallatin, May 28, 1816–May 16, 1902. Vol. 8, Pt. 1–591
Riddle, George Peabody, Sept. 22, 1851–Nov. 26, 1910. Vol. 8, Pt. 1–591
Riddle, Matthew Brown, Oct. 17, 1836–Aug. 30, 1916. Vol. 8, Pt. 1–592
Riddle, Samuel Doyle, July 1, 1861–Jan. 8, 1951. Supp. 5–568
Rideing, William Henry, Feb. 17, 1853–Aug. 22, 1918. Vol. 8, Pt. 1–593
Rideout, Henry Milner, Apr. 25, 1877–Sept. 17, 1927. Vol. 8, Pt. 1–594
Ridgaway, Henry Bascom, Sept. 7, 1830–Mar. 30, 1895. Vol. 8, Pt. 1–594
Ridge, Major, *c.* 1771–June 22, 1839. Vol. 8, Pt. 1–595
Ridgely, Charles Goodwin, July 2, 1784–Feb. 4, 1848. Vol. 8, Pt. 1–595
Ridgely, Daniel Bowly, Aug. 1, 1813–May 5, 1868. Vol. 8, Pt. 1–596
Ridgely, Nicholas, Sept. 30, 1762–Apr. 1, 1830. Vol. 8, Pt. 1–597
Ridgway, Robert, July 2, 1850–Mar. 25, 1929. Vol. 8, Pt. 1–598
Ridgway, Robert, Oct. 19, 1862–Dec. 19, 1938. Supp. 2–558
Ridpath, John Clark, Apr. 26, 1840–July 31, 1900. Vol. 8, Pt. 1–599
Riefler, Winfield William, Feb. 9, 1897–Apr. 5, 1974. Supp. 9–660
Rieger, Johann Georg Joseph Anton, Apr. 23, 1811–Aug. 20, 1869. Vol. 8, Pt. 1–599
Riegger, Wallingford, Apr. 29, 1885–Apr. 2, 1961. Supp. 7–647
Rigdon, Sidney, Feb. 19, 1793–July 14, 1876. Vol. 8, Pt. 1–600
Rigge, William Francis, Sept. 9, 1857–Mar. 31, 1927. Vol. 8, Pt. 1–601
Riggs, Elias, Nov. 19, 1810–Jan. 17, 1901. Vol. 8, Pt. 1–602
Riggs, George Washington, July 4, 1813–Aug. 24, 1881. Vol. 8, Pt. 1–603
Riggs, John Mankey, Oct. 25, 1810–Nov. 11, 1885. Vol. 8, Pt. 1–604
Riggs, Stephen Return, Mar. 23, 1812–Aug. 24, 1883. Vol. 8, Pt. 1–605
Riggs, William Henry, Mar. 22, 1837–Aug. 31, 1924. Vol. 8, Pt. 1–606
Riis, Jacob August, May 3, 1849–May 26, 1914. Vol. 8, Pt. 1–606
Riis, Mary Phillips, Apr. 29, 1877–Aug. 4, 1967. Supp. 8–534
Riley, Benjamin Franklin, July 16, 1849–Dec. 14, 1925. Vol. 8, Pt. 1–608
Riley, Bennet, Nov. 27, 1787–June 9, 1853. Vol. 8 Pt. 1–608
Riley, Charles Valentine, Sept. 18, 1843–Sept. 14, 1895. Vol. 8, Pt. 1–609
Riley, Isaac Woodbridge, May 20, 1869–Sept. 2, 1933. Vol. 8, Pt. 1–610
Riley, James Whitcomb, Oct. 7, 1849–July 22, 1916. Vol. 8, Pt. 1–611
Riley, William Bell, Mar. 22, 1861–Dec. 5, 1947. Supp. 4–691
Rimmer, William, Feb. 20, 1816–Aug. 20, 1879. Vol. 8, Pt. 1–613

Rindge, Frederick Hastings, Dec. 21, 1857–Aug. 29, 1905.
Vol. 8, Pt. 1–614
Rinehart, Mary Roberts, Aug. 12, 1876–Sept. 22, 1958.
Supp. 6–542
Rinehart, Stanley Marshall, Jr., Aug. 18, 1897–Apr. 26, 1969.
Supp. 8–535
Rinehart, William Henry, Sept. 13, 1825–Oct. 28, 1874.
Vol. 8, Pt. 1–615
Ringgold, Cadwalader, Aug. 20, 1802–Apr. 29, 1867.
Vol. 8, Pt. 1–617
Ringling, Charles, Dec. 2, 1863–Dec. 3, 1926.
Vol. 8, Pt. 1–618
Riordan, Patrick William, Aug. 27, 1841–Dec. 27, 1914.
Vol. 8, Pt. 1–619
Ripley, Edward Hastings, Nov. 11, 1839–Sept. 14, 1915.
Vol. 8, Pt. 1–619
Ripley, Edward Payson, Oct. 30, 1845–Feb. 4, 1920.
Vol. 8, Pt. 1–620
Ripley, Eleazar Wheelock, Apr. 15, 1782–Mar. 2, 1839.
Vol. 8, Pt. 1–621
Ripley, Ezra, May 1, 1751–Sept. 21, 1841.
Vol. 8, Pt. 1–622
Ripley, George, Oct. 3, 1802–July 4, 1880.
Vol. 8, Pt. 1–623
Ripley, James Wolfe, Dec. 10, 1794–Mar. 15, 1870.
Vol. 8, Pt. 1–625
Ripley, Robert LeRoy, Dec. 26, 1893–May 27, 1949.
Supp. 4–692
Ripley, Roswell Sabine, Mar. 14, 1823–Mar. 29, 1887.
Vol. 8, Pt. 1–625
Ripley, William Zebina, Oct. 13, 1867–Aug. 16, 1941.
Supp. 3–632
Rising, Johan Classon, 1617–Apr. 1672.
Vol. 8, Pt. 1–626
Rister, Carl Coke, June 30, 1889–Apr. 16, 1955.
Supp. 5–569
Ritchard, Cyril, Dec. 1, 1898–Dec. 18, 1977.
Supp. 10–673
Ritchey, George Willis, Dec. 31, 1864–Nov. 4, 1945.
Supp. 3–633
Ritchie, Albert Cabell, Aug. 29, 1876–Feb. 24, 1936.
Supp. 2–559
Ritchie, Alexander Hay, Jan. 14, 1822–Sept. 19, 1895.
Vol. 8, Pt. 1–627
Ritchie, Anna Cora. [*See* Mowatt, Anna Cora Ogden, 1819–1870.]
Ritchie, Thomas, Nov. 5, 1778–July 3, 1854.
Vol. 8, Pt. 1–628
Ritner, Joseph, Mar. 25, 1780–Oct. 16, 1869.
Vol. 8, Pt. 1–629
Rittenhouse, David, Apr. 8, 1732–June 26, 1796.
Vol. 8, Pt. 1–630
Rittenhouse, Jessie Belle, Dec. 8, 1869–Sept. 28, 1948.
Supp. 4–693
Rittenhouse, William, 1644–Feb. 17, 1708.
Vol. 8, Pt. 1–632
Ritter, Frédéric Louis, June 22, 1834–July 6, 1891.
Vol. 8, Pt. 1–632
Ritter, Joseph Elmer, July 20, 1892–June 10, 1967.
Supp. 8–536
Ritter, William Emerson, Nov. 19, 1856–Jan. 10, 1944.
Supp. 3–635
Ritter, Woodward Maurice ("Tex"), Jan. 23, 1905–Jan. 2, 1974.
Supp. 9–662
Rivera, Luis Muñoz. [*See* Muñoz-Rivera, Luis, 1859–1916.]
Rivers, Lucius Mendel, Sept. 28, 1905–Dec. 28, 1970.
Supp. 8–538
Rivers, Thomas Milton, Sept. 3, 1888–May 12, 1962.
Supp. 7–648
Rivers, William James, July 17, 1822–June 22, 1909.
Vol. 8, Pt. 1–633
Rives, George Lockhart, May 1, 1849–Aug. 18, 1917.
Vol. 8, Pt. 1–634
Rives, Hallie Erminie, May 2, 1876–Aug. 16, 1956.
Supp. 6–544
Rives, John Cook, May 24, 1795–Apr. 10, 1864.
Vol. 8, Pt. 1–635
Rives, William Cabell, May 4, 1793–Apr. 25, 1868.
Vol. 8, Pt. 1–635
Rivington, James, 1724–July 4, 1802.
Vol. 8, Pt. 1–637
Rix, Julian Walbridge, Dec. 30, 1850–Nov. 24, 1903.
Vol. 8, Pt. 1–638
Roach, John, Dec. 25, 1813–Jan. 10, 1887.
Vol. 8, Pt. 1–639
Roane, Archibald, 1759–Jan. 4, 1819.
Vol. 8, Pt. 1–640
Roane, John Selden, Jan. 8, 1817–Apr. 8, 1867.
Vol. 8, Pt. 1–641
Roane, Spencer, Apr. 4, 1762–Sept. 4, 1822.
Vol. 8, Pt. 1–642
Roark, Ruric Nevel, May 19, 1859–Apr. 14, 1909.
Vol. 8, Pt. 1–643
Robb, Inez Early Callaway, Nov. 29, 1900–Apr. 4, 1979.
Supp. 10–674
Robb, James, Apr. 2, 1814–July 30, 1881.
Vol. 8, Pt. 1–644
Robb, William Lispenard, May 9, 1861–Jan. 26, 1933.
Supp. 1–630
Robbins, Chandler, Feb. 14, 1810–Sept. 11, 1882.
Vol. 8, Pt. 1–644
Robbins, Thomas, Aug. 11, 1777–Sept. 13, 1856.
Vol. 8, Pt. 1–645
Roberdeau, Daniel, 1727–Jan. 5, 1795.
Vol. 8, Pt. 1–646
Roberdeau, Isaac, Sept. 11, 1763–Jan. 15, 1829.
Vol. 8, Pt. 1–647
Robert, Christopher Rhinelander, Mar. 23, 1802–Oct. 27, 1878.
Vol. 8, Pt. 2–1
Robert, Henry Martyn, May 2, 1837–May 11, 1923.
Supp. 1–631
Roberts, Benjamin Stone, Nov. 18, 1810–Jan. 29, 1875.
Vol. 8, Pt. 2–2
Roberts, Benjamin Titus, July 25, 1823–Feb. 27, 1893.
Vol. 8, Pt. 2–2
Roberts, Brigham Henry, Mar. 13, 1857–Sept. 27, 1933.
Vol. 8, Pt. 2–3
Roberts, Edmund, June 29, 1784–June 12, 1836.
Vol. 8, Pt. 2–4
Roberts, Elizabeth Wentworth, June 10, 1871–Mar. 12, 1927.
Vol. 8, Pt. 2–5
Roberts, Elizabeth Madox, Oct. 30, 1881–Mar. 13, 1941.
Supp. 3–636
Roberts, Ellis Henry, Sept. 30, 1827–Jan. 8, 1918.
Vol. 8, Pt. 2–6
Roberts, George Brooke, Jan. 15, 1833–Jan. 30, 1897.
Vol. 8, Pt. 2–6
Roberts, Howard, Apr. 9, 1843–Apr. 18, 1900.
Vol. 8, Pt. 2–7
Roberts, Issachar Jacob, Feb. 17, 1802–Dec. 28, 1871.
Vol. 8, Pt. 2–8
Roberts, Job, Mar. 23, 1756–Aug. 20, 1851.
Vol. 8, Pt. 2–8
Roberts, Jonathan, Aug. 16, 1771–July 21, 1854.
Vol. 8, Pt. 2–9
Roberts, Joseph Jenkins, Mar. 15, 1809–Feb 24, 1876.
Vol. 8, Pt. 2–10
Roberts, Kenneth Lewis, Dec. 8, 1885–July 21, 1957.
Supp. 6–545
Roberts, Marshall Owen, Mar. 22, 1814–Sept. 11, 1880.
Vol. 8, Pt. 2–11
Roberts, Nathan S., July 28, 1776–Nov. 24, 1852.
Vol. 8, Pt. 2–12
Roberts, Oran Milo, July 1815–May 19, 1898.
Vol. 8, Pt. 2–13
Roberts, Owen Josephus, May 2, 1875–May 17, 1955.
Supp. 5–571
Roberts, Robert Richford, Aug. 2, 1778–Mar. 26, 1843.
Vol. 8, Pt. 2–14
Roberts, Solomon White, Aug. 3, 1811–Mar. 22, 1882.
Vol. 8, Pt. 2–15
Roberts, Theodore, Oct. 8, 1861–Dec. 14, 1928.
Vol. 8, Pt. 2–16
Roberts, William Charles, Sept. 23, 1832–Nov. 27, 1903.
Vol. 8, Pt. 2–17
Roberts, William Henry, Jan. 31, 1844–June 26, 1920.
Vol. 8, Pt. 2–17
Roberts, William Milnor, Feb. 12, 1810–July 14, 1881.
Vol. 8, Pt. 2–18
Roberts, William Randall, Feb. 6, 1830–Aug. 9, 1897.
Vol. 8, Pt. 2–19

Robertson, Absalom Willis, May 27, 1887–Nov. 1, 1971.
Supp. 9–663
Robertson, Alice Mary, Jan. 2, 1854–July 1, 1931.
Vol. 8, Pt. 2–20
Robertson, Archibald, May 8, 1765–Dec. 6, 1835.
Vol. 8. Pt. 2–21
Robertson, Ashley Herman, Dec. 14, 1867–July 13, 1930.
Vol. 8, Pt. 2–22
Robertson, George, Nov. 18, 1790–May 16, 1874.
Vol. 8, Pt. 2–22
Robertson, James, b. 1740.
Vol. 8, Pt. 2–23
Robertson, James, June 28, 1742–Sept. 1, 1814.
Vol. 8, Pt. 2–24
Robertson, James Alexander, Aug. 19, 1873–Mar. 20, 1939.
Supp. 2–560
Robertson, Jerome Bonaparte, Mar. 14, 1815–Jan. 7, 1891
Vol. 8, Pt. 2–25
Robertson, John, Apr. 13, 1787–July 5, 1873.
Vol. 8, Pt. 2–26
Robertson, Morgan Andrew, Sept. 30, 1861–Mar. 24, 1915.
Vol. 8, Pt. 2–27
Robertson, Thomas Bolling, Feb. 27, 1779–Oct. 5, 1828.
Vol. 8, Pt. 2–28
Robertson, William Henry, Oct. 10, 1823–Dec. 6, 1898.
Vol. 8, Pt. 2–28
Robertson, William Joseph, Dec. 30, 1817–May 27, 1898.
Vol. 8, Pt. 2–29
Robertson, William Schenck, Jan. 11, 1820–June 26, 1881.
Vol. 8, Pt. 2–30
Robertson, William Spence, Oct. 7, 1872–Oct. 24, 1955.
Supp. 5–577
Robertson, Wyndham, Jan. 26, 1803–Feb. 11, 1888.
Vol. 8, Pt. 2–30
Robeson, George Maxwell, Mar. 16, 1829–Sept. 27, 1897.
Vol. 8, Pt. 2–31
Robeson, Paul Leroy, Apr. 9, 1898–Jan. 23, 1976.
Supp. 10–676
Robidou, Antoine, Sept. 24, 1794–Aug. 29, 1860.
Vol. 8, Pt. 2–32
Robins, Henry Ephraim, Sept. 30, 1827–Apr. 23, 1917.
Vol. 8, Pt. 2–32
Robins, Margaret Dreier, Sept. 6, 1868–Feb. 21, 1945.
Supp. 3–638
Robins, Raymond, Sept. 17, 1873–Sept. 26, 1954.
Supp. 5–578
Robinson, Albert Alonzo, Oct. 21, 1844–Nov. 7, 1918.
Vol. 8, Pt. 2–33
Robinson, Benjamin Lincoln, Nov. 8, 1864–July 27, 1935.
Supp. 1–631
Robinson, Beverley, Jan. 11, 1722 o.s.–Apr. 9, 1792.
Vol. 8, Pt. 2–34
Robinson, Bill (Bojangles), May 25, 1878–Nov. 25, 1949.
Supp. 4–695
Robinson, Boardman, Sept. 6, 1876–Sept. 5, 1952.
Supp. 5–580
Robinson, Charles, July 21, 1818–Aug. 17, 1894.
Vol. 8, Pt. 2–34
Robinson, Charles Mulford, Apr. 30, 1869–Dec. 30, 1917.
Vol. 8, Pt. 2–36
Robinson, Charles Seymour, Mar. 31, 1829–Feb. 1, 1899.
Vol. 8, Pt. 2–37
Robinson, Christopher, May 15, 1806–Oct. 3, 1889.
Vol. 8, Pt. 2–38
Robinson, Claude Everett, Mar. 22, 1900–Aug. 7, 1961.
Supp. 7–649
Robinson, Conway, Sept. 15, 1805–Jan. 30, 1884.
Vol. 8, Pt. 2–39
Robinson, Edward, Apr. 10, 1794–Jan. 27, 1863.
Vol. 8, Pt. 2–39
Robinson, Edward, Nov. 1, 1858–Apr. 18, 1931.
Vol. 8, Pt. 2–40
Robinson, Edward G., Dec. 12, 1893–Jan. 26, 1973.
Supp. 9–665
Robinson, Edward Mott, Jan. 8, 1800–June 14, 1865.
Vol. 8, Pt. 2–41
Robinson, Edward Stevens, Apr. 18, 1893–Feb. 27, 1937.
Supp. 2–561
Robinson, Edward Van Dyke, Dec. 20, 1867–Dec. 10, 1915.
Vol. 8, Pt. 2–42
Robinson, Edwin Arlington, Dec. 22, 1869–Apr. 6, 1935.
Supp. 1–632
Robinson, Ezekiel Gilman, Mar. 23, 1815–June 13, 1894.
Vol. 8, Pt. 2–43
Robinson, Frederick Byron, Apr. 11, 1855–Mar. 23, 1910.
Vol. 8, Pt. 2–44
Robinson, George Canby, Nov. 4, 1878–Aug. 31, 1960.
Supp. 6–546
Robinson, Harriet Jane Hanson, Feb. 8, 1825–Dec. 22, 1911.
Vol. 8, Pt. 2–44
Robinson, Henry Cornelius, Aug. 28, 1832–Feb. 14, 1900.
Vol. 8, Pt. 2–45
Robinson, Henry Morton, Sept. 7, 1898–Jan. 13, 1961.
Supp. 7–650
Robinson, James Harvey, June 29, 1863–Feb. 16, 1936.
Supp. 2–562
Robinson, John, Feb. 3, 1704–May 11, 1766.
Vol. 8, Pt. 2–46
Robinson, John Cleveland, Apr. 10, 1817–Feb. 18, 1897.
Vol. 8, Pt. 2–46
Robinson, John Mitchell, Dec. 6, 1827–Jan. 14, 1896.
Vol. 8, Pt. 2–47
Robinson, John Roosevelt ("Jackie"), Jan. 31, 1919–Oct. 24, 1972.
Supp. 9–667
Robinson, Joseph Taylor, Aug. 26, 1872–July 14, 1937.
Supp. 2–566
Robinson, Moncure, Feb. 2, 1802–Nov. 10, 1891.
Vol. 8, Pt. 2–48
Robinson, Moses, Mar. 26, 1742–May 26, 1813.
Vol. 8, Pt. 2–49
Robinson, Rowland Evans, May 14, 1833–Oct. 15, 1900.
Vol. 8, Pt. 2–50
Robinson, Ruby Doris Smith, Apr. 25, 1942–Oct. 7, 1967.
Supp. 8–539
Robinson, Solon, Oct. 21, 1803–Nov. 3, 1880.
Vol. 8, Pt. 2–50
Robinson, Stillman Williams, Mar. 6, 1838–Oct. 31, 1910.
Vol. 8, Pt. 2–52
Robinson, Stuart, Nov. 14, 1814–Oct. 5, 1881.
Vol. 8, Pt. 2–53
Robinson, Theodore, June 3, 1852–Apr. 2, 1896.
Vol. 8, Pt. 2–54
Robinson, Therese Albertine Louise von Jakob, Jan. 26, 1797–Apr 13, 1870.
Vol. 8, Pt. 2–55
Robinson, William, Nov. 22, 1840–Jan. 2, 1921.
Vol. 8, Pt. 2–56
Robinson, William Callyhan, July 26, 1834–Nov. 6, 1911.
Vol. 8, Pt. 2–56
Robinson, William Erigena, May 6, 1814–Jan. 23, 1892.
Vol. 8, Pt. 2–57
Robinson, William Stevens, Dec. 7, 1818–Mar. 11, 1876.
Vol. 8, Pt. 2–58
Robinson-Smith, Gertrude, July 13, 1881–Oct. 22, 1963.
Supp. 7–651
Robot, Isidore, July 18, 1837–Feb. 15, 1887.
Vol. 8, Pt. 2–59
Robson, May, Apr. 19, 1858–Oct. 20, 1942.
Supp. 3–639
Robson, Stuart, Mar. 4, 1836–Apr. 29, 1903.
Vol. 8, Pt. 2–59
Rochambeau, Jean Baptiste Donatien de Vimeur, Comte de, July 1, 1725–May 10, 1807.
Vol. 8, Pt. 2–60
Roche, Arthur Somers, Apr. 27, 1883–Feb. 17, 1935.
Supp. 1–634
Roche, James Jeffrey, May 31, 1847–Apr. 3, 1908.
Vol. 8, Pt. 2–63
Roche, Josephine Aspinwall, Dec. 2, 1886–July 29, 1976.
Supp. 10–681
Rochester, Nathaniel, Feb. 21, 1752–May 17, 1831.
Vol. 8, Pt. 2–63
Rock, John, Aug. 19, 1836–Aug. 9, 1904.
Vol. 8, Pt. 2–64
Rockefeller, Abby Greene Aldrich, Oct. 26, 1874–Apr. 5, 1948.
Supp. 4–696
Rockefeller, John Davison, July 8, 1839–May 23, 1937.
Supp. 2–568

Rockefeller, John Davison, Jr., Jan. 29, 1874–May 11, 1960.
Supp. 6–547
Rockefeller, John Davison, 3rd, Mar. 21, 1906–July 10, 1978.
Supp. 10–682
Rockefeller, Martha Baird, Mar. 15, 1895–Jan. 24, 1971.
Supp. 9–670
Rockefeller, Nelson Aldrich, July 8, 1908–Jan. 26, 1979.
Supp. 10–685
Rockefeller, William, May 31, 1841–June 24, 1922.
Vol. 8, Pt. 2–65
Rockefeller, Winthrop, May 1, 1912–Feb. 22, 1973.
Supp. 9–671
Rockhill, William Woodville, Apr. 1854–Dec. 8, 1914.
Vol. 8, Pt. 2–66
Rockne, Knute Kenneth, Mar. 4, 1888–Mar. 31, 1931.
Vol. 8, Pt. 2–67
Rockwell, Alphonso David, May 18, 1840–Apr. 12, 1933.
Vol. 8, Pt. 2–68
Rockwell, George Lincoln, Mar. 9, 1918–Aug. 25, 1967.
Supp. 8–540
Rockwell, Kiffin Yates, Sept. 20, 1892–Sept. 23, 1916.
Vol. 8, Pt. 2–69
Rockwell, Norman Perceval, Feb. 3, 1894–Nov. 8, 1978.
Supp. 10–688
Rockwell, Willard Frederick, Mar. 31, 1888–Oct. 16, 1978.
Supp. 10–691
Roddey, Philip Dale, 1820–Aug. 1897.
Vol. 8, Pt. 2–70
Rodenbough, Theophilus Francis, Nov. 5, 1838–Dec. 19, 1912.
Vol. 8, Pt. 2–71
Rodes, Robert Emmett, Mar. 29, 1829–Sept. 19, 1864.
Vol. 8, Pt. 2–71
Rodgers, Christopher Raymond Perry, Nov. 14, 1819–Jan. 8, 1892.
Vol. 8, Pt. 2–72
Rodgers, George Washington, Feb. 22, 1787–May 21, 1832.
Vol. 8, Pt. 2–73
Rodgers, George Washington, Oct. 30, 1822–Aug. 17, 1863.
Vol. 8, Pt. 2–74
Rodgers, John, Aug. 5, 1727–May 7, 1811.
Vol. 8, Pt. 2–74
Rodgers, John, 1773–Aug. 1, 1838.
Vol. 8, Pt. 2–75
Rodgers, John, Aug. 8, 1812–May 5, 1882.
Vol. 8, Pt. 2–77
Rodgers, John, Jan. 15, 1881–Aug. 27, 1926.
Vol. 8, Pt. 2–79
Rodgers, Richard Charles, June 28, 1902–Dec. 30, 1979.
Supp. 10–692
Rodman, Issac Peace, Aug. 18, 1822–Sept. 30, 1862.
Vol. 8, Pt. 2–79
Rodman, Thomas Jackson, July 30, 1815–June 7, 1871.
Vol. 8, Pt. 2–80
Rodney, Caesar, Oct. 7, 1728–June 26, 1784.
Vol. 8, Pt. 2–81
Rodney, Caesar Augustus, Jan. 4, 1772–June 10, 1824.
Vol. 8, Pt. 2–82
Rodney, Thomas, June 4, 1744–Jan. 2, 1811.
Vol. 8, Pt. 2–83
Rodzinski, Artur, Jan. 2, 1892–Nov. 27, 1958.
Supp. 6–549
Roe, Edward Payson, Mar. 7, 1838–July 19, 1888.
Vol. 8, Pt. 2–84
Roe, Francis Asbury, Oct. 4, 1823–Dec. 28, 1901.
Vol. 8, Pt. 2–85
Roe, Gilbert Ernstein, Feb. 7, 1865–Dec. 22, 1929.
Vol. 8, Pt. 2–86
Roebling, John Augustus, June 12, 1806–July 22, 1869.
Vol. 8, Pt. 2–86
Roebling, Washington Augustus, May 26, 1837–July 21, 1926.
Vol. 8, Pt. 2–89
Roeding, George Christian, Feb. 4, 1868–July 23, 1928.
Vol. 8, Pt. 2–90
Roemer, Karl Ferdinand, Jan. 5, 1818–Dec. 14, 1891.
Vol. 8, Pt. 2–91
Roethke, Theodore Huebner, May 25, 1908–Aug. 1, 1963.
Supp. 7–652
Rogers, Clara Kathleen Barnett, Jan. 14, 1844–Mar. 8, 1931.
Vol. 8, Pt. 2–92
Rogers, Edith Nourse, Mar. 19, 1881–Sept. 10, 1960.
Supp. 6–551
Rogers, Edward Staniford, June 28, 1826–Mar. 29, 1899.
Vol. 8, Pt. 2–92
Rogers, Harriet Burbank, Apr. 12, 1834–Dec. 12, 1919.
Vol. 8, Pt. 2–93
Rogers, Henry Darwin, Aug. 1, 1808–May 29, 1866.
Vol. 8, Pt. 2–94
Rogers, Henry Huttleston, Jan. 29, 1840–May 19, 1909.
Vol. 8, Pt. 2–95
Rogers, Henry J., Mar. 10, 1811–Aug. 20, 1879.
Vol. 8, Pt. 2–96
Rogers, Henry Wade, Oct. 10, 1853–Aug. 16, 1926.
Vol. 8, Pt. 2–97
Rogers, Isaiah, Aug. 17, 1800–Apr. 13, 1869.
Vol. 8, Pt. 2–98
Rogers, James Blythe, Feb. 11, 1802–June 15, 1852.
Vol. 8, Pt. 2–99
Rogers, James Gamble, Mar. 3, 1867–Oct. 1, 1947.
Supp. 4–697
Rogers, James Harris, July 13, 1856–Dec. 12, 1929.
Vol. 8, Pt. 2–100
Rogers, James Harvey, Sept. 25, 1886–Aug. 13, 1939.
Supp. 2–576
Rogers, John, Dec. 1, 1648–Oct. 17, 1721.
Vol. 8, Pt. 2–101
Rogers, John, Oct. 30, 1829–July 26, 1904.
Vol. 8, Pt. 2–102
Rogers, John Almanza Rowley, Nov. 12, 1828–July 22, 1906.
Vol. 8, Pt. 2–103
Rogers, John Ignatius, May 27, 1843–Mar. 13, 1910.
Vol. 8, Pt. 2–104
Rogers, John Rankin, Sept. 4, 1838–Dec. 26, 1901.
Vol. 8, Pt. 2–104
Rogers, John Raphael, Dec. 11, 1856–Feb. 18, 1934.
Vol. 8, Pt. 2–105
Rogers, Mary Josephine, Oct. 27, 1882–Oct. 9, 1955.
Supp. 5–581
Rogers, Moses, *c.* 1779–Oct. 15, 1821.
Vol. 8, Pt. 2–106
Rogers, Randolph, July 6, 1825–Jan. 15, 1892.
Vol. 8, Pt. 2–107
Rogers, Robert, Nov. 7, 1731 o.s.–May 18, 1795.
Vol. 8, Pt. 2–108
Rogers, Robert Empie, Mar. 29, 1813–Sept. 6, 1884.
Vol. 7, Pt. 2–109
Rogers, Robert William, Feb. 14, 1864–Dec. 12, 1930.
Vol. 8, Pt. 2–110
Rogers, Stephen, Jan. 1826–May 23, 1878.
Vol. 8, Pt. 2–111
Rogers, Thomas, Mar. 16, 1792–Apr. 19, 1856.
Vol. 8, Pt. 2–112
Rogers, Will, Nov. 4, 1879–Aug. 15, 1935.
Supp. 1–635
Rogers, William Crowninshield, July 26, 1823–July 2, 1888.
Vol. 8, Pt. 2–115
Rogers, William Allen, May 23, 1854–Oct. 20, 1931.
Vol. 8, Pt. 2–113
Rogers, William Augustus, Nov. 13, 1832–Mar. 1, 1898.
Vol. 8, Pt. 2–114
Rogers, William Barton, Dec. 7, 1804–May 30, 1882.
Vol. 8, Pt. 2–115
Rohde, Ruth Bryan Owen, Oct. 2, 1885–July 27, 1954.
Supp. 5–582
Rohé, George Henry, Jan. 26, 1851–Feb. 6, 1899.
Vol. 8, Pt. 2–116
Roheim, Geza, Sept. 12, 1891–June 7, 1953.
Supp. 5–583
Rohlfs, Anna Katharine Green, Nov. 11, 1846–Apr. 11, 1935.
Supp. 1–637
Rolette, Jean Joseph, Sept. 23, 1781–Dec. 1, 1842.
Vol. 8, Pt. 2–117
Rolf, Ida Pauline, May 19, 1896–Mar. 19, 1979.
Supp. 10–695
Rolfe, John, 1585–1622.
Vol. 8, Pt. 2–117
Rolfe, Robert Abial ("Red"), Oct. 1, 1908–July 8, 1969.
Supp. 8–541
Rolfe, William James, Dec. 10, 1827–July 7, 1910.
Vol. 8, Pt. 2–118

Rollins, Alice Marland Wellington, June 12, 1847–Dec. 5, 1897.
Vol. 8, Pt. 2–119
Rollins, Edward Henry, Oct. 3, 1824–July 31, 1889.
Vol. 8, Pt. 2–120
Rollins, Frank West, Feb. 24, 1860–Oct. 27, 1915.
Vol. 8, Pt. 2–120
Rollins, James Sidney, Apr. 19, 1812–Jan. 9, 1888.
Vol. 8, Pt. 2–121
Rollinson, William, Apr. 15, 1762–Sept. 21, 1842.
Vol. 8, Pt. 2–122
Rolph, James, Aug. 23, 1869–June 2, 1934.
Supp. 1–638
Rolshoven, Julius, Oct. 28, 1858–Dec. 7, 1930.
Vol. 8, Pt. 2–123
Rölvaag, Ole Edvart, Apr. 22, 1876–Nov. 5, 1931.
Vol. 8, Pt. 2–124
Roman, André Bienvenu, Mar. 5, 1795–Jan. 28, 1866.
Vol. 8, Pt. 2–125
Romanoff, Michael ("Prince Mike"), Feb. 1893?–Sept. 1, 1971.
Supp. 9–673
Romans, Bernard, *c.* 1720–*c.* 1784.
Vol. 8, Pt. 2–126
Romayne, Nicholas, Sept. 1756–July 21, 1817.
Vol. 8, Pt. 2–127
Rombauer, Irma Louise, Oct. 30, 1877–Oct. 14, 1962.
Supp. 7–656
Romberg, Sigmund, July 29, 1887–Nov. 9, 1951.
Supp. 5–584
Rombro, Jacob, Oct. 10, 1858–Nov. 28, 1922.
Vol. 8, Pt. 2–128
Romeike, Henry, Nov. 19, 1855–June 3, 1903.
Vol. 8, Pt. 2–129
Romer, Alfred Sherwood ("Al"), Dec. 28, 1894–Nov. 5, 1973.
Supp. 9–674
Rommel, Edwin Americus ("Eddie"), Sept. 13, 1897–Aug. 26, 1970.
Supp. 8–543
Romnes, Haakon Ingolf ("H. I."), Mar. 2, 1907–Nov. 19, 1973.
Supp. 9–676
Rondthaler, Edward, July 24, 1842–Jan. 31, 1931.
Vol. 8, Pt. 2–130
Rood, Ogden Nicholas, Feb. 3, 1831–Nov. 12, 1902.
Vol. 8, Pt. 2–131
Rooney, Pat, July 4, 1880–Sept. 9, 1962.
Supp. 7–657
Roosa, Damel Bennett St. John, Apr. 4, 1838–Mar. 8, 1908.
Vol. 8, Pt. 2–132
Roosevelt, (Anna) Eleanor, Oct. 11, 1884–Nov. 7, 1962.
Supp. 7–658
Roosevelt, Franklin Delano, Jan. 30, 1882–Apr. 12, 1945.
Supp. 3–641
Roosevelt, Hilborne Lewis, Dec. 21, 1849–Dec. 30, 1886.
Vol. 8, Pt. 2–133
Roosevelt, Kermit, Oct. 10, 1889–June 4, 1943.
Supp. 3–667
Roosevelt, Nicholas J., Dec. 27, 1767–July 30, 1854.
Vol. 8, Pt. 2–133
Roosevelt, Robert Barnwell, Aug. 7, 1829–June 14, 1906.
Vol. 8, Pt. 2–134
Roosevelt, Theodore, Oct. 27, 1858–Jan. 6, 1919.
Vol. 8, Pt. 2–135
Roosevelt, Theodore, Sept. 13, 1887–July 12, 1944.
Supp. 3–668
Root, Amos Ives, Dec. 9, 1839–Apr. 30, 1923.
Vol. 8, Pt. 2–144
Root, Elihu, Feb. 15, 1845–Feb. 7, 1937.
Supp. 2–577
Root, Elisha King, May 10, 1808–Aug. 31, 1865.
Vol. 8, Pt. 2–144
Root, Erastus, Mar. 16, 1773–Dec. 24, 1846.
Vol. 8, Pt. 2–145
Root, Frank Albert, July 3, 1837–June 20, 1926.
Vol. 8, Pt. 2–146
Root, Frederic Woodman, June 13, 1846–Nov. 8, 1916.
Vol. 8, Pt. 2–146
Root, George Frederick, Aug. 30, 1820–Aug. 6, 1895.
Vol. 8, Pt. 2–147
Root, Jesse, Dec. 28, 1736 o.s.–Mar. 29, 1822.
Vol. 8, Pt. 2–148
Root, John Wellborn, Jan. 10, 1850–Jan. 15, 1891.
Vol. 8, Pt. 2–149
Root, Joseph Pomeroy, Apr. 23, 1826–July 20, 1885.
Vol. 8, Pt. 2–150
Roper, Daniel Calhoun, Apr. 1, 1867–Apr. 11, 1943.
Supp. 3–669
Roper, Elmo Burns, Jr., July 31, 1900–Apr. 30, 1971.
Supp. 9–677
Ropes, James Hardy, Sept. 3, 1866–Jan. 7, 1933.
Vol. 8, Pt. 2–151
Ropes, John Codman, Apr. 28, 1836–Oct. 28, 1899.
Vol. 8, Pt. 2–152
Ropes, Joseph, Dec. 15, 1770–Sept. 29, 1850.
Vol. 8, Pt. 2–152
Rorer, David, May 12, 1806–July 7, 1884.
Vol. 8, Pt. 2–153
Rorimer, James Joseph, Sept. 7, 1905–May 11, 1966.
Supp. 8–544
Rorty, James Hancock, Mar. 30, 1890–Feb. 25, 1973.
Supp. 9–678
Rosa, Edward Bennett, Oct. 4, 1861–May 17, 1921.
Vol. 8, Pt. 2–154
Rosati, Joseph, Jan. 12, 1789–Sept. 25, 1843.
Vol. 8, Pt. 2–155
Rose, Alex, Oct. 15, 1898–Dec. 28, 1976.
Supp. 10–696
Rose, Aquila, *c.* 1695–1723.
Vol. 8, Pt. 2–156
Rose, Billy, Sept. 6, 1899–Feb. 10, 1966.
Supp. 8–545
Rose, Chauncey, Dec. 24, 1794–Aug. 13, 1877.
Vol. 8, Pt. 2–156
Rose, Edward, fl. 1811–1834.
Vol. 8, Pt. 2–157
Rose, Ernestine Louise Siismondi Potowski, Jan. 13, 1810–Aug. 4, 1892.
Vol. 8, Pt. 2–158
Rose, John Carter, Apr. 27, 1861–Mar. 26, 1927.
Vol. 8, Pt. 2–159
Rose, Joseph Nelson, Jan. 11, 1862–May 4, 1928.
Vol. 8, Pt. 2–159
Rose, Mary Davies Swartz, Oct. 31, 1874–Feb. 1, 1941.
Supp. 3–670
Rose, Uriah Milton, Mar. 5, 1834–Aug. 12, 1913.
Vol. 8, Pt. 2–161
Rose, Walter Malins, Nov. 25, 1872–Feb. 12, 1908.
Vol. 8, Pt. 2–161
Rose, Wickliffe, Nov. 19, 1862–Sept. 5, 1931.
Supp. 1–639
Rosebury, Theodor, Aug. 10, 1904–Nov. 25, 1976.
Supp. 10–698
Rosecrans, Sylvester Horton, Feb. 5, 1827–Oct. 21, 1878.
Vol. 8, Pt. 2–162
Rosecrans, William Starke, Sept. 6, 1819–Mar. 11, 1898.
Vol. 8, Pt. 2–163
Roselins, Christian, Aug. 10, 1803–Sept. 5, 1873.
Vol. 8, Pt. 2–164
Rosen, Joseph A., Feb. 15, 1878–Apr. 2, 1949.
Supp. 4–698
Rosenau, Milton Joseph, Jan. 1, 1869–Apr. 9, 1946.
Supp. 4–700
Rosenbach, Abraham Simon Wolf, July 22, 1876–July 1, 1952.
Supp. 5–586
Rosenbach, Philip Hyman, Sept. 29, 1863–Mar. 5, 1953.
Supp. 5–586
Rosenberg, Abraham Hayyim, Oct. 17, 1838–Aug. 5, 1925.
Vol. 8 Pt. 2–165
Rosenberg, Ethel, Sept. 28, 1915–June 19, 1953.
Supp. 5–588
Rosenberg, Henry, June 22, 1824–May 12, 1893.
Vol. 8 Pt. 2–166
Rosenberg, Julius, May 12, 1918–June 19, 1953.
Supp. 5–588
Rosenberg, Paul, Dec. 29, 1881–June 30, 1959.
Supp. 6–552
Rosenblatt, Bernard Abraham, June 15, 1886–Oct. 14, 1969.
Supp. 8–548
Rosenblatt, Joseph, May 9, 1882–June 19, 1933.
Vol. 8, Pt. 2–167

Rosenfeld, Morris, Dec. 28, 1862–June 22, 1923.
Vol. 8, Pt. 2–167
Rosenfeld, Paul Leopold, May 4, 1890–July 21, 1946.
Supp. 4–702
Rosenman, Samuel Irving, Feb. 13, 1896–June 24, 1973.
Supp. 9–679
Rosenstein, Nettie Rosencrans, Sept. 26, 1893–Mar. 13, 1980.
Supp. 10–699
Rosenstiel, Lewis Solon, July 21, 1891–Jan. 21, 1976.
Supp. 10–700
Rosenthal, Herman, Oct. 6, 1843–Jan. 27, 1917.
Vol. 8, Pt. 2–168
Rosenthal, Max, Nov. 23, 1833–Aug. 8, 1918.
Vol. 8, Pt. 2–169
Rosenthal, Toby Edward, Mar. 15, 1848–Dec. 23, 1917.
Vol. 8, Pt. 2–170
Rosenwald, Julius, Aug. 12, 1862–Jan. 6, 1932.
Vol. 8, Pt. 2–170
Rosenwald, Lessing Julius, Feb. 10, 1891–June 25, 1979.
Supp. 10–702
Rosewater, Edward, Jan. 28, 1841–Aug. 30, 1906.
Vol. 8, Pt. 2–171
Rosewater, Victor, Feb. 13, 1871–July 12, 1940.
Supp. 2–582
Ross, Abel Hastings, Apr. 28, 1831–May 13, 1893.
Vol. 8, Pt. 2–172
Ross, Alexander, May 9, 1783–Oct. 23, 1856.
Vol. 8, Pt. 2–173
Ross, Alexander Coffman, May 31, 1812–Feb. 26, 1883.
Vol. 8, Pt. 2–174
Ross, Araminta. [*See* Tubman, Harriet, *c.* 1821–1913]
Ross, Betsy, Jan. 1, 1752–Jan. 30, 1836.
Vol. 8, Pt. 2–174
Ross, Charles Griffith, Nov. 9, 1885–Dec. 5, 1950.
Supp. 4–703
Ross, Denman Waldo, Jan. 10, 1853–Sept. 12, 1935.
Supp. 1–640
Ross, Edmund Gibson, Dec. 7, 1826–May 8, 1907.
Vol. 8, Pt. 2–175
Ross, Edward Alsworth, Dec. 12, 1866–July 22, 1951.
Supp. 5–591
Ross, Erskine Mayo, June 30, 1845–Dec. 10, 1928.
Vol. 8, Pt. 2–176
Ross, George, May 10, 1730–July 14, 1779.
Vol. 8, Pt. 2–177
Ross, Harold Wallace, Nov. 6, 1892–Dec. 6, 1951.
Supp. 5–593
Ross, James, July 12, 1762–Nov. 27, 1847.
Vol. 8, Pt. 2–178
Ross, James Delmage McKenzie, Nov. 9, 1872–Mar. 14, 1939.
Supp. 2–583
Ross, John, Oct. 3, 1790–Aug. 1, 1866.
Vol. 8, Pt. 2–178
Ross, Lawrence Sullivan, Sept. 27, 1838–Jan. 3, 1898.
Vol. 8, Pt. 2–179
Ross, Martin, Nov. 27, 1762–1827.
Vol. 8, Pt. 2–180
Ross, Nellie Tayloe, Nov. 29, 1876–Dec. 20, 1977.
Supp. 10–703
Ross, Thomas Joseph, July 27, 1893–May 27, 1975.
Supp. 9–681
Rossen, Robert, Mar. 16, 1908–Feb. 18, 1966.
Supp. 8–550
Rosser, Thomas Lafayette, Oct. 15, 1836–Mar. 29, 1910.
Vol. 8, Pt. 2–181
Rossiter, Clinton Lawrence, III, Sept. 18, 1917–July 10, 1970.
Supp. 8–551
Rossiter, Thomas Prichard, Sept. 29, 1818–May 17, 1871.
Vol. 8, Pt. 2–182
Rossiter, William Sidney, Sept. 9, 1861–Jan. 23, 1929.
Vol. 8, Pt. 2–182
Rostovtzeff, Michael Ivanovitch, Nov. 10, 1870–Oct. 20, 1952.
Supp. 5–594
Rotch, Abbott Lawrence, Jan. 6, 1861–Apr. 7, 1912.
Vol. 8, Pt. 2–183
Rotch, Arthur, May 13, 1850–Aug. 15, 1894.
Vol. 8, Pt. 2–184
Rotch, Thomas Morgan, Dec. 9, 1849–Mar. 9, 1914.
Vol. 8, Pt. 2–185
Rotch, William, Dec. 4, 1734 o.s.–May 16, 1828.
Vol. 8, Pt. 2–186
Roth, Lillian, Dec. 13, 1910–May 12, 1980.
Supp. 10–704
Roth, Samuel, Nov. 17, 1894–July 3, 1974.
Supp. 9–682
Rothafel, Samuel Lionel, July 9, 1881–Jan. 13, 1936.
Supp. 2–584
Rothermel, Peter Frederick, July 8, 1817–Aug. 15, 1895.
Vol. 8, Pt. 2–187
Rothko, Mark, Sept. 25, 1903–Feb. 25, 1970.
Supp. 8–552
Rothrock, Joseph Trimble, Apr. 9, 1839–June 2, 1922.
Vol. 8, Pt. 2–188
Rothwell, Richard Pennefather, May 1, 1836–Apr. 17, 1901.
Vol. 8, Pt. 2–189
Roulston, Marjorie Hillis, May 25, 1890–Nov. 8, 1971.
Supp. 9–683
Roulstone, George, Oct. 8, 1767–1804.
Vol. 8, Pt. 2–190
Round, William Marshall Fitts, Mar. 26, 1845–Jan. 2, 1906.
Vol. 8, Pt. 2–190
Rouquette, Adrien Emmanuel, Feb. 13, 1813–July 15, 1887.
Vol. 8, Pt. 2–191
Rouquette, François Dominique, Jan. 2, 1810–May 1890.
Vol. 8, Pt. 2–192
Rourke, Constance Mayfield, Nov. 14, 1885–Mar. 23, 1941.
Supp. 3–672
Rous, Francis Peyton, Oct. 5, 1879–Feb. 16, 1970.
Supp. 8–555
Rousseau, Harry Harwood, Apr. 19, 1870–July 24, 1930.
Vol. 8, Pt. 2–193
Rousseau, Lovell Harrison, Aug. 4, 1818–Jan. 7, 1869.
Vol. 8 Pt. 2–194
Rovenstine, Emery Andrew, July 20, 1895–Nov. 9, 1960.
Supp. 6–553
Rovere, Richard Halworth, May 5, 1915–Nov. 23, 1979.
Supp. 10–706
Rowan, John, July 12, 1773–July 13, 1843.
Vol. 8, Pt. 2–195
Rowan, Stephen Clegg, Dec. 25, 1808–Mar. 31, 1890.
Vol. 8, Pt. 2–196
Rowe, Leo Stanton, Sept. 17, 1871–Dec. 5, 1946.
Supp. 4–705
Rowe, Lynwood Thomas, Jan. 11, 1912–Jan. 8, 1961.
Supp. 7–662
Roweli, George Presbury, July 4, 1838–Aug. 28, 1908.
Vol. 8, Pt. 2–197
Rowell, Chester Harvey, Nov. 1, 1867–Apr. 12, 1948.
Supp. 4–706
Rowland, Henry Augustus, Nov. 27, 1848–Apr. 16. 1901.
Vol. 8, Pt. 2–198
Rowland, Henry Cottrell, May 12, 1874–June 6, 1933.
Vol. 8, Pt. 2–199
Rowland, Thomas Fitch, Mar. 15, 1831–Dec. 13, 1907.
Vol. 8, Pt. 2–200
Rowlands, William, Oct. 10, 1807–Oct. 27, 1866.
Vol. 8, Pt. 2–201
Rowlandson, Mary White, *c.* 1635–*c.* 1678.
Vol. 8, Pt. 2–201
Rowse, Samuel Worcester, Jan. 29, 1822–May 24, 1901.
Vol. 8, Pt. 2–202
Rowson, Susanna Haswell, *c.* 1762–Mar. 2, 1824.
Vol. 8, Pt. 2–203
"Roxy." [*See* Rothafel, Samuel Lionel, 1881–1936.]
Royall, Anne Newport, June 11, 1769–Oct. 1, 1854.
Vol. 8, Pt. 2–204
Royce, Josiah, Nov. 20, 1855–Sept. 14, 1916.
Vol. 8, Pt. 2–205
Royce, Ralph, June 28, 1890–Aug. 7, 1965.
Supp. 7–663
Roye, Edward James, Feb. 3, 1815–Feb. 12, 1872.
Vol. 8, Pt. 2–212
Royster, James Finch, June 26, 1880–Mar. 21, 1930.
Vol. 8, Pt. 2–212
Ruark, Robert Chester, Dec. 29, 1915–July 1, 1965.
Supp. 7–665
Rubey, William Walden, Dec. 19, 1898–Apr. 12, 1974.
Supp. 9–685
Rubicam, Raymond, June 16, 1892–May 8, 1978.
Supp. 10–707
Rubin, Isidor Clinton, Jan. 8, 1883–July 10, 1958.
Supp. 6–554

Rubinow, Isaac Max, Apr. 19, 1875–Sept. 1, 1936.
Supp. 2–585
Rubinstein, Helena, Dec. 25, 1870–Apr. 1, 1965.
Supp. 7–666
Rublee, George, July 7, 1868–Apr. 26, 1957.
Supp. 6–556
Rublee, Horace, Aug. 19, 1829–Oct. 19, 1896.
Vol. 8, Pt. 2–213
Ruby, Jack L., Mar. 25, 1911–Jan. 3, 1967.
Supp. 8–557
Rucker, George ("Nap"), Sept. 30, 1884–Dec. 19, 1970.
Supp. 8–558
Ruckstull, Frederick Wellington, May 22, 1853–May 26, 1942.
Supp. 3–673
Rudge, William Edwin, Nov. 23, 1876–June 12, 1931.
Vol. 8, Pt. 2–214
Ruditsky, Barney, Jan. 3, 1898–Oct. 18, 1962.
Supp. 7–667
Rudkin, Margaret Fogarty, Sept. 14, 1897–June 1, 1967.
Supp. 8–559
Ruef, Abraham, Sept. 2, 1864–Feb. 29, 1936.
Supp. 2–587
Ruffin, Edmund, Jan. 5, 1794–June 18, 1865.
Vol. 8, Pt. 2–214
Ruffin, Thomas, Nov. 17, 1787–Jan. 15, 1870.
Vol. 8, Pt. 2–216
Ruffner, Henry, Jan. 16, 1790–Dec. 17, 1861.
Vol. 8, Pt. 2–217
Ruffner, William Henry, Feb. 11, 1824–Nov. 24, 1908.
Vol. 8, Pt. 2–218
Ruger, Thomas Howard, Apr. 2, 1833–June 3, 1907.
Vol. 8, Pt. 2–219
Rugg, Arthur Prentice, Aug. 20, 1862–June 12, 1938.
Supp. 2–588
Rugg, Harold Ordway, Jan. 17, 1886–May 17, 1960.
Supp. 6–557
Ruggles, Samuel Bulkley, Apr. 11, 1800–Aug. 28, 1881.
Vol. 8, Pt. 2–220
Ruggles, Timothy, Oct. 20, 1711–Aug. 4, 1795.
Vol. 8, Pt. 2–221
Ruhl, Arthur Brown, Oct. 1, 1876–June 7, 1935.
Supp. 1–642
Ruhräh, John, Sept. 26, 1872–Mar. 10, 1935.
Supp. 1–643
Rukeyser, Muriel, Dec. 15, 1913–Feb. 12, 1980.
Supp. 10–709
Rumford, Benjamin Thompson, Count. [*See* Thompson, Benjamin, 1753–1814.]
Ruml, Beardsley, Nov. 5, 1894–Apr. 18, 1960.
Supp. 6–558
Rummel, Joseph Francis, Oct. 14, 1876–Nov. 8, 1964.
Supp. 7–668
Rumsey, Charles Cary, Aug. 29, 1879–Sept. 21, 1922.
Vol. 8, Pt. 2–222
Rumsey, James, Mar. 1743–Dec. 20, 1792.
Vol. 8, Pt. 2–223
Rumsey, Mary Harriman, Nov. 17, 1881–Dec. 18, 1934.
Supp. 1–644
Rumsey, William, Oct. 18, 1841–Jan. 16, 1903.
Vol. 8, Pt. 2–223
Runcie, Constance Faunt Le Roy, Jan. 15, 1836–May 17, 1911.
Vol. 8, Pt. 2–224
Runkle, John Daniel, Oct. 11, 1822–July 8, 1902.
Vol. 8, Pt. 2–225
Runyon, Damon, Oct. 3, 1880–Dec. 10, 1946.
Supp. 4–708
Rupp, Adolph Frederick, Sept. 2, 1901–Dec. 10, 1977.
Supp. 10–710
Rupp, Israel Daniel, July 10, 1803–May 31, 1878.
Vol. 8, Pt. 2–225
Rupp, William, Apr. 17, 1839–Apr. 3, 1904.
Vol. 8, Pt. 2–226
Ruppert, Jacob, Aug. 5, 1867–Jan. 13, 1939.
Supp. 2–589
Rusby, Henry Hurd, Apr. 26, 1855–Nov. 18, 1940.
Supp. 2–590
Rush, Benjamin, Dec. 24, 1745 o.s.–Apr. 19, 1813.
Vol. 8, Pt. 2–227
Rush, James, Mar. 15, 1786–May 26, 1869.
Vol. 8, Pt. 2–231
Rush, Richard, Aug. 29, 1780–July 30, 1859.
Vol. 8, Pt. 2–231
Rush, William, July 4, 1756–Jan. 17, 1833.
Vol. 8, Pt. 2–234
Rushing, James Andrew, Aug. 26, 1903–June 8, 1972.
Supp. 9–686
Rusk, Jeremiah McClain, June 17, 1830–Nov. 21, 1893.
Vol. 8, Pt. 2–235
Rusk, Thomas Jefferson, Dec. 5, 1803–July 29, 1857.
Vol. 8, Pt. 2–236
Russ, John Dennison, Sept. 1, 1801–Mar. 1, 1881.
Vol. 8, Pt. 2–237
Russell, Annie, Jan. 12, 1864–Jan. 16, 1936.
Supp. 2–592
Russell, Benjamin, Sept. 13, 1761–Jan. 4, 1845.
Vol. 8, Pt. 2–238
Russell, Charles Edward, Sept. 25, 1860–Apr. 23, 1941.
Supp. 3–674
Russell, Charles Ellsworth ("Pee Wee"), Mar. 27, 1906–Feb. 15, 1969.
Supp. 8–561
Russell, Charles Taze, Feb. 16, 1852–Oct. 31, 1916.
Vol. 8, Pt. 2–240
Russell, Charles Wells, Mar. 16, 1856–Apr. 5, 1927.
Vol. 8, Pt. 2–241
Russell, David Allen, Dec. 10, 1820–Sept. 19, 1864.
Vol. 8, Pt. 2–241
Russell, Henry Norris, Oct. 25, 1877–Feb. 18, 1957.
Supp. 6–560
Russell, Irwin, June 3, 1853–Dec. 23, 1879.
Vol. 8, Pt. 2–242
Russell, Israel Cook, Dec. 10, 1852–May 1, 1906.
Vol. 8, Pt. 2–243
Russell, James Earl, July 1, 1864–Nov. 4, 1945.
Supp. 3–676
Russell, James Solomon, Dec. 20, 1857–Mar. 28, 1935.
Supp. 1–645
Russell, John Henry, July 4, 1827–Apr. 1, 1897.
Vol. 8, Pt. 2–244
Russell, Jonathan, Feb. 27, 1771–Feb. 17, 1832.
Vol. 8, Pt. 2–245
Russell, Joseph, Oct. 8, 1719 o.s.–Oct. 16, 1804.
Vol. 8, Pt. 2–245
Russell, Lillian, Dec. 4, 1861–June 6, 1922.
Vol. 8, Pt. 2–246
Russell, Mother Mary Baptist, Apr. 18, 1829–Aug. 6, 1898.
Vol. 8, Pt. 2–247
Russell, Osborne, June 12, 1814–*c.* 1865.
Vol. 8, Pt. 2–248
Russell, Richard Brevard, Jr. ("Dick"), Nov. 2, 1897–Jan. 21, 1971.
Supp. 9–688
Russell, Rosalind, June 4, 1912–Nov. 28, 1976.
Supp. 10–712
Russell, Sol Smith, June 15, 1848–Apr. 28, 1902.
Vol. 8, Pt. 2–249
Russell, William, Apr. 28, 1798–Aug. 16, 1873.
Vol. 8, Pt. 2–249
Russell, William Eustis, Jan. 6, 1857–July 16, 1896.
Vol. 8 Pt. 2–250
Russell, William Henry, Oct. 9, 1802–Oct. 13, 1873.
Vol. 8, Pt. 2–251
Russell, William Hepburn, Jan. 31, 1812–Sept. 10, 1872.
Vol. 8, Pt. 2–252
Russwurm, John Brown, Oct. 1, 1799–June 17, 1851.
Vol. 8, Pt. 2–253
Rust, John Daniel, Sept. 6, 1892–Jan. 20, 1954.
Supp. 5–596
Rust, RIchard Sutton, Sept. 12, 1815–Dec. 22, 1906.
Vol. 8, Pt. 2–253
Ruter, Martin, Apr. 3, 1785–May 16, 1838.
Vol. 8, Pt. 2–254
Rutgers, Henry, Oct. 7, 1745–Feb. 17, 1830.
Vol. 8, Pt. 2–255
Ruth, George Herman (Babe), Feb. 6, 1895–Aug. 17, 1948.
Supp. 4–709
Rutherford, Joseph Franklin, Nov. 8, 1869–Jan. 8, 1942.
Supp. 3–678
Rutherfurd, Lewis Morris, Nov. 25, 1816–May 30, 1892.
Vol. 8, Pt. 2–256

Rutledge, Edward, Nov. 23, 1749–Jan. 23, 1800.
Vol. 8, Pt. 2–257
Rutledge, John, Sept. 1739–July 18, 1800.
Vol. 8, Pt. 2–258
Rutledge, Wiley Blount, July 20, 1894–Sept. 10, 1949.
Supp. 4–712
Ryan, Abram Joseph, Feb. 5, 1838–Apr. 22, 1886.
Vol. 8, Pt. 2–260
Ryan, Arthur Clayton, Dec. 28, 1879–June 22, 1927.
Vol. 8, Pt. 2–261
Ryan, Cornelius John ("Connie"), June 5, 1920–Nov. 23, 1974.
Supp. 9–690
Ryan, Edward George, Nov. 13, 1810–Oct. 19, 1880.
Vol. 8, Pt. 2–262
Ryan, Harris Joseph, Jan. 8, 1866–July 3, 1934.
Supp. 1–645
Ryan, John Augustine, May 25, 1869–Sept. 16, 1945.
Supp. 3–679
Ryan, John Dennis, Oct. 10, 1864–Feb. 11, 1933.
Vol. 8, Pt. 2–262
Ryan, Patrick John, Feb. 20, 1831–Feb. 11, 1911.
Vol. 8, Pt. 2–263
Ryan, Robert Bushnell, Nov. 11, 1909–July 11, 1973.
Supp. 9–691
Ryan, Stephen Vincent, Jan. 1, 1825–Apr. 10, 1896.
Vol. 8, Pt. 2–264
Ryan, Thomas Fortune, Oct. 17, 1851–Nov. 23, 1928.
Vol. 8, Pt. 2–265
Ryan, Walter D'Arcy, Apr. 17, 1870–Mar. 14, 1934.
Vol. 8, Pt. 2–268
Rybner, Martin Cornelius, Oct. 26, 1853–Jan. 21, 1929.
Vol. 8, Pt. 2–269
Rydberg, Per Axel, July 6, 1860–July 25, 1931.
Vol. 8, Pt. 2–269
Ryder, Albert Pinkham, Mar. 19, 1847–Mar. 28, 1917.
Vol. 8, Pt. 2–270
Ryerson, Martin Antoine, Oct. 26, 1856–Aug. 11, 1932.
Vol. 8, Pt. 2–272
Ryland, Robert, Mar. 14, 1805–Apr. 23, 1899.
Vol. 8, Pt. 2–272
Rynning, Ole, Apr. 4, 1809–Sept. 1838.
Vol. 8, Pt. 2–273

Saarinen, Eero, Aug. 20, 1910–Sept. 1, 1961.
Supp. 7–669
Saarinen, Gottlieb Eliel, Aug. 20, 1873–July 1, 1950.
Supp. 4–713
Sabath, Adolph J., Apr. 4, 1866–Nov. 6, 1952.
Supp. 5–597
Sabin, Charles Hamilton, Aug. 24, 1868–Oct. 10, 1933.
Vol. 8, Pt. 2–274
Sabin, Florence Rena, Nov. 9, 1871–Oct. 3, 1953.
Supp. 5–600
Sabin, Joseph, Dec. 6?, 1821–June 5, 1881.
Vol. 8, Pt. 2–275
Sabine, Lorenzo, July 28, 1803–Apr. 14, 1877.
Vol. 8, Pt. 2–276
Sabine, Wallace Clement Ware, June 13, 1868–Jan. 10, 1919.
Vol. 8, Pt. 2–277
Sacagawea, *c.* 1787–Dec. 20, 1812.
Vol. 8, Pt. 2–278
Sacco, Nicola, Apr. 22, 1891–Aug. 23, 1927.
Vol. 8, Pt. 2–279
Sachs, Alexander, Aug. 1, 1893–June 23, 1973.
Supp. 9–695
Sachs, Bernard, Jan. 2, 1858–Feb. 8, 1944.
Supp. 3–682
Sachs, Hanns, Jan. 10, 1881–Jan. 10, 1947.
Supp. 4–716
Sachs, Julius, July 6, 1849–Feb. 2, 1934.
Vol. 8, Pt. 2–280
Sachs, Paul Joseph, Nov. 24, 1878–Feb. 17, 1965.
Supp. 7–673
Sachs, Theodore Bernard, May 2, 1868–Apr. 2, 1916.
Vol. 8, Pt. 2–281
Sachse, Julius Friedrich, Nov. 22, 1842–Nov. 14, 1919.
Vol. 8, Pt. 2–282
Sack, Israel, Sept. 15, 1883–May 4, 1959.
Supp. 6–562
Sackett, Henry Woodward, Aug. 31, 1853–Dec. 9, 1929.
Vol. 8, Pt. 2–282
Sadlier, Denis, 1817–Feb. 4, 1885.
Vol. 8, Pt. 2–283
Sadlier, Mary Anne Madden, Dec. 31, 1820–Apr. 5, 1903.
Vol. 8, Pt. 2–284
Sadtler, John Philip Benjamin, Dec. 25, 1823–Apr. 28, 1901.
Vol. 8, Pt. 2–284
Sadtler, Samuel Philip, July 18, 1847–Dec. 20, 1923.
Vol. 8, Pt. 2–285
Saenderl, Simon, Sept. 30, 1800–Feb. 22, 1879.
Vol. 8, Pt. 2–286
Safford, James Merrill, Aug. 13, 1822–July 3, 1907.
Vol. 8, Pt. 2–286
Safford, Truman Henry, Jan. 6, 1836–June 13, 1901.
Vol. 8, Pt. 2–287
Safford, William Edwin, Dec. 14, 1859–Jan. 10, 1926.
Vol. 8, Pt. 2–288
Sage, Bernard Janin, Feb. 5, 1821–Sept. 2, 1902.
Vol. 8, Pt. 2–289
Sage, Henry Williams, Jan. 31, 1814–Sept. 18, 1897.
Vol. 8, Pt. 2–290
Sage, Margaret Olivia Slocum, Sept. 8, 1828–Nov. 4, 1918.
Vol. 8, Pt. 2–291
Sage, Russell, Aug. 4, 1816–July 22, 1906.
Vol. 8, Pt. 2–292
St. Ange de Bellerive, Louis, *c.* Oct. 1698–Dec. 27, 1774.
Vol. 8, Pt. 2–293
St. Clair, Arthur, Mar. 23, 1736 o.s.–Aug. 31, 1818.
Vol. 8, Pt. 2–293
St. Denis (Denys), Louis Juchereau de, Sept. 17, 1676–June 11, 1744.
Vol. 8, Pt. 2–295
St. Denis, Ruth, Jan. 20, 1879–July 21, 1968.
Supp. 8–620
Saint-Gaudens, Augustus, Mar. 1, 1848–Aug. 3 1907.
Vol. 8, Pt. 2–296
St. John, Charles Edward, Mar 15, 1857–Apr. 26, 1935.
Supp. 1–646
St. John, Isaac Munroe, Nov. 19, 1827–Apr. 7, 1880.
Vol. 8, Pt. 2–302
St. John, John Pierce, Feb. 25, 1833–Aug. 31, 1916.
Vol. 8, Pt. 2–303
St. Lusson, Simon Francois Daumont, Sieur de, d. 1674.
Vol. 8, Pt. 2–304
Saint-Mémin, Charles Balthazar Julien Fevret de, Mar. 12, 1770–June 23, 1852.
Vol. 8, Pt. 2–305
Saint-Méry, Moreau de. [*See* Moreau de Saint-Méry, Médéric-Louis-Elie, 1750–1819.]
St. Vrain, Ceran de Hault de Lassus de, May 5, 1802–Oct. 28, 1870.
Vol. 8, Pt. 2–305
Sajous, Charles Euchariste de Médicis, Dec. 13, 1852–Apr. 27, 1929.
Vol. 8, Pt. 2–306
Sakel, Manfred Joshua, June 6, 1900–Dec. 2, 1957.
Supp. 6–563
Salisbury, Albert, Jan. 24, 1843–June 2, 1911.
Vol. 8, Pt. 2–307
Salisbury, Edward Elbridge, Apr. 6, 1814–Feb. 5, 1901.
Vol. 8, Pt. 2–308
Salisbury, James Henry, Oct. 13, 1823–Aug. 23, 1905.
Vol. 8, Pt. 2–309
Salisbury, Rollin D., Aug. 17, 1858–Aug. 15, 1922.
Vol. 8, Pt. 2–309
Salmon, Daniel Elmer, July 23, 1850–Aug. 30, 1914.
Vol. 8, Pt. 2–311
Salmon, Lucy Maynard, July 27, 1853–Feb. 14, 1927.
Vol. 8, Pt. 2–312
Salmon, Thomas William, Jan. 6, 1876–Aug. 13, 1927.
Vol. 8, Pt. 2–313
Salm-Salm, Agnes Elisabeth Winona Leclercq Joy, Princess, Dec. 25, 1840–Dec. 21, 1912.
Vol. 8, Pt. 2–310
Salomon, Haym, *c.* 1740–Jan. 6, 1785.
Vol. 8, Pt. 2–313
Salter, William, Nov. 17, 1821–Aug. 15, 1910.
Vol. 8, Pt. 2–314
Salter, William Mackintire, Jan. 30, 1853–July 18, 1931.
Vol. 8, Pt. 2–315

Saltonstall, Dudley, Sept. 8, 1738–1796.
Vol. 8, Pt. 2–316
Saltonstall, Gordon, Mar. 27, 1666 o.s.–Sept. 20, 1724 o.s.
Vol. 8, Pt. 2–317
Saltonstall, Leverett, Sept. 1, 1892–June 17, 1979.
Supp. 10–715
Saltonstall, Richard, *c.* 1610–Apr. 29, 1694.
Vol. 8, Pt. 2–318
Saltus, Edgar Evertson, Oct. 8, 1855–July 31, 1921.
Vol. 8, Pt. 2–319
Samaroff, Olga, Aug. 8, 1882–May 17, 1948.
Supp. 4–717
Sampson, Martin Wright, Sept. 7, 1866–Aug. 22, 1930.
Vol. 8, Pt. 2–320
Sampson, William, Jan. 1764–Dec. 28, 1836.
Vol. 8, Pt. 2–321
Sampson, William Thomas, Feb. 9, 1840–May 6, 1902.
Vol. 8, Pt. 2–321
Samuels, Edward Augustus, July 4, 1836–May 27, 1908.
Vol. 8, Pt. 2–323
Samuels, Samuel, Mar. 14, 1823–May 18, 1908.
Vol. 8, Pt. 2–324
Sanborn, Edwin David, May 14, 1808–Dec. 29, 1885.
Vol. 8, Pt. 2–325
Sanborn, Franklin Benjamin, Dec. 15, 1831–Feb. 24, 1917.
Vol. 8, Pt. 2–326
Sanborn, Katherine Abbott, July 11, 1839–July 9, 1917.
Vol. 8, Pt. 2–327
Sanborn, Walter Henry, Oct. 19, 1845–May 10, 1928.
Vol. 8, Pt. 2–328
Sandburg, Carl August, Jan. 6, 1878–July 22, 1967.
Supp. 8–562
Sande, Earl, Nov. 13, 1898–Aug. 20, 1968.
Supp. 8–565
Sandeman, Robert, Apr. 29, 1718–Apr. 2, 1771.
Vol. 8, Pt. 2–329
Sanders, Billington McCarter, Dec. 2, 1789–Mar. 12, 1854.
Vol. 8, Pt. 2–329
Sanders, Charles Walton, Mar. 24, 1805–July 5, 1889.
Vol. 8, Pt. 2–330
Sanders, Daniel Clarke, May 3, 1768–Oct. 18, 1850.
Vol. 8, Pt. 2–331
Sanders, Daniel Jackson, Feb. 15, 1847–Mar. 6, 1907.
Vol. 8, Pt. 2–332
Sanders, Elizabeth Elkins, Aug. 12, 1762–Feb. 19, 1851.
Vol. 8, Pt. 2–332
Sanders, Frank Knight, June 5, 1861–Feb. 20, 1933.
Vol. 8, Pt. 2–333
Sanders, George, July 3, 1906–Apr. 25, 1972.
Supp. 9–696
Sanders, George Nicholas, Feb. 27, 1812–Aug. 12, 1873.
Vol. 8, Pt. 2–334
Sanders, Harland David ("Colonel"), Sept. 9, 1890–Dec. 16, 1980.
Supp. 10–717
Sanders, James Harvey, Oct. 9, 1832–Dec. 22, 1899.
Vol. 8, Pt. 2–335
Sanders, Thomas, Aug. 18, 1839–Aug. 7, 1911.
Vol. 8, Pt. 2–336
Sanders, Wilbur Fisk, May 2, 1834–July 7, 1905.
Vol. 8, Pt. 2–336
Sanderson, Ezra Dwight, Sept. 25, 1878–Sept. 27, 1944.
Supp. 3–683
Sanderson, John, 1783–Apr. 5, 1844.
Vol. 8, Pt. 2–337
Sanderson, Robert, 1608–Oct. 7, 1693.
Vol. 8, Pt. 2–338
Sanderson, Sibyl, Dec. 7, 1865–May 16, 1903.
Vol. 8, Pt. 2–338
Sandham, Henry, May 24, 1842–June 21, 1910.
Vol. 8, Pt. 2–339
Sandler, Jacob Koppel, Aug. 6, 1856–Feb. 23, 1931.
Vol. 8, Pt. 2–340
Sandoz, Mari, May 11, 1896–Mar. 10, 1966.
Supp. 8–566
Sands, Benjamin Franklin, Feb. 11, 1812–June 30, 1883.
Vol. 8, Pt. 2–341
Sands, Comfort, Feb. 26, 1748–Sept. 22, 1834.
Vol. 8, Pt. 2–341
Sands, David, Oct. 4, 1745–June 4, 1818.
Vol. 8, Pt. 2–342
Sands, Diana Patricia, Aug. 22, 1934–Sept. 21, 1974.
Supp. 9–698
Sands, Joshua Ratoon, May 13, 1795–Oct. 2, 1883.
Vol. 8, Pt. 2–343
Sands, Robert Charles, May 11, 1799–Dec. 16, 1832.
Vol. 8, Pt. 2–344
Sandys, George, Mar. 2, 1577/78–Mar. 4, 1643/44.
Vol. 8, Pt. 2–344
Sanford, Edmund Clark, Nov. 10, 1859–Nov. 22, 1924.
Vol. 8, Pt. 2–346
Sanford, Edward Terry, July 23, 1865–Mar. 8, 1930.
Vol. 8, Pt. 2–347
Sanford, Elias Benjamin, June 6, 1843–July 3, 1932.
Vol. 8, Pt. 2–347
Sanford, Henry Shelton, June 15, 1823–May 21, 1891.
Vol. 8, Pt. 2–348
Sanford, Nathan, Nov. 5, 1777–Oct. 17, 1838.
Vol. 8, Pt. 2–349
Sanger, Charles Robert, Aug. 31, 1860–Feb. 25, 1912.
Vol. 8, Pt. 2–350
Sanger, George Partridge, Nov. 27, 1819–July 3, 1890.
Vol. 8 Pt. 2–350
Sanger, Margaret Higgins, Sept. 14, 1879–Sept. 6, 1966.
Supp. 8–567
Sangster, Margaret Elizabeth Munson, Feb. 22, 1838–June 4, 1912.
Vol. 8, Pt. 2–351
Sankey, Ira David, Aug. 28, 1840–Aug. 13, 1908.
Vol. 8, Pt. 2–352
Santayana, George, Dec. 16, 1863–Sept. 26, 1952.
Supp. 5–601
Sapir, Edward, Jan. 26, 1884–Feb. 4, 1939.
Supp. 2–593
Sappington, John, May 15, 1776–Sept. 7, 1856.
Vol. 8, Pt. 2–353
Sardi, Melchiorre Pio Vencenzo ("Vincent"), Dec. 23, 1885–Nov. 19, 1969.
Supp. 8–570
Sarg, Tony, Apr. 24, 1880–Mar. 7, 1942.
Supp. 3–484
Sargent, Aaron Augustus, Oct. 28, 1827–Aug. 14, 1887.
Vol. 8, Pt. 2–353
Sargent, Charles Sprague, Apr. 24, 1841–Mar. 22, 1927.
Vol. 8, Pt. 2–354
Sargent, Dudley Allen, Sept. 28, 1849–July 21, 1924.
Vol. 8, Pt. 2–355
Sargent, Epes, Sept. 27, 1813–Dec. 30, 1880.
Vol. 8, Pt. 2–356
Sargent, Fitzwilliam, Jan. 17, 1820–Apr. 25, 1889.
Vol. 8, Pt. 2–357
Sargent, Frank Pierce, Nov. 18, 1854–Sept. 4, 1908.
Vol. 8, Pt. 2–358
Sargent, Frederick, Nov. 11, 1859–July 26, 1919.
Vol. 8, Pt. 2–359
Sargent, George Henry, May 5, 1867–Jan. 14, 1931.
Vol. 8, Pt. 2–359
Sargent, Henry, *c.* Nov. 1770–Feb. 21, 1845.
Vol. 8, Pt. 2–360
Sargent, Henry Winthrop, Nov. 26, 1810–Nov. 11, 1882.
Vol. 8, Pt. 2–361
Sargent, James, Dec. 5, 1824–Jan. 12, 1910.
Vol. 8, Pt. 2–361
Sargent, John Osborne, Sept. 20, 1811–Dec. 28, 1891.
Vol. 8, Pt. 2–362
Sargent, John Singer, Jan. 12, 1856–Apr. 15, 1925.
Vol. 8, Pt. 2–363
Sargent, Lucius Manlius, June 25, 1786–June 2, 1867.
Vol. 8, Pt. 2–367
Sargent, Nathan, May 5, 1794–Feb. 2, 1875.
Vol. 8, Pt. 2–368
Sargent, Winthrop, May 1, 1753–Jan. 3, 1820.
Vol. 8, Pt. 2–368
Sargent, Winthrop, Sept. 23, 1825–May 18, 1870.
Vol. 8, Pt. 2–369
Sarnoff, David, Feb. 27, 1891–Dec. 12, 1971.
Supp. 9–699
Sarpy, Peter A., Nov. 3, 1805–Jan. 4, 1865.
Vol. 8, Pt. 2–370
Sartain, Emily, Mar. 17, 1841–June 18, 1927.
Vol. 8, Pt. 2–370

Sartain, John, Oct. 24, 1808–Oct. 25, 1897.
Vol. 8, Pt. 2–371
Sartain, Samuel, Oct. 8, 1830–Dec. 20, 1906.
Vol. 8, Pt. 2–372
Sartain, William, Nov. 21, 1843–Oct. 25, 1924.
Vol. 8, Pt. 2–373
Sarton, George Alfred Léon, Aug. 31, 1884–Mar. 22, 1956.
Supp. 6–564
Sartwell, Henry Parker, Apr. 18, 1792–Nov. 15, 1867.
Vol. 8, Pt. 2–374
Saslavsky, Alexander, Feb. 8, 1876–Aug. 2, 1924.
Vol. 8, Pt. 2–374
Sassacus, *c.* 1560–June 1637.
Vol. 8, Pt. 2–375
Satterlee, Henry Yates, Jan. 11, 1843–Feb. 22, 1908.
Vol. 8, Pt. 2–375
Satterlee, Richard Sherwood, Dec. 6, 1798–Nov. 10, 1880.
Vol. 8, Pt. 2–376
Sauer, Carl Ortwin, Dec. 24, 1889–July 18, 1975.
Supp. 9–702
Sauganash, *c.* 1780–Sept. 28, 1841.
Vol. 8, Pt. 2–376
Saugrain de Vigni, Antoine François, Feb. 17, 1763–*c.* May 19, 1820.
Vol. 8, Pt. 2–377
Saulsbury, Eli, Dec. 29, 1817–Mar. 22, 1893.
Vol. 8, Pt. 2–378
Saulsbury, Gove, May 29, 1815–July 31, 1881.
Vol. 8, Pt. 2–378
Saulsbury, Willard, June 2, 1820–Apr. 6, 1892.
Vol. 8, Pt. 2–379
Saulsbury, Willard, Apr. 17, 1861–Feb. 20, 1927.
Vol. 8, Pt. 2–380
Saunders, Alvin, July 12, 1817–Nov. 1, 1899.
Vol. 8, Pt. 2–380
Saunders, Clarence, Dec. 1881–Oct. 14, 1953.
Supp. 5–603
Saunders, Frederick, Aug. 14, 1807–Dec. 12, 1902.
Vol. 8, Pt. 2–381
Saunders, Prince, d. Feb. 1839.
Vol. 8, Pt. 2–382
Saunders, Romulus Mitchell, Mar. 3, 1791–Apr. 21, 1867.
Vol. 8, Pt. 2–382
Saunders, William, Dec 7, 1822–Sept. 11, 1900.
Vol. 8, Pt. 2–383
Saunders, William Laurence, July 30, 1835–Apr. 2, 1891.
Vol. 8, Pt. 2–384
Saunders, William Lawrence, Nov. 1, 1856–June 25, 1931.
Vol. 8, Pt. 2–385
Saur, Christopher. [*See* Sower, Christopher, 1693–1758.]
Sauveur, Albert, June 21, 1863–Jan. 26, 1939.
Supp. 2–594
Savage, Edward, Nov. 26, 1761–July 6, 1817.
Vol. 8, Pt. 2–386
Savage, Henry Wilson, Mar. 21, 1859–Nov. 29, 1927.
Vol. 8, Pt. 2–386
Savage, James, July 13, 1784–Mar. 8, 1873.
Vol. 8, Pt. 2–387
Savage, John, Dec. 13, 1828–Oct. 9, 1888.
Vol. 8, Pt. 2–388
Savage, John Lucian ("Jack"), Dec. 25, 1879–Dec. 28, 1967.
Supp. 8–572
Savage, Minot Judson, June 10, 1841–May 22, 1918.
Vol. 8, Pt. 2–389
Savage, Philip Henry, Feb. 11, 1868–June 4, 1899.
Vol. 8, Pt. 2–390
Savage, Thomas Staughton, June 7, 1804–Dec. 29, 1880.
Vol. 8, Pt. 2–391
Savery, William, 1721–May 1787.
Vol. 8, Pt. 2–392
Savery, William, Sept. 14, 1750 o.s.–June 19, 1804.
Vol. 8, Pt. 2–392
Saville, Marshall Howard, June 24, 1867–May 7, 1935.
Supp. 1–647
Sawyer, Leicester Ambrose, July 28, 1807–Dec. 29, 1898.
Vol. 8, Pt. 2–393
Sawyer, Lemuel, 1777–Jan. 9, 1852.
Vol. 8, Pt. 2–394
Sawyer, Lorenzo, May 23, 1820–Sept. 7, 1891.
Vol. 8, Pt. 2–395
Sawyer, Philetus, Sept. 22, 1816–Mar. 29, 1900.
Vol. 8, Pt. 2–396
Sawyer, Sylvanus, Apr. 15, 1822–Oct. 13, 1895.
Vol. 8, Pt. 2–397
Sawyer, Thomas Jefferson, Jan. 9, 1804–July 24, 1899.
Vol. 8, Pt. 2–397
Sawyer, Walter Howard. May 21, 1867–Dec. 21, 1923.
Vol. 8, Pt. 2–398
Sawyer, Wilbur Augustus, Aug. 7, 1879–Nov. 12, 1951.
Supp. 5–604
Saxe, John Godfrey, June 2, 1816–Mar. 31, 1887
Vol. 8, Pt. 2–399
Saxton, Eugene Francis, Aug. 11, 1884–June 26, 1943.
Supp. 3–685
Saxton, Joseph, Mar. 22, 1799–Oct. 26, 1873.
Vol. 8, Pt. 2–400
Say, Benjamin, Aug. 28, 1755–Apr. 23, 1813.
Vol. 8, Pt. 2–400
Say, Thomas, June 27, 1787–Oct. 10, 1834.
Vol. 8, Pt. 2–401
Sayles, John, Mar. 9, 1825–May 22, 1897.
Vol. 8, Pt. 2–402
Saypol, Irving Howard, Sept. 3, 1905–June 30, 1977.
Supp. 10–718
Sayre, Lewis Albert, Feb. 29, 1820–Sept. 21, 1900.
Vol. 8, Pt. 2–403
Sayre, Reginald Hall, Oct. 18, 1859–May 29, 1929.
Vol. 8, Pt. 2–404
Sayre, Robert Heysham, Oct. 13, 1824–Jan. 5, 1907.
Vol. 8, Pt. 2–405
Sayre, Stephen, June 12, 1736–Sept. 27, 1818.
Vol. 8, Pt. 2–406
Sayre, Wallace Stanley, June 24, 1905–May 14, 1972.
Supp. 9–704
Scammell, Alexander, Mar. 27, 1747–Oct. 6, 1781.
Vol. 8, Pt. 2–406
Scammon, Jonathan Young, July 27, 1812–Mar. 17, 1890.
Vol. 8, Pt. 2–407
Scanlan, Lawrence, Sept. 29, 1843–May 10, 1915.
Vol. 8, Pt. 2–408
Scarborough, Dorothy, Jan. 27, 1878–Nov. 7, 1935.
Supp. 1–648
Scarborough, Lee Rutland, July 4, 1870–Apr. 10, 1945.
Supp. 1–686
Scarborough, William Saunders, Feb. 16, 1852?–Sept. 9, 1926.
Vol. 8, Pt. 2–409
Scarbrough, William, Feb. 18, 1776–June 11, 1838.
Vol. 8, Pt. 2–410
Scattergood, Thomas, Jan.? 23, 1748–Apr. 24, 1814.
Vol. 8, Pt. 2–410
Schadle, Jacob Evans, June 23, 1849–May 29, 1908.
Vol. 8, Pt. 2–411
Schaeberle, John Martin, Jan. 10, 1853–Sept. 19, 1924.
Vol. 8, Pt. 2–412
Schaeffer, Charles Frederick, Sept. 3, 1807–Nov 23, 1879.
Vol. 8, Pt. 2–412
Schaeffer, Charles William, May 5, 1813–Mar. 15, 1896.
Vol. 8, Pt. 2–413
Schaeffer, David Frederick, July 22, 1787–May 5, 1837.
Vol. 8, Pt. 2–414
Schaeffer, Frederick Christian, Nov. 12, 1792–Mar. 26, 1831.
Vol. 8, Pt. 2–415
Schaeffer, Frederick David, Nov. 15, 1760–Jan. 27, 1836.
Vol. 8, Pt. 2–415
Schaeffer, Nathan Christ, Feb. 3, 1849–Mar. 15, 1919.
Vol. 8. Pt. 2–416
Schaff, Philip, Jan. 1, 1819–Oct. 20, 1893.
Vol. 8, Pt. 2–417
Schalk, Raymond William ("Cracker"), Aug. 12, 1892–May 19, 1970.
Supp. 8–573
Schall, Thomas David, June 4, 1877–Dec. 22, 1935.
Supp. 1–649
Schamberg, Jay Frank, Nov. 6, 1870–Mar. 30, 1934.
Vol. 8, Pt. 2–418
Scharf, John Thomas, May 1, 1843–Feb. 28, 1898.
Vol. 8, Pt. 2–419
Schary, Dore, Aug. 31, 1905–July 7, 1980.
Supp. 10–720
Schauffler, Henry Albert, Sept. 4, 1837–Feb. 15, 1905.
Vol. 8, Pt. 2–420

Schauffler, William Gottlieb, Aug. 22, 1798–Jan. 26, 1883.
Vol. 8, Pt. 2–420
Schechter, Solomon, Dec. 7, 1850–Nov. 15, 1915.
Vol. 8, Pt. 2–421
Scheel, Fritz, Nov. 7, 1852–Mar. 13, 1907.
Vol. 8, Pt. 2–423
Schele De Vere, Maximilian, Nov. 1, 1820–May 12, 1898.
Vol. 8, Pt. 2–423
Schell, Augustus, Aug. 1, 1812–Mar. 27, 1884.
Vol. 8, Pt. 2–424
Schelling, Ernest Henry, July 26, 1876–Dec. 8, 1939.
Supp. 2–595
Schelling, Felix Emanuel, Sept. 3, 1858–Dec. 15, 1945.
Supp. 3–688
Schem, Alexander Jacob, Mar. 16, 1826–May 21, 1881.
Vol. 8, Pt. 2–425
Schenck, Ferdinand Schureman, Aug. 6, 1845–Apr. 6, 1925.
Vol. 8, Pt. 2–426
Schenck, James Findlay, June 11, 1807–Dec. 21, 1882.
Vol. 8, Pt. 2–426
Schenck, Nicholas Michael, Nov. 14, 1881–Mar. 3, 1969.
Supp. 8–576
Schenck, Robert Cumming, Oct. 4, 1809–Mar. 23, 1890.
Vol. 8, Pt. 2–427
Schereschewsky, Samuel Isaac Joseph, May 6, 1831–Oct. 15, 1906.
Vol. 8, Pt. 2–428
Scherman, Harry, Feb. 1, 1887–Nov. 12, 1969.
Supp. 8–577
Scheve, Edward Benjamin, Feb. 13, 1865–June 18, 1924.
Vol. 8, Pt. 2–429
Schevill, Rudolph, June 18, 1874–Feb. 17, 1946.
Supp. 4–718
Schickillemy. [*See* Shikellamy, d. 1748.]
Schieren, Charles Adolph, Feb. 28, 1842–Mar. 10, 1915.
Vol. 8, Pt. 2–430
Schiff, Jacob Henry, Jan. 10, 1847–Sept. 25, 1920.
Vol. 8, Pt. 2–430
Schildkraut, Joseph, Mar. 22, 1896–Jan. 21, 1964.
Supp. 7–674
Schilling, Hugo Karl, Mar. 28, 1861–July 1931.
Vol. 8, Pt. 2–432
Schillinger, Joseph, Sept. 1, 1895–Mar. 23, 1943.
Supp. 3–689
Schindler, Kurt, Feb. 17, 1882–Nov. 16, 1935.
Supp. 1–650
Schindler, Rudolph Michael, Sept. 5, 1887–Aug. 22, 1953.
Supp. 5–605
Schindler, Solomon, Apr. 24, 1842–May 5, 1915.
Vol. 8, Pt. 2–433
Schinz, Albert, Mar. 9, 1870–Dec. 19, 1943.
Supp. 3–690
Schippers, Thomas, Mar. 9, 1930–Dec. 16, 1977.
Supp. 10–721
Schirmer, Gustav, Sept. 19, 1829–Aug. 6, 1893.
Vol. 8, Pt. 2–434
Schirmer, Rudolph Edward, July 22, 1859–Aug. 20, 1919.
Vol. 8, Pt. 2–435
Schlatter, Michael, July 14, 1716–Oct. 31, 1790.
Vol. 8, Pt. 2–435
Schlesinger, Arthur Meier, Feb. 27, 1888–Oct. 30, 1965.
Supp. 7–675
Schlesinger, Benjamin, Dec. 25, 1876–June 6, 1932.
Vol. 8, Pt. 2–436
Schlesinger, Frank, May 11, 1871–July 10, 1943.
Supp. 3–691
Schley, Winfield Scott, Oct. 9, 1839–Oct. 2, 1909.
Vol. 8, Pt. 2–437
Schmauk, Theodore Emanuel, May 30 1860–Mar. 23, 1920.
Vol. 8, Pt. 2–439
Schmidt, Arthur Paul, Apr. 1, 1846–May 5, 1921.
Vol. 8, Pt. 2–440
Schmidt, Carl Louis August, Mar. 7, 1885–Feb. 23, 1946.
Supp. 4–719
Schmidt, Friedrich August, Jan. 3, 1837–May 15, 1928.
Vol. 8, Pt. 2–440
Schmidt, Nathaniel, May 22, 1862–June 29, 1939.
Supp. 2–596
Schmucker, Beale Melanchthon, Aug. 26, 1827–Oct. 15, 1888.
Vol. 8, Pt. 2–441
Schmucker, John George, Aug. 18, 1771–Oct. 7, 1854.
Vol. 8, Pt. 2–442
Schmucker, Samuel Simon, Feb. 28, 1799–July 26, 1873.
Vol. 8, Pt. 2–443
Schnabel, Artur, Apr. 17, 1882–Aug. 15, 1951.
Supp. 5–607
Schnauffer, Carl Heinrich, July 4, 1823–Sept. 4, 1854.
Vol. 8, Pt. 2–444
Schneider, Albert, Apr. 13, 1863–Oct. 27, 1928.
Vol. 8, Pt. 2–445
Schneider, Benjamin, Jan. 18, 1807–Sept. 14, 1877.
Vol. 8, Pt. 2–446
Schneider, George, Dec. 13, 1823–Sept. 16, 1905.
Vol. 8, Pt. 2–446
Schneider, Herman, Sept. 12, 1872–Mar. 28, 1939.
Supp. 2–597
Schneider, Theodore, Apr. 7, 1703–July 10, 1764.
Vol. 8, Pt. 2–447
Schneiderman, Rose, Apr. 6, 1882–Aug. 11, 1972.
Supp. 9–705
Schneller, George Otto, Jan. 14, 1843–Oct. 20, 1895.
Vol. 8, Pt. 2–448
Schnerr, Leander, Sept. 27, 1836–Sept. 3, 1920.
Vol. 8, Pt. 2–448
Schocken, Theodore, Oct. 8, 1914–Mar. 20, 1975.
Supp. 9–706
Schodde, George Henry, Apr. 15, 1854–Sept. 15, 1917.
Vol. 8, Pt. 2–449
Schoenberg, Arnold, Sept. 13, 1874–July 13, 1951.
Supp. 5–608
Schoenheimer, Rudolf, May 10, 1898–Sept. 11, 1941.
Supp. 3–693
Schoenhof, Jacob, 1839–Mar. 14, 1903.
Vol. 8, Pt. 2–450
Schoeppel, Andrew Frank, Nov. 23, 1894–Jan. 21, 1962.
Supp. 7–677
Schoff, Stephen Alonzo, Jan. 16, 1818–May 6, 1904.
Vol. 8, Pt. 2–451
Schofield, Henry, Aug. 7, 1866–Aug. 15, 1918.
Vol. 8, Pt. 2–451
Schofield, John McAllister, Sept. 29, 1831–Mar. 4, 1906.
Vol. 8, Pt. 2–452
Schofield, William Henry, Apr. 6, 1870–June 24, 1920.
Vol. 8, Pt. 2–454
Scholte, Hendrik Peter, Sept. 25, 1805–Aug. 25, 1868.
Vol. 8, Pt. 2–455
Schomer, Nahum Meir, Dec. 18, 1849–Nov. 24, 1905.
Vol. 8, Pt. 2–456
Schoolcraft, Henry Rowe, Mar. 28, 1793–Dec. 10, 1864.
Vol. 8, Pt. 2–456
Schöpf, Johann David, Mar. 8, 1752–Sept. 10, 1800.
Vol. 8, Pt. 2–457
Schorer, Mark, May 17, 1908–Aug. 11, 1977.
Supp. 10–723
Schott, Charles Anthony, Aug. 7, 1826–July 31, 1901.
Vol. 8, Pt. 2–458
Schouler, James, Mar. 20, 1839–Apr. 16, 1920.
Vol. 8, Pt. 2–459
Schouler, William, Dec. 31, 1814–Oct. 24, 1872.
Vol. 8, Pt. 2–460
Schradieck, Henry, Apr. 29, 1846–Mar. 25, 1918.
Vol. 8, Pt. 2–461
Schrembs, Joseph, Mar. 12, 1866–Nov. 2, 1945.
Supp. 3–694
Schrieck, Sister Louise Van Der, Nov. 14, 1813–Dec. 3, 1886.
Vol. 8, Pt. 2–462
Schriver, Edmund, Sept. 16, 1812–Feb. 10, 1899.
Vol. 8, Pt. 2–463
Schroeder, John Frederick, Apr. 8, 1800–Feb. 26, 1857.
Vol. 8, Pt. 2–463
Schroeder, Rudolph William, Aug. 14, 1886–Dec. 29, 1952.
Supp. 5–610
Schroeder, Seaton, Aug. 17, 1849–Oct. 19, 1922.
Vol. 8, Pt. 2–464
Schuchert, Charles, July 3, 1858–Nov. 20, 1942.
Supp. 3–695
Schuessele, Christian. [*See* Schussele, Christian, 1826–1879.]
Schultz, Dutch. [*See* Flegenheimer, Arthur, 1902–1935.]
Schultz, Henry, Sept. 4, 1893–Nov. 26, 1938.
Supp. 2–599

Schultze, Augustus, Feb. 3, 1840–Nov. 12, 1918.
Vol. 8, Pt. 2–465
Schumann-Heink, Ernestine, June 15, 1861–Nov. 17, 1936.
Supp. 2–600
Schumpeter, Joseph Alois, Feb. 8, 1883–Jan. 8, 1950.
Supp. 4–720
Schurman, Jacob Gould, May 22, 1854–Aug. 13, 1942.
Supp. 3–696
Schurz, Carl, Mar. 2, 1829–May 14, 1906.
Vol. 8, Pt. 2–466
Schussele, Christian, Apr. 16, 1826–Aug. 21, 1879.
Vol. 8, Pt. 2–470
Schuster, Max Lincoln, Mar. 2, 1897–Dec. 20, 1970.
Supp. 8–578
Schuttler, Peter, Dec. 22, 1812–Jan. 16, 1865.
Vol. 8, Pt. 2–471
Schuyler, Eugene, Feb. 26, 1840–July 16, 1890.
Vol. 8, Pt. 2–471
Schuyler, George Washington, Feb. 2, 1810–Feb. 1, 1888.
Vol. 8, Pt. 2–472
Schuyler, James Dix, May 11, 1848–Sept. 13, 1912.
Vol. 8, Pt. 2–473
Schuyler, Louisa Lee, Oct. 26, 1837–Oct. 10, 1926.
Vol. 8, Pt. 2–474
Schuyler, Margarita, 1701–Aug. 1782.
Vol. 8, Pt. 2–475
Schuyler, Montgomery, Aug. 19, 1843–July 16, 1914.
Vol. 8, Pt. 2–475
Schuyler, Peter, Sept. 17, 1657–Feb. 19, 1724.
Vol. 8, Pt. 2–476
Schuyler, Philip John, Nov. 11, 1733–Nov. 18, 1804.
Vol. 8, Pt. 2–477
Schuyler, Robert Livingston, Feb. 26, 1883–Aug. 15, 1966.
Supp. 8–579
Schwab, Charles Michael, Feb. 18, 1862–Sept. 18, 1939.
Supp. 2–601
Schwab, John Christopher, Apr. 1, 1865–Jan. 12, 1916.
Vol. 8, Pt. 2–480
Schwartz, Delmore David, Dec. 8, 1913–July 11, 1966.
Supp. 8–581
Schwartz, Maurice, June 15, 1889–May 10, 1960.
Supp. 6–566
Schwarz, Engene Amandus, Apr. 21, 1844–Oct. 15, 1928.
Vol. 8, Pt. 2–480
Schwatka, Frederick, Sept. 29, 1849–Nov. 2, 1892.
Vol. 8, Pt. 2–481
Schweinitz, Edmund Alexander de, Mar. 20, 1825–Dec. 18, 1887.
Vol. 8, Pt. 2–482
Schweinitz, Emil Alexander de, Jan. 18, 1866–Feb. 15, 1904.
Vol. 8, Pt. 2–483
Schweinitz, George Edmund de, Oct. 26, 1858–Aug. 22, 1938.
Supp. 2–603
Schweinitz, Lewis David von, Feb. 13, 1780–Feb. 8, 1834.
Vol. 8, Pt. 2–483
Schwellenbach, Lewis Baxter, Sept. 20, 1894–June 10, 1948.
Supp. 4–723
Schwidetzky, Oscar Otto Rudolf, Dec. 31, 1874–Oct. 11, 1963.
Supp. 7–678
Schwimmer, Rosika, Sept. 11, 1877–Aug. 3, 1948.
Supp. 4–724
Scidmore, Eliza Ruhamah, Oct. 14, 1856–Nov. 3, 1928.
Vol. 8, Pt. 2–484
Scollard, Clinton, Sept. 18, 1860–Nov. 19, 1932.
Vol. 8, Pt. 2–485
Scopes, John Thomas, Aug. 3, 1900–Oct. 21, 1970.
Supp. 8–582
Scott, Allen Cecil, Aug. 16, 1882–May 1, 1964.
Supp. 7–679
Scott, Austin, Aug. 10, 1848–Aug. 15, 1922.
Vol. 8, Pt. 2–486
Scott, Charles, *c.* 1739–Oct. 22, 1813.
Vol. 8, Pt. 2–487
Scott, Colin Alexander, Feb. 11, 1861–Apr. 5, 1925.
Vol. 8, Pt. 2–487
Scott, Dred, *c.* 1795–Sept. 17, 1858.
Vol. 8, Pt. 2–488
Scott, Emmett Jay, Feb. 13, 1873–Dec. 12, 1957.
Supp. 6–567
Scott, Fred Newton, Aug. 20, 1860–May 29, 1931.
Vol. 8, Pt. 2–489
Scott, Gustavus, 1753–Dec. 25, 1800.
Vol. 8, Pt. 2–490
Scott, Harvey Whitefield, Feb. 1, 1838–Aug. 7, 1910.
Vol. 8, Pt. 2–491
Scott, Hugh Lenox, Sept. 22, 1853–Apr. 30, 1934.
Supp. 1–651
Scott, Irving Murray, Dec. 25, 1837–Apr. 28, 1903.
Vol. 8, Pt. 2–491
Scott, James Brown, June 3, 1866–June 25, 1943.
Supp. 3–699
Scott, James Wilmot, June 26, 1849–Apr. 14, 1895.
Vol. 8, Pt. 2–492
Scott, Job, Oct. 18, 1751–Nov. 22, 1793.
Vol. 8, Pt. 2–493
Scott, John, *c.* 1630–1696.
Vol. 8, Pt. 2–494
Scott, John Adams, Sept. 15, 1867–Oct. 27, 1947.
Supp. 4–728
Scott, John Morin, *c.* 1730–Sept. 14, 1784.
Vol. 8, Pt. 2–495
Scott, John Prindle, Aug. 16, 1877–Dec. 2, 1952.
Vol. 8, Pt. 2–496
Scott, Leroy, May 11, 1875–July 21, 1929.
Vol. 8, Pt. 2–496
Scott, Orange, Feb. 13, 1800–July 31, 1847.
Vol. 8, Pt. 2–497
Scott, Robert Kingston, July 8, 1826–Aug. 12, 1900.
Vol. 8, Pt. 2–498
Scott, Samuel Parsons, July 8, 1846–May 30, 1929.
Vol. 8, Pt. 2–499
Scott, Thomas Alexander, Dec. 28, 1823–May 21, 1881.
Vol. 8, Pt. 2–500
Scott, Thomas Fielding, Mar. 12, 1807–July 14, 1867.
Vol. 8, Pt. 2–501
Scott, Walter, Oct. 31, 1796–Apr. 23, 1861.
Vol. 8, Pt. 2–502
Scott, Walter Dill, May 1, 1869–Sept. 23, 1955.
Supp. 5–611
Scott, Walter Edward, 1870?–Jan. 5, 1954.
Supp. 5–613
Scott, William, June 7, 1804–May 18, 1862.
Vol. 8, Pt. 2–503
Scott, William Anderson, Jan. 31, 1813–Jan. 14, 1885.
Vol. 8, Pt. 2–503
Scott, William Berryman, Feb. 12, 1858–Mar. 29 1947.
Supp. 4–729
Scott, W(illiam) Kerr, Apr. 17, 1896–Apr. 16, 1958.
Supp. 6–568
Scott, William Lawrence, July 2, 1828–Sept. 19, 1891.
Vol. 8, Pt. 2–504
Scott, Winfield, June 13, 1786–May 29, 1866.
Vol. 8, Pt. 2–505
Scovel, Henry Sylvester, July 29, 1869–Feb. 11, 1905.
Vol. 8, Pt. 2–511
Scovel, Sylvester. [*See* Scovel, Henry Sylvester, 1869–1905.]
Scovell, Melville Amasa, Feb 26, 1855–Aug. 15, 1912.
Vol. 8, Pt. 2–512
Scoville, Joseph Alfred, Jan. 30, 1815–June 25, 1864.
Vol. 8, Pt. 2–513
Scranton, George Whitfield, May 23, 1811–Mar. 24, 1861.
Vol. 8 Pt. 2–513
Screws, William Wallace, Feb. 25, 1839–Aug. 7, 1913.
Vol. 8, Pt. 2–514
Scribner, Charles, Feb. 21, 1821–Aug. 26, 1871.
Vol. 8, Pt. 2–515
Scribner, Charles, Oct. 18, 1854–Apr. 19, 1930.
Vol. 8, Pt. 2–516
Scribner, Charles, Jan. 26, 1890–Feb. 11, 1952.
Supp. 5–614
Scripps, Edward Wyllis, June 18, 1854–Mar. 12, 1926.
Vol. 8, Pt. 2–517
Scripps, Ellen Browning, Oct. 18, 1836–Aug. 3, 1932.
Vol. 8, Pt. 2–518
Scripps, James Edmund, Mar. 19, 1835–May 29, 1906.
Vol. 8, Pt. 2–519
Scripps, Robert Paine, Oct. 27, 1895–Mar. 2, 1938.
Supp. 2–605
Scripps, William Edmund, May 6, 1882–June 12, 1952.
Supp. 5–615
Scruggs, William Lindsay, Sept. 14, 1836–July 18, 1912.
Vol. 8, Pt. 2–520

Scrymser, James Alexander, July 18, 1839–Apr. 21, 1918.
Vol. 8, Pt. 2–521
Scudder, Horace Elisha, Oct. 16, 1838–Jan. 11, 1902.
Vol. 8, Pt. 2–522
Scudder, John, Sept 3, 1793–Jan. 13, 1855.
Vol. 8, Pt. 2–523
Scudder, John Milton, Sept. 8, 1829–Feb. 17, 1894.
Vol. 8, Pt. 2–524
Scudder, (Julia) Vida Dutton, Dec. 15, 1861–Oct. 9, 1954.
Supp. 5–616
Scudder, Nathaniel, May 10?, 1733–Oct. 16, 1781.
Vol. 8, Pt. 2–524
Scudder, Samuel Hubbard, Apr. 13, 1837–May 17, 1911.
Vol. 8, Pt. 2–525
Scull, John, 1765–Feb. 8, 1828.
Vol. 8, Pt. 2–526
Scullin, John, Aug. 17, 1836–May 28, 1920.
Vol. 8, Pt. 2–527
Seabury, George John, Nov. 10, 1844–Feb. 13, 1909.
Vol. 8, Pt. 2–527
Seabury, Samuel, Nov. 30, 1729–Feb. 25, 1796.
Vol. 8, Pt. 2–528
Seabury, Samuel, June 9, 1801–Oct. 10, 1872.
Vol. 8, Pt. 2–530
Seabury, Samuel, Feb. 22, 1873–May 7, 1958.
Supp. 6–569
Seager, Henry Rogers, July 21, 1870–Aug. 23, 1930.
Vol. 8, Pt. 2–531
Seagrave, Gordon Stifler, Mar. 18, 1897–Mar. 28, 1965.
Supp. 7–679
Sealsfield, Charles, Mar. 3, 1793–May 26, 1864.
Vol. 8, Pt. 2–532
Seaman, Elizabeth Cochrane, May 5, 1867–Jan. 27, 1922.
Vol. 8, Pt. 2–533
Searing, Laura Catherine Redden, Feb. 9, 1840–Aug. 10, 1923.
Vol. 8, Pt. 2–534
Searle, Arthur, Oct. 21, 1837–Oct. 23, 1920.
Vol. 8, Pt. 2–534
Searle, James, 1733–Aug. 7, 1797.
Vol. 8, Pt. 2–535
Searle, John Preston, Sept. 12, 1854–July 26, 1922.
Vol. 8, Pt. 2–536
Sears, Barnas, Nov. 19, 1802–July 6, 1880.
Vol. 8, Pt. 2–537
Sears, Edmund Hamilton, Apr. 6, 1810–Jan. 16, 1876.
Vol. 8, Pt. 2–538
Sears, Isaac, *c.* July 1, 1730–Oct. 28, 1786.
Vol. 8, Pt. 2–539
Sears, Richard Dudley, Oct. 26, 1861–Apr. 8, 1943.
Supp. 3–701
Sears, Richard Warren, Dec. 7, 1863–Sept. 28, 1914.
Vol. 8, Pt. 2–540
Sears, Robert, June 28, 1810–Feb. 17, 1892.
Vol. 8, Pt. 2–541
Seashore, Carl Emil, Jan. 28, 1866–Oct. 16, 1949.
Supp. 4–730
Seaton, William Winston, Jan. 11, 1785–June 16, 1866.
Vol. 8, Pt. 2–541
Seattle, *c.* 1786–June 7, 1866.
Vol. 8, Pt. 2–542
Seawell, Molly Elliot, Oct. 23, 1860–Nov. 15, 1916.
Vol. 8, Pt. 2–543
Sebastian, Benjamin, *c.* 1745–Mar. 1834.
Vol. 8, Pt. 2–543
Seberg, Jean Dorothy, Nov. 13, 1938–*c.* Aug. 31, 1979.
Supp. 10–725
Seccomb, John, Apr. 25, 1708–Oct. 27, 1792.
Vol. 8, Pt. 2–544
Seddon, James Alexander, July 13, 1815–Aug. 19, 1880.
Vol. 8, Pt. 2–545
Sedella, Antoine. [*See* Antoine, Père, 1748–1829.]
Sedgwick, Anne Douglas, Mar. 28, 1873–July 19, 1935.
Supp. 1–652
Sedgwick, Arthur George, Oct. 6, 1844–July 14, 1915.
Vol. 8, Pt. 2–546
Sedgwick, Catharine Maria, Dec. 28, 1789–July 31, 1867.
Vol. 8, Pt. 2–547
Sedgwick, Ellery, Feb. 27, 1872–Apr. 21, 1960.
Supp. 6–571
Sedgwick, John, Sept. 13, 1813–May 9, 1864.
Vol. 8, Pt. 2–548
Sedgwick, Robert, *c.* 1613–May 24, 1656.
Vol. 8, Pt. 2–549
Sedgwick, Theodore, May 9, 1746–Jan. 24, 1813.
Vol. 8, Pt. 2–549
Sedgwick, Theodore, Dec. 1780–Nov. 7, 1839.
Vol. 8, Pt. 2–551
Sedgwick, Theodore, Jan. 27, 1811–Dec. 8, 1859.
Vol. 8, Pt. 2–551
Sedgwick, William Thompson, Dec. 29, 1855–Jan. 21, 1921.
Vol. 8, Pt. 2–552
Sedley, William Henry. [*See* Smith, William Henry, 1806–1872.]
See, Horace, July 17, 1835–Dec. 14, 1909.
Vol. 8, Pt. 2–553
Seed, Miles Ainscough, Feb. 24, 1843–Dec. 4, 1913.
Vol. 8, Pt. 2–554
Seeger, Alan, June 22, 1888–July 4, 1916.
Vol. 8, Pt. 2–555
Seelye, Julius Hawley, Sept. 14, 1824–May 12, 1895.
Vol. 8, Pt. 2–555
Seelye, Laurenus Clark, Sept. 20, 1837–Oct. 12, 1924.
Vol. 8, Pt. 2–557
Seevers, William Henry, Apr. 8, 1822–Mar. 24, 1895.
Vol. 8, Pt. 2–558
Seghers, Charles Jean, Dec. 26, 1839–Nov. 28, 1886.
Vol. 8, Pt. 2–558
Seguin, Edouard, Jan. 20, 1812–Oct. 28, 1880.
Vol. 8, Pt. 2–559
Seguin, Edward Constant, 1843–Feb. 19, 1898.
Vol. 8, Pt. 2–560
Seiberling, Frank Augustus, Oct. 6, 1859–Aug. 11, 1955.
Supp. 5–617
Seibold, Louis, Oct. 10, 1863–May 10, 1945.
Supp. 3–702
Seidel, George Lukas Emil, Dec. 13, 1864–June 24, 1947.
Supp. 4–732
Seidensticker, Oswald, May 3, 1825–Jan. 10, 1894.
Vol. 8, Pt. 2–561
Seidl, Anton, May 7, 1850–Mar. 28, 1898.
Vol. 8, Pt. 2–561
Seiler, Carl, Apr. 14, 1849–Oct. 11, 1905.
Vol. 8, Pt. 2–562
Seip, Theodore Lorenzo, June 25, 1842–Nov. 28, 1903.
Vol. 8, Pt. 2–563
Seiss, Joseph Augustus, Mar. 18, 1823–Jun. 20, 1904.
Vol. 8, Pt. 2–563
Seitz, Don Carlos, Oct. 4, 1862–Dec. 4, 1935.
Supp. 1–653
Seitz, William Chapin, June 19, 1914–Oct. 26, 1974.
Supp. 9–708
Seixas, Gershom Mendes, Jan. 15, 1746–July 2, 1816.
Vol. 8, Pt. 2–564
Séjour, Victor, June 2, 1817–Sept. 21, 1874.
Vol. 8, Pt. 2–565
Selby, William, 1739?–Dec. 1798.
Vol. 8, Pt. 2–566
Selden, George Baldwin, Sept. 14, 1846–Jan. 17, 1922.
Vol. 8, Pt. 2–567
Seldes, Gilbert Vivian, Jan. 3, 1893–Sept. 29, 1970.
Supp. 8–584
Selfridge, Thomas Oliver, Feb. 6, 1836–Feb. 4, 1924.
Vol. 8, Pt. 2–568
Selig, William Nicholas, Mar. 14, 1864–July 15, 1948.
Supp. 4–734
Seligman, Arthur, June 14, 1871–Sept. 25, 1933.
Vol. 8, Pt. 2–569
Seligman, Edwin Robert Anderson, Apr. 25, 1861–July 18, 1939.
Supp. 2–606
Seligman, Isaac Newton, July 10, 1855–Sept. 30, 1917.
Vol. 8, Pt. 2–570
Seligman, Jesse, Aug. 11, 1827–Apr. 23, 1894.
Vol. 8, Pt. 2–571
Seligman, Joseph, Nov. 22, 1819–Apr. 25, 1880.
Vol. 8, Pt. 2–571
Selijns, Henricus, 1636–1701.
Vol. 8, Pt. 2–572
Selikovitsch, Goetzel, May 23, 1863–Nov. 27, 1926.
Vol. 8, Pt. 2–573

Sellers, Coleman, Jan. 28, 1827–Dec. 28, 1907.
Vol. 8, Pt. 2–574
Sellers, Isaiah, *c.* 1802–Mar. 6, 1864.
Vol. 8, Pt. 2–575
Sellers, Matthew Bacon, Mar. 29, 1869–Apr. 5, 1932.
Vol. 8, Pt. 2–576
Sellers, William, Sept. 19, 1824–Jan. 24, 1905.
Vol. 8, Pt. 2–576
Sellstedt, Lars Gustaf, Apr. 30, 1819–June 4, 1911.
Vol. 8, Pt. 2–577
Selyns, Henricus. [*See* Selijns, Henricus, 1636–1701.]
Selznick, David O., May 10, 1902–June 22, 1965.
Supp. 7–681
Sembrich, Marcella, Feb. 15, 1858–Jan. 11, 1935.
Supp. 1–654
Semmes, Alexander Jenkins, Dec. 17, 1828–Sept. 20, 1898.
Vol. 8, Pt. 2–578
Semmes, Raphael, Sept. 27, 1809–Aug. 30, 1877.
Vol. 8, Pt. 2–579
Semmes, Thomas Jenkins, Dec. 16, 1824–June 23, 1899.
Vol. 8, Pt. 2–582
Semple, Ellen Churchill, Jan. 8, 1863–May 8, 1932.
Vol. 8, Pt. 2–583
Seney, George Ingraham, May 12, 1826–Apr. 7, 1893.
Vol. 8, Pt. 2–583
Senn, Nicholas, Oct. 31, 1844–Jan. 2, 1908.
Vol. 8, Pt. 2–584
Sennett, George Burritt, July 28, 1840–Mar. 18, 1900.
Vol. 8, Pt. 2–585
Sennett, Mack, Jan. 17, 1880–Nov. 5, 1960.
Supp. 6–572
Sequoyah, 1770?–Aug. 1843.
Vol. 8, Pt. 2–586
Sergeant, Henry Clark, Nov. 2, 1834–Jan. 30, 1907.
Vol. 8, Pt. 2–586
Sergeant, John, 1710–July 27, 1749.
Vol. 8, Pt. 2–587
Sergeant, John, Dec. 5, 1779–Nov. 23, 1852.
Vol. 8, Pt. 2–588
Sergeant, Jonathan Dickinson, 1746–Oct. 8, 1793.
Vol. 8, Pt. 2–589
Sergeant, Thomas, Jan. 14, 1782–May 5, 1860.
Vol. 8, Pt. 2–590
Serling, Rodman Edward ("Rod"), Dec. 25, 1924–June 28, 1975.
Supp. 9–710
Serra, Junípero, Nov. 24, 1713–Aug. 28, 1784.
Vol. 8, Pt. 2–591
Serrell, Edward Wellman, Nov. 5, 1826–Apr. 25, 1906.
Vol. 8, Pt. 2–592
Service, Robert William, Jan. 16, 1874–Sept. 11, 1958.
Supp. 6–574
Servoss, Thomas Lowery, Oct. 14, 1786–Nov. 30, 1866.
Vol. 8, Pt. 2–593
Sessions, Henry Howard, June 21, 1847–Mar. 14, 1915.
Vol. 8, Pt. 2–593
Sestini, Benedict, Mar. 20, 1816–Jan. 17, 1890.
Vol. 8, Pt. 2–594
Setchell, William Albert, Apr. 15, 1864–Apr. 5, 1943.
Supp. 3–703
Seth, James, May 6, 1860–July 24, 1924.
Vol. 8, Pt. 2–595
Seton, Elizabeth Ann Bayley, Aug. 28, 1774–Jan. 4, 1821.
Vol. 8, Pt. 2–596
Seton, Ernest Thompson, Aug. 14, 1860–Oct. 23, 1946.
Supp. 4–735
Seton, Grace Gallatin Thompson, Jan. 28, 1872–Mar. 19, 1959.
Supp. 6–575
Seton, Robert, Aug. 28, 1839–Mar. 22, 1927.
Vol. 8, Pt. 2–597
Seton, William, Jan. 28, 1835–Mar. 15, 1905.
Vol. 8, Pt. 2–598
Settle, Thomas, Jan. 23, 1831–Dec. 1, 1888.
Vol. 8, Pt. 2–598
Severance, Caroline Maria Seymour, Jan. 12, 1820–Nov. 10, 1914.
Vol. 8, Pt. 2–599
Severance, Frank Hayward, Nov. 28, 1856–Jan. 26, 1931.
Vol. 8, Pt. 2–600
Severance, Louis Henry, Aug. 1, 1838–June 25, 1913.
Vol. 8, Pt. 2–601
Sevier, Ambrose Hundley, Nov. 4, 1801–Dec. 31, 1848.
Vol. 8, Pt. 2–601
Sevier, John, Sept. 23, 1745–Sept. 24, 1815.
Vol. 8, Pt. 2–602
Sewall, Arthur, Nov. 25, 1835–Sept. 5, 1900.
Vol. 8, Pt. 2–605
Sewall, Frank, Sept. 24, 1837–Dec. 7, 1915.
Vol. 8, Pt. 2–606
Sewall, Harold Marsh, Jan. 3, 1860–Oct. 28, 1924.
Vol. 8, Pt. 2–606
Sewall, Jonathan, Aug. 17, 1728–Sept. 26, 1796.
Vol. 8, Pt. 2–607
Sewall, Jonathan Mitchell, 1748–Mar. 29, 1808.
Vol. 8, Pt. 2–608
Sewall, Joseph Addison, Apr. 20, 1830–Jan. 17, 1917.
Vol. 8, Pt. 2–609
Sewall, May Eliza Wright, May 27, 1844–July 22, 1920.
Vol. 8, Pt. 2–610
Sewall, Samuel, Mar. 28, 1652–Jan. 1, 1730.
Vol. 8, Pt. 2–610
Sewall, Stephen, Apr. 4, 1734–July 23, 1804.
Vol. 8, Pt. 2–612
Seward, Frederick William, July 8, 1830–Apr. 25, 1915.
Vol. 8, Pt. 2–612
Seward, George Frederick, Nov. 8, 1840–Nov. 28, 1910.
Vol. 8, Pt. 2–613
Seward, Theodore Frelinghuysen, Jan. 25, 1835–Aug. 30, 1902.
Vol. 8, Pt. 2–614
Seward, William Henry, May 16, 1801–Oct. 10, 1872.
Vol. 8, Pt. 2–615
Sewell, William Joyce, Dec. 6, 1835–Dec. 27, 1901.
Vol. 9, Pt. 1–1
Sexton, Anne Gray Harvey, Nov. 9, 1928–Oct. 4, 1974.
Supp. 9–711
Seybert, Adam, May 16, 1773–May 2, 1825.
Vol. 9, Pt. 1–2
Seybert, Henry, Dec. 23, 1801–Mar. 3, 1883.
Vol. 9, Pt 1–3
Seybert, John, July 7, 1791–Jan. 4, 1860.
Vol. 9, Pt. 1–3
Seyffarth, Gustavus, July 13, 1796–Nov. 17, 1885.
Vol 9, Pt. 1–4
Seymour, Charles, Jan. 1, 1885–Aug. 11, 1963.
Supp. 7–682
Seymour, George Franklin, Jan. 5, 1829–Dec. 8, 1906.
Vol. 9, Pt. 1–5
Seymour, Horatio, May 31, 1810–Feb. 12, 1886.
Vol. 9, Pt. 1–6
Seymour, Horatio Winslow, 1854–Dec. 17, 1920.
Vol. 9, Pt. 1–9
Seymour, Thomas Day, Apr. 1, 1848–Dec. 31, 1907.
Vol. 9, Pt. 1–10
Seymour, Thomas Hart, Sept. 29, 1807–Sept. 3, 1868.
Vol. 9, Pt. 1–11
Seymour, Truman, Sept. 24, 1824–Oct. 30, 1891.
Vol. 9, Pt. 1–12
Seymour, William, Dec. 19, 1855–Oct. 2, 1933.
Vol. 9, Pt. 1–13
Shabonee, *c.* 1775–July 1859.
Vol. 9, Pt. 1–13
Shafer, Helen Almira, Sept. 23, 1839–Jan. 20, 1894.
Vol. 9, Pt. 1–14
Shafroth, John Franklin, June 9, 1854–Feb. 20, 1922.
Vol. 9, Pt. 1–14
Shafter, William Rufus, Oct. 16, 1835–Nov. 12, 1906.
Vol. 9, Pt. 1–15
Shahan, Thomas Joseph, Sept. 11, 1857–Mar. 9, 1932.
Vol. 9, Pt. 1–16
Shahn, Benjamin ("Ben"), Sept. 12, 1898–Mar. 14, 1969.
Supp. 8–586
Shaikewitz, Nahum Meir. [*See* Schomer, Nahum Meir, 1849–1905]
Shakallamy. [*See* Shikellamy, d. 1748.]
Shaler, Nathaniel Southgate, Feb. 20, 1841–Apr. 10, 1906.
Vol. 9, Pt. 1–17
Shaler, William, *c.* 1773–Mar. 29, 1833.
Vol. 9, Pt. 1–19

Shannon, Fred Albert, Feb. 12, 1893–Feb. 4, 1963. Supp. 7–684
Shannon, Wilson, Feb. 24, 1802–Aug. 30, 1877. Vol. 9, Pt. 1–20
Shapley, Harlow, Nov. 2, 1885–Oct. 20, 1972. Supp. 9–712
Sharkey, William Lewis, July 12, 1798–Mar. 30, 1873. Vol. 9, Pt. 1–21
Sharp, Dallas Lore, Dec. 13, 1870–Nov. 29, 1929. Vol. 9, Pt. 1–22
Sharp, Daniel, Dec. 25, 1783–June 23, 1853. Vol. 9, Pt. 1–23
Sharp, John, Nov. 9, 1820–Dec. 23, 1891. Vol. 9, Pt. 1–23
Sharp, Katharine Lucinda, May 25, 1865–June 1, 1914. Vol. 9, Pt. 1–24
Sharp, William Graves, Mar. 14, 1859–Nov. 17, 1922. Vol. 9, Pt. 1–25
Sharpe, Horatio, Nov. 15, 1718–Nov. 9, 1790. Vol. 9, Pt. 1–25
Sharples, James, *c.* 1751–Feb. 26, 1811. Vol. 9, Pt. 1–26
Sharpless, Isaac, Dec. 16, 1848–Jan. 16, 1920. Vol. 9, Pt. 1–27
Sharswood, George, July 7, 1810–May 28, 1883. Vol. 9, Pt. 1–28
Shattuck, Aaron Draper, Mar. 9, 1832–July 30, 1928. Vol. 9, Pt. 1–29
Shattuck, Frederick Cheever, Nov. 1, 1847–Jan. 11, 1929. Vol. 9, Pt. 1–30
Shattuck, George Brune, Aug. 18, 1844–Mar. 12, 1923. Vol. 4, Pt. 1–31
Shattuck, George Cheyne, July 17, 1783–Mar. 18, 1854. Vol. 9, Pt. 1–31
Shattuck, George Cheyne, July 22, 1813–Mar. 22, 1893. Vol. 9, Pt. 1–32
Shattuck, Lemuel, Oct. 15, 1793–Jan. 17, 1859. Vol. 9, Pt. 1–33
Shaubena. [*See* Shabonee, *c.* 1775–1859.]
Shauck, John Allen, Mar. 26, 1841–Jan. 3, 1918. Vol. 9, Pt. 1–34
Shaughnessy, Clark Daniel, Mar. 6, 1892–May 15, 1970. Supp. 8–587
Shaw, Albert, July 23, 1857–June 25, 1947. Supp. 4–738
Shaw, Anna Howard, Feb. 14, 1847–July 2, 1919. Vol. 9, Pt. 1–35
Shaw, Clay L., Mar. 17, 1913–Aug. 15, 1974. Supp. 9–714
Shaw, Edward Richard, Jan. 13, 1850–Feb. 11, 1903. Vol. 9, Pt. 1–37
Shaw, Elijah, Dec. 19, 1793–May 5, 1851. Vol. 9, Pt. 1–37
Shaw, Henry, July 24, 1800–Aug. 25, 1889. Vol. 9, Pt. 1–38
Shaw, Henry Wheeler, Apr. 21, 1818–Oct. 14, 1885. Vol. 9, Pt. 1–39
Shaw, Howard Van Doren, May 7, 1869–May 6, 1926. Vol. 9, Pt. 1–40
Shaw, John, 1773–Sept. 17, 1823. Vol. 9 Pt. 1–41
Shaw, John, May 4, 1778–Jan. 10, 1809. Vol. 9, Pt. 1–41
Shaw, Lawrence Timothy ("Buck"), Mar. 28, 1899–Mar. 19, 1977. Supp. 10–726
Shaw, Lemuel, Jan. 9, 1781–Mar. 30, 1861. Vol. 9, Pt. 1–42
Shaw, Leslie Mortier, Nov. 2, 1848–Mar. 28, 1932. Vol. 9, Pt. 1–43
Shaw, Mary, Jan. 25, 1854–May 18, 1929. Vol. 9, Pt. 1–44
Shaw, Nathaniel, Dec. 5, 1735–Apr. 15, 1782. Vol. 9, Pt. 1–45
Shaw, Oliver, Mar. 13, 1779–Dec. 31, 1848. Vol. 9, Pt. 1–46
Shaw, Pauline Agassiz, Feb. 6, 1841–Feb. 10, 1917. Vol. 9, Pt. 1–46
Shaw, Samuel, Oct. 2, 1754–May 30, 1794. Vol. 9, Pt. 1–47
Shaw, Thomas, May 5, 1838–Jan. 19, 1901. Vol. 9, Pt. 1–48
Shaw, (Warren) Wilbur, Oct. 31, 1902–Oct. 30, 1954. Supp. 5–618
Shaw, WIlliam Smith, Aug. 12, 1778–Apr. 25, 1826. Vol. 9, Pt. 1–49
Shawn, Edwin Meyers ("Ted"), Oct. 21, 1891–Jan. 9, 1972. Supp. 9–716
Shays, Daniel, *c.* 1747–Sept. 29, 1825. Vol. 9, Pt. 1–49
Shea, John Dawson Gilmary, July 22, 1824–Feb. 22, 1892. Vol. 9, Pt. 1–50
Shean, Albert, May 12, 1868–Aug. 12, 1949. Supp. 4–739
Shear, Theodore Leslie, Aug. 11, 1880–July 3, 1945. Supp. 3–704
Shearman, Thomas Gaskell, Nov. 25, 1834–Sept. 29, 1900. Vol. 9, Pt. 1–52
Shecut, John Linnaeus Edward Whitridge, Dec. 4, 1770–June 1, 1836. Vol. 9, Pt. 1–53
Shedd, Fred Fuller, Feb. 9, 1871–Apr. 2, 1937. Supp. 2–609
Shedd, Joel Herbert, May 31, 1834–Nov. 27, 1915. Vol. 9, Pt. 1–53
Shedd, John Graves, July 20, 1850–Oct. 22, 1926. Vol. 9, Pt. 1–54
Shedd, William Greenough Thayer, June 21, 1820–Nov. 17, 1894. Vol. 9, Pt. 1–56
Shedd, William Ambrose, Jan. 24, 1865–Aug. 7, 1918. Vol. 9, Pt. 1–55
Sheean, James Vincent, Dec. 5, 1899–Mar. 15, 1975. Supp. 9–717
Sheedy, Dennis, Sept. 26, 1846–Oct. 16, 1923. Vol. 9, Pt. 1–57
Sheeler, Charles R., Jr., July 16, 1883–May 7, 1965. Supp. 7–685
Sheen, Fulton John, May 8, 1895–Dec. 9, 1979. Supp. 10–728
Sheffield, Devello Zelotes, Aug. 13, 1841–July 1, 1913. Vol. 9, Pt. 1–57
Sheffield, Joseph Earl, June 19, 1793–Feb. 16, 1882. Vol. 9, Pt. 1–58
Sheil, Bernard James, Feb. 18, 1886–Sept. 13, 1969. Supp. 8–588
Shelby, Evan, 1719–Dec. 4, 1794. Vol. 9, Pt. 1–59
Shelby, Isaac, Dec. 11, 1750–July 18, 1826. Vol. 9, Pt. 1–60
Shelby, Joseph Orville, Dec. 12, 1830–Feb. 13, 1897. Vol. 9, Pt. 1–62
Sheldon, Charles Monroe, Feb. 26, 1857–Feb. 24, 1946. Supp. 4–740
Sheldon, Edward Austin, Oct. 4, 1823–Aug. 26, 1897. Vol. 9, Pt. 1–63
Sheldon, Edward Stevens, Nov. 21, 1851–Oct. 16, 1925. Vol. 9, Pt. 1–64
Sheldon, Henry Newton, June 28, 1843–Jan. 14, 1926. Vol. 9, Pt. 1–65
Sheldon, Mary Downing. [*See* Barnes, Mary Downing Sheldon, 1850–1898.]
Sheldon, Walter Lorenzo, Sept. 5, 1858–June 5, 1907. Vol. 9, Pt. 1–66
Sheldon, William Evarts, Oct. 22, 1832–Apr. 16, 1900. Vol. 9, Pt. 1–66
Sheldon, William Herbert, Nov. 19, 1898–Sept. 16, 1977. Supp. 10–730
Shelekhov, Grigorii Ivanovich, 1747–July 31, 1795. Vol. 9, Pt. 1–67
Shellabarger, Samuel, May 18, 1888–Mar. 21, 1954. Supp. 5–619
Shelton, Albert Leroy, June 9, 1875–Feb. 17, 1922. Vol. 9, Pt. 1–68
Shelton, Edward Mason, Aug. 7, 1846–May 9, 1928. Vol. 9, Pt. 1–69
Shelton, Frederick William, May 20, 1815–June 20, 1881. Vol. 9, Pt. 1–70
Shepard, Charles Upham, June 29, 1804–May 1, 1886. Vol. 9, Pt. 1–71

Shepard, Edward Morse, July 23, 1850–July 28, 1911.
Vol. 9, Pt. 1–72
Shepard, Fred Douglas, Sept. 11, 1855–Dec. 18, 1915.
Vol. 9, Pt. 1–73
Shepard, James Edward, Nov. 3, 1875–Oct. 6, 1947.
Supp. 4–742
Shepard, James Henry, Apr. 14, 1850–Feb. 21, 1918.
Vol. 9, Pt. 1–73
Shepard, Jesse. [*See* Grierson, Francis, 1848–1927]
Shepard, Seth, Apr. 23, 1847–Dec. 3, 1917.
Vol. 9, Pt. 1–74
Shepard, Thomas, Nov. 5, 1605–Aug. 25, 1649.
Vol. 9, Pt. 1–75
Shepard, William, Dec. 1, 1737–Nov. 16, 1817.
Vol. 9, Pt. 1–76
Shepherd, Alexander Robey, Jan. 31, 1835–Sept. 12, 1902.
Vol. 9, Pt. 1–77
Shepherd, William Robert, June 12, 1871–June 7, 1934.
Supp. 1–655
Shepley, Ether, Nov. 2, 1789–Jan. 15, 1877.
Vol. 9, Pt. 1–78
Shepley, George Foster, Jan. 1, 1819–July 20, 1878.
Vol. 9, Pt. 1–78
Sheppard, John Morris, May 28, 1875–Apr. 9, 1941.
Supp. 3–706
Sheppard, Samuel Edward, July 29, 1882–Sept. 29, 1948.
Supp. 4–743
Sheridan, Philip Henry, Mar. 6, 1831–Aug. 5, 1888.
Vol. 9, Pt. 1–79
Sherman, Allan, Nov. 30, 1924–Nov. 20, 1973.
Supp. 9–719
Sherman, Forrest Percival, Oct. 30, 1896–July 22, 1951.
Supp. 5–620
Sherman, Frank Dempster, May 6, 1860–Sept. 19, 1916.
Vol. 9, Pt. 1–81
Sherman, Frederick Carl, May 27, 1888–July 27, 1957.
Supp. 6–576
Sherman, Henry Clapp, Oct. 16, 1875–Oct. 7, 1955.
Supp. 5–622
Sherman, James Schoolcraft, Oct. 24, 1855–Oct. 30, 1912.
Vol. 9, Pt. 1–82
Sherman, John, Dec. 26, 1613–Aug. 8, 1685.
Vol. 9, Pt. 1–83
Sherman, John, May 10, 1823–Oct. 22, 1900.
Vol. 9, Pt. 1–84
Sherman, Roger, Apr. 19, 1721 o.s.–July 23, 1793.
Vol. 9, Pt. 1–88
Sherman, Stuart Pratt, Oct. 1, 1881–Aug. 21, 1926.
Vol. 9, Pt. 1–91
Sherman, Thomas West, Mar. 26, 1813–Mar. 16, 1879.
Vol. 9, Pt. 1–92
Sherman, William Tecumseh, Feb. 8, 1820–Feb. 14, 1891.
Vol. 9, Pt. 1–93
Sherry, Louis, 1856–June 9, 1926.
Vol. 9, Pt. 1–97
Sherwin, Thomas, Mar. 26, 1799–July 23, 1869.
Vol. 9, Pt. 1–98
Sherwood, Adiel, Oct. 3, 1791–Aug. 18, 1879.
Vol. 9, Pt. 1–99
Sherwood, Isaac Ruth, Aug. 13, 1835–Oct. 15, 1925.
Vol. 9, Pt. 1–100
Sherwood, Katharine Margaret Brownlee, Sept. 24, 1841–Feb. 15, 1914.
Vol. 9, Pt. 1–100
Sherwood, Mary Elizabeth Wilson, Oct. 27, 1826–Sept. 12, 1903.
Vol. 9, Pt. 1–101
Sherwood, Robert Emmet, Apr. 4, 1896–Nov. 14, 1955.
Supp. 5–623
Sherwood, Thomas Adiel, June 2, 1834–Nov. 11, 1918.
Vol. 9, Pt. 1–102
Sherwood, William Hall, Jan 31, 1854–Jan. 75 1911.
Vol. 9, Pt. 1–103
Shick Calamys. [*See* Shikellamy, d. 1748.]
Shields, Charles Woodruff, Apr. 4, 1825–Aug. 26, 1904.
Vol. 9, Pt. 1–104
Shields, Francis Xavier ("Frank"), Nov. 17, 1909–Aug. 19, 1975.
Supp. 9–721
Shields, George Howell, June 19, 1842–Apr. 27, 1924.
Vol. 9, Pt. 1–105
Shields, George Oliver, Aug. 26, 1846–Nov. 11, 1925.
Vol. 9, Pt. 1–106
Shields, James, May 12, 1806–June 1, 1879.
Vol. 9, Pt. 1–106
Shields, John Knight, Aug. 15, 1858–Sept. 30, 1934.
Supp. 1–656
Shields, Thomas Edward, May 9, 1862–Feb. 15, 1921.
Vol. 9, Pt. 1–107
Shikellamy, d. Dec. 6, 1748.
Vol. 9, Pt. 1–109
Shillaber, Benjamin Penhallow, July 12, 1814–Nov. 25, 1890.
Vol. 9, Pt. 1–109
Shinn, Asa, May 3, 1781–Feb. 11, 1853.
Vol. 9, Pt. 1–110
Shinn, Everett, Nov. 6, 1876–May 1, 1953.
Supp. 5–624
Shipherd, John Jay, Mar. 28, 1802–Sept. 16, 1844.
Vol. 9, Pt. 1–111
Shipley, Ruth Bielaski, 1885–Nov. 3, 1966.
Supp. 8–589
Shipman, Andrew Jackson, Oct. 15, 1857–Oct. 17, 1915.
Vol. 9, Pt. 1–112
Shipp, Albert Micajah, June 15, 1819–June 27, 1887.
Vol. 9, Pt. 1–113
Shipp, Scott, Aug. 2, 1839–Dec. 4, 1917.
Vol. 9, Pt. 1–114
Shippen, Edward, 1639–Oct. 2, 1712.
Vol. 9, Pt. 1–115
Shippen, Edward, Feb. 16/26, 1728/29–Apr. 15, 1806.
Vol. 9, Pt. 1–116
Shippen, William, Oct. 21, 1736–July 11, 1808.
Vol. 9, Pt. 1–117
Shipstead, Henrik, Jan. 8, 1881–June 26, 1960.
Supp. 6–577
Shiras, George, Jan. 26, 1832–Aug. 2, 1924.
Vol. 9, Pt. 1–118
Shiras, Oliver Perry, Oct. 22, 1833–Jan. 7, 1916.
Vol. 9, Pt. 1–118
Shirlaw, Walter, Aug. 6, 1838–Dec. 26, 1909.
Vol. 9, Pt. 1–119
Shirley, William, Dec. 2, 1694–Mar. 24, 1771.
Vol. 9, Pt. 1–120
Shobonier. [*See* Shabonee, *c.* 1775–1859.]
Sholes, Christopher Latham, Feb. 14, 1819–Feb. 17, 1890.
Vol. 4, Pt. 1–122
Shonts, Theodore Perry, May 5, 1856–Sept. 21, 1919.
Vol. 9, Pt. 1–123
Shook, Alfred Montgomery, July 16, 1845–Mar. 18, 1923.
Vol. 9, Pt. 1–124
Shor, Bernard ("Toots"), May 6, 1903–Jan. 23, 1977.
Supp. 10–731
Shorey, Paul, Aug. 3, 1857–Apr. 24, 1934.
Vol. 9, Pt. 1–125
Short, Charles, May 28, 1821–Dec. 24, 1886.
Vol. 9, Pt. 1–126
Short, Charles Wilkins, Oct. 6, 1794–Mar. 7, 1863.
Vol. 9, Pt. 1–127
Short, Joseph Hudson, Jr., Feb. 11, 1904–Sept. 18, 1952.
Supp. 5–626
Short, Luke, Nov. 19, 1908–Aug. 18, 1975.
Supp. 9–722
Short, Sidney Howe, Oct. 8, 1858–Oct. 21, 1902.
Vol. 9, Pt. 1–128
Short, Walter Campbell, Mar. 30, 1880–Sept. 3, 1949.
Supp. 4–744
Short, William, Sept. 30, 1759–Dec. 5, 1849.
Vol. 9, Pt. 1–128
Shorter, John Gill, Apr. 23, 1818–May 29, 1872.
Vol. 9, Pt. 1–129
Shotwell, James Thomson, Aug. 6, 1874–July 15, 1965.
Supp. 7–687
Shoup, Francis Asbury, Mar. 22, 1834–Sept. 4, 1896.
Vol. 9, Pt. 1–130
Shoup, George Laird, June 15, 1836–Dec. 21, 1904.
Vol. 9, Pt. 1–131
Shouse, Jouett, Dec. 10, 1879–June 2, 1968.
Supp. 8–591
Showerman, Grant, Jan. 9, 1870–Nov. 13, 1935.
Supp. 1–657
Shrady, George Frederick, Jan. 14, 1837–Nov. 30, 1907.
Vol. 9, Pt. 1–132

Shrady, Henry Merwin, Oct. 24, 1871–Apr. 12, 1922.
Vol. 9, Pt. 1–132
Shreve, Henry Miller, Oct. 21, 1785–Mar. 6, 1851.
Vol. 9, Pt. 1–133
Shreve, Thomas Hopkins, Dec. 17, 1808–Dec. 22, 1853.
Vol. 9, Pt. 1–134
Shub, Abraham David, Sept. 13, 1887–May 27, 1973.
Supp. 9–723
Shubert, Lee, Mar. 15, 1873?–Dec. 25, 1953.
Supp. 5–626
Shubrick, John Templer, Sept. 12, 1788–July 1815.
Vol. 9, Pt. 1–135
Shubrick, William Branford, Oct. 31, 1790–May 27, 1874.
Vol. 9, Pt. 1–136
Shuck, Jehu Lewis, Sept. 4, 1812–Aug. 20, 1863.
Vol. 9, Pt. 1–137
Shuey, Edwin Longstreet, Jan. 3, 1857–Sept. 27, 1924.
Vol. 9, Pt. 1–138
Shuey, William John, Feb. 9, 1827–Feb. 2 1, 1920.
Vol. 9, Pt. 1–138
Shufeldt, Robert Wilson, Feb. 21, 1822–Nov. 7, 1895.
Vol. 9, Pt. 1–139
Shull, George Harrison, Apr. 15, 1874–Sept. 28, 1954.
Supp. 5–628
Shulze, John Andrew, July 19, 1775–Nov. 18, 1852.
Vol. 9, Pt. 1–140
Shumlin, Herman Elliott, Dec. 6, 1898–June 14, 1979.
Supp. 10–733
Shunk, Francis Rawn, Aug. 7, 1788–July 30, 1848.
Vol. 9, Pt. 1–141
Shurtleff, Nathaniel Bradstreet, June 29, 1810–Oct. 17, 1874.
Vol. 9, Pt. 1–141
Shurtleff, Roswell Morse, June 14, 1838–Jan. 6, 1915.
Vol. 9, Pt. 1–142
Shuster, George Nauman, Aug. 27, 1894–Jan. 25, 1977.
Supp. 10–734
Shuster, W(illiam) Morgan, Feb. 23, 1877–May 26, 1960.
Supp. 6–579
Shute, Samuel, Jan. 12, 1662–Apr. 15, 1742.
Vol. 9, Pt. 1–143
Siamese twins. [*See* Chang and Eng, 1811–1874.]
Sibert, William Luther, Oct. 12, 1860–Oct. 16, 1935.
Supp. 1–658
Sibley, George Champlain, Apr. 1, 1782–Jan. 31, 1863.
Vol. 9, Pt. 1–144
Sibley, Henry Hastings, Feb. 20, 1811–Feb. 18, 1891.
Vol. 9, Pt. 1–144
Sibley, Hiram, Feb. 6, 1807–July 12, 1888.
Vol. 9, Pt. 1–145
Sibley, John, May 19, 1757–Apr. 8, 1837.
Vol. 9, Pt. 1–146
Sibley, John Langdon, Dec. 29, 1804–Dec. 9, 1885.
Vol. 9, Pt. 1–147
Sibley, Joseph Crocker, Feb. 18, 1850–May 19, 1926.
Vol. 9, Pt. 1–148
Sicalamous. [*See* Shikellamy, d. 1748.]
Sicard, Montgomery, Sept. 30, 1836–Sept. 14, 1900.
Vol. 9, Pt. 1–148
Sickels, Frederick Ellsworth, Sept 20, 1819–Mar. 8, 1895.
Vol. 9, Pt. 1–149
Sickles, Daniel Edgar, Oct. 20, 1825–May 3, 1914.
Vol. 9, Pt. 1–150
Sidell, William Henry, Aug. 21, 1810–July 1, 1873.
Vol. 9, Pt. 1–151
Sidis, Boris, Oct. 12, 1867–Oct. 24, 1923.
Vol. 9, Pt. 1–152
Sidney, Margaret. [*See* Lothrop, Harriett Mulford Stone, 1844–1924.]
Sieber, Al, Feb. 29, 1844–Feb. 19, 1907.
Supp. 1–659
Sigel, Franz, Nov. 18, 1824–Aug. 21, 1902.
Vol. 9, Pt. 1–153
Sigerist, Henry Ernest, Apr. 7, 1891–Mar. 17, 1957.
Supp. 6–580
Sigman, Morris, May 15, 1881–July 20, 1931.
Vol. 9, Pt. 1–154
Sigourney, Lydia Howard Huntley, Sept. 1, 1791–June 10, 1865.
Vol. 9, Pt. 1–155
Sigsbee, Charles Dwight, Jan. 16, 1845–July 19, 1923.
Vol. 9, Pt. 1–156
Sikes, William Wirt, Nov. 23, 1836–Aug. 18, 1883.
Vol. 9, Pt. 1–157
Sikorsky, Igor Ivanovich, May 25, 1889–Oct. 26, 1972.
Supp. 9–725
Silcox, Ferdinand Augustus, Dec. 25, 1882–Dec. 20, 1939.
Supp. 2–610
Silkwood, Karen Gay, Feb. 19, 1946–Nov. 13, 1974.
Supp. 9–726
Sill, Anna Peck, Aug. 9, 1816–June 18, 1889.
Vol. 9, Pt. 1–157
Sill, Edward Rowland, Apr. 29, 1841–Feb. 27, 1887.
Vol. 9, Pt. 1–158
Silliman, Benjamin, Aug. 8, 1779–Nov. 24, 1864.
Vol. 9, Pt. 1–160
Silliman, Benjamin, Dec. 4, 1816–Jan. 14, 1885.
Vol. 9, Pt. 1–163
Sills, Milton, Jan. 12, 1882–Sept. 15, 1930.
Vol. 9, Pt. 1–164
Siloti, Alexander Ilyitch, Oct. 10, 1863–Dec. 8, 1945.
Supp. 3–707
Silsbee, Nathaniel, Jan. 14, 1773–July 14, 1850.
Vol. 4, Pt. 1–165
Silver, Abba Hillel, Jan. 28, 1893–Nov. 28, 1963.
Supp. 7–688
Silver, Gray, Feb. 17, 1871–July 28, 1935.
Supp. 1–660
Silver, Thomas, June 17, 1813–Apr. 12, 1888.
Vol. 9, Pt. 1–165
Silverheels, Jay, May 26, 1919–March 5, 1980.
Supp. 10–736
Silverman, Joseph, Aug. 25, 1860–July 26, 1930.
Vol. 9, Pt. 1–166
Silverman, Sime, May 18, 1873–Sept. 22, 1933.
Vol. 9, Pt. 1–167
Silvers, Louis, Sept. 6, 1889–Mar. 26, 1954.
Supp. 5–629
Simkhovitch, Mary Melinda Kingsbury, Sept. 8, 1867–Nov. 15, 1951.
Supp. 5–630
Simmons (Szymanski), Aloysius Harry, May 22, 1903–May 26, 1956.
Supp. 6–581
Simmons, Edward, Oct. 27, 1852–Nov. 17, 1931.
Vol. 9, Pt. 1–168
Simmons, Franklin, Jan. 11, 1839–Dec. 6, 1913.
Vol. 9, Pt. 1–169
Simmons, Furnifold McLendel, Jan. 20, 1854–Apr. 30, 1940.
Supp. 2–611
Simmons, George Henry, Jan. 2, 1852–Sept. 1, 1937.
Supp. 2–612
Simmons, James Stevens, June 7, 1890–July 31, 1954.
Supp. 5–631
Simmons, Roscoe Conkling Murray, June 20, 1878–Apr. 27, 1951.
Supp. 5–632
Simmons, Thomas Jefferson, June 25, 1837–Sept. 12, 1905.
Vol. 9, Pt. 1–169
Simmons, William Joseph, May 6, 1880–May 18, 1945.
Supp. 3–708
Simms, Ruth Hanna McCormick, Mar. 27, 1880–Dec. 31, 1944.
Supp. 3–710
Simms, William Elliott, Jan. 2, 1822–June 25, 1898.
Vol. 9, Pt. 1–170
Simms, William Gilmore, Apr. 17, 1806–June 11, 1870.
Vol. 9, Pt. 1–171
Simon, Richard Leo, Mar. 6, 1899–July 29, 1960.
Supp. 6–582
Simonds, Frank Herbert, Apr. 5, 1878–Jan. 23, 1936.
Supp. 2–613
Simons, Algie Martin, Oct. 9, 1870–Mar. 11, 1950.
Supp. 4–745
Simons, Henry Calvert, Oct. 9, 1899–June 19, 1946.
Supp. 4–747
Simonton, Charles Henry, July 11, 1829–Apr. 25, 1904.
Vol. 9, Pt. 1–174
Simonton, James William, Jan. 30, 1823–Nov. 2, 1882.
Vol. 9, Pt. 1–175
Simpson, Albert Benjamin, Dec. 15, 1843–Oct. 29, 1919.
Vol. 9, Pt. 1–176

Simpson, Charles Torrey, June 3, 1846–Dec. 17, 1932.
Supp. 1–661
Simpson, Edmund Shaw, 1784–July 31, 1848.
Vol. 9, Pt. 1–177
Simpson, Edward, Mar. 3, 1824–Dec. 1, 1888.
Vol. 9, Pt. 1–178
Simpson, James Hervey, Mar. 9, 1813–Mar. 2, 1883.
Vol. 9, Pt. 1–179
Simpson, Jerry, Mar. 31, 1842–Oct. 23, 1905.
Vol. 9, Pt. 1–179
Simpson, John Andrew, July 4, 1871–Mar. 15, 1934.
Vol. 9, Pt. 1–180
Simpson, Matthew, June 21, 1811–June 18, 1884.
Vol. 9, Pt. 1–181
Simpson, Michael Hodge, Nov. 15, 1809–Dec. 21, 1884.
Vol. 9, Pt. 1–182
Simpson, Stephen, July 24, 1789–Aug. 17, 1854.
Vol. 9, Pt. 1–183
Simpson, William Dunlap, Oct. 27, 1823–Dec. 26, 1890.
Vol. 9, Pt. 1–184
Simpson, William Kelly, Apr 10, 1855–Feb. 6, 1914.
Vol. 9, Pt. 1–185
Sims, Charles N., May 18, 1835–Mar. 27, 1908.
Vol. 9, Pt. 1–185
Sims, James Marion, Jan. 25, 1813–Nov. 13, 1883.
Vol. 9, Pt. 1–186
Sims, William Sowden, Oct. 15, 1858–Sept. 28, 1936.
Supp. 2–614
Sims, Winfield Scott, Apr. 6, 1844–Jan. 7, 1918.
Vol. 9, Pt. 1–188
Sinclair, Harry Ford, July 6, 1876–Nov. 10, 1956.
Supp. 6–584
Sinclair, Upton Beall, Jr., Sept. 20, 1878–Nov. 25, 1968.
Supp. 8–593
Singer, Charles H., Mar. 17, 1903–Mar. 26, 1972.
Supp. 9–727
Singer, Isaac Merrit, Oct. 27, 1811–July 23, 1875.
Vol. 9, Pt. 1–188
Singer, Israel Joshua, Nov. 30, 1893–Feb. 10, 1944.
Supp. 3–711
Singerly, William Miskey, Dec. 27, 1832–Feb. 27, 1898.
Vol. 9, Pt. 1–189
Singleton, Esther, Nov. 4, 1865–July 2, 1930.
Vol. 9, Pt. 1–190
Singleton, James Washington, Nov. 23, 1811–Apr. 4, 1892.
Vol. 9, Pt. 1–191
Sinnott, Edmund Ware, Feb. 5, 1888–Jan. 6, 1968.
Supp. 8–595
Siringo, Charles A., Feb. 7, 1855–Oct. 19, 1928.
Vol. 9, Pt, 1–191
Sisler, George Harold ("Gorgeous George"), Mar. 24, 1893–Mar. 26, 1973.
Supp. 9–729
Sissle, Noble Lee, July 10, 1889–Dec. 17, 1975.
Supp. 9–730
Sitting Bull, 1834?–Dec. 15, 1890.
Vol. 9, Pt. 1–192
Sizer, Nelson, May 27, 1812–Oct. 18, 1897.
Vol. 9, Pt. 1–193
Skaggs, Marion Barton, Apr. 5, 1888–May 8, 1976.
Supp. 10–737
Skaniadariio, *c.* 1735–Aug. 10, 1815.
Vol. 9, Pt. 1–194
Skenandoa, 1706?–Mar. 11, 1816.
Vol. 9, Pt. 1–194
Skene, Alexander Johnston Chalmers, June 17, 1837–July 4, 1900.
Vol. 9, Pt. 1–194
Skidmore, Louis, Apr. 8, 1897–Sept. 27, 1962.
Supp. 7–690
Skillern, Ross Hall, Nov. 13, 1875–Sept. 20, 1930.
Vol. 9, Pt. 1–195
Skinner, Aaron Nicols, Aug. 10, 1845–Aug. 14, 1918.
Vol. 9, Pt. 1–196
Skinner, Alanson Buck, Sept. 7, 1886–Aug. 17, 1925.
Vol. 9, Pt. 1–197
Skinner, Charles Rufus, Aug. 4, 1844–June 30, 1928.
Vol. 9, Pt. 1–197
Skinner, Cornelia Otis, May 30, 1901–July 9, 1979.
Supp. 10–739
Skinner Halcyon, Mar. 6, 1824–Nov. 28, 1900.
Vol. 9, Pt. 1–198
Skinner, Harry, May 25, 1855–May 19, 1929.
Vol. 9, Pt. 1–199
Skinner, John Stuart, Feb. 22, 1788–Mar. 21, 1851.
Vol. 9, Pt. 1–199
Skinner, Otis, June 28, 1858–Jan. 4, 1942.
Supp. 3–713
Skinner, Thomas Harvey, Mar. 7, 1791–Feb. 1, 1871.
Vol. 9, Pt. 1–201
Skinner, William, Nov. 14, 1824–Feb. 28, 1902.
Vol. 9, Pt. 1–202
Skouras, George Panagiotes, Apr. 23, 1896–Mar. 16, 1964.
Supp. 7–691
Skouras, Spyros Panagiotes, Mar. 28, 1893–Aug. 16, 1971.
Supp. 9–732
Slade, Joseph Alfred, *c.* 1824–Mar. 10, 1864.
Vol. 9, Pt. 1–202
Slade, William, May 9, 1786–Jan. 16, 1859.
Vol. 9, Pt. 1–203
Slafter, Edmund Farwell, May 30, 1816–Sept. 22, 1906.
Vol. 9, Pt. 1–204
Slater, John Clarke, Dec. 22, 1900–July 25, 1976.
Supp. 10–741
Slater, John Fox, Mar. 4, 1815–May 7, 1884.
Vol. 9, Pt. 1–205
Slater, Samuel, June 9, 1768–Apr. 21, 1835.
Vol. 9, Pt. 1–205
Slattery, Charles Lewis, Dec. 9, 1867–Mar. 12, 1930.
Vol. 9, Pt. 1–206
Slaughter, Philip, Oct. 26, 1808–June 12, 1890.
Vol. 9, Pt. 1–207
Sleeper, Jacob, Nov. 21, 1802–Mar. 31, 1889.
Vol. 9, Pt. 1–208
Slemp, Campbell Bascom, Sept. 4, 1870–Aug. 7, 1943.
Supp. 3–714
Slicer, Thomas Roberts, Apr. 16, 1847–May 29, 1916.
Vol. 9, Pt. 1–209
Slichter, Louis Byrne, May 19, 1896–Mar. 25, 1978.
Supp. 10–742
Slichter, Sumner Huber, Jan. 8, 1892–Sept. 27, 1959.
Supp. 6–585
Slidell, John, 1793–July 29, 1871.
Vol. 9, Pt. 1–209
Slipher, Vesto Melvin, Nov. 11, 1875–Nov. 8, 1969.
Supp. 8–597
Sloan, Alfred Pritchard, Jr., May 23, 1875–Feb. 17, 1966.
Supp. 8–598
Sloan, George Arthur, May 30, 1893–May 20, 1955.
Supp. 5–633
Sloan, Harold Paul, Dec. 12, 1881–May 22, 1961.
Supp. 7–693
Sloan, James Forman, Aug. 10, 1874–Dec. 21, 1933.
Vol. 9, Pt. 1–211
Sloan, John French, Aug. 2, 1871–Sept. 7, 1951.
Supp. 5–634
Sloan, Matthew Scott, Sept. 5, 1881–June 14, 1945.
Supp. 3–715
Sloan, Richard Elihu, June 22, 1857–Dec. 14, 1933.
Vol. 9, Pt. 1–212
Sloan, Samuel, Dec. 24, 1817–Sept. 22, 1907.
Vol. 9, Pt. 1–213
Sloan, Tod. [*See* Sloan, James Forman, 1874–1933.]
Sloane, Isabel Cleves Dodge, Feb. 26, 1896–Mar. 9, 1962.
Supp. 7–695
Sloane, William Milligan, Nov. 12, 1850–Sept. 11, 1928.
Vol. 9, Pt. 1–214
Sloat, John Drake, July 26, 1781–Nov. 28, 1867.
Vol. 9, Pt. 1–214
Slocum, Frances, Mar. 4, 1773–Mar. 9, 1847.
Vol. 9, Pt. 1–215
Slocum, Henry Warner, Sept. 24, 1827–Apr. 14, 1894.
Vol. 9, Pt. 1–216
Slocum, Joshua, Feb. 20, 1844–*c.* 1910.
Vol. 9, Pt. 1–217
Slocum, Samuel, Mar. 4, 1792–Jan. 26, 1861.
Vol. 9, Pt. 1–218
Sloss, James Withers, Apr. 7, 1820–May 4, 1890.
Vol. 9, Pt. 1–219
Sloss, Louis, July 13, 1823–June 4, 1902.
Vol. 9, Pt. 1–219

Slosson, Edwin Emery, June 7, 1865–Oct. 15, 1929.
Vol. 9, Pt. 1–220
Small, Albion Woodbury, May 11, 1854–Mar. 24, 1926.
Vol. 9, Pt. 1–221
Small, Alvan Edmond, Mar. 4, 1811–Dec. 31, 1886.
Vol. 9, Pt. 1–222
Smalley, Eugene Virgil, July 18, 1841–Dec. 30, 1899.
Vol. 9, Pt. 1–223
Smalley, George Washburn, June 2, 1833–Apr. 4, 1916.
Vol. 9, Pt. 1–223
Smalls, Robert, Apr. 5, 1839–Feb. 22, 1915.
Vol. 9, Pt. 1–224
Smallwood, William, 1732–Feb. 12, 1792.
Vol. 9, Pt. 1–225
Smart, David Archibald, Oct. 4, 1892–Oct. 16, 1952.
Supp. 5–637
Smart, James Henry, June 30, 1841–Feb. 21, 1900.
Vol. 9, Pt. 1–226
Smedley, Agnes, 1894–May 6, 1950.
Supp. 4–749
Smedley, William Thomas, Mar. 26, 1858–Mar. 26, 1920.
Vol. 9, Pt. 1–227
Smibert, John, 1688–Apr. 2, 1751.
Vol. 9, Pt. 1–228
Smiley, Albert Keith, Mar. 17, 1828–Dec. 2, 1912.
Vol. 9, Pt. 1–230
Smillie, George Henry, Dec. 29, 1840–Nov. 10, 1921.
Vol. 9, Pt. 1–231
Smillie, James, Nov. 23, 1807–Dec. 4, 1885.
Vol. 9, Pt. 1–232
Smillie, James David, Jan. 16, 1833–Sept. 14, 1909.
Vol. 9, Pt. 1–232
Smillie, Ralph, July 8, 1887–Feb. 16, 1960.
Supp. 6–587
Smith, Abby Hadassah, June 1, 1797–July 23, 1878.
Vol. 9, Pt. 1–233
Smith, Albert Holmes, July 19, 1835–Dec. 14, 1885.
Vol. 9, Pt. 1–234
Smith Albert Merriman, Feb. 10, 1913–Apr. 13, 1970.
Supp. 8–606
Smith, Alexander, Sept. 11, 1865–Sept. 8, 1922.
Vol. 9, Pt. 1–235
Smith, Alfred Emanuel, Dec. 30, 1873–Oct. 4, 1944.
Supp. 3–716
Smith, Alfred Holland, Apr. 26, 1863–Mar. 8, 1924.
Vol. 9, Pt. 1–235
Smith, Andrew Jackson, Apr. 28, 1815–Jan. 30, 1897.
Vol. 9, Pt. 1–236
Smith, Archibald Cary, Sept. 4, 1837–Dec. 8, 1911.
Vol. 9, Pt. 1–237
Smith, Arthur Henderson, July 18, 1845–Aug. 31, 1932.
Vol. 9, Pt. 1–238
Smith, Asa Dodge, Sept. 21, 1804–Aug. 16, 1877.
Vol. 9, Pt. 1–239
Smith, Ashbel, Aug. 13, 1805–Jan. 21, 1886.
Vol. 9, Pt. 1–239
Smith, Azariah, Feb. 16, 1817–June 3, 1851.
Vol. 9, Pt. 1–240
Smith, Benjamin Eli, Feb. 7, 1857–Feb. 24, 1913.
Vol. 9, Pt. 1–241
Smith, Benjamin Mosby, June 30, 1811–Mar. 14, 1893.
Vol. 9, Pt. 1–242
Smith, Bessie, Apr. 15, 1894–Sept. 26, 1937.
Supp. 2–616
Smith, Betty, Dec. 19, 1896–Jan. 17, 1972.
Supp. 9–735
Smith, Bruce, May 23, 1892–Sept. 18, 1955.
Supp. 5–638
Smith, Buckingham, Oct. 31, 1810–Jan. 5, 1871.
Vol. 9, Pt. 1–243
Smith, Byron Caldwell, Aug. 28, 1849–May 4, 1877.
Vol. 9, Pt. 1–244
Smith, Caleb Blood, Apr. 16, 1808–Jan. 7, 1864.
Vol. 9, Pt. 1–244
Smith, Charles Alphonso, May 28, 1864–June 13, 1924.
Vol. 9, Pt. 1–245
Smith, Charles Emory, Feb. 18, 1842–Jan. 19, 1908.
Vol. 9, Pt. 1–246
Smith, Charles Ferguson, Apr. 24, 1807–Apr. 25, 1862.
Vol. 9, Pt. 1–247
Smith, Charles Forster, June 30, 1852–Aug. 3, 1931.
Vol. 9, Pt. 1–247
Smith, Charles Henry, June 15, 1826–Aug. 24, 1903.
Vol. 9, Pt. 1–248
Smith, Charles Henry, Nov. 1, 1827–July 17, 1902.
Vol. 9, Pt. 1–249
Smith, Charles Perrin, Jan. 5, 1819–Jan. 27, 1883.
Vol. 9, Pt. 1–250
Smith, Charles Shaler, Jan. 16, 1836–Dec. 19, 1886.
Vol. 9, Pt. 1–251
Smith, Charles Sprague, Apr. 27, 1853–Mar. 30, 1910.
Vol. 9, Pt. 1–252
Smith, Chauncey, Jan. 11, 1819–Apr. 5, 1895.
Vol. 9, Pt. 1–253
Smith, Courtney Craig, Dec. 20, 1916–Jan. 16, 1969.
Supp. 8–600
Smith, Daniel, Oct. 29, 1748–June 16, 1818.
Vol. 9, Pt. 1–254
Smith, Daniel B., July 14, 1792–Mar. 29, 1883.
Vol. 9, Pt. 1–255
Smith, David Eugene, Jan. 21, 1860–July 29, 1944.
Supp. 3–721
Smith, David Roland, Mar. 9, 1906–May 23, 1965.
Supp. 7–696
Smith, Edgar Fahs, May 23, 1854–May 3, 1928.
Vol. 9, Pt. 1–255
Smith, Edmund Kirby. [*See* Kirby-Smith, Edmund, 1824–1893.]
Smith, Edmund Munroe, Dec. 8, 1854–Apr. 13, 1926.
Vol. 9, Pt. 1–256
Smith, Edward Hanson, Oct. 29, 1889–Oct. 29, 1961.
Supp. 7–698
Smith, Eli, Sept. 13, 1801–Jan. 11, 1857.
Vol. 9, Pt. 1–257
Smith, Elias, June 17, 1769–June 29, 1846.
Vol. 9, Pt. 1–258
Smith, Elihu Hubbard, Sept. 4, 1771–Sept. 19, 1798.
Vol. 9, Pt. 1–259
Smith, Elizabeth Oakes Prince, Aug. 12, 1806–Nov. 15, 1893.
Vol. 9, Pt. 1–260
Smith, Eliza Roxey Snow. [*See* Snow, Eliza Roxey, 1804–1887.]
Smith, Ellison DuRant, Aug. 1, 1864–Nov. 17, 1944.
Supp. 3–722
Smith, Erasmus Darwin, Oct. 10, 1806–Nov. 11, 1883.
Vol. 9, Pt. 1–261
Smith, Erminnie Adelle Platt, Apr. 26, 1836–June 9, 1886.
Vol. 9, Pt. 1–262
Smith, Erwin Frink, Jan. 21, 1854–Apr. 6, 1927.
Vol. 9, Pt. 1–262
Smith, Eugene Allen, Oct. 27, 1841–Sept. 7, 1927.
Vol. 9, Pt. 1–263
Smith, Francis Henney, Oct. 18, 1812–Mar. 21, 1890.
Vol. 9, Pt. 1–264
Smith, Francis Hopkinson, Oct. 23, 1838–Apr. 7, 1915.
Vol. 9, Pt. 1–265
Smith, Francis Marion, Feb. 2, 1846–Aug. 27, 1931.
Vol. 9, Pt. 1–267
Smith, Frank Leslie, Nov. 24, 1867–Aug. 30, 1950.
Supp. 4–751
Smith, Fred Burton, Dec. 24, 1865–Sept. 4, 1936.
Supp. 2–617
Smith, George, Feb. 10, 1806–Oct. 7, 1899.
Vol. 9, Pt. 1–267
Smith, George Albert, Apr. 4, 1870–Apr 4, 1951.
Supp. 5–639
Smith, George Henry, Oct. 20, 1873–Jan. 9, 1931.
Vol. 9, Pt. 1–268
Smith, George Otis, Feb. 22, 1871–Jan. 10, 1944.
Supp. 3–724
Smith, Gerald Birney, May 3, 1868–Apr. 3, 1929.
Vol. 9, Pt. 1–269
Smith, Gerald L. K., Feb. 27, 1898–Apr. 15, 1976.
Supp. 10–744
Smith, Gerrit, Mar. 6, 1797–Dec. 28, 1874.
Vol. 9, Pt. 1–270
Smith, Giles Alexander, Sept. 29, 1829–Nov. 5, 1876.
Vol. 9, Pt. 1–271
Smith, Gustavus Woodson, Mar. 1822–June 24, 1896.
Vol. 9, Pt. 1–272
Smith, Hamilton, July 5, 1840–July 4, 1900.
Vol. 9, Pt. 1–273

Smith, Hannah Whitall, Feb. 7, 1832–May 1, 1911.
Vol. 9, Pt. 1–274
Smith, Harold Babbitt, May 23, 1869–Feb. 9, 1932.
Vol. 9, Pt. 1–275
Smith, Harold Dewey, June 6, 1898–Jan. 23, 1947.
Supp. 4–753
Smith, Harry Allen, Dec. 19, 1907–Feb. 24, 1976.
Supp. 10–746
Smith, Harry Bache, Dec. 28, 1860–Jan. 1, 1936.
Supp. 2–618
Smith, Harry James, May 24, 1880–Mar. 16, 1918.
Vol. 9, Pt. 1–276
Smith, Henry Augustus Middleton, Apr. 30, 1853–Nov. 23, 1924.
Vol. 9, Pt. 1–276
Smith, Henry Boynton, Nov. 21, 1815–Feb. 7, 1877.
Vol. 9, Pt. 1–277
Smith, Henry Justin, June 19, 1875–Feb. 9, 1936.
Supp. 2–619
Smith, Henry Louis, July 30, 1859–Feb. 27, 1951.
Supp. 5–641
Smith, Henry Preserved, Oct. 23, 1847–Feb. 26, 1927.
Vol. 9, Pt. 1–278
Smith, Hezekiah, Apr. 21, 1737–Jan. 24, 1805.
Vol. 9, Pt. 1–279
Smith, Hiram, Feb. 19, 1817–May 15, 1890.
Vol. 9, Pt. 1–280
Smith, Hoke, Sept. 2, 1855–Nov. 27, 1931.
Vol. 9, Pt. 1–280
Smith, Holland McTyeire, Apr. 20, 1882–Jan. 12, 1967.
Supp. 8–602
Smith, Homer William, Jan. 2, 1895–Mar. 25, 1962.
Supp. 7–699
Smith, Horace, Oct. 28, 1808–Jan. 15, 1893.
Vol. 9, Pt. 1–282
Smith, Horatio Elwin, May 8, 1886–Sept. 9, 1946.
Supp. 4–754
Smith, Horton, May 22, 1908–Oct. 15, 1963.
Supp. 7–700
Smith, Howard Worth ("Judge"), Feb. 2, 1883–Oct. 3, 1976.
Supp. 10–747
Smith, Israel, Apr. 6, 1759–Dec. 2, 1810.
Vol. 9, Pt. 1–283
Smith, James, *c.* 1759–July 11, 1806.
Vol. 9, Pt. 1–283
Smith, James, *c.* 1737–*c.* 1814.
Vol. 9, Pt. 1–284
Smith, James, June 12, 1851–Apr. 1, 1927.
Vol. 9, Pt. 1–285
Smith, James Allen, May 5, 1860–Jan. 30, 1924.
Vol. 9, Pt. 1–286
Smith, James Francis, Jan. 28, 1859–June 29, 1928.
Vol. 9, Pt. 1–287
Smith, James McCune, Apr. 18, 1813–Nov. 17, 1865.
Vol. 9, Pt. 1–288
Smith, James Perrin, Nov. 27, 1864–Jan. 1, 1931.
Vol. 9, Pt. 1–289
Smith, Jedediah Strong, June 24, 1798–May 27, 1831.
Vol. 9, Pt. 1–290
Smith, Jeremiah, Nov. 29, 1759–Sept. 21, 1842.
Vol. 9, Pt. 1–291
Smith, Jeremiah, July 14, 1837–Sept. 3, 1921.
Vol. 9, Pt. 1–292
Smith, Jeremiah, Jan. 14, 1870–Mar. 12, 1935.
Supp. 1–662
Smith, Job Lewis, Oct. 15, 1827–June 9, 1897.
Vol. 9, Pt. 1–293
Smith, Joel West, Sept. 17, 1837–May 9, 1924.
Vol. 9, Pt. 1–294
Smith, John, 1579/80–June 21, 1631.
Vol. 9, Pt. 1–294
Smith, John, *c.* 1735–*c.* 1824.
Vol. 9, Pt. 1–296
Smith, John Augustine, Aug. 29, 1782–Feb. 9, 1865.
Vol. 9, Pt. 1–297
Smith, John Bernhard, Nov. 21, 1858–Mar. 12, 1912.
Vol. 9, Pt. 1–298
Smith, John Blair, June 12, 1756–Aug. 22, 1799.
Vol. 9, Pt. 1–299
Smith, John Cotton, Feb. 12, 1765–Dec. 7, 1845.
Vol. 9, Pt. 1–300
Smith, John Cotton, Aug. 4, 1826–Jan. 9, 1882.
Vol. 9, Pt. 1–300
Smith, John Eugene, Aug. 3, 1816–Jan. 29, 1897.
Vol. 9, Pt. 1–301
Smith, John Gregory, July 22, 1818–Nov. 6, 1891.
Vol. 9, Pt. 1–302
Smith, John Jay, June 16, 1798–Sept. 23, 1881.
Vol. 9, Pt. 1–303
Smith, John Lawrence, Dec. 17, 1818–Oct. 12, 1883.
Vol. 9, Pt. 1–304
Smith, John Merlin Powis, Dec. 28, 1866–Sept. 26, 1932.
Vol. 9, Pt. 1–305
Smith, John Rowson, May 11, 1810–Mar. 21, 1864.
Vol. 9, Pt. 1–306
Smith, John Rubens, Jan. 23, 1775–Aug. 21, 1849.
Vol. 9, Pt. 1–307
Smith, Jonas Waldo, Mar. 9, 1861–Oct. 14, 1933.
Vol. 9, Pt. 1–307
Smith, Jonathan Bayard, Feb. 21, 1742–June 16, 1812.
Vol. 9, Pt. 1–308
Smith, Joseph, Mar. 30. 1790–Jan. 17, 1877.
Vol. 9, Pt. 1–309
Smith, Joseph, Dec. 23, 1805–June 27, 1844.
Vol. 9, Pt. 1–310
Smith, Joseph, Nov. 6, 1832–Dec. 10, 1914.
Vol. 9, Pt. 1–312
Smith, Joseph Fielding, Nov. 13, 1838–Nov. 19, 1918.
Vol. 9, Pt. 1–312
Smith, Joseph Fielding, July 19, 1876–July 2, 1972.
Supp. 9–736
Smith, Judson, June 28, 1837–June 29, 1906.
Vol. 9, Pt. 1–314
Smith, Julia Evelina, 1792–1886. [*See* Smith, Abby Hadassah, 1797–1878.]
Smith, Junius, Oct. 2, 1780–Jan. 22, 1853.
Vol. 9, Pt. 1–315
Smith, Justin Harvey, Jan. 13, 1857–Mar. 21, 1930.
Vol. 9, Pt. 1–316
Smith, Lillian Eugenia, Dec. 12, 1897–Sept. 28, 1966.
Supp. 8–604
Smith, Lloyd Logan Pearsall, Oct. 18, 1865–Mar. 2, 1946.
Supp. 4–755
Smith, Lloyd Pearsall, Feb. 6, 1822–July 2, 1886.
Vol. 9, Pt. 1–317
Smith, Lucy Harth, Jan. 24, 1888–Sept. 20, 1955.
Supp. 5–641
Smith, Marcus. Jan. 7, 1829–Aug. 11, 1874.
Vol. 9, Pt. 1–318
Smith, Margaret Bayard, Feb. 20, 1778–June 7, 1844.
Vol. 9, Pt. 1–318
Smith, Martin Luther, Sept. 9, 1819–July 29, 1866.
Vol. 9, Pt. 1–319
Smith, Melancton, May 7, 1744–July 29, 1798.
Vol. 9, Pt. 1–319
Smith, Melancton, May 24, 1810–July 19, 1893.
Vol. 9, Pt. 1–320
Smith, Meriwether, 1730–Jan. 24, 1794.
Vol. 9, Pt. 1–321
Smith, Mildred Catharine, Mar. 9, 1891–Aug. 30, 1973.
Supp. 9–738
Smith, Milton Hannibal, Sept. 12, 1836–Feb. 22, 1921.
Vol. 9, Pt. 1–322
Smith, Morgan Lewis, Mar. 8, 1821–Dec. 28, 1874.
Vol. 9, Pt. 1–323
Smith, Nathan, Sept. 30, 1762–Jan. 26, 1829.
Vol. 9, Pt. 1–324
Smith, Nathan, Jan. 8, 1770–Dec. 6, 1835.
Vol. 9, Pt. 1–327
Smith, Nathaniel, Jan. 6, 1762–Mar. 9, 1822.
Vol. 9, Pt. 1–329
Smith, Nathan Ryno, May 21, 1797–July 3, 1877.
Vol. 9, Pt. 1–327
Smith, Oliver, Jan. 20, 1766–Dec. 22, 1845.
Vol. 9, Pt. 1–329
Smith, Oliver Hampton, Oct. 23, 1794–Mar. 19, 1859.
Vol. 9, Pt. 1–330
Smith, Ormond Gerald, Aug. 30, 1860–Apr. 17, 1933.
Supp. 1–664
Smith, Persifor Frazer, Nov. 16, 1798–May 17, 1858.
Vol. 9, Pt. 1–331

Smith, Peter, Nov. 15, 1768–Apr. 14, 1837.
Vol. 9, Pt. 1–332
Smith, Preserved, July 22, 1880–May 15, 1941.
Supp. 3–725
Smith, Ralph Tyler, Oct. 6, 1915–Aug. 13, 1972.
Supp. 9–739
Smith, Richard, Mar. 22, 1735–Sept. 17, 1803.
Vol. 9, Pt. 1–332
Smith, Richard Penn, Mar. 13, 1799–Aug. 12, 1854.
Vol. 9, Pt. 1–333
Smith, Richard Somers, Oct. 30, 1813–Jan. 23, 1877.
Vol. 9, Pt. 1–334
Smith, Robert, *c.* 1722–Feb. 11, 1777.
Vol. 9, Pt. 1–335
Smith, Robert, Aug. 14, 1732 o.s.–Oct. 28, 1801.
Vol. 9, Pt. 1–336
Smith, Robert, Nov. 3, 1757–Nov. 26, 1842.
Vol. 9, Pt. 1–337
Smith, Robert Alexander C., Feb. 22, 1857–July 27, 1933.
Vol. 9, Pt. 1–338
Smith, Robert Barnwell. [*See* Rhett, Robert Barnwell, 1800–1876.]
Smith, Robert Hardy, Mar. 21, 1813–Mar. 13, 1878.
Vol. 9, Pt. 1–339
Smith, Robert Sidney, Feb. 13, 1877–Oct. 20, 1935.
Supp. 1–665
Smith, Roswell, Mar. 30, 1829–Apr. 19, 1892.
Vol. 9, Pt. 1–339
Smith, Russell, Apr. 26, 1812–Nov. 8, 1896.
Vol. 9, Pt. 1–340
Smith, Samuel, July 27, 1752–Apr. 22, 1839.
Vol. 9, Pt. 1–341
Smith, Samuel Francis, Oct. 21, 1808–Nov. 16, 1895.
Vol. 9, Pt. 1–342
Smith, Samuel Harrison, 1772–Nov. 1, 1845.
Vol. 9, Pt. 1–343
Smith, Samuel Stanhope, Mar. 16, 1750–Aug. 21, 1819.
Vol. 9, Pt. 1–344
Smith, Seba, Sept. 14, 1792–July 28, 1868.
Vol. 9, Pt. 1–345
Smith, Solomon Franklin, Apr. 20, 1801–Feb. 14, 1869.
Vol. 9, Pt. 1–346
Smith, Sophia, Aug. 27, 1796–June 12, 1870.
Vol. 9, Pt. 1–347
Smith, Stephen, Feb. 19, 1823–Aug. 26, 1922.
Vol. 9, Pt. 1–348
Smith, Theobald, July 31, 1859–Dec. 10, 1934.
Supp. 1–665
Smith, Theodate Louise, Apr. 9, 1859–Feb. 16, 1914.
Vol. 9, Pt. 1–349
Smith, Thomas Adams, Aug. 12, 1781–June 25, 1844.
Supp. 1–667
Smith, Thomas Vernor, Apr. 26, 1890–May 24, 1964.
Supp. 7–701
Smith, Truman, Nov. 27, 1791–May 3, 1884.
Vol. 9, Pt. 1–350
Smith, Uriah, May 2, 1832–Mar. 6, 1903.
Vol. 9, Pt. 1–350
Smith, Walter Bedell, Oct. 5, 1895–Aug. 9, 1961.
Supp. 7–702
Smith, Walter Inglewood, July 10, 1862–Jan. 27, 1922.
Vol. 9, Pt. 1–351
Smith, William, Oct. 8, 1697–Nov. 22, 1769.
Vol. 9, Pt. 1–352
Smith, William, Sept. 7, 1727–May 14, 1803.
Vol. 9, Pt. 1–353
Smith, William, June 25, 1728–Dec. 3, 1793.
Vol. 9, Pt. 1–357
Smith, William, *c.* 1754–Apr. 6, 1821.
Vol. 9, Pt. 1–358
Smith, William, *c.* 1762–June 26, 1840.
Vol. 9, Pt. 1–359
Smith, William, Sept. 6, 1797–May 18, 1887.
Vol. 9, Pt. 1–361
Smith, William Andrew, Nov. 29, 1802–Mar. 1, 1870.
Vol. 9, Pt. 1–361
Smith, William Eugene, Dec. 30, 1918–Oct. 15, 1978.
Supp. 10–749
Smith, William Farrar, Feb. 17, 1824–Feb. 28, 1903.
Vol. 9, Pt. 1–362
Smith, William Henry, Dec. 4, 1806–Jan. 17, 1872.
Vol. 9, Pt. 1–363
Smith, William Henry, Dec. 1, 1833–July 27, 1896.
Vol. 9, Pt. 1–364
Smith, William Loughton, *c.* 1758–Dec. 19, 1812.
Vol. 9, Pt. 1–365
Smith, William Nathan Harrell, Sept. 24, 1812–Nov. 14, 1889.
Vol. 9, Pt. 1–366
Smith, William Russell, Mar. 27, 1815–Feb. 26, 1896.
Vol. 9, Pt. 1–366
Smith, William Sooy, July 22, 1830–Mar. 4, 1916.
Vol. 9, Pt. 1–367
Smith, William Stephens, Nov. 8, 1755–June 10, 1816.
Vol. 9, Pt. 1–368
Smith, William Waugh, Mar. 12, 1845–Nov. 29, 1912.
Vol. 9, Pt. 1–369
Smith, Winchell, Apr. 5, 1871–June 10, 1933.
Vol. 9, Pt. 1–370
Smith, Xanthus Russell, Feb. 26, 1839–Dec. 2, 1929.
Vol. 9, Pt. 1–371
Smith James Youngs, Sept. 15, 1809–Mar. 26, 1876.
Vol. 9, Pt. 1–289
Smohalla, *c.* 1815–1907.
Vol. 9, Pt. 1–371
Smoot, Reed Owen, Jan. 10, 1862–Feb. 9, 1941.
Supp. 3–726
Smyth, Albert Henry, June 18, 1863–May 4, 1907.
Vol. 9, Pt. 1–372
Smyth, Alexander, 1765–Apr. 17, 1830.
Vol. 9, Pt. 1–373
Smyth, Egbert Coffin, Aug. 24, 1829–Apr. 12, 1904.
Vol. 9, Pt. 1–374
Smyth, Herbert Weir, Aug. 8, 1857–July 16, 1937.
Supp. 2–620
Smyth, John Henry, July 14, 1844–Sept. 5, 1908.
Vol. 9, Pt. 1–375
Smyth, Julian Kennedy, Aug. 8, 1856–Apr. 4, 1921.
Vol. 9, Pt. 1–376
Smyth, Newman, June 25, 1843–Jan. 6, 1925.
Vol. 9, Pt. 1–376
Smyth, Thomas, June 14, 1808–Aug. 20, 1873.
Vol. 9, Pt. 1–377
Smyth, William, Feb. 2, 1797–Apr. 4, 1868.
Vol. 9, Pt. 1–378
Snead, Thomas Lowndes, Jan. 10, 1828–Oct. 17, 1890.
Vol. 9, Pt. 1–379
Snell, Bertrand Hollis, Dec. 9, 1870–Feb. 2, 1958.
Supp. 6–587
Snelling, Henry Hunt, Nov. 8, 1817–June 24, 1897.
Vol. 9, Pt. 1–379
Snelling, Josiah, 1782–Aug. 20, 1828.
Vol. 9, Pt. 1–380
Snelling, William Joseph, Dec. 26, 1804–Dec. 24, 1848.
Vol. 9, Pt. 1–381
Snethen, Nicholas, Nov. 15, 1769–May 30, 1845.
Vol. 9, Pt. 1–382
Snider, Denton Jaques, Jan. 9, 1841–Nov. 25, 1925.
Vol. 9, Pt. 1–383
Snow, Carmel White, Aug. 21, 1887–May 7, 1961.
Supp. 7–704
Snow, Edgar Parkes, July 19, 1905–Feb. 15, 1972.
Supp. 9–740
Snow, Eliza Roxey, Jan. 21, 1804–Dec. 5, 1887.
Vol. 9, Pt. 1–384
Snow, Francis Huntington, June 29, 1840–Sept. 20, 1908.
Vol. 9, Pt. 1–385
Snow, Jessie Baker, May 26, 1868–June 16, 1947.
Supp. 4–756
Snow, John Ben, June 16, 1883–Jan. 21, 1973.
Supp. 9–741
Snow, Lorenza, Apr. 3, 1814–Oct. 10, 1901.
Vol. 9, Pt. 1–386
Snow, William Freeman, July 13, 1874–June 12, 1950.
Supp. 4–758
Snowden, James Ross, Dec. 9, 1809–Mar. 21, 1878.
Vol. 9, Pt. 1–387
Snowden, Thomas, Aug. 12, 1857–Jan. 27, 1930.
Vol. 9, Pt. 1–387
Snyder, Edwin Reagan, Sept. 2, 1872–Jan. 13, 1925.
Vol. 9, Pt. 1–388

Snyder, Howard McCrum, Feb. 7, 1881–Sept. 22, 1970.
Supp. 8–608
Snyder, John Francis, Mar. 22, 1830–Apr. 30, 1921.
Vol. 9, Pt. 1–389
Snyder, Simon, Nov. 5, 1759–Nov. 9, 1819.
Vol. 9, Pt. 1–389
Sobeloff, Simon E., Dec. 3, 1895–July 11, 1973.
Supp. 9–743
Sobolewski, J. Friedrich Eduard, Oct. 1, 1808–May 17, 1872.
Vol. 9, Pt. 1–390
Sokolsky, George Ephraim, Sept. 5, 1893–Dec. 12, 1962.
Supp. 7–705
Soldan, Frank Louis, Oct. 20, 1842–Mar. 27, 1908.
Vol. 9, Pt. 1–391
Soley, James Russell, Oct. 1, 1850–Sept. 11, 1911.
Vol. 9, Pt. 1–392
Solger, Reinhold, July 17, 1817–Jan. 11, 1866.
Vol. 9, Pt. 1–392
Solis-Cohen, Jacob Da Silva. [*See* Cohen, Jacob Da Silva Solis, 1838–1927.]
Solomons, Adolphus Simeon, Oct. 26, 1826–Mar. 18, 1910.
Vol. 9, Pt. 1–393
Somers, Richard, Sept. 15, 1778–Sept. 4, 1804.
Vol. 9, Pt. 1–394
Somervell, Brehon Burke, May 9, 1892–Feb. 13, 1955.
Supp. 5–642
Sonneck, Oscar George Theodore, Oct. 6, 1873–Oct. 30, 1928.
Vol. 9, Pt. 1–395
Sonnichsen, Albert, May 5, 1878–Aug. 15, 1931.
Vol. 9, Pt. 1–396
Son of Many Beads, *c.* 1866–July 30, 1954.
Supp. 5–644
Sooysmith, Charles, July 20, 1856–June 1, 1916.
Vol. 9, Pt. 1–397
Sophocles, Evangelinus Apostolides, *c.* 1805–Dec. 17, 1883.
Vol. 9, Pt. 1–397
Sorensen, Charles, Sept. 27, 1881–Aug. 13, 1968.
Supp. 8–609
Sorge, Friedrich Adolph, Nov. 9, 1828–Oct. 26, 1906.
Vol. 9, Pt. 1–398
Sorin, Edward Frederick, Feb. 6, 1814–Oct. 31, 1893.
Vol. 9, Pt. 1–399
Sothern, Edward Askew, Apr. 1, 1826–Jan. 20, 1881.
Vol. 9, Pt. 1–400
Sothern, Edward Hugh, Dec. 6, 1859–Oct. 28, 1933.
Vol. 9, Pt. 1–401
Soto, Hernando De. [*See* De Soto, Hernando, *c.* 1500–1542.]
Souchon, Edmond, Dec. 1, 1841–Aug. 5, 1924.
Vol. 9, Pt. 1–402
Soulé, George, May 14, 1834–Jan. 26, 1926.
Vol. 9, Pt. 1–403
Soule, Joshua, Aug. 1, 1781–Mar. 6, 1867.
Vol. 9, Pt. 1–404
Soulé, Pierre, Aug. 31, 1801–Mar. 26, 1870.
Vol. 9, Pt. 1–405
Sousa, John Philip, Nov. 6, 1854–Mar. 6, 1932.
Vol. 9, Pt. 1–407
Southack, Cyprian, Mar. 25, 1662–Mar. 27, 1745.
Vol. 9 Pt. 1–408
Southall, James Cocke, Apr. 2, 1828–Sept. 13, 1897.
Vol. 9, Pt. 1–409
Southard, Elmer Ernest, July 28, 1876–Feb. 8, 1920.
Vol. 9, Pt. 1–410
Southard, Lucien H., Feb. 4, 1827–Jan. 10, 1881.
Vol. 9, Pt. 1–411
Southard, Samuel Lewis, June 9, 1787–June 26, 1842.
Vol. 9, Pt. 1–411
Southern, Julia Marlowe. [*See* Marlowe, Julia, 1866–1950.]
Southgate, Horatio, July 5, 1812–Apr. 12, 1894.
Supp. 1–668
Southmayd, Charles Ferdinand, Nov. 27, 1824–July 11, 1911.
Vol. 9, Pt. 1–412
Southwick, Solomon, Dec. 25, 1773–Nov. 18, 1839.
Vol. 9, Pt. 1–413
Southworth, Emma Dorothy Eliza Nevitte, Dec. 26, 1819–June 30, 1899.
Vol. 9, Pt. 1–414
Sower, Christopher, 1693–Sept. 25, 1758.
Vol. 9, Pt. 1–415
Sower, Christopher, September 1721–Aug. 26, 1784.
Vol. 9, Pt. 1–416
Sower, Christopher, Jan 27, 1754–July 3, 1799.
Vol. 9, Pt. 1–417
Soyer, Moses, Dec. 25, 1899–Sept. 2, 1974.
Supp. 9–744
Spaatz, Carl Andrew ("Tooey"), June 28, 1891–July 14, 1974.
Supp. 9–746
Spaeth, Adolph, Oct. 29, 1839–June 25, 1910.
Vol. 9, Pt. 1–418
Spaeth, John Duncan, Sept. 27, 1868–July 26, 1954.
Supp. 5–645
Spaeth, Sigmund, Apr. 10, 1885–Nov. 11, 1965.
Supp. 7–706
Spahr, Charles Barzillai, July 20, 1860–Aug 30, 1904.
Vol. 9, Pt. 1–418
Spaight, Richard Dobbs, Mar. 25, 1758–Sept. 6, 1802.
Vol. 9, Pt. 1–419
Spalding, Albert, Aug. 15, 1888–May 26, 1953.
Supp. 5–646
Spalding, Albert Goodwill, Sept. 2, 1850–Sept. 9, 1915.
Vol. 9, Pt. 1–420
Spalding, Catherine, Dec. 23, 1793–Mar. 20, 1858.
Vol. 9, Pt. 1–421
Spalding, Franklin Spencer, Mar. 13, 1865–Sept. 25, 1914.
Vol. 9, Pt. 1–422
Spalding, John Lancaster, June 2, 1840–Aug. 25, 1916.
Vol. 9, Pt. 1–422
Spalding, Lyman, June 5, 1775–Oct. 21, 1821.
Vol. 9, Pt. 1–423
Spalding, Martin John, May 23, 1810–Feb. 7, 1872.
Vol. 9, Pt. 1–424
Spalding, Thomas, Mar. 26, 1774–Jan. 4, 1851.
Vol. 9, Pt. 1–426
Spalding, Volney Morgan, Jan. 29, 1849–Nov. 12, 1918.
Vol. 9, Pt. 1–427
Spangenberg, Augustus Gottlieb, July 15, 1704–Sept. 18, 1792.
Vol. 9, Pt. 1–428
Spangler, Edward. [*See* Booth, John Wilkes, 1838–1865.]
Spangler, Henry Wilson, Jan. 18, 1858–Mar. 17, 1912.
Vol. 9, Pt. 1–429
Spargo, John, Jan. 31, 1876–Aug. 17, 1966.
Supp. 8–10
Sparks, Edwin Erle, July 16, 1860–June 15, 1924.
Vol. 9, Pt. 1–430
Sparks, Jared, May 10, 1789–Mar. 147 1866.
Vol. 9, Pt. 1–430
Sparks, William Andrew Jackson, Nov. 19, 1828–May 7, 1904.
Vol. 9, Pt. 1–434
Sparrow, William, Mar. 12, 1801–Jan. 17, 1874.
Vol. 9, Pt. 1–435
Spaulding, Charles Clinton, Aug. 1, 1874–Aug. 1, 1952.
Supp. 5–647
Spaulding, Edward Gleason, Aug. 6, 1873–Jan. 31, 1940.
Supp. 2–621
Spaulding, Elbridge Gerry, Feb. 24, 1809–May 5, 1897.
Vol. 9, Pt. 1–436
Spaulding, Levi, Aug. 22, 1791–June 18, 1873.
Vol. 9, Pt. 1–437
Spaulding, Oliver Lyman, Aug. 2, 1833–July 30, 1922.
Vol. 9, Pt. 1–438
Speaker, Tris E., Apr. 4, 1888–Dec. 8, 1958.
Supp. 6–588
Speaks, Oley, June 28, 1874–Aug. 27, 1948.
Supp. 4–759
Spear, Charles, May 1, 1801–Apr. 13, 1863.
Vol. 4, Pt. 1–438
Spear, William Thomas, June 3, 1834–Dec. 8, 1913.
Vol. 9, Pt. 1–439
Speck, Frank Gouldsmith, Nov. 8, 1881–Feb. 6, 1950.
Supp. 4–761
Speed, James, Mar. 11, 1812–June 25, 1887.
Vol. 9, Pt. 1–440
Speer, Emma Bailey, May 15, 1872–Apr. 25, 1961.
Supp. 7–707
Speer, Emory, Sept. 3, 1848–Dec. 13, 1918.
Vol. 4, Pt. 1–441
Speer, Robert Elliott, Sept. 10, 1867–Nov. 23, 1947.
Supp. 4–763

Speer, William, Apr. 24, 1822–Feb. 15, 1904.
Vol. 9, Pt. 1–442
Speir, Samuel Fleet, Apr. 9, 1838–Dec. 19, 1895.
Vol. 9, Pt. 1–443
Speiser, Ephraim Avigdor, Jan. 24, 1902–June 15, 1965.
Supp. 7–709
Spellman, Francis Joseph, May 4, 1889–Dec. 2, 1967.
Supp. 8–612
Spence, Brent, Dec. 24, 1874–Sept. 18, 1967.
Supp. 8–615
Spencer, Ambrose, Dec. 13, 1765–Mar. 13, 1848.
Vol. 9, Pt. 1–443
Spencer, Anna Garlin, Apr. 17, 1851–Feb. 12, 1931.
Vol. 4, Pt. 1–445
Spencer, Christopher Miner, June 20, 1833–Jan. 14, 1922.
Vol. 9, Pt. 1–446
Spencer, Cornelia Phillips, Mar. 20, 1825–Mar. 11, 1908.
Vol. 9, Pt. 1–447
Spencer, Elihu, Feb. 12, 1721–Dec. 27, 1784.
Vol. 9, Pt. 1–447
Spencer, Jesse Ames, June 17, 1816–Sept. 2, 1898.
Vol. 9, Pt. 1–448
Spencer, John Canfield, Jan. 8, 1788–May 17, 1855.
Vol. 9, Pt. 1–449
Spencer, Joseph, Oct. 3, 1714–Jan. 13, 1789.
Vol. 9, Pt. 1–450
Spencer, Pitman Clemens, July 28, 1793–Jan. 15, 1860.
Vol. 9, Pt. 1–451
Spencer, Platt Rogers, Nov. 7, 1800–May 16, 1864.
Vol. 9, Pt. 1–451
Spencer, Robert, Dec. 1, 1879–July 10, 1931.
Vol. 9, Pt. 1–452
Spencer, Samuel, Mar. 2, 1847–Nov. 29, 1906.
Vol. 9, Pt. 1–453
Sperry, Elmer Ambrose, Oct. 12, 1860–June 16, 1930.
Vol. 9, Pt. 1–454
Sperry, Nehemiah Day, July 10, 1827–Nov. 13, 1911.
Vol. 9, Pt. 1–456
Sperry, WiLlard Learoyd, Apr. 5, 1882–May 15, 1954.
Supp. 5–648
Spewack, Samuel, Sept. 16, 1899–Oct. 14, 1971.
Supp. 9–747
Speyer, James Joseph, July 22, 1861–Oct. 31, 1941.
Supp. 3–728
Spicker, Max, Aug. 16, 1858–Oct. 15, 1912.
Vol. 9, Pt. 1–456
Spier, Leslie, Dec. 13, 1893–Dec. 3, 1961.
Supp. 7–710
Spiering, Theodore, Sept. 5, 1871–Aug. 11, 1925.
Vol. 9, Pt. 1–457
Spillman, William Jasper, Oct. 23, 1863–July 11, 1931.
Vol. 9, Pt. 1–458
Spilsbury, Edmund Gybbon, Dec. 7, 1845–May 28, 1920.
Vol. 9, Pt. 1–459
Spingarn, Arthur Barnett, Mar. 28, 1878–Dec. 1, 1971.
Supp. 9–749
Spingarn, Joel Elias, May 17, 1875–July 26, 1939.
Supp. 2–622
Spink, John George Taylor, Nov. 6, 1888–Dec. 7, 1962.
Supp. 7–711
Spinner, Francis Elias, Jan. 21, 1802–Dec. 31, 1890.
Vol. 9, Pt. 1–460
Spitzka, Edward Anthony, June 17, 1876–Sept. 4, 1922.
Vol. 9, Pt. 1–461
Spitzka, Edward Charles, Nov. 10, 1852–Jan. 13, 1914.
Vol. 9, Pt. 1–461
Spivak, Charles David, Dec. 25, 1861–Oct. 16, 1927.
Vol. 9, Pt. 1–462
Spofford, Ainsworth Rand, Sept. 12, 1825–Aug. 11, 1908.
Vol. 9, Pt. 1–463
Spofford, Harriet Elizabeth Prescott, Apr. 3, 1835–Aug. 14, 1921.
Vol. 9, Pt. 1–464
Spooner, John Coit, Jan. 6, 1843–June 11, 1919.
Vol. 9, Pt. 1–465
Spooner, Lysander, Jan. 19, 1808–May 14, 1887.
Vol. 9, Pt. 1–466
Spooner, Shearjashub, Dec 3, 1809–Mar. 14, 1859.
Vol. 9, Pt. 1–467
Sporn, Philip, Nov. 25, 1896–Jan. 23, 1978.
Supp. 10–750
Spotswood, Alexander, 1676–June 7, 1740.
Vol. 9, Pt. 1–467
Spotted Tail, *c.* 1833–Aug. 5, 1881.
Vol. 9, Pt. 1–469
Spottswood, Stephen Gill, July 1897–Dec. 1, 1974.
Supp. 9–750
Sprague, Achsa W., *c.* 1828–July 6, 1862.
Vol. 9, Pt. 1–469
Sprague, Charles, Oct. 26, 1791–Jan. 22, 1875.
Vol. 9, Pt. 1–470
Sprague, Charles Arthur, Nov. 12, 1887–Mar. 13, 1969.
Supp. 8–616
Sprague, Charles Ezra, Oct. 9, 1842–Mar. 21, 1912.
Vol. 9, Pt. 1–471
Sprague, Frank Julian, July 25, 1857–Oct. 25, 1934.
Supp. 1–669
Sprague, Homer Baxter, Oct. 19, 1829–Mar. 23, 1918.
Vol. 9, Pt. 1–472
Sprague, Kate Chase, Aug. 13, 1840–July 31, 1899.
Vol. 9, Pt. 1–473
Sprague, Oliver Mitchell Wentworth, Apr. 22, 1873–May 24, 1953.
Supp. 5–650
Sprague, Peleg, Apr. 27, 1793–Oct. 13, 1880.
Vol. 9, Pt. 1–473
Sprague, William, June 5, 1773–Mar. 28, 1836.
Vol. 9, Pt. 1–474
Sprague, William, Sept. 12, 1830–Sept. 11, 1915.
Vol. 9, Pt. 1–475
Sprague, William Buell, Oct. 16, 1795–May 7, 1876.
Vol. 9, Pt. 1–476
Sprecher, Samuel, Dec. 28, 1810–Jan. 10, 1906.
Vol. 9, Pt. 1–477
Spreckels, Claus, July 9, 1828–Dec. 26, 1908.
Vol. 9, Pt. 1–478
Spreckels, John Diedrich, Aug. 16, 1853–June 7, 1926.
Vol. 9, Pt. 1–479
Spreckels, Rudolph, Jan. 1, 1872–Oct. 4, 1958.
Supp. 6–590
Spring, Gardiner, Feb. 24, 1785–Aug. 18, 1873.
Vol. 9, Pt. 1–479
Spring, Leverett Wilson, Jan. 5, 1840–Dec. 23, 1917.
Vol. 9, Pt. 1–480
Spring, Samuel, Feb. 27, 1746 o.s.–Mar. 4, 1819.
Vol. 9, Pt. 1–481
Springer, Charles, Dec. 19, 1857–Feb. 12, 1932.
Supp. 1–670
Springer, Frank, June 17, 1848–Sept. 22, 1927.
Vol. 9, Pt. 1–482
Springer, Reuben Runyan, Nov. 16, 1800–Dec. 11, 1884.
Vol. 9, Pt. 1–482
Springer, William McKendree, May 30, 1836–Dec. 4, 1903
Vol. 9, Pt. 1–483
Sproul, Allan, Mar. 9, 1896–Apr. 9, 1978.
Supp. 10–752
Sproul, Robert Gordon, May 22, 1891–Sept. 10, 1975.
Supp. 9–752
Sproul, William Cameron, Sept. 16, 1870–Mar. 21, 1928.
Vol. 9, Pt. 1–484
Sproule, William, Nov. 25, 1858–Jan. 1, 1935.
Supp. 1–671
Sproull, Thomas, Sept. 15, 1803–Mar. 21, 1892.
Vol. 9, Pt. 1–485
Spruance, Raymond Ames, July 3, 1886–Dec. 13, 1969.
Supp. 8–618
Sprunt, James, June 9, 1846–July 9, 1924.
Vol. 9, Pt. 1–486
Spurr, Josiah Edward, Oct. 1, 1870–Jan. 12, 1950.
Supp. 4–764
Squanto, d. 1622.
Vol. 9, Pt. 1–487
Squibb, Edward Robinson, July 4, 1819–Oct. 25, 1900.
Vol. 9, Pt. 1–487
Squier, Ephraim George, June 17, 1821–Apr. 17, 1888.
Vol. 9, Pt. 1–488
Squier, George Owen, Mar. 21, 1865–Mar. 24, 1934.
Vol. 9, Pt. 1–489
Squiers, Herbert Goldsmith, Apr. 20, 1859–Oct. 20, 1911.
Vol. 9, Pt. 1–490
Squire, Watson Carvosso, May 18, 1838–June 7, 1926.
Vol. 9, Pt. 1–491

Stacy, Walter Parker, Dec. 26, 1884–Sept. 13, 1951.
Supp. 5–651
Stager, Anson, Apr. 20, 1825–Mar. 26, 1885.
Vol. 9, Pt. 1–492
Stagg, Amos Alonzo, Aug. 16, 1862–Mar. 17, 1965.
Supp. 7–712
Stahel, Julius, Nov. 5, 1825–Dec. 4, 1912.
Vol. 9, Pt. 1–493
Stahlman, Edward Bushrod, Sept. 2, 1843–Aug. 12, 1930.
Vol. 9, Pt. 1–493
Stahr, John Summers, Dec. 2, 1841–Dec. 21, 1915.
Vol. 9, Pt. 1–494
Staley, Cady, Dec. 12, 1840–June 27, 1928.
Vol. 9, Pt. 1–495
Stallings, Laurence Tucker, Nov. 24, 1894–Feb. 28, 1968.
Supp. 8–621
Stallo, Johann Bernhard, Mar. 16, 1823–Jan. 6, 1900.
Vol. 9, Pt. 1–496
Stanard, Mary Mann Page Newton, Aug. 15, 1865–June 5, 1929.
Vol. 9, Pt. 1–497
Stanard, William Glover, Oct. 2, 1858–May 6, 1933.
Vol. 9, Pt. 1–497
Stanbery, Henry, Feb. 20, 1803–June 26, 1881.
Vol. 9, Pt. 1–498
Stanchfield, John Barry, Mar. 30, 1855–June 25, 1921.
Vol. 9, Pt. 1–499
Standerren, Ann Lees. [*See* Lee, Ann, 1736–1784.]
Standish, Burt L. [*See* Patten, Gilbert, 1866–1945.]
Standish, Myles, *c.* 1584–Oct. 3, 1656.
Vol. 9, Pt. 1–500
Standley, William Harrison, Dec. 18, 1872–Oct. 25, 1963.
Supp. 7–713
Stanford, John, Oct. 20, 1754–Jan. 14, 1834.
Vol. 9, Pt. 1–500
Stanford, Leland, Mar. 9, 1824–June 21, 1895.
Vol. 9, Pt. 1–501
Stang, William, Apr. 21, 1854–Feb. 2, 1907.
Vol. 9, Pt. 1–506
Stanley, Albert Augustus, May 25, 1851–May 19, 1932.
Vol. 9, Pt. 1–506
Stanley, Ann Lee. [*See* Lee, Ann, 1736–1784.]
Stanley, Augustus Owsley, May 21, 1867–Aug. 12, 1958.
Supp. 6–591
Stanley, David Sloane, June 1, 1828–Mar. 13, 1902.
Vol. 9, Pt. 1–507
Stanley, Francis Edgar, June 1, 1849–July 31, 1918.
Vol. 9, Pt. 1–508
Stanley, Harold, Oct. 2, 1885–May 14, 1963.
Supp. 7–714
Stanley, Henry Morton, 1841–May 10, 1904.
Vol. 9, Pt. 1–509
Stanley, John Mix, Jan. 17, 1814–Apr. 10, 1872.
Vol. 9, Pt. 1–513
Stanley, Robert Crooks, Aug. 1, 1876–Feb. 12, 1951.
Supp. 5–652
Stanley, Wendell Meredith, Aug. 16, 1904–June 15, 1971.
Supp. 9–753
Stanley, William, Nov. 22, 1858–May 14, 1916.
Vol. 9, Pt. 1–514
Stanly, Edward, July 13, 1810–July 12, 1872.
Vol. 9, Pt. 1–515
Stansbury, Howard, Feb. 8, 1806–Apr. 17, 1863.
Vol. 9, Pt. 1–516
Stansbury, Joseph, Jan. 9, 1742 o.s.?–Nov. 9, 1809.
Vol. 9, Pt. 2–516
Stanton, Edwin McMasters, Dec. 19, 1814–Dec. 24, 1869
Vol. 9, Pt. 1–517
Stanton, Elizabeth Cady, Nov. 12, 1815–Oct. 26, 1902.
Vol. 9, Pt. 1–521
Stanton, Frank Lebby, Feb 22, 1857–Jan. 7, 1927.
Vol. 9, Pt. 1–523
Stanton, Frederick Perry, Dec. 22, 1814–June 4, 1894.
Vol. 9, Pt. 1–523
Stanton, Henry Brewster, June 27, 1805–Jan. 14, 1887.
Vol. 9, Pt. 1–524
Stanton, Richard Henry, Sept. 9, 1812–Mar. 20, 1891.
Vol. 9, Pt. 1–525
Stanwood, Edward, Sept. 16, 1841–Oct. 11, 1923.
Vol. 9, Pt. 1–526
Staples, Waller Redd, Feb. 24, 1826–Aug. 20, 1897.
Vol. 9, Pt. 1–527
Staples, William Read, Oct. 10, 1798–Oct. 19, 1868.
Vol. 9, Pt. 1–528
Starbuck, Edwin Diller, Feb. 20, 1866–Nov. 19, 1947.
Supp. 4–766
Starin, John Henry, Aug. 27, 1825–Mar. 22, 1909.
Vol. 9, Pt. 1–529
Stark, Edward Josef, Apr. 29, 1858–Apr. 22, 1918.
Vol. 9, Pt. 1–530
Stark, Harold Raynsford, Nov. 12, 1880–Aug. 20, 1972.
Supp. 9–754
Stark, John, Aug. 28, 1728–May 8, 1822.
Vol. 9, Pt. 1–530
Stark, Lloyd Crow, Nov. 23, 1886–Sept. 17, 1972.
Supp. 9–756
Stark, Louis, May 1, 1888–May 17, 1954.
Supp. 5–653
Starks, Edwin Chapin, Jan. 25, 1867–Dec. 30, 1932.
Supp. 1–672
Starr, Eliza Allen, Aug. 29, 1824–Sept. 7, 1901.
Vol. 9, Pt. 1–531
Starr, Frederick, Sept. 2, 1858–Aug. 14, 1933.
Vol. 9, Pt. 1–532
Starr, Louis, Apr. 25, 1849–Sept. 12, 1925.
Vol. 9, Pt. 1–533
Starr, Merritt, Feb. 27, 1856–Aug. 2, 1931.
Vol. 9, Pt. 1–534
Starr, Moses Allen, May 16, 1854–Sept. 4, 1932.
Vol. 9, Pt. 1–534
Starrett, Laroy S., Apr. 25, 1836–Apr. 23, 1922.
Vol. 9, Pt. 1–535
Starrett, Paul, Nov. 25, 1866–July 5, 1957.
Supp. 6–592
Starrett, William Aiken, June 14, 1877–Mar. 26, 1932.
Vol. 9, Pt. 1–536
Statler, Ellsworth Milton, Oct. 26, 1863–Apr. 16, 1928.
Vol. 9, Pt. 1–537
Stauffer, David McNeely, Mar. 24, 1845–Feb. 5, 1913.
Vol. 9, Pt. 1–538
Staughton, William, Jan. 4, 1770–Dec. 12, 1829.
Vol. 9, Pt. 1–539
Stayton, John William, Dec. 24, 1830–July 5, 1894.
Vol. 9, Pt. 1–540
Steagall, Henry Bascom, May 19, 1873–Nov. 22, 1943.
Supp. 3–729
Stearman, Lloyd Carlton, Oct. 26, 1898–Apr. 3, 1975.
Supp. 9–757
Stearns, Abel, Feb. 9, 1798–Aug. 23, 1871.
Vol. 9, Pt. 1–540
Stearns, Asahel, June 17, 1774–Feb. 5, 1839.
Vol. 9, Pt. 1–541
Stearns, Eben Sperry, Dec. 23, 1819–Apr. 11, 1887.
Vol. 9, Pt. 1–542
Stearns, Frank Ballou, Nov. 6, 1878–July 5, 1955.
Supp. 5–654
Stearns, Frank Waterman, Nov. 8, 1856–Mar. 6, 1939.
Supp. 2–623
Stearns, Frederic Pike, Nov. 11, 1851–Dec. 1, 1919.
Vol. 9, Pt. 1–542
Stearns, George Luther, Jan. 8, 1809–Apr. 9, 1867.
Vol. 9, Pt. 1–543
Stearns, Harold Edmund, May 7, 1891–Aug. 13, 1943.
Supp. 3–730
Stearns, Henry Putnam, Apr. 18, 1828–May 27, 1905.
Vol. 9, Pt. 1–544
Stearns, Irving Ariel, Sept. 12, 1845–Oct. 5, 1920.
Vol. 9, Pt. 1–545
Stearns, John Newton, May 24, 1829–Apr. 21, 1895.
Vol. 9, Pt. 1–546
Stearns, Oliver, June 3, 1807–July 18, 1885.
Vol. 9, Pt. 1–546
Stearns, Robert Edwards Carter, Feb. 1, 1827–July 27, 1909.
Vol. 9, Pt. 1–547
Stearns, Shubal, Jan. 28, 1706–Nov. 20, 1771.
Vol. 9, Pt. 1–548
Stearns, William Augustus, Mar. 17, 1805–June 8, 1876.
Vol. 9, Pt. 1–549
Stebbins, Horatio, Aug. 8, 1821–Apr. 8, 1902.
Vol. 9. Pt. 1–549

Stebbins, Rufus Phineas, Mar. 3, 1810–Aug. 13, 1885.
Vol. 9, Pt. 1–550
Steck, George, July 19, 1829–Mar. 31, 1897.
Vol. 9, Pt. 1–551
Stedman, Edmund Clarence, Oct. 8, 1833–Jan. 18, 1908.
Vol. 9, Pt. 1–552
Steedman, Charles, Sept. 20, 1811–Nov. 13, 1890.
Vol. 9, Pt. 1–553
Steedman, James Blair, July 29, 1817–Oct. 18, 1883.
Vol. 9, Pt. 1–554
Steele, Daniel, Oct. 5, 1824–Sept. 2, 1914.
Vol. 9, Pt. 1–555
Steele, Frederick, Jan. 14, 1819–Jan. 12, 1868.
Vol. 9, Pt. 1–555
Steele, Joel Dorman, May 14, 1836–May 25, 1886.
Vol. 9, Pt. 1–556
Steele, John, Nov. 16, 1764–Aug. 14, 1815.
Vol. 9, Pt. 1–557
Steele, Wilbur Daniel, Mar. 17, 1886–May 26, 1970.
Supp. 8–622
Steendam, Jacob, 1616–*c.* 1672.
Vol. 9, Pt. 1–557
Steenwijck, Cornelis Van. [*See* Steenwyck, Cornelis, d. 1684.]
Steenwyck, Cornelis, d. 1684.
Vol. 9, Pt. 1–558
Steers, George, July 20, 1820–Sept. 25, 1856.
Vol. 9, Pt. 1–559
Stefansson, Vilhjalmur, Nov. 3, 1879–Aug. 26, 1962.
Supp. 7–715
Steffens, Lincoln, Apr. 6, 1866–Aug. 9, 1936.
Supp. 2–624
Stehle, Aurelius Aloysius, Apr. 30, 1877–Feb. 12, 1930.
Vol. 9, Pt. 1–560
Steichen, Edward Jean, Mar. 27, 1879–Mar. 25, 1973.
Supp. 9–759
Stein, Evaleen, Oct. 12, 1863–Dec. 11, 1923.
Vol. 9, Pt. 1–561
Stein, Gertrude, Feb. 3, 1874–July 27, 1946.
Supp. 4–767
Stein, Leo Daniel, May 11, 1872–July 29, 1947.
Supp. 4–770
Steinbeck, John Ernst, Jr., Feb. 27., 1902–Dec. 20, 1968.
Supp. 8–624
Steiner, Bernard Christian, Aug. 13, 1867–Jan. 12, 1926.
Vol. 9, Pt. 1–561
Steiner, Lewis Henry, May 4, 1827–Feb. 18, 1892.
Vol. 9, Pt. 1–562
Steiner, Maximilian Raoul Walter ("Max"), May 10, 1888–Dec. 28, 1971.
Supp. 9–761
Steinert, Morris, Mar. 9, 1831–Jan. 21, 1912.
Vol. 9, Pt. 1–563
Steinhardt, Laurence Adolph, Oct. 6, 1892–Mar. 28, 1950.
Supp. 4–771
Steinitz, William, May 17, 1836–Aug. 12, 1900.
Vol. 9, Pt. 1–564
Steinman, David Barnard, June 11, 1886–Aug. 21, 1960.
Supp. 6–593
Steinmetz, Charles Proteus, Apr. 9, 1865–Oct. 26, 1923.
Vol. 9, Pt. 1–565
Steinmeyer, Ferdinand. [*See* Farmer, Ferdinand, 1720–1786.].
Steinway, Christian Friedrich Theodore, Nov. 6, 1825–Mar. 26, 1889.
Vol. 9, Pt. 1–566
Steinway, Henry Engelhard, Feb. 15, 1797–Feb. 7, 1871.
Vol. 9, Pt. 1–567
Steinway, William, Mar. 5, 1835–Nov. 30, 1896.
Vol. 9, Pt. 1–568
Stejneger, Leonhard Hess, Oct. 30, 1851–Feb. 28, 1943.
Supp. 3–732
Stella, Joseph, June 13, 1877–Nov. 5, 1946.
Supp. 4–733
Stelze, Charles, June 4, 1896–Feb. 27, 1941.
Supp. 3–733
Stengel, Alfred, Nov. 3, 1868–Apr. 10, 1939.
Supp. 2–628
Stengel, Charles Dillon ("Casey"), July 30, 1890–Sept. 29, 1975.
Supp. 9–762
Stephens, Alexander Hamilton, Feb. 11, 1812–Mar. 4, 1883.
Vol. 9, Pt. 1–569
Stephens, Alice Barber, July 1, 1858–July 13, 1932.
Vol. 9, Pt. 1–575
Stephens, Ann Sophla, 1813–Aug. 20, 1886.
Vol. 9, Pt. 1–576
Stephens, Charles Asbury, Oct. 21, 1844–Sept. 22, 1931.
Vol. 9, Pt. 1–577
Stephens, Edwin William, Jan. 21, 1849–May 22, 1931.
Vol. 9, Pt. 1–577
Stephens, Henry Morse, Oct. 3, 1857–Apr. 16, 1919.
Vol. 9, Pt. 1–578
Stephens, John Lloyd, Nov. 28, 1805–Oct. 12, 1852.
Vol. 9, Pt. 1–579
Stephens, Linton, July 1, 1823–July 14, 1872.
Vol. 9, Pt. 1–580
Stephens, Uriah Smith, Aug. 3, 1821–Feb. 13, 1882.
Vol. 9, Pt. 1–581
Stephenson, Benjamin Franklin, Oct. 3, 1823–Aug. 30, 1871.
Vol. 9, Pt. 1–582
Stephenson, Carl, Aug. 10, 1886–Oct. 3, 1954.
Supp. 5–655
Stephenson, Isaac, June 18, 1829–Mar. 15, 1918.
Vol. 9, Pt. 1–582
Stephenson, John, July 4, 1809–July 31, 1893.
Vol. 9, Pt. 1–583
Stephenson, Nathaniel Wright, July 10, 1867–Jan. 17, 1935.
Supp. 1–673
Sterett, Andrew, Jan. 27, 1778–Jan. 9, 1807.
Vol. 9, Pt. 1–584
Sterki, Victor, Sept. 27, 1846–Jan. 25, 1933.
Vol. 9, Pt. 1–585
Sterling, George, Dec. 1, 1869–Nov. 17, 1926.
Vol. 9, Pt. 1–585
Sterling, James, 1701?–Nov. 10, 1763.
Vol. 9, Pt. 1–586
Sterling, John Whalen, July 17, 1816–Mar. 9, 1885.
Vol. 9, Pt. 1–587
Sterling, John William, May 12, 1844–July 5, 1918.
Vol. 9, Pt. 1–588
Sterling, Ross Shaw, Feb. 11, 1875–Mar. 25, 1949.
Supp. 4–775
Stern, Bill, July 1, 1907–Nov. 19, 1971.
Supp. 9–765
Stern, Joseph William, Jan. 11, 1870–Mar. 31, 1934.
Vol. 9, Pt. 1–589
Stern, Kurt Guenter, Sept. 19, 1904–Feb. 3, 1956.
Supp. 6–595
Stern, Otto, Feb. 17, 1888–Aug. 17, 1969.
Supp. 8–627
Sternberg, Constantin Ivanovich, Edler von, July 9, 1852–Mar. 31, 1924.
Vol. 9, Pt. 1–590
Sternberg, George Miller, June 8, 1838–Nov. 3, 1915.
Vol. 9, Pt. 1–590
Sterne, Maurice, July 13, 1878–July 23, 1957.
Supp. 6–596
Sterne, Simon, July 23, 1839–Sept. 22, 1901.
Vol. 9, Pt. 1–592
Sterne, Stuart. [*See* Bloede, Gertrude, 1845–1905.]
Sterrett, James Macbride, Jan. 13, 1847–May 31, 1923.
Vol. 9, Pt. 1–593
Sterrett, John Robert Sitlington, Mar. 4, 1851–June 15, 1914.
Vol. 9, Pt. 1–594
Stetefeldt, Carl August, Sept. 28, 1838–Mar. 17, 1896.
Vol. 9, Pt. 1–595
Stetson, Augusta Emma Simmons, *c.* 1842–Oct. 12, 1928.
Vol. 9, Pt. 1–595
Stetson, Charles Augustus, Apr. 1, 1810–Mar. 28, 1888.
Vol. 9, Pt. 1–596
Stetson, Charles Walter, Mar. 25, 1858–July 20, 1911.
Vol. 9, Pt. 1–597
Stetson, Francis Lynde, Apr. 23, 1846–Dec. 5, 1920.
Vol. 9, Pt. 1–598
Stetson, Henry Crosby, Oct. 10, 1900–Dec. 3, 1955.
Supp. 5–656
Stetson, John Batterson, May 5, 1830–Feb. 18, 1906.
Vol. 9, Pt. 1–599
Stetson, William Wallace, June 17, 1849–July 1, 1910.
Vol. 9, Pt. 1–599
Stettinius, Edward Reilly, Oct. 22, 1900–Oct. 31, 1949.
Supp. 4–776
Stettinius, Edward Riley, Feb. 15, 1865–Sept. 3, 1925.
Vol. 9, Pt. 1–600

Steuben, Friedrich Wilhelm Ludolf Gerhard Augustin, Baron von, Sept. 17, 1730–Nov. 28, 1794.
Vol. 9, Pt. 1–601
Steuben, John, Oct. 31, 1906–May 9, 1957.
Supp. 6–597
Steuer, Max David, Sept. 6, 1870?–Aug. 21, 1940.
Supp. 2–629
Stevens, Abel, Jan. 17, 1815–Sept. 11, 1897.
Vol. 9, Pt. 1–604
Stevens, Alexander Hodgdon, Sept. 4, 1789–Mar. 30, 1869.
Vol. 9, Pt. 1–605
Stevens, Ashton, Aug. 11, 1872–July 11, 1951.
Supp. 5–657
Stevens, Benjamin Franklin, Feb. 19, 1833–Mar. 5, 1902.
Vol. 9, Pt. 1–606
Stevens, Clement Hoffman, Aug. 21, 1821–July 25, 1864.
Vol. 9, Pt. 1–607
Stevens, Doris, Oct. 26, 1892–Mar. 22, 1963.
Supp. 7–717
Stevens, Edwin Augustus, July 28, 1795–Aug. 7, 1868.
Vol. 9, Pt. 1–608
Stevens, Emily, Feb. 27, 1882–Jan. 2, 1928.
Vol. 9, Pt. 1–609
Stevens, Frank Mozley, Aug. 10, 1880–Jan. 3, 1965.
Supp. 7–718
Stevens, George Cooper, Dec. 18, 1904–Mar. 8, 1975.
Supp. 9–766
Stevens, George Washington, Jan. 16, 1866–Oct. 29, 1926.
Vol. 9, Pt. 1–610
Stevens, George Barker, July 13, 1854–June 22, 1906.
Vol. 9, Pt. 1–610
Stevens, Harry Mozley, June 14, 1855–May 3, 1934.
Supp. 7–718
Stevens, Henry, Aug. 24, 1819–Feb. 28, 1886.
Vol. 9, Pt. 1–611
Stevens, Hiram Fairchild, Sept. 11, 1852–Mar. 9, 1904.
Vol. 9, Pt. 1–612
Stevens, Isaac Ingalls, Mar. 25, 1818–Sept. 1, 1862.
Vol. 9, Pt. 1–612
Stevens, John, 1749–Mar. 6, 1838.
Vol. 9, Pt. 1–614
Stevens, John Austin, Jan. 22, 1795–Oct. 19, 1874.
Vol. 9, Pt. 1–616
Stevens, John Austin, Jan. 21, 1827–June 16, 1910.
Vol. 9, Pt. 1–617
Stevens, John Frank, Apr. 25, 1853–June 2, 1943.
Supp. 3–735
Stevens, John Harrington, June 13, 1820–May 28, 1900.
Vol. 9, Pt. 1–617
Stevens, John Leavitt, Aug. 1, 1820–Feb. 8, 1895.
Vol. 9, Pt. 1–618
Stevens, Robert Livingston, Oct. 18, 1787–Apr 20, 1856.
Vol. 9, Pt. 1–619
Stevens, Thaddeus, Apr. 4, 1792–Aug. 11, 1868.
Vol. 9, Pt. 1–620
Stevens, Thomas Holdup, Feb. 22, 1795–Jan. 21, 1841.
Vol. 9, Pt. 1–625
Stevens, Thomas Holdup, May 27, 1819–May 15, 1896.
Vol. 9, Pt. 1–626
Stevens, Wallace, Oct. 2, 1879–Aug. 2, 1955.
Supp. 5–658
Stevens, Walter Husted, Aug. 24, 1827–Nov. 12, 1867.
Vol. 9, Pt. 1–627
Stevens, William Arnold, Feb. 5, 1839–Jan. 2, 1910.
Vol. 9, Pt. 1–627
Stevens, William Bacon, July 13, 1815–June 11, 1887.
Vol. 9, Pt. 1–628
Stevenson, Adlai Ewing, Oct. 23, 1835–June 14, 1914.
Vol. 9, Pt. 1–629
Stevenson, Adlai Ewing, II, Feb. 5, 1900–July 14, 1965.
Supp. 7–719
Stevenson, Andrew, Jan. 21, 1784–Jan. 25, 1857.
Vol. 9, Pt. 1–630
Stevenson, Carter Littlepage, Sept. 21. 1840–July 25, 1888.
Vol. 9, Pt. 1–631
Stevenson, James, Dec. 24, 1840–July 25, 1888.
Vol. 9, Pt. 1–631
Stevenson, John James, Oct. 10, 1841–Aug. 10, 1924.
Vol. 9, Pt. 1–632
Stevenson, John White, May 4, 1812–Aug. 10, 1886.
Vol. 9, Pt. 1–633
Stevenson, Matilda Coxe Evans, *c.* 1850–June 24, 1915.
Vol. 9, Pt. 1–634
Stevenson, Sara Yorke, Feb. 19, 1847–Nov. 14, 1921.
Vol. 9, Pt. 1–635
Steward, Ira, May 10, 1831–Mar. 13, 1883.
Vol. 9, Pt. 2–1
Stewardson, John, Mar. 21, 1858–Jan. 6, 1896.
Vol. 9, Pt. 2–2
Stewart, Alexander Peter, Oct. 2, 1821–Aug. 30, 1908.
Vol. 9, Pt. 2–3
Stewart, Alexander Turney, Oct. 12, 1803–Apr. 10, 1876.
Vol. 9, Pt. 2–3
Stewart, Alvan, Sept. 1, 1790–May 1, 1849.
Vol. 9, Pt. 2–5
Stewart, Andrew, June 11, 1791–July 16, 1872.
Vol. 9, Pt. 2–6
Stewart, Arthur Thomas ("Tom"), Jan. 11, 1892–Oct. 11, 1972.
Supp. 9–769
Stewart, Charles, July 28, 1778–Nov. 6, 1869.
Vol. 9, Pt. 2–6
Stewart, Donald Ogden, Nov. 30, 1894–Aug. 2, 1980.
Supp. 10–755
Stewart, Edwin, May 5, 1837–Feb. 28, 1933.
Vol. 9, Pt. 2–7
Stewart, Eliza Daniel, Apr. 25, 1816–Aug. 6, 1908.
Vol. 9, Pt. 2–8
Stewart, George Neil, Apr. 18, 1860–May 28, 1930.
Vol. 9, Pt. 2–9
Stewart, Humphrey John, May 22, 1854–Dec. 28, 1932.
Vol. 9, Pt. 2–10
Stewart, John Aikman, Aug. 26, 1822–Dec. 17, 1926.
Vol. 9, Pt. 2–10
Stewart, John George, June 2, 1890–May 24, 1970.
Supp. 8–629
Stewart, Philo Penfield, July 6, 1798–Dec. 13, 1868.
Vol. 9, Pt. 2–11
Stewart, Robert Marcellus, Mar. 12, 1815–Sept. 21, 1871.
Vol. 9, Pt. 2–13
Stewart, Robert, Jan. 31, 1839–Oct. 23, 1915.
Vol. 9, Pt. 2–12
Stewart, Walter Winne, May 24, 1885–Mar. 6, 1958.
Supp. 6–598
Stewart, William Rhinelander, Dec. 3, 1852–Sept. 4, 1929.
Vol. 9, Pt. 2–15
Stewart, William Morris, Aug. 9, 1827–Apr. 23, 1909.
Vol. 9, Pt. 2–13
Stickney, Alpheus Beede, June 27, 1840–Aug. 9, 1916.
Vol. 9, Pt. 2–15
Stiegel, Henry William, May 13, 1729–Jan. 10, 1785.
Vol. 9, Pt. 2–16
Stieglitz, Aifred, Jan. 1, 1864–July 13, 1946.
Supp. 4–778
Stieglitz, Julius, May 26, 1867–Jan. 10, 1937.
Supp. 2–630
Stigler, William Grady, July 7, 1891–Aug. 21, 1952.
Supp. 5–661
Stiles, Charles Wardell, May 15, 1867–Jan. 24, 1941.
Supp. 3–737
Stiles, Ezra, Nov. 29, 1727 o.s.–May 12, 1795.
Vol. 9, Pt. 2–18
Stiles, Henry Reed, Mar. 10, 1832–Jan. 7, 1909.
Vol. 9, Pt. 2–21
Still, Andrew Taylor, Aug. 6, 1828–Dec. 12, 1917.
Vol. 9, Pt. 2–21
Still, Clyfford, Nov. 30, 1904–June 23, 1980.
Supp. 10–757
Still, William, Oct. 7, 1821–July 14, 1902.
Vol. 9, Pt. 2–22
Still, William Grant, Jr., May 11, 1895–Dec. 3, 1978.
Supp. 10–760
Stillé, Alfred, Oct. 30, 1813–Sept. 24, 1900.
Vol. 9, Pt. 2–23
Stillé, Charles Janeway, Sept. 23, 1819–Aug. 11, 1899.
Vol. 9, Pt. 2–24
Stillman, James, June 9, 1850–Mar. 15, 1918.
Vol. 9, Pt. 2–25
Stillman, Samuel, Feb. 27, 1737 o.s.–Mar. 12, 1807.
Vol. 9, Pt. 1–26
Stillman, Thomas Bliss, May 24, 1852–Aug. 10, 1915.
Vol. 9, Pt. 2–27

Stillman, Thomas Edgar, Mar. 23, 1837–Sept. 4, 1906.
Vol. 9, Pt. 2–28
Stillman, William James, June 1, 1828–July 6, 1901.
Vol. 9, Pt. 2–29
Stilwell, Joseph Warren, Mar. 19, 1883–Oct. 12, 1946.
Supp. 4–781
Stilwell, Silas Moore, June 6, 1800–May 16, 1881.
Vol. 9, Pt. 2–30
Stilwell, Simpson Everett, Aug. 25, 1849–Feb. 17, 1903.
Vol. 9, Pt. 2–31
Stimpson, William, Feb. 14, 1832–May 26, 1872.
Vol. 9, Pt. 2–31
Stimson, Alexander Lovett, Dec. 14, 1816–Jan. 2, 1906.
Vol. 9, Pt. 2–32
Stimson, Frederic Jesup, July 20, 1855–Nov. 19, 1943.
Supp. 3–739
Stimson, Henry Lewis, Sept. 21, 1867–Oct. 20, 1950.
Supp. 4–784
Stimson, Julia Catherine, May 26, 1881–Sept. 29, 1948.
Supp. 4–788
Stimson, Lewis Atterbury, Aug. 24, 1844–Sept. 17, 1917.
Vol. 9, Pt. 2–33
Stine, Charles Milton Altland, Oct. 18, 1882–May 28, 1954.
Supp. 5–662
Stiness, John Henry, Aug. 9, 1840–Sept. 6, 1913.
Vol. 9, Pt. 2–34
Stirling, Lord William. [*See* Alexander, William, 1726–1783.]
Stith, William, 1707–Sept. 19, 1755.
Vol. 9, Pt. 2–34
Stitt, Edward Rhodes, July 22, 1867–Nov. 13, 1948.
Supp. 4–790
Stobo, Robert, 1727–*c.* 1772.
Vol. 9, Pt. 2–35
Stock, Frederick August, Nov. 11, 1872–Oct. 20, 1942.
Supp. 3–740
Stockard, Charles Rupert, Feb. 27, 1879–Apr. 7, 1939.
Supp. 2–631
Stockbridge, Henry, Sept. 18, 1856–Mar. 22, 1924.
Vol. 9, Pt. 2–36
Stockbridge, Henry Smith, Aug. 31, 1822–Mar. 11, 1895.
Vol. 9, Pt. 2–37
Stockbridge, Horace Edward, May 19, 1857–Oct. 30, 1930.
Vol. 9, Pt. 2–37
Stockbridge, Levi, Mar. 13, 1820–May 2, 1904.
Vol. 9, Pt. 2–38
Stockdale, Thomas Ringland, Mar. 28, 1828–Jan. 8, 1899.
Vol. 9, Pt. 2–39
Stöckhardt, Karl Georg, Feb. 17, 1842–Jan. 9, 1913.
Vol. 9, Pt. 2–40
Stockton, Charles G., Aug 27, 1853–Jan. 5, 1931.
Vol. 9, Pt. 2–41
Stockton, Charles Herbert, Oct. 13, 1845–May 31, 1924.
Vol. 9, Pt. 2–41
Stockton, Frank Richard, Apr. 5, 1834–Apr. 20, 1902.
Vol. 9, Pt. 2–42
Stockton, John Potter, Aug. 2, 1826–Jan. 22, 1900.
Vol. 9, Pt. 2–44
Stockton, Richard, Oct. 1, 1730–Feb. 28, 1781.
Vol. 9, Pt. 2–45
Stockton, Richard, Apr. 17, 1764–Mar. 7, 1828.
Vol. 9, Pt. 2–47
Stockton, Robert Field, Aug. 20, 1795–Oct. 7, 1866.
Vol. 9, Pt. 2–48
Stockton, Thomas Hewlings, June 4, 1808–Oct. 9, 1868.
Vol. 9, Pt. 2–49
Stockwell, John Nelson, Apr. 10, 1832–May 18, 1920.
Vol. 9, Pt. 2–50
Stoddard, Amos, Oct. 26, 1762–May 11, 1813.
Vol. 9, Pt. 2–51
Stoddard, Charles Warren, Aug. 7, 1843–Apr. 23, 1909.
Vol. 9, Pt. 2–52
Stoddard, David Tappan, Dec. 2, 1818–Jan. 22, 1857.
Vol. 9, Pt. 2–52
Stoddard, Elizabeth Drew Barstow, May 6, 1823–Aug. 1, 1902.
Vol. 9, Pt. 2–53
Stoddard, John Fair, July 20, 1825–Aug. 6, 1873.
Vol. 9, Pt. 2–54
Stoddard, John Lawson, Apr. 24, 1850–June 5, 1931.
Vol. 9, Pt. 2–55
Stoddard, John Tappan, Oct. 20, 1852–Dec. 9, 1919.
Vol. 9, Pt. 2–56
Stoddard, Joshua c., Aug. 26, 1814–Apr. 3, 1902.
Vol. 9, Pt. 2–56
Stoddard, Richard Henry, July 2, 1825–May 12, 1903.
Vol. 9, Pt. 2–57
Stoddard, Solomon, Sept. 1643–Feb. 11, 1728/29.
Vol. 9, Pt. 2–59
Stoddard, Theodore Lothrop, June 29, 1883–May 1, 1950.
Supp. 4–791
Stoddard, William Osborn, Sept. 24, 1835–Aug. 29, 1925.
Vol. 9, Pt. 2–60
Stoddart, James Henry, Oct. 13, 1827–Dec. 9, 1907.
Vol. 9, Pt. 2–61
Stoddart, Joseph Marshall, Aug. 10, 1845–Feb. 25, 1921.
Vol. 9, Pt. 2–62
Stoddert, Benjamin, 1751–Dec. 17, 1813.
Vol. 9, Pt. 2–62
Stoeckel, Carl, Dec. 7, 1858–Nov. 1, 1925.
Vol. 9, Pt. 2–64
Stoek, Harry Harkness, Jan. 16, 1866–Mar. 1, 1923.
Vol. 9, Pt. 2–64
Stoessel, Albert Frederic, Oct. 11, 1894–May 12, 1943.
Supp. 3–742
Stoever, Martin Luther, Feb. 17, 1820–July 22, 1870.
Vol. 9, Pt. 2–65
Stokes, Anson Phelps, Feb. 22, 1838–June 28, 1913.
Vol. 9, Pt. 2–66
Stokes, Anson Phelps, Apr. 13, 1874–Aug. 13, 1958.
Supp. 6–599
Stokes, Caroline Phelps, 1854–1909. [*See* Stokes, Olivia Eggleston Phelps, 1847–1927.]
Stokes, Frederick Abbot, Nov. 4, 1857–Nov. 15, 1939.
Supp. 2–633
Stokes, Isaac Newton Phelps, Apr. 11, 1867–Dec. 18, 1944.
Supp. 3–743
Stokes, Maurice, June 17, 1933–Apr. 6, 1970.
Supp. 8–631
Stokes, Montfort, Mar. 12, 1762–Nov. 4, 1842.
Vol. 9, Pt. 2–67
Stokes, Olivia Eggleston Phelps, Jan. 11, 1847–Dec. 14, 1927.
Vol. 9, Pt. 2–68
Stokes, Rose Harriet Pastor, July 18, 1879–June 20, 1933.
Vol. 9, Pt. 2–68
Stokes, Thomas Lunsford, Jr., Nov. 1, 1898–May 14, 1958.
Supp. 6–601
Stokes, William Earl Dodge, May 22, 1852–May 19, 1926.
Vol. 9, Pt. 2–69
Stokowski, Leopold Anthony, Apr. 18, 1882–Sept. 13, 1977.
Supp. 10–761
Stolberg, Benjamin, Nov. 30, 1891–Jan. 21, 1951.
Supp. 5–663
Stone, Abraham, Oct. 30, 1890–July 3, 1959.
Supp. 6–602
Stone, Amasa, Apr. 27, 1818–May 11, 1883.
Vol. 9, Pt. 2–70
Stone, Barton Warren, Dec. 24, 1772–Nov. 9, 1844.
Vol. 9, Pt. 2–71
Stone, Charles Augustus, Jan. 16, 1867–Feb. 25, 1941.
Supp. 3–744
Stone, Charles Pomeroy, Sept. 30, 1824–Jan. 24, 1887.
Vol. 9, Pt. 2–72
Stone, David, Feb. 17, 1770–Oct. 7, 1818.
Vol. 9, Pt. 2–72
Stone, David Marvin, Dec. 23, 1817–Apr. 2, 1895.
Vol. 9, Pt. 2–73
Stone, Edward Durell, Mar. 9, 1902–Aug. 6, 1978.
Supp. 10–764
Stone, Ellen Maria, July 24, 1846–Dec. 13, 1927.
Vol. 9, Pt. 2–74
Stone, George Washington, Oct. 24, 1811–Mar. 11, 1894.
Vol. 9, Pt. 2–74
Stone, Harlan Fiske, Oct. 11, 1872–Apr. 22, 1946.
Supp. 4–793
Stone, Horatio, Dec. 25, 1808–Aug. 25, 1875.
Vol. 9, Pt. 2, 75
Stone, James Kent, Nov. 10, 1840–Oct. 14, 1921.
Vol. 9, Pt. 2–76
Stone, John Augustus, Dec. 15, 1800–May 29, 1834.
Vol. 9, Pt. 2–77
Stone, John Marshall, Apr. 30, 1830–Mar. 26, 1900.
Vol. 9, Pt. 2–78
Stone, John Seely, Oct. 7, 1795–Jan. 13, 1882.
Vol. 9, Pt. 2–79

Stone, John Stone, Sept. 24, 1869–May 20, 1943.
Supp. 3–747
Stone, John Wesley, July 18, 1838–Mar. 24, 1922.
Vol. 9, Pt. 2–79
Stone, Lucy, Aug. 13, 1818–Oct. 18, 1893.
Vol. 9, Pt. 2–80
Stone, Melville Elijah, Aug. 22, 1848–Feb. 15, 1929.
Vol. 9, Pt. 2–81
Stone, Ormond, Jan. 11, 1847–Jan. 17, 1933.
Supp. 1–674
Stone, Richard French, Apr. 1, 1844–Oct. 3, 1913.
Vol. 9, Pt. 2–83
Stone, Samuel, July 1602–July 20, 1663.
Vol. 9, Pt. 2–83
Stone, Thomas, 1743–Oct. 5, 1787.
Vol. 9, Pt. 2–84
Stone, Warren, Feb. 3, 1808–Dec. 6, 1872.
Vol. 9, Pt. 2–85,
Stone, Warren Sanford, Feb. 1, 1860–June 12, 1925.
Vol. 9, Pt. 2–86
Stone, Wilbur Fisk, Dec. 28, 1833–Dec. 27, 1920.
Vol. 9, Pt. 2–86
Stone, William, *c.* 1603–*c.* 1660.
Vol. 9, Pt. 2–87
Stone, William Joel, May 7, 1848–Apr. 14, 1918.
Vol. 9, Pt. 2–88
Stone, William Leete, Apr. 20, 1792–Aug. 15, 1844.
Vol. 9, Pt. 2–89
Stone, William Leete, Apr. 4, 1835–June 11, 1908.
Vol. 9, Pt. 2–90
Stone, William Oliver, Sept. 26, 1830–Sept. 15, 1875.
Vol. 9, Pt. 2–91
Stone, Witmer, Sept. 22, 1866–May 23, 1939.
Supp. 2–633
Stoneman, George, Aug. 8, 1822–Sept. 5, 1894.
Vol. 9, Pt. 2–92
Stong, Phil(lip Duffield), Jan. 27, 1899–Apr. 26, 1957.
Supp. 6–603
Storer, Bellamy, Aug. 28, 1847–Nov. 12, 1922.
Vol. 9, Pt. 2–93
Storer, David Humphreys, Mar. 26, 1804–Sept. 10, 1891.
Vol. 9, Pt. 2–93
Storer, Francis Humphreys, Mar. 27, 1832–July 30, 1914.
Vol. 9, Pt. 2–94
Storer, Horatio Robinson, Feb. 27, 1830–Sept. 18, 1922.
Vol. 9, Pt. 2–95
Storey, Moorfield, Mar. 19, 1845–Oct. 24, 1929.
Vol. 9, Pt. 2–96
Storey, Wilbur Fisk, Dec. 19, 1819–Oct. 27, 1884.
Vol. 9, Pt. 2–97
Storrow, Charles Storer, Mar. 25, 1809–Apr. 30, 1904.
Vol. 9, Pt. 2–98
Storrow, James Jackson. July 29, 1837–Apr 15, 1897.
Vol. 9, Pt. 2–99
Storrs, Richard Salter, Feb. 6, 1787–Aug. 11, 1873.
Vol. 9, Pt. 2–100
Storrs, Richard Salter, Aug. 21, 1821–June 5, 1900.
Vol. 9, Pt. 2–101
Story, Isaac, Aug. 7, 1774–July 19, 1803.
Vol. 9, Pt. 2–102
Story, Joseph, Sept. 18, 1779–Sept. 10, 1845.
Vol. 9, Pt. 2–102
Story, Julian Russell, Sept. 8, 1857–Feb. 23, 1919.
Vol. 9, Pt. 2–108
Story, William Edward, Apr. 29, 1850–Apr. 10, 1930.
Vol. 9, Pt. 2–109
Story, William Wetmore, Feb. 12, 1819–Oct. 7, 1895.
Vol. 9, Pt. 2–109
Stotesbury, Edward Townsend, Feb. 26, 1849–May 16, 1938.
Supp. 2–634
Stott, Henry Gordon, May 13, 1866–Jan. 15, 1917.
Vol. 9, Pt. 2–111
Stouffer, Samuel Andrew, June 6, 1900–Aug. 24, 1960.
Supp. 6–604
Stouffer, Vernon Bigelow, Aug. 22, 1901–July 26, 1974.
Supp. 9–770
Stoughton, Edwin Wallace, May 1, 1818–Jan. 7, 1882.
Vol. 9, Pt. 2–112
Stoughton, William, Sept. 30, 1631–July 7, 1701.
Vol. 9, Pt. 2–113
Stout, Rex Todhunter, Dec. 1, 1886–Oct. 27, 1975.
Supp. 9–771
Stovall, Pleasant Alexander, July 10, 1857–May 14, 1935.
Supp. 1–675
Stow, Baron, June 16. 1801–Dec. 27, 1869.
Vol. 9, Pt. 2–114
Stowe, Calvin Ellis, Apr. 26, 1802–Aug. 22, 1886.
Vol. 9, Pt. 2–115
Stowe, Harriet Elizabeth Beecher, June 14, 1811–July 1, 1896.
Vol. 9, Pt. 2–115
Strachey, William, fl. 1606–1618.
Vol. 9, Pt. 2–120
Straight, Willard Dickerman, Jan. 31, 1880–Dec. 1, 1918.
Vol. 9, Pt. 2–121
Strain, Isaac G., Mar. 4, 1821–May 14, 1857.
Vol. 9, Pt. 2–122
Stranahan, James Samuel Thomas, Apr. 25, 1808–Sept. 3, 1898.
Vol. 9, Pt. 2–122
Strand, Paul, Oct. 16, 1890–Mar. 31, 1976.
Supp. 10–765
Strang, James Jesse, Mar. 21, 1813–July 9, 1856.
Vol. 9, Pt. 2–123
Strange, Michael, Oct. 1, 1890–Nov. 5, 1950.
Supp. 4–797
Stratemeyer, Edward, Oct. 4, 1862–May 10, 1930.
Vol. 9, Pt. 2–125
Stratemeyer, George Edward, Nov. 24, 1890–Aug. 9, 1969.
Supp. 8–632
Straton, John Roach, Apr. 6, 1875–Oct. 29, 1929.
Vol. 9, Pt. 2–125
Stratton, Charles Sherwood, Jan. 4, 1838–July 15, 1883.
Vol. 9, Pt. 2–126
Stratton, Samuel Wesley, July 18, 1861–Oct. 18, 1931.
Vol. 9, Pt. 2–127
Stratton-Porter, Gene. [*See* Porter, Gene Stratton, 1863–1924.]
Straus, Isidor, Feb. 6, 1845–Apr. 15, 1912.
Vol. 9, Pt. 2–128
Straus, Jesse Isidor, June 25, 1872–Oct. 4, 1936.
Supp. 2–635
Straus, Nathan, Jan. 31, 1848–Jan. 11, 1931.
Vol. 9, Pt. 2–129
Straus, Oscar Solomon, Dec. 23, 1850–May 3, 1926.
Vol. 9, Pt. 2–130
Straus, Percy Selden, June 27, 1876–Apr. 6, 1944.
Supp. 3–748
Straus, Roger W(illiams), Dec. 14, 1891–July 28, 1957.
Supp. 6–606
Straus, Simon William, Dec. 23, 1866–Sept. 7, 1930.
Vol. 9, Pt. 2–132
Strauss, Joseph Baermann, Jan. 9, 1870–May 16, 1938.
Supp. 2–636
Strauss, Lewis Lichtenstein, Jan. 31, 1896–Jan. 21, 1974.
Supp. 9–773
Stravinsky, Igor Fyodorovich, June 17, 1882–Apr. 6, 1971.
Supp. 9–774
Strawbridge, Robert, d. Aug. 1781.
Vol. 9, Pt. 2–132
Strawn, Jacob, May 30, 1800–Aug. 23, 1865.
Vol. 9, Pt. 2–133
Strawn, Silas Hardy, Dec. 15, 1866–Feb. 4, 1946.
Supp. 4–799
Street, Alfred Billings, Dec. 18, 1811–June 2, 1881.
Vol. 9, Pt. 2–134
Street, Augustus Russell, Nov. 5, 1791–June 12, 1866.
Vol. 9, Pt. 2–135
Street, Joseph Montfort, Dec. 18, 1782–May 5, 1840.
Vol. 9, Pt. 2–136
Streeter, George Linius, Jan. 12, 1873–July 27, 1948.
Supp. 4–800
Stribling, Thomas Sigismund, Mar. 4, 1881–July 8, 1965.
Supp. 7–724
Strickland, William, *c.* 1787–Apr. 6, 1854.
Vol. 9, Pt. 2–137
Stringfellow, Franklin, June 18, 1840–June 8, 1913.
Vol. 9, Pt. 2–138
Stringham, Silas Horton, Nov. 7, 1797–Feb. 7, 1876.
Vol. 9, Pt. 2–139
Stringham, Washington Irving, Dec. 10, 1847–Oct. 5, 1909.
Vol. 9, Pt. 2–140

Stritch, Samuel Alphonsus, Aug. 17, 1887–May 27, 1958.
Supp. 6–607
Strobel, Charles Louis, Oct. 6, 1852–Apr. 4, 1936.
Supp. 2–638
Strobel, Edward Henry, Dec 7, 1855–Jan. 15, 1908.
Vol. 9, Pt. 2–140
Stroheim, Erich Von. [*See* Von Stroheim, Erich, 1885–1957.]
Stromme, Peer Olsen, Sept. 15, 1856–Sept. 15, 1921.
Vol. 9, Pt. 2–141
Strong, Anna Louise, Nov. 24, 1885–Mar. 29, 1970.
Supp. 8–634
Strong, Augustus Hopkins, Aug. 3, 1836–Nov. 29, 1921.
Vol. 9, Pt. 2–142
Strong, Benjamin, Dec. 22, 1872–Oct. 16, 1928.
Vol. 9, Pt. 2–143
Strong, Caieb, Jan. 9, 1745–Nov. 7, 1819.
Vol. 9, Pt. 2–144
Strong, Charles Augustus, Nov. 28, 1862–Jan. 23, 1940.
Supp. 2–638
Strong, Charles Lyman, Aug. 15, 1826–Feb. 9, 1883.
Vol. 9, Pt. 2–146
Strong, Elmer Kenneth, Jr. ("Ken"), Aug. 6, 1906–Oct. 5, 1979.
Supp. 10–767
Strong, Harriet Williams Russell, July 23, 1844–Sept. 16, 1926.
Vol. 9, Pt. 2–147
Strong, James, Aug. 14, 1822–Aug. 7, 1894.
Vol. 9, Pt. 2–147
Strong, James Hooker, Apr. 26, 1814–Nov. 28, 1882.
Vol. 9, Pt. 2–148
Strong, James Woodward, Sept. 29, 1833–Feb. 24, 1913.
Vol. 9, Pt. 2–149
Strong, Josiah, Jan. 19, 1847–Apr. 28, 1916.
Vol. 9, Pt. 2–150
Strong, Moses McCure, May 20, 1810–July 20, 1894.
Vol. 9, Pt. 2–151
Strong, RIchard Pearson, Mar. 18, 1872–July 4, 1948.
Supp. 4–802
Strong, Theodore, July 26, 1790–Feb. 1, 1869.
Vol. 9, Pt. 2–152
Strong, Walter Ansel, Aug. 13, 1883–May 10, 1931.
Vol. 9, Pt. 2–152
Strong, William, May 6, 1808–Aug. 19, 1895.
Vol. 9, Pt. 2–153
Strong, William Barstow, May 16, 1837–Aug. 3, 1914.
Vol 9, Pt. 2–155
Strong, William Lafayette, Mar. 22, 1827–Nov. 2, 1900.
Vol. 9, Pt. 2–155
Strother, David Hunter, Sept. 26, 1816–Mar. 8, 1888.
Vol. 9, Pt. 2–156
Strubberg, Friedrich Armand, Mar. 18, 1806–Apr. 3, 1889.
Vol. 9, Pt. 2–157
Strudwick, Edmund Charles Fox, Mar. 25, 1802–Nov. 30, 1879.
Vol. 9, Pt. 2–158
Strunsky, Simeon, July 23, 1879–Feb. 5, 1948.
Supp. 4–803
Struve, Gustav, Oct. 11, 1805–Aug. 21, 1870.
Vol. 9, Pt. 2–158
Struve, Otto, Aug. 12, 1897–Apr. 6, 1963.
Supp. 7–726
Stryker, Lloyd Paul, June 5, 1885–June 21, 1955.
Supp. 1–664
Stryker, Merancthon Woolsey, Jan. 7, 1851–Dec. 6, 1929.
Vol. 9, Pt. 2–159
Stuart, Alexander Hugh Holmes, Apr. 2, 1807–Feb. 13, 1891.
Vol. 9, Pt. 2–160
Stuart, Archibald, Mar. 19, 1757–July 11, 1832.
Vol. 9, Pt. 2–161
Stuart, Charles Macaulay, Aug. 20, 1853–Jan. 26, 1932.
Vol. 9, Pt. 2–163
Stuart, Charles, 1783–1865.
Vol. 9, Pt. 2–162
Stuart, Charles Beebe, June 4, 1814–Jan. 4, 1881.
Vol. 9, Pt. 2–163
Stuart, Elbridge Amos, Sept. 10, 1856–Jan. 14, 1944.
Supp. 3–749
Stuart, Francis Lee, Dec. 3, 1866–Jan. 15, 1935.
Supp. 1–676
Stuart, Gilbert, Dec. 3, 1755–July 9, 1828.
Vol. 9, Pt. 2–164
Stuart, Granville, Aug. 27, 1834–Oct. 2, 1918.
Vol. 9, Pt. 2–168
Stuart, Henry Robson. [*See* Robson, Stuart, 1836–1903.]
Stuart, Isaac William, June 13, 1809–Oct. 2, 1861.
Vol. 9, Pt. 2–169
Stuart, James Ewell Brown, Feb. 6, 1833–May 12, 1864.
Vol. 9, Pt. 2–170
Stuart, John, *c.* 1700–Mar. 25, 1779.
Vol. 9, Pt. 2–172
Stuart, John Leighton, June 24, 1876–Sept. 19, 1962.
Supp. 7–727
Stuart, John Todd, Nov. 10, 1807–Nov. 28, 1885.
Vol. 9, Pt. 2–173
Stuart, Moses, Mar. 26, 1780–Jan. 4, 1852.
Vol. 9, Pt. 2–174
Stuart, Robert, Feb. 19, 1785–Oct. 29, 1848.
Vol. 9, Pt. 2–175
Stuart, Robert Leighton, July 21, 1806–Dec. 12, 1882.
Vol. 9, Pt. 2–176
Stuart, Ruth McEnery, May 21, 1849–May 6, 1917.
Vol. 9, Pt. 2–177
Stub, Hans Gerhard, Feb. 23, 1849–Aug. 1, 1931.
Vol. 9, Pt. 2–178
Stubbs, Walter Roscoe, Nov. 7, 1858–Mar. 25, 1929.
Supp. 1–677
Stuck, Hudson, Nov. 11, 1863–Oct. 10, 1920.
Vol. 9, Pt. 2–178
Stuckenberg, John Henry Wilbrandt, Jan. 6, 1835–May 28, 1903.
Vol. 9, Pt. 2–179
Studebaker, Clement, Mar. 12, 1831–Nov. 27, 1901.
Vol. 9, Pt. 2–180
Stuhldreher, Harry A., Oct. 14, 1901–Jan. 26, 1965.
Supp. 7–728
Sturges, Preston, Aug. 29, 1898–Aug. 6, 1959.
Supp. 6–608
Sturgis, Russell, Oct. 16, 1836–Feb. 11, 1909.
Vol. 9, Pt. 2–181
Sturgis, Samuel Davis, June 11, 1822–Sept. 28, 1889.
Vol. 9, Pt. 2–182
Sturgis, William, Feb. 25, 1782–Oct. 21, 1863.
Vol. 9, Pt. 2–183
Sturtevant, Benjamin Franklin, Jan. 18, 1833–Apr. 17, 1890.
Vol. 9, Pt. 2–184
Sturtevant, Edward Lewis, Jan. 23, 1842–July 30, 1898.
Vol. 9, Pt. 2–185
Sturtevant, Julian Monson, July 26, 1805–Feb. 11, 1886.
Vol. 9, Pt. 2–186
Stutz, Harry Clayton, Sept. 12, 1876–June 25, 1930.
Vol. 9, Pt. 2–186
Stuyvesant, Petrus, 1592–Feb. 1672.
Vol. 9, Pt. 2–187
Sublette, William Lewis, 1799?–July 23, 1845.
Vol. 9, Pt. 2–189
Sugiura, Kanematsu, June 5, 1892–Oct. 21, 1979.
Supp. 10–768
Sullavan, Margaret, May 16, 1909–Jan. 1, 1960.
Supp. 6–610
Sullivan, Edward Vincent ("Ed"), Sept. 28, 1901–Oct. 13, 1974.
Supp. 9–778
Sullivan, George, Aug. 29, 1771–June 14, 1838.
Vol. 9, Pt. 2–189
Sullivan, Harry Stack, Feb. 21, 1892–Jan. 14, 1949.
Supp. 4–805
Sullivan, James, Apr. 22, 1744–Dec. 10, 1808.
Vol. 9, Pt. 2–190
Sullivan, James Edward, Nov. 18, 1860–Sept. 16, 1914.
Vol. 9, Pt. 2–141
Sullivan, James William, Mar. 9, 1848–Sept. 27, 1938.
Supp. 2–640
Sullivan, John, Feb. 17, 1740–Jan. 23, 1795.
Vol. 9, Pt. 2–192
Sullivan, John Florence. [*See* Allen, Fred, 1894–1956.]
Sullivan, John Lawrence, Oct. 15, 1858–Feb. 2, 1918.
Vol. 9, Pt. 2–193
Sullivan, Louis Henri, Sept. 3, 1856–Apr. 14, 1924.
Vol. 9, Pt. 2–194
Sullivan, Louis Robert, May 21, 1892–Apr. 23, 1925.
Vol. 9, Pt. 2–197

Sullivan, Mark, Sept. 10, 1874–Aug. 13, 1952.
Supp. 5–666
Sullivan, Timothy Daniel, July 23, 1862–Aug. 31, 1913.
Vol. 9, Pt. 2–198
Sullivan, William, Nov. 1774–Sept. 3, 1839.
Vol. 9, Pt. 2–199
Sullivan, William Henry, Aug. 9, 1864–Jan. 26, 1929.
Vol. 9, Pt. 2–200
Sullivant, William Starling, Jan. 15, 1803–Apr. 30, 1873.
Vol. 9, Pt. 2–201
Sully, Daniel John, Mar. 9, 1861–Sept. 19, 1930.
Vol. 9, Pt. 2–201
Sully, Thomas, 1783–Nov. 5, 1872.
Vol. 9, Pt. 2–202
Sulzberger, Arthur Hays, Sept. 12, 1891–Dec. 11, 1968.
Supp. 8–636
Sulzberger, Cyrus Lindauer, July 11, 1858–Apr. 30, 1932.
Vol. 9, Pt. 2–205
Sulzberger, Mayer, June 22, 1843–Apr. 20, 1923.
Vol. 9, Pt. 2–205
Sulzer, William, Mar. 18, 1863–Nov. 6, 1941.
Supp. 3–751
Summerall, Charles Pelot, Mar. 4, 1867–May 14, 1955.
Supp. 5–668
Summerfield, Arthur Ellsworth, Mar. 17, 1899–Apr. 26, 1972.
Supp. 9–781
Summers, Edith. [*See* Kelley, Edith Summers, 1884–1956.]
Summers, George William, Mar. 4, 1804–Sept. 19, 1868.
Vol. 9, Pt. 2–206
Summers, Thomas Osmond, Oct. 11, 1812–May 6, 1882.
Vol. 9, Pt. 2–207
Summersby, Kathleen Helen ("Kay"), 1908–Jan. 20, 1975.
Supp. 9–782
Sumner, Charles, Jan. 6, 1811–Mar. 11, 1874.
Vol. 9, Pt. 2–208
Sumner, Edwin Vose, Jan. 30, 1797–Mar. 21, 1863.
Vol. 9, Pt. 2–214
Sumner, Francis Bertody, Aug. 1, 1874–Sept. 6, 1945.
Supp. 3–752
Sumner, Increase, Nov. 27, 1746–June 7, 1799.
Vol. 9, Pt. 2–215
Sumner, James Batcheller, Nov. 19, 1887–Aug. 12, 1955.
Supp. 1–669
Sumner, Jethro, *c.* 1733–Mar. 1785.
Vol. 9, Pt. 2–216
Sumner, Walter Taylor, Dec. 5, 1873–Sept. 4, 1935.
Supp. 1–678
Sumner, William Graham, Oct. 30, 1840–Apr. 12, 1910.
Vol. 9, Pt. 2–217
Sumners, Hatton William, May 30, 1875–Apr. 19, 1962.
Supp. 7–730
Sumter, Thomas, Aug. 14, 1734–June 1, 1832.
Vol. 9, Pt. 2–219
Sunday, William Ashley, Nov. 18, 1862–Nov. 6, 1935.
Supp. 1–679
Sunderland, Eliza Jane Read, Apr. 19, 1839–Mar. 3, 1910.
Vol. 9, Pt. 2–221
Sunderland, La Roy, Apr. 22, 1804–May 15, 1885.
Vol. 9, Pt. 2–222
Surratt, John H., b. 1844. [*See* Booth, John Wilkes, 1838–1865.]
Surratt, Mary E., 1820–1865. [*See* Booth, John Wilkes, 1838–1865.]
Susann, Jacqueline, Aug. 20, 1921–Sept. 21, 1974.
Supp. 9–784
Sutherland, Earl Wilbur, Jr., Nov. 19, 1915–Mar. 9, 1974.
Supp. 9–786
Sutherland, Edwin Hardin, Aug. 13, 1883–Oct. 11, 1950.
Supp. 4–808
Sutherland, George, Mar. 25, 1862–July 18, 1942.
Supp. 3–753
Sutherland, Joel Barlow, Feb. 26, 1792–Nov. 15, 1861.
Vol. 9, Pt. 2–222
Sutherland, Richard Kerens, Nov. 27, 1893–June 25, 1966.
Supp. 8–637
Sutro, Adolph Heinrich Joseph, Apr. 29, 1830–Aug. 8, 1898.
Vol. 9, Pt. 2–223
Sutter, John Augustus, Feb. 1803–June 18, 1880.
Vol. 9, Pt. 2–224
Sutton, William Francis, Jr. ("Willie"), June 30, 1901–Nov. 2, 1980.
Supp. 10–770
Sutton, William Seneca, Aug. 12, 1860–Nov. 26, 1928.
Vol. 9, Pt. 2–225
Suzzallo, Henry, Aug. 22, 1875–Sept. 25, 1933.
Vol. 9, Pt. 2–226
Svenson, Andrew Edward, May 8, 1910–Aug. 21, 1975.
Supp. 9–787
Sverdrup, Georg, Dec. 16, 1848–May 3, 1907.
Vol. 9, Pt. 2–229
Swain, Clara A., July 18, 1834–Dec. 25, 1910.
Vol. 9, Pt. 2–229
Swain, David Lowry, Jan. 4, 1801–Aug. 27, 1868.
Vol. 9, Pt. 2–230
Swain, George Fillmore, Mar. 2, 1857–July 1, 1931.
Supp. 1–680
Swain, James Barrett, July 30, 1820–May 27, 1895.
Vol. 9, Pt. 2–231
Swallow, George Clinton, Nov. 17, 1817–Apr. 20, 1899.
Vol. 9, Pt. 2–292
Swallow, Silas Comfort, Mar. 5, 1839–Aug. 13, 1930.
Vol. 9, Pt. 2–233
Swan, James, 1754–July 31, 1830.
Vol. 9, Pt. 2–234
Swan, Joseph Rockwell, Dec. 28, 1802–Dec. 18, 1884.
Vol. 9, Pt. 2–234
Swan, Timothy, July 23, 1758–July 23, 1842.
Vol. 9, Pt. 2–235
Swank, James Moore, July 12, 1832–June 21, 1914.
Vol. 9, Pt. 2–236
Swann, Thomas, *c.* 1806–July 24, 1883.
Vol. 9, Pt. 2–237
Swanson, Claude Augustus, Mar. 31, 1862–July 7, 1939.
Supp. 2–641
Swanton, John Reed, Feb. 19, 1873–May 2, 1958.
Supp. 6–611
Swartwout, Samuel, Nov. 17, 1783–Nov. 21, 1856.
Vol. 9, Pt. 2–238
Swasey, Ambrose, Dec. 19, 1846–June 15, 1937.
Supp. 2–642
Swayne, Noah Haynes, Dec. 7, 1804–June 8, 1884.
Vol. 9, Pt. 2–239
Swayne, Wager, Nov. 10, 1834–Dec. 18, 1902.
Vol. 9, Pt. 2–240
Sweeney, Martin Leonard, Apr. 15, 1885–May 1, 1960.
Supp. 6–613
Sweeny, Peter Barr, Oct. 9, 1825–Aug. 30, 1911.
Vol. 9, Pt. 2–241
Sweeny, Thomas William, Dec. 25, 1820–Apr. 10, 1892.
Vol. 9, Pt. 2–242
Sweet, John Edson, Oct. 21, 1832–May 8, 1916.
Vol. 9, Pt. 2–243
Swenson, David Ferdinand, Oct. 29, 1876–Feb. 11, 1940.
Supp. 2–643
Swensson, Carl Aaron, June 25, 1857–Feb. 16, 1904.
Vol. 9, Pt. 2–243
Swett, John, July 31, 1830–Aug. 22, 1913.
Vol. 9, Pt. 2–244
Swift, Gustavus Franklin, June 24, 1839–Mar. 29, 1903.
Vol. 9, Pt. 2–245
Swift, John Franklin, Feb. 28, 1829–Mar. 10, 1891.
Vol. 9, Pt. 2–246
Swift, Joseph Gardner, Dec. 31, 1783–July 23, 1865.
Vol. 9, Pt. 2–247
Swift, Lewis, Feb. 29, 1820–Jan. 4, 1913.
Vol. 9, Pt. 2–247
Swift, Linton Bishop, July 15, 1888–Apr. 11, 1946.
Supp. 4–810
Swift, Louis Franklin, Sept. 27, 1861–May 12, 1937.
Supp. 2–644
Swift, Lucius Burrie, July 31, 1844–July 3, 1929.
Vol. 9, Pt. 2–248
Swift, William Henry, Nov. 6, 1800–Apr. 7, 1879.
Vol. 9, Pt. 2–249
Swift, Zephaniah, Feb. 27, 1759–Sept. 27, 1823.
Vol. 9, Pt. 2–250
Swing, David, Aug. 23, 1830–Oct. 3, 1894.
Vol. 9, Pt. 2–251

Swing, Raymond Edwards (Gram), Mar. 25, 1887–Dec. 22, 1968.
Supp. 8–639
Swinton, John, Dec. 12, 1829–Dec. 15, 1901.
Vol. 9, Pt. 2–252
Swinton, William, Apr. 23, 1833–Oct. 24, 1892.
Vol. 9, Pt. 2–252
Swisshelm, Jane Grey Cannon, Dec. 6, 1815–July 22, 1884.
Vol. 9, Pt. 2–253
Switzer, Mary Elizabeth, Feb. 16, 1900–Oct. 16, 1971
Supp. 9–788
Switzler, William Franklin, Mar. 16, 1819–May 24, 1906.
Vol. 9, Pt. 2–254
Swope, Gerard, Dec. 1, 1872–Nov. 20, 1957.
Supp. 6–614
Swope, Herbert Bayard, Jan. 5, 1882–June 20, 1958.
Supp. 6–615
Sydenstricker, Edgar, July 15, 1881–Mar. 19, 1936.
Supp. 2–645
Sydnor, Charles Sackett, July 21, 1898–Mar. 2, 1954.
Supp. 5–671
Sykes, George, Oct. 9, 1822–Feb. 8, 1880.
Vol. 9, Pt. 2–255
Sylvester, Frederick Oakes, Oct. 8, 1869–Mar. 2, 1915.
Vol. 9, Pt. 2–255
Sylvester, James Joseph, Sept. 3, 1814–Mar. 15, 1897.
Vol. 9, Pt. 2–256
Sylvis, William H., Nov. 26, 1828–July 27, 1869.
Vol. 9, Pt. 2–257
Symes, James Miller, July 8, 1897–Aug. 3, 1976.
Supp. 10–771
Symmes, John Cleves, July 21, 1742–Feb. 26, 1814.
Vol. 9, Pt. 2–258
Symons, George Gardner, 1865–Jan. 12, 1930.
Vol. 9, Pt. 2–259
Symons, Thomas William, Feb. 7, 1849–Nov. 23, 1920.
Vol. 9, Pt. 2–260
Syms, Benjamin, 1591?–1642.
Vol. 9, Pt. 2–260
Syng, Philip, Sept. 29, 1703–May 8, 1789.
Vol. 9, Pt. 2–261
Szell, George, June 7, 1897–July 30, 1970.
Supp. 8–641
Szilard, Leo, Feb. 11, 1898–May 30, 1964.
Supp. 7–731
Szold, Benjamin, Nov. 15, 1829–July 31, 1902.
Vol. 9, Pt. 2–262
Szold, Henriett, Dec. 21, 1860–Feb. 13, 1945.
Supp. 3–756
Szyk, Arthur, June 3, 1894–Sept. 13, 1951.
Supp. 5–672

Tabb, John Banister, Mar. 22, 1845–Nov. 19, 1909.
Vol. 9, Pt. 2–262
Taber, John, May 5, 1880–Nov. 22, 1965.
Supp. 7–733
Tabor, Horace Austin Warner, Nov. 26, 1830–Apr. 10, 1899.
Vol. 9, Pt. 2–263
Taft, Alphonso, Nov. 5, 1810–May 21, 1891.
Vol. 9, Pt. 2–264
Taft, Charles Phelps, Dec. 21, 1843–Dec. 31, 1929.
Vol. 9, Pt. 2–265
Taft, Henry Waters, May 27, 1859–Aug. 11, 1945.
Supp. 3–758
Taft, Lorado Zadoc, Apr. 29, 1860–Oct. 30, 1936.
Supp. 2–647
Taft, Robert Alphonso, Sept. 8, 1889–July 31, 1953.
Supp. 5–673
Taft, William Howard, Sept. 15, 1857–Mar. 8, 1930.
Vol. 9, Pt. 2–266
Taggard, Genevieve, Nov. 28, 1894–Nov. 8, 1948.
Supp. 4–811
Taggart, Thomas, Nov. 17, 1856–Mar. 6, 1929.
Vol. 9, Pt. 2–272
Tagliabue, Giuseppe, Aug. 10, 1812–May 7, 1878.
Vol. 9, Pt. 2–273
Tait, Arthur Fitzwilliam, Aug. 5, 1819–Apr. 28, 1905.
Vol. 9, Pt. 2–273
Tait, Charles, Feb. 1, 1768–Oct. 7, 1835.
Vol. 9, Pt. 2–274
Takamine, Jokichi, Nov. 3, 1854–July 22, 1922.
Vol. 9, Pt. 2–275
Talbot, Arthur Neweul, Oct 21, 1857–Apr. 35 1942.
Supp. 3–759
Talbot, Emily Fairbanks, Feb. 22, 1834–Oct. 29 1900.
Vol. 9, Pt. 2–276
Talbot, Ethelbert, Oct. 9, 1848–Feb. 27, 1928.
Vol. 9, Pt. 2–276
Talbot, Francis Xavier, Jan. 25, 1889–Dec. 3, 1953.
Supp. 5–677
Talbot, Henry Paul, May 15, 1864–June 18, 1927.
Vol. 9, Pt. 2–277
Talbot, Israel Tisdale, Oct. 29, 1829–July 2, 1899.
Vol. 4, Pt. 2–278
Talbot, John, 1645–Nov. 29, 1727.
Vol. 9, Pt. 2–278
Talbot, Silas, Jan. 11, 1751–June 30, 1813.
Vol. 9, Pt. 2–280
Talbott, Harold Elstner, Mar. 31, 1888–Mar. 2, 1957.
Supp. 6–617
Talcott, Andrew, Apr. 20, 1797–Apr. 22, 1883.
Vol. 9, Pt. 2–281
Talcott, Eliza, May 23, 1836–Nov. 1, 1911.
Vol. 9, Pt. 2–281
Talcott, Joseph, Nov. 1669–Nov. 11, 1741.
Vol. 9, Pt. 2–282
Taliaferro, Lawrence, Feb. 28, 1794–Jan. 22, 1871.
Vol. 9, Pt. 2–283
Taliaferro, William Booth, Dec. 28, 1822–Feb. 27, 1898.
Vol. 9, Pt. 2–283
Tallmadge, Benjamin, Feb. 25, 1754–Mar. 7, 1835.
Vol. 9, Pt. 2–284
Tallmadge, James, Jan. 28, 1778–Sept. 29, 1853.
Vol. 9, Pt. 2–285
Talmadge, Constance, Apr. 19, 1900–Nov. 23, 1973.
Supp. 9–791
Talmadge, Eugene, Sept. 23, 1884–Dec. 21, 1946.
Supp. 4–812
Talmage, James Edward, Sept. 21, 1862–July 27, 1933.
Vol. 9, Pt. 2–286
Talmage, John Van Nest, Aug. 18, 1819–Aug. 19, 1892.
Vol. 9, Pt. 2–286
Talmadge, Norma, May 2, 1897–Dec. 24, 1957.
Supp. 6–618
Talmage, Thomas DeWitt, Jan. 7, 1832–Apr. 12, 1902.
Vol. 9, Pt. 2–287
Talvj. [*See* Robinson, Therese Albertine Louise von Jakob, 1797–1870.]
Tamarkin, Jacob David, July 11, 1888–Nov. 18, 1945.
Supp. 3–760
Tamarón, Pedro, d. Dec. 21, 1768.
Vol. 9, Pt. 2–288
Tamiris, Helen, Apr. 23, 1903–Aug. 4, 1966.
Supp. 8–642
Tamiroff, Akim, Oct. 29, 1899–Sept. 17, 1972.
Supp. 9–792
Tammany, fl. 1685.
Vol. 9, Pt. 2–289
Tammen, Harry Heye, Mar. 6, 1856–July 19, 1924.
Supp. 1–93
Tammen, Harry Heye. [*See* Bonfils, Frederick Gilmer, 1860–1933.]
Tandy, Charles David, May 15, 1918–Nov. 4, 1978.
Supp. 10–773
Taney, Roger Brooke, Mar. 17, 1777–Oct. 12, 1864.
Vol. 9, Pt. 2–289
Tanguay, Eva, Aug. 1, 1878–Jan. 11, 1947.
Supp. 4–814
Tanneberger, David, Mar. 21, 1728–May 19, 1804.
Vol. 9, Pt. 2–294
Tanner, Benjamin, Mar. 27, 1775–Nov. 14, 1848.
Vol. 9, Pt. 2–295
Tanner, Benjamin Tucker, Dec. 25, 1835–Jan. 15, 1923.
Vol. 9, Pt. 2–296
Tanner, Edward Everett, III ("Patrick Dennis"), May 18, 1921–Nov. 6, 1976).
Supp. 10–774
Tanner, Henry Ossawa, June 21, 1859–May 25, 1937.
Supp. 2–648
Tanner, Henry Schenck, 1786–1858.
Vol. 9, Pt. 2–296
Tanner, James, Apr. 4, 1844–Oct. 2, 1927.
Vol. 9, Pt. 2–297
Tansill, Charles Callan, Dec. 9, 1890–Nov. 12, 1964.
Supp. 7–734

Tappan, Arthur, May 22, 1786–July 23, 1865.
Vol. 9, Pt. 2–298
Tappan, Benjamin, May 25, 1773–Apr. 20, 1857.
Vol. 9, Pt. 2–300
Tappan, Eli Todd, Apr. 30, 1824–Oct. 23, 1888.
Vol. 9, Pt. 2–301
Tappan, Eva March, Dec. 26, 1854–Jan. 29, 1930.
Vol. 9, Pt. 2–301
Tappan, Henry Philip, Apr. 18, 1805–Nov. 15, 1881.
Vol. 9, Pt. 2–302
Tappan, Lewis, May 23, 1788–June 21, 1873.
Vol. 9, Pt. 2–303
Tappen, Frederick Dobbs, Jan. 29, 1829–Feb. 28, 1902.
Vol. 9, Pt. 2–304
Tapper, Bertha Feiring, Jan. 25, 1859–Sept. 2, 1915.
Vol. 9, Pt. 2–305
Tarbell, Edmund Charles, Apr. 26, 1862–Aug. 1, 1938.
Supp. 2–649
Tarbell, Frank Bigelow, Jan. 1, 1853–Dec. 4, 1920.
Vol. 9, Pt. 2–306
Tarbell, Ida Minerva, Nov. 5, 1857–Jan. 6, 1944.
Supp. 3–761
Tarbell, Joseph, *c.* 1780–Nov. 25, 1815.
Vol. 9, Pt. 2–306
Tarbox, Increase Niles, Feb. 11, 1815–May 3, 1888.
Vol. 9, Pt. 2–307
Tarkington, Booth, July 29, 1869–May 19, 1946.
Supp. 4–815
Tarr, Ralph Stockman, Jan. 15, 1864–Mar. 21, 1912.
Vol. 9, Pt. 2–308
Tashrak. [*See* Zevin, Israel Joseph, 1872–1926.]
Tashunca-Uitco. [*See* Crazy Horse, *c.* 1849–1877.]
Tate, George Henry Hamilton, Apr. 30, 1894–Dec. 24, 1953.
Supp. 5–678
Tate, John Orley Allen, Nov. 19, 1899–Feb. 9, 1979.
Supp. 10–775
Tate, John Torrence, July 28, 1889–May 27, 1950.
Supp. 4–817
Tatham, William, Apr. 13, 1752–Feb. 22, 1819.
Vol. 9, Pt. 2–309
Tatlock, John Strong Perry, Feb. 24, 1876–June 24, 1948.
Supp. 4–819
Tattnall, Josiah, Nov. 9, 1795–June 14, 1871.
Vol. 9, Pt. 2–310
Tatum, Art, Oct. 13, 1910–Nov. 5, 1956.
Supp. 6–619
Tatum, Edward Lawrie, Dec. 14, 1909–Nov. 5, 1975.
Supp. 9–793
Tauber, Maurice Falcolm, Feb. 14, 1908–Sept. 21, 1980.
Supp. 10–777
Taussig, Frank William, Dec. 28, 1859–Nov. 11, 1940.
Supp. 2–650
Taussig, Frederick Joseph, Oct. 26, 1872–Aug. 21, 1943.
Supp. 3–763
Taussig, Joseph Knefler, Aug. 30, 1877–Oct. 29, 1947.
Supp. 4–820
Taussig, William, Feb. 28, 1826–July 10, 1913.
Vol. 9, Pt. 2–311
Tawney, James Albertus, Jan 3, 1855–June 12, 1919.
Vol. 9, Pt. 2–312
Taylor, Alfred Alexander, Aug. 6, 1848–Nov. 24, 1931.
Vol. 9, Pt. 2–313
Taylor, Archibald Alexander Edward, Aug. 27, 1834–Apr. 23, 1903.
Vol. 9, Pt. 2–313
Taylor, Bayard, Jan. 11, 1825–Dec. 19, 1878.
Vol. 9, Pt. 2–314
Taylor, Benjamin Franklin, July 19, 1819–Feb. 24, 1887.
Vol. 9, Pt. 2–316
Taylor, Bert Leston, Nov. 13, 1866–Mar. 19, 1921.
Vol. 9, Pt. 2–317
Taylor, Charles Atonzo, Jan. 20, 1864–Mar. 20, 1942.
Supp. 3–764
Taylor, Charles Fayette, Apr. 25, 1827–Jan. 25, 1899.
Vol. 9, Pt. 2–317
Taylor, Charles Henry, July 14, 1846–June 22, 1921.
Vol. 9, Pt. 2–318
Taylor, Charlotte De Bernier, 1806–Nov. 26, 1861.
Vol. 9, Pt. 2–319
Taylor, Creed, 1766–Jan. 17, 1836.
Vol. 9, Pt. 2–320
Taylor, David Watson, Mar. 4, 1864–July 28, 1940.
Supp. 2–652
Taylor, Edward, *c.* 1645–June 24, 1729.
Supp. 1–681
Taylor, Edward Thompson, Dec. 25, 1793–Apr. 5, 1871.
Vol. 9, Pt. 2–321
Taylor, Francis Henry, Apr. 23, 1903–Nov. 22, 1957.
Supp. 6–620
Taylor, Frank Bursley, Nov. 23, 1860–June 12, 1938.
Supp. 2–653
Taylor, Frank Walter, Mar. 8, 1874–July 27, 1921.
Vol. 9, Pt. 2–322
Taylor, Frederick Winslow, Mar. 20, 1856–Mar. 21, 1915.
Vol. 9, Pt. 2–323
Taylor, Fred Manville, July 11, 1855–Aug. 7, 1932.
Vol. 9, Pt. 2–323
Taylor, George, 1716–Feb. 23, 1781.
Vol. 9, Pt. 2–324
Taylor, George Boardman, Dec. 27, 1832–Sept. 28, 1907.
Vol. 9, Pt. 2–325
Taylor, George William, July 10, 1901–Dec. 15, 1972.
Supp. 9–794
Taylor, Graham, May 2. 1851–Sept. 26, 1938.
Supp. 2–654
Taylor, Hannis, Sept. 12, 1851–Dec. 26, 1922.
Vol. 9, Pt. 2–326
Taylor, Harry, June 26, 1862–Jan. 28, 1930.
Vol. 9, Pt. 2–327
Taylor, Henry Osborn, Dec. 5, 1856–Apr. 13, 1941.
Supp. 3–765
Taylor, James Barnett, Mar. 19, 1804–Dec. 22, 1871.
Vol. 9, Pt. 2–328
Taylor, James Bayard. [*See* Taylor, Bayard, 1825–1878.]
Taylor, James Monroe, Aug. 5, 1848–Dec. 19, 1916.
Vol. 9, Pt. 2–329
Taylor, James Wickes, Nov. 6, 1819–Apr. 28, 1893.
Vol. 9, Pt. 2–330
Taylor, John, 1752–Apr. 12, 1835.
Vol. 9, Pt. 2–330
Taylor, John, Dec. 19?, 1753–Aug. 21, 1824.
Vol. 9, Pt. 2–331
Taylor, John, Nov. 1, 1808–July 25, 1887.
Vol. 9, Pt. 2–333
Taylor, John Louis, Mar. 1, 1769–Jan. 29, 1829.
Vol. 9, Pt. 2–334
Taylor, John W., Mar. 26, 1784–Sept. 18, 1854.
Vol. 9, Pt. 2–335
Taylor, Joseph Deems, Dec. 22, 1885–July 3, 1966.
Supp. 8–644
Taylor, Joseph Wright, Mar. 1, 1810–Jan. 18, 1880.
Vol. 9, Pt. 2–336
Taylor, Laurette, Apr. 1, 1884–Dec. 7, 1946.
Supp. 4–821
Taylor, Marshall William, July 1, 1846–Sept. 11, 1887.
Vol. 9, Pt. 2–337
Taylor, Moses, Jan. 11, 1806–May 23, 1882.
Vol. 9, Pt. 2–338
Taylor, Myron Charles, Jan. 18, 1874–May 6, 1959.
Supp. 6–622
Taylor, Nathaniel William, June 23, 1786–Mar. 10, 1858.
Vol. 9, Pt. 2–338
Taylor. Raynor. *c.* 1747–Aug. 17, 1825.
Vol. 9, Pt. 2–339
Taylor, Richard, Jan. 27, 1826–Apr. 12, 1879.
Vol. 9, Pt. 2–340
Taylor, Richard Cowling, Jan. 18, 1789–Oct. 27, 1851.
Vol. 9, Pt. 2–341
Taylor, Robert, Aug. 5, 1911–June 8, 1969.
Supp. 8–645
Taylor, Robert Love, July 31, 1850–Mar. 31, 1912.
Vol. 9, Pt. 2–341
Taylor, Robert Tunstall, Jan. 16, 1867–Feb. 21, 1929.
Vol. 9, Pt. 2–343
Taylor, Samuel Harvey, Oct. 3, 1807–Jan. 29, 1871.
Vol. 9, Pt. 2–343
Taylor, Stevenson, Feb. 12, 1848–May 19, 1926.
Vol. 9, Pt. 2–344
Taylor, Theodore Roosevelt ("Hound Dog"), Apr. 12, 1917–Dec. 17, 1975.
Supp. 9–796

Taylor, William, May 2, 1821–May 18, 1902.
Vol. 9, Pt. 2–345
Taylor, William Chittenden, Mar. 3, 1886–Nov. 2, 1958.
Supp. 6–623
Taylor, William Ladd, Dec. 10, 1854–Dec. 26, 1926.
Vol. 9, Pt. 2–346
Taylor, William Mackergo, Oct. 23, 1829–Feb. 8, 1895.
Vol. 9, Pt. 2–347
Taylor, William Rogers, Nov. 7, 1811–Apr. 14, 1889.
Vol. 9, Pt. 2–347
Taylor, William Vigneron, Apr. 11, 1780–Feb. 11, 1858.
Vol. 9, Pt. 2–348
Taylor, Zachary, Nov. 24, 1784–July 9, 1850.
Vol. 9, Pt. 2–349
Tazewell, Henry, Nov. 27, 1753–Jan. 24, 1799.
Vol. 9, Pt. 2–354
Tazewell, Littleton Waller, Dec. 17, 1774–May 6, 1860.
Vol. 9, Pt. 2–355
Tchelitchew, Pavel, Sept. 21, 1898–July 31, 1957.
Supp. 6–624
Teagarden, Weldon Leo ("Jack"), Aug. 20, 1905–Jan. 15, 1964.
Supp. 7–735
Teall, Francis Augustus, Aug. 16, 1822–Nov. 16, 1894.
Vol. 9, Pt. 2–357
Teasdale, Sara, Aug. 8, 1884–Jan. 29, 1933.
Vol. 9, Pt. 2–357
Tecumseh, Mar. 1768?–Oct. 5, 1813.
Vol. 9, Pt. 2–358
Tedyuskung, *c.* 1700–Apr. 19, 1763.
Vol. 9, Pt. 2–360
Teeple, John Edgar, Jan. 4, 1874–Mar. 23, 1931.
Supp. 1–682
Teggart, Frederick John, May 9, 1870–Oct. 12, 1946.
Supp. 4–823
Telfair, Edward, *c.* 1735–Sept. 19, 1807.
Vol. 9, Pt. 2–361
Teller, Henry Moore, May 23, 1830–Feb. 23, 1914.
Vol. 9, Pt. 2–362
Temple, Oliver Perry, Jan. 27, 1820–Nov. 2, 1907.
Vol. 9, Pt. 2–363
Temple, William Grenville, Mar. 23, 1824–June 28, 1894.
Vol. 9, Pt. 2–364
Templeton, Alec Andrew, July 4, 1910–Mar. 28, 1963.
Supp. 7–737
Ten Broeck, Abraham, May 13, 1734–Jan. 19, 1810.
Vol. 9, Pt. 2–365
Ten Broeck, Richard, May 1812–Aug. 1, 1892.
Vol. 9, Pt. 2–365
Tené-Angpóte. [*See* Kicking Bird, d. 1875.]
Tennent, Gilbert, Feb. 5, 1703–July 23, 1764.
Vol. 9, Pt. 2–366
Tennent, John, *c.* 1700–*c.* 1760.
Vol. 9, Pt. 2–369
Tennent, William, 1673–May 6, 1745.
Vol. 9, Pt. 2–369
Tennent, William, June 3, 1705–Mar. 8, 1777.
Vol. 9, Pt. 2–370
Tenney, Charles Daniel, June 29, 1857–Mar. 14, 1930.
Vol. 9, Pt. 2–371
Tenney, Edward Payson, Sept. 29, 1835–July 24, 1916.
Vol. 9, Pt. 2–373
Tenney, Tabitha Gilman, Apr. 7, 1762–May 2, 1837.
Vol. 9, Pt. 2–373
Tenney, William Jewett, 1811–Sept. 20, 1883.
Vol. 9, Pt. 2–374
Tenskwatawa, Mar. 1768?–1834?.
Vol. 9, Pt. 2–375
Teresa, Mother, *c.* 1766–Sept. 9, 1846.
Vol. 9, Pt. 2–376
Terhune, Albert Payson, Dec. 21, 1872–Feb. 18, 1942.
Supp. 3–766
Terhune, Mary Virginia Hawes, Dec. 21, 1830–June 3, 1922.
Vol. 9, Pt. 2–376
Terman, Lewis Madison, Jan. 15, 1877–Dec. 21, 1956.
Supp. 6–626
Terrell, Edwin Holland, Nov. 21, 1848–July 1, 1910.
Vol. 9, Pt. 2–377
Terrell, Mary Eliza Church, Sept. 23, 1863–July 24, 1954.
Supp. 5–679
Terry, Alfred Howe, Nov. 10, 1827–Dec. 16, 1890.
Vol. 9, Pt. 2–378
Terry, David Smith, Mar. 8, 1823–Aug. 14, 1889.
Vol. 9, Pt. 2–379
Terry, Eli, Apr. 13, 1772–Feb. 26, 1852.
Vol. 9, Pt. 2–380
Terry, Marshall Orlando, June 21, 1848–Oct. 11, 1933.
Vol. 9, Pt. 2–381
Terry, Milton Spenser, Feb. 22, 1840–July 13, 1914.
Vol. 9, Pt. 2–382
Terry, Paul Houlton, Feb. 19, 1887–Oct. 25, 1971.
Supp. 9–797
Tesla, Nikola, July 9, 1856–Jan. 7, 1943.
Supp. 3–767
Testut, Charles, *c.* 1818–July 1, 1892.
Vol. 9, Pt. 2–383
Teuber, Hans-Lukas ("Luke"), Aug. 7, 1916–Jan. 4, 1977.
Supp. 10–779
Teusler, Rudolf Bolling, Feb. 25, 1876–Aug. 10, 1934.
Vol. 9, Pt. 2–383
Tevis, Lloyd, Mar. 20, 1824–July 24, 1899.
Vol. 9, Pt. 2–384
Thacher, Edwin, Oct. 12, 1839–Sept. 21, 1920.
Vol. 9, Pt. 2–385
Thacher, George, Apr. 12, 1754–Apr. 6, 1824.
Vol. 9, Pt. 2–386
Thacher, James, Feb. 14, 1754–May 23, 1844.
Vol. 9, Pt. 2–387
Thacher, John Boyd, Sept. 11, 1847–Feb. 25, 1909.
Vol. 9, Pt. 2–388
Thacher, Peter, July 18, 1651–Dec. 17, 1727.
Vol. 9, Pt. 2–389
Thacher, Peter, Mar. 21, 1752–Dec. 16, 1802.
Vol. 9, Pt. 2–390
Thacher, Samuel Cooper, Dec. 14, 1785–Jan. 2, 1818.
Vol. 9, Pt. 2–391
Thacher, Thomas Anthony, Jan. 11, 1815–Apr. 7, 1886.
Vol. 9, Pt. 2–392
Thacher, Thomas Day, Sept. 10, 1881–Nov. 12, 1950.
Supp. 4–825
Thalberg, Irving Grant, May 30, 1899–Sept. 14, 1936.
Supp. 2–656
Thanet, Octave. [*See* French, Alice, 1850–1934.]
Thatcher, Benjamin Bussey, Oct. 8, 1809–July 14, 1840.
Vol. 9, Pt. 2–393
Thatcher, George. [*See* Thacher, George, 1754–1824.]
Thatcher, Henry Knox, May 26, 1806–Apr. 5, 1880.
Vol. 9, Pt. 2–393
Thatcher, Mahlon Daniel, Dec. 6, 1839–Feb. 22, 1916.
Vol. 9, Pt. 2–394
Thatcher, Roscoe Wilfred, Oct. 5, 1872–Dec. 6, 1933.
Vol. 9, Pt. 2–395
Thaw, Harry Kendall, Feb. 1, 1871–Feb. 22, 1947.
Supp. 4–826
Thaw, William, Oct. 12, 1818–Aug. 17, 1889.
Vol. 9, Pt. 2–396
Thaxter, Celia Laighton, June 29, 1835–Aug. 26, 1894.
Vol. 9, Pt. 2–397
Thaxter, Roland, Aug. 28, 1858–Apr. 22, 1932.
Vol. 9, Pt. 2–398
Thayer, Abbott Handerson, Aug. 12, 1849–May 29, 1921.
Vol. 9, Pt. 2–399
Thayer, Atexander Wheelock, Oct. 22, 1817–July 15, 1897.
Vol. 9, Pt. 2–401
Thaver, Amos Madden, Oct. 10, 1841–Apr. 24, 1905.
Vol. 9, Pt. 2–402
Thayer, Eli, June 11, 1819–Apr. 15, 1899.
Vol. 9, Pt. 2–402
Thayer, Ezra Ripley, Feb. 21, 1866–Sept. 14, 1915.
Vol. 9, Pt. 2–404
Thayer, Gideon French, Sept. 21, 1793–Mar. 27, 1864.
Vol. 9, Pt. 2–404
Thayer, James Bradley, Jan. 15, 1831–Feb. 14, 1902.
Vol. 9, Pt. 2–405
Thayer, John, May 15, 1758–Feb. 17, 1815.
Vol. 9, Pt. 2–406
Thayer, John Milton, Jan. 24, 1820–Mar. 19, 1906.
Vol. 9, Pt. 2–407
Thayer, Joseph Henry, Nov. 7, 1828–Nov. 26, 1901.
Vol. 9, Pt. 2–408

Thayer, Nathaniel, Sept. 11, 1808–Mar. 7, 1883.
Vol. 9, Pt. 2–409
Thayer, Sylvanus, June 9, 1785–Sept. 7, 1872.
Vol. 9, Pt. 2–410
Thayer, Thomas Baldwin, Sept. 10, 1812–Feb. 12, 1886.
Vol. 9, Pt. 2–411
Thayer, Tiffany Ellsworth, Mar. 1, 1902–Aug. 23, 1959.
Supp. 6–627
Thayer, Whitney Eugene, Dec. 11, 1838–June 27, 1889.
Vol. 9, Pt. 2–411
Thayer, William Makepeace, Feb. 23, 1820–Apr. 7, 1898.
Vol. 9, Pt. 2–412
Thayer, William Roscoe, Jan. 16, 1859–Sept. 7, 1923.
Vol. 9, Pt. 2–413
Thayer, William Sydney, June 23, 1864–Dec. 10, 1932.
Vol. 9, Pt. 2–414
Thébaud, Augustus J., Nov. 20, 1807–Dec. 17, 1885.
Vol. 9, Pt. 2–415
Theobald, Robert Alfred, Jan. 25, 1884–May 13, 1957.
Supp. 6–628
Theobald, Samuel, Nov. 12, 1846–Dec. 20, 1930.
Vol. 9, Pt. 2–416
Theus, Jeremiah, *c.* 1719–May 18, 1774.
Vol. 9, Pt. 2–416
Thierry, Camille, Oct. 1814–Apr. 1875.
Vol. 9, Pt. 2–417
Thilly, Frank, Aug. 18, 1865–Dec. 28, 1934.
Supp. 1–682
Thoburn, Isabella, Mar. 29, 1840–Sept. 1, 1901.
Vol. 9, Pt. 2–418
Thoburn, James Mills, Mar. 7, 1836–Nov. 28, 1922.
Vol. 9, Pt. 2–418
Thomas, Allen, Dec. 14, 1830–Dec. 3, 1907.
Vol. 9, Pt. 2–420
Thomas, Amos Russell, Oct. 3, 1826–Oct. 31, 1895.
Vol. 9, Pt. 2–420
Thomas, Augustus, Jan. 8, 1857–Aug. 12, 1934.
Vol. 9, Pt. 2–421
Thomas, Calvin, Oct. 28, 1854–Nov. 4, 1919.
Vol. 9, Pt. 2–422
Thomas, Charles Spalding, Dec. 6, 1849–June 24, 1934.
Vol. 9, Pt. 2–423
Thomas, Christian Friedrich Theodore, Oct. 11, 1835–Jan. 4, 1905.
Vol. 9, Pt. 2–424
Thomas, Cyrus, July 27, 1825–June 26, 1910.
Vol. 9, Pt. 2–426
Thomas, David, June 11, 1762–Nov. 27, 1831.
Vol. 9, Pt. 2–426
Thomas, David, Nov. 3, 1794–June 20, 1882.
Vol. 9, Pt. 2–427
Thomas, Edith Matilda, Aug. 12, 1854–Sept. 13, 1925.
Vol. 9 Pt. 2–428
Thomas, Elbert Duncan, June 17, 1883–Feb. 11, 1953.
Supp. 5–680
Thomas, Francis, Feb. 3, 1799–Jan. 22, 1876.
Vol. 9, Pt. 2–429
Thomas, Frederick William, Oct. 25, 1806–Aug. 27, 1866.
Vol. 9, Pt. 2–430
Thomas, George, *c.* 1695–Dec. 31, 1774.
Vol. 9, Pt. 2–431
Thomas, George Allison, 1911–Oct. 18, 1968.
Supp. 8–647
Thomas, George Clifford, Oct. 28, 1839–Apr. 21, 1909.
Vol. 9, Pt. 2–431
Thomas, George Henry, July 31, 1816–Mar. 28, 1870.
Vol. 9, Pt. 2–432
Thomas, Isaiah, Jan. 19, 1749 o.s.–Apr. 4, 1831.
Vol. 9, Pt. 2–435
Thomas, Jesse Burgess, 1777–May 3, 1853.
Vol. 9, Pt. 2–436
Thomas, Jesse Burgess, July 29, 1832–June 6, 1915.
Vol. 9, Pt. 2–437
Thomas, John, Nov. 9, 1724–June 2, 1776.
Vol. 9, Pt. 2–438
Thomas, John Charles, Sept. 6, 1891–Dec. 13, 1960.
Supp. 6–630
Thomas, John Jacobs, Jan. 8, 1810–Feb. 22, 1895.
Vol. 9, Pt. 2–439
Thomas, John Parnell, Jan. 16, 1895–Nov. 19, 1970.
Supp. 8–648
Thomas, (John William) Elmer, Sept. 8, 1876–Sept. 19, 1965.
Supp. 7–738
Thomas, John Wilson, Aug. 24, 1830–Feb. 12, 1906.
Vol. 9, Pt. 2–440
Thomas, Joseph, Sept. 23, 1811–Dec. 24, 1891.
Vol. 9, Pt. 2–440
Thomas, Lorenzo, Oct. 1804–Mar. 2, 1875.
Vol. 9, Pt. 2–441
Thomas, Martha Carey, Jan 2, 1857–Dec. 2, 1935.
Supp. 1–684
Thomas, Norman Mattoon, Nov. 20, 1884–Dec. 19, 1968.
Supp. 8–649
Thomas, Philip Evan, Nov. 11, 1776–Sept. 1, 1861.
Vol. 9, Pt. 2–442
Thomas, Philip Francis, Sept. 12, 1810–Oct. 2, 1890.
Vol. 9, Pt. 2–443
Thomas, Richard Henry, Jan. 26, 1854–Oct. 3, 1904.
Vol. 9, Pt. 2–443
Thomas, Robert Bailey, Apr. 24, 1766–May 19, 1846.
Vol. 9, Pt. 2–444
Thomas, Roland Jay, June 9, 1900–Apr. 18, 1967.
Supp. 8–651
Thomas, Seth, Aug. 19, 1785–Jan. 29, 1859.
Vol. 9, Pt. 2–445
Thomas, Theodore. [*See* Thomas, Christian Friedrich Theodore, 1835–1905.]
Thomas, Theodore Gaillard, Nov. 21, 1831–Feb. 28, 1903.
Vol. 9, Pt. 2–446
Thomas, William Isaac, Aug. 13, 1863–Dec. 6, 1947.
Supp. 4–827
Thomas, William Widgery, Aug. 26, 1839–Apr. 25, 1927.
Vol. 9, Pt. 2–447
Thomes, William Henry, May 5, 1824–Mar. 6, 1895.
Vol. 9, Pt. 2–447
Thompson, Alfred Wordsworth, May 26, 1840–Aug. 28, 1896.
Vol. 9, Pt. 2–448
Thompson, Arthur Webster, May 8, 1875–Nov. 9, 1930.
Vol. 9, Pt. 2–449
Thompson, Benjamin, July 14, 1642–Apr. 10?, 1714.
Vol. 9, Pt. 2–584
Thompson, Benjamin, Mar. 26, 1753–Aug. 21, 1814.
Vol. 9, Pt. 2–449
Thompson, Cephas Giovanni, Aug. 3, 1809–Jan. 5, 1888.
Vol. 9, Pt. 2–452
Thompson, Charles Oliver, Sept. 25, 1836–Mar. 17, 1885.
Vol. 9, Pt. 2–453
Thompson, Daniel Pierce, Oct. 1, 1795–June 6, 1868.
Vol. 9, Pt. 2–454
Thompson, David, Apr. 30, 1770–Feb. 10, 1857.
Vol. 9, Pt. 2–455
Thompson, David P., Nov. 8, 1834–Dec. 13, 1901.
Vol. 9, Pt. 2–455
Thompson, Denman, Oct. 15, 1833–Apr. 14, 1911.
Vol. 9, Pt. 2–456
Thompson, Dorothy, July 9, 1893–Jan. 30, 1961.
Supp. 7–739
Thompson, Edward Herbert, Sept. 28, 1856–May 11, 1935.
Supp. 1–685
Thompson, Egbert, June 6, 1822–Jan. 5, 1881.
Vol. 9, Pt. 2–457
Thompson, Hugh Miller, June 5, 1830–Nov. 18, 1902.
Vol. 9, Pt. 2–458
Thompson, Hugh Smith, Jan. 24, 1836–Nov. 20, 1904.
Vol. 9, Pt. 2–458
Thompson, Jacob, May 15, 1810–Mar. 24, 1885.
Vol. 9, Pt. 2–459
Thompson, James Maurice, Sept. 9, 1844–Feb. 15, 1901.
Vol. 9, Pt. 2–460
Thompson, Jeremiah, Dec. 9, 1784–Nov. 10, 1835.
Vol. 9, Pt. 2–461
Thompson, Jerome B., Jan. 30, 1814–May 1, 1886.
Vol. 9, Pt. 2–462
Thompson, John. [*See* Thomson, John, 1776–1799.]
Thompson, John, Nov. 2, 1802–Apr. 19, 1891.
Vol. 9, Pt. 2–462
Thompson, John Bodine, Oct. 14, 1830–Sept. 4, 1907.
Vol. 9, Pt. 2–463
Thompson, John Reuben, Oct. 23, 1823–Apr. 30, 1873.
Vol. 9, Pt. 2–464
Thompson, Joseph Parrish, Aug. 7, 1819–Sept. 20, 1879.
Vol. 9, Pt. 2–464

Thompson, Josiah Van Kirk, Feb. 15, 1854–Sept. 27, 1933.
Vol. 9, Pt. 2–465
Thompson, Launt, Feb. 8, 1833–Sept. 26, 1894.
Vol. 9, Pt. 2–466
Thompson, Llewellyn E. ("Tommy"), Jr., Aug. 24, 1904–Feb. 6, 1972.
Supp. 9–798
Thompson, Malvina Cynthia, Jan. 9, 1893–Apr. 12, 1953.
Supp. 5–682
Thompson, Martin E., *c.* 1786–July 24, 1877.
Vol. 9, Pt. 2–467
Thompson, Maurice. [*See* Thompson, James Maurice, 1844–1901.]
Thompson, Oscar Lee, Oct. 10, 1887–July 3, 1945.
Supp. 3–770
Thompson, Richard Wigginton, June 9, 1809–Feb. 9, 1900.
Vol. 9, Pt. 2–468
Thompson, Robert Ellis, Apr. 5, 1844–Oct. 19, 1924.
Vol. 9, Pt. 2–469
Thompson, Robert Means, Mar. 2, 1849–Sept. 5, 1930.
Supp. 1–687
Thompson, Samuel Rankin, Apr. 17, 1833–Oct. 28, 1896.
Vol. 9, Pt. 2–470
Thompson, Seymour Dwight, Sept. 18, 1842–Aug. 11, 1904.
Vol. 9, Pt. 2–471
Thompson, Slason, Jan. 5, 1849–Dec. 22, 1935.
Supp. 1–688
Thompson, Smith, Jan. 17, 1768–Dec. 18, 1843.
Vol. 9, Pt. 2–471
Thompson, Stith, Mar. 7, 1885–Jan. 10, 1976.
Supp. 10–780
Thompson, Thomas Larkin, May 31, 1838–Feb. 1, 1898.
Vol. 9, Pt. 2–473
Thompson, Waddy, Sept. 8, 1798–Nov. 23, 1868.
Vol. 9, Pt. 2–473
Thompson, Wiley, Sept. 23, 1781–Dec. 28, 1835.
Vol. 9, Pt. 2–474
Thompson, Will Lamartine, Nov. 7, 1847–Sept. 20, 1909.
Vol. 9, Pt. 2–475
Thompson, William, 1736–Sept. 3, 1781.
Vol. 9, Pt. 2–476
Thompson, William Boyce, May 13, 1869–June 27, 1930.
Vol. 9, Pt. 2–476
Thompson, William Gilman, Dec. 25, 1856–Oct. 27, 1927.
Vol. 9, Pt. 2–477
Thompson, William Hale, May 14, 1867–Mar. 19, 1944.
Supp. 3–771
Thompson, William Oxley, Nov. 5, 1855–Dec. 9, 1933.
Vol. 9, Pt. 2–478
Thompson, William Tappan, Aug. 31, 1812–Mar. 24, 1882.
Vol. 9, Pt. 2–479
Thompson, Zadock, May 23, 1796–Jan. 19, 1856.
Vol. 9, Pt. 2–480
Thomson, Charles, Nov. 29, 1729–Aug. 16, 1824.
Vol. 9, Pt. 2–481
Thomson, Edward, Oct. 12, 1810–Mar. 22, 1870.
Vol. 9, Pt. 2–482
Thomson, Edward William, Feb. 12, 1849–Mar. 5, 1924.
Vol. 9, Pt. 2–483
Thomson, Elihu, Mar. 29, 1853–Mar. 13, 1937.
Supp. 2–657
Thomson, Frank, July 5, 1841–June 5, 1899.
Vol. 9, Pt. 2–483
Thomson, John, Nov. 3, 1776–Jan. 25, 1799.
Vol. 9, Pt. 2–484
Thomson, John, Oct. 25, 1853–June 1, 1926.
Vol. 9, Pt. 2–485
Thomson, John Edgar, Feb. 10, 1808–May 27, 1874.
Vol. 9, Pt. 2–486
Thomson, Mortimer Neal, Sept. 2, 1831–June 25, 1875.
Vol. 9, Pt. 2–487
Thomson, Samuel, Feb. 9, 1769–Oct. 4, 1843.
Vol. 9, Pt. 2–488
Thomson, William, Jan. 16, 1727–Nov. 2, 1796.
Vol. 9, Pt. 2–489
Thomson, William McClure, Dec. 31, 1806–Apr. 8, 1894.
Vol. 9, Pt. 2–490
Thorburn, Grant, Feb. 18, 1773–Jan. 21, 1863.
Vol. 9, Pt. 2–490
Thoreau, Henry David, July 12, 1817–May 6, 1862.
Vol. 9, Pt. 2–491
Thorek, Max, Mar. 10, 1880–Jan. 25, 1960.
Supp. 6–631
Thorndike, Ashley Horace, Dec. 26, 1871–Apr. 17, 1933.
Vol. 9, Pt. 2–497
Thorndike, Edward Lee, Aug. 31, 1874–Aug. 9, 1949.
Supp. 4–831
Thorndike, Israel, Apr. 30, 1755–May 8, 1832.
Vol. 9, Pt. 2–498
Thorndike, Lynn, July 24, 1882–Dec. 28, 1965.
Supp. 7–741
Thorne, Charles Robert, *c.* 1814–Dec. 13, 1893.
Vol. 9, Pt. 2–499
Thorne, Charles Robert, 1840–Feb. 10, 1883.
Vol. 9, Pt. 2–500
Thornton, Daniel I. J., Jan. 31, 1911–Jan. 18, 1976.
Supp. 10–782
Thornton, Henry Worth, Nov. 6, 1871–Mar. 14, 1933.
Vol. 9, Pt. 2–501
Thornton, Jessy Quinn, Aug. 24, 1810–Feb. 5, 1888.
Vol. 9, Pt. 2–502
Thornton, John Wingate, Aug. 12, 1818–June 6, 1878.
Vol. 9, Pt. 2–503
Thornton, Matthew, *c.* 1714–June 24, 1803.
Vol. 9, Pt. 2–503
Thornton, William, May 20, 1759–Mar. 28, 1828.
Vol. 9, Pt. 2–504
Thornwell, James Henley, Dec. 9, 1812–Aug. 1, 1862.
Vol. 9, Pt. 2–507
Thorp, John, 1784–Nov. 15, 1848.
Vol. 9, Pt. 2–508
Thorpe, James Francis, May 28, 1888–Mar. 28, 1953.
Supp. 5–683
Thorpe Rose Alnora Hartwick, July 18, 1850–July 19, 1939.
Supp. 2–659
Thorpe, Thomas Bangs, Mar. 1, 1815–Sept. 20, 1878.
Vol. 9, Pt. 2–509
Thrasher, John Sidney, 1817–Nov. 10, 1879.
Vol. 9, Pt. 2–509
Throop, Enos Thompson, Aug. 21, 1784–Nov. 1, 1874.
Vol. 9, Pt. 2–510
Throop, Montgomery Hunt, Jan. 26, 1827–Sept. 11, 1892.
Vol. 9, Pt. 2–511
Thulstrup, Bror Thure, Apr. 5, 1848–June 9, 1930.
Vol. 9, Pt. 2–512
Thumb, Tom. [*See* Stratton, Charles Sherwood, 1838–1883.]
Thurber, Charles, Jan. 2, 1803–Nov. 7, 1886.
Vol. 9, Pt. 2–513
Thurber, Christopher Carson, May 19, 1880–May 31, 1930.
Vol. 4, Pt. 2–513
Thurber, George, Sept. 2, 1821–Apr. 2, 1890.
Vol. 9, Pt. 2–514
Thurber, James Grover, Dec. 8, 1894–Nov. 2, 1961.
Supp. 7–742
Thurber, Jeannette Meyer, Jan. 29, 1850–Jan. 2, 1946.
Supp. 4–834
Thurman, Allen Granberry, Nov. 13, 1813–Dec. 12, 1895.
Vol. 9, Pt. 2–515
Thursby, Emma Cecilia, Feb. 21, 1845–July 4, 1931.
Vol. 9, Pt. 2–516
Thurston, Howard, July 20, 1869–Apr. 13, 1936.
Supp. 2–660
Thurston, Lorrin Andrews, July 31, 1858–May 11, 1931.
Vol. 9, Pt. 2–517
Thurston, Robert Henry, Oct. 25, 1839–Oct. 25, 1903.
Vol. 9, Pt. 2–518
Thurston, Robert Lawton, Dec. 13, 1800–Jan. 13, 1874.
Vol. 9, Pt. 2–520
Thurstone, Louis Leon, May 29, 1887–Sept. 29, 1955.
Supp. 5–684
Thwaites, Reuben Gold, May 15, 1853–Oct. 22, 1913.
Vol. 9, Pt. 2–521
Thwing, Charles Franklin, Nov. 9, 1853–Aug. 29, 1937.
Supp. 2–663
Thye, Edward John, Apr. 26, 1896–Aug. 28, 1969.
Supp. 8–653
Tibbett, Lawrence Mervil, Nov. 16, 1896–July 15, 1960.
Supp. 6–632
Tibbles, Susette La Flesche. [*See* Bright Eyes, 1854–1903.]
Tibbles, Thomas Henry, May 22, 1838–May 14, 1928.
Vol. 9, Pt. 2–522

Tichenor, Isaac, Feb. 8, 1754–Dec. 11, 1838.
Vol. 9, Pt. 2–523
Tichenor, Isaac Taylor, Nov. 11, 1825–Dec. 2, 1902.
Vol. 9, Pt. 2–523
Ticknor, Elisha, Mar. 25, 1757–June 22, 1821.
Vol. 9, Pt. 2–524
Ticknor, Francis Orray, Nov. 13, 1822–Dec. 18, 1874.
Vol. 9, Pt. 2–525
Ticknor, George, Aug. 1, 1791–Jan. 26, 1871.
Vol. 9, Pt. 2–525
Ticknor, William Davis, Aug. 6, 1810–Apr. 10, 1864.
Vol. 9, Pt. 2–528
Tidball, John Caldwell, Jan. 25, 1825–May 15, 1906.
Vol. 9, Pt. 2–529
Tiebout, Cornelius, *c.* 1773–*c.* 1830.
Vol. 9, Pt. 2–530
Tiedeman, Christopher Gustavus, July 16, 1857–Aug. 25, 1903.
Vol. 9, Pt. 2–531
Tiernan, Frances Christine Fisher, July 5, 1846–Mar. 24, 1920.
Vol. 9, Pt. 2–531
Tierney, Richard Henry, Sept. 2, 1870–Feb. 10, 1928.
Vol. 9, Pt. 2–532
Tiffany, Charles Lewis, Feb. 15, 1812–Feb. 18, 1902.
Vol. 9, Pt. 2–533
Tiffany, Katrina Brandes Ely, Mar. 25, 1875–Mar. 11, 1927.
Vol. 9, Pt. 2–533
Tiffany, Louis Comfort, Feb. 18, 1848–Jan. 17, 1933.
Vol. 9, Pt. 2–534
Tiffany, Louis McLane, Oct. 10, 1844–Oct. 23, 1916.
Vol. 9, Pt. 2–535
Tiffin, Edward, June 19, 1766–Aug. 9, 1829.
Vol. 9, Pt. 2–535
Tigert, John James, Nov. 25, 1856–Nov. 21, 1906.
Vol. 9, Pt. 2–536
Tigert, John James, IV, Feb. 11, 1882–Jan. 21, 1965.
Supp. 7–744
Tikamthi. [*See* Tecumseh, 1768?–1813.]
Tilden, Samuel Jones, Feb. 9, 1814–Aug. 4, 1886.
Vol. 9, Pt. 2–537
Tilden, William Tatem ("Big Bill"), Feb. 10, 1893–June 5, 1953.
Supp. 5–686
Tileston, Thomas, Aug. 13, 1793–Feb. 29, 1864.
Vol. 9, Pt. 2–541
Tilghman, Edward, Feb. 11, 1750/51–Nov. 1, 1815.
Vol. 9, Pt. 2–542
Tilghman, Matthew, Feb. 17, 1718–May 4, 1790.
Vol. 9, Pt. 2–543
Tilghman, Richard Albert, May 24, 1824–Mar. 24, 1899.
Vol. 9, Pt. 2–544
Tilghman, Tench, Dec. 25, 1744–Apr. 18, 1786.
Vol. 9, Pt. 2–545
Tilghman, William, Aug. 12, 1756–Apr. 29, 1827.
Vol. 9, Pt. 2–545
Tilghman, William Matthew, July 4, 1854–Nov. 1, 1924.
Vol. 9, Pt. 2–546
Tillich, Paul, Aug. 20, 1886–Oct. 22, 1965.
Supp. 7–745
Tillman, Benjamin Ryan, Aug. 11, 1847–July 3, 1918.
Vol. 9, Pt. 2–547
Tilney, Frederick, June 4, 1875–Aug. 7, 1938.
Supp. 2–664
Tilson, John Quillin, Apr. 5, 1866–Aug. 14, 1958.
Supp. 6–633
Tilton, Edward Lippincott, Oct. 19, 1861–Jan. 5, 1933.
Vol. 9, Pt. 2–549
Tilton, James, June 1, 1745–May 14, 1822.
Vol. 9, Pt. 2–550
Tilton, John Rollin, June 8, 1828–Mar. 22, 1888.
Vol. 9, Pt. 2–551
Tilton, Theodore, Oct. 2, 1835–May 25, 1907.
Vol. 9, Pt. 2–551
Tilyou, George Cornelius, Feb. 3, 1862–Nov. 30, 1914.
Vol. 9, Pt. 2–553
Tilzer, Harry Von, July 8, 1872–Jan. 10, 1946.
Supp. 4–835
Timberlake, Gideon, Mar. 6, 1876–Mar. 1, 1951.
Supp. 5–688
Timberlake, Henry, 1730–Sept. 30, 1765.
Vol. 9, Pt. 2–553
Timby, Theodore Ruggles, Apr. 5, 1822–Nov. 9, 1909.
Vol. 9, Pt. 2–554
Timken, Henry, Aug. 16, 1831–Mar. 16, 1909.
Vol. 9, Pt. 2–555
Timm, Henry Christian, July 11, 1811–Sept. 5, 1892.
Vol. 9, Pt. 2–555
Timme, Walter, Feb. 24, 1874–Feb. 12, 1956.
Supp. 6–634
Timon, John, Feb. 12, 1797–Apr. 16, 1867.
Vol. 9, Pt. 2–556
Timothy, Lewis, d. Dec. 1738.
Vol. 9, Pt. 2–557
Timrod, Henry, Dec. 8, 1828–Oct. 6, 1867.
Vol. 9, Pt. 2–558
Tincker, Mary Agnes, July 18, 1831–Nov. 27, 1907.
Vol. 9, Pt. 2–560
Tingey, Thomas, Sept. 11, 1750–Feb. 23, 1829.
Vol. 9, Pt. 2–560
Tingley, Katherine Augusta Westcott, July 6, 1847–July 11, 1929.
Vol. 9, Pt. 2–561
Tinkham, George Holden, Oct. 20, 1870–Aug. 28, 1956.
Supp. 6–635
Tiomkin, Dimitri, May 10, 1894–Nov. 11, 1979.
Supp. 10–783
Tipton, John, Aug. 15, 1730–Aug. 1813.
Vol. 9, Pt. 2–562
Tipton, John, Aug. 14, 1786–Apr. 5, 1839.
Vol. 9, Pt. 2–563
Tishman, David, Apr. 22, 1889–June 18, 1980.
Supp. 10–785
Tisquantum. [*See* Squanto, d. 1622.]
Titchener, Edward Bradford, Jan. 11, 1867–Aug. 3, 1927.
Vol. 9, Pt. 2–564
Titcomb, John Wheelock, Feb. 24, 1860–Jan. 26, 1932.
Vol. 9, Pt. 2–565
Tittle, Ernest Fremont, Oct. 21, 1885–Aug. 3, 1949.
Supp. 4–836
Tobani, Theodore Moses, May 2, 1855–Dec. 12, 1933.
Vol. 9, Pt. 2–566
Tobey, Charles William, July 22, 1880–July 24, 1953.
Supp. 5–689
Tobey, Edward Silas, Apr. 5, 1813–Mar. 29, 1891.
Vol. 9, Pt. 2–567
Tobey, Mark, Dec. 11, 1890–Apr. 24, 1976.
Supp. 10–786
Tobias, Channing Heggie, Feb. 1, 1882–Nov. 5, 1961.
Supp. 7–748
Tobin, Austin Joseph, May 25, 1903–Feb. 8, 1978.
Supp. 10–788
Tobin, Daniel Joseph, Apr. 3, 1875–Nov. 14, 1955.
Supp. 5–690
Tobin, Maurice Joseph, May 22, 1901–July 19, 1953.
Supp. 5–691
Tod, David, Feb. 21, 1805–Nov. 13, 1868.
Vol. 9, Pt. 2–567
Tod, George, Dec. 11, 1773–Apr. 11, 1841.
Vol. 9, Pt. 2–568
Tod, John, Nov. 1779–Mar. 27, 1830.
Vol. 9, Pt. 2–569
Todd, Charles Stewart, Jan. 22, 1791–May 17, 1871.
Vol. 9, Pt. 2–569
Todd, Eli, July 22, 1769–Nov. 17, 1833.
Vol. 9, Pt. 2–570
Todd, Henry Alfred, Mar. 13, 1854–Jan. 3, 1925.
Vol. 9, Pt. 2–571
Todd, John, Oct. 9, 1800–Aug. 24, 1873.
Vol. 9, Pt. 2–572
Todd, Mabel Loomis, Nov. 10, 1856–Oct. 14, 1932.
Vol. 9, Pt. 2–573
Todd, Mike, June 22, 1909–Mar. 22, 1958.
Supp. 6–637
Todd, Sereno Edwards, June 3, 1820–Dec. 26, 1898.
Vol. 9, Pt. 2–574
Todd, Thomas, Jan. 23, 1765–Feb. 7, 1826.
Vol. 9, Pt. 2–574
Todd, Thomas Wingate, Jan. 15, 1885–Dec. 28, 1938.
Supp. 2–665
Todd, Walter Edmond Clyde, Sept. 6, 1874–June 25, 1969.
Supp. 8–654

Todman, William Selden ("Bill"), July 31, 1916–July 29, 1979.
Supp. 10–789
Toklas, Alice Babette, Apr. 30, 1877–Mar. 7, 1967.
Supp. 8–655
Toland, Hugh Huger, Apr. 16, 1806–Feb. 27, 1880.
Vol. 9, Pt. 2–575
Tolley, Howard Ross, Sept. 30, 1889–Sept. 18, 1958.
Supp. 6–638
Tolman, Edward Chace, Apr. 14, 1886–Nov. 19, 1959.
Supp. 6–639
Tolman, Herbert Cushing, Nov. 4, 1865–Nov. 24, 1923.
Vol. 9, Pt. 2–576
Tolman, Richard Chace, Mar. 4, 1881–Sept. 5, 1948.
Supp. 4–837
Tome, Jacob, Aug. 13, 1810–Mar. 16, 1898.
Vol. 9, Pt. 2–577
Tomkins, Floyd Williams, Feb. 7, 1850–Mar. 24, 1932.
Vol. 9, Pt. 2–578
Tomlin, Bradley Walker, Aug. 19, 1899–May 11, 1953.
Supp. 1–692
Tomlins, WIlliam Lawrence, Feb. 4, 1844–Sept. 26, 1930.
Vol. 9, Pt. 2–578
Tomlinson, Everett Titsworth, May 23, 1859–Oct. 30, 1931.
Vol. 9, Pt. 2–579
Tomochichi, 1650?–Oct. 5, 1739.
Vol. 9, Pt. 2–580
Tompkins, Arnold, Sept. 10, 1849–Aug. 12, 1905.
Vol. 9, Pt. 2–580
Tompkins, Daniel Augustus, Oct. 12, 1851–Oct. 18, 1914.
Vol. 9, Pt. 2–581
Tompkins, Daniel D., June 21, 1774–June 11, 1825.
Vol. 9, Pt. 2–583
Tompkins, Sally Louisa, Nov. 9, 1833–July 25, 1916.
Vol. 9, Pt. 2–584
Tondorf, Francis Anthony, July 17, 1870–Nov. 29, 1929.
Vol. 9, Pt. 2–585
Tone, Stanislas Pascal Franchot, Feb. 27, 1905–Sept. 18, 1968.
Supp. 8–657
Toner, Joseph Meredith, Apr. 30, 1825–July 30, 1896.
Vol. 9, Pt. 2–586
Tonty, Henry de, 1650–1704.
Vol. 9, Pt. 2–587
Toole, Edwin Warren, Mar. 24, 1839–May 17, 1905.
Vol. 9, Pt. 2–588
Toole, Joseph Kemp, May 12, 1851–Mar. 11, 1929.
Vol. 9, Pt. 2–589
Toombs, Robert Augustus, July 2, 1810–Dec. 15, 1885.
Vol. 9, Pt. 2–590
Topliff, Samuel, Apr. 25, 1789–Dec. 11, 1864.
Vol. 9, Pt. 2–592
Torbert, Alfred Thomas Archimedes, July 1, 1833–Aug. 29, 1880.
Vol. 9, Pt. 2–593
Torrence, Frederick Ridgely, Nov. 27, 1874–Dec. 25, 1950.
Supp. 4–840
Torrence, Joseph Thatcher, Mar. 15, 1843–Oct. 31, 1896.
Vol. 9, Pt. 2–594
Torrey, Bradford, Oct. 9, 1843–Oct. 7, 1912.
Vol. 9, Pt. 2–594
Torrey, Charles Cutler, Dec. 20, 1863–Nov. 12, 1956.
Supp. 6–641
Torrey, Charles Turner, Nov. 21, 1813–May 9, 1846.
Vol. 9, Pt. 2–595
Torrey, John, Aug. 15, 1796–Mar. 10, 1873.
Vol. 9, Pt. 2–596
Toscanini, Arturo, Mar. 25, 1867–Jan. 16, 1957.
Supp. 6–642
Totten, George Muirson, May 28, 1809–May 17, 1884.
Vol. 9, Pt. 2–598
Totten, Joseph Gilbert, Aug. 23, 1788–Apr. 22, 1864.
Vol. 9, Pt. 2–598
Tou, Erik Hansen, Oct. 11, 1857–Nov. 14, 1917.
Vol. 9, Pt. 2–599
Toucey, Isaac, Nov. 15, 1792–July 30, 1869.
Vol. 9, Pt. 2–600
Toulmin, Harry Theophilus, Mar. 4, 1838–Nov. 12, 1916.
Vol. 9, Pt. 2–602
Toulmin, Harry, Apr. 7, 1766–Nov. 11, 1823.
Vol. 9, Pt. 2–601
Toumey, James William, Apr. 17, 1865–May 6, 1932.
Vol. 9, Pt. 2–603
Tourel, Jennie, June 22, 1900–Nov. 23, 1973.
Supp. 9–800
Tourgée, Albion Winegar, May 2, 1838–May 21, 1905.
Vol. 9, Pt. 2–603
Tourjée, Eben, June 1, 1834–Apr. 12, 1891.
Vol. 9, Pt. 2–605
Tousard, Anne Louis de, Mar. 12, 1749–May 8, 1817.
Vol. 9, Pt. 2–605
Tousey, Sinclair, July 18, 1815–June 16, 1887.
Vol. 9, Pt. 2–606
Tower, Charlemagne, Apr. 17, 1848–Feb. 24, 1923.
Vol. 9, Pt. 2–607
Tower, Zealous Bates, Jan. 12, 1819–Mar. 20, 1900.
Vol. 9, Pt. 2–608
Towers, John Henry, Jan. 30, 1885–Apr. 30, 1955.
Supp. 5–694
Towle, George Makepeace, Aug. 27, 1841–Aug. 9, 1893.
Vol. 9, Pt. 2–609
Towler, John, June 20, 1811–Apr. 2, 1889.
Vol. 9, Pt. 2–609
Town, Ithiel, Oct. 3, 1784–June 13, 1844.
Vol. 9, Pt. 2–610
Towne, Benjamin, d. July 8, 1793.
Vol. 9, Pt. 2–611
Towne, Charles Arnette, Nov. 21, 1858–Oct. 22, 1928.
Vol. 9, Pt. 2–612
Towne, Charles Hanson, Feb. 2, 1877–Feb. 28, 1949.
Supp. 4–841
Towne, Henry Robinson, Aug. 28, 1844–Oct. 15, 1924.
Vol. 9, Pt. 2–613
Towne, John Henry, Feb. 20, 1818–Apr. 6, 1875.
Vol. 9, Pt. 2–614
Townley, Arthur Charles, Dec. 30, 1880–Nov. 7, 1959.
Supp. 6–644
Towns, George Washington Bonaparte, May 4, 1801–July 15, 1854.
Vol. 9, Pt. 2–615
Townsend, Edward Davis, Aug. 22, 1817–May 10, 1893.
Vol. 9, Pt. 2–615
Townsend, Francis Everett, Jan. 13, 1867–Sept. 1, 1960.
Supp. 6–645
Townsend, George Alfred, Jan. 30, 1841–Apr. 15, 1914.
Vol. 9, Pt. 2–616
Townsend, John Kirk, Aug. 10, 1809–Feb. 6, 1851.
Vol. 4, Pt. 2–617
Townsend, Luther Tracy, Sept. 27, 1838–Aug. 2, 1922.
Vol. 9, Pt. 2–618
Townsend, Mary Ashley, Sept. 24, 1832–June 7, 1901.
Vol. 9, Pt. 2–619
Townsend, Mira Sharpless, Sept. 26, 1798–Nov. 20, 1859.
Vol. 9, Pt. 2–619
Townsend, Robert, Oct. 21, 1819–Aug. 15, 1866.
Vol. 9, Pt. 2–620
Townsend, Virginia Frances, 1836–Aug. 11, 1920.
Vol. 9, Pt. 2–621
Townsend, Willard Saxby, Jr., Dec. 4, 1895–Feb. 3, 1957.
Supp. 6–647
Toy, Crawford Howell, Mar. 23, 1836–May 12, 1919.
Vol. 9, Pt. 2–621
Tracy, Benjamin Franklin, Apr. 26, 1830–Aug. 6, 1915.
Vol. 9, Pt. 2–622
Tracy, Joseph, Nov. 3, 1793–Mar. 24, 1874.
Vol. 9, Pt. 2–623
Tracy, Nathaniel, Aug. 11, 1751–Sept. 20, 1796.
Vol. 9, Pt. 2–624
Tracy, Spencer Bonaventure, Apr. 5, 1900–June 10, 1967.
Supp. 8–658
Tracy, Uriah, Feb. 2, 1755–July 19, 1807.
Vol. 9, Pt. 2–624
Traetta, Filippo. [*See* Trajetta, Philip, *c.* 1776–1854.]
Train, Arthur Cheney, Sept. 6, 1875–Dec. 22, 1945.
Supp. 3–723
Train, Enoch, May 2, 1801–Sept. 8, 1868.
Vol. 9, Pt. 2–625
Train, George Francls, May. 24, 1829–Jan. 19, 1904.
Vol. 9, Pt. 2–626
Trajetta, Philip, *c.* 1776–Jan. 9, 1854.
Vol. 9, Pt. 2–627

Trammell, Niles, July 6, 1894–Mar. 28, 1973.
Supp. 9–801
Trask, James Dowling, Aug. 21, 1890–May 24, 1942.
Supp. 3–774
Traubel, Helen, June 16, 1899–July 28, 1972.
Supp. 9–804
Traubel, Horace L., Dec. 19, 1858–Sept. 8, 1919.
Vol. 9. Pt. 2–627
Trautwine, John Cresson, Mar. 30, 1810–Sept. 14, 1883.
Vol. 9, Pt. 2–628
Travers, Jerome Dunstan, May 19, 1887–Mar. 30, 1951.
Supp. 5–695
Travis, Walter John, Jan. 10, 1862–July 31, 1927.
Vol. 9, Pt. 2–629
Travis, William Barret, Aug. 9, 1809–Mar. 6, 1836.
Vol. 9, Pt. 2–630
Traylor, Melvin Alvah, Oct. 21, 1878–Feb. 14, 1934.
Vol. 9, Pt. 2–631
Traynor, Harold Joseph ("Pie"), Nov. 11, 1899–Mar. 16, 1972.
Supp. 9–805
Treadwell, Daniel, Oct. 10, 1791–Feb. 27, 1872.
Vol. 9, Pt. 2–631
Treat, Robert, 1622?–July 12, 1710.
Vol. 9, Pt. 2–633
Treat, Samuel, Dec. 17, 1815–Aug. 31, 1902.
Vol. 9, Pt. 2–634
Treat, Samuel Hubbel, June 21, 1811–Mar. 27, 1887.
Vol. 9, Pt. 2–634
Tree, Lambert, Nov. 29, 1832–Oct. 9, 1910.
Vol. 9, Pt. 2–635
Trelease, William, Feb. 22, 1857–Jan. 1, 1945.
Supp. 3–775
Tremain, Henry Edwin, Nov. 14, 1840–Dec 9, 1910
Vol. 9, Pt. 2–636
Tremaine, Henry Barnes, July 20, 1866–May 13, 1932.
Vol. 9, Pt. 2–636
Trenchard, Stephen Decatur, July 10, 1818–Nov. 15, 1883.
Vol. 9, Pt. 2–637
Trenholm, George Alfred, Feb. 25, 1807–Dec. 9, 1876.
Supp. 1–689
Trent, William, Feb. 13, 1715–1787?.
Vol. 9, Pt. 2–638
Trent, William Peterfield, Nov. 10, 1862–Dec. 6, 1939.
Supp. 2–666
Tresca, Carlo, Mar. 9, 1879–Jan 11, 1943.
Supp. 3–776
Trescot, William Henry, Nov. 10, 1822–May 4, 1898.
Vol. 9, Pt. 2–639
Trevellick, Richard F., May 1830–Feb. 15, 1895.
Vol. 9, Pt. 2–640
Trilling, Lionel, July 4, 1905–Nov. 5, 1975.
Supp. 9–807
Trimble, Allen, Nov. 24, 1783–Feb. 3, 1870.
Vol. 9, Pt. 2–641
Trimble, Isaac Ridgeway, May 15, 1802–Jan. 2, 1888.
Vol. 9, Pt. 2–641
Trimble, Robert, 1777–Aug. 25, 1828.
Vol. 9, Pt. 2–642
Tripp, Bartlett, July 15, 1842–Dec. 8, 1911.
Vol. 9, Pt. 2–643
Tripp, Guy Eastman, Apr. 22, 1865–June 14, 1927.
Vol. 9, Pt. 2–644
Trippe, John, 1785–July 9, 1810.
Vol. 9, Pt. 2–645
Trist, Nicholas Philip, June 2, 1800–Feb. 11, 1874.
Vol. 9, Pt. 2–645
Tristano, Leonard Joseph ("Lennie"), Mar. 19, 1919–Nov. 18, 1978.
Supp. 10–791
Troland, Leonard Thompson, Apr. 26, 1889–May 27, 1932.
Vol. 9, Pt. 2–646
Troost, Gerard, Mar. 15, 1776–Aug. 14, 1850.
Vol. 9, Pt. 2–647
Trott, Benjamin, *c.* 1770–*c.* 1841.
Vol. 9, Pt. 2–648
Trott, Nicholas, Jan. 19, 1662/63–Jan. 21, 1739/40.
Vol. 9, Pt. 2–649
Troup, George Michael, Sept. 8, 1780–Apr. 26, 1856.
Vol. 9, Pt. 2–650
Troup, Robert, 1757–Jan. 14, 1832.
Vol. 9, Pt. 2–651
Trow, John Fowler, Jan. 30, 1810–Aug. 8, 1886.
Vol. 9, Pt. 2–652
Trowbridge, Augustus, Jan. 2, 1870–Mar. 14, 1934.
Vol. 9, Pt. 2–652
Trowbridge, Edmund, 1709–Apr. 2, 1793.
Vol. 9, Pt. 2–653
Trowbridge, John, Aug. 5, 1843–Feb. 18, 1923.
Vol. 9, Pt. 2–654
Trowbridge, John Townsend, Sept. 18, 1827–Feb. 12, 1916.
Vol. 9, Pt. 2–655
Trowbridge, William Petit, May 25, 1828–Aug. 12, 1892.
Vol. 9, Pt. 2–656
Troye, Edward, 1808–July 25, 1874.
Vol. 10, Pt. 1–1
Trude, Alfred Samuel, Apr. 21, 1847–Dec. 12, 1933.
Vol. 10, Pt. 1–2
Trudeau, Edward Livingston, Oct. 5, 1848–Nov. 15, 1915.
Vol. 10, Pt. 1–2
Trudeau, Jean Baptiste [*See* Truteau, Jean Baptiste, 1748–1827.]
True, Alfred Charles, June 5, 1853–Apr. 23, 1929.
Vol. 10, Pt. 1–4
True, Frederick William, July 8, 1858–June 25, 1914.
Vol. 10, Pt. 1–5
Trueblood, Benjamin Franklin, Nov. 25, 1847–Oct. 26, 1916.
Vol. 10, Pt. 1–5
Truett, George Washington, May 6, 1867–July 7, 1944.
Supp. 3–778
Truman, Benjamin Cummings, Oct. 25, 1835–July 18, 1916.
Vol. 10, Pt. 1–6
Truman, Harry S., May 8, 1884–Dec. 26, 1972.
Supp. 9–808
Trumbauer, Horace, Dec. 28, 1868–Sept. 18, 1938.
Supp. 2–667
Trumbo, James Dalton, Dec. 9, 1905–Sept. 10, 1976.
Supp. 10–793
Trumbull, Benjamin, Dec. 19, 1735–Feb. 2, 1820.
Vol. 10, Pt. 1–7
Trumbull, Henry Clay, June 8, 1830–Dec. 8, 1903.
Vol. 10, Pt. 1–8
Trumbull, James Hammond, Dec. 20, 1821–Aug. 5, 1897.
Vol. 10, Pt. 1–9
Trumbull, John, Apr. 13, 1750 o.s.–May 11, 1831.
Vol. 10, Pt. 1–10
Trumbull, John, June 6, 1756–Nov. 10, 1843.
Vol. 10, Pt. 1–11
Trumbull, Jonathan, Oct. 12, 1710–Aug. 17, 1785.
Vol. 10, Pt. 1–15
Trumbull, Jonathan, Mar. 26, 1740–Aug. 7, 1809.
Vol. 10, Pt. 1–17
Trumbull, Joseph, Mar. 11, 1737–July 23, 1778.
Vol. 10, Pt. 1–18
Trumbull, Lyman, Oct. 12, 1813–June 25, 1896.
Vol. 10, Pt. 1–19
Truteau, Jean Baptiste, Dec. 11, 1748–Jan. 30?, 1827.
Vol. 10, Pt. 1–20
Truxtun, Thomas, Feb. 17, 1755–May 5, 1822.
Vol. 10, Pt. 1–21
Truxtun, William Talbot, Mar. 11, 1824–Feb. 25, 1887.
Vol. 10, Pt. 1–22
Tryon, Dwight William, Aug. 13, 1849–July 1, 1925.
Vol. 10, Pt. 1–23
Tryon, George Washington, May 20, 1838–Feb. 5, 1888.
Vol. 10, Pt. 1–24
Tryon, William, 1729–Jan. 27, 1788.
Vol. 10, Pt. 1–25
Tubman, Harriet, *c.* 1821–Mar. 10, 1913.
Vol. 10, Pt. 1–27
Tuck, Amos, Aug. 2, 1810–Dec. 11, 1879.
Vol. 10, Pt. 1–27
Tucker, Allen, June 29, 1866–Jan. 26, 1939.
Supp. 2–669
Tucker, Benjamin Ricketson, Apr. 17, 1854–June 22, 1939.
Supp. 2–669
Tucker, George, Aug. 20, 1775–Apr. 10, 1861.
Vol. 10, Pt. 1–28

Tucker, Gilbert Milligan, Aug. 26, 1847–Jan. 13, 1932.
Vol. 10, Pt. 1–30
Tucker, Henry Holcombe, May 10, 1819–Sept. 9, 1889.
Vol. 10, Pt. 1–31
Tucker, Henry St. George, Dec. 29, 1780–Aug. 28, 1848.
Vol. 10, Pt. 1–32
Tucker, Henry St. George, Apr. 5, 1853–July 23, 1932.
Vol. 10, Pt. 1–33
Tucker, Henry St. George, July 16, 1874–Aug. 8, 1959.
Supp. 6–648
Tucker, John Randolph, Jan. 31, 1812–June 12, 1883.
Vol. 10, Pt. 1–33
Tucker, John Randolph, Dec. 24, 1823–Feb. 13, 1897.
Vol. 10, Pt. 1–34
Tucker, Luther, May 7, 1802–Jan. 26, 1873.
Vol. 10, Pt. 1–35
Tucker, Nathaniel Beverley, Sept. 6, 1784–Aug. 26, 1851.
Vol. 10, Pt. 1–36
Tucker, Nathaniel Beverley, June 8, 1820–July 4, 1890.
Vol. 10, Pt. 1–37
Tucker, Richard, Aug. 28, 1913–Jan. 8, 1975.
Supp. 9–815
Tucker, St. George, June 29, 1752 o.s.–Nov. 10, 1827.
Vol. 10, Pt. 1–38
Tucker, Samuel, Nov. 1, 1747–Mar. 10, 1833.
Vol. 10, Pt. 1–39
Tucker, Sophie, Jan. 13, 1887–Feb. 9, 1966.
Supp. 8–660
Tucker, Stephen Davis, Jan. 28, 1818–Oct. 9, 1902.
Vol. 10, Pt. 1–40
Tucker, William Jewett, July 13, 1839–Sept. 29, 1926.
Vol. 10, Pt. 1–41
Tuckerman, Bayard, July 2, 1855–Oct. 20, 1923.
Vol. 10, Pt. 1–42
Tuckerman, Edward, Dec. 7, 1817–Mar. 15, 1886.
Vol. 10, Pt. 1–42
Tuckerman, Frederick, May 7, 1857–Nov. 8, 1929.
Vol. 10, Pt. 1–44
Tuckerman, Frederick Goddard, Feb. 4, 1821–May 9, 1873.
Vol. 10, Pt. 1–44
Tuckerman, Henry Theodore, Apr. 20, 1813–Dec. 17, 1871.
Vol. 10, Pt. 1–45
Tuckerman, Joseph, Jan. 18, 1778–Apr. 20, 1840.
Vol. 10, Pt. 1–46
Tuckey, William, *c.* 1708–Sept. 14, 1781.
Vol. 10, Pt. 1–46
Tudor, Frederic, Sept. 4, 1783–Feb. 6, 1864.
Vol. 10, Pt. 1–47
Tudor, William, Jan. 28, 1779–Mar. 9, 1830.
Vol. 10, Pt. 1–48
Tufts, Charles, July 17, 1781–Dec. 24, 1876.
Vol. 10, Pt. 1–49
Tufts, Cotton, May 30, 1732–Dec. 8, 1815.
Vol. 10, Pt. 1–49
Tufts, James Hayden, July 9, 1862–Aug. 5, 1942.
Supp. 3–779
Tufts, John, May 5, 1689–Aug. 17, 1752.
Vol. 10, Pt. 1–50
Tugwell, Rexford Guy, July 10, 1891–July 21, 1979.
Supp. 10–794
Tulane, Paul, May 10, 1801–Mar. 27, 1887.
Vol. 10, Pt. 1–51
Tully, William, Nov. 18, 1785–Feb. 28, 1859.
Vol. 10, Pt. 1–51
Tumulty, Joseph Patrick, May 5, 1879–Apr. 8, 1954.
Supp. 5–696
Tunnell, Emlen, Mar. 29, 1925–July 23, 1975.
Supp. 9–817
Tunney, James Joseph ("Gene"), May 25, 1897–Nov. 7, 1978.
Supp. 10–796
Tupper, Benjamin, Mar. 11, 1738–June 7, 1792.
Vol. 10, Pt. 1–52
Tupper, Henry Allen, Feb. 29, 1828–Mar. 27, 1902.
Vol. 10, Pt. 1–53
Turell, Jane, Feb. 25, 1708–Mar. 26, 1735.
Vol. 10, Pt. 1–54
Turkevich, Leonid Ieronimovich. [*See* Leonty, Metropolitan, 1876–1965.]
Turnbull, Andrew, *c.* 1718–Mar. 13, 1792.
Vol. 10, Pt. 1–54
Turnbull, Robert James, Jan. 1775–June 15, 1833.
Vol. 10, Pt. 1–55
Turnbull, William, 1800–Dec. 9, 1857.
Vol. 10, Pt. 1–57
Turner, Asa, June 11, 1799–Dec. 13, 1885.
Vol. 10, Pt. 1–57
Turner, Charles Yardley, Nov. 25, 1850–Dec. 31, 1918.
Vol. 10, Pt. 1–59
Turner, Daniel, 1794–Feb. 4, 1850.
Vol. 10, Pt. 1–59
Turner, Edward, Nov. 25, 1778–May 23, 1860.
Vol. 10, Pt. 1–60
Turner, Edward Raymond, May 28, 1881–Dec. 31, 1929.
Vol. 10, Pt. 1–61
Turner, Fennell Parrish, Feb. 25, 1867–Feb. 10, 1932.
Vol. 10, Pt. 1–61
Turner, Frederick Jackson, Nov. 14, 1861–Mar. 14, 1932.
Vol. 10, Pt. 1–62
Turner, George, Feb. 25, 1850–Jan. 26, 1932.
Vol. 10, Pt. 1–64
Turner, George Kibbe, Mar. 23, 1869–Feb. 15, 1952.
Supp. 5–698
Turner, Henry McNeal, Feb. 1, 1834–May 8, 1915.
Vol. 10, Pt. 1–65
Turner, James Milton, May 16, 1840–Nov. 1, 1915.
Vol. 10, Pt. 1–66
Turner, John Wesley, July 19, 1833–Apr. 8, 1899.
Vol. 10, Pt. 1–67
Turner, Jonathan Baldwin, Dec. 7, 1805–Jan. 10, 1899.
Vol. 10, Pt. 1–68
Turner, Josiah, Dec. 27, 1821–Oct. 26, 1901.
Vol. 10, Pt. 1–68
Turner, Nat, Oct. 2, 1800–Nov. 11, 1831.
Vol. 10, Pt. 1–69
Turner, Richmond Kelly, May 27, 1885–Feb. 12, 1961.
Supp. 7–749
Turner Ross Sterling, June 29, 1847–Feb. 12, 1915.
Vol. 10, Pt. 1–70
Turner, Samuel Hulbeart, Jan. 23, 1790–Dec. 21, 1861.
Vol. 10, Pt. 1–71
Turner, Walter Victor, Apr. 3, 1866–Jan. 9, 1919.
Vol. 10, Pt. 1–71
Turner, William, Apr. 8, 1871–July 10, 1936.
Supp. 2–671
Turney, Peter, Sept. 22, 1827–Oct. 19, 1903.
Vol. 10, Pt. 1–72
Turpin, Ben, Sept. 19, 1869?–July 1, 1940.
Supp. 2–672
Tuthill, William Burnet, Feb. 11, 1855–Aug. 25, 1929.
Vol. 10, Pt. 1–73
Tuttle, Charles Wesley, Nov. 1, 1829–July 17, 1881.
Vol. 10, Pt. 1–74
Tuttle, Daniel Sylvester, Jan. 26, 1837–Apr. 17, 1923.
Vol. 10, Pt. 1–75
Tuttle, Herbert, Nov. 29, 1846–June 21, 1894.
Vol. 10, Pt. 1–75
Tutwiler, Henry, Nov. 16, 1807–Sept. 22, 1884.
Vol. 10, Pt. 1–76
Tutwiler, Julia Strudwick, Aug. 15, 1841–Mar. 24, 1916.
Vol. 10, Pt. 1–77
Twachtman, John Henry, Aug. 4, 1853–Aug. 8, 1902.
Vol. 10, Pt. 1–78
Twain, Mark. [*See* Clemens, Samuel Langhorne, 1835–1910.]
Tweed, Harrison, Oct. 18, 1885–June 16, 1969.
Supp. 8–662
Tweed, William Marcy, Apr. 3, 1823–Apr. 12, 1878.
Vol. 10, Pt. 1–79
Twichell, Joseph Hopkins, May 27, 1838–Dec. 20, 1918.
Vol. 7, Pt. 2–82
Twiggs, David Emanuel, 1790–July 15, 1862.
Vol. 10, Pt. 1–83
Twining, Alexander Catlin, July 5, 1801–Nov. 22, 1884.
Vol. 10, Pt. 1–83
Twitchell, Amos, Apr. 11, 1781–May 26, 1850.
Vol. 10, Pt. 1–84
Tydings, Millard Evelyn, Apr. 6, 1890–Feb. 9, 1961.
Supp. 7–750
Tyler, Bennet, July 10, 1783–May 14, 1858.
Vol. 10, Pt. 1–85
Tyler, Charles Mellen, Jan. 8, 1832–May 15, 1918.
Vol. 10, Pt. 1–86
Tyler, Daniel, Jan. 7, 1799–Nov. 30, 1882.
Vol. 10, Pt. 1–86

Tyler, George Crouse, Apr. 13, 1867–Mar. 13, 1946.
Supp. 4–842
Tyler, John, Feb. 28, 1747–Jan. 6, 1813.
Vol. 10, Pt. 1–87
Tyler, John, Mar. 29, 1790–Jan. 18, 1862.
Vol. 10, Pt. 1–88
Tyler, Lyon Gardiner, Aug. 1853–Feb. 12, 1935.
Supp. 1–691
Tyler, Moses Coit, Aug. 2, 1835–Dec. 28, 1900.
Vol. 10, Pt. 1–92
Tyler, Ransom Hubert, Nov. 18, 1815–Nov. 21, 1881.
Vol. 10, Pt. 1–93
Tyler, Robert, Sept. 9, 1816–Dec. 3, 1877.
Vol. 10, Pt. 1–94
Tyler, Robert Ogden, Dec. 22, 1831–Dec. 1, 1874.
Vol. 10, Pt. 1–94
Tyler, Royall, July 18, 1757–Aug. 26, 1826.
Vol. 10, Pt. 1–95
Tyler, Royall, May 4, 1884–Mar. 2, 1953.
Supp. 5–699
Tyler, Samuel, Oct. 22, 1809–Dec. 15, 1877.
Vol. 10, Pt. 1–97
Tyler, William, June 5, 1806–June 18, 1849.
Vol. 10, Pt. 1–98
Tyler, William Seymour, Sept. 2, 1810–Nov. 19, 1897.
Vol. 10, Pt. 1–99
Tyndale, Hector, Mar. 24, 1821–Mar. 19, 1880.
Vol. 10, Pt. 1–100
Tyng, Edward, 1683–Sept. 8, 1755.
Vol. 10, Pt. 1–100
Tyng, Stephen Higginson, Mar. 1, 1800–Sept. 3, 1885.
Vol. 10, Pt. 1–101
Tyson, George Emory, Dec. 15, 1829–Oct. 18, 1906.
Vol. 10, Pt. 1–102
Tyson, James, Oct. 26, 1841–Feb. 21, 1919.
Vol. 10, Pt. 1–103
Tyson, Job Roberts, Feb. 8, 1803–June 27, 1858.
Vol. 10, Pt. 1–103
Tyson, Lawrence Davis, July 4, 1861–Aug. 24, 1929.
Vol. 10, Pt. 1–104
Tyson, Stuart Lawrence, Nov. 12, 1873–Sept. 16, 1932.
Vol. 10, Pt. 1–105
Tytus, John Butler, Dec. 6, 1875–June 2, 1944.
Supp. 3–781

Udden, Johan August, Mar. 19, 1859–Jan. 5, 1932.
Vol. 10, Pt. 1–106
Uhler, Philip Reese, June 3, 1835–Oct. 21, 1913.
Vol. 10, Pt. 1–106
Ulloa, Antonio de, Jan. 12, 1716–July 5, 1795.
Vol. 10, Pt. 1–107
Ulmer, Edgar Georg, Sept. 17, 1904–Sept. 30, 1972.
Supp. 9–819
Ulrich, Edward Oscar, Feb. 1, 1857–Feb. 22, 1944.
Supp. 3–782
Unangst, Erias, Aug. 8, 1824–Oct. 12, 1903.
Vol. 10, Pt. 1–108
Uncas, *c.* 1588–*c.* 1683.
Vol. 10, Pt. 1–108
Underhill, Frank Pell, Dec. 21, 1877–June 28, 1932.
Vol. 10, Pt. 1–109
Underhill, John, *c.* 1597–Sept. 21, 1672.
Vol. 10, Pt. 1–110
Underwood, Benjamin Franklin, July 6, 1839–Nov. 10, 1914.
Vol. 10, Pt. 1–111
Underwood, Francis Henry, Jan. 12, 1825–Aug. 7, 1894.
Vol. 10, Pt. 1–112
Underwood, Frederick Douglas, Feb. 1, 1849–Feb. 18, 1942.
Supp. 3–783
Underwood, Horace Grant, July 19, 1859–Oct. 12, 1916.
Vol. 10, Pt. 1–113
Underwood, John Curtiss, Mar. 14, 1809–Dec. 7, 1873.
Vol. 10, Pt. 1–113
Underwood, John Thomas, Apr. 12, 1857–July 2, 1937.
Supp. 2–673
Underwood, Joseph Rogers, Oct. 24, 1791–Aug. 23, 1876.
Vol. 10, Pt. 1–114
Underwood, Loring, Feb. 15, 1874–Jan. 13, 1930.
Vol. 10, Pt. 1–115
Underwood, Lucien Marcus, Oct. 26, 1853–Nov. 16, 1907.
Vol. 10, Pt. 1–116
Underwood, Oscar Wilder, May 6, 1862–Jan. 25, 1929.
Vol. 10, Pt. 1–117
Untermeyer, Louis, Oct. 1, 1885–Dec. 17, 1977.
Supp. 10–799
Untermyer, Samuel, June 6, 1858–Mar. 16, 1940.
Supp. 2–674
Upchurch, John Jordan, Mar. 26, 1820–Jan. 18, 1887.
Vol. 10, Pt. 1–119
Updegraff, David Brainard, Aug. 23, 1830–May 23, 1894.
Vol. 10, Pt. 1–120
Updike, Daniel, *c.* 1693–May 15, 1757.
Vol. 10, Pt. 1–120
Updike, Daniel Berkeley, Feb. 24, 1860–Dec. 29, 1941.
Supp. 3–784
Upham, Charles Wentworth, May 4, 1802–June 15, 1875.
Vol. 10, Pt. 1–121
Upham, Samuel Foster, May 19, 1834–Oct. 5, 1904.
Vol. 10, Pt. 1–122
Upham, Thomas Cogswell, Jan. 30, 1799–Apr. 2, 1872.
Vol. 10, Pt. 1–123
Upham, Warren, Mar. 8, 1850–Jan. 29, 1934.
Vol. 10, Pt. 1–124
Upjohn, Richard, Jan. 22, 1802–Aug. 17, 1878.
Vol. 10, Pt. 1–125
Upjohn, Richard Michell, Mar. 7, 1828–Mar. 3, 1903.
Vol. 10 Pt. 1–126
Upshaw, William David, Oct. 15, 1866–Nov. 21, 1952.
Supp. 5–701
Upshur, Abel Parker, June 17, 1791–Feb. 28, 1844.
Vol. 10, Pt. 1–127
Upshur, John Henry, Dec. 5, 1823–May 30, 1917.
Vol. 10, Pt. 1–128
Upton, Emory, Aug. 27, 1839–Mar. 15, 1881.
Vol. 10, Pt. 1–128
Upton, George Bruce, Oct. 11, 1804–July 1, 1874.
Vol. 10, Pt. 1–130
Upton, George Putnam, Oct. 25, 1834–May 19, 1919.
Vol. 10, Pt. 1–131
Upton, Winslow, Oct. 12, 1853–Jan. 8, 1914.
Vol. 10, Pt. 1–132
Urban, Joseph, May 26, 1872–July 10, 1933.
Vol. 10, Pt. 1–132
U'Ren, William Simon, Jan. 10, 1859–Mar. 8, 1949.
Supp. 4–844
Urso, Camilla, June 13, 1842–Jan. 20, 1902.
Vol. 10, Pt. 1–134
Usher, John Palmer, Jan. 9, 1816–Apr. 13, 1889.
Vol. 10, Pt. 1–134
Usher, Nathaniel Reilly, Apr 7, 1855–Jan. 9, 1931.
Vol. 10, Pt. 1–135
Utley, Freda, Jan. 23, 1898–Jan. 21, 1978.
Supp. 10–800
Utley, George Burwelt, Dec. 3, 1876–Oct. 4, 1946.
Supp. 4–845

Vaca, Alvar Núñez Cabeza de. [*See* Núñez Cabeza de Vaca, Alvar, *c.* 1490–*c.* 1557.]
Vail, Aaron, Oct. 24, 1796–Nov. 4, 1878.
Vol. 10, Pt. 1–136
Vail, Alfred, Sept. 25, 1807–Jan. 18, 1859.
Vol. 10, Pt. 1–136
Vail, Robert William Glenroie, Mar. 26, 1890–June 21, 1966.
Supp. 8–663
Vail, Stephen Montfort, Jan. 15, 1816–Nov. 26, 1880.
Vol. 10, Pt. 1–137
Vail, Theodore Newton, July 16, 1845–Apr. 16, 1920.
Vol. 10, Pt. 1–138
Vaillant, George Clapp, Apr. 5, 1901–May 13, 1945.
Supp. 3–786
Valachi, Joseph Michael, Sept. 22, 1904–Apr. 3, 1971.
Supp. 9–820
Valentine, David Thomas, Sept. 15, 1801–Feb. 25, 1869.
Vol. 10, Pt. 1–140
Valentine, Edward Virginius, Nov. 12, 1838–Oct. 19, 1930.
Vol. 10, Pt. 1–140
Valentine, Milton, Jan. 1, 1825–Feb. 7, 1906.
Vol. 10, Pt. 1–141
Valentine, Robert Grosvenor, Nov. 29, 1872–Nov. 14, 1916.
Vol. 10, Pt. 1–142
Vallandigham, Clement Laird, July 29, 1820–June 17, 1871.
Vol. 10, Pt. 1–143

Vallejo, Mariano Guadalupe, July 7, 1808–Jan. 18, 1890.
Vol. 10, Pt. 1–145
Vallentine, Benjamin Bennaton, Sept. 7, 1843–Mar. 30, 1926.
Vol. 10, Pt. 1–146
Valliant, Leroy Branch, June 14, 1838–Mar. 3, 1913.
Vol. 10, Pt. 1–147
Van, Bobby, Dec. 6, 1930–July 30, 1980.
Supp. 10–801
Van Allen, Frank, Jan. 10, 1860–Aug. 28, 1923.
Vol. 10, Pt. 1–148
Van Alstyne, Fanny Crosby. [*See* Crosby, Fanny, 1820–1915.]
Van Amringe, John Howard, Apr. 3, 1835–Sept. 10, 1915.
Vol. 10, Pt. 1–148
Van Anda, Carr Vattel, Dec. 2, 1864–Jan. 28, 1945.
Supp. 3–787
Van Beuren, Johannes, *c.* 1680–July 27, 1755.
Vol. 10, Pt. 1–149
Van Brunt, Henry, Sept. 5, 1832–Apr. 8, 1903.
Vol. 10, Pt. 1–150
Van Buren, John, Feb. 10, 1810–Oct. 13, 1866.
Vol. 10, Pt. 1–151
Van Buren, Martin, Dec. 5, 1782–July 24, 1862.
Vol. 10, Pt. 1–152
Van Buren, William Holme, Apr. 4, 1819–Mar. 25, 1883.
Vol. 10, Pt. 1–157
Vance, Ap Morgan, May 24, 1854–Dec. 9, 1915.
Vol. 10, Pt. 1–157
Vance, Arthur Charres ("Dazzy"), Mar. 4, 1891–Feb. 16, 1961.
Supp. 7–751
Vance, Harold Sines, Aug. 22, 1890–Aug. 31, 1959.
Supp. 6–649
Vance, Louis Joseph, Sept. 19, 1879–Dec. 16, 1933.
Supp. 1–691
Vance, Vivian, July 26, 1912–Aug. 17, 1979.
Supp. 10–803
Vance, Zebulon Baird, May 13, 1830–Apr. 14, 1894.
Vol. 10, Pt. 1–158
Van Cortlandt, Olofft Stevenszen, 1600–Apr. 5, 1684.
Vol. 10, Pt. 1–161
Van Cortlandt, Philip, Aug. 21, 1749–Nov. 5, 1831.
Vol. 10, Pt. 1–162
Van Cortlandt, Pierre, Jan. 10, 1721–May 1, 1814.
Vol. 10, Pt. 1–163
Van Cortlandt, Stephanus, May 7, 1643–Nov. 25, 1700.
Vol. 10, Pt. 1–164
Van Curler. Arent, 1620–July 1667.
Vol. 10, Pt. 1–165
Van Dam, Rip, *c.* 1660–June 10, 1749.
Vol. 10, Pt. 1–166
Van de Graaff, Robert Jemison, Dec. 20, 1901–Jan. 16, 1967.
Supp. 8–665
Vandegrift, Alexander Archer, Mar. 13, 1887–May 8, 1973.
Supp. 9–822
Van Deman, Esther Boise, Oct. 1, 1862–May 3, 1937.
Supp. 2–676
Vandenberg, Arthur Hendrick, Mar. 22, 1884–Apr. 18, 1951.
Supp. 5–702
Vandenberg, Hoyt Sanford, Jan. 24, 1899–Apr. 2, 1954.
Supp. 5–705
Vandenhoff, George, 1813–June 16, 1885.
Vol. 10, Pt. 1–167
Van Depoele, Charles Joseph, Apr. 27, 1846–Mar. 18, 1892.
Vol. 10, Pt. 1–168
Vanderbilt, Amy, July 22, 1908–Dec. 27, 1974.
Supp. 9–824
Vanderbilt, Arthur T., July 7, 1888–June 16, 1957.
Supp. 6–650
Vanderbilt, Cornelius, May 27, 1794–Jan. 4, 1877.
Vol. 10, Pt. 1–169
Vanderbilt, Cornelius, Nov. 27, 1843–Sept. 12, 1899.
Vol. 10, Pt. 1–173
Vanderbilt, Cornelius, Jr. ("Cornelius IV," "Neil"), Apr. 30, 1898–July 7, 1974.
Supp. 9–825
Vanderbilt, George Washington, Nov. 14, 1862–Mar. 6, 1914.
Vol. 10, Pt. 1–174
Vanderbilt, Gloria Morgan, Aug. 23, 1904–Feb. 13, 1965.
Supp. 7–752
Vanderbilt, Grace Graham Wilson, Sept. 3, 1870–Jan. 7, 1953.
Supp. 5–707
Vanderbilt, Wilham Kissam, Dec. 12, 1849–July 22, 1920.
Vol. 10, Pt. 1–176
Vanderbilt, William Henry, May 8, 1821–Dec. 8, 1885.
Vol. 10, Pt. 1–175
Vanderburgh, William Henry, *c.* 1798–Oct. 14, 1832.
Vol. 10, Pt. 1–177
Van Der Donck, Adriaen, May 7, 1620–*c.* 1655.
Vol. 10, Pt. 1–178
Vandergrift, Jacob Jay, Apr. 10, 1827–Dec. 26, 1899.
Vol. 10, Pt. 1–179
Vandergrift, Margaret. [*See* Janvier, Margaret Thomson, 1844–1913.]
Van Der Kemp, Francis Adrian, May 4, 1752–Sept. 7, 1829.
Vol. 10, Pt. 1–179
Vanderlip, Frank Arthur, Nov. 17, 1864–June 29, 1937.
Supp. 2–677
Vanderlyn, John, Oct. 15, 1775–Sept. 23, 1852.
Vol. 10, Pt. 1–180
Van Der Stucken, Frank Valentin, Oct. 15, 1858–Aug. 16, 1929.
Vol. 10, Pt. 1–181
Vander Veer, Albert, July 10, 1841–Dec. 19, 1929.
Vol. 10, Pt. 1–182
Vander Wee, John Baptist, Feb. 20, 1824–Feb. 24, 1900.
Vol. 10, Pt. 1–183
Van Devanter, Willis, Apr. 17, 1859–Feb. 8, 1941.
Supp. 3–788
Van de Velde, James Oliver, Apr. 3, 1795–Nov. 13, 1855.
Vol. 10, Pt. 1–184
Van de Warker, Edward Ely, Nov. 27, 1841–Sept. 5, 1910.
Vol. 10, Pt. 1–184
Van Dine, S. S. [*See* Wright, Willard Huntington, 1888–1939.]
Van Doren, Carl Clinton, Sept. 10, 1884–July 18, 1950.
Supp. 4–846
Van Doren, Irita Bradford, Mar. 16, 1891–Dec. 18, 1966.
Supp. 8–666
Van Doren, Mark Albert, June 13, 1894–Dec. 10, 1972.
Supp. 9–827
Van Dorn, Earl, Sept. 17, 1820–May 8, 1863.
Vol. 10, Pt. 1–185
Van Druten, John William, June 1, 1901–Dec. 19, 1957.
Supp. 6–652
Van Dyck, Cornelius Van Alen, Aug. 13, 1818–Nov. 13, 1895.
Vol. 10, Pt. 1–186
Van Dyke, Henry, Nov. 10, 1852–Apr. 10, 1933.
Vol. 10, Pt. 1–186
Van Dyke, John Charles, Apr. 21, 1856–Dec. 5, 1932.
Vol. 10, Pt. 1–188
Van Dyke, John Wesley, Dec. 27, 1849–Sept. 13, 1939.
Supp. 2–679
Van Dyke, Nicholas, Sept. 25, 1738–Feb. 19, 1789.
Vol. 10, Pt. 1–189
Van Dyke, Nicholas, Dec. 20, 1770–May 21, 1826.
Vol. 10, Pt. 1–190
Van Dyke, Paul, Mar. 25, 1859–Aug. 30, 1933.
Vol. 10, Pt. 1–191
Vane, Sir Henry, 1613–June 14, 1662.
Vol. 10, Pt. 1–191
Van Fleet, Walter, June 18, 1857–Jan. 26, 1922.
Vol. 10, Pt. 1–193
Van Hise, Charles Richard, May 29, 1857–Nov. 19, 1918.
Vol. 10, Pt. 1–194
Van Hook, Weller, May 16, 1862–July 1, 1933.
Vol. 10, Pt. 1–195
Van Horn, Robert Thompson, May 19, 1824–Jan. 3, 1916.
Vol. 10, Pt. 1–196
Van Horne, William Cornelius, Feb. 3, 1843–Sept. 11, 1915.
Vol. 10, Pt. 1–197
Van Ilpendam, Jan Jansen, *c.* 1595–1647.
Vol. 10, Pt. 1–199
Van Lennep, Henry John, Mar. 18, 1815–Jan. 11, 1889.
Vol. 10, Pt. 1–199
Van Lennep, William Bird, Dec. 5, 1853–Jan. 9, 1919.
Vol. 10, Pt. 1–200
Van Loon, Hendrik Willem, Jan. 14, 1882–Mar. 11, 1944.
Supp. 3–789
Van Meter, John Blackford, Sept. 6, 1842–Apr. 8, 1930.
Vol. 10, Pt. 1–201
Van Name, Addison, Nov. 15, 1835–Sept. 29, 1922.
Vol. 10, Pt. 1–201

Van Ness, William Peter, *c.* 1778–Sept. 6, 1826.
Vol. 10, Pt. 1–202
Van Nest, Abraham Rynier, Feb. 16, 1823–June 1, 1892.
Vol. 10, Pt. 1–203
Van Nostrand, David, Dec. 5, 1811–June 14, 1886.
Vol. 10, Pt. 1–203
Van Osdel, John Mills, July 31, 1811–Dec. 21, 1891.
Vol. 10 Pt. 1–204
Van Quickenborne, Charles Felix, Jan. 21, 1788–Aug. 17, 1837.
Vol. 10, Pt. 1–205
Van Raalte, Albertus Christiaan, Oct. 17, 1811–Nov. 7, 1876.
Vol. 10, Pt. 1–206
Van Rensselaer, Cortlandt, May 26, 1808–July 25, 1860.
Vol. 10, Pt. 1–207
Van Rensselaer, Mariana Griswold, Feb. 25, 1851–Jan. 20, 1934.
Vol. 10, Pt. 1–207
Van Rensselaer, Martha, June 21, 1864–May 26, 1932.
Vol. 10, Pt. 1–208
Van Rensselaer, Nicholas, *c.* Sept. 25, 1636–1678.
Vol. 10, Pt. 1–209
Van Rensselaer, Solomon, Aug. 6, 1774–Apr. 23, 1852.
Vol. 10, Pt. 1–210
Van Rensselaer, Stephen, Nov. 1, 1764–Jan. 26, 1839.
Vol. 10, Pt. 1–211
Van Santvoord, George, Dec. 8, 1819–Mar. 6, 1863.
Vol. 10, Pt. 1–212
Van Schaack, Henry Cruger, Apr. 2, 1802–Dec. 16, 1887.
Vol. 10, Pt. 1–213
Van Schaack, Peter, Mar. 1747–Sept. 17, 1832.
Vol. 10, Pt. 1–213
Van Schaick, Goose, Sept. 5, 1736–July 4, 1789.
Vol. 10, Pt. 1–214
Van Slyke, Lucius Lincoln, Jan. 6, 1859–Sept 30, 1931.
Vol. 10, Pt. 1–215
Van Sweringen, Mantis James, July 8, 1881–Dec. 12, 1935.
Supp. 1–692
Van Twiller, Wouter, *c.* 1580–*c.* 1656.
Vol. 10, Pt. 1–216
Van Tyne, Claude Halstead, Oct. 16, 1869–Mar. 21, 1930.
Vol. 10, Pt. 1–217
Vanuxem, Lardner, July 23, 1792–Jan. 25, 1848.
Vol. 10, Pt. 1–218
Van Vechten, Abraham, Dec. 5, 1762–Jan. 6, 1837.
Vol. 10, Pt. 1–218
Van Vechten, Carl, June 17, 1880–Dec. 21, 1964.
Supp. 7–753
Van Vleck, Edward Burr, June 7, 1863–June 2, 1943.
Supp. 3–791
Van Vleck, John Hasbrouck, Mar. 13, 1899–Oct. 27, 1980.
Supp. 10–804
Van Winkle, Peter Godwin, Sept. 7, 1808–Apr. 15, 1872.
Vol. 10, Pt. 1–219
Van Wyck, Charles Henry, May 10, 1824–Oct. 24, 1895.
Vol. 10, Pt. 1–220
Vanzetti, Bartolomeo, 1888–1927. [*See* Sacco, Nicola, 1891–1927.]
Vardaman, James Kimble, July 26, 1861–June 25, 1930.
Vol. 10, Pt. 1–221
Vardill, John, 1749–Jan. 16, 1811.
Vol. 10, Pt. 1–222
Vare, William Scott, Dec. 24, 1867–Aug. 7, 1934.
Vol. 10, Pt. 1–223
Varela y Morales, Félix Francisco José María de la Concepción, Nov. 20, 1788–Feb. 18, 1853.
Vol. 10, Pt. 1–224
Varèse, Edgard, Dec. 22, 1883–Nov. 6, 1965.
Supp. 7–755
Varick, James, fl. 1796–1828.
Vol. 10, Pt. 1–225
Varick, Richard, Mar. 25, 1753–July 30, 1831.
Vol. 10, Pt. 1–226
Varnum, James Mitchell, Dec. 17, 1748–Jan. 10, 1789.
Vol. 10, Pt. 1–227
Varnum, Joseph Bradley, Jan 29, 1750/51–Sept 11, 1821.
Vol. 10, Pt. 1–228
Vasey, George, Feb. 28, 1822–Mar. 4, 1893.
Vol. 10, Pt. 1–224
Vasiliev, Alexander Alexandrovich, Oct. 5, 1867–May 30, 1953.
Supp. 5–708
Vassall, John, 1625–July ?, 1688.
Vol. 10, Pt. 1–230
Vassar, Matthew, Apr. 29, 1792–June 23, 1868.
Vol. 10, Pt. 1–230
Vattemare, Nicolas Marie Alexandre, Nov. 8, 1796–Apr. 7, 1864.
Vol. 10, Pt. 1–231
Vauclain, Samuel Matthews, May 18, 1856–Feb. 4, 1940.
Supp. 2–680
Vaudreuil-Cavagnal, Pierre de Rigaud, Marquis de, 1704–Aug. 4, 1778.
Vol. 10, Pt. 1–232
Vaughan, Benjamin, Apr. 30, 1751–Dec. 8, 1835.
Vol. 10, Pt. 1–233
Vaughan, Charles, June 30, 1759–May 15, 1839.
Vol. 10, Pt. 1–235
Vaughan, Daniel, *c.* 1818–Apr. 6, 1879.
Vol. 10, Pt. 1–235
Vaughan, Thomas Wayland, Sept. 20, 1870–Jan. 16, 1952.
Supp. 5–709
Vaughan, Victor Clarence, Oct. 27, 1851–Nov. 21, 1929.
Vol. 10, Pt. 1–236
Vaux, Calvert, Dec. 20, 1824–Nov. 19, 1895.
Vol. 10, Pt. 1–237
Vaux, Richard, Dec. 19, 1816–Mar. 22, 1895.
Vol. 10, Pt. 1–238
Vaux, Roberts, Jan. 21, 1786–Jan. 7, 1836.
Vol. 10, Pt. 1–239
Vawter, Charles Erastus, June 9, 1841–Oct. 27, 1905.
Vol. 10, Pt. 1–240
Veatch, Arthur Clifford, Oct. 26, 1878–Dec. 24, 1938.
Supp. 2–681
Veazey, Thomas Ward, Jan. 31, 1774–July 1, 1842.
Vol. 10, Pt. 1–240
Veblen, Oswald, Jan. 24, 1880–Aug. 10, 1960.
Supp. 6–653
Veblen, Thorstein Bunde, July 30, 1857–Aug. 3, 1929.
Vol. 10, Pt. 1–241
Vedder, Edward Bright, June 28, 1878–Jan. 30, 1952.
Supp. 5–710
Vedder, Elihu, Feb. 26, 1836–Jan. 29, 1923.
Vol. 10, Pt. 1–244
Vedder, Henry Clay, Feb. 26, 1853–Oct. 13, 1935.
Supp. 1–693
Veiller, Lawrence Turnure, Jan. 7, 1872–Aug. 30, 1959.
Supp. 6–654
Venable, Charles Scott, Apr. 19, 1827–Aug. 11, 1900.
Vol. 10, Pt. 1–245
Venable, Francis Preston, Nov. 17, 1856–Mar. 17, 1934.
Vol. 10, Pt. 1–246
Venable, William Henry, Apr. 29, 1836–July 6, 1920.
Vol. 10, Pt. 1–247
Venuti, Giuseppe ("Joe"), Sept. 16, 1903–Aug. 14, 1978.
Supp. 10–806
Verbeck, Guido Herman Fridolin, Jan. 23, 1830–Mar. 10, 1898.
Vol. 10, Pt. 1–248
Verbeck, William, Jan. 18, 1861–Aug. 24, 1930.
Vol. 10, Pt. 1–249
Verbrugghen, Henri, Aug. 1, 1873–Nov. 12, 1934.
Vol. 10, Pt. 1–250
Vérendrye, Pierre Gaultier de Varennes, Sieur de la. [*See* La Vérendrye, Pierre Gaultier de Varennes, Sieur de, 1685–1749.]
Verhaegen, Peter Joseph, June 21, 1800–July 21, 1868.
Vol. 10, Pt. 1–250
Verity, George Matthew, Apr. 22, 1865–Nov. 6, 1942.
Supp. 3–792
Vermilye, Kate Jordan. [*See* Jordan, Kate, 1862–1926.]
Vernon, Samuel, Dec. 6, 1683–Dec. 5, 1737.
Vol. 10, Pt. 1–251
Vernon, William, Jan. 17, 1719–Dec. 22, 1806.
Vol. 10, Pt. 1–251
Verot, Jean Marcel Pierre Auguste, May 23, 1805–June 10, 1876.
Vol. 10, Pt. 1–252
Verplanck, Gulian Crommelin, Aug. 6, 1786–Mar. 18, 1870.
Vol. 10, Pt. 1–253
Verrill, Addison Emery, Feb. 9, 1839–Dec. 10, 1926.
Vol. 10, Pt. 1–254

Verrill, Alpheus Hyatt, July 23, 1871–Nov. 14, 1954.
Supp. 5–711
Verwyst, Chrysostom Adrian, Nov. 23, 1841–June 23, 1925.
Vol. 10, Pt. 1–255
Very, Jones, Aug. 28, 1813–May 8, 1880.
Vol. 10, Pt. 1–256
Very, Lydia Louisa Ann, Nov. 2, 1823–Sept. 10, 1901.
Vol. 10, Pt. 1–257
Vesey, Denmark, *c.* 1767–July 2, 1822.
Vol. 10, Pt. 1–258
Vesey, Télémaque. [*See* Vesey, Denmark, *c.* 1767–1822.]
Vesey, William, Aug. 10, 1674–July 11, 1746.
Vol. 10, Pt. 1–259
Vest, George Craham, Dec. 6, 1830–Aug. 9, 1904.
Vol. 10, Pt. 1–260
Vetch, Samuel, Dec. 9, 1668–Apr. 30, 1732.
Vol. 10, Pt. 1–260
Vethake, Henry, 1792–Dec. 16, 1866.
Vol. 10, Pt. 1–262
Vezin, Hermann, Mar. 2, 1829–June 12, 1910.
Vol. 10, Pt. 1–262
Vibbard, Chauncey, Nov. 11, 1811–June 5, 1891.
Vol. 10, Pt. 1–263
Vick, James, Nov. 23, 1818–May 16, 1882.
Vol. 10, Pt. 1–264
Vickery, Howard Leroy, Apr. 20, 1892–Mar. 21, 1946.
Supp. 4–848
Victor, Frances Fuller, May 23, 1826–Nov. 14, 1902.
Vol. 10, Pt. 1–265
Victor, Orville James, Oct. 23, 1827–Mar. 14, 1910.
Vol. 10, Pt. 1–265
Vidor, Florence, July 23, 1895–Nov. 3, 1977.
Supp. 10–807
Viel, François Étienne Bernard Alexandre, Oct. 31, 1736–Dec. 16, 1821.
Vol. 10, Pt. 1–266
Viele, Aernout Cornelissen, 1640–1704.
Vol. 10, Pt. 1–267
Viele, Egbert Ludovicus, June 17, 1825–Apr. 22, 1902.
Vol. 10, Pt. 1–267
Viereck, George Sylvester, Dec. 31, 1884–March 18, 1962.
Supp. 7–756
Vignaud, Henry, Nov. 27, 1830–Sept. 16, 1922.
Vol. 10, Pt. 1–268
Vigo, Joseph Maria Francesco, Dec. 3, 1747–Mar. 22, 1836.
Vol. 10, Pt. 1–270
Vilas, William Freeman, July 9, 1840–Aug. 27, 1908.
Vol. 10, Pt. 1–270
Villagrá, Gasper Pérez de, *c.* 1555–*c.* 1620.
Vol. 10, Pt. 1–271
Villard, Fanny Garrison. [*See* Villard, Helen Frances Garrison, 1844–1928.]
Villard, Helen Frances Garrison, Dec. 16, 1844–July 5, 1928.
Vol. 10, Pt. 1–272
Villard, Henry, Apr. 10, 1835–Nov. 12, 1900.
Vol. 10, Pt. 1–273
Villard, Oswald Garrison, Mar. 13, 1872–Oct. 1, 1949.
Supp. 4–849
Villeré, Jacques Philippe, Apr. 28, 1761–Mar. 7, 1830.
Vol. 10, Pt. 1–275
Vincennes, François Marie Bissot, Sieur de, June 17, 1700–Mar. 25, 1736.
Vol. 10, Pt. 1–275
Vincennes, Jean Baptiste Bissot, Sieur de, Jan. 19, 1668–1719.
Vol. 10, Pt. 1–276
Vincent, Frank, Apr. 2, 1848–June 19, 1916.
Vol. 10, Pt. 1–277
Vincent, George Edgar, Mar. 21, 1864–Feb. 1, 1941.
Supp. 3–793
Vincent, John Carter, Aug. 19, 1900–Dec. 3, 1972.
Supp. 9–829
Vincent, John Heyl, Feb. 23, 1832–May 9, 1920.
Vol. 10, Pt. 1–277
Vincent, Marvin Richardson, Sept. 11, 1834–Aug. 18, 1922.
Vol. 10, Pt. 1–279
Vincent, Mary Ann, Sept. 18, 1818–Sept. 4, 1887.
Vol. 10, Pt. 1–280
Viner, Jacob, May 3, 1892–Sept. 12, 1970.
Supp. 8–668
Vinson, Fred(erick) Moore, Jan. 22, 1890–Sept. 8, 1953.
Supp. 5–711
Vinton, Alexander Hamilton, May 2, 1807–Apr. 26, 1881.
Vol. 10, Pt. 1–280
Vinton, Francis, Aug. 29, 1809–Sept. 29, 1872.
Vol. 10, Pt. 1–281
Vinton, Francis Laurens, June 1, 1835–Oct. 6, 1879.
Vol. 10, Pt. 1–282
Vinton, Frederic, Oct. 9, 1817–Jan. 1, 1890.
Vol. 10, Pt. 1–283
Vinton, Frederic Porter, Jan. 29, 1846–May 20, 1911.
Vol. 10, Pt. 1–283
Vinton, Samuel Finley, Sept. 25, 1792–May 11, 1862.
Vol. 10, Pt. 1–284
Visscher, William Lightfoot, Nov. 25, 1842–Feb. 10, 1924.
Vol. 10, Pt. 1–285
Vitale, Ferruccio, Feb. 5, 1875–Feb. 26, 1933.
Vol. 10, Pt. 1–285
Vizcaíino, Sebastián, *c.* 1550–*c.* 1628.
Vol. 10, Pt. 1–286
Vizetelly, Frank Horace, Apr. 2, 1864–Dec. 20, 1938.
Supp. 2–682
Vladeck, Baruch Charney, Jan. 13, 1886–Oct. 30, 1938.
Supp. 2–683
Vladimiroff, Pierre, Feb. 1, 1893–Nov. 25, 1970.
Supp. 8–669
Vogrich, Max Wilhelm Karl, Jan. 24, 1852–June 10, 1916.
Vol. 10, Pt. 1–287
Volck, Adalbert John, Apr. 14, 1828–Mar. 26, 1912.
Vol. 10, Pt. 1–288
Volk, Leonard Wells, Nov. 7, 1828–Aug. 19, 1895.
Vol. 10, Pt. 1–288
Volstead, Andrew John, Oct. 31, 1860–Jan. 20, 1947.
Supp. 4–852
Von Braun, Wernher. [*See* Braun, Wernher von, 1912–1977.]
Von Holst, Hermann Eduard. [*See* Holst, Hermann Eduard von, 1841–1904.]
Von Kármán, Theodore. [*See* Kármán, Theodore (Todor) Von, 1881–1963.]
Von Moschzisker, Robert, Mar. 6, 1870–Nov. 21, 1939.
Supp. 2–684
Von Neumann, John, Dec. 28, 1903–Feb. 8, 1957.
Supp. 6–655
Vonnoh, Robert William, Sept. 17, 1858–Dec. 28, 1933.
Vol. 10, Pt. 1–289
Von Ruck, Karl, July 10, 1849–Nov. 5, 1922.
Vol. 10, Pt. 1–290
Von Sternberg, Josef, May 29, 1894–Dec. 22, 1969.
Supp. 8–671
Von Stroheim, Erich, Sept. 22, 1885–May 12, 1957.
Supp. 6–656
Von Teuffel, Blanche Willis Howard. [*See* Howard, Blanche Willis, 1847–1898.]
Von Wiegand, Karl Henry, Sept. 11, 1874–June 7, 1961.
Supp. 7–758
Voorhees, Daniel Wolsey, Sept. 26, 1827–Apr. 10, 1897.
Vol. 10, Pt. 1–291
Voorhees, Edward Burnett, June 22, 1856–June 6, 1911.
Vol. 10, Pt. 1–201
Voorhees, Philip Falkerson, 1792–Feb. 23, 1862.
Vol. 10, Pt. 1–292
Voorsanger, Jacob, Nov. 13, 1852–Apr. 27, 1908.
Vol. 10, Pt. 1–293
Vopicka, Charles Joseph, Nov. 3, 1857–Sept. 3, 1935.
Supp. 1–694
Voris, John Ralph, June 6, 1880–Jan. 12, 1968.
Supp. 8–673
Vorse, Mary Heaton, Oct. 9, 1874–June 14, 1966.
Supp. 8–674
Vose, George Leonard, Apr. 19, 1831–Mar. 30, 1910.
Vol. 10, Pt. 1–294
Vought, Chance Milton, Feb. 26, 1890–July 25, 1930.
Vol. 10, Pt. 1–294
Vroom, Peter Dumont, Dec. 12, 1791–Nov. 18, 1873.
Vol. 10, Pt. 1–295

Wabasha, *c.* 1773–*c.* 1855.
Vol. 10, Pt. 1–296
Wachsmuth, Charles, Sept. 13, 1829–Feb. 7, 1896.
Vol. 10, Pt. 1–297
Wacker, Charles Henry, Aug. 29, 1856–Oct. 31, 1929.
Vol. 10, Pt. 1–298

Waddel, James, July 1739–Sept. 17, 1805.
Vol. 10, Pt. 1–298
Waddel, John Newton, Apr. 2, 1812–Jan. 9, 1895.
Vol. 10, Pt. 1–299
Waddel, Moses, July 29, 1770–July 21, 1840.
Vol. 10, Pt. 1–300
Waddell, Alfred Moore, Sept. 16, 1834–Mar. 17, 1912.
Vol. 10, Pt. 1–300
Waddell, Hugh, 1734?–Apr. 9, 1773.
Vol. 10, Pt. 1–301
Waddell, James Iredell, July 13, 1824–Mar. 15, 1886.
Vol. 10, Pt. 1–302
Waddell, John Alexander Low, Jan. 15, 1854–Mar. 3, 1938.
Supp. 2–685
Wade, Benjamin Franklin, Oct. 27, 1800–Mar. 2, 1878.
Vol. 10, Pt. 1–303
Wade, Decius Spear, Jan. 23, 1835–Aug. 3, 1905.
Vol. 10, Pt. 1–305
Wade, Jeptha Homer, Aug. 11, 1811–Aug. 9, 1890.
Vol. 10, Pt. 1–306
Wade, Jeptha Homer, Oct. 15, 1857–Mar. 6, 1926.
Supp. 1–695
Wade, Martin Joseph, Oct. 20, 1861–Apr. 16, 1931.
Vol. 10, Pt. 1–307
Wadsworth, Eliot, Sept. 10, 1876–May 29, 1959.
Supp. 6–659
Wadsworth, James, Apr. 20, 1768–June 7, 1844.
Vol. 10, Pt. 1–307
Wadsworth, James Samuel, Oct. 30, 1807–May 8, 1864.
Vol. 10, Pt. 1–308
Wadsworth, James Wolcott, Jr., Aug. 12, 1877–June 21, 1952.
Supp. 5–715
Wadsworth, Jeremiah, July 12, 1743–Apr. 30, 1804.
Vol. 10, Pt. 1–309
Wadsworth, Peleg, May 6, 1748–Nov. 12, 1829.
Vol. 10, Pt. 1–310
Waesche, Russell Randolph, Jan 6, 1886–Oct. 17, 1946.
Supp. 4–853
Wagener, John Andreas, July 23, 1816–Aug. 28, 1876.
Supp. 1–696
Waggaman, Mary Teresa McKee, Sept. 21, 1846–July 30, 1931.
Vol. 10, Pt. 1–311
Wagner, Clinton, Oct. 28, 1837–Nov. 25, 1914.
Vol. 10, Pt. 1–311
Wagner, John Peter, Feb. 24, 1874–Dec. 5, 1955.
Supp. 5–716
Wagner, Robert Ferdinand, June 8, 1877–May 4, 1953.
Supp. 5–717
Wagner, Webster, Oct. 2, 1817–Jan. 13, 1882.
Vol. 10, Pt. 1–312
Wagner, William, Jan. 15, 1796–Jan. 17, 1885.
Vol. 10, Pt. 1–313
Wahl, William Henry, Dec. 14, 1848–Mar. 23, 1909.
Vol. 10, Pt. 1–314
Waidner, Charles William, Mar. 6, 1873–Mar. 10, 1922.
Vol. 10, Pt. 1–315
Wailes, Benjamin Leonard Covington, Aug. 1, 1797–Nov. 16, 1862.
Vol. 10, Pt. 1–315
Wainwright, Jonathan Mayhew, Feb. 24, 1792–Sept. 21, 1854.
Vol. 10, Pt. 1–316
Wainwright, Jonathan Mayhew, July 21, 1821–Jan. 1, 1863.
Vol. 10, Pt. 1–317
Wainwright, Jonathan Mayhew, Aug. 23, 1883–Sept. 2, 1953.
Supp. 5–719
Wainwright, Richard, Jan. 5, 1817–Aug. 10, 1862.
Vol. 10, Pt. 1–318
Wainwright, Richard, Dec. 17, 1849–Mar. 6, 1926.
Vol. 10, Pt. 1–319
Wait, Samuel, Dec. 19, 1789–July 28, 1867.
Vol. 10, Pt. 1–320
Wait, William, Feb. 2, 1821–Dec. 29, 1880.
Vol. 10, Pt. 1–320
Wait, William Bell, Mar. 25, 1839–Oct. 25, 1916.
Vol. 10, Pt. 1–321
Waite, Henry Matson, May 15, 1869–Sept. 1, 1944.
Supp. 3–795
Waite, Morrison Remick, Nov. 29, 1816–Mar. 23, 1888.
Vol. 10, Pt. 1–322
Wakeley, Joseph Burton, Feb. 18, 1809–Apr. 27, 1875.
Vol. 10, Pt. 1–325
Waksman, Selman Abraham, July 22, 1888–Aug. 16, 1973.
Supp. 9–833
Walcot, Charles Metlton, *c.* 1816–May 15, 1868.
Vol. 10, Pt. 1–326
Walcot, Charles Melton, July 1, 1840–Jan. 1, 1921.
Vol. 10, Pt. 1–326
Walcott, Charles Doolittle, Mar. 31, 1850–Feb. 9, 1927.
Vol. 10, Pt. 1–327
Walcott, Henry Pickering, Dec. 23, 1838–Nov. 11, 1932.
Vol. 10, Pt. 1–329
Wald, Lillian D., Mar. 10, 1867–Sept. 1, 1940.
Supp. 2–687
Walden, Jacob Treadwell, Apr. 25, 1830–May 21, 1918.
Vol. 10, Pt. 1–330
Walden, John Morgan, Feb. 11, 1831–Jan. 21, 1914.
Vol. 10, Pt. 1–330
Walderne, Richard, *c.* 1615–June 1689.
Vol. 10, Pt. 1–331
Waldo, David, Apr. 30, 1802–May 20, 1878.
Vol. 10, Pt. 1–332
Waldo, Samuel, 1695–May 23, 1759.
Vol. 10, Pt. 1–333
Waldo, Samuel Lovett, Apr. 6, 1783–Feb. 16, 1861.
Vol. 10, Pt. 1–333
Waldo, Samuel Putnam, Mar. 12, 1779–Feb. 23, 1826.
Vol. 10, Pt. 1–334
Waldron, Richard. [*See* Walderne, Richard, 1615–1689.]
Wales, James Albert, Aug. 30, 1852–Dec. 6, 1886.
Vol. 10, Pt. 1–335
Wales, Leonard Eugene, Nov. 26, 1823–Feb. 8, 1897.
Vol. 10, Pt. 1–336
Walgreen, Charles Rudolph, Oct. 9, 1873–Dec. 11, 1939.
Supp. 2–688
Walke, Henry, Dec. 24, 1808–Mar. 8, 1896.
Vol. 10, Pt. 1–336
Walker, Alexander, Oct. 13, 1818–Jan. 24, 1893.
Vol. 10, Pt. 1–337
Walker, Amasa, May 4, 1799–Oct. 29, 1875.
Vol. 10, Pt. 1–338
Walker, Asa, Nov. 13, 1845–Mar. 7, 1916.
Vol. 10, Pt. 1–339
Walker, Madame C. J. [*See* Walker, Sarah Breedlove, 1867–1919.]
Walker, David, Sept. 28, 1785–June 28, 1830.
Vol. 10, Pt. 1–340
Walker, David, Feb. 19, 1806–Sept. 30, 1879.
Vol. 10, Pt. 1–340
Walker, David Shelby, May 2, 1815–July 20, 1891.
Vol. 10, Pt. 1–341
Walker, Francis Amasa, July 2, 1840–Jan. 5, 1897.
Vol. 10, Pt. 1–342
Walker, Frank Comerford, May 30, 1886–Sept. 13, 1959.
Supp. 6–660
Walker, Gilbert Carlton, Aug. 1, 1832–May 11, 1885.
Vol. 10, Pt. 1–344
Walker, Henry Oliver, May 14, 1843–Jan. 14, 1929.
Vol. 10, Pt. 1–345
Walker, James, Aug. 16, 1794–Dec. 23, 1874.
Vol. 10, Pt. 1–346
Walker, James Barr, July 29, 1805–Mar. 6, 1887.
Vol. 10, Pt. 1–347
Walker, James John, June 19, 1881–Nov. 18, 1946.
Supp. 4–854
Walker, John Brisben, Sept. 10, 1847–July 7, 1931.
Vol. 10, Pt. 1–347
Walker, John Grimes, Mar. 20, 1835–Sept. 15, 1907.
Vol. 10, Pt. 1–348
Walker, Jonathan Hoge, July 20, 1754–Jan. 1824.
Vol. 10, Pt. 1–349
Walker, Joseph Reddeford, Dec. 13, 1798–Oct. 27, 1876.
Vol. 10, Pt. 1–350
Walker, Leroy Pope, Feb. 7, 1817–Aug. 22, 1884.
Vol. 10, Pt. 1–351
Walker, Mary Edwards, Nov. 26, 1832–Feb. 21, 1919.
Vol. 10, Pt. 1–352
Walker, Pinkney Houston, June 18, 1815–Feb. 7, 1885.
Vol. 10, Pt. 1–352
Walker, Reuben Lindsay, May 29, 1827–June 7, 1890.
Vol. 10, Pt. 1–353
Walker, Robert Franklin, Nov. 29, 1850–Nov. 19, 1930.
Vol. 10, Pt. 1–354

Walker, Robert John, July 19, 1801–Nov. 11, 1869.
Vol. 10, Pt. 1–355
Walker, Sarah Breedlove, Dec. 23, 1867–May 25, 1919.
Vol. 10, Pt. 1–358
Walker, Sears Cook, Mar. 23, 1805–Jan. 30, 1853.
Vol. 10, Pt. 1–359
Walker, Stuart Armstrong, Mar. 4, 1880–Mar. 13, 1941.
Supp. 3–796
Walker, Thomas, Jan. 25, 1715–Nov. 9, 1794.
Vol. 10, Pt. 1–360
Walker, Thomas Barlow, Feb. 1, 1840–July 28, 1928.
Vol. 10, Pt. 1–361
Walker, Timothy, July 27, 1705–Sept. 1, 1782.
Vol. 10, Pt. 1–362
Walker, Timothy, Dec. 1, 1802–Jan. 15, 1856.
Vol. 10, Pt. 1–363
Walker, Walton Harris, Dec. 3, 1889–Dec. 23, 1950.
Supp. 4–856
Walker, William, May 8, 1824–Sept. 12, 1860.
Vol. 10, Pt. 1–363
Walker, William Henry Talbot, Nov. 26, 1816–July 22, 1864.
Vol. 10, Pt. 1–365
Walker, William Johnson, Mar. 15, 1790–Apr. 2, 1865.
Vol. 10, Pt. 1–366
Walker, Williston, July 1, 1860–Mar. 9, 1922.
Vol. 10, Pt. 1–366
Wallace, Charles William, Feb. 6, 1865–Aug. 7, 1932.
Vol. 10, Pt. 1–367
Wallace, David, Apr. 24, 1799–Sept. 4, 1859.
Vol. 10, Pt. 1–368
Wallace, Henry, Mar. 19, 1836–Feb. 22, 1916.
Vol. 10, Pt. 1–369
Wallace, Henry Agard, Oct. 7, 1888–Nov. 18, 1965.
Supp. 7–759
Wallace, Henry Cantwell, May 11, 1866–Oct 25 1924.
Vol. 10, Pt. 1–370
Wallace, Horace Binney, Feb. 26, 1817–Dec. 16, 1852.
Vol. 10, Pt. 1–370
Wallace, Hugh Campbell, Feb. 10, 1863–Jan. 1, 1931.
Vol. 10, Pt. 1–371
Wallace, John Findley, Sept. 10, 1852–July 3, 1921.
Vol. 10, Pt. 1–372
Wallace, John Hankins, Aug. 16, 1822–May 2, 1903.
Vol. 10, Pt. 1–373
Wallace, John William, Feb. 17, 1815–Jan. 12, 1884.
Vol. 10, Pt. 1–374
Wallace, Lewis, Apr. 10, 1827–Feb. 15, 1905.
Vol. 10, Pt. 1–375
Wallace, Lurleen Burns, Sept. 19, 1926–May 7, 1968.
Supp. 8–676
Wallace, William, Mar. 16, 1825–May 20, 1904.
Vol. 10, Pt. 1–376
Wallace, William Alexander Anderson, Apr. 3, 1817–Jan. 7, 1899.
Vol. 10, Pt. 1–377
Wallace, William James, Apr. 14, 1837–Mar. 11, 1917.
Vol. 10, Pt. 1–378
Wallace, William Ross, 1819–May 5, 1881.
Vol. 10, Pt. 1–378
Wallack, Henry John, 1790–Aug. 30, 1870.
Vol. 10, Pt. 1–379
Wallack, James William, *c.* 1795–Dec. 25, 1864.
Vol. 10, Pt. 1–380
Wallack, James William, Feb. 24, 1818–May 24, 1873.
Vol. 10, Pt. 1–381
Wallack, John Lester. [*See* Wallack, Lester, 1820–1888]
Wallack, Lester, Jan. 1, 1820–Sept. 6, 1888.
Vol. 10, Pt. 1–382
Wallenda, Karl, Jan. 21, 1905–Mar. 22, 1978.
Supp. 10–809
Waller, Emma, *c.* 1820–Feb. 28, 1899.
Vol. 10, Pt. 1–383
Waller, Fats. [*See* Waller, Thomas Wright 1904–1943]
Waller, Frederic, Mar. 10, 1886–May 18, 1954.
Supp. 5–721
Waller, John Lightfoot, Nov. 23, 1809–Oct. 10, 1854.
Vol. 10, Pt. 1–383
Waller, Thomas Macdonald, *c.* 1840–Jan. 25, 1924.
Vol. 10, Pt. 1–384
Waller, Thomas Wright, May 21, 1904–Dec. 15, 1943.
Supp. 3–797
Waller, Willard Walter, July 30, 1899–July 26, 1945.
Supp. 3–799
Wallgren, Mon[rad] C[harles], Apr. 17, 1891–Sept. 18, 1961.
Supp. 7–763
Walling, William English, Mar. 14, 1877–Sept. 12, 1936.
Supp. 2–689
Wallis, Severn Teackle, Sept. 8, 1816–Apr. 11, 1894.
Vol. 10, Pt. 1–385
Waln, Nicholas, Sept. 19, 1742–Sept. 29, 1813.
Vol. 10, Pt. 1–386
Waln, Robert, Feb. 22, 1765–Jan. 24, 1836.
Vol. 10, Pt. 1–387
Waln, Robert, Oct. 20, 1794–July 4, 1825.
Vol. 10, Pt. 1–387
Walsh, Benjamin Dann, Sept. 21, 1808–Nov. 18, 1869.
Vol. 10, Pt. 1–388
Walsh, Blanche, Jan. 4, 1873–Oct. 31, 1915.
Vol. 10, Pt. 1–389
Walsh, David Ignatius, Nov. 11, 1872–June 11, 1947.
Supp. 4–847
Walsh, Edmund Aloysius, Oct. 10, 1885–Oct. 31, 1956.
Supp. 6–661
Walsh, Edward Augustine, May 14, 1881–May 26, 1959.
Supp. 6–662
Walsh, Francis Patrick, July 20, 1864–May 2, 1939.
Supp. 2–690
Walsh, Henry Collins, Nov. 23, 1863–Apr. 29, 1927.
Vol. 10, Pt. 1–390
Walsh, James Anthony, Feb. 24, 1867–Apr. 14, 1936.
Supp. 2–691
Walsh, Michael, *c.* 1815–Mar. 17, 1859.
Vol. 10, Pt. 1–390
Walsh, Raoul, Mar. 11, 1887–Dec. 30, 1980.
Supp. 10–810
Walsh, Robert, Aug. 30, 1784–Feb. 7, 1859.
Vol. 10, Pt. 1–391
Walsh, Thomas, Oct. 14, 1871–Oct. 29, 1928.
Vol. 10, Pt. 1–392
Walsh, Thomas James, June 12, 1859–Mar. 2, 1933.
Vol. 10, Pt. 1–393
Walsh, Thomas Joseph, Dec. 6, 1873–June 6, 1952.
Supp. 5–722
Walter, Albert G., June 21, 1811–Oct. 14, 1876.
Vol. 10, Pt. 1–395
Walter, Bruno, Sept. 15, 1876–Feb. 17, 1962.
Supp. 7–764
Walter, Eugene, Nov. 27, 1874–Sept. 26, 1941.
Supp. 3–800
Walter, Francis Eugene, May 26, 1894–May 31, 1963.
Supp. 7–766
Walter, Thomas, *c.* 1740–Jan. 17, 1789.
Vol. 10, Pt. 1–396
Walter, Thomas, Dec. 13, 1696–Jan. 10, 1725.
Vol. 10, Pt. 1–395
Walter, Thomas Ustick, Sept. 4, 1804–Oct. 30, 1887.
Vol. 10, Pt. 1–397
Walters, Alexander, Aug. 1, 1858–Feb. 2, 1917.
Vol. 10, Pt. 1–398
Walters, Henry, Sept. 26, 1848–Nov. 30, 1931.
Vol. 10, Pt. 1–399
Walters, William Thompson, May 23, 1820–Nov. 22, 1894.
Vol. 10, Pt. 1–400
Walthall, Edward Cary, Apr. 4, 1831–Apr. 21, 1898.
Vol. 10, Pt. 1–401
Walthall, Henry Brazeal, Mar. 16, 1878–June 17, 1936.
Supp. 2–693
Walther, Carl Ferdinand Wilhelm, Oct. 25, 1811–May 7, 1887.
Vol. 10, Pt. 1–402
Walton, George, 1741–Feb. 2, 1804.
Vol. 10, Pt. 1–403
Walton, Lester Aglar, Apr. 20, 1882–Oct. 16, 1965.
Supp. 7–767
Walworth, Clarence Augustus, May 30, 1820–Sept. 19, 1900.
Vol. 10, Pt. 1–405
Walworth, Jeannette Ritchie Hadermann, Feb. 22, 1837–Feb. 4, 1918.
Vol. 10, Pt. 1–406
Walworth, Reuben Hyde, Oct. 26, 1788–Nov. 28, 1867.
Vol. 10, Pt. 1–406
Wambaugh, Sarah, Mar. 6, 1882–Nov. 12, 1955.
Supp. 5–723

Wanamaker, John, July 11, 1838–Dec. 12, 1922.
Vol. 10, Pt. 1–407
Wanamaker, Lewis Rodman, Feb. 13, 1863–Mar. 9, 1928.
Vol. 10, Pt. 1–409
Wanamaker, Reuben Melville, Aug. 2, 1866–June 18, 1924.
Vol. 10, Pt. 1–410
Waner, Paul Glee, Apr. 16, 1903–Aug. 29, 1965.
Supp. 7–768
Wanger, Walter, July 11, 1894–Nov. 18, 1968.
Supp. 8–677
Wanless, William James, May 1, 1865–Mar. 3, 1933.
Vol. 10, Pt. 1–411
Wanton, Joseph, Aug. 15, 1705–July 19, 1780.
Vol. 10, Pt. 1–412
Warbasse, James Peter, Nov. 22, 1866–Feb. 22, 1957.
Supp. 6–663
Warburg, Felix Moritz, Jan. 14, 1871–Oct. 20, 1937.
Supp. 2–694
Warburg, James Paul, Aug. 18, 1896–June 3, 1969.
Supp. 8–679
Warburg, Paul Moritz, Aug. 10, 1868–Jan. 24, 1932.
Vol. 10, Pt. 1–412
Ward, Aaron Montgomery, Feb. 17, 1843–Dec. 7, 1913.
Vol. 10, Pt. 1–414
Ward, Arch Burdette, Dec. 27, 1896–July 9, 1955.
Supp. 5–724
Ward, Artemas, Nov. 26, 1727–Oct. 28, 1800.
Vol. 10, Pt. 1–415
Ward, Artemus. [*See* Browne, Charles Farrar, 1834–1867.]
Ward, Charles Alfred, Oct. 12, 1883–Jan. 12, 1951.
Supp. 5–725
Ward, Charles Henshaw, Nov. 5, 1872–Oct. 9, 1935.
Supp. 1–697
Ward, Cyrenus Osborne, Oct. 28, 1831–Mar. 19, 1902.
Vol. 10, Pt. 1–416
Ward, Elizabeth Stuart Phelps, Aug. 31, 1844–Jan. 28, 1911.
Vol. 10, Pt. 1–417
Ward, Frederick Townsend, Nov. 29, 1831–Sept. 21, 1862.
Vol. 10, Pt. 1–419
Ward, Genevieve, Mar. 27, 1838–Aug. 18, 1922.
Vol. 10, Pt. 1–420
Ward, George Gray, Dec. 30, 1844–June 15, 1922.
Vol. 10, Pt. 1–421
Ward, Harry Frederick, Oct. 15, 1873–Dec. 9, 1966.
Supp. 8–680
Ward, Henry Augustus, Mar. 9, 1834–July 4, 1906.
Vol. 10, Pt. 1–421
Ward, Henry Baldwin, Mar. 4, 1865–Nov. 30, 1945.
Supp. 3–802
Ward, Henry Dana, Jan. 13, 1797–Feb. 29, 1884.
Vol. 10, Pt. 1–422
Ward, Herbert Dickinson, June 30, 1861–June 18, 1932.
Vol. 10, Pt. 1–423
Ward, James Edward, Feb. 25, 1836–July 23, 1894.
Vol. 10, Pt. 1–424
Ward, James Harmon, Sept. 25, 1806–June 27, 1861.
Vol. 10, Pt. 1–425
Ward, James Warner, June 5, 1816–June 28, 1897.
Vol. 10, Pt. 1–426
Ward, John Elliott, Oct. 2, 1814–Nov. 29, 1902.
Vol. 10, Pt. 1–426
Ward, John Quincy Adams, June 29, 1830–May 1, 1910.
Vol. 10, Pt. 1–427
Ward, Joseph, May 5, 1838–Dec. 11, 1889.
Vol. 10, Pt. 1–429
Ward, Lester Frank, June 18, 1841–Apr. 18, 1913.
Vol. 10, Pt. 1–430
Ward, Lydia Arms Avery Coonley, Jan. 31, 1845–Feb. 26, 1924.
Vol. 10, Pt. 1–432
Ward, Marcus Lawrence, Nov. 9, 1812–Apr. 25, 1884.
Vol. 10, Pt. 1–432
Ward, Montgomery. [*See* Ward, Aaron Montgomery, 1843–1913.]
Ward, Nancy, fl. 1776–1781.
Vol. 10, Pt. 1–433
Ward, Nathaniel, *c.* 1578–Oct. 1652.
Vol. 10, Pt. 1–433
Ward, Richard, Apr. 15, 1689–Aug. 21, 1763.
Vol. 10, Pt. 1–434
Ward, Richard Halsted, June 17, 1837–Oct. 28, 1917.
Vol. 10, Pt. 1–435
Ward, Robert De Courcy, Nov. 29, 1867–Nov. 12, 1931.
Vol. 10, Pt. 1–436
Ward, Samuel, May 27, 1725–Mar. 26, 1776.
Vol. 10, Pt. 1–437
Ward, Samuel, Nov. 17, 1756–Aug. 16, 1832.
Vol. 10, Pt. 1–437
Ward, Samuel, May 1, 1786–Nov. 27, 1839.
Vol. 10, Pt. 1–438
Ward, Samuel, Jan. 25, 1814–May 19, 1884.
Vol. 10, Pt. 1–439
Ward, Samuel Ringgold, Oct. 17, 1817–1866?.
Vol. 10, Pt. 1–440
Ward, Thomas, June 8, 1807–Apr. 13, 1873.
Vol. 10, Pt. 1–440
Ward, Thomas Wren, Nov. 20, 1786–Mar. 4, 1858.
Vol. 10, Pt. 1–441
Ward, William Hayes, June. 25, 1835–Aug. 28, 1916.
Vol. 10, Pt. 1–442
Warde, Frederick Barkham, Feb. 23, 1851–Feb. 7, 1935.
Supp. 1–698
Warden, David Bailie, 1772–Oct. 9, 1845.
Vol. 10, Pt. 1–443
Warden, Robert Bruce, Jan. 18, 1824–Dec. 3, 1888.
Vol. 10, Pt. 1–444
Warder, John Aston, Jan. 19, 1812–July 14, 1883.
Vol. 10, Pt. 1–444
Wardman, Ervin, Dec. 25, 1865–Jan. 13, 1923.
Vol. 10, Pt. 1–445
Ware, Ashur, Feb. 10, 1782–Sept. 10, 1873.
Vol. 10, Pt. 1–446
Ware, Edmund Asa, Dec. 22, 1837–Sept. 25, 1885.
Vol. 10, Pt. 1–446
Ware, Henry, Apr. 1, 1764–July 12, 1845.
Vol. 10, Pt. 1–447
Ware, Henry, Apr. 21, 1794–Sept. 22, 1843.
Vol. 10, Pt. 1–448
Ware, John, Dec. 19, 1795–Apr. 29, 1864.
Vol. 10, Pt. 1–449
Ware, John Fothergill Waterhouse, Aug. 31, 1818–Feb. 26, 1881.
Vol. 10, Pt. 1–450
Ware, Nathaniel A., d. 1854.
Vol. 10, Pt. 1–451
Ware, William, Aug. 3, 1797–Feb. 19, 1852.
Vol. 10, Pt. 1–451
Ware, William Robert, May 27, 1832–June 9, 1915.
Vol. 10, Pt. 1–452
Warfield, Benjamin Breckinridge, Nov. 5, 1851–Feb. 16, 1921.
Vol. 10, Pt. 1–453
Warfield, Catherine Ann Ware, June 6, 1816–May 21, 1877.
Vol. 10, Pt. 1–454
Warfield, David, Nov. 28, 1866–June 27, 1951.
Supp. 5–726
Warfield, Solomon Davies, Sept. 4, 1859–Oct. 24, 1927.
Vol. 10, Pt. 1–455
Waring, George Edwin, July 4, 1833–Oct. 29, 1898.
Vol. 10, Pt. 1–456
Waring, Julius Waties, July 27, 1880–Jan. 11, 1968.
Supp. 8–682
Warman, Cy, June 22, 1855–Apr. 7, 1914.
Vol. 10, Pt. 1–457
Warmoth, Henry Clay, May 9, 1842–Sept. 30, 1931.
Vol. 10, Pt. 1–457
Warner, Adoniram Judson, Jan. 13, 1834–Aug. 12, 1910.
Vol. 10, Pt. 1–459
Warner, Amos Griswold, Dec. 21, 1861–Jan. 17, 1900.
Vol. 10, Pt. 1–460
Warner, Anna Bartlett, Aug. 31, 1827–Jan. 22, 1915.
Vol. 10, Pt. 1–461
Warner, Anne Richmond, Oct. 14, 1869–Feb. 1, 1913.
Vol. 10, Pt. 1–461
Warner, Charles Dudley, Sept. 12, 1829–Oct. 20, 1900.
Vol. 10, Pt. 1–462
Warner, Edward Pearson, Nov. 9, 1894–July 12, 1958.
Supp. 6–665
Warner, Fred Maltby, July 21, 1865–Apr. 17, 1923.
Vol. 10, Pt. 1–463
Warner, Glenn Scobey ("Pop"), Apr. 5, 1871–Sept. 7, 1954.
Supp. 5–727
Warner, Harry Morris, Dec. 12, 1881–July 25, 1958.
Supp. 6–667

Warner, Hiram, Oct. 29, 1802–June 30, 1881.
Vol. 10, Pt. 1–464
Warner, Jack Leonard, Aug. 1892–Sept. 9, 1978.
Supp. 10–811
Warner, James Cartwright, Aug. 20, 1830–July 21, 1895.
Vol. 10, Pt. 1–465
Warner, Jonathan Trumbull, Nov. 20, 1807–Apr. 22, 1895.
Vol. 10, Pt. 1–466
Warner, Juan José. [*See* Warner, Jonathan Trumbull, 1807–1895.]
Warner, Langdon, Aug. 1, 1881–June 9, 1955.
Supp. 5–729
Warner, Olin Levi, Apr. 9, 1844–Aug. 14, 1896.
Vol. 10, Pt. 1–467
Warner, Seth, May 6, 1743 o.s.–Dec. 26, 1784.
Vol. 10, Pt. 1–468
Warner, Susan Bogert, July 11, 1819–Mar. 17, 1885.
Vol. 10, Pt. 1–469
Warner, Wiliiam, June 11, 1840–Oct. 4, 1916.
Vol. 10, Pt. 1–469
Warner, William Lloyd, Oct. 26, 1898–May 23, 1970.
Supp. 8–683
Warner, Worcester Reed, May 16, 1846–June 25, 1929.
Vol. 10, Pt. 1–470
Warren, Charles, Mar. 9, 1868–Aug. 16, 1954.
Supp. 5–730
Warren, Cyrus Moors, Jan. 15, 1824–Aug. 13, 1891.
Vol. 10, Pt. 1–471
Warren, Earl, Mar. 19, 1891–July 9, 1974.
Supp. 9–834
Warren, Francis Emroy, June 20, 1844–Nov. 24, 1929.
Vol. 10, Pt. 1–472
Warren, Fuller, Oct. 3, 1905–Sept. 23, 1973.
Supp. 9–838
Warren, George Frederick, Feb. 16, 1874–May 24, 1938.
Supp. 2–695
Warren, Gouverneur Kemble, Jan. 8, 1830–Aug. 8, 1882.
Vol. 10, Pt. 1–473
Warren, Henry Clarke, Nov. 18, 1854–Jan. 3, 1899.
Vol. 10, Pt. 1–474
Warren, Henry Ellis, May 21, 1872–Sept. 21, 1957.
Supp. 6–668
Warren, Henry White, Jan. 4, 1831–July 22, 1912.
Vol. 10, Pt. 1–475
Warren, Herbert Langford, Mar. 29, 1857–June 27, 1917.
Supp. 1–698
Warren, Howard Crosby, June 12, 1867–Jan. 4, 1934.
Vol. 10, Pt. 1–476
Warren, Israel Perkins, Apr. 8, 1814–Oct. 9, 1892.
Vol. 10, Pt. 1–477
Warren, James, Sept. 28, 1726–Nov. 28, 1808.
Vol. 10, Pt. 1–478
Warren, John, July 27, 1753–Apr. 4, 1815.
Vol. 10, Pt. 1–479
Warren, John Collins, Aug. 1, 1778–May 4, 1856.
Vol. 10, Pt. 1–480
Warren, John Collins, May 4, 1842–Nov. 3, 1927.
Vol. 10, Pt. 1–481
Warren, Joseph, June 11, 1741–June 17, 1775.
Vol. 10, Pt. 1–482
Warren, Josiah, *c.* 1798–Apr. 14, 1874.
Vol. 10, Pt. 1–483
Warren, Leonard, Apr. 21, 1911–Mar. 4, 1960.
Supp. 6–669
Warren, Lindsay Carter, Dec. 16, 1889–Dec. 28, 1976.
Supp. 10–814
Warren, Mercy Otis, Sept. 14, 1728 o.s.–Oct. 19, 1814.
Vol. 10, Pt. 1–484
Warren, Minton, Jan. 29, 1850–Nov. 26, 1907.
Vol. 10, Pt. 1–485
Warren, Sir Peter, Mar. 10, 1703–July 29, 1752.
Vol. 10, Pt. 1–485
Warren, Richard Henry, Sept. 17, 1859–Dec. 3, 1933.
Vol. 10, Pt. 1–487
Warren, Russell, Aug. 5, 1783–Nov. 16, 1860.
Vol. 10, Pt. 1–487
Warren, Samuel Prowse, Feb. 18, 1841–Oct. 7, 1915.
Vol. 10, Pt. 1–488
Warren, Shields, Feb. 26, 1898–July 1, 1980.
Supp. 10–815
Warren, William, May 10, 1767–Oct. 19. 1832.
Vol. 10, Pt. 1–489
Warren, William, Nov. 17, 1812–Sept. 21, 1888.
Vol. 10 Pt. 1–489
Warren, William Fairfield, Mar. 13, 1833–Dec. 6, 1929.
Vol. 10, Pt. 1–490
Warrington, Albert Powell, Aug. 27, 1886–June 16, 1939.
Supp. 2–697
Warrington, Lewis, Nov. 3, 1782–Oct. 12, 1851.
Vol. 10, Pt. 1–492
Warthin, Aldred Scott, Oct. 21, 1866–May 23, 1931.
Vol. 10, Pt. 1–493
Washakie, *c.* 1804–Feb. 15, 1900.
Vol. 10, Pt. 1–494
Washburn, Albert Henry, Apr. 11, 1866–Apr. 2, 1930.
Vol. 10, Pt. 1–494
Washburn, Cadwallader Colden, Apr. 22, 1818–May 14, 1882.
Vol. 10, Pt. 1–495
Washburn, Charles Grenfill, Jan. 28, 1857–May 25, 1928.
Vol. 10, Pt. 1–497
Washburn, Edward Abiel, Apr. 16, 1819–Feb. 2, 1881.
Vol. 10. Pt. 1–498
Washburn, Edward Wight, May 10, 1881–Feb. 6, 1934.
Vol. 10, Pt. 1–498
Washburn, Elihu Benjamin. [*See* Washburne, Elihu Benjamin, 1816–1887.]
Washburn, Emory, Feb. 14, 1800–Mar. 18, 1877.
Vol. 10, Pt. 1–499
Washburn, George, Mar.1, 1833–Feb. 15, 1915.
Vol. 10, Pt. 1–500
Washburn, Ichabod, Aug. 11, 1798–Dec. 30, 1868.
Vol. 10, Pt. 1–501
Washburn, Israel, June 6, 1813–May 12, 1883.
Vol. 10, Pt. 1–502
Washburn, Margaret Floy, July 25, 1871–Oct. 29, 1939.
Supp. 2–698
Washburn, Nathan, Apr. 22, 1818–Sept. 13, 1903.
Vol. 10, Pt. 1–503
Washburn, William Drew, Jan. 14, 1831–July 29, 1912.
Vol. 10, Pt. 1–504
Washburne, Elihu Benjamin, Sept. 23, 1816–Oct. 23, 1887.
Vol. 10, Pt. 1–504
Washington, Booker Taliaferro, Apr. 5, 1856–Nov. 14, 1915.
Vol. 10, Pt. 1–506
Washington, Bushrod, June 5, 1762–Nov. 26, 1829.
Vol. 10, Pt. 1–508
Washington, Dinah, Aug. 1924–Dec. 14, 1963.
Supp. 7–769
Washington, George, Feb. 11/22, 1732–Dec. 14, 1799.
Vol. 10, Pt. 1–509
Washington, Henry Stephens, Jan. 15, 1867–Jan. 7, 1934.
Vol. 10, Pt. 1–527
Washington, John Macrae, Oct. 1797–Dec. 24, 1853.
Vol. 10, Pt. 1–528
Washington, Kenneth Stanley ("The General"), Aug. 8, 1918–June 24, 1971.
Supp. 9–840
Waterhouse, Benjamin, Mar. 4, 1754–Oct. 2, 1846.
Vol. 10, Pt. 1–529
Waterhouse, Frank, Aug. 8, 1867–Mar. 20, 1930.
Vol. 10, Pt. 1–532
Waterhouse, Sylvester, Sept. 15, 1830–Feb. 12, 1902.
Vol. 10, Pt. 1–533
Waterman, Alan Tower, June 4, 1892–Dec. 1, 1967.
Supp. 8–685
Waterman, Lewis Edson, Nov. 20, 1837–May 1, 1901.
Vol. 10, Pt. 1–533
Waterman, Robert H., Mar. 4, 1808–Aug. 9, 1884.
Vol. 10, Pt. 1–534
Waterman, Thomas Whitney, June 28, 1821–Dec. 7, 1898.
Vol. 10, Pt. 1–535
Waters, Daniel, June 20, 1731–Mar. 26, 1816.
Vol. 10, Pt. 1–536
Waters, Ethel, Oct. 31, 1896–Sept. 1, 1977.
Supp. 10–817
Waters, William Everett, Dec. 20, 1856–Aug. 3, 1924.
Vol. 10, Pt. 1–537
Watie, Stand, Dec. 12, 1806–Sept. 9, 1871.
Vol. 10, Pt. 1–537
Watkins, Arthur Vivian, Dec. 18, 1886–Sept. 7, 1973.
Supp. 9–841

Watkins, George Claiborne, Nov. 25, 1815–Dec. 7, 1872.
Vol. 10, Pt. 1–538
Watkins, John Elfreth, May 17, 1852–Aug. 11, 1903.
Vol. 10, Pt. 1–539
Watson, Andrew, Feb. 15, 1834–Dec. 9, 1916.
Vol. 10, Pt. 1–539
Watson, Arthur Kittridge, Apr. 23, 1919–July 26, 1974.
Supp. 9–843
Watson, Charles Roger, July 17, 1873–Jan. 10, 1948.
Supp. 4–859
Watson, David Thompson, Jan. 2, 1844–Feb. 24, 1916.
Vol. 10, Pt. 1–540
Watson, Elkanah, Jan. 22, 1758–Dec. 5, 1842.
Vol. 10, Pt. 1–541
Watson, Henry Clay, 1831–June 24, 1867.
Vol. 10, Pt. 1–542
Watson, Henry Cood, Nov. 4, 1818–Dec. 2, 1875.
Vol. 10, Pt. 1–543
Watson, James Craig, Jan. 28, 1838–Nov. 22, 1880.
Vol. 10, Pt. 1–543
Watson, James Eli, Nov. 2, 1864–July 29, 1948.
Supp. 4–861
Watson, James Madison, Feb. 8, 1827–Sept. 29, 1900.
Vol. 10, Pt. 1–544
Watson, John Broadus, Jan. 9, 1878–Sept. 25, 1958.
Supp. 6–670
Watson, John Crittenden, Aug. 24, 1842–Dec. 14, 1923.
Vol. 10, Pt. 1–545
Watson, John Fanning, June 13, 1779–Dec. 23, 1860.
Vol. 10, Pt. 1–546
Watson, John William Clark, Feb. 27, 1808–Sept. 24, 1890.
Vol. 10, Pt. 1–547
Watson, Sereno, Dec. 1, 1826–Mar. 9, 1892.
Vol. 10, Pt. 1–547
Watson, Thomas Augustus, Jan. 18, 1854–Dec. 13, 1934.
Vol. 10, Pt. 1–548
Watson, Thomas Edward, Sept. 5, 1856–Sept. 26, 1922.
Vol. 10, Pt. 1–549
Watson, Thomas John, Feb. 17, 1874–June 19, 1956.
Supp. 6–673
Watson, William, Jan. 19, 1834–Sept. 30, 1915.
Vol. 10, Pt. 1–551
Watt, Donald Beates, May 3, 1893–Nov. 27, 1977.
Supp. 10–819
Watterson, Harvey Magee, Nov. 23, 1811–Oct. 1, 1891.
Vol. 10, Pt. 1–551
Watterson, Henry, Feb. 16, 1840–Dec. 22, 1921.
Vol. 10, Pt. 1–552
Watterston, George, Oct. 23, 1783–Feb. 4, 1854.
Vol. 10, Pt. 1–555
Watts, Alan Wilson, Jan. 6, 1915–Nov. 16, 1973.
Supp. 9–845
Watts, Franklin Mowry, June 11, 1904–May 21, 1978.
Supp. 10–820
Watts, Frederick, May 9, 1801–Aug. 17, 1889.
Vol. 10, Pt. 1–556
Watts, Thomas Hill, Jan. 3, 1819–Sept. 16, 1892.
Vol. 10, Pt. 1–557
Wattson, Lewis Thomas. [*See* Francis, Paul James, 1863–1940]
Waugh, Beverly, Oct. 25, 1789–Feb. 9, 1858.
Vol. 10, Pt. 1–558
Waugh, Frederick Judd, Sept. 13, 1861–Sept. 10, 1940.
Supp. 2–699
Waxman, Franz, Dec. 24, 1906–Feb. 24, 1967.
Supp. 8–688
Wayland, Francis, Mar. 11, 1796–Sept. 30, 1865.
Vol. 10, Pt. 1–558
Wayland, Francis, Aug. 23, 1826–Jan. 9, 1904.
Vol. 10, Pt. 1–560
Waymack, William Wesley, Oct. 18, 1888–Nov. 5, 1900.
Supp. 6–676
Wayman, Alexander Walker, Sept. 1821–Nov. 30, 1895.
Vol. 10, Pt. 1–561
Waymouth, George, fl. 1601–1612.
Vol. 10, Pt. 1–562
Wayne, Anthony, Jan. 1, 1745–Dec. 15, 1796.
Vol. 10, Pt. 1–563
Wayne, Arthur Trezevant, Jan. 1, 1863–May 5, 1930.
Vol. 10, Pt. 1–565
Wayne, James Moore, *c.* 1790–July 5, 1867.
Vol. 10, Pt. 1–565
Wayne, John, May 26, 1907–June 11, 1979.
Supp. 10–822
Weare, Meshech, Jan. 16, 1713–Jan. 14, 1786.
Vol. 10, Pt. 1–566
Weatherford, William, *c.* 1780–Mar. 9, 1824.
Vol. 10, Pt. 1–567
Weaver, Aaron Ward, July 1, 1832–Oct. 2, 1919.
Vol. 10, Pt. 1–568
Weaver, James Baird, June 12, 1833–Feb. 6, 1912.
Vol. 10, Pt. 1–568
Weaver, Philip, b. 1791.
Vol. 10, Pt. 1–570
Weaver, Warren, July 17, 1894–Nov. 24, 1978.
Supp. 10–824
Weaver, William Dixon, Aug. 30, 1857–Nov. 2, 1919.
Vol. 10, Pt. 1–570
Webb, Alexander Stewart, Feb. 15, 1835–Feb. 12, 1911.
Vol. 10, Pt. 1–571
Webb, Charles Henry, Jan. 24, 1834–May 24, 1905.
Vol. 10, Pt. 1–572
Webb, Clifton, Nov. 19, 1893–Oct. 13, 1966.
Supp. 8–690
Webb, Daniel, *c.* 1700–Nov. 11, 1773.
Vol. 10, Pt. 1–573
Webb, George James, June 24, 1803–Oct. 7, 1887.
Vol. 10, Pt. 1–574
Webb, Harry Howard, Aug. 15, 1853–June 2, 1939.
Supp. 2–700
Webb, James Watson, Feb. 8, 1802–June 7, 1884.
Vol. 10, Pt. 1–574
Webb, John Burkitt, Nov. 22, 1841–Feb. 17, 1912.
Vol. 10, Pt. 1–575
Webb, Thomas, *c.* 1724–Dec. 10, 1796.
Vol. 10, Pt. 1–576
Webb, Thomas Smlth, Oct. 30, 1771–July 6, 1819.
Vol. 10, Pt. 1–577
Webb, Walter Prescott, Apr. 3, 1888–Mar. 8, 1963.
Supp. 7–770
Webb, William Henry, June 19, 1816–Oct. 30, 1899.
Vol. 10, Pt. 1–578
Webb, William Robert, Nov. 11, 1842–Dec. 19, 1926.
Vol. 10, Pt. 1–579,
Webber, Charles Wilkens, May 29, 1819–April 1856.
Vol. 10, Pt. 1–580
Webber, Herbert John, Dec. 27, 1865–Jan. 18, 1946.
Supp. 4–862
Weber, Albert, July 8, 1828–June 25, 1879.
Vol. 10, Pt. 1–581
Weber, Gustav Carl Erich, May 26, 1828–Mar. 21, 1912.
Vol. 10, Pt. 1–581
Weber, Henry Adam, July 12, 1845–June 14, 1912.
Vol. 10, Pt. 1–582
Weber, Joseph Morris, Aug. 11, 1867–May 10, 1942.
Supp. 3–803
Weber, Max, Apr. 18, 1881–Oct. 4, 1961.
Supp. 7–772
Webster, Alice Jane Chandler, July 24, 1876–June 11, 1916.
Vol. 10, Pt. 1–583
Webster, Arthur Gordon, Nov. 28, 1863–May 15, 1923.
Vol. 10, Pt. 1–584
Webster, Benjamin ("Ben") Francis, Mar. 27, 1909–Sept. 20, 1973.
Supp. 9–846
Webster, Daniel, Jan. 18, 1782–Oct. 24, 1852.
Vol. 10, Pt. 1–585
Webster, Edwin Sibley, Aug. 26, 1867–May 10, 1950.
Supp. 3–744
Webster, Edwin Sibley. [*See* Stone, Charles Augustus, 1867–1941.]
Webster, Harold Tucker, Sept. 21, 1885–Sept. 22, 1952.
Supp. 5–731
Webster, Jean. [*See* Webster, Alice Jane Chandler, 1876–1916.]
Webster, John White, May 20, 1793–Aug. 30, 1850.
Vol. 10, Pt. 1–592
Webster, Joseph Dana, Aug. 25, 1811–Mar. 12, 1876.
Vol. 10, Pt. 1–593
Webster, Margaret ("Peggy"), Mar. 15, 1905–Nov. 13, 1972.
Supp. 9–848
Webster, Noah, Oct. 16, 1758–May 28, 1843.
Vol. 10, Pt. 1–594
Webster, Pelatiah, Nov. 24, 1726–Sept. 2, 1795.
Vol. 10, Pt. 1–597

Webster-Powell, Alma. [*See* Powell, Alma Webster, 1874–1930.]
Weddell, Alexander Wilbourne, Apr. 6, 1876–Jan. 1, 1948. Supp. 4–863
Weed, Lewis Hill, Nov. 15, 1886–Dec. 21, 1952. Supp. 5–733
Weed, Thurlow, Nov. 15, 1797–Nov. 22, 1882. Vol. 10, Pt. 1–598
Weede, Robert, Feb. 22, 1903–July 9, 1972. Supp. 9–849
Weeden, William Babcock, Sept. 1, 1834–Mar. 28, 1912. Vol. 10, Pt. 1–600
Weeks, Edwin Lord, 1849–Nov. 17, 1903. Vol. 10, Pt. 1–601
Weeks, John Elmer, Aug. 9, 1853–Feb. 2, 1949. Supp. 4–864
Weeks, John Wingate, Apr. 11, 1860–July 12, 1926. Vol. 10, Pt. 1–601
Weeks, Joseph Dame, Dec. 3, 1840–Dec. 26, 1896. Vol. 10, Pt. 1–602
Weeks, Sinclair, June 15, 1893–Feb. 7, 1972. Supp. 9–851
Weeks, Stephen Beauregard, Feb. 2, 1865–May 3, 1918. Vol. 10, Pt. 1–603
Weems, Mason Locke, Oct. 11, 1759–May 23, 1825. Vol. 10, Pt. 1–604
Weems, Ted, Sept. 26, 1901–May 6, 1963. Supp. 7–774
Wegmann, Edward, Nov. 27, 1850–Jan. 3, 1935. Supp. 1–699
Wehle, Louis Brandeis, Sept. 13, 1880–Feb. 13, 1959. Supp. 6–677
Weicker, Lowell Palmer, Oct. 14, 1903–Nov. 25, 1978. Supp. 10–826
Weidenmann, Jacob, Aug. 22, 1829–Feb. 6, 1893. Vol. 10, Pt. 1–605
Weidenreich, Franz, June 7, 1873–July 11, 1948. Supp. 4–866
Weidig, Adolf, Nov. 28, 1867–Sept. 23, 1931. Vol. 10, Pt. 1–606
Weidner, Revere Franklin, Nov. 22, 1851–Jan. 6, 1915. Vol. 10, Pt. 1–606
Weigel, Gustave, Jan. 15, 1906–Jan. 3, 1964. Supp. 7–775
Weightman, William, Sept. 30, 1813–Aug. 25, 1904. Vol. 10, Pt. 1–607
Weil, Richard, Oct. 15, 1876–Nov. 19, 1917. Vol. 10, Pt. 1–608
Weill, Kurt, Mar. 2, 1900–Apr. 3, 1950. Supp. 4–867
Weinberger, Jacob, Jan. 4, 1882–May 21, 1974. Supp. 9–852
Weir, Ernest Tener, Aug. 1, 1875–June 26, 1957. Supp. 6–678
Weir, John Ferguson, Aug. 28, 1841–Apr. 8, 1926. Vol. 10, Pt. 1–608
Weir, Julian Alden, Aug. 30, 1852–Dec. 8, 1919. Vol. 10, Pt. 1–609
Weir, Robert Fulton, Feb. 16, 1838–Apr. 6, 1927. Vol. 10, Pt. 1–611
Weir, Robert Walter, June 18, 1803–May 1, 1889. Vol. 10, Pt. 1–612
Weisenburg, Theodore Herman, Apr. 10, 1876–Aug. 3, 1934. Vol. 10, Pt. 1–613
Weiser, Johann Conrad, Nov. 2, 1696–July 13, 1760. Vol. 10, Pt. 1–614
Weiss, Ehrich. [*See* Houdini, Harry, 1874–1926.]
Weiss, George Martin, June 23, 1894–Aug. 13, 1972. Supp. 9–854
Weiss, John, June 28, 1818–Mar. 9, 1879. Vol. 10, Pt. 1–615
Weiss, Soma, Jan. 27, 1899–Jan. 31, 1942. Supp. 3–805
Weitzel, Godfrey, Nov. 1, 1835–Mar. 19, 1884. Vol. 10, Pt. 1–616
Welby, Amelia Ball Coppuck, Feb. 3, 1819–May 3, 1852. Vol. 10, Pt. 1–617
Welch, Adonijah Strong, Apr. 12, 1821–Mar. 14, 1889. Vol. 10, Pt. 1–617
Welch, Ashbel, Dec. 4, 1809–Sept. 25, 1882. Vol. 10, Pt. 1–618
Welch, Charles Clark, June 14, 1830–Feb. 1, 1908. Vol. 10, Pt. 1–619
Welch, John, Oct. 28, 1805–Aug. 5, 1891. Vol. 10, Pt. 1–620
Welch, Joseph Nye, Oct. 22, 1890–Oct. 6, 1960. Supp. 6–679
Welch, Leo Dewey, Apr. 22, 1898–Oct. 21, 1978. Supp. 10–827
Welch, Philip Henry, Mar. 1, 1849–Feb. 24, 1889. Vol. 10, Pt. 1–620
Welch, William Henry, Apr. 8, 1850–Apr. 30, 1934. Vol. 10, Pt. 1–621
Welch, William Wickham, Dec. 10, 1818–July 30, 1892. Vol. 10, Pt. 1–624
Weld, Arthur Cyril Gordon, Mar. 4, 1862–Oct. 11, 1914. Vol. 10, Pt. 1–625
Weld, Theodore Dwight, Nov. 23, 1803–Feb. 3, 1895. Vol. 10, Pt. 1–625
Weld, Thomas, 1595–Mar. 23, 1660/61. Vol. 10, Pt. 1–627
Welker, Herman, Dec. 11, 1906–Oct. 30, 1957. Supp. 6–681
Weller, John B., Feb. 22, 1812–Aug. 17, 1875. Vol. 10, Pt. 1–628
Welles, (Benjamin) Sumner, Oct. 14, 1892–Sept. 24, 1961. Supp. 7–776
Welles, Gideon, July 1, 1802–Feb. 11, 1878. Vol. 10, Pt. 1–629
Welles, Noah, Sept. 25, 1718–Dec. 31, 1776. Vol. 10, Pt. 1–632
Welles, Roger, Dec. 7, 1862–Apr. 26, 1932. Vol. 10, Pt. 1–632
Welling, James Clarke, July 14, 1825–Sept. 4, 1894. Vol. 10, Pt. 1–633
Welling, Richard Ward Greene, Aug. 27, 1858–Dec. 17, 1946. Supp. 4–869
Wellington, Arthur Mellen, Dec. 20, 1847–May 16, 1895. Vol. 10, Pt. 1–634
Wellman, Samuel Thomas, Feb. 5, 1847–July 11, 1919. Vol. 10, Pt. 1–635
Wellman, Walter, Nov. 3, 1858–Jan. 31, 1934. Vol. 10, Pt. 1–635
Wellman, William Augustus, Feb. 29, 1896–Dec. 9, 1975. Supp. 9–855
Wellons, William Brock, Nov. 9, 1821–Feb. 16, 1877. Vol. 10, Pt. 1–636
Wells, David Ames, June 17, 1828–Nov. 5, 1898. Vol. 10, Pt. 1–637
Wells, Erastus, Dec. 2, 1823–Oct. 2, 1893. Vol. 10, Pt. 1–638
Wells, Harriet Sheldon, 1873–Feb. 8, 1961. Supp. 7–778
Wells, Harry Gideon, July 21, 1875–Apr. 26, 1943. Supp. 3–806
Wells, Henry, Dec. 12, 1805–Dec. 10, 1878. Vol. 10, Pt. 1–639
Wells, Horace, Jan. 21, 1815–Jan. 24, 1848. Vol. 10, Pt. 1–640
Wells, James Madison, Jan. 8, 1808–Feb. 28, 1899. Vol. 10, Pt. 1–641
Wells, John, *c.* 1770–Sept. 7, 1823. Vol. 10, Pt. 1–642
Wells, Robert William, Nov. 29, 1795–Sept. 22, 1864. Vol. 10, Pt. 1–643
Wells, Samuel Roberts, Apr. 4, 1820–Apr. 13, 1875. Vol. 10, Pt. 1–643
Wells, William Charles, May 24, 1757–Sept. 18, 1817. Vol. 10, Pt. 1–644
Wells, William Harvey, Feb. 27, 1812–Jan. 21, 1885. Vol. 10, Pt. 1–645
Wells, William Vincent, Jan. 2, 1826–June 1, 1876. Vol. 10, Pt. 1–646
Welsh, John, Nov. 9, 1805–Apr. 10, 1886. Vol. 10, Pt. 1–647
Wemyss, Francis Courtney, May 13, 1797–Jan. 5, 1859. Vol. 10, Pt. 1–647
Wende, Ernest, July 23, 1853–Feb. 11, 1910. Vol. 10, Pt. 1–648
Wende, Grover William, Apr. 6, 1867–Feb. 9, 1926. Vol. 10, Pt. 1–649

Wendell, Barrett, Aug. 23, 1855–Feb. 8, 1921.
Vol. 10, Pt. 1–649
Wendte, Charles William, June 11, 1844–Sept. 9, 1931.
Vol. 10, Pt. 1–651
Wenley, Robert Mark, July 19, 1861–Mar. 29, 1929.
Vol 10, Pt. 1–652
Wenner, George Unangst, May 17, 1844–Nov. 1, 1934.
Vol. 10, Pt. 1–653
Wentworth, Benning, July 24, 1696–Oct. 14, 1770.
Vol. 10, Pt. 1–653
Wentworth, Cecile de, d. Aug. 28, 1933.
Vol. 10, Pt. 1–654
Wentworth, George Albert, July 31, 1835–May 24, 1906.
Vol. 10, Pt. 1–655
Wentworth, John, Aug. 20, 1737 N.S.–Apr. 8, 1820.
Vol. 10, Pt. 1–656
Wentworth, John, Mar. 5, 1815–Oct. 16, 1888.
Vol. 10, Pt. 1–657
Wentworth, Paul, d. Dec. 1793.
Vol. 10, Pt. 1–659
Werden, Reed, Feb. 28, 1818–July 11, 1886.
Vol. 10, Pt. 2–1
Wergeland, Agnes Mathilde, May 8, 1857–Mar. 6, 1914.
Vol. 10, Pt. 2–1
Wernwag, Lewis, Dec. 4, 1769–Aug. 12, 1843.
Vol. 10, Pt. 2–2
Wertenbaker, Charles Christian, Feb. 11, 1901–Jan. 8, 1955.
Supp. 5–734
Wertenbaker, Thomas Jefferson, Feb. 6, 1879–Apr. 22, 1966.
Supp. 8–691
Wertheimer, Max, Apr. 15, 1880–Oct. 12, 1943.
Supp. 3–808
Wesbrook, Frank Fairchild, July 12, 1868–oct. 20, 1918.
Vol. 10, Pt. 2–3
Wesselhoeft, Conrad, Mar. 23, 1834–Dec. 17, 1904.
Vol. 10, Pt. 2–4
Wesselhoeft, Walter, 1838–1920. [*See* Wesselhoeft, Conrad, 1834–1904.]
Wesson, Daniel Baird, May 18, 1825–Aug. 4, 1906.
Vol. 10, Pt. 2–4
West, Allen Brown, June 19, 1886–Sept. 18, 1936.
Supp. 2–701
West, Andrew Fleming, May 17, 1853–Dec. 27, 1943.
Supp. 3–809
West, Benjamin, Mar. 1730–Aug. 26, 1813.
Vol. 10, Pt. 2–5
West, Benjamin, Oct. 10, 1728–Mar. 11, 1820.
Vol. 10, Pt. 2–6
West, Francis, Oct. 28, 1586–1634.
Vol. 10, Pt. 2–9
West, George, Feb. 17, 1823–Sept. 20, 1901.
Vol. 10, Pt. 2–10
West, Henry Sergeant, Jan. 21, 1827–Apr. 1, 1876.
Vol. 10, Pt. 2–10
West, James Edward, May 16, 1876–May 15, 1948.
Supp. 4–871
West, Joseph, d. 1692?.
Vol. 10, Pt. 2–11
West, Mae, Aug. 17, 1893–Nov. 22, 1980.
Supp. 10–828
West, Oswald, May 20, 1873–Aug. 22, 1960.
Supp. 6–682
West, Roy Owen, Oct. 27, 1868–Nov. 29, 1958.
Supp. 6–683
West, Samuel, Mar. 3, 1730 O.S.–Sept. 24, 1807.
Vol. 10, Pt. 2–12
West, William Edward, Dec. 10, 1788–Nov. 2, 1857.
Vol. 10, Pt. 2–12
Westcott, Edward Noyes, Sept. 27, 1846–Mar. 31, 1898.
Vol. 10, Pt. 2–13
Westcott, Thompson, June 5, 1820–May 8, 1888.
Vol. 10, Pt. 2–14
Westergaard, Harald Malcolm, Oct. 9, 1888–June 22, 1950.
Supp. 4–873
Westermann, William Linn, Sept. 15, 1873–Oct. 4, 1954.
Supp. 5–735
Western, Lucille, Jan. 8, 1843–Jan. 11, 1877.
Vol. 10, Pt. 2–14
Westervelt, Jacob Aaron, Jan. 20, 1800–Feb. 21, 1879.
Vol. 10, Pt. 2–15
Westinghouse, George, Oct. 6, 1846–Mar. 12, 1914.
Vol. 10, Pt. 2–16
Westley, Helen, Mar. 28, 1875–Dec. 12, 1942.
Supp. 3–811
Weston, Edward, May 9, 1850–Aug. 20, 1936.
Supp. 2–702
Weston, Edward Henry, Mar. 24, 1886–Jan. 1, 1958.
Supp. 6–684
Weston, Edward Payson, Mar. 15, 1839–May 12, 1929.
Vol. 10, Pt. 2–18
Weston, Nathan Austin, Apr. 5, 1868–Nov. 29, 1933.
Vol. 10, Pt. 2–19
Weston, Thomas, *c.* 1575–*c.* 1644.
Vol. 10, Pt. 2–20
Weston, William, *c.* 1752–Aug. 29, 1833.
Vol. 10, Pt. 2–21
Wetherill, Charles Mayer, Nov. 4, 1825–Mar. 5, 1871.
Vol. 10, Pt. 2–22
Wetherill, Samuel, Apr. 12, 1736–Sept. 24, 1816.
Vol. 10, Pt. 2–23
Wetherill, Samuel, May 27, 1821–June 24, 1890.
Vol. 10, Pt. 2–23
Wetzel, Lewis, 1764–1808?.
Vol. 10, Pt. 2–24
Wexler, Irving ("Waxey Gordon"), 1888–June 24, 1952.
Supp. 5–736
Weyerhaeuser, Frederick Edward, Nov. 4, 1872–Oct. 18, 1945.
Supp. 3–812
Weyl, Hermann, Nov. 9, 1885–Dec. 1955.
Supp. 5–737
Weymouth, Frank Elwin, June 2, 1874–July 22, 1941.
Supp. 3–813
Whalen, Grover Aloysius, June 2, 1886–Apr. 20, 1962.
Supp. 7–779
Whalley, Edward, d. 1674 or 1675.
Vol. 10, Pt. 2–25
Wharton, Anne Hollingsworth, Dec. 15, 1845–July 29, 1928.
Vol. 10, Pt. 2–25
Wharton, Charles Henry, May 25, 1748 O.S.–July 23, 1833.
Vol. 10, Pt. 2–26
Wharton, Edith Newbold Jones, Jan. 24, 1862–Aug. 11, 1937.
Supp. 2–703
Wharton, Francis, Mar. 7, 1820–Feb. 21. 1889.
Vol. 10, Pt. 2–27
Wharton, Greene Lawrence, July 17, 1847–Nov. 4, 1906.
Vol. 10, Pt. 2–28
Wharton, Joseph, Mar. 3, 1826–Jan. 11, 1909.
Vol. 10, Pt. 2–29
Wharton, Richard, d. May 14, 1689.
Vol. 10, Pt. 2–30
Wharton, Robert, Jan. 12, 1757–Mar. 7, 1834.
Vol. 10, Pt. 2–31
Wharton, Samuel, May 3, 1732–1800.
Vol. 10, Pt. 2–32
Wharton, Thomas, 1735–May 22, 1778.
Vol. 10, Pt. 2–33
Wharton, Thomas Isaac, May 17, 1791–Apr. 7, 1856.
Vol. 10, Pt. 2–34
Wharton, William H., 1802–Mar. 14, 1839.
Vol. 10, Pt. 2–35
Whatcoat, Richard, Feb. 23, 1736–July 5, 1806.
Vol. 10, Pt. 2–36
Wheat, Zachariah Davis ("Buck"), May 23, 1888–Mar. 11, 1972.
Supp. 9–857
Wheatley, Phillis, *c.* 1753–Dec. 5, 1784.
Vol. 10, Pt. 2–36
Wheatley, William, Dec. 5, 1816–Nov. 3, 1876.
Vol. 10, Pt. 2–37
Wheaton, Frank, May 8, 1833–June 18, 1903.
Vol. 10, Pt. 2–38
Wheaton, Henry, Nov. 27, 1785–Mar. 11, 1848.
Vol. 10, Pt. 2–39
Wheaton, Nathaniel Sheldon, Aug. 20, 1792–Mar 18, 1862.
Vol. 10, Pt. 2–42
Whedon, Daniel Denison, Mar. 20, 1808–June 8, 1885.
Vol. 10, Pt. 2–43
Wheeler, Andrew Carpenter, June 4, 1835–Mar. 10, 1903.
Vol. 10, Pt. 2–44
Wheeler, Arthur Leslie, Aug. 12, 1872–May 22, 1932.
Supp. 1–700
Wheeler, Benjamin Ide, July 15, 1854–May 2, 1927.
Vol. 10, Pt. 2–44

Wheeler, Burton Kendall, Feb. 27, 1882–Jan. 6, 1975. Supp. 9–859
Wheeler, Daniel Denison, Mar. 20, 1808–June 8, 1885. Vol. 10, Pt. 2–43
Wheeler, Earle Gilmore, Jan. 13, 1908–Dec. 18, 1975. Supp. 9–860
Wheeler, Everett Pepperrell, Mar. 10, 1840–Feb. 8, 1925. Vol. 10, Pt. 2–46
Wheeler, George Montague, Oct. 9, 1842–May 3, 1905. Vol. 10, Pt. 2–47
Wheeler, (George) Post, Aug. 6, 1869–Dec. 23, 1956. Supp. 6–686
Wheeler, George Wakeman, Dec. 1, 1860–July 27, 1932. Vol. 10, Pt. 2–48
Wheeler, James Rignall, Feb. 15, 1859–Feb. 9, 1918. Vol. 10, Pt. 2–49
Wheeler, John Hill, Aug. 2, 1806–Dec. 7, 1882. Vol. 10, Pt. 2–50
Wheeler, John Martin, Nov. 10, 1879–Aug. 22, 1938. Supp. 2–706
Wheeler, Joseph, Sept. 10, 1836–Jan. 25, 1906. Vol. 10, Pt. 2–50
Wheeler, Nathaniel, Sept. 7, 1820–Dec. 31, 1893. Vol. 10, Pt. 2–52
Wheeler, Royall Tyler, 1810–April 1864. Vol. 10, Pt. 2–53
Wheeler, Schuyler Skaats, May 17, 1860–Apr. 20, 1923. Vol. 10, Pt. 2–53
Wheeler, Wayne Bidwell, Nov. 10, 1869–Sept. 5, 1927. Vol. 10, Pt. 2–54
Wheeler, William, Dec. 6, 1851–July 1, 1932. Vol. 10, Pt. 2–55
Wheeler, William Adolphus, Nov. 14, 1833–Oct. 28, 1874. Vol. 10, Pt. 2–56
Wheeler, Wiiliam Almon, June 30, 1819–June 4, 1887. Vol. 10, Pt. 2–57
Wheeler, William Morton, Mar. 19, 1865–Apr. 19, 1937. Supp. 2–707
Wheelock, Eleazar, Apr. 22, 1711–Apr. 24, 1779. Vol. 10, Pt. 2–58
Wheelock, John, Jan. 28, 1754–Apr. 4, 1817. Vol. 10, Pt. 2–59
Wheelock, John Hall, Sept. 9, 1886–Mar. 22, 1978. Supp. 10–830
Wheelock, Joseph Albert, Feb. 8, 1831–May 9, 1906. Vol. 10, Pt. 2–60
Wheelock, Lucy, Feb. 1, 1857–Oct. 2, 1946. Supp. 4–874
Wheelwright, Edmund March, Sept. 14, 1854–Aug. 14, 1912. Vol. 10, Pt. 2–61
Wheelwright, John, *c.* 1592–Nov. 15, 1679. Vol. 10, Pt. 2–62
Wheelwright, Mary Cabot, Oct. 2, 1878–July 19, 1958. Supp. 6–687
Wheelwright, William, Mar. 16, 1798–Sept. 26, 1873. Vol. 10, Pt. 2–63
Wheery, Elwood Morris, Mar. 26, 1843–Oct. 5, 1927. Vol. 10, Pt. 2–65
Whelpley, Henry Milton, May 24, 1861–June 26, 1926. Vol. 10, Pt. 2–64
Wherry, Kenneth Spicer, Feb. 28, 1892–Nov. 29, 1951. Supp. 5–738
Whetzel, Herbert Hice, Sept. 5, 1877–Nov. 30, 1944. Supp. 3–814
Whipple, Abraham, Sept. 26, 1733–May 27, 1819. Vol. 10, Pt. 2–66
Whipple, Amiel Weeks, 1816–May 7, 1863. Vol. 10, Pt. 2–66
Whipple, Edwin Percy, Mar. 8, 1819–June 16, 1886. Vol. 10, Pt. 2–67
Whipple, Frances Harriet. [*See* Green, Frances Harriet Whipple, 1805–1878.]
Whipple, Henry Benjamin, Feb. 15, 1822–Sept. 16, 1901. Vol. 10, Pt. 2–68
Whipple, Sherman Leland, Mar. 4, 1862–Oct. 20, 1930. Vol. 10, Pt. 2–69
Whipple, Squire, Sept. 16, 1804–Mar. 15, 1888. Vol. 10, Pt. 2–70
Whipple, William, Jan. 14, 1730–Nov. 10, 1785. Vol. 10, Pt. 2–71
Whistler, George Washington, May 19, 1800–Apr. 7, 1849. Vol. 10, Pt. 2–72
Whistler, James Abbott McNeill, July 10, 1834–July 17, 1903. Vol. 10, Pt. 2–73
Whitaker, Alexander, 1585–Mar. 1616/17. Vol. 10, Pt. 2–79
Whitaker, Charles Harris, May 19, 1872–Aug. 10, 1938. Supp. 2–708
Whitaker, Daniel Kimball, Apr. 13, 1801–Mar. 24, 1881. Vol. 10, Pt. 2–80
Whitaker, Nathaniel, Nov. 1730–Jan. 26, 1795. Vol. 10, Pt. 2–81
Whitcher, Frances Miriam Berry, Nov. 1, 1814–Jan. 4, 1852. Vol. 10, Pt. 2–82
Whitcomb, James, Dec. 1, 1795–Oct. 4, 1852. Vol. 10, Pt. 2–82
Whitcomb, Seldon Lincoln, July 19, 1866–Apr. 22, 1930. Vol. 10, Pt. 2–83
White, Albert Smith, Oct. 24, 1803–Sept. 4, 1864. Vol. 10. Pt. 2–84
White, Alexander, *c.* 1738–Oct. 9, 1804. Vol. 10, Pt. 2–85
White, Alexander, Mar. 30, 1814–Mar. 18, 1872. Vol. 10, Pt. 2–85
White, Alfred Tredway, May 28, 1846–Jan. 29, 1921. Vol. 10, Pt. 2–86
White, Alma Bridwell, June 16, 1862–June 26, 1946. Supp. 4–875
White, Andrew, 1579–Dec. 27, 1656. Vol. 10, Pt. 2–87
White, Andrew Dickson, Nov. 7, 1832–Nov. 4, 1918. Vol. 10, Pt. 2–88
White, Benjamin Franklin, Feb. 3, 1873–May 20, 1958. Supp. 6–688
White, Canvass, Sept. 8, 1790–Dec. 18, 1834. Vol. 10, Pt. 2–43
White, Charles Abiathar, Jan. 26, 1826–June 29, 1910. Vol. 10, Pt. 2–93
White, Charles Ignatius, Feb. 1, 1807–Apr. 1, 1878. Vol. 10, Pt. 2–94
White, Charles Wilbert, Apr. 2, 1918–Oct. 3, 1979. Supp. 10–832
White, Clarence Cameron, Aug. 10, 1880–June 30, 1960. Supp. 6–689
White, David, July 1, 1862–Feb. 7, 1935. Supp. 1–701
White, Edward Douglass, Mar. 1795–Apr. 18, 1847. Vol. 10, Pt. 2–95
White, Edward Douglass, Nov. 3, 1845–May 19, 1921. Vol. 10, Pt. 2–96
White, Edward Higgins, II, Nov. 14, 1930–Jan. 27, 1967. Supp. 8–693
White, Ellen Gould Harmon, Nov. 26, 1827–July 16, 1915. Vol. 10, Pt. 2–98
White, Emerson Elbridge, Jan. 10, 1829–Oct. 21, 1902. Vol. 10, Pt. 2–99
White, George, Mar. 12, 1802–Apr. 30, 1887. Vol. 10, Pt. 2–99
White, George, 1890–Oct. 11, 1968. Supp. 8–694
White, George Leonard, Sept. 20, 1838–Nov. 8. 1895. Vol. 10, Pt. 2–100
White, Henry, Mar. 28, 1732–Dec. 23, 1786. Vol. 10, Pt. 2–101
White, Henry, Mar. 29, 1850–July 15, 1927. Vol. 10, Pt. 2–102
White, Henry Clay, Dec. 30, 1848–Dec. 1, 1927. Vol. 10, Pt. 2–103
White, Horace, Aug. 10, 1834–Sept. 16, 1916. Vol. 10, Pt. 2–104
White, Hugh Lawson, Oct. 30, 1773–Apr. 10, 1840. Vol. 10, Pt. 2–105
White, Israel Charles, Nov. 1, 1848–Nov. 25, 1927. Vol. 10, Pt. 2–107
White, James, 1747–Aug. 14, 1821. Vol. 10, Pt. 2–108
White, James Clarke, July 7, 1833–Jan. 5, 1916. Vol. 10, Pt. 2–108
White, James William, Nov. 2, 1850–Apr. 24, 1916. Vol. 10, Pt. 2–109

White, John, fl. 1585–1593.
Vol. 10, Pt. 2–110
White, John Blake, Sept. 2, 1781–*c.* Aug. 2, 1859.
Vol. 10, Pt. 2–111
White, John De Haven, Aug. 19, 1815–Dec. 25, 1895.
Vol. 10, Pt. 2–112
White, John Williams, Mar. 5, 1849–May 9, 1417.
Vol. 10. Pt. 2–112
White, Joseph Malachy, Oct. 14, 1891–Feb. 28, 1959.
Supp. 6–691
White, Josh, Feb. 11, 1915–Sept. 5, 1969.
Supp. 8–695
White, Leonard Dupee, Jan. 17, 1891–Feb. 23, 1958.
Supp. 6–692
White, Minor Martin, July 9, 1908–June 24, 1976.
Supp. 10–833
White, Paul Dudley, June 6, 1886–Oct. 31, 1973.
Supp. 9–862
White, Pearl, Mar. 4, 1889–Aug. 4, 1938.
Supp. 2–710
White, Richard Grant, May 23, 1821–Apr. 8. 1885.
Vol. 10, Pt. 2–113
White, Samuel, Dec. 1770–Nov. 4, 1804.
Vol. 10, Pt. 2–114
White, Samuel Stockton, June 19, 1822–Dec. 30. 1879.
Vol. 10, Pt. 2–115
White, Stanford, Nov. 9, 1853–June 25, 1906.
Vol. 10, Pt. 2–116
White, Stephen Mallory, Jan. 19, 1853–Feb. 21, 1901.
Vol. 10, Pt. 2–118
White, Stephen Van Culen, Aug. 1, 1831–Jan. 18, 1913.
Vol. 10, Pt. 2–119
White, Stewart Edward, Mar. 12, 1873–Sept. 18, 1946.
Supp. 4–877
White, Thomas Willis, Mar. 28, 1788–Jan. 19, 1843.
Vol. 10, Pt. 2–120
White, Walter Francis, July 1, 1893–Mar. 21, 1955.
Supp. 5–740
White, William, Apr. 4, 1748 N.S.–July 17, 1836.
Vol. 10, Pt. 2–121
White, William Alanson, Jan. 24, 1870–Mar. 7, 1937.
Supp. 2–711
White, William Allen, Feb. 10, 1868–Jan. 29, 1944.
Supp. 3–815
White, William Nathaniel, Nov. 28, 1819–July 14, 1867.
Vol. 10, Pt. 2–122
White Eyes, d. 1778.
Vol. 10, Pt. 2–123
Whitefield, George, Dec. 16, 1714 O.S.–Sept. 30, 1770.
Vol. 10, Pt. 2–124
Whitehead, Alfred North, Feb. 15, 1861–Dec. 30, 1947.
Supp. 4–878
Whitehead, Walter Edward, May 20, 1908–Apr. 16, 1978.
Supp. 10–835
Whitehead, Wilbur Cherrier, May 22, 1866–June 27, 1931.
Vol. 10, Pt. 2–129
Whitehead, William Adee, Feb. 19, 1810–Aug. 8, 1884.
Vol. 10, Pt. 2–130
Whitehill, Clarence Eugene, Nov. 5, 1871–Dec. 18, 1932.
Vol. 10, Pt. 2–131
Whitehill, Robert, July 21, 1738–Apr. 7, 1813.
Vol. 10, Pt. 2–131
Whitehouse, Frederic Cope, Nov. 9, 1842–Nov. 16, 1911.
Vol. 10, Pt. 2–132
Whiteman, Paul Samuel ("Pops"), Mar. 28, 1890–Dec. 29, 1967.
Supp. 8–697
Whiteside, Arthur Dare, Sept. 15, 1882–June 17, 1960.
Supp. 6–693
Whitfield, Henry, 1597–*c.* 1657.
Vol. 10, Pt. 2–133
Whitfield, Owen, Oct. 9, 1892–Aug. 11, 1965.
Supp. 7–781
Whitfield, Robert Parr, May 27, 1828–Apr. 6, 1910.
Vol. 10, Pt. 2–134
Whiting, Arthur Battelle, June 20, 1861–July 20, 1936.
Supp. 2–712
Whiting, Charles Goodrich, Jan. 30, 1842–June 20, 1922.
Vol. 10, Pt. 2–135
Whiting, George Elbridge, Sept. 14, 1840–Oct. 14, 1923.
Vol. 10, Pt. 2–136
Whiting, William, Mar. 3, 1813–June 29, 1873.
Supp. 1–703
Whiting, William Henry Chase, Mar. 22, 1824–Mar. 10, 1865.
Vol. 10, Pt. 2–136
Whitlock, Brand, Mar. 4, 1869–May 24, 1934.
Vol. 10, Pt. 2–137
Whitman, Albery Allson, May 30, 1851–June 29, 1901.
Vol. 10, Pt. 2–138
Whitman, Charles Otis, Dec. 14, 1842–Dec. 6, 1910.
Vol. 10, Pt. 2–139
Whitman, Charles Seymour, Aug. 28, 1868–Mar. 29, 1947.
Supp. 4–884
Whitman, Ezekiel, Mar. 9, 1776–Aug. 1, 1866.
Vol. 10, Pt. 2–140
Whitman, Marcus, Sept. 4, 1802–Nov. 29, 1847.
Vol. 10, Pt. 2–141
Whitman, Royal, Oct. 24, 1857–Aug. 19, 1946.
Supp. 4–886
Whitman, Sarah Helen Power, Jan. 19, 1803–June 27, 1878.
Vol. 10, Pt. 2–143
Whitman, Walt, May 31, 1819–Mar. 26, 1892.
Vol. 10, Pt. 2–143
Whitmer, David, Jan. 7, 1805–Jan. 25, 1888.
Vol. 10, Pt. 2–152
Whitmore, Frank Clifford, Oct. 1, 1887–June 24, 1947.
Supp. 4–888
Whitmore, William Henry, Sept. 6, 1836–June 14, 1900.
Vol. 10, Pt. 2–153
Whitney, Adeline Dutton Train, Sept. 15, 1824–Mar. 20, 1906.
Vol. 10, Pt. 2–154
Whitney, Alexander Fell, Apr. 12, 1873–July 16, 1949.
Supp. 4–889
Whitney, Anne, Sept. 2, 1821–Jan. 23, 1915.
Vol. 10, Pt. 2–155
Whitney, Asa, Dec. 1, 1791–June 4, 1874.
Vol. 10, Pt. 2–155
Whitney, Asa, Mar. 14, 1797–Sept. 17, 1872.
Vol. 10, Pt. 2–156
Whitney, Caspar, Sept. 2, 1861–Jan. 18, 1929.
Supp. 1–704
Whitney, Charlotte Anita, July 7, 1867–Feb. 4, 1955.
Supp. 5–742
Whitney, Courtney, May 20, 1897–Mar. 21, 1969.
Supp. 8–698
Whitney, Eli, Dec. 8, 1765–Jan. 8, 1825.
Vol. 10, Pt. 2–157
Whitney, George, Oct. 9, 1885–July 22, 1963.
Supp. 7–782
Whitney, Gertrude Vanderbilt, Jan. 9, 1875–Apr. 18, 1942.
Supp. 3–818
Whitney, Harry Payne, Apr. 29, 1872–Oct. 26, 1930.
Vol. 10, Pt. 2–160
Whitney, James Lyman, Nov. 28, 1835–Sept. 25, 1910.
Vol. 10, Pt. 2–161
Whitney, Josiah Dwight, Nov. 23, 1819–Aug. 19, 1896.
Vol. 10, Pt. 2–161
Whitney, Mary Watson, Sept. 11, 1847–Jan. 21, 1920.
Vol. 10, Pt. 2–163
Whitney, Myron William, Sept. 6, 1836–Sept. 18, 1910.
Vol. 10, Pt. 2–164
Whitney, Richard, Aug. 1, 1888–Dec. 5, 1874.
Supp. 9–863
Whitney, William Collins, July 5, 1841–Feb. 2, 1904.
Vol. 10, Pt. 2–165
Whitney, William Dwight, Feb. 9, 1827–June 7, 1894.
Vol. 10, Pt. 2–166
Whitney, Willis Rodney, Aug. 22, 1868–Jan. 9, 1958.
Supp. 6–694
Whiton, James Morris, Apr. 11, 1833–Jan. 25, 1920.
Vol. 10, Pt. 2–169
Whitsitt, William Heth, Nov. 25, 1841–Jan. 20, 1911.
Vol. 10, Pt. 2–170
Whittaker, Charles Evans, Feb. 22, 1901–Nov. 26, 1973.
Supp. 9–865
Whittelsey, Abigail Goodrich, Nov. 29, 1788–July 16, 1858.
Vol. 10, Pt. 2–170
Whittemore, Amos, Apr. 19, 1759–Mar. 27, 1828.
Vol. 10, Pt. 2–171
Whittemore, Thomas, Jan. 1, 1800–Mar. 21, 1861.
Vol. 10, Pt. 2–172

Whittemore, Thomas, Jan. 2, 1871–June 8, 1950.
Supp. 4–890
Whittier, John Greenleaf, Dec. 17, 1807–Sept. 7, 1892.
Vol. 10, Pt. 2–173
Whittingham, William Rollinson, Dec. 2, 1805–Oct. 17, 1879.
Vol. 10, Pt. 2–176
Whittredge, Worthington, May 22, 1820–Feb. 25, 1910.
Vol. 10. Pt. 2–177
Whitworth, George Frederic, Mar. 15, 1816–Oct. 6, 1907.
Vol. 10, Pt. 2–177
Whorf, Benjamin Lee, Apr. 24, 1897–July 26, 1941.
Supp. 3–819
Whyte, William Pinkney, Aug. 9, 1824–Mar. 17, 1908.
Vol. 10, Pt. 2–178
Wickard, Claude Raymond, Feb. 28, 1893–Apr. 29, 1967.
Supp. 8–699
Wickersham, George Woodward, Sept. 19, 1858–Jan. 25, 1936.
Supp. 2–713
Wickersham, James Pyle, Mar. 5, 1825–Mar. 25, 1891.
Vol. 10, Pt. 2–179
Wickes, Lambert, 1735?–Oct. 1, 1777.
Vol. 10, Pt. 2–180
Wickes, Stephen, Mar. 17, 1813–July 8, 1889.
Vol. 10, Pt. 2–181
Wickham, John, June 6, 1763–Jan. 22, 1839.
Vol. 10, Pt. 2–181
Wickliffe, Charles Anderson, June 8, 1788–Oct. 31, 1869.
Vol. 10, Pt. 2–182
Wickliffe, Robert Charles, Jan. 6, 1819–Apr. 18, 1895.
Vol. 10, Pt. 2–183
Wickson, Edward James, Aug. 3, 1848–July 16, 1923.
Vol. 10, Pt. 2–184
Widener, George Dunton, Mar. 11, 1889–Dec. 8, 1971.
Supp. 9–866
Widener, Harry Elkins, Jan. 3, 1885–Apr. 15, 1912.
Vol. 10, Pt. 2–184
Widener, Peter Arrell Brown, Nov. 13, 1834–Nov. 6, 1915.
Vol. 10, Pt. 2–185
Widforss, Gunnar Mauritz, Oct. 21, 1879–Nov. 30, 1934.
Vol. 10, Pt. 2–186
Widney, Joseph Pomeroy, Dec. 26, 1841–July 4, 1938.
Supp. 2–715
Wiechmann, Ferdinand Gerhard, Nov. 12, 1858–Apr. 24, 1919.
Vol. 10, Pt. 2–187
Wieland, George Reber, Jan. 24, 1865–Jan. 18, 1953.
Supp. 5–742
Wiener, Alexander Solomon, Mar. 16, 1907–Nov. 6, 1976.
Supp. 10–836
Wiener, Leo, July 26, 1862–Dec. 12, 1939.
Supp. 2–716
Wiener, Norbert, Nov. 26, 1894–Mar. 18, 1964.
Supp. 7–783
Wigfall, Louis Trezevant, Apr. 21, 1816–Feb. 18, 1874.
Vol. 10, Pt. 2–187
Wigger, Winand Michael, Dec. 9, 1841–Jan. 5, 1901.
Vol. 10, Pt. 2–189
Wiggin, Albert Henry, Feb. 21, 1868–May 21, 1951.
Supp. 5–744
Wiggin, James Henry, May 14, 1836–Nov. 3, 1900.
Vol. 10, Pt. 2–189
Wiggin, Kate Douglas, Sept. 28, 1856–Aug. 24, 1923.
Vol. 10, Pt. 2–190
Wiggins, Carleton, Mar. 4, 1848–June 11, 1932.
Vol. 10, Pt. 2–191
Wigglesworth, Edward, *c.* 1693–Jan. 16, 1765.
Vol. 10, Pt. 2–191
Wigglesworth, Edward, Feb. 7, 1732–June 17, 1794.
Vol. 10, Pt. 2–192
Wigglesworth, Edward, Dec. 30, 1840–Jan. 23, 1896.
Vol. 10, Pt. 2–193
Wigglesworth, Michael, Oct. 18, 1631–May 27, 1705.
Vol. 10, Pt. 2–194
Wight, Frederick Coit, Apr. 30, 1859–Dec. 23, 1933.
Vol. 10, Pt. 2–195
Wight, Peter Bonnett, Aug. 1, 1838–Sept. 8, 1925.
Vol. 10, Pt. 2–195
Wightman, Hazel Virginia Hotchkiss, Dec. 20, 1886–Dec. 5, 1974.
Supp. 9–867
Wigmore, John Henry, Mar. 4, 1863–Apr. 20, 1943.
Supp. 3–820
Wignell, Thomas, *c.* 1753–Feb. 21, 1803.
Vol. 10, Pt. 2–196
Wikoff, Henry, *c.* 1813–May 2, 1884.
Vol. 10, Pt. 2–197
Wilbur, Cressy Livingston, Mar. 16, 1865–Aug. 9, 1928.
Vol. 10, Pt. 2–198
Wilbur, Curtis Dwight, May 10, 1867–Sept. 8, 1954.
Supp. 5–746
Wilbur, Hervey Backus, Aug. 18, 1820–May 1, 1883.
Vol. 10, Pt. 2–199
Wilbur, John, June 17, 1774–May 1, 1856.
Vol. 10, Pt. 2–200
Wilbur, Ray Lyman, Apr. 13, 1875–June 26, 1949.
Supp. 4–891
Wilbur, Samuel, *c.* 1585–July 29, 1656.
Vol. 10, Pt. 2–200
Wilcox, Cadmus Marcellus, May 29, 1824–Dec. 2, 1890.
Vol. 10, Pt. 2–201
Wilcox, Delos Franklin, Apr. 22, 1873–Apr. 4, 1928.
Vol. 10, Pt. 2–202
Wilcox, Ella Wheeler, Nov. 5, 1850–Oct. 30, 1919.
Vol. 10, Pt. 2–203
Wilcox, Reynold Webb, Mar. 29, 1856–June 6, 1931.
Vol. 10, Pt. 2–204
Wilcox, Stephen, Feb. 12, 1830–Nov. 27, 1893.
Vol. 10, Pt. 2–204
Wilczynski, Ernest Julius, Nov. 13, 1876–Sept. 14, 1932.
Vol. 10, Pt. 2–205
Wilde, George Francis Faxon, Feb. 23, 1845–Dec. 3, 1911.
Vol. 10, Pt. 2–206
Wilde, Richard Henry, Sept. 24, 1789–Sept. 10, 1847.
Vol. 10, Pt. 2–206
Wilder, Alexander, May 14, 1823–Sept. 18, 1908.
Vol. 10, Pt. 2–207
Wilder, Alexander Lafayette Chew ("Alec"), Feb. 16, 1907–Dec. 24, 1980.
Supp. 10–838
Wilder, Harris Hawthorne, Apr. 7, 1864–Feb. 27, 1928.
Vol. 10, Pt. 2–208
Wilder, John Thomas, Jan. 31, 1830–Oct. 20, 1917.
Vol. 10, Pt. 2–209
Wilder, Laura Ingalls, Feb. 7, 1867–Feb. 10, 1957.
Supp. 6–696
Wilder, Marshall Pinckney, Sept. 22, 1798–Dec. 16, 1886.
Vol. 10, Pt. 2–210
Wilder, Russell Morse, Nov. 24, 1885–Dec. 16, 1959.
Supp. 6–697
Wilder, Thornton Niven, Apr. 17, 1897–Dec. 7, 1975.
Supp. 9–869
Wildman, Murray Shipley, Feb. 22, 1868–Dec. 24, 1930.
Vol. 10, Pt. 2–211
Wildt, Rupert, June 25, 1905–Jan. 9, 1976.
Supp. 10–839
Wildwood, Will. [*See* Pond, Frederick Eugene, 1856–1925.]
Wiley, Alexander, May 26, 1884–Oct. 26, 1967.
Supp. 8–700
Wiley, Andrew Jackson, July 15, 1862–Oct. 8, 1931.
Vol. 10, Pt. 2–212
Wiley, Bell Irvin, Jan. 5, 1906–Apr. 4, 1980.
Supp. 10–841
Wiley, Calvin Henderson, Feb. 3, 1819–Jan. 11, 1887.
Vol. 10, Pt. 2–213
Wiley, David, d. *c.* 1813.
Vol. 10, Pt. 2–213
Wiley, Ephraim Emerson, Oct. 6, 1814–Mar. 13, 1893.
Vol. 10, Pt. 2–214
Wiley, Harvey Washington, Oct. 18, 1844–June 30, 1930.
Vol. 10, Pt. 2–215
Wilhelmina, May 11, 1939–Mar. 1, 1980.
Supp. 10–842
Wilkes, Charles, Apr. 3, 1798–Feb. 8, 1877.
Vol. 10, Pt. 2–216
Wilkes, George, 1817–Sept. 23, 1885.
Vol. 10, Pt. 2–218
Wilkeson, Samuel, June 1, 1781–July 7, 1848.
Vol. 10, Pt. 2–218
Wilkie, Franc Bangs, July 2, 1832–Apr. 12, 1892.
Vol. 10, Pt. 2–219

Wilkins, Ross, Feb. 19, 1799–May 17, 1872.
Vol. 10, Pt. 2–220
Wilkins, William, Dec. 20, 1779–June 23, 1865.
Vol. 10, Pt. 2–221
Wilkinson, David, Jan. 5, 1771–Feb. 3, 1852.
Vol. 10, Pt. 2–222
Wilkinson, James, 1757–Dec. 28, 1825.
Vol. 10, Pt. 2–222
Wilkinson, Jemima, Nov. 29, 1752–July 1, 1819.
Vol. 10, Pt. 2–226
Wilkinson, Jeremiah, July 6, 1741–Jan. 29, 1831.
Vol. 10, Pt. 2–227
Wilkinson, John, Nov. 6, 1821–Dec. 29, 1891.
Vol. 10, Pt. 2–228
Wilkinson, Robert Shaw, Feb. 18, 1865–Mar. 13, 1932.
Vol. 10, Pt. 2–229
Wilkinson, Theodore Stark, Dec. 22, 1888–Feb. 21, 1946.
Supp. 4–895
Will, Allan Sinclair, July 28, 1868–Mar. 10, 1934.
Vol. 10, Pt. 2–230
Willard, Daniel, Jan. 28, 1861–July 6, 1942.
Supp. 3–823
Willard, De Forest, Mar. 23, 1846–Oct. 14, 1910.
Vol. 10, Pt. 2–230
Willard, Emma Hart, Feb. 23, 1787–Apr. 15, 1870.
Vol. 10, Pt. 2–231
Willard, Frances Elizabeth Caroline, Sept. 28, 1839–Feb. 18, 1898.
Vol. 10, Pt. 2–233
Willard, Frank Henry, Sept. 21, 1893–Jan. 11, 1958.
Supp. 6–698
Willard, James Field, Dec. 30, 1876–Nov. 21, 1935.
Supp. 1–705
Willard, Joseph, Dec. 29, 1738–Sept. 25, 1804.
Vol. 10, Pt. 2–234
Willard, Joseph, Mar. 14, 1798–May 12, 1865.
Vol. 10, Pt. 2–235
Willard, Joseph Edward, May 1, 1865–Apr. 4, 1924.
Vol. 10, Pt. 2–236
Willard, Josiah Flint, Jan. 23, 1869–Jan. 20, 1907.
Supp. 1–706
Willard, Mary Hatch, Dec. 15, 1856–Mar. 29, 1926.
Vol. 10, Pt. 2–236
Willard, Samuel, Jan. 31, 1639/40–Sept. 12, 1707.
Vol. 10, Pt. 2–237
Willard, Samuel, Apr. 18, 1775–Oct. 8, 1859.
Vol. 10, Pt. 2–238
Willard, Sidney, Sept. 19, 1780–Dec. 6, 1856.
Vol. 10, Pt. 2–239
Willard, Simon, 1605–Apr. 24, 1676 O.S..
Vol. 10, Pt. 2–240
Willard, Simon, Apr. 3, 1753–Aug. 30, 1848.
Vol. 10, Pt. 2–240
Willard, Solomon, June 26, 1783–Feb. 27, 1861.
Vol. 10, Pt. 2–241
Willcox, Louise Collier, Apr. 24, 1865–Sept. 13, 1929.
Vol. 10, Pt. 2–242
Willcox, Orlando Bolivar, Apr. 16, 1823–May 10, 1907.
Vol. 10, Pt. 2–243
Willebrandt, Mabel Walker, May 23, 1889–Apr. 6, 1963.
Supp. 7–785
Willet, William, Nov. 1, 1867–Mar. 29, 1921.
Vol. 10, Pt. 2–243
Willett, Herbert Lockwood, May 5, 1864–Mar. 28, 1944.
Supp. 3–824
Willett, Marinus, July 31, 1740–Aug. 22, 1830.
Vol. 10, Pt. 2–244
Willey, Samuel Hopkins, Mar. 11, 1821–Jan. 21, 1914.
Vol. 10, Pt. 2–245
Willey, Waitman Thomas, Oct. 18, 1811–May 2, 1900.
Vol. 10, Pt. 2–246
Williams, Alpheus Starkey, Sept. 20, 1810–Dec. 21, 1878.
Vol. 10, Pt. 2–247
Williams, Aubrey Willis, Aug. 23, 1890–Mar. 3, 1965.
Supp. 7–786
Williams, Barney, July 20, 1823–Apr. 25, 1876.
Vol. 10, Pt. 2–248
Williams, Ben Ames, Mar. 7, 1889–Feb. 4, 1953.
Supp. 5–747
Williams, Bert, *c.* 1876–Mar. 4, 1922.
Vol. 10, Pt. 2–249
Williams, Catharine Read Arnold, Dec. 31, 1787–Oct. 11, 1872.
Vol. 10, Pt. 2–249
Williams, Channing Moore, July 18, 1829–Dec. 2, 1910.
Vol. 10, Pt. 2–250
Williams, Charles David, July 30, 1860–Feb. 14, 1923.
Vol. 10, Pt. 2–251
Williams, Charles Richard, Apr. 16, 1853–May 6, 1927.
Vol. 10, Pt. 2–252
Williams, Daniel Hale, Jan. 18, 1858–Aug. 4 1931.
Vol. 10, Pt. 2–252
Williams, David Rogerson, Mar. 8, 1776–Nov. 17. 1830.
Vol. 10, Pt. 2–253
Williams, Edward Thomas, Oct. 17, 1854–Jan. 27, 1944.
Supp. 3–825
Williams, Edwin, Sept. 25, 1797–Oct. 21, 1854.
Vol. 10, Pt. 2–254
Williams, Eleazar, *c.* 1789–Aug. 28, 1858.
Vol. 10, Pt. 2–255
Williams, Elisha, Aug. 24, 1694–July 24, 1755.
Vol. 10, Pt. 2–256
Williams, Elisha, Aug. 29, 1773–June 29, 1833.
Vol. 10, Pt. 2–257
Williams, Elkanah, Dec. 19, 1822–Oct. 5, 1888.
Vol. 10, Pt. 2–258
Williams, Ephraim, Mar. 7, 1714 N.S.–Sept. 8, 1755.
Vol. 10, Pt. 2–259
Williams, Fannie Barrier, Feb. 12, 1855–Mar. 4, 1944.
Supp. 3–827
Williams, Francis Henry, Apr. 15, 1852–June 22, 1936.
Supp. 2–717
Williams, Frank Martin, Apr. 11, 1873–Feb. 20, 1930.
Vol. 10, Pt. 2–260
Williams, Frederick Wells, Oct. 31, 1857–Jan. 22, 1928.
Vol. 10, Pt. 2–260
Williams, Gaar Campbell, Dec. 12, 1880–June 15, 1935.
Supp. 1–707
Williams, Gardner Fred, Mar. 14, 1842–Aug. 22, 1922.
Vol. 10, Pt. 2–261
Williams, George Huntington, Jan. 28, 1856–July 12, 1894.
Vol. 10, Pt. 2–263
Williams, George Henry, Mar. 26, 1820–Apr. 4, 1910.
Vol. 10, Pt. 2–262
Williams, George Washington, Oct. 16, 1849–Aug. 4, 1891.
Vol. 10, Pt. 2–263
Williams, Harrison Charles, Mar. 16, 1873–Nov. 10, 1953.
Supp. 5–749
Williams, Henry Shaler, Mar. 6, 1847–July 31, 1918.
Vol. 10, Pt. 2–264
Williams, Henry Willard, Dec. 11, 1821–June 13, 1895.
Vol. 10, Pt. 2–265
Williams, (Hiram) Hank, Sept. 17, 1923–Jan. 1, 1953.
Supp. 5–748
Williams, Israel, Nov. 30, 1709–Jan. 10, 1788.
Vol. 10, Pt. 2–266
Williams, James, July 1, 1796–Apr. 10, 1869.
Vol. 10, Pt. 2–267
Williams, James Douglas, Jan. 16, 1808–Nov. 20, 1880.
Vol. 10, Pt. 2–267
Williams, Jesse Lynch, May 6, 1807–Oct. 9, 1886.
Vol. 10, Pt. 2–268
Williams, Jesse Lynch, Aug. 17, 1871–Sept. 14, 1929.
Vol. 10, Pt. 2–269
Williams, John, Dec. 10, 1664–June 12, 1729.
Vol. 10, Pt. 2–270
Williams, John, Apr. 28, 1761–Oct. 12, 1818.
Vol. 10, Pt. 2–270
Williams, John, Jan. 29, 1778–Aug. 10, 1837.
Vol. 10, Pt. 2–271
Williams, John, Aug. 30, 1817–Feb. 7, 1899.
Vol. 10, Pt. 2–272
Williams, John Elias, June 11, 1871–Mar. 24, 1927.
Vol. 10, Pt. 2–274
Williams, John Elias, Oct. 28, 1853–Jan. 2, 1919.
Vol. 10, Pt. 2–273
Williams, John Fletcher, Sept. 25, 1834–Apr. 28, 1895.
Vol. 10, Pt. 2–275
Williams, John Foster, Oct. 12, 1743–June 24, 1814.
Vol. 10, Pt. 2–276
Williams, John Joseph, Apr. 27, 1822–Aug. 30, 1907.
Vol. 10, Pt. 2–276

Williams, John Sharp, July 30, 1854–Sept. 27, 1932.
Vol. 10, Pt. 2–277
Williams, John Skelton, July 6, 1865–Nov. 4, 1926.
Vol. 10, Pt. 2–279
Williams, John Whitridge, Jan. 26, 1866–Oct. 21, 1931.
Vol. 10, Pt. 2–280
Williams, Jonathan, May 26, 1750–May 16, 1815.
Vol. 10, Pt. 2–280
Williams, Linsly Rudd, Jan. 28, 1875–Jan. 8, 1934.
Vol. 10, Pt. 2–282
Williams, Marshall Jay, Feb. 22, 1837–July 7, 1902.
Vol. 10, Pt. 2–283
Williams, Nathaniel, Aug. 25, 1675–Jan. 10, 1737/38.
Vol. 10, Pt. 2–283
Williams, Otho Holland, March 1749–July 15, 1794.
Vol. 10, Pt. 2–284
Williams, Reuel, June 2, 1783–July 25, 1862.
Vol. 10, Pt. 2–285
Williams, Robert, *c.* 1745–Sept. 26, 1775.
Vol. 10, Pt. 2–286
Williams, Roger, *c.* 1603–1682/83.
Vol. 10, Pt. 2–286
Williams, Samuel May, Oct. 4, 1795–Sept. 13, 1858.
Vol. 10, Pt. 2–299
Williams, Samuel Wells, Sept. 22, 1812–Feb. 16, 1884.
Vol. 10, Pt. 2–290
Williams, Stephen West, Mar. 27, 1790–July 6, 1855.
Vol. 10, Pt. 2–291
Williams, Talcott, Juiv 20, 1849–Jan. 24, 1928.
Vol. 10, Pt. 2–291
Williams, Thomas Harry, May 19, 1909–July 6, 1979.
Supp. 10–843
Williams, Thomas Scott, June 26, 1777–Dec. 15, 1861.
Vol. 10, Pt. 2–292
Williams, Walter, July 2, 1864–July 29, 1935.
Supp. 1–708
Williams, William, Apr. 8, 1731–Aug. 2, 1811.
Vol. 10, Pt. 2–293
Williams, William, Oct. 12, 1787–June 10, 1850.
Vol. 10, Pt. 2–294
Williams, William Carlos, Sept. 17, 1883–Mar. 4, 1963.
Supp. 7–788
Williams, William R., Oct. 14, 1804–Apr. 1, 1885.
Vol. 10, Pt. 2–295
Williams, William Sherley, d. Mar. 1849.
Vol. 10, Pt. 2–296
Williamson, Andrew, *c.* 1730–Mar. 21, 1786.
Vol. 10, Pt. 2–296
Williamson, Charles, July 12, 1757–Sept. 4, 1808.
Vol. 10, Pt. 2–297
Williamson, Hugh, Dec. 5, 1735–May 22, 1819.
Vol. 10, Pt. 2–298
Williamson, Isaac Halsted, Sept. 27 1767–July 10, 1844.
Vol. 10, Pt. 2–300
Williamson, William Durkee, July 31, 1779–May 27, 1846.
Vol. 10, Pt. 2–301
Willie, Asa Hoxie, Oct. 11, 1829–Mar. 16, 1899.
Vol. 10, Pt. 2–302
Willing, Thomas, Dec. 19, 1731 o.s.–Jan. 19, 1821.
Vol. 10, Pt. 2–302
Willingham, Robert Josiah, May 15, 1854–Dec. 20, 1914.
Vol. 10, Pt. 2–304
Willis, Albert Shelby, Jan. 22, 1843–Jan. 6, 1897.
Vol. 10, Pt. 2–304
Willis, Bailey, May 31, 1857–Feb. 19, 1949.
Supp. 4–896
Willis, Henry Parker, Aug. 14, 1874–July 18, 1937.
Supp. 2–718
Willis, Nathaniel, June 6, 1780–May 26, 1870.
Vol. 10, Pt. 2–305
Willis, Nathaniel Parker, Jan. 20, 1806–Jan. 20, 1867.
Vol. 10, Pt. 2–306
Willis, Olympia Brown. [*See* Brown, Olympia, 1835–1926.]
Willis, William, Aug. 31, 1794–Feb. 17, 1870.
Vol. 10, Pt. 2–309
Williston, Samuel, June 17, 1795–July 18, 1874.
Vol. 10, Pt. 2–309
Williston, Samuel, Sept. 24, 1861–Feb. 18, 1963.
Supp. 7–791
Williston, Samuel Wendell, July 10, 1852–Aug. 30, 1918.
Vol. 10, Pt. 2–310
Williston, Seth, Apr. 4, 1770–Mar. 2, 1851.
Vol. 10, Pt. 2–311
Willkie, Wendell Lewis, Feb. 18, 1892–Oct. 8, 1944.
Supp. 3–828
Willoughby, Westel Woodbury, July 20, 1867–Mar. 26, 1945.
Supp. 3–830
Wills, Childe Harold, June 1, 1878–Dec. 30, 1940.
Supp. 2–720
Wills, Chill, July 18, 1902–Dec. 15, 1978.
Supp. 10–844
Wills, Harry, May 15, 1889?–Dec. 21, 1958.
Supp. 6–699
Wills, James Robert ("Bob"), Mar. 6, 1905–May 13, 1975.
Supp. 9–872
Willson, Augustus Everett, Oct. 13, 1846–Aug. 24, 1931.
Vol. 10, Pt. 2–312
Willys, John North, Oct. 25, 1873–Aug. 26, 1935.
Supp. 1–709
Wilmarth, Lemuel Everett, Mar. 11, 1835–July 27, 1918.
Vol. 10, Pt. 2–312
Wilmer, James Jones, Jan. 15, 1749/50–Apr. 14, 1814.
Vol. 10, Pt. 2–313
Wilmer, Joseph Père Bell, Feb. 11, 1812–Dec. 2, 1878.
Vol. 10, Pt. 2–314
Wilmer, Richard Hooker, Mar. 15, 1816–June 14, 1900.
Vol. 10, Pt. 2–315
Wilmer, William Holland, Oct. 29, 1782–July 24, 1827.
Vol. 10, Pt. 2–315
Wilmer, William Holland, Aug. 26, 1863–Mar. 12, 1936.
Supp. 2–721
Wilmot, David, Jan. 20, 1814–Mar. 16, 1868.
Vol. 10, Pt. 2–317
Wilson, Alexander, July 6, 1766–Aug. 23, 1813.
Vol. 10, Pt. 2–317
Wilson, Allen Benjamin, Oct. 18, 1824–Apr. 29, 1888.
Vol. 10, Pt. 2–319
Wilson, Augusta Jane Evans. [*See* Evans, Augusta Jane, 1835–1909.]
Wilson, Bird, Jan. 8, 1777–Apr. 14, 1859.
Vol. 10, Pt. 2–320
Wilson, Charles Edward, Nov. 18, 1886–Jan. 3, 1972.
Supp. 9–873
Wilson, Charles Erwin, July 18, 1890–Sept. 26, 1961.
Supp. 7–793
Wilson, Clarence True, Apr. 24, 1872–Feb. 16, 1939.
Supp. 2–722
Wilson, Edith Bolling, Oct. 15, 1872–Dec. 28, 1961.
Supp. 7–795
Wilson, Edmund, Jr., May 8, 1895–June 12, 1972.
Supp. 9–874
Wilson, Edmund Beecher, Oct. 19, 1856–Mar. 3, 1939.
Supp. 2–724
Wilson, Ernest Henry, Feb. 15, 1876–Oct. 15, 1930.
Vol. 10, Pt. 2–321
Wilson, Francis, Feb. 7, 1854–Oct. 7, 1935.
Supp. 1–710
Wilson, George Francis, Dec. 7, 1818–Jan. 19, 1883.
Vol. 10, Pt. 2–322
Wilson, George Grafton, Mar. 29, 1863–Apr. 30, 1951.
Supp. 5–751
Wilson, Halsey William, May 12, 1868–Mar. 1, 1954.
Supp. 5–752
Wilson, Harry Leon, May 1, 1867–June 28, 1939.
Supp. 2–725
Wilson, Henry, Feb. 16, 1812–Nov. 22, 1875.
Vol. 10, Pt. 2–322
Wilson, Henry Lane, Nov. 3, 1857–Dec. 22, 1932.
Vol. 10, Pt. 2–325
Wilson, Henry Parke Custis, Mar. 5, 1827–Dec. 27, 1897.
Vol. 10, Pt. 2–326
Wilson, Hugh Robert, Jan. 29, 1885–Dec. 29, 1946.
Supp. 4–897
Wilson, James, Sept. 14, 1742–Aug. 21, 1798.
Vol. 10, Pt. 2–326
Wilson, James, Aug. 16, 1836–Aug. 26, 1920.
Vol. 10, Pt. 2–330
Wilson, James Falconer, Oct. 19, 1828–Apr. 22 1895.
Vol. 10, Pt. 2–331
Wilson, J(ames) Finley, Aug. 28, 1881–Feb. 19, 1952.
Supp. 5–754

Wilson, James Grant, Apr. 28, 1832–Feb. 1, 1914.
Vol. 10, Pt. 2–333
Wilson, James Harrison, Sept. 2, 1837–Feb. 23, 1925.
Vol. 10, Pt. 2–334
Wilson, James Southall, Nov. 12, 1880–June 26, 1963.
Supp. 7–796
Wilson, John, *c.* 1591–Aug. 7, 1667.
Vol. 10, Pt. 2–336
Wilson, John Fleming, Feb. 22, 1877–Mar. 5, 1922.
Vol. 10, Pt. 2–337
Wilson, John Leighton, Mar. 25, 1809–July 13, 1886.
Vol. 10, Pt. 2–337
Wilson, John Lockwood, Aug. 7, 1850–Nov. 6, 1912.
Vol. 10, Pt. 2–338
Wilson, Joseph Chamberlain, Dec. 13, 1909–Nov. 22, 1971.
Supp. 9–877
Wilson, Joseph Miller, June 20, 1838–Nov. 24, 1902.
Vol. 10, Pt. 2–339
Wilson, Joshua Lacy, Sept. 22, 1774–Aug. 14, 1846.
Vol. 10, Pt. 2–340
Wilson, Louis Blanchard, Dec. 22, 1866–Oct. 5, 1943.
Supp. 3–831
Wilson, Marie, Aug. 19, 1916–Nov. 23, 1972.
Supp. 9–879
Wilson, Mortimer, Aug. 6, 1876–Jan. 27, 1932.
Vol. 10, Pt. 2–341
Wilson, Orlando Winfield ("Win," "O. W."), May 15, 1900–Oct. 18, 1972.
Supp. 9–880
Wilson, Peter, Nov. 23, 1746–Aug. 1, 1825.
Vol. 10, Pt. 2–341
Wilson, Robert Burns, Oct. 30, 1850–Mar. 31, 1916.
Vol. 10, Pt. 2–342
Wilson, Samuel, Sept. 13, 1766–July 31, 1854.
Vol. 10, Pt. 2–343
Wilson, Samuel Graham, Feb. 11, 1858–July 2, 1916.
Vol. 10, Pt. 2–343
Wilson, Samuel Mountford, *c.* 1823–June 4, 1892.
Vol. 10, Pt. 2–344
Wilson, Samuel Ramsay, June 4, 1818–Mar. 3, 1886.
Vol. 10, Pt. 2–345
Wilson, Samuel Thomas, 1761–May 23, 1824.
Vol. 10, Pt. 2–346
Wilson, Theodore Delavan, May 11, 1840–June 29, 1896.
Vol. 10, Pt. 2–346
Wilson, Thomas Woodrow. [*See* Wilson, Woodrow, 1856–1924.]
Wilson, Warren Hugh, May 1, 1867–Mar. 2, 1937.
Supp. 2–726
Wilson, William, Apr. 27, 1794–Apr. 29, 1857.
Vol. 10, Pt. 2–347
Wilson, William, Dec. 25, 1801–Aug. 25, 1860.
Vol. 10, Pt. 2–348
Wilson, William Bauchop, Apr. 2, 1862–May 25, 1934.
Vol. 10, Pt. 2–348
Wilson, William Dexter, Feb. 28, 1816–July 30, 1900.
Vol. 10, Pt. 2–349
Wilson, William Griffith ("Bill W."), Nov. 26, 1895–Jan. 24, 1971.
Supp. 9–882
Wilson, William Hasell, Nov. 5, 1811–Aug. 17, 1902.
Vol. 10, Pt. 2–350
Wilson, William Lyne, May 3, 1843–Oct. 17, 1900.
Vol. 10, Pt. 2–351
Wilson, Woodrow, Dec. 28, 1856–Feb. 3, 1924.
Vol. 10, Pt. 2–352
Wiltz, Louis Alfred, Oct. 22, 1843–Oct. 16, 1881.
Vol. 10, Pt. 2–368
Wimar, Carl, Feb. 19, 1828–Nov. 28, 1862.
Vol. 10, Pt. 2–369
Wimmer, Boniface, Jan. 14, 1809–Dec. 8, 1887.
Vol. 10, Pt. 2–370
Wimsatt, William Kurtz, Nov. 17, 1907–Nov. 10, 1973.
Supp. 9–883
Winans, Ross, Oct. 17, 1796–Apr. 11, 1877.
Vol. 10, Pt. 2–371
Winans, Thomas De Kay, Dec. 6, 1820–June 10, 1878.
Vol. 10, Pt. 2–372
Winans, William, Nov. 3, 1788–Aug. 31, 1857.
Vol. 10, Pt. 2–373
Winant, John Gilbert, Feb. 23, 1889–Nov. 3, 1947.
Supp. 4–899
Winchell, Alexander, Dec. 31, 1824–Feb. 19, 1891.
Vol. 10, Pt. 2–373
Winchell, Horace Vaughn, Nov. 1, 1865–July 28, 1923.
Vol. 10, Pt. 2–374
Winchell, Newton Horace, Dec. 17, 1839–May 2, 1914.
Vol. 10, Pt. 2–375
Winchell, Walter, Apr. 7, 1897–Feb. 20, 1972.
Supp. 9–885
Winchester, Caleb Thomas, Jan. 18, 1847–Mar. 24, 1920.
Vol. 10, Pt. 2–376
Winchester, Elhanan, Sept. 30, 1751–Apr. 18, 1797.
Vol. 10, Pt. 2–377
Winchester, James, Feb. 6, 1752–July 26, 1826.
Vol. 10, Pt. 2–378
Winchester, Oliver Fisher, Nov. 30, 1810–Dec. 11, 1880.
Vol. 10, Pt. 2–379
Winchevsky, Morris, Aug. 9, 1856–Mar. 18, 1932.
Vol. 10, Pt. 2–379
Winder, John Henry, Feb. 21, 1800–Feb. 8, 1865.
Vol. 10, Pt. 2–380
Winder, Levin, Sept. 4, 1757–July 1, 1819.
Vol. 10, Pt. 2–381
Winder, William Henry, Feb. 18, 1775–May 24, 1824.
Vol. 10, Pt. 2–382
Windom, William, May 10, 1827–Jan. 29, 1891.
Vol. 10, Pt. 2–383
Winebrenner, John, Mar. 25, 1797–Sept. 12, 1860.
Vol. 10, Pt. 2–384
Wines, Enoch Cobb, Feb. 17, 1806–Dec. 10, 1879.
Vol. 10, Pt. 2–385
Wines, Frederick Howard, Apr. 9, 1838–Jan. 31, 1912.
Vol. 10, Pt. 2–386
Wing, Joseph Elwyn, Sept. 14, 1861–Sept. 10, 1915.
Vol. 10, Pt. 2–386
Wingate, Paine, May 14, 1799–Mar. 7, 1838.
Vol. 10, Pt. 2–387
Wingfield, Edward Maria, fl. 1586–1613.
Vol. 10, Pt. 2–388
Winkler, Edwin Theodore, Nov. 13, 1823–Nov. 10, 1883.
Vol. 10, Pt. 2–389
Winlock, Herbert Eustis, Feb. 1, 1884–Jan. 26, 1950.
Supp. 4–901
Winlock, Joseph, Feb. 6, 1826–June 11, 1875.
Vol. 10, Pt. 2–389
Winn, Richard, 1750–Dec. 19, 1818.
Vol. 10, Pt. 2–390
Winnemucca, Sarah, *c.* 1844–Oct. 16, 1891.
Vol. 10, Pt. 2–391
Winship, Albert Edward, Feb. 24, 1845–Feb. 17, 1933.
Vol. 10, Pt. 2–391
Winship, Blanton, Nov. 23, 1869–Oct. 9, 1947.
Supp. 4–902
Winship, George Parker, July 29, 1871–June 22, 1952.
Supp. 5–755
Winslow, Cameron McRae, July 29, 1854–Jan. 2, 1932.
Vol. 10, Pt. 2–392
Winslow, Charles-Edward Amory, Feb. 4, 1877–Jan. 8, 1957.
Supp. 6–701
Winslow, Edward, Oct. 18, 1595–May 8, 1655.
Vol. 10, Pt. 2–393
Winslow, Edward, Nov. 1, 1669–Dec. 1, 1753.
Vol. 10, Pt. 2–394
Winslow, Edward Francis, Sept. 28, 1837–Oct. 22, 1914.
Vol. 10, Pt. 2–395
Winslow, Hubbard, Oct. 30, 1799–Aug. 13, 1864.
Vol. 10, Pt. 2–396
Winslow, John, May 10, 1703–Apr. 17, 1774.
Vol. 10, Pt. 1–396
Winslow, John Ancrum, Nov. 19, 1811–Sept. 29, 1873.
Vol. 10, Pt. 2–397
Winslow, John Bradley, Oct. 4, 1851–July 13, 1920.
Vol. 10, Pt. 2–398
Winslow, John Flack, Nov. 10, 1810–Mar. 10, 1892.
Vol. 10, Pt. 2–399
Winslow, Josiah, *c.* 1629–Dec. 18, 1680.
Vol. 10, Pt. 2–400
Winslow, Miron, Dec. 11, 1789–Oct. 22, 1864.
Vol. 10, Pt. 2–401

Winslow, Ola Elizabeth, Jan. 5, 1885–Sept. 27, 1977.
Supp. 10–846
Winslow, Sidney Wilmot, Sept. 20, 1854–June 18, 1917.
Vol. 10, Pt. 2–401
Winslow, William Copley, Jan. 13, 1840–Feb. 2, 1925.
Vol. 10, Pt. 2–402
Winsor, Justin, Jan. 2, 1831–Oct. 22, 1897.
Vol. 10, Pt. 2–403
Winston, Harry, Mar. 1, 1896–Dec. 8, 1978.
Supp. 10–847
Winston, John Anthony, Sept. 4, 1812–Dec. 21, 1871.
Vol. 10, Pt. 2–404
Winston, Joseph, June 17, 1746–Apr. 21, 1815.
Vol. 10, Pt. 2–405
Winter, William, July 15, 1836–June 30, 1917.
Vol. 10, Pt. 2–405
Winterhalter, Hugo, Aug. 15, 1909–Sept. 17, 1973.
Supp. 9–887
Winthrop, Fitz-John. [*See* Winthrop, John, 1638–1707.]
Winthrop, James, Mar. 28, 1752–Sept. 26, 1821.
Vol. 10, Pt. 2–407
Winthrop, John, Jan. 12, 1587/88 o.s.–Mar. 26, 1649.
Vol. 10, Pt. 2–408
Winthrop, John, Feb. 12, 1605/06 o.s.–Apr. 5, 1676.
Vol. 10, Pt. 2–411
Winthrop, John, Mar. 14, 1638–Nov. 27, 1707.
Vol. 10, Pt. 2–413
Winthrop, John, Dec. 19, 1714–May 3, 1779.
Vol. 10, Pt. 2–414
Winthrop, Robert Charles, May 12, 1809–Nov. 16, 1894.
Vol. 10, Pt. 2–416
Winthrop, Theodore, Sept. 28, 1828–June 10, 1861.
Vol. 10, Pt. 2–417
Winton, Alexander, June 20, 1860–June 21, 1932.
Vol. 10, Pt. 2–417
Wirt, William, Nov. 8, 1772–Feb. 18, 1834.
Vol. 10, Pt. 2–418
Wirt, William Albert, Jan. 21. 1874–Mar. 11, 1938.
Supp. 2–727
Wise, Aaron, May 2, 1844–Mar. 30, 1896.
Vol. 10, Pt. 2–421
Wise, Daniel, Jan. 10, 1813–Dec. 19, 1898.
Vol. 10, Pt. 2–422
Wise, Henry Alexander, Dec. 3, 1806–Sept. 12, 1876.
Vol. 10, Pt. 2–423
Wise, Henry Augustus, May 24, 1819–Apr. 2, 1869.
Vol. 10, Pt. 2–425
Wise, Isaac Mayer, Mar. 29, 1819–Mar. 26, 1900.
Vol. 10, Pt. 2–426
Wise, John, Aug. 1652–Apr. 8, 1725.
Vol. 10, Pt. 2–427
Wise, John, Feb. 24, 1808–Sept. 29, 1879.
Vol. 10, Pt. 2–428
Wise, John Sergeant, Dec. 27, 1846–May 12, 1913.
Vol. 10, Pt. 2–429
Wise, Stephen Samuel, Mar. 17, 1874–Apr. 19, 1949.
Supp. 4–903
Wise, Thomas Alfred, Mar. 23, 1865–Mar. 21, 1928.
Vol. 10, Pt. 2–430
Wislizenus, Frederick Adolph, May 21, 1810–Sept. 22, 1889.
Vol. 10, Pt. 2–430
Wislocki, George Bernays, Mar. 25, 1892–Oct. 22, 1956.
Supp. 6–703
Wisner, Henry, 1720–Mar. 4, 1790.
Vol. 10, Pt. 2–431
Wissler, Clark, Sept. 18, 1870–Aug. 25, 1947.
Supp. 4–906
Wistar, Caspar, Feb. 3, 1696–Mar. 21, 1752.
Vol. 10, Pt. 2–432
Wistar, Caspar, Sept. 13, 1761–Jan. 22, 1818.
Vol. 10, Pt. 2–433
Wister, Owen, July 14, 1860–July 21, 1938.
Supp. 2–728
Wister, Sarah, July 20, 1761–Apr. 21, 1804.
Vol. 10, Pt. 2–434
Withers, Frederick Clarke, Feb. 4, 1828–Jan. 7, 1901.
Vol. 10, Pt. 2–435
Witherspoon, Alexander Maclaren, Oct. 31, 1894–Mar. 4, 1964.
Supp. 7–797
Witherspoon, Herbert, July 21, 1873–May 10, 1935.
Supp. 1–711
Witherspoon, John, Feb. 5, 1723–Nov. 15, 1794.
Vol. 10, Pt. 2–435
Witherspoon, John Alexander, Sept. 13, 1864–Apr. 26, 1929.
Vol. 10, Pt. 2–438
Witmark, Isidore, June 15, 1869–Apr. 9, 1941.
Supp. 3–833
Witte, Edwin Emil, Jan. 4, 1887–May 20, 1960.
Supp. 6–705
Witthaus, Rudolph August, Aug. 30, 1846–Dec. 19, 1915.
Vol. 10, Pt. 2–439
Wodehouse, Pelham Grenville, Oct. 15, 1881–Feb. 14, 1975.
Supp. 9–888
Woerner, John Gabriel, Apr. 28, 1826–Jan. 20, 1900.
Vol. 10, Pt. 2–439
Wofford, William Tatum, June 28, 1823–May 22, 1884.
Vol. 10, Pt. 2–440
Wolcott, Edward Oliver, Mar. 26, 1848–Mar. 1, 1905.
Vol. 10, Pt. 2–441
Wolcott, Oliver, Nov. 20, 1726–Dec. 1, 1797.
Vol. 10, Pt. 2–442
Wolcott, Oliver, Jan. 11, 1760–June 1, 1833.
Vol. 10, Pt. 2–443
Wolcott, Roger, Jan. 4, 1679–May 17, 1767.
Vol. 10, Pt. 2–445
Wolf, George, Aug. 12, 1777–Mar. 11, 1840.
Vol. 10, Pt. 2–446
Wolf, Henry, Aug. 3, 1852–Mar. 18, 1916.
Vol. 10, Pt. 2–447
Wolf, Innocent William, Apr. 13, 1843–Oct. 14, 1922.
Vol. 10, Pt. 2–448
Wolf, Simon, Oct. 28, 1836–June 4, 1923.
Vol. 10, Pt. 2–449
Wolfe, Bertram David, Jan. 19, 1896–Feb. 21, 1977.
Supp. 10–848
Wolfe, Catharine Lorillard, Mar. 1828–Apr. 4, 1887.
Vol. 10, Pt. 2–449
Wolfe, Harry Kirke, Nov. 10, 1858–July 30, 1918.
Vol. 10, Pt. 2–450
Wolfe, John David, July 24, 1792–May 17, 1872.
Vol. 10, Pt. 2–451
Wolfe, Thomas Clayton, Oct. 3, 1900–Sept. 15, 1938.
Supp. 2–730
Wolff, Kurt August Paul, Mar. 3, 1887–Oct. 21, 1963.
Supp. 7–798
Wolfskill, William, Mar. 20, 1798–Oct. 3, 1866.
Vol. 10, Pt. 2–451
Wolfsohn, Carl, Dec. 14, 1834–July 30, 1907.
Vol. 10, Pt. 2–452
Wolfson, Erwin Service, Mar. 27, 1902–June 26, 1962.
Supp. 7–799
Wolfson, Harry Austryn, Nov. 2, 1887–Sept. 19, 1974.
Supp. 9–890
Wolheim, Louis Robert, Mar. 28, 1881–Feb. 18, 1931.
Supp. 1–712
Woll, Matthew, Jan. 25, 1880–June 1, 1956.
Supp. 6–706
Wolle, John Frederick, Apr. 4, 1863–Jan. 12, 1933.
Vol. 10, Pt. 2–453
Wolman, Leo, Feb. 24, 1890–Oct. 2, 1961.
Supp. 7–800
Wong, Anna May, Jan. 3, 1907–Feb. 3, 1961.
Supp. 7–801
Wood, Abraham, fl. 1638–1680.
Vol. 10, Pt. 2–454
Wood, Casey Albert, Nov. 21, 1856–Jan. 26, 1942.
Supp. 3–834
Wood, Charles Erskine Scott, Feb. 20, 1852–Jan. 22, 1944.
Supp. 3–836
Wood, Craig Ralph, *c.* 1901–May 7, 1968.
Supp. 8–702
Wood, David Duffle, Mar. 2, 1838–Mar. 27, 1910.
Vol. 10, Pt. 2–454
Wood, Edith Elmer, Sept. 24, 1871–Apr. 29, 1945.
Supp. 3–837
Wood, Edward Stickney, Apr. 28, 1846–July 11, 1905.
Vol. 10, Pt. 2–455
Wood, Fernando, June 14, 1812–Feb. 14, 1881.
Vol. 10, Pt. 2–456

Wood, Frederick Hill, Jan. 2, 1877–Dec. 28, 1943.
Supp. 3–839
Wood, Garfield Arthur ("Gar"), Dec. 4, 1880–June 19, 1971.
Supp. 9–891
Wood, George, Jan. 1789–Mar. 17, 1860.
Vol. 10, Pt. 2–457
Wood, George Bacon, Mar. 12, 1797–Mar. 30, 1879.
Vol. 10, Pt. 2–458
Wood, Grant, Feb. 13, 1892–Feb. 12, 1942.
Supp. 3–840
Wood, Henry Alexander Wise, Mar. 1, 1866–Apr. 9, 1939.
Supp. 2–733
Wood, Horatio Charles, Jan. 13, 1841–Jan. 3, 1920.
Vol. 10, Pt. 2–459
Wood, James, July 12, 1799–Apr. 7, 1867.
Vol. 10, Pt. 2–460
Wood, James, Nov. 12, 1839–Dec. 19, 1925.
Vol. 10, Pt. 2–460
Wood, James Frederick, Apr. 27, 1813–June 20, 1883.
Vol. 10, Pt. 2–461
Wood, James J., Mar. 25, 1856–Apr. 19, 1928.
Vol. 10, Pt. 2–462
Wood, James Rushmore, Sept. 14, 1813–May 4, 1882.
Vol. 10, Pt. 2–463
Wood, Jethro, Mar. 16, 1774–Sept. 18, 1834.
Vol. 10, Pt. 2–464
Wood, John, *c.* 1775–May 15, 1822.
Vol. 10, Pt. 2–464
Wood, John Stephens, Feb. 8, 1885–Sept. 12, 1968.
Supp. 8–703
Wood, John Taylor, Aug. 13, 1830–July 19, 1904.
Vol. 10, Pt. 2–465
Wood, Joseph, *c.* 1778–*c.* 1832.
Vol. 10, Pt. 2–466
Wood, Leonard, Oct. 9, 1860–Aug. 7, 1927.
Vol. 10, Pt. 2–467
Wood, Mary Elizabeth, Aug. 22, 1861–May 1, 1931.
Vol. 10, Pt. 2–46
Wood, Peggy, Feb. 9, 1892–Mar. 18, 1978.
Supp. 10–850
Wood, Reuben, *c.* 1792–Oct. 1, 1864.
Vol. 10, Pt. 2–470
Wood, Robert Elkington, June 13, 1879–Nov. 6, 1969.
Supp. 8–704
Wood, Samuel, July 17, 1760–May 5, 1844.
Vol. 10, Pt. 2–471
Wood, Sarah Sayward Barrell Keating, Oct. 1, 1759–Jan. 6, 1855.
Vol. 10, Pt. 2–472
Wood, Thomas, Aug. 22, 1813–Nov. 21, 1880.
Vol. 10, Pt. 2–473
Wood, Thomas Bond, Mar. 17, 1844–Dec. 18, 1922.
Vol. 10, Pt. 2–473
Wood, Thomas John, Sept. 25, 1823–Feb. 25, 1906.
Vol. 10, Pt. 2–474
Wood, Walter Abbott, Oct. 23, 1815–Jan. 15, 1892.
Vol. 10, Pt. 2–475
Wood. William, fl. 1629–1635.
Vol. 10, Pt. 2–476
Wood, William Burke, May 26, 1779–Sept. 23, 1861.
Vol. 10, Pt. 2–476
Wood, William Robert, Jan. 5, 1861–Mar. 7, 1933.
Vol. 10, Pt. 2–478
Woodberry, George Edward, May 12, 1855–Jan. 2, 1930.
Vol. 10, Pt. 2–478
Woodbridge, Frederick James Eugene, Mar. 26, 1867–June 1, 1940.
Supp. 2–734
Woodbridge, John, 1613–Mar. 17, 1695.
Vol. 10, Pt. 2–481
Woodbridge, Samuel Merrill, Apr. 5, 1819–June 24, 1905.
Vol. 10, Pt. 2–482
Woodbridge, William Channing, Dec. 18, 1794–Nov. 9, 1845.
Vol. 10, Pt. 2–484
Woodbridge, William, Aug. 20, 1780–Oct. 20, 1861.
Vol. 10, Pt. 2–483
Woodbury, Charles Jeptha Hill, May 4, 1851–Mar. 20, 1916.
Vol. 10, Pt. 2–485
Woodbury, Daniel Phineas, Dec. 16, 1812–Aug. 15, 1864.
Vol. 10, Pt. 2–485
Woodbury, Helen Laura Sumner, Mar. 12, 1876–Mar. 10, 1933.
Vol. 10, Pt. 2–486
Woodbury, Isaac Baker, Oct. 23, 1819–Oct. 26, 1858.
Vol. 10, Pt. 2–487
Woodbury, Levi, Dec. 22, 1789–Sept. 4, 1851.
Vol. 10, Pt. 2–488
Woodford, Stewart Lyndon, Sept. 3, 1835–Feb. 14, 1913.
Vol. 10, Pt. 2–489
Woodford, William, Oct. 6, 1734–Nov. 13, 1780.
Vol. 10, Pt. 2–490
Woodhouse, James, Nov. 17, 1770–June 4, 1809.
Vol. 10, Pt. 2–491
Woodhull, Alfred Alexander, Apr. 13, 1837–Oct. 18, 1921.
Vol. 10, Pt. 2–492
Woodhull, Nathaniel, Dec. 30, 1722–Sept. 20, 1776.
Vol. 10, Pt. 2–492
Woodhull, Victoria Claflin, Sept. 23, 1838–June 10, 1927.
Vol. 10, Pt. 2–493
Woodin, William Hartman, May 27, 1868–May 3, 1934.
Vol. 10, Pt. 2–494
Woodring, Harry Hines, May 31, 1887–Sept. 9, 1967.
Supp. 8–705
Woodrow, James, May 30, 1828–Jan. 17, 1907.
Vol. 10, Pt. 2–495
Woodruff, Charles Edward, Oct. 2, 1860–June 13, 1915.
Vol. 10, Pt. 2–496
Woodruff, Lorande Loss, July 14, 1879–June 23, 1947.
Supp. 4–909
Woodruff, Theodore Tuttle, Apr. 8, 1811–May 2, 1892.
Vol. 10, Pt. 2–497
Woodruff, Timothy Lester, Aug. 4, 1858–Oct. 12, 1913.
Vol. 10, Pt. 2–498
Woodruff, Wilford, Mar. 1, 1807–Sept. 2, 1898.
Vol. 10, Pt. 2–498
Woodruff, William Edward, Dec. 24, 1795–June 19, 1885.
Vol. 10, Pt. 2–500
Woods, Alva, Aug. 13, 1794–Sept. 6, 1887.
Vol. 10, Pt. 2–500
Woods, Charles Robert, Feb. 19, 1827–Feb. 26, 1885.
Vol. 10, Pt. 2–501
Woods, James Haughton, Nov. 27, 1864–Jan. 14, 1935.
Supp. 1–713
Woods, Leonard, June 19, 1774–Aug. 24, 1854.
Vol. 10, Pt. 2–502
Woods, Leonard, Nov. 24, 1807–Dec. 24, 1878.
Vol. 10, Pt. 2–502
Woods, Robert Archey, Dec. 9, 1865–Feb. 18, 1925.
Vol. 10, Pt. 2–503
Woods, William Allen, May 16, 1837–June 29, 1901.
Vol. 10, Pt. 2–504
Woods, William Burnham, Aug. 3, 1824–May 14, 1887.
Vol. 10, Pt. 2–505
Woodson, Carter Godwin, Dec. 19, 1875–Apr. 3, 1950.
Supp. 4–910
Woodward, Augustus Brevoort, 1774–June 12, 1827.
Vol. 10, Pt. 2–506
Woodward, Calvin Milton, Aug. 25, 1837–Jan. 12, 1914.
Vol. 10, Pt. 2–507
Woodward, Henry, *c.* 1646–*c.* 1686.
Vol. 8, Pt. 1–508
Woodward, Joseph Janvier, Oct. 30, 1833–Aug. 17, 1884.
Vol. 10, Pt. 2–509
Woodward, Robert Burns, Apr. 10, 1917–July 8, 1979.
Supp. 10–851
Woodward, Robert Simpson, July 21, 1849–June 29, 1924.
Vol. 10, Pt. 2–510
Woodward, Samuel Bayard, Jan. 10, 1787–Jan. 3, 1850.
Vol. 10, Pt. 2–511
Woodward, William, Apr. 7, 1876–Sept. 26, 1953.
Supp. 5–756
Woodworth, Jay Backus, Jan. 2, 1865–Aug. 4 1925.
Vol. 10, Pt. 2–511
Woodworth, Samuel, Jan. 13, 1784–Dec. 9, 1842.
Vol. 10, Pt. 2–512
Wool, Jolin Ellis, Feb. 29, 1784–Nov. 10, 1869.
Vol. 10, Pt. 2–513
Woolf, Benjamin Edward, Feb. 16, 1836–Feb. 7, 1901.
Vol. 10, Pt. 2–514

Woollcott, Alexander Humphreys, Jan. 19, 1887–Jan. 23, 1943.
Supp. 3–842
Woolley, Celia Parker, June 14, 1848–Mar. 9, 1918.
Vol. 10, Pt. 2–515
Woolley, Edgar Montillion ("Monty"), Aug. 17, 1888–May 6, 1963.
Supp. 7–802
Woolley, John Granville, Feb. 15, 1850–Aug. 13, 1922.
Vol. 10, Pt. 2–515
Woolley, Mary Emma, July 13, 1863–Sept. 5, 1947.
Supp. 4–912
Woolman, Collett Everman, Oct. 8, 1889–Sept. 11, 1966.
Supp. 8–707
Woolman, John, Oct. 19, 1720–Oct. 7, 1772.
Vol. 10, Pt. 2–516
Woolsey, John Munro, Jan. 3, 1877–May 4, 1945.
Supp. 3–843
Woolsey, Melancthon Taylor, June 5, 1780–May 19, 1838.
Vol. 10, Pt. 2–517
Woolsey, Sarah Chauncy, Jan. 29, 1835–Apr. 9, 1905.
Vol. 10, Pt. 2–518
Woolsey, Theodore Dwight, Oct. 31, 1801–July 1, 1889.
Vol. 10, Pt. 2–519
Woolsey, Theodore Salisbury, Oct. 22, 1852–Apr. 24, 1929.
Vol. 10, Pt. 2–520
Woolson, Abba Louisa Goold, Apr. 30, 1838–Feb. 6, 1921.
Vol. 10, Pt. 2–521
Woolson, Constance Fenimore, March 1840–Jan. 24, 1894.
Vol. 10, Pt. 2–522
Woolworth, Frank Winfield, Apr. 13, 1852–Aug. 8, 1919.
Vol. 10, Pt. 2–523
Wooster, Charles Whiting, 1780–1848.
Vol. 10, Pt. 2–524
Wooster, David, Mar. 2, 1711–May 2, 1777.
Vol. 10, Pt. 2–524
Wootassite. [*See* Outacity, fl. 1756–1777.]
Wootton, Richens Lacy, May 6, 1816–Aug. 21, 1893.
Vol. 10, Pt. 2–525
Worcester, Edwin Dean, Nov. 19, 1828–June 13, 1904.
Vol. 10, Pt. 2–526
Worcester, Elwood, May 16, 1862–July 19, 1940.
Supp. 2–735
Worcester, Joseph Emerson, Aug. 24, 1784–Oct. 27, 1865.
Vol. 10, Pt. 2–526
Worcester, Noah, Nov. 25, 1758–Oct. 31, 1837.
Vol. 10, Pt. 2–528
Worcester, Samuel, Nov. 1, 1770–June 7, 1821.
Vol. 10, Pt. 2–529
Worcester, Samuel Austin, Jan. 19, 1798–Apr. 20, 1859.
Vol. 10, Pt. 2–530
Worden, John Lorimer, Mar. 12, 1818–Oct. 18, 1897.
Vol. 10, Pt. 2–531
Work, Henry Clay, Oct. 1, 1832–June 8, 1884.
Vol. 10, Pt. 2–531
Work, Hubert, July 3, 1860–Dec. 14, 1942.
Supp. 3–845
Work, Milton Cooper, Sept. 15, 1864–June 27, 1934.
Vol. 10, Pt. 2–532
Workman, Fanny Bullock, Jan. 8, 1859–Jan. 22, 1925.
Vol. 10, Pt. 2–533
Wormeley, Katharine Prescott, Jan. 14, 1830–Aug. 4, 1908.
Vol. 10, Pt. 2–034
Wormeley, Mary Elizabeth. [*See* Latimer, Mary Elizabeth Wormeley, 1822–1904.]
Wormley, James, Jan. 16, 1819–Oct. 18, 1884.
Vol. 10, Pt. 2–534
Wormley, Theodore George, Apr. 1, 1826–Jan. 3, 1897.
Vol. 10, Pt. 2–535
Worth, Jonathan, Nov. 18, 1802–Sept. 5, 1869.
Vol. 10, Pt. 2–536
Worth, William Jenkins, Mar. 1, 1794–May 7, 1849.
Vol. 10, Pt. 2–536
Worthen, Amos Henry, Oct. 31, 1813–May 6, 1888.
Vol. 10, Pt. 2–537
Worthen, William Ezra, Mar. 14, 1819–Apr. 2, 1897.
Vol. 10, Pt. 2–538
Worthington, Henry Rossiter, Dec. 17, 1817–Dec. 17, 1880.
Vol. 10, Pt. 2–539
Worthington, John, Nov. 24, 1719–Apr. 25, 1800.
Vol. 10, Pt. 2–539
Worthington, Thomas, July 16, 1773–June 20, 1827.
Vol. 10, Pt. 2–540
Wovoka, *c.* 1856–Oct. 1932.
Vol. 10, Pt. 2–541
Woytinsky, Wladimir Savelievich, Nov. 12, 1885–June 11, 1960.
Supp. 6–708
Wragg, William, 1714–Sept. 2, 1777.
Vol. 10, Pt. 2–541
Wrather, William Embry, Jan. 20, 1883–Nov. 28, 1963.
Supp. 7–803
Wraxall, Peter, d. July 10, 1759.
Vol. 10, Pt. 2–542
Wright, Benjamin, Oct. 10, 1770–Aug. 24, 1842.
Vol. 10, Pt. 2–543
Wright, Carroll Davidson, July 25, 1840–Feb. 20, 1909.
Vol. 10, Pt. 2–544
Wright, Charles, Oct. 29, 1811–Aug. 11, 1885.
Vol. 10, Pt. 2–545
Wright, Charles Barstow, Jan. 8, 1822–Mar. 24, 1898.
Vol. 10, Pt. 2–546
Wright, Chauncey, Sept. 20, 1830–Sept. 12, 1875.
Vol. 10, Pt. 2–547
Wright, Elizur, Feb. 12, 1804–Nov. 21, 1885.
Vol. 10, Pt. 2–548
Wright, Fielding Lewis, May 16, 1895–May 4, 1956.
Supp. 6–710
Wright, Frances, Sept. 6, 1795–Dec. 13, 1852.
Vol. 10, Pt. 2–549
Wright, Frank Lloyd, June 8, 1867–Apr. 9, 1959.
Supp. 6–711
Wright, George, Jan. 28, 1847–Aug. 21, 1937.
Supp. 2–737
Wright, George Frederick, Jan. 22, 1838–Apr. 20, 1921.
Vol. 10, Pt. 2–550
Wright, George Grover, Mar. 24, 1820–Jan. 11, 1896.
Vol. 10, Pt. 2–551
Wright, Hamilton Kemp, Aug. 2, 1867–Jan. 9, 1917.
Vol. 10, Pt. 2–552
Wright, Harold Bell, May 4, 1872–May 24, 1944.
Supp. 3–846
Wright, Hendrick Bradley, Apr. 24, 1808–Sept. 2, 1881.
Vol. 10, Pt. 2–553
Wright, Henry, Jan. 10, 1835–Oct. 3, 1895.
Vol. 10, Pt. 2–554
Wright, Henry, July 2, 1878–July 9, 1936.
Supp. 2–737
Wright, Horatio Gouverneur, Mar. 6, 1820–July 2, 1899.
Vol. 10, Pt. 2–554
Wright, James Arlington, Dec. 13, 1927–Mar. 25, 1980.
Supp. 10–853
Wright, James Lendrew, Apr. 6, 1816–Aug. 3, 1893.
Vol. 10, Pt. 2–555
Wright, John Henry, Feb. 4, 1852–Nov. 25, 1908.
Vol. 10, Pt. 2–556
Wright, John Joseph, July 18, 1909–Aug. 10, 1979.
Supp. 10–855
Wright, John Kenneth Lloyd, Dec. 12, 1892–Dec. 20, 1972.
Supp. 9–893
Wright, John Stephen, July 16, 1815–Sept. 26, 1874.
Vol. 10, Pt. 2–557
Wright, Jonathan Jasper, Feb. 11, 1840–Feb. 18, 1885.
Vol. 10, Pt. 2–558
Wright, Joseph Jefferson Burr, Apr. 27, 1801–May 14, 1878.
Vol. 10, Pt. 2–560
Wright, Joseph, July 16, 1756–1793.
Vol. 10, Pt. 2–559
Wright, Joseph Albert, Apr. 17, 1810–May 11, 1867.
Vol. 10, Pt. 2–559
Wright, Luke Edward, Aug. 29, 1846–Nov. 17, 1922.
Vol. 10, Pt. 2–561
Wright, Marcus Joseph, June 5, 1831–Dec. 27, 1922.
Vol. 10, Pt. 2–561
Wright, Orville, Aug. 19, 1871–Jan. 30, 1948.
Supp. 4–913
Wright, Patience Lovell, 1725–Mar. 23, 1786.
Vol. 10, Pt. 2–562
Wright, Philip Green, Oct. 3, 1861–Sept. 4, 1934.
Vol. 10, Pt. 2–563
Wright, Richard Nathaniel, Sept. 4, 1908–Nov. 28, 1960.
Supp. 6–715

Wright, Richard Robert, May 16, 1853–July 2, 1947.
Supp. 4–915
Wright, Robert, Nov. 20, 1752–Sept. 7, 1826.
Vol. 10, Pt. 2–564
Wright, Robert William, Feb. 22, 1816–Jan. 9, 1885.
Vol. 10, Pt. 2–565
Wright, Silas, May 24, 1795–Aug. 27, 1847.
Vol. 10, Pt. 2–565
Wright, Theodore Lyman, Sept. 13, 1858–Oct. 4, 1926.
Vol. 10, Pt. 2–567
Wright, Theodore Paul, May 25, 1895–Aug. 21, 1970.
Supp. 8–708
Wright, Wilbur, Apr. 16, 1867–May 30, 1912.
Vol. 10, Pt. 2–568
Wright, Willard Huntington, Oct. 15, 1888–Apr. 11, 1939.
Supp. 2–739
Wright, William, Nov. 13, 1794–Nov. 1, 1866.
Vol. 10, Pt. 2–570
Wright, William, May 9, 1829–Mar. 16, 1898.
Supp. 1–714
Wrigley, Philip Knight, Dec. 5, 1894–Apr. 12, 1977.
Supp. 10–856
Wrigley, William, Sept. 30, 1861–Jan. 26, 1932.
Supp. 1–715
Wrosetasatow. [*See* Outacity, fl. 1756–1777.]
Wu P'an-Chao. [*See* Ng, Poon Chew, 1866–1931.]
Wurtz, Henry, *c.* 1828–Nov. 8, 1910.
Vol. 10, Pt. 2–571
Wyant, Alexander Helwig, Jan. 11, 1836–Nov. 29, 1892.
Vol. 10, Pt. 2–572
Wyatt, Sir Francis, 1588–August 1644.
Vol. 10, Pt. 2–573
Wyckoff, John Henry, Nov. 12, 1881–June 1, 1937.
Supp. 2–741
Wyckoff, Walter Augustus, Apr. 12, 1865–May 15, 1908.
Vol. 10, Pt. 2–574
Wyeth, John, Mar. 31, 1770–Jan. 23, 1858.
Vol. 10, Pt. 2–575
Wyeth, John Allan, May 26, 1845–May 28, 1922.
Vol. 10, Pt. 2–576
Wyeth, Nathaniel Jarvis, Jan. 29, 1802–Aug. 31, 1856.
Vol. 10, Pt. 2–576
Wyeth, Newell Convers, Oct. 22, 1882–Oct. 19, 1945.
Supp. 3–847
Wylie, Andrew, Apr. 12, 1789–Nov. 11, 1851.
Vol. 10, Pt. 2–577
Wylie, Elinor Morton Hoyt, Sept. 7, 1885–Dec. 16, 1928.
Vol. 10, Pt. 2–578
Wylie, Philip Gordon, May 12, 1902–Oct. 25, 1971.
Supp. 9–894
Wylie, Robert, 1839–Feb. 1877.
Vol. 10, Pt. 2–580
Wylie, Samuel Brown, May 21, 1773–Oct. 13, 1852.
Vol. 10, Pt. 2–581
Wyllys, George, Oct. 6, 1710–Apr. 24, 1796.
Vol. 10, Pt. 2–581
Wyman, Horace, Nov. 27, 1827–May 8, 1915.
Vol. 10, Pt. 2–582
Wyman, Jeffries, Aug. 11, 1814–Sept. 4, 1874.
Vol. 10, Pt. 2–583
Wyman, Morrill, July 25, 1812–Jan. 30, 1903.
Vol. 10, Pt. 2–584
Wyman, Robert Harris, July 12, 1822–Dec. 2, 1882.
Vol. 10, Pt. 2–585
Wyman, Seth, Mar. 4, 1784–Apr. 2, 1843.
Vol. 10, Pt. 2–586
Wynn, Ed, Nov. 9, 1886–June 19, 1966.
Supp. 8–710
Wythe, George, 1726–June 8, 1806.
Vol. 10, Pt. 2–586

Xántus, János, Oct. 5, 1825–Dec. 13, 1894.
Vol. 10, Pt. 2–589

Yale, Caroline Ardelia, Sept. 29, 1848–July 2, 1933.
Vol. 10, Pt. 2–590
Yale, Elihu, Apr. 5, 1649–July 8, 1721.
Vol. 10, Pt. 2–590
Yale, Linus, Apr. 4, 1821–Dec. 25, 1868.
Vol. 10, Pt. 2–591
Yancey, James Edward ("Jimmy"), 1894–Sept. 17, 1951.
Supp. 5–757
Yancey, William Lowndes, Aug. 10, 1814–July 27, 1863.
Vol. 10, Pt. 2–592
Yandell, David Wendell, Sept. 4, 1826–May 2, 1898.
Vol. 10, Pt. 2–595
Yandell, Lunsford Pitts, July 4, 1805–Feb. 4, 1878.
Vol. 10, Pt. 2–596
Yates, Abraham, 1724–June 30, 1796.
Vol. 10, Pt. 2–597
Yates, Herbert John, Aug. 24, 1880–Feb. 3, 1966.
Supp. 8–711
Yates, John Van Ness, Dec. 18, 1779–Jan. 10, 1839.
Vol. 10, Pt. 2–598
Yates, Matthew Tyson, Jan. 8, 1819–Mar. 17, 1888.
Vol. 10, Pt. 2–598
Yates, Richard, Jan. 18, 1815–Nov. 27, 1873.
Vol. 10, Pt. 2–599
Yates, Robert, Jan. 27, 1738–Sept. 9, 1801.
Vol. 10, Pt. 2–601
Yawkey, Thomas Austin ("Tom"), Feb. 21, 1903–July 9, 1976.
Supp. 10–859
Yeadon, Richard, Oct. 23, 1802–Apr. 25, 1870.
Vol. 10, Pt. 2–602
Yeager, Joseph, *c.* 1792–June 9, 1859.
Vol. 10, Pt. 2–602
Yeaman, William Pope, May 28, 1832–Feb. 19, 1904.
Vol. 10, Pt. 2–603
Yeamans, Sir John, 1610/11–Aug. 1674.
Vol. 10, Pt. 2–604
Yeardley, Sir George, *c.* 1587–Nov. 1627.
Vol. 10, Pt. 2–605
Yeates, Jasper, Apr. 17, 1745–Mar. 14, 1817.
Vol. 10, Pt. 2–606
Yeatman, James Erwin, Aug. 27, 1818–July 7, 1901.
Vol. 10, Pt. 2–606
Yell, Archibald, Aug. 1797–Feb. 23, 1847.
Vol. 10, Pt. 2–607
Yellin, Samuel, Mar. 2, 1885–Oct. 3, 1940.
Supp. 2–742
Yellowley, Edward Clements, Aug. 12, 1873–Feb. 8, 1962.
Supp. 7–805
Yeomans, John William, Jan. 7, 1800–June 22, 1863.
Vol. 10, Pt. 2–608
Yergan, Max, July 19, 1892–Apr. 11, 1975.
Supp. 9–897
Yerger, William, Nov. 22, 1816–June 7, 1872.
Vol. 10, Pt. 2–609
Yerkes, Charles Tyson, June 25, 1837–Dec. 29, 1905.
Vol. 10, Pt. 2–609
Yerkes, Robert Mearns, May 26, 1876–Feb. 3, 1956.
Supp. 6–717
Yoakum, Benjamin Franklin, Aug. 20, 1859–Nov. 28, 1929.
Vol. 10, Pt. 2–611
Yoakum, Henderson, Sept. 6, 1810–Nov. 30, 1856.
Vol. 10, Pt. 2–612
Yohn, Frederick Coffay, Feb–8, 1875–June 5, 1933.
Vol. 10, Pt. 2–613
Yon, Pietro Alessandro, Aug. 8, 1886–Nov. 22, 1943.
Supp. 3–849
York, Alvin Cullum, Dec. 13, 1887–Sept. 2, 1964.
Supp. 7–806
Yorke, Peter Christopher, Aug. 15, 1864–Apr. 5, 1925.
Vol. 10, Pt. 2–614
Yost, Casper Salathiel, July 1, 1864–May 30, 1941.
Supp. 3–850
Yost, Fielding Harris, Apr. 30, 1871–Aug. 20, 1946.
Supp. 4–917
You, Dominique, *c.* 1772–Nov. 14, 1830.
Vol. 10, Pt. 2–615
Youmans, Edward Livingston, June 3, 1821–Jan. 18, 1887.
Vol. 10, Pt. 2–615,
Youmans, Vincent Millie, Sept. 27, 1898–Apr. 5, 1946.
Supp. 4–918
Youmans, William Jay, Oct. 14, 1838–Apr. 10, 1901.
Vol. 10, Pt. 2–616
Young, Aaron, Dec. 19, 1819–Jan. 13, 1898.
Vol. 10, Pt. 2–617
Young, Alexander, Sept. 22, 1800–Mar. 16, 1854.
Vol. 10, Pt. 2–618
Young, Alfred, Jan. 21, 1831–Apr. 4, 1900.
Vol. 10, Pt. 2–619

Young, Allyn Abbott, Sept. 19, 1876–Mar. 7, 1929. Vol. 10, Pt. 2–619
Young, Ammi Burnham, June 19, 1798–Mar. 13, 1874. Supp. 1–716
Young, Art, Jan. 14, 1866–Dec. 29, 1943. Supp. 3–851
Young, Brigham, June 1, 1801–Aug. 29, 1877. Vol. 10, Pt. 2–620
Young, Charles Augustus, Dec. 15, 1834–Jan. 3, 1908. Vol. 10, Pt. 2–623
Young, Clarence Marshall, July 23, 1889–Apr. 10, 1973. Supp. 9–898
Young, Clark Montgomery, Sept. 3, 1856–Feb. 28, 1908. Vol. 10, Pt. 2–624
Young, David, Jan. 27, 1781–Feb. 13, 1852. Vol. 10, Pt. 2–625
Young, Denton True ("Cy"), Mar. 29, 1867–Nov. 4, 1955. Supp. 5–759
Young, Ella Flagg, Jan. 15, 1845–Oct. 26, 1918. Vol. 10, Pt. 2–626
Young, Ewing, d. Feb. 15, 1841. Vol. 10, Pt. 2–627
Young, George, Oct. 16, 1870–Apr. 16, 1935. Supp. 1–717
Young, Hugh Hampton, Sept. 18, 1870–Aug. 23, 1945. Supp. 3–853
Young, Jesse Bowman, July 5, 1844–July 30, 1914. Vol. 10, Pt. 2–627
Young, John, June 12, 1802–Apr. 23, 1852. Vol. 10, Pt. 2–628
Young, John Clarke, Aug. 12, 1803–June 23, 1857. Vol. 10, Pt. 2–629
Young, John Richardson, 1782–June 8, 1804. Vol. 10, Pt. 2–630
Young, John Russell, Nov. 20, 1840–Jan. 17, 1899. Vol. 10, Pt. 2–630
Young, John Wesley, Nov. 17, 1879–Feb. 17, 1932. Vol. 10, Pt. 2–631
Young, Josue Maria, Oct. 29, 1808–Sept. 18, 1866. Vol. 10, Pt. 2–632
Young, Karl, Nov. 2, 1879–Nov. 17, 1943. Supp. 3–854
Young, Lafayette, May 10, 1848–Nov. 15, 1926. Vol. 10, Pt. 2–632
Young, Mahonri Mackintosh, Aug. 9, 1877–Nov. 2, 1957. Supp. 6–719
Young, Owen D., Oct. 27, 1874–July 11, 1962. Supp. 7–808
Young, Pierce Manning Butler, Nov. 15, 1836–July 6, 1896. Vol. 10, Pt. 2–633
Young, Robert Ralph, Feb. 14, 1897–Jan. 25, 1958. Supp. 6–721
Young, Samuel Hall, Sept. 12, 1847–Sept. 2, 1927. Vol. 10, Pt. 2–634
Young, Stark, Oct. 11, 1881–Jan. 6, 1963. Supp. 7–811
Young, Thomas, Feb. 19, 1731/32–June 24, 1777. Vol. 10, Pt. 2–635
Young, Whitney Moore, Jr., July 31, 1921–Mar. 11, 1971. Supp. 9–900
Youngdahl, Luther Wallace, May 29, 1896–June 21, 1978. Supp. 10–862
Younger, Maud, Jan. 10, 1870–June 25, 1936. Supp. 2–743
Younger, Thomas Coleman, Jan. 15, 1844–Mar. 21, 1916. Vol. 10, Pt. 2–636
Youngs, John, Apr. 1623–Apr. 12, 1698. Vol. 10, Pt. 2–636
Yount, George Concepcíon, May 4, 1794–Oct. 5, 1865. Vol. 10, Pt. 2–637
Yulee, David Levy, June 12, 1810–Oct. 10, 1886. Vol. 10, Pt. 2–638
Yung Wing, Nov. 17, 1828–Apr. 21, 1912. Vol. 10, Pt. 2–638

Zach, Max Wilhelm, Aug. 31, 1864–Feb. 3, 1921. Vol. 10, Pt. 2–639
Zacharias, Ellis Mark, Jan. 1, 1890–June 28, 1961. Supp. 7–812
Zachos, John Celivergos, Dec. 20, 1820–Mar. 20, 1898. Vol. 10, Pt. 2–640
Zaharias, Mildred ("Babe") Didrikson, June 26, 1914–Sept. 27, 1956. Supp. 6–722
Zahm, John Augustine, Sept. 14, 1851–Nov. 10, 1921. Vol. 10, Pt. 2–641
Zahniser, Howard Clinton, Feb. 25, 1906–May 5, 1964. Supp. 7–813
Zakrzewska, Marie Elizabeth, Sept. 6, 1829–May 12, 1902. Vol. 10, Pt. 2–642
Zamorano, Agustin Juan Vicente, May 5, 1798–Sept. 16, 1842. Vol. 10, Pt. 2–642
Zane, Charles Shuster, Mar. 3, 1831–Mar. 29, 1915. Vol. 10, Pt. 2–643
Zane, Ebenezer, Oct. 7, 1747–Nov. 19, 1812. Vol. 10, Pt. 2–644
Zanuck, Darryl Francis, Sept. 5, 1902–Dec. 22, 1979. Supp. 10–863
Zeckendorf, William, June 30, 1905–Sept. 30, 1976. Supp. 10–866
Zeilin, Jacob, July 16, 1806–Nov. 18, 1880. Vol. 10, Pt. 2–645
Zeisberger, David, Apr. 11, 1721–Nov. 17, 1808. Vol. 10, Pt. 2–645
Zeisler, Fannie Bloomfield, July 16, 1863–Aug. 20, 1927. Vol. 10, Pt. 2–647
Zeisler, Sigmund, Apr. 11, 1860–June 4, 1931. Vol. 10, Pt. 2–648
Zellerbach, Harold Lionel, Mar. 25, 1894–Jan. 29, 1978. Supp. 10–867
Zellerbach, James David, Jan. 17, 1892–Aug. 3, 1963. Supp. 7–814
Zenger, John Peter, 1697–July 28, 1746. Vol. 10, Pt. 2–648
Zentmayer, Joseph, Mar. 27, 1826–Mar. 28, 1888. Vol. 10, Pt. 2–650
Zerrahn, Carl, July 28, 1826–Dec. 29, 1909. Vol. 10, Pt. 2–650
Zeuner, Charles, Sept. 20, 1795–Nov. 7, 1857. Vol. 10, Pt. 2–651
Zevin, Israel Joseph, Jan. 31, 1872–Oct. 6, 1926. Vol. 10, Pt. 2–652
Ziegemeier, Henry Joseph, Mar. 27, 1869–Oct. 15, 1930. Vol. 10, Pt. 2–653
Ziegfeld, Florenz, Mar. 21, 1869–July 22, 1932. Vol. 10, Pt. 2–653
Ziegler, David, 1748–Sept. 24, 1811. Vol. 10, Pt. 2–654
Ziegler, William, Sept. 1, 1843–May 24, 1905. Vol. 10, Pt. 2–655
Ziehn, Bernhard, Jan. 20, 1845–Sept. 8, 1912. Vol. 10, Pt. 2–656
Ziff, William Bernard, Aug. 1, 1898–Dec. 20, 1953. Supp. 5–760
Zilboorg, Gregory, Dec. 25, 1890–Sept. 17, 1959. Supp. 6–724
Zimmerman, Eugene, Dec. 17, 1845–Dec. 20, 1914. Vol. 10, Pt. 2–657
Zimmerman, Eugene, May 25, 1862–Mar. 26, 1935. Supp. 1–718
Zimmerman, Henry ("Heinie"), Feb. 10, 1886–Mar. 14, 1969. Supp. 8–712
Zinsser, Hans, Nov. 17, 1878–Sept. 4, 1940. Supp. 2–744
Zinzendorf, Nicolaus Ludwig, May 26, 1700–May 9, 1760. Vol. 10, Pt. 2–657
Znaniecki, Florian Witold, Jan. 15, 1882–Mar. 23, 1958. Supp. 6–725
Zogbaum, Rufus Fairchild, Aug. 28, 1849–Oct. 22, 1925. Vol. 10, Pt. 2–658
Zollars, Ely Vaughan, Sept. 19, 1847–Feb. 10, 1916. Vol. 10, Pt. 2–659
Zollicoffer, Felix Kirk, May 19, 1812–Jan. 19, 1862. Vol. 10, Pt. 2–659
Zook, George Frederick, Apr. 22, 1885–Aug. 17, 1951. Supp. 5–761
Zorach, William, Feb. 28, 1889–Nov. 15, 1966. Supp. 8–714
Zubly, John Joachim, Aug. 27, 1724–July 23, 1781. Vol. 10, Pt. 2–660

Zukofsky, Louis, Jan. 23, 1904–May 12, 1978.
Supp. 10–869
Zukor, Adolph, Jan. 7, 1873–June 10, 1976.
Supp. 10–870
Zunser, Eliakum, Oct. 28, 1836–Sept. 22, 1913.
Vol. 10, Pt. 2–661
Zuppke, Robert Carl, July 2, 1879–Dec. 22, 1957.
Supp. 6–727
Zwicky, Fritz, Feb. 14, 1898–Feb. 8, 1974.
Supp. 9–901

CONTRIBUTORS WITH SUBJECTS

The names in capitals are the contributors—the names listed below are the subjects of their contributions.

ABBAZIA, PATRICK
Ingram, Jonas Howard
ABBEY, KATHRYN T.
Law, Evander McIvor
ABBOT, CHARLES G.
Herring, Augustus Moore
Langley, Samuel Pierpont
Manly, Charles Matthews
Newcomb, Simon
ABBOT, WILIS J.
Nixon, William Penn
ABBOTT, CHARLES DAVID
Piatt, Donn
Pyle, Howard
Townsend, George Alfred
ABBOTT, CRAIG
Jackson, Charles Reginald
Motley, Willard Francis
ABBOTT, EDITH
Lathrop, Julia Clifford
ABBOTT, LAWRENCE F.
Kennan, George
ABBOTT, MATHER A.
Mackenzie, James Cameron
ABBOTT, WILBUR CORTEZ
Adams, George Burton
Scott, John
ABEL, THEODORE
Znaniecki, Florian Witold
ABELL, A. I.
Callahan, Patrick Henry
ABELSON, PHILIP H.
Fleming, John Adam
ABERNETHY, THOMAS P.
Bruce, Philip Alexander
Cloud, Noah Bartlett
Collier, Henry Walkins
Dibrell, George Gibbs
Donelson, Andrew Jackson
Eaton, John Henry
Evans, Henry Clay
Gordon, George Washington
Grundy, Felix
Jackson, Andrew
Johnson, James
Johnson, Richard Mentor
Lewis, William Berkeley
Mason, Stevens Thomson
Moore, Gabriel
Nicholas, George
Nicholas, John
Nicholas, Philip Norborne
Nicholas, Robert Carter
Nicholas, Wilson Cary
O'Neale, Margaret
Overton, John
Pendleton, Edmund
Pettus, Edmund Winston
Pickens, Israel
Pierpont, Francis Harrison
Pleasants, James
Pleasants, John Hampden
Randolph, Sarah Nicholas
Randolph, Thomas Jefferson
Randolph, Thomas Mann
Rives, William Cabell
Roane, Archibald
Robertson, Wyndham
Robinson, John
Stevenson, Andrew
Stuart, Alexander Hugh Holmes
Tyler, John, 1747–1813
Tyler, John, 1790–1862
Tyler, Robert
Walker, Thomas
Wayne, James Moore
White, Hugh Lawson
Wirt, William
ABRAHAM, EVELYN
Meason, Isaac
ABRAHAMSON, DAVID
Davis, Bernard George
ABRAHAMSON, IRVING
Crothers, Rachel
ABRAMS, LE ROY
Dudley, William Russel
ABRAMS, RICHARD M.
Eastman, Joseph Bartlett
ACHESON, SAM H.
Bailey, Joseph Weldon
Richardson, Willard
ACKERMAN, CARL WILLIAM
Williams, Talcott
ADAMS, ADELINE
Bartlett, Paul Wayland
Bitter, Karl Theodore Francis
Borglum, Solon Hannibal
Boyle, John J.
Brenner, Victor David
Browere, John Henri Isaac
Brown, Henry Kirke
Crawford, Thomas
Dexter, Henry, 1806–1876
Doyle, Alexander
Elwell, Frank Edwin
Ezekiel, Moses Jacob
Frazee, John
Gould, Thomas Ridgeway
Grafly, Charles
Greenough, Horatio
Greenough, Richard Saltonstall
Hart, Joel Tanner
Hartley, Jonathan Scott
Haseltine, James Henry
Hosmer, Harriet Goodhue
Hoxie, Vinnie Ream
Hughes, Robert Ball
Ives, Chauncey Bradley
Jackson, John Adams
Kemeys, Edward
Launitz, Robert Eberhard Schmidt Von Der
MacDonald, James Wilson Alexander
Martiny, Philip
Mead, Larkin Goldsmith
Mears, Helen Farnsworth
Mills, Clark
Milmore, Martin
Mozier, Joseph
Mulligan, Charles J.
O'Donovan, William Rudolf
Palmer, Erastus Dow
Partridge, William Ordway
Potter, Edward Clark
Potter, Louis McClellan
Powers, Hiram
Pratt, Bela Lyon
Quinn, Edmond Thomas
Rimmer, William
Rush, William
Thompson, Launt
Valentine, Edward Virginius
Volk, Leonard Wells
Ward, John Quincy Adams
Warner, Olin Levi
Whitney, Anne
Wright, Patience Lovell
ADAMS, ARTHUR
Pynchon, Thomas Ruggles
Stuart, Isaac William
Wheaton, Nathaniel Sheldon
Williams, John, 1817–1899
ADAMS, FRANKLIN P.
Taylor, Bert Leston
ADAMS, GRAHAM, JR.
Walsh, Francis Patrick
ADAMS, HARRY B.
Brown, Charles Reynolds
ADAMS, JAMES TRUSLOW
Ames, Nathaniel
Belcher, Jonathan
Bernard, Sir Francis
Blackstone, William
Bollan, William
Bradford, Alden
Burnet, William, 1688–1729
Canonicus
Checkley, John
Clarke, Richard
Clarke, Walter
Coffin, John
Colman, Benjamin
Conant, Roger
Cotton, John
Crandall, Prudence
Danforth, Thomas, 1623–1699
Dare, Virginia
Davenport, John
Dawes, William
Deane, Charles
DeBerdt, Dennys
Denning, William
Dexter, Henry Martyn
Dickinson, John
Dorr, Thomas Wilson
Drake, Samuel Gardner
Draper, Margaret Green
Draper, Richard
Dudley, Joseph
Dudley, Thomas
Dummer, Jeremiah, *c.* 1679–1739
Dunster, Henry
Dustin, Hannah

Dyer, Mary
Easton, John
Easton, Nicholas
Eaton, Nathaniel
Eaton, Samuel
Eaton, Theophilus
Eliot, John
Ellis, George Edward
Endecott, John
Everendon, Walter
Faneuil, Peter
Fanning, David
Fanning, Edmund, 1739–1818
Fiske, John, 1842–1901
Frothingham, Richard
Gage, Thomas
Gardiner, Sir Christopher
Gardiner, Lion
Gookin, Daniel
Gorham, Nathaniel
Gorton, Samuel
Green, Francis
Gridley, Jeremiah
Hancock, John, 1736–1793
Hibbins, Ann
Higginson, Francis
Higginson, John
Higginson, Stephen
Hooker, Thomas
Hopkins, Edward
Hutchinson, Anne
Johnson, Samuel
Leverett, John, 1616–1679
Lincoln, Benjamin
Lowell, John, 1743–1802
Massassoit
Maverick, Samuel
Miantonomo
Montgomery, Richard
Morton, Thomas
Norton, John
Oldham, John
Oliver, Andrew
Oliver, Peter
Palfrey, John Gorham
Parkman, Francis
Pepperell, Sir William
Popham, George
Putnam, Israel
Quincy, Josiah
Randolph, Edward
Sewall, Samuel
Shays, Daniel
Shirley, William
Shute, Samuel
Smith, John, 1579–1631
Sullivan, James
Uncas
Vane, Sir Henry
Warren, Joseph
Wheelwright, John
Winsor, Justin
Winthrop, John, 1587–1649
Winthrop, John, 1605–1676
Wise, John
ADAMS, RANDOLPH GREENFIELD
Arnold, Benedict
Clements, William Lawrence
Clinton, James
Conway, Thomas
Gates, Horatio
Gladwin, Henry
Greene, Nathanael
Harrisse, Henry
Lee, Charles, 1731–1782
Pontiac
Sullivan, John
ADAMS, RAYMOND L.
Green, Constance McLaughlin
ADAMS, RAYMOND WILLIAM
Hecker, Isaac Thomas
Hedge, Frederic Henry
Hewit, Augustine Francis
Lathrop, George Parsons
Peabody, Elizabeth Palmer
Ripley, George
Thoreau, Henry David
ADAMS, WALTER S.
Hale, George Ellery
Moody, (Arthur Edson) Blair
ADDISON, DANIEL DULANY
Hobart, John Henry
Huntington, William Reed
Mulford, Elisha
Nash, Henry Sylvester
Perry, William Stevens
ADKINS, NELSON F.
Davis, Oscar King
Inman, John
Irving, John Treat
Lardner, Ringgold Wilmer
McMaster, Guy Humphreys
Morford, Henry
Morris, George Pope
Picton, Thomas
Pond, George Edward
Porter, William Trotter
Ruhl, Arthur Brown
Sands, Robert Charles
Scollard, Clinton
Scoville, Joseph Alfred
Seton, William
Sikes, William Wirt
Sprague, Charles
Stillman, William James
Tuckerman, Henry Theodore
Woodworth, Samuel
ADLER, CYRUS
Dropsie, Moses Aaron
Jacobs, Joseph, 1854–1916
Lesser, Isaac
Malter, Henry
Margalis, Max Leopold
Morais, Sabato
Schechter, Solomon
Schiff, Jacob Henry
Sulzberger, Mayer
AGAR, HERBERT
Bingham, Robert Worth
AGARD, W. R.
Showerman, Grant
AGGER, EUGENE E.
Gilbert, Seymour Parker
Vanderlip, Frank Arthur
AHLSTROM, SYDNEY E.
Peabody, Francis Greenwood
AITKEN, HUGH G. J.
Crozier, William
AKERS, CHARLES W.
McMillin Alvin Nugent ("Bo")
AKIN, WILLIAM E.
Rautenstrauch, Walter
ALBERTSON, DEAN
Wickard, Claude Raymond
ALBION, ROBERT G.
Barker, Josiah
Bayard, William
Bell, Jacob
Bertram, John
Boyle, Thomas
Buchanan, Thomas
Chever, James W.
Cobb, Elijah
Collins, Edward Knight
Creesy, Josiah Perkins
Crowninshield, George
Earle, Ralph
Fanning, Edmund
Fanning, Nathaniel
Fish, Preserved
Forbes, Robert Bennet
Gardner, Caleb
Gibbons, Thomas
Grace, William Russell
Green, John Cleve
Green, Nathan
Griffiths, John Willis
Hall, Samuel, 1800–1870
Howland, Gardiner Greene
Jumel, Stephen
Knight, Edward Collings
Laurens, Henry
Law, George
McAllister, Charles Albert
Marshall, Charles Henry
Merry, William Lawrence
Minturn, Robert Bowne
Morgan, Charles
Munson, Walter David
Ogden, Aaron
Ogden, David Bayard
Olden, Charles Smith
Outerbridge, Eugenius Harvey
Palmer, Nathaniel Brown
Peabody, Joseph
Pintard, John
Pintard, Lewis
Price, Rodman McCamley
Quintard, George William
Roberts, Marshall Owen
Samuels, Samuel
Sands, Comfort
Scarbrough, William
Scudder, Nathaniel
Servoss, Thomas Lowery
Sewall, Arthur
Sewall, Harold Marsh
Sewell, William Joyce
Slocum, Joshua
Smith, Junius
Smith, Richard
Smith, Robert Alexander C.
Southard, Samuel Lewis
Starin, John Henry
Stephens, John Lloyd
Tileston, Thomas
Train, Enoch
Vaughan, Charles
Vernon, William
Ward, James Edward
Webb, William Henry
Westervelt, Jacob Aaron
Wheelwright, William
Williamson, Isaac Halsted
ALBRIGHT, WILLIAM F.
Bliss, Frederick Jones
Merrill, Selah
Paine, John Alsop
Robinson, Edward, 1794–1863

Smith, Eli
Stuart, Moses
ALDEN, CARROLL STORRS
Bailey, Theodorus
Dewey, George
Graham, James Duncan
Kearny, Lawrence
Lamberton, Benjamin Peffer
McCalla, Bowman Hendry
McGiffin, Philo Norton
Niblack, Albert Parker
Perkins, George Hamilton
Roe, Francis Asbury
ALDEN, EDMUND KIMBALL
Alden, Ichabod
Alden, John
Alexander, William
Anderson, George Thomas
Angell, Israel
Antes, Henry
Archer, James J.
Armistead, George
Armstrong, John
Arnold, Jonathan
Asboth, Alexander Sandor
Ashe, John
Ashe, John Baptista
Ashmead, Isaac
Attucks, Crispus
Auchmuty, Robert, d. 1750
Auchmuty, Robert, d. 1788
Auchmuty, Samuel
Avery, Isaac Wheeler
Bache, Benjamin Franklin
Bache, Richard
Bache, Theophylact
Bailey, Ann
Bailey, Anna Warner
Bailey, James Anthony
Bancroft, Edward
Banister, John, 1734–1788
Barber, Francis
Barclay, Thomas
Barnum, Henry A.
Barnwell, John
Barton, William
Bassett, Richard
Batcheller, George Sherman
Bates, John Coalter
Baxter, Henry
Baylor, George
Beall, John Yates
Beatty, John, 1749–1826
Bedford, Gunning, 1742–1797
Bedford, Gunning, 1747–1812
Berry, Hiram Gregory
Boyd, John Parker
Brearly, David
Brooke, Francis Taliaferro
Browne, Thomas
Buford, Abraham, 1749–1833
Cadwalader, John, 1742–1786
Cadwalader, Lambert
Caldwell, David
Caldwell, James
Campbell, William, 1745–1781
Caswell, Richard
Cilley, Joseph
Clarke, Elijah
Cobb, David
Crawford, William
Ewing, James
Frazer, Persifor, 1736–1792
Gansevoort, Peter
Harmar, Josiah
Hayne, Isaac
Hazen, Moses
Herkimer, Nicholas
Howard, John Eager
Ledyard, William
Parker, John
Parker, Josiah
Pierce, William Leigh
Ramsay, Nathaniel
ALDRICH, MICHELE L.
Berry, Edward Wilber
Darton, Nelson Horatio
Foshag, William Frederick
Stetson, Henry Crosby
ALDRICH, RICHARD
Paine, John Knowles
ALEX, WILLIAM
Olmsted, Frederick Law
ALEXANDER, CHARLES C.
Foxx, James Emory
Simmons, William Joseph
Warner, Glenn Scobey ("Pop")
ALFORD, L. P.
Gantt, Henry Laurence
ALGER, JOHN LINCOLN
Greene, Samuel Stillman
Leach, Daniel Dyer
Mowry, William Augustus
ALLARD, DEAN C.
Joy, Charles Turner
ALLBRAY, NEDDA C.
Leibowitz, Samuel Simon
ALLEMANN, ALBERT
Beck, Carl
Bozeman, Nathan
Caldwell, Eugene Wilson
ALLEN, ARTHUR A.
Fuertes, Louis Agassiz
ALLEN, EDWARD ELLIS
Anagnos, Michael
Campbell, Francis Joseph
Churchman, William Henry
Fisher, John Dix
Howe, Samuel Gridley
Smith, Joel West
ALLEN, FORREST C.
Naismith, James
ALLEN, THE REVEREND JACK
Niebuhr, Karl Paul Reinhold ("Reinie")
ALLEN, FREEMAN H.
Merrill, George Edmands
ALLEN, GARDNER W.
Haraden, Jonathan
Hinman, Elisha
Hopkins, John Burroughs
Hull, Isaac
McNeill, Daniel
McNeill, Hector
Maffitt, David
Preble, Edward
Ridgely, Charles Goodwin
Ropes, Joseph
Saltonstall, Dudley
ALLEN, GARLAND E.
Hart, Edwin Bret
ALLEN, HERVEY
Poe, Edgar Allan
ALLEN, HORACE NEWTON
Appenzeller, Henry Gerhard
Harris, Merriman Colbert
Underwood, Horace Grant
ALLEN, HOWARD W.
Poindexter, Miles
ALLEN, MARY BERNARD
Holt, Joseph
ALLEY, ROBERT S.
Gorcey, Leo
ALLIN, LAWRENCE CARROLL
Moscone, George Richard
Summerfield, Arthur Ellsworth
ALLING, ARTHUR N.
Thomson, Samuel
ALLINSON, FRANCIS G.
Gildersleeve, Basil Lanneau
Harkness, Albert
Lincoln, John Larkin
ALLISON, WILLIAM HENRY
Backus, Isaac
Burrage, Henry Sweetser
Cathcart, William
Chase, Irah
Church, Pharcellus
Clarke, John
Clarke, William Newton
Dodge, Ebenezer
Edwards, Morgan
Furman, Richard
Gano, John
Gano, Stephen
Going, Jonathan
Griffith, Benjamin
Hackett, Horatio Balch
Horr, George Edwin
Hovey, Alvah
Jeter, Jeremiah Bell
Johnson, Elias Henry
Judson, Adoniram
Judson, Ann Hasseltine
Judson, Edward
Judson, Sarah Hall Boardman
King, Henry Melville
Kneeland, Abner
Loguen, Jeremain Wesley
Love, Emanuel King
Pendleton, James Madison
Randall, Benjamin
Rhees, Morgan John
Rice, Luther
Smith, Hezekiah
Smith, Samuel Francis
Staughton, William
Stearns, Shubal
Stevens, William Arnold
Stillman, Samuel
Stow, Baron
Strong, Augustus Hopkins
ALLPORT, GORDON W.
Holt, Edwin Bissell
ALMACK, JOHN C.
Swett, John
ALPERN, SARA
Kirchwey, Freda
Meyer, Agnes Elizabeth Ernst
ALTER, DINSMORE
Alter, David
AMACHER, PETER
Coghill, George Ellett
AMBERSON, J. BURNS
Miller, James Alexander
AMBLER, CHARLES HENRY
Atkinson, George Wesley
Boreman, Arthur Ingram

Hunter, Robert Mercer Taliaferro

Amend, Katharine H.
Blitz, Antonio
Boelen, Jacob
Collins, John Anderson
Coney, John
Cooke, Henry David
Cummings, Amos Jay
Cushman, Pauline
Davenport, Ira Erastus
Edwards, John, *c.* 1671–1746
Forepaugh, Adam
Fox, Margaret
Gilbert, Anne Hartley
Gilbert, John Gibbs
Griffing, Josephine Sophie White
Hamlin, William
Harland, Thomas
Hart, James MacDougal
Hart, William
Henry, Edward Lamson
Herrmann, Alexander
Houdini, Harry
Howland, Alfred Cornelius
Hull, John
Hurd, Nathaniel
Palmer, William Henry

Ames, Joseph Sweetman
Alexander, John Henry
Rowland, Henry Augustus

Ames, William E.
Gilmer, Elizabeth Meriwether ("Dorothy Dix")
Post, Emily Price
Revell, Nellie MacAleney
Sokolsky, George Ephraim

Ames, Winslow
Lachaise, Gaston

Amoroso, E. C.
Wislocki, George Bernays

Amsterdam, Gustav G.
Wharton, Thomas Isaac

Anderson, Benjamin M., Jr.
Hepburn, Alonzo Barton

Anderson, Bern
Bristol, Mark Lambert

Anderson, Dave
Cannon, James Thomas

Anderson, David D.
Bromfield, Louis
Cohen, Octavus Roy
Gardner, Erle Stanley
Hillyer, Robert Silliman
Morley, Christopher Darlington
O'Connor, Mary Flannery
Paul, Elliot Harold
Rinehart, Mary Roberts
White, Josh

Anderson, Dice R.
Randolph, Edmund, 1753–1813

Anderson, Frank Maloy
Kendall, Amos

Anderson, George M.
Volck, Adalbert John

Anderson, George Pomeroy
Young, Thomas

Anderson, Harold M.
Mitchell, Edward Page

Anderson, J. Douglas
Geers, Edward Franklin
Johnson, William Ransom

Anderson, Lewis Flint
Hailmann, William Nicholas
Holbrook, Alfred
Lewis, Samuel
Lindley, Jacob
Lord, Asa Dearborn

Anderson, Neal L.
Murphy, Edgar Gardner

Anderson, Oscar E.
Carrier, Willis Haviland

Anderson, Oscar E., Jr.
Goddard, Robert Hutchings

Anderson, Peter J.
Byrd, Richard Evelyn
Smith, Edward Hanson

Anderson, Russell H.
Strawn, Jacob
Studebaker, Clement
Todd, Sereno Edwards
Warder, John Aston
Wing, Joseph Elwyn
Wood, Jethro
Wright, John Stephen

Andrews, Clarence
Robinson, Henry Morton

Andrews, Clarence A.
Aiken, Conrad Potter
Baldwin, Faith
Carr, John Dickson
Clark, Walter Van Tilburg
Colum, Padraic
Gallico, Paul William
Leopold, Nathan Freudenthal, Jr.
Stong, Phil(lip Duffield)
Sutton, William Francis, Jr. ("Willie")

Andrews, James Parkhill
Case, William Scoville

Andrews, J. D.
Ferree, Clarence Errol

Andrews, Wayne
Aldrich, Chester Holmes
Mackay, Clarence Hungerford
Saarinen, Gottlieb Eliel
Trumbauer, Horace

Angell, Patricia Vaughn
Morgan, Julia

Anger, Charles L.
Summerall, Charles Pelot

Angle, Paul M.
Horner, Henry
Lewis, Lloyd Downs
Thompson, William Hale

Anker, Roy M.
Fosdick, Harry Emerson

Annan, Gertrude L.
Polak, John Osborn
Purple, Samuel Smith
Roosa, Daniel Bennett St. John
Shrady, George Frederick
Skene, Alexander Johnston Chalmers
Smith, Stephen
Stevens, Alexander Hodgdon
Thomas, Theodore Gaillard
Thompson, William Gilman
Vander Veer, Albert
Van de Warker, Edward Ely
Wilcox, Reynold Webb
Witthaus, Rudolph August
Wyeth, John Allan

Annunziata, Frank
Bell, Bernard Iddings
Brace, Donald Clifford
Meyer, Frank Straus

Anthony, Katharine
Fuller, Sarah Margaret
Stowe, Harriet Elizabeth Beecher
Willard, Frances Elizabeth
Wright, Frances

Antone, George P.
Getty, George Franklin, II
Jarman, Walton Maxey
Noyes, William Albert, Jr.
Wilson, Charles Edward
Zellerbach, Harold Lionel

Appleton, Marguerite
Partridge, Richard
Ward, Richard
Ward, Samuel, 1725–1776
Ward, Samuel, 1756–1832
Wilbur, Samuel

Appleton, William M.
Janis, Elsie

Appleton, William W.
Adams, Maude
Clark, Bobby
Flynn, Errol Leslie
Gray, Gilda
Hardy, Oliver Norvell
Lawrence, Gertrude
Talmadge, Norma

Arbaugh, George B.
Smith, Joseph

Archer, John
Rudge, William Edwin

Archer, John Clark
Abeel, David
Agnew, Eliza
Ainslie, Peter
Allen, David Oliver
Allen, Young John
Anderson, David Lawrence
Andrews, Lorrin
Ashmore, William
Bassett, James
Bingham, Hiram, 1789–1869
Bingham, Hiram, 1831–1908
Bliss, Daniel
Bliss, Edwin Elisha
Bliss, Edwin Munsell
Bliss, Howard Sweetser
Butler, William, 1818–1899
Chandler, John Scudder
Clough, John Everett
Coan, Titus
Cushing, Josiah Nelson
De Forest, John Kinne Hyde
Dwight, Harrison Gray Otis
Dwight, Henry Otis
Ewing, James Caruthers Rhea
Fletcher, James Cooley
Heyer, John Christian Frederick
Hume, Robert Allen
Jessup, Henry Harris
Jones, John Peter
Kellogg, Samuel Henry
Loewenthal, Isidor
McLeen, Archibold
Mansell, William Albert
Mason, Francis
Mudge, James
Schauffler, William Gottlieb
Spaulding, Levi
Stewart, Robert

Van Allen, Frank
West, Henry Sergeant
Wharton, Greene Lawrence
Wheery, Elwood Morris
Winslow, Miron

Archibald, Raymond Clare
Armstead, George B.
Bowditch, Nathaniel
Byerly, William Elwood
Cajori, Florian
Clark, Charles Hopkins
Peirce, Benjamin
Peirce, Benjamin Osgood
Peirce, James Mills
Story, William Edward
Strong, Theodore
Upton, Winslow
West, Benjamin

Aretakis, Jonathan G.
Athenagoras I
Boyd, Louise Arner
Waters, Ethel

Arey, Leslie B.
Ranson, Stephen Walter

Armour, Robert
Lindsay, Howard

Armour, Robert A.
Miller, Gilbert Heron
Nagel, Conrad

Armstead, George B.
Clark, Charles Hopkins

Armstrong, Edward C.
Elliott, Aaron Marshall
Marden, Charles Carroll

Armstrong, Florence A.
Younger, Maud

Armstrong, Lisa M.
Chase, Ilka

Arnason, H. Harvard
Calder, Alexander Stirling

Arnaud, Leopold
Boring, William Alciphron

Arnon, Daniel I.
Hoagland, Dennis Robert

Arnould, Richard J.
Hormel, George Albert

Aronson, Sidney H.
Lazarsfeld, Paul Felix

Arrington, Leonard J.
Eccles, Marriner Stoddard
Jackling, Daniel Cowan
McKay, David Oman
Smith, George Albert
Smith, Joseph Fielding

Arrowood, Charles F.
Mercer, Charles Fenton
Palmer, Benjamin Morgan

Arvin, Newton
Sill, Edward Rowland

Ashburn, Frank D.
Peabody, Endicott

Ashburn, Percy M.
Dick, Elisha Cullen
Gihon, Albert Leary
Hoff, John Van Rensselaer
Kober, George Martin
Lawson, Thomas
Lovell, Joseph
McCaw, James Brown
McDowell, Ephraim
McGuire, Hunter Holmes
Mann, James
Mitchell, Thomas Duché
Moore, Samuel Preston
Otis, George Alexander
Peck, Charles Howard
Potts, Jonathan
Rauch, John Henry

Ashby, Clifford
Nazimova, Alla

Ashdown, Avery A.
Norris, James Flack

Ashhurst, Astley P. C.
Neill, John
Norris, George Washington
Packard, John Hooker

Ashley, Clifford W.
Macy, Joseph
Morrell, Benjamin

Ashley, Frederick Willlam
Brough, John
Cutter, Charles Ammi
Green, Samuel Swett
Grifiin, Appleton Prentiss Clark
Griswold, William McCrillis
Lowery, Woodbury
Nichols, Charles Lemuel
Watterson, George

Atherton, Lewis E.
Maytag, Frederick Louis

Atkinson, Brooks
Mantle, (Robert) Burns

Atwater, Helen W.
Richardson, Anna Euretta

Atwater, Katharine L.
Richards, Thomas Addison

Atwell, Charles B.
Locy, William Albert

Atwood, Albert W.
Morgan, John Pierpont
Morgan, Junius Spencer

Atwood, John Murray
Cone, Orello

Aub, Joseph C.
Edsall, David Linn

Aubrey, Edwin Ewart
Smith, Gerald Birney

Ault, Warren O.
Newton, Thomas, 1660–1721

Aurand, Harold W., Jr.
Leemans, Alphonse E. ("Tuffy")
Strong, Elmer Kenneth, Jr. ("Ken")

Austin, James B.
Johnston, John

Austin, Mary L.
Calkins, Gary Nathan

Austrian, Robert
Long, Perrin Hamilton

Avery, Glen E.
Black, Douglas MacRae
McCormack, Buren Herbert ("Mac")

Avinoff, A.
Holland, William Jacob

Axford, C. B.
Hayden, Charles

Aydt, Deborah
Hayward, Leland

Ayer, Joseph Cullen
Kemp, James
Kerfoot, John Barrett
Lay, Henry Champlin
Lee, Alfred
Newton, Richard
Newton, Richard Heber
Newton, William Wilberforce
Pilmore, Joseph
Potter, Alonzo
Potter, Eliphalet Nott
Potter, Henry Codman
Potter, Horatio
White, William

Ayres, Samuel Gardiner
Hurlbut, Jesse Lyman
Peck, Jesse Truesdell
Peirce, Bradford Kinney

Babcock, Harold D.
St. John, Charles Edward

Babcock, Kendric C.
Gregory, John Milton

Bach, C. A.
Bailey, Joseph
Baird, Absalom
Barnes, James
Barry, William Farquhar
Grant, Ulysses Simpson

Bachrack, Stanley D.
Kohlberg, Alfred

Back, E. A.
Emerton, James Henry

Bacon, Benjamin Wisner
Abbot, Ezra
Bissell, Edwin Cone
Bouton, Nathaniel
Burr, Enoch Fitch
Curtis, Edward Lewis
Edwards, Jonathan, 1745–1801
Emmons, Nathanael
Fisher, George Park
Hall, Isaac Hollister

Bacon, Elizabeth M.
Pemberton, Israel
Pemberton, James
Pemberton, John
Penington, Edward, 1667–1701
Penington, Edward, 1726–1796

Bacon, Harold M.
Blichfeldt, Hans Frederik

Bacon, Josephine Daskam
Wiggin, Kate Douglas

Bacon, Theodore D.
Abbott, Edward
Albright, Jacob
Bellamy, Joseph
Bradford, Amory Howe
Chadwick, John White
Chapin, Alonzo Bowen
Cook, Flavius Josephus

Bade, William F.
Muir, John

Bader-Borel, Phyllis
Davis, Meyer
Sanders, George
Sheean, James Vincent

Baehr, George
Sachs, Bernard

Bagby, Wesley M.
Rublee, George

Bailey, Edward M.
Norton, John Pitkin

Bailey, Fred A.
Durante, James Francis ("Jimmy")

Bailey, Joy Julian
Jennings, Jonathan

Bailey, Mabel Driscoll
Anderson, Maxwell

BAINTON, ROLAND H.
McGiffert, Arthur Cushman
Mitchell, Jonathan
Mombert, Jacob Isidor
Murdock, James
Walker, Williston
BAIRD, BIL
Sarg, Tony
BAKELESS, JOHN
Bellamy, Edward
Littell, Eliakim
Mabie, Hamilton Wright
Pratt, Richard Henry
Putnam, George Haven
Putnam, George Palmer
Spahr, Charles Barzillai
BAKER, CARLOS H.
Hemingway, Ernest Miller
Very, Jones
Very, Lydia Louisa Ann
BAKER, CHRISTINA H.
Dix, Dorothea Lynde
Gilman, Arthur
Peabody, Josephine Preston
BAKER, FRANK COLLINS
Gould, Augustus Addison
Kennicott, Robert
Sterki, Victor
Stimpson, William
Tryon, George Washington
BAKER, HORACE B.
Green, Jacob
Harshberger, John William
Meigs, James Aitkin
Michaux, André
Michaux, François André
Montgomery, Thomas G. Harrison
Parry, John Stubbs
Parvin, Theophilus
BAKER, JOHN H.
Cortissoz, Royal
Kuhn, Walt
Miller, Kenneth Hayes
Sloan, John French
BAKER, NEWTON B.
Johnson, Tom Loftin
BAKER, PAUL R.
Barnes, Albert Coombs
BAKER, RAY PALMER
Babcock, Washington Irving
Beman, Nathan Sidney Smith
Buck, Leffert Lefferts
Francis, Charles Spencer
Francis, John Morgan
Gardiner, James Terry
Geddes, James
Graff, Frederick
Greene, George Sears, 1837–1922
Griffin, Eugene
Griswold, John Augustus
Guthrie, Alfred
Menocal, Aniceto Garcia
Mills, Hiram Francis
Murphy, John W.
Nason, Henry Bradford
Ricketts, Palmer Chamberlaine
BAKER, RICHARD ALLAN
Anderson, Clinton Presba
BAKER, THERESE DUZINKIEWICZ
Fogarty, Anne Whitney
Norell, Norman
BAKER, WILLIAM J.
Owens, James Cleveland ("Jessie")
BAKER-CROTHERS, HAYES
Archdale, John
Bozman, John Leeds
Bull, William, 1683–1755
Bull, William, 1710–1791
Campbell, Lord William
Johnson, Sir Nathaniel
Johnson, Robert
Lowndes, Rawlins
Lyttelton, William Henry
Middleton, Arthur
Moore, James, d. 1706
West, Joseph
Yeamans, Sir John
BAKEWELL, CHARLES MONTAGUE
Alden, Timothy
Davidson, Thomas
Gardiner, Harry Norman
BALABKINS, NICHOLAS W.
Babson, Roger Ward
BALCH, MARSTON
Wheatley, William
Wood, William Burke
BALDWIN, CHARLES S.
Price, Thomas Randolph
BALDWIN, LELAND D.
Wetzel, Lewis
Ziegler, David
BALL, GORDON
Kerouac, Jack
BALL, WILLIAM W.
Manning, Richard Irvine
BALLAGH, JAMES CURTIS
Bradford, William, 1755–1795
Campbell, Charles
Chavis, John
Chew, Benjamin
Clymer, George
BALLARD, MICHAEL B.
Jackson, Mahalia
BALLARD, TERRY
Angeli, Pier
Hall, Leonard Wood
Renaldo, Duncan
BALLIET, THOMAS M.
Shaw, Edward Richard
BAMBERGER, WERNER
Isbrandtsen, Hans Jeppesen
Luckenbach, J(ohn) Lewis
BANNER, LOIS W.
Helburn, Theresa
BANNISTER, ROBERT C.
Odum, Howard Washington
BANNISTER, ROBERT C., JR.
Baker, Ray Stannard
BANNISTER, TURPIN C.
Mauran, John Lawrence
Mizner, Addison
BANNON, JOHN FRANCIS
Bolton, Herbert Eugene
BARBA, PRESTON A.
Sealsfield, Charles
Strubberg, Friedrich Armand
BARBEAU, ARTHUR E.
Alinsky, Saul David
Davis, Benjamin Oliver, Sr.
Snow, Edgar Parkes
BARBOUR, HENRY G.
Underhill, Franklin Pell
BARCLAY, ALBERT H.
Cook, Robert Johnson
Courtney, Charles Edward
BARCLAY, SHEPARD
Whitehead, Wilbur Cherrier
Work, Milton Cooper
BARCLAY, THOMAS S.
Adams, Ephraim Douglass
Blow, Henry Taylor
Bogy, Lewis Vital
Drake, Charles Daniel
Folk, Joseph Wingate
Gamble, Hamilton Rowan
Hardin, Charles Henry
Hatch, William Henry
Hitchcock, Ethan Allen, 1835–1909
King, Austin Augustus
Linn, Lewis Fields
Lucas, James H.
McBain, Howard Lee
McNeill, John Hanson
Noble, John Willock
Philips, John Finis
Preetorius, Emil
Price, Thomas Lawson
Ralston, William Chapman
Rollins, James Sidney
Rolph, James
Scott, Dred
Scott, William
Sherwood, Thomas Adiel
Shields, George Howell
BARCLAY, WADE CRAWFORD
Oldham, William Fitzjames
BARDEEN, CHARLES RUSSELL
Baxley, Henry Willis
Baynham, William
BARGER, A. CLIFFORD
Porter, William Townsend
BARKER, EUGENE CAMPBELL
Archer, Branch Tanner
Austin, Moses
Austin, Stephen Fuller
BARKER, LEWELLYS F.
McCrae, Thomas
Noguchi, Hideyo
Osler, William
Thayer, William Sydney
BARKER, VIRGIL
Bluemner, Oscar Florians
Frieseke, Frederick Carl
Lawson, Ernest
Tucker, Allen
BARNARD, ELLSWORTH
Willkie, Wendell Lewis
BARNARD, HARRY
Couzens, James
Mack, Julian William
BARNARD, JOHN
Vincent, George Edgar
BARNES, GILBERT H.
Lee, Luther
Lovejoy, Elijah Parish
Lovejoy, Owen
Nelson, David
Stewart, Alvan
Stockton, Thomas Hewlings
Stuart, Charles
Sutherland, La Roy
Torrey, Charles Turner
Weld, Theodore Dwight
Wright, Elizur

BARNES, HOWARD
Eagels, Jeanne
BARNES, JAMES
Thulstrup, Bror Thure
BARNES, VIOLA FLORENCE
Andros, Sir Edmund
Bradstreet, Simon
Glover, John
Greaton, John
Greene, Christopher
Hawley, Gideon, 1727–1807
Hubbard, William
Phips, Sir William
Wharton, Richard
BARNETT, CLARIBEL RUTH
Affleck, Thomas
Browne, Daniel Jay
Butterfield, Kenyon Leech
Capron, Horace
Dodge, Jacob Richards
Dufour, John James
Ellsworth, Henry Leavitt
Flint, Charles Louis
Gaylord, Willis
Goodall, Harvey L.
Johnson, Benjamin Pierce
Johnston, John
Klippart, John Hancock
Knapp, Samuel Asabel
Le Duc, William Gates
Mayo, Mary Anne Bryant
Newton, Isaac, 1800–1867
Oemler, Arminius
Pedder, James
Philips, Martin Wilson
Powell, George Harold
Stockbridge, Horace Edward
Tucker, Luther
Vick, James
Watts, Frederick
Wiley, David
BARNHART, JOHN DONALD
Willey, Waitman Thomas
BARNHART, JOHN H.
Rydberg, Per Axel
Torrey, John
BARNOUW, ADRIAAN J.
Megapolensis, Johannes
Michaelius, Jonas
Minuit, Peter
Selijns, Henricus
Steendam, Jacob
BARON, SALO W.
Bernstein, Herman
BARRETT, HARRY MCWHIRTER
Baker, James Hutchins
Gove, Aaron Estellus
BARRON, DONALD H.
Donaldson, Henry Herbert
BARROWS, ANNA
Lincoln, Mary Johnson Bailey
BARROWS, DAVID P.
Pacheco, Romualdo
BARROWS, HAROLD K.
Fitzgerald, Desmond
Henny, David Christiaan
Kay, Edgar Boyd
Koyl, Charles Herschel
Lundie, John
McNeill, William Gibbs
Sawyer, Walter Howard
Schuyler, James Dix
Shedd, Joel Herbert
Smith, Jonas Waldo
Stearns, Frederic Pike
Storrow, Charles Storer
Vose, George Leonard
Wheeler, William
Whistler, George Washington
Wiley, Andrew Jackson
Worthen, William Ezra
BARROWS, ROBERT G.
Handley, Harold Willis
BARTEE, ALICE FLEETWOOD
Davis, John Warren
BARTEE, WAYNE C.
Donnell, Forrest C.
Hartley, Fred Allen, Jr.
Long, Edward Vaughn
BARTHEL, THOMAS H.
Goslin, Leon Allen ("Goose")
Medwick, Joseph ("Ducky") Michael
Rice, Edgar Charles ("Sam")
BARTHOLD, ALLEN J.
Nancrède, Paul Joseph Guérard de
BARTLETT, CLARENCE
Hale, Edwin Moses
Hempel, Charles Julius
Hering, Constantine
Holcombe, William Henry
Jackson, Mercy Ruggles Bisbe
Janney, Oliver Edward
Neidhard, Charles
Peters, John Charles
Pulte, Joseph Hippolyt
Raue, Charles Gottlieb
Small, Alvan Edmond
Talbot, Israel Tisdale
Thomas, Amos Russell
Van Lennep, William Bird
BARTLETT, HOWARD R.
Penhallow, Samuel
BARTLETT, J. HENRY
Evans, Thomas
BARTLEY, NUMAN V.
Cox, Edward Eugene
BARTON, GEORGE A.
Clay, Albert Tobias
Gordon, George Byron
Harper, Robert Francis
Haupt, Paul
Haynes, John Henry
Hilprecht Herman Volrath
Jastrow, Morris
Müller, Wilhelm Max
Peters, John Punnett
Rogers, Robert William
Ward, William Hayes
BARTOW, STUART
Combs, Earle Bryan
Wright, James Arlington
BARTSCH, PAUL
Holmes, William Henry
Simpson, Charles Torrey
BASS, LAWRENCE W.
Levene, Phoebus Aaron Theodore
BASS, ROBERT DUNCAN
McCord, Louisa Susanna Cheves
McKinley, Carlyle
Moïse, Penina
BASSETT, JOHN SPENCER
Adams, Herbert Baxter
Bryan, William Jennings
BASSETT, T. D. SEYMOUR
Fisher, Dorothea Frances Canfield
Peattie, Donald Culross
BASTERT, RUSSELL H.
Barrett, John
BASTIN, EDSON S.
Penrose, Richard Alexander Fullerton
BATEMAN, ALAN M.
Pirsson, Louis Valentine
BATES, ERNEST SUTHERLAND
Albee, Ernest
Alcott, Amos Bronson
Alden, Henry Mills
Alger, Horatio
Allyn, Robert
Alsop, George
Ament, William Scott
Andrews, John
Andrews, Stephen Pearl
Apes, William
Bacon, Delia Salter
Baldwin, Matthias William
Bascom, John
Bates, Walter
Beasley, Frederick
Beers, Ethel Lynn
Blackwell, Antoinette Louisa Brown
Blavatsky, Helena Petrovna Hahn
Bleecker, Ann Eliza
Blood, Benjamin Paul
Bolton, Sarah Knowles
Booth, Edwin Thomas
Booth, John Wilkes
Booth, Junius Brutus
Bourne, Randolph Silliman
Bowen, Francis
Brace, Charles Loring
Brokmeyer, Henry C.
Brownell, William Crary
Brownson, Orestes Augustus
Buchanan, Joseph Rodes
Cammerhoff, John Christopher
Cartwright, Peter
Carus, Paul
Caruso, Enrico
Considérant, Victor Prosper
Crosby, Ernest Howard
Dowie, John Alexander
Duncan, Isadora
Foster, George Burman
Fowler, Orson Squire
Frederic, Harold
Gayarré, Charles Étienne Arthur
Grierson, Francis
Grimes, James Stanley
Harris, William Torrey
Hedge, Levi
Hickok, Laurens Perseus
Hitchcock, Ethan Allen, 1798–1870
Howison, George Holmes
Judge, William Quan
Lindsay, Nicholas Vachel
Lloyd, Alfred Henry
Miller, Cincinnatus Hiner
Olcott, Henry Steel
Quimby, Phineas Parkhurst
Reed, John, 1887–1920

Riley, Isaac Woodbridge
Russell, Charles Taze
Sherman, Stuart Pratt
Smith, Charles Sprague
Smith, Harry James
Snider, Denton Jaques
Stedman, Edmund Clarence
Stetson, Augusta Emma Simmons
Tingley, Katherine Augusta Westcott
Underwood, Benjamin Franklin
Wenley, Robert Mark
Wiggins, James Henry
Wilder, Alexander
Wilkinson, Jemima
Wilson, William Dexter
Wright, Chauncey

BATES, FRANCES
Newell, Peter Sheaf Hersey

BATTLE, GEORGE GORDON
Osborne, James Walker

BATTLE, WILLIAM JAMES
Fay, Edwin Whitfield

BAUER, G. PHILIP
Mason, John, *c.* 1600–1672
Sassacus
Walderne, Richard
Warren, James
Warren, Mercy Otis

BAUER, LOUIS AGRICOLA
Bache, Alexander Dallas

BAUER, THOMAS J.
Walsh, James Anthony

BAUGH, ALBERT C.
Mackenzie, Robert Shelton
McMichael, Morton
Markoe, Peter

BAUGHIN, WILLIAM A.
Dykstra, Clarence Addison

BAUGHMAN, JAMES L.
Cooper, Gary
Kovacs, Ernie
Luce, Henry Robinson

BAUGHMAN, JAMES P.
Mallory, Clifford Day

BAUR, JOHN I. H.
Grosz, George

BAUR, WILLIAM L.
Rieger, Johann Georg Joseph Anton

BAXANDALL, LEE
Corey, Lewis

BAXTER, ANNETTE K.
Woolley, Mary Emma

BAXTER, GREGORY P.
Richards, Theodore William

BAXTER, WILLIAM T.
Henchman, Daniel
Kilby, Christopher

BAYNE-JONES, STANHOPE
Jordan, Edwin Oakes
Zinsser, Hans

BAYOR, RONALD H.
Crump, Edward Hull

BEACH, ARTHUR GRANDVILLE
Andrews, Israel Ward

BEADLE, GEORGE W.
Morgan, Thomas Hunt

BEALE, HOWARD K.
Kavanagh, Edward
Welles, Gideon

BEAN, JOHN W.
Lombard, Warren Plimpton

BEAN, MALCOLM
Stephenson, Carl

BEAN, WALTON
Ruef, Abraham
Spreckels, Rudolph

BEAN, WILLIAM G.
Lee, George Washington Custis
Letcher, John
McCausland, John
Mason, John Young
O'Ferrall, Charles Triplett
Peyton, John Lewis
Shipp, Scott
Smith, Francis Henney
Tucker, Henry St. George, 1853–1932
Tucker, John Randolph, 1823–1897
Upshur, Abel Parker

BEARD, MARY R.
Maclay, William

BEARDSLEY, WILLIAM A.
Bass, Edward
Beardsley, Eben Edwards
Bowden, John
Brownell, Thomas Church
Burgess, Alexander
Burgess, George
Doolittle, Amos

BEATTY, WILLIAM K.
Bovie, William T.
Drinker, Cecil Kent

BEATY, JOHN O.
Cooke, John Esten

BEAVER, DONALD DEB.
De Forest, Lee

BEAVER, R. PIERCE
Cort, Edwin Charles
McKean, James William
Peabody, Lucy Whitehead
Reed, Mary

BECK, ROBERT W.
Ross, James Delmage McKenzie

BECKER, CARL LOTUS
Adams, Samuel
Franklin, Benjamin, 1706–1790
Hutchinson, Thomas

BECKER, CARL M.
Falk, Maurice
Tytus, John Butler
Verity, George Matthew

BECKER, DOROTHY G.
Morgan, Anne

BECKER, STANLEY L.
Schmidt, Carl Louis August

BECKER, STEPHEN
Field, Marshall, III

BECKHART, BENJAMIN HAGGOTT
Anderson, Benjamin McAlester
Fraser, Leon
Willis, Henry Parker

BECNEL, THOMAS A.
Ellender, Allen Joseph

BEDDIE, JAMES S.
Smith, Jeremiah

BEDE, JEAN-ALBERT
Smith, Horatio Elwin

BEEZLEY, WILLIAM H.
O'Doul, Francis Joseph ("Lefty")
Rucker, George ("Nap")

BEHLAR, PATRICIA A.
Hébert, Felix Edward ("Eddie")
Smith, Howard Worth ("Judge")

BEHRINGER, CLARA M.
Cowl, Jane
Robson, May

BELDEN, CHARLES F. D.
Benton, Josiah Henry
Chamberlain, Mellen

BELL, DANIEL
Vladeck, Baruch Charney

BELLINGER, ALFRED L.
Newell, Edward Theodore

BELLOWS, ROBERT P.
Peabody, Robert Swain

BELLUSH, BERNARD
Winant, John Gilbert

BEMIS, SAMUEL FLAGG
Fuller, Joseph Vincent
Jay, John

BENDER, HAROLD H.
Green, William Henry
Whitney, William Dwight

BENDER, W. J.
Morton, Charles

BENDIXEN, ALFRED
Forbes, Esther
Vorse, Mary Heaton

BENEDICT, H. Y.
Sutton, William Seneca

BENJAMIN, MARCUS
Dall, William Healey
Rathbun, Richard
Rhees, William Jones
Seabury, George John

BENNETT, DAVID H.
Langer, William
Townsend, Francis Everett

BENNETT, EDWARD
Grew, Joseph Clark

BENNETT, ORVAL
Niedringhaus, Frederick Gottlieb
Orthwein, Charles F.

BENNETT, WELLS
Blodget, Samuel

BENSON, ADOLPH B.
Henningsen, Charles Frederick
Morton, John
Poulson, Niels
Reeves, Arthur Middleton

BENSON, C. C.
Johnston, Albert Sidney
Ord, Edward Otho Cresap
Osterhaus, Peter Joseph
Parke, John Grubb
Pemberton, John Clifford
Phisterer, Frederick
Pickett, George Edward
Pleasonton, Alfred
Potter, Robert Brown
Reynolds, John Fulton
Schriver, Edmund
Shelby, Joseph Orville

BENSON, JACKSON J.
Steinbeck, John Ernst, Jr.

BENSON, JANE A.
Breckinridge, Aida de Acosta
Dingman, Mary Agnes
Williams, Harrison Charles

BENTINCK-SMITH, WILLIAM
Greene, Jerome Davis
BENTON, ELBERT JAY
Barber, Ohio Columbus
Brinkerhoff, Jacob
Brinkerhoff, Roeliff
Brown, Alexander Ephraim
Burke, Stevenson
Burton, Theodore Elijah
Case, Leonard, 1786–1864
Case, Leonard, 1820–1880
Cleaveland, Moses
Cowles, Edwin
Delano, Columbus
Devereux, John Henry
Eells, Dan Parmelee
Giddings, Joshua Reed
Grasselli, Caesar Augustin
Hinman, George Wheeler
Hinsdale, Burke Aaron
Holden, Liberty Emery
Johnson, Levi
Johnston, Seth Whitmore
Kelley, Alfred
Mather, Samuel
Mather, Samuel Holmes
Mather, Samuel Livingston
Ranney, Rufus Percival
Severance, Louis Henry
Stone, Amasa
Wade, Jeptha Homer
BERDAHL, CLARENCE
Garner, James Wilford
BERDAN, JOHN M.
Beers, Henry Augustin
BERGER, JEANNETTE L.
Young, John Russell
BERGMAN, J. PETER
Arnold, Edward
BERKELEY, FRANCIS L., JR.
Smith, Thomas Adams
BERKIN, CAROL R.
Auchincloss, Hugh Dudley, Jr.
Battle, John Stewart
Pulitzer, Margaret Leech
Vidor, Florence
BERMAN, HYMAN
Price, George Moses
BERNER, ROBERT L.
Abrams, Creighton Williams, Jr.
Bemelmans, Ludwig
Cooke, Samuel
Ferber, Edna Jessica
Kresge, Sebastian Spering
May, Morton Jay
Mayer, Oscar Gottfried
Sandoz, Mari
BERNSTEIN, ALISON
Madigan, Laverne
BERNSTEIN, DAVID
Crawford, Samuel Earl
Dressen, Charles Walter
Fleischer, Nathaniel Stanley ("Nat")
Harridge, William ("Will")
Hartnett, Charles Leo ("Gabby")
Kinter, Robert Edmonds
McKechnie, William Boyd
Schalk, Raymond William ("Cracker")
Sisler, George Harold ("Gorgeous George")
BERNSTEIN, ELDON
Gaisman, Henry Jaques
Hood, Clifford Firoved
Hughes, Albert William
Mortimer, Charles Greenough
Rosenstein, Nettie Rosencrans
BERRY, EDWARD W.
White, David
BERRY, LEMUEL
Taylor, Theodore Roosevelt ("Hound Dog")
BERRY, LEMUEL, JR.
Prima, Luigi ("Louis")
BERRY, S. STILLMAN
Stearns, Robert Edwards Carter
BERRYMAN, JACK W.
Hoppe, William Frederick ("Willie")
Jones, Benjamin Allyn
McCarthy, Charles Louis (Clem)
Mallory, Anna Margrethe ("Molla") Bjurstedt
Travers, Jerome Dunstan
BERTOCCI, PETER A.
Brightman, Edgar Sheffield
BETTEN, FRANCIS S.
Behrens, Henry
BETTS, JOHN R.
Hitchcock, Thomas
McGrath, Matthew J.
BETTS, THOMAS JEFFRIES
Wheeler, Joseph
Wood, Leonard
BEWER, JULIUS AUGUST
Smith, Henry Preserved
BEYER, RICHARD L.
Hunter, Robert
BEYERCHEN, ALAN
Franck, James
BEZILLA, MICHAEL
Clement, Martin Withington
Symes, James Miller
BEZOU, HENRY C.
Rummel, Joseph Francis
BICKEL, ALEXANDER M.
Van Devanter, Willis
BIDDLE, GEORGE
Borie, Adolphe
BIDWELL, PERCY W.
Callender, Guy Stevens
Emery, Henry Crosby
Holls, George Frederick William
Hourwich, Isaac Aaronovich
Jenks, Jeremiah Whipple
Leach, Shepherd
Lee, Henry, 1782–1867
Longley, Alcander
Luther, Seth
McFadden, Louis Thomas
McPherson, Logan Grant
Masquerier, Lewis
Maxwell, Hugh
Moore, Ely
Moss, Frank
Nordhoff, Charles
North, Simon Newton Dexter
Noyes, John Humphrey
Parsons, Frank
Pitkin, Timothy
Plant, Henry Bradley
Porter, Robert Percival
Stilwell, Silas Moore
Wilkeson, Samuel
BIEBER, RALPH PAUL
Bain, George Luke Scobie
Brannan, Samuel
BIEDER, ROBERT E.
Cohen, Felix Solomon
BIERLEY, PAUL E.
Pryor, Arthur W.
BIGELOW, BRUCE M.
Lopez, Aaron
BIGELOW, GORDON E.
Rawlings, Marjorie Kinnan
BILLARD, F. C.
Kimball, Sumner Increase
BILLINGTON, MONROE
Barrows, Alice Prentice
Gore, Thomas Pryor
Smith, Lucy Harth
BILSTEIN, ROGER E.
Buckley, Oliver Ellsworth
Howard, Henry
Schroeder, Rudolph William
Warner, Edward Pearson
BING, FRANKLIN C.
Lining, John
BINGHAM, EUGENE C.
Hart, Edward
BINGHAM, WOODBRIDGE
Williams, Edward Thomas
BINING, ARTHUR C.
McKinley, Albert Edward
BINKLEY, WILLIAM C.
Porter, James Davis
Stahlman, Edward Bushrod
Taylor, Alfred Alexander
Taylor, Robert Love
Thomas, John Wilson
Turney, Peter
BIRCH, FRANCIS
Daly, Reginald Aldworth
BIRNBAUM, GEORGE PHILIP
Arliss, George
Cohan, George Michael
Errol, Leon
Greenstreet, Sydney Hughes
Lord, Pauline
Skinner, Otis
Youmans, Vincent Millie
BIRR, KENDALL
Emmet, William Le Roy
Gherardi, Bancroft
Hill, Ernest Rowland
Kent, Arthur Atwater
BLACK, J. WILLIAM
Potter, Platt
BLACKBURN, GLEN A.
Tipton, John
BLACKMAR, FRANK WILSON
Anderson, John Alexander
Anthony, George Tobey
BLACKMER, ALAN ROGERS
Morrill, Justin Smith
Quincy, Edmund
Quincy, Josiah Phillips
BLACKORBY, EDWARD C.
Burdick, Usher Lloyd
Lemke, William Frederick
BLACKWELL, ROBERT EMORY
Smith, William Andrew
BLAKE, JOHN B.
Snow, William Freeman

Blake, Marion E.
Van Deman, Esther Boise
Blakeslee, George H.
Dennis, Alfred Lewis Pinneo
Blanchard, Arthur A.
Mulliken, Samuel Parsons
Talbot, Henry Paul
Blanchard, Edith R.
Garvin, Lucius Fayette Clark
Harris, Caleb Fiske
Hopkins, Esek
Hoppin, William Warner
Howell, David
Hunter, William
Jenckes, Joseph, 1632–1717
Jenckes, Joseph, 1656–1740
Jenks, Joseph
Lippitt, Henry
Potter, Elisha Reynolds
Redwood, Abraham
Smith, James Youngs
Sprague, William, 1830–1915
Stiness, John Henry
Updike, Daniel
Blanton, Wyndham B.
Smith, John Augustine
Tennent, John
Blantz, Thomas E.
Dooley, Thomas Anthony, III
Glennon, John Joseph
Haas, Francis Joseph
Stritch, Samuel Alphonsus
Blashfield, Edwin Howland
Alexander, John White
Blaut, Julia
Rothko, Mark
Blegen, Theodore C.
Andrews, Christopher Columbus
Baker, James Heaton
Bottineau, Pierre
Flandrau, Charles Eugene
Haugen, Nils Pederson
McLeod, Martin
Peerson, Cleng
Reierson, Johan Reinert
Rynning, Ole
Schall, Thomas David
Williams, John Fletcher
Blesh, Rudi
Harney, Benjamin Robertson
Blessing, Arthur R.
Cochrane, Henry Clay
Dyer, Nehemiah Mayo
Evans, Robley Dunglison
Gridley, Charles Vernon
Hamblin, Joseph Eldridge
Herndon, William Lewis
Hichborn, Philip
Loring, Charles Harding
Luce, Stephen Bleecker
Bleyer, Williard Grosvenor
Hale, David
Hallock, Charles
Hallock, Gerard
Peck, George Wilbur
Ralph, Julian
Rublee, Horace
Scripps, Edward Wyllis
Scripps, James Edmund
Smith, William Henry, 1833–1896
Storey, Wilbur Fisk
Tousey, Sinclair
Bliss, Gilbert A.
Moore, Eliakim Hastings
Bliss, John Alden
Doherty, Henry Latham
Mitchell, Sidney Zollicoffer
Bliven, Bruce
Straight, Willard Dickerman
Blodget, Louise Pearson
Linderman, Henry Richard
Park, James
Pitcairn, John
Russell, Lillian
Spencer, Samuel
Walsh, Thomas James
Blodgett, Geoffrey
Churchill, Winston
Hughes, Charles Evans
Moses, George Higgins
Tarbell, Ida Minerva
Bloom, Lansing B.
Larrazolo, Octaviano Ambrosio
Peralta, Pedro de
Rhodes, Eugene Manlove
Seligman, Arthur
Springer, Charles
Bloomfield, Maxwell H.
Day, George Parmly
Doran, George Henry
Golden, John
Guinzburg, Harold Kleinert
Knapp, Joseph Palmer
Odell, George Clinton Densmore
Scribner, Charles
Simon, Richard Leo
Blotner, Joseph
Faulkner (Falkner), William Cuthbert
Blue, George Verne
Robinson, Christopher
Root, Joseph Pomeroy
Scruggs, William Lindsay
Blum, Joe
Wills, James Robert ("Bob")
Blum, John Morton
Burleson, Albert Sidney
Morgenthau, Henry, Jr.
Tumulty, Joseph Patrick
Blum, Joseph
Mercer, John Herndon ("Johnny")
Blumenson, Martin
Patton, George Smith
Walker, Walton Harris
Blumer, G. Alder
Beard, George Miller
Beck, John Brodhead
Gallup, Joseph Adams
Holyoke, Edward Augustus
King, Dan
Ordronaux, John
Parsons, Usher
Ray, Isaac
Blumer, George
Barton, Benjamin Smith
Beck, Theodric Romeyn
Bell, Luther Vose
Brill, Nathan Edwin
Brown, William
Byrne, John
Cohen, Jacob da Silva Solis
Edebohls, George Michael
Emmet, Thomas Addis, 1828–1919
Boardman, Roger S.
Altman, Benjamin
Bailey, Gamaliel
Bailey, James Montgomery
Baldwin, John Denison
Ballou, Adin
Barnard, Charles Francis
Buffum, Arnold
Chace, Elizabeth Buffum
Colman, Lucy Newhall
Cox, Hannah Peirce
Boas, R. P.
Huntington, Edward Vermilye
Boatfield, Helen C.
Child, Robert
Fletcher, Benjamin
Hare, Robert
Hazen, Moses
Nolan, Philip
Noyan, Gilles-Augustin Payen de
Noyan, Pierre-Jacques Payen de
Radisson, Pierre Esprit
Stuart, Francis Lee
Walsh, Michael
Weed, Thurlow
Bochner, Salomon
Bateman, Harry
Weyl, Hermann
Bodayla, Stephen D.
Bliss, Robert Woods
Brooks, Overton
Brown, Clarence James
Cochrane, Gordon Stanley ("Mickey")
Cummings, Walter Joseph
Davis, Francis Breese, Jr.
Downey, Sheridan
Ford, Hannibal Choate
Goddard, Calvin Hooker
Hupp, Louis Gorham
Hutton, Edward Francis
Lasser, Jacob Kay
Lehman, Robert
Mead, James Michael
Murchison, Clinton Williams
Robinson, Claude Everett
Speaker, Tris E.
Stanley, Harold
Warburg, James Paul
Ward, Charles Alfred
Boddington, Ernest F.
Corcoran, James Andrew
Egan, Michael
Farmer, Ferdinand
Bode, Carl
Thorpe, Rose Alnora Hartwick
Bodian, David
Hoerr, Normand Louis
Bogart, Ernest Ludlow
Harahan, James Theodore
Harding, Abner Clark
Jewett, Hugh Judge
Joy, James Frederick
Matteson, Joel Aldrich
Oakes, Thomas Fletcher
Ogden, William Butler
Payne, Henry Clay
Perkins, Charles Elliott
Plumb, Glenn Edward
Stickney, Alpheus Beede
Traylor, Melvin Alvah

BOGUE, ALLAN G.
Gregory, Clifford Verne
BOHJALIAN, ANDREW
Barton, Bruce Fairchild
BOLANDER, LOUIS H.
Corbin, Henry Clark
Heintzelman, Stuart
McCawley, Charles Laurie
Morton, Charles Gould
Muir, Charles Henry
Read, George Windle
Reynolds, William
Rhind, Alexander Colden
Robertson, Ashley Herman
Russell, John Henry
Schenck, James Findlay
Schroeder, Seaton
Selfridge, Thomas Oliver
Sigsbee, Charles Dwight
Snowden, Thomas
Steedman, Charles
Strain, Isaac G.
Stringham, Silas Horton
Strong, James Hooker
Townsend, Robert
Trenchard, Stephen Decatur
Usher, Nathaniel Reilly
Voorhees, Philip Falkerson
Walker, Asa
Ward, James Harmon
Weaver, Aaron Ward
Welles, Roger
Wickes, Lambert
Wyman, Robert Harris
BOLT, JOSEPH S.
Nadelman, Elie
BOLT, JOSEPH SULLIVAN
Flannagan, John Bernard
BOLTON, CHARLES K.
Howe, Mark Anthony De Wolfe
Jewett, Clarence Frederick
Montgomery, David Henry
Poole, Fitch
Rindge, Frederick Hastings
Shaw, William Smith
Shurtleff, Nathaniel Bradstreet
Thornton, John Wingate
Tudor, William
Whipple, Edwin Percy
Whitmore, William Henry
Widener, Harry Elkins
Winthrop, Robert Charles
Young, Alexander
BOLTON, ETHEL STANWOOD
Topliff, Samuel
Tuckerman, Joseph
BOLTON, HERBERT EUGENE
Cabrillo, Juan Rodriguez
Cárdenas, García Lópéz de
Coronada, Francisco Vázquez
Crespi, Juan
De Mézières Y Chigny, Athanase
Kino, Eusebio Francisco
Palóu, Francisco
BOLTON, LAETITIA TODD
Dickinson, Anson
BOLTON, THEODORE
Alexander, Francis
Ames, Ezra
Ames, Joseph Alexander
Armstrong, David Maitland
Baker, George Augustus
Beard, James Carter
Beard, James Henry
Beard, William Holbrook
Bellows, George Wesley
Bounetheau, Henry Brintnell
BOLWELL, ROBERT W.
King, Edward Smith
Lawson, James
Lennox, Charlotte Ramsay
MacDowell, Katherine Sherwood Bonner
McGovern, John
Magruder, Julia
Parker, Jane Marsh
Pike, Mary Hayden Green
Prentiss, Elizabeth Payson
Reid, Thomas Mayne
Searing, Laura Catherine Redden
Shreve, Thomas Hopkins
Smith, Elizabeth Oakes Prince
Southworth, Emma Dorothy Eliza Nevitte
Stratemeyer, Edward
BOND, BEVERLEY W., JR.
Andrews, Sherlock James
Burnet, Jacob
Putnam, Rufus
Symmes, John Cleves
BOND, EARLE D.
Kirkbride, Thomas Story
BOND, W. H.
Jackson, William Alexander
BONHAM, MILLEDGE LOUIS
Brant, Joseph
Cambreleng, Churchill Caldom
Conkling, Alfred
Dickinson, Daniel Stevens
Dorsheimer, William Edward
Duryée, Abram
Dwight, William
Morgan, George Washington
Morgan, James Morris
BONSAL, STEPHEN
Bowen, Herbert Wolcott
Calhoun, William James
BOOKER, JOHN MANNING
Greenlaw, Edwin Almiron
BORCHARD, EDWIN M.
Penfield, William Lawrence
BORING, WILLIAM A.
Hamlin, Alfred Dwight Foster
BORIS, EILEEN C.
Scudder, (Julia) Vida Dutton
BORNEMANN, ALFRED
Laughlin, James Laurence
BOROME, JOSEPH A.
Bostwick, Arthur Elmore
Utley, George Burwell
BOSHA, FRANCIS J.
Chatterton, Ruth
Hardwicke, Cedric Webster
BOSTON, LEONARD NAPOLEON
Maury, Francis Fontaine
BOSTWICK, ARTHUR E.
Ives, Halsey Cooley
BOSWELL, WILLIAM E.
Moore, Grace
Samaroff, Olga
BOTEIN, STEPHEN
Crane, Frederick Evan
Cromwell, William Nelson
Hiscock, Frank Harris
Lewis, William Draper
Wigmore, John Henry
BOURNE, HENRY E.
Putnam, Ruth
Tuttle, Herbert
BOUTON, ARCHIBALD LEWIS
Cannon, Charles James
Clinch, Charles Powell
Cook, Martha Elizabeth Duncan Walker
Coombe, Thomas
Cozzens, Frederick Swartwout
Drake, Joseph Rodman
Janvier, Catharine Ann
Janvier, Thomas Allibone
Kimball, Richard Burleigh
McLellan, Isaac
Mayo, William Starbuck
BOVEY, SETH
Short, Luke
BOWDEN, WITT
Boies, Henry Martyn
Borie, Adolph Edward
Buckalew, Charles Rollin
Dickson, Thomas
Disston, Henry
Dolan, Thomas
Drexel, Anthony Joseph
Drexel, Francis Martin
Drexel, Joseph William
Hartranft, John Frederick
Hays, Alexander
Hopkinson, Joseph
Hoyt, Henry Martyn
Ingersoll, Charles Jared
Ingersoll, Jared, 1749–1822
Lewis, Lawrence
McKennan, Thomas McKean Thompson
Mercur, Ulysses
Mitchell, James Tyndale
Ward, Cyrenus Osborne
Wilson, William Bauchop
BOWERMAN, GEORGE F.
Noyes, Crosby Stuart
BOWERMAN, SARAH G.
Banister, Zilpah Polly Grant
Banvard, John
Banvard, Joseph
Barrett, Kate Waller
Bartlett, John
Bloede, Gertrude
Bouvet, Marie Marguerite
Bristed, Charles Astor
Bristed, John
Brockett, Linus Pierpont
Brooks, Elbridge Streeter
Brooks, James Gordon
Brown, Charlotte Emerson
Bulfinch, Thomas
Burleigh, William Henry
Burnham, Clara Louise Root
Burt, Mary Elizabeth
Carpenter, Frank George
Chandler, Elizabeth Margaret
Cheney, Ednah Dow Littlehale
Chesebrough, Caroline
Clarke, Rebecca Sophia
Clemmer, Mary
Cooke, Rose Terry
Cornwallis, Kinaban
Cratty, Mabel
Cummins, Maria Susanna
Cutter, George Washington
Dahlgren, Sarah Madeline Vinton

Darling, Flora Adams
Dodge, Grace Hoadley
Dodge, Mary Elizabeth Mapes
Elder, Susan Blanchard
Ellet, Elizabeth Fries Lummis
Finley, Martha Farquharson
Foster, Hannah Webster
French, Lucy Virginia Smith
Gardener, Helen Hamilton
Habberton, John
Hale, Lucretia Peabody
Hall, Florence Marion Howe
Harris, Miriam Coles
Harrison, Constance Cary
Holmes, Mary Jane Hawes
Howard, Blanche Willis
Janvier, Margaret Thomson
Jenks, Tudor Storrs
Johnson, Helen Louise Kendrick
Johnson, Virginia Wales
Jordan, Kate
Judson, Emily Chubbuck
Kelly, Myra
Lathbury, Mary Artemisia
Latimer, Mary Elizabeth Wormeley
Leslie, Eliza
Lewis, Estelle Anna Blanche Robinson
Lippincott, Sara Jane Clarke
McCutcheon, George Barr
Milburn, William Henry
Miller, Emily Clarke Huntington
Miller, Harriet Mann
Miner, Myrtilla
Morley, Margaret Warner
Moulton, Ellen Louise Chandler
Norris, Mary Harriott
Norton, Mary Alice Peloubet
Parton, Sara Payson Willis
Perry, Nora
Piatt, John James
Piatt, Sara Morgan Bryan
Powell, William Bramwell
Pratt, Eliza Anna Farman
Preston, Harriet Waters
Prud'homme, John Francis Eugene
Richards, Zalmon
Rollins, Alice Marland Wellington
Sangster, Margaret Elizabeth Munson
Seawell, Molly Elliot
Sherwood, Mary Elizabeth Wilson
Tiernan, Frances Christine Fisher
Wilkins, William
Wormley, Katharine Prescott

BOWERS, CLAUDE G.
Coleman, William
Duane, William

BOWIE, THEODORE
Warner, Langdon

BOWIE, WALTER RUSSELL
Meigs, John
Norwood, Robert Winkworth

BOWLERS, CLAUDE G.
Coleman, William
Duane, William

BOWMAN, F. E.
McLellan, Isaac

BOYD, BRIAN
Nabokov, Vladimir Vladimirovich

BOYD, CATHERINE E.
Taylor, Henry Osborn

BOYD, CHARLES N.
Archer, Frederic
Bergmann, Carl
Blodgett, Benjamin Colman
Bristow, George Frederick

BOYD, JULIAN P.
Maclay, Samuel
Murray, Louise Shipman Welles
Oliver, Paul Ambrose
Palmer, Henry Wilbur
Sergeant, John, 1779–1852
Sergeant, Jonathan Dickinson
Sergeant, Thomas
Sherman, Roger
Smith, Melancton, 1744–1798
Spencer, Ambrose
Stone, William Leete
Wilson, James
Wright, Hendrick Bradley

BOYD, LYLE G.
Richards, Laura Elizabeth Howe
Smith, David Eugene

BOYD, WILLIAM KENNETH
Alexander, Abraham
Bassett, John Spencer
Burke, Thomas, *c.* 1747–1783
Clingman, Thomas Lanier
Craven, Braxton
Ellis, John Willis
Graffenried, Christopher
Lawson, John
Morehead, John Motley
Murphey, Archibald De Bow
Overman, Lee Slater

BOYDEN, E. A.
Jackson, Clarence Martin

BOYDEN, WILLIAM L.
Mackey, Albert Gallatin
Morris, Robert, 1818–1888

BOYER, BLANCHE B.
Beeson, Charles Henry

BOYER, PAUL S.
Buck, Franklyn Howard
Crowninshield, Francis Welch
D'Olier, Franklin
Doubleday, Nelson
Harris, Paul Percy
Hines, Duncan
Holmes, Elias Burton
McGraw, James Herbert
McIntyre, Alfred Robert
Macrae, John
Oldfield, ("Barney") Berna Eli
Sheldon, Charles Monroe
Thaw, Harry Kendall
Towne, Charles Hanson
Woolsey, John Munro

BOYLAN, JAMES
Annenberg, Moses Louis
Dealey, George Bannerman
Gauvreau, Emile Henry
Gunther, John
Hearst, William Randolph
Kaempffiert, Waldemar Bernhard
Koenigsberg, Moses
Lait, Jacquin Leonard (Jack)
Manly, Basil Maxwell
Michelson, Charles
Rice, (Henry) Grantland
Seibold, Louis
Thompson, Dorothy

BOYLE, SHEILA TULLY
Robeson, Paul Leroy

BOYLE, THOMAS
Robinson, Edward G.

BOYLES, MARY
Connelly, Marcus Cook ("Marc")

BOYNTON, PERCY H.
Fuller, Henry Blake
Howard, Bronson Crocker
Hubbard, Elbert
Hutton, Laurence

BRACKETT, JEFFREY R.
Cummings, Edward
Hemenway, Mary Porter Tileston
Johnson, Ellen Cheney

BRADEN, CHARLES S.
Dittemore, John Valentine
Warrington, Albert Powell

BRADFORD, JANET B.
Steiner, Maximilian Raoul Walter ("Max")

BRADLEY, EDWARD SCULLEY
Ireland, Joseph Norton

BRADLEY, MICHAEL R.
Buttrick, George Arthur
Clay, Lucius DuBignon
Hershey, Lewis Blaine
Little, William Lawson, Jr.
McCarthy, Joseph Vincent ("Joe")
McDonald, David John
Meserve, Frederick Hill
Newsom, Herschel David

BRADLEY, WILLIAM JOSEPH
Mercer, Jesse

BRADNER, LEICESTER
Brooke, Charles Frederick Tucker

BRADWAY, JOHN S.
Goldman, Mayer C.

BRANDERIS, HERMAN
Joubert de la Muraille, James Hector Marie Nicholas

BRANDES, JOSEPH
Hoover, Herbert Clark
Hoover, Herbert William

BRANDT, ALLAN M.
Doull, James Angus
Gasser, Herbert Spencer
Kenyon, Josephine Hemenway

BRANDT, LILIAN
Anderson, Elizabeth Milbank
Baker, Harvey Humphrey

BRASCH, FREDERICK EDWARD
Alexander, Stephen
Winthrop, John

BRAUER, JERALD C.
Case, Shirley Jackson

BRAUER, KINLEY J.
Wilson, George Grafton

BRAUGH, PAT
Halsman, Philippe

BRAUN, WILLIAM A.
Thomas, Calvin

BRAVERMAN, SAUL
Hofmann, Josef Casimir
Kreisler, Fritz

BRAWLEY, BENJAMIN
Bell, James Madison
Cary, Lott
Cuffe, Paul
Delany, Martin Robinson
Dunbar, Paul Laurence
Forten, James
Hammon, Jupiter
Henson, Josiah
Holly, James Theodore
Holsey, Lucius Henry
Hood, James Walker
BREBNER, J. BARTLET
Hansen, Marcus Lee
Vetch, Samuel
BRECK, EDWARD
Abbot, Joel
Allen, William Henry
Aylwin, John Cushing
Badger, Oscar Charles
Bainbridge, William
Barker, Albert Smith
Barney, Joshua
Barron, James
Barry, John
Belknap, George Eugene
Bell, Henry Haywood
Biddle, James
Biddle, Nicholas
Blake, Homer Crane
Blakely, Johnston
Boggs, Charles Stuart
Breck, Samuel
Breese, Kidder Randolp
Bullard, William Hannum Grubb
Burrows, William
Caldwell, Charles Henry Bromedge
Clark, Charles Edgar
Cushing, William Barker
BRECKENRIDGE, ELIZABETH
Palmer, John McAuley
BRECKINRIDGE, SOPHONISBA P.
Kelley, Florence
BREESKIN, ADELYN D.
Avery, Milton Clark
BREEZLEY, WILLIAM H.
Crosley, Powel, Jr.
BREMNER, ROBERT H.
Abbott, Edith
BRETT, AGNES B.
Ingham, Charles Cromwell
Irving, John Beaufain
Jewett, William
BRETZ, J. HARLEN
Taylor, Frank Bursley
BREWER, HELENE MAXWELL
Pinchot, Amos Richards Eno
BRIAND, PAUL L., JR.
Hall, James Norman
Nordhoff, Charles Bernard
BRIDENBAUGH, CARL
Thatcher, Benjamin Bussey
Tucker, Nathaniel Beverley, 1784–1851
Weiser, Johann Conrad
BRIDENBAUGH, JESSICA HILL
Royall, Anne Newport
Sedgwick, Theodore, 1780–1839
Tenney, Tabitha Gilman
Woolson, Abba Louisa Goold
BRIDGES, ROBERT
Burlingame, Edward Livermore
Williams, Jesse Lynch, 1871–1929
BRIDGEWATER, WILLIAM
Laffite, Jean
Little Turtle
McLeod, Hugh
Navarre, Pierre
You, Dominique
BRIDGMAN, HOWARD ALLEN
Abbot, Lyman
BRIDGMAN, P. W.
Duane, William
Hall, Edwin Herbert
BRIEGER, GERT H.
Kelser, Raymond Alexander
Lewis, Dean De Witt
BRIGGS, GEORGE W.
Buck, Philo Melvin
BRIGGS, JOHN E.
Conger, Edwin Hurd
Hurd, John Codman
Koussevitzky, Serge Alexandrovich
McPherson, Smith
Rorer, David
Seevers, William Henry
Shiras, Oliver Perry
Smith, Walter Inglewood
Wade, Martin Joseph
Wright, George Grover
BRIGGS, LYMAN J.
Burgess, George Kimball
McNair, Fred Walter
BRIGHAM, ALBERT PERRY
Baker, Marcus
BRIGHAM, CLARENCE SAUNDERS
Arthur, William
Barnard, John
Bartlett, John Russell
Evans, Charles
BRIGHAM, HERBERT O.
Bourne, Benjamin
BRILL, A. A.
Kirby, George Hughes
BRINBAUM, GEORGE P.
George, Gladys
BRINCKERHOFF, FRED
Rockwell, Norman Perceval
BRINK, FRANK, JR.
Bronk, Detlev Wulf
BRINKMAN, JOHN A.
Olmstead, Albert Ten Eyck
BRINTON, CRANE
Noailles, Louis Marie, Viscomte de
Paine, Thomas
Robinson, James Harvey
BRISCOE, RUTH LEE
Massey, George Betton
Morris, Caspar
BRITT, ALBERT
Blanchard, Jonathan
BRITTAIN, JAMES E.
Baker, Walter Ransom Gail
Carlson, Chester Floyd
Dumont, Allen Balcom
Hogan, John Vincent Lawless
Jackson, Dugald Caleb
BRITTAIN, JOAN T.
Stallings, Laurence Tucker
BRITTON, W. E.
Jenkins, Edward Hopkins
BROCKETT, PAUL
Sellers, Matthew Bacon
BROCKUNIER, SAMUEL H.
Williams, Roger
BROCKWAY, GEORGE P.
Norton, William Warder
BROCKWAY, JEAN LAMBERT
Malbone, Edward Greene
Peale, Anna Claypoole
Peale, James
Peale, Raphael
Trott, Benjamin
BRODERICK, FRANCIS L.
Ryan, John Augustine
BRODIE, DONALD M.
Crane, Charles Richard
BRODY, DAVID
Boyle, Michael J.
Fitzpatrick, John
Green, William
Hillman, Sidney
Nestor, Agnes
Perkins, Frances
Perlman, Selig
Reuther, Walter Philip
Robins, Margaret Dreier
BROGAN, DENIS W.
Collins, Patrick Andrew
BRONNER, EDWIN B.
Jones, Rufus Matthew
BRONSON, ELSIE M. S.
Hitchcock, Enos
Johnston, Augustus
Jones, William
Kingsbury, John
BRONSON, WALTER COCHRAN
Caswell, Alexis
Child, Lydia Maria Francis
Halleck, Fitz-Greene
Longfellow, Henry Wadsworth
BROOKS, ALFRED G.
Gest, Morris
BROOKS, ALFRED MANSFIELD
Strickland, William
BROOKS, CHANDLER McC.
Bazett, Henry Cuthbert
BROOKS, JOHN
Heineman, Daniel Webster ("Dannie")
BROOKS, ROBERT C.
Penrose, Boies
Sproul, William Cameron
Vare, William Scott
BROOKS, ROBERT PRESTON
Austell, Alfred
Berrien, John Macpherson
Black, Eugene Robert
Brown, Joseph Emerson
Bullock, Rufus Brown
Clayton, Augustin Smith
Clements, Judson Claudius
Cobb, Howell
Cobb, Thomas Reade Rootes
Colquitt, Alfred Holt
Colquitt, Walter Terry
Cook, Philip
Cooper, Mark Anthony
Couper, James Hamilton
Crawford, George Walker
Crawford, Martin Jenkins
Crisp, Charles Frederick

Dawson, William Crosby
Early, Peter
Felton, Rebecca Latimer
Felton, William Harrell
Few, William
Flannery, John
Forsyth, John, 1780–1841
Gartrell, Lucius Jeremiah
Gibbons, William
Gordon, John Brown
Gordon, William Washington
Grant, John Thomas
Habersham, James
Habersham, Joseph
Hall, Lyman
Hammond, Nathaniel Job
Hammond, Samuel
Hardee, William Joseph
Harrison, George Paul
Hawkins, Benjamin
Hill, Joshua
Hill, Walter Barnard
Hillyer, Junius
Houstoun, John
Howley, Richard
Hughes, Dudley Mays
Lawton, Alexander Robert
McCay, Henry Kent
McDaniel, Henry Dickerson
McDonald, Charles James
Smith, Hoke

Brooks, Van Wyck
Melville, Herman

Broughton, T. Robert S.
Frank, Tenney
Marsh, Frank Burr

Brouwer, Dirk
Brown, Ernest William

Brown, Barbara Illingworth
Cori, Gerty Theresa Radnitz

Brown, Charles H.
Hare, James H.

Brown, E. Francis
Hawley, Joseph
Pomeroy, Seth
Williams, Israel
Worthington, John

Brown, Elmer Ellsworth
MacCracken, Henry Mitchell

Brown, Ernest W.
Hill, George William

Brown, Everett S.
Dickinson, Donald McDonald
Ferris, Woodbridge Nathan
Grant, Claudius Buchanan

Brown, F. Craighill
Graves, Frederick Rogers

Brown, Harper
Jamison, Cecilia Viets Dakin Hamilton

Brown, Harry James
Besse, Arthur Lyman
Blodgett, John Wood

Brown, James Douglas
Wyckoff, Walter Augustus

Brown, J. Thompson
Johnson, David Bancroft

Brown, Lawrason
Trudeau, Edward Livingston

Brown, Letitia
Barrett, Janie Porter

Brown, L. Parmly
Brown, Solyman
Fillebrown, Thomas
Garretson, James Edmund
Harris, Chapin Aaron
Hayden, Horace H.
Kingsley, Norman William
McQuillen, John Hugh
Miller, Willoughby Dayton
Parmly, Eleazar
Riggs, John Mankey
White, John De Haven
White, Samuel Stockton

Brown, Margaret Louise
Lyon, Caleb
McCormick, Richard Cunningham
Randall, Robert Richard
Root, Erastus
Whitney, Asa

Brown, Marshall S.
Gillett, Ezra Hall
Gordy, John Pancoast
Henry, Caleb Sprague

Brown, Oswald E.
Lambuth, James William
Lambuth, Walter Russell
McGready, James
McTyeire, Holland Nimmons
Merrill, James Griswold

Brown, Philip M.
Frelinghuysen, Frederick Theodore

Brown, Ralph Adams
Dobie, Gilmour
McLoughlin, Maurice Evans
Thorpe, James Francis
Zaharias, Mildred ("Babe") Didrikson

Brown, Robert M.
Ganett, Henry
Guyot, Arnold Henry

Brown, Rollo W.
Briggs, LeBaron Russell

Brown, Roscoe Conkling Ensign
Abell, Arunah Shepherdson

Brown, Samuel Horton
Pyle, Walter Lytle

Brown, Sterling A.
Johnson, James Weldon
Whitman, Albery Allson

Brown, Truesdell S.
Westermann, William Linn

Brown, William Adams
Hall, Charles Cuthbert
Hitchcock, Roswell Dwight

Browne, C. A.
Johnson, Samuel William
Smith, Edgar Fahs
Stillman, Thomas Bliss
Storer, Francis Humphreys
Thatcher, Roscoe Wilfred
Warren, Cyrus Moors
Weber, Henry Adam
Weichmann, Ferdinand Gerhard
Wetherill, Charles Mayer
White, Henry Clay
Wiley, Harvey Washington
Wurtz, Henry

Browne, Charles A.
Clarke, Frank Wigglesworth
Hooker, Samuel Cox

Browne, Henry J.
Curran, John Joseph
Hayes, Patrick Joseph

Browne, Richard G.
Fifer, Joseph Wilson

Browne, Waldo R.
Ward, Lydia Arms Avery Coonley

Browne, William F.
Hayden, Robert Earl
Rushing, James Andrew
Still, William Grant, Jr.

Brownson, Carleton L.
Mezes, Sidney Edward

Brubacher, Abram R.
Hawley, Gideon, 1785–1870

Brubacher, John S.
Brackett, Anna Callender
Bulkley, John Williams
Calkins, Norman Allison
Cooper-Poucher, Matilda S.
Lovell, John Epy
MacVicar, Malcolm
Marble, Albert Prescott
Maxwell, William Henry

Bruccoli, Matthew J.
O'Hara, John Henry

Bruce, Kathleen
Berkeley, John
Cabell, William
Cary, Archibald
Mallory, Stephen Russell

Bruce, Philip Alexander
Argall, Sir Samuel
Bacon, Nathaniel
Berkeley, Sir William
Botetourt, Norborne Berkeley, Baron de
Upton, Emory
Wilson, James Harrison

Bruce, Robert V.
Billings, Asa White Kenney
Hodgkinson, Francis
Klein, August Clarence
Mackenzie, Ranald Slidell
Moss, Sanford Alexander
North, Frank Joshua
Richards, Robert Hallowell
Terry, Alfred Howe
Upton, Emory
Wilson, James Harrison

Brunner, Edmund deS.
Wilson, Warren Hugh

Bruno, Frank J.
Eliot, William Greenleaf

Bruns, Robert T.
Bernstein, Theodore Menline

Bryan, George Sands
Batterson, James Goodwin
Bishop, William Darius
Boardman, Thomas Danford
Brandegee, Frank Bosworth
Brewster, James
Buckingham, William Alfred
Butler, Thomas Belden

Bryan, Paul E.
Pardee, Don Albert

Bryant, Lynwood
Kettering, Charles Franklin

Brydon, G. MacLaren
Madison, James
Meade, William
Pendleton, William Nelson
Penick, Charles Clifton
Peterkin, George William
Slaughter, Philip

Whitaker, Alexander
Wilmer, Richard Hooker
Wilmer, William Holland
BUCCO, MARTIN
Schorer, Mark
Steele, Wilbur Daniel
BUCHANAN, A. RUSSELL
Nelson, Donald Marr
Patterson, Robert Porter
BUCHANAN, JOHN
Bache, Jules Semon
BUCK, ELIZABETH HAWTHORN
Connolly, John
BUCK, OSCAR MACMILLAN
Bowen, George
Butler, John Wesley
Hoisington, Henry Richard
Strong, James
Taylor, William
Thoburn, Isabella
Thoburn, James Mills
Wood, Thomas Bond
BUCK, PAUL H.
Hallett, Benjamin Franklin
Holten, Samuel
Hooper, Samuel
Long, John Davis
Lowell, John, 1799–1836
Lyman, Theodore, 1792–1849
Meyer, George von Lengerke
BUCK, SOLON JUSTUS
Alvord, Clarence Walworth
Folwell, William Watts
Goodhue, James Madison
Green, Samuel Bowdlear
Hosmer, James Kendall
Hubbard, Lucius Frederick
Johnson, John Albert
Kelley, Oliver Hudson
Neill, Edward Duffield
Nelson, Knute
Nelson, Rensselaer Russell
Ramsey, Alexander
Rice, Edmund
Rice, Henry Mower
Scott, William Lawrence
Scull, John
Sibley, Henry Hastings
Sibley, Joseph Crocker
Stewart, Andrew
Thaw, William
Wilkins, William
BUCKHAM, JOHN W.
Nash, Charles Sumner
BUDD, RALPH
Gray, Carl Raymond
BUDER, STANLEY
Bassett, Edward Murray
Wood, Edith Elmer
BUENGER, WALTER L.
Hunt, Haroldson Lafayette
BUENKER, JOHN D.
Fitzgerald, John Francis
BUFFINGTON, ARTHUR H.
Willard, Simon
BUHITE, RUSSELL D.
Griswold, Alfred Whitney
Hurley, Patrick Jay
BULLARD, F. LAURISTON
Greene, Nathaniel
Kendall, George Wilkins
MacGahan, Januarius Aloysius
O'Reilly, John Boyle
Rice, Charles Allen Thorndike
Taylor, Charles Henry
BULLARD, FRED M.
Jaggar, Thomas Augustus, Jr.
BULMAN, RAYMOND F.
Tillich, Paul
BUNI, ANDREW
Dixon, Thomas
Robeson, Paul Leroy
Wright, Richard Robert
BURD, RACHEL
Bartlett, Francis Alonzo
BURDICK, CAROL
McGinley, Phyllis
Prouty, Olive Higgins
BURGESS, GEORGE K.
Rosa, Edward Bennett
BURKLEO, SANDRA F. VAN
Hays, Arthur Garfield
BURLINGAME, C. C.
Stearns, Henry Putnam
Todd, Eli
Woodward, Samuel Bayard
BURLINGAME, ROGER
Berliner, Emile
Edison, Thomas Alva
Fessenden, Reginald Aubrey
BURNER, DAVID
Smith, Alfred Emanuel
BURNET, DUNCAN
Burnet, William, 1730–1791
BURNET, ROBERTA B.
Eaton, William
Lear, Tobias
BURNETT, CHARLES T.
Hyde, William DeWitt
BURNETT, EDMUND C.
Hardy, Samuel
Harrison, Benjamin, 1726–1791
Harvie, John
Langworthy, Edward
Lee, Arthur
Lee, Richard Henry
Lee, William
L'Hommedieu, Ezra
Lovell, James
Osgood, Samuel
Smith, Meriwether
Thomson, Charles
BURNETT, ROBYN
Cooley, Harold Dunbar
Ellis, Clyde Taylor
Ramspeck, Robert C. Word ("Bob")
BURNHAM, ALAN
Flagg, Ernest
Pope, John Russell
BURNHAM, GUY H.
Blunt, Edmund March
Blunt, George William
Chaillé-Long, Charles
Danenhower, John Wilson
DeLong, George Washington
DeWitt, Simeon
Du Chaillu, Paul Belloni
Erskine, Robert
Evans, Lewis
Farmer, John, 1798–1859
BURNHAM, JOHN C.
Brill, Abraham Arden
Burrow, Trigant
Jelliffe, Smith Ely
Oberndorf, Clarence Paul
Watson, John Broadus
BURNHAM, WILLIAM H.
Smith, Theodate Louise
BURNS, CHARLES A.
Shields, Francis Xavier ("Frank")
BURNS, DAVID D.
Wilson, Orlando Winfield ("Win," "O.W.")
BURNS, JAMES ALOYSIUS
Angela, Mother
BURNS, MARGIE
Burnett, Chester Arthur ("Howlin' Wolf")
Thompson, Stith
BURR, CHARLES W.
Mitchell, John Kearsley
Mitchell, Silas Weir
BURR, GEORGE LINCOLN
White, Andrew Dickson
BURRAGE, WALTER LINCOLN
Agnew, Cornelius Rea
Agnew, David Hayes
Archer, John
Awl, William Maclay
Bard, John
Bard, Samuel
Bartlett, Elisha
Loring, Edward Greely
Reid, William Wharry
BURRETT, CLAUDE A.
Helmuth, William Tod
Wesselhoeft, Conrad
BURROWS, MILLAR
Schmidt, Nathaniel
BURSTYN, HAROLD L.
Wrather, William Embry
BURT, C. PAULINE
Stoddard, John Tappan
BURTON, DAVID H.
Binkley, Wilfred Ellsworth
Harlow, Ralph Volney
Muzzey, David Saville
Pringle, Henry Fowles
BURTON, ROBERT E.
Neuberger, Richard Lewis
BUSH, DOUGLAS
Lowes, John Livingston
BUSH, RONNIE BETH
Thorek, Max
BUSSEY, GERTRUDE C.
Calkins, Mary Whiton
BUSTER, ALAN
Abzner, Dorothy Emma
Browning, Tod
Carroll, Leo Grattan
Gipson, Frederick Benjamin
Hayes, Gabby
Mansfield, Jayne
Wanger, Walter
BUTLER, CHARLES HENRY
Bancroft, Edgar Addison
BUTLER, PIERCE
Bermudez, Edouard Edmond
Breaux, Joseph Arsenne
BUTLER, WILLIAM MILL
McTammany, John
O'Reilly, Henry
Rathbone, Justus Henry
BUTSCH, DAVID W.
O'Brian, John Lord
BUTTERFIELD, L. H.
Ford, Worthington Chauncey
BYERS, JANET LYNN
Edmondson, William
Lamb, William Frederick

BYRNE, FRANK L.
Flanagan, Edward Joseph

CADBURY, HENRY J.
Penn, John
Penn, Richard
Penn, Thomas
Thayer, Joseph Henry
CAFFEY, FRANCIS GORDON
Brown, William Garrott
CAHILL, CHARLES T.
Breed, Ebenezer
CAIN, LOUIS P.
Tolley, Howard Ross
CAIRNS, HUNTINGTON
Hornblower, William Butler
Howry, Charles Bowen
Ivins, William Mills
Lockwood, Ralph Ingersoll
Moseley, Edward Augustus
Nicholson, Joseph Hopper
Phelps, Charles Edward
Potts, Richard
Rayner, Isidor
Robinson, John Mitchell
Rose, John Carter
Whyte, William Pinkney
CAIRNS, WILLIAM B.
Benjamin, Park, 1809–1864
Buckingham, Joseph Tinker
Conway, Moncure Daniel
Field, Eugene
Gilder, Jeannette Leonard
Gilder, Richard Watson
Godwin, Parke
Goodrich, Samuel Griswold
Holland, Josiah Gilbert
Sargent, Epes
CALDER, ISABEL M.
Chipman, Ward
De La Warr, Thomas West, Baron
Dixwell, John
Dow, Henry
Fenwick, George
Gates, Sir Thomas
Goffe, William
Haynes, John
Jenkins, John Stilwell
Lane, Sir Ralph
Lechford, Thomas
Lothropp, John
MacSparran, James
Mansfield, Richard
Peter, Hugh
Peters, Samuel Andrew
Trumbull, James Hammond
Whalley, Edward
CALDER, WILLIAM M., III
Bieber, Margarete
Capps, Edward
Hadas, Moses
Jaeger, Werner Wilhelm
CALDWELL, ORESTES HAMPTON
Westinghouse, George
CALDWELL, ROBERT G.
Clark, William Thomas
Fannin, James Walker
Flanagan, Webster
Gaines, Reuben Reid
Gould, Robert Simonton
Hamilton, Andrew Jackson
Hancock, John, 1824–1893
Hogg, James Stephen
Houston, Samuel
Jones, Anson
King, Richard
Lamar, Mirabeau Buonaparte
Lane, Walter Page
McCulloch, Ben
Maxey, Samuel Bell
Mills, Roger Quarles
Rice, William Marsh
CALHOUN, CHARLES W.
McElroy, Robert McNutt
CALINGER, RONALD
Bliss, Gilbert Ames
Dickson, Leonard Eugene
CALKINS, EARNEST ELMO
Nitchie, Edward Bartlett
CALKINS, FRANK C.
Diller, Joseph Silas
CALLAHAN, JAMES MORTON
Bulloch, James Dunwody
Camden, Johnson Newlon
Davis, Henry Gassaway
Elkins, Stephen Benton
Faulkner, Charles James, 1847–1929
Fleming, Aretas Brooks
Holcombe, James Philemon
Lightburn, Joseph Andrew Jackson
Summers, George William
CALLEN, ALFRED COPELAND
Stoek, Harry Harkness
CALVERT, MONTE A.
Cooley, Mortimer Elwyn
Kimball, Dexter Simpson
CAMPBELL, CHRISTIANA MCFADYEN
Alexander, Will Winton
CAMPBELL, KILLIS
Lynch, James Daniel
CAMPBELL, LAWRENCE
Davidson, Jo
Dreier, Katherine Sophie
Fisher, Henry Conroy ("Bud")
Kuniyoshi, Yasuo
Robinson, Boardman
CAMPBELL, LEON
Bailey, Solon Irving
Rogers, William Augustus
CANBY, HENRY SEIDEL
Dodd, Lee Wilson
Thoreau, Henry David
CANBY, ROBERT C.
Arents, Albert
Church, John Adams
Daggett, Ellsworth
Eilers, Frederic Anton
Goetz, George Washington
Hill, Nathaniel Peter
Hofman, Heinrich Oscar
Howe, Henry Marion
Hunt, Robert Woolston
Raht, August Wilhelm
CANTOR, LOUIS
Hunter, Ivory Joe
Whitfield, Owen
CAPPELLETTI, J. S.
Harris, LeRoy Ellsworth ("Roy")
CAPPON, LESTER J.
Ginter, Lewis
Milner, John Turner
Noble, Samuel
Shook, Alfred Montgomery
Tyler, Daniel
Warner, James Cartwright
CARBONE, PETER F., JR.
Rugg, Harold Ordway
CARDOSO, JACK J.
Gray, William Scott, Jr.
Kalmus, Herbert Thomas
Kalmus, Natalie Mabelle Dunfee
Pickens, William
Royce, Ralph
Zook, George Frederick
CARDWELL, KENNETH H.
Draper, Dorothy
Gropius, Walter Adolf Georg
Maybeck, Bernard Ralph
Skidmore, Louis
CAREY, CHARLES F.
Benton, James Gilchrist
Browning, John Moses
Dahlgren, John Adolphus Bernard
Davidson, John Wynn
Dent, Frederick Tracy
Dyer, Alexander Brydie
Edwards, Oliver
Elliott, Washington Lafayette
Ellsworth, Elmer Ephraim
Emory, William Hemsley
Lewis, Isaac Newton
Sims, Winfield Scott
CAREY, GARY
Lombard, Carole
CARLETON, WILLIAM G.
Fletcher, Duncan Upshaw
CARLHIAN, JEAN PAUL
Coolidge, Charles Allerton
CARLIN, PHILIP H.
Perin, Charles Page
CARLSON, AVERY L.
Williams, Samuel May
CARLSON, ELOF AXEL
Muller, Hermann Joseph
CARLTON, FRANK T.
Duncan, James
CARMAN, HARRY J.
Bouck, William C.
Coker, David Robert
Colles, Christopher
De Forest, Robert Weeks
Finley, John Huston
Hall, Abraham Oakey
Hamilton, James Alexander
Higgins, Frank Wayland
Hill, David Bennett
Hunt, Washington
McCook, Anson George
Maclay, William Brown
Manning, Daniel
Morgan, Edwin Denison
CARMAN, J. ERNEST
Prosser, Charles Smith
CARMICHAEL, O. C.
Pritchett, Henry Smith
CARNES, MARK C.
Groves, Leslie Richard, Jr.
CAROSSO, VINCENT P.
Giannini, Amadeo Peter
Lamont, Thomas William
Whitney, George
Wiggin, Albert Henry
CARPENTER, BRIAN
Gore, Robert Hayes

Carpenter, Brian B.
Powers, Francis Gary
Carpenter, F. M.
Wheeler, William Morton
Carpenter, Frederic Ives
Reed, Elizabeth Armstrong
Carpenter, William S.
Livingston, Edward
Magie, William Jay
Murray, William Vans
Parker, James
Parker, John Cortlandt
Paterson, William
Carr, Irving J.
Squier, George Owen
Carr, William G.
Kefauver, Grayson Neikirk
Carroll, John B.
Whorf, Benjamin Lee
Carroll, John M.
Bartlett, Edward Lewis ("Bob")
Considine, Robert ("Bob") Bernard
Donaldson, Jesse Monroe
Donovan, James Britt
Eisler, Gerhart
Nevers, Ernest Alonzo ("Ernie")
Ruby, Jack L.
Young, Owen D.
Carroll, Patrick J.
Zahn, John Augustine
Carson, Gerald
Billingsley, John Sherman
Birdseye, Clarence
Brinkley, John Richard
Byoir, Carl Robert
Calkins, Earnest Elmo
Crumbine, Samuel Jay
Kellogg, Will Keith
Kiss, Max
Littledale, Clara Savage
Manville, Thomas Franklyn ("Tommy"), Jr.
Pew, Joseph Newton, Jr.
Carson, William Glascow Bruce
Dean, Julia
Drake, Frances Ann Denny
Drake, Samuel
Smith, Marcus
Smith, Solomon Franklin
Carson, William W.
Ridpath, John Clark
Carstensen, Fred V.
Gaisman, Henry Jaques
Hood, Clifford Firoved
Hughes, Albert William
Klein, Anne
Mortimer, Charles Greenough
Rosenstein, Nettie Rosencrans
Carstensen, Vernon
Horlick, William
Jessup, Walter Albert
Carter, Clarence Edwin
Allen, William
Ashley, James Mitchell
Bartley, Mordecai
Carter, Everett
Garland, Hamlin
Grey, Zane
Carter, Paul A.
Adams, Samuel Hopkins
McConnell, Francis John
Potter, Charles Francis
Thurber, James Grover
Carter, Warrick L.
Ellington, Edward Kennedy ("Duke")
Jordan, Louis
Kenton, Stanley Newcomb
Sissle, Noble Lee
Cartwright, Richard S.
Elliott, Walter Hackett Robert
Carver, W. O.
McGlothlin, William Joseph
Casada, James A.
Eklund, Carl Robert
Hubbard, Wynant Davis
Jacobs, Hirsch
Shaughnessy, Clark Daniel
Casamajor, Louis
Tilney, Frederick
Case, Arthur E.
Kaye, Frederick Benjamin
Lewis, Charlton Thomas
Lewis, Enoch
Case, Ermine Cowles
Williston, Samuel Wendell
Caskey, Marie
Booth, Evangeline Cory
Burroughs, Edgar Rice
Herriman, George Joseph
Rourke, Constance Mayfield
White, Alma Bridwell
Cassara, Charles
Casals, Pablo
Cassedy, James H.
Chapin, Charles Value
Hoffman, Frederick Ludwig
Stiles, Charles Wardell
Castañeda, Jim
Mangrum, Lloyd Eugene
Castle, W. B.
Minot, George Richards
Caswell, John E.
Ellsworth, Lincoln
Peary, Josephine Diebitsch
Catchings, Benjamin
Colby, Gardner
Corson, Robert Rodgers
Crozer, John Price
Cupples, Samuel
Cate, James Lea
Arnold, Henry Harley
Mitchell, William
Catterall, Louise Fontaine
Mettauer, John Peter
Spencer, Pitman Clemens
Cauthen, Irby B., Jr.
Wilson, James Southall
Cauthen, Kenneth
Macintosh, Douglas Clyde
Cavert, Samuel McCrea
Brown, William Adams
Sanford, Elias Benjamin
Cawley, F. Stanton
Schofield, William Henry
Chadwick, Charles W.
Juengling, Frederick
Chadwick, George I.
Ganss, Henry George
Chafee, Zechariah, Jr.
Heard, Franklin Fiske
Heywood, Ezra Hervey
Hilliard, Francis
Holmes, Nathaniel
Lowell, John, 1824–1897
Manatt, James Irving
Parsons, Theophilus
Pollak, Walter Heilprin
Schofield, Henry
Sedgwick, Theodore, 1746–1813
Shaw, Lemuel
Smith, Jeremiah, 1837–1921
Sumner, Increase
Washburn, Emory
Chaffin, Nora C.
Few, William Preston
Chalmers, W. Ellison
Cameron, Andrew Carr
Gronlund, Laurence
Chamberlain, Charles J.
Coulter, John Merle
Millspaugh, Charles Frederick
Chamberlain, Hope S.
Battle, Kemp Plummer
Battle, William Horn
Spencer, Cornelia Phillips
Chamberlain, Joseph Edgar
Stephens, Charles Asbury
Chamberlain, Joseph S.
Goessmann, Charles Anthony
Chambers, Clarke A.
Elliott, John Lovejoy
Hodson, William
Kellogg, Paul Underwood
Lindeman, Eduard Christian
Chambers, John Whiteclay, II
Andrews, Roy Chapman
McCarran, Patrick Anthony
Norton, Mary Teresa Hopkins
Pick, Lewis Andrew
Chambers, Will Grant
McCormick, Samuel Black
Chambliss, Hardee
Austen, Peter Townsend
Babcock, James Francis
Barker, George Frederick
Chandler, Alfred D., Jr.
Cortelyou, George Bruce
Du Pont, Pierre Samuel
Raskob, John Jakob
Sloan, Alfred Pritchard, Jr.
Chandler, Charles Lyon
Halsey, Thomas Lloyd
Jewett, David
Wooster, Charles Whiting
Chapelle, Howard I.
Herreshoff, Nathanael Greene
Chapman, Charles E.
Moses, Bernard
Chapman, Henry S.
Ford, Daniel Sharp
Stanwood, Edward
Thomson, Edward William
Torrey, Bradford
Chapman, J. Virgil
Roark, Ruric Nevel
Chase, Frank H.
Balestier, Charles Wolcott
Barton, Thomas Pennant
Benton, Joel
Chase, George H.
Hoppin, Joseph Clark
Chase, Gilbert
Cadman, Charles Wakefield
Carpenter, John Alden

Farwell, Arthur
Weill, Kurt
CHASE, LEW ALLEN
Hulbert, Edwin James
CHASE, STANLEY P.
Abbott, Jacob
Abbott, John Stevens Cabot
CHASE, WAYLAND J.
Beecher, Catharine Esther
Bingham, Caleb
Brooks, Charles
Colburn, Warren
Darby, John
Dickinson, John Woodbridge
O'Shea, Michael Vincent
Salisbury, Albert
Sterling, John Whalen
CHAVKIN, ALLAN
Menjou, Adolphe Jean
CHERNY, ROBERT W.
Howard, Edgar
CHESSMAN, G. WALLACE
Roosevelt, Kermit
CHESTERMAN, E. E.
Wright, William
CHEYNEY, EDWARD P.
Motley, John Lothrop
Munro, Dana Carleton
CHILDS, ARNEY R.
Elliott, Stephen
Gibbes, Robert Wilson
Gibbes, William Hasell
Michel, William Middleton
Porcher, Francis Peyre
Ravenel, Henry William
Ravenel, St. Julien
Shecut, John Linnaeus Edward Whitridge
CHILDS, JAMES B.
Martel, Charles
CHILTON, ALEXANDER W.
Hamilton, Schuyler
Hardie, James Allen
Hartsuff, George Lucas
Hascall, Milo Smith
Hatch, John Porter
CHINOY, HELEN KRICH
Craven, Frank
MacKaye, Percy Wallace
CHITTENDEN, RUSSELL HENRY
Brewer, William Henry
Curtis, John Green
Dalton, John Call
Dunglison, Robley
Hough, Theodore
Lusk, Graham
Martin, Henry Newell
Meltzer, Samuel James
Mendel, Lafayette Benedict
CHITWOOD, O. P.
Mathews, Henry Mason
Van Winkle, Peter Godwin
CHORLEY, E. CLOWES
Burleson, Hugh Latimer
Gailor, Thomas Frank
Thompson, Hugh Miller
Tyng, Stephen Higginson
CHRISTENSON, CORNELIA V.
Kinsey, Alfred Charles
CHRISTIAN, HENRY A.
Folin, Otto Knut Olof
CHRISTIE, FRANCIS ALBERT
Abbot, Francis Ellingwood
Ballon, Hosea, 1771–1852
Ballon, Hosea, 1796–1861
Bancroft, Aaron
Bixby, James Thompson
Edwards, Jonathan, 1703–1758
Huidekoper, Frederic
Huidekoper, Harm Jan
Jackson, Samuel Macauley
Livermore, Abiel Abbot
Longfellow, Samuel
Lowe, Charles
Murray, John, 1741–1815
Parker, Theodore
Stearns, Oliver
Stebbins, Rufus Phineas
CHRISTIE, JEAN
Cooke, Morris Llewellyn
CHRISTOPHER, PAUL
Bachrach, Louis Fabian
CHRISTY, ARTHUR E.
Sherman, Frank Dempster
CHURCH, ROBERT L.
Stimson, Frederic Jesup
CHURCH, SAMUEL HARDEN
Scott, Thomas Alexander
CHURCHILL, ALLEN L.
Belmont, August
Bliss, Cornelius Newton
Butterick, Ebenezer
CHYET, STANLEY F.
Szold, Henrietta
CIKOVSKY, NICOLAI, JR.
Beaux, Cecilia
CLAGETT, MARSHALL
Thorndike, Lynn
CLAPESATTLE, HELEN
Mayo, Charles Horace
Mayo, William James
CLAPP, MARGARET
Pendleton, Ellen Fitz
CLARK, BARRETT H.
Hazelton, George Cochrane
CLARK, CHARLES E.
Prentice, Samuel Oscar
Rogers, Henry Wade
Wayland, Francis, 1826–1904
Wheeler, George Wakeman
Williams, Thomas Scott
CLARK, DORA MAE
Boehler, Peter
Boehm, Martin
Egle, William Henry
Evans, Evan
Evans, John, fl. 1703–1731
Ewing, John
Jacobson, John Christian
Jungman, John George
Kolb, Dielman
CLARK, ELIOT
Hassam, Frederick Childe
Robinson, Theodore
Twachtman, John Henry
Waugh, Frederick Judd
Weir, Julian Alden
Wyant, Alexander Helwig
CLARK, ELIOT C.
Lie, Jonas
CLARK, GEORGE H.
Loomis, Mahlon
CLARK, HARRY HAYDEN
More, Paul Elmer
CLARK, HUBERT LYMAN
Allen, Timothy Field
Field, Herbert Haviland
Garman, Samuel
Girard, Charles Frederic
Holbrook, John Edwards
Hyatt, Alpheus
Marcou, Jules
Pourtalès, Louis François de
Samuels, Edward Augustus
Wyman, Jeffries
CLARK, JANE
Heron, William
Parsons, Samuel Holden
Robinson, Beverley
Stansbury, Joseph
CLARK, NORMAN H.
Willebrandt, Mabel Walker
CLARK, ROBERT C.
Curry, George Law
Deady, Matthew Paul
Dolph, Joseph Norton
Duniway, Abigail Jane Scott
Hume, William
Jackson, Charles Samuel
Ladd, William Sargent
Lord, William Paine
Lovejoy, Asa Lawrence
Mitchell, John Hipple
Pennoyer, Sylvester
Scott, Harvey Whitefield
Thompson, David P.
Williams, George Henry
CLARK, WALTER E.
Sheppard, Samuel Edward
Warren, Henry Clarke
CLARKE, PETER P.
Razaf, Andy
CLAYTON, BRUCE
Shellabarger, Samuel
CLAYTON, CHARLES C.
Birchall, Frederick Thomas
Haskell, Henry Joseph
Mott, Frank Luther
CLEAVER, CAROLE
Pippin, Horace
CLECAK, PETER
Mills, Charles Wright
CLELAND, ROBERT GLASS
Axtell, Samuel Beach
Beatty, William Henry
Bigler, John
Booth, Newton
McFarland, Thomas Bard
McKinstry, Elisha Williams
Miller, John Franklin
Ross, Erskine Mayo
Strong, Harriet Williams Russell
CLEMEN, RUDOLF A.
Cudahy, Michael
Dold, Jacob
Hammond, George Henry
Hubbard, Gurdon Saltonstall
Morris, Nelson
Swift, Louis Franklin
CLEMENT, ANTHONY C.
Conklin, Edwin Grant
CLEMENT, ERNEST W.
Greene, Daniel Crosby
Griffis, William Elliot
Hepburn, James Curtis
Murray, David
CLEMENT, RUFUS E.
Walters, Alexander

Clemons, Harry
Lowrie, James Walter
Nevius, John Livingston
Reid, Gilbert
Williams, John Elias
Wood, Mary Elizabeth
Clendinning, Katherine W.
Campbell, Allen
Carll, John Franklin
Childe, John
Cohen, Mendes
Cox, Lemuel
Crocker, Francis Bacon
Delamater, Cornelius Henry
Doane, Thomas
Dubois, Augustus Jay
Wheeler, Schuyler Skaats
Clippinger, D. A.
Tomlins, William Lawrence
Clippinger, Walter G.
Kephart, Ezekiel Boring
Kephart, Isaiah Lafayette
Clokie, Hugh McD.
Parker, Joel
Pennington, William
Randolph, Theodore Fitz
Stockton, John Potter
Clowes, George H. A.
Cutler, Elliott Carr
Clymer, Kenton J.
Barrows, David Prescott
Coad, Oral S.
Bernard, John
Bidwell, Barnabas
Cooper, Thomas Abthorpe
Dunlap, William
Everett, David
Fawcett, Edgar
Fennell, James
Field, Joseph M.
Finn, Henry James William
Hallam, Lewis
Hamblin, Thomas Sowerby
Hardenbergh, Jacob Rutsen
Henry, John, 1746–1794
Heron, Matilda Agnes
Hill, George Handel
Hodgkinson, John
Lord, William Wilberforce
Merry, Ann Brunton
Morris, Elizabeth
Price, Stephen
Simpson, Edmund Shaw
Wignell, Thomas
Coan, Charles F.
Cubero, Pedro Rodriguez
De Vargas Zapata Y. Lujan
Ponce de Leon, Diego
Cobb, Collier
Mitchell, Elisha
Cobb, W. Montague
Carson, Simeon Lewis
Coben, Stanley
Hays, Will H.
Coblentz, Virgil
Rice, Charles
Coburn, Frederick W.
Agate, Alfred T.
Agate, Frederick Styles
Ayer, James Cook
Badger, Joseph
Benbridge, Henry
Birch, Thomas
Birch, William Russell
Blackburn, Joseph
Boott, Kirk
Brown, Mather
Champney, Benjamin
Champney, James Wells
Church, Frederick Stuart
Closson, William Baxter
Coffin, William Anderson
Cole, Joseph Foxcroft
Copley, John Singleton
Cornoyer, Paul
Cranch, Christopher Pearse
Crowninshield, Frederic
Cummings, Thomas Seir
Ditson, Oliver
Dummer, Jeremiah, 1645–1718
Dunham, Henry Morton
Feke, Robert
Field, Robert
Flagg, Josiah
Gardner, Isabella Stewart
Glidden, Charles Jasper
Goodrich, William Marcellus
Gould, Nathaniel Duren
Hall, George Henry
Harding, Chester
Hawthorne, Charles Webster
Higginson, Henry Lee
Hin, Thomas, 1829–1908
Huntington, Elisha
Jordan, Eben Dyer
Jouett, Matthew Harris
King, Samuel
Kirchmayer, John
Lang, Benjamin Johnson
Leavitt, Joshua
Listemann, Bernhard
Lockwood, Robert Wilton
Longfellow, Ernest Wadsworth
Longfellow, William Pitt Preble
Low, John Gardner
Lyon, James
Mason, Frank Stuart
Miles, Henry Adolphus
Morse, Edward Sylvester
Mount, William Sidney
Nesmith, John
Norman, John
Parker, James Cutler Dunn
Pelham, Henry
Pelham, Peter
Perkins, Charles Callahan
Pratt, Matthew
Quartley, Arthur
Ranger, Henry Ward
Richards, William Trost
Roberts, Elizabeth Wentworth
Rolshoven, Julius
Rowse, Samuel Worcester
Sargent, Henry
Savage, Edward
Schouler, William
Sellstedt, Lars Gustaf
Shattuck, Aaron Draper
Simmons, Edward
Smith, John Rowson
Smith, John Rubens
Stetson, Charles Walter
Taylor, William Ladd
Theus, Jeremiah
Thompson, Cephas Giovanni
Thompson, Jerome B.
Tourjée, Eben
Tufts, John
Turner, Ross Sterling
Varnum, James Mitchell
Varnum, Joseph Bradley
Vonnoh, Robert William
Walter, Thomas, 1696–1725
Woolf, Benjamin Edward
Coburn, F. W.
Clark, Walter Leighton
Clarke, Thomas Benedict
Dodge, William De Leftwich
Hart, George Overbury
Kane, John
Luks, George Benjamin
Perry, Walter Scott
Cochran, Charles F.
Armstrong, John, 1755–1816
Cochran, Thomas C.
Chrysler, Walter Percy
Cochrane, Edward L.
Taylor, David Watson
Code, Joseph B.
Seton, Elizabeth Ann Bayley
Seton, Robert
Coe, Samuel Gwynn
Carmichael, William
Coe, Wesley R.
Verrill, Addison Emery
Coffee, Rudolph I.
Meyer, Martin Abraham
Coffey, Hobart
Stone, John Wesley
Wilkins, Ross
Coffin, Henry Sloane
Hall, John
Coffin, Robert P. Tristram
Nack, James M.
Paine, Robert Treat
Coffman, Edward M.
Harbord, James Guthrie
March, Peyton Conway
Cogley, John
Gillis, James Martin
Cohen, Libby Okun
Singer, Israel Joshua
Cohen, Sol
Irwin, Elisabeth Antoinette
Cohen, Warren I.
Greene, Roger Sherman
Colbert, Thomas Burnell
Barton, James Edward
Fay, Francis Anthony ("Frank")
Garst, Roswell ("Bob")
Hickenlooper, Bourke Blakemore
Colby, Elbridge
Winthrop, Theodore
Colby, James Fairbanks
Atherton, Joshua
Bartlett, Josiah
Poland, Luke Potter
Colby, Ursula Sybille
Clapp, Margaret Antoinette
Millett, Fred Benjamin
Prouty, Charles Tyler
Schocken, Theodore
Colby, William E.
Lindley, Curtis Holbrook
Cole, Arthur C.
Hanna, Marcus Alonzo
Harmon, Judson
Keifer, Joseph Warren
Webster, Daniel

Cole, Charles William
Reid, Thomas Mayne
Cole, Esther
Cabet, Étienne
Swift, Gustavus Franklin
Cole, Fannie L. Gwinner
Adams, Charles R.
Apthorp, William Foster
Baermann, Carl
Baker, Benjamin Franklin
Billings, William
Emmett, Daniel Decatur
Fillmore, John Comfort
Finck, Henry Theophilus
Fry, William Henry
Goldbeck, Robert
Goodrich, Alfred John
Gottschalk, Louis Moreau
Graupner, Johann Christian Gottlieb
Griffes, Charles Tomlinson
Jarvis, Charles H.
Joseffy, Rafael
Klein, Bruno Oscar
Kneisel, Franz
Krehbiel, Henry Edward
Liebling, Emil
Mees, Arthur
Merz, Karl
Mollenhauer, Emil
Pearce, Stephen Austen
Pease, Alfred Humphreys
Perabo, Johann Ernst
Perry, Edward Baxter
Pratt, Silas Gamaliel
Rice, Fenelon Bird
Root, Frederic Woodman
Scheve, Edward Benjamin
Sherwood, William Hall
Spiering, Theodore
Wolfsohn, Carl
Cole, Fay-Cooper
Dorsey, George Amos
Starr, Frederick
Cole, Rossetter Gleason
Buck, Dudley
Lutkin, Peter Christian
Nevin, Ethelbert Woodbridge
Stanley, Albert Augustus
Upton, George Putnam
Weidig, Adolf
Zeisler, Fannie Bloomfield
Cole, Wayne S.
Shipstead, Henrik
Colegrove, Kenneth Wallace
Bond, Shadrach
Breese, Sidney
Coleman, Christopher B.
Foulke, William Dudley
Law, John
McCulloch, Oscar Carleton
Merrill, Samuel
Morris, Thomas Armstrong
Whitcomb, James
Williams, Charles Richard
Williams, James Douglas
Coleman, Mary C.
Rogers, Mary Josephine
Coleman, Melvin E.
Stone, Melville Elijah
Coleman, Norman F.
Reed, Simeon Gannett

Coleman, R. V.
Ludlow, Roger
Colestock, Henry T.
Malcom, Howard
Coletta, Paolo E.
Bryan, Charles Wayland
Moreell, Ben
Raulston, John Tate
Rohde, Ruth Bryan Owen
Colgrove, Kenneth Wallace
Breese, Sidney
Coll, Blanche D.
Brackett, Jeffrey Richardson
Glenn, John Mark
Hersey, Evelyn Weeks
Switzer, Mary Elizabeth
Collier, James Lincoln
Armstrong, Louis ("Satchmo")
Collier, Theodore
Lawrence, William Beach
Wayland, Francis, 1796–1865
Collingwood, G. Harris
Silcox, Ferdinand Augustus
Collins, Edward H.
Mills, Ogden Livingston
Collins, Guy N.
Rock, John
Roeding, George Christian
Collins, John W.
Marshall, Frank James
Collins, Patrick W.
Weigel, Gustave
Colman, Edna Mary
Brent, Margaret
Colman, Gould P.
Ladd, Carl Edwin
Commager, Henry Steele
McLaughlin, Andrew Cunningham
Commons, John R.
Gompers, Samuel
Kellogg, Edward
Lennon, John Brown
McNeill, George Edwin
Mitchell, John, 1870–1919
Compton, W. D.
Chaffee, Roger Bruce
Grissom Virgil Ivan ("Gus")
White, Edward Higgins, II
Conant, Kenneth J.
Warren, Herbert Langford
Conboy, Kenneth
Angell, Ernest
Condit, Carl W.
Graham, Ernest Robert
Moisseiff, Leon Solomon
Parker, Theodore Bissell
Perkins, Dwight Heald
Pond, Irving Kane
Purdy, Corydon Tyler
Rogers, James Gamble
Waite, Henry Matson
Cone, Thomas E., Jr.
Cooley, Thomas Benton
Conger, George P.
Swenson, David Ferdinand
Coniglione, Richard
Bennett, Earl W.
Coe, Virginius ("Frank")
McCreary, Conn
Wood, Garfield Arthur ("Gar")

Conn, Stetson
McNair, Lesley James
Short, Walter Campbell
Connelley, William E.
Hickok, James Butler
Connick, Charles Jay
Willit, William
Connor, R. D. W.
Gaston, William
Hall, James, 1744–1826
Harnett, Cornelius
Hogun, James
Hyde, Edward
Vance, Zebulon Baird
Connors, Richard J.
Hague, Frank
Connorton, Judy
Church, Thomas Dolliver
Conrad, Henry C.
Bennett, Caleb Prew
Constance, Lincoln
Jepson, Willis Linn
Converse, Florence
Bates, Katharine Lee
Palmer, Alice Elvira Freeman
Shafer, Helen Almira
Conwell, Ralph E.
Kendrick, John Benjamin
Cook, Delia Crutchfield
Gordon, Kermit
Lippincott, Joseph Wharton
Roulston, Marjorie Hillis
Smith, Mildred Catharine
Cooke, Jacob E.
Bancroft, Frederic
Coolidge, Charles A.
Perkins, Thomas Nelson
Coolidge, Mary Roberts
Warner, Amos Griswold
Cooper, Diane E.
Britton, Barbara
Kelly, Emmett Leo
Wallenda, Karl
Cooper, G. Arthur
Ulrich, Edward Oscar
Cooper, Lane
Bartram, William
Cook, Albert Stanburrough
Cooper, William J., Jr.
Percy, William Alexander
Corbett, John
Campbell, Thomas Joseph
Goupil, René
Cordery, Stacy A.
Longworth, Alice Lee Roosevelt
Corey, David
Hopkins, Miriam
Howe, James Wong
Johnson, Nunnally Hunter
Cornell, Greta A.
Wentworth, Cecile de
Cornell, Thomas David
Van de Graaff, Robert Jemison
Corner, George V.
Landsteiner, Karl
Corner, George W.
Auer, John
Carrel, Alexis
Cullen, Thomas Stephen
Flexner, Simon
Hoagland, Charles Lee
Hooker, Donald Russell
Howell, William Henry

Hume, Edgar Erskine
Kelly, Howard Atwood
Loeb, Leo
Murphy, James Bumgardner
Pepper, William, III
Rivers, Thomas Milton
Sabin, Florence Rena
Stockard, Charles Rupert
Streeter, George Linius
Weed, Lewis Hill
CORNWELL, ELMER E., JR.
Key, Valdimer Orlando, Jr.
CORONITI, JOSEPH
Stokowski, Leopold Anthony
Stravinsky, Igor Fyodorovich
CORTISSOZ, ROYAL
Isham, Samuel
La Farge, John
Melchers, Gari
Saint-Gaudens, Augustus
Scribner, Charles, 1821–1871
Scribner, Charles, 1854–1930
Whistler, James Abbott McNeill
CORWIN, EDWARD S.
Bradley, Joseph P.
Chase, Samuel
Field, Stephen Johnson
Ford, Henry Jones
Marshall, John
CORY, DANIEL M.
Strong, Charles Augustus
COSTA, ALBERT B.
Bachmann, Werner Emmanuel
Ellis, Carleton
Johnson, Treat Baldwin
Michael, Arthur
Noyes, William Albert
Sherman, Henry Clapp
Stine, Charles Milton Altland
COTNER, ROBERT C.
Murray, William Henry David
COTNER, ROBERT CRAWFORD
Macune, Charles William
COTTERILL, R. S.
Beattie, Francis Robert
Biddle, Clement
Blackburn, Joseph Clay Styles
Boyle, Jeremiah Tilford
Bullitt, Alexander Scott
Clark, James
Combs, Leslie
Cooper, Joseph Alexander
Covode, John
Durrett, Reuben Thomas
Evans, Walter
Filson, John
Garrard, James
Goebel, William
Goodloe, William Cassius
Green, Norvin
Guthrie, James
Hamtranck, John Francis
Harlan, James, 1800–1863
Hay, George
Henderson, Leonard
Henderson, Richard
Letcher, Robert Perkins
Lewis, Joseph Horace
Littell, William
Logan, Benjamin
Maxwell, Augustus Emmett
Mills, Benjamin
Milton, John
Moore, Thomas Patrick
Morrow, Edwin Porch
Pasco, Samuel
Perry, Edward Aylesworth
Raney, George Pettus
Walker, David Shelby
Watterson, Harvey Magee
Wickliffe, Charles Anderson
Willson, Augustus Everett
Woods, Alva
Yulee, David Levy
COTTMAN, GEORGE S.
Maxwell, David Hervey
Milroy, Robert Huston
Parke, Benjamin
Perkins, Samuel Elliott
Posey, Thomas
COTTON, ROBERT C.
Jesup, Thomas Sidney
Parsons, Lewis Baldwin
Patterson, Robert
Prentiss, Benjamin Mayberry
COULTER, ELLIS MERTON
Adair, John
Anderson, Richard Clough, 1750–1826
Anderson, Richard Clough, 1788–1826
Barry, William Taylor
Bedinger, George Michael
Bibb, George Mortimer
Blackburn, Luke Pryor
Boyd, Lynn
Boyle, John
Bradley, William O'Connell
Bramlette, Thomas E.
Breckinridge, John
Breckinridge, John Cabell
Breckinridge, Robert Jefferson
Breckinridge, William Campbell Preston
Brown, John
Brown, John Young
Buckner, Simon Bolivar
Butler, William Orlando
Carlisle, John Griffin
Church, Alonzo
Clay, Cassius Marcellus
Clay, Green
Clay, Henry
Cofer, Martin Hardin
Crittenden, George Bibb
Crittenden, John Jordan
Crittenden, Thomas Leonidas
Davis, Garrett
Desha, Joseph
Edwards, John, 1748–1837
Greenup, Christopher
Hardin, Ben
Hardin, Martin D.
Harrod, James
Hopkins, Samuel, 1753–1819
Howard, Benjamin
Jacob, Richard Taylor
Jones, Noble Wymberley
King, John Pendleton
King, Thomas Butler
Magoffin, Beriah
Marshall, Humphrey, 1760–1841
Marshall, Humphrey, 1812–1872
Marshall, James Markham
Marshall, Louis
Marshall, Thomas Alexander
Mell, Patrick Hues, 1814–1888
Orr, Gustavus John
Peters, Richard
Phinizy, Ferdinand
Powell, Lazarus Whitehead
Preston, William
Procter, John Robert
Robertson, George
Rousseau, Lovell Harrison
Rowan, John
Simmons, Thomas Jefferson
Simms, William Elliott
Speed, James
Stevens, William Bacon
Stevenson, John White
Telfair, Edward
Underwood, Joseph Rogers
White, George
White, William Nathaniel
COULTER, E. MERTON
Hunt, Benjamin Weeks
Knight, Lucian Lamar
Phillips, Ulrich Bonnell
COULTER, STANLEY
Bailey, Jacob Whitman
COUPER, WALTER J.
Lloyd, Henry Demarest
COURSAULT, JESSE H.
Jesse, Richard Henry
Lathrop, John Hiram
Laws, Samuel Spahr
Read, Daniel, 1805–1878
Soldan, Frank Louis
COURT, W. H. B.
Catesby, Mark
COVERT, WILLIAM C.
Speer, William
COWAN, LOUISE
Tate, John Orley Allen
COWAN, RUTH SCHWARTZ
McClung, Clarence Erwin
COWDREY, MARY BARTLETT
Dewing, Thomas Wilmer
COWIE, ALEXANDER
Trumbull, John, 1750–1831
COX, ISAAC JOSLIN
Blennerhassett, Harman
Bollman, Justus Erich
Burr, Aaron
Claiborne, William Charles Coles
Clark, Daniel, 1776–1813
Daveiss, Joseph Hamilton
Kemper, Reuben
Mathews, George
Sebastian, Benjamin
Smith, John, 1735–1824
Swartwout, Samuel
Toulmin, Harry
Wilkinson, James
Williamson, Charles
COX, JOHN, JR.
Bowne, John
Wood, Samuel
COX, THEODORE S.
Lomax, John Tavloe
Minor, John Barbee
Minor, Raleigh Colston
Moncure, Richard Cassius Lee
Munford, William
Parker, Marsena Rudolph
Parker, Richard Elliot

Patrick, Marsena Rudolph
Patton, John Mercer
Wickham, John
Wythe, George
COY, OWEN C.
Marshall, James Wilson
CRABB, A. L.
Priestley, James
CRAIG, FRANK A.
Flick, Lawrence Francis
CRAM, MARSHALL P.
Cleaveland, Parker
CRANE, ESTHER
Shaw, Pauline Agassiz
Syms, Benjamin
CRANE, KATHARINE ELIZABETH
Hopkins, Edward Augustus
Kamaikan
Kicking Bird
Leschi
Livingston, James
McKee, John
Mathews, John
Menewa
Middleton, Arthur
Morgan, William
Oconostota
Osceola
Outacity
Palmer, Joel
Pushmataha
Reed, James, 1722–1807
Ridge, Major
Riggs, George Washington
Scammell, Alexander
Seattle
Shabonee
Shepard, William
Shikellamy
Skenandoa
Spencer, Joseph
Sprague, Kate Chase
Sprague, William, 1830–1915
Street, Joseph Montfort
Tecumseh
Tedyuskung
Tenskwatawa
Thompson, John Bodine
Tomochichi
Tucker, Nathaniel Beverley, 1820–1890
Vassall, John
Ward, Nancy
Weatherford, William
Wovoka
CRANE, VERNER W.
Bray, Thomas
Coram, Thomas
Cross, Arthur Lyon
Cuming, Sir Alexander
Hughes, Price
McCrady, Edward
Marchant, Henry
Nairne, Thomas
Priber, Christian
Purry, Jean Pierre
Woodward, Henry
CRANEFIELD, PAUL F.
Cohn, Alfred Einstein
CRATTY, ROBERT IRVIN
Pammel, Louis Hermann
CRAVEN, AVERY
Dodd, William Edward
CRAVEN, AVERY O.
Aime, Valcour
Binns, John Alexander
Boré, Jean Étienne
Botts, Charles Tyler
Brigham, Joseph Henry
Garnett, James Mercer
Ruffin, Edmund
Taylor, John
CRAVEN, WAYNE
Dallin, Cyrus Edwin
MacNeil, Hermon Atkins
Ruckstull, Frederick Wellington
CRAVEN, WESLEY FRANK
West, Francis
White, John, 1585–1593
Wingfield, Edward Maria
Wyatt, Sir Francis
Yeardley, Sir George
CRAVENS, HAMILTON
Bush, Vannevar ("Van")
Dobzhansky, Theodosius Grigorievich
Prescott, Samuel Cate
Waterman, Alan Tower
Yerkes, Robert Mearns
CRAWFORD, NELSON ANTRIM
Ainslie, Hew
Atkinson, Wilmer
Buel, Jesse
Fuller, Andrew S.
CRAWFORD, RICHARD
Romberg, Sigmund
CREER, LELAND HARGRAVE
Dern, George Henry
CREMIN, LAWRENCE A.
Dewey, John
McMurry, Frank Morton
Thorndike, Edward Lee
CRESSEY, DONALD R.
Sutherland, Edwin Hardin
CRESSON, MARGARET FRENCH
MacMonnies, Frederick William
CREW, HENRY
Bell, Louis
CRIPPS, THOMAS R
McDaniel, Hattie
Moore, Frederick Randolph
Robinson, Bill (Bojangles)
CRITTENDEN, CHARLES C.
McLean, Angus Wilton
CROCKETT, WALTER HILL
Bradley, Stephen Row
Brainerd, Lawrence
Buck, Daniel
Butler, Ezra
Haselton, Seneca
Holbrook, Frederick
CROFTON, BARBARA MCCARTHY
Conover, Harry Sayles
Petri, Angelo
CRONEIS, CAREY
Worthen, Amos Henry
CRONON, E. DAVID
Daniels, Josephus
Garvey, Marcus Moziah
CROOKS, JAMES B.
Bruce, William Cabell
CROSBIE, LAURENCE MURRAY
Abbot, Benjamin
CROSBY, DOUGLAS R.
Eisenhart, Luther Pfahler
CROSBY, ELIZABETH
Huber, Gotthelf Carl
CROSS, ARTHUR LYON
Van Tyne, Claude Halstead
CROSS, HARDY
Lindenthal, Gustav
Swain, George Fillmore
CROSS, JENNIFER
Saunders, Clarence
CROSS, ROBERT D.
Cushing, Richard James
Gambrell, Mary Latimer
Herberg, Will
Schlesinger, Arthur Meier
Shuster, George Nauman
Smith, Courtney Craig
CROSS, WHITMAN
Washington, Henry Stephens
CROTHERS, SAMUEL M.
Channing, William Ellery
CROWL, PHILIP A.
Forrestal, James Vincent
CROWNFIELD, FREDERIC R.
Mercer, Lewis Pyle
Reed, James, 1834–1921
Sewall, Frank
CROWTHER, BOSLEY
Allen, Kelcey
Jones, Robert Edmond
Laemmle, Carl
Mayer, Louis Burt
Thalberg, Irving Grant
CROWTHER, SIMEON J.
Holt, William Franklin
Kraft, James Lewis
Moore, Henry Ludwell
CRUNDEN, ROBERT M.
Nock, Albert Jay
CRUSE, HAROLD W.
Lee, Canada
CUDDIHY, PAUL R.
Vizetelly, Frank Horace
CUFF, ROBERT D.
Baruch, Bernard Mannes
CUMBERLAND, SHARON
Hansburg, George Bernard
Lawson, John Howard
CUMMINS, GEORGE B.
Arthur, Joseph Charles
CUNLIFFE, MARCUS
Freeman, Douglas Southall
CUNNINGHAM, C. C.
Tarbell, Edmund Charles
CUNNINGHAM, FRANK R.
Gold, Michael
Odets, Clifford
CUNNINGHAM, G. WATTS
Thilly, Frank
CUNNINGHAM, SUSAN J.
Higgins, Marguerite
CUNNINGHAM, WILLIAM JAMES
Baldwin, William Henry
Brown, William Carlos
Callaway, Samuel Rodger
Hill, James Jerome
Lovett, Robert Scott
Newman, William H.
Sproule, William
Thornton, Henry Worth
Van Horne, William Cornelius
CURLEE, ABIGAIL
Mills, Robert, 1809–1888

Curran, Grace Wickham
Wilmarth, Lemuel Everett
Current, Richard N.
Underwood, John Thomas
Curti, Merle E.
Brattle, William
Brazer, John
Buchanan, Joseph
Burritt, Elihu
Grimké, Angelina Emily
Grimké, Sarah Moore
Grimké, Thomas Smith
Ladd, William
Love, Alfred Henry
Rantoul, Robert, 1778–1858
Rantoul, Robert, 1805–1852
Sanders, George Nicholas
Trueblood, Benjamin Franklin
Curtis, Edward E.
Cornell, Ezekiel
Crane, John
Durkee, John
Learned, Ebenezer
Lynde, Benjamin
Meade, Richard Kidder
Mercer, Hugh
Nixon, John, 1727–1815
North, William
Oliver, Andrew
Paterson, John
Pitcairn, John
Poor, Enoch
Prescott, Oliver
Prescott, William
Shaw, Samuel
Smith, William Stephens
Stark, John
Thomas, John
Thompson, William
Trumbull, Jonathan, 1740–1809
Trumbull, Joseph
Wadsworth, Jeremiah
Wadsworth, Peleg
Ward, Artemas
Warner, Seth
Williams, Otho Holland
Williams, William, 1731–1811
Woodford, William
Curtiss, Thomas Quinn
Von Stroheim, Erich
Cushman, Robert E.
Brewer, David Josiah
Dill, James Brooks
Dillon, John Forrest
Dodd, Samuel Calvin Tate
Harlan, John Marshall
Hunt, Ward
Lansing, John
Lindabury, Richard Vliet
Livingston, Henry Brockholst
Nelson, Samuel
Nott, Charles Cooper
Noyes, Walter Chadwick
Pound, Cuthbert Winfred
Thompson, Smith
Throop, Montgomery Hunt
Cutler, Carl C.
Rogers, William Crowninshield
Waterman, Robert H.
Cutler, Dorothy P.
Farabee, William Curtis
Cutter, R. Ammi
Field, Fred Tarbell
Dabney, Charles William
McBryde, John McLaren
Vawtor, Charles Erastus
Venable, Charles Scott
Dabney, Virginius
Chandler, Julian Alvin Carroll
Martin, Thomas Staples
Underwood, Oscar Wilder
Da Boll, Raymond Franklin
Cooper, Oswald Bruce
Da Costa, J. Chalmers
Gross, Samuel David
Gross, Samuel Weissell
Daggett, Stuart
Hine, Charles De Lano
Huntington, Collis Potter
Judah, Theodore Dehone
Markham, Charles Henry
Ripley, Edward Payson
Stanford, Leland
Strong, William Barstow
Daher, Michael
Connolly, Thomas H.
Dahl, George
Kent, Charles Foster
Daigle, Lennet J.
Redman, Ben Ray
Dain, Norman
Beers, Clifford Whittingham
Dain, Phyllis
Lydenberg, Harry Miller
Wilson, Halsey William
Dains, Frank Burnett
Long, John Harper
Dale, Edward E.
Haskell, Charles Nathaniel
McCoy, Isaac
Mayes, Joel Bryan
Pitchlynn, Peter Perkins
Posey, Alexander Lawrence
Robertson, Alice Mary
Robertson, William Schenck
Ross, John
Watie, Stand
Worcester, Samuel Austin
Dale, Harrison Clifford
Ashley, William Henry
Becknell, William
Beckwourth, James P.
Bozeman, John M.
Bridger, James
Hawley, James Henry
Hutton, Levi William
Long, Stephen Harriman
Daley, Arthur J.
Sullivan, James Edward
Dalfiume, Richard M.
Crosswaith, Frank Rudolph
Dalrymple, Candice
Norden, Carl Lukas
Daly, John C. K.
Lear, William Powell
Daly, Lloyd W.
Oldfather, William Abbott
Daly, Reginald Aldworth
Woodworth, Jay Backus
Damon, Allan L.
Bemis, Samuel Flagg
Berryman, John
Bickel, Alexander Mordecai
Blanshard, Paul
Browder, Earl Russell
Catton, Charles Bruce
Cole, Charles Woolsey
Gleason, Ralph Joseph
Hayden, Carl Trumbull
Huntley, Chester ("Chet") Robert
Krock, Arthur
Marshall, Samuel Lyman Atwood ("Slam")
Murphy, Audie Leon
Trumbo, James Dalton
Van Doren, Mark Albert
Winchell, Walter
Damon, S. Foster
Chivers, Thomas Holley
Damon, Theron J.
Cole, George Watson
Dance, Helen Oakley
Bailey, Mildred
Holiday, Billie
Dance, Stanley
Bechet, Sidney
Catlett, Sidney
Henderson, Fletcher Hamilton
Lunceford, James Melvin ("Jimmie")
Page, Oran Thaddeus ("Lips")
Dandy, Walter E.
Bloodgood, Joseph Colt
Daniel, Marjorie
Zubly, John Joachim
Daniels, David I.
Culbertson, Josephine Murphy
Lenz, Sidney Samuel
Daniels, Roger
Glassford, Pelham Davis
Ickes, Harold Le Clair
Kennedy, Joseph Patrick
Lehman, Herbert Henry
Sherwood, Robert Emmet
Daniels, Winthrop M.
Prouty, Charles Azro
Dantzler, Jeff
Butts, James Wallace ("Wally")
Danzig, Allison
Tilden, William Tatem ("Big Bill")
Dargan, Marion
Drayton, William Henry
D'Arienzo, Camille
Haymes, Richard Benjamin ("Dick")
Darling, Arthur Burr
Appleton, Nathan
Appleton, Samuel
Henshaw, David
Newlands, Francis Griffith
Darnell, Regna
MacCurdy, George Grant
Spier, Leslie
Daughrity, Kenneth L.
Willis, Nathaniel
Willis, Nathaniel Parker
Davenport, Charles B.
Mall, Franklin Paine
Mayor, Alfred Goldsborough
Davenport, Lesley
Tatum, Edward Lawrie
Davidman, Richard
Darin, Bobby
Davidson, Abraham A.
Gropper, William
Reinhardt, Ad
Shahn, Benjamin ("Ben")

Soyer, Moses
Tobey, Mark

DAVIDSON, CHALMERS G.
Fayssoux, Peter
Gaston, James McFadden
Irvine, William

DAVIDSON, DONALD
Malone, Walter
Marling, John Leake
Moore, John Trotwood

DAVIDSON, MARSHALL B.
Taylor, Francis Henry

DAVIES, CLARENCE E.
Main, Charles Thomas

DAVIES, WALLACE EVAN
Bara, Theda
White, Pearl

DAVIS, ALLEN
Simkhovitch, Mary Melinda Kingsbury

DAVIS, ALLEN F.
Bowen, Louise De Koven
Breckenridge, Sophonisba Preston

DAVIS, ARTHUR KYLE, JR.
Smith, Charles Alphonso

DAVIS, ARTHUR POWELL
Newell, Frederick Haynes

DAVIS, AUDREY B.
Osterhout, Winthrop John Vanleuven
Schwidetzky, Oscar Otto Rudolf

DAVIS, CHARLES B.
Peck, James Hawkins

DAVIS, CHERYL L.
Lee, Manfred B.

DAVIS, ELMER
Jones, George
Raymond, Henry Jarvis

DAVIS, HENRY C.
Marks, Elias

DAVIS, JEROME
Gough, John Bartholomew

DAVIS, KENNETH S.
Post, Augustus

DAVIS, MARJORY HENDRICKS
Chase, Pliny Earle

DAVIS, TENNEY L.
Thompson, Benjamin
Watson, William

DAVIS, WILLIAM W.
Haskell, Dudley Chase

DAVISON, ELIZABETH THOMPSON
Bowie, Oden
Bowie, Richard Johns
Bowie, Robert
Bradford, Augustus Williamson

DAVOL, RALPH
Boylies, Francis
Leonard, Daniel
Paine, Robert Treat

DAWES, CHESTER L.
Kennelly, Arthur Edwin

DAWES, NORMAN H.
Saltonstall, Richard

DAWSON, GILES E.
Adams, Joseph Quincy

DAWSON, JOSEPH MARTIN
Newman, Albert Henry

DAWSON, NELSON L.
Sweeney, Martin Leonard

DAY, CLIVE
Farnam, Henry
Schwab, John Christopher
Sheffield, Joseph Earl

DAY, RICHARD E.
Hasenclever, Peter
Jamison, David
McElrath, Thomas
Macfarlane, Robert
Munsell, Joel
Murray, John, 1737–1808
Murray, Robert
Ogden, Samuel
Onderdonk, Henry
Philipse, Frederick
Pratt, Zadock
Schuyler, Peter
Steenwyck, Cornelis
Van Curler, Arent
Van Dam, Rip
Van der Kemp, Francis Adrian
Van Rensselaer, Nicholas
Viele, Aernout Cornelissen

DAY, ROY
Fleming, William Maybury
Ford, John Thomson
Fox, Charles Kemble
Fox, George Washington Lafayette

DEALEY, JAMES QUAYLE
Ward, Lester Frank

DEAN, VERA MICHELES
Simonds, Frank Herbert

DEARBORN, NED H.
Kraus-Boelté, Maria
Krauss, John
Krüsi, Johann Heinrich Hermann

DEARDORFF, NEVA R.
Cabot, Richard Clarke
Lee, Joseph
Rubinow, Isaac Max

DEARING, MARY R.
Boardman, Mabel Thorp

DEBO, ANGIE
Hastings, William Wirt

DE BRUHL, MARSHALL
Carson, Rachel Louise
Hatlo, Jimmy
Johnson, Edward
Metalious, Grace

DEFORD, RONALD K.
Bryan, Kirk

DEGRAAF, LEONARD
Lubin, Isador

DE GREGORIO, VINCENT J.
Glackens, William James

DEGREGORIO, WILLIAM A.
Biffle, Leslie L.
Brucker, Wilber Marion
Duffy, Edmund
Perez, Leander Henry

DEITSCH, RICHARD G.
Albright, William Foxwell
Fahy, Charles

DEKAY, CHARLES
Bierstadt, Albert
Blakelock, Ralph Albert

DE KIEWIET, C. W.
Rhees, Rush

DELAPLAINE, EDWARD S.
Johnson, Thomas
Martin, Luther

DELAVAN, D. BRYSON
Leland, George Adams
Mackenzie, John Noland
Simpson, William Kelly
Wagner, Clinton

DELL, FLOYD
Cook, George Cram

DE LONG, IRWIN H.
Dubbs, Joseph Henry

DEMAREST, WILLIAM H. S.
Livingston, John Henry
Milledoler, Philip
Riddle, Matthew Brown
Schenck, Ferdinand Schureman
Scott, Austin
Searle, John Preston
Van Nest, Abraham Rynier
Woodbridge, Samuel Merrill

DENNES, WILLIAM R.
Prall, David Wight

DENNETT, TYLER
Burlingame, Anson
Harris, Townsend

DENNIS, ALFRED L. P.
Hay, John Milton

DENNIS, EVERETTE E.
Berryman, Clifford Kennedy
Dille, John Flint
Fisher, Hammond Edward
Fox, Fontaine Talbot, Jr.
Gross, Milt
Raymond, Alexander Gillespie

DENTAN, ROBERT C.
Barton, George Aaron

DE PORTE, JOSEPH V.
Wilbur, Cressy Livingston

DERISH, JUDITH
Brenon, Herbert

DERLETH, AUGUST
Gale, Zona

DESCHAMPS, CHRISTIANE L.
Adler, Polly

DETLEFSEN, ELLEN GAY
Neal, Josephine Bicknell
Pfahler, George Edward
Stone, Abraham

DE TURK, ERNEST E.
Hopkins, Cyril George

DEUTSCH, BABETTE
Oppenheim, James

DEUTSCH, HERMAN J.
Atwood, David
Carpenter, Matthew Hale
Jones, Wesley Livsey
Lander, Edward
Leary, John
Meany, Edmond Stephen
Rogers, John Rankin
Squire, Watson Carvosso

DE VENCENTES, PHILIP
Bowes, Edward J.
Burnham, Frederick Russell
Gregg, John Robert
Morton, Ferdinand Quintin
Whitney, Alexander Fell

DEVINE, MICHAEL J.
Bundy, Harvey Hollister
Smith, Ralph Tyler

DEVORKIN, DAVID H.
Adams, Walter Sydney
Russell, Henry Norris
Struve, Otto

DE VOTO, BERNARD
Smith, Joseph, 1805–1844
Young, Brigham

DEWEY, DAVIS R.
Colman, John
Conant, Charles Arthur
Davis, Andrew McFarland
Del Mar, Alexander
Dunbar, Charles Franklin
Gouge, William M.
Gunton, George
DEWEY, EDWARD H.
Prince, Thomas
Shepard, Thomas
Sherman, John, 1613–1685
Talbot, John
Thacher, Peter, 1651–1727
Thacher, Peter, 1752–1802
Thacher, Samuel Cooper
Walker, Timothy, 1705–1782
Ward, Nathaniel
West, Samuel
Whitefield, Henry
Wigglesworth, Edward, 1693–1765
Wigglesworth, Edward, 1732–1794
DEWEY, FRED H.
Baldwin, Matthias William
DEWULF, BERNARD G.
Burnham, William Henry
DIAMOND, LOUIS K.
Blackfan, Kenneth Daniel
DIBACCO, THOMAS V.
Davis, Arthur Vining
Knauth, Oswald Whitman
DIBBLE, ROY FLOYD
Fitzsimmons, Robert Prometheus
DICK, EVERETT N.
Himes, Joshua Vaughan
Miller, William
Smith, Uriah
Ward, Henry Dana
White, Ellen Gould Harman
DICKE, THOMAS S.
Lazarus, Fred, Jr.
Pew, John Howard
DICKINSON, HOBERT CUTLER
Waidner, Charles William
DICKINSON, JOHN
Clifford, Nathan
Curtis, Benjamin Robbins
Cushing, William
DICKINSON, Z. C.
Taylor, Fred Manville
DICKSON, CHARLES ELLIS
Hoyt, John Sherman
DICKSON, HAROLD E.
Flagg, James Montgomery
Karfiol, Bernard
Shinn, Everett
DIDLAKE, MARY LE GRAND
Short, Charles Wilkins
DIEKE, SALLY H.
Hubble, Edwin
DIERLAM, ROBERT J.
Fiske, Harrison Grey
DIETZ, F. C.
Larson, Laurence Marcellus
DILLER, THEODORE
Atlee, John Light
Atlee, Washington Lemuel
Walter, Albert G.
DILLER, WILLIAM F.
Woodruff, Lorande Loss
DILLIARD, IRVING
Abbot, Willis John
Ameringer, Oscar
Anderson, Paul Y.
Andrews, Bert
Angle, Paul McClelland
Bent, Silas
Berger, Meyer
Biddle, Anthony Joseph Drexel, Jr.
Billikopf, Jacob
Bok, Edward William
Bonfils, Frederick Gilmer
Bovard, Oliver Kirby
Bowker, Richard Rogers
Breckinridge, Desha
Brisbane, Arthur
Broun, Heywood Campbell
Busch, Adolphus
Cesare, Oscar Edward
Clapper, Raymond Lewis
Cleghorn, Sarah Norcliffe
Cobb, Irvin Shrewsbury
Cowles, Gardner
Darling, Jay Norwood ("Ding")
Duvall, Gabriel
Fairlie, John Archibald
Gibbons, Floyd
Gitt, Josiah Williams ("Jess")
Goldberg, Reuben Lucius ("Rube")
Gray, Harold Lincoln
Guest, Edgar Albert
Hannegan, Robert Emmet
Heaton, John Langdon
Hill, Edwin Conger
Howard, Roy Wilson
Howe, Edgar Watson
Hutchinson, Paul
Irwin, William Henry
Jackson, Charles Douglas
Jacobs, Paul
Kirby, Rollin
Lane, William Carr
Lehmann, Frederick William
Lewis, James Hamilton
Liggett, Walter William
Lord, Chester Sanders
Lorimer, William
Love, Robertus Donnell
McAdams, Clark
McClure, Robert Alexis
McClure, Samuel Sidney
McIntyre, Oscar Odd
McKinley, William Brown
McManus, George
Mallinckrodt, Edward
Mason, Walt
Minton, Sherman
Nieman, Lucius William
Older, Fremont
Patterson, Alicia
Piggott, James
Powell, John Benjamin
Pulitzer, Joseph, Jr.
Pulitzer, Ralph
Pyle, Ernest Taylor
Reed, James Alexander
Ripley, Robert LeRoy
Ross, Charles Griffith
Scripps, Robert Paine
Scullin, John
Sellers, Isaiah
Sheldon, Walter Lorenzo
Smith, Frank Leslie
Stephens, Edwin William
Sutherland, George
Switzler, William Franklin
Sylvester, Frederick Oakes
Tammen, Harry Heye
Taussig, William
Thompson, Slason
Turner, George Kibbe
Turner, James Milton
Tuttle, Daniel Sylvester
Villard, Oswald Garrison
Walthall, Henry Brazeal
Walton, Lester Aglar
Waterhouse, Sylvester
Waymack, William Wesley
Webster, Harold Tucker
Wells, Erastus
White, William Allen
Widforss, Gunnar Mauritz
Willard, Frank Henry
Williams, Gaar Campbell
Wimar, Carl
Woerner, John Gabriel
Woodward, Calvin Milton
Yeatman, James Erwin
Yost, Casper Salathiel
Young, Art
Zuppke, Robert Carl
DINNEEN, MARCIA B.
Hathaway, Donny
McCoy, Tim
D'INNOCENZO, MICHAEL
Sprague, Oliver Mitchell Wentworth
DINSMORE, CHARLES ALLEN
Bacon, Leonard
Beecher, Lyman
Botta, Vincenzo
Brooks, Phillips
Bushnell, Horace
Carleton, Will
Cary, Alice
Cary, Phoebe
Davenport, James
Dinsmoor, Robert
Harris, Samuel
Hopkins, Samuel, 1721–1803
Munger, Theodore Thornton
Stevens, George Barker
Taylor, Nathaniel William
Tyler, Bennet
DISNEY, DONALD B., JR.
Hewitt, Henry Kent
DITTES, JAMES E.
Starbuck, Edwin Diller
DITZION, SIDNEY
Flexner, Jennie Maas
DIVEN, BENJAMIN C.
Graves, Alvin Cushman
DIVEN, ROBERT JOSEPH
Jackson, Sheldon
DIVINE, ROBERT A.
Tansill, Charles Callan
DIXON, A. IMRIE
Lovewell, John
DIXON, FRANK HAIGH
Cassatt, Alexander Johnston
Corning, Erastus
Harriman, Edward Henry
Randolph, Epes
Smith, Alfred Holland

Thomson, Frank
Thomson, John Edgar
Worcester, Edwin Dean
Wright, Charles Barston
DIXON, ROLAND B.
Newell, William Wells
Putnam, Frederic Ward
DOANE, GILBERT H.
Allen, Ethan
Allen, Ira
Baker, Remember
Chipman, Nathaniel
Chittenden, Martin
Chittenden, Thomas
Fairfield, Edmund Burke
Fay, Jonas
DOBBIE, ELLIOTT V. K.
Krapp, George Philip
DOBIE, ARMISTEAD M.
Tucker, Henry St. George, 1780–1848
Tucker, St. George
DOBIE, EDITH
White, Stephen Mallory
DOBSON, ELEANOR ROBINETTE
Audubon, John James
Bickmore, Albert Smith
Brown, John, 1744–1780
Browne, John
Browne, William
Bryan, George
Burleigh, Charles Calistus
Burr, Theodosia
Connelly, Pierce Francis
Cuming, Fortescue
Darley, Felix Octavius Carr
Dwight, John Sullivan
Estaugh, Elizabeth Haddon
Frémont, Jessie Benton
Holmes, David
Jemison, Mary
Nolan, Philip
Putnam, Arthur
Radisson, Pierre Esprit
Shaler, Nathaniel Southgate
DOBSON, MELISSA A.
Glueck, Nelson
Kunitz, Moses
Rickard, Clinton
Slater, John Clarke
Teuber, Hans-Lukas ("Luke")
DODD, LEE WILSON
Miller, Henry
DODD, WILIAM E.
Davis, Henry Winter
Henry, Patrick
Stringfellow, Franklin
DODGE, CHARLES WRIGHT
Dewey, Chester
Sartwell, Henry Parker
DODGE, ERNEST S.
Benson, Frank Weston
DODGE, MARY DANFORTH
Danforth, Moseley Isaac
DODGE, RICHARD E.
Brigham, Albert Perry
DODGE, ROBERT G.
Rugg, Arthur Prentice
DODSON, LEONIDAS
Mayo, William
Spotswood, Alexander
DOENECKE, JUSTUS D.
Borchard, Edwin Montefiore
Knutson, Harold
DOETSCH, RAYMOND N.
Henrici, Arthur Trautwein
DOIG, JAMESON W.
Tobin, Austin Joseph
DOLAN, JOHN J.
Guthrie, William Dameron
Pinkney, William
Tyler, Samuel
Zane, Charles Schuster
DOLMETSCH, CARL R.
Nathan, George Jean
DONALD, DAVID HERBERT
Randall, James Garfield
DONALDSON, SCOTT
Tarkington, Booth
Torrence, Frederick Ridgely
DONDORE, DOROTHY ANN
Catherwood, Mary Hartwell
Chopin, Kate O'Flaherty
Flint, Timothy
Howe, Henry
Ingraham, Joseph Holt
Ingraham, Prentiss
Kirkland, Caroline Matilda Stansbury
Kirkland, Joseph
McConnel, John Ludlum
McKenney, Thomas Loraine
DONNAN, ELIZABETH
Capen, Samuel Billings
Durant, Henry Fowle
Elder, William
Emerson, Joseph
Fry, Richard
Harnden, William Frederick
Howard, Ada Lydia
Hunnewell, Horatio Hollis
Livermore, Mary Ashton Rice
Lowell, Josephine Shaw
Raguet, Condy
Sabine, Lorenzo
Sewall, Jonathan
Sullivan, William
Walker, Amasa
Webster, Pelatiah
DONNELLY, HAROLD I.
Packard, Frederick Adolphus
DONOVAN, ROBERT J.
Johnson, Louis Arthur
DORFMAN, JOSEPH
Mitchell, Wesley Clair
Seligman, Edwin Robert Anderson
DORN, HAROLD
Davis, Harvey Nathaniel
DORN, JACOB H.
Holt, Arthur Erastus
DORSETT, LYLE W.
Pendergast, Thomas Joseph
DORSON, RICHARD M.
Read, Opie Pope
Swanton, John Reed
DOTY, WILLIAM KAVANAUGH
Henley, Robert
Hollins, George Nichols
Holmes, Daniel Henry
DOUGLAS, DOROTHY W.
Steward, Ira
DOW, MARGARET ELDER
Kane, Elisha Kent
DOWLINC, JOHN E.
Parker, George Howard
DOWNER, ALAN S.
Ames, Winthrop
Beck, Martin
Faversham, William Alfred
Howard, Sidney Coe
Irwin, May
DOWNES, EDWARD O. D.
Aldrich, Richard
Henderson, William James
DOWNES, RANDOLPH C.
St. Clair, Arthur
Slocum, Frances
Tupper, Benjamin
Wayne, Anthony
White Eyes
Zane, Ebenezer
DOWNES, WILLIAM HOWE
Bridgman, Frederic Arthur
De Camp, Joseph Rodefer
Doughty, Thomas
Durand, Asher Brown
Duveneck, Frank
Eakins, Thomas
Fuller, George
Garrett, Edmund Henry
Gaul, William Gilbert
Gay, Winckworth Allan
Gifford, Robert Swain
Gifford, Sanford Robinson
Gray, Henry Peters
Guy, Seymour Joseph
Hale, Philip Leslie
Harrison, Lovell Birge
Harrison, Thomas Alexander
Hayden, Charles Henry
Hays, William Jacob
Hennessy, William John
Henri, Robert
Homer, Winslow
Hoppin, Augustus
Howe, William Henry
Hunt, William Morris
Inman, Henry, 1801–1846
Inness, George
Jarvis, John Wesley
Johnson, Jonathan Eastman
Johnston, Henrietta
Jones, Hugh Bolton
Kensett, John Frederick
Lathrop, Francis Augustus
Le Clear, Thomas
Leslie, Charles Robert
Leutze, Emanuel
Lewis, Edmund Darch
Loeb, Louis
Loop, Henry Augustus
McEntee, Jervis
Macomber, Mary Lizzie
Matteson, Tompkins Harrison
May, Edward Harrison
Mayer, Constant
Maynard, George Willoughby
Merritt, Anna Lea
Metcalf, Willard Leroy
Mignot, Louis Remy
Miller, Charles Henry
Minor, Robert Crannell
Moran, Edward
Moran, Peter
Moran, Thomas
Mosler, Henry

Mowbray, Henry Siddons
Murphy, John Francis
Neagle, John
Neal, David Dalhoff
Newman, Henry Roderick
Newman, Robert Loftin
Nicoll, James Craig
Norton, William Edward
Oertel, Johannes Adam Simon
Page, William
Palmer, Walter Launt
Pearce, Charles Sprague
Picknell, William Lamb
Porter, Benjamin Curtis
Powell, William Henry
Prendergast, Maurice Brazil
Quidor, John
Ranney, William Tylee
Reid, Robert
Reinhart, Benjamin Franklin
Reinhart, Charles Stanley
Reuterdahl, Henry
Ritchie, Alexander Hay
Rosenthal, Toby Edward
Rossiter, Thomas Prichard
Ryder, Albert Pinkham
Sandham, Henry
Sargent, John Singer
Shirlaw, Walter
Shurtleff, Roswell Morse
Smedley, William Thomas
Smillie, George Henry
Smillie, James
Smillie, James David
Stone, William Oliver
Symons, George Gardner
Tait, Arthur Fitzwilliam
Thompson, Alfred Wordsworth
Tilton, John Rollin
Vanderlyn, John
Vedder, Elihu
Vinton, Frederic Porter
Waldo, Samuel Lovett
Walker, Henry Oliver
Weeks, Edwin Lord
West, William Edward
Wiggins, Carleton
Wylie, Robert
Zogbaum, Rufus Fairchild
DOWS, OLIN
Bruce, Edward Bright
DOYLE, HENRY GRATTAN
Winship, Albert Edward
DOYLE, J. KAAZ
Dies, Martin
DOZER, DONALD MARQUAND
Brickell, Henry Herschel
Myles, John
DREW, JOSEPH
Hobson, Julius Wilson
DRINKER, SOPHIE H.
Mussey, Ellen Spencer
DRIVER, CARL S.
Robertson, James, 1742–1814
Smith, Daniel
White, James
Williams, John, 1778–1837
Wright, Marcus Joseph
DROZE, WILMON H.
Crowe, Francis Trenholm
DRUMM, STELLA M.
Cerré, Jean Gabriel
Chouteau, Pierre
Crunden, Frederick Morgan
Doniphan, Alexander William
Glenn, Hugh
Hall, Willard Preble
Harrison, James
Hogan, John
Lange, Louis
Lorimier, Pierre Louis
McCoy, Joseph Geating
Mackay, James
Mackenzie, Donald
Mackenzie, Kenneth
McKnight, Robert
Majors, Alexander
Mitchell, David Dawson
Pilcher, Joshua
Pratte, Bernard
Provost, Etienne
St. Ange De Bellerive, Louis
St. Vrain, Ceran DeHault de Lassus de
Saugrain de Vigni, Antoine François
Sublette, William Lewis
Truteau, Jean Baptiste
Vigo, Joseph Maria Francesco
Waldo, David
DRURY, AUGUSTUS WALDO
Berger, Daniel
DUBOFSKY, MELVYN
Bellanca, Dorothy Jacobs
Chaplin, Ralph Hosea
Hunter, Robert
Lewis, John Llewellyn
Mahler, Herbert
O'Hare, Kate (Richards) Cunningham
Potofsky, Jacob Samuel
Taylor, George William
DU BOIS, W. E. BURGHARDT
De Wolf, James
Douglass, Frederick
Johnson, Elijah
Roberts, Joseph Jenkins
Roye, Edward James
Russwurm, John Brown
DUBRIDGE, LEE A.
Millikan, Robert Andrews
DUDDEN, ARTHUR POWER
Fels, Samuel Simeon
DUDDY, EDWARD A.
Farwell, John Villiers
Field, Marshall
Forgan, James Berwick
Henrotin, Charles
Hutchinson, Benjamin Peters
Hutchinson, Charles Lawrence
Lawson, Victor Freemont
Leiter, Levi Zeigler
Patten, James A.
Raymond, Benjamin Wright
Ream, Norman Bruce
Ryerson, Martin Antoine
Schuttler, Peter
Sears, Richard Warren
Shedd, John Graves
Torrence, Joseph Thatcher
Ward, Aaron Montgomery
DUFF, JOHN B.
Douglas, Helen Gahagan
Hughes, Howard Robard, Jr.
DUFFEY, BERNARD
Monroe, Harriet
DUFFY, JOHN
Emerson, Haven
Goldwater, Sigismund Schulz
Matas, Rudolph
DUGAN, RAYMOND SMITH
Barnard, Edward Emerson
Bond, George Phillips
Bond, William Cranch
Boss, Lewis
Brooks, William Robert
Burnham, Sherburne Wesley
Chandler, Seth Carlo
Clark, Alvan
Clark, Alvan Graham
Davidson, George
Doolittle, Charles Leander
Doolittle, Eric
Draper, Henry
Eastman, John Robie
Fleming, Williamina Paton Stevens
Flint, Albert Stowell
Gillis, James Melville
Gould, Benjamin Apthorp
Hall, Asaph
Harkness, William
Holden, Edward Singleton
Hough, George Washington
Hubbard, Joseph Stillman
Hussey, William Joseph
Keeler, James Edward
Kirkwood, Daniel
Leavenworth, Francis Preserved
Leavitt, Henrietta Swan
Lord, Henry Curwen
Lowell, Percival
Metcalf, Joel Hastings
Parkhurst, John Adelbert
Peters, Christian Henry Frederick
Rees, John Krom
Rutherfurd, Lewis Morris
Young, Charles Augustus
DUKE, ESCAL F.
Sheppard, John Morris
DU MEZ, ANDREW G.
Jacobs, Joseph, 1859–1929
Kraemer, Henry
Parrish, Edward
Proctor, William
Smith, Daniel B.
Spalding, Lyman
Squibb, Edward Robinson
Weightman, William
DUMKE, GLENN S.
Widney, Joseph Pomeroy
DUMOND, DWIGHT L.
Yancey, William Lowndes
DUNBAR, B. A.
Shepard, James Henry
DUNBAR, LOUISE B.
Nicola, Lewis
DUNHAM, DOROTHY KNIGHT
Roche, Arthur Somers
DUNHAM, DOWS
Reisner, George Andrew
DUNHAM, HAROLD H.
Sparks, William Andrew Jackson
DUNIWAY, CLYDE AUGUSTUS
Adams, Alva
Baker, Edward Dickinson
Strong, James Woodward

DUNN, JOSEPH
Currier, Charles Warren
DUNN, WALDO H.
Mitchell, Donald Grant
DUNNE, GERALD T.
Black, Hugo Lafayette
DUNNE, W. M. P.
MacArthur, John Donald
Mason, Francis Van Wyck
Reeves, Daniel F.
Ryan, Cornelius John ("Connie")
Vanderbilt, Amy
Wylie, Philip Gordon
DUNNING, WILLIAM B.
Brophy, Truman William
Flagg, Josiah Foster
Hudson, Edward
DUNNINGTON, JOHN H.
Weeks, John Elmer
DUPONT, DAVID
Hammond, Laurens
Tristano, Leonard Joseph ("Lennie")
DUR, PHILIP F.
Caffery, Jefferson
DURAND, WILLIAM FREDERICK
Allen, Jeremiah Mervin
Copeland, Charles W.
Dickie, George William
Eckart, William Roberts
Ericsson, John
Thurston, Robert Henry
Timby, Theodore Ruggles
DUREL, LIONEL C.
Canonge, Louis Placide
Deléry, François Charles
Dugué, Charles Oscar
Dupratz, Antoine Simon Le Page
Garreau, Armand
Humbert, Jean Joseph Amable
Mercier, Charles Alfred
Moreau-Lislet, Louis Casimir Elisabeth
DUTCHER, GEORGE MATTHEW
Stephens, Henry Morse
DUTTON, GEORGE B.
Nelson, Henry Loomis
DWIGHT, HARRISON GRISWOLD
Adee, Alvey Augustus
Ellicott, Andrew
James, George Wharton
Whitlock, Brand
DWYER, DONALD HARRIS
Atterbury, Grosvenor
DYER, FRANK L.
Martin, Thomas Commerford
DYER, WALTER A.
Phyfe, Duncan
Stiegel, Henry William
DYKES, DE WITT S., JR.
Bethune, Mary McLeod
DYKSTRA, ROBERT R.
Scott, Walter Edward

EARL, POLLY ANNE
Dennison, Henry Sturgis
EARLE, A. SCOTT
Crile, George Washington
EARLE, ROSAMONDE HOPKINS
Payne, William Harold
Pierce, John Davis
EASTERBY, J. H.
Adams, James Hopkins
Aiken, David Wyatt
Aiken, William
Allston, Robert Francis Withers
Alston, Joseph
Bratton, John
Brumby, Richard Trapier
Chestnut, James
Conner, James
De Saussure, Henry William
Drayton, John
Drayton, Thomas Fenwick
Drayton, William, 1732–1790
Drayton, William, 1776–1846
Hampton, Wade, 1751–1835
Hampton, Wade, 1818–1902
Pinckney, Charles
Pinckney, Henry Laurens
Pringle, John Julius
Stephenson, Nathaniel Wright
EASTERLY, SUSAN
Gabo, Naum
Nabokov, Nicolas
EASTMAN, EDWARD R.
Harris, Joseph
EASTMAN, LINDA ANNE
Brett, William Howard
Galbreath, Charles Burleigh
EATON, ARTHUR WENTWORTH HAMILTON
Winslow, William Copley
EATON, EDWARD DWIGHT
Chapin, Aaron Lucius
Fairchild, James Harris
Hallock, William Allen
Hammond, Edward Payson
Hand, Daniel
Hillis, Newell Dwight
Hopkins, John Henry
McKenzie, Alexander
Mahan, Asa
Mead, Charles Marsh
Mears, David Otis
Morris, Edward Dafydd
Morrison, Nathan Jackson
Noble, Frederick Alphonso
Pearsons, Daniel Kimball
Post, Truman Marcellus
Rankin, Jeremiah Eames
Robinson, Charles Seymour
Smith, Judson
Stewart, Philo Penfield
Stowe, Calvin Ellis
Warren, Israel Perkins
Wright, Theodore Lyman
EATON, LEONARD K.
Jensen, Jens
EATON, WALTER PRICHARD
Baker, George Pierce
Belasco, David
Booth, Agnes
Boucicault, Dion
Brougham, John
Burk, John Daly
Burton, William Evans
Clifton, Josephine
Coghlan, Rose
Conway, Frederick Bartlett
Cushman, Charlotte Saunders
Cushman, Susan Webb
Daly, Peter Christopher Arnold
Daniels, Frank Albert
Drew, John, 1827–1862
Drew, John, 1853–1927
Drew, Louisa Lane
Fiske, Minnie Maddern
Forrest, Edwin
Goodwin, Nathaniel Carll
Hackett, James Henry
Hackett, James Keteltas
Herne, James A.
Hopper, DeWolf
Janauschek, Franziska Magdalena Romance
Jefferson, Joseph, 1774–1832
Jefferson, Joseph, 1829–1905
Keene, Thomas Wallace
Kemble, Frances Anne
Long, John Luther
MacKaye, James Morrison Steele
Mansfield, Richard
Modjeska, Helena
Moody, William Vaughn
Olcott, Chauncey
Power, Frederick Tyrone
Rehan, Ada
Silverman, Sime
Smith, Winchell
Sothern, Edward Askew
Sothern, Edward Hugh
Stevens, Emily
Stoddart, James Henry
Thomas, Augustus
Thompson, Denman
Thorne, Charles Robert, 1814–1893
Thorne, Charles Robert, 1840–1883
Urban, Joseph
Vandenhoff, George
Walcot, Charles Melton, *c.* 1816–1868
Walcot, Charles Melton, 1840–1921
Ward, Genevieve
Wemyss, Francis Courtney
Williams, Barney
Williams, Bert
Wilson, Francis
Winter, William
Wise, Thomas Alfred
Ziegfeld, Florenz
ECKENRODE, H. J.
Lee, Francis Lightfoot
Lee, Henry, 1756–1818
Lee, Richard Bland
EDEL, LEON
Wharton, Edith Newbold Jones
EDELMAN, EDWARD
Hancock, Thomas
EDER, DORIS L.
Rockefeller, Martha Baird
EDGELL, GEORGE H.
Lowell, Guy
EDGERTON, FRANKLIN
Hodgson, William Brown
Hopkins, Edward Washburn
EDGERTON, MILTON T.
Davis, John Staige
EDGETT, EDWIN FRANCIS
Bacon, Frank
Ballou, Maturin Murray
Barrett, Lawrence
Bernard, William Bayle
Bonstelle, Jessie

Burgess, Neil
Burke, Charles St. Thomas
Cayvan, Georgia
Chaney, Lon
Christy, Edwin P.
Claxton, Kate
Dana, Richard Henry, 1787–1879
Dana, Richard Henry, 1815–1882
De Angelis, Thomas Jefferson
Deering, Nathaniel
De Mille, Henry Churchill
Ditrichstein, Leo
Dressler, Marie
Durivage, Francis Alexander
Edes, Benjamin
Edeson, Robert
Estes, Dana
Field, Mary Katherine Keemle
Hale, Louise Closser
Hale, Nathan
Hale, Philip
Harrison, Richard Berry
Hitchcock, Raymond
Hodge, William Thomas
Hudson, Charles
Illington, Margaret
James, Louis
Jones, Joseph Stevens
Kester, Paul
Kirby, J. Hudson
Klein, Charles
Lackaye, Wilton
Le Moyne, William J.
Lewis, Arthur
Liveright, Horace Brisbin
Logan, Cornelius Ambrosius
Logan, Olive
McCullough, John
Manners, John Hartley
Mantell, Robert Bruce
Mason, John, 1858–1919
Megrue, Roi Cooper
Mitchell, William, 1798–1856
Montague, Henry James
O'Neill, James
Osborn, Laughton
Owen, William Florence
Owens, John Edmond
Parker, Henry Taylor
Placide, Henry
Potter, Paul Meredith
Powell, Snelling
Powell, Thomas
Pray, Isaac Clark
Presbrey, Eugene Wiley
Proctor, Joseph
Rankin, McKee
Raymond, John T.
Richings, Peter
Riddle, George Peabody
Roberts, Theodore
Robson, Stuart
Russell, Sol Smith
Sargent, George Henry
Seymour, William
Shaw, Mary
Sills, Milton
Smith, William Henry, 1806–1872
Vezin, Hermann
Vincent, Mary Ann
Waller, Emma
Warde, Frederick Barkham
Warren, William, 1767–1832
Warren, William, 1812–1888
Western, Lucille
Wolheim, Louis Robert

EDMINSTER, LYNN R.
Page, Thomas Walker

EDMONDS, ANTHONY O.
Jacobs, Michael Strauss

EDMONDS, JOHN H.
Bonner, John
Burgis, William

EDSALL, JOHN T.
Cohn, Edwin Joseph
Henderson, Lawrence Joseph

EDSON, HOWARD A.
Pritchard, Frederick John

EDWARD, BROTHER
Azarias, Brother

EDWARDS, ANNE
Leigh, Vivien

EDWARDS, EVERETT E.
Periam, Jonathan
Reid, James L.
Scovell, Melville Amasa
Silver, Gray
Spillman, William Jasper
Sturtevant, Edward Lewis
True, Alfred Charles

EDWARDS, G. FRANKLIN
Frazier, Edward Franklin

EDWARDS, GRANVILLE D.
Moore, William Thomas

EDWARDS, HERBERT J.
Herne, Chrystal Katharine

EGAN, MARTIN
Morrow, Dwight Whitney

EGGERT, GERALD
Gimbel, Bernard Feustman

EGGERT, GERALD G.
Cabot, Godfrey Lowell
Fairless, Benjamin F.
Girdler, Tom Mercer
Randall, Clarence Belden

EGGLESTON, JOSEPH D.
Foote, William Henry
Hoge, Moses
Hoge, Moses Drury
Lacy, Drury
McIlwaine, Richard
Maxwell, William

EGLI, CLARA
Southack, Cyprian

EHRENZWEIG, ALBERT A.
Radin, Max

EHRLICH, EVELYN
Bennett, Constance Campbell

EISELEN, FREDERICK C.
Raymond, Miner
Ridgaway, Henry Bascom

EISENHART, KATHARINE S.
Marquand, Henry Gurdon

EISENHART, LUTHER P.
Minto, Walter

EISENSTADT, A. S.
Adams, James Truslow

EKBLAW, W. ELMER
Greely, Adolphus Washington

ELIOT, ALEXANDER
Frankfurter, Alfred Moritz
McBride, Henry

ELIOT, MARTHA M.
Abbott, Grace

ELIOT, SAMUEL ATKINS
Armstrong, Samuel Chapman
Bartol, Cyrus Augustus
Batchelor, George
Bellows, Henry Whitney

ELKINS, ELIZABETH A.
Moore, Hugh Everett
Penfold, Joseph Weller

ELKUS, ABRAM I.
Straus, Oscar Solomon

ELLIOTT, EDWARD C.
Purdue, John

ELLIOTT, THOMPSON C.
Ogden, Peter Skene
Thompson, David

ELLIOTT, WILLIAM G.
Griffith, William
Haines, Charles Glidden
Haines, Lynn
Hanson, Alexander Contee, 1749–1806
Hayes, John Lord
Howard, Benjamin Chew

ELLIS, ELIZABETH BRECKENRIDGE
Oglesby, Richard James
Pope, Nathaniel
Springer, William McKendree
Thomas, Jesse Burgess

ELLIS, ELMER
Teller, Henry Moore
Williams, Walter

ELLIS, JOHN TRACY
Guilday, Peter Keenan

ELLIS, L. ETHAN
Judd, Norman Buel
Kellogg, Frank Billings
Madden, Martin Barnaby
Mann, James Robert
Mason, William Ernest
Rutgers, Henry
Trumbull, Lyman
Washburne, Elihu Benjamin

ELLIS, MILTON
Brown, William Hill
Day, Holman Francis
Fessenden, Thomas Green
Mellen, Grenville
Morton, Sarah Wentworth Apthorp
Murray, Judith Sargent Stevens
Neal, John
Rowson, Susanna Haswell
Smith, Elihu Hubbard
Wood, Sarah Sayward Barrell Keating

ELLIS, WILLIAM E.
Hess, Victor Franz
Szilard, Leo

ELSON, ARTHUR
Carr, Benjamin
Coerne, Louis Adolphe
Converse, Charles Crozat
Edwards, Julian
Eichberg, Julius
Emery, Stephen Albert

ELSROAD, LINDA
Carter, Maybelle Addington

ELTSCHER, LOUIS R.
Hurley, Roy T.
Stearman, Lloyd Carlton

ELZAS, BARNETT A.
Mordecai, Moses Cohen

Pinto, Isaac
Poznanski, Gustavus
Elzy, Martin I.
Verrill, Alpheus Hyatt
Emerson, Horton W., Jr.
Baker, John Franklin
Sande, Earl
Stagg, Amos Alonzo
Emerson, Kendall
Coolidge, Archibald Cary
Crothers, Samuel McChord
Emerton, Ephraim
Felton, Cornelius Conway
Frothingham, Paul Revere
Gross, Charles
Gurney, Ephraim Whitman
Thayer, William Roscoe
Williams, Linsly Rudd
Emerton, Ephraim
Coolidge, Archibald Cary
Crothers, Samuel McChord
Felton, Cornelius Conway
Frothingham, Paul Revere
Gross, Charles
Gurney, Ephraim Whitman
Thayer, William Roscoe
Emery, Edwin
Noyes, Frank Brett
Reid, Ogden Mills
Van Anda, Carr Vattel
Emery, William M.
Banks, Charles Edward
Putnam, Eben
Ricketson, Daniel
Robinson, Edward Mott
Rotch, William
Sturgis, William
Warren, Russell
Williams, Catharine Read Arnold
Emmons, William Harvey
Upham, Warren
Engel, Carl
Schirmer, Gustav
Schirmer, Rudolph Edward
Sonneck, Oscar George Theodore
Engel, William J.
Lower, William Edgar
Engelbrecht, Lloyd C.
Eames, Charles Ormand, Jr.
English, John P.
Macdonald, Charles Blair
Ennis, J. Harold
Dallas, Alexander James
Ensign, Forest Chester
Benton, Thomas Hart
Epstein, Dena J.
Stock, Frederick August
Erdman, Charles R., Jr.
Abbett, Leon
Blair, John Insley
Dickerson, Mahlon
Dryden, John Fairfield
Field, Richard Stockton
Frelinghuysen, Frederick
Frelinghuysen, Theodore
Kinney, William Burnet
Robeson, George Maxwell
Erickson, Alana J.
Disney, Roy Oliver
Rankin, Jeannette Pickering
Stewart, Arthur Thomas ("Tom")
Erickson, Erling A.
Morgan, John Pierpont
Ermarth, Margaret Sittler
Tipton, John
Erskine, John
MacDowell, Edward Alexander
Erskine, Marjory
Duchesne, Rose Philippine
Esarey, Logan
Benton, Allen Richardson
Bright, Jesse David
Espenschied, Lloyd
Carson, John Renshaw
Esposito, David M.
Champion, Gower
Dana, Charles Anderson
Firestone, Harvey Samuel, Jr.
Naish, Joseph Carrol
Rennie, Michael
Wills, Chill
Esposito, William E.
Carey, Max George ("Scoops")
Hubbard, Robert C. ("Cal")
O'Brien, Robert David ("Davey")
Estes, J. A.
Locke, David Ross
Ettenberg, Eugene M.
Dwiggins, William Addison
Ettinger, Amos A.
Oglethorpe, James Edward
Soulé, Pierre
Eugenia, Sister
Guérin, Ann-Thérèse
Eula, Michael J.
De Seversky, Alexander Procofieff
Franzblau, Rose Nadler
Wolfe, Bertram David
Wright, John Joseph
Eurich, Alvin C.
Coffman, Lotus Delta
Evans, Austin P.
Burr, George Lincoln
Evans, Daniel
Fenn, William Wallace
Park, Edwards Amasa
Porter, Ebenezer
Evans, G. Heberton, Jr.
Barnett, George Ernest
Evans, Howard E.
Howard, Leland Ossian
Evans, James F.
Butler, Burridge Davenal
Evans, John Norris
Noyes, Henry Drury
Evans, Lawrence Boyd
Bacon, John
Briggs, George Nixon
Evans, Paul D.
Cazenove, Théophile
Ellicott, Joseph
Everett, Robert
Harpur, Robert
Ludlow, Thomas William
Mappa, Adam Gerard
Mitchell, Stephen Mix
Morris, Luzon Burritt
Morrison, William McCutchan
Niles, Nathaniel, 1741–1828
Olney, Jesse
Paine, Charles
Paine, Elijah
Painter, Gamaliel
Palmer, William Adams
Phelps, Oliver
Prentiss, Samuel
Pringle, Cyrus Guernsey
Rowlands, William
Sanders, Daniel Clarke
Slade, William
Slafter, Edmund Farwell
Smith, John Gregory
Evensen, Bruce J.
March, Frederic
Tunney, James Joseph ("Gene")
Everett, Walter G.
Seth, James
Evermann, Barton Warren
Jordan, David Starr
Evjens, John O.
Johnsen, Erik Kristian
Oftedal, Sven
Preus, Christian Keyser
Richard, James William
Schmauk, Theodore Emanuel
Schmidt, Friedrich August
Schodde, George Henry
Seyffarth, Gustavus
Stromme, Peer Olsen
Stub, Hans Gerhard
Stuckenberg, John Henry Wilbrandt
Sverdrup, Georg
Tou, Erik Hansen
Weidner, Revere Franklin
Ewan, Joseph
McLaren, John
Trelease, William
Ewen, David
Baccaloni, Salvatore
Bloch, Ernest
Bori, Lucrezia
De Rose, Peter
De Sylva, George Gard "Buddy"
Farrar, Geraldine
Gatti-Casazza, Giulio
Gershwin, George
Hammerstein, Oscar, II
Kahn, Gustav Gerson
Martinelli, Giovanni
Melton, James
Pinza, Ezio
Riegger, Wallingford
Schnabel, Artur
Schoenberg, Arnold
Tibbett, Lawrence Mervil
Toscanini, Arturo
Ewing, George Henry
Lorimer, George Claude
Ezell, John S.
Beaty, Amos Leonidas
Berry, Martha McChesney
Cullinan, Joseph Stephen
Marland, Ernest Whitworth
Phillips, Frank
Truett, George Washington

Fabre, Michel
Wright, Richard Nathaniel
Fagley, Frederick L.
Cadman, Samuel Parkes

Failing, Patricia
Arno, Peter
Epstein, Jacob
Halpert, Edith Gregor
Lewisohn, Sam Adolph
Marsh, Reginald
Moses, Anna Mary Robertson ("Grandma")
Newman, Barnett
Tomlin, Bradley Walker
Zorach, William
Failing, Patricia Stipe
Stein, Leo Daniel
Fairchild, Fred R.
Adams, Thomas Sewall
Fairchild, Henry Pratt
Holt, Henry
Richmond, Mary Ellen
Fairchild, Herman L.
Perkins, George Henry
Fairman, Charles
Butler, Pierce
Jackson, Charles
Knowlton, Marcus Perrin
Lord, Otis Phillips
Loring, Ellis Gray
McCullough, John Griffith
Merrick, Pliny
Metcalf, Theron
Miller, Samuel Freeman
Montefiore, Joshua
Parker, Joel
Parsons, Theophilus
Phillips, Willard
Pierce, Edward Lillie
Richardson, William Adams
Ruggles, Timothy
Falconer, John I.
Root, Amos Ives
Falk, Stanley L.
Wilbur, Curtis Dwight
Fanger, Donald
Cross, Samuel Hazzard
Faris, Ellsworth
Small, Albion Woodbury
Faris, Paul Patton
McAfee, John Armstrong
McLeod, Alexander
Mason, John Mitchell
Miller, James Russell
Miller, Samuel
Neill, William
Nevin, Alfred
Nevin, Edwin Henry
Parker, Joel
Patterson, Robert Mayne
Patton, William
Pentecost, George Frederick
Peters, Madison Clinton
Roberts, William Charles
Scott, William Anderson
Shedd, William Greenough Thayer
Simpson, Albert Benjamin
Skinner, Thomas Harvey
Farish, Hunter D.
Tait, Charles
Farmer, Hallie
Clayton, Henry De Lamar
Fry, Birkett Davenport
Hamilton, Peter
Herbert, Hilary Abner
Hilliard, Henry Washington
Hopkins, Arthur Francis
Hopkins, Juliet Ann Opie
Houston, George Smith
Lane, James Henry
Lyon, Francis Strother
McKinstry, Alexander
Oates, William Calvin
O'Neal, Edward Asbury
Owen, Thomas McAdory
Parsons, Lewis Eliphalet
Perry, William Flake
Pickett, Albert James
Screws, William Wallace
Shorter, John Gill
Smith, Robert Hardy
Smith, William Russell
Stone, George Washington
Tutwiler, Henry
Tutwiler, Julia Strudwick
Watts, Thomas Hill
Winston, John Anthony
Farnham, Willard
Tatlock, John Strong Perry
Farnum, Grace C.
Swanson, Claude Augustus
Farr, Albert M.
Hoffman, Eugene Augustus
Farr, Finis
Johnson, Jack
Farrar, Clarence B.
Dewey, Richard Smith
Faulk, Odie B.
Croy, Homer
Mulford, Clarence Edward
Faulkner, Ethel Webb
Dwight, Benjamin Woodbridge
Dwight, Nathaniel
Dwight, Sereno Edwards
Parker, Richard Green
Smith, Sophia
Steele, Joel Dorman
Stoddard, John Fair
Faulkner, Harold Underwood
Abbott, Horace
Alger, Cyrus
Ames, James Tyler
Ames, Nathan Peabody
Babbitt, Benjamin Talbot
Bates, Joshua
Benner, Philip
Bent, Josiah
Bliss, Eliphalet Williams
Borden, Richard
Bradley, Milton
Bridges, Robert, d. 1656
Brooker, Charles Frederick
Brown, Ebenezer
Burrowes, Edward Thomas
Butler, Simeon
Candee, Leverett
Chapin, Chester William
Cheney, Ward
Chickering, Jonas
Chisholm, Hugh Joseph
Cobb, Jonathan Holmes
Combs, Moses Newell
Coney, Jabez
Crocker, Alvah
Cummings, John
Dennison, Aaron Lufkin
Douglas, Benjamin
Downer, Samuel
Draper, Eben Sumner
Draper, William Franklin
Dwight, Edmund
Eastman, Arthur MacArthur
Fordney, Joseph Warren
Gary, Elbert Henry
Gilbert, William Lewis
Jackson, Patrick Tracy
James, Charles Tillinghast
Lowell, Francis Cabot
Mackay, John William
Merriam, Charles
Merrill, Joshua
Perry, William
Phelps, Anson Greene
Phelps, Guy Rowland
Pope, Albert Augustus
Sperry, Nehemiah Day
Ward, George Gray
Faulkner, John Alfred
Atkinson, John
Baker, Osmon Cleander
Bashford, James Whitford
Faulkner, William H.
Harrison, James Albert
Fausold, Martin L.
Gannett, Frank Ernest
Wadsworth, James Wolcott, Jr.
Faust, Albert Bernhardt
Bartholdt, Richard
Brachvogel, Udo
Brentano, Lorenz
Brühl, Gustav
Dorsch, Eduard
Grund, Francis Joseph
Hart, James Morgan
Hecker, Friedrich Karl Franz
Heinzen, Karl Peter
Hewett, Waterman Thomas
Hilgard, Theodor Erasmus
Learned, Marion Dexter
Rapp, Wilhelm
Rattermann, Heinrich Armin
Fawcett, Ellen Douglass
Cunningham, Ann Pamela
Fawcett, James Waldo
Scott, Thomas Fielding
Slattery, Charles Lewis
Faxon, Harriet
Robinson, Edward, 1858–1931
Fee, Walter R.
Stockton, Richard
Feinberg, Gerald
Einstein, Albert
Feinberg, Renee
Shub, Abraham David
Feinstein, Estelle F.
Bingham, Hiram
Feleky, Charles
Haraszthy de Mokcsa, Agoston
Xántus, János
Fellner, Felix
Schnerr, Leander
Stehle, Aurelius Aloysius
Wimmer, Boniface
Wolf, Innocent William
Fellows, Frederick
Van Vleck, John Hasbrouck
Fellows, George Emory
Cannon, George Quayle
Feltus, George Haws
House, Samuel Reynolds
Jones, John Taylor
McFarland, Samuel Gamble

McGilvary, Daniel
Matton, Stephen
FENN, WILLIAM PURVIANCE
Fee, John Gregg
FENN, WILLIAM W.
Chauncy, Charles, 1592–1671/2
Chauncy, Charles, 1705–1787
Clarke, James Freeman
Gordon, George Angier
Hodges, George
Hopkins, Mark
FENTON, NORMAN
Southard, Elmer Ernest
FERGUSON, EUGENE S.
Kingsbury, Albert
FERGUSON, WALLACE K.
Smith, Preserved
FERLING, JOHN E.
Ward, Arch Burdette
FERM, ROBERT L.
McPherson, Aimee Semple
FERM, VERGILIUS
Krauth, Charles Porterfield
Schmucker, Samuel Simon
FERN, ALAN M.
Ganso, Emil
FERRELL, ROBERT H.
Carr, Wilbur John
Clark, Joshua Reuben, Jr.
Eisenhower, Dwight David
Hull, Cordell
Levinson, Salmon Oliver
Stark, Lloyd Crow
Truman, Harry S.
FERRELL, SARAH
Bolm, Adolph Rudolphovitch
FERRIS, WILLIAM R.
Lomax, John Avery
FERRIS, WILLIAM R., JR.
Ledbetter, Huddie ("Leadbelly")
FERRY, W. HAWKINS
Kahn, Albert
FERTIG, WALTER L.
Nicholson, Meredith
FETTER, FRANK W.
Kemmerer, Edwin Walter
FIEBEGER, GUSTAVE JOSEPH
Anderson, James Patton
Anderson, Richard Heron
Barnard, John Gross
Burnside, Ambrose Everett
Crook, George
Duane, James Chatham
Humphreys, Andrew Atkinson
Mahan, Dennis Hart
Mansfield, Joseph King Fenno
Marshall, William Louis
Merrill, William Emery
Michie, Peter Smith
Talcott, Andrew
Thayer, Sylvanus
Tower, Zealous Bates
Trimble, Isaac Ridgeway
Turnbull, William
Turner, John Wesley
FIEDLER, LESLIE A.
Leonard, William Ellery
FIELD, CORINNE T.
Davis, Abraham Lincoln, Jr.
Evola, Natale ("Joe Diamond")
Heald, Henry Townley
Martinez, Maria
Shaw, Clay L.
Wilson, William Griffith ("Bill W.")
FIELD, JAMES A., JR.
Mitscher, Marc Andrew
Sims, William Sowden
FIELDING, MANTLE
Anderson, Alexander
Sully, Thomas
West, Benjamin, 1728–1820
FIESER, LOUIS F.
Kohler, Elmer Peter
FILLER, LOUIS
Armstrong, Hamilton Fish
Bennett, Hugh Hammond
Boole, Ella Alexander
Clark, Grenville
Coulter, Ernest Kent
Dunne, Finley Peter
Filene, Edward Albert
Flandrau, Charles Macomb
Hall, Bolton
Hapgood, Hutchins
Hapgood, Norman
Kellor, Frances (Alice)
Lovett, Robert Morss
Markham, Edwin
Morgan, Arthur Ernest
Myers, Gustavus
Pinchot, Cornelia Elizabeth Bryce
Rittenhouse, Jessie Belle
Spaeth, John Duncan
Steffens, Lincoln
Tugwell, Rexford Guy
Van Loon, Hendrik Willem
FINCH, JAMES KIP
Bates, Onward
Burr, William Hubert
Cooper, Hugh Lincoln
Davies, John Vipond
Fletcher, Robert
Mead, Elwood
Modjeski, Ralph
Moran, Daniel Edward
Parsons, William Barclay
Ridgway, Robert
Symons, Thomas William
Thacher, Edwin
Thompson, Charles Oliver
Totten, George Muirson
Waddell, John Alexander Low
Whipple, Squire
White, Canvass
Wright, Benjamin
FINDLING, JOHN E.
Allen, George Venable
Bullitt, William Christian
Castle, William Richards, Jr.
Clayton, William Lockhart
FINE, SIDNEY
Murphy, Frank
FINGER, CHARLES J.
Reedy, William Marion
Woodruff, William Edward
FINNEY, BYRON A.
Davis, Raymond Cazallis
FIRKINS, OSCAR W.
Howells, William Dean
Northrop, Cyrus
FIROR, WARFIELD M.
Reid, Mont Rogers
FISCHER, LE ROY H.
Gurowski, Adam
FISCHER, WILLIAM E., JR.
Chapman, Oscar Littleton
Widener, George Dunton
FISH, CARL RUSSELL
Blaine, James Gillespie
Buchanan, James
Butler, Benjamin Franklin, 1818–1893
Curtis, George Ticknor
FISH, PETER GRAHAM
Parker, John Johnston
FISHBEIN, MORRIS
Blalock, Nelson Gales
DeLee, Joseph Bolivar
Simmons, George Henry
FISHER, GALEN R.
Chessman, Caryl Whittier
FISHER, G. CLYDE
Akeley, Carl Ethan
FISHER, H. H.
Golder, Frank Alfred
FISHER, JAMES
Koenig, George Augustus
FISHER, WALTER
Dett, Robert Nathaniel
FISK, DANIEL M.
Harlan, Richard
Morton, Samuel George
FISKE, HERBERT H.
Warden, David Bailie
FITCH, EDWARD
Mears, John William
North, Edward
North, Simeon, 1802–1884
FITCH, JAMES M.
Whitaker, Charles Harris
FITCH, JOHN A.
Lee, Porter Raymond
FITCH, NÖEL RILEY
Nin, Anaïs
FITE, GILBERT C.
Murphy, Frederick E.
Norbeck, Peter
Peek, George Nelson
FITTRO, MARY ELIZABETH
Leeds, John
Paca, William
Stone, Thomas
Stone, William
FITZPATRICK, EDWARD A.
Katzer, Frederic Xavier
FITZPATRICK, JOHN
Greenwood, John
Jackson, William, 1759–1828
Tilghman, Tench
Varick, Richard
Washington, George
FITZPATRICK, JOHN F.
Herrmann, Bernard
Tiomkin, Dimitri
Waxman, Franz
FITZPATRICK, PAUL J.
Falkner, Roland Post
FITZSIMONS, NEAL
Hovey, Otis Ellis
Stevens, John Frank
FLACK, J. KIRKPATRICK
Kaltenborn, Hans Von
Patrick, Edwin Hill ("Ted")
FLAHERTY, DAVID HARRIS
Train, Arthur Cheney

FLANNERY-HERZFELD, REGINA
Cooper, John Montgomery
FLEET, SUSAN
Biggs, Edward George Power
Levant, Oscar
Schippers, Thomas
FLEMING, DONALD
Cannon, Walter Bradford
FLEMING, WALTER LYNWOOD
Barrow, Washington
Bate, William Brimage
Baxter, John
Brown, John Calvin
Brown, Neill Smith
Carmack, Edward Ward
Catron, John
FLETCHER, ROBERT S.
Shipherd, John Jay
FLEXNER, SIMON
Councilman, William Thomas
Rose, Wickliffe
FLICK, ALEXANDER CLARENCE
Barnard, Daniel Dewey
Beardsley, Samuel
Betts, Samuel Rossiter
Black, Frank Swett
Fernow, Berthold
Stone, William Leete
Tilden, Samuel Jones
FLIPPIN, PERCY SCOTT
Culpeper, Thomas Lord
Ellis, Henry
Fauquier, Francis
Gooch, Sir William
Hewat, Alexander
Heyward, Thomas
Hyrne, Edmund Massingberd
Johnson, Herschel Vespasian
FLITCROFT, JOHN E.
Gilchrist, Robert
Hobart, Garret Augustus
Murphy, Franklin
Rix, Julian Walbridge
Thompson, Daniel Pierce
FLOM, GEORGE T.
Eielsen, Elling
Janson, Kristofer Nagel
FLOOD, NANCY V.
Budenz, Louis Francis
Lyons, Leonard
FLOWER, DEAN
Arlen, Michael
Arvin, Newton
Atherton, Gertrude Franklin (Horn)
Bacon, Leonard
Cabell, James Branch
Coffin, Robert Peter Tristram
La Farge, Christopher Grant
McNulty, John Augustine
Parker, Dorothy Rothschild
Stribling, Thomas Sigismund
FLYNN, GEORGE Q.
Niles, David K.
Walker, Frank Comerford
FLYNN, JOHN T.
Rockefeller, William
FOERSTER, NORMAN
Babbitt, Irving
Burroughs, John
FOGARTY, GERALD P., S.J.
Spellman, Francis Joseph
FOIK, PAUL J.
Padilla, Juan de
FOLLIARD, EDWARD T.
McLean, Edward Beale
FOLMSBEE, STANLEY J.
Byrns, Joseph Wellington
FOLSOM, JOSEPH FULFORD
Young, David
FOOTE, ARTHUR
Schmidt, Arthur Paul
FOOTE, FRANKLIN M.
Lewis, Francis Park
FOOTE, HARRY W.
Silliman, Benjamin, 1816–1885
FOOTE, HENRY WILDER
Norton, Andrews
Phillips, George
FORBES, ALLYN B.
Newman, Henry
FORD, AMELIA C.
Mortimer, Mary
Waldo, Samuel
FORD, JEREMIAH D. M.
Hills, Elijah Clarence
Lang, Henry Roseman
Sheldon, Edward Stevens
Ticknor, George
FORD, WORTHINGTON CHAUNCEY
Adams, Brooks
Adams, Charles Francis, 1807–1886
Adams, Charles Francis, 1835–1915
Adams, John
Adams, John Quincy
FORSYTH, KING LOGAN
Quesnay, Alexandre-Marie
FORTSON, BLANTON
Benning, Henry Lewis
Bleckley, Logan Edwin
Campbell, John Archibald
Charlton, Thomas Usher Pulaski
Clay, Joseph, 1741–1804
Cobb, Andrew Jackson
Erskine, John
Jackson, James, 1819–1887
Lamar, Joseph Rucker
Lumpkin, Joseph Henry
Warner, Hiram
FOSBROKE, HUGHELL E. W.
Moore, Clement Clarke
Turner, Samuel Hulbeart
FOSTER, WILLIAM
Maclean, John
FOWKES, FREDERICK M.
Harkins, William Draper
FOWLER, HAROLD L.
Bryan, John Stewart
FOWLER, HAROLD NORTH
Abbott, Frank Frost
Allen, Frederic De Forest
Allen, William Francis
Anthon, Charles
Beck, Charles
Bennett, Charles Edwin
Bingham, William
Botsford, George Willis
Burnam, John Miller
Carter, Jesse Benedict
Chase, Thomas
Dennison, Walter
Mitchell, Lucy Myers Wright
Platner, Samuel Ball
FOWLER, HENRY THATCHER
Sanders, Frank Knight
FOX, DANIEL M.
Ayres, Leonard Porter
Bliss, Cornelius Newton
Embree, Edwin Rogers
Leathers, Waller Smith
Rockefeller, Abby Greene Aldrich
Sawyer, Wilbur Augustus
Strong, Richard Pearson
FOX, DIXON RYAN
Clinton, DeWitt
Hammond, Jabez Delano
Heathcote, Caleb
Osgood, Herbert Levi
FOX, EARLY LEE
Bocock, Thomas Stanley
Boteler, Alexander Robinson
Clay, Matthew
Clopton, John
Dawson, John
FOX, GEORGE HENRY
Jackson, George Thomas
FOX, JOHN DAVID
Chambers, Whittaker
FOX, LOUIS H.
Farnum, Dustin Lancy
Lander, Jean Margaret Davenport
Lewis, James
Ludlow, Noah Miller
FOX, L. WEBSTER
Burnett, Swan Moses
Littell, Squier
Norris, William Fisher
Oliver, Charles Augustus
FOX, WILLIAM LLOYD
Dandy, Walter Edward
Elsberg, Charles Albert
FOYE, WILBUR G.
Rice, William North
FRAME, JAMES EVERETT
Vincent, Marvin Richardson
FRANCIS, JOHN, JR.
Verbeck, William
FRANCKE, KUNO
Follen, Charles
FRANK, BENIS M.
Higgins, Andrew Jackson
FRANK, ELIZABETH
Bogan, Louise Marie
FRANKEL, CHARLES
Edman, Irwin
FRANKENSTEIN, ALFRED V.
Hartley, Marsden
Hertz, Alfred
FRANKFURTER, FELIX
Cardozo, Benjamin Nathan
Holmes, Oliver Wendell
Valentine, Robert Grosvenor
FRANKLIN, FABIAN
Heilprin, Michael
FRANKLIN, JOHN HOPE
Lynch, John Roy
FRANKLIN, PHILIP
Moore, Clarence Lemuel Elisha
FRANKLIN, WILLIAM M.
Welles, (Benjamin) Sumner
FRANTZ, JOE B.
Richardson, Sid Williams
FRASER, RUSSELL
Blackmur, Richard Palmer

FRAZER, JOSEPH C. W.
Morse, Harmon Northrop
FRAZIER, E. FRANKLIN
Miller, Kelly
FREDERICK, JOHN H.
Burrall, William Porter
Cass, George Washington
Clark, Horace Francis
Crocker, Charles
Dillon, Sidney
Eastman, Timothy Corser
Eckert, Thomas Thompson
Elkins, William Lukens
Fitler, Edwin Henry
Florence, Thomas Birch
Fraley, Frederick
Griscom, Clement Acton
Guthrie, George Wilkins
Habersham, Alexander Wylly
Harding, Jesper
Harding, William White
Harrah, Charles Jefferson
Harrison, John
Harrison, Joseph
Haupt, Herman
Hillegas, Michael
Houston, Henry Howard
Humphreys, Joshua
Huston, Charles
Hutchinson, James
Ingham, Samuel Delucenna
Johnson, John Graver
Jones, Jehu Glancy
Jones, Joel
Jones, Thomas P.
Jones, William
Kane, John Kintzing
Kane, Thomas Leiper
Keating, William Hypolitus
Keep, Henry
Knight, Jonathan
Leiper, Thomas
Lewis, William
Lippincott, Joshua Ballinger
Lukens, Rebecca Webb Pennock
Macalester, Charles, 1765–1832
Macalester, Charles, 1798–1873
Martin, John Hill
Meade, George
Meade, Richard Worsam
Meredith, Samuel
Merrick, Samuel Vaughan
Miner, Charles
Mitten, Thomas Eugene
Morris, Anthony, 1766–1860
Morris, Cadwalader
Moxham, Arthur James
Nesbitt, John Maxwell
Nixon, John, 1733–1808
Packer, William Fisher
Parrish, Charles
Patterson, Morris
Pattison, Robert Emory
Pollock, James
Porter, David Rittenhouse
Post, George Adams
Preston, Jonas
Rea, Samuel
Read, John, 1769–1854
Roach, John
Roberts, George Brooke
Roberts, Solomon White
Sayre, Robert Heysham
Scranton, George Whitfield
FREDERIKSON, EDNA TUTT
St. John, John Pierce
FREEDLEY, GEORGE
Anderson, Mary
FREEDMAN, DAVID NOEL
Montgomery, James Alan
FREEDMAN, ESTELLE B.
Blair, Emily Newell
Phillips, Lena Madesin
FREEHAFER, EDWARD G.
Anderson, Edwin Hatfield
FREEMAN, DOUGLAS SOUTHALL
Alexander, Edward Porter
Allen, Henry Watkins
Hill, Ambrose Powell
Hood, John Bell
Jackson, Thomas Jonathan
Lee, Fitzhugh
Lee, Robert Edward
Longstreet, James
Stuart, James Ewell Brown
FREEMAN, JOSHUA B.
Quill, Michael Joseph
FREEMAN-WITTHOFT, BONITA
Lomax, Louis Emanuel
FREIDEL, FRANK
Howe, Louis McHenry
Roosevelt, Franklin Delano
FRENCH, JOHN C.
Beadle, Erastus Flavel
Chambers, Robert William
Comfort, Will Levington
Harrison, Henry Sydnor
Hewitt, John Hill
Kennedy, William Sloane
Lynde, Francis
Mathews, William
Mifflin, Lloyd
Miles, George Henry
Norris, Benjamin Franklin
Parke, John
Phillips, Henry
Pinkney, Edward Coote
Preston, Margaret Junkin
Prime, Benjamin Youngs
Randall, James Ryder
Reese, Lizette Woodworth
Requier, Augustus Julian
Scarborough, Dorothy
Sedgwick, Anne Douglas
Thomas, Frederick William
Visscher, William Lightfoot
FRENCH, ROBERT D.
Cochran, Alexander Smith
Hadley, Arthur Twining
Jocelyn, Nathaniel
Lounsbury, Thomas Raynesford
FREUND, PAUL A.
Brandeis, Louis Dembitz
Frankfurter, Felix
Powell, Thomas Reed
FRIDLINGTON, ROBERT J.
Bamberger, Louis
Ladd, Kate Macy
FRIED, RICHARD M.
Millikin, Eugene Donald
Welch, Joseph Nye
FRIEDENWALD, HARRY
Reuling, George
FRIEDMAN, B. H.
Kline, Franz Josef
Pollock, (Paul) Jackson
FRIEDMANN, HERBERT
Nelson, Edward William
Ober, Frederick Albion
Richmond, Charles Wallace
Sennett, George Burritt
FRIERSON, J. NELSON
Johnstone, Job
FRIERSON, WILLIAM LITTLE
Andrews, Garnett
Brown, John Calvin
Brown, Neill Smith
Carmack, Edward Ward
Catron, John
Jackson, Howell Edmunds
Key, David McKendree
Lurton, Horace Harmon
FRIESS, HORACE L.
Adler, Felix
FRIGUGLIETTI, JAMES
Brinton, Clarence Crane
Gottschalk, Louis Reichenthal
Notestein, Wallace
FRIIS, HERMAN R.
Abert, John James
Davis, William Morris
FRIO, DANIEL
Rowe, Lynwood Thomas
FRISCH, PAUL A.
Geer, William Aughe ("Will")
Skaggs, Marion Barton
Todman, Wiliam Selden ("Bill")
FROST, RICHARD H.
Mooney, Thomas Joseph
FRUTON, JOSEPH S.
Bergmann, Max
Meyerhof, Otto
FRYKMAN, GEORGE A.
Howard, Joseph Kinsey
Johnson, Albert
Wallgren, Mon[rad] C[harles]
FUCHS, RALPH F.
Cook, Walter Wheeler
Rutledge, Wiley Blount
FUESS, CLAUDE MOORE
Adams, John
Bacon, Edwin Munroe
Bancroft, Cecil Franklin Patch
Bartlet, William
Bishop, Robert Roberts
Bradley, Charles Henry
Brown, Moses, 1738–1836
Brown, Moses, 1742–1827
Brown, Obadiah
Carter, Franklin
Carter, Robert, 1819–1879
Choate, Rufus
Clifford, John Henry
Cushing, Caleb
Cushing, John Perkins
Cushing, Luther Stearns
Cutler, Manasseh
Davis, John, 1787–1854
Davis, John Chandler Bancroft
Dawes, Henry Laurens
Devens, Charles
Dexter, Timothy
Douglas, William Lewis
Earle, Alice Morse
Edwards, Bela Bates

Edwards, Justin
Eliot, Samuel Atkins
Endicott, Charles Moses
Endicott, William Crowninshield
Eustis, Henry Lawrence
Eustis, William
Fields, Annie Adams
Fields, James Thomas
Fox, Gustavus Vasa
Gardner, Henry Joseph
Garrison, William Lloyd
Gaston, William
Ginn, Edwin
Gray, William
Greenhalge, Frederic Thomas
Guild, Curtis, 1827–1911
Guild, Curtis, 1860–1915
Houghton, Henry Oscar
Keep, Robert Porter
King, Rufus
Knox, Henry
Mallary, Rollin Carolas
Mason, Jeremiah
Mattocks, John
Morrill, Justin Smith
Morton, Marcus, 1819–1891
Pearson, Eliphalet
Phillips, John
Phillips, Samuel
Phillips, Wendell
Phillips, William
Stearns, Frank Waterman

FULLER, GEORGE W.
Dennis, Graham Barclay
McGraw, John Harte
Turner, George
Waterhouse, Frank
Wilson, John Lockwood

FULLER, JOSEPH V.
Fish, Hamilton
Fish, Nicholas
MacVeagh, Isaac Wayne
Olney, Richard
Penfield, Frederic Courtland
Phelps, William Walter
Porter, Horace
Pruyn, Robert Hewson
Read, John Meredith, 1837–1896

FULLER, RAYMOND GARFIELD
Angell, George Thorndike
Auchmuty, Richard Tylden

FULLERTON, KEMPER
Bosworth, Edward Increase
Wright, George Frederick

FULTON, JOHN F.
Alden, Ebenezer
Allen, Nathan
Appleton, Nathaniel Walker
Beach, Wooster
Bean, Tarleton Hoffman
Bigelow, Henry Jacob
Bigelow, Jacob
Bigelow, William Sturgis
Bishop, Seth Scott
Blackwell, Elizabeth
Bosworth, Francke Huntington
Bowditch, Henry Ingersoll
Boylston, Zabdiel
Brown, Frederic Tilden
Bryant, Joseph Decatur
Buck, Albert Henry
Buck, Gurdon
Buckler, Thomas Hepburn
Bull, William Tillinghast
Bushnell, George Ensign
Cabot, Arthur Tracy
Capen, Nahum
Colton, Gardner Quincy
Cushing, Harvey Williams
Cushny, Arthur Robertson
Darling, Samuel Taylor
Davis, Henry Gassett
Delafield, Edward
Delafield, Francis
Douglass, William
Duane, Alexander
Dusser de Barenne, Joannes Gregorius
Dwight, Thomas
Fitz, Reginald Heber
Foster, John Pierrepont Codrington
Gale, Benjamin
Gardiner, Silvester
Gerhard, William Wood
Green, Horace
Harrington, Charles
Hayward, George
Horsfield, Thomas
Jackson, Charles Thomas
Jackson, James, 1777–1867
Knapp, Philip Coombs
Kneeland, Samuel
Langford, Nathaniel Pitt
Long, Crawford Williamson
Martin, Henry Austin
Morton, William Thomas Green
Parker, Willard
Pearce, Richard Mills
Post, Wright
Priestley, Joseph
Wells, Horace

FUMOSA, RICHARD
Bowles, Jane Auer
Still, Clyfford

FUNK, ELMER H.
Keating, John Marie

FURCRON, THOMAS
Lehmann, Lotte
Melchior, Lauritz Lebrecht Hommel
Tucker, Richard

FURFEY, PAUL HANLY
Regan, Agnes Gertrude
Teresa, Mother

FURLONG, PATRICK J.
Hodes, Henry Irving
Hoffman, Paul Gray
Jones, John Price
Keller, Kaufman Thuma

FURLONG, PHILIP J.
Kohlmann, Anthony

FURMAN, FRANKLIN DE R.
Mayer, Alfred Marshall
Morton, Henry

FURNESS, CAROLINE E.
Mitchell, Maria
Whitney, Mary Watson

FURNESS, CLIFTON JOSEPH
Gilbert, Henry Franklin Belknap

FUTRELL, ROBERT FRANK
Fairchild, Muir Stephen
Gorrell, Edgar Staley

GAAR, GILLIAN G.
Rolf, Ida Pauline

GABARD, WILLIAM M.
Hardwick, Thomas William

GABRIEL, RALPH HENRY
Cross, Wilbur Lucius
Dana, Samuel Whittlesey
Gardiner, Robert Hallowell
Hale, Benjamin
Hawley, Joseph Roswell
Holmes, Ezekiel
Loring, George Bailey
Lubin, David
Lyman, Joseph Bardwell

GAFFEY, JAMES P.
Hanna, Edward Joseph

GAGEY, EDMOND M.
Bennett, Richard
Westley, Helen

GAINES, FRANCIS PENDLETON
Barnwell, Robert Woodward
Butler, Andrew Pickens
Butler, Matthew Calbraith
Butler, Pierce Mason
Capers, Ellison
Chamberlain, Daniel Henry
Coker, James Lide
Hagood, Johnson
Hilt, Daniel Harvey
Holmes, Isaac Edward

GALBREATH, CHARLES BURLEIGH
Carrington, Henry Beebee
Maxwell, William
Ross, Alexander Coffman

GALE, ESSON M.
Rockhill, William Woodville
Tenney, Charles Daniel

GALLAGHER, KATHARINE JEANNE
Chase, Philander
De Koven, James
Hamilton, William Thomas, 1820–1888
Hanson, Alexander Contee, 1786–1819
Kemper, Jackson

GALLAHER, RUTH A.
Curtis, Samuel Ryan

GALLINGER, HERBERT P.
Moore, Zephaniah Swift

GALLOWAY, EILENE MARIE
Hegeman, John Rogers
Proctor, Lucien Brock
Rambaut, Mary Lucinda Bonney

GALLUP, CLARENCE M.
Benedict, David

GALPIN, W. FREEMAN
Miller, Warner
Smith, Peter

GALVIN, JOHN T.
Green, William Joseph, Jr.
Lawrence, David Leo
Tinkham, George Holden
Weeks, Sinclair

GAMBRELL, HERBERT P.
Ellet, Charles
Hyer, Robert Stewart
Menard, Michel Branamour
Yoakum, Henderson

GANFIELD, DOROTHY
Husting, Paul Oscar

GANNON, DAVID
Francis, Paul James

Ganoe, William A.
Halleck, Henry Wager
Hooker, Joseph
Mason, Richard Barnes
Meade, George Gordon
Scott, Winfield
Totten, Joseph Gilbert
Twiggs, David Emanuel
Warren, Gouverneur Kemble
Washington, John Macrae
Wool, John Ellis
Worth, William Jenkins
Garber, Paul N.
Lane, John
Olin, Stephen
Paine, Robert
Pierce, George Foster
Soule, Joshua
Waugh, Beverly
Whatcoat, Richard
Wiley, Ephraim Emerson
Williams, Robert
Winans, William
Garby, Lee
Mapes, Charles Victor
Mapes, James Jay
Piper, Charles Vancouver
Voorhees, Edward Burnett
Gardner, Albert Ten Eyck
Barnard, George Grey
Gardner, Lloyd C.
Dulles, John Foster
Gardner, Peter S.
Piston, Walter Hamor
Gardner, W. U.
Allen, Edgar
Gardy, Alison
Cochran, Jacqueline
Cort, Stewart Shaw
Cushman, Austin Thomas ("Joe")
Fernós Isern, Antonio
Forman, Celia Adler
Ingelfinger, Franz Joseph
Iturbi, José
Limón, José Arcadio
Lopez, Vincent Joseph
Muñoz Marín, Luis
Perdue, Arthur William
Reid, Rose Marie
Warren, Shields
Gargan, William M.
Anderson, Margaret Carolyn
Morrison, Jim
Ochs, Phil
Porter, Katherine Anne
Garlich, Richard Cecil, Jr.
Mazzei, Philip
Garraghan, Gilbert J.
Cataldo, Joseph Maria
O'Fallon, John
Garratt, George A.
Bryant, Ralph Clement
Record, Samuel James
Garraty, John A.
Mondell, Frank Wheeler
Woytinsky, Wladimir Savelievich
Garren, Sarah R.
Evans, Bergen Baldwin
Garrett, C. G. B.
Bensley, Robert Russell
Carlson, Anton Julius
Novy, Frederick George
Steinman, David Barnard
Warren, Henry Ellis
Wiener, Norbert
Garrett, Charles
Thacher, Thomas Day
Garrett, Shirley Stone
Ferguson, John Calvin
Frame, Alice Seymour Browne
Lyon, David Willard
Pott, Francis Lister Hawks
Garrett, Wendell D.
Nutting, Wallace
Sack, Israel
Garrison, Curtis W.
Brown, George William
Calvert, Charles Benedict
Carroll, Daniel
Chambers, Ezekiel Forman
Clayton, Joshua
Clayton, Thomas
Gist, Mordecai
Hall, Willard
Hambleton, Thomas Edward
Handy, Alexander Hamilton
Harrington, Samuel Maxwell
Hughes, George Wurtz
Johns, Kensey, 1759–1848
Johns, Kensey, 1791–1857
McDonogh, John
McLane, Allan
Mitchell, Nathaniel
Morgan, John Tyler
Stoddert, Benjamin
Swain, James Barrett
Tome, Jacob
Wyeth, John
Garrison, Fielding H.
Bowditch, Henry Pickering
Handerson, Henry Ebenezer
Garrison, F. Lynwood
Neilson, William George
Outerbridge, Alexander Ewing
Trautwine, John Cresson
Vanuxem, Lardner
Wahl, William Henry
Garrison, Hazel Shields
Semple, Ellen Churchill
Taylor, Richard Cowling
Garrison, Winifred Ernest
Richardson, Robert
Scott, Walter
Garsoian, Nina G.
Vasiliev, Alexander Alexandrovich
Gaston, Edwin W., Jr.
Richter, Conrad Michael
Gates, Paul W.
Buley, Roscoe Carlyle
Farrand, Livingston
Shannon, Fred Albert
Warren, George Frederick
Gates, Sylvester
Sacco, Nicola
Gatewood, Willard B., Jr.
Harrison, Francis Burton
Ironside, Henry Allan
Upshaw, William David
Gaudio, Sybil Del
Hubley, John
Gauld, Charles A.
Farquhar, Percival
Gaustad, Edwin S.
Stokes, Anson Phelps
Gavin, Donald P.
Schrembs, Joseph
Gaylord, Winfield R.
Sargent, Frank Pierce
Sorge, Friedrich Adolph
Gebhard, David
Schindler, Rudolph Michael
Gehrenbeck, Richard K.
Davisson, Clinton Joseph
Frank, Philipp G.
Germer, Lester Halbert
Goudsmit, Samuel Abraham
Millikan, Clark Blanchard
Rademacher, Hans
Shapley, Harlow
Stern, Otto
Geiling, E. M. K.
Abel, John Jacob
Geiser, Karl Frederick
Brice, Calvin Stewart
Geiser, Samuel W.
Boll, Jacob
Lincecum, Gideon
Lindheimer, Ferdinand Jacob
Mohr, Charles Theodore
Montgomery, Edmund Duncan
Munson, Thomas Volney
Ney, Elisabet
Wright, Charles
Geist, Christopher D.
O'Brien, Willis Harold
Geitner, Paul
Elliot, Cass ("Mama")
Hayward, Susan
Moorehead, Agnes
Serling, Rodman Edward ("Rod")
Gelb, Barbara
O'Neill, Eugene
Gelfand, Lawrence E.
Polk, Frank Lyon
Gentile, Richard H.
Bailey, John Moran
Clement, Frank Goad
Cutler, Robert
Elliott, William Yandell, III
Herter, Christian Archibald
McCormack, John William
Murtaugh, Daniel Edward ("Danny")
Radcliffe, George Lovic Pierce
Shipley, Ruth Bielaski
Yawkey, Thomas Austin ("Tom")
Genzmer, George H.
Acrelius, Israel
Adler, George J.
Agnus, Felix
Alden, Raymond Macdonald
Ayer, Francis Wayland
Barr, Charles
Bateman, Newton
Baugher, Henry Louis
Benjamin, Samuel Greene Wheeler
Bennett, de Robigne Mortimer
Bennett, Floyd
Berkenmeyer, Wilhelm Christoph
Bewley, Anthony
Bimeler, Joseph Michael
Bingham, Amelia
Bingham, George Caleb
Bird, Frederic Mayer

Birkbeck, Morris
Bixby, Horace Ezra
Blake, John Lauris
Blinn, Holbrook
Boehm, John Philip
Bolles, Frank
Boltzius, Johann Martin
Bonaparte, Elizabeth Patterson
Bourne, Nehemiah
Boynton, Charles Brandon
Bradford, Gamaliel
Brady, Cyrus Townsend
Brattle, Thomas
Brown, Goold
Browne, Benjamin Frederick
Bryant, John Howard
Bryce, Lloyd Stephens
Bucher, John Conrad
Buford, Napoleon Bonaparte
Bunce, Oliver Bell
Burleigh, George Shepard
Cabell, James Lawrence
Campanius, John
Campbell, William Henry
Capers, William
Carpenter, Francis Bicknell
Carryl, Guy Wetmore
Chambers, Talbot Wilson
Chang and Eng
Channing, William Ellery, 1818–1901
Child, Francis James
Clark, Charles Heber
Clarke, Helen Archibald
Clarke, Joseph Ignatius Constantine
Clarke, Mary Francis
Cleveland, Aaron
Cleveland, Richard Jeffry
Cobb, Sylvanus
Cobbett, William
Codman, John
Coggeshall, George
Coit, Henry Augustus
Coit, Henry Leber
Coit, Thomas Winthrop
Colby, Frank Moore
Condon, Thomas
Converse, Edmund Cogswell
Converse, James Booth
Coppens, Charles
Copway, George
Crafts, William
Crane, Frank
Crane, Jonathan Townley
Crapsey, Algernon Sidney
Creamer, David
Crosby, Fanny
Crowninshield, Benjamin Williams
Crowninshield, Jacob
Cutler, Carroll
Dall, Caroline Wells Healey
Dana, John Cotton
Davidson, Lucretia Maria
Davidson, Margaret Miller
Davidson, Robert
Davis, Matthew Livingston
Day, Henry Noble
Day, James Roscoe
Deindörfer, Johannes
Demme, Charles Rudolph
Derby, Elias Hasket, 1766–1826
Derby, Elias Hasket, 1803–1880
Disbrow, William Stephen
Doane, George Washington
Dockstader, Lew
Dod, Albert Baldwin
Dole, Charles Fletcher
Downing, George
Drury, John Benjamin
Duganne, Augustine Joseph Hickey
Durand, Elie Magloire
Duryea, Hermanes Barkulo
Dwight, Francis
Dwight, Theodore, 1796–1866
Dylander, John
Eastman, Charles Gamage
Eastman, Harvey Gridley
Eddy, Daniel Clarke
Eliot, Samuel
Elliot, James
Embury, Emma Catherine
Emerson, Edward Waldo
Emerson, Mary Moody
Emerson, Oliver Farrar
Evans, Edward Payson
Fairbank, Calvin
Falckner, Daniel
Falckner, Justus
Fay, Theodore Sedgwick
Fechter, Charles Albert
Fernald, James Champlin
Ferris, Isaac
Finotti, Joseph Maria
Fitz, Henry
Fleischmann, Charles Louis
Fletcher, Horace
Flower, George
Flower, Richard
Flügel, Ewald
Folger, Henry Clay
Folger, Peter
Forsyth, John, 1810–1886
Fosdick, Charles Austin
Fox, Richard Kyle
Francke, Kuno
Frankland, Lady Agnes Surriage
Franklin, James
Freedman, Andrew
Freeman, Bernardus
Frelinghuysen, Theodorus Jacobus
Frey, Joseph Samuel Christian Frederick
Frisbie, Levi
Fritschel, Conrad Sigmund
Fritschel, Gottfried Leonhard Wilhelm
Frothingham, Nathaniel Langdon
Frothingham, Octavius Brooks
Fuller, Hiram
Furness, Horace Howard, 1833–1912
Furness, Horace Howard, 1865–1930
Fussell, Bartholomew
Gaylor, Charles
Gerhart, Emanuel Vogel
Gibbons, James Sloan
Gibbons, William
Giesler-Anneke, Mathilde Franziska
Gillespie, William Mitchell
Godfrey, Benjamin
Goetschius, John Henry
Good, James Isaac
Good, Jeremiah Haak
Goodall, Thomas
Goodrich, Charles Augustus
Goodrich, Chauncey
Goodwin, John Noble
Gould, Benjamin Apthorp
Gould, Hannah Flagg
Grabau, Johannes Andreas August
Gräbner, August Lawrence
Graham, George Rex
Gray, Asa
Greene, Albert Gorton
Greenwald, Emanuel
Griffin, Edward Dorr
Griffin, Solomon Bulkley
Griswold, Rufus Wilmot
Gros, John Daniel
Grossmann, Georg Martin
Grube, Bernhard Adam
Guild, Reuben Aldridge
Guiney, Louise Imogen
Gummere, Francis Barton
Gummere, John
Gummere, Samuel James
Gunter, Archibald Clavering
Hammett, Samuel Adams
Harbaugh, Henry
Harby, Isaac
Hardy, Arthur Sherburne
Harpster, John Henry
Harris, Joel Chandler
Hartwig, Johann Christoph
Hay, Charles Augustus
Hazelius, Ernest Lewis
Helffenstein, John Albert Conrad
Helmuth, Justus Henry Christian
Hendel, John William
Henkel, Paul
Hentz, Caroline Lee Whiting
Herman, Lebrecht Frederick
Herr, John
Hillard, George Stillman
Holland, Edwin Clifford
Horn, Edward Traill
Hosmer, William Howe Cuyler
Hubbs, Rebecca
Hummel, Abraham Henry
Jacobs, Michael
Jacoby, Ludwig Sigmund
Jones, Sybil
Judson, Edward Zane Carroll
Keimer, Samuel
Kelpius, Johann
Kettell, Samuel
Klipstein, Louis Frederick
Knapp, Samuel Lorenzo
Kocherthal, Josua von
Kollack, Shepard
Krauth, Charles Philip
Krez, Konrad
Kroeger, Adolf Ernst
Kunze, John Christopher
Kurtz, Benjamin
Latrobe, Charles Hazlehurst
Leighton, William
Leland, Charles Godfrey
Leonard, Levi Washburn
Lewis, Alfred Henry

Lochman, John George
Loy, Matthias
Lyon, Harris Merton
Mann, Mary Tyler Peabody
Mann, William Julius
Mason, Stevens Thomson
Maxim, Hiram Stevens
Mayer, Lewis
Mayer, Philip Frederick
Mayo, Frank
Melsheimer, Friedrich Valentin
Miller, George
Miller, John Peter
Moldehnke, Edward Frederick
Morris, John Gottlieb
Morse, Henry Dutton
Morse, Samuel Finley Breese
Muhlenberg, Frederick Augustus
Muhlenberg, Frederick Augustus Conrad
Muhlenberg, Gotthilf Henry Ernest
Muhlenberg, Henry Augustus Philip
Mühlenberg, Henry Melchior
Muhlenberg, John Peter Gabriel
Muhlenberg, William Augustus
Murdock, Frank Hitchcock
Murray, Lindley
Notz, Frederick William Augustus
Oakley, Annie
O'Brien, Frederick
O'Connor, William Douglas
O'Hara, Theodore
Otterbein, Philip William
Parrington, Vernon Louis
Parton, James
Passavant, William Alfred
Pastorius, Francis Daniel
Patch, Sam
Peabody, Oliver William Bourn
Peabody, William Bourn Oliver
Peck, Harry Thurston
Pickering, John
Pierpont, John
Pilkington, James
Pinkham, Lydia Estes
Plumbe, John
Plummer, Henry
Pond, Frederick Eugene
Pratt, Daniel
Printz, Johan Björnsson
Quick, John Herbert
Rafinesque, Constantine Samuel
Rapp, George
Read, Thomas Buchanan
Reed, Henry Hope
Reed, Myrtle
Reed, Sampson
Rice, Dan
Richardson, Albert Deane
Richardson, Charles Francis
Ricord, Frederick William
Rising, Johan Classon
Robinson, Rowland Evans
Roe, Edward Payson
Rolfe, William James
Rose, Aquila
Ross, Betsy
Roulstone, George
Rupp, Israel Daniel
Sachse, Julius Friedrich
Sadtler, John Philip Benjamin
Sanborn, Franklin Benjamin
Saxe, John Godfrey
Schaeffer, Charles Frederick
Schaeffer, Charles William
Schaeffer, David Frederick
Schaeffer, Frederick Christian
Schaeffer, Frederick David
Schmucker, Beale Melanchthon
Schmucker, John George
Schöpf, Johann David
Seidensticker, Oswald
Seip, Theodore Lorenzo
Seiss, Joseph Augustus
Seybert, John
Shaw, Henry Wheeler
Shaw, John, 1778–1809
Short, Charles
Smith, Benjamin Eli
Smith, Byron Caldwell
Sower, Christopher, 1693–1758
Sower, Christopher, 1721–1784
Spaeth, Adolph
Spencer, Platt Rogers
Stöckhardt, Karl Georg
Stoever, Martin Luther
Stokes, Caroline Phelps
Stokes, Olivia Egleston Phelps
Stratton, Charles Sherwood
Tanneberger, David
Teall, Francis Augustus
Tenney, William Jewett
Thompson, Joseph Parrish
Traubel, Horace L.
Trowbridge, John Townsend
Victor, Frances Fuller
Victor, Orville James
Walther, Carl Ferdinand Wilhelm
Weiss, John
White, Richard Grant
Wilkes, George
Williams, Ephraim
Winebrenner, John
Zinzendorf, Nicolaus Ludwig

GENZMER, MARGARET WADSWORTH
Graham Sylvester
McCann, Alfred Watterson

GEORGINI, SUSAN J.
Friedlaender, Walter Ferdinand

GERBER, BARBARA
Revson, Charles Haskell
Winston, Harry

GERBER, WILLIAM
O'Brien, Thomas James
O'Shaughnessy, Nelson Jarvis Waterbury

GERIG, JOHN LAWRENCE
Todd, Henry Alfred

GEROULD, JAMES THAYER
Vinton, Frederic

GEROULD, JOHN H.
Patten, William

GERRY, MARGARITA S.
Howe, Julia Ward

GERSON, VIRGINIA
Fitch, William Clyde

GESELL, BEATRICE CHANDLER
Blow, Susan Elizabeth
Harrison, Elizabeth

GETTLEMAN, MARVIN E.
Stokes, Isaac Newton Phelps

GHENT, W. J.
Adair, James
Addicks, John Edward O'Sullivan
Allerton, Samuel Waters
Ambler, James Markham Marshall
Armour, Philip Danforth
Armstrong, George Buchanan
Astor, John Jacob, 1763–1848
Astor, John Jacob, 1822–1890
Astor, John Jacob, 1864–1912
Astor, William Backhouse
Astor, William Waldorf
Atkinson, Henry
Atwater, Caleb
Avery, Benjamin Parke
Ayer, Edward Everett
Baer, George Frederick
Baird, Matthew
Baker, James
Baldwin, John
Ballard, Bland Williams
Bard, William
Barker, Jacob
Barker, Wharton
Barlow, John Whitney
Barnum, Zenus
Bass, Sam
Bates, Barnabas
Beale, Edward Fitzgerald
Belden, Josiah
Bell, James Stroud
Bent, Charles
Bent, William
Bidwell, John
Billy the Kid
Bliss, William Dwight Porter
Boas, Emil Leopold
Bonneville, Benjamin Louis Eulalie de
Boone, Daniel
Bowie, James
Brady, Mathew B.
Breen, Patrick
Bridgman, Herbert Lawrence
Bright Eyes
Broderick, David Colbreth
Buchanan, Joseph Ray
Burden, Henry
Burgess, Edward
Burnett, Henry Lawrence
Burnett, Peter Hardeman
Californa Joe
Cameron, Robert Alexander
Campbell, Robert
Carson, Christopher
Carter, William Samuel
Chisum, John Simpson
Chittenden, Hiram Martin
Chouteau, Auguste Pierre
Chouteau, Jean Pierre
Chouteau, René Auguste
Clyman, James
Cody, William Frederick
Coleman, William Tell
Colgate, James Boorman
Colgate, William
Colter, John
Connelly, Henry
Connor, Patrick Edward
Crawford, John Wallace (Captain Jack)

Crazy Horse
Crockett, David
Crooks, Ramsay
Cumming, Alfred
Custer, George Armstrong
Dalton, Robert
Debs, Eugene Victor
De Leon, Daniel
Dixon, William
Dorion, Marie
Farnham, Russel
Fitzpatrick, Thomas
Fonda, John H.
Friday
Gall
Geronimo
Girty, Simon
Gist, Christopher
Glass, Hugh
Grass, John
Gratiot, Charles
Gregg, Josiah
Grouard, Frank
Gunnison, John Williams
Harmon, Daniel Williams
Haywood, William Dudley
Henry, Andrew
Horn, Tom
Hunt, Wilson Price
Inman, Henry, 1837–1899
James, Jesse Woodson
James, Thomas
Joseph
Kearney, Stephen Watts
Kenton, Simon
La Barge, Joseph
Laclede, Pierre
Langworthy, James Lyon
Laramie, Jacques
Larpenteur, Charles
Leavenworth, Henry
Ledyard, John
Lee, Jason
Leonard, Zenas
Little Crow V
Lynch, James Mathew
McClellan, Robert
McLaughlin, James
Marsh, Grant Prince
Mason, Samuel
Masterson, William Barclay
Maus, Marion Perry
Maxwell, Lucien Bonaparte
Meek, Joseph L.
Meeker, Ezra
Menard, Pierre
Morrison, William
Murrieta, Joaquin
Newell, Robert
Ouray
Parsons, Albert Richard
Pattie, James Ohio
Pryor, Nathaniel
Quanah
Red Cloud
Red Wing
Reynolds, Charles Alexander
Richardson, Wilds Preston
Robidou, Antoine
Ross, Alexander
Russell, Osborne
Russell, William Henry
Russell, William Hepburn
Sacagawea
Sauganash
Sequoyah
Sibley, George Champlain
Sitting Bull
Slade, Joseph Alfred
Spotted Tail
Stansbury, Howard
Stearns, Abel
Stilwell, Simpson Everett
Stokes, Montford
Stone, Warren Sanford
Stuart, Granville
Stuart, Robert
Swinton, John
Tammany
Thornton, Tessy Quinn
Tibbles, Thomas Henry
Tilghman, William Matthew
Truman, Benjamin Cummings
Wabasha
Walker, Joseph Reddeford
Warner, Jonathan Trumbull
Warren, Josiah
Washakie
Williams, William Sherley
Winemucca, Sarah
Wislizenus, Frederick Adolph
Wolfskill, William
Wootton, Richens Lacy
Young, Ewing
Younger, Thomas Coleman
Yount, George Concepcíon

GIESE, WILLIAM FREDERIC
Owen, Edward Thomas

GIFFEN, M. B.
Sanford, Henry Shelton

GIFFORD, ALICE J.
Beard, Mary

GIGLIO, FRANCES T.
Byington, Spring
Randolph, Lillian

GIGLIO, JAMES N.
Brown, Walter Folger
Daugherty, Harry Micajah
Edison, Charles
O'Donnell, Kenneth Patrick
Rich, Robert
Taber, John

GILBERT, DANIEL R.
Cheyney, Edward Potts
Davis, Ernest R. ("Ernie")
Lombardi, Vincent Thomas
Marciano, Rocky
Neyland, Robert Reese, Jr.

GILCREEST, EDGAR L.
Toland, Hugh Huger

GILES, HOWARD E.
Hambridge, Jay

GILL, BRENDAN
Ross, Harold Wallace

GILL, MERTON M.
Rapaport, David

GILL, TOM
Pack, Charles Lathrop

GILLIAM, J. F.
Rostovtzeff, Michael Ivanovitch

GILLOOLY, JOHN
Cabot, Charles Sebastian Thomas
McCoy, George Braidwood

GILMARTIN, MICHAEL
Berg, Morris ("Moe")

GILMORE, C. W.
Gidley, James Williams

GILMORE, MYRON P.
Berenson, Bernard

GINGER, RAY
Darrow, Clarence Seward

GINGERICH, OWEN
Baade, Wilhelm Heinrich Walter

GIOIA, DANA
Auden, Wystan Hugh

GIPSON, LAWRENCE H.
Clewell, John Henry
Coppée, Henry
Ettwein, John
Fisher, Sydney George, 1856–1927
Ingersoll, Jared, 1722–1781
Packer, Asa
Schweinitz, Edmund Alexander de

GIROUX, ROBERT
Farrar, John Chipman

GLASRUD, BRUCE A.
Dean, William Henry, Jr.

GLASS, H. BENTLEY
Shull, George Harrison

GLASSER, OTTO
Williams, Francis Henry

GLEASON, H. A.
Britton, Nathaniel Lord
Hollick, Charles Arthur

GLEASON, PHILIP
Noll, John Francis

GLENN, LEONIDAS CHALMERS
Troost, Gerard

GLUECK, NELSON
Fisher, Clarence Stanley

GNEUHS, GEOFFREY B.
Day, Dorothy

GOBLE, GEORGE W.
Grier, Robert Cooper
Hohfeld, Wesley Newcomb
Todd, Thomas
Treat, Samuel Hubbel
Trimble, Robert
Walker, Pinkney Houston
Washington, Bushrod
Wilson, William, 1794–1857
Woods, William Allen
Zeisler, Sigmund

GODDARD, HAROLD C.
Emerson, William

GODWIN, BLAKE-MORE
Libbey, Edward Drummond
Stevens, George Washington

GOEBEL, DOROTHY BURNE
Harrison, William Henry

GOEBEL, JULIUS
Körner, Gustav Philipp

GOEN, C. C.
Hughes, Edwin Holt
Newton, Joseph Fort
Scarborough, Lee Rutland

GOLD, HARRY
Hatcher, Robert Anthony

GOLDBERG, MICHAEL
Arquette, Clifford
Barker, Alexander Crichlow ("Lex")
Berkeley, Busby
Brennan, Walter
Cassidy, Jack

Chaney, Lon, Jr.
Conte, Richard
Cox, Wallace Maynard ("Wally")
Haley, Jack
Nielsen, Arthur Charles
Oberon, Merle
Sherman, Allan
Susann, Jacqueline
GOLDER, FRANK A.
Baranov, Alexander Andreevich
GOLDMAN, EDWARD A.
Henshaw, Henry Wetherbee
GOLDMAN, RICHARD FRANKO
Damrosch, Frank Heino
Goldmark, Rubin
GOLDSTEIN, MALCOLM
Beery, Wallace Fitzgerald
Blackton, James Stuart
Epstein, Philip G.
Garfield, John
Kaufman, George S.
Rossen, Robert
GOLDSTONE, RICHARD
Wilder, Thornton Niven
GOLENBOCK, PETER J.
Bender, Charles Albert ("Chief")
Walsh, Edward Augustine
GOLER, GEORGE W.
Moore, Edward Mott
GOMERY, DOUGLAS
Warner, Harry Morris
GOMES, PETER J.
Sperry, Willard Learoyd
GOOD, CARTER V.
McAndrew, William
Wirt, William Albert
GOOD, HARRY GEHMAN
Picket, Albert
Youmans, Edward Livingston
Youmans, William Jay
GOODLOE, ROBERT W.
Harrell, John
McAnally, David Rice
McFerrin, John Berry
Marvin, Enoch Mather
GOODMAN, WALTER
Rankin, John Elliott
GOODSELL, FRED FIELD
Barton, James Levi
GOODSTEIN, JUDITH R.
Ascoli, Max
Courant, Richard
Guggenheim, Harry Frank
Tolman, Richard Chace
GOODWIN, CARDINAL
Browne, John Ross
Mills, Cyrus Taggart
Mills, Susan Lincoln Tolman
GOODWIN, G. F.
Del Ruth, Roy
Dumont, Margaret
Horton, Edward Everett, Jr.
Matthews, Joseph Brown
Taylor, Robert
Tracy, Spencer Bonaventure
GOODWIN, WILLARD E.
Young, Hugh Hampton
GOODYKOONTZ, COLIN B.
Ammons, Elias Milton
Bowen, Thomas Meade
Brown, Henry Cordis
Costigan, Edward Prentiss
Hulbert, Archer Butler
O'Donnell, Thomas Jefferson
Patterson, Thomas MacDonald
Pitkin, Frederick Walker
Sewall, Joseph Addison
Willard, James Field
GOOSSEN, E. C.
Davis, Stuart
GORDON, ARMISTEAD CHURCHILL, JR.
Banister, John
Cabell, Joseph Carrington
Cameron, William Evelyn
Claiborne, Nathaniel Herbert
Cocke, John Hartwell
Cocke, Philip St. George
Dabney, Richard
Dabney, Thomas Smith Gregory
Doddridge, Joseph
Ewell, Benjamin Stoddert
Ewell, Richard Stoddert
Fleming, William
Garnett, James Mercer
Garnett, Muscoe Russell Hunter
Garnett, Robert Selden
Gholson, Thomas Saunders
Gholson, William Yates
Gilmer, Thomas Walker
Goode, John
Graham, John
Green, James Stephens
Griffin, Cyrus
Grigsby, Hugh Blair
Hardin, John
Hayne, Paul Hamilton
Heath, James Ewell
Hening, William Waller
Innes, James
Jackson, John George
Janney, Samuel McPherson
Johnston, Peter
Jones, Hugh
Jones, John Beauchamps
Jones, John William
Jones, John Winston
Jones, Joseph
Jouett, John
Keith, James
Law, Sallie Chapman Gordon
McCabe, John Collins
McCabe, William Gordon
Mathews, Samuel
Munford, Robert
Percy, George
Pory, John
Pott, John
Robertson, John
Sandys, George
Schele De Vere, Maximilian
Southall, James Cocke
Stanard, Mary Mann Page Newton
Stanard, William Glover
Stith, William
Strachey, William
Ticknor, Francis Orray
Timrod, Henry
Tompkins, Sally Louisa
GORDON, RITA WERNER
De Priest, Oscar Stanton
GOREN, ARTHUR A.
Magnes, Judah Leon
GORTNER, ROSS AIKEN
Harris, James Arthur
GOTTLIEB, JANE
Ganz, Rudolph
Lhévinne, Rosina
Rodgers, Richard Charles
Tourel, Jennie
GOTWALS, VERNON
De Luca, Giuseppe
Speaks, Oley
Yon, Pietro Alessandro
GOUGH, ROBERT
Bell, James Ford
GOULD, HARRIS PERLEY
Campbell, George Washington, 1817–1898
Coxe, William
Gale, Elbridge
Garey, Thomas Andrew
Kendrick, William
GOULD, KENNETH M.
McClintock, Oliver
Murphy, Francis
Nation, Carry Amelia Moore
Noss, Theodore Bland
Oliver, Henry William
Porter, Stephen Geyer
GOULD, LEWIS L.
Breckinridge, Henry Skillman
Connally, Thomas Terry ("Tom")
Johnson, Lyndon Baines
Lanham, Frederick Garland ("Fritz")
McNutt, Paul Vories
Pool, Joe Richard
Ross, Nellie Tayloe
Stanley, Augustus Owsley
Sumners, Hatton William
GOULD, OLIVIA H.
Wilder, Laura Ingalls
GOULD, STEPHEN JAY
Cushman, Joseph Augustine
GOWANS, ALAN
Maginnis, Charles Donagh
GOWEN, HERBERT H.
Shelton, Edward Mason
GRACY, DAVID B., II
Bennett, Henry Garland
GRAD, FRANK P.
Chamberlain, Joseph Perkins
GRAEBNER, ALAN
Maier, Walter Arthur
GRAEBNER, NORMAN A.
George, Walter Franklin
GRAEBNER, WILLIAM
Atlas, Charles S.
Coyle, Grace Longwell
Kilpatrick, William Heard
Rice, John Andrew
Spargo, John
Steichen, Edward Jean
GRAF, LEROY P.
McReynolds, Samuel Davis
GRAFF, HENRY F.
Cobb, Tyrus Raymond ("Ty")
Gehrig, Henry Louis
Hornsby, Rogers
Ott, Melvin Thomas ("Mel")
Robinson, John Roosevelt ("Jackie")
Ruppert, Jacob
Stengel, Charles Dillon ("Casey")

Wagner, John Peter
Zimmerman, Henry ("Heinie")
GRAFLY, DOROTHY
Knight, Daniel Ridgway
Krimmel, John Lewis
Lambdin, James Reid
Miller, Leslie William
Rehn, Frank Knox Morton
Roberts, Howard
Rothermel, Peter Frederick
Sartain, Emily
Sartain, John
Sartain, Samuel
Sartain, William
Schussele, Christian
Sharples, James
Smith, Russell
Smith, Xanthus Russell
Spencer, Robert
Stephens, Alice Barber
Taylor, Frank Walter
Wood, Joseph
Wright, Joseph
GRAHAM, ALICE ARCHER
Prentiss, Elizabeth Payson
GRAHAM, FRANK
Rickard, George Lewis
GRAHAM, GLADYS
Bingham, Anne Willing
Crapsey, Adelaide
Dodge, Mary Abigail
Doubleday, Neltje de Graff
Douglas, Amanda Minnie
Dupuy, Eliza Ann
Jeffrey, Rosa Griffith Vertner Johnson
Kinney, Elizabeth Clementine Dodge Stedman
Lazarus, Emma
GRAHAM, HUGH DAVIS
Wright, Fielding Lewis
GRAHAM, JOHN A.
Morley, Sylvanus Griswold
GRAHAM, OTIS L., JR.
McAdoo, William Gibbs
Russell, Charles Edward
GRAHAM, PATRICIA ALBJERG
Caldwell, Otis William
GRAHAM, THEODORA R.
Williams, William Carlos
GRAHAM, WILLIAM CREIGHTON
Smith, John Merlin Powis
GRAM, LEWIS M.
Greene, Charles Ezra
GRANCSAY, STEPHEN V.
Riggs, William Henry
GRANGER, WALTER
Lucas, Frederic Augustus
Matthew, William Diller
Ward, Henry Augustus
GRANNISS, RUCH SHEPARD
Gilliss, Walter
Matthews, William
GRANT, E. ALLISON
Payne, John Howard
GRANT, FRANCIS C.
Frazier, Charles Harrison
GRANT, H. ROGER
Seiberling, Frank Augustus
Stearns, Frank Ballou
GRANT, WALTER S.
Anderson, Joseph Reid
Armstrong, Frank C.
Ashby, Turner
Benham, Henry Washington
GRANTHAM, DEWEY W.
Bilbo, Theodore Gilmore
Lea, Luke
Owen, Robert Latham
GRANTHAM, G. E.
Nichols, Edward Leamington
GRAS, N. S. B.
Baker, George Fisher
Flint, Charles Ranlett
GRATON, L. C.
Ransome, Frederick Leslie
GRAVES, CHARLES
Alger, William Rounseville
Allen, Joseph Henry
Ames, Charles Gordon
Peabody, Andrew Preston
Potter, William James
Powell, Edward Payson
Sears, Edmund Hamilton
Thayer, Thomas Baldwin
Whittemore, Thomas
GRAVES, HENRY SOLON
Fernow, Bernhard Edward
Hough, Franklin Benjamin
Toumey, James William
GRAY, JAMES
Burton, Richard Eugene
GRAY, LOUIS HERBERT
Bradley, Charles William
Brown, John Porter
Mills, Lawrence Heyworth
Nies, James Buchanan
GRAY, RALPH D.
Ball, George Alexander
GRAY, VIRGINIA
Richardson, Tobias Gibson
Riddell, John Leonard
GRAY, VIRGINIA GEARHART
Haarstick, Henry Christian
Hall, Luther Egbert
Souchon, Edmond
Stone, Warren
GRAYBAR, LLOYD J.
Blandy, William Henry Purnell
Denfield, Louis Emil
Eichelberger, Robert Lawrence
Ingersoll, Royal Eason
Kimball, Dan Able
McWilliams, Carey
Millis, Walter
Nimitz, Chester William
Ryan, Robert Bushnell
Saltonstall, Leverett
Shaw, Albert
Snyder, Howard McCrum
Talbott, Harold Elstner
Turner, Richmond Kelly
Vandegrift, Alexander Archer
Weiss, George Martin
Zukor, Adolph
GREBSTEIN, SHELDON NORMAN
Lewis, Harry Sinclair
GREELEY, W. B.
Donovan, John Joseph
Griggs, Everett Gallup
GREELY, A. W.
Hall, Charles Francis
Hayes, Isaac Israel
Lockwood, James Booth
GREELY, JOHN N.
Merritt, Wesley
Mordecai, Alfred
Myer, Albert James
GREEN, EDWIN L.
Middleton, John Izard
Nott, Henry Junius
Rivers, William James
GREEN, FLETCHER M.
Fleming, Walter Lynwood
Green, Benjamin Edwards
Green, Duff
Reed, John, 1757–1845
Spalding, Thomas
Stephens, Linton
Thompson, Wiley
Towns, George Washington Bonaparte
Troup, George Michael
Walton, George
Wofford, William Tatum
Young, Pierce Manning Butler
GREEN, PAUL M.
Arvey, Jacob M.
GREENE, EVARTS B.
James, Edmund Janes
Johnson, William Samuel
GREENE, JEROME DAVIS
Buttrick, Wallace
GREENE, LARRY A.
Malcolm X
GREENLEAF, WILLIAM
Budd, Edward Gowen
Fisher, Frederic John
Ford, Henry
Knudsen, William S.
Newberry, Truman Handy
Norton, Charles Hotchkiss
Selig, William Nicholas
GREENOUGH, CHESTER N.
Wendell, Barrett
GREENSLET, FERRIS
Lodge, George Cabot
GREENSTEIN, JESSE L.
Jansky, Karl Guthe
GREENWALD, DOROTHY
Scott, Fred Newton
Tarbox, Increase Niles
GREEP, ROY O.
Howe, Percy Rogers
GREEVER, GARLAND
Cheney, John Vance
GREGORIE, ANNE KING
Hill, William
Howe, George
Kinlock, Cleland
LaBorde, Maximilian
Ladd, Catherine
Lee, Thomas
Lucas, Jonathan, 1754–1821
Lucas, Jonathan, 1775–1832
Pickens, Andrew
Pinckney, Elizabeth Lucas
Ravenel, Edmund
Ravenel, Harriott Horry Rutledge
Read, Jacob
Smith, Henry Augustus Middleton
Smith, William Loughton
Sumter, Thomas
Thomson, William
Vesey, Denmark, *c.* 1767–1822
Wayne, Arthur Trezevant
Williamson, Andrew

Wilson, John Leighton
Winn, Richard
GREGORY, WILLIAM B.
Harrod, Benjamin Morgan
Hébert, Louis
GREINER, DONALD J.
Frost, Robert Lee
GRENIER, JUDSON A.
Chandler, Harry
GRICE, WARREN
Akerman, Amos Tappan
Bacon, Augustus Octavius
GRIEVES, BERENICE ELAINE
Southworth, Emma Dorothy Eliza Nevitte
GRIFFITH, ERNEST S.
Matthews, Nathan
Parker, Isaac
Pierce, Henry Lillie
GRIFFITH, IVOR
Remington, Joseph Price
GRIFFITH, JEAN W., JR.
Lilly, Eli
GRIFFITH, RICHARD
Gilbert, John
Mix, Tom
GRIFFITH, ROBERT
McCarthy, Joseph Raymond
GRIGG, E. R. N.
Coutard, Henri
GRILL, FREDERICK
Schneider, Albert
GRIMES, ALAN P.
Graham, Frank Porter
Ogg, Frederic Austin
Rossiter, Clinton Lawrence, III
Smith, Thomas Vernor
GRINNELL, FRANK W.
Sheldon, Henry Newton
Sprague, Peleg
Stearns, Asahel
GRINNELL, JOSEPH
Cooper, James Graham
GRINSTEAD, WREN JONES
Colton, Elizabeth Avery
GRINSTEIN, HYMAN B.
Revel, Bernard
GROAT, GEORGE GORHAM
Arthur, Peter M.
GROSVENOR, GILBERT
Bell, Alexander Melville
GRUBAR, FRANCIS S.
Archipenko, Alexander
GRUENING, ERNEST
Macy, John Albert
GRUENING, MARTHA
Stokes, Rose Harriet Pastor
Walker, David, 1785–1830
Walker, Sarah Breedlove
Ware, Edmund Asa
White, George Leonard
GRUENSTEIN, S. E.
Eddy, Clarence
GRUSD, EDWARD E.
Monsky, Henry
GUE, GURNEY C.
Hildreth, Samuel Clay
Morgan, Justin
Rarey, John Solomon
Ten Broeck, Richard
GUEST, IVOR
Fokine, Michel
GUILDAY, PETER
Bayley, James Roosevelt
GULICK, CHARLES BURTON
Dyer, Louis
Goodwin, William Watson
Greenough, James Bradstreet
Leach, Abby
Moore, Clifford Herschel
Sophocles, Evangelinus Apostolides
White, John Williams
Wright, John Henry
GUMMERE, AMELIA MOTT
Benezet, Anthony
GUMMERE, RICHARD M.
Parrish, Anne
GUNN, SIDNEY
Johnston, Thomas
Joy, Thomas
Kneeland, Samuel
Knight, Sarah Kemble
Lapham, William Berry
Leavitt, Mary Greenleaf Clement
Lee, Eliza Buckminster
Lee, Hannah Farnham Sawyer
Lewis, Winslow
Lindsey, William
Little, Charles Coffin
Lothrop, Daniel
Paine, Charles Jackson
Peck, George Washington
Perkins, Thomas Handasyd
Pidgin, Charles Felton
Prang, Louis
Prang, Mary Amelia Dana Hicks
Rand, Edward Sprague
Russell, Joseph
Sargent, John Osborne
Sargent, Lucius Manlius
Savage, James
Sharp, Dallas Lore
Silsbee, Nathaniel
Simpson, Michael Hodge
Storey, Moorfield
Thayer, Nathaniel
Thorndike, Israel
Tobey, Edward Silas
Towle, George Makepeace
Train, George Francis
Upton, George Bruce
Ward, Samuel, 1814–1884
Winslow, Sidney Wilmot
Wyman, Seth
GUNTHER, GERALD
Hand, Learned
GURLEY, FRANKLIN L.
Devers, Jacob Loucks
GUTFREUND, OWEN D.
Levitt, Arthur
Levy, Gustave Lehmann
Sayre, Wallace Stanley
Zeckendorf, William
GUTMAN, JUDITH MARA
Austen, (Elizabeth) Alice
Johnston, Frances Benjamin
GUY, JAMES SAMUEL
Jones, Harry Clary
Pendleton, Edmund Monroe
GUZDA, HENRY P.
Mitchell, James Paul

HAAS, EDWARD F.
Maestri, Robert Sidney
HAAS, ROBERT BARTLETT
Eilshemius, Louis Michel
Gorky, Arshile
HABEL, SUE
Adler, Felix
Burns, Bob
HACHTEN, WILLIAM A.
Grant, Harry Johnston
HACKETT, BYRNE
Andrews, William Loring
HACKETT, CHARLES W.
Croix, Teodoro de
Escalante, Silvestre Velez De
Niza, Marcos de
Oñate, Juan de
Otermin, Antonio de
Peñalosa, Briceño Diego Dioniso de
Tamarón, Pedrol
Villagrá, Gasper Pérez de
HADDON, RAWSON W.
Davis, Charles Harold
Low, Will Hicok
HADLOCK, RICHARD B.
Waller, Thomas Wright
HAEHN, OLIVIA A.
Bacheller, Irving
Brown, Margaret Wise
White, Stewart Edward
HAFEN, LEROY R.
Adams, Andy
Adams, Charles
Butterfield, John
Chorpenning, George
Holladay, Ben
Holliday, Cyrus Kurtz
McCreery, James Work
Mears, Otto
Nicholson, Samuel Danford
Pike, Zebulon Montgomery
Shafroth, John Franklin
Sheedy, Dennis
Stone, Wilbur Fisk
Tabor, Horace Austin Warner
Welch, Charles Clark
HAGAN, HORACE H.
Terry, David Smith
HAIGHT, GORDON S.
Sigourney, Lydia Howard Huntley
Witherspoon, Alexander Maclaren
HAIL, WILLIAM J.
Burgevine, Henry Andrea
McCartee, Divie Bethune
Ward, Frederick Townsend
HAINES, MICHAEL F.
Bierwirth, John Edward
Condon, Edward Uhler
Mirsky, Alfred Ezra
HAINES, SAMUEL F.
Plummer, Henry Stanley
HALE, EDWARD E.
Lewis, Tayler
HALE, NANCY
Hinkle, Beatrice Moses
HALE, ROBERT
Appleton, John, 1804–1891
Appleton, John, 1815–1864
HALEY, J. EVETTS
Goodnight, Charles

Lasater, Edward Cunningham
Littlefield, George Washington
Siringo, Charles A.
HALL, CLIFTON L.
Payne, Bruce Ryburn
HALL, COURTNEY R.
Seybert, Adam
Seybert, Henry
HALL, DAVID D.
Appleton, William Sumner
HALL, EDWIN H.
Lovering, Joseph
Sabine, Wallace Clement Ware
Trowbridge, John
HALL, JOHN PHILIP
Furuseth, Andrew
HALL, LAURENCE P.
Gibbs, Oliver Wolcott
HALL, PERCIVAL
Clarke, Francis Devereux
Clerc, Laurent
Crouter, Albert Louis Edgerton
Fay, Edward Allen
Gallaudet, Edward Miner
Gallaudet, Thomas
Gallaudet, Thomas Hopkins
Peet, Harvey Prindle
Peet, Isaac Lewis
Porter, Samuel
HALL, THOMAS B.
Sappington, John
HALLER, MARK H.
Capone, Alphonse
Guzik, Jack
Laughlin, Harry Hamilton
HALLION, RICHARD P.
Pangborn, Clyde Edward
HAM, MARY C.
Biard, Pierre
HAM, ROBERT EDMOND
Abbott, John Stevens Cabot
HAMBY, ALONZO L.
Barkley, Alben William
Dirksen, Everett McKinley
McGranery, James Patrick
Rayburn, Samuel Taliaferro ("Sam")
HAMER, MARGUERITE BARTLETT
McGhee, Charles McClung
McMinn, Joseph
Phelan, James
Rhea, John
HAMER, PHILIP M.
Beard, Richard
Bell, John
Blount, William
Blount, Willie
Campbell, George Washington, 1769–1848
Campbell, William Bowen
Cannon, Newton
Carrick, Samuel
Carroll, William
Cocke, William
Cravath, Erastus Milo
Embree, Elihu
Fitzpatrick, Morgan Cassius
Foster, Ephraim Hubbard
Garrett, William Robertson
Gillem, Alvan Cullem
Humes, Thomas William
Maynard, Horace
Meigs, Return Jonathan
Nicholson, Alfred Osborne Pope
Peay, Austin
Pillow, Gideon Johnson
Ramsey, James Gettys McGready
HAMILTON, CHARLES V.
Powell, Adam Clayton, Jr.
HAMILTON, EARL J.
Gay, Edwin Francis
HAMILTON, EDWARD P.
Frizell, Joseph Palmer
HAMILTON, GEORGE L.
Crane, Thomas Frederick
HAMILTON, HOLMAN
Bowers, Claude Gernade
HAMILTON, J. G. DE ROULHAC
Ashe, Thomas Samuel
Badger, George Edmund
Barringer, Daniel Moreau
Bickett, Thomas Walter
Connor, Henry Groves
Dick, Robert Paine
Dobbin, James Cochran
Dobbs, Arthur
Dunning, William Archibald
Edwards, Weldon Nathaniel
Elmore, Franklin Harper
Fowler, Joseph Smith
Franklin, Jesse
Fuller, Thomas Charles
Gaines, Edmund Pendleton
Gilmer, John Adams
Goodloe, Daniel Reaves
Graham, Joseph
Hale, Edward Joseph
Hamilton, James, 1786–1857
Hammond, James Henry
Harper, Robert Goodloe
Harper, William
Hawks, Francis Lister
Helper, Hinton Rowan
Henderson, James Pinckney
Henderson, John Brooks
Hewes, Joseph
Holden, William Woods
Hooper, William
Howard, Oliver Otis
Howe, Robert
Husbands, Hermon
Iredell, James
Jarvis, Thomas Jordan
Johnson, Joseph
Johnson, William
Johnston, Samuel
Jones, Willie
Kirby-Smith, Edmund
Kitchin, Claude
Legaré, Hugh Swinton
McDuffie, George
McKay, James Iver
Macon, Nathaniel
Mangum, Willie Person
Martin, François-Xavier
Merrimon, Augustus Summerfield
Moore, Bartholomew Figures
Pearson, Richmond Mumford
Penn, John
Perry, Benjamin Franklin
Person, Thomas
Petigru, James Louis
Pinckney, Charles Cotesworth
Pinckney, Thomas
Polk, William
Pollard, Edward Alfred
Pool, John
Preston, John Smith
Preston, William Campbell
Pritchard, Jeter Connelly
Quintard, Charles Todd
Ransom, Matt Whitaker
Rayner, Kenneth
Reade, Edwin Godwin
Reid, David Settle
Revels, Hiram Rhoades
Ripley, Roswell Sabine
Ross, Edmund Gibson
Ruffin, Thomas
Saunders, Romulus Mitchell
Saunders, William Laurence
Settle, Thomas
Skinner, Harry
Smith, Robert, 1732 o.s.–1801
Smith, William, *c.* 1762–1840
Smith, William Nathan Harrell
Spaight, Richard Dobbs
Sprunt, James
Stanly, Edward
Steele, John
Stone, David
Swain, David Lowry
Tourgée, Albion Winegar
Turnbull, Robert James
Turner, Josiah
Turner, Nat
Walker, Leroy Pope
Wheeler, John Hill
Williamson, Hugh
Worth, Jonathan
Wragg, William
HAMILTON, PETER JOSEPH
Bankhead, John Hollis
HAMILTON, VIRGINIA V.
Heflin, James Thomas
HAMILTON, WALTON H.
Hoxie, Robert Franklin
HAMLIN, TALBOT F.
Albro, Lewis Colt
Atwood, Charles B.
Audsley, George Ashdown
Banner, Peter
Barber, Donn
Benjamin, Asher
Brunner, Arnold William
Cabot, Edward Clarke
Carrère, John Merven
Carter, Elias
Cope, Walter
Dakin, James Harrison
Davis, Alexander Jackson
Day, Frank Miles
Fenner, Burt Leslie
Gallier, James
Gilman, Arthur Delevan
Greenough, Henry
Haight, Charles Coolidge
Hardenbergh, Henry Janeway
Hastings, Thomas
Hood, Raymond Mathewson
Lafever, Minard
Lienau, Detlef
McComb, John
Magonigle, Harold Van Buren
Mangin, Joseph François
Marshall, Henry Rutgers
Parris, Alexander

Pelz, Paul Johannes
Post, George Browne
Price, Bruce
Ramée, Joseph Jacques
Renwick, James, 1818–1895
Richardson, Henry Hobson
Rogers, Isaiah
Root, John Wellborn
Rotch, Arthur
Starrett, William Aiken
Stewardson, John
Sturgis, Russell
Thompson, Martin E.
Tilton, Edward Lippincott
Tuthill, William Burnet
Upjohn, Richard
Upjohn, Richard Michell
Van Brunt, Henry
Van Rensselaer, Mariana Griswold
Ware, William Robert
Wheelwright, Edmund March
Willard, Solomon
Withers, Frederick Clarke
Young, Ammi Burnham

HAMMERSMITH, JACK L.
Borzage, Frank

HAMMOND, J. W.
Ryan, Walter D'Arcy

HAMMOND, WILLIAM A.
Laguna, Theodore de Leo de
Moore, Addison Webster
Sackett, Henry Woodward

HAMOR, WILLIAM A.
Duncan, Robert Kennedy

HAMPSON, RICK
Adonis, Joe
Colombo, Joseph Anthony
Costello, Frank
Gambino, Carlo
Giancana, Sam ("Mooney")
Hogan, Frank Smithwick
McIntyre, James Francis Aloysius
Ricca, Paul
Valachi, Jospeh Michael

HAND, IRVING F.
Gregg, Willis Ray

HANDLIN, OSCAR
Morse, John Torrey

HANDY, ROBERT T.
Jefferson, Charles Edward
Stelzle, Charles
Wilson, Clarence True

HANEY, JOHN LOUIS
Armstrong, Paul
Barnard, Charles
Brown, David Paul
Coates, Florence Earle
Conrad, Robert Taylor

HANEY, LYNN
Baker, Josephine

HANKE, LEWIS
Rowlandson, Mary White

HANKIN, JOSEPH N.
Folsom, Marion Bayard
Grossinger, Jennie

HANLEY, MILES L.
Wheeler, William Adolphus
Worcester, Joseph Emerson

HANNA, ALFRED J.
Trenholm, George Alfred

HANSCOM, ELIZABETH DEERING
Freeman, Mary Eleanor Wilkins
Larcom, Lucy
Pool, Maria Louise
Sanborn, Katherine Abbott
Ward, Elizabeth Stuart Phelps
Yale, Caroline Ardelia

HANSEN, VAGN K.
Ellington, Earl Buford
Hartsfield, William Berry
Metcalf, Lee Warren

HANSON, HOWARD
Goetschius, Percy

HANSON, JOSEPH MILLS
Rosser, Thomas Lafayette
Stevens, Clement Hoffman
Taliaferro, William Booth
Vanderburgh, William Henry
Whiting, William Henry Chase
Wilcox, Cadmus Marcellus
Wood, Thomas John
Wright, Horatio Gouverneur

HARBAGE, ALFRED
Schelling, Felix Emanuel

HARBAUGH, WILIAM H.
Davis, John William

HARBESON, JOHN F.
Klauder, Charles Zeller

HARDING, GEORGE L.
Zamorano, Agustin Juan Vicente

HARDY, EDWARD ROCHIE, JR.
Rainsford, William Stephen
Seabury, Samuel, 1801–1872
Seymour, George Franklin
Southgate, Horatio
Talbot, Ethelbert
Walden, Jacob Treadwell
Wilson, Bird

HARDY, E. R.
Coffin, Henry Sloane
Gavin, Frank Stanton Burns
Manning, William Thomas

HARDY, STEPHEN
Owen, Stephen Joseph

HARE, LLOYD C. M.
Mayhew, Thomas
Wainwright, Jonathan Mayhew, 1792–1854

HARKNESS, R. E. E.
Vedder, Henry Clay

HARLAN, ROBERT D.
Nash, John Henry

HARLEY, L. GIBB
Longyear, John Munroe

HARLOW, ALVIN E.
Alden, Cynthia May Westover

HARLOW, ALVIN F.
Adams, Edward Dean
Atterbury, William Wallace
Belmont, Alva Ertskin Smith Vanderbilt
Borden, Lizzie Andrew
Brann, William Cowper
Burns, William John
Collier, Barron Gift
Corbett, James John
Corey, William Ellis
Crane, William Henry
Cutting, Robert Fulton
Dillinger, John
Dillingham, Charles Bancroft
Doheny, Edward Laurence
Dollar, Robert
Du Pont, Thomas Coleman
Flegenheimer, Arthur
Foy, Eddie
George, William Reuben
Heath, Thomas Kurton
Hires, Charles Elmer
Hitchcock, James Ripley Wellman
Hopwood, Avery
Hough, Emerson
Hurlbert, William Henry
Jerome, William Travers
Johnston, William Andrew
Kahn, Otto Herman
Keenan, James Francis
Kingsley, Darwin Pearl
Kroger, Bernhard Henry
Kunz, George Frederick
Lawson, Thomas William
Lee, Ivy Ledbetter
Leiter, Joseph
Littleton, Martin Wiley
McGeehan, William O'Connell
McGraw, John Joseph
McIntyre, James
Mann, Louis
Marbury, Elisabeth
Marling, Alfred Erskine
Maxim, Hiram Percy
Mercer, Henry Chapman
Moffett, Cleveland Langston
Morawetz, Victor
Muldoon, William
Myrick, Herbert
O'Leary, Daniel
Post, Wiley
Price, Theodore Hazeltine
Price, William Thompson
Quantrill, William Clarke
Redpath, James
Reick, William Charles
Rice, Calvin Winsor
Ringling, Charles
Rogers, Henry Huttleston
Romeike, Henry
Rumsey, Mary Harriman
Ryan, John Dennis
Sage, Russell
Saunders, Frederick
Savage, Henry Wilson
Sherry, Louis
Sonnichsen, Albert
Statler, Ellsworth Milton
Stetson, Charles Augustus
Stewart, Alexander Turney
Stewart, John Aikman
Stewart, William Rhinelander
Stimson, Alexander Lovett
Stokes, William Earl Dodge
Stone, David Marvin
Straus, Jesse Isidor
Straus, Simon William
Strong, William Lafayette
Sullivan, Timothy Daniel
Sully, Daniel John
Sweeny, Peter Barr
Talmage, Thomas De Witt
Tevis, Lloyd
Thorburn, Grant
Tiffany, Charles Lewis
Tiffany, Louis Comfort
Tilyou, George Cornelius
Tripp, Guy Eastman
Tweed, William Marcy
Vanderbilt, Cornelius, 1794–1877

Vanderbilt, Cornelius, 1843–1899
Vanderbilt, George Washington
Vanderbilt, William Henry
Vanderbilt, William Kissam
Van Nostrand, David
Van Sweringen, Mantis James
Vibbard, Chauncey
Viele, Egbert Ludovicus
Wallack, Henry John
Wallack, James William, *c.* 1795–1864
Wallack, James William, 1818–1873
Wallack, Lester
Walsh, Blanche
Whitney, Caspar
Whitney, Harry Payne
Willard, Josiah Flint
Wood, Henry Alexander Wise
Woodhull, Victoria Claflin
Woolworth, Frank Winfield
Wrigley, William
Young, George
Ziegler, William

HARLOW, RALPH V.
Dana, Francis
Deane, Silas
Elliot, Jonathan
Force, Peter
Hathorne, William
Heath, William
Smith, Gerrit

HARPER, GEORGE M.
Maclean, John
Murray, James Ormsbee

HARPER, GEORGE MCLEAN
Patton, Francis Landey
Shields, Charles Woodruff

HARPER, IDA HUSTED
Shaw, Anna Howard

HARPER, LAWRENCE A.
Gillette, King Camp

HARRADON, H. D.
Bauer, Louis Agricola

HARRELL, ISAAC S.
Andrews, Sidney

HARRINGTON, KEVIN
Mies Van Der Rohe, Ludwig

HARRIS, BRICE
Westcott, Edward Noyes

HARRIS, CHARLES M.
Mitchell, Margaret Munnerlyn
Williams, Ben Ames

HARRIS, GILBERT DENNISON
Williams, Henry Shaler

HARRIS, MICHAEL R.
Flexner, Abraham

HARRIS, REBECCA S.
Lamoureux, Andrew Jackson

HARRIS, ROBERT L., JR.
Robinson, Ruby Doris Smith

HARRIS, THOMAS LE GRAND
Caldwell, Alexander
Carney, Thomas
Conway, Martin Franklin
Crawford, Samuel Johnson
Deitzler, George Washington
Usher, John Palmer

HARRIS, WILLIAM H.
Randolph, Asa Philip
Townsend, Willard Saxby, Jr.

HARRISON, FAIRFAX
Beverley, Robert
Fairfax, Thomas

HARRISON, JOHN M.
Blakeslee, Howard Walter

HARRISON, MARJORIE FREEMAN
Rose, Alex

HARRISON, RICHARD A.
Choate, Anne Hyde Clarke
Harriman, Florence Jaffray Hurst
Miller, David Hunter

HARROW, BENJAMIN
Atwater, Wilbur Olin
Baruch, Simon
Baskerville, Charles
Biggs, Hermann Michael

HARROWER, MOLLY
Koffka, Kurt

HARSHBERGER, JOHN W.
Meehan, Thomas

HART, ALBERT BUSHNELL
Oakes, George Washington Ochs

HART, EDWARD
Bolton, Henry Carrington
McMurtrie, William

HART, EDWIN B.
Babcock, Stephen Moulton

HART, FANCHON
Rusby, Henry Hurd

HART, FREEMAN H.
Johnston, Zachariah
Jones, Gabriel
McClurg, James
Mason, Thomson
Moore, Andrew
Stuart, Archibald
White, Alexander

HART, JOHN E.
Crouse, Russel McKinley
Dell, Floyd James
Farrell, James Thomas
Jones, James Ramon
Kreymborg, Alfred Francis
McFee, William
O'Connor, Edwin Greene
Toklas, Alice Babette

HARTLEY, E. NEAL
Schwab, Charles Michael

HARTT, MARY BRONSON
Dean, Bashford
Eytinge, Rose
Fisher, Clara
Florence, William Jermyn
Foster, Benjamin
Gill, Laura Drake
Gillespie, Mabel
Goodyear, William Henry
Hall, Arethusa
Hall, Henry Bryan
Hapgood, Isabel Florence
Harrison, Gabriel
Havell, Robert
Haworth, Joseph
Heinemann, Ernst
Herter, Christian
Hill, John
Holder, Joseph Bassett
Holland, Edmund Milton
Holland, George
Holland, Joseph Jefferson
Hollyer, Samuel
Hunt, Mary Hannah Hanchett
Jacobi, Mary Corinna Putnam
Kehew, Mary Morton Kimball
Keller, Arthur Ignatius
Keppel, Frederick
Lawrie, Alexander
Leney, William Satchwell
Loeb, Sophie Irene Simon
Lothrop, Alice Louise Higgins
Marshall, William Edgar
Mitchell, Margaret Julia
Terhune, Mary Virginia Hawes

HARTWELL, JOHN AUGUSTUS
Weir, Robert Fulton

HARVEY, A. MCGEHEE
Blalock, Alfred
Longcope, Warfield Theobald
Robinson, George Canby

HARVEY, GEORGE C.
Gould, George Milbry
Haldeman, Samuel Steman
Hart, Charles Henry

HARVEY, SAMUEL C.
Da Costa, John Chalmers
Judd, Edward Starr

HARWOOD, MARGARET
Mitchell, William, 1791–1869
Searle, Arthur
Winlock, Joseph

HASKELL, DANIEL C.
McDougall, Alexander
Moore, Sir Henry
Morgan, Daniel

HAST, ADELE
Briggs, Lyman James
Cooke, Robert Anderson
Fejos, Paul
Kidder, Alfred Vincent
Nelson, Nels Christian

HASTINGS, GEORGE E.
Duché, Jacob
Ferguson, Elizabeth Graeme
Hopkinson, Francis

HATCH, LOUIS C.
Allen, Elisha Hunt
Bates, James
Boutelle, Charles Addison
Bradbury, James Ware
Coburn, Abner

HATCHER, WILLIAM H.
Willoughby, Westel Woodbury

HAUGEN, EINAR R.
Rölvaag, Ole Edvart

HAUPTMAN, LAURENCE M.
Beatty, Willard Walcott
Jemison, Alice Mae Lee
Silverhills, Jay
Thomas, George Allison

HAUPTMAN, ROBERT
McCullers, Carson

HAUSER, PHILIP M.
Ogburn, William Fielding

HAVENS, GEORGE R.
Armstrong, Edward Cooke

HAVENS, W. W., JR.
Pegram, George Braxton

HAVIG, ALAN R.
Carrington, Elaine Stern
Denny, George Vernon, Jr.
Hooper, Claude Ernest
Husing, Edward Britt ("Ted")

HAWKINS, HUGH
Ames, Joseph Sweetman

Butler, Nicholas Murray
Lowell, Abbott Lawrence
HAWKINS, RICHARD A.
Loeb, Milton B.
Welch, Leo Dewey
HAWLEY, ELLIS W.
Arnold, Thurman Wesley
Biggers, John David
Swope, Gerard
HAWLEY, FRANCES B.
Cesnola, Luigi Palma di
Clarke, Sir Caspar Purdon
Cook, Clarence Chatham
Vincent, Frank
HAWORTH, PAUL L.
Davis, John Wesley
Dunn, William McKee
Dunn, Williamson
English, William Hayden
Judah, Samuel
Julian, George Washington
Kern, John Worth
Kimball, Nathan
Lane, Henry Smith
Lanier, James Franklin Doughty
HAY, CHARLES C., III
Barnes, Julius Howland
Reynolds, Richard Samuel, Sr.
Reynolds, William Neal
Thomas, John Parnell
Thomas, (John William) Elmer
HAY, MELBA PORTER
Andrus, Ethel Percy
Brewster, Ralph Owen
Dole, James Drummond
Hale, Frederick
Hamilton, Alice
Hoffman, Clare Eugene
Pope, James Pinckney
Wiley, Alexander
HAY, THOMAS ROBSON
Beatty, John
HAYCRAFT, ROBERT
Arensberg, Walter Conrad
Lancaster, Henry Carrington
HAYES, CARLTON J. H.
Moon, Parker Thomas
HAYES, DOREMUS A.
Little, Charles Joseph
Lunt, Orrington
Terry, Milton Spenser
HAYES, JOHN D.
Gleaves, Albert
Reeves, Joseph Mason
Taussig, Joseph Knefler
HAYES, ROBERT C.
Livingston, Robert R., 1718–1775
Livingston, Robert R., 1746–1813
HAYLOR, ADA P.
Morehead, John Motley
HAYNES, FRED E.
Clarkson, Coker Fifield
Cole, Chester Cicero
Cummins, Albert Baird
Dawson, Thomas Cleland
Deemer, Horace Emerson
Ellis, Seth Hockett
Evans, George Henry
Larrabee, William
Lewelling, Lorenzo Dow
Perkins, George Douglas
Pettigrew, Richard Franklin
Price, Hiram
HAYNES, GEORGE HENRY
Ashmun, George
Banks, Nathaniel Prentiss
Crane, Winthrop Murray
Gillett, Frederick Huntington
Hoar, Ebenezer Rockwood
Hoar, George Frisbie
Hoar, Samuel
Sumner, Charles
Thompson, Edward Herbert
Washburn, Charles Grenfill
Wilson, Henry
HAYNES, RICHARD F.
Matthews, Francis Patrick
Tucker, Henry St. George
HAYWOOD, MARSHALL DELANCEY
Atkinson, Thomas
Burrington, George
Eden, Charles
Ludwell, Philip
HAZLITT, HENRY
Pollak, Gustav
HEAD, WILLIAM
Bergen, Edgar
Blackmer, Sydney Alderman
Buck, Pearl Comfort Sydenstricker
Butterworth, William Walton ("Walt")
Conrad, Maximilian Arthur, Jr.
Daley, Cass
Dunn, Michael
Egtvedt, Clairmont ("Claire") Leroy
Hires, Charles Elmer, Jr.
Leonard, Jack E.
McElroy, Neil Hosler
Ritchard, Cyril
HEALY, DAVID F.
Griscom, Lloyd Carpenter
HEALY, JOHN DAVID
Brophy, Thomas D'Arcy
Burnett, Leo
Cross, Milton John
Dickinson, Edwin De Witt
Goodman, Louis Earl
Hays, Paul R.
Reed, Stanley Forman
Saypol, Irving Howard
Whittaker, Charles Evans
HEBARD, GRACE RAYMOND
Carey, Joseph Maull
Wergeland, Agnes Mathilde
HECHT, STUART J.
Guthrie, Sir Tyrone
HECK, EARL L. W.
Hack, George
Hawks, John
Hayes, William Henry
Herrman, Augustine
Hunt, William Gibbes
Johnston, Gabriel
Palmer, Joseph
Peirce, William
Pound, Thomas
Sedgwick, Theodore, 1811–1859
Van der Donck, Adriaen
HECK-RABI, LOUISE
Templeton, Alec Andrew
HEDGES, JAMES B.
Villard, Henry
Weeden, William Babcock
HEEFNER, DANIEL
Irvine, William Mann
HEFELBOWER, SAMUEL G.
Sprecher, Samuel
Unangst, Erias
Wenner, George Unangst
HEFTON, JOHN M.
Murray, Mae
HEIDER, GRACE M.
Lewin, Kurt
Wertheimer, Max
HEIDNER, SAMUEL J.
Page, Richard Lucian
Pender, William Dorsey
Ramsay, George Douglas
Ramseur, Stephen Dodson
Reynolds, Joseph Jones
Richardson, Israel Bush
Ricketts, James Brewerton
Riley, Bennett
Ripley, James Wolfe
Russell, David Allen
St. John, Isaac Munroe
Sidell, William Henry
Sigel, Franz
Smith, Charles Henry, 1827–1902
Smith, John Eugene
Stahel, Julius
HEILBRONER, ROBERT L.
Morgenthau, Henry
HEILBRONNER, HANS
Rosen, Joseph A.
HEILMAN, ELIZABETH WILTBANK
Scidmore, Eliza Ruhamah
Shields, George Oliver
Stuck, Hudson
Workman, Fanny Bullock
HEILMAN, ROBERT B.
Roethke, Theodore Huebner
HEIM, KEITH M.
Ammann, Othmar Hermann
HEINL, ROBERT DEBS, JR.
Lejeune, John Archer
HELLMAN, GEOFFREY T.
Guggenheim, Solomon Robert
Lehman, Arthur
Lewisohn, Adolph
HELLMAN, GEORGE S.
Curtis, George William
Spingarn, Joel Elias
HELLWEG, J. F.
Skinner, Aaron Nichols
HENCH, ATCHESON L.
Eggleston, George Cary
Johnson, Chapman
HENDERSON, EDWARD P.
Cross, Charles Whitman
HENDERSON, RICHARD B.
Maverick, (Fontaine) Maury
HENDERSON, VIRGINIA
Goodrich, Annie Warburton
HENDERSON, WILLIAM J.
Huneker, James Gibbons
HENDRICK, BURTON JESSE
Carnegie, Andrew
HENDRICK, ELLWOOD
Chandler, Charles Frederick
Draper, John William
Freas, Thomas Bruce
HENDRICKSON, G. L.
Hale, William Gardner
Warren, Minton

HENDRICKSON, KENNETH E., JR.
Lunn, George Richard
HENLEY, R. R.
Dorset, Marion
HENLINE, H. H.
Perrine, Frederic Auten Combs
HENMON, VIVIAN ALLEN CHARLES
Carpenter, Stephen Haskins
Conover, Obadiah Milton
HENNESEY, JAMES, S.J.
Talbot, Francis Xavier
HENRY, BRUCE
Collier, Constance
HENSON, PAMELA M.
Akeley, Mary Leonore
Chase, (Mary) Agnes Merrill
Dorn, Harold Fred
HERBEN, STEPHEN J.
Kynett, Alpha Jefferson
Nelson, Reuben
HERBERT P. GALLINGER
Moore, Zephaniah Swift
HEROLD, AMOS L.
Paulding, James Kirke
HERON, DAVID W.
Chester, Colby Mitchell
Patchen, Kenneth
Patterson, Richard Cunningham, Jr.
Sproul, Robert Gordon
Wrigley, Philip Knight
HERON, DAVID WINSTON
Gilbert, Alfred Carlton
Kirkus, Virginia
Langlie, Arthur Bernard
HERRICK, GLENN W.
Comstock, John Henry
HERRICK, ROBERT
Tarbell, Frank Bigelow
HERRING, GEORGE C.
Fall, Bernard B.
HERRINGTON, NANCY J.
Dunning, John Ray
Evans, Herbert McLean
Richards, Dickinson Woodruff
Weaver, Warren
HERRIOT, FRANK I.
Drake, Francis Marion
HERRNSTEIN, R. J.
Lashley, Karl Spencer
HERRON, STELLA
Blanc, Antoine
Blenk, James Hubert
Janssens, Francis
HERSEY, FRANK WILSON CHENEY
Malcolm, Daniel
Prescott, Samuel
HERSEY, JOHN
Wertenbaker, Charles Christian
HERTY, CHARLES H.
Venable, Francis Preston
HERTZBERG, ARTHUR
Haas, Jacob Judah Aaron de
Masliansky, Zvi Hirsch
Wise, Stephen Samuel
HERVEY, JOHN L.
Madden, John Edward
Sloan, James Forman
Wallace, John Hankins
HESS, GARY R.
Hamilton, Maxwell McGaughey
HESSEN, ROBERT
Grace, Eugene Gifford
Rand, James Henry
HEWES, EDWIN B.
Higginson, Nathaniel
HEWES, JAMES E., JR.
Somervell, Brehon Burke
HEWLETT, RICHARD G.
Dean, Gordon Evans
Murray, Thomas Edward
HEXTER, MAURICE B.
Warburg, Felix Moritz
HEY, KENNETH R.
Skouras, George Panagiotes
HIBBARD, RUFUS P.
Miles, Manly
HIBBEN, JOHN GRIER
McCosh, James
HICKERSON, JOHN D.
Moffat, Jay Pierrepont
HICKMAN, EMILY
Fargo, William George
Wells, Henry
HICKMAN, RUSSELL
Block, Adriaen
HICKS, FREDERICK CHARLES
Boston, Charles Anderson
Carter, James Coolidge
Choate, Joseph Hodges
Coudert, Frederic René
Emmet, Thomas Addis, 1764–1827
Evarts, William Maxwell
Field, David Dudley, 1805–1894
Gummere, William Stryker
Hutchins, Thomas
Kent, James
Kirby, Ephraim
O'Conor, Charles
Wheaton, Henry
HICKS, GRANVILLE
Boyd, Thomas Alexander
Glass, Montague Marsden
Gregory, Eliot
Ladd, Joseph Brown
Meneely, Andrew
Nadal, Ehrman Syme
Phillips, David Graham
Rohlfs, Anna Katharine Green
Saltus, Edgar Evertson
Scott, Leroy
Vance, Louis Joseph
Warner, Anna Bartlett
Warner, Susan Bogert
Wilcox, Ella Wheeler
HICKS, JOHN DONALD
Allen, William Vincent
Barrett, Charles Simon
Billings, Frederick
Blaine, John James
Creighton, John Andrew
Crounse, Lorenzo
Donnelly, Ignatius
Fairbanks, Charles Warren
Frank, Glenn
Furnas, Robert Wilkinson
Hitchcock, Phineas Warrener
Holcomb, Silas Alexander
McDonald, Joseph Ewing
Manderson, Charles Frederick
Marquett, Turner Mastin
Marshall, Thomas Riley
Matthews, Claude
Maxwell, Samuel
Morton, Julius Sterling
Morton, Oliver Perry
New, Harry Stewart
Paddock, Algernon Sidney
Polk, Leonidas Lafayette
Rosewater, Edward
Stevenson, Adlai Ewing
Washburn, Cadwallader Colden
Weaver, James Baird
HIDY, MURIEL E.
Claflin, John
HIDY, RALPH WILLARD
Van Dyke, John Wesley
Ward, Thomas Wren
Weyerhaeuser, Frederick Edward
HIGGINS, ROGER WOLCOTT
Plummer, Jonathan
HIGGS, ROBERT J.
Hagen, Walter Charles
HIGHAM, CHARLES
DeMille, Cecil Blount
HIGHAM, ROBIN
Bell, Lawrence Dale
Lockheed, Malcolm
Martin, Glenn Luther ("Cy")
Scott, Allen Cecil
HIGHTOWER, RAYMOND L.
Wilson, Joshua Lacy
Wilson, Samuel Ramsay
HILDEBRAND, JOEL H.
Latimer, Wendell Mitchell
HILGARD, ERNEST R.
Robinson, Edward Stevens
Tolman, Edward Chace
HILL, CHARLES E.
Erving, George William
Foster, John Watson
HILL, DAVID JAYNE
Herrick, Myron Timothy
HILL, FRANK ERNEST
Duryea, Charles Edgar
Firestone, Harvey Samuel
Ford, Edsel Bryant
Wills, Childe Harold
HILL, HAMLIN
Faust, Frederick Shiller
HILL, HELEN
Mason, Georg
HILL, JIM DAN
Waddell, James Iredell
Wilkinson, John
Winslow, John Ancrum
HILL, LEWIS WEBB
Morse, John Lovett
HILL, MARILYN WOOD
Alsop, Mary O'Hara
Bayh, Marvella Belle Hern
Cavert, Samuel McCrea
Mesta, Perle Reid Skirvin
Mitchell, Martha Elizabeth Beall
Priest, Ivy Maude Baker
HILLE, EINAR
Tamarkin, Jacob David
HILLER, E. T.
Hayes, Edward Carey
HIMES, NORMAN E.
Knowlton, Charles
HINES, THOMAS S.
Neutra, Richard Joseph
HINKE, WILLIAM J.
Schlatter, Michael

HINMAN, EDGAR L.
Wolfe, Harry Kirke
HINTON, EDWARD M.
Grimké, Archibald Henry
McAllister, Samuel Ward
McCarroll, James
McHenry, James
Marden, Orison Swett
Martin, Frederick Townsend
Mathews, Albert
Matthews, Franklin
HIRSCH, ARTHUR H.
Le Jau, Francis
HIRSCH, FOSTER
Hopper, Edna Wallace
Kelly, George Edward
Lloyd, Harold Clayton
Wayne, John
HIRSCH, MARK D.
Copeland, Royal Samuel
O'Brien, Morgan Joseph
HIRSCHHORN, BERNARD
Childs, Richard Spencer
Eichelberger, Clark Mell
Ewing, Oscar Ross
Youngdahl, Luther Wallace
HIRSCHLAND, ELLEN B.
Cone, Claribel
Cone, Etta
Dale, Chester
Dale, Maud Murray Thompson
HIRSH, FREDERICK R., JR.
Richtmyer, Floyd Karker
HISE, FRANK L.
Abbott, Frank
Allen, John
Black, Greene Vardiman
Bonwill, William Gibson Arlington
HITCHINGS, SINCLAIR
Wyeth, Newell Convers
HOBBS, JOSEPH P.
Hodges, Courtney Hicks
Puller, Lewis Burwell ("Chesty")
Russell, Richard Brevard, Jr. ("Dick")
Smith, Walter Bedell
HOBBS, WILLIAM H.
Russell, Israel Cook
HOCKETT, CHARLES F.
Bloomfield, Leonard
HOCKETT, HOMER CAREY
Buckland, Ralph Pomeroy
Bushnell, Asa Smith
Corwin, Thomas
Cox, Jacob Dolson
Cox, Samuel Sullivan
Day, William Rufus
Dennison, William
Foster, Charles
Hamer, Thomas Lyon
Hickenlooper, Andrew
Hitchcock, Peter
Hoadly, George
HOCKING, WILLIAM ERNEST
Palmer, George Herbert
HODDER, FRANK H.
Eldridge, Shalor Winchell
HODGE, FREDERICK W.
Hough, Walter
Morgan, Lewis Henry
HODGES, GRAHAM
Lewis, John Henry
Mabley, Jackie ("Moms")
HODGES, JAMES A.
Berry, George Leonard
Haywood, Allan Shaw
HODGES, PAUL C.
Brown, Percy
Hirsch, Isaac Seth
HOFF, SYLVIA G.
Fromm-Reichmann, Frieda
HOFFMAN, M. M.
Crétin, Joseph
Hennessy, John
Loras, Jean Mathias Pierre
Mazzuchelli, Samuel Charles
HOFFMAN, RAND
Holly, Charles Hardin ("Buddy")
HOFMANN, GEORGE F.
Christie, John Walter
HOHNER, ROBERT A.
Cannon, James
Cherrington, Ernest Hurst
LaFarge, John
HOLCOMBE, ARTHUR N.
Lawrence, Abbott
Lawrence, Amos
Lawrence, Amos Adams
Lawrence, William, 1783–1848
HOLDEN, RAYMOND
MacCameron, Robert
Mitchell, John Ames
Morgan, Matthew Somerville
HOLLANDER, STANLEY C.
Hartford, George Huntington
Hartford, George Ludlum
Hartford, John Augustine
HOLLEY, I. B., JR.
Hines, John Leonard ("Birdie")
Palmer, John McAuley
HOLLI, MELVIN G.
Cobo, Albert Eugene
HOLLIS, DANIEL WALKER
Blease, Coleman Livingston
Smith, Ellison DuRant
HOLLON, W. EUGENE
Rister, Carl Coke
HOLLORAN, PETER C.
Glueck, Eleanor Touroff
Watts, Alan Wilson
HOLLY, MICHAEL ANN
Panofsky, Erwin
HOLMAN, C. HUGH
Glasgow, Ellen Anderson Gholson
HOLMES, BURNHAM
Roth, Samuel
Tanner, Edward Everett, III ("Patrick Dennis")
HOLMES, EUGENE C.
Locke, Alain Leroy
HOLMES, HARRY N.
Hall, Charles Martin
HOLMES, JOHN HAYNES
Grant, Percy Stickney
Haven, Joseph
Janes, Lewis George
Levermore, Charles Herbert
Lowell, Robert Traill Spence
Lyman, Albert Josiah
Moxom, Philip Stafford
Parkhurst, Charles Henry
Riis, Jacob August
Spencer, Anna Garlin
Straton, John Roach
Strong, Josiah
Tyson, Stuart Lawrence
Villard, Helen Frances Garrison
HOLMES, OLIVER W.
Keith, Minor Cooper
Litchfield, Electus Backus
McCarren, Patrick Henry
Maxwell, George Hebard
Meiggs, Henry
Munro, George
Murphy, Henry Cruse
Murrell, John A.
Newton, Henry Jotham
Newton, Isaac, 1794–1858
Orr, Alexander Ector
Payne, Oliver Hazard
Pinkerton, Allan
Revell, Fleming Hewitt
Richmond, Dean
Rogers, Moses
Schell, Augustus
HOLT, IVAN LEE
Palmore, William Beverly
HOLT, JEAN MACKINNON
Breck, George William
Brevoort, James Renwick
Davenport, Homer Calvin
Dearth, Henry Golden
Dewing, Maria Richards Oakey
Earle, James
Eaton, Joseph Oriel
Eaton, Wyatt
Edmonds, Francis William
Eichholtz, Jacob
Elliott, Charles Loring
Elliott, John
Enneking, John Joseph
Farrer, Henry
Fassett, Cornelia Adèle Strong
Fisher, Alvan
Flagg, George Whiting
Flagg, Jared Bradley
HOLT, LUCIUS H.
Goodrich, Frank Boott
Hoffman, Charles Fenno
Hoffman, John Thompson
Hoffman, Wickham
Kelly, John
Kernan, Francis
Kinsella, Thomas
Knickerbocker, Herman
HOLT, W. STULL
Scharf, John Thomas
HOLTER, MARY FRANCES
Yerkes, Charles Tyson
HOLTHAUS, PHILIP G.
Aldrich, Winthrop William
HOMER, WILLIAM I.
Stieglitz, Alfred
HONEYMAN, A. VAN DOREN
Maxwell, William
Neilson, John
Nelson, William, 1847–1914
Newell, William Augustus
Odell, Jonathan
Ogden, David
Vroom, Peter Dumont
Ward, Marcus Lawrence
Whitehead, William Adee

Honig, Joel
Livingstone, Belle
Hoogenboom, Ari
Bloom, Sol
Cudahy, Edward Aloysius, Jr.
Ellmaker, (Emmett) Lee
Gibbs, (Oliver) Wolcott
Littauer, Lucius Nathan
Reed, David Aiken
Rovere, Richard Halworth
Volstead, Andrew John
Hoogenboom, Lynn
Johnson, Malcolm Malone
Lippmann, Walter
Hoogenboom, Olive
Arden, Elizabeth
Castle, Irene Foote
Chase, Edna Woolman
Garden, Mary
Hopper, Hedda
Kilgallen, Dorothy Mae
Luhan, Mabel Dodge
Norris, Kathleen Thompson
Rose, Billy
Vanderbilt, Gloria Morgan
Hooker, Helene Maxwell
Heney, Francis Joseph
Hooker, Henry D.
Husmann, George
Longworth, Nicholas, 1782–1863
Hooker, Marjorie
Keith, Arthur
Hooker, Roland Mather
Talcott, Joseph
Trumbull, Benjamin
Winthrop, John
Wyllys, George
Hoover, Dwight W.
Matthes, Gerard Hendrik
Micheaux, Oscar
Hoover, Harvey D.
Hunton, William Lee
Hope, Arthur J.
Hudson, Daniel Eldred
Hopf, Rita Hilborn
Barth, Carl Georg Lange
Hopkins, Albert A.
Adams, Isaac
Beach, Alfred Ely
Blanchard, Thomas
Hopkins, B. Smith
Parr, Samuel Wilson
Hopkins, C. Howard
Mott, John R.
Smith, Fred Burton
Hopkins, E. Washburn
Hall, Fitzedward
Hopkins, L. Thomas
Newlon, Jesse Homer
Hoppenstand, Gary
Pal, George
Horack, Frank E.
Kinne, La Vega George
Kirkwood, Samuel Jordan
Horgan, Paul
Saxton, Eugene Francis
Horgan, Stephen Henry
Levy, Louis Edward
Moss, John Calvin
Hormell, Orren C.
Kent, Edward

Hornblow, Arthur
Adams, Edwin
Aldrich, Louis
Aldridge, Ira Frederick
Arden, Edwin Hunter Pendleton
Blake, William Rufus
Bowers, Elizabeth Crocker
Chanfrau, Francis S.
Chanfrau, Henrietta Baker
Horner, Harlan H.
Randall, Samuel Sidwell
Rice, Victor Moreau
Horowitz, Murray M.
Levenson, Samuel ("Sam")
Horton, Walter M.
King, Henry Churchill
Hosay, Philip M.
Graves, David Bibb
Sanderson, Ezra Dwight
Hoskins, Halford Lancaster
Tufts, Charles
Hough, Henry Beetle
Lincoln, Joseph Crosby
Hough, Walter
Barber, Edwin Atlee
Bourke, John Gregory
Brower, Jacob Vradenberg
Byington, Cyrus
Casanowicz, Immanuel Moses
Churchill, William
Curtin, Jeremiah
Cushing, Frank Hamilton
Davis, Edwin Hamilton
Dorsey, James Owen
Emerson, Ellen Russell
Fewkes, Jesse Walter
Gatschet, Albert Samuel
Goddard, Pliny Earle
Hale, Horatio Emmons
Jones, William
McGee, William John
McGuire, Joseph Deakins
Mallery, Garrick
Mason, Otis Tufton
Matthews, Washington
Mooney, James
Pilling, James Constantine
Rau, Charles
Schoolcraft, Henry Rowe
Skinner, Alanson Buck
Smith, Erminnie Adelle Platt
Stevenson, James
Stevenson, Matilda Coxe Evans
Thomas, Cyrus
Hounshell, David A.
Gunnison, Foster
House, Albert V., Jr.
Randall, Samuel Jackson
Howard, Harvey J.
Green, John
Howard, James L.
Harding, Seth
Howard, Jane
Mead, Margaret
Howard, John Tasker
Braslau, Sophie
Chadwick, George Whitefield
Fairchild, Blair
Hadley, Henry Kimball
Johns, Clayton
Kroeger, Ernest Richard
Loeffler, Charles Martin
Nevin, George Balch

Oberhoffer, Emil Johann
Oehmler, Leo Carl Martin
Parsons, Albert Ross
Peters, William Cumming
Pratt, Waldo Selden
Root, George Frederick
Runcie, Constance Faunt Le Roy
Sanderson, Sibyl
Saslavsky, Alexander
Scheel, Fritz
Schindler, Kurt
Schradieck, Henry
Seidl, Anton
Selby, William
Sembrich, Marcella
Seward, Theodore Frelinghuysen
Shaw, Oliver
Sousa, John Philip
Southard, Lucien H.
Spicker, Max
Steck, George
Steinway, Christian Friedrich Theodore
Steinway, Henry Engelhard
Steinway, William
Stern, Joseph William
Sternberg, Constantin Ivanovich, Edler von
Stewart, Humphrey John
Stoeckel, Carl
Tapper, Bertha Feiring
Taylor, Raynor
Thayer, Alexander Wheelock
Thayer, Whitney Eugene
Thomas, Christian Friedrich Theodore
Thursby, Emma Cecilia
Timm, Henry Christian
Tobani, Theodore Moses
Trajetta, Philip
Tremaine, Henry Barnes
Tuckey, William
Urso, Camilla
Van der Stucken, Frank Valentin
Verbrugghen, Henri
Vogrich, Max Wilhelm Karl
Warren, Richard Henry
Watson, Henry Cood
Webb, George James
Webb, Thomas Smith
Weber, Albert
Weld, Arthur Cyril Gordon
Whitehill, Clarence Eugene
Whiting, George Elbridge
Whitney, Myron William
Wight, Frederick Coit
Wilson, Mortimer
Witherspoon, Herbert
Wood, David Duffle
Woodbury, Isaac Baker
Work, Henry Clay
Zerrahn, Carl
Howard, Leland Ossian
Ashmead, William Harris
Coquillett, Daniel William
Cresson, Ezra Townsend
Dyar, Harrison Gray
Edwards, William Henry
Fernald, Charles Henry
Fitch, Asa

Forbes, Stephen Alfred
Glover, Townend
Grote, Augustus Radcliffe
Hagen, Hermann August
Harris, Thaddeus William
Horn, George Henry
Hubbard, Henry Guernsey
Hunter, Walter David
Knab, Frederick
LeConte, John Lawrence
Lintner, Joseph Albert
McCook, Henry Christopher
Osten Sacken, Carl Robert Romanovich, Von Der
Packard, Alpheus Spring
Peck, William Dandridge
Peckham, George Williams
Riley, Charles Valentine
Say, Thomas
Schwarz, Eugene Amandus
Scudder, Samuel Hubbard
Smith, John Bernhard
Snow, Francis Huntington
Uhler, Philip Reese
Walsh, Benjamin Dann
HOWARD, MARGARET A.
Pei, Mario Andrew
HOWARD, SAMUEL F., JR.
Untermyer, Samuel
HOWAY, F. W.
Gray, Robert
Ingraham, Joseph
Kendrick, John
HOWE, HARRISON E.
Dow, Herbert Henry
Slosson, Edwin Emery
Teeple, John Edgar
HOWE, M. A. DEWOLFE
Bancroft, George
Bradford, Gamaliel
Chapman, John Jay
Hale, Edward Everett
Higginson, Thomas Wentworth
Holmes, Abiel
Holmes, Oliver Wendell
Lowell, James Russell
Rideing, William Henry
Scudder, Horace Elisha
HOWE, WALTER
Quelch, John
HOWE, WILL D.
Doubleday, Frank Nelson
Riley, James Whitcomb
HOWER, RALPH M.
Straus, Percy Selden
HOWLAND, HAROLD
Booth, Mary Louise
Bowen, Henry Chandler
Briggs, Charles Frederick
Brooks, Erastus
Brooks, Noah
Browne, Junius Henri
Bundy, Jonas Mills
Burchard, Samuel Dickinson
HOWLETT, CHARLES F.
Connolly, Maureen Catherine
Lapchick, Joseph Bohomiel
Stokes, Maurice
Waner, Paul Glee
HOXIE, ELIZABETH F.
Brady, William Aloysius
Pollock, Channing
HUBBARD, CLIFFORD CHESLEY
Ellery, William
HUBBARD, G. EVANS
Nicholson, John
HUBBARD, JOSEPH B.
Persons, Warren Milton
HUBBARD, THEODORA KIMBALL
Cleveland, Horace William Shaler
Eliot, Charles
Olmsted, Frederick Law
Olmsted, John Charles
HUBBELL, HARRY M.
Kingsley, James Luce
Perrin, Bernadotte
HUBBS, CARL L.
Sumner, Francis Bertody
HUDSON, JAMES J.
Andrews, Frank Maxwell
Patrick, Mason Mathews
HUDSON, WINWRHROP S.
Barbour, Clarence Augustus
HUGHES, ELIZABETH S.
Gossett, Benjamin Brown
HUGHES, THOMAS PARKE
Bendix, Vincent
Cottrell, Frederick Gardner
Jewett, Frank Baldwin
Lewis, George William
Stone, Charles Augustus
Webster, Edwin Sibley
HUGHES, WILLIAM
Bankhead, Tallulah
Begley, Edward James ("Ed")
Burke, Billie
Clift, Edward Montgomery
Keaton, Joseph Francis ("Buster"), V
Laurel, Stan
Muni, Paul
Novarro, Ramon
Pitts, Zasu
Wilson, Marie
HUHNER, LEON
Kohler, Max James
HULBERT, ARCHER B.
Tenney, Edward Payson
HULBERT, J. R.
Manly, John Matthews
Rickert, Martha Edith
HULL, CHARLES H.
Cornell, Alonzo B.
HULL, HANNAH CLOTHIER
Bond, Elizabeth Powell
HULL, WILLIAM I.
Magill, Edward Hicks
HUME, EDWARD ERSKINE
Bullitt, Henry Massie
Caldwell, Charles
Campbell, Henry Fraser
Chisolm, John Julian
Davidge, John Beale
De Rosset, Moses John
Dickson, Samuel Henry
Doughty, William Henry
Dowell, Greensville
Dudley, Benjamin Winslow
Dyer, Isadore
Eberle, John
HUMMEL, ARTHUR W.
Hunter, William C.
Ng Poon Chew
HUMPHREY, EDWARD FRANK
Bulkeley, Morgan Gardner
Camp, Hiram
Colton, Calvin
HUMPHREYS, R. A.
Robertson, William Spence
HUMPHREYS, WILLIAM JACKSON
Abbe, Cleveland
Bentley, Wilson Alwyn
Bigelow, Frank Hagar
Blodget, Lorin
Coffin, James Henry
Espy, James Pollard
Ferrel, William
Harrington, Mark Walrod
Hazen, Henry Allen
Redfield, William C.
Ward, Robert De Courcy
HUNGARLAND, ROBERT L.
Dillingham, Walter Francis
Parkinson, Thomas Ignatius
HUNGERFORD, EDWARD BUELL
Sizer, Nelson
Thompson, Arthur Webster
Wells, Samuel Roberts
HUNLEY, J. D.
Braun, Wernher Von
HUNT, J. RAMSAY
Starr, Moses Allen
HUNTER, ADELAIDE MEADOR
McKenzie, Robert Tait
HUNTER, LOUIS C.
Howe, Samuel
Mills, Elijah Hunt
HUNTER, THOMAS MARSHALL
Foster, Thomas Jefferson
HUNTER, W. C.
McCumber, Porter James
HUREWITZ, J. C.
Speiser, Ephraim Avigdor
HURLEY, ALFRED F.
Vandenberg, Hoyt Sanford
HUTCHINSON, WILLIAM T.
Lowden, Frank Orren
McArthur, John, 1826–1906
McClernand, John Alexander
HUTCHISON, WILLIAM R.
Lyman, Eugene William
HUTHMACHER, J. JOSEPH
Walsh, David Ignatius
HUYGHE, PATRICK
Goldmark, Peter Carl
Stanley, Wendell Meredith
HYDE, CHARLES GILMAN
Fuller, George Warren
HYDE, FRANCIS EDWIN
Perham, Josiah
HYDE, GRANT M.
Bleyer, Willard Grosvenor
HYMA, ALBERT
Campbell, James Valentine
Christiancy, Isaac Peckham
Crary, Isaac Edwin
Felch, Alpheus
Ferry, Thomas White
Kieft, Willem
Lothrop, George Van Ness
Palmer, Thomas Witherell
Van Cortlandt, Oloff Stevenszen
Van Raalte, Albertus Christiaan
Van Twiller, Wouler
HYMAN, HERBERT H.
Stouffer, Samuel Andrew

Ibbotson, Joseph D.
Kirkland, Samuel
Ihde, Aaron J.
Adkins, Homer Burton
Baekeland, Leo Hendrik
Bancroft, Wilder Dwight
Chittenden, Russell Henry
Cluett, Sanford Lockwood
Elvehjem, Conrad Arnold
Gomberg, Moses
Gortner, Ross Aiken
Haynes, Williams
Hudson, Claude Silbert
Kendall, Edward Calvin
Kirkwood, John Gamble
Koch, Fred Conrad
Kohler, Walter Jodok, Jr.
Onsager, Lars
Schoenheimer, Rudolf
Sheldon, William Herbert
Stern, Kurt Guenter
Waksman, Selman Abraham
Immerman, Richard H.
Dulles, Allen Welsh
Ingalls, Daniel H. H.
Lanman, Charles Rockwell
Ingersoll, L. R.
Mendenhall, Charles Elwood
Inglis, William O.
Sullivan, John Lawrence
Ingraham, Mark H.
Birge, Edward Asahel
Ingram, Augustus E.
Halderman, John A.
Le Gendre, Charles William
McCormick, Robert Sanderson
Magoffin, James Wiley
Maney, George Earl
Morris, Edward Joy
Murphy, Dominic Ignatius
Ireland, John, 1827–1896
Long, James
Irwin, Ray W.
Morris, Richard Valentine
O'Brien, Richard
Shaw, John, 1773–1823
Somers, Richard
Spencer, John Canfield
Sterett, Andrew
Stewart, Charles
Tallmadge, Benjamin
Tallmadge, James
Throop, Enos Thompson
Trippe, John
Tyndale, Hector
Underwood, John Curtiss
Valentine, David Thomas
Irwin, Raymond D.
Winslow, Ola Elizabeth
Isaacs, Asher
Donnell, James C.
Ford, John Baptiste
French, Aaron
Guffey, James McClurg
Heinz, Henry John
Hogg, George
Horton, Valentine Baxter
Jones, Benjamin Franklin
Jones, William Richard
Leishman, John G. A.
Lockhart, Charles
Lyon, James Benjamin
Metcalf, William
Moorhead, James Kennedy
Mowbray, George Mordey
Nevin, Robert Peebles
O'Hara, James
Oliver, George Tener
Reed, James Hay
Rees, James
Vandergrift, Jacob Jay
Isaacs, Edith J. R.
Bloomgarden, Solomon
Gordin, Jacob
Niblo, William
Palmer, Albert Marshman
Pastor, Antonio
Isaacs, Lewis M.
Conried, Heinrich
Israel, Fred L.
Long, Breckinridge
Israel, Jerry
Davis, Dwight Filley
Ives, Samuel A.
Plimpton, George Arthur

Jack, John G.
Sargent, Charles Sprague
Wilson, Ernest Henry
Jack, Olive M.
Jewell, Harvey
Jack, Theodore Henley
Bagby, Arthur Pendleton
Candler, Asa Griggs
Clay, Clement Claiborne
Clay, Clement Comer
Clemens, Jeremiah
Jackson, Henry Rootes
Johnston, Joseph Forney
Jones, Thomas Goode
Lewis, Dixon Hall
Jackson, A. V. Williams
Bloomfield, Maurice
Jackson, Barbara B.
Payne-Gaposchkin, Cecilia Helena
Jackson, Daniel D.
Hendrick, Ellwood
Jackson, Dugald C.
Behrend, Bernard Arthur
Jackson, George Stuyvesant
Lowell, John, 1769–1840
Jackson, Joseph
Archer, Samuel
Bailey, Lydia R.
Carbutt, John
Charles, William
Childs, Cephas Grier
Childs, George William
Clay, Edward Williams
Currier, Nathaniel
Cushman, George Hewett
Dawkins, Henry
Drake, Alexander Wilson
Dunlap, John
Du Simitière, Pierre Eugène
Eckstein, John
Edwin, David
Ehninger, John Whetten
Fitzgerald, Thomas
Folwell, Samuel
Fox, Gilbert
Girsch, Frederick
Gobrecht, Christian
Goddard, Paul Beck
Godfrey, Thomas, 1704–1749
Goodman, Charles
Gostelowe, Jonathan
Hall, David
Hall, Sarah Ewing
Hart, Abraham
Heilprin, Angelo
Hill, Richard
Humphreys, James
Ives, James Merritt
Jackson, David
Jansen, Reinier
Jenkins, John, 1728–1785
Jenkins, John, 1751–1827
Jennings, John
Johnston, David Claypoole
Jordan, John Woolf
Kearney, Francis
Kneass, Samuel Honeyman
Kneass, Strickland
Kneass, William
Lawson, Alexander
Leaming, Thomas
Leavitt, Dudley
Leeds, Daniel
Lewis, Wilfred
Lippard, George
Longacre, James Barton
Ludwick, Christopher
MacKellar, Thomas
Malcolm, James Peller
Markoe, Abraham
Mease, James
Melish, John
Miles, Edward
Miller, John Henry
Morwitz, Edward
Newsam, Albert
Nicholson, James Bartram
Otis, Bass
Pease, Joseph Ives
Pendleton, John B.
Piggot, Robert
Rosenthal, Max
Savery, William, 1721–1787
Smith, John Jay
Smith, Lloyd Pearsall
Snowden, James Ross
Stoddart, Joseph Marshall
Tanner, Benjamin
Tiebout, Cornelius
Wagner, William
Watson, John Fanning
Westcott, Thompson
Wetherill, Samuel
Wharton, Robert
Jackson, Kenneth T.
Flynn, Edward Joseph
Jackson, Luther P., Jr.
Ottley, Roi
Jackson, Richard
Goldman, Edwin Franko
Jackson, Russell Leigh
Jackson, Hall
Tracy, Nathaniel
Jacobs, Travis Beal
Steinhardt, Laurence Adolph
Jacobs, Wilbur R.
Farrand, Max
Jacobsen, Edna L.
Southwick, Solomon
Ten Broeck, Abraham
Vesey, William
West, George

Wisner, Henry
Woodhull, Nathaniel
Young, John
JACOBSON, ARTHUR C.
Kearsley, John
JACOBSON, LESLIE S.
Du Vigneaud, Vincent
Wiener, Alexander Solomon
JACOBSON, WENDEE
Rukeyser, Muriel
JAFFÉ, ERNST R.
Davidoff, Leo Max
JAFFE, IRMA B.
Stella, Joseph
JAMES, ALFRED P.
Negley, James Scott
Olmsted, Marlin Edgar
JAMES, D. CLAYTON
Friedman, William Frederick
MacArthur, Douglas
Sutherland, Richard Kerens
Whitney, Courtney
JAMES, EDWARD T.
Coxey, Jacob Sechler
Hayes, John William
U'Ren, William Simon
JAMES, JAMES ALTON
Bissell, William Henry
Black, John Charles
Clark, George Rogers
Gibault, Pierre
Pollock, Oliver
JAMES, M. C.
Green, Seth
Henshall, James Alexander
Mather, Fred
Titcomb, John Wheelock
JAMESON, J. FRANKLIN
Hunt, Gaillard
Johnson, Allen
JANOWITZ, MORRIS
Thomas, William Isaac
JARVIS, ERIC
Boring, Edwin Garrigues
Evers, Medgar Wiley
Holland, Spessard Lindsey
Kelly, Walter ("Walt") Crawford, Jr.
Malin, Patrick Murphy
Warren, Fuller
JAY, MARTIN
Neumann, Franz Leopold
JEANSONNE, GLEN
Smith, Gerald L. K.
JEBSEN, HARRY, JR.
Cromwell, Dean Bartlett
Jones, Robert Tyre, Jr.
Vance, Arthur Charles ("Dazzy")
JEFFERSON, PAUL
Reid, Ira De Augustine
JELLIFFE, SMITH ELY
Dana, Charles Loomis
Morton, William James
JELLINEK, GEORGE
Nevada, Emma
JENKINS, CHARLES F.
Matlack, Timothy
JENKINS, EDWARD HOPKINS
Adams, Dudley W.
Adlum, John
Armsby, Henry Prentiss
Arnold, Lauren Briggs
Budd, Joseph Lancaster
Chamberlain, William Isaac
Coburn, Foster Dwight
Collier, Peter
Colman, Henry
Deane, Samuel
Dickson, David
Eliot, Jared
Emerson, George Barrell
Fairchild, George Thompson
JENKINS, EDWARD S.
Julian, Percy Lavon
JENKINS, REESE V.
Mees, Charles Edward Kenneth
Watson, Thomas John
JENKINS, WALTER S.
Beach, Amy Marcy Cheney
JENKS, WILLIAM L.
Woodward, Augustus Brevoort
JENNINGS, WALTER LOUIS
Hill, Henry Barker
Kinnicutt, Leonard Parker
JENSEN, GORDON M.
Easley, Ralph Montgomery
JENSEN, PAUL M.
Nichols, Dudley
JENSON, CAROL ELIZABETH
Adams, Annette Abbott
JEPSON, WILLIS L.
Greene, Edward Lee
Hansen, George
Holder, Charles Frederick
Howell, Thomas Jefferson
Kellogg, Albert
Knowlton, Frank Hall
Kuhn, Adam
Kunze, Richard Ernest
Lemmon, John Gill
Parry, Charles Christopher
Wickson, Edward James
JERVEY, THEODORE D.
Trott, Nicholas
JESSUP, MARY E.
Bush, Lincoln
Eddy, Harrison Prescott
Strauss, Joseph Baermann
JESSUP, PHILIP C.
Root, Elihu
JESSUP, WALTER E.
Hill, Louis Clarence
JEWELL, EDWARD ALDEN
Raymond, George Lansing
JEWELL, WILLIAM M.
Brush, George de Forest
Gardner, Helen
JEWETT, FRANK B.
Carty, John Joseph
JOERG, W. L. G.
Adams, Cyrus Cornelius
Bien, Julius
Hoen, August
Tanner, Henry Schenck
JOHANNINGMEIER, ERWIN V.
Bagley, William Chandler
JOHANNINGMEIER, E. V.
Day, Edmund Ezra
JOHANSEN, DOROTHY O.
Foster, William Trufant
JOHNSON, ALLEN
Adams, Henry Brooks
Asbury, Francis
Boucher, Jonathan
Brown, John, 1800–1859
Bryan, William Jennings
Claghorn, George
Cooper, Myles
Douglas, Stephen Arnold
Eddy, Mary Morse Baker
Evans, Warren Felt
JOHNSON, ALLEN S.
Hoover, Charles Franklin
JOHNSON, ALONZO
Belo, Alfred Horatio
JOHNSON, ALVIN
Clark, John Bates
JOHNSON, ARTHUR M.
Mellon, William Larimer
JOHNSON, CECIL
Lowrey, Mark Perrin
Lowry, Robert
JOHNSON, CECIL M.
Durfee, Zoheth Sherman
JOHNSON, CLAUDIUS O.
Harrison, Carter Henry
JOHNSON, DIANE
Duggar, Benjamin Minge
JOHNSON, EDGAR A. J.
Amory, Thomas
Cook, Elisha
Cushing, Thomas
JOHNSON, EDGAR HUTCHINSON
Bumstead, Horace
Candler, Allen Daniel
Haygood, Atticus Green
Hopkins, Isaac Stiles
JOHNSON, EDWIN LEE
Tolman, Herbert Cushing
JOHNSON, GUY B.
Gonzales, Ambrose Elliott
JOHNSON, H. EARLE
Fisher, William Arms
Homer, Louise Dilworth Beatty
Mason, Daniel Gregory
JOHNSON, HENRY
De Costa, Benjamin Franklin
Dutton, Samuel Train
JOHNSON, KAREN E.
Mayer, Maria Goeppert
JOHNSON, JAMES P.
Oswald, Lee Harvey
JOHNSON, JOHN R.
Carothers, Wallace Hume
JOHNSON, JOSEPH E.
Taylor, George
JOHNSON, PETER LEO
Heiss, Michael
Henni, John Martin
JOHNSON, ROGER T.
La Follette, Robert Marion, Jr.
JOHNSON, T. CARY, JR.
Millington, John
Robertson, William Joseph
Robinson, Conway
Smith, John Blair
Smith, John Lawrence
Waddel, James
JOHNSON, THOMAS H.
Taylor, Edward
JOHNSON, WALTER
Stettinius, Edward Reilly
Stevenson, Adlai Ewing, II
JOHNSTON, J. WESLEY
Ames, Edward Raymond
Andrews, Edward Gayer
JOHNSTON, PAUL
Bateson, Gregory

Eiseley, Loren Corey
Wilson, Edmund, Jr.
JOHNSTONE, D. BRUCE
Hutchins, Robert Maynard
JONES, D. F.
East, Edward Murray
JONES, H. G.
Connor, Robert Digges Wimberly
JONES, HORACE LEONARD
Sterrett, John Robert Sitlington
JONES, HOWARD MUMFORD
Murat, Achille
Royster, James Finch
Tyler, Moses Coit
JONES, JAMES H.
Gregg, Alan
JONES, LAWRENCE N.
Powell, Adam Clayton, Sr.
JONES, PETER D'A.
Coit, Stanton
Gerber, (Daniel) Frank
Gerber, Daniel (Frank)
JONES, PHILLIP S.
Jackson, Dunham
Miller, George Abram
JONES, ROBERT L.
Sedgwick, Robert
JONES, RUFUS M.
Coffin, Charles Fisher
Comstock, Elizabeth L.
Gibbons, Abigail Hopper
Hicks, Elias
Hoag, Joseph
Hopper, Isaac Tatem
Hunt, Nathan
Jay, Allen
Keith, George
Kelsey, Rayner Wickersham
Owen, Griffith
Sands, David
Scattergood, Thomas
Smith, Hannah Whitall
Thomas, Richard Henry
Updegraff, David Brainard
Waln, Nicholas
Wilbur, John
Wood, James, 1839–1925
JONES, STEVEN D.
Wilhelmina
Winterhalter, Hugo
JONES, THEODORE F.
Brown, Elmer Ellsworth
Mathews, Cornelius
JONES, WILLARD LEONARD
Jacobs, William Plumer
JONES, WILLIAM
Cranston, John
Van Beuren, Johannes
Van Buren, William Holme
JORDAN, DANIEL P.
Stacy, Walter Parker
JORDAN, DAVID STARR
Agassiz, Jean Louis Rodolphe
Baird, Spencer Fullerton
Gilbert, Charles Henry
Gill, Theodore Nicholas
Goode, George Brown
Lesueur, Charles Alexandre
JORDAN, FREDERICK W.
Kuhlman, Kathryn
JORDAN, H. DONALDSON
Helm, Charles John
Huse, Caleb
Murphy, William Sumter
Thayer, Eli
Voorhees, Daniel Wolsey
Walker, Robert John
JORDAN, JESSIE KNIGHT
Agassiz, Jean Louis Rodolphe
Baird, Spencer Fullerton
JORDAN, PHILIP D.
Salter, William
Salter, William Mackintire
Winslow, Edward Francis
Wylie, Andrew
JORDAN, WHITMAN H.
Goodale, Stephen Lincoln
JOSEPHSON, HAROLD
Gitlow, Benjamin
Shotwell, James Thomson
JOY, JAMES R.
Cranston, Earl
Fowler, Charles Henry
Hamilton, John William
Hartzell, Joseph Crane
Haven, Erastus Otis
Haven, Gilbert
Kidder, Daniel Parish
McFarland, John Thomas
Mattison, Hiram
Merrick, Frederick
Merrill, Stephen Mason
Mudge, Enoch
Neely, Thomas Benjamin
Newman, John Philip
Salm-Salm, Agnes Elisabeth Winona Leclercq Joy, Princess
Vincent, John Heyl
JOYNER, DAVID L.
Ford, Mary
Haynes, Henry Doyle ("Homer")
JUDD, CHARLES H.
Colvin, Stephen Sheldon
Jackman, Wilbur Samuel
Parker, Francis Wayland
Parker, Samuel Chester
Young, Ella Flagg
JUDSON, SHELDON
Johnson, Douglas Wilson
JUNGEBLUT, CLAUS W.
Gay, Frederick Parker

KAESE, HAROLD
Sears, Richard Dudley
Wright, George
KAHN, JEFFREY A.
Ewing, James
Libman, Emanuel
MacCallum, William George
KAHN, LOTHAR
Feuchtwanger, Lion
KAHRL, GEORGE MORROW
Stobo, Robert
KALK, DANIEL S.
Fairchild, David Grandison
Merrill, Elmer Drew
KAMMETT, LAWRENCE
Will, Allen Sinclair
KANE, HOPE FRANCES
Arnold, Samuel Greene
Bowler, Metcalf
Richmond, John Wilkes
KARL, BARRY D.
Merriam, Charles Edward, Jr.
KARPINSKI, LOUIS C.
Loyd, Samuel
Mackenzie, George Henry
Morphy, Paul Charles
Pike, Nicolas
Pillsbury, Harry Nelson
Steinitz, William
KASTEN, MARIE A.
Bacon, Alice Mabel
Beard, Thomas Francis
Beatty, Charles Clinton
Beauchamp, William
Bennet, Sanford Fillmore
Blake, Lillie Devereux
Bloomer, Amelia Jenks
Boissevain, Inez Milholland
Bond, Hugh Lennox
Booth-Tucker, Emma Moss
Bottome, Margaret McDonald
Bourne, George
Boyd, Belle
Bradford, Edward Green
Bradley, Lydia Moss
Bridgman, Laura Dewey
Brigham, Mary Ann
Bromfield, John
Brown, George, 1823–1892
Brown, Isaac Van Arsdale
Bucknell, William
Burnett, Joseph
Burns, Anthony
Burroughs, John Curtis
Capen, Elmer Hewitt
Chaplin, Jeremiah
Chapman, Maria Weston
Cheney, Oren Burbank
Church, William Conant
Coffin, Levi
Coffin, Lorenzo S.
Crosby, Howard
KATZ, IRVING
Dodge, Joseph Morrell
Wolfson, Erwin Service
KATZMAN, DAVID M.
Binga, Jesse
Hutcheson, William Levi
Pelham, Robert A.
KAUFMAN, PAUL
Knox, Thomas Wallace
Lea, Homer
Poore, Benjamin Perley
Scovel, Henry Sylvester
Simonton, James William
KAUFMANN, EDGAR, JR.
Wright, Frank Lloyd
KAY, DELBERT
Nordberg, Bruno Victor
KAZIN, ALFRED
Van Doren, Carl Clinton
KEATS, SHEILA
Stoessel, Albert Frederic
KEBLER, LYMAN F.
Beck, Lewis Caleb
Craigie, Andrew
KEEP, ROBERT PORTER
Porter, Sarah
KEHL, GEORGE L.
Campbell, William
KELLAR, HERBERT ANTHONY
Atkins, Jearum
Bement, Caleb N.
Downing, Andrew Jackson
Downing, Charles

McCormick, Cyrus Hall
McCormick, Leander James
McCormick, Robert
McCormick, Stephen
Robinson, Solon
Skinner, John Stuart
Wilder, Marshall Pinckney
Wood, Walter Abbott

Kellar, Lucile O'connor
McCormick, Cyrus Hall

Keller, Albert G.
Day, Clarence Shepard

Keller, David S.
Duncan, Donald Franklin

Keller, Deane
Fisher, Harrison

Keller, Franklin J.
Bloomfield, Meyer

Keller, Morton
Beck, James Montgomery
Richberg, Donald Randall

Kelley, Donald R.
Mattingly, Garrett

Kellner, Douglas
Marcuse, Herbert

Kellock, Katharine Amend
Revere, Paul
Richardson, Joseph
Sanderson, Robert
Syng, Philip
Vernon, Samuel
Winslow, Edward

Kellogg, Louise Phelps
Alemany, José Sadoc
Altham, John
André, Louis
Badin, Stephen Theodore
Bapst, John
Baraga, Frederic
Bienville, Jean Baptiste Le Moyne, Sieur de
Bourgmont, Étienne Venyard, Sieur de
Brodhead, Daniel
Brulé, Etienne
Cadillac, Antoine de la Mother, Sieur
Carver, Jonathan
Céleron, de Blainville, Pierre Joseph de
Champlain, Samuel de
Charlevoix, Pierre François, Xavier de
Chaumonot, Pierre Joseph Marie
Clark, William
Cornstalk
Dablon, Claude
De Langlade, Charles Michel
Druillettes, Gabriel
Duluth, Daniel Greysolon, Sieur
Dunmore, John Murray
Faribault, Jean Baptiste
Fish, Carl Russell
Forsyth, Thomas
Garakonthie, Daniel
Gass, Patrick
Gravier, Jacques
Guignas, Michel
Hennepin, Louis
Henry, Alexander
Hooper, Jessie Annette Jack
Iberville, Pierre Le Moyne, Sieur d'
Joques, Isaac
Jolliet, Louis
Joutel, Henri
Juneau, Solomon Laurent
Kinzie, John
Lahontan, Louis-Armand de Lom d'Arce, Baron de
Lapham, Increase Allen
La Ronde, Louis Denis, Sieur de
La Salle, Robert Cavelier, Sieur de
Laudaonnière, René Goulaine de
La Vérendrye, Pierre Gaultier De Varennes, Sieur de
Legler, Henry Eduard
Léry, Joseph Gaspard Chaussegros de
Le Sueur, Pierre
Lewis, Meriwether
L'Halle, Constantin de
Marest, Pierre Gabriel
Marquette, Jacques
Membré, Zenobius
Ménard, René
Monette, John Wesley
Nicolet, Jean
Nicollet, Joseph Nicolas
Ordway, John
Perrot, Nicolas
Pond, Peter
Râle, Sébastien
Ribaut, Jean
Rolette, Jean Joseph
Saenderl, Simon
St. Denis (Denys), Louis Juchereau de
St. Lusson, Simon François Daumont, Sieur de
Thwaites, Reuben Gold
Tonty, Henry de
Vaudreuil-Cavagnal, Pierre de Rigaud, Marquis de
Verwyst, Chrysostom Adrian
Vincennes, François Marie Bissot, Sieur de
Vincennes, Jean Baptiste Bissot, Sieur de
Williams, Eleazar

Kellogg, Remington
Savage, Thomas Staughton

Kellogg, Vernon Lyman
Burbank, Luther

Kelly, Alfred H.
Jackson, Robert Houghwout

Kelly, Howard A.
Burrage, Walter Lincoln
Howard, William Travis
Sims, James Marion
Williams, John Whitridge
Wilson, Henry Parke Custis

Kelly, Robert J.
Abel, Rudolf Ivanovich
Bruno, Angelo
Cohen, Meyer Harris ("Mickey")
Gold, Harry ("Raymond")

Kelsey, Harry
Abel-Henderson, Annie Heloise

Kelsey, Rayner W.
Chalkley, Thomas
Cox, Henry Hamilton
Eddy, Thomas
Hallowell, Richard Price
Larkin, Thomas Oliver
Mifflin, Warner
Morris, Anthony, 1654–1721
Penn, William
Savery, William, 1750–1804
Scott, Job
Sharpless, Isaac

Kemmerer, Donald L.
Andrew, Abram Piatt
Crissinger, Daniel Richard
Hamlin, Charles Sumner
Noyes, Alexander Dana
Reynolds, George McClelland

Kemp, William Webb
Burk, Frederic Lister
Cooper, Sarah Brown Ingersoll
Lange, Alexis Frederick
Le Conte, John

Kempton, J. H.
Collins, Guy N.

Kendall, Isoline Rodd
Beer, William

Kendall, Lane C.
Franklin, Philip Albright Small
Hague, Robert Lincoln

Kendle, Burton
Campbell, William Edward March

Kendrick, Alexander
Murrow, Edward (Egbert) Roscoe
Swing, Raymond Edwards (Gram)

Kendrick, Benjamin B.
McIver, Charles Duncan

Kendrick, M. Slade
Davenport, Herbert Joseph

Kennedy, Albert Joseph
Addams, Jane
Woods, Robert Archey

Kennedy, David M.
Dickinson, Robert Latou
Moley, Raymond Charles
Rosenman, Samuel Irving
Sanger, Margaret Higgins
Sullivan, Mark

Kennedy, Richard S.
Wolfe, Thomas Clayton

Kennedy, Susan Estabrook
Anderson, Mary
Crowley, Leo Thomas
Dodd, Bella Visono
Dreier, Mary Elisabeth
Farley, James Aloysius
Goldenweiser, Emanuel Alexander
Marcus, Bernard Kent
Maybank, Burnet Rhett
Strauss, Lewis Lichtenstein
Wadsworth, Eliot

Kennelly, Karen, C.S.J.
Brown, Charlotte Hawkins

Kennelly, Karen M.
Mitchell, Lucy Sprague
Voris, John Ralph

Kenney, Ruth
Talmadge, Constance

Kenny, Robert W.
Ralph, James

Kent, Frank Richardson
Brown, Alexander, 1764–1834
Brown, George, 1787–1859
Brown, James, 1791–1877
Brown, John A.

Kent, G. C.
Whetzel, Herbert Hice

KENT, ROLAND G.
Newbold, William Romaine
KENYON, BERNICE
Gluck, Alma
KEOGH, ANDREW
Van Name, Addison
KEPLEY, DAVID R.
Reynolds, Robert Rice
KEPPEL, FREDERICK P.
Suzzallo, Henry
KERBY, WILLIAM JOSEPH
Alphonsa, Mother
Anthony, Sister
Bouquillon, Thomas Joseph
Conaty, Thomas James
Keane, John Joseph
KERN, JOHN D.
Woolson, Constance Fenimore
KERN, LOUIS J.
Jackson, Shirley Hardie
Kelland, Clarence Budington
KERNAN, WARWICK J.
Roberts, Ellis Henry
KERR, SARAH
Ulmer, Edgar Georg
KERWIN, JEROME G.
Walgreen, Charles Rudolph
KESLER, JOHN C.
Braden, Spruille
KETRING, RUTH ANNA
Osborn, Charles
KEY, JACK D.
Craig, Winchell McKendree
KEY, J. B.
Bankhead, John Hollis
Steagall, Henry Bascom
KEY, PIERRE VAN RENSSELAER
Cary, Annie Louise
KEYES, CHARLES R.
Wachsmuth, Charles
KEYES, EDWARD L.
Otis, Fessenden Nott
KEYS, ALICE M.
Colden, Cadwallader
KIDDER, ALFRED VINCENT
Bandelier, Adolph Francis Alphonse
KIERAN, JOHN
Huggins, Miller James
Johnson, Byron Bancroft
Mathewson, Christopher
Morrissey, John
Rockne, Knute Kenneth
Spalding, Albert Goodwill
Travis, Walter John
Weston, Edward Payson
Wright, Henry
KIERSTEAD, CAROLINE HEMINWAY
Scott, William Berryman
KIGER, JOSEPH C.
French, Paul Comly
Keppel, Frederick Paul
Smith, Henry Louis
KILLEFFER, D. H.
Herty, Charles Holmes
Landis, Walter Savage
KILPATRICK, CARROLL
Bankhead, William Brockman
KIMBALL, FISKE
Bulfinch, Charles
Godefroy, Maximilian
Goodhue, Bertram Grosvenor
Hadfield, George
Hallet, Étienne Sulpice
Harrison, Peter
Haviland, John
Hoban, James
Latrobe, Benjamin Henry, 1764–1820
L'Enfant, Pierre Charles
McIntire, Samuel
Mills, Robert, 1781–1855
Thornton, William
KIMBALL, MARIE GOEBEL
Short, William
KIMBALL, WARREN F.
Jones, Jesse Holman
KINDILIEN, CARLIN T.
Fite, Warner
Pitkin, Walter Boughton
Runyon, Damon
KING, ALMA DEXTA
Oldham, Williamson Simpson
KING, EDWARD S.
Pickering, Edward Charles
KING, JAMES GORE
Parmentier, Andrew
KING, JAMES GORE, JR.
Mayhew, Thomas
Strong, Caleb
KING, JOHN O.
Gregory, Thomas Barger
KING, PHILIP B.
Willis, Bailey
KING, ROY T.
Wells, Robert William
KING, WILLIAM BRUCE
Corcoran, William Wilson
KINLEY, DAVID
Weston, Nathan Austin
KIRBY, RICHARD S.
Cain, William
Weston, William
KIRK, GRAYSON L.
Reinsch, Paul Samuel
KIRK, RICHARD R.
King, Grace Elizabeth
Stuart, Ruth McEnery
KIRKENDALL, RICHARD S.
Baker, Oliver Edwin
Cannon, Clarence
Klem, William J. (Bill)
McMahon, Brien
Pressman, Lee
KIRKLAND, EDWARD CHASE
Daniels, Winthrop More
Gilmore, James Roberts
Jaquess, James Frazier
Jewett, William Cornell
King, Samuel Ward
Willis, William
KIRSCH, FELIX M.
Antoine, Père
KIRSHNER, RALPH
Asbury, Herbert
Baroody, William Joseph
Blackstone, Harry
Bush, Prescott Sheldon
Cerf, Bennett Alfred
Fitzsimmons, James Edward ("Sunny Jim")
George, Grace
Hirsch, Maximilian Justice
Kiphuth, Robert John Herman
McAuliffe, Anthony Clement
Ouimet, Francis Desales
Robertson, Absalom Willis
Sarnoff, David
Sloane, Isabel Cleves Dodge
Stuart, John Leighton
Wiley, Bell Irvin
Williams, Thomas Harry
KIRWAN, ALBERT D.
Harrison, Byron Patton
KISH, DOROTHY
Chase, Mary Ellen
Francis, Kay
Tanguay, Eva
KLEBANOFF, SHOSHANA
Brown, George Scratchley
Monroe, Vaughn Wilton
Skouras, Spyros Panagiotes
Stevens, George Cooper
Vanderbilt, Cornelius, Jr. ("Cornelius IV," "Neil")
KLEENE, GUSTAV A.
McCook, John James
KLEIN, LOUIS A.
Pearson, Leonard
KLEIN, MAURY
Calhoun, Patrick
KLEINFIELD, H. L.
Barrymore, John
Barrymore, Lionel
Huston, Walter
Marlowe, Julia
Woollcott, Alexander Humphreys
KLEMIN, ALEXANDER
Chanute, Octave
Vought, Chance Milton
Wellman, Walter
Wise, John
Wright, Wilbur
KLINE, ALLEN MARSHALL
Dillingham, William Paul
Fairbanks, Erastus
Fuller, Levi Knight
Hall, Hiland
Hammond, Edwin
KLINE, JOHN R.
Patterson, Robert
KLINGBERG, FRANK J.
Tappan, Arthur
Tappan, Lewis
KNAPP, CHARLES M.
James, Ollie Murray
KNAPP, JOSEPH G.
Babcock, Howard Edward
KNAUSS, JAMES O.
Duval, William Pope
Hackley, Charles Henry
Howard, Jacob Merritt
Howard, William Alanson
Sower, Christopher, 1754–1799
KNIGHT, ARTHUR
Fairbanks, Douglas
Turpin, Ben
KNIGHT, EDGAR WALLACE
Aycock, Charles Brantley
Caldwell, Joseph
Wiley, Calvin Henderson
KNIGHT, GRANT C.
Bowman, John Bryan
Cawein, Madison Julius
Loos, Charles Louis
Patterson, James Kennedy
Peers, Benjamin Orrs
Prentice, George Dennison
Warfield, Catherine Ann Ware
Wilson, Robert Burns

KNIGHT, OLIVER
Block, Paul
Copley, Ira Clifton
KNITTLE, RHEA MANSFIELD
Danforth, Thomas, 1703–1788
Dyott, Thomas W.
Hewes, Robert
Jarves, Deming
Wistar, Caspar
KNOEFEL, PETER K.
Barbour, Henry Gray
KNOTT, H. W. HOWARD
Abbott, Austin
Abbott, Benjamin Vaughan
Aldrich, Edgar
Allen, Charles
Allen, John James
Ames, Samuel
Andrews, Charles
Andrews, George Pierce
Angel, Benjamin Franklin
Angell, Joseph Kinnicutt
Anthon, John
Arrington, Alfred W.
Baldwin, John Brown
Bangs, Francis Nehemiah
Barbour, Oliver Lorenzo
Barlow, Samuel Latham Mitchill
Barradall, Edward
Barton, Robert Thomas
Bates, Daniel Moore
Bates, George Handy
Beach, William Augustus
Beall, Samuel Wootton
Beaman, Charles Cotesworth
Beaupré, Arthur Matthias
Bell, Clark
Bemis, George
Benedict, Erastus Cornelius
Benjamin, Judah Philip
Bennett, Edmund Hatch
Bennett, Nathaniel
Bidwell, Marshall Spring
Bigelow, Melville Madison
Bingham, Harry
Binney, Horace
Bishop, Joel Prentiss
Blackford, Charles Minor
Blatchford, Richard Milford
Bliss, George
Bliss, Jonathan
Blowers, Sampson Salter
Bonney, Charles Carroll
Bradbury, Theophilus
Bradford, Alexander Warfield
Bradwell, James Bolesworth
Bradwell, Myra
Brady, James Topham
Brannon, Henry
Brewster, Frederick Carroll
Brightly, Frederick Charles
Brown, Addison
Brown, Henry Billings
Browne, Irving
Burdick, Francis Marion
Burke, Thomas, 1849–1925
Burrill, Alexander Mansfield
Butterworth, Benjamin
Bynum, William Preston
Cadwalader, John, 1805–1879
Cady, Daniel
Caines, George
Caldwell, Henry Clay
Carlisle, James Mandeville
Casey, Joseph
Caton, John Dean
Chambers, George
Champlin, John Wayne
Chandler, Peleg Whitman
Chase, George
Chilton, William Paris
Chipman, Daniel
Chisolm, Alexander Robert
Clagett, Wyseman
Clark, Greenleaf
Clopton, David
Clough, William Pitt
Comstock, George Franklin
Conrad, Holmes
Cooke, John Rogers
Cowley, Charles
Cox, Rowland
Coxe, Richard Smith
Cranch, William
Cross, Edward
Crump, William Wood
Curtis, Edwin Upton
Cuyler, Theodore
Daly, Charles Patrick
Dana, Richard
Dane, Nathan
Daniel, Peter Vivian
Dargan, Edmund Strother
Daveis, Charles Stewart
D'Avezac, Auguste Geneviève Valentin
Davis, George Breckenridge
Davis, John, 1761–1847
Davis, Noah, 1818–1902
Davis, William Thomas
Day, James Gamble
Day, Luther
Dean, Amos
Dearborn, Henry Alexander Scammell
Delmas, Delphin Michael
Deming, Henry Champion
Denver, James William
Dexter, Franklin
Dexter, Samuel, 1761–1816
Dexter, Wirt
Dickerson, Edward Nicoll
Dickerson, Philemon
Dickey, Theophilus Lyle
Diven, Alexander Samuel
Dixon, Luther Swift
Doddridge, Philip
Doe, Charles
Donnelly, Charles Francis
Dos Passos, John Randolph
Douglas, Henry Kyd
Doyle, John Thomas
Duane, William John
Dudley, Paul
Duer, John
Duer, William
Dunlop, James
DuPonceau, Pierre Étienne
Durant, Thomas Jefferson
Durell, Edward Henry
Durfee, Job
Durfee, Thomas
Dutton, Henry
Dwight, Theodore William
Dyer, Eliphalet
Earle, Thomas
Edmonds, John Worth
Edwards, Charles
Elliott, Benjamin
Ellis, George Washington
Ellsworth, Henry William
Emery, Lucilius Alonzo
Emott, James, 1771–1850
Emott, James, 1823–1884
Evarts, Jeremiah
Ewing, Charles
Farrar, Edgar Howard
Farrar, Timothy
Fenner, Charles Erasmus
Field, Maunsell Bradhurst
Field, Walbridge Abner
Fitzhugh, William
Flagg, Azariah Cutting
Flanders, Henry
Fletcher, Calvin
Fletcher, Richard
Fletcher, William Asa
Folger, Walter
Ford, Gordon Lester
Foster, Roger Sherman Baldwin
Francis, Tench
Gardiner, John
Garrison, Cornelius Kingsland
Garrison, William Re Tallack
Gerard, James Watson
Gerry, Elbridge Thomas
Gibson, John Bannister
Gilpin, Edward Woodward
Glover, Samuel Taylor
Goddard, Luther Marcellus
Goff, John William
Goudy, William Charles
Gould, James
Graham, David
Graham, John Andrew
Gray, Francis Calley
Gray, George
Gray, John Chipman
Green, Andrew Haswell
Green, Henry Woodhull
Green, William
Greenleaf, Simon
Gregory, Stephen Strong
Grinnell, Henry
Grinnell, Joseph
Grinnell, Moses Hicks
Howe, William F.
KNOWLES, MORRIS
Herschel, Clemens
Hill, Frank Alpine
Holbrook, Josiah
Knowlton, Daniel C.
KNUDSON, ALBERT C.
Townsend, Luther Tracy
KOCH, G. ADOLF
Palmer, Elihu
KOELSCH, WILLIAM A.
Atwood, Wallace Walter
Brown, Ralph Hall
Fenneman, Nevin Melancthon
KOENIG, HARRY C.
Mundelein, George William
KOGAN, HERMAN
Kelly, Edward Joseph
Smith, Henry Justin
KOHLER, MAX J.
Marshall, Louis
Peixotto, Benjamin Franklin
Seligman, Isaac Newton

Seligman, Jesse
Seligman, Joseph
Kolb, Harold H., Jr.
Ade, George
Kolb, Harold H., Jr.
Patten, Gilbert
Kolmer, John A.
Schamberg, Jay Frank
Koopman, Harry Lyman
Faunce, William Herbert Perry
Foss, Sam Walter
Langdon, Courtney
Kopf, Edwin W.
Fackler, David Parks
Harris, Elisha
McCay, Charles Francis
Kopperl, Sheldon J.
Dakin, Henry Drysdale
Korhonen, Cynthia S.
Burton, Harold Hitz
Korman, Gerd
Commons, John Rogers
Kornhauser, Anne
Schneiderman, Rose
Kornwolf, James D.
Elmslie, George Grant
Koudelka, Janet B.
Freeman, Allen Weir
Kovaleff, Theodore P.
McCulloch, Robert Paxton
Kovarik, Alois F.
Boltwood, Bertram Borden
Hastings, Charles Sheldon
Mansfield, Jared
Olmsted, Denison
Pupin, Michael Idvorsky
Kozinn, Allan
Lennon, John Winston Ono
Kraemer, Caspar John, Jr.
Waters, William Everett
Kramer, Paul J.
Livingston, Burton Edward
Kraut, Alan M.
Hines, James J.
Shaw, (Warren) Wilbur
Krayer, Otto
Hunt, Reid
Krehbiel, C. E.
Goerz, David
Krempel, Daniel S.
Boyer, Charles
Clurman, Harold Edgar
Colman, Ronald Charles
Cornell, Katharine
Goldwyn, Samuel
Langner, Lawrence
Laughton, Charles
Mielziner, Jo
Parks, Larry
Rains, Claude
Kreuter, Gretchen von Loewe
Simons, Algie Martin
Kreuter, Kent
Mitchell, William DeWitt
Krey, A. C.
Haggerty, Melvin Everett
Krock, Arthur
Watterson, Henry
Kroeber, Alfred L.
Dixon, Roland Burrage
Krogman, W. M.
Todd, Thomas Wingate
Krohn, Ernst C.
Reinagle, Alexander
Sobolewski, J. Friedrich Edward
Warren, Samuel Prowse
Zach, Max Wilhelm
Ziehn, Bernard
Krooss, Herman E.
Berwind, Edward Julius
McGarrah, Gates White
Speyer, James Joseph
Krout, John A.
Fox, Dixon Ryan
Livingston, Peter Van Brugh
Livingston, Philip
Livingston, Robert
Livingston, William, 1723–1790
Morris, Lewis, 1671–1746
Morris, Lewis, 1726–1798
Morris, Richard
Morris, Robert, 1745–1815
Morris, Robert Hunter
Raines, John
Schuyler, George Washington
Schuyler, Margarita
Schuyler, Philip John
Van Cortlandt, Philip
Van Cortlandt, Pierre
Van Cortlandt, Stephanus
Krueger, Leonard B.
Mitchell, Alexander
Smith, George
Krum, Gracie Brainerd
Gillman, Henry
Krumbhaar, E. B.
Otto, John Conrad
Krusen, Wilmer
Leffmann, Henry
Kubler, Ernest A.
Reisinger, Hugo
Robinson, Therese Albertine Louise Von Jakob
Kuehl, Olga Llano
Siloti, Alexander Ilyitch
Kuehl, Warren F.
Atkinson, Henry Avery
Holt, Hamilton Bowen
Hyde, Charles Cheney
McDonald, James Grover
Marburg, Theodore
Scott, James Brown
Wambaugh, Sarah
Kuhlmann, Charles B.
Pillsbury, Charles Alfred
Kummer, George
O'Neill, Rose Cecil
Kunkel, Beverley Waugh
Porter, Thomas Conrad
Kurland, Gerald
Duffy, Hugh
Kilpatrick, John Reed
Kingsley, Elizabeth Seelman
Lajoie, Napoleon ("Larry")
Richards, Vincent
Kutulas, Judy
Bliven, Bruce Ormsby
De Kruif, Paul Henry
Kent, Rockwell
Rorty, James Hancock
Kuykendall, Ralph S.
Baldwin, Henry Perrine
Bishop, Charles Reed
Cooper, Henry Ernest
Dole, Sanford Ballard
Farrington, Wallace Rider
Judd, Gerrit Parmele
Kalanianaole, Jonah Kuhio
Restarick, Henry Bond
Richards, William
Thurston, Lorrin Andrews
Willis, Albert Shelby

Labaree, Leonard W.
Andrews, Charles McLean
Clinton, George
Douglas, William, 1742–1777
Fitch, Thomas
Law, Jonathan
Nicholson, Francis
Nicolls, Matthias
Nicolls, Richard
Nicolls, William
Pownall, Thomas
Saltonstall, Gurdon
Treat, Robert
Trumbull, Jonathan, 1710–1785
Tryon, William
Lach, Donald F.
MacNair, Harley Farnsworth
Lacher, J. H. A.
Hoffmann, Francis Arnold
Ladd, Harry S.
Vaughan, Thomas Wayland
Ladd, William Palmer
Hart, Samuel
Leaming, Jeremiah
Smith, William, 1754–1821
La Follette, Robert
Swan, James
La Follette, Suanne
Hibben, Paxton Pattison
La Forte, Robert Sherman
Bristow, Joseph Little
Lagemann, Ellen Condliffe
Bryson, Lyman Lloyd
Lahue, Kalton C.
Sennett, Mack
Laing, Gordon J.
Shorey, Paul
Lakin, Pamela
Clemente, Roberto
Lamb, Arthur B.
Sanger, Charles Robert
Lambert, Walter D.
Bowie, William
Lamont, Corliss
Flynn, Elizabeth Gurley
Lampl, Paul
Higgins, Daniel Paul
Land, Robert H.
Fitzpatrick, John Clement
Land, Robert Hunt
Tyler, Lyon Gardiner
Land, William G.
Hill, Thomas, 1818–1891
Robbins, Thomas
Robinson, Henry Cornelius
Root, Jesse
Seymour, Thomas Hart
Waller, Thomas MacDonald
Landau, Sarah Bradford
Delano, William Adams
Landman, J. H.
Stoughton, Edwin Wallace
Landon, Fred
Lay, Benjamin
Lundy, Benjamin

Realf, Richard
Ward, Samuel Ringgold
LANE, ANN J.
Beard, Mary Ritter
LANE, ELBERT C.
Mitchell, Edwin Knox
Paton, Lewis Bayles
LANE, ERNEST PRESTON
Wilczynski, Ernest Julius
LANE, WILLIAM C.
Cogswell, Joseph Green
Folsom, Charles
Jewett, Charles Coffin
LANE, WINTHROP D.
Round, William Marshall Fitts
LANG, JOHN W.
Field, Charles William
Morell, George Webb
Morton, James St. Clair
North, Simeon, 1765–1852
LANGDON, WILLIAM CHAUNCY
Bell, Alexander Graham
Hubbard, Gardiner Greene
Orton, William
Sanders, Thomas
Smith, Chauncey
Storrow, James Jackson
Vail, Theodore Newton
Watson, Thomas Augustus
Woodbury, Charles Jeptha Hill
LANGFELD, HERBERT S.
Baldwin, James Mark
Hamilton, Edward John
McDougall, William
Münsterberg, Hugo
Sidis, Boris
Warren, Howard Crosby
LANGSDORF, ALEXANDER S.
Nipher, Francis Eugene
LANKEVICH, GEORGE J.
Carlson, Richard Dutoit
Cordier, Andrew Wellington
Dale, Charles Marks
Devine, Andrew ("Andy")
LANZA, CONRAD H.
Barlow, Francis Channing
Beaver, James Addams
Bragg, Braxton
Buell, Don Carlos
Heintzelman, Samuel Peter
Hunt, Henry Jackson
Hunter, David
Johnston, Joseph Eggleston
Jones, David Rumph
Morgan, John Hunt
Mosby, John Singleton
Sickles, Daniel Edgar
Smith, William Farrar
Stanley, David Sloane
Sykes, George
Taylor, Harry
Townsend, Edward Davis
Tyler, Robert Ogden
Wheaton, Frank
Woods, Charles Robert
LARKIN, FREDERICK V.
Halsey, Frederick Arthur
Haswell, Charles Haynes
Herr, Herbert Thacker
Porter, Holbrook Fitz-John
Spangler, Henry Wilson
Wetherill, Samuel, 1821–1890
LARROWE, C. PATRIC
King, Carol Weiss
LARSEN, CHARLES E.
Heatter, Gabriel
Kruger, Otto
Lindsey, Benjamin Barr
Pegler, Westbrook
LARSON, CEDRIC A.
Marquis, Albert Nelson
LARSON, HENRIETTA M.
Farish, William Stamps
Gallagher, Ralph W.
LARSON, OLAF F.
Galpin, Charles Josiah
LARSON, T. A.
Hunt, Lester Callaway
LA SALA, LINDA
Holliday, Judy
LASH, JOSEPH P.
Roosevelt, (Anna) Eleanor
LASSER, MICHAEL
Crisp, Donald
Fiedler, Arthur
LATANE, JOHN H.
Lathrop, Barnes F.
Schouler, James
LATHROP, BARNES F.
Hoover, James Matthews
Ireland, John, 1827–1896
Long, James
LATIMER, MARGARET
Coudert, Frederic René, Jr.
Erpf, Armand Grover
Hodgins, Eric Francis
Jordan, Benjamin Everett
Parker, Edward Pickering
Weinberger, Jacob
LATOURETTE, KENNETH S.
Beach, Harlan Page
Graves, Rosewell Hobart
Happer, Andrew Patton
Hart, Virgil Chittenden
Holcombe, Chester
Hoover, James Matthews
Kerr, John Glascow
Laufer, Berthold
Lowry, Hiram Harrison
Martin, William Alexander Parsons
Mateer, Calvin Wilson
Olyphant, David Washington Cincinnatus
Parker, Alvin Pierson
Parker, Peter
Pye, Watts Orson
Schereschewsky, Samuel Isaac Joseph
Sheffield, Devello Zelotes
Shelton, Albert Leroy
Shuck, Jehu Lewis
Smith, Arthur Henderson
Stoddard, David Tappan
Stone, Ellen Maria
Talmage, John Van Nest
Teusler, Rudolf Bolling
Turner, Fennell Parrish
Verbeck, Guido Herman Fridolin
Watson, Andrew
Williams, Channing Moore
Williams, Frederick Wells
Williams, Samuel Wells
Yates, Matthew Tyson
Yung, Wing
LAUB, JOHN H.
Glueck, Sheldon ("Sol")
LAUDERDALE, KEVIN
Cain, James Mallahan
LAW, ROBERT ADGER
Callaway, Morgan
LAWALL, CHARLES H.
Chapman, Nathaniel
Maisch, John Michael
LAWRENCE, A. A.
Walker, William Johnson
LAWRENCE, BARBARA
Allen, Glover Morrill
LAWRENCE, WILLIAM
Stone, John Seely
LAWSON, MICHAEL L.
Artzybasheff, Boris
Parrish, Maxfield
LAWTON, GEORGE
Post, Isaac
LAYTON, EDWIN
Bedaux, Charles Eugene
Harrington, John Lyle
LAYTON, TERESA L.
Paul, Alice
Thompson, Llewellyn E. ("Tommy"), Jr.
LEAB, DANIEL J.
Berle, Adolf Augustus, Jr.
Boudin, Louis Boudinoff
Kracauer, Siegfried
Lasky, Jesse Louis
Newhouse, Samuel Irving
Parsons, Louella Rose Oettinger
Von Sternberg, Josef
Weicker, Lowell Palmer
LEACOCK, STEPHEN
Browne, Charles Farrar
Newell, Robert Henry
Nye, Edgar Wilson
LEAKE, CHAUNCEY D.
Miller, William Snow
LEARNED, H. BARRETT
Marcy, William Learned
LEARY, JOHN J., JR.
Conboy, Sara Agnes McLaughlin
LEARY, WILLIAM M.
Arnold, Leslie Philip
Balchen, Bernt
Foulois, Benjamin Delahauf
Ide, John Jay
Krueger, Walter
MacNider, Hanford
Patterson, William Allan ("Pat")
Wright, Theodore Paul
Young, Clarence Marshall
LEARY, WILLIAM M., JR.
Bellanca, Giuseppe Mario
LEAVY, MARVIN D.
Marquard, Richard William ("Rube")
LEDOUX, LOUIS V.
Robinson, Edwin Arlington
LEDUC, THOMAS
Aydelotte, Frank
King, Stanley
Meiklejohn, Alexander
Todd, Walter Edmond Clyde
LEDUC, THOMAS, II
Andrews, Israel DeWolf
LEE, ALGERNON
London, Meyer

LEE, AMY
Jones, Lindley Armstrong ("Spike")
Weems, Ted
LEE, EDWIN A.
Snyder, Edwin Reagan
LEE, JAMES MELVIN
Barsotti, Charles
Bonner, Robert
Bradford, Andrew
Bradford, John
Bradford, Joseph
Bradford, Thomas
Carroll, Howard
Chamberlain, Henry Richardson
Charless, Joseph
Clark, Willis Gaylord
Cobb, Frank Irving
Cockerill, John Albert
Congdon, Charles Taber
Cooper, William
Creelman, James
Cunliffe-Owen, Philip Frederick
Curtis, William Eleroy
De Young, Michel Harry
Grasty, Charles Henry
LEE, R. ALTON
Schwellenbach, Lewis Baxter
Wherry, Kenneth Spicer
LEE, RENSSELAER W.
Mather, Frank Jewett, Jr.
LEFFERT, HENRY
Hovey, Richard
Russell, Irwin
LEFLER, HUGH T.
Kelley, William Darrah
Pou, Edward William
LEHMANN, PHYLLIS WILLIAMS
Hawes, Harriet Ann Boyd
LEICESTER, HENRY M.
Browne, Charles Albert
LEIGHTON, RICHARD M.
Chennault, Claire Lee
Hodge, John Reed
Zacharias, Ellis Mark
LEIGHTON, RICHARD N.
Stratemeyer, George Edward
LEINBACH, PAUL S.
Beissel, Johann Conrad
LEISY, ERNEST E.
Johnston, Mary
Krehbiel, Christian
LEITCH, ALEXANDER
Burr, Aaron, 1716–1757
LEITER, SAMUEL L.
Bloomgarden, Kermit
Hurok, Solomon Isaievitch
Inge, William Motter
Lunt, Alfred David, Jr.
Pickford, Mary
Russell, Rosalind
Sands, Diana Patricia
Shumlin, Herman Elliott
Spewack, Samuel
Webster, Margaret ("Peggy")
LELAND, WALDO G.
Vignaud, Henry
LELAND, WALDO GIFFORD
Jameson, John Franklin
LEMMON, SARAH MCCULLOH
Talmadge, Eugene
LEMON, HARVEY B.
Michelson, Albert Abraham
LEMONS, J. STANLEY
Brown, Gertrude Foster
Park, Maud Wood
Stevens, Doris
LENNIG, ARTHUR
Lorre, Peter
Lugosi, Bela
LEONARD, IDA REID
Poston, Charles Debrill
LEONARD, NEIL
Morton, Ferdinand Joseph ("Jelly Roll")
LEONARD, THOMAS C.
Creel, George
Duranty, Walter
Farson, Negley
Flynn, John Thomas
McGill, Ralph Emerson
Wagner, Robert Ferdinand
LEONARD, WILLIAM ELLERY
Leonard, Sterling Andrus
LEONARD, WILLIAM R.
Jarvis, Edward
Kennedy, Joseph Camp
Mayo-Smith, Richmond
LEOPOLD, W. F.
Curme, George Oliver
LEPPARD, H. M.
Goode, John Paul
LERNER, EDNA ALBERS
Alexander, Franz Gabriel
Berger, Victor Louis
Frank, Lawrence Kelso
Hillquit, Morris
Lynd, Robert Staughton
Reik, Theodor
Roheim, Geza
LERNER, MAX
Gates, John Warne
Greene, William Cornell
Guggenheim, Daniel
Guggenheim, Meyer
Hamilton, Walton Hale
Moore, William Henry
Morse, Charles Wyman
Ryan, Thomas Fortune
Swope, Herbert Bayard
Veblen, Thorstein Bunde
Yerkes, Charles Tyson
LESLIE, JOHN KENNETH
Crawford, James Pyle Wickersham
LESLIE, J. PAUL
Long, Earl Kemp
Morrison, Delesseps Story
LESSER, ALLEN F.
Menken, Adah Isaacs
LESSER, SOL
McLaglen, Victor
LESSER, STEPHEN O.
Costello, Lou
LESSING, LAWRENCE
Armstrong, Edwin Howard
LESTER, H. H.
Sauveur, Albert
LESTER, ROBIN D.
Yost, Fielding Harris
LETTIERI, RONALD
Dodd, Thomas Joseph
Lasswell, Harold Dwight
LEUCHTENBURG, WILLIAM E.
Borah, William Edgar
Johnson, Hugh Samuel
McReynolds, James Clark
LEVENSON, J. C.
Dreiser, Theodore
LEVIN, GAIL
Hopper, Edward
LEVINE, STUART
Cloud, Henry Roe
LEVSTIK, FRANK R.
Barthelmess, Richard
Morton, Rogers Clark Ballard
Nichols, Roy Franklin
Niles, John Jacob
Sanders, Harland David ("Colonel")
Schuster, Max Lincoln
Vedder, Edward Bright
Young, Whitney Moore, Jr.
LEVY, EUGENE
Cook, Will Marion
LEVY, MILTON
Michaelis, Leonor
LEWENSTEIN, BRUCE V.
Davis, Watson
LEWINSON, EDWIN R.
Johnson, Edward Austin
LEWIS, CHARLES LEE
Balch, George Beall
Brooke, John Mercer
Buchanan, Franklin
Cheever, Henry Theodore
Colton, Walter
Dromgoole, William Allen
Jones, Catesby Ap Roger
Jones, George
Jones, Thomas Ap Catesby
Murfree, Mary Noailles
Porter, John Luke
Queen, Walter W.
Ramsay, Francis Munroe
Rideout, Henry Milner
Ridgely, Daniel Bowly
Robert, Henry Martyn
Robertson, Morgan Andrew
Rowan, Stephen Clegg
Wilson, John Fleming
LEWIS, DAVID L.
Hershey, Milton Snavely
LEWIS, EDWARD S.
Tobias, Channing Heggie
LEWIS, FRANK GRANT
Dagg, John Leadley
LEWIS, FREDERIC THOMAS
Minot, Charles Sedgwick
LEWIS, GEORGE M.
Fordyce, John Addison
Morrow, Prince Albert
Palmer, Alonzo Benjamin
Pilcher, Paul Monroe
Ranney, Ambrose Loomis
Wende, Ernest
Wende, Grover William
LEWIS, H. G.
Schultz, Henry
LEWIS, JOHN V.
Coffey, James Vincent
Hastings, Serranus Clinton
LEWIS, W. DAVID
Hunter, Croil
Jensen, Peter Laurits
Kirchwey, George Washington
Lawes, Lewis Edward
Rickenbacker, Edward Vernon ("Eddie")
Taylor, William Chittenden

LEWIS, WILLIAM S.
Garry, Spokane
MacDonald, Ranald
LEWIS, WINSTON B.
Leahy, William Daniel
LEWIS, W. LEE
Nef, John Ulric
LEYDENBERG, HARRY MILLER
Plummer, Mary Wright
LEYS, WAYNE A. R.
Tufts, James Hayden
LIBBEY, JAMES K.
Fletcher, Henry Prather
LIBBY, ORIN G.
Belcourt, George Antoine
Pierce, Gilbert Ashville
LICH, GLEN E.
Dobie, J(ames) Frank
O'Daniel, Wilbert Lee ("Pappy")
Peterkin, Julia Mood
LICHLITER, WILLIAM F.
Gibson, Charles Dana
LICHTENSTEIN, NELSON
Davis, William Hammatt
Leiserson, William Morris
Stolberg, Benjamin
LICHTENWANGER, WILLIAM
Gabrilowitsch, Ossip
Godowsky, Leopold
McCormack, John Francis
Schelling, Ernest Henry
Whiting, Arthur Battelle
LIEBERT, HERMAN W.
Isham, Ralph Heyward
LIEN, ARNOLD J.
Hammond, William Gardiner
Jameson, John Alexander
Judson, Frederick Newton
Keener, William Albert
Minor, Virginia Louisa
LIESTMAN, DANIEL
Cain, Harry Pulliam
Dill, Clarence Cleveland
Fosdick, Raymond Blaine
Penney, James Cash ("J. C.")
Sachs, Alexander
LIKNESS, CRAIG S.
Duke, Vernon
Rooney, Pat
LILLIE, FRANK RATTRAY
Whitman, Charles Otis
LINCOLN, CHARLES H.
Adams, Robert
Allen, Andrew
Allen, William, 1704–1780
Anderson, William
Bailey, Francis
Bayard, James Ash(e)ton, 1767–1815
Bayard, James Asheton, 1799–1880
Bayard, John Bubenheim
Bayard, Richard Henry
Bingham, William
LINDLEY, HARLOW
Kennedy, Robert Patterson
Kilbourne, James
Riddle, Albert Gallatin
LINDSAY, R. B.
Barus, Carl
LINEHAN, PAUL H.
Herbermann, Charles George
LINFORTH, IVAN MORTIMER
Wheeler, Benjamin Ide
LINGELBACH, ANNA LANE
Jenkins, Howard Malcolm
Klingelsmith, Margaret Center
Lockrey, Sarah Hunt
Logan, Deborah Norris
Logan, George
Martin, Elizabeth Price
Oberholtzer, Sara Louisa Vickers
Penniman, James Hosmer
Pepper, George Seckel
Poulson, Zachariah
Price, Eli Kirk
Proud, Robert
Sanderson, John
Smyth, Albert Henry
Stevenson, Sara Yorke
Stillé, Charles Janeway
Townsend, Mira Sharpless
Wallace, David
Wallace, Lewis
Wharton, Anne Hollingsworth
Wister, Sarah
LINGELBACH, WILLIAM E.
Ames, Herman Vandenburg
Carson, Hampton Lawrence
Girard, Stephen
Jarvis, William
McMaster, John Bach
LINGLE, WALTER LEE
Plumer, William Swan
Reed, Richard Clark
Rice, David
Rice, Nathan Lewis
Smyth, Thomas
Waddel, John Newton
LINGLEY, CHARLES RAMSDELL
Babcock, Orville E.
Badeau, Adam
Belknap, William Worth
Dingley, Nelson
Frye, William Pierce
LINK, A. S.
Houston, David Franklin
LINK, EUGENE P.
Putnam, Helen Cordelia
LIPPMAN, MONROE
Klaw, Marc
LIPSEY, ROGER
Coomaraswamy, Ananda Kentish
LITTELL, JOHN STOCKTON, II
Roberts, Issachar Jacob
LITTLEHALES, GEORGE W.
Green, Francis Mathews
Hilgard, Julius Erasmus
Jones, Ernest Lester
Trowbridge, William Petit
Walker, Sears Cook
LIVINGSTON, ARTHUR
Coltrane, John William
LIVINGSTON, ARTHUR P.
Bruce, Lenny
Russell, Charles Ellsworth ("Pee Wee")
LIVINGSTON, ARTHUR PAUL
Cole, Nat ("King")
LLOYD, CRAIG
Hinshaw, David Schull
LLOYD, JOHN URI
Howe, Andrew Jackson
LLOYD, TREVOR
Cook, Frederick Albert
LOBDELL, GEORGE H., JR.
Knox, Frank
LOBINGIER, CHARLES SUMNER
Hosmer, Hezekiah Lord
Ingraham, Edward Duffield
Jay, Peter Angustus
Paine, Henry Warren
Peckham, Rufus Wheeler
Peckham, Wheeler Hazard
Penrose, Charles Bingham
Pitney, Mahlon
Pomeroy, John Norton
Price, Eli Kirk
Quitman, John Anthony
Rawle, Francis (1846–1930)
Rawle, William
Rawle, William Henry
Redfield, Amasa Angell
Redfield, Isaac Fletcher
Richardson, James Daniel
Richardson, William Merchant
Robinson, William Callyhan
Rose, Walter Malins
Russell, Charles Wells
Sanborn, Walter Henry
Sanford, Edward Terry
Sanger, George Partridge
Saulsbury, Eli
Saulsbury, Gove
Saulsbury, Willard, 1820–1892
Saulsbury, Willard, 1861–1927
Scott, Samuel Parsons
Sloan, Richard Elihu
Trude, Alfred Samuel
Wales, Leonard Eugene
Watson, David Thompson
LOCKE, L. LELAND
Baldwin, Frank Stephen
Grant, George Barnard
LOCKMILLER, DAVID A.
Crowder, Enoch Herbert
LOCKWOOD, FRANK C.
Greenway, John Campbell
Hubbell, John Lorenzo
McClintock, James Harvey
Sieber, Al
LOEB, ROBERT F.
Palmer, Walter Walker
LOETSCHER, FREDERICK WILLIAM
Alexander, Archibald
Alexander, Joseph Addison
Alexander, Samuel Davies
LOETSCHER, LEFFERTS A.
Machen, John Gresham
Speer, Robert Elliott
LOGAN, ANDY
Whitman, Charles Seymour
LOGAN, RAYFORD W.
Drew, Charles Richard
Hope, John
Houston, Charles Hamilton
Woodson, Carter Godwin
LOHR, LENOX R.
Dawes, Rufus Cutler
LOMASK, MILTON
Guggenheim, Simon
LOMBARD, GEORGE F. F.
Mayo, George Elton
LOMBARD, MILDRED E.
Peters, John Andrew
Sayre, Stephen

- Searle, James
- Wentworth, Paul
- White, Henry
- Williams, Jonathan

LONDON, HARVEY
- Martin, Everett Dean

LONDON, HERBERT I.
- Duchin, Edward Frank ("Eddy")
- Tilzer, Harry Von

LONG, C. N. H.
- Henderson, Yandell

LONG, ESMOND R.
- Baldwin, Edward Robinson
- Brown, Lawrason
- Gardner, Leroy Upson
- Krause, Allen Kramer

LONG, FRANCIS TAYLOR
- Johnston, Richard Malcolm

LONGCOPE, WARFIELD T.
- Baetjer, Frederick Henry
- Smith, Nathan, 1762–1829
- Smith, Nathan Ryno

LONGWELL, CHESTER R.
- Dana, Edward Salisbury

LONN, ELLA
- Ames, Adelbert
- Darke, William
- Garrett, John Work
- Garrett, Robert
- Garrett, Thomas
- Griffith, Goldsborough Sappington
- Hicks, Thomas Holliday
- Kellogg, William Pitt
- Latrobe, John Hazlehurst Boneval
- Lee, Thomas Sim
- Ligon, Thomas Watkins
- Lloyd, Edward, 1744–1796
- Lloyd, Edward, 1779–1834
- Lowndes, Lloyd
- Nelson, Roger
- Nicholls, Francis Redding Tillou
- Pearce, James Alfred
- Pinchback, Pinckney Benton
- Plater, George
- Pratt, Thomas George
- Roman, André Bienvenu
- Semmes, Thomas Jenkins
- Sharpe, Horatio
- Stockbridge, Henry
- Stockbridge, Henry Smith
- Swann, Thomas
- Thomas, Francis
- Thomas, Philip Francis
- Wallis, Severn Teackle
- Warmoth, Henry Clay
- Wells, James Madison
- Wickliffe, Robert Charles
- Wilmer, Joseph Père Bell
- Winans, Ross
- Winans, Thomas De Kay

LOOMIS, FREDERIC B.
- Shepard, Charles Upham

LOOMIS, LOUISE R.
- Howland, Emily

LOPATA, ROY HAYWOOD
- Fullam, Frank L.
- Knappen, Theodore Temple
- Nessler, Karl Ludwig
- Smillie, Ralph

LORD, ALBERT B.
- Scott, John Adams

LORD, C. W.
- Wigfall, Louis Trezevant

LORD, MILTON EDWARD
- Whitney, James Lyman

LORENCE, JAMES J.
- Duffy, Francis Ryan

LORENZ, LINCOLN
- Gould, Edward Sherman
- Green, Asa

LORIMER, FRANK
- Lotka, Alfred James

LOUGHRAN, JAMES N., S.J.
- Sheen, Fulton John

LOUIS, JAMES P.
- Simms, Ruth Hanna McCormick

LOUNSBURY, RALPH G.
- McNutt, Alexander

LOVETT, ROBERT W.
- Kirstein, Louis Edward
- Liggett, Louis Kroh

LOWE, VICTOR
- Whitehead, Alfred North

LOWENS, IRVING
- Chotzinoff, Samuel
- Kelley, Edgar Stillman
- Thompson, Oscar Lee

LOWERY, CHARLES D.
- Boggs, Thomas Hale
- Clark, Tom Campbell
- Feis, Herbert
- Gipson, Lawrence Henry
- Labaree, Leonard Woods
- Muhammad, Elijah
- Nevins, Joseph Allan

LOWES, JOHN LIVINGSTON
- Lowell, Amy

LOWITT, RICHARD
- Aandahl, Fred George
- Ashurst, Henry Fountain
- Case, Francis Higbee
- Monroney, Almer Stillwell ("Mike")
- Norris, George William
- Sabath, Adolph J.
- Shouse, Jouett
- Thye, Edward John

LOWREY, LAWRENCE T.
- Davis, Joseph Robert
- Davis, Reuben
- Ellis, Powhatan
- Proctor, William Cooper

LOWRIE, SELDEN GALE
- Mansfield, Edward Deering
- Matthews, Stanley

LOWRY, W. MCNEIL
- Gaither, Horace Rowan, Jr.

LOWTHER, LELAND S.
- Digges, Dudley

LUBOVE, ROY
- Bettman, Alfred
- Devine, Edward Thomas
- Dinwiddie, Courtenay
- Perry, Clarence Arthur
- Purdy, Lawson
- Veiller, Lawrence Turnure
- West, James Edward

LUBS, HERBERT A.
- Reese, Charles Lee

LUCE, ROBERT
- Evans, Lawrence Boyd
- McCall, Samuel Walker

LUDINGTON, TOWNSEND
- Dos Passos, John Roderigo

LUDMERER, KENNETH M.
- Davenport, Charles Benedict
- Erlanger, Joseph

LUEBBERING, KEN
- Haagen-Smit, Arie Jan
- Link, Theodore Carl
- Roche, Josephine Aspinwall

LUEDERS, EDWARD
- Van Vechten, Carl

LUFT, ERIC V. D.
- Békésy, Georg von
- Dyer, Rolla Eugene
- Kaufmann, Walter Arnold
- Knowles, John Hilton
- Kolb, Lawrence
- Sugiura, Kanematsu

LUISI, CARMINE
- Galante, Carmine

LUKER, RALPH E.
- Brennan, Francis James
- Holmes, John Haynes
- Oxnam, Garfield Bromley
- Sheil, Bernard James

LULL, CHARLES E. T.
- Palfrey, John Carver
- Pennypacker, Galusha

LULL, RICHARD S.
- Hay, Oliver Perry

LUNDEEN, EARNEST W.
- Saunders, Alvin

LUQUER, THATCHER T. P.
- Pellew, Henry Edward

LUTHER, PHILIP
- Costain, Thomas Bertram
- Garis, Howard Roger
- Kerr, Sophie
- Koch, Vivienne

LUTZ, ALMA
- Blatch, Harriot Eaton Stanton
- Willard, Emma Hart

LYDENBERG, HARRY MILLER
- Allen, William Frederick
- Bjerregaard, Carl Henrik Andreas
- Lenox, James
- Morse, Sidney Edwards
- Stevens, Benjamin Franklin
- Stevens, Henry
- Wilson, James Grant

LYDENBERG, H. M.
- Dewey, Melvil
- Eames, Wilberforce

LYLE, WILLIAM T.
- Mason, Claibourne Rice
- Robinson, Moncure

LYNCH, WILLIAM O.
- Hannegan, Edward Allen
- Hillis, David
- Holman, Jesse Lynch
- Hughes, James

LYNN, MARGARET
- Whitcomb, Seldon Lincoln

LYON, RALPH M.
- Waddel, Moses

LYTTLE, CHARLES H.
- Johnson, Franklin
- Jones, Jenkin Lloyd
- Mann, Newton

Savage, Minot Judson
Wendte, Charles William

MABBOTT, THOMAS OLLIVE
Brooks, Maria Gowen
Cliffton, William
Osgood, Francis Sargent Locke
Redfield, Justus Starr
MCADAM, JOANNE F.
Clothier, William Jackson
MACADAM, VIRGINIA
Morris, Clara
MCADIE, ALEXANDER
Durant, Charles Ferson
Jeffries, John
King, Samuel Archer
La Mountain, John
Lowe, Thaddeus Sobieski Coulincourt
Rotch, Abbott Lawrence
MCAFFEE, HELEN
Mowatt, Anna Cora Ogden
MACARTNEY, THOMAS B.
Holley, Horace
MCAVOY, THOMAS T.
Nieuwland, Julius Arthur
MCBAIN, HOWARD LEE
White, Edward Douglass, 1845–1921
MCBRIDE, FRANCIS R.
Coughlin, Charles Edward
Leahy, Francis William ("Frank")
MCBRIDE, SARAH
Guggenheim, Marguerite ("Peggy")
MCCAFFREY, KATHRINE R.
Johnstone, Edward Ransom
MACCAFFREY, WALLACE T.
Read, Conyers
MCCALLUM, JAMES DOW
Wheelock, Eleazar
Wheelock, John
MACCALLUM, WILLIAM G.
Halsted, William Stewart
Welch, William Henry
Welch, William Wickham
MCCANN, WILLIAM
Adamic, Louis
Allen, Hervey
Beach, Rex
Bridges, Thomas Jefferson Davis ("Tommy")
Freeman, Joseph
Gernsback, Hugo
Gibbs, Arthur Hamilton
Haldeman-Julius, Emanuel
Hergesheimer, Joseph
Johnson, Owen McMahon
King, Alexander
Knopf, Blanche Wolf
Kyne, Peter Bernard
Lewisohn, Ludwig
Liebling, Abbott Joseph
MacArthur, Charles Gordon
MacDonald, Betty
Moore, (Austin) Merrill
Rice, Elmer
Rommel, Edwin Americus ("Eddie")
Sandburg, Carl August
Sedgwick, Ellery
Sinclair, Upton Beall, Jr.
Thayer, Tiffany Ellsworth
Ziff, William Bernard
MCCARTHY, JAMES
Strawn, Silas Hardy
Vinson, Fred(erick) Moore
MCCARTHY, JOSEPH M.
Capen, Samuel Paul
Irwin, Robert Benjamin
MCCARTHY, RAYMOND G.
Cooke, Elisha
MCCARTIN, JOSEPH A.
Hoffa, James Riddle ("Jimmy")
MCCARTY, MACLYN
MacLeod, Colin Munro
MCCAUGHEY, ROBERT A.
Gildersleeve, Virginia Crocheron
Meyer, Annie Nathan
MCCAUL, ROBERT L.
Judd, Charles Hubbard
MCCAUSLAND, ELIZABETH
Cary, Elisabeth Luther
Myers, Jerome
MCCLEAN, ALBERT F.
Fields, Lewis Maurice
MCCLELLAN, LAWRENCE, JR.
Ory, Edward ("Kid")
MCCLURE, CLARENCE H.
Fletcher, Thomas Clement
MCCLURE, N. E.
Linn, John Blair
Neal, Joseph Clay
MCCLUSKEY, NEIL G.
Johnson, George
MACCOLL, MARY
Webster, Alice Jane Chandler
MCCOLLESTER, LEE SULLIVAN
Adams, John Coleman
Amherst, Jeffery
MCCOLLUM, E. V.
Hess, Alfred Fabian
MCCONNELL, J. W.
Weisenburg, Theodore Herman
MCCORD, DAVID
Copeland, Charles Townsend
MCCORMAC, EUGENE I.
McLane, Louis
Polk, James Knox
MCCORMICK, SAMUEL BLACK
Bruce, Robert
MCCORMICK, THOMAS DENTON
Baker, La Fayette Curry
Bingham, John Armor
Blount, Thomas
Buchanan, John
Bulloch, Archibald
Burrowes, Thomas Henry
Cameron, Archibald
Christian, William
De Haas, John Philip
Faulk, Andrew Jackson
Fenno, John
Frazer, John Fries
Frazer, Persifor
Fries, John
Gibson, George
Gibson, John
Goss, James Walker
MCCOY, DONALD R.
Dawes, Charles Gates
Garner, John Nance
Hoover, Herbert Clark, Jr.
Kefauver, (Carey) Estes
O'Mahoney, Joseph Christopher
Reece, Brazilla Carroll
Scopes, John Thomas
Wallace, Lurleen Burns
Wood, John Stephens
MCCOY, GARNETT
Smith, David Roland
MCCOY, SONDRA VAN METER
Allen, Forrest Clare ("Phog")
Hope, Clifford Ragsdale
MACCRACKEN, HENRY N.
Jewett, Milo Parker
Raymond, John Howard
Taylor, James Monroe
Vassar, Matthew
MCCRACKEN, ROBERT T.
Von Moschzisker, Robert
MCCRAE, THOMAS
Da Costa, Jacob Mendez
Dewees, William Potts
Dorsey, John Syng
Gibson, William
Hartshorne, Henry
Hays, Isaac
Hodge, Hugh Lenox
McClellan, George, 1796–1847
McClellan, George, 1849–1913
Pepper, William
Physick, Philip Syng
Smith, Albert Holmes
MCCRAW, THOMAS K.
McKellar, Kenneth Douglas
Morgan, John Harcourt Alexander
Olds, Leland
MCCREA, NELSON GLENN
Merriam, Augustus Chapman
Wilson, Peter
MCCREA, ROSWELL CHENEY
Atkinson, Edward
Bergh, Henry
MCCUE, WILLIAM T.
Rice, Alice Caldwell Hegan
MCCUTCHEON, ROGER P.
Dinwiddie, Albert Bledsoe
Hunt, Carleton
Nicholson, Eliza Jane Poitevent Holbrook
Pinney, Norman
Poydras, Julien De Lalande
Soulé, George
Townsend, Mary Ashley
Walker, Alexander
Walworth, Jeannette Ritchie Hadermann
MCDANIEL, ARTHUR S.
Hale, Robert Safford
Johnson, Alexander Smith
Jones, Samuel
Loomis, Arphaxed
Lord, Daniel
MCDANIEL, W. B., 2D
Landis, Henry Robert Murray
Schweinitz, George Edmund de
MCDONAGH, DON
Draper, Ruth
Humphrey, Doris
MCDONALD, ARCHIE P.
Hobby, William Pettus
MCDONALD, FORREST
Carlisle, Floyd Leslie
Couch, Harvey Crowley

Insull, Samuel
Sloan, Matthew Scott
McDONALD, GERALD D.
Harlow, Jean
McDONALD, PHILIP B.
Argall, Philip
Balbach, Edward
Bayles, James Copper
Billings, Charles Ethan
Boyden, Uriah Atherton
Brunton, David William
Coxe, Eckley Brinton
Day, David Talbot
Douglas, James
Field, Cyrus West
Frick, Henry Clay
Fritz, John
Holmes, Joseph Austin
Humphreys, Alexander Crombie
Hyatt, John Wesley
Janin, Louis
Jennings, James Hennen
Kirchhoff, Charles William
Raymond, Charles Walker
Raymond, Rossiter Worthington
Rothwell, Richard Pennefather
Winchell, Horace Vaughn
MACDONALD, WILLIAM L.
Bigelow, John
Birney, James
Birney, James Gillespie
Birney, William
Brayton, Charles Ray
Cannon, Joseph Gurney
Chamberlain, Joshua Lawrence
Chandler, Zachariah
Clark, Champ
Colfax, Schuyler
Whittemore, Thomas
MACDOUGALL, DIANNE NEWELL
Snow, Jessie Baker
McDOUGALL, RICHARD
Beach, Sylvia Woodbridge
McDOWELL, FREDERICK P. W.
Roberts, Elizabeth Madox
McDOWELL, GEORGE TREMAINE
Boner, John Henry
MACE, RUTH LOWENS
Nolen, John
MACE, WILLIAM HARRISON
Bardeen, Charles William
MACELWANE, JAMES B.
Odenbach, Frederick Louis
MACFARLAND, FRANK M.
Starks, Edwin Chapin
McFARLAND, JOSEPH
Meigs, Arthur Vincent
Meigs, Charles Delucena
Meigs, John Forsyth
Pancoast, Joseph
Pancoast, Seth
Stillé, Alfred
White, James William
Wood, George Bacon
Wood, Horatio Charles
Wormley, Theodore George
Young, John Richardson
McFARLAND, KEITH D.
Woodring, Harry Hines
McFARLAND, MARVIN W.
Wright, Orville
McFARLAND, WALTER MARTIN
Babcock, George Herman
Bailey, Frank Harvey
Canaga, Alfred Bruce
Hoxie, William Dixie
Kafer, John Christian
Mattice, Asa Martines
Taylor, Stevenson
Wilcox, Stephen
McGIFFERT, ARTHUR CUSHMAN
Briggs, Charles Augustus
Brown, Francis, 1849–1916
McGILL, RALPH
Howell, Clark
McGLANNAN, ALEXIUS
Tiffany, Louis McLane
McGLOTHLIN, W. J.
Johnson, William Bullein
Manly, Basil
Marshal, Daniel
Mullins, Edgar Young
Murrow, Joseph Samuel
Riley, Benjamin Franklin
Sanders, Billington McCarter
Sherwood, Adiel
Tucker, Henry Holcombe
McGOLDRICK, JOSEPH D.
Hylan, John Francis
McGRANE, REGINALD C.
Christy, David
Cist, Charles, 1738–1805
Cist, Charles, 1792–1868
Clarke, Robert
Cox, George Barnsdale
Edgerton, Alfred Peck
Elder, William Henry
Ellis, John Washington
Ewing, Hugh Boyle
Ewing, Thomas, 1789–1871
Ewing, Thomas, 1829–1896
Faran, James John
Findlay, James
Foraker, Joseph Benson
Force, Manning Ferguson
Gage, Lyman Judson
Galloway, Samuel
Greenwood, Miles
Guilford, Nathan
Gunther, Charles Frederick
Hammond, Charles
Hovey, Charles Edward
Ingalls, Melville Ezra
Langston, John Mercer
Lawrence, William, 1819–1899
Leaming, Jacob Spicer
Leavitt, Humphrey Howe
Lytle, William Haines
McLean, John
Pattison, John M.
Pendleton, George Hunt
Schneider, Herman
Springer, Reuben Runyan
Thurman, Allen Granberry
Warden, Robert Bruce
Zimmerman, Eugene
McGRATH, CHARLOTTE
De Wilde, Brandon
McGREGOR, MALCOLM F.
West, Allen Brown
MACINTOSH, DOUGLAS CLYDE
Beckwith, Clarence Augustine
MACK, WARREN B.
Landreth, David
Lippincott, James Starr
Powel, John Hare
McKAY, ELIZABETH
Buchanan, Edgar
McGraw, Donald Cushing
Pierce, Edward Allen
Snow, John Ben
McKAY, ERNEST A.
Boyd, William
Cohn, Alfred A.
Cohn, Harry
Fox, William
Garland, Judy
Heflin, Van
Lake, Veronica
MacDonald, Jeanette Anna
Morehouse, Ward
Nichols, Ruth Rowland
Raft, George
Rathbone, Basil
Sturges, Preston
Tucker, Sophie
West, Mae
McKAY, SETH SHEPARD
Camp, John Lafayette, 1828–1891
Camp, John Lafayette, 1855–1918
Davis, Edmund Jackson
Gary, Martin Witherspoon
Gregg, Maxcy
Reagan, John Henninger
Ross, Lawrence Sullivan
Rusk, Thomas Jefferson
Shepard, Seth
McKAY, STEPHEN
Blue, Ben
MACKAY-SMITH, ALEXANDER
Woodward, William
McKEE, OLIVER, JR.
Fisher, Walter Lowrie
Garrison, Lindley Miller
Lane, Franklin Knight
Longworth, Nicholas, 1869–1931
Payne, John Barton
Wood, William Robert
Woodin, William Hartman
McKELVEY, BLAKE
Bausch, Edward
Eastman, George
Gleason, Kate
Spear, Charles
Wines, Enoch Cobb
Wines, Frederick Howard
McKELVEY, JEAN TREPP
Davis, Katharine Bement
McKENNA, MARIAN C.
May, Andrew Jackson
McKENZIE, KENNETH
Parsons, Thomas William
McKENZIE, R. TAIT
Murphy, Michael Charles
McKERNS, JOSEPH P.
Brokenshire, Norman Ernest
Freed, Alan J.
McKINNEY, GORDON B.
Jeffries, James Jackson
Simmons (Szymanski), Aloysius Harry
McKINSTRY, H. E.
Lindgren, Waldemar
MCLAUCHLIN, ANDREW C.
Cooley, Thomas McIntyre
Judson, Harry Pratt

McClaughlin, Charles Capen
Moore, Charles
McLean, Albert F.
Bogart, Humphrey DeForest
Bragdon, Claude Fayette
Curry, John Steuart
Dean, James Byron
Howard, Willie
Monroe, Marilyn
Shean, Albert
Strange, Michael
Weber, Joseph Morris
McLean, Albert F., Jr.
Carroll, Earl
Jolson, Al
Taylor, Charles Alonzo
Wood, Grant
MacLear, Anne Bush
Cochrane, John
Curtis, Newton Martin
Hunter, Thomas
MacMahon, Arthur W.
Goodnow, Frank Johnson
McMahon, Edward
Smith, James Allen
McMillan, Douglas J.
Baker, Dorothy Dodds
Ruark, Robert Chester
McMahon, Robert J.
Merchant, Livingston Tallmadge
Murphy, Robert Daniel
McMurray, Donald L.
Cattell, William Cassaday
Eaton, John
McCartney, Washington
Pardee, Ario
Porter, James Madison
McMurtrie, Douglas C.
Meeker, Jotham
Timothy, Lewis
MacNair, Harley Farnsworth
King, Charles William
McNally, Michael J.
Hurley, Joseph Patrick
McNamara, Katherine
Pilat, Ignaz Anton
Robinson, Charles Mulford
Sargent, Henry Winthrop
Underwood, Loring
Vaux, Calvert
Vitale, Ferruccio
Weidenmann, Jacob
McNamara, William
Sorin, Edward Frederick
McNaugher, John
Moorehead, William Gallogly
McNeill, T. F.
Poe, Orlando Metcalfe
Quinby, Isaac Ferdinand
Ransom, Thomas Edward Greenfield
Ripley, Edward Hastings
Rodes, Robert Emmett
Seymour, Truman
Sherman, Thomas West
Smith, Charles Ferguson
Smith, Giles Alexander
Smith, Morgan Lewis
Smith, Persifor Frazer
Tidball, John Caldwell
Torbert, Alfred Thomas Archimedes
Macnie, John P.
Wheeler, John Martin
MacNiven, Ian S.
Miller, Henry Valentine
McPheeters, W. E.
King, Rufus
McPherson, John Hanson Thomas
Ashmun, Jehudi
Atkinson, William Yates
Blount, James Henderson
Clark, John
Gilmer, George Rockingham
Milledge, John
Mitchell, David Brydie
Newman, William Truslow
Nisbet, Eugenius Aristides
Northen, William Jonathan
Speer, Emory
McShane, Larry
Charles, Ezzard Mack
Fine, Larry
Liston, Charles ("Sonny")
Nelson, Oswald George ("Ozzie")
McWilliams, Carey
Sterling, George
Madaras, Lawrence H.
Roosevelt, Theodore
Madden, Eva Anne
Elliott, Sarah Barnwell
Maddox, Jerald C.
Genthe, Arnold
Maddox, Robert Franklin
Kilgore, Harley Martin
Maddox, Robert James
Slemp, Campbell Bascom
Madison, Charles A.
Harcourt, Alfred
Madison, James H.
Whiteside, Arthur Dare
Magee, James D.
Johnson, Alexander Bryan
Johnson, Joseph French
Magee, M. D'Arcy
Magruder, George Lloyd
Magie, William Francis
Fine, Henry Burchard
Henry, Joseph
Loomis, Elmer Howard
Magill, Roswell
Cravath, Paul Drennan
Mahan, Bruce E.
Carpenter, Cyrus Clay
Chambers, John
Davenport, George
Dubuque, Julien
Eastman, Enoch Worthen
Leffler, Isaac
Leffler, Shepard
Mahoney, Joseph F.
Walsh, Edmund Aloysius
Walsh, Thomas Joseph
Makinson, Randell L.
Greene, Charles Sumner
Greene, Henry Mather
Maland, Charles J.
Brackett, Charles William
Chaplin, Charles Spencer ("Charlie")
Curtiz, Michael
Johnston, Eric Allen
Malin, James C.
Curtis, Charles
Lease, Mary Elizabeth Clyens
Logan, Cornelius Ambrose
Martin, John Alexander
Morrill, Edmund Needham
Phillips, William Addison
Root, Frank Albert
Stubbs, Walter Roscoe
Mallalieu, W. C.
Gary, James Albert
Goldsborough, Charles
Goldsborough, Louis Malesherbes
Goldsborough, Robert
Grimké, John Faucheraud
Hunter, Whiteside Godfrey
Johnson, Bradley Tyler
Kent, Joseph
Key, Philip Barton
Lindsay, William
McAfee, Robert Breckinridge
McCreary, James Bennett
Metcalfe, Thomas
Morehead, Charles Slaughter
Morehead, James Turner
Owsley, William
Mallison, A. G.
Gregory, Thomas Watt
Malloch, Archibald C.
Church, Benjamin
Craik, James
Malone, Dumas
Alderman, Edwin Anderson
Baldwin, Abraham
Barbour, James
Barbour, Philip Pendelton
Callender, James Thomson
Cooper, Thomas
Drayton, John
Drayton, William, 1732–1790
Drayton, William, 1776–1846
Fulton, Robert Burwell
Giles, William Branch
Gilmer, Francis Walker
Henry, William Wirt
Humphreys, Benjamin Grubb
Jefferson, Thomas
Madison, Dolly Payne
Randolph, John, 1773–1833
Rhodes, James Ford
Malone, Kemp
March, Francis Andrew, 1825–1911
March, Francis Andrew, 1863–1928
Webster, Noah
Maloney, Wendy Hall
Abernathy, Roy
McDonnell, James Smith, Jr.
Pratt, John Lee
Manchester, Mary E.
Adams, Andrew
Andrews, Charles Bartlett
Baldwin, Roger Sherman
Baldwin, Simeon
Mandel, Bernard
Hayes, Max Sebastian
Mandelbaum, David G.
Sapir, Edward
Mangione, Jerre
Cahill, Holger
Mann, Arthur T.
La Guardia, Fiorello Henry
Mead, Edwin Doak

Moore, James Edward
Walker, James John
MANN, HELEN JO SCOTT
De Young, Michel Harry
Freeman, Frederick Kemper
Sprague, Charles Ezra
MANN, LOUIS LEOPOLD
Adler, Samuel
Asher, Joseph Mayor
Hirsch, Emil Gustav
Rosenwald, Julius
MANN, ROBERT S.
Lee, James Melvin
MANN, RUTH J.
Funk, Casimir
Hench, Philip Showalter
MANNING, HELEN TAFT
Rhoades, James E.
Taylor, Joseph Wright
Thomas, Martha Carey
MANNING, MARTIN J.
Allen, George Edward
Grant, William Thomas, Jr.
Purtell, William Arthur
Svenson, Andrew Edward
MANROSS, WILLIAM W.
Schroeder, John Frederick
MANVILLE, RICHARD H.
Merriam, Clinton Hart
MARCOSSON, ISAAC F.
Frohman, Charles
MARCUS, ROBERT D.
Man Ray
MARCUSON, ISAAC E.
Grossman, Louis
MARGOLIS, JOHN D.
Eliot, T(homas) S(tearns)
Krutch, Joseph Wood
MARGULIES, HERBERT F.
Lenroot, Irvine Luther
MARKHAM, JESSE WILLIAM
Fetter, Frank Albert
MARKOE, ARNOLD
Shor, Bernard ("Toots")
Washington, Kenneth Stanley ("The General")
MARKS, HENRY SEYMOUR
Kearns, Jack
Maranville, Walter James Vincent ("Rabbit")
MARKS, LIONEL S.
Hollis, Ira Nelson
MARMARELLI, RONALD S.
Covici, Pascal ("Pat")
Funk, Wilfred John
Hard, William
High, Stanley Hoflund
Sulzberger, Arthur Hays
MARMER, HARRY A.
Bent, Silas
Eimbeck, William
Harris, Rollin Arthur
Hassler, Ferdinand Rudolph
Hayford, John Fillmore
Lindenkohl, Adolph
Martin, Artemas
Maury, Matthew Fontaine
Mendenhall, Thomas Corwin
Mitchell, Henry
Pavy, Octave
Peary, Robert Edwin
Schott, Charles Anthony
MARRARO, HOWARD R.
Foresti, Eleutario Felice
MARSDEN, BRIAN G.
Moulton, Forest Ray
Perrine, Charles Dillon
MARSHALL, GEORGE
Williams, John Elias
Yoakum, Benjamin Franklin
MARSHALL, JAMES TRIMBLE, JR.
Brown, John Appleton
Brown, John George
Bunce, William Gedney
MARSHALL, S. L. A.
McAlexander, Ulysses Grant
MARSHALL, STEPHEN G.
Craig, Cleo Frank
Freed, Arthur
Kyes, Roger Martin
McHugh, Keith Stratton
McLean, Robert
Mauchly, John William
Murchison, John Dabney
Potter, Charles Edward
Riefler, Winfield William
Romnes, Haakon Ingolf ("H. I.")
Singer, Charles H.
Sporn, Philip
Sproul, Allan
Thornton, Daniel I. J.
Van, Bobby
Whitehead, Walter Edward
MARSHALL, THOMAS M.
Bates, Edward
Bates, Frederick
MARSHALL, WILLIAM B.
Lea, Isaac
MARSZALEK, JOHN F.
Brundage, Avery
Capp, Al
Connor, Theophilus ("Bull") Eugene
Hamer, Fannie Lou
Harlan, John Marshall
Michaux, Lightfoot Solomon
Perkins, Marion
Spingarn, Arthur Barnett
Wilson, J(ames) Finley
MARTENS, FREDERICK HERMAN
Abbott, Emma
Bispham, David Scull
Damrosch, Leopold
Dannreuther, Gustav
Davis, John, *c.* 1780–1825
De Coppet, Edward J.
De Koven, Henry Louis Reginald
Dresel, Otto
Estey, Jacob
Fairlamb, James Remington
Fischer, Emil Friedrich August
Fletcher, Alice Cunningham
Gemünder, August Martin Ludwig
Gericke, Wilhelm
Gilchrist, William Wallace
Gilmore, Patrick Sarsfield
Gleason, Frederic Grant
Hamlin, Emmons
Hammerstein, Oscar
Hanchett, Henry Granger
Harris, Charles Kassell
Hauk, Minnie
Heinrich, Max
Herbert, Victor
Hewitt, James
Hill, Ureli Corelli
Hoffman, Richard
Humiston, William Henry
Kellogg, Clara Louise
Knabe, Valentine Wilhelm
Kobbé, Gustav
Koemmenich, Louis
Maretzek, Max
Marzo, Eduardo
Mason, Henry
Mason, Lowell
Mason, Luther Whiting
Mason, William
Mathews, William Smythe Babcock
Moore, Annie Aubertine Woodward
Moore, John Weeks
Musin, Ovide
Neuendorff, Adolph Heinrich Anton Magnus
Nordica, Lillian
Nunó, Jamie
Osgood, George Laurie
Phillips, Philip
Powell, Alma Webster
Powell, Maud
Presser, Theodore
Ritter, Frédéric Louis
Rogers, Clara Kathleen Barnett
Roosevelt, Hilborne Lewis
Rybner, Martin Cornelius
MARTIN, ALBERT R.
Munroe, Charles Edward
MARTIN, ALBRO
Cowen, Joshua Lionel
Damon, Ralph Shepard
Frye, William John ("Jack")
Gifford, Walter Sherman
Moody, John
Moran, Eugene Francis
Rockefeller, John Davison, Jr.
Skinner, Cornelia Otis
Starrett, Paul
MARTIN, ASA EARL
Dinwiddie, Edwin Courtland
Findley, William
Fitzsimmons, or Fitzsimins, Thomas
Forward, Walter
Shulze, John Andrew
Shunk, Francis Rawn
Sparks, Edwin Erle
Swallow, Silas Comfort
Wolf, George
MARTIN, BERNARD
Philipson, David
MARTIN, GEOFFREY
Bowman, Isaiah
MARTIN, GEOFFREY I.
Jefferson, Mark Sylvester William
MARTIN, GEOFFREY J.
Huntington, Ellsworth
MARTIN, JAMES J.
Berkman, Alexander
Goldman, Emma
Tucker, Benjamin Ricketson
MARTIN, KAREN
Tarr, Ralph Stockman

Martin, Lawrence
Mitchell, John, d. 1768
Marvuglio, Matthew
Adderley, Julian Edwin ("Cannonball")
Wilder, Alexander Lafayette Chew ("Alec")
Marx, Paul B.
Michel, Virgil George
Mason, Alpheus Thomas
Corwin, Edward Samuel
Haines, Daniel
Hornblower, Joseph Coerten
Roberts, Owen Josephus
Stone, Harlan Fiske
Mason, Christine Gibbons
Masters, Edgar Lee
Mason, Daniel Gregory
Savage, Philip Henry
Mason, Edward S.
Taussig, Frank William
Mason, Lester B.
Verplanck, Gulian Crommelin
Masson, Thomas L.
Bangs, John Kendrick
Matas, Rudolph
Prevost, François Marie
Richardson, Tobias Gibson
Riddell, John Leonard
Mates, Julian
Harris, Sam Henry
Mather, Anne D.
McCormick, Anne Elizabeth O'Hare
Mather, Frank Jewett, Jr.
Abbey, Edwin Austin
Davies, Arthur Bowen
Marquand, Allan
Martin, Homer Dodge
Tryon, Dwight William
Van Dyke, John Charles
Mathews, Albert P.
Drake, Benjamin
Drake, Daniel
Elwell, John Johnson
Gaillard, Edwin Samuel
Garlick, Theodatus
Goforth, William
Goldsmith, Middleton
Hildreth, Samuel Prescott
Jackson, John Davies
Keyt, Alonzo Thrasher
King, John
Rachford, Benjamin Knox
Ransohoff, Joseph
Mathews, Shailer
Barrows, John Henry
Miller, Lewis
Moulton, Richard Green
Mathews, Thomas G.
Winship, Blanton
Matteson, David M.
Adams, Abijah
Brown, Jameson, 1800–1855
Campbell, John
Draper, John
Fitch, Samuel
Fleming, John, 1764–1800
Gill, John
Green, Bartholomew
Green, Samuel
Johnson, Marmaduke
Matthews, Brander
Bunner, Henry Cuyler
Matthews, Fred H.
Park, Robert Ezra
Matthiessen, Francis O.
Crane, Harold Hart
Jewett, Sarah Orne
Maury, Jean West
Sprague, Kate Chase
Maxcy, Kenneth F.
Frost, Wade Hampton
Maxcy, Spencer J.
Baziotes, William
Louis, Morris
Maxon, William R.
Eaton, Daniel Cady
Peck, Charles Horton
Perrine, Henry
Pursh, Fredrick
Rose, Joseph Nelson
Safford, William Edwin
Spalding, Volney Morgan
Sullivant, William Starling
Tuckerman, Edward
Underwood, Lucien Marcus
Vasey, George
Walter, Thomas
Maxwell, Robert S.
Esch, John Jacob
La Follette, Philip Fox
May, Joseph
Bender, George Harrison
Lucas, Scott Wike
Mayall, Margaret W.
Cannon, Annie Jump
Mayberry, Susan Neal
Bontemps, Arna Wendell
Fromm, Erich
Ransom, John Crowe
Mayer, Andre
Lahey, Frank Howard
Mayer, Emil
Asch, Morris Joseph
Gruening, Emil
Mayer, George H.
Lundeen, Ernest
Olson, Floyd Bjerstjerne
Mayer, George Louis
Liebling, Estelle
Mayer, Martin
Buckner, Emory Roy
Mayhew, Theodore L.
Astor, William Vincent
Kelley, Edith Summers
Whalen, Grover Aloysius
Mayo, Bernard
Dunlap, Robert Pinckney
Hamlin, Charles
Hubbard, John
King, Horatio
Mayo, Laurence Shaw
Belknap, Jeremy
Dexter, Samuel, 1726–1810
Dowse, Thomas
Farmer, John, 1789–1838
Felt, Joseph Barlow
Goodhue, Benjamin
Hoyt, Albert Harrison
Langdon, Samuel
Langdon, Woodbury
Lathrop, John
Livermore, George
Lossing, Benson John
Lovell, John
Lowell, Edward Jackson
Lunt, George
Mason, Jonathan
Maycock, Thomas J.
Mason, Arthur John
Moser, Christopher Otto
Mazuzan, George T.
Austin, Warren Robinson
Bridges, (Henry) Styles
Mazzaro, Jerome
Jarrell, Randall
Ley, Willy
Lowell, Robert Traill Spence, Jr.
Meade, Julian R.
Whitaker, Daniel Kimball
Meade, Robert Douthat
Jenkins, Albert Gallatin
Jenkins, Micah
Lee, William Henry Fitzhugh
Logan, Thomas Muldrup, 1840–1914
Long, Armistead Lindsay
McClellan, Henry Brainerd
Magruder, John Bankhead
Martin, James Green
Maury, Dabney Herndon
Northrop, Lucius Bellinger
Pelham, John
Polk, Leonidas
Polk, Lucius Eugene
Randolph, Alfred Magill
Randolph, George Wythe
Ravenscroft, John Stark
Seddon, James Alexander
Shoup, Francis Asbury
Walker, Reuben Lindsay
Walker, William Henry Talbot
Winder, John Henry
Wise, Henry Alexander
Wise, Henry Augustus
Wise, John Sergeant
Means, Stewart
Allen, Alexander Viets Griswold
Meany, Edmond S.
Ferry, Elisha Peyre
Mechlin, Leila
Brackett, Edward Augustus
Bradford, William, 1823–1892
Bristol, John Bunyan
Brooks, Richard Edwin
Burroughs, Bryson
Bush-Brown, Henry Kirke
Dielman, Frederick
Evans, William Thomas
Ffoulke, Charles Mather
Freer, Charles Lang
French, William Merchant Richardson
Lukeman, Henry Augustus
Niehaus, Charles Henry
Paris, Walter
Pattison, James William
Pine, Robert Edge
Powell, Lucien Whiting
White, John Blake
Whittridge, Worthington
Wolf, Henry
Medina, Harold R.
Steuer, Max David
Meeks, Carroll L. V.
Ford, George Burdett
Granger, Alfred Hoyt
Meenes, Max
Jastrow, Joseph

Megargee, Richard
Moore, John Bassett
Mein, William Wallace
Webb, Harry Howard
Meine, Franklin J.
Harris, George Washington, 1814–1869
Pomeroy, Marcus Mills
Shillaber, Benjamin Penhallow
Thomson, Mortimer Neal
Thorpe, Thomas Bangs
Meland, Bernard E.
Mathews, Shailer
Melcher, Frederic G.
Brett, George Platt
Mendel, Lafayette B.
Osborne, Thomas Burr
Mendell, Clarence W.
Hadley, James
Peck, Tracy
Seymour, Thomas Day
Thacher, Thomas Anthony
Wheeler, Arthur Leslie
Mendenhall, John C.
Waln, Robert, 1794–1825
Meneely, A. Howard
Cameron, James Donald
Cameron, Simon
Harvey, George Brinton McClellan
Kerney, James
Page, Walter Hines
Redfield, William Cox
Smith, James, 1851–1927
Stanbery, Henry
Stanton, Edwin McMasters
Thomas Lorenzo
Wade, Benjamin Franklin
Mennel, Robert M.
Flexner, Bernard
Swift, Linton Bishop
Mensh, Mark
Fischer, Louis
Menzel, Donald H.
Campbell, William Wallace
Howe, Herbert Alonzo
Lewis, Exum Percival
Schaeberle, John Martin
Meredith, Albert B.
Northrop, Birdsey Grant
Mereness, Newton D.
Calvert, Charles
Calvert, George
Calvert, Leonard
Claiborne, William
Coode, John
Copley, Lionel
Copley, Thomas
Dulany, Daniel, 1685–1753
Dulany, Daniel, 1722–1797
Eddis, William
Eden, Robert
Fendall, Josias
Hanson, John
Henry, John, 1750–1798
Hindman, William
McMahon, John Van Lear
Ogle, Samuel
Scott, Gustavus
Smallwood, William
Smith, Caleb Blood
Smith, Oliver Hampton
Tilghman, Matthew
Vinton, Samuel Finley
White, Albert Smith
Winder, Levin
Wright, Joseph Albert
Wright, Robert
Mergen, Bernard
Piper, William Thomas
Merino, Barbara B.
Lybrand, William Mitchell
Meriwether, Robert Lee
Burke, AEdanus
Butler, Pierce
Butler, William, 1759–1821
Gadsden, Christopher
Gaillard, John
Garden, Alexander, 1757–1829
Hutson, Richard
Jamison, David Flavel
Keitt, Lawrence Massillon
McCord, David James
Marion, Francis
Moultrie, William
Ramsay, David
Rutledge, Edward
Rutledge, John
Merriam, Charles E.
Burgess, John William
Freund, Ernst
Merriam, John Campbell
Chamberlin, Thomas Chrowder
Merrill, George Perkins
Ashburner, Charles Albert
Barrell, Joseph
Becker, George Ferdinand
Beecher, Charles Emerson
Blake, William Phipps
Bradley, Frank Howe
Branner, John Casper
Broadhead, Garland Carr
Brooks, Alfred Hulse
Brooks, Thomas Benton
Brush, George Jarvis
Calvin, Samuel
Clark, William Bullock
Clarke, John Mason
Claypole, Edward Waller
Cook, George Hammell
Cope, Edward Drinker
Crosby, William Otis
Dana, James Dwight
Dutton, Clarence Edward
Eaton, Amos
Emmons, Ebenezer
Emmons, Samuel Franklin
Gilbert, Grove Karl
Hague, Arnold
Hague, James Duncan
Hall, James, 1811–1898
Hayden, Ferdinand Vandiveer
Hayes, Charles Willard
Hilgard, Eugene Woldemar
Hitchcock, Charles Henry
Hitchcock, Edward, 1793–1864
Houghton, Douglass
Iddings, Joseph Paxon
Irving, Roland Duer
Jackson, Charles Thomas
Kemp, James Furman
Kerr, Washington Caruthers
King, Clarence
LeConte, Joseph
Leidy, Joseph
Lesley, Peter
Lesquereux, Leo
Maclure, William
Marsh, Othniel Charles
Mather, William Williams
Meek, Fielding Bradford
Newberry, John Strong
Orton, Edward Francis Baxter
Owen, David Dale
Powell, John Wesley
Pumpelly, Raphael
Rogers, Henry Darwin
Rogers, William Barton
Safford, James Merrill
Salisbury, Rollin D.
Shaler, Nathaniel Southgate
Smith, Eugene Allen
Springer, Frank
Stevenson, John James
Swallow, George Clinton
Van Hise, Charles Richard
Walcott, Charles Doolittle
White, Israel Charles
Whitney, Josiah Dwight
Williams, George Huntington
Winchell, Alexander
Winchell, Newton Horace
Merrill, Marion
Becket, Frederick Mark
Merrill, Milton R.
Smoot, Reed Owen
Merriman, Roger B.
Bigelow, Erastus Brigham
Prescott, William Hickling
Merritt, Ernest
Anthony, William Arnold
Merritt, James Douglas
Sullivan, Edward Vincent ("Ed")
Merritt, Raymond Harland
Blakeley, George Henry
Howell, Albert Summers
Talbot, Arthur Newell
Meryman, Richard S.
Mankiewicz, Herman Jacob
Meserve, Walter J.
Anglin, Margaret Mary
Mesick, Jane Louise
Butterworth, Hezekiah
Messbarger, Paul R.
Repplier, Agnes
Messer, Helaine
Goodyear, Anson Conger
Metcalf, Frank J.
Holden, Oliver
Holyoke, Samuel
Jackson, George K.
Keller, Mathias
Kemp, Robert H.
Law, Andrew
Oatman, Johnson
Oliver, Henry Kemble
Palmer, Horatio Richmond
Palmer, Ray
Read, Daniel, 1757–1836
Scott, John Prindle
Swan, Timothy
Thompson, Will Lamartine
Willard, Samuel
Metcalf, John Calvin
Cooke, Philip Pendleton
Mets, David R.
Spaatz, Carl Andrew ("Tooey")
Metzger, Bruce M.
Lake, Kirsopp

MEYER, ADOLF
Brush, Edward Nathaniel
Phipps, Henry
MEYER, DONALD
Carnegie, Dale
Fillmore, Charles
Oursler, (Charles) Fulton
MEYER, HERMAN H. B.
Flint, Weston
Lanman, Charles
Sabin, Joseph
MEYER, LEO J.
Platt, Orville Hitchcock
MEYLAN, GEORGE L.
Gulick, Luther Halsey, 1865–1918
Sargent, Dudley Allen
MEZZACAPPA, ANTONIO L.
Grandgent, Charles Hall
MICHELSON, TRUMAN
Brinton, Daniel Garrison
MIDDLEBROOK, DIANE WOOD
Sexton, Anne Gray Harvey
MIDDLEKAUFF, ROBERT
Miller, Perry Gilbert Eddy
MIDDLETON, CHARLES R.
Armour, Thomas Dickson ("Tommy")
Fox, Jacob Nelson ("Nellie")
Giles, Warren Crandall
Gilliam, James William ("Junior")
Merrill, Gretchen Van Zandt
Prefontaine, Steve Roalnd ("Pre")
Rupp, Adolph Frederick
Smith, Horton
Wood, Craig Ralph
MILES, EDWIN A.
Carson, Jack
Fazenda, Louise Marie
Schenck, Nicholas Michael
Yates, Herbert John
MILES, WYNDHAM D.
Lamb, Arthur Becket
MILLER, DARLIS A.
Dworshak, Henry Clarence
Ferguson, Miriam Amanda Wallace
Johnson, Edwin Carl
MILLER, DOUGLASS W.
Craig, Daniel H.
Dexter, Henry 1813–1910
Dickinson, Charles Monroe
Fiske, Stephen Ryder
Gallagher, William Davis
Gray, Joseph W.
MILLER, FRED D.
Just, Ernest Everett
MILLER, GENEVIEVE
Sigerist, Henry Ernest
MILLER, GERRIT S.
Mearns, Edgar Alexander
MILLER, HAROLD P.
Hawthorne, Julian
MILLER, JAMES P.
Nash, Frederick Ogden
MILLER, JAMES R.
Hamilton, Clayton
Tyler, George Crouse
MILLER, JANE A.
Mallinckrodt, Edward, Jr.
MILLER, JERRY L.
Meredith, Edna C. Elliott
Putnam, Nina Wilcox
MILLER, JOHN PERRY
Fisher, Irving
MILLER, JOHN VEIL, JR.
Johnson, Eldridge Reeves
MILLER, KAREN S.
Hill, John Wiley
MILLER, J. RONALD
Eaton, Charles Aubrey
MILLER, LILLIAN B.
Whitney, Gertrude Vanderbilt
MILLER, LINDA PATTERSON
Burchfield, Charles Ephraim
Manship, Paul Howard
Murphy, Gerald Clery
Stewart, Donald Ogden
MILLER, PERRY
Nurse, Rebecca
Walker, James
MILLER, PHILIP LIESON
Galli-Curci, Amelita
White, Joseph Malachy
MILLER, RANDALL M.
Carter, William Hodding, Jr.
Smith, Lillian Eugenia
MILLER, RAYMOND C.
Dow, Alex
Harris, William Alexander
Ingalls, John James
Peffer, William Alfred
Pingree, Hazen Stuart
Simpson, Jerry
MILLER, ROBERT MOATS
Fisher, Frederick Bohn
Tittle, Ernest Fremont
MILLER, T. GRIER
Stengel, Alfred
MILLER, WILLIAM D.
Maurin, Peter Aristide
MILLER, WILLIAM SNOW
Godman, John Davidson
Horner, William Edmonds
Kempster, Walter
MILLER, WILLIAM THOMAS
Beals, Ralph Albert
MILLETT, ALLAN R.
Bullard, Robert Lee
Ely, Hanson Edward
MILLICAN, C. BOWIE
Van Depoele, Charles Joseph
MILLIGAN, FLORENCE
Osborn, William Henry
MILLIKEN, WILLIAM M.
Dickinson, Preston
MILLSTEIN, BARBARA HEAD
Kanaga, Consuelo Delesseps
MIMS, EDWIN
Ayres, Brown
Bledsoe, Albert Taylor
Kirkland, James Hampton
Lanier, Sidney
MIMS, EDWIN, JR.
Erlanger, Abraham Lincoln
Gansevoort, Leonard
Grau, Maurice
Hawkins, Dexter Arnold
Hill, Frederick Trevor
Holley, Marietta
McVicker, James Hubert
Marble, Danforth
Murdoch, James Edward
MINDIL, CLINTON
Clark, Lewis Gaylord
Coates, George Henry
MINER, LOUIE M.
Deming, Philander
MINNICH, HARVEY C.
Mcguffey, William Holmes
Osborn, Henry Stafford
Tappan, Eli Todd
Thompson, William Oxley
White, Emerson Elbridge
MITCHELL, BROADUS
Alvey, Richard Henry
Archer, Stevenson
Baird, Henry Carey
Basso, (Joseph) Hamilton
Cardozo, Jacob Newton
Carey, Henry Charles
Carey, Mathew
Catchings, Waddill
Clark, John Maurice
Colwell, Stephen
Cone, Moses Herman
Coxe, Tench
Dawson, Francis Warrington
De Bow, James Dunwoody Brownson
Dew, Thomas Roderick
Dugdale, Richard Louis
Duke, Benjamin Newton
Duke, James Buchanan
Du Pont, Eleuthère Irénée
Du Pont, Henry
Du Pont, Henry Algernon
Du Pont, Victor Marie
Fitzhugh, George
Fries, Francis
George, Henry, 1839–1897
George, Henry, 1862–1916
Gray, George Alexander
Gregg, William
Hammett, Henry Pinckney
Hammond, Bray
Hollander, Jacob Harry
Holt, Edwin Michael
Hopkins, Johns
Hughes, Henry
Jordan, Virgil Justin
Niles, Hezekiah
Nugent, John Frost
Owen, Robert Dale
Pasvolsky, Leo
Patten, Simon Nelson
Patterson, William
Perry, Arthur Latham
Post, Louis Freeland
Pratt, Enoch
Rae, John
Ravmond, Daniel
Robinson, Edward Van Dyke
Ruml, Beardsley
Schoenhof, Jacob
Simpson, Stephen
Spooner, Lysander
Thomas, Philip Evan
Thompson, Robert Ellis
Tompkins, Daniel Augustus
Tucker, George
Vethake, Henry
Walters, Henry
Walters, William Thompson
Ware, Nathaniel A.
Warfield, Solomon Davies

Wells, David Ames
Wildman, Murray Shipley
Wolman, Leo
Wright, Carroll Davidson
MITCHELL, CATHERINE PALMER
Frazer, Oliver
Freeman, James Edwards
French, Edwin Davis
Frost, Arthur Burdett
Gibson, William Hamilton
Gillam, Bernhard
Gilpin, Charles Sidney
Goodridge, Sarah
Gutherz, Carl
Keppler, Joseph
MITCHELL, FRANKLIN D.
Hyde, Arthur Mastick
MITCHELL, LARRY R.
Waller, Willard Walter
MITCHELL, MARY HEWITT
Brace, John Pierce
Cady, Sarah Louise Ensign
MITCHELL, ROBERT J.
Zellerbach, James David
MITCHELL, SAMUEL CHILES
Curry, Jabez Lamar Monroe
Gilman, Daniel Coit
Hatcher, William Eldridge
Henry, Robert
Holmes, George Frederick
Maxcy, Jonathan
Puryear, Bennet
MITCHELL, STEWART
Minot, George Richards
Mitchell, Nahum
Russell, Jonathan
Russell, William Eustis
Seymour, Horatio
MITCHELL, WALTER, JR.
Rowell, George Presbury
MITCHELL, WILMOT B.
Kellogg, Elijah
Newman, Samuel Phillips
Pickard, Samuel Thomas
MITGANG, HERBERT
Seabury, Samuel
MITMAN, CARL W.
Abbott, William Hawkins
Allen, Horatio
Arnold, Aza
Babbitt, Isaac
Ball, Albert
Beach, Frederick Converse
Benjamin, George Hillard
Blake, Eli Whitney
Blake, Francis
Bogardus, James
Borden, Gail
Borden, Simeon
Brown, Fayette
Brown, James Salisbury
Brown, Joseph Emerson
Buckland, Cyrus
Bullock, William A.
Burson, William Worth
Burt, John
Burt, William Austin
Bushnell, David
Campbell, Andrew
Case, Jerome Increase
Channing, William Francis
Cist, Jacob
Clymer, George E.
Colburn, Irving Wightman
Colt, Samuel
Conant, Hezekiah
Corliss, George Henry
Cottrell, Calvert Byron
Craven, John Joseph
Crowell, Luther Childs
Cutler, James Goold
Cutting, James Ambrose
Daft, Leo
Dalzell, Robert M.
Dancel, Christian
Danforth, Charles
Daniels, Fred Harris
Davenport, Thomas
Davis, Phineas
Davis, William Augustine
Deere, John
Deering, William
Delany, Patrick Bernard
Detmold, Christian Edward
Dixon, Joseph
Dod, Daniel
Dow, Lorenzo, 1825–1899
Drake, Edwin Laurentine
Dripps, Isaac L.
Dunbar, Robert
Dunwoody, William Hood
Durand, Cyrus
Durham, Caleb Wheeler
Eads, James Buchanan
Earle, Pliny
Edgar, Charles
Edwards, Talmadge
Edwards, William
Eickemeyer, Rudolf
Emerson, James Ezekiel
Emerson, Ralph
Emery, Albert Hamilton
Esterbrook, Richard
Esterly, George
Evans, Oliver
Ewbank, Thomas
Fairbanks, Henry
Fairbanks, Thaddeus
Farmer, Hannah Tobey Shapleigh
Farmer, Moses Gerrish
Field, Stephen Dudley
Fitch, John
Flad, Henry
Forney, Matthias Nace
Francis, James Bicheno
Francis, Joseph
Fulton, Robert
Furlow, Floyd Charles
Gally, Merritt
Gaskill, Harvey Freeman
Gatling, Richard Jordan
Gayley, James
Gibbs, James Ethan Allen
Gilbert, Rufus Henry
Glidden, Joseph Farwell
Goddard, Calvin Luther
Goddu, Louis
Good, John
Goodrich, Benjamin Franklin
Goodwin, Hannibal Williston
Goodyear, Charles, 1800–1860
Goodyear, Charles, 1833–1896
Gordon, George Phineas
Gorrie, John
Grav, Elisha
Greist, John Milton
Grinnell, Frederick
Gunn, James Newton
Haish, Jacob
Hall, Thomas
Hall, Thomas Seavey
Hallidie, Andrew Smith
Hammond, James Bartlett
Harvey, Hayward Augustus
Hayden, Joseph Shepard
Hayward, Nathaniel Manley
Henry, William
Herdic, Peter
Herreshoff, James Brown
Heywood, Levi
Hoe, Richard March
Hoe, Robert, 1784–1833
Hoe, Robert, 1839–1909
Holland, John Philip
Holley, Alexander Lyman
Hotchkiss, Benjamin Berkeley
House, Henry Alonzo
House, Royal Earl
Howe, Elias
Howe, Frederick Webster
Howe, John Ireland
Howe, William
Howell, John Adams
Hubbard, Henry Griswold
Hubert, Conrad
Hudson, William Smith
Hughes, David Edward
Hughes, Howard Robard
Hussey, Obed
Ingersoll, Simon
Janney, Eli Hamilton
Jeffrey, Joseph Andrew
Jenkins, Nathaniel
Jenney, William Le Baron
Jerome, Chauncey
Johnston, Samuel
Jones, Amanda Theodosia
Keen, Morris Longstreth
Kent, William
Kier, Samuel M.
Kingsford, Thomas
Knight, Edward Henry
Kruesi, John
Lamb, Isaac Wixom
Lamme, Benjamin Garver
Lampson, Sir Curtis Miranda
Langley, John Williams
Lanston, Tolbert
Larned, Joseph Gay Eaton
Latta, Alexander Bonner
Lawrence, Richard Smith
Lay, John Louis
Leavitt, Erasmus Darwin
Leavitt, Frank McDowell
Leffel, James
Leggett, Mortimer Dormer
Levy, Max
Leyner, John George
Lieb, John William
Lloyd, Marshall Burns
Locke, John
Longstreet, William
Lucas, Anthony Francis
Lyall, James
Lyman, Benjamin Smith
McCoy, Elijah
McDougall, Alexander
McKay, Gordon

Marks, Amasa Abraham
Marsh, Charles Wesley
Marsh, Sylvester
Marsh, William Wallace
Mason, William
Mast, Phineas Price
Masury, John Wesley
Matthews, John
Matzeliger, Jan Ernst
Maxim, Hudson
Maynard, Edward
Melville, David
Mergenthaler, Ottmar
Merritt, Israel John
Miller, Ezra
Moody, Paul
Morey, Samuel
Morgan, Charles Hill
Munger, Robert Sylvester
Munn, Orson Desaix
Murray, Thomas Edward
Muybridge, Eadweard
Newcomb, Charles Leonard
Nicholson, William Thomas
Norris, William
Noyes, La Verne
Ogden, Francis Barber
Oliver, James
Orr, Hugh
Otis, Charles Rollin
Otis, Elisha Graves
Packard, James Ward
Page, Charles Grafton
Painter, William
Parrott, Robert Parker
Peek, Frank William
Perkins, Jacob
Perry, Stuart
Pitts, Hiram Avery
Pope, Franklin Leonard
Porter, Rufus
Pratt, Francis Ashbury
Pratt, John
Prescott, George Bartlett
Priest, Edward Dwight
Pullman, George Mortimer
Read, Nathan
Reese, Abram
Reese, Isaac
Reese, Jacob
Remington, Eliphalet
Remington, Philo
Renwick, Edward Sabine
Renwick, Henry Brevoort
Reynolds, Edwin
Reynolds, Samuel Godfrey
Rice, Richard Henrv
Roberts, William Milnor
Robinson, Stillman Williams
Robinson, William
Rogers, Henry J.
Rogers, James Harris
Rogers, John Raphael
Rogers, Thomas
Roosevelt, Nicholas J.
Root, Elisha King
Rowland, Thomas Fitch
Rumsey, James
Sargent, James
Saunders, William Lawrence
Sawyer, Sylvanus
Saxton, Joseph
Schieren, Charles Adolph
Schneller, George Otto
Scott, Irving Murray
See, Horace
Seed, Miles Ainscough
Selden, George Baldwin
Sellers, Coleman
Sellers, William
Sergeant, Henry Clark
Sessions, Henry Howard
Shaw, Thomas
Sholes, Christopher Latham
Short, Sidney Howe
Sickels, Frederick Ellsworth
Silver, Thomas
Singer, Isaac Merrit
Skinner, Halcyon
Slater, Samuel
Slocum, Samuel
Smith, Horace
Spencer, Christopher Miner
Sperry, Elmer Ambrose
Sprague, William, 1773–1836
Stager, Anson
Stanley, Francis Edgar
Stanley, William
Starrett, Laroy S.
Steinmetz, Charles Proteus
Stephenson, John
Stevens, Edwin Augustus
Stevens, John
Stevens, Robert Livingston
Stoddard, Joshua C.
Sturtevant, Benjamin Franklin
Stutz, Harry Clayton
Sweet, John Edson
Tagliabue, Giuseppe
Taylor, Fredrick Winslow
Terry, Eli
Thomas, Seth
Thomson, John
Thorp, John
Thurber, Charles
Thurston, Robert Lawton
Timken, Henry
Towne, Henry Robinson
Treadwell, Daniel
Turner, Walter Victor
Twining, Alexander Catlin
Vail, Alfred
Wagner, Webster
Wallace, William
Warner, Worcester Reed
Washburn, Ichabod
Washburn, Nathan
Waterman, Lewis Edson
Watkins, John Elfreth
Weaver, William Dixon
Webb, John Burkitt
Welch, Ashbel
Wellman, Samuel Thomas
Wesson, Daniel Baird
Wheeler, Nathaniel
Whitney, Asa
Whitney, Eli
Whittemore, Amos
Wilkinson, David
Wilkinson, Jeremiah
Willard, Simon
Wilson, Allen Benjamin
Wilson, George Francis
Winchester, Oliver Fisher
Winslow, John Flack
Winton, Alexander
Wood, James J.
Woodruff, Theodore Tuttle
Worthington, Henry Rossiter
Wyman, Horace
Yale, Linus

MIZENER, ARTHUR
Fitzgerald, Francis Scott Key

MOEHLMAN, CONRAD HENRY
MacArthur, Robert Stuart
Morehouse, Henry Lyman
Morgan, Thomas Jefferson
Moss, Lemuel
Osgood, Howard
Robins, Henry Ephraim

MOFFETT, E. V.
Hill, James
Livermore, Arthur
Livermore, Edward St. Loe
Livermore, Samuel, 1732–1803
Morril, David Lawrence

MOHLER, JOHN FREDERICK
Himes, Charles Francis

MOHLER, JOHN R.
Moore, Veranus Alva

MOLESWORTH, CHARLES
Moore, Marianne Craig

MOLEY, RAYMOND
Murphy, Charles Francis

MONAGHAN, FRANK
Bierce, Ambrose Gwinett
Bohm, Max
Burns, Otway
Clinton, George
Coffin, Sir Isaac
Coke, Thomas
Coxe, Daniel
Crowne, John
Crowne, William
Devoy, John
Dewing, Francis
Donn-Byrne, Brian Oswald
Dove, David James
Evans, Thomas Wiltberger
Field, David Dudley, 1781–1867
Field, Henry Martyn
Field, Thomas Warren
Fox, Harry
Foxall, Henry
Gaillardet, Théodore Frédéric
Gay, Sydney Howard
Gibbs, George, 1815–1873
Gilder, William Henry
Gordon, George Henry
Gordon, William
Goucher, John Franklin
Graydon, Alexander
Greene, George Washington
Grover, Cuvier
Hagner, Peter
Hall, Samuel Read
Halpine, Charles Graham
Halsey, John
Halstead, Murat
Hanaford, Phoebe Ann Coffin
Harris, Benjamin
Hart, John Seely
Hastings, Samuel Dexter
Haven, Henry Philemon
Haverly, Christopher
Hazeltine, Mayo Williamson
Headley, Joel Tyler
Holley, Myron
Hollister, Gideon Hiram

Hunt, Isaac
Huntington, Jabez
Huntington, Jedediah
Ingle, Richard
Jackson, James Caleb
Kalb, Johann
Kapp, Friedrich
Kidd, William
Kirk, John Foster
Kosciuszko, Tadeusz Andrezej Bonaventura
Lafayette, Marie Joseph Paul Yves Roch Gilbert du Motier Marquis de
Littlepage, Lewis
Mitchel, John
Moylan, Stephen
O'Brien, Fitz-James
Pollard, Joseph Percival
Pulaski, Casimir
Robinson, William Erigena
Rochambeau, Jean Baptiste Donatien De Vimeur, Comte de
Sargent, Winthrop, 1825–1870
Savage, John
Schwatka, Frederick
Seaman, Elizabeth Cochrane
Shepherd, William Robert
Spooner, Shearjashub
Stearns, John Newton
Tuckerman, Bayard
Ward, Charles Henshaw
Watson, Elkanah
Wikoff, Henry
Wood, Abraham

MONROE, HARRIET
Teasdale, Sara
Trowbridge, Augustus

MONTGOMERY, THOMAS L.
Edmonds, John

MONTGOMERY, WALTER A.
Harrison, Gessner

MOOD, FULMER
Brierton, John
Fiske, John, 1744–1797
Freeman, Nathaniel
Gosnold, Bartholomew
Inman, George
Jewett, John Punchard
Josselyn, John
May, Samuel Joseph
Mayhew, Jonathan
Mood, Francis Asbury

MOODY, HERBERT R.
Doremus, Robert Ogden

MOODY, RICHARD
Walker, Stuart Armstrong

MOODY, ROBERT E.
Allan, John
Chandler, John
Claflin, William
Clapp, Asa
Cushman, Joshua
Dawson, Henry Barton
Frye, Joseph
Greenleaf, Moses
Hall, Samuel, 1740–1807
Holmes, John
Huntington, William Edwards
Jackson, William, 1783–1855
Jewell, Marshall
Kidder, Frederic
King, William
Longfellow, Stephen
Manley, Joseph Homan
Mellen, Prentiss
Morrill, Anson Peaslee
Morrill, Lot Myrick
Morse, Freeman Harlow
Parris, Albion Keith
Plaisted, Harris Merrill
Preble, William Pitt
Putnam, William LeBaron
Rice, Alexander Hamilton
Rich, Isaac
Shepley, Ether
Shepley, George Foster
Shepley, George Foster
Sleeper, Jacob
Thacher, George
Ware, Ashur
Warren, William Fairfield
Whitman, Ezekiel
Williamson, William Durkee

MOONEY, HUGHSON
Hart, Lorenz Milton
Kern, Jerome David
Morgan, Helen
Witmark, Isidore

MOORE, ALBERT B.
Chapman, Reuben
Comer, Braxton Bragg
Deas, Zachariah Cantey
Fitzpatrick, Benjamin
Forney, William Henry
Gaines, George Strother
Gayle, John
Goldthwaite, George
Goldthwaite, Henry Barnes
Goold, William A.
Gracie, Archibald
Hubbard, David
Kolb, Reuben Francis
McKinley, John
Meek, Alexander Beaufort
Murfee, James Thomas

MOORE, AUSTIN L.
Noyes, William Curtis
Oakley, Thomas Jackson
Ogden, Thomas Ludlow
Radcliff, Jacob

MOORE, C. EARL
Stotesbury, Edward Townsend

MOORE, CHARLES
Baldwin, Henry Porter
Blair, Austin
Bliss, Aaron Thomas
Brewer, Mark Spencer
Burnham, Daniel Hudson
Burrows, Julius Caesar
French, Daniel Chester
McKim, Charles Follen
McKim, James Miller
McMillan, James
Mead, William Rutherford
Medary, Milton Bennett
Millet, Francis Davis
Norton, Charles Eliot
Platt, Charles Adams
Richardson, Charles Williamson
Shrady, Henry Merwin
White, Stanford

MOORE, DEBORAH DASH
Rosenblatt, Bernard Abraham
Schary, Dore

MOORE, EDWARD CALDWELL
Harris, George
Ropes, James Hardy

MOORE, GEORGE T.
Engelmann, George
Shaw, Henry

MOORE, JACK B.
Bodenheim, Maxwell
Cayton, Horace Roscoe
Viereck, George Sylvester

MOORE, JAMES G.
Goff, Emmet Stull

MOORE, JOHN ROBERT
Bailey, Josiah William

MOORE, LOUISE M.
Smith, Elizabeth Oakes Prince

MOORE, MARY ATWELL
Carpenter, Stephen Cullen
Cheetham, James
Croswell, Harry

MOORE, ROSS H.
Lattimore, William

MOORE, STEPHEN C.
Bishop, John Peale

MOORE, WILLIAM HOWARD
Barrett, Frank Aloysius
Engle, Clair William Walter
Leedom, Boyd Stewart

MOOREHEAD, WARREN KING
Peet, Stephen Denison
Snyder, John Francis

MORA, GEORGE
Horney, Karen Danielssen
Zilboorg, Gregory

MORAIS, HERBERT M.
Leland, John

MORAN, HUGH A.
Klopsch, Louis
Lord, Eleazar

MORAN, KEVIN J.
Young, Stark

MORAN, THOMAS F.
Biddle, Horace P.

MORBY, EDWIN S.
Schevill, Rudolph

MORDELL, ALBERT
Whittier, John Greenleaf

MORGAN, ALFRED L.
Grundy, Joseph Ridgway
Lewis, Ed ("Strangler")
Luchese, Thomas
Pepper, George Wharton
Walter, Francis Eugene

MORGAN, ANNE HODGES
Kerr, Robert Samuel

MORGAN, JOHN HILL
Ramage, John
Stuart, Gilbert

MORGAN, THEODORE H.
Smith, Harold Babbitt

MORIARTY, G. ANDREWS, JR.
Hasket, Elias

MORISON, ELTING E.
Baker, Newton Diehl
Disney, Walter Elias ("Walt")
Fiske, Bradley Allen
Hobson, Richmond Pearson
Jones, Hilary Pollard
Stimson, Henry Lewis

MORISON, SAMUEL ELIOT
Ames, Fisher
Austin, Benjamin
Austin, Jonathan Loring

Bradford, William, 1589–1657
Brooks, John
Brooks, Peter Chardon
Cabot, George
Clark, Arthur Hamilton
Day, Stephen
Gerry, Elbridge
Hart, Albert Bushnell
Harvard, John
Hoar, Leonard
Johnson, Edward
Kirkland, John Thornton
Leverett, John, 1662–1724
McKay, Donald
Oakes, Urian
Otis, Harrison Gray
Otis, James
Parker, Thomas
Pynchon, William
Quincy, Josiah, 1772–1864
Sparks, Jared
Squanto
Wilkinson, Theodore Stark

MORLAN, ROBERT L.
Townley, Arthur Charles

MORRIS, HARRISON S.
Ferris, Jean Léon Gérôme

MORRIS, JAMES POLK
Rovenstine, Emery Andrew
Seagrave, Gordon Stifler
Timberlake, Gideon
Timme, Walter

MORRIS, RICHARD B.
Campbell, William W.
Cockran, William Bourke
Colden, Cadwallader David
Cramer, Michael John
Fassett, Jacob Sloat
Fenton, Reuben Eaton
Floyd, William
Folger, Charles James
Gaynor, William Jay
Glynn, Martin Henry
Hoffman, David Murray
Hoffman, Josiah Ogden
Hoffman, Ogden
Low, Abiel Abbot
Low, Isaac
Low, Nicholas
Low, Seth
Mitchel, John Purroy
Murray, Joseph
Read, John, 1679/80–1749
Reed, Joseph
Scott, John Morin
Smith, William, 1697–1769
Smith, William, 1728–1793
Stockton, Richard
Trowbridge, Edmund
Van Santvoord, George
Van Vechten, Abraham
Walworth, Reuben Hyde
Wells, John
Williams, Elisha, 1773–1833
Zenger, John Peter

MORRIS, RICHARD KNOWLES
Cable, Frank Taylor
Lake, Simon

MORRIS, WILLIAM ALFRED
Bancroft, Hubert Howe

MORRISON, FRANK B.
Henry, William Arnon

MORRISON, JOSEPH L.
Cash, Wilbur Joseph

MORROW, FRANK
Ernst, Max
Prinze, Freddie

MORSE, JARVIS M.
Dixon, James
Edwards, Henry Waggaman
Ellsworth, William Wolcott
English, James Edward
Foot, Samuel Augustus
Foster, Lafayette Sabine
Green, Thomas
Loomis, Dwight
Niles, John Milton
Toucey, Isaac
Wanton, Joseph

MORSE, JOSIAH
Ogilvie, James

MORSE, SAMUEL FRENCH
Stevens, Wallace

MORSE, SIDNEY G.
Stoughton, William

MORTON, LOUIS
Buckner, Simon Bolivar
Earle, Edward Mead
Wainwright, Jonathan Mayhew

MORTON, RICHARD L.
Barbour, John Strode, Jr.
Bayly, Thomas Henry
Braxton, Carter
Cabell, Nathaniel Francis
Cabell, Samuel Jordan
Cabell, William H.
Cabell, William Lewis
Camm, John
Carr, Dabney
Carrington, Paul
Fry, Joshua
Holloway, John
Horrocks, James
Johns, John
Lee, Richard
Lewis, Andrew
Lewis, Fielding
Mercer, James

MOSES, MONTROSE J.
Bangs, Frank C.
Barnabee, Henry Clay
Barrett, George Horton
Barrymore, Georgiana Emma Drew
Barrymore, Maurice
Bateman, Kate Josephine

MOSS, ALFRED
Clement, Rufus Early

MOTT, FRANK LUTHER
Hudson, Frederic
Perkins, James Handasyd
Peterson, Charles Jacobs
Peterson, Henry
Walker, John Brisben
Young, Lafayette

MOTT, PETER
Cummings, E. E.

MOULTON, HAROLD G.
Brookings, Robert Somers

MOUNTCASTLE, HARRY W.
Stockwell, John Nelson

MOWER, EDMUND C.
Phelps, Edward John
Robinson, Moses

MOWRY, GEORGE E.
Johnson, Hiram Warren
Wickersham, George Woodward

MOYER, ALBERT E.
Bridgman, Percy Williams

MUCCIGROSSO, ROBERT
Dewey, Thomas Edmund
Lindbergh, Charles Augustus, Jr.
McClellan, John Little
Welling, Richard Ward Greene

MUGLESTON, WILLIAM F.
Farago, Ladislas
Harris, Julian La Rose
Hindus, Maurice Gerschon
Pearson, Drew
Smith, Albert Merriman

MUGRIDGE, DONALD H.
Newport, Christopher

MULDER, RONALD A.
Crosser, Robert
Scott, W(illiam) Kerr
Stigler, William Grady
Thompson, Malvina Cynthia

MULDER, WILLIAM
Thomas, Elbert Duncan

MULHOLLAND, JAMES A.
De Forest, Alfred Victor
Gillett, Horace Wadsworth

MULHOLLAND, JOHN
Goldin, Horace
Leipzig, Nate
Thurston, Howard

MULL, GEORGE FULMER
Apple, Thomas Gilmore
Bausman, Benjamin
Bomberger, John Henry Augustus
Rauch, Frederic Augustus
Rupp, William

MULLIGAN, WILLIAM H., JR.
Bushman, Francis Xavier
Carpenter, Walter Samuel, Jr.
Cavanagh, Jerome Patrick ("Jerry")
Gerber, Daniel Frank
Gibson, Edmund Richard ("Hoot")
Hart, Philip Aloysius
Marx, Adolf Arthur ("Harpo")
Marx, Leonard ("Chico")
Mott, Charles Stewart

MUMFORD, LEWIS
Behrendt, Walter Curt
Wright, Henry

MUNRO, DANA C.
Lea, Henry Charles

MUNRO, WILLIAM BENNETT
Eaton, Dorman Bridgman
Jenckes, Thomas Allen
Lodge, Henry Cabot

MUNROE, CHARLES E.
Dudley, Charles Benjamin

MURCHISON, CARL
Sanford, Edmund Clark

MURDOCK, EUGENE C.
Rolfe, Robert Abial ("Red")

MURDOCK, KENNETH BALLARD
Byles, Mather
Green, Joseph
Hildreth, Richard
Mather, Cotton
Mather, Increase
Mather, Richard

Mather, Samuel
Wigglesworth, Michael
Wilson, John
Wood, William
MURNAGHAN, F. D.
Morley, Frank
MURPHY, EARL FINBAR
Kephart, John William
MURPHY, JEANNE R.
Wightman, Hazel Virginia Hotchkiss
MURPHY, LAWRENCE R.
Watson, Charles Roger
MURPHY, PAUL L.
Devaney, John Patrick
MURPHY, ROBERT CUSHMAN
Stone, Witmer
MURRAY, CHARLES
Bemis, Harold Edward
MURRAY, J. FLORENCE
Searing, Laura Catherine Redden
MURRAY, ROBERT K.
Hanson, Ole
Palmer, Alexander Mitchell
MURRELL, WILLIAM
Briggs, Clare A.
Demuth, Charles
Opper, Frederick Burr
Smith, Robert Sidney
Zimmerman, Eugene
MURRIN, JOHN M.
Wertenbaker, Thomas Jefferson
MUSSER, PAUL H.
Barker, James Nelson
MUSSEY, H. R.
Barrows, Samuel June
MUZZEY, DAVID SAVILLE
Butler, Benjamin Franklin, 1795–1858
Butler, Charles
Butler, William Allen
Gallatin, Abraham Alfonse Albert
Morris, Gouverneur
MYCUE, DAVID JOHN
Moore, Anne Carroll
Vail, Robert William Glenroie
MYERS, GEORGE B.
Du Bose, William Porcher
MYERS, GEORGE S.
Eigenmann, Carl H.

NACHLAS, I. WILLIAM
Taylor, Robert Tunstall
NADWORNY, MILTON J.
Alford, Leon Pratt
NAGEL, ERNEST
Cohen, Morris Raphael
Lewis, Clarence Irving
NASH, EDWIN G.
Akers, Benjamin Paul
Amateis, Louis
Augur, Hezekiah
Bailly, Joseph Alexis
Ball, Thomas
Bartholomew, Edward Sheffield
Bissell, George Edwin
Calverley, Charles
Clarke, Thomas Shields
Clevenger, Shobal Vail
Cogdell, John Stevens
Connelly, Pierce Francis
Donaghue, John

NASH, FRANK
Brooks, George Washington
Graham, William Alexander
NASH, GERALD D.
Andrews, John Bertram
Epstein, Abraham
Sinclair, Harry Ford
NASH, RAY
Goudy, Frederic William
NASH, RODERICK
Leopold, (Rand) Aldo
McFarland, John Horace
NATHANS, ELIZABETH S.
Hatcher, Orie Latham
NAVIN, THOMAS R.
Straus, Roger W(illiams)
NAYLOR, NATALIE A.
Monroe, Paul
NEAL, DONN C.
Donovan, William Joseph
Munro, William Bennett
Reed, Daniel Alden
NEAL, NEVIN E.
Robinson, Joseph Taylor
NEAL, STEVE
Bingay, Malcolm Wallace
Bliss, George William
Bowen, Catherine Drinker
Braddock, James J.
Burpee, David
Byrd, Harry Flood
Cordon, Guy
Daley, Richard Joseph
Dilworth, Richardson
Driscoll, Alfred Eastlack
Eisenhower, Mamie Geneva Doud
Fischetti, John
Goldfine, Bernard
Hamilton, John Daniel Miller, II
Howe, Quincy
Ives, Irving McNeil
Kantor, MacKinlay
Lisagor, Peter Irvin
Martin, Joseph William, Jr.
Shaw, Lawrence Timothy ("Buck")
Sprague, Charles Arthur
Summersby, Kathleen Helen ("Kay")
Van Doren, Irita Bradford
West, Oswald
NEFF, FRANK HOWARD
Staley, Cady
NEIDLE, CECYLE S.
Lehman, Adele Lewisohn
NEILSON, WILLIAM ALLAN
Seelye, Laurenus Clark
Thorndike, Ashley Horace
NELLI, HUMBERT S.
Giovannitti, Arturo
NELSON, ALLAN
Crosby, Percy Lee
Eddy, Nelson
Highet, Gilbert
Keller, James Gregory
Kenny, John V.
Kirby, Allan Price
Luciano, Charles ("Lucky")
Madden, Owen Victor ("Owney")
McBride, Mary Margaret
Profaci, Joseph
Wolff, Kurt August Paul

NELSON, CLARK W.
Wilson, Louis Blanchard
NELSON, CLIFFORD M.
Wieland, George Reber
NELSON, DAVID HART
Allen, James Browning
NELSON, ELIZABETH R.
Ace, Jane
Beavers, Louise
Blondell, Joan
Dailey, Dan, Jr.
Dresser, Louise Kerlin
Farnum, Franklyn
Gish, Dorothy
Johnson, Harold Ogden ("Chic")
Joplin, Janis Lyn
Kane, Helen
Lynn, Diana ("Dolly")
Olsen, John Sigvard ("Ole")
Stout, Rex Todhunter
NELSON, JOHN HERBERT
Allen, James Lane
Baldwin, Joseph Glover
Page, Thomas Nelson
Thompson, William Tappan
NELSON, LOWRY
Ivins, Anthony Woodward
Roberts, Brigham Henry
Talmage, James Edward
NELSON, THOMAS K.
Packard, Joseph
NELSON, WALDO E.
Mitchell, Albert Graeme
NETTLES, H. EDWARD
Geyer, Henry Sheffie
Jackson, Claiborne Fox
Kerens, Richard C.
Lyon, Nathaniel
McClurg, Joseph Washington
McNair, Alexander
Marmaduke, John Sappington
Miller, John
Napton, William Barclay
Norton, Elijah Hise
Phelps, John Smith
Polk, Trusten
Price, Sterling
Stewart, Robert Marcellus
Stone, William Joel
Sweeny, Thomas William
Van Horn, Robert Thompson
Vest, George Graham
Warner, William
NEU, IRENE D.
Lilly, Josiah Kirby
Stuart, Elbridge Amos
NEUMAN, ABRAHAM A.
Adler, Cyrus
NEVINS, ALLAN
Ames, Oakes
Arthur, Timothy Shay
Bennett, James Gordon, 1795–1872
Bennett, James Gordon, 1841–1918
Bowles, Samuel, 1797–1851
Bowles, Samuel, 1826–1878
Bowles, Samuel, 1851–1915
Bristow, Benjamin Helm
Brooks, James
Bryant, William Cullen
Coolidge, Calvin
Cornell, Ezra
Dana, Charles Anderson

Dix, John Adams
Drew, Daniel
Fisk, James, 1834–1872
Ford, Paul Leicester
Franklin, Fabian
Frémont, John Charles
Gould, Jay
Greeley, Horace
Hamilton, Alexander, 1757–1804
Harding, Warren Gamaliel
Hayes, Rutherford Birchard
Hone, Philip
Johnson, Willis Fletcher
Leupp, Francis Ellington
Mellon, Andrew William
Nast, Thomas
Ogden, Rollo
Payne, Sereno Elisha
Platt, Thomas Collier
Reid, Whitelaw
Rockefeller, John Davison
Stevens, Thaddeus
Strunsky, Simeon
Tilton, Theodore
White, Henry, 1850–1927
Wilson, William Lyne

NEVIUS, BLAKE
Herrick, Robert Welch

NEWELL, FRANK W.
Jackson, Edward

NEWELL, LYMAN C.
Booth, James Curtis
Cooke, Josiah Parsons
Dana, James Freeman
Dana, Samuel Luther
Genth, Frederick Augustus
Gorham, John
Guthrie, Samuel
Hayes, Augustus Allen
Horsford, Eben Norton
Hunt, Thomas Sterry
James, Charles
Loeb, Morris
Mabery, Charles Frederic
Metcalfe, Samuel Lytler
Mitchill, Samuel Latham
Moore, Richard Bishop
Morfit, Campbell
Nichols, James Robinson
Peckham, Stephen Farnum
Phillips, Francis Clifford
Porter, John Addison
Power, Frederick Belding
Prescott, Albert Benjamin
Randall, Wyatt William
Rogers, Robert Empie

NEWHALL, BEAUMONT
Hine, Lewis Wickes
Jackson, William Henry

NEWLIN, CLAUDE M.
Brackenridge, Henry Marie
Brackenridge, Hugh Henry

NEWMAN, LOUIS I.
Gottheil, Richard James Horatio

NEWMAN, ROGER K.
Cahn, Edmond Nathaniel
Ernst, Morris Leopold
Sobeloff, Simon E.
Tweed, Harrison

NEWMAN, RONALD B.
Benchley, Robert Charles

NEWMARK, NATHAN M.
Westergaard, Harald Malcolm

NEWQUIST, ROY
Crawford, Joan

NEWSOME, A. R.
Henderson, Archibald
Jones, Allen
Locke, Matthew
Martin, Alexander
Martin, Josiah
Moore, Alfred
Moore, James, 1737–1777
Moore, Maurice
Nash, Abner
Nash, Francis
Nash, Frederick
Polk, Thomas
Sawyer, Lemuel
Sumner, Jethro
Taylor, John Louis
Waddell, Alfred Moore
Waddell, Hugh
Weeks, Stephen Beauregard

NEWTON, WESLEY PHILLIPS
Acosta, Bertram Blanchard ("Bert")
Henderson, Paul
Woolman, Collett Everman

NEYMAN, CLINTON ANDREW
Shreve, Thomas Hopkins

NICHOLS, CHARLES L.
Fowle, Daniel

NICHOLS, FRANKLIN T.
Stone, Samuel

NICHOLS, FREDERICK D.
Kimball, (Sidney) Fiske

NICHOLS, JEANNETTE P.
Allison, William Boyd
Dalzell, John
Dolliver, Jonathan Prentiss
Harvey, William Hope
Meigs, William Montgomery
Pittman, Key
Ritner, Joseph
Roberts, Jonathan
Sherman, John, 1823–1900
Thomas, George Clifford
Walker, Francis Amasa

NICHOLS, ROBERT H.
Cooper, Jacob
Curtis, Olin Alfred
Darling, Henry
Davis, Henry
Dennis, James Shepard
Donnell, Robert
Ewing, Finis
Green, Ashbel
Green, Jacob
Hatfield, Edwin Francis
Hodge, Archibald Alexander
Hodge, Charles
Lane, Horace M.
Lansing, Gulian
Lindsley, John Berrien
Lindsley, Philip
Loughridge, Robert McGill
Marquis, John Abner
Moffat, James Clement
Morgan, Edwin Barber
Nassau, Robert Hamill
Prime, Samuel Irenaeus
Roberts, William Henry
Smith, Henry Boynton
Spring, Gardiner
Sproull, Thomas
Stryker, Melancthon Woolsey
Taylor, Archibald Alexander Edward
Thomson, William McClure
Walker, James Barr
Warfield, Benjamin Breckinridge
Williston, Seth
Wood, James, 1799–1867
Yeomans, John William
Young, Samuel Hall

NICHOLS, ROY F.
Bigler, William
Black, Jeremiah Sullivan
Cambell, James
Dallas, George Mifflin
Forney, John Wien
Geary, John White
Gilpin, Henry Dilworth
Grow, Galusha Aaron
King, William Rufus Devane
McClelland, Robert
Meredith, William Morris
Oberholtzer, Ellis Paxson
Pierce, Benjamin
Pierce, Franklin
Reed, William Bradford
Sutherland, Joel Barlow
Tyson, Job Roberts
Welsh, John
Wilmot, David

NICOLSON, MARJORIE
Neilson, William Allan

NIEMCZYK, CAROLINE
Reid, Helen Miles Rogers

NIEMEYER, GLENN A.
Olds, Ransom Eli

NIEMTZOW, ANNETTE
Dawley, Almena
Hepburn, Katharine Houghton
Whitney, Charlotte Anita

NISBET, ROBERT
Teggart, Frederick John

NISSENBAUM, STEPHEN
Bond, Carrie Jacobs

NIXON, HERMAN C.
Gaut, John McReynolds
Robb, James
Robertson, Thomas Bolling
Roselius, Christian
Sage, Bernard Janin
Tulane, Paul
Villeré, Jacques Philippe
White, Edward Douglas
Wiltz, Louis Alfred

NOBLE, A. B.
Beardshear, William Miller
Welch, Adonijah Strong

NOBLE, CHARLES
Bacon, David
Bacon, Leonard Woolsey
Bangs, Nathan
Barnes, Albert
Bartlett, Samuel Colcord
Bates, Arlo
Baxter, William
Behrends, Adolphus Julius

NOBLE, FREDERICK PERRY
Whitworth, George Frederic

NOBLE, HAROLD J.
Dye, William McEntyre

Foulk, George Clayton
Greathouse, Clarence Ridgeby
Heard, Augustine
Jones, George Heber
Nolan, Hugh J.
Dougherty, Dennis Joseph
Nolan, J. Bennett
Otto, Bodo
Noland, Lowell E.
Juday, Chancey
Noland, Stephen
Hubbard, Frank McKinney
Noll, John F.
Dwenger, Joseph
Nollen, John Scholte
Edgren, August Hjalmar
Gates, George Augustus
Magoun, George Frederic
Scholte, Hendrik Peter
Norfleet, Fillmore
Saint-Mémin, Charles Balthazar
Norris, Joe L.
Niblack, William Ellis
Noble, James
Orth, Godlove Stein
Otto, William Tod
Norris, Walter B.
Dornin, Thomas Aloysius
Downer, Eliphalet
Ellery, Frank
Endicott, Mordecai Thomas
Entwistle, James
Jouett, James Edward
Kempff, Louis
Knight, Austin Melvin
Lee, Samuel Phillips
Lenthall, John
Livingston, John William
McCann, William Penn
McCauley, Edward Yorke
McDougal, David Stockton
McKean, William Wister
Palmer, James Shedden
Pillsbury, John Elliott
Norton, Elliot
Geddes, Norman Bel
Norton, Nancy P.
Knox, Rose Markward
Litchfield, Paul Weeks
Notz, William
List, Georg Friedrich
Noyes, Alexander D.
Harding, William Procter Gould
McCulloch, Hugh
Mills, Darius Ogden
Tappen, Frederick Dobbs
Warburg, Paul Moritz
Noyes, Clara D.
Delano, Jane Arninda
Noyes, Hermon M.
Niles, Samuel
Noyes, W. A.
Remsen, Ira
Smith, Alexander
Nugent, W. T. K.
Murdock, Victor
Numbers, Ronald L.
Price, George Edward McCready
Nute, Grace Lee
Dickson, Robert
Hall, Sherman
Pierz, Franz
Pond, Samuel William
Ravoux, Augustin
Riggs, Stephen Return
Taliaferro, Lawrence
Whipple, Henry Benjamin
Nutter, E. J. M.
Breck, James Lloyd
Nutting, Wallace
Goddard, John

Oates, Stephen B.
King, Martin Luther, Jr.
Oberholtzer, Ellis P.
Cooke, Jay
Harrison, Charles Custis
Morris, Robert, 1734–1806
O Brien, David J.
Dietz, Peter Ernest
O'Connell, William Henry
O'Brien, Frank M.
Beach, Moses Sperry
Beach, Moses Yale
Day, Benjamin Henry
Laffan, William Mackay
Locke, Richard Adams
O'Malley, Frank Ward
O'Connor, Raymond G.
Cone, Hutchinson Ingham
O'Daniel, V. F.
Connolly, John
Odell, George C. D.
Matthews, James Brander
Oesper, Ralph E.
Midgley, Thomas
Oestreich, Thomas
Haid, Leo
Offner, Arnold A.
Wilson, Hugh Robert
Ogden, Charles J.
Jackson, Abraham Valentine Williams
Ogden, Henry N.
Fuertes, Estevan Antonio
Ogden, Rollo
Godkin, Edwin Lawrence
Ogilby, Remsen B.
Brent, Charles Henry
O'Grady, John
Burke, John Joseph
Ohl, John Kennedy
Drum, Hugh Aloysius
Eddy, Manton Sprague
Hines, Frank Thomas
O'Callahan, Joseph Timothy
O'Donnell, Emmett, Jr. ("Rosy")
Rudkin, Margaret Fogarty
Theobald, Robert Alfred
Ohman, Lynne E.
Burns, Raymond Joseph
Rosebury, Theodor
O'Keefe, Kevin J.
Chapman, John Arthur
Daley, Arthur John
Grant, Jane Cole
Olby, Robert
Avery, Oswald Theodore
Campbell, Douglas Houghton
Jeffrey, Edward Charles
Olch, Peter D.
Elman, Robert
Graham, Evarts Ambrose
Olin, Reuel K.
McCracken, Joan
Olin, Spencer C., Jr.
Rowell, Chester Harvey
Oliphant, Herman
Mechem, Floyd Russell
Oliver, John Chadwick
Mussey, Reuben Dimond
Oliver, John Rathbone
Crawford, John
Jackson, Samuel
James, Thomas Chalkley
Jameson, Horatio Gates
Kerlin, Isaac Newton
Oliver, John W.
Black, James
Brown, William Hughey
Vauclain, Samuel Matthews
Olivier, Charles P.
Stone, Ormond
Olmsted, A. J.
Snelling, Henry Hunt
Olney, Louis A.
Matthews, Joseph Merritt
Olson, Frederick I.
Hoan, Daniel Webster
Seidel, George Lukas Emil
Ward, Harry Frederick
Olson, James C.
Rosewater, Victor
Olson, Kenneth E.
Shedd, Fred Fuller
O'Neal, Stephanie
Stouffer, Vernon Bigelow
O'Neill, William L.
Barth, Alan
Crosby, Harry Lillis ("Bing")
Eastman, Max Forrester
Getty, Jean Paul
Morgenthau, Hans Joachim
Thomas, Norman Mattoon
Utley, Freda
Wheeler, Burton Kendall
Onigman, Marc
Stuhldreher, Harry A.
Orrok, George A.
Hammer, William Joseph
Sargent, Frederick
Osborn, Henry Fairfield
Allen, Joel Asaph
Butler, Howard Crosby
Grant, Madison
Grinnell, George Bird
Hornaday, William Temple
Osborn, Norris Galpin
Bromley, Isaac Hill
Camp, Walter Chauncey
Osborne, James Harvey
Baldwin, Elihu Whittlesey
Osgood, Robert B.
Bradford, Edward Hickling
Lovett, Robert Williamson
Sayre, Lewis Albert
Sayre, Reginald Hall
Taylor, Charles Fayette
Osterhout, Winthrop J. V.
Loeb, Jacques
Ostrander, Gilman M.
McBride, F(rancis) Scott
O'Sullivan, John
Finletter, Thomas Knight
O'Sullivan, Vincent
Merrill, Stuart Fitz Randolph
Overholser, Winfred
White, William Alanson

OVERTON, RICHARD C.
Budd, Ralph
Holden, Hale
OWEN, DAVID EDWARD
Ferry, Orris Sanford
Gillette, Francis
OWEN, MARIE BANKHEAD
Bibb, William Wyatt
Brickell, Robert Coman
OWSLEY, FRANK LAWRENCE
Anderson, Joseph
Brown, Aaron Venable
Harney, William Selby
Harris, Isham Green
Helm, John Larue
Houk, Leonidas Campbell
Mann, Ambrose Dudley
Mason, James Murray
Williams, James
OXNAM, G. BROMLEY
McDowell, William Fraser

PACH, WALTER
Healy, George Peter Alexander
Hicks, John, 1823–1890
Hovenden, Thomas
PACHTER, MARC
De Wolfe, Elsie
Smith, Lloyd Logan Pearsall
Stearns, Harold Edmund
PACKARD, FRANCIS RANDOLPH
Allen, Harrison
Ashhurst, John
Atkinson, William Biddle
Bartholow, Roberts
Bond, Thomas
Bridges, Robert, 1806–1882
Burnett, Charles Henry
Cadwalader, Thomas
Carson, Joseph
Chapman, Henry Cadwalader
Chovet, Abraham
Coakley, Cornelius Godfrey
Coxe, John Redman
Keen, William Williams
Knight, Frederick Irving
Kyle, David Braden
Mayer, Emil
Parrish, Joseph
Pascalis-Ouvrière, Felix
Randall, Burton Alexander
Sajous, Charles Euchariste De Médicis
Sargent, Fitzwilliam
Say, Benjamin
Seiler, Carl
Shippen, William
Skillern, Ross Hall
Tyson, James
Wistar, Caspar
PACKARD, HYLAND
Hackett, Francis
PACKARD, LAURENCE B.
Perkins, James Breck
PAGE, LEIGH
Bumstead, Henry Andrews
Nichols, Ernest Fox
PAHLOW, EDWIN WILLIAM
Brodhead, John Romeyn
PAINTER, PATRICIA
Brady, Mildred Alice Edie
PAINTER, PATRICIA SCOLLARD
Chapelle, Dickey
Nesbit, Evelyn Florence
PALLISTER, JOHN C.
Lutz, Frank Eugene
PALMER, CATHERINE W.
Ferguson, William Jason
Forbes, Edwin
Foster, Stephen Collins
Fowler, Frank
PALMER, FREDERICK
Bliss, Tasker Howard
PALMER, HENRY R.
Colt, Le Baron Bradford
PALMER, JOHN MCAULEY
Steuben, Friedrich Wilhelm Ludolf Gerhard Augustin, Baron von
PALMER, MILDRED B.
Earle, Ralph
Godbe, William Samuel
Hill, Robert Andrews
Kimball, Heber Chase
Pratt, Parley Parker
Smiley, Albert Keith
PALMER, PATRICIA
Hawks, Howard Winchester
Maxwell, Marvel Marilyn
PALMER, THEODORE SHERMAN
Buckley, Samuel Botsford
PALTSITS, VICTOR HUGO
Allibone, Samuel Austin
Bradford, William, 1663–1752
Bradford, William, 1721/22–1791
Duyckinck, Evert Augustus
Duyckinck, George Long
Fleet, Thomas
Foster, John
Gaine, Hugh
Goddard, William
Green, Jonas
Greenleaf, Thomas
Holt, John
Hudson, Henry
Lovelace, Francis
Mecom, Benjamin
Parker, James
Rivington, James
Robertson, James, b. 1740
Stuyvesant, Petrus
PANCOAST, HENRY K.
Leonard, Charles Lester
PAPADEMETRIOU, PETER C.
Saarinen, Eero
PAPENFUSS, GEORGE F.
Setchell, William Albert
PARADISE, SCOTT H.
Fowle, William Bentley
Gardiner, John Sylvester John
Gilman, Caroline Howard
Gilman, Samuel
Morton, Marcus, 1784–1864
Peabody, George
Taylor, Samuel Harvey
PARCEL, JOHN I.
Flather, John Joseph
McAlpine, William Jarvis
McDonald, John Bartholomew
Morison, George Shattuck
Okerson, John Augustus
Pratt, Thomas Willis
Smith, Charles Shaler
Smith, William Sooy
Sooysmith, Charles
PARE, GEORGE W.
Lefevere, Peter Paul
PARET, J. PARMLY
Larned, William Augustus
PARGELLIS, STANLEY M.
Abercromby, James
Bouquet, Henry
Braddock, Edward
Bradstreet, John
Forbes, John, 1710–1759
Howe, George Augustus, Viscount
Leisler, Jacob
Loudoun, John Campbell, Earl of
Lyman, Phineas
Mackellar, Patrick
Meserve, Nathaniel
Monckton, Robert
Montrésor, James Gabriel
Montrésor, John
Morris, Roger
Reynolds, John, 1713–1788
Rogers, Robert
Shaw, Nathaniel
Webb, Daniel
Winslow, John
Wolcott, Oliver, 1726–1797
Wolcott, Roger
Wooster, David
Yale, Elihu
PARISH, JOHN C.
Dodge, Augustus Caesar
Dodge, Henry
Lucas, Robert
Lummis, Charles Fletcher
O'Fallon, James
PARK, EDWARDS A.
Holt, Luther Emmett
Howland, John
PARK, FRANCES FENTON
Lockwood, Belva Ann Bennett
PARK, JULIAN
Putnam, James Osborne
PARK, STEPHEN A.
Liggett, Hunter
PARK, THOMAS
Pearl, Raymond
PARKER, ARTHUR C.
Skaniadariio
PARKER, CHARLES W.
Nixon, John Thompson
Pennington, William Sandford
Rellstab, John
PARKER, FRANKLIN
Blaine, Anita (Eugenie) McCormick
Chase, Harry Woodburn
Locke, Bessie
PARKER, GAIL THAIN
Blackwell, Alice Stone
PARKER, JAMES REID
Hokinson, Helen Elna
PARKER, WILLIAM BELMONT
Aldrich, Thomas Bailey
Andrew, John Albion
Anthony, Henry Bowen
Cooper, Edward
Cooper, Peter
Curtin, Andrew Gregg

Hewitt, Abram Stevens
Hewitt, Peter Cooper
PARKES, HENRY B.
Harris, Thaddeus Mason
Marsh, James
Merrill, Daniel
Mills, Samuel John
Nason, Elias
Norris, Edward
Osgood, Jacob
Rogers, John, 1648–1721
Seccomb, John
Stoddard, Solomon
PARKMAN, FRANCIS
Menéndez De Avilés, Pedro
PARKS, EDD WINFIELD
Stearns, Eben Sperry
Webb, William Robert
Winchester, James
Zollicoffer, Felix Kirk
PARKS, GARY
De Cuevas, Marquis
PARMELEE, JULIUS H.
Bernet, John Joseph
Fink, Albert
Hines, Walker Downer
Messler, Thomas Doremus
Poor, Henry Varnum
Poor, John Alfred
PARMENTER, CLARENCE E.
Dargan, Edwin Preston
PARMET, HERBERT S.
McKay, (James) Douglas
PAROT, JOSEPH J.
Hodur, Francis
PARRIS, LAROSE
Boyle, Harold Vincent ("Hal")
Muse, Clarence
Yergan, Max
PARRY, ELLWOOD C., III
Leyendecker, Joseph Christian
Sheeler, Charles R., Jr.
Weston, Edward Henry
PARRY, JOHN JAY
Morgan, Abel
Pugh, Ellis
PARSHLEY, HOWARD M.
Wilder, Harris Hawthorne
PARSONS, EDWARD L.
Kip, William Ingraham
Nichols, William Ford
PARSONS, GEOFFREY
Hammond, Percy Hunter
PASCHALL, CLARENCE
Schilling, Hugo Karl
PASCHALL, JOHN
Cohen, John Sanford
PASSER, HAROLD C.
Thomson, Elihu
Weston, Edward
PATERSON, THOMAS G.
Gauss, Clarence Edward
PATTEE, FRED LEWIS
Atherton, George Washington
Burnett, Francis Eliza Hodgson
Cable, George Washington
Crawford, Francis Marion
Davis, Rebecca Blaine Harding
Davis, Richard Harding
Freneau, Philip Morin
Pugh, Evan
PATTEN, WILLIAM
Wales, James Albert
Yohn, Frederick Coffay
PATTERSON, GEORGE W.
Guthe, Karl Eugen
PATTERSON, JAMES T.
Taft, Robert Alphonso
PATTERSON, MERRILL R.
Fairfield, Sumner Lincoln
PATTERSON, S. HOWARD
Macfarlane, Charles William
PATTON, JAMES W.
Jasper, William
Magrath, Andrew Gordon
Manigault, Arthur Middleton
Nott, Abraham
O'Neall, John Belton
Williams, David Rogerson
PATTTON, W. KENNETH
Stitt, Edward Rhodes
PAUL, JOHN R.
Trask, James Dowling
PAUL, RODMAN W.
Fleming, Arthur Henry
PAULING, LINUS
Lewis, Gilbert Newton
Noyes, Arthur Amos
PAULLIN, CHARLES OSCAR
Baldwin, Evelyn Briggs
Benson, William Shepherd
Black, William Murray
Boucher, Horace Edward
Brownson, Willard Herbert
Brush, Charles Francis
Burroughs, William Seward
Capps, Washington Lee
Caraway, Thaddeus Horatius
Carter, John, 1737–1781
Carter, Landon
Carter, Robert
Carter, Samuel Powhatan
Chadwick, French Ensor
Chauncey, Isaac
Conyngham, Gustavus
Craven, Thomas Tingey
Craven, Tunis Augustus MacDonough
Curtiss, Glenn Hammond
Cutting, Bronson Murray
Dale, Richard
Davison, Gregory Caldwell
De Haven, Edwin Tesse
Dellenbaugh, Frederick Samuel
Downes, John
Drayton, Percival
Duncan, James
Du Pont, Samuel Francis
Edwards, Clarence Ransom
Elliott, Jesse Duncan
Emerson, Benjamin Kendall
Emmons, George Foster
Farragut, David Glasgow
Farragut, George
Frost, Holloway Halstead
Gherardi, Bancroft
Greene, Samuel Dana
Greer, James Augustin
Hurley, Edward Nash
Jones, John Paul
Kuhn, Joseph Ernst
Landais, Pierre
Lawrence, James
Legge, Alexander
Little, George
Lull, Edward Phelps
McCall, Edward Rutledge
McCauley, Charles Stewart
MacDonough, Thomas
MacKenzie, Alexander Slidell
Maclay, Edgar Stanton
Manley, John
Marchand, John Bonnett
Melville, George Wallace
Mervine, William
Michler, Nathaniel
Mills, Enos Abijah
Minnigerode, Lucy
Moore, Edwin Ward
Mullany, James Robert Madison
Murray, Alexander
Nicholson, James
Nicholson, James William Augustus
Nicholson, Samuel
O'Brien, Jeremiah
O'Shaughnessy, Michael Maurice
Peabody, Cecil Hobart
Perry, Christopher Raymond
Perry, Matthew Calbraith
Perry, Oliver Hazard
Piez, Charles
Porter, David
Porter, David Dixon
Rainey, Henry Thomas
Raymond, Harry Howard
Rodgers, Christopher Raymond Perry
Rodgers, George Washington, 1787–1832
Rodgers, George Washington, 1822–1863
Rodgers, John, 1773–1838
Rodgers, John, 1812–1882
Scott, Hugh Lenox
Sloat, John Drake
Smith, Joseph, 1790–1877
Stockton, Charles Herbert
Stockton, Robert Field
Talbot, Silas
Tarbell, Joseph
Tattnall, Josiah
Thatcher, Henry Knox
Thompson, Robert Means
Tucker, Samuel
Turner, Daniel
Tyng, Edward
Wagener, John Andreas
Wainwright, Jonathan Mayhew, 1821–1863
Wainwright, Richard, 1817–1862
Wainwright, Richard, 1849–1926
Warrington, Lewis
Whipple, Abraham
Wilkes, Charles
Williams, John Foster
Woolsey, Melancthon Taylor
Zeilin, Jacob
PAXSON, FREDERICK LOGAN
Alger, Russell Alexander
Altgelt, John Peter
Arthur, Chester Alan
Babcock, Joseph Weeks
Ballinger, Richard Achilles

Barnum, Phineas Taylor
Barstow, William Augustus
Bashford, Coles
Bissell, Wilson Shannon
Brewster, Benjamin Harris
Chandler, William Eaton
Cleveland, Stephen Grover
Conkling, Roscoe
Denby, Edwin
Fair, James Graham
Fairchild, Charles Stebbins
Fairchild, Lucius
Fisk, Clinton Bowen
Flower, Roswell Pettibone
Funston, Frederick
Garfield, James Abram
Grant, Ulysses Simpson
Hazen, William Babcock
Ingersoll, Robert Green
Kohlstaat, Herman Henry
La Follette, Robert Marion
Lamont, Daniel Scott
Lincoln, Robert Todd
Logan, John Alexander
McKinley, William
Morton, Levi Parsons
Morton, Paul
Roosevelt, Theodore
Sawyer, Philetus
Spaulding, Elbridge Gerry
Spooner, John Coit
Stephenson, Isaac
Turner, Frederick Jackson
Vilas, William Freeman
Whitney, William Collins
PAYNE, CECILIA H.
King, Edward Skinner
PAYNE, CHARLES E.
Grinnell, Josiah Bushnell
Jones, George Wallace
Lacey, John Fletcher
Lowe, Ralph Phillips
McCrary, George Washington
McDill, James Wilson
Macy, Jesse
Main, John Hanson Thomas
PEABODY, ROBERT E.
Derby, Elias Hasket, 1739–1799
Derby, Richard
PEARCE, HAYWOOD J., JR.
Hill, Benjamin Harvey
Iverson, Alfred
Jenkins, Charles Jones
Lamar, Lucius Quintus Cincinnatus
Lumpkin, Wilson
McIntosh, William
PEARCE, KATHARINE S.
Patrick, Mary Mills
PEARCE, WILLIAM M.
Mackenzie, Murdo
PEARSON, C. C.
Abbott, Joseph Carter
Biggs, Asa
Bragg, Thomas
Bridgers, Robert Rufus
Brown, Bedford
Carlile, John Snyder
Carr, Elias
Clark, Walter
Cox, William Ruffin
Daniel, John Warwick
Davie, William Richardson
Davis, George
Dudley, Edward Bishop
Hoke, Robert Frederick
Holmes, Theophilus Hunter
Hughes, Robert William
Hunter, Eppa
Jones, Samuel Porter
Kemper, James Lawson
Kitchin, William Walton
Lee, James Wideman
Lewis, John Francis
Mahone, William
Massey, John Edward
Minor, Lucian
Ritchie, Thomas
Roane, Spencer
Ross, Martin
Ruffner, Henry
Ruffner, William Henry
Wait, Samuel
Walker, Gilbert Carlton
PEARSON, EDMUND L.
Jenks, George Charles
Webster, John White
PEARSON, HENRY G.
Boutwell, George Sewall
Everett, Alexander Hill
Everett, Edward
Forbes, John Murray, 1813–1898
McElwaine, William Howe
Tudor, Frederic
PEARSON, NORMAN HOLMES
Wright, Robert William
PEARY, GERALD
Anderson, Edward ("Eddie")
Walsh, Raoul
PEASE, ARTHUR STANLEY
Smyth, Herbert Weir
PEASE, THEODORE CALVIN
Allen, William Joshua
Arnold, Isaac Newton
Browning, Orville Hickman
Edwards, Ninian Wirt
Farnsworth, John Franklin
Farwell, Charles Benjamin
Ford, Thomas
Hardin, John J.
Herndon, William Henry
Hitt, Robert Roberts
Hurlbut, Stephen Augustus
Peck, John Mason
Raum, Green Berry
PEATMAN, JOHN G.
Murphy, Gardner
PEATTIE, DONALD CULROSS
Agassiz, Alexander
Agassiz, Elizabeth Cabot Cary
Atkinson, George Francis
Audubon, John James
Bachman, John
Barnes, Charles Reid
Barton, William Paul Crillon
Bartram, John
Beal, William James
Bessey, Charles Edwin
Bigelow, Jacob
Brackenridge, William D.
Brainerd, Ezra
Brandegee, Townshend Stith
Bull, Ephraim Wales
Burrell, Thomas Jonathan
Chapman, Alvan Wentworth
Chapman, John
Clayton, John
Collins, Frank Shipley
Curtis, Moses Ashley
Darlington, William
Farlow, William Gilson
Garden, Alexander
PECK, EPAPHRODITUS
Dunbar, Moses
PECK, LILLIE M.
Wald, Lillian D.
PECK, MORTON E.
Luelling, Henderson
PEDDLE, JOHN B.
Rose, Chauncey
PEEBLES, BERNARD M.
Rand, Edward Kennard
PEELING, JAMES H.
Gregg, Andrew
Hamilton, James, *c.* 1710–1783
Hand, Edward
Harris, John
Hartley, Thomas
Hazelwood, John
Hemphill, Joseph
Hiester, Daniel
Hiester, Joseph
Irvine, James
Kinsey, John
Lacock, Abner
Leib, Michael
Levin, Lewis Charles
Lowrie, Walter
McKean, Joseph Borden
McKean, Samuel
McKean, Thomas
Marshall, Christopher
Mifflin, Thomas
Moore, William, 1735–1793
Morgan, John
Peters, Richard, *c.* 1704–1776
Peters, Richard, 1744–1828
Pettit, Charles
Pettit, Thomas McKean
Porter, Andrew
Potter, James
Read, George
Roberdeau, Daniel
Ross, George
Ross, James
Salomon, Haym
Smith, James, 1719–1806
Smith, Jonathan Bayard
Snyder, Simon
Tilghman, Edward
Tilghman, William
Tod, John
Van Dyke, Nicholas, 1738–1789
Van Dyke, Nicholas, 1770–1826
Walker, Jonathan Hoge
Wharton, Thomas
Whitehill, Robert
Yeates, Jasper
PEERS, SUSIE M.
Evermann, Barton Warren
PEIRCE, GEORGE J.
Goodale, George Lincoln
PELLS, RICHARD H.
Agee, James Rufus
PENDERGRASS, EUGENE P.
Pancoast, Henry Khunrath
PENICK, JAMES, JR.
Pinchot, Gifford
Smith, George Otis

PENKOWER, MONTY N.
Flanagan, Hallie
PENNIMAN, JOSIAH H.
Pepper, William
PENNINGTON, EDGAR LEGARE
Forbes, John, d. 1783
PENZL, HERBERT
Prokosch, Eduard
PERKIN, ROBERT L.
Penrose, Spencer
PERKINS, DEXTER
Gillet, Ransom Hooker
Granger, Francis
Greenleaf, Halbert Stevens
Hill, David Jayne
Johnston, Robert Matteson
Kasson, John Adam
Monroe, James
Rochester, Nathaniel
Rush, Richard
Seward, Frederick William
Seward, William Henry
Sibley, Hiram
PERKINS, EDWIN J.
Merrill, Charles Edward
PERKINS, ERNEST RALPH
Wharton, Francis
PERKINS, FRANCIS D.
Bodanzky, Artur
Gilman, Lawrence
Schumann-Heink, Ernestine
PERKINS, HENRY F.
Thompson, Zadock
PERLMAN, MARK
Slichter, Sumner Huber
PERRI, MARY ELLEN SWEENEY
Gibbons, Euell
O'Neill, C. William ("Bill")
PERRY, ANNA B.
Campbell, John Wood, Jr.
Keating, Kenneth Barnard
McGrath, James Howard
Smith, Harry Allen
PERRY, CHARNER
Mead, George Herbert
PERRY, EDWARD DELAVAN
Wheeler, James Rignall
Whitehouse, Frederick
PERRY, HELEN SWICK
Sullivan, Harry Stack
PERRY, HOBART S.
Converse, John Heman
Cramp, Charles Henry
Cramp, William
Parry, Charles Thomas
Pearse, John Barnard Swett
Thomas, David
Towne, John Henry
Waln, Robert, 1765–1836
Wharton, Joseph
Widener, Peter Arrell Brown
PERRY, LAWRENCE
Haughton, Percy Duncan
PERRY, RALPH BARTON
Eliot, Charles William
James, Henry, 1811–1882
James, William
Royce, Josiah
Woods, James Haughton
PERSHEY, EDWARD
Booth, Albert James, Jr. ("Albie")
PERSHING, BENJAMIN H.
Cowan, Edgar
Sargent, Winthrop, 1753–1820
PERSONS, CHARLES E.
Hyde, Henry Baldwin
Park, Trenor William
Phillips, Thomas Wharton
Post, Charles William
PERSONS, FREDERICK TORREL
Adams, Nehemiah
Adams, William
Barton, William Eleazar
Benjamin, Nathan
Berg, Joseph Frederic
Bethune, George Washington
Bidwell, Walter Hilliard
Blakeslee, Erastus
Brady, John Green
Brownlee, William Craig
Burton, Asa
Chamberlain, Jacob
Chapin, Calvin
Cheever, George Barrell
Child, Frank Samuel
Clark, Joseph Sylvester
Cobb, William Henry
Coleman, Leighton
Coleman, Lyman
Collyer, Robert
Conant, Hannah O'Brien Chaplin
Conant, Thomas Jefferson
Conwell, Russell Herman
Cooper, Samuel
Corby, William
Dean, Sidney
Dempster, John
Dewey, Orville
Doane, William Croswell
Dorchester, Daniel
Doty, Elihu
Dunning, Albert Elijah
Everett, Charles Carroll
Fleming, John, 1807–1894
Follett, Mary Parker
Freeman, James
Furness, William Henry
Good, Adolphus Clemens
Goodrich, Chauncey
Hallett, Benjamin
Hiacoomes
Hogue, Wilson Thomas
Jackson, Edward Payson
Jenks, William
Jones, Abner
Lawrance, Uriah Marion
McClure, Alexander Wilson
Newcomb, Harvey
North, Frank Mason
Noyes, George Rapall
Paine, Robert Treat
Parkhurst, Charles
Peloubet, Francis Nathan
Perkins, Justin
Peters, Absalom
Pond, Enoch
Poor, Daniel
Purnell, Benjamin
Rice, Edwin Wilbur
Richards, Charles Herbert
Ripley, Ezra
Ross, Abel Hastings
Sawyer, Leicester Ambrose
Schauffler, Henry Albert
Scudder, John
Shedd, William Ambrose
Smith, Elias
Smyth, Egbert Coffin
Spring, Samuel
Steele, Daniel
Sunday, William Ashley
Talcott, Eliza
Todd, John
Tracy, Joseph
Whiton, James Morris
Williams, William R.
Williston, Samuel
Woods, Leonard, 1774–1854
PETERS, JAMES A.
Stejneger, Leonhard Hess
PETERS, JEAN
Melcher, Frederic Gershom
PETERSEN, PETER L.
Henie, Sonja
Jensen, Benton Franklin ("Ben")
Jones, John Marvin
Reynolds, Quentin James
PETERSON, A. EVERETT
Aikens, Andrew Jackson
Alvord, Corydon Alexis
Appleton, Daniel
Appleton, William Henry
Appleton, William Worthen
Armstrong, Samuel Turell
Baker, Peter Carpenter
Bartlett, John Sherren
Bayard, Nicholas
Bayard, Samuel
Bell, Robert
Bladen, William
Brewster, Osmyn
Chester, Joseph Lemuel
Cochran, John
Corwin, Edward Tanjore
Crocker, Uriel
Cruger, Henry
De Peyster, Abraham
De Peyster, John Watts
Folsom, George
Francis, Charles Stephen
Fraunces, Samuel
Frissell, Hollis Burke
Gowans, William
Graham, James
Grim, David
Harper, Fletcher
Harper, James
Herring, James
Homes, Henry Augustus
Hooker, William
Hunt, Freeman
Imbert, Antoine
Inglis, Charles
Jay, John
Jay, William
Johnston, Henry Phelps
Johnston, John Taylor
Joline, Adrian Hoffman
Jones, Thomas
Kearny, Philip
Lamb, Martha Joanna Reade Nash
Le Roux, Bartholomew
Le Roux, Charles
Leslie, Frank

Leslie, Miriam Florence Folline
Loudon, Samuel
Ludlow, Daniel
O'Callaghan, Edmund Bailey
Osborn, Selleck
Pennington, James W. C.
Stanford, John
PETERSON, BARBARA BENNETT
Grable, Betty
PETERSON, F. ROSS
Chavez, Dennis
Clyde, George Dewey
Hatch, Carl A.
Krug, Julius Albert
Morse, Wayne Lyman
Watkins, Arthur Vivian
Welker, Herman
PETERSON, HAROLD F.
Weddell, Alexander Wilbourne
PETERSON, HENRY J.
Hoyt, John Wesley
Warren, Francis Emroy
PETERSON, ROBERT
Gibson, Joshua
PETERSON, THEODORE
Lane, Gertrude Battles
PETTIJOHN, FRANCIS J.
Lawson, Andrew Cowper
PFAFF, CAROLINE S.
Shreve, Henry Miller
PFEFFERKORN, BLANCHE
Noyes, Clara Dutton
PFEIFFER, ROBERT H.
Lyon, David Gordon
Mitchell, Hinckley Gilbert Thomas
PHALEN, JAMES M.
Agramonte Y Simoni, Aristides
Ainsworth, Frederick Crayton
Allison, Nathaniel
Allison, Richard
Ashford, Bailey Kelly
Barnes, Joseph K.
Bernays, Augustus Charles
Billings, Frank
Brainard, Daniel
Brown, Samuel
Bruce, Archibald
Byford, William Heath
Carroll, James
Carter, Henry Rose
Cooper, Elias Samuel
Davis, Nathan Smith
Dennis, Frederic Shepard
Emerson, Gouverneur
Engelmann, George Julius
Eve, Paul Fitzsimons
Faget, Jean Charles
Favill, Henry Baird
Fenger, Christian
Ferguson, Alexander Hugh
Finlay, Carlos Juan
Fletcher, Robert
Fletcher, William Baldwin
Forwood, William Henry
Garrison, Fielding Hudson
Goldberger, Joseph
Gorgas, William Crawford
Gradle, Henry
Guild, La Fayette
Guiteras, Juan
Hammond, William Alexander
Henrotin, Fernand
Holmes, Bayard Taylor
Husk, Charles Ellsworth
Hyde, James Nevins
Ingals, Ephraim Fletcher
Johnston, George Ben
Jones, Joseph
Kilty, William
King, Albert Freeman Africanus
Kinloch, Robert Alexander
Lane, Levi Cooper
Lawson, Leonidas Menon
Lazear, Jesse William
Letterman, Jonathan
Linde, Christian
Logan, Thomas Muldrup, 1808–1876
Lydston, George Frank
Lyster, Henry Francis Le Hunte
McCormack, Joseph Nathaniel
McCreery, Charles
Manson, Otis Frederick
Martin, Franklin Henry
Mastin, Claudius Henry
Maxwell, George Troup
Merrill, James Cushing
Miller, Henry
Morrow, Thomas Vaughan
Murphy, John Benjamin
Nancrède, Charles Beylard Guérard de
Newton, Robert Safford
Ochsner, Albert John
O'Reilly, Robert Maitland
Palmer, Daniel David
Pilcher, Lewis Stephen
Pitcher, Zina
Powell, William Byrd
Quine, William Edward
Reed, Walter
Robinson, Frederick Byron
Rockwell, Alfonso David
Sachs, Theodore Bernard
Salisbury, James Henry
Salmon, Daniel Elmer
Satterlee, Richard Sherwood
Schadle, Jacob Evans
Scudder, John Milton
Semmes, Alexander Jenkins
Senn, Nicholas
Smith, James McCune
Smith, Theobald
Speir, Samuel Fleet
Spitzka, Edward Anthony
Spitzka, Edward Charles
Steiner, Lewis Henry
Stephenson, Benjamin Franklin
Sternberg, George Miller
Stockton, Charles G.
Stone, Richard French
Terry, Marshall Orlando
Tilton, James
Toner, Joseph Meredith
Vance, Ap Morgan
Van Hook, Weller
Von Ruck, Karl
Ward, Richard Halsted
Weil, Richard
Wickes, Stephen
Wilbur, Hervey Backus
Williams, David Hale
Williams, Elkanah
Wood, James Rushmore
Wood, Thomas
Woodhull, Alfred Alexander
Woodruff, Charles Edward
Woodward, Joseph Janvier
Wright, Hamilton Kemp
Wright, Joseph Jefferson Burr
Yandell, David Wendell
Yandell, Lunsford Pitts
PHELPS, ISAAC KING
Frear, William
PHELPS, ORME W.
Millis, Harry Alvin
PHELPS, REGINALD H.
Conant, James Bryant
Fay, Sidney Bradshaw
Jones, Howard Mumford
PHILBRICK, FRANCIS SAMUEL
Blodgett, Henry Williams
Boutell, Henry Sherman
Bowers, Lloyd Wheaton
Buchanan, William Insco
Cullom, Shelby Moore
Dickinson, Jacob McGavock
Fry, James Barnet
Fuller, Melville Weston
Hall, John Elihu
Harding, George
Hare, John Innes Clark
Hoffman, David
Lockwood, Samuel Drake
McClain, Emlin
McKenna, Joseph
Pennypacker, Samuel Whitaker
Read, John Meredith, 1797–1874
Sharswood, George
Shiras, George
Strong, William
Wallace, John William
PHILBRICK, NORMAN
Bates, Blanche
PHILIPSON, DAVID
Berkowitz, Henry
Blaustein, David
Deutsch, Gotthard
Gratz, Barnard
Gratz, Michael
Gratz, Rebecca
Lilienthal, Max
Neumark, David
Wice, Isaac Mayer
PHILLIPS, CLIFTON J.
Luce, Henry Winters
McFarland, George Bradley
PHILLIPS, J. O. C.
Stoddard, Theodore Lothrop
PHILLIPS, LOUIS
Bishop, Elizabeth
Dean, Jay Hanna ("Dizzy")
Ford, John
Harris, Jed
Hitchcock, Alfred Joseph
PHILLIPS, PAUL CHRISLER
Brantley, Theodore
Carter, Thomas Henry
Clark, William Andrews
Craighead, Edwin Boone
Daly, Marcus
De Lacy, Walter Washington
Edgerton, Sidney
Gibson, Paris
Hamilton, William Thomas, 1822–1908
Haskell, Ella Louise Knowles

Hauser, Samuel Thomas
Heinze, Frederick Augustus
Maginnis, Martin
Mullan, John
Nelson, John
Potts, Benjamin Franklin
Sanders, Wilbur Fisk
Toole, Edwin Warren
Toole, Joseph Kemp
Wade, Dennis Spear
PHILLIPS, PAUL CHRYSOSTOM
Hitchcock, Edward, 1828–1911
PHILLIPS, ROBERT
Geismar, Maxwell David
Schwartz, Delmore David
Wheelock, John Hall
PHILLIPS, ULRICH BONNELL
Calhoun, John Caldwell
Crawford, William Harris
Hayne, Robert Young
Stephens, Alexander Hamilton
Toombs, Robert Augustus
PHILP, KENNETH R.
Collier, John
PICKEN, ROBERT A.
Guthrie, Ramon
PICKENS, DONALD K.
Johnson, Osa
PIEHL, CHARLES K.
Hodges, Luther Hartwell
PIERCE, BESSIE LOUISE
Cermak, Anton Joseph
PIERSOL, GEORGE MORRIS
Kelly, Aloysius Oliver Joseph
PIERSON, WILLIAM WHATLEY, JR.
Branch, John
Branch, Lawrence O'Bryan
Burton, Hutchins Gordon
PILCHER, LEWIS FREDERICK
Caffin, Charles Henry
Cook, Walter
Cummings, Charles Amos
PILSBRY, HENRY AUGUSTUS
Adams, Charles Baker
Anthony, John Gould
Binney, Amos
Brooks, William Keith
PINCKNEY, JOSEPHINE
Heyward, DuBose
PINKETT, HAROLD T.
Baker, Hugh Potter
Carver, George Washington
Drury, Newton Bishop
Fly, James Lawrence
Gabrielson, Ira Noel
MacKaye, Benton
Spottswood, Stephen Gill
Zahniser, Howard Clinton
PIPES, NELLIE B.
Isom, Mary Frances
PITKIN, HARVEY
Kroeber, Alfred Louis
PITMAN, FRANK W.
Bourne, Edward Gaylord
PLACZEK, ADOLF K.
Hamlin, Talbot Faulkner
PLEADWELL, FRANK L.
Pinkney, Ninian
PLEASANTS, J. HALL
Hesselius, Gustavus
Hesselius, John
Wilmer, James Jones
PLUMB, CHARLES S.
Renick, Felix
Sanders, James Harvey
PLUMMER, W. C.
Gowen, Franklin Benjamin
POFFENBERGER, A. T.
Hollingworth, Leta Stetter
POGEL, NANCY
Fitzpatrick, Daniel Robert
POGUE, FORREST C.
Marshall, George Catlett, Jr.
POLENBERG, RICHARD
Smith, Harold Dewey
POLLARD, JOHN A.
Alsop, Richard
Brainard, John Gardiner Calkins
Warner, Charles Dudley
POLLEY, MICHAEL J.
Vincent, John Carter
POLLOCK, JAMES K.
Quay, Matthew Stanley
POLLOCK, LEWIS J.
Patrick, Hugh Talbot
POMEROY, EARL
Bourne, Jonathan
McNary, Charles Linza
POMFRET, JOHN E.
Carnahan, James
Davies, Samuel
Dickinson, Jonathan
Smith, Samuel Stanhope
Witherspoon, John
Woodrow, James
Woolman, John
POOL, DAVID DE SOLA
Ehrlich, Arnold Bogumil
Einhorn, David
Felsenthal, Bernhard
Friedlaender, Israel
Gottheil, Gustav
Harris, Maurice Henry
Isaacs, Abram Samuel
Isaacs, Samuel Myer
Jastrow, Marcus
Kaiser, Alois
Kalisch, Isador
Kalisch, Samuel
Kohler, Kaufmann
Kohut, Alexander
Krauskopf, Joseph
Levy, Joseph Leonard
Mendes, Frederic de Sola
Mosessohn, David Nehemiah
Nordheimer, Isaac
Raphall, Morris Jacob
Sandler, Jacob Koppel
Schindler, Solomon
Silverman, Joseph
Solomons, Adolphus Simeon
Stark, Edward Josef
Straus, Isador
Straus, Nathan
Szold, Benjamin
Voorsanger, Jacob
Wise, Aaron
POOL, D. DE SOLA
Enelow, Hyman Gerson
Hirschensohn, Chaim
Kohut, George Alexander
Mendes, Henry Pereira
POOR, JOHN M.
Lundin, Carl Axel Robert
Paul, Henry Martyn
Safford, Truman Henry
Swift, Lewis
Tuttle, Charles Wesley
POPE, ARTHUR
Moore, Charles Herbert
POPE, CLIFFORD H.
Ditmars, Raymond Lee
Noble, Gladwyn Kingsley
POPE, DANIEL A.
Durstine, Roy Sarles
Resor, Stanley Burnet
POPE, JENNIE BARNES
Washburn, Israel
Williams, Reuel
Wright, William
POPE, RICHARD M.
Ames, Edward Scribner
PORTENIER, LILLIAN
Downey, June Etta
PORTER, DAVID L.
Bible, Dana Xenophon
Bierman, Bernard William ("Bernie")
Brown, Prentiss Marsh
Cassidy, Marshall Whiting
Douglas, Paul Howard
Gillette, Guy Mark
Harris, Stanley Raymond ("Bucky")
Hastings, Daniel Oren
Hooper, Harry Bartholomew
Lewis, Fulton, Jr.
Munson, Thurman Lee
Murray, James Edward
Warren, Lindsay Carter
PORTER, DOROTHY B.
Sanders, Daniel Jackson
Tubman, Harriet
PORTER, FRANK C.
Bacon, Benjamin Wisner
PORTER, JERMAIN G.
Mitchel, Ormsby MacKnight
PORTER, KENNETH WIGGINS
Rose, Edward
Sterling, Ross Shaw
PORTER, LUCIUS C.
Rawlinson, Frank Joseph
PORTER, WILLIAM E.
Davenport, Russell Wheeler
PORTER, WILLIAM R.
Hovgaard, William
POSEY, WALTER B.
Candler, Warren Akin
POSTIGLIONE, COREY
Calder, Alexander
POTTER, ALFRED C.
Sibley, John Langdon
POTTER, BARRETT G.
Elman, Harry ("Ziggy")
Gray, Glen ("Spike")
Lombardo, Gaetano Albert ("Guy")
Teagarden, Weldon Leo ("Jack")
Venuti, Giuseppe ("Joe")
Whiteman, Paul Samuel ("Pops")
Yancey, James Edward ("Jimmy")
POTTER, DAVID M.
Long, Huey Pierce
POTTLE, FREDERICK A.
Phelps, William Lyon

POTTS, CHARLES SHIRLEY
Batts, Robert Lynn
Harris, John Woods
Hemphill, John
Hubbard, Richard Bennett
Limpscomb, Abner Smith
Moore, George Fleming
Parker, Edwin Brewington
Pease, Elisha Marshall
Roberts, Oran Milo
Sayles, John
Stayton, John William
Wheeler, Royall Tyler
Willie, Asa Hoxie
POUND, ARTHUR
Barron, Clarence Walker
POUND, LOUISE
French, Alice
Jackson, Helen Maria Fiske Hunt
MacLean, George Edwin
Wallace, Charles William
POWELL, ALDEN L.
Schneider, George
Stoddard, William Osborn
POWELL, ARTHUR CHILTON
Murray, John Gardner
POWELL, ARTHUR G.
Hanus, Paul Henry
POWELL, DAPHNE
Vladimiroff, Pierre
POWELL, ROBERT CHARLES
Boisen, Anton Theophilus
Dunbar, (Helen) Flanders
McCarthy, Daniel Joseph
Sakel, Manfred Joshua
POWER, RICHARD LYLE
Calef, Robert
POWERS, RICHARD GID
Presley, Elvis Aron
PRATT, ANNE S.
Leypoldt, Frederick
PRATT, JULIUS W.
Armstrong, John
Dearborn, Henry
Fillmore, Millard
Hull, William
Johnson, Oliver
Jones, David
Lansing, Robert
McClure, George
Macomb, Alexander
Madison, James
O'Sullivan, John Louis
Porter, Peter Buell
Tompkins, Daniel D.
Van Rensselaer, Solomon
Van Rensselaer, Stephen
PRATT, ROBERT A.
Young, Karl
PRATT, WALDO SELDEN
Adgate, Andrew
Allen, Nathan H.
PREBLE, EDWARD
Abrams, Albert
Bulkley, Lucius Duncan
Bumstead, Freeman Josiah
Carnochan, John Murray
Clevenger, Shobal Vail, 1843–1920
Cooke, John Esten, 1783–1853
Davis, Charles Henry Stanley
Earle, Pliny, 1809–1892
Elsberg, Louis
Evans, George Alfred
Fisher, George Jackson
Flint, Austin, 1812–1886
Flint, Austin, 1836–1915
Foster, Frank Pierce
Fowler, George Ryerson
Francis, John Wakefield
Friedenwald, Aaron
Fuller, Robert Mason
Garcelon, Alonzo
Gerrish, Frederic Henry
Gerster, Arpad Geyza Charles
Gilliam, David Tod
Gray, John Purdue
Guernsey, Egbert
Hall, William Whitty
Hamilton, Allan McLane
Hamilton, Frank Hastings
Hartley, Frank
Haviland, Clarence Floyd
Henry, Morris Henry
Herter, Christian Archibald
Hoch, August
Hosack, Alexander Eddy
Hosack, David
Hutchinson, Woods
Jackson, Abraham Reeves
Jacobi, Abraham
Janeway, Edward Gamaliel
Janeway, Theodore Caldwell
Jarvis, William Chapman
Jones, Calvin
Jones, John
Jones, William Palmer
Judson, Adoniram Brown
Kedzie, Robert Clark
Keeley, Leslie E.
Keyes, Edward Lawrence
Kolle, Frederick Strange
Lee, Charles Alfred
Lefferts, George Morewood
Letchworth, William Pryor
Lincoln, Rufus Pratt
Lozier, Clemence Sophia Harned
Lumbrozo, Jacob
Lusk, William Thompson
McBurney, Charles
McCosh, Andrew James
MacNeven, William James
March, Alden
Miller, Edward
Mott, Valentine
PRENTICE, WILLIAM K.
Frothingham, Arthur Lincoln
PRESCOTT, FREDERICK CLARKE
Finch, Francis Miles
PRESCOTT, SAMUEL C.
Stratton, Samuel Wesley
PRICE, DAVID E.
Mahoney, John Friend
PRICHARD, WALTER
Dymond, John
PRIDE, ARMISTEAD S.
Abbott, Robert Sengstacke
PRIDE, LEO B.
Couldock, Charles Walter
PRIESTLEY, HERBERT INGRAM
Alvarado, Juan Bautista
Benavides, Alonzo de
Costansó, Miguel
De Soto, Hernando
Espejo, Antonio de
Fages, Pedro
Hittell, John Shertzer
Hittell, Theodore Henry
Luna Y Arellano, Tristan de
Moscoso De Alvarado, Luis de
PRIMER, BEN
Sloan, Harold Paul
PRINCE, LEON C.
Kline, George
McClure, Alexander Kelly
Nisbet, Charles
PRINGLE, HENRY F.
Taft, Alphonso
Taft, Charles Phelps
Taft, William Howard
PROSCHANSKY, HARRIS
Huebner, Solomon Stephen
PRUITT, BETTYE H.
Frary, Francis Cowles
PRUITT, WILLIAM
Pettengill, Samuel Barrett
PUCKETTE, CHARLES McD.
Sulzberger, Cyrus Lindauer
PULLEY, RAYMOND H.
Glass, Carter
PURCELL, EDWARD
Conboy, Martin
PURCELL, EDWARD A., JR.
Clark, Bennett Champ
Wood, Frederick Hill
PURCELL, J. M.
Keeler, Ralph Olmstead
PURCELL, RICHARD J.
Adams, Alvin
Ames, Frederick Lothrop
Ames, Oliver, 1779–1863
Ames, Oliver, 1807–1877
Ames, Oliver, 1831–1895
Armstrong, George Washington
Aspinwall, William Henry
Blanchet, François Norbet
Bradley, Denis Mary
Brondel, John Baptist
Bruté de Rémur, Simon William Gabriel
Cabrini, Francis Xavier
Carroll, John
Chatard, Francis Silas
Cheverus, John Louis Ann Magdalen Lefebre de
Corrigan, Michael Augustine
Cotton, Joseph Potter
Curtis, Alfred Allen
Daeger, Albert Thomas
David, John Baptist Mary
Dowling, Austin
Doyle, Alexander Patrick
Duffy, Francis Patrick
Engelhardt, Zephyrin
England, John
Feehan, Patrick Augustine
Fenwick, Edward Dominic
Ffrench, Charles Dominic
Fitzgerald, Edward
Flaget, Benedict Joseph
Galberry, Thomas
Gallagher, Hugh Patrick
Gallitzin, Demetrius Augustine
Garrigan, Philip Joseph
Gasson, Thomas Ignatius
Gilmour, Richard
Gmeiner, John

Graessl, Lawrence
Greaton, Joseph
Griffin, Martin Ignatius Joseph
Hassard, John Rose Greene
Heenan, John Carmel
Helbron, Peter
Helmpraecht, Joseph
Hughes, John Joseph
Huntington, Jedediah Vincent
Ireland, John, 1838–1918
Ives, Levi Silliman
Judge, Thomas Augustine
Julia, Sister
Keane, James John
Kelly, Eugene
Kenedy, Patrick John
Kenrick, Francis Patrick
Kirlin, Joseph Louis Jerome
Larkin, John
Lemke, Peter Henry
Levins, Thomas C.
Maas, Anthony J.
McCaffrey, John
McCloskey, John
McCloskey, William George
McElroy, John
McFaul, James Augustine
McGill, John
McGivney, Michael Joseph
McGrath, James
McGuire, Charles Bonaventure
Machebeuf, Joseph Projectus
McHenry, James
McKenna, Charles Hyacinth
McMaster, James Alphonsus
McQuaid, Bernard John
Maes, Camillus Paul
Malone, Sylvester
Maloney, Martin
Maréchal, Ambrose
Marty, Martin
Matignon, Francis Anthony
Meeschaert, Théophile
Menetrey, Joseph
Mengarini, Gregory
Messmer, Sebastian Gebhard
Middleton, Thomas Cooke
Miles, Richard Pius
Ming, John Joseph
Moeller, Henry
Molyneux, Robert
Moore, John, 1834–1901
Moosmüller, Oswald William
Moriarity, Patrick Eugene
Morini, Austin John
Mulry, Thomas Maurice
Murphy, John
Neale, Leonard
Nerinckx, Charles
Neumann, John Nepomucene
Nobili, John
O'Brien, Matthew Anthony
O'Callaghan, Jeremiah
O'Connor, James
O'Connor, Michael
Odin, John Mary
O'Gorman, Thomas
Ortynsky, Stephen Soter
Palladino, Lawrence Benedict
Pardow, William O'Brien
Peter, Sarah Worthington King
Phelan, David Samuel
Pise, Charles Constantine
Portier, Michael
Potamian, Brother
Power, John
Preston, Thomas Scott
Price, Thomas Frederick
Purcell, John Baptist
Quarter, William
Quigley, James Edward
Raffeiner, John Stephen
Ravalli, Antonio
Rese, Frederick
Reuter, Dominic
Richard, Gabriel
Riordan, Patrick William
Robot, Isidore
Roche, James Jeffrey
Rosecrans, Sylvester Horton
Russell, Mother Mary Baptist
Ryan, Abram Joseph
Ryan, Patrick John
Ryan, Stephen Vincent
Sadlier, Denis
Sadlier, Mary Anne Madden
Scanlan, Lawrence
Schneider, Theodore
Schrieck, Sister Louise Van der
Seghers, Charles Jean
Shahan, Thomas Joseph
Shea, John Dawson Gilmary
Shields, James
Shields, Thomas Edward
Shipman, Andrew Jackson
Smith, John Cotton, 1765–1845
Smith, Nathan, 1770–1835
Smith, Nathaniel
Spalding, Catherine
Spalding, John Lancaster
Spalding, Martin John
Stang, William
Starr, Eliza Allen
Stone, James Kent
Swift, Zephaniah
Thayer, John
Thébaud, Augustus J.
Tierney, Richard Henry
Timon, John
Tracy, Uriah
Tyler, William
Vander Wee, John Baptist
Van de Velde, James Oliver
Van Quickenborne, Charles Felix
Varela Y Morales, Felix Francisco José María de la Concepción
Verhaegen, Peter Joseph
Verot, Jean Marcel Pierre Auguste
Walsh, Robert
Walworth, Clarence Augustus
White, Andrew
White, Charles Ignatius
Whiting, William
Wigger, Winand Michael
Williams, John Joseph
Wilson, Samuel Thomas
Wood, James Frederick
Yorke, Peter Christopher
Young, Alfred
Young, Josue Maria

PURCELL, SALLEE MCNAMARA
Malone, Dudley Field

PURDY, LAWSON
Ensley, Enoch

PURSELL, CARROLL
Borg, George William
Merriam, John Campbell
Ritter, William Emerson
Rust, John Daniel

PUSEY, MERLO J.
Graham, Philip Leslie
Meyer, Eugene Isaac

QUAIFE, MILO MILTON
Barry, John Stewart
Campau, Joseph

QUIGLEY, MARTIN, JR.
Rothafel, Samuel Lionel

QUILL, J. MICHAEL
Bow, Clara Gordon
Powell, Richard Ewing ("Dick")
Power, Tyrone
Waller, Frederic
Webb, Clifton
Wong, Anna May

QUINN, ARTHUR HOBSON
Aiken, George L.
Baker, Benjamin A.
Bannister, Nathaniel Harrington
Barnes, Charlotte Mary Sanford
Bateman, Sidney Frances Cowell
Bird, Robert Montgomery
Boker, George Henry
Campbell, Bartley
Custis, George Washington Parke
Daly, John Augustin
Godfrey, Thomas, 1736–1763
Harrigan, Edward
Hoyt, Charles Hale
Mitchell, Langdon Elwyn
Mitchell, Silas Weir
Stone, John Augustus
Tyler, Royall

RAACKE, I. D.
Nelson, Marjorie Maxine

RABINOWITZ, ISAAC
Torrey, Charles Cutler

RADBILL, SAMUEL X.
Brennemann, Joseph
Gesell, Arnold Lucius

RADER, BENJAMIN G.
Bell, De Benneville ("Bert")
Heffelfinger, William Walter ("Pudge")
Riddle, Samuel Doyle
Stewart, Walter Winne

RAE, JOHN B.
Boeing, William Edward
Braniff, Thomas Elmer
Chapin, Roy Dikeman
Coffin, Howard Earle
Durant, William Crapo
Duryea, James Frank
Fisher, Alfred J.
Fisher, Charles T.
Joy, Henry Bourne
Kellett, William Wallace
Keys, Clement Melville
Lawrance, Charles Lanier
Lockheed, Allan Haines
Nash, Charles Williams
Sorensen, Charles
Swasey, Ambrose

Vance, Harold Sines
Wilson, Charles Erwin
RAGATZ, LOWELL JOSEPH
Hatton, Frank
McComas, Louis Emory
Miller, Oliver
Moran, Benjamin
Shepherd, Alexander Robey
Welling, James Clarke
RAINE, JAMES WATT
Rogers, John Almanza Rowley
RAINGER, RONALD
Farnsworth, Philo Taylor
Menninger, William Claire
Osborn, Henry Fairfield
Romer, Alfred Sherwood ("Al")
Sinnott, Edmund Ware
RAINWATER, P. L.
Watson, John William Clark
RAMAKER, ALBERT J.
Kendrick, Asahel Clark
RAMMELKAMP, CHARLES HENRY
Baldwin, Theron
Beecher, Edward
Bradley, John Edwin
Sturtevant, Julian Monson
RAMMELKAMP, JULIAN S.
McCormick, Robert Rutherford
RAMPERSAD, ARNOLD
Du Bois, William Edward Burghardt
Hughes, James Langston
RAMSDELL, CHARLES WILLIAM
Baker, Daniel
Baker, William Mumford
Baylor, Robert Emmet Bledsoe
Bell, Peter Hansborough
Burleson, Edward
Burleson, Rufus Clarence
Burnet, David Gouverneur
Coke, Richard
Culberson, Charles Allen
Gulberson, David Browning
Gorgas, Josiah
Lubbock, Francis Richard
Memminger, Christopher Gustavus
Myers, Abraham Charles
Neighbors, Robert Simpson
RAMSEY, FREDERIC, JR.
Oliver, Joseph
RAMSEY, GEORGE H.
Nott, Josiah Clark
RANDALL, J. G.
Calhoun, John
Chase, Salmon Portland
Davis, David
Lamon, Ward Hill
Lincoln, Abraham
Lincoln, Mary Todd
Logan, Stephen Trigg
Nicolay, John George
Reynolds, John, 1788–1865
Singleton, James Washington
Stuart, John Todd
Yates, Richard
RANDALL, JOHN HERMAN, JR.
Woodbridge, Frederick James Eugene
RANDEL, WILLIAM PEIRCE
Hagedorn, Hermann Ludwig Gebhard
Hart, Moss
RANDOLPH, HARRISON
Middleton, Nathaniel Russell
RANKIN, BELLE
Blackburn, Gideon
Corson, Juliet
Doak, Samuel
Farmer, Fannie Merritt
Gordon, Laura De Force
Hay, Mary Garrett
Huntington, Margaret Jane Evans
Low, Juliette Gordon
Pitman, Benn
Severance, Caroline Maria Seymour
Skinner, William
RANKIN, DANIEL S.
Mitchell, Isaac
RAPHAEL, HONORA
Smith, Betty
RAPHAEL, MARC LEE
Liebman, Joshua Loth
RASKIN, A. H.
Stark, Louis
RASKIN, EUGENE
La Farge, Christopher Grant
Yellin, Samuel
RASMUSSEN, R. KENT
Crane, Bob Edward
McQueen, Terence Stephen ("Steve")
Oakie, Jack
Seberg, Jean Dorothy
RASMUSSEN, WAYNE D.
Edwards, Everett Eugene
Hansen, Niels Ebbesen
Webber, Herbert John
RATHBONE, PERRY T.
Sachs, Paul Joseph
RATNER, SIDNEY
Bentley, Arthur Fisher
RAU, ALBERT G.
Heckewelder, John Gottlieb Ernestus
Levering, Joseph Mortimer
Loskiel, George Henry
Nitschmann, David
Peter, John Frederick
Post, Christian Frederick
Reichel, Charles Gotthold
Reichel, William Cornelius
Rondthaler, Edward
Schultze, Augustus
Schweinitz, Emil Alexander de
Schweinitz, Lewis David von
Spangenberg, Augustus Gottlieb
Zeisberger, David
RAUB, WILLIAM L.
Gale, George Washington
Garman, Charles Edward
RAUCHER, ALAN
Hannagan, Stephen Jerome
RAUP, HUGH M.
James Thomas Potts
RAVITCH, MARK M.
Bevan, Arthur Dean
Finney, John Miller Turpin
RAWLEY, JAMES A.
Benton, William Burnett
Cox, James Middleton, Jr.
Flanders, Ralph Edward
Ford, Guy Stanton
Green, Theodore Francis
Gruening, Ernest
Holbrook, Stewart Hall
Hughes, Rupert
West, Roy Owen
Wood, Peggy
RAY, P. ORMAN
Atchison, David Rice
Brown, Benjamin Gratz
Davis, Horace
Donohue, Peter
Gerstle, Lewis
Haggin, James Ben Ali
Kahn, Julius
Kearney, Denis
King of Williams, James
McAllister, Hall
McAllister, Matthew Hall
Marsh, John
Morrow, William W.
Otis, Harrison Gray
Perkins, George Clement
Phelan, James
Phelan, James Duval
Price, William Cecil
Randolph, Edmund, 1819–1861
Sargent, Aaron Augustus
Sawyer, Lorenzo
Scripps, Ellen Browning
Sloss, Louis
Smith, Francis Marion
Spreckels, Claus
Spreckels, John Diedrich
Stewart, William Morris
Sutro, Adolph Heinrich Joseph
Swift, John Franklin
Weller, John B.
Wilson, Samuel Mountford
RDEN, GEORGE H.
Burton, William
Cannon, William
Gilbert, Eliphalet Wheeler
McKinly, John
Purnell, William Henry
Ridgely, Nicholas
Rodney, Caesar
Rodney, Caesar Augustus
Rodney, Thomas
White, Samuel
READ, HELEN APPLETON
Force, Juliana Rieser
READ, PATRICIA
Eustis, Dorothy Leib Harrison Wood
Frohman, Daniel
Tanner, Henry Ossawa
READ, THOMAS T.
Bassett, William Hastings
Bradley, Frederick Worthen
Manning, Vannoy Hartrog
Mathews, John Alexander
Matthiessen, Frederick William
Maynard, George William
Merritt, Leonidas
Moore, Philip North
Olcott, Eben Erskine
Overman, Frederick
Smith, Hamilton
Stetefeldt, Carl August
Vinton, Francis Laurens
Wellington, Arthur Mellen
Williams, Gardner Fred

REARDON, M. E.
McNicholas, John Timothy
REDE, WYLLYS
Hotz, Ferdinand Carl
Whittingham, William Rollinson
REDFIELD, RUTH
Colby, Luther
Davis, Andrew Jackson
Dods, John Bovee
REDMAN, NICK
Fielding, Jerry
REDMAN, TIM
Zukofsky, Louis
REED, AMY LOUISE
Wilson, William
REED, HENRY HOPE, JR.
Blashfield, Edwin Howland
REED, JAMES
Bryant, Louise Frances Stevens
Pincus, Gregory Goodwin ("Goody")
REED, JAMES W.
Guttmacher, Alan Frank
Rockefeller, John Davison
REED, WALT
Birch, Reginald Bathurst
REEDS, CHESTER A.
Whitefield, Robert Parr
REESE, LIZETTE WOODWORTH
Henderson, Daniel McIntyre
REEVES, JESSE SIDDALL
Angell, James Burrill
REGUER, SARA
Belkin, Samuel
Wolfson, Harry Austryn
REICH, SHELDON
Marin, John (Cheri)
REICHARD, GARY W.
Kerner, Otto, Jr.
REICHELDERFER, F. W.
McAdie, Alexander George
REICHLE, HERBERT S.
Mundé, Paul Fortunatus
Noeggerath, Emil Oscar Jacob Bruno
Peaslee, Edmund Randolph
Polk, William Mecklenburg
Richmond, John Lambert
Smith, Job Lewis
Starr, Louis
Weber. Gustav Carl Erich
REID, JOSEPH H.
Brace, Charles Loring
REID, W. T.
Bolza, Oskar
REIDER, NORMAN
Fenichel, Otto
REIFF, ROBERT F.
Christy, Howard Chandler
Held, John, Jr.
Rosenberg, Paul
Sterne, Maurice
Szyk, Arthur
Tchelitchew, Pavel
REILLY, KEVIN P.
Allen, James Edward, Jr.
REINERS, JOHN C.
Casadesus, Robert Marcel
Koussevitzky, Olga Naumoff
Piatigorsky, Gregor
REITT, BARBARA B.
Loveman, Amy
REMALEY, PETER P.
Fowler, Gene
Service, Robert William
REMINI, ROBERT V.
James, Marquis
REN, WEN-HUA
Gordon, John Franklin
Watts, Franklin Mowry
RESTOUT, DENISE
Landowska, Wanda Aleksandra
Robinson-Smith, Gertrude
RETHERFORD, J. E.
Shoup, George Laird
REYNOLDS, CLARK G.
Adams, Charles Francis
Barbey, Daniel Edward
Bloch, Claude Charles
Brereton, Lewis Hyde
Burgess, W(illiam) Starling
Hackett, Robert Leo ("Bobby")
Halsey, William Frederick, Jr.
Kimmel, Husband Edward
Kincaid, Thomas Cassin
Kirk, Alan Goodrich
Morison, Samuel Eliot
Nolan, Bob
Radford, Arthur William
Ricketts, Claude Vernon
Sherman, Forrest Percival
Sherman, Frederick Carl
Spruance, Raymond Ames
Standley, William Harrison
Stark, Harold Raynsford
Towers, John Henry
REYNOLDS, JOHN HENRY
Leete, William
RHINELANDER, PHILIP M.
Satterlee, Henry Yates
RHODES, CHARLES DUDLEY
Averell, William Woods
Birney, David Bell
Blunt, James Gillpatrick
Brannan, John Milton
Brooks, William Thomas Harbaugh
Buchanan, Robert Christie
Buford, Abraham, 1820–1884
Butterfield, Daniel
Ernst, Oswald Herbert
Farnsworth, Ebon John
Gaillard, David Du Bose
Garrard, Kenner
Gillmore, Quincy Adams
Goethals, George Washington
Graham, William Montrose
Haan, William George
Hancock, Winfield Scott
Hodges, Harry Foote
Howze, Robert Lee
Imboden, John Daniel
Irwin, George Le Roy
Jadwin, Edgar
Johnson, Bushrod Rust
Johnson, Edward
Johnson, Richard W.
Jordan, Thomas
Kautz, August Valentine
Kelton, John Cunningham
Kershaw, Joseph Brevard
Keyes, Erasmus Darwin
Kilpatrick, Hugh Judson
Lander, Frederick West
Lewis, William Gaston
Loring, William Wing
Ludlow, William
McCallum, Daniel Craig
McCawley, Charles Grymes
McCook, Alexander McDowell
McCook, Edward Moody
Magoon, Charles Edward
Meade, Robert Leamy
Meagher, Thomas Francis
Meigs, Montgomery Cunningham
Menoher, Charles Thomas
Merriam, Henry Clay
Miles, Nelson Appleton
Minty, Robert Horatio George
Morgan, James Dada
Mulholland, St. Clair Augustin
Nicholson, William Jones
Noble, Alfred
Roberts, Benjamin Stone
Rodman, Thomas Jackson
Rogers, John Ignatius
Ruger, Thomas Howard
Sedgwick, John
Shafter, William Rufus
Sheridan, Philip Henry
Simpson, James Hervey
Smith, James Francis
RHODES, TIMOTHY
Mosely, Philip Edward
Ridder, Bernard Herman
RIBBLE, F. D. G.
Lile, William Minor
RICE, HERBERT W.
Chalmers, William James
Falk, Otto Herbert
Kohler, Walter Jodok
RICE, WILLIAM NORTH
Cummings, Joseph
RICH, DANIEL CATTON
Harshe, Robert Bartholow
RICHARDS, ALFRED E.
Paine, Ralph Delahaye
RICHARDS, ELIZABETH M.
Vattemare, Nicholas Marie Alexandre
RICHARDS, THOMAS COLE
Calkins, Phineas Wolcott
Chamberlain, Nathan Henry
Chapin, Edwin Hubbell
Chapman, John Wilbur
Clark, George Whitefield
Cobb, Sylvanus
Dike, Samuel Warren
RICHARDSON, EDWARD E.
Sterrett, James Macbride
RICHARDSON, GEORCE L.
Hall, Arthur Crawshay Alliston
Littlejohn, Abram Newkirk
RICHARDSON, HESTER DORSEY
Hamilton, Alexander, 1712–1756
RICHARDSON, LEON B.
Occom, Samson
Sanborn, Edwin David
Smith, Asa Dodge
Tucker, William Jewett
Whitaker, Nathaniel
RICHARDSON, LEON J.
Kellogg, Martin
RICHARDSON, LYON N.
Bradstreet, Anne
Thwing, Charles Franklin

RICHMAN, IRVING BERDINE
Aco, Michel
Alarcón, Hernando De
Allefonsce, Jean
Amadas, Philip
Anza, Juan Bautista De
Ayala, Juan Manuel De
Ayllon, Lucas Vasquez De
Black Hawk
Coddington, William
Collins, John
Cranston, Samuel
Fenner, Arthur
Fenner, James
Font, Pedro
Foster, Theodore
Francis, John Brown
Garcés, Francisco Tomás Hermenegildo
Greene, William, 1695/96–1758
Greene, William, 1731–1809
Groseilliers, Médart Chouart
Hopkins, Stephen
Keokuk
Lisa, Manuel
Ponce de León, Juan
RICKARD, THOMAS A.
Pearce, Richard
RIDEOUT, WALTER B.
Anderson, Sherwood
Calverton, Victor Francis
RIDGELY, JOSEPH V.
Chandler, Raymond Thornton
Erskine, John
Hammett, Samuel Dashiell
Quinn, Arthur Hobson
Roberts, Kenneth Lewis
Van Druten, John William
RIDGLEY, RONALD H.
Howard, Moe
Josephson, Matthew
RIDGEWAY, GEORGE L.
Marvin, Dudley
RIDGLEY, RONALD H.
Bell, Eric Temple
Blair, William Richards
Gunn, Ross
Jeffers, William Martin
Mendelsohn, Samuel
RIEGEL, ROBERT E.
Gould, George Jay
Hubbard, Thomas Hamlin
Jeffery, Edward Turner
Kirkman, Marshall Monroe
Marvin, Dudley
Mellen, Charles Sanger
Moffat, David Halliday
Palmer, William Jackson
Pearson, Edward Jones
Reigel, Robert E.
Smith, Milton Hannibal
Wallace, John Findley
RIESS, STEVEN A.
Heilmann, Harry
Klein, Charles Herbert ("Chuck")
RIFE, CLARENCE W.
Kittson, Norman Wolfred
RILEY, FRANKLIN LAFAYETTE
Alcorn, James Lusk
Barry, William Taylor Sullivan
Brown, Albert Gallatin
Campbell, Josiah A. Patterson
Chalmers, James Ronald
Claiborne, John Francis Hamtramck
Clark, Charles
Dunbar, William
Fulton, Robert Burwell
RILEY, HARRIS D., JR.
Papanicolaou, George Nicholas
Rous, Francis Peyton
Smith, Homer William
Sutherland, Earl Wilbur, Jr.
RINGENBERG, WILLIAM C.
Buchman, Frank Nathan Daniel
Erdman, Charles Rosenbury
Jones, Robert Reynolds ("Bob")
Kagan, Henry Enoch
Pierce, Robert Willard
Ritter, Joseph Elmer
RIPPY, J. FRED
Gadsden, James
Poinsett, Joll Roberts
Thompson, Waddy
Trist, Nicholas Philip
RISCHIN, MOSES
Cahan, Abraham
RISTINE, FRANK H.
Brown, Samuel Gilman
Thompson, James Maurice
RITCHIE, DONALD A.
Duff, James Henderson
Knowland, William Fife
Landis, James McCauley
Pecora, Ferdinand
RITCHIE, WILLIAM A.
Parker, Arthur Caswell
RITVO, LUCILLE B.
Mejer, Adolf
RIVLIN, BENJAMIN
Bunche, Ralph Johnson
ROBBINS, RICHARD
Johnson, Charles Spurgeon
ROBBINS, ROSSELL HOPE
Brown, Carleton
ROBBINS, WILLIAM J.
Crocker, William
ROBERSON, GLORIA GRANT
Dyett, Thomas Ben
ROBERT, JOSEPH C.
Patterson, Rufus Lenoir
ROBERTS, DONALD A.
Grinnell, Henry Walton
Harland, Henry
Major, Charles
Moses, Montrose Jonas
O'Higgins, Harvey Jerrold
Shepard, Edward Morse
Tremain, Henry Edwin
Webb, Alexander Stewart
Wheeler, Everett Pepperrell
Youngs, John
ROBERTS, GEORGE B.
Perkins, James Handasyd
Peter, Robert
ROBERTS, JOHN D.
Cope, Arthur Clay
ROBERTSON, DAVID A.
Goodspeed, Thomas Wakefield
Gunsaulus, Frank Wakeley
Leonard, Robert Josselyn
MacAlister, James
Mayo, Amory Dwight
ROBERTSON, H. E.
Wesbrook, Frank Fairchild
ROBERTSON, JAMES ALEXANDER
Call, Richard Keith
Narváez, Pánfilo de
Nüñez Cabeza De Vaca, Alvar
Smith, Buckingham
ROBIE, EDWARD HODGES
Hammond, John Hays
ROBINETT, PAUL M.
Chaffee, Adna Romanza
Craig, Malin
ROBINSON, BENJAMIN L.
Watson, Sereno
ROBINSON, BURR A.
Bristol, William Henry
Church, Irving Porter
Gotshall, William Charles
Irving, John Duer
McCullough, Ernest
Meyer, Henry Coddington
Miller, Kempster Blanchard
Moldenke, Richard George Gottlob
Mulholland, William
Nettleton, Edwin S.
Newhouse, Samuel
Pearson, Fred Stark
Peters, Edward Dyer
Rafter, George W.
Rand, Addison Crittenden
Randolph, Isham
Richards, Charles Brinckerhoff
Richards, Joseph William
Robb, William Lispenard
Roberts, Nathan S.
Robinson, Albert Alonzo
Serrell, Edward Wellman
Smith, Jonas Waldo
Spilsbury, Edmund Gybbon
Stauffer, David McNeely
Stearns, Irving Ariel
Stott, Henry Gordon
Strong, Charles Lyman
Stuart, Charles Beebe
Wegmann, Edward
Wernag, Lewis
Williams, Frank Martin
Williams, Jesse Lynch
Wilson, Joseph Miller
Wilson, William Hasell
ROBINSON, C. A., JR.
Allinson, Francis Greenleaf
ROBINSON, CERVIN
Corbett, Harvey Wiley
ROBINSON, DAVID MOORE
Bright, James Wilson
ROBINSON, DOANE
Fetterman, William Judd
Kyle, James Henderson
Ladd, Edwin Freemont
Loucks, Henry Langford
Mellette, Arthur Calvin
ROBINSON, EDGAR E.
Hager, John Sharpenstein
Haight, Henry Huntly
Hearst, George
Hearst, Phoebe Apperson
Latham, Milton Slocum
Lick, James
ROBINSON, EDGAR EUGENE
Requa, Mark Lawrence
ROBINSON, EDWIN ARLINGTON
Perry, Thomas Sergeant

Robinson, Elwyn B.
Amidon, Charles Fremont
Robinson, George W.
Emerton, Ephraim
Robinson, Gregory
Fields, Dorothy
Robinson, Henry Morton
Dorgan, Thomas Aloysius
Rogers, William Allen
Thomas, Robert Bailey
Robinson, Herbert Spencer
Smith, Roswell
Tomlinson, Everett Titsworth
Watson, Henry Clay
Webber, Charles Wilkins
Zachos, John Celivergos
Robinson, Marion O.
Cushman, Vera Charlotte Scott
Robinson, William Alexander
Atherton, Charles Gordon
Barlett, Ichabod
Bayard, Thomas Francis
Bell, Charles Henry
Bell, Samuel
Bentley, William
Berry, Nathaniel Springer
Bishop, Abraham
Blair, Henry William
Bowdoin, James, 1726–1790
Bowdoin, James, 1752–1811
Brown, Francis, 1784–1820
Cheney, Person Colby
Clark, Daniel
Corbin, Daniel Chase
Currier, Moody
Daggett, David
Dwight, Theodore, 1764–1846
Edmunds, George Franklin
Edwards, Pierpont
Evans, George
Fairfield, John
Fessenden, Francis
Fessenden, James Deering
Fessenden, Samuel
Fessenden, William Pitt
Fisk, James, 1763– 1844
Fogg, George Gilman
Folsom, Nathaniel
Foot, Solomon
Foster, Abiel
Foster, Abigail Kelley
Foster, John Gray
Foster, Stephen Symonds
Gallinger, Jacob Harold
Gilman, John Taylor
Gilman, Nicholas
Gilmore, Joseph Albree
Goodrich, Chauncey
Goodrich, Elizur
Goodwin, Ichabod
Granger, Gideon
Griswold, Matthew
Griswold, Roger
Griswold, Stanley
Hale, Eugene
Hale, John Parker
Hamlin, Hannibal
Harriman, Walter
Hill, Isaac
Hinds, Asher Crosby
Holman, William Steele
Langdon, John
Lincoln, Enoch
Lincoln, Levi, 1749–1820
Lincoln, Levi, 1782–1868
Lord, Nathan
Lyon, Matthew
Metcalf, Henry Harrison
Patterson, James Willis
Peabody, Nathaniel
Perley, Ira
Pickering, John
Pickering, Timothy
Plumer, William
Reed, Thomas Brackett
Rollins, Edward Henry
Rollins, Frank West
Smith, Israel
Smith, Jeremiah, 1759–1842
Sullivan, George
Thornton, Matthew
Tichenor, Isaac
Tuck, Amos
Washburn, Albert Henry
Weare, Meshech
Whipple, William
Wingate, Paine
Robinson, William M., Jr.
Coxetter, Louis Mitchell
Lamar, Gazaway Bugg
Maffitt, John Newland
Rains, George Washington
Read, Charles William
Semmes, Raphael
Smith, Gustavus Woodson
Tucker, John Randolph, 1812–1883
Wood, John Taylor
Robison, Daniel M.
McMillin, Benton
Shields, John Knight
Witherspoon, John Alexander
Rochester, Anna
Woodbury, Helen Laura Sumner
Rockwell, William Walker
Prentiss, George Lewis
Rodabaugh, James H.
Bishop, Robert Hamilton
Jones, Samuel Milton
Roden, Carl B.
McClurg, Alexander Caldwell
Poole, William Frederick
Rodionoff, Nicholas R.
Shelekhov, Grigorii Ivanovich
Roe, Joseph W.
Hartness, James
Roever, William H.
Chauvenet, William
Rogan, Octavia F.
Rosenberg, Henry
Rogers, Allen
Sadtler, Samuel Philip
Rogers, James Grafton
Long, Joseph Ragland
Thatcher, Mahlon Daniel
Rogers, L. Harding, Jr.
Warren, Sir Peter
Rogers, Lindsay
Baldwin, Henry
Blatchford, Samuel
Rogers, Max Gray
Moffatt, James
Rogosin, William Donn
Dundee, Johnny
Langford, Samuel
Leavitt, Frank Simmons (Man Mountain Dean)
Rohne, J. Magnus
Clausen, Claus Lauritz
Dahl, Theodore Halvorson
Dietrichson, Johannes Wilhelm Christian
Hoenecke, Gustav Adolf Felix Theodor
Hove, Elling
Hoyme, Gjermund
Kildahl, Johan Nathan
Koren, Ulrik Vilhelm
Larsen, Peter Laurentius
Lenker, John Nicholas
Lindberg, Conrad Emil
Norelius, Eric
Pieper, Franz August Otto
Roland, Charles G.
Wilder, Russell Morse
Rolbiecki, John J.
Barzynski, Vincent
Dabrowski, Joseph
Rollins, Alfred B., Jr.
Hopkins, Harry Lloyd
Roper, Daniel Calhoun
Rollins, Carl P.
De Vinne, Theodore Low
Rollins, Reed C.
Fernald, Merritt Lyndon
Romanofsky, Peter
Potter, Ellen Culver
Romanus, Charles F., Sr.
Patch, Alexander McCarrell
Romasco, Albert U.
Brookhart, Smith Wildman
Watson, James Eli
Rome, Roman
Kiewit, Peter
Marx, Herbert ("Zeppo")
Marx, Julius Henry ("Groucho")
Marx, Milton ("Gummo")
Rockefeller, Winthrop
Seitz, William Chapin
Romer, Alfred S.
Barbour, Thomas
Ronsaville, Virginia
Corbin, Margaret
Curwen, Samuel
McCauley, Mary Ludwig Hays
Rooney, Miriam Theresa
Fitzpatrick, John Bernard
Root, Edward W.
Hooker, Philip
Root, Ernest Rob
Langstroth, Lorenzo Lorraine
Root, Robert K.
Hudson, Henry Norman
Root, Walter S.
Lee, Frederic Schiller
Root, Winfred Trexler
Keith, Sir William
Ropes, James H.
Gregory, Caspar René
Moore, George Foot
Roppolo, Joseph Patrick
Barry, Philip James Quinn
Rorabaugh, W. J.
Alsop, Stewart Johonnot Oliver
Genovese, Vito
Jones, Jim
Poling, Daniel Alfred

Ruditsky, Barney
Yellowley, Edward Clements
ROSE, FLORA
Van Rensselaer, Martha
ROSE, GEORGE, III
Alexander, James
Bouvier, John
ROSE, KATHERINE
Gates, Caleb Frank
ROSE, LISLE A.
Messersmith, George Strausser
ROSEBOOM, EUGENE H.
Tod, David
Wood, Reuben
ROSEN, ELLIOTT
Edge, Walter Evans
ROSEN, GEORGE
Baker, Sara Josephine
Blake, Francis Gilman
Park, William Hallock
Rosenau, Milton Joseph
ROSEN, JEFF
Webster, Benjamin ("Ben") Francis
ROSEN, ROBERT S.
Hirschbein, Peretz
ROSENAU, WILLIAM
Mielziner, Moses
ROSENBACH, A. S. W.
Bement, Clarence Sweet
Mackenzie, William
Polock, Moses
ROSENBERG, J. MITCHELL
Frank, Jerome
ROSENBERG, NATHAN
De Leeuw, Adolph Lodewyk
ROSENBERRY, LOIS K. M.
Helmer, Bessie Bradwell
Meeker, Moses
Mosher, Eliza Maria
Nichols, Clarina Irene Howard
Parrish, Celestia Susannah
Sewall, May Eliza Wright
Talbot, Emily Fairbanks
Tiffany, Katrina Brandes Ely
ROSENBERRY, MARVIN B.
Cassoday, John Bolivar
Jenkins, James Graham
Larrabee, Charles Hathaway
Lyon, William Penn
Orton, Harlow South
Ryan, Edward George
Strong, Moses McCure
Winslow, John Bradley
ROSENBLATT, MILTON B.
Wells, Harry Gideon
ROSENFELD, ALBERT
Langmuir, Irving
ROSENFELD, LULLA
Adler, Sara
Schwartz, Maurice
ROSENFELD, SUSAN
Hoover, John Edgar
Keeney, Barnaby Conrad
ROSENKRANTZ, BARBARA GUTMANN
Briggs, Lloyd Vernon
Brunswick, Ruth Mack
Gunn, Selskar Michael
ROSENOF, THEODORE
Amlie, Thomas Ryum
ROSENZWEIG, ROY
Brophy, John
Foster, William Z.
Mason, Lucy Randolph
Muste, Abraham Johannes
Steuben, John
ROSEWATER, VICTOR
Creighton, Edward
Hale, William Bayard
McLean, William Leppard
McRae, Milton Alexander
Nelson, William Rockhill
Phillips, Walter Polk
Prime, William Cowper
Singerly, William Miskey
ROSS, BARBARA
Guthrie, Edwin Ray, Jr.
ROSS, DOROTHY
Cattell, James McKeen
ROSS, EARLE DUDLEY
Gear, John Henry
Geddes, James Loraine
Harlan, James, 1820–1899
Haugen, Gilbert Nelson
Herron, Francis Jay
Howell, James Bruen
Kenyon, William Squire
Knapp, Bradford
Pearson, Raymond Allen
Shaw, Leslie Mortier
Wilson, James Falconer
ROSS, ELIZABETH D.
Hill, Patty Smith
Wheelock, Lucy
ROSS, FRANK A.
Giddings, Franklin Henry
ROSS, FRANK EDWARD
Allen, Philip
Austin, James Trecothick
Bland, Thomas
Brown, John Porter
Bryant, Gridley
Burrill, James
Butler, John
Butler, Richard
Butler, Walter N.
Butler, Zebulon
Cathcart, James Leander
Chafin, Eugene Wilder
Childs, Thomas
Clarke, John Sleeper
Cleveland, Benjamin
Cleveland, Chauncey Fitch
Darby, William
Davidson, William Lee
Dickinson, Philemon
Elbert, Samuel
Febiger, Christian
Forman, David
Grayson, William
Gridley, Richard
Gulick, Luther Halsey, 1828–1891
Harlan, Josiah
Hite, Jost
Howard, Volney Erskine
Ives, Joseph Christmas
James, Edwin
Knowlton, Thomas
Lamb, John
Laurens, John
Lewis, William David
McArthur, William Pope
McDowell, Charles
McDowell, Joseph
Neville, John
ROSS, HAROLD E.
Van Slyke, Lucius Lincoln
ROSS, MARC
Eno, William Phelps
ROSS, MARVIN CHAUNCEY
Porter, Arthur Kingsley
ROSS, PHILIP
Hall, Paul
ROSS, RODNEY A.
Leland, Waldo Gifford
ROSS, SUE FIELDS
Bernstein, Aline
ROSSINI, FREDERICK D.
Washburn, Edward Wight
ROSSITER, FRANK R.
Downes, (Edwin) Olin
ROSTOW, W. W.
Rogers, James Harvey
ROTH, JOHN K.
Bode, Boyd Henry
Buchanan, Scott Milross
Carnap, Rudolf
Divine, Father
Hocking, William Ernest
Latourette, Kenneth Scott
Montague, William Pepperell
Niebuhr, Helmut Richard
Perry, Ralph Barton
Santayana, George
ROTHENSTEINER, JOHN E.
Hoecken, Christian
Kenrick, Peter Richard
ROUDER, WENDY
Hampden, Walter
Leiber, Fritz
Taylor, Laurette
ROURKE, CONSTANCE M.
Crabtree, Lotta
Keene, Laura
ROUS, PEYTON
Warthin, Aldred Scott
ROWE, HENRY KALLOCH
Anderson, Martin Brewer
Bowne, Borden Parker
Boyce, James Petigru
Bright, Edward
Broadus, John Albert
Brown, Charles Rufus
Brown, John Newton
Callender, John
Campbell, Alexander
Campbell, Thomas
Mitchell, Edward Cushing
Sharp, Daniel
Thomas, Jesse Burgess
ROWE, J. P.
Clapp, Charles Horace
ROWE, ROBERT R.
Barker, James William
Boldt, George C.
Boorman, James
Bruce, George
ROWLAND, DUNBAR
Adams, William Wirt
Brandon, Gerard Chittocque
Gholson, Samuel Jameson
Hardy, William Harris
Harris, Nathaniel Harrison
Harris, Wiley Pope
Harris, William Littleton
Henderson, John
ROZAKIS, LAURIE
Barrie, Wendy

Hayakawa, Sessue
Vance, Vivian
RUBIN, JOAN SHELLEY
Canby, Henry Seidel
Rinehart, Stanley Marshall, Jr.
RUBIN, JOSEPH L.
Murphy, William Walton
RUDOLPH, FREDERICK
Dennett, Tyler (Wilbur)
Garfield, Harry Augustus
RUFUS, W. CARL
Rittenhouse, David
Watson, James Craig
RUHRAH, JOHN
Hemmeter, John Conrad
RUNDELL, WALTER, JR.
Webb, Walter Prescott
RUPPENTHAL, ROLAND G.
Lee, John Clifford Hodges
RUSH, N. ORWIN
Fraser, James Earle
Leigh, William Robinson
RUSK, GEORGE Y.
Miller, John
RUSK, RALPH L.
Bennett, Emerson
Coggeshall, William Turner
Eggleston, Edward
Imlay, Gilbert
RUSK, WILLIAM SENER
Adams, Herbert Samuel
Polk, Willis Jefferson
Rinehart, William Henry
Rogers, John, 1829–1904
Rogers, Randolph
Rumsey, Charles Cary
Simmons, Franklin
Stone, Horatio
Story, Julian Russell
Story, William Wetmore
Thayer, Abbott Handerson
Turner, Charles Yardley
Walter, Thomas Ustick
Weir, John Ferguson
Weir, Robert Walter
RUSSELL, ROSS
Parker, Charlie ("Bird")
RUSSELL, WILLIAM L.
Salmon, Thomas William
RUTLAND, ROBERT A.
Benton, Thomas Hart
Dryfoos, Orvil E.
Gaylord, Edward King
Kiplinger, Willard Monroe
Reynolds, Julian Sargeant
Scherman, Harry
Scripps, William Edmund
Shuster, W(illiam) Morgan
RUTLAND, ROBERT ALLEN
McClatchy, Charles Kenny
RYAN, EDWIN
Dubois, John
RYAN, JOHN A.
McGlynn, Edward
RYAN, JOHN K.
Pace, Edward Aloysius
Turner, William
RYAN, PAT M.
Allen, Viola Emily
Brice, Fanny
Pemberton, Brock
Perry, Antoinette
Shubert, Lee
Warfield, David
RYDEN, GEORGE H.
Burton, William
Cannon, William
Gilbert, Eliphalet Wheeler
McKinly, John
Purnell, William Henry
Ridgely, Nicholas
Rodney, Caesar
Rodney, Caesar Augustus
Rodney, Thomas
White, Samuel

SABLOSKY, IRVING L.
Damrosch, Walter Johannes
Spalding, Albert
SACHS, BERNARD
Seguin, Edouard
Seguin, Edward Constant
SAFFORD, JEFFREY
Vickery, Howard Leroy
SAFFORD, JEFFREY J.
Douglas, Lewis Williams
SAFFRON, MORRIS H.
Fowler, Russell Story
Haupt, Alma Cecelia
Rubin, Isidor Clinton
Warbasse, James Peter
SAFIER, DAVID
Cunningham, Imogen
Strand, Paul
SAKOLSKI, A. M.
Hendrix, Joseph Clifford
Hotchkiss, Horace Leslie
Jones, Frank
Keith, Benjamin Franklin
SALES, JANE
McCord, James Bennett
SALMON, WESLEY C.
Reichenbach, Hans
SALMOND, JOHN
McEntee, James Joseph
SALON, MARLENE
Farrand, Beatrix Cadwalader Jones
SALOUTOS, THEODORE
Butler, Marion
Callimachos, Panos Demetrios
Frazier, Lynn Joseph
Goss, Albert Simon
Hirth, William Andrew
Jardine, William Marion
Johnson, Magnus
Reno, Milo
Sloan, George Arthur
SALSBURY, STEPHEN
Du Pont, Lammot
SALTER, SUMNER
Bartlett, Homer Newton
Bradbury, William Batchelder
SAMINSKY, LAZARE
Rosenblatt, Joseph
SAMPLE, DANA L.
Morón, Alonzo Graseano
Wildt, Rupert
SAMSON, VERNE LOCKWOOD
Johnston, Annie Fellows
Rowland, Henry Cottrell
Singleton, Esther
Smith, George Henry
Stein, Evaleen
Stiles, Henry Reed
Tappan, Eva March
Thayer, William Makepeace
Waggaman, Mary Teresa McKee
Warner, Anne Richmond
Wormley, James
SAMUELSON, PAUL A.
Schumpeter, Joseph Alois
SANBORN, ASHTON ROLLINS
Loeb, James
SANDBURG, CARL
Wentworth, John
Wright, Philip Green
SANDIFER, DURWARD V.
Johnson, William
Jones, Samuel
Kirkpatrick, Andrew
Kneeland, Stillman Foster
Knott, Aloysius Leo
Mitchell, William, 1801–1886
SANTORA, JOSEPH C.
Engelhard, Charles William
Rosenwald, Lessing Julius
SAPIENZA, MADELINE
Adams, Frank Ramsay
Bohlen, Charles Eustis ("Chip")
Brent, George
Bruce, David Kirkpatrick Este
Monteux, Pierre Benjamin
Munch, Charles
Reiner, Fritz
Spaeth, Sigmund
Warner, Jack Leonard
Zanuck, Darryl Francis
SAPOSS, DAVID J.
Schlesinger, Benjamin
Sigman, Morris
SARASOHN, DAVID
Marcosson, Isaac Frederick
Von Wiegand, Karl Henry
SARDY, HYMAN
Hill, Arthur Middleton
SARGENT, GEORGE HENRY
Mosher, Thomas Bird
SAUL, RICHARD S.
Johnson, George Francis
SAVAGE, CARLTON
Foote, Lucius Harwood
Ide, Henry Clay
Jackson, John Brinckerhoff
SAVAGE, GEORGE
Walter, Eugene
SAVELLE, MAX
Morgan, George
SAWYER, RALPH A.
Lyman, Theodore
SAYRE, WALLACE S.
Kenna, John Edward
Roe, Gilbert Ernstein
SCAASI, ARNOLD
Adrian, Gilbert
Carnegie, Hattie
SCARBOROUGH, DOROTHY
Barr, Amelia Edith Huddleston
SCHAFER, JOSEPH
Abernethy, George
Adams, William Lysander
Applegate, Jesse
Atkinson, George Henry
Boise, Reuben Patrick
Campbell, Prince Lucien
Corbett, Henry Winslow
De Smet, Pierre-Jean

Doolittle, James Rood
Doty, James Duane
Draper, Lyman Copeland
Farnham, Thomas Jefferson
Gaines, John Pollard
Greenhow, Robert
Grover, La Fayette
Jackson, Mortimer Melville
Kelley, Hall Jackson
Keyes, Elisha Williams
Lane, Joseph
McLoughlin, John
Nesmith, James Willis
Parker, Samuel
Randall, Alexander Williams
Rusk, Jeremiah McClain
Smith, Jedediah Strong
Stevens, Isaac Ingalls
Whitman, Marcus
Wyeth, Nathaniel Jarvis
SCHAFFER, ALAN L.
Marcantonio, Vito Anthony
SCHAMBERG, JAY FRANK
Duhring, Louis Adolphus
SCHAPIRO, ISRAEL
Imber, Naphtali Herz
Paley, John
Rombro, Jacob
Rosenberg, Abraham Hayyim
Rosenfeld, Morris
Rosenthal, Herman
Schomer, Nahum Meir
Selikovitsch, Goetzel
Spivak, Charles David
Winchevsky, Morris
Wolf, Simon
Zevin, Israel Joseph
Zunser, Eliakum
SCHARNHORST, GARY
Forester, Cecil Scott
Howard, Elston Gene ("Ellie")
SCHEIN, JEROME D.
Keller, Helen Adams
SCHELL, HERBERT S.
Young, Clark Montgomery
SCHELLENBERG, T. R.
Binkley, Robert Cedric
SCHENE, MICHAEL G.
Stefansson, Vilhjalmur
SCHEUER, JEFFREY
Lang, Fritz
Stafford, Jean
SCHEVILL, FERDINAND
Holst, Hermann Eduard von
SCHEWEL, AMY
Robb, Inez Early Callaway
Trammell, Niles
SCHEYER, ERNST
Hofmann, Hans
Weber, Max
SCHIEDT, RICHARD C.
Stahr, John Summers
SCHILLER, A. ARTHUR
Smith, Edmund Munroe
SCHILLER, FRANCIS
Kennedy, Robert Foster
SCHLABACH, THERON F.
Ely, Richard Theodore
Witte, Edwin Emil
SCHLESINGER, ARTHUR M., JR.
Kennedy, John Fitzgerald
Kennedy, Robert Francis
SCHLESINGER, FRANK
Elkin, William Lewis
SCHLESINGER, H. I.
Stieglitz, Julius
SCHLUNDT, CHRISTENA L.
Shawn, Edwin Meyers ("Ted")
Tamiris, Helen
SCHMEHL, LAWRENCE H.
Hinman, Joel
Hosmer, Titus
James, Edward Christopher
Knapp, Martin Augustine
SCHMIDT, DOROTHY S. ("DOREY")
Benson, Sally
Blocker, Dan
Grosvenor, Gilbert Hovey
King, Richard, Jr.
Kleberg, Robert Justus, Jr.
Reese, Heloise Bowles
Ritter, Woodward Maurice ("Tex")
Tandy, Charles David
SCHMIDT, DWIGHT L.
Warner, William Lloyd
SCHMIDT, LESTER F.
Ball, Frank Clayton
SCHMIDT, LOUIS BERNARD
Henderson, David Bremner
Hepburn, William Peters
Meredith, Edwin Thomas
Simpson, John Andrew
Wallace, Henry
Wallace, Henry Cantwell
Wilson, James
SCHNEER, CECIL J.
Bowen, Norman Levi
Spurr, Josiah Edward
SCHNEIDER, DAVID M.
Adie, David Craig
SCHNEIDER, HERBERT W.
Colby, Luther
Davis, Andrew Jackson
Dods, John Bovee
Harris, Thomas Lake
Hudson, Thomas Jay
Hyslop, James Hervey
Lee, Ann
Newbrough, John Ballou
Pratt, James Bissett
Sandeman, Robert
SCHOBINGER, GEORGE
McConnell, Ira Welch
SCHOEN, ELIN
Miranda, Carmen
SCHOENBERGER, H. W.
Hill, Frederic Stanhope
Hillhouse, James Abraham
Ingersoll, Edward
Judah, Samuel Benjamin Helbert
Noah, Mordecai Manuel
Smith, Richard Penn
SCHOENFELD, DOROTHY BRIGSTOCK
Kiam, Omar
McCardell, Claire
Maxwell, Elsa
Orry-Kelly
Snow, Carmel White
SCHOFIELD, ANN
Lang, Lucy Fox Robins
SCHOFIELD, CARLETON F.
Dodge, Raymond
SCHOTT, THOMAS E.
Hawley, Paul Ramsey
Pate, Maurice
SCHRADER, FRANZ
Wilson, Edmund Beecher
SCHREIBER, CARL F.
English, Thomas Dunn
Hirst, Henry Beck
Möllhausen, Heinrich Balduin
SCHROEDER, FRED E. H.
Hartmann, Carl Sadakichi
Norris, Charles Gilman Smith
Terhune, Albert Payson
SCHROM, NANCY
Nathan, Maud
SCHRUBEN, FRANCIS W.
Allen, Henry Justin
SCHUCHERT, CHARLES
Gabb, William More
Gibbs, George
Merrill, George Perkins
SCHUETTE, H. A.
Reid, David Boswell
SCHUKER, STEPHEN A.
Avery, Sewell Lee
Davison, George Willets
Goldschmidt, Jakob
Leffingwell, Russell Cornell
Prince, Frederick Henry
SCHULTES, RICHARD EVANS
Ames, Oakes
SCHULTZ, JACK
Bridges, Calvin Blackman
SCHULTZ, STANLEY K.
Curley, James Michael
Curran, Thomas Jerome
SCHULZE, ELDOR PAUL
James, Thomas Lemuel
Kemble, Gouverneur
SCHUSKY, ERNEST L.
Cantril, Albert Hadley
Densmore, Frances
Heye, George Gustav
La Farge, Oliver Hazard Perry
MacIver, Robert Morrison
Powdermaker, Hortense
Radin, Paul
Sauer, Carl Ortwin
Son of Many Beads
SCHUSKY, MARY SUE DILLIARD
Abbott, Eleanor Hallowell
Aldrich, Bess Genevra Streeter
Anthony, Katharine Susan
Bailey, (Irene) Temple
Baum, Hedwig ("Vicki")
Carr, Charlotte Elizabeth
Fauset, Jessie Redmon
Hill, Grace Livingston
Hobart, Alice Nourse Tisdale
Leaf, Wilbur Munro
Orton, Helen Fuller
Rives, Hallie Erminie
Wheeler, (George) Post
SCHUYLER, HAMILTON
Morris, Edmund
Ogden, Uzal
Smith, Charles Perrin
SCHUYLER, MONTGOMERY
Bacon, Robert
Eidlitz, Cyrus Lazelle Warner
Eidlitz, Leopold
Le Brun, Napoléon Eugène Henry Charles

SCHUYLER, ROBERT LIVINGSTON
Beer, George Louis
SCHWANTES, ROBERT S.
Fleisher, Benjamin Wilfrid
Gulick, Sidney Lewis
SCHWARTZ, ARTHUR
Koller, Carl
SCHWARTZ, CHARLES
Porter, Cole
SCHWARTZ, ELI
Hansen, Alvin Harvey
Johnson, Harry Gordon
SCHWARZ, JORDAN A.
Bunker, Arthur Hugh
Byrnes, James Francis
Doughton, Robert Lee
Guffey, Joseph F.
Kaiser, Henry John
Neely, Matthew Mansfield
Patman, John William Wright
SCHWARZ, RICHARD W.
Kellogg, John Harvey
SCOBIE, INGRID WINTHER
Bloor, Ella Reeve
SCOON, ROBERT
Spaulding, Edward Gleason
SCOTT, CHARLES F.
Sprague, Frank Julian
SCOTT, EDITH
Hanson, James Christian Meinich
SCOTT, FRANKLIN WILLIAM
Brownlow, William Ganaway
Hall, James, 1793–1868
Morrison, William Ralls
Russell, Benjamin
SCOTT, JONATHAN FRENCH
Backus, Truman Jay
Bailey, Ebenezer
Bailey, Rufus William
Barnes, Mary Downing Sheldon
SCOTT, KENNETH
Fiske, George Converse
SCOTT, LESLIE M.
Pittock, Henry Lewis
SCROGGS, WILLIAM O.
Walker, William
SEARS, FREDERIC C.
Manning, Robert
SEARS, J. D.
Campbell, Marius Robinson
SEARS, LOUIS M.
Benton, Thomas Hart, 1782–1858
Brown, Ethan Allen
Cass, Lewis
Smart, James Henry
SEARS, PAUL B.
Clements, Frederic Edward
Cowles, Henry Chandler
SEARS, ROBERT R.
Hull, Clark Leonard
Terman, Lewis Madison
SEELIG, M. G.
Hodgen, John Thompson
Still, Andrew Taylor
Whelpley, Henry Milton
SEITZ, DON C.
Depew, Chauncey Mitchell
SELDEN, SAMUEL
Koch, Frederick Henry
SELEMENT, GEORGE
Dodd, Monroe Elmon
SELLARDS, ELIAS HOWARD
Udden, Johan August
SELLARS, ROY W.
Morris, George Sylvester
Tappan, Henry Philip
SELLERS, HORACE WELLS
McArthur, John, 1823–1890
Peale, Charles Willson
Peale, Rembrandt
Peale, Sarah Miriam
Peale, Titian Ramsay
SELLERS, JAMES LEE
Paine, Halbert Eleazer
Philipp, Emanuel Lorenz
Sarpy, Peter A.
Thayer, John Milton
Van Wyck, Charles Henry
SELLERS, J. L.
Hitchcock, Gilbert Monell
Holdrege, George Ward
SELLIN, THORSTEN
Brockway, Zebulon Reed
Hart, Hastings Hornell
Koren, John
Lewis, Orlando Faulkland
Lynds, Elam
Osborne, Thomas Mott
Pilsbury, Amos
Vaux, Richard
Vaux, Roberts
SEMONCHE, JOHN E.
Phillips, John Sanburn
SENIOR, CLARENCE
Iglesias, Santiago
SENNETT, TED
Benny, Jack
Donlevy, Brian
Janssen, David
Tamiroff, Akim
Wellman, William Augustus
SENSABAUGH, GEORGE F.
Jones, Richard Foster
SENTURIA, JOSEPH J.
Wanamaker, John
Wanamaker, Lewis Rodman
Williams, John Skelton
SERONDE, JOSEPH
Knapp, William Ireland
SEVERANCE, FRANK HAYWARD
Alexander, De Alva Stanwood
SEWALL, HENRY
Vaughan, Victor Clarence
SEYBOLT, ROBERT FRANCIS
Cook, John Williston
Grew, Theophilus
Morrison, John Irwin
Neef, Francis Joseph Nicholas
Northend, Charles
Nott, Eliphalet
Orcutt, Hiram
Park, Roswell
Peabody, Selim Hobart
Peirce, Cyrus
Pormort, Philemon
Russell, William
Sheldon, Edward Austin
Sheldon, William Evarts
Sherwin, Thomas
Stetson, William Wallace
Thayer, Gideon French
Ticknor, Elisha
Tompkins, Arnold
Turner, Asa
Turner, Jonathan Baldwin
Watson, James Madison
Wells, William Harvey
Wickersham, James Pyle
SEYMOUR, CHARLES
House, Edward Mandell
Wilson, Woodrow
SEYMOUR, GEORGE DUDLEY
Austin, Henry
Hale, Nathan
Hoadley, David
Niemeyer, John Henry
Town, Ithiel
SEYMOUR, HAROLD
Alexander, Grover Cleveland
Griffith, Clark Calvin
SHACHTMAN, TOM
Wilson, Edith Bolling
SHAFER, ROBERT
Boies, Horace
Dodge, Grenville Mellen
Grimes, James Wilson
Gue, Benjamin F.
Mason, Charles
Nichols, George Ward
Parvin, Theodore Sutton
Payne, William Morton
SHAMBAUGH, BENJAMIN F.
Boies, Horace
Dodge, Grenville Mellen
Grimes, James Wilson
Gue, Benjamin F.
Mason, Charles
Parvin, Thieodore Sutton
SHAMBAUGH, BERTHA M. H.
Metz, Christian
SHANDS, ALFRED R., JR.
Whitman, Royal
SHANE, C. D.
Curtis, Heber Doust
Moore, Joseph Haines
SHANE, MARY LEA
Aitken, Robert Grant
SHANKLAND, R. S.
Allison, Samuel King
Miller, Dayton Clarence
SHANLEY, ESTELLE M.
Cozzens, James Gould
SHANNON, DAVID A.
Walling, William English
SHANNON, FRED A.
Spring, Leverett Wilson
SHANNON, WILLIAM H.
Merton, Thomas
SHANNON, WILLIAM V.
Patterson, Joseph Medill
SHAOUL, ROSALYN
Tishman, David
SHAPIRO, EDWARD S.
Burgess, Frank Gelett
De Palma, Ralph
Lambeau, Earl Louis ("Curly")
Lawson, Robert Ripley
White, Benjamin Franklin
Wills, Harry
SHAPIRO, HARRY L.
Hooton, Earnest Albert
Weidenreich, Franz
SHAPIRO, JAN
Boswell, Connie (Connee)
Callas, Maria
Etting, Ruth

Froman, Ellen Jane
Pons, Lily

SHAPLEN, ROBERT
Musica, Philip Mariano Fausto

SHARLIN, HAROLD I.
Gale, Henry Gordon

SHARP, NICHOLAS A.
Anthony, John J.
Correll, Charles James

SHAVER, MURIEL
Baum, Lyman Frank
Blackwell, Henry Brown
Bliss, Porter Cornelius
Brainerd, Erastus
Bross, William
Brown, Olympia
Brown, Simon
Browne, Francis Fisher
Bryan, Mary Edwards
Castle, Vernon Blythe
Chambers, James Julius
Chandler, Joseph Ripley
Child, David Lee
Cox, Palmer
Croly, David Goodman
Croly, Jane Cunningham
Davidge, William Pleater
Davis, Paulina Kellogg Wright
Delavan, Edward Cornelius
Duff, Mary Ann Dyke
Farnham, Eliza Woodson Burham
Flower, Lucy Louisa Coues
Fuller, Loie
Gilbert, Linda
Goodnow, Isaac Tichenor

SHAW, ARNOLD
Armstrong, Henry Worthington ("Harry")
Guthrie, Woody
Handy, William Christopher
Hendrix, Jimi
Silvers, Louis
Taylor, Joseph Deems
Washington, Dinah
Williams, (Hiram) Hank

SHAW, EDWIN B.
Lewis, Ellis

SHAW, HARRY, JR.
Joynes, Edward Southey
Stoddard, Elizabeth Drew Bartow
Stoddard, Richard Henry
Thomas, Edith Matilda
Tincker, Mary Agnes

SHAW, ROBERT K.
Norcross, Orlando Whitney

SHAW, WILFRED B.
Hutchins, Harry Burns

SHAW, WILLIAM BRISTOL
Abbey, Henry Eugene
Aborn, Milton
Adams, Henry Carter
Albee, Edward Franklin
Allis, Edward Phelps
Andrews, Chauncey Hummason
Andrews, Stephen Pearl
Arbuckle, John
Archbold, John Dustin
Avery, Samuel Putnam
Baker, Lorenzo Dow
Barber, Amzi Lorenzo
Benjamin, George Hillard
Bergh, Christian
Bragg, Edward Stuyvesant
Brayman, Mason
Butts, Isaac
Byrnes, Thomas F.
Cary, Edward
Chittenden, Simeon Baldwin
Claflin, Horace Brigham
Clark, Jonas Gilman
Clark, Myron Holley
Collier, Peter Fenelon
Corbin, Austin
Crimmins, John Daniel
Croker, Richard
Davey, John
Davison, Henry Pomeroy
Day, Horace H.
De Kay, George Colman
De Kay, James Ellsworth
Delafield, John, 1748–1824
Delafield, John, 1786–1853
Delmonico, Lorenzo
Dodd, Frank Howard
Dodge, David Low
Dodge, William Earl
Doremus, Sarah Platt Haines
Douglass, David Bates
Dudley, Charles Edward
Dun, Robert Graham
Eckford, Henry
Englis, John
Faber, John Eberhard
Fahnestock, Harris Charles
Fayerweather, Daniel Burton
Fels, Joseph
Field, Benjamin Hazard
Fish, Stuyvesant
Fisher, Joshua Francis
Fiske, Haley
Foster, Judith Ellen Horton
Francis, Samuel Ward
Genin, John Nicholas
Gorham, Jabez
Grant, Lewis Addison
Green, Henrietta Howland Robinson
Harris, William
Hasbrouck, Abraham Bruyn
Hatch, Rufus
Havemeyer, Henry Osborne
Havemeyer, William Frederick
Heath, Perry Sanford
Herring, Silas Clark
Hicks, John, 1847–1917
Higinbotham, Harlow Niles
Irene, Sister
James, Daniel Willis
Jesup, Morris Ketchum
Jones, Alexander
Jordan, William George
Judd, Orange
Juilliard, Augustus D.
Keely, John Ernst Worrell
Keene, James Robert
Kennedy, John Stewart
King, James Gore
King, John Alsop
Lefferts, Marshall
Lexow, Clarence
Loew, Marcus
Lord, David Nevins
Lorillard, Pierre
McCall, John Augustine
McCurdy, Richard Aldrich
Macy, Valentine Everit
Masson, Thomas Lansing
Moskowitz, Belle Lindner Israels
Odell, Benjamin Barker
Ogden, Robert Curtis
Packard, Silas Sadler
Paine, Byron
Pond, James Burton
Proctor, Frederick Francis
Putnam, Gideon
Quigg, Lemuel Ely
Reed, Lumar
Rice, Isaac Leopold
Ruggles, Samuel Bulkley
Sabin, Charles Hamilton
Schuyler, Louisa Lee
Scrymser, James Alexander
Sears, Robert
Seney, George Ingraham
Shonts, Theodore Perry
Sloan, Samuel
Smith, Ormond Gerald
Spinner, Francis Elias
Sterling, John William
Stetson, John Batterson
Stettinius, Edward Riley
Stevens, John Austin, 1795–1874
Stillman, James
Stranahan, James Samuel Thomas
Stuart, Robert Leighton
Taylor, Moses
Thompson, John
Thompson, William Boyce
White, Alfred Tredway
Willard, Mary Hatch
Willys, John North
Wolfe, John David

SHEA, WILLIAM E.
Squiers, Herbert
Thompson, Richard Wigginton
Walker, Mary Edwards
Weeks, John Wingate
Wheeler, Wayne Bidwell
Woodford, Stewart Lyndon
Woolley, John Granville
Wright, Luke Edward

SHEAFER, LOUIS
Glaspell, Susan Keating

SHEAFFER, LOUIS
Douglas, Lloyd Cassel

SHEAR, CORNELIUS LOTT
Ellis, Job Bicknell

SHEARER, AUGUSTUS H.
Lacey, John
Larned, Josephus Nelson
Severance, Frank Hayward
Ward, James Warner

SHEDD, SOLON
Smith, James Perrin

SHEEHAN, DONAL
Wyckoff, John Henry

SHELDON, HENRY D.
Hall, Granville Stanley

SHELDON, MARION
Wright, Silas

SHELLEY, WALTER BROWN
Pusey, William Allen

SHELTON, SUZANNE
St. Denis, Ruth

Shenk, Hiram H.
Bates, Samuel Penniman
Shenton, James P.
Kerby, William Joseph
Shepard, Arthur MacC.
Alden, James
Almy, John Jay
Shepard, Morris G.
Ostromislensky, Iwan Iwanowich
Shepherd, Rebecca
Mannes, Leopold Damrosch
Shepherd, Rebecca Ann
Rubinstein, Helena
Shepherd, William R.
Rives, George Lockhart
Sloane, William Milligan
Sheridan, Eugene R.
Boyd, Julian Parks
Sherman, Clifton Lucien
Burr, Alfred Edmund
Sherman, Jay J.
Livingstone, William
Newberry, John Stoughton
Newberry, Oliver
Sherwood, Garrison P.
Carter, Caroline Louise Dudley
Sherwood, Henry Noble
Brown, George Pliny
Sherwood, Morgan
Jones, Lewis Ralph
Shetrone, H. C.
Fowke, Gerard
Shewmaker, Kenneth E.
Carlson, Evans Fordyce
Smedley, Agnes
Shinn, Owen L.
Tilghman, Richard Albert
Shipler, Guy Emery
Hale, Charles Reuben
Houghton, George Hendric
Huntington, Frederic Dan
Langdon, William Chauncy
McLaren, William Edward
Odenheimer, William Henry
Onderdonk, Benjamin Tredwell
Onderdonk, Henry Ustick
Provoost, Samuel
Smith, John Cotton, 1826–1882
Spencer, Jesse Ames
Shipman, Fred W.
Gardner, Charles Kitchell
Hood, Washington
Kelly, Luther Sage
Lederer, John
Loring, Frederick Wadsworth
Needham, James
O'Fallon, Benjamin
Ogden, Herbert Gouverneur
Shippee, Lester Burrell
Davis, Cushman Kellogg
Gorman, Willis Arnold
Loring, Charles Morgridge
Lowry, Thomas
Marshall, William Rainey
Merriam, William Rush
Mitchell, William, 1832–1900
Nettleton, Alvred Bayard
Otis, Charles Eugene
Peavey, Frank Hutchinson
Pillsbury, John Sargent
Smalley, Eugene Virgil
Stevens, Hiram Fairchild
Stevens, John Harrington
Tawney, James Albertus
Towne, Charles Arnette
Walker, Thomas Barlow
Washburn, William Drew
Wheelock, Joseph Albert
Windom, William
Shipton, Clifford K.
Pring, Martin
Willard, Joseph, 1738–1804
Willard, Joseph, 1798–1865
Willard, Samuel
Williams, Nathaniel
Winthrop, James
Shirley, Glenn
Lillie, Gordon William
Shirley, Wayne
Mannes, Clara Damrosch
Shively, Charles
O'Sullivan, Mary Kenney
Shiver, Peter, Jr.
Lewis, William Henry
Shoemaker, Floyd Calvin
Broadhead, James Overton
Cockrell, Francis Marion
Colman, Norman Jay
Crittenden, Thomas Theodore
Shor, Elizabeth Noble
Bigelow, Henry Bryant
Bowen, Ira Sprague
Ewing, William Maurice
Heezen, Bruce Charles
Hubbard, Bernard Rosecrans
Kofoid, Charles Atwood
Rubey, William Walden
Shorey, Paul
Harper, William Rainey
Shout, John D.
Blitzstein, Marc
Dandridge, Dorothy Jean
Loesser, Frank
Shover, John L.
Ayres, William Augustus
Benson, Oscar Herman
O'Neal, Edward Asbury, III
Showalter, Elaine C.
Taggard, Genevieve
Shriver, Phillip Raymond
Pomerene, Atlee
Shryock, Richard H.
Abbott, Samuel Warren
Arnold, Richard Dennis
Deaver, John Blair
Rush, Benjamin
Rush, James
Strudwick, Edmund Charles Fox
Taylor, Charlotte de Bernier
Wells, William Charles
Shurcliff, William A.
Pfund, August Herman
Shuster, George N.
Donahue, Patrick
Finn, Francis James
Kilmer, Alfred Joyce
Lambert, Louis Aloisius
Lambing, Andrew Arnold
Lamy, John Baptist
Lynch, Patrick Neeson
Walsh, Henry Collins
Walsh, Thomas
Sicherman, Barbara
Coriat, Isador Henry
Sickels, Eleanor M.
Schuyler, Montgomery
Smalley, George Washburn
Vallentine, Benjamin Bennaton
Ward, Thomas
Wardman, Ervin
Warman, Cy
Webb, James Watson
Welch, Philip Henry
Wheeler, Andrew Carpenter
Siebert, Wilbur H.
De Brahm, William Gerard
Graham, John
Leonard, George
Moody, James
Moultrie, John
Romans, Bernard
Stuart, John
Turnbull, Andrew
Siegel, Katherine A. S.
Eaton, Cyrus Stephen
Mundt, Karl Earl
Sievers, Harry J., S.J.
Drexel, Katharine Mary
Sikes, E. W.
Clemson, Thomas Green
Siler, Joseph F.
Garnett, Alexander Yelverton Peyton
Hullihen, Simon P.
Sills, Kenneth C. M.
Avery, John
Goodwin, Daniel Raynes
Johnson, Henry
McKeen, Joseph
Packard, Alpheus Spring
Smyth, William
Upham, Thomas Cogswell
Woods, Leonard, 1807–1878
Silver, Rollo G.
Stokes, Frederick Abbot
Silverman, Alexander
Owens, Michael Joseph
Silverman, S. Richard
Goldstein, Max Aaron
Silveus, Marian
Thompson, Josiah Van Kirk
Warner, Adoniram Judson
Weeks, Joseph Dame
Simkins, Francis Butler
Gist, William Henry
Lever, Asbury Francis
McGowan, Samuel
Miles, William Porcher
Montague, Andrew Jackson
Moses, Franklin J.
Orr, James Lawrence
Pickens, Francis Wilkinson
Rainey, Joseph Hayne
Scott, Robert Kingston
Simpson, William Dunlap
Smalls, Robert
Thompson, Hugh Smith
Thornwell, James Henley
Tillman, Benjamin Ryan
Trescot, William Henry
Wilkinson, Robert Shaw
Simmons, Jerold L.
Burlingham, Charles Culp
Dickinson, John
Stryker, Lloyd Paul
Simms, L. Moody, Jr.
Barrymore, Ethel
Blue, Gerald Montgomery ("Monte")

Darwell, Jane
Gable, (William) Clark
Hull, Josephine
Jackson, Joseph Henry
Karloff, Boris
Schildkraut, Joseph
Stevens, Ashton
Todd, Mike
Tone, Stanislas Pascal Franchot
White, Clarence Cameron
SIMON, GEORGE T.
Miller, Glenn
SIMONDS, FREDERIC W.
Roemer, Karl Ferdinand
SIMONS, CORINNE MILLER
Lloyd, John Uri
SIMPSON, B. M., III
McCormick, Lynde Dupuy
SIMPSON, GEORGE GAYLORD
Granger, Walter
Osborn, Henry Fairfield
SIMPSON, LESLEY BYRD
Vallejo, Mariano Guadalupe
Vizcaino, Sebastían
SIMPSON, LEWIS P.
Bradford, Roark Whitney Wickliffe
SIMPSON, SARAH H. J.
Duane, James
SIMPSON, WILLIAM KELLY
Winlock, Herbert Eustis
SIMSON, RENNIE
Douglas, Aaron
Du Bois, Shirley Lola Graham
Griffin, John Howard
White, Charles Wilbert
SINCLAIR, BRUCE
Rice, George Samuel
Weymouth, Frank Elwin
SINGER, EDGAR A., JR.
Fullerton, George Stuart
SINGER, JAMES
Veblen, Oswald
SINGH, RAGHU N.
Kennedy, George Clayton
SIOUSSAT, ST. GEORGE L.
Johnson, Andrew
Smith, Justin Harvey
SIPLEY, LOUIS WALTON
Ives, Frederic Eugene
SISSON, CHARLES P.
Moody, William Henry
SITKOFF, HARVARD
Brownlee, James Forbis
Cooper, (Leon) Jere
Dawson, William Levi
Gaston, Herbert Earle
Lowenstein, Allard Kenneth
Nye, Gerald Prentice
Roper, Elmo Burns, Jr.
Tilson, John Quillin
Tobin, Maurice Joseph
Tydings, Millard Evelyn
SIZER, THEODORE
Jarves, James Jackson
Parton, Arthur
Penfield, Edward
Ross, Denman Waldo
Smibert, John
Street, Augustus Russell
Trumbull, John, 1756–1843
SKEEL, EMILY E. F.
Weems, Mason Locke
SKEHAN, PATRICK W.
Hyvernat, Henri
SKILLING, HAZEL
Ryan, Harris Joseph
SKINNER, CLARENCE A.
Brace, Dewitt Bristol
SKINNER, CLARENCE R.
Miner, Alonzo Ames
SKINNER, CONSTANCE LINDSAY
Franchère, Gabriel
Stanley, Henry Morton
SKLAR, ROBERT
Bitzer, George William
Fields, William Claude
Flaherty, Robert Joseph
Griffith, David Wark
Hart, William Surrey
Langdon, Harry Philmore
Lubitsch, Ernst
Porter, Edwin Stanton
SKLARIN, GLENN N.
Frick, Ford Christopher
Stern, Bill
SLADE, MARY B.
Saunders, Prince
SLADE, WILLIAM ADAMS
Andrews, Elisha Benjamin
Carpenter, Edmund Janes
Hazard, Jonathan J.
Hazard, Rowland Gibson
Hazard, Thomas
Hazard, Thomas Robinson
Spofford, Ainsworth Rand
SLATTERY, THOMAS C.
Grainger, George Percy
SLAUGHTER, GERTRUDE
Allinson, Anne Crosby Emery
SLOANE, DAVID C.
Milk, Harvey Bernard
SLOCUM, ADELE
Rhoads, Cornelius Packard
SLONIMSKY, NICOLAS
Foote, Arthur William
Ives, Charles Edward
Korngold, Erich Wolfgang
Mitropoulos, Dimitri
Schillinger, Joseph
SMALL, MELVIN
Davies, Joseph Edward
Houghton, Alanson Bigelow
SMERTENKO, CLARA MILLERD
Herron, George Davis
SMITH, ALBERT WILLIAM
Kerr, Walter Craig
SMITH, ALICE KIMBALL
Oppenheimer, Julius Robert
SMITH, ALICE R. HUGER
Fraser, Charles
SMITH, CARLETON SPRAGUE
Converse, Frederick Shepherd
SMITH, CHARLES FORSTER
Adams, Charles Kendall
SMITH, DANIEL M.
Colby, Bainbridge
Cox, James Middleton
SMITH, DAVID
Bates, Theodore Lewis ("Ted")
Johnson, Howard Deering
Whitney, Richard
SMITH, DAVID C.
Eckstorm, Fannie Hardy
SMITH, DAVID EUGENE
Adrain, Robert
Bôcher, Maxime
Cole, Frank Nelson
Craig, Thomas
De Forest, Erastus Lyman
Farrar, John
Green, Gabriel Marcus
Greenwood, Isaac
Halsted, George Bruce
Johnson, William Woolsey
Loomis, Elias
McClintock, Emory
Maschke, Heinrich
Newton, Hubert Anson
Runkle, John Daniel
Stringham, Washington Irving
Sylvester, James Joseph
Wentworth, George Albert
SMITH, DAVID STANLEY
Parker, Horatio William
Steinert, Morris
SMITH, EDGAR FAHS
Bache, Franklin
Boyé, Martin Hans
Cutbush, James
Griscom, John
Hare, Robert
Lea, Mathew Carey
Woodhouse, James
SMITH, EDWARD CONRAD
Hitchcock, Frank Harris
MacVeagh, Franklin
Mooney, William
Nicoll, De Lancey
Olyphant, Robert Morrison
Opdyke, George
Parker, Alton Brooks
Parker, Amasa Junius
Parsons, John Edward
Pierrepont, Edwards
Robertson, William Henry
Roosevelt, Robert Barnwell
Rumsey, William
Sampson, William
Sanford, Nathan
Sedgwick, Arthur George
Shearman, Thomas Gaskell
Sherman, James Schoolcraft
Smith, Charles Emory
Smith, Erasmus Darwin
Smith, Truman
Stanchfield, John Barry
Sterne, Simon
Tanner, James
Tracy, Benjamin Franklin
Wheeler, William Almon
Wood, Fernando
Wood, George
Woodruff, Timothy Lester
SMITH, EDWIN W.
Aggrey, James Emman Kwegyir
Lindley, Daniel
SMITH, FRED M.
Lucas, Daniel Bedinger
Post, Melville Davisson
Strother, David Hunter
SMITH, GADDIS
Acheson, Dean Gooderham
SMITH, GERALD BIRNEY
Anderson, Galusha
SMITH, GERTRUDE
Merrill, Elmer Truesdell
SMITH, HAROLD S.
Ghent, William James

SMITH, HARRY WORCESTER
Troye, Edward
SMITH, HENRY CLAY
Allport, Gordon Willard
Bingham, Walter Van Dyke
Fryer, Douglas Henry
Maslow, Abraham H.
Otis, Arthur Sinton
SMITH, J. M. POWIS
Curtiss, Samuel Ives
SMITH, JOE PATTERSON
Grierson, Benjamin Henry
SMITH, JOHN DAVID
Owsley, Frank Lawrence
SMITH, MARION PARRIS
Colden, Jane
Logan, James, 1674–1751
Logan, James Harvey
Marshall, Humphry
Reilly, Marion
Rittenhouse, William
Roberts, Job
Rothrock, Joseph Trimble
SMITH, PAUL A.
Veatch, Arthur Clifford
SMITH, RALPH C.
Adams, Joseph Alexander
Aitken, Robert
Andrews, Joseph
Barber, John Warner
SMITH, RALPH G.
Edmunds, Charles Wallis
SMITH, ROLAND M.
Simmons, Roscoe Conkling Murray
SMITH, RONALD A.
Berenson, Senda
SMITH, WALTER M.
Dunn, Charles
Durrie, Daniel Steele
SMITH, WARREN HUNTING
Towler, John
SMITH, WILLIAM
Finlay, Hugh
SMITH, WILLIAM E.
Blair, Francis Preston, 1791–1876
Blair, Francis Preston, 1821–1875
Blair, Montgomery
Cassidy, William
Croswell, Edwin
Gales, Joseph, 1761–1841
Gales, Joseph, 1786–1860
King, Preston
Medary, Samuel
Morris, Thomas
Rives, John Cook
Sargent, Nathan
Seaton, William Winston
Smith, Margaret Bayard
Smith, Samuel Harrison
Vallandigham, Clement Laird
Van Buren, John
Van Buren, Martin
Van Ness, William Peter
Venable, William Henry
Walden, John Morgan
Williams, George Washington
Woodbury, Levi
SMITH, WILLIAM ROY
Hazard, Ebenezer
Hazard, Samuel
Holme, Thomas
Lloyd, David
Lloyd, Thomas
Markham, William
Moore, John, 1659–1732
Moore, William, 1699–1783
More, Nicholas
Norris, Isaac, 1671–1735
Norris, Isaac, 1701–1766
Pusey, Caleb
Rawie, Francis, *c.* 1662–1726/27
Shippen, Edward, 1639–1712
Shippen, Edward, 1728/29–1806
Thomas, George
SMITHER, HARRIET
Smith, Ashbel
SMULLYAN, ARTHUR
Rand, Benjamin
SMYTH, HERBERT WEIR
Lane, George Martin
Morgan, Morris Hicky
Richardson, Rufus Byam
SMYTHE, GEORGE FRANKLIN
Andrews, Lorin
Leonard, William Andrew
McIlvaine, Charles Pettit
SNYDER, JOHN KIMBALL
Abbott, Jacob
SNYDER, LOUIS L.
Hayes, Carlton Joseph Huntley
SNYDER, MERRILL J.
Plotz, Harry
SNYDER, W. E.
Newcomer, Christian
SOARES, JANET
Horst, Louis
SOBEL, ROBERT
Black, Eli
Chandler, Norman
Coleman, John Aloysius
Cordiner, Ralph Jarron
Cuppia, Jerome Chester
Dykstra, John
Frazer, Joseph Washington
Gray, Harold Edwin
Hilton, Conrad Nicholson
Homer, Arthur Bartlett
Jacoby, Neil Herman
Meyer, André Benoit Mathieu
Reynolds, Milton
Watson, Arthur Kittridge
Wilson, Joseph Chamberlain
Young, Robert Ralph
SOBOL, ROBERT
Hopson, Howard Colwell
SOCOLOFSKY, HOMER E.
Bean, Leon Lenwood
Capper, Arthur
Hertz, John Daniel
Schoeppel, Andrew Frank
SOHON, F. W.
Tondorf, Francis Anthony
SOKAL, MICHAEL M.
Scott, Walter Dill
Seashore, Carl Emil
SOLBERG, CARL
Humphrey, Hubert Horatio, Jr.
SOLBERG, WINTON U.
Davenport, Eugene
SOLLMAN, TORALD
Stewart, George Neil
SOLOMON, BARBARA MILLER
Brooks, John Graham
SOLOMON, HARRY C.
Campbell, Charles Macfie
SOLOMON, IRVIN D.
James, Daniel, Jr. ("Chappie")
SOLOMON, MELISSA
Flanner, Janet
SOLON, LEONARD R.
Gödel, Kurt Friedrich
SOLOW, HERBERT
Parker, Carleton Hubbell
Seixas, Gershom Mendes
Stephens, Uriah Smith
Sylvis, William H.
Trevellick, Richard F.
Upchurch, John Jordan
Wright, James Lendrew
SOLVICK, STANLEY D.
Hawley, Willis Chatman
Taft, Henry Waters
SOMMER, LEO H.
Whitmore, Frank Clifford
SONNEBORN, T. M.
Jennings, Herbert Spencer
SONNECK, OSCAR G. T.
Heinrich, Antony Philip
SONNICHSEN, ALBERT
Kelly, Edmond
SONTAG, RAYMOND J.
Van Dyke, Paul
SOPER, GEORGE A.
McMath, Robert Emmet
Waring, George Edwin
SOSNA, MORTON
Williams, Aubrey Willis
SOULE, BYRON A.
Acheson, Edward Goodrich
SOULE, SHERROD
Andrews, Samuel James
Andrews, William Watson
Badger, Joseph, 1757–1846
SOUTHALL, JAMES P. C.
Maclaurin, Richard Cockburn
Renwick, James, 1792–1863
Rood, Ogden Nicholas
Troland, Leonard Thompson
Zentmayer, Joseph
SOUTHERN, DAVID W.
Hunton, George Kenneth
Waring, Julius Waties
SOUTHERN, EILEEN
Burleigh, Henry Thacker
SOUVAY, CHARLES L.
Andreis, Andrew James Felix Bartholomew De
Du Bourg, Louis Guillaume Valentin
Rosati, Joseph
SPAETH, J. DUNCAN
Hibben, John Grier
Hunt, Theodore Whitefield
Lacy, Ernest
Van Dyke, Henry
SPALDING, JAMES ALFRED
Aspinwall, William
Barker, Jeremiah
Batchelder, John Putnam
SPALDING, M. E.
Neville, Wendell Cushing
SPANTON, A. I.
Buchtel, John Richards
SPARGO, JOHN
Haswell, Anthony

SPATT, HARTLEY
Kahn, Louis I.
Sikorsky, Igor Ivanovich
Stone, Edward Durrell
SPAULDING, E. WILDER
Law, Richard
Morris, Lewis Richard
Olds, Robert Edwin
Partridge, James Rudolph
Pendleton, John Strother
Pickett, James Chamberlayne
Pitkin, William, 1635–1694
Pitkin, William, 1694–1769
Pitkin, William, 1725–1789
Plumley, Frank
Roberts, Edmund
Schenck, Robert Cumming
Schuyler, Eugene
Seward, George Frederick
Sharp, William Graves
Storer, Bellamy
Taylor, Hannis
Tower, Charlemagne
Tripp, Bartlett
Vail, Aaron
Van Schaick, Goose
Willard, Joseph Edward
Willett, Marinus
Wilson, Henry Lane
Yates, Abraham
Yates, John Van Ness
Yates, Robert
SPAULDING, FRANK E.
Inglis, Alexander James
SPAULDING, OLIVER L.
MacArthur, Arthur
SPAULDING, OLIVER L., JR.
Lawton, Henry Ware
McClellan, George Brinton
McDowell, Irvin
McPherson, James Birdseye
Marcy, Randolph Barnes
Otis, Elwell Stephen
Pope, John
Porter, Fitz-John
Rawlins, John Aaron
Ropes, John Codman
Rosecrans, William Starke
Schofield, John McAllister
Sherman, William Tecumseh
Slocum, Henry Warner
Stoneman, George
Thomas, George Henry
Weitzel, Godfrey
Wilcox, Orlando Bolivar
SPAULDING, THOMAS MARSHALL
Alexander, Barton Stone
Alexander, William Dewitt
Allen, Henry Tureman
Allen, Robert
Alvord, Benjamin
Ammen, Jacob
Anderson, Robert
Andrews, George Leonard
Armistead, Lewis Addison
Arnold, Lewis Golding
Arnold, Richard
Ayres, Romeyn Beck
Baker, Laurence Simmons
Barksdale, William
Barringer, Rufus
Barton, Seth Maxwell
Battle, Cullen Andrews
Beale, Richard Lee Turberville
Beauregard, Pierre Gustave Toutant
Bee, Barnard Elliott
Bee, Hamilton Prioleau
Bernard, Simon
Birge, Henry Warner
Bomford, George
Bonaparte, Jerome Napoleon
Bowers, Theodore Shelton
Boynton, Edward Carlisle
Brooke, John Rutter
Brown, Jacob Jennings
Burbridge, Stephen Gano
Bussey, Cyrus
Canby, Edward Richard Sprigg
Carr, Eugene Asa
Carr, Joseph Bradford
Carroll, Samuel Sprigg
Casey, Silas
Chaffee, Adna Romanza
Cheatham, Benjamin Franklin
Chetlain, Augustus Louis
Cist, Henry Martyn
Colston, Raleigh Edward
Cooke, Philip St. George
Cooper, Samuel, 1798–1876
Corse, John Murray
Couch, Darius Nash
Crozet, Claude
Cullum, George Washington
Dana, Napoleon Jackson Tecumseh
Davies, Henry Eugene
Davis, George Whitefield
Davis, Jefferson Columbus
Devin, Thomas Casimer
Dickman, Joseph Theodore
Dodge, Theodore Ayrault
Doubleday, Abner
Duke, Basil Wilson
Early, Jubal Anderson
Evans, Clement Anselm
Evans, Nathan George
Ferrero, Edward
Forrest, Nathan Bedford
Foster, Robert Sanford
Franklin, William Buel
French, William Henry
Fuller, John Wallace
Gardner, John Lane
Getty, George Washington
Gibbon, John
Gilmor, Harry
Graham, Charles Kinnaird
Granger, Gordon
Grant, Frederick Dent
Greene, Francis Vinton
Greene, George Sears
Gregg, John
Griflin, Charles
Griffin, Simon Goodell
King, Edward Leonard
Lee, William Little
Mills, Anson
Partridge, Alden
Ripley, Eleazar Wheelock
Roberdeau, Isaac
Smith, Andrew Jackson
Smith, Martin Luther
Smith, Richard Somers
Snelling, Josiah
Steedman, James Blair
Steele, Frederick
Stevens, John Leavitt
Stevens, Walter Husted
Stevenson, Carter Littlepage
Stone, Charles Pomeroy
Sturgis, Samuel Davis
Sumner, Edwin Vose
Swayne, Wager
Swift, Joseph Gardner
Swift, William Henry
Swinton, William
Thomas, Allen
Tucker, Stephen Davis
Van Dorn, Earl
Wadsworth, James Samuel
Webster, Joseph Dana
Wheeler, George Montague
Whipple, Amiel Weeks
Williams, Alpheus Starkey
Winder, William Henry
Woodbury, Daniel Phineas
SPEAR, ALLAN H.
Jackson, Robert R.
Williams, Fannie Barrier
SPEAR, JOHN W.
Heard, Dwight Bancroft
SPECTOR, RONALD
Knox, Dudley Wright
SPEER, ROBERT ELLIOTT
Wanless, William James
SPEERT, HAROLD
Taussig, Frederick Joseph
SPENCE, CLARK C.
Dwight, Arthur Smith
Mathewson, Edward Payson
SPENCER, CHARLES WORTHEN
Benson, Egbert
Clarke, George
Clarkson, Matthew
Coote, Richard
Cruger, John
De Lancey, James, 1703–1760
De Lancey, James, 1732–1800
De Lancey, James, 1746–1804
De Lancey, Oliver
De Lancey, William Heathcote
Hamilton, Andrew, d. 1741
Hobart, John Sloss
Horsmanden, Daniel
Kennedy, Archibald
Laurance, John
Lewis, Francis
Lewis, Morgan
Thomas, David
SPICEHANDLER, DANIEL
Trilling, Lionel
Untermeyer, Louis
SPIEGEL, SHALOM
Davidson, Israel
SPIELHOLTZ, GERALD I.
Woodward, Robert Burns
SPILLER, ROBERT E.
Shelton, Frederick William
Thomas, Joseph
Wallace, Horace Binney
SPINCARN, J. E.
Woodberry, George Edward
SPOFFORD, CHARLES M.
Freeman, John Ripley
SPRENG, SAMUEL PETER
Esher, John Jacob
SPRING, LA VERNE WARD
Kelley, William

SPURLIN, PAUL M.
Schinz, Albert
SQUIRES, JAMES DUANE
Sprague, Homer Baxter
SRB, ADRIAN R.
Emerson, Rollins Adams
STACEY, C. P.
O'Mahony, John
O'Neill, John
Roberts, William Randall
Smith, Robert, 1722–1777
STAHL, LISA A.
Faith, Percy
Hutton, Barbara Woolworth
STANARD, MARY NEWTON
Archer, William Segar
Breckenridge, James
STANLEY, GEORGE M.
Leverett, Erank
STANLEY, PETER W.
Forbes, William Cameron
Quezon, Manuel Luis
STANLEY, RICHARD J.
Waymouth, George
STANTON, TIMOTHY WILLIAM
White, Charles Abiathar
STAROBIN, JOSEPH R.
Minor, Robert
STARR, HARRIS ELWOOD
Abbey, Henry
Abbot, Gorham Dummer
Abbott, Benjamin
Adams, Daniel
Adams, Ebenezer
Adams, Eliphalet
Adams, Hannah
Adams, Jasper
Aiken, Charles Augustus
Akers, Elizabeth Chase
Alden, Isabella Macdonald
Alden, Joseph
Allen, Paul
Allen, Thomas M.
Allen, William, 1784–1868
Alline, Henry
Altsheler, Joseph Alexander
Anderson, Henry Tompkins
Andrew, Samuel
Anthon, Charles Edward
Anthony, Susan Brownell
Appleton, James
Appleton, Jesse
Appleton, Thomas Gold
Armstrong, George Dod
Atwater, Lyman Hotchkiss
Augustus, John
Austin, David
Austin, Jane Goodwin
Austin, Samuel
Austin, William
Ayres, Anne
Babcock, Maltbie Davenport
Backus, Azel
Bacon, Thomas
Bailey, Jacob
Barnard, Henry
Bartlett, Joseph
Barton, Clara
Beecher, Charles
Beecher, Henry Ward
Beecher, Thomas Kinnicut
Bickel, Luke Washington
Bickerdyke, Mary Ann Ball
Blaikie, William
Bliss, Philip Paul
Bolton, Sarah Tittle Barrett
Bonard, Louis
Bouton, John Bell
Bowman, Thomas
Brainerd, David
Brainerd, John
Breckinridge, John
Bridgman, Elijah Coleman
Bronson, Walter Cochrane
Brooks, Charles Timothy
Brown, Phoebe Hinsdale
Brown, Samuel Robbins
Brownell, Henry Howard
Buckley, James Monroe
Burnap, George Washington
Burrell, David James
Burton, Nathaniel Judson
Bush, George
Byrne, Andrew
Cannon, Harriet Starr
Channing, Edward Tyrrell
Channing, William Henry
Chapman, Victor Emmanuel
Cheney, Charles Edward
Clap, Thomas
Clark, Jonas
Clark, Sheldon
Clark, Thomas March
Clay, Joseph, 1764–1811
Colver, Nathaniel
Cone, Spencer Houghton
Connelly, Cornelia
Cooke, George Willis
Cooper, Ezekiel
Cox, Samuel Hanson
Coxe, Arthur Cleveland
Craig, Austin
Creath, Jacob, 1777–1854
Creath, Jacob, 1799–1886
Crittenton, Charles Nelson
Crocker, Hannah Mather
Crooks, George Richard
Cummins, George David
Cutler, Timothy
Cuyler, Theodore Ledyard
Daboll, Nathan
Daggett, Naphtali
Dana, James
Day, Jeremiah
Dearing, John Lincoln
De Forest, John William
Dickins, John
Diman, Jeremiah Lewis
Dix, Morgan
Dole, Nathan Haskell
Dorrell, William
Doyle, Sarah Elizabeth
Drinkwater, Jennie Maria
Duffield, George, 1732–1790
Duffield, George, 1794–1868
Duffield, Samuel Augustus Willoughby
Durbin, John Price
Dwight, Timothy, 1752–1817
Dwight, Timothy, 1828–1916
Eaton, Homer
Embury, Philip
Emory, John
Errett, Isaac
Evans, Hugh Davey
Evans, Nathaniel
Ewer, Ferdinand Cartwright
Fallows, Samuel
Fanning, Tolbert
Farley, Harriet
Fenwick, Benedict Joseph
Ferguson, William Porter Frisbee
Finley, James Bradley
Finley, Robert
Finley, Samuel
Finney, Charles Grandison
Fisher, Daniel Webster
Fisher, Ebenezer
Fisk, Wilbur
Fiske, Fidelia
Fitton, James
Flickinger, Daniel Kumler
Flower, Benjamin Orange
Floy, James
Follen, Eliza Lee Cabot
Foss, Cyrus David
Foster, Charles James
Foster, Frank Hugh
Foster, Randolph Sinks
Fowler, Orin
Francis, Convers
Franklin, Benjamin, 1812–1878
Gaines, Wesley John
Gammon, Elijah Hedding
Gannett, Ezra Stiles
Gannett, William Channing
Garrettson, Freeborn
Gates, Frederick Taylor
Gay, Ebenezer
Gibbons, Herbert Adams
Gladden, Washington
Goodell, William, 1792–1867
Goodrich, Chauncey Allen
Goodrich, Elizur, 1734–1797
Goodwin, Elijah
Gordon, Andrew
Graham, Isabella Marshall
Grant, Asahel
Green, Lewis Warner
Greenleaf, Benjamin
Greer, David Hummell
Grellet, Stephen
Griswold, Alexander Viets
Gunn, Frederick William
Hall, Charles Henry
Hall, Hazel
Hallowell, Benjamin
Hamline, Leonidas Lent
Hardey, Mother Mary Aloysia
Hare, George Emlen
Hare, William Hobart
Harper, Ida Husted
Harris, William Logan
Harrison, William Pope
Hartranft, Chester David
Hawes, Charles Boardman
Hayden, Amos Sutton
Hayden, William
Haygood, Laura Askew
Headley, Phineas Camp
Heck, Barbara
Hedding, Elijah
Hendrix, Eugene Russell
Hepworth, George Hughes
Herbert, Henry William
Herford, Oliver Brooke
Herrick, Edward Claudius
Hibbard, Freeborn Garrettson

Hooker, Isabella Beecher
Hopkins, Lemuel
Hoshour, Samuel Klinefelter
Hosmer, Frederick Lucian
Hunt, Robert
Hunter, Andrew
Ingalls, Marilla Baker
Inskip, John Swanel
Jarratt, Devereux
Jarvis, Abraham
Jeanes, Anna T.
Johnson, Samuel, 1822–1882
Joyce, Isaac Walton
Judd, Sylvester
Junkin, George
Kelly, Michael J.
King, Thomas Starr
Kingsley, Calvin
Kirk, Edward Norris
Kumler, Henry
Lamont, Hammond
Lane, Tidence
Lard, Moses E.
Lee, Jesse
Lord, John
Lothrop, Harriett Mulford Stone
Lufbery, Raoul Gervais Victor
McAuley, Jeremiah
McAuley, Thomas
McCabe, Charles Cardwell
McCalla, William Latta
M'Clintock, John
McDowell, John, 1751–1820
McDowell, John, 1780–1863
McGarvey, John William
McKendree, William
McVickar, William Neilson
MacWhorter, Alexander
Mahan, Milo
Manning, James
Marsh, John, 1788–1868
Meigs, Josiah
Messer, Asa
Milligan, Robert
Moore, James, 1764–1814
Moore, Richard Channing
Nash, Daniel
Nettleton, Asahel
Nott, Samuel
Ochs, Julius
Ogilvie, John, 1724–1774
O'Kelly, James
Osborn, Norris Galpin
Paddock, Benjamin Henry
Paddock, John Adams
Parker, Edwin Pond
Parker, Edwin Wallace
Payson, Edward
Peck, George
Pendleton, William Kimbrough
Phelps, Austin
Pierpont, James
Pierson, Abraham, 1609–1678
Pierson, Abraham, *c.* 1645–1707
Pierson, Arthur Tappan
Pierson, Hamilton Wilcox
Pike, Albert
Pinkerton, Lewis Letig
Porter, Noah
Power, Frederick Dunglison
Purviance, David
Reach, Alfred James
Reed, David
Reid, John Morrison
Robbins, Chandler
Roberts, Benjamin Titus
Roberts, Robert Richford
Robinson, Ezekiel Gilman
Rockwell, Kiffin Yates
Rodgers, John, 1727–1811
Rodgers, John, 1881–1926
Rogers, James Blythe
Russell, James Solomon
Ruter, Martin
Sage, Henry Williams
Sankey, Ira David
Sawyer, Thomas Jefferson
Schaff, Philip
Sears, Barnas
Seeger, Alan
Sergeant, John, 1710–1749
Shaw, Elijah
Shuey, William John
Simpson, Matthew
Sims, Charles N.
Slicer, Thomas Roberts
Smith, Oliver
Smith, William, 1727–1803
Smyth, Newman
Spalding, Franklin Spencer
Sparrow, William
Spencer, Elihu
Sprague, William Buell
Stebbins, Horatio
Stiles, Ezra
Stokes, Anson Phelps
Stone, Barton Warren
Storrs, Richard Salter, 1787–1873
Storrs, Richard Salter, 1821–1900
Strawbridge, Robert
Sumner, Walter Taylor
Sumner, William Graham
Swain, Clara A.
Swing, David
Taylor, Edward Thompson
Taylor, William Mackergo
Tennent, Gilbert
Tennent, William, 1673–1745
Tennent, William, 1705–1777
Tichenor, Isaac Taylor
Tomkins, Floyd Williams
Twichell, Joseph Hopkins
Tyler, Charles Mellen
Upham, Samuel Foster
Vail, Stephen Montfort
Van Rensselaer, Cortlandt
Varick, James
Vinton, Alexander Hamilton
Vinton, Francis
Wadsworth, James
Wakeley, Joseph Burton
Ware, Henry, 1764–1845
Ware, Henry, 1794–1843
Ware, John Fothergill Waterhouse
Ware, William
Warren, Henry White
Washburn, Edward Abiel
Wayman, Alexander Walker
Webb, Thomas
Welles, Noah
Wellons, William Brock
Wharton, Charles Henry
Whedon, Daniel Denison
Whitefield, George
Willard, Sidney
Willey, Samuel Hopkins
Williams, Charles David
Williams, Elisha, 1694–1755
Winchester, Elhanan
Winslow, Hubbard
Wise, Daniel
Woodbridge, William Channing
Woolsey, Theodore Dwight
Worcester, Noah
Worcester, Samuel
Wylie, Samuel Brown
Young, Jessie Bowman
Zollars, Ely Vaughan

STARR, LOUIS M.
Carvalho, Solomon Solis
Earhart, Amelia Mary
Goddard, Morrill
Johnson, Robert Underwood
Martin, Edward Sandford
Means, Gaston Bullock
Miller, Webb
Patterson, Eleanor Medill

STARRETT, VINCENT
Biggers, Earl Derr

STAVE, BRUCE M.
McLevy, Jasper

STEAD, EUGENE A., JR.
Weiss, Soma

STEADMAN, J. M., JR.
Smith, Charles Henry, 1826–1903
Stanton, Frank Lebby
Wilde, Richard Henry

STEARNS, BERTHA MONICA
Godey, Louis Antoine
Hale, Sarah Josepha Buell
Hasbrouck, Lydia Sayer
Haven, Emily Bradley Neal
Herrick, Sophia McIlvaine Bledsoe
Hooper, Lucy Hamilton
Martyn, Sarah Towne Smith
Mayo, Sarah Carter Edgarton
Nichols, Mary Sargeant Neal Gove
Nichols, Thomas Low
Sanders, Elizabeth Elkins
Sedgwick, Catharine Maria
Sherwood, Katharine Margaret Brownlee
Spofford, Harriet Elizabeth Prescott
Stephens, Ann Sophia
Swisshelm, Jane Grey Cannon
Townsend, Virginia Frances
Welby, Amelia Ball Coppuck
Whitcher, Frances Miriam Berry
Whitney, Adeline Dutton Train
Whittelsey, Abigail Goodrich
Woolsey, Sarah Chauncy

STEARNS, HENRY P.
Bellingham, Richard
Canonchet
Church, Benjamin, 1639–1718
Philip

STEARNS, MARSHALL W.
Rainey, Gertrude Malissa Nix Pridgett
Smith, Bessie

Stearns, Raymond P.
Parris, Samuel
Underhill, John
Weld, Thomas
Williams, John, 1664–1729
Stebbins, Joel
Comstock, George Cary
Stebenne, David L.
Meany, William George
Rockefeller, Nelson Aldrich
Steck, Francis Borgia
Serra, Junipero
Steele, Richard W.
Early, Stephen Tyree
Steffek, Edwin F.
Pyle, Robert
Steffen, Nancy L.
Burgess, Thornton Waldo
Cooper, Kent
Dreyfus, Max
Field, Marshall, IV
Stegner, Wallace
DeVoto, Bernard Augustine
Wister, Owen
Stein, Leon
Henry, Alice
Stein, Stanley J.
Haring, Clarence
Steiner, Fred
Newman, Alfred
Steiner, Gotthold
Cobb, Nathan Augustus
Steiner, Walter Ralph
Baer, William Stevenson
Brigham, Amariah
Brinton, John Hill
Bronson, Henry
Steiner, William F., Jr.
Morton, Charles Walter
Steirer, William E., Jr.
Greenslet, Ferris
Steirer, William F.
Adams, Franklin Pierce
Steirer, William F., Jr.
Howey, Walter Crawford
O'Brien, Robert Lincoln
Phillips, Harry Irving
Stenerson, Douglas C.
Mencken, Henry Louis
Stenstrom, Christine
Albers, Josef
White, Minor Martin
Stephens, Edna B.
Fletcher, John Gould
Stephens, Ferris J.
Dougherty, Raymond Philip
Stephens, George W.
Nelson, Nelson Olsen
Stephens, John
Alexander, Hartley Burr
Stephenson, George M.
Esbjörn, Lars Paul
Hasselquist, Tuve Nilsson
Lind, John
Lindbergh, Charles Augustus
Mattson, Hans
Swensson, Carl Aaron
Thomas, William Widgery
Stephenson, Martha Tucker
Adams, Abigail
Davis, Varina Anne Jefferson
Davis, Varina Howell
Stephenson, Nathaniel Wright
Aldrich, Nelson Wilmarth
Benjamin, Judah Philip
Davis, Jefferson
Stephenson, Wendell H.
Boyd, Thomas Duckett
Lane, James Henry, 1814–1866
Mitchell, Robert Byington
Montgomery, James
Plumb, Preston B.
Pomeroy, Samuel Clarke
Porter, Alexander
Reeder, Andrew Horatio
Richardson, Edmund
Robinson, Charles
Shannon, Wilson
Slidell, John
Stanton, Frederick Perry
Taylor, Richard
Taylor, Zachary
Sterling, Keir B.
Allen, Arthur Augustus
Beary, Donald Bradford
Beebe, (Charles) William
Blodgett, Katherine Burr
Chapin, James Paul
Child, Charles Manning
Griscom, Ludlow
Jones, Lynds
Kostelanetz, Andre
Lear, Ben
McKeldin, Theodore Roosevelt
Miller, Gerrit Smith, Jr.
Oberholser, Harry Church
Seton, Grace Gallatin Thompson
Smith, Holland McTyeire
Tate, George Henry Hamilton
Wheeler, Earle Gilmore
Sternstein, Jerome L.
Diat, Louis Felix
Rombauer, Irma Louise
Sardi, Melchiorre Pio Vencenzo ("Vincent")
Stevens, Raymond
Little, Arthur Dehon
Stevens, S. K.
Farrell, James Augustine
Stevens, Thomas Wood
Goodman, Kenneth Sawyer
Stevens, Walter B.
Francis, David Rowland
Stevens, Wayne E.
Coles, Edward
Dongan, Thomas
Duncan, Joseph
Edwards, Ninian
Hendrick
Johnson, Guy
Johnson, Sir John
Johnson, Sir William
Munro, Henry
Trent, William
Wentworth, John, 1737–1820
Wharton, Samuel
Wraxall, Peter
Stevens, William Oliver
Adams, William Taylor
Stevenson, John A.
Galloway, Beverly Thomas
Kauffman, Calvin Henry
Smith, Erwin Frink
Steward, Helen R.
Rust, Richard Sutton
Stoddard, Amos
Stewart, Charles C.
Tauber, Maurice Falcolm
Stewart, De Lisle
Vaughan, Daniel
Stewart, Edgar I.
Ward, Joseph
Stewart, George R., Jr.
Derby, George Horatio
Harte, Francis Brett
McBurney, Robert Ross
Thomes, William Henry
Webb, Charles Henry
Wells, William Vincent
Stewart, Randall
Kester, Vaughan
King, William Benjamin Basil
Ticknor, William Davis
Upham, Charles Wentworth
Stewart, William J.
McIntire, Ross
Stigler, George J.
Simons, Henry Calvert
Stillwell, Margaret B.
Hawkins, Rush Christopher
Stillwell, Paul
Martin, Johnny Leonard Roosevelt ("Pepper")
Stine, Jeffrey K.
Cone, Russell Glenn
Houdry, Eugene Jules
Savage, John Lucian ("Jack")
Stock, Leo F.
Pallen, Condé Benoist
Stocking, George W., Jr.
Benedict, Ruth Fulton
Boas, Franz
Redfield, Robert
Wissler, Clark
Stokes, Anson Phelps
Dexter, Franklin Bowditch
Dillard, James Hardy
Washington, Booker Taliaferro
Stone, Alan
Perlman, Philip Benjamin
Stone, Donald L.
Hackett, Frank Warren
Haddock, Charles Brickett
Stone, Marshall H.
Birkhoff, George David
Stone, Richard G.
Weaver, Philip
Stone, Witmer
Abbott, Charles Conrad
Brewer, Thomas Mayo
Brewster, William
Cassin, John
Cory, Charles Barney
Coues, Elliott
Elliot, Daniel Giraud
Forbush, Edward Howe
Lawrence, George Newbold
Maynard, Charles Johnson
Nehrling, Henry
Nuttall, Thomas
Ord, George
Ridgway, Robert
Townsend, John Kirk
Wilson, Alexander
Stones, Elleine H.
Burton, Clarence Monroe
Storrs, Harry C.
Little, Charles Sherman

STORY, RONALD
Beatty, Clyde Raymond
Breen, Joseph Ignatius
Selznick, David O.
Woolley, Edgar Montillion ("Monty")
STOVER, JOHN F.
Harrison, Fairfax
Willard, Daniel
STRATTON, DAVID H.
Fall, Albert Bacon
STRAYER, JOSEPH R.
Haskins, Charles Homer
STREVEY, TRACY E.
McCormick, Joseph Medill
Medill, Joseph
Scott, James Wilmot
Seymour, Horatio Winslow
STRICKLAND, ARVARH E.
Spaulding, Charles Clinton
STRINGER-HYE, RICHARD
Busch, Hermann
STRINGFIELD, V. T.
Meinzer, Oscar Edward
STRITZLER, HELEN S.
Sullavan, Margaret
STROBEL, MARIAN ELIZABETH
Wells, Harriet Sheldon
STROTHMAN, STUART W.
Mostel, Samuel Joel ("Zero")
STROUP, HERBERT
Rutherford, Joseph Franklin
STROUT, CUSHING
Beard, Charles Austin
STROVEN, CARL G.
Stoddard, Charles Warren
STRUIK, D. J.
Van Vleck, Edward Burr
STRUNK, OLIVER
Zeuner, Charles
STRUNK, WILLLIAM, JR.
Sampson, Martin Wright
STRUVE, OTTO
Frost, Edwin Brant
STUEWER, ROGER H.
Compton, Arthur Holly
Compton, Karl Taylor
Fermi, Enrico
Gamow, George
Lawrence, Ernest Orlando
Tate, John Torrence
STUNKARD, HORACE W.
Ward, Henry Baldwin
STURCHIO, JEFFREY L.
Pfister, Alfred
SUBER, EDNA SWENSON
Stratemeyer, Edward
SUDDS, R. H.
Hart, Edmund Hall
Henderson, Peter
Hovey, Charles Mason
McMahon, Bernard
Miller, Samuel, 1820–1901
Parsons, Samuel Bowne
Prince, Willim, *c.* 1725–1802
Prince William, 1766–1842
Prince, William Robert
Rogers, Edward Staniford
SUID, LAWRENCE H.
Ladd, Alan Walbridge
SULLIVAN, FRANK
Marquis, Donald Robert Perry
SULLIVAN, JAMES
Draper, Andrew Sloan
Leipziger, Henry Marcus
Page, David Perkins
Phelps, William Franklin
Pruyn, John Van Schaick Lansing
SULMAN, A. MICHAEL
Anderson, Victor Vance
SUMMERS, LIONEL M.
Jones, Leonard Augustus
Southmayd, Charles Ferdinand
Stetson, Francis Lynde
Stillman, Thomas Edgar
Tiedeman, Christopher Gustavus
Toulmin, Harry Theophilus
Tyler, Ransom Hubert
Wallace, William James
SUMMERS, U. T. MILLER
Matthiessen, Francis Otto
SUMMERSON, WILLIAM H.
Benedict, Stanley Rossiter
SUMNER, WILLIAM A.
Hoard, William Dempster
King, Franklin Hiram
Smith, Hiram
SUSMAN, WARREN I.
Howard, Leslie
SUSSKIND, CHARLES
Conrad, Frank
Page, Leigh
Stone, John Stone
Tesla, Nikola
SUSSKIND, JACOB L.
Carmichael, Oliver Cromwell
Clark, Felton Grandison
Gauss, Christian Frederick
McHale, Kathryn
Patri, Angelo
Watt, Donald Beates
SUTHERLAND, ARTHUR E.
Beale, Joseph Henry
SUTTIE, ROSCOE H.
Hazen, Allen
SUTTON, WALTER A.
Allen, Florence Ellinwood
SUTTON, WILLIAM SENECA
Baldwin, Joseph
SWAIN, DONALD C.
Allen, Edward Tyson
SWAIN, MARTHA H.
Altmeyer, Arthur Joseph
Short, Joseph Hudson, Jr.
SWAIN, ROBERT E.
Franklin, Edward Curtis
SWAN, WILLIAM U.
Herreshoff, John Brown
Lawley, George Frederick
Smith, Archibald Cary
Steers, George
SWANBERG, W. A.
Davies, Marion Cecilia
SWANN, W. F. G.
McClenahan, Howard
SWANSON, FREDERICK C.
Campbell, James Hepburn
Cooper, James
SWARTWOUT, EGERTON
Gilbert, Cass
SWEENEY, J. K.
Dickson, Earle Ensign
Holmes, Julius Cecil
SWEET, ALFRED H.
Dod, Thaddeus
SWEET, WILLLAM WARREN
De Pauw, Washington Charles
Gray, Isaac Pusey
Grose, William
Henderson, Charles Richmond
Hovey, Alvin Peterson
Howard, Timothy Edward
Larrabee, William Clark
McCaine, Alexander
Nast, William
Nevin, John Williamson
Quayle, William Alfred
Scott, Orange
Shinn, Asa
Snethen, Nicholas
Stevens, Abel
Stuart, Charles Macaulay
Taylor, John, 1752–1835
Thomson, Edward
SWEETLAND, WILLIAM VIRGIL
Randall, Samuel
SWEM, EARL GREGG
Blair, James
Blair, John, 1687–1771
Blair, John, 1732–1800
Bland, Richard
Bland, Theodorick
SWENDER, PHILLIP THARP
Davis, Adelle
Fieser, Louis Frederick
White, Paul Dudley
SWIFT, EBEN
Augur, Christopher Columbus
Buford, John
SWIFT, FLETCHER HARPER
Durant, Henry
Mann, Horace
Marwedel, Emma Jacobina Christiana
SWINDLER, HENRY O.
Neill, Thomas Hewson
Nelson, William, 1824–1862
SWISHER, CARL BRENT
Boyden, Roland William
Gregory, Charles Noble
Taney, Roger Brooke
SYDNOR, CHARLES S.
Featherston, Winfield Scott
Foote, Henry Stuart
George, James Zachariah
Gordon, James
Leflore, Greenwood
McLaurin, Austin Joseph
McLean, Walter
Martin, William Thompson
Mayes, Edward
Money, Hernando De Soto
Orr, Juhu Amaziah
Poindexter, George
Prentiss, Seargent Smith
Sharkey, William Lewis
Stewart, Alexander Peter
Stockdale, Thomas Ringland
Stone, John Marshall
Thompson, Jacob
Turner, Edward
Vardaman, James Kimble
Wailes, Benjamin Leonard Covington
Walthall, Edward Cary

Williams, John Sharp
Yerger, William
SYREK, TAMMY ANN
Haworth, Leland John
Slichter, Louis Byrne
Zwicky, Fritz
SYRETT, HAROLD C.
McClellan, George Brinton
SZASZ, FERENC M.
Riley, William Bell

TAFT, PHILIP
Frayne, Hugh
Garretson, Austin Bruce
Howard, Charles Perry
Johnston, William Hugh
Maurer, James Hudson
Murray, Philip
Sullivan, James William
Woll, Matthew
TAFT, WILLIAM H.
James, Edwin Leland
TALBERT, CHARLES GANO
McVey, Frank Lerond
TALBOT, HENRY P.
Crafts, James Mason
Drown, Thomas Messinger
TALBOT, MARION
Richards, Ellen Henrietta Swallow
TALLMADGE, THOMAS E.
Holabird, William
Pond, Allen Bartlit
Shaw, Howard Van Doren
Sullivan, Louis Henri
Van Osdel, John Mills
Wight, Peter Bonnett
TANDY, JEANNETTE R.
Burdette, Robert Jones
Cooper, Susan Fenimore
TANNER, EDWIN PLATT
Anson, Adrian Constantine
Basse, Jeremiah
Beauchamp, William Martin
Carter, William Samuel
Chadwick, Henry
Clarkson, John Gibson
Cornbury, Edward Hyde Viscount
Cosby, William
Deerfoot
Fenwick, John
Franklin, William
Hamilton, Andrew, d. 1703
TANSELLE, G. THOMAS
Huebsch, Benjamin W.
TANSILL, CHARLES C.
Hurst, John Fletcher
TARBELL, ROBERTA K.
Young, Mahonri Mackintosh
TARR, JOEL ARTHUR
Harrison, Carter Henry, Jr.
TASHER, LUCY LUCILE
Snead, Thomas Lowndes
TASSINARI, EDWARD J.
Bartlett, Dewey Follett
Easter, Luscious Luke
Hodge, Albert Elmer ("Al")
Page, Joseph Francis ("Joe")
TATE, MERZE
Farrington, Joseph Rider
TATLOCK, JOHN S. P.
Hempl, George
TATUM, GEORGE B.
Cret, Paul Philippe
TAUSSIG, FRANK WILLIAM
Young, Allyn Abbott
TAYLOR, FRANK A.
Appleby, John Francis
Atwood, Lewis John
Bachelder, John
Bacon, Edward Payson
Ball, Ephraim
Bissell, George Henry
Blake, Lyman Reed
Blodget, Samuel
Boyden, Seth
Brooks, Byron Alden
Brown, Sylvanus
Coe, Israel
Crompton, George
Crompton, William
Draper, Ira
Graff, Frederic
Harper, John Lyell
Harris, Daniel Lester
Hayden, Hiram Washington
Hazard, Augustus George
Henck, John Benjamin
Hering, Carl
Hering, Rudolph
Hoadley, John Chipman
Hobbs, Alfred Charles
Holcomb, Amasa
Holland, Clifford Milburn
Holloway, Joseph Flavius
Holmes, Israel
Houston, Edwin James
Hunt, Alfred Ephraim
Hunt, Charles Wallace
Hussey, Curtis Grubb
Hutton, Frederick Remsen
Ingersoll, Robert Hawley
Isherwood, Benjamin Franklin
Jervis, John Bloomfield
Johnson, Edwin Ferry
Johnson, John Butler
Jones, Evan William
Judson, Egbert Putnam
Katte, Walter
Kinnersley, Ebenezer
Klein, Joseph Frederic
Knowles, Lucius, James
Latrobe, Benjamin Henry, 1806–1878
Laurie, James
Leonard, Harry Ward
Lyman, Chester Smith
TAYLOR, FRANK O.
Takamine, Jokichi
TAYLOR, JOHN R. M.
Adams, Daniel Weissiger
Adams, John, 1825–1864
TAYLOR, LLOYD C., JR.
Holt, Winifred
TAYLOR, RICHARD S.
Norris, John Franklyn
TAYLOR, WILLIAM A.
Gideon, Peter Miller
Kellerman, Karl Frederic
Lyon, Theodatus Timothy
Saunders, William
Thomas, John Jacobs
Van Fleet, Walter
TAYLOR, WILLIAM S.
Prince, Morton
TEBBEL, JOHN
Lorimer, George Horace
TEDLOW, RICHARD S.
Lasker, Albert Davis
Link, Henry Charles
TEETER, A. GRACE
Johnson, Oliver
Jones, David
TEFFT, SHELDON
Bigelow, Harry Augustus
TEN HOOR, MARTEN
Heller, Maximilian
Lynch, Robert Clyde
TEPPER, ALBERT
Grauer, Benjamin Franklin ("Ben")
TERMAN, FREDERICK EMMONS
Durand, William Frederick
Hansen, William Webster
TESAR, ANTHONY V.
Hessoun, Joseph
THAYER, CHARLES HIRAM
Stockbridge, Levi
"THE EDITORS"
Bentley, Elizabeth Terrill
THEOHARIS, ATHAN
Dennis, Eugene
Fischer, Ruth
Perry, Pettis
Remington, William Walter
THILLY, FRANK
Creighton, James Edwin
THODY, P. M. W.
Abbott, William A. ("Bud")
Cobb, Lee J.
Huxley, Aldous Leonard
Lee, Bruce
O'Brien, Justin
Wimsatt, William Kurtz
Wodehouse, Pelham Grenville
THOM, CHARLES
Marbut, Curtis Fletcher
THOMAS, CHARLES M.
Towne, Benjamin
THOMAS, C. R. WALTHER
Nies, Konrad
THOMAS, DAVID Y.
Battle, Burrell Bunn
Baxter, Elisha
Berry, James Henderson
Borland, Solon
Boudinot, Elias, *c.* 1803–1839
Boudinot, Elias Cornelius
Brough, Charles Hillman
Churchill, Thomas James
Clarke, James Paul
Clayton, Powell
Cleburne, Patrick Ronayne
Conway, Elias Nelson
Conway, James Sevier
Davis, Jeff
Dorsey, Stephen Wallace
English, Elbert Hartwell
Fagan, James Fleming
Fishback, William Meade
Flanagin, Harris
Garland, Augustus Hill
Govan, Daniel Chevilette
Hindman, Thomas Carmichael
Izard, George
Johnson, Robert Ward
Jones, James Kimbrough
McRae, Thomas Chipman

Murphy, Isaac
Parker, Isaac Charles
Rector, Henry Massey
Roane, John Selden
Rose, Uriah Milton
Sevier, Ambrose Hundley
Walker, David, 1806–1879
Watkins, George Claiborne
Yell, Archibald

THOMAS, EVAN
Bartlett, William Holmes Chambers

THOMAS, LOUIS R.
Bauer, Harold Victor
De Paolis, Alessio
Elman, Mischa
Friml, Charles Rudolf
Katchen, Julius
Rodzinski, Artur
Szell, George
Traynor, Harold Joseph ("Pie")
Walter, Bruno
Warren, Leonard
Weede, Robert

THOMAS, MILTON HALSEY
Buckminster, Joesph Stevens
Jay, Sir James
Jones, William Alfred
Kemp, John
King, Charles
McVickar, John
Middleton, Peter
Moore, Benjamin
Moore, Nathaniel Fish
Romayne, Nicholas
Van Amringe, John Howard
Vardill, John

THOMAS, NORMAN F.
Bell, Frederic Somers

THOMAS, ROBERT E.
Hooker, Elon Huntington

THOMAS, R. S.
Bell, James Franklin
Casey, Thomas Lincoln
Johnston, William Hartshorne

THOMAS, THEODORE N.
Heschel, Abraham Joshua
Paul, William Darwin ("Shorty")

THOMPSON, BRUCE
Beall, James Glenn

THOMPSON, C. MILDRED
McPherson, Edward
Palmer, Bertha Honoré
Palmer, Potter
Salmon, Lucy Maynard

THOMPSON, ERNEST TRICE
Makemie, Francis
Peck, Thomas Ephraim
Reid, William Shields
Rice, John Holt
Robinson, Stuart
Smith, Benjamin Mosby

THOMPSON, FREDERIC L.
Humphrey, Heman
Morse, Anson Daniel
Sachs, Julius
Seelye, Julius Hawley
Stearns, William Augustus

THOMPSON, GERALD
Allen, Gracie
Harrah, William Fisk ("Bill")
Knight, Goodwin Jess ("Goodie")
McClintic, Guthrie

THOMPSON, HOLLAND
Durant, Thomas Clark
Flagler, Henry Morrison
Flagler, John Haldane
Forman, Joshua
Hall, Nathan Kelsey
Harris, Ira
Havens, James
Inman, John Hamilton
Inman, Samuel Martin

THOMPSON, HOMER A.
Shear, Theodore Leslie

THOMPSON, J. A.
Gerard, James Watson

THOMPSON, JOHN
Rosenfeld, Paul Leopold

THOMPSON, RANDALL
Mannes, David

THOMPSON, SUSAN OTIS
Adams, Randolph Greenfield

THOMS, HERBERT
Alcott, William Andrus
Graves, William Phillips
Hirst, Barton Cooke
Hooker, Worthington
Ives, Eli
Knight, Jonathan
North, Elisha
Perkins, Elisha
Tully, William

THOMSON, ELIZABETH H.
Fulton, John Farquhar

THOMSON, IRVING L.
Child, Richard Washburn
Egan, Patrick
Heap, Samuel Davies
King, Jonas
McKim, Isaac
McRae, Duncan Kirkland
MacVeagh, Charles
Maxcy, Virgil
Meigs, Return Jonathan
Mitchell, George Edward
Morgan, Edwin Vernon
Nelson, Thomas Henry
Newel, Stanford
Niles, Nathaniel, 1791–1869
O'Brien, Edward Charles
Osborn, Thomas Andrew
Osborn, Thomas Ogden
Stovall, Pleasant Alexander
Strobel, Edward Henry
Terrell, Edwin Holland
Thompson, Thomas Larkin
Todd, Charles Stewart
Tree, Lambert
Vopicka, Charles Joseph
Wallace, Hugh Campbell
Ward, John Elliott

THORINGTON, J. MONROE
Mitchell, Samuel Augustus

THORNTON, HARRISON JOHN
Chandler, Thomas Bradbury

THORP, WILLARD
Tabb, John Banister

THORPE, EDWARD S.
Pepper, William

THURMOND, DENNIS
Evans, William John ("Bill")
Garner, Erroll Louis

THWING, CHARLES FRANKLIN
Barnard, Frederick Augustus Porter
Burton, Ernest DeWitt
Burton, Marion LeRoy

TICKNOR, CAROLINE
Alcott, Louisa May

TILDEN, CHARLES J.
Hughes, Hector James
Roebling, John Augustus
Roebling, Washington Augustus

TILLETT, WILBUR FISK
Alexander, Gross
Andrew, James Osgood
Bascom, Henry Bidleman

TINDALL, GEORGE B.
Parker, John Milliken

TINGLEY, DONALD F.
Humphries, George Rolfe
Mason, Max
Metcalfe, Ralph Harold
Mitchell, Stephen Arnold
Rivers, Lucius Mendel

TINKER, EDWARD LAROCQUE
Hearn, Lafcadio
Latil, Alexandre
Marigny, Bernard
Mazureau, Étienne
Moreau De Saint-Méry, Médéric Louis Élie
Pennell, Joseph
Perché, Napoleon Joseph
Perry, Enoch Wood
Rémy, Henri
Rouquette, Adrien Emmanuel
Rouquette, François Dominique
Séjour, Victor
Testut, Charles
Thierry, Camille
Tousard, Anne Louis de
Viel, François Étienne Bernard Alexandre

TINO, RICHARD L.
Cone, Fairfax Mastick
Lawrence, David
Ross, Thomas Joseph
Rubicam, Raymond

TINSLEY, JAMES A.
Ferguson, James Edward

TIPPLE, EZRA SQUIER
Boehm, Henry
Buttz, Henry Anson

TISCHLER, BARBARA L.
Fox, Virgil Keel
Silkwood, Karen Gay
Traubel, Helen

TISHLER, HACE
Johnson, Alexander

TOBEY, CHARLES
Tunnell, Emlen

TOBEY, JAMES A.
Sedgwick, William Thompson

TOBIN, EUGENE M.
Fagan, Mark Matthew

TODD, ELIZABETH
Ormsby, Waterman Lilly
Outcault, Richard Felton

TODD, FREDERICK P.
Sibert, William Luther

TOEPFER, KENNETH H.
Russell, James Earl

TOLMAN, R. P.
Catlin, George

Chapman, John Gadsby
Cheney, John
Cheney, Seth Wells
Stanley, John Mix
TOLMAN, RUEL P.
Gellatly, John
TOMLINSON, DAVID O.
Fearing, Kenneth Flexner
Jeffers, John Robinson
TOMPKINS, C. DAVID
Vandenberg, Arthur Hendrick
TONDORF, FRANCIS A.
Bayma, Joseph
Rigge, William Francis
Sestini, Benedict
TONKS, OLIVER S.
Hubbard, Richard William
Huntington, Daniel
TOPPIN, EDGAR ALLAN
Haynes, George Edmund
Scott, Emmett Jay
TORODASH, MARTIN
Keyes, Frances Parkinson
Mitchell, Thomas Gregory
Spence, Brent
TORREY, CHARLES C.
Gibbs, Josiah Willard, 1790–1861
Orne, John
Salisbury, Edward Elbridge
Toy, Crawford Howell
TOULMIN, HARRY A., JR.
Patterson, John Henry
TOURSCHER, F. E.
Carr, Thomas Matthew
Conwell, Henry
TOWER, OLIN F.
Morley, Edward Williams
TOWER, WILLIAM B., JR.
Winchester, Caleb Thomas
TOWNER, LAWRENCE W.
Graff, Everett Dwight
Phillips, William
TOWNSEND, LEAH
Eve, Joseph
TOZZER, ALFRED M.
Bowditch, Charles Pickering
TRACHTENBERG, ALAN
Evans, Walker
Frank, Waldo David
Goldmark, Henry
TRANI, EUGENE
Work, Hubert
TRATTNER, WALTER I.
Folks, Homer
Heckscher, August
Lovejoy, Owen Reed
TRAYNOR, ROGER J.
Costigan, George Purcell
TREADWELL, AARON L.
Orton, James
TREAT, PAYSON J.
Low, Frederick Ferdinand
TREFOUSSE, HANS L.
Cole, Arthur Charles
Milton, George Fort
TREXLER, HARRISON A.
DeBardeleben, Henry Fairchild
Hillman, Thomas Tennessee
Pratt, Daniel
Sloss, James Withers
TRIMBLE, BRUSE R.
Waite, Morrison Remick
TRISCO, ROBERT F.
Meyer, Albert Gregory
TROLANDER, JUDITH ANN
Balch, Emily Greene
Binford, Jessie Florence
Dock, Lavinia Lloyd
Lingelbach, Anna Lane
Peck, Lillie
Riis, Mary Phillips
TRUE, ALFRED CHARLES
Allen, Richard Lamb
Alvord, Henry Elijah
Barry, Patrick
Beatty, Adam
Bordley, John Beale
TRUESDELL, LEON E.
Hill, Joseph Adna
TRUSCOTT, ALAN
Culbertson, Ely
TSCHAN, FRANCIS J.
Chanche, John Mary Joseph
Chapelle, Placide Louis
Harding, Robert
TUCHMAN, BARBARA W.
Stilwell, Joseph Warren
TUCKER, WILLIAM E.
Willett, Herbert Lockwood
TUCKERMAN, FREDERICK
Chadbourne, Paul Ansel
Clark, Henry James
Clark, William Smith
Goodell, Henry Hill
Gulick, John Thomas
TUGWELL, REXFORD G.
Seager, Henry Rogers
TULCHIN, JOSEPH S.
Rowe, Leo Stanton
TUNSTALL, ROBERT B.
Leigh, Benjamin Watkins
Taylor, Creed
Tazewell, Henry
Tazewell, Littleton Waller
TURCK, CHARLES J.
Knott, James Proctor
Young, John Clarke
TURK, MILTON HAIGHT
Norton, John Nicholas
TURNBULL, ANDREW
Perkins, Maxwell Evarts
TURNER, ALBERT L.
Morton, Robert Russa
TURNER, CHARLES W.
Harahan, William Johnson
TURNER, DARWIN T.
McKay, Claude
TURNER, JEAN-RAE
Mich, Daniel Danforth
TURNER, THOMAS B.
Moore, Joseph Earle
TUTHILL, EDWARD
Hanson, Roger Weightman
Hobson, Edward Henry
TUTOROW, NORMAN E.
Gaxton, William
Paul, Josephine Bay
Rockwell, George Lincoln
TUTTLE, ALONZO H.
Kinkead, Edgar Benton
Nash, Simeon
Okey, John Waterman
Richards, John Kelvey
Shauck, John Allen
Spear, William Thomas
Swan, Joseph Rockwell
Swayne, Noah Haynes
Walker, Timothy, 1802–1856
Wanamaker, Reuben Melville
Welch, John
Williams, Marshall Jay
Woods, William Burnham
TUTTLE, ANN LESLIE
Post, Marjorie Merriweather
TUTTLE, JULIUS H.
Green, Samuel Abbott
TWEEDY, HENRY H.
Hoppin, James Mason
Proctor, Henry Hugh
TWYNHAM, LEONARD
Sprague, Achsa W.
TYACK, DAVID B.
Cubberley, Ellwood Patterson
TYLER, ALICE FELT
Elliott, Charles Burke
TYLER, GUS
Kelly, Machine Gun (George Kelly Barnes, Jr.)
Wexler, Irving ("Waxey Gordon")
TYNER, RICHARD F. F.
Mayhew, Experience
TYOR, PETER L.
Goddard, Henry Herbert
TYTELL, JOHN
Pound, Ezra Loomis

UHL, A. H.
Kremers, Edward
UPSON, LENT DAYTON
Wilcox, Delos Franklin
UPTON, WILLIAM TREAT
Beck, Johann Heinrich
Bird, Arthur
Burlin, Natalie Curtis
Burton, Frederick Russell
Hanby, Benjamin Russell
Hastings, Thomas
UROFF, MARGARET DICKIE
Plath, Sylvia
UROFSKY, MELVIN I.
Ballantine, Arthur Atwood
Chafee, Zechariah, Jr.
Cline, Genevieve Rose
Curtis, Charles Pelham
Davis, Pauline Morton Sabin
Douglas, William Orville
Dowling, Noel Thomas
Goldsborough, Thomas Alan
Grady, Henry Francis
Greenbaum, Edward Samuel
Howe, Mark De Wolfe
Lane, Arthur Bliss
Llewellyn, Karl Nickerson
Miller, Nathan Lewis
Montague, Gilbert Holland
Musmanno, Michael Angelo
Rogers, Edith Nourse
Silver, Abba Hillel
Snell, Bertrand Hollis
Vanderbilt, Arthur T.
Warren, Charles
Warren, Earl
Williston, Samuel
USHER, ROLAND GREENE
Allerton, Isaac
Brewster, William, 1567–1644
Carver, John

Cushman, Robert
Morton, George
Morton, Nathaniel
Standish, Myles
Weston, Thomas
Winslow, Edward
Winslow, Josiah
USSELMAN, STEVEN W.
Fairchild, Sherman Mills
UTLAUT, ROBERT L.
Bestor, Arthur Eugene
UTLEY, GEORGE B.
Gardner, Gilson
Newberry, Walter Loomis
Perkins, Frederic Beecher
Rich, Obadiah
Scammon, Jonathan Young
Sharp, Katharine Lucinda
Strong, Walter Ansel
Taylor, Benjamin Franklin
White, Alexander, 1814–1872
Wilkie, Franc Bangs
Woolley, Celia Parker
UTTER, WILLIAM T.
Campbell, John Wilson
Campbell, Lewis Davis
Cook, Isaac
Creighton, William
Drake, John Burroughs
Eckels, James Herron
Goodenow, John Milton
Groesbeck, William Slocum
Grosvenor, Charles Henry
Huntington, Samuel, 1765–1817
McArthur, Duncan
Meigs, Return Jonathan, 1764–1824
Morrow, Jeremiah
Pease, Calvin
Tiffin, Edward
Tod, George
Worthington, Thomas

VAIL, DERRICK T.
Gifford, Sanford Robinson
Wood, Casey Albert
VAIL, ROBERT W. G.
Thomas, Isaiah
VANCE, CLARENCE H.
Seabury, Samuel, 1729–1796
Sears, Isaac
VANCE, JOHN R.
McIntosh, John Baillie
McLaws, Lafayette
McMillan, James Winning
Martindale, John Henry
VANCE, JOHN T.
Griggs, John William
Grosscup, Peter Stenger
Paschal, George Washington
VANCE, MAURICE M.
Debye, Peter Joseph William
Kharasch, Morris Selig
Piccard, Jean Felix
Thurstone, Louis Leon
White, Leonard Dupee
VANCE, WILLIAM REYNOLDS
Woolsey, Theodore Salisbury
VAN CLEVE, EDWARD M.
Russ, John Dennison
Wait, William Bell
VAN CLEVE, THOMAS C.
Pike, James Shepherd
VAN DE KAMP, PETER
Schlesinger, Frank
VAN DER KLOOT, WILLIAM
Loewi, Otto
VANDERSEE, CHARLES
Poole, Ernest Cook
VANDER VELDE, LEWIS G.
Warner, Fred Maltby
Woodbridge, William
VAN DEUSEN, JOHN G.
Hamilton, Paul
Huger, Benjamin
Huger, Daniel Elliott
Huger, Francis Kinloch
Huger, Isaac
Huger, John
Kennedy, John Doby
Loring, Joshua, 1716–1781
Loring, Joshua, 1744–1789
Ludlow, Gabriel George
Ludlow, George Duncan
Lynch, Thomas, 1727–1776
Lynch, Thomas, 1749–1779
Manning, Richard Irvine
Middleton, Henry, 1717–1784
Middleton, Henry, 1770–1846
Miller, Stephen Decatur
Taylor, John W.
Troup, Robert
VANDIVER, FRANK E.
Pershing, John Joseph
York, Alvin Cullum
VAN DOREN, CARL
Brown, Charles Brockden
Clemens, Samuel Langhorne
Cooper, James Fenimore
Hawthorne, Nathaniel
James, Henry, 1843–1916
Porter, William Sydney
Simms, William Gilmore
Stockton, Frank Richard
Taylor, Bayard
Wylie, Elinor Morton Hoyt
VAN DOREN, HAROLD L.
Koehler, Robert
VAN DOREN, MARK
Comstock, Anthony
Dibble, Roy Floyd
Emerson, Ralph Waldo
Whitman, Walt
VAN DOREN, SANDRA SHAFFER
Eglevsky, André Yevgenyevich
Helpern, Milton
Martin, Warren Homer
Thomas, Roland Jay
VAN DYKE, PAUL
Baird, Charles Washington
Baird, Henry Martyn
Baird, Robert
VAN FOSSEN, IRENE
Laimbeer, Nathalie Schenck
Matheson, William John
Mulford, Prentice
VAN HOOSEN, BERTHA
Mergler, Marie Josepha
VAN LAER, ARNOLD J. F.
Bogardus, Everardus
De Vries, David Pietersen
Hudde, Andries
Krol, Bastiaen Jansen
Van Ilpendam, Jan Jansen
VAN LENNEP, WILLIAM
Brady, Alice
Elliott, Maxine
Gillette, William Hooker
Russell, Annie
Smith, Harry Bache
VAN METER, SONDRA
Barnard, Chester Irving
VAN PELT, JOHN V.
Hunt, Richard Morris
VAN RAVENSWAAY, CHARLES
Barton, David
VAN SANTVOORD, GEORGE
Buehler, Huber Gray
Van Schaack, Henry Cruger
Van Schaack, Peter
VAN SLYCK, DEFOREST
Harrison, Henry Baldwin
Hillhouse, James
Huntington, Samuel, 1731–1796
VAN TASSEL, DAVID D.
McHugh, Rose John
Shepard, James Edward
VAN TINE, WARREN R.
Frey, John Philip
Lundeberg, Harry
Morrison, Frank
Tobin, Daniel Joseph
VARGA, NICHOLAS
Cullen, Hugh Roy
VARRELL, H. M.
Lyman, Theodore, 1833–1897
VAUGHN, SUSAN
Ohrbach, Nathan M. ("N. M.")
Rockwell, Willard Frederick
VAUGHN, VICTOR C.
Beaumont, William
VECOLI, RUDOLPH J.
Tresca, Carlo
VEEDER, BORDEN S.
Marriott, Williams McKim
VEEDER, VAN VECHTEN
Hough, Charles Merrill
VEITH, ILZA
Menninger, Charles Frederick
VENABLE, FRANCIS PRESTON
Mallet, John William
VESTAL, S. C.
Newton, John
VEYSEY, LAURENCE R.
Angell, James Rowland
Reinhardt, Aurelia Isabel Henry
Schurman, Jacob Gould
West, Andrew Fleming
Wilbur, Ray Lyman
VIETS, HENRY R.
Babcock, James Woods
Baker, Frank
Baldwin, William
Barker, Benjamin Fordyce
Barton, John Rhea
Battey, Robert
Bayley, Richard
Chadwick, James Read
Channing, Walter
Cullis, Charles
Dix, John Homer
Edes, Robert Thaxter
Ellis, Calvin
Ernst, Harold Clarence
Fisher, Theodore Willis
Hale, Enoch
Harrington, Thomas Francis

Hunt, Harriot Kezia
Kimball, Gilman
Lewis, Dioclesian
Lloyd, James
Marcy, Henry Orlando
Mumford, James Gregory
Oliver, Fitch Edward
Putnam, Charles Pickering
Putnam, James Jackson
Ramsay, Alexander
Randolph, Jacob
Redman, John
Reese, John James
Richardson, Maurice Howe
Richardson, William Lambert
Rogers, Stephen
Rotch, Thomas Morgan
Shattuck, Frederick Cheever
Shattuck, George Brune
Shattuck, George Cheyne, 1783–1854
Shattuck, George Cheyne, 1813–1893
Storer, David Humphreys
Storer, Horatio Robinson
Thacher, James
Tuckerman, Frederick
Tuckerman, Frederick Goddard
Tufts, Cotton
Twitchell, Amos
Walcott, Henry Pickering
Ware, John
Warren, John
Warren, John Collins, 1778–1856
Warren, John Collins, 1842–1927
Waterhouse, Benjamin
White, James Clarke
Wigglesworth, Edward
Williams, Henry Willard
Williams, Stephen West
Wood, Edward Stickney
Wyman, Morrill
Young, Aaron
Zakrzewska, Marie Elizabeth

VILES, JONAS
Allen, Thomas
Bland, Richard Parks
Bliss, Philemon
Boggs, Lillburn W.

VILLARD, HAROLD G.
Horton, Samuel Dana
Knox, John Jay
Nell, William Cooper
Payne, Christopher Harrison
Payne, Daniel Alexander
Perkins, George Walbridge
Perry, Rufus Lewis
Powers, Daniel William
Pratt, Charles
Pratt, Sereno Stansbury
Rankine, William Birch
Ray, Charles Bennett
Remond, Charles Lenox
Scarborough, William Saunders
Slater, John Fox
Smyth, John Henry
Still, William
Tanner, Benjamin Tucker
Taylor, Marshall William
Turner, Henry McNeal
Ward, Samuel, 1786–1839
White, Stephen Van Culen

VILLARD, OSWALD GARRISON
Croly, Herbert David
Curtis, Cyrus Hermann Kotzschmar
Linn, William Alexander
Munsey, Frank Andrew
Pulitzer, Joseph
Ridder, Herman
Schurz, Carl
Seitz, Don Carlos
White, Horace

VINCENT, JOHN MARTIN
Browne, William Hand
Huntington, Henry Edwards
Lieber, Francis

VINCENT, WILLIAM L.
Parsons, Talcott

VINOKOUROFF, MICHAEL Z.
Innokentii
Ioasaf
Kuskov, Ivan Aleksandrovich

VINSON, BETTY B.
Knight, Frank Hyneman
Lowell, Ralph

VIOLETTE, EUGENE M.
Blanchard, Newton Crain
Bouligny, Dominique
Boyd, David French
Caffery, Donelson
Conrad, Charles Magill
Foster, Murphy James
Gibson, Randall Lee
La Tour, Le Blond de
McCaleb, Theodore Howard
Merrick, Edwin Thomas
Moore, Thomas Overton
Mouton, Alexander
Pauger, Adrien de
Sullivan, William Henry

VISELTEAR, ARTHUR J.
Winslow, Charles-Edward Amory

VITELLI, JAMES R.
Adler, Elmer
Brown, John Mason, Jr.
Seldes, Gilbert Vivian

VIZETELLY, FRANK HORACE
Champlin, John Denison
Funk, Isaac Kauffman
Gregory, Daniel Seelye

VOGEL, MORRIS J.
Cannon, Ida Maud
Simmons, James Stevens

VOIGT, DAVID QUENTIN
Barrow, Edward Grant
Cicotte, Edward Victor
Collins, Edward Trowbridge
Comiskey, Grace Elizabeth Reidy
Grove, Robert Moses ("Lefty")
Johnson, Walter Perry
Kelly, John Brendan
Landis, Kenesaw Mountain
Mack, Connie
MacPhail, Leland Stanford ("Larry")
O'Malley, Walter Francis
Rickey, Wesley Branch
Ruth, George Herman (Babe)
Spink, John George Taylor
Stevens, Frank Mozley
Stevens, Harry Mozley
Young, Denton True ("Cy")

VOIGT, JOHN
Condon, Albert Edwin ("Eddie")
Grofé, Ferde
Krupa, Eugene Bertram ("Gene")
Mingus, Charles, Jr.

VOLWILER, ALBERT T.
Croghan, George, d. 1782
Croghan, George, 1791–1849
Harrison, Benjamin, 1833–1901
Miller, William Henry Harrison
Porter, Albert Gallatin
Proctor, Redfield
Swank, James Moore
Swift, Lucius Burrie

VON ECKARDT, WOLF
Mendelsohn, Erich (or Eric)

VOORHEES, DAVID WILLIAM
O'Dwyer, William

VOORHEES, DAYTON
Beasley, Mercer

VOSPER, EDNA
Vaughan, Benjamin

VOSS, FREDERICK
Diller, Burgoyne
Lebrun, Federico ("Rico")

VOSS, FREDERICK S.
Biddle, George
Bourke-White, Margaret
Chaliapin, Boris Fyodorovich
Gilbreth, Lillian Evelyn Moller
Laurence, William Leonard
Rorimer, James Joseph
Smith, William Eugene
Wynn, Ed

VOTH, PAUL D.
Chamberlain, Charles Joseph

WADDELL, LOUIS M.
Earle, George Howard, III
Fine, John Sydney
James, Arthur Horace

WADE, JOHN DONALD
Ashe, Samuel
Ashe, William Shepperd
Avery, William Waigstill
Bass, William Capers
Baylor, Frances Courtenay
Behan, William James
Bellamy, Elizabeth W. Croom
Binns, John
Blake, Mary Elizabeth McGrath
Bloodworth, Timothy
Bohune, Lawrence
Bryan, Thomas Barbour
Bulkeley, Peter
Carleton, Henry Guy
Caruthers, William Alexander
Chappell, Absalom Harris
Clapp, William Warland
Clarke, Mary Bayard Devereux
Clement, Edward Henry
Colburn, Zerah
Conant, Alban Jasper
Cook, Russell S.
Coolbrith, Ina Donna
Corrothers, James David
Corson, Hiram
Crandall, Charles Henry
Crane, Anne Moncure

Crawford, John Martin
Crerar, John
Cromwell, Gladys Louise Husted
Crosby, John Schuyler
Curwood, James Oliver
Cutler, Lizzie Petit
Dabney, Robert Lewis
Dabney, Virginius
Dalcho, Frederick
Dale, Samuel
Daniel, John Moncure
Davidson, James Wood
Daviess, Maria Thompson
Davis, Jerome Dean
Davis, Mary Evelyn Moore
Davis, Noah Knowles
Deems, Charles Force
De Fontaine, Felix Gregory
De Lamar, Joseph Raphael
Delano, Amassa
De Leon, Thomas Cooper
Derbigny, Pierre Auguste Charles Bourguignon
De Trobriand, Régis Denis de Keredern
Diaz, Abby Morton
Didier, Eugene Lemoine
Dimitry, Alexander
Dimitry, Charles Patton
Disturnell, John
Ditson, George Leighton
Donnelly, Eleanor Cecilia
Dorr, Julia Caroline Ripley
Dorsey, Anna Hanson McKenney
Dorsey, Sarah Anne Ellis
Dow, Lorenzo, 1777–1834
Drake, Francis Samuel
Drake, Samuel Adams
Drumgoole, John Christopher
Du Bois, William Ewing
Early, John
Elliott, Charles
Elliott, William
Ellis, Edward Sylvester
Elwyn, Alfred Langdon
Estabrook, Joseph
Evans, Augusta Jane
Fairfax, Donald McNeill
Few, Ignatius Alphonso
Field, Roswell Martin
Fisher, Sidney George, 1809–1871
Fiske, Amos Kidder
Fitzgerald, Oscar Penn
Flagg, Edmund
Flagg, Thomas Wilson
Ford, Patrick
Forman, Justus Miles
Fosdick, William Whiteman
Foster, David Skaats
Fox, John William
Fuller, Richard
Fulton, Justin Dewey
Furman, James Clement
Galloway, Charles Betts
Gambrell, James Bruton
Garland, Landon Cabell
Gilmore, Joseph Henry
Girardeau, John Lafayette
Goodsell, Daniel Ayres
Goulding, Francis Robert
Grady, Henry Woodfin
Grafton, Charles Chapman
Graves, James Robinson
Graves, John Temple
Graves, Zuinglius Calvin
Green, Alexander Little Page
Grieve, Miller
Grimes, Absalom Carlisle
Gwin, William McKendree
Gwinnett, Button
Harben, William Nathaniel
Hargrove, Robert Kennon
Haughery, Margaret Gaffney
Hays, William Shakespeare
Holcombe, Henry
Hooper, Johnson Jones
Hope, James Barron
Howell, Evan Park
Hubner, Charles William
Jones, Charles Colcock
Lipscomb, Andrew Adgate
Longstreet, Augustus Baldwin

WADE, LOUISE CARROLL
McDowell, Mary Eliza
Taylor, Graham
Terrell, Mary Eliza Church

WAGENKNECHT, EDWARD
Grant, Robert
Paine, Albert Bigelow

WAGGONER, RAYMOND W.
Barrett, Albert Moore

WAGLEY, CHARLES
Lewis, Oscar

WAGNER, CHARLES F.
Fortescue, Charles LeGeyt

WAGNER, R. RICHARD
Everleigh, Ada
Everleigh, Minna

WAGNER, THEODORE B.
Frasch, Herman

WAGNON, WILLIAM O., JR.
Fairburn, William Armstrong
Gates, Thomas Sovereign
Hill, George Washington
James, Arthur Curtiss

WAGONER, C. D.
Faccioli, Giuseppe
Potter, William Bancroft
Rice, Edwin Wilbur

WAIT, WILLIAM CUSHING
Elder, Samuel James

WAITE, FREDERICK C.
Kirtland, Jared Potter

WAITE, J. HERBERT
Howe, Lucien
Jeffries, Benjamin Joy
Knapp, Herman

WALBRIDGE, EARLE F.
Pearson, Edmund Lester
Wright, Willard Huntington

WALCUTT, CHARLES CHILD
Beer, Thomas

WALD, GEORGE
Hecht, Selig

WALDEN, DANIEL
Hecht, Ben
Hurst, Fannie

WALKER, BUZ M.
Montgomery, William Bell

WALKER, FRANKLIN DICKERSON
Wilson, Harry Leon

WALKER, FRANKLIN TRENABY
Trent, William Peterfield

WALKER, J. SAMUEL
Wallace, Henry Agard

WALKER, S. JAY
Hurston, Zora Neale

WALL, ALEXANDER J.
Moore, Frank
Moore, George Henry
Moore, Jacob Bailey
Robertson, Archibald
Stevens, John Austin, 1827–1910
Trow, John Fowler

WALL, BENNETT H.
Barden, Graham Arthur
Johnston, Olin DeWitt Talmadge
Kress, Samuel Henry
Rathbone, Monroe Jackson ("Jack")

WALL, JOSEPH F.
Lipchitz, Jacques

WALL, JOSEPH FRAZIER
Biddle, Francis Beverley
Hendrick, Burton Jesse
Humphrey, George Magoffin
Olds, Irving Sands
Phipps, Lawrence Cowle
Taylor, Myron Charles
Weir, Ernest Tener

WALL, JOSEPH S.
Foote, John Ambrose

WALLACE, D. D.
Shipp, Albert Micajah
Yeadon, Richard

WALLACE, W. STEWART
Henry, John, 1807–1820

WALLER, INGRID NELSON
Lipman, Jacob Goodale

WALMSLEY, JAMES ELLIOTT
Bonham, Milledge Luke
Botts, John Minor
Brawley, William Hiram
Brooks, Preston Smith
Cheves, Langdon
Echols, John
Elzey, Arnold
Eppes, John Wayles
Faulkner, Charles James, 1814–1898
Floyd, John
Floyd, John Buchanan
Lomax, Lunsford Lindsay
Lowndes, William
McDowell, James
Preston, William Ballard
Pryor, Roger Atkinson
Smith, William, 1797–1887
Smith, William Waugh
Smyth, Alexander
Staples, Waller Redd

WALSH, JAMES J.
Farley, John Murphy
O'Dwyer, Joseph
Paine, Martyn
Pattison, Granville Sharp
Quinan, John Russell
Ricord, Philippe
Rohé, George Henry

WALSH, J. L.
Osgood, William Fogg

WALTER, FRANK K.
Jones, Herschel Vespasian

WALTER, PAUL ALFRED FRANCIS
Prince, Le Baron Bradford
WALTER, RICHARD D.
Myerson, Abraham
WALTERS, EVERETT
Fess, Simeon Davidson
WALTERS, RAYMOND
Wolle, John Frederick
WALTON, J. BARNARD
Cresson, Elliott
WARBEKE, JOHN M.
Scott, Colin Alexander
WARD, CHARLES S.
Wehle, Louis Brandeis
WARD, ESTELLE FRANCES
Jones, William Patterson
WARD, HARRY F.
Rauschenbusch, Walter
WARD, PATRICIA SPAIN
Aldrich, Charles Anderson
Cabot, Hugh
Chapin, Henry Dwight
Nutting, Mary Adelaide
Stimson, Julia Catherine
WARE, EDITH E.
Sage, Margaret Olivia Slocum
Skinner, Charles Rufus
WARE, EDITH W.
Breasted, James Henry
WARE, LOUISE
Peabody, George Foster
WARFEL, HARRY R.
Carruth, Fred Hayden
Grosset, Alexander
Percival, James Gates
Porter, Gene Stratton
WARNER, HOYT LANDON
Clarke, John Hessin
Garfield, James Rudolph
WARNER, LANDON
Howe, Frederic Clemson
WARNER, LANGDON
Fenollosa, Ernest Francisco
WARNER, MARJORIE F.
Brincklé, William Draper
WARNER, ROBERT A.
Red Jacket
Smohalla
WARNER, ROBERT M.
Osborn, Chase Salmon
WARREN, CHARLES H.
Silliman, Benjamin, 1779–1864
WARREN, DONALD R.
Tigert, John James, IV
WARREN, SHIELDS
Christian, Henry Asbury
Mallory, Frank Burr
WARTHIN, ALDRED S.
Ohlmacher, Albert Philip
WASHBURN, FREDERIC A.
Mixter, Samuel Jason
WASHBURN, HENRY B.
Worcester, Elwood
WASHBURN, MARGARET F.
Titchener, Edward Bradford
WASHINGTON, JOSEPH R., JR.
Gregg, John Andrew
WASSER, HENRY
Kronenberger, Louis, Jr.
Langer, William Leonard
WASSERSTROM, WILLIAM
Brooks, Van Wyck
Deland, Margaret
WATERHOUSE, EDWARD J.
Allen, Edward Ellis
WATERMAN, W. RANDALL
Brisbane, Albert
Dow, Neal
Evans, Frederick William
Gage, Frances Dana Barker
Gage, Matilda Joslyn
Goodell, William
Green, Beriah
Green, Frances Harriet Whipple
Gurley, Ralph Randolph
Miller, Jonathan Peckham
Morse, Jedidiah
Parish, Elijah
Payson, Seth
Robinson, Harriet Jane Hanson
Robinson, William Stevens
Stearns, George Luther
WATERS, CAMPBELL EASTER
Hillebrand, William Francis
WATERS, EDWARD N.
Engel, Carl
Nielsen, Alice
Putnam, (George) Herbert
Rachmaninoff, Sergei Vasilyevich
WATKINS, SAMUEL S.
Gibbs, George
WATSON, EDWARD H.
Bascom, Florence
WATSON, MARK S.
Ritchie, Albert Cabell
WATSON, RICHARD L., JR.
Gardner, Oliver Maxwell
Simmons, Furnifold McLendel
WATT, JAMES CRAWFORD
McMurrich, James Playfair
WATTEL, HAROLD L.
Cambridge, Godfrey MacArthur
Chamberlin, Edward Hastings
Fairchild, Fred Rogers
Harriman, Edward Roland Noel
Harris, Seymour Edwin
Johnson, Alvin Saunders
Levitt, Abraham
Nourse, Edwin Griswold
Overstreet, Harry Allen
Rosenstiel, Lewis Solon
WATTS, EMILY STIPES
Millay, Edna St. Vincent
WATTS, EUGENE J.
Smith, Bruce
WAY, ROYAL B.
Harvey, Louis Powell
Howe, Timothy Otis
WEATHERBY, C. A.
Robinson, Benjamin Lincoln
WEATHERFORD, DORIS
Blanchfield, Florence Aby
Bolton, Frances Payne Bingham
WEAVER, RAYMOND
Allston, Washington
WEAVER, RUFUS W.
Waller, John Lightfoot
Whitsitt, William Heth
Willingham, Robert Josiah
Winkler, Edwin Theodore
Yeaman, William Pope
WEBB, GEORGE E.
Kuiper, Gerard Peter
Libby, Willard Frank
WEBB, GEORGE ERNEST
Douglass, Andrew Ellicott
Nicholson, Seth Barnes
Slipher, Vesto Melvin
WEBB, R. K.
Schuyler, Robert Livingston
WEBB, ROBERT H.
Humphreys, Milton Wylie
WEBB, W. P.
Jones, John B.
Wharton, William H.
WEBBER, MABEL L.
Izard, Ralph
Manigault, Gabriel
Manigault, Peter
Manigault, Pierre
WEBER, WILLIAM A.
Cockerell, Theodore Dru Alison
WEBSTER, HUTTON
Howard, George Elliott
WECHSLER, HARRY L.
Jackson, Chevalier
WECTER, DIXON
Rogers, Will
WEEKS, EDWARD
Allen, Fred
Allen, Frederick Lewis
WEEKS, MANGUM
Cheshire, Joseph Blount
WEEMS, JOHN EDWARD
Henson, Matthew Alexander
WEHLE, LOUIS B.
McCarthy, Charles
WEIGLE, LUTHER ALLAN
Clark, Francis Edward
Mills, Benjamin Fay
Moody, Dwight Lyman
Trumbull, Henry Clay
Valentine, Milton
WEIGLEY, EMMA SEIFRIT
Marlatt, Abby Lillian
Rose, Mary Davies Swartz
WEIGLEY, RUSSELL F.
Merrill, Frank Dow
WEIGOLD, MARILYN E.
Fitzgerald, Alice Louise Florence
Speer, Emma Bailey
WEINBERG, JULIUS
Ross, Edward Alsworth
WEINBERG, MEYER
Carter, Boake
McNamee, Graham
WEINBERG, SYDNEY STAHL
Bonsal, Stephen
Davis, Elmer Holmes
Lange, Dorothea
Lardner, John Abbott
Stokes, Thomas Lunsford, Jr.
WEINBERGER, CASPAR W., JR.
Curtis, Edward Sheriff
WEINSTEIN, ALLEN
Rosenberg, Ethel
Rosenberg, Julius
WEINSTEIN, STEPHEN
Frisch, Frank Francis ("The Fordham Flash")
Hodges, Gilbert Ray
Meusel, Robert William
Wheat, Zachariah Davis ("Buck")
WEISBLAT, TINKY ("DAKOTA")
Bailey, Bill
Balaban, Barney

Brown, Johnny Mack
Landis, Jessie Royce
Main, Marjorie
Romanoff, Michael ("Prince Mike")
Roth, Lillian
Terry, Paul Houlton

WEISENBURG, THEODORE H.
Mills, Charles Karsner
Potts, Charles Sower

WEISENBURGER, FRANCIS P.
Hoey, Clyde Roark
Noyes, Edward Follansbee
Payne, Henry B.
Pugh, George Ellis
Sherwood, Isaac Ruth
Shuey, Edwin Longstreet
Tappan, Benjamin
Taylor, James Wickes
Trimble, Allen

WEISMAN, AVERY D.
Sachs, Hanns

WEISS, BENJAMIN P.
Dercum, Francis Xavier

WEISS, GAIL GARFINKEL
Henderson, Ray

WEISS, HARRY B.
Yeager, Joseph

WEISS, NANCY J.
Caraway, Hattie Ophelia Wyatt
Kahn, Florence Prag
Sulzer, William
White, Walter Francis

WEISS, PAUL
Peirce, Charles Sanders

WEITENKAMPF, FRANK
Anthony, Andrew Varick Stout
Bacher, Otto Henry
Bellew, Frank Henry Temple
Bowen, Abel
Brennan, Alfred Laurens
Cole, Timothy
Linton, William James
Maverick, Peter
Mielatz, Charles Frederick William
Rollinson, William
Schoff, Stephen Alonzo

WELCH, WILLIAM HENRY
Welch, William Wickham

WELKER, ROBERT H.
Bailey, Florence Augusta Merriam
Chapman, Frank Michler
Pearson, Thomas Gilbert
Seton, Ernest Thompson

WELLINGTON, RAYNOR G.
Beadle, William Henry Harrison

WELLS, CHARLES L.
Otey, James Hervey
Patillo, Henry
Pettigrew, Charles

WELLS, F. ESTELLE
Jayne, Horace Fort
Marshall, Clara
Michener, Ezra
Ott, Isaac
Pickering, Charles
Preston, Ann
Price, Joseph
Willard, De Forest

WELLS, H. GIDEON
Ricketts, Howard Taylor

WELLS, JAMES M.
McMurtrie, Douglas Crawford

WELLS, WALTER A.
Cutter, Ephraim

WELSH, S. JANE
Ramsay, Erskine
Stanley, Robert Crooks

WENTZ, ABDEL ROSS
Day, David Alexander
Jacobs, Henry Eyster

WERNER, RAYMOND C.
Galloway, Joseph

WERTENBAKER, THOMAS JEFFERSON
Brown, Alexander, 1843–1906
Byrd, William, 1652–1704
Byrd, William, 1674–1744
Dale, Sir Thomas
Dinwiddie, Robert
Pocahontas
Powhatan
Rolfe, John

WERTHEIM, TOBY
Ireland, Charles Thomas, Jr. ("Chick")

WEST, ELIZABETH HOWARD
Forbes, John, 1769–1823
Hays, John Coffee
Panton, William
Wallace, William Alexander Anderson

WESTCOTT, ALLAN
Ammen, Daniel
Badger, Charles Johnston
Barron, Samuel
Beaumont, John Colt
Blue, Victor
Calvert, George Henry
Champlin, Stephen
Chester, Colby Mitchell
Chester, George Randolph
Coffin, Charles Carleton
Collier, Hiram Price
Collins, Napoleon
Colvocoresses, George Musalas
Conner, David
Coontz, Robert Edward
Crane, Stephen
Crane, William Montgomery
Crosby, Peirce
Davis, Charles Henry, 1807–1877
Davis, Charles Henry, 1845–1921
Davis, John Lee
Decatur, Stephen, 1752–1808
Decatur, Stephen, 1779–1820
Eberle, Edward Walter
Egan, Maurice Francis
Ewell, James
Ewell, Thomas
Foote, Andrew Hull
Forrest, French
Gillon, Alexander
Glynn, James
Gorringe, Henry Honeychurch
Grant, Albert Weston
Griffin, Robert Stanislaus
Hayden, Edward Everett
Hughes, Charles Frederick
Ingersoll, Royal Rodney
Ingraham, Duncan Nathaniel
Jeffers, William Nicholson
Jenkins, Thornton Alexander
Jones, Jacob
Kelley, James Douglas Jerrold
Key, Francis Scott
Kimball, William Wirt
Landon, Melville de Lancy
Lanigan, George Thomas
Lanman, Joseph
Lardner, James Lawrence
Leggett, William
Lester, Charles Edwards
Loomis, Charles Battell
Ludlow, Fitz Hugh
Lynch, William Francis
McNair, Frederick Vallette
Mahan, Alfred Thayer
Mayo, William Kennon
Meade, Richard Worsam, 1807–1870
Meade, Richard Worsam, 1837–1897
Milligan, Robert Wiley
Moffett, William Adger
Montgomery, John Berrien
Morris, Charles
Murdock, Joseph Ballard
Olmsted, Gideon
Page, Thomas Jefferson
Palmer, James Croxall
Palmer, John Williamson
Parker, Foxhall Alexander
Parker, William Harwar
Parrott, Enoch Greenleafe
Patterson, Daniel Todd
Patterson, Thomas Harman
Pattison, Thomas
Paulding, Hiram
Pennock, Alexander Mosely
Percival, John
Phelps, Thomas Stowell
Philip, John Woodward
Plunkett, Charles Peshall
Poor, Charles Henry
Preble, George Henry
Pringle, Joel Roberts Poinsett
Quackenbush, Stephen Platt
Raby, James Joseph
Radford, Wiiliam
Read, George Campbell
Read, Thomas
Reid, Samuel Chester
Remey, George Collier
Revere, Joseph Warren
Ringgold, Cadwalader
Rousseau, Harry Harwood
Sampson, William Thomas
Sands, Benjamin Franklin
Sands, Joshua Ratoon
Schley, Winfield Scott
Shubrick, John Templer
Shubrick, William Branford
Shufeldt, Robert Wilson
Sicard, Montgomery
Simpson, Edward
Smith, Melancton, 1810–1893
Soley, James Russell
Stevens, Thomas Holdup, 1795–1841
Stevens, Thomas Holdup, 1819–1896
Stewart, Edwin
Stoddard, John Lawson
Taylor, William Rogers

Taylor, William Vigneron
Temple, William Grenville
Thompson, Egbert
Tingey, Thomas
Truxtun, Thomas
Truxtun, William Talbot
Tyson, George Emory
Upshur, John Henry
Waldo, Samuel Putnam
Walke, Henry
Walker, John Grimes
Waters, Daniel
Watson, John Crittenden
Werden, Reed
Wilde, George Francis Faxon
Wilson, Theodore Delavan
Winslow, Cameron McRae
Worden, John Lorimer
Ziegemeier, Henry Joseph
WESTERFIELD, RAY B.
Farnam, Henry Walcott
WESTERHOFF, JOHN HENRY, III
Coe, George Albert
WESTON, ARTHUR D.
Goodnough, Xanthus Henry
WESTON, MARY ANN
Mowrer, Edgar Ansel
WESTON, PETER J.
Rhine, Joseph Banks
WESTON, WILLIAM H., JR.
Thaxter, Roland
WETMORE, ALEXANDER
True, Frederick William
WETTEREAU, JAMES O.
Willing, Thomas
Wolcott, Oliver, 1760–1833
WEYER, EDWARD M.
Ladd, George Trumbull
Le Moyne, Francis Julius
WHEELER, GERALD E.
Pratt, William Veazie
WHEELER, GERARD E.
Lee, Willis Augustus
WHEELER, JESSIE F.
Wilson, Samuel
WHEELER, JOSEPH L.
Mayer, Brantz
WHICHER, GEORGE F.
Adams, Charles Follen
Alden, William Livingston
Arnold, George
Dennie, Joseph
Dickinson, Emily Elizabeth
Genung, John Franklin
Lewis, Charles Bertrand
Sewall, Jonathan Mitchell
Story, Isaac
Thaxter, Celia Laighton
Todd, Mabel Loomis
Turell, Jane
Tyler, William Seymour
Underwood, Francis Henry
Wallace, William Ross
Ward, Herbert Dickinson
Whiting, Charles Goodrich
WHIPPLE, THOMAS K.
London, Jack
WHISNANT, DAVID E.
Boyd, James
WHITAKER, ARTHUR P.
Bowles, William Augustus
Carondelet, Francisco Luis Hector, Baron de
Fanning, Alexander Campbell Wilder
Forbes, John Murray, 1771–1831
Gálvez, Bernardo de
Gayoso de Lemos, Manuel
Jackson, James, 1757–1806
McGillivray, Alexander
McIntosh, Lachlan
Miró, Esteban Rod
O'Reilly, Alexander
Robertson, James Alexander
Sevier, John
Ulloa, Antonio de
WHITAKER, CHARLES HARRIS
Bacon, Henry
WHITE, CHARLES ADAMS
Elson, Louis Charles
WHITE, COURTLAND Y., III
Smith, Francis Hopkinson
WHITE, G. EDWARD
Pound, (Nathan) Roscoe
WHITE, HORATIO S.
Fiske, Daniel Willard
WHITE, LAURA A.
Rhett, Robert Barnwell
WHITE, LESLIE A.
Goldenweiser, Alexander Alexandrovich
Parsons, Elsie Worthington Clews
WHITE, MELVIN JOHNSON
Brown, James, 1766–1835
Bullard, Henry Adams
Eustis, George, 1796–1858
Eustis, George, 1828–1872
Eustis, James Biddle
Hahn, George Michael Decker
Hall, Dominick Augustin
Hays, Harry Thompson
Hébert, Paul Octave
Howe, William Wirt
Hunt, William Henry
Johnston, Josiah Stoddard
Johnston, William Preston
Kenner, Duncan Farrar
Lafon, Thomy
Livermore, Samuel, 1786–1833
Lucas, John Baptiste Charles
Ludeling, John Theodore
McEnery, Samuel Douglas
Manning, Thomas Courtland
Morgan, Philip Hicky
Newcomb, Josephine Louise Le Monnier
Provosty, Olivier Otis
WHITE, ROBERT
Thomas, John Charles
WHITE, WILLIAM A.
Nichols, Charles Henry
WHITEHILL, WALTER MUIR
Browne, Herbert Wheildon Cotton
Carnegie, Mary Crowninshield Endicott Chamberlain
Colcord, Lincoln Ross
Connick, Charles Jay
Coolidge, Julian Lowell
Coolidge, Thomas Jefferson
Cram, Ralph Adams
Edwards, Richard Stanislaus
Howe, Mark Antony De Wolfe
Kean, Jefferson Randolph
King, Ernest Joseph
Lawrence, William
Lodge, John Ellerton
Marquand, John Phillips
Mayo, Henry Thomas
Perry, Bliss
Tyler, Royall
Updike, Daniel Berkeley
Wheelwright, Mary Cabot
Winship, George Parker
WHITEHOUSE, VIRGINIA
Bickel, Karl August
WHITELAW, JOHN L.
Graves, William Sidney
WHITELEY, EMILY STONE
Hughes, Christopher
WHITEMAN, HAROLD B., JR.
Davis, Norman Hezekiah
WHITFIELD, STEPHEN J.
Berg, Gertrude Edelstein
Cantor, Eddie
Goodman, Paul
Kallen, Horace Meyer
Moore, Victor Frederick
Rahv, Philip
WHITING, BARTLETT JERE
Kittredge, George Lyman
WHITLEY, MARY T.
Norsworthy, Naomi
WHITMAN, ALDEN
Herbst, Josephine Frey
Manning, Marie
Smart, David Archibald
Strong, Anna Louise
WHITMORE, ALLAN R.
Beard, Daniel Carter
WHITNAH, DONALD R.
Marvin, Charles Frederick
WHITTIER, ISABEL M. S.
Wentworth, Benning
WHITTLESEY, WALTER LINCOLN
Bloomfield, Joseph
Boudinot, Elias, 1740–1821
Cattell, Alexander Gilmore
Clark, Abraham
Condit, John
Dayton, Elias
Dayton, Jonathan
Dayton, William Lewis
Elmer, Ebenezer
Elmer, Jonathan
Elmer, Lucius Quintius Cincinnatus
Faesch, John Jacob
Fell, John
Ford, Jacob
Hart, John
Henderson, Thomas
Hornblower, Josiah
Houston, William Churchill
Howell, Richard
WHORTON, JAMES C.
Sumner, James Batcheller
WICKENDEN, ROBERT J.
Anshutz, Thomas Pollock
Beckwith, James Carroll
Blum, Robert Frederick
Casilear, John William
Chase, William Merritt
Church, Frederick Edwin
Cole, Thomas
Cox, Kenyon

WICKERSHAM, GEORGE W.
Grosvenor, Edwin Prescott
WICKHAM, HENRY F.
Nutting, Charles Cleveland
WIDICK, B. J.
Durkin, Martin Patrick
WIEBE, ROBERT
Hofstadter, Richard
WIECEK, WILLIAM MICHAEL
Lehman, Irving
WIEHL, DOROTHY G.
Sydenstricker, Edgar
WIENEFELD, ROBERT H.
Turner, Edward Raymond
WIER, JEANNE ELIZABETH
Blasdel, Henry Goode
Comstock, Henry Tompkins Paige
Jones, John Percival
Nye, James Warren
O'Brien, William Shoney
WIEST, EDWARD
Innes, Harry
WIGHT, FREDERICK S.
Dove, Arthur Garfield
WIGMORE, JOHN H.
Bruce, Andrew Alexander
WIGNER, EUGENE P.
Von Neumann, John
WILCOX, E. V.
Allen, Anthony Benezet
Allen, Lewis Falley
WILCOX, JEROME K.
Peck, George Record
Starr, Merritt
Wacker, Charles Henry
WILD, ESTELLE PARTHENIA
Pike, Mary Hayden Green
WILD, ROBERT
Hamilton, Charles Smith
Hopkins, James Campbell
WILDER, CHARLES E.
Young, John Wesley
WILDES, HARRY EMERSON
House, Edward Howard
Knox, George William
MacCauley, Clay
Maclay, Robert Samuel
WILENS, SALLY
Harrison, Ross Granville
WILEY, HARVEY W.
Adams, Henry Cullen
WILGUS, A. CURTIS
Thrasher, John Sidney
WILKINS, BURLEIGH TAYLOR
Baker, Carl Lotus
WILKINS, ROBERT P.
Libby, Orin Grant
WILKINS, THURMAN
Borglum, John Gutzon de la Mothe
James, Will Roderick
Wood, Charles Erskine Scott
Wright, Harold Bell
WILKINSON, VERNON L.
Wait, William
Waterman, Thomas Whitney
WILL, ALLEN SINCLAIR
Gibbons, James
McKelway, St. Clair
Marble, Manton Malone
Merrill, William Bradford
Miller, Charles Ransom
WILLARD, JAMES FIELD
Chaffee, Jerome Bonaparte
Eaton, Benjamin Harrison
Evans, John, 1814–1897
Gilpin, William
Grant, James Benton
Hallett, Moses
Loveland, William Austin Hamilton
Meeker, Nathan Cook
Thomas, Charles Spalding
Wolcott, Edward Oliver
WILLCOX, WALTER F.
Billings, John Shaw
Hollerith, Herman
Rossiter, William Sidney
Shattuck, Lemuel
WILLETT, HURD C.
Humphreys, Wiliam Jackson
WILLEY, GORDON R.
Vaillant, George Clapp
WILLIAMS, AMELIA
Robertson, Jerome Bonaparte
Travis, William Barret
WILLIAMS, CLARENCE RUSSELL
Bradley, William Czar
Collamer, Jacob
Larrinaga, Tulio
Muñoz-Rivera, Luis
WILLIAMS, DEAN E.
Johnson, Wendell Andrew Leroy
WILLIAMS, ERNEST W., JR.
Loree, Leonor Fresnel
Underwood, Frederick Douglas
WILLIAMS, HERBERT M.
Park, Roswell
WILLIAMS, LEWIS W., II
Taft, Lorado Zadoc
WILLIAMS, MARY WILHELMINE
Carroll, John Lee
Clayton, John Middleton
Cowen, John Kissig
Creswell, John Angel James
Gilman, Charlotte Perkins Stetson
Hise, Elijah
Jenifer, Daniel of St. Thomas
Johnson, Reverdy
Kennedy, John Pendleton
McLane, Robert Milligan
Mercer, John Francis
Mercer, Margaret
Mott, James
Mott, Lucretia Coffin
Pillsbury, Parker
Rose, Ernestine Louise Siismondi Potowski
Smith, Abby Hadassah
Smith, Robert, 1757–1842
Smith, Samuel
Squier, Ephraim George
Stanton, Elizabeth Cady
Stanton, Henry Brewster
Stewart, Eliza Daniel
Stone, Lucy
Sunderland, Eliza Jane Read
Van Meter, John Blackford
Veazey, Thomas Ward
WILLIAMS, SAMUEL C.
Haywood, John
Humphreys, West Hughes
Jackson, William Hicks
Johnson, Cave
Jones, James Chamberlayne
Tatham, William
Temple, Oliver Perry
Timberlake, Henry
Tyson, Lawrence Davis
Wilder, John Thomas
WILLIAMS, STANLEY THOMAS
Alsop, Richard
Barlow, Joel
Brainard, John Gardiner Calkins
Crèvecoeur, Michel
Humphreys, David
Irving, John Treat
Irving, Peter
Irving, Pierre Munro
Irving, Washington
Irving, William
Montgomery, George Washington
Payne, John Howard
WILLIAMS, TYRRELL
Hadley, Herbert Spencer
Hitchcock, Henry
Hough, Warwick
Thayer, Amos Madden
Thompson, Seymour Dwight
Treat, Samuel
Valliant, Leroy Branch
Walker, Robert Franklin
WILLIAMS, VERNON L.
Clark, Joseph James ("Jocko")
WILLIAMS, WALTER
Cortambert, Louis Richard
Grosvenor, William Mason
Keating, John McLeod
King, Henry
Knapp, George
McCullagh, Joseph Burbridge
WILLIAMS, WILLIAM APPLEMAN
Robins, Raymond
WILLIAMS, WILLIAM H.
Abt, Isaac Arthur
Kirk, Norman Thomas
WILLIAMSON, CHARLES C.
Nelson, Charles Alexander
WILLIAMSON, FRANCIS T.
Newton, Thomas, 1768–1847
WILLIAMSON, MILDRED E.
Knight, Henry Cogswell
WILLIS, EOLA
Ioor, William
WILLIS, H. PARKER
Bell, Isaac
Bliss, George
Brady, Anthony Nicholas
Cannon, James Graham
Clews, Henry
Coe, George Simmons
Cook, James Merrill
Curtis, George
Strong, Benjamin
WILLISTON, SAMUEL
Ames, James Barr
Gray, Horace
Langdell, Christopher Columbus
Thayer, Ezra Ripley
Thayer, James Bradley
Whipple, Sherman Leland
WILLOCK, ROGER
Butler, Smedley Darlington
Geiger, Roy Stanley

WILLOUGHBY, MALCOLM F.
Waesche, Russell Randolph
WILLOUGHBY, WILLIAM F.
Lord, Herbert Mayhew
WILLS, ALBERT POTTER
Webster, Arthur Gordon
WILMER, WILLIAM H.
Theobald, Samuel
WILMETH, DON B.
Aronson, Boris Solomon
Lahr, Bert
Rand, Sally
White, George
WILMOT, SYDNEY
Strobel, Charles Louis
WILMUTH, DON B.
Lee, Gypsy Rose
WILSON, DANIEL J.
Lovejoy, Arthur Oncken
WILSON, DONALD D.
Burdick, Eugene Leonard
WILSON, EDWIN B.
Gibbs, Josiah Willard
WILSON, GEORGE GRAFTON
Coolidge, Thomas Jefferson
WILSON, JAMES SOUTHALL
Bagby, George William
Minor, Benjamin Blake
Thompson, John Reuben
White, Thomas Willis
Whitman, Sarah Helen Power
Willcox, Louise Collier
WILSON, JOAN HOFF
Martin, Anne Henrietta
WILSON, JOHN A.
Chiera, Edward
WILSON, JOHN S.
Celestin, Oscar ("Papa")
Dorsey, Thomas Francis ("Tommy")
Tatum, Art
WILSON, LOUIS B.
Mayo, William Worrell
WILSON, LOUIS R.
Graham, Edward Kidder
WILSON, MARY TOLFORD
Bevier, Isabel
Coolidge, Elizabeth Penn Sprague
Greene, Belle Da Costa
Thurber, Teannette Meyer
Vanderbilt, Grace Graham Wilson
WILSON, NETTA W.
Owre, Alfred
WILSON, OTTO
Andrews, Alexander Boyd
Armstrong, Robert
WILSON, RICHARD GUY
Stewart, John George
Wright, John Kenneth Lloyd
WILSON, SAMUEL M.
Scott, Charles
Shelby, Evan
Shelby, Isaac
Smith, James, 1737–1814
Stanton, Richard Henry
WILSON, WILLIAM
Arnold, Harold DeForest
WILSTACH, PAUL
Davenport, Edward Loomis
Davenport, Fanny Lily Gypsy
WIMER, KURT
Seymour, Charles
WINBUSH, SAMUEL VON
Ashford, Emmett Littleton
Daniels, Farrington
WINCH, DONALD
Viner, Jacob
WINNER, VIOLA HOPKINS
Cather, Willa
Stein, Gertrude
WINPENNY, THOMAS R.
Behn, Sosthenes
Dumaine, Frederic Christopher
Prentis, Henning Webb, Jr.
WINSHIP, GEORGE P.
Channing, Edward
WINSLOW, NATHAN
Potter, Nathaniel
WINSTON, JAMES E.
Carleton, Henry
Collens, Thomas Wharton
WINSTON, MICHAEL R.
Johnson, Mordecai Wyatt
WINSTON, ROBERT W.
Potter, Robert
Winston, Joseph
WINTER, JOHN GARRETT
D'Ooge, Martin Luther
WINTERICH, JOHN T.
Emmett, Burton
WINTERS, DONALD L.
Bailey, Liberty Hyde
WINTON, GEORGE B.
Summers, Thomas Osmond
Tigert, John James
WIRTS, KRISTINE
Elder, Ruth
WISBEY, HERBERT A., JR.
Booth, Ballington
WISE, GEORGE
Colpitts, Edwin Henry
Ferguson, Samuel
Whitney, Willis Rodney
WISER, VIVIAN
Dabney, Charles William
WISSLER, CLARK
Chamberlain, Alexander Francis
Saville, Marshall Howard
Sullivan, Louis Robert
WITBECK, ALBERT T.
Freeman, Thomas
Sibley, John
WITEK, JOSEPH
Mullin, Willard Harlan
WITHAM, BARRY B.
Behrman, Samuel Nathaniel ("S. N.")
Davis, Owen Gould
Hall, Juanita Armethea
Hansberry, Lorraine Vivian
Herbert, Frederick Hugh
Janney, Russell Dixon
WITHERSPOON, GARY J.
Dodge, Henry Chee
WITTHOFT, JOHN
Hamilton, Edith
Linton, Ralph
Lowie, Robert Harry
Speck, Frank Gouldsmith
WITTKE, CARL
Rice, Thomas Dartmouth
WOLF, EDWIN, II
Rosenbach, Abraham Simon Wolf
Rosenbach, Philip Hyman
WOLF, THOMAS P.
Capehart, Homer Earl
McKinney, Frank Edward, Sr.
Montoya, Joseph Manuel
WOLFSON, HARRY A.
Monis, Judah
Sewall, Stephen
WOLPER, JOANNA
Paley, Barbara Cushing ("Babe")
WOOD, FRANCIS CARTER
Prudden, Theophil Mitchell
WOODALL, ALLEN E.
Snelling, William Joseph
WOODBINE, GEORGE EDWARD
Baldwin, Simeon Eben
Ellsworth, Oliver
Reeve, Tapping
Story, Joseph
WOODBURN, JAMES A.
Beveridge, Albert Jeremiah
Hall, Baynard Rush
Hendricks, Thomas Andrews
Hendricks, William
Johnston, Alexander
WOODBURY, HELEN SUMNER
Gould, Elgin Ralston Lovell
Jones, Mary Harris
Keefe, Daniel Joseph
Lee, William Granville
McNulty, Frank Joseph
Mailly, William
Most, Johann Joseph
Nash, Arthur
Noonan, James Patrick
Pike, Robert
Powderly, Terence Vincent
WOODBURY, ROBERT M.
Pike, Robert
WOODFIN, MAUDE H.
Genet, Edmond Charles
Harvey, Sir John
Lee, Charles, 1758–1815
Lee, Henry, 1787–1837
Marshall, Thomas
Mason, George
Nelson, Hugh
Nelson, Thomas
Nelson, William, 1711–1772
Page, John
Page, Mann
Randolph, John, 1728–1784
Randolph, Sir John
Randolph, Peyton
Randolph, William
Ryland, Robert
Taylor, George Boardman
Taylor, James Barnett
Thomson, John
Tupper, Henry Allen
Wood, John
WOODRUFF, CLINTON ROGERS
Blankenburg, Rudolph
WOODS, ALAN C.
Wilmer, William Holland
WOODSON, CARTER GODWIN
Allen, Richard
Boyd, Richard Henry
Brown, John Mifflin
Brown, Morris
Brown, William Wells
Bruce, Blanche K.
Cain, Richard Harvey

Clinton, George Wylie
Garnet, Henry Highland
Greener, Richard Theodore
WOODWARD, CARL R.
Nelson, Julius
Read, Charles
Thurber, George
WOODWARD, SHERMAN M.
Davis, Arthur Powell
WOODWARD, VANN
Watson, Thomas Edward
WOODWARD, WALTER C.
Nicholson, Timothy
WOODWORTH, ROBERT S.
Franz, Shepherd Ivory
Ladd-Franklin, Christine
Washburn, Margaret Floy
WOODY, ROBERT H.
Boyd, William Kenneth
Moses, Franklin, Jr.
Simonton, Charles Henry
Sydnor, Charles Sackett
Wright, Jonathan Jasper
WOODY, THOMAS
Alison, Francis
Allen, George
Allen, William Henry
Bishop, Nathan
Burton, Warren
Calhoun, William Barron
Camp, David Nelson
Carter, James Gordon
Cheever, Ezekiel
Cobb, Lyman
Colburn, Dana Pond
Cooley, Edwin Gilbert
Cooper, William John
Dock, Christopher
Downey, John
Furst, Clyde Bowman
Keagy, John Miller
Knox, Samuel
Pennypacker, Elijah Funk
Phelps, Almira Hart Lincoln
Poor, John
Schaeffer, Nathan Christ
Sill, Anna Peck
WOOLLEY, MARY E.
Lyon, Mary
WOOLSEY, GEORGE
Stimson, Lewis Atterbury
WOOSTER, JAMES W., JR.
Harkness, Edward Stephen
WORCESTER, WILLIAM LORING
Barrett, Benjamin Fiske
Giles, Chauncey
WORRELL, WILLIAM H.
Frieze, Henry Simmons
Kelsey, Francis Willey
WORTH, DEAN S.
Wiener, Leo
WORTHY, JAMES C.
Wood, Robert Elkington
WRIGHT, C. P.
Marshall, Benjamin
Thompson, Jeremiah
WRIGHT, ERNEST H.
Boyesen, Hjalmar Hjorth
Canfield, James Hulme
Carpenter, George Rice
Da Ponte, Lorenzo
Drisler, Henry
Duer, William Alexander
Earle, Mortimer Lamson
WRIGHT, FREDERICK E.
Woodward, Robert Simpson
WRIGHT, HARRY A.
Pynchon, John
WRIGHT, HELEN
Benson, Eugene
Brumidi, Constantino
Cassatt, Mary
Coleman, Charles Caryl
Colman, Samuel
Coman, Charlotte Buell
Cropsey, Jasper Francis
Haskell, Ernest
Hyde, Helen
Jones, Alfred
Keith, William
Kingsley, Elbridge
Koehler, Sylvester Rosa
Koopman, Augustus
Kruell, Gustav
Mackubin, Florence
Nicholls, Rhoda Holmes
Plowman, George Taylor
Porter, Russell Williams
Reed, Earl Howell
Ritchey, George Willis
WRIGHT, HERBERT F.
Balch, Thomas Willing
Bidlack, Benjamin Alden
Denby, Charles
Eames, Charles
Farman, Elbert Eli
Fearn, John Walker
Fisher, George Purnell
Fox, Williams Carlton
Gorman, Arthur Pue
Gresham, Walter Quintin
Jones, Walter
Knox, Philander Chase
WRIGHT, JAMES
Tobey, Charles William
WRIGHT, JOHN W.
Hatch, Edward
Howe, Albion Parris
Spaulding, Oliver Lyman
WRIGHT, NELDA E.
Hay, Oliver Perry
WRIGHT, WALTER L., JR.
Bradish, Luther
Brewer, Charles
Carr, Dabney Smith
Carter, Henry Alpheus Peirce
De Forest, David Curtis
English, George Bethune
Ferguson, Thomas Barker
Gibson, Walter Murray
Green, Beniamin Edwards
Gregg, David McMurtrie
Gummere, Samuel René
Hale, Charles
Hamlin, Cyrus
Hassaurek, Friedrich
Hill, John Henry
Hunnewell, James
Marsh, George Perkins
Marshall, James Fowle Baldwin
Offley, David
Peirce, Henry Augustus
Post, George Edward
Prime, Edward Dorr Griffin
Rhind, Charles
Riggs, Elias
Robert, Christopher Rhinelander
Ryan, Arthur Clayton
Schneider, Benjamin
Shaler, William
Shepard, Fred Douglas
Smith, Azariah
Thurber, Christopher Carson
Van Dyck, Cornelius Van Alen
Van Lennep, Henry John
Washburn, George
Wilson, Samuel Graham
WROTH, LAWRENCE COUNSELMAN
Brown, John, 1736–1803
Brown, John Carter
Brown, Joseph
Brown, Nicholas, 1729 o.s.–1791
Brown, Nicholas, 1769–1841
Carroll, Charles
Cooke, Ebenezer
Cresap, Michael
Cresap, Thomas
Logan, James, 1725–1780
Nuthead, William
Parks, William
Staples, William Read
Steiner, Bernard Christian
Sterling, James
WUNSCH, WILLIAM F.
Smyth, Julian Kennedy
WYER, JAMES INGERSOLL
Eastman, William Reed
Fairchild, Mary Salome Cutler
Randall, Henry Stephens
Sanders, Charles Walton
Street, Alfred Billings
Thacher, John Boyd
Thompson, Samuel Rankin
Tucker, Gilbert Milligan
Williams, Edwin
Williams, John, 1761–1818
Williams, William, 1787–1850
WYLLIE, JOHN C.
Gordon, William Fitzhugh
Levy, Uriah Phillips
Lynch, Charles
Lyons, Peter
WYLLYS, RUFUS KAY
Hunt, George Wylie Paul
WYLY, M. VIRGINIA
Apgar, Virginia
WYLY, VIRGINIA
Perelman, Sidney Joseph
WYMAN, MARY ALICE
Botta, Anne Charlotte Lynch
Smith, Seba
WYNN, DUDLEY
Austin, Mary
WYNNE, JOHN J.
Allouez, Claude Jean
WYNNER, EDITH
Schwimmer, Rosika
WYZANSKI, CHARLES E., JR.
Hand, Augustus Noble

YALE, CAROLINE A.
Rogers, Harriet Burbank
YANS, VIRGINIA MCLAUGHLIN
Antin, Mary
YARD, ROBERT STERLING
Mather, Stephen Tyng

YARMOLINSKY, AVRAHM
Rezanov, Nikolai Petrovich
YATES, NORRIS
Cuppy, William Jacob (Will)
YEAGER, MARY A.
Hormel, Jay Catherwood
YEUELL, DONOVAN
Heth, Henry
Lee, Stephen Dill
Lovell, Mansfield
McElroy, John
Morris, William Hopkins
Mott, Gershom
Mower, Joseph Anthony
Palmer, Innis Newton
Parker, Ely Samuel
Peck, John James
Pettigrew, James Johnston
Rains, Gabriel James
Reno, Jesse Lee
Reynolds, Alexander Welch
Robinson, John Cleveland
Roddey, Philip Dale
Rodenbough, Theophilus Francis
Rodman, Isaac Peace
YNTEMA, HESSEL E.
Oliphant, Herman
YOCHELSON, ELLIS L.
Schuchert, Charles
YOCHELSON, ELLIS Y.
Grabau, Amadeus William
YODER, H. S., JR.
Day, Arthur Louis
YONGE, JULIEN C.
Bloxham, William Dunnington
Broward, Napoleon Bonaparte
YOST, EDNA
Abbot, Henry Larcom
Alden, John Ferris
Allaire, James Peter
Allen, John F.
Angell, William Gorham
Benjamin, Park, 1849–1922
Bettendorf, William Peter
Bogart, John
Bogne, Virgil Gay
Boller, Alfred Pancoast
Bonzano, Adolphus
Brashear, John Alfred
Brown, William Henry
Buckhout, Isaac Craig
Canfield, Richard A.
Carpenter, Franklin Reuben
Cheesman, Forman
Cheney, Benjamin Pierce
Church, George Earl
Coates, Samuel
Coffin, Charles Albert
Cogswell, William Browne
Colton, George Radcliffe
Colver, William Byron
Cook, Zebedee
Cooley, Lyman Edgar
Cooper, Theodore
Cope, Caleb
Cope, Thomas Pym
Corthell, Elmer Lawrence
Delafield, Richard
Durfee, William Franklin
Egleston, Thomas
Emery, Charles Edward
Evans, Anthony Walton Whyte
Fanning, John Thomas
Felton, Samuel Morse
Ferris, George Washington Gale
Fisher, Clark
YOUNG, CHESTER RAYMOND
Kuykendall, Ralph Simpson
YOUNG, FREDERIC GEORGE
Chamberlain, George Earle
YOUNG, GEORGE B.
Baker, Jehu
YOUNG, JAMES HARVEY
Dickinson, Anna Elizabeth
Macfadden, Bernarr
Merck, George Wilhelm
YOUNG, KIMBALL
Lee, John Doyle
Pratt, Orson
Rigdon, Sidney
Sharp, John
Smith, Joseph Fielding
Snow, Eliza Roxey
Snow, Lorenzo
Strang, James Jesse
Taylor, John
Whitmer, David
Woodruff, Wilford
YOUNG, LOUISE M.
Catt, Carrie Clinton Lane Chapman
YOUNG, MAHONRI M.
Remington, Frederic
YOUNG, RICHARD
Hudson, Manley Ottmer
YOUNG-BRUEHL, ELISABETH
Arendt, Hannah
YOWELL, EVERETT I.
Porter, Jermain Gildersleeve

ZACCANO, JOSEPH P., JR.
Garrett, Finis James
ZACEK, JOSEPH FREDERICK
Leonty, Metropolitan
ZANTZINGER, CLARENCE CLARK
Barber, Donn
ZDANOWICZ, CASIMIR DOUGLASS
Smith, Charles Forster
ZELENY, JOHN
Eddy, Henry Turner
ZENOS, ANDREW C.
Baird, Samuel John
Blackburn, William Maxwell
Blair, Samuel
Brainerd, Thomas
ZEYDEL, EDWIN H.
Ottendorfer, Anna Behr Uhl
Ottendorfer, Oswald
ZIEGER, ROBERT H.
Davis, James John
ZINK, HAROLD
McLaughlin, Hugh
McManes, James
Magee, Christopher Lyman
Ralston, Samuel Moffett
Taggart, Thomas
ZUBER, OSBURN
Glass, Franklin Potts
ZUCKER, ADOLF EDWARD
Reitzel, Robert
Schem, Alexander Jacob
Schnauffer, Carl Heinrich
Solger, Reinhold
Stallo, Johann Bernhard
Struve, Gustav
ZUNDER, THEODORE A.
Barlow, Joel

BIRTHPLACES—UNITED STATES

ALABAMA

Allen, James Browning
Allen, Viola Emily
Bankhead, John Hollis, 1842–1920
Bankhead, John Hollis, 1872–1946
Bankhead, Tallulah
Bankhead, William Brockman
Belmont, Alva Ertskin Smith Vanderbilt
Berry, James Henderson
Birney, David Bell
Birney, William
Black, Hugo Lafayette
Bozeman, Nathan
Brickell, Robert Coman
Bridgman, Frederic Arthur
Brown, Johnny Mack
Brown, William Garrott
Bullard, Robert Lee
Burleson, Rufus Clarence
Camp, John Lafayette
Campbell, William Edward March
Carmichael, Oliver Cromwell
Clay, Clement Claiborne
Clayton, Henry De Lamar
Clemens, Jeremiah
Cole, Nat ("King")
Comer, Braxton Bragg
Connor, Theophilus ("Bull") Eugene
Culberson, Charles Allen
Davis, Mary Evelyn Moore
De Bardeleben, Henry Fairchild
De Priest, Oscar Stanton
Dowling, Noel Thomas
Duggar, Benjamin Minge
Elder, Ruth
English, Elbert Hartwell
Ernst, Morris Leopold
Fearn, John Walker
Fitzpatrick, Morgan Cassius
Fleming, Walter Lynwood
Fulton, Robert Burwell
Gaines, Reuben Reid
Glass, Franklin Potts
Gorgas, William Crawford
Grant, James Benton
Graves, David Bibb
Greenway, John Campbell
Gregg, John
Guild, La Fayette
Hall, Paul
Hamilton, Andrew Jackson
Hancock, John
Handy, William Christopher
Harding, William Procter Gould
Hardy, William Harris
Hargrove, Robert Kennon
Heflin, James Thomas
Hitchcock, Ethan Allen, 1835–1909
Hitchcock, Henry
Hobson, Julius Wilson
Hobson, Richmond Pearson
Jones, Robert Reynolds ("Bob")
Jones, Samuel Porter
Julian, Percy Lavon
Keller, Helen Adams
Kolb, Reuben Francis
Lambrith, James William
Lile, William Minor
Love, Emanuel King
Lyon, David Gordon
McKellar, Kenneth Douglas
Manly, John Matthews
Mastin, Claudius Henry
Mitchell, Sidney Zollicoffer
Moore, John Trotwood
Morgan, John Hunt
Murphy, Edgar Gardner
Oates, William Calvin
O'Neal, Edward Asbury, 1818–1890
O'Neal, Edward Asbury, III, 1875–1958
Owen, Thomas McAdory
Owens, James Cleveland ("Jesse")
Owsley, Frank Lawrence
Parsons, Albert Richard
Pelham, John
Perry, Pettis
Pettus, Edmund Winston
Pou, Edward William
Riley, Benjamin Franklin
Roddey, Philip Dale
Screws, William Wallace
Sibert, William Luther
Simmons, William Joseph
Sloan, Matthew Scott
Sloss, James Withers
Smith, Eugene Allen
Smith, Holland McTyeire
Steagall, Henry Bascom
Tomochichi
Toulmin, Harry Theophilus
Tutwiler, Julia Strudwick
Valliant, Leroy Branch
Van de Graaff, Robert Jemison
Van Doren, Irita Bradford
Vincent, John Heyl
Walker, Leroy Pope
Wallace, Lurleen Burns
Walthall, Henry Brazeal
Washington, Dinah
Watts, Thomas Hill
Weatherford, William
Williams, Aubrey Willis
Williams, (Hiram) Hank
Winston, John Anthony
Wyeth, John Allan

ARIZONA

Devine, Andrew ("Andy")
Douglas, Lewis Williams
Geronimo
Hayden, Carl Trumbull
Mingus, Charles, Jr.
Patch, Alexander McCarrell

ARKANSAS

Adler, Cyrus
Anthony, Katharine Susan
Barnes, Julius Howland
Baylor, Frances Courtenay
Bennett, Henry Garland
Biffle, Leslie L.
Brady, Mildred Alice Edie
Burns, Bob
Couch, Harvey Crowley
Davis, Jefferson
Dean, Jay Hanna ("Dizzy")
Ellis, Clyde Taylor
Fletcher, John Gould
Gray, Carl Raymond
Haynes, George Edmund
Jordan, Louis
Ladd, Alan Walbridge
Liston, Charles ("Sonny")
MacArthur, Douglas
McClellan, John Little
McRae, Thomas Chipman
Mitchell, Martha Elizabeth Beall
Perkins, Marion
Powell, Richard Ewing ("Dick")
Robinson, Joseph Taylor
Somervell, Brehon Burke
Stone, Edward Durell
Sutton, William Seneca

CALIFORNIA

Aborn, Milton
Abrams, Albert
Acosta, Bertram Blanchard ("Bert")
Adams, Annette Abbott
Aitken, Robert Grant
Allen, Gracie
Alvarado, Juan Bautista
Anderson, Edward ("Eddie")
Anderson, Mary
Andrus, Ethel Percy
Arzner, Dorothy Emma
Ashford, Emmett Littleton
Atherton, Gertrude Franklin (Horn)
Atkinson, Henry Avery
Bacon, Frank
Beatty, Willard Walcott
Belasco, David
Berkeley, Busby
Blinn, Holbrook
Bowes, Edward J.
Boyd, Louise Arner
Bradley, Frederick Worthen
Brady, William Aloysius
Britton, Barbara
Brownlee, James Forbis
Burton, Clarence Monroe
Chandler, Norman

Cone, Fairfax Mastick
Connolly, Maureen Catherine
Cooper, William John
Corbett, Harvey Wiley
Corbett, James John
Cottrell, Frederick Gardner
De Angelis, Thomas Jefferson
Dorgan, Thomas Aloysius
Doyle, Alexander Patrick
Drury, Newton Bishop
Duncan, Isadora
Engle, Clair William Walter
Erlanger, Joseph
Evans, Herbert McLean
Fay, Francis Anthony ("Frank")
Fisher, William Arms
Ford, Mary
Frost, Robert Lee
Gaxton, William
George, Henry
Getty, George Franklin, II
Gherardi, Bancroft
Giannini, Amadeo Peter
Gilbreth, Lillian Evelyn Moller
Goldberg, Reuben Lucius ("Rube")
Goodman, Louis Earl
Grady, Henry Francis
Guthrie, William Dameron
Hammond, John Hays
Hansen, William Webster
Harrah, William Fisk ("Bill")
Hearst, William Randolph
Heilmann, Harry
Hinkle, Beatrice Moses
Hohfeld, Wesley Newcomb
Hooper, Harry Bartholomew
Hopper, Edna Wallace
Howard, Sidney T. Coe
Hubbard, Bernard Rosecrans
Jackson, Shirley Hardie
Jepson, Willis Linn
Jewett, Frank Baldwin
Johnson, Hiram Warren
Jones, Lindley Armstrong ("Spike")
Keller, James Gregory
Kirchoff, Charles William Henry
Kohlberg, Alfred
Knowland, William Fife
Kuykendall, Ralph Simpson
Kyne, Peter Bernard
Laguna, Theodore de Leo de
Lasky, Jesse Louis
Lawson, Ernest
Lee, Bruce
Leonard, Robert Josselyn
Leonard, Sterling Andrus
Lewis, John Henry
Lindley, Curtis Holbrook
Lockheed, Allan Haines
Lockheed, Malcolm
London, Jack
Lord, Pauline
Lydston, George Frank
Lynn, Diana ("Dolly")
McClatchy, Charles Kenny
McClintock, James Harvey
McClung, Clarence Erwin
McGeehan, William O'Connell
Mack, Julian William
Mackay, Clarence Hungerford
Magnes, Judah Leon
Mather, Stephen Tyng
Matthiessen, Francis Otto
Maxwell, George Hebard
Meusel, Robert William
Meyer, Eugene Isaac
Meyer, Martin Abraham
Mezes, Sidney Edward
Mizner, Addison
Monroe, Marilyn
Morgan, Julia
Moscone, George Richard
Moss, Sanford Alexander
Nevada, Emma
Norris, Kathleen Thompson
O'Brien, Willis Harold
O'Doul, Francis Joseph ("Lefty")
Overstreet, Harry Allen
Oxnam, Garfield Bromley
Pacheco, Romualdo
Palón, Francisco
Parker, Carleton Hubbell
Patton, George Smith
Peek, Frank William
Phelan, James Duval
Regan, Agnes Gertrude
Reinhardt, Aurelia Isabel Henry
Ripley, Robert LeRoy
Robb, Inez Early Callaway
Roberts, Theodore
Rockefeller, Martha Baird
Roeding, George Christian
Rolph, James
Royce, Josiah
Ruef, Abraham
Sanderson, Sibyl
Sanford, Edmund Clark
Scripps, Robert Paine
Seton, Grace Gallatin Thompson
Smith, James Francis
Spreckels, Rudolph
Sproul, Allan
Sproul, Robert Gordon
Stafford, Jean
Standley, William Harrison
Steffens, Lincoln
Steinbeck, John Ernst, Jr.
Stevens, Ashton
Stevens, George Cooper
Stevenson, Adlai Ewing, II
Suzzallo, Henry
Swain, George Fillmore
Taylor, William Chittenden
Terry, Paul Houlton
Theobald, Robert Alfred
Tibbett, Lawrence Mervil
Toklas, Alice Babette
Vallejo, Mariano Guadalupe
Wanger, Walter
Warfield, David
Warner, William Lloyd
Warren, Earl
Washington, Kenneth Stanley ("The General")
Webb, Harry Howard
White, Stephen Mallory
Whitney, Charlotte Anita
Wightman, Hazel Virginia Hotchkiss
Wigmore, John Henry
Wilson, Marie
Wislocki, George Bernays
Wong, Anna May
Younger, Maud
Zellerbach, Harold Lionel
Zellerbach, James David

COLORADO

Allen, Edgar
Andrews, Bert
Bliss, George William
Byington, Spring
Chaney, Lon
Chapman, John Arthur
Fairbanks, Douglas
Fowler, Gene
Gipson, Lawrence Henry
Gregg, Alan
Herr, Herbert Thacker
Hoagland, Dennis Robert
Holt, Arthur Erastus
Lea, Homer
Leyner, John George
Libby, Willard Frank
MacDonald, Betty
McDonnell, James Smith, Jr.
McHugh, Keith Stratton
McWilliams, Carey
May, Morton Jay
Otis, Arthur Sinton
Parsons, Talcott
Perry, Antoinette
Ross, Harold Wallace
Sabin, Florence Rena
Shumlin, Herman Elliott
Smith, Homer William
Tatum, Edward Lawrie
Thompson, Llewellyn E. ("Tommy"), Jr.
Trumbo, James Dalton
Whiteman, Paul Samuel ("Pops")

CONNECTICUT

Abbot, Willis John
Abbott, Frank Frost
Abbott, William Hawkins
Acheson, Dean Gooderham
Adams, Andrew
Adams, John
Adams, William
Adrian, Gilbert
Alcott, Amos Bronson
Alcott, William Andrus
Alexander, Francis
Alford, Leon Pratt
Allen, Edward Tyson
Allen, Ethan
Allen, Ira
Allen, Jeremiah Mervin
Allyn, Robert
Alsop, Richard
Alsop, Stewart Johonnot Oliver
Alvord, Corydon Alexis
Andrews, Charles McLean
Andrews, Israel Ward
Andrews, Lorrin
Andrews, Samuel James

Andrews, Sherlock James
Andrews, William Watson
Arnold, Benedict
Arnold, Harold DeForest
Arnold, Leslie Philip
Atwater, Lyman Hotchkiss
Atwood, Lewis John
Augur, Hezekiah
Austin, David
Austin, Henry
Austin, Moses
Austin, Samuel
Ayer, James Cook
Ayres, Leonard Porter
Babcock, Washington Irving
Backus, Azel
Backus, Isaac
Bacon, Alice Mabel
Bacon, Benjamin Wisner
Bacon, David
Bacon, John
Bacon, Leonard Woolsey
Badger, Oscar Charles
Bailey, Anna Warner
Bailey, Ebenezer
Bailey, John Moran
Baker, Remember
Baldwin, Abraham
Baldwin, Edward Robinson
Baldwin, Frank Stephen
Baldwin, Henry
Baldwin, John
Baldwin, John Denison
Baldwin, Roger Sherman
Baldwin, Simeon
Baldwin, Simeon Eben
Baldwin, Theron
Bangs, Nathan
Banister, Zilpah Polly Grant
Barber, John Warner
Barbour, Clarence Augustus
Barbour, Henry Gray
Barlow, Joel
Barnard, Daniel Dewey
Barnard, Henry
Barnum, Phineas Taylor
Barstow, William Augustus
Bartholomew, Edward Sheffield
Bartlett, Paul Wayland
Batchelor, George
Bates, Theodore Lewis ("Ted")
Bates, Walter
Batterson, James Goodwin
Bayley, Richard
Beach, Moses Yale
Beach, Wooster
Beard, George Miller
Beardsley, Eben Edwards
Beaumont, William
Beecher, Charles
Beecher, Henry Ward
Beecher, Lyman
Beecher, Thomas Kinnicut
Beers, Clifford Whittingham
Begley, Edward James ("Ed")
Belden, Josiah
Bell, Jacob
Bellamy, Joseph
Benedict, David
Benedict, Erastus Cornelius
Bentley, Elizabeth Terrill
Besse, Arthur Lyman
Bidwell, Walter Hilliard
Bingham, Caleb
Birge, Henry Warner
Bishop, Abraham
Bissell, George Edwin
Blakeslee, Erastus
Blatchford, Richard Milford
Blatchford, Samuel
Bliss, Philemon
Boardman, Thomas Danforth
Bolton, Sarah Knowles
Booth, Albert James, Jr. ("Albie")
Bostwick, Arthur Elmore
Bouton, Nathaniel
Bowen, Henry Chandler
Bowers, Elizabeth Crocker
Bowles, Samuel, 1797–1851
Bowles, Samuel, 1826–1878
Bowles, Samuel, 1851–1915
Brace, Charles Loring
Brace, John Pierce
Bradley, Frank Howe
Bradley, Stephen Row
Brainard, John Gardiner Calkins
Brainerd, David
Brainerd, Erastus
Brainerd, John
Brainerd, Lawrence
Brandegee, Frank Bosworth
Brandegee, Townshend Stith
Brewster, James
Brinton, Clarence Crane
Bristol, William Henry
Brockway, Zebulon Reed
Bromley, Isaac Hill
Bronson, Henry
Brooker, Charles Frederick
Brown, Ethan Allen
Brown, John
Brown, John Newton
Brown, Samuel Robbins
Brown, Solymon
Buck, Daniel
Buck, Dudley
Buckingham, Joseph Tinker
Buckingham, William Alfred
Buckland, Cyrus
Buel, Jesse
Buell, Abel
Bulkeley, Morgan Gardner
Bulkley, John Williams
Bunce, William Gedney
Burleigh, Charles Calistus
Burleigh, George Shepard
Burleigh, William Henry
Burr, Aaron
Burr, Alfred Edmund
Burr, Enoch Fitch
Burr, William Hubert
Burrall, William Porter
Burritt, Elihu
Burton, Asa
Burton, Nathaniel Judson
Burton, Richard Eugene
Bushnell, David
Bushnell, Horace
Butler, John
Butler, Simeon
Butler, Thomas Belden
Cable, Frank Taylor
Calkins, Mary Whiton
Camp, David Nelson
Camp, Hiram
Camp, Walter Chauncey
Candee, Leverett
Capp, Al
Carrington, Henry Beebee
Carter, Franklin
Case, William Scoville
Chamberlain, Jacob
Chamberlain, William Isaac
Chandler, Thomas Bradbury
Chapin, Aaron Lucius
Chapin, Alonzo Bowen
Chauncey, Isaac
Cheney, John
Cheney, Seth Wells
Cheney, Ward
Chester, Colby Mitchell
Chester, Joseph Lemuel
Childs, Richard Spencer
Chipman, Daniel
Chipman, Nathaniel
Chittenden, Martin
Chittenden, Russell Henry
Chittenden, Simeon Baldwin
Chittenden, Thomas
Church, Frederick Erwin
Church, Irving Porter
Clark, Charles Hopkins
Clark, Horace Francis
Clark, Sheldon
Clark, William Thomas
Cleaveland, Moses
Cleveland, Chauncey Fitch
Coan, Titus
Coe, Israel
Coggeshall, George
Coit, Thomas Winthrop
Cole, George Watson
Colt, Samuel
Comstock, Anthony
Cooke, Rose Terry
Copeland, Charles W.
Corbin, Austin
Corning, Erastus
Cowles, Henry Chandler
Cox, Jacob Dolson
Crane, Bob Edward
Crary, Isaac Edwin
Cross, Wilbur Lucius
Croswell, Harry
Curtiss, Samuel Ives
Cushman, George Hewitt
Cutler, Manasseh
Daboll, Nathan
Dana, Edward Salisbury
Dana, Samuel Whittelsey
Danforth, Moseley Isaac
Davenport, Charles Benedict
Davenport, James
Davis, Charles Henry Stanley
Davis, George Whitefield
Day, Henry Noble
Day, Jeremiah
Dean, Sidney
Deane, Silas
De Forest, David Curtis

De Forest, John Kinne Hyde
De Forest, John William
De Koven, Henry Louis Reginald
De Koven, James
Deming, Henry Champion
De Vinne, Theodore Low
Dickinson, Anson
Dickinson, Daniel Stevens
Dike, Samuel Warren
Dillingham, Charles Bancroft
Dixon, James
Dockstader, Lew
Dodd, Thomas Joseph
Dodge, David Low
Dodge, William Earl
Doolittle, Amos
Douglas, Benjamin
Douglas, William
Dow, Lorenzo
Downer, Eliphalet
Dudley, William Russel
Dunbar, Moses
Dunning, Albert Elijah
Durand, William Frederick
Durkee, John
Dutton, Clarence Edward
Dutton, Henry
Dwight, Benjamin Woodbridge
Dwight, Sereno Edwards
Dwight, Theodore, 1764–1846
Dwight, Theodore, 1796–1866
Dwight, Timothy
Dyer, Eliphalet
Eaton, William
Edwards, Henry Waggaman
Edwards, Jonathan, 1703–1758
Eliot, Jared
Ellsworth, Henry Leavitt
Ellsworth, Henry William
Ellsworth, Oliver
Ellsworth, William Wolcott
Emmons, Nathanael
English, James Edward
Falkner, Roland Post
Fanning, Edmund
Fanning, John Thomas
Fanning, Nathaniel
Farnam, Henry Walcott
Farrell, James Augustine
Fayerweather, Daniel Burton
Ferry, Orris Sanford
Fetterman, William Judd
Field, David Dudley, 1781–1867
Field, David Dudley, 1805–1894
Field, Stephen Johnson
Fillmore, John Comfort
Finney, Charles Grandison
Fiske, John
Fitch, John
Fitch, Samuel
Fitch, Thomas
Flagg, George Whiting
Flagg, Jared Bradley
Fleming, William Maybury
Foot, Samuel Augustus
Foote, Andrew Hull
Foote, William Henry
Ford, Gordon Lester
Forward, Walter
Foster, John Pierrepont Codrington
Foster, Lafayette Sabine
Foulois, Benjamin Delahauf
Fryer, Douglas Henry
Gallaudet, Edward Miner
Gallaudet, Thomas
Gallup, Joseph Adams
Gardner, Leroy Upson
Gary, James Albert
Gauvreau, Emile Henry
Gaylord, Willis
Gibbs, Josiah Willard
Gibson, William Hamilton
Giddings, Franklin Henry
Gilbert, William Lewis
Gillett, Ezra Hall
Gillette, Francis
Gillette, William Hooker
Gilman, Charlotte Perkins Stetson
Gilman, Daniel Coit
Gleason, Frederic Grant
Goddard, William
Goodhue, Bertram Grosvenor
Goodrich, Charles Augustus
Goodrich, Chauncey
Goodrich, Chauncey Allen
Goodrich, Elizur, 1734–1797
Goodrich, Elizur, 1761–1849
Goodrich, Samuel Griswold
Goodyear, Charles
Goodyear, William Henry
Gould, Edward Sherman
Gould, George Jay
Gould, James
Graham, John Andrew
Graham, Sylvester
Granger, Francis
Granger, Gideon
Green, Beriah
Green, Thomas
Griffin, Edward Dorr
Griffing, Josephine Sophie White
Griswold, Alexander Viets
Griswold, Matthew
Griswold, Roger
Griswold, Stanley
Grosvenor, Charles Henry
Grow, Galusha Aaron
Guernsey, Egbert
Gunn, Frederick William
Gurley, Ralph Randolph
Hadley, Arthur Twining
Hale, David
Hale, Nathan
Hall, Asaph
Hall, Isaac Hollister
Hall, Lyman
Halleck, Fitz-Greene
Hamline, Leonidas Lent
Hammett, Samuel Adams
Hammond, Edward Payson
Hand, Daniel
Harding, Abner Clark
Harris, William Torrey
Harrison, Henry Baldwin
Hart, John
Hart, Samuel
Harvey, Louis Powell
Haskell, Ernest
Hastings, Thomas
Haven, Henry Philemon
Hawley, Gideon, 1727–1809
Hawley, Gideon, 1785–1870
Hayden, Horace H.
Hendrick, Burton Jesse
Herrick, Edward Claudius
Herter, Christian Archibald
Hewit, Augustine Francis
Hickok, Laurens Perseus
Higginson, Nathaniel
Hill, Ureli Corelli
Hillhouse, James
Hillhouse, James Abraham
Hinman, Elisha
Hinman, Joel
Hitchcock, Peter
Hoadley, David
Hoadly, George
Hobart, John Sloss
Hogan, Frank Smithwick
Holbrook, Alfred
Holbrook, Frederick
Holbrook, Josiah
Holcomb, Amasa
Holley, Alexander Lyman
Holley, Horace
Holley, Myron
Hollister, Gideon Hiram
Holmes, Abiel
Holmes, Israel
Hooker, Donald Russell
Hooker, Isabella Beecher
Hopkins, Lemuel
Hopkins, Samuel, 1721–1803
Hosmer, Titus
Hotchkiss, Benjamin Berkeley
Howe, Henry
Howe, John Ireland
Howland, Gardiner Greene
Hubbard, Henry Griswold
Hubbard, Joseph Stillman
Hubbard, Richard William
Hull, Isaac
Hull, William
Humphrey, Heman
Humphreys, David
Hunt, Mary Hannah Hanchett
Hunt, Thomas Sterry
Huntington, Collis Potter
Huntington, Jabez
Huntington, Jedediah
Huntington, Samuel, 1731–1796
Huntington, Samuel, 1765–1817
Hyde, James Nevins
Ingersoll, Jared, 1722–1781
Ingersoll, Jared, 1749–1822
Ingersoll, Simon
Inglis, Alexander James
Ives, Charles Edward
Ives, Chauncey Bradley
Ives, Eli
Ives, Frederic Eugene
Ives, Levi Silliman
Jarvis, Abraham
Jenkins, John, 1728–1785
Jenkins, John, 1751–1827
Jerome, Chauncey
Jesup, Morris Ketchum
Jewett, David
Jewett, William
Jocelyn, Nathaniel

Johnson, Samuel
Johnson, Seth Whitmore
Johnson, Treat Baldwin
Johnson, William
Johnson, William Samuel
Johnston, Josiah Stoddard
Jones, Joel
Judah, Theodore Detton
Keeler, James Edward
Keep, Robert Porter
Kelley, Alfred
Kellogg, Albert
Kellogg, Edward
Kellogg, Martin
Kellogg, William Pitt
Kendall, Edward Calvin
Kensett, John Frederick
Kilbourne, James
King, Dan
Kingsbury, John
Kingsley, James Luce
Kirby, Ephraim
Kirkland, Samuel
Kirtland, Jared Potter
Knight, Jonathan
Ladd-Franklin, Christine
Lanman, Charles Rockwell
Lanman, Joseph
Larned, Joseph Gay Eaton
Larrabee, William
Law, Andrew
Law, John
Law, Jonathan
Law, Richard
Leaming, Jeremiah
Leavenworth, Henry
Leavitt, Humphrey Howe
Ledyard, John
Ledyard, William
Lee, Charles Alfred
Leonard, William Andrew
Lester, Charles Edwards
Levermore, Charles Herbert
Lockwood, Ralph Ingersoll
Lockwood, Robert Wilton
Loomis, Arphaxed
Loomis, Dwight
Loomis, Elias
Lord, Daniel
Lord, David Nevins
Lord, Eleazar
Lothrop, Harriett Mulford Stone
Lusk, Graham
Lusk, William Thompson
Lyman, Chester Smith
Lyman, Phineas
Lynds, Elam
Lyon, Nathaniel
McClellan, George, 1796–1847
McGwney, Michael Joseph
MacKaye, Benton
MacLean, George Edwin
McLevy, Jasper
McMahon, Brien
Mallary, Rollin Carolas
Mansfield, Edward Deering
Mansfield, Jared
Mansfield, Joseph King Fenno
Mansfield, Richard
Marble, Danforth
Marks, Amasa Abraham
Marsh, John
Marshall, Daniel
Marvin, Dudley
Mason, Jeremiah
Mason, William
Masson, Thomas Lansing
Mather, Frank Jewett, Jr.
Mather, Samuel Livingston
Mather, William Williams
Mattocks, John
Meigs, Josiah
Meigs, Return Jonathan, 1740–1823
Meigs, Return Jonathan, 1764–1824
Merrill, Selah
Miller, Emily Clark Huntington
Miller, Oliver
Mills, Samuel John
Miner, Charles
Mitchell, Donald Grant
Mitchell, Elisha
Mitchell, Samuel Augustus
Mitchell, Stephen Mix
Moody, (Arthur Edson) Blair
Morey, Samuel
Morgan, Charles
Morgan, John Pierpont
Morris, Charles
Morris, Luzon Burritt
Morse, Jedidiah
Moses, Bernard
Moulton, Ellen Louise Chandler
Munson, Walter David
Murdock, James
Murdock, Joseph Ballard
Nettleton, Asahel
Newberry, John Strong
Newberry, Oliver
Newberry, Walter Loomis
Newcomb, Charles Leonard
Newman, Alfred
Niles, John Milton
North, Edward
North, Elisha
North, Simeon, 1765–1852
North, Simeon, 1802–1884
Northrop, Birdsey Grant
Northrop, Cyrus
Norton, Charles Hotchkiss
Nott, Abraham
Nott, Eliphalet
Nott, Samuel
Noyes, Walter Chadwick
Occom, Samson
Olmsted, Denison
Olmsted, Frederick Law
Olmsted, Gideon
Olney, Jesse
Ormsby, Waterman Lilly
Osborn, Henry Fairfield
Osborn, Norris Galpin
Osborn, Selleck
Osborne, Thomas Burr
Owen, Edward Thomas
Packer, Asa
Paddock, Benjamin Henry
Paddock, John Adams
Paine, Elijah
Painter, Gamaliel
Palmer, Albert Marshman
Palmer, Elihu
Palmer, Nathaniel Brown
Palmer, William Adams
Parish, Elijah
Park, Roswell, 1807–1869
Park, Roswell, 1852–1914
Parker, Amasa Junius
Parsons, Samuel Holden
Paterson, John
Pease, Calvin
Pease, Elisha Marshall
Pease, Joseph Ives
Peck, Charles Howard
Peck, Harry Thurston
Peck, John Mason
Peck, Tracy
Peet, Harvey Prindle
Peet, Isaac Lewis
Penfield, Frederic Courtland
Percival, James Gates
Perkins, Elisha
Perkins, Frederic Beecher
Perrin, Bernadotte
Peters, Samuel Andrew
Phelps, Almira Hart Lincoln
Phelps, Anson Greene
Phelps, Guy Rowland
Phelps, John Smith
Phelps, Oliver
Phelps, William Lyon
Phillips, Harry Irving
Picket, Albert
Pierpont, John
Pierrepont, Edwards
Piggott, James
Pinchot, Gifford
Pinney, Norman
Pitkin, Frederick Walker
Pitkin, Timothy
Pitkin, William, 1694–1769
Pitkin, William, 1725–1789
Plant, Henry Bradley
Platt, Charles Adams
Platt, Orville Hitchcock
Platver, Samuel Ball
Pond, Peter
Pond, Samuel William
Porter, Arthur Kingsley
Porter, Ebenezer
Porter, Noah
Porter, Peter Buell
Porter, Samuel
Porter, Sarah
Potter, Edward Clark
Potter, Ellen Culver
Potter, William Bancroft
Powell, Adam Clayton, Jr.
Pratt, Bela Lyon
Prentice, Samuel Oscar
Prentiss, Samuel
Preston, Thomas Scott
Prudden, Theophil Mitchell
Purtell, William Arthur
Putnam, Nina Wilcox
Pynchon, Thomas Ruggles
Quintard, Charles Todd
Quintard, George William
Ranney, William Tylee

Raymond, Charles Walker
Raymond, Daniel
Read, John, 1679/80–1749
Redfield, Justus Starr
Redfield, William C.
Reid, Samuel Chester
Remington, Eliphalet
Reynolds, Edwin
Riggs, John Markey
Ripley, James Wolfe
Robbins, Thomas
Robins, Henry Ephraim
Robinson, Edward, 1794–1863
Robinson, Henry Cornelius
Robinson, Solon
Robinson, William Callyhan
Rockwell, Alphonso David
Rogers, John, 1648–1721
Rogers, John Almanza Rowley
Rogers, Moses
Rogers, Thomas
Rogers, William Augustus
Rood, Ogden Nicholas
Root, Erastus
Root, Jesse
Rose, Chauncey
Rosenthal, Toby Edward
Rossiter, Thomas Prichard
Rowland, Thomas Fitch
Ruggles, Samuel Bulkley
Russell, Rosalind
Sage, Bernard Janin
Sage, Henry Williams
Saltonstall, Dudley
Sanford, Elias Benjamin
Sanford, Henry Shelton
Sassacus
Saunders, Prince
Savage, Thomas Staughton
Sawyer, Walter Howard
Scoville, Joseph Alfred
Scranton, George Whitfield
Seabury, Samuel, 1729–1796
Seabury, Samuel, 1801–1872
Sedgwick, John
Sedgwick, Theodore, 1746–1813
Sedgwick, William Thompson
Seelye, Julius Hawley
Seelye, Laurenus Clark
Setchell, William Albert
Seymour, Charles
Seymour, Thomas Hart
Shaler, William
Shaw, Nathaniel
Sheffield, Joseph Earl
Sigourney, Lydia Howard Huntley
Sill, Edward Rowland
Silliman, Benjamin, 1779–1864
Silliman, Benjamin, 1816–1885
Sloan, Alfred Pritchard, Jr.
Smith, Abby Hadassah
Smith, Arthur Henderson
Smith, Ashbel
Smith, Charles Emory
Smith, Eli
Smith, Elias
Smith, Elihu Hubbard
Smith, Harry James
Smith, Israel
Smith, James Youngs
Smith, Joel West
Smith, John Cotton, 1765–1845
Smith, Junius
Smith, Nathan, 1770–1835
Smith, Nathaniel
Smith, Roswell
Smith, Truman
Smith, Winchell
Sonnichsen, Albert
Sparks, Jared
Spencer, Ambrose
Spencer, Christopher Miner
Spencer, Elihu
Spencer, Joseph
Sperry, Nehemiah Day
Sprague, Frank Julian
Sprague, William Buell
Stanton, Henry Brewster
Stedman, Edmund Clarence
Steiner, Bernard Christian
Stephens, Ann Sophia
Sterling, John William
Stevens, Clement Hoffman
Stevens, Thomas Holdup, 1819–1896
Steward, Ira
Stewart, Philo Penfield
Stiles, Ezra
Stine, Charles Milton Altland
Stoddard, Amos
Stoeckel, Carl
Stone, David Marvin
Stone, Wilbur Fisk
Stone, William Oliver
Stowe, Harriet Elizabeth Beecher
Stratton, Charles Sherwood
Street, Augustus Russell
Strong, Elmer Kenneth, Jr. ("Ken")
Strong, William
Stuart, Isaac William
Stuart, Moses
Sturtevant, Julian Monson
Sumner, Francis Bertody
Talcott, Andrew
Talcott, Eliza
Talcott, Joseph
Tarbox, Increase Niles
Tatlock, John Strong Perry
Taylor, Nathaniel William
Terry, Alfred Howe
Terry, Eli
Thacher, Thomas Anthony
Thomas, Seth
Thompson, Charles Oliver
Thurber, Christopher Carson
Ticknor, Elisha
Tiffany, Charles Lewis
Tod, George
Tod, John
Todd, Eli
Totten, George Muirson
Totten, Joseph Gilbert
Toucey, Isaac
Tousey, Sinclair
Town, Ithiel
Townsend, Virginia Frances
Tracy, Uriah
Troland, Leonard Thompson
True, Alfred Charles
True, Frederick William
Trumbull, Benjamin
Trumbull, Henry Clay
Trumbull, James Hammond
Trumbull, John, 1750–1831
Trumbull, John, 1756–1843
Trumbull, Jonathan, 1710–1785
Trumbull, Jonathan, 1740–1809
Trumbull, Joseph
Trumbull, Lyman
Tryon, Dwight William
Tucker, William Jewett
Tully, William
Twichell, Joseph Hopkins
Twining, Alexander Catlin
Tyler, Bennet
Tyler, Daniel
Tyler, Moses Coit
Utley, George Burwell
Van Vleck, Edward Burr
Van Vleck, John Hasbrouck
Verrill, Alpheus Hyatt
Vonnoh, Robert William
Wadsworth, James
Wadsworth, Jeremiah
Waite, Morrison Remick
Wakeley, Joseph Burton
Waldo, Samuel Lovett
Waldo, Samuel Putnam
Walker, Amasa
Walworth, Reuben Hyde
Ward, James Harmon
Warner, Jonathan Trumbull
Warner, Olin Levi
Warner, Seth
Warren, Israel Perkins
Washburn, Nathan
Watson, Sereno
Webster, Pelatiah
Weicker, Lowell Palmer
Weiss, George Martin
Welch, Adonijah Strong
Welch, William Henry
Welch, William Wickham
Weld, Theodore Dwight
Welles, Gideon
Welles, Noah
Welles, Roger
Wells, Harry Gideon
Wells, Horace
Wells, Samuel Roberts
Wells, William Harvey
Wheaton, Nathaniel Sheldon
Wheeler, Arthur Leslie
Wheeler, Nathaniel
Wheelock, Eleazar
Wheelock, John
White, William Nathaniel
Whitman, Charles Seymour
Whitney, Asa
Whittelsey, Abigail Goodrich
Wight, Frederick Coit
Wilcox, Reynold Webb
Willard, De Forest
Willard, Emma Hart
Williams, Alpheus Starkey
Williams, Edwin
Williams, Elisha
Williams, Thomas Scott
Williams, William

Williamson, William Durkee
Williston, Seth
Wilson, George Grafton
Winchester, Caleb Thomas
Winthrop, Theodore
Wolcott, Oliver, 1726–1797
Wolcott, Oliver, 1760–1833
Wolcott, Roger
Woodbridge, William
Woodruff, Timothy Lester
Woodruff, Wilford
Woodward, Samuel Bayard
Woolley, Mary Emma
Woolsey, Theodore Salisbury
Wooster, Charles Whiting
Wooster, David
Work, Henry Clay
Wright, Benjamin
Wright, Charles
Wright, Elizur
Wright, Horatio Gouverneur
Wyllys, George

DELAWARE

Bates, Daniel Moore
Bates, George Handy
Bayard, James Asheton
Bayard, Richard Henry
Bayard, Thomas Francis
Beauchamp, William
Bedford, Gunning
Bird, Robert Montgomery
Brown, John Mifflin
Budd, Edward Gowen
Burton, William
Canby, Henry Seidel
Cannon, Annie Jump
Cannon, William
Chandler, Elizabeth Margaret
Clayton, John Middleton
Coit, Henry Augustus
Cummins, George David
Davies, Samuel
Du Pont, Henry
Du Pont, Henry Algernon
Du Pont, Lammot
Du Pont, Pierre Samuel
Emerson, Gouverneur
Evans, Oliver
Fisher, George Purnell
Forwood, William Henry
Garretson, James
Gibbons, James Sloan
Gilpin, Edward Woodward
Gray, George
Harrington, Samuel Maxwell
Howell, Richard
Johns, Clayton
Johns, John
Johns, Kensey
Johnson, Eldridge Reeves
Jones, David
Jones, Jacob
Keating, William Hypolitus
Kollock, Shepard
Lea, Isaac
Learned, Marion Dexter
Lewis, William David
Lord, William Paine
McCullough, John Griffith
Macdonough, Thomas
McKean, Joseph Borden
McKennan, Thomas McKean Thompson
McLane, Louis
McLane, Robert Milligan
MacWhorter, Alexander
Marquand, John Phillips
Miller, Edward
Miller, Samuel
Mitchell, Nathaniel
Moore, John Bassett
Newbold, William Romaine
Palmer, William Jackson
Parke, John
Polk, Trusten
Pyle, Howard
Read, John, 1769–1854
Read, Thomas
Ridgely, Nicholas
Rodney, Caesar
Rodney, Caesar Augustus
Rodney, Thomas
Ross, George
Saulsbury, Eli
Saulsbury, Gove
Saulsbury, Willard, 1820–1892
Saulsbury, Willard, 1861–1927
Smyth, Herbert Weir
Squibb, Edward Robinson
Stewart, John George
Sykes, George
Thomas, Lorenzo
Tilton, James
Torbert, Alfred Thomas Archimedes
Townsend, George Alfred
Van Dyke, Nicholas, 1738–1789
Van Dyke, Nicholas, 1770–1826
Wales, Leonard Eugene
White, Samuel
Wiley, Andrew Jackson
Wilson, Clarence True

DISTRICT OF COLUMBIA

Ashford, Bailey Kelly
Baker, William Mumford
Barber, Donn
Beale, Edward Fitzgerald
Bowie, Richard Johns
Brannan, John Milton
Breck, George William
Broderick, David Colbreth
Burke, Billie
Carroll, Samuel Sprigg
Cassidy, Marshall Whiting
Colby, Frank Moore
Considine, Robert ("Bob") Bernard
Cook, Will Marion
Corcoran, William Wilson
Cranch, Christopher Pearse
Craven, Thomas Tingey
Da Costa, John Chalmers
Davis, Benjamin Oliver, Sr.
Davis, Watson
Dimitry, Charles Patton
Dorsey, Anna Hanson McKenney
Drew, Charles Richard
Dulles, John Foster
Ellington, Edward Kennedy ("Duke")
Ewell, Benjamin Stoddert
Ewell, Richard Stoddert
Farrington, Joseph Rider
Fay, Sidney Bradshaw
Fitzpatrick, John Clement
Force, Manning Ferguson
Garrison, Fielding Hudson
Gauss, Clarence Edward
Getty, George Washington
Gibbons, Floyd
Gilliss, James Melville
Goldsborough, Louis Malesherbes
Graham, William Montrose
Graves, Alvin Cushman
Hartley, Frank
Hodes, Henry Irving
Hodgson, William Brown
Holly, James Theodore
Hoover, John Edgar
Houston, Charles Hamilton
Hunter, David
Hyatt, Alpheus
Ingersoll, Royal Eason
Janney, Oliver Edward
Johnson, Robert Underwood
Johnston, Eric Allen
Kelser, Raymond Alexander
King of William, James
Lenthall, John
Lewis, Fulton, Jr.
Lipscomb, Andrew Adgate
Lovell, Mansfield
McAuliffe, Anthony Clement
McCormick, Cyrus Hall
McGuire, Joseph Deakins
McLean, Edward Beale
McNamee, Graham
Magruder, George Lloyd
Manning, Marie
Mason, James Murray
Mattingly, Garrett
Maynard, George Willoughby
Meade, Robert Leamy
Nicholson, William Jones
Noyes, Frank Brett
O'Neale, Margaret
Peary, Josephine Diebitsch
Pilling, James Constantine
Pleasonton, Alfred
Plunkett, Charles Peshall
Pollock, Channing
Pratt, Thomas George
Prouty, Charles Tyler
Queen, Walter W.
Ramsay, Francis Munroe
Rawlings, Marjorie Kinnan
Razaf, Andy
Richardson, Charles Williamson
Riggs, George Washington
Rodgers, John, 1881–1926
Schroeder, Seaton
Scott, William Lawrence
Seibold, Louis
Semmes, Alexander Jenkins
Semmes, Thomas Jenkins
Shellabarger, Samuel

Shepherd, Alexander Robey
Shuster, W(illiam) Morgan
Slicer, Thomas Roberts
Sousa, John Philip
Southworth, Emma Dorothy Eliza Nevitte
Steers, George
Stoek, Harry Harkness
Swann, Thomas
Towle, George Makepeace
Tree, Lambert
Vance, Louis Joseph
Wainwright, Richard, 1849–1926
Watterson, Henry
Weaver, Aaron Ward
West, James Edward
Wheeler, Earle Gilmore
Willard, Joseph Edward
Winlock, Herbert Eustis
Winslow, Cameron McRae
Wormley, James

FLORIDA

Adderley, Julian Edwin ("Cannonball")
Avery, Isaac Wheeler
Bellamy, Elizabeth Whitfield Croom
Bloxham, William Dunnington
Brooke, John Mercer
Broward, Napoleon Bonaparte
Bryan, Mary Edwards
Cochran, Jacqueline
Davis, Edmund Jackson
Drayton, William
Forbes, John Murray
Geiger, Roy Stanley
Holland, Spessard Lindsey
Hurston, Zora Neale
James, Daniel, Jr. ("Chappie")
Johnson, James Weldon
Kirby-Smith, Edmund
McCoy, George Braidwood
McIntosh, John Bailie
Merrill, Charles Edward
Morrison, Jim
Pace, Edward Aloysius
Randolph, Asa Philip
Raney, George Pettus
Smith, Lillian Eugenia
Summerall, Charles Pelot
Turnbull, Robert James
Warren, Fuller
Zacharias, Ellis Mark

GEORGIA

Abbott, Robert Sengstacke
Aiken, Conrad Potter
Alexander, Edward Porter
Allen, Young John
Anderson, George Thomas
Andrew, James Osgood
Andrews, Garnett
Arnold, Richard Dennis
Atkinson, William Yates
Bacon, Augustus Octavius
Baker, Daniel
Barrett, Charles Simon
Barrett, Janie Porter
Bass, William Capers
Battey, Robert
Battle, Cullen Andrews
Benning, Henry Lewis
Benson, William Shepherd
Berry, Martha McChesney
Bibb, William Wyatt
Black, Eugene Robert
Blalock, Alfred
Bleckley, Logan Edwin
Blount, James Henderson
Boudinot, Elias
Boudinot, Elias Cornelius
Bowie, James
Bozeman, John M.
Bulloch, James Dunwody
Butts, James Wallace ("Wally")
Callaway, Morgan
Campbell, Henry Fraser
Campbell, John Archibald
Candler, Allen Daniel
Candler, Asa Griggs
Candler, Warren Akin
Cardozo, Jacob Newton
Carnochan, John Murray
Charles, Ezzard Mack
Chivers, Thomas Holley
Clay, Joseph
Clay, Lucius DuBignon
Clements, Judson Claudius
Clopton, David
Cobb, Andrew Jackson
Cobb, Howell
Cobb, Thomas Reade Rootes
Cobb, Tyrus Raymond ("Ty")
Cohen, John Sanford
Collier, John
Colquitt, Alfred Holt
Cook, Philip
Couper, James Hamilton
Cox, Edward Eugene
Crawford, George Walker
Crawford, Martin Jenkins
Culberson, David Browning
Cumming, Alfred
Curry, Jabez Lamar Monroe
Davis, John Warren
Dawson, William Crosby
Dawson, William Levi
Dickson, David
Divine, Father
Doughty, William Henry
Elliott, Sarah Barnwell
Evans, Augusta Jane
Evans, Clement Anselm
Eve, Paul Fitzsimons
Fahy, Charles
Fannin, James Walker
Felton, Rebecca Latimer
Felton, William Harrell
Few, Ignatius Alphonso
Fitzpatrick, Benjamin
Fletcher, Duncan Upshaw
Folsom, Marion Bayard
Frémont, John Charles
Furlow, Floyd Charles
Gaines, Wesley John
Gartrell, Lucius Jeremiah
George, James Zachariah
George, Walter Franklin
Gibbons, Thomas
Gibson, Joshua
Gordon, John Brown
Gordon, William Washington
Goulding, Francis Robert
Grady, Henry Woodfin
Grant, John Thomas
Habersham, Joseph
Hadas, Moses
Hale, William Gardner
Hall, Charles Henry
Hammond, Nathaniel Job
Harben, William Nathaniel
Hardee, William Joseph
Hardwick, Thomas William
Hardy, Oliver Norvell
Harris, Joel Chandler
Harris, Julian La Rose
Harris, William Littleton
Harrison, George Paul
Harrison, William Pope
Hartsfield, William Berry
Haygood, Atticus Green
Haygood, Laura Askew
Henderson, Fletcher Hamilton
Herring, Augustus Moore
Herty, Charles Holmes
Hill, Beniamin Harvey
Hill, Walter Barnard
Hillyer, Junius
Hodges, Courtney Hicks
Holsey, Lucius Henry
Hope, John
Hopkins, Isaac Stiles
Hopkins, Miriam
Houston, John
Howell, Evan Park
Howley, Richard
Hubbard, Richard Bennett
Hudson, Claude Silbert
Hughes, Dudley Mays
Hyer, Robert Stewart
Iverson, Alfred
Jackson, Henry Rootes
Jackson, James, 1819–1887
Jacobs, Joseph, 1859–1929
Johnson, Herschel Vespasian
Johnson, Malcolm Malone
Johnson, Nunnally Hunter
Johnston, Richard Malcolm
Jones, Charles Colcock
Jones, Joseph
Jones, Robert Tyre, Jr.
Jones, Thomas Goode
Judson, Frederick Newton
Keener, William Albert
Kerneys, Edward
Kilpatrick, William Heard
King, Martin Luther, Jr.
Knight, Lucian Lamar
Lamar, Gazaway Bugg
Lamar, Joseph Rucker
Lamar, Lucius Quintus Cincinnatus
Lamar, Mirabeau Buonaparte
Langworthy, Edward
Le Conte, John
Le Conte, Joseph

Lee, Ivy Ledbetter
Lee, James Wideman
Lincecum, Gideon
Lomax, Louis Emanuel
Long, Crawford Williamson
Longstreet, Augustus Baldwin
Lumpkin, Joseph Henry
McAdoo, William Gibbs
McAllister, Hall
McAllister, Matthew Hall
McAllister, Samuel Ward
McCullers, Carson
McDaniel, Henry Dickerson
McDuffie, George
McGillivray, Alexander
McIntosh, William
McKinley, Carlyle
McKinstry, Alexander
McLaws, Lafayette
Maxwell, Augustus Emmett
Maxwell, George Troup
Mayes, Joel Bryan
Meigs, Montgomery Cunningham
Mell, Patrick Hues, 1814–1888
Mell, Patrick Hues, 1850–1918
Melton, James
Mercer, John Herndon ("Johnny")
Metcalfe, Ralph Harold
Milledge, John
Millis, Walter
Milner, John Turner
Milton, John
Mitchell, Margaret Munnerlyn
Moore, George Fleming
Morehouse, Ward
Muhammad, Elijah
Murrow, Joseph Samuel
Nisbet, Eugenius Aristides
Northen, William Jonathan
O'Connor, Mary Flannery
Odum, Howard Washington
Oemler, Arminius
Ogburn, William Fielding
Osceola
Paschal, George Washington
Peabody, George Foster
Pendleton, Edmund Monroe
Perry, William Flake
Phillips, Ulrich Bonnell
Phinizy, Ferdinand
Pierce, George Foster
Pierce, William Leigh
Pinchback, Pinckney Benton Stewart
Rainey, Gertrude Malissa Nix Pridgett
Ramspeck, Robert C. Word ("Bob")
Riegger, Wallingford
Rivers, Thomas Milton
Robinson, John Roosevelt ("Jackie")
Robinson, Ruby Doris Smith
Root, John Wellborn
Rucker, George ("Nap")
Russell, Richard Brevard, Jr. ("Dick")
St. John, Isaac Munroe
Sanders, Billington McCarter
Saunders, William Lawrence, 1856–1931
Scarborough, William Saunders
Sherwood, Thomas Adiel
Shorter, John Gill
Silcox, Ferdinand Augustus
Simmons, Thomas Jefferson
Smith, Albert Merriman
Smith, Buckingham
Smith, Charles Henry, 1826–1903
Spalding, Thomas
Speer, Emory
Spencer, Samuel
Stallings, Laurence Tucker
Stephens, Alexander Hamilton
Stephens, Linton
Stokes, Thomas Lunsford, Jr.
Stovall, Pleasant Alexander
Sydnor, Charles Sackett
Talmadge, Eugene
Tattnall, Josiah
Taylor, Charlotte De Bernier
Tensler, Rudolf Bolling
Thomas, Charles Spalding
Ticknor, Francis Orray
Tobias, Channing Heggie
Toombs, Robert Augustus
Towers, John Henry
Towns, George Washington Bonaparte
Trammell, Niles
Troup, George Michael
Tucker, Henry Holcombe
Twiggs, David Emanuel
Upshaw, William David
Wailes, Benjamin Leonard Covington
Walker, William Henry Talbot
Ward, John Elliott
Watie, Stand
Watson, Thomas Edward
Wayne, James Moore
Wheeler, Joseph
White, Walter Francis
Willie, Asa Hoxie
Winkler, Edwin Theodore
Winship, Blanton
Wofford, William Tatum
Wood, John Stephens
Wright, Richard Robert
Yancey, William Lowndes

HAWAII

Alexander, William Dewitt
Armstrong, Samuel Chapman
Baldwin, Henry Perrine
Bingham, Hiram
Carter, Henry Alpheus Peirce
Castle, William Richards, Jr.
Dillingham, Walter Francis
Dole, Sanford Ballard
Gulick, John Thomas
Gulick, Luther Halsey, 1828–1891
Gulick, Luther Halsey, 1865–1918
Hillebrand, William Francis
Kalanianaole, Jonah Kuhio
Lathrop, George Parsons
Patterson, William Allan ("Pat")
Thurston, Lorrin Andrews

IDAHO

Borglum, John Gutzon de la Mothe
Jardine, William Marion
Kamaiakan
Pound, Ezra Loomis
Sacagawea
Welker, Herman

ILLINOIS

Abbott, Emma
Abt, Isaac Arthur
Adams, Cyrus Cornelius
Adams, Frank Ramsay
Adams, Franklin Pierce
Addams, Jane
Alcorn, James Lusk
Alinsky, Saul David
Allison, Samuel King
Arvey, Jacob M.
Atwood, Wallace Walter
Austin, Mary
Ayres, William Augustus
Bacon, Henry
Baker, James
Balaban, Barney
Bancroft, Edgar Addison
Bancroft, Frederic
Barrett, Albert Moore
Barrow, Edward Grant
Barrows, David Prescott
Barton, William Eleazar
Beaupré, Arthur Matthias
Bendix, Vincent
Benny, Jack
Bentley, Arthur Fisher
Bergen, Edgar
Bernays, Augustus Charles
Bestor, Arthur Eugene
Bettendorf, William Peter
Bevan, Arthur Dean
Bickel, Karl August
Black, Greene Vardiman
Black Hawk
Blackstone, Harry
Bliss, Gilbert Ames
Bloom, Sol
Bloomfield, Leonard
Bode, Boyd Henry
Borah, William Edgar
Boring, William Alciphron
Bosworth, Edward Increase
Bovard, Oliver Kirby
Bowen, Louise De Koven
Brann, William Cowper
Breasted, James Henry
Breckinridge, Henry Skillman
Brennemann, Joseph
Brophy, Truman William
Brown, Gertrude Foster
Brunswick, Ruth Mack
Bryan, Charles Wayland
Bryan, William Jennings
Bryant, Ralph Clement
Bumstead, Henry Andrews
Burroughs, Edgar Rice
Bush, Lincoln
Calkins, Earnest Elmo

Capps, Edward
Carpenter, John Alden
Chalmers, William James
Chamberlain, Henry Richardson
Chamberlin, Thomas Chrowder
Champion, Gower
Chandler, Raymond Thornton
Chase, (Mary) Agnes Merrill
Coghill, George Ellett
Cohn, Alfred A.
Colton, George Radcliffe
Comiskey, Grace Elizabeth Reidy
Conger, Edwin Hurd
Conover, Harry Sayles
Coolbrith, Ina Donna
Coolidge, Elizabeth Penn Sprague
Copley, Ira Clifton
Coquillett, Daniel William
Correll, Charles James
Cort, Edwin Charles
Costigan, George Purcell
Cozzens, James Gould
Crane, Charles Richard
Crane, Frank
Crothers, Rachel
Crothers, Samuel McChord
Cudahy, Edward Aloysius, Jr.
Cummings, Walter Joseph
Cushman, Vera Charlotte Scott
Daley, Richard Joseph
Danenhower, John Wilson
Davis, Arthur Powell
Davis, Pauline Morton Sabin
Davisson, Clinton Joseph
Dell, Floyd James
Dille, John Flint
Dirksen, Everett McKinley
Disney, Roy Oliver
Disney, Walter Elias ("Walt")
Donaldson, Jesse Monroe
Donoghue, John
Dos Passos, John Roderigo
Doubleday, Neltje de Graff
Downes (Edwin) Olin
Drake, Francis Marion
Dressen, Charles Walter
Dunbar, (Helen) Flanders
Duniway, Abigail Jane Scott
Dunne, Finley Peter
Durkin, Martin Patrick
Duryea, Charles Edgar
Duryea, James Frank
Du Vigneaud, Vincent
Dyer, Louis
Easley, Ralph Montgomery
East, Edward Murray
Eddy, Manton Sprague
Eichelberger, Clark Mell
Elliott, John Lovejoy
Ellsworth, Lincoln
Emmett, Burton
Farrell, James Thomas
Fearing, Kenneth Flexner
Ferris, George Washington Gale
Field, Marshall, III
Finley, John Huston
Firestone, Harvey Samuel, Jr.
Fisher, Henry Conroy ("Bud")
Flower, Benjamin Orange
Forbes, Stephen Alfred
Fox, Virgil Keel
Frankfurter, Alfred Moritz
Fry, James Barnet
Fuller, Henry Blake
Fuller, Loie
Gale, Henry Gordon
Gardner, Gilson
Gary, Elbert Henry
Gates, Caleb Frank
Gates, John Warne
Germer, Lester Halbert
Giancana, Sam ("Mooney")
Gibbs, George
Gilbert, Charles Henry
Giles, Warren Crandall
Gilman, Arthur
Goodman, Kenneth Sawyer
Goodnight, Charles
Goudy, Frederic William
Graham, Evarts Ambrose
Gray, Glen ("Spike")
Gray, Harold Lincoln
Gray, William Scott, Jr.
Greenlaw, Edwin Almiron
Gunther, John
Hale, George Ellery
Hale, Louise Closser
Hallett, Moses
Hammond, Laurens
Hansberry, Lorraine Vivian
Hapgood, Hutchins
Hapgood, Norman
Harbord, James Guthrie
Harlan, James
Harlan, John Marshall
Harridge, William ("Will")
Harrington, Mark Walrod
Harrison, Carter Henry, Jr.
Hart, George Overbury
Hartzell, Joseph Crane
Hathaway, Donny
Hawthorne, Charles Webster
Helmer, Bessie Bradwell
Hemingway, Ernest Miller
Hibben, John Grier
Hickok, James Butler
High, Stanley Hoflund
Higinbotham, Harlow Niles
Hills, Elijah Clarence
Hodge, John Reed
Hoerr, Normand Louis
Hoffman, Paul Gray
Hokinson, Helen Elna
Holmes, Elias Burton
Hood, Clifford Firoved
Horner, Henry
Hovey, Richard
Howard, Charles Perry
Howard, Leland Ossian
Hubbard, Elbert
Humphrey, Doris
Hunt, Haroldson Lafayette
Hunt, Lester Callaway
Huntington, Ellsworth
Huntington, William Edwards
Hurley, Edward Nash
Husk, Charles Ellsworth
Hyde, Charles Cheney
Illington, Margaret
Ingals, Ephraim Fletcher
Jackson, Robert R.
James, Edmund Janes
James, Louis
Jennings, Herbert Spencer
Johnson, Albert
Johnson, Harold Ogden ("Chic")
Jones, James Ramon
Jones, Wesley Livsey
Keane, James John
Keefe, Daniel Joseph
Kelly, Edward Joseph
Kelsey, Rayner Wickersham
Kempff, Louis
Keokuk
Kerner, Otto, Jr.
Kilgallen, Dorothy Mae
Kingsbury, Albert
Kirby, Rollin
Kirkman, Marshall Monroe
Knight, Frank Hyneman
Knowles, John Hilton
Koch, Fred Conrad
Kofoid, Charles Atwood
Kohlsaat, Herman Henry
Krupa, Eugene Bertram ("Gene")
Landis, Jessie Royce
Lardner, John Abbott
Lasswell, Harold Dwight
Lathrop, Julia Clifford
Lawson, Victor Freemont
Lee, John Doyle
Lee, William Granville
Leiber, Fritz
Leiter, Joseph
Lenz, Sidney Samuel
Leonard, Jack E.
Leopold, Nathan Freudenthal, Jr.
Lewis, Dean De Witt
Lillie, Gordon William
Lincoln, Robert Todd
Lindsay, Nicholas Vachel
Lingelbach, Anna Lane
Logan, John Alexander
Loree, Leonor Fresnel
Lowry, Thomas
Lucas, Scott Wike
McAdams, Clark
MacCameron, Robert
McClure, Robert Alexis
McConnel, John Ludlum
McCord, James Bennett
McCormick, Joseph Medill
McCormick, Robert Rutherford
McCoy, Joseph Geating
McCumber, Porter James
McKinley, William Brown
McLaughlin, Andrew Cunningham
Mann, James Robert
Marquis, Donald Robert Perry
Martin, Everett Dean
Martin, Warren Homer
Mason, Francis Van Wyck
Masterson, William Barclay
Maxwell, Lucien Bonaparte
Mayer, Oscar Gottfried
Maytag, Frederick Louis
Meinzer, Oscar Edward
Mendelsohn, Samuel
Micheaux, Oscar
Miller, Perry Gilbert Eddy

Millikan, Clark Blanchard
Millikan, Robert Andrews
Mitchell, James Tyndale
Mitchell, John, 1870–1919
Mitchell, Lucy Sprague
Mitchell, Wesley Clair
Monroe, Harriet
Mooney, Thomas Joseph
Morgan, Helen
Morrison, William Ralls
Motley, Willard Francis
Mowrer, Edgar Ansel
Mulford, Clarence Edward
Munson, Thomas Volney
Nash, Charles Williams
Nevins, Joseph Allan
Newell, Peter Sheaf Hersey
Nicholson, Seth Barnes
Nielsen, Arthur Charles
Norris, Benjamin Franklin
Norris, Charles Gilman Smith
Novy, Frederick George
Nutting, Charles Cleveland
O'Brien, Justin
Paine, Ralph Delahaye
Palmer, John McAuley
Parkhurst, John Adelbert
Parr, Samuel Wilson
Parrington, Vernon Louis
Parsons, Louella Rose Oettinger
Patten, James A.
Patten, Simon Nelson
Patterson, Alicia
Patterson, Eleanor Medill
Patterson, Joseph Medill
Pearson, Drew
Pearson, Thomas Gilbert
Peattie, Donald Culross
Peek, George Nelson
Pentecost, George Frederick
Perkins, George Walbridge
Poole, Ernest Cook
Post, Charles William
Post, Marjorie Merriweather
Powell, Alma Webster
Powell, Maud
Radford, Arthur William
Rainey, Henry Thomas
Raum, Green Berry
Rawlins, John Aaron
Raymond, George Lansing
Redfield, Robert
Reed, Earl Howell
Reed, Myrtle
Reeves, Joseph Mason
Revell, Fleming Hewitt
Revell, Nellie MacAleney
Rhees, Rush
Richmond, Mary Ellen
Ridgway, Robert
Robertson, Ashley Herman
Robinson, Benjamin Lincoln
Robinson, Edward Van Dyke
Robinson, James Harvey
Rockwell, George Lincoln
Rogers, John Raphael
Rohde, Ruth Bryan Owen
Rosenwald, Julius
Rosenwald, Lessing Julius
Ross, Edward Alsworth
Roulston, Marjorie Hillis
Rowell, Chester Harvey
Ruby, Jack L.
Ruhl, Arthur Brown
Ryan, Robert Bushnell
Sandburg, Carl August
Schalk, Raymond William ("Cracker")
Schneider, Albert
Schroeder, Rudolph William
Schwatka, Frederick
Scott, Harvey Whitefield
Scott, John Adams
Scott, Walter Dill
Scripps, Edward Wyllis
Selig, William Nicholas
Sharp, Katharine Lucinda
Shaw, Howard Van Doren
Sheean, James Vincent
Sheen, Fulton John
Sheil, Bernard James
Sherman, Allan
Short, Luke
Short, Walter Campbell
Sills, Milton
Simons, Henry Calvert
Simpson, Charles Torrey
Skinner, Cornelia Otis
Slade, Joseph Alfred
Slater, John Clarke
Smith, Frank Leslie
Smith, Harry Allen
Smith, Henry Justin
Smith, Ralph Tyler
Smith, Robert Sidney
Snow, William Freeman
Snyder, John Francis
Spalding, Albert
Spalding, Albert Goodwill
Stephenson, Benjamin Franklin
Stettinius, Edward Reilly
Stone, Melville Elijah
Stone, Ormond
Stratton, Samuel Wesley
Strawn, Silas Hardy
Strong, Josiah
Strong, Walter Ansel
Stryker, Lloyd Paul
Sturges, Preston
Sunderland, Eliza Jane Read
Symons, George Gardner
Taft, Lorado Zadoc
Talbot, Arthur Newell
Tanner, Edward Everett, III ("Patrick Dennis")
Teeple, John Edgar
Thayer, Tiffany Ellsworth
Thomas, Jesse Burgess
Thompson, Seymour Dwight
Thurstone, Louis Leon
Todd, Henry Alfred
Tompkins, Arnold
Townsend, Francis Everett
Tristano, Leonard Joseph ("Lennie")
Turner, George Kibbe
Vanderlip, Frank Arthur
Van Doren, Carl Clinton
Van Horne, William Cornelius
Vincent, George Edgar
Wacker, Charles Henry
Walgreen, Charles Rudolph
Wallace, Henry Cantwell
Waller, Willard Walter
Ward, Arch Burdette
Ward, Lester Frank
Warman, Cy
Warmoth, Henry Clay
Waymack, William Wesley
West, Roy Owen
Westermann, William Linn
Weston, Edward Henry
Weston, Nathan Austin
Weyerhaeuser, Frederick Edward
White, Charles Wilbert
Willard, Frank Henry
Willcox, Louise Collier
Williams, Jesse Lynch
Williams, Thomas Harry
Wilson, Edmund Beecher
Wilson, Harry Leon
Wilson, Hugh Robert
Wilson, James Harrison
Wolfe, Harry Kirke
Wright, John Kenneth Lloyd
Wright, Theodore Paul
Wrigley, Philip Knight
Yancey, James Edward ("Jimmy")
Young, Art
Zeckendorf, William
Ziegfeld, Florenz
Ziff, William Bernard

INDIANA

Acker, Charles Ernest
Adams, Andy
Ade, George
Allport, Gordon Willard
Anderson, Edwin Hatfield
Anderson, Margaret Carolyn
Andrew, Abram Piatt
Arvin, Newton
Atterbury, William Wallace
Aydelotte, Frank
Barnes, Charles Reid
Bass, Sam
Beadle, William Henry Harrison
Beard, Charles Austin
Beard, Mary Ritter
Beeson, Charles Henry
Bell, Lawrence Dale
Bement, Charles Sweet
Bennett, Richard
Billings, John Shaw
Blackburn, William Maxwell
Blasdel, Henry Goode
Blue, Gerald Montgomery ("Monte")
Boisen, Anton Theophilus
Booth, Newton
Bowers, Claude Gernade
Bradley, Lydia Moss
Budenz, Louis Francis
Buley, Roscoe Carlyle
Burnside, Ambrose Everett
Caldwell, Otis William
Calkins, Gary Nathan
Capehart, Homer Earl
Carey, Max George ("Scoops")

Catlett, Sidney
Chapman, John Wilbur
Chase, William Merritt
Coffman, Lotus Delta
Condon, Albert Edwin ("Eddie")
Cooper, Henry Ernest
Cooper, Kent
Cope, Arthur Clay
Crawford, Samuel Johnson
Cubberley, Ellwood Patterson
Cuppy, William Jacob (Will)
Curme, George Oliver
Daeger, Albert Thomas
Davis, Adelle
Davis, Elmer Holmes
Davis, Jefferson Columbus
Davis, John Lee
Dean, James Byron
Debs, Eugene Victor
Deemer, Horace Emerson
Denby, Edwin
De Pauw, Washington Charles
Dillinger, John
Dodge, Henry
Doolittle, Charles Leander
Doolittle, Eric
Douglas, Lloyd Cassel
Dreiser, Theodore
Dresser, Louise Kerlin
Du Bois, Shirley Lola Graham
Dunn, William McKee
Eads, James Buchanan
Eggleston, Edward
Eggleston, George Cary
English, William Hayden
Ewing, Oscar Ross
Fazenda, Louise Marie
Fetter, Frank Albert
Flanner, Janet
Fletcher, James Cooley
Fletcher, William Baldwin
Fordney, Joseph Warren
Foster, John Watson
Foster, Robert Sanford
Frick, Ford Christopher
Geer, William Aughe ("Will")
Ghent, William James
Gimbel, Bernard Feustman
Girdler, Tom Mercer
Goode, George Brown
Goudy, William Charles
Green, Norvin
Gresham, Walter Quintin
Gridley, Charles Vernon
Grissom Virgil Ivan ("Gus")
Haan, William George
Hackley, Charles Henry
Haggerty, Melvin Everett
Hale, William Bayard
Hamtrauck, John Francis
Handley, Harold Willis
Hannagan, Stephen Jerome
Harper, Ida Husted
Hawks, Howard Winchester
Hawley, Paul Ramsey
Hay, John Milton
Hay, Mary Garrett
Hay, Oliver Perry
Hays, Will H.
Heath, Perry Sanford
Henderson, Charles Richmond
Herron, George Davis
Hershey, Lewis Blaine
Hibben, Paxton Pattison
Hill, Edwin Conger
Hill, John Wiley
Hodges, Gilbert Ray
Hoffa, James Riddle ("Jimmy")
Holcomb, Silas Alexander
Hollis, Ira Nelson
Holman, William Steele
Hornaday, William Temple
Hovey, Alvin Peterson
Howe, Edgar Watson
Howe, Louis McHenry
Hunter, Robert
Ingram, Jonas Howard
Jaquess, James Frazier
Jessup, Walter Albert
Johnston, Annie Fellows
Jones, George Wallace
Jones, Jim
Juday, Chancey
Julian, George Washington
Kern, John Worth
Kimball, Nathan
Klein, Charles Herbert ("Chuck")
Lane, James Henry
Leavenworth, Francis Preserved
Levinson, Salmon Oliver
Lewis, Lloyd Downs
Lilly, Eli
Lilly, Josiah Kirby
Little Turtle
Loeb, Milton B.
Logan, James Harvey
Lombard, Carole
Lowes, John Livingston
Lynd, Robert Staughton
McCormack, Buren Herbert ("Mac")
McCrary, George Washington
McCutcheon, George Barr
McFarland, John Thomas
McHale, Kathryn
McKinney, Frank Edward, Sr.
McMurry, Frank Morton
McNutt, Paul Vories
McPherson, Smith
McQueen, Terence Stephen ("Steve")
Macy, Jesse
Main, Marjorie
Major, Charles
Marshall, Thomas Riley
Martin, William Alexander Parsons
Mead, Elwood
Meek, Fielding Bradford
Mellette, Arthur Calvin
Menninger, Charles Frederick
Miller, Cincinnatus Hiner
Miller, John Franklin
Millis, Harry Alvin
Mills, Anson
Milroy, Robert Huston
Minton, Sherman
Monroe, Paul
Moody, William Vaughn
Mooney, James
Moore, Addison Webster
Moore, Philip North
Morgan, Thomas Jefferson
Morrow, William W.
Morton, Oliver Perry
Nash, Arthur
Nathan, George Jean
Nelson, William Rockhill
New, Harry Stewart
Newlon, Jesse Homer
Newsom, Herschel David
Niblack, Albert Parker
Niblack, William Ellis
Nicholson, Meredith
Nixon, William Penn
Noll, John Francis
Norell, Norman
Noyes, William Albert, Jr.
Ogg, Frederic Austin
Oliphant, Herman
Olsen, John Sigvard ("Ole")
Osborn, Chase Salmon
Pearson, Edward Jones
Pearson, Leonard
Pearson, Raymond Allen
Philipson, David
Phillips, David Graham
Piatt, John James
Plummer, Mary Wright
Porter, Albert Gallatin
Porter, Cole
Porter, Gene Stratton
Pyle, Ernest Taylor
Randall, James Garfield
Record, Samuel James
Reisner, George Andrew
Rice, Edgar Charles ("Sam")
Ridpath, John Clark
Riley, James Whitcomb
Riley, William Bell
Ritter, Joseph Elmer
Rodman, Thomas Jackson
Rose, Joseph Nelson
Rovenstine, Emery Andrew
Runcie, Constance Faunt Le Roy
St. John, John Pierce
Sanders, Harland David ("Colonel")
Schelling, Felix Emanuel
Scott, Fred Newton
Scott, Leroy
Shaw, (Warren) Wilbur
Shelton, Albert Leroy
Shields, Charles Woodruff
Shoup, Francis Asbury
Sims, Charles N.
Sissle, Noble Lee
Skidmore, Louis
Slipher, Vesto Melvin
Sloan, James Forman
Smith, David Roland
Smith, Walter Bedell
Sparks, William Andrew Jackson
Spooner, John Coit
Springer, William McKendree
Stanley, Wendell Meredith
Starbuck, Edwin Diller
Stein, Evaleen
Stephenson, Carl
Stout, Rex Todhunter
Straton, John Roach

Straus, Simon William
Stubbs, Walter Roscoe
Tarkington, Booth
Taylor, Frank Bursley
Terman, Lewis Madison
Terrell, Edwin Holland
Thomas, (John William) Elmer
Thompson, James Maurice
Thompson, Oscar Lee
Thornton, Henry Worth
Thorpe, Rose Alnora Hartwick
Tolley, Howard Ross
Trueblood, Benjamin Franklin
Usher, Nathaniel Reilly
Vanderburgh, William Henry
Van Devanter, Willis
Van Doren, Mark Albert
Van Hook, Weller
Veatch, Arthur Clifford
Voris, John Ralph
Wallace, Lewis
Warthin, Aldred Scott
Watson, James Eli
Webb, Clifton
Wharton, Greene Lawrence
Whetzel, Herbert Hice
Whistler, George Washington
Wickard, Claude Raymond
Wiley, Harvey Washington
Williams, Elkanah
Williams, Gaar Campbell
Willkie, Wendell Lewis
Wills, Childe Harold
Wilson, Henry Lane
Wilson, John Lockwood
Wirt, William Albert
Wissler, Clark
Wood, Thomas Bond
Wood, William Robert
Woolman, Collett Everman
Wright, George Grover
Wright, Wilbur
Yohn, Federick Coffay

IOWA

Adams, Ephraim Douglass
Adams, Henry Carter
Adler, Felix
Alden, Cynthia May Westover
Aldrich, Bess Genevra Streeter
Anson, Adrian Constantine
Baker, Carl Lotus
Ballinger, Richard Achilles
Beer, Thomas
Bell, Frederic Somers
Benson, Oscar Herman
Binford, Jessie Florence
Bingham, Walter Van Dyke
Bliven, Bruce Ormsby
Borg, George William
Botsford, George Willis
Bowen, Thomas Meade
Buckley, Oliver Ellsworth
Buckner, Emory Roy
Budd, Ralph
Burdick, Eugene Leonard
Burton, Marion Le Roy
Byoir, Carl Robert
Campbell, Marius Robinson
Carothers, Wallace Hume
Case, Francis Higbee
Cody, William Frederick
Collier, Hiram Price
Cone, Russell Glenn
Cook, George Cram
Cooley, Edwin Gilbert
Cowles, Gardner
De Forest, Lee
Devaney, John Patrick
Devine, Edward Thomas
Dickinson, Edwin De Witt
Dickson, Leonard Eugene
Eisenhower, Mamie Geneva Doud
Ely, Hanson Edward
Emerson, Oliver Farrar
Evermann, Barton Warren
Gabrielson, Ira Noel
Garretson, Austin Bruce
Garst, Roswell ("Bob")
Gidley, James Williams
Gillette, Guy Mark
Glaspell, Susan Keating
Graff, Everett Dwight
Gray, Harold Edwin
Gregory, Clifford Verne
Hall, James Norman
Hamilton, John Daniel Miller, II
Hawley, James Henry
Hays, Paul R.
Heezen, Bruce Charles
Herbst, Josephine Frey
Hickenlooper, Bourke Blakemore
Hillis, Newell Dwight
Hooper, Jessie Annette Jack
Hoover, Herbert Clark
Hope, Clifford Ragsdale
Hopkins, Harry Lloyd
Hough, Emerson
Hove, Elling
Howard, Edgar
Howard, Joseph Kinsey
Howey, Walter Crawford
Hutton, Levi William
Irwin, Robert Benjamin
Jackson, Clarence Martin
Jensen, Benton Franklin ("Ben")
Kantor, MacKinlay
Keenan, James Francis
Kerby, William Joseph
Knapp, Bradford
Koren, John
Langdon, Harry Philmore
Laughlin, Harry Hamilton
Leahy, William Daniel
Leedom, Boyd Stewart
Leopold, (Rand) Aldo
Leverett, Frank
Lewelling, Lorenzo Dow
Lewis, John Llewellyn
Lunn, George Richard
McGee, William John
McKean, James William
MacNider, Hanford
Mall, Franklin Paine
Martin, Glenn Luther ("Cy")
Maxwell, Elsa
Maxwell, Marvel Marilyn
Meredith, Edna C. Elliott
Meredith, Edwin Thomas
Merriam, Charles Edward, Jr.
Merriam, John Campbell
Miller, Glenn
Mitchell, Stephen Arnold
Morley, Margaret Warner
Mott, Frank Luther
Nagel, Conrad
Noyes, William Albert
Paul, Josephine Bay
Phillips, John Sanburn
Pierce, Robert Willard
Plumb, Glenn Edward
Pritchard, Frederick John
Quick, John Herbert
Read, George Windle
Remey, George Collier
Reno, Milo
Reynolds, George McClelland
Ringling, Charles
Ross, Lawrence Sullivan
Rowe, Leo Stanton
Ruml, Beardsley
Russell, Charles Edward
Russell, Lillian
Ryan, Arthur Clayton
Salter, William Mackintire
Seberg, Jean Dorothy
Shaw, Lawrence Timothy ("Buck")
Sherman, Stuart Pratt
Shorey, Paul
Smith, Courtney Craig
Smith, Fre Burton
Smith, Walter Inglewood
Springer, Charles
Springer, Frank
Stone, Warren Sanford
Stong, Phil(lip Duffield)
Stouffer, Samuel Andrew
Sunday, William Ashley
Tate, John Torrence
Tilghman, William Matthew
Van Allen, Frank
Vance, Arthur Charles ("Dazzy")
Van Vechten, Carl
Veblen, Oswald
Wallace, Henry Agard
Wallgren, Mon(rad) C(harles)
Warner, Amos Griswold
Watts, Franklin Mowry
Wayne, John
Welch, Joseph Nye
Whitcomb, Selden Lincoln
Whitehill, Clarence Eugene
Whitney, Alexander Fell
Wilbur, Curtis Dwight
Wilbur, Ray Lyman
Wilson, Mortimer
Wood, Garfield Arthur ("Gar")
Wood, Grant
Young, Clarence Marshall
Young, Karl
Young, Lafayette

KANSAS

Bemis, Harold Edward
Braniff, Thomas Elmer
Browder, Earl Russell
Capper, Arthur

Chaffee, Adna Romanza
Chaplin, Ralph Hosea
Chrysler, Walter Percy
Clapper, Raymond Lewis
Cobb, Frank Irving
Curry, John Steuart
Curtis, Charles
Douglas, Aaron
Earhart, Amelia Mary
Fisher, Dorothea Frances Canfield
Frank, Tenney
Franklin, Edward Curtis
Friday
Gaylord, Edward King
Gregg, John Andrew
Hadley, Herbert Spencer
Harrington, John Lyle
Hatch, Carl A.
Henderson, Paul
Hinshaw, David Schull
Holmes, Julius Cecil
Inge, William Motter
Johnson, Edwin Carl
Johnson, Hugh Samuel
Johnson, Osa
Johnson, Walter Perry
Johnson, Wendell Andrew Leroy
Keaton, Joseph Francis ("Buster"), V
Kelly, Emmett Leo
Kenton, Stanley Newcomb
Kuhn, Joseph Ernst
Latimer, Wendell Mitchell
Lee, John Clifford Hodges
Livingstone, Belle
McDaniel, Hattie
Marlatt, Abby Lillian
Masters, Edgar Lee
Menninger, William Claire
Mills, Enos Abijah
Moore, Hugh Everett
Murdock, Victor
Nichols, Ernest Fox
O'Hare, Kate (Richards) Cunningham
Parker, Charlie ("Bird")
Parks, Larry
Peabody, Lucy Whitehead
Pemberton, Brock
Pitts, Zasu
Runyon, Damon
Rupp, Adolph Frederick
Schoeppel, Andrew Frank
Slosson, Edwin Emery
Smith, Harold Dewey
Smith, William Eugene
Sprague, Charles Arthur
Starrett, Paul
Starrett, William Aiken
Stearman, Lloyd Carlton
Stewart, Walter Winne
Sutherland, Earl Wilbur, Jr.
Vance, Vivian
Vincent, John Carter
White, William Allen
Whittaker, Charles Evans
Willebrandt, Mabel Walker
Woodring, Harry Hines
Wright, Henry
Zook, George Frederick

KENTUCKY

Adams, William Wirt
Alexander, Barton Stone
Alexander, Gross
Allen, Henry Tureman
Allen, James Lane
Altsheler, Joseph Alexander
Anderson, Richard Clough
Anderson, Robert
Anderson, Victor Vance
Anshutz, Thomas Pollock
Applegate, Jesse
Atchison, David Rice
Baker, Jehu
Barkley, Alben William
Baylor, Robert Emmet Bledsoe
Becknell, William
Bell, James Franklin
Bent, Silas
Berryman, Clifford Kennedy
Birney, James
Birney, James Gillespie
Blackburn, Joseph Clay Styles
Blackburn, Luke Pryor
Blair, Francis Preston
Blair, Montgomery
Bland, Richard Parks
Bledsoe, Albert Taylor
Bloch, Claude Charles
Boggs, Lillburn W.
Bolton, Sarah Tittle Barrett
Bowman, John Bryan
Boyle, Jeremiah Tilford
Bradley, William O'Connell
Bramlette, Thomas E.
Brandeis, Louis Dembitz
Breckenridge, Sophonisba Preston
Breckinridge, Desha
Breckinridge, John
Breckinridge, John Cabell
Breckinridge, Robert Jefferson
Brennan, Alfred Laurens
Bristow, Benjamin Helme
Bristow, Joseph Little
Brown, Benjamin Gratz
Brown, John Mason, Jr.
Brown, John Young
Brown, William Wells
Browning, Orville Hickman
Browning, Tod
Buchanan, Joseph Rodes
Buckner, Simon Bolivar, 1823–1914
Buckner, Simon Bolivar, 1886–1945
Buford, Abraham
Buford, John
Buford, Napoleon Bonaparte
Bullitt, Henry Massie
Burbridge, Stephen Gano
Burnam, John Miller
Butler, Burridge Davenal
Butler, William Orlando
California Joe
Canby, Edward Richard Sprigg
Carlisle, John Griffin
Carson, Christopher
Carter, Caroline Louise Dudley
Cawein, Madison Julius
Chilton, William Paris
Churchill, Thomas James
Clark, Champ
Clay, Cassius Marcellus
Cobb, Irvin Shrewsbury
Cofer, Martin Hardin
Coleman, William Tell
Combs, Earle Bryan
Combs, Leslie
Connelly, Henry
Cooper, Joseph Alexander
Corwin, Thomas
Crittenden, George Bibb
Crittenden, John Jordan
Crittenden, Thomas Leonidas
Crittenden, Thomas Theodore
Croghan, George
Cullom, Shelby Moore
Davies, William Augustine
Daviess, Maria Thompson
Davis, Garrett
Davis, Jefferson
Dickey, Theophilus Lyle
Dinwiddie, Atbert Bledsoe
Doniphan, Alexander William
Drake, Benjamin
Duke, Basil Wilson
Duncan, Joseph
Dunn, Charles
Dunn, Williamson
Du Pont, Thomas Coleman
Durbin, John Price
Durrett, Reuben Thomas
Duveneck, Frank
Edwards, Ninian Wirt
Evans, Walter
Everleigh, Ada
Everleigh, Minna
Fagan, James Fleming
Fall, Albert Bacon
Fee, John Gregg
Field, Charles William
Flanagan, Webster
Flexner, Abraham
Flexner, Bernard
Flexner, Jennie Maas
Flexner, Simon
Floyd, John
Ford, John Baptiste
Foster, Ephraim Hubbard
Fowke, Gerard
Fox, Fontaine Talbot, Jr.
Fox, John William
Francis, David Rowland
Frazer, Oliver
Garrard, Kenner
Gholson, Samuel Jameson
Gibson, Randall Lee
Gilliss, Walter
Goldman, Edwin Franko
Goodloe, William Cassius
Gore, Robert Hayes
Gorman, Willis Arnold
Greathouse, Clarence Ridgeby
Green, Benjamin Edwards
Green, Duff
Green, Lewis Warner
Greene, George Sears
Griffith, David Wark
Grimes, Absalom Carlisle

Guthrie, James
Haggin, James Ben Ali
Halderman, John A.
Hall, William Whitty
Hanson, Roger Weightman
Hardin, Charles Henry
Hardin, John J.
Harlan, James
Harlan, John Marshall
Harney, Benjamin Robertson
Harrison, Carter Henry
Harrison, Elizabeth
Harrison, James
Hart, Joel Tanner
Hatch, William Henry
Hauser, Samuel Thomas
Hays, William Shakespeare
Helm, John Larue
Henderson, Yandell
Herndon, William Henry
Hill, Patty Smith
Hines, Duncan
Hines, Walker Downer
Hobson, Edward Henry
Hodgen, John Thompson
Holladay, Ben
Holman, Jesse Lynch
Holt, Joseph
Hood, John Bell
Hume, Edgar Erskine
Hunter, William C.
Ireland, John, 1827–1896
Jackson, Claiborne Fox
Jackson, John Davies
Jacob, Richard Taylor
James, Ollie Murray
Jennings, James Hennen
Johnson, Richard Mentor
Johnson, Richard W.
Johnson, Robert Ward
Johnson, Tom Loftin
Johnston, Albert Sidney
Johnston, William Preston
Jones, William Palmer
Jouett, James Edward
Jouett, Matthew Harris
Kimmel, Husband Edward
King, John Pendleton
Klaw, Marc
Knott, James Proctor
Koch, Frederick Henry
Krock, Arthur
Lane, Henry Smith
Lawson, Leonidas Merion
Lee, Willis Augustus
Lewis, Joseph Horace
Lincoln, Abraham
Lincoln, Mary Todd
Linn, Lewis Fields
Logan, Stephen Trigg
Lorimer, George Horace
Lurton, Horace Harmon
McAfee, Robert Breckinridge
McCalla, William Latta
McCann, William Penn
McClernand, John Alexander
McCormack, Joseph Nathaniel
McCreary, James Bennett
McCreery, Charles
McElroy, John
McElroy, Robert McNutt
McGarvey, John William
McMillan, James Winning
McMillin, Benton
McReynolds, James Clark
Magoffin, Beriah
Magoffin, James Wiley
Majors, Alexander
Marcosson, Isaac Frederick
Marshall, Humphrey
Marshall, Thomas Alexander
Marshall, William Louis
Martin, William Thompson
Masquerier, Lewis
Matthews, Claude
Matthews, Joseph Brown
Maury, Francis Fontaine
Maxey, Samuel Bell
Maxwell, David Hervey
May, Andrew Jackson
Meigs, Return Jonathan
Miller, Henry
Miller, Samuel Freeman
Mills, Robert, 1809–1888
Mills, Roger Quarles
Mitchel, Ormsby MacKnight
Moore, William Thomas
Morehead, Charles Slaughter
Morehead, James Turner
Morgan, Thomas Hunt
Morris, Thomas Armstrong
Morrow, Edwin Porch
Morrow, Prince Albert
Morrow, Thomas Vaughan
Morton, Rogers Clark Ballard
Moss, Lemuel
Nation, Carry Amelia Moore
Nelson, Thomas Henry
Nelson, William, 1824–1862
Niles, John Jacob
Nolan, Philip
Norton, Elijah Hise
O'Fallon, Benjamin
O'Fallon, John
Oglesby, Richard James
O'Hara, Theodore
Palmer, Bertha Honoré
Palmer, John McAuley
Pattie, James Ohio
Peay, Austin
Phillips, Lena Madesin
Piatt, Sarah Morgan Bryan
Polk, Willis Jefferson
Pope, John
Pope, Nathaniel
Poston, Charles Debrill
Powell, Lazarus Whitehead
Powell, William Byrd
Powers, Francis Gary
Preston, William
Price, William Thompson
Proctor, John Robert
Purnell, Benjamin
Pusey, William Allen
Rachford, Benjamin Knox
Rector, Henry Massey
Reed, Stanley Forman
Reynolds, Charles Alexander
Reynolds, Joseph Jones
Rice, Alice Caldwell Hegan
Rice, Nathan Lewis
Richardson, Tobias Gibson
Ridgely, Daniel Bowly
Rives, Hallie Erminie
Roark, Ruric Nevel
Roberts, Elizabeth Madox
Robertson, George
Robertson, Jerome Bonaparte
Rogers, James Gamble
Rollins, James Sidney
Rose, Uriah Milton
Rousseau, Lovell Harrison
Russell, William Henry
Rutledge, Wiley Blount
Sanders, George Nicholas
Saunders, Alvin
Scopes, John Thomas
Scott, Hugh Lenox
Scott, Walter Edward
Semple, Ellen Churchill
Shaler, Nathaniel Southgate
Shelby, Joseph Orville
Shields, George Howell
Short, Charles Wilkins
Shouse, Jouett
Simms, William Elliott
Smith, Gustavus Woodson
Smith, William Russell
Spalding, John Lancaster
Spalding, Martin John
Speed, James
Spence, Brent
Springer, Reuben Runyan
Stanley, Augustus Owsley
Stayton, John William
Stevenson, Adlai Ewing
Stevenson, James
Stone, Richard French
Stone, William Joel
Stuart, John Todd
Sublette, William Lewis
Switzler, William Franklin
Tate, John Orley Allen
Taylor, Marshall William
Taylor, Richard
Terry, David Smith
Tevis, Lloyd
Thompson, Stith
Tichenor, Isaac Taylor
Todd, Charles Stewart
Towne, Charles Hanson
Traylor, Melvin Alvah
Underwood, Oscar Wilder
Vest, George Graham
Vinson, Fred(erick) Moore
Visscher, William Lightfoot
Walker, David, 1806–1879
Walker, David Shelby
Walker, Pinkney Houston
Walker, Stuart Armstrong
Wallace William Ross
Waller, John Lightfoot
Walling, William English
Walters, Alexander
Warden, Robert Bruce
Warfield, Benjamin Breckinridge
Watkins, George Claiborne
Watson, John Crittenden
Webber, Charles Wilkins
Wehle, Louis Brandeis

West, William Edward
White, Alma Bridwell
Whitman, Albery Allson
Wickliffe, Charles Anderson
Wickliffe, Robert Charles
Willis, Albert Shelby
Willson, Augustus Everett
Winlock, Joseph
Witherspoon, Alexander Maclaren
Wood, Thomas John
Wrather, William Embry
Yates, Richard
Yeaman, William Pope
Young, Whitney Moore, Jr.

LOUISIANA

Aime, Valcour
Armstrong, Louis ("Satchmo")
Basso, (Joseph) Hamilton
Beauregard, Pierre Gustave Toutant
Bechet, Sidney
Behan, William James
Bermudez, Edouard Edmond
Blanchard, Newton Crain
Bontemps, Arna Wendell
Bouligny, Dominique
Bouvet, Marie Marguerite
Breaux, Joseph Arsenne
Brooks, Overton
Butterworth, William Walton ("Walt")
Cable, George Washington
Caffery, Donelson
Caffery, Jefferson
Cahn, Edmond Nathaniel
Canonge, Louis Placide
Carter, William Hodding, Jr.
Celestin, Oscar ("Papa")
Chouteau, Jean Pierre
Chouteau, René Auguste
Clark, Felton Grandison
Collens, Thomas Wharton
Connelly, Pierre Francis
Cushman, Pauline
Davis, Abraham Lincoln, Jr.
Deléry, François Charles
Dimitry, Alexander
Dugué, Charles Oscar
Edeson, Robert
Elder, Susan Blanchard
Elkin, William Lewis
Ellender, Allen Joseph
Eustis, George
Eustis, James Biddle
Faget, Jean Charles
Farrar, Edgar Howard
Fay, Edwin Whitfield
Fiske, Minnie Maddern
Fortier, Alcée
Foster, Murphy James
Gayarré, Charles Étienne Arthur
Gherardi, Bancroft
Goldman, Mayer C.
Gottschalk, Louis Moreau
Hall, Luther Egbert
Harrod, Benjamin Morgan
Hébert, Felix Edward ("Eddie")
Hébert, Louis
Hébert, Paul Octave
Herriman, George Joseph
Hunt, Carleton
Hunt, Gaillard
Jackson, Mahalia
Janin, Louis
Janvier, Margaret Thomson
Kenner, Duncan Farrar
Kennicott, Robert
King, Grace Elizabeth
Koenigsberg, Moses
La Barge, Joseph
Lafon, Thomy
Latil, Alexandre
Ledbetter, Huddie ("Lead-belly")
Lejeune, John Archer
Leslie, Miriam Florence Folline
Levy, Gustave Lehmann
Lisa, Manuel
Long, Earl Kemp
Long, Huey Pierce
Ludeling, John Theodore
Lynch, John Roy
McEnery, Samuel Douglas
Maestri, Robert Sidney
Marigny, Bernard
Matas, Rudolph
Matthews, James Brander
Menken, Adah Isaacs
Mercier, Charles Alfred
Morgan, James Morris
Morgan, Philip Hicky
Morphy, Paul Charles
Morrison, Delesseps Story
Morton, Ferdinand Joseph ("Jelly Roll")
Mouton, Alexander
Nicholls, Francis Redding Tillou
Oliver, Joseph
Ory, Edward ("Kid")
Osgood, Howard
Oswald, Lee Harvey
Ott, Melvin Thomas ("Mel")
Patterson, Thomas Harman
Pavy, Octave
Perez, Leander Henry
Pope, James Pinckney
Prima, Luigi ("Louis")
Provosty, Olivier Otis
Richardson, Henry Hobson
Roman, André Bienvenu
Rouquette, Adrien Emmanuel
Rouquette, François Dominique
Scarborough, Lee Rutland
Séjour, Victor
Shaw, Clay L.
Smith, Marcus
Sothern, Edward Hugh
Souchon, Edmond
Stuart, Ruth McEnery
Thierry, Camille
Turpin, Ben
Viel, François Étienne Bernard Alexandre
Vignaud, Henry
Vileré, Jacques Philippe
Walker, Sarah Breedlove
Wells, James Madison
White, Edward Douglass
Wills, Harry
Wiltz, Louis Alfred

MAINE

Abbot, Ezra
Abbot, Gorham Dummer
Abbott, Edward
Abbott, Frank
Abbott, Jacob
Abbott, John Stevens Cabot
Akers, Benjamin Paul
Akers, Elizabeth Chase
Albee, Edward Franklin
Alden, James
Alexander, De Alva Stanwood
Allen, William Henry
Allinson, Anne Crosby Emery
Ames, Adelbert
Anderson, Martin Brewer
Andrew, John Albion
Andrews, George Pierce
Andrews, Israel DeWolf
Bailey, Rufus William
Baker, James Hutchins
Banks, Charles Edward
Barker, Benjamin Fordyce
Barker, Jacob
Barrett, Benjamin Fiske
Bartol, Cyrus Augustus
Bates, Arlo
Bates, James
Beaman, Charles Cotesworth
Bean, Leon Lenwood
Berry, Hiram Gregory
Berry, Nathaniel Springer
Bickmore, Albert Smith
Black, Frank Swett
Blunt, James Gillpatrick
Bogan, Louise Marie
Bond, William Cranch
Boutelle, Charles Addison
Brackett, Edward Augustus
Bradbury, James Ware
Bradbury, William Batchelder
Bradley, Milton
Brannan, Samuel
Brewster, Ralph Owen
Bridges, (Henry) Styles
Brooks, Erastus
Brooks, James
Brooks, Noah
Brooks, Peter Chardon
Brown, Samuel Gilman
Browne, Charles Farrar
Cary, Annie Louise
Cayvan, Georgia
Chadbourne, Paul Ansel
Chamberlain, Joshua Lawrence
Chandler, Peleg Whitman
Chase, George
Chase, Mary Ellen
Cheever, George Barrell
Cheever, Henry Theodore
Clark, Walter Van Tilburg
Clarke, McDonald
Clarke, Rebecca Sophia
Clarkson, Coker Fifield
Cobb, Sylvanus, 1798–1866
Cobb, Sylvanus, 1823–1887

Coburn, Abner
Coffin, Charles Albert
Coffin, Robert Peter Tristram
Colby, Gardner
Cole, Joseph Foxcroft
Colman, Samuel
Cook, Walter Wheeler
Copeland, Charles Townsend
Cross, Arthur Lyon
Cummings, Joseph
Curtis, Cyrus Hermann Kotzschmar
Curtis, Olin Alfred
Cutler, Elliott Carr
Dana, Napoleon Jackson Tecumseh
Daveis, Charles Stewart
Davis, Henry Gassett
Davis, Owen Gould
Davis, Raymond Cazallis
Davis, William Hammatt
Day, Holman Francis
Day, James Roscoe
Deane, Charles
Dearing, John Lincoln
Deering, Nathaniel
Deering, William
Dennison, Aaron Lufkin
Dingley, Nelson
Dix, Dorothea Lynde
Dole, Charles Fletcher
Dow, Lorenzo
Dow, Neal
Drinkwater, Jennie Maria
Dryden, John Fairfield
Dunlap, Robert Pinckney
Eastman, Charles Gamage
Eckstorm, Fannie Hardy
Edes, Robert Thaxter
Elliott, Maxine
Emerson, Ellen Russell
Emerson, George Barrell
Emerson, James Ezekiel
Emery, Henry Crosby
Emery, Lucilius Alonzo
Emery, Stephen Albert
Estes, Dana
Evans, George
Everett, Charles Carroll
Fairfield, John
Farmer, Hannah Tobey Shapleigh
Farrington, Wallace Rider
Felch, Alpheus
Fernald, Charles Henry
Fernald, James Champlin
Fernald, Merritt Lyndon
Fessenden, Francis
Fessenden, James Deering
Fessenden, Samuel
Fillebrown, Thomas
Fisher, Clark
Fisher, Ebenezer
Flagg, Edmund
Flint, Charles Ranlett
Folsom, George
Ford, John
Foster, Benjamin
Freeman, John Ripley
Frye, William Pierce
Fuller, Melville Weston
Gammon, Elijah Hedding
Gannett, Henry
Garcelon, Alonzo
Garman, Charles Edward
George, Gladys
Gerrish, Frederic Henry
Gibson, Paris
Gill, Laura Drake
Ginn, Edwin
Goddard, Henry Herbert
Goddard, Morrill
Goddard, Pliny Earle
Goodale, George Lincoln
Goodale, Stephen Lincoln
Goodwin, Daniel Raynes
Goodwin, Ichabod
Goodwin, John Noble
Gould, George Milbry
Grant, Albert Weston
Grant, Claudius Buchanan
Grant, George Barnard
Greenough, James Bradstreet
Griffin, Eugene
Griswold, William McCrillis
Grover, Cuvier
Grover, La Fayette
Hale, Eugene
Hall, Edwin Herbert
Hamlin, Alfred Dwight Foster
Hamlin, Charles
Hamlin, Cyrus
Hamlin, Hannibal
Harris, George
Harris, Samuel
Hartford, George Huntington
Hartley, Marsden
Hatch, Edward
Hatch, Rufus
Hawkins, Dexter Arnold
Hayes, Edward Carey
Hayes, John Lord
Hill, Frank Alpine
Hill, James
Hillard, George Stillman
Hinds, Asher Crosby
Hitchcock, Roswell Dwight
Holden, Liberty Emery
Howard, Blanche Willis
Howard, Oliver Otis
Howard, Volney Erskine
Howe, Albion Parris
Howe, Lucien
Howe, Timothy Otis
Hubbard, John
Hubbard, Thomas Hamlin
Hughes, Charles Frederick
Hume, William
Hussey, Obed
Ingalls, Melville Ezra
Ingraham, Joseph Holt
Jackson, John Adams
Jewett, Charles Coffin
Jewett, John Punchard
Jewett, Sarah Orne
Johnson, Henry
Johnson, Jonathan Eastman
Jones, Rufus Matthew
Jones, Sybil
Jordan, Edwin Oakes
Kavanagh, Edward
Kellogg, Elijah
Kimball, Sumner Increase
Kimball, William Wirt
King, Henry Melville
King, Horatio
King, Rufus
King, William
Klingelsmith, Margaret Center
Ladd, Edwin Fremont
Lane, Gertrude Battles
Lane, Horace M.
Lapham, William Berry
Larrabee, William Clark
Little, Charles Coffin
Littledale, Clara Savage
Long, John Davis
Longfellow, Henry Wadsworth
Longfellow, Samuel
Longfellow, Stephen
Longfellow, William Pitt Preble
Lord, Herbert Mayhew
Lord, Nathan
Loring, Charles Morgridge
Lovejoy, Elijah Parish
Lovejoy, Owen
Low, Frederick Ferdinand
Lunt, Orrington
Mabery, Charles Frederic
McCulloch, Hugh
McGraw, John Harte
McLellan, Isaac
Magoun, George Frederic
Malcolm, Daniel
Manley, Joseph Homan
Marble, Albert Prescott
Mason, Luther Whiting
Mason, Otis Tufton
Mathews, Shailer
Mathews, William
Maxim, Hiram Stevens
Maxim, Hudson
Mellen, Grenville
Merriam, Henry Clay
Merrick, Samuel Vaughan
Merrill, Elmer Drew
Merrill, George Perkins
Millay, Edna St. Vincent
Mills, Hiram Francis
Mitchell, Edward Page
Moore, Anne Carroll
Morrill, Anson Peaslee
Morrill, Edmund Needham
Morrill, Lot Myrick
Morse, Charles Wyman
Morse, Edward Sylvester
Morse, Freeman Harlow
Morton, Charles Gould
Moses, George Higgins
Mosher, Thomas Bird
Munsey, Frank Andrew
Neal, John
Neal, Josephine Bicknell
Nelson, Charles Alexander
Nichols, Charles Henry
Nichols, George Ward
Noble, Frederick Alphonso
Norcross, Orlando Whitney
Nordica, Lillian
North, William
Noyes, Crosby Stuart

Nye, Edgar Wilson
O'Brien, Jeremiah
O'Brien, Richard
Osgood, Herbert Levi
Packard, Alpheus Spring
Packard, Joseph
Paine, Henry Warren
Paine, John Knowles
Parker, Edwin Pond
Parris, Albion Keith
Parris, Alexander
Parsons, Usher
Parton, Sara Payson Willis
Patten, Gilbert
Peavey, Frank Hutchinson
Pepperrell, Sir William
Perham, Josiah
Perkins, George Clement
Peters, John Andrew
Phelps, Thomas Stowell
Phips, Sir William
Pierce, Edward Allen
Pike, James Shepherd
Pike, Mary Hayden Green
Pingree, Hazen Stuart
Piston, Walter Hamor
Poor, Henry Varnum
Poor, John Alfred
Pratt, William Veazie
Preble, Edward
Preble, George Henry
Preble, William Pitt
Prentiss, Elizabeth Payson
Prentiss, George Lewis
Prentiss, Seargent Smith
Proctor, Frederick Frances
Putnam, George Palmer
Putnam, William Le Baron
Reed, Elizabeth Armstrong
Reed, Thomas Brackett
Richards, Robert Hallowell
Richardson, Charles Francis
Rideout, Henry Milner
Roberts, Kenneth Lewis
Robinson, Edwin Arlington
Rockefeller, Nelson Aldrich
Rogers, Edith Nourse
Rogers, John Rankin
Rowse, Samuel Worcester
Russell, Osborne
Sargent, Dudley Allen
Savage, Minot Judson
Scammon, Jonathan Young
Sewall, Arthur
Sewall, Frank
Sewall, Harold Marsh
Sewall, Joseph Addison
Sewall, Stephen
Sheldon, Edward Stevens
Sheldon, Henry Newton
Shepley, George Foster
Sibley, John Langdon
Simmons, Franklin
Sleeper, Jacob
Small, Albion Woodbury
Small, Alvan Edmond
Smiley, Albert Keith
Smith, Charles Henry, 1827–1902
Smith, Elizabeth Oakes Prince
Smith, George Otis
Smith, Henry Boynton
Smith, Seba
Smith, Theodate Louise
Smyth, Egbert Coffin
Smyth, Newman
Smyth, William
Soule, Joshua
Southgate, Horatio
Spofford, Harriet Elizabeth Prescott
Stanley, Francis Edgar
Stanwood, Edward
Starrett, Laroy S.
Stearns, Frederic Pike
Stephens, Charles Asbury
Stetson, Augusta Emma Simmons
Stetson, William Wallace
Stevens, John Frank
Stevens, John Leavitt
Stevens, William Bacon
Stickney, Alpheus Beede
Storer, David Humphreys
Sturtevant, Benjamin Franklin
Sullivan, James
Sullivan, Louis Robert
Sullivan, William
Swallow, George Clinton
Swanton, John Reed
Talbot, Emily Fairbanks
Thatcher, Benjamin Bussey
Thatcher, Henry Knox
Thomas, William Widgery
Thomes, William Henry
Thorndike, Ashley Horace
Thornton, John Wingate
Thrasher, John Sidney
Thwing, Charles Franklin
Tincker, Mary Agnes
Townsend, Luther Tracy
Tripp, Bartlett
Tripp, Guy Eastman
Tuck, Amos
Tuttle, Charles Wesley
Tyler, Charles Mellen
Upton, George Bruce
Verrill, Addison Emery
Vinton, Francis Laurens
Vinton, Frederic Porter
Vose, George Leonard
Walker, Williston
Washburn, Cadwallader Colden
Washburn, Israel
Washburn, William Drew
Washburne, Elihu Benjamin
Waters, William Everett
Weymouth, Frank Elwin
Whipple, William
White, Ellen Gould Harmon
White, James Clarke
Whitman, Charles Otis
Whitman, Royal
Wilder, Harris Hawthorne
Willard, Joseph
Williams, Reuel
Willis, Nathaniel Parker
Winslow, Edward Francis
Wood, Frederick Hill
Wood, Sarah Sayward Barrell Keating
Woolson, Abba Louisa Goold
Young, Aaron
Young, Josue Maria

MARYLAND

Adams, Thomas Sewall
Alexander, John Henry
Alvey, Richard Henry
Andrews, John
Archer, James J.
Archer, John
Archer, Stevenson
Bachrach, Louis Fabian
Badger, Charles Johnston
Baer, William Stevenson
Baetjer, Frederick Henry
Baker, John Franklin
Bamberger, Louis
Bannister, Nathaniel Harrington
Barber, Edwin Atlee
Barnett, George Ernest
Barney, Joshua
Bartholow, Roberts
Bassett, Richard
Baxley, Henry Willis
Bayard, James Ash(e)ton
Bayard, John Bubenheim
Beach, Sylvia Woodbridge
Beall, James Glenn
Beall, Samuel Wootton
Beatty, Adam
Bonaparte, Charles Joseph
Bonaparte, Elizabeth Patterson
Bonaparte, Jerome Napoleon
Bond, Hugh Lennox
Bond, Shadrach
Bond, Thomas
Bonsal, Stephen
Booth, Edwin Thomas
Booth, John Wilkes
Bordley, John Beale
Boston, Charles Anderson
Bowie, Oden
Bowie, Robert
Bowie, William
Bowles, William Augustus
Bozman, John Leeds
Bradford, Augustus Williamson
Bradford, Edward Green
Breckinridge, William Campbell Preston
Brookings, Robert Somers
Brown, George William
Brown, Lawrason
Browne, William Hand
Bruce, David Kirkpatrick Este
Buchanan, Franklin
Buchanan, John
Buchanan, Robert Christie
Buckler, Thomas Hepburn
Burns, William John
Bushman, Francis F. Xavier
Cain, James Mallahan
Calvert, Charles Benedeict
Calvert, George Henry
Calverton, Victor Francis
Campbell, William Henry
Cannon, James
Carmichael, William
Carroll, Charles

Carroll, Daniel
Carroll, John
Carroll, John Lee
Carvalho, Solomon Solis
Casey, Joseph
Caswell, Richard
Chaillé-Long, Charles
Chambers, Ezekiel Forman
Chanche, John Mary Joseph
Chappell, Absalom Harris
Chase, Samuel
Chatard, Francis Silas
Chester, Colby Mitchell
Chew, Benjamin
Childs, George William
Churchman, William Henry
Clark, Charles Heber
Clarke, John Sleeper
Clayton, Joshua
Clayton, Thomas
Cohen, Mendes
Cone, Claribel
Conway, Martin Franklin
Cooke, Ebenezer
Cooper, Ezekiel
Cooper, James
Cooper, John Montgomery
Councilman, William Thomas
Crane, Anne Moncure
Creamer, David
Cresap, Michael
Creswell, John Angel James
Curtis, Alfred Allen
Davidge, John Beale
Davidson, Robert
Davis, David
Davis, Henry Gassaway
Davis, Henry Winter
Davis, Meyer
Deady, Matthew Paul
Decatur, Stephen
Deems, Charles Force
Dew, Thomas Roderick
Dickinson, John, 1732–1808
Dickinson, John, 1894–1952
Dickinson, Philemon
Didier, Eugene Lemoine
Dorsey, James Owen
Douglass, Frederick
Dulany, Daniel
Duvall, Gabriel
Eberle, John
Edwards, Minian
Elder, William Henry
Elliot, Cass ("Mama")
Elliott, Jesse Duncan
Elzey, Arnold
Emory, John
Emory, William Hemsley
Evans, Hugh Davey
Ewing, John
Fenwick, Benedict Joseph
Fenwick, Edward Dominic
Ferguson, William Jason
Few, William
Flynn, John Thomas
Ford, Henry Jones
Ford, John Thomson
Forrest, French
Foxx, James Emory
Francis, Paul James
Franklin, Philip Albright Small
Frazier, Edward Franklin
French, William Henry
Friedenwald, Aaron
Galloway, Joseph
Gantt, Henry Laurence
Garnet, Henry Highland
Garrett, John Work
Garrettson, Freeborn
Geyer, Henry Sheffie
Gibbons, Herbert Adams
Gibbons, James
Gibson, William
Gilmor, Harry
Gist, Christopher
Gist, Mordecai
Glenn, John Mark
Goddard, Calvin Hooker
Goddard, Paul Beck
Godman, John Davidson
Goldsborough, Charles
Goldsborough, Robert
Goldsborough, Thomas Alan
Goldsmith, Middleton
Gordy, John Pancoast
Gorman, Arthur Pue
Gorrell, Edgar Staley
Graves, Rosewell Hobart
Greene, Samuel Dana
Greenwald, Emanuel
Griffith, Goldsborough Sappington
Grove, Robert Moses ("Lefty")
Gruening, Ernest
Guttmacher, Alan Frank
Hambleton, Thomas Edward
Hamilton, William Thomas
Hammett, Samuel Dashiell
Hammond, Charles
Hammond, William Alexander
Handy, Alexander Hamilton
Hanson, Alexander Contee, 1749–1806
Hanson, Alexander Contee, 1786–1819
Hanson, John
Hardey, Mother Mary Aloysia
Hastings, Daniel Oren
Hemmeter, John Conrad
Henry, John
Henshall, James Alexander
Henson, Josiah
Henson, Matthew Alexander
Hesselius, John
Hicks, Thomas Holliday
Hill, Richard
Hindman, William
Hoffman, David
Holiday, Billie
Hollander, Jacob Harry
Hollins, George Nichols
Holt, Henry
Hopkins, Johns
Howard, Benjamin Chew
Howard, John Eager
Howell, William Henry
Howison, George Holmes
Hubner, Charles William
Hughes, Christopher
Hughes, James
Hurst, John Fletcher
Husbands, Hermon
Iddings, Joseph Paxon
James, Thomas
Jenifer, Daniel of St. Thomas
Jewett, Hugh Judge
Johns, Kensey
Johnson, Reverdy
Johnson, Thomas
Jones, Harry Clary
Jones, Hugh Bolton
Jones, John Beauchamp
Kefauver, Grayson Neikirk
Kennedy, John Pendleton
Kent, Joseph
Kerr, Sophie
Key, Francis Scott
Key, Philip Barton
Kirk, Norman Thomas
Kirkwood, Daniel
Kirkwood, Samuel Jordan
Knott, Aloysius Leo
Kolb, Lawrence
Lane, Tidence
Latrobe, Charles Hazlehurst
Lazear, Jesse William
Leaf, Wilbur Munro
Lee, Thomas Sim
Leeds, John
Leiter, Levi Zeigler
Lewis, Estelle Ann Blanche Robinson
Lloyd, Edward, 1744–1796
Lloyd, Edward, 1779–1834
Lockwood, James Booth
Logan, Cornelius Ambrosius
Longcope, Warfield Theobald
Louis, Morris
McCaffrey, John
McCardell, Claire
McClenahan, Howard
McComas, Louis Emory
McCormick, Lynde Dupuy
McDonogh, John
Machen, John Gresham
McKeldin, Theodore Roosevelt
McKenney, Thomas Loraine
Mackenzie, John Noland
McMahon, John Van Lear
Marburg, Theodore
Marden, Charles Carroll
Marriott, Williams McKim
Massey, George Betton
Maus, Marion Perry
Mayer, Alfred Marshall
Mayer, Brantz
Mayor, Alfred Goldsborough
Mencken, Henry Louis
Mercer, Margaret
Miles, George Henry
Miles, Richard Pius
Mills, Benjamin
Mitchell, George Edward
Moore, Henry Ludwell
Morawetz, Victor
Murray, Alexander
Murray, John Gardner
Murray, William Vans
Muse, Clarence

Neale, Leonard
Nelson, Roger
Newcomb, Josephine Louise Le Monnier
Nicholson, James
Nicholson, Joseph Hopper
Nicholson, Samuel
Norris, James Flack
Norris, William
Noyes, Clara Dutton
O'Brien, Frederick
Ord, Edward Otho Cresap
Otis, Elwell Stephen
Oursler, (Charles) Fulton
Paca, William
Painter, William
Palmer, James Croxall
Palmer, John Williamson
Partridge, James Rudolph
Pattison, Robert Emory
Peale, Charles Willson
Peale, James
Peale, Raphael
Pennington, James W. C.
Perdue, Arthur William
Perlman, Philip Benjamin
Peterkin, George William
Pinkerton, Lewis Letig
Pinkney, Ninian
Pinkney, William
Pise, Charles Constantine
Plater, George
Porter, Nathaniel
Post, Emily Price
Potts, Richard
Price, Bruce
Proctor, William
Purnell, William Henry
Quigg, Lemuel Ely
Radcliffe, George Lovic Pierce
Randall, Burton Alexander
Randall, James Ryder
Randall, Wyatt William
Rayner, Isidor
Read, George
Reese, Charles Lee
Reese, Lizette Woodworth
Ricketts, Palmer Chamberlaine
Ricord, Philippe
Ridgaway, Henry Bascom
Ridgely, Charles Goodwin
Riley, Bennet
Rinehart, William Henry
Ringgold, Cadwalader
Roberts, Robert Richford
Robinson, George Canby
Robinson, John Mitchell
Robson, Stuart
Rodgers, George Washington, 1787–1832
Rodgers, John, 1773–1838
Rodgers, John, 1812–1882
Rogers, Henry J.
Rogers, Robert Empie
Rohé, George Henry
Rommel, Edwin Americus ("Eddie")
Rose, John Carter
Rous, Francis Peyton
Royall, Anne Newport
Rumsey, James
Russell, John Henry
Ruth, George Herman ("Babe")
Ryan, Abram Joseph
Sachs, Bernard
Sachs, Julius
Sadtler, John Philip Benjamin
Sands, Ben Jamin Franklin
Sappington, John
Saxton, Eugene Francis
Schaeffer, Charles William
Scharf, John Thomas
Schley, Winfield Scott
Schmucker, Samuel Simon
Schroeder, John Frederick
Scott, Irving Murray
Searing, Laura Catherine Redden
Seiss, Joseph Augustus
Sellers, Matthew Bacon
Semmes, Raphael
Shaw, John, 1778–1809
Shelby, Isaac
Shipley, Ruth Bielaski
Sinclair, Upton Beall, Jr.
Singleton, Esther
Skinner, John Stuart
Smallwood, William
Smith, Francis Hopkinson
Sobeloff, Simon E.
Spalding, Catherine
Sprecher, Samuel
Spruance, Raymond Ames
Steiner, Lewis Henry
Sterett, Andrew
Stockbridge, Henry
Stoddert, Benjamin
Stone, Barton Warren
Stone, Thomas
Sturgis, Russell
Sutherland, Richard Kerens
Szold, Henrietta
Tammen, Harry Heye
Taney, Roger Brooke
Theobold, Samuel
Thomas, Allen
Thomas, Francis
Thomas, Martha Carey
Thomas, Philip Evan
Thomas, Philip Francis
Thomas, Richard Henry
Thompson, Alfred Wordsworth
Tiffany, Louis McLane
Tilghman, Edward
Tilghman, Matthew
Tilghman, Tench
Tilghman, William
Tipton, John
Trippe, John
Tubman, Harriet
Turner, Charles Yardley
Turner, Edward Raymond
Tydings, Millard Evelyn
Tyler, Samuel
Uhler, Philip Reese
Valentine, Milton
Van Osdel, John Mills
Veazey, Thomas Ward
Waesche, Russell Randolph
Waggaman, Mary Teresa McKee
Wagner, Clinton
Waidner, Charles William
Wallis, Severn Teackle
Walsh, Robert
Walters, Henry
Ward, Samuel Ringgold
Warfield, Solomon Davies
Warrington, Albert Powell
Watson, Henry Clay
Wayman, Alexander Walker
Weede, Robert
Weems, Mason Locke
Welby, Ameli Ball Coppuck
Wharton, Charles Henry
White, Charles Ignatius
White, Henry
White, Henry Clay
Whitney, Courtney
Wickes, Lambert
Wilkinson, James
Wilkinson, Theodore Stark
Williams, John Whitridge
Williams, Otho Holland
Wilmer, James Jones
Wilmer, William Holland
Winchester, James
Winder, John Henry
Winder, Levin
Winder, William Henry
Winebrenner, John
Wolman, Leo
Wright, Robert
Young, John Richardson

MASSACHUSETTS

Abbot, Benjamin
Abbot, Francis Ellingwood
Abbot, Henry Larcom
Abbot, Joel
Abbott, Austin
Abbott, Benjamin Vaughan
Abbott, Eleanor Hallowell
Abbott, Horace
Abbott, Lyman
Abbott, Samuel Warren
Abrams, Creighton Williams, Jr.
Adams, Abigail
Adams, Abijah
Adams, Brooks
Adams, Charles Baker
Adams, Charles Follen
Adams, Charles Francis, 1807–1886
Adams, Charles Francis, 1835–1915
Adams, Charles Francis, 1866–1954
Adams, Charles R.
Adams, Daniel
Adams, Dudley W.
Adams, Edward Dean
Adams, Edwin
Adams, Eliphant
Adams, Frederick Upham
Adams, Hannah
Adams, Henry Brooks
Adams, Herbert Baxter
Adams, John
Adams, Jasper
Adams, John Coleman

Adams, John Quincy
Adams, Jehemiah
Adams, Samuel
Adams, William Taylor
Agassiz, Elizabeth Cabot Cary
Aiken, George L.
Albro, Lewis Colt
Alden, Ebenezer
Alden, Ichabod
Alden, Timothy
Alden, William Livingston
Aldrich, Charles Anderson
Alger, Cyrus
Alger, Horatio
Alger, William Rounseville
Allen, Alexander Viets Griswold
Allen, Anthony Benezet
Allen, Charles
Allen, David Oliver
Allen, Edward Ellis
Allen, Fred
Allen, Frederick Lewis
Allen, Joel Asaph
Allen, Joseph Henry
Allen, Lewis Falley
Allen, Nathan
Allen, Nathan H.
Allen, Richard Lamb
Allen, Thomas
Allen, William
Allen, William Francis
Alphonsa, Mother
Alvord, Clarence Walworth
Alvord, Henry Elijah
Ames, Charles Gordon
Ames, Edward Raymond
Ames, Ezra
Ames, Fisher
Ames, Frederick Lothrop
Ames, Herman Vandenburg
Ames, James Barr
Ames, James Tyler
Ames, Joseph Alexander
Ames, Nathan Peabody
Ames, Nathaniel
Ames, Oakes, 1804–1873
Ames, Oakes, 1874–1950
Ames, Oliver, 1779–1863
Ames, Oliver, 1807–1877
Ames, Oliver, 1831–1895
Ames, Winthrop
Andrew, Samuel
Andrews, Charles Bartlett
Andrews, George Leonard
Andrews, Joseph
Andrews, Sidney
Andrews, Stephen Pearl
Angell, George Thorndike
Anthony, Susan Brownell
Apes, William
Appleton, Daniel
Appleton, James
Appleton, John
Appleton, Nathaniel Walker
Appleton, Thomas Gold
Appleton, William Henry
Appleton, William Sumner
Apthorp, William Foster
Armsby, Henry Prentiss
Armstrong, George Washington
Armstrong, Henry Worthington ("Harry")
Armstrong, Samuel Turell
Ashmun, George
Aspinwall, William
Atherton, George Washington
Atherton, Joshua
Atkinson, Edward
Atkinson, George Henry
Atwater, Caleb
Atwood, Charles B.
Auchmuty, Robert
Auchmuty, Samuel
Augustus, John
Austin, Benjamin
Austin, James Trecothick
Austin, Jane Goodwin
Austin, Jonathan Loring
Austin, William
Avery, John
Babbitt, Irving
Babbitt, Isaac
Babcock, James Francis
Babson, Roger Ward
Bacon, Robert
Badger, Joseph, 1708–1765
Badger, Joseph, 1757–1846
Bailey, Jacob
Bailey, Jacob Whitman
Baker, Benjamin Franklin
Baker, Harvey Humphrey
Baker, Lorenzo Dow
Balch, Emily Greene
Baldwin, Loammi, 1740–1807
Baldwin, Loammi, 1780–1838
Baldwin, William Henry
Ball, Albert
Ball, Thomas
Ballou, Maturin Murray
Bancroft, Aaron
Bancroft, Edward
Bancroft, George
Banks, Nathaniel Prentiss
Barbour, Thomas
Bardeen, Charles William
Barker, Albert Smith
Barker, George Frederick
Barker, Jeremiah
Barker, Josiah
Barlow, Samuel Latham Mitchill
Barnard, Charles
Barnard, Charles Francis
Barnard, Chester Irving
Barnard, Frederick Augustus Porter
Barnard, John
Barnard, John Gross
Barnes, Charlotte Mary Sanford
Barnes, James
Barron, Clarence Walker
Barrows, Alice Prentice
Bartlet, William
Bartlett, Francis Alonzo
Bartlett, John
Bartlett, Joseph
Bartlett, Josiah
Barton, Clara
Bascom, Florence
Bass, Edward
Bassett, William Hastings
Bates, Joshua
Bates, Katharine Lee
Bates, Samuel Penniman
Baylies, Francis
Beach, Alfred Ely
Beach, Moses Sperry
Beale, Joseph Henry
Beckwith, Clarence Augustine
Behrman, Samuel Nathaniel ("S. N.")
Belcher, Jonathan
Belknap, Jeremy
Bellamy, Edward
Bellows, Albert Fitch
Bellows, Henry Whitney
Bemis, George
Bemis, Samuel Flagg
Benchley, Robert Charles
Benjamin, Asher
Bennett, Emerson
Benson, Frank Weston
Bent, Josiah
Bentley, William
Berle, Adolf Augustus, Jr.
Bernard, William Bayle
Betts, Samuel Rossiter
Bidwell, Barnabas
Bidwell, Marshall Spring
Bigelow, Erastus Brigham
Bigelow, Frank Hagar
Bigelow, Harry Augustus
Bigelow, Henry Bryant
Bigelow, Henry Jacob
Bigelow, Jacob
Bigelow, William Sturgis
Billings, William
Binney, Amos
Bird, Arthur
Bishop, Elizabeth
Bishop, Robert Roberts
Bitzer, George William
Bixby, James Thompson
Blackmur, Richard Palmer
Blake, Eli Whitney
Blake, Francis
Blake, Lyman Reed
Blanchard, Thomas
Bliss, Cornelius Newton
Bliss, George, 1816–1896
Bliss, George, 1830–1897
Bliss, Jonathan
Blodget, Samuel
Blodgett, Benjamin Colman
Blodgett, Henry Williams
Blowers, Sampson Salter
Blunt, George William
Bôcher, Maxine
Boies, Henry Martyn
Boise, Reuben Patrick
Bolles, Frank
Boltwood, Bertram Borden
Bond, George Phillips
Bonham, Milledge Luke
Borden, Lizzie Andrew
Borden, Richard
Borden, Simeon
Bourne, Jonathan
Boutell, Henry Sherman
Boutwell, George Sewall
Bowditch, Henry Ingersoll

Bowditch, Henry Pickering
Bowditch, Nathaniel
Bowdoin, James, 1726–1790
Bowdoin, James, 1752–1811
Bowen, Francis
Bowers, Lloyd Wheaton
Bowker, Richard Rogers
Boyd, John Parker
Boyden, Roland William
Boyden, Seth
Boyden, Uriah Atherton
Boyle, Thomas
Boylston, Zabdiel
Boynton, Charles Brandon
Brackett, Jeffrey Richardson
Bradbury, Theophilus
Bradford, Alden
Bradford, Edward Hickling
Bradford, Gamaliel, 1831–1911
Bradford, Gamaliel, 1863–1932
Bradford, William
Bradish, Luther
Bradley, John Edwin
Brattle, Thomas
Brattle, William
Brazer, John
Breck, Samuel
Breed, Ebenezer
Brennan, Walter
Brewer, Charles
Brewer, Thomas Mayo
Brewster, Osmyn
Brewster, William
Bridgman, Elijah Coleman
Bridgman, Herbert Lawrence
Bridgman, Percy Williams
Briggs, Charles Frederick
Briggs, George Nixon
Briggs, LeBaron Russell
Briggs, Lloyd Vernon
Brigham, Amariah
Brigham, Mary Ann
Brightman, Edgar Sheffield
Bromfield, John
Bronson, Walter Cochrane
Brooks, Charles
Brooks, Charles Timothy
Brooks, Elbridge Streeter
Brooks, John
Brooks, Maria Gowen
Brooks, Phillips
Brooks, Richard Edwin
Brown, Addison
Brown, Charlotte Emerson
Brown, Ebenezer
Brown, Henry Billings
Brown, Henry Kirke
Brown, James
Brown, John
Brown, John Appleton
Brown, Mather
Brown, Moses
Brown, Percy
Brown, Ralph Hall
Brown, Simon
Brown, William Hill
Browne, Benjamin Frederick
Browne, Charles Albert
Browne, Herbert Wheildon Cotton
Browne, William
Brownell, Thomas Church
Bryant, Gridley
Bryant, John Howard
Bryant, William Cullen
Bulfinch, Charles
Bulfinch, Thomas
Bull, Ephraim Wales
Bullard, Henry Adams
Bumstead, Freeman Josiah
Bumstead, Horace
Burbank, Luther
Burgess, Edward
Burgess, Frank Gelett
Burgess, George Kimball
Burgess, Neil
Burgess, Thornton Waldo
Burgess, W(illiam) Starling
Burlingame, Edward Livermore
Burnett, Joseph
Burnham, Clara Louise Root
Burrage, Henry Sweetser
Burrage, Walter Lincoln
Burrill, Thomas Jonathan
Burroughs, Bryson
Burt, William Austin
Burton, Harold Hitz
Bush, Vannevar ("Van")
Bushnell, George Ensign
Butler, Ezra
Butler, John Wesley
Butler, Zebulon
Butterick, Ebenezer
Byington, Cyrus
Byles, Mather
Cabot, Arthur Tracy
Cabot, Edward Clarke
Cabot, George
Cabot, Godfrey Lowell
Cabot, Hugh
Cabot, Richard Clarke
Cady, Sarah Louise Ensign
Caldwell, Charles Henry Bromedge
Calhoun, William Barron
Callender, John
Canfield, Richard A.
Capen, Elmer Hewitt
Capen, Nahum
Capen, Samuel Billings
Capen, Samuel Paul
Capron, Horace
Carnegie, Mary Crowninshield Endicott
Carpenter, Edmund Janes
Carter, Elias
Carter, James Coolidge
Carter, James Gordon
Carty, John Joseph
Caiver, Jonathan
Caswell, Alexis
Chadwick, George Whitefield
Chadwick, James Read
Chadwick, John White
Chamberlain, Daniel Henry
Chamberlain, Nathan Henry
Champney, James Wells
Chandler, Charles Frederick
Chandler, Joseph Ripley
Chandler, Seth Carlo
Channing, Edward
Channing, William Ellery
Channing, William Francis
Channing, William Henry
Chapin, Calvin
Chapin, Chester William
Chaplin, Jeremiah
Chapman, Alvan Wentworth
Chapman, John
Chapman, Maria Weston
Chase, Harry Woodburn
Chase, Pliny Earle
Chase, Thomas
Chauncy, Charles
Checkley, John
Cheney, Ednah Dow Littlehale
Chever, James W.
Child, David Lee
Child, Francis James
Child, Lydia Maria Francis
Child, Richard Washburn
Childe, John
Childs, Thomas
Chipman, Ward
Choate, Joseph Hodges
Choate, Rufus
Church, Benjamin
Church, George Earl
Church, Thomas Dolliver
Claflin, Horace Brigham
Claflin, William
Claghorn, George
Clap, Thomas
Clapp, Asa
Clapp, Charles Horace
Clapp, William Warland
Clark, Alvan
Clark, Alvan Graham
Clark, Arthur Hamilton
Clark, Henry James
Clark, John Maurice
Clark, Jonas
Clark, Jonas Gilman
Clark, Joseph Sylvester
Clark, Thomas March
Clark, William Smith
Clarke, Frank Wigglesworth
Clarke, Richard
Clarkson, John Gibson
Cleaveland, Parker
Clement, Edward Henry
Cleveland, Aaron
Cleveland, Horace William Shaler
Cleveland, Richard Jeffry
Cobb, David
Cobb, Elijah
Cobb, Jonathan Holmes
Cobb, Lyman
Cobb, Nathan Augustus
Cobb, William Henry
Cochrane, Gordon Stanley ("Mickey")
Codman, John
Coffin, Charles Fisher
Coffin, Sir Isaac
Coffin, James Henry
Coffin, John
Cogswell, Joseph Green
Colburn, Dana Pond
Colburn, Irving Wightman
Colburn, Warren

Colby, Luther
Cole, Frank Nelson
Coleman, Lyman
Coleman, William
Collins, Edward Knight
Collins, Frank Shipley
Colman, Benjamin
Colman, Henry
Colman, John
Colman, Lucy Newhall
Colt, LeBaron Bradford
Colton, Calvin
Conant, Charles Arthur
Conant, Hannah O'Brien Chaplin
Conant, Hezekiah
Conant, James Bryant
Conboy, Sara Agnes McLaughlin
Coney, John
Congdon, Charles Taber
Conly, Jabez
Converse, Charles Crozat
Converse, Edmund Cogswell
Converse, Frederick Shepherd
Conwell, Russell Herman
Cook, Clarence Chatham
Cook, Russell S.
Cook, Zebedee
Cooke, Elisha, 1637–1715
Cooke, Elisha, 1678–1737
Cooke, Josiah Parsons
Coolidge, Archibald Cary
Coolidge, Charles Allerton
Coolidge, Julian Lowell
Coolidge, Thomas Jefferson, 1831–1920
Coolidge, Thomas Jefferson, 1893–1959
Cooper, Samuel
Copley, John Singleton
Corbett, Henry Winslow
Corson, Juliet
Corthell, Elmer Lawrence
Cory, Charles Barney
Cowl, Jane
Cox, Lemuel
Coyle, Grace Longwell
Crafts, James Mason
Craigie, Andrew
Cranch, William
Crane, John
Crane, William Henry
Crane, Winthrop Murray
Craven, Frank
Creesy, Josiah Perkins
Crocker, Alvah
Crocker, Hannah Mather
Crocker, Uriel
Cross, Charles Whitman
Crowell, Luther Childs
Crowninshield, Benjamin Williams
Crowninshield, Frederic
Crowninshield, George
Crowninshield, Jacob
Cuffe, Paul
Cullis, Charles
Cummings, Charles Amos
Cummings, E. E.
Cummings, Edward
Cummings, John
Cummins, Maria Susanna
Curley, James Michael
Currier, Nathaniel
Curtis, Benjamin Robbins
Curtis, Charles Pelham
Curtis, Edwin Upton
Curtis, George
Curtis, George Ticknor
Curtis, Moses Ashley
Curwen, Samuel
Cushing, Caleb
Cushing, John Perkins
Cushing, Josiah Nelson
Cushing, Luther Stearns
Cushing, Richard James
Cushing, Thomas
Cushing, William
Cushman, Charlotte Saunders
Cushman, Joseph Augustine
Cushman, Joshua
Cushman, Susan Webb
Cutler, Charles Ammi
Cutler, Ephraim
Cutler, Robert
Cutler, Timothy
Daggett, David
Daggett, Naphtali
Dall, Caroline Wells Healey
Dall, William Healey
Dalton, John Call
Dana, Francis
Dana, James
Dana, Richard
Dana, Richard Henry, 1787–1879
Dana, Richard Henry, 1815–1882
Dane, Nathan
Danforth, Charles
Danforth, Thomas
Darby, John
Davenport, Edward Loomis
Davis, Andrew McFarland
Davis, Arthur Vining
Davis, Charles Harold
Davis, Charles Henry, 1807–1877
Davis, Charles Henry, 1845–1921
Davis, George Breckenridge
Davis, Horace
Davis, John, 1761–1847
Davis, John, 1780–1838
Davis, John Chandler Bancroft
Davis, William Thomas
Dawes, Henry Laurens
Dawes, William
Day, Arthur Louis
Day, Benjamin Henry
Day, Horace H.
Deane, Samuel
De Costa, Benjamin Franklin
De Fontaine, Felix Gregory
Delano Amassa
DeMille, Cecil Blount
Denfield, Louis Emil
Dennie, Joseph
Dennison, Henry Sturgis
Derby, Elias Hasket, 1736–1826
Derby, Elias Hasket, 1761–1799
Derby, Elias Hasket, 1803–1880
Derby, George Horatio
Derby, Richard
Devens, Charles
Dewey, Chester
Dewey, Orville
Dewing, Thomas Wilmer
Dexter, Franklin
Dexter, Franklin Bowditch
Dexter, Henry
Dexter, Henry Martyn
Dexter, Samuel, 1726–1810
Dexter, Samuel, 1761–1816
Dexter, Timothy
Diaz, Abby Morton
Dickinson, Emily Elizabeth
Dickinson, John Woodbridge
Dickinson, Jonathan
Ditson, George Leighton
Ditson, Oliver
Dix, John Homer
Dixon, Joseph
Dixon, Roland Burrage
Doane, Thomas
Doane, William Craswell
Dodge, Ebenezer
Dodge, Grenville Mellon
Dodge, Mary Abigail
Dodge, Raymond
Dodge, Theodore Ayrault
Dole, James Drummond
Dole, Nathan Haskell
Dorchester, Daniel
Douglas, Paul Howard
Douglas, William Lewis
Downer, Samuel
Downes, John
Dowse, Thomas
Drake, Samuel Adams
Draper, Eben Sumner
Draper, Ira
Draper, William Franklin
Du Bois, William Edward Burghardt
Duchin, Edward Frank ("Eddy")
Dudley, Joseph
Dudley, Paul
Duganne, Augustine Joseph Hickey
Dumaine, Frederic Christopher
Dummer, Jeremiah, 1645–1718
Dummer, Jeremiah, 1679–1739
Dunbar, Charles Franklin
Dunham, Henry Morton
Durant, Henry
Durant, Thomas Clark
Durant, William Crapo
Durfee, William Franklin
Durfee, Zobeth Sherman
Durivage, Francis Alexander
Dwight, Arthur Smith
Dwight, Edmund
Dwight, Francis
Dwight, Harrison Gray Otis
Dwight, John Sullivan
Dwight, Nathaniel
Dwight, Theodore
Dwight, Thomas
Dwight, Timothy
Dwight, William
Dyer, Nehemiah Mayo
Eagels, Jeanne
Eames, Charles
Earle, Alice Morse
Earle, James

Earle, Pliny, 1762–1832
Earle, Pliny, 1809–1892
Earle, Ralph, 1751–1801
Earle, Ralph, 1874–1939
Earle, Thomas
Eddy, Clarence
Eddy, Daniel Clarke
Eddy, Harrison Prescott
Eddy, Henry Turner
Edes, Benjamin
Edmonds, John
Edwards, Bela Bates
Edwards, Jonathan, 1745–1801
Edwards, Justin
Edwards, Oliver
Edwards, Pierpont
Eldridge, Shalor Winchell
Eliot, Charles
Eliot, Charles William
Eliot, Samuel
Eliot, Samuel Atkins
Eliot, William Greenleaf
Elliot, James
Ellis, Calvin
Ellis, George Edward
Elman, Robert
Elson, Louis Charles
Elwell, Frank Edwin
Emerson, Edward Waldo
Emerson, Mary Moody
Emerson, Ralph
Emerson, Ralph Waldo
Emerson, William
Emerton, Ephraim
Emerton, James Henry
Emmons, Ebenezer
Emmons, Samuel Franklin
Endicott, Charles Moses
Endicott, William Crowninshield
English, George Bethune
Erving, George William
Eustis, George
Eustis, Henry Lawrence
Eustis, William
Evans, Charles
Evarts, William Maxwell
Everett, Alexander Hill
Everett, David
Everett, Edward
Ewer, Ferdinand Cartwright
Fairbanks, Erastus
Fairbanks, Thaddeus
Fairchild, Blair
Fairchild, James Harris
Fairchild, Mary Salome Cutler
Fairfield, Sumner Lincoln
Fanning, Alexander Campbell Wilder
Farlow, William Gilson
Farmer, Fannie Merritt
Farmer, John
Farnham, Russel
Farnum, Franklyn
Farrar, Geraldine
Farrar, John
Faunce, William Herbert Perry
Fay, Jonas
Felt, Joseph Barlow
Felton, Cornelius Conway
Felton, Samuel Morse
Fenn, William Wallace
Fenno, John
Fenollosa, Ernest Francisco
Fewkes, Jesse Walter
Fiedler, Arthur
Field, Cyrus West
Field, Henry Martyn
Field, Marshall
Field, Stephen Dudley
Field, Walbridge Abner
Fields, Annie Adams
Filene, Edward Albert
Fisher, Alvan
Fisher, George Park
Fisher, John Dix
Fisher, Theodore Willis
Fisk, James
Fiske, Fidelia
Fiske, George Converse
Fiske, John
Fitton, James
Fitz, Henry
Fitz, Reginald Heber
Fitzgerald, John Francis
Fitzpatrick, John Bernard
Flagg, Josia
Flagg, Josiah Foster
Flagg, Thomas Wilson
Fletcher, Horace
Flint, Albert Stowell
Flint, Austin, 1812–1886
Flint, Austin, 1836–1915
Flint, Charles Louis
Flint, Timothy
Flower, Lucy Louisa Coues
Folger, Charles James
Folger, Walter
Follen, Eliza Lee Cabot
Follett, Mary Parker
Foote, Arthur William
Forbes, Esther
Forbes, Robert Bennet
Forbes, William Cameron
Forbush, Edward Howe
Ford, Daniel Sharp
Ford, George Burdett
Foster, Abiel
Foster, Abigail Kelley
Foster, Frank Hugh
Foster, Hannah Webster
Foster, John
Foster, Judith Ellen Horton
Foster, Roger Sherman Baldwin
Foster, Theodore
Foster, William Trufant
Foster, William Z.
Fowle, Daniel
Fowle, William Bentley
Fox, Charles Kemble
Fox, George Washington Lafayette
Fox, Gustavus Vasa
Fox, Harry
Francis, Charles Stephen
Francis, Convers
Francis, Joseph
Frankland, Lady Agnes Surriage
Franklin, Benjamin
Franklin, James
Fraser, Leon
Freeman, James
Freeman, Mary Eleanor Wilkins
Freeman, Nathaniel
French, Alice
French, Edwin Davis
Frieze, Henry Simmons
Frisbie, Levi
Frothingham, Arthur Lincoln
Frothingham, Nathaniel Langdon
Frothingham, Octavius Brooks
Frothingham, Paul Revere
Frothingham, Richard
Frye, Joseph
Fullam, Frank L.
Fuller, Hiram
Fuller, Sarah Margaret
Furness, William Henry
Gannett, Ezra Stiles
Gannett, William Channing
Gardiner, John
Gardner, Erle Stanley
Gardner, Henry Joseph
Gardner, John Lane
Garrison, William Lloyd
Gay, Ebenezer
Gay, Frederick Parker
Gay, Sydney Howard
Gay, Winckworth Allan
Gerry, Elbridge
Gibbs, Josiah Willard
Gibson, Charles Dana
Gifford, Robert Swain
Gifford, Walter Sherman
Gilbert, Henry Franklin Belknap
Gilbert, John Gibbs
Giles, Chauncey
Gill, John
Gillett, Frederick Huntington
Gillis, James Martin
Gilman, Arthur Delevan
Gilman, Caroline Howard
Gilman, Samuel
Gilmore, James Roberts
Gilmore, Joseph Henry
Glidden, Charles Jasper
Glover, John
Goddard, John
Goddard, Robert Hutchings
Godfrey, Benjamin
Goldthwaite, George
Goodell, William
Goodhue, Benjamin
Goodnough, Xanthus Henry
Goodrich, Chauncey, 1759–1815
Goodrich, Chauncey, 1798–1858
Goodrich, Frank Boott
Goodrich, William Marcellus
Goodridge, Sarah
Goodwin, Nathaniel Carll
Goodwin, William Watson
Gordon, George Henry
Gorham, John
Gorham, Nathaniel
Gould, Benjamin Apthorp, 1787–1859
Gould, Benjamin Apthorp, 1824–1896
Gould, Hannah Flagg
Gould, Thomas Ridgeway
Grafton, Charles Chapman
Grandgent, Charles Hall

Grant, Percy Stickney
Grant, Robert
Graves, William Phillips
Gray, Francis Calley
Gray, Horace
Gray, John Chipman
Gray, William
Greaton, John
Greely, Adolphus Washington
Green, Andrew Haswell
Green, Asa
Green, Bartholomew
Green, Francis
Green, Francis Matthews
Green, Henrietta Howland Robinson
Green, Jacob
Green, John
Green, Jonas
Green, Joseph
Green, Nathan
Green, Samuel Abbott
Green, Samuel Bowdlear
Green, Samuel Swett
Greene, Charles Ezra
Greene, Daniel Crosby
Greene, Roger Sherman
Greene, Samuel Stillman
Greenleaf, Benjamin
Greenleaf, Moses
Greenleaf, Simon
Greenleaf, Thomas
Greenough, Henry
Greenough, Horatio
Greenough, Richard Saltonstall
Greenwood, Isaac
Greenwood, John
Grew, Joseph Clark
Gridley, Jeremiah
Gridley, Richard
Griffin, Solomon Bulkley
Grimes, James Stanley
Grinnell, Frederick
Grinnell, Henry
Grinnell, Joseph
Grinnell, Moses Hicks
Grosvenor, William Mason
Guild, Curtis, 1827–1911
Guild, Curtis, 1860–1915
Guild, Reuben Aldridge
Guilford, Nathan
Guiney, Louise Imogen
Gurney, Ephraim Whitman
Guthrie, Samuel
Hackett, Horatio Balch
Hadley, Henry Kimball
Hague, Arnold
Hague, James Duncan
Hale, Benjamin
Hale, Charles
Hale, Edward Everett
Hale, Enoch
Hale, Lucretia Peabody
Hale, Nathan
Hale, Philip Leslie
Haley, Jack
Hall, Arethusa
Hall, Florence Marion Howe
Hall, Granville Stanley
Hall, James
Hall, Samuel, 1740–1807
Hall, Samuel, 1800–1870
Hall, Willard
Hallett, Benjamin
Hallett, Benjamin Franklin
Hallock, Gerard
Hallock, William Allen
Halsey, John
Hamblin, Joseph Eldridge
Hamlin, Charles Sumner
Hammond, George Henry
Hammond, Jabez Delano
Hammond, James Bartlett
Hanaford, Phoebe Ann Coffin
Hancock, John
Hancock, Thomas
Hapgood, Isabel Florence
Haraden, Jonathan
Harahan, James Theodore
Harding, Chester
Harding, Seth
Hardy, Arthur Sherburne
Harkness, Albert
Harnden, William Frederick
Harrington, Charles
Harrington, Thomas Francis
Harris, Thaddeus Mason
Harris, Thaddeus William
Harris, William
Hart, John Seely
Hasket, Elias
Hassam, Frederick Childe
Hastings, Samuel Dexter
Haven, Erastus Otis
Haven, Gilbert
Haven, Joseph
Hawes, Harriet Ann Boyd
Hawley, Joseph
Hawthorne, Julian
Hawthorne, Nathaniel
Hayden, Charles
Hayden, Charles Henry
Hayden, Edward Everett
Hayden, Ferdinand Vaudiveer
Hayden, Hiram Washington
Hayden, Joseph Shepard
Haynes, John Henry
Hayward, George
Hayward, Nathaniel Manley
Hazeltine, Mayo Williamson
Hazen, Moses
Healy, George Peter Alexander
Heard, Augustine
Heard, Dwight Bancroft
Heard, Franklin Fiske
Heath, William
Hedge, Frederic Henry
Hedge, Levi
Henchman, Daniel
Henderson, Lawrence Joseph
Henry, Caleb Sprague
Henshaw, David
Henshaw, Henry Wetherbee
Hentz, Caroline Lee Whiting
Hepworth, George Hughes
Herne, Chrystal Katharine
Herrick, Robert Welch
Herschel, Clemens
Hersey, Evelyn Weeks
Hewes, Robert
Heywood, Ezra Hervey
Heywood, Levi
Hiacoomes
Hichborn, Philip
Higginson, Stephen
Higginson, Thomas Wentworth
Hildreth, Richard
Hildreth, Samuel Prescott
Hill, Frederic Stanhope
Hill, George Handel
Hill, Henry Barker
Hill, Isaac
Hilliard, Francis
Hitchcock, Charles Henry
Hitchcock, Edward, 1793–1864
Hitchcock, Edward, 1828–1911
Hitchcock, Enos
Hitchcock, James Ripley Wellman
Hoar, Ebenezer Rockwood
Hoar, George Frisbie
Hoar, Samuel
Hobbs, Alfred Charles
Hodges, Harry Foote
Holden, Oliver
Holder, Charles Frederick
Holder, Joseph Bassett
Holland, Clifford Milburn
Holland, Josiah Gilbert
Holmes, Ezekiel
Holmes, John
Holmes, Mary Jane Hawes
Holmes, Oliver Wendell, 1809–1894
Holmes, Oliver Wendell, 1841–1935
Holt, Edwin Bissell
Holten, Samuel
Holyoke, Edward Augustus
Holyoke, Samuel
Homer, Arthur Bartlett
Homer, Winslow
Homes, Henry Augustus
Hooker, Joseph
Hooker, Philip
Hooker, Worthington
Hooper, Samuel
Hooper, William
Hopkins, Edward Washburn
Hopkins, Mark
Horr, George Edwin
Hosmer, Frederick Lucian
Hosmer, Harriet Goodhue
Hosmer, James Kendall
Houghton, Alanson Bigelow
Houghton, George Hendric
House, Edward Howard
Hovey, Charles Mason
Howard, Henry
Howe, Andrew Jackson
Howe, Elias
Howe, Frederick Webster
Howe, George
Howe, Henry Marion
Howe, Mark De Wolfe
Howe, Quincy
Howe, Samuel
Howe, Samuel Gridley
Howe, William
Howe, William F.
Hubbard, Gardiner Greene

Hudson, Charles
Hudson, Daniel Eldred
Hudson, Frederic
Hull, Josephine
Hummel, Abraham Henry
Hunnewell, Horatio Hollis
Hunnewell, James
Hunt, Alfred Ephraim
Hunt, Freeman
Hunt, Harriot Kezia
Hunt, William Gibbes
Huntington, Elisha
Huntington, Frederic Dan
Huntington, William Reed
Hurd, John Codman
Hurd, Nathaniel
Huse, Caleb
Hutchinson, Beniamin Peters
Hutchinson, Charles Lawrence
Hutchinson, Thomas
Hyde, William DeWitt
Ingalls, John James
Ingraham, Joseph
Inman, George
Ireland, Charles Thomas, Jr. ("Chick")
Jackson, Charles
Jackson, Charles Thomas
Jackson, Dunham
Jackson, Helen Maria Fiske Hunt
Jackson, James, 1777–1867
Jackson, Mercy Ruggles Bisbe
Jackson, Patrick Tracy
Jackson, William
Jameson, John Franklin
Jarves, Deming
Jarves, James Jackson
Jarvis, Edwar
Jarvis, William
Jefferson, Mark Sylvester William
Jeffries, Benjamin Joy
Jeffries, John
Jenkins, Edward Hopkins
Jenkins, Nathaniel
Jenks, William
Jenney, William Le Baron
Johnson, Allen
Johnson, Ellen Cheney
Johnson, George Francis
Johnson, Howard Deering
Johnson, Joseph French
Johnson, Samuel
Johnston, Thomas
Jones, Abner
Jones, Anson
Jones, Calvin
Jones, Joseph Stevens
Jones, Leonard Augustus
Jordan, Eben Dyer
Judd, Sylvester
Judge, Thomas Augustine
Judson, Adoniram
Judson, Ann Hasseltine
Kalmus, Herbert Thomas
Kehew, Mary Morton Kimball
Kellett, William Wallace
Kelley, Oliver Hudson
Kemp, Robert H.
Kendall, Amos
Kendrick, John
Kennedy, John Fitzgerald
Kennedy, Joseph Patrick
Kennedy, Robert Francis
Kenrick, William
Kerouac, Jack
Kettell, Samuel
Keyes, Erasmus Darwin
Kilby, Christopher
Kimball, (Sidney) Fiske
King, Edward Leonard
King, Edward Smith
King, Jonas
King, Thomas Butter
Kinnicutt, Leonard Parker
Kittredge, George Lyman
Knapp, Philip Coombs
Knapps Samuel Lorenzo
Kneeland, Abner
Kneeland, Samuel, 1697–1769
Kneeland, Samuel, 1821–1888
Kneeland, Stillman Foster
Knight, Austin Melvin
Knight, Frederick Irving
Knight, Henry Cogswell
Knight, Sarah Kemble
Knowles, Lucius James
Knowlton, Charles
Knowlton, Marcus Perrin
Knowlton, Thomas
Knox, Frank
Knox, Henry
Lahey, Frank Howard
Lamb, Arthur Becket
Lamb, Martha Joanna Reade Nash
Lander, Edward
Lander, Frederick West
Lane, George Martin
Lang, Benjamin Johnson
Langdon, Samuel
Langer, William Leonard
Langley, John Williams
Langley, Samuel Pierpont
Larcom, Lucy
Larkin, Thomas Oliver
Lathrop, John
Lawrance, Charles Lanier
Lawrence, Abbott
Lawrence, Amos
Lawrence, Amos Adams
Lawrence, William, 1783–1848
Lawrence, William, 1819–1899
Lawrence, William, 1850–1941
Lawson, Thomas William
Leach, Abby
Leach, Daniel Dyer
Leach, Shepherd
Learned, Ebenezer
Leavitt, Erasmus Darwin
Leavitt, Henrietta Swan
Leavitt, Joshua
Lee, Alfred
Lee, Hannah Farnham Sawyer
Lee, Henry, 1782–1867
Lee, Joseph
Leland, George Adams
Leland, John
Leland, Waldo Gifford
Le Moyne, William J.
Leonard, Charles Lester
Leonard, Daniel
Leonard, George
Leonard, Levi Washburn
Leverett, John, 1662–1724
Lewis, Clarence Irving
Lewis, Gilbert Newton
Lewis, Orlando Faulkland
Lewis, Samuel
Lewis, Winslow
Libbey, Edward Drummond
Lincoln, Benjamin
Lincoln, Enoch
Lincoln, John Larkin
Lincoln, Joseph Crosby
Lincoln, Levi, 1749–1820
Lincoln, Levi, 1782–1868
Lincoln, Mary Johnson Bailey
Lincoln, Rufus Pratt
Lindsey, William
Litchfield, Paul Weeks
Little, Arthur Dehon
Little, George
Livermore, George
Livermore, Mary Ashton Rice
Livermore, Samuel, 1732–1803
Locke, Bessie
Lodge, George Cabot
Lodge, Henry Cabot
Lodge, John Ellerton
Logan, Cornelius Ambrose
Lombard, Warren Plimpton
Longfellow, Ernest Wadsworth
Lord, Otis Phillips
Loring, Charles Harding
Loring, Edward Greely
Loring, Ellis Gray
Loring, Frederick Wadsworth
Loring, George Bailey
Loring, Joshua, 1716–1781
Loring, Joshua, 1744–1789
Lothrop, Alice Louise Higgins
Lothrop, George Van Ness
Lovejoy, Asa Lawrence
Loveland, William Austin Hamilton
Lovell, James
Lovell, John
Lovell, Joseph
Lovering, Joseph
Lovett, Robert Morss
Lovett, Robert Williamson
Low, Abiel Abbot
Low, John Gardner
Lowell, Abbott Lawrence
Lowell, Amy
Lowell, Edward Jackson
Lowell, Francis Cabot
Lowell, Guy
Lowell, James Russell
Lowell, John, 1743–1802
Lowell, John, 1769–1840
Lowell, John, 1799–1836
Lowell, John, 1824–1897
Lowell, Josephine Shaw
Lowell, Percival
Lowell, Ralph
Lowell, Robert Traill Spence
Lowell, Robert Traill Spence, Jr.
Lubin, Isador
Lucas, Frederic Augustus
Lummis, Charles Fletcher

Lunt, George
Lyman, Benjamin Smith
Lyman, Eugene William
Lyman, Joseph Bardwell
Lyman, Theodore, 1792–1849
Lyman, Theodore, 1833–1897
Lyman, Theodore, 1874–1954
Lynde, Benjamin
Lyon, Mary
MacArthur, Arthur
McBurney, Charles
McCarren, Patrick Henry
McCarthy, Charles
McCawley, Charles Laurie
McClure, Alexander Wilson
McCormack, John William
McElwain, William Howe
McIntire, Samuel
McIntyre, Alfred Robert
Mack, Connie
McKay, Gordon
McKenzie, Alexander
MacNeil, Hermon Atkins
McNeill, Daniel
McNeill, George Edwin
McNulty, John Augustine
Macomber, Mary Lizzie
Macy, Josiah
Maier, Walter Arthur
Main, Charles Thomas
Manley, John
Mann, Horace
Mann, James
Mann, Mary Tyler Peabody
Mann, Newton
Manning, Robert
Maranville, Walter James Vincent ("Rabbit")
Marble, Manton Malone
March, Alden
March, Francis Andrew
Marchant, Henry
Marciano, Rocky
Marcy, Henry Orlando
Marcy, Randolph Barnes
Marcy, William Learned
Marsh, John
Marshall, Charles Henry
Marshall, James Fowle Baldwin
Martin, Joseph William, Jr.
Mason, Daniel Gregory
Mason, Frank Stuart
Mason, Henry
Mason, Jonathan
Mason, Lowell
Mason, William
Massassoit
Masury, John Wesley
Mather, Cotton
Mather, Increase
Mather, Samuel
Matthews, Nathan
Maxcy, Jonathan
Maxcy, Virgil
May, Samuel Joseph
Mayhew, Experience
Mayhew, Jonathan
Maynard, Charles Johnson
Mayo, Frank
Mayo, Sarah Carter Edgarton
Mead, George Herbert
Mears, David Otis
Mecom, Benjamin
Melcher, Frederic Gershom
Mellen, Charles Sanger
Mellen, Prentiss
Merriam, Charles
Merrick, Edwin Thomas
Merrick, Frederick
Merrick, Pliny
Merrill, Daniel
Merrill, Elmer Truesdell
Merrill, Frank Dow
Merrill, George Edwards
Merrill, Gretchen Van Zandt
Merrill, James Cushing
Merrill, James Griswold
Merrill, Joshua
Meserve, Frederick Hill
Messer, Asa
Metcalf, Theron
Metcalf, Willard Leroy
Meyer, George Von Lengerke
Miles, Henry Adolphus
Miles, Nelson Appleton
Miller, Kempster Blanchard
Miller, William
Miller, William Snow
Millett, Fred Benjamin
Mills, Elijah Hunt
Minot, Charles Sedgwick
Minot, George Richards, 1758–1802
Minot, George Richards, 1885–1950
Mitchell, Albert Graeme
Mitchell, Edward Cushing
Mitchell, Henry
Mitchell, Maria
Mitchell, Nahum
Mitchell, William, 1791–1869
Mixter, Samuel Jason
Montague, Gilbert Holland
Montague, William Pepperell
Moody, Dwight Lyman
Moody, Paul
Moody, William Henry
Moore, Clifford Herschel
Moore, Zephaniah Swift
Moorehead, Agnes
Morgan, Edwin Denison
Morgan, James Dada
Morgan, Junius Spencer
Morgan, Justin
Morison, George Shattuck
Morison, Samuel Eliot
Morris, Robert, 1818–1888
Morse, Henry Dutton
Morse, John Lovett
Morse, John Torrey
Morse, Samuel Finley Breese
Morse, Sidney Edwards
Morton, Marcus, 1784–1864
Morton, Marcus, 1819–1891
Morton, Sarah Wentworth Apthorp
Morton, William James
Morton, William Thomas Green
Moseley, Edward Augustus
Mosely, Philip Edward
Motley, John Lothrop
Mott, Lucretia Coffin
Mudge, Enoch
Mudge, James
Mulliken, Samuel Parsons
Munn, Orson Desaix
Munroe, Charles Edward
Munsell, Joel
Murdoch, Frank Hitchcock
Murphy, Gerald Clery
Murphy, Michael Charles
Murray, Judith Sargent Stevens
Muzzey, David Saville
Myrick, Herbert
Nash, Charles Sumner
Nash, Daniel
Nash, Simeon
Nason, Elias
Nason, Henry Bradford
Neagle, John
Neal, David Dalhoff
Nell, William Cooper
Newell, William Wells
Newman, Henry
Newman, Samuel Phillips
Nichols, Charles Lemuel
Nichols, James Robinson
Nicholson, James William Augustus
Niles, David K.
Nixon, John, 1727–1815
Northend, Charles
Norton, Andrews
Norton, Charles Eliot
Norton, Mary Alice Peloubet
Norton, William Edward
Noyes, Arthur Amos
Noyes, Edward Follansbee
Noyes, George Rapall
Nutting, Wallace
Oakes, Thomas Fletcher
Ober, Frederick Albion
O'Brien, Robert Lincoln
O'Callahan, Joseph Timothy
O'Connell, William Henry
O'Connor, William Douglas
O'Donnell, Kenneth Patrick
O'Gorman, Thomas
Oliver, Andrew, 1706–1774
Oliver, Andrew, 1731–1799
Oliver, Fitch Edward
Oliver, Henry Kemble
Oliver, Peter
Olney, Richard
O'Mahoney, Joseph Christopher
Orne, John
Osborn, William Henry
Osgood, Frances Sargent Locke
Osgood, George Laurie
Osgood, Samuel
Osgood, William Fogg
Otis, Bass
Otis, George Alexander
Otis, Harrison Gray
Otis, James
Ouimet, Francis Desales
Packard, Alpheus Spring
Packard, Frederick Adolphus
Packard, Silas Sadler
Page, Charles Grafton

Paine, Albert Bigelow
Paine, Charles Jackson
Paine, Robert Treat, 1731–1814
Paine, Robert Treat, 1773–1811
Paine, Robert Treat, 1835–1910
Paley, Barbara Cushing ("Babe")
Palfrey, John Carver
Palfrey, John Gorham
Palmer, George Herbert
Palmer, Walter Walker
Park, Maud Wood
Parker, Edward Pickering
Parker, Henry Taylor
Parker, Horatio William
Parker, Isaac
Parker, James Cutler Dunn
Parker, John
Parker, Peter
Parker, Richard Green
Parker, Samuel
Parker, Theodore
Parker, Theodore Bissell
Parkhurst, Charles Henry
Parkman, Francis
Parsons, Theophilus, 1750–1813
Parsons, Theophilus, 1797–1882
Parsons, Thomas William
Patten, William
Pattison, James William
Paul, Elliot Harold
Paul, Henry Martyn
Payne, Henry Clay
Payne, William Morton
Payson, Seth
Peabody, Andrew Preston
Peabody, Elizabeth Palmer
Peabody, Endicott
Peabody, Francis Greenwood
Peabody, George
Peabody, Joseph
Peabody, Nathaniel
Peabody, Robert Swain
Pearce, Charles Sprague
Pearson, Edmund Lester
Pearson, Eliphalet
Pearson, Fred Stark
Peck, George Washington
Peck, William Dandridge
Peirce, Benjamin
Peirce, Benjamin Osgood
Peirce, Charles Sanders
Peirce, Cyrus
Peirce, Henry Augustus
Peirce, James Mills
Pelham, Henry
Percival, John
Perkins, Charles Callahan
Perkins, Frances
Perkins, George Henry
Perkins, Jacob
Perkins, James Handasyd, 1810–1849
Perkins, James Handasyd, 1876–1940
Perkins, Justin
Perkins, Thomas Handasyd
Perkins, Thomas Nelson
Perley, Ira
Perry, Bliss
Perry, Edward Aylesworth
Perry, Edward Baxter
Perry, Enoch Wood
Perry, Nora
Perry, Walter Scott
Perry, William
Peters, Edward Dyer
Phelps, Austin
Phillips, John
Phillips, Samuel
Phillips, Walter Polk
Phillips, Wendell
Phillips, Willard
Phillips, William, 1750/51–1827
Phillips, William, 1824–1893
Phillips, William Addison
Pickard, Samuel Thomas
Pickering, Edward Charles
Pickering, John
Pickering, Timothy
Pidgin, Charles Felton
Pierce, Benjamin
Pierce, Edward Lillie
Pierce, Henry Lillie
Pierpont, James
Pierson, Abraham
Pike, Albert
Pillsbury, Harry Nelson
Pillsbury, John Elliott
Pillsbury, Parker
Pinkham, Lydia Estes
Plath, Sylvia
Plimpton, George Arthur
Plumer, William
Plummer, Jonathan
Poe, Edgar Allan
Pomeroy, Samuel Clarke
Pomeroy, Seth
Pond, Enoch
Pond, George Edward
Pool, Maria Louise
Poole, Fitch
Poole, William Frederick
Poor, Charles Henry
Poor, Daniel
Poor, Enoch
Poore, Benjamin Perley
Pope, Albert Augustus
Pope, Franklin Leonard
Porter, Benjamin Curtis
Porter, David
Porter, Rufus
Potter, Charles Francis
Potter, William James
Pratt, Charles
Pratt, Daniel, 1809–1887
Pratt, Enoch
Pratt, Thomas Willis
Pray, Isaac Clark
Prendergast, Maurice Brazil
Prentice, George Dennison
Presbrey, Eugene Wiley
Prescott, Oliver
Prescott, Samuel
Prescott, William
Prescott, William Hickling
Preston, Harriet Waters
Priest, Edward Dwight
Prince, Frederick Henry
Prince, Morton
Prince, Thomas
Proctor, Joseph
Prouty, Olive Higgins
Putnam, Charles Pickering
Putnam, Eben
Putnam, Frederic Ward
Putnam, Gideon
Putnam, Israel
Putnam, James Jackson
Putnam, Rufus
Quincy, Edmund
Quincy, Josiah, 1744–1775
Quincy, Josiah, 1772–1864
Quincy, Josiah Phillips
Rand, Addison Crittenden
Rand, Edward Kennard
Rand, Edward Sprague
Randall, Samuel
Ranney, Ambrose Loomis
Ranney, Rufus Percival
Rantoul, Robert, 1778–1858
Rantoul, Robert, 1805–1852
Ray, Charles Bennett
Ray, Isaac
Read, Daniel, 1757–1836
Read, Nathan
Reed, David
Reed, James, 1722–1807
Reed, James, 1834–1921
Reed, Sampson
Reed, Simeon Gannett
Reid, Robert
Remond, Charles Lenox
Revere, Joseph Warren
Revere, Paul
Revson, Charles Haskell
Rhoads, Cornelius Packard
Rice, Alexander Hamilton
Rice, Calvin Winsor
Rice, Charles Allen Thorndike
Rice, Luther
Rice, William Marsh
Rice, William North
Rich, Isaac
Rich, Obadiah
Richards, Ellen Henrietta Swallow
Richards, Laura Elizabeth Howe
Richards, William
Richards, Zalmon
Richardson, Albert Deane
Richardson, Maurice Howe
Richardson, Rufus Byam
Richardson, Willard
Richardson, William Adams
Richardson, William Lambert
Richmond, John Lambert
Ricketson, Daniel
Riddell, John Leonard
Riddle, Albert Gallatin
Riddle, George Peabody
Rindge, Frederick Hastings
Ripley, Edward Payson
Ripley, Ezra
Ripley, George
Ripley, William Zebina
Robbins, Chandler
Robinson, Charles
Robinson, Edward, 1858–1931
Robinson, Ezekiel Gilman
Robinson, Harriet Jane Hanson
Robinson, Henry Morton

Robinson, Moses
Robinson, William Stevens
Roche, Arthur Somers
Rockwell, Willard Frederick
Rodgers, John, 1727–1811
Rogers, Edward Staniford
Rogers, Harriet Burbank
Rogers, Henry Huttleston
Rogers, Isaiah
Rogers, John, 1829–1904
Rogers, Mary Josephine
Rogers, Robert
Rozers, William Crowninshield
Rolfe, William James
Rollins, Alice Marland Wellington
Root, Elisha King
Root, Frederic Woodman
Root, George Frederick
Root, Joseph Pomeroy
Ropes, James Hardy
Ropes, Joseph
Ross, Abel Hastings
Rossiter, William Sidney
Rotch, Abbott Lawrence
Rotch, Arthur
Rotch, William
Roth, Lillian
Roulstone, George
Rugg, Arthur Prentice
Rugg, Harold Ordway
Ruggles, Timothy
Russ, John Dennison
Russell, Benjamin
Russell, Joseph
Russell, William Eustis
Rust, Richard Sutton
Ruter, Martin
Ryder, Albert Pinkham
Sabin, Charles Hamilton
Salisbury, Edward Elbridge
Saltonstall, Gurdon
Saltonstall, Leverett
Samuels, Edward Augustus
Sanders, Daniel Clarke
Sanders, Elizabeth Elkins
Sanders, Thomas
Sanger, Charles Robert
Sanger, George Partridge
Sargent, Aaron Augustus
Sargent, Charles Sprague
Sargent, Epes
Sargent, Fitzwilliam
Sargent, Henry
Sargent, Henry Winthrop
Sargent, John Osborne
Sargent, Lucius Manlius
Sargent, Winthrop, 1753–1820
Sartwell, Henry Parker
Savage, Edward
Savage, James
Savage, Philip Henry
Saville, Marshall Howard
Sawyer, Sylvanus
Scammell, Alexander
Schofield, Henry
Schouler, James
Scudder, Horace Elisha
Scudder, Samuel Hubbard
Sears, Barnas
Sears, Edmund Hamilton
Sears, Isaac
Sears, Richard Dudley
Seccomb, John
Sedgwick, Catharine Maria
Sedgwick, Theodore, 1780–1839
Selfridge, Thomas Oliver
Severance, Frank Hayward
Sewall, Jonathan
Sewall, Jonathan Mitchell
Sexton, Anne Gray Harvey
Shattuck, Frederick Cheever
Shattuck, George Brune
Shattuck, George Cheyne, 1783–1854
Shattuck, George Cheyne, 1813–1893
Shattuck, Lemuel
Shaw, Henry Wheeler
Shaw, Lemuel
Shaw, Mary
Shaw, Oliver
Shaw, Samuel
Shaw, William Smith
Shays, Daniel
Shedd, Joel Herbert
Shedd, William Greenough Thayer
Shepard, William
Shepley, Ether
Sherman, Roger
Short, Charles
Shurtleff, Nathaniel Bradstreet
Sibley, George Champlain
Sibley, Hiram
Sibley, John
Silsbee, Nathaniel
Simkhovitch, Mary Melinda Kingsbury
Simmons, Edward
Simonds, Frank Herbert
Simpson, Michael Hodge
Sinnott, Edmund Ware
Sizer, Nelson
Skinner, Aaron Nichols
Skinner, Otis
Smalley, George Washburn
Smith, Cale Blood
Smith, Charles Sprague
Smith, Edward Hanson
Smith, Geral Birney
Smith, Harold Babbitt
Smith, Horace
Smith, Horatio Elwin
Smith, John Cotton, 1826–1882
Smith, John Rowson
Smith, Jonas Waldo
Smith, Joseph, 1790–1877
Smith, Judson
Smith, Nathan, 1762–1829
Smith, Oliver
Smith, Samuel Francis
Smith, Sophia
Snelling, Josiah
Snelling, William Joseph
Snow, Eliza Roxey
Snow, Francis Huntington
Snow, Jessie Baker
Soley, James Russell
Southard, Elmer Ernest
Sparrow, William
Spear, Charles
Spellman, Francis Joseph
Spencer, Anna Garlin
Sperry, Willard Learoyd
Spooner, Lysander
Spottswood, Stephen Gill
Sprague, Charles
Sprague, Homer Baxter
Sprague, Oliver Mitchell Wentworth
Sprague, Peleg
Spring, Gardiner
Spring, Samuel
Spurr, Josiah Edward
Stanley, Harold
Starr, Eliza Allen
Stearns, Abel
Stearns, Asahel
Stearns, Eben Sperry
Stearns, Frank Waterman
Stearns, George Luther
Stearns, Harold Edmund
Stearns, Henry Putnam
Stearns, Oliver
Stearns, Robert Edwards Carter
Stearns, Shubal
Stearns, William Augustus
Stebbins, Horatio
Stebbins, Rufus Phineas
Stetson, Charles Augustus
Stetson, Henry Crosby
Stevens, Isaac Ingalls
Stimpson, William
Stimson, Alexander Lovett
Stimson, Frederic Jesup
Stimson, Julia Catherine
Stockbridge, Henry Smith
Stockbridge, Horace Edward
Stockbridge, Levi
Stockwell, John Nelson
Stoddard, David Tappan
Stoddard, Elizabeth Drew Barstow
Stoddard, John Lawson
Stoddard, John Tappan
Stoddard, Richard Henry
Stoddard, Solomon
Stoddard, Theodore Lothrop
Stone, Amasa
Stone, Charles Augustus
Stone, Charles Pomeroy
Stone, Ellen Maria
Stone, James Kent
Stone, John Augustus
Stone, John Seely
Stone, Lucy
Storer, Francis Humphreys
Storer, Horatio Robinson
Storey, Moorfield
Storrow, James Jackson
Storrs, Richard Salter, 1787–1873
Storrs, Richard Salter, 1821–1900
Story, Isaac
Story, Joseph
Story, William Edward
Story, William Wetmore
Stowe, Calvin Ellis
Strong, Caleb
Strong, Charles Augustus
Strong, Theodore
Sturgis, William
Sturtevant, Edward Lewis

Sullivan, John Lawrence
Sullivan, Louis Henri
Sumner, Charles
Sumner, Edwin Vose
Sumner, Increase
Sumner, James Batcheller
Swan, Timothy
Swift, Gustavus Franklin
Swift, Joseph Gardner
Swift, Louis Franklin
Swift, William Henry
Swift, Zephaniah
Switzer, Mary Elizabeth
Sylvester, Frederick Oakes
Talbot, Henry Paul
Talbot, Israel Tisdale
Talbot, Silas
Tappan, Arthur
Tappan, Benjamin
Tappan, Lewis
Tarbell, Edmund Charles
Tarbell, Frank Bigelow
Tarbell, Joseph
Tarr, Ralph Stockman
Taylor, Bert Leston
Taylor, Charles Alonzo
Taylor, Charles Henry
Taylor, William Ladd
Tenney, Charles Daniel
Thacher, George
Thacher, James
Thacher, Peter, 1651–1727
Thacher, Peter, 1752–1802
Thacher, Samuel Cooper
Thaxter, Roland
Thayer, Abbott Handerson
Thayer, Alexander Wheelock
Thayer, Eli
Thayer, Ezra Ripley
Thayer, Gideon French
Thayer, James Bradley
Thayer, John
Thayer, John Milton
Thayer, Joseph Henry
Thayer, Nathaniel
Thayer, Sylvanus
Thayer, Thomas Baldwin
Thayer, Whitney Eugene
Thayer, William Makepeace
Thayer, William Roscoe
Thayer, William Sydney
Thomas, David
Thomas, Isaiah
Thomas, John
Thompson, Benjamin
Thompson, Cephas Giovanni
Thompson, Daniel Pierce
Thompson, Edward Herbert
Thompson, Jerome B.
Thompson, John
Thompson, William Hale
Thoreau, Henry David
Thorndike, Edward Lee
Thorndike, Israel
Thorndike, Lynn
Thorp, John
Thorpe, Thomas Bangs
Thurber, Charles
Thwaites, Reuben Gold
Ticknor, George
Tileston, Thomas
Tingley, Katherine Augusta Westcott
Tinkham, George Holden
Tobey, Charles William
Tobey, Edward Silas
Tobin, Maurice Joseph
Todd, Mabel Loomis
Tolman, Edward Chace
Tolman, Herbert Cushing
Tolman, Richard Chace
Tondorf, Francis Anthony
Topliff, Samuel
Torrey, Bradford
Torrey, Charles Turner
Tower, Zealous Bates
Townsend, Edward Davis
Tracy, Nathaniel
Train, Arthur Cheney
Train, Enoch
Train, George Francis
Traynor, Harold Joseph ("Pie")
Treadwell, Daniel
Trott, Benjamin
Trow, John Fowler
Trowbridge, Edmund
Trowbridge, John
Tucker, Benjamin Ricketson
Tucker, Samuel
Tuckerman, Edward
Tuckerman, Frederick
Tuckerman, Frederick Goddard
Tuckerman, Henry Theodore
Tuckerman, Joseph
Tudor, Frederic
Tudor, William
Tufts, Charles
Tufts, Cotton
Tufts, James Hayden
Tufts, John
Tupper, Benjamin
Turell, Jane
Turner, Asa
Turner, Jonathan Baldwin
Tyler, Ransom Hubert
Tyler, Royall, 1757–1826
Tyler, Royall, 1884–1953
Tyler, William Seymour
Tyng, Edward
Tyng, Stephen Higginson
Underwood, Francis Henry
Underwood, Loring
Upham, Samuel Foster
Upton, George Putnam
Upton, Winslow
Vaillant, George Clapp
Valentine, Robert Grosvenor
Van Brunt, Henry
Varnum, James Mitchell
Varnum, Joseph Bradley
Very, Jones
Very, Lydia Louisa Ann
Villard, Helen Frances Garrison
Vinton, Frederic
Vinton, Samuel Finley
Wade, Benjamin Franklin
Wadsworth, Eliot
Wadsworth, Peleg
Wainwright, Richard, 1817–1862
Walcot, Charles Melton, 1840–1921
Walcott, Henry Pickering
Waldo, Samuel
Walker, Francis Amasa
Walker, Henry Oliver
Walker, Sears Cook
Walker, Timothy, 1705–1782
Walker, Timothy, 1802–1856
Walker, William Johnson
Wallace, John Findley
Walsh, David Ignatius
Walsh, Edmund Aloysius
Walsh, James Anthony
Walter, Thomas, 1696–1725
Ward, Artemas
Ward, Charles Henshaw
Ward, Elizabeth Stuart Phelps
Ward, Frederick Townsend
Ward, Henry Dana
Ward, Herbert Dickinson
Ward, Robert De Courcy
Ward, Thomas Wren
Ward, William Hayes
Ware, Ashur
Ware, Edmund Asa
Ware, Henry, 1764–1845
Ware, Henry, 1794–1843
Ware, John
Ware, John Fothergill Waterhouse
Ware, William
Ware, William Robert
Warner, Charles Dudley
Warner, Hiram
Warner, Langdon
Warner, Worcester Reed
Warren, Charles
Warren, Cyrus Moors
Warren, Francis Emroy
Warren, Henry Clarke
Warren, Henry Ellis
Warren, Henry White
Warren, James
Warren, John
Warren, John Collins, 1778–1856
Warren, John Collins, 1842–1927
Warren, Joseph
Warren, Josiah
Warren, Mercy Otis
Warren, Shields
Warren, William Fairfield
Washburn, Albert Henry
Washburn, Charles Grenfill
Washburn, Edward Abiel
Washburn, Emory
Washburn, George
Washburn, Ichabod
Waters, Daniel
Watson, Elkanah
Watson, Thomas Augustus
Watson, William
Wayland, Francis, 1826–1904
Webb, Thomas Smith
Webster, Arthur Gordon
Webster, Edwin Sibley
Webster, John White
Webster, Noah
Weeks, Edwin Lord
Weeks, Joseph Dame
Weeks, Sinclair

Weiss, John
Weld, Arthur Cyril Gordon
Wellington, Arthur Mellen
Wellman, Samuel Thomas
Wellman, William Augustus
Wells, David Ames
Wells, William Vincent
Wendell, Barrett
Wendte, Charles William
Wesson, Daniel Baird
West, Benjamin
West, Samuel
Wheeler, Benjamin Ide
Wheeler, Burton Kendall
Wheeler, George Montague
Wheeler, William
Wheeler, William Adolphus
Wheelwright, Edmund March
Wheelwright, Mary Cabot
Wheelwright, William
Whipple, Amiel Weeks
Whipple, Edwin Percy
Whipple, Squire
Whistler, James Abbott McNeill
Whitaker, Daniel Kimball
White, Charles Abiathar
White, Leonard Dupee
White, Paul Dudley
Whiting, Arthur Battelle
Whiting, George Elbridge
Whiting, William
Whiting, William Henry Chase
Whitman, Ezekiel
Whitmore, Frank Clifford
Whitmore, William Henry
Whitney, Anne
Whitney, Asa
Whitney, Caspar
Whitney, Eli
Whitney, George
Whitney, James Lyman
Whitney, Josiah Dwight
Whitney, Mary Watson
Whitney, Myron William
Whitney, Richard
Whitney, William Collins
Whitney, William Dwight
Whiton, James Morris
Whittemore, Amos
Whittemore, Thomas, 1800–1861
Whittemore, Thomas, 1871–1950
Whittier, John Greenleaf
Whorf, Benjamin Lee
Wiggin, Albert Henry
Wiggin, James Henry
Wigglesworth, Edward, 1693–1765
Wigglesworth, Edward, 1732–1794
Wigglesworth, Edward, 1840–1896
Wilbur, Hervey Backus
Wilde, George Francis Faxon
Wiley, Ephraim Emerson
Willard, Joseph
Willard, Samuel, 1639/40–1707
Willard, Samuel, 1775–1859
Willard, Sidney
Willard, Simon
Willard, Solomon
Williams, Elisha
Williams, Ephraim
Williams, Francis Henry
Williams, Henry Willard
Williams, Israel
Williams, John, 1664–1729
Williams, John, 1817–1899
Williams, John Foster
Williams, John Joseph
Williams, Jonathan
Williams, Nathaniel
Williams, Stephen West
Williams, William
Willis, Nathaniel
Willis, William
Williston, Samuel, 1795–1874
Williston, Samuel, 1861–1963
Williston, Samuel Wendell
Wilmarth, Lemuel Everett
Wilson, George Francis
Wilson, Samuel
Winchester, Elhanan
Winchester, Oliver Fisher
Wingate, Paine
Winship, Albert Edward
Winship, George Parker
Winslow, Charles-Edward Amory
Winslow, Edward
Winslow, John
Winslow, Josiah
Winslow, Sidney Wilmot
Winslow, William Copley
Winsor, Justin
Winter, William
Winthrop, James
Winthrop, John, 1638–1707
Winthrop, John, 1714–1779
Winthrop, Robert Charles
Wise, John
Wolcott, Edward Oliver
Wood, Edward Stickney
Wood, Jethro
Woodberry, George Edward
Woodbridge, Samuel Merrill
Woodbridge, William Channing
Woodbury, Charles Jeptha Hill
Woodbury, Isaac Baker
Woods, James Haughton
Woods, Leonard, 1774–1854
Woods, Leonard, 1807–1878
Woodward, Calvin Milton
Woodward, Robert Burns
Woodworth, Samuel
Worcester, Samuel Austin
Workman, Fanny Bullock
Worthen, William Ezra
Worthington, John
Wright, Chauncey
Wright, John Joseph
Wright, John Stephen
Wright, Philip Green
Wright, Silas
Wyeth, John
Wyeth, Newell Convers
Wylie, Philip Gordon
Wyman, Horace
Wyman, Jeffries
Wyman, Morrill
Yale, Elihu
Yeomans, John William
Young, Alexander

MICHIGAN

Ament, William Scott
Anthon, John
Atkinson, George Francis
Atterbury, Grosvenor
Avery, Sewell Lee
Bachmann, Werner Emmanuel
Bacon, Leonard
Bagley, William Chandler
Bailey, James Anthony
Bailey, Liberty Hyde
Baker, Ray Stannard
Barrows, John Henry
Beach, Rex
Beal, William James
Bennett, Earl W.
Bigelow, Melville Madison
Binga, Jesse
Birkhoff, George David
Blodgett, John Wood
Boeing, William Edward
Bovie, William T.
Brewer, Mark Spencer
Briggs, Lyman James
Brooks, Alfred Hulse
Brower, Jacob Vradenberg
Brown, Olympia
Brown, Prentiss Marsh
Brucker, Wilber Marion
Brundage, Avery
Bunche, Ralph Johnson
Bundy, Harvey Hollister
Burnett, Leo
Burton, Frederick Russell
Butterfield, Kenyon Leech
Campaw, Joseph
Campbell, Douglas Houghton
Carleton, Will
Catton, Charles Bruce
Cavanagh, Jerome Patrick ("Jerry")
Chaffee, Roger Bruce
Chapin, Roy Dikeman
Chessman, Caryl Whittier
Child, Charles Manning
Church, Frederick Stuart
Cicotte, Edward Victor
Clements, William Lawrence
Cobo, Albert Eugene
Cole, Arthur Charles
Comfort, Will Levington
Cooke, George Willis
Cooley, Thomas Benton
Copeland, Royal Samuel
Corby, William
Corrothers, James David
Corwin, Edward Samuel
Cox, Wallace Maynard ("Wally")
Curtis, Edward Lewis
Curtis, Heber Doust
Curwood, James Oliver
Darling, Jay Norwood ("Ding")
Davenport, Eugene
De Kruif, Paul Henry
De Langlade, Charles Michel
Dennison, Walter
Dewey, Thomas Edmund
Dodge, Joseph Morrell
Drum, Hugh Aloysius

Eaton, Daniel Cady
Elliott, Walter Hackett Robert
Fairchild, David Grandison
Farnsworth, Elon John
Ferber, Edna Jessica
Ferry, Elisha Peyre
Ferry, Thomas White
Flaherty, Robert Joseph
Folks, Homer
Ford, Edsel Bryant
Ford, Henry
Forsyth, Thomas
Frieseke, Frederick Carl
Gauss, Christian Frederick
Gay, Edwin Francis
Geddes, Norman Bel
Gerber, (Daniel) Frank
Gerber, Daniel (Frank)
Gräbner, August Lawrence
Graham, Ernest Robert
Green, Constance McLaughlin
Hale, Frederick
Haworth, Leland John
Hayden, Robert Earl
Haynes, Williams
Hill, Louis Clarence
Hodgins, Eric Francis
Howard, Brownson Crocker
Howard, Timothy Edward
Howell, Albert Summers
Hubbard, Henry Guernsey
Hulbert, Edwin James
Humphrey, George Magoffin
Hunt, Henry Jackson
Hupp, Louis Gorham
Hutcheson, William Levi
Ingersoll, Robert Hawley
Ingersoll, Royal Rodney
Irwin, George Le Roy
Jenks, Jeremiah Whipple
Jones, Howard Mumford
Joy, Henry Bourne
Kearns, Jack
Kelland, Clarence Budington
Kellogg, John Harvey
Kellogg, Paul Underwood
Kellogg, Will Keith
Kidder, Alfred Vincent
King, Henry Churchill
Kirchwey, George Washington
Kohler, Max James
Krehbiel, Henry Edward
Lacy, William Albert
Lamb, Isaac Wixom
Lamoureux, Andrew Jackson
Lanman, Charles
Lardner, Ringgold Wilmer
Lemmon, John Gill
Levy, Max
Liggett, Louis Kroh
Lindbergh, Charles Augustus, Jr.
Lindeman, Eduard Christian
Livingston, Burton Edward
Longyear, John Munroe
Lovejoy, Owen Reed
McAndrew, William
McCoy, Tim
McHugh, Rose John
McKinstry, Elisha Williams
Macomb, Alexander
MacPhail, Leland Stanford ("Larry")
McRae, Milton Alexander
Macy, John Albert
Marsh, Frank Burr
Matthews, Franklin
Mayo, Mary Anne Bryant
Meany, Edmond Stephen
Melchers, Gari
Mesta, Perle Reid Skirvin
Miller, Webb
Moore, Charles
Morton, Paul
Moulton, Forest Ray
Muir, Charles Henry
Murphy, Frank
Navarre, Pierre
Nestor, Agnes
Newberry, Truman Handy
Noble, Alfred
O'Brien, Thomas James
Otis, Charles Eugene
Pack, Charles Lathrop
Palmer, Thomas Witherell
Penfield, William Lawrence
Pilcher, Lewis Stephen
Pitkin, Walter Boughton
Pond, Allen Bartlit
Pond, Irving Kane
Potter, Charles Edward
Prall, David Wight
Raby, James Joseph
Roethke, Theodore Huebner
Rolshoven, Julius
Royce, Ralph
Ryan, John Dennis
Ryerson, Martin Antoine
St. John, Charles Edward
Sanderson, Ezra Dwight
Schall, Thomas David
Schippers, Thomas
Scripps, William Edmund
Seager, Henry Rogers
Shafter, William Rufus
Shepard, James Henry
Sherman, Frederick Carl
Sibley, Henry Hastings
Sloane, Isabel Cleves Dodge
Squier, George Owen
Summerfield, Arthur Ellsworth
Taylor, Fred Manville
Thomas, Calvin
Tilzer, Harry Von
Toumey, James William
Towne, Charles Arnette
Vance, Harold Sines
Vandenberg, Arthur Hendrick
Van Tyne, Claude Halstead
Webber, Herbert John
Whelpley, Henry Milton
White, Stewart Edward
Wilbur, Cressy Livingston
Wilcox, Delas Franklin
Willcox, Orlando Bolivar
Willett, Herbert Lockwood
Williams, Gardner Fred
Winchell, Horace Vaughn
Woodward, Robert Simpson
Yawkey, Thomas Austin ("Tom")

MINNESOTA

Bender, Charles Albert ("Chief")
Benton, William Burnett
Bierman, Bernard William ("Bernie")
Bottineau, Pierre
Boyle, Michael J.
Burdick, Usher Lloyd
Burleson, Hugh Latimer
Burnham, Federick Russell
Butler, Pierce
Carlson, Richard Dutoit
Carruth, Fred Hayden
Conrad, Maximilian Arthur, Jr.
Cooper, Hugh Lincoln
Daniels, Farrington
Densmore, Frances
Dobie, Gilmour
Douglas, William Orville
Dworshak, Henry Clarence
Edwards, Everett Eugene
Farwell, Arthur
Fillmore, Charles
Fitzgerald, Francis Scott Key
Flandrau, Charles Macomb
Frary, Francis Cowles
Fraser, James Earle
Frazier, Lynn Joseph
Frey, John Philip
Fulton, Johnt Farquhar
Garland, Judy
Getty, Jean Paul
Gillespie, Mabel
Goode, John Paul
Griggs, Everett Gallup
Haines, Lynn
Hall, Hazel
Haupt, Alma Cecelia
Heffelfinger, William Walter ("Pudge")
Hodson, William
Hopkins, Cyril George
Hormel, Jay Catherwood
Johnson, John Albert
Judd, Edward Starr
Kerr, Walter Craig
Knappen, Theodore Temple
Langlie, Arthur Bernard
Lemke, William Frederick
Lewis, Harry Sinclair
Liggett, Walter William
Little Crow V
Lloyd, Marshall Burns
Lowden, Frank Orren
McAlexander, Ulysses Grant
McNair, Lesley James
Magoon, Charles Edward
Manship, Paul Howard
Mayo, Charles Horace
Mayo, William James
Mich, Daniel Danforth
Michel, Virgil George
Mitchell, William DeWitt
Nevers, Ernest Alonzo ("Ernie")
Olds, Robert Edwin
Olson, Floy Bjerstjerne
Oppenheim, James
Pegler, Westbrook

Plowman, George Taylor
Plummer, Henry Stanley
Putnam, Helen Cordelia
Pye, Watts Orson
Ranson, Stephen Walter
Red Wing
Reynolds, Milton
Rothafel, Samuel Lionel
Ryan, John Augustine
Sears, Richard Warren
Shaughnessy, Clark Daniel
Shields, Thomas Edward
Shipstead, Henrik
Swift, Linton Bishop
Todd, Mike
Townley, Arthur Charles
Volstead, Andrew John
Wabasha
Warner, Anne Richmond
White, Minor Martin
Wood, John Taylor
Youngdahl, Luther Wallace

MISSISSIPPI

Allen, George Edward
Bailey, Joseph Weldon
Barry, William Taylor Sullivan
Baskerville, Charles
Battle, Burrell Bunn
Bilbo, Theodore Gilmore
Black, John Charles
Bodenheim, Maxwell
Boggs, Thomas Hale
Boyd, Richard Henry
Brandon, Gerard Chittocque
Burnett, Chester Arthur ("Howlin' Wolf")
Brickell, Henry Herschel
Brough, Charles Hillman
Chamberlain, George Earle
Claiborne, John Francis Hamtramck
Clarke, James Paul
Clayton, William Lockhart
Davis, Joseph Robert
Davis, Varina Howell
Dickinson, Jacob McGavock
Dorsey, Sarah Anne Ellis
Easter, Luscious Luke
Ellington, Earl Buford
Evers, Medgar Wiley
Farish, William Stamps
Faulkner (Falkner), William Cuthbert
Finney, John Miller Turpin
Gailor, Thomas Frank
Gaither, Horace Rowan, Jr.
Galloway, Charles Betts
Garner, James Wilford
Gordon, James
Gore, Thomas Pryor
Gregory, Thomas Watt
Hamer, Fannie Lou
Harris, Nathaniel Harrison
Harris, Wiley Pope
Harrison, Byron Patton
Harrison, James Albert
Howry, Charles Bowen
Hughes, Henry
Humphreys, Benjamin Grubb
Ingraham, Prentiss
Jeffrey, Rosa Griffith Vertner Johnson
Jones, James Kimbrough
Leflore, Greenwood
Littlefield, George Washington
Lomax, John Avery
MacDowell, Katherine Sherwood Bonner
McLaurin, Anselm Joseph
Manning, Vannoy Hartrog
Mayes, Edward
Money, Hernando De Soto
Morton, Ferdinand Quintin
Mullins, Edgar Young
Newlands, Francis Griffith
Nicholson, Eliza Jane Poitevent Holbrook
Parker, John Milliken
Percy, William Alexander
Phelan, James
Pitchlynn, Peter Perkins
Pittman, Key
Presley, Elvis Aron
Pushmataha
Putnam, Arthur
Rankin, John Elliott
Read, Charles William
Russell, Irwin
Short, Joseph Hudson, Jr.
Simmons, Roscoe Conkling Murray
Still, William Grant, Jr.
Stockard, Charles Rupert
Taylor, Theodore Roosevelt ("Hound Dog")
Van Dorn, Earl
Warfield, Catherine Ann Ware
Wheeler, George Wakeman
Whitfield, Owen
Williams, Ben Ames
Wright, Fielding Lewis
Wright, Richard Nathaniel
Yellowley, Edward Clements
Young, Stark
Zimmerman, Eugene

MISSOURI

Ace, Jane
Alexander, Will Winton
Allen, Forrest Clare ("Phog")
Allison, Nathaniel
Anderson, Benjamin McAlester
Arden, Edwin Hunter Pendleton
Armstrong, Paul
Asbury, Herbert
Baker, Josephine
Baldwin, Evelyn Briggs
Bates, John Coalter
Bates, Onward
Beckwith, James Carroll
Beery, Wallace Fitzgerald
Benson, Sally
Bent, Silas
Bent, William
Benton, Thomas Hart
Blair, Emily Newell
Bliss, Robert Woods
Blow, Susan Elizabeth
Bogy, Lewis Vital
Bonfils, Frederick Gilmer
Boswell, Connie ("Connee")
Boyd, William Kenneth
Boyle, Harold Vincent ("Hal")
Brookhart, Smith Wildman
Buchanan, Edgar
Buchanan, Joseph Ray
Caldwell, Eugene Wilson
Campbell, Prince Lucien
Cannon, Clarence
Caraway, Thaddeus Horatius
Carnegie, Dale
Carver, George Washington
Chetlain, Augustus Louis
Chopin, Kate O'Flaherty
Chouteau, Auguste Pierre
Chouteau, Pierre
Churchill, Winston
Clark, Bennett Champ
Clemens, Samuel Langhorne
Cockrell, Francis Marion
Colby, Bainbridge
Coontz, Robert Edward
Cornoyer, Paul
Craig, Cleo Frank
Craig, Malin
Craighead, Edwin Boone
Creel, George
Crowder, Enoch Herbert
Croy, Homer
Dalton, Robert
Dandy, Walter Edward
Darwell, Jane
Davis, Dwight Filley
Davison, Gregory Caldwell
Dent, Frederick Tracy
De Young, Michel Harry
Dodge, Augustus Caesar
Donnell, Forrest C.
Dooley, Thomas Anthony, III
Eames, Charles Ormand, Jr.
Eliot, T(homas) S(tearns)
Ellis, George Washington
Engelmann, George Julius
Evans, Walker
Field, Eugene
Field, Mary Katherine Keemle
Field, Roswell Martin
Finck, Henry Theophilus
Finn, Francis James
Fletcher, Thomas Clement
Fox, Williams Carlton
Frank, Glenn
Froman, Ellen Jane
Galloway, Beverly Thomas
Goldstein, Max Aaron
Gotshall, William Charles
Grable, Betty
Grant, Frederick Dent
Grant, Harry Johnston
Grant, Jane Cole
Griffith, Clark Calvin
Hammond, Bray
Hannegan, Robert Emmet
Harlow, Jean
Harshe, Robert Bartholow
Hatcher, Robert Anthony
Hearst, George

Hearst, Phoebe Apperson
Hendrix, Eugene Russell
Hendrix, Joseph Clifford
Hewett, Waterman Thomas
Hildreth, Samuel Clay
Holden, Edward Singleton
Holden, Hale
Holt, William Franklin
Horn, Tom
Horst, Louis
Howard, Elston Gene ("Ellie")
Howell, Thomas Jefferson
Hubbard, Robert C. ("Cal")
Hubbard, Wynant Davis
Hubble, Edwin
Hudson, Manley Ottmer
Hughes, Howard Robard
Hughes, James Langston
Hughes, Rupert
Hunt, George Wylie Paul
Hyde, Arthur Mastick
Jackling, Daniel Cowan
James, Jesse Woodson
James, Marquis
Jones, Benjamin Allyn
Joy, Charles Turner
Keith, Arthur
Kimball, Dan Able
Kroeger, Ernest Richard
Kuhlman, Kathryn
Lange, Alexis Frederick
Lear, William Powell
Link, Theodore Carl
Long, Breckinridge
Long, Edward Vaughn
Love, Robertus Donnell
Lunceford, James Melvin ("Jimmie")
McAfee, John Armstrong
McArthur, William Pope
McBride, Mary Margaret
McCausland, John
McClurg, Joseph Washington
McConnell, Ira Welch
McCreary, Conn
McCulloch, Robert Paxton
MacCurdy, George Grant
Macfadden, Berharr
McIntyre, Oscar Odd
McManus, George
Malin, Patrick Murphy
Mallinckrodt, Edward
Mallinckrodt, Edward, Jr.
Marbut, Curtis Fletcher
Marmaduke, John Sappington
Marshall, William Rainey
Marvin, Enoch Mather
Mondell, Frank Wheeler
Moore, Marianne Craig
More, Paul Elmer
Morfit, Campbell
Nelson, Donald Marr
Nelson, Marjorie Maxine
Nicholson, James Bartram
Niebuhr, Helmut Richard
Niebuhr, Karl Paul Reinhold ("Reinie")
Noonan, James Patrick
Oakie, Jack
O'Sullivan, Mary Kenney
Pallen, Condé Benoist
Parker, Edward Brewington
Pendergast, Thomas Joseph
Penney, James Cash ("J. C.")
Pershing, John Joseph
Philips, John Finis
Powell, John Benjamin
Pratte, Bernard
Prentis, Henning Webb, Jr.
Pritchett, Henry Smith
Pryor, Arthur W.
Pulitzer, Ralph
Quayle, William Alfred
Rand, Sally
Rautenstrauch, Walter
Reedy, William Marion
Rickard, George Lewis
Robidon, Antoine
Rombauer, Irma Louise
Ross, Charles Griffith
Ross, Nellie Tayloe
Roth, Lillian
Rubey, William Walden
Russell, Charles Ellsworth ("Pee Wee")
Russell, Sol Smith
Rutherford, Joseph Franklin
St. Vrain, Ceran De Hault De Lassus de
Sarpy, Peter A.
Sauer, Carl Ortwin
Shafroth, John Franklin
Shannon, Fred Albert
Shapley, Harlow
Shawn, Edwin Meyers ("Ted")
Skaggs, Marion Barton
Smedley, Agnes
Smith, Horton
Smith, James Allen
Smith, Joseph Fielding
Snow, Edgar Parkes
Spiering, Theodore
Spillman, William Jasper
Spink, John George Taylor
Stark, Lloyd Crow
Stengel, Charles Dillon ("Casey")
Stephens, Edwin William
Stettinius, Edward Riley
Stoessel, Albert Frederic
Swift, John Franklin
Swope, Gerard
Swope, Herbert Bayard
Talbot, Ethelbert
Taussig, Frank William
Teasdale, Sara
Thomas, Augustus
Toole, Edwin Warren
Toole, Joseph Kemp
Traubel, Helen
Truman, Harry S.
Turner, George
Turner, James Milton
Vaughn, Victor Clarence
Walker, Robert Franklin
Wallace, Charles William
Wallace, Hugh Campbell
Walsh, Francis Patrick
Walton, Lester Aglar
Webster, Benjamin ("Ben") Francis
Wheat, Zachariah Davis ("Buck")
White, Pearl
Wiener, Norbert
Williams, Walter
Winslow, Ola Elizabeth
Wood, Robert Elkington
Yost, Casper Salathiel
Younger, Thomas Coleman

MONTANA

Baker, Dorothy Dodds
Beary, Donal Bradford
Braden, Spruille
Brophy, Thomas D'Arcy
Cooper, Gary
Huntley, Chester ("Chet") Robert
Kennedy, George Clayton
Metcalf, Lee Warren
Rankin, Jeannette Pickering
Thompson, William Boyce
Washakie

NEBRASKA

Abbott, Edith
Abbott, Grace
Alexander, Grover Cleveland
Alexander, Hartley Burr
Barrett, Frank Aloysius
Billings, Asa White Kenney
Bright Eyes
Bryson, Lyman Lloyd
Clements, Frederic Edward
Clift, Edward Montgomery
Cloud, Henry Roe
Crawford, Samuel Earl
Dern, George Henry
Dunning, John Ray
Eiseley, Loren Corey
Embree, Edwin Rogers
Etting, Ruth
Fairchild, Fred Rogers
Gibson, Edmund Richard ("Hoot")
Gifford, Sanford Robinson
Gortner, Ross Aiken
Guthrie, Edwin Ray, Jr.
Hayward, Leland
Heald, Henry Townley
Higgins, Andrew Jackson
Hitchcock, Gilbert Monell
Hoagland, Charles Lee
Hollingworth, Leta Stetter
Hunter, Walter David
Janssen, David
Jeffers, William Martin
Johnson, Alvin Saunders
Kiewit, Peter
Leahy, Francis William ("Frank")
Lloyd, Harold Clayton
Malcolm X
Matthews, Francis Patrick
Monsky, Henry
Morton, Charles Walter
Pate, Maurice
Patterson, Richard Cunningham, Jr.
Phillips, Frank
Pound, (Nathan) Roscoe

Red Cloud
Rhodes, Eugene Manlove
Roche, Josephine Aspinwall
Roper, Elmo Burns, Jr.
Rosewater, Victor
Sandoz, Mari
Scott, Allen Cecil
Simpson, John Andrew
Smart, David Archibald
Spencer, Robert
Stevens, Doris
Strong, Anna Louise
Sutherland, Edwin Hardin
Taylor, Robert
Warren, George Frederick
Washburn, Edward Wight
Wherry, Kenneth Spicer
Zanuck, Darryl Francis

NEVADA

Ashurst, Henry Fountain
Lynch, Robert Clyde
McCarran, Patrick Anthony
McLoughlin, Maurice Evans
Martin, Anne Henrietta
Michelson, Charles
Requa, Mark Lawrence
Winnemucca, Sarah
Wovoka

NEW HAMPSHIRE

Abbott, Joseph Carter
Adams, Ebenezer
Adams, Isaac
Akerman, Amos Tappan
Albee, Ernest
Aldrich, Edgar
Aldrich, Thomas Bailey
Allen, Glover Morrill
Andrews, Christopher Columbus
Andrews, Elish Benjamin
Appleton, John
Appleton, Nathan
Appleton, Samuel
Atherton, Charles Gordon
Atwood, David
Bachelder, John
Bailey, Solon Irving
Baker, Osmon Cleander
Ballon, Hosea
Bancroft, Cecil Franklin Patch
Barnabee, Henry Clay
Baroody, William Joseph
Barry, John Stewart
Bartlett, Ichabod
Bartlett, Samuel Colcord
Batchelder, John Putnam
Batchelder, Samuel
Beach, Amy Marcy Cheney
Beard, Mary
Belknap, George Eugene
Bell, Charles Henry
Bell, Louis
Bell, Luther Vose
Bell, Samuel
Benton, James Gilchrist
Bissell, George Henry
Blair, Henry William
Blake, John Lauris
Blodget, Samuel
Blunt, Edmund March
Bonton, John Bell
Bridgman, Laura Dewey
Brooks, John Graham
Brown, Charles Rufus
Brown, Francis, 1784–1820
Brown, Francis, 1849–1916
Brown, George
Browne, Daniel Jay
Buckminster, Joseph Stevens
Bundy, Jonas Mills
Burnap, George Washington
Burnham, William Henry
Burton, Warren
Butler, Benjamin Franklin
Cass, Lewis
Chamberlain, Mellen
Champney, Benjamin
Chandler, Harry
Chandler, John
Chandler, William Eaton
Chandler, Zachariah
Chase, Philander
Chase, Salmon Portland
Cheney, Benjamin Pierce
Cheney, Oren Burbank
Cheney, Person Colby
Chickering, Jonas
Cilley, Joseph
Clark, Daniel
Clark, Greenleaf
Clarke, James Freeman
Clifford, Nathan
Coffin, Charles Carleton
Coffin, Lorenzo S.
Cones, Elliott
Corbin, Daniel Chase
Craig Daniel H.
Cram, Ralph Adams
Craven, Tunis Augustus Macdonough
Currier, Moody
Cutler, Carroll
Cutting, James Ambrose
Damon, Ralph Shepard
Dana, Charles Anderson
Dana, James Freeman
Dana, Samuel Luther
Daniels, Fred Harris
Darling, Flora Adams
Davis, Noah
Davis, Phineas
Day, Edmund Ezra
Dearborn, Henry
Dearborn, Henry Alexander Scammell
Dodge, Jacob Richards
Doe, Charles
Donovan, John Joseph
Drake, Francis Samuel
Drake, Samuel Gardner
Durant, Henry Fowle
Durell, Edward Henry
Dutton, Samuel Train
Eastman, Arthur MacArthur
Eastman, Enoch Worthen
Eastman, John Robie
Eastman, Timothy Corser
Eaton, John
Eddy, Mary Morse Baker
Ellis, Carleton
Elwyn, Alfred Langdon
Emerson, Benjamin Kendall
Emerson, Joseph
Estabrook, Joseph
Estey, Jacob
Farley, Harriet
Farmer, Moses Gerrish
Farnum, Dustin Lancy
Farrar, Timothy
Ferguson, Samuel
Fessenden, Thomas Green
Fessenden, William Pitt
Fields, James Thomas
Fiske, Amos Kidder
Flanders, Henry
Fletcher, William Asa
Flynn, Elizabeth Gurley
Fogg, George Gilman
Folsom, Charles
Folsom, Nathaniel
Foss, Sam Walter
Foster, Frank Pierce
Foster, John Gray
Foster, Stephen Symonds
French, Daniel Chester
French, William Merchant Richardson
Fuller, Levi Knight
Gardner, Helen
Gilman, John Taylor
Gilman, Nicholas
Glidden, Joseph Farwell
Goldthwaite, Henry Barnes
Goodenow, John Milton
Goodhue, James Madison
Gordon, George Phineas
Gould, Augustus Addison
Gove, Aaron Estellus
Greeley, Horace
Greene, Nathaniel
Griffin, Appleton Prentiss Clark
Griffin, Simon Goodell
Grimes, James Wilson
Gunnison, John Williams
Hackett, Frank Warren
Haddock, Charles Brickett
Haines, Charles Glidden
Hale, Edwin Moses
Hale, Horatio Emmons
Hale, John Parker
Hale, Sarah Joseph Buell
Hall, Charles Francis
Hall, George Henry
Hall, Samuel Read
Hall, Thomas Seavey
Harlow, Ralph Volney
Harriman, Walter
Haskell, Ella Louise Knowles
Hill, Joseph Adna
Holmes, Nathaniel
Howard, Ada Lydia
Howland, Alfred Cornelius
Hoyt, Albert Harrison
Hoyt, Charles Hale
Hunton, George Kenneth
Hutchins, Harry Burns
Jackson, Hall

Jewell, Harvey
Jewell, Marshall
Jewett, Clarence Frederick
Jones, Frank
Jones, John Taylor
Jones, Robert Edmond
Joy, James Frederick
Judson, Sarah Hall Boardman
Keith, Benjamin Franklin
Kelley, Hall Jackson
Kendall, George Wilkins
Kent, Edward
Kidder, Frederic
Kimball, Gilman
Kimball, Richard Burleigh
Kinkaid, Thomas Cassin
Knox, Thomas Wallace
Ladd, William
Langdell, Christopher Columbus
Langdon, John
Langdon, Woodbury
Lear, Tobias
Leavitt, Dudley
Leavitt, Mary Greenleaf Clement
Lee, Eliza Buckminster
Little, Charles Sherman
Livermore, Abiel Abbot
Livermore, Arthur
Livermore, Edward St. Loe
Livermore, Samuel, 1786–1833
Locke, John
Long, Stephen Harriman
Lord, John
Lothrop, Daniel
Lovewell, John
Lowe, Charles
Lowe, Thaddeus Sobieski Coulincourt
McKeen, Joseph
Marden, Orison Sweet
Marsh, Sylvester
Martyn, Sarah Towne Smith
Mather, Samuel Holmes
Mathews, William Smythe Babcock
Mead, Edwin Doak
Mead, Larkin Goldsmith
Merrill, William Bradford
Meserve, Nathaniel
Metalious, Grace
Metcalf, Henry Harrison
Miller, Charles Ransom
Miner, Alonzo Ames
Moore, Frank
Moore, George Henry
Moore, Jacob Bailey
Moore, John Weeks
Morril, David Lawrence
Morrison, Nathan Jackson
Mussey, Reuben Dimond
Neal, Joseph Clay
Nelson, Edward William
Nesmith, John
Nichols, Mary Sargeant Neal Gove
Nichols, Thomas Low
Orcutt, Hiram
Ordway, John
Osgood, Jacob
Page, David Perkins
Parker, Francis Wayland
Parker, Joel
Parker, Willard
Parrott, Enoch Greenleafe
Parrott, Robert Parker
Partridge, Richard
Patrick, Mary Mills
Patterson, James Willis
Payson, Edward
Peabody, Oliver William Bourn
Peabody, William Bourn Oliver
Pearl, Raymond
Peaslee, Edmund Randolph
Perkins, George Hamilton
Perry, Arthur Latham
Peters, Absalom
Pickering, John
Pierce, Franklin
Pierce, John Davis
Pike, Nicholas
Pillsbury, Charles Alfred
Pillsbury, John Sargent
Pilsbury, Amos
Plaisted, Harris Merrill
Poor, John
Porter, Fitz-John
Pratt, Daniel, July 20, 1799–May 13, 1873
Prescott, George Bartlett
Prescott, Samuel Cate
Proctor, Lucien Brock
Quimby, Phineas Parkhurst
Randall, Benjamin
Rankin, Jeremiah Eames
Rice, Georze Samuel
Richards, Charles Herbert
Richardson, William Merchant
Ripley, Eleazar Wheelock
Roberts, Edmund
Rolfe, Robert Abial ("Red")
Rollins, Edward Henry
Rollins, Frank West
Sabine, Lorenzo
Sanborn, Edwin David
Sanborn, Franklin Benjamin
Sanborn, Katherine Abbott
Sanborn, Walter Henry
Sargent, George Henry
Savage, Henry Wilson
Shahan, Thomas Joseph
Shattuck, Aaron Draper
Shaw, Elijah
Shear, Theodore Leslie
Shedd, Fred Fuller
Shedd, John Graves
Sherman, Forrest Percival
Sherwin, Thomas
Sherwood, Mary Elizabeth Wilson
Shillaber, Benjamin Penhallow
Shurtleff, Roswell Morse
Smart, James Henry
Smith, Asa Dodge
Smith, Hamilton
Smith, Jeremiah, 1759–1842
Smith, Jeremiah, 1837–1921
Smith, Jeremiah, 1870–1935
Smith, Justin Harvey
Smith, Nathan Ryno
Smith, Uriah
Spalding, Lyman
Spaulding, Levi
Spaulding, Oliver Lyman
Spofford, Ainsworth Rand
Stark, John
Stearns, John Newton
Stone, Harlan Fiske
Stow, Baron
Sullivan, George
Sullivan, John
Sumner, Walter Taylor
Swasey, Ambrose
Swett, John
Taylor, Harry
Taylor, Samuel Harvey
Tenney, Edward Payson
Tenney, Tabitha Gilman
Thaxter, Celia Laighton
Thomson, Samuel
Ticknor, William Davis
Tilton, John Rollin
Titcomb, John Wheelock
Treat, Samuel
Twitchell, Amos
Upham, Thomas Cogswell
Upham, Warren
Walker, Asa
Walker, John Grimes
Waterhouse, Sylvester
Weare, Meshech
Webster, Daniel
Webster, Joseph Dana
Weeks, John Wingate
Wentworth, Benning
Wentworth, George Albert
Wentworth, John, 1737 N.S.–1820
Wentworth, John, 1815–1888
Wentworth, Paul
Whipple, Sherman Leland
White, Horace
Wilder, Marshall Pinckney
Willey, Samuel Hopkins
Wilson, Henry
Wilson, William Dexter
Wood, Edith Elmer
Wood, Leonard
Wood, Walter Abbott
Woodbury, Daniel Phineas
Woodbury, Levi
Woolson, Constance Fenimore
Worcester, Joseph Emerson
Worcester, Noah
Worcester, Samuel
Wright, Carroll Davidson
Wyman, Robert Harris
Wyman, Seth
Young, Ammi Burnham
Young, Charles Augustus

NEW JERSEY

Abbott, Charles Conrad
Abbott, William A. ("Bud")
Abeel, David
Adams, Joseph Alexander
Alexander, Samuel Davies
Allen, William Frederick
Allinson, Francis Greenleaf
Alsop, Mary O'Hara
Apgar, Virginia
Archer, Samuel
Armstrong, George Dod
Armstrong, John

Arnold, Lewis Golding
Bailey, Gamaliel
Bainbridge, William
Baird, Charles Washington
Baldwin, Matthias William
Barber, Francis
Bard, John
Barrell, Joseph
Barrett, Lawrence
Barton, James Edward
Bateman, Newton
Beach, Harlan Page
Berrien, John MacPherson
Berry, Edward Wilber
Bishop, William Darius
Blackford, Charles Minor
Blackwell, Alice Stone
Blair, John Insley
Blakeley, George Henry
Bloomfield, Joseph
Boggs, Charles Stuart
Bourke-White, Margaret
Bourne, Randolph Silliman
Brearly, David
Breckinridge, Aida de Acosta
Brewster, Benjamin Harris
Bristol, Mark Lambert
Brooks, Van Wyck
Bross, William
Brown, George Scratchley
Brown, Isaac Van Arsdale
Buckley, James Monroe
Burlingham, Charles Culp
Burnet, David Gouverneur
Burnet, Jacob
Burnet, William
Burr, Aaron
Butler, Nicholas Murray
Cadwalader, Lambert
Caldwell, Joseph
Campbell, Andrew
Campbell, John Wood, Jr.
Cattell, Alexander Gilmore
Cattell, William Cassaday
Chambers, John
Chapman, Frank Michler
Chase, Edna Woolman
Christie, John Walter
Clapp, Margaret Antoinette
Clark, Abraham
Clark, George Whitefield
Claxton, Kate
Cleveland, Stephen Grover
Coerne, Louis Adolphe
Coit, Henry Leber
Cole, Charles Woolsey
Combs, Moses Newell
Condit, John
Cone, Spencer Houghton
Conte, Richard
Cook, Albert Stanburrough
Cook, George Hammell
Cook, Isaac
Cooke, Robert Anderson
Cooper, James Fenimore
Cooper, Samuel
Corrigan, Michael Augustine
Costello, Lou
Cox, Samuel Hanson
Coxe, Arthur Cleveland
Coxe, John Redman
Coxe, Richard Smith
Craig, Austin
Crane, Jonathan Townley
Crane, Stephen
Crane, William Montgomery
Craven, John Joseph
Darling, Samuel Taylor
Dayton, Elias
Dayton, Jonathan
Dayton, William Lewis
Dennis, Frederic Shepard
Dennis, James Shepard
Dickerson, Edward Nicoll
Dickerson, Mahlon
Dickerson, Philemon
Dickinson, Robert Latou
Dingman, Mary Agnes
Disbrow, William Stephen
Ditmars, Raymond Lee
Doane, George Washington
Dod, Albert Baldwin
Dod, Thaddeus
Dodd, Frank Howard
D'Olier, Franklin
Douglas, Helen Gahagan
Douglass, David Bates
Drake, Alexander Wilson
Drake, Daniel
Duffy, Edmund
Dunlap, William
Dunning, William Archibald
Du Pont, Samuel Francis
Durand, Asher Brown
Durand, Cyrus
Eames, Wilberforce
Edgar, Charles
Edison, Charles
Edsall, David Linn
Edwards, William
Eilshemius, Louis Michel
Elmer, Ebenezer
Elmer, Jonathan
Elmer, Lucius Quintius Cincinnatus
Endicott, Mordecai Thomas
Entwistle, James
Evans, Anthony Walton Whyte
Evans, William John ("Bill")
Ewing, Charles
Fagan, Mark Matthew
Farrand, Livingston
Farrand, Max
Farson, Negley
Fauset, Jessie Redmon
Fay, Edward Allen
Fields, Dorothy
Filed, Richard Stockton
Finley, Robert
Fiske, Haley
Fiske, Stephen Ryder
Flanagin, Harris
Force, Peter
Ford, Jacob
Forman, David
Frank, Waldo David
Franz, Shepherd Ivory
Frazee, John
Frelinghuysen, Frederick
Frelinghuysen, Frederick Theodore
Frelinghuysen, Theodore
Gano, John
Gardner, Charles Kitchell
Garrison, Lindley Miller
Gaul, William Gilbert
Gilbert, Seymour Parker
Gilchrist, Robert
Gilchrist, William Wallace
Gilder, Richard Watson
Gitlow, Benjamin
Godwin, Parke
Goetschius, Percy
Goodrich, Annie Warburton
Goslin, Leon Allen ("Goose")
Grace, Eugene Gifford
Green, Ashbel
Green, Henry Woodhull
Green, John Cleve
Green, William Henry
Greenwood, Miles
Griffith, William
Griggs, John William
Griscom, John
Griscom, Lloyd Carpenter
Griswold, Alfred Whitney
Grundy, Joseph Ridgway
Guggenheim, Harry Frank
Gummere, Francis Barton
Gummere, Samuel James
Gummere, Samuel René
Gummere, William Stryker
Hager, John Sharpenstein
Hague, Frank
Hall, Juanita Armethea
Halsey, William Frederick, Jr.
Halsted, George Bruce
Hardenbergh, Henry Janeway
Hare, William Hobart
Harris, Jed
Hart, James Morgan
Hartford, John Augustine
Hartley, Fred Allen, Jr.
Hatfield, Edwin Francis
Henderson, John
Henderson, Thomas
Henderson, William James
Henry, Alexander
Hewes, Joseph
Hewitt, Henry Kent
Higgins, Daniel Paul
Hill, David Jayne
Hill, Ernest Rowland
Hill, Thomas, 1818–1891
Hillyer, Robert Silliman
Hires, Charles Elmer
Hobart, Garret Augustus
Hodge, Archibald Alexander
Hoffman, Josiah Ogden
Hopper, Isaac Tatem
Hornblower, Joseph Coerten
Hornblower, William Butler
Howell, David
Howell, James Bruen
Hubbs, Rebecca
Hunt, Theodore Whitefield
Hunt, Wilson Price
Hutchins, Thomas
Hutchinson, Paul
Imlay, Gilbert
Ivins, Anthony Woodward

Ivins, William Mills
Jackson, Charles Reginald
Jackson, John Brinckerhoff
Jackson, Joseph Henry
Janeway, Edward Gamaliel
Jay, Peter Augustus
Jeffers, William Nicholson
Jennings, Jonathan
Johnson, Elijah
Johnston, Augustus
Jones, Ernest Lester
Kafer, John Christian
Katchen, Julius
Kearney, Francis
Kearney, Lawrence
Kearny, Stephen Watts
Keater, Vaughan
Kelly, Howard Atwood
Kenny, John V.
Kerlin, Isaac Newton
Kerney, James
Kilmer, Alfred Joycen
Kilpatrick, Hugh Judson
Kinney, William Burnet
Kinsey, Alfred Charles
Kinsey, John
Kirkpatrick, Andrew
Klein, August Clarence
Knight, Edward Coleings
Kovacs, Ernie
Kroeber, Alfred Louis
Lafever, Minard
Lake, Simon
Lange, Dorothea
Larned, William Augustus
Lasser, Jacob Kay
Lawrence, James
Leaming, Thomas
Leonard, William Ellery
Lieb, John William
Lindabury, Richard Vliet
Lindsey, John Berrien
Lindsley, Philip
Linn, William Alexander
Lippincott, Joshua Ballinger
Littell, Eliakim
Littell, Squier
Littell, William
Lloyd, Alfred Henry
Longstreet, William
Longworth, Nicholas, 1782–1863
Low, Isaac
Low, Nicholas
Lowenstein, Allard Kenneth
Lozier, Clemence Sophia Harned
Lundy, Benjamin
Lyon, James
McAllister, Charles Albert
McCalla, Bowman Hendry
McCauley, Mary Ludwig Hays
McDowell, John
McEntee, James Joseph
McGraw, Donald Cushing
McIlvaine, Charles Pettit
Maclean, John
McLean, John
McLean, Walter
McMichael, Morton
McMurtrie, Douglas Crawford
McMurtrie, William
Madigan, Laverne
Magie, William Jay
Magonigle, Harold Van Buren
Manning, James
Marin, John (Cheri)
Marshall, James Wilson
Marten, Alexander
Marten, Luther
Mason, John
Matlack, Timothy
Medwick, Joseph ("Ducky") Michael
Meeker, Moses
Messler, Thomas Doremus
Meyer, Frank Straus
Miller, Ezra
Miller, James Alexander
Miller, John
Mills, Benjamin Fay
Mitchell, James Paul
Mitchell, Thomas Gregory
Montgomery, John Berrien
Mooey, James
Moody, John
Moore, Edward Mott
Moore, Ely
Moore, Victor Frederick
Moran, Daniel Edward
Morford, Henry
Morgan, Daniel
Morley, Edward Williams
Morris, Edmund
Morris, Robert, 1745–1815
Mott, Charles Stewart
Mott, Gershom
Murphy, Franklin
Myers, Gustavus
Napton, William Barclay
Neilson, John
Nelson, Oswald George ("Ozzie")
Nelson, William, 1847–1914
Newton, Isaac, 1800–1867
Nichols, Roy Franklin
Nies, James Buchanan
Nixon, John Thompson
Norris, Mary Harriott
Norton, Mary Teresa Hopkins
Noyes, Alexander Dana
Oatman, Johnson
Odell, Jonathan
O'Donnell, Thomas Jefferson
Ogden, Aaron
Ogden, David
Ogden, Francis Barber
Ogden, Samuel
Ogden, Thomas Ludlow
Ogden, Uzal
Olcott, Henry Steel
Opdyke, George
Osborn, Henry Fairfield
Otto, John Conrad
Oxden, Charles Smith
Page, Leigh
Paine, John Alsop
Palmer, James Shedden
Pancoast, Joseph
Parke, Benjamin
Parker, Dorothy Rothschild
Parker, James, *c.* 1714–1770
Parker, James, 1776–1868
Parker, Joel
Parker, John Cortlandt
Parsons, Frank
Parvin, Theodore Sutton
Patrick, Edwin Hill ("Ted")
Paul, Alice
Pennington, William
Pennington, William Sandford
Periam, Jonathan
Perrine, Frederic Auten Combs
Perrine, Henry
Pettit, Charles
Pike, Zebulon Montgomery
Pincus, Gregory Goodwin ("Goody")
Pitney, Mahlon
Plotz, Harry
Pollak, Walter Heilprin
Post, Louis Freeland
Price, Rodman McCamley
Quinby, Isaac Ferdinand
Ralph, James
Randall, Robert Richard
Randolph, Theodore Fitz
Reed, Joseph
Rellstab, John
Richards, Dickinson Woodruff
Riggs, Elias
Roberts, Nathan S.
Robeson, George Maxwell
Robeson, Paul Leroy
Rovere, Richard Halworth
Rusby, Henry Hurd
St. Denis, Ruth
Salmon, Daniel Elmer
Sayre, Lewis Albert
Scattergood, Thomas
Schary, Dore
Schelling, Ernest Henry
Scovell, Melville Amasa
Scudder, John
Scudder, Nathaniel
Sedgwick, Anne Douglas
Seldes, Gilbert Vivian
Sergeant, John, 1710–1749
Sergeant, Jonathan Dickinson
Shafer, Helen Almira
Sharp, Dallas Lore
Shinn, Asa
Shinn, Everett
Shreve, Henry Miller
Sickels, Frederick Ellsworth
Silver, Thomas
Simpson, James Hervey
Singer, Charles H.
Sloan, Harold Paul
Smith, James, 1851–1927
Smith, John Jay
Smith, Lloyd Logan Pearsall
Smith, Richard
Somers, Richard
Sonneck, Oscar George Theodore
Southard, Samuel Lewis
Stagg, Amos Alonzo
Stanley, Robert Crooks
Stephens, Alice Barber
Stephens, John Lloyd
Stephens, Uriah Smith
Stetson, John Batterson
Stevens, Edwin Augustus

Stevens, Robert Livingston
Stieglitz, Alfred
Stieglitz, Julius
Still, William
Stillman, Thomas Bliss
Stimson, Lewis Atterbury
Stockton, John Potter
Stockton, Richard, 1730–1781
Stockton, Richard, 1764–1828
Stockton, Robert Field
Stockton, Thomas Hewlings
Stratemeyer, Edward
Sulzer, William
Sumner, William Graham
Sutherland, Joel Barlow
Svenson, Andrew Edward
Talmadge, Norma
Talmage, John Van Nest
Talmage, Thomas DeWitt
Taylor, Joseph Wright
Tedyuskung
Terhune, Albert Payson
Thacher, Thomas Day
Thomas, John Parnell
Thompson, John Bodine
Tichenor, Isaac
Tomlinson, Everett Titsworth
Traubel, Horace L.
Tucker, Stephen Davis
Tumulty, Joseph Patrick
Tyson, George Emory
Vail, Alfred
Vanderbilt, Arthur T.
Vanderbilt, William Henry
Van Dyke, John Charles
Van Santvoord, George
Varick, Richard
Veiller, Lawrence Turnure
Voorhees, Edward Burnett
Voorhees, Philip Falkerson
Vroom, Peter Dumont
Warbasse, James Peter
Ward, Aaron Montgomery
Ward, James Warner
Ward, Marcus Lawrence
Ward, Richard Halsted
Ward, Thomas
Warren, Howard Crosby
Washington, Henry Stephens
Watson, Arthur Kittridge
Watson, John Fanning
Waugh, Frederick Judd
Welling, James Clarke
Westervelt, Jacob Aaron
Wetherill, Samuel
Whitehead, William Adee
Whiteside, Arthur Dare
Willard, Mary Hatch
Williams, William Carlos
Williamson, Isaac Halsted
Wilson, Edmund, Jr.
Winans, Ross
Winans, Thomas De Kay
Wines, Enoch Cobb
Wood, George
Wood, George Bacon
Woodhull, Alfred Alexander
Woollcott, Alexander Humphreys
Woolman, John
Wright, Joseph
Wright, Patience Lovell
Wylie, Elinor Morton Hoyt
Young, David
Zane, Charles Shuster

NEW MEXICO

Beals, Ralph Albert
Bryan, Kirk
Carleton, Henry Guy
Chavez, Dennis
Condon, Edward Uhler
Cushman, Austin Thomas ("Joe")
Dodge, Henry Chee
Glassford, Pelham Davis
Hilton, Conrad Nicholson
Hubbell, John Lorenzo
Lyon, Harris Merton
Martinez, Maria
Montoya, Joseph Manuel
Ouray
Seligman, Arthur
Son of Many Beads

NEW YORK

Abbe, Cleveland
Abbey, Henry
Abernethy, George
Adams, Henry Cullen
Adams, James Truslow
Adams, Samuel Hopkins
Adee, Alvey Augustus
Adler, Elmer
Agate, Alfred T.
Agate, Frederick Styles
Agnew, Cornelius Rea
Agnew, Eliza
Akeley, Carl Ethan
Alden, Isabella Macdonald
Alden, John Ferris
Alden, Joseph
Alden, Raymond MacDonald
Aldridge, Ira Frederick
Alexander, Stephen
Alexander, William
Allaire, James Peter
Allen, Arthur Augustus
Allen, Horatio
Allen, John
Allen, Kelcey
Allerton, Samuel Waters
Allis, Edward Phelps
Allison, Richard
Altman, Benjamin
Amidon, Charles Fremont
Anderson, Alexander
Anderson, Elizabeth Milbank
Anderson, Galusha
Andrews, Charles
Andrews, Edward Gayer
Andrews, William Loring
Angel, Benjamin Franklin
Anthon, Charles
Anthon, Charles Edward
Anthony, Andrew Varick Stout
Anthony, George Tobey
Anthony, John J.
Appleby, John Francis
Appleton, William Worthen
Armour, Philip Danforth
Armstrong, David Maitland
Armstrong, Edwin Howard
Armstrong, Hamilton Fish
Arno, Peter
Arnold, Edward
Arnold, George
Arnold, Isaac Newton
Arnold, Lauren Briggs
Arthur, Joseph Charles
Arthur, Timothy Shay
Ashmun, Jehudi
Aspinwall, William Henry
Astor, John Jacob, 1822–1890
Astor, John Jacob, 1864–1912
Astor, William Backhouse
Astor, William Vincent
Astor, William Waldorf
Atkinson, John
Atwater, Wilbur Olin
Auchmuty, Richard Tylden
Auer, John
Augur, Christopher Columbus
Austen, (Elizabeth) Alice
Austen, Peter Townsend
Averell, William Woods
Avery, Benjamin Parke
Avery, Milton Clark
Avery, Samuel Putnam
Ayres, Romeyn Beck
Babbitt, Benjamin Talbot
Babcock, George Herman
Babcock, Howard Edward
Babcock, Maltbie Davenport
Babcock, Stephen Moulton
Bache, Jules Semon
Bacheller, Irving
Bachman, John
Backus, Truman Jay
Bacon, Edward Payson
Bacon, Leonard
Badeau, Adam
Bailey, Florence Augusta Merriam
Bailey, James Montgomery
Bailey, Theodorus
Baker, Benjamin A.
Baker, Frank
Baker, George Augustus
Baker, George Fisher
Baker, La Fayette Curry
Baker, Peter Carpenter
Baker, Sara Josephine
Baker, Walter Ransom Gail
Baldwin, Elihu Whittlesey
Baldwin, Faith
Balestier, Charles Wolcott
Bangs, Francis Nehemiah
Bangs, John Kendrick
Banvard, John
Banvard, Joseph
Barbour, Oliver Lorenzo
Barclay, Thomas
Barker, Alexander Crichlow ("Lex")
Barker, James William
Barlow, Francis Channing
Barlow, John Whitney
Barnes, Albert
Barnes, Mary Downing Sheldon

Barnum, Henry A.
Barrows, Samuel June
Barry, Philip James Quinn
Barry, William Farquhar
Barth, Alan
Barthelmess, Richard
Bartlett, Homer Newton
Bascom, Henry Bidleman
Bascom, John
Bashford, Coles
Bassett, Edward Murray
Batcheller, George Sherman
Baum, Lyman Frank
Bausch, Edward
Baxter, Henry
Bayard, William
Bayles, James Copper
Bayley, James Roosevelt
Beach, Frederick Converse
Beach, William Augustus
Beadle, Erastus Flavel
Beard, James Henry
Beardsley, Samuel
Beauchamp, William Martin
Beck, John Brodhead
Beck, Lewis Caleb
Beck, Theodric Romeyn
Becker, George Ferdinand
Beebe, (Charles) William
Beecher, Catharine Esther
Beecher, Charles Emerson
Beecher, Edward
Beer, George Louis
Beers, Ethel Lynn
Beers, Henry Augustin
Belknap, William Worth
Bell, Clark
Bell, Isaac
Beman, Nathan Sidney Simth
Bement, Caleb N.
Benedict, Ruth Fulton
Benjamin, George Hillard
Benjamin, Nathan
Benjamin, Park
Bennet, Sanford Fillmore
Bennett, Constance Campbell
Bennett, de Robigne Mortimer
Bennett, Floyd
Bennett, James Gordon
Bennett, Nathaniel
Benson, Eugene
Benton, Allen Richardson
Benton, Joel
Berg, Gertrude Edelstein
Berg, Morris ("Moe")
Berger, Meyer
Bergh, Christian
Bergh, Henry
Bernet, John Joseph
Bernstein, Aline
Bernstein, Theodore Menline
Bethune, George Washington
Bidlack, Benjamin Alden
Bidwell, John
Bierwirth, John Edward
Bigelow, John
Biggs, Hermann Michael
Billy The Kid (Bonney, William H.)
Birdseye, Clarence
Birge, Edward Asahel
Bishop, Charles Reed
Bishop, Joel Prentiss
Bishop, Nathan
Bissell, Edwin Cone
Bissell, William Henry
Bissell, Wilson Shannon
Bixby, Horace Ezra
Black, Douglas MacRae
Blackfan, Kenneth Daniel
Blackwell, Antoinette Louisa Brown
Blaikie, William
Blair, Austin
Blake, Homer Crane
Blake, William Phipps
Blakelock, Ralph Albert
Blandy, William Henry Purnell
Blashfield, Edwin Howland
Blatch, Harriot Eaton Stanton
Bleecker, Ann Eliza
Bliss, Aaron Thomas
Bliss, Cornelius Newton
Bliss, Eliphalet Williams
Bliss, Porter Cornelius
Block, Paul
Blodget, Lorin
Blodgett, Katharine Burr
Blondell, Joan
Blood, Benjamin Paul
Bloomer, Amelia Jenks
Bloomgarden, Kermit
Bloor, Ella Reeve
Bogardus, James
Bogart, Humphrey DeForest
Bogart, John
Bogue, Virgil Gay
Bohlen, Charles Eustis ("Chip")
Boies, Horace
Boissevain, Inez Milholland
Bolton, Henry Carrington
Bomford, George
Bond, Elizabeth Powell
Bonney, Charles Carroll
Bonstelle, Jessie
Booth, Mary Louise
Borchard, Edwin Montefiore
Borden, Gail
Bottome, Margaret McDonald
Bouch, William C.
Bourne, Edward Gaylord
Bow, Clara Gordon
Bowen, Abel
Bowen, Herbert Wolcott
Bowen, Ira Sprague
Bowles, Jane Auer
Boyle, John J.
Brace, Charles Loring
Brace, Dewitt Bristol
Brace, Donald Clifford
Brackett, Charles William
Braddock, James J.
Bradford, Alexander Warfield
Bradford, Amory Howe
Bradford, William
Bradley, Joseph P.
Brady, Alice
Brady, James Topham
Brady, John Green
Brady, Mathew B.
Bragg, Edward Stuyvesant
Brainard, Daniel
Brainerd, Thomas
Braslau, Sophie
Brayman, Mason
Breese, Sidney
Brevoort, James Renwick
Brewer, William Henry
Brice, Fanny
Bridges, Calvin Blackman
Briggs, Charles Augustus
Brigham, Albert Perry
Bright, Jesse David
Brill, Nathan Edwin
Brinkerhoff, Jacob
Brinkerhoff, Roeliff
Brisbane, Albert
Brisbane, Arthur
Bristed, Charles Astor
Bristol, John Bunyan
Bristow, George Frederick
Britton, Nathaniel Lord
Brodhead, Daniel
Bronk, Detlev Wulf
Brooks, Byron Alden
Brooks, James Gordon
Brooks, Thomas Benton
Broun, Heywood Campbell
Browere, John Henri Isaac
Brown, Elmer Ellsworth
Brown, Frederic Tilden
Brown, Margaret Wise
Brown, Phoebe Hinsdale
Brown, William Adams
Brown, William Carlos
Browne, Irving
Browne, Junius Henri
Brownell, William Crary
Brownson, Willard Herbert
Bruce, Archibald
Bruce, Edward Bright
Bruce, Lenny
Brunner, Arnold William
Brush, Edward Nathaniel
Brush, George Jarvis
Bryce, Lloyd Stephens
Buck, Albert Henry
Buck, Gurdon
Buck, Leffert Lefferts
Buck, Philo Melvin
Buckhout, Isaac Craig
Buckley, Samuel Botsford
Budd, Joseph Lancaster
Bulkley, Lucius Duncan
Bullock, Rufus Brown
Bullock, William A.
Bunce, Oliver Bell
Bunker, Arthur Hugh
Bunner, Henry Cuyler
Burchard, Samuel Dickinson
Burdick, Francis Marion
Burke, John Joseph
Burke, Stevenson
Burke, Thomas
Burlin Natalie Curtis
Burlingame, Anson
Burnham, Daniel Hudson
Burr, George Lincoln
Burr, Theodosia
Burrill, Alexander Mansfield

Burroughs, John
Burroughs, John Curtis
Burroughs, William Seward
Burt, John
Bush-Brown, Henry Kirke
Bushnell, Asa Smith
Butler, Benjamin Franklin
Butler, Charles
Butler, Howard Crosby
Butler, Walter N.
Butler, William Allen
Butterfield, Daniel
Butterfield, John
Buttrick, Wallace
Butts, Isaac
Cady, Daniel
Calkins, Norman Allison
Calkins, Phineas Wolcott
Callas, Maria
Calverley, Charles
Cambridge, Godfrey MacArthur
Cameron, Robert Alexander
Campbell, Allen
Campbell, George Washington
Campbell, James Valentine
Campbell, Thomas Joseph
Campbell, William W.
Cannon, Charles James
Cannon, James Graham
Cannon, James Thomas
Cantor, Eddie
Capone, Alphonse
Cardozo, Benjamin Nathan
Carlisle, Floyd Leslie
Carll, John Franklin
Carlson, Evans Fordyce
Carpenter, Francis Bicknell
Carpenter, Stephen Haskins
Carr, Eugene Asa
Carr, Joseph Bradford
Carrier, Willis Haviland
Carrington, Elaine Stern
Carroll, Howard
Carryl, Guy Wetmore
Carter, Jesse Benedict
Carter, Robert
Cary, Edward
Cary, Elisabeth Luther
Case, Jerome Increase
Casey, Thomas Lincoln
Casilear, John William
Cassidy, Jack
Cassidy, William
Cassoday, John Bolivar
Castle, Irene Foote
Cavert, Samuel McCrea
Cerf, Bennett Alfred
Chaffee, Jerome Bonaparte
Chambers, Robert William
Champlin, John Wayne
Chanfrau, Francis S.
Chapin, Edwin Hubbell
Chapin, James Paul
Chapman, John Jay
Chapman, Victor Emmanuel
Chase, Ilka
Chatterton, Ruth
Cheesman, Forman
Cheney, John Vance
Chesebrough, Caroline
Chevey, Charles Edward
Child, Frank Samuel
Chittenden, Hiram Martin
Choate, Anne Hyde Clarke
Christiancy, Isaac Peckham
Church, John Adams
Church, Pharcellus
Church, William Conant
Churchill, William
Claflin, John
Clark, Grenville
Clark, Lewis Gaylord
Clark, Myron Holley
Clark, Willis Gaylord
Clarke, John Mason
Clarke, Thomas Benedict
Clarke, William Newton
Clarkson, Matthew
Clemmer, Mary
Clifton, Josephine
Clinch, Charles Powell
Clinton DeWitt
Clinton, George
Clinton, James
Clough, John Everett
Clough, William Pitt
Cluett, Sanford Lockwood
Clurman, Harold Edgar
Coakley, Cornelius Godfrey
Cobb, Lee J.
Cochran, Alexander Smith
Cochrane, John
Coe, George Albert
Coffey, James Vincent
Coffin, Henry Sloane
Cogswell, William Browne
Cohen, Felix Solomon
Cohen, Jacob De Silva Solis
Cohen, Meyer Harris ("Mickey")
Cohn, Alfred Einstein
Cohn, Edwin Joseph
Cohn, Harry
Colden, Cadwallader David
Cole, Chester Cicero
Coleman, Charles Caryl
Coleman, John Aloysius
Colfax, Schuyler
Colgate, James Boorman
Collamer, Jacob
Collier, Peter
Collins, Edward Trowbridge
Collins, Guy N.
Colman, Norman Jay
Colombo, Joseph Anthony
Coman, Charlotte Buell
Comstock, George Franklin
Conboy, Martin
Cone, Hutchinson Ingham
Cone, Orello
Conkling, Alfred
Conkling, Roscoe
Cook, Flavius Josephus
Cook, Frederick Albert
Cook, James Merrill
Cook, John Williston
Cook, Walter
Cooley, Lyman Edgar
Cooley, Mortimer Elwyn
Cooley, Thomas McIntyre
Cooper, Edward
Cooper, James Graham
Cooper, Peter
Cooper, Sarah Brown Ingersoll
Cooper, Susan Fenimore
Cooper, Theodore
Cooper-Poucher, Matilda S.
Corliss, George Henry
Cornell, Alonzo B.
Cornell, Ezra
Cortelyou, George Bruce
Cortissoz, Royal
Corwin, Edward Tanjore
Couch, Darius Nash
Coudert, Frederic René
Coudert, Frederic René, Jr.
Courtney, Charles Edward
Cowen, Joshua Lionel
Cozzens, Frederick Swartwout
Crabtree, Lotta
Crandall, Charles Henry
Crane, Frederick Evan
Crane, Thomas Frederick
Crapsey, Adelaide
Cravath, Erastus Milo
Crawford, Thomas
Crerar, John
Crimmins, John Daniel
Crittenton, Charles Nelson
Crocker, Charles
Crocker, Francis Bacon
Croly, Herbert David
Cromwell, Gladys Louise Husted
Cromwell, William Nelson
Cropsey, Jaspar Francis
Crosby, Ernest Howard
Crosby, Founy
Crosby, Howard
Crosby, John Schuyler
Crosby, Percy Lee
Cross, Milton John
Croswell, Edwin
Crounse, Lorenzo
Cruger, Henry
Cruger, John
Culbertson, Josephine Murphy
Cullum, George Washington
Cummings, Amos Jay
Cuppia, Jerome Chester
Curran, Thomas Jerome
Curtis, John Green
Curtis, Newton Martin
Curtis, Samuel Ryan
Curtiss, Glenn Hammond
Cutler, James Goold
Cutting, Bronson Murray
Cutting, Robert Fulton
Cuyler, Theodore Ledyard
Daggett, Ellsworth
Dailey, Dan, Jr.
Dakin, James Harrison
Dale, Charles Marks
Dale, Chester
Dale, Maud Murray Thompson
Daley, Arthur John
Daly, Peter Christopher Arnold
Dalzell, John
Dana, Charles Anderson
Dana, James Dwight
Darin, Bobby
Darton, Nelson Horatio

Davidson, Jo
Davidson, Lucretia Maria
Davidson, Margaret Miller
Davies, Arthur Bowen
Davies, Henry Eugene
Davies, Marion Cecilia
Davis, Alexander Jackson
Davis, Andrew Jackson
Davis, Cushman Kellogg
Davis, Francis Breese, Jr.
Davis, Henry
Davis, Jerome Dean
Davis, Katharine Bement
Davis, Matthew Livingston
Davis, Nathan Smith
Davis, Oscar King
Davis, Paulina Kellogg Wright
Davison, George Willets
Dawley, Almena
Day, Clarence Shepard
Day, Dorothy
Day, George Parmly
Day, Luther
Dean, Bashford
Dean, Julia
Deerfoot
De Forest, Alfred Victor
De Forest, Robert Weeks
De Kay, George Colman
Delafield, Edward
Delafield, Francis
Delafield, John
Delafield, Richard
De Lancey, James, 1703–1760
De Lancey, James, 1732–1800
De Lancey, James, 1746–1804
De Lancey, William Heathcote
Delano, Jane Arminda
Delano, William Adams
Delavan, Edward Cornelius
Delawater, Cornelius Henry
DeLee, Joseph Bolivar
De Long, George Washington
Del Mar, Alexander
Deming, Philander
Dempster, John
Depew, Chauncey Mitchell
De Peyster, Abraham
De Peyster, John Watts
De Rose, Peter
De Sylva, George Gard "Buddy"
Devin, Thomas Casimer
Dewey, Melvil
Dewey, Richard Smith
De Wilde, Brandon
Dewing, Maria Richards Oakey
De Witt, Simeon
De Wolfe, Elsie
Dexter, Henry
Dibble, Ray Floyd
Dickinson, Charles Monroe
Dickinson, Donald McDonald
Dickinson, Preston
Dietz, Peter Ernest
Dill, James Brooks
Diller, Burgoyne
Dillon, John Forrest
Dillon, Sidney
Disturnell, John
Diven, Alexander Samuel
Dix, Morgan
Dodge, Grace Hoadley
Dodge, Mary Elizabeth Mapes
Dods, John Bovee
Dolph, Joseph Norton
Donaldson, Henry Herbert
Donn-Byrne, Brian Oswald
Donovan, James Britt
Donovan, William Joseph
Doolittle, James Rood
Doremus, Robert Ogden
Doremus, Sarah Platt Haines
Dorn, Harold Fred
Dorsheimer, William Edward
Doty, Elihu
Doty, James Duane
Doubleday, Abner
Doubleday, Frank Nelson
Doubleday, Nelson
Douglas, Amanda Minnie
Dove, Arthur Garfield
Dowling, Austin
Downing, Andrew Jackson
Downing, Charles
Doyle, John Thomas
Drake, Edwin Laurentine
Drake, Francis Ann Denny
Drake, Joseph Rodman
Draper, Andrew Sloan
Draper, Dorothy
Draper, Lyman Copeland
Draper, Ruth
Dreier, Katherine Sophie
Dreier, Mary Elisabeth
Drew, Daniel
Drisler, Henry
Drury, John Benjamin
Dryfoos, Orvil E.
Duane, Alexander
Duane, James
Duane, James Chatham
Duane, William
Dudley, Charles Benjamin
Duer, John
Duffield, Samuel Augustus Willoughby
Dulles, Allen Welsh
Dumont, Allen Balcom
Dumont, Margaret
Durant, Charles Ferson
Durante, James Francis ("Jimmy")
Durrie, Daniel Steele
Duryea, Hermanes Barkulo
Duryée, Abram
Duyckinck, Evert Augustus
Dwight, Theodore William
Dyar, Harrison Gray
Earle, Edward Mead
Earle, Mortimer Lamson
Eastman, George
Eastman, Harvey Gridley
Eastman, Joseph Bartlett
Eastman, Max Forrester
Eastman, William Reed
Eaton, Amos
Edebohls, George Michael
Edgerton, Alfred Peck
Edgerton, Sidney
Edman, Irwin
Edmonds, Francis William
Edmonds, John Worth
Edwards, William Henry
Eells, Dan Parmelee
Egleston, Thomas
Ehuinger, John Whelten
Eidlitz, Cyrus Lazelle Warner
Ellet, Elizabeth Fries Lummis
Elliot, Daniel Giraud
Elliott, Charles Loring
Ellis, Jo Bicknell
Ellsworth, Elmer Ephraim
Elsberg, Charles Atbert
Ely, Richard Theodore
Embury, Emma Catherine
Emerson, Haven
Emerson, Rollins Adams
Emery, Albert Hamilton
Emery, Charles Edward
Emmet, William Le Roy
Emott, James, 1771–1850
Emott, James, 1823–1884
Engelhard, Charles William
Englis, John
Eno, William Phelps
Epstein, Jacob
Epstein, Philip G.
Erdman, Charles Rosenbury
Erlanger, Abraham Lincoln
Erpf, Armand Grover
Errett, Isaac
Erskine, John
Esterly, George
Evans, Edward Payson
Evans, George Alfred
Evola, Natale ("Joe Diamond")
Fairbank, Calvin
Fairchild, Charles Stebbins
Fairchild, Sherman Mills
Faneuil, Peter
Fanning, Edmund
Fargo, William George
Farley, James Aloysius
Farman, Elbert Eli
Farmer, John
Farnam, Henry
Farnham, Eliza Woodson Burhans
Farrand, Beatrix Cadwalader Jones
Farwell, Charles Benjamin
Farwell, John Villiers
Fassett, Cornelia Adèle Strong
Fassett, Jacob Sloat
Fawcett, Edgar
Fay, Theodore Sedgwick
Feis, Herbert
Feke, Robert
Fell, John
Fenner, Burt Leslie
Fenton, Reuben Eaton
Ferguson, William Porter Frisbee
Ferris, Isaac
Ferris, Woodbridge Nathan
Field, Benjamin Hazard
Field, Herbert Haviland
Field, Marshall, IV
Field, Maunsell Bradhurst
Field, Thomas Warren
Fields, Lewis Maurice
Fillmore, Millard
Finch, Francis Miles
Fischetti, John

Fish, Hamilton
Fish, Nicholas
Fish, Stuyvesant
Fisher, George Jackson
Fisher, Harrison
Fisher, Irving
Fisk, Clinton Bowen
Fiske, Bradley Allen
Fiske, Daniel Willard
Fiske, Harrison Grey
Fitch, Asa
Fitch, William Clyde
Fitzgerald, Thomas
Fitzsimmons, James Edward ("Sunny Jim")
Flagg, Ernest
Flagg, James Montgomery
Flagler, Henry Morrison
Flagler, John Haldane
Flandrau, Charles Eugene
Flegenheimer, Arthur
Fleischer, Nathaniel Stanley ("Nat")
Fletcher, Robert
Flint, Weston
Florence, William Jermyn
Flower, Roswell Pettibone
Floy, James
Floyd, William
Flynn, Edward Joseph
Folger, Henry Clay
Folwell, William Watts
Fonda, John H.
Foote, Lucius Harwood
Forbes, Edwin
Ford, Hannibal Choate
Ford, Paul Leicester
Ford, Worthington Chauncey
Forman, Celia Adler
Forman, Joshua
Forman, Justus Miles
Forrestal, James Vincent
Forsyth, John
Fosdick, Charles Austin
Fosdick, Harry Emerson
Fosdick, Raymond Blaine
Foshag, William Frederick
Foster, David Skaats
Foulke, William Dudley
Fowler, Frank
Fowler, George Ryerson
Fowler, Orson Squire
Fowler, Russell Story
Fox, Dixon Ryan
Foy, Eddie
Francis, Charles Spencer
Francis, John Morgan
Francis, John Wakefield
Francis, Samuel Ward
Frank, Jerome
Frederic, Harold
Freedman, Andrew
Freer, Charles Lang
Freneau, Philip Morin
Freund, Ernst
Frisch, Frank Francis ("The Fordham Flash")
Frissell, Hollis Burke
Frost, Holloway Halstead
Fuertes, Louis Agassiz
Fuller, Andrew S.
Fuller, George
Fuller, George Warren
Fuller, Robert Mason
Fulton, Justin Dewey
Funk, Wilfred John
Furman, Richard
Gage, Lyman Judson
Gage, Matilda Joslyn
Galante, Carmine
Gale, Benjamin
Gale, George Washington
Gallagher, Ralph W.
Gallico, Paul William
Gally, Merritt
Galpin, Charles Josiah
Gannett, Frank Ernest
Gano, Stephen
Gansevoort, Leonard
Gansevoort, Peter
Gardiner, James Terry
Gardner, Isabella Stewart
Garfield, John
Garis, Howard Roger
Garrett, Edmund Henry
Garrison, Cornelius Kingsland
Gaskill, Harvey Freeman
Gayler, Charles
Gaynor, William Jay
Gear, John Henry
Gehrig, Henry Louis
Geismar, Maxwell David
Gellatly, John
Genin, John Nicholas
Genung, John Franklin
George, Grace
George, William Reuben
Gerard, James Watson, 1794–1874
Gerard, James Watson, 1867–1951
Gerry, Elbridge Thomas
Gershwin, George
Gibbs, George
Gibbs, Oliver Wolcott, 1822–1908
Gibbs, (Oliver) Wolcott, 1902–1958
Gifford, Sanford Robinson
Gilbert, Eliphalet Wheeler
Gilbert, Grove Karl
Gilbert, Linda
Gilbert, Rufus Henry
Gilder, Jeannette Leonard
Gildersleeve, Virginia Crocheron
Gill, Theodore Nicholas
Gillespie, William Mitchell
Gillet, Ransom Hooker
Gillett, Horace Wadsworth
Gilman, Lawrence
Ginter, Lewis
Gleason, Kate
Gleason, Ralph Joseph
Glueck, Eleanor Touroff
Glynn, Martin Henry
Goddard, Calvin Luther
Goddard, Luther Marcellus
Godey, Louis Antoine
Goethals, George Washington
Goff, Emmet Stull
Goforth, William
Gold, Michael
Golden, John
Goldmark, Henry
Goldmark, Rubin
Goldwater, Sigismund Schulz
Goodell, William
Goodman, Paul
Goodnow, Frank Johnson
Goodrich, Benjamin Franklin
Goodsell, Daniel Ayres
Goodspeed, Thomas Wakefield
Goodwin, Hannibal Williston
Goodyear, Anson Conger
Gorcey, Leo
Gordon, Andrew
Goss, Albert Simon
Gottschalk, Louis Reichenthal
Gould, Jay
Gracie, Archibald
Graham, Charles Kinnaird
Granger, Gordon
Grant, Asahel
Grant, Madison
Grauer, Benjamin Franklin ("Ben")
Graves, Frederick Rogers
Gray, Asa
Gray, Henry Peters
Green, Gabriel Marcus
Green, Seth
Greenbaum, Edward Samuel
Greene, William Cornell
Greenslet, Ferris
Gregg, Willis Ray
Gregory, Charles Noble
Gregory, Daniel Seelye
Gregory, Eliot
Gregory, John Milton
Griffes, Charles Tomlinson
Griffiths, John Willis
Grinnell, George Bird
Grinnell, Henry Walton
Griscom, Ludlow
Griswold, John Augustus
Groesbeck, William Slocum
Grofé, Ferde
Gropper, William
Gross, Charles
Gross, Milt
Groves, Leslie Richard, Jr.
Gue, Benjamin F.
Guggenheim, Marguerite ("Peggy")
Guinzburg, Harold Kleinert
Gunnison, Foster
Guthrie, Alfred
Guthrie, Ramon
Habberton, John
Habersham, Alexander Wylly
Hackett, James Henry
Hadley, James
Hagedorn, Hermann Ludwig Gebhard
Hagen, Walter Charles
Haight, Charles Coolidge
Haight, Henry Huntly
Haines, Daniel
Hall, Abraham Oakley
Hall, Charles Cuthbert
Hall, Fitzedward
Hall, Leonard Wood
Hall, Nathan Kelsey

Halleck, Henry Wager
Hallock, Charles
Halsey, Frederick Arthur
Halsted, William Stewart
Hamilton, Alice
Hamilton, Allan McLane
Hamilton, Charles Smith
Hamilton, Clayton
Hamilton, James Alexander
Hamilton, Schuyler
Hamlin, Emmons
Hamlin, Talbot Faulkner
Hammerstein, Oscar, II
Hammon, Jupiter
Hampden, Walter
Hanchett, Henry Granger
Hand, Augustus Noble
Hand, Learned
Hanna, Edward Joseph
Harcourt, Alfred
Hard, William
Hardenbergh, Jacob Rutsen
Hardie, James Allen
Harland, Henry
Harper, Fletcher
Harper, James
Harper, John Lyell
Harrigan, Edward
Harriman, Edward Henry
Harriman, Edward Roland Noel
Harriman, Florence Jaffray Hurst
Harris, Chapin Aaron
Harris, Charles Kassell
Harris, Ira
Harris, Miriam Coles
Harris, Rollin Arthur
Harris, Sam Henry
Harris, Seymour Edwin
Harris, Stanley Raymond ("Bucky")
Harris, Townsend
Harrison, Fairfax
Harrison, Francis Burton
Hart, Edmund Hall
Hart, Lorenz Milton
Hart, Moss
Hart, Virgil Chittenden
Hart, Wilbiam Surrey
Harte, Francis Brett
Hartford, George Ludlum
Hartley, Jonathan Scott
Hartness, James
Hartsuff, George Lucas
Harvey, Hayward Augustus
Hasbrouck, Abraham Bruyn
Hasbrouck, Lydia Sayer
Hascall, Milo Smith
Hassard, John Rose Greene
Hastings, Charles Sheldon
Hastings, Serranus Clinton
Hastings, Thomas
Haswell, Charles Haynes
Hatch, John Porter
Haughton, Percy Duncan
Hauk, Minnie
Havemeyer, Henry Osborne
Havemeyer, William Frederick
Haven, Emily Bradley Neal
Havens, James Smith
Haviland, Clarence Floyd
Hawes, Charles Boardman
Hayes, Carlton Joseph Huntley
Hayes, Gabby
Hayes, Patrick Joseph
Hayford, John Fillmore
Hays, Arthur Garfield
Hays, William Jacob
Hayward, Susan
Headley, Joel Tyler
Headley, Phineas Camp
Heaton, John Langdon
Heatter, Gabriel
Hecht, Ben
Hecker, Isaac Thomas
Hedding, Elijah
Heenan, John Carmel
Hegeman, John Rogers
Heintzelman, Stuart
Heinze, Frederick Augustus
Helburn, Theresa
Helm, Charles John
Helpern, Milton
Hemenway, Mary Porter Tileston
Henderson, Ray
Hendrick
Hendrick, Ellwood
Heney, Francis Joseph
Henry, Joseph
Hepburn, Alonzo Barton
Hepburn, Katharine Houghton
Herdic, Peter
Herkimer, Nicholas
Herne, James A.
Herrmann, Bernard
Hess, Alfred Fabian
Hewitt, Abram Stevens
Hewitt, John Hill
Hewitt, Peter Cooper
Heye, George Gustav
Hibbard, Freeborn Garrettson
Hicks, Elias
Hicks, John, 1847–1917
Higgins, Frank Wayland
Higginson, Henry Lee
Hill, David Bennett
Hill, Frederick Trevor
Hill, George William
Hill, Grace Livingston
Hill, John Henry
Hill, Nathaniel Peter
Hines, James J.
Hinman, George Wheeler
Hirsch, Isaac Seth
Hirth, William Andrew
Hiscock, Frank Harris
Hitchcock, Phineas Warrener
Hitchcock, Raymond
Hoadley, John Chipman
Hoag, Joseph
Hoard, William Dempster
Hobart, Alice Nourse Tisdale
Hodge, William Thomas
Hodges, George
Hoe, Richard March
Hoe, Robert, 1839–1909
Hoff, John Van Rensselaer
Hoffman, Charles Fenno
Hoffman, David Murray
Hoffman, Eugene Augustus
Hoffman, John Thompson
Hoffman, Ogden
Hoffman, Wickham
Hofstadter, Richard
Hogue, Wilson Thomas
Holabird, William
Holcombe, Chester
Holdrege, George Ward
Holland, Edmund Milton
Holland, Joseph Jefferson
Hollerith, Herman
Hollev, Marietta
Hollick, Charles Arthur
Holliday, Judy
Holmes, Daniel Henry
Holt, Hamilton Bowen
Holt, Luther Emmett
Holt, Winifred
Hone, Philip
Hooker, Elon Huntington
Hoppe, William Frederick ("Willie")
Hopper, DeWolf
Hopper, Edward
Hormel, George Albert
Horsford, Eben Norton
Horton, Edward Everett, Jr.
Hosack, Alexander Eddy
Hosack, David
Hosmer, Hezekiah Lord
Hosmer, William Howe Cuyler
Hotchkiss, Horace Leslie
Hough, Franklin Benjamin
Hough, George Washington
Houghton, Douglass
House, Henry Alonzo
House, Samuel Reynolds
Hovey, Alvah
Howard, George Elliott
Howard, Moe
Howe, Herbert Alonzo
Howe, Julia Ward
Howe, William Wirt
Howell, John Adams
Howland, Emily
Howland, John
Hoxie, Robert Franklin
Hoxie, William Dixie
Hoyt, John Sherman
Hubbard, Lucius Frederick
Huebsch, Benjamin W.
Hughes, Albert William
Hughes, Charles Evans
Hughes, George Wurtz
Hull, Clark Leonard
Hunt, Benjamin Weeks
Hunt, Charles Wallace
Hunt, Ward
Hunt, Washington
Huntington, Daniel
Huntington, Edward Vermilye
Huntington, Henry Edwards
Huntington, Jedediah Vincent
Huntington, Margaret Jane Evans
Hurlbut, Jesse Lyman
Hurley, Roy T.
Husing, Edward Britt ("Ted")
Hutchins, Robert Maynard
Hutton, Barbara Woolworth
Hutton, Edward Francis
Hutton, Frederick Remsen
Hutton, Laurence

Hyatt, John Wesley
Hyde, Helen
Hyde, Henry Baldwin
Hylan, John Francis
Ingalls, Marilla Baker
Ingersoll, Robert Green
Inman, Henry, 1801–1846
Inman, Henry, 1837–1899
Inman, John
Inness, George
Ireland, Joseph Norton
Irving, John Treat
Irving, Peter
Irving, Pierre Munro
Irving, Roland Duer
Irving, Washington
Irving, William
Irwin, Elisabeth Antoinette
Irwin, William Henry
Isaacs, Abram Samuel
Isham, Ralph Heyward
Isham, Samuel
Isherwood, Benjamin Franklin
Ives, Halsey Cooley
Ives, Irving McNeil
Ives, James Merritt
Ives, Joseph Christmas
Jackson, Abraham Valentine Williams
Jackson, Charles Douglas
Jackson, George Thomas
Jackson, James Caleb
Jackson, Mortimer Melville
Jackson, Samuel Macauley
Jackson, Sheldon
Jackson, William Henry
Jacobs, Hirsch
Jacobs, Michael Strauss
Jacobs, Paul
James, Arthur Curtiss
James, Edward Christopher
James, Henry, 1811–1882
James, Henry, 1843–1916
James, Thomas Lemuel
James, William
Janeway, Theodore Caldwell
Jay, Sir James
Jay, John, 1745–1829
Jay, John, 1817–1894
Jay, William
Jelliffe, Smith Ely
Jemison, Alice Mae Lee
Jenkins, James Graham
Jenkins, John Stilwell
Jenks, Tudor Storrs
Jerome, William Travers
Jervis, John Bloomfield
Jewett, William Cornell
Johnson, Alexander Smith
Johnson, Benjamin Pierce
Johnson, Elias Henry
Johnson, Helen Louise Kendrick
Johnson, Sir John
Johnson, Levi
Johnson, Owen McMahon
Johnson, Samuel William
Johnson, Virginia Wales
Johnson, William Woolsey
Johnson, Willis Fletcher
Johnston, Alexander
Johnston, John Taylor
Johnston, Samuel
Joline, Adrian Hoffman
Jones, Amanda Theodosia
Jones, George Heber
Jones, Herschel Vespasian
Jones, John
Jones, Samuel, 1734–1819
Jones, Samuel, 1770–1853
Jones, Thomas
Jones, William Alfred
Jordan, David Starr
Jordan, Virgil Justin
Jordan, William George
Josephson, Matthew
Judah, Samuel
Judah, Samuel Benjamin Helbert
Judd, Gerrit Parmele
Judd, Norman Buel
Judd, Orange
Judson, Edward Zane Carroll
Judson, Egbert Putnam
Judson, Emily Chubbuck
Judson, Harry Pratt
Kaempffert, Waldemar Bernhard
Kaiser, Henry John
Kane, Helen
Kane, John Kintzing
Kaye, Frederick Benjamin
Kearny, Philip
Keating, Kenneth Barnard
Kedzie, Robert Clark
Keeley, Leslie E.
Keene, Thomas Wallace
Keep, Henry
Keith, Minor Cooper
Keller, Arthur Ignatius
Kelley, James Douglas Jerrold
Kellogg, Frank Billings
Kellogg, Samuel Henry
Kelly, John
Kelly, Luther Sage
Kelly, Michael J.
Kelsey, Francis Willey
Kemble, Gouverneur
Kemp, James Furman
Kemper, Jackson
Kenedy, Patrick John
Kent, Charles Foster
Kent, James
Kent, Rockwell
Kenyon, Josephine Hemenway
Keppel, Frederick Paul
Kern, Jerome David
Kernan, Francis
Kert, Charles Foster
Kidder, Daniel Parish
Kilpatrick, John Reed
King, Carol Weiss
King, Charles
King, Edward Skinner
King, James Gore
King, John
King, John Alsop
King, Preston
King, Richard
King, Rufus
King, Stanley
King, Thomas Starr
Kingsley, Calvin
Kingsley, Elizabeth Seelman
Kingsley, Norman William
Kinne, La Vega George
Kinney, Elizabeth Clementine Dodge Stedman
Kip, William Ingraham
Kiphuth, Robert John Herman
Kirchwey, Freda
Kirk, Edward Norris
Kirkland, Caroline Matilda Stansbury
Kirkland, John Thornton
Kirkland, Joseph
Kirstein, Louis Edward
Klein, Anne
Klem, William J. ("Bill")
Knapp, Joseph Palmer
Knapp, Martin Augustine
Knapp, Seaman Asahel
Knapp, William Ireland
Knauth, Oswald Whitman
Knickerbocker, Herman
Knopf, Blanche Wolf
Knox, George William
Knox, John Jay
Kobbé, Gustav
Koch, Vivienne
Kreymborg, Alfred Francis
Kuhn, Walt
Kunz, George Frederick
Ladd, Carl Edwin
Ladd, Kate Macy
La Farge, Christopher Grant
La Farge, John
La Farge, Oliver Hazard Perry
La Guardia, Fiorello Henry
Lahr, Bert
Laimbeer, Natalie Schenk
Lait, Jacquin Leonard ("Jack")
Lake, Veronica
Lamb, John
Lamb, William Frederick
Lamont, Daniel Scott
Lamont, Hammond
Lamont, Thomas William
La Mountain, John
Landon, Melville de Lancey
Lane, Arthur Bliss
Langford, Nathaniel Pitt
Langmuir, Irving
Lansing, Gulian
Lansing, John
Lansing, Robert
Lapchick, Joseph Bohomiel
Lapham, Increase Allen
Larrabee, Charles Hathaway
Lathbury, Mary Artemisia
Lathrop, John Hiram
Law, George
Lawes, Lewis Edward
Lawrence, George Newbold
Lawrence, William Beach
Lawrie, Alexander
Lawson, John Howard
Lawson, Robert Ripley
Lay, John Louis
Lazarus, Emma
Le Clear, Thomas
Le Conte, John Lawrence

Leavitt, Frank Simmons (Man Mountain Dean)
Lee, Canada
Lee, Frederic Schiller
Lee, James Melvin
Lee, Luther
Lee, Manfred B.
Lee, Porter Raymond
Lee, William Little
Lefferts, George Morewood
Lefferts, Marshall
Leffingwell, Russell Cornell
Leggett, Mortimer Dormer
Leggett, William
Lehman, Adele Lewisohn
Lehman, Arthur
Lehman, Herbert Henry
Lehman, Irving
Lehman, Robert
Lennox, Charlotte Ramsay
Lenox, James
Le Roux, Charles
Letchworth, William Pryor
Leupp, Francis Ellington
Levenson, Samuel ("Sam")
Levitt, Abraham
Levitt, Arthur
Lewis, Dioclesian
Lewis, George William
Lewis, James
Lewis, Morgan
Lewis, Oscar
Lewis, Taylor
Lewisohn, Sam Adolph
Lexow, Clarence
L'Hommedieu, Ezra
Libman, Emanuel
Liebling, Abbott Joseph
Liebling, Estelle
Lindsay, Howard
Link, Henry Charles
Lintner, Joseph Albert
Lippincott, Sara Jane Clarke
Lippmann, Walter
Litchfield, Electus Backus
Littauer, Lucius Nathan
Littlejohn, Abram Newkirk
Livingston, Edward
Livingston, Henry Brockholst
Livingston, John Henry
Livingston, John William
Livingston, Peter VanBrugh
Livingston, Philip
Livingston, Robert R., 1718–1775
Livingston, Robert R., 1746–1813
Livingston, William
Lloyd, Henry Demarest
Lloyd, James
Lloyd, John Uri
Locke, David Ross
Lockwood, Belva Ann Bennett
Lockwood, Samuel Drake
Loeb, James
Loesser, Frank
Loew, Marcus
Logan, Olive
Lombardi, Vincent Thomas
Longworth, Alice Lee Roosevelt
Loomis, Charles Battell
Loomis, Elmer Howard
Loomis, Mahlon
Loop, Henry Augustus
Lopez, Vincent Joseph
Lord, Asa Dearborn
Lord, Chester Sanders
Lord, William Wilberforce
Lorillard, Pierre
Lossing, Benson John
Lounsbury, Thomas Raynesford
Loveman, Amy
Low, Seth
Low, Will Hicok
Lowery, Woodbury
Luce, Stephen Bleecker
Luckenbach, J(ohn) Lewis
Ludlow, Daniel
Ludlow, Fitz Hugh
Ludlow, Gabriel George
Ludlow, George Duncan
Ludlow, Noah Miller
Ludlow, Thomas William
Ludlow, William
Luhan, Mabel Dodge
Lynch, James Mathew
Lynde, Francis
Lyon, Caleb
Lyon, Theodatus Timothy
Lyon, William Penn
Lyons, Leonard
Mabie, Hamilton Wright
McAdie, Alexander George
McAlpine, William Jarvis
McArthur, Duncan
McCall, John Augustine
McCarthy, Charles Louis (Clem)
McCloskey, John
McCloskey, William George
McComb, John
McCormick, Richard Cunningham
McCullough, Ernest
McCurdy, Richard Aldrich
MacDowell, Edward Alexander
McEntee, Jervis
McGarrah, Gates White
McGiffert, Arthur Cushman
McGlyn, Edward
McGovern, John
McGraw, James Herbert
McGraw, John Joseph
McIntyre, James Francis Aloysius
MacKaye, James Morrison Steele
MacKaye, Percy Wallace
Mackenzie, Alexander Slidell
Mackenzie, Ranald Slidell
McLaren, William Edward
McLaughlin, Hugh
Maclay, William Brown
McLeod, Hugh
McMaster, Guy Humphreys
McMaster, James Alphonsus
McMaster, John Bach
McMath, Robert Emmet
MacMonnies, Frederick William
McQuaid, Bernard John
McVickar, William Neilson
McVicker, James Hubert
Macy, Valentine Everit
Maginnis, Martin
Mahan, Alfred Thayer
Mahan, Asa
Mahan, Dennis Hart
Mallory, Clifford Day
Malone, Dudley Field
Mankiewicz, Herman Jacob
Mann, Louis
Mannes, David
Mannes, Leopold Damrosch
Manning, Daniel
Mantle, (Robert) Burns
Mapes, Charles Victor
Mapes, James Jay
Marbury, Elisabeth
Marcantonio, Vito Anthony
Marcus, Bernard Kent
Marquand, Allan
Marquand, Henry Gurdon
Marsh, Grant Prince
Marsh, Othniel Charles
Marshall, Frank James
Marshall, Henry Rutgers
Marshall, Louis
Marshall, Samuel Lyman Atwood ("Slam")
Marshall, William Edgar
Martin, Artemas
Martin, Edward Sandford
Martin, Frederick Townsend
Martin, Homer Dodge
Martindale, John Henry
Marx, Adolf Arthur ("Harpo")
Marx, Herbert ("Zeppo")
Marx, Julius Henry ("Groucho")
Marx, Leonard ("Chico")
Marx, Milton ("Gummo")
Maslow, Abraham H.
Mason, Charles
Mason, John Mitchell
Mason, William Ernest
Mather, Fred
Mathews, Albert
Mathews, Cornelius
Matteson, Joel Aldrich
Matteson, Tompkins Harrison
Mattice, Asa Martines
Mattison, Hiram
Mattoon, Stephen
Maverick, Peter
Maxim, Hiram Percy
Maxwell, Samuel
Maybeck, Bernard Ralph
Mayer, Emil
Mayer, Philip Frederick
Maynard, Edward
Maynard, George William
Mayo, William Starbuck
Mead, James Michael
Meade, Richard Worsam
Meany, William George
Mearns, Edgar Alexander
Mechem, Floyd Russell
Megrue, Roi Cooper
Meiggs, Henry
Melville, George Wallace
Melville, Herman
Mendel, Lafayette Benedict
Meneely, Andrew
Merchant, Livingston Tallmadge
Merck, George Wilhelm
Merriam, Augustus Chapman
Merriam, Clinton Hart

Merriam, William Rush
Merrill, Stuart Fitz Randolph
Merritt, Israel John
Merritt, Leonidas
Merry, William Lawrence
Meyer, Agnes Elizabeth Ernst
Meyer, Annie Nathan
Michael, Arthur
Miles, Manly
Milk, Harvey Bernard
Milledoler, Philip
Miller, Charles Henry
Miller, David Hunter
Miller, Gerrit Smith, Jr.
Miller, Gilbert Heron
Miller, Harriet Mann
Miller, Henry Valentine
Miller, Kenneth Hayes
Miller, Nathan Lewis
Miller, Warner
Miller, William Henry Harrison
Mills, Clark
Mills, Cyrus Taggart
Mills, Darius Ogden
Mills, Lawrence Heyworth
Millspaugh, Charles Frederick
Miner, Myrtilla
Minor, Robert Crannell
Minturn, Robert Bowne
Mirsky, Alfred Ezra
Mitchel, John Purroy
Mitchell, Hinckley Gilbert Thomas
Mitchell, Isaac
Mitchell, John Ames
Mitchell, Margaret Julia
Mitchell, William, 1801–1886
Mitchill, Samuel Latham
Moffat, David Halliday
Moffat, Jay Pierrepont
Moffett, Cleveland Langston
Mollenhauer, Emil
Montgomery, David Henry
Montgomery, Thomas Harrison
Moon, Parker Thomas
Mooney, William
Moore, Benjamin
Moore, Charles Herbert
Moore, Clement Clarke
Moore, Nathaniel Fish
Moore, Richard Channing
Moore, Veranus Alva
Moore, William Henry
Moran, Eugene Francis
Morehouse, Henry Lyman
Morell, George Webb
Morgan, Anne
Morgan, Charles Hill
Morgan, Edwin Barber
Morgan, Edwin Vernon
Morgan, John Pierpont
Morgan, Lewis Henry
Morgenthau, Henry, Jr.
Morrell, Benjamin
Morris, Edward Dafydd
Morris, Gouverneur
Morris, Lewis, 1671–1746
Morris, Lewis, 1726–1798
Morris, Lewis Richard
Morris, Richard
Morris, Richard Valentine
Morris, Robert Hunter
Morris, William Hopkins
Mortimer, Charles Greenough
Morton, Henry
Morton, Julius Sterling
Moses, Anna Mary Robertson ("Grandma")
Moses, Montrose Jonas
Mosher, Eliza Maria
Moskowitz, Belle Lindner Israels
Mosler, Henry
Moss, Frank
Mostel, Samuel Joel ("Zero")
Mott, James
Mott, John R.
Mott, Valentine
Mount, William Sidney
Muldoon, William
Mulford, Prentice
Mullany, James Robert Madison
Muller, Hermann Joseph
Mulry, Thomas Maurice
Mumford, James Gregory
Mundelein, George William
Munger, Theodore Thornton
Murphy, Charles Francis
Murphy, Henry Cruse
Murphy, John Francis
Murphy, John W.
Murray, David
Murray, Thomas Edward, 1860–1929
Murray, Thomas Edward, 1891–1961
Musica, Philip Mariano Fausto
Myer, Albert James
Nack, James M.
Naish, Joseph Carrol
Nash, Frederick Ogden
Nathan, Maud
Nelson, Henry Loomis
Nelson, Rensselaer Russell
Nelson, Reuben
Nelson, Samuel
Nevins, John Livingston
Newberry, John Stoughton
Newell, Robert Henry
Newhouse, Samuel
Newhouse, Samuel Irving
Newman, Barnett
Newman, Henry Roderick
Newman, John Philip
Newton, Hubert Anson
Newton, Isaac, 1794–1858
Nichols, Ruth Rowland
Nichols, William Ford
Nicoll, De Lancey
Nicoll, James Craig
Nipher, Francis Eugene
Nitchie, Edwar Bartlett
Noble, Gladwyn Kingsley
Norsworthy, Naomi
North, Frank Joshua
North, Frank Mason
North, Simon Newton Dexter
Norton, John Nicholas
Norton, John Pitkin
Nott, Charles Cooper
Nourse, Edwin Griswold
Noyes, Henry Drury
Noyes, La Verne
Noyes, William Curtis
Nye, James Warren
Oakley, Thomas Jackson
Oberholser, Harry Church
Oberndorf, Clarence Paul
O'Brian, John Lord
O'Brien, Edward Charles
O'Brien, Morgan Joseph
O'Conor, Charles
Odell, Benjamin Barker
Odell, George Clinton Densmore
Odenbach, Frederick Louis
O'Donnell, Emmett, Jr. ("Rosy")
Ogden, David Bayard
Ogden, Herbert Gouverneur
Ogden, Rollo
Ogden, William Butler
Ogilvie, John
Olcott, Chauncey
Olcott, Eben Erskine
Olds, Leland
Olmstead, Albert Ten Eyck
Olmsted, Frederick Law
Olyphant, Robert Morrison
O'Malley, Walter Francis
Onderdonk, Benjamin Tredwell
Onderdonk, Henry
Onderdonk, Henry Ustick
O'Neill, Eugene
Oppenheimer, Julius Robert
Ordronaux, John
Orton, Edward Francis Baxter
Orton, Harlow South
Orton, Helen Fuller
Orton, James
Orton, William
Osborn, Laughton
Osborne, Thomas Mott
O'Shaughnessy, Nelson Jarvis Waterbury
O'Shea, Michael Vincent
Osterhout, Winthrop John Vanleuven
Otis, Charles Rollin
Otis, Fessenden Nott
Ottley, Roi
Paddock, Algernon Sidney
Page, William
Palmer, Alice Elvira Freeman
Palmer, Alonzo Benjamin
Palmer, Erastus Dow
Palmer, Horatio Richmond
Palmer, Innis Newton
Palmer, Potter
Palmer, Walter Launt
Pardee, Ario
Pardow, William O'Brien
Park, William Hallock
Parker, Alton Brooks
Parker, Arthur Caswell
Parker, Ely Samuel
Parker, Foxhall Alexander
Parker, Jane Marsh
Parker, William Harwar
Parsons, Elsie Worthington Clews
Parsons, John Edward
Parsons, Lewis Baldwin
Parsons, Lewis Eliphalet
Parsons, Samuel Bowne

Parsons, William Barclay
Parton, Arthur
Pastor, Antonio
Paton, Lewis Bayles
Patrick, Marsena Rudolph
Patterson, Daniel Todd
Patterson, Robert Porter
Pattison, Thomas
Paul, William Darwin ("Shorty")
Paulding, Hiram
Paulding, James Kirke
Payne, Henry B.
Payne, John Howard
Payne, Sereno Elisha
Payne, William Harold
Peabody, Josephine Preston
Peck, Charles Horton
Peck, George
Peck, George Record
Peck, George Wilbur
Peck, Jesse Truesdell
Peck, John James
Peck, Lillie
Peckham, George Williams
Peckham, Rufus Wheeler
Peckham, Wheeler Hazard
Peixotto, Benjamin Franklin
Peloubet, Francis Nathan
Pendleton, John B.
Penfield, Edward
Pennoyer, Sylvester
Perelman, Sidney Joseph
Perin, Charles Page
Perkins, George Douglas
Perkins, Maxwell Evarts
Perry, Clarence Arthur
Perry, Stuart
Peters, John Charles
Peters, John Punnett
Phelps, William Franklin
Philip, John Woodward
Phillips, Philip
Picton, Thomas
Pierce, Gilbert Ashville
Pierson, Arthur Tappan
Pierson, Hamilton Wilcox
Piggot, Robert
Pilcher, Paul Monroe
Pintard, John
Pintard, Lewis
Piper, William Thomas
Pirsson, Louis Valentine
Pitcher, Zina
Platt, Thomas Collier
Polak, John Osborn
Polk, Frank Lyon
Pomeroy, John Norton
Pomeroy, Marcus Mills
Pond, James Burton
Pope, John Russell
Porter, Holbrook Fitz-John
Porter, Jermain Gildersleeve
Porter, John Addison
Post, Augustus
Post, George Adams
Post, George Browne
Post, George Edward
Post, Isaac
Post, Wright
Pott, Francis Lister Hawks
Potter, Alonzo
Potter, Eliphalet Nott
Potter, Henry Codman
Potter, Horatio
Potter, Louis McClellan
Potter, Platt
Potter, Robert Brown
Pound, Cuthbert Winfred
Powell, Edward Payson
Powell, George Harold
Powell, John Wesley
Powell, William Bramwell
Powell, William Henry
Power, Frederick Belding
Powers, Daniel William
Prang, Mary Amelia Dana Hicks
Pratt, Eliza Ann Farman
Pratt, James Bissett
Pratt, Orson
Pratt, Parley Parker
Pratt, Richard Henry
Pratt, Sereno Stansbury
Pratt, Tadock
Prescott, Albert Benjamin
Pressman, Lee
Price, Stephen
Price, Theodore Hazeltine
Prime, Benjamin Youngs
Prime, Edward Dorr Griffin
Prime, Samuel Irenaeus
Prime, William Cowper
Prince, Le Baron Bradford
Prince, William, *c.* 1725–1802
Prince, William, 1766–1842
Prince, William Robert
Pringle, Henry Fowles
Prinze, Freddie
Prosser, Charles Smith
Provoost, Samuel
Pruyn, John Van Schaick Lansing
Pruyn, Robert Hewson
Pulitzer, Joseph, Jr.
Pulitzer, Margaret Leech
Pullman, George Mortimer
Pumpelly, Raphael
Purdy, Lawson
Purple, Samuel Smith
Putnam, (George) Herbert
Putnam, James Osborne
Putnam, Ruth
Quackenbush, Stephen Platt
Quidor, John
Quitman, John Anthony
Radcliff, Jacob
Raft, George
Rafter, George W.
Raines, John
Ralph, Julian
Rambaut, Mary Lucinda Bonney
Rand, James Henry
Randall, Alexander Williams
Randall, Clarence Belden
Randall, Henry Stephens
Randall, Samuel Sidwell
Ranger, Henry Ward
Rankine, William Birch
Raskob, John Jakob
Rathbone, Justus Henry
Rathbun, Richard
Rauschenbusch, Walter
Raymond, Alexander Gillespie
Raymond, Benjamin Wright
Raymond, Henry Jarvis
Raymond, John Howard
Raymond, John T.
Raymond, Miner
Red Jacket
Redfield, Amasa Angell
Redfield, William Cox
Redman, Ben Ray
Reed, Daniel Alden
Reed, Luman
Rees, John Krom
Reeve, Tapping
Reeves, Daniel F.
Reid, Gilbert
Reid, John Morrison
Reid, Ogden Mills
Reid, William Wharry
Reinhardt, Ad
Remington, Frederic
Remington, Philo
Remington, William Walter
Remsen, Ira
Renwick, Edward Sabine
Renwick, Henry Brevoort
Renwick, James, 1818–1895
Reynolds, Julian Sargeant
Reynolds, Quentin James
Rhind, Alexander Colden
Rice, Dan
Rice, Edwin Wilbur
Rice, Elmer
Rice, Thomas Dartmouth
Rice, Victor Moreau
Richards, Charles Brinkerhoff
Richards, Vincent
Richtmyer, Floyd Karker
Rickard, Clinton
Ricketts, James Brewerton
Ridder, Bernard Herman
Ridder, Herman
Ridgway, Robert
Riefler, Winfield William
Riggs, William Henry
Riley, Isaac Woodbridge
Rittenhouse, Jessie Belle
Rives, George Lockhart
Robb, William Lispenard
Robert, Christopher Rhinelander
Roberts, Benjamin Titus
Roberts, Ellis Henry
Roberts, Marshall Owen
Robertson, Morgan Andrew
Robertson, William Henry
Robertson, William Schenck
Robins, Margaret Dreier
Robins, Raymond
Robinson, Charles Mulford
Robinson, John Cleveland
Robinson-Smith, Gertrude
Rockefeller, John Davison
Rockefeller, John Davison, 3d
Rockefeller, William
Rockefeller, Winthrop
Rockwell, Norman Perceval
Rodgers, Christopher Raymond Perry
Rodgers, George Washington, 1822–1863

Rodgers, Richard Charles
Roe, Edward Payson
Roe, Francis Asbury
Rogers, Henry Wade
Rogers, Randolph
Rogers, Stephen
Rohlfs, Anna Katharine Green
Rolf, Ida Pauline
Romayne, Nicholas
Romer, Alfred Sherwood ("Al")
Rooney, Pat
Roosa, Daniel Bennett St. John
Roosevelt, (Anna) Eleanor
Roosevelt, Franklin Delano
Roosevelt, Hilborne Lewis
Roosevelt, Kermit
Roosevelt, Nicholas J.
Roosevelt, Robert Barnwell
Roosevelt, Theodore, 1858–1919
Roosevelt, Theodore, 1887–1944
Root, Elihu
Root, Frank Albert
Rorty, James Hancock
Rosa, Edward Bennett
Rose, Billy
Rosenberg, Ethel
Rosenberg, Julius
Rosenfeld, Paul Leopold
Ross, Thomas Joseph
Rossen, Robert
Rousseau, Harry Harwood
Rowland, Henry Cottrell
Rubicam, Raymond
Rudge, William Edwin
Rudkin, Margaret Fogarty
Ruger, Thomas Howard
Rukeyser, Muriel
Rumsey, Charles Cary
Rumsey, Mary Harriman
Rumsey, William
Runkle, John Daniel
Ruppert, Jacob
Russell, David Allen
Russell, Henry Norris
Russell, Israel Cook
Russell, James Earl
Rutgers, Henry
Rutherfurd, Lewis Morris
Sachs, Paul Joseph
Sackett, Henry Woodward
Sage, Margaret Olivia Slocum
Sage, Russell
Salisbury, James Henry
Salmon, Lucy Maynard
Salmon, Thomas William
Salter, William
Saltus, Edgar Evertson
Sampson, William Thomas
Sanders, Charles Walton
Sanders, Wilbur Fisk
Sands, Comfort
Sands, David
Sands, Diana Patricia
Sands, Joshua Ratoon
Sands, Robert Charles
Sanford, Nathan
Sanger, Margaret Higgins
Sangster, Margaret Elizabeth Munson
Satterlee, Henry Yates
Satterlee, Richard Sherwood
Sawyer, Leicester Ambrose
Sawyer, Lorenzo
Sayles, John
Saypol, Irving Howard
Sayre, Reginald Hall
Sayre, Stephen
Schell, Augustus
Schenck, Ferdinand Schureman
Schirmer, Rudolph Edward
Schlesinger, Frank
Schofield, John McAllister
Schoolcraft, Henry Rowe
Schuyler, Eugene
Schuyler, George Washington
Schuyler, James Dix
Schuyler, Louisa Lee
Schuyler, Margarita
Schuyler, Montgomery
Schuyler, Peter
Schuyler, Philip John
Schuyler, Robert Livingston
Schwab, John Christopher
Schwartz, Delmore David
Scollard, Clinton
Scott, John Morin
Scott, John Prindle
Scribner, Charles, 1821–1871
Scribner, Charles, 1854–1930
Scribner, Charles, 1890–1952
Scrymser, James Alexander
Scullin, John
Seabury, George John
Seabury, Samuel
Searle, James
Searle, John Preston
Sedgwick, Arthur George
Sedgwick, Ellery
Sedgwick, Theodore, 1811–1859
Seeger, Alan
Seitz, William Chapin
Seixas, Gershom Mendes
Selden, George Baldwin
Seligman, Edwin Robert Anderson
Seligman, Isaac Newton
Seney, George Ingraham
Sennett, George Burritt
Sergeant, Henry Clark
Serling, Rodman Edward ("Rod")
Sessions, Henry Howard
Seton, Elizabeth Ann Bayley
Seton, William
Severance, Caroline Maria Seymour
Seward, Frederick William
Seward, George Frederick
Seward, Theodore Frelinghuysen
Seward, William Henry
Seymour, George Franklin
Seymour, Horatio
Seymour, Horatio Winslow
Seymour, William
Shaw, Edward Richard
Shea, John Dawson Gilmary
Sheffield, Devello Zelotes
Sheldon, Charles Monroe
Sheldon, Edward Austin
Shelton, Frederick William
Shepard, Edward Morse
Shepard, Fred Douglas
Sheridan, Philip Henry
Sherman, Frank Dempster
Sherman, James Schoolcraft
Sherwood, Adiel
Sherwood, Isaac Ruth
Sherwood, Robert Emmet
Sherwood, William Hall
Shields, Francis Xavier ("Frank")
Shipherd, John Jay
Shrady, George Frederick
Shrady, Henry Merwin
Shufeldt, Robert Wilson
Sibley, Joseph Crocker
Sicard, Montgomery
Sickles, Daniel Edgar
Sidell, William Henry
Sigsbee, Charles Dwight
Sikes, William Wirt
Sill, Anna Peck
Silverman, Sime
Silvers, Louis
Simon, Richard Leo
Simonton, James William
Simpson, Edward
Simpson, William Kelly
Sims, Winfield Scott
Singer, Isaac Merrit
Skaniadariio
Skinner, Alanson Buck
Skinner, Charles Rufus
Slidell, John
Sloat, John Drake
Slocum, Henry Warner
Smillie, George Henry
Smillie, James David
Smillie, Ralph
Smith, Alfred Emanuel
Smith, Archibald Cary
Smith, Azariah
Smith, Betty
Smith, Bruce
Smith, David Eugene
Smith, Edmund Munroe
Smith, Erasmus Darwin
Smith, Erminnie Adelle Platt
Smith, Erwin Frink
Smith, Gerrit
Smith, Giles Alexander
Smith, Harry Bache
Smith, Hezekiah
Smith, James McCune
Smith, Jedediah Strong
Smith, Job Lewis
Smith, John Bernhard
Smith, Martin Luther
Smith, Melancton, 1744–1898
Smith, Melancton, 1810–1893
Smith, Milton Hannibal
Smith, Morgan Lewis
Smith, Ormond Gerald
Smith, Peter
Smith, Solomon Franklin
Smith, Stephen
Smith, Theobald
Smith, William, 1728–1793
Smith, William Henry, 1833–1896
Smith, William Stephens
Smyth, Julian Kennedy
Snell, Bertrand Hollis
Snelling, Henry Hunt

Snethen, Nicholas
Snow, John Ben
Snowden, Thomas
Sokolsky, George Ephraim
Solomons, Adolphus Simeon
Sooysmith, Charles
Soulé, George
Southmayd, Charles Ferdinand
Spalding, Volney Morgan
Spaulding, Elbridge Gerry
Speck, Frank Gouldsmith
Speir, Samuel Fleet
Spencer, Cornelia Phillips
Spencer, Jesse Ames
Spencer, John Canfield
Spencer, Platt Rogers
Sperry, Elmer Ambrose
Speyer, James Joseph
Spier, Leslie
Spingarn, Arthur Barnett
Spingarn, Joel Elias
Spinner, Francis Elias
Spitzka, Edward Anthony
Spitzka, Edward Charles
Sprague, Charles Ezra
Squier, Ephraim George
Squire, Watson Carvosso
Stager, Anson
Staley, Cady
Stanbery, Henry
Stanchfield, John Barry
Stanford, Leland
Stanley, John Mix
Stanley, William
Stansbury, Howard
Stanton, Elizabeth Cady
Starin, John Henry
Starr, Frederick
Starr, Merritt
Starr, Moses Allen
Stearns, Irving Ariel
Steele, Daniel
Steele, Frederick
Steele, Joel Dorman
Steinhardt, Laurence Adolph
Steinman, David Barnard
Stelzle, Charles
Sterling, George
Stern, Bill
Stern, Joseph William
Sternberg, George Miller
Stetson, Francis Lynde
Stevens, Alexander Hodgdon
Stevens, Emily
Stevens, George Barker
Stevens, George Washington
Stevens, John
Stevens, John Austin
Stevens, Walter Husted
Stevenson, John James
Stewart, Alvan
Stewart, Edwin
Stewart, John Aikman
Stewart, Robert Marcellus
Stewart, William Morris
Stewart, William Rhinelander
Stiles, Charles Wardell
Stiles, Henry Reed
Stillman, Thomas Edgar
Stillman, William James
Stilwell, Joseph Warren
Stilwell, Silas Moore
Stimson, Henry Lewis
Stoddard, Charles Warren
Stoddard, John Fair
Stoddard, William Osborn
Stokes, Anson Phelps, 1838–1913
Stokes, Anson Phelps, 1874–1958
Stokes, Caroline Phelps
Stokes, Frederick Abbot
Stokes, Isaac Newton Phelps
Stokes, Olivia Egleston Phelps
Stokes, William Earl Dodge
Stone, Horatio
Stone, William Leete, 1792–1844
Stone, William Leete, 1835–1908
Stoneman, George
Straight, Willard Dickermam
Stranahan, James Samuel Thomas
Strand, Paul
Strang, James Jesse
Strange, Michael
Straus, Jesse Isidor
Straus, Percy Selden
Straus, Roger W(illiams)
Street, Alfre Billings
Streeter, George Linius
Stringham, Silas Horton
Stringham, Washington Irving
Strong, Augustus Hopkins
Strong, Benjamin
Strong, Harriet Williams Russell
Strong, James
Strong, James Hooker
Stryker, Melancthon Woolsey
Stuart, Charles Beebe
Stuart, Robert Leighton
Sullivan, Edward Vincent ("Ed")
Sullivan, Harry Stack
Sullivan, James Edward
Sullivan, Timothy Daniel
Sulzberger, Arthur Hays
Sutton, William Francis, Jr. ("Willie")
Swain, Clara A.
Swain, James Barrett
Swan, Joseph Rockwell
Swartwout, Samuel
Sweeny, Peter Barr
Sweet, John Edson
Swift, Lewis
Swift, Lucius Burrie
Swing, Raymond Edwards (Gram)
Symmes, John Cleves
Symons, Thomas William
Taber, John
Tallmadge, Benjamin
Tallmadge, James
Talmadge, Constance
Tamiris, Helen
Tanner, Benjamin
Tanner, Henry Schenck
Tanner, James
Tappan, Henry Philip
Tappen, Frederick Dobbs
Taussig, Frederick Joseph
Taylor, Benjamin Franklin
Taylor, Graham
Taylor, Henry Osborn
Taylor, James Monroe
Taylor, James Wickes
Taylor, John W.
Taylor, Joseph Deems
Taylor, Laurette
Taylor, Moses
Taylor, Myron Charles
Taylor, Stevenson
Teall, Francis Augustus
Teller, Henry Moore
Ten Broeck, Abraham
Ten Broeck, Richard
Terry, Marshall Orlando
Terry, Milton Spenser
Thacher, Edwin
Thacher, John Boyd
Thalberg, Irving Grant
Thayer, Amos Madden
Thomas, Amos Russell
Thomas, George Allison
Thomas, John Jacobs
Thomas, Joseph
Thompson, Dorothy
Thompson, Egbert
Thompson, Malvina Cynthia
Thompson, Martin E.
Thompson, Smith
Thompson, William Gilman
Thomson, Mortimer Neal
Thorne, Charles Robert, 1814–1893
Thorne, Charles Robert, 1840–1883
Throop, Enos Thompson
Throop, Montgomery Hunt
Thurber, Jeannette Meyer
Thursby, Emma Cecilia
Tiebout, Cornelius
Tierney, Richard Henry
Tiffany, Louis Comfort
Tilden, Samuel Jones
Tilney, Frederick
Tilton, Edward Lippincott
Tilton, Theodore
Tilyou, George Cornelius
Timby, Theodore Ruggles
Timme, Walter
Tishman, David
Tobin, Austin Joseph
Todd, Sereno Edwards
Todman, William Selden ("Bill")
Tomkins, Floyd Williams
Tomlin, Bradley Walker
Tompkins, Daniel D.
Tone, Stanislas Pascal Franchot
Torrey, John
Townsend, Mary Ashley
Townsend, Robert
Tracy, Benjamin Franklin
Trask, James Dowling
Travers, Jerome Dunstan
Treat, Samuel Hubbel
Trelease, William
Tremain, Henry Edwin
Tremaine, Henry Barnes
Trenchard, Stephen Decatur
Trilling, Lionel
Trowbridge, Augustus
Trowbridge, John Townsend
Trowbridge, William Petit
Trude, Alfred Samuel

Trudeau, Edward Livingston
Truxtun, Thomas
Tucker, Allen
Tucker, Gilbert Milligan
Tucker, Richard
Tuckerman, Bayard
Tugwell, Rexford Guy
Tunney, James Joseph ("Gene")
Turner, Daniel
Turner, John Wesley
Turner, Ross Sterling
Tuthill, William Burnet
Tuttle, Daniel Sylvester
Tweed, Harrison
Tweed, William Marcy
Tyler, Robert Ogden
Underhill, Franklin Pell
Underwood, Benjamin Franklin
Underwood, John Curtiss
Underwood, Lucien Marcus
Untermeyer, Louis
Upton, Emory
Usher, John Palmer
Vail, Robert William Glenroie
Vail, Stephen Montfort
Valachi, Joseph Michael
Valentine, David Thomas
Van, Bobby
Van Buren, John
Van Buren, Martin
Van Cortlandt, Philip
Van Cortlandt, Pierre
Van Cortlandt, Stephanus
Van Dam, Rip
Vanderbilt, Amy
Vanderbilt, Cornelius, 1794–1877
Vanderbilt, Cornelius, 1843–1899
Vanderbilt, Cornelius, Jr. ("Cornelius IV," "Neil")
Vanderbilt, George Washington
Vanderbilt, Grace Graham Wilson
Vanderbilt, William Kissam
Vanderlyn, John
Vander Veer, Albert
Van de Warker, Edward Ely
Van Dyck, Cornelius Van Alen
Van Dyke, Paul
Van Fleet, Walter
Van Name, Addison
Van Ness, William Peter
Van Nest, Abraham Rynier
Van Nostrand, David
Van Rensselaer, Cortlandt
Van Rensselaer, Mariana Griswold
Van Rensselaer, Martha
Van Rensselaer, Solomon
Van Rensselaer, Stephen
Van Schaack, Henry Cruger
Van Schaack, Peter
Van Schaick, Goose
Van Slyke, Lucius Lincoln
Van Vechten, Abraham
Van Winkle, Peter Godwin
Van Wyck, Charles Henry
Vardill, John
Varick, James
Vedder, Edward Bright
Vedder, Elihu
Vedder, Henry Clay
Verplanck, Julian Crommelin
Vesey, William
Vibbard, Chauncey
Victor, Frances Fuller
Viele, Aernout Cornelissen
Viele, Egbert Ludovicus
Vincent, Frank
Vincent, Marvin Richardson
Volk, Leonard Wells
Vorse, Mary Heaton
Vought, Chance Milton
Wade, Jeptha Homer
Wadsworth, James Samuel
Wadsworth, James Wolcott, Jr.
Wagner, Webster
Wainwright, Jonathan Mayhew, 1821–1863
Wait, Samuel
Wait, William
Wait, William Bell
Walcott, Charles Doolittle
Walden, Jacob Treadwell
Walker, Gilbert Carlton
Walker, James John
Walker, Mary Edwards
Wallace, William James
Wallack, Lester
Waller, Frederic
Waller, Thomas Macdonald
Waller, Thomas Wright
Walsh, Blanche
Walsh, Raoul
Walsh, Thomas
Walworth, Clarence Augustus
Ward, Cyrenus Osborne
Ward, Genevieve
Ward, Henry Augustus
Ward, Henry Baldwin
Ward, James Edward
Ward, Joseph
Ward, Samuel, 1814–1884
Waring, George Edwin
Warner, Adoniram Judson
Warner, Anna Bartlett
Warner, Glenn Scobey ("Pop")
Warner, Susan Bogert
Warren, Gouverneur Kemble
Warren, Leonard
Warren, Richard Henry
Washburn, Margaret Floy
Waterman, Alan Tower
Waterman, Lewis Edson
Waterman, Robert H.
Waterman, Thomas Whitney
Watson, James Madison
Watson, Thomas John
Watterston, George
Wayland, Francis, 1796–1865
Webb, Alexander Stewart
Webb, Charles Henry
Webb, James Watson
Webb, William Henry
Weber, Joseph Morris
Webster, Alice Jane Chandler
Webster, Margaret ("Peggy")
Weed, Thurlow
Weigel, Gustave
Weil, Richard
Weir, John Ferguson
Weir, Julian Alden
Weir, Robert Fulton
Weir, Robert Walter
Welch, Ashbel
Welch, Charles Clark
Welch, Leo Dewey
Welch, Philip Henry
Welles, (Benjamin) Sumner
Wells, Erastus
Wells, Harriet Sheldon
Wells, John
Wende, Ernest
Wende, Grover William
Wentworth, Cecile de
West, Mae
Westcott, Edward Noyes
Westinghouse, George
Westley, Helen
Wexler, Irving ("Waxey Gordon")
Whalen, Grover Aloysius
Wharton, Edith Newbold Jones
Wheatley, William
Whedon, Daniel Denison
Wheeler, Andrew Carpenter
Wheeler, Everett Pepperrell
Wheeler, (George) Post
Wheeler, Schuyler Skaats
Wheeler, William Almon
Wheelock, John Hall
Whipple, Henry Benjamin
Whitaker, Nathaniel
Whitcher, Frances Miriam Berry
White, Alfred Tredway
White, Andrew Dickson
White, Canvass
White, David
White, George
White, George Leonard
White, Joseph Malachy
White, Richard Grant
White, Stanford
White, William Alanson
Whitehouse, Frederic Cope
Whitfield, Robert Parr
Whitman, Marcus
Whitman, Walt
Whitney, Gertrude Vanderbilt
Whitney, Harry Payne
Whitney, Willis Rodney
Whittingham, William Rollinson
Wickes, Stephen
Wickham, John
Wickson, Edward James
Wiechmann, Ferdinand Gerhard
Wiener, Alexander Solomon
Wigger, Winand Michael
Wiggins, Carleton
Wight, Peter Bonnett
Wilder, Alexander
Wilder, Alexander Lafayette Chew ("Alec")
Wilder, John Thomas
Wilkes, Charles
Wilkes, George
Wilkie, Franc Bangs
Willard, Frances Elizabeth Caroline
Willet, William
Willett, Marinus
Williams, Charles Richard
Williams, Fannie Barrier
Williams, Frank Martin

Williams, George Henry
Williams, George Huntington
Williams, Henry Shaler
Williams, Linsly Rudd
Williams, Samuel Wells
Williams, William R.
Willis, Bailey
Willis, Henry Parker
Willys, John North
Wilson, Allen Benjamin
Wilson, Charles Edward
Wilson, Joseph Chamberlain
Wilson, Theodore Delavan
Winant, John Gilbert
Winchell, Alexander
Winchell, Newton Horace
Winchell, Walter
Wing, Joseph Elwyn
Winslow, John Bradley
Winston, Harry
Wise, Henry Augustus
Wisner, Henry
Witherspoon, Herbert
Witmark, Isidore
Witthaus, Rudolph August
Wolfe, Bertram David
Wolfe, Catharine Lorillard
Wolfe, John David
Wolheim, Louis Robert
Wood, Craig Ralph
Wood, Henry Alexander Wise
Wood, James, 1799–1867
Wood, James, 1839–1925
Wood, James Rushmore
Wood, Joseph
Wood, Mary Elizabeth
Wood, Peggy
Wood, Samuel
Woodford, Stewart Lyndon
Woodhull, Nathaniel
Woodruff, Lorande Loss
Woodruff, Theodore Tuttle
Woodruff, William Edward
Woodward, Augustus Brevoort
Woodward, William
Woodworth, Jay Backus
Wool, John Ellis
Woolley, Edgar Montillion ("Monty")
Woolsey, Melancthon Taylor
Woolsey, Theodore Dwight
Woolworth, Frank Winfield
Worcester, Edwin Dean
Worden, John Lorimer
Worth, William Jenkins
Worthington, Henry Rossiter
Wright, George
Wright, George Frederick
Wright, Harold Bell
Wright, William
Yale, Linus
Yates, Abraham
Yates, Herbert John
Yates, John Van Ness
Yates, Robert
Youmans, Edward Livingston
Youmans, Vincent Millie
Youmans, William Jay
Young, Ella Flagg
Young, Owen D.
Young, Thomas
Zimmerman, Henry ("Heinie")
Zinsser, Hans
Zukofsky, Louis

NORTH CAROLINA

Alderman, Edwin Anderson
Allen, George Venable
Allen, William
Ammons, Elias Milton
Andrews, Alexander Boyd
Armistead, Lewis Addison
Arrington, Alfred W.
Ashe, John
Ashe, John Baptista
Ashe, Samuel
Ashe, Thomas Samuel
Ashe, William Shepperd
Atkinson, Henry
Avery, William Waigstill
Aycock, Charles Brantley
Badger, George Edmund
Bailey, Josiah William
Baker, Laurence Simmons
Barden, Graham Arthur
Barringer, Daniel Moreau
Barringer, Rufus
Bassett, John Spencer
Battle, Kemp Plummer
Battle, William Horn
Baxter, Elisha
Baxter, John
Beasley, Frederick
Bell, Henry Haywood
Belo, Alfred Horatio
Bennett, Hugh Hammond
Benton, Thomas Hart
Bickett, Thomas Walter
Biggs, Asa
Bingham, Robert Worth
Bingham, William
Blackmer, Sydney Alderman
Blake, Lillie Devereux
Blalock, Nelson Gates
Bloodworth, Timothy
Blount, Thomas
Blount, Willie
Blue, Victor
Bonner, John Henry
Bragg, Braxton
Bragg, Thomas
Branch, John
Branch, Lawrence O'Bryan
Bridgers, Robert Rufus
Brinkley, John Richard
Brooks, George Washington
Brown, Bedford
Burgevine, Henry Andrea
Burleson, Edward
Burns, Otway
Burton, Hutchins Gordon
Butler, Marion
Bynum, William Preston
Cain, William
Caldwell, Charles
Cambreleng, Churchill Caldom
Cannon, Joseph Gurney
Cannon, Newton
Carr, Elias
Carson, Simeon Lewis
Cheshire, Joseph Blount
Clark, John
Clark, Walter
Clarke, Francis Devereux
Clarke, Mary Bayard Devereux
Clement, Rufus Early
Clewell, John Henry
Clingman, Thomas Lanier
Coffin, Levi
Colton, Elizabeth Avery
Coltrane, John William
Connor, Henry Graves
Connor, Robert Digges Wimberly
Cooley, Harold Dunbar
Cox, William Ruffin
Craven, Braxton
Daly, John Augustin
Daniels, Josephus
Dargan, Edmund Strother
Davis, George
De Mille, Henry Churchill
Denny, George Vernon, Jr.
De Rosset, Moses John
Dick, Robert Paine
Dixon, Thomas
Dobbin, James Cochran
Dodd, William Edward
Donnell, Robert
Doughton, Robert Lee
Dudley, Edward Bishop
Duke, Benjamin Newton
Duke, James Buchanan
Eaton, John Henry
Edwards, Weldon Nathaniel
Elliott, Aaron Marshall
Ellis, John Willis
Fels, Samuel Simeon
Finley, James Bradley
Fitzgerald, Oscar Penn
Forney, William Henry
Fries, Francis
Fuller, Thomas Charles
Gaines, George Strother
Gardner, Oliver Maxwell
Gaston, William
Gatling, Richard Jordan
Gilmer, John Adams
Gould, Robert Simonton
Govan, Daniel Chevilette
Graham, Edward Kidder
Graham, Frank Porter
Graham, William Alexander
Gray, George Alexander
Hale, Edward Joseph
Harnett, Cornelius
Harrell, John
Hawkins, Benjamin
Hawks, Francis Lister
Hawley, Joseph Roswell
Haywood, John
Heineman, Daniel Webster ("Dannie")
Helper, Hinton Rowan
Henderson, Archibald
Henderson, James Pinckney
Henderson, Leonard
Henkel, Paul
Hill, Robert Andrews
Hilliard, Henry Washington

Hoey, Clyde Roark
Hoke, Robert Frederick
Holden, William Woods
Holmes, Theophilus Hunter
Holt, Edwin Michael
Hooper, Johnson Jones
Houston, David Franklin
Houston, William Churchill
Howe, Robert
Howell, Robert Boyté Crawford
Hunt, Nathan
Jarvis, Thomas Jordan
Jasper, William
Johnson, Andrew
Johnson, Edward Austin
Johnson, William Ransom
Johnston, Joseph Forney
Jones, Alexander
Jones, Allen
Jones, Willie
Jordan, Benjamin Everett
Kerr, Washington Caruthers
King, William Rufus Devane
Kirby, George Hughes
Kitchin, Claude
Kitchin, William Walton
Koopman, Augustus
Lane, Joseph
Lanier, James Franklin Doughty
Law, Sallie Chapman Gordon
Lewis, Exum Percival
Lewis, William Gaston
Long, James
Loring, William Wing
Luelling, Henderson
Lyon, Francis Strother
Mabley, Jackie ("Moms")
McGilvary, Daniel
McIver, Charles Duncan
McKay, James Iver
McLean, Angus Wilton
McNeill, William Gibbs
Macon, Nathaniel
McRae, Duncan Kirkland
Madison, Dolly Payne
Mangum, Willie Person
Manly, Basil
Manning, Thomas Courtland
Martin, James Green
Means, Gaston Bullock
Mercer, Jesse
Merrimon, Augustus Summerfield
Moore, Alfred
Moore, Bartholomew Figures
Moore, Gabriel
Moore, James, 1737–1777
Moore, Maurice
Moore, Thomas Overton
Mordecai, Alfred
Morehead, John Motley
Murphey, Archibald De Bow
Murphy, James Bumgardner
Murrow, Edward (Egbert) Roscoe
Nash, Frederick
Nicholson, Timothy
Osborn, Charles
Osborne, James Walker
Overman, Lee Slater
Page, Walter Hines
Paine, Robert
Parker, John Johnston
Patterson, Rufus Lenoir
Payne, Bruce Ryburn
Pearson, Richmond Mumford
Pegram, George Braxton
Pender, William Dorsey
Pettigrew, James Johnston
Pickens, Israel
Pickett, Albert James
Polk, James Knox
Polk, Leonidas
Polk, Leonidas Lafayette
Polk, Lucius Eugene
Polk, William
Pool, John
Porter, William Sydney
Potter, Robert
Price, Thomas Frederick
Purviance, David
Rains, Gabriel James
Rains, George Washington
Ramseur, Stephen Dodson
Ransom, Matt Whitaker
Rayner, Kenneth
Reade, Edwin Godwin
Reichel, William Cornelius
Reid, David Settle
Revels, Hiram Rhoades
Reynolds, Robert Rice
Richardson, Edmund
Rivers, Lucius Mendel
Ross, Martin
Royster, James Finch
Ruark, Robert Chester
Saunders, Romulus Mitchell
Saunders, William Laurence, 1835–1891
Sawyer, Lemuel
Schweinitz, Emil Alexander de
Scott, Thomas Fielding
Scott, W(illiam) Kerr
Sellers, Isaiah
Settle, Thomas
Shepard, James Edward
Shipp, Albert Micajah
Simmons, Furnifold McLendel
Simmons, James Stevens
Skinner, Harry
Skinner, Thomas Harvey
Smith, Charles Alphonso
Smith, Henry Louis
Smith, Hoke
Smith, Robert Hardy
Smith, William, 1762–1840
Smith, William Nathan Harrell
Spaight, Richard Dobbs
Spaulding, Charles Clinton
Stacy, Walter Parker
Stanly, Edward
Steele, John
Steele, Wilbur Daniel
Stitt, Edward Rhodes
Stone, David
Strudwick, Edmund Charles Fox
Stuart, Elbridge Amos
Swain, David Lowry
Taylor, Hannis
Thompson, Jacob
Tiernan, Frances Christine Fisher
Truett, George Washington
Turner, Josiah
Tyson, Lawrence Davis
Upchurch, John Jordan
Vance, Zebulon Baird
Waddel, Moses
Waddell, Alfred Moore
Waddell, James Iredell
Walker, David, 1785–1830
Warren, Lindsay Carter
Webb, William Robert
Weeks, Stephen Beauregard
Wheeler, John Hill
White, Hugh Lawson
White, James
White, Stephen Van Culen
Wilcox, Cadmus Marcellus
Wiley, Calvin Henderson
Williams, Jesse Lynch
Williams, John
Winslow, John Ancrum
Wolfe, Thomas Clayton
Worth, Jonathan
Yell, Archibald
Yergan, Max
Yount, George Concepcíon

NORTH DAKOTA

Aandahl, Fred George
Amlie, Thomas Ryum
Durstine, Roy Sarles
Flannagan, John Bernard
Hunter, Croil
Langer, William
Still, Clyfford

OHIO

Abbey, Henry Eugene
Abel, John Jacob
Adams, William Lysander
Adkins, Homer Burton
Akeley, Mary Leonore
Aldrich, Louis
Alger, Russell Alexander
Allen, Frederic de Forest
Allen, Robert
Allen, William Vincent
Allison, William Boyd
Anderson, Sherwood
Andrews, Chauncey Hummason
Andrews, Lorin
Angell, Ernest
Angle, Paul McClelland
Archbold, John Dustin
Arquette, Clifford
Ashmore, William
Axtell, Samuel Beach
Bacher, Otto Henry
Bacon, Delia Salter
Bailey, Joseph
Baird, Samuel John
Baker, James Heaton
Baker, Oliver Edwin
Ball, Ephraim
Ball, Frank Clayton
Ball, George Alexander
Ballantine, Arthur Atwood

Bancroft, Hubert Howe
Bara, Theda
Barber, Ohio Columbus
Bartlett, Dewey Follett
Barus, Carl
Bauer, Louis Agricola
Beard, Daniel Carter
Beard, James Carter
Beard, Thomas Francis
Beard, William Holbrook
Beardshear, William Miller
Beatty, Clyde Raymond
Beatty, John
Beatty, William Henry
Beavers, Louise
Beck, Johann Heinrich
Bell, Bernard Iddings
Bell, James Madison
Bellows, George Wesley
Bender, George Harrison
Benedict, Stanley Rossiter
Bessey, Charles Edwin
Bettman, Alfred
Beveridge, Albert Jeremiah
Bevier, Isabel
Bickel, Luke Washington
Bickerdyke, Mary Ann Ball
Biddle, Horace P.
Bierce, Ambrose Gwinett
Biggers, Earl Derr
Bingham, Amelia
Binkley, Wilfred Ellsworth
Blanshard, Paul
Blum, Robert Frederick
Boardman, Mabel Thorp
Bohm, Max
Bolton, Frances Payne Bingham
Boole, Ella Alexander
Bosworth, Francke Huntington
Boyd, Thomas Alexander
Boyd, William
Bragdon, Claude Fayette
Brett, William Howard
Brice, Calvin Stewart
Brigham, Joseph Henry
Bromfield, Louis
Brooks, William Keith
Brooks, William Thomas Harbaugh
Brough, John
Brown, Carleton
Brown, Clarence James
Brown, Fayette
Brown, George Pliny
Brown, Henry Cordis
Brown, John Porter
Brown, Walter Folger
Brush, Charles Francis
Buchanan, William Insco
Buchtel, John Richards
Buckland, Ralph Pomeroy
Buell, Don Carlos
Burchfield, Charles Ephraim
Burnett, Henry Lawrence
Burns, Raymond Joseph
Burton, Ernest De Witt
Burton, Theodore Elijah
Bush, Prescott Sheldon
Bussey, Cyrus
Butterworth, Benjamin
Byford, William Heath
Callahan, Patrick Henry
Callender, Guy Stevens
Campbell, Lewis Davis
Campbell, William Wallace
Canaga, Alfre Bruce
Canfield, James Hulme
Carney, Thomas
Carpenter, Frank George
Carr, Charlotte Elizabeth
Carr, Wilbur John
Carter, Thomas Henry
Cary, Alice
Cary, Phoebe
Case, Leonard
Cass, George Washington
Catherwood, Mary Hartwell
Chaffee, Adna Romanza
Chamberlain, Charles Joseph
Chamberlain, Joseph Perkins
Chambers, James Julius
Chapin, Henry Dwight
Cherrington, Ernest Hurst
Chester, George Randolph
Christy, David
Christy, Howard Chandler
Cist, Henry Martyn
Clark, Bobby
Clark, Charles
Clarke, John Hessin
Clevenger, Shobal Vail
Cline, Genevieve Rose
Cockerill, John Albert
Coffin, Howard Earle
Coit, Stanton
Colver, William Byron
Commons, John Rogers
Compton, Arthur Holly
Compton, Karl Taylor
Conklin, Edwin Grant
Conover, Obadiah Milton
Cooke, Henry David
Cooke, Jay
Cooper, Elias Samuel
Cooper, Jacob
Cooper, Oswald Bruce
Corbin, Henry Clark
Cordier, Andrew Wellington
Coulter, Ernest Kent
Cowen, John Kissig
Cowles, Edwin
Cox, Georges Barnsdale
Cox, James Middleton
Cox, James Middleton, Jr.
Cox, Kenyon
Cox, Samuel Sullivan
Craig, Winchell McKendree
Crane, Harold Hart
Cranston, Earl
Crapsey, Algernon Sidney
Cratty, Mabel
Cravath, Paul Drennan
Creighton, Edward
Creighton, John Andrew
Crile, George Washington
Crissinger, Daniel Richard
Crocker, William
Crook, George
Crosby, William Otis
Crosley, Powel, Jr.
Crouse, Russel McKinley
Crozier, William
Curtis, William Eleroy
Cushing, Harvey Williams
Custer, George Armstrong
Dahlgren, Sarah Madeleine Vinton
Dandridge, Dorothy Jean
Daniels, Frank Albert
Daniels, Winthrop More
Darrow, Clarence Seward
Daugherty, Harry Micajah
Davis, Edwin Hamilton
Dawes, Charles Gates
Dawes, Rufus Cutler
Day, David Talbot
Day, James Gamble
Day, William Rufus
De Camp, Joseph Rodefer
Dellenbaugh, Frederick Samuel
Dennison, William
Dickman, Joseph Theodore
Dill, Clarence Cleveland
Dinwiddie, Edwin Courtland
Dittemore, John Valentine
Doherty, Henry Latham
Dorsey, George Amos
Doyle, Alexander
Drake, John Burroughs
Du Bois, Augustus Jay
Dun, Robert Graham
Dunbar, Paul Laurence
Duncan, Donald Franklin
Dwenger, Joseph
Dwiggins, William Addison
Dyer, Rolla Eugene
Dykstra, Clarence Addison
Eaton, Benjamin Harrison
Eaton, Joseph Oriel
Eckart, William Roberts
Eckert, Thomas Thompson
Edison, Thomas Alva
Edwards, Clarence Ransom
Eichelberger, Robert Lawrence
Elkins, Stephen Benton
Elliott, Charles Burke
Ellis, Edward Sylvester
Ellis, John Washington
Ellis, Seth Hockett
Elwell, John Johnson
Emmett, Daniel Decatur
Enneking, John Joseph
Ernst, Harold Clarence
Ernst, Oswald Herbert
Evans, Bergen Baldwin
Evans, John
Evans, Lawrence Boyd
Ewing, Hugh Boyle
Ewing, Thomas
Fairbanks, Charles Warren
Fairchild, George Thompson
Fairchild, Lucius
Fairless, Benjamin F.
Faran, James John
Fenneman, Nevin Melancthon
Ferree, Clarence Errol
Fess, Simeon Davidson
Fieser, Louis Frederick
Finley, Martha Farquharson
Firestone, Harvey Samuel
Fisher, Alfred J.

Fisher, Charles T.
Fisher, Frederic John
Fleming, John Adam
Flickinger, Daniel Kumler
Foraker, Joseph Benson
Fordyce, John Addison
Fosdick, William Whiteman
Foster, Charles
Foster, Randolph Sinks
Fowler, Joseph Smith
Frank, Lawrence Kelso
Franklin, Benjamin
Freas, Thomas Bruce
French, Aaron
Frohman, Charles
Frohman, Daniel
Funk, Isaac Kauffman
Funston, Frederick
Furnas, Robert Wilkinson
Gable, (William) Clark
Gage, Frances Dan Barker
Galbreath, Charles Burleigh
Garey, Thomas Andrew
Garfield, Harry Augustus
Garfield, James Abram
Garfield, James Rudolph
Gavin, Frank Stanton Burns
Gideon, Peter Miller
Gilbert, Cass
Gilliam, David Tod
Gillmore, Quincy Adams
Gish, Dorothy
Glueck, Nelson
Goodrich, Alfred John
Goodwin, Elijah
Gordon, John Franklin
Granger, Alfred Hoyt
Grant, Ulysses Simpson
Grasselli, Caesar Augustin
Gray, Elisha
Green, William
Greene, Charles Sumner
Greene, Henry Mather
Greer, James Augustin
Grey, Zane
Griffin, Charles
Grose, William
Gross, Samuel Weissell
Grosscup, Peter Stenger
Gunn, James Newton
Gunn, Ross
Gunsaulus, Frank Wakeley
Hall, Charles Martin
Halstead, Murat
Hammond, Percy Hunter
Hanby, Benjamin Russel
Handerson, Henry Ebenezer
Hanna, Marcus Alonzo
Hannegan, Edward Allen
Harding, Warren Gamaliel
Harkness, Edward Stephen
Harmon, Judson
Harper, Robert Francis
Harper, William Rainey
Harris, James Arthur
Harris, Merriman Colbert
Harris, William Logan
Harrison, Benjamin
Hart, Edwin Bret
Hart, Hastings Hornell
Haskell, Charles Nathaniel
Haskell, Henry Jospeh
Hatton, Frank
Hayden, Amos Sutton
Hayes, Charles Willard
Hayes, Max Sebastian
Hayes, Rutherford Birchard
Hayes, William Henry
Hendricks, Thomas Andrews
Henri, Robert
Henry, William Arnon
Hepburn, William Peters
Herrick, Myron Timothy
Herrick, Sophia McIlvaine Bledsoe
Hickenlooper, Andrew
Hinsdale, Burke Aaron
Hitchcock, Frank Harris
Hitt, Robert Roberts
Hocking, William Ernest
Hodge, Albert Elmer ("Al")
Holloway, Joseph Flavius
Holmes, William Henry
Hooper, Claude Ernest
Hoover, Charles Franklin
Hoover, Herbert William
Hopwood, Avery
Horton, Samuel Dana
Howard, Roy Wilson
Howe, William Henry
Howells, William Dean
Hoyt, John Wesley
Hubbard, Frank McKinney
Hudson, Thomson Jay
Huggins, Miller James
Humiston, William Henry
Hunt, Reid
Hurley, Joseph Patrick
Hurst, Fannie
Hussey, William Joseph
Hyslop, James Hervey
Jackman, Wilbur Samuel
Janis, Elsie
Janney, Russell Dixon
Jay, Allen
Jefferson, Charles Edward
Jeffrey, Joseph Andrew
Jeffries, James Jackson
Johnson, Bushrod Rust
Johnson, Byron Bancroft
Johnson, Franklin
Johnson, George
Johnson, John Butler
Johnston, William Hartshorne
Jones, Lynds
Joyce, Isaac Wilson
Kalisch, Samuel
Keeler, Ralph Olmstead
Keifer, Joseph Warren
Kellor, Frances (Alice)
Kennan, George
Kennedy, Robert Patterson
Kennedy, William Sloane
Kenyon, William Squire
Kerr, John Glasgow
Kester, Paul
Kettering, Charles Franklin
Keyt, Alonzo Thrasher
King, Ernest Joseph
King, Henry
Kingsley, Elbridge
Kinkead, Edgar Benton
Kiplinger, Willard Monroe
Klippart, John Hancock
Knox, Rose Markward
Krapp, George Philip
Kroger, Bernhard Henry
Kronenberger, Louis, Jr.
Kruger, Otto
Kyes, Roger Martin
Kyle, David Braden
Kyle, James Henderson
Ladd, George Trumbull
Lamme, Benjamin Garver
Landis, Henry Robert Murray
Landis, Kenesaw Mountain
Lane, Levi Cooper
Lanston, Tolbert
Latham, Milton Slocum
Latta, Alexander Bonner
Laughlin, James Laurence
Lawrance, Uriah Marion
Lawrence, William, 1819–1899
Lawton, Henry Ware
Lazarus, Fred, Jr.
Leaming, Jacob Spicer
Leavitt, Frank McDowell
Le Duc, William Gates
Leonard, Harry Ward
Lewis, Alfred Henry
Lewis, Charles Bertrand
Liebman, Joshua Loth
Loeb, Louis
Loeb, Morris
Long, John Harper
Long, Perrin Hamilton
Longley, Alcander
Longworth, Nicholas, 1869–1931
Lord, Henry Curwen
Lowe, Ralph Phillips
Lower, William Edgar
Lowry, Hiram Harrison
Lydenberg, Harry Miller
Lytle, William Haines
McBride, (Francis) Scott
McCabe, Charles Cardwell
McClain, Emlin
McConnell, Francis John
McCook, Alexander McDowell
McCook, Anson George
McCook, Edward Moody
McCook, Henry Christopher
McCook, John James
MacCracken, Henry Mitchell
McCulloch, Oscar Carleton
McDill, James Wilson
McDonald, James Grover
MacDonald, James Wilson Alexander
McDonald, Joseph Ewing
McDougal, David Stockton
McDowell, Irvin
McDowell, Mary Eliza
McDowell, William Fraser
McElroy, Neil Hosler
MacGahan, Januarius Aloysius
McKinley, William
McPherson, James Birdseye
McPherson, Logan Grant
McVey, Frank Lerond
Main, John Hanson Thomas

Mallory, Frank Burr
Manatt, James Irving
Marquard, Richard William ("Rube")
Marquett, Turner Mastin
Marquis, Albert Nelson
Marvin, Charles Frederick
Mather, Samuel
Matthews, Stanley
Mauchly, John William
Mayo-Smith, Richmond
Meeker, Ezra
Meeker, Jotham
Meeker, Nathan Cook
Mees, Arthur
Mendenhall, Charles Elwood
Mendenhall, Thomas Corwin
Merrill, Stephen Mason
Miller, Dayton Clarence
Miller, Lewis
Miller, Willoughby Dayton
Millikin, Eugene Donald
Mitchell, Edwin Knox
Mitchell, Robert Byington
Moeller, Henry
Moley, Raymond Charles
Monroe, Vaughn Wilton
Montgomery, James
Moore, Clarence Lemuel Elisha
Moore, Eliakim Hastings
Moore, Joseph Haines
Moore, Richard Bishop
Moorehead, William Gallogly
Morgan, Arthur Ernest
Mullin, Willard Harlan
Munson, Thurman Lee
Murphy, Gardner
Mussey, Ellen Spencer
Nash, Henry Sylvester
Nettleton, Alvred Bayard
Nettleton, Edwin S.
Newbrough, John Ballou
Newell, Robert
Newell, William Augustus
Newsam, Albert
Newton, Robert Safford
Nichols, Dudley
Niehaus, Charles Henry
Noble, John Willock
Norris, George William
Norton, William Warder
Notestein, Wallace
Nugent, John Frost
Oalies, George Washington Ochs
Oakley, Annie
O'Daniel, Wilbert Lee ("Pappy")
O'Dwyer, Joseph
Ohlmacher, Albert Philip
Okey, John Waterman
Oldfield, ("Barney")Berna Eli
Olds, Ransom Eli
Oliver, Charles Augustus
O'Neill, C. William ("Bill")
Opper, Frederick Burr
Osborn, Thomas Ogden
Otis, Harrison Gray
Outcault, Richard Felton
Packard, James Ward
Paine, Byron
Paine, Halbert Eleazer
Pardee, Don Albert
Parker, Isaac Charles
Parker, Samuel Chester
Parsons, Albert Ross
Patchen, Kenneth
Patrick, Hugh Talbot
Patterson, John Henry
Pattison, John M.
Payne, Oliver Hazard
Pease, Alfred Humphreys
Peet, Stephen Denison
Pendleton, George Hunt
Perkins, Charles Elliott
Perrine, Charles Dillon
Peter, Sarah Worthington King
Plumb, Preston B.
Poe, Orlando Metcalfe
Pomerene, Atlee
Porter, Stephen Geyer
Porter, William Townsend
Potts, Benjamin Franklin
Power, Tyrone
Pratt, Donn
Proctor, William Cooper
Pugh, George Ellis
Quantrill, William Clarke
Ralston, Samuel Moffett
Ralston, William Chapman
Ransohoff, Joseph
Rarey, John Solomon
Raymond, Rossiter Worthington
Read, Daniel, 1805–1878
Reed, James Alexander
Reed, Mary
Reeves, Arthur Middleton
Reid, James L.
Reid, Whitelaw
Resor, Stanley Burnet
Rhodes, James Ford
Rice, Felelon Bird
Richards, John Kelvey
Rickenbacker, Edward Vernon ("Eddie")
Rickert, Martha Edith
Ricketts, Howard Taylor
Rickey, Wesley Branch
Rigge, William Francis
Riggs, Stephen Return
Riprey, Roswell Sabine
Ritchey, George Willis
Robinson, Edward Stevens
Rockefeller, John Davison, Jr.
Rogers, William Allen
Root, Amos Ives
Rorimer, James Joseph
Rose, Mary Davies Swartz
Rosecrans, Sylvester Horton
Rosecrans, William Starke
Rosenstiel, Lewis Solon
Ross, Alexander Coffman
Ross, Denman Waldo
Ross, Edmund Gibson
Rourke, Constance Mayfield
Roye, Edward James
Rusk, Jeremiah McClain
Sabine, Wallace Clement Ware
Safford, James Merrill
Safford, William Edwin
Sampson, Martin Wright
Sanders, James Harvey
Schenck, James Findlay
Schenck, Robert Cumming
Schevill, Rudolph
Schlesinger, Arthur Meier
Schuchert, Charles
Scott, Austin
Scott, Samuel Parsons
Scott, William Berryman
Scudder, John Milton
Seiberling, Frank Augustus
Seitz, Don Carlos
Severance, Louis Henry
Seymour, Thomas Day
Shabonee
Shannon, Wilson
Sharp, William Graves
Shauck, John Allen
Shaw, Albert
Sherman, John, 1823–1900
Sherman, William Tecumseh
Sherwood, Katharine Margaret Brownlee
Shields, George Oliver
Short, Sidney Howe
Shuey, Edwin Longstreet
Shuey, William John
Shull, George Harrison
Silverman, Joseph
Simms, Ruth Hanna McCormick
Simpson, Matthew
Sisler, George Harold ("Gorgeous George")
Skinner, Halcyon
Sloan, Richard Elihu
Sloane, William Milligan
Smalley, Eugene Virgil
Smith, Alfred Holland
Smith, Byron Caldwell
Smith, Henry Preserved
Smith, Joseph, 1832–1914
Smith, Preserved
Smith, William Sooy
Snider, Denton Jaques
Snow, Lorenzo
Spahr, Charles Barzillai
Sparks, Edwin Erle
Speaks, Oley
Spear, William Thomas
Sprague, Kate Chase
Stanley, David Sloane
Stanton, Edwin McMasters
Stearns, Frank Ballou
Stephenson, Nathaniel Wright
Stevens, William Arnold
Stewart, Donald Ogden
Stewart, Eliza Daniel
Stewart, Robert
Stockton, Charles G.
Stone, John Wesley
Storer, Bellamy
Stouffer, Vernon Bigelow
Stratemeyer, George Edward
Strauss, Joseph Baermann
Strobel, Charles Louis
Strong, William Lafayette
Stuhldreher, Harry A.
Stutz, Harry Clayton
Sullivant, William Starling
Swayne, Wager
Sweeney, Martin Leonard

Swing, David
Taft, Charles Phelps
Taft, Henry Waters
Taft, Robert Alphonso
Taft, William Howard
Talbott, Harold Elstner
Tappan, Eli Todd
Tatum, Art
Taylor, Archibald Alexander Edward
Tecumseh
Tenskwatawa
Thatcher, Roscoe Wilfred
Thilly, Frank
Thoburn, Isabella
Thoburn, James Mills
Thomas, Edith Matilda
Thomas, Norman Mattoon
Thomas, Roland Jay
Thompson, David P.
Thompson, William Oxley
Thompson, William Tappan
Thomson, William McClure
Thurber, James Grover
Thurston, Howard
Tibbles, Thomas Henry
Tittle, Ernest Fremont
Tod, David
Todd, Walter Edmond Clyde
Torrence, Frederick Ridgely
Tourgée, Albion Winegar
Townsend, Willard Saxby, Jr.
Twachtman, John Henry
Tyler, George Crouse
Tytus, John Butler
Ulrich, Edward Oscar
Updegraff, Davi Brainard
Vail, Theodore Newton
Vallandigham, Clement Laird
Van Anda, Carr Vattel
Van Deman, Esther Boise
Van Sweringen, Mantis James
Venable, William Henry
Verity, George Matthew
Vickery, Howard Leroy
Victor, Orville James
Voorhees, Daniel Wolsey
Wade, Decius Spear
Wade, Jeptha Homer
Waite, Henry Matson
Wald, Lillian D.
Walden, John Morgan
Wales, James Albert
Walker, Thomas Barlow
Walter, Eugene
Wambaugh, Sarah
Wanamaker, Reuben Melville
Ward, Charles Alfred
Ward, John Quincy Adams
Weaver, James Baird
Weber, Henry Adam
Weed, Lewis Hill
Weeks, John Elmer
Weitzel, Godfrey
Welch, John
Weller, John B.
Wellman, Walter
Wheeler, Wayne Bidwell
White, Emerson Elbridge
White Eyes
Whitehead, Wilbur Cherrier
Whitlock, Brand
Whittredge, Worthington
Widney, Joseph Pomeroy
Wilder, Russell Morse
Wildman, Murray Shipley
Williams, Charles David
Williams, Edward Thomas
Williams, Harrison Charles
Williams, James Douglas
Williams, John Elias
Williams, John Fletcher
Williams, Marshall Jay
Wilson, Charles Erwin
Wilson, James Falconer
Wilson, Samuel Mountford
Wilson, Samuel Ramsay
Windom, William
Wolfson, Erwin Service
Woodhull, Victoria Claflin
Woods, Charles Robert
Woods, William Burnham
Woolley, Celia Parker
Woolley, John Granville
Woolsey, Sarah Chauncy
Worcester, Elwood
Wright, Hamilton Kemp
Wright, James Arlington
Wright, Orville
Wright, William
Wyant, Alexander Helwig
Young, Allyn Abbott
Young, Clark Montgomery
Young, Denton True ("Cy")
Young, John Wesley
Zahm, John Augustine
Zollars, Ely Vaughan

OKLAHOMA

Armstrong, Frank C.
Bayh, Marvella Belle Hern
Berryman, John
Billingsley, John Sherman
Chaney, Lon, Jr.
Clark, Joseph James ("Jocko")
Dunn, Michael
Francis, Kay
Guthrie, Woody
Hamilton, Maxwell McGaughey
Harris, LeRoy Ellsworth ("Roy")
Hastings, William Wirt
Heflin, Van
Hurley, Patrick Jay
Jansky, Karl Guthe
Jones, William
Kerr, Robert Samuel
Kirkwood, John Gamble
Martin, Johnny Leonard Roosevelt ("Pepper")
Monroney, Almer Stillwell ("Mike")
Owen, Stephen Joseph
Posey, Alexander Lawrence
Robertson, Alice Mary
Rogers, Will
Rushing, James Andrew
Stigler, William Grady
Thorpe, James Francis
Waner, Paul Glee

OREGON

Barbey, Daniel Edward
Bates, Blanche
Cromwell, Dean Bartlett
Cunningham, Imogen
Davenport, Homer Calvin
Gaston, Herbert Earle
Gilbert, Alfred Carlton
Hawley, Willis Chatman
Joseph
Kanaga, Consuelo Delesseps
Keeney, Barnaby Conrad
Latourette, Kenneth Scott
MacDonald, Ranald
McGinley, Phyllis
McIntire, Ross
McKay, (James) Douglas
McNary, Charles Linza
Markham, Edwin
Neuberger, Richard Lewis
Pettengill, Samuel Barrett
Poling, Daniel Alfred
Prefontaine, Steve Roland ("Pre")
Reed, John, 1887–1920
Robinson, Claude Everett
Turner, Richmond Kelly

PENNSYLVANIA

Abbett, Leon
Abbey, Edwin Austin
Abbott, Benjamin
Abernethy, Roy
Acheson, Edward Goodrich
Adams, Randolph Greenfield
Adams, Robert
Addicks, John Edward O'Sullivan
Adlum, John
Agnew, David Hayes
Albright, Jacob
Alcott, Louisa May
Alexander, John White
Alexander, Joseph Addison
Allen, Andrew
Allen, Harrison
Allen, Henry Justin
Allen, Hervey
Allen, Richard
Allen, William
Allibone, Samuel Austin
Alter, David
Anderson, John Alexander
Anderson, Joseph
Anderson, Maxwell
Angela, Mother
Appenzeller, Henry Gerhard
Apple, Thomas Gilmore
Arbuckle, John
Arensberg, Walter Conrad
Armstrong, John
Arnold, Henry Harley
Asch, Morris Joseph
Ashburner, Charles Albert
Ashhurst, John
Ashley, James Mitchell
Ashmead, Isaac
Ashmead, William Harris
Atkinson, William Biddle
Atkinson, Wilmer

Atlee, John Light
Atlee, Washington Lemuel
Awl, William Maclay
Bache, Alexander Dallas
Bache, Benjamin Franklin
Bache, Franklin
Baer, George Frederick
Bailey, Francis
Bailey, Frank Harvey
Bailey, Lydia R.
Baird, Absalom
Bairds Henry Carey
Baird, Henry Martyn
Baird, Robert
Baird, Spencer Fullerton
Baldwin, Joseph
Baldwin, William
Bard, Samuel
Bard, William
Barker, James Nelson
Barker, Wharton
Barnard, George Grey
Barnes, Albert Coombs
Barnes, Joseph K.
Barnum, Zenus
Barrymore, Ethel
Barrymore, Georgiana Emma Drew
Barrymore, John
Barrymore, Lionel
Bartlett, William Holmes Chambers
Bartley, Mordecai
Barton, Benjamin Smith
Barton, John Rhea
Barton, Thomas Pennant
Barton, William Paul Crillon
Bartram, John
Bartram, William
Baugher, Henry Louis
Bausman, Benjamin
Bayard, Samuel
Baziotes, William
Bean, Tarleton Hoffman
Beasley, Mercer
Beatty, John
Beaumont, John Colt
Beaux, Cecilia
Beaver, James Addams
Beck, James Montgomery
Bedford, Gunning
Bedinger, George Michael
Bell, De Benneville ("Bert")
Bell, James Ford
Bell, James Stroud
Benbridge, Henry
Benner, Philip
Bennett, Caleb Prew
Berger, Daniel
Berkowitz, Henry
Berwind, Edward Julius
Biddle, Anthony Joseph Drexel, Jr.
Biddle, Clement
Biddle, George
Biddle, James
Biddle, Nicholas, 1750–1778
Biddle, Nicholas, 1786–1844
Bigler, John
Bigler, William
Bingham, Anne Willing
Bingham, John Armor
Bingham, William
Binkley, Robert Cedric
Binney, Horace
Bird, Frederic Mayer
Bisphan, David Scull
Black, James
Black, Jeremiah Sullivan
Black, William Murray
Blaine, James Gillespie
Blake, Francis Gilman
Bliss, Philip Paul
Bliss, Tasker Howard
Blitzstein, Marc
Boehm, Henry
Boker, George Henry
Boller, Alfred Pancoast
Bomberger, John Henry Augustus
Boone, Daniel
Booth, James Curtis
Boreman, Arthur Ingram
Borie, Adolph Edward
Borie, Adolphe
Boring, Edwin Garrigues
Boudinot, Elias
Bourke, John Gregory
Bowen, Catherine Drinker
Bowers, Theodore Shelton
Bowman, Thomas
Boyd, James
Brackenridge, Henry Marie
Bradford, William
Brady, Cyrus Townsend
Brashear, John Alfred
Breck, James Lloyd
Breen, Joseph Ignatius
Breese, Kidder Randolph
Brennan, Francis James
Brereton, Lewis Hyde
Brewster, Frederick Carroll
Bridges, Robert
Bright, James Wilson
Brinton, Daniel Garrison
Brinton, John Hill
Brodhead, John Romeyn
Brooke, John Rutter
Brown, Charles Brockden
Brown, David Paul
Brown, Jacob Jennings
Brown, William Henry
Brown, William Hughey
Buchanan, James
Buchman, Frank Nathan Daniel
Buckalew, Charles Rollin
Bucknell, William
Buehler, Huber Gray
Bullard, William Hannum Grubb
Bullitt, William Christian
Burdette, Robert Jones
Burleigh, Henry Thacker
Burnett, Charles Henry
Burpee, David
Burrell, David James
Burrowes, Thomas Henry
Burrows, Julius Caesar
Burrows, William
Burson, William Worth
Butler, Smedley Darlington
Buttz, Henry Anson
Byerly, William Elwood
Cadman, Charles Wakefield
Cadwalader, John, 1742–1786
Cadwalader, John, 1805–1879
Cadwalader, Thomas
Calder, Alexander
Calder, Alexander Stirling
Caldwell, Alexander
Caldwell, David
Calhoun, William James
Cameron, James Donald
Cameron, Simon
Campbell, Bartley
Campbell, James
Campbell, James Hepburn
Carey, Henry Charles
Carnahan, James
Carpenter, Cyrus Clay
Carpenter, Walter Samuel, Jr.
Carr, John Dickson
Carrick, Samuel
Carroll, Earl
Carroll, William
Carson, Hampton Lawrence
Carson, John Renshaw
Carson, Joseph
Carson, Rachel Louise
Carter, John
Case, Leonard
Cassatt, Alexander Johnston
Cassatt, Mary
Cassin, John
Catlin, George
Catron, John
Cattell, James McKeen
Chambers, George
Chambers, Talbot Wilson
Chambers, Whittaker
Chanfrau, Henrietta Baker
Chapman, Henry Cadwalader
Chauvenet, William
Cheyney, Edward Potts
Childs, Cephas Grier
Chorpenning, George
Christy, Edwin P.
Cist, Charles
Cist, Jacob
Clark, Walter Leighton
Clark, William Andrews
Clarke, Helen Archibald
Clarke, Thomas Shields
Clay, Albert Thomas
Clay, Edward Williams
Clayton, Powell
Clement, Martin Withington
Clemson, Thomas Green
Cliffton, William
Clothier, William Jackson
Clymer, George
Clymer, George E.
Coates, Florence Earle
Coates, Samuel
Cochran, John
Cochrane, Henry Clay
Coffin, William Anderson
Coggeshall, William Turner
Coleman, Leighton
Collins, Napoleon
Connelly, Cornelia
Connelly, Marcus Cook ("Marc")
Conner, David

Connick, Charles Jay
Connolly, John
Conrad, Frank
Conrad, Robert Taylor
Converse, James Booth
Cook, Martha Elizabeth Duncan Walker
Cook, Robert Johnson
Cooke, Morris Llewellyn
Coombe, Thomas
Cooper, William
Cope, Caleb
Cope, Edward Drinker
Cope, Thomas Pym
Cope, Walter
Corbin, Margaret
Corey, William Ellis
Coriat, Isador Henry
Cornstalk
Corse, John Murray
Corson, Hiram
Corson, Robert Rodgers
Cort, Stewart Shaw
Cowan, Edgar
Cox, Hannah Peirce
Cox, Rowland
Coxe, Eckley Brinton
Coxe, Tench
Coxe, William
Coxey, Jacob Sechler
Craig, Thomas
Cramp, Charles Henry
Cramp, William
Crawford, James Pyle Wickersham
Crawford, John Martin
Cresson, Elliott
Cresson, Ezra Townsend
Crooks, George Richard
Crosby, Peirce
Crozer, John Price
Crumbine, Samuel Jay
Cullinan, Joseph Stephen
Cummins, Albert Baird
Cupples, Samuel
Curran, John Joseph
Curry, George Law
Curtin, Andrew Gregg
Cushing, Frank Hamilton
Cutbush, James
Dahlgren, John Adolphus Bernard
Daley, Cass
Dallas, George Mifflin
Darby, William
Darke, William
Darley, Felix Octavius Carr
Darling, Henry
Darlington, William
Davenport, Russell Wheeler
Davidson, William Lee
Davis, Bernard George
Davis, Ernest R. ("Ernie")
Davis, John Wesley
Davis, Noah Knowles
Davis, Rebecca Blaine Harding
Davis, Richard Harding
Davis, Stuart
Davis, William Morris
Davison, Henry Pomeroy
Day, David Alexander
Day, Frank Miles
Deaver, John Blair
De Haren, Edwin Jesse
Deitzler, George Washington
Del Ruth, Roy
Deland, Margaret
Demuth, Charles
Dercum, Francis Xavier
Desha, Joseph
Devers, Jacob Loucks
Dewees, William Potts
Dick, Elisha Cullen
Dickinson, Anna Elizabeth
Diller, Joseph Silas
Dilworth, Richardson
Dock, Lavinia Lloyd
Dodd, Lee Wilson
Dodd, Samuel Calvin Tate
Doddridge, Joseph
Doddridge, Philip
Dolan, Thomas
Donnelly, Eleanor Cecilia
Donnelly, Ignatius
Dorsey, John Syng
Dorsey, Thomas Francis ("Tommy")
Dos Passas, John Randolph
Dougherty, Dennis Joseph
Dougherty, Raymond Philip
Doughty, Thomas
Downey, John
Drew, John
Drexel, Anthony Joseph
Drexel, Joseph William
Drexel, Katharine Mary
Drinker, Cecil Kent
Driscoll, Alfred Eastlack
Dropsie, Moses Aaron
Drown, Thomas Messinger
Duane, William
Dubbs, Joseph Henry
Du Bois, William Ewing
Duff, James Henderson
Duffield, George, 1732–1790
Duffield, George, 1794–1868
Dunlop, James
Dunwoody, William Hood
Durant, Thomas Jefferson
Durham, Caleb Wheeler
Dye, William McEntyre
Eakins, Thomas
Earle, George Howard, III
Eckels, James Herron
Eddy, Thomas
Edge, Walter Evans
Edwards, Richard Stanislaus
Egan, Maurice Francis
Egle, William Henry
Eichholtz, Jacob
Eisenhart, Luther Pfahler
Elder, William
Ellet, Charles
Ellicott, Andrew
Ellicott, Joseph
Ellicott, Washington Lafayette
Ellmaker, (Emmett) Lee
Elman, Harry ("Ziggy")
English, Thomas Dunn
Espy, James Pollard
Eustis, Dorothy Leib Harrison Wood
Evans, Henry Clay
Evans, Lewis
Evans, Nathaniel
Evans, Thomas
Evans, Thomas Wiltberger
Eve, Joseph
Ewing, James, 1736–1806
Ewing, James, 1866–1943
Ewing, James Caruthers Rhea
Eytinge, Rose
Fahnestock, Harris Charles
Fairlamb, James Remington
Falk, Maurice
Farabee, William Curtis
Farquhar, Percival
Faulk, Andrew Jackson
Ferguson, Elizabeth Graeme
Ferrel, William
Ferris, Jean Léon Gérôme
Ffoulke, Charles Mather
Fielding, Jerry
Fields, William Claude
Filson, John
Findlay, James
Fine, Henry Burchard
Fine, John Sydney
Fine, Larry
Finletter, Thomas Knight
Fischer, Louis
Fisher, Clarence Stanley
Fisher, Daniel Webster
Fisher, Frederick Bohn
Fisher, Hammond Edward
Fisher, Joshua Francis
Fisher, Sidney George
Fisher, Sydney George
Fite, Warner
Fitler, Edwin Henry
Flather, John Joseph
Fleisher, Benjamin Wilfrid
Fleming, John
Fletcher, Henry Prather
Flick, Lawrence Francis
Florence, Thomas Birch
Fogarty, Anne Whitney
Folwell, Samuel
Foote, John Ambrose
Force, Juliana Rieser
Ford, Thomas
Forepaugh, Adam
Forney, John Wien
Forney, Matthias Nace
Forrest, Edwin
Forten, James
Foster, Stephen Collins
Foster, Thomas Jefferson
Foulk, George Clayton
Fox, Jacob Nelson ("Nellie")
Fraley, Frederick
Francis, John Brown
Franklin, William
Franklin, William Buel
Frayne, Hugh
Frazer, John Fries
Frazer, Persifor, 1736–1792
Frazer, Persifor, 1844–1909
Frazier, Charles Harrison
Frear, William
Freed, Alan J.
French, Paul Comly

Frick, Henry Clay
Fries, John
Fritz, John
Frost, Arthur Burdett
Fry, William Henry
Fulton, Robert
Furness, Horace Howard, 1732–1790
Furness, Horace Howard, 1794–1868
Furst, Clyde Bowman
Fussell, Bartholomew
Gabb, William More
Gallagher, William Davis
Gallaudet, Thomas Hopkins
Galloway, Samuel
Garman, Samuel
Garner, Erroll Louis
Garrett, Thomas
Gass, Patrick
Gates, Thomas Sovereign
Gayley, James
Geary, John White
Geddes, James
George, Henry
Gerhard, William Wood
Gerhart, Emanuel Vogel
Gibbon, John
Gibbons, Abigail Hopper
Gibbons, William
Gibson, George
Gibson, John
Gibson, John Bannister
Giddings, Joshua Reed
Gihon, Albert Leary
Gilder, William Henry
Gilpin, William
Girty, Simon
Gitt, Josiah Williams ("Jess")
Glackens, William James
Gladden, Washington
Glynn, James
Gobrecht, Christian
Godfrey, Thomas, 1704–1749
Godfrey, Thomas, 1736–1763
Goebel, William
Good, Adolphus Clemens
Good, James Isaac
Good, Jeremiah Haak
Goodman, Charles
Goodyear, Charles
Gordon, Kermit
Gordon, Laura De Force
Gorgas, Josiah
Gostelowe, Jonathan
Goucher, John Franklin
Gouge, William M.
Gowen, Franklin Benjamin
Graff, Frederic
Graff, Frederick
Grafly, Charles
Graham, George Rex
Graham, Joseph
Grant, William Thomas, Jr.
Gratz, Rebecca
Gray, Isaac Pusey
Gray, John Purdue
Graydon, Alexander
Green, Jacob
Green, William Joseph, Jr.
Greener, Richard Theodore
Gregg, Andrew
Gregg, David McMurtrie
Gregory, Casper René
Gregory, Thomas Barger
Grier, Robert Cooper
Grierson, Benjamin Henry
Griffin, Martin Ignatius Joseph
Griffis, William Elliot
Griscom, Clement Acton
Gross, Samuel David
Guffiey, James McClurg
Guffey, Joseph F.
Guggenheim, Daniel
Guggenheim, Simon
Guggenheim, Solomon Robert
Guilday, Peter Keenan
Gummere, John
Guthrie, George Wilkins
Hagner, Peter
Haid, Leo
Haldeman, Samuel Steman
Haldeman-Julius, Emanuel
Hale, Charles Reuben
Hall, Baynard Rush
Hall, James, 1744–1826
Hall, James, 1793–1868
Hall, John Elihu
Hall, Sarah Ewing
Hall, Thomas
Hallowell, Benjamin
Hallowell, Richard Price
Hamer, Thomas Lyon
Hamilton, Peter
Hammer, William Joseph
Hancock, Winfield Scott
Happer, Andrew Patton
Harbaugh, Henry
Hardin, Ben
Hardin, Martin D.
Harding, George
Harding, Jesper
Harding, William White
Hare, George Emlen
Hare, John Innes Clark
Hare, Robert
Haring, Clarence
Harkins, William Draper
Harlan, Josiah
Harlan, Richard
Harmar, Josiah
Harpster, John Henry
Harrah, Charles Jefferson
Harris, George Washington
Harris, John
Harrison, Charles Custis
Harrison, Gabriel
Harrison, John
Harrison, Joseph
Harrison, Lovell Birge
Harrison, Ross Granville
Harrison, Thomas Alexander
Harrod, James
Harshberger, John William
Hart, Abraham
Hart, Albert Bushnell
Hart, Charles Henry
Hart, Edward
Hart, Philip Aloysius
Hartley, Thomas
Hartranft, Chester David
Hartranft, John Frederick
Hartshorne, Henry
Haseltine, James Henry
Haskins, Charles Homer
Haupt, Herman
Haverly, Christopher
Hay, Charles Augustus
Hayden, William
Hayes, Isaac Israel
Hayes, John William
Hays, Alexander
Hays, Isaac
Hazard, Ebenezer
Hazard, Samuel
Heap, Samuel Davies
Heath, Thomas Kurton
Heintzelman, Samuel Peter
Heinz, Henry John
Helmuth, William Tod
Hemphill, Joseph
Hench, Philip Showalter
Henck, John Benjamin
Hendricks, William
Henrici, Arthur Trautwein
Henry, Andrew
Henry, William
Hepburn, James Curtis
Hergesheimer, Joseph
Hering, Carl
Hering, Rudolph
Herr, John
Herron, Francis Jay
Hershey, Milton Snavely
Hicks, John, 1823–1890
Hiester, Daniel
Hiester, Joseph
Hill, George Washington
Hillegas, Michael
Hillis, David
Himes, Charles Francis
Hires, Charles Elmer, Jr.
Hirst, Barton Cooke
Hirst, Henry Beck
Hise, Elijah
Hittell, John Shertzer
Hittell, Theodore Henry
Hobart, John Henry
Hodge, Charles
Hodge, Hugh Lenox
Hoffman, Clare Eugene
Hogan, John Vincent Lawless
Holliday, Cyrus Kurtz
Holls, George Frederick William
Holmes, David
Holmes, John Haynes
Homer, Louise Dilworth Beatty
Hood, James Walker
Hood, Washington
Hooper, Lucy Hamilton
Hoover, James Matthews
Hopkins, Edward Augustus
Hopkinson, Francis
Hopkinson, Joseph
Hopper, Hedda
Horn, Edward Traill
Horn, George Henry
Horsfield, Thomas
Hoshour, Samuel Klinefelter
Hough, Charles Merrill

Houston, Henry Howard
Howe, Frederic Clemson
Hoyt, Henry Martyn
Hughes, Hector James
Huidekoper, Frederic
Hullihen, Simon P.
Humphreys, Andrew Atkinson
Humphreys, James
Humphreys, Joshua
Humphries, George Rolfe
Huneker, James Gibbons
Hunt, Robert Woolston
Hunter, Andrew
Hussey, Curtis Grubb
Huston, Charles
Hutchinson, James
Ickes, Harold Le Clair
Ingersoll, Charles Jared
Ingersoll, Edward
Ingham, Samuel Delucenna
Ingraham, Edward Duffield
Irvine, James
Irvine, William Mann
Jackson, Abraham Reeves
Jackson, Chevalier
Jackson, David
Jackson, Dugald Caleb
Jackson, Edward
Jackson, Robert Houghwout
Jackson, Samuel
Jacobs, Henry Eyster
Jacobs, Michael
Jadwin, Edgar
Jaggar, Thomas Augustus, Jr.
James, Arthur Horace
James, Thomas Chalkley
James, Thomas Potts
Jameson, Horatio Gates
Janvier, Catharine Ann
Janvier, Thomas Allibone
Jarvis, Charles H.
Jayne, Horace Fort
Jeanes, Anna T.
Jeffers, John Robinson
Jefferson, Joseph
Jenkins, Howard Malcolm
Jennings, John
Jessup, Henry Harris
Johnson, John Graver
Johnston, David Claypoole
Johnston, William Andrew
Jones, Benjamin Franklin
Jones, George
Jones, Jehu Glancy
Jones, John Price
Jones, William
Jones, William Patterson
Jones, William Richard
Jordon, John Woolf
Junkin, George
Kagan, Henry Enoch
Kane, Elisha Kent
Kane, Thomas Leiper
Kauffman, Calvin Henry
Kaufman, George S.
Kay, Edgar Boyd
Keagy, John Miller
Keating, John Marie
Keely, John Ernst Worrell
Keen, Morris Longstreth
Keen, William Williams
Keller, Kaufman Thuma
Kelley, Florence
Kelley, William Darrah
Kelly, Aloysius Oliver Joseph
Kelly, George Edward
Kelly, John Brendan
Kelly, Walter ("Walt") Crawford, Jr.
Kelly, William
Kelton, John Cunningham
Kemmerer, Edwin Walter
Kennedy, Joseph Camp Griffith
Kent, William
Kephart, Ezekial Boring
Kephart, Isaiah La Fayette
Kephart, John William
Kier, Samuel M.
King, Samuel Archer
Kintner, Robert Edmonds
Kirby, Allan Price
Kirk, Alan Goodrich
Kirkbride, Thomas Story
Kirkus, Virginia
Kirlin, Joseph Louis Jerome
Klauder, Charles Zeller
Kline, Franz Josef
Kneass, Samuel Honeyman
Kneass, Strickland
Kneass, William
Knight, Daniel Ridgway
Knight, Jonathan
Knox, Philander Chase
Kohler, Elmer Peter
Kraemer, Henry
Krause, Allen Kramer
Krauth, Charles Philip
Kresge, Sebastian Spering
Kress, Samuel Henry
Kuhn, Adam
Kumler, Henry
Kurtz, Benjamin
Kynett, Alpha Jefferson
Lacey, John
Lacy, Ernest
Lambdin, James Reid
Lambert, Louis Aloisius
Lamberton, Benjamin Jeffer
Lambing, Andrew Arnold
Landis, Walter Savage
Lane, William Carr
Langstroth, Lorenzo Lorraine
Lardner, James Lawrence
La Roche, Rene
Latrobe, Benjamin Henry, 1806–1878
Latrobe, John Hazlehurst Boneval
Lawrence, David
Lawrence, David Leo
Lea, Henry Charles
Lea, Mathew Carey
Lease, Mary Elizabeth Clyens
Le Brun, Napoléon Eugène Henry Charles
Leffler, Isaac
Leffler, Shepherd
Leffmann, Henry
Leib, Michael
Leidy, Joseph
Leishman, John G. A.
Leland, Charles Godfrey
Le Moyne, Francis Julius
Lenker, John Nicholas
Leonard, Zenas
Lesley, Peter
Leslie, Eliza
Letterman, Jonathan
Levant, Oscar
Levy, Uriah Phillips
Lewis, Charlton Thomas
Lewis, Edmund Darch
Lewis, Ellis
Lewis, Enoch
Lewis, Isaac Newton
Lewis, Lawrence
Lewis, Wilfred
Lewis, William
Lewis, William Draper
Lick, James
Liggett, Hunter
Lightburn, Joseph Andrew Jackson
Linderman, Henry Richard
Lindley, Daniel
Lindley, Jacob
Linn, John Blair
Linton, Ralph
Lippard, George
Lippincott, James Starr
Lippincott, Joseph Wharton
Little, Charles Joseph
Liveright, Horace Brisbin
Lochman, John George
Locke, Alain Leroy
Locke, Matthew
Lockrey, Sarah Hunt
Logan, Deborah Norris
Logan, George
Logan, James, *c.* 1725–1780
Long, John Luther
Longacre, James Barton
Love, Alfred Henry
Loy, Matthias
Loyd, Samuel
Lucas, James H.
Luce, Henry Winters
Lukens, Rebecca Webb Pennock
Luks, George Benjamin
Lutz, Frank Eugene
Lybrand, William Mitchell
Lyon, James Benjamin
Macalester, Charles, 1798–1873
MacArthur, Charles Gordon
MacArthur, John Donald
McBride, Henry
McCall, Samuel Walker
McCann, Alfred Watterson
McCartee, Divie Bethune
McCarthy, Daniel Joseph
McCarthy, Joseph Vincent ("Joe")
McCartney, Washington
McCauley, Charles Stewart
MacCauley, Clay
McCauley, Edward Yorke
McCawley, Charles Grymes
McCay, Charles Francis
McCay, Henry Kent
McClellan, George, 1849–1913
McClellan, George Brinton
McClellan, Henry Brainerd
McClellan, Robert

McClelland, Robert
McClintock, Emory
McClintock, John
McClintock, Oliver
McClure, Alexander Kelly
McClurg, Alexander Caldwell
McCormick, Samuel Black
McCoy, Isaac
McCracken, Joan
McCreery, James Work
MacDonald, David John
MacDonald, Jeanette Anna
McDowell, John
McElrath, Thomas
McFadden, Louis Thomas
McFarland, John Horace
McFarland, Samuel Gamble
McFarland, Thomas Bard
Macfarlane, Charles William
McGiffin, Philo Norton
McGill, John
McGranery, James Patrick
McGready, James
McGuffey, William Holmes
McKean, Samuel
McKean, Thomas
McKean, William Wister
McKechnie, William Boyd
McKenna, Joseph
Mackenzie, William
McKim, Charles Follen
McKim, Isaac
McKim, James Miller
McKinley, Albert Edward
McLane, Allan
Maclay, Robert Samuel
Maclay, Samuel
Maclay, William
McLean, Robert
McLean, William Lippard
McMinn, Joseph
McNair, Alexander
McNair, Frederick Valette
MacNair, Harley Farnsworth
McPherson, Edward
McQuillen, John Hugh
MacVeagh, Charles
MacVeagh, Franklin
MacVeagh, Isaac Wayne
Madden, John Edward
Magee, Christopher Lyman
Magill, Edward Hicks
Mailly, William
Malcolm, James Peller
Malcom, Howard
Mallery, Garrick
Man Ray
Manderson, Charles Frederick
Mansfield, Jayne
March, Francis Andrew
March, Peyton Conway
Marchand, John Bonnett
Marland, Ernest Whitworth
Marquis, John Abner
Marshall, Clara
Marshall, George Catlett, Jr.
Marshall, Humphry
Martin, Elizabeth Price
Martin, John Alexander
Martin, John Hill
Mast, Phineas Price
Mateer, Calvin Wilson
Mathews, John Alexander
Mathewson, Christopher
Matthews, Joseph Merritt
Maurer, James Hudson
Mayer, Lewis
Mead, Margaret
Meade, George
Meade, Richard Worsam
Mears, John William
Mease, James
Medary, Milton Bennett
Medary, Samuel
Meigs, Arthur Vincent
Meigs, James Aitken
Meigs, John
Meigs, John Forsyth
Meigs, William Montgomery
Mellon, Andrew William
Mellon, William Larimer
Menjou, Adolphe Jean
Menoher, Charles Thomas
Mercer, Henry Chapman
Mercer, Lewis Pyle
Mercur, Ulysses
Meredith, Samuel
Meredith, William Morris
Merritt, Anna Lea
Mervine, William
Messersmith, George Strausser
Metcalf, Joel Hastings
Metcalf, William
Michener, Ezra
Michler, Nathaniel
Middleton, Thomas Cooke
Midgley, Thomas
Mifflin, Lloyd
Mifflin, Thomas
Milburn, William Henry
Miller, George
Miller, George Abram
Miller, James Russell
Miller, Samuel
Milligan, Robert Wiley
Mills, Charles Karsner
Mitchell, John Hipple
Mitchell, Langdon Elwyn
Mitchell, Silas Weir
Mitchell, Thomas Duché
Mix, Tom
Montgomery, James Alan
Moore, Annie Aubertine Woodward
Moore, George Foot
Moore, James Edward
Moore, Joseph Earle
Moore, William, 1699–1783
Moore, William, 1735–1793
Moorhead, James Kennedy
Moran, Benjamin
Morgan, George
Morgan, George Washington
Morgan, John
Morley, Christopher Darlington
Morley, Sylvanus Griswold
Morris, Anthony, 1766–1860
Morris, Cadwalader
Morris, Caspar
Morris, Edward Joy
Morris, George Pope
Morris, John Gottlieb
Morris, Thomas
Morrison, John Irwin
Morrison, William
Morrow, Jeremiah
Morton, James St. Clair
Morton, John
Morton, Samuel George
Moss, John Calvin
Muhlenberg, Frederick Augustus
Mühlenberg, Frederick Augustus Conrad
Mühlenberg, Gotthilf Henry Ernest
Mühlenberg, Henry Augustus Philip
Muhlenberg, John Peter Gabriel
Muhlenberg, William Augustus
Mulford, Elisha
Murdock, James Edward
Murphy, Dominic Ignatius
Murphy, Isaac
Murray, John, 1737–1808
Murray, Lindley
Murray, Louise Shipman Welles
Murtaugh, Daniel Edward ("Danny")
Musmanno, Michael Angelo
Nancrède, Charles Beylard Guérard de
Nassau, Robert Hamill
Neely, Thomas Benjamin
Negley, James Scott
Neill, Edward Duffield
Neill, John
Neill, Thomas Hewson
Neill, William
Neilson, William George
Nesbit, Evelyn Florence
Nevin, Alfred
Nevin, Edwin Henry
Nevin, Ethelbert Woodbridge
Nevin, George Balch
Nevin, John Williamson
Nevin, Robert Peebles
Newcomer, Christian
Newell, Frederick Haynes
Newton, Henry Jotham
Newton, Richard Heber
Newton, William Wilberforce
Niles, Hezekiah
Nixon, John, 1733–1808
Noah, Mordecai Manuel
Nock, Albert Jay
Nolen, John
Norris, George Washington
Norris, Isaac, 1701–1766
Norris, William Fisher
Noss, Theodore Bland
Oberholtzer, Ellis Paxson
Oberholtzer, Sara Louisa Vickers
Odenheimer, William Henry
Odets, Clifford
Oehmler, Leo Carl Martin
Offley, David
Ogden, Robert Curtis
O'Hara, John Henry
Olds, Irving Sands
Olmsted, Marlin Edgar
O'Malley, Frank Ward

O'Neill, Rose Cecil
Ord, George
O'Reilly, Robert Maitland
Ortle, Godlove Stein
Osborn, Henry Stafford
Osborn, Thomas Andrew
Ott, Isaac
Otto, William Tod
Outerbridge, Alexander Ewing
Outerbridge, Eugenius Harvey
Packard, John Hooker
Packer, William Fisher
Page, Joseph Francis ("Joe")
Palmer, Alexander Mitchell
Palmer, Henry Wilbur
Pancoast, Henry Khunrath
Pancoast, Seth
Park, James
Park, Robert Ezra
Parke, John Grubb
Parker, George Howard
Parkinson, Thomas Ignatius
Parrish, Anne
Parrish, Charles
Parrish, Edward
Parrish, Joseph
Parrish, Maxfield
Parry, Charles Thomas
Parry, John Stubbs
Passavant, William Alfred
Patterson, Morris
Patterson, Robert Mayne
Patton, William
Peale, Anna Claypoole
Peale, Rembrandt
Peale, Sarah Miriam
Peale, Titian Ramsay
Pearse, John Barnard Swett
Peary, Robert Edwin
Peffer, William Alfred
Pemberton, Israel
Pemberton, James
Pemberton, John
Pemberton, John Clifford
Penington, Edward
Penn, John
Penn, Richard
Pennell, Joseph
Pennypacker, Elijah Funk
Pennypacker, Galusha
Pennypacker, Samuel Whitaker
Penrose, Boies
Penrose, Charles Bingham
Penrose, Richard Alexander Fullerton
Penrose, Spencer
Pepper, George Seckel
Pepper, George Wharton
Pepper, William, 1810–1864
Pepper, William, 1843–1898
Pepper, William, III, 1874–1947
Peters, Madison Clinton
Peters, Richard, 1744–1828
Peters, Richard, 1810–1889
Peterson, Charles Jacobs
Peterson, Henry
Pettigrew, Charles
Pettit, Thomas McKean
Pew, John Howard
Pew, Joseph Newton, Jr.
Pfahler, George Edward
Phelps, William Walter
Phillips, Francis Clifford
Phillips, Henry
Phillips, Thomas Wharton
Phipps, Henry
Phipps, Lawrence Cowle
Physick, Philip Syng
Pickens, Andrew
Pickering, Charles
Pippin, Horace
Plumer, William Swan
Polk, Thomas
Polock, Moses
Porter, Andrew
Porter, David Dixon
Porter, David Rittenhouse
Porter, Edwin Stanton
Porter, Horace
Porter, James Madison
Porter, Thomas Conrad
Potts, Charles Sower
Potts, Jonathan
Poulson, Zachariah
Powderly, Terence Vincent
Powdermaker, Hortense
Powel, John Hare
Pratt, Matthew
Pratt, Waldo Selden
Presser, Theodore
Preston, Ann
Preston, Jonas
Preston, Margaret Junkin
Preston, William Campbell
Price, Eli Kirk, 1797–1884
Price, Eli Kirk, 1860–1933
Price, Hiram
Pugh, Evan
Purdue, John
Pyle, Robert
Pyle, Walter Lytle
Quay, Matthew Stanley
Quinan, John Russell
Quinn, Arthur Hobson
Quinn, Edmond Thomas
Raguet, Condy
Ramsay, David
Ramsay, Erskine
Ramsay, Nathaniel
Ramsey, Alexander
Randall, Samuel Jackson
Randolph, Jacob
Rauch, John Henry
Rawle, Francis, 1846–1930
Rawle, William
Rawle, William Henry
Rea, Samuel
Read, Charles
Read, Conyers
Read, John Meredith, 1797–1874
Read, John Meredith, 1837–1896
Read, Thomas Buchanan
Ream, Norman Bruce
Redman, John
Reed, David Aiken
Reed, Henry Hope
Reed, James Hay
Reed, William Bradford
Reeder, Andrew Horatio
Reese, John James
Rehn, Frank Knox Morton
Reick, William Charles
Reid, William Shields
Reilly, Marion
Reinhart, Benjamin Franklin
Reinhart, Charles Stanley
Remington, Joseph Price
Repplier, Agnes
Reynolds, John
Reynolds, John Fulton
Reynolds, William
Rhees, William Jones
Rhine, Joseph Banks
Rhoades, James E.
Rich, Robert
Richards, Theodore William
Richards, William Trost
Richardson, Joseph
Richardson, Robert
Richter, Conrad Michael
Riddle, Matthew Brown
Riddle, Samuel Doyle
Rigdon, Sidney
Rinehart, Mary Roberts
Rinehart, Stanley Marshall, Jr.
Ritner, Joseph
Rittenhouse, David
Roane, Archibald
Robb, James
Roberdeau, Isaac
Roberts, Elizabeth Wentworth
Roberts, George Brooke
Roberts, Howard
Roberts, Job
Roberts, Jonathan
Roberts, Owen Josephus
Roberts, Solomon White
Roberts, William Milnor
Robertson, James Alexander
Robinson, Edward Mott
Rockhill, William Woodville
Rodenbough, Theophilus Francis
Roebling, Washington Augustus
Rogers, Henry Darwin
Rogers, James Blythe
Rogers, John Ignatius
Rogers, Robert William
Rogers, William Barton
Rondthaler, Edward
Rosenau, Milton Joseph
Rosenbach, Abraham Simon Wolf
Rosenbach, Philip Hyman
Ross, Betsy
Ross, James
Rossiter, Clinton Lawrence, III
Rotch, Thomas Morgan
Rothermel, Peter Frederick
Rothrock, Joseph Trimble
Rowan, John
Rowland, Henry Augustus
Rupp, Israel Daniel
Rupp, William
Rush, Benjamin
Rush, James
Rush, Richard
Rush, William
Russell, Charles Taze
Ryan, Harris Joseph
Sachse, Julius Friedrich
Sadtler, Samuel Philip

Samuels, Samuel
Sanderson, John
Sankey, Ira David
Sargent, Winthrop, 1825–1870
Sartain, Emily
Sartain, Samuel
Sartain, William
Savery, William, 1750–1804
Saxton, Joseph
Say, Benjamin
Say, Thomas
Sayre, Robert Heysham
Schadle, Jacob Evans
Schaeffer, Charles Frederick
Schaeffer, David Frederick
Schaeffer, Frederick Christian
Schaeffer, Nathan Christ
Schamberg, Jay Frank
Schmauk, Theodore Emanuel
Schmucker, Beale Melanchthon
Schneider, Benjamin
Schneider, Herman
Schodde, George Henry
Schriver, Edmund
Schwab, Charles Michael
Schweinitz, Edmund Alexander de
Schweinitz, George Edmund de
Schweinitz, Lewis David von
Scott, Robert Kingston
Scott, Thomas Alexander
Scovel, Henry Sylvester
Scull, John
Seaman, Elizabeth Cochrane
See, Horace
Seidel, George Lukas Emil
Seip, Theodore Lorenzo
Sellers, Coleman
Sellers, William
Selznick, David O.
Sergeant, John, 1779–1852
Sergeant, Thomas
Servoss, Thomas Lowery
Seybert, Adam
Seybert, Henry
Seybert, John
Sharpless, Isaac
Sharswood, George
Shaw, Thomas
Sheeler, Charles R., Jr.
Shippen, Edward, 1728/29–1806
Shippen, William
Shiras, George
Shiras, Oliver Perry
Sholes, Christopher Latham
Shonts, Theodore Perry
Shor, Bernard ("Toots")
Shoup, George Laird
Shulze, John Andrew
Shunk, Francis Rawn
Simpson, Stephen
Singerly, William Miskey
Skillern, Ross Hall
Slattery, Charles Lewis
Sloan, John French
Smedley, William Thomas
Smith, Albert Holmes
Smith, Andrew Jackson
Smith, Charles Ferguson
Smith, Charles Perrin
Smith, Charles Shaler
Smith, Daniel B.
Smith, Edgar Fahs
Smith, Hannah Whitall
Smith, Hiram
Smith, James, 1737–1814
Smith, John Blair
Smith, Jonathan Bayard
Smith, Lloyd Pearsall
Smith, Margaret Bayard
Smith, Mildred Catharine
Smith, Oliver Hampton
Smith, Persifor Frazer
Smith, Richard Penn
Smith, Richard Somers
Smith, Robert, 1757–1842
Smith, Samuel
Smith, Samuel Harrison
Smith, Samuel Stanhope
Smith, Xanthus Russell
Smyth, Albert Henry
Snowden, James Ross
Snyder, Edwin Reagan
Snyder, Simon
Sower, Christopher, 1754–1799
Spaatz, Carl Andrew ("Tooey")
Spaeth, John Duncan
Spaeth, Sigmund
Spalding, Franklin Spencer
Spangler, Henry Wilson
Speer, Emma Bailey
Speer, Robert Elliott
Speer, William
Sproul, William Cameron
Sproull, Thomas
Stahr, John Summers
Stark, Harold Raynsford
Starr, Louis
Statler, Ellsworth Milton
Stauffer, David McNeely
Steedman, James Blair
Stehle, Aurelius Aloysius
Stein, Gertrude
Stein, Leo Daniel
Stengel, Alfred
Sterling, John Whalen
Sterne, Simon
Sterrett, James Macbride
Stevens, Abel
Stevens, Wallace
Stewardson, John
Stewart, Andrew
Stillé, Alfred
Stillé, Charles Janeway
Stillman, Samuel
Stockdale, Thomas Ringland
Stockton, Charles Herbert
Stockton, Frank Richard
Stoddart, Joseph Marshall
Stoever, Martin Luther
Stokes, Maurice
Stone, Witmer
Stotesbury, Edward Townsend
Strain, Isaac G.
Strawn, Jacob
Strickland, William
Studebaker, Clement
Sturgis, Samuel Davis
Sullivan, James William
Sullivan, Mark
Sulzberger, Cyrus Lindauer
Susann, Jacqueline
Swallow, Silas Comfort
Swank, James Moore
Swensson, Carl Aaron
Swisshelm, Jane Grey Cannon
Sylvis, William H.
Symes, James Miller
Talbot, Francis Xavier
Tanner, Benjamin Tucker
Tanner, Henry Ossawa
Tarbell, Ida Minerva
Tawney, James Albertus
Taylor, Bayard
Taylor, Francis Henry
Taylor, Frank Walter
Taylor, Frederick Winslow
Taylor, George William
Thatcher, Mahlon Daniel
Thaw, Harry Kendall
Thaw, William
Thomas, George Clifford
Thomas, John Charles
Thompson, Arthur Webster
Thompson, Denman
Thompson, Joseph Parrish
Thompson, Josiah Van Kirk
Thompson, Robert Means
Thompson, Samuel Rankin
Thompson, Will Lamartine
Thomson, Frank
Thomson, John Edgar
Thomson, William
Tiffany, Katrina Brandes Ely
Tilden, William Tatem ("Big Bill")
Tilghman, Richard Albert
Timon, John
Tome, Jacob
Toner, Joseph Meredith
Torrence, Joseph Thatcher
Tower, Charlemagne
Towne, Henry Robinson
Towne, John Henry
Townsend, John Kirk
Townsend, Mira Sharpless
Trautwine, John Cresson
Trent, William
Trumbauer, Horace
Truxtun, William Talbot
Tryon, George Washington
Tunnell, Emlen
Turnbull, William
Turner, Samuel Hulbeart
Tyndale, Hector
Tyson, James
Tyson, Job Roberts
Tyson, Stuart Lawrence
Unangst, Erias
Van Amringe, John Howard
Van Buren, William Holme
Vandergrift, Jacob Jay
Van Dyke, Henry
Van Dyke, John Wesley
Van Horn, Robert Thompson
Van Meter, John Blackford
Vanuxem, Lardner
Vare, William Scott
Vauclain, Samuel Matthews
Vaux, Richard
Vaux, Roberts
Venuti, Giuseppe ("Joe")

Vezin, Hermann
Von Moschzisker, Robert
Wagner, John Peter
Wagner, William
Wahl, William Henry
Walker, Frank Comerford
Walker, James Barr
Walker, John Brisben
Walker, Jonathan Hoge
Walker, Robert John
Wallace, David
Wallace, Henry
Wallace, Horace Binney
Wallace, John Hankins
Wallace, John William
Waln, Nicholas
Waln, Robert, 1765–1836
Waln, Robert, 1794–1825
Walsh, Edward Augustine
Walsh, Thomas Joseph
Walter, Francis Eugene
Walter, Thomas Ustick
Walters, William Thompson
Walworth, Jeannette Ritchie Hodermann
Wanamaker, John
Wanamaker, Lewis Rodman
Warden, John Aston
Warner, Edward Pearson
Warren, William, 1812–1888
Waters, Ethel
Watson, David Thompson
Watt, Donald Beates
Watts, Frederick
Wayne, Anthony
Weaver, William Dixon
Webb, John Burkitt
Weems, Ted
Weidner, Revere Franklin
Weir, Ernest Tener
Welsh, John
Wenner, George Unangst
Werdin, Reed
West, Andrew Fleming
West, Benjamin
Westcott, Thompson
Wetherill, Charles Mayer
Wetherill, Samuel
Wetzel, Lewis
Wharton, Anne Hollingsworth
Wharton, Francis
Wharton, Joseph
Wharton, Robert
Wharton, Samuel
Wharton, Thomas
Wharton, Thomas Isaac
Wherry, Elwood Morris
White, James William
White, John De Haven
White, Samuel Stockton
White, William
Whitehill, Robert
Wickersham, George Woodward
Wickersham, James Pyle
Widener, George Dunton
Widener, Harry Elkins
Widener, Peter Arrell Brown
Wieland, George Reber
Wiggin, Kate Douglas
Wikoff, Henry
Wiley, David
Wilkins, Ross
Wilkins, William
Willard, James Field
Williams, Daniel Hale
Williams, George Washington
Williamson, Hugh
Willing, Thomas
Wilmot, David
Wilson Bird
Wilson, Francis
Wilson, John Fleming
Wilson, Joseph Miller
Wilson, Louis Blanchard
Wilson, Robert Burns
Wilson, Samuel Graham
Wilson, Warren Hugh
Winans, Williams
Wines, Frederick Howard
Winterhalter, Hugo
Wise, John
Wistar, Caspar
Wister, Owen
Wister, Sarah
Wolf, George
Wolle, John Frederick
Wood, Charles Erskine Scott
Wood, David Duffle
Wood, Fernando
Wood, Horatio Charles
Wood, James Frederick
Woodhouse, James
Woodin, William Hartman
Woodruff, Charles Edward
Woods, Robert Archey
Woodward, Joseph Janvier
Work, Hubert
Work, Milton Cooper
Wormley, Theodore George
Wright, Charles Barstow
Wright, Hendrick Bradley
Wright, Jonathan Jasper
Wright, Joseph Albert
Wright, Joseph Jefferson Burr
Wrigley, William
Wurtz, Henry
Wylie, Andrew
Wynn, Ed
Yeager, Joseph
Yeates, Jasper
Yerkes, Charles Tyson
Yerkes, Robert Mearns
Young, Jesse Bowman
Young, John Clarke
Young, Samuel Hall
Zahniser, Howard Clinton
Zeilin, Jacob
Ziegemeier, Henry Joseph
Ziegler, William

PUERTO RICO

Clemente, Roberto
Fernós Isern, Antonio
Muñoz Marín, Luis

RHODE ISLAND

Abell, Arunah Shepherdson
Aldrich, Chester Holmes
Aldrich, Nelson Wilmarth
Aldrich, Richard
Aldrich, Winthrop William
Allen, Paul
Allen, Philip
Allen, William Henry
Allen, Zachariah
Alline, Henry
Almy, John Jay
Ames, Samuel
Angell, Israel
Angell, James Burrill
Angell, Joseph Kinnicutt
Angell, William Gorham
Anthony, Henry Bowen
Anthony, John Gould
Anthony, William Arnold
Arnold, Aza
Arnold, Jonathan
Arnold, Richard
Arnold, Samuel Greene
Auchincloss, Hugh Dudley, Jr.
Bacon, Edwin Munroe
Baker, George Pierce
Baldwin, Henry Porter
Ballou, Adin
Bancroft, Wilder Dwight
Bartlett, Elisha
Bartlett, John Russell
Barton, William
Bennett, Charles Edwin
Boss, Lewis
Bourne, Benjamin
Brayton, Charles Ray
Brown, Goold
Brown, James Salisbury
Brown, John
Brown, John Carter
Brown, Joseph
Brown, Joseph Rogers
Brown, Moses
Brown, Nicholas, 1729–1791
Brown, Nicholas, 1769–1841
Brown, Obadiah
Brown, Sylvanus
Brownell, Henry Howard
Buffum, Arnold
Bull, William Tillinghast
Burgess, Alexander
Burgess, George
Burrill, James
Butterworth, Hezekiah
Casey, Silas
Chace, Elizabeth Buffum
Chafee, Zechariah, Jr.
Champlin, John Denison
Champlin, Stephen
Channing, Edward Tyrell
Channing, Walter
Channing, William Ellery
Chapin, Charles Value
Church, Benjamin
Clark, John Bates
Clarke, Walter
Clifford, John Henry
Coe, George Simmons
Cohan, George Michael
Collins, John
Colvin, Stephen Sheldon
Cornell, Ezekiel

Cotton, Joseph Potter
Cottrell, Calvert Byron
Crandall, Prudence
Cranston, Samuel
Cross, Samuel Hazzard
Curtis, George William
Davis, Harvey Nathaniel
Dearth, Henry Golden
Decatur, Stephen
De Wolf, James
Diman, Jeremiah Lewis
Dorr, Thomas Wilson
Doyle, Sarah Elizabeth
Duffy, Hugh
Durfee, Job
Durfee, Thomas
Eddy, Nelson
Elder, Samuel James
Ellery, Frank
Ellery, William
Fenner, Arthur
Fenner, James
Fish, Carl Russell
Fish, Preserved
Gardiner, Silvester
Gardner, Caleb
Gibbs, George
Gorham, Jabez
Green, Theodore Francis
Greene, Albert Gorton
Greene, Christopher
Greene, Edward Lee
Greene, Francis Vinton
Greene, George Sears
Greene, George Washington
Greene, Nathanael
Greene, William, 1695/96–1758
Greene, William, 1731–1809
Hackett, Robert Leo ("Bobby")
Hague, Robert Lincoln
Halsey, Thomas Lloyd
Hamlin, William
Hammond, William Gardiner
Harris, Caleb Fiske
Harris, Daniel Lester
Hartnett, Charles Leo ("Gabby")
Hatlo, Jimmy
Haworth, Joseph
Hazard, Augustus George
Hazard, Jonathan J.
Hazard, Rowland Gibson
Hazard, Thomas
Hazard, Thomas Robinson
Herreshoff, James Brown
Herreshoff, John Brown
Herreshoff, Nathanael Greene
Himes, Joshua Vaughan
Hood, Raymond Mathewson
Hopkins, Esek
Hopkins, John Burroughs
Hopkins, Stephen
Hoppin, Augustus
Hoppin, James Mason
Hoppin, Joseph Clark
Hoppin, William Warner
Howe, Mark Anthony De Wolfe
Howe, Mark Antony De Wolfe
Howe, Percy Rogers
Hunter, William
Ide, John Jay
James, Charles Tillinghast
Janes, Lewis George
Jenckes, Joseph
Jenckes, Thomas Allen
Jones, William
King, Charles William
King, Clarence
King, Samuel
King, Samuel Ward
Ladd, Joseph Brown
La Farge, Christopher Grant
LaFarge, John
Lajoie, Napoleon ("Larry")
Lippitt, Henry
Little, William Lawson, Jr.
Lomax, Lunsford Lindsay
Luther, Seth
Malbone, Edward Greene
Mauran, John Lawrence
McGrath, James Howard
Melville, David
Mills, Ogden Livingston
Morgan, Morris Hicky
Munro, Dana Carleton
Newel, Stanford
Nicholson, William Thomas
Niles, Nathaniel, 1741–1828
Niles, Samuel
O'Connor, Edwin Greene
Olyphant, David Washington Cincinnatus
Palmer, Ray
Park, Edwards Amasa
Patch, Sam
Peckham, Stephen Farnum
Pendleton, Ellen Fitz
Perry, Christopher Raymond
Perry, Matthew Calbraith
Perry, Oliver Hazard
Perry, Thomas Sergeant
Perry, William Stevens
Pinchot, Cornelia Elizabeth Bryce
Potter, Elisha Reynolds
Reynolds, Samuel Godfrey
Richmond, John Wilkes
Robinson, Christopher
Rockefeller, Abby Greene Aldrich
Rodman, Isaac Peace
Round, William Marshall Fitts
Russell, Jonathan
Scott, Job
Sheldon, William Herbert
Shepard, Charles Upham
Sherman, Thomas West
Slater, John Fox
Slocum, Frances
Slocum, Samuel
Southwick, Solomon
Sprague, William, 1773–1836
Sprague, William, 1830–1915
Stanley, Albert Augustus
Staples, William Read
Stetson, Charles Walter
Stiness, John Henry
Stuart, Gilbert
Sully, Daniel John
Sunderland, La Roy
Taylor, William Rogers
Taylor, William Vigneron
Tenney, William Jewett
Thomas, Frederick William
Thurber, George
Thurston, Robert Henry
Thurston, Robert Lawton
Tourjée, Eben
Truman, Benjamin Cummings
Updike, Daniel
Updike, Daniel Berkeley
Vernon, Samuel
Vernon, William
Vinton, Alexander Hamilton
Vinton, Francis
Wanton, Joseph
Ward, Richard
Ward, Samuel, 1725–1776
Ward, Samuel, 1756–1832
Ward, Samuel, 1786–1839
Warren, Minton
Warren, Russell
Waterhouse, Benjamin
Weaver, Philip
Weeden, William Babcock
Welling, Richard Ward Greene
Weston, Edward Payson
Wheaton, Frank
Wheaton, Henry
Whipple, Abraham
Whitaker, Charles Harris
Whitman, Sarah Helen Power
Wilbur, John
Wilcox, Stephen
Wilkinson, David
Wilkinson, Jemima
Wilkinson, Jeremiah
Williams, Catharine Read Arnold
Williams, Samuel May

SOUTH CAROLINA

Adair, John
Adams, Joseph Quincy
Aiken, David Wyatt
Aiken, William
Allston, Robert Francis Withers
Allston, Washington
Alston, Joseph
Anderson, David Lawrence
Anderson, Richard Heron
Babcock, James Woods
Baldwin, James Mark
Barnwell, Robert Woodward
Baruch, Bernard Mannes
Bee, Barnard Elliott
Bee, Hamilton Prioleau
Bethune, Mary McLeod
Blease, Coleman Livingston
Bounethean, Henry Brintnell
Boyce, James Petigru
Boyd, Julian Parks
Bratton, John
Brawley, William Hiram
Brooks, Preston Smith
Brown, Albert Gallatin
Brown, Charlotte Hawkins
Brown, Joseph Emerson
Brown, Morris
Brumby, Richard Trapier
Bull, William, 1683–1755
Bull, William, 1710–1791
Bulloch, Archibald

Butler, Andrew Pickens
Butler, Matthew Calbraith
Butler, Pierce Mason
Byrnes, James Francis
Calhoun, John Caldwell
Calhoun, Patrick
Campbell, Josiah A. Patterson
Cannon, Harriet Starr
Capers, Ellison
Capers, William
Cash, Wilbur Joseph
Charlton, Thomas Usher Pulaski
Chestnut, James
Cheves, Langdon
Chisolm, Alexander Robert
Chisolm, John Julian
Clarke, Etijah
Clinton, George Wylie
Cloud, Noah Bartlett
Cogdell, John Stevens
Cohen, Octavus Roy
Coker, David Robert
Coker, James Lide
Conner, James
Corcoran, James Andrew
Crafts, William
Cunningham, Ann Pamela
Davidson, James Wood
Deas, Zachariah Cantey
De Bow, James Dunwoody Brownson
De Leon, Thomas Cooper
De Saussure, Henry William
Dickson, Samuel Henry
Dorr, Julia Caroline Ripley
Drayton, John
Drayton, Percival
Drayton, Thomas Fenwich
Drayton, William
Drayton, William Henry
Du Bose, William Porcher
Elbert, Samuel
Elliott, Benjamin
Elliott, Stephen
Elliott, William
Elmore, Franklin Harper
Evans, Nathan George
Fayssoux, Peter
Ferguson, Thomas Barker
Few, William Preston
Fraser, Charles
Freed, Arthur
Fuller, Richard
Furman, James Clement
Gadsden, Christopher
Gadsden, James
Gaillard, David Du Bose
Gaillard, Edwin Samuel
Gaillard, John
Gambrell, James Bruton
Gambrell, Mary Latimer
Garden, Alexander
Gary, Martin Witherspoon
Gaston, James McFadden
Gayle, John
Gibbes, Robert Wilson
Gibbes, William Hasell
Gibbons, William
Gildersleeve, Basil Lanneau
Girardeau, John Lafayette
Gist, William Henry
Gonzales, Ambrose Elliott
Gorrie, John
Gossett, Benjamin Brown
Graves, John Temple
Gregg, Maxcy
Grimké, Angelina Emily
Grimké Archibald Henry
Grimké, John Faucheraud
Grimké, Sara Moore
Grimké, Thomas Smith
Hagood, Johnson
Hall, Dominick Augustin
Hamilton, James
Hamilton, Paul
Hammett, Henry Pinckney
Hammond, James Henry
Hampton, Wade
Harper, William
Hayne, Isaac
Hayne, Paul Hamilton
Hayne, Robert Young
Hemphill, John
Henry, Edward Lamson
Henry, Robert
Herbert, Hilary Abner
Heyward, DuBose
Heyward, Thomas
Hill, Daniel Harvey
Hill, Joshua
Hitchcock, Thomas
Holbrook, John Edwards
Holland, Edwin Clifford
Holmes, Isaac Edward
Holmes, Joseph Austin
Howell, Clark
Huger, Benjamin
Huger, Daniel Elliott
Huger, Francis Kinloch
Huger, Isaac
Huger, John
Hunt, William Henry
Hurlbert, William Henry
Hurlbut, Stephen Augustus
Hutson, Richard
Hyrne, Edmund Massingberd
Ingraham, Duncan Nathaniel
Ioor, William
Irving, John Beaufain
Izard, Ralph
Jackson, Andrew
Jacobs, William Plumer
Jamison, David Flavel
Jenkins, Charles Jones
Jenkins, Micah
Johnson, Joseph
Johnson, William
Johnson, William Bullein
Johnston, Henrietta
Johnston, Olin DeWitt Talmadge
Johnstone, Job
Jones, David Rumph
Jones, John B.
Just, Ernest Everett
Keitt, Lawrence Massillon
Kellogg, Clara Louise
Kennedy, John Doby
Kershaw, Joseph Brevard
Keyes, Edward Lawrence
Kinloch, Cleland
Kirkland, James Hampton
La Borde, Maximilian
Laurens, Henry
Laurens, John
Law, Evander McIvor
Lawton, Alexander Robert
Lee, Stephen Dill
Lee, Thomas
Legaré, Hugh Swinton
Lever, Asbury Francis
Levin, Lewis Charles
Lipscomb, Abner Smith
Logan, Thomas Muldrup, 1808–1876
Logan, Thomas Muldrup, 1840–1914
Longstreet, James
Loughridge, Robert McGill
Lowndes, William
Lowry, Robert
Lubbock, Francis Richard
Lynch, Thomas, 1727–1776
Lynch, Thomas, 1749–1779
McBryde, John McLaren
McCaleb, Theodore Howard
McCall, Edward Rutledge
McCord, David James
McCord, Louisa Susanna Cheves
McCrady, Edward
McDonald, Charles James
McGowan, Samuel
Mackey, Albert Gallatin
McTyeire, Holland Nimmons
Magrath, Andrew Gordon
Manigault, Arthur Middleton
Manigault, Gabriel
Manigault, Peter
Manly, Basil
Manly, Basil Maxwell
Manning, Richard Irvine, 1789–1836
Manning, Richard Irvine, 1859–1931
Marion, Francis
Marks, Elias
Mathews, John
Maybank, Burnet Rhett
Meek, Alexander Beaufort
Michel, William Middleton
Middleton, Arthur, 1681–1737
Middleton, Arthur, 1742–1787
Middleton, Henry
Middleton, John Izard
Middleton, Nathaniel Russell
Mignot, Louis Remy
Miles, William Porcher
Miller, Kelly
Miller, Stephen Decatur
Mills, Robert, 1781–1855
Moffett, William Adger
Moïse, Penina
Montgomery, William Bell
Mood, Francis Asbury
Moore, Samuel Preston
Mordecai, Moses Cohen
Moses, Franklin J.
Moultrie, John
Moultrie, William
Murphy, William Sumter
Murray, James Ormsbee

Myers, Abraham Charles
Newman, Albert Henry
Northrop, Lucius Bellinger
Nott, Henry Junius
Nott, Josiah Clark
O'Neall, John Belton
Orr, Gustavus John
Orr, James Lawrence
Orr, John Amaziah
Palmer, Benjamin Morgan
Payne, Daniel Alexander
Peck, Thomas Ephraim
Perry, Benjamin Franklin
Peterkin, Julia Mood
Petigru, James Louis
Philips, Martin Wilson
Pickens, Francis Wilkinson
Pickens, William
Pinckney, Charles
Pinckney, Charles Cotesworth
Pinckney, Henry Laurens
Pinckney, Thomas
Poinsett, Joel Roberts
Porcher, Francis Peyre
Pratt, John
Pringle, Joel Roberts Poinsett
Pringle, John Julius
Rainey, Joseph Hayne
Ravenel, Edmund
Ravenel, Harriott Horry Rutledge
Ravenel, Henry William
Ravenel, St. Julien
Read, Jacob
Requier, Augustus Julian
Rhett, Robert Barnwell
Rice, John Andrew
Richardson, Anna Euretta
Rivers, William James
Robert, Henry Martyn
Roberts, Oran Milo
Rogers, James Harvey
Roper, Daniel Calhoun
Rusk, Thomas Jefferson
Rutledge, Edward
Rutledge, John
Sanders, Daniel Jackson
Scarbrough, William
Shecut, John Linnaeus Edward Whitridge
Shepherd, William Robert
Shubrick, John Templer
Shubrick, William Branford
Simms, William Gilmore
Simonton, Charles Henry
Simpson, William Dunlap
Sims, James Marion
Smalls, Robert
Smith, Charles Forster
Smith, Ellison DuRant
Smith, Henry Augustus Middleton
Smith, James Perrin
Smith, John Lawrence
Smith, William Loughton
Spreckels, John Diedrich
Stanton, Frank Lebby
Steedman, Charles
Stevens, Thomas Holdup, 1795–1841
Strobel, Edward Henry
Stuart, Francis Lee
Thomas, Theodore Gaillard
Thompson, Hugh Smith
Thompson, Waddy
Thornwell, James Henley
Tiedeman, Christopher Gustavus
Tillman, Benjamin Ryan
Timrod, Henry
Toland, Hugh Huger
Tompkins, Daniel Augustus
Travis, William Barret
Trenholm, George Alfred
Trescot, William Henry
Trott, Nicholas
Tupper, Henry Allen
Turner, Henry McNeal
Waddel, John Newton
Waring, Julius Waties
Watson, John Broadus
Wayne, Arthur Trezevant
Wells, William Charles
White, George
White, John Blake
White, Josh
Wigfall, Louis Trezevant
Wilkinson, Robert Shaw
Williams, David Rogerson
Willingham, Robert Josiah
Wilson, John Leighton
Wilson, William Hasell
Woolsey, John Munro
Wragg, William
Yeadon, Richard
Young, Pierce Manning Butler
Zogbaum, Rufus Fairchild

SOUTH DAKOTA

Anderson, Clinton Presba
Flanagan, Hallie
Gall
Graham, Philip Leslie
Grass, John
Hansen, Alvin Harvey
Humphrey, Hubert Horatio, Jr.
Lawrence, Ernest Orlando
Lundeen, Ernest
Mundt, Karl Earl
Norbeck, Peter
Sande, Earl
Schmidt, Carl Louis August
Sitting Bull
Thye, Edward John
Wilson, Orlando Winfield ("Win," "O. W.")

TENNESSEE

Adams, John
Agee, James Rufus
Allen, William Joshua
Anderson, James Patton
Anderson, Paul Y.
Andrews, Frank Maxwell
Austell, Alfred
Ayres, Brown
Balch, George Beall
Barksdale, William
Barnard, Edward Emerson
Barrow, Washington
Barton, Bruce Fairchild
Barton, David
Bate, William Brimage
Beard, Richard
Bell, John
Benton, Thomas Hart
Berry, George Leonard
Bewley, Anthony
Bible, Dana Xenophon
Boyd, Lynn
Bradford, Joseph
Bradford, Roark Whitney Wickliffe
Branner, John Casper
Brantley, Theodore
Bridges, Thomas Jefferson Davis ("Tommy")
Brown, John Calvin
Brown, Neill Smith
Brush, George de Forest
Burgess, John William
Burnet, Peter Hardeman
Burnett, Swan Moses
Byrns, Joseph Wellington
Cain, Harry Pulliam
Campbell, Francis Joseph
Campbell, William Bowen
Caraway, Hattie Ophelia Wyatt
Carmack, Edward Ward
Carter, Samuel Powhatan
Catchings, Waddill
Cheatham, Benjamin Franklin
Chisum, John Simpson
Clement, Frank Goad
Collier, Barron Gift
Cone, Moses Herman
Conway, Elias Nelson
Conway, James Sevier
Cooper, (Leon) Jere
Crockett, David
Crump, Edward Hull
Davis, Norman Hezekiah
Davis, Reuben
Dibrell, George Gibbs
Dickson, Earle Ensign
Dodd, Monroe Elmon
Dorset, Marion
Dromgoole, William Allen
Edmondson, William
Elliott, William Yandell, III
Embree, Elihu
Ensley, Enoch
Fanning, Tolbert
Farragut, David Glasgow
Featherston, Winfield Scott
Fenner, Charles Erasmus
Folk, Joseph Wingate
Forrest, Nathan Bedford
Frazer, Joseph Washington
Fuller, Joseph Vincent
Gaisman, Henry Jaques
Garland, Augustus Hill
Garrett, Finis James
Garvin, Lucius Fayette Clark
Gaut, John McReynolds
Geers, Edward Franklin
Gillem, Alvan Cullem
Gilliam, James William ("Junior")
Gilmer, Elizabeth Meriwether ("Dorothy Dix")
Gleaves, Albert
Gordon, George Washington

Green, Alexander Little Page
Gregg, Josiah
Gwin, William McKendree
Hamilton, Walton Hale
Harahan, William Johnson
Harney, William Selby
Harris, Isham Green
Harrison, Henry Sydnor
Haynes, Henry Doyle ("Homer")
Hays, Harry Thompson
Hays, John Coffee
Hillman, Thomas Tennessee
Hindman, Thomas Carmichael
Hogg, James Stephen
Houk, Leonidas Campbell
Houston, George Smith
Howze, Robert Lee
Hull, Cordell
Humes, Thomas William
Humphreys, West Hughes
Inman, John Hamilton
Inman, Samuel Martin
Isom, Mary Frances
Jackson, Howell Edmunds
Jackson, William Hicks
Jarman, Walton Maxey
Jarrell, Randall
Johnson, Cave
Johnson, David Bancroft
Johnson, Mordecai Wyatt
Jones, James Chamberlayne
Jones, Jesse Holman
Kefauver, (Carey) Estes
Kelly, Machine Gun (George Kelly Barnes, Jr.)
Key, David McKendree
King, Austin Augustus
Krutch, Joseph Wood
Lard, Moses E.
Lea, Luke
Levering, Joseph Mortimer
Lindsey, Benjamin Barr
Littleton, Martin Wiley
Loguen, Jermain Wesley
Lowrey, Mark Perrin
McAnally, David Rice
McCulloch, Ben
McFerrin, John Berry
McGhee, Charles McClung
McGill, Ralph Emerson
McGlothlin, William Joseph
McReynolds, Samuel Davis
Malone, Walter
Maney, George Earl
Markham, Charles Henry
Marling, John Leake
Milton, George Fort
Moore, (Austin) Merrill
Moore, Grace
Morgan, John Tyler
Murfree, Mary Noailles
Murrell, John A.
Nelson, David
Newman, William Truslow
Nicholson, Alfred Osborne Pope
Nielsen, Alice
Oconostota
Oldham, Williamson Simpson
Palmore, William Beverly
Peck, James Hawkins
Perkins, Dwight Heald
Perry, Rufus Lewis
Pillow, Gideon Johnson
Poindexter, Miles
Polk, William Mecklenburg
Porter, James Davis
Pritchard, Jeter Connelly
Proctor, Henry Hugh
Ramsey, James Gettys McGready
Randolph, Lillian
Ransom, John Crowe
Raulston, John Tate
Rayburn, Samuel Taliaferro ("Sam")
Read, Opie Pope
Reagan, John Henninger
Reece, Brazilla Carroll
Reed, Richard Clark
Reynolds, Richard Samuel, Sr.
Rice, (Henry) Grantland
Richardson, James Daniel
Richberg, Donald Randall
Ridge, Major
Riis, Mary Phillips
Roane, John Selden
Roberts, Issachar Jacob
Rockwell, Kiffin Yates
Rogers, James Harris
Rose, Edward
Rose, Wickliffe
Ross, John
Sanford, Edward Terry
Scott, William Anderson
Scruggs, William Lindsay
Sequoyah
Sevier, Ambrose Hundley
Sharkey, William Lewis
Shields, John Knight
Shook, Alfred Montgomery
Sloan, George Arthur
Smith, Bessie
Smith, George Henry
Stewart, Arthur Thomas ("Tom")
Stilwell, Simpson Everett
Stone, John Marshall
Stribling, Thomas Sigismund
Stritch, Samuel Alphonsus
Sumners, Hatton William
Taylor, Alfred Alexander
Taylor, Robert Love
Temple, Oliver Perry
Terrell, Mary Eliza Church
Thomas, Cyrus
Thomas, John Wilson
Tigert, John James, IV
Tilson, John Quillin
Tipton, John
Turner, Fennell Parrish
Turney, Peter
Vance, Ap Morgan
Walker, William
Ward, Nancy
Warner, James Cartwright
Watterson, Harvey Magee
White, Clarence Cameron
White, Edward Douglass
Whitsitt, William Heth
Wiley, Bell Irvin
Williams, James
Williams, John Sharp
Wilson, J(ames) Finley
Witherspoon, John Alexander
Woods, William Allen
Wright, Luke Edward
Wright, Marcus Joseph
Yandell, David Wendell
Yandell, Lunsford Pitts
Yeatman, James Erwin
Yerger, William
Yoakum, Henderson
York, Alvin Cullum
Young, Ewing
Zollicoffer, Felix Kirk

TEXAS

Batts, Robert Lynn
Beaty, Amos Leonidas
Blocker, Dan
Buck, Franklyn Howard
Burleson, Albert Sidney
Camp, John Lafayette
Carter, William Samuel
Chennault, Claire Lee
Clark, Tom Campbell
Connally, Thomas Terry ("Tom")
Cordon, Guy
Crawford, Joan
Cullen, Hugh Roy
Dies, Martin
Dobie, J(ames) Frank
Dyer, Isadore
Eberle, Edward Walter
Eisenhower, Dwight David
Ewing, William Maurice
Ferguson, James Edward
Ferguson, Miriam Amanda Wallace
Fly, James Lawrence
Frye, William John ("Jack")
Garner, John Nance
Gibbons, Euell
Gipson, Frederick Benjamin
Graves, William Sidney
Griffin, John Howard
Hirsch, Maximilian Justice
Hobby, William Pettus
Holly, Charles Hardin ("Buddy")
Hornsby, Rogers
House, Edward Mandell
Hughes, Howard Robard, Jr.
Hunter, Ivory Joe
Johnson, Jack
Johnson, Lyndon Baines
Jones, John Marvin
Jones, Richard Foster
Joplin, Janis Lyn
Kendrick, John Benjamin
Key, Valdimer Orlando, Jr.
King, Richard, Jr.
Kleberg, Robert Justus, Jr.
Lanham, Frederick Garland ("Fritz")
Lasater, Edward Cunningham
Lovett, Robert Scott
Mangrum, Lloyd Eugene
Maverick, (Fontaine) Maury
McMillin Alvin Nugent ("Bo")

Mills, Charles Wright
Minor, Robert
Moser, Christopher Otto
Munger, Robert Sylvester
Murchison, Clinton Williams
Murchison, John Dabney
Murphy, Audie Leon
Murray, William Henry David
Newton, Joseph Fort
Neyland, Robert Reese, Jr.
Nimitz, Chester William
Norris, John Franklyn
O'Brien, Robert David ("Davey")
Ochs, Phil
Page, Oran Thaddeus ("Lips")
Parker, Alvin Pierson
Patman, John William Wright
Pool, Joe Richard
Porter, Katherine Anne
Post, Wiley
Quanah
Reese, Heloise Bowles
Richardson, Sid Williams
Richardson, Wilds Preston
Rister, Carl Coke
Ritter, Woodward Maurice ("Tex")
Rosenman, Samuel Irving
Rowe, Lynwood Thomas
Rust, John Daniel
Samaroff, Olga
Scarborough, Dorothy
Scott, Emmett Jay
Shepard, Seth
Sheppard, John Morris
Silkwood, Karen Gay
Siringo, Charles A.
Smith, Thomas Vernor
Speaker, Tris E.
Sterling, Ross Shaw
Stevenson, Matilda Coxe Evans
Stillman, James
Tandy, Charles David
Tansill, Charles Callan
Teagarden, Weldon Leo ("Jack")
Thornton, Daniel I. J.
Van Der Stucken, Frank Valentin
Vardaman, James Kimble
Vaughan, Thomas Wayland
Vidor, Florence
Walker, Walton Harris
Webb, Walter Prescott
White, Edward Higgins, II
Wills, Chill
Wills, James Robert ("Bob")
Yoakum, Benjamin Franklin
Young, Hugh Hampton
Young, Robert Ralph
Zaharias, Mildred ("Babe") Didrikson

UTAH

Adams, Maude
Allen, Florence Ellinwood
Borglum, Solon Hannibal
Borzage, Frank
Browning, John Moses
Cantril, Albert Hadley
Clark, Joshua Reuben, Jr.
Clyde, George Dewey
Dallin, Cyrus Edwin
DeVoto, Bernard Augustine
Eccles, Marriner Stoddard
Farnsworth, Philo Taylor
Gilbert, John
Haywood, William Dudley
Held, John, Jr.
Hines, Frank Thomas
Kahn, Florence Prag
Knight, Goodwin Jess ("Goodie")
McKay, David Oman
Moreell, Ben
Priest, Ivy Maude Baker
Smith, George Albert
Smith, Jospeh Fielding
Smoot, Reed Owen
Thomas, Elbert Duncan
Wardman, Ervin
Watkins, Arthur Vivian
Young, Mahonri Mackintosh

VERMONT

Adams, Alvin
Adams, Charles Kendall
Adams, George Burton
Adams, Herbert Samuel
Aiken, Charles Augustus
Aikens, Andrew Jackson
Ainsworth, Frederick Crayton
Alden, Henry Mills
Allen, Elisha Hunt
Allen, George
Allen, Timothy Field
Alvord, Benjamin
Ames, Joseph Sweetman
Angell, James Rowland
Arthur, Chester Alan
Atkins, Jearum
Austin, Warren Robinson
Babcock, Joseph Weeks
Babcock, Orville E.
Ballou, Hosea
Barber, Amzi Lorenzo
Barrett, John
Barton, James Levi
Bennett, Edmund Hatch
Bentley, Wilson Alwyn
Benton, Josiah Henry
Billings, Charles Ethan
Billings, Frederick
Bingham, Harry
Bingham, Hiram
Blaine, Anita (Eugenie) McCormick
Blanchard, Jonathan
Bliss, Daniel
Bliss, Edwin Elisha
Botta, Anne Charlotte Lynch
Bowen, George
Boynton, Edward Carlisle
Bradley, William Czar
Bradwell, Myra
Brainerd, Ezra
Browne, Francis Fisher
Brownson, Orestes Augustus
Burnham, Sherburne Wesley
Bush, George
Carpenter, Matthew Hale
Chase, Irah
Church, Alonzo
Clark, Charles Edgar
Clark, William Bullock
Closson, William Baxter
Coates, George Henry
Colburn, Zerah
Collins, John Anderson
Colton, Gardner Quincy
Colton, Walter
Colver, Nathaniel
Conant, Alban Jasper
Conant, Thomas Jefferson
Converse, John Heman
Coolidge, Calvin
Dana, Charles Loomis
Dana, John Cotton
Davenport, Herbert Joseph
Davenport, Thomas
Dean, Amos
Deere, John
Delano, Columbus
Dewey, George
Dewey, John
Dillingham, William Paul
Dixon, Luther Swift
Dorsey, Stephen Wallace
Douglas, Stephen Arnold
Douglass, Andrew Ellicott
Eaton, Dorman Bridgman
Eaton, Homer
Edmunds, George Franklin
Emmons, George Foster
Evans, Warren Felt
Evarts, Jeremiah
Fairbanks, Henry
Farnham, Thomas Jefferson
Farrar, John Chipman
Field, Fred Tarbell
Fisk, James
Fisk, Wilbur
Flagg, Azariah Cutting
Flanders, Ralph Edward
Fletcher, Calvin
Fletcher, Richard
Foot, Solomon
Frost, Edwin Brant
Gale, Elbridge
Garlick, Theodatus
Gates, George Augustus
Gilmore, Joseph Albree
Going, Jonathan
Goodall, Harvey L.
Goodnow, Isaac Tichenor
Granger, Walter
Grant, Lewis Addison
Graves, James Robinson
Graves, Zuinglius Calvin
Gray, Joseph W.
Green, Horace
Greenleaf, Halbert Stevens
Grinnell, Josiah Bushnell
Griswold, Rufus Wilmot
Hale, Philip
Hale, Robert Safford
Hall, Hiland
Hall, Sherman
Hamilton, Frank Hastings
Hammond, Edwin
Harmon, Daniel Williams

Harris, Elisha
Harvey, George Brinton McClellan
Haselton, Seneca
Haskell, Dudley Chase
Hawkins, Rush Christopher
Hayes, Augustus Allen
Hazen, Allen
Hazen, William Babcock
Herring, Silas Clark
Hitchcock, Ethan Allen, 1798–1870
Hoisington, Henry Richard
Holbrook, Stewart Hall
Holmes, Bayard Taylor
Hopkins, James Campbell
Horton, Valentine Baxter
Houghton, Henry Oscar
House, Royal Earl
Hovey, Charles Edward
Hovey, Otis Ellis
Howard, Jacob Merritt
Howard, William Alanson
Hubbard, Gurdon Saltonstall
Hudson, Henry Norman
Hulbert, Archer Butler
Hunt, Richard Morris
Hunt, William Morris
Ide, Henry Clay
Jackson, William Alexander
James, Edwin
Jameson, John Alexander
Jewett, Milo Parker
Johnson, Edwin Ferry
Johnson, Oliver
Jones, George
Kasson, John Adam
Kendrick, Asahel Clark
Kent, Arthur Atwater
Keyes, Elisha Williams
Kimball, Heber Chase
Kingsley, Darwin Pearl
Knowlton, Frank Hall
Ladd, William Sargent
Lampson, Sir Curtis Miranda
Langdon, William Chauncy
Langworthy, James Lyon
Lawrence, Richard Smith
Lull, Edward Phelps
Lyman, Albert Josiah
Marsh, George Perkins
Marsh, James
Mayo, Henry Thomas
Mead, Charles Marsh
Mead, William Rutherford
Merrill, Samuel
Miller, Jonathan Peckham
Miller, Leslie William
Mills, Susan Lincoln Tolman
Morrill, Justin Smith
Morris, George Sylvester
Morse, Anson Daniel
Morse, Harmon Northrop
Morton, Levi Parsons
Mower, Joseph Anthony
Mozier, Joseph
Newcomb, Harvey
Nichols, Clarina Irene Howard
Niles, Nathaniel, 1791–1869
Noyes, John Humphrey
Olin, Stephen
Otis, Elisha Graves
Paine, Charles
Paine, Martyn
Park, Trenor William
Parker, Edwin Wallace
Parker, Joel
Parkhurst, Charles
Parmly, Eleazar
Partridge, Alden
Peabody, Cecil Hobart
Peabody, Selim Hobart
Pearsons, Daniel Kimball
Peirce, Bradford Kinney
Perkins, Samuel Elliott
Perry, Ralph Barton
Pettigrew, Richard Franklin
Phelps, Charles Edward
Phelps, Edward John
Picknell, William Lamb
Pilkington, James
Plumley, Frank
Poland, Luke Potter
Porter, Russell Williams
Porter, William Trotter
Post, Truman Marcellus
Powell, Thomas Reed
Powers, Hiram
Pratt, Francis Ashbury
Pratt, Silas Gamaliel
Pringle, Cyrus Guernsey
Proctor, Redfield
Prouty, Charles Azro
Ransom, Thomas Edward Greenfield
Redfield, Isaac Fletcher
Rice, Edmund
Rice, Henry Mower
Richardson, Israel Bush
Richmond, Dean
Ripley, Edward Hastings
Rix, Julian Walbridge
Roberts, Benjamin Stone
Robinson, Albert Alonzo
Robinson, Charles Seymour
Robinson, Rowland Evans
Robinson, Stillman Williams
Robinson, Theodore
Rowell, George Presbury
Rublee, Horace
Russell, William Hepburn
Safford, Truman Henry
Salm-Salm, Agnes Elisabeth Winona Leclercq Joy, Princess
Sargent, Frank Pierce
Sargent, James
Sargent, Nathan
Sawyer, Philetus
Sawyer, Thomas Jefferson
Saxe, John Godfrey
Schoff, Stephen Alonzo
Scott, Orange
Seymour, Truman
Shaw, Leslie Mortier
Sheldon, Walter Lorenzo
Sheldon, William Evarts
Sherry, Louis
Slade, William
Slafter, Edmund Farwell
Smith, Chauncey
Smith, John Gregory
Smith, Joseph, 1805–1844
Smith, William Farrar
Southard, Lucien H.
Spaulding, Edward Gleason
Spooner, Shearjashub
Sprague, Achsa W.
Spring, Leverett Wilson
Stevens, Benjamin Franklin
Stevens, Henry
Stevens, Hiram Fairchild
Stevens, Thaddeus
Stoddard, Joshua C.
Stone, Warren
Storey, Wilbur Fisk
Stoughton, Edwin Wallace
Strong, Charles Lyman
Strong, James Woodward
Strong, Moses McCure
Strong, William Barstow
Tabor, Horace Austin Warner
Taft, Alphonso
Taylor, Charles Fayette
Temple, William Grenville
Thompson, Zadock
Todd, John
Torrey, Charles Cutler
Tracy, Joseph
Tucker, Luther
Tuttle, Herbert
Tyler, William
Vilas, William Freeman
Wade, Martin Joseph
Wells, Henry
Wheeler, James Rignall
Wheeler, John Martin
Wheeler, Royall Tyler
Wheelock, Lucy
Whitcomb, James
Whiting, Charles Goodrich
Willard, Daniel
Wilson, Halsey William
Wilson, William Griffith ("Bill W.")
Winslow, Hubbard
Winslow, John Flack
Winslow, Miron
Wood, Reuben
Woods, Alva
Worthen, Amos Henry
Wright, Robert William
Yale, Caroline Ardelia
Young, Brigham
Young, John

VIRGINIA

Abert, John James
Adams, Daniel Weissiger
Adams, James Hopkins
Ainslie, Peter
Alexander, Archibald
Allen, Henry Watkins
Allen, John James
Allen, Thomas M.
Ambler, James Markham Marshall
Ammen, Daniel
Ammen, Jacob
Anderson, Henry Tompkins
Anderson, Joseph Reid
Anderson, Richard Clough

Anderson, William
Archer, Branch Tanner
Archer, William Segar
Armistead, George
Armstrong, Edward Cooke
Armstrong, Robert
Ashby, Turner
Ashley, William Henry
Atkinson, George Wesley
Atkinson, Thomas
Austin, Stephen Fuller
Bagby, Arthur Pendleton
Bagby, George William
Bailey, Bill
Bailey, (Irene) Temple
Baldwin, John Brown
Baldwin, Joseph Glover
Ballard, Bland Williams
Bangs, Frank C.
Banister, John
Barbour, James
Barbour, John Strode, Jr.
Barbour, Philip Pendleton
Barrett, Kate Waller
Barron, James
Barron, Samuel
Barry, William Taylor
Barton, Robert Thomas
Barton, Seth Maxwell
Bates, Edward
Bates, Frederick
Battle, John Stewart
Baylor, George
Bayly, Thomas Henry
Beale, Richard Lee Turberville
Beall, John Yates
Beckwourth, James P.
Bell, Peter Hansborough
Beverley, Robert
Bibb, George Mortimer
Bingham, George Caleb
Binns, John Alexander
Bitter, Karl Theodore Francis
Blackburn, Gideon
Blair, Francis Preston
Blair, John, 1687–1771
Blair, John, 1732–1800
Blanchfield, Florence Aby
Bland, Richard
Bland, Theodorick
Blow, Henry Taylor
Bocock, Thomas Stanley
Borland, Solon
Botts, Charles Tyler
Botts, John Minor
Boyd, Belle
Boyd, David French
Boyd, Thomas Duckett
Boyle, John
Bradford, John
Brannon, Henry
Braxton, Carter
Breckenridge, James
Breckenridge, John
Bridger, James
Broadhead, Garland Carr
Broadus, John Albert
Brodhead, James Overton
Brooke, Francis Taliaferro
Brown, Aaron Venable
Brown, James
Brown, John, 1757–1837
Brown, Samuel
Brownlow, William Gannaway
Bruce, Blanche K.
Bruce, Philip Alexander
Bruce, William Cabell
Bryan, John Stewart
Bryan, Thomas Barbour
Buchanan, Joseph
Buford, Abraham
Bullitt, Alexander Scott
Burns, Anthony
Burrow, Trigant
Butler, William
Byrd, Richard Evelyn
Byrd, William
Cabell, James Branch
Cabell, James Lawrence
Cabell, Joseph Carrington
Cabell, Nathaniel Francis
Cabell, Samuel Jordan
Cabell, William
Cabell, William H.
Cabell, William Lewis
Cain, Richard Harvey
Caldwell, Henry Clay
Caldwell, James
Call, Richard Keith
Camden, Johnson Newlon
Cameron, William Evelyn
Campbell, Charles
Campbell, John Wilson
Campbell, William
Capps, Washington Lee
Carleton, Henry
Carlile, John Snyder
Carlisle, James Mandeville
Carr, Dabney
Carr, Dabney Smith
Carrington, Paul
Carter, Henry Rose
Carter, John
Carter, Landon
Carter, Maybelle Addington
Carter, Robert
Cartwright, Peter
Caruthers, William Alexander
Cary, Archibald
Cary, Lott
Cather, Willa
Chalmers, James Ronald
Chandler, Julian Alvin Carroll
Chapman, John Gadsby
Chapman, Oscar Littleton
Chapman, Reuben
Christian, Henry Asbury
Christian, William
Claiborne, Nathaniel Herbert
Claiborne, William Charles Coles
Clark, George Rogers
Clark, James
Clark, William
Clay, Clement Comer
Clay, Green
Clay, Henry
Clay, Matthew
Clayton, Augustin Smith
Cleghorn, Sarah Norcliffe
Cleveland, Benjamin
Clopton, John
Clyman, James
Cocke, John Hartwell
Cocke, Philip St. George
Cocke, William
Coe, Virginius ("Frank")
Coke, Richard
Coles, Edward
Collier, Henry Watkins
Colquitt, Walter Terry
Colter, John
Colwell, Stephen
Cone, Etta
Conrad, Charles Magill
Conrad, Holmes
Conway, Moncure Daniel
Cooke, John Esten
Cooke, Philip St. George
Cooper, Mark Anthony
Costigan, Edward Prentiss
Crawford, William
Crawford, William Harris
Creath, Jacob
Creighton, William
Cross, Edward
Crump, William Wood
Cutler, Lizzie Petit
Dabney, Charles William
Dabney, Richard
Dabney, Robert Lewis
Dabney, Thomas Smith Gregory
Dabney, Virginius
Dagg, John Leodley
Dale, Richard
Dale, Samuel
Daniel, John Moncure
Daniel, John Warwick
Daniel, Peter Vivian
Dare, Virginia
Dargan, Edwin Preston
Daveiss, Joseph Hamilton
Davidson, John Wynn
Davis, John Staige
Davis, Varina Anne Jefferson
Dawson, John
Dean, William Henry, Jr.
De Lacy, Walter Washington
Denby, Charles
Denver, James William
Dillard, James Hardy
Dinwiddie, Courtenay
Doak, Samuel
Dod, Daniel
Dodge, William De Leftwich
Dowell, Greensville
Dudley, Benjamin Winslow
Dupuy, Eliza Ann
Duval, William Pope
Dyer, Alexander Brydie
Early, John
Early, Jubal Anderson
Early, Peter
Early, Stephen Tyree
Echols, John
Edwards, John, 1748–1837
Ellis, Powhatan
Emmet, Thomas Addis
Eppes, John Wayles
Evans, Robley Dunglison
Ewell, James

Ewell, Thomas
Ewing, Finis
Ewing, Thomas
Ezekiel, Moses Jacob
Fackler, David Parks
Fairfax, Donald McNeill
Fanning, David
Faulkner, Charles James, 1806–1884
Faulkner, Charles James, 1847–1929
Fels, Joseph
Fifer, Joseph Wilson
Fishback, William Meade
Fitzhugh, George
Fleming, Aretas Brooks
Floyd, John Buchanan
Foote, Henry Stuart
Forsyth, John
Franklin, Jesse
Freeman, Allen Weir
Freeman, Douglas Southall
Freeman, Frederick Kemper
Frémont, Jessie Benton
French, Lucy Virginia Smith
Frost, Wade Hampton
Fry, Birkett Davenport
Gaines, Edmund Pendleton
Gaines, John Pollard
Gamble, Hamilton Rowan
Gardener, Helen Hamilton
Garland, Landon Cabell
Garnett, Alexander Yelverton Peyton
Garnett, James Mercer, 1770–1843
Garnett, James Mercer, 1840–1916
Garnett, Muscoe Russell Hunter
Garnett, Robert Selden
Garrard, James
Garrett, William Robertson
Gholson, Thomas Saunders
Gholson, William Yates
Gibbs, James Ethan Allen
Giles, William Branch
Gilmer, Francis Walker
Gilmer, George Rockingham
Gilmer, Thomas Walker
Gilpin, Charles Sidney
Glasgow, Ellen Anderson Gholson
Glass, Carter
Glenn, Hugh
Glover, Samuel Taylor
Goode, John
Gordon, William Fitzhugh
Goss, James Walker
Graham, James Duncan
Graham, John
Grasty, Charles Henry
Grayson, William
Green, James Stephens
Green, William
Greene, Belle Da Costa
Greenhow, Robert
Greenup, Christopher
Griffin, Cyrus
Griffin, Robert Stanislaus
Grigsby, Hugh Blair
Grundy, Felix
Hall, Willard Preble
Hamilton, James
Hammond, Samuel
Hampton, Wade
Hardin, John
Hardy, Samuel
Harper, Robert Goodloe
Harris, John Woods
Harris, William Alexander
Harrison, Benjamin
Harrison, Constance Cary
Harrison, Gessner
Harrison, William Henry
Harvie, John
Hatcher, Orie Latham
Hatcher, William Eldridge
Hay, George
Heath, James Ewell
Henderson, John Brooks
Henderson, Richard
Hening, William Waller
Henley, Robert
Henry, Patrick
Henry, William Wirt
Herndon, William Lewis
Heth, Henry
Hill, Ambrose Powell
Hine, Charles De Lano
Hodges, Luther Hartwell
Hoge, Moses
Hoge, Moses Drury
Holcombe, Henry
Holcombe, James Philemon
Holcombe, William Henry
Holt, John
Hope, James Barron
Hopkins, Arthur Francis
Hopkins, Juliet Ann Opie
Hopkins, Samuel, 1753–1819
Horner, William Edmonds
Hough, Theodore
Hough, Warwick
Houston, Edwin James
Houston, Samuel
Howard, Benjamin
Howard, William Travis
Hubbard, David
Hughes, Robert William
Humphreys, Milton Wylie
Hunter, Robert Mercer Taliaferro
Hunton, Eppa
Imboden, John Daniel
Innes, Harry
Innes, James
Jackson, Charles Samuel
Jackson, John George
James, Edwin Leland
Janney, Eli Hamilton
Janney, Samuel McPherson
Jarratt, Devereux
Jarvis, William Chapman
Jefferson, Thomas
Jenkins, Albert Gallatin
Jenkins, Thornton Alexander
Jesse, Richard Henry
Jesup, Thomas Sidney
Jeter, Jeremiah Bell
Johnson, Ames
Johnson, Chapman
Johnson, Charles Spurgeon
Johnson, Edward
Johnson, Louis Arthur
Johnston, George Ben
Johnston, Joseph Eggleston
Johnston, Mary
Johnston, Peter
Johnston, Zachariah
Jones, Catesby ap Roger
Jones, Gabriel
Jones, Hilary Pollard
Jones, John William
Jones, John Winston
Jones, Joseph
Jones, Thomas ap Catesby
Jones, Walter
Jordan, Thomas
Jouett, John
Joynes, Edward Southey
Kalmus, Natalie Mabelle Dunfee
Kean, Jefferson Randolph
Keith, James
Kemper, James Lawson
Kemper, Reuben
Kenna, John Edward
Kenton, Simon
Keyes, Frances Parkinson
Kilgore, Harley Martin
Klipstein, Louis Frederick
Krauth, Charles Porterfield
Lackaye, Wilton
Lacock, Abner
Lacy, Drury
Ladd, Catherine
Lamon, Ward Hill
Lancaster, Henry Carrington
Lane, James Henry
Lane, John
Langston, John Mercer
Lanier, Sidney
Lattimore, William
Laws, Samuel Spahr
Lawson, Thomas
Lay, Henry Champlin
Leathers, Waller Smith
Lee, Arthur
Lee, Charles, 1758–1815
Lee, Fitzhugh
Lee, Francis Lightfoot
Lee, George Washington Custis
Lee, Henry, 1756–1818
Lee, Henry, 1787–1837
Lee, Jesse
Lee, Richard Bland
Lee, Richard Henry
Lee, Robert Edward
Lee, Samuel Phillips
Lee, William
Lee, William Henry Fitzhugh
Leffel, James
Leigh, Benjamin Watkins
Letcher, John
Letcher, Robert Perkins
Lewis, Dixon Hall
Lewis, Fielding
Lewis, James Hamilton
Lewis, John Francis
Lewis, Meriwether
Lewis, William Berkeley
Lewis, William Henry

Ligon, Thomas Watkins
Lindsay, William
Littlepage, Lewis
Logan, Benjamin
Lomax, John Tayloe
Long, Armistead Lindsay
Long, Joseph Ragland
Low, Juliette Gordon
Lukeman, Henry Augustus
Lumpkin, Wilson
Lynch, Charles
Lynch, James Daniel
Lynch, William Francis
McCabe, John Collins
McCabe, William Gordon
McCaw, James Brown
McClurg, James
McCormick, Cyrus Hall
McCormick, Leander James
McCormick, Robert
McCormick, Robert Sanderson
McCormick, Stephen
McDowell, Charles
McDowell, Ephraim
McDowell, James
McDowell, Joseph
McGuire, Hunter Holmes
McIlwaine, Richard
McKee, John
McKinley, John
McKnight, Robert
McNeill, John Hanson
Macrae, John
Madison, James
Magruder, John Bankhead
Magruder, Julia
Mahan, Milo
Mahone, William
Manly, Charles Matthews
Mann, Ambrose Dudley
Manson, Otis Frederick
Marshall, Humphrey
Marshall, James Markham
Marshall, John
Marshall, Louis
Marshall, Thomas
Martin, Thomas Staples
Mason, Claibourne Rice
Mason, George
Mason, John Young
Mason, Lucy Randolph
Mason, Richard Barnes
Mason, Samuel
Mason, Stevens Thomson, 1760–1803
Mason, Stevens Thomson, 1811–1843
Mason, Thomson
Massey, John Edward
Mathews, George
Maury, Dabney Herndon
Maury, Matthew Fontaine
Maxwell, William
Mayo, William Kennon
Meade, Richard Kidder
Meade, William
Meason, Isaac
Meek, Joseph L.
Mercer, Charles Fenton
Mercer, James
Mercer, John Francis
Metcalfe, Samuel Lytler
Metcalfe, Thomas
Mettauer, John Peter
Michaux, Lightfoot Solomon
Mifflin, Warner
Minnigerode, Lucy
Minor, Benjamin Blake
Minor, John Barbee
Minor, Lucian
Minor, Raleigh Colston
Minor, Virginia Louisa
Mitchell, David Dawson
Mitchell, John Kearsley
Moncure, Richard Cassius Lee
Monette, John Wesley
Monroe, James
Montague, Andrew Jackson
Moore, Andrew
Moore, Edwin Ward
Moore, Frederick Randolph
Moore, James, 1764–1814
Moore, Thomas Patrick
Morehead, John Motley
Morgan, William
Morrison, William McCutchan
Morton, Robert Russa
Mosby, John Singleton
Mullan, John
Munford, Robert
Munford, William
Murfee, James Thomas
Murray, Mae
Myers, Jerome
Nash, Abner
Nash, Francis
Neighbors, Robert Simpson
Nelson, Hugh
Nelson, Thomas
Nelson, William, 1711–1772
Neville, John
Neville, Wendell Cushing
Newman, Robert Loftin
Newman, William H.
Newton, John
Newton, Thomas, 1768–1847
Nicholas, George
Nicholas, John
Nicholas, Philip Norborne
Nicholas, Robert Carter
Nicholas, Wilson Cary
Noble, James
O'Donovan, William Rudolf
O'Ferrall, Charles Triplett
Otey, James Hervey
Overton, John
Owen, Robert Latham
Owsley, William
Page, John
Page, Mann
Page, Richard Lucian
Page, Thomas Jefferson
Page, Thomas Nelson
Page, Thomas Walker
Parker, Josiah
Parker, Richard Elliot
Parrish, Celestia Susannah
Patton, John Mercer
Pearce, James Alfred
Peers, Benjamin Orrs
Pelham, Robert A.
Pendleton, Edmund
Pendleton, James Madison
Pendleton, John Strother
Pendleton, William Kimbrough
Pendleton, William Nelson
Penick, Charles Clifton
Penn, John
Penniman, James Hosmer
Pennock, Alexander Mosely
Person, Thomas
Peyton, John Lewis
Pick, Lewis Andrew
Pickett, George Edward
Pickett, James Chamberlayne
Pierpont, Francis Harrison
Pilcher, Joshua
Pleasants, James
Pleasants, John Hampden
Pocahontas
Poindexter, George
Pollard, Edward Alfred
Porter, John Luke
Posey, Thomas
Powell, Adam Clayton, Sr.
Powell, Lucien Whiting
Power, Frederick Dunglison
Pratt, John Lee
Prentiss, Benjamin Mayberry
Preston, John Smith
Preston, William Ballard
Price, Joseph
Price, Sterling
Price, Thomas Lawson
Price, Thomas Randolph
Price, William Cecil
Pryor, Nathaniel
Pryor, Roger Atkinson
Puller, Lewis Burwell ("Chesty")
Puryear, Bennet
Radford, William
Ramsay, George Douglas
Randolph, Alfred Magill
Randolph, Edmund, 1753–1813
Randolph, Edmund, 1819–1861
Randolph, Epes
Randolph, George Wythe
Randolph, Isham
Randolph, Sir John
Randolph, John, 1727 or 1728–1784
Randolph, John, 1773–1833
Randolph, Peyton
Randolph, Sarah Nicholas
Randolph, Thomas Jefferson
Randolph, Thomas Mann
Ravenscroft, John Stark
Reed, Walter
Reid, Ira De Augustine
Reid, Mont Rogers
Renick, Felix
Reynolds, Alexander Welch
Reynolds, William Neal
Rice, David
Rice, John Holt
Richard, James William
Ritchie, Albert Cabell

Ritchie, Thomas
Rives, John Cook
Rives, William Cabell
Roane, Spencer
Roberts, Joseph Jenkins
Robertson, James, 1742–1814
Robertson, John
Robertson, Thomas Bolling
Robertson, William Joseph
Robertson, Wyndham
Robinson, Beverley
Robinson, Bill (Bojangles)
Robinson, Conway
Robinson, John
Robinson, Moncure
Rochester, Nathaniel
Rodes, Robert Emmett
Rorer, David
Ross, Erskine Mayo
Rosser, Thomas Lafayette
Ruffin, Edmund
Ruffin, Thomas
Ruffner, Henry
Ruffner, William Henry
Russell, James Solomon
Ryan, Thomas Fortune
Ryland, Robert
Saunders, Clarence
Scott, Charles
Scott, Dred
Scott, Gustavus
Scott, William
Scott, Winfield
Seaton, William Winston
Seawell, Molly Elliot
Sebastian, Benjamin
Seddon, James Alexander
Seevers, William Henry
Sevier, John
Sherman, Henry Clapp
Shipman, Andrew Jackson
Shipp, Scott
Short, William
Shreve, Thomas Hopkins
Shuck, John Lewis
Silver, Gray
Singleton, James Washington
Slaughter, Philip
Slemp, Campbell Bascom
Smith, Benjamin Mosby
Smith, Daniel
Smith, Francis Henney
Smith, Howard Worth ("Judge")
Smith, John, 1735–1824
Smith, John Augustine
Smith, Lucy Harth
Smith, Meriwether
Smith, Thomas Adams
Smith, William, 1797–1887
Smith, William Andrew
Smith, William Waugh
Smythe, John Henry
Snead, Thomas Lowndes
Southall, James Cocke
Spencer, Pitman Clemens
Stanard, Mary Mann Page Newton
Stanard, William Glover
Stanton, Frederick Perry
Stanton, Richard Henry
Staples, Waller Redd
Sterrett, John Robert Sitlington
Stevenson, Andrew
Stevenson, Carter Littlepage
Stevenson, John White
Still, Andrew Taylor
Stith, William
Stokes, Montfort
Stone, George Washington
Stone, John Stone
Street, Joseph Montfort
Stringfellow, Franklin
Strong, Richard Pearson
Stuart, Alexander Hugh Holmes
Stuart, Archibald
Stuart, Granville
Stuart, James Ewell Brown
Sullavan, Margaret
Summers, George William
Sumner, Jethro
Sumter, Thomas
Swanson, Claude Augustus
Swayne, Noah Haynes
Tabb, John Banister
Tait, Charles
Taliaferro, Lawrence
Taliaferro, William Booth
Tauber, Maurice Falcolm
Taylor, Creed
Taylor, David Watson
Taylor, Edward Thompson
Taylor, George Boardman
Taylor, John, 1752–1835
Taylor, John, 1753–1824
Taylor, Robert Tunstall
Taylor, William
Taylor, Zachary
Tazewell, Henry
Tazewell, Littleton Waller
Terhune, Mary Virginia Hawes
Thomas, George Henry
Thomas, Jesse Burgess
Thomas, William Isaac
Thompson, John Reuben
Thompson, Richard Wigginton
Thompson, Thomas Larkin
Thompson, Wiley
Thomson, John
Thornton, Jesse Quinn
Thurman, Allen Granberry
Timberlake, Gideon
Timberlake, Henry
Todd, Thomas
Tompkins, Sally Louisa
Toy, Crawford Howell
Trent, William Peterfield
Trimble, Allen
Trimble, Isaac Ridgeway
Trimble, Robert
Trist, Nicholas Philip
Tucker, Henry St. George, 1780–1848
Tucker, Henry St. George, 1853–1932
Tucker, Henry St. George, 1874–1959
Tucker, John Randolph, 1812–1883
Tucker, John Randolph, 1823–1897
Tucker, Nathaniel Beverley, 1784–1851
Tucker, Nathaniel Beverley, 1820–1890
Turner, Edward
Turner, Nat
Tutwiler, Henry
Tyler, John, 1747–1813
Tyler, John, 1790–1862
Tyler, Lyon Gardiner
Tyler, Robert
Underwood, Joseph Rogers
Untermyer, Samuel
Upshur, Abel Parker
Upshur, John Henry
Valentine, Edward Virginius
Vandegrift, Alexander Archer
Venable, Charles Scott
Venable, Francis Preston
Walke, Henry
Walker, Alexander
Walker, Joseph Reddeford
Walker, Reuben Lindsay
Walker, Thomas
Wallace, William Alexander Anderson
Walthall, Edward Cary
Walton, George
Ward, Lydia Arms Avery Cooney
Warrington, Lewis
Washington, Booker Taliaferro
Washington, Bushrod
Washington, George
Washington, John Macrae
Watkins, John Elfreth
Watson, John William Clark
Waugh, Beverly
Weddell, Alexander Wilbourne
Wellons, William Brock
Wells, Robert William
Wertenbaker, Charles Christian
Wertenbaker, Thomas Jefferson
Wharton, William H.
White, Alexander
White, Thomas Willis
Wilkinson, John
Will, Allen Sinclair
Williams, Channing Moore
Williams, John Skelton
Willoughby, Westel Woodbury
Wilmer, Joseph Pére Bell
Wilmer, Richard Hooker
Wilmer, William Holland
Wilson, Edith Bolling
Wilson, James Southall
Wilson, Joshua Lacy
Wilson, William
Wilson, Woodrow
Winn, Richard
Winston, Joseph
Wise, Henry Alexander
Woodford, William
Woodson, Carter Godwin
Wootton, Richens Lacy
Wright, Willard Huntington
Wythe, George
Young, George

WASHINGTON

Bailey, Mildred
Bartlett, Edward Lewis ("Bob")
Blakeslee, Howard Walter
Buchanan, Scott Milross
Carlson, Chester Floyd
Cayton, Horace Roscoe
Chamberlin, Edward Hastings
Cordiner, Ralph Jarron
Crosby, Harry Lillis ("Bing")
Dean, Gordon Evans
Dennis, Eugene
Fairchild, Muir Stephen
Faust, Frederick Shiller
Garry, Spokane
Hendrix, Jimi
Knox, Dudley Wright
Lee, Gypsy Rose
Leschi
Llewellyn, Karl Nickerson
McClintic, Guthrie
Pangborn, Clyde Edward
Seattle
Smohalla
Taggard, Genevieve
Wainwright, Jonathan Mayhew

WEST VIRGINIA

Allen, James Edward, Jr.
Baker, Newton Diehl
Bent, Charles
Bishop, John Peale
Brooke, Charles Frederick Tucker
Brown, Charles Reynolds
Buck, Pearl Comfort Sydenstricker
Byrd, Harry Flood
Carpenter, Franklin Reuben
Chadwick, French Ensor
Cooke, Philip Pendleton
Davis, John William
Delany, Martin Robinson
Dixon, William
Dolliver, Jonathan Prentiss
Douglas, Henry Kyd
Elkins, William Lukens
Fairfield, Edmund Burke
Fisher, Walter Lowrie
Foster, George Burman
Greer, David Hummell
Gregg, William
Hamilton, John William
Harvey, William Hope
Hill, Arthur Middleton
Hines, John Leonard ("Birdie")
Hough, Walter
Hughes, Edwin Holt
Humphreys, Wiliam Jackson
Jackson, Thomas Jonathan
Johnson, Douglas Wilson
Johnston, Frances Benjamin
Lacey, John Fletcher
Lashley, Karl Spencer
Leigh, William Robinson
Lisagor, Peter Irvin
Lowndes, Lloyd
Lucas, Daniel Bedinger
Lucas, Robert
Miller, John
Morrow, Dwight Whitney
Nadal, Ehrman Syme
Neely, Matthew Mansfield
Owens, Michael Joseph
Patrick, Mason Mathews
Payne, Christopher Harrison
Payne, John Barton
Post, Melville Davisson
Rathbone, Monroe Jackson ("Jack")
Reno, Jesse Lee
Reuther, Walter Philip
Robertson, Absalom Willis
Russell, Charles Wells
Sayre, Wallace Stanley
Sinclair, Harry Ford
Strauss, Lewis Lichtenstein
Strother, David Hunter
Tidball, John Caldwell
Vawtor, Charles Erastus
Waldo, David
Webster, Harold Tucker
White, Israel Charles
Willey, Wartman Thomas
Wilson, William Lyne
Worthington, Thomas
Yost, Fielding Harris
Zane, Ebenezer

WISCONSIN

Adams, Alva
Altmeyer, Arthur Joseph
Ames, Edward Scribner
Andrews, John Bertram
Andrews, Roy Chapman
Ayer, Edward Everett
Baker, Hugh Potter
Bashford, James Whitford
Billings, Frank
Bishop, Seth Scott
Blaine, John James
Bleyer, Willard Grosvenor
Bloodgood, Joseph Colt
Bolton, Herbert Eugene
Bond, Carrie Jacobs
Briggs, Clare A.
Bryant, Joseph Decatur
Burt, Mary Elizabeth
Cannon, Ida Maud
Cannon, Walter Bradford
Catt, Carrie Clinton Lane Chapman
Chafin, Eugene Wilder
Chapelle, Dickey
Coburn, Foster Dwight
Comstock, George Cary
Comstock, John Henry
Crowley, Leo Thomas
Curtin, Jeremiah
Curtis, Edward Sheriff
Cushing, William Barker
Davies, Joseph Edward
Dawson, Thomas Cleland
Dennett, Tyler (Wilbur)
Dexter, Wirt
Doheny, Edward Laurence
Duffy, Francis Ryan
Egtvedt, Clairmont ("Claire") Leroy
Eklund, Carl Robert
Elvehjem, Conrad Arnold
Esch, John Jacob
Falk, Otto Herbert
Favill, Henry Baird
Fitzpatrick, Daniel Robert
Ford, Guy Stanton
Gale, Zona
Garland, Hamlin
Gasser, Herbert Spencer
Gesell, Arnold Lucius
Gillette, King Camp
Goetz, George Washington
Grabau, Amadeus William
Haas, Francis Joseph
Hansen, Marcus Lee
Hanson, Ole
Harris, Paul Percy
Haugen, Gilbert Nelson
Hazelton, George Cochrane
Hempl, George
Hine, Lewis Wickes
Hoan, Daniel Webster
Hooton, Earnest Albert
Hopson, Howard Colwell
Houdini, Harry
Hoxie, Vinnie Ream
Hubley, John
Huebner, Solomon Stephen
Husting, Paul Oscar
Irving, John Duer
Jones, Lewis Ralph
Kaltenborn, Hans Von
Kelley, Edgar Stillman
King, Franklin Hiram
Kohler, Walter Jodok
Kohler, Walter Jodok, Jr.
Kremers, Edward
Krug, Julius Albert
La Follette, Philip Fox
La Follette, Robert Marion
La Follette, Robert Marion, Jr.
Lambeau, Earl Louis ("Curly")
Leemans, Alphonse E. ("Tuffy")
Legge, Alexander
Lennon, John Brown
Lenroot, Irvine Luther
Lewis, Ed ("Strangler")
Libby, Orin Grant
Lunt, Alfred David, Jr.
Lutkin, Peter Christian
McCarthy, Joseph Raymond
McIntyre, James
McNair, Fred Walter
Macune, Charles William
Mahoney, John Friend
Manville, Thomas Franklyn ("Tommy"), Jr.
March, Frederic
Martin, Franklin Henry
Mason, Max
Matheson, William John
Mears, Helen Farnsworth
Merrill, William Emery
Meyer, Albert Gregory
Mitscher, Marc Andrew
Moldenke, Richard George Gottlob
Morse, Wayne Lyman
Murphy, Frederick E.

Murphy, John Benjamin
Murphy, Robert Daniel
Nehrling, Henry
Newell, Edward Theodore
Nieman, Lucius William
Nye, Gerald Prentice
Ochsner, Albert John
Older, Fremont
Pammel, Louis Hermann
Penfold, Joseph Weller
Perkins, James Breck
Persons, Warren Milton
Pfund, August Herman
Philipp, Emanuel Lorenz
Pond, Frederick Eugene
Preus, Christian Keyser
Purdy, Corydon Tyler
Reid, Helen Miles Rogers
Reinsch, Paul Samuel
Rice, Edwin Wilbur
Richmond, Charles Wallace
Ritter, William Emerson
Robinson, Frederick Byron
Roe, Gilbert Ernstein
Romnes, Haakon Ingolf ("H. I.")
Rublee, George
Salisbury, Albert
Salisbury, Rollin D.
Savage, John Lucian ("Jack")
Sawyer, Wilbur Augustus
Schorer, Mark
Schwellenbach, Lewis Baxter
Scidmore, Eliza Ruhamah
Scott, James Wilmot
Sewall, May Eliza Wright
Showerman, Grant
Shuster, George Nauman
Simmons (Szymanski), Aloysius Harry
Simons, Algie Martin
Slichter, Louis Byrne
Slichter, Sumner Huber
Smith, Francis Marion
Smith, Gerald L. K.
Starks, Edwin Chapin
Stromme, Peer Olsen
Stub, Hans Gerhard
Tobey, Mark
Tracy, Spencer Bonaventure
Turner, Frederick Jackson
Underwood, Frederick Douglas
U'Ren, William Simon
Vandenberg, Hoyt Sanford
Van Hise, Charles Richard
Veblen, Thorstein Bunde
Walsh, Thomas James
Warner, William
Weaver, Warren
West, Allen Brown
Wheeler, William Morton
Wilcox, Ella Wheeler
Wilder, Laura Ingalls
Wilder, Thornton Niven
Wiley, Alexander
Willard, Josiah Flint
Witte, Edwin Emil
Woodbury, Helen Laura Sumner
Wright, Frank Lloyd
Wright, Theodore Lyman

WYOMING

Arnold, Thurman Wesley
Downey, June Etta
Downey, Sheridan
Pollock, (Paul) Jackson
Snyder, Howard McCrum
Spotted Tail

STATE NOT SPECIFIED

Attucks, Crispus
Baynham, William
Black, Eli
Glass, Hugh
Grew, Theophilus
Johnson, Robert
Kicking Bird
Plummer, Henry
Pontiac
Powhatan
Squanto
Tammany
Uncas
Vesey, Denmark
Ware, Nathaniel A.
Wimsatt, William Kurtz

BIRTHPLACES—FOREIGN COUNTRIES

ARGENTINA

Haymes, Richard Benjamin ("Dick")
Parvin, Theophilus

AUSTRALIA

Booth, Agnes
Errol, Leon
Flynn, Errol Leslie
Grainger, George Percy
Henry, Alice
Jacobs, Joseph, 1854–1916
Mason, Arthur John
Mayo, George Elton
Oberon, Merle
Orry-Kelly
Ritchard, Cyril
Robson, May
Travis, Walter John

AUSTRIA

(Including Austria-Hungary)

Baraga, Frederic
Baum, Hedwig ("Vicki")
Berger, Victor Louis
Bloomfield, Maurice
Bodanzky, Artur
Brill, Abraham Arden
Carnegie, Hattie
Conried, Heinrich
Deutsch, Gotthard
Drexel, Francis Martin
Fall, Bernard B.
Fenichel, Otto
Frank, Philipp G.
Frankfurter, Felix
Franzblau, Rose Nadler
Gericke, Wilhelm
Goldberger, Joseph
Grau, Maurice
Grossmann, Louis
Grund, Francis Joseph
Hassaurek, Friedrich
Herbert, Frederick Hugh
Hess, Victor Franz
Katzer, Frederic Xavier
Keppler, Joseph
King, Alexander
Korngold, Erich Wolfgang
Kreisler, Fritz
Landsteiner, Karl
Lang, Fritz
Lazarsfeld, Paul Felix
Lowie, Robert Harry
Lucas, Anthony Francis
Malter, Henry
Muni, Paul
Neutra, Richard Joseph
Ohrbach, Nathan M. ("N. M.")
Ortynsky, Stephen Soter
Pierz, Franz
Pilat, Ignaz Anton
Pollak, Gustav
Pupin, Michael Idvorsky
Raffeiner, John Stephen
Reik, Theodor
Rosenstein, Nettie Rosencrans
Roth, Samuel
Rubin, Isidor Clinton
Sachs, Hanns
Sakel, Manfred Joshua
Schildkraut, Joseph
Schindler, Rudolph Michael
Schnabel, Artur
Schoenberg, Arnold
Schuster, Max Lincoln
Sporn, Philip
Stark, Edward Josef
Steiner, Maximilian Raoul Walter ("Max")
Ulmer, Edgar Georg
Urban, Joseph
Von Sternberg, Josef
Von Stroheim, Erich
Weinberger, Jacob
Weisenburg, Theodore Herman
Zeisler, Fannie Bloomfield
Zeisler, Sigmund

BELGIUM

(Including Flanders)

Baekeland, Leo Hendrik
Bouquillon, Thomas Joseph
Brondel, John Baptist
Carondelet, Francisco Luis Hector, Baron de
Coppens, Charles
Croix, Teodoro de
De Smet, Pierre-Jean
Hennepin, Louis
Heurotin, Charles
Heurotin, Fernand
Janssens, Francis
Lefevere, Peter Paul
Maes, Camillus Paul
Meerschaert, Théophile
Musin, Ovide
Nerinckx, Charles
Nieuwland, Julius Arthur
Parmentier, Andrew
Rau, Charles
Sauveur, Albert
Seghers, Charles Jean
Van Depoele, Charles Joseph
Vander Wee, John Baptist
Van de Velde, James Oliver
Van Quickenborne, Charles Felix
Verbrugghen, Henri
Verhaegen, Peter Joseph

BERMUDA

Cooke, John Esten
Cooke, John Rogers
Meigs, Charles Delucena
Patton, Francis Landey
Tucker, George
Tucker, St. George

BOHEMIA

Heinrich, Antony Philip
Heller, Maximilian
Herrman, Augustine
Hessoun, Joseph
Janauschek, Franziska Magdalena Romance
Levy, Louis Edward
Neumann, John Nepomucene
Prokosch, Eduard
Rosewater, Edward
Steinitz, William
Taussig, William
Vopicka, Charles Joseph
Wise, Isaac Mayer

BRAZIL

Carrère, John Merven
Glover, Townend
Wegmann, Edward
Wise, John Sergeant

BRITISH GUIANA

Benjamin, Park
Holmes, George Frederick
Vethake, Henry

BULGARIA

Arlen, Michael
Zwicky, Fritz

BURMA

Seagrave, Gordon Stifler

CANADA

Anglin, Margaret Mary
Arden, Elizabeth
Avery, Oswald Theodore
Aylwin, John Cushing
Barton, George Aaron
Bassett, James
Beattie, Francis Robert
Becket, Frederick Mark
Belcourt, George Antoine
Benham, Henry Washington
Bensley, Robert Russell
Bingay, Malcolm Wallace
Blake, William Rufus
Blanchet, François Norbert
Blue, Ben
Bowen, Norman Levi
Bowman, Isaiah
Brent, Charles Henry
Brokenshire, Norman Ernest

Brunton, David William
Burk, Frederic Lister
Burrowes, Edward Thomas
Callaway, Samuel Rodger
Carpenter, George Rice
Carson, Jack
Case, Shirley Jackson
Céloron de Blainville, Pierre Joseph de
Cerré, Jean Gabriel
Chisholm, Hugh Joseph
Clark, Francis Edward
Colpitts, Edwin Henry
Comstock, Henry Tompkins Paige
Copway, George
Costain, Thomas Bertram
Coughlin, Charles Edward
Couzens, James
Cox, Palmer
Coxetter, Louis Mitchell
Creath, Jacob
Creelman, James
Creighton, James Edwin
Crouter, Albert Louis Edgerton
Crowe, Francis Trenholm
Cullen, Thomas Stephen
Cutter, George Washington
Daly, Reginald Aldworth
Dett, Robert Nathaniel
Doran, George Henry
Douglas, James
Doull, James Angus
Dow, Herbert Henry
Dressler, Marie
Dubuque, Julien
Duffy, Francis Patrick
Duncan, Robert Kennedy
Dymond, John
Eaton, Charles Aubrey
Eaton, Cyrus Stephen
Eaton, Wyatt
Faith, Percy
Faribault, Jean Baptiste
Farnsworth, John Franklin
Ferguson, Alexander Hugh
Ferguson, John Calvin
Fessenden, Reginald Aubrey
Finn, Henry James William
Fleming, Arthur Henry
Fortescue, Charles LeGeyt
Fowler, Charles Henry
Fox, Margaret
Franchére, Gabriel
Freeman, James Edwards
Frizell, Joseph Palmer
Gallinger, Jacob Harold
Garrison, William Re Tallack
Gibault, Pierre
Goddu, Louis
Gordon, George Byron
Gould, Elgin Ralston Lovell
Grosset, Alexander
Hackett, James Keteltas
Hambidge, Jay
Harrison, Richard Berry
Hill, James Jerome
Hunton, William Lee
Huston, Walter
Iberville, Pierre Le Moyne, Sieur d'
Ironside, Henry Allan
Irwin, May
Jacoby, Neil Herman
James, Will Roderick
Jamison, Cecilia Viets Dakin Hamilton
Jeffrey, Edward Charles
Johnson, Edward
Johnson, Harry Gordon
Johnston, William Hugh
Johnstone, Edward Ransom
Jolliet, Louis
Juneau, Solomon Laurent
Kelley, Edith Summers
Keys, Clement Melville
Kimball, Dexter Simpson
King, William Benjamin Basil
Kinzie, John
Kirk, John Foster
Kittson, Norman Wolfred
Koyl, Charles Herschel
Kraft, James Lewis
Lane, Franklin Knight
Langford, Samuel
Lanigan, George Thomas
Laramie, Jacques
Larned, Josephus Nelson
La Ronde, Louis Denis, Sieur de
Lear, Ben
Leary, John
Lee, Jason
Léry, Joseph Gaspard Chaussegros de
Lewis, Francis Park
Lillie, Frank Rattray
Livingston, James
Livingstone, William
Lombardo, Gaetano Albert ("Guy")
Lorimier, Pierre Louis
Loucks, Henry Langford
MacArthur, Robert Stuart
McBain, Howard Lee
MacCallum, William George
McCoy, Elijah
McCrae, Thomas
Macdonald, Charles Blair
McKay, Donald
McKenzie, Robert Tait
McLaughlin, James
McLean, Archibald
MacLeod, Colin Munro
McLeod, Martin
McLoughlin, John
McMillan, James
McMurrich, James Playfair
McPherson, Aimee Semple
Mahler, Herbert
Marling, Alfred Erskine
Marsh, Charles Wesley
Marsh, William Wallace
Mason, Walt
Mathewson, Edward Payson
Matthew, William Diller
Medill, Joseph
Menard, Michel Branamour
Menard, Pierre
Mitchell, William, 1832–1900
Morgan, John Harcourt Alexander
Morris, Clara
Morrison, Frank
Moxom, Philip Stafford
Munro, George
Munro, William Bennett
Murphy, William Walton
Murray, James Edward
Naismith, James
Nash, John Henry
Nesmith, James Willis
Newcomb, Simon
Nicholson, Samuel Danford
Nolan, Bob
Norwood, Robert Winkworth
Noyan, Pierre-Jacques Payen de
Nutting, Mary Adelaide
Ogden, Peter Skene
O'Higgins, Harvey Jerrold
Osler, William
Palmer, Daniel David
Palmer, Joel
Pearce, Richard Mills
Phelan, David Samuel
Pickford, Mary
Piper, Charles Vancouver
Price, George Edward McCready
Provost, Etienne
Quigley, James Edward
Rand, Benjamin
Rankin, McKee
Raymond, Harry Howard
Reid, Rose Marie
Riordan, Patrick William
Robinson, Boardman
Rolette, Jean Joseph
Rose, Walter Malins
Ross, James Delmage McKenzie
Rothwell, Richard Pennefather
Ryan, Stephen Vincent
Ryan, Walter D'Arcy
St. Ange De Bellerive, Louis
St. Denis (Denys), Louis Juchereau de
Sandham, Henry
Sauganash
Scherman, Harry
Schofield, William Henry
Schurman, Jacob Gould
Scott, Colin Alexander
Scott, James Brown
Sears, Robert
Sennett, Mack
Shikellamy
Shotwell, James Thomson
Silverheels, Jay
Simpson, Albert Benjamin
Simpson, Jerry
Sims, William Sowden
Slocum, Joshua
Squiers, Herbert Goldsmith
Stefansson, Vilhjalmur
Stephenson, Isaac
Stevens, John Harrington
Stewart, George Neil
Storrow, Charles Storer
Sullivan, William Henry
Tanguay, Eva
Thompson, Slason
Thomson, Edward William
Truteau, Jean Baptiste
Upham, Charles Wentworth

Vaudreuil-Cavagnal, Pierre de Rigaud, Marquis de
Vincennes, Jean Baptiste Bissot
Viner, Jacob
Waddell, John Alexander Low
Wanless, William James
Warner, Jack Leonard
Warren, Samuel Prowse
Watson, James Craig
Wesbrook, Frank Fairchild
West, Oswald
Wheelock, Joseph Albert
White, Benjamin Franklin
Williams, Eleazar
Wood, Casey Albert
Wood, William Burke
Woodbridge, Frederick James Eugene

CEYLON

Coomaraswamy, Ananda Kentish
Sanders, Frank Knight

CHILE

Albright, William Foxwell
De Cuevas, Marquis
Murrieta, Joaquin

CHINA

Coulter, John Merle
Howe, James Wong
Lambuth, Walter Russell
Lowrie, James Walter
Luce, Henry Robinson
Lyon, David Willard
Maclay, Edgar Stanton
Ng Poon Chew
Stuart, John Leighton
Sydenstricker, Edgar
Williams, Frederick Wells
Yung Wing

CUBA

Agramonte Y Simoni, Aristides

CZECHOSLOVAKIA

(*See also* Bohemia; Moravia; Silesia)
Cermak, Anton Joseph
Cori, Gerty Theresa Radnitz
Gerster, Arpad Geyza Charles
Friml, Charles Rudolf
Hertz, John Daniel
Koller, Carl
Ottendorfer, Oswald
Sabath, Adolph J.
Schumann-Heink, Ernestine
Schumpeter, Joseph Alois
Steuer, Max David
Wertheimer, Max

DENMARK

Bierregaard, Carl Henrik Andreas
Blichfeldt, Hans Frederik
Boyé, Martin Hans
Clausen, Claus Lauritz
Febiger, Christian
Fenger, Christian
Gronlund, Laurence
Hansen, Niels Ebbesen
Hovgaard, William
Isbrandtsen, Hans Jeppesen
Jacobson, John Christian
Jensen, Jens
Jensen, Peter Laurits
Knudsen, William S.
Linde, Christian
Melchior, Lauritz Lebrecht Hommel
Nelson, Julius
Nelson, Nels Christian
Poulson, Niels
Riis, Jacob August
Rybner, Martin Cornelius
Sorensen, Charles
Westergaard, Harald Malcolm

DUTCH GUIANA

Matzeliger, Jan Ernst

EGYPT

Forester, Cecil Scott
Mowbray, Henry Siddons
Watson, Charles Roger

ENGLAND

(Including Channel Islands, Isle of Man, Isle of Wight, Orkney Islands, Scilly Isles)

Abel-Henderson, Annie Heloise
Alden, John
Allen, John F.
Allerton, Isaac
Alsop, George
Altham, John
Amadas, Philip
Amherst, Jeffery
Andros, Sir Edmund
Archdale, John
Archer, Frederic
Argall, Sir Samuel
Arliss, George
Asbury, Francis
Asher, Joseph Mayor
Auden, Wystan Hugh
Ayer, Francis Wayland
Ayres, Anne
Bache, Richard
Bache, Theophylact
Bacon, Nathaniel
Bacon, Thomas
Bailey, Ann
Baker, Edward Dickinson
Banister, John
Banner, Peter
Barr, Amelia Edith Huddleston
Barradall, Edward
Barrett, George Horton
Bartlett, John Sherren
Bateman, Harry
Bates, Barnabas
Bateson, Gregory
Bauer, Harold Victor
Baxter, William
Bazett, Henry Cuthbert
Beer, William
Bellingham, Richard
Berkeley, John
Berkeley, Sir William
Bernard, John
Bernard, Sir Francis
Bertram, John
Biggs, Edward George Power
Birch, Reginald Bathurst
Birch, Thomas
Birch, William Russell
Birchall, Frederick Thomas
Birkbeck, Morris
Blackstone, William
Blackton, James Stuart
Blackwell, Elizabeth
Blackwell, Henry Brown
Bladen, William
Bland, Thomas
Blennerhassett, Harman
Blitz, Antonio
Bollan, William
Boorman, James
Booth, Ballington
Booth, Evangeline Cory
Booth, Junius Brutus
Booth-Tucker, Emma Moss
Boucher, Jonathan
Bourne, George
Bourne, Nehemiah
Bowler, Metcalf
Bowne, John
Bradford, William, 1589/90–1657
Bradford, William, 1663–1752
Bradstreet, Anne
Bradstreet, Simon
Bradwell, James Bolesworth
Bray, Thomas
Brent, Margaret
Brett, George Platt
Brewster, William
Brierton, John
Bright, Edward
Brightly, Frederick Charles
Bristed, John
Brooks, William Robert
Brophy, John
Brown, Ernest William
Brown, John George
Browne, John
Bulkeley, Peter
Burgis, William
Burnett, Frances Eliza Hodgson
Burrington, George
Burton, William Evans
Buttrick, George Arthur
Byrd, William
Cabot, Charles Sebastian Thomas
Cadman, Samuel Parkes
Caffin, Charles Henry
Calef, Robert
Calvert, Charles
Calvert, George
Calvert, Leonard
Cameron, Andrew Carr
Camm, John

Campbell, Lord William
Campbell, William
Cannon, George Quayle
Carbutt, John
Carr, Benjamin
Carroll, James
Carroll, Leo Grattan
Carteret, Philip
Castle, Vernon Blythe
Catesby, Mark
Chadwick, Henry
Chalkley, Thomas
Chamberlain, Alexander Francis
Chaplin, Charles Spencer ("Charlie")
Chauncy, Charles, 1592–1671/72
Cheetham, James
Cheever, Ezekiel
Child, Robert
Chovet, Abraham
Clagett, Wyseman
Claiborne, William
Clarke, George
Clarke, John
Clay, Joseph
Claypole, Edward Waller
Clayton, John
Clews, Henry
Clinton, George
Cobbett, William
Cockerell, Theodore Dru Alison
Coddington, William
Coghlan, Rose
Cole, Thomas
Cole, Timothy
Colgate, William
Collier, Constance
Collyer, Robert
Colman, Ronald Charles
Comstock, Elizabeth L.
Conant, Roger
Connolly, Thomas H.
Conway, Frederick Bartlett
Cooper, Myles
Cooper, Thomas
Cooper, Thomas Abthorpe
Copley, Lionel
Coram, Thomas
Cornbury, Edward Hyde, Viscount
Cornwallis, Kinahan
Cotton, John
Couldock, Charles Walter
Cowley, Charles
Coxe, Daniel
Cranston, John
Cresop, Thomas
Crisp, Charles Frederick
Croly, Jane Cunningham
Crompton, George
Crompton, William
Crowne, John
Crowne, William
Crunden, Frederick Morgan
Culpeper, Thomas, Lord
Cuming, Sir Alexander
Cummings, Thomas Seirs
Cunliffe-Owen, Philip Frederick
Cushman, Robert
Daft, Leo
Dakin, Henry Drysdale
Dalcho, Frederick
Danforth, Thomas
Davenport, Fanny Lily Gypsy
Davenport, George
Davenport, John
Davey, John
Davidge, William Pleater
Davidson, George
Davie, William Richardson
Dawkins, Henry
Dawson, Francis Warrington
Dawson, Henry Barton
Day, Stephen
Dealey, George Bannerman
De Berdt, Dennys
Delafield, John
De La Warr, Thomas West, Baron
Dennis, Graham Barclay
Dickins, John
Dickson, Thomas
Disston, Henry
Dixwell, John
Dorrell, William
Dove, David James
Dow, Henry
Downing, George
Drake, Samuel
Draper, John William
Dudley, Charles Edward
Dudley, Thomas
Duer, William
Duff, Mary Ann Dyke
Dunglison, Robley
Dunster, Henry
Duranty, Walter
Dyer, Mary
Dyott, Thomas W.
Eaton, Nathaniel
Eaton, Samuel
Eaton, Theophilus
Eddis, William
Eden, Charles
Eden, Robert
Edmunds, Charles Wallis
Edwards, Charles
Edwards, John, 1671–1746
Edwards, Julian
Edwards, Morgan
Edwards, Talmadge
Edwin, David
Eliot, John
Elliot, Jonathan
Elliott, John
Ellis, Henry
Endecott, John
Estaugh, Elizabeth Haddon
Esterbrook, Richard
Evans, Frederick William
Evans, George Henry
Everendon, Walter
Ewbank, Thomas
Fairburn, William Armstrong
Fairfax, Thomas
Fallows, Samuel
Farrer, Henry
Fauquier, Francis
Faversham, William Alfred
Fechter, Charles Albert
Fendall, Josias
Fennell, James
Fenwick, George
Fenwick, John
Field, Robert
Fisher, Clara
Fitzhugh, William
Fitzsimmons, Robert Prometheus
Fleet, Thomas
Fletcher, Benjamin
Fletcher, Robert
Flower, George
Flower, Richard
Folger, Peter
Foster, Charles James
Fox, Gilbert
Foxall, Henry
Francis, James Bicheno
Fry, Joshua
Fry, Richard
Fuller, John Wallace
Gage, Thomas
Gales, Joseph, 1761–1841
Gales, Joseph, 1786–1860
Gardiner, Sir Christopher
Gardiner, Harry Norman
Gardiner, Lion
Gardiner, Robert Hallowell
Gasson, Thomas Ignatius
Gates, Horatio
Gates, Sir Thomas
Gibbs, Arthur Hamilton
Gilbert, Anne Hartley
Gillam, Bernhard
Gilpin, Henry Dilworth
Gladwin, Henry
Glass, Montague Marsden
Godbe, William Samuel
Goffe, William
Gompers, Samuel
Gooch, Sir William
Goodall, Thomas
Gookin, Daniel
Gordon, William
Gorton, Samuel
Gosnold, Bartholomew
Gottheil, Richard James Horatio
Gough, John Bartholomew
Graham, David
Greaton, Joseph
Green, Samuel
Greenhalge, Frederic Thomas
Greenstreet, Sydney Hughes
Grierson, Francis
Grote, Augustus Radcliffe
Guest, Edgar Albert
Gunn, Selskar Michael
Gunter, Archibald Clavering
Gunton, George
Guthrie, Sir Tyrone
Guy, Seymour Joseph
Gwinnett, Button
Haas, Jacob Judah Aaron de
Habersham, James
Hall, Arthur Crawshay Alliston
Hall, Henry Bryan
Hallam, Lewis
Hallidie, Andrew Smith
Hamblin, Thomas Sowerby
Hamilton, Andrew
Hamilton, William Thomas
Harding, Robert

Hardwicke, Cedric Webster
Hare, James H.
Harland, Thomas
Harris, Benjamin
Harris, Joseph
Harris, Maurice Henry
Harris, Thomas Lake
Harrison, Peter
Harvard, John
Harvey, Sir John
Haswell, Anthony
Hathorne, William
Havell, Robert
Haviland, John
Hawks, John
Haynes, John
Haywood, Allan Shaw
Hazelwood, John
Heathcote, Caleb
Heckewelder, John Gottlieb Ernestus
Henningsen, Charles Frederick
Henry, Morris Henry
Herbert, Henry William
Herford, Oliver Brooke
Herring, James
Hewitt, James
Hibbins, Ann
Higginson, Francis
Higginson, John
Hill, John
Hill, Thomas, 1829–1908
Hitchcock, Alfred Joseph
Hoar, Leonard
Hodgkinson, Francis
Hodgkinson, John
Hoe, Robert, 1784–1833
Hoffman, Richard
Hogg, George
Holland, George
Holloway, John
Hollyer, Samuel
Holme, Thomas
Hooker, Samuel Cox
Hooker, Thomas
Hooker, William
Hoover, Herbert Clark, Jr.
Hopkins, Edward
Horlick, William
Hornblower, Josiah
Horrocks, James
Horsmanden, Daniel
Howard, Leslie
Howe, George Augustus, Viscount
Hubbard, William
Hudson, Henry
Hudson, William Smith
Hughes, David Edward
Hughes, Robert Ball
Hull, John
Hunt, Robert
Hutchinson, Anne
Hutchinson, Woods
Huxley, Aldous Leonard
Hyde, Edward
Ingle, Richard
Inskip, John Swanel
Insull, Samuel
Iredell, James
Irene, Sister
Izard, George
Jackson, George K.
Jackson, James, 1757–1806
Jackson, William
Jacobi, Mary Corinna Putnam
James, Charles
James, Daniel Willis
James, George Wharton
Jarvis, John Wesley
Jefferson, Joseph
Jeffery, Edward Turner
Jenckes, Joseph
Jenks, George Charles
Jenks, Joseph
Johnson, Alexander
Johnson, Alexander Bryan
Johnson, Edward
Johnson, Marmaduke
Johnson, Sir Nathaniel
Jones, Alfred
Jones, Hugh
Jones, John Percival
Jones, Noble Wymberley
Jones, Thomas P.
Josselyn, Hugh
Joy, Thomas
Karloff, Boris
Katte, Walter
Kearsley, John
Keene, James Robert
Keene, Laura
Keimer, Samuel
Kemble, Frances Anne
Kempster, Walter
Kilty, William
King, Albert Freeman Africanus
Kingsford, Thomas
Kinnersley, Ebenezer
Klein, Charles
Knight, Edward Henry
Lake, Kirsopp
Lander, Jean Margaret Davenport
Landreth, David
Lane, Sir Ralph
Larkin, John
Latimer, Mary Elizabeth Wormeley
Latrobe, Benjamin Henry, 1764–1820
Laughton, Charles
Laurance, John
Laurel, Stan
Lawley, George Frederick
Lawrence, Gertrude
Lawson, John
Lay, Benjamin
Lechford, Thomas
Lee, Ann
Lee, Charles, 1731–1782
Lee, Richard
Leeds, Daniel
Leete, William
Leipziger, Henry Marcus
Leney, William Satchwell
Lennon, John Winston Ono
Leslie, Charles Robert
Leslie, Frank
Leverett, John, 1616–1679
Levy, Joseph Leonard
Lewis, Arthur
Linton, William James
Locke, Richard Adams
Lorimer, William
Lothropp, John
Lovelace, Francis
Lovell, John Epy
Lucas, Jonathan, 1754–1821
Lucas, Jonathan, 1775–1832
Ludlow, Roger
Ludwell, Philip
Lyttelton, William Henry
McCormick, Anne Elizabeth O'Hare
McDougall, William
McLaglen, Victor
Madden, Martin Barnaby
Madden, Owen Victor ("Owney")
Manners, John Hartley
Manning, William Thomas
Markham, William
Marlowe, Julia
Marshall, Benjamin
Martin, Henry Austin
Martin, Thomas Commerford
Mason, Francis
Mason, George
Mason, John
Mather, Richard
Mathews, Samuel
Matthews, John
Maverick, Samuel
May, Edward Harrison
Mayhew, Thomas, 1593–1682
Mayhew, Thomas, 1621–1657
Mayo, William
Mayo, William Worrell
Meehan, Thomas
Mees, Charles Edward Kenneth
Meiklejohn, Alexander
Mendes, Henry Pereira
Merry, Ann Brunton
Middleton, Henry
Middleton, Peter
Miles, Edward
Miller, Henry
Millington, John
Mitchell, John, d. 1768
Mitchell, Jonathan
Mitchell, William, 1798–1856
Mitten, Thomas Eugene
Molyneux, Robert
Monckton, Robert
Montague, Henry James
Montefiore, Joshua
Moore, John, *c.* 1569–1732
Moran, Edward
Moran, Peter
Moran, Thomas
More, Nicholas
Morgan, Matthew Somerville
Morley, Frank
Morris, Anthony, 1654–1721
Morris, Elizabeth
Morris, Robert, 1734–1806
Morris, Roger
Mortimer, Mary
Morton, Charles
Morton, George
Morton, Thomas
Moulton, Richard Green
Mowbray, George Mordey

Murray, John, 1741–1815
Muybridge, Eadweard
Myles, John
Needham, James
Nelson, John
Newport, Christopher
Newton, Richard
Newton, Thomas, 1660–1721
Nicholls, Rhoda Holmes
Nichols, Edward Leamington
Nicholson, Francis
Nicolls, Matthias
Nicolls, Richard
Nicolls, William
Noble, Samuel
Nordhoff, Charles Bernard
Norman, John
Norris, Edward
Norris, Isaac, 1671–1735
Norton, John
Nurse, Rebecca
Nuthead, William
Nuttall, Thomas
Oakes, Urian
Ogle, Samuel
Oglethorpe, James Edward
Oldham, John
Owens, John Edmond
Paine, Thomas
Palmer, Joseph
Palmer, William Henry
Paris, Walter
Parks, William
Parris, Samuel
Parry, Charles Christopher
Parton, James
Pasco, Samuel
Payne-Gaposchkin, Cecilia Helena
Pearce, Richard
Pearce, Stephen Austen
Pedder, James
Peirce, William
Pelham, Peter
Pellew, Henry Edward
Penhallow, Samuel
Penington, Edward
Penn, Thomas
Penn, William
Peter, Hugh
Peter, Robert
Peters, Richard
Peters, William Cumming
Phillips, George
Pierson, Abraham
Pike, Robert
Pilmore, Joseph
Pine, Robert Edge
Pinkney, Edward Coote
Pitkin, William, 1635–1694
Pitman, Benn
Pittock, Henry Lewis
Popham, George
Pormort, Philemon
Porter, Robert Percival
Pory, James
Pott, John
Potter, Paul Meredith
Pound, Thomas
Powell, Thomas
Power, Frederick Tyrone
Pownall, Thomas
Priestley, James
Priestley, Joseph
Pring, Martin
Proud. Robert
Pusey, Caleb
Putnam, George Haven
Pynchon, John
Pynchon, William
Quelch, John
Quine, William Edward
Rains, Claude
Randolph, Edward
Randolph, William
Ransome, Frederick Leslie
Rawle, Francis, 1662–1726/27
Rawlinson, Frank Joseph
Reach, Alfred James
Realf, Richard
Reinagle, Alexander
Rennie, Michael
Renwick, James, 1792–1863
Restarick, Henry Bond
Reynolds, John
Richards, Joseph William
Richards, Thomas Addison
Richings, Peter
Rideing, William Henry
Riley, Charles Valentine
Rimmer, William
Rivington, James
Roberts, Brigham Henry
Rogers, Clara Kathleen Barnett
Rolfe, John
Rollinson, William
Rose, Aquila
Rosebury, Theodor
Rowlands, William
Rowlandson, Mary White
Rowson, Susanna Haswell
Ruditsky, Barney
Russell, Annie
Sabin, Joseph
Saltonstall, Richard
Sanderson, Robert
Sandys, George
Sargent, Frederick
Sartain, John
Saunders, Frederick
Savery, William, 1721–1787
Scott, John
Scripps, Ellen Browning
Scripps, James Edmund
Searle, Arthur
Sedgwick, Robert
Seed, Miles Ainscough
Selby, William
Serrell, Edward Wellman
Service, Robert William
Seton, Ernest Thompson
Sewall, Samuel
Sharp, Daniel
Sharpe, Horatio
Sharples, James
Shaw, Anna Howard
Shaw, Henry
Shearman, Thomas Gaskell
Shelton, Edward Mason
Shepard, Thomas
Sheppard, Samuel Edward
Sherman, John, 1613–1685
Shippen, Edward, 1639–1712
Shirley, William
Shute, Samuel
Simmons, George Henry
Simpson, Edmund Shaw
Skinner, William
Slater, Samuel
Smith, John, 1579–1631
Smith, John Merlin Powis
Smith, John Rubens
Smith, Robert, 1732–1801
Smith, Robert Alexander
Smith, William, 1697–1769
Sothern, Edward Askew
Southack, Cyprian
Spargo, John
Spilsbury, Edmund Gybbon
Standish, Myles
Stanford, John
Stansbury, Joseph
Staughton, William
Stevens, Frank Mozley
Stevens, Harry Mozley
Stewart, Humphrey John
Stoddart, James Henry
Stokowski, Leopold Anthony
Stone, Samuel
Stone, William
Story, Julian Russell
Stott, Henry Gordon
Stoughton, William
Strachey, William
Stuck, Hudson
Sully, Thomas
Summers, Thomas Osmond
Sutherland, George
Sylvester, James Joseph
Syms, Benjamin
Tait, Arthur Fitzwilliam
Talbot, John
Talmage, James Edward
Tate, George Henry Hamilton
Tatham, William
Taylor, Edward
Taylor, James Barnett
Taylor, John
Taylor, John Louis
Taylor, Raynor
Taylor, Richard Cowling
Tennent, John
Thompson, David
Thompson, Jeremiah
Thomson, Elihu
Tiffin, Edward
Tingey, Thomas
Titchener, Edward Bradford
Todd, Thomas Wingate
Tomlins, William Lawrence
Toulmin, Harry
Towler, John
Towne, Benjamin
Treat, Robert
Trevellick, Richard F.
Troup, Robert
Tryon, William
Tuckey, William
Turner, Walter Victor
Underhill, John
Underwood, Horace Grant

Underwood, John Thomas
Upjohn, Richard
Upjohn, Richard Michell
Utley, Freda
Vallentine, Benjamin Bennaton
Vandenhoff, George
Van Druten, John William
Vane, Sir Henry
Vasey, George
Vassall, John
Vassar, Matthew
Vaughan, Charles
Vaux, Calvert
Vick, James
Vincent, Mary Ann
Vizetelly, Frank Horace
Wainwright, Jonathan Mayhew, 1792–1854
Walcot, Charles Melton, 1816–1868
Walderne, Richard
Wallace, William
Wallack, Henry John
Wallack, James William, 1795–1864
Wallack, James William, 1818–1873
Waller, Emma
Walsh, Benjamin Dann
Walter, Thomas, *c.* 1740–1789
Ward, George Gray
Ward, Harry Frederick
Ward, Nathaniel
Warde, Frederick Barkham
Warner, Fred Maltby
Warren, Herbert Langford
Warren, William, 1767–1832
Waterhouse, Frank
Watson, Henry Cood
Watts, Alan Wilson
Waymouth, George
Webb, Daniel
Webb, George James
Webb, Thomas
Weightman, William
Weld, Thomas
Wemyss, Francis Courtney
West, Francis
West, George
West, Joseph
Weston, Edward
Weston, Thomas
Weston, William
Whalley, Edward
Wharton, Richard
Whatcoat, Richard
Wheelwright, John
Whitaker, Alexander
White, Andrew
White, John
Whitefield, George
Whitehead, Alfred North
Whitehead, Walter Edward
Whitfield, Henry
Whitworth, George Frederic
Wigglesworth, Michael
Wignell, Thomas
Wilbur, Samuel
Willard, Simon
Williams, John
Williams, Robert
Williams, Roger
Wilson, Ernest Henry
Wilson, John
Wilson, Samuel Thomas
Wingfield, Edward Maria
Winslow, Edward
Winthrop, John, 1587/88–1649
Winthrop, John, 1605/06 o.s.–1676
Wise, Daniel
Wise, Thomas Alfred
Withers, Frederick Clarke
Wodehouse, Pelham Grenville
Wood, Abraham
Wood, William
Woodbridge, John
Woodrow, James
Woolf, Benjamin Edward
Wormeley, Katharine Prescott
Wraxall, Peter
Wright, Henry
Wyatt, Sir Francis
Wylie, Robert
Yeamans, Sir John
Yeardley, Sir George
Young, Alfred
Youngs, John

ESTONIA

Holst, Hermann Eduard von, 1841–1904
Kahn, Louis I.
Leiserson, William Morris

FINLAND

Nordberg, Bruno Victor
Saarinen, Eero
Saarinen, Gottlieb Eliel

FRANCE

Aca, Michel
Agnus, Felix
Allefonsce, John
Allouez, Claude Jean
André, Louis
Badin, Stephen Theodore
Bailly, Joseph Alexis
Bedaux, Charles Eugene
Benezet, Anthony
Bernard, Simon
Biard, Pierre
Biddle, Francis Beverley
Bienville, Jean Baptiste le Moyne, Sieur de
Blanc, Antoine
Bonard, Louis
Bonneville, Benjamin Louis Eulalie de
Bouvier, John
Boyer, Charles
Brady, Anthony Nicholas
Brulé, Étienne
Bruté de Rémur, Simon William Gabriel
Bryant, Louise Frances Stevens
Cabet, Étienne
Cadillac, Antoine de la Mothe
Carrel, Alexis
Casadesus, Robert Marcel
Champlain, Samuel de
Chanute, Octave
Chapelle, Placide Louis
Charlevoix, Pierre François Xavier de
Chaumonot, Pierre Joseph Marie
Cheverus, John Louis Ann Magdalen Lefebre de
Clerc, Laurent
Colston, Raleigh Edward
Considérant, Victor Prosper
Cortambert, Louis Richard
Coutard, Henri
Cret, Paul Philippe
Crétin, Joseph
Crèvecoeur, Michel-Guillaume Jean de
Crowninshield, Francis Welch
Crozet, Claude
Dablon, Claude
Dannreuther, Gustav
David, John Baptist Mary
Delmas, Delphin Michael
De Mézières y Clugny, Athanase
Derbigny, Pierre Auguste Charles Bourguignon
De Trobriand, Régis Denis de Keredern
De Vries, David Pietersen
Diat, Louis Felix
Du Bois, John
Duchesne, Rose Philippine
Dugdale, Richard Louis
Duluth, Daniel Greysolon, Sieur
Du Ponceau, Pierre Étienne
Du Pont, Eleuthère Irénée
Du Pont, Victor Marie
Durand, Élie Magloire
Engel, Carl
Esher, John Jacob
Flaget, Benedict Joseph
Forbes, John Murray
Gaillardet, Théodore Frédéric
Garreau, Armand
Genet, Edmond Charles
Girard, Stephen
Gravier, Jacques
Grellet, Stephen
Groseilliers, Médart Chouart, Sieur de
Guérin, Anne-Thérèse
Guignas, Michel
Hallet, Étienne Sulpice
Harrisse, Henry
Herrmann, Alexander
Herter, Christian Archibald
Hite, Jost
Houdry, Eugene Jules
Humbert, Jean Joseph Amable
Hyvernat, Henri
Imbert, Antoine
Jogues, Isaac
Johnston, Robert Matteson
Joubert de la Maraille, James Hector Marie Nicholas
Joutel, Henri
Jumel, Stephen

Kelly, Edmond
Klein, Joseph Frederic
Kohlmann, Anthony
Lachaise, Gaston
Laclede, Pierre
Lafayette, Marie Joseph Paul Yves Roch Gilbert du Motier, Marquis de
Laffite, Jean
Lahontan, Louis-Armand de Lom D'Arce, Baron de
Lamy, John Baptist
Landais, Pierre
Larpenteur, Charles
La Salle, Robert Cavelier, Sieur de
La Tour, Le Blond de
Laudonnière, René Goulaine de
Le Gendre, Charles William
Le Jau, Francis
L'Enfant, Pierre Charles
Lesueur, Charles Alexandre
Le Sueur, Pierre
L'Halle, Constantin de
Loeffler, Charles Martin
Loos, Charles Louis
Loras, Jean Mathias Pierre
Lucas, John Baptiste Charles
Lufbery, Raoul Gervais Victor
Machebeuf, Joseph Projectus
Mangin, Joseph François
Manigautt, Pierre
Marcow, Jules
Maréchal, Ambrose
Marest, Pierre Gabriel
Marquette, Jacques
Marsh, Reginald
Martin, François-Xavier
Martiny, Philip
Matignon, Francis Anthony
Maurin, Peter Aristide
Mayer, Constant
Mazureau, Étienne
Membré, Zenobius
Ménard, René
Merton, Thomas
Meyer, André Benoit Mathieu
Michaux, André
Michaux, François André
Mielziner, Jo
Mitchell, William
Monteux, Pierre Benjamin
Mowatt, Anna Cora Ogden
Murat, Achille
Nancrède, Paul Joseph Guérard de
Neef, Francis Joseph Nicholas
Nicola, Lewis
Nicolet, Jean
Nicollet, Joseph Nicolas
Nin, Anaïs
Niza, Marcos de
Noailles, Louis Marie, Vicomte de
Noyan, Gilles-Augustin Payen de
Odin, John Mary
Partridge, William Ordway
Pascalis-Ouvrière, Felix
Pauger, Adrien de
Perché, Napoleon Joseph
Perrot, Nicolas
Petri, Angelo
Pinchot, Amos Richards Eno
Pons, Lily
Portier, Michael
Poydras, Julien de Lelande
Prevost, François Marie
Quartley, Arthur
Quesnay, Alexandre-Marie
Radisson, Pierre Esprit
Râle, Sébastien
Ramée, Joseph Jacques
Ravoux, Augustin
Rémy, Henri
Ribaut, Jean
Richard, Gabriel
Ritter, Frédéric Louis
Robot, Isidore
Rochambeau, Jean Baptiste Donatien de Vimeur, Comte de
Rosenberg, Paul
Ruckstull, Frederick Wellington
St. Lusson, Simon François Daumont, Sieur de
Saint-Mémin, Charles Balthazar Julien Fevret de
Saugrain de Vigni, Antoine François
Schussele, Christian
Seguin, Edouard
Seguin, Edward Constant
Sigerist, Henry Ernest
Sorin, Edward Frederick
Soulé, Pierre
Stevenson, Sara Yorke
Testut, Charles
Thébaud, Augustus J.
Timothy, Lewis
Tonty, Henry de
Tousard, Anne Louis de
Tulane, Paul
Urso, Camilla
Vail, Aaron
Vattemare, Nicolas Marie Alexandre
Verot, Jean Marcel Pierre Auguste
Wolf, Henry
You, Dominique

GALICIA

Grossinger, Jennie
Imber, Naphtali Herz
Neumark, David
Sembrich, Marcella
Speiser, Ephraim Avigdor
Zach, Max Wilhelm

GERMANY

(Including Bavaria and Prussia)

Adams, Charles
Adler, Felix
Adler, George J.
Adler, Samuel
Albers, Josef
Ameringer, Oscar
Antes, Henry
Arendt, Hannah
Arents, Albert
Astor, John Jacob
Baade, Wilhelm Heinrich Walter
Baermann, Carl
Balbach, Edward
Balch, Thomas Willing
Bartholdt, Richard
Beck, Carl
Beck, Charles
Behrendt, Walter Curt
Behrens, Henry
Beissel, Johann Conrad
Belmont, August
Bergmann, Max
Berkenmeyer, Wilhelm Christoph
Berliner, Emile
Bieber, Margarete
Bien, Julius
Bierstadt, Albert
Bimeler, Joseph Michael
Blankenburg, Rudolph
Blenk, James Hubert
Bloede, Gertrude
Bluemner, Oscar Florians
Boas, Emil Leopold
Boas, Franz
Boehler, Peter
Boehm, John Philip
Boldt, George C.
Bollman, Justus Erich
Bolza, Oskar
Bonzano, Adolphus
Brachvogel, Udo
Braun, Wernher von
Brentano, Lorenz
Brokmeyer, Henry C.
Brühl, Gustav
Busch, Adolphus
Busch, Hermann
Cammerhoff, John Christopher Frederick
Carnap, Rudolf
Carus, Paul
Cornell, Katharine
Damrosch, Walter Johannes
Dancel, Christian
Deindörfer, Johannes
Demme, Charles Rudolph
Detmold, Christian Edward
Dielman, Frederick
Dold, Jacob
Dorsch, Eduard
Dresel, Otto
Dreyfus, Max
Duhring, Louis Adolphus
Eckstein, John
Eichberg, Julius
Eickemeyer, Rudolf
Eigenmann, Carl H.
Eilers, Frederic Anton
Eimbeck, William
Einhorn, David
Einstein, Albert
Eisler, Gerhart
Elsberg, Louis
Engelhardt, Zephyrin
Engelmann, George
Ernst, Max
Ettwein, John
Faber, John Eberhard
Falckner, Daniel
Falckner, Justus

Farmer, Ferdinand
Felsenthal, Bernhard
Fernow, Bernhard Eduard
Fernow, Berthold
Feuchtwanger, Lion
Fink, Albert
Fischer, Emil Friedrick August
Fischer, Ruth
Flad, Henry
Flügel, Ewald
Follen, Charles
Franck, James
Francke, Kuno
Frasch, Herman
Frelinghuysen, Theodorus Jacobus
Frey, Joseph Samuel Christian Frederick
Friedlaender, Walter Ferdinand
Fritschel, Conrad Sigmund
Fritschel, Gottfried Leonhard Wilhelm
Fromm, Erich
Fromm-Reichmann, Frieda
Ganso, Emil
Ganss, Henry George
Gemünder, August Martin Ludwig
Genth, Frederick Augustus
Genthe, Arnold
Gerstle, Lewis
Giesler-Anneke, Mathilde Franziska
Girsch, Frederick
Gmeiner, John
Goessmann, Charles Anthony
Goldbeck, Robert
Goldschmidt, Jakob
Gottheil, Gustav
Grabau, Johannes Andreas August
Gradle, Henry
Graessl, Lawrence
Graupner, Johann Christian Gottlieb
Grim, David
Gropius, Walter Adolf Georg
Gros, John Daniel
Grossmann, Georg Martin
Grosz, George
Grube, Bernhard Adam
Gruening, Emil
Gunther, Charles Frederick
Guthe, Karl Eugen
Haarstick, Henry Christian
Hack, George
Hagen, Hermann August
Hahn, Georg Michael Decker
Haish, Jacob
Hamilton, Edith
Hammerstein, Oscar
Hansen, George
Hanus, Paul Henry
Hartwig, Johann Christoph
Hasenclever, Peter
Haupt, Paul
Hazelius, Ernest Lewis
Hecker, Friedrich Karl Franz
Heckscher, August
Heinemann, Ernst
Heinrich, Max
Heinzen, Karl Peter
Heiss, Michael
Helbron, Peter
Helffenstein, John Albert Conrad
Helmpraecht, Joseph
Helmuth, Justus Henry Christian
Hempel, Charles Julius
Hendel, John William
Herbermann, Charles George
Hering, Constantine
Herman, Lebrecht Frederick
Herter, Christian
Hertz, Alfred
Heyer, John Christian Frederick
Hilgard, Eugene Woldemar
Hilgard, Julius Erasmus
Hilgard, Theodor Erasmus
Hilprecht, Herman Volrath
Hirsch, Emil Gustav
Hoecken, Christian
Hoen, August
Hoenecke, Gustav Adolf Felix Thedor
Hoffman, Frederick Ludwig
Hoffmann, Francis Arnold
Hofman, Heinrich Oscar
Hofmann, Hans
Horney, Karen Danielssen
Hotz, Ferdinand Carl
Howard, Willie
Husmann, George
Ingelfinger, Franz Joseph
Jacobi, Abraham
Jacoby, Ludwig Sigmund
Jaeger, Werner Wilhelm
Juengling, Frederick
Jungman, John George
Kahn, Albert
Kahn, Gustav Gerson
Kahn, Julius
Kahn, Otto Herman
Kalb, Johann
Kalisch, Isidor
Kallen, Horace Meyer
Kapp, Friedrich
Kaufmann, Walter Arnold
Kautz, August Valentine
Keller, Mathias
Kellerman, Karl Frederic
Kelpius, Johann
Kiehbiel, Christian
Kirchmayer, John
Klein, Bruno Oscar
Kline, George
Klopsch, Louis
Knab, Frederick
Knabe, Valentine Wilhelm Ludwig
Knapp, Herman
Kober, George Martin
Kocherthal, Josua von
Koehler, Robert
Koehler, Sylvester Rosa
Koemmenich, Louis
Koenig, George Augustus
Koffka, Kurt
Kohler, Kaufmann
Kolb, Dielman
Kolle, Frederick Strange
Korner, Gustav Philipp
Kracauer, Siegfried
Kraus, John
Kraus-Boelté, Maria
Krauskopf, Joseph
Krez, Konrad
Krimmel, John Lewis
Kroeger, Adolph Ernst
Kruell, Gustav
Kunze, John Christopher
Kunze, Richard Ernest
Laemmle, Carl
Lange, Louis
Lasker, Albert Davis
Laufer, Berthold
Lederer, John
Leeser, Isaac
Lehmann, Frederick William
Lehmann, Lotte
Leisler, Jacob
Lemke, Peter Henry
Leutze, Emanuel
Lewin, Kurt
Lewisohn, Adolph
Lewisohn, Ludwig
Ley, Willy
Leyendecker, Joseph Christian
Leypoldt, Frederick
Lieber, Francis
Liebling, Emil
Lienau, Detlef
Lilienthal, Max
Lindenkohl, Adolph
Lindheimer, Ferdinand Jacob
List, Georg Friedrich
Listemann, Bernhard
Loeb, Jacques
Loeb, Leo
Loewi, Otto
Lovejoy, Arthur Oncken
Lubitsch, Ernst
Ludwick, Christopher
Maas, Anthony J.
McClellan, George Brinton
Maisch, John Michael
Mann, William Julius
Mansfield, Richard
Marcuse, Herbert
Marwedel, Emma Jacobina Christiana
Maschke, Heinrich
Mattheissen, Frederick William
Melsheimer, Friedrick Valentin
Memminger, Christopher Gustavus
Mendelsohn, Erich (*or* Eric)
Mergenthaler, Ottmar
Mergler, Marie Josepha
Merz, Karl
Metz, Christian
Meyer, Henry Coddington
Meyerhof, Otto
Michaelis, Leonor
Michelson, Albert Abraham
Mies van der Rohe, Ludwig
Miller, John Henry
Miller, John Peter
Mohr, Charles Theodore
Moldehuke, Edward Frederick
Möllhausen, Heinrich Baldwin
Mombert, Jacob Isidor
Moosmüller, Oswald William
Morgenthau, Hans Joachim
Morgenthau, Henry
Morris, Nelson

Morwitz, Edward
Most, Johann Joseph
Mühlenberg, Henry Melchior
Müller, Wilhelm Max
Munch, Charles
Mundé, Paul Fortunatus
Münsterberg, Hugo
Nast, Thomas
Nast, William
Neidhard, Charles
Nessler, Karl Ludwig
Neuendorff, Adolph Heinrich Anton Magnus
Ney, Elisabet
Nicolay, John George
Niedringhaus, Frederick Gottlieb
Niemeyer, John Henry
Nies, Konrad
Noeggerath, Emil Oscar Jacob Bruno
Nordheimer, Isaac
Nordhoff, Charles
Notz, Frederick William Augustus
Oberhoffer, Emil Johann
Ochs, Julius
Oertel, Johannes Adam Simon
Orthwein, Charles F.
Osterhaus, Peter Joseph
Ottendorfer, Anna Behr Uhl
Otterbein, Philip William
Otto, Bodo
Overman, Frederick
Panofsky, Erwin
Pastorius, Francis Daniel
Perabo, Johann Ernst
Peters, Christian Henry Frederick
Phisterer, Frederick
Pieper, Franz August Otto
Piez, Charles
Pollard, Joseph Percival
Post, Christian Frederick
Preetorius, Emil
Priber, Christian
Pulte, Joseph Hippolyt
Pursh, Frederick
Rademacher, Hans
Raht, August Wilhelm
Rapp, George
Rapp, Wilhelm
Rattermann, Heinrich Armin
Rauch, Frederick Augustus
Raue, Charles Gottlieb
Reed, John, 1757–1845
Reichenbach, Hans
Reisinger, Hugo
Reitzel, Robert
Rese, Frederick
Reuling, George
Reuter, Dominic
Rice, Charles
Rice, Isaac Leopold
Rieger, Johann Georg Joseph Anton
Rittenhouse, William
Robinson, Therese Albertine Louise Von Jakob
Rock, John
Roebling, John Augustus
Roemer, Karl Ferdinand
Roselius, Christian
Rummel, Joseph Francis
Saenderl, Simon
Sapir, Edward
Schaeberle, John Martin
Schaeffer, Frederick David
Schauffler, William Gottlieb
Scheel, Fritz
Schem, Alexander Jacob
Scheve, Edward Benjamin
Schieren, Charles Adolph
Schiff, Jacob Henry
Schilling, Hugo Karl
Schindler, Kurt
Schindler, Solomon
Schirmer, Gustav
Schmidt, Arthur Paul
Schmidt, Friedrich August
Schmucker, John George
Schnauffer, Carl Heinrich
Schneider, George
Schneider, Theodore
Schneller, George Otto
Schnerr, Leander
Schocken, Theodore
Schoenheimer, Rudolf
Schoenhof, Jacob
Schöpf, Johann David
Schott, Charles Anthony
Schradieck, Henry
Schrembs, Joseph
Schultze, Augustus
Schurz, Carl
Schuttler, Peter
Seidensticker, Oswald
Seligman, Jesse
Seligman, Joseph
Seyffarth, Gustavus
Shean, Albert
Sieber, Al
Sigel, Franz
Sloss, Louis
Sobolewski, J. Friedrich Eduard
Soldan, Frank Louis
Solger, Reinhold
Sorge, Friedrich Adolph
Sower, Christopher, 1693–1758
Sower, Christopher, 1721–1784
Spaeth, Adolph
Spangenberg, Augustus Gottlieb
Spicker, Max
Spreckels, Claus
Stahlman, Edward Bushrod
Stallo, Johann Bernard
Stang, William
Steck, George
Steinert, Morris
Steinmetz, Charles Proteus
Steinway, Christian Friedrich Theodore
Steinway, Henry Engelhard
Steinway, William
Stern, Kurt Guenter
Stern, Otto
Stetefeldt, Carl August
Steuben, Friedrich Wilhelm Ludolf Gerhard Augustin, Baron von
Stiegel, Henry William
Stock, Frederick August
Stockhardt, Karl Georg
Stolberg, Benjamin
Straus, Isidor
Straus, Nathan
Straus, Oscar Solomon
Strubberg, Friedrich Armand
Struve, Gustav
Stuckenberg, John Henry Wilbrandt
Sulzberger, Mayer
Tannenberger, David
Taussig, Joseph Knefler
Teuber, Hans-Lukas ("Luke")
Thomas, Christian Friedrich Theodore
Tillich, Paul
Timken, Henry
Timm, Henry Christian
Tobani, Theodore Moses
Viereck, George Sylvester
Villard, Henry
Villard, Oswald Garrison
Volsk, Adalbert John
Von Wiegand, Karl Henry
Wachsmuth, Charles
Wagener, John Andreas
Wagner, Robert Ferdinand
Wallenda, Karl
Walter, Albert G.
Walter, Bruno
Walther, Carl Ferdinand Wilhelm
Warburg, Felix Moritz
Warburg, James Paul
Warburg, Paul Moritz
Waxman, Franz
Weber, Albert
Weber, Gustav Carl Erich
Weidenreich, Franz
Weidig, Adolf
Weill, Kurt
Weiser, Johann Conrad
Wernawag, Lewis
Wesselhoeft, Conrad
Weyl, Hermann
Wilczynski, Ernest Julius
Wildt, Rupert
Wimar, Carl
Wimmer, Boniface
Wislizenus, Frederick Adolph
Wistar, Caspar
Woerner, John Gabriel
Wolf, Innocent William
Wolf, Simon
Wolff, Kurt August Paul
Wolfsohn, Carl
Zakrzewska, Marie Elizabeth
Zenger, John Peter
Zentmayer, Joseph
Zeuner, Charles
Ziegler, David
Ziehn, Bernhard
Zinzendorf, Nicolaus Ludwig
Zuppke, Robert Carl

GHANA

Aggrey, James Emman Kwegyir

GIBRALTAR

Montrésor, John

GREECE

Anagnos, Michael
Athenagoras I
Benjamin, Samuel Greene Wheeler
Colvocoresses, George Musalas
Hearn, Lafcadio
Mitropoulos, Dimitri
Papanicolaou, George Nicholas
Skouras, George Panagiotes
Skouras, Spyros Panagiotes
Sophocles, Evangelinus Apostolides

GUATEMALA

Sarg, Tony

HONG KONG

Barrie, Wendy
Higgins, Marguerite

HUNGARY

Alexander, Franz Gabriel
Asboth, Alexander Sandor
Beck, Martin
Békésy, Georg Von
Curtiz, Michael
Ditrichstein, Leo
Farago, Ladislas
Fejos, Paul
Fleischmann, Charles Louis
Fox, William
Franklin, Fabian
Goldmark, Peter Carl
Haraszthy de Mokcsa, Agoston
Heilprin, Angelo
Joseffy, Rafael
Kaiser, Alvis
Karfiol, Bernard
Kiss, Max
Kohnt, Alexander
Kohut, George Alexander
Lorre, Peter
Lugosi, Bela
Pal, George
Pulitzer, Joseph
Rapaport, David
Reiner, Fritz
Roheim, Geza
Romberg, Sigmund
Schwimmer, Rosika
Seidl, Anton
Stahel, Julius
Stark, Louis
Szell, George
Szilard, Leo
Szold, Benjamin
Thorek, Max
Von Neumann, John
Weiss, Soma
Wise, Aaron
Wise, Stephen Samuel
Xántus, Jánas
Zukor, Adolph

ICELAND

Cahill, Holger

INDIA

Barrymore, Maurice
Bellew, Frank Henry Temple
Bruce, Andrew Alexander
Chandler, John Scudder
Fullerton, George Stuart
Hazen, Henry Allen
Huber, Gotthelf Carl
Hume, Robert Allen
Judd, Charles Hubbard
Judson, Adoniram Brown
Judson, Edward
Kennelly, Arthur Edwin
Leigh, Vivien
Mansell, William Albert
Oldham, William Fitzjames
Scudder, (Julia) Vida Dutton
Wyckoff, John Henry
Wyckoff, Walter Augustus

INDONESIA

(*See* Java)

IRAN

(*See* Persia)

IRELAND

Adair, James
Adrain, Robert
Alison, Francis
Amory, Thomas
Anthony, Sister
Argall, Philip
Armstrong, George Buchanan
Armstrong, John
Arthur, William
Azarias, Brother
Baird, Matthew
Barnwell, John
Barry, John
Barry, Patrick
Beatty, Charles Clinton
Binns, John
Blair, Samuel
Blair, William Richards
Blake, Mary Elizabeth McGrath
Blakely, Johnston
Bonner, Robert
Boucicault, Dion
Bowden, John
Breen, Patrick
Brenon, Herbert
Brent, George
Brougham, John
Brown, Alexander
Brown, George
Brown, James
Brown, John A.
Browne, John Ross
Bryan, George
Burk, John Daly
Burke, AEdanus
Burke, Thomas
Butler, Pierce
Butler, Richard
Butler, William
Byrne, Andrew
Byrne, John
Byrnes, Thomas F.
Campbell, Alexander
Campbell, Robert
Campbell, Thomas
Carey, Mathew
Carpenter, Stephen Cullen
Carr, Thomas Matthew
Cathcart, James Leander
Cathcart, William
Charless, Joseph
Clark, Daniel
Clarke, Sir Caspar Purdon
Clarke, Joseph Ignatius Constantine
Clarke, Mary Francis
Cleburne, Patrick Ronayne
Coate, Richard
Cockran, William Bourke
Colden, Cadwallader
Colles, Christopher
Collier, Peter Fenelon
Collins, Patrick Andrew
Colum, Padraic
Conaty, Thomas James
Condon, Thomas
Connolly, John
Connor, Patrick Edward
Conway, Thomas
Conwell, Henry
Conyngham, Gustavus
Cosby, William
Cox, Henry Hamilton
Crawford, John
Crawford, John Wallace
Croghan, George
Croker, Richard
Croly, David Goodman
Cudahy, Michael
Cuming, Fortescue
Daly, Charles Patrick
Daly, Marcus
Dalzell, Robert M.
Delany, Patrick Bernard
Devoy, John
Digges, Dudley
Dinsmoor, Robert
Dobbs, Arthur
Donahue, Patrick
Dongan, Thomas
Donlevy, Brian
Donnelly, Charles Francis
Dornin, Thomas Aloysius
Drew, John
Dripps, Isaac L.
Drumgoole, John Christopher
Duane, William John
Dulany, Daniel
Dunlap, John
Egan, Michael
Elliott, Charles
Embury, Philip
Emmet, Thomas Addis
England, John
Erskine, John
Evans, William Thomas
Fair, James Graham
Farley, John Murphy
Feehan, Patrick Augustine

Ffrench, Charles Dominic
Field, Joseph M.
Findley, William
Finley, Samuel
Fitzgerald, Edward
Fitzpatrick, John
Fitzpatrick, Thomas
Fitzsimmons or Fitzsimins, Thomas
Flanagan, Edward Joseph
Flannery, John
Ford, Patrlck
Fox, Richard Kyle
Francis, Tench
Gaine, Hugh
Galberry, Thomas
Gallagher, Hugh Patrick
Gallier, James
Garrett, Robert
Garrigan, Philip Joseph
Gillman, Henry
Gilmore, Patrick Sarsfield
Glennon, John Joseph
Godkin, Edwin Lawrence
Goff, John William
Good, John
Grace, William Russell
Gregg, John Robert
Hackett, Francis
Hall, Bolton
Hall, John
Halpine, Charles Graham
Hamilton, Edward John
Hand, Edward
Harpur, Robert
Haughery, Margaret Gaffney
Heck, Barbara
Hennessy, John
Hennessy, William John
Henry, John, 1746–1794
Henry, John, fl. 1807–1820
Herbert, Victor
Heron, Matilda Agnes
Heron, William
Hill, William
Hoban, James
Hogan, John
Hogun, James
Holland, John Philip
Hopkins, John Henry
Hovenden, Thomas
Hudson, Edward
Hughes, John Joseph
Hunter, Thomas
Hunter, Whiteside Godfrey
Ingham, Charles Cromwell
Inglis, Charles
Ireland, John, 1838–1918
Irvine, William
Johnson, Guy
Johnson, Sir William
Jones, Mary Harris
Jordan, Kate
Judge, William Quan
Julia, Sister
Keane, John Joseph
Kearney, Denis
Keating, John McLeod
Kelley, Eugene
Kelly, Myra
Kennedy, Robert Foster
Kenrick, Francis Patrick
Kenrick, Peter Richard
Keppel, Frederick
Kerens, Richard C.
Kerfoot, John Barrett
Kinsella, Thomas
Knox, Samuel
Laffan, William Mackay
Lane, Walter Paye
Leighton, William
Levins, Thomas C.
Lewis, Andrew
Logan, James, 1674–1751
Loudon, Samuel
Lynch, Patrick Neeson
Lyon, Matthew
Lyons, Peter
Lyster, Henry Francis Le Hunte
McAuley, Jeremiah
McAuley, Thomas
McBurney, Robert Ross
McCaine, Alexander
McCarroll, James
McClure, George
McClure, Samuel Sidney
McCormack, John Francis
McCosh, Andrew James
McCullagh, Joseph Burbridge
McCullough, John
McDonald, John Bartholomew
McElroy, John
McFaul, James Augustine
McGrath, James
McGrath, Matthew J.
McGuire, Charles Bonaventure
McHenry, James, 1753–1816
McHenry, James, 1785–1845
Mackay, John William
McKenna, Charles Hyacinth
Mackenzie, Robert Shelton
McKinly, John
McMahon, Bernard
McManes, James
McNeill, Hector
MacNeven, William James
McNicholas, John Timothy
McNulty, Frank Joseph
McNutt, Alexander
MacSparran, James
McVickar, John
Maginnis, Charles Donagh
Makemie, Francis
Mallet, John William
Malone, Sylvester
Maloney, Martin
Marshall, Christopher
Martin, Henry Newell
Matthews, Washington
Maxwell, William
Maxwell, William Henry
Meagher, Thomas Francis
Milligan, Robert
Milmore, Martin
Minty, Robert Horatio George
Mitchel, John
Montgomery, Richard
Moore, James, d. 1706
Moore, John, 1834–1901
Moriarity, Patrick Eugene
Morrissey, John
Moylan, Stephen
Mulholland St. Clair Augustin
Mulholland William
Mulligan, Charles J.
Murphy, Francis
Murphy, John
Murray, Joseph
Nesbitt, John Maxwell
Niblo, William
O'Brien, Fitz-James
O'Brien, Matthew Anthony
O'Brien, William Shoney
O'Callaghan, Edmund Bailey
O'Callaghan, Jeremiah
O'Connor, James
O'Connor, Michael
O'Dwyer, William
O'Fallon, James
O'Hara, James
O'Leary, Daniel
Oliver, George Tener
Oliver, Henry William
O'Mahony, John
O'Neill, James
O'Neill, John
O'Reilly, Alexander
O'Reilly, Henry
O'Reilly, John Boyle
Orr, Alexander Ector
O'Shaughnessy, Michael Maurice
Owen, William Florence
Paterson, William
Patterson, Robert, 1743–1824
Patterson, Robert, 1792–1881
Patterson, Thomas MacDonald
Patterson, William
Phelan, James
Pollock, Oliver
Porter, Alexander
Potamian, Brother
Potter, James
Power, John
Purcell, John Baptist
Quarter, William
Quill, Michael Joseph
Rainsford, William Stephen
Ramage, John
Read, George Campbell
Rehan, Ada
Reid, Thomas Mayne
Rhea, John
Roach, John
Roberts, William Randall
Robinson, Stuart
Robinson, William
Robinson, William Erigena
Roche, James Jeffrey
Rowan, Stephen Clegg
Russell, Mother Mary Baptist
Ryan, Cornelius John ("Connie")
Ryan, Edward George
Ryan, Patrick John
Sadlier, Denis
Sadlier, Mary Anne Madden
Saint-Gaudens, Augustus
Sampson, William
Savage, John
Scantan, Lawrence
Sewall, William Joyce
Shaw, John, 1773–1823

Sheedy, Dennis
Shields, James
Sloan, Samuel
Smith, James, 1719–1806
Smyth, Alexander
Smyth, Thomas
Snow, Carmel White
Sproule, William
Stephenson, John
Sterling, James
Stewart, Alexander Turney
Strawbridge, Robert
Summersby, Kathleen Helen ("Kay")
Sweeny, Thomas William
Syng, Philip
Taggart, Thomas
Teggart, Frederick John
Tennent, Gilbert
Tennent, William, 1673–1745
Tennent, William, 1705–1777
Teresa, Mother
Thompson, Hugh Miller
Thompson, Launt
Thompson, Robert Ellis
Thompson, William
Thomson, Charles
Thornton, Matthew
Tobin, Daniel Joseph
Turner, William
Vaughan, Daniel
Waddel, James
Waddell, Hugh
Walsh, Michael
Warden, David Bailie
Warren, Sir Peter
Wilde, Richard Henry
Williams, Barney
Wood, James J.
Wright, James Lendrew
Wylie, Samuel Brown
Yorke, Peter Christopher
Young, John Russell

ITALY

Adonis, Joe
Amateis, Louis
Andreis, Andrew James Felix Bartholomew de
Angeli, Pier
Ascoli, Max
Atlas, Charles S.
Baccaloni, Salvatore
Barsotti, Charles
Bayma, Joseph
Bellanca, Giuseppe Mario
Bemelmans, Ludwig
Botta, Vincenzo
Boucher, Horace Edward
Brumidi, Constantino
Bruno, Angelo
Cabrini, Francis Xavier
Caruso, Enrico
Cataldo, Joseph Maria
Cesnola, Luigi Palma di
Chiera, Edward
Clevenger, Shobal Vail
Corey, Lewis
Costello, Frank
Crawford, Francis Marion
Da Ponte, Lorenzo
De Luca, Giuseppe
De Palma, Ralph
De Paolis, Alessio
Dodd, Bella Visono
Dundee, Johnny
Faccioli, Giuseppe
Fermi, Enrico
Finotti, Joseph Maria
FitzgeraJd, Alice Louise Florence
Foresti, Eleutario Felice
Galli-Curci, Amelita
Gambino, Carlo
Gatti-Casazza, Giulio
Genovese, Vito
Giovannitti, Arturo
Hadfield. George
Kino, Eusebio Francisco
Langdon, Courtney
Lebrun, Federico ("Rico")
Legler, Henry Eduard
Luchese, Thomas
Luciano, Charles ("Lucky")
Mackubin, Florence
Martinelli, Giovanni
Marzo, Eduardo
Mazzachelli, Samuel Charles
Mazzei, Philip
Mengarini, Gregory
Morais, Sabato
Morini, Austin John
Nobili, John
Palladino, Lawrence Benedict
Patri, Angelo
Pecora, Ferdinand
Pei, Mario Andrew
Pinza, Ezio
Profaci, Joseph
Ravalli, Antonio
Ricca, Paul
Rosati, Joseph
Sacco, Nicola
Sardi, Melchiorre Pio Vencenzo ("Vincent")
Sargent, John Singer
Sestini, Benedict
Seton, Robert
Stella, Joseph
Tagliabue, Giuseppe
Toscanini, Arturo
Trajetta, Philip
Tresca, Carlo
Vanzetti, Bartolomeo
Vigo, Joseph Maria Francesco
Vitale, Ferruccio
Walsh, Henry Collins
Yon, Pietro Alessandro

JAMAICA

Garvey, Marcus Moziah
McKay, Claude

JAPAN

Greene, Jerome Davis
Hartmann, Carl Sadakichi
Hayakawa, Sessue
Kuniyoshi, Yasuo
Landis, James McCauley
Noguchi, Hideyo
Sugiura, Kanematsu
Takamine, Jokichi
Verbeck, William

JAVA

Norden, Carl Lukas

LATVIA

Bellanca, Dorothy Jacobs
Davidoff, Leo Max
Halsman, Philippe
Moisseiff, Leon Solomon
Sterne, Maurice

LITHUANIA

Berenson, Bernard
Berenson, Senda
Bloomgarden, Solomon
Godowsky, Leopold
Goldman, Emma
Hillman, Sidney
Laurence, William Leonard
Lipchitz, Jacques
Myerson, Abraham
Sachs, Alexander
Sack, Israel
Schereschewsky, Samuel Isaac Joseph
Schlesinger, Benjamin
Shahn, Benjamin ("Ben")
Silver, Abba Hillel
Winchevsky, Morris
Wolfson, Harry Austryn
Zorach, William

LUXEMBOURG

Gernsback, Hugo
Steichen, Edward Jean
Woll, Matthew

MARSHALL ISLANDS

Gulick, Sidney Lewis

MEXICO

Font, Pedro
Kiam, Omar
Larrazolo, Octaviano Ambrosio
Limón, José Arcadio
Novarro, Ramon
Oñate, Juan de

MORAVIA

Gödel, Kurt Friedrich
Lindenthal, Gustav
Maretzek, Max
Nitschmann, David
Sealsfield, Charles
Zeisberger, David

NETHERLANDS

Bayard, Nicholas
Behrends, Adolphus Julius Frederick
Block, Adriaen
Boelen, Jacob
Bogardus, Everardus
Bok, Edward William
Burnet, William
Cazenove, Théophile
Covode, John
Cuyler, Theodore
Debye, Peter Joseeh William
De Haas, John Philip
De Lamar, Joseph Raphael
De Leeuw, Adolph Lodewyk
D'ooge, Martin Luther
Dupratz, Antoine Simon Le Page
Dusser de Barenne, Joannes Gregorius
Dykstra, John
Freeman, Bernardus
Gallitzin, Demetrius Augustine
Goudsmit, Samuel Abraham
Haagen-Smit, Arie Jan
Henny, David Christiaan
Hudde, Andries
Huidekoper, Harm Jan
Isaacs, Samuel Myer
Jansen, Reinier
Kieft, Willem
Krol, Bastiaen Jansen
Kuiper, Gerard Peter
Le Roux, Bartholomew
Mappa, Adam Gerard
Matthes, Gerard Hendrik
Megapolensis, Johannes
Michaëlius, Jonas
Minuit, Peter
Morton, Nathaniel
Muste, Abraham Johannes
Peter, John Frederick
Philipse, Frederick
Romans, Bernard
Scholte, Hendrik Peter
Schrieck, Sister Louise Van Der
Selijns, Henricus
Steendam, Jacob
Steenwyck, Cornelis
Stuyvesant, Petrus
Troost, Gerard
Van Beuren, Johannes
Van Cortlandt, Oloff Stevenszen
Van Curler, Arent
Van Der Donck, Adriaen
Van Der Kemp, Francis Adrian
Van Ilpendam, Jan Jansen
Van Loon, Hendrik Willem
Van Raalte, Albertus Christiaan
Van Rensselaer, Nicholas
Van Twiller, Wouter
Verbeck, Guido Herman Fridolin
Verwyst, Chrysostom Adrian
Voorsanger, Jacob
Wilhelmina

NORWAY

Balchen, Bernt
Barth, Carl Georg Lange
Boyesen, Hjalmar Hjorth
Dahl, Theodor Halvorson
Dietrichson, Johannes Wilhelm Christian
Eielsen, Elling
Furuseth, Andrew
Hanson, James Christian Meinich
Haugen, Nils Pederson
Henie, Sonja
Hoyme, Gjermund
Janson, Kristofer Nagel
Johnsen, Erik Kristian
Kildahl, Johan Nathan
Knutson, Harold
Koren, Ulrik Vilhelm
Larsen, Peter Laurentius
Larson, Laurence Marcellus
Lie, Jonas
Lundeberg, Harry
Mallory, Anna Margrethe ("Molla") Bjurstedt
Nelson, Knute
Nelson, Nelson Olsen
Oftedal, Sven
Onsager, Lars
Owre, Alfred
Peerson, Cleng
Reiersen, Johan Reinert
Rockne, Knute Kenneth
Rõlvaag, Ole Edvart
Rynning, Ole
Stejneger, Leonhard Hess
Sverdrup, Georg
Tapper, Bertha Feiring
Tou, Erik Hansen
Wergeland, Agnes Mathilde

PALESTINE

Hirschensohn, Chaim

PERSIA

Labaree, Leonard Woods
Mitchell, Lucy Myers Wright
Oldfather, William Abbott
Shedd, William Ambrose
Wright, John Henry

PERU

Peñalosa Briceño, Diego Dioniso de

PHILIPPINES

Quezon, Manuel Luis

POLAND

(*See also* Silesia)

Baruch, Simon
Barzynski, Vincent
Belkin, Samuel
Blaustein, David
Dabrowski, Joseph
Damrosch, Leopold
Friedlaender, Israel
Funk, Casimir
Glueck, Sheldon ("Sol")
Goldin, Horace
Goldwyn, Samuel
Gray, Gilda
Gurowski, Adam
Hecht, Selig
Heilprin, Michael
Heschel, Abraham Joshua
Hodur, Francis
Hofmann, Josef Casimir
Jastrow, Joseph
Jastrow, Marcus
Jastrow, Morris
Kosciuszko, Tadeusz Andrzej Bonawentura
Krueger, Walter
Landowska, Wanda Aleksandra
Loewenthal, Isidor
London, Meyer
Lotka, Alfred James
Lubin, David
Modjeska, Helena
Modjeski, Ralph
Nadelman, Elie
Neumann, Franz Leopold
Perlman, Selig
Poznanski, Gustavus
Pulaski, Casimir
Radin, Max
Radin, Paul
Rose, Alex
Rose, Ernestine Louise Siismondi Potowski
Rosenblatt, Bernard Abraham
Rosenfeld, Morris
Rosenthal, Max
Rubinstein, Helena
Salomon, Haym
Schneiderman, Rose
Schultz, Henry
Schwidetzky, Oscar Otto Rudolf
Singer, Israel Joshua
Stokes, Rose Harriet Pastor
Szyk, Arthur
Warner, Harry Morris
Wiener, Leo
Znaniecki, Florian Witold

PORTUGAL

Benavides, Alonzo de
Cabrillo, Juan Rodriguez
De Kay, James Ellsworth
Lopez, Aaron
Lumbrozo, Jacob
Miranda, Carmen

ROMANIA

Bickel, Alexander Mordecai
Bloomfield, Meyer
Covici, Pascal ("Pat")
Culbertson, Ely
Gluck, Alma
Kneisel, Franz
Liebowitz, Samuel Simon
Renaldo, Duncan
Robinson, Edward G.
Schechter, Solomon

RUSSIA

Abel, Rudolf Ivanovich
Adler, Polly
Adler, Sara
Annenberg, Moses Louis
Antin, Mary
Archipenko, Alexander
Aronson, Boris Solomon
Artzybasheff, Boris
Baranov, Alexander Andreevich
Berkman, Alexander
Bernstein, Herman
Billikopf, Jacob
Blavatsky, Helena Petrovna Hahn
Bolm, Adolph Rudolphovitch
Boudin, Louis Boudinoff
Brenner, Victor David
Cahan, Abraham
Carter, Boake
Casanowicz, Immanuel Moses
Chaliapin, Boris Fyodorovich
Chotzinoff, Samuel
Cist, Charles
Cohen, Morris Raphael
Cooke, Samuel
Davidson, Israel
De Seversky, Alexander Procofieff
Dobzhansky, Theodosius Grigorievich
Duke, Vernon
Eglevsky, André Yevgenyevich
Ehrlich, Arnold Bogamil
Elman, Mischa
Enelow, Hyman Gerson
Epstein, Abraham
Fokine, Michel
Freeman, Joseph
Friedman, William Frederick
Gabo, Naum
Gabrilowitsch, Ossip
Gamow, George
Gest, Morris
Goerz, David
Goldenweiser, Alexander Alexandrovich
Goldenweiser, Emanuel Alexander
Golder, Frank Alfred
Goldfine, Bernard
Gomberg, Moses
Gordin, Jacob
Guzik, Jack
Halpert, Edith Gregor
Hansburg, George Bernard
Herberg, Will
Hillquit, Morris
Hindus, Maurice Gerschon
Hirschbein, Peretz
Hourwich, Isaac Aaronovich
Hubert, Conrad
Hurok, Solomon Isaievitch
Ioasaf
Innokentiĭ
Jolson, Al
Kharasch, Morris Selig
Kostelanetz, Andre
Koussevitzky, Olga Naumoff
Koussevitzky, Serge Alexandrovich
Kunitz, Moses
Kuskov, Ivan Aleksandrovich
Lang, Lucy Fox Robins
Launitz, Robert Eberhard Schmidt Von Der
Leonty, Metropolitan
Levene, Phoebus Aaron Theodore
Lhévinne, Rosina
Lipman, Jacob Goodale
Loeb, Sophie Irene Simon
Loskiel, George Henry
Margalis, Max Leopold
Masliansky, Zvi Hirsch
Mayer, Louis Burt
Mears, Otto
Meltzer, Samuel James
Mosessohn, David Nehemiah
Nabokov, Nicolas
Nabokov, Vladimir Vladimirovich
Nazimova, Alla
Osten Sacken, Carl Robert Romanovich Von Der
Ostromislensky, Iwan Iwanowich
Paley, John
Pasvolsky, Leo
Piatigorsky, Gregor
Potofsky, Jacob Samuel
Price, George Moses
Rachmaninoff, Sergei Vasilyevich
Rahv, Philip
Revel, Bernard
Rezanov, Nikolai Petrovich
Romanoff, Michael ("Prince Mike")
Rombro, Jacob
Romeike, Henry
Ropes, John Codman
Rosen, Joseph A.
Rosenberg, Abraham Hayyim
Rosenblatt, Joseph
Rosenthal, Herman
Rostovtzeff, Michael Ivanovitch
Rothko, Mark
Rubinow, Isaac Max
Sachs, Theodore Bernard
Sanders, George
Sandler, Jacob Koppel
Sarnoff, David
Saslavsky, Alexander
Schenck, Nicholas Michael
Schillinger, Joseph
Schomer, Nahum Meir
Schwartz, Maurice
Selikovitsch, Goetzel
Shelekhov, Grigorii Ivanovich
Shub, Abraham David
Shubert, Lee
Sidis, Boris
Sikorsky, Igor Ivanovich
Siloti, Alexander Ilyitch
Soyer, Moses
Spewack, Samuel
Spivak, Charles David
Sternberg, Constantin Ivanovich Edler von
Steuben, John
Stone, Abraham
Stravinsky, Igor Fyodorovich
Strunsky, Simeon
Struve, Otto
Tamarkin, Jacob David
Tamiroff, Akim
Tchelitchew, Pavel
Tiomkin, Dimitri
Tourel, Jennie
Tucker, Sophie
Vasiliev, Afexander Alexandrovich
Vladeck, Baruch Charney
Vladimiroff, Pierre
Vogrich, Max Wilhelm Karl
Waksman, Selman Abraham
Weber, Max
Woytinsky, Wladimir Savelievich
Yellin, Samuel
Zevin, Israel Joseph
Zilboorg, Gregory
Zunser, Eliakum

SCOTLAND

Abercromby, James
Adie, David Craig
Affleck, Thomas
Ainslie, Hew
Aitken, Robert
Alexander, Abraham
Alexander, James
Allan, John
Armour, Thomas Dickson ("Tommy")
Arthur, Peter M.
Auchmuty, Robert
Audsley, George Ashdown
Bain, George Luke Scobie
Barr, Charles
Bell, Alexander Graham
Bell, Alexander Melville
Bell, Eric Temple
Bell, Robert
Bennett, James Gordon
Bishop, Robert Hamilton
Blair, James
Brackenridge, Hugh Henry
Brackenridge, William D.
Brown, William
Brownlee, William Craig
Bruce, George
Bruce, Robert
Buchanan, Thomas
Burden, Henry
Callender, James Thomson
Calvin, Samuel
Cameron, Archibald
Campbell, Charles Macfie
Campbell, George Washington
Campbell, John
Carnegie, Andrew
Clarke, Robert
Craik, James
Crisp, Donald
Crooks, Ramsay
Crosser, Robert
Cushny, Arthur Robertson
Davidson, Thomas
Dickie, George William
Dickson, Robert
Dollar, Robert
Donahue, Peter
Douglass, William
Dow, Alex
Dowie, John Alexander
Dunbar, Robert

Dunbar, William
Duncan, James
Dunmore, John Murray
Dunwiddie, Robert
Eckford, Henry
Elmslie, George Grant
Erskine, Robert
Fairlie, John Archibald
Finlay, Hugh
Fleming, John
Fleming, William
Fleming, Williamina Paton Stevens
Forbes, John, 1710–1759
Forbes, John, d. 1783
Forbes, John, 1769–1823
Forgan, James Berwick
Garden, Alexander
Garden, Mary
Geddes, James Loraine
Gilmour, Richard
Goold, William A.
Gordon, George Angier
Gowans, William
Graham, Isabella Marshall
Graham, James
Graham, John
Grieve, Miller
Hall, David
Hamilton, Alexander
Hamilton, Andrew
Harkness, William
Hart, James MacDougal
Hart, William
Henderson, Daniel McIntyre
Henderson, David Bremner
Henderson, Peter
Hewat, Alexander
Highet, Gilbert
Humphreys, Alexander Crombie
Hunter, Robert
Jamison, David
Johnston, Gabriel
Johnston, John, 1791–1880
Johnston, John, 1881–1950
Johnston, Samuel
Jones, John Paul
Kane, John
Keith, George
Keith, Sir William, 1680–1749
Keith, William, 1839–1911
Kemp, James
Kemp, John
Kennedy, Archibald
Kennedy, John Stewart
Kidd, William
Laurie, James
Lawson, Alexander
Lawson, Andrew Cowper
Lawson, James
Leiper, Thomas
Lining, John
Livingston, Robert
Lockhart, Charles
Lorimer, George Claude
Loudoun, John Campbell, Earl of
Lowrie, Walter
Lundie, John
Lyall, James
Macalester, Charles, 1765–1832
MacAlister, James
McArthur, John, 1823–1890
McArthur, John, 1826–1906
McCallum, Daniel Craig
McCosh, James
McDougall, Alexander, 1732–1786
McDougall, Alexander, 1845–1923
Macintosh, Douglas Clyde
McIntosh, Lachlan
MacIver, Robert Morrison
Mackay, James
Mackellar, Patrick
Mackenzie, Donald
Mackenzie, George Henry
Mackenzie, James Cameron
Mackenzie, Kenneth
Mackenzie, Murdo
McLaren, John
Maclaurin, Richard Cockburn
Maclean, John
McLeod, Alexander
Maclure, William
McTammany, John
MacVicar, Malcolm
Mantell, Robert Bruce
Matthews, William
Maxwell, Hugh
Melish, John
Mercer, Hugh
Michie, Peter Smith
Minto, Walter
Mitchell, Alexander
Mitchell, David Brydie
Moffat, James Clement
Moffatt, James
Montgomery, Edmund Duncan
Montrésor, James Gabriel
Muir, John
Munro, Henry
Murray, Philip
Murray, Robert
Nairne, Thomas
Neilson, William Allan
Nisbet, Charles
Ogilvie, James
Oliver, James
Orr, Hugh
Owen, David Dale
Owen, Robert Dale
Panton, William
Patillo, Henry
Patterson, James Kennedy
Pattison, Granville Sharp
Phillips, William Addison
Phyfe, Duncan
Pinkerton, Allan
Pitcairn, John, 1722–1775
Pitcairn, John, 1841–1916
Rae, John
Ramsay, Alexander
Redpath, James
Reid, David Boswell
Rhind, Charles
Ritchie, Alexander Hay
Robertson, Archibald
Robertson, James, b. 1740
Robertson, William Spence
Ross, Alexander
Russell, William
St. Clair, Arthur
Sandeman, Robert
Saunders, William
Schouler, William
Scott, Walter
Seth, James
Sharp, John
Shirlaw, Walter
Skene, Alexander Johnston Chalmers
Smibert, John
Smillie, James
Smith, Alexander
Smith, George
Smith, Robert, 1722–1777
Smith, Russell
Smith, William, 1727–1803
Smith, William, 1754–1821
Sprunt, James
Stephens, Henry Morse
Stobo, Robert
Stuart, Charles Macaulay
Stuart, John
Stuart, Robert
Swan, James
Swinton, John
Swinton, William
Taylor, William Mackergo
Telfair, Edward
Thomson, John
Thorburn, Grant
Turnbull, Andrew
Vetch, Samuel
Watson, Andrew
Wenley, Robert Mark
White, Alexander
William, Charles
Williamson, Andrew
Williamson, Charles
Wilson, Alexander
Wilson, James, 1742–1798
Wilson, James, 1836–1920
Wilson, James Grant
Wilson, Peter
Wilson, William
Wilson, William Bauchop
Winton, Alexander
Witherspoon, John
Wood, John
Wright, Frances

SIAM

Chang and Eng

SILESIA

Courant, Richard
Damrosch, Frank Heino
Gratz, Barnard
Gratz, Michael
Mannes, Clara Damrosch
Mayer, Maria Goeppert
Pelz, Paul Johannes
Prang, Louis
Reichel, Charles Gotthold
Schwarz, Eugene Amandus

SOUTH AFRICA

Rathbone, Basil

SOVIET UNION

(*See* Russia)

SPAIN

Alemany, José Sadoc
Antoine, Père
Anza, Juan Bautista de
Ayala, Juan Manuel de
Ayllon, Lucas Vasquez de
Bori, Lucrezia
Cárdenas, García Lópéz de
Casals, Pablo
Copley, Thomas
Coronado, Francisco Vásquez
Costansó, Miguel
Cubero, Pedro Rodríquez
De Soto, Hernando
De Vargas, Zapata y Lujan Ponce de Leon, Diego
Escalante, Silvestre Velez de
Espejo, Antonio de
Fages, Pedro
Ferrero, Edward
Garcés, Francisco Tomás Hermenegildo
Gálvez, Bernardo de
Gayoso de Lemos, Manuel
Iglesias, Santiago
Iturbi, José
Luna y Arellano, Tristan de
Meade, George Gordon
Meade, Richard Worsam
Menéndez, De Aviles Pedro
Miró, Esteban Rodríquez
Montgomery, George Washington
Moscoso De Alvarado, Luis de
Narváez, Panfilo de
Núñez, Cabeza De Vaca, Alvar
Nunó, Jaime
Ponce De León, Juan
Portolá, Gaspar de
Santayana, George
Tamarón, Pedro
Ulloa, Antonio de
Villagrá, Gaspar Pérez de
Viccaíno, Sebastián

SRI LANKA

(*See* Ceylon)

SURINAM

(*See* Dutch Guiana)

SWEDEN

Acrelius, Israel
Anderson, Mary
Campanius, John
Carlson, Anton Julius
Cesare, Oscar Edward
Dylander, John
Edgren, August Hjalmar
Ericsson, John
Esbjörn, Lars Paul
Fersen, Hans Axel, Count Von
Folin, Otto Knut Olof
Hasselquist, Tuve Nilsson
Hesselius, Gustavus
Johnson, Magnus
Leipzig, Nate
Lind, John
Lindberg, Charles Augustus
Lindberg, Conrad Emil
Lindgren, Waldemar
Lundin, Carl Axel Robert
Mattson, Hans
Norelius, Eric
Ockerson, John Augustus
Printz, Johan Björnsson
Raphall, Morris Jacob
Reuterdahl, Henry
Rising, Johan Classon
Rydberg, Per Axel
Schele De Vere, Maximilian
Schmidt, Nathaniel
Seashore, Carl Emil
Sellstedt, Lars Gustaf
Swenson, David Ferdinand
Thulstrup, Bror Thure
Udden, Johan August
Widforss, Gunnar Mauritz

SWITZERLAND

Agassiz, Alexander
Agassiz, Jean Louis Rodolphe
Ammann, Othmar Hermann
Bandelier, Adolph Francis Alphonse
Bapst, John
Behrend, Bernard Arthur
Bloch, Ernest
Boll, Jacob
Bouquet, Henry
Bucher, John Conrad
Cajori, Florian
Cramer, Michael John
Delmonico, Lorenzo
Dufour, John James
Du Simitière, Pierre Eugène
Faesch, John Jacob
Gallatin, Abraham Alfonse Albert
Ganz, Rudolph
Gatschet, Albert Samuel
Goetschius, John Henry
Gold, Harry ("Raymond")
Graffenried, Christopher
Gratiot, Charles
Guggenheim, Meyer
Gutherz, Carl
Guyot, Arnold Henry
Hailmann, William Nicholas
Hassler, Ferdinand Rudolph
Henni, John Martin
Hoch, August
Kruesi, John
Krüsi, Johann Heinrich Hermann
Lang, Henry Roseman
Lesquereux, Leo
Martel, Charles
Marty, Martin
Menetrey, Joseph
Messmer, Sebastian Gebhard
Meyer, Adolf
Ming, John Joseph
Nef, John Ulric
Olmsted, John Charles
Pfister, Alfred
Piccard, Jean Félix
Pourtalès, Louis François de
Purry, Jean Pierre
Rosenberg, Henry
Schaff, Philip
Schinz, Albert
Schlatter, Michael
Seiler, Carl
Senn, Nicholas
Shaw, Pauline Agassiz
Smith, John Eugene
Sterki, Victor
Theus, Jeremiah
Troye, Edward
Vanderbilt, Gloria Morgan
Weidenmann, Jacob
Wirt, William
Zimmerman, Eugene
Zubly, John Joachim

SYRIA

Adams, Walter Sydney
Bliss, Frederick Jones
Bliss, Howard Sweetser
Dennis, Alfred Lewis Pinneo
Smith, Benjamin Eli

THAILAND

(*See also* Siam)

McFarland, George Bradley

TURKEY

Bliss, Edwin Munsell
Bliss, William Dwight Porter
Brewer, David Josiah
Callimachos, Panos Demetrios
Dwight, Henry Otis
Frame, Alice Seymour Browne
Goodell, Henry Hill
Gorky, Arshile
Gregory, Menas Sarkas Boulgourjian
Grosvenor, Edwin Prescott
Grosvenor, Gilbert Hovey
Jackson, Edward Payson
Johnston, Henry Phelps
Rafinesque, Constantine Samuel
Schauffler, Henry Albert
Van Lennep, Henry John
Van Lennep, William Bird
Von Ruck, Karl
Williams, Talcott
Zachos, John Celivergos

VIRGIN ISLANDS

Behn, Sosthenes
Crosswaith, Frank Rudolph
Morón, Alonzo Graseano

WALES

Coke, Thomas
Davies, John Vipond

Davis, James John
Easton, John
Easton, Nicholas
Evans, Evan
Evans, John
Everett, Robert
Gardiner, John Sylvester John
Griffith, Benjamin
Hughes, Price
Jones, Evan William
Jones, Jenkin Lloyd
Jones, John Peter
Jones, Samuel Milton
Langner, Lawrence
Lewis, Francis
Lloyd, David
Lloyd, Thomas
Morgan, Abel
Moxham, Arthur James
Nicholson, John
Owen, Griffith
Plumbe, John
Powell, Snelling
Pugh, Ellis
Rees, James
Reese, Abram
Reese, Isaac
Reese, Jacob
Rhees, Morgan John
Roberts, William Charles
Roberts, William Henry
Shelby, Evan
Smith, William Henry, 1806–1872
Stanley, Henry Morton
Templeton, Alec Andrew
Thomas, David
Williams, John Elias

WEST INDIES

Alarcón, Hernando De
Audubon, John James
Benjamin, Judah Philip
Berg, Joseph Frederic
Currier, Charles Warren
Da Costa, Jacob Mendez
Dallas, Alexander James
D'avezac, Auguste Geneviève Valentin
Davis, John
Du Bourg, Louis Guillaume Valentin
Dyett, Thomas Ben
Finlay, Carlos Juan
Fitzgerald, Desmond
Fletcher, Alice Cunningham
Fraunces, Samuel
Fuertes, Estevan Antonio
Gorringe, Henry Honeychurch
Guiteras, Juan
Hamilton, Alexander
Holland, William Jacob
Hunt, Isaac
Larrínaga, Tulio
Lowndes, Rawlins
Mallory, Stephen Russell
Markoe, Abraham
Markoe, Peter
Martin, Josiah
Mendes, Frederic De Sola
Menocal, Aniceto Garcia
Moore, Sir Henry
Moreau de Saint-Méry, Médéric-Louis-Élie
Moreau-Lislet, Louis Casimir Elisabeth
Muñoz-Rivera, Luis
Pinckney, Elizabeth Lucas
Prud'homme, John Francis Eugene
Redwood, Abraham
Ricord, Frederick William
Roberdeau, Daniel
Russwurm, John Brown
Stuart, Charles
Thomas, George
Thornton, William
Varela y Morales, Félix Francisco José María de la Concepción
Vaughan, Benjamin
Williams, Bert
Woodward, Henry
Yulee, David Levy

YUGOSLAVIA

Adamic, Louis
Rodzinski, Artur
Tesla, Nikola

AT SEA

Colcord, Lincoln Ross
Gibson, Walter Murray
Jemison, Mary
Juilliard, Augustus D.
Kirby, J. Hudson
Lathrop, Francis Augustus
McFee, William
Sajous, Charles Euchariste De Médicis

SCHOOLS AND COLLEGES

Listed below are the schools, colleges, and universities, followed, in each case, by the names of those persons in the Dictionary who have attended the respective institutions.

Academic and Commercial College (Wis.)
Haugen, Gilbert Nelson
Académie Carmen (France)
Frieseke, Frederick Carl
Académie Colarossi (France)
Robinson, Boardman
Académie Delacluse (France)
Young, Mahonri Mackintosh
Académie Julien (France)
Benson, Frank Weston
Benton, Thomas Hart
Biddle, George
Borglum, John Gutzon de la Mothe
Calder, Alexander Stirling
Eilshemius, Louis Michel
Karfiol, Bernard
Lipchitz, Jacques
MacNeil, Hermon Atkins
Ruckstull, Frederick Wellington
Szyk, Arthur
Weber, Max
Wood, Grant
Young, Art
Académie Ozenfant (France)
Bouché, René Robert
Academy of Arts and Sciences (Austria)
Ulmer, Edgar Georg
Academy of Commerce and Consular Affairs (Hungary)
Farago, Ladislas
Academy of Fine Arts, Chicago (Ill.)
Etting, Ruth
Academy of Fine Arts in Rome (Italy)
Baccaloni, Salvatore
Acadia University (Canada)
Case, Shirley Jackson
Eaton, Chartes Aubrey
Rand, Benjamin
Graduate Study
Case, Shirley Jackson
Eaton, Charles Aubrey
Adelphi Academy (Brooklyn, N.Y.)
Folger, Henry Clay
Fowler, Frank
Harland, Henry
Ivins, William Mills
Kemp, James Furman
Nitchie, Edward Bartlett
Partridge, William Ordway
Agricultural College of Utah
Hines, Frank Thomas
Jardine, William Marion
Alabama Polytechnic Institute
Fleming, Walter Lynwood
Owsley, Frank Lawrence
Sloan, Matthew Scott
Graduate Study
Duggar, Benjamin Minge
Fleming, Walter Lynwood
Sloan, Matthew Scott
Alabama Presbyterian College
Carmichael, Oliver Cromwell
Albany Academy (N.Y.)
Bogart, John
Boltwood, Bertram Borden
Bradford, Alexander Warfield
Brodhead, John Romeyn
Campbell, Allen
Cassidy, William
Cutler, James Goold
Draper, Andrew Sloan
Durrie, Daniel Steele
Hartley, Jonathan Scott
Henry, Joseph
Isherwood, Benjamin Franklin
James, Henry, 1811–1882
Marble, Manton Malone
Martin, Frederick Townsend
Pruyn, Robert Hewson
Smith, Charles Emory
Tucker, Gilbert Milligan
Viele, Egbert Ludovicus
Welch, Ashbel
Albany Law School (N.Y.)
Benjamin, Park, 1849–1922
Benton, Josiah Henry
Brewer, David Josiah
Brown, Irving
Cassoday, John Bolivar
Converse, Charles Crozat
Deming, Philander
Draper, Andrew Sloan
Eckels, James Herron
Jackson, Robert Houghwout
Kirchwey, George Washington
Kneeland, Stillman Foster
MacAlister, James
McKinley, William
Manley, Joseph Homan
Martin, Frederick Townsend
Parker, Alton Brooks
Peckham, George Williams
Peckham, Wheeler Hazard
Pitkin, Frederick Walker
Plaisted, Harris Merrill
Raines, John
Schenck, Ferdinand Schureman
Stone, William Leete
Tripp, Bartlett
Albany Medical College (N.Y.)
Benjamin, George Hillard
Blackfan, Kenneth Daniel
Duane, Alexander
Durant, Thomas Clark
Fuller, Robert Mason
Gregory, Menas Sarkas Boulgourjian
Hayden, Ferdinand Vandiveer
House, Samuel Reynolds
Salisbury, James Henry
Salmon, Thomas William
Smith, Theobald
Albany State College for Teachers (N.Y.)
Milk, Harvey Bernard
Albertus University (Germany)
Fromm-Reichmann, Frieda
Albion College (Mich.)
Adams, Henry Cullen
Bovie, William T.
Brown, Prentiss Marsh
Folks, Homer
Greene, Edward Lee
Lovejoy, Owen Reed
Moulton, Forest Ray
Nelson, Knute
Shaw, Anna Howard
Shepard, James Henry
Graduate Study
Lovejoy, Owen Reed
Albright Art School (N.Y.)
Seitz, William Chapin
Albright College (Pa.)
Spottswood, Stephen Gill
Alcorn Agricultural and Mechanical College (Miss.)
Evers, Medgar Wiley
Alfred Academy (*See* Alfred University)
Alfred University (N.Y.)
Anderson, Galusha
Cassoday, John Bolivar
Flint, Weston
Rogers, William Augustus
Stillman, Thomas Bliss
Stillman, Thomas Edgar
Willson, Augustus Everett
Graduate Study
Pearson, Raymond Allen
Allegheny College (Pa.)
Allison, William Boyd
Cooke, Henry David
Darrow, Clarence Seward
Dibble, Roy Floyd
Fogarty, Anne Whitney
Gary, James Albert
Harris, Merriman Colbert
Haskins, Charles Homer
Hays, Alexander
Holliday, Cyrus Kurtz
Howe, Frederic Clemson
Jackman, Wilbur Samuel
Jones, William Patterson
Kennedy, Joseph Camp Griffith
Kingsley, Calvin
Lowndes, Lloyd
McKinley, William
Metcalf, Joel Hastings
Oldham, William Fitzjames
Pierpont, Francis Harrison
Rice, Victor Moreau
Tarbell, Ida Minerva
Thoburn, James Mills
Thompson, Arthur Webster

ALLEGHENY SEMINARY (*See* WESTERN THEOLOGICAL SEMINARY)
ALLEGHENY THEOLOGICAL SEMINARY
Miller, James Russell
Moorehead, William Gallogly
ALLENTOWN SEMINARY (*See* MUHLENBERG COLLEGE)
ALMA COLLEGE (MICH.)
Knox, Frank
ALMA COLLEGE (N.Y.)
Hull, Clark Leonard
AMENIA SEMINARY (N.Y.)
Benton, Joel
Foss, Cyrus David
Pirsson, Louis Valentine
Winchell, Alexander
AMERICAN ACADEMY IN ROME (ITALY)
Graduate Study
Van Deman, Esther Boise
AMERICAN ACADEMY OF DRAMATIC ARTS (N.Y.)
DeMille, Cecil Blount
Lindsay, Howard
McClintic, Guthrie
Robinson, Edward G.
Russell, Rosalind
Schildkraut, Joseph
Tracy, Spencer Bonaventure
AMERICAN BUSINESS COLLEGE (MINN.)
Thye, Edward John
AMERICAN CONSERVATORY OF MUSIC (ILL.)
Gray, Glen
Tristano, Leonard Joseph ("Lennie")
AMERICAN INSTITUTE OF BANKING
Patterson, William Allan ("Pat")
AMERICAN UNIVERSITY (D.C.)
Graduate Study
Baroody, William Joseph
Lomax, Louis Emanuel
Zahniser, Howard Clinton
AMERICAN UNIVERSITY (TENN.)
Knight, Frank Hyneman
AMHERST ACADEMY (MASS.)
Blodgett, Henry Williams
Chamberlain, Daniel Henry
Clark, Joseph Sylvester
Dickinson, Emily Elizabeth
Graham, Sylvester
Hitchcock, Edward, 1828–1911
Loomis, Dwight
Lyon, Mary
Pope, Franklin Leonard
Riggs, Elias
AMHERST COLLEGE (MASS.)
Adams, Charles Baker
Adams, Herbert Baxter
Allen, David Oliver
Allen, Nathan
Allen, Timothy Field
Ames, Herman Vandenburg
Andrews, Charles Bartlett
Andrews, Israel Ward
Avery, John
Bancroft, Frederic
Barton, Bruce Fairchild
Bassett, Edward Murray
Bayley, James Roosevelt
Beecher, Henry Ward
Birdseye, Clarence
Bissell, Edwin Cone
Bliss, Daniel
Bliss, Edwin Elisha
Bliss, Edwin Munsell
Bliss, Frederick Jones
Bliss, Howard Sweetser
Bliss, William Dwight Porter
Bridgman, Elijah Coleman
Bridgman, Herbert Lawrence
Broun, Addison
Brownell, William Crary
Buchanan, Scott Milross
Burgess, John William
Chapman, Alvan Wentworth
Clark, George Whitefield
Clark, John Bates
Clark, John Maurice
Clark, Joseph Sylvester
Clark, Thomas March
Clark, William Bullock
Clark, William Smith
Clarke, John Mason
Cobb, William Henry
Codman, John
Coffin, James Henry
Cohn, Edwin Joseph
Coit, Stanton
Cole, Charles Woolsey
Coolidge, Calvin
Cross, Charles Whitman
Curtiss, Samuel Ives
Darling, Henry
Davis, Arthur Vining
Dewey, Melvil
Douglas, Lewis Williams
Drew, Charles Richard
Eastman, Joseph Bartlett
Edwards, Bela Bates
Emerson, Benjamin Kendall
Ewing, James
Farman, Elbert Eli
Fitch, William Clyde
Flint, Austin
Folger, Henry Clay
Fowler, Orson Squire
Gardiner, Harry Norman
Garman, Charles Edward
Garvin, Lucius Fayette Clark
Gillett, Frederick Huntington
Goodale, George Lincoln
Goodell, Henry Hill
Goodhue, James Madison
Goodnow, Frank Johnson
Grosvenor, Edwin Prescott
Grosvenor, Gilbert Hovey
Grow, Galusha Aaron
Hackett, Horatio Balch
Hallock, Charles
Hamlin, Alfred Dwight Foster
Hamlin, Talbot Faulkner
Hammond, William Gardiner
Hardy, Arthur Sherburne
Harris, George
Haven, Joseph
Hewett, Waterman Thomas
Hewit, Augustine Francis
Hitchcock, Charles Henry
Hitchcock, Edward, 1828–1911
Hitchcock, Roswell Dwight
Holland, William Jacob
Holt, Edwin Bissell
Hooper, Claude Ernest
Houston, Charles Hamilton
Humphries, George Rolfe
Huntington, Frederick Dan
Jackson, Edward Payson
James, Arthur Curtiss
Jameson, John Franklin
Jerome, William Travers
Johnson, Allen
Jones, John Taylor
Kemp, James Furman
King, Stanley
Landis, Henry Robert Murray
Lansing, Robert
Leland, George Adams
Lewis, William Henry
Lincoln, Rufus Pratt
Lord, Otis Phillips
Lyman, Eugene William
McClure, Alexander Wilson
March, Francis Andrew, 1825–1911
Marcy, Henry Orlando
Maynard, Horace
Mayo, Amory Dwight
Mayo-Smith, Richmond
Mead, William Rutherford
Mears, David Otis
Mell, Patrick Hues, 1814–1888
Merrill, Charles Edward
Merrill, James Griswold
Millett, Fred Benjamin
Moore, William Henry
Morrow, Dwight Whitney
Morse, Anson Daniel
Morse, Harmon Northrop
Nash, Charles Sumner
Nash, Simeon
Nason, Henry Bradford
Neill, Edward Duffield
Nitchie, Edward Bartlett
Northend, Charles
Noyes, Alexander Dana
Olds, Leland
Orne, John
Osgood, Herbert Levi
Palmer, Benjamin Morgan
Palmer, Walter Walker
Parker, Peter
Parkhurst, Charles Henry
Parsons, Talcott
Perkins, Justin
Plimpton, George Arthur
Pomeroy, Samuel Clarke
Potter, Edward Clark
Pray, Isaac Clark
Rainey, Henry Thomas
Rhees, Rush
Riefler, Winfield William
Riggs, Elias
Robinson, Charles Mulford
Robinson, Stuart
Rolfe, William James
Romer, Alfred Sherwood ("Al")
Rossiter, William Sidney
Rugg, Arthur Prentice
Schneider, Benjamin
Seelye, Jullus Hawley
Shepard, Charles Upham
Smith, Benjamin Eli

Smith, Charles Sprague
Smith, Edward Munroe
Smith, Henry Preserved
Smith, Horatio Elwin
Smith, Judson
Smith, Preserved
Snell, Bertrand Hollis
Sophocles, Evangelinus Apostolides
Spahr, Charles Barzillai
Stanchfield, John Barry
Stearns, Frank Waterman
Stebbins, Rufus Phineas
Stockbridge, Henry
Stockbridge, Henry Smith
Stoddard, John Tappan
Stone, Harlan Fiske
Storrs, Richard Salter, 1821–1900
Swinton, William
Taft, Alphonso
Tufts, James Hayden
Tyler, William Seymour
Van Lennep, Henry John
Vinton, Frederic
Walker, Francis Amasa
Walker, Williston
Ward, Herbert Dickinson
Ward, John Elliott
Ward, William Hayes
Washburn, George
Whipple, Amiel Weeks
Wilbur, Hervey Backus
Wilder, Harris Hawthorne
Williams, George Huntington
Williams, Talcott
Woodbridge, Frederick James Eugene
Woods, Robert Archey

Graduate Study
Bliss, Frederick Jones
Clark, George Whitefield
Grosvenor, Edwin Prescott
Grosvenor, Gilbert Hovey
March, Francis Andrew, 1825–1911
Osgood, Herbert Levi
Post, Augustus
Rainey, Henry Thomas
Wilbur, Henry Backus

AMMENDALE COLLEGE (MD.)
Bushman, Francis Xavier

ANDOVER (*See* PHILLIPS ACADEMY, ANDOVER, MASS.)

ANDOVER THEOLOGICAL SEMINARY (MASS.)
Abbott, Edward
Abbott, Gorham Dummer
Abbott, Jacob
Abbott, John Stevens Cabot
Adams, Charles Baker
Adams, Henry Carter
Adams, Jasper
Adams, Nehemiah
Adams, William
Aiken, Charles Augustus
Alden, Henry Mills
Allen, David Oliver
Ament, William Scott
Atkinson, George Henry
Bacon, Leonard
Bacon, Leonard Woolsey
Baldwin, Elihu Whittlesey
Barrows, John Henry
Bartlett, Samuel Colcord
Beach, Harlan Page
Beecher, Edward
Benjamin, Nathan
Bingham, Hiram, 1789–1869
Bingham, Hiram, 1831–1908
Blakeslee, Erastus
Blanchard, Tonathan
Bliss, Daniel
Bliss, Edwin Elisha
Bouton, Nathaniel
Brainerd, Ezra
Brainerd, Thomas
Bridgman, Elijah Coleman
Brown, Carleton
Brown, Samuel Gilman
Bumstead, Horace
Byington, Cyrus
Chase, Irah
Cheever, George Barrell
Cheever, Henry Theodore
Clark, Francis Edward
Clark, Joseph Sylvester
Cobb, William Henry
Coit, Thomas Winthrop
Collins, John Anderson
Colton, Calvin
Colton, Walter
Cook, Flavius Josephus
Dewey, Orville
Dike, Samuel Warren
Diman, Teremiah Lewis
Dole, Charles Fletcher
Dunning, Albert Elijah
Dwight, Harrison Gray Otis
Eaton, John
Edwards, Bela Bates
Edwards, Justin
Fairbanks, Henry
Farrar, John
Fisher, George Park
Foster, Frank Hugh
Gallaudet, Thomas Hopkins
Gates, George Augustus
Gibbs, Josiah Willard, 1790–1861
Goodell, William, 1792–1867
Goodrich, Chauncey, 1836–1925
Goodwin, Daniel Raynes
Green, Beriah
Greene, Daniel Crosby
Hackett, Horatio Balch
Haddock, Charles Brickett
Hale, Benjamin
Hall, Sherman
Hallock, Gerard
Hallock, William Allen
Harris, George
Harris, Samuel
Hart, Hastings Hornell
Hatfield, Edwin Francis
Haven, Joseph
Henry, Caleb Sprague
Hitchcock, Charles Henry
Hitchcock, Roswell Dwight
Homes, Henry Augustus
Hoppin, James Mason
Howe, George
Hume, Robert Allen
Jewett, Charles Coffin
Jones, John Taylor
Judson, Adoniram
Kellogg, Elijah
Kellogg, Martin
King, Jones
Ladd, George Trumbull
Lawrence, William, 1850–1941
Leach, Daniel Dyer
Loomis, Elias
Lord, Eleazar
Lord, John
Lord, Nathan
McClure, Alexander Wilson
McKenzie, Alexander
McKim, James Miller
Magoun, George Frederic
Mahan, Asa
Marsh, James
Mead, Charles Marsh
Merrill, James Griswold
Mulford, Elisha
Munger, Theodore Thornton
Murray, James Ormsbee
Neill, Edward Duffield
Noble, Frederick Alphonso
Noyes, John Humphrey
Ogden, Rollo
Orton, James
Packard, Joseph
Paine, John Alsop
Palmer, George Herbert
Park, Edwards Amasa
Parker, Samuel
Parkhurst, Charles
Peet, Stephen Denison
Perkins, Justin
Pillsbury, Parker
Post, Truman Marcellus
Rankin, Jeremiah Eames
Richards, William
Riggs, Elias
Ropes, James Hardy
Ross, Abel Hastings
Sanborn, Edwin David
Schauffler, Henry Albert
Schneider, Benjamin
Shedd, William Greenough Thayer
Sheldon, Charles Monroe
Sherwood, Adiel
Slafter, Edmund Farwell
Smith, Arthur Henderson
Smith, Asa Dodge
Smith, Eli
Smith, Henry Boynton
Smyth, Newman
Smyth, William
Snow, Francis Huntington
Southgate, Horatio
Spaulding, Levi
Spring, Gardiner
Spring, Leverett Wilson
Stearns, William Augustus
Stoddard, David Tappan
Storrs, Richard Salter, 1787–1873
Storrs, Richard Salter, 1821–1900
Stowe, Calvin Ellis
Taylor, Samuel Harvey
Thayer, Joseph Henry

Thwing, Charles Franklin
Todd, John
Torrey, Charles Cutler
Torrey, Charles Turner
Townsend, Luther Tracy
Winship, Albert Edward
Winslow, Hubbard
Winslow, Miron
Woods, Alva
Woods, Leonard, 1807–1878
Woods, Robert Archey
Worcester, Samuel Austin
Yeomans, John William

ANNAPOLIS (*See* UNITED STATES NAVAL ACADEMY)

ANTIOCH COLLEGE (OHIO)
Binkley, Wilfred Ellsworth
Brown, Olympia
Herford, Oliver Brooke
Jay, Allen
Keifer, Joseph Warren
Lawrance, Uriah Marion
Serling, Rodman Edward ("Rod")
Sherwood, Isaac Ruth
Shull, George Harrison
Terrell, Mary Eliza Church
Wilson, Edmund Beecher

APPLETON ACADEMY (N.H.)
Bancroft, Cecil Franklin Patch
Champney, Benjamin
Fiske, Amos Kidder
Mathews, William Smythe Babcock
Shattuck, Lemuel

ARIZONA TEACHERS COLLEGE
Devine, Andrew ("Andy")

ARKANSAS BAPTIST COLLEGE
Jordan, Louis

ARMOUR INSTITUTE OF TECHNOLOGY (ILL.)
Howell, Albert Summers
Lardner, Ringgold Wilmer
Wood, Garfield Arthur ("Gar")

ARMY MEDICAL SCHOOL
Ashford, Bailey Kelly

ARNOLD COLLEGE (ENGLAND)
Vizetelly, Frank Horace

ART CENTER OF LOS ANGELES (CALIF.)
Hubley, John

ART INSTITUTE OF BUFFALO (N.Y.)
Seitz, William Chapin

ART INSTITUTE OF CHICAGO (ILL.)
Leyendecker, Joseph Christian
Tanner, Edward Everett, III ("Patrick Dennis")
Tobey, Mark
Williams, Gaar Campbell
Ziff, William Bernard

ARTISTS' AND ARTISANS' INSTITUTE (N.Y.)
McBride, Henry

ART STUDENTS' LEAGUE (D.C.)
Hansburg, George Bernard
Johnston, Frances Benjamin

ART STUDENTS' LEAGUE (N.Y.)
Tobey, Mark
Bachrach, Louis Fabian
Barrymore, John
Barrymore, Lionel
Beard, Daniel Carter
Breck, George William
Burroughs, Bryson
Chambers, Robert William
Christy, Howard Chandler
Clarke, Thomas Shields
Curry, John Steuart
Davidson, Jo
Dickinson, Preston
Dreier, Katherine Sophie
Duffy, Edmund
Eilshemius, Louis Michel
Epstein, Jacob
French, Edwin Davis
Frieseke, Frederick Carl
Gág, Wanda (Hazel)
Gaul, William Gilbert
Gibson, Charles Dana
Gilman, Lawrence
Hambidge, Jay
Hartley, Marsden
Hawthorne, Charles Webster
Holt, Winifred
Hyde, Helen
Juengling, Frederick
Kirby, Rollin
Koehler, Robert
Kuniyoshi, Yasuo
Lawson, Ernest
Lie, Jonas
Lockwood, Robert Wilton
Loeb, Louis
McBride, Henry
MacMonnies, Frederick William
Manship, Paul Howard
Marsh, Reginald
Meière, Marie Hildreth
Miller, Kenneth Hayes
Newman, Barnett
O'Malley, Frank Ward
Penfield, Edward
Pollock, (Paul) Jackson
Potter, Ellen Culver
Pratt, Bela Lyon
Pyle, Howard
Reid, Robert
Remington, Frederic
Rockwell, Norman Perceval
Rothko, Mark
Smith, David Roland
Stella, Joseph
Still, Clyfford
Taylor, William Ladd
Tucker, Allen
Vance, Louis, Joseph
White, Charles Wilbert
Yohn, Frederic Coffay
Young, Art
Zogbaum, Rufus Fairchild

ASBURY COLLEGE (KY.)
Matthews, Joseph Brown
Wiley, Bell Irvin

ASBURY UNIVERSITY (*See* DE PAUW UNIVERSITY)

ASHFIELD ACADEMY (MASS.)
Fowler, Orson Squire
Hall, Granville Stanley
Lyon, Mary

ATHENÉE ROYALE (BELGIUM)
Sauveur, Albert

ATHENS CONSERVATORY OF MUSIC (GREECE)
Mitropoulos, Dimitri

ATHENS ACADEMY (GA.)
English, Elbert Hartwell
Paschal, George Washington
Wright, Charles Barstow

ATKINSON ACADEMY (N.H.)
Brown, Francis, 1784–1820
Clark, Greenleaf
Woodbury, Levi

ATLANTA BAPTIST COLLEGE
Johnson, Mordecai Wyatt

ATLANTA CONSERVATORY OF MUSIC (GA.)
Hardy, Oliver Norvell

ATLANTA LAW SCHOOL (GA.)
Ramspeck, Robert C. Word ("Bob")

ATLANTA UNIVERSITY (GA.)
Henderson, Fletcher Hamilton
Johnson, Edward Austin
Johnson, James Weldon
White, Walter Francis
Wright, Richard Robert

AUBURN THEOLOGICAL SEMINARY (N.Y.)
Babcock, Maltbie Davenport
Bascom, John
Benjamin, Nathan
Cloud, Henry Roe
Coan, Titus
Condon, Thomas
Cook, Russell S.
Darling, Henry
Fisher, George Park
Gally, Merritt
Grinnell, Josiah Bushnell
Headley, Joel Tyler
Headley, Phineas Camp
Hoisington, Henry Richard
Knox, George William
Logan, Cornelius Ambrose, 1832–1899
Lord, William Wilberforce
Morris, George Sylvester
Parker, Joel, 1799–1873
Roe, Edward Payson
Seelye, Julius Hawley
Sheffield, Devello Zelotes
Stryker, Melancthon Woolsey
Tappan, Henry Philip
Williams, John Elias, 1871–1927

AUBURN UNIVERSITY (ALA.)
Bullard, Robert Lee
Heflin, James Thomas
Smith, Holland McTyeire

AUGSBURG COLLEGE (MINN.)
Wiley, Alexander

AUGUSTA COLLEGE (KY.)
Browning, Orville Hickman
Doniphan, Alexander William
Fee, John Gregg
Foster, Randolph Sinks
Groesbeck, William Slocum
Preston, William
Wickliffe, Robert Charles

AUGUSTA COLLEGE (*See* WASHINGTON AND LEE UNIVERSITY, VA.)

AUGUSTANA COLLEGE (ILL.)
Borg, George William
Carlson, Anton Julius

Graduate Study
Carlson, Anton Julius

BABSON INSTITUTE OF BUSINESS ADMINISTRATION (MASS.)
Gerber, Daniel (Frank)
BACON ACADEMY (MAINE)
Bartholomew, Edward Sheffield
Crary, Isaac Edwin
Fowler, Orin
Gillett, Ezra Hall
Morgan, Edwin Denison
Trumbull, Lyman
BACONE COLLEGE (OKLA.)
Hurley, Patrick Jay
BAKER UNIVERSITY (KANS.)
Allen, Henry Justin
Bristow, Joseph Little
BALDWIN COLLEGE (OHIO)
Miller, Dayton Clarence
Graduate Study
Miller, Dayton Clarence
BALDWIN-WALLACE COLLEGE (OHIO)
Cline, Genevieve Rose
Moley, Raymond Charles
Norris, George William
Ulrich, Edward Oscar
Law
Sweeney, Martin Leonard
BALTIMORE CITY COLLEGE
Adams, Thomas Sewall
Boston, Charles Anderson
Gorrell, Edgar Staley
Hemmeter, John Conrad
Kennedy, John Pendleton
Latané, John Holladay
McKeldin, Theodore Roosevelt
Perlman, Philip Benjamin
Rose, John Carter
Ryan, Harris Joseph
Slicer, Thomas Roberts
Uhler, Philip Reese
Van Meter, John Blackford
Williams, John Whitridge
BALTIMORE POLYTECHNIC INSTITUTE
Bachrach, Louis Fabian
Hammett, Samuel Dashiell
BANGOR THELOGICAL SEMINARY (MAINE)
Beckwith, Clarence Augustine
Chamberlain, Joshua Lawrence
Chandler, Peleg Whitman
Cheever, Henry Theodore
Hamlin, Cyrus
Parker, Edwin Pond
Peloubet, Francis Nathan
Savage, Minot Judson
Smyth, Egbert Coffin
Tenney, Edward Payson
BAPTIST COLLEGE (IOWA)
Springer, Charles
BAPTIST COLLEGE (MO.)
Asbury, Herbert
BARBER-SCOTIA COLLEGE (N.C.)
Bethune, Mary McLeod
BARD COLLEGE (N.Y.)
Francis, Paul James
Nock, Albert Jay
Pecora, Ferdinand
Rovere, Richard Halworth
Graduate Study
Francis, Paul James
BARNARD COLLEGE (N.Y.)
Antin, Mary
Douglas, Helen Gahagan
Gildersleeve, Virginia Crocheron
Glueck, Eleanor Touroff
Hurston, Zora Neale
King, Carol Weiss
Kirchwey, Freda
Lehman, Adele Lewisohn
Loveman, Amy
Mead, Margaret
Meyer, Agnes Elizabeth Ernst
Parsons, Elsie Worthington Clews
Reid, Helen Miles Rogers
Rolf, Ida Pauline
Rumsey, Mary Harriman
BATES COLLEGE (MAINE)
Baker, James Hutchins
Dennett, Tyler (Wilbur)
Haskell, Ella Louise Knowles
Hayes, Edward Carey
Hewett, Waterman Thomas
Howe, Percy Rogers
Neal, Josephine Bicknell
Simmons, Franklin
Sullivan, Louis Robert
BATTLE CREEK COLLEGE (MICH.)
Price, George Edward McCready
BAYLOR FEMALE COLLEGE (TEX.)
Ferguson, Miriam Amanda Wallace ("Ma")
BAYLOR UNIVERSITY (TEX.)
Burleson, Albert Sidney
Connally, Thomas Terry ("Tom")
Norris, John Franklyn
Scarborough, Dorothy
Scarborough, Lee Rutland
Truett, George Washington
Graduate Study
Eaton, Charles Aubrey
Scarborough, Dorothy
BEAUMONT COLLEGE (ENGLAND)
Mackay, Clarence Hungerford
BELLEVUE COLLEGE (NEBR.)
Lunn, George Richard
BELLEVUE HOSPITAL MEDICAL COLLEGE (*See* NEW YORK UNIVERSITY, *Medicine*)
BELLEVUE TRAINING SCHOOL FOR NURSES (N.Y.)
Dock, Lavinia Lloyd
BELMONT COLLEGE (OHIO)
Cist, Henry Martyn
Halstead, Murat
Harrison, Benjamin, 1833–1901
Nixon, William Penn
Walden, John Morgan
Zimmerman, Eugene
BELOIT ACADEMY (WIS.)
Bishop, Seth Scott
Keyes, Elisha Williams
Williams, Jesse Lynch, 1871–1929
BELOIT COLLEGE (WIS.)
Adams, George Burton
Andrews, Roy Chapman
Bingham, Walter Van Dyke
Bishop, Seth Scott
Bundy, Jonas Mills
Bushnell, George Ensign
Chamberlin, Thomas Chrowder
Clark, Felton Grandison
Curtis, Edward Lewis
Davis, Jerome Dean
Gates, Caleb Frank
Hallett, Moses
Huntington, Ellsworth
MacPhail, Leland Stanford ("Larry")
Meinzer, Oscar Edward
Peet, Stephen Denison
Pettigrew, Richard Franklin
Salisbury, Rollin D.
Scott, James Wilmot
Skinner, Aaron Nichols
Smith, Arthur Henderson
Strong, James Woodward
Strong, Walter Ansel
White, Horace
Wright, Theodore Lyman
BEREA COLLEGE (KY.)
Barton, Bruce Fairchild
Barton, William Eleazar
Combs, Earle Bryan
Woodson, Carter Godwin
BERKELEY DIVINITY SCHOOL (CONN.)
Hart, Samuel
Leonard, William Andrew
Nichols, William Ford
Nock, Albert Jay
Potter, Eliphalet Nott
BERKSHIRE MEDICAL INSTITUTION (MASS.)
Green, Asa
Hopkins, Mark
Lee, Charles Alfred
Root, Joseph Pomeroy
Stone, Warren
BERLIN-CHARLOTTENBURG TECHNISCHE HOCHSCHULE (GERMANY)
Braun, Wernher von
Graduate Study
Kracauer, Siegfried
BERLIN HOCHSCHULE FÜR MUSIK
Nabokov, Nicolas
BERLIN POLYTECHNICUM (GERMANY)
Wiener, Leo
BETHANY COLLEGE (W. VA.)
Adams, William Lysander
Baldwin, Joseph
Baxter, William
Benton, Allen Richardson
Clark, Champ
Dennis, Graham Barclay
Ferrel, William
Hodgen, John Thompson
Lamar, Joseph Rucker
Lard, Moses E.
Loos, Charles Louis
McGarvey, John William
McLean, Archibald
Mayes, Edward
Moore, William Thomas
Odell, Benjamin Barker
Oliver, George Tener
Power, Frederick Dunglison
Wharton, Greene Lawrence
Willett, Herbert Lockwood

Williams, Edward Thomas
Zollars, Ely Vaughan
BETHEL COLLEGE (KY.)
Dargan, Edwin Preston
McGlothlin, William Joseph
BETHEL COLLEGE (TENN.)
Garrett, Finis James
BIALYSTOK SCHOOL OF COMMERCE (POLAND)
Perlman, Selig
BINGHAM SCHOOL (N.C.)
Ashe, Thomas Samuel
Dobbin, James Cochran
Page, Walter Hines
Waddell, Alfred Moore
Warren, Lindsay Carter
Webb, William Robert
BIRMINGHAM SOUTHERN UNIVERSITY (ALA.)
Jones, Robert Reynolds ("Bob")
BIRMINGHAM UNIVERSITY (ENGLAND)
Lotka, Alfred James
Graduate Study
Lotka, Alfred James
BISHOP PAINE DIVINITY SCHOOL (VA.)
Russell, James Solomon
BISHOP'S COLLEGE (CANADA)
Fessenden, Reginald Aubrey
BLACKBURN UNIVERSITY (ILL.)
Austin, Mary
BLACK HILLS COLLEGE (S.D.)
Gidley, James Williams
BLACK HILLS TEACHERS COLLEGE (S. DAK.)
Leedom, Boyd Stewart
BLOOMFIELD ACADEMY (MAINE)
Coburn, Abner
Coffin, Charles Albert
Howard, Volney Erskine
BLOOMFIELD ACADEMY (NJ.)
Dodd, Frank Howard
Hoisington, Henry Richard
Peloubet, Francis Nathan
Ward, Richard Halsted
BLOOMSBURG STATE NORMAL SCHOOL (PA.)
Pfahler, George Edward
BOLOGNA CONSERVATORY OF MUSIC (ITALY)
Spalding, Albert
BONEBRAKE THEOLOGICAL SEMINARY (OHIO)
Dougherty, Raymond Philip
BOSTON, ENGLISH HIGH SCHOOL
Ballou, Maturin Murray
Chandler, Seth Carlo
Child, Francis James
Cummings, Charles Amos
Green, Francis Mathews
Guild, Curtis, 1827–1911
Haley, Jack
Sullivan, Louis Henri
Whitmore, William David
BOSTON COLLEGE
Cushing, Richard James
O'Connell, William Henry
Tobin, Maurice Joseph
Walsh, James Anthony
Wright, John Joseph
BOSTON CONSERVATORY OF MUSIC
Berenson, Senda
BOSTON GIRLS LATIN SCHOOL
Berenson, Senda
Scudder, (Julia) Vida Dutton
BOSTON LATIN SCHOOL
Abbot, Henry Larcom
Adams, Charles Francis, 1807–1886
Adams, Charles Francis, 1835–1915
Ames, James Barr
Appleton, Thomas Gold
Austin, James Trecothick
Austin, Jonathan Loring
Barnard, Charles Francis
Barnes, James
Beecher, Charles
Bigelow, Henry Jacob
Blaikie, William
Bowditch, Henry Ingersoll
Breck, Samuel
Brooks, Phillips
Bulfinch, Thomas
Bumstead, Horace
Butler, John Wesley
Byles, Mather
Channing, William Ellery, 1818–1901
Channing, William Henry
Chauncy, Charles
Checkley, John
Child, Francis James
Clark, Arthur Hamilton
Clarke, James Freeman
Coerne, Louis Adolphe
Coffin, Sir Isaac
Converse, Edmund Cogswell
Crafts, James Mason
Craigie, Andrew
Crowninshield, Frederic
Dall, William Healey
Davis, Charles Henry, 1807–1877
Derby, Elias Hasket, 1803–1880
Devens, Charles
Dwight, John Sullivan
Eliot, Charles William
Ellis, George Edward
Emerson, Ralph Waldo
Eustis, William
Evarts, William Maxwell
Fenn, William Wallace
Fiedler, Arthur
Fiske, George Converse
Fitzpatrick, John Bernard
Ford, Patrick
Foster, Roger Sherman Baldwin
Fowle, William Bentley
Freeman, James
Furness, William Henry
Gardiner, Robert Hallowell
Goldthwaite, George
Gould, Benjamin Apthorp
Grafton, Charles Chapman
Gray, John Chipman
Greenough, James Bradstreet
Greenough, Richard Saltonstall
Hale, Charles
Hale, Edward Everett
Hammond, James Bartlett
Hancock, John, 1736–1793
Hardy, Arthur Sherburne
Hayden, Edward Everett
Hepworth, George Hughes
Hodges, Harry Foote
Hooper, William
Howe, Henry Marion
Hunt, Richard Morris
Jackson, Charles
Jackson, James, 1777–1867
Jenks, William
Kneeland, Samuel
Langley, Samuel Pierpont
Leland, George Adams
Leverett, John, 1662–1724
Lincoln, John Larkin
Loring, Edward Greely
Loring, Ellis Gray
MacKaye, Benton
McClure, Alexander Wilson
Mather, Cotton
Merrill, William Bradford
Milmore, Martin
Morton, William James
Mundé, Paul Fortunatus
Oliver, Henry Kemble
Osgood, William Fogg
Otis, George Alexander
Otis, Harrison Gray, 1765–1848
Paine, Charles Jackson
Paine, Robert Treat, 1731–1814
Paine, Robert Treat, 1773–1811
Paine, Robert Treat, 1835–1910
Palfrey, John Carver
Parker, Isaac
Parker, James Cutler Dunn
Parker, Richard Green
Parsons, Thomas William
Peabody, Selim Hobart
Pearce, Charles Sprague
Pearce, Richard Mills
Pelham, Henry
Phillips, Wendell
Phillips, William
Pickering, Edward Charles
Pond, George Edward
Pynchon, Thomas Ruggles
Quincy, Josiah Phillips
Reed, James, 1834–1921
Richardson, Wilrlam Lambert
Robinson, Edward, 1858–1931
Salisbury, Edward Elbridge
Sargent, Epes
Sargent, Henry Winthrop
Sargent, John Osborne
Scudder, Horace Elisha
Shattuck, Frederick Cheever
Shattuck, George Cheyne, 1813–1899
Shurtleff, Nathaniel Bradstreet
Smith, Samuel Francis
Southard, Elmer Ernest
Stimpson, William
Storey, Moorfield
Sumner, Charles
Thayer, Joseph Henry
Thayer, Thomas Baldwin
Townsend, Edward Davis
True, Alfred Charles
Tuckerman, Edward
Tuckerman, Henry Theodore
Tuckerman, Joseph

Van Brunt, Henry
Waldo, Samuel
Warren, John Collins, 1778–1856
Warren, John Collins, 1842–1927
Washburn, Edward Abiel
Wellington, Arthur Mellen
Whitmore, William David
Whiton, James Morris
Wigglesworth, Edward, c. 1693–1765
Wigglesworth, Edward, 1840–1896
Williams, Henry Willard
Willis, Nathaniel Parker
Winslow, William Copley
Winsor, Justin
Winthrop, John, 1714–1779
Wright, John Joseph

BOSTON NORMAL SCHOOL
Rogers, Mary Josephine

BOSTON NORMAL SCHOOL OF GYMNASTICS
Berenson, Senda

BOSTON SCHOOL OF ART
Kalmus, Natalie Mabelle Dunfee

BOSTON SCHOOL OF ORATORY
Blatch, Harriot Eaton Stanton

BOSTON (SIMMONS) SCHOOL OF SOCIAL WORK
Cannon, Ida Maud

BOSTON UNIVERSITY
Ayres, Leonard Porter
Bailey, Solon Irving
Bartlett, Francis Alonzo
Blackwell, Alice Stone
Bogan, Louise Marie
Brace, Dewitt Bristol
Cochrane, Gordon Stanley ("Mickey")
Drum, Hugh Aloysius
Ferguson, John Calvin
Hale, William Bayard
Jefferson, Mark Sylvester William
Kline, Franz Josef
Leonard, William Ellery
Libbey, Edward Drummond
Maier, Walter Arthur
Marden, Orison Swett
Myrick, Herbert
Oldham, William Fitzjames
Oxnam, Garfield Bromley
Sexton, Anne Gray Harvey
Simkhovitch, Mary Melinda Kingsbury
Tuckerman, Frederick
Warren, Shields
Watts, Franklin Mowry

Graduate Study
Ayres, Leonard Porter
Bailey, Solon Irving
Brightman, Edgar Sheffield
King, Martin Luther, Jr.
McConnell, Francis John
Stockbridge, Horace Edward

Law
Bloomfield, Meyer
Cooper, Henry Ernest
Dyett, Thomas Ben
Emerton, Ephraim
Laurence, William Leonard
McGrath, James Howard
Morton, Ferdinand Quintin
Roche, Arthur Somers
Rugg, Arthur Prentice
Russell, William Eustis
Stoddard, Theodore Lothrop
Walsh, David Ignatius
Young, Owen D.

Medicine
Shaw, Anna Howard

Music
Dunham, Henry Morton

Theology
Bashford, James Whitford
Brightman, Edgar Sheffield
Brown, Charles Reynolds
Butler, John Wesley
Coe, George Albert
Curtis, Olin Alfred
Ferguson, John Calvin
Fisher, Frederick Bohn
Hamilton, John William
High, Stanley Hoflund
Hughes, Edwin Holt
Huntington, William Edwards
Jefferson, Charles Edward
McDowell, William Fraser
McFarland, John Thomas
Mansell, William Albert
Mitchell, Hinckley Gilbert Thomas
Mudge, James
Sharp, Dallas Lore
Shaw, Anna Howard

BOWDOIN COLLEGE (MAINE)
Abbot, Ezra
Abbot, Gorham Dummer
Abbott, Jacob
Abbott, John Stevens Cabot
Alexander, De Alva Stanwood
Allen, William Henry
Andrew, John Albion
Appleton, John, 1804–1801
Appleton, John, 1815–1864
Barker, Benjamin Fordyce
Barrett, Benjamin Fiske
Bartol, Cyrus Augustus
Bates, Arlo
Beecher, Charles
Bell, Luther Vose
Bradbury, James Ware
Brewster, Ralph Owen
Burton, Harold Hitz
Carter, William Hodding, Jr.
Chamberlain, Joshua Lawrence
Chandler, Peleg Whitman
Cheever, George Barrell
Cheever, Henry Theodore
Coffin, Robert Peter Tristram
Curtis, Edwin Upton
Davies, Charles Stewart
Day, James Roscoe
Dean, William Henry, Jr.
Douglas, Paul Howard
Dunlap, Robert Pinckney
Emery, Henry Crosby
Emery, Lucilius Alonzo
Evans, George
Everett, Charles Carroll
Felch, Alpheus
Fernald, Charles Henry
Fessenden, Francis
Fessenden, James Deering
Fessenden, William Pitt
Fillebrown, Thomas
Flagg, Edmund
Frye, William Pierce
Fuller, Melville Weston
Garcelon, Alonzo
Gardner, Henry Joseph
Gerrish, Frederic Henry
Gibson, Paris
Goddard, Morrill
Goodwin, Daniel Raynes
Grover, La Fayette
Hale, Benjamin
Hale, John Parker
Hall, Edwin Herbert
Hamlin, Charles
Hamlin, Cyrus
Harrington, Charles
Harris, Samuel
Hawes, Charles Boardman
Hawkins, Dexter Arnold
Hawthorne, Nathaniel
Hill, Frank Alpine
Howard, Oliver Otis
Howe, Lucien
Hubbard, Thomas Hamlin
Ingalls, Melville Ezra
Ingraham, Joseph Holt
Ireland, Charles Thomas, Jr. ("Chick")
Johnson, Henry
Kellogg, Elijah
Kimball, Sumner Increase
King, Henry Melville
Kinsey, Alfred Charles
Larrabee, William Clark
Longfellow, Henry Wadsworth
Lord, Nathan
Lovejoy, Owen
McCulloch, Hugh
McLellan, Isaac
Magoun, George Frederic
Mitchell, Edward Page
Morse, Charles Wyman
Packard, Alpheus Spring, 1798–1884
Packard, Alpheus Spring, 1839–1905
Packard, Joseph
Parker, Edwin Pond
Peary, Robert Edwin
Pierce, Edward Allen
Pierce, Franklin
Poor, Henry Varnum
Prentiss, George Lewis
Prentiss, Seargent Smith
Putnam, William Le Baron
Ray, Isaac
Reed, Thomas Brackett
Rhoads, Cornelius Packard
Russwurm, John Brown
Sargent, Dudley Allen
Sewall, Frank
Sheldon, Henry Newton
Smith, Henry Boynton
Smith, John Cotton, 1826–1882
Smith, Seba
Smyth, Egbert Coffin

Smyth, William
Southgate, Horatio
Stanwood, Edward
Stephens, Charles Asbury
Storer, David Humphreys
Stowe, Calvin Ellis
Sturtevant, Edward Lewis
Swallow, George Clinton
Thatcher, Benjamin Bussey
Thomas, William Widgery
Torrey, Charles Cutler
Vail, Stephen Montfort
Washburn, William Drew
Wheeler, William Adolphus
Whitman, Charles Otis
Young, Aaron
Graduate Study
Hall, Edwin Herbert
Packard, Alpheus Spring, 1839–1905
Sewall, Frank
Medicine
Barker, Benjamin Fordyce
Everett, Charles Carroll
Gerrish, Frederic Henry
Holmes, Ezekiel
Ray, Isaac
BOWLING GREEN BUSINESS COLLEGE (KY.)
Hines, Duncan
BRADFORD ACADEMY (MASS.)
Atkinson, George Henry
Judson, Ann Hesseltine
Perley, Ira
Poole, Fitch
BRADFORD ACADEMY (VT.)
Benton, Josiah Henry
Jewett, Milo Parker
Pearsons, Daniel Kimball
Worthen, Amos Henry
BRADLEY UNIVERSITY (ILL.)
Hoerr, Normand Louis
Skidmore, Louis
BRANDEIS UNIVERSITY
Sexton, Anne Gray Harvey
BRECKINRIDGE COLLEGE (IOWA)
Haugen, Gilbert Nelson
BRIDGEWATER ACADEMY (MASS.)
Leach, Daniel Dyer
Phillips, Willard
Pierce, Edward Lillie
Pierce, Henry Lillie
Sanger, George Partridge
Shedd, Joel Herbert
BRIDGEWATER STATE NORMAL SCHOOL (MASS.)
Cushman, Joseph Augustine
O'Brien, Robert Lincoln
BRIDGTON ACADEMY (MAINE)
Grant, George Barnard
Hamlin, Charles
Hamlin, Cyrus
Hawkins, Dexter Arnold
Ingalls, Melville Ezra
BRIGHAM YOUNG UNIVERSITY (UTAH)
Farnsworth, Philo Taylor
Smith, George Albert
Smoot, Reed Owen
Watkins, Arthur Vivian
BRIGHTON COLLEGE (ENGLAND)
Sanders, George
BRIMMER SCHOOL (BOSTON, MASS.)
Ames, James Barr
Crane, William Henry
Milmore, Martin
Pearce, Charles Sprague
Sullivan, Louis Henri
BRISTOL ACADEMY (MASS.)
Baylies, Francis
Brownell, Thomas Church
Hill, George Handel
Shaw, Oliver
BROOKINGS INSTITUTION (D.C.)
Graham, Frank Porter
Lubin, Isador
BROOKLYN COLLEGE
Levenson, Samuel ("Sam")
BROOKLYN LAW SCHOOL (N.Y.)
Blanshard, Paul
Reynolds, Quentin James
Saypol, Irving Howard
Wilson, William Griffith ("Bill W.")
BROOKLYN POLYTECHNIC INSTITUTE (N.Y.)
Adams, James Truslow
Babcock, Washington Irving
Bowen, Herbert Wolcott
Brown, Alexander Ephraim
Canfield, James Hulme
Chambers, Robert William
Davenport, Charles Benedict
Dickinson, Robert Latou
Doubleday, Frank Nelson
Dwight, Arthur Smith
Field, Herbert Haviland
Flint, Charles Ranlett
Ford, Worthington Chauncey
Fowler, Russell Story
Gherardi, Bancroft
Gibson, William Hamilton
Hamilton, Clayton
Hampden, Walter
Hegeman, John Rogers
Heinze, Frederick Augustus
Hill, Frederick Trevor
Jelliffe, Smith Ely
Jenks, Tudor Storrs
Johnston, Alexander
Knapp, Joseph Palmer
Loomis, Charles Battell
Low, Seth
Melville, George Wallace
Pilcher, Paul Monroe
Post, Augustus
Raymond, Rossiter Worthington
Scollard, Clinton
Sloan, Alfred Pritchard, Jr.
Speir, Samuel Fleet
Sugiura, Kanematsu
Waller, Frederic
Wegmann, Edward
Wood, James J.
BROOKS MILITARY ACADEMY (OHIO)
Gregory, Thomas Barger
BROWN UNIVERSITY (R.I.)
Abbott, Samuel Warren
Adams, Jasper
Alden, Joseph
Allen, Edgar
Allen, Paul
Allen, Philip
Allen, Zachariah
Ames, Oliver, 1831–1895
Ames, Samuel
Andrews, Elisha Benjamin
Angell, George Thorndike
Angell, James Burrill
Angell, Joseph Kinnicutt
Anthony, Henry Bowen
Anthony, William Arnold
Arnold, Samuel Greene
Barbour, Clarence Augustus
Bates, Samuel Penniman
Benedict, David
Belkin, Samuel
Bennett, Charles Edwin
Binney, Amos
Bishop, Nathan
Blake, John Lauris
Blaustein, David
Boyce, James Petigru
Brayton, Charles Ray
Brightman, Edgar Sheffield
Brockett, Linus Pierpont
Brokmeyer, Henry C.
Bronson, Walter Cochrane
Brooks, Erastus
Brown, Nicholas, 1769–1841
Brownell, Thomas Church
Burgess, Alexander
Burgess, George
Burrage, Henry Sweetser
Burrill, James
Carpenter, Edmund Janes
Caswell, Alexis
Chafee, Zechariah, Jr.
Chapin, Charles Value
Chaplin, Jeremiah
Claflin, William
Clark, John Bates
Clifford, John Henry
Coghill, George Ellett
Colvin, Stephen Sheldon
Congdon, Charles Taber
Corthill, Elmer Lawrence
Cox, Samuel Sullivan
Cushing, Josiah Nelson
Davis, Harvey Nathaniel
Dexter, Henry Martyn
Dinau, Jeremiah Lewis
Dodge, Ebenezer
Durfee, Job
Durfee, Thomas
Durrett, Reuben Thomas
Ewing, Thomas
Fairfield, Sumner Lincoln
Faunce, William Herbert Perry
Fenner, James
Field, Fred Tarbell
Fish, Carl Russell
Fisher, George Park
Fisher, John Dix
Fisk, Wilbur
Fletcher, James Cooley
Foss, Sam Walter
Foster, Lafayette Sabine
Foster, Theodore
Francis, John Brown
French, Edwin Davis
Frieze, Henry Simmons
Fryer, Douglas Henry
Gale, Elbridge

Gaston, William, 1820–1894
Gifford, Sanford Robinson
Gilmore, Joseph Henry
Going, Jonathan
Gorky, Arshile
Green, Theodore Francis
Greene, Albert Gorton
Greene, George Washington
Greene, Samuel Stillman
Guild, Reuben Aldridge
Hallett, Benjamin Franklin
Halsey, Thomas Lloyd
Harkness, Albert
Harris, Caleb Fiske
Hay, John Milton
Herreshoff, James Brown
Heywood, Ezra Hervey
Hill, Nathaniel Peter
Himes, Joshua Vaughan
Holbrook, John Edwards
Holley, Alexander Lyman
Holmes, Ezekiel
Holmes, John
Homer, Arthur Bartlett
Hood, Raymond Mathewson
Hope, John
Hoppin, Augustus
Horr, George Edwin
Howe, Mark Anthony de Wolfe
Howe, Samuel Gridley
Hughes, Charles Evans
Hunter, William
Jenckes, Thomas Allen
Jewett, Charles Coffin
Jones, John Taylor
Judson, Adoniram
Judson, Adoniram Brown
Judson, Edward
Keen, William Williams
Kerner, Otto, Jr.
King, Charles William
King, Samuel Ward
Kingsbury, John
Knight, Henry Cogswell
Krause, Allen Kramer
Law, Andrew
Leach, Daniel Dyer
Leland, Waldo Gifford
Lincoln, John Larkin
Lothrop, George Van Ness
MacAlister, James
McCarthy, Charles
Magill, Edward Hicks
Mann, Horace
Marcy, William Learned
Maxcy, Jonathan
Maxcy, Virgil
Meiklejohn, Alexander
Messer, Asa
Metcalf, Theron
Miles, Henry Adolphus
Montgomery, David Henry
Moody, (Arthur Edson) Blair
Morón, Alonzo Graseano
Morton, Marcus, 1784–1864
Morton, Marcus, 1819–1891
Mowry, William Augustus
Munro, Dana Carleton
Murray, James Ormsbee
Nason, Elias
Nichols, Charles Lemuel
Nott, Eliphalet
Olney, Richard
Osterhout, Winthrop John Vanleuven
Park, Edwards Amasa
Peck, George Washington
Peckham, Stephen Farnum
Perelman, Sidney Joseph
Perry, William Stevens
Pierce, Edward Lillie
Pierce, John Davis
Pond, Enoch
Prentice, George Dennison
Randall, Samuel
Read, John Meredith, 1837–1896
Reed, David
Reynolds, Quentin James
Richmond, John Wilkes
Robinson, Christopher
Robinson, Ezekiel Gilman
Rockefeller, John Davison, Jr.
Rockwell, George Lincoln
Rogers, William Augustus
Russell, Jonathan
Sears, Barnas
Sharp, Dallas Lore
Sheldon, Charles Monroe
Sheldon, William Herbert
Shepard, Charles Upham
Smith, Gerald Birney
Smith, Roswell
Staples, William Read
Stiness, John Henry
Stone, William Leete
Tallmadge, James
Thayer, Eli
Thayer, John Milton
Thayer, William Makepeace
Thurber, Charles
Thurston, Robert Henry
Upton, George Putnam
Upton, Winslow
Utley, George Burwell
Varnum, James Mitchell
Ward, Joseph
Ward, Samuel, 1756–1832
Wayland, Francis, 1826–1904
Wheaton, Frank
Wheaton, Henry
Wheeler, Benjamin Ide
Whitman, Ezekiel
Williams, David Rogerson
Williamson, William Durkee
Wilson, George Grafton
Winkler, Edwin Theodore
Woolley, Mary Emma

Graduate Study

Allen, Edgar
Belkin, Samuel
Brightman, Edgar Sheffield
Coxhill, George Ellett
Corvin, Stephen Sheldon
Davis, Harvey Nathaniel
Gilbreth, Lillian Evelyn Moller
Green, Theodore Francis
Howell, David
Krause, Allen Kramer
Magill, Edward Hicks
Maxcy, Virgil
Meiklejohn, Alexander
Osterhout, Winthrop John Vanleuven
Rogers, William Augustus
Thurber, Charles
Thurston, Robert Henry
Wilson, George Grafton
Woolley, Mary Emma

Medicine

Allen, Zachariah
Bartlett, Elisha
Green, Asa
March, Alden

BRYANT AND STRATTON BUSINESS COLLEGE (ILL.)

Bennett, Earl W.
Sabath, Adolph J.

BRYN MAWR COLLEGE (PA.)

Allinson, Anne Crosby Emery
Balch, Emily Greene
Blodgett, Katharine Burr
Dunbar, (Helen) Flanders
Hamilton, Edith
Helburn, Theresa
Hepburn, Katharine Houghton
Moore, Marianne Craig
Reilly, Marion
Skinner, Cornelia Otis
Speer, Emma Bailey
Strong, Anna Louise
Tiffany, Katrina Brandes Ely

Graduate Study

Akeley, Mary Leonore
Allinson, Anne Crosby Emery
Hepburn, Katharine Houghton
Kenyon, Josephine Hemenway

BUCKNELL UNIVERSITY (PA.)

Bliss, Tasker Howard
Frear, William
Golder, Frank Alfred
Gregg, David McMurtrie
Hall, Thomas
Hill, David Jayne
Mathewson, Christopher ("Christy")
Potter, Charles Francis
Rawlinson, Frank Joseph
Thomas, Norman Mattoon

Graduate Study

Hill, David Jayne
Potter, Charles Francis

BUDAPEST ACADEMY OF ARTS (HUNGARY)

Pal, George

BUDAPEST ACADEMY OF MUSIC (HUNGARY)

Reiner, Fritz

BUDAPEST INSTITUTE OF TECHNOLOGY (HUNGARY)

Szilard, Leo

BUFFALO MEDICAL COLLEGE (N.Y.)

Brush, Edward Nathaniel
Myer, Albert James
Smith, Stephen

BURLESON COLLEGE (TEX.)

Neyland, Robert Reese, Jr.

BURR AND BURTON SEMINARY (MANCHESTER, VT.)

Cheney, John Vance
Roe, Edward Payson
Sheldon, William Evarts
Spring, Leverett Wilson

BUTLER UNIVERSITY (IND.)

Cope, Arthur Clay
Jones, Jim

Randall, James Garfield
Sissle, Noble Lee
Thompson, Stith

CALIFORNIA INSTITUTE OF TECHNOLOGY
Acosta, Bertram Blanchard ("Bert")
Carlson, Chester Floyd
Hawks, Howard Winchester
Hughes, Howard Robard, Jr.
Jewett, Frank Baldwin
Kirkwood, John Gamble
Graduate Study
Bowen, Ira Sprague
Millikan, Clark Blanchard
Zwicky, Fritz
CALIFORNIA STATE NORMAL SCHOOL AT CHICO
Adams, Annette Abbott
CAMBRIDGE HIGH AND LATIN SCHOOL (MASS.)
Bixby, James Thompson
Bôcher, Maxime
Greene, Charles Ezra
Holland, Clifford Milburn
Merrill, George Edmands
Nelson, Charres Alexander
Peirce, Charles Sanders
CAMBRIDGE UNIVERSITY (ENGLAND)
Bateman, Harry
Bateson, Gregory
Berryman, John
Boyd, James
Brown, Ernest William
Buchman, Frank Nathan Daniel
Carter, Boake
Child, Robert
Duranty, Walter
Field, Marshall, III
Guggenheim, Harry Frank
Howe, Quincy
Johnson, Harry Gordon
Kerner, Otto, Jr.
McDougall, William
Morley, Frank
Nabokov, Vladimir Vladimirovich
Payne-Gaposchkin, Cecilia Helena
Peabody, Endicott
Prouty, Charles Tyler
Rainsford, William Stephen
Rennie, Michael
Seymour, Charles
Whitehead, Alfred North
Graduate Study
Auchincloss, Hugh Dudley, Jr.
Blodgett, Katherine Burr
Brown, Ernest William
Farrand, Livingston
Guggenheim, Harry Frank
Johnson, Harry Gordon
McDougall, William
Mirsky, Alfred Ezra
Morley, Frank
Osborn, Henry Fairfield
Russell, Henry Norris
Whitehead, Alfred North
CANANDAIGUA ACADEMY (N.Y.)
Ball, Frank Clayton
Ball, George Alexander
Bennett, Nathaniel
Chesebrough, Caroline
Clarke, John Mason
Emery, Charles Edward
Rafter, George W.
Rankine, William Birch
Squires, Herbert Goldsmith
CANISIUS COLLEGE (N.Y.)
Odenbach, Frederick Louis
CAPITAL UNIVERSITY (OHIO)
Loy, Matthias
Norelius, Eric
Piatt, John James
Schodde, George Henry
Short, Sidney Howe
CAPITOL COLLEGE OF PHARMACY (COLO.)
Humphrey, Hubert Horatio, Jr
CARLETON COLLEGE (MINN.)
Benton, William Burnett
Brown, Carleton
Burton, Marion Le Roy
Butler, Pierce
Carson, Jack
Dickinson, Edwin De Witt
Edwards, Everett Eugene
Eklund, Carl Robert
Holmes, Bayard Taylor
Lundeen, Ernest
Mundt, Karl Earl
Pye, Watts Orson
Veblen, Thorstein Bunde
CARLETON COLLEGE (MO.)
Asbury, Herbert
CARLISLE INDIAN SCHOOL (PA.)
Bender, Charles Albert ("Chief")
Thorpe, James Francis
CARNEGIE INSTITUTE OF TECHNOLOGY (PA.)
Abernethy, Roy
Fogarty, Anne Whitney
McDonald, David John
Monroe, Vaughn Wilton
Svenson, Andrew Edward
Symes, James Miller
Wilson, Charles Erwin
Graduate Study
Robinson, Edward Stevens
CARROLL COLLEGE (WIS.)
Curtin, Jeremiah
Davis, Cushman Kellogg
Fairchild, Lucius
Lunt, Alfred David, Jr.
Showerman, Grant
Watson, Andrew
CARSON-NEWMAN COLLEGE (TENN.)
Bible, Dana Xenophon
Reece, Brazilla Carroll
Tilson, John Quillin
CASE INSTITUTE OF TECHNOLOGY (OHIO)
Stearns, Frank Ballou
CASE SCHOOL OF APPLIED SCIENCE (OHIO)
Bevier, Isabel
Dow, Herbert Henry
East, Edward Murray
CASE-WESTERN RESERVE UNIVERSITY (OHIO)
Hughes, Rupert
Graduate Study
Hughes, Rupert
CATHOLIC UNIVERSITY OF AMERICA (D.C.)
Bailey, John Moran
Dietz, Peter Ernest
Dowling, Austin
Duffy, Francis Patrick
Grady, Henry Francis
Keller, James Gregory
Tansill, Charles Callan
Graduate Study
Burke, John Joseph
Haas, Francis Joseph
Hayes, Patrick Joseph
Johnson, George
Keller, James Gregory
Kerby, William Joseph
Michel, Virgil George
Nieuwland, Julius Arthur
Ryan, John Augustine
Sheen, Fulton John
Tansill, Charles Callan
Wimsatt, William Kurtz
CATHOLIC UNIVERSITY OF LOUVAIN (BELGIUM)
Graduate Study
Kerby, William Joseph
CATHOLIC UNIVERSITY OF SANTIAGO (CHILE)
De Cuevas, Marquis
CAZENOVIA SEMINARY (N.Y.)
Andrews, Charles
Andrews, Edward Gayer
Armsur, Philip Danforth
Blair, Austin
Bowman, Thomas
Burdick, Francis Marion
Clarke, William Newton
Condon, Thomas
Cone, Orello
Cooper, Sarah Brown Ingersoll
Davis, Nathan Smith
Dexter, Wirt
Fairchild, Charles Stebbins
Fiske, Daniel Willard
Longyear, John Munroe
Mann, Newton
Newman, John Philip
Peck, Jesse Truesdell
Remington, Philo
Slocum, Henry Warner
Stanford, Leland
Stranahan, James Samuel Thomas
Throop, Montgomery Hunt
Underwood, Lucien Marcus
Vail, Stephen Montfort
CENTENARY COLLEGE (L.A.)
Hubbard, Robert C. ("Cal")
CENTENARY COLLEGE (N.J.)
McClenahan, Howard
CENTRAL COLLEGE (MO.)
Craighead, Edwin Boone
Hendrix, Joseph Clifford
Hirth, William Andrew
Parker, Edwin Brewington
Shafroth, John Franklin
Stuart, John Todd
Vest, George Graham
Wickliffe, Robert Charles
Yandell, David Wendell

CENTRAL HIGH SCHOOL (PHILA.)
Abbett, Leon
Allen, Harrison
Ashburner, Charles Albert
Atkinson, William Biddle
Bell, James Stroud
Brown, William Henry
Cochrane, Henry Clay
Cohen, Jacob Da Silva Solis
Cramp, Charles Henry
Davidson, George
Ffoulke, Charles Mather
Gabb, William More
Gihon, Albert Leary
Hartranft, Chester David
Houston, Edwin James
Jackson, Abraham Reeves
Kahn, Louis I.
Leffmann, Henry
Macfarlane, Charles William
Mills, Charles Karsner
Mitchell, James Tyndale
Murphy, Dominic Ignatius
Newhouse, Samuel
Oliver, Charles Augustus
Patterson, Robert Mayne
Pattison, Robert Emory
Potts, Charles Sower
Pyle, Walter Lytle
Rhees, William Tones
Rice, Edwin Wilbur
Rogers, John Ignatius
Rogers, Robert William
Smith, Eugene Allen
Smyth, Albert Henry
Stockton, Frank Richard
Sulzberger, Cyrus Lindauer
Sulzberger, Mayer
Townsend, George Alfred
Tryon, George Washington
Tyson, James
Widener, Peter Arrell Brown
Woodruff, Charles Edward
Woodward, Joseph Janvier
Yerkes, Charles Tyson
CENTRAL MISSOURI STATE TEACHERS COLLEGE
Hill, Arthur Middleton
CENTRAL NORMAL COLLEGE (ILL.)
Thomas, (John William) Elmer
CENTRAL NORMAL COLLEGE (IND.)
Menninger, Charles Frederick
CENTRAL NORMAL SCHOOL (IND.)
Terman, Lewis Madison
CENTRAL TURKEY COLLEGE (TURKEY)
Gregory, Menas Sarkas Boulgourjian
CENTRAL WESLEYAN COLLEGE (MO.)
Sauer, Carl Ortwin
CENTRE COLLEGE (KY.)
Baird, Samuel John
Birney, James
Blackburn, Joseph Clay Styles
Boyle, Jeremiah Tilford
Breckinridge, John Cabell
Breckinridge, William Campbell Preston
Brown, John Young
Buford, Abraham, 1820–1884
Burchard, Samuel Dickinson
Crittenden, Thomas Theodore
Duke, Basil Wilson
Green, Lewis Warner
Hall, William Whitty
Harlan, John Marshall
Holt, Joseph
Hume, Edgar Erskine
Jackson, John Davies
Johnston, William Preston
Lewis, Joseph Horace
McCreary, James Bennett
McMillin Alvin Nugent ("Bo")
Magoffin, Beriah
Martin, William Thompson
Matthews, Claude
Maury, Francis Fontaine
Norton, Elijah Hise
Peay, Austin
Philips, John Finis
Rice, Nathan Lewis
Stanley, Augustus Owsley
Stevenson, Adlai Ewing
Vinson, Fred(erick) Moore
West, Andrew Fleming
Graduate Study
Bible, Dana Xenophon
Hume, Edgar Erskine
CHAFFEE JUNIOR COLLEGE (CAL.)
Jones, Lindley Armstrong ("Spike")
CHAPMAN COLLEGE (CAL.)
Ashford, Emmett Littleton
CHARLESTON COLLEGE (S.C.)
Boyce, James Petigru
Frémont, John Charles
Hayne, Paul Hamilton
Jacobs, William Plumer
Johnson, Joseph
Kinlock, Robert Alexander
Logan, Thomas Muldrup, 1808–1876
CHARLOTTENBURG INSTITUTE OF TECHNOLOGY, BERLIN (GERMANY)
Braun, Wernher Von
CHATHAM COLLEGE (PA.)
Carson, Rachel Louise
CHAUNCY HALL SCHOOL (MASS.)
Bacon, Henry
Bumstead, Freeman Josiah
Guild, Curtis, 1860–1915
Jarves, James Jackson
Lovett, Robert Williamson
Riddle, George Peabody
Ropes, John Codman
Thayer, Abbott Handerson
Towne, John Henry
CHEROKEE MALE SEMINARY (OKLA.)
Hastings, William Wirt
CHESTER ACADEMY
Burnett, Henry Lawrence
Evans, Warren Felt
Forwood, William Henry
Grant, Lewis Addison
CHICAGO ACADEMY OF FINE ARTS
Hokinson, Helen Elna
CHICAGO ART INSTITUTE *(See also* ART INSTITUTE OF CHICAGO)
Barnard, George Grey
Chaplin, Ralph Hosea
Curry, John Steuart
Fraser, James Earle
Frieseke, Frederick Carl
Harshe, Robert Bartholow
Howey, Walter Crawford
White, Charles Weibert
CHICAGO COLLEGE OF LAW
Levinson, Salmon Oliver
Sabath, Adolph J.
CHICAGO COLLEGE OF MEDICINE AND SURGERY
Sullivan, Harry Stack
CHICAGO COLLEGE OF PHARMACY
Breasted, James Henry
CHICAGO CONSERVATORY OF MUSIC
Henderson, Ray
CHICAGO HEBREW INSTITUTE
Potofsky, Jacob Samuel
CHICAGO-KENT COLLEGE OF LAW
Dawson, William Levi
Horner, Henry
CHICAGO MEDICAL COLLEGE
Billings, Frank
Holmes, Bayard Taylor
Quine, William Edward
Senn, Nicholas
CHICAGO THEOLOGICAL SCHOOL
Gates, Caleb Frank
CHICAGO THEOLOGICAL SEMINARY
Breasted, James Henry
Davis, Jerome Dean
Greene, Daniel Crosby
Lyman, Albert Josiah
McCulloch, Oscar Carleton
CHRISTIAN COLLEGE (CAL.)
Markham, Edwin
CHRISTIAN COLLEGE (MO.)
Froman, Ellen Jane
Rand, Sally
CINCINNATI ART SCHOOL
Hill, Grace Livingston
CINCINNATI COLLEGE
Chase, Salmon Portland
Durbin, John Price
Fosdick, William Whiteman
Lytle, William Haines
Pendleton, George Hunt
Pugh, George Ellis
Law
Butterworth, Benjamin
Cannon, Joseph Gurney
Case, Leonard
Clark, Champ
Crawford, Samuel Johnson
Dawson, Thomas Cleland
Day, James Gamble
Denver, James William
Edgerton, Sidney
Ewing, Thomas
Goebel, William
Hine, Charles de Lano
Holmes, Daniel Henry
Hoyt, John Wesley
Lawrence, William, 1819–1899
Longworth, Nicholas
Morton, Oliver Perry
Noble, John Willock
Noyes, Edward Follansbee
Sherwood, Thomas Adiel
Storer, Bellamy
Swayne, Wager
Taft, William Howard

CINCINNATI COLLEGE OF MEDICINE AND SURGERY
Crumbine, Samuel Jay
CINCINNATI CONSERVATORY OF MUSIC
Niles, John Jacob
CINCINNATI LAW SCHOOL
Crosser, Robert
Dawes, Charles Gates
Pomerene, Atlee
Van Devanter, Willis
CITY COLLEGE OF NEW YORK
Abbe, Cleveland
Agramonte y Simoni, Aristides
Bangs, Francis Nehemiah
Baruch, Bernard Mannes
Bickel, Alexander Mordecai
Blackton, James Stuart
Bloomfield, Meyer
Borchard, Edwin Montefiore
Bowker, Richard Rogers
Brill, Abraham Arden
Brill, Nathan Edwin
Brooks, Elbridge Streeter
Brown, George, 1823–1892
Cambridge, Godfrey MacArthur
Carvalho, Solomon Solis
Claflin, John
Coakley, Cornelius Godfrey
Cobb, Lee J.
Cohen, Felix Solomon
Cohen, Morris Raphael
Corwin, Edward Tanjore
Croly, Herbert David
Damrosch, Frank Heino
Davidson, Israel
Dean, Bashford
Elsberg, Charles Albert
Epstein, Philip G.
Evans, William Thomas
Fackler, David Parks
Fleischer, Nathaniel Stanley ("Nat")
Fletcher, Robert
Frankfurter, Felix
Glass, Montague Marsden
Goethals, George Washington
Goldberger, Joseph
Goldmark, Rubin
Goodman, Paul
Grau, Maurice
Grauer, Benjamin Franklin ("Ben")
Green, Gabriel Marcus
Grinnell, Henry Walton
Hackett, James Keteltas
Harland, Henry
Hays, Arthur Garfield
Hecht, Selig
Helpern, Milton
Herberg, Will
Hirsch, Isaac Seth
Jackson, George Thomas
Jackson, Samuel Macauley
Jacobs, Paul
Jordan, Virgil Justin
Jordon, William George
Kaempffert, Waldemar Bernhard
Kohler, Max James
Leipziger, Henry Marcus
Lewis, Oscar
Libman, Emanuel
Lowie, Robert Harry
Lyons, Leonard
McAdie, Alexander George
McMaster, John Bach
Maslow, Abraham H.
Maybeck, Bernard Ralph
Mayer, Emil
Miller, Henry Valentine
Morgenthau, Henry
Moses, Montrose Jonas
Moss, Frank
Mostel, Samuel Joel ("Zero")
Newman, Barnett
Olcott, Eben Erskine
Park, William Hallock
Pasvolsky, Leo
Patri, Angelo
Pecora, Ferdinand
Pei, Mario Andrew
Pope, John Russell
Post, George Edward
Powell, Adam Clayton, Jr.
Radin, Max
Radin, Paul
Randolph, Asa Philip
Remsen, Ira
Rice, George Samuel
Roberts, William Henry
Robinson, Edward G.
Rosebury, Theodor
Rosenberg, Julius
Rosenman, Samuel Irving
Rubin, Isidor Clinton
Schlesinger, Frank
Schultz, Henry
Shahn, Benjamin ("Ben")
Shepard, Edward Morse
Sinclair, Upton Beall, Jr.
Spier, Leslie
Spingarn, Joel Elias
Spitzka, Edward Anthony
Spitzka, Edward Charles
Steinman, David Barnard
Steuer, Max David
Stieglitz, Alfred
Stillman, Thomas Edgar
Sturgis, Russell
Taylor, Bert Leston
Taylor, Stevenson
Tilton, Theodore
Timme, Walter
Towne, Charles Hanson
Tremain, Henry Edwin
Tuthill, William Burnet
Untermyer, Samuel
Veiller, Lawrence Turnure
Viereck, George Sylvester
Wagner, Robert Ferdinand
Weir, Robert Fulton
Wheeler, Everett Pepperrell
Wight, Peter Bonnett
Wise, Stephen Samuel
Wolfe, Bertram David
Wolheim, Louis Robert
Woodruff, Lorande Loss
Graduate Study
Coakley, Cornelius Godfrey
McAdie, Alexander George
CLAFLIN UNIVERSITY (S.C.)
Abbott, Robert Sengstacke
CLARK UNIVERSITY (MASS.)
Behrman, Samuel Nathaniel ("S.N.")
Bemis, Samuel Flagg
Dibble, Roy Floyd
Fryer, Douglas Henry
Goddard, Robert Hutchings
Harris, Rollin Arthur
Lubin, Isador
Graduate Study
Albee, Ernest
Bemis, Samuel Flagg
Burk, Frederic Lister
Calkins, Mary Whiton
Chamberlain, Alexander Francis
Chase, Harry Woodburn
Duncan, Robert Kennedy
Frazier, Edward Franklin
Fryer, Douglas Henry
Gesell, Arnold Lucius
Goddard, Henry Herbert
Jordan, Edwin Oakes
Odum, Howard Washington
Smith, Theodate Louise
Starbuck, Edwin Diller
Terman, Lewis Madison
CLEMSON COLLEGE (S.C.)
Cohen, Octavus Roy
Gossett, Benjamin Brown
Vincent, John Carter
CLEVELAND MEDICAL COLLEGE
Elwell, John Johnson
Goodrich, Benjamin Franklin
Newberry, John Strong
CLEVELAND SCHOOL OF ART (OHIO)
Burchfield, Charles Ephraim
CLINTON LIBERAL INSTITUTE (N.Y.)
Gage, Matilda Joslyn
McEntee, Jervis
Scollard, Clinton
Skinner, Charles Rufus
Stanford, Leland
COAST GUARD ACADEMY (N.Y.)
Waesche, Russell Randolph
COBB DIVINITY SCHOOL (MAINE)
Hayes, Edward Carey
COE COLLEGE (IOWA)
Reed, James Alexander
Ross, Edward Alsworth
COKESBURY INSTITUTE (S.C.)
Bass, William Capers
Capers, Ellison
De Bow, James Dunwoody Brownson
Gary, Martin Witherspoon
McTyeire, Holland Nimmons
Pratt, John
White, Samuel
COLBY COLLEGE (MAINE)
Anderson, Martin Brewer
Brooks, James
Butler, Benjamin Franklin, 1818–1893
Day, Holman Francis
Dearing, John Lincoln
Dingley, Nelson
Emery, Stephen Albert
Hinds, Asher Crosby
Holden, Liberty Emery
Howard, Volney Erskine

Lapham, William Berry
Lord, Herbert Mayhew
Lovejoy, Elijah Parish
McNulty, John Augustine
Marble, Albert Prescott
Mathews, Shailer
Mathews, William
Merriam, Henry Clay
Mitchell, Edward Cushing
Morrill, Lot Myrick
Paine, Henry Warren
Plaistead, Harris Merrill
Scammon, Jonathan Young
Sheldon, Edward Stevens
Small, Albion Woodbury
Smith, Charles Henry, 1827–1902
Smith, George Otis
Tripp, Bartlett

Graduate Study
Smith, Charles Henry, 1827–1902

COLGATE UNIVERSITY
Avery, Oswald Theodore
Bonney, Charles Carroll
Brigham, Albert Perry
Brown, John Newton
Burroughs, John Curtis
Carpenter, Stephen Haskins
Church, Pharcellus
Clarke, William Newton
Davis, Oscar King
Fosdick, Harry Emerson
Fosdick, Raymond Blaine
Galpin, Charles Josiah
Hindus, Maurice Gerschon
Hughes, Albert William
Hughes, Charles Evans
Judson, Edward
Knapp, William Ireland
Landon, Melville de Lancey
Loomis, Elmer Howard
Orton, Harlow South
Powell, Adam Clayton, Jr.
Rathbone, Justus Henry
Stillman, Thomas Edgar
Taylor, Benjamin Franklin
Tupper, Henry Allen
Utley, George Burwell
Williams, Frank Martin

Graduate Study
Davis, Oscar King
Fosdick, Harry Emerson
Galpin, Charles Josiah
Hindus, Maurice Gerschon
Schmidt, Nathaniel

Theology
Brigham, Albert Perry
Clarke, William Newton
Johnson, Franklin
Raymond, John Howard

COLLEGE CHAMPOLLION, FIGEAC (FRANCE)
Boyer, Charles

COLLEGE DE GENEVE (SWITZERLAND)
Bacon, Benjamin Wisner

COLLEGE OF CHARLESTON (S.C.)
De Bow, James Dunwoody Brownson
Fraser, Charles
Furman, James Clement
Gildersleeve, Basil Lanneau
Girardeau, John Lafayette
Lewisohn, Ludwig
McCrady, Edward
Maybank, Burnet Rhett
Middleton, Nathaniel Russell
Miles, William Porcher
Mills, Robert, 1781–1855
Mood, Francis Asbury
Rivers, Lucius Mendel
Silcox, Ferdinand Augustus
Simonton, Charles Henry
Smith, Henry Augustus Middleton
Smith, John Lawrence
Tiedeman, Christopher Gustavus
Trescot, William Henry
Waring, Julius Waties

Graduate Study
Lewisohn, Ludwig
Mood, Francis Asbury

COLLEGE OF EMPORIA (KANS.)
Pemberton, Brock

COLLEGE OF MEDICAL EVANGELISTS (CAL.)
Price, George Edward McCready

COLLEGE OF NEW JERSEY (*See* PRINCETON UNIVERSITY)

COLLEGE OF NEW ROCHELLE (N.Y.)
Kilgallen, Dorothy Mae

COLLEGE OF PHARMACY OF NEW YORK
Kunze, Richard Ernest
Mayer, Emil
Ziegler, William

COLLEGE OF PHILADELPHIA (*See* UNIVERSITY OF PENNSYLVANIA)

COLLEGE OF PHYSICIANS AND SURGEONS (MD.)
Hunt, Reid

COLLEGE OF PHYSICIANS AND SURGEONS (*See* COLUMBIA UNIVERSITY, *Medicine*)

COLLEGE OF ST. FRANCIS XAVIER
Malone, Dudley Field

COLLEGE OF ST. MARY OF THE SPRINGS (OHIO)
McCormick, Anne Elizabeth O'Hare

COLLEGE OF ST. XAVIER (N.Y.) (*See also* ST. FRANCIS XAVIER COLLEGE)
Campbell, Thomas Joseph
Crimmins, John Daniel
Drumgoole, John Christopher
Duffy, Francis Patrick
Edebohls, George Michael
Herbermann, Charles George
Keane, James John
McFaul, James Augustine
Moeller, Henry
Pardow, William O'Brien
Tierney, Richard Henry
Wixler, Winand Michael

COLLEGE OF SOUTH CAROLINA (*See* UNIVERSITY OF SOUTH CAROLINA)

COLLEGE OF THE CITY OF NEW YORK (*See* CITY COLLEGE OF NEW YORK)

COLLEGE OF THE PACIFIC (CAL.)
Kuykendall, Ralph Simpson
Widney, Joseph Pomeroy

COLLEGE OF WILLIAM AND MARY (VA.)
Anderson, Richard Clough
Archer, William Segar
Barbour, Philip Pendleton
Barry, William Taylor
Bibb, George Mortimer
Blair, John, 1687–1771
Blair, John, 1732–1800
Bland, Richard
Bloxham, William Dunnington
Brandon, Gerard Chittocque
Braxton, Carter
Breckenridge, James
Breckinridge, John, 1760–1806
Brown, James, 1766–1835
Brown, John, 1757–1837
Cabell, James Branch
Cabell, Joseph Carrington
Cabell, Samuel Jordan
Cabell, William H.
Cary, Archibald
Chandler, Julian Alvin Carroll
Claiborne, William Charles Coles
Cocke, John Hartwell
Coke, Richard
Coles, Edward
Crittenden, John Jordan
Croghan, George, 1791–1849
Crump, William Wood
Dabney, Thomas Smith Gregory
Dearborn, Henry Alexander Sammell
Dew, Thomas Roderick
Garrett, William Robertson
Gilmer, Francis Walker
Greenhow, Robert
Hardy, Samuel
Harrison, Benjamin, 1726–1791
Henley, Robert
Hope, James Barron
Innes, James
Jefferson, Thomas
Johnson, Chapman
Jones, John Winston
Lee, Henry, 1787–1837
Leigh, Benjamin Watkms
Littlepage, Lewis
McRae, Duncan Kirkland
Madison, James, 1749–1812
Mason, Stevens Thomson, 1760–1803
Mercer, James
Mercer, John Francis
Minor, Benjamin Blake
Minor, Lucian
Monroe, James
Munford, William
Nelson, Hugh
Nelson, Roger
Newton, Thomas, 1768–1847
Nicholas, George
Nicholas, John
Nicholas, Philip Norborne
Nicholas, Robert Carter
Nicholas, Wilson Cary
Page, John
Plater, George

Pleasants, James
Pleasants, John Hampden
Randolph, Alfred Magill
Randolph, Edmund, 1753–1813
Randolph, Edmund, 1819–1861
Randolph, Sir John
Randolph, Peyton
Randolph, Thomas Mann
Rives, William Cabell
Roane, Spencer
Robertson, John
Robertson, Thomas Bolling
Robertson, Wyndham
Robinson, John
Robinson, Moncure
Rogers, James Blythe
Rogers, William Barton
Ruffin, Edmund
Scott, Winfield
Short, William
Smith, Daniel
Smith, John Augustine
Stanard, William Glover
Staples, Walter Redd
Stevenson, Andrew
Stuart, Alexander Hugh Holmes
Stuart, Archibald
Taliaferro, William Booth
Taylor, John
Taylor, John Louis
Tazewell, Henry
Tazewell, Littleton Waller
Thomson, John, 1776–1799
Todd, Charles Stewart
Tucker, George
Tucker, Henry St. George
Tucker, Nathaniel Beverley
Tucker, St. George
Tyler, John, 1747–1813
Tyler, John, 1790–1862
Tyler, Robert
Walker, Thomas
Warrington, Lewis
Washington, Bushrod
Williams, Channing Moore
Wilson, James Southall
Wythe, George

Graduate Study
Chandler, Julian Alvin Carroll
Garrett, William Robertson

Law
Cooke, John Rogers
Ellis, Powhatan
Marshall, John
Mason, James Murray
Ravenscroft, John Stark

COLLEGE OF WOOSTER (OHIO)
Bevier, Isabel
Boole, Ella Alexander
Compton, Arthur Holly
Compton, Karl Taylor
Fairless, Benjamin F.
Lyon, David Willard
Notestein, Wallace
Patrick, Hugh Talbot
Rhine, Joseph Banks
Thomas, Roland Jay

Graduate Study
Bevier, Isabel
Boole, Ella Alexander
Compton, Karl Taylor

COLLEGE ST. GERVAIS (BELGIUM)
Feininger, Lyonel (Charles Léonell Adrian)

COLLEGIATE INSTITUTE OF CHATHAM (CANADA)
Ross, James Delmage McKenzie

COLOGNE CONSERVATORY (GERMANY)
Busch, Hermann

COLORADO COLLEGE
Gaylord, Edward King
Holt, Arthur Erastus
Leverett, Frank
Paul, Josephine Bay

COLORADO SCHOOL OF MINES
Fairbanks, Douglas

COLORADO STATE COLLEGE OF AGRICULTURE
Jones, Benjamin Allyn

COLUMBIA COLLEGE (S.C.)
Peterkin, Julia Mood

COLUMBIAN UNIVERSITY (*See* GEORGE WASHINGTON UNIVERSITY)

COLUMBIA THEOLOGICAL SEMINARY (S.C.)
Jacobs, William Plumer
McKinley, Carlyle
Palmer, Benjamin Morgan
Wilson, John Leighton

COLUMBIA UNIVERSITY (N.Y.)
Adler, Felix
Aggrey, James Emman Kwegyir
Allen, Horatio
Anthon, Charles
Anthon, Charles Edward
Anthon, John
Armstrong, Edwin Howard
Astor, John Jacob, 1822–1890
Auchmuty, Richard Tylden
Bangs, John Kendrick
Barclay, Thomas
Bard, Samuel
Bard, William
Beck, John Brodhead
Beebe, (Charles) William
Beer, George Louis
Benson, Egbert
Bergh, Henry
Bernstein, Theodore Menline
Berryman, John
Bethune, George Washington
Black, Douglas MacRae
Blatchford, Samuel
Blount, Willie
Bolton, Henry Carrington
Borchard, Edwin Montefiore
Bourke-White, Margaret
Bourne, Randolph Silliman
Bowden, John
Brace, Donald Clifford
Bridges, Calvin Blackman
Browere, John Henri Isaac
Brown, Margaret Wise
Bruce, Archibald
Bruce, Edward Bright
Burrill, Alexander Mansfield
Butler, Nicholas Murray
Cahill, Holger
Cardozo, Benjamin Nathan
Carrington, Elaine Stern
Carryl, Guy Wetmore
Cerf, Bennett Alfred
Chambers, Whittaker
Chapin, James Paul
Chapman, John Arthur
Chisolm, Alexander Robert
Chotzinoff, Samuel
Clinton, De Witt
Clurman, Harold Edgar
Cohn, Alfred Einstein
Coit, Stanton
Colby, Frank Moore
Cole, George Watson
Collins, Edward Trowbridge
Cook, Walter Wheeler
Cooper, Edward
Copeland, Charles W.
Coudert, Frederic René
Coudert, Frederic René, Jr.
Cowen, Joshua Lionel
Cruger, Henry
Cutting, Robert Fulton
Dana, Charles Anderson
Davies, Henry Eugene
Davis, Bernard George
De Koven, James
Delafield, John, 1786–1853
De Mille, Henry Churchill
De Peyster, John Watts
De Wilde, Brandon
Dix, Morgan
Doremus, Robert Ogden
Drisler, Henry
Dunning, John Ray
Dunning, William Archibald
Duyckinck, Evert Augustus
Earhart, Amelia Mary
Earle, Edward Mead
Earle, Mortimer Lamson
Edman, Irwin
Ehninger, John Whetten
Ely, Richard Theodore
Emott, James, 1823–1884
Erpf, Armand Grover
Erskine, John
Fairchild, Sherman Mills
Fawcett, Edgar
Ferris, Isaac
Fish, Hamilton
Fish, Stuyvesant
Floy, James
Ford, Worthington Chauncey
Foulke, William Dudley
Fox, Dixon Ryan
Francis, John Wakefield
Francis, Samuel Ward
Frank, Lawrence Kelso
Franz, Shepherd Ivory
Fraser, Leon
Freeman, Joseph
Gallico, Paul William
Gehrig, Henry Louis
Geismar, Maxwell David
Gerard, James Watson, 1794–1874
Gerard, James Watson 1867–1951
Gerry, Elbridge Thomas
Gibbs, Oliver Wolcott
Gillespie, William Mitchell
Gleason, Ralph Joseph
Goldenweiser, Alexander Alexandrovich

Goldenweiser, Emanuel Alexander
Goldwater, Sigismund Schulz
Gottheil, Richard James Horatio
Graham, John, 1774–1820
Griscom, Ludlow
Hackett, James Henry
Haight, Charles Coolidge
Hamilton, Alexander, 1757–1804
Hamilton, James Alexander
Hammerstein, Oscar, II
Harcourt, Alfred
Harris, Maurice Henry
Harrison, Fairfax
Harrison, Henry Sydnor
Hart, Lorenz Milton
Hastings, Thomas, 1860–1929
Havemeyer, William Frederick
Hayes, Carlton Joseph Huntley
Hays, Arthur Garfield
Hays, Paul R.
Hewitt, Abram Stevens
Hewitt, Peter Cooper
Hill, John Henry
Hine, Lewis Wickes
Hobson, Julius Wilson
Hoffman, Charles Fenno
Hoffman, David Murray
Hoffman, Ogden
Hogan, Frank Smithwick
Holls, George Frederick William
Holt, Hamilton Bowen
Hopkins, Edward Washburn
Horton, Edward Everett, Jr.
Hosack, David
Hughes, James Langston
Hurd, John Codman
Hutton, Frederick Remsen
Irving, John Duer
Irving, John Treat
Irving, Pierre Munro
Irving, Roland Duer
Jackson, Abraham Valentine Williams
Jackson, George Thomas
Jay, John, 1745–1829
Jay, John, 1817–1894
Jay, Peter Augustus
Jenks, Tudor Storrs
Johnson, Allen
Jones, Samuel
Jones, William
Jones, William Alfred
Josephson, Matthew
Kearny, Philip
Kearny, Stephen Watts
Kellogg, Paul Underwood
Kelly, Edmond
Kemble, Gouverneur
Kemp, James Furman
Kemper, Jackson
Kendall, Edward Calvin
Kent, Rockwell
Keppel, Frederick Paul
Kerouac, Jack
Kilmer, Alfred Joyce
Knapp, Joseph Palmer
Kobbé, Gustav
Kroeber, Alfred Louis
Langer, William
Lathrop, Francis Augustus
Lawrence, William Beach
Lee, Ivy Ledbetter
Lehman, Irving
Lenox, James
Leonar, Robert Josselyn
Levitt, Arthur
Linn, John Blair
Livingston, Robert R., 1746–1813
Lloyd, Henry Demarest
Locke, Bessie
Low, Seth
Ludlow, Thomas William
McCartee, Divie Bethune
McHale, Kathryn
McNulty, John Augustine
McVickar, John
McVickar, William Neilson
Macy, Valentine Everit
Mahan, Alfred Thayer
Mankiewicz, Herman Jacob
Marcus, Bernard Kent
Margolis, Max Leopold
Marshall, Henry Rutgers
Mason, John, 1858–1919
Mason, John Mitchell
Matthews, James Brander
Maxwell, Hugh
Mayer, Philip Frederick
Maynard, George William
Megrue, Roi Cooper
Merriam, Augustus Chapman
Merton, Thomas
Meyer, Annie Nathan
Milledoler, Philip
Mitchel, John Purroy
Mitchell, William, 1801–1886
Moisseiff, Leon Solomon
Moldenke, Richard George Gottlob
Moon, Parker Thomas
Moore, Benjamin
Moore, Clement Clarke
Moore, Nathaniel Fish
Morris, Gouverneur
Muller, Hermann Joseph
Murphy, Henry Cruse
Nadal, Ehrman Syme
Nies, Tames Buchanan
Oberholser, Harry Church
Odell, Benjamin Barker
Odell, George Clinton Densmore
Ogden, Thomas Ludlow
Olyphant, Robert Morrison
O'Mahoney, Joseph Christopher
Onderdonk, Benjamin Tredwell
Onderdonk, Henry
Onderdonk, Henry Ustick
Oppenheim, James
Osborn, Laughton
O'Sullivan, John Louis
Parsons, William Barclay
Partridge, William Ordway
Pasvolsky, Leo
Patchen, Kenneth
Patterson, Richard Cunningham, Jr.
Peck, Harry Thurston
Plotz, Harry
Pollak, Walter Heilprin
Pott, Francis Lister Hawks
Price, Stephen
Provoost, Samuel
Pupin, Michael Idvorsky
Raymond, John Howard
Redman, Ben Ray
Rees, John Krom
Reinhardt, Ad
Renwick, Edward Sabine
Renwick, Henry Brevoort
Renwick, James, 1792–1863
Renwick, James, 1818–1895
Reynolds, Richard Samuel, Sr.
Richardson, Anna Euretta
Ridder, Bernard Herman
Rives, George Lockhart
Robb, William Lispenard
Robinson, Henry Morton
Rodgers, Richard Charles
Rosenblatt, Bernard Abraham
Rosenman, Samuel Irving
Rosewater, Victor
Roth, Samuel
Rubinow, Isaac Max
Rukeyser, Muriel
Rutgers, Henry
Sachs, Alexander
Sachs, Julius
Sands, Robert Charles
Sapir, Edward
Satterlee, Henry Yates
Sayre, Reginald Hall
Schlesinger, Arthur Meier
Schuster, Max Lincoln
Schuyler, Robert Livingston
Sedgwick, Theodore, 1811–1859
Seligman, Edwin Robert Anderson
Seligman, Isaac Newton
Seymour, George Franklin
Shepherd, William Robert
Sherman, Frank Dempster
Shrady, Henry Merwin
Simkhovitch, Mary Melinda Kingsbury
Simon, Richard Leo
Slidell, John
Sloane, William Milligan
Smillie, Ralph
Smith, Bruce
Sokolsky, George Ephraim
Sparrow, William
Speck, Frank Gouldsmith
Spencer, Jesse Ames
Spewak, Samuel
Spingarn, Arthur Barnett
Spingarn, Joel Elias
Sporn, Philip
Steinhardt, Laurence Adolph
Stephens, John Lloyd
Stevens, John
Stewart, John Aikman
Stokes, Isaac Newton Phelps
Straus, Oscar Solomon
Strunsky, Simeon
Sulzberger, Arthur Hays
Sweeny, Peter Barr
Tate, George Henry Hamilton
Tauber, Maurice Falcolm
Terhune, Albert Payson
Tompkins, Daniel D.
Trilling, Lionel

Troup, Robert
Trowbridge, Augustus
Trudeau, Edward Livingston
Tucker, Allen
Tuttle, Daniel Sylvester
Van Amringe, John Howard
Van Ness, William Peter
Verplanck, Julian Crommelin
Vethake, Henry
Vincent, Marvin Richardson
Vroom, Peter Dumont
Weil, Richard
Weiss, Soma
Wheeler, Schuyler Skaats
Whitehouse, Frederic Cope
Williams, William R.
Willis, Bailey
Wise, Stephen Samuel
Witthaus, Rudolph August
Woodford, Stewart Lyndon
Woodward, Augustus Brevoort
Worcester, Elwood
Youmans, William Jay
Young, John Clarke
Zilboorg, Gregory
Zinsser, Hans
Zukofsky, Louis

Architecture

Atterbury, Grosvenor
Delano, William Adams
Hamlin, Talbot Faulkner
Ide, John Jay
Lamb, William Frederick
Porter, Arthur Kingsley

Graduate Study

Akeley, Mary Leonore
Alexander, Hartley Burr
Ames, Herman Vandenburg
Anderson, Benjamin McAlester
Andrews, Roy Chapman
Baker, Carl Lotus
Baker, Oliver Edwin
Bancroft, Frederic
Barber, Donn
Barrows, Alice Prentice
Beard, Charles Austin
Beary, Donald Bradford
Becket, Frederick Mark
Behrman, Samuel Nathaniel ("S.N.")
Bell, Eric Temple
Benedict, Ruth Fulton
Bentley, Elizabeth Terrill
Blanshard, Paul
Borchard, Edwin Montefiore
Boyd, William Kenneth
Britton, Nathaniel Lord
Butler, Howard Crosby
Butler, Nicholas Murray
Calkins, Gary Nathan
Campbell, William
Carter, William Hodding, Jr.
Cavert, Samuel McCrea
Chapin, James Paul
Clapp, Margaret Antonette
Clark, Felton Grandison
Clark, John Maurice
Coffman, Lotus Delta
Cohen, Morris Raphael
Cole, Charles Woolsey
Cutting, Robert Fulton
Davidson, Israel
Davis, Adelle
Dean, Bashford
Dennis, Alfred Lewis Pinneo
Dibble, Roy Floyd
Dobie, J(ames) Frank
Dodd, Bella Visono
Douglas, Aaron
Douglas, Paul Howard
Dowling, Noel Thomas
Dunbar, (Helen) Flanders
Dunning, John Ray
Dunning, William Archibald
Dyar, Harrison Gray
Earle, Edward Mead
Earle, Mortimer Lamson
Eastman, Max Forrester
Edman, Irwin
Emery, Henry Crosby
Erskine, John
Fairlie, John Archibald
Fauset, Jessie Redmon
Fisher, Dorothea Frances Canfield
Fleming, Walter Lynwood
Ford, Guy Stanton
Fox, Dixon Ryan
Franz, Shepherd Ivory
Franzblau, Rose Nadler
Fraser, Leon
Furst, Clyde Bowman
Gambrell, Mary Latimer
Garner, James Wilford
Gavin, Frank Stanton Burns
Geer, William Aughe ("Will")
Geismar, Maxwell David
Gerard, James Watson (1867–1951)
Gilbreth, Lillian Evelyn Moller
Gildersleeve, Virginia Crocheron
Goldenweiser, Alexander Alexandrovich
Gortner, Ross Aiken
Grady, Henry Francis
Graham, Edward Kidder
Graham, Frank Porter
Green, Gabriel Marcus
Greenslet, Ferris
Hadas, Moses
Hamilton, Clayton
Hayes, Carlton Joseph Huntley
Hays, Paul R.
Heezen, Bruce Charles
Hofstadter, Richard
Holt, Edwin Bissell
Hourwich, Isaac Aaronovich
Inglis, Alexander James
Irving, John Duer
Irwin, Elisabeth Antoinette
Jackson, Abraham Valentine Williams
Jelliffe, Smith Ely
Johnson, Alvin Saunders
Johnson, Douglas Wilson
Jones, Richard Foster
Jordan, Virgil Justin
Kagan, Henry Enoch
Kelly, Myra
Kendall, Edward Calvin
Knauth, Oswald Whitman
Koch, Vivienne
Kohler, Max James
Kroeber, Alfred Louis
Krutch, Joseph Wood
Kunitz, Moses
La Farge, Oliver Hazard Perry
Lee, Porter Raymond
Leiserson, William Morris
Leonard, Robert Josselyn
Leonard, Sterling Andrus
Leonard, William Ellery
Levenson, Samuel ("Sam")
Lewis, Oscar
Lewisohn, Ludwig
Linton, Ralph
Lowie, Robert Harry
McBain, Howard Lee
McClung, Clarence Erwin
McHale, Kathryn
MacNair, Harley Farnsworth
Malin, Patrick Murphy
Margolis, Max Leopold
Marshall, Henry Rutgers
Martin, Anne Henrietta
Mathews, John Alexander
Matthew, William Diller
Matthews, Joseph Brown
Maxwell, Hugh
Mead, Margaret
Menninger, William Claire
Merriam, Charles Edward, Jr.
Merton, Thomas
Millikan, Robert Andrews
Moldenke, Richard George Gottlob
Moley, Raymond Charles
Moon, Parker Thomas
Mott, Frank Luther
Muller, Hermann Joseph
Mundt, Karl Earl
Murphy, Gardner
Muzzey, David Saville
Nichols, Roy Franklin
Nies, James Buchanan
Noble, Gladwyn Kingsley
Odell, George Clinton Densmore
Odum, Howard Washington
Ogburn, William Fielding
Olds, Leland
O'Sullivan, John Louis
Parker, Samuel Chester
Parsons, Elsie Worthington Clews
Patri, Angelo
Payne, Bruce Ryburn
Peck, Harry Thurston
Pegram, George Braxton
Pei, Mario Andrew
Phillips, Ulrich Bonnell
Pope, John Russell
Powell, Thomas Reed
Radin, Max
Radin, Paul
Reinhardt, Ad
Remington, William Walter
Renwick, Edward Sabine
Ripley, William Zebina
Robinson, Claude Everett
Robinson, Henry Morton
Roche, Josephine Aspinwall
Rolf, Ida Pauline
Romer, Alfred Sherwood ("Al")
Rosenblatt, Bernard Abraham
Rosewater, Victor

Rupp, Adolph Frederick
Sachs, Alexander
Sachs, Julius
Sapir, Edward
Scarborough, Dorothy
Schlesinger, Arthur Meier
Schlesinger, Frank
Schultz, Henry
Schuyler, Robert Livingston
Seligman, Edwin Robert Anderson
Shepherd, William Robert
Sherman, Henry Clapp
Shotwell, James Thomson
Sinclair, Upton Beall, Jr.
Smith, Bruce
Smith, Preserved
Snyder, Edwin Reagan
Spahr, Charles Barzillai
Spaulding, Edward Gleason
Speck, Frank Gouldsmith
Spier, Leslie
Spingarn, Arthur Barnett
Spingarn, Joel Elias
Steinhardt, Laurence Adolph
Steinman, David Barnard
Stimson, Julia Catherine
Stockard, Charles Rupert
Stong, Phil(lip Duffiefd)
Sugiura, Kanematsu
Sullivan, Louis Robert
Sumner, Francis Bertody
Suzzallo, Henry
Swenson, David Ferdinand
Thorndike, Lynn
Trilling, Lionel
Van Doren, Carl Clinton
Van Doren, Irita Bradford
Van Doren, Mark Albert
Voris, John Ralph
Whitcomb, Selden Lincoln
White, Israel Charles
Whitehouse, Frederic Cope
Wiechmann, Ferdinand Gerhard
Wilcox, Delos Franklin
Wise, Stephen Samuel
Wissler, Clark
Woodruff, Lorande Loss
Young, Stark
Zinsser, Hans

Journalism

Berstein, Theodore Menline
Bromfield, Louis
Higgins, Marguerite
Liebling, Abbott Joseph
Richards, Vincent
Rosenfeld, Paul Leopold

Law

Astor, William Waldorf
Bancroft, Edgar Addison
Bassett, Edward Murray
Beer, Thomas
Black, Douglas MacRae
Bowen, Herbert Wolcott
Bowers, Lloyd Wheaton
Bruce, Edward Bright
Burlingham, Charles Culp
Byoir, Carl Robert
Cardozo, Benjamin Nathan
Chase, George
Clark, Walter
Cohen, Felix Solomon
Colby, Bainbridge
Colt, LeBaron Bradford
Cook, Walter Wheeler
Coudert, Frederic René
Coudert, Frederic René, Jr.
Crane, Frederick Evan
Crane, Thomas Frederick
Cravath, Paul Drennan
Cromwell, William Nelson
Crosby, Ernest Howard
Dana, Charles Anderson
De Forest, Robert Weeks
De Leon, Daniel
Dewey, Thomas Edmund
Dickinson, Jacob McGavock
Donovan, William Joseph
Douglas, William Orville
Dowling, Noel Thomas
Folger, Henry Clay
Foster, Roger Sherman Baldwin
Foulke, William Dudley
Fox, John William
Garfield, Harry Augustus
Garfield, James Rudolph
Goodnow, Frank Johnson
Grant, Madison
Grau, Maurice
Greenbaum, Edward Samuel
Grosvenor, Edwin Prescott
Guthrie, William Dameron
Hale, Frederick
Hall, Bolton
Hall, Isaac Hollister
Hays, Paul R.
Hoffman, David Murray
Hogan, Frank Smithwick
Holls, George Frederick William
Hornblower, William Butler
Hughes, Charles Evans
Ivins, William Mills
Jerome, William Travers
Joline, Adrian Hoffman
Kalisch, Samuel
Kelly, Edmond
Kobbé, Gustav
Kohler, Max James
Lea, Luke
Leffingwell, Russell Cornell
Lehman, Irving
Leipziger, Henry Marcus
Leupp, Francis Ellington
Levitt, Arthur
Lewisohn, Sam Adolph
Lexow, Clarence
Lowery, Woodbury
Mabie, Hamilton Wright
MacVeagh, Charles
MacVeagh, Franklin
Marshall, Louis, 1856–1929
Matthews, James Brander
Mitchell, Langdon Elwyn
Morgenthau, Henry
Morrow, Dwight Whitney
Nelson, Henry Loomis
Nicoll, De Lancey
O'Brien, Morgan Joseph
Osborne, James Walker
Phelps, William Walter
Pinchot, Amos Richards Eno
Polk, Frank Lyon
Pratt, James Bissett
Prince, Le Baron Bradford
Putnam, (George) Herbert
Reed, Stanley Forman
Rice, Charles Allen Thorndike
Rice, Isaac Leopold
Rives, George Lockhart
Robeson, Paul Leroy
Roosevelt, Franklin Delano
Rosenblatt, Bernard Abraham
Rosenman, Samuel Irving
Saltus, Edgar Evertson
Schirmer, Rudolph Edward
Schuyler, Eugene
Smith, Edmund Munroe
Springarn, Arthur Barnett
Sterling, John William
Steuer, Max David
Stevens, Hiram Fairchild
Stevens, John
Stewart, William Rhinelander
Stone, Harlan Fiske
Straus, Oscar Solomon
Taft, Charles Phelps
Taft, Henry Waters
Taylor, Henry Osborn
Thurston, Lorrin Andrews
Tiedeman, Christopher Gustavus
Tremain, Henry Edwin
Untermyer, Samuel
Vanderbilt, Arthur T.
Van Dyke, John Charles
Watkins, Arthur Vivian
White, Stewart Edward
Whitney, Harry Payne
Wood, Charles Erskine Scott
Woolsey, John Munro

Medicine

Agnew, Cornelius Rea
Agramonte y Simoni, Aristides
Apgar, Virginia
Avery, Oswald Theodore
Beach, Wooster
Beard, George Miller
Beck, John Brodhead
Beck, Lewis Caleb
Beck, Theodric Romeyn
Brill, Abraham Arden
Brown, Frederic Tilden
Bruce, Archibald
Buck, Albert Henry
Buck, Gurdon
Buckley, Samuel Botsford
Bulkley, Lucius Duncan
Bull, William Tillinghast
Carnochan, John Murray
Chamberlain, Jacob
Chapin, Charles Value
Chapin, Henry Dwight
Cohn, Alfred Einstein
Cook, Frederick Albert
Cooke, Robert Anderson
Cooper, James Graham
Curtis, John Green
Dana, Charles Loomis
Delafield, Edward
Delafield, Francis
Duane, Alexander
Edebohls, George Michael
Elsberg, Charles Albert
Emerson, Haven
Ewing, James
Farrand, Livingston

Fletcher, William Baldwin
Foster, Frank Pierce
Fowler, Russell Story
Francis, John Wakefield
Gibbs, Oliver Wolcott
Gilbert, Rufus Henry
Goldsmith, Middleton
Gorrie, John
Greenhow, Robert
Gruening, Emil
Guthrie, Samuel
Halsted, William Stewart
Hamilton, Allan McLane
Hamilton, Frank Hastings
Handerson, Henry Ebenezer
Harris, Elisha
Hartley, Frank
Herter, Christian Archibald
Hess, Alfred Fabian
Hirsch, Isaac Seth
Hoff, John Van Rensselaer
Holmes, Bayard Taylor
House, Samuel Reynolds
Howe, John Ireland
Husk, Charles Ellsworth
Hyde, James Nevins
Irving, Peter
Janeway, Edward Gamaliel
Janeway, Theodore Caldwell
Jelliffe, Smith Ely
Johnstone, Job
Judson, Adoniram Brown
Lazear, Jesse Williams
Le Conte, John
Le Conte, John Lawrence
Le Conte, Joseph
Lefferts, George Morewood
Levene, Phoebus Aaron Theodore
Lewis, Dean De Witt
Libman, Emanuel
Lincoln, Rufus Pratt
McBurney, Charles
McCosh, Andrew James
Marks, Elias
Mayo, William Starbuck
Mearns, Edgar Alexander
Merriam, Clinton Hart
Miller, James Alexander
Mirsky, Alfred Ezra
Moore, Edward Mott
Morton, Rogers Clark Ballard
Mott, Valentine
Myerson, Abraham
Nott, Josiah Clark
Noyes, Henry Drury
O'Dwyer, Joseph
Osborn, Henry Fairfield
Owre, Alfred
Palmer, Alonzo Benjamin
Park, William Hallock
Parry, Charles Christopher
Peck, Charles Howard
Pilcher, Paul Monroe
Plotz, Harry
Remsen, Ira
Richards, Dickinson Woodruff
Rolf, Ida Pauline
Romayne, Nicholas
Rubin, Isidor Clinton
Rubinow, Isaac Max
Rusby, Henry Hurd
Sayre, Lewis Albert
Schneider, Albert
Seguin, Edward Constant
Shrady, George Frederick
Simpson, William Kelly
Smith, Arthur Henderson
Smith, Stephen
Spitzka, Edward Anthony
Spooner, Shearjashub
Starr, Moses Allen
Sternberg, George Miller
Streeter, George Linius
Taylor, Robert Tunstall
Thompson, William Gilman
Timme, Walter
Torrey, John
Warbasse, James Peter
West, Henry Sergeant
Whitman, Marcus
Williams, Linsly Rudd
Williams, Stephen West
Wood, James Rushmore
Zilboorg, Gregory

Pharmacy
Kiss, Max

School of Mines
Aldrich, Chester Holmes
Austen, Peter Townsend
Barus, Carl
Britton, Nathaniel Lord
Church, John Adams
Crocker, Francis Bacon
Dwight, Arthur Smith
Ellsworth, Lincoln
Ferguson, Samuel
Heinze, Frederick Augustus
Heye, George Gustav
Hollerith, Herman
Hollick, Charles Arthur
Hoyt, John Sherman
Hutton, Frederick Remsen
Irving, Roland Duer
Kraemer, Henry
Kunitz, Moses
Langmuir, Irving
Levene, Phoebus Aaron Theodore
Lusk, Graham
Matthew, William Diller
Moldenke, Richard George Gottlob
Moore, Philip North
Moran, Daniel Edward
Olcott, Eben Erskine
Paine, John Alsop
Parsons, William Barclay
Piez, Charles
Rees, John Krom
Rice, George Samuel
Russell, Israel Cook
Stanley, Robert Crooks
Stone, John Stone
Thompson, William Boyce
Wiechmann, Ferdinand Gerhard
Woodin, William Hartman

Teachers College (*See* TEACHERS COLLEGE, COLUMBIA UNIVERSITY (N.Y.)

COMMONWEALTH COLLEGE (ARK.)
Patchen, Kenneth

CONCORDIA COLLEGE (IND.)
Carey, Max George ("Scoops")

CONCORDIA SEMINARY (MO.)
Gräbner, August Lawrence
Hanson, James Christian Meinich
Hoenecke, Gustav Adolf Felix Theodor
Hove, Elling
Koren, John
Pieper, Franz August Otto
Preus, Christian Keyser
Schmidt, Friedrich August
Stromme, Peer Olsen
Stub, Hans Gerhard

CONCORDIA THEOLOGICAL SEMINARY (MO.)
Maier, Walter Arthur

CONNECTICUT LITERARY INSTITUTE (*See* SUFFIELD SCHOOL)

CONSERVATOIRE DE MUSIQUE, PARIS (FRANCE)
Iturbi, José

CONVERSE COLLEGE (S.C.)
Peterkin, Julia Mood

CONSERVATOIRE NATIONALE (FRANCE)
Boyer, Charles

COOK COUNTY NORMAL SCHOOL (ILL.)
Nelson, Edward William

COOPERATIVE SCHOOL FOR STUDENT TEACHERS (N.Y.)
Brown, Margaret Wise

COOPER MEDICAL COLLEGE (CAL.)
Snow, William Freeman
Wilbur, Ray Lyman

COOPER UNION (N.Y.)
Bitzer, George William
Christie, John Walter
Cowen, Joshua Lionel
Deland, Margaret
King, Alexander
Kunitz, Moses
Kunz, George Frederick
Lukeman, Henry Augustvus
Opper, Frederick Burr

CORCORAN SCIENTIFIC SCHOOL (D.C.)
Davis, William Hammatt

CORNELL COLLEGE (IOWA)
Baker, Carl Lotus
Devine, Edward Thomas

CORNELL UNIVERSITY (N.Y.)
Acker, Charles Ernest
Allen, Arthur Augustus
Atkinson, George Francis
Babcock, Stephen Moulton
Balestier, Charles Wolcott
Bausch, Edward
Berkowitz, Henry
Biggs, Herman Michael
Boring, Edwin Garrigues
Botsford, George Willis
Bourke-White, Margaret
Branner, John Casper
Bromfield, Louis
Bryant, Ralph Clement
Burpee, David
Burr, George Lincoln
Carlisle, Floyd Leslie

Carpenter, Walter Samuel, Jr.
Carrier, Willis Haviland
Chambers, James Julius
Chittenden, Hiram Martin
Church, Irving Porter
Comstock, John Henry
Creighton, James Edwin
Cushing, Frank Hamilton
Dorn, Harold Fred
Dove, Arthur Garfield
Dudley, William Russel
Edgren, August Hjalmar
Eilshemius, Louis Michel
Elliott, John Lovejoy
Fauset, Jessie Redmon
Flather, John Joseph
Foraker, Joseph Benson
Ford, Hannibal Choate
Francis, Charles Spencer
Fuertes, Louis Agassiz
Gannett, Frank Ernest
Germer, Lester Halbert
Gherardi, Bancroft
Gifford, Sanford Robinson
Gillett, Horace Wadsworth
Gleason, Kate
Gottschalk, Louis Reichenthal
Grant, James Benton
Gregg, Willis Ray
Halsey, Frederick Arthur
Hammond, Laurens
Harper, John Lyell
Harris, Rollin Arthur
Hawks, Howard Winchester
Hayford, John Fillmore
Hendrix, Joseph Clifford
Henry, William Arnon
Hill, Ernest Rowland
Hillebrand, William Francis
Hills, Elijah Clarence
Hiscock, Frank Harris
Hodgins, Eric Francis
Holmes, Joseph Austin
House, Edward Mandell
Howard, Leland Ossian
Hoxie, Robert Franklin
Isham, Ralph Heyward
Jackson, Dugald Caleb
Jordan, David Starr
Kellerman, Karl Frederic
Kelley, Florence
Kellor, Frances (Alice)
Kerr, Walter Craig
King, Franklin Hiram
Kingsbury, Albert
Knight, Goodwin Jess
("Goodie")
Ladd, Carl Edwin
Laguna, Theodore de Leo de
Lamoureux, Andrew Jackson
Larned, William Augustus
Lee, Porter Raymond
Lewis, George William
McAllister, Charles Albert
McConnell, Ira Welch
Matthews, Franklin
Menjou, Adolphe Jean
Midgley, Thomas
Miller, Kempster Blanchard
Millspaugh, Charles Frederick
Moore, Veranus Alva
Morgenthau, Henry, Jr.
Mott, John R.
Nathan, George Jean
Nichols, Edward Leamington
Nourse, Edwin Griswold
Noyes, Walter Chadwick
Oberndorf, Clarence Paul
Olmstead, Albert Ten Eyck
O'Shea, Michael Vincent
Parsons, Frank
Pearson, Edward Jones
Pearson, Leonard
Pearson, Raymond Allen
Perry, Clarence Arthur
Pew, Joseph Newton, Jr.
Pincus, Gregory Goodwin
("Goody")
Pound, Cuthbert Winfred
Powell, George Harold
Pressman, Lee
Pringle, Henry Fowles
Prosser, Charles Smith
Putnam, Ruth
Rafter, George W.
Rathbun, Richard
Reed, Daniel Alden
Reeves, Arthur Middleton
Richtmyer, Floyd Karker
Riegger, Wallingford
Roberts, Kenneth Lewis
Rosenwald, Lessing Julius
Rossiter, Clinton Lawrence, III
Russell, James Earl
Ryan, Harris Joseph
Sackett, Henry Woodward
Salmon, Daniel Elmer
Sanderson, Ezra Dwight
Severance, Frank Haywood
Shepard, Fred Douglas
Simpson, William Kelly
Smith, Harold Babbitt
Smith, Theobald
Sperry, Elmer Ambrose
Stevens, George Barker
Straight, Willard Dickerman
Sullivan, Harry Stack
Teeple, John Edgar
Thomas, Martha Carey
Thurstone, Louis Leon
Tone, Stanislas Pascal Franchot
Trelease, William
Vail, Robert William Glenroie
Van Loon, Hendrik Willem
Veatch, Arthur Clifford
Warner, Glenn Scobey
("Pop")
Washburn, Albert Henry
White, David
White, William Alanson
Wiener, Alexander Solomon
Wolheim, Louis Robert

Graduate Study

Adams, Joseph Quincy
Albee, Ernest
Allen, Arthur Augustus
Arthur, Joseph Charles
Bagley, Wilham Chandler
Bode, Boyd Henry
Boring, Edwin Garrigues
Bronson, Walter Cochrane
Buckley, Oliver Ellsworth
Dorn, Harold Fred
Emerson, Oliver Farrar
Ferree, Clarence Errol
Fetter, Frank Albert
Friedman, William Frederick
Gherardi, Bancroft
Gillett, Horace Wadsworth
Goldenweiser, Emanuel
Alexander
Gottschalk, Louis Reichenthal
Griscom, Ludlow
Hanson, James Christian
Meinich
Hewett, Waterman Thomas
Hooker, Elon Huntington
Hopkins, Cyril George
Howard, Leland Ossian
Kemmerer, Edwin Walter
Ladd, Carl Edwin
Lewis, George William
Lipman, Jacob Goodale
Lotka, Alfred James
Manly, Charles Matthews
Meiklejohn, Alexander
Moore, Addison Webster
Moore, Clarence Lemuel
Elisha
Morgan, John Harcourt
Alexander
Moss, Sanford Alexander
Nichols, Ernest Fox
Olmstead, Albert Ten Eyck
Parr, Samuel Wilson
Pearson, Raymond Allen
Pincus, Gregory Goodwin
("Goody")
Powell, George Harold
Pritchard, Frederick John
Prosser, Charles Smlth
Rautenstrauch, Walter
Richtmyer, Floyd Karker
Smith, Theobald
Thilly, Frank
Warren, George Frederick
Washburn, Margaret Floy
Whetzel, Herbert Hice
Whitcomb, Selden Lincoln
Wiener, Norbert
Young, John Wesley
Zook, George Frederick

Law

Leibowitz, Samuel Simon
Mussey, Ellen Spencer
Reed, Daniel Alden
Rose, Walter Malins
Taylor, Myron Charles
Warner, Glenn Scobey
("Pop")

Medicine

Helpern, Milton
Marriott, Williams McKim
Menninger, William Claire
Muller, Hermann Joseph
Neal, Josephine Bicknell
Oberndorf, Clarence Paul
Trask, James Dowling
Weiss, Soma

CORNISH SCHOOL OF ALLIED ARTS (WA.)

Huntley, Chester ("Chet") Robert

CORTLAND STATE TEACHERS COLLEGE (N.Y.)

Ladd, Carl Edwin

Creighton University (Neb.)
Barrett, Frank Aloysius
Cudahy, Edward Aloysius, Jr.
Matthews, Francis Patrick
Mitchell, Stephen Arnold
Shaw, Lawrence Timothy ("Buck")
Law
Barrett, Frank Aloysius
Monsky, Henry
Crozer Theological Seminary (Pa.)
Chiera, Edward
King, Martin Luther, Jr.
Sloan, Harold Paul
Culver Military Academy (Ind.)
Burpee, David
Cushman, Austin Thomas ("Joe")
Ingram, Jonas Howard
O'Malley, Walter Francis
Weicker, Lowell Palmer
Culver-Stockton College (Mo.)
Long, Edward Vaughn
Cumberland College (Ky.)
Alcorn, James Lusk
Morrow, Edwin Porch
Roane, John Selden
Scott, William Anderson
Watterson, Harvey Magee
Cumberland University (Tenn.)
Allen, George Edward
Battle, Burrell Bunn
Beard, Richard
Brantley, Theodore
Clement, Frank Goad
Dyer, Rolla Eugene
Ensley, Enoch
Foster, Murphy James
Hardy, William Harris
Hatch, Carl A.
McReynolds, Samuel Davis
Graduate Study
Miller, George Abram
Peck, Harry Thurston
Law
Bate, William Brimage
Clements, Judson Claudius
Cooper, (Leon) Jere
Davis, Jeff
Fitzpatrick, Morgan Cassius
Gaines, Reuben Reid
Gordon, George Washington
Gore, Thomas Pryor
Hull, Cordell
Lurton, Horace Harmon
McCreary, James Bennett
Patman, John William Wright
Stewart, Arthur Thomas ("Tom")
Valliant, Leroy Branch
Warren, Fuller
Curry School of Expressionism (Mass.)
Kalmus, Natalie Mabelle Dunfee
Curtis Institute of Music (Pa.)
Blitzstein, Marc
Schippers, Thomas
Cutler School (N.Y.)
Carryl, Guy Wetmore
Coffin, Henry Sloane
Howland, John
Janeway, Theodore Caldwell

Dakota Wesleyan University (S. Dak.)
Anderson, Clinton Presba
Case, Francis Higbee
Dalhousie University (Canada)
Doull, James Angus
Medicine
Doull, James Angus
Dallas College (Ore.)
Poling, Daniel Alfred
Damrosch Institute of Music
Cross, Milton John
Dane Law School (*See* Harvard University, *Law*)
Danish Naval Academy (Denmark)
Hovgaard, William
Dartmouth College (N.H.)
Adams, Daniel
Adams, Ebenezer
Adams, Henry Carter
Adams, Walter Sydney
Aiken, Charles Augustus
Akerman, Amos Tappan
Angell, George Thorndike
Appleton, Jesse
Atkinson, George Henry
Bailey, Rufus William
Bancroft, Cecil Franklin Patch
Barlow, Joel
Barrett, John
Bartlett, Ichabod
Bartlett, Samuel Colcord
Bell, Charles Henry
Bell, Louis
Bell, Samuel
Bickmore, Albert Smith
Bingham, Caleb
Bingham, Harry
Bissell, George Henry
Black, Frank Swett
Blake, Francis Gilman
Boss, Lewis
Bouton, John Bell
Brown, Francis, 1784–1820
Brown, Francis, 1849–1916
Brown, George William
Brown, Samuel Gilman
Burton, Asa
Bush, George
Cantril, Albert Hadley
Chamberlain, Mellen
Chase, Harry Woodburn
Chase, Philander
Chase, Salmon Portland
Cheney, Oren Burbank
Chipman, Daniel
Choate, Rufus
Clark, Daniel, 1809–1891
Clark, Francis Edward
Clark, Greenleaf
Cluttenden, Martin
Colman, Henry
Currier, Moody
Dana, Charles Loomis
Dana, John Cotton
Day, Edmund Ezra
Dingley, Nelson
Doe, Charles
Dryfoos, Orvil E.
Dunning, William Archibald
Eastman, John Robie
Eaton, John
Eaton, William
Ely, Richard Theodore
Estabrook, Joseph
Evans, Warren Felt
Everett, David
Fairbanks, Henry
Farmer, Moses Gerrish
Farrar, Timothy
Felt, Joseph Barlow
Fessenden, Samuel
Fessenden, Thomas Green
Field, Walbridge Abner
Fletcher, Horace
Fletcher, Richard
Fogg, George Gilman
Forrestal, James Vincent
Foster, Stephen Symonds
Frost, Edwin Brant
Frost, Robert Lee
Gates, George Augustus
Goddard, Morrill
Goodell, William, 1792–1867
Goodwin, John Noble
Grant, George Barnard
Greene, Daniel Crosby
Greenleaf, Benjamin
Grimes, James Wilson
Gulick, Sidney Lewis
Haddock, Charles Brickett
Hall, Sherman
Hayes, John Lord
Hazen, Henry Allen
Henry, Caleb Sprague
Hough, Charles Merrill
House, Samuel Reynolds
Hovey, Alvah
Hovey, Charles Edward
Hovey, Otis Ellis
Hovey, Richard
Hubbard, Gardiner Greene
Hubbard, John
Huntington, Samuel 1765–1817
Huntington Elisha
Hutchins, Harry Burns
Ide, Henry Clay
Jackson, Edward Payson
Jewell, Harvey
Jewett, Milo Parker
Joy, James Frederick
Just, Ernest Everett
Kendall, Amos
Kiewit, Peter
Kimball, Richard Burleigh
Knapp, Samuel Lorenzo
Ledyard, John
Liebling, Abbott Joseph
Little, Charles Sherman
Long, Stephen Harriman
Lord, John
McCall, Samuel Walker
McKeen, Joseph
Marsh, George Perkins
Marsh, James
Mather, Samuel Holmes
Merrill, Daniel
Merrill, Samuel
Miller, Charles Ransom
Miller, Jonathan Peckham

Miller, Oliver
Moore, George Henry
Moore, Zephaniah Swift
Morris, George Sylvester
Morrison, Nathan Jackson
Moses, George Higgins
Mussey, Reuben Dimond
Nichols, Thomas Low
Noyes, Edward Follansbee
Noyes, John Humphrey
O'Brien, Robert Lincoln
Oliver, Fitch Edward
Oliver, Henry Kemble
Orcutt, Hiram
Ordronaux, John
Palmer, Elihu
Parish, Elijah
Parker, Joel, 1795–1875
Parris, Albion Keith
Partridge, Alden
Patterson, James Willis
Patterson, John Henry
Paul, Henry Martyn
Pearl, Raymond
Pearsons, Daniel Kimball
Peaslee, Edmund Randolph
Perley, Ira
Peters, Absalom
Pillsbury, Charles Alfred
Poor, Daniel
Porter, Ebenezer
Procter, Redfield
Prouty, Charles Azro
Prouty, Charles Tyler
Ranney, Ambrose Loomis
Redfield, Isaac Fletcher
Remington, William Walter
Richardson, Charles Francis
Ripley, Eleazar Wheelock
Robinson, William Callyhan
Rockefeller, Nelson Aldrich
Rolfe, Robert Abial ("Red")
Root, Erastus
Rugg, Harold Ordway
Ruml, Beardsley
Ryan, Robert Bushnell
Sanborn, Edwin David
Sanborn, Walter Henry
Shattuck, George Cheyne, 1783–1854
Shepley, Ether
Shepley, George Foster
Shurtleff, Roswell Morse
Slafter, Edmund Farwell
Smith, Asa Dodge
Smith, Justin Harvey
Spaulding, Levi
Stevens, Thaddeus
Strong, Moses McCure
Sumner, Walter Taylor
Talbot, Ethelbert
Taylor, Samuel Harvey
Tenney, Charles Daniel
Tenney, Edward Payson
Thompson, Charles Oliver
Ticknor, Elisha
Ticknor, George
Townsend, Luther Tracy
Tracy, Joseph
Tuck, Amos
Tucker, William Jewett
Twitchell, Amos
Upham, Thomas Cogswell
Upham, Warren
Wanger, Walter
Webster, Daniel
Webster, Joseph Dana
Wentworth, John, 1815–1888
Wheelock, John
White, Leonard Dupee
Willey, Samuel Hopkins
Williams, Ben Ames
Williston, Seth
Woodbury, Daniel Phineas
Woodbury, Levi
Woods, Leonard, 1807–1878
Worcester, Samuel
Wright, John Henry
Young, Charles Augustus

Graduate Study
Andrews, John Bertram
Chase, Harry Woodburn
Day, Edmund Ezra
Dickinson, Edwin De Witt
Hale, Nathan, 1784–1863
Paul, Henry Martyn
White, Leonard Dupee

Medicine
Adams, Daniel
Alden, Ebenezer
Banks, Charles Edward
Bell, Luther Vose
Cheney, Oren Burbank
Dana, Charles Loomis
Gallup, Joseph Adams
Garcelon, Alonzo
Hayes, Augustus Allen
Kimball, Gilman
Knowlton, Charles
Little, Charles Sherman
Nichols, James Robinson
Peaslee, Edmund Randolph

DAVIDSON COLLEGE (N.C.)
Bynum, William Preston
Campbell, Josiah A. Patterson
Carter, Landon
Osborne, James Walker
Ramseur, Stephen Dodson
Simmons, James Stevens
Smith, Charles Alphonso
Smith, Henry Louis
Wilson, Woodrow

DAVIS AND ELKINS COLLEGE
Allen, James Edward, Jr.

DAY'S ACADEMY (MASS.)
Parker, Peter
Pond, Enoch
Sunderland, La Roy
Towle, George Makepeace

DECORAH INSTITUTE (MINN.)
Volstead, Andrew John

DEERFIELD ACADEMY (MASS.)
Allen, Charles
Fuller, George
Howe, Samuel
Mayo, Amory Dwight
Williamson, William Durkee

DELAWARE COLLEGE (DEL.)
Blandy, William Henry Purnell

DELAWARE LITERARY INSTITUTE (N.Y.)
Champlin, John Wayne
Jones, Herschel Vespasian
White, William Nathaniel

DELAWARE STATE COLLEGE (DEL.)
Messersmith, George Strausser

DENISON UNIVERSITY (OHIO)
Adkins, Homer Burton
Ashmore, William
Behrends, Adolphus Julius Frederick
Burton, Ernest De Witt
Dorsey, George Amos
Fairfield, Edmund Burke
Harmon, Judson
Johnson, Douglas Wilson
Kerr, John Glasgow
Larrabee, Charles Hathaway
Rose, Mary Davies Swartz
Seagrave, Gordon Stifler
Stevens, William Arnold

DE PAUL UNIVERSITY (ILL.)
Daley, Richard Joseph
Farrell, James Thomas

DE PAUW UNIVERSITY (IND.)
Beard, Charles Austin
Beard, Mary Ritter
Beveridge, Albert Jeremiah
Booth, Newton
Curme, George Oliver
Eggleston, George Cary
Fisher, Frederick Bohn
Frick, Ford Christopher
Harlan, James, 1820–1899
Hitt, Robert Roberts
Jaquess, James Frazier
Julian, Percy Lavon
McCormack, Buren Herbert ("Mac")
McDonald, Joseph Ewing
Mead, Margaret
Moore, Addison Webster
Ogg, Frederic Austin
Patterson, Thomas MacDonald
Phillips, David Graham
Porter, Albert Gallatin
Ridpath, John Clark
Shoup, Francis Asbury
Sims, Charles N.
Sissle, Noble Lee
Stephenson, Carl
Stone, Wilbur Fisk
Terrell, Edwin Holland
Van Devanter, Willis
Voorhees, Daniel Wolsey
Watson, James Eli
West, Roy Owen
Williams, Elkanah
Wirt, William Albert
Wood, Thomas Bond

Graduate Study
Curme, George Oliver
Stephenson, Carl
West, Roy Owen
Wirt, William Albert

Law
West, Roy Owen

DERBY ACADEMY (MASS.)
Carter, James Coolidge
Gardiner, Robert Hatlowell
Savage, James

DES MOINES COLLEGE (IOWA)
McVey, Frank Lerond

DETROIT COLLEGE OF LAW (MICH.)
Kelland, Clarence Budington

DETROIT JUNIOR COLLEGE (MICH.)
Bachmann, Werner Emmanuel
DICKINSON COLLEGE (PA.)
Allen, John James
Baird, Spencer Fullerton
Bates, Daniel Moore
Baugher, Henry Louis
Beale, Richard Lee Turberville
Bender, Charles Albert ("Chief")
Bethune, George Washington
Bigler, John
Bowman, Thomas
Bridges, Robert, 1806–1882
Brown, Samuel
Buchanan, James
Campbell, William Henry
Chambers, Talbot Wilson
Conway, Moncure Daniel
Creighton, William
Creswell, John Angel James
Crooks, George Richard
Cummins, George David
Deems, Charles Force
Dunlop, James
Edwards, Ninian
Elliott, Washington Lafayette
Ellis, Powhatan
Fisher, George Purnell
Fisher, Sidney George
Floyd, John
Furst, Clyde Bowman
Gerhard, William Wood
Gibson, John Bannister
Goucher, John Franklin
Grier, Robert Cooper
Haldeman, Samuel Steman
Hare, George Emlen
Himes, Charles Francis
Hurst, John Fletcher
Lamberton, Benjamin Peffer
Lane, William Carr
Learned, Marion Dexter
MacCauley, Clay
McClelland, Robert, 1807–1880
McComas, Louis Emory
McKim, James Miller
Maclay, Robert Samuel
Neely, Thomas Benjamin
Palmer, James Croxall
Ridgaway, Henry Bascom
Robinson, John Mitchell
Saulsbury, Eli
Saulsbury, Willard, 1820–1892
Snowden, James Ross
Taney, Roger Brooke
Thomas, Philip Francis
Wahl, William Henry
Walker, Jonathan Hodge
Watts, Frederick
Wilkins, Ross
Wilkins, William
Wormley, Theodore George
Wright, Hendrick Brodley
Young, Jesse Bowman
Young, John Clarke
Graduate Study
Furst, Clyde Bowman
Gray, John Purdue
Law
Curtin, Andrew Gregg
Fine, John Sydney
James, Arthur Horace
Kephart, John William
Muse, Clarence
Nevin, Alfred
Medicine
Campbell, James Hepburn
DICKINSON SEMINARY (PA.)
Parker, Arthur Caswell
DICKSON COLLEGE (TENN.)
Caraway, Thaddeus Horatius
DICKSON NORMAL COLLEGE (TENN.)
Caraway, Hattie Ophelia Wyatt
DIXON COLLEGE AND NORMAL SCHOOL (ILL.)
Parsons, Louella Rose Oettinger
DIXWELL'S LATIN SCHOOL (MASS.)
Adams, Henry Brooks
Emmons, Samuel Franklin
Lodge, Henry Cabot
Longfellow, Ernest Wadsworth
Lowell, Edward Jackson
Matthews, Nathan
Peabody, Robert Swain
Peirce, Charles Sanders
Rotch, Arthur
Stone, James Kent
DOANE COLLEGE (NEB.)
Fairchild, Fred Rogers
Taylor, Robert
DRAKE UNIVERSITY (IOWA)
Ames, Edward Scribner
Gillette, Guy Mark
Glaspell, Susan Keating
Larson, Laurence Marcellus
Nicholson, Seth Barnes
Stong, Phil(lip Duffield)
Young, Clarence Marshall
DREW THEOLOGICAL SEMINARY (N.J.)
Alexander, Gross
Appenzeller, Henry Gerhard
Ferguson, William Porter Frisbee
Murray, John Gardner
Sloan, Harold Paul
Tittle, Ernest Fremont
Tobias, Channing Heggie
DREW UNIVERSITY (N.J.)
Matthews, Joseph Brown
DREXEL UNIVERSITY (PA.)
Cable, Frank Taylor
Gold, Harry ("Raymond")
Shor, Bernard ("Toots")
DROPSIE COLLEGE (PA.)
Graduate Study
Revel, Bernard
Speiser, Ephraim Avigdor
DUKE UNIVERSITY (N.C.)
Allen, George Venable
Boyd, Julian Parks
Boyd, William Kenneth
Campbell, John Wood, Jr.
Payne, Bruce Ryburn
Pegram, George Braxton
Roper, Daniel Calhoun
Simmons, Furnifold McLendel
Graduate Study
Boyd, William Kenneth
DULWICH COLLEGE (ENGLAND)
Chandler, Raymond Thornton
Wodehouse, Pelham Grenville
DUMMER ACADEMY (MASS.)
Bromfield, John
Cleaveland, Parker
Emerson, George Barrell
Jackson, Charles
Jackson, James, 1777–1867
Jackson, Patrick Tracy
King, Rufus, 1755–1827
Knight, Henry Cogswell
Lander, Frederick West
Parsons, Theophilus, 1750–1813
Phillips, Samuel
Poore, Benjamin Perley
Preble, Edward
Smyth, Egbert Coffin
DURHAM UNIVERSITY COLLEGE OF SCIENCE (ENGLAND)
Campbell, William

EARLHAM COLLEGE (IND.)
Goddard, Pliny Earle
Jessup, Walter Albert
Johnson, Robert Underwood
Kelsey, Rayner Wickersham
Nixon, William Penn
Stanley, Wendell Meredith
Trueblood, Benjamin Franklin
Wildman, Murray Shipley
EAST CENTRAL NORMAL SCHOOL (OKLA.)
Kerr, Robert Samuel
EASTERN KENTUCKY NORMAL SCHOOL
Combs, Earle Bryan
EASTERN SHORE COLLEGE (MD.)
Perdue, Arthur William
EASTERN TEACHERS' COLLEGE (KY.)
Combs, Earle Bryan
EAST FLORIDA MILITARY AND AGRICULTURAL COLLEGE
Cone, Hutchinson Ingham
EAST GREENWICH ACADEMY (R.I.)
Aldrich, Nelson Wilmarth
Tourjée, Eben
Upham, Samuel Foster
Warren, William Fairfield
Winship, Albert Edward
EAST HARTMAN SCHOOL OF DESIGN (PA.)
Fogarty, Anne Whitney
EASTMAN BUSINESS COLLEGE (N.Y.)
Kresge, Sebastian Spering
EASTMAN SCHOOL OF MUSIC
Wilder, Alexander Lafayette Chew ("Alec")
EAST TEXAS STATE UNIVERSITY
Rayburn, Samuel Taliaferro ("Sam")
ECLECTIC MEDICAL COLELGE (N.Y.)
Hrdlicka, Ales
ECLECTIC MEDICAL INSTITUTE (OHIO)
Henshall, James Alexander
Hoyt, John Wesley
Kunze, Richard Ernest
Morrow, Prince Albert
Scudder, John Milton

ECLECTIC MEDICAL UNIVERSITY OF KANSAS
Brinkley, John Richard
ÉCOLE BERNARD PALISSY (FRANCE)
Lachaise, Gaston
ÉCOLE DES ARTS ET METIERS (FRANCE)
Houdry, Eugene Jules
ÉCOLE DES BEAUX-ARTS (FRANCE)
Aldrich, Chester Holmes
Atterbury, Grosvenor
Barnard, George Grey
Borglum, John Gutzon de la Mothe
Brush, Geore de Forest
Burroughs, Bryson
Calder, Alexander Stirling
Corbet, Harvey-Wiley
Cret, Paul Philippe
Davidson, Jo
Dickinson, Preston
Flagg, Ernest
Fraser, James Earle
Granger, Alfred Hoyt
Hood, Raymond Mathewson
Ide, John Jay
Lachaise, Gaston
Lamb, William Frederick
Lawrance, Charles Lanier
Lipchitz, Jacques
Lukeman, Henry Augustus
MacMonnies, Frederick William
MacNeil, Hermon Atkins
Maybeck, Bernard Ralph
Morgan, Julia
Robinson, Boardman
Rogers, James Gamble
Stokes, Isaac Newton Phelps
Taft, Lorado Zadoç
ÉCOLE DES HAUTES ÉTUDES (FRANCE)
Mather, Frank Jewett, Jr.
ÉCOLE DES MINES (BELGIUM)
Sauveur, Albert
ÉCOLE DES MINES (FRANCE)
Perin, Charles Page
ÉCOLES DES PONTS ET CHAUSÉES (FRANCE)
Modjeski, Ralph
ÉCOLE LIBRE DES SCIENCES POLITIQUES (FRANCE)
Wilson, Hugh Robert
ÉCOLE NORMALE DE MUSIQUE
Piston, Walter Hamor
ECUMENICAL PATRIARCHATE THEOLOGICAL SEMINARY (TURKEY)
Athenagoras I
EDEN THEOLOGICAL SEMINARY (MO.)
Neibuhr, Helmut Richard
EDGEFIELD ACADEMY (S.C.)
Bonham, Milledge Luke
La Borde, Maximilian
Tompkins, Daniel Augustus
EDGEHILL SCHOOL (N.J.)
Bagby, George William
Miller, John, 1819–1895
Stillé, Charles Janeway
EDINBURGH UNIVERSITY (SCOTLAND) (*See also* UNIVERSITY OF EDINBURGH)
Campbell, Charles Macfie
MacIver, Robert Morrison
Neilson, William Allan
Graduate Study
MacIver, Robert Morrison
Medicine
Campbell, Charles Macfie
ELGIN ACADEMY (ILL.)
Boyd, Thomas Alexander
ELMHURST COLLEGE (ILL.)
Niebuhr, Helmut Richard
Niebuhr, Karl Paul Reinhold ("Reinie")
ELMIRA COLLEGE (N.Y.)
Hill, Grace Livingston
ELMIRA FREE ACADEMY (N.Y.)
Farwell, Charles Benjamin
Goff, Emmet Stull
Roe, Francis Asbury
Stanchfield, John Barry
Wing, Joseph Elwyn
EMERSON COLLEGE OF ORATORY (MASS.)
Lunt, Alfred David, Jr.
EMORY AND HENRY COLLEGE (VA.)
Allen, Young John
Comer, Braxton Bragg
Goode, John
Lambuth, Walter Russell
Stuart, James Ewell Brown
Vawter, Charles Erastus
EMORY COLLEGE (GA.)
Allen, Young John
Barkley, Alben William
Bass, William Capers
Callaway, Morgan
Candler, Warren Akin
Hadas, Moses
Harrison, William Pope
Haygood, Atticus Green
Holland, Spessard Lindsey
Hopkins, Isaac Stiles
Hyer, Robert Stewart
Keener, William Albert
Lamar, Lucius Quintus Cincinnatus
Lee, Ivy Ledbetter
Lee, James Wideman
Odum, Howard Washington
Orr, Gustavus John
Rivers, Thomas Milton
Stewart, Arthur Thomas ("Tom")
EPISCOPAL ACADEMY (PHILA.)
Boller, Alfred Pancoast
Coleman, Leighton
Decatur, Stephen, 1779–1820
Drew, John, 1853–1927
George, Henry, 1839–1897
Harrison, Charles Custis
Hirsch, Emil Gustav
Hobart, John Henry
Lewis, Lawrence
Montgomery, Thomas Harrison
Morton, Henry
Outerbridge, Alexander Ewing
Penrose, Boies
Wheaton, Nathaniel Sheldon
EPISCOPAL THEOLOGICAL SCHOOL (MASS.)
Bigelow, Frank Hagar
Lawrence, William
Livermore, Abiel Abbot
Nash, Henry Sylvester
Peabody, Endicott
Rand, Edward Kennard
Slattery, Charles Lewis
Sterrett, James MacBride
Woods, James Haughton
EPWORTH SEMINARY AND JUNIOR COLLEGE (IOWA)
Benson, Oscar Herman
ERSKINE COLLEGE (S.C.)
Montgomery, William Bell
Orr, Jehu Amaziah
Riley, Benjamin Frnaklin
ETLINGER DRAMATIC SCHOOL (ENGLAND)
Webster, Margaret ("Peggy")
EWING COLLGE (ILL.)
Martin, Warren Homer
EXCELSIOR COLLEGE (TEXAS)
Batts, Robert Lynn
EXETER ACADEMY (*See* PHILLIPS EXETER ACADEMY)

FAIRFIELD ACADEMY (N.Y.)
Arnold, Lauren Briggs
Dickinson, Charles Monroe
Dwight, Harrison Gray Otis
Gray, Asa
Hadley, James
Kelley, Alfred
Loomis, Arphaxed
Lord, Chester Sanders
Satterlee, Richard Sherwood
Whipple, Squire
FARMER'S COLLEGE (*See* BELMONT COLLEGE)
FEDERAL INSTITUTE OF TECHNOLOGY (SWITZERLAND)
Norden, Carl Lukas
Zwicky, Fritz
FEMALE MEDICAL COLLEGE (*See* WOMAN'S MEDICAL COLLEGE)
FERRIS INSTITUTE (MICH.)
Bowman, Isaiah
FIRST STATE COLLEGE OF BRNO (CZECHOSLOVAKIA)
Sakel, Manfred Jsohua
FISK UNIVERSITY (TENN.)
Dawson, William Levi
Du Bois, William Edward Burghardt
Haynes, George Edmund
Lunceford, James Melvin ("Jimmie")
Wilson, J(ames) Finley
Graduate Study
Pickens, William
FLORIDA A&M UNIVERSITY
Adderley, Julian Edwin ("Cannonball")
FLORIDA STATE COLLEGE FOR WOMEN
Van Doren, Irita Bradford
Graduate Study
Van Doren, Irita Bradford
FLORIDA STATE NORMAL SCHOOL
Geiger, Roy Stanley

FLORIDA STATE UNIVERSITY
Morrison, Jim
FORDHAM UNIVERSITY (N.Y.)
Burrow, Trigant
Coppens, Charles
Curran, Thomas Jerome
Daley, Arthur John
Donovan, James Britt
Drumgoole, John Christopher
Edebohls, George Michael
Farley, John Murphy
Flynn, Edward Joseph
Flynn, Martin Henry
Frisch, Frank Francis ("The Fordham Flash")
Hasard, John Rose Greene
Herbermann, Charles George
La Farge, John
Lombardi, Vincent Thomas
McMahon, Brien
O'Brien, Morgan Joseph
Richards, Vincent
Rosecrans, Sylvester Horton
Seton, William
Shea, John Dawson Gilmary
Spellman, Francis Joseph
Wigger, Winand Michael
Law
Hunton, George Kenneth
Lombardi, Vincent Thomas
O'Dwyer, William
O'Malley, Walter Francis
Tobin, Austin Joseph
FORT WORTH POLYTECHNIC INSTITUTE (TEX.)
Speaker, Tris E.
FRAMINGHAM ACADEMY (MASS.)
Clark, Thomas March
Gordon, George Henry
Peirce, Cyrus
Pike, Albert
Weiss, John
FRANK HOLME SCHOOL OF ILLUSTRATION (ILL.)
Dwiggins, William Addison
FRANKLIN AND MARSHALL COLLEGE (PA.)
Appenzeller, Henry Gerhard
Apple, Thomas Gilmore
Baer, George Frederick
Bausman, Benjamin
Black, William Murray
Bomberger, John Henry Augustus
Clay, Albert Tobias
Douglas, Henry Kyd
Dubbs, Joseph Henry
Ferrel, William
Gerhart, Emanuel Vogel
Gitt, Josiah Williams ("Jess")
Harbaugh, Henry
Hartranft, John Frederick
McFarland, Thomas Bard
Miller, George Abram
Peters, Madison Clinton
Rupp, William
Schaeffer, Nathan Christ
Sayre, Wallace Stanley
Stahr, John Summers
Stauffer, David McNeely
Steiner, Lewis Henry
FRANKLIN COLLEGE (*See* UNIVERSITY OF GEORGIA)
FRANKLIN COLLEGE (IND.)
Caldwell, Otis William
Davis, Elmer Holmes
Main, Marjorie
Monroe, Paul
Voris, John Ralph
FRANKLIN COLLEGE (OHIO)
Hammond, Percy Hunter
FREDERICKSBURG COLLEGE (VA.)
Sydenstricker, Edgar
FREDONIA ACADEMY (N. Y.)
Barbour, Oliver Lorenzo
Houghton, Douglass
Orton, Edward Francis Baxter
Strang, James Jesse
FREMONT NORMAL COLLEGE (NEB.)
Dern, George Henry
FRIEDRICH-WILHELMS UNIVERSITY (GERMANY)
Bieber, Margarete
Jaeger, Werner Wilhelm
Stern, Kurt Guenter
FRIENDS UNIVERSITY (KANS.)
Ayres, William Augustus
Graduate Study
Ayres, William Augustus
FURMAN UNIVERSITY (S.C.)
Watson, John Broadus
Graduate Study
Manly, John Matthews

GARRETT BIBLE INSTITUTE (CAL.)
Atkinson, Henry Avery
GARRETT BIBLICAL INSTITUTE (ILL.)
Clement, Rufus Early
Fowler, Charles Henry
Hart, Virgil Chittenden
Hartzell, Joseph Crane
Hutchinson, Paul
Stuart, Charles Macaulay
GENERAL THEOLOGICAL SEMINARY (N.Y.)
Bradley, Charles William
Breck, James Lloyd
Burgess, Alexander
Burleson, Hugh Latimer
Coleman, Leighton
Crapsey, Algernon Sidney
De Koven, James
Dix, Morgan
Doane, George Washington
Fite, Warner
Francis, Paul James
Gailor, Thomas Frank
Gavin, Frank Stanton Burns
Goodwin, Hannibal Williston
Graves, Frederick Rogers
Hall, Charles Henry
Hare, George Emlen
Hoffman, Eugene Augustus
Kip, William Ingraham
Lee, Alfred
McVickar, William Neilson
Murphy, Edgar Gardner
Newton, Richard
Nies, James Buchanan
Odenheimer, William Henry
Paddock, Benjamin Henry
Paddock, John Adams
Pott, Francis Lister Hawks
Preston, Thomas Scott
Robinson, William Callyhan
Schroeder, John Frederick
Seymour, George Franklin
Spalding, Franklin Spencer
Spencer, Jesse Ames
Stone, John Seely
Talbot, Ethelbert
Whitehouse, Frederic Cope
Whittingham, William Rollinson
Winslow, William Copley
Worcester, Elwood
GENESEE COLLEGE (*See* SYRACUSE UNIVERSITY)
GENESEE WESLEYAN SEMINARY (N.Y.)
Keating, Kenneth Barnard
Rittenhouse, Jessie Belle
GENEVA COLLEGE (N.Y.) (*See* HOBART COLLEGE)
GENEVA COLLEGE (PA.)
Curry, John Steuart
Hubbard, Robert C. ("Cal")
GENEVA MEDICAL SCHOOL (N.Y.)
Blackwell, Elizabeth
Purple, Samuel Smith
Smith, Azariah
Smith, Stephen
GEORGE PEABODY COLLEGE FOR TEACHERS (TENN.)
Inge, William Motter
GEORGETOWN COLLEGE (KY.)
Breaux, Joseph Arsenne
Golden, Frank Alfred
Lorimer, George Claude
Loring, William Wing
Pentecost, George Frederick
GEORGETOWN UNIVERSITY (D.C.)
Ashford, Bailey Kelly
Beale, Edward Fitzgerald
Blease, Coleman Livingston
Bowie, Richard Johns
Bradley, Denis Mary
Bryce, Lloyd Stephens
Burbridge, Stephen Gano
Childe, John
Corcoran, William Wilson
De Leon, Thomas Cooper
Denby, Charles
Dimitry, Alexander
Dimitry, Charles Patton
Doyle, John Thomas
Egan, Maurice Francis
Fahy, Charles
Faulkner, Charles James
Fenwick, Benedict Joseph
Foote, John Ambrose
Gaston, William, 1778–1844
Glueck, Sheldon ("Sol")
Green, Benjamin Edwards
Hart, Philip Aloysius
Heth, Henry
Kavaugh, Edward
Kober, George Martin
Lackaye, Wilton
Latrobe, Benjamin Henry
Latrobe, John Hazlehurst Boneval

Leggett, William
Longyear, John Munroe
Magruder, George Lloyd
Mengarini, Gregory
Montoya, Joseph Manuel
Mouton, Alexander
Muñoz Marín, Luis
Musmanno, Michael Angelo
Nast, Condé Montrose
O'Shaughnessy, Nelson Jarvis Waterbury
Pallen, Conde Benoist
Pise, Charles Constantine
Provosty, Olivier Otis
Randall, James Ryder
Reeves, Daniel F.
Russell, Charles Wells
Saxton, Eugene Francis
Semmes, Alexander Jenkins
Semmes, Thomas Jenkins
Shipman, Andrew Jackson
Walsh, Henry Collins
Walsh, Thomas
Walters, Henry
White, Edward Douglass, 1845–1921
Whiting, William Henry Chase
Wimsatt, William Kurtz

Graduate Study
Musmanno, Michael Angelo
Nast, Condé Montrose

Law
Bankhead, John Hollis
Bankhead, William Brockman
Carr, Wilbur John
Chavez, Dennis
Conboy, Martin
Cortelyou, George Bruce
Flynn, John Thomas
Hall, Leonard Wood
Lever, Asbury Francis
Mitchell, Stephen Arnold
Muñoz Marín, Luis
Musmanno, Michael Angelo
Walter, Francis Eugene

Medicine
Dana, Charles Loomis
Foote, John Ambrose
Garrison, Fielding Hudson

George Washington University (D.C.)
Alden, Raymond MacDonald
Baker, Frank
Considine, Robert ("Bob") Bernard
Coves, Elliott
Cranch, Christopher Pearse
Davis, Arthur Powell
Davis, Meyer
Davis, Watson
Eliot, William Greenleaf
Franklin, Fabian
Glueck, Sheldon ("Sol")
Harris, William Alexander
Hazelton, George Cochrane
Hitchcock, Frank Harris
Howell, Robert Boyte Crawford
Kelser, Raymond Alexander
Leemans, Alphonse E. ("Tuffy")
Lewis, Exum Percival
Mason, Otis Tufton
Mitchell, William
Morfit, Campbell
Richardson, Charles Williamson
Ryland, Robert
Shuster, W(illiam) Morgan
Stanton, Frederick Perry
Stow, Baron
Tucker, Henry Holcombe
Walter, Francis Eugene
Weddell, Alexander Wilbourne
Wheeler, John Hill
Wilson, William Lyne

Graduate Study
Clark, Bennett Champ
Gidley, James Williams
Moore, Charles
Munroe, Charles Edward
Rister, Carl Coke
Simmons, James Stevens
Wilkinson, Theodore Stark
Zahniser, Howard Clinton

Law
Carr, Wilbur John
Cortelyou, George Bruce
Davis, William Hammatt
Dulles, John Foster
Flint, Weston
Guthrie, George Wilkins
Hastings, Daniel Oren
Hoover, John Edgar
Hopson, Howard Colwell
McCawley, Charles Laurie
MacPhail, Leland Stanford ("Larry")
Murphy, Robert Daniel
Newlands, Francis Griffith
Robins, Raymond
Weddell, Alexander Wilbourne
Wilson, William Lyne

Medicine
Bean, Tarleton Hoffman
Coues, Elliott
Dana, Charles Loomis
Dorset, Marion
Moore, Veranus Alva
Vander Veer, Albert

Georgia Augusta University (Germany)
Mayer, Maria Goeppert

Georgia College
O'Connor, Mary Flannery

Georgia Law School
Black, Eugene Robert

Georgia Military Institute
Harrison, George Paul
Howell, Evan Park
Russell, Richard Brevard, Jr.
Spencer, Samuel
Young, Pierce Manning Butler

Georgia School of Technology
Towers, John Henry

Germantown Academy (Pa.)
Bird, Robert Montgomery
Downey, John
Schaefter, Charles William
Schaeffer, Frederick Christian
Stockton, Charles Herbert

German University of Prague (Czechoslovakia)
Cori, Gerty Theresa Radnitz
Prokosch, Eduard

Gettysburg College (Pa.)
Beall, James Glenn
Buehler, Huber Gray
Clay, Albert Tobias
Eisenhart, Luther Pfahler
Hay, Charles Augustus
Horn, Edward Traill
Hunton, William Lee
Jacobs, Henry Eyster
McPherson, Edward
Muhlenberg, Frederick Augustus
Orth, Godlove Stein
Payne, Daniel Alexander
Richard, James William
Sadtler, John Philip Benjamin
Sadtler, Samuel Philip
Schmucker, Beale Melancthon
Seip, Theodore Lorenzo
Seiss, Joseph Augustus
Smith, Edgar Fahs
Sprecher, Samuel
Stine, Charles Milton Altland
Stoever, Martin Luther
Unangst, Erias
Valentine, Milton

Graduate Study
Stine, Charles Milton Altland

Gettysburg Theological Seminary (Pa.)
Harpster, John Henry
Hay, Charles Augustus
Jacobs, Henry Eyster
Morris, John Gottlieb
Passavant, William Alfred
Richard, James William
Schaeffer, Charles William

Glasgow University (Scotland) (*See* University of Glasgow)

Gonzaga College (D.C.)
Conboy, Martin

Gonzaga College (Wash.)
Brophy, Thomas D'Arcy

Gonzaga University (Wash.)
Crosby, Harry Lillis ("Bing")
Hubbard, Bernard Rosecrans
Walker, Frank Comerford

Gordon Military Institute
Russell, Richard Brevard, Jr. ("Dick")

Gordon School of Theology (Ma.)
Spottswood, Stephen Gill

Gorham Academy (Maine)
Andrew, John Albion
Bradbury, James Ware
Peters, John Andrew
Prentiss, George Lewis
Smyth, William
Stowe, Calvin Ellis
Young, Aaron

Goucher College (Md.)
Blair, Emily Newell
Phillips, Lena Madesin
Powdermaker, Hortense

Graduate Study
Adams, Joseph Quincy

Grand Island College (Neb.)
Abbott, Grace
Sutherland, Edwin Hardin

GRAND SEMINAIRE, MONTREAL (CANADA)
Schrembs, Joseph
GRAND SEMINARY (CANADA)
Curran, John Joseph
GRANVILLE COLLEGE (*See* DENISON UNIVERSITY)
GREENSBORO LAW SCHOOL (N.C.)
Dixon, Thomas
GREENVILLE ACADEMY (TENN.)
Barton, David
GREENVILLE COLLEGE (ILL.)
Zahniser, Howard Clinton
GREENVILLE MILITARY INSTITUTE (S.C.)
Manly, John Matthews
GREENVILLE WOMEN'S COLLEGE (S.C.)
Gambrell, Mary Latimer
GREYLOCK INSTITUTE (MASS.)
Davison, Henry Pomeroy
Dickinson, John Woodbridge
Hazelton, George Cochrane
Sabin, Charles Hamilton
GRINNELL COLLEGE (IOWA)
Adams, Ephraim Douglass
Buckley, Oliver Ellsworth
Burton, Theodore Elijah
Cooper, Gary
Cowles, Gardner
Emerson, Oliver Farrar
Flanagan, Hallie
Hall, James Norman
Hopkins, Harry Lloyd
Hughes, Edwin Holt
Jones, Lynds
Kenyon, William Squire
Macy, Jesse
Manatt, James Irving
Noyes, William Albert
Noyes, William Albert, Jr.
Ryan, Arthur Clayton
Shaw, Albert
Welch, Joseph Nye
Whitcomb, Selden Lincoln
Wilson, James
Graduate Study
Noyes, William Albert
GRISWOLD COLLEGE (IOWA)
Restarick, Henry Bond
GROTON SCHOOL (MASS.)
Acheson, Dean Gooderham
Allen, Frederick Lewis
Alsop, Stewart Johnnet Oliver
Auchincloss, Hugh Dudley, Jr.
Biddle, George
Burnap, George Washington
Carter, James Gordon
Cutting, Bronson Murray
Farrar, Timothy
Harriman, Edward Roland Noel
Haughton, Percy Duncan
Heintzelman, Stuart
Holbrook, Alfred
Hoppin, Joseph Clark
McCormick, Joseph Medill
McCormick, Robert Rutherford
Osborn, Henry Fairfield, 1887–1969
Parker, Joel, 1795–1875
Todd, Sereno Edwards
GROVE CITY COLLEGE (PA.)
Pew, John Howard
GUILFORD COLLEGE (N.C.)
Pearson, Thomas Gilbert
GUSTAVUS ADOLPHUS COLLEGE (MINN.)
Seashore, Carl Emil
Youngdahl, Luther Wallace

HAHNEMANN MEDICAL SCHOOL (ILL.)
Menninger, Charles Frederick
Simmons, George Henry
HALLOWELL ACADEMY (MAINE)
Abbott, Jacob
Abbott, John Stevens Cabot
Cheever, George Barrell
Cheever, Henry Theodore
Hubbard, Thomas Hamlin
Williams, Reuel
HAMBURG SCHOOL OF APPLIED ARTS (GERMANY)
Feininger, Lyonel (Charles Léonell Adrian)
HAMILTON ACADEMY (N.Y.)
Bishop, Nathan
Bonney, Charles Carroll
Cogswell, William Browne
Maynard, Edward
Orton, Harlow South
Park, Roswell, 1807–1869
Smith, Erasmus Darwin
Sterling, John Whalen
HAMILTON COLLEGE (N.Y.)
Adams, Samuel Hopkins
Amidon, Charles Fremont
Barnes, Albert
Bassett, Edward Murray
Bennett, Nathaniel
Blair, Austin
Bliss, Philemon
Bliss, Porter Cornelius
Bradford, Amory Howe
Breese, Sidney
Burdick, Francis Marion
Child, Frank Samuel
Cochrane, John
Dwight, Benjamin Woodbridge
Dwight, Harrison Gray Otis
Dwight, Theodore William
Eells, Dan Parmelee
Fiske, Daniel Willard
Grant, Asabel
Hall, Isaac Hollister
Hawley, Joseph Roswell
Hinman, George Wheeler
Hodges, George
Howe, William Wirt
Hunt, Ward
Huntington, Daniel
Ives, Irving McNeil
Ives, Levi Silliman
Jenkins, John Stilwell
Kendrick, Asahel Clark
Kidder, Daniel Parish
King, Edward Skinner
Knox, George William
Knox, John Jay
Lathrop, John Hiram
Lord, Chester Sanders
McMaster, Guy Humphreys
Mahan, Asa
Miller, William Henry Harrison
North, Edward
North, Simon Newton Dexter
Orton, Edward Francis Baxter
Paine, John Alsop
Parker, Joel, 1799–1873
Payne, Henry B.
Pierson, Arthur Tappan
Pomeroy, John Norton
Porter, Jermain Gildersleeve
Pound, Ezra
Powell, Edward Payson
Putnam, James Osborne
Randall, Samuel Sidwell
Reid, Gilbert
Robinson, Edward, 1794–1863
Root, Elihu
Sawyer, Leicester Ambrose
Sayles, John
Schneider, Benjamin
Scollard, Clinton
Shaw, Henry Wheeler
Sheldon, Edward Austin
Sherman, James Schoolcraft
Sherman, James Schoolcraft
Smith, Erasmus Darwin
Smith, Gerrit
Stryker, Lloyd Paul
Stryker, Melancthon Woolsey
Taylor, James Wickes
Thayer, Amos Madden
Underwood, John Curtiss
Walker, Gilbert Carlton
Wallace, William James
Warner, Charles Dudley
Whedon, Daniel Denison
White, William Nathaniel
Wickson, Edward James
Winslow, William Copley
Woollcott, Alexander Humphreys
Graduate Study
Stryker, Lloyd Paul
HAMILTON LITERARY AND THEOLOGICAL INSTITUTION (*See* COLGATE UNIVERSITY)
HAMILTON SCHOOL OF DRAMATIC EXPRESSION (KY.)
Main, Marjorie
HAMLINE UNIVERSITY (MINN.)
Schall, Thomas David
HAMMA SCHOOL OF THEOLOGY OF WITTENBERG UNIVERSITY (OHIO)
Douglas, Lloyd Cassel
Graduate Study
Douglas, Lloyd Cassel
HAMPDEN-SYDNEY COLLEGE (VA.)
Atkinson, Thomas
Baker, Daniel
Bibb, George Mortimer
Bocock, Thomas Stanley
Cabell, Nathaniel Francis
Cabell, William H.
Carr, Dabney
Coles, Edward
Dabney, Charles William
Dabney, Robert Lewis
Gamble, Hamilton Rowan
Giles, William Branch
Harrison, William Henry

Howard, William Travis
Johnston, Peter
Klipstein, Louis Frederick
Ligon, Thomas Watkins
McGready, James
McIlwaine, Richard
Manson, Otis Frederick
Mettauer, John Peter
Penick, Charles Clifton
Pollard, Edward Alfred
Preston, John Smith
Preston, William Ballard
Price, Sterling
Pryor, Roger Atkinson
Rives, William Cabell
Smith, Benjamin Mosby
Stevenson, John White
Stuart, John Leighton
Sydnor, Charles Sackett
Venable, Charles Scott
Waddel, Moses
Theology
Lindley, Daniel
HAMPTON INSTITUTE (VA.)
Abbott, Robert Sengstacke
Barrett, Janie Porter
Morón, Alonzo Graseano
Morton, Robert Russa
Smith, Lucy Harth
HANNIBAL-LA GRANGE COLLEGE (MO.)
Cannon, Clarence
HANOVER COLLEGE (IND.)
Barnes, Charles Reid
Blackburn, William Maxwell
Coulter, John Merle
Dawson, Thomas Cleland
English, William Hayden
Fisher, Walter Lowrie
Goldsmith, Middleton
Hamilton, Edward John
Hendricks, Thomas Andrews
Jacob, Richard Taylor
Monroe, Paul
Oldfather, William Abbott
Patterson, James Kennedy
Porter, Albert Gallatin
Riley, William Bell
Wallace, William Ross
Whitworth, George Frederic
Wiley, Harvey Washington
Wilson, Samuel Ramsey
Graduate Study
Jessup, Walter Albert
HARDIN-SIMMONS UNIVERSITY (TEX.)
Blocker, Dan
Richardson, Sid Williams
Rister, Carl Coke
HARTFORD THEOLOGICAL SEMINARY (CONN.)
Barton, James Levi
Frame, Alice Seymour Browne
Nutting, Wallace
Pitkin, Walter Boughton
Rhees, Rush
HARVARD UNIVERSITY (MASS.)
Abbot, Benjamin
Abbot, Francis Ellingwood
Adams, Brooks
Adams, Charles Francis, 1807–1886
Adams, Charles Francis, 1835–1915
Adams, Eliphalet
Adams, Henry Brooks
Adams, John, 1735–1826
Adams, John Quincy
Adams, Nehemiah
Adams, Samuel
Agassiz, Alexander
Agee, James Rufus
Aiken, Conrad Potter
Alden, Ebenezer
Alden, Timothy
Aldrich, Richard
Aldrich, Winthrop William
Alger, Horatio
Allen, Charles
Allen, Edward Ellis
Allen, Frederick Lewis
Allen, Glover Morrill
Allen, James Edward, Jr.
Allen, Joel Asaph
Allen, Joseph Henry
Allen, William
Allen, William Francis
Allison, Nathaniel
Allport, Gordon Willard
Allston, Washington
Ames, Fisher
Ames, Frederick Lothrop
Ames, James Barr
Ames, Oakes
Ames, Winthrop
Andrew, Samuel
Angell, Ernest
Appleton, Nathaniel Walker
Appleton, Thomas Gold
Appleton, William Sumner
Apthorp, William Foster
Arensberg, Walter Conrad
Arvin, Newton
Aspinwall, William
Astor, John Jacob, 1864–1912
Astor, William Vincent
Atherton, Charles Gordon
Atherton, Joshua
Atwood, Charles B.
Auchmuty, Samuel
Austin, James Trecothick
Austin, Jonathan Loring
Austin, William
Babbitt, Irving
Babcock, James Francis
Babcock, James Woods
Bacon, Robert
Bailey, Jacob
Baker, George Pierce
Baker, Harvey Humphrey
Balch, Thomas Willing
Baldwin, Loammi, 1780–1838
Baldwin, William Henry
Ballantine, Arthur Atwood
Bancroft, Aaron
Bancroft, Wilder Dwight
Bancroft. George
Barbour, Thomas
Barlow, Francis Channing
Barnard, Charles Francis
Barnard, Chester Irving
Barnard, John
Barnes, Joseph K.
Barnwell, Robert Woodward
Bartlett, Joseph
Bass, Edward
Batchelor, George
Beal, William James
Beale, Joseph Henry
Beaman, Charles Cotesworth
Becker, George Ferdinand
Behrman, Samuel Nathaniel ("S.N.")
Belcher, Jonathan
Belkin, Samuel
Belknap, Jeremy
Bellows, Henry Whitney
Bemis, George
Benchley, Robert Charles
Benjamin, Park, 1809–1864
Bentley, William
Berenson, Bernard
Berle, Adolf Augustus, Jr.
Besse, Arthur Lyman
Bettman, Alfred
Bickmore, Albert Smith
Biddle, Francis Beverley
Biddle, George
Bigelow, Frank Hagar
Bigelow, Harry Augustus
Bigelow, Henry Bryant
Bigelow, Henry Jacob
Bigelow, Jacob
Bigelow, William Sturgis
Biggers, Earl Derr
Billings, Asa White Kenney
Binney, Horace
Birkhoff, George David
Bixby, James Thompson
Blaikie, William
Blaustein, David
Bliss, Cornelius Newton
Bliss, George, 1830–1897
Bliss, Jonathan
Bliss, Robert Woods
Bloomfield, Leonard
Bloomfield, Meyer
Blowers, Sampson Salter
Bôcher, Maxime
Bohlen, Charles Eustis ("Chip")
Bonaparte, Charles Joseph
Bonaparte, Jerome Napoleon
Bond, George Phillips
Boott, Kirk
Bourne, Benjamin
Bourne, Jonathan
Boutell, Henry Sherman
Bowditch, Charles Pickering
Bowditch, Henry Ingersoll
Bowditch, Henry Pickering
Bowdoin, James, 1726–1790
Bowdoin, James, 1752–1811
Bowen, Francis
Bowman, Isaiah
Boyden, Roland William
Brackett, Jeffrey Richardson
Bradford, Alden
Bradford, Edward Hickling
Bradford, Gamaliel
Bradley, Milton
Bradley, Theophilus
Brainerd, Erastus
Brattle, Thomas
Brattle, William
Brazer, John

Brewer, Thomas Mayo
Bridgman, Percy Williams
Briggs, LeBaron Russell
Brinton, Clarence Crane
Brooks, Alfred Hulse
Brooks, Charles
Brooks, Charles Timothy
Brooks, Phillips
Brooks, Van Wyck
Broun, Heywood Campbell
Brown, Addison
Brown, Charles Rufus
Brown, Frederic Tilden
Brown, John Mason, Jr.
Brown, Walter Folger
Brown, William Garrott
Browne, Daniel Jay
Browne, William
Brownlee, James Forbis
Buckminster, Joseph Stevens
Bulfinch, Charles
Bulfinch, Thomas
Bull, William Tillinghast
Bullard, Henry Adams
Burgess, Edward
Burgess, W(illiam) Starling
Burlingame, Edward Livermore
Burlingham, Charles Culp
Burnap, George Washington
Burnham, William Henry
Burrage, Walter Lincoln
Burton, Frederick Russell
Burton, Warren
Byerly, William Elwood
Byles, Mather
Cabot, Arthur Tracy
Cabot, George
Cabot, Godfrey Lowell
Cabot, Hugh
Cabot, Richard Clarke
Callender, John
Calvert, George Henry
Campbell, Prince Lucien
Cannon, Walter Bradford
Capen, Samuel Paul
Carpenter, George Rice
Carpenter, John Alden
Carter, James Coolidge
Carter, James Gordon
Castle, William Richards, Jr.
Catchings, Waddill
Chadwick, James Read
Chamberlain, Joseph Perkins
Chamberlain, Nathan Henry
Chandler, Charles Frederick
Chandler, Seth Carlo
Channing, Edward
Channing, Edward Tyrrell
Channing, Walter
Channing, William Ellery, 1780–1842
Channing, William Ellery, 1818–1901
Channing, William Francis
Channing, William Henry
Chapman, John Jay
Chapman, Victor Emmanuel
Chase, Pliny Earle
Chase, Thomas
Chauncy, Charles
Child, David Lee
Child, Francis James
Child, Richard Washburn
Chipman, Ward
Choate, Joseph Hodges
Clap, Thomas
Clark, Grenville
Clark, Henry James
Clark, Jonas
Clarke, Frank Wigglesworth
Clarke, James Freeman
Clarke, Richard
Cleaveland, Parker
Cleveland, Aaron
Clothier, William Jackson
Cobb, David
Cobb, Jonathan Holmes
Coerne, Louis Adolphe
Cogswell, Joseph Green
Coker, James Lide
Colburn, Warren
Cole, Frank Nelson
Colman, Benjamin
Colpitts, Edwin Henry
Conant, James Bryant
Converse, Frederick Shepherd
Cook, Clarence Chatham
Cook, Flavius Josephus
Cook, George Cram
Cook, Walter
Cooke, Elisha, 1637–1715
Cooke, Elisha, 1678–1737
Cooke, Josiah Parsons
Coolidge, Archibald Cary
Coolidge, Charles Allerton
Coolidge, Julian Lowell
Coolidge, Thomas Jefferson
Cooper, Samuel, 1725–1783
Copeland, Charles Townsend
Cory, Charles Barney
Costigan, Edward Prentiss
Costigan, George Purcell
Cotton, Joseph Potter
Cozzens, James Gould
Crafts, James Mason
Crafts, William
Cranch, Christopher Pearse
Cranch, William
Croly, Herbert David
Cross, Arthur Lyon
Cross, Samuel Hazzard
Crowne, John
Crowninshield, Frederic
Cummings, Edward
Cummings, E. E.
Curtin, Jeremiah
Curtis, Benjamin Robbins
Curtis, Charles Pelham
Curtis, George Ticknor
Curtis, John Green
Curwen, Samuel
Cushing, Caleb
Cushing, Luther Stearns
Cushing, Thomas
Cushing, William
Cushman, Joseph Augustine
Cushman, Joshua
Cutler, Elliott Carr
Cutler, Robert
Cutler, Timothy
Cutter, Charles Ammi
Cutting, Bronson Murray
Dalton, John Coll
Damon, Ralph Shepard
Dana, Charles Anderson
Dana, Francis
Dana, James
Dana, James Freeman
Dana, Richard
Dana, Richard Henry, 1787–1879
Dana, Richard Henry, 1815–1882
Dana, Samuel Luther
Dane, Nathan
Danforth, Thomas, 1703–c. 1786
Davenport, Charles Benedict
Davidoff, Leo Max
Davies, Henry Eugene
Davis Andrew McFarland
Davis Charles Henry, 1807–1877
Davis, Dwight Filley
Davis, Horace
Davis, John, 1761–1847
Davis, John Chandler Bancroft
Davis, Owen Gould
Davis, William Morris
Davis, William Thomas
Dawson, John
Deane, Samuel
Deering, Nathaniel
Dennie, Joseph
Dennison, Henry Sturgis
Derby, Elias Hasket, 1766–1826
Derby, Elias Hasket, 1803–1880
Dett, Robert Nathaniel
Devens, Charles
DeVoto, Bernard Augustine
Dexter, Franklin
Dexter, Samuel, 1761–1816
Diller, Joseph Silas
Dillingham, Walter Francis
Dix, John Homer
Dixon, Roland Burrage
Doe, Charles
Dole, Charles Fletcher
Dole, James Drummond
Dole, Nathan Haskell
Dorr, Thomas Wilson
Dorsheimer, William Edward
Dos Passos, John Roderigo
Downing, George
Dudley, Joseph
Dudley, Paul
Dummer, Jeremiah, c. 1679–1739
Dunbar, Charles Franklin
Durant, Henry Fowle
Durell, Edward Henry
Durfee, William Franklin
Dwight, Francis
Dwight, John Sullivan
Dwight, Thomas
Dyer, Louis
Eames, Charles
Earhart, Amelia Mary
Earle, George Howard, III
Edes, Robert Thaxter
Eliot, Charles
Eliot, Charles William
Eliot, Samuel
Eliot, Samuel Atkins
Eliot, T(homas) S(tearns)
Elleny, William

Elliott, Aaron Marshall
Elliott, William
Ellis, Calvin
Ellis, George Edward
Elman, Robert
Elwyn, Alfred Langdon
Emerson, Edward Waldo
Emerson, George Barrell
Emerson, Haven
Emerson, Joseph
Emerson, Ralph Waldo
Emerson, William
Emerton, Ephraim
Emmons, Samuel Franklin
Endicott, William Crowninshield
English, George Bethune
Ernst, Harold Clarence
Ernst, Oswald Herbert
Eustis, George, 1796–1858
Eustis, George, 1828–1872
Eustis, Henry Lawrence
Eustis, James Biddle
Eustis, William
Everett, Alexander Hill
Everett, Edward
Ewer, Ferdinand Cartwright
Fairchild, Blair
Fairchild, Charles Stebbins
Fairchild, Sherman Mills
Fairlie, John Archibald
Farlow, William Gilson
Farrar, John
Fay, Sidney Bradshaw
Feis, Herbert
Felton, Cornelius Conway
Felton, Samuel Morse
Fenn, William Wallace
Fenollosa, Ernest Francisco
Fernald, James Champlin
Fernald, Merritt Lyndon
Fessenden, Francis
Fewkes, Jesse Walter
Field, Herbert Haviland
Field, Marshall, IV
Finck, Henry Theophilus
Fisher, Joshua Francis
Fiske, Amos Kidder
Fiske, George Converse
Fiske, John
Fitz, Reginald Heber
Flagg, Thomas Wilson
Flandrau, Charles Macomb
Fletcher, John Gould
Flint, Albert Stowell
Flint, Austin
Flint, Charles Louis
Flint, Timothy
Folsom, Charles
Folsom, George
Foote, Arthur William
Forbes, John Murray
Forbes, William Cameron
Force, Manning Ferguson
Ford, George Burdett
Foster, Abiel
Foster, Frank Hugh
Foster, John
Foster, John Watson
Foster, William Trufant
Fox, John William
Francis, Convers
Frear, William
Freeman, James
French, William Merchant Richardson
Frisbie, Levi
Frothingham, Nathaniel Langdon
Frothingham, Octavius Brooks
Frothingham, Paul Revere
Fullam, Frank L.
Fuller, Joseph Vincent
Fuller, Richard
Fulton, John Farquhar
Furness, Horace Howard, 1833–1912
Furness, Horace Howard, 1865–1930
Furness, William Henry
Gannett, Ezra Stiles
Gannett, Henry
Gannett William Channing
Gardiner, Robert Hallowell
Garrard, Kenner
Garrison, Lindley Miller
Gary, Martin Witherspoon
Gay, Ebenezer
Gay, Frederick Parker
Gay, Sydney Howard
Gerry, Elbridge
Gibbs, George, 1815–1873
Gifford, Walter Sherman
Gilman, Samuel
Golder, Frank Alfred
Goldmark, Henry
Goodhue, Benjamin
Goodnough, Xanthus Henry
Goodrich, Frank Boott
Goodwin, William Watson
Gordon, George Angier
Gordon, George Byron
Gorham, John
Gould, Augustus Addison
Gould, Benjamin Apthorp, 1787–1859
Grandgent, Charles Hall
Grant, George Barnard
Grant, Harry Johnston
Grant, Percy Stickney
Grant, Robert
Gray, Francis Calley
Gray, Horace
Gray, John Chipman
Green, Francis
Green, Jacob, 1722–1790
Green, John
Green, Joseph
Green, Samuel Abbott
Green, Samuel Swett
Greene, Charles Ezra
Greene, George Sears
Greene, Jerome Davis
Greene, Roger Sherman
Greener, Richard Theodore
Greenhalge, Frederic Thomas
Greenlaw, Edwin Almiron
Greenough, Henry
Greenough, Horatio
Greenough, James Bradstreet
Greenwood, Isaac
Gregg, Alan
Grew, Joseph Clark
Gridley, Jeremiah
Griswold, William McCrillis
Gruening, Ernest
Guild, Curtis, 1860–1915
Guinzburg, Harold Kleinert
Gummere, Francis Barton
Gurney, Ephraim Whitman
Hackett, Frank Warren
Hagedorn, Hermann Ludwig Gebhard
Hague, James Duncan
Hale, Charles
Hale, Edward Everett
Hale, Frederick
Hale, Horatio Emmons
Hale, William Bayard
Hale, William Gardner
Hall, Fitzedward
Hall, Willard
Hamlin, Charles Sumner
Hancock, John, 1736–1793
Hand, Augustus Noble
Hand, Learned
Hapgood, Hutchins
Hapgood, Norman
Haring, Clarence
Harrington, Charles
Harris, Seymour Edwin
Harris, Thaddeus Mason
Harris, Thaddeus William
Harris, William
Harrod, Benjamin Morgan
Hart, Albert Bushnell
Haughton, Percy Duncan
Hawthorne, Julian
Hayward, George
Hazeltine, Mayo Williamson
Heard, Franklin Fiske
Hearst, William Randolph
Hedge, Frederic Henry
Hedge, Levi
Henck, John Benjamin
Henderson, Lawrence Joseph
Herrick, Robert Welch
Herschel, Clemens
Herter, Christian Archibald
Hess, Alfred Fabian
Higginson, Henry Lee
Higginson, Nathaniel
Higginson, Thomas Wentworth
Hildreth, Richard
Hill, Henry Barker
Hill, Joseph Adna
Hill, Thomas, 1818–1891
Hillard, George Stillman
Hillyer, Robert Silliman
Hitchcock, Enos
Hitchcock, Frank Harris
Hitchcock, James Ripley Wellman
Hitchcock, Thomas
Hoar, Ebenezer Rockwood
Hoar, George Frisbie
Hoar, Leonard
Hoar, Samuel
Hocking, William Ernest
Hoer, Ebenezer Rockwood
Hoffman, Wickham
Holdrege, George Ward
Holland, Clifford Milburn
Holmes, John Haynes
Holmes, Nathaniel
Holmes, Oliver Wendell, 1809–1894

Holmes, Oliver Wendell, 1841–1935
Holt, Edwin Bissell
Holyoke, Edward Augustus
Holyoke, Samuel
Hooper, William
Hoover, Charles Franklin
Hoppin, Joseph Clark
Horton, Samuel Dana
Hosmer, Frederick Lucian
Hosmer, James Kendall
Houghton, Alanson Bigelow
Howe, Andrew Jackson
Howe, Henry Marion
Howe, Mark De Wolfe
Howe, Quincy
Hubbard, Henry Guernsey
Hubbard, William
Hubbard, Wynant Davis
Hughes, Hector James
Hughes, Howard Robard
Huidekoper, Frederic
Hunt, Carleton
Hunt, William Gibbes
Hunt, William Morris
Huntington, Edward Vermilye
Huntington, Jeddediah
Huntington, William Reed
Hurlbert, William Henry
Hutchinson, Thomas
Hyatt, Alphaeus
Hyde, William DeWitt
Inman, George
Jackman, Wilbur Samuel
Jackson, Charles
Jackson, Dunham
Jackson, James, 1777–1867
Jaggar, Thomas Augustus, Jr.
James, Edmund Janes
James, William
Jarvis, Edward
Jeffries, Benjamin Joy
Jeffries, John
Jenks, William
Jenney, William LeBaron
Jennings, James Herman
Johns, Clayton
Johnson, Joseph French
Johnson, Samuel
Jones, John Price
Jones, Leonard Augustus
Jones, Robert Edmond
Jones, William
Jordan, Eben Dyer
Kallen, Horace Meyer
Kauffman, Calvin Henry
Keith, Arthur
Kennedy, George Clayton
Kennedy, John Fitzgerald
Kennedy, Joseph Patrick
Kennedy, Robert Francis
Kent, Edward
Kerr, Washington Caruthers
Kidder, Alfred Vincent
Kimball, (Sidney) Fiske
King, Henry Churchill
King, James Gore
King, Rufus, 1755–1827
Kirkland, John Thornton
Kittredge, George Lyman
Knapp, Philip Coombs
Knauth, Oswald Whitman
Kneeland, Samuel
Knight, Henry Cogswell
Knowles, John Hilton
Kyes, Roger Martin
Ladd, William
La Farge, Christopher Grant
La Farge, John
La Farge, Oliver Hazard Perry
Lamont, Hammond
Lamont, Thomas William
Lander, Edward
Lane, George Martin
Langdell, Christopher Columbus
Langdon, Courtney
Langer, William Leonard
Langley, John Williams
Lardner, John Abbott
Lathrop, John
Laughlin, James Laurence
Laurence, William Leonard
Law, Jonathan
Lawrence, Amos Adams
Lawrence, William
Lear, Tobias
Lee, Alfred
Lee, Joseph
Lee, William Henry Fitzhugh
Lehman, Arthur
Leiter, Joseph
Leonard, Charles Lester
Leonard, Daniel
Leonard, Levi Washburn
Leverett, John, 1662–1724
Lewis, Clarence Irving
Lewis, Gilbert Newton
Lincoln, Enoch
Lincoln, Levi, 1749–1820
Lincoln, Levi, 1782–1868
Lincoln, Robert Todd
Lindsay, Howard
Lippmann, Walter
Littauer, Lucius Nathan
Livermore, Abiel Abbot
Livermore, Samuel, 1786–1833
Lloyd, Alfred Henry
Locke, Alain Leroy
Lodge, George Cabot
Lodge, John Ellerton
Loeb, James
Loeb, Morris
Lombard, Warren Plimpton
Long, John Davis
Longfellow, Ernest Wadsworth
Longfellow, Samuel
Longfellow, Stephen
Longfellow, William Pitt Preble
Longworth, Nicholas
Loring, Edward Greely
Loring, Ellis Gray
Loring, Frederick Wadsworth
Loring, George Bailey
Lovell, James
Lovell, John
Lovell, Joseph
Lovering, Joseph
Lovett, Robert Morss
Lovett, Robert Williamson
Lowe, Charles
Lowell, Abbott Lawrence
Lowell, Edward Jackson
Lowell, Francis Cabot
Lowell, Guy
Lowell, James Russell
Lowell, John, 1743–1802
Lowell, John, 1769–1840
Lowell, John, 1799–1836
Lowell, John, 1824–1897
Lowell, Percival
Lowell, Ralph
Lowell, Robert Traill Spence
Lowell, Robert Traill Spence, Jr.
Lowery, Woodbury
Lummis, Charles Fletcher
Lunt, George
Lydenberg, Harry Miller
Lyman, Benjamin Smith
Lyman, Theodore, 1792–1849
Lyman, Theodore, 1833–1897
Lynde, Benjamin
Mabery, Charles Frederic
McBurney, Charles
MacCurdy, George Grant
McElroy, Neil Hosler
McIntyre, Alfred Robert
MacKaye, Benton
McKenzie, Alexander
McKim, Charles Follen
MacNider, Hanford
MacVeagh, Charles
Macy, John Albert
Mallinckrodt, Edward, Jr.
Mallory, Frank Burr
Mann, James
Mannes, Leopold Damrosch
Mapes, Charles Victor
Marmaduke, John Sappington
Marquand, John Phillips
Marsh, John, 1799–1856
Martin, Edward Sandford
Mason, Daniel Gregory
Mason, Francis Van Wyck
Mather, Cotton
Mather, Increase
Mather, Samuel, 1706–1785
Matthews, Nathan
Mattingly, Garrett
Mayer, Oscar Gottfried
Mayhew, Jonathan
Mead, George Herbert
Mellen, Grenville
Mellen, Prentiss
Mercer, Henry Chapman
Merck, George Wilhelm
Merrick, Pliny
Merrill, George Edmands
Merrill, William Bradford
Meyer, George von Lengerke
Mezes, Sidney Edward
Miller, Gerrit Smith, Jr.
Millet, Francis Davis
Mills, Ogden Livingston
Minot, George Richards
Mirsky, Alfred Ezra
Mitchell, James Tyndale
Mitchell, John Ames
Mitchell, Jonathan
Mitchell, Nahum
Moffat, Jay Pierrepont
Montague, Gilbert Holland
Montague, William Pepperell
Moody, William Henry
Moody, William Vaughn
Moore, Charles

Moore, Clifford Herschel
Moore, Hugh Everett
Morgan, Edwin Vernon
Morgan, John Pierpont
Morgan, Morris Hicky
Morison, George Shattuck
Morison, Samuel Eliot
Morley, Sylvanus Griswold
Morris, Edward Joy
Morse, Edward Sylvester
Morse, John Lovett
Morse, John Torrey
Morton, Ferdinand Quintin
Morton, William James
Mosely, Philip Edward
Motley, John Lothrop
Mumford, James Gregory
Munro, William Bennett
Munroe, Charles Edward
Muzzey, David Saville
Nash, Frederick Ogden
Nash, Henry Sylvester
Nef, John Ulric
Nelson, Charles Alexander
Newell, William Wells
Newman, Henry
Newman, Samuel Phillips
Niles, Nathaniel, 1741–1828
Niles, Samuel
Noble, Gladwyn Kingsley
Nordhoff, Charles Bernard
Norton, Andrews
Norton, Charles Eliot
Noyes, George Repall
Nutting, Wallace
O'Brian, John Lord
O'Brien, Robert Lincoln
O'Donnell, Kenneth Patrick
Olds, Robert Edwin
Oliver, Andrew, 1706–1774
Oliver, Andrew, 1731–1799
Oliver, Henry Kemble
Oliver, Peter
Olmsted, Frederick Law
Oppenheimer, Julius Robert
Osborne, Thomas Mott
Osgood, George Laurie
Osgood, Howard
Osgood, Samuel
Osgood, William Fogg
Otis, Harrison Gray, 1765–1848
Otis, James
Packard, Frederick Adolphus
Page, Charles Grafton
Paine, Charles
Paine, Charles Jackson
Paine, Elijah
Paine, Martyn
Paine, Robert Treat, 1731–1814
Paine, Robert Treat, 1773–1811
Paine, Robert Treat, 1835–1910
Palfrey, John Carver
Palfrey, John Gorham
Palmer, George Herbert
Parker, Carleton Hubbell
Parker, Edward Pickering
Parker, George Howard
Parker, Henry Taylor
Parker, Isaac
Parker, James Cutler Dunn
Parker, Richard Green
Parker, Theodore
Parker, Willard
Parkman, Francis
Parrington, Vernon Louis
Parris, Samuel
Parsons, Samuel Holden
Parsons, Theophilus, 1750–1813
Parsons, Theophilus, 1797–1882
Partridge, James Rudolph
Pasco, Samuel
Patten, William
Payson, Edward
Payson, Seth
Peabody, Andrew Preston
Peabody, Francis Greenwood
Peabody, Oliver William Bourn
Peabody, Robert Swain
Peabody, William Bourn Oliver
Pearson, Edmund Lester
Pearson, Eliphalet
Peattie, Donald Culross
Peck, William Dandridge
Peirce, Benjamin
Peirce, Benjamin Osgood
Peirce, Charles Sanders
Peirce, Cyrus
Peirce, James Mills
Penrose, Boies
Penrose, Richard Alexander Fullerton
Penrose, Spencer
Perin, Charles Page
Perkins, Charles Callahan
Perkins, James Handasyd
Perkins, Maxwell Evarts
Perkins, Thomas Nelson
Perry, Thomas Sergeant
Perry, William
Perry, William Stevens
Phillips, John
Phillips, John Sanburn
Phillips, Samuel
Phillips, Wendell
Phillips, Willard
Phillips, William
Pickering, Charles
Pickering, Edward Charles
Pickering, John, *c.* 1738–1805
Pickering, John, 1777–1846
Pickering, Timothy
Pierpont, James
Pierson, Abraham, *c.* 1645–1707
Pike, Albert
Pike, Nicolas
Piper, William Thomas
Piston, Walter Hamor
Pollak, Walter Heilprin
Pond, George Edward
Poor, John
Potter, Elisha Reynolds
Pray, Isaac Clark
Preble, William Pitt
Prescott, Oliver
Prescott, William Hickling
Prince, Frederick Henry
Prince, Morton
Prince, Thomas
Pulitzer, Joseph, Jr.
Pulitzer, Ralph
Putnam, Charles Pickering
Putnam, Frederic Ward
Putnam, (George) Herbert
Putnam, Helen Cordelia
Putnam, James Jackson
Pynchon, Thomas Ruggles
Quincy, Edmund
Quincy, Josiah, 1744–1775
Quincy, Josiah, 1772–1864
Quincy, Josiah Phillips
Rand, Benjamin
Rand, Edward Kennard
Randall, Clarence Belden
Rantoul, Robert, 1805–1852
Rawle, Francis, 1846–1930
Read, Conyers
Read, John, 1679/80–1749
Read, Nathan
Reed, James, 1834–1921
Reed, John, 1887–1920
Reed, Sampson
Reisner, George Andrew
Richards, John Kelvey
Richards, Theodore William
Richardson, Henry Hobson
Richardson, William Adams
Richardson, William Merchant
Riddle, George Peabody
Rideout, Henry Milner
Rindge, Frederick Hastings
Rinehart, Stanley Marshall, Jr.
Ripley, Ezra
Ripley, George
Robbins, Chandler
Robinson, Benjamin Lincoln
Robinson, Edward, 1858–1931
Robinson, Edwin Arlington
Robinson, James Harvey
Roethke, Theodore Huebner
Rogers, William Crowninshield
Roosevelt, Franklin Delano
Roosevelt, Kermit
Roosevelt, Theodore
Ropes, James Hardy
Ropes, John Codman
Rorimer, James Joseph
Ross, Denman Waldo
Rotch, Arthur
Rotch, Thomas Morgan
Rothrock, Joseph Trimble
Rublee, George
Ruggles, Timothy
Ruhl, Arthur Brown
Rumsey, Charles Cary
Runkle, John Daniel
Russell, William Eustis
Sachs, Bernard
Sachs, Paul Joseph
Safford, Truman Henry
Saltonstall, Gurdon
Saltonstall, Leverett
Sanborn, Franklin Benjamin
Sanders, Daniel Clarke
Sanford, Edward Terry
Sanger, Charles Robert
Sanger, George Partridge
Santayana, George
Sargent, Charles Sprague
Sargent, Henry Winthrop
Sargent, John Osborne
Sargent, Lucius Manlius
Sargent, Winthrop, 1753–1820
Savage, Henry Wilson
Savage, James
Savage, Philip Henry

Sawyer, Wilbur Augustus
Scammell, Alexander
Schofield, Henry
Schorer, Mark
Schouler, James
Scott, James Brown
Searle, Arthur
Sears, Richard Dudley
Seccomb, John
Sedgwick, Arthur George
Sedgwick, Ellery
Seeger, Alan
Seldes, Gilbert Vivian
Sewall, Harold Marsh
Sewall, Jonathan
Sewall, Jonathan Mitchell
Sewall, Joseph Addison
Sewall, Samuel
Sewall, Stephen
Shaler, Nathaniel Southgate
Sharpless, Isaac
Shattuck, Frederick Cheever
Shattuck, George Brune
Shattuck, George Cheyne, 1783–1854
Shattuck, George Cheyne, 1813–1893
Shaw, Lemuel
Shaw, William Smith
Sheldon, Edward Stevens
Shepley, George Foster
Sherwin, Thomas
Sherwood, Robert Emmet
Shorey, Paul
Short, Charles
Shubrick, William Branford
Shurtleff, Nathaniel Bradstreet
Sibley, John Langdon
Sidis, Boris
Simmons, Edward
Simonds, Frank Herbert
Sinnott, Edmund Ware
Slattery, Charles Lewis
Smith, Courtney Craig
Smith, Jeremiah, 1759–1842
Smith, Jeremiah, 1837–1921
Smith, Lloyd Logan Pearsall
Smith, Ormond Gerald
Smith, Samuel Francis
Smyth, Herbert Weir
Soley, James Russell
Southard, Elmer Ernest
Spalding, Lyman
Sparks, Jared
Spearns, William Augustus
Spencer, Ambrose
Sprague, Oliver Mitchell Wentworth
Sprague, Peleg
Spurr, Josiah Edward
Starr, Merritt
Stearns, Asahel
Stearns, Eben Sperry
Stearns, Harold Edmund
Stearns, Oliver
Stearns, William Augustus
Stebbins, Horatio
Stein, Leo Daniel
Stephenson, Nathaniel Wright
Stetson, Henry Crosby
Stevens, John Austin, 1827–1910
Stevens, Wallace
Stewardson, John
Stimson, Frederic Jesup
Stoddard, Solomon
Stoddard, Theodore Lothrop
Stokes, Isaac Newton Phelps
Stolberg, Benjamin
Stone, Edward Durell
Stone, James Kent
Storer, Bellamy
Storer, Francis Humphreys
Storer, Horatio Robinson
Storey, Moorfield
Storrow, Charles Storer
Storrow, James Jackson
Story, Isaac
Story, Joseph
Story, Wilham Edward
Story, William Wetmore
Stoughton, William
Straus, Jesse Isidor
Straus, Percy Selden
Stringham, Washington Irving
Strobel, Edward Henry
Strong, Caleb
Strong, Charles Augustus
Sullivan, George
Sullivan, Mark
Sullivan, William
Sumner, Charles
Sumner, James Batcheller
Swanton, John Reed
Tarr, Ralph Stockman
Tatlock, John Strong Perry
Taussig, Frank William
Taussig, Frederick Joseph
Taylor, Edward
Taylor, Frank Bursley
Taylor, Henry Osborn
Taylor, Richard
Thacher, George
Thacher, Peter, 1651–1727
Thacher, Peter, 1752–1802
Thacher, Samuel Cooper
Thaw, Harry Kendall
Thaxter, Roland
Thayer, Alexander Wheelock
Thayer, Ezra Ripley
Thayer, James Bradley
Thayer, Joseph Henry
Thayer, Wilham Roscoe
Thayer, William Sydney
Thompson, Benjamin
Thoreau, Henry David
Thorndike, Edward Lee
Thwing, Charles Franklin
Tinkham, George Holden
Tompkins, Floyd Williams
Tompson, Benjamin
Tower, Charlemagne
Townsend, Edward Davis
Tracy, Nathaniel
Train, Arthur Cheney
Treat, Samuel
Trowbridge, Edmund
Trowbridge, John
Trumbull, John, 1756–1843
Trumbull, Jonathan, 1710–1785
Trumbull, Jonathan, 1740–1809
Trumbull, Joseph
Tuckerman, Bayard
Tuckerman, Edward
Tuckerman, Frederick Goddard
Tuckerman, Henry Theodore
Tuckerman, Joseph
Tudor, William
Tufts, Cotton
Tufts, John
Tweed, Harrison
Tyler, Royall
Tyng, Stephen Higginson
Underwood, Loring
Upham, Charles Wentworth
Vaillant, George Clapp
Valentine, Robert Grosvenor
Van Brunt, Henry
Vaughan, Thomas Wayland
Veblen, Oswald
Verrill, Addison Emery
Very, Jones
Vesey, William
Villard, Oswald Garrison
Wadsworth, Eliot
Wadsworth, James Samuel
Wadsworth, Peleg
Wainwright, Jonathan Mayhew
Walcott, Henry Pickering
Walker, James
Walker, Sears Cook
Walker, Timothy, 1705–1782
Walker, Timothy, 1802–1856
Walker, William Johnson
Walsh, James Anthony
Walter, Thomas
Walters, Henry
Warburg, James Paul
Ward, Artemas
Ward, Henry Dana
Ward, Robert DeCourcey
Wardman, Ervin
Ware, Ashur
Ware, Henry, 1764–1845
Ware, Henry, 1794–1843
Ware, John
Ware, John Fothergill Waterhouse
Ware, William
Ware, William Robert
Warner, Edward Pearson
Warner, Langdon
Warren, Charles
Warren, Cyrus Moors
Warren, Henry Clarke
Warren, Herbert Langford
Warren, James
Warren, John
Warren, John Collins, 1778–1856
Warren, John Collins, 1842–1927
Warren, Joseph
Washburn, Charles Grenfill
Washburn, Edward Abiel
Watson, William
Weeks, Sinclair
Wehle, Louis Brandeis
Welles, (Benjamin) Sumner
Welling, Richard Ward Greene
Wheelock, John Hall
White, David
White, Paul Dudley
Whiting, William
Whitmore, Frank Clifford
Whitney, George

Whitney, Richard
Wigmore, John Henry
Wirliston, Samuel
Winlock, Herbert Eustis
Winship, George Parker
Wister, Owen
Wolfson, Harry Austryn
Woods, James Haughton
Woodward, William
Wright, Willard Huntington

Divinity School
Alger, Horatio
Alger, William Rounseville
Bancroft, George
Barnard, Charles Francis
Barrett, Benjamin Fiske
Barrows, Samuel June
Bartol, Cyrus Augustus
Bass, Edward
Bellows, Henry Whitney
Bixby, James Thompson
Bronson, Walter Cochrane
Brooks, Charles Timothy
Brooks, John Graham
Burnap, George Washington
Burton, Warren
Chadwick, John White
Chamberlam, Nathan Henry
Channing, William Henry
Clarke, James Freeman
Collier, Hiram Price
Conway, Moncure Daniel
Cranch, Christopher Pearse
Crothers, Samuel McChord
Cummings, Edward
Cutler, Charles Ammi
Dwight, John Sullivan
Eliot, Samuel Atkins
Eliot, William Greenleaf
Ellis, George Edward
Emerson, Ralph Waldo
English, George Bethune
Everett, Charles Carroll
Everett, Edward
Fenn, William Wallace
Frothingham, Octavius Brooks
Gannett, Ezra Stiles
Gannett, William Channing
Gould, George Milbry
Green, Samuel Swett
Harland, Henry
Hedge, Frederic Henry
Hepworth, George Hughes
Holmes, John Haynes
Hosmer, Frederick Lucian
Hosmer, James Kendall
Huidekoper, Frederic
Huntington, Frederick Dan
Hurlbert, William Henry
Johnson, Samuel
Judd, Sylvester
Kennedy, William Sloane
Leonard, Levi Washburn
Longfellow, Samuel
Lovering, Joseph
Lowe, Charles
Maier, Walter Arthur
Metcalf, Joel Hastings
Miles, Henry Adolphus
Montgomery, David Henry
Newell, William Wells
Noyes, George Rapall
Parker, Theodore
Peabody, Andrew Preston
Peabody, Francis Greenwood
Peabody, William Bowin Oliver
Peirce, Cyrus
Peirce, James Mills
Potter, William James
Rand, Edward Kennard
Reed, Sampson
Ripley, George
Robbins, Chandler
Salter, William Mackintire
Sibley, John Langdon
Sparks, Jared
Stearns, Oliver
Stebbins, Horatio
Stebbins, Rufus Phineas
Stevens, William Arnold
Wendte, Charles William
Wigglesworth, Edward, *c.* 1693–1765
Willard, Sidney
Wilson, William Dexter
Young, Alexander

Graduate Study
Allen, Frederick Lewis
Allen, George Venable
Allen, Glover Morrill
Allen, Hervey
Allen, James Edward, Jr.
Allinson, Francis Greenleaf
Allport, Gordon Willard
Ames, Herman Vandenburg
Ames, Oakes
Andrew, Abram Piatt
Angell, James Rowland
Appleton, William Sumner
Arensberg, Walter Conrad
Babbitt, Irving
Bailey, Liberty Hyde
Barbour, Thomas
Barton, George Aaron
Bazett, Henry Cuthbert
Beals, Ralph Albert
Bemis, Samuel Flagg
Bennett, Charles Edwin
Berle, Adolf Augustus, Jr.
Bigelow, Henry Bryant
Billings, Asa White Kenney
Bingham, Hiram
Bingham, Walter Van Dyke
Binkley, Wilfred Ellsworth
Birge, Edward Asahel
Birkhoff, George David
Blanshard, Paul
Bovie, William T.
Bowditch, Charles Pickering
Bridgman, Percy Williams
Briggs, LeBaron Russell
Brigham, Albert Perry
Brooks, William Keith
Brown, Carleton
Buchanan, Scott Milross
Bunche, Ralph Johnson
Burrage, Walter Lincoln
Bush, Vannevar ("Van")
Byerly, William Elwood
Byles, Mather
Calkins, Mary Whiton
Cannon, Walter Bradford
Cantril, Albert Hadley
Carpenter, John Alden
Chamberlin, Edward Hastings
Channing, Edward
Chauncy, Charles
Christian, Henry Asbury
Church, Thomas Dolliver
Cohen, Felix Solomon
Cohen, Morris Raphael
Cole, Frank Nelson
Collender, Guy Stevens
Colman, Benjamin
Colpitts, Edwin Henry
Conant, James Bryant
Cook, Walter
Cope, Arthur Clay
Cort, Stewart Shaw
Crafts, William
Cross, Arthur Lyon
Cross, Samuel Hazzard
Cullen, Countée Porter
Cummings, Edward
Cummings, E. E.
Curtis, John Green
Daly, Reginald Aldworth
Daniels, Farrington
Davenport, Charles Benedict
Davis, Harvey Nathaniel
Day, Edmund Ezra
Dean, William Henry, Jr.
Dickinson, Edwin De Witt
Dixon, Roland Burrage
Dorsey, George Amos
Douglas, Paul Howard
Duane, William
Du Bois, William Edward Burghardt
Eaton, Daniel Cady
Edwards, Everett Eugene
Eigenmann, Carl H.
Eliot, T(homas) S(tearns)
Emery, Henry Crosby
Evans, Bergen Baldwin
Fairlie, John Archibald
Farabee, William Curtis
Fay, Sidney Bradshaw
Feis, Herbert
Few, William Preston
Fieser, Louis Frederick
Fish, Carl Russell
Folks, Homer
Folsom, Marion Bayard
Foster, William Trufant
Frothingham, Paul Revere
Fuller, Joseph Vincent
Galpin, Charles Josiah
Geismar, Maxwell David
Gilman, Daniel Coit
Gilman, Samuel
Glueck, Eleanor Touroff
Glueck, Sheldon ("Sol")
Goode, George Brown
Goode, John Paul
Goodwin, William Watson
Gordon, Kermit
Grabau, Amadeus William
Grant, Percy Stickney
Grant, Robert
Green, John
Greene, Roger Sherman
Greenlaw, Edwin Almiron
Gummere, Francis Barton
Haggerty, Melvin Everett
Hall, Fitzedward

Hansen, Marcus Lee
Hapgood, Hutchins
Harris, Seymour Edwin
Hawes, Charles Boardman
Hecht, Selig
Hibben, Paxton Pattison
Hill, Joseph Adna
Hillard, George Stillman
Hindus, Maurice Gerschon
Hitchcock, James Ripley Wellman
Hoar, Leonard
Hobson, Julius Wilson
Hocking, William Ernest
Hoffman, Eugene Augustus
Holt, Edwin Bissell
Hooper, Claude Ernest
Hoover, Herbert Clark, Jr.
Horton, Samuel Dana
Hough, George Washington
Houston, David Franklin
Howe, Mark Antony De Wolfe
Huntington, Edward Vermilye
Huntington, Ellsworth
Hutchinson, Thomas
Hyde, Charles Cheney
Kallen, Horace Meyer
Keeney, Barnaby Conrad
Irwin, Robert Benjamin
Jackson, Dunham
Jaggar, Thomas Augustus, Jr.
Jefferson, Mark Sylvester William
Jeffrey, Edward Charles
Jennings, Herbert Spencer
Johnson, Harry Gordon
Johnson, William Samuel
Julian, Percy Lavon
Kallen, Horace Meyer
Kaufmann, Walter Arnold
Keith, Arthur
Kennedy, George Clayton
Kidder, Alfred Vincent
Kinsey, Alfred Charles
Koch, Frederick Henry
Kofoid, Charles Atwood
La Farge, Oliver Hazard Perry
Lamb, Arthur Becket
Lander, Edward
Langer, William Leonard
Lathrop, John
Laughlin, James Laurence
Law, Jonathan
Lawrence, William
Leaf, Wilbur Munro
Leland, Waldo Gifford
Leonard, William Ellery
Leverett, John
Lewis, Clarence Irving
Lewis, Gilbert Newton
Linton, Ralph
Lloyd, Alfred Henry
Locke, Alain Leroy
Locy, William Albert
Lodge, Henry Cabot
Lomax, John Avery
Longfellow, William Pitt Preble
Lovejoy, Arthur Oncken
Lovell, James
Lowery, Woodbury
Lowes, John Livingston
Lyman, Theodore, 1833–1897
McAdie, Alexander George
MacCurdy, George Grant
McDonald, James Grover
McKaye, Benton
McKeen, Joseph
Maier, Walter Arthur
Mallinckrodt, Edward, Jr.
Manly, John Matthews
Marbut, Curtis Fletcher
Mather, Cotton
Matthiessen, Francis Otto
Mattingly, Garrett
Mayor, Alfred Goldsborough
Mezes, Sidney Edward
Minot, Charles Sedgwick
Minot, George Richards
Montague, Gilbert Holland
Montague, William Pepperell
Moody, William Vaughn
Morgan, Edwin Vernon
Morgan, Morris Hicky
Morison, Samuel Eliot
Morley, Sylvanus Griswold
Mosely, Philip Edward
Munro, William Bennett
Murphy, Gardner
Neilson, William Allan
Nelson, Charles Alexander
Newman, Henry
O'Brien, Justin
Osrg, Frederic Austin
Oldfather, William Abbott
Olds, Leland
Osgood, William Fogg
Otis, Harrison Gray, 1765–1848
Oxnam, Garfield Bromley
Parker, George Howard
Parsons, Samuel Holden
Peirce, Charles Sanders
Penrose, Richard Alexander Fullerton
Perin, Charles Page
Perry, Ralph Barton
Phelps, William Lyon
Phillips, John
Pike, Nicholas
Pratt, James Bissett
Procter, John Robert
Quincy, Edmund
Quincy, Josiah, 1744–1775
Rand, Benjamin
Read, Conyers
Reisner, George Andrew
Richards, Theodore William
Richardson, William Lambert
Ritter, William Emerson
Robinson, James Harvey
Ross, Denman Waldo
Runkle, John Daniel
Sabine, Wallace Clement Ware
Sachs, Alexander
Sadtler, Samuel Philip
St. John, Charles Edward
Sanger, Charles Robert
Santayana, George
Schocken, Theodore
Schofield, William Henry
Schwartz, Delmore David
Scollard, Clinton
Scott, James Brown
Scudder, Samuel Hubbard
Setchell, William Albert
Shellabarger, Samuel
Sherman, Frank Dempster
Sherman, Stuart Pratt
Sidis, Boris
Simmons, James Stevens
Sinnott, Edmund Ware
Slater, John Clarke
Smith, Charles Forster
Smith, Courtney Craig
Smith, Harry James
Southard, Elmer Ernest
Sparks, Jared
Sprague, Oliver Mitchell Wentworth
Spurr, Josiah Edward
Starbuck, Edwin Diller
Stearns, Eben Sperry
Stefansson, Vilhjalmur
Stephenson, Carl
Stetson, Henry Crosby
Stith, Thompson
Stoddard, Theodore Lothrop
Storer, Francis Humphreys
Stouffer, Samuel Andrew
Sumner, James Batcheller
Swanton, John Reed
Tandy, Charles David
Tatlock, John Strong Perry
Taussig, Frank William
Teuber, Hans-Lukas ("Luke")
Thaxter, Roland
Thayer, William Roscoe
Thompson, Stith
Thorndike, Ashley Horace
Tolman, Edward Chace
Tracy, Nathaniel
Trelease, William
Troland, Leonard Thompson
Vaillant, George Clapp
Van Vleck, John Hasbrouck
Vaughan, Thomas Wayland
Villard, Oswald Garrison
Viner, Jacob
Ward, Harry Frederick
Ward, Henry Baldwin
Waterhouse, Sylvester
Wheeler, James Rignall
Whitaker, Daniel Kimball
Whitcomb, Selden Lincoln
White, John Williams
Whitmore, Frank Clifford
Whittemore, Thomas
Wiener, Norbert
Wigglesworth, Edward, 1732–1794
Wigglesworth, Michael
Wigmore, John Henry
Willard, Samuel, 1639–1707
Wilson, Joseph Chamberlain
Wolfe, Thomas Clayton
Wolfson, Harry Austryn
Woodrow, James
Woodson, Carter Godwin
Woodward, William
Woolley, Edgar Montillion ("Monty")
Wright, Philip Green
Wright, Theodore Lyman
Wurtz, Henry
Yerkes, Robert Mearns
Young, Karl

Landscape Architecture
Church, Thomas Dolliver
Murphy, Gerald Clery
Law School
Abbott, Benjamin Vaughan
Acheson, Dean Gooderham
Adams, Brooks
Adams, Charles Francis
Aldrich, Winthrop William
Allen, Charles
Allen, Henry Watkins
Ames, James Barr
Andrews, Christopher Columbus
Angell, Ernest
Appleton, John, 1815–1864
Arnold, Samuel Greene
Arnold, Thurman Wesley
Astor, John Jacob, 1822–1890
Bailey, John Moran
Baker, Harvey Humphrey
Ballantine, Arthur Atwood
Batcheller, George Sherman
Bates, George Handy
Beale, Joseph Henry
Beaman, Charles Cotesworth
Bemis, George
Benjamin, Park, 1809–1864
Berle, Adolf Augustus, Jr.
Bettman, Alfred
Bickel, Alexander Mordecai
Biddle, Francis Beverley
Biddle, George
Bigelow, Harry Augustus
Bishop, Robert Roberts
Blaikie, William
Bliss, George, 1830–1897
Bolles, Frank
Bonaparte, Charles Joseph
Boyden, Roland William
Brackett, Charles William
Brandeis, Louis Dembitz
Breckinridge, Henry Skillman
Brewster, Ralph Owen
Brown, Addison
Brown, Henry Billings
Brown, Walter Folger
Bruce, Philip Alexander
Bryan, John Stewart
Bryan, Thomas Barbour
Buckner, Emory Roy
Buford, Napoleon Bonaparte
Bundy, Harvey Hollister
Bundy, Jonas Mills
Burlingame, Anson
Burton, Harold Hitz
Cabell, Nathaniel Francis
Carroll, John Lee
Carter, James Coolidge
Catchings, Waddill
Chafee, Zechariah, Jr.
Chamberlain, Daniel Henry
Chamberlain, Mellen
Chandler, Peleg Whitman
Chandler, Wilham Eaton
Chapman, John Jay
Child, Richard Washburn
Choate, Joseph Hodges
Choate, Rufus
Clark, Greenleaf
Clark, Grenville
Cole, Chester Cicero
Copeland, Charles Townsend
Corbin, Austin
Costigan, George Purcell
Cotton, Joseph Potter
Curry, Jabez Lamar Monroe
Curtis, Benjamin Robbins
Curtis, Charles Pelham
Curtis, George Ticknor
Cushing, Caleb
Cutler, Robert
Davenport, Herbert Joseph
Davis, Horace
Deming, Henry Champion
Dennis, James Shepard
Devens, Charles
Dickinson, John
Doe, Charles
Donnelly, Charles Francis
Donovan, James Britt
Driscoll, Alfred Eastlack
Dunbar, Charles Franklin
Dwight, Francis
Eames, Charles
Eaton, Dorman Bridgman
Echols, John
Endicott, William Crowninshield
Evans, Lawrence Boyd
Evarts, William Maxwell
Ewing, Oscar Ross
Fairchild, Charles Stebbins
Field, Fred Tarbell
Field, Walbridge Abner
Fisher, Sydney George
Fly, James Lawrence
Fogg, George Gilman
Frankfurter, Felix
Fuller, Melville Weston
Gilbert, Seymour Parker
Gillett, Frederick Huntington
Gordon, George Henry
Grafton, Charles Chapman
Graham, Philip Leslie
Gray, George
Gray, Horace
Gray, John Chipman
Green, Theodore Francis
Greene, Jerome Davis
Grimké, Archibald Henry
Hackett, Frank Warren
Hall, Abraham Oakey
Hamlin, Charles Sumner
Hand, Augustus Noble
Hand, Learned
Hapgood, Norman
Hawkins, Dexter Arnold
Hayes, John Lord
Hayes, Rutherford Birchard
Hillard, George Stillman
Hilliard, Francis
Hoadly, George
Hoar, Ebenezer Rockwood
Hoar, George Frisbie
Hodson, William
Hohfeld, Wesley Newcomb
Holden, Hale
Holmes, Nathaniel
Holmes, Oliver Wendell
Hoppin, Augustus
Hoppin, James Mason
Horton, Samuel Dana
Houston, Charles Hamilton
Howe, Mark De Wolfe
Hudson, Manley Ottmer
Ingalls, Melville Ezra
James, Henry, 1843–1916
Jenkins, Albert Gallatin
Jones, Charles Colcock
Jones, Leonard Augustus
Joy, James Frederick
Keating, Kenneth Barnard
Keener, William Albert
King, Stanley
Lander, Edward
Landis, James McCauley
Langde, Christopher Columbus
Lawton, Alexander Robert
Lawton, Henry Ware
Lee, Ivy Ledbetter
Lee, Joseph
Lee, William Little
Lewis, William Henry
Lincoln, Robert Todd
Lodge, Henry Cabot
Long, John Davis
Longworth, Nicholas
Lord, Otis Phillips
Lowell, Abbott Lawrence
Lowell, James Russell
McCurdy, Richard Aldrich
Mack, Julian William
McNutt, Paul Vories
Magrath, Andrew Gordon
Matthews, Albert
Matthews, William
Mellen, Grenville
Mills, Ogden Livingston
Mitchell, Langdon Elwyn
Montague, Gilbert Holland
Moody, William Henry
Morawetz, Victor
Morison, George Shattuck
Morón, Alonzo Graseano
Morton, Marcus, 1819–1891
Newel, Stanford
Olds, Irving Sands
Olds, Robert Edwin
Olney, Richard
Ordronaux, John
Otis, Elwell Stephen
Paine, Henry Warren
Paine, Robert Treat, 1835–1910
Parkman, Francis
Parsons, Lewis Baldwin
Partridge, James Rudolph
Patterson, Robert Porter
Peabody, Oliver William Bourn
Peirce, James Mills
Pennoyer, Sylvester
Percy, William Alexander
Perkins, Thomas Nelson
Peters, John Andrew
Phelps, Charles Edward
Phillips, Wendell
Phillips, William
Pierce, Edward Lillie
Plimpton, George Arthur
Plumb, Glenn Edward
Pollak, Walter Heilprin
Post, Augustus
Pound, (Nathan) Roscoe
Powell, Thomas Reed
Pressman, Lee
Preston, John Smith
Preston, William
Quincy, Josiah Phillips

Randall, Clarence Belden
Rawle, Francis, 1846–1930
Richardson, William Adams
Richberg, Donald Randall
Rollins, Frank West
Ropes, John Codman
Rublee, George
Ryerson, Martin Antoine
Saltonstall, Leverett
Sanford, Edward Terry
Sanger, George Partridge
Sargent, Winthrop, 1825–1870
Schauffler, Henry Albert
Schofield, Henry
Sedgwick, Arthur George
Sellers, Matthew Bacon
Semmes, Thomas Jenkins
Shattuck, George Cheyne, 1813–1893
Shellabarger, Samuel
Simpson, William Dunlap
Smalley, George Washburn
Smith, Buckingham
Smith, Jeremiah, 1759–1842
Smith, Jeremiah, 1837–1921
Spear, William Thomas
Starr, Merritt
Stevens, Henry
Stevenson, Adlai Ewing, II
Stimson, Frederic Jesup
Stimson, Henry Lewis
Storey, Moorfield
Storrow, James Jackson
Story, William Wetmore
Strobel, Edward Henry
Sullivan, Mark
Sumner, Charles
Taft, Robert Alphonso
Taliaferro, William Booth
Taussig, Frank William
Taylor, Frederick Winslow
Terrell, Edwin Holland
Thayer, Alexander Wheelock
Thayer, Ezra Ripley
Thayer, James Bradley
Thompson, Robert Means
Thornton, John Wingate
Tinkham, George Holden
Towle, George Makepeace
Train, Arthur Cheney
Tuttle, Charles Wesley
Tweed, Harrison
Warren, Charles
Wehle, Louis Brandeis
Welch, Joseph Nye
Welling, Richard Ward Greene
Wheeler, Everett Pepperrell
Wherry, Kenneth Spicer
White, David
Whiting, William
Whitney, William Collins
Whyte, William Pinkney
Wigmore, John Henry
Willard, Joseph, 1798–1865
Williston, Samuel
Willson, Augustus Everett
Winter, William
Wolcott, Edward Oliver

Medical School

Abbott, Samuel Warren
Allen, Edward Ellis
Allison, Nathaniel
Babcock, James Woods
Batchelder, John Putnam
Bates, James
Bigelow, Henry Jacob
Bigelow, William Sturgis
Binney, Amos
Blake, Francis Gilman
Bowditch, Henry Ingersoll
Bowditch, Henry Pickering
Bradford, Edward Hickling
Brewer, Thomas Mayo
Brown, Percy
Bumstead, Freeman Josiah
Burrage, Walter Lincoln
Cabot, Arthur Tracy
Cabot, Hugh
Cabot, Richard Clarke
Cannon, Walter Bradford
Chadwick, James Read
Channing, Walter
Cushing, Harvey Williams
Cutler, Elliott Carr
Cutter, Ephraim
Dall, William Healey
Dalton, John Call
Davidoff, Leo Max
Dixon, John Homer
Edes, Robert Thaxter
Ellis, Calvin
Ernst, Harold Clarence
Farlow, William Gilson
Fillebrown, Thomas
Finney, John Miller Turpin
Fisher, John Dix
Fisher, Theodore Willis
Fitzgerald, John Francis
Flagg, Thomas Wilson
Garvin, Lucius Fayette Clark
Goodale, George Lincoln
Gorham, John
Gould, Augustus Addison
Graves, William Phillips
Green, John
Green, Samuel Abbott
Gregg, Alan
Gruening, Ernest
Hale, Enoch
Harrington, Charles
Harrington, Thomas Francis
Henderson, Lawrence Joseph
Holder, Joseph Bassett
Hooker, Worthington
Hoover, Charles Franklin
Howe, Lucien
Ingelfinger, Franz Joseph
Jackson, Charles Thomas
Jackson, James, 1777–1867
James, William
Jarvis, Edward
Jeffries, Benjamin Joy
Judson, Adoniram Brown
Knapp, Philip Coombs
Lahey, Frank Howard
Leland, George Adams
Lewis, Dioclesian
Lincoln, Rufus Pratt
Lombard, Warren Plimpton
Loring, Edward Greely
Loring, George Bailey
Lovell, Joseph
Lovett, Robert Williamson
Mallory, Frank Burr
Marcy, Henry Orlando
Marden, Orison Swett
Martin, Henry Austin
Minot, Charles Sedgwick
Minot, George Richards
Mixter, Samuel Jason
Morse, John Lovett
Morton, William James
Morton, William Thomas Green
Mumford, James Gregory
Mundé, Paul Fortunatus
Nichols, Charles Lemuel
Niles, Nathaniel, 1791–1869
Norton, William Edward
Oliver, Fitch Edward
Paine, Martyn
Palmer, Walter Walker
Parker, Willard
Parsons, Thomas William
Pearce, Richard Mills
Perry, William
Peters, Edward Dyer
Pickering, Charles
Prince, Morton
Putnam, Charles Pickering
Putnam, James Jackson
Rhoads, Cornelius Packard
Richardson, Maurice Howe
Richardson, William Lambert
Rotch, Thomas Morgan
Round, William Marshall Fitts
Sawyer, Wilbur Augustus
Shattuck, Frederick Cheever
Shattuck, George Brune
Shattuck, George Cheyne, 1813–1893
Shurtleff, Nathaniel Bradstreet
Smith, Nathan, 1762–1829
Southard, Elmer Ernest
Spalding, Lyman
Stearns, Henry Putnam
Storer, David Humphreys
Storer, Horatio Robinson
Sturtevant, Edward Lewis
Talbot, Israel Tisdale
Taylor, Robert Tunstall
Thaxter, Roland
Thayer, William Sydney
Warren, Shields
Weare, Meshech
Webster, Arthur Gordon
Webster, John White
Weiss, John
Wendell, Barrett
Wentworth, Benning
Wentworth, George Albert
Wentworth, John, 1737–1820
Wesselhoeft, Conrad
West, Samuel
Wheelwright, Edmund March
Whitaker, Daniel Kimball
White, James Clarke
White, Paul Dudley
Whitman, Royal
Widener, Harry Elkins
Wigglesworth, Edward, c. 1693–1765
Wigglesworth, Edward, 1732–1794
Wigglesworth, Edward, 1840–1896

Wigglesworth, Michael
Wircox, Reynold Webb
Wiley, Harvey Washington
Willard, Joseph, 1738–1804
Willard, Joseph, 1798–1865
Willard, Samuel, 1639–1707
Willard, Samuel, 1775–1859
Willard, Sidney
Williams, Elisha, 1694–1755
Williams, Franas Henry
Williams, Henry Willard
Williams, Israel
Williams, John, 1664–1729
Williams, John, 1817–1899
Williams, Nathaniel
Williams, William, 1731–1811
Willis, William
Willson, Augustus Everett
Wingate, Paine
Winslow, Josiah
Winsor, Justin
Winthrop, James
Winthrop, John, 1638–1707
Winthrop, John, 1714–1779
Winthrop, Robert Charles
Wise, John
Wood, Edward Stickney
Wood, Leonard
Woodberry, George Edward
Woods, Alva
Woods, Leonard, 1774–1854
Woodward, Calvin Milton
Woodworth, Jay Backus
Worthen, William Ezra
Wright, Chauncey
Wyman, Jeffries
Wyman, Morrill
Young, Alexander
HAVERFORD COLLEGE (PA.)
Allinson, Francis Greenleaf
Barton, George Aaron
Carr, John Dickson
Drinker, Cecil Kent
Elliott, Aaron Marshall
Fite, Warner
Gates, Thomas Sovereign
Goddard, Henry Herbert
Gummere, Francis Barton
Hallowell, Richard Price
Hartshorne, Henry
Hinshaw, David Schull
Hires, Charles Elmer, Jr.
Jones, Rufus Matthew
Katchen, Julius
Lewis, William Draper
Lippincott, James Storr
Lutz, Frank Eugene
Morley, Christopher Darlington
Parrish, Maxfield
Richards, Theodore William
Rogers, Robert William
Smiley, Albert Keith
Smith, Lloyd Logan Pearsall
Smith, Lloyd Pearsall
Spaeth, Sigmund
Starr, Louis
Thomas, Richard Henry
Tyson, James
Updegraff, David Brainard
Wood, James, 1839–1925
Graduate Study
Goddard, Henry Herbert
Jones, Rufus Matthew
Spaeth, Sigmund
HEATHERLEY'S ART SCHOOL (ENGLAND)
Kline, Franz Jose
HEBREW UNION COLLEGE (OHIO)
Berkowitz, Henry
Enelow, Hyman Gerson
Gavin, Frank Stanton Burns
Glueck, Nelson
Grossmann, Louis
Heller, Maximilian
Krauskopf, Joseph
Liebman, Joshua Loth
Magnes, Judah Leon
Meyer, Martin Abraham
Philipson, David
Silver, Abba Hillel
Silverman, Joseph
Graduate Study
Liebman, Joshua Loth
Philipson, David
Theology
Kagan, Henry Enoch
HEBRON ACADEMY (MAINE)
Hale, Eugene
Hamlin, Hannibal
Long, John Davis
HEIDELBERG COLLEGE (OHIO)
Fenneman, Nevin Melancthon
Seiberling, Frank Augustus
HEIDELBERG UNIVERSITY (OHIO)
Baker, Oliver Edwin
Graduate Study
Baker, Oliver Edwin
Glueck, Nelson
HICKMAN SCHOOL OF SPEECH AND EXPRESSION (D.C.)
Dies, Martin
HIGHLAND PARK COLLEGE (IOWA)
Budd, Ralph
Nagel, Conrad
HILDESHEIMER SEMINAR
Heschel, Abraham Joshua
HILLSDALE COLLEGE (MICH.)
Carleton, Will
King, Henry Churchill
Rice, Fenelon Bird
Wilbur, Cressy Livingston
HIRAM COLLEGE (OHIO)
Garfield, James Abram
Hinsdale, Burke Aaron
Hoover, Herbert William
Lindsay, Nicholas Vachel
Young, Allyn Abbott
Young, Clark Montgomery
HOBART COLLEGE (N.Y.)
Blodget, Lorin
Brogg, Edward Stuyvesant
Brooks, William Keith
Cheney, Charles Edward
Doolittle, James Rood
Dove, Arthur Garfield
Duyckinck, George Long
Folger, Charles James
Folwell, William Watts
Graves, Frederick Rogers
Handerson, Henry Ebenezer
Hosmer, William Howe Cuyler
Myer, Albert James
Norton, John Nicholas
Phelps, Austin
Randall, Henry Stephens
Rankine, William Birch
Ricord, Frederick William
Schuyler, Montgomery
Seymour, Horatio
Throop, Montgomery Hunt
HOCHSCHULE FÜR MUSIK, BERLIN (GERMANY)
Stoessel, Albert Frederic
HOCHSCHULE FÜR DIE WISSENSCHAFT DES JUDENTUMS (GERMANY)
Heschel, Abraham Joshua
HOFSTRA UNIVERSITY (N.Y.)
Cambridge, Godfrey MacArthur
HOLLINS COLLEGE (VA.)
Brown, Margaret Wise
HOLY CROSS COLLEGE (MASS.)
Armstrong, Frank C.
Bradley, Denis Mary
Conaty, Thomas James
Hudson, Daniel Eldred
Hunton, George Kenneth
McNulty, John Augustine
Tobin, Austin Joseph
Walsh, David Ignatius
HOMEOPATHIC MEDICAL COLLEGE (PA.)
Helmuth, William Tod
Hilgard, Eugene Woldemar
Talbot, Israel Tisdale
HOMER ACADEMY (N.Y.)
Harris, Ira
Nye, James Warren
Pennoyer, Sylvester
Salisbury, James Henry
Sanders, Charles Walton
Smith, Job Lewis
Smith, Stephen
Sterling, John Whalen
Stoddard, William Osborn
HOOD COLLEGE (MD.)
Kerr, Sophie
McCardell, Claire
HOPE COLLEGE (MICH.)
Muste, Abraham Johannes
HOPEWELL ACADEMY
Howell, David
Jewett, Hugh Judge
Jones, David
Smith, Hezekiah
HOPEWELL ACADEMY (PA.)
Jewett, Hugh Judge
HOPKINS ACADEMY (MASS.)
HOOKER, JOSEPH
Judd, Sylvester
Kingsley, Elbridge
Nash, Simeon
Stockbridge, Levi
HOPKINS GRAMMAR SCHOOL (CONN.)
Baldwin, Roger Sherman
Baldwin, Simeon Eben
Barnard, Henry
Camp, Walter Chauncey
Case, William Scoville
Champlin, John Denison
Cutler, Charles Ammi
Day, Henry Noble
Dwight, Sereno Edwards
Dwight, Timothy, 1828–1916

Hadley, Arthur Twining
Holmes, Isaac Edward
Hunt, Gaillard
Huntington, Frederick Dan
Levermore, Charles Herbert
Mansfield, Richard, 1723–1820
Osborn, Norris Galpin
Stoeckel, Carl
Thacher, Thomas Anthony
Thompson, William Gilman
Totten, George Muirson
Wales, Leonard Eugene
Williams, Frederick Wells
Woolsey, Theodore Dwight

HOPKINTON ACADEMY (N.H.)
Currier, Moody
Gunnison, John Williams
Harriman, Walter
Perkins, George Hamilton
Woodbury, Daniel Phineas

HOUGHTON WESLEYAN METHODIST SEMINARY
Bowen, Ira Sprague

HOWARD COLLEGE (ALA.)
Brown, William Garrott
Johnson, John Butler
Lyon, David Gordon
Moore, John Trotwood

HOWARD COLLEGE (IND.)
Evermann, Barton Warren

HOWARD SCHOOL OF MUSIC (D.C.)
Du Bois, Shirley Lola Graham

HOWARD UNIVERSITY (D.C.)
Davis, Benjamin Oliver, Sr.
Dyett, Thomas Ben
Frazier, Edward Franklin
Hathaway, Donny
Hobson, Julius Wilson
Hurston, Zora Neale
Miller, Kelly
Pelham, Robert A.
White, Clarence Cameron

Graduate Study
Miller, Kelly

HUDSON RIVER INSTITUTE (N.Y)
Abbey, Henry
Draper, Lyman Copeland
Evans, George Alfred
Sherwood, Isaac Ruth

HUMBOLDT UNIVERSITY (GERMANY)
Heschel, Abraham Joshua

HUNTER COLLEGE (N.Y.)
Bernstein, Aline
Dodd, Bella Visono
Franzblau, Rose Nadler

IGNATIUS COLLEGE (AUSTRIA)
Hubbard, Bernard Rosecrans

ILLINOIS COLLEGE
Bateman, Newton
Beecher, Thomas Kinnicut
Bryan, William Jennings
Capps, Edward
Carson, Jack
Goudy, William Charles
Greenlaw, Edwin Almiron
Martin, Everett Dean
Smith, Byron Caldwell
Smith, Ralph Tyler
Yates, Richard

ILLINOIS COLLEGE OF PHOTOGRAPHY
Weston, Edward Henry

ILLINOIS INDUSTRIAL UNIVERSITY
(*See* UNIVERSITY OF ILLINOIS)

ILLINOIS INSTITUTE OF TECHNOLOGY
Andrus, Ethel Percy
Chaffee, Roger Bruce
Lait, Jacquin Leonard (Jack)

ILLINOIS NORMAL UNIVERSITY
Crocker, William

ILLINOIS STATE NORMAL SCHOOL
Burrill, Thomas Jonathan
Cook, John Williston
Garman, Samuel
Gove, Aaron Estellus
Jennings, Herbert Spencer
McMurry, Frank Morton
Scott, Walter Dill

ILLINOIS STATE NORMAL UNIVERSITY
Gray, William Scott, Jr.

ILLINOIS WESLEYAN COLLEGE
Fifer, Joseph Wilson

ILLINOIS WESLEYAN UNIVERSITY
Crane, Frank
Frear, William
Gray, Glen
Hogue, Wilson Thomas
Hunt, Lester Callaway
Illington, Margaret
Lucas, Scott Wike
Stevenson, Adlai Ewing
Talmage, James Edward

IMPERIAL ACADEMY OF MUSIC (AUSTRIA)
Steiner, Maximilian Raoul Walter ("Max")

IMPERIAL COLLEGE OF SCIENCE AND TECHNOLOGY (ENGLAND)
Tate, George Henry Hamilton

IMPERIAL CONSERVATORY AT MOSCOW (RUSSIA)
Piatigorsky, Gregor

IMPERIAL CONSERVATORY AT ST. PETERSBURG (RUSSIA)
Gabrilowitsch, Ossip
Schillinger, Joseph

IMPERIAL INSTITUTE OF ENGINEERING (AUSTRIA)
Schindler, Rudolph Michael

IMPERIAL MILITARY MEDICAL ACADEMY (RUSSIA)
Levene, Phoebus Aaron Theodore

IMPERIAL NAVAL ACADEMY (RUSSIA)
De Seversky, Alexander Procofieff

INDIANAPOLIS ART INSTITUTE
Norell, Norman

INDIANAPOLIS LAW SCHOOL
Budenz, Louis Francis

INDIANA STATE NORMAL SCHOOL
Howard, George Elliott
Juday, Chancey
McCreery, James Work
Tompkins, Arnold

INDIANA STATE TEACHERS COLLEGE
Shannon, Fred Albert

INDIANA STATE UNIVERSITY
Bayh, Marvella Belle Hern
Dunn, William McKee
Eigenmann, Carl H.
Evermann, Barton Warren
Foster, John Watson
Gresham, Walter Quintin
Hardin, Charles Henry
Harper, Ida Husted
Leavenworth, Francis Preserved
Martin, William Alexander Parsons
Mellette, Arthur Calvin
Niblack, William Ellis
Parvin, Theophilus
Rollins, James Sidney
Scott, Leroy
Springer, William McKendree
Stone, Wilbur Fisk
Tompkins, Arnold
Warthin, Alfred Scott
Wright, George Grover
Wright, Joseph Albert

Graduate Study
Coulter, John Merle
Eigenmann, Carl H.
Evermann, Barton Warren
Gilbert, Charles Henry

Law
Gorman, Willis Arnold
Mellette, Arthur Calvin

INDIANA UNIVERSITY
Aydelotte, Frank
Bayh, Marvella Belle Hern
Beeson, Charles Henry
Boisen, Anton Theophilus
Buley, Roscoe Carlyle
Coffman, Lotus Delta
Cooper, Kent
Cubberley, Ellwood Patterson
Dreiser, Theodore
Edmunds, Charles Wallis
Ewing, Oscar Ross
Fetter, Frank Albert
Fox, Fontaine Talbot, Jr.
Haggerty, Melvin Everett
Handley, Harold Willis
Hawley, Paul Ramsey
Haworth, Leland John
Hill, Edwin Conger
Hill, John Wiley
Hunter, Robert
Jones, Jim
Juday, Chancey
Lingelbach, Anna Lane
McDonald, James Grover
McNutt, Paul Vories
Millis, Harry Alvin
Minton, Sherman
Newlon, Jesse Homer
Newsom, Herschel David
Oliphant, Herman
Pyle, Ernest Taylor
Slipher, Vesto Melvin
Starbuck, Edwin Diller
Stephenson, Nathaniel Wright
Tolley, Howard Ross
Veatch, Arthur Clifford

Willkie, Wendell Lewis
Wissler, Clark
Graduate Study
Beeson, Charles Henry
Buley, Roscoe Carlyle
Coffman, Lotus Delta
Haworth, Leland John
Juday, Chancey
Lingelbach, Anna Lane
McDonald, James Grover
Millis, Harry Alvin
Ogg, Frederic Austin
Shannon, Fred Albert
Slipher, Vesto Melvin
Terman, Lewis Madison
Wissler, Clark
Law
Willkie, Wendell Lewis
Medicine
Rovenstine, Emery Andrew
INSTITUTE FOR ART HISTORY (GERMANY)
Frankfurter, Alfred Moritz
INSTITUTE HEUBI (SWITZERLAND)
Vanderbilt, Amy
INSTITUTE OF MUSICAL ART (N.Y.)
Bowen, Catherine Drinker
Riegger, Wallingford
Rodgers, Richard Charles
INTERNATIONAL SCHOOL FOR SOCIAL AND RELIGIOUS STUDIES (ENGLAND)
Pyle, Robert
INTERNATIONAL YMCA COLLEGE (MASS.)
Stagg, Amos Alonzo
IOWA, UNIVERSITY OF (*See* UNIVERSITY OF IOWA)
IOWA COLLEGE OF LAW
Howard, Edgar
IOWA COLLEGE (*See* GRINNELL COLLEGE)
IOWA STATE AGRICULTURAL COLLEGE
Hornaday, William Temple
IOWA STATE COLLEGE
Catt, Carrie Clinton Lane Chapman
Garst, Roswell ("Bob")
Hansen, Niels Ebbesen
Graduate Study
Hansen, Niels Ebbesen
IOWA STATE COLLEGE OF AGRICULTURE
Arthur, Joseph Charles
Bemis, Haroad Edward
Carver, George Washington
Fairchild, David Grandison
Gregory, Clifford Verne
Graduate Study
Arthur, Joseph Charles
Carver, George Washington
IOWA STATE TEACHERS COLLEGE
Benson, Oscar Herman
IOWA STATE UNIVERSITY
Barrett, Albert Moore
Dykstra, Clarence Addison
Gabrielson, Ira Noel
Gray, Harold Edwin
Hansen, Marcus Lee
Hickenlooper, Bourke Blakemore
Leverett, Frank
Mead, Elwood
Meredith, Edna C. Elliott
Smith, Fred Burton
Veblen, Oswald
Wallace, Henry Agard
Graduate Study
Hansen, Marcus Lee
Law
Harris, Paul Percy
Kenyon, William Squire
Springer, Charles
Medicine
Barrett, Albert Moore
IOWA WESLEYAN COLLEGE
Graduate Study
Cowles, Gardner
IRISH ACADEMY OF MUSIC (IRELAND)
Ryan, Cornelius John ("Connie")
INSTITUTO TECNICO OF MILAN (ITALY)
Bellanca, Giuseppe Mario
ITHACA ACADEMY (N.Y.)
Brewer, William Henry
Finch, Francis Miles
Sackett, Henry Woodward
Stevens, George Barker

JAGIELLONIAN UNIVERSITY OF KRAKOW (POLAND)
Znaniecki, Florian Witold
JEFFERSON COLLEGE (LA.)
Eustis, George, 1828–1872
Hébert, Louis
Hébert, Paul Octave
JEFFERSON COLLEGE (MISS.)
Brown, Albert Gallatin
Inzraham, Prentiss
Wailes, Benjamin Leonard Covington
JEFFERSON MEDICAL COLLEGE (PA.)
Asch, Morris Joseph
Atkinson, William Biddle
Atlee, Washington Lemuel
Bailey, Gamaliel
Battey, Robert
Bissell, William Henry
Blalock, Nelson Gales
Bonwill, William Gibson Arlington
Brainard, Daniel
Brinton, Daniel Garrison
Brinton, John Hill
Brown, George, 1823–1892
Cohen, Jacob Da Silva Solis
Da Costa, Jacob Mendez
Da Costa, John Chalmers
Dix, John Homer
Dowell, Greensville
Elder, William
Elsberg, Louis
Emmet, Thomas Addis, 1828–1919
Evans, Thomas Wiltberger
Finlay, Carlos Juan
Flick, Lawrence Francis
Flint, Austin
Gould, George Milbuy
Green, Samuel Abbott
Gross, Samuel David
Gross, Samuel Weissell
Guild, La Fayette
Heap, Samuel Davies
Howard, William Travis
Howe, Andrew Jackson
Huston, Charles
Jackson, Chevalier
Jones, Anson
Judson, Adoniram Brown
Keen, William Williams
Kerr, John Glasgow
Kyle, David Braden
Landis, Henry Robert Murray
Lane, Levi Cooper
Leffmann, Henry
Le Moyne, Francis Julius
Letterman, Jonathan
McClellan, George, 1849–1913
McGuire, Hunter Holmes
McQuillen, John Hugh
Maury, Francis Fontaine
Meigs, James Aitken
Mitchell, Silas Weir
Nicholson, Alfred Osborne Pope
Northrop, Lucius Bellinger
Pinkney, Ninian
Richardson, Robert
Riggs, John Mankey
Sajous, Charles Euchariste de Médicis
Schadle, Jacob Evans
Sims, James Marion
Snyder, Howard McCrum
Spitka, Edward Anthony
Squibb, Edward Robinson
Stockton, Thomas Hewlings
Thomson, Edward
Tiffin, Edward
Toner, Joseph Meredith
Van Dyck, Cornelius Van Alen
Warder, John Aston
White, John De Haven
Willard, De Forest
Woodruff, Charles Edward
Young, Aaron
JEWISH THEOLOGICAL SEMINARY
Graduate Study
Hadas, Moses
JOHN CARROLL UNIVERSITY (OHIO)
Hurley, Joseph Patrick
JOHN MARSHALL LAW SCHOOL (ILL.)
Arvey, Jacob M.
JOHNS HOPKINS UNIVERSITY (MD.)
Abt, Isaac Arthur
Adams, Thomas Sewall
Ames, Joseph Sweetman
Auer, John
Baer, William Stevenson
Baetjer, Frederick Henry
Baker, Newton Diehl
Bassett, John Spencer
Bell, Louis
Bentley, Arthur Fisher
Berry, Edward Wilber
Boston, Charles Anderson
Botsford, George Willis
Brown, Lawrason
Bumstead, Henry Andrews
Calverton, Victor Francis

Casanowicz, Immanuel Moses
Cattell, James McKeen
Davis, Richard Harding
Day, David Talbot
Dickinson, John
Fall, Bernard B.
Fay, Edwin Whitfield
Fitzgerald, Alice Louise Florence
Flexner, Abraham
Gantt, Henry Laurence
Garrison, Fielding Hudson
Goddard, Calvin Hooker
Guttmacher, Alan Frank
Halsted, George Bruce
Harrison, Ross Granville
Hoerr, Normand Louis
Hollander, Jacob Harry
Hough, Theodore
Howell, William Henry
Hunt, Reid
Jayne, Horace Fort
Jones, Harry Clary
Keeler, James Edward
Koyl, Charles Herschel
Ladd-Franklin, Christine
Latané, John Holladay
Lazear, Jesse William
Longcope, Warfield Theobald
Machen, John Gresham
Marburg, Theodore
Marden, Charles Carroll
Marquand, Allan
Mauchly, John William
Nelson, Edward William
Norris, James Flack
Noyes, Clara Dutton
Perlman, Philip Benjamin
Radcliffe, George Lovic Pierce
Reese, Charles Lee
Ritchie, Albert Cabell
Robinson, George Canby
Rogers, Robert William
Rosewater, Victor
Rous, Francis Peyton
Smyth, Albert Henry
Stem, Leo Daniel
Stone, John Stone
Stringham, Washington Irving
Talmage, James Edward
Taylor, Robert Tunstall
Todman, William Selden ("Bill")
Tondorf, Francis Anthony
Waidner, Charles William
Williams, John Whitridge
Willoughby, Westel Woodbury
Wolman, Leo

Graduate Study

Abel, John Jacob
Adams, Thomas Sewall
Adler, Cyrus
Albright, William Foxwell
Allinson, Francis Greenleaf
Ames, Joseph Sweetman
Andrews, Charles McLean
Armstrong, Edward Cooke
Baer, William Stevenson
Baetjer, Frederick Henry
Barnett, George Ernest
Bascom, Florence
Bateman, Harry
Bentley, Arthur Fisher
Bloomfield, Maurice
Brackett, Jeffrey Richardson
Briggs, Lyman James
Bright, James Wilson
Brough, Charles Hillman
Burnham, William Henry
Burrow, Trigant
Burton, Richard Eugene
Cajori, Florian
Calverton, Victor Francis
Carson, Rachel Louise
Chandler, Julian Alvin Carroll
Commons, John Rogers
Conklin, Edwin Grant
Craig, Thomas
Dargan, Edwin Preston
Dewey, John
Dixon, Thomas
Donaldson, Henry Herbert
Eisenhart, Luther Pfahler
Finley, John Huston
Franklin, Edward Curtis
Franklin, Fabian
Freeman, Douglas Southall
Frothingham, Arthur Lincoln
Furst, Clyde Bowman
Glenn, John Mark
Gould, Elgin Ralston Lovell
Hall, Edwin Herbert
Hamilton, Alice
Harrison, Ross Granville
Hart, Edward
Haskins, Charles Homer
Hayes, Charles Willard
Hemmeter, John Conrad
Herter, Christian Archibald
Herty, Charles Holmes
Hollander, Jacob Harry
Howe, Frederic Clemson
Howell, William Henry
Humphreys, Wiliam Jackson
Hunt, Reid
Jameson, John Franklin
Jarvis, William Chapman
Jastrow, Joseph
Kilpatrick William Heard
Kohler, Elmer Peter
Krapp, George Philip
Lancaster, Henry Carrington
Lashley, Karl Spencer
Latané, John Holladay
Learned, Marion Dexter
Lee, Frederic Schiller
Levermore, Charles Herbert
Lewis, Exum Percival
Machen, John Gresham
McMurrich, James Playfair
Main, John Hanson Thomas
Marden, Charles Carroll
Marquand, Allan
Mather, Frank Jewett, Jr.
Mauchly, John William
Mendenhall, Charles Elwood
Miller, Kelly
Moore, Henry Ludwell
Moore, Joseph Haines
Morgan, Thomas Hunt
Nichols, Edward Leamington
Norris, James Flack
Noyes, William Albert
Page, Walter Hines
Pfund, August Herman
Philipson, David
Pratt, Waldo Selden
Radcliffe, George Lovic Pierce
Randall, Wyatt William
Rosa, Edward Bennett
Ross, Edward Alsworth
Royce, Josiah
Rubey, William Walden
Ruhräh, John
Sanford, Edmund Clark
Scott, John Adams
Seager, Henry Rogers
Shaw, Albert
Shear, Theodore Leslie
Shields, Thomas Edward
Smith, Charles Alphonso
Smith, George Otis
Smith, Homer William
Smith, Horatio Elwin
Smith, Theobald
Squier, George Owen
Steiner, Bernard Christian
Stine, Charles Milton Altland
Sydnor, Charles Sackett
Thomas, Martha Carey
Thomas, Richard Henry
Timberlake, Gideon
Trent, William Peterfield
Van Vleck, Edward Burr
Willoughby, Westel Woodbury
Wilson, Edmund Beecher
Wilson, Woodrow
Wolman, Leo

Medical School

Barbour, Henry Gray
Blalock, Alfred
Brown, Lawrason
Callaway, Morgan
Christian, Henry Asbury
Cort, Edwin Charles
Craig, Winchell McKendree
Dandy, Walter Edward
Davis, John Staige
Du Vigneaud, Vincent
Elman, Robert
Erlanger, Joseph
Evans, Herbert McLean
Flexner, Simon
Freeman, Allen Weir
Gasser, Herbert Spencer
Gay, Frederick Parker
Goddard, Calvin Hooker
Guttmacher, Alan Frank
Hooker, Donald Russell
Hume, Edgar Erskine
Kenyon, Josephine Hemenway
Krause, Allen Kramer
Longcope, Warfield Theobald
MacCallum, William George
Moore, Joseph Earle
Murphy, James Bumgardner
Reid, Mont Rogers
Rivers, Thomas Milton
Robinson, George Canby
Rous, Francis Peyton
Sabin, Florence Rena
Seagrave, Gordon Stifler
Stein, Gertrude
Strong, Richard Pearson
Weed, Lewis Hill
Wislocki, George Bernays

Johnson College (Ill.)
- Easley, Ralph Montgomery

Jones Commercial College (Mo.)
- Skouras, Spyros Panagiotes

Jubilee College (Ill.)
- Giles, Warren Crandall

Juilliard School
- Bowen, Catherine Drinker
- Herrmann, Bernard

Julien Academy (*See* Académie Julien, France)

Junior College of Kansas City (Mo.)
- Snow, Edgar Parks

Juridicial Seminary of St. Apollinaire (Italy)
- Brennan, Francis James

Kaiser Wilhelm Institute, Dresden (Germany)
- Du Vigneaud, Vincent

Kansas, University of (*See* University of Kansas)

Kansas City Baptist Theological Seminary (Kan.)

Graduate Study
- Martin, Warren Homer

Kansas City Junior College
- Boyle, Harold Vincent ("Hal")
- Snow, Edgar Parkes

Kansas City University
- Brady, Mildred Alice Edie

Kansas City School of Osteopathy
- Allen, Forrest Clare ("Phog")

Kansas State Agricultural College
- Harbord, James Guthrie
- Stearman, Lloyd Carlton

Graduate Study
- Harbord, James Guthrie

Kansas State College of Agriculture
- Fairchild, David Grandison
- Marlatt, Abby Lillian

Graduate Study
- Fairchild, David Grandison
- Marlatt, Abby Lillian

Kansas State Normal School
- Davis, Arthur Powell

Kansas Wesleyan University
- Martin, Glenn Luther ("Cy")

Kent College of Law (Ill.)
- Abbott, Robert Sengstacke

Kent State University (Ohio)
- Munson, Thurman Lee

Kentucky, University of (*See* University of Kentucky)

Kentucky Agricultural and Mechanical College
- McMillin, Benton
- Stanley, Augustus Owsley

Kentucky Military Institute
- Burbridge, Stephen Gano
- Hoke, Robert Frederick
- McClure, Robert Alexis
- Phelan, James, 1856–1891
- Williams, John Sharp

Kentucky State College
- Smith, Lucy Harth

Kentucky State Industrial College
- Young, Whitney Moore, Jr.

Kentucky Wesleyan College
- Reed, Stanley Forman

Kenyon College (Ohio)
- Allen, Alexander Viets Griswold
- Andrews, Lorin
- Bledsoe, Albert Taylor
- Buckland, Ralph Pomeroy
- Crosser, Robert
- Davis, David
- Davis, Edwin Hamilton
- Davis, Henry Winter
- Dyer, Rolla Eugene
- Ellis, John Washington
- Goebel, William
- Granger, Alfred Hoyt
- Hayes, Rutherford Birchard
- Jones, Jehu Glancy
- Le Duc, William Gates
- Lowell, Robert Traill Spence, Jr.
- McKinstry, Elisha Williams
- Marshall, William Louis
- Matthews, Stanley
- Minor, John Barbee
- Pease, Alfred Humphreys
- Piatt, John James
- Rockwell, Alphonso David
- Rosecrans, Sylvester Horton
- Smith, John Cotton, 1826–1882
- Speer, William
- Stanton, Edwin McMasters
- Thomas, Jesse Burgess, 1832–1915
- Trenchard, Stephen Decatur
- Williams, Charles David
- Wright, James Arlington
- Zachos, John Celivergos

Keystone State Normal School (Pa.)
- Messersmith, George Strausser

Kiev Art Institute (Russia)
- Archipenko, Alexander

Kiev Theological Academy (Russia)
- Leonty, Metropolitan

Kiev University (Russia)
- Dobzhansky, Theodosius Grigorievich

Kimball Union Academy (N.H.)
- Bissell, George Henry
- Clark, Francis Edward
- Dillingham, William Paul
- Field, Walbridge Abner
- Flanders, Henry
- Hall, Samuel Read
- Hough, Charles Merrill
- Just, Ernest Everett
- Mather, Samuel Holmes
- Miller, Charles Ransom
- Morris, George Sylvester
- Noble, Frederick Alphonso
- Parkhurst, Charles
- Richards, Charles Herbert
- Smith, Asa Dodge
- Stevens, Hiram Fairchild
- Tucker, William Jewett

King College (Tenn.)
- Reynolds, Richard Samuel, Sr.
- Reynolds, William Neal

King's College (*See* Columbia University)

Kirkland School (Ill.)
- Blaine, Anita (Eugenie) McCormick

Kitchener College (Canada)
- Murray, James Edward

Knox College (Ill.)
- Bancroft, Edgar Addison
- Bancroft, Frederic
- Bradwell, James Bolesworth
- Calkins, Earnest Elmo
- Field, Eugene
- Finley, John Huston
- Foote, Lucius Harwood
- McClure, Samuel Sidney
- McCoy, Joseph Gesting
- Perkins, George Henry
- Phillips, John Sanburn
- Rainey, Henry Thomas
- Revels, Hiram Rhoades
- Salter, William Mackintire
- Scripps, Ellen Browning
- Severance, Frank Hayward
- White, Stephen Van Culen

Königliche Akademie Der Tonkunst (Germany)
- Converse, Frederick Shepherd

Königliche Bergakademie At Freiberg (Germany)
- Lindgren, Waldemar

Königliche Kunstschule in Berlin (Germany)
- Albers, Josef

Lafayette College (Pa.)
- Barber, Edwin Atlee
- Bright, James Wilson
- Cattell, James McKeen
- Craig, Austin
- Craig, Thomas
- Crawford, John Martin
- Garrett, John Work
- Gayley, James
- Good, James Isaac
- Green, William Henry
- Griggs, John William
- Harkness, William
- Hart, Edward
- Hench, Philip Showalter
- Hoyt, Henry Martyn
- Hutchinson, Paul
- Jackson, Joseph Henry
- Jadwin, Edgar
- Kirby, Allan Price
- Macfarlane, Charles William
- Mackenzie, James Cameron
- McMurtrie, William
- March, Francis Andrew, 1863–1928
- March, Peyton Conway
- Meigs, John
- Michler, Nathaniel
- Nassau, Robert Hamill
- Nevin, George Balch
- Ott, Isaac
- Porter, Thomas Conrad
- Ramsey, Alexander
- Rodenbough, Theophilus Francis
- Shaw, Edward Richard

Starr, Frederick
Watkins, John Elfreth
Graduate Study
March, Francis Andrew, 1863–1928
Meigs, John
Shaw, Edward Richard
LAKE ERIE COLLEGE FOR WOMEN (PA.)
Mussey, Ellen Spencer
LAKE FOREST COLLEGE (ILL.)
Chapman, John Wilbur
Graff, Everett Dwight
Hillis, Newell Dwight
Humiston, William Henry
Lewis, Dean De Witt
Mills, Benjamin Fay
Sabath, Adolph J.
Law
Woll, Matthew
LAKE FOREST UNIVERSITY
Law
Morrison, Frank
LAMAR STATE COLLEGE OF TECHNOLOGY (TEX.)
Joplin, Janis Lyn
Silkwood, Karen Gay
LANCASTER THEOLOGICAL COLLEGE (ENGLAND)
Buttrick, George Arthur
LANE THEOLOGICAL SEMINARY (OHIO)
Andrews, Samuel James
Bateman, Newton
Beecher, Charles
Beecher, Henry Ward
Beecher, Thomas Kinnicut
Blanchard, Jonathan
Chapman, John Wilbur
Fee, John Gregg
Howlson, George Holmes
Noble, Frederick Alphonso
Orton, Edward Francis Baxter
Smith, Henry Preserved
Stanton, Henry Brewster
Strong, Josiah
LAWRENCE ACADEMY (MASS.)
Barker, George Frederick
Beecher, Charles
Green, Samuel Abbott
Jones, Leonard Augustus
Richardson, Rufus Byam
Richardson, William Adams
Tarbell, Frank Bigelow
Towle, George Makepeace
Walker, James
LAWRENCE SCIENTIFIC SCHOOL
Brown, Percy
LAWRENCE UNIVERSITY (WIS.)
Curtis, Olin Alfred
Davis, Jerome Dean
Hooton, Earnest Albert
Huntington, Margaret Jane Evans
LAWRENCEVILLE SCHOOL (N.J.)
Bartlett, Dewey Follett
Besse, Arthur Lyman
Borie, Adolphe
Breckinridge, Desha
Butterworth, William Walton ("Walt")
Green, Henry Woodhull
Green, John Cleve
Gross, Samuel David
Gummere, Samuel René
Gummere, William Stryker
Kirby, Allan Price
McGraw, Donald Cushing
Maclean, John, 1800–1886
Mallory, Clifford Day
Porter, Horace
Price, Rodman McCamley
Rodgers, John, 1881–1926
Watt, Donald Beates
Weicker, Lowell Palmer
Woodhull, Alfred Alexander
LEBANON SCHOOL OF LAW (TENN.)
Bailey, Joseph Weldon
LEBANON VALLEY COLLEGE (PA.)
Dougherty, Raymond Philip
Ryan, Harris Joseph
Graduate Study
Dougherty, Raymond Philip
LEHRERSEMINAR, BÜREN (GERMANY)
Albers, Josef
LEHIGH UNIVERSITY (PA.)
Barrell, Joseph
Cooke, Morris Llewellyn
Davis, Richard Harding
Doolittle, Eric
Girdler, Tom Mercer
Grace, Eugene Gifford
Howe, Mark Antony De Wolfe
Landis, Walter Savage
Macfarlane, Charles William
Packard, James Ward
Patch, Alexander McCarrell
Porter, Holbrook Fitz-John
Rathbone, Monroe Jackson ("Jack")
Richards, Joseph William
Schneider, Herman
Stoek, Harry Harkness
Talmage, James Edward
Walter, Francis Eugene
Wickersham, George Woodward
Graduate Study
Bowie, William
Landis, Walter Savage
Richards, Joseph Williams
Sadtler, Samuel Philip
LEHMAN COLLEGE (N.Y.)
Darin, Bobby
LEICESTER ACADEMY (MASS.)
Ames, Oliver, 1831–1895
Davis, John, 1787–1854
Eames, Charles
Earle, Pliny, 1809–1892
Earle, Thomas
Guilford, Nathan
Henshaw, David
Hill, Thomas, 1818–1891
Knowles, Lucius James
Marcy, William Learned
Merrick, Pliny
Morton, William Thomas Green
Olney, Richard
Poole, William Frederick
Rice, Luther
Washburn, Emory
Whitney, Eli
Woods, Leonard, 1774–1854
LEIPZIG INSTITUTE FOR THE HISTORY OF MEDICINE (GERMANY)
Sigerist, Henry Ernest
LELAND COLLEGE (LA.)
Davis, Abraham Lincoln, Jr.
LELAND STANFORD UNIVERSITY (CAL.)
Blinn, Holbrook
Freas, Thomas Bruce
Harper, Ida Husted
Lea, Homer
Peek, Frank William
LENOX COLLEGE (IOWA)
McKean, James William
Merriam, Charles Edward, Jr.
Merriam, John Campbell
LEWIS INSTITUTE (ILL.)
Krock, Arthur
Nourse, Edwin Griswold
LIBERTY HALL ACADEMY (*See* WASHINGTON AND LEE UNIVERSITY)
LINFIELD COLLEGE (OREG.)
Latourette, Kenneth Scott
LITCHFIELD LAW SCHOOL (CONN.)
Angell, Joseph Kinnicutt
Baldwin, Roger Sherman
Blake, Eli Whitney
Brace, John Pierce
Bradley, Stephen Row
Burrall, William Porter
Calhoun, John Caldwell
Clayton, John Middleton
Edwards, Henry Waggaman
Ellsworth, Henry Leavitt
Ellsworth, William Wolcott
Francis, John Brown
Gould, James
Green, Henry Woodhull
Hasbrouck, Abraham Bruyn
Hawks, Francis Lester
Hollister, Gideon Hiram
Howe, Samuel
Hull, William
Hunt, Ward
Johns, Kensey
King, James Gore
Lawrence, William Beach
Longstreet, Augustus Baldwin
Lord, Daniel
Mann, Horace
Mansfield, Edward Deering
Mason, John Young
Metcalf, Theron
Morse, Sidney Edwards
Morton, Marcus, 1784–1864
Nisbet, Eugenius Aristides
Pierpont, John
Platt, Orville Hitchcock
Porter, Peter Buell
Raymond, Daniel
Schell, Augustus
Smith, Junius
Smith, Nathan, 1770–1835
Smith, Nathaniel
Smith, Truman
Sprague, Peleg
Stephens, John Lloyd
Strong, Moses McCure
Tod, George
Williams, Elisha, 1773–1833

Williams, Thomas Scott
Wolcott, Oliver
Woodbridge, William
Woodbury, Levi
LITTLE ROCK COLLEGE (ARK.)
Powell, Richard Ewing ("Dick")
LIVERPOOL COLLEGE OF ART (ENGLAND)
Lennon, John
LIVINGSTONE COLLECE (N.C.)
Aggrey, James Emman Kwegyir
Clement, Rufus Early
LOMBARD COLLEGE (ILL.)
Sandburg, Carl August
Wright, Theodore Paul
LONDON SCHOOL OF ECONOMICS (ENGLAND)
Abbott, Edith
Neumann, Franz Leopold
Graduate Study
Graham, Frank Porter
Meyer, Frank Straus
Parsons, Talcott
Powdermaker, Hortense
Schultz, Henry
Utley, Freda
LONDON SCHOOL OF MINES (ENGLAND)
Herbert, Frederick Hugh
LONDON UNIVERSITY (ENGLAND)
Utley, Freda
LONG BEACH JUNIOR COLLEGE (CALIF.)
Britton, Barbara
LONG ISLAND COLLEGE HOSPITAL (N.Y.)
Medicine
Tilney, Frederick
White, William Alanson
LONG ISLAND COLLEGE OF MEDICINE (N.Y.)
Dickinson, Robert Latou
Wiener, Alexander Solomon
LONG ISLAND MEDICAL COLLEGE (N.Y.)
Kirby, George Hughes
LORAS COLLEGE (IOWA)
Kerby, William Joseph
Ward, Arch Burdette
LOS ANGELES CITY COLLEGE (CAL.)
Ashford, Emmett Littleton
Hubley, John
LOS ANGELES COLLEGE (CAL.)
Hubbard, Bernard Rosecrans
LOS ANGELES SCHOOL OF ART
Kuniyoshi, Yasuo
LOUISIANA, UNIVERSITY OF (*See* TULANE UNIVERSITY)
LOUISIANA POLYTECHNIC INSTITUTE
Pope, James Pinckney
LOUISIANA STATE UNIVERSITY
Boyd, Thomas Duckett
Brooks, Overton
Chennault, Claire Lee
Harrison, Byron Patton
Lowell, Robert Traill Spence, Jr.
Morrison, Delesseps Story
Perez, Leander Henry
Graduate
Humphrey, Hubert Horatio, Jr.
Lowell, Robert Traill Spence, Jr.
Law
Brooks, Overton
Morrison, Delesseps Story
LOUISVILLE, UNIVERSITY OF (*See* UNIVERSITY OF LOUISVILLE)
LOUISVILLE COLLEGE OF PHARMACY (KY.)
Flexner, Simon
LOUISVILLE COLLEGIATE INSTITUTE (KY.)
Hill, Patty Smith
LOUISVILLE LAW SCHOOL (KY.)
Klaw, Marc
LOWELL TEXTILE INSTITUTE
Dickson, Earle Ensign
LOWVILLE ACADEMY (N.Y.)
Bartlett, John Russell
Dickinson, Charles Monroe
Doty, James Duane
Hough, Franklin Benjamin
Johnson, Samuel William
Strong, James
LOYOLA COLLEGE (MD.)
Saxton, Eugene Francis
LOYOLA UNIVERSITY (CAL.)
Wright, Willard Huntington
LOYOLA UNIVERSITY (LA.)
Law
Long, Earl Kemp
LOYOLA UNIVERSITY OF CHICAGO
Harrison, Carter Henry, Jr.
LUTHERAN THEOLOGICAL SEMINARY (*See* GETTYSBURG COLLEGE)
LUTHER COLLEGE (IOWA)
Hanson, James Christian Meinich
Haugen, Nils Pederson
Kildahl, John Nathan
Koren, John
Preus, Christian Keyser
Stromme, Peer Olsen
Stub, Hans Gerhard
LYONS COLLEGIATE INSTITUTE (IOWA)
Patrick, Mary Mills

MACALESTER COLLEGE (MINN.)
Baker, Hugh Potter
MCCORMICK THEOLOGICAL SEMINARY (ILL.)
Holt, Arthur Erastus
Lyon, David Willard
Martin, Everett Dean
Scott, Walter Dill
MCGEE COLLEGE (MO.)
Hirth, William Andrew
MCGILL UNIVERSITY (CANADA)
Becket, Frederick Mark
McKenzie, Robert Tait
MacLeod, Colin Munro
Mathewson, Edward Payson
Naismith, James
Viner, Jacob
Graduate Study
Harrington, John Lyle
Medicine
Drew, Charles Richard
McKenzie, Robert Tait
MacLeod, Colin Munro
Wood, Casey Albert
MCKENDREE COLLEGE (ILL.)
Baker, Jehu
Bernays, Augustus Charles
Loveland, William Austin Hamilton
Morrison, William Ralls
Snyder, John Francis
Sparks, William Andrew Jackson
Waller, Willard Walter
Wilson, James Harrison
Zane, Charles Shuster
MCMASTER UNIVERSITY (CANADA)
Eaton, Charles Aubrey
Eaton, Cyrus Stephen
Macintosh, Douglas Clyde
Graduate Study
Eaton, Charles Aubrey
MCMURRY COLLEGE (TEX.)
Key, Valdimer Orlando, Jr.
MCPHERSON COLLEGE (KANS.)
Johnson, Wendell Andrew Leroy
MADISON UNIVERSITY (*See* COLGATE UNIVERSITY)
MADRAS CHRISTIAN COLLEGE (INDIA)
Oldham, William Fitzjames
MAINE STATE SEMINARY (*See* BATES COLLEGE)
MAINE WESLEYAN SEMINARY
Burrowes, Edward Thomas
Fernald, Charles Henry
Fillebrown, Thomas
Howe, Timothy Otis
Maxim, Hudson
Stevens, John Leavitt
MANCHESTER COLLEGE (IND.)
Cordier, Andrew Wellington
MANCHESTER TECHNICAL SCHOOL (ENGLAND)
Sanders, George
MANHATTAN COLLEGE (N.Y.)
Dowling, Austin
Hayes, Patrick Joseph
Mundelein, George William
MANNES COLLEGE OF MUSIC (N.Y.)
Evans, William John ("Bill")
MARIAHILFE MILITARY ACADEMY (AUSTRIA)
Von Stroheim, Erich
MARIETTA COLLEGE (OHIO)
Bosworth, Francke Huntington
Dawes, Charles Gates
Dawes, Rufus Cutler
Elliott, Charles Burke
Fairfield, Edmund Burke
Howison, George Holmes
Hulbert, Archer Butler
Johnson, Byron Bancroft
Kinkead, Edgar Benton
Mitchell, Edwin Knox
O'Neill, C. William ("Bill")
Quinan, John Russell
Shedd, William Ambrose
Williams, John Elias, 1871–1927
Graduate Study
Dawes, Charles Gates
MARION INSTITUTE (ALA.)
Short, Joseph Hudson, Jr.
MARQUETTE UNIVERSITY (WIS.)
Conrad, Maximilian Arthur, Jr.

McCarthy, Joseph Raymond
Metcalfe, Ralph Harold
Murphy, Robert Daniel
Medicine
Mahoney, John Friend
MARSHALL COLLEGE (*See* FRANKLIN AND MARSHALL COLLEGE)
MARSHALL COLLEGE (W. VA.)
Harvey, William Hope
Sayre, Wallace Stanley
MARVIN COLLEGE (KY.)
Barkley, Alben William
MARYKNOLL SEMINARY (N.Y.)
Keller, James Gregory
MARYLAND INSTITUTE, COLLEGE OF ART
Leigh, William Robinson
MARYLAND INSTITUTE OF FINE AND APPLIED ARTS
Louis, Morris
MARYMOUNT COLLEGE (N.Y.)
Russell, Rosalind
MARYVILLE COLLEGE (TENN.)
Rutledge, Wiley Blount
Williams, Aubrey Willis
MASSACHUSETTS AGRICULTURAL COLLEGE
Bartlett, Francis Alonzo
Stone, Harlan Fiske
MASSACHUSETTS COLLEGE OF PHARMACY
Duchin, Edward Frank ("Eddy")
MASSACHUSETTS INSTITUTE OF TECHNOLOGY
Adams, Edward Dean
Babson, Roger Ward
Bassett, William Hastings
Blashfield, Edwin Howland
Bowen, Norman Levi
Brophy, Thomas D'Arcy
Browne, Herbert Wheildon Cotton
Brunner, Arnold William
Burgess, Frank Gelett
Burgess, George Kimball
Cabot, Godfrey Lowell
Calkins, Gary Nathan
Campbell, John Wood, Jr.
Chapelle, Dickey
Clapp, Charles Horace
Coolidge, Charles Allerton
De Forest, Alfred Victor
Draper, Eben Sumner
Du Pont, Alfred Irénée
Du Pont, Irénée
Du Pont, Lammot
Du Pont, Pierre Samuel
Du Pont, Thomas Coleman
Dyar, Harrison Gray
Edison, Charles
Ellis, Carleton
Farwell, Arthur
Fenner, Burt Leslie
Flint, Albert Stowell
Ford, George Burdett
Freeman, John Ripley
French, Daniel Chester
French, William Merchant Richardson
Fuller, George Warren
Gilbert, Cass
Grabau, Amadeus William
Granger, Alfred Hoyt
Greene, Charles Ezra
Greene, Charles Sumner
Greene, Henry Mather
Groves, Leslie Richard, Jr.
Gunn, Selskar Michael
Hale, George Ellery
Hamlin, Alfred Dwight Foster
Harkins, William Draper
Hayden, Charles
Hazen, Allen
Herreshoff, Nathanael Greene
Hodgins, Eric Francis
Hood, Raymond Mathewson
Howard, Henry
Howe, Henry Marion
Hunt, Alfred Ephraim
Jarman, Walton Maxey
Jordan, Edwin Oakes
Kalmus, Herbert Thomas
Kinnicutt, Leonard Parker
La Farge, Christopher Grant
Leonard, Harry Ward
Lewis, Wilfred
Litchfield, Paul Weeks
Little, Arthur Dehon
Lowell, Guy
McMurtrie, Douglas Crawford
Main, Charles Thomas
Matthes, François Emile
Matthes, Gerard Hendrik
Mauran, John Lawrence
Maxim, Hiram Percy
Merrill, Frank Dow
Meserve, Frederick Hill
Minot, Charles Sedgwick
Mixter, Samuel Jason
Mulliken, Samuel Parsons
Newell, Frederick Haynes
Noyes, Arthur Amos
Parker, Theodore Bissell
Peabody, Cecil Hobart
Pearson, Fred Stark
Perkins, Dwight Heald
Prescott, Samuel Cate
Rice, Calvin Winsor
Richards, Ellen Henrietta Swallow
Richards, Robert Hallowell
Ripley, William Zebina
Rockwell, Willard Frederick
Rollins, Frank West
Rotch, Abbott Lawrence
Rotch, Arthur
Sauveur, Albert
Shaw, Howard Van Doren
Sherman, Forrest Percival
Skidmore, Louis
Sloan, Alfred Pritchard, Jr.
Smith, Edward Hanson
Smith, Jonas Waldo
Stone, Charles Augustus
Stone, Edward Durell
Sullivan, Louis Henry
Swain, George Fillmore
Swope, Gerard
Talbot, Henry Paul
Taylor, William Chittenden
Tolman, Edward Chace
Tolman, Richard Chace
Troland, Leonard Thompson
Tucker, Benjamin Ricketson
Vickery, Howard Leroy
Waite, Henry Matson
Warner, Edward Pearson
Warren, Henry Ellis
Warren, Herbert Langford
Washburn, Edward Wight
Webster, Edwin Sibley
Wheelwright, Edmund March
Whitney, Willis Rodney
Whorf, Benjamin Lee
Williams, Francis Henry
Winslow, Charles-Edward Amory
Woodbury, Charles Jeptha Hill
Woodward, Robert Burns
Wright, Theodore Paul
Graduate Study
Bush, Vannevar ("Van")
Clapp, Charles Horace
Douglas, Lewis Williams
Du Pont, Irénée
Ford, George Burdett
Gorrell, Edgar Staley
Graves, Alvin Cushman
Kalmus, Herbert Thomas
Kirkwood, John Gamble
McDonnell, James Smith, Jr.
Oxnam, Garfield Bromley
Pew, John Howard
Ripley, William Zebina
Tolman, Richard Chace
Whitney, Willis Rodney
Winslow, Charles-Edward Amory
Woodward, Robert Burns
MASSACHUSETTS NORMAL ART SCHOOL
Adams, Herbert Samuel
MacNeil, Hermon Atkins
Metcalf, Willard Leroy
Miller, Leslie William
Perry, Walter Scott
Robinson, Boardman
Sylvester, Frederick Oakes
Vonnoh, Robert William
MASSACHUSETTS STATE COLLEGE
Brown, Ralph Hall
Green, Samuel Bowdlear
Myrick, Herbert
Stockbridge, Horace Edward
Tuckerman, Frederick
Tydings, Millard Evelyn
Wheeler, William
MASSACHUSETTS STATE NORMAL SCHOOL
Cortelyou, George Bruce
MASSACHUSETTS STATE NORMAL SCHOOL AT WESTFIELD
Diller, Joseph Silas
MAYVILLE STATE COLLEGE (N.D.)
Burdick, Usher Lloyd
MEADVILLE THEOLOGICAL SCHOOL (PA.)
Abbot, Francis Ellingwood
Batchelor, George
Cooke, George Willis
Jones, Jenkin Lloyd
Kennedy, William Sloane
Metcalf, Joel Hastings
Wiggin, James Henry
MECHANICS INSTITUTE (N.Y.)
Rose, Mary Davies Swartz

Medical College of Ohio
Billings, John Shaw
Newton, Robert Safford
Oliver, Fitch Edward
Rachford, Benjamin Knox
Ransohoff, Joseph
Medical College of South Carolina
Chisolm, John Julian
Logan, Thomas Muldrup, 1808–1876
Massey, George Betton
Pendleton, Edmund Monroe
Ravenel, Mazyck Porcher
Smith, John Lawrence
Stevens, William Bacon
Thomas, Theodore Gaillard
Medical College of Virginia
Briggs, Lloyd Vernon
Medico-Chirurgical College of Philadelphia
Pfahler, George Edward
Melbourne Conservatory (Australia)
Grainger, George Percy
Mercersburg Theological Seminary (Pa.)
Bausman, Benjamin
Gerhart, Emanuel Vogel
Harbaugh, Henry
Mercer University (Ga.)
Butts, James Wallace ("Wally")
Candler, Allen Daniel
Cox, Edward Eugene
Crawford, Martin Jenkins
Davis, Noah Knowles
George, Walter Franklin
Hardwick, Thomas William
Hubbard, Richard Bennett
Johnson, Malcolm Malone
Johnston, Richard Malcolm
Kilpatrick, William Heard
McDaniel, Henry Dickerson
Murrow, Joseph Samuel
Newman, Albert Henry
Ogburn, William Fielding
Sherwood, Thomas Adiel
Straton, John Roach
Upshaw, William David
Vincent, John Carter
Winship, Blanton
Wood, John Stephens
Law
George, Walter Franklin
Metropolitan Business College, Chicago (Ill.)
Thompson, William Hale
Mexico Academy (N.Y.)
Emery, Albert Hamilton
Moore, Veranus Alva
Skinner, Charles Rufus
Watson, James Madison
Miami University (Ohio)
Anderson, John Alexander
Angle, Paul McClelland
Billings, John Shaw
Birney, James
Brice, Calvin Stewart
Davis, Joseph Robert
Dennison, William
Dickey, Theophilus Lyle
Durbin, John Price
Evans, Bergen Baldwin
Faran, James John
Fee, John Gregg
Galloway, Samuel
Groesbeck, William Slocum
Hardin, Charles Henry
Harrison, Benjamin, 1833–1901
Hittell, John Shertzer
Hittell, Theodore Henry
Hodge, Albert Elmer ("Al")
Howell, James Bruen
Kennedy, William Sloane
Kenner, Duncan Farrar
Laws, Samuel Spahr
Loughridge, Robert McGill
Lowe, Ralph Phillips
McClurg, Alexander Caldwell
McClurg, Joseph Washington
McCracken, Henry Mitchell
McDill, James Witson
Moore, Philip North
Morrison, John Irwin
Morton, Oliver Perry
Noble, John Willock
Patterson, John Henry
Reid, Whitelaw
Schenck, Robert Cumming
Scott, Samuel Parsons
Smith, Caleb Blood
Swing, David
Thomson, William McClure
Torrence, Frederick Ridgely
Venable, William Henry
Weller, John B.
Wilson, Samuel Ramsay
Medicine
Burnett, Swan Moses
McCormack, Joseph Nathaniel
Zachos, John Celivergos
Michigan, University of (*See* University of Michigan)
Michigan Agricultural College
Bagley, William Chandler
Baker, Hugh Potter
Baker, Ray Stannard
Friedman, William Frederick
Sanderson, Ezra Dwight
Michigan College of Mines
Flaherty, Robert Joseph
Michigan State Agricultural College
Bessey, Charles Edwin
Butterfield, Kenyon Leech
Davenport, Eugene
Lewis, Charles Bertrand
Lindeman, Eduard Christian
St. John, Charles Edward
Shelton, Edward Mason
Symons, Thomas William
Toumey, James William
Graduate Study
Davenport, Eugene
Michigan State Normal College
Bowman, Isaiah
Potter, Charles Edward
Michigan State Normal School
Kellogg, John Harvey
St. John, Charles Edward
Michigan State University
Bailey, Liberty Hyde
Briggs, Lyman James
Copeland, Royal Samuel
Diller, Burgoyne
Graduate Study
McAndrew, William
Middlebury College (Vt.)
Ashmun, Jehudi
Barton, James Levi
Beman, Nathan Sidney Smith
Bingham, Hiram, 1789–1869
Blanchard, Jonathan
Brainerd, Ezra
Chase, Irah
Church, Alonzo
Collins, John Anderson
Conant, Thomas Jefferson
Day, Luther
Evans, Warren Felt
Foot, Solomon
Glidden, Joseph Farwell
Green, Beriah
Haines, Charles Glidden
Hall, Thomas Seavey
Hatfield, Edwin Francis
Hepburn, Alonzo Barton
Howard, William Alanson
Howe, George
Howe, Mark Anthony de Wolfe
Hudson, Henry Norman
James, Edwin
Kelley, Hall Jackson
Knowlton, Frank Hall
Mallary, Rollin Carolas
Mead, Charles Marsh
Nelson, Samuel
Olin, Stephen
Patton, William
Pettengill, Samuel Barrett
Phelps, Edward John
Pitcher, Zina
Post, Truman Marcellus
Rankin, Jeremiah Eames
Sawyer, Thomas Jefferson
Saxe, John Godfrey
Schoolcraft, Henry Rowe
Sheffield, Devello Zelotes
Sheldon, Walter Lorenzo
Sheldon, William Evarts
Sherwood, Adiel
Slade, William
Stevens, Henry
Strong, Moses McCure
Thompson, Daniel Pierce
Tyler, Samuel
Ward, Henry Augustus
Wines, Enoch Cobb
Winslow, Hubbard
Winslow, Miron
Wright, Silas
Milan Conservatory (Italy)
Galli-Curci, Amelita
Milan Politecnico (Italy)
Bellanca, Giuseppe Mario
Millersburg Female College (Ky.)
White, Alma Bridwell
Miller School of Commerce (N.Y.)
Watson, Thomas John
Milligan College (Tenn.)
Knight, Frank Hyneman
Powers, Francis Gary

MILLS COLLEGE (CAL.)
Nevada, Emma
MILLSAPS COLLEGE (MISS.)
Ellington, Earl Buford
MILTON COLLEGE (WIS.)
West, Allen Brown
MILTON ACADEMY (MASS.)
Child, Richard Washburn
Cobb, Jonathan Holmes
Forbes, Robert Bennet
Pierce, Henry Lillie
MILWAUKEE ART STUDENTS LEAGUE (WIS.)
Steichen, Edward Jean
MILWAUKEE NORMAL SCHOOL (WIS.)
Bolton, Herbert Eugene
Zuppke, Robert Carl
MILWAUKEE UNIVERSITY
Mahoney, John Friend
MINNESOTA COLLEGE OF LAW
Youngdahl, Luther Wallace
MISSISSIPPI AGRICULTURAL AND MECHANICAL COLLEGE
Stockard, Charles Rupert
MISSISSIPPI COLLEGE
Brough, Charles Hillman
MISSISSIPPI STATE COLLEGE
Duggar, Benjamin Minge
MISSISSIPPI STATE UNIVERSITY
Garner, James Wilford
MISSOURI, UNIVERSITY OF (*See* UNIVERSITY OF MISSOURI)
MISSOURI SCHOOL OF MINES
Jackling, Daniel Cowan
MISSOURI STATE TEACHERS COLLEGE
Smith, Horton
MISSOURI WESLEYAN COLLEGE
Jones, Benjamin Allyn
MOHEGAN LAKE MILITARY ACADEMY (N.Y.)
Berkeley, Busby
MONMOUTH COLLEGE (ILL.)
Howard, Oliver Otis
Shonts, Theodore Perry
Sloan, Richard Elihu
Sprague, Charles Arthur
Wallace, John Findley
MONSON ACADEMY (MASS.)
Barnard, Henry
Bennett, Emerson
Bissell, Edwin Cone
Brown, Samuel Robbins
Colton, Calvin
Knowlton, Marcus Perrin
Loomis, Dwight
Munn, Orson Desaix
Sophocles, Evangelinus Apostolides
Storrs, Richard Salter, 1821–1900
Yung, Wing
MONTANA STATE COLLEGE
Huntley, Chester ("Chet") Robert
MONTCLAIR STATE TEACHERS COLLEGE (N.J.)
Svenson, Andrew Edward
MONTVALE INSTITUTE (TENN.)
Hull, Cordell

MOODY BIBLE INSTITUTE (ILL.)
Stelzle, Charles
MOORE'S HILL COLLEGE (IND.)
Main, John Hanson Thomas
Graduate Study
Main, John Hanson Thomas
MORAVIAN COLLEGE AND THEOLOGICAL SEMINARY (PA.)
Clewell, John Henry
Holland, William Jacob
Levering, Joseph Mortimer
Reichel, William Cornelius
Thursby, Emma Cecilia
MORAVIAN COLLEGE (PA.)
Badè, William Frederic
Beck, James Montgomery
Schweinitz, George Edmund de
MOREHOUSE COLLEGE (GA.)
Davis, John Warren
King, Martin Luther, Jr.
Reid, Ira De Augustine
MORNINGSIDE COLLEGE (IOWA)
Gabrielson, Ira Noel
Stouffer, Samuel Andrew
Waymack, William Wesley
MOSCOW CONSERVATORY (RUSSIA)
Lhévinne, Rosina
Rachmaninoff, Sergei Vasilyevich
MOSCOW PHILHARMONIC SCHOOL (RUSSIA)
Koussevitzky, Serge Alexandrovich
MOUNT ALLISON UNIVERSITY (CANADA)
Colpitts, Edwin Henry
MOUNT HOLYOKE COLLEGE (MASS.)
Apgar, Virginia
Brigham, Mary Ann
Colton, Elizabeth Avery
Dickinson, Emily Elizabeth
Fairchild, Mary Salome Cutler
Fiske, Fidelia
Frame, Alice Seymour Browne
Freeman, Mary Eleanor Wilkins
Hersey, Evelyn Weeks
Howard, Ada Lydia
Mills, Susan Lincoln Tolman
Mitchell, Lucy Myers Wright
Perkins, Frances
Sunderland, Eliza Jane Read
Yale, Caroline Ardelia
Graduate Study
Green, Constance McLaughlin
MOUNT PLEASANT CLASSICAL INSTITUTE (MASS.)
Beecher, Henry Ward
Clark, Horace Francis
Frick, Henry Clay
Prime, William Cowper
MOUNT PLEASANT COLLEGE (*See* OTTERBEIN COLLEGE)
MOUNT ST. MARY'S COLLEGE (MD.)
Chatard, Francis Silas
Cooper, James
Corrigan, Michael Augustine
Elder, William Henry
Fitzgerald, Edward

Flanagan, Edward Joseph
Fry, William Henry
Gilmour, Richard
La Farge, John
Le Conte, John Lawrence
McCann, Alfred Watterson
McCloskey, John
McCloskey, William George
McCoffery, John
Miles, George Henry
Pise, Charles Constantine
Purcell, John Baptist
Quarter, William
Seton, Robert
Seton, William
Toner, Joseph Meredith
White, Charles Ignatius
White, Edward Douglass, 1845–1921
Winterhalter, Hugo
Graduate Study
Flanagan, Edward Joseph
MOUNT ST. MARY'S OF THE WEST (OHIO)
Dwenger, Joseph
Enneking, John Joseph
Fitzgerald, Edward
Noll, John Francis
Rosecrans, Sylvester Horton
Spalding, John Lancaster
MOUNT UNION COLLEGE (OHIO)
Atkinson, George Wesley
Galbreath, Charles Burleigh
Hamilton, John William
Knox, Philander Chase
Laughlin, James Laurence
Presser, Theodore
Thompson, Will Lamartine
Tibbles, Thomas Henry
MOUNT VERNON SEMINARY (D.C.)
Post, Marjorie Merriweather
MOUNT WASHINGTON COLLEGIATE INSTITUTE (N.Y.)
Conkling, Roscoe
Miller, Charles Henry
Mitchell, Edward Page
Phelps, William Walter
Pierson, Arthur Tappan
MOUNT ZION ACADEMY (S.C.)
Aiken, David Wyatt
Bratton, John
Chappell, Absalom Harris
Du Bose, William Porcher
Gaillard, David Du Bose
Jones, John B.
Lewis, Dixon Hall
Porcher, Francis Peyre
MT. AIRY LUTHERAN THEOLOGICAL SEMINARY
Buchman, Frank Nathan Daniel
MUHLENBERG COLLEGE (PA.)
Buchman, Frank Nathan Daniel
Kohler, Elmer Peter
Peters, Madison Clinton
Rupp, William
Weidner, Revere Franklin
Graduate Study
Miller, George Abram
MUNGRET COLLEGE (IRELAND)
Turner, William

MUSEUM OF FINE ARTS SCHOOL (MASS.)
Benson, Frank Weston
Davis, Charles Harold
Tarbell, Edmund Charles
MUSKINGUM COLLEGE (OHIO)
Harper, Robert Francis
Harper, William Rainey
Kyle, David Braden
McBride, F(rancis) Scott
Moorehead, Agnes
Moorehead, William Gallogly
Thompson, William Oxley

NAPLES ACADEMY OF FINE ARTS (ITALY)
Lebrun, Federico ("Rico")
NASSAU HALL (*See* PRINCETON UNIVERSITY)
NATIONAL ACADEMY OF DESIGN (N.Y.)
Anshutz, Thomas Pollock
Baziotes, William
Beckwith, James Carroll
Benson, Eugene
Brevoort, James Renwick
Brush, George de Forest
Bush-Brown, Henry Kirke
Chase, William Merritt
Christy, Howard Chandler
Dewing, Maria Richards Oakey
Eaton, Wyatt
Freeman, James Edwards
Gaul, William Gilbert
Gray, Henry Peters
Hartley, Marsden
Hennessy, William John
Hicks, John, 1823–1890
Jones, Alfred
Karfiol, Bernard
Keller, Arthur Ignatius
Koehler, Robert
Lawrie, Alexander
Lie, Jonas
Lukeman, Henry Augustus
MacMonnies, Frederick William
Maynard, George Willoughby
Ormsby, Waterman Lilly
Page, William
Platt, Charles Adams
Reinhart, Benjamin Franklin
Richards, Thomas Addison
Robinson, Theodore
Ryder, Albert Pinkham
Soyer, Moses
Shattuck, Aaron Draper
Shurtleff, Roswell Morse
Spencer, Robert
Sterne, Maurice
Wiggins, Carleton
NATIONAL CONSERVATORY OF MUSIC (N.Y.)
Burleigh, Henry Thacker
Cook, Will Marion
Downes, (Edwin) Olin
Goldman, Edwin Franko
NATIONAL NORMAL UNIVERSITY (OHIO)
Hull, Cordell
NATIONAL TECHNICAL INSTITUTE, NAPLES (ITALY)
Lebrun, Federico ("Rico")
NATIONAL UNIVERSITY (D.C.)
Dies, Martin
West, James Edward
Whitney, Courtney
Law
Dies, Martin
Glueck, Sheldon ("Sol")
West, James Edward
NATIONAL UNIVERSITY, DUBLIN (IRELAND)
Brent, George
NATURAL SCIENCE ESTABLISHMENT (N.Y.)
Wheeler, William Morton
NAVAL ENGINEERING SCHOOL (ITALY)
Gatti-Casazza, Giulio
NAVAL TECHNICAL SCHOOL (NORWAY)
Barth, Carl Georg Lange
NAZARETH HALL (PA.)
Berg, Joseph Frederic
Cist, Jacob
Fries, Francis
McCalla, Bowman Hendry
McCawley, Charles Grymes
Mallory, Stephen Russell
Rondthaler, Edward
Schweinitz, Edmund Alexander de
Schweinitz, Emil Alexander de
NEBRASKA WESLEYAN UNIVERSITY
Dunning, John Ray
Gortner, Ross Aiken
High, Stanley Hoflund
Hope, Clifford Ragsdale
NEOPHEGEN COLLEGE (TENN.)
Read, Opie Pope
NEWARK ACADEMY (N.J.)
Clayton, Thomas
Frelinghuysen, Frederick Theodore
Gregg, Andrew
Hamilton, Peter
Jones, Ernest Lester
Lieb, John William
Murphy, Franklin
Parke, John
Platner, Samuel Ball
Shields, Charles Woodruff
Whitehead, William Adee
Wiley, Andrew Jackson
NEWBERRY COLLEGE (S.C.)
Blease, Coleman Livingston
Lever, Asbury Francis
NEW BRUNSWICK THEOLOGICAL SEMINARY (N.J.)
Chambers, Talbot Wilson
Corwin, Edward Tanjore
Drury, John Benjamin
Ferris, Isaac
Muste, Abraham Johannes
Schenck, Ferdinand Schureman
Searle, John Preston
Talmage, John Van Nest
Talmage, Thomas De Witt
Woodbridge, Samuel Merrill
NEWBURY SEMINARY (VT.)
Dillingham, William Paul
Flanders, Henry
Hoyt, Albert Harrison
Pearsons, Daniel Kimball
NEW COLLEGE OF EDINBURGH (SCOTLAND)
Coffin, Henry Sloane
NEW ENGLAND CONSERVATORY OF MUSIC (MASS.)
Brady, Alice
Brown, Gertrude Foster
Chadwick, George Whitefield
Cortelyou, George Bruce
Daniels, Frank Albert
Dunham, Henry Morton
Gilbert, Henry Franklin Belknap
Hadley, Henry Kimball
Hull, Josephine
Lodge, John Ellerton
Mason, Frank Stuart
Nordica, Lillian
Presser, Theodore
Rockefeller, Martha Baird
Williams, Fannie Barrier
Winterhalter, Hugo
NEW HAMPSHIRE COLLEGE OF AGRICULTURE AND MECHANICAL ARTS
Hazen, Allen
NEW HAMPTON ACADEMY (N.H.)
Fogg, George Gilman
Haven, Emily Bradley Neal
Morrison, Nathan Jackson
Plaisted, Harris Merrill
Robinson, Ezekiel Gilman
NEW HAMPTON LITERARY AND THEOLOGICAL INSTITUTION (N.H.)
Cheney, Oren Burbank
Eddy, Daniel Clarke
Gale, Elbridge
McCall, Samuel Walker
Marden, Orison Swett
NEW IPSWICH ACADEMY (N.H.)
Allen, David Oliver
Bell, Samuel
Everett, David
Howard, Ada Lydia
Payson, Edward
Sherwin, Thomas
Stearns, John Newton
Stearns, Oliver
Wilder, Marshall Pinckney
Worcester, Samuel
NEW JERSEY COLLEGE OF LAW (NEW JERSEY LAW SCHOOL)
Kenny, John V.
Nelson, Oswald George ("Ozzie")
Newhouse, Samuel Irving
NEW MEXICO SCHOOL OF MINES
Hilton, Conrad Nicholson
NEW PALTZ STATE NORMAL SCHOOL (N.Y.)
Harcourt, Alfred
NEW SALEM ACADEMY (MASS.)
Allen, David Oliver
Going, Jonathan
Heywood, Levi
Howe, Samuel
NEW SCHOOL FOR SOCIAL RESEARCH (N.Y.)
Cahill, Holger
De Wilde, Brandon
Rorty, James Hancock
NEW SCHOOL OF DESIGN (MASS.)
Gorky, Arshile

NEWTON COLLEGIATE INSTITUTE (N.J.)
Warbasse, James Peter
NEWTON THEOLOGICAL INSTITUTION (MASS.)
Anderson, Martin Brewer
Andrews, Elisha Benjamin
Banvard, Joseph
Brown, Charles Rufus
Burrage, Henry Sweetser
Cushing, Josiah Nelson
Dearing, John Lincoln
Dodge, Ebenezer
Eaton, Charles Aubrey
Faunce, William Herbert Perry
Fernald, James Champlin
Gilmore, Joseph Henry
Horr, George Edwin
Hovey, Alvah
Jones, John Taylor
King, Henry Melville
Lincoln, John Larkin
Manly, Basil, 1825–1892
Mason, Francis
Mathews, Shailer
Merrill, George Edmands
Mitchell, Edward Cushing
Robins, Henry Ephraim
Robinson, Ezekiel Gilman
Small, Albion Woodbury
Stevens, William Arnold
Williams, George Washington
Winkler, Edwin Theodore
NEW YORK COLLEGE OF PHARMACY
Coit, Henry Leber
Disbrow, William Stephen
Jacobi, Mary Corinna Putnam
NEW YORK FREE ACADEMY (*See* CITY COLLEGE OF NEW YORK)
NEW YORK HOMEOPATHIC MEDICAL COLLEGE
Gallinger, Jacob Harold
Hanchett, Henry Granger
Harkness, William
Hrdlicka, Ales
Miller, Charles Henry
Millspaugh, Charles Frederick
NEW YORK HOSPITAL SCHOOL OF NURSING
Beard, Mary
Goodrich, Annie Warburton
NEW YORK HOSPITAL TRAINING SCHOOL FOR NURSES
Stimson, Julia Catherine
Wald, Lillian D.
NEW YORK INSTITUTE OF PHOTOGRAPHY
Smith, William Eugene
NEW YORK LAW SCHOOL
Borchard, Edwin Montefiore
Chester, Colby Mitchell
Colby, Bainbridge
Coulter, Ernest Kent
Dodd, Lee Wilson
Ernst, Morris Leopold
Fosdick, Raymond Blaine
Griscom, Lloyd Carpenter
Harlan, John Marshall
Harrison, Francis Burton
Heatter, Gabriel
Hylan, John Francis
McClellan, George Brinton
Miller, David Hunter
Pecora, Ferdinand
Pinchot, Amos Richards Eno
Purdy, Lawson
Rice, Elmer
Seabury, Samuel
Stevens, Wallace
Taber, John
Wagner, Robert Ferdinand
Walker, James John
Whalen, Grover Aloysius
NEW YORK MEDICAL COLLEGE
Byrne, John
Lapham, William Berry
Otis, Fessenden Nott
Spooner, Shearjashub
Taylor, Charles Fayette
NEW YORK SCHOOL FOR APPLIED DESIGN
Bernstein, Aline
NEW YORK SCHOOL OF APPLIED DESIGN FOR WOMEN
Meière, Marie Hildreth
NEW YORK SCHOOL OF ART
Hooper, Edward
Kent, Rockwell
Miller, Kenneth Hayes
Stella, Joseph
NEW YORK SCHOOL OF FINE AND APPLIED ARTS
Adrian, Gilbert
Gropper, William
Lawson, Robert Ripley
Norell, Norman
NEW YORK SCHOOL OF PHILANTHROPY
Paul, Alice
Perkins, Frances
Rankin, Jeannette Pickering
Graduate Study
Billikopf, Jacob
NEW YORK SCHOOL OF SOCIAL WORK
Coyle, Grace Longwell
Glueck, Eleaner Touroff
NEW YORK SCHOOL OF THEATER
Kovacs, Ernie
NEW YORK STATE LIBRARY SCHOOL AT ALBANY
Anderson, Edwin Hatfield
Pearson, Edmund Lester
NEW YORK TRAINING SCHOOL FOR TEACHERS
Lange, Dorothea
Stark, Louis
NEW YORK UNIVERSITY
Abbott, Austin
Abbott, Benjamin Vaughan
Abbott, Edward
Abbott, Lyman
Adderley, Julian Edwin ("Cannonball")
Adler, George J.
Baird, Charles Washington
Baird, Henry Martyn
Bloomgarden, Kermit
Bond, Hugh Lennox
Bowne, Borden Parker
Brill, Abraham Arden
Buehler, Huber Gray
Butler, William Allen
Carter, Jesse Benedict
Clark, Henry James
Clay, Albert Tobias
Cox, Wallace Maynard ("Wally")
Coxe Arthur Cleveland
Croly, David Goodman
Crosby, Ernest Howard
Crosby, Howard
Crosby, John Schuyler
Cullen, Countée Porter
Doubleday, Nelson
Duyckinck, George Long
Fiske, Harrison Grey
Fleischer, Nathaniel Stanley ("Nat")
Goodsell, Daniel Ayres
Hall, Abraham Oakey
Hay, Charles Augustus
Herrmann, Bernard
Higgins, Daniel Paul
Hine, Lewis Wickes
Horn, Edward Traill
Houghton, George Hendric
Huntington, Jedediah Vincent
Hunton, William Lee
Isaacs, Abram Samuel
Johnson, Willis Fletcher
Johnston, Jalen Taylor
Jones, James Ramon
Koch, Vivienne
Lasser, Jacob Kay
Lee, Manfred B.
Levy, Gustave Lehmann
Ludlow, William
Maclay, William Brown
Madigan, Laverne
Mathews, Cornelius
Mills, Lawrence Heyworth
Moore, George Henry
Mostel, Samuel Joel ("Zero")
Noyes, Henry Drury
Olcott, Henry Steel
Orth, Godlove Stein
Parsons, John Edward
Paton, Lewis Bayles
Payne, Daniel Alexander
Picton, Thomas
Post, George Browne
Pressman, Lee
Redfield, Amasa Angell
Reid, John Morrison
Rorty, James Hancock
Rosebury, Theodor
Rossen, Robert
Russell, Israel Cook
Salter, William
Schuyler, George Washington
Shahn, Benjamm ("Ben")
Shear, Theodore Leslie
Sickles, Daniel Edgar
Smillie, James David
Snow, John Ben
Speir, Samuel Fleet
Sprecher, Samuel
Stevenson, John James
Stoever, Martin Luther
Strong, Elmer Kenneth, Jr. ("Ken")
Taylor, Joseph Deems
Tilden, Samuel Jones

Todman, William Selden ("Bill")
True, Frederick William
Unangst, Erias
Underwood, Horace Grant
Vail, Alfred
Valentine, Milton
Vanderbilt, Amy
Wegmann, Edward
White, Richard Grant
Whitman, Charles Seymour
Woodbridge, Samuel Merrill
Youmans, William Jay
Young, Alfred
Zeckendorf, William

Graduate Study
Davison, George Willets
Hine, Lewis Wickes
Isaacs, Abram Samuel
Kingsley, Elizabeth Seelman
Madigan, Laverne
Noyes, Henry Drury
Parsons, John Edward
Reece, Brazilla Carroll
Revel, Bernard
Sayre, Wallace Stanley
Shaw, Edward Richard
Shear, Theodore Leslie
Stevenson, John James
Stoddard, John Fair
Watkins, Arthur Vivian

Law
Allen, Florence Ellinwood
Boissevain, Inez Milholland
Boudin, Louis Boudinoff
Dill, James Brooks
Dodd, Bella Visono
Glass, Montague Marsden
Golden, John
Goldman, Mayer C.
Hillquit, Morris
Kaempffert, Waldemar Bernhard
King, Carol Weiss
La Guardia, Fiorello Henry
Levitt, Abraham
Marcantonio, Vito Anthony
Murray, James Edward
Palmer, Albert Marshman
Radin, Max
Robeson, Paul Leroy
Root, Elihu
Talmage, Thomas DeWitt
Thomas, John Parnell
Tilden, Samuel Jones
Tishman, David

Medicine
Abbott, Frank
Ainsworth, Frederick Crayton
Allen, Timothy Field
Biggs, Hermann Michael
Bishop, Seth Scott
Bosworth, Franke Huntington
Brill, Nathan Edwin
Bryant, Joseph Decatur
Burnett, Swan Moses
Caldwell, Eugene Wilson
Carroll, James
Chapin, Charles Value
Coakley, Cornelius Godfrey
Davis, Charles Henry Stanley
Dennis, Frederic Shepard
De Rosset, Moses John
Disbrow, William Stephen
Doremus, Robert Ogden
Draper, Henry
Evans, George Alfred
Fisher, George Jackson
Fowler, George Ryerson
Francis, Samuel Ward
Goldberger, Joseph
Goldwater, Sigismund Schulz
Guernsey, Egbert
Gulick, Luther Halsey, 1828–1891
Gulick, Luther Halsey, 1865–1918
Hammond, William Alexander
Hempel, Charles Julius
Howland, John
Johnston, George Ben
Kellogg, John Harvey
Lambuth, Walter Russell
Lydston, George Frank
McCaw, James Brown
McKean, James William
Mackenzie, John Noland
Maxwell, George Troup
Mayer, Emil
Mendes, Henry Pereira
Morrow, Prince Albert
Nichols, Charles Henry
Osborn, Henry Fairfield
Patrick, Hugh Talbot
Price, George Moses
Purple, Samuel Smith
Pusey, William Allen
Quintard, Charles Todd
Ranney, Ambrose Loomis
Reed, Walter
Rockwell, Alphonso David
Roosa, Daniel Bennett St. John
Rubinow, Isaac Max
Rusby, Henry Hurd
Sayre, Reginald Hall
Spitka, Edward Charles
Stiles, Henry Reed
Stone, Abraham
Wanless, William James
Wilbur, Cressy Livingston
Witthaus, Rudolph August
Wyckoff, John Henry
Wyeth, John Allan

NIAGARA UNIVERSITY (N.Y.)
Donovan, William Joseph
McCarthy, Joseph Vincent ("Joe")

NOBLE AND GREENOUGH SCHOOL (MASS.)
Lovett, Robert Williamson
Lowell, Guy
Lowell, Percival
Saltonstall, Leverett
Underwood, Loring
Ward, Robert De Courcy

NORGES TEKNISKE HOGSKOLE (NORWAY)
Onsager, Lars

NORMAL ART SCHOOL (MASS.)
Piston, Walter Hamor

NORMAL SCHOOL OF MARYVILLE (N. DAK.)
Frazier, Lynn Joseph

NORMAL SCHOOL OF ARIZONA
Hayden, Carl Trumbull

NORTH AMERICAN COLLEGE, ROME (ITALY)
Spellman, Francis Joseph
Stritch, Samuel Alphonsus
Turner, William

Graduate Study
Pace, Edward Aloysius

NORTH AMERICAN COLLEGE (ITALY)
Dougherty, Dennis Joseph
Meyer, Albert Gregory
O'Connell, William Henry
Rummel, Joseph Francis

Theology
Cooper, John Montgomery

NORTH CAROLINA MILITARY AND POLYTECHNIC INSTITUTE
Cain, William

NORTH CAROLINA STATE UNIVERSITY
Scott, W(illiam) Kerr

NORTH CAROLINA STATE UNIVERSITY AT RALEIGH
Gardner, Oliver Maxwell

NORTH CENTRAL COLLEGE (ILL.)
Baldwin, Evelyn Briggs
Breasted, James Henry
Link, Henry Charles

NORTHEASTERN STATE COLLEGE (OKLA.)
Stigler, William Grady

NORTHEAST MISSOURI STATE COLLEGE
Laughlin, Harry Hamilton

NORTH GEORGIA AGRICULTURAL COLLEGE
Wood, John Stephens

NORTH GEORGIA COLLEGE
Morehouse, Ward

NORTH PACIFIC DENTAL COLLEGE (OREG.)
Buchanan, Edgar

NORTHWESTERN MILITARY AND NAVAL ACADEMY (WIS.)
Tracy, Spencer Bonaventure

NORTHWESTERN UNIVERSITY (ILL.)
Aldrich, Charles Anderson
Bemis, Harold Edward
Bergen, Edgar
Bliss, George William
Boutell, Henry Sherman
Corrothers, James David
Eichelberger, Clark Mell
Emmett, Burton
Frank, Glenn
Garst, Roswell ("Bob")
Gates, John Warne
Greenlaw, Edwin Almiron
Hamilton, John Daniel Miller, II
Hard, William
Harrington, Mark Walrod
Hart, Virgil Chittenden
Helmer, Bessie Bradwell
Hoffman, Clare Eugene
James, Edmund Janes
Johnson, Harold Ogden ("Chic")
Johnson, Joseph French
Lisagor, Peter Irvin
Olsen, John Sigvard ("Ole")
Patten, Simon Nelson

Peek, George Nelson
Pieper, Franz August Otto
Ricketts, Howard Taylor
Scott, John Adams
Scott, Walter Dill
Sewall, May Eliza Wright
Shipstead, Henrik
Taylor, Fred Manville
Ward, Harry Frederick
Graduate Study
Case, Francis Higbee
Clement, Rufus Early
Greenlaw, Edwin Almiron
Helmer, Bessie Bradwell
Sauer, Carl Ortwin
Sharp, Katharine Lucinda
Watts, Alan Wilson
Law
Dawson, William Levi
Gardner, Gilson
Hadley, Herbert Spencer
Hamilton, John Daniel Miller, II
Kerner, Otto, Jr.
McCormick, Robert Rutherford
Olson, Floyd Bjerstjerne
Plumb, Glenn Edward
Zeisler, Sigmund
Medicine
Abt, Isaac Arthur
Aldrich, Charles Anderson
Bishop, Seth Scott
Brennemann, Joseph
DeLee, Joseph Bolivar
Fordyce, John Addison
Gradle, Henry
McCord, James Bennett
Martin, Franklin Henry
Mayo, Charles Horace
Ohlmacher, Albert Philip
Park, Roswell, 1852–1914
Plummer, Henry Stanley
Ricketts, Howard Taylor
Williams, Daniel Hale
NORTHWICK COLLEGE (ENGLAND)
Mendes, Henry Pereira
NORWALK ACADEMY (OHIO)
Gilmore, Quincy Adams
Harris, William Logan
Hayes, Rutherford Birchard
Victor, Orville James
NORWICH FREE ACADEMY (CONN.)
Bourne, Edward Gaylord
Bryant, Joseph Decatur
Colvocoresses, George Musalas
Dorchester, Daniel
Gilman, Daniel Coit
Prentice, Samuel Oscar
Thurber, Christopher Carson
Ware, Edmund Asa
NORWICH UNIVERSITY (VT.)
Adams, Edward Dean
Adams, James Hopkins
Alvord, Henry Elijah
Beach, William Augustus
Boggs, Charles Stuart
Bragg, Thomas
Dixon, Luther Swift
Dodge, Grenville Mellen
Frazer, John Fries
Hatch, Edward
Hayes, Augustus Allen
Horton, Valentine Baxter
Hubbard, Henry Griswold
Huntington, William Reed
Kellogg, William Pitt
Lee, William Little
Lyon, Caleb
Milroy, Robert Huston
Morgan, Junius Spencer
Mower, Joseph Anthony
Porter, Russell Williams
Ransom, Thomas Edward Greenfield
Seymour, Horatio
Seymour, Thomas Hart
Seymour, Truman
Totten, George Muirson
Ward, Frederick Townsend
Ward, James Harmon
Welles, Gideon
Wellman, Samuel Thomas
Wheeler, William Adolphus
Wilson, William Griffith ("Bill W.")
NOTRE DAME CONVENT (MD.)
Johnston, Frances Benjamin
NOTRE DAME UNIVERSITY
Corby, William
Dooley, Thomas Anthony, III
Elliott, Walter Hackett Robert
Fahy, Charles
Howard, Timothy Edward
Lambeau, Earl Louis ("Curly")
Leahy, Francis William ("Frank")
Murphy, Frederick E.
Nelson, William Rockhill
Nieuwland, Julius Arthur
O'Connor, Edwin Greene
Riordan, Patrick William
Rockne, Knute Kenneth
Shaw, Lawrence Timothy ("Buck")
Shuster, George Nauman
Smith, William Eugene
Stuhldreher, Harry A.
Ward, Arch Burdette
Zahm, John Augustine
Law
Walker, Frank Comerford

OAHU COLLEGE (HAWAII)
Baldwin, Henry Perrine
OAKLAND CITY COLLEGE (IND.)
Hodges, Gilbert Ray
OBERLIN ACADEMY (OHIO)
Ament, William Scott
Gray, Elisha
Gulick, Luther Halsey
Haskell, Henry Jospeh
Herrick, Myron Timothy
Powell, William Bramwell
OBERLIN COLLEGE (OHIO)
Allen, Frederic de Forest
Ament, William Scott
Angle, Paul McClelland
Barber, Amzi Lorenzo
Bickerdyke, Mary Ann Ball
Blackwell, Antoinette Louisa Brown
Bosworth, Edward Increase
Bowen, Ira Sprague
Brooks, John Graham
Brown, John Mifflin
Bruce, Blanche K.
Burns, Anthony
Burt, Mary Elizabeth
Burton, Theodore Elijah
Callender, Guy Stevens
Catton, Charles Bruce
Chamberlain, Charles Joseph
Chapman, John Wilbur
Cloud, Henry Roe
Coffin, Lorenzo S.
Commons, John Rogers
Cowles, Henry Chandler
Cravath, Erastus Milo
Cravath, Paul Drennan
Dawley, Almena
Dill, James Brooks
Du Bois, Shirley Lola Graham
Ells, Dan Parmelee
Fairbanks, Calvin
Fairchild, George Thompson
Fairchild, James Harris
Fairfield, Edmund Burke
Fillmore, John Comfort
Gray, Elisha
Gunn, Ross
Hall, Charles Martin
Hart, Hastings Hornell
Haskell, Henry Jospeh
Hayden, Ferdinand Vandiveer
Hayes, Charles Willard
Hutchins, Robert Maynard
Johnson, Byron Bancroft
Jones, Lynds
Kedzie, Robert Clark
King, Henry Churchill
Kofoid, Charles Atwood
Kyle, James Henderson
Langston, John Mercer
McCord, James Bennett
Mead, George Herbert
Miller, Emily Clark Huntington
Millikan, Robert Andrews
Nettleton, Alvred Bayard
Nettleton, Edwin S.
Plumb, Glenn Edward
Powell, John Wesley
Rogers, John Almanza Rowley
Rogers, John Raphael
Ross, Abel Hastings
Roye, Edward James
Ryan, Arthur Clayton
Scarborough, William Saunders
Scidmore, Eliza Ruhamah
Scott, John Prindle
Shafer, Helen Almira
Smith, Judson
Snider, Denton Jaques
Snow, Lorenzo
Spaulding, Oliver Lyman
Starr, Merritt
Stevens, Doris
Still, William Grant, Jr.
Stone, Lucy
Strong, Anna Louise
Swing, Raymond Edwards (Gram)
Terrell, Mary Eliza Church
Thomas, Edith Matilda
Turner, James Milton
Wheeler, Wayne Bidwell
Whipple, Henry Benjamin
Wilder, Thornton Niven

Wilkinson, Robert Shaw
Willard, Frances Elizabeth Caroline
Wilson, Warren Hugh
Wright, George Frederick
Graduate Study
Chamberlain, Charles Joseph
Du Bois, Shirley Lola Graham
Jones, Lynds
Millikan, Robert Andrews
Moley, Raymond Charles
Plumb, Glenn Edward
Terrell, Mary Eliza Church
Music
Cook, Will Marion
Densmore, Frances
Dett, Robert Nathaniel
Theology
Blackwell, Antoinette Louisa Brown
Bosworth, Edward Increase
Fairchild, George Thompson
Fairchild, James Harris
Fairfield, Edmund Burke
King, Henry Churchill
Morrison, Nathan Jackson
Pye, Watts Orson
Rogers, John Almanza Rowley
Ryan, Arthur Clayton
Smith, Judson
Tenney, Charles Daniel
Wright, George Frederick
OBERLIN CONSERVATORY OF MUSIC (OHIO)
White, Clarence Cameron
OBERLIN THEOLOGICAL SEMINARY (OHIO)
Barton, William Eleazar
OCCIDENTAL COLLEGE (CAL.)
Baker, Dorothy Dodds
Cromwell, Dean Bartlett
Jeffers, John Robinson
Rockefeller, Martha Baird
ODEON ATHENON (GREECE)
Callas, Maria
OGDEN COLLEGE (KY.)
Bent, Silas
Bloch, Claude Charles
Hines, Walker Downer
Witherspoon, Alexander Maclaren
OGLETHORPE UNIVERSITY (GA.)
Smith, Albert Merriman
OHIO MEDICAL COLLEGE
Byford, William Heath
Gates, Richard Jordan
Gilliam, David Tod
Jones, William Palmer
Keyt, Alonzo Thrasher
Owen, David Dale
OHIO NORTHERN UNIVERSITY
Binkley, Wilfred Ellsworth
Bromfield, Louis
Crile, George Washington
Fairless, Benjamin F.
Fess, Simeon Davidson
Lower, William Edgar
Yost, Fielding Harris
Law
Fess, Simeon Davidson
OHIO STATE NORMAL SCHOOL
Reed, Mary
OHIO STATE UNIVERSITY
Ames, Edward Raymond
Bellows, George Wesley
Brough, John
Butterworth, Benjamin
Campbell, Marius Robinson
Coulter, Ernest Kent
Cox, Samuel Sullivan
Dickey, Theophilus Lyle
Eichelberger, Robert Lawrence
Fisher, Dorothea Frances Canfield
Fowke, Gerard
Freed, Alan J.
Kellerman, Karl Frederic
Kettering, Charles Franklin
Kingsbury, Albert
Kiplinger, Willard Monroe
Lamme, Benjamin Carver
Landis, Henry Robert Murray
Lazarus, Fred, Jr.
Lord, Henry Curwen
Marquett, Turner Mastin
Marvin, Charles Frederick
Moore, Clarence Lemuel Elisha
Norton, William Warder
Ochs, Phil
Osborn, Thomas Ogden
Owens, James Cleveland ("Jesse")
Read, Daniel, 1805–1878
Sabine, Wallace Clement Ware
Safford, James Merrill
Shannon, Wilson
Shiras, George
Shiras, Oliver Perry
Short, Sidney Howe
Smith, William Sooy
Sparks, Edwin Erle
Sullivant, William Starling
Summers, George William
Thurber, James Grover
Young, John Wesley
Graduate Study
Adkins, Homer Burton
Bible, Dana Xenophon
Homeopathic Medicine
Lewis, Francis Park
Law
Burns, Raymond Joseph
Colver, William Byron
Cox, Samuel Sullivan
O'Neill, C. William ("Bill")
OHIO UNIVERSITY
Cranston, Earl
Lindley, Daniel
Smith, David Roland
OHIO WESLEYAN COLLEGE
Hughes, Edwin Holt
Tittle, Ernest Fremont
OHIO WESLEYAN UNIVERSITY
Atkinson, George Wesley
Baker, James Heaton
Binzham, Amelia
Burie, Stevenson
Conklin, Edwin Grant
Craig, Winchell McKendree
Cramer, Michael John
Cratty, Mabel
Dill, Clarence Cleveland
Dwight, Henry Otis
Fairbanks, Charles Warren
Foraker, Joseph Benson
Freas, Thomas Bruce
Gould, George Milbry
Gunsaulus, Frank Wakeley
Henry, William Arnon
Herrick, Myron Timothy
Hoyt, John Wesley
Jefferson, Charles Edward
Koch, Frederick Henry
Lowry, Hiram Harrison
McCabe, Charles Cordwell
McConnell, Francis John
McDowell, William Fraser
McVey, Frank Lerond
Mansell, William Albert
Mast, Phineas Price
Pattison, John M.
Rickey, Wesley Branch
Sparks, Edwin Erle
White, John Williams
Williams, John Fletcher
Williams, Marshall Jay
Woolley, John Granvlle
Graduate Study
Ferree, Clarence Errol
McDowell, William Fraser
OKLAHOMA AGRICULTURAL AND MECHANICAL COLLEGE
Clark, Joseph James ("Jocko")
OKLAHOMA STATE UNIVERSITY
Bayh, Marvella Belle Hern
OKOLONA COLLEGE (MISS.)
Whitfield, Owen
OLIVET COLLEGE (MICH.)
Beckwith, Clarence Augustine
Sperry, Willard Learoyd
OMAHA MEDICAL COLLEGE (NEB.)
Townsend, Francis Everett
ONEIDA INSTITUTE (N.Y.)
Bishop, Joel Prentiss
Bliss, Philemon
Brainard, Daniel
Garnet, Henry Highland
Grinnell, Josiah Bushnell
Janney, Eli Hamilton
Warner, Charles Dudley
Weld, Theodore Dwight
ONEIDA SEMINARY (N.Y.)
Alden, Isabella Macdonald
OREGON STATE UNIVERSITY
McKay, James Douglas
OSKALOOSA COLLEGE (IOWA)
Hornaday, William Temple
Reno, Milo
OTTERBEIN COLLEGE (OHIO)
Beardshear, William Miller
Frick, Henry Clay
Hanby, Benjamin Russel
Kephart, Isaiah Lafayette
Shauck, John Allen
Shuey, Edwin Longstreet
Weber, Henry Adam
OUACHITA BAPTIST UNIVERSITY (ARK.)
Bennett, Henry Garland
OWEGO ACADEMY (N.Y.)
Genung, John Franklin
Gladden, Washington
Pumpelly, Raphael
Rockefeller, William
Tracy, Benjamin Franklin

OXFORD ACADEMY (N.Y.)
Park, Roswell, 1807–1869
Randall, Samuel Sidwell
Robinson, John Cleveland
Seymour, Horatio
OXFORD UNIVERSITY (ENGLAND)
Auden, Wystan Hugh
Bazett, Henry Cuthbert
Brinton, Clarence Crane
Brooke, Charles Frederick Tucker
Buchanan, Scott Milross
Burdick, Eugene Leonard
Butterworth, William Walton ("Walt")
Campbell, William
Coffin, Robert Peter Tristram
Coolidge, Julian Lowell
Crisp, Donald
Fulton, John Farquhar
Getty, Jean Paul
Gibbs, Arthur Hamilton
Gipson, Lawrence Henry
Gordon, Kermit
Guthrie, Sir Tyrone
Harlan, John Marshall
Highet, Gilbert
Hooton, Earnest Albert
Hubble, Edwin
Huxley, Aldous Leonard
Lake, Kirsopp
Locke, Alain Leroy
Luce, Henry Robinson
Meyer, Frank Straus
O'Shaughnessy, Nelson Jarvis Waterbury
Overstreet, Harry Allen
Rice, John Andrew
Smith, Lloyd Logan Pearsall
Stokowski, Leopold Anthony
Tyler, Royall
Graduate Study
Beard, Charles Austin
Berenson, Bernard
Davis, Elmer Holmes
Elliot, William Yandell, III
Evans, Bergen Baldwin
Fieser, Louis Frederick
Guthrie, Tyrone
Haring, Clarence
Lake, Kirsopp
Kallen, Horace Meyer
MacIver, Robert Morrison
Matthiessen, Francis Otto
Morley, Christopher Darlington
Page, Thomas Walker
Ransom, John Crowe
Scarborough, Dorothy
Scudder, (Julia) Vida Dutton
Smith, Courtney Craig
Sperry, Willard Learoyd
Tigert, John James, IV
Van de Graaff, Robert Jemison
West, Allen Brown
Medicine
Bazett, Henry Cuthbert

PACIFIC METHODIST COLLEGE (CAL.)
Atkinson, Henry Avery
PACIFIC UNION COLLEGE (CAL.)
Bontemps, Arna Wendell
PACIFIC UNIVERSITY (ORE.)
Gilbert, Alfred Carlton
PACKARD BUSINESS COLLEGE (N.Y.)
Norton, Mary Teresa Hopkins
PACKARD COLLEGIATE INSTITUTE (N.Y.)
Vanderbilt, Amy
PACKARD COMMERCIAL COLLEGE (N.Y.)
Farley, James Aloysius
Whalen, Grover Aloysius
PACKER COLLEGIATE INSTITUTE (N.Y.)
Vanderbilt, Amy
PAINE COLLEGE (GA.)
Lomax, Louis Emanuel
Tobias, Channing Heggie
PALATINE JOSEPH POLYTECHNIC (HUNGARY)
Kármán, Theodore (Todor) Von
PARIS CONSERVATORY (FRANCE)
Casadesus, Robert Marcel
Kreisler, Fritz
Pons, Lily
Varèse, Edgard
Wister, Owen
PARK COLLEGE (MO.)
Willebrandt, Mabel Walker
PARMA CONSERVATORY (ITALY)
Toscanini, Arturo
PARSONS SCHOOL OF DESIGN (N.Y.)
McCardell, Claire
PARTRIDGE'S MILITARY ACADEMY (*See* NORWICH UNIVERSITY)
PASADENA JUNIOR COLLEGE
Robinson, John Roosevelt ("Jackie")
PASADENA NAZARENE COLLEGE (CAL.)
Pierce, Robert Willard
PATON CONGREGATIONAL COLLEGE (ENGLAND)
Booth, Ballington
PEABODY CONSERVATORY OF MUSIC (MD.)
Bowen, Catherine Drinker
Fox, Virgil Keel
Phillips, Lena Madesin
Smith, Lillian Eugenia
Thomas, John Charles
Weede, Robert
PEABODY NORMAL COLLEGE (TENN.)
Anthony, Katharine Susan
Bilbo, Theodore Gilmore
PEIRCE BUSINESS COLLEGE (PA.)
Stotesbury, Edward Townsend
PEMBROKE ACADEMY (N.H.)
Alger, William Rounseville
Bell, Charles Henry
Brown, Simon
Chamberlain, Mellen
Eastman, Enoch Worthen
Swett, John
Tenney, Edward Payson
PENN CHARTER SCHOOL (PA.)
Allison, Nathaniel
PENNINGTON SEMINARY (NJ.)
Bowne, Borden Parker
Buckley, James Monroe
Taylor, Alfred Alexander
Taylor, Robert Love
PENNSYLVANIA ACADEMY OF FINE ARTS
Abbey, Edwin Austin
Anshutz, Thomas Pollock
Biddle, George
Bingham, George Caleb
Borie, Adolphe
Boyle, John J.
Calder, Alexander Stirling
Chapman, John Gadsby
Cox, Kenyon
Demuth, Charles
Eakins, Thomas
Frost, Arthur Burdett
Grafly, Charles
Harrison, Lovell Birge
Harrison, Thomas Alexander
Haseltine, James Henry
Henri, Robert
Henry, Edward Lamson
Hergesheimer, Joseph
Hicks, John, 1823–1890
Hill, Thomas, 1829–1908
Korpman, Augustus
Luks, George Benjamin
Marin, John (Cheri)
Mielziner, Jo
Mifflin, Lloyd
O'Malley, Frank Ward
Parton, Arthur
Pennell, Joseph
Rehn, Frank Knox Morton
Roberts, Elizabeth Wentworth
Roberts, Howard
Rothermel, Peter Frederick
Sartain, Emily
Sartain, William
Sheeler, Charles R., Jr.
Shinn, Everett
Smedley, William Thomas
Smith, Xanthus Russell
Smyth, John Henry
Stephens, Alice Barber
Stetson, Charles Walter
Tanner, Henry Ossawa
Taylor, Frank Walter
Waugh, Frederick Judd
Wilmarth, Lemuel Everett
PENNSYLVANIA MILITARY COLLEGE
Morley, Sylvanus Griswold
Stern, Bill
PENNSYLVANIA SCHOOL OF SOCIAL WORK
Hersey, Evelyn Weeks
PENNSYLVANIA STATE COLLEGE
Lasser, Jacob Kay
Graduate Study
Lasser, Jacob Kay
PENNSYLVANIA STATE NORMAL SCHOOL AT BLOOMSBURG
Fernós Isern, Antonio
PENNSYLVANIA STATE NORMAL SCHOOL AT SHIPPENSBURG
Hoover, James Matthews
PENNSYLVANIA STATE UNIVERSITY
Epstein, Philip G.
Jackson, Dugald Caleb
Wieland, George Reber
Graduate Study
Jackson, Dugald Caleb

PHILADELPHIA COLLEGE OF PHARMACY (PA.)
Battey, Robert
Hatcher, Robert Anthony
Jacobs, Joseph, 1859–1929
Kraemer, Henry
Lilly, Eli
Lilly, Josiah Kirby
Parrish, Edward
Power, Frederick Belding
Procter, William
Remington, Joseph Price
Stitt, Edward Rhodes

PHILADELPHIA DENTAL COLLEGE (PA.)
Howe, Percy Rogers

PHILADELPHIA DIVINITY SCHOOL (PA.)
Montgomery, James Alan

PHILADELPHIA SCHOOL OF INDUSTRIAL ART (PA.)
Sheeler, Charles R., Jr.

PHILADELPHIA SCHOOL OF PEDAGOGY (PA.)
Fischer, Louis

PHILLIPS ACADEMY (ANDOVER, MASS.)
Abbot, Benjamin
Abbott, Joseph Carter
Abbott, Samuel Warren
Adams, Charles Baker
Adams, Henry Carter
Alden, Timothy
Allen, Nathan H.
Alvord, Clarence Walworth
Ames, Samuel
Austin, James Trecothick
Barth, Alan
Bates, Theodore Lewis ("Ted")
Battey, Robert
Beard, George Miller
Benjamin, George Hillard
Birney, David Bell
Bishop, Robert Roberts
Bliss, William Dwight Porter
Brown, George, 1823–1892
Burrell, David James
Carpenter, George Rice
Carter, Franklin
Chamberlain, Daniel Henry
Clark, Thomas March
Coleman, William
Cook, Flavius Josephus
Cook, Robert Johnson
Cutler, Carroll
Daveis, Charles Stewart
De Forest, John Kinne Hyde
Dennis, Frederic Shepard
Doe, Charles
Dole, Nathan Haskell
Dorsheimer, William Edward
Durant, Henry
Edmands, John
Emerson, Ralph
Evans, Walker
Farmer, Moses Gerrish
Farrar, Timothy
Fisher, Theodore Willis
Fitzgerald, Desmond
Flagg, Thomas Wilson
Flint, Charles Louis
Flint, Timothy
Fox, Gustavus Vasa
Frisbie, Levi
Frissell, Hollis Burke
Gannett, Ezra Stiles
Gardiner, Robert Hallowell
Gilmore, Joseph Henry
Goodell, William, 1792–1867
Grafton, Charles Chapman
Graves, William Phillips
Greener, Richard Theodore
Greenway, John Campbell
Guernsey, Egbert
Hackett, Horatio Balch
Hall, Charles Henry
Hall, Sherman
Halsted, William Stewart
Hamilton, John Daniel Miller, II
Hammond, Edward Payson
Hammond, James Bartlett
Hardy, Arthur Sherburne
Harris, William Torrey
Hewit, Augustine Francis
Hildreth, Samuel Prescott
Holmes, Oliver Wendell
Homes, Henry Augustus
Howe, Mark Anthony de Wolfe
Hyde, James Nevins
Ingelfinger, Franz Joseph
Isham, Samuel
Jackson, Edward Payson
Jenkins, Edward Hopkins
Jenney, William Le Baron
Johnson, Henry
Jones, William
Kaye, Frederick Benjamin
King, William
Kirkland, John Thornton
Knight, Henry Cogswell
Kohler, Walter Jodok, Jr.
Lawson, Victor Freemont
Lee, Henry, 1782–1867
Leonard, William Andrew
Linn, William Alexander
Loring, Frederick Wadsworth
McKenzie, Alexander
McLellan, Isaac
Marsh, John, 1799–1856
Marsh, Othniel Charles
Mears, David Otis
Mills, Benjamin Fay
Moody, William Henry
Morse, Samuel Finley Breese
Mowry, William Augustus
Newman, Samuel Phillips
Oliver, Henry Kemble
Orcutt, Hiram
Packard, Joseph
Palmer, George Herbert
Palmer, Ray
Payne, Oliver Hazard
Peet, Harvey Prindle
Poor, Daniel
Quincy, Edmund
Quincy, Josiah, 1772–1864
Rantoul, Robert, 1805–1852
Ray, Isaac
Raymond, George Lansing
Reid, Robert
Ropes, James Hardy
Rowland, Henry Augustus
Rust, Richard Sutton
Short, Charles
Smith, Charles Sprague
Smith, John Cotton, 1826–1882
Smith, Jonas Waldo
Smith, Jonas Waldo
Smyth, Newman
Stearns, Eben Sperry
Stearns, William Augustus
Stevens, Isaac Ingalls
Stevens, William Bacon
Stewart, Edwin
Storrow, James Jackson
Taft, Charles Phelps
Thayer, Alexander Wheelock
Torrey, Charles Turner
Trow, John Fowler
Tyler, Charles Mellen
Van Name, Addison
Walker, William Johnson
Ward, Herbert Dickinson
Ward, Joseph
Ward, William Hayes
Ware, Henry, 1794–1843
Washburn, George
Wheelwright, William
Whitney, Josiah Dwight
Willis, Nathaniel Parker
Williston, Samuel
Winslow, Hubbard
Woods, Alva
Woods, Leonard, 1807–1878
Worcester, Joseph Emerson
Wrigley, Philip Knight

PHILLIPS EXETER ACADEMY (N.H.)
Abbot, Ezra
Akerman, Amos Tappan
Ames, Frederick Lothrop
Angel, Benjamin Franklin
Atherton, George Washington
Babcock, James Wood
Bancroft, George
Barker, Alexander Crichlow ("Lex")
Bell, Charles Henry
Bell, Louis
Blake, John Lauris
Bowen, Francis
Boyden, Roland William
Brown, Charles Rufus
Buckminster, Joseph Stevens
Bulfinch, Thomas
Cass, Lewis
Chadbourne, Paul Ansel
Chadwick, John White
Cogswell, Joseph Green
Coolidge, Julian Lowell
Curtin, Jeremiah
Dana, James Freeman
Deering, Nathaniel
Dix, John Adams
Doe, Charles
Dorr, Thomas Wilson
Dunbar, Charles Franklin
Durell, Edward Henry
Dwight, Francis
Elwyn, Alfred Langdon
Felch, Alpheus
Field, Roswell Martin
Fletcher, James Cooley
Folsom, Charles
Folsom, George
Freed, Arthur
French, William Merchant Richardson

Gardner, Henry Joseph
Garrison, Lindley Miller
Greene, Charles Ezra
Griswold, William McCrillis
Hackett, Frank Warren
Hale, John Parker
Hale, William Gardner
Hawks, Howard Winchester
Heard, Augustine
Hildreth, Richard
Holmes, Nathaniel
Howland, John
Hyde, William DeWitt
Irwine, William Mann
Langdell, Christopher Columbus
Lincoln, Robert Todd
Lincoln, Rufus Pratt
Livermore, Abiel Abbot
Lowe, Charles
Lunt, George
Lyman, Theodore, 1792–1849
McCaleb, Theodore Howard
Mackenzie, James Cameron
MacVeagh, Charles
Mitchell, John Ames
Morison, George Shattuck
Morril, David Lawrence
Moses, George Higgins
Nutting, Wallace
Packard, Alpheus Spring, 1798–1884
Paine, Charles
Palfrey, John Gorham
Parker, Edward Pickering
Peabody, William Bourn Oliver
Perkins, James Handasyd
Porter, Fitz-John
Rawle, Francis, 1846–1930
Sanborn, Franklin Benjamin
Sargent, Lucius Manlius
Sibley, John Langdon
Sill, Edward Rowland
Smith, Jeremiah, 1837–1921
Smith, Uriah
Sparks, Jared
Stebbins, Horatio
Stewart, Donald Ogden
Sullivan, George
Taylor, Frederick Winslow
Thompson, William Boyce
Titcomb, John Wheelock
Tower, Charlemagne
Wardman, Ervin
Ware, William Robert
Waterhouse, Sylvester
Webster, Daniel
Wentworth, George Albert
Willard, Joseph, 1798–1865
Willis, William
Woodberry, George Edward
Woodruff, Timothy Lester
Wyman, Jeffries
Wyman, Morrill

PHILLIPS UNIVERSITY (OKLA.)
James, Marquis
Owen, Stephen Joseph

PIEDMONT COLLEGE (GA.)
Smith, Lillian Eugenia

PINKERTON ACADEMY (N.H.)
Bartlett, Samuel Colcord
Derby, Elias Hasket, 1803–1880
Fairbanks, Henry
Richardson, William Adams
Spofford, Harriet Elizabeth Prescott
Taylor, Samuel Harvey

PITTSBURGH THEOLOGICAL SEMINARY (PA.)
McBride, F(rancis) Scott

PITTSBURGH TRAINING SCHOOL FOR NURSES (PA.)
Rinehart, Mary Roberts

PITTSBURG STATE UNIVERSITY (KAN.)
Haldeman-Julius, Emanuel

PLAINFIELD ACADEMY (CONN.)
Burleigh, Charles Calistus
Burleigh, William Henry
Gaston, William, 1820–1894
Harris, Daniel Lester
Kingsley, James Luce
Moore, Addison Webster
Nott, Eliphalet
Parish, Elijah
Slater, John Fox
Smith, William, 17971–1887
Tyler, Daniel

PLATTEVILLE STATE TEACHERS COLLEGE (WIS.)
Williams, Thomas Harry

POLYTECHNIC ENGINEERING SCHOOL, MUNICH (GERMAN)
Gabo, Naum

POLYTECHNIC INSTITUTE IN HELSINKI (FINLAND)
Saarinen, Gottlieb Eliel

POLYTECHNIC INSTITUTE IN KIEV (RUSSIA)
Sikorsky, Igor Ivanovich

POLYTECHNIC INSTITUTE OF CHARLOTTENBURG (GERMANY)
Behrend, Bernard Arthur

POLYTECHNIC SCHOOL OF DELFT (NETHERLANDS)
Henny, David Christiaan

POLYTECHNICUM OF MOSCOW (RUSSIA)
Ostromislensky, Iwan Iwanowich

POMONA COLLEGE (CAL.)
Barrows, David Prescott
Taylor, Robert
Ward, Charles Henshaw
Wright, Willard Huntington

PONTIFICAL ATHENAEUM ANGELICO (ITALY)
Graduate Study
Sheen, Fulton John

PONTIFICAL BIBLICAL INSTITUTE (ITALY)
Graduate Study
Meyer, Albert Gregory

PONTIFICAL GREGORIAN UNIVERSITY (ITALY)
Graduate Study
Weigel, Gustave
Wright, John Joseph

PORTER'S SCHOOL, FARMINGTON (CONN.)
Dodge, Grace Hoadley
Hapgood, Isabel Florence
Stokes, Caroline Phelps
Talcott, Eliza

PORTLAND ACADEMY (MAINE)
Abbott, John Stevens Cabot
Fessenden, Francis
Longfellow, Samuel
Mellen, Grenville
Peary, Robert Edwin

PRAGUE CONSERVATORY OF MUSIC (AUSTRIA-HUNGARY)
Friml, Charles Rudolf

PRATT INSTITUTE (N.Y.)
Fischetti, John
Hill, Ernest Rowland
Karfiol, Bernard
Luckenbach, J(ohn) Lewis
Moore, Anne Carroll
Norell, Norman
Rockwell, George Lincoln
Weber, Max

PRESBYTERIAN COLLEGE (CANADA)
Naismith, James

PRINCETON THEOLOGICAL SEMINARY (N.J.)
Cannon, James
Foote, William Henry
Gibbons, Herbert Adams
Hibben, John Grier
Holland, William Jacob
Knight, Lucian Lamar
Luce, Henry Winters
Lunn, George Richard
Machen, John Gresham
Speer, Robert Elliott
Watson, Charles Roger

PRINCETON UNIVERSITY (N.J.)
Alexander, Joseph Addison
Alexander, Samuel Davies
Alston, Joseph
Andrew, Abram Piatt
Archer, James J.
Archer, John
Archer, Stevenson
Armstrong, George Dod
Armstrong, Hamilton Fish
Armstrong, John, 1758–1843
Arnold, Richard Dennis
Arnold, Thurman Wesley
Bacon, John
Baker, Daniel
Baker, William Mumford
Baldwin, James Mark
Barber, Francis
Barker, Alexander Crichlow ("Lex")
Bartlett, Dewey Follett
Barton, William Paul Crillon
Bayard, James Asheton, 1767–1815
Bayard, James Asheton, 1799–1880
Bayard, Richard Henry
Bayard, Samuel
Beasley, Frederick
Beasley, Mercer
Beatty, John, 1749–1826
Bedford, Gunning
Belknap, William Worth
Berg, Morris ("Moe")
Berrien, John Macpherson
Biddle, Nicholas, 1786–1844
Birney, James Gillespie
Bishop, John Peale

Blair, Francis Preston, 1821–1875
Blount, Willie
Boker, George Henry
Boteler, Alexander Robinson
Bowden, John
Boyd, James
Boyle, Jeremiah Tilford
Brackenridge, Hugh Henry
Bradford, William, 1755–1795
Branch, Lawrence O'Bryan
Brandon, Gerard Chittocque
Breckinridge, Desha
Breckinridge, Henry Skillman
Breckinridge, John, 1797–1841
Breckinridge, John Cabell
Brewster, Benpamin Harris
Brincklé, William Draper
Brown, Isaac Van Arsdale
Bruce, David Kirkpatrick Este
Burnet, Jacob
Burnet, William, 1730–1791
Burr, Aaron, 1756–1836
Butler, Howard Crosby
Butterworth, William Walton ("Walt")
Buttz, Henry Anson
Caldwell, David
Caldwell, James
Caldwell, Joseph
Cameron, James Donald
Campbell, Charles
Campbell, George Washington, 1769–1848
Carnahan, James
Carson, John Renshaw
Carter, Jesse Benedict
Carter, Samuel Powhatan
Cattell, William Cassaday
Chambers, George
Chapin, Henry Dwight
Chavis, John
Chesnut, James
Clarke, Thomas Shields
Clay, Joseph, 1764–18
Colquitt, Alfred Holt
Colquitt, Walter Terry
Cone, Spencer Houghton
Conover, Obadiah Milton
Converse, James Booth
Cooke, Philip Pendleton
Cowen, John Kissig
Cox, Rowland
Coxe, Richard Smith
Crane, Jonathan Townley
Crane, Thomas Frederick
Crawford, George Walker
Crothers, Samuel McChord
Custis, George Washington Parke
Cuyler, Theodore Ledyard
Dallas, George Mifflin
Daniel, Peter Vivian
Daniels, Winthrop More
Dayton, Jonathan
Dayton, William Lewis
Dennis, Alfred Lewis Pinneo
Dennis, James Shepard
Dickerson, Edward Nicoll
Dickerson, Mahlon
Doak, Samuel
Dod, Albert Baldwin
Dod, Thaddeus
D'Olier, Franklin
Drayton, John
Duft, James Henderson
Duffield, George, 1732–1790
Dulles, Allen Welsh
Dulles, John Foster
Durstine, Roy Sarles
Early, Peter
Edsall, David Linn
Edwards, Henry Waggaman
Edwards, Jonathan, 1745–1801
Edwards, Pierpont
Elliott, Benjamin
Ellsworth, Oliver
Engelhard, Charles William
Erdman, Charles Rosenbury
Ewing, Charles
Ewing, John
Farrand, Livingston
Farrand, Max
Few, Ignatius Alphonso
Field, Richard Stockton
Fine, Henry Burchard
Finley, Robert
Finn, Henry James William
Finney, John Miller Turpin
Firestone, Harvey Samuel, Jr.
Fish, Nicholas
Fitzgerald, Francis Scott Key
Flint, Albert Stowell
Forman, David
Forrestal, James Vincent
Forsyth, John
Fosdick, Raymond Blaine
Frankfurter, Alfred Moritz
Frelinghuysen, Frederick
Frelinghuysen, Theodore
Freneau, Philip Morin
Funk, Wilfred John
Gano, John
Gaston, William, 1778–1844
Getty, George Franklin, II
Gholson, William Yates
Gibson, William
Gidley, James Williams
Gildersleeve, Basil Lanneau
Giles, William Branch
Glass, Franklin Potts
Godwin, Parke
Goodman, Kenneth Sawyer
Graham, Evarts Ambrose
Gray, George
Green, Ashbel
Green, Henry Woodhull
Gregory, Daniel Seelye
Guffey, Joseph F.
Gummere, Samuel René
Gummere, William Stryker
Hager, John Sharpenstein
Haines, Daniel
Hall, Bolton
Hall, James, 1744–1826
Hall, John Elihu
Halsted, George Bruce
Hamilton, Maxwell McGaughey
Hamilton, Peter
Harlan, John Marshall
Harper, Robert Goodloe
Hart, James Morgan
Hart, John Seely
Hartley, Frank
Hawkins, Benjamin
Hayward, Leland
Hazard, Ebenezer
Henderson, Thomas
Henderson, William James
Henry, John, 1750–1798
Hepburn, James Curtis
Hibben, John Grier
Hibben, Paxton Pattison
Hobart, John Henry
Hodge, Archibald Alexander
Hodge, Charles
Hodge, Hugh Lenox
Hormel, Jay Catherwood
Hornblower, William Butler
Hosack, David
Houston, William Churchill
Howard, Benjamin Chew
Howell, David
Hudson, Claude Silbert
Huger, Daniel Elliott
Hunt, Theodore Whitefield
Hunter, Andrew
Hutson, Richard
Ingersoll, Charles Jared
Inman, Samuel Martin
Irvine, William Mann
Iverson, Alfred
Jackson, Charles Douglas
Johns, John
Johns, Kensey
Johnson, Bradley Tyler
Johnson, William, 1771–1834
Joline, Adnan Hoffman
Jones, Charles Colcock
Jones, Joseph
Kellett, William Wallace
Kellogg, Samuel Henry
Kirk, Edward Norris
Kirkland, Samuel
Kirkpatrick, Andrew
Krock, Arthur
Landis, James McCauley
Lawrence, David
Lee, Charles
Lee, Henry, 1756–1818
Lee, Ivy Ledbetter
Leland, Godfrey Charles
Lewis, Morgan
Lewisohn, Sam Adolph
Lindley, Jacob
Lindsley, Philip
Livermore, Samuel, 1732–1803
Livingston, Edward
Livingston, Henry Brockholst
Long, Breckinridge
Lowrie, James Walter
Luckenbach, J(ohn) Lewis
Ludlow, Fitz Hugh
Lumpkin, Joseph Henry
Lynd, Robert Staughton
Lyon, James
McAllister, Matthew Hall
MacCauley, Clay
McCay, Henry Kent
McClellan, George Brinton
McClenahan, Howard
McCormick, Cyrus Hall
McCosh, Andrew James
McDonnell, James Smith, Jr.
McDowell, James
McDowell, John, 1780–1863

McElroy, Robert McNutt
McGraw, Donald Cushing
McGuire, Joseph Deakins
McIlvaine, Charles Pettit
Maclean, John, 1800–1886
McLean, Robert
McMahon, John Van Lear
Macon, Nathaniel
MacWhorter, Alexander
Madison, James, 1750/51–1836
Magie, William Jay
Manning, James
Mansfield, Edward Deering
Marquand, Allan
Martin, Alexander
Martin, Luther
Mason, Jonathan
Meade, William
Mercer, Charles Fenton
Merchant, Livingston Tallmadge
Meyer, Frank Straus
Miller, James Alexander
Miller, John, 1819–1895
Moffat, James Clement
Montgomery, William Bell
Morris, John Gottlieb
Napton, William Barclay
Nash, Frederick
Nassau, Robert Hamill
Neill, William
Nicoll, DeLancey
Niles, Nathaniel, 1741–1828
Nixon, John Thompson
Odell, Jonathan
O'Neill Eugene
Orr, Jehu Amaziah
Osborn, Henry Fairfield, 1857–1935
Osborn, Henry Fairfield, 1887–1969
Otis, George Alexander
Otto, John Conrad
Parker, Joel, 1816–1888
Pate, Maurice
Paterson, William
Patton, John Mercer
Pearce, James Alfred
Pennington, William
Pepper, William, 1810–1864
Perrine, Frederic Auten Combs
Perry, Ralph Barton
Phelps, Charles Edward
Phillips, David Graham
Pintard, John
Pitney, Mahlon
Pollock, James
Pomerene, Atlee
Poole, Ernest Cook
Potter, Nathaniel
Pratt, Thomas George
Price, Bruce
Price, Rodman McCamley
Prime, Benjamin Youngs
Prime, William Cowper
Proctor, William Cooper
Radcliff, Jacob
Ramsay, David
Ramsay, Nathaniel
Read, John, 1769–1854
Reed, David Aiken
Reed, Joseph
Reeve, Tapping
Reid, Wilham Shields
Reynolds, Julian Sargeant
Rhea, John
Rice, David
Roberts, William Charles
Robeson, George Maxwell
Rockefeller, John Davison, 3d
Rood, Ogden Nicholas
Root, Jesse
Ruffin, Thomas
Rush, Benjamin
Rush, James
Rush, Richard
Russell, Henry Norris
Sayre, Stephen
Schenck, Ferdinand Schureman
Schirmer, Rudolph Edward
Schroeder, John Frederick
Scott, William Berryman
Scribner, Charles, 1821–1871
Scribner, Charles, 1854–1930
Scribner, Charles, 1890–1952
Scudder, John
Scudder, Nathaniel
Sergeant, John, 1779–1852
Sergeant, Jonathan Dickinson
Sergeant, Thomas
Sheldon, Walter Lorenzo
Shellabarger, Samuel
Shelton, Frederick William
Shields, Charles Woodruff
Shippen, William
Skinner, Thomas Harvey
Smith, Hezekiah
Smith, John Blair
Smith, Jonathan Bayard
Smith, Persifor Frazer
Smith, Samuel Stanhope
Smith, William Stephens
Southard, Samuel Lewis
Spalding, Franklin Spencer
Speer, Robert Elliott
Spring, Samuel
Starr, Moses Allen
Sterling, John Whalen
Stevenson, Adlai Ewing, II
Stockton, John Potter
Stockton, Richard, 1730–1781
Stockton, Richard, 1764–1828
Stockton, Robert Field
Stone, David
Straus, Roger W(illiams)
Tarkington, Booth
Taylor, Archibald Alexander Edward
Thomas, Allen
Thomas, Norman Mattoon
Thompson, Smith
Tichenor, Isaac
Todd, Henry Alfred
Torrence, Frederick Ridgely
Troup, George Michael
Van Dyke, Henry
Van Dyke, Nicholas
Van Dyke, Paul
Van Lennep, William Bird
Wallace, Horace Binney
Wanamaker, Lewis Rodman
Ward, Thomas
Warfield, Benjamin Breckinridge
Warren, Howard Crosby
Waterman, Alan Tower
Watson, Charles Roger
Watt, Donald Beates
Wayne, James Moore
Welling, James Clarke
Wells, John
West, Andrew Fleming
Wheeler, (George) Post
Whitaker, Nathaniel
Whiteside, Arthur Dare
Wiley, David
Williams, Charles Richard
Williams, Jesse Lynch, 1871–1929
Williams, Linsly Rudd
Wilson, Edmund, Jr.
Wilson, Henry Parke Custis
Wilson, John Fleming
Wilson, Samuel Graham
Wilson, Woodrow
Winant, John Gilbert
Wood, George
Woodhull, Alfred Alexander
Wurtz, Henry
Wyckoff, Walter Augustus
Wylie, Philip Gordon
Young, Alfred
Young, John Richardson

Graduate Study

Baldwin, James Mark
Brackenridge, Hugh Henry
Butler, Howard Crosby
Cannon, James
Carson, John Renshaw
Coffin, Robert Peter Tristram
Compton, Arthur Holly
Compton, Karl Taylor
Crane, Thomas Frederick
Daniels, Winthrop More
Davisson, Clinton Joseph
Dickinson, John
Farrand, Max
Fosdick, Raymond Blaine
Fullerton, George Stuart
Gummere, William Stryker
Hibben, John Grier
Hudson, Claude Silbert
Irvine, William Mann
Kallen, Horace Meyer
Laughlin, Harry Hamilton
Lord, William Wilberforce
Lowrie, James Walter
McElroy, Robert McNutt
Miller, Dayton Clarence
Miller, James Alexander
Otis, George Alexander
Paterson, William
Perrine, Frederic Auten Combs
Rossiter, Clinton Lawrence, III
Russell, Henry Norris
Shellabarger, Samuel
Seitz, William Chapin
Shapley, Harlow
Spaeth, Sigmund
Taylor, Francis Henry
Waterman, Alan Tower
Wheeler, (George) Post
Wilson, James Southall
Woodhull, Alfred Alexander

Theology

Alden, Joseph
Alexander, Samuel Davies

Andrews, Lorrin
Baird, Henry Martyn
Baird, Robert
Baker, William Mumford
Barnes, Albert
Baugher, Henry Louis
Bethune, George Washington
Blackburn, William Maxwell
Boyce, James Petigru
Breckinridge, John, 1797–1841
Bush, George
Campbell, William Henry
Cattell, William Cassaday
Chambers, Talbot Wilson
Clark, Thomas March
Cobb, William Henry
Conover, Obadiah Milton
Cuyler, Theodore Ledyard
Dennis, James Shepard
Dod, Albert Baldwin
Estabrook, Joseph
Fleming, John
Fletcher, James Cooley
Gale, George Washington
Galloway, Samuel
Gilbert, Eliphalet Wheeler
Green, Lewis Warner
Green, William Henry
Gregory, Caspar René
Gregory, Daniel Seelye
Hall, Baynard Rush
Hart, John Seely
Hodge, Archibald Alexander
Hodge, Charles
Howard, Benjamin Chew
Humes, Thomas William
Hunt, Theodore Whitefield
Jackson, Samuel Macauley
Jackson, Sheldon
James, Henry, 1811–1882
Kellogg, Samuel Henry
Kirk, Edward Norris
Laws, Samuel Spahr
Lesley, Peter
Lindsley, Philip
Lord, Eleazer
Lord, William Wilberforce
Loughridge, Robert McGill
Lovejoy, Elijah Parish
Lowrie, James Walter
MacCracken, Henry Mitchell
McGilvary, Daniel
McIlvaine, Charles Pettit
McKim, James Miller
Maclean, John, 1800–1886
Manly, Basil, 1825–1892
Marquand, Allan
Mattoon, Stephen
Merrill, James Griswold
Miller, John, 1819–1895
Morris, John Gottlieb
Muhlenberg, Frederick Augustus
Nassau, Robert Hamill
Nevin, Edwin Henry
Nevin, John Williamson
Parvin, Theophilus
Paton, Lewis Bayles
Patterson, Robert Mayne
Patton, Francis Landey
Patton, William
Peers, Benjamin Orrs
Peters, Absalom
Pierce, John Davis
Plumer, William Swan
Porter, Thomas Conrad
Prime, Edward Dorr Griffin
Prime, Samuel Irenaeus
Raymond, George Lansing
Roberts, William Charles
Roberts, William Henry
Robinson, Charles Seymour
Robinson, Stuart
Ruffner, William Henry
Sawyer, Leicester Ambrose
Scott, William Anderson
Shedd, William Ambrose
Shields, Charles Woodruff
Smyth, Thomas
Sprague, William Buell
Sterling, John Whalen
Taylor, Archibald Alexander Edward
Wilson, Samuel Graham
Wilson, Samuel Ramsay
Wines, Frederick Howard
Wood, James, 1799–1867
Woodbridge, William Channing
Woolsey, Theodore Dwight
Wyckoff, Walter Augustus
Young, John Clarke
Young, Samuel Hall

PRITCHETT COLLEGE (MO.)
Kenyon, Josephine Hemenway
Pritchett, Henry Smith
Graduate Study
Kenyon, Josephine Hemenway

PROVIDENCE COLLEGE (R.I.)
Dodd, Thomas Joseph
McGrath, James Howard

PURDUE UNIVERSITY (IND.)
Ade, George
Bourke-White, Margaret
Chaffee, Roger Bruce
Davis, Adelle
Gray, Harold Lincoln
Grissom, Virgil Ivan ("Gus")
Hannagan, Stephen Jerome
Mead, Elwood
Osborn, Chase Salmon
Tarkington, Booth
Waesche, Russell Randolph
Wickard, Claude Raymond

QUEEN'S COLLEGE (*See* RUTGERS UNIVERSITY)

QUEEN'S MUSEUM COLLEGE (N.C.)
Davidson, William Lee
Davie, William Richardson
Graham, Joseph
Polk, William

QUEEN'S UNIVERSITY (CANADA)
Bowen, Norman Levi
Fortescue, Charles LeGeyt
Graduate Study
Fortescue, Charles LeGeyt

QUEEN'S UNIVERSITY (IRELAND)
Kennedy, Robert Foster

RACINE COLLEGE (WIS.)
Burleson, Hugh Latimer
Gailor, Thomas Frank

RADCLIFFE COLLEGE (MASS.)
Abbott, Eleanor Hallowell
Balch, Emily Greene
Brunswick, Ruth Mack
Cleghorn, Sarah Norcliffe
Follett, Mary Parker
Gillespie, Mabel
Hull, Josephine
Keller, Helen Adams
Leavitt, Henrietta Swan
Mitchell, Lucy Sprague
Park, Maud Wood
Peabody, Josephine Preston
Simkhovitch, Mary Melinda Kingsbury
Smith, Mildred Catharine
Stein, Gertrude
Switzer, Mary Elizabeth
Wambaugh, Sarah
Graduate Study
Flanagan, Hallie
Payne-Gaposchkin, Cecilia Helena
Prouty, Olive Higgins

RANDOLPH-MACON ACADEMY (VA.)
Chapman, Oscar Littleton

RANDOLPH-MACON COLLEGE (VA.)
Armstrong, Edward Cooke
Barnett, George Ernest
Buck, Pearl Comfort Sydenstricker
Cannon, James
Christian, Henry Asbury
Clopton, David
Craven, Braxton
Ellis, John Willis
Evans, Nathan George
Gartrell, Lucius Jeremiah
Howard, William Travis
James, Edwin Leland
Jarvis, Thomas Jordan
McTyeire, Holland Nimmons
Moore, Henry Ludwell
Page, Thomas Walker
Page, Walter Hines
Pratt, John Lee
Puryear, Bennet
Smith, William Waugh
Swanson, Claude Augustus
Taylor, David Watson

RAND SCHOOL OF SOCIAL SCIENCE (N.Y.)
Brent, George
Crosswaith, Frank Rudolph
Randolph, Asa Philip

REGIS COLLEGE
Montoya, Joseph Manuel

RENSSELAER POLYTECHNIC INSTITUTE (N.Y.)
Alden, John Ferris
Bogue, Virgil Gay
Boner, Alfred Pancoast
Booth, James Curtis
Buck, Leffert Lefferts
Burr, William Hubert
Cassatt, Alexander Johnston
Cluett, Sanford Lockwood
Cogswell, William Browne
Cook, George Hammell
Cooley, Lyman Edgar
Cooper, Theodore
Cummings, Charles Amos
Dumont, Allen Balcom
Emery, Albert Hamilton
Emmons, Ebenezer

Endicott, Mordecai Thomas
Evans, Anthony Walton Whyte
Ferris, George Washington Gale
Fisher, Clark
Fitch, Asa
Fuertes, Estevan Antonio
Gardiner, James Terry
Grinnell, Frederick
Hall, Fitzedward
Hall, James, 1811–1898
Horsford, Eben Norton
Houghton, Douglass
House, Samuel Reynolds
Judah, Theodore Dehone
Kay, Edgar Boyd
Knappen, Theodore Temple
Kneass, Strickland
Larrínaga, Tulio
Menocal, Aniceto Garcia
Metcalf, William
Mills, Hiram Francis
Moore, Edward Mott
Murphy, John W.
Peter, Robert
Pratt, Thomas Willis
Ricketts, Palmer Chamberlaine
Riddell, John Leonard
Roberts, George Brooke
Roebling, Washington Augustus
Rousseau, Henry Harwood
Rowland, Henry Augustus
Salisbury, James Henry
Sooysmith, Charles
Stearns, Irving Ariel
Thacher, Edwin
Thomas, Joseph
Tompkins, Daniel Augustus
Van de Warker, Edward Ely
Waddell, John Alexander Low
White, Alfred Tredway
Wickes, Stephen
Williams, Samuel Wells
Wilson, Joseph Miller

RHODE ISLAND COLLEGE (*See* BROWN UNIVERSITY)

RHODE ISLAND SCHOOL OF DESIGN
Gorky, Arshile
Homer, Arthur Bartlett

RICE UNIVERSITY
Ewing, William Maurice
Tandy, Charles David

RICHMOND COLLEGE (VA.)
Freeman, Allen Weir
Freeman, Douglas Southall
Long, Joseph Ragland
McBain, Howard Lee
Montague, Andrew Jackson

RIPON COLLEGE (WIS.)
Jones, Lewis Ralph
Tracy, Spencer Bonaventure

RIVERSIDE JUNIOR COLLEGE (CAL.)
Carlson, Chester Floyd

ROANOKE COLLEGE (VA.)
Reid, Mont Rogers

ROBERT BROOKINGS GRADUATE SCHOOL (D.C.)
Riefler, Winfield William

ROCHESTER INSTITUTE OF TECHNOLOGY (N.Y.)
Hooker, Elon Huntington

ROCHESTER THEOLOGICAL SCHOOL (MO.)
Ruckstull, Frederick Wellington

ROCHESTER THEOLOGICAL SEMINARY (N.Y.)
Anderson, Galusha
Barbour, Clarence Augustus
Behrends, Adolphus Julius Frederick
Burton, Ernest De Witt
Buttrick, Wallace
Clark, George Whitefield
Foster, George Burman
Fulton, Justin Dewey
Gates, Frederick Taylor
Genung, John Franklin
Goodspeed, Thomas Wakefield
Johnson, Elias Henry
Johnson, Mordecai Wyatt
MacArthur, Robert Stuart
Morehouse, Henry Lyman
Moss, Lemuel
Moxom, Philip Stafford
Newman, Albert Henry
Rawlinson, Frank Joseph
Stevens, George Barker
Stevens, William Arnold
Strong, Augustus Hopkins
Strong, Charles Augustus
Taylor, James Monroe
Thomas, Jesse Burgess, 1832–1915
Vedder, Henry Clay

ROCKFORD COLLEGE (ILL.)
Binford, Jessie Florence
Mussey, Ellen Spencer

ROCK RIVER SEMINARY (ILL.)
Hallett, Moses
Hitt, Robert Roberts
Ingals, Ephraim Fletcher
Jones, William Patterson
Rawlins, John Aaron
Thompson, Seymour Dwight

ROLLINS COLLEGE (FLA.)
Beach, Rex

ROSE-HULLMAN INSTITUTE OF TECHNOLOGY (IND.)
Mendenhall, Charles Elwood

ROUND HILL SCHOOL (MASS.)
Appleton, Thomas Gold
Barnes, Joseph K.
Bellows, Henry Whitney
Ellis, George Edward
Gibbs, George, 1815–1873
Hillard, George Stillman
Kearny, Philip
Lowell, Robert Traill Spence
Perkins, James Handasyd
Riggs, George Washington
Shattuck, George Cheyne, 1813–1893
Shurtleff, Nathaniel Bradstreet
Stoddard, David Tappan
Storrow, Charles Storer
Ward, Samuel
Whitney, Josiah Dwight

ROXBURY LATIN SCHOOL (MASS.)
Allen, William Francis
Baker, Harvey Humphrey
Baldwin, William Henry
Bancroft, Wilder Dwight
Bradford, Edward Hickling
Cabot, Hugh
Conant, James Bryant
Dyar, Harrison Gray
Grant, Percy Stickney
Hale, Philip Leslie
Hunt, Alfred Ephraim
McBurney, Charles
Scudder, Horace Elisha
Soley, James Russell
Sumner, Increase
Sumner, James Batcheller
Thorndike, Ashley Horace
Tobey, Charles William
Upton, George Bruce
Wheelwright, Edmund March
Williams, John, 1664–1729

ROYAL ACADEMY AT MUNICH (GERMANY)
Birch, Reginald Bathurst
Dielman, Frederick

ROYAL ACADEMY AT TAIN (SCOTLAND)
Mackenzie, Murdo

ROYAL ACADEMY OF ART IN BERLIN (GERMANY)
Feininger, Lyonel (Charles Léonell Adrian)

ROYAL ACADEMY OF DESIGN (GERMANY)
Bluemner, Oscar Florians

ROYAL ACADEMY OF DRAMATIC ARTS (ENGLAND)
Hardwicke, Cedric Webster
Laughton, Charles
Leigh, Vivien

ROYAL ACADEMY OF FINE ARTS IN MUNICH (GERMANY)
Leigh, William Robinson

ROYAL ACADEMY OF MUSIC, BERLIN (GERMANY)
Fiedler, Arthur

ROYAL ACADEMY OF MUSIC (ENGLAND)
Biggs, Edward George Power

ROYAL ACADEMY OF THEATER AND ART (HUNGARY)
Curtiz, Michael

ROYAL ARTS AND CRAFTS SCHOOL IN BERLIN (GERMANY)
Grosz, George

ROYAL CENTRAL INSTITUTE OF GYMNASTICS (SWEDEN)
Berenson, Senda

ROYAL COLLEGE OF SCIENCE, TORONTO (CANADA)
Townsend, Willard Saxby, Jr.

ROYAL CONSERVATORY OF MUSIC (BELGIUM)
Bloch, Ernest

ROYAL CONSERVATORY OF MUSIC (SPAIN)
Casals, Pablo

ROYAL HIGH SCHOOL OF MUSIC, BERLIN (GERMANY)
Lehmann, Lotte

ROYAL HUNGARIAN MEDICAL UNIVERSITY (HUNGARY)
Fejos, Paul

ROYAL HUNGARIAN UNIVERSITY (HUNGARY)
Graduate Study
Rapaport, David

Royal Institute of Technology, Stuttgart (Germany)
Strobel, Charles Louis
Royal Irish University
Kennedy, Robert Foster
O'Shaughnessy, Michael Maurice
Royal Naval College (England)
Hovgaard, William
Royal Opera School (Denmark)
Melchior, Lauritz Lebrecht Hommel
Royal Polytechnic Institute of Milan (Italy)
Faccioli, Giuseppe
Royal Polytechnic School At Stuttgart (Germany)
Elkin, William Lewis
Royal Saxon Academy of the Fine Arts in Dresden (Germany)
Grosz, George
Royal School of Mines At Freiberg (Germany)
Hammond, John Hays
Royal School of Mines (London)
Graduate Study
Webb, Harry Howard
Royal Technical College (Denmark)
Westergaard, Harald Malcolm
Royal University of Ireland
Hackett, Francis
Turner, William
Rush Medical College (Ill.)
Bevan, Arthur Dean
Brophy, Truman William
Cameron, Robert Alexander
Favill, Henry Baird
Forbes, Stephen Alfred
Graham, Evarts Ambrose
Henrotin, Fernand
Ingals, Ephraim Fletcher
Keeley, Leslie E.
Lewis, Dean De Witt
Miles, Manly
Murphy, John Benjamin
Ochsner, Albert John
Ranson, Stephen Walter
Robinson, Frederick Byron
Stephenson, Benjamin Franklin
Thorek, Max
Wells, Harry Gideon
White, Charles Abiathar
Wilder, Russell Morse
Russell's Military School (Conn.)
Bogue, Virgil Gay
Daggett, Ellsworth
Lusk, William Thompson
Penfield, Frederic Courtland
Russian Military School of Aeronautics
De Seversky, Alexander Procofieff
Russian Naval Academy
Sikorsky, Igor Ivanovich

Rutgers University (N.J.)
Blakeley, George Henry
Bogart, John
Bradley, Joseph P.
Brodhead, John Romeyn
Brown, George William
Chamberlain, Jacob
Chambers, Talbot Wilson
Cook, Albert Stanburrough
Cook, Walter Wheeler
Cooke, Robert Anderson
De Witt, Simeon
Dod, Daniel
Doty, Elihu
Drury, John Benjamin
Fairchird, David Grandison
Fiske, Haley
Fiske, Stephen Ryder
Fitch, Asa
Forsyth, John
Frelinghuysen, Frederick Theodore
Frelinghuysen, Theodore
Gaut, John McReynolds
Gilbert, Seymour Parker
Griffis, William Elliot
Hartley, Fred Allen, Jr.
Hill, George William
Hobart, Garret Augustus
Hoffman, Eugene Augustus
Janeway, Edward Gamaliel
Johnston, Alexander
Judah, Samuel
Kilmer, Alfred Joyce
Kip, William Ingraham
Lipman, Jacob Goodale
Loree, Leonor Fresnel
Nelson, Oswald George ("Ozzie")
Newell, William Augustus
Nichols, Roy Franklin
Parker, John Cortlandt
Polak, John Osborn
Pruyn, Robert Hewson
Ricord, Frederick William
Robeson, Paul Leroy
Searle, John Preston
Smith, Jeremiah, 1759–1842
Stillman, Thomas Bliss
Talmage, John Van Nest
Taylor, Graham
Thompson, John Bodine
Van Nest, Abraham Rynier
Van Wyck, Charles Henry
Voorhees, Edward Burnett
Waksman, Selman Abraham
Wilson, Peter
Wyckoff, John Henry
Graduate Study
Cooke, Robert Anderson
Loree, Leonor Fresnel
Nichols, Roy Frankliin
Waksman, Selman Abraham

St. Aloysius College (Australia)
Ritchard, Cyril
St. Anselm's College (N.H.)
Baroody, William Joseph
Rummel, Joseph Francis
St. Bernard Seminary (N.Y.)
Hurley, Joseph Patrick

St. Bonaventure College (N.Y.)
Dietz, Peter Ernest
Walsh, Thomas Joseph
Graduate Study
Walsh, Thomas Joseph
St. Charles Borromeo Seminary (Pa.)
Brennan, Francis James
Guilday, Peter Keenan
St. Charles College (Md.)
Cooper, John Montgomery
Garrigan, Philip Joseph
Gibbons, James
Gillis, James Martin
Keane, John Joseph
O'Connell, William Henry
Pace, Edward Aloysius
Price, Thomas Frederick
Sterling, George
St. Charles Seminary (Pa.)
Dougherty, Dennis Joseph
St. Francis College (Pa.)
Stokes, Maurice
St. Francis Seminary (Wis.)
Haas, Francis Joseph
Kerby, William Joseph
St. Francis Seraphic College (Ohio)
Daeger, Albert Thomas
Engelhardt, Zephyrin
St. Francis Xavier College (N.Y.)
Burke, John Joseph
Dietz, Peter Ernest
Ross, Thomas Joseph
Walker, James John
Graduate Study
O'Brien, Morgan Joseph
St. Gregory's Preparatory Seminary (Ohio)
Stritch, Samuel Alphonsus
St. Ignatius College (Ill.)
McCoy, Tim
St. Johnsbury Academy (Vt.)
Coolidge, Calvin
Fairbanks, Henry
Gates, George Augustus
Lloyd, Alfred Henry
Parker, Edwin Wallace
Russell, Charles Edward
St. John's College (La.)
Harahan, William Johnson
St. John's College (Md.)
Alexander, John Henry
Brereton, Lewis Hyde
Chester, Colby Mitchell
Councilman, William Thomas
Davidge, John Beale
Gibson, William
Hanson, Alexander Contee, 1785–1819
Hoffman, David
Johnson, Reverdy
Key, Francis Scott
Lockwood, James Booth
Lomax, John Tayloe
Mullan, John
Pinkney, Ninian
Randall, Burton Alexander
Randall, Wyatt William

Shaw, John, 1778–1809
Thomas, Francis
Turner, Edward Raymond
Will, Allen Sinclair
Wilson, Clarence True
ST. JOHN'S COLLEGE (*See* FORDHAM UNIVERSITY)
ST. JOHN'S SEMINARY (MASS.)
Cushing, Richard James
Dowling, Austin
Gillis, James Martin
Walsh, James Anthony
Wright, John Joseph
ST. JOHN'S UNIVERSITY (MINN.)
Michel, Virgil George
Graduate Study
Michel, Virgil George
ST. JOHN'S UNIVERSITY (N.Y.)
Law
Curran, Thomas Jerome
Lyons, Leonard
ST. JOHN'S UNIVERSITY (OHIO)
Johnson, George
ST. JOSEPH'S COLLEGE (AUSTRALIA)
Errol, Leon
ST. JOSEPH'S COLLEGE (IND.)
Hodges, Gilbert Ray
Krupa, Eugene Bertram ("Gene")
ST. JOSEPH'S COLLEGE (KY.)
Clay, Cassius Marcellus
Garland, Augustus Hill
Holt, Joseph
Johnson, Robert Ward
McGill, John
O'Hara, Theodore
Powell, Lazarus Whitehead
Preston, William
Speed, James
Wells, James Madison
Wickliffe, Robert Charles
ST. JOSEPH'S COLLEGE (PA.)
Breen, Joseph Ignatius
Green, William Joseph, Jr.
ST. JOSEPH'S PROVINCIAL SEMINARY (N.Y.)
Hayes, Patrick Joseph
ST. JOSEPH'S SEMINARY (N.Y.)
Rummel, Joseph Francis
McIntyre, James Francis Aloysius
ST. LAWRENCE COLLEGE (WIS.)
Noll, John Francis
ST. LAWRENCE UNIVERSITY (N.Y.)
Bacheller, Irving
Gunnison, Foster
Heaton, John Langdon
Lee, Frederic Schiller
Saypol, Irving Howard
Young, Owen D.
Graduate Study
Lee, Frederic Schiller
ST. LOUIS UNIVERSITY (MO.)
Blow, Henry Taylor
Coleman, William Tell
Cooper, Elias Samuel
Coppens, Charles
Finn, Francis James
Ludeling, John Theodore
Pallen, Condé Benoist
Reedy, William Marion
Russell, Irwin
Snyder, John Francis
Stettinius, Edward Riley
Taussig, William
Dentistry
Hunt, Lester Callaway
Law
Hannegan, Robert Emmet
Medicine
Dooley, Thomas Anthony, III
ST. MARKS SCHOOL (MASS.)
Dilworth, Richardson
Duane, Alexander
Lowell, Robert Traill Spence, Jr.
Mather, Samuel, 1851–1931
Morgan, Morris Hicky
ST. MARY'S COLLEGE (CAL.)
Heilmann, Harry
Hooper, Harry Bartholomew
ST. MARY'S COLLEGE (IND.)
Gore, Robert Hayes
ST. MARY'S COLLEGE (KS.)
Budenz, Louis Francis
ST. MARY'S COLLEGE (KY.)
Morrow, Edwin Porch
ST. MARY'S COLLEGE (MD.)
Baxley, Henry Willis
Bowie, Oden
Bradford, Augustus Williamson
Buckler, Thomas Hepburn
Caffery, Donelson
Chanche, John Mary Joseph
Churchill, Thomas James
Corrigan, Michael Augustine
De Lacy, Walter Washington
Dornin, Thomas Aloysius
Fisher, George Purnell
Gibbons, James
Graves, Rosewell Hobart
Hambleton, Thomas Edward
Hays, Harry Thompson
Kavanagh, Edward
Knott, Aloysius Leo
La Barge, Joseph
Latrobe, Benjamin Henry
Latrobe, Charles Hazlehurst
Latrobe, John Hazlehurst Boneval
Logan, Cornelius Ambrosius, 1806–1853
McGivney, Michael Joseph
Mayer, Alfred Marshall
Mayer, Brantz
Meade, Richard Worsam, 1807–1870
Norris, William
Pinkney, Edward Coote
Rogers, Henry J.
Roman, André Bienvenu
Smith, James, 1851–1927
Spalding, John Lancaster
Spalding, Martin John
Tappan, Eli Todd
Wallis, Severn Teackle
ST. MARY'S COLLEGE (PA.)
Dietz, Peter Ernest
ST. MARY'S SEMINARY (MD.)
Chapelle, Placide Louis
Curtis, Alfred Allen
Dietz, Peter Ernest
Keane, John Joseph
Portier, Michael
Price, Thomas Frederick
Shields, Thomas Edward
Tabb, John Banister
Walsh, Robert
Yorke, Peter Christopher
ST. MARY'S SEMINARY (OHIO)
Hurley, Joseph Patrick
ST. MARY'S UNIVERSITY (MD.)
Grady, Henry Francis
ST. MATTHEW'S COLLEGE (CAL.)
Whitney, Caspar
ST. MEINRAD COLLEGE (IND.)
Ritter, Joseph Elmer
ST. MEINRAD SCHOOL OF THEOLOGY (IND.)
Ritter, Joseph Elmer
ST. MICHAEL'S COLLEGE (CANADA)
Coughlin, Charles Edward
ST. OLAF COLLEGE (MINN.)
Lawrence, Ernest Orlando
Volstead, Andrew John
ST. PAUL COLLEGE OF LAW (MINN.)
Schall, Thomas David
Swift, Linton Bishop
ST. PAUL SEMINARY (MINN.)
Ryan, John Augustine
Sheen, Fulton John
ST. PAUL'S SCHOOL (N.H.)
Bohlen, Charles Eustis ("Chip")
Bonsal, Stephen
Brown, William Adams
Chapman, John Jay
Chapman, Victor Emmanuel
Crawford, Francis Marion
Engelhard, Charles William
Fisher, Sydney George
Garfield, Harry Augustus
Hearst, William Randolph
Hoyt, John Sherman
Kirtin, Joseph Louis Jerome
Leiter, Joseph
Marquand, Allan
Mitchell, Langdon Elwyn
Morison, Samuel Eliot
Mumford, James Gregory
Nicoll, De Lancey
Norton, William Warder
Porter, Holbrook Fitz-John
Saltus, Edgar Evertson
Shattuck, George Brune
Thayer, William Roscoe
Thornton, Henry Worth
ST. PETERSBURG CONSERVATORY (RUSSIA)
Kostelanetz, Andre
Tiomkin, Dimitri
ST. PETERSBURG JUNIOR COLLEGE (FLA.)
Morrison, Jim
ST. PETERSBURG UNIVERSITY (RUSSIA)
Stravinsky, Igor Fyodorovich
Vasiliev, Alexander Alexandrovich
Graduate Study
Vasiliev, Alexander Alexandrovich
ST. PETER'S COLLEGE (N.J.)
Tumulty, Joseph Patrick

St. Stephen's Normal Training School (Va.)
Russell, James Solomon
St. Viator's College (Ill.)
Sheen, Fulton John
Sheil, Bernard James
St. Viator's Seminary (Ill.)
Sheen, Fulton John
Sheil, Bernard James
St. Vincent's College (Pa.)
Curran, John Joseph
Flick, Lawrence Francis
Ganss, Henry George
Lambert, Louis Aloisius
McFaul, James Augustine
Ramsay, Erskine
Stehle, Aurelius Aloysius
Wolf, Innocent William
St. Vincent Seminary (Pa.)
Hodur, Francis
Judge, Thomas Augustine
Mundelein, George William
St. Xavier College (N.Y.)
Ross, Thomas Joseph
St. Xavier College (Ohio)
Browne, Junius Henri
Budenz, Louis Francis
Hickenlooper, Andrew
Piatt, Donn
Pugh, George Ellis
Rigge, William Francis
Ste. Barbe College (France)
Behn, Sosthenes
Sainte-Marie College (Canada)
Dougherty, Dennis Joseph
Salado College (Tex.)
Ferguson, Miriam Amanda Wallace
Salem Collegiate Institute (N.J.)
Baldwin, James Mark
Salem Latin School (Mass.)
Adams, Nehemiah
Brooks, Charles Timothy
Dodge, Ebenezer
Endicott, William Crowninshield
Rogers, William Crowninshield
Williams, Henry Willard
Salt Lake College (Utah)
Allen, Florence Ellinwood
San Francisco Normal School (Cal.)
Regan, Agnes Gertrude
San Joaquin Valley College (Cal.)
Wilson, Clarence True
Santa Clara College (Cal.)
Carleton, Henry Guy
Delmas, Delphin Michael
Hubbard, Bernard Rosecrans
Smith, James Francis
White, Stephen Mallory
Santa Clara University (Cal.)
Devine, Andrew ("Andy")
McClatchy, Charles Kenny
Santa Monica College (Cal.)
Burdick, Eugene Leonard
Santa Rosa Junior College
Nevers, Ernest Alonzo ("Ernie")
Scarritt-Morrisville College (Tenn.)
Alexander, Will Winton
School of Engineering and Navigation (England)
Hitchcock, Alfred Joseph
School of Fine and Applied Art (N.Y.)
Gropper, William
School of Fine Arts (D.C.)
Williams, Fannie Barrier
School of Industrial Art of the Pennsylvania Museum
Yellin, Samuel
School of Modern Painting, Moscow (Russia)
Aronson, Boris Solomon
School of Philanthropy (N.Y.)
Dreier, Mary Elisabeth
School of the Theater, Kiev (Russia)
Aronson, Boris Solomon
Schola Cantorum (France)
Niles, John Jacob
Scio College (Ohio)
Akeley, Mary Leonore
Seabury-Western Theological Seminary (Ill.)
Watts, Alan Wilson
Seneca Collegiate Institute (N.Y.)
Alden, Isabella Macdonald
Seton Hall College (N.J.)
Barrymore, John
Keating, John Marie
Kelley, James Douglas Jerrold
McFaul, James Augustine
Messmer, Sebastian Gebhard
Walsh, Raoul (?)
Wigger, Winand Michael
Seward Institute (N.Y.)
Baker, George Fisher
Shaw University (N.C.)
Shepard, James Edward
Yergan, Max
Law
Johnson, Edward Austin
Sherwood School of Music (Ill.)
Mesta, Perle Reid Skirvin
Shurtleff College (Ill.)
Applegate, Jesse
Coghill, George Ellett
Loveland, William Austin Hamilton
McAdams, Clark
Moxom, Philip Stafford
Palmer, John McAuley
Sherwood, Thomas Adiel
Simmons College (Mass.)
Peck, Lillie
Simpson College (Iowa)
Carver, George Washington
Mott, Frank Luther
Smith College (Mass.)
Bailey, Florence Augusta Merriam
Binford, Jessie Florence
Bryant, Louise Frances Stevens
Calkins, Mary Whiton
Cushman, Vera Charlotte Scott
Eckstorm, Fannie Hardy
Gill, Laura Drake
Green, Constance McLaughlin
Hawes, Harriet Ann Boyd
Irwin, Elisabeth Antoinette
Littledale, Clara Savage
Norton, Mary Alice Peloubet
Plath, Sylvia
Prouty, Olive Higgins
Rogers, Mary Josephine
Sabin, Florence Rena
Scudder, (Julia) Vida Dutton
Smith, Theodate Louise
Wood, Edith Elmer
Graduate Study
Calkins, Mary Whiton
Scudder, (Julia) Vida Dutton
Sorbonne (France)
Babbitt, Irving
Boyer, Charles
Carr, John Dickson
Clurman, Harold Edgar
Eliot, T(homas) S(tearns)
Elliott, William Yandell, III
Halsman, Philippe
King, Alexander
Lingelbach, Anna Lane
Morawetz, Victor
Nabokov, Nicolas
Reed, Stanley Forman
Skinner, Cornelia Otis
Van de Graaff, Robert Jemison
Znaniecki, Florian Witold
Graduate Study
Liebling, Abbott Joseph
Lovejoy, Arthur Oncken
Kallen, Horace Meyer
Marsh, Frank Burr
Sheen, Fulton John
Steffens, Lincoln
Wheeler, (George) Post
South Berwick Academy (Maine)
Goodwin, Daniel Raynes
Goodwin, Ichabod
Hayes, John Lord
Lord, John
Lord, Nathan
Tripp, Guy Eastman
South Carolina College (*See* University of South Carolina)
South Carolina Medical College
Bratton, John
Gaillard, Edwin Samuel
Gaston, James McFadden
La Borde, Maximilian
Mackey, Albert Gallatin
Michael, William Middleton
Moore, Samuel Preston
South Carolina Military Institute
Capers, Ellison
Coker, James Lide
Ferguson, Thomas Barker
Jenkins, Micah
Southeast Alabama Agricultural School
Steagall, Henry Bascom
Southeastern Louisiana College
Evans, William John ("Bill")
Southern Baptist Theological Seminary (Ky.)
Coghill, George Ellett
Lyon, David Gordon

McGlothlin, William Joseph
Newton, Joseph Fort
Norris, John Franklyn
Riley, William Bell
Scarborough, Lee Rutland
SOUTHERN BAPTIST THEOLOGICAL SEMINARY (S.C.)
Newman, Albert Henry
SOUTHERN ILLINOIS TEACHERS COLLEGE
Hodge, John Reed
SOUTHERN ILLINOIS UNIVERSITY
Jones, Wesley Livsey
SOUTHERN METHODIST UNIVERSITY (TEX.)
Pool, Joe Richard
SOUTHERN NORMAL COLLEGE (TENN.)
Stribling, Thomas Sigismund
SOUTHERN NORMAL UNIVERSITY LAW SCHOOL (TENN.)
May, Andrew Jackson
SOUTHERN UNIVERSITY (ALA.)
Heflin, James Thomas
Hobson, Richmond Pearson
SOUTH SIDE HOSPITAL TRAINING SCHOOL FOR NURSES (PA.)
Blanchfield, Florence Aby
SOUTHWESTERN PRESBYTERIAN UNIVERSITY (TENN.)
Dinwiddie, Courtenay
Gregory, Thomas Watt
Pittman, Key
SOUTHWESTERN UNIVERSITY (TEX.)
Dobie, J(ames) Frank
Jones, John Marvin
SOUTHWEST MISSOURI STATE TEACHERS COLLEGE
Hoagland, Charles Lee
SOUTHWEST TEXAS STATE TEACHERS COLLEGE
Johnson, Lyndon Baines
SPELMAN COLLEGE (GA.)
Robinson, Ruby Doris Smith
SPOKANE UNIVERSITY
Still, Clyfford
SPRINGFIELD TRAINING COLLEGE (MASS.)
Yergan, Max
SPRING GARDEN INSTITUTE (N.J.)
Shinn, Everett
SPRING HILL COLLEGE (ALA.)
Bermudez, Edouard Edmond
Gordon, William Fitzhugh
McEnery, Samuel Douglas
Morphy, Paul Charles
STANFORD UNIVERSITY (CAL.)
Andrews, Bert
Bell, Eric Temple
Bickel, Karl August
Binkley, Robert Cedric
Blichfeldt, Hans Frederik
Bliven, Bruce Ormsby
Burdick, Eugene Leonard
Burk, Frederic Lister
Chandler, Norman
Davis, Norman Hezekiah
Hammond, Bray
Hansen, William Webster
Harkins, William Draper
Hayden, Carl Trumbull
Hoagland, Dennis Robert
Hoover, Herbert Clark
Hoover, Herbert Clark, Jr.
Humphries, George Rolfe
Irwin, William Henry
Kimball, Dexter Simpson
Knight, Goodwin Jess ("Goodie")
Kuykendall, Ralph Simpson
Little, William Lawson, Jr.
McCulloch, Robert Paxton
McNary, Charles Linza
Martin, Anne Henrietta
Metcalf, Lee Warren
Nevers, Ernest Alonzo ("Ernie")
Nordhoff, Charles Bernard
Otis, Arthur Sinton
Perry, Clarence Arthur
Rose, Walter Malins
Snow, William Freeman
Starks, Edwin Chapin
Steinbeck, John Ernst, Jr.
Suzzallo, Henry
Teggart, Frederick John
Wilbur, Ray Lyman
Winslow, Ola Elizabeth
Wrigley, Philip Knight
Graduate Study
Anderson, Maxwell
Binkley, Robert Cedric
Blichfeldt, Hans Frederik
Hansen, William Webster
Harkins, William Draper
Kefauver, Grayson Neikirk
Otis, Arthur Sinton
Snow, William Freeman
Wilbur, Ray Lyman
Winslow, Ola Elizabeth
Medicine
Hinkle, Beatrice Moses
STATE HIGHER ARTS AND TECHNOLOGY WORKSHOPS, MOSCOW (RUSSIA)
Chaliapin, Boris Fyodorovich
STATE NORMAL SCHOOL, FARMINGTON (MAINE)
Stevens, John Frank
STATE NORMAL SCHOOL AT CALIFORNIA (PA.)
Wilson, Louis Blanchard
STATE NORMAL SCHOOL AT FREDONIA (N.Y.)
McGraw, James Herbert
STATE NORMAL SCHOOL (ILL.)
Brown, Elmer Ellsworth
STATE NORMAL SCHOOL IN KIRKSVILLE (MO.)
Pershing, John Joseph
STATE NORMAL SCHOOL IN WARRENSBURG (MO.)
MacCurdy, George Grant
STATE NORMAL SCHOOL (MASS.)
Brown, Charlotte Hawkins
STATE NORMAL SCHOOL (WIS.)
Ritter, William Emerson
STATE TEACHERS COLLEGE (ARIZ.)
McClintock, James Harvey
STATE TEACHERS COLLEGE AT ADA (OKLA.)
Waner, Paul Glee
STATE TEACHERS COLLEGE AT WARRENSBURG (MO.)
Carnegie, Dale
STATE UNIVERSITY OF IOWA
Benson, Oscar Herman
Merriam, Charles Edward, Jr.
Law
Hyde, Arthur Mastick
STATE UNIVERSITY OF KENTUCKY
Morgan, Thomas Hunt
STAUNTON MILITARY ACADEMY (VA.)
Giles, Warren Crandell
Ohs, Phil
STETSON UNIVERSITY (FLA.)
Geiger, Roy Stanley
Kalmus, Natalie Mabelle Dunfee
STEPHENS COLLEGE (MO.)
Crawford, Joan
Mitchell, Martha Elizabeth Beall
STEVENS INSTITUTE OF TECHNOLOGY (N.J.)
Ayres, Brown
Bristol, William Henry
Calder, Alexander
De Palma, Ralph
Gantt, Henry Laurence
Gibbs, George
Herring, Augustus Moore
Hewitt, Peter Cooper
Hoxie, William Dixie
Humphreys, Alexander Crombie
Kent, William
Klein, August Clarence
Leavitt, Frank McDowell
Lieb, John William
Marin, John (Cheri)
Mayor, Alfred Goldsborough
Mortimer, Charles Greenough
Mott, Charles Stewart
Rice, Richard Henry
Stanley, Robert Crooks
STOCKHOLM UNIVERSITY (SWEDEN)
Schmidt, Nathaniel
STOCKTON BUSINESS COLLEGE (CAL.)
Ashurst, Henry Fountain
STRASBOURG CONSERVATORY (GERMANY)
Ganz, Rudolph
STUTTGART CONSERVATORY (GERMANY)
Nabokov, Nicolas
SUFFIELD SCHOOL (CONN.)
Andrews, Elisha Benjamin
Brockett, Linus Pierpont
French, Edwin Davis
Weeden, William Babock
SULLINS COLLEGE (VA.)
Sullavan, Margaret
SUL ROSS STATE COLLEGE (TEXAS)
Blocker, Dan
SWARTHMORE COLLEGE
Bronk, Detlev Wulf
Clothier, William Jackson
Gordon, Kermit
Grundy, Joseph Ridgway
Kintner, Robert Edmonds
Lewis, Lloyd Downs
Linton, Ralph
Palmer, Alexander Mitchell

Paul, Alice
Pearson, Drew
Pyle, Robert
Richards, John Kelvey
Smyth, Herbert Weir
Sproul, William Cameron
SWISS FEDERAL POLYTECHNIC INSTITUTE IN ZURICH
Ammann, Othmar Hermann
SWISS INSTITUTE OF TECHNOLOGY
Piccard, Jean Felix
SYDNEY UNIVERSITY (AUSTRALIA)
Errol, Leon
SYRACUSE UNIVERSITY
Babcock, Howard Edward
Babcock, Maltbie Davenport
Brokenshire, Norman Ernest
Collins, Guy N.
Davis, Ernest R. ("Ernie")
Dolph, Joseph Norton
Farman, Elbert Eli
Fowler, Charles Henry
Haviland, Clarence Floyd
Hopkins, Miriam
Jackson, Charles Reginald
Jackson, Shirley Hardie
Kelly, Luther Sage
Kidder, Daniel Parish
Lockwood, Belva Bennett
Lozier, Clemence Sophia Harned
Maclay, Edgar Stanton
Morehouse, Henry Lyman
Noss, Theodore Bland
Ranger, Henry Ward
Raymond, Henry Jarvis
Smith, David Eugene
Steele, Joel Dorman
Thomas, Amos Russell
Thompson, Dorothy
Tomlin, Bradley Walker
Underwood, Lucien Marcus
Wilder, Alexander
Williams, Frank Martin
Graduate Study
Brokenshire, Norman Ernest
Fall, Bernard B.
Smith, David Eugene

TABOR COLLEGE (IOWA)
Simmons, George Henry
TALLADEGA COLLEGE (ALA.)
Pickens, William
TARKIO COLLEGE (MO.)
Carothers, Wallace Hume
TEACHERS COLLEGE, COLUMBIA UNIVERSITY (N.Y.)
Antin, Mary
Ayres, Leonard Porter
Cubberley, Ellwood Patterson
Dingman, Mary Agnes
Gray, William Scott, Jr.
Harshe, Robert Bartholow
Jessup, Walter Albert
Kirkus, Virginia
Moskowitz, Belle Lindner Israels
Newlon, Jesse Homer
Powell, Adam Clayton, Jr.
Rose, Mary Davies Swartz
Graduate Study
Hollingworth, Leta Stetter
Payne, Bruce Ryburn

TECHNICAL UNIVERSITY IN AACHEN (GERMANY)
Debye, Peter Joseph William
Graduate Study
Debye, Peter Joseph William
TECHNICAL UNIVERSITY OF KARLSRUHE (GERMANY)
Harkins, William Draper
TECHNISCHE HOCHSCHULE, VIENNA (AUSTRIA)
Lang, Fritz
Neutra, Richard Joseph
TECHNISCHE HOCHSCHULE IN BERLIN (GERMANY)
Mendelsohn, Erich (or Eric)
TECHNISCHE HOCHSCHULE IN DRESDEN (GERMANY)
Halsman, Philippe
TECHNISCHE HOCHSCHULE IN MUNICH (GERMANY)
Mott, Charles Stewart
TECHNISCHE HOCHSCHULE IN STUTTGART (GERMANY)
Reichenbach, Hans
TECHNISCHE HOCHSCHULE IN ZURICH (SWITZERLAND)
Graduate Study
Von Neumann, John
TEMPLE UNIVERSITY
McKinley, Albert Edward
Tauber, Maurice Falcolm
Law
McGranery, James Patrick
TENNESEE A. & M. COLLEGE
Kelly, Machine Gun (George Kelly Barnes, Jr.)
TENNESSEE WESLEYAN COLLEGE
Raulston, John Tate
TEXAS AGRICULTURAL AND MECHANICAL COLLEGE
Burleson, Albert Sidney
Mills, Charles Wright
Moser, Christopher Otto
Neyland, Robert Reese, Jr.
TEXAS CHRISTIAN UNIVERSITY
O'Brien, Robert David ("Davey")
Tandy, Charles David
TEXAS COLLEGE OF MINES
Marshall, Samuel Lyman Atwood ("Slam")
TEXAS SCHOOL OF FINE ARTS
Reese, Heloise Bowles
TEXAS TECHNOLOGICAL UNIVERSITY
Thornton, Daniel I.J.
THEOLOGICAL SEMINARY OF THE ECUMENICAL PATRIARCHATE (TURKEY)
Athenagoras I
THEOLOGICAL SEMINARY OF THE REFORMED CHURCH IN AMERICA (N.J.)
Taylor, Graham
THEOLOGICAL SEMINARY OF VIRGINIA
Kip, William Ingraham
Lay, Henry Champlin
Perry, William Stevens
Peterkin, George William
Randolph, Alfred Magill
Savage, Thomas Staughton

Slaughter, Philip
Tucker, Henry St. George
Williams, Channing Moore
Wilmer, Joseph Père Bell
Wilmer, Richard Hooker
THETFORD ACADEMY (VT.)
Eaton, John
Leavitt, Mary Greenleaf Clement
Perry, Arthur Latham
Slafter, Edmund Farwell
TORONTO CONSERVATORY OF MUSIC (CANADA)
Faith, Percy
TRANSYLVANIA COLLEGE (KY.)
Allen, James Lane
Atchison, David Rice
Austin, Stephen Fuller
Birney, James Gillespie
Blair, Francis Preston, 1791–1876
Bogy, Lewis Vital
Breckinridge, John Cabell
Brown, Benjamin Gratz
Buchanan, Joseph
Butler, William Orlando
Cameron, Archibald
Chambers, John
Clay, Cassius Marcellus
Connelly, Henry
Cooke, Henry David
Crittenden, George Bibb
Davis, Jefferson
Espy, James Pollard
Ford, Thomas
Fosdick, William Whiteman
Fox, John William
Goodloe, William Cassius
Green, Lewis Warner
Hardin, John J.
Hardin, Martin D.
Hise, Elijah
Humphreys, West Hughes
Johnston, Josiah Stoddard
Jones, George Wallace
Kellogg, Albert
Kerr, John Glasgow
Langdon, William Chauncey
McAfee, Robert Breckinridge
Mason, Stevens Thomson, 1811–1843
Monette, John Wesley
Morehead, Charles Slaughter
Morehead, James Turner
Morrow, Thomas Vaughan
Peers, Benjamin Orrs
Pope, Nathaniel
Powell, Lazarus Whitehead
Powell, William Byrd
Robertson, George
Sayre, Lewis Albert
Shannon, Wilson
Shelby, Joseph Orville
Short, Charles Wilkins
Todd, Charles Stewart
Turner, Edward
Underwood, Joseph Rogers
Vest, George Graham
Waldo, David
Whitcomb, James
Law
Allen, Thomas M.
Barry, William Taylor

Blair, Francis Preston, 1821–1876
Blair, Montgomery
Boyle, Jeremiah Tilford
Churchill, Thomas James
Clemens, Jeremiah
Donelson, Andrew Jackson
Duke, Basil Wilson
Edwards, Minian Wirt
Harlan, John Marshall
Harrison, Carter Henry
Long, Crawford Williamson
McConnel, John Ludlum
Magoffin, Beriah
Morehead, Charles Slaughter
Norton, Elijah Hise
Rollins, James Sidney
Rose, Uriah Milton
Simms, William Elliott
Speed, James
Yates, Richard
Medicine
Blackburn, Luke Pryor
Chivers, Thomas Holley
Gwin, William McKendree
Hall, William Whitty
Lawson, Leonidas Merion
Metcalfe, Samuel Lytler
Miller, Henry, 1800–1874
Miller, Samuel Freeman
Peter, Robert
Robertson, Jerome Bonaparte
Toland, Hugh Huger
Yandell, Lunsford Pitts
TRANSYLVANIA COLLEGE (VA.)
Ainslie, Peter
TRENTON ACADEMY (N.J.)
Abbott, Benjamin Vaughan
Fisher, Clark
Gummere, Samuel René
Roebling, Washington Augustus
Welling, James Clarke
TRINITY COLLEGE (CANADA)
Brent, Charles Henry
TRINITY COLLECE (CONN.)
Andrews, Charles McLean
Armstrong, David Maitland
Ashe, William Shepperd
Barbour, Henry Gray
Barthelmess, Richard
Bayley, James Roosevelt
Beardsley, Eben Edwards
Benjamin, Park, 1809–1864
Bowie, William
Bradley, Charles William
Buck, Dudley
Burton, Richard Eugene
Cheshire, Joseph Blount
Clement, Martin Withington
Crary, Isaac Edwin
Douglass, Andrew Ellicott
Ferguson, Samuel
Fisher, Sydney George
Flagg, Jared Bradley
Gallaudet, Edward Miner
Gallaudet, Thomas
Gilman, Arthur Delevan
Goddard, Paul Beck
Hart, Samuel
Nichols, William Ford
Nies, James Buchanan
Paddock, Benjamin Henry
Paddock, John Adams
Phelps, John Smith
Preston, Thomas Scott
Purdy, Lawson
Pynchon, Thomas Ruggles
Riggs, John Mankey
Sanford, Henry Shelton
Smith, Buckingham
Southard, Lucien H.
Thurber, Christopher Carson
Williams, John, 1817–1899
Graduate Study
Purdy, Lawson
TRINITY COLLEGE (N.C.)
Jordan, Benjamin Everett
Reynolds, William Neal
TRI-STATE COLLEGE (IND.)
Hershey, Lewis Blaine
TROY FEMALE ACADEMY (N.Y.)
Rohlfs, Anna Katharine Green
TROY FEMALE SEMINARY (N.Y.)
Cooper, Sarah Brown Ingersoll
Davidson, Lucretia Maria
Lewis, Estelle Anna Blanche Robinson
Moulton, Ellen Louise Chandler
Phelps, Almira Hart Lincoln
Rambaut, Mary Lucinda Bonney
Sage, Margaret Olivia Slocum
Smith, Erminnie Adelle Platt
Stanton, Elizabeth Cady
TUFTS UNIVERSITY (MASS.)
Adams, John Coleman
Babcock, Stephen Moulton
Bush, Vannevar ("Van")
Capen, Elmer Hewitt
Capen, Samuel Paul
Clement, Edward Henry
Ginn, Edwin
Lamb, Arthur Becket
Lewis, Orlando Faulkland
Pearce, Richard Mills
Pearson, Fred Stark
Rorty, James Hancock
Warren, Minton
Whittemore, Thomas
Wiener, Norbert
Wiggin, James Henry
Wright, Philip Green
Graduate Study
Bush, Vannevar ("Van")
Lamb, Arthur Becket
Medicine
Brunswick, Ruth Mack
Coriat, Isador Henry
Myerson, Abraham
TULANE UNIVERSITY (LA.)
Basso, (Joseph) Hamilton
Behan, William James
Boggs, Thomas Hale
Breaux, Joseph Arsenne
Caffery, Jefferson
Cahn, Edmond Nathaniel
Ellender, Allen Joseph
Farrar, Edgar Howard
Foster, Murphy James
Hall, Luther Egbert
Harris, Nathaniel Harrison
Hébert, Felix Edward ("Eddie")
Levy, Gustave Lehman
Lynch, Robert Clyde
Matas, Rudolph
Rice, John Andrew
Toulmin, Harry Theophilus
Vaughan, Thomas Wayland
Law
Bermudez, Edouard Edmond
Blanchard, Newton Crain
Boggs, Thomas Hale
Cahn, Edmond Nathaniel
Ellender, Allen Joseph
Fenner, Charles Erasmus
Gibson, Randall Lee
Hahn, Georg Michael Decker
Hunt, Carleton
Long, Huey Pierce
Lyman, Joseph Bardwell
Morphy, Paul Charles
Perez, Leander Henry
Provosty, Olivier Otis
Medicine
Dyer, Isadore
Handerson, Henry Ebenezer
Hatcher, Robert Anthony
Lynch, Robert Clyde
Riddell, John Leonard
Souchon, Edmond
TUSKEGEE INSTITUTE (ALA.)
Hobson, Julius Wilson
James, Daniel, Jr. ("Chappie")
Simmons, Roscoe Conkling Murray

UNION BAPTIST THEOLOGICAL SEMINARY (LA.)
Davis, Abraham Lincoln, Jr.
UNION COLLEGE (KY.)
Anderson, Victor Vance
UNION COLLEGE (N.Y.)
Alden, Joseph
Alexander, Stephen
Allen, David Oliver
Allen, Thomas
Allis, Edward Phelps
Andrews, Sherlock James
Arnold, Lauren Briggs
Arthur, Chester Alan
Baker, Walter Ransom Gail
Baldwin, Frank Stephen
Bayard, James Asheton, 1799–1880
Beall, Samuel Wootton
Beck, Lewis Caleb
Beck, Theodric Romeyn
Bellamy, Edward
Benjamin, George Hillard
Bigelow, John
Blair, Austin
Blatchford, Richard Milford
Blood, Benjamin Paul
Bradford, Alexander Warfield
Breckinridge, Robert Jefferson
Breese, Sidney
Brooks, James Gordon
Brooks, Thomas Benton
Brownell, Thomas Church
Butterfield, Daniel
Campbell, William W.
Carey, Joseph Maull
Cary, Edward
Cassidy, William
Cavert, Samuel McCrea

Cochrane, John
Comstock, George Franklin
Conkling, Alfred
Dean, Amos
Doane, George Washington
Duane, Alexander
Duane, James Chatham
Edmonds, John Worth
Ellis, Job Bicknell
Flint, Weston
Forman, Joshua
Fuller, Robert Mason
Gale, George Washington
Genung, John Franklin
Giddings, Franklin Henry
Gilbert, Eliphalet Wheeler
Goodwin, Hannibal Williston
Gregory, John Milton
Hall, Baynard Rush
Halleck, Henry Wager
Hamilton, Frank Hastings
Hare, George Emlen
Harris, Ira
Hartranft, John Frederick
Hawley, Gideon, 1785–1870
Headley, Joel Tyler
Hickok, Laurens Perseus
Hoff, John Van Rensselaer
Hoffman, John Thompson
Holcombe, Chester
Hough, Franklin Benjamin
Hough, George Washington
House, Samuel Reynolds
Hunt, Ward
Jackson, Edward
Jackson, Sheldon
James, Henry, 1811–1882
Jenkins, Charles Jones
Johnson, Benjamin Pierce
King, Preston
Knapp, Seaman Asahel
Lamont, Daniel Scott
Landon, Milville de Lancey
Lane, Levi Cooper
Lewis, Tayler
Littlejohn, Abram Newkirk
Ludlow, Fitz Hugh
McAuley, Thomas
McLeod, Alexander
McMaster, James Alphonsus
Mattoon, Stephen
Miller, Warner
Morgan, Lewis Henry
Morton, Julius Sterling
Murray, David
Nevin, John Williamson
Nevius, John Livingston
Nott, Charles Cooper
Paddock, Algernon Sidney
Park, Roswell, 1807–1869
Parker, Amasa Junius
Parry, Charles Christopher
Patterson, Robert Porter
Peck, Charles Horton
Peckham, Wheeler Hazard
Perry, Stuart
Perry, William
Pierson, Hamilton Wilcox
Potter, Alonzo
Potter, Eliphalet Nott
Potter, Horatio
Potter, Robert Brown
Price, Joseph
Prime, Edward Dorr Griffin
Randall, Henry Stephens
Rankine, William Birch
Raymond, John Howard
Reid, William Wharry
Rice, Alexander Hamilton
Rice, Edwin Wilbur
Ripley, Edward Hastings
Robertson, William Schenck
Salisbury, James Henry
Schell, Augustus
Schoolcraft, Henry Rowe
Sears, Edmund Hamilton
Seward, Frederick William
Seward, George Frederick
Seward, William Henry
Sherwood, Adiel
Smith, Charles Emory
Snow, Jessie Baker
Spencer, John Canfield
Sprague, Charles Ezra
Staley, Cady
Stillman, William James
Stone, John Seely
Streeter, George Linius
Tappan, Henry Philip
Taylor, John W.
Thomas, John Wilson
Toombs, Robert Augustus
Townsend, Robert
Tuckerman, Edward
Van de Warker, Edward Ely
Van Santvoord, George
Walworth, Clarence Augustus
Wayland, Francis, 1796–1865
Westinghouse, George
Whipple, Squire
White, Albert Smith
Whitsitt, William Heth
Wickes, Stephen
Wikoff, Henry
Wilkie, Franc Bangs
Wilson, John Leighton
Wood, James, 1799–1867
Woods, Leonard, 1807–1878
UNION COLLEGE OF LAW (ILL.)
Copley, Ira Clifton
Landis, Kenesaw Mountain
Lowden, Frank Orren
Rainey, Henry Thomas
UNION THEOLOGICAL SEMINARY (N.Y.)
Ament, William Scott
Armstrong, George Dod
Baird, Charles Washington
Baird, Henry Martyn
Bancroft, Cecil Franklin Patch
Barrows, John Henry
Bird, Frederic Mayer
Bissell, Edwin Cone
Blanshard, Paul
Bliss, Howard Sweetser
Boisen, Anton Theophilus
Bowen, George
Brady, John Green
Briggs, Charles Augustus
Brown, Charles Rufus
Brown, Francis, 1849–1916
Brown, Samuel Robbins
Brown, William Adams
Burrell, David James
Calkins, Phineas Wolcott
Cavert, Samuel McCrea
Chamberlain, Jacob
Chapin, Aaron Lucius
Child, Frank Samuel
Clewell, John Henry
Coffin, Henry Sloane
Converse, Tames Booth
Crothers, Samuel McChord
Curtis, Edward Lewis
Curtiss, Samuel Ives
Cutler, Carroll
Dabney, Robert Lewis
Darling, Henry
Dennett, Tyler (Wilbur)
D'Ooge, Martin Luther
Eastman, William Reed
Fosdick, Harry Emerson
Foster, Stephen Symonds
Gardiner, Harry Norman
Gillett, Ezra Hall
Gladden, Washington
Good, James Isaac
Goodnch, Chauncey, 1836–1925
Gulick, John Thomas
Gulick, Sidney Lewis
Hall, Charles Cuthbert
Hall, Granville Stanley
Hamilton, Edward John
Hammond, Edward Payson
Hammond, James Bartlett
Haven, Joseph
Hendrix, Eugene Russell
Hoge, Moses Drury
Hoppin, James Mason
Horr, George Edwin
Hunt, Theodore Whitefield
Hyde, William De Witt
Jackson, Samuel Macauley
Kellogg, Martin
Klipstein, Louis Frederick
Luce, Henry Winters
Lunn, George Richard
Lyman, Albert Josiah
Lyman, Chester Smith
Lynd, Robert Staughton
McGiffert, Arthur Cushman
McIlwaine, Richard
McMaster, James Alphonsus
Marquand, Allan
Mills, Cyrus Taggart
Mitchell, Edwin Knox
Moore, George Foot
Morris, George Sylvester
Mulford, Elisha
Muste, Abraham Johannes
Muzzey, David Saville
Nutting, Wallace
Ogden, Rollo
Olds, Leland
Osborn, Henry Stafford
Peet, Isaac Lewis
Phelps, Austin
Pierson, Arthur Tappan
Pierson, Hamilton Wilcox
Post, George Edward
Powell, Adam Clayton, Jr.
Powell, Edward Payson
Reed, Richard Clark
Reid, Gilbert
Reid, John Morrison
Richards, Charles Herbert

Robinson, Charles Seymour
Robinson, Stuart
Salter, William
Schuyler, George Washington
Smith, Arthur Henderson
Smith, Benjamin Mosby
Smith, Gerald Birney
Strong, James Woodward
Stuart, John Leighton
Thomas, Norman Mattoon
Willey, Samuel Hopkins
Wilson, Warren Hugh
Woodbridge, Frederick James Eugene
Graduate Study
Matthews, Joseph Brown
UNION UNIVERSITY (TENN.)
Dodd, Monroe Elmon
UNITED STATES COAST GUARD ACADEMY (CONN.)
Smith, Edward Hanson
UNITED STATES MILITARY ACADEMY (N.Y.)
Abbot, Henry Larcom
Abert, John James
Abrams, Creighton Williams, Jr.
Adams, John, 1825–1864
Alexander, Barton Stone
Alexander, Edward Porter
Allen, Henry Tureman
Allen, Robert
Allison, Nathaniel
Allston, Robert Francis Withers
Alvord, Benjamin
Ames, Adelbert
Ammen, Daniel
Ammen, Jacob
Anderson, Joseph Reid
Anderson, Richard Heron
Anderson, Robert
Andrews, Frank Maxwell
Andrews, George Leonard
Armistead, Lewis Addison
Arnold, Henry Harley
Arnold, Lewis Golding
Arnold, Richard
Augur, Christopher Columbus
Averell, William Woods
Avres, Romeyn Beck
Babcock, Orville E.
Bache, Alexander Dallas
Bailey, Jacob Whitman
Baird, Absalom
Baker, Laurence Simmons
Barlow, John Whitney
Barnard, John Gross
Barnes, James
Barry, William Farquhar
Bartlett, William Holmes Chambers
Barton, Seth Maxwell
Beauregard, Pierre Gustave Toutant
Bee, Barnard Elliott
Bell, James Franklin
Benham, Henry Washington
Benton, James Gilchrist
Black, William Murray
Blair, Montgomery
Bledsoe, Albert Taylor
Bliss, Tasker Howard
Bonaparte, Jerome Napoleon
Bonfils, Frederick Gilmer
Bonneville, Benjamin Louis Eulalie de
Bourke, John Gregory
Boynton, Edward Carlisle
Bragg, Braxton
Brannan, John Milton
Brooks, William Thomas Harbaugh
Brown, George Scratchley
Buchanan, Robert Christie
Buckner, Simon Bolivar, 1823–1914
Buckner, Simon Bolivar, 1886–1945
Buell, Don Carlos
Buford, Abraham, 1820–1884
Buford, John
Buford, Napoleon Bonaparte
Bullard, Robert Lee
Burnside, Ambrose Everett
Cabell, William Lewis
Camden, Johnson Newlon
Campbell, John Archibald
Canby, Edward Richard Sprigg
Carpenter, Matthew Hale
Carr, Eugene Asa
Carroll, Samuel Sprigg
Casey, Silas
Casey, Thomas Lincoln
Cass, George Washington
Chaffee, Adna Romanza
Childe, John
Childs, Thomas
Chittenden, Hiram Martin
Chouteau, Auguste Pierre
Clay, Lucius DuBignon
Cocke, Philip St. George
Cooke, Philip St. George
Cooper, Samuel
Coppée, Henry
Couch, Darius Nash
Craig, Malin
Crittenden, George Bibb
Crook, George
Crowder, Enoch Herbert
Crozier, William
Cullum, George Washington
Curtis, Samuel Ryan
Custer, George Armstrong
Dana, Napoleon Jackson Tecumseh
Davidson, John Wynn
Davis, George Breckinridge
Davis, Jefferson
Delafield, Richard
Dent, Frederick Tracy
Derby, George Horatio
Devers, Jacob Loucks
Dickman, Joseph Theodore
Donelson, Andrew Jackson
Doubleday, Abner
Drayton, Thomas Fenwick
Duane, James Chatham
Du Pont, Henry
Du Pont, Henry Algernon
Dwight, William
Dye, William McEntyre
Dyer, Alexander Brydie
Early, Jubal Anderson
Edwards, Clarence Ransom
Eichelberger, Robert Lawrence
Eisenhower, Dwight David
Elliott, Washington Lafayette
Ely, Hanson Edward
Elzey, Arnold
Emory, William Hemsley
Ernst, Oswald Herbert
Eustis, Henry Lawrence
Evans, Nathan George
Ewell, Benjamin Stoddert
Ewell, Richard Stoddert
Ewing, Hugh Boyle
Fannin, James Walker
Fanning, Alexander Campbell Wilder
Field, Charles William
Fletcher, Robert
Foote, Andrew Hull
Foster, John Gray
Franklin, William Buel
French, William Henry
Fry, Birkett Davenport
Fry, James Barnet
Gaillard, David Du Bose
Garnett, Robert Selden
Garrard, Kenner
Getty, George Washington
Gibbon, John
Gillem, Alvan Cullem
Gillmore, Quincy Adams
Gilpin, Wilham
Glassford, Pelham Davis
Goethals, George Washington
Goldthwaite, George
Gordon, George Henry
Gordon, William Washington
Gorgas, Josiah
Gorrell, Edgar Staley
Gracie, Archibald
Graham, James Duncan
Granger, Gordon
Grant, Frederick Dent
Grant, Ulysses Simpson
Graves, William Sidney
Greene, Francis Vinton
Greene, George Sears
Greene, David McMurtrie
Griffin, Charles
Griffin, Eugene
Grover, Cuvier
Groves, Leslie Richard, Jr.
Gunnison, John Williams
Haan, William George
Halleck, Henry Wager
Hamilton, Charles Smith
Hamilton, Schuyler
Hamtramck, John Francis
Hancock, Winfield Scott
Hardee, William Joseph
Hardie, James Allen
Hardy, Arthur Sherburne
Hartsuff, George Lucas
Hascall, Milo Smith
Hatch, John Porter
Haupt, Herman
Hays, Alexander
Hazen, William Babcock
Hébert, Louis
Hébert, Paul Octave
Heintzelman, Samuel Peter
Heintzelman, Stuart
Heth, Henry
Hewitt, John Hill

Hill, Ambrose Powell
Hill, Daniel Harvey
Hine, Charles de Lano
Hines, John Leonard ("Birdie")
Hitchcock, Ethan Allen, 1798–1870
Hodes, Henry Irving
Hodges, Courtney Hicks
Hodges, Harry Foote
Holabird, William
Holden, Edward Singleton
Holmes, Theophilus Hunter
Hood, John Bell
Hood, Washington
Hooker, Joseph
Howe, Albion Parris
Howze, Robert Lee
Huger, Benjamin
Hughes, George Wurtz
Humphreys, Andrew Atkinson
Humphreys, Benjamin Grubb
Hunt, Henry Jackson
Hunter, David
Huse, Caleb
Irwin, George Le Roy
Ives, Joseph Christmas
Jackson, Thomas Jonathan ("Stonewall")
Jackson, William Hicks
Jadwin, Edgar
Johnson, Bushrod Rust
Johnson, Edward
Johnson, Hugh Samuel
Johnson, Richard W.
Johnston, Albert Sidney
Johnston, Joseph Eggleston
Jones, David Rumph
Jordan, Thomas
Kautz, August Valentine
Kelton, John Cunningham
Keyes, Erasmus Darwin
Kilpatrick, Hugh Judson
King, Edward Leonard
King, Rufus, 1814–1876
Kinney, William Burnet
Kirby-Smith, Edmund
Knappen, Theodore Temple
Kuhn, Joseph Ernst
Lawton, Alexander Robert
Lee, Fitzhugh
Lee, George Washington Custis
Lee, John Clifford Hodges
Lee, Robert Edward
Lee, Stephen Dill
Lewis, Isaac Newton
Liggett, Hunter
Lomax, Lunsford Lindsay
Long, Armistead Lindsay
Longstreet, James
Lovell, Mansfield
Ludlow, William
Lyon, Nathaniel
McAlexander, Ulysses Grant
MacArthur, Douglas
McAuliffe, Anthony Clement
McClellan, George Brinton
McCook, Alexander McDowell
McDowell, Irvin
Mackenzie, Ranald Slidell
McLane, Robert Milligan
McLaws, Lafayette
McLeod, Hugh
McNair, Lesley James
McNeill, William Gibbs
McPherson, James Birdseye
Magruder, John Bankhead
Mahan, Dennis Hart
Mann, Ambrose Dudley
Mansfield, Edward Deering
Mansfield, Joseph King Fenno
March, Peyton Conway
Marmaduke, John Sappington
Marshall, Humphrey
Marshall, William Louis
Martin, James Green
Martin, John Hill
Martindale, John Henry
Mason, Charles
Mather, William Williams
Maury, Dabney Herndon
Maus, Marion Perry
Maxey, Samuel Bell
Maynard, Edward
Meade, George Gordon
Meigs, Montgomery Cunningham
Menoher, Charles Thomas
Merrill, Frank Dow
Merrill, William Emery
Merritt, Wesley
Michie, Peter Smith
Michler, Nathaniel
Mills, Anson
Mitchel, Ormsby MacKnight
Mordecai, Alfred
Morell, George Webb
Morris, Thomas Armstrong
Morris, William Hopkins
Morton, Charles Gould
Morton, James St. Clair
Mowbray, Henry Siddons
Muir, Charles Henry
Mullan, John
Myers, Abraham Charles
Neill, Thomas Hewson
Newton, John
Neyland, Robert Reese, Jr.
Nicholls, Francis Redding Tillow
Northrop, Lucius Bellinger
O'Donnell, Emmett, Jr. ("Rosy")
Ord, Edward Otho Cresap
Palfrey, John Carver
Palmer, Innis Newton
Palmer, John McAuley
Park, Roswell, 1807–1869
Parke, John Grubb
Parrott, Robert Parker
Partridge, Alden
Patch, Alexander McCarrell
Patrick, Marsena Rudolph
Patrick, Mason Mathews
Patton, George Smith
Peck, John James
Pelham, John
Pemberton, John Clifford
Pender, William Dorsey
Pendleton, William Nelson
Pershing, John Joseph
Pickett, George Edward
Pleasonton, Alfred
Poe, Edgar Allan
Poe, Orlando Metcalfe
Polk, Leonidas
Pope, John
Porter, Fitz-John
Quinby, Isaac Ferdinand
Rains, Gabriel James
Rains, George Washington
Ramsay, George Douglas
Ramseur, Stephen Dodson
Raymond, Charles Walker
Read, George Windle
Reno, Jesse Lee
Reynolds, Alexander Welch
Reynolds, John Fulton
Reynolds, Joseph Jones
Richardson, Israel Bush
Richardson, Wilds Preston
Ricketts, James Brewerton
Ripley, James Wolfe
Ripley, Roswell Sabine
Robert, Henry Martyn
Roberts, Benjamin Stone
Robinson, John Cleveland
Rodman, Thomas Jackson
Rosecrans, William Starke
Rosser, Thomas Lafayette
Royce, Ralph
Ruger, Thomas Howard
Russell, David Allen
Schenck, James Findlay
Schofield, John McAllister
Schriver, Edmund
Schwatka, Frederick
Scott, Hugh Lenox
Sedgwick, John
Seymour, Truman
Sheridan, Philip Henry
Sherman, Thomas West
Sherman, William Tecumseh
Shoup, Francis Asbury
Sibert, William Luther
Sidell, William Henry
Simpson, James Hervey
Slocum, Henry Warner
Smith, Charles Ferguson
Smith, Francis Henney
Smith, Gustavus Woodson
Smith, Martin Luther
Smith, Richard Somers
Smith, Robert Hardy
Smith, William Farrar
Smith, William Sooy
Snelling, William Joseph
Somervell, Brehon Burke
Spaatz, Carl Andrew ("Tooey")
Squier, George Owen
Stanley, David Sloane
Steele, Frederick
Stevens, Isaac Ingalls
Stevens, Walter Husted
Stevenson, Carter Littlepage
Stewart, Alexander Peter
Stilwell, Joseph Warren
Stone, Charles Pomeroy
Stoneman, George
Stratemeyer, George Edward
Stuart, James Ewell Brown
Sturgis, Samuel Davis
Summerall, Charles Pelot
Swift, Joseph Gardner
Swift, William Henry
Sykes, George
Symons, Thomas William

Talcott, Andrew
Taylor, Harry
Ten Broeck, Richard
Thatcher, Henry Knox
Thayer, Sylvanus
Thomas, George Henry
Thomas, Lorenzo
Tidball, John Caldwell
Torbert, Alfred Thomas Archimedes
Totten, Joseph Gilbert
Tower, Zealous Bates
Townsend, Edward Davis
Trimble, Isaac Ridgeway
Trist, Nicholas Philip
Trowbridge, William Petit
Turnbull, William
Turner, John Wesley
Tyler, Daniel
Tyler, Robert Ogden
Tyson, Lawrence Davis
Vandenberg, Hoyt Sanford
Vanderburgh, William Henry
Van Dorn, Earl
Vinton, Francis
Vinton, Francis Laurens
Wainwright, Jonathan Mayhew
Walker, John Brisben
Walker, Walton Harris
Walker, William Henry Talbot
Wallace, David
Warren, Gouverneur Kemble
Washington, John Macrae
Webb, Alexander Stewart
Weitzel, Godfrey
Wheeler, Earle Gilmore
Wheeler, George Montague
Wheeler, Joseph
Whipple, Amiel Weeks
Whistler, George Washington
Whistler, James Abbott McNeill
White, Edward Higgins, II
Whiting, William Henry Chase
Wilcox, Cadmus Marcellus
Willcox, Orlando Bolivar
Wilson, James Harrison
Winder, John Henry
Wood, Charles Erskine Scott
Wood, Robert Elkington
Wood, Thomas John
Woodbury, Daniel Phineas
Woods, Charles Robert
Wright, Horatio Gouverneur
Yoakum, Henderson
Young, Pierce Manning Butler
Zeilin, Jacob

UNITED STATES NAVAL ACADEMY (MD.)

Allen, Hervey
Badger, Charles Johnston
Badger, Oscar Charles
Bailey, Frank Harvey
Barbey, Daniel Edward
Barker, Albert Smith
Beale, Edward Fitzgerald
Beary, Donald Bradford
Benjamin, Park, 1849–1922
Benson, William Shepherd
Berwind, Edward Julius
Blake, Homer Crane
Blandy, William Henry Purnell
Bloch, Claude Charles
Blue, Victor
Bradford, Joseph
Brady, Cyrus Townsend
Brereton, Lewis Hyde
Bristol, Mark Lambert
Brown, Charles Rufus
Brownson, Willard Herbert
Bullard, William Hannum Grubb
Byrd, Richard Evelyn
Canaga, Alfred Bruce
Capps, Washington Lee
Chadwick, French Ensor
Chester, Colby Mitchell
Churchill, Winston
Clark, Charles Edgar
Clark, Joseph James ("Jocko")
Cohen, John Sanford
Cone, Hutchinson Ingham
Cooley, Mortimer Elwyn
Coontz, Robert Edward
Danenhower, John Wilson
Davis, Andrew McFarland
Davis, Charles Henry, 1845–1921
Davis, John Lee
Davison, Gregory Caldwell
De Long, George Washington
Denfield, Louis Emil
Dewey, George
Donlevy, Brian
Drake, Charles Daniel
Durand, William Frederick
Earle, Ralph
Eberle, Edward Walter
Edwards, Richard Stanislaus
Emmet, William Le Roy
Evans, Robley Dunglison
Fiske, Bradley Allen
Fly, James Lawrence
Foulk, George Clayton
Fox, Gustavus Vasa
Frost, Holloway Halstead
Gherodi, Bancroft
Gleaves, Albert
Gordon, John Franklin
Gossett, Benjamin Brown
Grant, Albert Weston
Greene, Samuel Dana
Greer, James Augustin
Gridley, Charles Vernon
Griffin, Robert Stanislaus
Gunnison, Foster
Habersham, Alexander Wylly
Halsey, William Frederick, Jr.
Hayden, Edward Everett
Hewitt, Henry Kent
Hobson, Richmond Pearson
Holder, Charles Frederick
Hollis, Ina Nelson
Homer, Arthur Bartlett
Howell, John Adams
Hughes, Charles Frederick
Ingersoll, Royal Eason
Ingersoll, Royal Rodney
Ingram, Jonas Howard
Jackson, John Brinckerhoff
Jeffers, William Nicholson
Jones, Hilary Pollard
Jouett, James Edward
Joy, Charles Turner
Kelley, James Douglas Jerrold
Kempff, Louis
Kimball, William Wirt
Kimmel, Husband Edward
King, Ernest Joseph
Kinkaid, Thomas Cassin
Kirk, Alan Goodrich
Knight, Austin Melvin
Knox, Dudley Wright
Lamberton, Benjamin Peffer
Leahy, William Daniel
Lee, Willis Augustus
Lejeune, John Archer
Luce, Stephen Bleecker
Lull, Edward Phelps
McCalla, Bowman Henry
McCauley, Edward Yorke
McCormick, Lynde Dupuy
McEnery, Samuel Douglas
McGiffin, Philo Norton
McLean, Walter
McNair, Frederick Vallette
Mahan, Alfred Thayer
Mattice, Asa Martines
Maury, Matthew Fontaine
Mayo, Henry Thomas
Mayo, William Kennon
Meade, Richard Worsam, 1837–1897
Meade, Robert Leamy
Michelson, Albert Abraham
Mitchell, Sidney Zollicoffer
Mitscher, Marc Andrew
Moffett, William Adger
Morgan, James Morris
Murdock, Joseph Ballard
Neville, Wendell Cushing
Niblack, Albert Parker
Nimitz, Chester William
Pardee, Don Albert
Parker, William Harwar
Perkins, George Hamilton
Phelps, Thomas Stowell
Philip, John Woodward
Pillsbury, John Elliott
Plunkett, Charles Peshall
Pratt, William Veazie
Raby, James Joseph
Radford, Arthur William
Ramsay, Francis Munroe
Read, Charles William
Reeves, Joseph Mason
Remey, George Collier
Ricketts, Claude Vernon
Robertson, Ashley Herman
Rockwell, Kiffin Yates
Rodgers, John, 1881–1926
Roe, Francis Asbury
Russell, John Henry
Safford, William Edwin
Sampson, William Thomas
Schley, Winfield Scott
Schroeder, Seaton
Selfridge, Thomas Oliver
Sherman, Forrest Percival
Sherman, Frederick Carl
Sicard, Montgomery
Sigsbee, Charles Dwight
Simpson, Edward
Sims, William Sowden
Smyth, Newman
Snowden, Thomas
Spangler, Henry Wilson

Sprague, Frank Julian
Spruance, Raymond Ames
Standley, William Harrison
Stark, Harold Raynsford
Stark, Lloyd Crow
Stockton, Charles Herbert
Taussig, Joseph Knefler
Taylor, David Watson
Theobald, Robert Alfred
Thompson, Robert Means
Towers, John Henry
Townsend, Robert
Trenchard, Stephen Decatur
Turner, Richmond Kelly
Vickery, Howard Leroy
Wainwright, Richard
Walker, Asa
Walker, John Grimes
Watson, John Crittenden
Weaver, Aaron Ward
Weaver, William Dixon
Weeks, John Wingate
Welles, Roger
Wilbur, Curtis Dwight
Wilde, George Francis Faxon
Wilkinson, Theodore Stark
Winslow, Cameron McRae
Wood, John Taylor
Woodruff, Charles Edward
Zacharias, Ellis Mark
Ziegemier, Henry Joseph

UNIVERSITY COLLEGE, LONDON (ENGLAND)
Du Vigneaud, Vincent
Mees, Charles Edward Kenneth
Mendes, Henry Pereira
Sheppard, Samuel Edward
Sigerist, Henry Ernest

Graduate Study
Sheppard, Samuel Edward

UNIVERSITY MEDICAL COLLEGE (N.Y.)
Cook, Frederick Albert

UNIVERSITY OF ADELAIDE (AUSTRALIA)
Mayo, George Elton

Graduate Study
Mayo, George Elton

UNIVERSITY OF AKRON (OHIO)
Crissinger, Daniel Richard
Kingsbury, Albert

UNIVERSITY OF ALABAMA
Allen, James Browning
Bankhead, John Hollis
Bankhead, William Brockman
Battle, Cullen Andrews
Brown, Johnny Mack
Campbell, William Edward March
Carmichael, Oliver Cromwell
Clay, Clement Claiborne
Clayton, Henry De Lamar
Clemens, Jeremiah
Comer, Braxton Bragg
Duggar, Benjamin Minge
Forney, William Henry
Gaines, Reuben Reid
Gould, Robert Simonton
Graves, David Bibb
Guild, La Fayette
Harding, William Procter Gould
Hargrove, Robert Kennon
Herbert, Hilary Abner
McKellar, Kenneth Douglas
Manly, Basil, 1825–1892
Meek, Alexander Beaufort
Moore, George Fleming
Owen, Thomas McAdory
Roberts, Oran Milo
Sibert, William Luther
Smith, Eugene Allen
Smith, William Russell
Toulmin, Harry Theophilus
Van de Graaff, Robert Jemison

Graduate Study
Carmichael, Oliver Cromwell
McKellar, Kenneth Douglas
Van de Graaff, Robert Jemison

Law
Allen, James Browning
Black, Hugo Lafayette
Clayton, Henry De Lamar
Smith, Holland McTyeire
Steagall, Henry Bascom
Wright, Fielding Lewis

Medicine
Black, Hugo Lafayette

UNIVERSITY OF ALASKA
Bartlett, Edward Lewis ("Bob")

UNIVERSITY OF AMSTERDAM (NETHERLANDS)

Medicine
Dusser de Barenne, Joannes Gregorius

UNIVERSITY OF ARIZONA
Fairchild, Sherman Mills
Kefauver, Grayson Neikirk

UNIVERSITY OF ARKANSAS
Burns, Bob
Ellis, Clyde Taylor
Mitchell, Martha Elizabeth Beall
Robinson, Joseph Taylor
Stone, Edward Durell

UNIVERSITY OF ATHENS (GREECE)
Callimachos, Panos Demetrios

Medicine
Papanicolaou, George Nicholas

UNIVERSITY OF BASEL (SWITZERLAND)
Pfister, Alfred
Piccard, Jean Felix
Teuber, Hans-Lukas ("Luke")

UNIVERSITY OF BERLIN (GERMANY)
Bauer, Louis Agricola
Beckwith, Clarence Augustine
Behrend, Bernard Arthur
Bolza, Oskar
Braun, Wernher Von
Brightman, Edgar Sheffield
Coe, George Albert
Franck, James
Freund, Ernst
Friedlaender, Walter Ferdinand
Fuller, George Warren
Goldmark, Peter Carl
Hammer, William Joseph
Horney, Karen Danielssen
Koffka, Kurt
Köhler, Wolfgang
Lasswell, Harold Dwight
Laufer, Berthold
Lewin, Kurt
Ley, Willy
Mather, Frank Jewett, Jr.
Mead, George Herbert
Michael, Arthur
Santayana, George
Schindler, Kurt
Simkhovitch, Mary Melinda Kingsbury
Stieglitz, Alfred
Stiles, Charles Wardell
Tillich, Paul
Von Neumann, John
Willard, Josiah Flint

Graduate Study
Allen, Florence Ellinwood
Balch, Emily Greene
Bentley, Arthur Fisher
Bergmann, Max
Brown, William Adams
Coit, Stanton
Falkner, Roland Post
Franklin, Edward Curtis
Gay, Edwin Francis
Glueck, Nelson
Gottheil, Richard James Horatio
Hayes, Edward Carey
Herty, Charles Holmes
Hibben, John Grier
Hoyt, John Sherman
Merrill, Elmer Truesdell
Millikan, Robert Andrews
Morgan, Edwin Vernon
Muzzey, David Saville
Rhees, Rush
Robb, William Lispenard
Schinz, Albert
Schmidt, Nathaniel
Stieglitz, Julius
Szilard, Leo
Tate, John Torrence
Thilly, Frank
Westermann, William Linn
Wheelock, John Hall
Wildt, Rupert
Woods, James Haughton

Medicine
Michaelis, Leonor
Schoenheimer, Rudolf

UNIVERSITY OF BERN (SWITZERLAND)
Békésy, Georg Von
Funk, Casimir

UNIVERSITY OF BESANÇON (FRANCE)
Laurence, William Leonard

UNIVERSITY OF BONN (GERMANY)
Bieber, Margarete
De Forest, Robert Weeks
Ernst, Max
Wolff, Kurt August Paul

Graduate Study
Coolidge, Julian Lowell
Harrison, Ross Granville
Spaulding, Edward Gleason

UNIVERSITY OF BORDEAUX (FRANCE)
Williams, Aubrey Willis

UNIVERSITY OF BRESLAU (GERMANY)
Courant, Richard

Graduate Study
Tillich, Paul

UNIVERSITY OF BUDAPEST (HUNGARY)
Békésy, Georg Von
Moholy-Nagy, László
Rapaport, David
Reiner, Fritz
Roheim, Geza
Graduate Study
Von Neumann, John
Medicine
Alexander, Franz Gabriel
UNIVERSITY OF BUFFALO (N.Y.)
Fisher, George Jackson
Hofstadter, Richard
Holt, Luther Emmett
O'Brian, John Lord
Seitz, William Chapin
Stockton, Charles G.
Wende, Ernest
Wende, Grover William
UNIVERSITY OF CALIFORNIA
Beals, Ralph Albert
Beatty, Willard Walcott
Bradley, Frederick Worthen
Burk, Frederic Lister
Chamberlain, Joseph Perkins
Church, Thomas Dolliver
Clyde, George Dewey
Condon, Edward Uhler
Cone, Fairfax Mastick
Conrad, Maximilian Arthur, Jr.
Cooper, William John
Corbett, Harvey Wiley
Cottrell, Frederick Gardner
Cushman, Austin Thomas ("Joe")
Davis, Adelle
Drury, Newton Bishop
Erlanger, Joseph
Evans, Herbert McLean
Faust, Frederick Shiller
Foshag, William Frederick
Gaither, Horace Rowan, Jr.
Gaxton, William
Gilbreth, Lillian Evelyn Moller
Goldberg, Reuben Lucius ("Rube")
Goodman, Louis Earl
Gunter, Archibald Clavering
Harris, LeRoy Ellsworth ("Roy")
Heney, Francis Joseph
Herbst, Josephine Frey
Higgins, Marguerite
Hohfield, Wesley Newcomb
Howard, Sidney Coe
Jepson, Willis Linn
Johnson, Hiram Warren
Kahn, Florence Prag
Knappen, Theodore Temple
Knowland, William Fife
Kohlberg, Alfred
Laguna, Theodore de Leo de
Lane, Franklin Knight
Libby, Willard Frank
Lindley, Curtis Holbrook
Lovejoy, Arthur Oncken
McLoughlin, Maurice Evans
Mann, Louis
Mather, Stephen Tyng
Merriam, John Campbell
Meyer, Eugene Isaac
Mezes, Sidney Edward
Morgan, Julia
Moss, Sanford Alexander
Nelson, Nels Christian
Norris, Benjamin Franklin
Norris, Charles Gilman Smith
Overstreet, Harry Allen
Parker, Carleton Hubbell
Phelan, James Duval
Ransome, Frederick Leslie
Reinhardt, Aurelia Isabel Henry
Ritter, William Emerson
Royce, Josiah
Ruef, Abraham
Sajous, Charles Euchariste de Médicis
Sanford, Edmund Clark
Sawyer, Wilbur Augustus
Schmidt, Carl Louis August
Sproul, Allan
Sproul, Robert Gordon
Steffens, Lincoln
Stein, Leo Daniel
Stoddard, Charles Warren
Taggard, Genevieve
Theobald, Robert Alfred
Warner, William Lloyd
Warren, Earl
Webb, Harry Howard
Wightman, Hazel Virginia Hotchkiss
Williams, Gardner Fred
Wilson, Orlando Winfield ("Win," "O.W.")
Zellerbach, James David
Zellerbach, Harold Lionel
Graduate Study
Baker, Dorothy Dodds
Barrows, David Prescott
Clyde, George Dewey
Condon, Edward Uhler
Cooper, William John
Foshag, William Frederick
Gilbreth, Lillian Evelyn Moller
Grady, Henry Francis
Jepson, Willis Linn
Kelsey, Rayner Wickersham
Kuykendall, Ralph Simpson
Latimer, Wendell Mitchell
Libby, Willard Frank
MacNair, Harley Farnsworth
Moss, Sanford Alexander
Nelson, Marjorie Maxine
Nelson, Nels Christian
Nicholson, Seth Barnes
Prall, David Wight
Ransome, Frederick Leslie
Schmidt, Carl Louis August
Stith, Thompson
Thomas, Elbert Duncan
Thompson, Stith
Waksman, Selman Abraham
Law
Adams, Annette Abbott
Chamberlain, Joseph Perkins
Engle, Clair William Walter
Gaither, Horace Rowan, Jr.
Goodman, Louis Earl
Heney, Francis Joseph
Moscone, George Richard
Ruef, Abraham
Warren, Earl
Medicine
Widney, Joseph Pomeroy
UNIVERSITY OF CALIFORNIA, LOS ANGELES
Baker, Dorothy Dodds
Bartlett, Edward Lewis ("Bob")
Bunche, Ralph Johnson
Harrah, William Fisk ("Bill")
Harris, LeRoy Ellsworth ("Roy")
Limón, José Arcadio
Morrison, Jim
Robinson, John Roosevelt ("Jackie")
Thornton, Daniel I. J.
Trumbo, James Dalton
Washington, Kenneth Stanley ("The General")
Graduate Study
Davis, Adelle
UNIVERSITY OF CHATTANOOGA
Raulston, John Tate
UNIVERSITY OF CHICAGO (ILL.)
Adams, Cyrus Cornelius
Adams, Frank Ramsay
Alinsky, Saul David
Allison, Samuel King
Andrus, Ethel Percy
Anthony, Katharine Susan
Atwood, Wallace Walter
Beal, William James
Bell, Bernard Iddings
Benson, Oscar Herman
Bestor, Arthur Eugene
Billikopf, Jacob
Birkhoff, George David
Blair, William Richards
Bliss, Gilbert Ames
Bloomfield, Maurice
Bontemps, Arna Wendell
Bryan, Charles Wayland
Chase, (Mary) Agnes Merrill
Coe, Virginius ("Frank")
Cohn, Edwin Joseph
Covici, Pascal ("Pat")
Cuppy, William Jacob (Will)
Davenport, Herbert Joseph
Davisson, Clinton Joseph
Dille, John Flint
Eichelberger, Clark Mell
Enelow, Hyman Gerson
Farrell, James Thomas
Fisher, Henry Conroy ("Bud")
Flanner, Janet
Frank, Jerome
Gale, Henry Gordon
Gardner, Helen
Gaston, Herbert Earle
Geer, William Aughe ("Will")
Goodspeed, Thomas Wakefield
Graham, Evarts Ambrose
Gray, William Scott, Jr.
Green, Constance McLaughlin
Greenlaw, Edwin Almiron
Gunther, John
Harper, Robert Francis
Henderson, Charles Richmond
Hine, Lewis Wickes
Hobart, Alice Nourse Tisdale
Hoffman, Paul Gray
Howe, Herbert Alonzo
Hubble, Edwin

Ickes, Harold Le Clair
Johnson, Charles Spurgeon
Johnson, Mordecai Wyatt
Kellor, Frances (Alice)
Kharasch, Morris Selig
Kirkwood, John Gamble
Lasswell, Harold Dwight
Leopold, Nathan Freudenthal, Jr.
Levinson, Salmon Oliver
Lurton, Horace Harmon
McHugh, Rose John
McKinley, Albert Edward
Miller, Perry Gilbert Eddy
Millikan, Clark Blanchard
Mitchell, Wesley Clair
Moore, Richard Bishop
Mott, Frank Luther
Mowrer, Edgar Ansel
O'Brien, Justin
Peattie, Donald Culross
Redfield, Robert
Rhine, Joseph Banks
Richberg, Donald Randall
Sheean, James Vincent
Sills, Milton
Smith, Henry Justin
Stone, Ormond
Tatum, Edward Lawrie
Thorek, Max
Van Vechten, Carl
Walling, William English
Wilder, Russell Morse
Wilson, Edmund Beecher
Wrigley, Philip Knight

Graduate Study

Abbott, Edith
Abbott, Grace
Adams, Joseph Quincy
Adams, Walter Sydney
Alinsky, Saul David
Allison, Samuel King
Alvord, Clarence Walworth
Atwood, Wallace Walter
Balch, Emily Greene
Barrows, David Prescott
Beeson, Charles Henry
Bestor, Arthur Eugene
Billikopf, Jacob
Bingham, Walter Van Dyke
Birkhoff, George David
Blair, William Richards
Bliss, Gilbert Ames
Blodgett, Katharine Burr
Bloomfield, Leonard
Bowen, Ira Sprague
Breckenridge, Sophonisba Preston
Brooke, Charles Frederick Tucker
Caldwell, Otis William
Cayton, Horace Roscoe
Chamberlain, Charles Joseph
Cohn, Edwin Joseph
Cordier, Andrew Wellington
Cowles, Henry Chandler
Crocker, William
Cuppy, William Jacob (Will)
Davis, John Warren
Davis, Katharine Bement
Dawley, Almena
Dickson, Leonard Eugene
Doolittle, Eric
Downey, June Etta
Dykstra, Clarence Addison
Evans, Lawrence Boyd
Fenneman, Nevin Melancthon
Folin, Otto Knut Olof
Frank, Tenney
Frazier, Edward Franklin
Gale, Henry Gordon
Gardner, Helen
Garner, James Wilford
Goode, John Paul
Goodman, Paul
Graham, Frank Porter
Graves, Alvin Cushman
Gray, William Scott, Jr.
Hatcher, Orie Latham
Hayakawa, Sessue
Hayes, Edward Carey
Hoerr, Normand Louis
Hoxie, Robert Franklin
Hubble, Edwin
Jacoby, Neil Herman
Jewett, Frank Baldwin
Jones, Howard Mumford
Jones, Lynds
Just, Ernest Everett
Key, Valdimer Orlando, Jr.
Kharasch, Morris Selig
Koch, Fred Conrad
Laswell, Harold Dwight
Lillie, Frank Rattray
Lingelbach, Anna Lane
Livingston, Burton Edward
Locy, William Albert
Lutz, Frank Eugene
McClung, Clarence Erwin
Macintosh, Douglas Clyde
Meinzer, Oscar Edward
Millett, Fred Benjamin
Millis, Harry Alvin
Mitchell, Wesley Clair
Monroe, Paul
Moulton, Forest Ray
Nourse, Edwin Griswold
Owsley, Frank Lawrence
Parker, Samuel Chester
Prokosch, Eduard
Randall, James Garfield
Ranson, Stephen Walter
Rhine, Joseph Banks
Rice, John Andrew
Rickert, Martha Edith
Robinson, Edward Stevens
Rogers, James Harvey
Royster, James Finch
Ruml, Beardsley
Sauer, Carl Ortwin
Scarborough, Dorothy
Sheldon, William Herbert
Shull, George Harrison
Sills, Milton
Simons, Henry Calvert
Skinner, Aaron Nichols
Slichter, Sumner Huber
Slosson, Edwin Emery
Smith, John Merlin Powis
Smith, Thomas Vernor
Stolberg, Benjamin
Stone, Ormond
Stouffer, Samuel Andrew
Strong, Anna Louise
Struve, Otto
Sutherland, Edwin Hardin
Sydenstricker, Edgar
Tauber, Maurice Falcolm
Thurstone, Louis Leon
Van Deman, Esther Boise
Veblen, Oswald
Waller, Willard Walter
Walling, William English
Watson, John Broadus
Webb, Walter Prescott
Wells, Harry Gideon
Whitcomb, Selden Lincoln
White, Leonard Dupee
Wilder, Russell Morse
Wildman, Murray Shipley
Willett, Herbert Lockwood
Willis, Henry Parker
Wirt, William Albert
Woodson, Carter Godwin
Young, Ella Flagg

Law

Allen, Florence Ellinwood
Breckenridge, Sophonisba Preston
Frank, Jerome
Goddard, Luther Marcellus
Ickes, Harold Le Clair
Oliphant, Herman
Pierce, Gilbert Ashville
Pope, James Pinckney
Redfield, Robert
Wrather, William Embry

Theology

Holt, Arthur Erastus
McClung, Clarence Erwin
Voris, John Ralph

UNIVERSITY OF CINCINNATI (OHIO)

Bara, Theda
Bauer, Louis Agricola
Benedict, Stanley Rossiter
Berkowitz, Henry
Crosley, Powel, Jr.
Fleming, John Adam
Gavin, Frank Stanton Burns
Glueck, Nelson
Grossmann, Louis
Heller, Maximilian
Howe, Herbert Alonzo
Huggins, Miller James
Kagan, Henry Enoch
Kronenberger, Louis, Jr.
Liebman, Joshua Loth
Magnes, Judah Leon
Meyer, Martin Abraham
Parker, Samuel Chester
Paul, William Darwin ("Shorty")
Philipson, David
Ritchey, George Willis
Robinson, Edward Stevens
Sampson, Martin Wright
Silver, Abba Hillel
Silverman, Joseph
Sloan, Richard Elihu
Spence, Brent
Stephenson, Nathaniel Wright
Strauss, Joseph Baermann
Thilly, Frank
Walker, Stuart Armstrong
Williams, Aubrey Willis
Wolfson, Erwin Service

Graduate Study
Prentis, Henning Webb, Jr.
Law
Crissinger, Daniel Richard
Morrow, Edwin Porch
Medicine
Hawley, Paul Ramsey
Paul, William Darwin ("Shorty")
UNIVERSITY OF CITY OF NEW YORK
(*See* NEW YORK UNIVERSITY)
UNIVERSITY OF COLORADO
Alden, Cynthia May Westover
Chapman, John Arthur
Conrad, Maximilian Arthur, Jr.
Fowler, Gene
May, Morton Jay
Miller, Glenn
Millikin, Eugene Donald
Morgan, Arthur Ernest
Snyder, Howard McCrum
Stafford, Jean
Thompson, Llewellyn E. ("Tommy"), Jr.
Trumbo, James Dalton
Graduate Study
Hills, Elijah Clarence
Sheldon, William Herbert
Stafford, Jean
Law
Rutledge, Wiley Blount
Weinberger, Jacob
Medicine
Naismith, James
UNIVERSITY OF CONNECTICUT
Rovere, Richard Halworth
UNIVERSITY OF CRACOW (POLAND)
(*See* UNIVERSITY OF KRAKOW)
UNIVERSITY OF DELAWARE
Agnew, David Hayes
Bagby, George William
Bradford, Edward Green
Joynes, Edward Southey
McCullough, John Griffith
Mears, John William
Purnell, William Henry
Saulsbury, Willard, 1820–1892
Stewart, John George
Townsend, George Alfred
Wiley, Andrew Jackson
UNIVERSITY OF DENVER (COLO.)
Chapman, Oscar Littleton
McWilliams, Carey
Shawn, Edwin Meyers ("Ted")
Smith, Homer William
Steele, Wilbur Daniel
UNIVERSITY OF DETROIT (MICH.)
Cavanagh, Jerome Patrick ("Jerry")
Gray, Harold Edwin
UNIVERSITY OF DUBLIN (IRELAND)
Fine, John Sydney
UNIVERSITY OF EDINBURGH (SCOTLAND) (*See also* EDINBURGH UNIVERSITY)
Arlen, Michael
Bishop, Robert Hamilton
Du Vigneaud, Vincent
Loeb, Leo
Roper, Elmo Burns, Jr.
UNIVERSITY OF FERRARA (ITALY)
Ascoli, Max
UNIVERSITY OF FLORENCE (ITALY)
Graduate Study
Bentley, Elizabeth Terrill
UNIVERSITY OF FLORIDA
Graham, Philip Leslie
Holland, Spessard Lindsey
Melton, James
Warren, Fuller
UNIVERSITY OF FRANKFURT (GERMANY)
Morgenthau, Hans Joachim
Neumann, Franz Leopold
UNIVERSITY OF FREIBURG (GERMANY)
Horney, Karen Danielssen
Marcuse, Herbert
Panofsky, Erwin
Graduate Study
Hart, Albert Bushnell
Marcuse, Herbert
Robinson, James Harvey
Tufts, James Hayden
Webb, Harry Howard
UNIVERSITY OF GENEVA (SWITZERLAND)
Lasswell, Harold Dwight
Znaniecki, Florian Witold
Graduate Study
Noyes, William Albert, Jr.
Rogers, James Harvey
UNIVERSITY OF GEORGIA
Bacon, Augustus Octavius
Benning, Henry Lewis
Black, Eugene Robert
Blalock, Alfred
Blount, James Henderson
Campbell, Henry Fraser
Campbell, John Archibald
Carleton, Henry
Clayton, Augustin Smith
Cobb, Andrew Jackson
Cobb, Howell
Cobb, Thomas Reade Rootes
Comer, Braxton Bragg
Cooper, Mark Anthony
Curry, Jabez Lamar Mun
Dawson, William Crosby
Doughty, William Henry
Eve, Paul Fitzsimons
Felton, William Harrell
Folsom, Marion Bayard
Fowler, Joseph Smith
Gartrell, Lucius Jeremiah
Gordon, John Brown
Grady, Henry Woodfin
Grant, John Thomas
Graves, John Temple
Hammond, Nathaniel Job
Hardy, Oliver Norvell
Harris, William Littleton
Herty, Charles Holmes
Hill, Benjamin Harvey
Hill, Walter Barnard
Hillyer, Junius
Hopkins, Isaac Stiles
Howell, Clark
Hughes, Dudley Mayo
Jackson, James, 1819–1887
Jacobs, Joseph, 1859–1929
Johnson, Herschel Vespasian
Knight, Lucian Lamar
Lamar, Joseph Rucker
Lane, John
Le Conte, John
Le Conte, Joseph
Long, Crawford Williamson
Lumpkin, Joseph Henry
Meigs, Charles Delucena
Mell, Patrick Hues, 1850–1918
Milner, John Turner
Nisbet, Eugenius Aristides
Orr, Gustavus John
Palmer, Benjamin Morgan
Phillips, Ulrich Bonnell
Phinizy, Ferdinand
Pickens, Francis Wilkinson
Pierce, George Foster
Sanders, Billington McCarter
Scott, Thomas Fielding
Shorter, John Gill
Smith, Charles Henry, 1826–1903
Speer, Emory
Spencer, Samuel
Stephens, Alexander Hamilton
Stephens, Linton
Stokes, Thomas Lunsford, Jr.
Stovall, Pleasant Alexander
Talmadge, Eugene
Timrod, Henry
Toombs, Robert Augustus
Waddel, John Newton
Willingham, Robert Josiah
Graduate Study
McCarthy, Charles
Mell, Patrick Hues, 1850–1918
Phillips, Ulrich Bonnell
Law
Andrews, Garnett
Atkinson, William Yates
Cobb, Andrew Jackson
Hardwick, Thomas William
Howell, Evan Park
Knight, Lucian Lamar
Russell, Richard Brevard, Jr. ("Dick")
Winship, Blanton
UNIVERSITY OF GHENT (BELGIUM)
Baekeland, Leo Hendrik
Sarton, George Alfred Léon
Graduate Study
Baekeland, Leo Hendrik
UNIVERSITY OF GLASGOW (SCOTLAND)
Capps, Washington Lee
Fairburn, William Armstrong
Highet, Gilbert
Moffatt, James
UNIVERSITY OF GÖTTINGEN (GERMANY)
Alexander, Franz Gabriel
Baade, Wilhelm Heinrich Walter
Browne, Charles Albert
Courant, Richard
Horney, Karen Danielssen
Rademacher, Hans
Graduate Study
Babcock, Stephen Moulton
Bliss, Gilbert Ames
Bolza, Oskar
Dabney, Charles William
Emerson, Benjamin Kendall
Jackson, Dunham

Kármán, Theodore (Todor) Von
Kremers, Edward
Langmuir, Irving
McCrae, Thomas
Mason, Max
Nichols, Edward Leamington
Oppenheimer, Julius Robert
Osgood, William Fogg
Rademacher, Hans
Smyth, Herbert Weir
Van Vleck, Edward Burr
Weyl, Hermann
Wheelock, John Hall

UNIVERSITY OF GRAZ (AUSTRIA)
Hess, Victor Franz

UNIVERSITY OF GRENOBLE (FRANCE)
Stigler, William Grady

UNIVERSITY OF HALLE (GERMANY)
Elliott, John Lovejoy

Graduate Study
Dodge, Raymond
Ely, Richard Theodore
Falkner, Roland Post
Fetter, Frank Albert
Hill, Joseph Adna
Howe, Frederic Clemson
Jackson, Abraham Valentine Williams
McMurry, Frank Morton
Peabody, Francis Greenwood
Rowe, Leo Stanton

UNIVERSITY OF HAWAII
Gibbons, Euell
Jones, James Ramon

UNIVERSITY OF HEIDELBERG (GERMANY)
Arendt, Hannah
Bonsal, Stephen
Franck, James
Freund, Ernst
Fromm, Erich
Gurowski, Adam
Hart, Edwin Bret
Michael, Arthur

Graduate Study
Clark, John Bates
Ely, Richard Theodore
Fromm, Erich
Glueck, Nelson
Magnes, Judah Leon
Parsons, Talcott
Reese, Charles Lee
Scott, William Berryman
Seligman, Edwin Robert Anderson
Stafford, Jean
Thilly, Frank

Medicine
Meyerhof, Otto

UNIVERSITY OF IDAHO
Gipson, Lawrence Henry
Pangborn, Clyde Edward
Robb, Inez Early Callaway
Welker, Herman

Law
Welker, Herman

UNIVERSITY OF ILLINOIS
Boring, William Alciphron
Brown, Prentiss Marsh
Brundage, Avery
Bryant, Ralph Clement
Bush, Lincoln
Cone, Russell Glenn
Crocker, William
Day, Dorothy
Du Vigneaud, Vincent
East, Edward Murray
Fearing, Kenneth Flexner
Hodge, John Reed
Hood, Clifford Firoved
Koch, Fred Conrad
Kyle, James Henderson
McKinley, William Brown
Mann, James Robert
Nevins, Joseph Allan
Noyes, William Albert, Jr.
Ockerson, John Augustus
Parks, Larry
Parr, Samuel Wilson
Post, Charles William
Sachs, Theodore Bernard
Scopes, John Thomas
Scovell, Melville Amasa
Sherman, Allan
Short, Luke
Short, Walter Campbell
Stratton, Samuel Wesley
Taft, Lorado Zadoc
Talbot, Arthur Newell
Vanderlip, Frank Arthur
Van Doren, Carl Clinton
Van Doren, Mark Albert
Van Hook, Weller
Waller, Willard Walter
Weston, Nathan Austin
Woolman, Collett Everman

Graduate Study
Anderson, Benjamin McAlester
Angle, Paul McClelland
Brown, Prentiss Marsh
Carothers, Warlace Hume
Crocker, William
Du Vigneaud, Vincent
East, Edward Murray
Heald, Henry Townley
Koch, Fred Conrad
Nevins, Joseph Allan
O'Neal, Edward Asbury, III
Rugg, Harold Ordway
Stanley, Wendell Meredith
Taft, Lorado Zadoc
Van Doren, Mark Albert
Westergaard, Harald Malcolm

UNIVERSITY OF INNSBRUCK (AUSTRIA)
Flanagan, Edward Joseph
La Farge, John

UNIVERSITY OF IOWA
Brown, Charles Reynolds
Byoir, Carl Robert
Chamberlin, Edward Hastings
Cook, George Cram
Heezen, Bruce Charles
Hough, Emerson
Johnson, Wendell Andrew Leroy
Johnston, Annie Fellows
Lowden, Frank Orren
McClain, Emlin
Nipher, Francis Eugene
Seberg, Jean Dorothy
Springer, Frank
Stefansson, Vilhjalmur
Tunnell, Emlen
Wade, Martin Joseph

Graduate Study
Johnson, Wendell Andrew Leroy
McClain, Emlin
Nipher, Francis Eugene
Shannon, Fred Albert

Law
Elliott, Charles Burke
Hickenlooper, Bourke Blakemore
Hughes, Howard Robard
McPherson, Smith

Medicine
Dillon, John Forrest
Matthews, Washington

UNIVERSITY OF JENA (GERMANY)
Genthe, Arnold
Glueck, Nelson

Graduate Study
Cobb, Nathan Augustus
Glueck, Nelson
McMurry, Frank Morton

UNIVERSITY OF KANSAS
Abel-Henderson, Annie Heloise
Allen, Forrest Clare ("Phog")
Binghatn, Walter Van Dyke
Borah, William Edgar
Brady, Mildred Alice Edie
Caldwell, Eugene Wilson
Douglas, Aaron
Ellis, George Washington
Frank, Tenney
Franklin, Edward Curtis
Gregg, John Andrew
Hadley, Herbert Spencer
Harrington, John Lyle
Harris, James Arthur
Holmes, Julius Cecil
Inge, William Motter
Latimer, Wendell Mitchell
Long, John Harper
McClung, Clarence Erwin
Moore, Joseph Earle
Pemberton, Brock
Rupp, Adolph Frederick
Schoeppel, Andrew Frank
Simpson, John Andrew
Slosson, Edwin Emery
Smith, Harold Dewey
White, William Allen
Wood, Frederick Hill
Zook, George Frederick

Graduate Study
Abeln-Henderson, Annie Heloise
Frank, Tenney
Franklin, Edward Curtis
Zook, George Frederick

Law
Wood, Frederick Hill

Medicine
Menninger, Charles Frederick

UNIVERSITY OF KANSAS CITY LAW SCHOOL (MO.)
Whittaker, Charles Evans

UNIVERSITY OF KENTUCKY
Carr, Wilbur John
Clark, Champ
Flower, Benjamin Orange
Goulding, Francis Robert
Munson, Thomas Volney

Scopes, John Thomas
Shelton, Albert Leroy
Skinner, Harry
Wiley, Bell Irvin
UNIVERSITY OF KHARKOV (RUSSIA)
Struve, Otto
UNIVERSITY OF KÖNIGSBURG (GERMANY)
Ley, Willy
UNIVERSITY OF KRAKOW (POLAND)
Hodur, Francis
Rubinstein, Helena
UNIVERSITY OF KRISTIANA (NORWAY)
Stejneger, Leonhard Hess
Law
Stejneger, Leonhard Hess
UNIVERSITY OF LEIPZIG (GERMANY)
Bancroft, Wilder Dwight
Mead, George Herbert
Schoenheimer, Rudolf
Graduate Study
Abel, John Jacob
Blichfeldt, Hans Frederik
Cattell, James McKeen
Child, Charles Manning
Cross, Charles Whitman
Daniels, Winthrop More
Dodd, William Edward
Emerton, Ephraim
Foster, Frank Hugh
Gottheil, Richard James Horatio
Hopkins, Edward Washburn
Judd, Charles Hubbard
Kirkland, James Hampton
Laufer, Berthold
Lotka, Alfred James
Lyon, David Gordon
Mulliken, Samuel Parsons
Noyes, Arthur Amos
Pace, Edward Aloysius
Page, Thomas Walker
Prokosch, Eduard
Scott, Walter Dill
Smyth, Herbert Weir
Spaeth, John Duncan
Stiles, Charles Wardell
Thomas, Martha Carey
Worcester, Elwood
UNIVERSITY OF LENINGRAD (RUSSIA)
Gamow, George
UNIVERSITY OF LEWISBURG (*See* BUCKNELL UNIVERSITY)
UNIVERSITY OF LEYDEN (NETHERLANDS)
De Leeuw, Adolph Lodewyk
Goudsmit, Samuel Abraham
Kuiper, Gerard Peter
UNIVERSITY OF LONDON (CANADA)
Schurman, Jacob Gould
Graduate Study
Schurman, Jacob Gould
UNIVERSITY OF LONDON (ENGLAND)
Adams, Joseph Quincy
Brenon, Herbert
Cadman, Samuel Parkes
Coomaraswamy, Ananda Kentish
Davies, John Vipond
Hitchcock, Alfred Joseph
Lasswell, Harold Dwight
Van Druten, John William
Graduate Study
Coomaraswamy, Ananda Kentish
Reece, Brazilla Carroll
Schultz, Henry
UNIVERSITY OF LOUISVILLE (KY.)
Dowell, Greensville
Flint, Austin
Visscher, William Lightfoot
Law
Bingham, Robert Worth
Bozeman, Nathan
Breckinridge, William Campbell Preston
Colman, Norman Jay
Durrett, Reuben Thomas
Flexner, Bernard
Johnston, William Preston
Shields, George Howell
Stayton, John William
Strubberg, Friedrich Armand
Willis, Albert Shelby
Medicine
Anderson, Victor Vance
Buchanan, Joseph Rodes
Flexner, Simon
Green, Norvin
Jackson, John Davies
Richardson, Tobias Gibson
Vance, Ap Morgan
Williams, Elkanah
Wyeth, John Allan
Yandell, David Wendell
UNIVERSITY OF LOUVAIN (BELGIUM)
Graduate Study
Sheen, Fulton John
UNIVERSITY OF LVOV (POLAND)
Rodzinski, Artur
UNIVERSITY OF LYONS (FRANCE)
Niles, John Jacob
Medicine
Carrel, Alexis
UNIVERSITY OF MADRID (SPAIN)
Law
Houston, Charles Hamilton
UNIVERSITY OF MAINE
Bridges, (Henry) Styles
Chase, Mary Ellen
Colcord, Lincoln Ross
Crowe, Francis Trenholm
Farrington, Wallace Rider
Fernald, Merritt Lyndon
Merrill, Elmer Drew
Paul, Elliot Harold
Weymouth, Frank Elwin
Graduate Study
Merrill, Elmer Drew
UNIVERSITY OF MARBURG (GERMANY)
Arendt, Hannah
Brightman, Edgar Sheffield
Coffin, Henry Sloane
Hart, Edwin Bret
Wolff, Kurt August Paul
Graduate Study
McGiffert, Arthur Cushman
UNIVERSITY OF MARYLAND
Browne, William Hand
Buckler, Thomas Hepburn
Carroll, James
Carter, Henry Rose
Godman, John Davidson
Krauth, Charles Philip
Leaf, Wilbur Munro
Palmer, James Croxall
Rayner, Isidor
Rose, John Carter
Sherman, Henry Clapp
Yandell, Lunsford Pitts
Graduate Study
Koch, Vivienne
Law
Boston, Charles Anderson
Bruce, David Kirkpatrick Este
Bruce, William Cabell
Glenn, John Mark
Goldsborough, Thomas Alan
McKeldin, Theodore Roosevelt
Mayer, Brantz
Perlman, Philip Benjamin
Ritchie, Albert Cabell
Sobeloff, Simon E.
Steiner, Bernard Christian
Stockbridge, Henry
Tydings, Millard Evelyn
Medicine
Ambler, James Markham Marshall
Bartholow, Roberts
Baxley, Henry Willis
Cabell, James Lawrence
Chatard, Francis Silas
Councilman, William Thomas
Davis, Charles Henry Stanley
Davis, John Wesley
Fernós Isern, Antonio
Freidenwald, Aaron
Fussell, Bartholomew
Garlick, Theodatus
Graves, Rosewell Hobart
Hemmeter, John Conrad
Hoch, August
Jameson, Horatio Gates
Janney, Oliver Edward
Jarvis, William Chapman
Kirk, Norman Thomas
Kolb, Lawrence
Palmer, John Williamson
Rogers, James Blythe
Rohé, George Henry
Ruhräh, John
Theobald, Samuel
Thomas, Richard Henry
Tiffany, Louis McLane
Wagner, Clinton
Williams, John Whitridge
Wilson, Henry Parke Custis
UNIVERSITY OF MIAMI (FLA.)
Dunn, Michael
Mitchell, Martha Elizabeth Beall
UNIVERSITY OF MICHIGAN
Abbot, Willis John
Abel, John Jacob
Adams, Charles Kendall
Adams, Ephraim Douglass
Adams, Franklin Pierce
Aldrich, Edgar
Anderson, Clinton Presba
Andrews, Sidney
Angell, James Rowland
Auer, John

Baker, Marcus
Barnes, Mary Downing Sheldon
Beadle, William Henry Harrison
Beal, William James
Beecher, Charles Emerson
Bell, Frederic Somers
Bennett, Sanford Fillmore
Bigelow, Melville Madison
Biggers, John David
Blakeslee, Howard Walter
Blanshard, Paul
Bourke-White, Margaret
Bovie, William T.
Brennemann, Joseph
Brett, William Howard
Bronk, Detlev Wulf
Brown, Elmer Ellsworth
Brunton, David William
Brush, Charles Francis
Bryson, Lyman Lloyd
Burlingame, Anson
Burnett, Leo
Burton, Clarence Monroe
Campbell, Douglas Houghton
Campbell, William Wallace
Carson, Simeon Lewis
Cassoday, John Bolivar
Chapin, Roy Dikeman
Clements, William Lawrence
Coffin, Howard Earle
Cole, Arthur Charles
Comstock, George Cary
Cooley, Thomas Benton
Corwin, Edward Samuel
Covici, Pascal ("Pat")
Curme, George Oliver
Curtis, Heber Doust
Curwood, James Oliver
Davis, Cushman Kellogg
Davis, Raymond Cazallis
Day, William Rufus
De Kruif, Paul Henry
Denby, Edwin
Dennison, Walter
Dewey, Thomas Edmund
D'Ooge, Martin Luther
Doolittle, Charles Leander
Dunn, Michael
Durham, Caleb Wheeler
Edmunds, Charles Wallis
Evans, Edward Payson
Evans, Lawrence Boyd
Farnsworth, Elon John
Fay, Edward Allen
Ferris, Woodbridge Nathan
Fulton, Justin Dewey
Gauss, Christian Frederick
Gay, Edwin Francis
Gomberg, Moses
Grant, Claudius Buchanan
Gunn, Ross
Hall, Asaph
Hamilton, Alice
Hanus, Paul Henry
Hapgood, Hutchins
Harrington, Mark Walrod
Hart, Edwin Bret
Hempl, George
Hill, Louis Clarence
Holden, Liberty Emery
Hopwood, Avery
Howard, Timothy Edward
Hull, Clark Leonard
Humphrey, George Magoffin
Hupp, Louis Gorham
Hussey, William Joseph
Hutchins, Harry Burns
Hyde, Arthur Mastick
Jenks, Jeremiah Whipple
Jennings, Herbert Spencer
Kinne, La Vega George
Lange, Alexis Frederick
Lemmon, John Gill
Leonard, Sterling Andrus
Lindbergh, Charles Augustus
Lisagor, Peter Irvin
Livingston, Burton Edward
Locy, William Albert
Long, Perrin Hamilton
Lyster, Peter Francis Le Hunte
McAndrew, William
McLaughlin, Andrew Cunningham
McMurry, Frank Morton
Mall, Franklin Paine
Marland, Ernest Whitworth
Marsh, Frank Burr
Miller, Willoughby Dayton
Morton, Julius Sterling
Moses, Bernard
Mowrer, Edgar Ansel
Newberry, John Stoughton
Nichols, Dudley
Noble, Alfred
Novy, Frederick George
Otis, Charles Eugene
Palmer, Alice Elvira Freeman
Park, Robert Ezra
Penfield, William Lawrence
Pilcher, Lewis Stephen
Pilcher, Paul Monroe
Pitkin, Walter Boughton
Plumley, Frank
Pond, Allen Bartlit
Pond, Irving Kane
Prall, David Wight
Robinson, Albert Alonzo
Robinson, Edward Van Dyke
Robinson, Stillman Williams
Roethke, Theodore Huebner
Rogers, Henry Wade
Rosen, Joseph A.
Rowell, Chester Harvey
Salmon, Lucy Maynard
Schaeberle, John Martin
Scott, Fred Newton
Scovel, Henry Sylvester
Seager, Henry Rogers
Shafroth, John Franklin
Shepard, Fred Douglas
Shepard, James Henry
Simons, Henry Calvert
Sisler, George Harold ("Gorgeous George")
Skene, Alexander Johnston Chalmers
Smith, Betty
Smith, Erwin Frank
Spalding, Volney Morgan
Starrett, William Aiken
Swift, Lucius Burrie
Thomas, Calvin
Thomson, Mortimer Neal
Towne, Charles Arnette
Van Deman, Esther Boise
Vandenberg, Arthur Hendrick
Van Hook, Weller
Van Slyke, Lucius Lincoln
Vaughan, Victor Clarence
Von Ruck, Karl
Watson, James Craig
Webb, John Burkitt
Welch, Adonijah Strong
White, Stewart Edward
Wilbur, Cressy Livingston
Wilcox, Delos Franklin
Winchell, Horace Vaughn
Winchell, Newton Horace
Woodward, Robert Simpson
Woolley, John Granville
Work, Hubert
Young, Karl

Graduate Study

Adams, Ephraim Douglass
Angell, James Rowland
Bachmann, Werner Emmanuel
Briggs, Lyman James
Bronk, Detlev Wulf
Bryson, Lyman Lloyd
Butterfield, Kenyon Leech
Campbell, Douglas Houghton
Chamberlin, Edward Hastings
Chamberlin, Thomas Chrowder
Cole, Arthur Charles
Curtis, Heber Doust
De Kruif, Paul Henry
Gauss, Christian Frederick
Gomberg, Moses
Gordon, John Franklin
Gunn, Ross
Harrington, Mark Walrod
Hayden, Robert Earl
Holden, Liberty Emery
Kimball, (Sidney) Fiske
Leonard, Sterling Andrus
Lubin, Isador
Lyster, Henry Francis Le Hunte
Marsh, Frank Burr
Pearl, Raymond
Pilcher, Lewis Stephen
Robinson Albert Alonzo
Robinson Edward Van Dyke
Roethke, Theodore Huebner
Rogers, Henry Wade
St. John, Charles Edward
Salmon, Lucy Maynard
Scott, Austin
Scott, Fred Newton
Shepard, James Henry
Smith, Erwin Frank
Smith, Harold Dewey
Taylor, Fred Manville
Van Deman, Esther Boise
White, Edward Higgins, II

Law

Abbot, Willis John
Ashurst, Henry Fountain
Avery, Sewell Lee
Beadle, William Henry Harrison
Bigelow, Melville Madison
Birbo, Theodore Gilmore
Brice, Calvin Stewart
Brooks, John Graham
Browne, Francis Fisher
Brucker, Wilber Marion
Burke, Thomas, 1849–1925

Burton, Clarence Monroe
Cowen, John Kissig
Darrow, Clarence Seward
Daugherty, Harry Micajah
Day, William Rufus
Dewey, Thomas Edmund
Dickinson, Donald McDonald
Downey, Sheridan
Hart, Philip Aloysius
Haselton, Seneca
Haugen, Nils Pederson
Hitchcock, Gilbert Monell
Humphrey, George Magoffin
Kern, John Worth
Knapp, Bradford
Loeb, Milton B.
McCumber, Porter James
McLaughlin, Andrew Cunningham
MacPhail, Leland Stanford ("Larry")
Metcalf, Henry Harrison
Murphy, Frank
O'Brien, Thomas James
Rickey, Wesley Branch
Sharp, William Graves
Shauck, John Allen
Smith, James Allen
Sutherland, George
Wheeler, Burton Kendall
Wood, William Robert

Medicine

Carson, Simeon Lewis
Cooley, Thomas Benton
Copeland, Royal Samuel
Dewey, Richard Smith
Edmunds, Charles Wallis
Huber, Gotthelf Carl
Hutchinson, Woods
Kellogg, John Harvey
Long, Perrin Hamilton
Mall, Franklin Paine
Mayo, William James
Moore, James Edward
Mosher, Eliza Maria
Novy, Frederick George
Peckham, George Williams
Pilcher, Lewis Stephen
Prescott, Albert Benjamin
Rockwell, Alphonso David
Weeks, John Elmer
White, Charles Abiathar

UNIVERSITY OF MINNESOTA

Adams, Cyrus Cornelius
Amlie, Thomas Ryum
Bell, James Ford
Bierman, Bernard William ("Bernie")
Cannon, Ida Maud
Carlson, Richard Dutoit
Carruth, Fred Hayden
Conrad, Maximilian Arthur, Jr.
Daniels, Farrington
Devaney, John Patrick
Dobie, Gilmour
Folin, Otto Knut Olof
Forman, Justus Miles
Frary, Francis Cowles
Fulton, John Farquhar
Goode, John Paul
Haupt, Alma Cecelia
Hodson, William
Humphrey, Hubert Horatio, Jr.
Jacobs, Paul
Liggett, Walter William
Mitchell, William DeWitt
Olson, Floyd Bjerstjerne
Owre, Alfred
Park, Robert Ezra
Plowman, George Taylor
Plummer, Henry Stanley
Ranson, Stephen Walter
Roper, Elmo Burns, Jr.
Schall, Thomas David
Shaughnessy, Clark Daniel
Sumner, Francis Bertody
Swenson, David Ferdinand
Swift, Linton Bishop
White, Minor Martin
Wilson, Halsey William
Winchell, Horace Vaughn
Youngdahl, Luther Wallace

Dentistry

Owre, Alfred

Graduate Study

Daniels, Farrington
Elliott, Charles Burke
Frary, Francis Cowles
Kefauver, Grayson Neikirk
Lawrence, Ernest Orlando
Swenson, David Ferdinand
Young, Whitney Moore, Jr.

Law

Burdick, Usher Lloyd
Devaney, John Patrick
Dobie, Gilmour
Lundeen, Ernest
Morse, Wayne Lyman
Youngdahl, Luther Wallace

Medicine

Judd, Edward Starr
Wilson, Louis Blanchard

UNIVERSITY OF MISSISSIPPI

Bailey, Joseph Weldon
Baskerville, Charles
Brickell, Henry Herschel
Fulton, Robert Burwell
Galloway, Charles Betts
Gordon, James
Howry, Charles Bowen
Lambuth, James William
Malone, Walter
Manning, Vannoy Hartrog
Mayes, Edward
Valliant, Leroy Branch
Wright, Luke Edward
Young, Stark

Graduate Study

Odum, Howard Washington

Law

Brough, Charles Hillman
Farish, William Stamps
Mayes, Edward
Money, Hernando de Soto
Rankin, John Elliott
Stockdale, Thomas Ringland

UNIVERSITY OF MISSOURI

Anderson, Benjamin McAlester
Boyle, Harold Vincent ("Hal")
Brady, Mildred Alice Edie
Broadhead, Garland Carr
Brown, George Scratchley
Clark, Bennett Champ
Craig, Cleo Frank
Croy, Homer
Dandy, Walter Edward
Donnell, Forrest C.
Elkins, Stephen Benton
Field, Eugene
Field, Roswell Martin
Froman, Ellen Jane
Galloway, Beverly Thomas
Grasty, Charles Henry
Hodgen, John Thompson
Hough, Warwick
Jackson, Clarence Martin
King, Richard, Jr.
Long, Edward Vaughn
Lyon, Harris Merton
McBride, Mary Margaret
Manly, Basil Maxwell
Marbut, Curtis Fletcher
Mayo, William Worrell
Nelson, Donald Marr
Powell, John Benjamin
Prentis, Henning Webb, Jr.
Rautenstrauch, Walter
Robb, Inez Early Callaway
Ross, Charles Griffith
Rubey, William Walden
Shapley, Harlow
Short, Luke
Shouse, Jouett
Smith, James Allen
Snow, Edgar Parkes
Spillman, William Tasper
Stewart, Walter Winne
Stone, William Joel
Walker, Robert Franklin

Graduate Study

Lubin, Isador
Rautenstrauch, Walter
Shapley, Harlow

Law

Cannon, Clarence
Crowder, Enoch Herbert
Donnell, Forrest C.

Medicine

Jackson, Clarence Martin

UNIVERSITY OF MONTANA

Metcalf, Lee Warren
Rankin, Jeannette Pickering

UNIVERSITY OF MONTREAL (CANADA)

Graduate Study

Tate, George Henry Hamilton

UNIVERSITY OF MUNICH (GERMANY)

Bergmann, Max
Gabo, Naum
Morgenthau, Hans Joachim
Schindler, Kurt
Shellabarger, Samuel
Stanley, Wendell Meredith
Weidenreich, Franz
Weyl, Hermann
Wolff, Kurt August Paul

Graduate Study

Baker, Hugh Potter
Fromm, Erich
Hooker, Samuel Cox
Noyes, William Albert
Oldfather, William Abbott
Piccard, Jean Felix
Pritchett, Henry Smith
Quinn, Arthur Hobson

Rand, Edward Kennard
Schevill, Rudolph
Van Loon, Hendrik Willem
UNIVERSITY OF MUNSTER (GERMANY)
Baade, Wilhelm Heinrich Walter
UNIVERSITY OF NASHVILLE (TENN.)
Barksdale, William
Bell, John
Dickinson, Jacob McGavock
Donelson, Andrew Jackson
Fanning, Tolbert
Foster, Ephraim Hubbard
Hitchcock, Henry
Johnson, Cave
Lindsley, John Berrien
Maney, George Earle
Paine, Robert
Pillow, Gideon Johnson
Porter, James Davis
Rose, Wickliffe
Walker, William
Winston, John Anthony
Yerger, William
Graduate Study
Rose, Wickliffe
UNIVERSITY OF NEBRASKA
Abbott, Edith
Alexander, Hartley Burr
Botsford, George Willis
Briggs, Clare A.
Buckner, Emory Roy
Cather, Willa
Clements, Frederic Edward
Dern, George Henry
Douglas, Aaron
Eiseley, Loren Corey
Emerson, Rollins Adams
Fisher, Dorothea Frances Canfield
Guthrie, Edwin Ray, Jr.
Hollingworth, Leta Stetter
Howard, George Elliott
Hunter, Walter David
Johnson, Alvin Saunders
Lewis, Gilbert Newton
Magoon, Charles Edward
Patterson, Richard Cunningham, Jr.
Pound, (Nathan) Roscoe
Pritchard, Frederick John
Ricketts, Howard Taylor
Rohde, Ruth Bryan Owen
Rydberg, Per Axel
Simmons, George Henry
Tate, John Torrence
Thatcher, Roscoe Wilfred
Wallace, Charles William
Warner, Amos Griswold
Warren, George Frederick
Webber, Herbert John
Westermann, William Linn
Wherry, Kenneth Spicer
Wolfe, Harry Kirke
Graduate Study
Abbott, Grace
Clements, Frederic Edward
Guthrie, Edwin Ray, Jr.
Johnson, Alvin Saunders
Pearson, Raymond Allen
Pound, (Nathan) Roscoe
Tate, John Torrence
Webber, Herbert John
Westermann, William Linn
Law
Schoeppel, Andrew Frank
Medicine
Gifford, Sanford Robinson
UNIVERSITY OF NEUCHATEL (SWITZERLAND)
Schinz, Albert
UNIVERSITY OF NEVADA
Clark, Walter Van Tilburg
McCarran, Patrick Anthony
Martin, Anne Henrietta
UNIVERSITY OF NEW HAMPSHIRE
Graduate Study
Baroody, William Joseph
UNIVERSITY OF NEW MEXICO
Bryan, Kirk
Chapman, Oscar Littleton
Johnson, Douglas Wilson
Graduate Study
Coghill, George Ellett
UNIVERSITY OF NORTH CAROLINA
Alderman, Edwin Anderson
Ashe, Thomas Samuel
Avery, William Waigstill
Aycock, Charles Brantley
Barden, Graham Arthur
Barringer, Daniel Moreau
Barringer, Rufus
Baskerville, Charles
Battle, Kemp Plummer
Battle, William Horn
Bennett, Hugh Hammond
Benton, Thomas Hart
Bingham, Robert Worth
Bingham, William, 1835–1873
Blackmer, Sydney Alderman
Blakely, Johnston
Branch, John
Branch, Lawrence O'Bryan
Bridgers, Robert Rufus
Brown, Aaron Venable
Brown, Bedford
Burton, Hutchins Gordon
Butler, Marion
Carr, Elias
Clark, Walter
Clingman, Thomas Lanier
Connor, Robert Digges Wimberly
Denny, George Vernon, Jr.
Dick, Robert Paine
Dobbin, James Cochran
Eaton, John Henry
Ellis, John Willis
Fuller, Thomas Charles
Gales, Joseph
Graham, Edward Kidder
Graham, Frank Porter
Graham, William Alexander
Hale, Edward Joseph
Hawks, Francis Lister
Henderson, James Pinckney
Hodges, Luther Hartwell
Hoey, Clyde Roark
Hopkins, Arthur Francis
Keeney, Barnaby Conrad
King, William Rufus Devane
Kirby, George Hughes
Kolb, Reuben Francis
Lewis, William Gaston
Lowenstein, Allard Kenneth
Lynch, James Daniel
McIver, Charles Duncan
McRae, Duncan Kirkland
Mangum, Willie Person
Manning, Thomas Courtland
Marriott, Williams McKim
Mason, John Young
Means, Gaston Bullock
Moore, Bartholomew Figures
Morehead, John Motley
Murphey, Archibald De Bow
Murphy, James Bumgardner
Nicholson, Alfred Osborne Pope
Otey, James Hervey
Parker, John Johnston
Patterson, Rufus Lenoir
Pearson, Richmond Mumford
Pearson, Thomas Gilbert
Pettigrew, James Johnston
Polk, James Knox
Polk, Leonidas
Pool, John
Pou, Edward William
Ransom, Matt Whitaker
Reynolds, Robert Rice
Ruark, Robert Chester
Saunders, Romulus Mitchell
Saunders, William Laurence, 1835–1891
Sawyer, Lemuel
Schweinitz, Emil Alexander de
Settle, Thomas
Shipp, Albert Micajah
Stacy, Walter Parker
Staples, Waller Redd
Swain, David Lowry
Taylor, Hannis
Thompson, Jacob
Waddell, Alfred Moore
Warren, Lindsay Carter
Webb, William Robert
Weeks, Stephen Beauregard
Wiley, Calvin Henderson
Wolfe, Thomas Clayton
Graduate Study
Bible, Dana Xenophon
Wheeler, John Hill
Law
Battle, Kemp Plummer
Bickett, Thomas Walter
Blackman, Sydney Alderman
Cooley, Harold Dunbar
Gardner, Oliver Maxwell
Graham, Frank Porter
McLean, Angus Wilton
Parker, John Johnston
Reynolds, Robert Rice
Vance, Zebulon Baird
Warren, Lindsay Carter
Medicine
Simmons, James Stevens
UNIVERSITY OF NORTH DAKOTA
Aandahl, Fred George
Amlie, Thomas Ryum
Anderson, Maxwell
Frazier, Lynn Joseph
Lemke, William Frederick
Law
Langer, William

UNIVERSITY OF NORTHERN IOWA
Aldrich, Bess Genevra Streeter
UNIVERSITY OF OKLAHOMA
Heflin, Van
Kerr, Robert Samuel
Monroney, Almer Stillwell ("Mike")
Stigler, William Grady
Law
Long, Huey Pierce
UNIVERSITY OF OREGON
Buchanan, Edgar
Leemans, Alphonse E. ("Tuffy")
Neuberger, Richard Lewis
Prefontaine, Steve Roland ("Pre")
Robinson, Claude Everett
Medicine
McIntire, Ross
UNIVERSITY OF PADUA (ITALY)
Child, Robert
UNIVERSITY OF PARIS (FRANCE)
Chamberlain, Joseph Perkins
Graduate Study
Hills, Elijah Clarence
Noyes, William Albert, Jr.
Page, Thomas Walker
Medicine
Coutard, Henri
UNIVERSITY OF PENNSYLVANIA
Abbott, Charles Conrad
Adams, Randolph Greenfield
Adams, Robert
Adler, Cyrus
Alden, Raymond MacDonald
Alexander, Hartley Burr
Allen, Andrew
Andrews, John
Asch, Morris Joseph
Ashhurst, John
Bache, Franklin
Barker, Wharton
Barton, Benjamin Smith
Bates, George Handy
Battey, Robert
Bell, De Benneville ("Bert")
Bibb, William Wyatt
Biddle, James
Biddle, Nicholas, 1786–1844
Bingham, William, 1752–1804
Bird, Frederic Mayer
Blitzstein, Marc
Bloor, Ella Reeve
Boller, Alfred Pancoast
Booth, James Curtis
Borie, Adolphe
Borie, Adolph Edward
Bozman, John Leeds
Bradford, Thomas
Breck, James Lloyd
Brewster, Frederick Carroll
Brinton, John Hill
Brooks, Thomas Benton
Brown, Ralph Hall
Buehler, Huber Gray
Bullitt, Henry Massie
Cadwalader, John, 1742–1786
Cadwalader, John, 1805–1879
Cadwalader, Lambert
Carson, Hampton Lawrence
Carson, Joseph
Chandler, Joseph Ripley
Chapman, Henry Cadwalader
Cheyney, Edward Potts
Clayton, Joshua
Clopton, John
Coit, Henry Augustus
Cole, Arthur Charles
Coombe, Thomas
Cope, Edward Drinker
Coxe, Eckley Brinton
Coxe, Tench
Crawford, James Pyle Wickersham
Cuyler, Theodore Da
Costa, John Chalmers
Davidson, Robert
Davis, Bernard George
Decatur, Stephen, 1779–1820
Dewees, William Potts
Dick, Elisha Cullen
Dickinson, Philemon
Duane, William
Duché, Jacob
Duffield, George 1794–1868
Duhring, Louis Adotphus
Du Pont, Francis Irénée
Du Pont, Henry Algernon
Durant, Thomas Jefferson
Eberle, John
Elmer, Lucius Quintius Cincinnatus
Falkner, Roland Post
Farson, Negley
Finletter, Thomas Knight
Fisher, Clarence Stanley
Fleisher, Benjamin Wilfrid
Floyd, John
Frazer, John Fries
Frazer, Persifor
Frazier, Charles Harrison
Fullerton, George Stuart
Furness, Horace Howard, 1865–1930
Garnett, Alexander Yelverton Peyton
Garrison, Lindley Miller
Gibbons, Herbert Adams
Gilpin, Henry Dilworth
Gilpin, William
Goldsborough, Charles
Graydon, Alexander
Grayson, William
Green, Jacob, 1790–1841
Gregory, Caspar René
Grey, Zane
Griscom, Lloyd Carpenter
Hagner, Peter
Hare, Charles Reuben
Hanson, Alexander Contee, 1749–1806
Harding, George
Hare, John Innes Clark
Hare, William Hobart
Harrison, Charles Custis
Harshberger, John William
Hart, Charles Henry
Hartranft, Chester David
Hays, Isaac
Hemphill, Joseph
Hering, Carl
Hindman, William
Hirsch, Emil Gustav
Hirst, Barton Cooke
Hobart, John Henry
Hoch, August
Hodge, Hugh Lenox
Hopkinson, Francis
Hopkinson, Joseph
Humphreys, James
Hunt, Isaac
Huston, Charles
Hutchinson, James
Ingersoll, Edward
Jackson, David
James, Thomas Chalkley
Jastrow, Joseph
Jastrow, Morris
Jayne, Horace Fort
Kahn, Louis I.
Keating, John Marie
Keating, William Hypolitus
Kelly, Aloysius Oliver Joseph
Kelly, Howard Atwood
Lane, William Carr
La Roche, René
Leonard, Charles Lester
Lesley, Peter
Leslie, Charles Robert
Lewis, Lawrence
Little, Charles Joseph
Lochman, John George
Long, Joseph Ragland
McCletlan, George, 1849–1913
McClellan, George Brinton
M'Clintock, John
McDowell, John, 1751–1820
McGuire, Hunter Holmes
McKean, Joseph Borden
Malin, Patrick Murphy
Marchant, Henry
Mason, James Murray
Matthews, Joseph Merritt
Mease, James
Medary, Milton Bennett
Meigs, Arthur Vincent
Meigs, John Forsyth
Meigs, Montgomery Cunningham
Meigs, William Montgomery
Meredith, William Morris
Merrill, James Cushing
Mifflin, Thomas
Miller, Samuel, 1769–1850
Mitchell, Silas Weir
Montgomery, James Alan
Montgomery, Thomas Harrison
Morgan, John
Morris, Anthony, 1766–1860
Morris, Edward Joy
Morton, Henry
Morton, James St. Clair
Muhlenberg, William Augustus
Neidhard, Charles
Neill, Edward Duflield
Neill, John
Neill, Thomas Hewson
Newbold, William Romaine
Newton, Richard
Newton, Richard Heber
Newton, William Wilberforce
Nichols, Charles Henry
Nolen, John
Norris, George Washington
Norris, William Fisher

North, Elisha
Oberholtzer, Ellis Paxson
Odenheimer, William Henry
Ogden, David Bayard
O'Malley, Walter Francis
Osborn, Henry Stafford
Otto, John Conrad
Otto, William Tod
Paca, William
Packard, John Hooker
Pancoast, Henry Khunrath
Parke, John
Parke, John Grubb
Pemberton, Brock
Pepper, George Wharton
Pepper, William, III
Pepper, William, 1843–1898
Peters, Richard
Peterson, Charles Jacobs
Pettit, Thomas McKean
Phelps, Austin
Phillips, Francis Clifford
Phillips, Henry
Physick, Philip Syng
Piñero Jiménez, Jesus Toribio
Pound, Ezra
Price, Eli Kirk
Procter, John Robert
Quinn, Arthur Hobson
Rawle, William Henry
Read, John Meredith, 1797–1874
Reed, Henry Hoke
Reed, William Bradford
Reese, John James
Revel, Bernard
Reynolds, Julian Sargeant
Roberts, Owen Josephus
Rodney, Caesar Augustus, 1772–1824
Rogers, Robert William
Rosenbach, Abraham Simon Wolf
Sargent, Winthrop, 1825–1870
Saunders, William Lawrence, 1856–1931
Schaeffer, Charles Frederick
Schaeffer, Charles William
Schaeffer, David Frederick
Schelling, Ernest Henry
Schelling, Felix Emanuel
Scherman, Harry
Schmauk, Theodore Emanuel
Schmucker, Samuel Simon
Sergeant, Jonathan Dickinson
Sharswood, George
Skillern, Ross Hall
Sloan, Harold Paul
Smith, Albert Holmes
Smith, Samuel Harrison
Smith, Xanthus Russell
Spaeth, John Duncan
Speiser, Ephraim Avigdor
Stengel, Alfred
Stillé, Alfred
Stone, Witmer
Taylor, Francis Henry
Thomas, John Parnell
Thompson, Robert Ellis
Thornton, Henry Worth
Tilden, William Tatem ("Big Bill")
Tilghman, Edward
Tilghman, Richard Albert
Tilghman, Tench
Tilghman, William
Towne, Henry Robinson
Turner, Samuel Hulbeart
Vezin, Hermann
Walker, Robert John
Wallace, John William
Weems, Ted
Weisenburg, Theodore Herman
Wetherill, Charles Mayer
Wetherill, Samuel, 1821–1890
Wharton, Thomas Isaac
White, William
Willard, De Forest
Willard, James Field
Williamson, Hugh
Wilson, Bird
Wood, George Bacon
Woodhouse, James
Work, Milton Cooper
Wright, Henry
Zellerbach, Harold Lionel

Architecture

La Farge, Christopher Grant

Dentistry

Rosebury, Theodor

Graduate Study

Adams, Randolph Greenfield
Bolton, Herbert Eugene
Bronk, Detlev Wulf
Capen, Samuel Paul
Chiera, Edward
Clay, Albert Tobias
Cole, Arthur Charles
Corwin, Edward Samuel
Coxe, Eckley Brinton
Crawford, James Pyle Wickersham
Day, Frank Miles
Devine, Edward Thomas
Eiseley, Loren Corey
Fauset, Jessie Redmon
Fite, Warner
Goldsborough, Charles
Goode, John Paul
Guthrie, Edwin Ray, Jr.
Huebner, Solomon Stephen
Lee, Porter Raymond
Lewis, Lawrence
Lewis, Orlando Faulkland
Lewis, William Draper
Lingelbach, Anna Lane
Linton, Ralph
Locy, William Albert
Macfarlane, Charles William
McKinley, Albert Edward
Matthews, Joseph Merritt
Meigs, William Montgomery
MIller, Edward
Miller, Willoughby Dayton
Mills, Charles Karsner
Montgomery, James Alan
Munro, Dana Carleton
Newbold, William Romaine
Oberholtzer, Ellis Paxson
Parke, John
Paul, Alice
Pearson, Leonard
Perkins, Frances
Pound, Ezra
Quinn, Arthur Hobson
Ravenel, Mazyck Porcher
Reese, John James
Rosenbach, Abraham Simon Wolf
Schelling, Felix Emanuel
Speck, Frank Gouldsmith
Taylor, George William
Vedder, Edward Bright
Waller, Willard Walter
Watt, Donald Beates
Wheeler, (George) Post
White, James Williams
Wieland, George Reber
Willard, James Field
Woodhouse, James

Law

Balch, Thomas Willing
Carey, Joseph Maull
Carson, Hampton Lawrence
Duff, James Henderson
Finletter, Thomas Knight
Gates, Thomas Sovereign
Johnson, John Graver
Klingelsmith, Margaret Center
Lewis, William Draper
Long, Crawford Williamson
Lowndes, Lloyd
McCullough, John Griffith
Mitchell, James Tyndale
Nixon, William Penn
Parkinson, Thomas Ignatius
Pennypacker, Samuel Whitaker
Pepper, George Wharton
Price, Eli Kirk
Roberts, Owen Josephus
Schelling, Felix Emanuel
Sterne, Simon
Tauber, Maurice Falcolm
Wickersham, George Woodward
Work, Milton Cooper

Medicine

Agnew, David Hayes
Abden, Ebenezer
Allen, Harrison
Allen, Nathan
Archer, John
Arnold, Richard Dennis
Ashhurst, John
Atlee, John Light
Awl, William Maclay
Ayer, James Cook
Bagby, George William
Baldwin, William
Barnes, Albert Coombs
Barnes, Joseph K.
Barton, John Rhea
Barton, William Paul Crillon
Bigelow, Jacob
Bird, Robert Montgomery
Bloodgood, Joseph Colt
Boyé, Martin Hans
Bridges, Robert, 1806–1882
Brincklé, William Draper
Burnett, Charles Henry
Burton, William
Caldwell, Charles
Carson, Joseph
Channing, Walter
Channing, William Francis
Chapman, Henry Cadwalader
Chapman, Nathaniel

Cohen, Jacob Da Silva Solis
Cooke, John Esten
Coxe, John Redman
Cutter, Ephraim
Darlington, William
Deaver, John Blair
Dercum, Francis Xavier
Dewees, William Potts
Dickson, Samuel Henry
Dorset, Marion
Dorsey, John Syng
Drake, Daniel
Drinker, Cecil Kent
Drown, Thomas Messenger
Dudley, Benjamin Winslow
Earle, Pliny
Edsall, David Linn
Egle, William Henry
Elmer, Jonathan
Elwyn, Alfred Langdon
Emerson, Gouverneur
English, Thomas Dunn
Eve, Paul Fitzsimons
Ewell, Thomas
Forwood, William Henry
Frazier, Charles Harrison
Garretson, James Edmund
Gerhard, William Wood
Gibbons, William, 1781–1845
Gibson, William
Gihon, Albert Leary
Goddard, Paul Beck
Gray, John Purdue
Guiteras, Juan
Guthrie, Samuel
Hamilton, Frank Hastings
Happer, Andrew Patton
Harlan, Richard
Hartshorne, Henry
Hayes, Isaac Israel
Hays, Isaac
Hayward, George
Hepburn, James Curtis
Holbrook, John Edwards
Horn, George Henry
Horner, William Edmonds
Horsfield, Thomas
Hosack, Alexander Eddy
House, Samuel Reynolds
Hubbard, John
Huger, Francis Kinloch
Huntington, Jedediah Vincent
Jackson, Abraham Reeves
Jackson, Edward
Jackson, Henry Rootes
Jackson, John Davies
Jackson, Samuel
Johnson, Joseph
Jones, Alexander
Jones, Jacob
Jones, Joseph
Kane, Elisha Kent
King, Albert Freeman Africanus
Kintoch, Robert Alexander
Kirkbride, Thomas Story
Kutland, Jared Potter
Leidy, Joseph
Leonard, Charles Lester
Lindsley, John Berrien
Littell, Squier
McCartee, Divie Bethune
McCarthy, Daniel Joseph
McClellan, George, 1796–1847
McFarland, George Bradley
McMahon, Bernard
Massey, George Betton
Mastin, Claudius Henry
Mease, James
Meigs, Arthur Vincent
Meigs, Charles Delucena
Meigs, William Montgomery
Mettauer, John Peter
Michener, Ezra
Miller, Edward
Mills, Charles Karsner
Mitchell, Albert Graeme
Mitchell, George Edward
Mitchell, John Kearsley
Mitchell, Thomas Duché
Moore, Edward Mott
Morris, Caspar
Morton, Samuel George
Mussey, Reuben Dimond
Nancrède, Charles Beylard Guérard de
Nassau, Robert Hamill
Neill, John
Newell, William Augustus
Norris, George Washington
Norris, William Fisher
Oliver, Charles Augustus
O'Reilly, Robert Maitland
Otis, George Alexander
Ott, Isaac
Packard, John Hooker
Pancoast, Henry Khunrath
Pancoast, Joseph
Pancoast, Seth
Parrish, Joseph
Parry, John Stubbs
Patton, John Mercer
Peale, Titian Ramsay
Pepper, William, III
Pepper, William, 1810–1864
Percival, James Gates
Philips, Martin Wilson
Potter, Nathaniel
Potts, Charles Sower
Potts, Jonathan
Pyle, Walter Lytle
Ramsey, James Gettys McGready
Randall, Burton Alexander
Randolph, Jacob
Rauch, John Henry
Ravener, Edmund
Richardson, Charles Williamson
Richardson, Robert
Rogers, Robert Empie
Rosenau, Milton Joseph
Rush, James
Sargent, Fitz William
Saulsbury, Gove
Schamberg, Jay Frank
Schweinitz, George Edmund de
Seiler, Carl
Seybert, Adam
Shattuck, George Cheyne, 1783–1854
Short, Charles Wilkins
Simmons, James Stevens
Skillern, Ross Hall
Small, Alvan Edmond
Smith, Albert Holmes
Spencer, Pitman Clemens
Starr, Louis
Steiner, Lewis Henry
Stengel, Alfred
Stevens, Alexander Hodgdon
Stitt, Edward Rhodes
Strudwick, Edmund Charles Fox
Sutherland, Joel Barlow
Taylor, Joseph Wright
Thomas, Amos Russell
Thomas, Joseph
Ticknor, Francis Orray
Van Buren, William Holme
White, James William
Wickes, Stephen
Williams, William Carlos
Wistar, Caspar, 1761–1818
Witherspoon, John Alexander
Wood, George Bacon
Wood, Horatio Charles
Wood, Thomas
Woodhouse, James
Woodhull, Alfred Alexander
Woodward, Joseph Janvier
Work, Hubert
Wormley, Theodore George
Wright, Joseph Jefferson Burr
Young, John Richardson

Wharton School
Cheyney, Edward Potts
Gates, Thomas Sovereign
Gimbel, Bernard Feustman
Lippincott, Joseph Wharton
Reynolds, Julian Sargeant
Rowe, Leo Stanton
Shor, Bernard ("Toots")
Stouffer, Vernon Bigelow
Taylor, George William
Tugwell, Rexford Guy

UNIVERSITY OF PISA (ITALY)
Fermi, Enrico

Graduate Study
Fermi, Enrico

UNIVERSITY OF PITTSBURGH (PA.)
Allen, Hervey
Davis, Bernard George
Epstein, Abraham
Guthrie, George Wilkins
Herron, Francis Jay
Jackson, Chevalier
Jeffers, John Robinson
Johnston, William Andrew
Kaufman, George S.
Mellon, Andrew William
Negley James Scott
Oehmler, Leo Carl Martin
Reed, James Hay
Svenson, Andrew Edward
Thaw, Harry Kendall
Thaw, William

Graduate Study
Epstein, Abraham
Lashley, Karl Spencer
Morón, Alonzo Graseano
Reid, Ira De Augustine

Law
Duff, James Henderson
Gitt, Josiah Williams ("Jess")
Reed, David Aiken

Medicine
Hench, Philip Showalter
Henrici, Arthur Trautwein

UNIVERSITY OF POITIERS (FRANCE)
Shuster, George Nauman
UNIVERSITY OF PUERTO RICO
Piñero Jiménez, Jesús Toribio
UNIVERSITY OF RAVENNA (ITALY)
Pinza, Ezio
UNIVERSITY OF REDLANDS (CAL.)
Dean, Gordon Evans
MacNair, Harley Farnsworth
UNIVERSITY OF RICHMOND (VA.)
Day, James Gamble
Eggleston, George Cary
Hatcher, William Eldridge
Massey, John Edward
Robertson, Absalom Willis
Snead, Thomas Lowndes
Stanard, William Glover
Taylor, George Boardman
Law
Robertson, Absalom Willis
UNIVERSITY OF ROCHESTER (N.Y.)
Anderson, Galusha
Ayer, Francis Wayland
Backus, Truman Jay
Carpenter, Stephen Haskins
Coe, George Albert
Du Vigneaud, Vincent
Fassett, Jacob Sloat
Fenner, Burt Leslie
Fulton, Justin Dewey
Gally, Merritt
Gates, Frederick Taylor
Gilbert, Grove Karl
Goodspeed, Thomas Wakefield
Harkness, William
Holt, Luther Emmett
Hooker, Elon Huntington
Jackson, Shirley Hardie
Johnson, Elias Henry
Keating, Kenneth Barnard
Kelsey, Francis Willey
MacArthur, Robert Stuart
MacVicar, Malcolm
Marble, Manton Malone
Morehouse, Henry Lyman
Moss, Lemuel
Moxom, Philip Stafford
Otis, Elwell Stephen
Payne, Sereno Elisha
Perkins, James Breck
Rauschenbusch, Walter
Robinson, Charles Mulford
Selden, George Baldwin
Slater, John Clarke
Sterrett, James MacBride
Stevens, George Parker
Stoddard, William Osborn
Strong, Charles Augustus
Taylor, James Monroe
Tourgée, Albion Winegar
Vedder, Edward Bright
Vedder, Henry Clay
Welch, Leo Dewey
Williams, Charles Richard
Wilson, Joseph Chamberlain
UNIVERSITY OF ROME (ITALY)
Graduate Study
Ascoli, Max
UNIVERSITY OF ST. ANDREWS (SCOTLAND)
Johnston, John
Graduate Study
Johnston, John
UNIVERSITY OF ST. PETERSBURG (RUSSIA)
Rostovtzeff, Michael Ivanovitch
Stravinsky, Igor Fyodorovich
Tamarkin, Jacob David
Woytinsky, Wladimir Savelievich
UNIVERSITY OF SANTO TOMAS (PHILIPPINES)
Quezon, Manuel Luis
UNIVERSITYOF SASKATCHEWAN (CANADA)
Jacoby, Neil Herman
UNIVERSITY OF SOUTH CAROLINA
Aiken, David Wyatt
Aiken, William
Bonham, Milledge Luke
Bratton, John
Brawley, William Hiram
Brooks, Preston Smith
Brumby, Richard Trapier
Butler, Andrew Pickens
Butler, Matthew Calbraith
Capers, William
Clinton, George Wylie
Coker, David Robert
Conner, James
Cooper, Mark Anthony
Davidson, James Wood
Davis, George
Elmore, Franklin Harper
Floyd, John Buchanan
Gaillard, Edwin Samuel
Gary, Martin Witherspoon
Gaston, James McFadden
Gayle, John
Gibbes, Robert Wilson
Gist, William Henry
Gordon, George Byron
Govan, Daniel Chevilette
Hammond, James Henry
Hampton, Wade, 1818–1902
Harper, William
Harrisse, Henry
Hilliard, Henry Washington
Houston, David Franklin
Jamison, David Flavel
Johnstone, Job
Jones, Charles Colcock
Keitt, Lawrence Massillon
Kennedy, John Doby
Kerr, Washington Caruthers
La Borde, Maximilian
Legaré, Hugh Swinton
Levin, Lewis Charles
Lewis, Dixon Hall
Logan, Thomas Muldrup, 1840–1914
McBryde, John McLaren
McCord, David James
McDonald, Charles James
McDuffie, George
McGowan, Samuel
McGrath, Andrew Gordon
Manly, Basil, 1798–1868
Manning, Richard Irvine, 1789–1836
Miller, Stephen Decatur
Moses, Franklin J.
Nisbet, Eugenius Aristides
Nott, Henry Junius
Nott, Josiah Clark
O'Neall, John Belton
Petigru, James Louis
Philips, Martin Wilson
Pickens, Francis Wilkinson
Pinckney, Henry Laurens
Porcher, Francis Peyre
Preston, William Campbell
Ravenel, Henry William
Richardson, Willard
Rivers, William James
Rogers, James Harvey
Sanders, Billington McCarter
Simonton, Charles Henry
Simpson, William Dunlap
Sims, James Marion
Smith, Ellison DuRant
Stitt, Edward Rhodes
Thompson, Waddy
Thornwell, James Henley
Tompkins, Daniel Augustus
Wigfall, Louis Trezevant
Yeadon, Richard
Graduate Study
Johnston, Olin DeWitt Talmadge
Rogers, James Harvey
Law
Blease, Coleman Livingston
Rivers, Lucius Mendel
UNIVERSITY OF SOUTH DAKOTA
Davenport, Herbert Joseph
Lawrence, Ernest Orlando
Norbeck, Peter
Law
Leedom, Boyd Stewart
UNIVERSITY OF SOUTHERN CALIFORNIA
Arzner, Dorothy Emma
De Sylva, George Gard ("Buddy")
Earhart, Amelia Mary
McGinley, Phyllis
McWilliams, Carey
Oxnam, Garfield Bromley
Trumbo, James Dalton
Wayne, John
Wilson, Clarence True
Wright, Willard Huntington
Graduate Study
Andrus, Ethel Percy
Davis, Adelle
Metcalfe, Ralph Harold
Law
Dean, Gordon Evans
McWilliams, Carey
Willebrandt, Mabel Walker
Medicine
Jeffers, John Robinson
Theology
Wilson, Clarence True
UNIVERSITY OF STRASBOURG (FRANCE/GERMANY)
Graduate Study
Elkin, William Lewis
Huntington, Edward Vermilye
Lang, Henry Roseman
Sachs, Bernard
Torrey, Charles Cutler
Woods, James Haughton

Medicine
Abel, John Jacob
Loewi, Otto
UNIVERSITY OF SYDNEY (AUSTRALIA)
Ritchard, Cyril
UNIVERSITY OF TENNESSEE
Bridges, Thomas Jefferson Davis ("Tommy")
Camp, John Lafayette, 1828–1891
Clay, Clement Comer
Davis, Owen Gould
Dorset, Marion
Kefauver, (Carey) Estes
Knight, Frank Hyneman
Krutch, Joseph Wood
McAdoo, William Gibbs
McGhee, Charles McClung
Milton, George Fort
Oakes, George Washington Ochs
Sanford, Edward Terry
Thomas, William Isaac
Graduate Study
Knight, Frank Hyneman
Thomas, William Isaac
UNIVERSITY OF TEXAS
Batts, Robert Lynn
Clark, Tom Campbell
Dickson, Leonard Eugene
Dies, Martin
Gipson, Frederick Benjamin
Hamilton, Walton Hale
Jones, Richard Foster
Joplin, Janis Lyn
Key, Valdimer Orlando, Jr.
Lanham, Frederick Garland ("Fritz")
Lomax, John Avery
Maverick, (Fontaine) Maury
Mills, Charles Wright
Pool, Joe Richard
Ritter, Woodward Maurice ("Tex")
Sheppard, John Morris
Smith, Thomas Vernor
Webb, Walter Prescott
Graduate Study
Burleson, Albert Sidney
Dickson, Leonard Eugene
Key, Valdimer Orlando, Jr.
Lomax, John Avery
Mills, Charles Wright
Smith, Thomas Vernor
Webb, Walter Prescott
Law
Clark, Tom Campbell
Connally, Thomas Terry ("Tom")
Graves, David Bibb
Gregory, Thomas Watt
Jones, John Marvin
Lanham, Frederick Garland ("Fritz")
Rayburn, Samuel Taliaferro ("Sam")
Sheppard, John Morris
UNIVERSITY OF TEXAS MEDICAL BRANCH AT GALVESTON
Dyer, Rolla Eugene
UNIVERSITY OF THE PACIFIC (CAL.)
Rhodes, Eugene Manlove
Moscone, George Richard
UNIVERSITY OF THE SOUTH (TENN.)
Cain, Harry Pulliam
Gorgas, William Crawford
Lea, Luke
Manning, William Thomas
Murphy, Edgar Gardner
Percy, William Alexander
Ravenel, Mazyck Porcher
Trammell, Niles
Williams, John Sharp
Graduate Study
Lea, Luke
UNIVERSITY OF TOLEDO (OHIO)
Tunnell, Emlen
UNIVERSITY OF TORONTO (CANADA)
Bensley, Robert Russell
Cullen, Thomas Stephen
Daly, Reginald Aldworth
Duffy, Francis Patrick
Jeffrey, Edward Charles
Johnson, Harry Gordon
Kelley, Edith Summers
Keys, Clement Melville
Lawson, Andrew Cowper
Lillie, Frank Rattray
MacCallum, William George
McCrae, Thomas
McMurrich, James Playfair
Morgan, John Harcourt Alexander
Shotwell, James Thomson
Townsend, Willard Saxby, Jr.
Graduate Study
Gortner, Ross Aiken
Jeffrey, Edward Charles
Johnson, Harry Gordon
Lawson, Andrew Cowper
McCrae, Thomas
McMurrich, James Playfair
Smith, Theobald
Medicine
Bensley, Robert Russell
McCrae, Thomas
UNIVERSITY OF TOULOUSE (FRANCE)
Guthrie, Ramon
UNIVERSITY OF TÜBINGEN (GERMANY)
Graduate Study
Gottheil, Richard James Horatio
Goudsmit, Samuel Abraham
UNIVERSITY OF UTRECHT (NETHERLANDS)
Haagen-Smit, Arie Jan
UNIVERSITY OF UTAH
Clark, Joshua Reuben, Jr.
DeVoto, Bernard Augustine
McGinley, Phyllis
McKay, David Oman
Smith, George Albert
Thomas, Elbert Duncan
UNIVERSITY OF VERMONT
Albee, Ernest
Allen, George
Ashmun, Jehudi
Atwater, Wilbur Olin
Austin, Warren Robinson
Bennett, Edmund Hatch
Brown, George, 1823–1892
Collamer, Jacob
Converse, John Heman
Deming, Philander
Dewey, John
Ditson, George Leighton
Eastman, Charles Gamage
Eaton, Dorman Bridgman
Fisk, Wilbur
Hale, Robert Safford
Hammond, James Bartlett
Harris, Paul Percy
Haselton, Seneca
Houghton, Henry Oscar
Jameson, John Alexander
Kasson, John Adam
Kingsley, Darwin Pearl
Miller, Jonathan Peckham
Peabody, Selim Hobart
Polak, John Osborn
Porter, Russell Williams
Powell, Thomas Reed
Pratt, Sereno Stansbury
Raymond, Henry Jarvis
Shedd, William Greenough Thayer
Smith, Chauncey
Smith, John Gregory
Spaulding, Edward Gleason
Stevens, Benjamin Franklin
Stevens, Hiram Fairchild
Stevens, Thaddeus
Stewart, Alvan
Thompson, Zadock
Tuttle, Herbert
Wheeler, James Rignall
Wheeler, John Martin
Wheeler, William Almon
Worcester, Samuel Austin
Graduate Study
Clark, Walter Van Tilburg
Kerr, Sophie
Medicine
Wheeler, John Martin
UNIVERSITY OF VIENNA (AUSTRIA)
Bonsal, Stephen
Fenichel, Otto
Frank, Philipp G.
Gödel, Kurt Friedrich
Goldmark, Peter Carl
Grund, Francis Joseph
Julian, Percy Lavon
Koller, Carl
Landsteiner, Karl
Lazarsfeld, Paul Felix
Prokosch, Eduard
Reik, Theodor
Schumpeter, Joseph Alois
Graduate Study
Goldmark, Peter Carl
Julian, Percy Lavon
Lazarsfeld, Paul Felix
Moore, Henry Ludwell
Park, William Hallock
Reik, Theodor
Wright, James Arlington
Medicine
Sakel, Manfred Joshua
UNIVERSITY OF VIRGINIA
Adams, Daniel Weissiger

Bailey, Joseph Weldon
Baldwin, John Brown
Barbour, John Strode, Jr.
Bayly, Thomas Henry
Beale, Richard Lee Turberville
Beall, John Yates
Beatty, William Henry
Blackford, Charles Minor
Boyd, David French
Brannon, Henry
Breckinridge, Desha
Briggs, Charles Augustus
Broadhead, James Overton
Broadus, John Albert
Bruce, Philip Alexander
Bruce, William Cabell
Bryan, John Stewart
Byrd, Richard Evelyn
Cabell, James Lawrence
Calvert, Charles Benedict
Carr, Elias
Carter, Henry Rose
Chalmers, James Ronald
Cocke, Philip St. George
Conrad, Holmes
Dabney, Robert Lewis
Dabney, Virginius
Davis, William Augustine
Dinwiddie, Albert Bledsoe
Farrar, Edgar Howard
Faulkner, Charles James
Fenner, Charles Erasmus
Fishback, William Meade
Fleming, Aretas Brooks
Fortier, Alcée
Frost, Wade Hampton
Garnett, James Mercer
Garnett, Muscoe Russell Hunter
Gholson, Thomas Saunders
Gilliss, James Melville
Goss, James Walker
Graves, Alvin Cushman
Greenway, John Campbell
Halsey, William Frederick, Jr.
Harris, John Woods
Harris, Wiley Pope
Harrison, Gessner
Harrison, James Albert
Henry, William Wirt
Herbert, Hilary Abner
Holcombe, James Philemon
Humphreys, Wiliam Jackson
Hunter, Robert Mercer Taliaferro
Jackson, Howell Edmunds
Jesse, Richard Henry
Johnston, George Ben
Jones, John William
Joynes, Edward Southey
Kane, Elisha Kent
Keith, James
Lancaster, Henry Carrington
Lane, James Henry
Lay, Henry Champlin
Leathers, Waller Smith
Lewis, Fulton, Jr.
Lewis, James Hamilton
Ligon, Thomas Watkins
Lucas, Daniel Bedinger
McBryde, John McLaren
McCabe, William Gordon
McCausland, John
McCormick, Robert Sanderson
McEnery, Samuel Douglas
Mackenzie, John Noland
Manning, Richard Irvine
Martin, Thomas Staples
Mastin, Claudius Henry
Mathews, Henry Mason
Maury, Dabney Herndon
Maxwell, Augustus Emmett
Milton, George Fort
Minor, Benjamin Blake
Minor, John Barbee
Minor, Raleigh Colston
Moore, John Bassett
Mosby, John Singleton
Page, Thomas Walker
Pendleton, William Kimbrough
Peterkin, George William
Poe, Edgar Allan
Polk, Lucius Eugene
Pollard, Edward Alfred
Pratt, John Lee
Preston, John Smith
Randolph, George Wythe
Raney, George Pettus
Reed, Walter
Reese, Charles Lee
Robertson, William Joseph
Rodgers, John, 1812–1882
Rood, Ogden Nicholas
Saulsbury, Willard, 1861–1927
Slaughter, Philip
Smith, Howard Worth ("Judge")
Smith, John Lawrence
Smith, William Waugh
Southall, James Cocke
Sterrett, John Robert Sitlington
Stettinius, Edward Reilly
Stevenson, John White
Stuart, Alexander Hugh Holmes
Swann, Thomas
Taylor, George Boardman
Thompson, John Reuben
Timberlake, Gideon
Toulmin, Harry Theophilus
Toy, Crawford Howell
Trent, William Peterfield
Tucker, Henry St. George
Tucker, John Randolph
Tucker, Nathaniel Beverley
Tutwiler, Henry
Underwood, Oscar Wilder
Vandegrift, Alexander Archer
Vawter, Charles Erastus
Venable, Charles Scott
Venable, Francis Preston
Walker, Alexander
Watson, John William Clark
Watts, Thomas Hill
Wertenbaker, Charles Christian
Wertenbaker, Thomas Jefferson
White, Henry Clay
Whitsitt, William Heth
Wigfall, Louis Trezevant
Wilson, William Lyne
Young, Hugh Hampton
Young, Robert Ralph

Graduate Study

Bryan, John Stewart
Cabell, James Lawrence
Curtis, Heber Doust
Dabney, Charles William
Dargan, Edwin Preston
Dinwiddie, Albert Bledsoe
Dinwiddie, Courtenay
Du Bose, William Porcher
Lancaster, Henry Carrington
Mathews, Henry Mason
Smith, Henry Louis
Spencer, Samuel
Taylor, Robert Tunstall
Trent, William Peterfield
Tyler, Lyon Gardiner
Wertenbaker, Thomas Jefferson
Wilson, James Southall
Young, Hugh Hampton

Law

Battle, John Stewart
Bingham, Robert Worth
Blackford, Charles Minor
Bruce, David Kirkpatrick Este
Clarke, James Paul
Clay, Clement Claiborne
Cook, Philip
Culberson, Charles Allen
Davis, Henry Winter
Field, Marshall, IV
Flexner, Bernard
Garnett, Muscoe Russell Hunter
Grady, Henry Woodfin
Green, Benjamin Edwards
Gregory, Thomas Watt
Hines, Walker Downer
Hubbard, Richard Bennett
Johnson, Louis Arthur
Kennedy, Robert Francis
Lile, William Minor
Long, Joseph Ragland
McIlwaine, Richard
McReynolds, James Clark
Minor, Raleigh Colston
Montague, Andrew Jackson
Moore, George Fleming
Orr, James Lawrence
Page, Thomas Nelson
Peyton, John Lewis
Preston, William Ballard
Pryor, Roger Atkinson
Randolph, Edmund, 1819–1861
Reed, Stanley Forman
Reynolds, Richard Samuel, Sr.
Seddon, James Alexander
Slemp, Campbell Bascom
Snead, Thomas Lowndes
Stephens, Linton
Swanson, Claude Augustus
Thornton, Jessy Quinn
Tree, Lambert
Tyler, Lyon Gardiner
Warrington, Albert Powell
Willard, Joseph Edward
Williams, John Sharp
Wilson, Woodrow
Wise, John Sergeant

Medicine

Burrow, Trigant
Dyer, Isadore
Frost, Wade Hampton
Kean, Jefferson Randolph
Leathers, Waller Smith
Mackenzie, John Noland
Reed, Walter

Wilmer, William Holland
Young, Hugh Hampton

UNIVERSITY OF WARSAW (POLAND)
Wiener, Leo
Znaniecki, Florian Witold

UNIVERSITY OF WASHINGTON
Bartlett, Edward Lewis ("Bob")
Bell, Eric Temple
Biggers, John David
Cayton, Horace Roscoe
Cunningham, Imogen
Egtvedt, Clairmont ("Claire") Leroy
Fairchild, Muir Stephen
Gaston, Herbert Earle
Groves, Leslie Richard, Jr.
Huntley, Chester ("Chet") Robert
Irwin, Robert Benjamin
Langlie, Arthur Bernard
MacDonald, Betty
Meany, Edmond Stephen
Toklas, Alice Babette

Graduate Study
Jeffers, John Robinson
Meany, Edmond Stephen
Nelson, Marjorie Maxine
Wright, James Arlington

Law
Johnston, Eric Allen
Langlie, Arthur Bernard
Schwellenbach, Lewis Baxter

UNIVERSITY OF WESTERN ONTARIO (CANADA)
Johnson, Edward

UNIVERSITY OF WISCONSIN
Adams, Henry Cullen
Altmeyer, Arthur Joseph
Andrews, John Bertram
Baker, Carl Lotus
Bascom, Florence
Bashford, James Whitford
Bleyer, Willard Grosvenor
Bloodgood, Joseph Colt
Bolton, Herbert Eugene
Bruce, Andrew Alexander
Cajori, Florian
Chafin, Eugene Wilder
Crowley, Leo Thomas
Davies, Joseph Edward
Duffy, Francis Ryan
Elvehjem, Conrad Arnold
Esch, John Jacob
Fallows, Samuel
Farrington, Joseph Rider
Favill, Henry Baird
Fearing, Kenneth Flexner
Ford, Guy Stanton
Gale, Zona
Garst, Roswell ("Bob")
Gasser, Herbert Spencer
Gesell, Arnold Lucius
Goetz, George Washington
Gregory, Charles Noble
Gregory, Stephen Strong
Hansberry, Lorraine Vivian
Hoan, Daniel Webster
Hooton, Earnest Albert
Hopson, Howard Colwell
Hoyme, Gjermund
Huebner, Solomon Stephen
Huntington, William Edmonds
Jansky, Karl Guthe
Johnson, Hugh Samuel
Jones, Howard Mumford
Kleberg, Robert Justus, Jr.
Kremers, Edward
Krug, Julius Albert
La Follette, Philip Fox
La Follette, Robert Marion
La Follette, Robert Marion, Jr.
Leiserson, William Morris
Libby, Orin Grant
Lindbergh, Charles Augustus, Jr.
Lord, Henry Curwen
McHugh, Keith Stratton
McNair, Fred Walter
March, Fredric
Maslow, Abraham H.
Mason, Max
Mich, Daniel Danforth
Morse, Wayne Lyman
Muir, John
Nelson, Julius
Nielsen, Arthur Charles
Ochsner, Albert John
Pammel, Louis Hermann
Patchen, Kenneth
Perlman, Selig
Persons, Warren Milton
Pfund, August Herman
Purdy, Corydon Tyler
Rawlins, Marjorie Kinnan
Reinsch, Paul Samuel
Robertson, William Spence
Robinson, Frederick Byron
Roe, Gilbert Ernstein
Romnes, Haakon Ingolf ("H. I.")
Rublee, Horace
Rutledge, Wiley Blount
Savage, John Lucian ("Jack")
Schorer, Mark
Schwartz, Delmore David
Showerman, Grant
Simons, Algie Martin
Slichter, Louis Byrne
Slichter, Sumner Huber
Spooner, John Coit
Tatum, Edward Lawrie
Thompson, Stith
Turner, Frederick Jackson
Van Hise, Charles Richard
Van Vleck, John Hasbrouck
Vilas, William Freeman
Walsh, Thomas James
Weaver, Warren
Wilcox, Ella Wheeler
Witte, Edwin Emil
Wright, Frank Lloyd
Wright, John Kenneth Lloyd
Zuppke, Robert Carl

Graduate Study
Altmeyer, Arthur Joseph
Andrews, John Bertram
Bagley, William Chandler
Baker, Carl Lotus
Baker, Oliver Edwin
Bascom, Florence
Bleyer, Willard Grosvenor
Bloomfield, Leonard
Bolton, Herbert Eugene
Brown, Ralph Hall
Buley, Roscoe Carlyle
Cope, Arthur Clay
Dorn, Harold Fred
Elvehjem, Conrad Arnold
Ford, Guy Stanton
Gale, Zona
Hansen, Alvin Harvey
Haworth, Leland John
Hoagland, Dennis Robert
Hooton, Earnest Albert
Huebner, Solomon Stephen
Hull, Clark Leonard
Jansky, Karl Guthe
Johnson, Hugh Samuel
Jordan, Virgil Justin
Krug, Julius Albert
Libby, Orin Grant
McCarthy, Charles
Maslow, Abraham H.
Morehead, Agnes
Morse, Wayne Lyman
Mills, Charles Wright
Nelson, Julius
Perlman, Selig
Persons, Warren Milton
Pritchard, Frederick John
Purdy, Corydon Tyler
Reinsch, Paul Samuel
Robertson, William Spence
Schorer, Mark
Showerman, Grant
Slichter, Louis Byrne
Slichter, Sumner Huber
Tatum, Edward Lawrie
Weaver, Warren
West, Allen Brown
Willard, James Field
Williams, Thomas Harry
Witte, Edwin Emil
Woodbury, Helen Laura Sumner
Young, Allyn Abbott

Law
Amlie, Thomas Ryum
Bruce, Andrew Alexander
Comstock, George Cary
Davies, Joseph Edward
Duffy, Francis Ryan
Esch, John Jacob
Gregory, Charles Noble
Gregory, Stephen Strong
La Follette, Philip Fox
Pettigrew, Richard Franklin
Roe, Gilbert Ernstein
Tawney, James Albertus
Wiley, Alexander
Winslow, John Bradley

UNIVERSITY OF WURZBURG (GERMANY)
Barus, Carl
Wertheimer, Max

Graduate Study
Robb, William Lispenard

UNIVERSITY OF WYOMING
Downey, June Etta
Downey, Sheridan

UNIVERSITY OF ZURICH (SWITZERLAND)
Cabot, Godfrey Lowell
Courant, Richard
Loeb, Leo
Sigerist, Henry Ernest
Znaniecki, Florian Witold

Graduate Study
Clark, John Bates
Herty, Charles Holmes
Ostromislensky, Iwan Iwanowich
Medicine
Ostromislensky, Iwan Iwanowich
UPPER IOWA UNIVERSITY
Albright, William Foxwell
Mott, John R.
URBANA UNIVERSITY (OHIO)
Du Pont, Thomas Coleman
URBAN COLLEGE OF PROPAGANDA, ROME (ITALY)
Mundelein, George William
URBANIA COLLEGE OF THE SACRED CONGREGATION DE PROPAGANDA FIDE (ITALY)
Meyer, Albert Gregory
URSINUS ACADEMY AND COLLEGE (PA.)
Yerkes, Robert Mearns
UTAH STATE UNIVERSITY
Clyde, George Dewey
UTICA ACADEMY (N.Y.)
Butterfield, Daniel
Caton, John Dean
Dwight, Harrison Gray Otis
Hoadley, John Chipman
James, Thomas Lemuel
Seymour, Horatio
Stevens, George Washington
Walcott, Charles Doolittle
Williams, George Huntington

VALPARAISO NORMAL SCHOOL (IND.)
Gerber, (Daniel) Frank
VALPARAISO UNIVERSITY (IND.)
Blaine, John James
Campbell, William Edward March
Hunt, Haroldson Lafayette
Norris, George William
Smith, Gerald L. K.
Teeple, John Edgar
VANCEBURG SEMINARY (KY.)
White, Alma Bridwell
VANDERBILT UNIVERSITY (TENN.)
Alexander, Will Winton
Altsheler, Joseph Alexander
Barnard, Edward Emerson
Craighead, Edwin Boone
Davis, Jeff
Davis, Norman Hezekiah
Dowling, Noel Thomas
Elliott, William Yandell, III
Fletcher, Duncan Upshaw
Folk, Joseph Wingate
Hamilton, Walton Hale
Jarrell, Randall
Knapp, Bradford
Lanham, Frederick Garland ("Fritz")
McGill, Ralph Emerson
McReynolds, James Clark
Melton, James
Moore, (Austin) Merrill
Pusey, William Allen
Ransom, John Crowe
Rice, (Henry) Grantland
Sloan, George Arthur
Smith, James Perrin
Tate, John Orley Allen
Tigert, John James
Tigert, John James, IV
Turner, Fennell Parrish
Graduate Study
Elliott, William Yandell, III
Jarrell, Randall
Pusey, William Allen
Law
Bilbo, Theodore Gilmore
Byrns, Joseph Wellington
Clement, Frank Goad
Fletcher, Duncan Upshaw
Hastings, William Wirt
Medicine
Moore, (Austin) Merrill
VASSAR COLLEGE (N.Y.)
Barrows, Alice Prentice
Benedict, Ruth Fulton
Bentley, Elizabeth Terrill
Bishop, Elizabeth
Blatch, Harriot Eaton Stanton
Boissevain, Inez Milholland
Carr, Charlotte Elizabeth
Crapsey, Adelaide
Davis, Katharine Bement
Hatcher, Orie Latham
Kirkus, Virginia
Ladd-Franklin, Christine
Lathrop, Julia Clifford
Leach, Abby
Millay, Edna St. Vincent
Norris, Mary Harriott
Pulitzer, Margaret Leech
Putnam, Helen Cordelia
Richards, Ellen Henrietta Swallow
Rickert, Martha Edith
Roche, Josephine Aspinwall
Rourke, Constance Mayfield
Rukeyser, Muriel
Semple, Ellen Churchill
Stimson, Julia Catherine
Tappan, Eva March
Tutwiler, Julia Strudwick
Washburn, Margaret Floy
Webster, Alice Jane Chandler
Whitney, Mary Watson
VICTORIA COLLEGE (ENGLAND)
Graduate Study
Dakin, Henry Drysdale
VICTORIA UNIVERSITY (ENGLAND)
Buttrick, George Arthur
Todd, Thomas Wingate
VIDUS VACU SKOLA (LATIVIA)
Halsman, Philippe
VIENNA ACADEMY OF FINE ARTS (AUSTRIA)
Mestrovic, Ivan
Schindler, Rudolph Michael
VIENNA ACADEMY OF MUSIC (AUSTRIA)
Busch, Hermann
Rodzinski, Artur
VIENNA CONSERVATORY (AUSTRIA)
Bodanzky, Artur
Goldmark, Rubin
VILNA TEACHERS INSTITUTE (RUSSIA)
Cahan, Abraham
VIRGINIA MILITARY INSTITUTE
Buckner, Simon Bolivar
Clark, Tom Campbell
Colston, Raleigh Edward
Conrad, Holmes
Culberson, Charles Allen
Echols, John
Ezekiel, Moses Jacob
Faulkner, Charles James
Fry, Birkett Davenport
Harris, William Alexander
Jones, Thomas Goode
Kemper, James Lawson
Lane, James Henry
McCausland, John
Mahone, William
Marshall, George Catlett, Jr.
Martin, Thomas Staples
Maverick, (Fontaine) Maury
Murfee, James Thomas
Patton, George Smith
Peyton, John Lewis
Polk, William Mechlenburg
Puller, Lewis Burwell ("Chesty")
Rockwell, Kiffin Yates
Rodes, Robert Emmett
Ross, Erskine Mayo
Shipp, Scott
Short, Joseph Hudson, Jr.
Slemp, Campbell Bascom
Walker, Reuben Lindsay
Willard, Joseph Edward
Wise, John Sergeant
VIRGINIA POLYTECHNIC INSTITUTE
Dodd, William Edward
Pick, Lewis Andrew
Graduate Study
Dodd, William Edward
VIRGINIA UNION UNIVERSITY
Johnson, Charles Spurgeon
Powell, Adam Clayton, Sr.
VOLHYNIAN THEOLOGICAL SEMINARY (RUSSIA)
Leonty, Metropolitan

WABASH COLLEGE (IND.)
Acker, Charles Ernest
Anderson, Edwin Hatfield
Arnold, Thurman Wesley
Bassett, James
Black, John Charles
Hays, Will H.
McDonald, Joseph Ewing
Marshall, Thomas Riley
Patterson, Thomas MacDonald
Record, Samuel James
Reynolds, Joseph Jones
Rose, Joseph Nelson
Rovenstine, Emery Andrew
Whetzel, Herbert Hice
Wilson, Henry Lane
Wilson, John Lockwood
Woods, William Allen
WADDEL'S ACADEMY (S.C.)
Butler, Andrew Pickens
Calhoun, John Caldwell
Collier, Henry Watkins
Curry, Jabez Lamar Monroe
Gilmer, George Rockingham
Legaré, Hugh Swinton
Longstreet, Augustus Baldwin
Petigru, James Louis

WAKE FOREST COLLEGE (N.C.)
Adams, Joseph Quincy
Bailey, Josiah William
Battle, John Stewart
Bickett, Thomas Walter
Cash, Wilbur Joseph
Dixon, Thomas
Kitchin, Claude
Kitchin, William Walton
Royster, James Finch
Simmons, Furnifold McLendel
Stallings, Laurence Tucker
Yates, Matthew Tyson
Graduate Study
Adams, Joseph Quincy
Law
Cash, Wilbur Joseph
WAR COLLEGE (D.C.)
Vanderbuilt, Cornelius, Jr.
WARSAW CONSERVATORY (POLAND)
Landowska, Wanda Aleksandra
WASHBURN COLLEGE (KAN.)
Menninger, William Claire
Sutherland, Earl Wilbur, Jr.
WASHBURN UNIVERSITY (KAN.)
Hope, Clifford Ragsdale
WASHINGTON ACADEMY (*See* WASHINGTON AND LEE UNIVERSITY)
WASHINGTON AND JEFFERSON COLLEGE (PA.)
Agnew, David Hayes
Anden, William Livingston
Andrews, Lorrin
Baird, Absalom
Baird, Robert
Beaver, James Addams
Bissell, George Henry
Blaine, James Gillespie
Breckinridge, Robert Jefferson
Breckinridge, William Campbell Preston
Bristow, Benjamin Helm
Brown, Fayette
Chambers, Ezekiel Forman
Colwell, Stephen
Cooper, James
Cort, Edwin Charles
Dodd, Samuel Calvin Tate
Ewing, James Caruthers Rhea
Fisher, Daniel Webster
Fleming, John
Foster, Stephen Collins
Fry, Birkett Davenport
Geary, John White
Gildersleeve, Basil Lanneau
Good, Adolphus Clemens
Greer, David Hummell
Hamilton, Maxwell McGaughey
Hamilton, William Thomas
Hemphill, John
Hendricks, William
Imboden, John Daniel
Jacobs, Michael
Jenkins, Albert Gallatin
Kemper, James Lawson
Lane, William Carr
Latham, Milton Slocum
Leffler, Shepherd
Letterman, Jonathan
Lowes, John Livingston
Lowndes, Lloyd
Lucas, James H.
Lyon, James Benjamin
McCartney, Washington
McCay, Charles Francis
McCook, Henry Christopher
McCook, John James
McCormick, Samuel Black
McFarland, George Bradley
McFarland, Samuel Gamble
McGuffey, William Holmes
McKennan, Thomas McKean Thompson
McLaren, William Edward
Marquis, John Abner
Mateer, Calvin Wilson
Mathews, John Alexander
Mercur, Ulysses
Milligan, Robert
Mitchell, William, 1832–1900
Morgan, George Washington
Muhlenberg, Frederick Augustus
Nevin, Alfred
Nevin, Edwin Henry
Nevin, Robert Peebles
Passavant, William Alfred
Pickens, Israel
Quay, Matthew Stanley
Riddle, Matthew Brown
Riggs, Stephen Return
Rollins, James Sidney
Sargent, Fitz William
Speer, William
Stanbery, Henry
Stewart, Robert
Stockdale, Thomas Ringland
Strother, David Hunter
Swank, James Moore
Thompson, Josiah Van Kirk
Vallandigham, Clement Laird
Wallace, Henry
Watson, David Thompson
Wherry, Elwood Morris
Wines, Frederick Howard
Wise, Henry Alexander
Woodrow, James
Wright, Joseph Jefferson Burr
Wylie, Andrew
Graduate Study
Cort, Edwin Charles
Lowes, John Livingston
WASHINGTON AND LEE UNIVERSITY (VA.)
Alexander, Archibald
Allen, John James
Ambler, James Markham Marshall
Anderson, David Lawrence
Ayres, Brown
Brown, Clarence James
Caruthers, William Alexander
Chamberlain, George Earle
Chavis, John
Davis, John William
Dillard, James Hardy
Echols, John
Ellis, Powhatan
Foote, Henry Stuart
Foster, Murphy James
Giles, Warren Crandall
Glenn, John Mark
Hall, Luther Egbert
Harris, John Woods
Hoge, Moses
Holcombe, William Henry
Humphreys, Milton Wylie
Humphreys, Wiliam Jackson
Lamar, Joseph Rucker
Le Moyne, Francis Julius
Letcher, John
McDowell, James
McKee, John
McRae, Thomas Chipman
Manly, Basil Maxwell
Moore, Andrew
Morrison, William McCutchan
Nelson, David
O'Ferrall, Charles Triplett
O'Neal, Edward Asbury, III
Owen, Robert Latham
Page, Thomas Nelson
Parker, Richard Elliott
Plumer, William Swan
Poindexter, Miles
Preston, William Campbell
Priestley, James
Rice, John Holt
Ruffner, Henry
Ruffner, William Henry
Shepard, Seth
Summers, George William
Sydenstricker, Edgar
Tucker, Henry St. George
Graduate Study
Davis, John William
Dillard, James Hardy
Glenn, John Mark
Sydenstricker, Edgar
Law
Baker, Newton Diehl
Dillard, James Hardy
WASHINGTON COLLEGE (CONN.) (*See* TRINITY COLLEGE)
WASHINGTON COLLEGE (MD.)
Cain, James Mallahan
Emory, John
Goldsborough, Thomas Alan
Harrington, Samuel Maxwell
Townsend, George Alfred
Veazey, Thomas Ward
Wilmer, William Holland
WASHINGTON COLLEGE (TENN.)
Carter, Samuel Powhatan
Ramsey, James Gettys McGready
Temple, Oliver Perry
Vance, Zebulon Baird
WASHINGTON COLLEGIATE INSTITUTE (N.Y.)
Clarke, Thomas Benedict
WASHINGTON STATE COLLEGE
Heald, Henry Townley
Murrow, Edward (Egbert) Roscoe
Graduate
Still, Clyfford
WASHINGTON STATE SCHOOL OF OPTOMETRY
Wallgren, Mon[rad] C[harles]
WASHINGTON UNIVERSITY (MO.)
Anderson, Paul Y.
Bates, John Coalter
Biggers, John David
Burman, John Miller
Cameron, William Evelyn

Crunden, Frederick Morgan
Eames, Charles Ormand, Jr.
Engelmann, George Julius
Fox, William Carlton
Francis, David Rowland
Harris, James Arthur
Hoagland, Charles Lee
Holden, Edward Singleton
Hurst, Fannie
Johnston, William Hartshorne
Link, Theodore Carl
More, Paul Elmer
Moreell, Ben
Stolberg, Benjamin
Taussig, Frank William
Wislocki, George Bernays
Graduate Study
More, Paul Elmer
Niebuhr, Helmut Richard
Webber, Herbert John
Law
Davis, Dwight Filley
Long, Breckinridge
Nast, Condé Montrose
Smith, Ralph Tyler
Medicine
Goldstein, Max Aaron
Hoagland, Charles Lee
Knowles, John Hilton
Porter, William Townsend
Sutherland, Earl Wilbur, Jr.
Taussig, Frederick Joseph
WATERVILLE COLLEGE (*See* COLBY COLLEGE)
WAYNE STATE UNIVERSITY (MICH.)
Hayden, Robert Earl
Reuther, Walter Philip
WEATHERFORD COLLEGE (TEX.)
Lanham, Frederick Garland ("Fritz")
WEBB INSTITUTE OF NAVAL ARCHITECTURE (N.Y.)
Ward, Charles Alfred
WELLESLEY COLLEGE
Bates, Katharine Lee
Breckenridge, Sophonisba Preston
Cannon, Annie Jump
Clapp, Margaret Antoinette
Coyle, Grace Longwell
Davies, Maria Thompson
Isom, Mary Frances
Kingsley, Elizabeth Seelman
Nichols, Ruth Rowland
Pendleton, Ellen Fitz
Plummer, Mary Wright
Smith, Mildred Catharine
Whitney, Charlotte Anita
Woodbury, Helen Laura Sumner
Graduate Study
Bates, Katharine Lee
Pendleton, Ellen Fitz
WESLEY COLLEGE (TEX.)
Dies, Martin
WESLEYAN COLLEGE (ENGLAND)
Davies, John Vipond
WESLEYAN COLLEGE (MONT.)
Cooper, Gary
WESLEYAN UNIVERSITY (CONN.)
Allyn, Robert
Andrews, Edward Gayer
Arnold, Harold DeForest
Atwater, Wilbur Olin
Baker, Osmon Cleander
Bangs, Francis Nehemiah
Brewer, David Josiah
Brooks, Byron Alden
Buckley, James Monroe
Buckley, Samuel Botsford
Burrowes, Edward Thomas
Burton, Nathaniel Hudson
Child, Charles Manning
Cummings, Joseph
Davison, George Willets
Dorchester, Daniel
Dow, Lorenzo
Foss, Cyrus David
Goode, George Brown
Gordy, John Pancoast
Greenslet, Ferris
Harris, Daniel Lester
Haven, Erastus Otis
Haven, Gilbert
Hendrix, Eugene Russell
Hoyt, Albert Harrison
Hubbard, Henry Griswold
Hurlbut, Jesse Lyman
Inglis, Alexander James
Judd, Charles Hubbard
Judd, Orange
Kemmerer, Edwin Walter
Kidder, Daniel Parish
Knapp, Martin Augustine
Lee, James Melvin
Mather, Samuel Livingston
Merrick, Frederick
Merrill, Elmer Truesdell
Mitchell, Hinckley Gilbert Thomas
Mudge, James
Peirce, Bradford Kinney
Pitkin, Frederick Walker
Ray, Charles Bennett
Rice, William North
Roberts, Benjamin Titus
Robinson, William
Robinson, William Callyhan
Rosa, Edward Bennett
Rust, Richard Sutton
Sanford, Elias Benjamin
Saxe, John Godfrey
Smith, Bruce
Squire, Watson Carvosso
Steele, Daniel
Stevens, Abel
Stiles, Charles Wardell
Strong, James
Thorndike, Ashley Horace
Thorndike, Edward Lee
Thorndike, Lynn
Thorpe, Thomas Bangs
True, Alfred Charles
Upham, Samuel Foster
Vanderbilt, Arthur T.
Van Vleck, Edward Burr
Warren, Henry White
Warren, William Fairfield
Weeks, Joseph Dame
Wiley, Ephraim Emerson
Winchell, Alexander
Winchester, Caleb Thomas
Wood, Thomas Bond
Graduate Study
Child, Charles Manning
Merrill, Elmer Truesdell
WESTERN COLLEGE (N. MEX.)
Rust, John Daniel
WESTERN COLLEGE FOR WOMEN (OHIO)
Anderson, Margaret Carolyn
WESTERN COLLEGIATE INSTITUTE (IOWA)
Howard, Edgar
WESTERN DENTAL COLLEGE (MO.)
Stengel, Charles Dillon ("Casey")
WESTERN RESERVE ECLECTIC INSTITUTE (*See* HIRAM COLLEGE)
WESTERN RESERVE UNIVERSITY (OHIO)
Allen, Florence Ellinwood
Allison, William Boyd
Axtell, Samel Beach
Bourke-White, Margaret
Brett, William Howard
Chamberlain, Jacob
Chamberlain, William Isaac
Clarke, John Hessin
Curtis, William Eleroy
Elwell, John Johnson
Flexner, Jennie Maas
Foote, Lucius Harwood
Hanna, Marcus Alonzo
Harvey, Louis Powell
Hoadly, George
Hough, Franklin Benjamin
Ladd, George Trumbull
Leggett, Mortimer Dormer
Lord, Asa Dearborn
McGiffert, Arthur Cushman
Newberry, John Strong
Paine, Halbert Eleazer
Ranney, Ruffus Percival
Robertson, James Alexander
Seymour, Thomas Day
Strong, Josiah
Wheeler, Wayne Bidwell
Willis, Henry Parker
Woods, William Burnham
Graduate Study
Allen, Florence Ellinwood
Medicine
Crile, George Washington
Lower, William Edgar
WESTERN THEOLOGICAL SEMINARY (ILL.)
Bell, Bernard Iddings
Sumner, Walter Taylor
WESTERN THEOLOGICAL SEMINARY (OHIO)
Ewing, James Caruthers Rhea
Fisher, Daniel Webster
Good, Adolphus Clemens
Happer, Andrew Patton
Jones, John Percival
Kyle, James Henderson
Lowes, John Livingston
McCook, Henry Christopher
McCormick, Samuel Black
McFarland, Samuel Gamble
Marquis, John Abner
Mateer, Calvin Wilson

Nevin, Alfred
Nevin, Edwin Henry
Riddle, Matthew Brown
Riggs, Stephen Return
Schereschewsky, Samuel Isaac Joseph
Speer, William
Tanner, Benjamin Tucker
Thompson, William Oxley
Wilson, Samuel Graham
Young, Samuel Hall

WESTFIELD ACADEMY (MASS.)
Allen, Jeremiah Mervin
Allen, Richard Lamb
Chapin, Chester William
Clemmer, Mary
Ditson, George Leighton
Goodrich, Benjamin Franklin
Hall, Arethusa
King, Thomas Butler
Orton, Edward Francis Baxter
Pease, Elisha Marshall
Perkins, Justin
Stockton, Charles G.
Thayer, Amos Madden
Williston, Samuel

WESTMINSTER COLLEGE (MO.)
McAfee, John Armstrong
Shields, George Howell
Shipp, Scott

WESTMINSTER COLLEGE (PA.)
Miller, James Russell
Potts, Benjamin Franklin
Thompson, Samuel Rankin

WESTON COLLEGE (MASS.)
O'Callahan, Joseph Timothy
Graduate Study
O'Callahan, Joseph Timothy

WEST POINT (*See* UNITED STATES MILITARY ACADEMY)

WESTTOWN BOARDING SCHOOL (PA.)
Cope, Edward Drinker
Cox, Hannah Peirce
Cox, Samuel Hanson
Emerson, Gouverneur
Gummere, John
Hayes, Isaac Israel
Hazard, Rowland Gibson
Hazard, Thomas Robinson
Magill, Edward Hicks
Morton, Samuel George
Say, Thomas
Sharpless, Isaac
Smith, Albert Holmes
Smith, John Joy
Wood, James, 1839–1925

WEST VIRGINIA UNIVERSITY
Brooke, Charles Frederick Tucker
Hough, Walter
Kilgore, Harley Martin
Lashley, Karl Spencer
McAuliffe, Anthony Clement
Neely, Matthew Mansfield
Graduate Study
Brooke, Charles Frederick Tucker
Hough, Walter
Kagan, Henry Enoch
Law
Yost, Fielding Harris

WHEATON COLLEGE (MASS.)
Lincoln, Mary Johnson Bailey
Parkhurst, John Adelbert
Stoddard, Elizabeth Drew Barstow
Woolley, Mary Emma

WHITESTOWN SEMINARY (N.Y.)
Child, Frank Samuel
Deming, Philander
Gaynor, William Jay
Morris, Edward Dafydd
Roberts, Ellis Henry

WHITMAN COLLEGE (WASH.)
Cordiner, Ralph Jarron
Douglas, William Orville
Nelson, Marjorie Maxine

WIDENER COLLEGE (PA.)
Riddle, Samuel Doyle

WILBERFORCE UNIVERSITY (OHIO)
Rushing, James Andrew
Still, William Grant, Jr.
Webster, Benjamin ("Ben") Francis

WILBRAHAM ACADEMY (MASS.)
Andrews, Elisha Benjamin
Baker, Lorenzo Dow
Baker, Osmon Cleander
Bowman, Thomas
Brown, John Mifflin
Burton, Nathaniel Judson
Conwell, Russell Herman
Crane, Winthrop Murray
Dean, Sidney
Goodnow, Isaac Tichenor
Haven, Gilbert
Ladd-Franklin, Christine
Lee, Jason
Marcy, Henry Orlando
Merrick, Edwin Thomas
Peirce, Bradford Kinney
Phelps, Austin
Pratt, Charles
Prudden, Theophil Mitchell
Ray, Charles Bennett
Raymond, Miner
Rushing, James Andrew
Rust, Richard Sutton
Slater, John Fox
Stebbins, Rufus Phineas
Steele, Daniel
Stevens, Abel
Warren, Henry White
Winchester, Caleb Thomas

WILEY UNIVERSITY (TEX.)
Scott, Emmett Jay

WILLAMETTE UNIVERSITY (ORE.)
Hawley, Willis Chatman
Graduate Study
Hawley, Willis Chatman

WILLARD'S FEMALE SEMINARY (*See* TROY FEMALE SEMINARY)

WILLIAM AND MARY (*See* COLLEGE OF WILLIAM AND MARY)

WILLIAM JEWELL COLLEGE (MO.)
Hudson, Manley Ottmer
Martin, Warren Homer
Graduate Study
Cannon, Clarence
Hudson, Manley Ottmer

WILLIAMS COLLEGE (MASS.)
Aitken, Robert Grant
Alden, Henry Mills
Allen, David Oliver
Allen, Elisha Hunt
Alvord, Clarence Walworth
Andrews, Israel Ward
Andrews, Samuel James
Armstrong, Samuel Chapman
Atwater, Caleb
Bachman, John
Ballinger, Richard Achilles
Barnard, Daniel Dewey
Bascom, John
Beman, Nathan Sidney Smith
Benedict, Erastus Cornelius
Benjamin, Nathan
Benjamin, Samuel Greene Wheeler
Betts, Samuel Rossiter
Birge, Edward Asahel
Boise, Reuben Patrick
Boynton, Charles Brandon
Brace, John Pierce
Brackett, Charles William
Bradish, Luther
Bradley, John Edwin
Brooks, William Keith
Bross, William
Browne, Charles Albert
Bryant, William Cullen
Bumstead, Freeman Josiah
Canfield, James Hulme
Carter, Franklin
Chadbourne, Paul Ansel
Clark, Horace Francis
Colby, Bainbridge
Curtis, Moses Ashley
Darby, John
Davies, Henry Eugene
Dearborn, Henry Alexander Scammell
Dennett, Tyler (Wilbur)
Dewey, Chester
Dewey, Orville
Dickinson, John Woodbridge
Dike, Samuel Warren
Dixon, James
Dodge, Raymond
Dole, Sanford Ballard
Driscoll, Alfred Eastlack
Eastman, Max Forrester
Eaton, Amos
Edmonds, John Worth
Edwards, Bela Bates
Edwards, Justin
Edwards, William Henry
Emmons, Ebenezer
Ernst, Morris Leopold
Evans, Walker
Field, David Dudley, 1805–1894
Field, Eugene
Field, Henry Martyn
Field, Stephen Dudley
Field, Stephen Johnson
Fieser, Louis Frederick
Fowler, Orin
Gardner, Gilson
Garfield, Harry Augustus
Garfield, James Abram
Garfield, James Rudolph
Giles, Chauncey
Gladden, Washington
Goodrich, Chauncey, 1836–1925

Green, Asa
Greenbaum, Edward Samuel
Griffin, Solomon Bulkley
Gross, Charles
Gulick, John Thomas
Hale, Nathan, 1784–1863
Hall, Charles Cuthbert
Hall, Granville Stanley
Hallock, Gerard
Hallock, William Allen
Hammond, Edward Payson
Haynes, John Henry
Hill, George Washington
Hitchcock, Phineas Warrener
Hoisington, Henry Richard
Holden, Hale
Holley, Myron
Hopkins, Mark
Howard, Jacob Merritt
Howe, Samuel
Hoyt, Henry Martyn
Ingalls, John James
Jackson, William Alexander
Judson, Harry Pratt
Kaufmann, Walter Arnold
Kellogg, Samuel Henry
King, Jonas
Kingsley, James Luce
Lamb, William Frederick
Labaree, Leonard Woods
Lawson, John Howard
Lee, Charles Alfred
Lehman, Herbert Henry
Leupp, Francis Ellington
Mabie, Hamilton Wright
McClellan, Henry Brainerd
MacLean, George Edwin
McMath, Robert Emmet
Mather, Frank Jewett, Jr.
Mills, Cyrus Taggart
Mills, Elijah Hunt
Mills, Samuel John
Morton, Chartes Walter
Nelson, Henry Loomis
Ogden, Rollo
Orton, James
Parker, Samuel
Peloubet, Francis Nathan
Perry, Arthur Latham
Perry, Bliss
Pratt, James Bissett
Pratt, Waldo Selden
Prime, Samuel Irenaeus
Raymond, George Lansing
Rice, Luther
Richards, William
Richards, Zalmon
Robbins, Thomas
Robinson, Benjamin Lincoln
Robinson, Charles Seymour
Roe, Edward Payson
Rowland, Henry Cottrell
Rumsey, William
Rutherford, Lewis Morris
Schauffler, Henry Albert
Scudder, Horrace Elisha
Scudder, Samuel Hubbard
Sherman, Stuart Pratt
Smith, Harry James
Snow, Francis Huntington
Spencer, John Canfield
Spring, Leverett Wilson
Stetson, Francis Lynde
Stewart, Edwin
Stiles, Henry Reed
Stoddard, David Tappan
Stoddard, John Lawson
Storrs, Richard Salter, 1787–1873
Thacher, John Boyd
Tomlinson, Everett Tilsworth
Tucker, Gilbert Milligan
Turner, George Kibbe
Vinton, Samuel Finley
Ward, Henry Augustus
Ward, Henry Baldwin
Ward, Richard Halsted
Washburn, Emory
Wells, David Ames
Whitman, Charles Seymour
Whitney, William Dwight
Williamson, William Durkee
Yancey, William Lowndes
Yeomans, John William
Graduate Study
Pratt, Waldo Selden
WILLIE HALSELL COLLEGE (OKLA.)
Clark, Joseph James ("Jocko")
WILLISTON SEMINARY (MASS.)
Andrews, George Pierce
Avery, John
Barber, Edwin Atlee
Bingham, Hiram, 1831–1908
Blakeslee, Erastus
Clark, William Smith
Crane, Winthrop Murray
Dexter, Franklin Bowditch
Dickinson, John Woodbridge
Durham, Caleb Wheeler
Goodell, Henry Hill
Hall, Granville Stanley
Hitchcock, Charles Henry
Hitchcock, Edward, 1828–1911
Hume, Robert Allen
Kellogg, Martin
Lincoln, Rufus Pratt
Lyman, Albert Josiah
Magill, Edward Hicks
Merrill, Selah
Nason, Henry Bradford
Northrop, Cyrus
Peck, Tracy
Smith, Judson
Spofford, Ainsworth Rand
Stanley, William
Stockbridge, Henry
Strong, Charles Lyman
Swinton, John
Wheeler, George Wakeman
WILMINGTON COLLEGE (OHIO)
Moore, Joseph Haines
WINONA STATE TEACHERS COLLEGE (IND.)
Rovenstine, Emery Andrew
WISCONSIN STATE NORMAL SCHOOL
Libby, Orin Grant
WITTENBERG COLLEGE (OHIO)
Anderson, Sherwood
Crothers, Samuel McChord
Dinwiddie, Edwin Courtland
Douglas, Lloyd Cassel
Funk, Isaac Kauffman
Grosscup, Peter Stenger
Krapp, George Philip
Lenker, John Nicholas
Marquett, Turner Mastin
Stuckenberg, John Henry Wilbrandt
Tittle, Ernest Fremont
WOFFORD COLLEGE (S.C.)
Cash, Wilbur Joseph
Few, William Preston
Johnston, Olin DeWitt Talmadge
Kirkland, James Hampton
Lever, Asbury Francis
Roper, Daniel Calhoun
Smith, Ellison DuRant
WOMAN'S MEDICAL COLLEGE (MD.)
Cone, Claribel
WOMAN'S MEDICAL COLLEGE (N.Y.)
Baker, Sara Josephine
WOMAN'S MEDICAL COLLEGE (PA.)
Addams, Jane
Jacobi, Mary Corinna Putnam
Lockrey, Sarah Hunt
Marshall, Clara
Potter, Ellen Culver
Putnam, Helen Cordelia
Swain, Clara A.
WOODSTOCK COLLEGE (CANADA)
Eaton, Cyrus Stephen
WOODSTOCK COLLEGE (MD.)
Campbell, Thomas Joseph
Rigge, William Francis
Talbot, Francis Xavier
Tondorf, Francis Anthony
Walsh, Edmund Aloysius
Weigel, Gustave
Graduate Study
La Farge, John
Walsh, Edmund Aloysius
WOODWARD COLLEGE (OHIO)
Clarke, Robert
Hickenlooper, Andrew
Parvin, Theodore Sutton
WORCESTER ACADEMY (MASS.)
Bates, Samuel Penniman
Colvin, Stephen Sheldon
Fullam, Frank L.
Green, Andrew Haswell
Harris, William Torrey
Lord, Chester Sanders
Meade, Richard Worsam, 1837–1897
Talbot, Israel Tisdale
Thayer, Eli
WORCESTER POLYTECHNIC INSTITUTE (MASS.)
Adams, Herbert Samuel
Alford, Leon Pratt
Armsby, Henry Prentiss
Coates, George Henry
Cobb, Nathan Augustus
Daniels, Fred Harris
Donovan, John Joseph
Eddy, Harrison Prescott
Furlow, Floyd Charles
Goddard, Robert Hutchings
Hague, Robert Lincoln
Kent, Arthur Atwater
Newcomb, Charles Leonard
Priest, Edward Dwight

Thompson, Edward Herbert
Washburn, Charles Grenfill

WORRALL'S ACADEMY (KY.)
Beard, Daniel Carter

XAVIER UNIVERSITY (OHIO)
Gold, Harry ("Raymond")

YALE UNIVERSITY (CONN.)
Abbott, Frank Frost
Acheson, Dean Gooderham
Adams, Andrew
Adams, Charles Baker
Adams, James Hopkins
Adams, John, 1772–1863
Adams, William
Alexander, William Dewitt
Alsop, Richard
Alsop, Stewart Johonnet Oliver
Andrews, George Pierce
Andrews, William Watson
Anthony, William Arnold
Armsby, Henry Prentiss
Arno, Peter
Ashmun, George
Atherton, George Washington
Atkinson, Thomas
Atterbury, Grosvenor
Atterbury, William Wallace
Atwater, Lyman Hotchkiss
Auchincloss, Hugh Dudley, Jr.
Austin, David
Austin, Samuel
Backus, Azel
Bacon, Benjamin Wisner
Bacon, Leonard
Bacon, Leonard Woolsey
Badger, George Edmund
Badger, Joseph, 1757–1846
Bailey, Ebenezer
Baldwin, Abraham
Baldwin, Elihu Whittlesey
Baldwin, Henry
Baldwin, John Denison
Baldwin, Roger Sherman
Baldwin, Simeon
Baldwin, Simeon Eben
Baldwin, Theron
Barber, Donn
Bardeen, Charles William
Barker, George Frederick
Barlow, Joel
Barnard, Frederick Augustus Porter
Barnard, Henry
Barry, Philip James Quinn
Barry, William Taylor Sullivan
Barth, Alan
Bates, Theodore Lewis ("Ted")
Beach, Frederick Converse
Beach, Harlan Page
Beard, George Miller
Beecher, Edward
Beecher, Lyman
Beer, Thomas
Beers, Clifford Whittingham
Beers, Henry Augustin
Bellamy, Joseph
Benét, Stephen Vincent
Benham, Henry Washington
Benjamin, Judah Philip
Bennett, Nathaniel
Benton, William Burnett
Bevan, Arthur Dean
Bidwell, Barnabas
Bidwell, Walter Hilliard
Bierwirth, John Edward
Bingham, Hiram, 1831–1908
Bishop, Abraham
Bishop, William Darius
Bissell, Wilson Shannon
Blake, Eli Whitney
Blake, William Phipps
Blakeslee, Erastus
Bliss, Porter Cornelius
Boies, Henry Martyn
Boisen, Anton Theophilus
Boltwood, Bertram Borden
Bostwick, Arthur Elmore
Bosworth, Edward Increase
Bosworth, Francke Huntington
Bourne, Edward Gaylord
Bouton, Nathaniel
Bowen, Herbert Wolcott
Bowers, Lloyd Wheaton
Bowles, Samuel, 1851–1915
Brace, Charles Loring
Bradley, Frank Howe
Bradley, Stephen Row
Bradley, William Czar
Brady, John Green
Brainard, John Gardiner Calkins
Brainerd, John
Brandegee, Frank Bosworth
Brandegee, Townshend Stith
Breckinridge, Robert Jefferson
Brewer, David Josiah
Brewer, William Henry
Brinton, Daniel Garrison
Bristead, Charles Astor
Bromley, Isaac Hill
Brown, Benjamin Gratz
Brown, Henry Billings
Brown, John, 1744–1780
Brown, Samuel Robbins
Brown, Solyman
Brown, William Adams
Bryan, Kirk
Buck, Albert Henry
Bulkley, Lucius Duncan
Bullitt, William Christian
Bumstead, Horace
Bundy, Harvey Hollister
Bunker, Arthur Hugh
Burnam, John Miller
Burnett, Charles Henry
Burr, Aaron, 1715/16–1757
Burr, Enoch Fitch
Burrall, William Porter
Burrell, David James
Burroughs, John Curtis
Burrowes, Thomas Henry
Bush, Prescott Sheldon
Bushnell, David
Bushnell, George Ensign
Bushnell, Horace
Calhoun, John Caldwell
Calhoun, William Barron
Calkins, Phineas Wolcott
Camp, Walter Chauncey
Carleton, Henry
Carrington, Henry Beebee
Carter, Franklin
Case, Leonard
Case, William Scoville
Chamberlain, Daniel Henry
Champlin, John Denison
Chandler, John Scudder
Chandler, Thomas Bradbury
Chapin, Aaron Lucius
Chapin, Calvin
Chase, George
Chauvenet, William
Chester, Colby Mitchell
Childs, Richard Spencer
Chipman, Nathaniel
Chittenden, Russell Henry
Churchill, William
Clark, Charles Hopkins
Clark, Sheldon
Clark, Thomas March
Clay, Cassius Marcellus
Clayton, John Middleton
Cleaveland, Moses
Cloud, Henry Roe
Cochran, Alexander Smith
Coffin, Henry Sloane
Coffin, William Anderson
Coit, Thomas Winthrop
Coleman, Lyman
Collier, Peter
Colt, LeBaron Bradford
Colton, Calvin
Colton, Walter
Conwell, Russell Herman
Cook, Flavius Josephus
Cook, Robert Johnson
Cook, Walter
Cooper, Jacob
Cooper, James Fenimore
Copley, Ira Clifton
Coppée, Henry
Cort, Stewart Shaw
Couper, James Hamilton
Cox, James Middleton, Jr.
Cross, Wilbur Lucius
Culbertson, Ely
Curtis, Edward Lewis
Cushing, Harvey Williams
Cutler, Carroll
Cutler, Manasseh
Cutter, Ephraim
Daggett, David
Daggett, Ellsworth
Daggett, Naphtali
Dalzell, John
Dana, Edward Salisbury
Dana, James Dwight
Dana, Samuel Whittelsey
Davenport, James
Davenport, Russell Wheeler
Davis, Henry
Davis, John, 1787–1854
Dawes, Henry Laurens
Day, Clarence Shepard
Day, George Parmly
Day, Henry Noble
Day, Jeremiah
Deane, Silas
De Forest, Erastus Lyman
De Forest, John Kinne Hyde
De Forest, Robert Weeks
Delafield, Edward
Delafield, Francis
De Lancey, William Heathcote
Delano, William Adams

Deming, Henry Champion
Dennis, Frederic Shepard
Depew, Chauncey Mitchell
Dexter, Franklin Bowditch
Dexter, Henry Martyn
Dickinson, Jonathan
Dickson, Earle Ensign
Dickson, Samuel Henry
Dill, James Brooks
Dilworth, Richardson
Dodd, Lee Wilson
Donaldson, Henry Herbert
Douglass, David Bates
Dryden, John Fairfield
Dubois, Augustus Jay
Dudley, Charles Benjamin
Duffield, Samuel Augustus Willoughby
Dunning, Albert Elijah
Du Pont, Francis Irénée
Durant, Henry
Dutton, Clarence Edward
Dutton, Henry
Dutton, Samuel Train
Dwight, Edmund
Dwight, Sereno Edwards
Dwight, Theodore
Dwight, Timothy, 1752–1817
Dwight, Timothy, 1828–1916
Dyer, Eliphalet
Dyer, Isadore
Eastman, William Reed
Eaton, Daniel Cady
Eddy, Henry Turner
Edmands, John
Edwards, Jonathan, 1703–1758
Egleston, Thomas
Elder, Samuel James
Eliot, Jared
Elliott, Stephen
Ellsworth, Henry Leavitt
Ellsworth, Henry William
Ellsworth, Oliver
Ellsworth, William Wolcott
Embree, Edwin Rogers
Emmons, Nathaniel
Eno, William Phelps
Evarts, Jeremiah
Evarts, William Maxwell
Fanning, Edmund, 1739–1818
Farnam, Henry Walcott
Farquhar, Percival
Farragut, David Glasgow
Farrar, John Chipman
Fearn, John Walker
Ferry, Orris Sanford
Field, David Dudley, 1781–1867
Field, Maunsell Bradhurst
Finch, Francis Miles
Fisher, Irving
Fitch, Samuel
Fitch, Thomas
Flather, John Joseph
Fleischer, Nathaniel Stanley ("Nat")
Foot, Samuel Augustus
Foote, William Henry
Forman, Justus Miles
Foster, John Pierrepont Codrington
Foster, Roger Sherman Baldwin
Fowler, Orin
Frank, Waldo David
Frazer, Joseph Washington
Frissell, Hollis Burke
Gadsden, James
Gale, Benjamin
Gallaudet, Thomas Hopkins
Gardiner, James Terry
Gardner, Leroy Upson
Gibbs, Josiah Willard, 1790–1861
Gibbs, Josiah Willard, 1839–1903
Gibson, Randall Lee
Gillett, Ezra Hall
Gillette, Francis
Gilman, Daniel Coit
Goddard, Calvin Luther
Goodrich, Charles Augustus
Goodrich, Chauncey, 1759–1815
Goodrich, Chauncey Allen
Goodrich, Elizur, 1734–1797
Goodrich, Elizur, 1761–1849
Goodyear, Anson Conger
Goodyear, William Henry
Gould, James
Granger, Francis
Granger, Gideon
Grant, Madison
Graves, William Phillips
Greenway, John Campbell
Gregory, Eliot
Gregory, Samuel
Griffin, Edward Dorr
Griggs, Everett Gallup
Grigsby, Hugh Blair
Grimké, Thomas Smith
Grinnell, George Bird
Griswold, Alfred Whitney
Griswold, Roger
Griswold, Stanley
Grosvenor, William Mason
Gugggenheim, Harry Frank
Guilford, Nathan
Gunn, Frederick William
Gurley, Ralph Randolph
Hadley, Arthur Twining
Hadley, James
Hague, Arnold
Haight, Henry Huntly
Hale, Nathan, 1755–1776
Hale, Philip
Hall, Charles Henry
Hall, Lyman
Hall, Willard Preble
Hallock, Charles
Halsted, William Stewart
Harkness, Edward Stephen
Harlow, Ralph Volney
Harper, William Rainey
Harriman, Edward Roland Noel
Harris, Jed
Harris, William Torrey
Harrison, Carter Henry
Harrison, Fairfax
Harrison, Francis Burton
Harrison, Henry Baldwin
Hasbrouck, Abraham Bruyn
Haskell, Dudley Chase
Hastings, Charles Sheldon
Havens, James Smith
Hawley, Gideon, 1727–1807
Hawley, Joseph
Hazard, Thomas
Henderson, Yandell
Hendrick, Burton Jesse
Herr, Herbert Thacker
Herrick, Edward Claudius
Hill, Frederick Trevor
Hillhouse, James
Hillhouse, James Abraham
Hitchcock, Henry
Hitchcock, Peter
Hittell, Theodore Henry
Hobart, John Sloss
Holbrook, Josiah
Holley, Horace
Hollister, Gideon Hiram
Holmes, Abiel
Holmes, Isaac Edward
Holt, Hamilton Bowen
Holt, Henry
Hooker, Donald Russell
Hooker, Worthington
Hopkins, Samuel, 1721–1803
Hoppin, James Mason
Hoppin, William Warner
Hosmer, Titus
Howland, John
Hubbard, Joseph Stillman
Hubbard, Richard William
Hull, William
Hume, Robert Allen
Humphrey, Heman
Humphreys, David
Hunt, Thomas Sterry
Hunt, William Henry
Hunter, Croil
Huntington, Daniel
Huntington, Jabez
Huntington, Jedediah Vincent
Huntington, Samuel, 1765–1817
Hurd, John Codman
Hutchins, Robert Maynard
Hyatt, Alphaeus
Hyde, Charles Cheney
Hyde, James Nevins
Iddings, Joseph Paxon
Ingersoll, Jared, 1722–1781
Ingersoll, Jared, 1749–1822
Ingelfinger, Franz Joseph
Isham, Ralph Heyward
Isham, Samuel
Ives, Charles Edward
Ives, Eli
Jackson, Henry Rootes
Janeway, Theodore Caldwell
Janney, Russell Dixon
Jarvis, Abraham
Jay, William
Jenkins, Edward Hopkins
Jenks, Tudor Storrs
Jessup, Henry Harris
Johnson, Alexander Smith
Johnson, Owen McMahon
Johnson, Samuel
Johnson, Samuel William
Johnson, William, 1769–1848
Johnson, William Samuel
Johnson, William Woolsey
Johnston, Henry Phelps
Johnston, William Preston
Jones, George

Jones, Joel
Jones, Samuel
Jones, Thomas
Judd, Orange
Judd, Sylvester
Judson, Frederick Newton
Kane, John Kintzing
Kaye, Frederick Benjamin
Keep, Robert Porter
Kellogg, Martin
Kennedy, William Sloane
Kent, Charles Foster
Kent, James
Keyes, Edward Lawrence
Kilpatrick, John Reed
King, Clarence
Kingsley, James Luce
Kip, William Ingraham
Kirchwey, George Washington
Klein, Joseph Frederic
Knight, Frederick Irving
Knight, Jonathan
Knowlton, Marcus Perrin
Kohler, Walter Jodok, Jr.
Lane, Arthur Bliss
Lanman, Charles Rockwell
Larned, Joseph Gay Eaton
Lathrop, John Hiram
Latourette, Kenneth Scott
Law, John
Law, Richard
Lawrance, Charles Lanier
Leaming, Jeremiah
Leavitt, Joshua
Leffingwell, Russell Cornell
Lehman, Robert
Levermore, Charles Herbert
Levinson, Salmon Oliver
Lewis, Charlton Thomas
Lewis, Harry Sinclair
L'Hommedieu, Ezra
Link, Henry Charles
Linn, William Alexander
Livingston, John Henry
Livingston, Peter Van Brugh
Livingston, Philip
Livingston, William, 1723–1790
Llewellyn, Karl Nickerson
Locke, John
Lockwood, Ralph Ingersoll
Longstreet, Augustus Baldwin
Loomis, Elias
Lord, Daniel
Lord, David Nevins
Lorimer, George Horace
Lounsbury, Thomas Raynesford
Luce, Henry Robinson
Luce, Henry Winters
Lusk, William Thompson
Lyman, Chester Smith
Lyman, Joseph Bardwell
Lyman, Phineas
McAllister, Hall
McCaleb, Theodore Howard
McClellen, George, 1796–1847
McClure, Alexander Wilson
McCormick, Joseph Medill
McCormick, Robert Rutherford
McDowell, James
MacVeagh, Franklin
MacVeagh, Isaac Wayne
Magill, Edward Hicks
Mallery, Garrick
Mansfield, Jared
Mansfield, Richard, 1723–1820
Marmaduke, John Sappington
Marsh, John, 1788–1868
Marsh, Othniel Charles
Marsh, Reginald
Marshall, Thomas Alexander
Mason, Jeremiah
Mathews, Albert
Matthiessen, Francis Otto
Maxwell, William, 1784–1857
Meigs, Josiah
Meigs, Return Jonathan, 1764–1824
Mendel, Lafayette Benedict
Merrill, Selah
Millikan, Clark Blanchard
Millis, Walter
Mitchell, Donald Grant
Mitchell, Elisha
Mitchell, Stephen Mix
Mitchell, William DeWitt
Moffett, Cleveland Langston
Moore, Eliakim Hastings
Moore, George Foot
Morris, Edward Dafydd
Morris, Lewis 1726–1798
Morris, Luzon Burritt
Morris, Richard
Morse, Jedidiah
Morse, Samuel Finlay Breese
Morse, Sidney Edwards
Morton, Rogers Clark Ballard
Mulford, Elisha
Munger, Theodore Thornton
Murchison, John Dabney
Murdock, James
Murphy, Gardner
Murphy, Gerald Clery
Nadal, Ehrman Syme
Nash, Daniel
Nelson, Rensselaer Russell
Nettleton, Asahel
Newel, Stanford
Newell, Edward Theodore
Newlands, Francis Griffith
Newton, Hubert Anson
Noble, Frederick Alphonso
Noble, John Willock
North, Simeon, 1802–1884
Northrop, Birdsey Grant
Northrop, Cyrus
Norton, John Pitkin
Nott, Abraham
Nott, Samuel
Oakley, Thomas Jackson
Ogden, David
Ogilvie, John
Olds, Irving Sands
Olmsted, Denison
Olmsted, John Charles
Osborn, Norris Galpin
Osborne, Thomas Burr
Owen, Edward Thomas
Paine, Ralph Delahaye
Palmer, Ray
Parker, Peter
Parsons, Lewis Baldwin
Paterson, John
Patterson, Joseph Medill
Payne, Oliver Hazard
Pearse, John Barnard Swett
Peck, Tracy
Peet, Harvey Prindle
Peet, Isaac Lewis
Penfold, Joseph Weller
Penniman, James Hosmer
Perkins, Elisha
Perkins, Frederic Beecher
Perkins, George Henry
Perrin, Bernadotte
Perry, Edward Aylesworth
Peters, John Andrew
Peters, John Punnett
Peters, Samuel Andrew
Phelps, William Lyon
Phelps, William Walter
Pickens, William
Pierpont, John
Pierrepont, Edwards
Pinchot, Amos Richards Eno
Pinchot, Gifford
Pinney, Norman
Pirsson, Louis Valentine
Pitkin, Timothy
Platner, Samuel Ball
Platt, Thomas Collier
Polk, Frank Lyon
Polk, Trusten
Poole, William Frederick
Porter, Arthur Kingsley
Porter, Cole
Porter, John Addison
Porter, Noah
Porter, Peter Buell
Porter, Samuel
Pratt, Bela Lyon
Prentice, Samuel Oscar
Prudden, Theophil Mitchell
Putnam, James Osborne
Reed, Stanley Forman
Reid, Ogden Mills
Remington, Frederic
Resor, Stanley Burnet
Richards, Charles Herbert
Richards, Dickinson Woodruff
Richardson, Rufus Byam
Riley, Isaac Woodbridge
Robbins, Thomas
Roberts, Ellis Henry
Robinson, Henry Cornelius
Robinson, William Erigena
Rockefeller, Winthrop
Rogers, James Gamble
Rogers, James Harvey
Rood, Ogden Nicholas
Rosenfeld, Paul Leopold
Rothko, Mark
Rowland, Henry Cottrell
Ruggles, Samuel Bulkley
Russ, John Dennison
Saarinen, Eero
St. John, Isaac Munroe
Salisbury, Edward Elbridge
Saltus, Edgar Evertson
Savage, Thomas Staughton
Schevill, Rudolph
Schippers, Thomas
Schuyler, Eugene
Schwab, John Christopher
Scott, Austin
Scott, John Morin
Seabury, Samuel, 1729–1796

Sedgwick, Theodore, 1746–1813
Sedgwick, Theodore, 1780–1839
Sedgwick, William Thompson
Selden, George Baldwin
Sergeant, John, 1710–1749
Setchell, William Albert
Seymour, Charles
Shaw, Howard Van Doren
Shiras, George
Sill, Edward Rowland
Silliman, Beniamin, 1779–1864
Silliman, Benjamin, 1816–1885
Smalley, George Washburn
Smillie, Ralph
Smith, Ashbel
Smith, Azariah
Smith, Eli
Smith, Elihu Hubbard
Smith, George Henry
Smith, Israel
Smith, Job Lewis
Smith, John Cotton, 1765–1845
Smith, Junius
Smith, Nathan Ryno
Smith, Truman
Smith, William, 1697–1769
Smith, William, 1728–1793
Smith, William Nathan Harrell
Spencer, Ambrose
Spencer, Elihu
Sprague, Homer Baxter
Sprague, William Buell
Spring, Gardiner
Stagg, Amos Alonzo
Stanley, Harold
Stanley, William
Stearns, Henry Putnam
Stedman, Edmund Clarence
Steiner, Bernard Christian
Sterling, John William
Stevens, Alexander Hodgdon
Stevens, Henry
Stevens, John Austin, 1795–1874
Stewart, Donald Ogden
Stewart, William Morris
Stiles, Ezra
Stillé, Alfred
Stillé, Charles Janeway
Stimson, Henry Lewis
Stimson, Lewis Atterbury
Stoddard, David Tappan
Stokes, Anson Phelps
Stokes, Frederick Abbot
Stokes, William Earl Dodge
Storrs, Richard Salter, 1787–1873
Street, Augustus Russell
Strong, Augustus Hopkins
Strong, Theodore
Strong, William
Stuart, Isaac William
Stuart, Moses
Sturtevant, Julian Monson
Sullivant, William Starling
Sumner, William Graham
Sutherland, Richard Kerens
Swayne, Wager
Swift, Zephaniah
Taber, John
Taft, Alphonso
Taft, Charles Phelps
Taft, Henry Waters
Taft, Robert Alphonso
Taft, William Howard
Tallmadge, Benjamin
Tarbell, Frank Bigelow
Tarbox, Increase Niles
Taylor, Nathaniel William
Taylor, Richard
Tenney, William Jewett
Thacher, Thomas Anthony
Thacher, Thomas Day
Thayer, John
Thomas, Joseph
Thompson, Joseph Parrish
Thompson, William Gilman
Thwaites, Reuben Gold
Tilden, Samuel Jones
Tilson, John Quillin
Tod, George
Todd, Eli
Todd, John
Tolman, Herbert Cushing
Torrey, Charles Turner
Towle, George Makepeace
Tracy, Uriah
Trumbull, Benjamin
Trumbull, James Hammond
Trumbull, John, 1750 o.s.–1831
Tully, William
Turner, Asa
Turner, Jonathan Baldwin
Twichell, Joseph Hopkins
Twining, Alexander Catlin
Tyler, Bennet
Tyler, Charles Mellen
Tyler, Moses Coit
Tytus, John Butler
Underhill, Frank Pell
Van Allen, Frank
Van Buren, John
Van Buren, William Holme
Van Name, Addison
Van Rensselaer, Cortlandt
Veblen, Thorstein Bunde
Verrill, Alpheus Hyatt
Vincent, Frank
Vincent, George Edgar
Vinton, Alexander Hamilton
Wadsworth, James
Wadsworth, James Wolcott, Jr.
Waite, Morrison Remick
Wales, Leonard Eugene
Ware, Edmund Asa
Warren, Israel Perkins
Washington, Henry Stephens
Waterman, Thomas Whitney
Waters, William Everett
Watson, Arthur Kittridge
Watson, Sereno
Webster, Noah
Webster, Pelatiah
Weed, Lewis Hill
Weicker, Lowell Palmer
Weiss, George Martin
Welch, William Henry
Welch, William Wickham
Welles, Noah
Wenner, George Unangst
West, Henry Sergeant
Weyerhaeuser, Frederick Edward
Wharton, Francis
Wheaton, Nathaniel Sheldon
Wheeler, Arthur Leslie
Wheeler, George Wakeman
Wheelock, Eleazar
Wheelock, John
Whipple, Sherman Leland
White, Andrew Dickson
Whitney, Eli
Whitney, Harry Payne
Whitney, James Lyman
Whitney, Josiah Dwight
Whitney, William Collins
Whitney, William Dwight
Whiton, James Morris
Wikoff, Henry
Wilcox, Reynold Webb
Wilder, Thornton Niven
Willard, De Forest
Williams, Alpheus Starkey
Williams, Frederick Wells
Williams, Henry Shaler
Williams, Thomas Scott
Willis, Nathaniel Parker
Wilmer, Richard Hooker
Wilson, Hugh Robert
Winslow, Hubbard
Winthrop, Theodore
Witherspoon, Alexander Maclaren
Witherspoon, Herbert
Wolcott, Edward Oliver
Wolcott, Oliver, 1726–1797
Wolcott, Oliver, 1760–1833
Woodbridge, William Channing
Woodruff, Timothy Lester
Woods, William Burnham
Woolley, Edgar Montillion ("Monty")
Woolsey, John Munro
Woolsey, Theodore Dwight
Woolsey, Theodore Salisbury
Wooster, David
Worcester, Joseph Emerson
Worthington, John
Wright, Charles
Wright, Elizur
Wright, Robert William
Wrigley, Philip Knight
Wyllys, George
Youmans, William Jay
Yung, Wing

Divinity

Niebuhr, Karl Paul Reinhold ("Reinie")

Drama

Smith, Betty

Forestry

Baker, Oliver Edwin
Record, Samuel James

Graduate Study

Abel-Henderson, Annie Heloise
Adams, James Truslow
Baker, Hugh Potter
Benedict, Stanley Rossiter
Benét, Stephen Vincent
Bloomfield, Maurice
Bostwick, Arthur Elmore
Bourne, Edward Gaylord
Bowman, Isaiah

Brown, William Adams
Bryan, Kirk
Bumstead, Henry Andrews
Burnam, John Miller
Burr, Aaron 1715/16–1757
Canby, Henry Seidel
Capps, Edward
Case, Shirley Jackson
Chittenden, Russell Henry
Cloud, Henry Roe
Collier, Peter
Cross, Wilbur Lucius
Cutler, Manasseh
Dana, Edward Salisbury
Day, Arthur Louis
De Forest, Lee
Dougherty, Raymond Philip
Dubois, Augustus Jay
Dudley, Charles Benjamin
Eastman, William Reed
Eddy, Henry Turner
Edgren, August Hjalmar
Embree, Edwin Rogers
Fairchild, Fred Rogers
Farnam, Henry Walcott
Fisher, Irving
Frank, Waldo David
Fullerton, George Stuart
Gipson, Lawrence Henry
Green, Constance McLaughlin
Grinnell, George Bird
Griswold, Alfred Whitney
Gunn, Ross
Hadley, Arthur Twining
Hadley, James
Harlow, Ralph Volney
Hastings, Charles Sheldon
Hay, Oliver Perry
Haynes, George Edmund
Henderson, Yandell
Hendrick, Burton Jesse
Hillhouse, James Abraham
Hooker, Donald Russell
Hume, Robert Allen
Humphreys, David
Huntington, Ellsworth
Hyde, Charles Cheney
Jackson, William Alexander
Jenkins, Edward Hopkins
Johnson, Treat Baldwin
Kent, Charles Foster
Labaree, Leonard Woods
Lanman, Charles Rockwell
Latourette, Kenneth Scott
Lawrence, Ernest Orlando
Leopold, (Rand) Aldo
Link, Henry Charles
Lomax, Louis Emanuel
MacCurdy, George Grant
McVey, Frank Lerond
Manatt, James Irving
Marsh, Othniel Charles
Mendel, Lafayette Benedict
Merrill, Elmer Truesdell
Moore, Eliakim Hastings
Newell, Edward Theodore
Niebuhr, Helmut Richard
Notestein, Wallace
Olmsted, Denison
Osborne, Thomas Burr
Owen, Edward Thomas
Page, Leigh
Paine, John Alsop
Peck, Tracy
Perkins, George Henry
Peters, John Punnett
Peters, Samuel Andrew
Phelps, William Lyon
Pirsson, Louis Valentine
Platner, Samuel Ball
Reid, Ogden Mills
Reinhardt, Aurelia Isabel Henry
Richardson, Rufus Byam
Riley, Isaac Woodbridge
Robertson, William Spence
Rogers, James Harvey
Rogers, William Augustus
Rood, Ogden Nicholas
Rose, Mary Davies Swartz
Rubey, William Walden
Safford, James Merrill
Salisbury, Edward Elbridge
Schuyler, Eugene
Seashore, Carl Emil
Seymour, Charles
Silcox, Ferdinand Augustus
Smalley, George Washburn
Smillie, Ralph
Smith, Theodate Louise
Smith, William, 1697–1769
Sperry, Willard Learoyd
Steiner, Bernard Christian
Taft, Charles Phelps
Tarbell, Frank Bigelow
Tolman, Herbert Cushing
Ward, Charles Henshaw
Watson, Arthur Kittridge
Watt, Donald Beates
Wheeler, Arthur Leslie
White, Andrew Dickson
Whitney, James Lyman
Whiton, James Morris
Wieland, George Reber
Wiley, Bell Irvin
Williams, Henry Shaler
Williston, Samuel Wendell
Wimsatt, William Kurtz
Witherspoon, Alexander Maclaren

Law

Baldwin, Simeon Eben
Bangs, Francis Nehemiah
Birney, James
Brown, Henry Billings
Brown, Joseph Emerson
Carrington, Henry Beebee
Cummings, Homer Stillé
Davis, David
Delmas, Delphin Michael
Dilworth, Richardson
Dodd, Thomas Joseph
Dwight, Theodore William
Goodrich, Chauncey, 1759–1815
Goodwin, Hannibal Williston
Graves, David Bibb
Harrison, Carter Henry, Jr.
Hoppin, William Warner
Hunt, William Henry
Hurd, John Codman
Hutchins, Robert Maynard
Ireland, Charles Thomas, Jr. ("Chick")
Johnston, John Taylor
Kefauver, (Carey) Estes
Lathrop, John Hiram
Lemke, William Frederick
Ligon, Thomas Watkins
Llewellyn, Karl Nickerson
Loomis, Dwight
Lowenstein, Allard Kenneth
McMahon, Brien
Minton, Sherman
Pettengill, Samuel Barrett
Phelps, Edward John
Prentice, Samuel Oscar
Scarborough, Lee Rutland
Sheppard, John Morris
Shiras, George
Shiras, Oliver Perry
Strong, William
Thacher, Thomas Day
Tilson, John Quillin
Wheeler, George Wakeman
Whipple, Sherman Leland
Williams, Alpheus Starkey
Woolsey, Theodore Salisbury
Young, Clarence Marshall

Medicine

Bacon, Leonard Woolsey
Baldwin, Edward Robinson
Brockett, Linus Pierpont
Bronson, Henry
Bushnell, George Ensign
Butler, Thomas Belden
Camp, Walter Chauncey
Cutter, Ephraim
Davidson, Jo
Davis, Henry Gassett
Gardner, Leroy Upson
Gilbert, Alfred Carlton
Gregory, Samuel
Homes, Henry Augustus
Huntington, Elisha
King, Dan
Kirtland, Jared Potter
Locke, John
Miller, William Snow
Parker, Peter
Peaslee, Edmund Randolph
Percival, James Gates
Phelps, Guy Rowland
Prudden, Theophil Mitchell
Rowland, Henry Cottrell
Russ, John Dennison
Sargent, Dudley Allen
Savage, Thomas Staughton
Smith, Ashbel
Smith, Azariah
Smith, Nathan Ryno
Stearns, Henry Putnam
Williston, Samuel Wendell

Sheffield Scientific School

Benét, William Rose
Boeing, William Edward
Booth, Albert James, Jr. ("Albie")
Brace, Charles Loring
Braden, Spruille
Canby, Henry Seidel
Cummings, Homer Stillé
Davis, Francis Breese, Jr.
Davis, John Staige
Day, Arthur Louis
De Forest, Lee
Ellsworth, Lincoln

Frazer, Joseph Washington
Guggenheim, Harry Frank
Hammond, John Hays
Heffelfinger, William Walter ("Pudge")
Hogan, John Vincent Lawless
Johnson, Treat Baldwin
Joy, Henry Bourne
Leopold, (Rand) Aldo
Merriam, Clinton Hart
Murray, Thomas Edward
Newberry, Truman Handy
Page, Leigh
Strong, Richard Pearson
Talbott, Harold Elstner
Trask, James Dowling
Wells, Harry Gideon
Wilson, Edmund Beecher
Yawkey, Thomas Austin ("Tom")

Theology

Adams, George Burton
Ames, Edward Scribner
Atwater, Lyman Hotchkiss
Badè, William Frederic
Baldwin, John Denison
Baldwin, Theron
Barrows, John Henry
Beardshear, William Miller
Beckwith, Clarence Augustine
Beecher, Lyman
Bidwell, Walter Hilliard
Bliss, Edwin Munsell
Brace, Charles Loring
Brainerd, David
Burr, Enoch Fitch
Burton, Marion Le Roy
Burton, Nathaniel Judson
Bushnell, Horace
Case, Shirley Jackson
Chandler, John Scudder
Coleman, Lyman
De Forest, John Kinne Hyde
Durant, Henry
Dwight, Benjamin Woodbridge
Dwight, Timothy, 1828–1916
Edmands, John
Edwards, Jonathan, 1703–1758
Fisher, George Park
Garman, Charles Edward
Green, Lewis Warner
Hadley, James
Henry, Caleb Sprague
Hitchcock, Charles Henry
Hitchcock, Edward, 1793–1864
Hume, Robert Allen
Lyman, Chester Smith
Lyman, Eugene William
MacLean, George Edwin
Magoun, George Frederick
Mears, John William
Merrill, Selah
Munger, Theodore Thornton
Niebuhr, Karl Paul Reinhold, ("Reinie")
North, Simeon, 1802–1884
Northdrop, Birdsey Grant
Noyes, John Humphrey
Olmsted, Denison
Parker, Peter
Patterson, James Willis
Peet, Stephen Denison
Perrin, Bernadotte
Peters, John Punnett
Phelps, Austin
Powell, Adam Clayton, Sr.
Proctor, Henry Hugh
Salter, William Mackintire
Sanders, Frank Knight
Smith, Azariah
Spottswood, Stephen Gill
Stevens, George Barker
Stoddard, John Lawson
Sturtevant, Julian Monson
Tarbox, Increase Niles
Terry, Milton Spenser
Tufts, James Hayden
Wheelock, Eleazar
Willett, Herbert Lockwood
Winslow, Hubbard
Woolsey, Theodore Dwight

YANKTON COLLEGE (S. DAK.)

Bode, Boyd Henry
Darling, Jay Norwood ("Ding")
Hansen, Alvin Harvey

YESHIVA UNIVERSITY

Black, Eli
Wolfson, Harry Austryn

YORKSHIRE COLLEGE (ENGLAND)

Dakin, Henry Drysdale

YOUNG LADIES INSTITUTE (N.Y.)

Alden, Isabella Macdonald

ZURICH CONSERVATORY (SWITZERLAND)

Ganz, Rudolph

ZURICH EIDGENOSSICHE TECHNISCHE HOCHSCHULE (SWITZERLAND)

Einstein, Albert

ZURICH POLYTECHNICUM (SWITZERLAND)

Cabot, Godfrey Lowell

OCCUPATIONS

Abolitionist
Bailey, Gamaliel
Birney, James Gillespie
Bourne, George
Bowditch, Henry Ingersoll
Brown, John
Buffum, Arnold
Burleigh, Charles Calistus
Chace, Elizabeth Buffum
Child, Lydia Maria Francis
Christy, David
Clay, Cassius Marcellus
Coffin, Levi
Coles, Edward
Collins, John Anderson
Colman, Lucy Newhall
Cooper, Thomas
Cox, Hannah Peirce
Deitzler, George Washington
Douglass, Frederick
Edgerton, Sidney
Embree, Elihu
Fairbank, Calvin
Fee, John Gregg
Fessenden, Samuel
Follen, Charles
Follen, Eliza Lee Cabot
Foster, Abigail Kelley
Foster, Stephen Symonds
Garnet, Henry Highland
Garrett, Thomas
Gibbons, Abigail Hopper
Gibbons, James Sloan
Giddings, Joshua Reed
Grimké, Angelina Emily
Grimké, Sarah Moore
Grinnell, Josiah Bushnell
Hallowell, Richard Price
Haven, Gilbert
Hazard, Thomas
Holley, Myron
Hopper, Isaac Tatem
Jackson, James Caleb
Johnson, Oliver
Julian, George Washington
Leavitt, Joshua
Lee, Luther
LeMoyne, Francis Julius
Loring, Ellis Gray
Lovejoy, Elijah Parish
Lovejoy, Owen
Lundy, Benjamin
McKim, James Miller
Mercer, Margaret
Miller, Jonathan Peckham
Mott, James
Nelson, David
Osborn, Charles
Post, Isaac
Realf, Richard
Sands, David
Scott, Orange
Stewart, Alvan
Stuart, Charles
Sumner, Charles
Sunderland, La Roy
Tappan, Arthur
Tappan, Benjamin
Tappan, Lewis
Taylor, John W.
Torrey, Charles Turner
Tubman, Harriet
Ward, Samuel Ringgold
Weld, Theodore Dwight
Whittier, John Greenleaf
Woolman, John
Accountant (See also Tax Expert)
Lasser, Jacob Kay
Lybrand, William Mitchell
Actor (See also Entertainer)
Abbott, William A. ("Bud")
Adams, Edwin
Aiken, George L.
Aldrich, Louis
Aldridge, Ira Frederick
Anderson, Edward ("Eddie")
Arden, Edwin Hunter Pendleton
Arliss, George
Arnold, Edward
Bacon, Frank
Baker, Benjamin A.
Bangs, Frank C.
Bannister, Nathaniel Harrington
Barker, Alexander Chrichlow ("Lex")
Barnabee, Henry Clay
Barrett, George Horton
Barrett, Lawrence
Barrymore, John
Barrymore, Lionel
Barrymore, Maurice
Barthelmess, Richard
Beery, Wallace Fitzgerald
Begley, Edward James ("Ed")
Belasco, David
Benchley, Robert Charles
Bennett, Richard
Benny, Jack
Bergen, Edgar
Bernard, John
Blackmer, Sydney Alderman
Blake, William Rufus
Blinn, Holbrook
Blocker, Dan
Blue, Ben
Blue, Gerald Montgomery ("Monte")
Bogart, Humphrey DeForest
Booth, Edwin Thomas
Booth, John Wilkes
Booth, Junius Brutus
Boucicault, Dion
Boyd, William
Boyer, Charles
Bradford, Joseph
Brennan, Walter
Brent, George
Brougham, John
Brown, Johnny Mack
Browning, Tod
Buchanan, Edgar
Burgess, Neil
Burke, Charles St. Thomas
Burns, Bob
Burton, William Evans
Bushman, Francis Xavier
Cabot, Charles Sebastian Thomas
Cambridge, Godfrey MacArthur
Carlson, Richard Dutoit
Carroll, Leo Grattan
Carson, Jack
Cassidy, Jack
Chaney, Lon
Chaney, Lon, Jr.
Chanfrau, Francis S.
Chaplin, Charles Spencer ("Charlie")
Clarke, John Sleeper
Clift, Edward Montgomery
Cobb, Lee J.
Cohan, George Michael
Colman, Ronald Charles
Conried, Heinrich
Conte, Richard
Conway, Frederick Bartlett
Cooper, Gary
Cooper, Thomas Abthorpe
Couldock, Charles Walter
Cox, Wallace Maynard ("Wally")
Crane, Bob Edward
Crane, William Henry
Craven, Frank
Crisp, Donald
Crosby, Harry Lillis ("Bing")
Dailey, Dan, Jr.
Dale, Charles Marks
Daly, Peter Christopher Arnold
Darin, Bobby
Davenport, Edward Loomis
Davidge, William Pleater
Dean, James Byron
De Angelis, Thomas Jefferson
DeMille, Cecil Blount
Devine, Andrew ("Andy")
DeWilde, Brandon
Digges, Dudley
Ditrichstein, Leo
Dockstader, Lew
Donlevy, Brian
Drake, Samuel
Drew, John, 1827–1862
Drew, John, 1853–1927
Dunn, Michael
Eddy, Nelson
Edeson, Robert
Fairbanks, Douglas
Farnum, Charles Albert
Farnum, Dustin Lancy
Farnum, Franklyn
Faversham, William Alfred
Fay, Francis Anthony ("Frank")
Fennell, James
Ferguson, William Jason
Field, Joseph M.
Fine, Larry
Finn, Henry James William
Fitzsimmons, Robert Prometheus

Fleming, William Maybury
Florence, William Jermyn
Flynn, Errol Leslie
Ford, John
Forrest, Edwin
Fox, Charles Kemble
Fox, George Washington Lafayette
Fox, Gilbert
Gable, (William) Clark
Garfield, John
Gaxton, William
Geer, William Aughe ("Will")
Gibson, Edmund Richard ("Hoot")
Gilbert, John
Gilbert, John Gibbs
Gillette, William Hooker
Gilpin, Charles Sidney
Goodwin, Nathaniel Carll
Gorcey, Leo
Greenstreet, Sydney Hughes
Hackett, James Henry
Hackett, James Keteltas
Haley, Jack
Hallam, Lewis
Hamblin, Thomas Sowerby
Hampden, Walter
Hardwicke, Cedric Webster
Harrigan, Edward
Harrison, Gabriel
Harrison, Richard Berry
Hart, William Surrey
Haworth, Joseph
Hayakawa, Sessue
Hayes, Gabby
Haymes, Richard Benjamin ("Dick")
Hazelton, George Cochrane
Heflin, Van
Henry, John, 1746–1794
Herne, James A.
Hill, Frederic Stanhope
Hill, George Handel
Hitchcock, Raymond
Hodge, Albert Elmer ("Al")
Hodge, William Thomas
Hodgkinson, John
Holland, Edmund Milton
Holland, Joseph Jefferson
Hopper, DeWolf
Horton, Edward Everett, Jr.
Howard, Leslie
Huston, Walter
James, Louis
Janssen, David
Jefferson, Joseph, 1774–1832
Jefferson, Joseph, 1829–1905
Johnston, David Claypoole
Jones, Joseph Stevens
Karloff, Boris
Keenan, James Francis
Keene, Thomas Wallace
Kirby, J. Hudson
Kruger, Otto
Lackaye, Wilton
Ladd, Alan Walbridge
Lahr, Bert
Laughton, Charles
Leavitt, Frank Simmons ("Man Mountain Dean")
Lee, Bruce
Lee, Canada
Leiber, Fritz
Le Moyne, William J.
Lewis, Arthur
Lewis, James
Lindsay, Howard
Lloyd, Harold Clayton
Logan, Cornelius Ambrosius
Lorre, Peter
Ludlow, Noah Miller
Lugosi, Bela
Lunt, Alfred David, Jr.
McCoy, George Braidwood
McCoy, Tim
McCullough, John
MacKaye, James Morrison Steele
McLaglen, Victor
McQueen, Terence Stephen ("Steve")
McVicker, James Hubert
Mann, Louis
Manners, John Hartley
Mansfield, Richard
Mantell, Robert Bruce
Marble, Danforth
March, Frederic
Marx, Herbert ("Zeppo")
Marx, Julius Henry ("Groucho")
Marx, Milton ("Gummo")
Mason, John
Mayo, Frank
Menjou, Adolphe Jean
Miller, Henry
Mitchell, Thomas Gregory
Mitchell, William, 1798–1856
Mix, Tom
Montague, Henry James
Moore, Victor Frederick
Mostel, Samuel Joel ("Zero")
Muni, Paul
Murdoch, Frank Hitchcock
Murdoch, James Edward
Murphy, Audi Leon
Muse, Clarence
Nagel, Conrad
Naish, Joseph Carrol
Novarro, Ramon
Oakie, Jack
Odets, Clifford
Olcott, Chauncey
O'Neill, James
Owen, William Florence
Owens, John Edmond
Parks, Larry
Pastor, Antonio
Payne, John Howard
Placide, Henry
Powell, Richard Ewing ("Dick")
Powell, Snelling
Power, Frederick Tyrone
Power, Tyrone
Pray, Isaac Clark
Presley, Elvis Aron
Prinze, Freddie
Proctor, Joseph
Raft, George
Rains, Claude
Rankin, McKee
Rathbone, Basil
Raymond, John T.
Renaldo, Duncan
Rennie, Michael
Richings, Peter
Riddle, George Peabody
Ritchard, Cyril
Ritter, Woodward Maurice ("Tex")
Roberts, Theodore
Robeson, Paul Leroy
Robinson, Edward G.
Robson, Stuart
Rogers, Will
Rooney, Pat
Russell, Sol Smith
Ryan, Robert Bushnell
Sanders, George
Schildkraut, Joseph
Schwartz, Maurice
Sennett, Mack
Seymour, William
Shean, Albert
Sills, Milton
Silverheels, Jay
Simpson, Edmund Shaw
Skinner, Otis
Smith, Marcus
Smith, William Henry, 1806–1872
Sothern, Edward Askew
Sothern, Edward Hugh
Stoddart, James Henry
Stone, John Agustus
Tamiroff, Akim
Taylor, Robert
Thayer, Tiffany Ellsworth
Thompson, Denman
Thorne, Charles Robert, 1814–1893
Thorne, Charles Robert, 1840–1883
Tone, Stanislas Pascal Franchot
Tracy, Spencer Bonaventure
Van, Bobby
Vandenhoff, George
Vezin, Hermann
Visscher, William Lightfoot
Von Stroheim, Erich
Walcot, Charles Melton, 1816–1868
Walcot, Charles Melton, 1840–1921
Wallack, Henry John
Wallack, James William 1795–1864
Wallack, James William, 1818–1873
Wallack, Lester
Walsh, Raoul
Walthall, Henry Brazeal
Warde, Frederick Barkham
Warfield, David
Warren, William, 1767–1832
Warren, William, 1812–1888
Wayne, John
Webb, Clifton
Wemyss, Francis Courtney
Wheatley, William
White, George
Wignell, Thomas
Williams, Barney
Williams, Bert
Wills, Chill
Wilson, Francis
Wise, Thomas Alfred

Wolheim, Louis Robert
Wood, William Burke
Woolley, Edgar Montillion ("Monty")
Wynn, Ed

ACTRESS (See also ENTERTAINER)
Adams, Maude
Adler, Sara
Allen, Viola Emily
Anderson, Mary
Angeli, Pier
Anglin, Margaret Mary
Bankhead, Tallulah
Bara, Theda
Barnes, Charlotte Mary Sanford
Barrie, Wendy
Barrymore, Ethel
Barrymore, Georgiana Emma Drew
Bateman, Kate Josephine
Bateman, Sidney Francis Cowell
Bates, Blanche
Beavers, Louise
Bennett, Constance Campbell
Berg, Gertrude Edelstein
Bingham, Amelia
Blondell, Joan
Bonstelle, Jessie
Booth, Agnes
Bow, Clara Gordon
Bowers, Elizabeth Crocker
Brady, Alice
Britton, Barbara
Burke, Billie
Byington, Spring
Carter, Caroline Louise Dudley
Castle, Irene Foote
Cayvan, Georgia
Chanfrau, Henrietta Baker
Chase, Ilka
Chatterton, Ruth
Claxton, Kate
Clifton, Josephine
Coghlan, Rose
Collier, Constance
Cornell, Katharine
Cowl, Jane
Crabtree, Lotta
Crawford, Joan
Cushman, Charlotte Saunders
Cushman, Pauline
Cushman, Susan Webb
Dandridge, Dorothy Jean
Darwell, Jane
Davenport, Fanny Lily Gypsy
Davies, Marion Cecilia
Dean, Julia
De Wolfe, Elsie
Dickinson, Anna Elizabeth
Douglas, Helen Gahagan
Drake, Frances Ann Denny
Dresser, Louise Kerlin
Dressler, Marie
Duff, Mary Ann Dyke
Dumont, Margaret
Eagels, Jeanne
Elliott, Maxine
Eytnige, Rose
Fazenda, Louise Marie
Field, Mary Katherine Kemble
Fisher, Clara
Fiske, Minnie Maddern
Forman, Celia Adler
Francis, Kay
Garland, Judy
George, Gladys
George, Grace
Gilbert, Anne Hartley
Gish, Dorothy
Grable, Betty
Hale, Louise Closser
Hall, Juanita Armethea
Harlow, Jean
Hayward, Susan
Henie, Sonja
Herne, Chrystal Katharine
Heron, Matilda Agnes
Holliday, Judy
Hopkins, Miriam
Hopper, Hedda
Hull, Josephine
Illington, Margaret
Irwin, May
Jananschek, Franziska Magdalena Romance
Kane, Helen
Keene, Laura
Kemble, Frances Anne
Lake, Veronica
Lander, Jean Margaret Davenport
Landis, Jessie Royce
Lawrence, Gertrude
Leigh, Vivien
Logan, Olive
Lombard, Carole
Lord, Pauline
Lynn, Diana ("Dolly")
McCracken, Joan
McDaniel, Hattie
MacDonald, Jeanette Anna
Main, Marjorie
Mansfield, Jayne
Marlowe, Julia
Maxwell, Marvel Marilyn
Menken, Adah Isaacs
Merry, Ann Brunton
Mitchell, Margaret Julia
Modjeska, Helena
Monroe, Marilyn
Moorehead, Agnes
Morgan, Helen
Morris, Clara
Morris, Elizabeth
Mowatt, Anna Cora Ogden
Murray, Mae
Nazimova, Alla
Oberon, Merle
Perry, Antoinette
Pickford, Mary
Pitts, Zasu
Rand, Sally
Rehan, Ada
Robson, May
Roth, Lillian
Rowson, Susanna Haswell
Russell, Annie
Russell, Rosalind
Sands, Diana Patricia
Seberg, Jean Dorothy
Shaw, Mary
Skinner, Cornelia Otis
Stevens, Emily
Strange, Michael
Sullavan, Margaret
Susann, Jacqueline
Talmadge, Constance
Talmadge, Norma
Taylor, Laurette
Tucker, Sophie
Vance, Vivian
Vidor, Florence
Vincent, Mary Ann
Waller, Emma
Walsh, Blanche
Ward, Genevieve
Waters, Ethel
Webster, Margaret ("Peggy")
West, Mae
Western, Lucille
Westley, Helen
White, Pearl
Wilson, Marie
Wong, Anna May
Wood, Peggy

ACTUARY (See also INSURANCE EXECUTIVE)
Fackler, David Parks
McCay, Charles Francis
McClintock, Emory
Wright, Elizur

ADMINISTRATOR (See also COLLEGE ADMINISTRATOR, PRISON ADMINISTRATOR)
Abernethy, George
Adams, Jasper
Angle, Paul McClelland
Cloud, Henry Roe
Coburn, Foster Dwight
Crafts, James Mason
Dinwiddie, Robert
Geddes, James Loraine
Goethals, George Washington
Goode, George Brown
Hatfield, Edwin Francis
Hawley, Gideon, 1785–1870
King, Clarence
Landis, James McCauley
Lynds, Elam
Magoon, Charles Edward
Mendenhall, Thomas Corwin
Nelson, Reuben
Perkins, George Henry
Pickering, Timothy
Pilsbury, Amos
Powell, John Wesley
Randall, Alexander Williams
Richmond, Mary Ellen
Runkle, John Daniel
Sargent, Winthrop, 1753–1820
Smith, Edgar Fahs
Smith, James Francis
Taylor, James Barnett
Thacher, Thomas Anthony
Tompkins, Sally Louisa
Valentine, Robert Grosvenor
Vaughan, Victor Clarence
Walcott, Charles Doolittle
Wilson, Peter
Woodward, Robert Simpson

ADVENTURER (See also COLONIZER, EXPLORER, FILIBUSTER, FUR TRADER, PRIVATEER, SPY, SWINDLER, TRADER, TRAVELER)
Argall, Sir Samuel

Bartlett, Joseph
Bowles, William Augustus
Boyd, John Parker
Burgevine, Henry Andrea
Clarke, Elijah
Coode, John
Crowne, William
Gibson, Walter Murray
Graffenried, Christopher, Baron de
Harlan, Josiah
Hayes, William Henry ("Bully")
Henry, John, fl. 1807–1820
Judson, Edward Zane Carroll
Laffite, Jean
Long, James
MacDonald, Ranald
Morton, Thomas
Peñalosa Briceño, Diego Dioniso de
Revere, Joseph Warren
Scott, John
Smith, John, 1579/80–1631
Thrasher, John Sidney
Walker, William
Ward, Frederick Townsend
Wikoff, Henry
Wingfield, Edward Maria
Yeardley, Sir George

ADVENTURESS
Livingstone, Belle

ADVERTISING AGENT
Ayer, Francis Wayland
Post, Charles William
Rowell, George Presbury

ADVERTISING EXECUTIVE
Ayer, Francis Wayland
Barton, Bruce Fairchild
Bates, Theodore Lewis ("Ted")
Benton, William Burnett
Block, Paul
Brophy, Thomas D'Arcy
Burnett, Leo
Calkins, Earnest Elmo
Cone, Fairfax Mastick
Durstine, Roy Sarles
Emmett, Burton
Lasker, Albert Davis
Resor, Stanley Burnet
Rubicam, Raymond
Watson, John Broadus

AERONAUT (See also AVIATOR, BALLOONIST)
Chanute, Octave
Durant, Charles Ferson
Herring, Augustus Moore
King, Samuel Archer
La Mountain, John
Langley, Samuel Pierpont
Lowe, Thaddeus Sobieski Coulincourt
Sellers, Matthew Bacon
Vought, Chance Milton
Wellman, Walter

AERONAUTICAL CONSULTANT
Ide, John Jay

AERONAUTICAL DESIGNER
Bellanca, Giuseppe Mario

AERONAUTICAL ENGINEER
Egtvedt, Clairmont ("Clair") Leroy
Lear, William Powell
McDonnell, James Smith, Jr.

AEROSPACE PIONEER
Bell, Lawrence Dale

AGENT, LITERARY (see LITERARY AGENT)

AGITATOR (See also PAMPHLETEER, PROPAGANDIST, RADICAL, REVOLUTIONIST)
Beach, Wooster
Cooper, Thomas
McCord, David James
McDougall, Alexander
Paine, Thomas
Struve, Gustav

AGRARIAN LEADER (See also AGRICULTURAL LEADER, AGRICULTURIST, FARM LEADER)
Johnson, Magnus
Lemke, William Frederick

AGRICULTURAL CHEMIST (See also AGRICULTURIST, CHEMIST)
Armsby, Henry Prentiss
Atwater, Wilbur Olin
Babcock, Stephen Moulton
Carver, George Washington
Collier, Peter
Frear, William
Hopkins, Cyril George
Jenkins, Edward Hopkins
Johnson, Samuel William
King, Franklin Hiram
Mapes, Charles Victor
Ravenel, St. Julien
Stockbridge, Horace Edward
Thatcher, Roscoe Wilfred
Van Slyke, Lucius Lincoln

AGRICULTURAL ECONOMIST (See also ECONOMIST)
Tolley, Howard Ross
Warren, George Frederick

AGRICULTURAL EDUCATOR (See also AGRICULTURIST, EDUCATOR)
Babcock, Howard Edward
Davenport, Eugene
Ladd, Carl Edwin

AGRICULTURAL HISTORIAN (See also HISTORIAN)
Edwards, Everett Eugene

AGRICULTURAL JOURNALIST (See also AGRICULTURIST, JOURNALIST)
Gregory, Clifford Verne
Sanders, James Harvey
Tucker, Luther
Wallace, Henry Cantwell
Wing, Joseph Elwyn

AGRICULTURAL LEADER (See also Agrarian Leader, Farm Leader)
Goss, Albert Simon
Haugen, Gilbert Nelson
Lowden, Frank Orren
Newsom, Herschel David

AGRICULTURAL SCIENTIST
Wallace, Henry Agard

AGRICULTURE, COMMISSIONER OF (See also AGRICULTURIST)
Le Duc, William Gates
Newton, Isaac, 1800–1867
Pearson, Raymond Allen

AGRICULTURIST (See also AGRICULTURAL CHEMIST, EDITOR, EDUCATOR, JOURNALIST; AGRICULTURE, COMMISSIONER OF; AGRONOMIST; ARBORICULTURIST; BOTANIC PHYSICIAN; BOTANIST; FARM COOPERATIVE LEADER; FARMER; FORESTER; GRANGER; HORTICULTURIST; NURSERYMAN; PLANT BREEDER; PLANTER; POMOLOGIST; SECRETARY OF AGRICULTURE; SEEDSMAN; SILVICULTURIST; SOIL EXPERT; SOIL SCIENTIST; SUGAR PLANTER; TREE SURGEON; TREE-CARE EXPERT; VITICULTURIST)
Allen, Richard Lamb
Bement, Caleb N.
Blalock, Nelson Gales
Bordley, John Beale
Brigham, Joseph Henry
Buel, Jesse
Capron, Horace
Chamberlain, William Isaac
Coker, David Robert
Dabney, Charles William
Eaton, Benjamin Harrison
Ellsworth, Henry Leavitt
Emerson, Gouverneur
Flint, Charles Louis
Furnas, Robert Wilkinson
Gardiner, Robert Hallowell
Garnett, James Mercer
Garst, Roswell ("Bob")
Goodale, Stephen Lincoln
Hazard, Thomas Robinson
Henry, William Arnon
Holmes, Ezekiel
Jarvis, William
Johnson, Benjamin Pierce
Johnston, John
Knapp, Bradford
Knapp, Seaman Asahel
Landreth, David
Leaming, Jacob Spicer
Le Duc, William Gates
L'Hommedieu, Ezra
Loring, George Bailey
Lubin, David
Lyman, Joseph Bardwell
McBryde, John McLaren
Mapes, James Jay
Mason, Arthur John
Miles, Manly
Mitchell, Donald Grant
Montgomery, William Bell
Morton, Julius Sterling
Murphy, Frederick E.
Oemler, Arminius
O'Neal, Edward Asbury, III
Patrick, Marsena Rudolph
Pedder, James
Peters, Richard, 1810–1889
Powel, John Hare
Randall, Henry Stephens
Roberts, Job
Robinson, Solon
Ruffin, Edmund

Shelton, Edward Mason
Smith, Hiram
Stockbridge, Levi
Sturtevant, Edward Lewis
Taylor, John
Todd, Sereno Edwards
Trimble, Allen
True, Alfred Charles
Turner, Jonathan Baldwin
Vanderbilt, George Washington
Vaughan, Benjamin
Voorhees, Edward Burnett
Waring, George Edwin
Watson, Elkanah
Watts, Frederick
Wilder, Marshall Pinckney
Wilson, James
AGRONOMIST (See also AGRICULTURIST)
Cobb, Nathan Augustus
Hopkins, Cyril George
Piper, Charles Vancouver
Rosen, Joseph A.
AIRCRAFT DESIGNER
Stearman, Lloyd Carlton
AIR FORCE CHIEF OF STAFF
Spaatz, Carl Andrew ("Tooey")
Vandenberg, Hoyt Sanford
AIR FORCE OFFICER
Brown, George Scratchley
Chennault, Claire Lee
Fairchild, Muir Stephen
Grissom, Virgil Ivan ("Gus")
James, Daniel, Jr. ("Chappie")
O'Donnell, Emmett, Jr. ("Rosy")
Royce, Ralph
Stratemeyer, George Edward
White, Edward Higgins, II
AIRLINE EXECUTIVE (See AVIATION EXECUTIVE)
AIRMAIL PIONEER
Henderson, Paul
ALCOHOLICS ANONYMOUS CO-FOUNDER
Wilson, William Griffith ("Bill W.")
ALIENIST (See also PHYSICIAN; PSYCHIATRIST; PSYCHOANALYST)
Awl, William Maclay
Flint, Austin
Gray, John Purdue
Hamilton, Allan McLane
ALMANAC MAKER
Ames, Nathaniel
Daboll, Nathan
Franklin, Benjamin
Leavitt, Dudley
Leeds, Daniel
Pierce, William
West, Benjamin
Young, David
AMERICAN CIVIL LIBERTIES UNION CHAIRMAN
Angell, Ernest
AMERICAN INDIAN POTTER
Matinez, Maria
AMERICAN INDIAN RIGHTS ADVOCATE
Madigan, Laverne
AMERICAN RED CROSS OFFICIAL
Boardman, Mabel Thorp
Olds, Robert Edwin
Payne, John Barton
AMUSEMENT PARK CREATOR
Disney, Walter Elias ("Walt")
ANARCHIST
Berkman, Alexander
Goldman, Emma
Most, Johann Joseph
Parsons, Albert Richard
Tucker, Benjamin Ricketson
Warren, Josiah
ANATOMIST (SEE ALSO PHYSICIAN)
Allen, Edgar
Allen, Harrison
Baker, Frank
Bensley, Robert Russell
Brödel, Max
Chovet, Abraham
Coghill, George Ellett
Davidge, John Beale
Dorsey, John Syng
Dwight, Thomas
Evans, Herbert McLean
Gerrish, Frederic Henry
Goddard, Paul Beck
Godman, John Davidson
Horner, William Edmonds
Huber, Gotthelf Carl
Jackson, Clarence Martin
McClellan, George, 1796–1847
McClellan, George, 1849–1913
McMurrich, James Playfair
Mall, Franklin Paine
March, Alden
Miller, William Snow
Nelson, Marjorie Maxine
Pancoast, Joseph
Pancoast, Seth
Papanicolaou, George Nicholas
Pattison, Granville Sharp
Ramsay, Alexander
Ranson, Stephen Walter
Robinson, Frederick Byron
Sabin, Florence Rena
Souchon, Edmond
Spitzka, Edward Anthony
Stockard, Charles Rupert
Todd, Thomas Wingate
Tuckerman, Frederick
Weed, Lewis Hill
Wislocki, George Bernays
Wyman, Jeffries
ANESTHESIOLOGIST (PHYSICIAN)
Colton, Gardner Quincy
Long, Crawford Williamson
Morton, William Thomas Green
Rovenstine, Emery Andrew
Wells, Horace
ANIMAL PSYCHOLOGIST
Yerkes, Robert Mearns
ANIMATED FILMMAKER
Hubley, John
ANIMATOR
Disney, Walter Elias ("Walt")
Terry, Paul Houlton
ANTHOLOGIST
Bronson, Walter Cochrane
Griswold, Rufus Wilmot
Kennedy, William Sloane
Tappan, Eva March
Untermeyer, Louis
ANTHROPOGEOGRAPHER (See also ANTHROPOLOGIST)
Semple, Ellen Churchill
ANTHROPOLOGIST (See also ETHNOLOGIST, FOLKLORIST)
Alexander, Hartley Burr
Bandelier, Adolph Francis Alphonse
Barrows, David Prescott
Benedict, Ruth Fulton
Boas, Franz
Brinton, Daniel Garrison
Chamberlain, Alexander Francis
Dixon, Roland Burrage
Dorsey, George Amos
Farabee, William Curtis
Farrand, Livingston
Fejos, Paul
Goldenweiser, Alexander Alexandrovich
Hooton, Earnest Albert
Hough, Walter
Hrdlicka, Ales
Hurston, Zora Neale
Kroeber, Alfred Louis
La Farge, Oliver Hazard Perry
Lewis, Oscar
Linton, Ralph
MacCurdy, George Grant
McGee, William John
McGuire, Joseph Deakins
Mead, Margaret
Meigs, James Aitken
Nelson, Nels Christian
Parker, Arthur Caswell
Parsons, Elsie Worthington Clews
Powdermaker, Hortense
Radin, Paul
Redfield, Robert
Roheim, Geza
Sapir, Edward
Skinner, Alanson Buck
Spier, Leslie
Starr, Frederick
Sullivan, Louis Robert
Swanton, John Reed
Todd, Thomas Wingate
Warner, William Lloyd
Weidenreich, Franz
Wheelwright, Mary Cabot
Wissler, Clark
ANTIQUARIAN
Alden, Timothy
Appleton, William Sumner
Arthur, William
Bartlett, John Russell
Campbell, Charles
Chester, Joseph Lemuel
Davis, Andrew McFarland
Dexter, Franklin Bowditch
Drake, Samuel Gardner
Du Simitière, Pierre Eugène
Earle, Alice Morse
Endicott, Charles Moses
Farmer, John
Felt, Joseph Barlow
Folsom, George
Green, Samuel Abbott
Grim, David
Hazard, Samuel

Hoyt, Albert Harrison
Jordan, John Woolf
Livermore, George
McCabe, John Collins
Malcolm, James Peller
Mercer, Henry Chapman
Munsell, Joel
Nutting, Wallace
Robbins, Thomas
Sachse, Julius Friedrich
Sargent, Lucius Manlius
Savage, James
Shurtleff, Nathaniel Bradstreet
Smith, Buckingham
Stanard, William Glover
Stevens, Benjamin Franklin
Taylor, Richard Cowling
Van Schaack, Henry Cruger
Watson, John Fanning
Whitmore, William Henry
Young, Alexander

ANTI-COMMUNIST WITNESS
Budenz, Louis Francis

ANTIQUE DEALER
Rosenbach, Abraham Simon Wolf
Rosenbach, Philip Hyman
Sack, Israel

ANTISUFFRAGIST
Meyer, Annie Nathan

APIARIST
Langstroth, Lorenzo Lorraine
Root, Amos Ives

APOTHECARY (See also DRUGGIST, PHARMACIST)
Craigie, Andrew
Jackson, David

ARACHNOLOGIST
Emerton, James Henry

ARBITRATOR
Morse, Wayne Lyman

ARBORICULTURIST (See also AGRICULTURIST, BOTANIST, FORESTER, HORTICULTURIST, NURSERYMAN, PLANT BREEDER, POMOLOGIST, SILVICULTURIST, TREE-CARE EXPERT, TREE SURGEON)
Sargent, Charles Sprague

ARCHABBOT (See also BISHOP, RELIGIOUS LEADER)
Schnerr, Leander
Stehle, Aurelius Aloysius

ARCHBISHOP (See also BISHOP, RELIGIOUS LEADER)
Alemany, José Sadoc
Blanc, Antoine
Blanchet, François Norbert
Blenk, James Hubert
Chapelle, Placide Louis
Corrigan, Michael Augustine
Dowling, Austin
Feehan, Patrick Augustine
Glennon, John Joseph
Hanna, Edward Joseph
Janssens, Francis
McNicholas, John Timothy
O'Connell, William Henry
Rummel, Joseph Francis
Stritch, Samuel Alphonsus

ARCHEOLOGIST (See also SCHOLAR)
Abbott, Charles Conrad
Albright, William Foxwell
Badè, William Frederic
Barber, Edwin Atlee
Beauchamp, William Martin
Bliss, Frederick Jones
Bowditch, Charles Pickering
Breasted, James Henry
Brower, Jacob Vradenberg
Butler, Howard Crosby
Casanowicz, Immanuel Moses
Cesnola, Luigi Palma di
Clarke, Sir Caspar Purdon
Conant, Alban Jasper
Davis, Edwin Hamilton
Fisher, Clarence Stanley
Fowke, Gerard
Glueck, Nelson
Goodyear, William Henry
Gordon, George Byron
Hawes, Harriet Ann Boyd
Haynes, John Henry
Holmes, William Henry
Hoppin, Joseph Clark
Kelsey, Francis Willey
Kidder, Alfred Vincent
MacCurdy, George Grant
Mercer, Henry Chapman
Merriam, Augustus Chapman
Merrill, Selah
Middleton, John Izard
Morley, Sylvanus Griswold
Murray, Louise Shipman Welles
Nies, James Buchanan
Paine, John Alsop
Parker, Arthur Caswell
Paton, Lewis Bayles
Peet, Stephen Denison
Peters, John Punnett
Porter, Arthur Kingsley
Putnam, Frederic Ward
Rau, Charles
Richardson, Rufus Byam
Rostovtzeff, Michael Ivanovitch
Saville, Marshall Howard
Seyffarth, Gustavus
Shear, Theodore Leslie
Snyder, John Francis
Speiser, Ephraim Avigdor
Squier, Ephraim George
Sterrett, John Robert Sitlington
Stevenson, Sara Yorke
Tarbell, Frank Bigelow
Thompson, Edward Herbert
Upham, Warren
Vaillant, George Clapp
Van Deman, Esther Boise
Wheeler, James Rignall
Whitehouse, Frederic Cope
Whittemore, Thomas
Winchell, Newton Horace
Winslow, William Copley

ARCHITECT (See also NAVAL ARCHITECT)
Albro, Lewis Colt
Aldrich, Chester Holmes
Atterbury, Grosvenor
Atwood, Charles B.
Audsley, George Ashdown
Austin, Henry
Bacon, Henry
Banner, Peter
Barber, Donn
Behrendt, Walter Curt
Benjamin, Asher
Blodget, Samuel
Bluemner, Oscar Florians
Boring, William Alciphron
Boucher, Horace Edward
Bragdon, Claude Fayette
Browne, Herbert Wheildon Cotton
Brunner, Arnold William
Bulfinch, Charles
Burnham, Daniel Hudson
Cabot, Edward Clarke
Carrère, John Merven
Carter, Elias
Clarke, Sir Caspar Purdon
Cook, Walter
Coolidge, Charles Allerton
Cope, Walter
Corbett, Harvey Wiley
Cram, Ralph Adams
Cret, Paul Philippe
Culter, James Goold
Cummings, Charles Amos
Dakin, James Harrison
Davis, Alexander Jackson
Day, Frank Miles
Delano, William Adams
Downing, Andrew Jackson
Eames, Charles Ormand, Jr.
Eidlitz, Cyrus Lazelle Warner
Eidlitz, Leopold
Elmslie, George Grant
Fenner, Burt Leslie
Flagg, Ernest
Ford, George Burdett
Gallier, James
Gilbert, Cass
Gilman, Arthur Delevan
Godefroy, Maximilian
Goodhue, Bertram Grosvenor
Graham, Ernest Robert
Granger, Alfred Hoyt
Greene, Charles Sumner
Greene, Henry Mather
Greenough, Henry
Gropius, Walter Adolf Georg
Hadfield, George
Haight, Charles Coolidge
Hallet, Étienne Sulpice
Hamlin, Alfred Dwight Foster
Hamlin, Talbot Faulkner
Hardenberg, Henry Janeway
Harrison, Peter
Hastings, Thomas
Haviland, John
Hawks, John
Higgins, Daniel Paul
Hoadley, David
Hoban, James
Holabird, William
Hood, Raymond Mathewson
Hooker, Philip
Hunt, Richard Morris
Jefferson, Thomas
Jenney, William Le Baron
Joy, Thomas
Kahn, Albert
Kahn, Louis I.
Kearsley, John
Kimball, (Sidney) Fiske
Klauder, Charles Zeller

Kneass, Samuel Honeyman
La Farge, Christopher Grant
Lafever, Minard
Lamb, William Frederick
Latrobe, Benjamin Henry, 1764–1820
Le Brun, Napoléon Eugène Henry Charles
Lienau, Detlef
Longfellow, William Pitt Preble
Lowell, Guy
McArthur, John, 1823–1890
McComb, John
McIntire, Samuel
McKim, Charles Folley
Maginnis, Charles Donagh
Magonigle, Harold Van Buren
Mangin, Joseph François
Marshall, Henry Rutgers
Mauran, John Lawrence
Maybeck, Bernard Ralph
Mazzuchelli, Samuel Charles
Mead, William Rutherford
Medary, Milton Bennett
Mendelsohn, Erich (or Eric)
Mies van der Rohe, Ludwig
Mills, Robert, 1781–1855
Mizner, Addison
Morgan, Julia
Neutra, Richard Joseph
Parris, Alexander
Peabody, Robert Swain
Pelz, Paul Johannes
Perkins, Dwight Heald
Platt, Charles Adams
Polk, Willis Jefferson
Pond, Allen Bartlit
Pond, Irving Kane
Pope, John Russell
Post, George Browne
Poulson, Niels
Price, Bruce
Ramée, Joseph Jacques
Renwick, James, 1818–1895
Richardson, Henry Hobson
Rogers, Isaiah
Rogers, James Gamble
Root, John Wellborn
Rotch, Arthur
Saarinen, Eero
Saarinen, Gottlieb Eliel
Schindler, Rudolph Michael
Shaw, Howard Van Doren
Sherman, Frank Dempster
Skidmore, Louis
Smith, Robert, 1722–1777
Starrett, William Aiken
Stewardson, John
Stewart, John George
Stokes, Isaac Newton Phelps
Stone, Edward Durell
Strickland, William
Sturgis, Russell
Sullivan, Louis Henri
Thompson, Martin E.
Thornton, William
Tilton, Edward Lippincott
Town, Ithiel
Trumbauer, Horace
Tucker, Allen
Tuthill, William Burnet
Upjohn, Richard
Upjohn, Richard Michell
Urban, Joseph
Van Brunt, Henry
Van Osdel, John Mills
Walter, Thomas Ustick
Ware, William Robert
Warren, Herbert Langford
Warren, Russell
Wheelwright, Edmund March
White, Stanford
Wight, Peter Bonnett
Willard, Soloman
Wilson, Joseph Miller
Withers, Frederick Clarke
Wright, Frank Lloyd
Wright, Henry
Wright, John Kenneth Lloyd
Young, Ammi Burnham

ARCHIVIST (See also LIBRARIAN, SCHOLAR)
Connor, Robert Digges Wimberly
Fernow, Berthold
Force, Peter
Ford, Worthington Chauncey
Knight, Lucian Lamar
Leland, Waldo Gifford
Owen, Thomas McAdory

ARCTIC EXPLORER
Boyd, Louise Arner

ARMOR EXPERT
Dean, Bashford

ARMY AIR CORPS OFFICER
Andrews, Frank Maxwell

ARMY MEDICAL OFFICER (See also PHYSICIAN, SOLDIER)
Hume, Edgar Erskine
Simmons, James Stevens

ARMY NURSE CORPS COMMANDER
Blanchfield, Florence Aby

ARMY OFFICER (See also GENERAL, SOLDIER)
Abrams, Creighton Williams, Jr.
Ainsworth, Frederick Crayton
Ames, Adelbert
Arnold, Henry Harley
Bell, James Franklin
Black, William Murray
Brereton, Lewis Hyde
Buckner, Simon Bolivar
Bullard, Robert Lee
Casey, Thomas Lincoln
Chaffee, Adna Romanza
Clay, Lucius DuBignon
Craig, Malin
Crowder, Enoch Herbert
Crozier, William
Davis, Benjamin Oliver, Sr.
Devers, Jacob Loucks
Drum, Hugh Aloysius
Eddy, Manton Sprague
Edwards, Clarence Ransom
Eichelberger, Robert Lawrence
Eisenhower, Dwight David
Ely, Hanson Edward
Fairchild, Muir Stephen
Foulois, Benjamin Delahauf
Glassford, Pelham Davis
Graves, William Sidney
Groves, Leslie Richard, Jr.
Guild, La Fayette
Harbord, James Guthrie
Hawley, Paul Ramsey
Heintzelman, Stuart
Hines, Frank Thomas
Hines, John Leonard ("Birdie")
Hodes, Henry Irving
Hodge, John Reed
Hodges, Courtney Hicks
Johnson, Hugh Samuel
Johnston, William Hartshorne
King, Edward Leonard
Krueger, Walter
Kuhn, Joseph Ernst
Lear, Ben
Lee, John Clifford Hodges
Liggett, Hunter
Lynch, John Roy
McAlexander, Ulysses Grant
MacArthur, Arthur
MacArthur, Douglas
McAuliffe, Anthony Clement
McClure, Robert Alexis
McNair, Lesley James
MacNider, Hanford
Marshall, George Catlett, Jr.
Michler, Nathaniel
Mitchell, William
Morton, Charles Gould
Muir, Charles Henry
Neyland, Robert Reese, Jr.
Palmer, John McAuley
Patch, Alexander McCarrell
Patrick, Mason Mathews
Patton, George Smith
Pick, Lewis Andrew
Read, George Windle
Roosevelt, Kermit
Roosevelt, Theodore
Schroeder, Rudolph William
Scott, Hugh Lenox
Short, Walter Campbell
Smith, Walter Bedell
Snyder, Howard McCrum
Somervell, Brehon Burke
Stilwell, Joseph Warren
Sutherland, Richard Kerens
Vedder, Edward Bright
Wagener, John Andreas
Wainwright, Jonathan Mayhew
Walker, Walton Harris
Wheeler, Earle Gilmore
Whitney, Courtney
Winship, Blanton
Wood, Charles Erskine Scott
Wood, Robert Elkington

ART COLLECTOR (See also COLLECTOR)
Arensberg, Walter Conrad
Bache, Jules Semon
Barnes, Albert Coombs
Berenson, Bernard
Cone, Claribel
Cone, Etta
Dale, Chester
Dale, Maud Murray Thompson
Emmett, Burton
Freer, Charles Lang
Gardner, Isabella Stewart
Gellatly, John
Goodyear, Anson Conger
Guggenheim, Marguerite ("Peggy")

Jarves, James Jackson
Johnson, John Graver
Johnston, John Taylor
Kress, Samuel Henry
Lasker, Albert Davis
Lehman, Adele Lewisohn
Lewisohn, Adolph
Mellon, Andrew William
Reisinger, Hugo
Rosenberg, Paul
Rosenwald, Lessing Julius
Ross, Denman Waldo
Ryerson, Martin Antoine
Walker, Thomas Barlow
Walters, Henry
Walters, William Thompson
White, Alexander

ART CONNOISSEUR
Avery, Samuel Putnam
Berenson, Bernard
Cahill, Holger
Clarke, Sir Caspar Purdon
Frankfurter, Alfred Moritz
Hart, Charles Henry
Laffan, William Mackay
Lyon, Caleb

ART CRITIC
Berenson, Bernard
Cary, Elisabeth Luther
Coffin, William Anderson
Cook, Clarence Chatham
Cortissoz, Royal
Cox, Kenyon
Foster, Benjamin
Frankfurter, Alfred Moritz
Hartmann, Carl Sadakichi
Hitchcock, James Ripley Wellman
Keppel, Frederick
Perkins, Charles Callahan
Rosenfeld, Paul Leopold
Stein, Leo Daniel
Van Dyke, John Charles
Van Rensselaer, Mariana Griswold
Wallace, Horace Binney

ART DEALER
Avery, Samuel Putnam
Halpert, Edith Gregor
Rosenberg, Paul

ART DIRECTOR
Hubley, John

ART EDUCATOR
Sachs, Paul Joseph

ART HISTORIAN
Berenson, Bernard
Bieber, Margarete
Coomaraswamy, Ananda Kentish
Friedlaender, Walter Ferdinand
Gardner, Helen
Kimball, (Sidney) Fiske
Panofsky, Erwin
Seitz, William Chapin
Warner, Langdon

ART PATRON
Altman, Benjamin
Crowninshield, Francis Welch
De Cuevas, Marquis
Dreier, Katherine Sophie
Evans, William Thomas
Guggenheim, Marguerite ("Peggy")
Kahn, Otto Herman
Lewisohn, Sam Adolph
Libbey, Edward Drummond
Luhan, Mabel Dodge
Murphy, Gerald Clery
Reed, Luman
Stieglitz, Alfred
Whitney, Gertrude Vanderbilt
Wolfe, Catharine Lorillard
Zellerbach, Harold Lionel

ART THEORETICIAN
Gabo, Naum

ARTIST (CARTOONIST, CRAFTSMAN, GRAPHIC ARTIST, ILLUSTRATOR, MODELER, MURALIST, PAINTER, SCULPTOR)
Allston, Washington
Appleton, Thomas Gold
Artzybasheff, Boris
Audubon, John James
Avery, Milton Clark
Baziotes, William
Beard, James Henry
Beard, William Holbrook
Bemelmans, Ludwig
Benton, Thomas Hart
Biddle, George
Birch, Reginald Bathurst
Burroughs, Bryson
Cassatt, Mary
Catlin, George
Cesare, Oscar Edward
Chaliapin, Boris Fyodorovich
Chaplin, Ralph Hosea
Chase, William Merritt
Cheney, Seth Wells
Cole, Thomas
Coman, Charlotte Buell
Conant, Alban Jasper
Connick, Charles Jay
Crosby, Percy Lee
Davis, Charles Harold
Davis, Stuart
Dellenbaugh, Frederick Samuel
Demuth, Charles
Dodge, William de Leftwich
Douglas, Aaron
Drake, Alexander Wilson
Dreier, Katherine Sophie
Du Simitière, Pierre Eugène
Emerton, James Henry
Ernst, Max
Flagg, Josiah Foster
Fuertes, Louis Agassiz
Fulton, Robert
Gág, Wanda (Hazel)
Gibson, William Hamilton
Gutherz, Carl
Hambridge, Jay
Harshe, Robert Bartholow
Hassam, Frederick Childe
Hokinson, Helen Elna
Holmes, William Henry
Howland, Alfred Cornelius
Hyde, Helen
Imbert, Antoine
Isham, Samuel
Ives, Halsey Cooley
James, Will Roderick
Jamison, Cecilia Viets Dakin Hamilton
Johnston, Henrietta
Kent, Rockwell
Koehler, Sylvester Rosa
Lanman, Charles
Lawrie, Alexander
Lesueur, Charles Alexandre
Leyendecker, Joseph Christian
Louis, Morris
Low, Will Hicok
Man Ray
Marin, John (Cheri)
Mitchell, John Ames
Moholy-Nagy, László
Moore, Charles Herbert
Morse, Samuel Finley Breese
Nicholls, Rhoda Holmes
Niemeyer, John Henry
Oertel, Johannes Adam Simon
Outcault, Richard Felton
Parrish, Maxfield
Peale, Titian Ramsay
Perry, Walter Scott
Pippin, Horace
Pyle, Howard
Rehn, Frank Knox Morton
Ripley, Robert LeRoy
Robinson, Boardman
Robinson, Theodore
Rothermel, Peter Frederick
Saint-Mémin, Charles Balthazar Julien Fevret de
Shahn, Benjamin ("Ben")
Sheeler, Charles R., Jr.
Smibert, John
Smith, Francis Hopkinson
Stein, Evaleen
Stillman, William James
Thorpe, Thomas Bangs
Thulstrup, Bror Thure
Tiffany, Louis Comfort
Tobey, Mark
Weber, Max
Weir, John Ferguson
White, Charles Wilbert
White, John
White, John Blake
Widforss, Gunnar Mauritz
Willet, William

ASSASSIN
Booth, John Wilkes
Oswald, Lee Harvey
Ruby, Jack L.

ASSASSIN (ACCUSED)
Shaw, Clay L.

ASSYRIOLOGIST (See also SCHOLAR)
Dougherty, Raymond Philip
Harper, Robert Francis
Haupt, Paul
Hilprecht, Herman Volrath

ASTRONAUT (See AERONAUT, AVIATOR, BALLOONIST)
Chaffee, Roger Bruce
Grissom, Virgil Ivan ("Gus")
White, Edward Higgins, II

ASTRONOMER
Abbe, Cleveland
Adams, Walter Sydney
Aitken, Robert Grant
Alexander, Stephen
Baade, Wilhelm Heinrich Walter
Bailey, Solon Irving
Barnard, Edward Emerson

Bond, George Phillips
Bond, William Cranch
Boss, Lewis
Bowditch, Nathaniel
Bowen, Ira Sprague
Brooks, William Robert
Burnham, Sherburne Wesley
Campbell, William Wallace
Cannon, Annie Jump
Chandler, Seth Carlo
Chauvenet, William
Clark, Alvan
Clark, Alvan Graham
Comstock, George Cary
Curtis, Heber Doust
Davidson, George
Doolittle, Charles Leander
Doolittle, Eric
Douglass, Andrew Ellicott
Draper, Henry
Eastman, John Robie
Elkin, William Lewis
Farrar, John
Fleming, Williamina Paton Stevens
Flint, Albert Stowell
Freeman, Thomas
Frost, Edwin Brant
Gilliss, James Melville
Gould, Benjamin Apthorp
Grew, Theophilus
Hale, George Ellery
Hall, Asaph
Harkness, William
Harrington, Mark Walrod
Holden, Edward Singleton
Hough, George Washington
Howe, Herbert Alonzo
Hubbard, Joseph Stillman
Hubble, Edwin
Hussey, William Joseph
Keeler, James Edward
King, Edward Skinner
Kirkwood, Daniel
Kuiper, Gerard Peter
Leavenworth, Francis Preserved
Leavitt, Henrietta Swan
Leeds, John
Loomis, Elias
Lord, Henry Curwen
Lowell, Percival
Lyman, Chester Smith
Metcalf, Joel Hastings
Mitchel, Ormsby MacKnight
Mitchell, Maria
Mitchell, William, 1791–1869
Moore, Joseph Haines
Moulton, Forest Ray
Newcomb, Simon
Nicholson, Seth Barnes
Parkhurst, John Adelbert
Paul, Henry Martyn
Payne-Gaposchkin, Cecilia Helena
Peirce, Benjamin
Perrine, Charles Dillon
Peters, Christian Henry Frederick
Pickering, Edward Charles
Porter, Jermain Gildersleeve
Pritchett, Henry Smith
Rees, John Krom
Rigge, William Francis
Ritchey, George Willis
Rittenhouse, David
Rogers, William Augustus
Russell, Henry Norris
Safford, Truman Henry
St. John, Charles Edward
Schaeberle, John Martin
Schlesinger, Frank
Searle, Arthur
Sestini, Benedict
Shapley, Harlow
Skinner, Aaron Nichols
Slipher, Vesto Melvin
Stockwell, John Nelson
Stone, Ormond
Struve, Otto
Swift, Lewis
Tuttle, Charles Wesley
Twining, Alexander Catlin
Upton, Winslow
Vaughan, Daniel
Walker, Sears Cook
Watson, James Craig
West, Benjamin
Whitney, Mary Watson
Winlock, Joseph
Winthrop, John
Young, Charles Augustus
Young, David

Astronomical Lensmaker
Brashear, John Alfred
Clark, Alvan
Clark, Alvan Graham

Astronomical Photographer (See also Astronomer, Photographer)
Draper, Henry

Astrophysicist (See also Astronomer, Physicist)
Mason, Max
Rutherfurd, Lewis Morris
Wildt, Rupert
Zwicky, Fritz

Athlete (See also Specific Sports)
Blaikie, William
Brown, Johnny Mack
Clothier, William Jackson
Hubbard, Robert C. ("Cal")
McGrath, Matthew J.
Metcalfe, Ralph Harold
Nevers, Ernest Alonzo ("Ernie")
O'Brien, Robert David ("Davey")
Owens, James Cleveland ("Jesse")
Pilkington, James
Prefontaine, Steve Roland ("Pre")
Thorpe, James Francis
Washington, Kenneth Stanley ("The General")
Zaharias, Mildred ("Babe") Didrikson

Athletic Coach
Lapchick, Joseph Bohomiel

Athletic Director
Allen, Forrest Clare ("Phog")
Butts, James Wallace ("Wally")

Athletic Trainer
Murphy, Michael Charles

Atom-Bomb Spy
Gold, Harry ("Raymond")

Attorney (See Lawyer)

Attorney General (Confederate)
Benjamin, Judah Philip
Davis, George
Watts, Thomas Hill

Attorney General (Federal)
Beck, James Montgomery
Biddle, Francis Beverley
Black, Jeremiah Sullivan
Bonaparte, Charles Joseph
Brewster, Benjamin Harris
Cummings, Homer Stillé
Daugherty, Harry Micajah
Devens, Charles
Garland, Augustus Hill
Gilpin, Henry Dilworth
Gregory, Thomas Watt
Harmon, Judson
Hoar, Ebenezer Rockwood
Kennedy, Robert Francis
Lee, Charles, 1758–1815
Legaré, Hugh Swinton
McGranery, James Patrick
McGrath, James Howard
Miller, William Henry Harrison
Moody, William Henry
Murphy, Frank
Olney, Richard
Palmer, Alexander Mitchell
Perlman, Philip Benjamin
Pierrepont, Edwards
Randolph, Edmund, 1753–1813
Speed, James
Stanbery, Henry
Stanton, Edwin McMasters
Stockton, John Potter
Taft, Alphonso
Taney, Roger Brooke
Thacher, Thomas Day
Toucey, Isaac
Wickersham, George Woodward
Williams, George Henry
Wirt, William

Attorney General (State)
Conner, James
Gilchrist, Robert
Johnston, Augustus
Martin, Luther
Pringle, John Julius
Robeson, George Maxwell
Trott, Nicholas
Updike, Daniel

Author (See also Biographer, Critic, Diarist, Dramatist, Essayist, Litterateur, Novelist, Poet, Writer)
Abbot, Willis John
Abbott, Austin
Abbott, Benjamin Vaughan
Abbott, Charles Conrad
Abbott, Edith
Abbott, Jacob
Abbott, Lyman
Acheson, Dean Gooderham
Acrelius, Israel
Adair, James
Adams, Andy
Adams, Frederick Upham

Adams, John Coleman
Adams, Samuel Hopkins
Ade, George
Adler, Polly
Aiken, Conrad Potter
Akeley, Mary Leonore
Akers, Elizabeth Chase
Alcott, Amos Bronson
Alcott, Louisa May
Alden, Henry Mills
Alden, Isabella Macdonald
Alden, Joseph
Alexander, Archibald
Alexander, Edward Porter
Alexander, Joseph Addison
Alger, William Rounseville
Alinsky, Saul David
Allen, Alexander Viets Griswold
Allen, Anthony Benezet
Allen, Ethan
Allen, George
Allen, Joel Asaph
Allen, Joseph Henry
Allen, William
Allen, Zachariah
Allston, Washington
Alsop, Charles
Alsop, Mary O'Hara
Altsheler, Joseph Alexander
Anderson Margaret Carolyn
Anderson, Sherwood
Anderson, Victor Vance
Andrews, Christopher Columbus
Andrews, Roy Chapman
Angle, Paul McClelland
Antin, Mary
Apes, William
Arthur, Timothy Shay
Artzybasheff, Boris
Ashhurst, John
Atkinson, George Wesley
Atwater, Caleb
Audsley, George Ashdown
Austin, Jane Goodwin
Austin, Mary
Austin, William
Azarias, Brother
Babbitt, Irving
Babcock, Maltbie Davenport
Babson, Roger Ward
Bacon, Alice Mabel
Bacon, Delia Salter
Bacon, Edwin Munroe
Badeau, Adam
Bagby, George William
Baird, Samuel John
Baker, Ray Stannard
Baker, William Mumford
Baldwin, Faith
Baldwin, Joseph
Baldwin, Joseph Glover
Baldwin, Loammi
Balestier, Charles Wolcott
Ballou, Hosea
Ballou, Maturin Murray
Bancroft, Aaron
Bancroft, Edward
Banvard, John
Banvard, Joseph
Barbour, Oliver Lorenzo
Bardeen, Charles William
Barnard, Charles
Barnes, Albert
Barr, Amelia Edith Huddleston
Barth, Alan
Bartholow, Roberts
Bartlett, Elisha
Bartlett, Joseph
Barton, Bruce Fairchild
Barton, Robert Thomas
Bates, Arlo
Bates, Katharine Lee
Baum, Lyman Frank
Bausman, Benjamin
Baylor, Frances Courtenay
Beard, Daniel Carter
Beard, James Carter
Beard, Mary Ritter
Beatty, John
Beers, Henry Augustin
Bell, Bernard Iddings
Bell, Charles Henry
Bell, Eric Temple
Bellamy, Edward
Bellamy, Elizabeth Whitfield Croom
Benét, William Rose
Benezet, Anthony
Benjamin, Asher
Benjamin, Park
Benjamin, Samuel Greene Wheeler
Bennett, Charles Edwin
Bentley, William
Benton, Thomas Hart
Berg, Gertrude Edelstein
Berger, Meyer
Berkman, Alexander
Berle, Adolf Augustus, Jr.
Biddle, Horace P.
Bidwell, Barnabas
Bierce, Ambrose Gwinett
Bigelow, John
Binkley, Wilfred Ellsworth
Binns, John
Bishop, John Peale
Bixby, James Thompson
Blackmur, Richard Palmer
Blake, John Lauris
Blake, Lillie Devereux
Blake, Mary Elizabeth McGrath
Blanshard, Paul
Bledsoe, Albert Taylor
Bleyer, Willard Grosvenor
Bloomgarden, Solomon
Bodenheim, Maxwell
Bok, Edward William
Bolton, Sarah Knowles
Bond, Elizabeth Powell
Bonsal, Stephen
Bontemps, Arna Wendell
Booth, Mary Louise
Botta, Anne Charlotte Lynch
Bottome, Margaret McDonald
Botts, John Minor
Boudin, Louis Boudinoff
Bouton, John Bell
Bouvet, Marie Marguerite
Bowen, Herbert Wolcott
Bowker, Richard Rogers
Boyesen, Hjalmar Hjorth
Boynton, Charles Brandon
Brace, John Pierce
Brachvogel, Udo
Brackenndge, Henry Marie
Brackenridge, Hugh Henry
Brackett, Charles William
Bradford, Alden
Brady, Cyrus Townsend
Bragdon, Claude Fayette
Brierton, John
Briggs, Charles Frederick
Brigham, Amariah
Brightly, Frederick Charles
Bristed, Charles Astor
Bristed, John
Brockett, Linus Pierpont
Bromfield, Louis
Brooks, Elbridge Streeter
Brooks, Noah
Broun, Heywood Campbell
Browder, Earl Russell
Brown, Addison
Brown, Benjamin Frederick
Brown, Margaret Wise
Brown, William Garrott
Brown, William Hill
Browne, John Ross
Browne, William Hand
Brownson, Orestes Augustus
Bruce, Andrew Alexander
Brühl, Gustav
Bryan, Mary Edwards
Bryce, Lloyd Stephens
Bryson, Lyman Lloyd
Buchanan, Joseph Rodes
Buchanan, Scott Milross
Buckminster, Joseph Stevens
Bulfinch, Thomas
Bunce, Oliver Bell
Bunner, Henry Cuyler
Buntline, Ned (See Judson, Edward Zane Carroll)
Burdick, Usher Lloyd
Burgess, John William
Burgess, Thornton Waldo
Burnap, George Washington
Burnett, Frances Eliza Hodgson
Burnham, Clara Louisa Root
Burrage, Walter Lincoln
Burrill, Alexander Mansfield
Burroughs, Edgar Rice
Burroughs, John
Burt, Mary Elizabeth
Burton, William Evans
Butler, William Allen
Butterworth, Hezekiah
Byrd, William
Cabell, Nathaniel Francis
Cable, George Washington
Caffin, Charles Henry
Cahill, Holger
Cain, James Mallahan
Cain, William
Caines, George
Calef, Robert
Calkins, Earnest Elmo
Calkins, Norman Allison
Callimachos, Panos Demetrios
Campbell, John Wood, Jr.
Cannon, Charles James
Capen, Nahum
Carleton, Henry
Carlson, Evans Fordyce
Carnegie, Dale
Carpenter, Edmund Janes

Carpenter, Frank George
Carpenter, George Rice
Carr, John Dickson
Carrington, Henry Beebee
Carroll, Howard
Carruth, Fred Hayden
Carryl, Guy Wetmore
Carter, Robert
Carter, William Hodding, Jr.
Caruthers, William Alexander
Cash, Wilbur Joseph
Castle, William Richards, Jr.
Cather, Willa
Catlin, George
Catton, Charles Bruce
Chadwick, John White
Chamberlain, Nathan Henry
Champlin, John Denison
Chandler, Elizabeth Margaret
Chandler, Raymond Thornton
Charlton, Thomas Usher Pulaski
Chase, Ilke
Chase, Mary Ellen
Cheney, Ednah Dow Littlehale
Cheney, John Vance
Chesebrough, Caroline
Chessman, Caryl Whittier
Chester, George Randolph
Child, Frank Samuel
Child, Lydia Maria Francis
Child, Richard Washburn
Chipman, Daniel
Chopin, Kate O'Flaherty
Church, Benjamin
Church, George Earl
Church, Irving Porter
Clapp, Margaret Antoinette
Clapp, William Warland
Clark, Charles Heber
Clarke, Helen Archibald
Clarke, Mary Bayard Devereux
Clemmer, Mary
Cleveland, Horace William Shaler
Clews, Henry
Clinch, Charles Powell
Clurman, Harold Edgar
Cobb, Irvin Shrewsbury
Cobb, Lyman
Coburn, Foster Dwight
Codman, John
Coffin, Charles Carleton
Coggeshall, George
Coggeshall, William Turner
Colburn, Warren
Colby, Frank Moore
Cole, Charles Woolsey
Collens, Thomas Wharton
Collier, Hiram Price
Colton, Calvin
Colton, Walter
Colvin, Stephen Sheldon
Conant, Charles Arthur
Conant, Hannah O'Brien Chaplin
Cone, Orello
Congdon, Charles Taber
Conkling, Alfred
Converse, James Booth
Conway, Moncure Daniel
Cook, Clarence Chatham
Cook, Martha Elizabeth Duncan Walker
Cooke, George Willis
Cooke, Josiah Parsons
Cooke, Philip St. George
Copway, George
Cornwallis, Kinahan
Corson, Hiram
Cortambert, Louis Richard
Cory, Charles Barney
Cotton, John
Cowley, Charles
Cox, Jacob Dolson
Cox, Palmer
Cox, Rowland
Cox, Samuel Sullivan
Coxe, Arthur Cleveland
Cozzens, Frederick Swartwout
Crafts, William
Crane, Anne Moncure
Crane, Stephen
Crane, Thomas Frederick
Crapsey, Algernon Sidney
Crocker, Hannah Mather
Croly, Herbert David
Crosby, Ernest Howard
Crothers, Samuel McChord
Crouse, Russel McKinley
Crowninshield, Frederic
Cullum, George Washington
Cuming, Fortescue
Cummins, Maria Susanna
Currier, Charles Warren
Curry, Jabez Lamar Monroe
Curtis, Charles Pelham
Curtis, George Ticknor
Curtis, George William
Curwen, Samuel
Cushing, Luther Stearns
Cutler, Lizzie Petit
Cuyler, Theodore Ledyard
Dabney, Robert Lewis
Dabney, Virginius
Dagg, John Leadley
Dahlgren, Sarah Madeleine Vinton
Daley, Arthur John
Dall, Caroline Wells Healey
Daly, Charles Patrick
Dana, John Cotton
Dana, Richard Henry
Daniels, Farrington
Darby, John
Darling, Flora Adams
Davenport, John
Davidson, James Wood
Davies, Joseph Edward
Davies, Maria Thompson
Davis, Adele
Davis, Andrew McFarland
Davis, Mary Evelyn Moore
Davis, Noah Knowles
Davis, Oscar King
Davis, Richard Harding
Davis, Varina Anne Jefferson
Davis, Varina Howell
Davis, William Thomas
Day, Clarence Shepard
Dean, Sidney
Dearborn, Henry Alexander Scammell
De Costa, Benjamin Franklin
Deems, Charles Force
Deering, Nathaniel
De Fontaine, Felix Gregory
De Forest, John William
De Kay, James Ellsworth
DeKruif, Paul Henry
Deland, Margaret
Delano, Amassa
De Leon, Thomas Cooper
Deléry, François Charles
Dellenbaugh, Frederick Samuel
Deming, Philander
De Peyster, John Watts
Detmold, Christian Edward
De Trobriand, Régis Denis de Keredern
Dewey, Orville
Diat, Louis Felix
Diaz, Abby Morton
Dibble, Roy Floyd
Didier, Eugene Lemoine
Dimitry, Charles Patton
Ditson, George Leighton
Dixon, Thomas
Dodd, Lee Wilson
Doddridge, Joseph
Dodge, Mary Abigail
Dodge, Mary Elizabeth Mapes
Dole, Nathan Haskell
Donnelly, Eleanor Cecilia
Dorchester, Daniel
Dorr, Julia Caroline Ripley
Dorsey, Anna Hanson McKenney
Dorsey, George Amos
Dorsey, Sarah Anne Ellis
Douglas, Amanda Minnie
Downey, June Etta
Downing, Charles
Drayton, John
Dromgoole, William Allen
Du Bois, Shirley Lola Graham
Duganne, Augustine Joseph Hickey
Dummer, Jeremiah
Dunlop, James
Du Ponceau, Pierre Étienne
Durfee, Job
Durivage, Francis Alexander
Dwight, Benjamin Woodbridge
Dwight, Theodore, 1764–1846
Dwight, Theodore, 1796–1866
Dwight, Timothy
Dyer, Louis
Earle, Alice Morse
Eckstorm, Fannie Hardy
Eddy, Daniel Clarke
Edes, Robert Thaxter
Edwards, Charles
Egan, Maurice Francis
Elder, Susan Blanchard
Elder, William
Eliot, Charles
Ellet, Elizabeth Fries Lummis
Elliott, Benjamin
Elliott, Sarah Barnwell
Elliott, Walter Hackett Robert
Ellis, Edward Sylvester
Ellis, George Washington
Elson, Louis Charles
Embree, Edwin Rogers
Embury, Emma Catherine

Emerson, Edward Waldo
Emerson, Ellen Russell
Erskine, John
Evans, Augusta Jane
Evans, Bergen Baldwin
Evans, Warren Felt
Everett, David
Ewbank, Thomas
Ewing, Hugh Boyle
Eytinge, Rose
Fairchild, David Grandison
Farago, Ladislas
Farley, Harriet
Farnham, Eliza Woodson Burhans
Farnham, Thomas Jefferson
Farrar, Timothy
Farwell Arthur
Faust, Frederick Shiller
Fawcett, Edgar
Fay, Edwin Whitefield
Fay, Theodore Sedgwick
Felton, Rebecca Latimer
Fernold, James Champlin
Fernow, Bernhard Eduard
Feuchtwanger, Lion
Field, Eugene
Field, Henry Martyn
Field, Mary Katherine Kemble
Field, Maunsell Bradhurst
Field, Richard Stockton
Field, Roswell Martin
Field, Thomas Warren
Fields, Annie Adams
Fields, James Thomas
Fieser, Louis Frederick
Fillebrown, Thomas
Finck, Henry Theophilus
Finley, John Huston
Finley, Martha Farquharson
Finn, Francis James
Fisher, Dorothea Frances Canfield
Fisher, Sidney George
Fiske, Amos Kidder
Fitzgerald, Oscar Penn
Flagg, Edmund
Flagg, James Montgomery
Flagg, Thomas Wilson
Flanders, Henry
Flandrau, Charles Eugene
Flint, Timothy
Florence, William Jermyn
Floy, James
Follen, Eliza Lee Cabot
Follett, Mary Parker
Folsom, George
Forbes, Edwin
Forbes, Robert Bennett
Force, Manning Ferguson
Forman, Justus Miles
Fortier, Alcée
Fosdick, Charles Austin
Fosdick, Harry Emerson
Fosdick, William Whiteman
Foster, David Skaats
Foster, Hannah Webster
Foster, Roger Sherman Baldwin
Foulke, William Dudley
Fowle, Daniel
Fowler, Gene
Francis, Samuel Ward
Frank, Jerome
Frank, Lawrence Kelso
Franklin, Benjamin
Freeman, James Edwards
Freeman, Mary Eleanor Wilkins
Frémont, Jessie Benton
French, Alice
French, Lucy Virginia Smith
Frothingham, Arthur Lincoln
Frothingham, Octavius Brooks
Frothingham, Paul Revere
Fry, James Barnet
Fulton, John Farquhar
Gage, Frances Dana Barker
Gage, Matilda Joslyn
Gaillardet, Théodore Frédéric
Gale, Zona
Gallico, Paul William
Garden, Alexander
Gardener, Helen Hamilton
Garis, Howard Roger
Garretson, James
Garrett, Edmund Henry
Gass, Patrick
Gay, Sydney Howard
Gernsback, Hugo
Ghent, William James
Gholson, William Yates
Gibbes, Robert Wilson
Gibbons, Euell
Gibbons, Herbert Adams
Gibbons, James Sloan
Gibbs, Arthur Hamilton
Gibbs, (Oliver) Wolcott
Giesler-Anneke, Mathilde Franziska
Gildersleeve, Basil Lanneau
Giles, Chauncey
Gillett, Ezra Hall
Gillman, Henry
Gilman, Arthur
Gilman, Caroline Howard
Gilman, Daniel Coit
Gilman, Samuel
Gilmer, Francis Walker
Gilmer, George Rockingham
Gilmore, James Roberts
Gilpin, Henry Dilworth
Gitlow, Benjamin
Glaspell, Susan Keating
Glass, Montague Marsden
Godwin, Parke
Goode, George Brown
Goodrich, Alfred John
Goodrich, Charles Augustus
Goodrich, Frank Boott
Goodrich, Samuel Griswold
Goodyear, William Henry
Gordon, George Angier
Gordon, George Henry
Gordon, William
Gould, Edward Sherman
Gould, George Milbry
Goulding, Francis Robert
Graham, David
Graham, John Andrew
Gray, John Chipman
Graydon, Alexander
Greely, Adolphus Washington
Green, Asa
Green, Frances Harriet Whipple
Green, Joseph
Green, Samuel Abbott
Greene, George Washington
Greenleaf, Moses
Greenleaf, Simon
Greenough, Henry
Gregg, Josiah
Grew, Joseph Clark
Grey, Zane
Grierson, Francis
Griffin, John Howard
Griffis, William Elliot
Grimké Archibald Henry
Griswold, Rufus Wilmot
Gross, Milt
Gross, Samuel David
Gruening, Ernest
Grund, Francis Joseph
Guild, Curtis, 1827–1911
Gulick, Luther Halsey, 1865–1918
Gunther, John
Gurowski, Adam
Habberton, John
Hackett, Frank Warren
Haines, Charles Glidden
Haldeman-Julius, Emanuel
Hale, Louise Closser
Hale, Lucretia Peabody
Hale, Sarah Josepha Buell
Hales, Edward Everett
Hall, Abraham Oakey
Hall, Arethusa
Hall, Baynard Rush
Hall, Florence Marion Howe
Hall, James, 1793–1868
Hall, James Norman
Halleck, Henry Wager
Hallock, Charles
Hamilton, Allan McLane
Hamilton, Edith
Hammett, Samuel Adams
Hammett, Samuel Dashiell
Hanaford, Phoebe Ann Coffin
Hanchett, Henry Granger
Hapgood, Hutchins
Hapgood, Isabel Florence
Harbaugh, Henry
Harland, Henry
Harper, Ida Husted
Harris, Benjamin
Harris, Joel Chandler
Harris, Joseph
Harrison, Constance Cary
Harrison, Gabriel
Hart, Charles Henry
Harte, Francis Brett
Hartmann, Carl Sadakichi
Hatcher, William Eldridge
Haupt, Herman
Haven, Emily Bradley Neal
Hawthorne, Julian
Hayes, John Lord
Hays, Arthur Garfield
Hazard, Thomas Robinson
Headley, Joel Tyler
Hearn, Lafcadio
Heath, James Ewell
Heilprin, Michael
Heinzen, Karl Peter
Helmuth, William Tod
Helper, Hinton Rowan
Hempel, Charles Julius

Henderson, Peter
Hendrick, Ellwood
Hennepin, Louis
Henningsen, Charles Frederick
Henry, Caleb Sprague
Hentz, Caroline Lee Whiting
Herbermann, Charles George
Herbert, Henry William
Herford, Oliver Brooke
Herrick, Sophia McIlvaine Bledsoe
Herron, George Davis
Higginson, Thomas Wentworth
Hildreth, Richard
Hilgard, Theodor Erasmus
Hill, Frederick Trevor
Hill, Grace Livingston
Hilliard, Henry Washington
Hillis, Newell Dwight
Hillquit, Morris
Hine, Charles De Lano
Hinsdale, Burke Aaron
Hinshaw, David Schull
Hirst, Barton Cooke
Hitchcock, Enos
Hitchcock, Ethan Allen, 1798–1870
Hitchcock, James Ripley Wellman
Hittell, John Shertzer
Hittell, Theodore Henry
Hodges, George
Hodgins, Eric Francis
Hofstadter, Richard
Hogue, Wilson Thomas
Hoisington, Henry Richard
Holcombe, William Henry
Holder, Joseph Bassett
Holland, Edwin Clifford
Holland, Josiah Gilbert
Holley, Alexander Lyman
Hollister, Gideon Hiram
Holmes, George Frederick
Holt, Henry
Hooker, Worthington
Hopkinson, Francis
Hosmer, Hezekiah Lord
Hosmer, James Kendall
Houdini, Harry
Hough, Emerson
House, Edward Howard
Howard, Blanche Willis
Howe, Edgar Watson
Howe, Julia Ward
Hoyt, Henry Martyn
Hubbard, Elbert
Hubbard, Wynant Davis
Hudson, Charles
Hudson, Thomson Jay
Hughes, Henry
Hughes, Rupert
Huneker, James Gibbons
Hunt, Isaac
Hunt, Theodore Whitefield
Hunter, William C.
Huntington, William Reed
Hunton, William Lee
Hurlbert, William Henry
Hurlbut, Jesse Lyman
Husmann, George
Hutchinson, Woods
Hutton, Laurence
Hyde, William De Witt
Ickes, Harold Le Clair
Ide, John Jay
Imlay, Gilbert
Ingersoll, Charles Jared
Ingersoll, Edward
Inglis, Alexander James
Ingraham, Edward Duffield
Ingraham, Joseph Holt
Ingraham, Prentiss
Inman, Henry
Irving, John Treat
Irving, Peter
Irving, Pierre Munro
Irving, Washington
Irwin, William Henry
Isham, Samuel
Jackson, Edward Payson
Jacobi, Mary Cerinna Putnam
James, Marquis
James, Thomas
James, Will Roderick
Jamison, Cecilia Viets Dakin Hamilton
Jamison, David Flavel
Janes, Lewis George
Janney, Russell Dixon
Janney, Samuel McPherson
Janvier, Catharine Ann
Janvier, Margaret Thomson
Janvier, Thomas Allibone
Jarves, James Jackson
Jay, John
Jay, William
Jefferson, Thomas
Jenkins, John Stilwell
Jenks, Tudor Storrs
Jewett, Sarah Orne
Johnson, Alexander Bryan
Johnson, Alvin Saunders
Johnson, Franklin
Johnson, Helen Louise Kendrick
Johnson, James Weldon
Johnson, Joseph
Johnson, Osa
Johnson, Richard W.
Johnson, Samuel
Johnson, Samuel William
Johnson, Viriginia Wales
Johnston, Richard Malcolm
Johnston, William Andrew
Joline, Adrian Hoffman
Jones, Alexander
Jones, Amanda Theodosia
Jones, George
Jones, Howard Mumford
Jones, John Beauchamp
Jones, William Alfred
Jordan, William George
Josephson, Matthew
Josselyn, John
Joutel, Henri
Joynes, Edward Southey
Judah, Samuel Benjamin Helbert
Judd, Sylvester
Judson, Edward Zane Carroll ("Ned Buntline")
Judson, Emily Chubbuck
Kaempffert, Waldemar Bernhard
Kaye, Frederick Benjamin
Keating, John McLeod
Keating, John Marie
Keener, William Albert
Keller, Helen Adams
Kelley, Edith Summers
Kelley, James Douglas Jerrold
Kellogg, Elijah
Kelly, Aloysius Oliver Joseph
Kelly, Myra
Kemble, Frances Anne
Kennan, George
Kennedy, John Pendleton
Kent, Charles Foster
Kidder, Frederic
Kimball, Richard Burleigh
King, Alexander
King, Clarence
King, Edward Smith
King, Grace Elizabeth
King, Thomas Starr
Kinsey, Alfred Charles
Kirk, John Foster
Kirkland, Caroline Matilda Stansbury
Kirkland, Joseph
Kirkman, Marshall Monroe
Kirkus, Virginia
Kirlin, Joseph Louis Jerome
Klingelsmith, Margaret Center
Knapp, Samuel Lorenzo
Knapp, William Ireland
Kneeland, Stillman Foster
Knight, Edward Henry
Knight, Henry Cogswell
Knox, George William
Knox, Thomas Wallace
Kobbé, Gustav
Koebler, Sylvester Rosa
Kohler, Max James
Krapp, George Philip
Krauth, Charles Porterfield
Krehbiel, Henry Edward
Kyne, Peter Bernard
La Borde, Maximilian
La Farge, John
La Farge, Oliver Hazard Perry
Lamb, Martha Joanna Reade Nash
Lambert, Louis Aloisius
Landon, Melville de Lancey
Landreth, David
Lane, Arthur Bliss
Langley, Samuel Pierpont
Lanman, Charles
Larcom, Lucy
Lardner, Ringgold Wilmer
Larned, Josephus Nelson
Larpenteur, Charles
Lathbury, Mary Artemisia
Lathrop, George Parsons
Latimer, Mary Elizabeth Wormeley
Lawson, James
Lawson, John
Lawson, Robert Ripley
Lawson, Thomas William
Lea, Homer
Leach, Daniel Dyer
Leavitt, Dudley
Lee, Eliza Buckminster
Lee, Hannah Farnham Sawyer
Lee, Henry, 1787–1837

Lee, James Melvin
Lee, James Wideman
Leeds, Daniel
Leeser, Isaac
Legler, Henry Eduard
Leigh, William Robinson
Leland, Charles Godfrey
Leonard, Sterling Andrus
Leonard, Zenas
Leopold, Nathan Freudenthal, Jr.
Leslie, Charles Robert
Leslie, Eliza
Lester, Charles Edwards
Levant, Oscar
Levy, Louis Edward
Lewis, Alfred Henry
Lewis, Estelle Anna Blanche Robinson
Lewis, Lawrence
Lewis, Orlando Faulkland
Liebling, Abbott Joseph
Liebman, Joshua Loth
Lincoln, John Larkin
Lincoln, Mary Johnson Bailey
Lindsey, William
Linn, William Alexander
Lippincott, Joseph Wharton
Lippincott, Sara Jane Clarke
Littell, William
Little, Arthur Dehon
Livermore, Abiel Abbot
Livermore, Mary Ashton Rice
Lloyd, Henry Demarest
Lockwood, Ralph Ingersoll
Lodge, Henry Cabot
Loeb, Sophie Irene Simon
Logan, Olive
Lomax, Louis Emanuel
London, Jack
Long, John Luther
Longfellow, William Pitt Preble
Longstreet, Augustus Baldwin
Lord, Eleazar
Loring, Frederick Wadsworth
Lossing, Benson John
Lounsbury, Thomas Raynesford
Love, Robertus Donnell
Loveman, Amy
Lowell, James Russell
Lowell, Percival
Lowell, Robert Traill Spence
Lucas, Daniel Bedinger
Ludlow, Fitz Hugh
Ludlow, Noah Miller
Luhan, Mabel Dodge
Lummis, Charles Ftetcher
Lunt, George
Lyman, Albert Josiah
Lyman, Theodore, 1792–1849
Lynch, James Daniel
Lynd, Robert Staughton
Lyon, Harris Merton
Lyttelton, William Henry
MacArthur, Robert Stuart
McBride, Mary Margaret
McCabe, William Gordon
McClure, Alexander Wilson
McClure, Samuel Sidney
McConnel, John Ludlum
McCrae, Thomas
McCullough, Ernest
MacDonald, Betty
McGarvey, John William
McGinley, Phyllis
McGovern, John
McKenney, Thomas Loraine
Mackenzie, Alexander Slidell
Mackenzie, Robert Shelton
Maclay, Edgar Stanton
McLeod, Alexander
McPherson, Edward
McQuillen, John Hugh
MacVicar, Malcolm
Macy, John Albert
Malcolm, James Peller
Malcom, Howard
Mann, Mary Tyler Peabody
Mann, Newton
Mann, William Julius
Mansfield, Edward Deering
Marble, Albert Prescott
Marden, Orison Swett
Margalis, Max Leopold
Marshall, Henry Rutgers
Martin, Anne Henrietta
Martin, François-Xavier
Martin, Frederick Townsend
Martin, John Hill
Martin, Thomas Commerford
Martin, William Alexander Parsons
Martyn, Sarah Towne Smith
Mason, Daniel Gregory
Mason, Francis Van Wyck
Mather, Cotton
Mather, Frank Jewett, Jr.
Mather, Fred
Mather, Increase
Mather, Richard
Mather, Samuel
Mathews, Albert
Mathews, Cornelius
Mathews, William
Matthews, Franklin
Matthews, Joseph Brown
Maxwell, Elsa
Maxwell, Samuel
Mayer, Brantz
Mayes, Edward
Mayhew, Experience
Mayo, Sarah Carter Edgarton
Mayo, William Starbuck
Mead, Edwin Doak
Mears, John William
Mease, James
Mechem, Floyd Russell
Meehan, Thomas
Meek, Alexander Beaufort
Meigs, Arthur Vincent
Meigs, Charles Delucena
Meigs, John Forsyth
Mell, Patrick Hues
Mellen, Grenville
Melville, Herman
Mercier, Charles Alfred
Merrill, Stephen Mason
Metcalf, Henry Harrison
Micheaux, Oscar
Mielziner, Moses
Miller, Emily Clark Huntington
Miller, Harriet Mann
Miller, James Russell
Miller, Samuel
Millet, Francis Davis
Mills, Enos Abijah
Minor, Raleigh Colston
Mitchell, Donald Grant
Mitchell, John, d. 1768
Mitchell, Margaret Munnerlyn
Mitchell, Nahum
Moffett, Cleveland Langston
Möllhausen, Heinrich Baldwin
Mombert, Jacob Isidor
Montefiore, Joshua
Moore, Annie Aubertine Woodward
Moore, Frank
Moore, Jacob Bailey
Moore, John Trotwood
Moran, Benjamin
Morford, Henry
Morgan, James Morris
Morley, Christopher Darlington
Morley, Margaret Warner
Morris, Edward Joy
Morris, William Hopkins
Morse, Sidney Edwards
Morse, Wayne Lyman
Morton, Charles Walter
Morton, Nathaniel
Mott, Frank Luther
Moulton, Richard Green
Mowatt, Anna Cora Ogden
Mowrer, Edgar Ansel
Mowry, William Augustus
Mulford, Clarence Edward
Mulford, Elisha
Mullins, Edgar Young
Mumford, James Gregory
Murat, Achille
Murdock, James
Murray, David
Murray, Judith Sargent Stevens
Nadal, Ehrman Syme
Nash, Henry Sylvester
Nash, Simeon
Nason, Elias
Nathan, George Jean
Neal, John
Neely, Thomas Benjamin
Nelson, Henry Loomis
Neuberger, Richard Lewis
Nevin, Alfred
Nevin, Edwin Henry
Newcomb, Harvey
Newman, Samuel Phillips
Newton, Joseph Fort
Nichols, Charles Lemuel
Nichols, Mary Sargeant Neal Gove
Nichols, Thomas Low
Nicholson, Meredith
Nin, Anaïs
Niza, Marcos de
Nock, Albert Jay
Nordhoff, Charles
Nordhoff, Charles Bernard
Norris, Marv Harriott
Northen, William Jonathan
Norton, Charles Eliot
Nott, Henry Junius
Nourse, Edwin Griswold
Oberholtzer, Sara Louisa Vickers
O'Brien, Fitz-James

O'Brien, Frederick
O'Callaghan, Jeremiah
O'Connor, William Douglas
Ogg, Frederic Austin
Okey, John Waterman
O'Malley, Frank Ward
O'Neall, John Belton
O'Neill, Rose Cecil
O'Reilly, Henry
Orton, Helen Fuller
Osborn, Henry Stafford
Osgood, Howard
O'Shea, Michael Vincent
Otis, Arthur Sinton
Ott, Isaac
Ottley, Roi
Owen, Robert Dale
Oxnam, Garfield Bromley
Paine, Ralph Delahaye
Paine, Thomas
Paley, John
Pallen, Condé Benoist
Palmer, Horatio Richmond
Palmer, Joel
Palmer, John McAuley
Palmer, John Williamson
Parish, Elijah
Parker, Jane Marsh
Parker, William Harwar
Parton, James
Parton, Sara Payson Willis
Partridge, William Ordway
Paschal, George Washington
Pastorius, Francis Daniel
Patterson, Robert Mayne
Pattie, James Ohio
Pattison, James William
Patton, William
Paulding, James Kirke
Peabody, Andrew Preston
Peabody, Elizabeth Palmer
Pearson, Edmund Lester
Peattie, Donald Culross
Peck, George Washington
Peck, John Mason
Pedder, James
Peloubet, Francis Nathan
Penfield, Edward
Penfield, Frederic Courtland
Penniman, James Hosmer
Pennington, James W. C.
Pentecost, George Frederick
Percy, George
Percy, William Alexander
Perelman, Sidney Joseph
Perkms, Frederic Beecher
Perkins, James Handasyd
Perry, Bliss
Perry, Edward Baxter
Perry, Thomas Sergeant
Peterkin, Julia Mood
Peters, Absalom
Peters, Madison Clinton
Peterson, Charles Jacobs
Peyton, John Lewis
Phelan, James, 1856–1891
Phelps, Almira Hart Lincoln
Phelps, Charles Edward
Phillips, Willard
Phillips, William Addison
Phisterer, Frederick
Pickard, Samuel Thomas
Picket, Albert
Pidgin, Charles Felton
Pierce, Gilbert Ashville
Pierson, Arthur Tappan
Pierson, Hamilton Wilcox
Pike, Albert
Pike, James Shepherd
Pise, Charles Constantine
Pollard, Edward Alfred
Pollard, Joseph Percival
Pollock, Channing
Pond, Enoch
Pond, Frederick Eugene
Pool, Maria Louise
Poore, Benjamin Perley
Porter, Robert Percival
Post, Louis Freeland
Poston, Charles Debrill
Potter, Elisha Reynolds
Powel, John Hare
Powell, Edward Payson
Prang, Mary Amelia Dana Hicks
Pratt, Sereno Stansbury
Preble, George Henry
Prentiss, George Lewis
Prescott, George Bartlett
Preston, Harriet Waters
Preston, Margaret Junkin
Preston, Thomas Scott
Price, William Thompson
Prime, Edward Dorr Griffin
Prime, Samuel Irenaeus
Prime, William Cowper
Proctor, William
Pugh, Ellis
Pulte, Joseph Hippolyt
Putnam, George Haven
Putnam, Nina Wilcox
Putnam, Ruth
Pyle, Howard
Quick, John Herbert
Quincy, Edmund
Quincy, Josiah Phillips
Rains, George Washington
Ramsey, James Gettys McGready
Randall, Henry Stephens
Randolph, Sarah Nicholas
Randolph, Thomas Jefferson
Ravenel, Harriott Horry Rutledge
Rawle, Francis, 1846–1930
Raymond, George Lansing
Read, Opie Pope
Redfield, Isaac Fletcher
Redman, Ben Ray
Reed, Earl Howell
Reed, Myrtle
Reed, Richard Clark
Reed, William Bradford
Reese, Heloise Bowles
Reid, Gilbert
Reiersen, Johan Reinert
Remington, Frederic
Rémy, Henri
Renwick, James, 1792–1863
Reuterdahl, Henry
Revere, Joseph Warren
Reynolds, Quentin James
Rhodes, Eugene Manlove
Rice, Alice Caldwell Hegan
Rice, Nathan Lewis
Richards, Laura Elizabeth Howe
Richards, Thomas Addison
Richardson, Charles Francis
Richardson, Robert
Richmond, Mary Ellen
Rickert, Martha Edith
Riddle, Albert Gallatin
Rideing, William Henry
Rideout, Henry Milner
Riis, Jacob August
Riley, Benjamin Franklin
Rivers, William James
Roberts, Elizabeth Madox
Roberts, Kenneth Lewis
Robertson, George
Robertson, John
Robertson, Morgan Andrew
Robinson, Charles Mulford
Robinson, Conway
Robinson, Henry Morton
Robinson, Rowland Evans
Robinson, Solon
Robinson, Stillman Williams
Robinson, Therese Albertine Louise Von Jakob
Robinson, William Callyhan
Rodenbough, Theophilus Francis
Roe, Edward Payson
Roe, Gilbert Ernstein
Rogers, Clara Kathleen Barnett
Rollins, Alice Marland Wellington
Rölvaag, Ole Edvart
Romans, Bernard
Rombro, Jacob
Roosevelt, Robert Barnwell
Root, Frank Albert
Rorty, James Hancock
Rose, John Carter
Rosenberg, Abraham Hayyim
Rosenthal, Herman
Ross, Alexander
Rowland, Henry Cottrell
Rowlandson, Mary White
Royall, Anne Newport
Ruffner, Henry
Rugg, Harold Ordway
Ruhl, Arthur Brown
Rukeyser, Muriel
Russell, Charles Edward
Russell, Osborne
Ryan, Cornelius John ("Connie")
Rynning, Ole
Sachs, Hanns
Sachse, Julius Friedrich
Sadlier, Mary Anne Madden
Sadtler, Samuel Philip
Sage, Bernard Janin
Salter, William
Salter, William Mackintire
Sanborn, Franklin Benjamin
Sanborn, Katherine Abbott
Sanders, Elizabeth Elkins
Sanders, Frank Knight
Sanderson, John
Sands, Robert Charles
Sangster, Margaret Elizabeth Munson
Sarg, Tony
Sargent, Epes
Sargent, John Osborne

Sargent, Lucius Manlius
Sargent, Winthrop, 1825–1870
Saunders, Frederick
Saunders, Prince
Savage, Minot Judson
Sawyer, Lemuel
Schechter, Solomon
Schofield, William Henry
Schroeder, John Frederick
Schultze, Augustus
Schuyler, George Washington
Schuyler, Montgomery
Scidmore, Eliza Ruhamah
Scott, Leroy
Scott, Samuel Parsons
Scott, William Anderson
Scruggs, William Lindsay
Scudder, Horace Elisha
Sears, Edmund Hamilton
Seawell, Molly Elliot
Sedgwick, Catharine Maria
Sedgwick, Theodore, 1780–1839
Sedgwick, Theodore, 1811–1859
Seiss, Joseph Augustus
Selikovitsch, Goetzel
Semmes, Raphael
Seton, Grace Gallatin Thompson
Seton, William
Severance, Frank Hayward
Sewall, Jonathan
Seward, Theodore Frelinghuysen
Shaler, William
Sharp, Dallas Lore
Shecut, John Linnaeus Edward Whitridge
Shedd, William Greenough Thayer
Sheen, Fulton John
Sheldon, Charles Monroe
Shelton, Frederick William
Sherwood, Katharine Margaret Brownlee
Sherwood, Mary Elizabeth Wilson
Shields, Charles Woodruff
Shields, George Oliver
Showerman, Grant
Shreve, Thomas Hopkins
Shub, Abraham David
Shuey, Edwin Longstreet
Shuster, George Nauman
Sigourney, Lydia Howard Huntley
Sikes, William Wirt
Simpson, James Hervey
Simpson, Stephen
Singleton, Esther
Siringo, Charles A.
Skinner, Cornelia Otis
Skinner, John Stuart
Skinner, Thomas Harvey
Slafter, Edmund Farwell
Sloan, Harold Paul
Sloan, Richard Elihu
Slocum, Joshua
Slosson, Edwin Emery
Smedley, Agnes
Smith, Alexander
Smith, Arthur Henderson
Smith, Charles Alphonso
Smith, Edmund Munroe
Smith, Elias
Smith, Elihu Hubbard
Smith, Elizabeth Oakes Prince
Smith, Francis Hopkinson
Smith, Hannah Whitall
Smith, Harry Allen
Smith, Henry Justin
Smith, James McCune
Smith, James, 1737–1814
Smith, John, 1579–1631
Smith, John Augustine
Smith, John Cotton, 1826–1882
Smith, Margaret Bayard
Smith, Richard Penn
Smith, Samuel Harrison
Smith, William Andrew
Smith, William Russell
Smythe, Albert Henry
Smythe, Thomas
Snead, Thomas Lowndes
Snider, Denton Jaques
Snyder, John Francis
Sobolewski, J. Friedrich Eduard
Sokolsky, George Ephraim
Solger, Reinhold
Sounichsen, Albert
Spalding, Thomas
Spangler, Henry Wilson
Spencer, Cornelia Phillips
Spencer, Jesse Ames
Spivak, Charles David
Spofford, Harriet Elizabeth Prescott
Sprague, Achsa W.
Sprague, Oliver Mitchell Wentworth
Sprunt, James
Starr, Eliza Allen
Stauffer, David McNeely
Steele, Daniel
Steffens, Lincoln
Stein, Evaleen
Stein, Gertrude
Stein, Leo Daniel
Stephens, Ann Sophia
Stephens, Charles Asbury
Stephens, John Lloyd
Sterling, James
Stevens, George Washington
Stevens, John Austin, 1827–1910
Stimson, Alexander Lovett
Stimson, Frederic Jesup
Stitt, Edward Rhodes
Stoddard, Charles Warren
Stoddard, John Lawson
Stoddard, William Osborn
Stoever, Martin Luther
Stong, Phil(lip Duffield)
Storey, Moorfield
Story, Isaac
Stout, Rex Todhunter
Stowe, Harriet Elizabeth Beecher
Straus, Oscar Solomon
Stromme, Peer Olsen
Strong, Josiah
Strother, David Hunter
Stuart, Charles Beebe
Stuart, Ruth McEnery
Sturgis, Russell
Sullivan, James William
Sullivan, William
Sunderland, Eliza Jane Read
Susann, Jacqueline
Svenson, Andrew Edward
Swensson, Carl Aaron
Swift, Lucius Burrie
Swinton, William
Tappan, Eli Todd
Tarbox, Increase Niles
Taylor, Bert Leston
Taylor, George Boardman
Taylor, James Wickes
Taylor, Joseph Deems
Temple, Oliver Perry
Tennent, John
Tenney, Edward Payson
Terhune, Albert Payson
Terhune, Mary Virginia Hawes
Thacher, John Boyd
Thacher, Samuel Cooper
Thatcher, Benjamin Bussey
Thayer, Thomas Baldwin
Thayer, William Makepeace
Thomas, John Jacobs
Thomas, Richard Henry
Thomes, William Henry
Thompson, Benjamin
Thompson, Daniel Pierce
Thompson, Edward William
Thompson, James Maurice
Thompson, Joseph Parrish
Thompson, Richard Wigginton
Thompson, Slason
Thorburn, Grant
Thorpe, Rose Alnora Hartwick
Thorpe, Thomas Bangs
Thrasher, John Sidney
Thurber, George
Ticknor, George
Tiernan, Frances Christine Fisher
Todd, John
Todd, Mabel Loomis
Todd, Sereno Edwards
Tolman, Herbert Cushing
Tomlinson, Everett Titsworth
Toner, Joseph Meredith
Topliff, Samuel
Torrey, Bradford
Tourgée, Albion Winegar
Towle, George Makepeace
Towne, Charles Hanson
Townsend, George Alfred
Townsend, Luther Tracy
Townsend, Mary Ashley
Townsend, Virginia Frances
Tracy, Joseph
Train, Arthur Cheney
Train, George Francis
Traubel, Horace L.
Trilling, Lionel
Trowbridge, John Townsend
Truman, Benjamin Cummings
Trumbull, Henry Clay
Tucker, George
Tucker, Gilbert Milligan
Tucker, Nathaniel Beverley, 1784–1851
Tuckerman, Bayard

Tudor, William
Turner, George Kibbe
Turner, Henry McNeal
Turner, William
Tyler, Samuel
Underwood, Francis Henry
Upham, Thomas Cogswell
Upton, Emory
Upton, George Putnam
Utley, Freda
Van Brunt, Henry
Vance, Louis Joseph
Vanderbilt, Amy
Van Der Kemp, Francis Adrian
Van Dyke, Henry
Van Rensselaer, Mariana Griswold
Van Schaack, Henry Cruger
Venable, William Henry
Verplanck, Gulian Crommelin
Verrill, Alpheus Hyatt
Very, Lydia Louisa Ann
Victor, Frances Fuller
Victor, Orville James
Villard, Oswald Garrison
Vincent, Frank
Vorse, Mary Heaton
Waddell, Alfred Moore
Waggaman, Mary Teresa McKee
Wakeley, Joseph Burton
Walden, Jacob Treadwell
Waldo, Samuel Putnam
Walker, Alexander
Wallace, John William
Wallace, Lewis
Wallis, Severn Teackle
Waln, Robert, 1794–1825
Walsh, Edmund Aloysius
Walsh, Henry Collins
Walworth, Jeannette Ritchie Hadermann
Warburg, James Paul
Ward, Cyrenus Osborne
Ward, Elizabeth Stuart Phelps
Ward, Harry Frederick
Ward, Herbert Dickinson
Ward, James Harmon
Ward, James Warner
Ward, Lydia Arms Avery Coonley
Ward, Nathaniel
Ward, Samuel, 1814–1884
Warden, David Bailie
Warden, Robert Bruce
Ware, Nathaniel A.
Ware, William
Waring, George Edwin
Warman, Cy
Warren, Israel Perkins
Washburn, Charles Grenfill
Washburn, Emory
Watson, Thomas Edward
Watts, Franklin Mowry
Webb, Charles Henry
Webber, Charles Wilkins
Webster, Alice Jane Chandler
Weems, Mason Locke
Wehle, Louis Brandeis
Weiss, John
Welby, Amelia Ball Coppuck
Wells, William Vincent
Wendte, Charles William
Wertenbaker, Charles Christian
West, Samuel
Westcott, Edward Noyes
Wharton, Anne Hollingsworth
Wharton, Francis
Wharton, Thomas Isaac
Wheeler, Andrew Carpenter
Wheeler, (George) Post
Wilhelmina
Whipple, Edwin Percy
Whipple, Squire
Whitcher, Frances Miram Berry
Whitcomb, Selden Lincoln
White, Emerson Elbridge
White, George
White, Stewart Edward
White, William Allen
Whitlock, Brand
Whitney, Adeline Dutton Train
Whitney, Caspar
Whiton, James Morris
Whittelsey, Abigail Goodrich
Whittemore, Thomas
Wiggin, Kate Douglas
Wigglesworth, Michael
Wikoff, Henry
Wilder, Laura Ingalls
Willard, Sidney
William, John
Williams, Charles Richard
Williams, Edwin
Williams, Frederick Wells
Williams, George Washington
Williams, Jesse Lynch
Williams, John
Williams, William R.
Wilson, George Grafton
Wilson, James Grant
Wilson, James Harrison
Wilson, James Southall
Wilson, John
Wilson, John Fleming
Wilson, Samuel Graham
Winchell, Alexander
Winkler, Edwin Theodore
Winslow, Edward
Winslow, Hubbard
Winthrop, Theodore
Wise, Daniel
Wise, Henry Augustus
Wister, Owen
Woerner, John Gabriel
Wolfe, Bertram David
Wood, Charles Erskine Scott
Wood, William
Woodbridge, John
Woodbury, Helen Laura Sumner
Woollcott, Alexander Humphreys
Woolley, Celia Parker
Woolsey, Sarah Chauncy
Woolson, Abba Louisa Goold
Woolson, Constance Fenimore
Workman, Fanny Bullock
Wormeley, Katherine Prescott
Wright, Marcus Joseph
Wright, Richard Nathaniel
Wright, Willard Huntington
Wright, William
Wyckoff, Walter Augustus
Wylie, Philip Gordon
Youmans, Edward Livingston
Young, Art
Young, Jesse Bowman
Zachos, John Celiverzos
Ziff, William Bernard
Zinsser, Hans

AUTHOR'S AGENT
Marbury, Elisabeth

AUTOMOBILE EXECUTIVE (See also MANUFACTURER, AUTOMOBILE)
Abernethy, Roy
Dykstra, John
Frazer, Joseph Washington
Hoffman, Paul Gray
Keller, Kaufman Thuma
McDonnell, James Smith, Jr.

AUTOMOBILE RACER
Oldfield, Berna Eli ("Barney")
Shaw, (Warren) Wilbur

AUTOMOTIVE DESIGNER
Wills, Childe Harold

AVIATION EXECUTIVE
Arnold, Leslie Philip
Boeing, William Edward
Chennault, Claire Lee
Damon, Ralph Shepard
Frye, William John ("Jack")
Gray, Harold Edwin
Hunter, Croil
Kellett, William Wallace
Keys, Clement Melville
Patterson, William Allan ("Pat")
Rickenbacker, Edward Vernon ("Eddie")
Schroeder, Rudolph William
Stearman, Lloyd Carlton
Woolman, Collett Everman
Young, Clarence Marshall

AVIATOR
Acosta, Bertram Blanchard ("Bert")
Arnold, Henry Harley ("Hap")
Arnold, Leslie Philip
Balchen, Bernt
Bennett, Floyd
Brereton, Lewis Hyde
Byrd, Richard Evelyn
Castle, Vernon Blythe
Chapman, Victor Emmanuel
Chennault, Claire Lee
Cochran, Jacqueline
Conrad, Maximilian Arthur, Jr.
Curtiss, Glenn Hammond
De Seversky, Alexander Procofieff
Earhart, Amelia Mary
Elder, Ruth
Foulois, Benjamin Delahauf
Geiger, Roy Stanley
Glidden, Charles Jasper
Gorrell, Edgar Staley
Hitchcock, Thomas
Hughes, Howard Robard, Jr.
Lindbergh, Charles Augustus, Jr.
Lufbery, Raoul Gervais Victor
Martin, Glenn Luther ("Cy")
Mitchell, William
Mitscher, Marc Andrew
Nichols, Ruth Rowland
Pangborn, Clyde Edward

Patrick, Mason Mathews
Post, Augustus
Post, Wiley
Powers, Francis Gary
Rickenbacker, Edward Vernon ("Eddie")
Rockwell, Kiffin Yates
Rodgers, John, 1881–1926
Royce, Ralph
Schroeder, Rudolph William
Spaatz, Carl Andrew ("Tooey")
Stearman, Lloyd Carlton
Wright, Orville
Wright, Wilbur

BACTERIOLOGIST (See also PHYSICIAN, SCIENTIST)
Avery, Oswald Theodore
Carroll, James
DeKruif, Paul Henry
Ernst, Harold Clarence
Gay, Frederick Parker
Henrici, Arthur Trautwein
Jordan, Edwin Oakes
Libman, Emanuel
Moore, Veranus Alva
Noguchi, Hideyo
Park, William Hallock
Plotz, Harry
Prescott, Samuel Cate
Prudden, Theophil Mitchell
Ravenel, Mazyck Porcher
Rosebury, Theodor
Schneider, Albert
Simmons, James Stevens
Smith, Erwin Frink
Sternberg, George Miller
Winslow, Charles-Edward Amory
Zinsser, Hans

BAKER
Ludwick, Christopher

BALLADIST (See also COMPOSER, LYRICIST, MUSICIAN, SONGWRITER)
Haswell, Anthony
Hays, William Shakespeare
Plummer, Jonathan
Prime, Benjamin Youngs

BALLET DANCER
Eglevsky, André Yevgenyevich

BALLET IMPRESARIO
De Cuevas, Marquis

BALLOONIST (See also AERONAUT, AVIATOR)
Wise, John

BANDIT (See also BRIGAND, BUCCANEER, BURGLAR, DESPERADO, OUTLAW, PIRATE)
Dillinger, John
Plummer, Henry

BANDLEADER (See also CONDUCTOR, MUSICIAN)
Davis, Meyer
Dorsey, Thomas Francis ("Tommy")
Ellington, Edward Kennedy ("Duke")
Elman, Harry ("Ziggy")
Fielding, Jerry
Gilmore, Patrick Sarsfield
Goldman, Edwin Franko
Gray, Glen
Handy, William Christopher
Henderson, Fletcher Hamilton
Jones, Lindley Armstrong ("Spike")
Kenton, Stanley Newcomb
Krupa, Eugene Bertram ("Gene")
Lombardo, Gaetano Albert ("Guy")
Lopez, Vincent Joseph
Lunceford, James Melvin ("Jimmie")
Miller, Glenn
Monroe, Vaughn Wilton
Nelson, Oswald George ("Ozzie")
Page, Oran Thaddeus ("Lips")
Pryor, Arthur W.
Sissle, Noble Lee
Sousa, John Philip
Teagarden, Weldon Leo ("Jack")
Venuti, Giuseppe ("Joe")
Weems, Ted
Whiteman, Paul Samuel ("Pops")
Wills, James Robert ("Bob")

BANKER (See also CAPITALIST, FINANCIER)
Adams, Edward Dean
Appleton, Nathan
Armstrong, Samuel Turell
Bacon, Robert
Baker, George Fisher
Beatty, John
Belmont, August
Binga, Jesse
Bingham, William
Bishop, Charles Reed
Black, Eugene Robert
Bliss, George
Bradford, Gamaliel
Brinkerhoff, Roeliff
Brown, Alexander
Brown, Fayette
Brown, James
Brown, John A.
Bush, Prescott Sheldon
Cannon, James Graham
Catchings, Waddill
Cattell, Alexander Gilmore
Chaffee, Jerome Bonaparte
Chetlain, Augustus Louis
Clark, Horace Francis
Coe, George Simmons
Cooke, Henry David
Cooke, Jay
Corbett, Henry Winslow
Corcoran, William Wilson
Creighton, Edward
Crowley, Leo Thomas
Cummings, Walter Joseph
Cutler, James Goold
Cutler, Robert
Dale, Chester
Davis, Norman Hezekiah
Davison, George Willets
Davison, Henry Pomeroy
Dawes, Charles Gates
De Coppet, Edward J.
Dodge, Joseph Morrell
Drexel, Anthony Joseph
Drexel, Francis Martin
Drexel, Joseph William
Eccles, Marriner Stoddard
Eells, Dan Parmelee
Ellis, John Washington
Elmore, Franklin Harper
Erpf, Armand Grover
Fahnestock, Harris Charles
Fenton, Reuben Eaton
Few, William
Fish, Stuyvesant
Flannery, John
Fletcher, Calvin
Forbes, William Cameron
Forgan, James Berwick
Forrestal, James Vincent
Fraley, Frederick
Fraser, Leon
Gage, Lyman Judson
Garrett, John Work
Gaston, Herbert Earle
Gates, Thomas Sovereign
Giannini, Amadeo Peter
Goldschmidt, Jakob
Grant, James Benton
Greene, Jerome Davis
Hall, James 1793–1868
Hammond, Bray
Hammond, Samuel
Harding, William Procter Gould
Hascall, Milo Smith
Heard, Dwight Bancroft
Hendrix, Joseph Clifford
Henrotin, Charles
Hepburn, Alonzo Barton
Herrick, Myron Timothy
Higginson, Henry Lee
Hunnewell, Horatio Hollis
Hutchinson, Charles Lawrence
Jeffrey, Joseph Andrew
Johnson, Alexander Bryan
Jones, Jesse Holman
Kahn, Otto Herman
Kelly, Eugene
King, Richard, Jr.
Ladd, William Sargent
Laimbeer, Nathalie Schenck
Lamar, Gazaway Bugg
Lamont, Thomas William
Lee, Thomas
Leffingwell, Russell Cornell
Lehman, Arthur
Lehman, Herbert Henry
Lehman, Robert
Levy, Gustave Lehmann
Lewis, William David
Littlefield, George Washington
Livingstone, William
Loeb, James
Long, Edward Vaughn
Low, Frederick Ferdinand
Lowell, Ralph
Lucas, James H.
Ludlow, Daniel
McFadden, Louis Thomas
McGarrah, Gates White
Marcus, Bernard Kent
Mather, Samuel Holmes
McKinney, Frank Edward, Sr.
Merriam, William Rush
Merrill, Charles Edward
Meyer, Eugene Isaac
Mills, Darius Ogden

Mitchell, Alexander
Morgan, James Dada
Morgan, John Pierpont
Morgan, Junius Spencer
Morrow, Dwight Whitney
Newberry, Walter Loomis
Peabody, George Foster
Perkins, George Clement
Perkins, George Walbridge
Perkins, James Handasyd
Powers, Daniel William
Price, Hiram
Prince, Frederick Henry
Ralston, William Chapman
Reynolds, George McClelland
Riggs, George Washington
Robb, James
Rollins, Frank West
Rosenberg, Henry
Sabin, Charles Hamilton
Salomon, Haym
Sayre, Stephen
Schneider, George
Seligman, Arthur
Seligman, Isaac Newton
Seligman, Jesse
Seney, George Ingraham
Shaw, Leslie Mortier
Smith, George
Smith, Samuel Harrison
Spaulding, Charles Clinton
Spaulding, Elbridge Gerry
Sprague, Charles
Sprague, Charles Ezra
Spreckels, Rudolph
Sproul, Allan
Stanley, Harold
Stevens, John Austin, 1795–1874
Stewart, John Aikman
Stillman, James
Stokes, Anson Phelps
Stotesbury, Edward Townsend
Straus, Simon William
Strong, Benjamin
Taggart, Thomas
Tappen, Frederick Dobbs
Taylor, Moses
Thatcher, Mahlon Daniel
Thomas, George Clifford
Thompson, David P.
Thompson, John
Thompson, Josiah Van Kirk
Tome, Jacob
Traylor, Melvin Alvah
Vanderlip, Frank Arthur
Waldo, David
Warburg, Paul Moritz
Ward, Samuel, 1786–1839
Welch, Leo Dewey
Westcott, Edward Noyes
White, Stephen Van Culen
Whitney, George
Whitney, Richard
Wiggin, Albert Henry
Williams, Samuel May
Willing, Thomas
Woodward, William
Wright, Richard Robert
Yeatman, James Erwin
BANK ROBBER
Sutton, William Francis, Jr. ("Willie")
BARITONE (see SINGER)
BASEBALL CLUB OWNER
Comiskey, Grace Elizabeth Reidy
Crosley, Powel, Jr.
O'Malley, Walter Francis
Yawkey, Thomas Austin ("Tom")
BASEBALL COMMISSIONER
Landis, Kenesaw Mountain
BASEBALL EXECUTIVE
Barrow, Edward Grant
Frick, Ford Christopher
Giles, Warren Crandall
Griffith, Clark Calvin
Harridge, William ("Will")
Johnson, Byron Bancroft
McKinney, Frank Edward, Sr.
MacPhail, Leland Stanford ("Larry")
Rickey, Wesley Branch
Weiss, George Martin
Wrigley, Philip Knight
BASEBALL MANAGER
Collins, Edward Trowbridge
Dressen, Charles Walter
Griffith, Clark Calvin
Harris, Stanley Raymond ("Bucky")
McCarthy, Joseph Vincent ("Joe")
McGraw, John Joseph
Mack, Connie
McKechnie, William Boyd
Murtaugh, Daniel Edward ("Danny")
Rolfe, Robert Abial ("Red")
Stengel, Charles Dillon ("Casey")
BASEBALL ORIGINATOR
Doubleday, Abner
BASEBALL PLAYER
Alexander, Grover Cleveland
Anson, Adrian Constantine
Baker, John Franklin
Bender, Charles Albert ("Chief")
Berg, Morris ("Moe")
Bridges, Thomas Jefferson Davis ("Tommy")
Carey, Max George ("Scoops")
Cicotte, Edward Victor
Clarkson, John Gibson
Clemente, Roberto
Cobb, Tyrus Raymond ("Ty")
Cochrane, Gordon Stanley ("Mickey")
Collins, Edward Trowbridge
Combs, Earle Bryan
Crawford, Samuel Earl
Dean, Jay Hannah ("Dizzy")
Dressen, Charles Walter ("Chuck")
Duffy, Hugh
Easter, Luscious Luke
Fox, Jacob Nelson ("Nellie")
Foxx, James Emory
Frisch, Frank Francis
Gehrig, Henry Louis ("Lou")
Gibson, Joshua
Gilliam, James William ("Junior")
Goslin, Leon Allen ("Goose")
Griffith, Clark Calvin
Grove, Robert Moses ("Lefty")
Harris, Stanley Raymond ("Bucky")
Hartnett, Charles Leo ("Gabby")
Heilmann, Harry
Hodges, Gilbert Ray
Hooper, Harry Bartholomew
Hornsby, Rogers
Howard, Elston Gene ("Ellie")
Huggins, Milrer James
Johnson, Walter Perry
Kelly, Michael J.
Klein, Charles Herbert ("Chuck")
Lajoie, Napoleon ("Larry")
McGraw, John Joseph
Maranville, Walter James Vincent ("Rabbit")
Marquard, Richard William ("Rube")
Martin, Johnny Leonard Roosevelt ("Pepper")
Mathewson, Christopher ("Christy")
Medwick, Joseph ("Ducky") Michael
Meusel, Robert William
Munson, Thurman Lee
Murtaugh, Daniel Edward ("Danny")
O'Doul, Francis Joseph ("Lefty")
Ott, Melvin Thomas ("Mel")
Page, Joseph Francis ("Joe")
Reach, Alfred James
Rice, Edgar Charles ("Sam")
Robinson, John Roosevelt ("Jackie")
Rolfe, Robert Abial ("Red")
Rommel, Edwin Americus ("Eddie")
Rowe, Lynwood Thomas
Rucker, George ("Nap")
Ruth, George Herman ("Babe")
Schalk, Raymond William ("Cracker")
Simmons (Szymanski), Aloysius Harry
Sisler, George Harold ("Gorgeous George")
Speaker, Tris E.
Strong, Elmer Kenneth, Jr. ("Ken")
Traynor, Harold Joseph ("Pie")
Vance, Arthur Charles ("Dazzy")
Wagner, John Peter
Walsh, Edward Augustine
Waner, Paul Glee
Wheat, Zachariah Davis ("Buck")
Wright, George
Wright, Henry
Young, Denton True ("Cy")
Zimmerman, Henry ("Heinie")
BASEBALL UMPIRE
Ashford, Emmett Littleton
Connolly, Thomas H.
Klem, William J. (Bill)

BASKETBALL COACH
Allen, Forrest Clare ("Phog")
Rupp, Adolph Frederick
BASKETBALL ORIGINATOR
Naismith, James
BASKETBALL PLAYER
Lapchick, Joseph Bohomiel
Stokes, Maurice
BATHING SUIT DESIGNER
Reid, Rose Marie
BEAUTY EXPERT
Arden, Elizabeth
Rubinstein, Helena
BELL FOUNDER (see IRON FOUNDER)
BIBLICAL ARCHAEOLOGIST
Albright, William Foxwell
BIBLICAL SCHOLAR
Barton, George Aaron
Lake, Kirsopp
Moffatt, James
Montgomery, James Alan
Speiser, Ephraim Avigdor
Willett, Herbert Lockwood
BIBLIOGRAPHER (See also SCHOLAR)
Bartlett, John Russell
Bolton, Henry Carrington
Bowker, Richard Rogers
Cole, George Watson
Eames, Wilberforce
Evans, Charles
Field, Herbert Haviland
Finotti, Joseph Maria
Fletcher, Robert
Ford, Worthington Chauncey
Garrison, Fielding Hudson
Greene, Belle Da Costa
Griffin, Appleton Prentiss Clark
Griswold, William McCrillis
Harrisse, Henry
Jackson, William Alexander
Jewett, Charles Coffin
Leypoldt, Frederick
McMurtrie, Douglas Crawford
Moore, George Henry
Nelson, Charles Alexander
Rand, Benjamin
Rhees, William Jones
Rich, Obadiah
Sabin, Joseph
Sargent, George Henry
Trumbull, James Hammond
Vail, Robert William Glenroie
Weeks, Stephen Beauregard
Wilson, Halsey William
Winship, George Parker
BIBLIOPHILE (See also BOOK COLLECTOR, COLLECTOR)
Adler, Elmer
Alden, Ebenezer
Andrews, William Loring
Ayer, Edward Everett
Barton, Thomas Pennant
Dowse, Thomas
Fisher, George Jackson
Ford, Gordon Lester
Fulton, John Farquhar
Gowans, William
Harris, Caleb Fiske
Hoe, Robert, 1839–1909
Hutton, Laurence
Jones, Herschel Vespasian
Mackenzie, William
Nichols, Charles Lemuel
Penniman, James Hosmer
Pennypacker, Samuel Whitaker
Polock, Moses
Prince, Thomas
Sabin, Joseph
Thacher, John Boyd
Wood, Casey Albert
Young, George
BILLIARD PLAYER
Hoppe, William Frederick ("Willie")
BIOCHEMIST (See also CHEMIST, PHYSICIAN, SCIENTIST)
Bergmann, Max
Chittenden, Russell Henry
Cohn, Edwin Joseph
Cori, Gerty Theresa Radnitz
Dakin, Henry Drysdale
Du Vigneaud, Vincent
Elvehjem, Conrad Arnold
Funk, Casimir
Haagen-Smit, Arie Jan
Gortner, Ross Aiken
Hart, Edwin Bret
Henderson, Lawrence Joseph
Herter, Christian Archibald
Hoagland, Charles Lee
Kendall, Edward Calvin
Koch, Fred Conrad
Kunitz, Moses
Levene, Phoebus Aaron Theodore
Marriott, Williams McKim
Meyerhof, Otto
Mirsky, Alfred Ezra
Osborne, Thomas Burr
Rolf, Ida Pauline
Schmidt, Carl Louis August
Schoenheimer, Rudolf
Schweinitz, Emil Alexander de
Stern, Kurt Guenter
Sugiura, Kanematsu
Sumner, James Batcheller
Tatum, Edward Lawrie
Vaughan, Victor Clarence
BIOGRAPHER (See also AUTHOR, WRITER)
Allen, Hervey
Anthony, Katharine Susan
Atkinson, William Biddle
Beer, Thomas
Bernard, William Bayle
Bowen, Catherine Drinker
Bradford, Gamaliel
Brooks, Van Wyck
Bruce, William Cabell
Drake, Benjamin
Du Bois, Shirley Lola Graham
Duyckinck, Evert Augustus
Duyckinck, George Long
Forester, Cecil Scott
Greenslet, Ferris
Hagedorn, Hermann Ludwig Gebhard
Hendrick, Burton Jesse
Hergesheimer, Joseph
Howe, Mark Antony De Wolfe
Johnson, Allen
Josephson, Matthew
Kennedy, William Sloane
Lewis, Lloyd Downs
Long, Armistead Lindsay
Morse, John Torrey
Nicolay, John George
Paine, Albert Bigelow
Parton, James
Pickard, Samuel Thomas
Pierce, Edward Lillie
Pringle, Henry Fowles
Proctor, Lucien Brock
Quinn, Arthur Hobson
Sandburg, Carl August
Sheean, James Vincent
Shellabarger, Samuel
Sprague, William Buell
Thayer, Alexander Wheelock
Thayer, William Roscoe
Van Doren, Carl Clinton
Winslow, Ola Elizabeth
BIOLOGIST (See also BOTANIST, SCIENTIST, ZOOLOGIST)
Carrel, Alexis
Chapman, Henry Cadwalader
Coghill, George Ellett
Conklin, Edwin Grant
Davenport, Charles Benedict
Harrison, Ross Granville
Jayne, Horace Fort
Jennings, Herbert Spencer
Lillie, Frank Rattray
Loeb, Leo
McClung, Clarence Erwin
McMurrich, James Playfair
Mayor, Alfred Goldsborough
Minot, Charles Sedgwick
Nelson, Julius
Noble, Gladwyn Kingsley
Pearl, Raymond
Pincus, Gregory Goodwin ("Goody")
Sedgwick, William Thompson
Stockard, Charles Rupert
Whitman, Charles Otis
Wilson, Edmund Beecher
Woodruff, Lorande Loss
BIOMEDICAL SCIENTIST
Sutherland, Earl Wilbur, Jr.
BIOMETRICIAN (See also BIOLOGIST, PHYSICIAN, SCIENTIST, STATISTICIAN)
Harris, James Arthur
BIOPHYSICIST (See also BIOLOGIST, PHYSICIST, SCIENTIST)
Bovie, William T.
Hecht, Selig
BIRTH CONTROL ADVOCATE
Hepburn, Katharine Houghton
Sanger, Margaret Higgins
Stone, Abraham
BISHOP (See also RELIGIOUS LEADER)
African Methodist Episcopal
Allen, Richard
Brown, John Mifflin
Brown, Morris
Clinton, George Wylie
Gaines, Wesley John
Gregg, John Andrew
Holsey, Lucius Henry
Hood, James Walker
Loguen, Jermain Wesley

Payne, Daniel Alexander
Tanner, Benjamin Tucker
Turner, Henry McNeal
Walters, Alexander
Wayman, Alexander Walker
Anglican
Inglis, Charles
Episcopal
Atkinson, Thomas
Bass, Edward
Brooks, Phillips
Brownell, Thomas Church
Burgess, Alexander
Burgess, George
Burleson, Hugh Latimer
Capers, Ellison
Chase, Philander
Cheney, Charles Edward
Clark, Thomas March
Coleman, Leighton
Coxe, Arthur Cleveland
De Lancey, William Heathcote
Doane, George Washington
Doane, William Croswell
Fallows, Samuel
Grafton, Charles Chapman
Graves, Frederick Rogers
Greer, David Hummell
Griswold, Alexander Viets
Hale, Charles Reuben
Hall, Arthur Crawshay Alliston
Hare, William Hobart
Hobart, John Henry
Holly, James Theodore
Hopkins, John Henry
Howe, Mark Anthony De Wolfe
Huntington, Frederic Dan
Ives, Levi Silliman
Jarvis, Abraham
Johns, John
Kemp, James
Kemper, Jackson
Kerfoot, John Barrett
Kip, William Ingraham
Lay, Henry Champlin
Lee, Alfred
Leonard, William Andrew
Littlejohn, Abram Newkirk
McIlvaine, Charles Pettit
McLaren, William Edward
McVickar, William Neilson
Madison, James
Meade, William
Moore, Benjamin
Moore, Richard Channing
Murray, John Gardner
Nichols, William Ford
Odenheimer, William Henry
Onderdonk, Benjamin Tredwell
Onderdonk, Henry Ustick
Otey, James Hervey
Paddock, Benjamin Henry
Paddock, John Adams
Penick, Charles Clifton
Perry, William Stevens
Peterkin, George William
Polk, Leonidas
Potter, Alonzo
Potter, Henry Codman
Potter, Horatio
Provoost, Samuel
Quintard, Charles Todd
Randolph, Alfred Magill
Ravenscroft, John Stark
Satterlee, Henry Yates
Schereschewsky, Samuel Isaac Joseph
Scott, Thomas Fielding
Seabury, Samuel, 1729–1796
Seymour, George Franklin
Slattery, Charles Lewis
Smith, Robert, 1732–1801
Spalding, Franklin Spencer
Stevens, William Bacon
Talbot, Ethelbert
Thompson, Hugh Miller
Tucker, Henry St. George
Tuttle, Daniel Sylvester
Wainwright, Jonathan Mayhew, 1792–1854
Whipple, Henry Benjamin
White, William
Whittingham, William Rollinson
Williams, Channing Moore
Williams, Charles David
Williams, John, 1817–1899
Wilmer, Joseph Père Bell
Wilmer, Richard Hooker
Evangelical
Esher, John Jacob
Seybert, John
German Baptist Brethren
Sower, Christopher, 1721–1784
Mennonite
Boehm, Martin
Methodist
Ames, Edward Raymond
Andrew, James Osgood
Andrews, Edward Gayer
Asbury, Francis
Baker, Osmon Cleander
Bascom, Henry Bidleman
Bashford, James Whitford
Bowman, Thomas
Capers, William
Coke, Thomas
Early, John
Emory, John
Fitzgerald, Oscar Penn
Foss, Cyrus David
Foster, Randolph Sinks
Fowler, Charles Henry
Galloway, Charles Betts
Goodsell, Daniel Ayres
Hamline, Leonidas Lent
Hargrove, Robert Kennon
Harris, Merriman Colbert
Harris, William Logan
Hartzell, Joseph Crane
Haven, Erastus Otis
Haven, Gilbert
Haygood, Atticus Green
Hedding, Elijah
Hendrix, Eugene Russell
Hurst, John Fletcher
Joyce, Isaac Wilson
Kingsley, Calvin
Lambuth, Walter Russell
McCabe, Charles Cardwell
McKendree, William
McTyeire, Holland Nimmons
Marvin, Enoch Mather
Merrill, Stephen Mason
Neely, Thomas Benjamin
Newman, John Phihp
Oxnam, Garfield Bromley
Paine, Robert
Parker, Edwin Wallace
Peck, Jesse Truesdell
Pierce, George Foster
Quayle, William Alfred
Roberts, Robert Richford
Simpson, Matthew
Soule, Joshua
Taylor, William
Thoburn, James Mills
Thomson, Edward
Tigert, John James
Vincent, John Heyl
Walden, John Morgan
Warren, Henry White
Waugh, Beverly
Whatcoat, Richard
Methodist Episcopal
Cranston, Earl
Fisher, Frederick Bohn
Hamilton, John William
Hughes, Edwin Holt
McConnell, Francis John
McDowell, William Fraser
Oldham, William Fitzjames
Moravian
Boehler, Peter
Boehm, Martin
Ettwein, John
Jacobson, John Christian
Kephart, Ezekiel Boring
Kumler, Henry
Laskiel, George Henry
Levering, Joseph Mortimer
Nitschmann, David
Reichel, Charles Gotthold
Rondthaler, Edward
Schweinitz, Edmund Alexander de
Spangenberg, Augustus Gottlieb
Polish National Catholic
Hodur, Francis
Protestant Episcopal
Brent, Charles Henry
Cheshire, Joseph Blount
Gailor, Thomas Frank
Lawrence, William
Manning, William Thomas
Restarick, Henry Bond
Southgate, Horatio
Sumner, Walter Taylor
Roman Catholic
Bayley, James Roosevelt
Bradley, Denis Mary
Byrne, Andrew
Carroll, John
Chanche, John Mary Joseph
Chatard, Francis Silas
Cheverus, John Louis Ann Magdalen Lefebre de
Connolly, John
Conwell, Henry
Crétin, Joseph
Curtis, Alfred Allen
David, John Baptist Mary
Dougherty, Dennis Joseph
Du Bois, John
Egan, Michael
England, John
Fenwick, Edward Dominic

Fitzpatrick, John Bernard
Flaget, Benedict Joseph
Galberry, Thomas
Haas, Francis Joseph
Haid, Leo
Heiss, Michael
Lefevere, Peter Paul
McQuaid, Bernard John
Noll, John Francis
Stritch, Samuel Alphonsus
Tamarón, Pedro
Russian
Ioasaf
BLACK MUSLIM LEADER
Muhammad, Elijah
BLIND, DEAF, MUTE
Bridgman, Laura Dewey
BLOCKADE RUNNER (See also NAVAL OFFICER)
Hambleton, Thomas Edward
BOOKBINDER
Matthews, William
Nicholson, James Bartram
BOOK COLLECTOR (See also ANTIQUARIAN, COLLECTOR)
Adler, Elmer
Ayer, Edward Everett
Brown, John Carter
Carson, Hampton Lawrence
Clements, William Lawrence
Emmett, Burton
Fiske, Daniel Willard
Folger, Henry Clay
Graff, Everett Dwight
Greene, Albert Gorton
Gunther, Charles Frederick
Jacobs, Joseph
Joline, Adrian Hoffman
Lenox, James
Mackenzie, William
Montague, Gilbert Holland
Pancoast, Seth
Plimpton, George Arthur
Toner, Joseph Meredith
Warden, David Bailie
Widener, Harry Elkins
Young, George
BOOK DESIGNER
Dwiggins, William Addison
Seton, Grace Gallatin Thompson
BOOKSELLER (See also PUBLISHER)
Beach, Sylvia Woodbridge
Bell, Robert
Brown, James
Francis, Charles Stephen
Fry, Richard
Gaine, Hugh
Goodrich, Chauncey
Green, Asa
Hall, David
Harris, Benjamin
Henchman, Daniel
Henderson, Daniel McIntyre
Kenedy, Patrick John
McClurg, Alexander Caldwell
Melcher, Frederic Gershom
Nancrède Paul Joseph Guérard de
Polock, Moses
Rivington, James
Stevens, Benjamin Franklin
Stevens, Henry
Trow, John Fowler
Weems, Mason Locke
Wilson, William
BOOTLEGGER
Capone, Alphonse ("Al")
Wexler, Irving ("Waxey Gordon")
BOTANIC PHYSICIAN (See also AGRICULTURIST, BOTANIST, PHYSICIAN)
Bickerdyke, Mary Ann Ball
Thomson, Samuel
BOTANICAL EXPLORER
Rusby, Henry Hurd
BOTANIST (See also AGRICULTURIST, BIOLOGIST)
Allen, Timothy Field
Alvan, Wentworth Chapman
Ames, Oakes
Arthur, Joseph Charles
Atkinson, George Francis
Bailey, Jacob Whitman
Bailey, Liberty Hyde
Baldwin, William
Banister, John
Barnes, Charles Reid
Barton, William Paul Crillon
Bartram, John
Beal, William James
Bessey, Charles Edwin
Bigelow, Jacob
Brackenridge, William D.
Brainerd, Ezra
Brandegee, Townshend Stith
Bridges, Robert
Britton, Nathaniel Lord
Buckley, Samuel Botsford
Burrill, Thomas Jonathan
Campbell, Douglas Houghton
Carver, George Washington
Chamberlain, Charles Joseph
Chase, (Mary) Agnes Merrill
Clark, Henry James
Clayton, John
Clements, Frederic Edward
Colden, Jane
Collins, Frank Shipley
Coulter, John Merle
Cowles, Henry Chandler
Curtis, Moses Ashley
Cutler, Manasseh
Darlington, William
Dudley, William Russel
Duggar, Benjamin Minge
Durand, Élie Magloire
Eaton, Daniel Cady
Elliott, Stephen
Ellis, Job Bicknell
Engelmann, George
Fairchild, David Grandison
Farlow, William Gilson
Fernald, Merritt Lyndon
Goodale, George Lincoln
Gray, Asa
Greene, Edward Lee
Harris, James Arthur
Harshberger, John William
Hollick, Charles Arthur
Howell, Thomas Jefferson
James, Thomas Potts
Jeffrey, Edward Charles
Jepson, Willis Linn
Kauffman, Calvin Henry
Kellogg, Albert
Knowlton, Frank Hall
Kraemer, Henry
Kuhn, Adam
Lemmon, John Gill
Lindheimer, Ferdinand Jacob
Marshall, Humphry
Meehan, Thomas
Michaux, André
Michaux, François André
Michener, Ezra
Millspaugh, Charles Frederick
Mitchell, Elisha
Mitchell, John, d. 1768
Mohr, Charles Theodore
Mühlenberg, Gotthilf Henry Ernest
Nieuwland, Julius Arthur
Nuttall, Thomas
Paine, John Alsop
Pammel, Louis Hermann
Parry, Charles Christopher
Porcher, Francis Peyre
Porter, Thomas Conrad
Pound, (Nathan) Roscoe
Pursh, Frederick
Ravenel, Henry William
Riddell, John Leonard
Robinson, Benjamin Lincoln
Rose, Joseph Nelson
Rothrock, Joseph Trimble
Rydberg, Per Axel
Safford, William Edwin
Sartwell, Henry Parker
Schweinitz, Lewis David von
Setchell, William Albert
Shecut, John Linnaeus Edward Whitridge
Short, Charles Wilkins
Sinnott, Edmund Ware
Smith, Edwin Frink
Spalding, Volney Morgan
Sullivant, William Starting
Thaxter, Roland
Thurber, George
Torrey, John
Trelease, William
Tuckerman, Edward
Underwood, Lucien Marcus
Vasey, George
Walter, Thomas, *c.* 1740–1789
Watson, Sereno
White, David
Wilson, Ernest Henry
Wright, Charles
BOXER (See also ATHLETE, PUGILIST)
Braddock, James J.
Charles, Ezzard Mack
Dundee, Johnny
Jeffries, James Jackson
Johnson, Jack
Langford, Samuel
Lewis, John Henry
Liston, Charles ("Sonny")
Marciano, Rocky
Tunney, James Joseph
Wills, Harry
BOY SCOUT LEADER
West, James Edward

BREEDER OF DOGS
Sloane, Isabel Cleves Dodge
BREEDER OF RACEHORSES (See also HORSEMAN)
Jones, Benjamin Allyn
Lorillard, Pierre
Madden, John Edward
White, Benjamin Franklin
BREWER
Busch, Adolphus
Jones, Frank
Ruppert, Jacob
Vassar, Matthew
Wacker, Charles Henry
BRIDGE BUILDER (See also ENGINEER [BRIDGE], ENGINEER [CIVIL])
Harrington, John Lyle
Lindenthal, Gustav
BRIDGE PLAYER (CONTRACT)
Culbertson, Ely
Culbertson, Josephine Murphy
Lenz, Sidney Samuel
Whitehead, Wilbur Cherrier
Work, Milton Cooper
BRIGAND (See also BANDIT, DESPERADO, OUTLAW)
Murrieta, Joaquin
BRITISH WOMEN'S AUXILIARY CORPS DRIVER
Summersby, Kathleen Helen ("Kay")
BROADCAST AUDIENCE ANALYST
Hooper, Claude Ernest
BROADCAST COMPANY EXECUTIVE
Kintner, Robert Edmonds
BRONZE FOUNDER (See also IRON FOUNDER)
Mills, Clark
BRYOLOGIST (See BOTANIST, BIOLOGIST)
BUCCANEER (See also BANDIT, BRIGAND, CRIMINAL, DESPERADO, OUTLAW, PIRATE)
You, Dominique
BUCK ROGERS ORIGINATOR
Dille, John Flint
BUFFERED ASPIRIN INVENTOR
Paul, William Darwin ("Shorty")
BUILDER (See also CANAL BUILDER, RAILROAD BUILDER, SHIPBUILDER)
Allaire, James Peter
Hawks, John
Hoban, James
Hooker, Philip
Joy, Thomas
Macfarlane, Charles William
Parris, Alexander
Starrett, Paul
Starrett, William Aiken
Wolfson, Erwin Service
BUILDING CONTRACTOR (See also CONTRACTOR)
Kelly, John Brendan
BURGLAR (See also BANDIT, BRIGAND, BUCCANEER, CRIMINAL, DESPERADO, OUTLAW, PIRATE)
Wyman, Seth
BUSINESS FORECASTER
Babson, Roger Ward
BUSINESSMAN (See also BUSINESSWOMAN, CAPITALIST, ENTREPRENEUR, EXECUTIVE, FACTOR, INDUSTRIALIST, MANUFACTURER, MERCHANT)
Abernethy, George
Adams, Charles Francis
Aldrich, Nelson Wilmarth
Allen, George Edward
Baldwin, Henry Porter
Batterson, James Goodwin
Bean, Leon Lenwood
Behn, Sosthenes
Bement, Clarence Sweet
Besse, Arthur Lyman
Bierwirth, John Edward
Bliss, Cornelius Newton
Borg, George William
Braden, Spruille
Brady, Anthony Nicholas
Bruce, Edward Bright
Brundage, Avery
Buchanan, William Insco
Buchtel, John Richards
Bucknell, William
Bunker, Arthur Hugh
Caldwell, Alexander
Camden, Johnson Newlon
Capehart, Homer Earl
Caroll, Howard
Chester, Colby Mitchell
Childs, Richard Spencer
Clay, Lucius DuBignon
Cobo, Albert Eugene
Coburn, Abner
Comer, Braxton Bragg
Cooke, Samuel
Cooper, Mark Anthony
Coxey, Jacob Sechler
Crane, Charles Richard
Cushman, Austin Thomas ("Joe")
Dana, Napoleon Jackson Tecumseh
Dawes, Rufus Cutler
Dexter, Henry
Dow, Lorenzo
Early, Stephen Tyree
Eastman, Harvey Gridley
Edison, Charles
Emery, Henry Crosby
Farwell, Charles Benjamin
Folsom, Marion Bayard
Forbes, John Murray
Franklin, William Buel
Garst, Roswell ("Bob")
Goldfine, Bernard
Gorham, Nathaniel
Grady, Henry Francis
Hamlin, Charles
Hartford, George Huntington
Hartford, George Ludlum
Hartford, John Augustine
Haugen, Gilbert Nelson
Hiester, Daniel
Hires, Charles Elmer, Jr.
Hogan, John
Holt, William Franklin
Hoyt, John Sherman
Huidekoper, Harm Jan
Keyes, Erasmus Darwin
Kimball, Dan Able
Knauth, Oswald Whitman
Kraft, James Lewis
Ladd, William Sargent
Lasater, Edward Cunningham
Lilly, Eli
Lowell, Percival
McCormick, Richard Cunningham
MacNider, Hanford
Maestri, Robert Sidney
Manigault, Peter
Matthews, Francis Patrick
Miller, David Hunter
Millikin, Eugene Donald
Mills, Cyrus Taggart
Mitchell, James Paul
Morton, Paul
Mosessohn, David Nehemiah
Murphy, Gerald Clery
Newberry, Truman Handy
Niles, Nathaniel, 1741–1828
O'Daniel, Wilbert Lee ("Pappy")
Olds, Irving Sands
Pate, Maurice
Peek, George Nelson
Penney, James Cash ("J.C.")
Perdue, Arthur William
Petri, Angelo
Phelps, William Walter
Pierce, Edward Allen
Radcliffe, George Lovic Pierce
Rand, James Henry
Reece, Brazilla Carroll
Rich, Robert
Richmond, Dean
Rockefeller, Nelson Aldrich
Roosevelt, Theodore
Scammon, Jonathan Young
Schell, Augustus
Scott, Allen Cecil
Shaw, Clay L.
Shuey, Edwin Longstreet
Sibley, Hiram
Smoot, Reed Owen
Snell, Bertrand Hollis
Snow, John Ben
Sprunt, James
Stouffer, Vernon Bigelow
Strawn, Silas Hardy
Stuart, Elbridge Amos
Taussig, William
Thomas, John Parnell
Thomas, (John William) Elmer
Tishman, David
Walker, Amasa
Whalen, Grover Aloysius
Wherry, Kenneth Spicer
Whitehead, Walter Edward
Wrigley, Philip Knight
Zellerbach, Harold Lionel
BUSINESSWOMAN
Arden, Elizabeth
Cochran, Jacqueline
Gleason, Kate
Post, Marjorie Merriweather
Rubinstein, Helena
Walker, Sarah Breedlove
Willard, Mary Hatch

Byzantine Scholar
Vasiliev, Alexander Alexandrovich

Cabalist (See also Religious Leader)
Pancoast, Seth
Cabinetmaker (See Carpenter)
Cable Promoter
Eastman, Arthur MacArthur
Field, Cyrus West
Scrymser, James Alexander
Calligrapher (See also Penman)
Dwiggins, William Addison
Canal Builder
Goethals, George Washington
Lacock, Abner
Moorhead, James Kennedy
Canal Promoter
Shonts, Theodore Perry
Watson, Elkanah
Cancer Research Pioneer
Sugiura, Kanematsu
Cannon Maker (See also Iron Founder)
Denning, William
Cantor (See also Singer)
Kaiser, Alois
Rosenblatt, Joseph
Stark, Edward Josef
Capitalist (See also Financier)
Allerton, Samuel Waters
Ames, Frederick Lothrop
Ames, Oakes
Ames, Oliver
Archbold, John Dustin
Astor, John Jacob, 1763–1848
Astor, John Jacob, 1822–1890
Astor, John Jacob, 1864–1914
Astor, William Backhouse
Astor, William Waldorf
Ayer, James Cook
Baldwin, Henry Perrine
Barber, Amzi Lorenzo
Barnum, Zenus
Bennett, James Gordon
Berwind, Edward Julius
Blair, John Insley
Blow, Henry Taylor
Boies, Henry Martyn
Brainerd, Lawrence
Brown, Henry Cordis
Burt, John
Campbell, Robert
Collier, Barron Gift
Converse, Edmund Cogswell
Cook, James Merrill
Corbin, Austin
Cornell, Ezra
Crimmins, John Daniel
Crocker, Charles
Daly, Marcus
De Lamar, Joseph Raphael
Dennis, Graham Barclay
Dickson, Thomas
Dolan, Thomas
Donahue, Peter
Drew, Daniel
Du Pont, Thomas Coleman
Eells, Dan Parmelee
Elkins, William Lukens
Field, Cyrus West
Fisk, James
Fiske, John
Flagler, Henry Morrison
Flagler, John Haldane
Fleischmann, Charles Louis
Folger, Henry Clay
Freedman, Andrew
Frick, Henry Clay
Gerstle, Lewis
Gilbert, William Lewis
Glidden, Joseph Farwell
Grace, William Russell
Grant, John Thomas
Guggenheim, Daniel
Haggin, James Ben Ali
Halleck, Henry Wager
Hanna, Marcus Alonzo
Harrah, Charles Jefferson
Hauser, Samuel Thomas
Havemeyer, Henry Osborne
Havemeyer, William Frederick
Huntington, Collis Potter
Jesup, Morris Ketchum
Jones, Frank
Juilliard, Augustus D.
Keith, Minor Cooper
Kennedy, John Stewart
Knight, Edward Collings
Leach, Shepherd
Leary, John
Leiter, Joseph
Lewisohn, Adolph
Logan, Thomas Muldrup, 1840–1914
Longyear, John Munroe
Lowry, Thomas
Lucas, James H.
Mackay, Clarence Hungerford
Mackay, John William
Macy, Valentine Everit
Markoe, Abraham
Marquand, Henry Gurdon
Mather, Samuel Livingston
Moffat, David Halliday
Moore, William Henry
O'Brien, William Shoney
Paine, Charles Jackson
Patten, James A.
Payne, Oliver Hazard
Phelan, James, 1824–1892
Pratt, Enoch
Ralston, William Chapman
Raymond, Benjamin Wright
Ream, Norman Bruce
Reed, Simeon Gannett
Roberts, Marshall Owen
Rogers, Henry Huttleston
Ryan, John Dennis
Ryerson, Martin Antoine
Scrymser, James Alexander
Severance, Louis Henry
Sheedy, Dennis
Simpson, Michael Hodge
Sloss, Louis
Smith, Francis Marion
Smith, Robert Alexander C.
Spreckels, Claus
Spreckles, John Diedrich
Squire, Watson Carvosso
Stewart, William Rhinelander
Stillman, James
Stokes, William Earl Dodge
Stone, Amasa
Stranahan, James Samuel Thomas
Taylor, Moses
Tevis, Lloyd
Thaw, William
Tobey, Edward Silas
Tod, David
Upton, George Bruce
Vanderbilt, George Washington
Vanderbilt, William Kissam
Vibbard, Chauncey
Waldo, Samuel
Walters, Henry
Waterhouse, Frank
Welch, Charles Clark
Winslow, Sidney Wilmot
Zimmerman, Eugene
Car Collector
Harrah, William Fisk ("Bill")
Cardinal
Brennan, Francis James
Cushing, Richard James
Glennon, John Joseph
Meyer, Albert Gregory
Ritter, Joseph Elmer
Spellman, Francis Joseph
Wright, John Joseph
Cardiologist (See also Physician)
Libman, Emanuel
White, Paul Dudley
CARE Executive Director
French, Paul Comly
Caricaturist (See Cartoonist)
Carpenter
Goddard, John
Gostelowe, Jonathan
Holden, Oliver
Luther, Seth
Phyfe, Duncan
Savery, William, 1721–1787
Carpetbagger (See also Adventurer, Speculator)
Clarke, William Thomas
Tourgée, Albion Winegar
Carriage Builder
Brewster, James
Cartographer (See also Mapmaker)
Farmer, John
Herrman, Augustine
Kino, Eusebio Francisco
Lindenkohl, Adolph
Ogden, Herbert Gouverneur
Pelham, Henry
Pound, Thomas
Romans, Bernard
Southack, Cyprian
Tanner, Henry Schenck
White, John
Cartoonist (See also Artist, Illustrator)
Arno, Peter
Bellew, Frank Henry Temple
Berryman, Clifford Kennedy
Briggs, Clare A.
Capp, Al
Cesare, Oscar Edward
Charles, William
Clay, Edward Williams
Crosby, Percy Lee

Darling, Jay Norwood ("Ding")
Davenport, Homer Calvin
Dorgan, Thomas Aloysius
Duffy, Edmund
Fischetti, John
Fisher, Hammond Edward
Fisher, Henry Conroy ("Bud")
Fitzpatrick, Daniel Robert
Fox, Fontaine Talbot, Jr.
Gibson, Charles Dana
Gillam, Bernhard
Goldberg, Reuben Lucius ("Rube")
Gray, Harold Lincoln
Gropper, William
Gross, Milt
Grosz, George
Hatlo, Jimmy
Held, John, Jr.
Herriman, George Joseph
Hubbard, Frank McKinney
Kelly, Walter ("Walt") Crawford, Jr.
Keppler, Joseph
Kirby, Rollin
McManus, George
Minor, Robert
Morgan, Matthew Somerville
Mullin, Willard Harlan
Nast, Thomas
Newell, Peter Sheaf Hersey
Opper, Frederick Burr
Raymond, Alexander Gillespie
Rogers, William Allen
Smith, Robert Sidney
Szyk, Arthur
Thurber, James Grover
Volck, Adalbert John
Wales, James Albert
Webster, Harold Tucker
Willard, Frank Henry
Williams, Gaar Campbell
Young, Art
Zimmerman, Eugene

CASINO OWNER
Harrah, William Fisk ("Bill")

CATERER (See RESTAURATEUR)

CATHOLIC PACIFIST
Day, Dorothy

CATHOLIC WORKER MOVEMENT COFOUNDER
Day, Dorothy

CATTLEMAN (See also DAIRY HUSBANDMAN, RANCHER, STOCK BREEDER)
Chisum, John Simpson
Goodnight, Charles
Lasater, Edward Cunningham
Littlefield, George Washington
McCoy, Joseph Geating
Mackenzie, Murdo
Renick, Felix
Springer, Charles
Strawn, Jacob

CAVALRY OFFICER
McCoy, Tim

CELLIST
Busch, Hermann
Casals, Pablo

CENSUS DIRECTOR
Kennedy, Joseph Camp Griffith
Merriam, William Rush

CHANCELLOR (STATE)
Harrington, Samuel Maxwell
Livingston, Robert R., 1746–1813
Saulsbury, Willard, 1820–1892
Walworth, Reuben Hyde

CHANDLER
Jackson, William, 1783–1855

CHAPLAIN (See also CLERGYMAN, RELIGIOUS LEADER)
Hunter, Andrew
Jones, David
Jones, George
Munro, Henry

CHEF
Diat, Louis Felix

CHEMIST (See also BIOCHEMIST, SCIENTIST)
Abel, John Jacob
Adkins, Homer Burton
Austen, Peter Townsend
Babcock, James Francis
Bache, Franklin
Bailey, Jacob Whitman
Bancroft, Wilder Dwight
Barker, George Frederick
Baskerville, Charles
Beck, Lewis Caleb
Benedict, Stanley Rossiter
Bolton, Henry Carrington
Boltwood, Bertram Borden
Booth, James Curtis
Boyé, Martin Hans
Browne, Charles Albert
Burnett, Joseph
Carothers, Wallace Hume
Chandler, Charles Frederick
Clarke, Frank Wigglesworth
Cooke, Josiah Parsons
Cope, Arthur Clay
Cottrell, Frederick Gardner
Crafts, James Mason
Cutbush, James
Dabney, Charles William
Dana, James Freeman
Dana, Samuel Luther
Daniels, Farrington
Day, David Talbot
Debye, Peter Joseph William
Doremus, Robert Ogden
Dorset, Marion
Dow, Herbert Henry
Draper, John William
Drown, Thomas Messinger
Dudley, Charles Benjamin
Duncan, Robert Kennedy
Du Pont, Francis Irénée
Ellis, Carleton
Fieser, Louis Frederick
Folin, Otto Knut Olof
Franklin, Edward Curtis
Freas, Thomas Bruce
Fullam, Frank L.
Genth, Frederick Augustus
Gibbs, Oliver Wolcott
Goessmann, Charles Anthony
Gomberg, Moses
Gorham, John
Grasselli, Caesar Augustin
Green, Jacob
Griscom, John
Guthrie, Samuel
Hall, Charles Martin
Hare, Robert
Harkins, William Draper
Hart, Edward
Hayes, Augustus Allen
Hendrick, Ellwood
Herty, Charles Holmes
Hill, Henry Barker
Hillebrand, William Francis
Hooker, Samuel Cox
Horsford, Eben Norton
Hudson, Claude Silbert
Hunt, Thomas Sterry
Jackson, Charles Thomas
James, Charles
Jarves, Deming
Johnson, Treat Baldwin
Johnston, John
Jones, Harry Clary
Keating, William Hypolitus
Kedzie, Robert Clark
Kharasch, Morris Selig
Kinnicutt, Leonard Parker
Kirkwood, John Gamble
Koenig, George Augustus
Kohler, Elmer Peter
Ladd, Edwin Fremont
Lamb, Arthur Becket
Langley, John Williams
Langmuir, Irving
Latimer, Wendell Mitchell
Lea, Mathew Carey
Leffmann, Henry
Levy, Louis Edward
Lewis, Gilbert Newton
Libby, Willard Frank
Loeb, Morris
Long, John Harper
Mabery, Charles Frederic
Maclean, John
McMurtrie, William
Mallet, John William
Mallinckrodt, Edward, Jr.
Matheson, William John
Matthews, Joseph Merritt
Merrill, Joshua
Metcalfe, Samuel Lytler
Michael, Arthur
Michaelis, Leonor
Midgley, Thomas
Mitchell, John Kearsley
Moore, Richard Bishop
Morfit, Campbell
Morley, Edward Williams
Mulliken, Samuel Parsons
Munroe, Charles Edward
Nef, John Ulric
Nichols, James Robinson
Nieuwland, Julius Arthur
Norris, James Flack
Norton, John Pitkin
Noyes, Arthur Amos
Noyes, William Albert
Noyes, William Albert, Jr.
Onsager, Lars
Ostromislensky, Iwan Iwanowich
Parr, Samuel Wilson
Peckham, Stephen Farnum
Pendleton, Edmund Monroe
Peter, Robert
Phillips, Francis Clifford
Piccard, Jean Felix

Porter, John Addison
Power, Frederick Belding
Prescott, Albert Benjamin
Pugh, Evan
Randall, Wyatt William
Reese, Charles Lee
Reid, David Boswell
Remsen, Ira
Rice, Charles
Richards, Ellen Henrietta Swallow
Richards, Theodore William
Rogers, James Blythe
Rogers, Robert Empie
Sadtler, Samuel Philip
Sanger, Charles Robert
Scovell, Melville Amasa
Seabury, George John
Shepard, James Henry
Sheppard, Samuel Edward
Silliman, Benjamin, 1816–1885
Slosson, Edwin Emery
Smith, Alexander
Smith, Edgar Fahs
Smith, John Lawrence
Squibb, Edward Robinson
Stern, Otto
Stieglitz, Julius
Stillman, Thomas Bliss
Stine, Charles Milton Altland
Stoddard, John Tappan
Storer, Francis Humphreys
Takamine, Jokichi
Talbot, Henry Paul
Taylor, William Chittenden
Teeple, John Edgar
Tilghman, Richard Albert
Tolman, Richard Chace
Torrey, John
Vaughan, Daniel
Warren, Cyrus Moors
Washburn, Edward Wight
Weber, Henry Adam
Weightman, William
Wetherill, Charles Mayer
White, Henry Clay
Whitmore, Frank Clifford
Whitney, Josiah Dwight
Whitney, Willis Rodney
Wiechmann, Ferdinand Gerhard
Wiley, Harvey Washington
Witthaus, Rudolph August
Wood, Edward Stickney
Woodhouse, James
Woodward, Robert Burns
Wurtz, Henry

CHESS PLAYER
Loyd, Samuel
Mackenzie, George Henry
Marshall, Frank James
Morphy, Paul Charles
Pillsbury, Harry Nelson
Rice, Isaac Leopold
Steinitz, William

CHIEF JUSTICE (STATE) (See also JUDGE, JURIST, LAWYER, SUPREME COURT JUSTICE)
De Lancey, James
Gaines, Reuben Reid
Horsmanden, Daniel
Livermore, Arthur
Lloyd, David
Lowe, Ralph Phillips
Lumpkin, Joseph Henry
Mellen, Prentiss
More, Nicholas
Morris, Lewis, 1671–1746
Morris, Robert Hunter
Morton, Marcus, 1819–1891
Nicholls, Francis Redding Tillon
Read, George
Rusk, Thomas Jefferson
Shippen, Edward, 1728–1806
Simpson, William Dunlap

CHINESE ART SPECIALIST
Ferguson, John Calvin

CHOIRMASTER (See also CONDUCTOR)
Dett, Robert Nathaniel
Tuckey, William

CHOREOGRAPHER
Berkeley, Busby
Bolm, Adolph Rudolphovitch
Champion, Gower
Fokine, Michel
Humphrey, Doris
Limón, José Arcadio
Shawn, Edwin Meyers ("Ted")
Tamiris, Helen

CHRISTIAN SCIENCE LEADER (See also RELIGIOUS LEADER)
Eddy, Mary Morse Baker
Stetson, Augusta Emma Simmons

CHRONICLER (See also DIARIST, HISTORIAN)
Clyman, James
Johnson, Edward

CHURCH HISTORIAN (See also HISTORIAN)
Dubbs, Joseph Henry
Edwards, Morgan
Guilday, Peter Keenan
Jackson, Samuel Macauley
Moffatt, James
Perry, William Stevens
Schaff, Philip
Walker, Williston
Whitsitt, William Heth

CINEMATOGRAPHER
Howe, James Wong

CIRCUS CLOWN (See CLOWN)

CIRCUS PROPRIETOR (See SHOWMAN)

CITY PLANNER
Atterbury, Grosvenor
Bassett, Edward Murray
Bettman, Alfred
Brunner, Arnold William
Ford, George Burdett
Moore, Charles
Nolen, John
Robinson, Charles Mulford
Saarinen, Gottlieb Eliel
Wacker, Charles Henry
Wright, Henry

CIVIC LEADER
Adams, Charles Francis, 1835–1915
Blodgett, John Wood
Breckinridge, Desha
Burlingham, Charles Culp
Chandler, Harry
Clement, Rufus Early
Cutting, Robert Fulton
Dawes, Rufus Cutler
Donovan, John Joseph
Fallows, Samuel
Fortier, Alcée
Foulke, William Dudley
Haskell, Henry Joseph
Hay, Mary Garrett
Hirsch, Emil Gustav
Jackson, Robert R.
Kirstein, Louis Edward
Lazarus, Fred, Jr.
Lingelbach, Anna Lane
Loring, Charles Morgridge
Marburg, Theodore
Martin, Elizabeth Price
Mosher, Eliza Maria
Ochs, Julius
O'Connor, William Douglas
Outerbridge, Eugenius Harvey
Price, Eli Kirk
Seligman, Isaac Newton
Seligman, Joseph
Sloan, George Arthur
Spaulding, Oliver Lyman
Stranahan, James Samuel Thomas
Strong, Harriet Williams Russell
Sullivan, William Henry
Sulzberger, Cyrus Lindauer
Taussig, William
Thacher, Thomas Day
Tiffany, Katrina Brandes Ely
Wagener, John Andreas
Waterhouse, Sylvester
Widney, Joseph Pomeroy
Williams, Fannie Barrier

CIVIC REFORMER (See also POLITICAL REFORMER, REFORMER, SOCIAL REFORMER)
Coulter, Ernest Kent

CIVIC WORKER
Bayh, Marvella Belle Hern
Coulter, Ernest Kent

CIVIL LIBERTARIAN
Chafee, Zechariah, Jr.
Flynn, Elizabeth Gurley
Malin, Patrick Murphy

CIVIL RIGHTS ACTIVIST
Bunche, Ralph Johnson
Hamer, Fannie Lou
Hobson, Julius Wilson
Spingarn, Arthur Barnett
Yergan, Max

CIVIL RIGHTS LEADER
Davis, Abraham Lincoln, Jr.
Evers, Medgar Wiley
Garvey, Marcus Moziah
Houston, Charles Hamilton
Howe, Mark De Wolfe
Hunton, George Kenneth
Jackson, Robert R.
Johnson, James Weldon
King, Martin Luther, Jr.
Malcolm X
Muhammad, Elijah
Randolph, Asa Philip
Remond, Charles Lenox
Robinson, Ruby Doris Smith
Smith, Lillian Eugenia
Spottswood, Stephen Gill

Still, William
Terrell, Mary Eliza Church
Turner, James Milton
Walker, David, 1785–1830
Waring, Julius Waties
White, Walter Francis
Young, Whitney Moore, Jr.
CIVIL SERVICE REFORMER (See also REFORMER)
Bonaparte, Charles Joseph
Eaton, Dorman Bridgman
Proctor, John Robert
Swift, Lucius Burrie
Wheeler, Everett Pepperrell
CLASSICIST (See also SCHOLAR)
Allinson, Francis Greenleaf
Beeson, Charles Henry
Capps, Edward
Ezekiel, Cheever
Fiske, George Converse
Frank, Tenney
Hadas, Moses
Hamilton, Edith
Harrison, Gessner
Highet, Gilbert
Jaeger, Werner Wilhelm
Kelsey, Francis Willey
Kendall, Asabel Clark
Lane, George Martin
Leach, Abby
Lewis, Charlton Thomas
Manatt, James Irving
Moore, Clifford Herschel
Morgan, Morris Hicky
Munford, William
North, Edward
Oldfather, William Abbott
Peck, Tracy
Rand, Edward Kennard
Scott, John Adams
Sewall, Stephen
Seymour, Thomas Day
Shorey, Paul
Showerman, Grant
Sophocles, Evangelinus Apostolides
Thacher, Thomas Anthony
Waters, William Everett
West, Andrew Fleming
Wheeler, Arthur Leslie
Wheeler, James Rignall
CLERGYMAN (See also ARCHABBOT, ARCHBISHOP, BISHOP, CARDINAL, CHAPLAIN, EVANGELIST, FOUNDER, RELIGIOUS LEADER)
Adventist
Himes, Joshua Vaughan
Miller, William
Ward, Henry Dana
White, Ellen Gould Harmon
African Methodist Episcopal
Gaines, Wesley John
Gregg, John Andrew
Spottswood, Stephen Gill
Whitman, Albery Allson
Anglican (See also EPISCOPAL)
Auchmuty, Samuel
Bacon, Thomas
Boucher, Jonathan
Bowden, John
Bray, Thomas
Camm, John
Chandler, Thomas Bradbury
Checkley, John
Coombe, Thomas
Davenport, John
Duché, Jacob
Evans, Evan
Evans, Nathaniel
Forbes, John, d. 1783
Heathcote, Caleb
Hunt, Isaac
Hunt, Robert
Inglis, Charles
Johnson, Samuel
Le Jau, Francis
Munro, Henry
Ogilvie, John
Peters, Richard, *c.* 1704–1776
Peters, Samuel Andrew
Smith, William, 1727–1803
Sterling, James
Talbot, John
Vesey William
Whitaker, Alexander
Baptist
Anderson, Galusha
Arthur, William
Backus, Isaac
Banvard, Joseph
Barbour, Clarence Augustus
Benedict, David
Boyce, James Petigru
Boyd, Richard Henry
Broadus, John Albert
Brown, Charles Rufus
Brown, John Newton
Burdette, Robert Jones
Burleson, Rufus Clarence
Burroughs, John Curtis
Buttrick, Wallace
Callender, John
Cathcart, William
Chaplin, Jeremiah
Cheney, Oren Burbank
Church, Pharcellus
Clark, George Whitefield
Clarke, John
Clarke, William Newton
Clay, Joseph
Colver, Nathaniel
Cone, Spencer Houghton
Conwell, Russell Herman
Creath, Jacob, 1777–1854
Creath, Jacob, 1799–1886
Dagg, John Leadley
Dixon, Thomas
Dodge, Ebenezer
Eaton, Charles Aubrey
Eddy, Daniel Clarke
Edwards, Morgan
Faunce, William Herbert Perry
Fermald, James Champlin
Fosdick, Harry Emerson
Foster, George Burman
Frey, Joseph Samuel Christian Frederick
Fuller, Richard
Fulton, Justin Dewey
Furman, James Clement
Furman, Richard
Gale, Elbridge
Gambrell, James Bruton
Gano, John
Gano, Stephen
Garrard, James
Gilmore, Joseph Henry
Going, Jonathan
Goodspeed, Thomas Wakefield
Graves, James Robinson
Gregory, John Milton
Griffith, Benjamin
Hatcher, William Eldridge
Henderson, Charles Richmond
Holcombe, Henry
Holman, Jesse Lynch
Horr, George Edwin
Hovey, Alvah
Howell, Robert Boyté Crawford
Jeter, Jeremiah Bell
Johnson, Franklin
Johnson, Mordecai Wyatt
Johnson, William Bullein
Jones, David
Judson, Edward
King, Henry Melville
King, Martin Luther, Jr.
Lamb, Isaac Wixom
Lane, Tidence
Leland, John
Lightburn, Joseph Andrew Jackson
Lorimer, George Claude
Love, Emanuel King
Lowrey, Mark Perrin
MacArthur, Robert Stuart
McGlothlin, William Joseph
Macintosh, Douglas Clyde
Malcolm, Howard
Manly, Basil, 1798–1868
Manly, Basil, 1825–1892
Manning, James
Marshall, Daniel
Martin, Warren Homer
Massey, John Edward
Mell, Patrick Hues
Mercer, Jesse
Merrill, Daniel
Merrill, George Edmands
Morehouse, Henry Lyman
Morgan, Abel
Morgan, Thomas Jefferson
Moss, Lemuel
Moxom, Philip Stafford
Mullins, Edgar Young
Myles, John
Osgood, Howard
Payne, Christopher Harrison
Peck, John Mason
Pendleton, James Madison
Pentecost, George Frederick
Perry, Rufus Lewis
Potter, Charles Francis
Powell, Adam Clayton, Jr.
Powell, Adam Clayton, Sr.
Rauschenbusch, Walter
Rhees, Morgan John
Rhees, Rush
Rice, Luther
Richmond, John Lambert
Riley, Benjamin Franklin
Riley, William Bell
Robins, Henry Ephraim
Robinson, Ezekiel Gilman
Ross, Martin

Ryland, Robert
Sanders, Billington McCarter
Sears, Barnas
Sharp, Daniel
Sherwood, Adiel
Smith, Hezekiah
Smith, John, *c.* 1735–1824
Smith, Samuel Francis
Stanford, John
Staughton, William
Stearns, Shubal
Stillman, Samuel
Stow, Baron
Straton, John Roach
Taylor, George Boardman
Taylor, James Barnett
Taylor, James Monroe
Taylor, John
Thomas, Jesse Burgess
Tichenor, Isaac Taylor
Tomlinson, Everett Titsworth
Tucker, Henry Holcombe
Tupper, Henry Allen
Vedder, Henry Clav
Waller, John Lightfoot
Wayland, Francis, 1796–1865
Whitfield, Owen
Whitsitt, William Heth
Williams, George Washington
Williams, William R.
Willingham, Robert Josiah
Winchester, Elhanan
Winkler, Edwin Theodore
Woods, Alva
Yeaman, William Pope
Campbellite (See Disciples of Christ)
Catholic (See Roman Catholic)
Christian Connection
Shaw, Elijah
Smith, Elias
Wellons, William Brock
Church of England (See Anglican)
Church of God
Michaux, Lightfoot Solomon
Church of the New Jerusalem (See Swedenborgian)
Congregational
Abbott, Edward
Abbott, Jacob
Abbott, John Stevens Cabot
Abbott, Lyman
Adams, Nehemiah
Alden, Timothy
Allen, William
Ament, William Scott
Andrew, Samuel
Atkinson, George Henry
Atkinson, Henry Avery
Atwater, Lyman Hotchkiss
Austin, David
Austin, Samuel
Backus, Azel
Bacon, Benjamin Wisner
Bacon, David
Bacon, John
Bacon, Leonard
Bacon, Leonard Woolsey
Bailey, Rufus William
Bancroft, Aaron
Barnard, John
Barrows, John Henry
Bartlett, Samuel Colcord
Barton, James Levi
Barton, William Eleazar
Beecher, Charles
Beecher, Edward
Beecher, Henry Ward
Beecher, Thomas Kinnicut
Behrends, Adolphus Julius Frederick
Belknap, Jeremy
Bissell, Edwin Cone
Blakeslee, Erastus
Bosworth, Edward Increase
Boynton, Charles Brandon
Bradford, Amory Howe
Brattle, William
Brown, Charles Reynolds
Bumstead, Horace
Burr, Enoch Fitch
Burton, Asa
Burton, Marion Le Roy
Burton, Nathaniel Judson
Bushnell, Horace
Byles, Mather
Calkins, Phineas Wolcott
Chapin, Aaron Lucius
Chapin, Calvin
Cheever, George Barrell
Child, Frank Samuel
Clap, Thomas
Clark, Francis Edward
Clark, Jonas
Clark, Joseph Sylvester
Cleveland, Aaron
Cobb, William Henry
Condon, Thomas
Cook, Russell S.
Cooper, Samuel, 1725–1783
Crane, Frank
Cravath, Erastus Milo
Cushman, Joshua
Cutler, Carroll
Cutler, Manasseh
Daggett, Naphtali
Dana, James
Davenport, James
Davis, Jerome Dean
Day, Henry Noble
Deane, Samuel
Dewey, Chester
Dexter, Henry Martyn
Dike, Samuel Warren
Diman, Jeremiah Lewis
Dole, Charles Fletcher
Douglas, Lloyd Cassel
Dunning, Albert Elijah
Durant, Henry
Dwight, Sereno Edwards
Dwight, Timothy, 1752–1817
Dwight, Timothy, 1828–1916
Eastman, William Reed
Edwards, Jonathan
Edwards, Justin
Eliot, Jared
Emerson, Joseph
Emmons, Nathanael
Everett, Robert
Fairbanks, Henry
Field, David Dudley
Fisher, George Park
Fowler, Orin
Gay, Ebenezer
Gladden, Washington
Goodrich, Charles Augustus
Goodrich, Chauncey Allen
Goodrich, Elizur
Gordon, George Angier
Gordon, William
Griffin, Edward Dorr
Griffis, William Elliot
Grinnell, Josiah Bushnell
Gulick, Sidney Lewis
Gunsaulus, Frank Wakeley
Hall, Sherman
Harris, George
Haven, Joseph
Hepworth, George Hughes
Herron, George Davis
Hiacoomes
Higginson, John
Hillis, Newell Dwight
Hitchcock, Edward, 1793–1864
Hitchcock, Enos
Hitchcock, Roswell Dwight
Hoisington, Henry Richard
Holmes, Abiel
Holt, Arthur Erastus
Hooker, Thomas
Hubbard, William
Hume, Robert Allen
Humphrey, Heman
Jefferson, Charles Edward
Jenks, William
Kellogg, Elijah
Kellogg, Martin
Kyle, James Henderson
Langdon, Samuel
Leavitt, Joshua
L'Halle, Constantin de
Lord, Nathan
Lovejoy, Owen Reed
Lyman, Albert Josiah
McCulloch, Oscar Carleton
McKeen, Joseph
McKenzie, Alexander
Magoun, George Frederic
Mahan, Asa
Marsh, John
Mather, Samuel
Mayhew, Thomas
Mead, Charles Marsh
Mears, David Otis
Merrill, Selah
Mills, Samuel John
Mitchell, Jonathan
Moore, Zephaniah Swift
Morril, David Lawrence
Morrison, Nathan Jackson
Morse, Jedidiah
Munger, Theodore Thornton
Murdock, James
Nash, Charles Sumner
Nason, Elias
Newcomb, Harvey
Newman, Samuel Phillips
Niles, Samuel
Noble, Frederick Alphonso
Norris, Edward
North, Simeon, 1802–1884
Nott, Samuel
Nutting, Wallace
Oakes, Urian
Palmer, Ray
Parish, Elijah
Parker, Edwin Pond

Parker, Samuel
Payson, Edward
Payson, Seth
Peet, Stephen Denison
Peloubet, Francis Nathan
Pennington, James W. C.
Peter, Hugh
Phelps, Austin
Phillips, George
Pierce, John Davis
Pierpont, James
Pierson, Abraham, 1645–1707
Pond, Enoch
Porter, Ebenezer
Porter, Noah
Post, Truman Marcellus
Proctor, Henry Hugh
Rankin, Jeremiah Eames
Rice, Edwin Wilbur
Richards, Charles Herbert
Robbins, Thomas
Rogers, John Almanza Rowley
Ross, Abel Hastings
Salter, William
Saltonstall, Gurdon
Sanders, Daniel Clarke
Sanford, Elias Benjamin
Schauffler, Henry Albert
Seccomb, John
Sheldon, Charles Monroe
Shepard, Thomas
Smyth, Egbert Coffin
Smyth, Newman
Sperry, Willard Learoyd
Sprague, William Buell
Spring, Leverett Wilson
Spring, Samuel
Stearns, William Augustus
Stiles, Ezra
Stoddard, Solomon
Storrs, Richard Salter, 1787–1873
Storrs, Richard Salter, 1821–1900
Strong, James Woodward
Strong, Josiah
Stuart, Moses
Sturtevant, Julian Monson
Tappan, Henry Philip
Tarbox, Increase Niles
Taylor, William Mackergo
Tenney, Edward Payson
Thacher, Peter
Thayer, Joseph Henry
Thayer, William Makepeace
Thompson, Joseph Parrish
Todd, John
Tracy, Joseph
Trumbull, Benjamin
Tucker, William Jewett
Tufts, John
Turner, Asa
Twichell, Joseph Hopkins
Tyler, Charles Mellen
Walker, Timothy, 1705–1782
Walter, Thomas, 1696–1725
Ward, Joseph
Ware, Henry, 1764–1845
Warren, Israel Perkins
Welles, Noah
Wheelock, Eleazar
Whiton, James Morris
Willard, Samuel, 1775–1859
Williams, Elisha
Williams, John, 1664–1729
Williston, Seth
Wines, Enoch Cobb
Wingate, Paine
Winship, Albert Edward
Winslow, Hubbard
Wise, John
Woods, Leonard, 1774–1854
Worcester, Noah
Worcester, Samuel
Wright, George Frederick
Yeomans, John William

Disciples of Christ
Adams, William Lysander
Ainslie, Peter
Allen, Thomas M.
Ames, Edward Scribner
Anderson, Henry Tompkins
Baxter, William
Campbell, Alexander
Creath, Jacob, 1777–1854
Creath, Jacob, 1799–1886
Errett, Isaac
Fanning, Tolbert
Franklin, Benjamin
Goodwin, Elijah
Goss, James Walker
Hayden, Amos Sutton
Hoshour, Samuel Klinefelter
Lard, Moses E.
Loos, Charles Louis
McGarvey, John William
McLean, Archibald
Milligan, Robert
Moore, William Thomas
Pendleton, William Kimbrough
Pinkerton, Lewis Letig
Power, Frederick Dunglison
Scott, Walter
Smith, Gerald L. K.
Willett, Herbert Lockwood
Zollars, Ely Vaughn

Dutch Reformed
Berg, Joseph Frederic
Bethune, George Washington
Bourne, George
Chambers, Talbot Wilson
Corwin, Edward Tanjore
Drury, John Benjamin
Ferris, Isaac
Freeman, Bernardus
Frelinghuysen, Theodorus Jacobus
Goetschius, John Henry
Hardenbergh, Jacob Rutsen
Hartranft, Chester David
Livingston, John Henry
McClure, Alexander Wilson
Megapolensis, Johannes
Michaëlius, Jonas
Milledoler, Philip
Riddle, Matthew Brown
Seelye, Julius Hawley
Selijns, Henricus
Talmage, Thomas DeWitt
Taylor, Graham
Van Rensselaer, Nicholas

Eastern Orthodox
Athenagoras I

Episcopal (See also Anglican)
Abbott, Edward
Adams, Jasper
Allen, Alexander Viets Griswold
Allen, George
Andrews, John
Beardsley, Eben Edwards
Beasley, Frederick
Bell, Bernard Iddings
Bird, Frederic Mayer
Blake, John Lauris
Brady, Cyrus Townsend
Breck, James Lloyd
Briggs, Charles Augustus
Bristed, John
Chamberlain, Nathan Henry
Chapin, Alonzo Bowen
Coit, Henry Augustus
Coit, Thomas Winthrop
Cooper, Myles
Crapsey, Algernon Sidney
Croswell, Harry
Cummins, George David
Curtis, Moses Ashley
Cutler, Timothy
Dalcho, Frederick
De Costa, Benjamin Franklin
De Koven, James
Dix, Morgan
Doddridge, Joseph
Ewer, Ferdinand Cartwright
Flagg, Jared Bradley
Francis, Paul James
Gavin, Frank Stanton Burns
Goodwin, Hannibal Williston
Grant, Percy Stickney
Griswold, Alexander Viets
Hall, Charles Henry
Hare, George Emlen
Harris, William
Hawks, Francis Lister
Henry, Caleb Sprague
Hodges, George
Hoffman, Eugene Augustus
Houghton, George Hendric
Humes, Thomas William
Huntington, William Reed
Ingraham, Joseph Holt
Jarratt, Devereux
Jarvis, Abraham
Jones, Hugh
Kilbourne, James
King, William Benjamin Basil
Knight, Henry Cogswell
Langdon, William Chauncy
Leach, Daniel Dyer
Leaming, Jeremiah
Le Jau, Francis
Lord, William Wilberforce
Lowell, Robert Traill Spence
McCabe, John Collins
McCook, John James
MacSparran, James
McVickar, John
Mahan, Milo
Mansfield, Richard
Mombert, Jacob Isidor
Montgomery, James Alan
Moore, James, 1764–1814
Muhlenberg, William Augustus
Mulford, Elisha
Murphy, Edgar Gardner
Nash, Daniel

Nash, Henry Sylvester
Newton, Richard
Newton, Richard Heber
Newton, William Wilberforce
Nies, James Buchanan
Norton, John Nicholas
Norwood, Robert Winkworth
Oertel, Johannes Adam Simon
Ogden, Uzal
Packard, Joseph
Park, Roswell
Pendleton, William Nelson
Penick, Charles Clifton
Peterkin, George William
Peters, John Punnett
Pettigrew, Charles
Piggot, Robert
Pilmore, Joseph
Pinney, Norman
Pott, Francis Lister Hawks
Potter, Eliphalet Nott
Pynchon, Thomas Ruggles
Rainsford, William Stephen
Russell, James Solomon
Satterlee, Henry Yates
Savage, Thomas Staughton
Schroeder, John Frederick
Scott, Thomas Fielding
Seabury, Samuel, 1801–1872
Shelton, Frederick William
Shields, Charles Woodruff
Shoup, Francis Asbury
Slafter, Edmund Farwell
Slaughter, Philip
Smith, John Cotton, 1826–1882
Smith, William, 1754–1821
Sparrow, William
Spencer, Jesse Ames
Sterrett, James Macbride
Stokes, Anson Phelps
Stone, John Seely
Stuck, Hudson
Tolman, Herbert Cushing
Tomkins, Floyd Williams
Tucker, Henry St. George
Turner, Samuel Hulbeart
Tyng, Stephen Higginson
Tyson, Stuart Lawrence
Vesey, William
Vinton, Alexander Hamilton
Vinton, Francis
Walden, Jacob Treadwell
Ward, Henry Dana
Washburn, Edward Abiel
Weems, Mason Locke
Wharton, Charles Henry
Wharton, Francis
Wheaton, Nathaniel Sheldon
White, George
Wilmer, James Jones
Wilmer, William Holland
Wilson, Bird
Wilson, William Dexter
Winslow, William Copley
Worcester, Elwood

Evangelical Lutheran
Dinwiddie, Edwin Courtland

Friends (See Quaker)

German Reformed
Bausman, Benjamin
Boehm, John Philip
Bomberger, John Henry
Bucher, John Conrad
Dubbs, Joseph Henry
Good, James Isaac
Good, Jeremiah Haak
Gros, John Daniel
Harbaugh, Henry
Helffenstein, John Albert Conrad
Hendel, John William
Herman, Lebrecht Frederick
Mayer, Lewis
Miller, John Peter
Otterbein, Philip William
Rupp, William
Schlatter, Michael
Stahr, John Summers

Greek Orthodox
Callimachos, Panos Demetrios

Jewish
Adler, Samuel
Asher, Joseph Mayor
Berkowitz, Henry
Blaustein, David
Einhorn, David
Enelow, Hyman Gerson
Felsenthal, Bernhard
Gottheil, Gustav
Grossmann, Louis
Harris, Maurice Henry
Heller, Maximilian
Hirsch, Emil Gustav
Hirschensohn, Chaim
Isaacs, Samuel Myer
Jastrow, Marcus
Kagan, Henry Enoch
Kalisch, Isidor
Kohler, Kaufmann
Kohut, Alexander
Kohut, George Alexander
Krauskopf, Joseph
Leeser, Isaac
Levy, Joseph Leonard
Liebman, Joshua Loth
Lilienthal, Max
Magnes, Judah Leon
Mendes, Frederic De Sola
Mendes, Henry Pereira
Meyer, Martin Abraham
Mielziner, Moses
Morais, Sabato
Philipson, David
Raphall, Morris Jacob
Schindler, Solomon
Seixas, Gershom Mendes
Silver, Abba Hillel
Silverman, Joseph
Szold, Benjamin
Voorsanger, Jacob
Wise, Aaron
Wise, Isaac Mayer
Wise, Stephen Samuel

Latter-Day Saints (See Mormon)

Lutheran
Acrelius, Israel
Bachman, John
Baugher, Henry Louis
Berkenmeyer, Wilhelm Christoph
Bird, Frederic Mayer
Boltzius, Johann Martin
Campanius, John
Clausen, Claus Lauritz
Dahl, Theodor Halvorson
Deindörfer, Johannes
Demme, Charles Rudolph
Dietrichson, Johannes Wilhelm Christian
Douglas, Lloyd Cassel
Dylander, John
Eielsen, Erling
Esbjörn, Lars Paul
Falckner, Daniel
Falckner, Justus
Funk, Isaac Kauffman
Grabau, Johannes Andreas August
Greenwald, Emanuel
Grossmann, Georg Martin
Hartwig, Johann Christoph
Hasselquist, Tuve Nilsson
Hay, Charles Augustus
Hayme, Gjermund
Hazelius, Ernest Lewis
Helmuth, Justus Henry Christian
Henkel, Paul
Hoenecke, Gustav Adolf Felix Theodor
Hoffmann, Francis Arnold
Horn, Edward Traill
Hunton, William Lee
Jacobs, Michael
Kildahl, Johan Nathan
Kocherthal, Josua von
Koren, John
Koren, Ulrik Vihelm
Krauth, Charles Philip
Krauth, Charles Porterfield
Kunze, John Christopher
Kurtz, Benjamin
Larsen, Peter Laurentius
Lenker, John Nicholas
Lindberg, Conrad Emil
Lochman, John George
Loy, Matthias
Maier, Walter Arthur
Mann, William Julius
Mayer, Philip Frederick
Melsheimer, Friedrich Valentin
Moldehnke, Edward Frederick
Morris, John Gottlieb
Muhlenberg, Frederick Augustus
Muhlenberg, Frederick Augustus Conrad
Mühlenberg, Gotthilf Henry Ernest
Muhlenberg, Henry Augustus Philip
Mühlenberg, Henry Melchior
Muhlenberg, John Peter Gabriel
Norelius, Eric
Oftedal, Sven
Passavant, William Alfred
Preus, Christian Keyser
Richard, James William
Sadtler, John Philip Benjamin
Schaeffer, Charles Frederick
Schaeffer, Charles William
Schaeffer, David Frederick
Schaeffer, Frederick Christian
Schaeffer, Frederick David
Schmauk, Theodore Emanuel
Schmucker, Beale Melanchthon
Schmucker, John George
Schmucker, Samuel Simon

Schodde, George Henry
Seip, Theodore Lorenzo
Seiss, Joseph Augustus
Spaeth, Adolph
Sprecher, Samuel
Stöckhardt, Karl Georg
Stub, Hans Gerhard
Swensson, Carl Aaron
Walther, Carl Ferdinand Wilhelm
Wenner, George Unangst

Mennonite
Goerz, David
Kolb, Dielman
Krehbiel, Christian
Rittenhouse, William

Methodist
Alexander, Gross
Asbury, Francis
Atkinson, John
Bangs, Nathan
Beauchamp, William
Bewley, Anthony
Boehm, Henry
Brown, Ebenezer
Buckley, James Monroe
Buttz, Henry Anson
Cadman, Samuel Parkes
Cain, Richard Harvey
Candler, Warren Akin
Cannon, James
Cartwright, Peter
Collyer, Robert
Cooper, Ezekiel
Cramer, Michael John
Crane, Frank
Crane, Jonathan Townley
Crooks, George Richard
Cummings, Joseph
Day, James Roscoe
Dean, Sidney
Deems, Charles Force
Dickins, John
Dorchester, Daniel
Durbin, John Price
Eaton, Homer
Elliott, Charles
Embury, Philip
Evans, Warren Felt
Fairbank, Calvin
Finley, James Bradley
Fisk, Wilbur
Floy, James
Foss, Cyrus David
Gammon, Elijah Hedding
Garrettson, Freeborn
Green, Alexander Little Page
Hamline, Leonidas Lent
Harrell, John
Harrison, William Pope
Hibbard, Freeborn Garrettson
Hogan, John
Hogue, Wilson Thomas
Hopkins, Isaac Stiles
Huntington, William Edwards
Hurlbut, Jesse Lyman
Inskip, John Swanel
Jaquess, James Frazier
Kidder, Daniel Parish
Kynett, Alpha Jefferson
Lane, John
Larrabee, William Clark
Lee, Jesse
Lee, Luther
Lipscomb, Andrew Adgate
McAnally, David Rice
McCaine, Alexander
M'Clintock, John
McFarland, John Thomas
McFerrin, John Berry
Mattison, Hiram
Merrick, Frederick
Milburn, William Henry
Mitchell, Hinckley Gilbert Thomas
Mood, Francis Asbury
Mudge, Enoch
Mudge, James
Nast, William
Nelson, Reuben
O'Kelly, James
Olin, Stephen
Palmore, William Beverly
Parkhurst, Charles
Peck, George
Peirce, Bradford Kinney
Ray, Charles Bennett
Reid, John Morrison
Revels, Hiram Rhoades
Ridgaway, Henry Bascom
Roberts, Benjamin Titus
Rowlands, William
Rust, Richard Sutton
Ruter, Martin
Shaw, Anna Howard
Shinn, Asa
Shipp, Albert Micajah
Sims, Charles N.
Sloan, Harold Paul
Smith, William Andrew
Snethen, Nicholas
Steele, Daniel
Stevens, Abel
Stockton, Thomas Hewlings
Strawbridge, Robert
Stuart, Charles Macaulay
Summers, Thomas Osmond
Swallow, Silas Comfort
Taylor, Marshall William
Terry, Milton Spenser
Tigert, John James
Tittle, Ernest Fremont
Townsend, Luther Tracy
Upham, Samuel Foster
Vail, Stephen Montfort
Van Meter, John Blackford
Wakeley, Joseph Burton
Warren, William Fairfield
Webb, Thomas
Whedon, Daniel Denison
Wiley, Ephraim Emerson
Williams, Robert
Winans, William
Wise, Daniel
Young, Jesse Bowman

Methodist Episcopal
North, Frank Mason
Wilson, Clarence True

Moravian (See United Brethren)

Mormon
Cannon, George Quayle
Clark, Joshua Reuben, Jr.
Godbe, William Samuel
Kimball, Heber Chase
Lee, John Doyle
Pratt, Parley Parker
Rigdon, Sidney
Roberts, Brigham Henry
Sharp, John
Smith, Joseph, 1805–1844
Smith, Joseph, 1832–1914
Snow, Lorenzo
Strang, James Jesse
Taylor, John
Whitmer, David
Woodruff, Wilford
Young, Brigham

Nonconformist
Chauncy, Charles 1592–1671/2
Chauncy, Charles 1705–1787
Eaton, Samuel
Higginson, Francis
Lothropp, John
Ward, Nathaniel

Presbyterian
Abbot, Gorham Dummer
Adams, William
Alexander, Archibald
Alexander, Samuel Davies
Alison, Francis
Anderson, John Alexander
Armstrong, George Dod
Babcock, Maltbie Davenport
Baird, Charles Washington
Baird, Henry Martyn
Baird, Robert
Baird, Samuel John
Baker, Daniel
Baker, William Mumford
Baldwin, Elihu Whittlesey
Barnes, Albert
Beard, Richard
Beattie, Francis Robert
Beatty, Charles Clinton
Beecher, Lyman
Beman, Nathan Sidney Smith
Bishop, Robert Hamilton
Blackburn, Gideon
Blackburn, William Maxwell
Blair, Samuel
Blanchard, Jonathan
Bourne, George
Boynton, Charles Brandon
Brainerd, Thomas
Breckinridge, John, 1797–1841
Breckinridge, Robert Jefferson
Brown, Isaac Van Arsdale
Brown, William Adams
Brownlee, William Craig
Bruce, Robert
Burchard, Samuel Dickinson
Burr, Aaron
Burrell, David James
Bush, George
Caldwell, David
Caldwell, James
Cameron, Archibald
Campbell, William Henry
Carrick, Samuel
Cattell, William Cassaday
Cavert, Samuel McCrea
Chavis, John
Coffin, Henry Sloane
Colman, Benjamin
Converse, James Booth
Corrothers, James David

Cox, Samuel Hanson
Crosby, Howard
Curtis, Edward Lewis
Cuyler, Theodore Ledyard
Darling, Henry
Davidson, Robert
Doak, Samuel
Dod, Albert Baldwin
Dod, Thaddeus
Donnell, Robert
Duffield, George, 1732–1790
Duffield, George, 1794–1868
Duffield, Samuel Augustus Willoughby
Dwight, Benjamin Woodbridge
Ewing, John
Field, Henry Martyn
Finley, Robert
Finley, Samuel
Fisher, Daniel Webster
Foote, William Henry
Frey, Joseph Samuel Christian Frederick
Frissell, Hollis Burke
Gale, George Washington
Gally, Merritt
Garnet, Henry Highland
Gaut, John McReynolds
Gilbert, Eliphalet Wheeler
Gillett, Ezra Hall
Girardeau, John Lafayette
Goulding, Francis Robert
Green, Ashbel
Green, Jacob
Green, Lewis Warner
Gregory, Daniel Seelye
Hall, Baynard Rush
Hall, Charles Cuthbert
Hall, James, 1744–1826
Hall, John
Hatfield, Edwin Francis
Headley, Phineas Camp
Henry, Robert
Hewat, Alexander
Hickok, Laurens Perseus
Hoge, Moses
Hoge, Moses Drury
House, Samuel Reynolds
Howe, George
Hunter, Andrew
Jackson, Samuel Macauley
Jacobs, William Plumer
Junkin, George
Kellogg, Samuel Henry
Kirk, Edward Norris
Knox, Samuel
Lacy, Drury
Lindley, Daniel
Lindsley, John Berrien
Lindsley, Philip
Linn, John Blair
Lunn, George Richard
Lyon, James
McAfee, John Armstrong
McAuley, Thomas
McBride, F(rancis) Scott
McCalla, William Latta
McCook, Henry Christopher
McCormick, Samuel Black
MacCracken, Henry Mitchell
McDowell, John
McFarland, Samuel Gamble
McGready, James
McIlwaine, Richard
McLeod, Alexander
MacWhorter, Alexander
Makemie, Francis
Marquis, John Abner
Mason, John Mitchell
Mattoon, Stephen
Mears, David Otis
Mears, John William
Miller, James Russell
Miller, John
Miller, Samuel
Mitchell, Edwin Knox
Moorehead, William Gallogly
Morris, Edward Dafydd
Morrison, William McCutchan
Murray, James Ormsbee
Neill, Edward Duffield
Neill, William
Nelson, David
Nevin, Alfred
Nevin, Edwin Henry
Nisbet, Charles
Noble, Frederick Alphonso
Nott, Eliphalet
Osborn, Henry Stafford
Palmer, Benjamin Morgan
Parker, Joel
Parker, Thomas
Parkhurst, Charles Henry
Patillo, Henry
Patterson, Robert Mayne
Patton, Francis Landey
Patton, William
Peck, Thomas Ephraim
Peters, Absalom
Peters, Madison Clinton
Pierson, Arthur Tappan
Pierson, Hamilton Wilcox
Plumer, William Swan
Prentiss, George Lewis
Prime, Edward Dorr Griffin
Prime, Samuel Irenaeus
Purviance, David
Reed, Richard Clark
Reid, William Shields
Rice, David
Rice, John Holt
Rice, Nathan Lewis
Roberts, William Charles
Roberts, William Henry
Robinson, Charles Seymour
Robinson, Stuart
Rodgers, John, 1727–1811
Ruffner, Henry
Ruffner, William Henry
Sanders, Daniel Jackson
Sawyer, Leicester Ambrose
Scott, William Anderson
Simpson, Albert Benjamin
Skinner, Thomas Harvey
Smith, Asa Dodge
Smith, Benjamin Mosby
Smith, Henry Boynton
Smith, Henry Preserved
Smith, John Blair
Smith, Samuel Stanhope
Smyth, Thomas
Speer, Robert Elliott
Spencer, Elihu
Spring, Gardiner
Sproull, Thomas
Stelzle, Charles
Stryker, Melancthon Woolsey
Swing, David
Taylor, Archibald Alexander Edward
Tennent, Gilbert
Tennent, William, 1673–1745
Tennent, William, 1705–1777
Thacher, Peter
Thompson, William Oxley
Thornwell, James Henley
Van Dyke, Henry
Van Rensselaer, Cortlandt
Vincent, Marvin Richardson
Voris, John Ralph
Waddel, James
Waddel, John Newton
Waddel, Moses
Walker, James Barr
Warfield, Benjamin Breckinridge
Whitaker, Nathaniel
Whitworth, George Frederic
Wiley, David
Willey, Samuel Hopkins
Wilson, Joshua Lacy
Wilson, Samuel Ramsay
Wilson, Warren Hugh
Witherspoon, John
Wood, James
Woodrow, James
Woods, Leonard, 1807–1878
Yeomans, John William
Young, John Clarke
Zubly, John Joachim

Protestant Episcopal (See Episcopal)

Puritan

Bulkeley, Peter
Cotton, John
Holden, Oliver
Mather, Cotton
Mather, Increase
Mather, Richard
Mayhew, Jonathan
Morton, Charles
Norton, John
Parris, Samuel
Sherman, John, 1613–1685
Stone, Samuel
Taylor, Edward
Weld, Thomas
Whitfield, Henry
Wigglesworth, Michael
Williams, Roger
Wilson, John
Woodbridge, John

Quaker

Chalkley, Thomas
Coffin, Charles Fisher
Comstock, Elizabeth L.
Evans, Thomas
Grellet, Stephen
Hallowell, Benjamin
Hicks, Elias
Hoag, Joseph
Hubbs, Rebecca
Hunt, Nathan
Janney, Samuel McPherson
Jay, Allen
Jones, Sybil
Kelsey, Rayner Wickersham

Mott, Lucretia Coffin
Muste, Abraham Johannes
Owen, Griffith
Pemberton, John
Pugh, Ellis
Sands, David
Savery, William, 1750–1804
Scattergood, Thomas
Scott, Job
Updegraff, David Brainard
Waln, Nicholas
Wilbur, John

Reformed Church in America
Schenck, Ferdinand Schureman
Searle, John Preston
Thompson, John Bodine
Van Nest, Abraham Rynier
Woodbridge, Samuel Merrill

Roman Catholic
Andreis, Andrew James Felix Bartholomew de
Andrews, Samuel James
Andrews, William Watson
Antoine, Père
Barzyndski, Vincent
Bayma, Joseph
Behrens, Henry
Benavides, Alonzo de
Burke, John Joseph
Campbell, Thomas Joseph
Carr, Thomas Matthew
Conaty, Thomas James
Cooper, John Montgomery
Coppens, Charles
Corcoran, James Andrew
Cosby, William
Coughlin, Charles Edward
Curran, John Joseph
Currier, Charles Warren
Cushing, Richard James
Dabrowski, Joseph
Dietz, Peter Ernest
Dougherty, Dennis Joseph
Drumgoole, John Christopher
Du Bois, John
Du Bourg, Louis Guillaume Valentin
Duffy, Francis Patrick
Dwenger, Joseph
Elder, William Henry
Elliott, Walter Hacket Robert
Farley, John Murphy
Fenwick, Benedict Joseph
Ffrench, Charles Dominic
Finn, Francis James
Finotti, Joseph Maria
Fitzgerald, Edward
Flanagan, Edward Joseph
Francis, Paul James
Gallagher, Hugh Patrick
Ganss, Henry George
Garrigan, Philip Joseph
Gasson, Thomas Ignatius
Gibbons, James
Gilmour, Richard
Gmeiner, John
Goupil, René
Greaton, Joseph
Guilday, Peter Keenan
Haid, Leo
Harding, Robert
Hayes, Patrick Joseph
Hecker, Isaac Thomas
Hennepin, Louis
Hennessy, John
Henni, John Martin
Hessoun, Joseph
Hewit, Augustine Francis
Hubbard, Bernard Rosecrans
Hudson, Daniel Eldred
Hughes, John Joseph
Hurley, Joseph Patrick
Ireland, John, 1838–1918
Johnson, George
Joubert de la Muraille, James Hector Marie Nicholas
Judge, Thomas Augustine
Katzer, Frederic Xavier
Keane, James John
Keane, John Joseph
Keller, James Gregory
Kenrick, Francis Patrick
Kenrick, Peter Richard
Kerby, William Joseph
Kirlin, Joseph Louis Jerome
Kohlmann, Anthony
LaFarge, John
Lambert, Louis Aloisius
Lambing, Andrew Arnold
Lamy, John Baptist
Larkin, John
Lee, James Wideman
Levins, Thomas C.
Loras, Jean Mathias Pierre
Lynch, Patrick Neeson
Maas, Anthony J.
McCaffrey, John
McCloskey, John
McCloskey, William George
McElroy, John, 1782–1877
McFaul, James Augustine
McGill, John
McGivney, Michael Joseph
McGlynn, Edward
McGrath, James
McGuire, Charles Bonaventure
McIntyre, James Francis Aloysius
Machebeuf, Joseph Provectus
Maes, Camillus Paul
Malone, Sylvester
Maréchal, Ambrose
Marest, Pierre Gabriel
Marty, Martin
Matignon, Francis Anthony
Meerschaert, Théophile
Merton, Thomas
Messmer, Sebastian Gebhard
Meyer, Albert Gregory
Michel, Virgil George
Miles, Richard Pius
Ming, John Joseph
Moeller, Henry
Molyneux, Robert
Moore, John, 1834–1901
Moosmüller, Oswald William
Moriarity, Patrick Eugene
Morini, Austin John
Mundelein, George William
Neale, Leonard
Nerinckx, Charles
Neumann, John Nepomucene
Nieuwland, Julius Arthur
Nobili, John
O'Brien, Matthew Anthony
O'Callaghan, Jeremiah
O'Callahan, Joseph Timothy
O'Connor, James
O'Connor, Michael
Odenbach, Frederick Louis
Odin, John Mary
O'Gorman, Thomas
Ortynsky, Stephen Soter
Pace, Edward Aloysius
Pardow, William O'Brien
Patrick, John Ryan
Perché, Napoleon Joseph
Phelan, David Samuel
Pise, Charles Constantine
Portier, Michael
Power, John
Preston, Thomas Scott
Price, Thomas Frederick
Purcell, John Baptist
Quarter, William
Quigley, James Edward
Rese, Frederick
Reuter, Dominic
Rigge, William Francis
Riordan, Patrick William
Ritter, Joseph Elmer
Robot, Isidore
Rosati, Joseph
Rosecrans, Sylvester Horton
Rouquette, Adrien Emmanuel
Ryan, Abram Joseph
Ryan, John Augustine
Ryan, Patrick John
Ryan, Stephen Vincent
Saenderl, Simon
Scanlan, Lawrence
Schnerr, Leander
Schrembs, Joseph
Seghers, Charles Jean
Semmes, Alexander Jenkins
Sestini, Benedict
Seton, Robert
Shahan, Thomas Joseph
Sheen, Fulton John
Sheil, Bernard James
Shields, Thomas Edward
Sorin, Edward Frederick
Spalding, John Lancaster
Spalding, Martin John
Spellman, Francis Joseph
Stang, William
Stehle, Aurelius Aloysius
Stone, James Kent
Tabb, John Banister
Talbot, Francis Xavier
Thébaud, Augustus J.
Tierney, Richard Henry
Timon, John
Tondorf, Francis Anthony
Turner, William
Tyler, William
Van de Velde, James Oliver
Varela y Morales, Félix Francisco José María de la Concepción
Verot, Jean Marcel Pierre Auguste
Viel, François Étienne Bernard Alexandre
Walsh, Edmund Aloysius
Walsh, James Anthony
Walsh, Thomas Joseph

White, Charles Ignatius
Wigger, Winand Michael
Williams, John Joseph
Wilson, Samuel Thomas
Wimmer, Boniface
Wolf, Innocent William
Wood, James Frederick
Wright, John Joseph
Yorke, Peter Christopher
Young, Alfred
Young, Josue Maria
Zahm, John Augustine
Russian Orthodox
Leonty, Metropolitan
Society of Friends (See Quaker)
Southern Baptist
Dodd, Monroe Elmon
Norris, John Franklyn
Rawlinson, Frank Joseph
Scarborough, Lee Rutland
Truett, George Washington
Swedenborgian
Barrett, Benjamin Fiske
Brown, Solyman
Giles, Chauncey
Mercer, Lewis Pyle
Reed, James, 1834–1921
Sewall, Frank
Smyth, Julian Kennedy
Unaffiliated
Craig, Austin
Newton, Joseph Fort
Spencer, Anna Garlin
Unitarian
Abbot, Francis Ellingwood
Alger, William Rounseville
Allen, Joseph Henry
Ames, Charles Gordon
Barnard, Charles Francis
Barrows, Samuel June
Bartol, Cyrus Augustus
Batchelor, George
Bellows, Henry Whitney
Bentley, William
Bixby, James Thompson
Brazer, John
Brooks, Charles
Brooks, Charles Timothy
Buckminster, Joseph Stevens
Burnap, George Washington
Burton, Warren
Chadwick, John White
Channing, William Ellery
Channing, William Henry
Clarke, James Freeman
Colman, Henry
Conway, Moncure Daniel
Cooke, George Willis
Cranch, Christopher Pearse
Crothers, Samuel McChord
Cummings, Edward
Dewey, Orville
Ellis, George Edward
Emerson, William
Everett, Edward
Fenn, William Wallace
Follen, Charles
Francis, Convers
Freeman, James
Frothingham, Nathaniel Langdon
Frothingham, Octavius Brooks
Frothingham, Paul Revere
Furness, William Henry
Gannett, Ezra Stiles
Gannett, William Channing
Gilman, Samuel
Hale, Edward Everett
Harris, Thaddeus Mason
Hedge, Frederic Henry
Hill, Thomas
Holley, Horace
Holmes, John Haynes
Hosmer, Frederick Lucian
Huntington, Frederic Dan
Janson, Kristofer Nagel
Jones, Jenkin Lloyd
Judd, Sylvester
King, Thomas Starr
Leonard, Levi Washburn
Livermore, Abiel Abbot
Longfellow, Samuel
Lowe, Charles
MacCauley, Clay
Mann, Newton
May, Samuel Joseph
Mayo, Amory Dwight
Metcalf, Joel Hastings
Miles, Henry Adolphus
Noyes, George Rapall
Palfrey, John Gorham
Parker, Theodore
Peabody, Andrew Preston
Peabody, Francis Greenwood
Peabody, Oliver William Bourn
Peabody, William Bourn Oliver
Pierpont, John
Potter, William James
Powell, Edward Payson
Reed, David
Ripley, Ezra
Robbins, Chandler
Savage, Minot Judson
Sears, Edmund Hamilton
Slicer, Thomas Roberts
Stearns, Oliver
Stebbins, Horatio
Stebbins, Rufus Phineas
Tuckerman, Joseph
Upham, Charles Wentworth
Walker, James
Ware, Henry, 1794–1843
Ware, John Fothergill Waterhouse
Ware, William
Weiss, John
Wendte, Charles William
West, Samuel
Wheelwright, John
Wiggin, James Henry
Willard, Samuel, 1775–1859
Woolley, Celia Parker
Young, Alexander
Zachos, John Celivergos
United Brethren
Beardshear, William Miller
Berger, Daniel
Clewell, John Henry
Flickinger, Daniel Kumler
Holland, William Jacob
Jungman, John George
Kephart, Isaiah Lafayette
Peter, John Frederick
Reichel, William Cornelius
Schultze, Augustus
Schweinitz, Lewis David von
Shuey, William John
Zinzendorf, Nicolaus Ludwig
United Evangelical
Poling, Daniel Alfred
Universalist
Adams, John Coleman
Ballou, Adin
Ballou, Hosea
Cobb, Sylvanus
Edwin, Hubbell Chapin
Ferguson, William Porter Frisbee
Fisher, Ebenezer
Hanaford, Phoebe Ann Coffin
Hudson, Charles
Kneeland, Abner
Miner, Alonzo Ames
Sawyer, Thomas Jefferson
Spear, Charles
Thayer, Thomas Baldwin
Whittemore, Thomas
CLIMATOLOGIST (See also METEOROLOGIST)
De Brahm, William Gerard
Logan, Thomas Muldrup, 1808–1876
Ward, Robert De Courcy
CLOCKMAKER (See also MANUFACTURER, WATCH)
Camp, Hiram
Harland, Thomas
Jerome, Chauncey
Terry, Eli
Thomas, Seth
Willard, Simon
CLOWN
Adler, Felix
Kelly, Emmett Leo
Rice, Dan
CLUB WOMAN
Choate, Anne Hyde Clarke
COAL MERCHANT
Clothier, William Jackson
COAL MINER
Haywood, Allan Shaw
COAL OPERATOR (See also INDUSTRIALIST)
Brown, William Hughey
Horton, Valentine Baxter
Pardee, Ario
Parrish, Charles
Roche, Josephine Aspinwall
Scott, William Lawrence
Thompson, Josiah Van Kirk
COAST GUARD OFFICER (See also NAVAL OFFICER)
Smith, Edward Hanson
Waesche, Russell Randolph
COLLECTOR (See also ART COLLECTOR, BOOK COLLECTOR, NUMISMATIST)
Bement, Clarence Sweet (minerals)
Clarke, Thomas Benedict (art)
Cone, Claribel (art)
Cone, Etta (art)
Disbrow, William Stephen (misc.)
Draper, Lyman Copeland (frontier history)

Emmett, Burton (prints)
Ffoulke, Charles Mather (tapestries)
Fisher, George Jackson (anatomical illustrations)
Folger, Henry Clay (Shakespeareana)
Guggenheim, Solomon Robert (art)
Harrah, William Fisk ("Bill") (cars)
Hawkins, Rush Christopher (incunabula)
Horner, Henry (Lincolniana)
Isham, Ralph Heyward (manuscripts)
Jacobs, Joseph, 1859–1929 (Burnsiana)
Lewis, Edmund Darch (misc.)
Lomax, John Avery (folk songs)
Lowery, Woodbury (maps)
Meserve, Frederick Hill (Lincolniana)
Miles, John Jacob (music)
Nutting, Wallace (antiques)
Pringle, Cyrus Guernsey (plants)
Riggs, William Henry (armor)
Rindge, Frederick Hastings (coins)
Scharf, John Thomas (Americana)
Sprague, William Buell (autographs)
Stauffer, David McNeely (autographic historical material)
Steinert, Morris (musical instruments)
Thomas, George Clifford (autographic historical material)
Vincent, Frank (antiquities)
Wilson, Ernest Henry (plants)

College Administrator
Fulton, Robert Burwell
Geddes, James Lorraine
Keppel, Frederick Paul
Perkins, George Henry
Royster, James Finch
Small, Albion Woodbury

College President
Adams, Charles Kendall
Adams, Jasper
Alden, Timothy
Alderman, Edwin Anderson
Allen, William Henry
Ames, Joseph Sweetman
Anderson, Galusha
Anderson, John Alexander
Anderson, Martin Brewer
Andrews, Elisha Benjamin
Andrews, Israel Ward
Andrews, Lorin
Angell, James Burrill
Angell, James Rowland
Atherton, George Washington
Atwood, Wallace Walter
Aydelotte, Frank
Ayres, Brown
Backus, Azel
Bailey, Rufus William
Baker, Hugh Potter
Baker, James Hutchins
Baldwin, Elihu Whittlesey
Ballou, Hosea
Barnard, Frederick Augustus Porter
Barrows, David Prescott
Barrows, John Henry
Bartlett, Samuel Colcord
Bascom, Henry Bidleman
Bascom, John
Bashford, James Whitford
Bass, William Capers
Battle, Kemp Plummer
Baugher, Henry Louis
Beardshear, William Miller
Beecher, Edward
Beman, Nathan Sidney Smith
Bennett, Henry Garland
Benton, Allen Richardson
Bethune, Mary McLeod
Blackburn, Gideon
Blackburn, William Maxwell
Blanchard, Jonathan
Bomberger, John Henry Augustus
Bowman, Isaiah
Bradley, John Edwin
Breckinridge, Robert Jefferson
Bronk, Detlev Wulf
Brown, Elmer Ellsworth
Brown, Francis
Brown, Samuel Gilman
Brownell, Thomas Church
Bryan, John Stewart
Burr, Aaron
Burton, Ernest DeWitt
Burton, Marion Le Roy
Butler, Nicholas Murray
Butterfield, Kenyon Leech
Cain, Richard Harvey
Caldwell, Joseph
Camm, John
Campbell, Prince Lucien
Campbell, William Henry
Candler, Warren Akin
Capen, Elmer Hewitt
Carnahan, James
Carrick, Samuel
Carter, Franklin
Caswell, Alexis
Cattell, William Cassaday
Chadbourne, Paul Ansel
Chandler, Julian Alvin Carroll
Chapin, Aaron Lucius
Chaplin, Jeremiah
Chase, Harry Woodburn
Chase, Thomas
Chauncey, Charles
Cheney, Oren Burbank
Clapp, Charles Horace
Clark, William Smith
Coffman, Lotus Delta
Compton, Karl Taylor
Conant, James Bryant
Cooper, Myles
Corby, William
Cordier, Andrew Wellington
Crafts, James Mason
Cravath, Erastus Milo
Craven, Braxton
Cummings, Joseph
Cutler, Carroll
Daggett, Naphtali
Darling, Henry
Davies, Samuel
Davis, Harvey Nathaniel
Davis, Henry
Day, Jeremiah
Dennett, Tyler (Wilbur)
Dickinson, Jonathan
Dunster, Henry
Durant, Henry
Dwight, Timothy, 1752–1817
Dwight, Timothy, 1828–1916
Dykstra, Clarence Addison
Eaton, Nathaniel
Eisenhower, Dwight D.
Eliot, Charles William
Estabrook, Joseph
Fairchild, George Thompson
Fairchild, James Harris
Farrand, Livingston
Faunce, William Herbert Perry
Ferris, Isaac
Few, Ignatius Alphonso
Fisher, Daniel Webster
Folwell, William Watts
Foster, William Trufant
Fox, Dixon Ryan
Fraley, Samuel
Frank, Glenn
Frelinghuysen, Theodore
Frieze, Henry Simmons
Furman, James Clement
Gambrell, Mary Latimer
Garfield, Harry Augustus
Garland, Landon Cabell
Gates, Caleb Frank
Gates, Thomas Sovereign
Gerhart, Emanuel Vogel
Gilbert, Eliphalet Wheeler
Gilman, Daniel Coit
Glueck, Nelson
Goodell, Henry Hill
Goodnow, Frank Johnson
Goodwin, Daniel Raynes
Goucher, John Franklin
Graham, Edward Kidder
Graves, Zuinglius Calvin
Green, Ashbel
Gregg, John Andrew
Gregory, John Milton
Griffin, Edward Dorr
Griswold, Alfred Whitney
Gummere, Samuel James
Hadley, Arthur Twining
Hadley, Herbert Spencer
Hardenbergh, Jacob Rutsen
Harris, William
Hasbrouck, Abraham Bruyn
Hibben, John Grier
Hickok, Laurens Perseus
Hill, David Jayne
Hill, Thomas
Hinman, George Wheeler
Hoar, Leonard
Holt, Hamilton Bowen
Horrocks, James
Howard, Ada Lydia
Humes, Thomas William
Humphrey, Heman
Huntington, William Edwards
Hutchins, Harry Burns

Hyer, Robert Stewart
James, Edmund Janes
Jessup, Walter Albert
Johns, John
Johnson, Mordecai Wyatt
Johnson, Samuel
Jordan, David Starr
Kephart, Ezekiel Boring
King, Charles
King, Stanley
Kirkland, James Hampton
Kirkland, John Thornton
Knapp, Bradford
Krauth, Charles Philip
Langdon, Samuel
Lathrop, John Hiram
Leverett, John, 1662–1724
Lipscomb, Andrew Adgate
Livermore, Abiel Abbot
Loos, Charles Louis
Lord, Nathan
Low, Seth
Lowell, Abbott Lawrence
McBryde, John McLaren
McCosh, James
McGlothlin, William Joseph
McIlwaine, Richard
McKeen, Joseph
Maclean, John
McNair, Fred Walter
McVey, Frank Lerond
Madison, James
Magill, Edward Hicks
Magnes, Judah Leon
Magoun, George Frederic
Mahan, Asa
Main, John Hanson Thomas
Manning, James
Marquis, John Abner
Marsh, James
Maxcy, Jonathan
Maxwell, William
Mayes, Edward
Mendenhall, Thomas Corwin
Merrill, George Edmands
Middleton, Nathaniel Russell
Miner, Alonzo Ames
Mitchell, Edward Cushing
Moore, Benjamin
Moore, Nathaniel Fish
Moore, Zephaniah Swift
Morgan, Arthur Ernest
Morgan, John Harcourt Alexander
Morrison, Nathan Jackson
Mortimer, Mary
Morton, Henry
Muhlenberg, Frederick Augustus
Neilson, William Allan
Nichols, Ernest Fox
Nisbet, Charles
Northrop, Cyrus
Nott, Eliphalet
Oakes, Urian
Parrish, Edward
Patrick, Mary Mills
Patton, Francis Landey
Payne, Bruce Ryburn
Payne, Daniel Alexander
Pearson, Raymond Allen
Pendleton, Ellen Fitz
Pendleton, William Kimbrough
Porter, Noah
Pott, Francis Lister Hawks
Potter, Eliphalet Nott
Preus, Christian Keyser
Pritchett, Henry Smith
Pugh, Evan
Purnell, William Henry
Pynchon, Thomas Ruggles
Quincy, Josiah, 1772–1864
Rankin, Jeremiah Eames
Raymond, John Howard
Reid, John Morrison
Reinhardt, Aurelia Isabel Henry
Rhees, Rush
Rhoades, James E.
Robinson, Ezekiel Gilman
Runkle, John Daniel
Sadtler, John Philip Benjamin
Sanford, Edmund Clark
Scarborough, William Saunders
Schurman, Jacob Gould
Scott, Austin
Scott, Walter Dill
Seelye, Laurenus Clark
Seip, Theodore Lorenzo
Sewall, Joseph Addison
Seymour, Charles
Shafer, Helen Almira
Sharpless, Isaac
Shepard, James Edward
Shuster, George Nauman
Sims, Charles N.
Smart, James Henry
Smith, Asa Dodge
Smith, John Augustine
Smith, John Blair
Smith, Samuel Stanhope
Smith, William Andrew
Smith, William Waugh
Sparks, Edwin Erle
Sproul, Robert Gordon
Stearns, William Augustus
Stewart, Alexander Peter
Stiles, Ezra
Stith, William
Stockbridge, Horace Edward
Strong, James Woodward
Stryker, Melancthon Woolsey
Stuart, John Leighton
Swain, David Lowry
Tappan, Henry Philip
Taylor, James Monroe
Thatcher, Roscoe Wilfred
Thomas, Martha Carey
Thompson, William Oxley
Thomson, Edward
Thornwell, James Henley
Thwing, Charles Franklin
Tigert, John James, IV
Tyler, Lyon Gardiner
Van Hise, Charles Richard
Venable, Francis Preston
Vincent, George Edgar
Waddel, Moses
Wait, Samuel
Walker, James
Warren, William Fairfield
Wayland, Francis, 1796–1865
Webb, Alexander Stewart
Wheeler, Benjamin Ide
Wheelock, Eleazar
Wheelock, John
White, Andrew Dickson
White, Henry Clay
Whitsitt, William Heth
Wilbur, Ray Lyman
Willard, Joseph
Willard, Samuel
Williams, Walter
Wilson, Woodrow
Woods, Alva
Woods, Leonard
Woolley, Mary Emma
Woolsey, Theodore Dwight
Wylie, Andrew

COLONIAL AGENT
Argall, Sir Samuel
Ashmun, Jehudi
Barnwell, John
Bollan, William
De Berdt, Dennys
Dummer, Jeremiah
Partridge, Richard
Randolph, Edward
Sebastian, Benjamin
Vassall, John
Weld, Thomas

COLONIAL LEADER
Bacon, Nathaniel
Byrd, William
Carter, Robert
Clarke, George
Dinwiddie, Robert
Gayoso de Lemos, Manuel
Habersham, James
Hathorne, William
Holloway, John
Jenifer, Daniel of St. Thomas
Kennedy, Archibald
Minuit, Peter
Moore, John, *c.* 1659–1732
Newton, Thomas, 1660–1721
Nicholas, Robert Carter
Norris, Isaac, 1671–1735
Núñez Cabeza De Vaca, Alvar
Owen, Griffith
Pike, Robert
Randolph, William
Schuyler, Peter
Stuyvesant, Petrus
Van Cortlandt, Stephanus
Weare, Meshech
Wharton, Richard
Wingfield, Edward Maria
Wragg, William
Yeardley, Sir George
Youngs, John

COLONIST
Blackstone, William
Claiborne, William
Fenwick, George
Fenwick, John
Gardiner, Lion
Gookin, Daniel
Gorton, Samuel
Hack, George
Lane, Sir Ralph
Mason, George
Maverick, George
Oldham, John
Popham, George
Rolfe, John
Saltonstall, Richard
Sandys, George

Scholte, Hendrik Peter
Sedgwick, Robert
Van Curler, Arent
Van Der Donck, Adriaen
Weston, Thomas
Wilbur, Samuel
Willard, Simon
COLONIZER
Cameron, Robert Alexander
Coram, Thomas
Cutler, Manasseh
Dale, Sir Thomas
De Vries, David Pietersen
Durkee, John
Eaton, Theophilus
Finley, Robert
Gosnold, Bartholomew
Graffenried, Christopher, Baron de
Henderson, Richard
Hite, Jost
Krehbiel, Christian
Oñate, Juan de
Peerson, Cleng
Purry, Jean Pierre
Ribaut, Jean
St. Denis (Denys), Louis Juchereau de
Smith, Robert, 1722–1777
Turnbull, Andrew
Wingfield, Edward Maria
Young, Brigham
COLOR CINEMATOGRAPHER
Kalmus, Natalie Mabelle Dunfee
COMEDIAN (See also ACTOR, CLOWN, COMEDIENNE, ENTERTAINER, HUMORIST, WIT)
Abbott, William A. ("Bud")
Allen, Fred
Anderson, Edward ("Eddie")
Arquette, Clifford
Barton, James Edward
Benny, Jack
Blue, Ben
Bruce, Lenny
Cambridge, Godfrey MacArthur
Cantor, Eddie
Carson, Jack
Costello, Lou
Dale, Charles Marks
Daniels, Frank Albert
Durante, James Francis ("Jimmy")
Errol, Leon
Fields, Lewis Maurice
Fields, William Claude
Fine, Larry
Foy, Eddie
Hardy, Oliver Norvell
Hayes, Gabby
Haynes, Henry Doyle ("Homer")
Holland, George
Howard, Moe
Howard, Willie
Johnson, Harold Ogden ("Chic")
Jones, Lindley Armstrong ("Spike")
Keaton, Joseph Francis, V ("Buster")
Langdon, Harry Philmore
Laurel, Stan
Leonard, Jack E.
Marx, Adolf Arthur ("Harpo")
Marx, Leonard ("Chico")
Mostel, Samuel Joel ("Zero")
Olsen, John Sigvard ("Ole")
Prinze, Freddie
Shean, Albert
Smith, Solomon Franklin
Turpin, Ben
Weber, Joseph Morris
Wynn, Ed
COMEDIENNE (See also ACTRESS, ENTERTAINER, HUMORIST)
Ace, Jane
Brice, Fanny
Daley, Cass
Fazenda, Louise Marie
Mabley, Jackie ("Moms")
COMIC ARTIST (See CARTOONIST)
COMMERCIAL COUNSELOR
Kuskov, Ivan Aleksandrovich
COMMISSIONER OF EDUCATION
Tigert, John James, IV
COMMUNICATIONS EXECUTIVE
Newhouse, Samuel Irving
Sarnoff, David
COMMUNICATIONS EXPERT
Singer, Charles H.
COMMUNIST (See also MARXIST THEORIST)
Cabet, Étienne
Dennis, Eugene
Eisler, Gerhart
Fischer, Ruth
Minor, Robert
COMMUNIST LEADER
Bloor, Ella Reeve
Browder, Earl Russell
Foster, William Z.
Perry, Pettis
COMMUNITY BUILDER (See also CITY PLANNER, CIVIC LEADER)
Atkinson, George Henry
Kelley, Alfred
Wadsworth, James
COMMUNITY ORGANIZER
Alinsky, Saul David
Collier, John
COMPILER (See also BIBLIOGRAPHER, SCHOLAR)
Adams, Hannah
Disturnell, John
Law, Andrew
Sears, Robert
Swan, Timothy
Tenney, Tabitha Gilman
Tufts, John
Valentine, David Thomas
COMPOSER (See also HYMNOLOGIST, MUSICIAN, SONGWRITER)
Allen, Nathan H.
Alsop, Mary O'Hara
Armstrong, Henry Worthington ("Harry")
Baker, Benjamin Franklin
Bartlett, Homer Newton
Beach, Amy Marcy Cheney
Beck, Johann Heinrich
Bird, Arthur
Blitzstein, Marc
Bloch, Ernest
Blodgett, Benjamin Colman
Bond, Carrie Jacobs
Bristow, George Frederick
Buck, Dudley
Burleigh, Henry Thacker
Burton, Frederick Russell
Cadman, Charles Wakefield
Carpenter, John Alden
Casadesus, Robert Marcel
Casals, Pablo
Carr, Benjamin
Chadwick, George Whitefield
Chaplin, Charles Spencer ("Charlie")
Coerne, Louis Adolphe
Cohan, George Michael
Coltrane, John William
Converse, Charles Crozat
Converse, Frederick Shepherd
Cook, Will Marion
Damrosch, Leopold
Damrosch, Walter Johannes
De Koven, Henry Louis Reginald
De Rose, Peter
Dett, Robert Nathaniel
Dresel, Otto
Du Bois, Shirley Lola Graham
Duke, Vernon
Dunham, Henry Morton
Edwards, Julian
Eichberg, Julius
Ellington, Edward Kennedy ("Duke")
Elman, Harry ("Ziggy")
Emery, Stephen Albert
Engel, Cart
Evans, William John ("Bill")
Fairchild, Blair
Fairlamb, James Remington
Faith, Percy
Farwell, Arthur
Fielding, Jerry
Fisher, William Arms
Foote, Arthur William
Foster, Stephen Collins
Friml, Charles Rudolf
Fry, William Henry
Ganss, Henry George
Ganz, Rudolph
Garner, Erroll Louis
Gershwin, George
Gilbert, Henry Franklin Belknap
Gilchrist, William Wallace
Gleason, Frederic Grant
Godowsky, Leopold
Goldbeck, Robert
Goldman, Edwin Franko
Goldmark, Rubin
Gottschalk, Louis Moreau
Grainger, George Percy
Griffes, Charles Tomlinson
Grofé, Ferde
Hadley, Henry Kimball
Hammerstein, Oscar
Harney, Benjamin Robertson
Harris, LeRoy Ellsworth ("Roy")
Hastings, Thomas
Hathaway, Donny

Hays, William Shakespeare
Heinrich, Antony Philip
Hemmeter, John Conrad
Henderson, Ray
Herrmann, Bernard
Hewitt, James
Hoffman, Richard
Hofmann, Josef Casimir
Holyoke, Samuel
Humiston, William Henry
Hunter, Ivory Joe
Ives, Charles Edward
Jackson, George K.
Johns, Clayton
Jones, Lindley Armstrong ("Spike")
Kaiser, Alois
Keller, Mathias
Kelley, Edgar Stillman
Kenton, Stanley Newcomb
Kern, Jerome David
Klein, Bruno Oscar
Koemmenich, Louis
Korngold, Erich Wolfgang
Kreisler, Fritz
Kroeger, Ernest Richard
Landowska, Wanda Aleksandra
Lang, Benjamin Johnson
Law, Andrew
Ledbetter, Huddie ("Leadbelly")
Levant, Oscar
Liebling, Emil
Liebling, Estelle
Loeffler, Charles Martin
Loesser, Frank
Lutkin, Peter Christian
MacDowell, Edward Alexander
Mannes, Leopold Damrosch
Maretzek, Max
Marzo, Eduardo
Mason, Daniel Gregory
Mason, William
Mercer, John Herndon ("Johnny")
Mingus, Charles, Jr.
Mitchell, Nahum
Mitropoulos, Dimitri
Morton, Ferdinand Joseph ("Jelly Roll")
Musin, Ovide
Nabokov, Nicolas
Nevin, Ethelbert Woodbridge
Nevin, George Balch
Newman, Alfred
Niles, John Jacob
Nolan, Bob
Nunó, Jaime
Oehmler, Leo Carl Martin
Oliver, Joseph
Ory, Edward ("Kid")
Osgood, George Laurie
Paine, John Knowles
Palmer, Horatio Richmond
Parker, Charlie ("Bird")
Parker, Horatio William
Parker, James Cutler Dunn
Pease, Alfred Humphreys
Perabo, Johann Ernst
Phillips, Philip
Piston, Walter Hamor
Porter, Cole
Pratt, Silas Gamaliel
Prima, Luigi ("Louis")
Pryor, Arthur W.
Rachmaninoff, Sergei Vasilyevich
Razaf, Andy
Reinagle, Alexander
Riegger, Wallingford
Ritter, Frédéric Louis
Rodgers, Richard Charles
Rogers, Clara Kathleen Barnett
Romberg, Sigmund
Root, Frederic Woodman
Root, George Frederick
Rosenblatt, Joseph
Runcie, Constance Faunt Le Roy
Rybner, Martin Cornelius
Sandler, Jacob Koppel
Schelling, Ernest Henry
Schillinger, Joseph
Schindler, Kurt
Schnabel, Artur
Schoenberg, Arnold
Scott, John Prindle
Selby, William
Shaw, Oliver
Sherwood, William Hall
Silvers, Louis
Sobolewski, J. Friedrich Eduard
Sousa, John Philip
Southard, Lucien H.
Speaks, Oley
Spicker, Max
Stanley, Albert Augustus
Stark, Edward Josef
Steiner, Maximilian Raoul Walter ("Max")
Sternberg, Constantin Ivanovich, Edler von
Stewart, Humphrey John
Still, William Grant, Jr.
Stoessel, Albert Frederic
Stokowski, Leopold Anthony
Stravinsky, Igor Fyodorovich
Swan, Timothy
Taylor, Joseph Deems
Taylor, Raynor
Thayer, Whitney Eugene
Tilzer, Harry Von
Tiomkin, Dimitri
Tobani, Theodore Moses
Trajetta, Philip
Tristano, Leonard Joseph ("Lennie")
Tuckey, William
Van Der Stucken, Frank Valentin
Varèse, Edgard
Vogrich, Max Wilhelm Karl
Waller, Thomas Wright ("Fats")
Warren, Richard Henry
Warren, Samuel Prowse
Waxman, Franz
Webb, George James
Weems, Ted
Weidig, Adolf
Weill, Kurt
Weld, Arthur Cyril Gordon
White, Clarence Cameron
White, Joseph Malachy
Whiting, Arthur Battelle
Whiting, George Elbridge
Wight, Frederick Coit
Wilder, Alexander Lafayette Chew ("Alec")
Wilson, Mortimer
Winterhalter, Hugo
Witmark, Isidore
Wolle, John Frederick
Woodbury, Isaac Baker
Woolf, Benjamin Edward
Yon, Pietro Alessandro
Youmans, Vincent Millie
Zach, Max Wilhelm
Zeuner, Charles

COMPTROLLER GENERAL
Warren, Lindsay Carter

COMPTROLLER OF CURRENCY (See also BANKER, ECONOMIST, FINANCIER)
Crissinger, Daniel Richard
Eckels, James Herron
Knox, John Jay
McCulloch, Hugh
Steele, John

COMPUTER SCIENTIST
Mauchly, John William

CONCESSIONAIRE
Grace, William Russell
Tilyou, George Cornelius

CONCHOLOGIST (See also BIOLOGIST, ZOOLOGIST)
Gould, Augustus Addison
Say, Thomas
Tryon, George Washington

CONDUCTOR (See also BANDLEADER, MUSICIAN)
Barrère, Georges
Beck, Johann Heinrich
Bergman, Carl
Bodanzky, Artur
Casals, Pablo
Damrosch, Leopold
Damrosch, Walter Johannes
Dannreuther, Gustav
Duchin, Edward Frank ("Eddy")
Faith, Percy
Fiedler, Arthur
Gabrilowitsch, Ossip
Ganz, Rudolph
Gericke, Wilhelm
Gilchrist, William Wallace
Gould, Nathaniel Duren
Hadley, Henry Kimball
Herrmann, Bernard
Hertz, Alfred
Hill, Ureli Corelli
Iturbi, José
Kostelanetz, Andre
Koussevitzky, Serge Alexandrovich
Kroeger, Ernest Richard
Lang, Benjamin Johnson
Listemann, Bernhard
Lunceford, James Melvin ("Jimmie")
Lutkin, Peter Christian
Mannes, David
Mees, Arthur
Miller, Glenn
Mitropoulos, Dimitri

Mollenhauer, Emil
Monteux, Pierre Benjamin
Munch, Charles
Neuendorff, Adolph Heinrich Anton Magnus
Newman, Alfred
Nunó, Jaime
Oberhoffer, Emil Johann
Osgood, George Laurie
Palmer, Horatio Richmond
Pratt, Silas Gamaliel
Rachmaninoff, Sergei Vasilyevich
Reiner, Fritz
Rodzinski, Artur
Root, Frederic Woodman
Saslavsky, Alexander
Scheel, Fritz
Schelling, Ernest Henry
Schippers, Thomas
Schradieck, Henry
Seidl, Anton
Siloti, Alexander Ilyitch
Silvers, Louis
Sobolewski, J. Friedrich Eduard
Spicker, Max
Spiering, Theodore
Stanley, Albert Augustus
Steiner, Maximilian Raoul Walter ("Max")
Stravinsky, Igor Fyodorovich
Stock, Frederick August
Stoessel, Albert Frederic
Stokowski, Leopold Anthony
Szell, George
Thomas, Christian Friedrich Theodore
Timm, Henry Christian
Toscanini, Arturo
Van Der Stucken, Frank Valentin
Verbrugghen, Henri
Walter, Bruno
Waxman, Franz
Weidig, Adolf
White, George Leonard
Whiteman, Paul Samuel ("Pops")
Wilson, Mortimer
Winterhalter, Hugo
Woolle, John Frederick
Zach, Max Wilhelm
Zerralin, Carl

CONFEDERATE AGENT (See also SPY)
Bulloch, James Dunwody
Clay, Clement Claiborne
Helm, Charles John
Holcombe, James Philemon
Kenner, Duncan Farrar
Lamar, Gazaway Bugg
Peyton, John Lewis
Sanders, George Nicholas
Thompson, Jacob
Tucker, Nathaniel Beverley, 1820–1890

CONGRESSIONAL INVESTIGATOR
Pecora, Ferdinand

CONGRESSMAN (CONFEDERATE) (See also CONGRESSMAN)
Bridgers, Robert Rufus
Shorter, John Gill
Smith, Robert Hardy
Staples, Waller Redd

CONGRESSMAN (CONTINENTAL) (See also CONGRESSMAN)
Burnet, William
Clay, Joseph
Deane, Silas
Goldsborough, Robert
Grayson, William
Griffin, Cyrus
Hanson, John
Henry, John, 1750–1798
Howell, David
Huntington, Samuel, 1731–1796
Johnson, Thomas
Jones, Allen
Langworthy, Edward
Low, Isaac
Lynch, Thomas, 1727–1776
McClurg, James
Marchant, Henry
Mathews, John
Mercer, James
Middleton, Henry
Mifflin, Thomas
Nash, Abner
Neilson, John
Pierce, William Leigh
Randolph, Peyton
Read, Jacob
Root, Jesse
Scudder, Nathaniel
Searle, James
Smith, Jonathan Bayard
Smith, Melancton, 1744–1798
Smith, Richard
Telfair, Edward
Tilghman, Matthew
Van Dyke, Nicholas, 1738–1789
Ward, Samuel, 1725–1776
Wisner, Henry
Zubly, John Joachim

CONGRESSMAN (See also CONGRESSMAN [CONFEDERATE], CONGRESSMAN [CONTINENTAL], CONGRESSWOMAN)
Aandahl, Fred George
Adams, Henry Cullen
Aiken, David Wyatt
Alexander, de Alva Stanwood
Allen, Elisha Hunt
Allen, Thomas
Allen, William
Allen, William Joshua
Allison, William Boyd
Amlie, Thomas Ryum
Anderson, Clinton Presba
Anderson, John Alexander
Andrew, Abram Piatt
Andrews, Sherlock James
Appleton, John
Archer, Wllliam Segar
Arnold, Isaac Newton
Ashe, William Shepperd
Ashley, James Mitchell
Ashley, William Henry
Ashmun, George
Ayres, William Augustus
Babcock, Joseph Weeks
Bailey, Joseph Weldon
Baker, Jehu
Banks, Nathaniel Prentiss
Barbour, John Strode
Barden, Graham Arthur
Barkley, Alben William
Barksdale, William
Barrett, Frank Aloysius
Barringer, Daniel Moreau
Barrow, Washington
Bartholdt, Richard
Barton, Bruce Fairchild
Bates, James
Bayly, Thomas Henry
Beall, James Glenn
Beardsley, Samuel
Beck, James Montgomery
Bedinger, George Michael
Bell, Peter Hansborough
Bender, George Harrison
Berger, Victor Louis
Berrien, John Macpherson
Bissell, William Henry
Blair, Henry William
Bland, Richard Parks
Bliss, Philemon
Bloom, Sol
Blount, James Henderson
Blow, Henry Taylor
Bocock, Thomas Stanley
Boggs, Thomas Hale
Bolton, Frances Payne Bingham
Boteler, Alexander Robinson
Botts, John Minor
Boutelle, Charles Addison
Boyd, Lynn
Bradley, William Czar
Bragg, Edward Stuyvesant
Branch, Lawrence O'Bryan
Brawley, William Hiram
Breckenridge, James
Breckinridge, William Campbell Preston
Brewer, Mark Spencer
Broadhead, James Overton
Brooks, Overton
Brooks, Preston Smith
Brown, Aaron Venable
Brown, Albert Gallatin
Brown, Clarence James
Brown, John Young
Brown, Prentiss Marsh
Burdick, Usher Lloyd
Burke, Aedanus
Burleson, Albert Sidney
Burlingame, Anson
Burton, Theodore Elijah
Butler, Benjamin Franklin
Butler, Ezra
Butler, William
Butler, William Orlando
Cabell, Samuel Jordan
Calvert, Charles Benedict
Cambreleng, Churchill Caldom
Campbell, James Hepburn
Campbell, John Wilson
Campbell, Lewis Davis
Campbell, William Bowen
Campbell, William W.
Candler, Allen Daniel
Cannon, Clarence
Cannon, Joseph Gurney

Cannon, Newton
Case, Francis Higbee
Chalmers, James Ronald
Chambers, John
Chandler, Joseph Ripley
Cheves, Langdon
Chittenden, Simeon Baldwin
Claiborne, John Francis Hamtramck
Claiborne, Nathaniel Herbert
Clark, James
Clay, Henry
Clay, Matthew
Clayton, Augustin Smith
Clayton, Henry De Lamar
Clements, Judson Claudius
Cleveland, Chauncey Fitch
Clopton, John
Cockran, William Bourke
Condit, John
Conger, Edwin Hurd
Conkling, Alfred
Connally, Thomas Terry ("Tom")
Conway, Martin Franklin
Cook, Philip
Cooley, Harold Dunbar
Cooper, (Leon) Jere
Copley, Ira Clifton
Coudert, Frederic René, Jr.
Covode, John
Cox, Edward Eugene
Cox, Samuel Sullivan
Crawford, Martin Jenkins
Creighton, William
Crisp, Charles Frederick
Crosser, Robert
Crowninshield, Jacob
Crump, Edward Hull
Cummings, Amos Jay
Curtis, Charles
Cushman, Joshua
Dalzell, John
Davis, Garret
Davis, Horace
Davis, John Wesley
Davis, John William
Dawes, Henry Laurens
Dawson, William Levi
Dayton, Jonathan
Dean, Sidney
Dearborn, Henry
Delano, Columbus
De Priest, Oscar Stanton
Desha, Joseph
Dickinson, Philemon
Dies, Martin
Dingley, Nelson
Dirksen, Everett McKinley
Dixon, James
Doughton, Robert Lee
Douglas, Lewis Williams
Drayton, William
Dudley, Edward Bishop
Dunn, William McKee
Duval, William Pope
Duvall, Gabriel
Dworshak, Henry Clarence
Eaton, Charles Aubrey
Edgerton, Sidney
Edwards, Henry Waggaman
Ellis, Clyde Taylor
Ellsworth, William Wolcott
Engle, Clair William Walter
English, William Hayden
Eppes, John Wayles
Esch, John Jacob
Evans, Walter
Ewing, Thomas
Ferry, Orris Sanford
Fess, Simeon Davidson
Findlay, James
Findley, William
Fitzpatrick, Morgan Cassius
Fitzsimmons, Thomas
Florence, Thomas Birch
Floyd, William
Foot, Samuel Augustus
Fordney, Joseph Warren
Forney, William Henry
Forward, Walter
Foster, Abiel
Foster, Charles
Fowler, Orin
Frye, William Pierce
Galloway, Samuel
Garfield, James Abram
Garrett, Finis James
Gear, John Henry
Gillett, Frederick Huntington
Gillette, Guy Mark
Gilmer, George Rockingham
Gilmer, John Adams
Glynn, Martin Henry
Goldsborough, Charles
Goldsborough, Thomas Alan
Goodenow, John Milton
Green, James Stephens
Green, William Joseph, Jr.
Greenhalge, Frederic Thomas
Greenup, Christopher
Griswold, John Augustus
Groesbeck, William Slocum
Grosvenor, Charles Henry
Hahn, Georg Michael Decker
Hale, Robert Safford
Hamer, Thomas Lyon
Hamilton, William Thomas
Hampton, Wade, 1751–1835
Hancock, John, 1824–1893
Hanson, Alexander Contee, 1786–1819
Hardin, Ben
Hardin, John J.
Harding, Abner Clark
Hardwick, Thomas William
Harlan, James
Harris, Wiley Pope
Harrison, Byron Patton
Harrison, Francis Burton
Hartley, Fred Allen, Jr.
Hartley, Thomas
Hasbrouck, Abraham Bruyn
Hastings, William Wirt
Hatch, William Henry
Haugen, Gilbert Nelson
Haugen, Nils Pederson
Havens, James Smith
Hawley, Willis Chatman
Hébert, Felix Edward ("Eddie")
Heflin, James Thomas
Hemphill, Joseph
Henderson, Archibald
Hendricks, Thomas Andrews
Hendricks, William
Hendrix, Joseph Clifford
Hepburn, William Peters
Herbert, Hilary Abner
Herter, Christian Archibald
Hiester, Daniel
Hiester, Joseph
Hillhouse, James
Hilliard, Henry Washington
Hillyer, Junius
Hinds, Asher Crosby
Hitt, Robert Roberts
Hoar, Ebenezer Rockwood
Hoar, George Frisbie
Hoar, Samuel
Hobson, Richmond Pearson
Hoey, Clyde Roark
Hoffman, Clare Eugene
Hoffman, Ogden
Hogan, John
Holman, William Steele
Holmes, Isaac Edward
Hope, Clifford Ragsdale
Hopkinson, Joseph
Houghton, Alanson Bigelow
Houk, Leonidas Campbell
Howard, Benjamin
Howard, Jacob Merritt
Howard, Volney Erskine
Hubbard, David
Hughes, Dudley Mays
Hull, Cordell
Hunt, Carleton
Hunter, Whiteside Godfrey
Hurlbut, Stephen Augustus
Ingersoll, Charles Jared
Ingham, Samuel Delucenna
Iverson, Alfred
Jackson, James, 1819–1887
Jackson, John George
Jackson, William, 1783–1855
James, Ollie Murray
Jenkins, Albert Gallatin
Jensen, Benton Franklin ("Ben")
Johns, Kensey
Johnson, Cave
Johnson, James
Johnson, Magnus
Johnson, Robert Ward
Johnson, Tom Loftin
Jones, Frank
Jones, Jehu Glancy
Jones, John Marvin
Jones, John Winston
Jones, William
Judd, Norman Buel
Kahn, Julius
Keating, Kenneth Barnard
Keifer, Joseph Warren
Keitt, Lawrence Massillon
Kelley, William Darrah
Kelly, John
Kenna, John Edward
Kennedy, John Fitzgerald
Kennedy, Robert Patterson
Kent, Joseph
Key, Philip Barton
Kilbourne, James
King, Austin Augustus
King, John Alsop

King, Thomas Butler
King, William Rufus Devane
Kitchin, Claude
Kitchin, William Walton
Knickerbocker, Herman
Knott, James Proctor
Knutson, Harold
Lacey, John Fletcher
Lacock, Abner
La Guardia, Fiorello Henry
Lane, Henry Smith
Lanham, Frederick Garland ("Fritz")
Lattimore, William
Law, John
Lawrence, William, 1819–1899
Leavitt, Humphrey Howe
Lee, William Henry Fitzhugh
Leffler, Isaac
Leffler, Shepherd
Leib, Michael
Lemke, William Frederick
Lenroot, Irvine Luther
Letcher, John
Letcher, Robert Perkins
Lever, Asbury Francis
Levin, Lewis Charles
Lewis, Dixon Hall
Lewis, James Hamilton
Lewis, Joseph Horace
Ligon, Thomas Watkins
Lind, John
Lindbergh, Charles Augustus
Littauer, Lucius Nathan
Littleton, Martin Wiley
Livermore, Arthur
Livermore, Edward St. Loe
Livermore, Samuel, 1732–1803
Lloyd, Edward, 1779–1834
Locke, Matthew
Long, John Davis
Longfellow, Stephen
Loomis, Arphaxed
Loomis, Dwight
Lorimer, William
Lowndes, William
Lucas, John Baptiste Charles
Lucas, Scott Wike
Lundeen, Ernest
Lynch, John Roy
Lyon, Francis Strother
McArthur, Duncan
McCall, Samuel Walker
McClelland, Robert
McClernand, John Alexander
McClurg, Joseph Washington
McComas, Louis Emory
McCook, Anson George
McCormack, John William
McCrary, George Washington
McCreary, James Bennett
McFadden, Louis Thomas
McGranery, James Patrick
McKay, James Iver
McKean, Samuel
McKee, John
McKennan, Thomas McKean Thompson
McKim, Isaac
McKinley, John
McKinley, William Brown
McLane, Robert Milligan
Maclay, Samuel
McLean, John
McMillin, Benton
McNulty, Frank Joseph
McPherson, Edward
McPherson, Smith
McRae, Thomas Chipman
McReynolds, Samuel Davis
Madden, Martin Barnaby
Maginnis, Martin
Mallary, Rollin Carolas
Mann, James Robert
Marcantonio, Vito Anthony
Marland, Ernest Whitworth
Marshall, Thomas Alexander
Martin, Joseph William, Jr.
Marvin, Dudley
Mason, John Young
Mathews, George
Mattocks, John
Maverick, (Fontaine) Maury
Maxwell, Augustus Emmett
Maxwell, Samuel
May, Andrew Jackson
Maynard, Horace
Mercee, John Francis
Mercer, Charles Fenton
Mercier, Ulysses
Metcalfe, Ralph Harold
Miles, William Porcher
Miller, John
Mills, Elijah Hunt
Mills, Roger Quarles
Miner, Charles
Mitchell, Alexander
Mitchell, George Edward
Mitchell, Nahum
Mitchill, Samuel Latham
Mondell, Frank Wheeler
Money, Hernando De Soto
Monroney, Almer Stillwell ("Mike")
Montague, Andrew Jackson
Montoya, Joseph Manuel
Moody, William Henry
Moore, Andrew
Moore, Ely
Moore, Gabriel
Moore, Thomas Patrick
Moorhead, James Kennedy
Morehead, Charles Slaughter
Morgan, George Washington
Morrill, Anson Peaslee
Morrill, Edmund Needham
Morrill, Justin Smith
Morris, Lewis Richard
Morrison, William Ralls
Morrissey, John
Morrow, Jeremiah
Morrow, William W.
Morse, Freeman Harlow
Morton, Rogers Clark Ballard
Murdock, Victor
Murray, William Henry David
Neely, Matthew Mansfield
Negley, James Scott
Nelson, Roger
Newberry, John Stoughton
Newell, William Augustus
Newlands, Francis Griffith
Newton, Thomas, 1768–1847
Niblack, William Ellis
Nicholas, John
Nicholas, Wilson Cary
Nicholson, Joseph Hopper
Niedringhaus, Frederick Gottlieb
Nisbet, Eugenius Aristides
Norris, George William
Norton, Elijah Hise
Nott, Abraham
Oates, William Calvin
O'Ferrall, Charles Triplett
Olmsted, Marlin Edgar
Orth, Godlove Stein
Pacheco, Romualdo
Packer, Asa
Page, John
Paine, Halbert Eleazer
Palmer, Alexander Mitchell
Palmer, Henry Wilbur
Parker, Isaac Charles
Patman, John William Wright
Pattison, John M.
Payne, Henry B.
Pearce, James Alfred
Pendleton, George Hunt
Pennington, William
Perkins, George Douglas
Perkins, James Breck
Pettengill, Samuel Barrett
Phelan, James, 1856–1891
Phelps, Charles Edward
Phelps, John Smith
Phelps, William Walter
Philips, John Finis
Phillips, Thomas Wharton
Phillips, William Addison
Pickens, Francis Wilkinson
Pierce, Henry Lillie
Pinckney, Henry Laurens
Plaisted, Harris Merrill
Plumley, Frank
Poindexter, George
Poland, Luke Potter
Pollock, James
Pool, Joe Richard
Porter, Albert Gallatin
Porter, Peter Buell
Porter, Stephen Geyer
Potter, Elisha Reynolds
Potter, Robert
Pou, Edward William
Powell, Adam Clayton, Jr.
Pratt, Zadock
Prentiss, Seargent Smith
Preston, William
Preston, William Ballard
Price, Hiram
Price, Sterling
Price, Thomas Lawson
Pryor, Roger Atkinson
Pujo, Arsène Paulin
Quigg, Lemuel Ely
Rainey, Joseph Hayne
Ramspeck, Robert C. Word ("Bob")
Randall, Samuel Jackson
Randolph, Thomas Mann
Rankin, John Elliott
Rayner, Kenneth
Read, Nathan
Reagan, John Henninger
Reece, Brazilla Carroll

Reed, Daniel Alden
Rhea, John
Rice, Alexander Hamilton
Rice, Edmund
Rich, Robert
Riddle, Albert Gallatin
Rivers, Lucius Mendel
Roberts, Ellis Henry
Roberts, Jonathan
Roberts, William Randall
Robertson, Alice Mary
Robertson, George
Robertson, John
Robinson, Joseph Taylor
Rollins, James Sidney
Rousseau, Lovell Harrison
Rowan, John
Rusk, Jeremiah McClain
Sabath, Adolph J.
Sage, Russell
Saunders, Romulus Mitchell
Sawyer, Lemuel
Schenck, Robert Cumming
Seddon, James Alexander
Sergeant, John, 1779–1852
Sergeant, Jonathan Dickinson
Sevier, Ambrose Hundley
Seybert, Adam
Seymour, Thomas Hart
Shafroth, John Franklin
Shepard, William
Sheppard, John Morris
Sherwood, Isaac Ruth
Shouse, Jouett
Sibley, Joseph Crocker
Sickles, Daniel Edgar
Simms, William Elliott
Simpson, Jerry
Singleton, James Washington
Skinner, Harry
Slemp, Campbell Bascom
Smalls, Robert
Smith, Caleb Blood
Smith, Howard Worth ("Judge")
Smith, Jeremiah, 1759–1842
Smith, Oliver Hampton
Smith, Truman
Smith, Walter Inglewood
Smith, William, 1797–1887
Smith, William Loughton
Smith, William Nathan Harrell
Smith, William Russell
Smyth, Alexander
Snell, Bertrand Hollis
Spaight, Richard Dobbs
Spalding, Thomas
Sparks, William Andrew Jackson
Spaulding, Elbridge Gerry
Speer, Emory
Spence, Brent
Spencer, Ambrose
Spencer, John Canfield
Sperry, Nehemiah Day
Springer, William McKendree
Stanley, Augustus Owsley
Stanly, Edward
Stanton, Frederick Perry
Stanton, Richard Henry
Starin, John Henry
Steagall, Henry Bascom
Steele, John
Stephens, Alexander Hamilton
Stephenson, Andrew
Stephenson, Isaac
Stevens, Thaddeus
Stevenson, Adlai Ewing
Stevenson, John White
Stewart, Andrew
Stigler, William Grady
Stockdale, Thomas Ringland
Stone, David
Stone, William Joel
Storer, Bellamy
Stuart, Alexander Hugh Holmes
Stuart, John Todd
Sullivan, George
Sulzer, William
Summers, George William
Sumners, Hatton William
Sumter, Thomas
Sutherland, Joel Barlow
Swann, Thomas
Swanson, Claude Augustus
Sweeney, Martin Leonard
Taber, John
Tallmadge, Benjamin
Tawney, James Albertus
Taylor, Alfred Alexander
Thacher, George
Thayer, Eli
Thomas, David
Thomas, Francis
Thomas, John Parnell
Thomas, Philip Francis
Thompson, Jacob
Thompson, Thomas Larkin
Thompson, Waddy
Thompson, Wiley
Throop, Enos Thompson
Thurman, Allen Granberry
Tilson, John Quillin
Tinkham, George Holden
Tod, John
Toucey, Isaac
Towne, Charles Arnette
Towns, George Washington Bonaparte
Tracy, Uriah
Troup, George Michael
Trumbull, Jonathan, 1740–1809
Tuck, Amos
Tucker, Henry St. George, 1853–1932
Tucker, John Randolph, 1823–1897
Tyson, Job Roberts
Upham, Charles Wentworth
Van Cortlandt, Philip
Van Horn, Robert Thompson
Van Rensselaer, Solomon
Van Rensselaer, Stephen
Verplanck, Julian Crommelin
Vibbard, Chauncey
Vinson, Fred(erick) Moore
Vinton, Samuel Finley
Volstead, Andrew John
Vroom, Peter Dumont
Waddell, Alfred Moore
Wadsworth, James Wolcott, Jr.
Wadsworth, Jeremiah
Wadsworth, Peleg
Walker, Amasa
Walker, Gilbert Carlton
Wallace, David
Wallgren, Mon(rad) C(harles)
Walter, Francis Eugene
Ward, Marcus Lawrence
Warner, Adoniram Judson
Warner, Hiram
Warner, William
Warren, Lindsay Carter
Washburn, Cadwallader Colden
Washburn, Charles Grenfill
Washburn, Israel
Washburn, William Drew
Washburne, Elihu Benjamin
Watson, James Eli
Watterson, Harvey Magee
Weaver, James Baird
Weeks, John Wingate
Welch, John
Weller, John B.
Wells, Erastus
Wentworth, John, 1815–1888
West, George
Wheeler, Joseph
White, Alexander
White, Stephen Van Culen
Whitehill, Robert
Whitman, Ezekiel
Wickliffe, Charles Anderson
Wilde, Richard Henry
Williams, David Rogerson
Willis, Albert Shelby
Wilmot, David
Wilson, James
Wilson, James Falconer
Wilson, William Bauchop
Wilson, William Lyne
Windom, William
Winn, Richard
Winthrop, Robert Charles
Wise, Henry Alexander
Wolf, George
Wood, Fernando
Wood, John Stephens
Wood, William Robert
Wright, Hendrick Bradley
Wright, Joseph Albert
Wright, Robert
Yates, Abraham
Yell, Archibald
Young, Pierce Manning Butler
Zollicoffer, Felix Kirk

CONGRESSWOMAN

Kahn, Florence Prag
Norton, Mary Teresa Hopkins
Rankin, Jeannette Pickering
Rogers, Edith Nourse
Rohde, Ruth Bryan Owen
Simms, Ruth Hanna McCormick

CONSERVATIONIST (See also ECOLOGIST)

Darling, Jay Norwood ("Ding")
Drury, Newton Bishop
Gabrielson, Ira Noel
Grinnell, George Bird
McAdams, Clark
McFarland, John Horace
Maxwell, George Hebard
Merriam, John Campbell
Morgan, Arthur Ernest
Olmsted, Frederick Law
Osborn, Henry Fairfield
Pack, Charles Lathrop
Pammel, Louis Hermann

Pearson, Thomas Gilbert
Penfold, Joseph Weller
Pinchot, Gifford
Roosevelt, Robert Barnwell
Shields, George Oliver
Silcox, Ferdinand Augustus
Zahniser, Howard Clinton
CONSTITUTIONAL LAWYER
O'Brian, John Lord
CONSTITUTIONAL SCHOLAR
Warren, Charles
CONSTRUCTION MAGNATE
Kiewit, Peter
CONSUL (See also DIPLOMAT, STATESMAN)
Andrews, Israel DeWolf
Cathcart, James Leander
De Forest, David Curtis
Foresti, Eleutario Felice
Gillman, Henry
Hale, Charles
Halsey, Thomas Lloyd
Heap, Samuel Davies
Helm, Charles John
Jarvis, William
Jones, William Patterson
King, Jonas
Lear, Tobias
McRae, Duncan Kirkland
Magoffin, James Wiley
Merrill, Selah
Morse, Freeman Harlow
Murphy, Dominic Ignatius
Murphy, William Walton
O'Brien, Richard
Offley, David
Ogden, Francis Barber
Osterhaus, Peter Joseph
Shaler, William
Stahel, Julius
Taylor, James Wickes
Thayer, Alexander Wheelock
Underwood, Francis Henry
Wood, Leonard
CONSUMER ADVOCATE
Brady, Mildred Alice Edie
CONTRACTOR (See also BUILDING CONTRACTOR)
Crimmins, John Daniel
Faesch, John Jacob
Fox, Harry
Glenn, Hugh
Haish, Jacob
Law, George
Levitt, Abraham
Stubbs, Walter Roscoe
Thompson, David P.
Vare, William Scott
Wolfson, Erwin Service
CONTROVERSIALIST (See also CLERGYMAN, PAMPHLETEER, PROPAGANDIST, WRITER)
Breckinridge, John, 1797–1841
Graves, James Robinson
McCaine, Alexander
McCalla, William Latta
Niles, Samuel
Ogden, Uzal
Pickering, Timothy
Yorke, Peter Christopher
CORNETIST
Handy, William Christopher
Oliver, Joseph
CORPORATE OFFICIAL
Crowley, Leo Thomas
CORPORATION LAWYER
Ewing, Oscar Ross
COSMOGRAPHER
Constansó, Miguel
COUNCILLOR (COLONIAL)
Nelson, William, 1711–1772
Page, Mann
Peters, Richard, *c.* 1704–1776
COUNTRY SINGER
Hunter, Ivory Joe
COURT REPORTER
Deming, Philander
Munford, William
Otto, William Tod
COWBOY (See also RANGER)
Adams, Andy
Gibson, Edmund Richard ("Hoot")
McCoy, Tim
Rhodes, Eugene Manlove
Rogers, Will
Siringo, Charles A.
CRAFTSMAN (See also ARTIST, CABINETMAKER, DIAMOND CUTTER, GOLDSMITH, PEWTERER, SILVERSMITH, TOOLMAKER, VIOLIN MAKER, WOOD-CARVER, WOOD-ENGRAVER)
Armstrong, David Maitland
Fitch, John
Hubbard, Elbert
La Farge, John
Revere, Paul
Wright, Philip Green
CRIMINAL (See also BOOTLEGGER, GANGSTER, ORGANIZED CRIME LEADER, RACKETEER)
Capone, Alphonse ("Al")
Chessman, Caryl Whittier
Wexler, Irving ("Waxey Gordon")
CRIMINOLOGIST (See also PENOLOGIST, PRISON REFORMER, SOCIOLOGIST)
Glueck, Eleanor Touroff
Goddard, Calvin Hooker
Kirchwey, George Washington
Smith, Bruce
Spitzka, Edward Anthony
Sutherland, Edwin Hardin
Wilson, Orlando Winfield ("Win," "O.W.")
CRITIC (See also ART, DRAMATIC, LITERARY, MUSIC, POLITICAL, SOCIAL CRITIC)
Agee, James Rufus
Bacon, Leonard
Bent, Silas
Bogan, Louise Marie
Bontemps, Arna Wendell
Bradford, Gamaliel
Brooks, Van Wyck
Brownell, William Crary
Clark, Walter Van Tilburg
Cranch, Christopher Pearse
DeVoto, Bernard Augustine
Farrell, James Thomas
Fowler, Frank
Fuller, Sarah Margaret
Gilder, Jeannette Leonard
Hale, Philip Leslie
Hamilton, Clayton
Hillyer, Robert Silliman
Humiston, William Henry
Huneker, James Gibbons
Jacobs, Joseph, 1854–1916
Jarves, James Jackson
Kilmer, Alfred Joyce
Kobbé, Gustav
Koch, Vivienne
Lanier, Sidney
Lowell, Amy
Mabie, Hamilton Wright
Magonigle, Harold Van Buren
Mencken, Henry Louis
Morehouse, Ward
Nathan, George Jean
Parker, Dorothy Rothschild
Poe, Edgar Allan
Pollak, Gustav
Pound, Ezra Loomis
Price, William Thompson
Rahv, Philip
Redman, Ben Ray
Reitzel, Robert
Rittenhouse, Jessie Belle
Seldes, Gilbert Vivian
Stedman, Edmund Clarence
Stoddard, Richard Henry
Sturgis, Russell
Trilling, Lionel
Tuckerman, Henry Theodore
Van Vechten, Carl
Wallace, Horace Binney
Walsh, Thomas
Wheeler, Andrew Carpenter
Wheelock, John Hall
Whitaker, Charles Harris
Willcox, Louise Collier
Williams, John
Woodberry, George Edward
Woollcott, Alexander Humphreys
Zukofsky, Louis
CRYPTOLOGIST
Friedman, William Frederick
CULT LEADER
Jones, Jim
CURATOR (See also MUSEUM DIRECTOR)
Burroughs, Bryson
Fitzpatrick, John Clement
Goodyear, William Henry
Koehler, Sylvester Rosa
Lutz, Frank Eugene
Rau, Charles
Seitz, William Chapin
Steichen, Edward Jean
Todd, Walter Edmond Clyde
Watkins, John Elfreth
CUSTOMS EXPERT
Colton, George Radcliffe
Keith, Sir William
Sterling, James
CYTOLOGIST
Wilson, Edmund Beecher

DAIRY HUSBANDMAN (See also CATTLEMAN)
Alvord, Henry Elijah
Arnold, Lauren Briggs
Hoard, William Dempster
DANCE EDUCATOR
Eglevsky, André Yevgenyevich
Horst, Louis
DANCER
Bailey, Bill
Barton, James Edward
Bolm, Adolph Rudolphovitch
Castle, Irene Foote
Castle, Vernon Blythe
Champion, Gower
Dailey, Dan, Jr.
Daley, Cass
Duncan, Isadora
Fokine, Michel
Fuller, Loie
Gilbert, Anne Hartley
Gray, Gilda
Humphrey, Doris
Limón, José Arcadio
McCracken, Joan
Murray, Mae
Rand, Sally
Robinson, Bill ("Bojangles")
Rooney, Pat
St. Denis, Ruth
Shaw, Edwin Meyers ("Ted")
Tamiris, Helen
Van, Bobby
Vladimiroff, Pierre
Webb, Clifton
DEAF EDUCATION SCHOLAR
Goldstein, Max Aaron
DEFENSE LAWYER
Leibowitz, Samuel Simon
DEMOCRATIC NATIONAL CHAIRMAN
Bailey, John Moran
DEMOGRAPHER (See also STATISTICIAN)
Lotka, Alfred James
DENDROCHRONOLOGIST
Douglass, Andrew Ellicott
DENTIST (See also PHYSICIAN)
Abbott, Frank
Allen, John
Black, Greene Vardiman
Bonwill, William Gibson Arlington
Brown, Solyman
Buchanan, Edgar
Evans, Thomas Wiltberger
Fillebrown, Thomas
Flagg, Josiah Foster
Garretson, James
Greenwood, John
Harris, Chapin Aaron
Hayden, Horace H.
Howe, Percy Rogers
Hudson, Edward
Hullihen, Simon P.
Kingsley, Norman William
Loomis, Mahlon
McQuillen, John Hugh
Miller, Willoughby Dayton
Morton, William Thomas Green
Owre, Alfred
Parsons, Thomas William
Riggs, John Mankey
Spooner, Shearjashub
Volck, Adalbert John
Wells, Horace
White, John de Haven
DEPARTMENT STORE EXECUTIVE (See also MERCHANT)
Lazarus, Fred, Jr.
Rosenwald, Lessing Julius
Straus, Percy Selden
DERMATOLOGIST (See also PHYSICIAN)
Duhring, Louis Adolphus
Jackson, George Thomas
Pusey, William Allen
Schamberg, Jay Frank
Wende, Ernest
Wende, Grover William
White, James Clarke
Wigglesworth, Edward
DESIGNER (CINEMATOGRAPHIC EQUIPMENT)
Howell, Albert Summers
DESIGNER (COSTUME)
Bernstein, Aline
DESIGNER (FASHION)
Adrian, Gilbert
Carnegie, Hattie
Fogarty, Anne Whitney
Kiam, Omar
Klein, Anne
McCardell, Claire
Norell, Norman
Orry-Kelly
Rosenstein, Nettie Rosencrans
DESIGNER (INTERIOR)
Eames, Charles Ormand, Jr.
Herter, Christian
DESIGNER (SCENIC)
Aronson, Boris Solomon
Bernstein, Aline
DESPERADO (See also BANDIT, BRIGAND, BUCCANEER, BURGLAR, CRIMINAL, OUTLAW, PIRATE)
Bass, Sam
Billy the Kid
Dalton, Robert
James, Jesse Woodson
Mason, Samuel
Slade, Joseph Alfred
Younger, Thomas Coleman
DETECTIVE
Burns, William John
Means, Gaston Bullock
Pinkerton, Allan
Ruditsky, Barney
Siringo, Charles A.
DIAMOND CUTTER (See also CRAFTSMAN)
Morse, Henry Dutton
DIARIST (See also CHRONICLER)
Breen, Patrick
Hone, Philip
Knight, Sarah Kemble
Laudonnière, René Goulaine de
Maclay, William
Marshall, Christopher
Nin, Anaïs
Sewall, Samuel
Smith, Richard
Wister, Sarah
DIESINKER (See also ENGRAVER)
Gobrecht, Christian
Kneass, William
Wright, Joseph
DIETICIAN (See also NUTRITIONIST, PHYSICIAN)
Nichols, Thomas Low
DIPLOMAT (See also CONSUL, STATESMAN)
Adams, Charles
Adams, Charles Francis
Adee, Alvey Augustus
Aldrich, Winthrop William
Allen, Elisha Hunt
Allen, George Venable
Anderson, Richard Clough
Angel, Benjamin Franklin
Angell, James Burrill
Appleton, John
Armstrong, John
Avery, Benjamin Parke
Bacon, Robert
Badeau, Adam
Bagby, Arthur Pendleton
Baker, Jehu
Bancroft, Edgar Addison
Bancroft, George
Barrett, John
Barringer, Daniel Moreau
Barton, Thomas Pennant
Bayard, James Ach(e)ton
Bayard, Thomas Francis
Beaupré, Arthur Matthias
Belmont, August
Benjamin, Samuel Greene Wheeler
Bernstein, Herman
Biddle, Anthony Joseph Drexel, Jr.
Bidlack, Benjamin Alden
Bigelow, John
Bingham, Robert Worth
Birney, James
Bliss, Robert Woods
Bliss, Tasker Howard
Blount, James Henderson
Blow, Henry Taylor
Bogardus, Everardus
Boker, George Henry
Bonsal, Stephen
Borland, Solon
Boutell, Henry Sherman
Bowdoin, James
Bowen, Herbert Wolcott
Bowers, Claude Gernade
Braden, Spruille
Bradish, Luther
Bradley, Charles William
Bristol, Mark Lambert
Broadhead, James Overton
Brown, James
Brown, John Porter
Bruce, David Kirkpatrick Este
Buchanan, William Insco
Bullitt, William Christian
Burlingame, Anson
Butterworth, William Walton ("Walt")
Caffery, Jefferson
Calhoun, William James
Cambreleng, Churchill Caldom
Cameron, Simon

Campbell, George Washington
Campbell, Lewis Davis
Carmichael, William
Carr, Dabney Smith
Carter, Henry Alpheus Peirce
Cass, Lewis
Castle, William Richards, Jr.
Child, Richard Washburn
Choate, Joseph Hodges
Clark, Joshua Reuben, Jr.
Clay, Clement Claiborne
Cole, Charles Woolsey
Conant, James Bryant
Conger, Edwin Hurd
Coolidge, Thomas Jefferson
Cooper, Henry Ernest
Cordier, Andrew Wellington
Cramer, Michael John
Crowder, Enoch Herbert
Dallas, George Mifflin
Dana, Francis
Daniel, John Moncure
Daniels, Josephus
D'Avezac, Auguste Geneviève Valentin
Davies, Joseph Edward
Davis, John Chandler Bancroft
Davis, John William
Davis, Norman Hezekiah
Dawson, Thomas Cleland
Dayton, William Lewis
Deane, Silas
Denby, Charles
Dickinson, Charles Monroe
Dodd, William Edward
Dodge, Augustus Caesar
Donelson, Andrew Jackson
Donovan, William Joseph
Douglas, Lewis Williams
Draper, William Franklin
Dulles, Allen Welsh
Dulles, John Foster
Du Pont, Victor Marie
Eames, Charles
Eaton, William
Edge, Walter Evans
Egan, Maurice Francis
Egan, Patrick
Ellis, Powhatan
Ellsworth, Henry William
Erving, George William
Eustis, George
Eustis, James Biddle
Eustis, William
Everett, Alexander Hill
Fairchild, Lucius
Farman, Elbert Eli
Fay, Theodore Sedgwick
Fearn, John Walker
Ferguson, Thomas Barker
Flagg, Edmund
Fletcher, Henry Prather
Fogg, George Gilman
Foote, Lucius Harwood
Forbes, John Murray
Foster, John Watson
Foulk, George Clayton
Fox, Williams Carleton
Francis, Charles Spencer
Francis, John Morgan
Franklin, Benjamin
Gadsden, James
Gallatin, Abraham Alfonse Albert
Gauss, Clarence Edward
Genet, Edmond Charles
Gerard, James Watson
Gifford, Walter Sherman
Grady, Henry Francis
Graham, John
Gray, Isaac Pusey
Greathouse, Clarence Ridgeby
Green, Benjamin Edwards
Greene, Roger Sherman
Grew, Joseph Clark
Grieve, Miller
Griscom, Lloyd Carpenter
Guggenheim, Harry Frank
Gummere, Samuel René
Guthrie, George Wilkins
Halderman, John A.
Hale, Edward Joseph
Hale, John Parker
Hamilton, Maxwell McGaughey
Hardy, Arthur Sherburne
Harriman, Florence Jaffray Hurst
Harris, Townsend
Harvey, George Brinton McClellan
Hassaurek, Friedrich
Hay, John Milton
Hayes, Carlton Joseph Huntley
Herrick, Myron Timothy
Hibben, Paxton Pattison
Hicks, John, 1847–1917
Hill, David Jayne
Hise, Elijah
Hoffman, Wickham
Holcombe, Chester
Holmes, Julius Cecil
Hoover, Herbert Clark, Jr.
Hopkins, Harry Lloyd
Houghton, Alanson Bigelow
Hughes, Christopher
Hunt, William Henry
Hunter, William
Hurley, Patrick Jay
Ide, Henry Clay
Izard, Ralph
Jackson, Charles Douglas
Jackson, Henry Rootes
Jackson, John Brinckerhoff
Jackson, Mortimer Melville
Jardine, William Marion
Jay, John, 1745–1829
Jay, John, 1817–1894
Jefferson, Thomas
Johnson, Reverdy
Judd, Norman Buel
Kasson, John Adam
Kavanagh, Edward
Keating, Kenneth Barnard
Kilpatrick, Hugh Judson
King, Rufus
King, Thomas Butler
King, William Rufus Devane
Kinney, William Burnet
Kirk, Alan Goodrich
Lane, Arthur Bliss
Langston, John Mercer
Larkin, Thomas Oliver
Larrínaga, Tulio
Laurens, John
Lawrence, Abbott
Lee, Arthur
Lee, William
LeGendre, Charles William
Leishman, John G. A.
Lincoln, Robert Todd
Lind, John
Livingston, Robert R., 1746–1813
Long, Breckinridge
Lothrop, George Van Ness
Low, Frederick Ferdinand
McCartee, Divie Bethune
McCook, Edward Moody
McCormick, Robert Sanderson
McDonald, James Grover
McLane, Louis
McLane, Robert Milligan
McMillin, Benton
McNutt, Paul Vories
MacVeagh, Charles
MacVeagh, Isaac Wayne
Maney, George Earl
Mann, Ambrose Dudley
Marling, John Leake
Marsh, George Perkins
Marshall, Humphrey
Marshall, James Fowle Baldwin
Mason, James Murray
Mason, John Young
Maxcy, Virgil
Merchant, Livingston Tallmadge
Merry, William Lawrence
Messersmith, George Strausser
Meyer, George Von Lengerke
Miller, David Hunter
Moffat, Jay Pierrepont
Montgomery, George Washington
Moore, Thomas Patrick
Moran, Benjamin
Morgan, Edwin Vernon
Morgan, Philip Hicky
Morgenthau, Henry
Morris, Edward Joy
Morris, Gouverneur
Morris, Richard Valentine
Morrison, Delesseps Story
Morrow, Dwight Whitney
Morton, Levi Parsons
Motley, John Lothrop
Muhlenberg, Henry Augustus Philip
Muñoz-Rivera, Luis
Murphy, Robert Daniel
Murray, William Vans
Nelson, Donald Marr
Nelson, Hugh
Nelson, Thomas Henry
Newel, Stanford
Nicholson, Meredith
Niles, Nathaniel, 1791–1869
Noyes, Edward Follansbee
O'Brien, Edward Charles
O'Brien, Thomas James
Offley, David
Osborn, Thomas Andrew
Osborn, Thomas Ogden
O'Shaughnessy, Nelson Jarvis Waterbury
Osten Sacken, Carl Robert Romanovich von der

O'Sullivan, John Louis
Pacheco, Romualdo
Page, Thomas Nelson
Page, Walter Hines
Palmer, Thomas Witherell
Parker, Peter
Partridge, James Rudolph
Patterson, Richard Cunningham, Jr.
Payne, John Howard
Peirce, Henry Augustus
Peixotto, Benjamin Franklin
Pendleton, George Hunt
Pendleton, John Strother
Penfield, Frederic Courtland
Phelps, Edward John
Phelps, William Walter
Phillips, William
Pickett, James Chamberlayne
Pierrepont, Edwards
Pinckney, Charles
Pinckney, Charles Cotesworth
Pinckney, Thomas
Pinkney, William
Poinsett, Joel Roberts
Polk, Frank Lyon
Porter, Horace
Preble, William Pitt
Preston, William
Pruyn, Robert Hewson
Putnam, James Osborne
Putnam, William LeBaron
Randolph, Sir John
Read, John Meredith, 1837–1896
Reed, William Bradford
Reid, Whitelaw
Reinsch, Paul Samuel
Rhind, Charles
Richards, William
Rives, William Cabell
Roberts, Edmund
Robinson, Christopher
Rockhill, William Woodville
Rodney, Caesar Augustus
Rohde, Ruth Bryan Owen
Root, Joseph Pomeroy
Rowe, Leo Stanton
Rublee, Horace
Rush, Richard
Russell, Charles Wells
Russell, Jonathan
Sanford, Henry Shelton
Saunders, Romulus Mitchell
Sayre, Stephen
Schenck, Robert Cumming
Schurman, Jacob Gould
Schurz, Carl
Schuyler, Eugene
Scruggs, William Lindsay
Sedgwick, Theodore, 1811–1859
Sewall, Harold Marsh
Seward, Frederick William
Seward, George Frederick
Seymour, Charles
Seymour, Thomas Hart
Shannon, Wilson
Sharp, William Graves
Short, William
Sickles, Daniel Edgar
Slidell, John
Smith, Charles Emory
Smith, Walter Bedell
Smith, William Loughton
Smyth, John Henry
Soulé, Pierre
Squier, Ephraim George
Squiers, Herbert Goldsmith
Stallo, Johann Bernhard
Standley, William Harrison
Steinhardt, Laurence Adolph
Stevens, John Leavitt
Stevenson, Andrew
Stillman, William James
Stimson, Frederic Jesup
Storer, Bellamy
Stovall, Pleasant Alexander
Straight, Willard Dickerman
Straus, Jesse Isidor
Straus, Oscar Solomon
Strobel, Edward Henry
Stuart, John Leighton
Swift, John Franklin
Taft, Alphonso
Taylor, Hannis
Taylor, Myron Charles
Tenney, Charles Daniel
Terrell, Edwin Holland
Thomas, Allen
Thomas, William Widgery
Thompson, Llewellyn E. ("Tommy"), Jr.
Thompson, Thomas Larkin
Thompson, Waddy
Tod, David
Todd, Charles Stewart
Torbert, Alfred Thomas Archimedes
Tower, Charlemagne
Tree, Lambert
Trescot, William Henry
Tripp, Bartlett
Trist, Nicholas Philip
Turner, James Milton
Vail, Aaron
Van Dyke, Henry
Vaughan, Benjamin
Vignaud, Henry
Vincent, John Carter
Vopicka, Charles Joseph
Wallace, Hugh Campbell
Walton, Lester Aglar
Ward, John Elliott
Warden, David Bailie
Washburn, Albert Henry
Washburne, Elihu Benjamin
Webb, James Watson
Weddell, Alexander Wilbourne
Welles, (Benjamin) Sumner
Wheaton, Henry
Wheeler, (George) Post
Wheeler, John Hill
White, Andrew Dickson
White, Henry
Whitlock, Brand
Wikoff, Henry
Wilkins, William
Willard, Joseph Edward
Williams, Edward Thomas
Williams, James
Williams, John
Williams, Samuel Wells
Willis, Albert Shelby
Wilson, Henry Lane
Wilson, Hugh Robert
Winant, John Gilbert
Woodford, Stewart Lyndon
Wright, Joseph Albert
Young, Owen D.
Zellerbach, James David

DIRECTOR (See also MOTION PICTURE DIRECTOR, STAGE DIRECTOR, THEATRICAL DIRECTOR)
Blackmer, Sydney Alderman
Brenon, Herbert
Carroll, Leo Grattan
Champion, Gower
Chaplin, Charles Spencer ("Charlie")
Clurman, Harold Edgar
Craven, Frank
Crisp, Donald
DeMille, Cecil Blount
Griffith, David Wark
Hampden, Walter
Hart, William Surrey
Hitchcock, Alfred Joseph
Lindsay, Howard
Lubitsch, Ernst
Miller, Gilbert Heron
Mitchell, Thomas Gregory
Muse, Clarence
Nagel, Conrad
Nichols, Dudley
Pemberton, Brock
Perry, Antoinette
Rice, Elmer
Ritchard, Cyril
Rossen, Robert
Schwartz, Maurice
Von Sternberg, Josef
White, George

DIRECTOR OF U.S. MINT (See also COMPTROLLER OF CURRENCY)
DeSaussure, Henry William
Linderman, Henry Richard
Ross, Nellie Tayloe
Snowden, James Ross

DISARMAMENT ADVOCATE
Dingman, Mary Agnes

DISK JOCKEY
Freed, Alan J.

DISCOVERER (See also EXPLORER, FRONTIERSMAN, GUIDE, PIONEER, SCOUT)
Cárdenas, García López de
De Soto, Hernando
Gray, Robert
Ingraham, Joseph
Ponce, Juan de León

DISTRICT ATTORNEY (See PROSECUTOR)

DIVER
Patch, Sam

DIXIE CUP CORPORATION FOUNDER
Moore, Hugh Everett

DOCTOR (See PHYSICIAN)

DRAFTSMAN
Sterne, Maurice

DRAMA CRITIC
Allen, Kelcey
Benchley, Robert Charles
Brown, John Mason, Jr.

Gibbs, (Oliver) Wolcott
Hale, Philip
Hammond, Percy Hunter
Kronenberger, Louis, Jr.
Laffan, William Mackay
Mailly, William
Mantle, (Robert) Burns
Moses, Montrose Jonas
Parker, Henry Taylor
Pollard, Joseph Percival
Stevens, Ashton
Winter, William
Young, Stark

DRAMATIST
Adams, Frank Ramsay
Ade, George
Aiken, George L.
Akins, Zoë
Anderson, Maxwell
Arden, Edwin Hunter Pendleton
Arliss, George
Armstrong, Paul
Auden, Wystan Hugh
Bacon, Frank
Baker, Benjamin A.
Bannister, Nathaniel Harrington
Barker, James Nelson
Barnes, Charlotte Mary Sanford
Barry, Philip James Quinn
Bateman, Sidney Frances Cowell
Baum, Lyman Frank
Behrman, Samuel Nathaniel ("S.N.")
Belasco, David
Bernard, William Bayle
Biggers, Earl Derr
Bird, Robert Montgomery
Blitzstein, Marc
Boker, George Henry
Boucicault, Dion
Bradford, Gamaliel
Bradford, Joseph
Brougham, John
Brown, David Paul
Burgess, Frank Gelett
Burk, John Daly
Burke, Charles St. Thomas
Campbell, Bartley
Canonge, Louis Placide
Carleton, Henry Guy
Chase, Ilke
Clarke, Joseph Ignatius Constantine
Cohan, George Michael
Cohen, Octavus Roy
Colum, Padraic
Connelly, Marcus Cook ("Marc")
Conrad, Robert Taylor
Cowl, Jane
Craven, Frank
Crothers, Rachel
Crouse, Russel McKinley
Crowne, John
Custis, George Washington Parke
Daly, John Augustin
Davis, Owen Gould
Davis, Richard Harding
Deering, Nathaniel
Dell, Floyd James
DeMille, Cecil Blount
De Mille, Henry Churchill
Dickinson, Anna Elizabeth
Ditrichstein, Leo
Dodd, Lee Wilson
Dunlap, William
Durivage, Francis Alexander
Elliott, Sarah Barnwell
English, Thomas Dunn
Epstein, Philip G.
Ferber, Edna Jessica
Field, Joseph M.
Finn, Henry James William
Fitch, William Clyde
Fitzgerald, Thomas
Flanagan, Hallie
Gayler, Charles
Gillette, William Hooker
Godfrey, Thomas
Golden, John
Goodman, Kenneth Sawyer
Goodrich, Frank Boott
Gordin, Jacob
Gunter, Archibald Clavering
Hamilton, Clayton
Hansberry, Lorraine Vivian
Harby, Isaac
Harrigan, Edward
Hart, Moss
Hazelton, George Cochrane
Hecht, Ben
Helburn, Theresa
Herbert, Frederick Hugh
Herne, James A.
Heyward, DuBose
Hill, Frederic Stanhope
Hirschbein, Peretz
Hodge, William Thomas
Hopwood, Avery
Howard, Bronson Crocker
Howard, Sidney Coe
Hoyt, Charles Hale
Hughes, James Langston
Inge, William Motter
Ioor, William
Jones, Joseph Stevens
Jordan, Kate
Judah, Samuel Benjamin Helbert
Kaufman, George S.
Kelly, George Edward
Kester, Paul
Klein, Charles
Kreymborg, Alfred Francis
Lacy, Ernest
Langner, Lawrence
Lennox, Charlotte Ramsay
Lindsay, Howard
Lindsey, William
Logan, Cornelius Ambrosius
Long, John Luther
MacArthur, Charles Gordon
McCarroll, James
McCullers, Carson
MacKaye, James Morrison Steele
MacKaye, Percy Wallace
Mankiewicz, Herman Jacob
Mann, Louis
Manners, John Hartley
Markoe, Peter
Marquis, Donald Robert Perry
Megrue, Roi Cooper
Miles, George Henry
Mitchell, Langdon Elwyn
Mitchell, Thomas Gregory
Mitchell, William, 1798–1856
Moody, William Vaughn
Morehouse, Ward
Munford, Robert
Murdoch, Frank Hitchcock
Nash, Frederick Ogden
Noah, Mordecai Manuel
Odets, Clifford
O'Neill, Eugene
Osborn, Laughton
Parker, Dorothy Rothschild
Payne, John Howard
Peabody, Josephine Preston
Pollock, Channing
Potter, Paul Meredith
Powell, Thomas
Pray, Isaac Clark
Presbrey, Eugene Wiley
Price, William Thompson
Randall, Samuel
Rice, Elmer
Sargent, Epes
Schomer, Nahum Meir
Séjour, Victor
Sherwood, Robert Emmet
Skinner, Cornelia Otis
Smith, Betty
Smith, Harry James
Smith, Richard Penn
Smith, Winchell
Spewack, Samuel
Stewart, Donald Ogden
Stone, John Augustus
Sturges, Preston
Tarkington, Booth
Thomas, Augustus
Thompson, Denman
Torrence, Frederick Ridgely
Tyler, Royall
Vallentine, Benjamin Bennaton
Van Druten, John William
Walcott, Charles Melton, 1816–1868
Walker, Stuart Armstrong
Wallack, Lester
Walter, Eugene
Ward, Thomas
Warren, Mercy Otis
West, Mae
White, John Blake
Wilder, Thornton Niven
Williams, Jesse Lynch
Willis, Nathaniel Parker
Wilson, Harry Leon
Wodehouse, Pelham Grenville
Woodworth, Samuel
Young, Stark

DRUG ADDICTION RESEARCH PIONEER
Kolb, Lawrence

DRUGGIST (See also APOTHECARY, PHARMACIST)
Browne, Benjamin Frederick
Lawrence, George Newbold

DRUMMER
Jones, Lindley Armstrong ("Spike")
Krupa, Eugene Bertram ("Gene")

EAST ASIAN AFFAIRS EXPERT
Greene, Roger Sherman
ECOLOGIST (See also CONSERVATIONIST)
Carson, Rachel Louise
Clements, Frederic Edward
Leopold, (Rand) Aldo
ECONOMIC ADVISER
Coe, Virginius ("Frank")
ECONOMIST (See also HOME ECONOMIST)
Adams, Henry Carter
Adams, Thomas Sewall
Anderson, Benjamin McAlester
Andrew, Abram Piatt
Andrews, John Bertram
Atkinson, Edward
Ayres, Leonard Porter
Barnett, George Ernest
Bigelow, Eratus Brigham
Blodget, Samuel
Callender, Guy Stevens
Cardozo, Jacob Newton
Carey, Henry Charles
Carey, Mathew
Catchings, Waddill
Chamberlin, Edward Hastings
Clark, John Bates
Clark, John Maurice
Commons, John Rogers
Conant, Charles Arthur
Corey, Lewis
Daniels, Winthrop More
Davenport, Herbert Joseph
Day, Edmund Ezra
Dean, William Henry, Jr.
Del Mar, Alexander
Dew, Thomas Roderick
Douglas, Paul Howard
Dunbar, Charles Franklin
Ely, Richard Theodore
Emery, Henry Crosby
Ensley, Enoch
Fairchild, Fred Rogers
Falkner, Roland Post
Farnam, Henry Walcott
Feis, Herbert
Fetter, Frank Albert
Fisher, Irving
Foster, William Trufant
George, Henry
Goldenweiser, Emanuel Alexander
Gordon, Kermit
Gould, Elgin Ralston Lovell
Gunton, George
Hadley, Arthur Twining
Hamilton, Walton Hale
Hansen, Alvin Harvey
Harris, Seymour Edwin
Haynes, Williams
Hollander, Jacob Harry
Horton, Samuel Dana
Hoxie, Robert Franklin
Jacoby, Neil Herman
James, Edmund James
Jenks, Jeremiah Whipple
Johnson, Harry Gordon
Jordan, Virgil Justin
Kemmerer, Edwin Walter
Knauth, Oswald Whitman
Knight, Frank Hyneman
Laughlin, James Laurence
Leiserson, William Morris
List, Georg Friedrich
Lubin, Isador
Macfarlane, Charles William
McPherson, Logan Grant
McVey, Frank Lerond
McVickar, John
Mayo-Smith, Richmond
Millis, Harry Alvin
Mitchell, Wesley Clair
Moore, Henry Ludwell
Nourse, Edwin Griswold
Olds, Leland
Page, Thomas Walker
Parker, Carleton Hubbell
Pasvolsky, Leo
Patten, Simon Nelson
Perlman, Selig
Perry, Arthur Latham
Persons, Warren Milton
Pitkin, Timothy
Poor, Henry Varnum
Rae, John
Raguet, Condy
Remington, William Walter
Riefler, Winfield William
Ripley, William Zebina
Robinson, Edward Van Dyke
Rogers, James Harvey
Sachs, Alexander
Schoenhof, Jacob
Schultz, Henry
Schumpeter, Joseph Alois
Schwab, John Christopher
Seager, Henry Rogers
Seligman, Edwin Robert Anderson
Shearman, Thomas Gaskell
Simons, Algie Martin
Simons, Henry Calvert
Slichter, Sumner Huber
Spahr, Charles Brazillai
Spillman, William Jasper
Stewart, Walter Winne
Sumner, William Graham
Taussig, Frank William
Taylor, Fred Manville
Thompson, Robert Ellis
Tucker, George
Tugwell, Rexford Guy
Vaughan, Benjamin
Veblen, Thorstein Bunde
Vethake, Henry
Viner, Jacob
Walker, Amasa
Walker, Francis Amasa
Webster, Pelatiah
Wells, David Ames
Weston, Nathan Austin
White, Horace
Wildman, Murray Shipley
Willis, Henry Parker
Wolman, Leo
Woodbury, Helen Laura Sumner
Woytinsky, Wladimir Savelievich
Wright, Philip Green
Young, Allyn Abbott
ECUMENICAL MOVEMENT LEADER
Brown, William Adams
Cavert, Samuel McCrea
ECUMENICAL PIONEER
Mott, John R.
EDITOR
Abbott, Lyman
Adams, Cyrus Cornelius
Adams, William Lysander
Aikens, Andrew Jackson
Alden, Henry Mills
Aldrich, Thomas Bailey
Allen, Frederick Lewis
Allen, Joseph Henry
Allen, Paul
Allen, Richard Lamb
Altsheler, Joseph Alexander
Ameringer, Oscar
Ames, Charles Gordon
Anderson, Margaret Carolyn
Armstrong, Hamilton Fish
Arthur, Timothy Shay
Atwood, David
Bagby, George William
Bangs, John Kendrick
Barron, Clarence Walker
Barrow, Washington
Barrows, Samuel June
Barsotti, Charles
Bartholdt, Richard
Bartlett, John
Bausman, Benjamin
Bayles, James Copper
Benét, William Rose
Benjamin, Park
Bennett, James Gordon
Bidwell, Walter Hilliard
Bigelow, John
Bird, Frederic Mayer
Bird, Robert Montgomery
Blackwell, Alice Stone
Blackwell, Henry Brown
Bledsoe, Albert Taylor
Bliss, Edwin Munsell
Bok, Edward William
Boner, John Henry
Booth, Mary Louise
Botts, Charles Tyler
Boudinot, Elias
Bowen, Henry Chandler
Bowker, Richard Rogers
Bowles, Samuel, 1797–1851
Bowles, Samuel, 1826–1878
Bowles, Samuel, 1851–1915
Brace, John Pierce
Bradwell, Myra
Brainerd, Erastus
Brainerd, Thomas
Brann, William Cowper
Brayman, Mason
Breckinridge, Desha
Breckinridge, William Campbell Preston
Brickell, Henry Herschel
Bright, Edward
Brisbane, Arthur
Bronson, Walter Cochrane
Brooks, James Gordon
Browne, Francis Fisher
Bryant, Louise Frances Stevens
Bryant, William Cullen
Buckingham, Joseph Tinker
Burlingame, Edward Livermore
Burr, Alfred Edmund
Burrage, Henry Sweetser

Butts, Isaac
Calverton, Victor Francis
Cameron, William Evelyn
Campbell, Charles
Campbell, John Wood, Jr.
Campbell, Lewis Davis
Canby, Henry Seidel
Cardozo, Jacob Newton
Carruth, Fred Hayden
Carter, John
Carter, Robert
Carter, William Hodding, Jr.
Cary, Edward
Catton, Charles Bruce
Chamberlain, Henry Richardson
Champlin, John Denison
Channing, Edward Tyrrell
Chase, Edna Woolman
Childs, Cephas Grier
Church, William Conant
Cist, Charles
Claiborne, John Francis Hamtramck
Clark, Charles Hopkins
Clark, Lewis Gaylord
Clark, Willis Gaylord
Clarke, Helen Archibald
Clarkson, Coker Fifield
Cobb, Frank Irving
Coffin, Robert Peter Tristram
Cohen, John Sanford
Colby, Frank Moore
Colver, William Byron
Cook, Martha Elizabeth Duncan Walker
Corcoran, James Andrew
Cornwallis, Kinahan
Costain, Thomas Bertram
Covici, Pascal ("Pat")
Croly, Herbert David
Crooks, George Richard
Croswell, Harry
Crowninshield, Francis Welch
Cunliffe-Owen, Philip Frederick
Dana, Charles Anderson
Dana, Edward Salisbury
Daniels, Josephus
Dart, Henry Paluché
Davenport, Russell Wheeler
Davis, Paulina Kellogg Wright
Davis, Watson
Dawson, Henry Barton
De Bow, James Dunwoody Brownson
Deering, Nathaniel
Dell, Floyd James
Dennie, Joseph
De Young, Michel Harry
Dingley, Nelson
Dodge, Mary Elizabeth Mapes
Dole, Nathan Haskell
Doyle, Alexander Patrick
Drake, Benjamin
Drury, John Benjamin
Du Bois, William Edward Burghardt
Dunbar, Charles Franklin
Dunning, Albert Elijah
Duyckinck, Evert Augustus
Duyckinck, George Long
Dwight, Henry Otis
Dwight, John Sullivan
Dwight, Theodore
Dymond, John
Edwards, Bela Bates
Elliot, Jonathan
Elliott, Charles
Ellmaker, (Emmett) Lee
Elwell, John Johnson
English, Thomas Dunn
Errett, Isaac
Evans, George Henry
Evans, Thomas
Everett, Alexander Hill
Fanning, Tolbert
Faran, James John
Farley, Harriet
Farrar, John Chipman
Fauset, Jessie Redmon
Fenno, John
Fernald, James Champlin
Fernow, Berthold
Finley, John Huston
Fiske, Amos Kidder
Fiske, Daniel Willard
Fitzgerald, Thomas
Fitzpatrick, John Clement
Flagg, Azariah Cutting
Fleisher, Benjamin Wilfrid
Florence, Thomas Birch
Flower, Benjamin Orange
Floy, James
Fogg, George Gilman
Folsom, Charles
Ford, Daniel Sharp
Ford, Guy Stanton
Ford, Henry Jones
Forney, Matthias Nace
Foster, Charles James
Foster, Frank Pierce
Foster, John Watson
Foster, Lafayette Sabine
Francis, Charles Spencer
Francis, John Morgan
Frank, Glenn
Frazer, John Fries
Freneau, Philip Morin
Fuller, Andrew S.
Fuller, Joseph Vincent
Funk, Isaac Kauffman
Gaillard, Edwin Samuel
Gallagher, William Davis
Gambrell, James Bruton
Gernsback, Hugo
Gibbs, (Oliver) Wolcott
Gilder, Jeannette Leonard
Gilder, Richard Watson
Gildersleeve, Basil Lanneau
Giles, Chauncey
Gillis, James Martin
Gilpin, Henry Dilworth
Gitt, Josiah Williams ("Jess")
Glass, Franklin Potts
Glynn, Martin Henry
Godkin, Edwin Lawrence
Godman, John Davison
Godwin, Parke
Goodhue, James Madison
Goodwin, Elijah
Gordon, Laura De Force
Gould, George Milbry
Graham, George Rex
Grasty, Charles Henry
Greeley, Horace
Green, Thomas
Greene, Nathaniel
Gregory, Daniel Seelye
Griffin, Solomon Bulkley
Griswold, Stanley
Grosvenor, Gilbert Hovey
Gruening, Ernest
Gunton, George
Habberton, John
Hackett, Francis
Hahn, Georg Michael Decker
Haines, Lynn
Haldeman-Julius, Emanuel
Hale, Edward Joseph
Hale, Sarah Josepha Buell
Hall, John Elihu
Hall, William Whitty
Hallett, Benjamin Franklin
Hanson, Alexander Contee, 1786–1819
Hapgood, Norman
Harris, Chapin Aaron
Harris, Joseph
Hart, Edward
Hart, John Seely
Harvey, George Brinton McClellan
Hasbrouck, Lydia Sayer
Hasselquist, Tuve Nilsson
Haswell, Anthony
Haven, Emily Bradley Neal
Hawley, Joseph Roswell
Hayes, Max Sebastian
Hays, Isaac
Hazard, Ebenezer
Hazard, Samuel
Heaton, John Langdon
Helmer, Bessie Bradwell
Hepworth, George Hughes
Herbermann, Charles George
Herrick, Sophia McIlvaine Bledsoe
Hewett, Waterman Thomas
Hicks, John, 1847–1917
High, Stanley Hoflund
Hildreth, Richard
Hill, Isaac
Hinman, George Wheeler
Hinsdale, Burke Aaron
Hoard, William Dempster
Hobby, William Pettus
Hodgins, Eric Francis
Hoffman, Charles Fenno
Holland, Josiah Gilbert
Holmes, Ezekiel
Holt, Hamilton Bowen
Hooker, Donald Russell
Hooper, Lucy Hamilton
Horr, George Edwin
Howard, Edgar
Howe, Mark Antony De Wolfe
Howell, Evan Park
Howell, James Bruen
Hubbard, Elbert
Hudson, Daniel Eldred
Hughes, Robert William
Hunt, Freeman
Hunt, William Gibbes
Huntington, Jedediah Vincent
Hunton, George Kenneth
Hunton, William Lee
Hurlbut, Jesse Lyman

Hutchinson, Paul
Hutton, Laurence
Inman, John
Jackson, Henry Rootes
Jackson, Joseph Henry
Jameson, John Franklin
Jarves, James Jackson
Jenkins, Howard Malcolm
Jenkins, John Stilwell
Jeter, Jeremiah Bell
Johnson, Allen
Johnson, John Albert
Johnson, Oliver
Johnson, Robert Underwood
Johnson, Willis Fletcher
Jones, Jenkins Lloyd
Jones, Thomas P.
Jordan, John Woolf
Jordan, William George
Joseffy, Rafael
Kaempffert, Waldemar
Bernhard
Keating, John Marie
Kellogg, Paul Underwood
Kent, William
Kephart, Isaiah Lafayette
Kerney, James
Kettell, Samuel
Keyes, Frances Parkinson
King, Alexander
King, Charles
King, Horatio
King, Rufus
King of William, James
Kinsella, Thomas
Kirchoff, Charles William Henry
Kirk, John Foster
Kline, George
Knopf, Blanche Wolf
Kohlsaat, Herman Henry
Kreymborg, Alfred Francis
Kronenberger, Louis, Jr.
Kurtz, Benjamin
LaFarge, John
Lamb, Martha Joanna Reade
Nash
Lamont, Hammond
Lane, Gertrude Battles
Lange, Louis
Lathrop, George Parsons
Lawrence, David
Lawson, James
Learned, Marion Dexter
Leavitt, Joshua
Lee, James Melvin
Lee, James Wideman
Leeser, Isaac
Levin, Lewis Charles
Lewis, Charlton Thomas
Lewis, Enoch
Lewisohn, Ludwig
Liggett, Walter William
Linn, William Alexander
Littell, Eliakim
Littledale, Clara Savage
Loos, Charles Louis
Lord, Chester Sanders
Lossing, Benson John
Loveman, Amy
Lovett, Robert Morss
Luce, Henry Robinson
Lummis, Charles Fletcher
Mabie, Hamilton Wright
McAdams, Clark
MacArthur, Robert Stuart
McCaw, James Brown
M'Clintock, John
McClure, Alexander Kelly
McClure, Alexander Wilson
McClure, Samuel Sidney
McCord, David James
McCullough, Ernest
McElroy, John
McKelway, St. Clair
McKinley, Albert Edward
Maclay, William Brown
McLeod, Alexander
McMichael, Morton
McPherson, Edward
McQuillen, John Hugh
Mansfield, Edward Deering
Marble, Manton Malone
Marsh, Charles Wesley
Martin, Franklin Henry
Martin, Thomas Commerford
Masson, Thomas Lansing
Mead, Edwin Doak
Medary, Samuel
Meigs, Josiah
Melcher, Frederic Gershom
Mencken, Henry Louis
Merrill, William Bradford
Metcalf, Henry Harrison
Mich, Daniel Danforth
Miller, Charles Ransom
Miller, David Hunter
Miller, Emily Clark Huntington
Miller, James Russell
Miller, John Henry
Miner, Charles
Minor, Benjamin Blake
Mitchell, Edward Page
Mitchell, Isaac
Mitchell, John Ames
Money, Hernando De Soto
Monroe, Harriet
Montgomery, William Bell
Moody, John
Moore, Frank
Moore, John Weeks
Morley, Christopher Darlington
Morris, Edmund
Morse, John Torrey
Morton, Charles Walter
Moses, Montrose Jonas
Mosessohn, David Nehemiah
Moss, Lemuel
Munn, Orson Desaix
Muñoz-Rivera, Luis
Nancrède, Paul Joseph Guérard
de
Nast, William
Nathan, George Jean
Neal, John
Nelson, Henry Loomis
Nevin, Alfred
Newcomb, Harvey
Newell, William Wells
Newton, Robert Safford
Ng Poon Chew
Nichols, Clarina Irene Howard
Nichols, Thomas Low
Nicola, Lewis
Nieman, Lucius William
Niles, Hezekiah
Niles, John Milton
Nock, Albert Jay
North, Simon Newton Dexter
Northen, William Jonathan
Norton, Charles Eliot
Oakes, George Washington
Ochs
O'Brien, Robert Lincoln
Ogg, Frederic Austin
Older, Fremont
O'Reilly, Henry
O'Reilly, John Boyle
Osborn, Norris Galpin
Otis, George Alexander
Oursler, (Charles) Fulton
Packard, Frederick Adolphus
Packer, William Fisher
Paley, John
Palfrey, John Gorham
Pallen, Condé Benoist
Palmore, William Beverly
Parkhurst, Charles
Passavant, William Alfred
Patterson, Robert Mayne
Patterson, Thomas MacDonald
Paul, Elliot Harold
Payne, John Howard
Peck, George
Peck, Harry Thurston
Pedder, James
Peirce, Bradford Kinney
Peloubet, Francis Nathan
Pendleton, William Kimbrough
Perché, Napoleon Joseph
Perkins, Frederic Beecher
Perkins, George Douglas
Perkins, Maxwell Evarts
Perry, Bliss
Peters, Absalom
Peterson, Charles Jacobs
Peterson, Henry
Phillips, John Sanburn
Pickard, Samuel Thomas
Pierson, Arthur Tappan
Pilcher, Lewis Stephen
Pinckney, Henry Laurens
Pinkerton, Lewis Letig
Pinkney, Edward Coote
Polk, Leonidas Lafayette
Pollak, Gustav
Pomeroy, Marcus Mills
Pond, George Edward
Poore, Benjamin Perley
Potter, William James
Powell, John Benjamin
Pratt, Eliza Anna Farman
Pratt, Sereno Stansbury
Presser, Theodore
Price, Thomas Frederick
Prime, Samuel Irenaeus
Pulitzer, Joseph, Jr.
Purple, Samuel Smith
Putnam, Eben
Quick, John Herbert
Raguet, Condy
Rahv, Philip
Raymond, Henry Jarvis
Raymond, Rossiter Worthington
Redman, Ben Ray
Redpath, James
Reed, David

Reid, Gilbert
Reid, John Morrison
Reiersen, Johan Reinert
Reitzel, Robert
Rémy, Henri
Rhoades, James E.
Rice, Edwin Wilbur
Rideing, William Henry
Ripley, George
Robertson, James Alexander
Robinson, Charles Seymour
Robinson, Stuart
Rombro, Jacob
Rorty, James Hancock
Ross, Charles Griffith
Ross, Harold Wallace
Rothwell, Richard Pennefather
Rowlands, William
Rublee, Horace
Rupp, William
Sanders, Daniel Jackson
Sanger, George Partridge
Sangster, Margaret Elizabeth Munson
Saunders, William Laurence
Sawyer, Thomas Jefferson
Saxton, Eugene Francis
Schem, Alexander Jacob
Schnauffer, Carl Heinrich
Schouler, William
Schultze, Augustus
Schuster, Max Lincoln
Schuyler, Robert Livingston
Schwimmer, Rosika
Scott, Harvey Whitefield
Screws, William Wallace
Scudder, Horace Elisha
Scull, John
Seymour, Horatio Winslow
Shattuck, George Brune
Shea, John Dawson Gilmary
Sherwood, Isaac Ruth
Shields, George Oliver
Shreve, Thomas Hopkins
Sigel, Franz
Silverman, Sime
Simpson, Stephen
Singerly, William Miskey
Singleton, Esther
Sloan, Harold Paul
Smalley, Eugene Virgil
Smith, Benjamin Eli
Smith, Charles Perrin
Smith, Edmund Munroe
Smith, Elias
Smith, Elihu Hubbard
Smith, John Augustine
Smith, John Cotton, 1826–1882
Smith, John Jay
Smith, Lillian Eugenia
Smith, Lloyd Pearsall
Smith, Mildred Catharine
Smith, Samuel Francis
Smith, Uriah
Smyth, Albert Henry
Snow, Carmel White
Spahr, Charles Barzillai
Sparks, Jared
Spivak, Charles David
Spooner, Shearjashub
Sprague, Charles Arthur
Stanard, William Glover
Stanwood, Edward
Stauffer, David McNeely
Stedman, Edmund Clarence
Stephens, Ann Sophia
Stephens, Edwin William
Steuben, John
Stevens, Abel
Stoddard, Richard Henry
Stoddart, Joseph Marshall
Stone, David Marvin
Stone, Richard French
Storey, Wilbur Fisk
Stovall, Pleasant Alexander
Street, Joseph Montfort
Stuart, Charles Macaulay
Summers, Thomas Osmond
Swisshelm, Jane Grey Cannon
Talmage, Thomas De Witt
Taylor, Marshall William
Teall, Francis Augustus
Tenney, William Jewett
Thatcher, Benjamin Bussey
Thayer, Thomas Baldwin
Thayer, William Makepeace
Thomas, John Jacobs
Thomas, Robert Bailey
Thompson, John Reuben
Thompson, Joseph Parrish
Thompson, Thomas Larkin
Thompson, William Tappan
Thomson, Edward
Thomson, Edward William
Thrasher, John Sidney
Thurber, George
Thurston, Lorrin Andrews
Thwaites, Reuben Gold
Tigert, John James
Tilton, Theodore
Todd, Henry Alfred
Torrence, Frederick Ridgely
Towne, Charles Hanson
Tracy, Joseph
Trumbull, Henry Clay
Tucker, Gilbert Milligan
Turner, George Kibbe
Turner, Henry McNeal
Turner, Josiah
Tyler, Robert
Underwood, Benjamin Franklin
Untermeyer, Louis
Updegraff, David Brainard
Vanderlip, Frank Arthur
Van Doren, Irita Bradford
Villard, Oswald Garrison
Vizetelly, Frank Horace
Vogrich, Max Wilhelm Karl
Walker, James Barr
Wallace, Henry
Waller, John Lightfoot
Walsh, Henry Collins
Walsh, Michael
Walsh, Thomas
Ward, Cyrenus Osborne
Ware, Ashur
Ware, John
Warner, Charles Dudley
Warren, Israel Perkins
Watson, Henry Clay
Watson, Henry Cood
Watterson, Harvey Magee
Watterson, Henry
Wellington, Arthur Mellen
Wentworth, John, 1815–1888
Wertenbaker, Charles Christian
Wharton, Francis
Whedon, Daniel Denison
Wheelock, John Hall
Wheelock, Joseph Albert
Whelpley, Henry Milton
Whitaker, Charles Harris
Whitaker, Daniel Kimball
White, Charles Ignatius
White, William Allen
White, William Nathaniel
Whitney, Caspar
Whittelsey, Abigail Goodrich
Whittemore, Thomas
Wiggin, James Henry
Willcox, Louise Collier
Williams, Charles Richard
Williams, Jesse Lynch
Willis, Henry Parker
Willis, Nathaniel
Willis, Nathaniel Parker
Wilson, George Grafton
Wilson, James Grant
Wilson, James Southall
Winchester, Caleb Thomas
Winchevsky, Morris
Winkler, Edwin Theodore
Winship, Albert Edward
Wise, Daniel
Woodruff, Lorande Loss
Woodruff, William Edward
Worcester, Noab
Wright, John Stephen
Wright, Marcus Joseph
Wright, Robert William
Wurtz, Henry
Wyeth, John
Yeadon, Richard
Yost, Casper Salathiel
Youmans, Edward Livingston
Youmans, William Jay
Young, Jesse Bowman
Young, Lafayette
Zahniser, Howard Clinton
Zevin, Israel Joseph
Ziff, William Bernard

EDITOR (AGRICULTURAL) (See also AGRICULTURIST)
Aiken, David Wyatt
Brown, Simon
Coburn, Foster Dwight
Gaylord, Willis
Judd, Orange
Myrick, Herbert
Skinner, John Stuart
Stockbridge, Horace Edward
Wiley, David

EDITOR (ANARCHIST)
Goldman, Emma

EDITOR (MAGAZINE)
Bliven, Bruce Ormsby
Brady, Mildred Alice Edie
Goodman, Paul
Kirchwey, Freda
Lorimer, George Horace
Patrick, Edwin Hill ("Ted")
Patterson, Alicia
Sedgwick, Ellery
Woodward, Robert Simpson

EDITOR (MEDICAL)
Ingelfinger, Franz Joseph

Jelliffe, Smith Ely
Simmons, George Henry
EDITOR (NEWSPAPER)
Abbott, Robert Sengstacke
Bingay, Malcolm Wallace
Bovard, Oliver Kirby
Brokenshire, Norman Ernest
Freeman, Douglas Southall
Gauvreau, Emile Henry
Goddard, Morrill
Howard, Joseph Kinsey
Howe, Edgar Watson
Howell, Clark
Johnson, Albert
Lait, Jacquin Leonard (Jack)
McClatchy, Charles Kenny
Ogden, Rollo
Patterson, Eleanor Medill
Pulitzer, Ralph
Reid, Ogden Mills
Shedd, Fred Fuller
Smith, Henry Justin
EDITOR (SCIENCE)
Blakeslee, Howard Walter
Cattell, James McKeen
Woodward, Robert Simpson
EDUCATOR (See also COLLEGE PRESIDENT, PROFESSOR, SCHOLAR, TEACHER)
Abbot, Benjamin
Abbot, Gorham Dummer
Abbott, Edith
Abbott, Jacob
Adams, Daniel
Adams, Ebenezer
Adams, John
Adler, Felix
Agassiz, Elizabeth Cabot Cary
Aggrey, James Emman Kwegyir
Aiken, Charles Augustus
Akeley, Mary Leonore
Alcott, Amos Bronson
Alcott, William Andrus
Alden, Joseph
Alderman, Edwin Anderson
Aldrich, Charles Anderson
Alexander, Archibald
Alexander, Joseph Addison
Alison, Francis
Allen, Alexander Viets Griswold
Allen, George
Allen, James Edward, Jr.
Allen, William
Allen, Young John
Allinson, Anne Crosby Emery
Allyn, Robert
Alvord, Henry Elijah
Ames, Herman Vandenburg
Ames, James Barr
Anderson, David Lawrence
Anderson, Victor Vance
Andrews, John
Andrews, Lorrin
Andrus, Ethel Percy
Angela, Mother
Anthon, Charles Edward
Apple, Thomas Gilmore
Appleton, Jesse
Armstrong, Samuel Chapman
Arnold, Thurman Wesley
Atkinson, George Henry
Atwater, Lyman Hotchkiss
Azarias, Brother
Backus, Truman Jay
Bagley, William Chandler
Bailey, Ebenezer
Bailey, Liberty Hyde
Baker, Daniel
Baldwin, Elihu Whittlesey
Baldwin, Joseph
Baldwin, Theron
Bancroft, Cecil Franklin Patch
Banister, Zilpah Polly Grant
Bapst, John
Barbour, Clarence Augustus
Bardeen, Charles William
Barnard, Henry
Barnes, Mary Downing Sheldon
Barnwell, Robert Woodward
Barrett, Janie Porter
Bateman, Newton
Bates, Arlo
Bates, Katharine Lee
Bates, Samuel Penniman
Baxter, William
Beadle, William Henry Harrison
Beals, Ralph Albert
Beard, Mary
Beard, Richard
Beatty, Willard Walcott
Beckwith, Clarence Augustine
Beecher, Catharine Esther
Beers, Henry Augustin
Belkin, Samuel
Bell, Alexander Graham
Bell, Alexander Melville
Bell, Bernard Iddings
Bell, Eric Temple
Bemis, Harold Edward
Benedict, Erastus Cornelius
Benson, Oscar Herman
Benton, Thomas Hart
Berry, Edward Wilber
Berry, Martha McChesney
Bestor, Arthur Eugene
Bickel, Alexander Mordecai
Bickmore, Albert Smith
Bigelow, Harry Augustus
Bigelow, Melville Madison
Bingham, William
Binkley, Wilfred Ellsworth
Bishop, Nathan
Bishop, Robert Hamilton
Blalock, Alfred
Blaustein, David
Bliss, Daniel
Bliss, Gilbert Ames
Bliss, Howard Sweetser
Bode, Boyd Henry
Bond, Elizabeth Powell
Bonney, Charles Carroll
Bontemps, Arna Wendell
Bosworth, Edward Increase
Bourne, Edward Gaylord
Bowden, John
Bowman, Thomas
Boyce, James Petigru
Boyd, David French
Boyd, Thomas Duckett
Boyesen, Hjalmar Hjorth
Brace, John Pierce
Brackett, Anna Callender
Brackett, Jeffrey Richardson
Bradford, Edward Hickling
Bradley, Charles Henry
Brainard, Daniel
Brainerd, Ezra
Brattle, William
Breaux, Joseph Arsenne
Briggs, LeBaron Russell
Brigham, Mary Ann
Brightman, Edgar Sheffield
Bronson, Walter Cochrane
Brookings, Robert Somers
Brooks, Charles
Brough, Charles Hillman
Brown, Charles Rufus
Brown, Charlotte Hawkins
Brown, George
Brown, George Pliny
Brown, Samuel Robbins
Browne, William Hand
Bruce, Robert
Brumby, Richard Trapier
Bryant, Joseph Decatur
Bryant, Ralph Clement
Bryson, Lyman Lloyd
Buchanan, Joseph
Buchanan, Scott Milross
Budenz, Louis Francis
Buehler, Huber Gray
Bulkley, John Williams
Bumstead, Horace
Bunche, Ralph Johnson
Burk, Frederic Lister
Burleson, Rufus Clarence
Burnam, John Miller
Burr, William Hubert
Burroughs, John Curtis
Burrowes, Thomas Henry
Burt, Mary Elizabeth
Buttrick, Wallace
Buttz, Henry Anson
Cabell, James Lawrence
Cady, Sarah Louise Ensign
Caldwell, Otis William
Calhoun, William Barron
Calkins, Norman Allison
Camp, David Nelson
Canby, Henry Seidel
Canfield, James Hulme
Cannon, James
Capen, Samuel Paul
Carmichael, Oliver Cromwell
Carnap, Rudolf
Carpenter, George Rice
Carpenter, Stephen Haskins
Carter, James Gordon
Carver, George Washington
Chamberlain, Joshua Lawrence
Chamberlin, Edward Hastings
Chandler, Julian Alvin Carroll
Channing, Edward Tyrrell
Chase, Harry Woodburn
Chase, Irah
Chase, Mary Ellen
Chavis, John
Cheever, Ezekiel
Church, Alonzo
Church, Irving Porter
Clapp, Margaret Antoinette
Clark, Felton Grandison
Clark, Walter Van Tilburg
Claypole, Edward Waller
Clement, Rufus Early
Clewell, John Henry

Cloud, Henry Roe
Clyde, George Dewey
Cobb, Lyman
Coe, George Albert
Coffin, Henry Sloane
Coffman, Lotus Delta
Colburn, Dana Pond
Cole, Charles Woolsey
Coleman, Lyman
Colton, Elizabeth Avery
Colvin, Stephen Sheldon
Conklin, Edwin Grant
Conover, Obadiah Milton
Cook, George Hammell
Cook, John Williston
Cooley, Edwin Gilbert
Cooley, Mortimer Elwyn
Cooper, Thomas
Cooper, William John
Cooper-Poucher, Matilda S.
Coppée, Henry
Coppens, Charles
Cordier, Andrew Wellington
Cox, Samuel Hanson
Craig, Austin
Craighead, Edwin Boone
Crandall, Prudence
Crary, Isaac Edwin
Crooks, George Richard
Crunden, Frederick Morgan
Cubberley, Ellwood Patterson
Curry, Jabez Lamar Monroe
Curtis, Edwards Lewis
Dagg, John Leadley
Daniels, Farrington
Darby, John
Davis, John Warren
Dawley, Almena
Day, Edmund Ezra
Day, Henry Noble
Day, James Roscoe
Day, Jeremiah
Dean, Amos
Denny, George Vernon, Jr.
Deutsch, Gotthard
Dewey, Chester
Dewey, John
Dickinson, John
Dickinson, John Woodbridge
Dickson, Leonard Eugene
Dillard, James Hardy
Diman, Jeremiah Lewis
Dimitry, Alexander
Dinwiddie, Albert Bledsoe
Doak, Samuel
Dod, Thaddeus
Dodge, Ebenezer
Donovan, James Britt
Dorchester, Daniel
Douglas, Aaron
Dove, David James
Downey, John
Draper, Andrew Sloan
Drinker, Cecil Kent
Drisler, Henry
Drown, Thomas Messinger
Dunham, Henry Morton
Dutton, Samuel Train
Dwight, Benjamin Woodbridge
Dwight, Francis
Dwight, Nathaniel
Dwight, Sereno Edwards
Dwight, Theodore, 1796–1866
Dwight, Theodore WIlliam
Dwight, Timothy
Dyer, Isadore
Dykstra, Clarence Addison
Earle, Edward Mead
Earle, Mortimer Lamson
Earle, Ralph
Eastman, Harvey Gridley
Eaton, Amos
Eaton, John
Edwards, Ninian Wirt
Eigenmann, Carl H.
Eiseley, Loren Corey
Eliot, Charles William
Elliott, William Yandell, III
Elman, Robert
Elvehjem, Conrad Arnold
Emerson, Benjamin Kendall
Emerson, George Barrell
Emerson, Joseph
Emerton, Ephraim
Erdman, Charles Rosenbury
Esbjörn, Lars Paul
Espy, James Pollard
Ewell, Benjamin Stoddert
Fairchild, Fred Rogers
Fairchild, George Thompson
Fairchild, James Harris
Fairfield, Edmund Burke
Fairlie, John Archibald
Fanning, Tolbert
Fay, Sidney Bradshaw
Ferguson, John Calvin
Ferris, Woodbridge Nathan
Fess, Simeon Davidson
Few, William Preston
Fieser, Louis Frederick
Fillebrown, Thomas
Finley, John Huston
Finley, Robert
Finn, Francis James
Finney, Charles Grandison
Fisher, Ebenezer
Fisk, Wilbur
Fiske, George Converse
Fite, Warner
Fitzpatrick, Morgan Cassius
Fleming, Walter Lynwood
Fletcher, Robert
Flexner, Abraham
Follen, Charles
Ford, Guy Stanton
Fortier, Alcée
Foss, Cyrus David
Foster, George Burman
Fowle, William Bentley
Frame, Alice Seymour Browne
Francis, Convers
Frank, Philipp G.
Frazier, Edward Franklin
Frear, William
Friedlaender, Walter Ferdinand
Frissell, Hollis Burke
Fuertes, Estevan Antonio
Furman, Richard
Furst, Clyde Bowman
Gale, George Washington
Galloway, Samuel
Gambrell, James Bruton
Garland, Landon Cabell
Garnet, Henry Highland
Garnett, James Mercer
Garrett, William Robertson
Gasson, Thomas Ignatius
Gates, George Augustus
Gauss, Christian Frederick
Giddings, Franklin Henry
Giesler-Anneke, Mathilde Franziska
Gildersleeve, Virginia Crocheron
Gill, Laura Drake
Gillespie, William Mitchell
Gillett, Ezra Hall
Gilman, Arthur
Gilmer, Francis Walker
Gödel, Kurt Friedrich
Going, Jonathan
Goldbeck, Robert
Goodale, George Lincoln
Goodell, Henry Hill
Goodnow, Isaac Tichenor
Goodrich, Annie Warburton
Goodrich, Chauncey Allen
Goodrich, Elizur
Goodspeed, Thomas Wakefield
Gordy, John Pancoast
Goss, James Walker
Gottschalk, Louis Reichenthal
Gove, Aaron Estellus
Grady, Henry Francis
Graham, Evarts Ambrose
Graham, Frank Porter
Gray, John Chipman
Gray, William Scott, Jr.
Green, Lewis Warner
Green, Samuel Bowdlear
Greene, Charles Ezra
Greene, George Washington
Greene, Samuel Stillman
Greener, Richard Theodore
Greenlaw, Edwin Almiron
Greenleaf, Benjamin
Gregg, Alan
Gregory, Charles Noble
Gregory, Daniel Seelye
Gregory, John Milton
Griffis, William Elliot
Grimké, Thomas Smith
Gros, John Daniel
Gross, Charles
Grossmann, Louis
Guérin, Anne-Thérèse
Guilford, Nathan
Gurney, Ephraim Whitman
Guthe, Karl Eugen
Haagen-Smit, Arie Jan
Haas, Francis Joseph
Haddock, Charles Brickett
Hale, Benjamin
Hall, Arethusa
Hall, Baynard Rush
Hall, Granville Stanley
Hall, Samuel Read
Hall, Willard
Hallowell, Benjamin
Hamlin, Cyrus
Hamlin, Talbot Faulkner
Hammond, William Gardiner
Hanus, Paul Henry
Hare, George Emlen
Harlow, Ralph Volney
Harper, William Rainey
Harpur, Robert

Harrell, John
Harrington, Charles
Harris, George
Harris, Samuel
Harris, William Torrey
Harrison, Charles Custis
Hart, Edward
Hart, John Seely
Hartranft, Chester David
Hasselquist, Tuve Nilsson
Haven, Erastus Otis
Hawkins, Dexter Arnold
Hawley, Gideon, 1785–1870
Hawley, Willis Chatman
Hayden, Amos Sutton
Haygood, Atticus Green
Heiss, Michael
Henck, John Benjamin
Henry, Caleb Sprague
Henry, Robert
Hewett, Waterman Thomas
Hibben, John Grier
Hill, Daniel Harvey
Hill, Frank Alpine
Hill, Henry Barker
Hill, John Henry
Hill, Patty Smith
Hill, Walter Barnard
Hills, Elijah Clarence
Himes, Charles Francis
Hinman, George Wheeler
Hinsdale, Burke Aaron
Hitchcock, Edward, 1793–1864
Hitchcock, Edward, 1828–1911
Hitchcock, Roswell Dwight
Hocking, William Ernest
Hoerr, Normand Louis
Hoffman, Eugene Augustus
Hoge, Moses
Hogue, Wilson Thomas
Horbrook, Alfred
Holcombe, James Philemon
Holland, William Jacob
Holley, Horace
Hollis, Ira Nelson
Holmes, Ezekiel
Holmes, George Frederick
Hope, John
Hopkins, Isaac Stiles
Hopkins, Mark
Horr, George Edwin
Hoshour, Samuel Klinefelter
Houston, David Franklin
Houston, Edwin James
Hovey, Alvah
Hovey, Charles Edward
Howard, Ada Lydia
Howe, George
Howe, Herbert Alonzo
Howland, Emily
Hoyt, John Wesley
Huber, Gotthelf Carl
Humphreys, Alexander Crombie
Hunt, Carleton
Hunt, Mary Hannah Hanchett
Hunt, Nathan
Hunter, Thomas
Huntington, Margaret Jane Evans
Hutchins, Harry Burns
Hutchins, Robert Maynard
Hyde, William DeWitt
Inglis, Alexander James
Irvine, William Mann
Irwin, Elisabeth Antoinette
Irwin, Robert Benjamin
Jackman, Wilbur Samuel
Jackson, Dugald Caleb
Jackson, Edward Payson
Jackson, Mercy Ruggles Bisbe
Jacobi, Mary Corinna Putnam
Jacobs, Michael
Jacobson, John Christian
Janes, Lewis George
Jaquess, James Frazier
Jardine, William Marion
Jay, Allen
Jeffrey, Edward Charles
Jesse, Richard Henry
Jessup, Walter Albert
Jewett, Milo Parker
Johnson, Alvin Saunders
Johnson, Charles Spurgeon
Johnson, David Bancroft
Johnson, Edward Austin
Johnson, Ellen Cheney
Johnson, Franklin
Johnson, George
Johnson, James Weldon
Johnson, Joseph French
Johnson, Wendell Andrew Leroy
Johnson, William Bullein
Johnston, Henry Phelps
Johnston, Richard Malcolm
Johnston, Robert Matteson
Johnston, William Preston
Johnstone, Edward Ransom
Jones, Richard Foster
Jones, William Patterson
Joynes, Edward Southey
Judson, Harry Pratt
Julia, Sister
Junkin, George
Kafer, John Christian
Kallen, Horace Meyer
Keagy, John Miller
Keener, William Albert
Keeney, Barnaby Conrad
Keep, Robert Porter
Kefauver, Grayson Neikirk
Kennedy, George Clayton
Kent, Charles Foster
Key, Valdimer Orlando, Jr.
Kidder, Daniel Parish
Kilpatrick, William Heard
Kimball, Dexter Simpson
King, Henry Churchill
Kingsbury, John
Kingsley, James Luce
Kinnicutt, Leonard Parker
Kirby-Smith, Edmund
Kirchwey, George Washington
Kirkland, James Hampton
Knox, George William
Knox, Samuel
Kohlmann, Anthony
Krapp, George Philip
Kraus, John
Kraus-Boelté, Maria
Krauth, Charles Porterfield
Krüsi, Johann Heinrich Hermann
Labaree, Leonard Woods
La Borde, Maximilian
Lacy, Drury
Lacy, Ernest
Lamont, Hammond
Lane, James Henry
Langdon, Courtney
Lange, Alexis Frederick
Langley, John Williams
Langston, John Mercer
Larkin, John
Larrabee, William Clark
Larsen, Peter Laurentius
Latané, John Holladay
Lathrop, John Hiram
Latourette, Kenneth Scott
Law, Evander McIvor
Laws, Samuel Spahr
Lawson, Andrew Cowper
Leach, Daniel Dyer
Leathers, Waller Smith
Lee, George Washington Custis
Lee, Stephen Dill
Leipziger, Henry Marcus
Leland, George Adams
Leonard, Levi Washburn
Leonard, Robert Josselyn
Leonard, Sterling Andrus
Levermore, Charles Herbert
Lewis, Clarence Irving
Lewis, Enoch
Lewis, Exum Percival
Lewis, Oscar
Lewis, Samuel
Lieber, Francis
Lindeman, Eduard Christian
Lindsley, John Berrien
Lindsley, Philip
Lipman, Jacob Goodale
Listemann, Bernhard
Littlefield, George Washington
Livingston, John Henry
Locke, Alain Leroy
Locke, Bessie
Longcope, Warfield Theobald
Longstreet, Augustus Baldwin
Lord, Asa Dearborn
Lord, Chester Sanders
Loughridge, Robert McGill
Lovell, John Epy
Lovett, Robert Morss
Lowes, John Livingston
Lowrey, Mark Perrin
Lubin, Isador
Luce, Henry Winters
Lutkin, Peter Christian
Lyon, David Gordon
Lyon, Mary
Maas, Anthony J.
McAfee, John Armstrong
MacAlister, James
McAnally, David Rice
McAndrew, William
McAuley, Thomas
McCaleb, Theodore Howard
McCartee, Divie Bethune
McCartney, Washington
McClellan, Henry Brainerd
McClenahan, Howard
M'Clintock, John
McCook, John James
McCormick, Samuel Black
MacCracken, Henry Mitchell
McDonald, James Grover

McDowell, John
McFarland, John Thomas
McFarland, Samuel Gamble
McGarvey, John William
McGuffey, William Holmes
McHale, Kathryn
McIver, Charles Duncan
Mackenzie, James Cameron
McKenzie, Robert Tait
MacLean, George Edwin
Maclean, John
McMurry, Frank Morton
MacVicar Malcolm
Mahan, Dennis Hart
Mahan, Milo
Main, John Hanson Thomas
Malcom, Howard
Manly, Basil, 1798–1868
Manly, Basil, 1825–1892
Mann, Horace
Mann, Mary Tyler Peabody
Mannes, Clara Damrosch
Mannes, David
Marble, Albert Prescott
Marks, Elias
Marshall, James Fowle Baldwin
Martin, Everett Dean
Martin, William Alexander Parsons
Mason, John Mitchell
Maxwell, William Henry
Mayo, Amory Dwight
Meany, Edmond Stephen
Mears, John William
Meigs, John
Meigs, Josiah
Meiklejohn, Alexander
Mell, Patrick Hues
Mendenhall, Thomas Corwin
Menetrey, Joseph
Mengarini, Gregory
Mercer, Margaret
Merrick, Frederick
Merrill, James Griswold
Messer, Asa
Mezes, Sidney Edward
Michel, Virgil George
Michie, Peter Smith
Middleton, Thomas Cooke
Milledoler, Philip
Miller, Emily Clark Huntington
Miller, Kelly
Miller, Leslie William
Miller, Samuel
Millet, Fred Benjamin
Milligan, Robert
Millikan, Robert Andrews
Mills, Cyrus Taggart
Mills, Susan Lincoln Tolman
Miner, Myrtilla
Minor, Benjamin Blake
Minot, Charles Sedgwick
Mitchell, Albert Graeme
Mitchell, Lucy Sprague
Molyneux, Robert
Monis, Judah
Monroe, Paul
Montague, William Pepperell
Mood, Francis Asbury
Moody, William Vaughn
Moore, James, 1764–1814
Moore, Joseph Earle
Morgan, Thomas Jefferson
Morison, Samuel Eliot
Morley, Margaret Warner
Morón, Alonzo Graseano
Morris, Edward Dafydd
Morris, George Sylvester
Morrison, John Irwin
Morse, Anson Daniel
Morse, Wayne Lyman
Morton, Robert Russa
Mosher, Eliza Maria
Moss, Lemuel
Mott, Frank Luther
Mowry, William Augustus
Mullins, Edgar Young
Munro, William Bennett
Murfee, James Thomas
Murray, David
Muste, Abraham Johannes
Muzzey, David Saville
Nabokov, Nicolas
Nash, Charles Sumner
Nason, Henry Bradford
Neef, Francis Joseph Nicholas
Neill, Edward Duffield
Neill, William
Nelson, David
Nelson, Reuben
Nevin, Edwin Henry
Nevin, John Williamson
Nevins, Joseph Allan
Newlon, Jesse Homer
Newman, Albert Henry
Nicholls, Rhoda Holmes
Nichols, Roy Franklin
Niebuhr, Helmut Richard
Nobili, John
Norris, Mary Harriott
Norsworthy, Naomi
North, Edward
North, Simeon, 1802–1884
Northend, Charles
Northrop, Birdsey Grant
Norton, John Pitkin
Noss, Theodore Bland
Notestein, Wallace
Nott, Henry Junius
Notz, Frederick William Augustus
Noyes, Clara Dutton
Nutting, Mary Adelaide
O'Callahan, Joseph Timothy
Odell, George Clinton Densmore
Ogden, Robert Curtis
O'Gorman, Thomas
Olin, Stephen
Orcutt, Hiram
Orr, Gustavus John
Orton, Edward Francis Baxter
Orton, James
Osborn, Henry Fairfield
O'Shea, Michael Vincent
Overstreet, Harry Allen
Owen, Edward Thomas
Owre, Alfred
Pace, Edward Aloysius
Packard, Silas Sadler
Page, David Perkins
Page, Leigh
Palmer, Alice Elvira Freeman
Palmer, Walter Walker
Pardow, William O'Brien
Park, Roswell
Parker, Amasa Junius
Parker, Francis Wayland
Parker, Samuel Chester
Parrish, Celestia Susannah
Partridge, Alden
Patri, Angelo
Patterson, James Kennedy
Patterson, James Willis
Payne, Bruce Ryburn
Payne, William Harold
Peabody, Cecil Hobart
Peabody, Elizabeth Palmer
Peabody, Endicott
Peabody, Selim Hobart
Pearce, Richard Mills
Pearson, Eliphalet
Peers, Benjamin Orrs
Peirce, Cyrus
Peirce, James Mills
Pei, Mario Andrew
Pendleton, James Madison
Penniman, James Hosmer
Pepper, William
Perkins, George Henry
Perry, Ralph Barton
Perry, Rufus Lewis
Perry, Thomas Sergeant
Perry, Walter Scott
Perry, William Flake
Phelps, Almira Hart Lincoln
Phelps, William Franklin
Pickens, William
Pierce, George Foster
Pierce, John Davis
Pinney, Norman
Poor, John
Porter, Ebenezer
Porter, James Davis
Porter, Noah
Post, Truman Marcellus
Potamian, Brother
Powell, John Wesley
Powell, William Bramwell
Pratt, Richard Henry
Priestley, James
Priestley, Joseph
Prosser, Charles Smith
Proud, Robert
Prouty, Charles Tyler
Puryear, Bennet
Putnam, Helen Cordelia
Quinby, Isaac Ferdinand
Quinn, Arthur Hobson
Rademacher, Hans
Rahv, Philip
Rambaut, Mary Lucinda Bonney
Randall, Henry Stephens
Randall, Samuel Sidwell
Rauch, Frederick Augustus
Rautenstrauch, Walter
Raymond, George Lansing
Raymond, Miner
Read, Daniel, 1805–1878
Redfield, Robert
Regan, Agnes Gertrude
Reichel, Charles Gotthold
Reichel, William Cornelius
Reichenbach, Hans
Reid, David Boswell

Reid, Ira De Augustine
Reid, William Shields
Reilly, Marion
Reinsch, Paul Samuel
Remsen, Ira
Reuter, Dominic
Revel, Bernard
Revels, Hiram Rhoades
Rice, John Holt
Rice, Luther
Rice, Victor Moreau
Rice, William North
Richard, Gabriel
Richard, James William
Richards, Zalmon
Richardson, Tobias Gibson
Ricketts, Palmer Chamberlaine
Ridpath, John Clark
Riley, Benjamin Franklin
Roark, Rurio Nevel
Robb, William Lispenard
Roberts, William Charles
Robertson, Alice Mary
Robertson, William Schenck
Robins, Henry Ephraim
Robinson, Ezekiel Gilman
Robinson, George Canby
Robinson, Stillman Williams
Robinson, William Callyhan
Rogers, Henry Darwin
Rogers, Henry Wade
Rogers, James Blythe
Rogers, John Almanza Rowley
Rogers, Robert Empie
Rogers, William Barton
Rohé, George Henry
Rölvaag, Ole Edvart
Ross, Denman Waldo
Rowson, Susanna Haswell
Ruffner, Henry
Ruffner, William Henry
Rugg, Harold Ordway
Russell, James Earl
Russell, James Solomon
Russell, William
Russwurm, John Brown
Rust, Richard Sutton
Ruter, Martin
Ryland, Robert
Saarinen, Gottlieb Eliel
Sachs, Julius
Safford, James Merrill
St. John, Charles Edward
Salisbury, Albert
Salisbury, Rollin D.
Salmon, Lucy Maynard
Sanborn, Edwin David
Sanders, Billington McCarter
Sanders, Charles Walton
Sanders, Daniel Clarke
Sanders, Daniel Jackson
Sartain, Emily
Sawyer, Thomas Jefferson
Scarborough, Lee Rutland
Schaeffer, Nathan Christ
Schlatter, Michael
Schmucker, Samuel Simon
Schodde, George Henry
Schultze, Augustus
Schuyler, Robert Livingston
Scopes, John Thomas
Scott, Austin
Scott, Emmett Jay
Scott, Walter Dill
Scott, William Anderson
Scovell, Melville Amasa
Sears, Barnas
Seelye, Julius Hawley
Shafer, Helen Almira
Shahan, Thomas Joseph
Shaler, Nathaniel Southgate
Sharp, Dallas Lore
Shaw, Edward Richard
Sheldon, Edward Austin
Sheldon, William Evarts
Shellabarger, Samuel
Sherman, Stuart Pratt
Sherwin, Thomas
Sherwood, Adiel
Shields, Thomas Edward
Shipp, Albert Micajah
Shipp, Scott
Shoup, Francis Asbury
Skinner, Charles Rufus
Skinner, Thomas Harvey
Slade, William
Sloane, William Milligan
Smart, James Henry
Smiley, Albert Keith
Smith, Alexander
Smith, Benjamin Mosby
Smith, Charles Alphonso
Smith, Charles Sprague
Smith, Courtney Craig
Smith, Daniel B.
Smith, David Eugene
Smith, Francis Henney
Smith, Harold Babbitt
Smith, Henry Louis
Smith, Judson
Smith, Lucy Harth
Smith, Richard Somers
Smith, William, 1727–1803
Smith, William Waugh
Smyth, Albert Henry
Smyth, John Henry
Snider, Denton Jaques
Snow, Francis Huntington
Snyder, Edwin Reagan
Soldan, Frank Louis
Son of Many Beads
Sorin, Edward Frederick
Soulé, George
Spaeth, John Duncan
Spalding, John Lancaster
Spangler, Henry Wilson
Sparrow, William
Spencer, Anna Garlin
Spencer, Jesse Ames
Sperry, Willard Learoyd
Sprague, Homer Baxter
Sprecher, Samuel
Stahr, John Summers
Stang, William
Stanley, Albert Augustus
Staughton, William
Stearns, Eben Sperry
Steele, Joel Dorman
Stengel, Alfred
Stephens, Henry Morse
Sterling, John Whalen
Stetson, William Wallace
Stevens, George Barker
Stevens, George Washington
Stillé, Charles Janeway
Stillman, Thomas Bliss
Stockbridge, Levi
Stoddard, John Fair
Stoek, Harry Harkness
Stoever, Martin Luther
Stokes, Anson Phelps
Stone, James Kent
Stone, John Seely
Stowe, Calvin Ellis
Strong, Richard Pearson
Stuart, Charles Macaulay
Sturtevant, Julian Monson
Summerall, Charles Pelot
Sumner, William Graham
Sunderland, Eliza Jane Read
Sutton, William Seneca
Suzzallo, Henry
Sverdrup, Georg
Swensson, Carl Aaron
Swett, John
Talbot, Arthur Newell
Tappan, Eli Todd
Taylor, Archibald Alexander Edward
Taylor, George William
Taylor, Nathaniel William
Taylor, Samuel Harvey
Tenney, Charles Daniel
Tenney, Edward Payson
Terrell, Mary Eliza Church
Terry, Milton Spenser
Thayer, Eli
Thayer, Gideon French
Thayer, Sylvanus
Thébaud, Augustus J.
Thoburn, Isabella
Thomas, Elbert Duncan
Thomas, Joseph
Thomas, Martha Carey
Thompson, Benjamin
Thompson, Charles Oliver
Thompson, Hugh Smith
Thompson, John Bodine
Thompson, Robert Ellis
Thompson, Samuel Rankin
Thurston, Robert Henry
Tichenor, Isaac Taylor
Ticknor, Elisha
Ticknor, George
Tomlinson, Everett Titsworth
Tompkins, Arnold
Toulmin, Harry
Townsend, Luther Tracy
Trowbridge, John
Trowbridge, William Petit
Trueblood, Benjamin Franklin
Tucker, William Jewett
Turner, Asa
Turner, Jonathan Baldwin
Turner, Samuel Hulbeart
Turner, William
Tutwiler, Henry
Tutwiler, Julia Strudwick
Tyler, Bennet
Tyler, Moses Coit
Vail, Stephen Montfort
Valentine, Milton
Van Lennep, Henry John
Van Meter, John Blackford
Van Quickenborne, Charles Felix

Varela y Morales, Félix Francisco José María de la Concepción
Vawtor, Charles Erastus
Venable, Charles Scott
Verbeck, William
Verhaegen, Peter Joseph
Vincent, George Edgar
Vincent, John Heyl
Vose, George Leonard
Waddel, John Newton
Wadsworth, James
Walker, Francis Amasa
Wallace, Charles William
Walsh, Edmund Aloysius
Ward, Harry Frederick
Ward, Joseph
Ware, Edmund Asa
Ware, John
Warren, William Fairfield
Warthin, Aldred Scott
Washburn, Edward Wight
Washburn, George
Washington, Booker Taliaferro
Waterhouse, Sylvester
Waters, William Everett
Watson, Charles Roger
Watson, William
Watt, Donald Beates
Wayland, Francis, 1796–1865
Webb, William Robert
Welch, Adonijah Strong
Welling, James Clarke
Welling, Richard Ward Greene
Wells, William Harvey
Wergeland, Agnes Mathilde
Wesbrook, Frank Fairchild
Wesselhoeft, Conrad
Wheaton, Nathaniel Sheldon
Wheeler, William
White, Emerson Elbridge
Whiton, James Morris
Whitworth, George Frederic
Wickersham, James Pyle
Widney, Joseph Pomeroy
Wigglesworth, Edward, 1693–1765
Wigglesworth, Edward, 1732–1794
Wigmore, John Henry
Wilbur, Hervey Backus
Wilczynski, Ernest Julius
Wilder, Russell Morse
Wildt, Rupert
Wiley, Calvin Henderson
Wiley, Ephraim Emerson
Wilkinson, Robert Shaw
Will, Allen Sinclair
Willard, Emma Hart
Willard, Samuel
Willard, Sidney
Willebrandt, Mabel Walker
Willey, Samuel Hopkins
Williams, John Elias
Williams, Robert
Williston, Samuel
Wilson, James Southall
Wilson, Orlando Winfield ("Win," "O.W.")
Wilson, Peter
Wilson, William Dexter
Wilson, William Lyne
Wines, Enoch Cobb
Wirt, William Albert
Witherspoon, Alexander Maclaren
Witherspoon, John Alexander
Wolfe, Harry Kirke
Wood, James
Wood, Thomas Bond
Woodbridge, Frederick James Eugene
Woodbridge, William Channing
Woodward, Calvin Milton
Woolsey, Theodore Dwight
Woolsey, Theodore Salisbury
Wright, Jonathan Jasper
Wright, Richard Robert
Wyckoff, John Henry
Wyeth, John Allan
Wylie, Andrew
Wylie, Samuel Brown
Yale, Caroline Ardelia
Yeomans, John William
Yergan, Max
Youmans, Edward Livingston
Young, Clark Montgomery
Young, Ella Flagg
Young, John Clarke
Zachos, John Celivergos
Zollars, Ely Vaughn
Zook, George Frederick

EFFICIENCY EXPERT
Bedaux, Charles Eugene

EGYPTOLOGIST (See also SCHOLAR)
Breasted, James Henry
McCauley, Edward Yorke
Reisner, George Andrew
Selikovitsch, Goetzel
Winlock, Herbert Eustis

ELECTRIC COMPANY EXECUTIVE
Sporn, Philip

ELECTRIC POWER ADMINISTRATOR
Ross, James Delmage McKenzie

ELECTRICAL ENGINEER (see ENGINEER, ELECTRICAL)

ELECTRICIAN (See also ENGINEER, ELECTRICAL)
Farmer, Moses Gerrish
Pope, Franklin Leonard

ELECTROTHERAPIST (See also PHYSICIAN)
Rockwell, Alphonso David

EMBEZZLER
Whitney, Richard

EMBRYOLOGIST (See also BIOLOGIST, PHYSICIAN, ZOOLOGIST)
Mall, Franklin Paine
Streeter, George Linius
Wilson, Edmund Beecher

EMIGRATION AGENT
Mattson, Hans

ENCYCLOPEDIST (See also COMPILER, SCHOLAR)
Heilprin, Michael
Mackey, Albert Gallatin
Schem, Alexander Jacob

ENDOCRINOLOGIST (See also PHYSICIAN)
Evans, Herbert McLean
Timme, Walter

ENGINEER (See also SPECIFIC TYPES)
Allen, Jeremiah Mervin
Allen, John F.
Argall, Philip
Babcock, George Herman
Babcock, Orville E.
Bailey, Frank Harvey
Bailey, Joseph
Ball, Albert
Barnes, James
Barrell, Joseph
Bayles, James Copper
Bell, Louis
Benham, Henry Washington
Benjamin, George Hillard
Black, William Murray
Bogart, John
Bonzano, Adolphus
Boyden, Uriah Atherton
Broadhead, Garland Carr
Burr, William Hubert
Cass, George Washington
Colles, Christopher
Coney, Jabez
Crozet, Claude
Curtis, Samuel Ryan
Daniels, Fred Harris
Davis, George Whitefield
De Lacy, Walter Washington
De Leeuw, Adolph Lodewyk
Dickie, George William
Dod, Daniel
Douglass, David Bates
Dripps, Isaac L.
Dunbar, Robert
Durfee, William Franklin
Durham, Caleb Wheeler
Eads, James Buchanan
Eastman, William Reed
Eckart, William Roberts
Eimbeck, William
Ellicott, Joseph
Emery, Albert Hamilton
Emery, Charles Edward
Ericsson, John
Ernst, Oswald Herbert
Eustis, Henry Lawrence
Field, Charles William
Flad, Henry
Ford, Hannibal Choate
Forney, Matthias Nace
Frasch, Herman
Fuertes, Estevan Antonio
Furlow, Floyd Charles
Gaillard, David Du Bose
Gantt, Henry Laurence
Gardiner, James Terry
Gaskill, Harvey Freeman
Gayley, James
Goethals, George Washington
Graff, Frederick
Greene, Francis Vinton
Grinnell, Frederick
Guthrie, Alfred
Hallidie, Andrew Smith
Hamilton, Schuyler
Harris, Daniel Lester
Haswell, Charles Haynes
Hebert, Louis
Henck, John Benjamin
Hickenlooper, Andrew
Hornblower, Josiah
Humphreys, Andrew Atkinson
Hunt, Alfred Ephraim

Hutton, Frederick Remsen
Jadwin, Edgar
James, Charles Tillinghast
Jervis, John Bloomfield
Jones, William Richard
Judah, Theodore Dehone
Kafer, John Christian
Kármán, Theodore (Todor) Von
Kerr, Walter Craig
Lamme, Benjamin Garver
La Tour, Le Blond de
Latrobe, Benjamin Henry, 1764–1820
Lefferts, Marshall
L'Enfant, Pierre Charles
Léry, Joseph Gaspard Chaussegros de
Lewis, William Gaston
Long, Stephen Harriman
Lucas, Anthony Francis
Ludlow, William
Lundie, John
McCallum, Daniel Craig
Macfarlane, Charles William
Mangin, Joseph François
Marshall, William Louis
Mason, Arthur John
Maxim, Hiram Stevens
Meigs, Montgomery Cunningham
Merrill, William Emery
Miller, Ezra
Millington, John
Mills, Robert, 1781–1855
Mitchell, Henry
Mordecai, Alfred
Moreell, Ben
Morell, George Webb
Morgan, Charles Hill
Morris, Thomas Armstrong
Morton, James St. Clair
Murray, Thomas Edward
Newton, John
Ockerson, John Augustus
Ogden, Francis Barber
Packard, James Ward
Painter, William
Palfrey, John Carver
Pardee, Ario
Parker, Ely Samuel
Parsons, William Barclay
Patterson, Richard Cunningham, Jr.
Pauger, Adrien de
Paul, Henry Martyn
Pearson, Fred Stark
Peters, Edward Dyer
Poe, Orlando Metcalfe
Reid, David Boswell
Renwick, Henry Brevoort
Renwick, James, 1792–1863
Reynolds, Edwin
Rice, Richard Henry
Ricketts, Palmer Chamberlaine
Roberts, Benjamin Stone
Robinson, Stillman Williams
Robinson, William
Roebling, John Augustus
Roosevelt, Nicholas J.
Rosser, Thomas Lafayette
Rousseau, Harry Harwood
Ryan, Walter D'Arcy
St. John, Isaac Munroe
Sargent, Frederick
Saunders, William Lawrence
Sawyer, Walter Howard
Scovel, Henry Sylvester
Sellers, Coleman
Sidell, William Henry
Simpson, James Hervey
Smith, Francis Hopkinson
Smith, William Farrar
Spangler, Henry Wilson
Sperry, Elmer Ambrose
Starrett, William Aiken
Stevens, Edwin Augustus
Stevens, John
Stevens, Robert Livingston
Storrow, Charles Storer
Strickland, William
Strong, Harriet Williams Russel
Stuart, Charles Beebe
Swift, Joseph Gardner
Swift, William Henry
Talcott, Andrew
Thompson, Charles Oliver
Thurston, Robert Henry
Tompkins, Daniel Augustus
Totten, George Muirson
Totten, Joseph Gilbert
Tower, Zealous Bates
Towne, Henry Robinson
Towne, John Henry
Trautwine, John Cresson
Trimble, Isaac Ridgeway
Troland, Leonard Thompson
Trowbridge, William Petit
Turnbull, William
Turner, Walter Victor
Twining, Alexander Catlin
Viele, Egbert Ludovicus
Vose, George Leonard
Ward, George Gray
Warren, Gouverneur Kemble
Warren, Russell
Watkins, John Elfreth
Watson, William
Webb, John Burkitt
Webster, Joseph Dana
Weitzel, Godfrey
Wellman, Samuel Thomas
Wheeler, William
Whistler, George Washington
White, Canvass
Wilcox, Stephen
Wilson, James Harrison
Winans, Thomas De Kay
Wood, James J.
Woodbury, Daniel Phineas
Woodward, Robert Simpson
Worthington, Henry Rossiter
Wright, Horatio Gouverneur

ENGINEER (AERONAUTICAL)
Acosta, Bertram Blanchard ("Bert")
Durand, William Frederick
Lawrance, Charles Lanier
Lewis, George William
Millikan, Clark Blanchard
Piccard, Jean Felix
Sikorsky, Igor Ivanovich
Warner, Edward Pearson
Wright, Theodore Paul

ENGINEER (ARMY)
Casey, Thomas Lincoln
Robert, Henry Martyn
Sibert, William Luther

ENGINEER (AUTOMOTIVE)
Coffin, Howard Earle
Gordon, John Franklin

ENGINEER (BRIDGE)
Cooper, Theodore
Cox, Lemuel
Hovey, Otis Ellis
Mason, Claibourne Rice
Modjeski, Ralph
Moisseiff, Leon Solomon
Morison, George Shattuck
Murphy, John W.
Roebling, John Augustus
Smith, Charles Shaler
Steinman, David Barnard
Strauss, Joseph Baermann
Wernwag, Lewis

ENGINEER (CHEMICAL)
Frary, Francis Cowles
Howard, Henry
Landis, Walter Savage
Little, Arthur Dehon
Morehead, John Motley
Whorf, Benjamin Lee

ENGINEER (CIVIL)
Alden, John Ferris
Allen, Horatio
Ammann, Othmar Hermann
Baldwin, Loammi, 1740–1807
Baldwin, Loammi, 1780–1838
Bates, Onward
Billings, Asa White Kenney
Bogue, Virgil Gay
Boller, Alfred Pancoast
Borden, Simeon
Brown, William Henry
Bryant, Gridley
Buck, Leffert Lefferts
Buckhout, Isaac Craig
Bush, Lincoln
Cambpell, Allen
Carll, John Franklin
Cassatt, Alexander Johnston
Chanute, Octave
Childe, John
Church, George Earl
Cohen, Mendes
Cone, Russell Glenn
Cooley, Lyman Edgar
Cooper, Theodore
Corthell, Elmer Lawrence
Crowe, Francis Trenholm
Davies, John Vipond
Detmold, Christian Edward
Devereux, John Henry
Dodge, Grenville Mellon
Duane, James Chatham
Dubois, Augustus Jay
Ellet, Charles
Ellsworth, Lincoln
Evans, Anthony Walton Whyte
Felton, Samuel Morse
Ferris, George Washington Gale
Freeman, John Ripley
Freeman, Thomas
Fulton, Robert
Geddes, James
Gillespie, William Mitchell

Goldmark, Henry
Graff, Frederic
Graham, Charles Kinnaird
Greene, Charles Ezra
Greene, George Sears, 1801–1899
Greene, George Sears, 1837–1922
Harrington, John Lyle
Harrod, Benjamin Morgan
Haupt, Herman
Hayford, John Fillmore
Hill, Louis Clarence
Hoadley, John Chipman
Holland, Clifford Milburn
Hooker, Elon Huntington
Hovey, Otis Ellis
Hughes, Hector James
Johnson, Edwin Ferry
Johnson, John Butler
Katte, Walter
Knappen, Theodore Temple
Kneass, Samuel Honeyman
Kneass, Strickland
Knight, Jonathan
Koyl, Charles Herschel
Latrobe, Benjamin Henry, 1806–1878
Latrobe, Charles Hazlehurst
Laurie, James
Lindenthal, Gustav
Lovell, Mansfield
McAlpine, William Jarvis
McConnell, Ira Welch
McCullough, Ernest
McMath, Robert Emmet
McNeill, William Gibbs
Menocal, Aniceto Garcia
Milner, John Turner
Moran, Daniel Edward
Morgan, Arthur Ernest
Nettleton, Edwin S.
Newell, Frederick Haynes
Noble, Alfred
Norcross, Orlando Whitney
Parker, Theodore Bissell
Peters, Richard, 1810–1889
Pick, Lewis Andrew
Pratt, Thomas Willis
Rafter, George W.
Randolph, Isham
Rea, Samuel
Ridgway, Robert
Roberdeau, Isaac
Roberts, Nathan S.
Roberts, Solomon White
Roberts, William Milnor
Robinson, Albert Alonzo
Robinson, Moncure
Roebling, Washington Augustus
Romans, Bernard
Rugg, Harold Ordway
Savage, John Lucian ("Jack")
Sayre, Robert Heysham
Schneider, Herman
Serrell, Edward Wellman
Silver, Thomas
Smillie, Ralph
Smith, Gustavus Woodson
Smith, Jonas Waldo
Smith, Jonas Waldo
Smith, William Sooy
Snow, Jessie Baker
Sooysmith, Charles
Staley, Cady
Stauffer, David McNeely
Stearns, Frederic Pike
Stevens, John Frank
Strobel, Charles Louis
Stuart, Francis Lee
Swain, George Fillmore
Talbot, Arthur Newell
Tatham, William
Thacher, Edwin
Waddell, John Alexander Low
Waite, Henry Matson
Walker, Reuben Lindsay
Wallace, John Findley
Wegmann, Edward
Welch, Ashbel
Wellington, Arthur Mellen
Westergaard, Harald Malcolm
Weston, William
Whipple, Squire
Williams, Frank Martin
Williams, Jesse Lynch
Wilson, Joseph Miller
Wilson, William Hasell
Worthen, William Ezra
Wright, Benjamin

ENGINEER (COMMUNICATIONS)
Colpitts, Edwin Henry
Business Man
Hoover, Herbert Clark, Jr.

ENGINEER (ELECTRICAL)
Anthony, William Arnold
Armstrong, Edwin Howard
Baker, Walter Ransom Gail
Behrend, Bernard Arthur
Billings, Asa White Kenney
Cable, Frank Taylor
Carson, John Renshaw
Carty, John Joseph
Conrad, Frank
Crocker, Francis Bacon
Daft, Leo
Delaney, Patrick Bernard
Dumont, Allen Balcom
Emmet, William Le Roy
Faccioli, Giuseppe
Field, Stephen Dudley
Fortescue, Charles LeGeyt
Gotshall, William Charles
Griffin, Eugene
Hammer, William Joseph
Harper, John Lyell
Heineman, Daniel Webster ("Dannie")
Hering, Carl
Hill, Ernest Rowland
Hogan, John Vincent Lawless
Houston, Edwin James
Jackson, Dugald Caleb
Jansky, Karl Guthe
Kennelly, Arthur Edwin
Kettering, Charles Franklin
Leonard, Harry Ward
Loomis, Mahlon
Moorhead, James Kennedy
O'Reilly, Henry
Peek, Frank William
Perrine, Frederic Anten Combs
Potter, William Bancroft
Prescott, George Bartlett
Priest, Edward Dwight
Rice, Edwin Wilbur
Robb, William Lispenard
Rogers, Henry J.
Rosenberg, Julius
Ross, James Delmage McKenzie
Ryan, Harris Joseph
Sargent, Frederick
Short, Sidney Howe
Smith, Harold Babbitt
Sprague, Frank Julian
Squier, George Owen
Stanley, William
Steinmetz, Charles Proteus
Stone, Charles Augustus
Stott, Henry Gordon
Swope, Gerard
Tesla, Nikola
Van Depoele, Charles Joseph
Weaver, William Dixon
Webster, Edwin Sibley
Weston, Edward

ENGINEER (HIGHWAY)
Merrill, Frank Dow

ENGINEER (HYDRAULIC)
Davis, Arthur Powell
Fanning, John Thomas
Fitzgerald, Desmond
Francis, James Bicheno
Frizell, Joseph Palmer
Hazen, Allen
Henny, David Christiaan
Herschel, Clemens
Hill, Louis Clarence
Knappen, Theodore Temple
Matthes, Gerard Hendrik
Mills, Hiram Francis
O'Shaughnessy, Michael Maurice
Schuyler, James Dix
Shedd, Joel Herbert
Weymouth, Frank Elwin

ENGINEER (HYDROELECTRIC)
Cooper, Hugh Lincoln

ENGINEER (INDUSTRIAL)
Gilbreth, Lillian Evelyn Moller
Gunn, James Newton
Hine, Charles De Lano
Porter, Holbrook Fitz-John
Rautenstrauch, Walter
Taylor, Frederick Winslow
Woodbury, Charles Jeptha Hill

ENGINEER (IRRIGATION)
Clyde, George Dewey
Eaton, Benjamin Harrison
Mead, Elwood
Nettleton, Edwin S.
Wiley, Andrew Jackson

ENGINEER (MARINE)
Fairburn, William Armstrong
Herreshoff, Nathanael Greene

ENGINEER (MECHANICAL)
Barth, Carl Georg Lange
Bristol, William Henry
Carrier, Willis Haviland
Clark, Walter Leighton
Cooke, Morris Llewellyn
Delamater, Cornelius Henry
Doane, Thomas
Durand, William Frederick
Emmet, William Le Roy
Faccioli, Giuseppe

Flanders, Ralph Edward
Flather, John Joseph
Fritz, John
Gibbs, George
Grant, George Barnard
Halsey, Frederick Arthur
Harper, John Lyell
Harrington, John Lyle
Harrison, Joseph
Herr, Herbert Thacker
Hoadley, John Chipman
Hobbs, Alfred Charles
Hodgkinson, Francis
Holley, Alexander Lyman
Holloway, Joseph Flavius
Hudson, William Smith
Humphreys, Alexander Crombie
Hunt, Charles Wallace
Isherwood, Benjamin Franklin
Jones, Evan William
Kent, William
Kimball, Dexter Simpson
Kingsbury, Albert
Klein, August Clarence
Klein, Joseph Frederic
Leavitt, Erasmus Darwin
Leavitt, Frank McDowell
Lewis, Wilfred
Lieb, John William
Main, Charles Thomas
Manly, Charles Matthews
Mattice, Asa Martines
Miller, Kempster Blanchard
Moss, Sanford Alexander
Murray, Thomas Edward
Newcomb, Charles Leonard
Nordberg, Bruno Victor
Norden, Carl Lukas
Norton, Charles Hotchkiss
Porter, Holbrook Fitz-John
Rice, Calvin Winsor
Richards, Charles Brinckerhoff
Sessions, Henry Howard
Swasey, Ambrose
Sweet, John Edson

ENGINEER (METALLURGICAL)
Bassett, William Hastings
Dwight, Arthur Smith

ENGINEER (MILITARY)
Abbot, Henry Larcom
Barlow, John Whitney
Bernard, Simon
Chittenden, Hiram Martin
Costansó, Miguel
De Brahm, William Gerard
Delafield, Richard
Duane, James Chatham
Gardiner, Lion
Gillmore, Quincy Adams
Godefroy, Maximilian
Gridley, Richard
Gunnison, John Williams
Hodges, Harry Foote
Hutchins, Thomas
Mackellar, Patrick
Mansfield, Joseph King Fenno
Montrésor, James Gabriel
Montrésor, John
Raymond, Charles Walker
Roberdeau, Isaac
Serrell, Edward Wellman
Smith, Gustavus Woodson
Symons, Thomas William
Thayer, Sylvanus

ENGINEER (MINING)
Blake, William Phipps
Bradley, Frederick Worthen
Brooks, Thomas Benton
Brunton, David William
Carpenter, Franklin Reuben
Clemson, Thomas Green
Cogswell, William Browne
Coxe, Eckley Brinton
Daggett, Ellsworth
Del Mar, Alexander
Douglas, James
Dwight, Arthur Smith
Emmons, Samuel Franklin
Greenway, John Campbell
Hague, James Duncan
Hammond, John Hays
Holmes, Joseph Austin
Hoover, Herbert Clark
Hulbert, Edwin James
Irving, Roland Duer
Jackling, Daniel Cowan
Janin, Louis
Jennings, James Hennen
Kemp, James Furman
King, Clarence
Lyman, Benjamin Smith
Manning, Vannoy Hartrog
Mathewson, Edward Payson
Maynard, George William
Moore, Philip North
Neilson, William George
Olcott, Eben Erksine
Peters, Edward Dyer
Ramsay, Erskine
Raymond, Rossiter Worthington
Requa, Mark Lawrence
Rice, George Samuel
Richards, Robert Hallowell
Rothwell, Richard Pennefather
Smith, Hamilton
Spilsbury, Edmund Gybbon
Stearns, Irving Ariel
Stoek, Harry Harkness
Strong, Charles Lyman
Vinton, Francis Laurens
Webb, Harry Howard
Williams, Gardner Fred
Winchell, Horace Vaughn

ENGINEER (NAVAL)
Canaga, Alfred Bruce
Copeland, Charles W.
Endicott, Mordecai Thomas
Entwistle, James
Fisher, Clark
Hollis, Ira Nelson
Hoxie, William Dixie
McAllister, Charles Albert
Taylor, Stevenson

ENGINEER (PUBLIC UTILITY)
Doherty, Henry Latham

ENGINEER (RADIO)
Conrad, Frank
Stone, John Stone

ENGINEER (RESEARCH)
Buckley, Oliver Ellsworth

ENGINEER (SANITARY)
Eddy, Harrison Prescott
Fuller, George Warren
Goodnough, Xanthus Henry
Hazen, Allen
Hering, Rudolph
Kay, Edgar Boyd
Kinnicutt, Leonard Parker
Meyer, Henry Coddington
Mills, Hiram Francis
Shedd, Joel Herbert
Waring, George Edwin

ENGINEER (STEEL)
Blakeley, George Henry
Perin, Charles Page

ENGINEER (STRUCTURAL)
Pond, Irving Kane
Purdy, Corydon Tyler

ENGINEER (TELEPHONE)
Gherardi, Bancroft
Jewett, Frank Baldwin
Stone, John Stone

ENGINEER (TOPOGRAPHICAL)
Abert, John James
Hood, Washington
Hughes, George Wurtz
Wheeler, George Montague
Whipple, Amiel Weeks

ENGINEER (WATER-SUPPLY)
Mulholland, William

ENGRAVER (See also ARTIST, DIESINKER, ETCHER, PHOTOENGRAVER)
Aitken, Robert
Alexander, Anderson
Andrews, Joseph
Barber, John Warner
Birch, William Russell
Buell, Abel
Burgis, William
Casilear, John William
Charles, William
Cheney, John
Cheney, Seth Wells
Childs, Cephas Grier
Clay, Edward Williams
Closson, William Baxter
Cushman, George Hewitt
Danforth, Moseley Isaac
Dawkins, Henry
Dewing, Francis
Doolittle, Amos
Dummer, Jeremiah
Durand, Asher Brown
Durand, Cyrus
Eckstein, John
Edwin, David
Field, Robert
Folwell, Samuel
Foster, John
Fox, Gilbert
French, Edwin Davis
Girsch, Frederick
Gobrecht, Christian
Goodman, Charles
Hall, Henry Bryan
Hamlin, William
Havell, Robert
Hill, John
Hollyer, Samuel
Hooker, William
Hurd, Nathaniel
Jocelyn, Nathaniel
Johnston, David Claypoole
Johnston, Thomas
Jones, Alfred

Kearny, Francis
Keith, William
Kensett, John Frederick
Kingsley, Elbridge
Kneass, William
Lawson, Alexander
Leney, William Satchwell
Le Roux, Charles
Longacre, James Barton
Malcolm, James Peller
Maverick, Peter
Norman, John
Ormsby, Waterman Lilly
Otis, Bass
Pease, Joseph Ives
Pelham, Henry
Pelham, Peter
Piggot, Robert
Prud'homme, John Francis Eugene
Ritchie, Alexander Hay
Rollinson, William
Rosenthal, Max
Saint-Mémin, Charles Balthazar Julien Fevret de
Sartain, Emily
Sartain, John
Sartain, Samuel
Savage, Edward
Schoff, Stephen Alonzo
Shirlaw, Walter
Smillie, James
Smillie, James David
Smith, John Rubens
Strickland, William
Tanner, Benjamin
Tiebout, Cornelius
Yeager, Joseph

ENGRAVER (WOOD) (See also ARTIST)
Adams, Joseph Alexander
Anthony, Andrew Varick Stout
Bowen, Abel
Cole, Timothy
Drake, Alexander Wilson
Heinemann, Ernst
Juengling, Frederick
Kruell, Gustav
Leslie, Frank
Linton, William James
Lossing, Benson John
Wolf, Henry

ENTERTAINER (See also ACTOR, ACTRESS, CLOWN, COMEDIAN, COMEDIENNE, HUMORIST, WIT)
Allen, Gracie
Armstrong, Louis ("Satchmo")
Baker, Josephine
Clark, Bobby
Gray, Gilda
Hopper, Edna Wallace
Janis, Elsie
Lee, Gypsy Rose
Mansfield, Jayne
Maxwell, Elsa
Nesbit, Evelyn Florence
Randolph, Lillian
Palmer, William Henry
Rooney, Pat
Waller, Thomas Wright ("Fats")

ENTOMOLOGIST (See also ZOOLOGIST)
Ashmead, William Harris
Burgess, Edward
Comstock, John Henry
Coquillett, Daniel William
Cresson, Ezra Townsend
Dyar, Harrison Gray
Edwards, William Henry
Fernald, Charles Henry
Fitch, Asa
Forbes, Stephen Alfred
Glover, Townend
Grote, Augustus Radcliffe
Hagen, Hermann August
Harris, Thaddeus William
Horn, George Henry
Howard, Leland Ossian
Hubbard, Henry Guernsey
Hunter, Walter David
Kinsey, Alfred Charles
Knab, Frederick
LeConte, John Lawrence
Lintner, Joseph Albert
Lutz, Frank Eugene
Melsheimer, Friedrich Valentin
Morgan, John Harcourt Alexander
Osten Sacken, Carl Robert Romanovich von der
Packard, Alpheus Spring
Peckham, George Williams
Riley, Charles Valentine
Sanderson, Ezra Dwight
Say, Thomas
Schwarz, Eugene Amandus
Scudder, Samuel Hubbard
Smith, John Bernhard
Taylor, Charlotte De Bernier
Thomas, Cyrus
Uhler, Philip Reese
Walsh, Benjamin Dann
Wheeler, William Morton
Williston, Samuel Wendell

ENTREPRENEUR (See also BUSINESSMAN, CAPITALIST, INDUSTRIALIST, MANUFACTURER, MERCHANT)
Condon, Albert Edwin ("Eddie")
Fairchild, Sherman Mills
Farquhar, Percival
Johnson, Howard Deering
Kennedy, Joseph Patrick
Pincus, Gregory Goodwin ("Goody")
Sanders, Harland David ("Colonel")
Tandy, Charles David

EPIDEMIOLOGIST (See also PHYSICIAN)
Carter, Henry Rose
Chapin, Charles Value
Doull, James Angus
Dyer, Rolla Eugene
Frost, Wade Hampton
Rosenau, Milton Joseph
Sedgwick, William Thompson
Sternberg, George Miller

ESPIONAGE AGENT
Berg, Morris ("Moe")
Gold, Harry ("Raymond")
Powers, Francis Gary

ESSAYIST (See also AUTHOR, WRITER)
Agee, James Rufus
Appleton, Thomas Gold
Auden, Wystan Hugh
Behrman, Samuel Nathaniel ("S.N.")
Bourne, Randolph Silliman
Calvert, George Henry
Colum, Padraic
Crévecoeur, Michel-Guillaume Jean de
Crothers, Samuel McChord
Dana, Richard Henry
Dennie, Joseph
Douglas, Lloyd Cassel
Downey, John
Emerson, Ralph Waldo
Goodman, Paul
Gregory, Eliot
Guiney, Louise Imogen
Hall, Sarah Ewing
Holley, Marietta
Holmes, Oliver Wendell
Kinney, Elizabeth Clementine Dodge Stedman
Lazarus, Emma
McKinley, Carlyle
Miller, Henry Valentine
Porter, Katherine Anne
Saltus, Edgar Evertson
Sperry, Willard Learoyd
Story, William Wetmore
Tate, John Orley Allen
Thoreau, Henry David
Tuckerman, Henry Theodore
Warner, Charles Dudley
Willcox, Louise Collier
Winchevsky, Morris
Winter, William

ETCHER (See also ARTIST, ENGRAVER)
Bacher, Otto Henry
Bellows, Albert Fitch
Benson, Frank Weston
Charles, William
Clay, Edward Williams
Dielman, Frederick
Duveneck, Frank
Farrer, Henry
Forbes, Edwin
Garrett, Edmund Henry
Gifford, Robert Swain
Hart, George Overbury
Haskell, Ernest
Koopman, Augustus
Merritt, Anna Lea
Mielatz, Charles Frederick William
Miller, Charles Henry
Moran, Peter
Moran, Thomas
Nicoll, James Craig
Pennell, Joseph
Platt, Charles Adams
Plowman, George Taylor
Reed, Earl Howell
Rix, Julian Walbridge
Smillie, James David
Whistler, James Abbott McNeill
Young, Mahonri Mackintosh

ETHICAL CULTURE LEADER
Coit, Stanton
Elliott, John Lovejoy
ETHNOLOGIST (See also ANTHROPOLOGIST)
Bourke, John Gregory
Churchill, William
Cooper, John Montgomery
Cushing, Frank Hamilton
Dorsey, James Owen
Emerson, Ellen Russell
Farabee, William Curtis
Fewkes, Jesse Walter
Fletcher, Alice Cunningham
Gatschet, Albert Samuel
Gibbs, George
Goddard, Pliny Earle
Hale, Horatio Emmons
Henshaw, Henry Wetherbee
Jones, William
Lowie, Robert Harry
Mallery, Garrick
Mason, Otis Tufton
Matthews, Washington
Mooney, James
Morgan, Lewis Henry
Nott, Josiah Clark
Pilling, James Constantine
Safford, William Edwin
Schoolcraft, Henry Rowe
Skinner, Alanson Buck
Smith, Erminnie Adelle Platt
Speck, Frank Gouldsmith
Stevenson, James
Stevenson, Matilda Coxe Evans
Thomas, Cyrus
Woodruff, Charles Edward
Wyman, Jeffries
ETHNOMUSICOLOGIST
Densmore, Frances
ETIQUETTE AUTHORITY
Post, Emily Price
Vanderbilt, Amy
ETYMOLOGIST
Vizetelly, Frank Horace
EUGENICIST
Davenport, Charles Benedict
Laughlin, Harry Hamilton
EVANGELIST (See also CLERGYMAN, RELIGIOUS LEADER)
Chapman, John Wilbur
Crittenden, Charles Nelson
Dow, Lorenzo
Durant, Henry Fowle
Hammond, Edward Payson
Hayden, William
Ironside, Henry Allan
Jones, Robert Reynolds ("Bob")
Jones, Samuel Porter
McPherson, Aimee Semple
Miller, George
Mills, Benjamin Fay
Moody, Dwight Lyman
Nettleton, Asahel
Pierce, Robert Willard
Rieger, Johann Georg Joseph Anton
Riley, William Bell
Smith, Fred Burton
Stone, Barton Warren
Sunday, William Ashley ("Billy")
Taylor, William
Updegraff, David Brainard
Upshaw, William David
Waters, Ethel
Whitefield, George
EXECUTIVE (See also BUSINESSMAN, BUSINESSWOMAN, CAPITALIST, ENTREPRENEUR, INDUSTRIALIST, MANUFACTURER, MERCHANT)
Avery, Sewell Lee
Barton, Bruce Fairchild
Berwind, Edward Julius
Black, Eli
Boeing, William Edward
Braniff, Thomas Elmer
Brookings, Robert Somers
Brownlee, James Forbis
Brush, George Jarvis
Carpenter, John Alden
Clayton, William Lockhart
Copley, Ira Clifton
Cordiner, Ralph Jarron
Davis, Francis Breese, Jr.
Dean, Gordon Evans
Dillingham, Walter Francis
Dittemore, John Valentine
D'Olier, Franklin
Drum, Hugh Aloysius
Dyer, Isadore
Fairburn, William Armstrong
Ferguson, Samuel
Flint, Charles Ranlett
French, Paul Comly
Gaisman, Henry Jaques
Getty, George Franklin, II
Gherardi, Bancroft
Gifford, Walter Sherman
Gordon, John Franklin
Gossett, Benjamin Brown
Green, Norvin
Gregory, Thomas Barger
Guggenheim, Simon
Harbord, James Guthrie
Hartford, George Huntington
Hartford, George Ludlum
Hartford, John Augustine
Henderson, Paul
Hill, George Washington
Homer, Arthur Bartlett
Hopson, Howard Corwell
Hurley, Roy T.
Hutton, Edward Francis
Ireland, Charles Thomas, Jr. ("Chick")
Jarman, Walton Maxey
Johnson, Eldridge Reeves
Kirby, Allan Price
Kyes, Roger Martin
Lawrance, Charles Lanier
Loeb, Milton B.
McElroy, Neil Hosler
McHugh, Keith Stratton
Marshall, Charles Henry
Mellon, William Larimer
Mitchell, Sidney Zollicoffer
Mortimer, Charles Greenough
Murphy, Robert Daniel
Murray, Thomas Edward
Nelson, Donald Marr
Newhouse, Samuel Irving
Nielsen, Arthur Charles
Olcott, Eben Erskine
Orton, William
Patterson, Richard Cunningham, Jr.
Pew, John Howard
Pratt, John Lee
Prentis, Henning Webb, Jr.
Ramspeck, Robert C. Word ("Bob")
Reid, Helen Miles Rogers
Reynolds, Richard Samuel, Sr.
Robinson, John Roosevelt ("Jackie")
Romnes, Haakon Ingolf ("H.I.")
Rudkin, Margaret Fogarty
Schenck, Nicholas Michael
Simmons, George Henry
Sloan, George Arthur
Sloan, Matthew Scott
Somervell, Brehon Burke
Stettinius, Edward Reilly
Swope, Gerard
Talbott, Harold Elstner
Thalberg, Irving Grant
Vail, Theodore Newton
Vance, Harold Sines
Wacker, Charles Henry
Watson, Arthur Kittridge
Watson, Thomas John
Weicker, Lowell Palmer
Welch, Leo Dewey
Whiteside, Arthur Dare
Willkie, Wendell Lewis
Wilson, Charles Edward
Wilson, Charles Erwin
Wilson, Joseph Chamberlain
Yates, Herbert John
Yerkes, Charles Tyson
EXPERIMENTER (See also AGRICULTURIST, AGRICULTURAL CHEMIST, CHEMIST, PHYSIOLOGIST, PHYSICIST, SCIENTIST)
Johnson, Samuel William
Kinnersley, Ebenezer
Lining, John
Livingston, Robert R., 1746–1813
Loomis, Mahlon
Page, Charles Grafton
Reid, James L.
Thatcher, Roscoe Wilfred
EXPLORER (See also DISCOVERER, FRONTIERSMAN, GUIDE, PIONEER, SCOUT)
Aco, Michel
Akeley, Carl Ethan
Akeley, Mary Leonore
Alarcón, Hernando de
Ambler, James Markham Marshall
Andrews, Roy Chapman
Anza, Juan Bautista de
Armstrong, John
Ashley, William Henry
Ayllon, Lucas Vasquez de
Baldwin, Evelyn Briggs
Bandelier, Adolph Francis Alphonse
Becknell, William
Bingham, Hiram

Bourgmont, Étienne Venyard, Sieur de
Bridgman, Herbert Lawrence
Brower, Jacob Vradenberg
Brulé, Étienne
Burnham, Frederick Russell
Byrd, Richard Evelyn
Cabrillo, Juan Rodriguez
Céloron de Blainville, Pierre Joseph de
Chaillé-Long, Charles
Champlain, Samuel de
Charlevoix, Pierre François Xavier de
Church, George Earl
Clark, William
Colter, John
Cook, Frederick Albert
Coronado, Francisco Vázquez
Crespi, Juan
Danenhower, John Wilson
De Long, George Washington
De Mézlères y Clugny, Athauase
Du Chaillu, Paul Belloni
Duluth, Daniel Greysolon, Sieur de
Eklund, Carl Robert
Ellsworth, Lincoln
Escalante, Silvestre Velez de
Fanning, Edmund
Filson, John
Forsyth, Thomas
Freeman, Thomas
Frémont, John Charles
Garcés, Francisco Tomás Hermenegildo
Gass, Patrick
Gist, Christopher
Greely, Adolphus Washington
Groseilliers, Médart Chouart, Sieur de
Hall, Charles Francis
Harmon, Daniel Williams
Hayes, Isaac Israel
Heilprin, Angelo
Henry, Alexander
Henson, Matthew Alexander
Horsfield, Thomas
Hubbard, Bernard Rosecrans
Iberville, Pierre Le Moyne, Sieur d'
Ives, Joseph Christmas
James, Edwin
Johnson, Osa
Jolliet, Louis
Kane, Elisha Kent
Kennan, George
Kennicott, Robert
Kino, Eusebio Francisco
Lander, Frederick West
Langford, Nathaniel Pitt
Lanman, Charles
La Salle, Robert Cavelier, Sieur de
La Vérendrye, Pierre Gaultier de Varennes, Sieur de
Lederer, John
Ledyard, John
Le Sueur, Pierre
Lewis, Meriwether
Lockwood, James Booth
Long, Stephen Harriman
Luna y Arellano, Tristan de
Mackay, James
Marquette, Jacques
Menéndez de Avilés, Pedro
Michaux, André
Morrell, Benjamin
Muir, John
Mullan, John
Needham, James
Nicolet, Jean
Nicollet, Joseph Nicolas
Niza, Marcos de
Núñez Cabeza de Vaca, Alvar
Ogden, Peter Skene
Ordway, John
Orton, James
Page, Thomas Jefferson
Palmer, Nathaniel Brown
Parker, Samuel
Pavy, Octave
Peary, Robert Edwin
Perrot, Nicolas
Pike, Zebulon Montgomery
Ponce de León, Juan
Pond, Peter
Porter, Russell Williams
Poston, Charles Debrill
Pring, Martin
Pumpelly, Raphael
Pursh, Frederick
Radisson, Pierre Esprit
Roosevelt, Kermit
Ross, Alexander
St. Denis (Denys), Louis Juchereau de
St. Lusson, Simon François Daumont, Sieur de
Schoolcraft, Henry Rowe
Sibley, George Champlain
Smith, Jedediah Strong
Smith, John, 1579–1631
Stanley, Henry Morton
Stansbury, Howard
Stefansson, Vilhjalmur
Stevenson, James
Strain, Isaac G.
Thompson, David
Thompson, Edward Herbert
Tonty, Henry de
Truteau, Jean Baptiste
Tyson, George Emory
Verrill, Alpheus Hyatt
Vincennes, Jean Baptiste Bissot, Sieur de
Vizcaíno, Sabastián
Walker, Joseph Reddeford
Walker, Thomas
Walsh, Henry Collins
Waymouth, George
Webber, Charles Wilkins
Welles, Roger
Wellman, Walter
Wilkes, Charles
Wood, Abraham
Workman, Fanny Bullock
Wyeth, Nathaniel Jarvis

EXPRESSMAN (See also TRANSPORTER)
Adams, Alvin
Armstrong, George Washington
Butterfield, John
Cheney, Benjamin Pierce
Fargo, William George
Harnden, William Frederick
Stimson, Alexander Lovett
Wells, Henry

FACTOR (See also MERCHANT)
Flannery, John
McLoughlin, John
Richardson, Edmund

FAITH HEALER
Kuhlman, Kathryn

FAMILY PLANNING ADVOCATE
Guttmacher, Alan Frank

FARM COOPERATIVE LEADER
Babcock, Howard Edward

FARMER (See also AGRICULTURIST)
Allen, Anthony Benezet
Binns, John Alexander
Bromfield, Louis
Clark, Abraham
Clayton, John Middleton
Cox, Henry Hamilton
Delafield, John
Dickson, David
Frazier, Lynn Joseph
Glidden, Joseph Farwell
Gregg, Andrew
Harris, Joseph
Hart, John
Haugen, Gilbert Nelson
Heard, Dwight Bancroft
Hecker, Friedrich Karl Franz
Hiester, Daniel
Hughes, Dudley Mays
Jardine, William Marion
Johnson, Edward
Lacock, Abner
Leaming, Jacob Spicer
Livingston, Robert R., 1746–1813
Magoffin, Beriah
Northen, William Jonathan
Paine, Elijah
Palmer, William Adams
Peters, Richard, 1744–1828
Polk, Leonidas Lafayette
Potter, James
Reed, John, 1757–1845
Rodney, Thomas
Silver, Gray
Stockton, Richard
Strawn, Jacob
Wadsworth, James Wolcott, Jr.
Wilkinson, Jeremiah
Wing, Joseph Elwyn
Wood, James

FARM LEADER (See also AGRICULTURAL LEADER, AGRICULTURIST)
Barrett, Charles Simon
Butler, Marion
Gregory, Clifford Verne
Hirth, William Andrew
Kolb, Reuben Francis
Macune, Charles William
Moser, Christopher Otto
Peek, George Nelson
Reno, Milo
Silver, Gray
Simpson, John Andrew

FASCIST COLLABORATOR
Bedaux, Charles Eugene

Fashion Authority
Snow, Carmel White
Fashion Model
Wilhelmina
Fashion Retailer
Carnegie, Hattie
FBI Informer
Bentley, Elizabeth Terrill
Federal Art Administrator
Bruce, Edward Bright
Federal Art Project Director
Cahill, Holger
Federal Bureau of Investigation Director
Hoover, John Edgar
Federal Official
Carr, Wilbur
Matthews, Francis Patrick
Willebrandt, Mabel Walker
Williams, Aubrey Willis
Wrather, William Embry
Federal Reserve Board Governor
Crissinger, Daniel Richard
Federal Reserve Board Member
Hamlin, Charles Sumner
Federal Theatre Project Director
Flanagan, Hallie
Federal Trade Commissioner
Ayres, William Augustus
Feminist
Allen, Florence Ellinwood
Anthony, Katharine Susan
Bloor, Ella Reeve
Breen, Margaret
Brown, Charlotte Emerson
Brown, Olympia
Catt, Carrie Clinton Lane Chapman
Chace, Elizabeth Buffum
Crocker, Hannah Mather
Doyle, Sarah Elizabeth
Duniway, Abigail Jane Scott
Foster, Abigail Kelley
Gage, Matilda Joslyn
Grant, Jane Cole
Grimké, Angelina Emily
Grimké, Sarah Moore
Harper, Ida Husted
Haskell, Ella Louise Knowles
Hepburn, Katharine Houghton
Hooker, Isabella Beecher
Huntington, Margaret Jane Evans
Kehew, Mary Morton Kimball
Lozier, Clemence Sophia Harned
Martin, Anne Henrietta
Mussey, Ellen Spencer
Nathan, Maud
Park, Maud Wood
Robinson, Harriet Jane Hanson
Schwimmer, Rosika
Sewall, May Eliza Wright
Sill, Anna Peck
Smith, Abby Hadassah
Snow, Eliza Roxey
Stanton, Elizabeth Cady
Stevens, Doris
Stone, Lucy
Terrell, Mary Eliza Church
Walker, Mary Edwards
Zakrzewska, Maria Elizabeth
Fencer
Hewes, Robert
Fenian Leader
Devoy, John
O'Mahony, John
O'Neill, John
Roberts, William Randall
Sweeny, Thomas William
Filibuster
Walker, William
Ward, Frederick Townsend
Film Animator
O'Brien, Willis Harold
Terry, Paul Houlton
Film Censor
Breen, Joseph Ignatius
Filmmaker (See also Motion Picture Director)
Eames, Charles Ormand, Jr.
Flaherty, Robert Joseph
Hughes, Howard Robard, Jr.
Micheaux, Oscar
Morrison, Jim
Porter, Edwin Stanton
Selig, William Nicholas
Strand, Paul
Financier (See also Banker, Capitalist, Stockbroker)
Adams, Charles Francis
Aldrich, Nelson Wilmarth
Aldrich, Winthrop William
Astor, William Vincent
Austell, Alfred
Bache, Jules Semon
Barbour, John Strode
Barker, Jacob
Barker, Wharton
Baruch, Bernard Mannes
Bates, Joshua
Biddle, Nicholas
Borie, Adolph Edward
Brooker, Charles Frederick
Butterfield, John
Calhoun, Patrick
Canfield, Richard H.
Carlisle, Floyd Leslie
Cazenove, Théophile
Cheves, Langdon
Chisolm, Alexander Robert
Chouteau, Pierre
Clews, Henry
Cooke, Jay
Coolidge, Thomas Jefferson
Corbin, Daniel Chase
Craigie, Andrew
Crerar, John
Currier, Moody
Cutting, Robert Fulton
Dana, Charles Anderson
Day, George Parmly
Dillon, Sidney
Duer, William
Dunwoody, William Hood
Durant, William Crapo
Eckels, James Herron
Fair, James Graham
Fairchild, Charles Stebbins
Fessenden, William Pitt
Garrett, Robert
Garrison, Cornelius Kingsland
Garrison, William Re Tallack
Gary, Elbert Henry
Giannini, Amadeo Peter
Gilbert, Seymour Parker
Gilman, John Taylor
Girard, Stephen
Godfrey, Benjamin
Goodwin, Ichabod
Gould, George Jay
Gould, Jay
Green, Henrietta Howland Robinson
Green, John Cleve
Griscom, Clement Acton
Guggenheim, Meyer
Hambleton, Thomas Edward
Harding, Abner Clark
Harding, William Procter Gould
Harriman, Edward Roland Noel
Harrison, Charles Custis
Harvie, John
Hatch, Rufus
Hayden, Charles
Hertz, John Daniel
Hill, James Jerome
Holden, Liberty Emery
Holladay, Ben
Hopson, Howard Colwell
Hotchkiss, Horace Leslie
Huntington, Henry Edwards
Inman, John Hamilton
James, Arthur Curtiss
Joy, Henry Bourne
Keep, Henry
Keys, Clement Melville
Kirby, Allan Price
King, James Gore
Knox, John Jay
Lamont, Daniel Scott
Lamont, Thomas William
Lanier, James Franklin Doughty
Lewisohn, Sam Adolph
Lord, Herbert Mayhew
Ludlow, Thomas William
Macalester, Charles, 1798–1873
McGhee, Charles McClung
Mather, Samuel
Matheson, William John
Mellon, Andrew William
Meredith, Samuel
Meyer, André Benoit Mathieu
Mitchell, Alexander
Morgan, John Pierpont
Morgan, Junius Spencer
Morris, Robert, 1734–1806
Murchison, John Dabney
Nettleton, Alvred Bayard
Newhouse, Samuel
Nixon, John, 1733–1808
Park, Trenor WIlliam
Peabody, George
Pearsons, Daniel Kimball
Peters, Richard, 1810–1889
Phinizy, Ferdinand
Pollock, Oliver
Randolph, Thomas Jefferson
Raskob, John Jakob
Rice, Isaac Leopold
Ripley, Edward Hastings
Roberts, Ellis Henry
Rockefeller, William

Rollins, Edward Henry
Rose, Chauncey
Ryan, Thomas Fortune
Sage, Russell
Salomon, Haym
Sanders, Thomas
Scarbrough, William
Schiff, Jacob Henry
Seligman, Joseph
Shuster, W(illiam) Morgan
Smith, George
Smith, Jeremiah
Speyer, James Joseph
Sprague, Oliver Mitchell Wentworth
Starrett, William Aiken
Stevens, Edwin Augustus
Stevens, John Austin, 1827–1910
Straight, Willard Dickerman
Straus, Lewis Lichtenstein
Straus, Simon William
Swan, James
Taylor, Myron Charles
Thatcher, Mahlon Daniel
Thayer, Nathaniel
Thompson, Robert Means
Thompson, William Boyce
Trenholm, George Alfred
Vanderbilt, Cornelius, 1794–1877
Vanderbilt, Cornelius, 1843–1899
Vanderbilt, William Henry
Villard, Henry
Wade, Jeptha Homer
Wadsworth, Eliot
Walker, William Johnson
Wallace, Hugh Campbell
Warburg, Felix Moritz
Warburg, James Paul
Ward, Samuel, 1814–1884
Warfield, Solomon Davies
Watson, John Fanning
Weightman, William
Weyerhaeuser, Frederick Edward
Whitney, Harry Payne
Whitney, William Collins
Whittemore, Thomas
Widener, Peter Arrell Brown
Williams, John Skelton
Wright, Charles Barston
Yerkes, Charles Tyson

FIRE PREVENTION EXPERT
Woodbury, Charles Jeptha Hill

FIRST LADY
Adams, Abigail
Eisenhower, Mamie Geneva Doud
Lincoln, Mary Todd
Madison, Dolly Payne
Roosevelt, (Anna) Eleanor
Wilson, Edith Bolling

FISH CULTURIST (see PISCICULTURIST)

FLORIST (See NURSEYMAN)

FLUTIST
Barrère, Georges

FOLK HUMORIST
Levenson, Samuel ("Sam")

FOLKLORIST (*See also* ANTHROPOLOGIST, ETHNOLOGIST)
Dobie, J(ames) Frank
Hurston, Zora Neale
Jacobs, Joseph, 1854–1916
Newell, William Wells
Rourke, Constance Mayfield
Sandburg, Carl August
Scarborough, Dorothy
Swanton, John Reed
Thompson, Stith

FOLK PLAYS SPECIALIST
Koch, Frederick Henry

FOLK SINGER
Niles, John Jacob

FOOD ADMINISTRATOR
Lasater, Edward Cunningham

FOOD CHEMIST (See also CHEMIST)
Sherman, Henry Clapp

FOOD INDUSTRY EXECUTIVE
Mortimer, Charles Greenough

FOOTBALL COACH (See also ATHLETIC DIRECTOR)
Bible, Dana Xenophon
Bierman, Bernard William ("Bernie")
Butts, James Wallace ("Wally")
Dobie, Gilmour
Haughton, Percy Duncan
Lambeau, Earl Louis ("Curly")
Leahy, Francis William ("Frank")
Lombardi, Vincent Thomas
McMillin, Alvin Nugent ("Bo")
Murphy, Michael Charles
Neyland, Robert Reese, Jr.
Owen, Stephen Joseph
Rockne, Knute Kenneth
Shaughnessy, Clark Daniel
Shaw, Lawrence Timothy ("Buck")
Stagg, Amos Alonzo
Warner, Glenn Scobey ("Pop")
Yost, Fielding Harris
Zuppke, Robert Carl

FOOTBALL PLAYER
Bell, De Benneville ("Bert")
Booth, Albert James, Jr. ("Albie")
Davis, Ernest R. ("Ernie")
Heffelfinger, William Walter "Pudge"
Lambeau, Earl Louis ("Curly")
Leavitt, Frank Simmons ("Man Mountain Dean")
Leemans, Alphonse E. ("Tuffy")
McMillin, Alvin Nugent ("Bo")
Strong, Elmer Kenneth, Jr. ("Ken")
Stuhldreher, Harry A.
Tunnell, Emlen

FOOTBALL PROMOTER
Camp, Walter Chauncey

FORD FOUNDATION PRESIDENT
Heald, Henry Townley

FOREIGN-AID ADMINISTRATOR
Hoffman, Paul Gray

FOREIGN CORRESPONDENT (See also JOURNALIST, NEWSPAPER CORRESPONDENT, NEWSPAPER REPORTER)
Gibbons, Herbert Adams
Hébert, Felix Edward ("Eddie")
Miller, Webb
Sheean, James Vincent
Swing, Raymond Edwards (Gram)
Von Wiegand, Karl Henry

FOREIGN POLICY ADVISER
Coudert, Frederic René

FOREIGN SERVICE OFFICER
Bohlen, Charles Eustis ("Chip")

FORENSIC PATHOLOGIST
Helpern, Milton

FORESTER (See also AGRICULTURIST, SILVICULTURIST)
Allen, Edward Tyson
Baker, Hugh Potter
Bryant, Ralph Clement
Fernow, Bernhard Eduard
Hough, Franklin Benjamin
MacKaye, Benton
Pinchot, Gifford
Record, Samuel James
Rothrock, Joseph Trimble
Silcox, Ferdinand Augustus
Toumey, James William
Vanderbilt, George Washington
Warder, John Aston

FOUNDATION EXECUTIVE
Embree, Edwin Rogers
Gaither, Horace Rowan, Jr.
Glenn, John Mark
Greene, Roger Sherman
Keppel, Frederick Paul
Knowles, John Hilton
Scott, James Brown

FOUNDER
Addams, Jane (Hull-House, Chicago, Ill.)
Allen, Richard (African Methodist Episcopal Church)
Andrew, Samuel (Yale College)
Andrus, Ethel Percy (American Association of Retired Persons, National Retired Teachers Association)
Anza, Juan Bautista de (San Francisco, Cal.)
Archer, John (Medical and Chirurgical Faculty of Maryland)
Austin, Stephen Fuller (Texas)
Baker, George Pierce (47 Workshop)
Baldwin, John (Baldwin-Wallace College, Baker University)
Ballou, Adin (Hopedale Community)
Beers, Clifford Whittingham (mental hygiene movement)
Black, James (National Prohibition Party)
Blair, James (College of William and Mary)
Blavatsky, Helena Petrovna Hahn (Theosophical Society)
Bliss, Daniel (Syrian Protestant College)

Boisen, Anton Theophilus (clinical pastoral education movement)
Booth, Ballington (Volunteers of America)
Bowman, John Bryan (Kentucky University)
Buchman, Frank Nathan Daniel (Moral Re-Armament)
Cabell, Joseph Carrington (University of Virginia)
Cabrini, Francis Xavier (Mother Cabrini) (Missionary Sisters of the Sacred Heart)
Cadillac, Antoine de la Mothe (Detroit, Mich.)
Campbell, Thomas (Disciples of Christ)
Cannon, Harriet Starr (Sisterhood of St. Mary)
Champlain, Samuel de (Canada)
Clark, Francis Edward (Young People's Society of Christian Endeavor)
Coit, Stanton (America's first social settlement)
Connelly, Cornelia (Society of the Holy Child Jesus)
Conover, Harry Sayles (Harry Conover Modeling Agency)
Considérant, Victor Prosper (utopian community in Texas)
Cook, George Cram (Provincetown Players)
Cooke, Samuel (Penn Fruit Company)
Cooper, Sarah Brown Ingersoll (kindergartens)
Cornell, Ezra (Cornell University)
Coulter, Ernest Kent (Big Brother Movement)
Crittenton, Charles Nelson (Florence Crittenton Missions)
Cummins, George David (Reformed Episcopal Church)
Cunningham, Ann Pamela (Mount Vernon Ladies' Association of the Union)
Dabrowski, Joseph (S.S. Cyril and Methodius Seminary)
Darling, Flora Adams (patriotic organizations)
Davenport, George (Davenport, Iowa)
Davidge, John Beale (Univ. of Maryland)
Dempster, John (Methodist theological seminaries)
Dodge, David Low (New York Peace Society)
Dole, James Drummond (Hawaiian Pineapple Company)
Donahue, Peter (Union Iron Workers)
Dooley, Thomas Anthony, III (Medical International Corporation Organization, MEDICO)
Dorrell, William (Dorrellites)
Dowie, John Alexander (Christian Catholic Apostolic Church in Zion)
Drexel, Katharine Mary (Sisters of the Blessed Sacrament for Indians and Colored People)
Dufour, John James (Swiss vineyards in America)
Easley, Ralph Montgomery (National Civic Federation)
Eddy, Mary Morse Baker (Christian Science)
Eggleston, Thomas (School of Mines, Columbia Univ.)
Eielsen, Elling (Norwegian Evangelical Church of North America)
Eliot, William Greenleaf (Washington University of St. Louis)
Estaugh, Elizabeth Haddon (Haddonfield home for travelling ministers)
Eustis, Dorothy Leib Harrison Wood (The Seeing Eye)
Evans, John (Northwestern University, Colorado Seminary)
Ewing, Finis (Cumberland Presbyterian Church)
Fee, John Gregg (Berea College)
Few, Ignatius Alphonso (Emory College)
Fillmore, Charles (Unity School of Christianity)
Flanagan, Edward Joseph (Boys Town)
Foster, Thomas Jefferson (International Correspondence Schools)
Francis, Paul James (Society of the Atonement)
George, William Reuben (George Junior Republic)
Goodall, Harvey L. (livestock market paper)
Guérin, Anne-Thérèse (Mother Theodore) (Sisters of Providence of Saint Mary-of-the-Woods)
Hallett, Benjamin (Seamen's Bethels)
Harris, John (Harrisburg, Pa.)
Harris, Paul Percy (Rotary International)
Harvard, John (Harvard College)
Haynes, George Edmund (Urban League)
Hecker, Isaac Thomas (Paulists)
Herr, John (Reformed Mennonites)
Higginson, Henry Lee (Boston Symphony Orchestra)
Hodur, Francis (Polish National Catholic Church in America)
Holmes, Joseph Austin (U.S. Bureau of Mines)
Houghton, George Hendric (Church of the Transfiguration, N.Y.C.)
Hubbard, Gardiner Greene (National Geographic Society)
Huidekoper, Harm Jan (Meadville Theological School)
Huntington, Henry Edwards (Huntington Library and Art Gallery)
Hyde, Henry Baldwin (Equitable Life Assurance Society of the U.S.)
Jackson, Patrick Tracy (cotton factories at Lowell, Mass.)
Jansky, Karl Guthe (science of radio astronomy)
Jenckes, Joseph (Pawtucket, R.I.)
Johnson, Elijah (Liberia)
Jones, Robert Reynolds ("Bob") (Bob Jones University)
Joubert de la Muraille, James Hector Marie Nicholas (Oblate Sisters of Providence)
Juneau, Solomon Laurent (Milwaukee, Wis.)
Kalmus, Herbert Thomas (Technicolor Incorporated)
Keeley, Oliver Hudson (Grange)
Keith, George ("Christian Quakers")
Keith, Minor Cooper (American Fruit Company)
Keppler, Joseph (*Puck*)
King, John (eclectic school of medicine)
King, Richard (ranch)
Kneisel, Franz (Kneisel Quartet)
Knight, Jonathan (American Medical Association, Yale Medical School)
Kroger, Bernhard Henry (Kroger grocery store chain)
Kuskov, Ivan Aleksandrovich (Russian settlement in California)
Laclede, Pierre (St. Louis, Mo.)
Lambeau, Earl Louis ("Curly") (Green Bay Packers football team)
Lane, John (Vicksburg, Miss.)
Lee, Ann (Shakers in America)
Lewis, Samuel (free public school system of Ohio)
Liggett, Louis Kroh (United Drug Company)
Lindley, Jacob (Ohio University)
Lippard, George (Brotherhood of the Union)
Lorimier, Pierre Louis (Cape Girardeau, Mo.)
Lovejoy, Asa Lawrence (Portland, Oreg.)
Low, Juliette Gordon (Girl Scouts of America)
Lowell, John, 1799–1836 (Lowell Institute)

Lyon, David Willard (YMCA in China)
McClellan, George, 1796–1847 (Jefferson Medical College)
Maclay, Robert Samuel (colleges)
McPherson, Aimee Semple (International Church of the Foursquare Gospel)
Mannes, David (Mannes College of Music)
Marquis, Albert Nelson (*Who's Who in America*)
Maslow, Abraham H. (humanistic psychology)
Maurin, Peter Aristide (Catholic Worker Movement)
Meeker, Nathan Cook (Union Colony of Colorado)
Menninger, Charles Frederick (Menninger Clinic)
Meyer, Annie Nathan (Barnard College)
Mooney, William (New York Society of Tammany)
Morgan, John (University of Penn. Medical School)
Muller, Hermann Joseph (radiation genetics)
Murray, John, 1741–1815 (Universalism in America)
Myer, Albert James (Weather Bureau)
Nast, William (first German Methodist church in the U.S.)
Newbrough, John Ballou (Shalam religious community)
Newcomer, Christian (Church of the United Brethren in Christ)
Noble, Samuel (Anniston, Ala.)
Noyes, John Humphrey (Oneida Community)
Oglethorpe, James Edward (colony of Georgia)
Osgood, Jacob (Osgoodites)
Otterbein, Philip William (Church of the United Brethren in Christ)
Painter, Gamaliel (Middlebury College)
Palmer, Daniel David (chiropractic)
Parmly, Eleazer (dentistry, as an organized profession)
Pastorius, Francis Daniel (Germantown, Pa.)
Peirce, Charles Sanders (pragmatism)
Penn, William (Pennsylvania)
Peralta, Pedro de (Santa Fé, New Mex.)
Phelps, Guy Rowland (Connecticut Mutual Life Insurance Company)
Phillips, Frank (Phillips Petroleum Company)
Phillips, John (Phillips Exeter Academy)
Phillips, Lena Madesin (International Federation of Business and Professional Women, National Federation of Business and Professional Women's Clubs)
Phillips, Samuel (Phillips Academy, Andover)
Pierpont, James (Yale College)
Plant, Henry Bradley (Plant system of railroads)
Porter, James Madison (Lafayette College)
Porter, Rufus (*Scientific American*)
Portolá, Gaspar de (San Diego and Monterey, Cal.)
Purnell, Benjamin (House of David)
Purviance, David (Christian denomination)
Putnam, Gideon (Saratoga Springs, N.Y.)
Quimby, Phineas Parkhurst (mental healing)
Radcliff, Jacob (Jersey City, N.J.)
Randall, Benjamin (Free-Will Baptists)
Rapp, George (Harmony Society)
Rathbone, Justus Henry (Order of Knights of Pythias)
Rezanov, Nikolai Petrovich (Russian-American Company)
Rice, John Andrew (Black Mountain College)
Rice, William Marsh (William Marsh Rice Institute)
Robinson-Smith, Gertrude (Berkshire Symphony Festival, Inc., Tanglewood)
Rochester, Nathaniel (Rochester, N.Y.)
Rogers, John, 1648–1721 (Rogerenes)
Rogers, Mary Josephine (Maryknoll Sisters)
Ross, Harold Wallace (*New Yorker*)
Rowell, George Presbury (*Printer's Ink*)
Russell, Mother Mary Baptist (Sisters of Mercy in California)
Russell, William Hepburn (Pony Express)
Sanford, Henry Shelton (Sanford, Fla.)
Scherman, Harry (Book-of-the-Month Club)
Schneider, Herman (cooperative system of education)
Schrieck, Sister Louise Van der (Sisters of Notre Dame de Namur)
Seton, Elizabeth Ann Bayley (American Society of Charity)
Severance, Caroline Maria Seymour (women's clubs)
Shaw, Henry (Missouri Botanical Garden)
Shelekhov, Grigori Ivanovich (first Russian colony in America)
Shinn, Asa (Methodist Protestant Church)
Shipherd, John Jay (Oberlin College)
Simmons, William Joseph (Ku Klux Klan)
Simpson, Albert Benjamin (Christian and Missionary Alliance)
Slater, Samuel (American cotton industry)
Smith, Sophia (Smith College)
Snethen, Nicholas (Methodist Protestant Church)
Sorin, Edward Frederick (University of Notre Dame)
Spalding, Catherine (Sisters of Charity of Nazareth)
Spring, Samuel (American Board of Commissioners for Foreign Missions)
Spring, Samuel (Andover Theological Seminary)
Stephenson, Benjamin Franklin (Grand Army of the Republic)
Stewart, Philo Penfield (Oberlin College)
Still, Andrew Taylor (osteopathy)
Taylor, Joseph Wright (Bryn Mawr College)
Teresa, Mother (Visitation Order in U.S.)
Teusler, Rudolf Bolling (St. Luke's Hospital, Tokyo)
Thomas, Isaiah (American Antiquarian Society)
Thomas, Robert Bailey (*Farmer's Almanack*)
Tonty, Henry de (Mississippi Valley settlements)
Tourjée, Eben (New England Conservatory of Music)
Townley, Arthur Charles (Nonpartisan League)
Townsend, Francis Everett (Old Age Revolving Pension Plan)
Tufts, Charles (Tufts College)
Upchurch, John Jordan (Ancient Order of United Workmen)
Valentine, Robert Grosvenor (industrial counseling)
Van Raalte, Albertus Christiaan (Dutch settlement in Holland, Mich.)
Varick, James (African Methodist Episcopal Zion Church)
Vassar, Matthew (Vassar College)
Vattemare, Nicholas Marie Alexandre (system of international exchanges)
Vincennes, François Marie Bissot, Sieur de (Vincennes, Ind.)
Wade, Jeptha Homer (American commercial telegraph system)

Walgreen, Charles Rudolph (Walgreen drugstore chain)
Werthelmer, Max (Gestalt movement)
Wetherill, Samuel (Free Quakers)
White, Alma Bridwell (Pillar of Fire Church)
White, Thomas Willis (*Southern Literary Messenger*)

FRATERNAL ORDER LEADER
Davis, James John
Wilson, J(ames) Finley

FREEMASON
Morgan, William
Pike, Albert

FREE-SOILER
Stearns, George Luther

FREE-STATE ADVOCATE
Conway, Martin Franklin
Pomeroy, Samuel Clarke

FREETHINKER
Bennett, De Robigne Mortimer
Underwood, Benjamin Franklin
Wright, Frances

FREIGHTER (See also TRANSPORTER)
Majors, Alexander
Russell, William Hepburn

FRONTIERSMAN (See also DISCOVERER, EXPLORER, GUIDE, PIONEER, SCOUT)
Bridger, James
Burleson, Edward
California Joe
Crockett, David
Dixon, William
Fonda, John H.
Hughes, Price
Kenton, Simon
Lillie, Gordon William
Maxwell, Lucien Bonaparte
North, Frank Joshua
Oñate, Juan de
Shelby, Evan
Wallace, William Alexander Anderson

FROZEN FOOD PROCESS INVENTOR
Birdseye, Clarence

FUNAMBULIST
Wallenda, Karl

FUNDAMENTALIST ADVOCATE
Price, George Edward McCready

FUND RAISER
Jones, John Price

FUR TRADER (See also FUR TRAPPER, MERCHANT, TRADER, TRAPPER)
Ashely, William Henry
Astor, John Jacob
Baranov, Alexander Andreevich
Bent, Charles
Bent, William
Bridger, James
Cerré, Jean Gabriel
Chouteau, Auguste Pierre
Chouteau, Jean Pierre
Chouteau, Pierre
Crooks, Ramsay
Dickson, Robert
Farnham, Russel
Franchère, Gabriel
Gray, Robert
Harmon, Daniel Williams
Henry, Alexander
Hubbard, Gurdon Saltonstall
Kinzie, John
Kittson, Norman Wolfred
La Barge, Joseph
Larpenteur, Charles
Lisa, Manuel
Mackenzie, Donald
Mackenzie, Kenneth
McLeod, Martin
Menard, Pierre
Mitchell, David Dawson
Morton, Thomas
Navarre, Pierre
Ogden, Peter Skene
Pilcher, Joshua
Pond, Peter
Pratte, Bernard
Provost, Etienne
Rolette, Jean Joseph
Ross, Alexander
Sarpy, Peter A.
Sibley, Henry Hastings
Stuart, Robert
Sublette, William Lewis
Thompson, David
Vanderburgh, William Henry
Willard, Simon

FUR TRAPPER (See also FUR TRADER, MERCHANT, TRADER, TRAPPER)
Campbell, Robert
Henry, Andrew

GAMBLER
Canfield, Richard A.
Morrissey, John

GANGSTER (See also BOOTLEGGER, CRIMINAL)
Capone, Alphonse ("Al")
Flegenheimer, Arthur
Galante, Carmine
Kelly, Machine Gun (George Kelly Barnes, Jr.)
Madden, Owen Victor ("Owney")

GAS PRODUCER
Gregory, Thomas Barger

GASTROENTEROLOGIST
Ingelfinger, Franz Joseph

GAY RIGHTS ACTIVIST
Milk, Harvey Bernard

GEM MERCHANT
Winston, Harry

GEMOLOGIST
Kunz, George Frederick

GENEALOGIST
Alden, Ebenezer
Banks, Charles Edward
Chester, Joseph Lemuel
Farmer, John
Lapham, William Berry
Putnam, Eben
Shattuck, Lemuel
Sherman, Frank Dempster
Smith, Charles Perrin
Stiles, Henry Reed
Tyler, Lyon Gardiner

GENERAL (See also AVIATOR, SOLDIER)
Abercromby, James
Allen, Henry Tureman
Arnold, Henry Harley
Arnold, Lewis Golding
Braddock, Edward
Colston, Raleigh Edward
Conway, Thomas
Cooper, Samuel
Corse, John Murray
Couch, Darius Nash
Cox, Jacob Dolson
Eisenhower, Dwight David
Evans, Clement Anselm
Evans, Nathan George
Floyd, John Buchanan
Forrest, Nathan Bedford
Gartrell, Lucius Jeremiah
Grant, Ulysses Simpson
Greene, Nathaniel
Gregg, John
Hanson, Roger Weightman
Herron, Francis Jay
Hodges, Courtney Hicks
Howe, George Augustus, third Viscount Howe
Humbert, Jean Joseph Amable
Jackson, William Hicks
Kalb, Johann
Kelser, Raymond Alexander
Knox, Henry
Krueger, Walter
Lee, Charles, 1731–1782
Logan, Thomas Muldrup, 1840–1914
Loudoun, John Campbell, Fourth Earl of
MacArthur, Douglas
McIntosh, William
Manigault, Arthur Middleton
March, Peyton Conway
Marion, Francis
Maxey, Samuel Bell
Monckton, Robert
Moultrie, William
Nicholls, Francis Redding Tillou
O'Donnell, Emmett, Jr. ("Rosy")
Patton, George Smith
Pershing, John Joseph
Polk, Leonidas
Porter, Peter Buell
St. John, Isaac Munroe
Slocum, Henry Warner
Steuben, Friedrich Wilhelm Ludolf Gerhard Augustin, Baron von
Stevenson, Carter Littlepage
Sullivan, John
Trumbull, Joseph
Vandegrift, Alexander Archer
Van Dorn, Earl
Wadsworth, Peleg
Wainwright, Jonathan Mayhew
Walthall, Edward Cary
Ward, Artemas
Watie, Stand
Webb, Daniel
Wigfall, Louis Trezevant
Wise, Henry Alexander
Woodhull, Nathaniel
Wooster, David

GENETICIST (See also BIOLOGIST, CYTOLOGIST, ZOOLOGIST)
Bridges, Calvin Blackman
Collins, Guy N.
Emerson, Rollins Adams
Morgan, Thomas Hunt
Muller, Hermann Joseph
Sinnott, Edmund Ware
Tatum, Edward Lawrie
GEODESIST (See also SURVEYOR)
Bowie, William
Davidson, George
Hassler, Ferdinand Rudolph
Hayford, John Fillmore
Hilgard, Julius Erasmus
Rees, John Krom
GEOGRAPHER (See also CARTOGRAPHER, MAPMAKER)
Atwood, Wallace Walter
Baker, Marcus
Baker, Oliver Edwin
Bowman, Isaiah
Boyd, Louise Arner
Brigham, Albert Perry
Brooks, Alfred Hulse
Brown, Ralph Hall
Cowles, Henry Chandler
Darby, William
Davidson, George
Davis, William Morris
De Brahm, William Gerard
Erskine, Robert
Evans, Lewis
Fenneman, Nevin Melancthon
Gannett, Henry
Goode, John Paul
Guyot, Arnold Henry
Huntington, Ellsworth
Hutchins, Thomas
Jefferson, Mark Sylvester William
Johnson, Douglas Wilson
Melish, John
Mitchell, Samuel Augustus
Morse, Jedidiah
Pory, John
Robinson, Edward, 1794–1863
Sauer, Carl Ortwin
Schott, Charles Anthony
Tanner, Henry Schenck
Tarr, Ralph Stockman
Tatham, William
Thompson, David
Worcester, Joseph Emerson
GEOLOGIST (See also GEOMORPHOLOGIST, GEOPHYSICIST)
Agassiz, Jean Louis Rodolphe
Ashburner, Charles Albert
Atwood, Wallace Walter
Bailey, Jacob Whitman
Barrell, Joseph
Bascom, Florence
Becker, George Ferdinand
Blake, William Phipps
Boll, Jacob
Bowen, Norman Levi
Boyé, Martin Hans
Bradley, Frank Howe
Brainerd, Ezra
Branner, John Casper
Broadhead, Garland Carr
Brooks, Alfred Hulse
Brooks, Thomas Benton
Bryan, Kirk
Calvin, Samuel
Campbell, Marius Robinson
Carll, John Franklin
Chamberlin, Thomas Chrowder
Christy, David
Clapp, Charles Horace
Clark, William Bullock
Claypole, Edward Waller
Condon, Thomas
Cook, George Hammell
Crosby, William Otis
Cross, Charles Whitman
Daly, Reginald Aldworth
Dana, James Dwight
Darton, Nelson Horatio
Davis, William Morris
Day, David Talbot
Diller, Joseph Silas
Dutton, Clarence Edward
Emerson, Benjamin Kendall
Emmons, Ebenezer
Emmons, Samuel Franklin
Fenneman, Nevin Melancthon
Foshag, William Frederick
Gilbert, Grove Karl
Grabau, Amadeus William
Hague, Arnold
Hall, James, 1811–1898
Hayden, Ferdinand Vandiveer
Hayden, Horace H.
Hayes, Charles Willard
Heilprin, Angelo
Hilgard, Eugene Woldemar
Hitchcock, Charles Henry
Hitchcock, Edward, 1793–1864
Houghton, Douglass
Hunt, Thomas Sterry
Iddings, Joseph Paxon
Irving, John Duer
Irving, Roland Duer
Jackson, Charles Thomas
Jaggar, Thomas Augustus, Jr.
Johnson, Douglas Wilson
Keith, Arthur
Kemp, James Furman
Kerr, Washington Caruthers
King, Clarence
Lawson, Andrew Cowper
LeConte, Joseph
Lesley, Peter
Leverett, Frank
Lindgren, Waldemar
Lucas, Anthony Francis
Lyman, Benjamin Smith
McGee, William John
Maclure, William
Marbut, Curtis Fletcher
Marcou, Jules
Mather, William Williams
Matthes, François Emile
Meinzer, Oscar Edward
Merrill, George Perkins
Mitchell, Elisha
Newberry, John Strong
Orton, Edward Francis Baxter
Owen, David Dale
Penrose, Richard Alexander Fullerton
Percival, James Gates
Perin, Charles Page
Perkins, George Henry
Pirsson, Louis Valentine
Powell, John Wesley
Price, George Edward McCready
Proctor, John Robert
Prosser, Charles Smith
Pumpelly, Raphael
Ransome, Frederick Leslie
Rice, William North
Roemer, Karl Ferdinand
Rogers, Henry Darwin
Rogers, William Barton
Rubey, William Walden
Russell, Israel Cook
Safford, James Merrill
Salisbury, Rollin D.
Scopes, John Thomas
Scott, William Berryman
Shaler, Nathaniel Southgate
Smith, Erminnie Adelle Platt
Smith, Eugene Allen
Smith, George Otis
Smith, James Perrin
Spurr, Josiah Edward
Stetson, Henry Crosby
Stevenson, John James
Swallow, George Clinton
Talmage, James Edward
Tarr, Ralph Stockman
Taylor, Frank Bursley
Taylor, Richard Cowling
Troost, Gerard
Udden, Johan August
Ulrich, Edward Oscar
Upham, Warren
Van Hise, Charles Richard
Vanuxem, Lardner
Vaughan, Thomas Wayland
Veatch, Arthur Clifford
White, Charles Abiathar
White, David
White, Israel Charles
Whitney, Josiah Dwight
Willis, Bailey
Winchell, Alexander
Winchell, Horace Vaughn
Winchell, Newton Horace
Woodworth, Jay Backus
Worthen, Amos Henry
Wright, George Frederick
GEOMORPHOLOGIST
Bryan, Kirk
Johnson, Douglas Wilson
GEOPHYSICIST
Day, Arthur Louis
Ewing, William Maurice
Fleming, John Adam
Kennedy, George Clayton
Slichter, Louis Byrne
GIRL SCOUT LEADER
Choate, Anne Hyde Clarke
Low, Juliette Gordon
GLASSMAKER (See also GLAZIER)
Hewes, Robert
Leighton, William
Libbey, Edward Drummond
Stiegel, Henry William
Tiffany, Louis Comfort
GLAZIER (See also GLASSMAKER)
Godfrey, Thomas

GOLDSMITH (See also CRAFTSMAN)
Le Roux, Bartholomew
GOLF-COURSE DESIGNER
Macdonald, Charles Blair
GOLFER
Armour, Thomas Dickson ("Tommy")
Hagen, Walter Charles
Jones, Robert Tyre, Jr.
Little, William Lawson, Jr.
Macdonald, Charles Blair
Mangrum, Lloyd Eugene
Ouimet, Francis Desales
Smith, Horton
Travers, Jerome Dunstan
Travis, Walter John
Wood, Craig Ralph
GOSPEL SINGER
Jackson, Mahalia
GOSSIP COLUMNIST
Hopper, Hedda
Lyons, Leonard
Parsons, Louella Rose Oettinger
GOVERNMENT ADVISER
Elliott, William Yandell, III
GOVERNMENT OFFICIAL (See also PUBLIC OFFICIAL)
Altmeyer, Arthur Joseph
Ames, Joseph Sweetman
Arnold, Thurman Wesley
Ballantine, Arthur Atwood
Bennett, Henry Garland
Bethune, Mary McLeod
Biffle, Leslie L.
Breckinridge, Henry Skillman
Bundy, Harvey Hollister
Bunker, Arthur Hugh
Bush, Vannevar ("Van")
Chapman, Oscar Littleton
Clayton, William Lockhart
Coolidge, Thomas Jefferson
Cooper, William John
Creel, George
Crowley, Leo Thomas
Cutler, Robert
Dennett, Tyler (Wilbur)
Dodge, Joseph Morrell
Dorn, Harold Fred
Early, Stephen Tyree
Finletter, Thomas Knight
Flint, Weston
Fly, James Lawrence
Gaston, Herbert Earle
Haas, Francis Joseph
Hannegan, Robert Emmet
Herrick, Robert Welch
Hill, Arthur Middleton
Hines, Frank Thomas
Hopkins, Harry Lloyd
Hunt, Gaillard
Johnson, Hugh Samuel
Kennedy, Joseph Patrick
Knudsen, William S.
Krug, Julius Albert
Leffingwell, Russell Cornell
Legge, Alexander
Lubin, Isador
McEntee, James Joseph
McHugh, Keith Stratton
Manly, Basil Maxwell
Merchant, Livingston Tallmadge
Merriam, Charles Edward, Jr.
Meyer, Eugene Isaac
Mitchell, William DeWitt
Nelson, Donald Marr
Niles, David K.
Pasvolsky, Leo
Payne, Christopher Harrison
Pelham, Robert A.
Pickens, William
Post, Louis Freeland
Powderly, Terence Vincent
Richberg, Donald Randall
Roche, Josephine Aspinwall
Russell, Charles Wells
Sargent, Frank Pierce
Sherwood, Robert Emmet
Strauss, Lewis Lichtenstein
Talbott, Harold Elstner
Tobin, Austin Joseph
Vance, Harold Sines
Vanderlip, Frank Arthur
Wadsworth, Eliot
Warburg, James Paul
Warner, Edward Pearson
Waterman, Alan Tower
Waymack, William Wesley
Wharton, Francis
Zook, George Frederick
GOVERNOR (ACTING)
Argall, Sir Samuel (Va.)
Blair, John (Va.)
Danforth, Thomas (Mass.)
Evans, John (Pa.)
Hamilton, Andrew, d.1703 (Pa.)
Hamilton, Andrew Jackson (Tex.)
Hamilton, James, 1710–1783 (Pa.)
Lloyd, Thomas (Pa.)
Nelson, William, 1711–1772 (Va.)
Paddock, Algernon Sidney (Nebr.)
Parsons, Lewis Eliphalet (Ala.)
St. Ange de Bellerive, Louis (La.)
Sharkey, William Lewis (Miss.)
Shippen, Edward, 1639–1712 (Pa.)
Stanton, Frederick Perry (Kans.)
Stoddard, Amos (La.)
GOVERNOR (COLONIAL)
Andros, Sir Edmund
Archdale, John
Basse, Jeremiah
Belcher, Jonathan
Bellingham, Richard
Berkeley, Sir William
Bernard, Sir Francis
Botetourt, Norborne Berkeley, Baron de
Burnet, William
Burrington, George
Calvert, Leonard
Campbell, Lord William
Clarke, Walter
Clinton, George
Coote, Richard
Copley, Lionel
Cosby, William
Cranston, John
Cranston, Samuel
Cubero, Pedro Rodriguez
Culpeper, Thomas, Lord
Dobbs, Arthur
Dongan, Thomas
Dudley, Joseph
Dudley, Thomas
Dunmore, John Murray, Earl of
Eden, Robert
Ellis, Henry
Fendall, Josias
Fitch, Thomas
Fletcher, Benjamin
Franklin, William
Gage, Thomas
Gates, Sir Thomas
Gooch, Sir William
Greene, William
Hamilton, Andrew, d. 1703
Harvey, Sir John
Hopkins, Stephen
Hunter, Robert
Hutchinson, Thomas
Hyde, Edward
Johnson, Robert
Johnson, Sir Nathaniel
Johnston, Gabriel
Keith, Sir William
Kieft, Willem
Law, Jonathan
Leete, William
Leverett, John, 1616–1679
Lovelace, Francis
Ludwell, Philip
Lyttelton, William Henry
Markham, William
Martin, Josiah
Mayhew, Thomas
Middleton, Arthur
Miró, Esteban Rodríguez
Moore, James, d. 1706
Moore, Sir Henry
Nicholson, Francis
Nicolls, Richard
Ogle, Samuel
Phips, Sir William
Pierpont, Francis Harrison
Pott, John
Pownall, Thomas
Printz, Johan Björnsson
Reynolds, John
Rising, Johan Classon
Russwurm, John Brown
Saltonstall, Gurdon
Sharpe, Horatio
Shirley, William
Shute, Samuel
Stone, William
Talcott, Joseph
Thomas, George
Treat, Robert
Trumbull, Jonathan, 1710–1785
Tryon, William
Ulloa, Antonio de
Vane, Sir Henry
Van Twiller, Wouter
Villeré, Jacques Philippe
Ward, Richard
Ward, Samuel, 1725–1776
Wentworth, Benning
Wentworth, John, 1737 N.S.–1820
West, Joseph

Winslow, Josiah
Winthrop, John, 1587/88 o.s.–1649
Winthrop, John, 1605/06 o.s.–1676
Winthrop, John, 1638–1707
Wolcott, Oliver, 1726–1797
Wolcott, Roger
Wyatt, Sir Francis
Yeamans, Sir John
Yeardley, Sir George

GOVERNOR (GENERAL)
Alvarado, Juan Bautista (Mexican California)
Brown, William (Bermuda)
Coddington, William (Aquidneck)
Colton, George Radcliffe (Puerto Rico)
Corondo, Francisco Vázquez (Nueva Galicia)
Gore, Robert Hayes (Puerto Rico)
Hasket, Elias (Bahamas)
Minuit, Peter (New Sweden)
Muñoz Marín, Luis (Puerto Rico)
Vandreuli-Cavagnal, Pierre de Riguad, Marquis de (Canada)
Wright, Luke Edward (Philippines)

GOVERNOR (STATE)
Aandahl, Fred George (N.Dak.)
Abbett, Leon (N.J.)
Adams, Alva (Colo.)
Adams, James Hopkins (S.C.)
Alcorn, James Lusk (Miss.)
Alger, Russell Alexander (Mich.)
Allen, Henry Justin (Kans.)
Allen, Henry Watkins (La.)
Allen, Philip (R.I.)
Allen, William (Ohio)
Allston, Robert Francis Withers (S.C.)
Altgeld, John Peter (Ill.)
Ames, Adelbert (Miss.)
Ames, Oliver (Mass.)
Ammons, Elias Milton (Colo.)
Andrew, John Albion (Mass.)
Anthony, George Tobey (Kans.)
Ashe, Samuel (N.C.)
Atkinson, William Yates (Ga.)
Aycock, Charles Brantley (N.C.)
Bagby, Arthur Pendleton (Ala.)
Baldwin, Henry Porter (Mich.)
Baldwin, Roger Sherman (Conn.)
Baldwin, Simeon Eben (Conn.)
Banks, Nathaniel Prentiss (Mass.)
Barrett, Frank Aloysius (Wyo.)
Barry, John Stewart (Mich.)
Barstow, William Augustus (Wis.)
Bartlett, Josiah (N.H.)
Bartley, Mordecai (Ohio)
Bashford, Coles (Wis.)
Bate, William Brimage (Tenn.)
Bates, Frederick (Mo.)
Battle, John Stewart (Va.)
Beaver, James Addams (Pa.)
Bell, Peter Hansborough (Tex.)
Bell, Samuel (N.H.)
Bennett, Caleb Prew (Del.)
Berry, James Henderson (Ark.)
Berry, Nathaniel Springer (N.H.)
Bibb, William Wyatt (Ala.)
Bickett, Thomas Walter (N.C.)
Bienville, Jean Baptiste Le Moyne, Sieur de (La.)
Bigler, John (Calif.)
Bigler, William (Pa.)
Birbo, Theodore Gilmore (Miss.)
Bissell, William Henry (Ill.)
Black, Frank Swett (N.Y.)
Blackburn, Luke Pryor (Ky.)
Blaine, John James (Wis.)
Blair, Austin (Mich.)
Blanchard, Newton Crain (La.)
Blasdel, Henry Goode (Nev.)
Blease, Coleman Livingston (S.C.)
Bliss, Aaron Thomas (Mich.)
Blount, Willie (Tenn.)
Bloxham, William Dunnington (Fla.)
Boggs, Lillburn W. (Mo.)
Boies, Horace (Iowa)
Bond, Shadrach (Ill.)
Bonham, Milledge Lake (S.C.)
Booth, Newton (Calif.)
Boreman, Arthur Ingram (W.Va.)
Bouck, William C. (N.Y.)
Bowdoin, James (Mass.)
Bowie, Oden (Md.)
Bowie, Robert (Md.)
Bradford, Augustus Williamson (Md.)
Bradly, William O'Connell (Ky.)
Bramlette, Thomas E. (Ky.)
Branch, John (N.C.)
Brandon, Gerard Chittocque (Miss.)
Brewster, Ralph Owen (Maine)
Bridges, (Henry) Styles (N.H.)
Brough, John (Ohio)
Broward, Napoleon Bonaparte (Fla.)
Brown, Aaron Venable (Tenn.)
Brown, Albert Gallatin (Miss.)
Brown, Benjamin Gratz (Mo.)
Brown, John Calvin (Tenn.)
Brown, John Young (Ky.)
Brownlow, William Gannaway (Tenn.)
Bryan, Charles Wayland (Nebr.)
Buckingham, William Alfred (Conn.)
Bulkeley, Morgan Gardner (Conn.)
Bull, William (S.C.)
Bullock, Rufus Brown (Ga.)
Burke, Thomas (N.C.)
Burton, Hutchins Gordon (N.C.)
Burton, William (Del.)
Bushnell, Asa Smith (Ohio)
Butler, Benjamin Franklin (Mass.)
Butler, Ezra (Vt.)
Butler, Pierce Mason (S.C.)
Byrd, Harry Flood (Va.)
Cabell, William H. (Va.)
Cadillac, Antoine de la Mothe (La.)
Call, Richard Keith (Fla.)
Cameron, William Evelyn (Va.)
Campbell, William Bowen (Tenn.)
Candler, Allen Daniel (Ga.)
Cannon, Newton (Tenn.)
Cannon, William (Del.)
Capper, Arthur (Kans.)
Carney, Thomas (Kans.)
Carondelet, Francisco Luis Hector, Baron de (La.)
Carpenter, Cyrus Clay (Iowa)
Carr, Elias (N.C.)
Carroll, John Lee (Md.)
Carroll, William (Tenn.)
Carteret, Philip (N.J.)
Chamberlain, Daniel Henry (S.C.)
Chamberlain, George Earle (Oreg.)
Chamberlain, Joshua Lawrence (Maine)
Chambers, John (Iowa)
Chapman, Reuben (Ala.)
Cheney, Person Colby (N.H.)
Chittenden, Martin (Vt.)
Chittenden, Thomas (Vt.)
Churchill, Thomas James (Ark.)
Claflin, William (Mass.)
Claiborne, William Charles Coles (La.)
Clark, Charles (Miss.)
Clark, James (Ky.)
Clark, John (Ga.)
Clark, Myron Holley (N.Y.)
Clarke, James Paul (Ark.)
Clay, Clement Comer (Ala.)
Clayton, Joshua (Del.)
Clayton, Powell (Ark.)
Clement, Frank Goad (Tenn.)
Cleveland, Chauncey Fitch (Conn.)
Cleveland, Stephen Grover (N.Y.)
Clyde, George Dewey (Utah)
Coburn, Abner (Maine)
Coke, Richard (Tex.)
Coles, Edward (Ill.)
Collier, Henry Watkins (Ala.)
Comer, Braxton Bragg (Ala.)
Conway, James Sevier (Ark.)
Cornbury, Edward Hyde (N.Y. and N.J.)
Cornell, Alonzo B. (N.Y.)
Corwin, Thomas (Ohio)
Cox, Jacob Dolson (Ohio)
Crane, Winthrop Murray (Mass.)
Crawford, George Walker (Ga.)
Crawford, Samuel Johnson (Kans.)
Crittenden, Thomas Theodore (Mo.)
Cross, Wilbur Lucius (Conn.)
Crounse, Lorenzo (Nebr.)
Curtin, Andrew Gregg (Pa.)
Davie, William Richardson (N.C.)

Davis, Cushman Kellogg (Minn.)
Davis, Edmund Jackson (Tex.)
Davis, Jeff (Ark.)
De La Warr, Thomas West, Baron (Va.)
Dennison, William (Ohio)
Derbigny, Pierre Auguste Charles Bourguignon (La.)
Dern, George Henry (Utah)
Desha, Joseph (Ky.)
Dewey, Thomas Edward (N.Y.)
Dickerson, Mahlon (N.J.)
Dingley, Nelson (Maine)
Dix, John Adams (N.Y.)
Donnell, Forrest C. (Mo.)
Douglas, William Lewis (Mass.)
Drake, Francis Marion (Iowa)
Drayton, John (S.C.)
Driscoll, Alfred Eastlack (N.J.)
Dudley, Edward Bishop (N.C.)
Duff, James Henderson (Pa.)
Duncan, Joseph (Ill.)
Dunlap, Robert Pinckney (Maine)
Duval, William Pope (Fla.)
Earle, George Howard, III (Pa.)
Easton, John (R.I.)
Easton, Nicholas (R.I.)
Eden, Charles (N.C.)
Edge, Walter Evans (N.J.)
Edison, Charles (N.J.)
Edwards, Henry Waggaman (Conn.)
Edwards, Ninian (Ill.)
Elbert, Samuel (Ga.)
Ellis, John Willis (N.C.)
Ellsworth, William Wolcott (Conn.)
Endecott, John (Mass.)
Fages, Pedro (Calif.)
Fairbanks, Erastus (Vt.)
Fairchild, Lucius (Wis.)
Fauquier, Francis (Va.)
Felch, Alpheus (Mich.)
Fenner, Arthur (R.I.)
Fenner, James (R.I.)
Fenton, Reuben Eaton (N.Y.)
Ferguson, James Edward (Tex.)
Ferguson, Miriam Amanda Wallace (Tex.)
Ferris, Woodbridge Nathan (Mich.)
Ferry, Elisha Peyre (Wash.)
Fifer, Joseph WIlson (Ill.)
Fishback, William Meade (Ark.)
Fitzpatrick, Benjamin (Ala.)
Flanagin, Harris (Ark.)
Fleming, Aretas Brooks (W.Va.)
Flower, Roswell Pettibone (N.Y.)
Floyd, John (Va.)
Floyd, John Buchanan (Va.)
Folk, Joseph Wingate (Mo.)
Foot, Samuel Augustus (Conn.)
Foote, Henry Stuart (Miss.)
Foraker, Joseph Benson (Ohio)
Ford, Thomas (Ill.)
Foster, Charles (Ohio)
Foster, Murphy James (La.)
Francis, David Rowland (Mo.)
Francis, John Brown (R.I.)
Frazier, Lynn Joseph (N.Dak.)
Fuller, Levi Knight (Vt.)
Furnas, Robert Wilkinson (Nebr.)
Gamble, Hamilton Rowan (Mo.)
Gardner, Henry Joseph (Mass.)
Gardner, Oliver Maxwell (N.C.)
Garrard, James (Ky.)
Garvin, Lucius Fayette Clark (R.I.)
Gayle, John (Ala.)
Gear, John Henry (Iowa)
Geary, John White (Pa.)
Gilmer, George Rockingham (Ga.)
Gilmore, Joseph Albree (N.H.)
Gist, William Henry (S.C.)
Glynn, Martin Henry (N.Y.)
Goebel, William (Ky.)
Goldsborough, Charles (Md.)
Grant, James Benton (Colo.)
Graves, David Bibb (Ala.)
Gray, Isaac Pusey (Ind.)
Green, Theodore Francis (R.I.)
Greene, William (R.I.)
Greenhalge, Frederic Thomas (Mass.)
Greenup, Christopher (Ky.)
Grimes, James Wilson (Iowa)
Griswold, Matthew (Conn.)
Guild, Curtis, 1860–1915 (Mass.)
Hadley, Herbert Spencer (Mo.)
Hagood, Johnson (S.C.)
Hahn, Georg Michael Decker (La.)
Haight, Henry Huntly (Calif.)
Haines, Daniel (N.J.)
Hall, Hiland (Vt.)
Hall, Luther Egbert (La.)
Hall, Willard Preble (Mo.)
Hamilton, James, 1786–1857 (S.C.)
Hamilton, Paul (S.C.)
Hamilton, William Thomas (Md.)
Hammond, James Henry (S.C.)
Hampton, Wade, 1818–1902 (S.C.)
Handley, Harold Willis (Ind.)
Hardin, Charles Henry (Mo.)
Hardwick, Thomas William (Ga.)
Harmon, Judson (Ohio)
Harriman, Walter (N.H.)
Harrison, Benjamin, 1726–1791 (Va.)
Harrison, Henry Baldwin (Conn.)
Hartness, James (Vt.)
Harvey, Louis Powell (Wis.)
Haskell, Charles Nathaniel (Okla.)
Hawley, James Henry (Idaho)
Hayne, Robert Young (S.C.)
Haynes, John (Conn. and Mass.)
Hébert, Paul Octave (La.)
Helm, John Larue (Ky.)
Henderson, James Pinckney (Tex.)
Hendricks, Thomas Andrews (Ind.)
Hendricks, William (Ind.)
Henry, John, 1750–1798 (Md.)
Herter, Christian Archibald (Mass.)
Hicks, Thomas Holliday (Md.)
Hiester, Joseph (Pa.)
Hoadly, George (Ohio)
Hoard, William Dempster (Wis.)
Hobby, William Pettus (Tex.)
Hoey, Clyde Roark (N.C.)
Hoffman, John Thompson (N.Y.)
Hogg, James Stephen (Tex.)
Horbrook, Frederick (Vt.)
Holden, William Woods (N.C.)
Holland, Spessard Lindsey (Fla.)
Holmes, David (Miss.)
Hopkins, Edward (Conn.)
Hoppin, William Warner (R.I.)
Horner, Henry (Ill.)
Houston, George Smith (Ala.)
Houstoun, John (Ga.)
Hovey, Alvin Peterson (Ind.)
Howell, Richard (N.J.)
Hubbard, John (Maine)
Hubbard, Lucius Frederick (Minn.)
Hubbard, Richard Bennett (Tex.)
Hughes, Charles Evans (N.Y.)
Humphreys, Benjamin Grubb (Miss.)
Hunt, George Wylie Paul (Ariz.)
Hunt, Lester Callaway (Wyo.)
Hunt, Washington (N.Y.)
Huntington, Samuel, 1731–1796 (Conn.)
Huntington, Samuel, 1765–1817 (Ohio)
Hyde, Arthur Mastick (Mo.)
Ireland, John, 1827–1896 (Tex.)
Jackson, Claiborne Fox (Mo.)
Jackson, James, 1757–1806 (Ga.)
James, Arthur Horace (Pa.)
Jarvis, Thomas Jordan (N.C.)
Jenckes, Joseph (R.I.)
Jenkins, Charles Jones (Ga.)
Jennings, Jonathan (Ind.)
Jewell, Marshall (Conn.)
Johnson, Edwin Carl (Colo.)
Johnson, Hiram Warren (Calif.)
Johnson, John Albert (Minn.)
Johnson, Thomas (Md.)
Johnston, Joseph Forney (Ala.)
Jones, James Chamberlayne (Tenn.)
Jones, Thomas Goode (Ala.)
Jones, William (R.I.)
Kavanagh, Edward (Maine)
Kellogg, William Pitt (La.)
Kemper, James Lawson (Va.)
Kendrick, John Benjamin (Wyo.)
Kent, Edward (Maine)
Kent, Joseph (Md.)
Kerner, Otto, Jr. (Ill.)
Kerr, Robert Samuel (Okla.)
King, Austin Augustus (Mo.)

King, John Alsop (N.Y.)
King, Samuel Ward (R.I.)
King, William (Maine)
Kirkwood, Samuel Jordan (Iowa)
Kitchin, William Walton (N.C.)
Knight, Goodwin Jess ("Goodie") (Calif.)
Knott, James Proctor (Ky.)
Kohler, Walter Jodok (Wis.)
Kohler, Walter Jodok, Jr. (Wis.)
La Follette, Philip Fox (Wis.)
La Follette, Robert Marion (Wis.)
Langlie, Arthur Bernard (Wash.)
Larrabee, William (Iowa)
Larrazolo, Octaviano Ambrosio (N.Mex.)
Lawrence, David Leo (Pa.)
Lee, Thomas Sim (Md.)
Lehman, Herbert Henry (N.Y.)
Letcher, John (Va.)
Letcher, Robert Perkins (Ky.)
Lewelling, Lorenzo Dow (Kans.)
Lewis, Morgan (N.Y.)
Ligon, Thomas Watkins (Md.)
Lind, John (Minn.)
Lippitt, Henry (R.I.)
Lloyd, Edward, 1779–1834 (Md.)
Long, Earl Kemp (La.)
Long, Huey Pierce (La.)
Long, John Davis (Mass.)
Lord, William Paine (Oreg.)
Low, Frederick Ferdinand (Calif.)
Lowden, Frank Orren (Ill.)
Lowe, Ralph Phillips (Iowa)
Lowndes, Lloyd (Md.)
Lowry, Robert (Miss.)
Lubbock, Francis Richard (Tex.)
Lucas, Robert (Ohio)
McArthur, Duncan (Ohio)
McCall, Samuel Walker (Mass.)
McClelland, Robert (Mich.)
McClurg, Joseph Washington (Mo.)
McCreary, James Bennett (Ky.)
McCullough, John Griffith (Vt.)
McDaniel, Henry Dickerson (Ga.)
McDonald, Charles James (Ga.)
McDowell, James (Va.)
McEnery, Samuel Douglas (La.)
McGrath, James Howard (R.I.)
McGraw, John Harte (Wash.)
McKay, (James) Douglas (Oreg.)
McKeldin, Theodore Roosevelt (Md.)
McLaurin, Anselm Joseph (Miss.)
McLean, Angus Wilton (N.C.)
McMillin, Benton (Tenn.)
McMinn, Joseph (Tenn.)
McNair, Alexander (Mo.)
McNutt, Paul Vories (Ind.)
McRae, Thomas Chipman (Ark.)
Magoffin, Beriah (Ky.)
Magrath, Andrew Gordon (S.C.)
Manning, Richard Irvine, 1789–1836 (S.C.)
Manning, Richard Irvine, 1859–1931 (S.C.)
Marland, Ernest Whitworth (Okla.)
Marmaduke, John Sappington (Mo.)
Marshall, Thomas Riley (Ind.)
Marshall, William Rainey (Minn.)
Martin, Alexander (N.C.)
Martin, John Alexander (Kans.)
Mason, Richard Barnes (Calif.)
Mason, Stevens Thomson (Mich.)
Mathews, Henry Mason (W.Va.)
Mathews, John (S.C.)
Mathews, Samuel (Va.)
Matteson, Joel Aldrich (Ill.)
Matthews, Claude (Ind.)
Mattocks, John (Vt.)
Maybank, Burnet Rhett (S.C.)
Meigs, Return Jonathan (Ohio)
Mellette, Arthur Calvin (S.D.)
Mercer, John Francis (Md.)
Metcalfe, Thomas (Ky.)
Mifflin, Thomas (Pa.)
Milledge, John (Ga.)
Miller, John (Mo.)
Miller, Nathan Lewis (N.Y.)
Milton, John (Fla.)
Mitchell, David Brydie (Ga.)
Mitchell, Nathaniel (Del.)
Montague, Andrew Jackson (Va.)
Moore, Gabriel (Ala.)
Moore, Thomas Overton (La.)
Morehead, Charles Slaughter (Ky.)
Morehead, James Turner (Ky.)
Morehead, John Motley (N.C.)
Morgan, Edwin Denison (N.Y.)
Morril, David Lawrence (N.H.)
Morrill, Anson Peaslee (Maine)
Morrill, Edmund Needham (Kans.)
Morrill, Lot Myrick (Maine)
Morris, Lewis, 1671–1746 (N.J.)
Morris, Luzon Burritt (Conn.)
Morris, Robert Hunter (Pa.)
Morrow, Edwin Porch (Ky.)
Morrow, Jeremiah (Ohio)
Morton, Levi Parsons (N.Y.)
Morton, Marcus, 1784–1864 (Mass.)
Morton, Oliver Perry (Ind.)
Moses, Franklin J. (S.C.)
Moultrie, William (S.C.)
Mouton, Alexander (La.)
Murphy, Franklin (N.J.)
Murphy, Frank (Mich.)
Murphy, Isaac (Ark.)
Nash, Abner (N.C.)
Neely, Matthew Mansfield (W.Va.)
Nelson, Knute (Minn.)
Nelson, Thomas (Va.)
Newell, William Augustus (N.J.)
Nicholas, Wilson Cary (Va.)
Nicholls, Francis Redding Tillou (La.)
Norbeck, Peter (S.Dak.)
Northen, William Jonathan (Ga.)
Noyes, Edward Follansbee (Ohio)
Oates, William Calvin (Ala.)
O'Daniel, Wilbert Lee ("Pappy") (Tex.)
Odell, Benjamin Barker (N.Y.)
O'Ferrall, Charles Triplett (Va.)
Ogden, Aaron (N.J.)
Oglesby, Richard James (Ill.)
Olden, Charles Smith (N.J.)
Olson, Floyd Bjerstjerne (Minn.)
O'Neal, Edward Asbury (Ala.)
O'Neill, C. William ("Bill") (Ohio)
Orr, James Lawrence (S.C.)
Osborn, Chase Salmon (Mich.)
Otermín, Antonio de (N.Mex.)
Owsley, William (Ky.)
Paca, William (Md.)
Pacheco, Romualdo (Calif.)
Page, John (Va.)
Paine, Charles (Vt.)
Palmer, John McAuley (Ill.)
Parker, John Milliken (La.)
Parris, Albion Keith (Maine)
Pattison, John M. (Ohio)
Pease, Elisha Marshall (Tex.)
Peay, Austin (Tenn.)
Peck, George Wilbur (Wis.)
Peñalosa Briceño, Diego Dioniso de (N.Mex.)
Pennington, William (N.J.)
Pennington, William Sandford (N.J.)
Pennoyer, Sylvester (Oreg.)
Pennypacker, Samuel Whitaker (Pa.)
Peralta, Pedro de (N.Mex.)
Percy, George (Va.)
Perkins, George Clement (Calif.)
Perry, Benjamin Franklin (S.C.)
Perry, Edward Aylesworth (Fla.)
Phelps, John Smith (Mo.)
Philipp, Emanuel Lorenz (Wis.)
Pickens, Francis Wilkinson (S.C.)
Pickens, Israel (Ala.)
Pierce, Benjamin (N.H.)
Pillsbury, John Sargent (Minn.)
Pinchot, Gifford (Pa.)
Pinckney, Charles (S.C.)
Pinckney, Thomas (S.C.)
Pingree, Hazen Stuart (Mich.)
Pitkin, Frederick Walker (Colo.)
Pitkin, William, 1694–1769 (Conn.)
Plaisted, Harris Merrill (Maine)
Plater, George (Md.)
Pleasants, James (Va.)
Pollock, James (Pa.)
Porter, Albert Gallatin (Ind.)
Porter, James Davis (Tenn.)
Pratt, Thomas George (Md.)
Price, Rodman McCamley (N.J.)
Price, Sterling (Mo.)
Proctor, Redfield (Vt.)
Ralston, Samuel Moffett (Ind.)

Ramsey, Alexander (Minn.)
Randall, Alexander Williams (Wis.)
Randolph, Theodore Fitz (N.J.)
Randolph, Thomas Mann (Va.)
Rector, Henry Massey (Ark.)
Reid, David Settle (N.C.)
Reynolds, John (Ill.)
Rice, Alexander Hamilton (Mass.)
Ritchie, Albert Cabell (Md.)
Ritner, Joseph (Pa.)
Roane, Archibald (Tenn.)
Robertson, Thomas Bolling (La.)
Robertson, Wyndham (Va.)
Robinson, Charles (Kans.)
Rockefeller, Nelson Aldrich (N.Y.)
Rogers, John Rankin (Wash.)
Roman, Andé Bienvenu (La.)
Ross, Lawrence Sullivan (Tex.)
Ross, Nellie Tayloe
Rusk, Jeremiah McClain (Wis.)
Russell, Richard Brevard, Jr. ("Dick") (Ga.)
Russell, William Eustis (Mass.)
Rutledge, Edward (S.C.)
St. John, John Pierce (Kans.)
Saulsbury, Gove (Del.)
Scott, Charles (Ky.)
Scott, Robert Kingston (S.C.)
Scott, W(illiam) Kerr (N.C.)
Seligman, Arthur (N.Mex.)
Sevier, John (Tenn.)
Seymour, Horatio (N.Y.)
Seymour, Thomas Hart (Conn.)
Shafroth, John Franklin (Colo.)
Shaw, Leslie Mortier (Iowa)
Shelby, Isaac (Ky.)
Shorter, John Gill (Ala.)
Shoup, George Laird (Idaho)
Shulze, John Andrew (Pa.)
Shunk, Francis Rawn (Pa.)
Sibley, Henry Hastings (Minn.)
Simpson, William Dunlap (S.C.)
Smallwood, William (Md.)
Smith, Alfred Emanuel (N.Y.)
Smith, Hoke (Ga.)
Smith, James Youngs (R.I.)
Smith, Jeremiah, 1759–1842 (N.H.)
Smith, John Cotton, 1765–1845 (Conn.)
Smith, John Gregory (Vt.)
Smith, William, 1797–1887 (Va.)
Snyder, Simon (Pa.)
Southard, Samuel Lewis (N.J.)
Spaight, Richard Dobbs (N.C.)
Sprague, Charles Arthur (Oreg.)
Sprague, William, 1830–1915 (R.I.)
Sproul, William Cameron (Pa.)
Stanford, Leland (Calif.)
Stark, Lloyd Crow (Mo.)
Sterling, Ross Shaw (Tex.)
Stevenson, Adlai Ewing, II (Ill.)
Stevenson, John White (Ky.)
Stewart, Robert Marcellus (Mo.)
Stokes, Montfort (N.C.)
Stone, John Marshall (Miss.)
Stone, William Joel (Mo.)
Stoneman, George (Calif.)
Stubbs, Walter Roscoe (Kans.)
Sulzer, William (N.Y.)
Sumner, Increase (Mass.)
Swain, David Lowry (N.C.)
Swann, Thomas (Md.)
Swanson, Claude Augustus (Va.)
Talmadge, Eugene (Ga.)
Taylor, Alfred Alexander (Tenn.)
Taylor, Robert Love (Tenn.)
Tazewell, Littleton Waller (Va.)
Telfair, Edward (Ga.)
Thomas, Francis (Md.)
Thomas, Philip Francis (Md.)
Thompson, Hugh Smith (S.C.)
Throop, Enos Thompson (N.Y.)
Thye, Edward John (Minn.)
Tiffin, Edward (Ohio)
Tilden, Samuel Jones (N.Y.)
Tillman, Benjamin Ryan (S.C.)
Tobey, Charles William (N.H.)
Tobin, Maurice Joseph (Mass.)
Tod, David (Ohio)
Tompkins, Daniel D. (N.Y.)
Toole, Joseph Kemp (Mont.)
Toucey, Isaac (Conn.)
Towns, George Washington Bonaparte (Ga.)
Trimble, Allen (Ohio)
Trumbull, Jonathan, 1740–1809 (Conn.)
Tugwell, Rexford Guy (P.R.)
Turney, Peter (Tenn.)
Tyler, John, 1747–1813 (Va.)
Vance, Zebulon Baird (N.C.)
Vardaman, James Kimble (Miss.)
Veazey, Thomas Ward (Md.)
Vroom, Peter Dumont (N.J.)
Walker, David Shelby (Fla.)
Walker, Gilbert Carlton (Va.)
Wallace, David (Ind.)
Wallace, Lurleen Burns (Ala.)
Waller, Thomas Macdonald (Conn.)
Wallgren, Mon(rad) C(harles) (Wash.)
Walsh, David Ignatius (Mass.)
Wanton, Joseph (R.I.)
Ward, Marcus Lawrence (N.J.)
Warmoth, Henry Clay (La.)
Warner, Fred Maltby (Mich.)
Warren, Earl (Calif.)
Warren, Fuller (Fla.)
Washburn, Cadwallader Colden (Wis.)
Washburn, Emory (Mass.)
Washburn, Israel (Maine)
Watts, Thomas Hill (Ala.)
Weller, John B. (Calif.)
Wells, James Madison (La.)
West, Francis (Va.)
West, Oswald (Oreg.)
Whitcomb, James (Ind.)
White, John (Va.)
Whitman, Charles Seymour (N.Y.)
Wickliffe, Robert Charles (La.)
Williams, David Rogerson (S.C.)
Williams, James Douglas (Ind.)
Williamson, Isaac Halsted (N.J.)
Williamson, William Durkee (Maine)
Willson, Augustus Everett (Ky.)
Wiltz, Louis Alfred (La.)
Winant, John Gilbert (N.H.)
Winder, Levin (Md.)
Winston, John Anthony (Ala.)
Wise, Henry Alexander (Va.)
Wolcott, Oliver, 1760–1833 (Conn.)
Wolf, George (Pa.)
Wood, Reuben (Ohio)
Woodbridge, William (Mich.)
Woodring, Harry Hines (Kans.)
Worth, Jonathan (N.C.)
Worthington, Thomas (Ohio)
Wright, Fielding Lewis (Miss.)
Wright, Joseph Albert (Ind.)
Wright, Robert (Md.)
Wright, Silas (N.Y.)
Yates, Richard (Ill.)
Yell, Archibald (Ark.)
Youngdahl, Luther Wallace (Minn.)

GOVERNOR (TERRITORIAL)

Blount, William (Tenn.)
Brady, John Green (Alaska)
Clark, William (Mo.)
Cotton, George Radcliff (P.R.)
Connelly, Henry (N.Mex.)
Cumming, Alfred (Utah)
Curry, George Law (Oreg.)
Davis, Dwight Filley (Philippines)
De Vargas Zapata y Lujan Ponce De Leon, Diego (N.Mex.)
Dodge, Henry (Wis.)
Dole, Sanford Ballard (Hawaii)
Edgerton, Sidney (Mont.)
Farrington, Wallace Rider (Hawaii)
Fine, John Sydney (Pa.)
Forbes, William Cameron (Philippines)
Gaines, John Pollard (Oreg.)
Geary, John White (Kans.)
Gilpin, William (Colo.)
Gorman, Willis Arnold (Minn.)
Hammond, Samuel (Mo.)
Hauser, Samuel Thomas (Mont.)
Howard, Benjamin (La.)
Hoyt, John Wesley (Wyo.)
Izard, George (Ark.)
Lane, Joseph (Oreg.)
Lewis, Meriwether (La.)
Lyon, Caleb (Idaho)
McCook, Edward Moody (Colo.)
Magoon, Charles Edward (C.Z.)
Mathews, George (Miss.)
Mitchell, Robert Byington (N.Mex.)
Muñoz Marín, Luis (P.R.)
Murphy, Frank (Philippines)
Nye, James Warren (Nev.)
Peñalosa Briceñ, Diego Dionisio (N.Mex.)
Pierce, Gilbert Ashville (Dakota)
Piñero Jiménez, Jesás Toribio (P.R.)

Portolá , Gaspar de (Upper Calif.)
Posey, Thomas (Indian Terr.)
Potts, Benjamin Franklin (Mont.)
Prince, Le Baron Bradford (N.Mex.)
Reeder, Andrew Horatio (Kans.)
St. Clair, Arthur (Northwest)
Sargent, Winthrop, 1753–1820 (Miss.)
Saunders, Alvin (Nebr.)
Shepherd, Alexander Robey (D.C.)
Shepley, George Foster (La.)
Sloan, Richard Elihu (Ariz.)
Squire, Watson Carvosso (Wash.)
Stevens, Isaac Ingalls (Wash.)
Walker, Robert John (Kans.)
Winship, Blanton (P.R.)

GRAMMARIAN
Brown, Goold
Murray, Lindley
Scott, Fred Newton

GRANGE (See also AGRICULTURIST)
Adams, Dudley W.
Ellis, Seth Hockett
Mayo, Mary Anne Bryant

GRAPHIC ARTIST
Archipenko, Alexander
Marsh, Reginald

GROCER
Skaggs, Marion Barton

GUERRILLA CHIEFTAIN
Quantrill, William Clarke
Sumter, Thomas

GUIDE (See also SCOUT)
Baker, James
Bottineau, Pierre
Carson, Christopher ("Kit")
Fitzpatrick, Thomas
Provost, Etienne
Reynolds, Charles Alexander
Rose, Edward
Walker, Joseph Reddeford
Williams, William Sherley

GUITARIST
Carter, Maybelle Addington
Condon, Albert Edwin ("Eddie")
Ford, Mary
Hendrix, Jimi
Lennon, John Winston Ono
Taylor, Theodore Roosevelt ("Hound Dog")
White, Josh
Williams, (Hiram) Hank

GUNSMITH (See also ORDNANCE EXPERT)
Henry, William
Lawrence, Richard Smith
Pomeroy, Seth
Whittemore, Amos

GYNECOLOGIST (See also PHYSICIAN)
Byford, William Heath
Cullen, Thomas Stephen
Dickinson, Robert Latou
Engelmann, George Julius
Gilliam, David Tod
Graves, William Phillips
Howard, William Travis
Jackson, Abraham Reeves
Kelly, Howard Atwood
Marcy, Henry Orlando
Parry, John Stubbs
Parvin, Theophilus
Polak, John Osborn
Rubin, Isidor Clinton
Sims, James Marion
Skene, Alexander Johnston Chalmers
Smith, Albert Holmes
Storer, Horatio Robinson
Taussig, Frederick Joseph
Thomas, Theodore Gaillard
Van de Warker, Edward Ely
Wilson, Henry Parke Custis

HARNESS MAKER (See MANUFACTURER, *Saddles and Harnesses*

HARNESS RACER
White, Benjamin Franklin

HARPSICHORDIST
Landowska, Wanda Aleksandra

HATTER (See MANUFACTURER, *Hats*)

HEALTH CARE ADMINISTRATOR
Fitzgerald, Alice Louise Florence

HEALTH PROPAGANDIST
Kellogg, John Harvey

HEBRAIST (See also SEMITIST, SCHOLAR)
Davidson, Israel
Harper, William Rainey
Revel, Bernard
Schechter, Solomon
Sewall, Stephen
Wolfson, Harry Austryn

HEIRESS
Hutton, Barbara Woolworth

HELLENIST (See also CLASSICIST, SCHOLAR)
Callimachos, Panos Demetrios
Goodwin, William Watson
Smyth, Herbert Weir
White, John William
Wright, John Henry

HEROINE
Bailey, Anna Warner
Corbin, Margaret
McCauley, Mary Ludwig Hays

HERPETOLOGIST (See also ZOOLOGIST)
Barbour, Thomas
Ditmars, Raymond Lee

HIGH WIRE WALKER (See FUNAMBULIST)

HISPANIST
Crawford, James Pyle Wickersham

HISTOLOGIST (See also ANATOMIST, PHYSICIAN)
Hoerr, Normand Louis

HISTORIAN (See also CHRONICLER, CHURCH HISTORIAN, LITERARY HISTORIAN, MEDICAL HISTORIAN, MEDIEVALIST)
Abbott, John Stevens Cabot
Abel-Henderson, Annie Heloise
Absalom, Harris Chappell
Adams, Brooks
Adams, Charles Francis
Adams, Charles Kendall
Adams, Ephraim Douglass
Adams, George Burton
Adams, Henry Brooks
Adams, James Truslow
Adams, Randolph Greenfield
Alexander, de Alva Stanwood
Alexander, William Dewitt
Allen, Frederick Lewis
Alvord, Clarence Walworth
Ames, Herman Vandenburg
Andrews, Charles McLean
Angle, Paul McClelland
Arendt, Hannah
Arnold, Isaac Newton
Arnold, Samuel Greene
Asbury, Herbert
Atkinson, John
Backus, Isaac
Baird, Charles Washington
Baird, Henry Martyn
Baker, Carl Lotus
Baker, Frank
Bancroft, Frederic
Bancroft, George
Bancroft, Hubert Howe
Bandelier, Adolph Francis Alphonse
Banks, Charles Edward
Barber, John Warner
Bassett, John Spencer
Bayley, James Roosevelt
Beard, Charles Austin
Beard, Mary Ritter
Beauchamp, William Martin
Beer, George Louis
Bemis, Samuel Flagg
Benedict, David
Berenson, Bernard
Beveridge, Albert Jeremiah
Beverley, Robert
Binkley, Robert Cedric
Bolton, Herbert Eugene
Botsford, George Willis
Bourne, Edward Gaylord
Bouton, Nathaniel
Bowers, Claude Gernade
Boyd, Julian Parks
Boyd, William Kenneth
Bozman, John Leeds
Breasted, James Henry
Brinton, Clarence Crane
Brodhead, John Romeyn
Bronson, Henry
Brown, Alexander
Brown, William Wells
Bruce, Philip Alexander
Buley, Roscoe Carlyle
Burr, George Lincoln
Burrage, Henry Sweetser
Burton, Clarence Monroe
Cabell, James Branch
Cajori, Florian
Callender, Guy Stevens
Campbell, Charles
Campbell, William W.
Carson, Hampton Lawrence
Case, Shirley Jackson
Cathcart, William

Chamberlain, Mellen
Channing, Edward
Charlevoix, Pierre François Xavier de
Cheyney, Edward Potts
Chittenden, Hiram Martin
Cist, Henry Martyn
Claiborne, John Francis Hamtramck
Clark, Arthur Hamilton
Colcord, Lincoln Ross
Cole, Arthur Charles
Colum, Padraic
Connor, Robert Digges Wimberly
Cooke, John Esten
Coolidge, Archibald Cary
Corwin, Edward Samuel
Corwin, Edwin Tanjore
Crawford, Francis Marion
Cross, Arthur Lyon
Dart, Henry Paluché
Dawson, Henry Barton
Deane, Charles
Del Mar, Alexander
Dennett, Tyler (Wilbur)
Dennis, Alfred Lewis Pinneo
Dennis, James Shepard
DeVoto, Bernard Augustine
Dexter, Franklin Bowditch
Dodd, William Edward
Dodge, Theodore Ayrault
Dos Passos, John Roderigo
Drake, Francis Samuel
Drake, Samuel Adams
Drake, Samuel Gardner
Draper, John William
Draper, Lyman Copeland
Du Bois, William Edward Burghardt
Dunlap, William
Dunning, William Archibald
Dupratz, Antoine Simon Le Page
Durrett, Reuben Thomas
Eggleston, Edward
Egle, William Henry
Eliot, Samuel
Elliott, Charles
Ellis, George Edward
Emerton, Ephraim
Engelhardt, Zephyrin
English, William Hayden
Evans, Clement Anselm
Fall, Bernard B.
Farrand, Max
Fay, Sidney Bradshaw
Feis, Herbert
Fernow, Berthold
Field, David Dudley
Filson, John
Finney, Charles Grandison
Fish, Carl Russell
Fisher, George Park
Fisher, Sydney George
Fiske, John
Fleming, Walter Lynwood
Folwell, William Watts
Forbes, Esther
Force, Peter
Ford, Henry Jones
Ford, Paul Leicester
Fortier, Alcée
Fox, Dixon Ryan
Francis, Joshua Francis
Francke, Kuno
Frank, Tenney
Freeman, Douglas Southall
Frothingham, Richard
Fulton, John Farquhar
Gambrell, Mary Latimer
Garrett, William Robertson
Garrison, Fielding Hudson
Gavin, Frank Stanton Burns
Gay, Edwin Francis
Gayarré, Charles Étienne Arthur
Gipson, Lawrence Henry
Goddard, Calvin Hooker
Golder, Frank Alfred
Good, James Isaac
Gordy, John Pancoast
Gottschalk, Louis Reichenthal
Gräbner, August Lawrence
Green, Constance McLaughlin
Greene, Francis Vinton
Greenhow, Robert
Griffin, Martin Ignatius Joseph
Grigsby, Hugh Blair
Gross, Charles
Hall, Hiland
Hamilton, Alexander, 1712–1756
Hammond, Bray
Hammond, Jabez Delano
Hansen, Marcus Lee
Haring, Clarence
Harlow, Ralph Volney
Harrisse, Henry
Hart, Albert Bushnell
Haskins, Charles Homer
Hawks, Francis Lister
Hay, John Milton
Hayes, Carlton Joseph Huntley
Haynes, Williams
Haywood, John
Hendrick, Burton Jesse
Henry, William Wirt
Hewat, Alexander
Hildreth, Samuel Prescott
Hill, Frederick Trevor
Hoffman, David
Hofstadter, Richard
Holbrook, Stewart Hall
Holmes, Abiel
Holst, Hermann Eduard von
Howard, Joseph Kinsey
Howe, George
Howe, Henry
Howe, Mark De Wolfe
Howe, Quincy
Hubbard, William
Hulbert, Archer Butler
Hunt, Gaillard
Ireland, Joseph Norton
Jacobs, Joseph, 1854–1916
Jameson, John Franklin
Jenkins, Howard Malcolm
Jewett, Clarence Frederick
Johnson, Allen
Johnston, Alexander
Johnston, Henry Phelps
Johnston, Robert Matteson
Jones, Charles Colcock
Jones, Howard Mumford
Jones, Hugh
Kapp, Friedrich
Keeney, Barnaby Conrad
Kelsey, Rayner Wickersham
Knight, Lucian Lamar
Knox, Dudley Wright
Kobbé, Gustav
Körner, Gustav Philip
Krehbiel, Henry Edward
Kuykendall, Ralph Simpson
Labaree, Leonard Woods
Lacy, William Albert
Lambing, Andrew Arnold
Langer, William Leonard
Larson, Laurence Marcellus
Latané, John Holladay
Latourette, Kenneth Scott
Lea, Henry Charles
Learned, Marion Dexter
Lee, Jesse
Leland, Waldo Gifford
Lenker, John Nicholas
Levering, Joseph Mortimer
Libby, Orin Grant
Lingelbach, Anna Lane
Logan, Deborah Norris
Lovejoy, Arthur Oncken
Lowell, Edward Jackson
Lowery, Woodbury
McAfee, Robert Breckinridge
McCrady, Edward
McElroy, Robert McNutt
McGiffert, Arthur Cushman
McKinley, Albert Edward
McLaughlin, Andrew Cunningham
McMahon, John Van Lear
McMaster, John Bach
MacNair, Harley Farnsworth
Mahan, Alfred Thayer
Marquand, Allan
Marsh, Frank Burr
Marshall, Humphrey
Marshall, Samuel Lyman Atwood ("Slam")
Mattingly, Garrett
Meigs, William Montgomery
Merrill, Elmer Truesdell
Miles, Henry Adolphus
Miller, David Hunter
Miller, William Snow
Milton, George Fort
Minot, George Richards
Mitchell, Lucy Myers Wright
Moffat, James Clement
Monette, John Wesley
Moon, Parker Thomas
Moore, George Foot
Moore, George Henry
Moreau De Saint-Méry, Médéric-Louis-Élie
Morison, Samuel Eliot
Morse, Anson Daniel
Moses, Bernard
Motley, John Lothrop
Munro, Dana Carleton
Murray, Louise Shipman Welles
Muzzey, David Saville
Myers, Gustavus
Neill, Edward Duffield
Nelson, William, 1847–1914
Nevins, Joseph Allan

Newman, Albert Henry
Nichols, Roy Franklin
Niles, Samuel
Notestein, Wallace
Oberholtzer, Ellis Paxson
O'Callaghan, Edmund Bailey
Odell, George Clinton Densmore
Oliver, Fitch Edward
Olmstead, Albert Ten Eyck
Onderdonk, Henry
Osgood, Herbert Levi
Owen, Thomas McAdory
Owsley, Frank Lawrence
Palfrey, John Gorham
Palón, Francisco
Parkman, Francis
Parrington, Vernon Louis
Penhallow, Samuel
Pennypacker, Samuel Whitaker
Perkins, James Breck
Phillips, Ulrich Bonnell
Pickett, Albert James
Pitkin, Timothy
Poole, William Frederick
Prescott, William Hickling
Proud, Robert
Pulitzer, Margaret Leech
Putnam, Eben
Quincy, Josiah Phillips
Quinn, Arthur Hobson
Ramsay, David
Rand, Edward Kennard
Randall, James Garfield
Rattermann, Heinrich Armin
Read, Conyers
Reeves, Arthur Middleton
Reichel, William Cornelius
Rhodes, James Ford
Ricketson, Daniel
Ridpath, John Clark
Rister, Carl Coke
Rives, George Lockhart
Robertson, James Alexander
Robertson, William Spence
Robinson, James Harvey
Ropes, John Codman
Rostovtzeff, Michael Ivanovitch
Rourke, Constance Mayfield
Rupp, Israel Daniel
Sabine, Lorenzo
Salmon, Lucy Maynard
Salter, William
Sandoz, Mari
Sarton, George Alfred Léon
Saunders, William Laurence
Scharf, John Thomas
Schlesinger, Arthur Meier
Schmidt, Nathaniel
Schouler, James
Schouler, William
Schuyler, Robert Livingston
Schweinitz, Edmund Alexander de
Seidensticker, Oswald
Severance, Frank Hayward
Seymour, Charles
Shannon, Fred Albert
Shea, John Dawson Gilmary
Shepherd, William Robert
Shotwell, James Thomson
Simonds, Frank Herbert
Slaughter, Philip
Sloane, William Milligan
Smith, David Eugene
Smith, Henry Augustus Middleton
Smith, Justin Harvey
Smith, Preserved
Smith, William, 1728–1793
Sonneck, Oscar George Theodore
Spargo, John
Sparks, Edwin Erle
Sparks, Jared
Spring, Leverett Wilson
Stanard, Mary Mann Page Newton
Stanwood, Edward
Staples, William Read
Steiner, Bernard Christian
Stephens, Henry Morse
Stephenson, Nathaniel Wright
Stevens, Abel
Stevens, William Bacon
Stiles, Henry Reed
Stillé, Charles Janeway
Stith, William
Stone, William Leete, 1792–1844
Stone, William Leete, 1835–1908
Strachey, William
Stuart, Isaac William
Swank, James Moore
Switzler, William Franklin
Sydnor, Charles Sackett
Tansill, Charles Callan
Taylor, Henry Osborn
Teggart, Frederick John
Thacher, James
Thayer, William Roscoe
Thomas, Isaiah
Thompson, Zadock
Thornton, John Wingate
Trent, William Peterfield
Trescot, William Henry
Trumbull, Benjamin
Trumbull, James Hammond
Turner, Edward Raymond
Turner, Frederick Jackson
Tuttle, Charles Wesley
Tuttle, Herbert
Tyler, Lyon Gardiner
Tyler, Moses Coit
Tyler, Royall
Tyson, Job Roberts
Upham, Charles Wentworth
Upham, Warren
Vail, Robert William Glenroie
Van Dyke, Paul
Van Loon, Hendrik Willem
Van Tyne, Claude Halstead
Vedder, Henry Clay
Victor, Frances Fuller
Vignaud, Henry
Warren, Charles
Warren, Herbert Langford
Warren, Mercy Otis
Washburne, Elihu Benjamin
Webb, Walter Prescott
Weeden, William Babcock
Weeks, Stephen Beauregard
Wergeland, Agnes Mathilde
Wertenbaker, Thomas Jefferson
West, Allen Brown
Westcott, Thompson
Westermann, William Linn
Wheaton, Henry
Wheeler, John Hill
White, Andrew Dickson
White, Leonard Dupee
Whitehead, William Adee
Wickes, Stephen
Wiener, Leo
Wiley, Bell Irvin
Willard, James Field
Willard, Joseph
Williams, Thomas Harry
Williamson, William Durkee
Willis, William
Wilson, Edmund, Jr.
Winsor, Justin
Woodson, Carter Godwin
Worcester, Joseph Emerson
Yoakum, Henderson
Zook, George Frederick

HOME ECONOMIST (See also ECONOMIST)
Bevier, Isabel
Marlatt, Abby Lillian
Norton, Mary Alice Peloubet
Richards, Ellen Henrietta Swallow
Richardson, Anna Euretta
Van Rensselaer, Martha

HOMEOPATHIST (See also PHYSICIAN)
Hering, Constantine
Neidhard, Charles
Thomas, Amos Russell

HORSE BREEDER (See also HORSEMAN)
Jacobs, Hirsch

HORSEMAN (See also HORSE BREEDER, RACEHORSE OWNER)
Breckinridge, Desha
Ten Broeck, Richard
Woodward, William

HORSE TAMER (See also COWBOY, HORSEMAN)
Rarey, John Solomon

HORSE TRAINER
Fitzsimmons, James Edward ("Sunny Jim")
Hirsch, Maximilian Justice
Jacobs, Hirsch
Jones, Benjamin Allyn
McCreary, Conn
Sande, Earl
White, Benjamin Franklin

HORTICULTURIST (See also AGRICULTURIST)
Adams, Dudley W.
Bailey, Liberty Hyde
Barry, Patrick
Budd, Joseph Lancaster
Bull, Ephraim Wales
Burrill, Thomas Jonathan
Campbell, George Washington
Cook, Zebedee
Downing, Andrew Jackson
Downing, Charles
Fuller, Andrew S.
Gale, Elbridge

Garey, Thomas Andrew
Goff, Emmet Stull
Goodrich, Chauncey
Green, Samuel Bowdlear
Hansen, George
Hansen, Niels Ebbesen
Haraszthy De Mokcsa, Agoston
Hart, Edmund Hall
Henderson, Peter
Hilgard, Theodor Erasmus
Hovey, Charles Mason
Hunnewell, Horatio Hollis
Hunt, Benjamin Weeks
Lippincott, James Starr
Logan, James Harvey
Longworth, Nicholas, 1782–1863
McFarland, John Horace
McLaren, John
McMahon, Bernard
Mazzei, Philip
Meehan, Thomas
Miller, Samuel
Munson, Thomas Volney
Nehrling, Henry
Parmentier, Andrew
Parsons, Samuel Bowne
Periam, Jonathan
Powell, George Harold
Pursh, Frederick
Pyle, Robert
Roeding, George Christian
Rogers, Edward Staniford
Sargent, Henry Winthrop
Saunders, William
Strong, Harriet Williams Russell
Thurber, George
Van Fleet, Walter
Warder, John Aston
White, William Nathaniel
Wickson, Edward James

HOSPITAL ADMINISTRATOR
Goldwater, Sigismund Schulz
McFarland, George Bradley
White, William Alanson

HOSTESS (See also SOCIALITE)
Botta, Anne Charlotte Lynch
Carnegie, Mary Crowninshield Endicott Chamberlain
De Wolfe, Elsie
Madison, Dolly Payne
Maxwell, Elsa
Meredith, Edna C. Elliott
Mesta, Perle Reid Skirvin
Schuyler, Margarita
Sprague, Kate Chase

HOTELMAN
Barnum, Zenus
Boldt, George C.
Drake, John Burroughs
Fraunces, Samuel
Grim, David
Hilton, Conrad Nicholson
Niblo, William
Statler, Ellsworth Milton
Stetson, Charles Augustus
Stokes, William Earl Dodge
Taggart, Thomas
Wormley, James

HOUSING EXPERT
Veiller, Lawrence Turnure

HOUSING REFORMER
Stokes, Isaac Newton Phelps
Wood, Edith Elmer

HUMANIST
Loeb, James

HUMANITARIAN (See also REFORMER, SETTLEMENT WORKER, SOCIAL REFORMER, SOCIAL WORKER)
Blackwell, Alice Stone
Carson, Robert Rodgers
Dix, Dorothea Lynde
Eustis, Dorothy Leib Harrison Wood
Fisher, Joshua Francis
Hopper, Isaac Tatem
Howe, Samuel Gridley
Klopsch, Louis
Nicholson, Timothy
Pierce, Robert Willard
Pond, Allen Bartlit
Roosevelt, (Anna) Eleanor
Rush, Benjamin
Seward, Theodore Frelinghuysen
Smiley, Albert Keith
Smith, George Albert
Stanford, John
Stewart, Eliza Daniel
Stowe, Harriet Elizabeth Beecher

HUMAN RELATIONS ADVISER
Anthony, John T.

HUMORIST (See also CLOWN, COMEDIAN, COMEDIENNE, WIT)
Bangs, John Kendrick
Benchley, Robert Charles
Brown, Charles Farrar
Burdette, Robert Jones
Burgess, Frank Gelett
Clemens, Samuel Langhorne
Cobb, Irvin Shrewsbury
Cuppy, William Jacob ("Will")
Derby, George Horatio
Dunne, Finley Peter
Foss, Sam Walter
Frost, Arthur Burdett
Harris, George Washington
Holley, Marietta
Hooper, Johnson Jones
Hubbard, Frank McKinney
Landon, Melville de Lancey
Lewis, Charles Bertrand
Loomis, Charles Battell
McAdams, Clark
Marquis, Donald Robert Perry
Mason, Walt
Masson, Thomas Lansing
Nash, Frederick Ogden
Neal, Joseph Clay
Newell, Robert Henry
Nye, Edgar Wilson
Peck, George Wilbur
Perelman, Sidney Joseph
Pomeroy, Marcus Mills
Poole, Fitch
Read, Opie Pope
Rogers, Will
Shaw, Henry Wheeler (Josh Billings)
Shillaber, Benjamin Penhallow
Smith, Charles Henry ("Bill Arp"), 1826–1903
Smith, Harry Allen
Stewart, Donald Ogden
Thompson, William Tappan
Thomson, Mortimer Neal
Thorpe, Thomas Bangs
Welch, Philip Henry
Williams, Gaar Campbell
Zevin, Israel Joseph

HUNTER (See also FRONTIERSMAN, GUIDE, SCOUT)
Beckwourth, James P.
Provost, Etienne
Reynolds, Charles Alexander
Tinkham, George Holden

HYDROGRAPHER (See also GEODESIST, SURVEYOR)
Blunt, Edmund March
Blunt, George William
Ellis, Henry
Green, Francis Mathews
McArthur, William Pope
Mitchell, Henry

HYDROLOGIST (See also GEOLOGIST)
McGee, William John

HYDROTHERAPIST (See also PHYSICIAN)
Nichols, Thomas Low

HYGIENIST (See also PHYSICIAN)
Harrington, Thomas Francis
Ravenel, Mazyck Porcher
Thompson, William Gilman
Vaughan, Victor Clarence

HYMNOLOGIST (See also COMPOSER, LYRICIST, MUSICIAN)
Beissel, Johann Conrad
Billings, William
Bird, Frederic Mayer
Brown, Phoebe Hinsdale
Creamer, David
Crosby, Fanny
Duffield, Samuel Augustus Willoughby
Floy, James
Gilmore, Joseph Henry
Hastings, Thomas
Hatfield, Edwin Francis
Hosmer, Frederick Lucian
Lathbury, Mary Artemisia
Mason, Lowell
Oatman, Johnson
Palmer, Ray
Robinson, Charles Seymour
Thompson, Will Lamartine
Wendte, Charles William
Willard, Samuel

ICE SKATER
Henie, Sonja
Merrill, Gretchen Van Zandt

ICHTHYOLOGIST (See also PISCICULTURIST, ZOOLOGIST)
Bean, Tarleton Hoffman
Evermann, Barton Warren
Goode, George Brown
Starks, Edwin Chapin

ILLUSTRATOR (See also ARTIST, CARTOONIST, PAINTER)
Agate, Alfred T.

Artzybasheff, Boris
Bacher, Otto Henry
Beard, Daniel Carter
Beard, James Carter
Beard, Thomas Francis
Bellew, Frank Henry Temple
Bellows, George Wesley
Birch, Reginald Bathurst
Bouché, René Robert
Brennan, Alfred Laurens
Burgess, Frank Gelett
Chambers, Robert William
Champney, James Wells
Christy, Howard Chandler
Cox, Palmer
Curry, John Steuart
Darley, Felix Octavius Carr
Dielman, Frederick
Douglas, Aaron
Ehninger, John Whetton
Fisher, Harrison
Flagg, James Montgomery
Frost, Arthur Burdett
Garrett, Edmund Henry
Gaul, William Gilbert
Gibson, Charles Dana
Gifford, Robert Swain
Glackens, William James
Gross, Milt
Held, John, Jr.
Hennessy, William John
Herford, Oliver Brooke
Hoppin, Augustus
Keller, Arthur Ignatius
King, Alexander
Kirby, Rollin
Lawson, Robert Ripley
Leaf, Wilbur Munro
Leigh, William Robinson
Leyendecker, Joseph Christian
Loeb, Louis
Newell, Peter Sheaf Hersey
O'Neill, Rose Cecil
Penfield, Edward
Raymond, Alexander Gillespie
Reinhart, Charles Stanley
Remington, Frederic
Reuterdahl, Henry
Richards, Thomas Addison
Rockwell, Norman Perceval
Rowse, Samuel Worcester
Sandham, Henry
Sarg, Tony
Seton, Ernest Thompson
Shinn, Everett
Smedley, William Thomas
Stephens, Alice Barber
Strother, David Hunter
Taylor, Frank Walter
Taylor, William Ladd
Van Loon, Hendrik Willem
Vedder, Elihu
Verrill, Alpheus Hyatt
Wyeth, Newell Convers
Yohn, Frederick Coffay
Zogbaum, Rufus Fairchild

IMMIGRATION LEADER (See also LABOR LEADER)
Keefe, Daniel Joseph
Peerson, Cleng
Reiersen, Johan Reinert
Rynning, Ole

IMMIGRATION RESTRICTION ADVOCATE
Grant, Madison

IMMUNOLOGIST (See also PHYSICIAN)
Avery, Oswald Theodore
Foster, Frank Pierce
Landsteiner, Karl
Noguchi, Hideyo

IMPERSONATOR
Vattemare, Nicolas Marie Alexandre

IMPORTER
Kohlberg, Alfred

IMPOSTER
Keely, John Ernst Worrell

IMPRESARIO (See also THEATRICAL MANAGER)
Abbey, Henry Eugene
Aborn, Milton
Beck, Martin
Conried, Heinrich
Grau, Maurice
Hammerstein, Oscar
Hurok, Solomon Isaievitch
Maretzek, Max
Neuendorff, Adolph Heinrich Anton Magnus
Nunó, Jaime
Shawn, Edwin Meyers ("Ted")

INDEXER
Nelson, Charles Alexander

INDIAN AGENT
Butler, John
Butler, Richard
Carson, Christopher ("Kit")
Chouteau, Jean Pierre
Clark, William
Cocke, William
Croghan, George
De Mézières y Clugny, Athanase
Fitzpatrick, Thomas
Forsyth, Thomas
Gaines, George Strother
Hamtramck, John Francis
Hawkins, Benjamin
McCoy, Isaac
McKee, John
McLaughlin, James
Meeker, Nathan Cook
Milroy, Robert Huston
Mitchell, David Brydie
Morgan, George
Nairne, Thomas
Neighbors, Robert Simpson
O'Fallon, Benjamin
Pryor, Nathaniel
Sibley, George Champlain
Sibley, John
Street, Joseph Montfort
Taliaferro, Lawrence
Thompson, Wiley
Weiser, Johann Conrad

INDIAN AUTHORITY
Curtis, Edward Sheriff
McKenney, Thomas Loraine

INDIAN CAPTIVE
Rowlandson, Mary White
Slocum, Frances

INDIAN CHIEF
Black Hawk
Brant, Joseph
Canonchet
Canonicus
Captain Jack
Comstalk
Copway, George
Crazy Horse
Friday
Gall
Garakonthie, Daniel
Geronimo
Hendrick
Joseph
Kamaiakan
Keokuk
Kicking Bird
Leflore, Greenwood
Leschi
Little Crow V
Little Turtle
McGillwray, Alexander
McIntosh, William
Massassoit
Mayes, Joel Bryan
Menewa
Miantonomo
Oconostota
Ouray
Outacity
Parker, Ely Samuel
Philip
Pitchlynn, Peter Perkins
Pontiac
Powhatan
Pushmataha
Quanah
Red Cloud
Red Jacket
Red Wing
Ross, John
Sanganash
Sassacus
Seattle
Shabonee
Shikellamy
Sitting Bull
Skaniadariio
Spotted Tail
Tammany
Tecumseh
Tedyskung
Thomas, George Allison
Tomochichi
Uncas
Wabasha
Washakie
Weatherford, William
White Eyes

INDIAN FIGHTER (See also PIONEER, SOLDIER)
Ballard, Bland Williams
Boone, Daniel
Connor, Patrick Edward
Gilpin, William
Hardin, John
Kenton, Simon
Lovewell, John
Sieber, Al
Wetzel, Lewis

INDIAN INTERPRETER (See INTERPRETER)

INDIAN LEADER
Dodge, Henry Chee

Rickard, Clinton
Son of Many Beads
Ward, Nancy
Watie, Stand
Williams, Eleazar
Wraxall, Peter

INDIAN MUSIC TRANSCRIBER
Burlin, Natalie Curtis
Burton, Frederick Russell

INDIAN NEGOTIATOR (See also DIPLOMAT)
Ridge, Major
Viele, Aermont Cornelissen

INDIAN PROPHET (See also RELIGIOUS LEADER)
Smohalla
Tenskwatawa
Wovoka

INDIAN RUNNER (See also ATHLETE)
Deerfoot

INDIAN TRADER (See TRADER)

INDUSTRIAL CHEMIST
Baekeland, Leo Hendrik

INDUSTRIAL CONSULTANT
Sokolsky, George Ephraim

INDUSTRIAL DESIGNER
Geddes, Norman Bel

INDUSTRIAL ENGINEER (See ENGINEER, INDUSTRIAL)

INDUSTRIALIST (See also BUSINESSMAN, BUSINESSWOMAN, CAPITALIST, EXECUTIVE, MANUFACTURER)
Adams, Edward Dean
Atkinson, Edward
Ball, Frank Clayton
Barnes, Julius Howland
Bausch, Edward
Bell, James Ford
Bendix, Vincent
Bennett, Earl W.
Budd, Edward Gowen
Cabot, Godfrey Lowell
Carpenter, Walter Samuel Jr.
Clements, William Lawrence
Cluett, Sanford Lockwood
Coffin, Charles Albert
Coffin, Howard Earle
Cordiner, Ralph Jarron
Crowley, Leo Thomas
Cummings, Walter Joseph
Dana, Charles Anderson
Davis, Arthur Vining
De Bardeleben, Henry Fairchild
Dibrell, George Gibbs
Douglas, James
Drake, Edwin Laurentine
Duke, Benjamin Newton
Duke, James Buchanan
Dumaine, Frederic Christopher
Du Pont, Henry Algernon
Du Pont, Irénée
Du Pont, Lammot
Du Pont, Pierre Samuel
Eaton, Cyrus Stephen
Eccles, Marriner Stoddard
Elkins, Stephen Benton
Engelhard, Charles William
Evans, Henry Clay
Fairless, Benjamin F.
Falk, Maurice
Falk, Otto Herbert
Firestone, Harvey Samuel
Ford, Henry
Gantt, Henry Laurence
Gates, John Warne
Gerber, Daniel Frank
Girdler, Tom Mercer
Goldfine, Bernard
Goodrich, Benjamin Franklin
Goodyear, Anson Conger
Goodyear, Charles
Grace, Eugene Gifford
Green, Duff
Greenleaf, Halbert Stevens
Grinnell, Frederick
Guggenheim, Harry Frank
Heineman, Daniel Webster ("Dannie")
Heinze, Frederick Augustus
Higgins, Andrew Jackson
Hillman, Thomas Tennessee
Hooker, Elon Huntington
Houdry, Eugene Jules
Hughes, Howard Robard, Jr.
Hume, William
Humphrey, George Magoffin
Hurley, Edward Nash
Hurley, Roy T.
Jackling, Daniel Cowan
Johnson, Tom Loftin
Jones, Benjamin Franklin
Jones, William Richard
Joy, Henry Bourne
Kaiser, Henry John
Kier, Samuel M.
King, Stanley
Kohler, Walter Jodok, Jr.
Larned, Joseph Gay Eaton
Lewisohn, Sam Adolph
McCulloch, Robert Paxton
McDaniel, Henry Dickerson
McKay, Gordon
Maloney, Martin
Mellon, Andrew William
Milner, John Turner
Morehead, John Motley
Mott, Charles Stewart
Murchison, Clinton Williams
Patterson, Robert
Peavey, Frank Hutchinson
Pew, Joseph Newton, Jr.
Phipps, Lawrence Cowle
Pratt, Daniel, 1799–1873
Prince, Frederick Henry
Pullman, George Mortimer
Pynchon, John
Randall, Clarence Belden
Reynolds, Milton
Rockefeller, John Davison
Rockefeller, John Davison, Jr.
Rockefeller, William
Rockwell, Willard Frederick
Roebling, Washington Augustus
Rosenstiel, Lewis Solon
Schwab, Charles Michael
Shook, Alfred Montgomery
Sloan, Alfred Pritchard, Jr.
Sloss, James Withers
Sorensen, Charles
Stettinius, Edward Riley
Straus, Roger W(illiams)
Swank, James Moore
Takamine, Jokichi
Tompkins, Daniel Augustus
Tripp, Guy Eastman
Tudor, Frederic
Tyler, Daniel
Valentine, Robert Grosvenor
Vance, Harold Sines
Warner, Adoniram Judson
Warner, James Cartwright
Washburn, Cadwallader Colden
Weston, Edward
Wetherill, Samuel
Wilder, John Thomas
Willys, John North
Winslow, John Flack
Wood, Garfield Arthur ("Gar")
Young, Owen D.
Zellerbach, James David

INDUSTRIAL PIONEER, ELECTROTHERMAL
Acheson, Edward Goodrich

INDUSTRIAL PSYCHOLOGIST
Link, Henry Charles

INDUSTRIAL RELATIONS CONSULTANT
Eaton, Charles Aubrey
Taylor, George William

INDUSTRIAL RESEARCH PIONEER
Little, Arthur Dehon

INFLUENCE PEDDLER
Goldfine, Bernard

INSTRUMENT MAKER (See MANUFACTURER)

INSURANCE EXECUTIVE
Kingsley, Darwin Pearl
MacArthur, John Donald
Parkinson, Thomas Ignatius
Spaulding, Charles Clinton

INSURANCE EXPERT (See also STATISTICIAN)
Allen, Jeremiah Mervin
Bard, William
Cook, Zebedee
D'Olier, Franklin
Dryden, John Fairfield
Epstein, Abraham
Fiske, Haley
Hegeman, John Rogers
Lawson, James
McCall, John Augustine
McCurdy, Richard Aldrich

INSURGENT (See also AGITATOR, REBEL, REVOLUTIONIST)
Fries, John
Shays, Daniel

INTELLIGENCE OFFICIAL
Dulles, Allen Welsh

INTERIOR DECORATOR (See also ARTIST, LANDSCAPE GARDENER)
De Wolfe, Elsie
Draper, Dorothy
Herter, Christian

INTERNATIONALIST
Catt, Carrie Clinton Lane Chapman
Crane, Charles Richard
Holt, Hamilton Bowen
McDonald, James Grover
Marburg, Theodore
Shotwell, James Thomson
Wambaugh, Sarah

INTERNATIONAL LAW SCHOLAR
Wilson, George Grafton
INTERPRETER (See also LINGUIST)
Dorian, Marie
Horn, Tom
Lorimier, Pierre Louis
Sacagawea
Squanto
Viele, Clermont Cornelissen
Winnemucca, Sarah
INTERSTATE COMMERCE COMMISSIONER
Lane, Franklin Knight
Morrison, William Ralls
Prouty, Charles Azro
INTERSTATE COMMERCE COMMISSION MEMBER
Daniels, Winthrop More
Esch, John Jacob
INTERVIEWER
Marcosson, Isaac Frederick
INVENTOR (See also EXPERIMENTER)
Acheson, Edward Goodrich
Acker, Charles Ernest
Adams, Frederick Upham
Adams, Isaac
Adams, Joseph Alexander
Akeley, Carl Ethan
Alger, Cyrus
Allen, Horatio
Allen, John F.
Allen, Zachariah
Angell, William Gorham
Appleby, John Francis
Armstrong, Edwin Howard
Arnold, Aza
Astor, John Jacob
Atkins, Jearum
Atwood, Lewis John
Babbitt, Benjamin Talbot
Babbitt, Isaac
Babcock, George Herman
Bachelder, John
Baekeland, Leo Hendrik
Baldwin, Frank Stephen
Ball, Albert
Ball, Ephraim
Bancroft, Edward
Barnes, Albert Coombs
Batchelder, John Putnam
Batchelder, Samuel
Bausch, Edward
Beach, Moses Yale
Bell, Alexander Graham
Bement, Caleb N.
Bendix, Vincent
Berliner, Emile
Bettendorf, William Peter
Bigelow, Erastus Brigham
Blair, William Richards
Blake, Eli Whitney
Blake, Francis
Blake, Lyman Reed
Blanchard, Thomas
Bogardus, James
Bonard, Louis
Bonwill, William Gibson Arlington
Bonzano, Adolphus
Borden, Gail
Borg, George William
Bovie, William T.
Boyden, Seth
Boyden, Uriah Atherton
Brooks, Byron Alden
Brown, Alexander Ephraim
Brown, Fayette
Brown, James Salisbury
Brown, Joseph Rogers
Brown, Sylvanus
Browning, John Moses
Brunton, David William
Brush, Charles Francis
Bryant, Gridley
Buchanan, Joseph
Buckland, Cyrus
Bullock, William A.
Burden, Henry
Burgess, W(illiam) Starling
Burroughs, William Seward
Burrowes, Edward Thomas
Burson, William Worth
Burt, John
Burt, William Austin
Bushnell, David
Butterick, Ebenezer
Campbell, Andrew
Carlson, Chester Floyd
Carothers, Wallace Hume
Channing, William Francis
Christie, John Walter
Cist, Jacob
Cluett, Sanford Lockwood
Clymer, George E.
Coates, George Henry
Colburn, Irving Wightman
Colles, Christopher
Colt, Samuel
Conant, Hezekiah
Converse, Edmund Cogswell
Cooper, Peter
Corliss, George Henry
Cottrell, Calvert Byron
Cottrell, Frederick Gardner
Cowen, Joshua Lionel
Craven, John Joseph
Crompton, George
Crompton, William
Crowell, Luther Childs
Crozier, William
Curtiss, Gelnn Hammond
Cutler, James Goold
Cutting, James Ambrose
Daft, Leo
Dahlgren, John Adolphus Bernard
Dalzell, Robert M.
Dancel, Christian
Danforth, Charles
Daniels, Fred Harris
Davenport, Thomas
Davis, Phineas
Davis, William Augustine
Davison, Gregory Caldwell
De Forest, Lee
Delany, Patrick Bernard
Dickson, Earle Ensign
Dixon, Joseph
Dod, Daniel
Doremus, Robert Ogden
Dow, Lorenzo
Draper, Ira
Dripps, Isaac L.
Dunbar, Robert
Du Pont, Francis Irénée
Durand, Cyrus
Durfee, William Franklin
Durfee, Zoheth Sherman
Durham, Caleb Wheeler
Duryea, Cahrles Edgar
Duryea, James Frank
Dymond, John
Eads, James Buchanan
Earle, Pliny
Eastman, George
Edgar, Charles
Edison, Thomas Alva
Edwards, Oliver
Edwards, William
Eickemeyer, Rudolf
Ellis, Carleton
Emerson, James Ezekiel
Emerson, Ralph
Emery, Albert Hamilton
Ericsson, John
Esterly, George
Evans, Oliver
Eve, Joseph
Ewbank, Thomas
Fairbanks, Henry
Fairbanks, Thaddeus
Fairchild, Sherman Mills
Farmer, Moses Gerrish
Farnsworth, Philo Taylor
Ferris, George Washington Gale
Fessenden, Reginald Aubrey
Fessenden, Thomas Green
Field, Stephen Dudley
Fisher, Clark
Fitch, John
Flad, Henry
Ford, Hannibal Choate
Ford, John Baptiste
Forney, Matthias Vace
Fortescue, Charles LeGeyt
Francis, Joseph
Franklin, Benjmain
Frash, Herman
French, Aaron
Fuller, Levi Knight
Fuller, Robert Mason
Fulton, Robert
Furlow, Floyd Charles
Gaisman, Henry Jaques
Gally, Merritt
Gaskill, Harvey Freeman
Gatling, Richard Jordan
Gayley, James
Gernsback, Hugo
Gibbs, James Ethan Allen
Gilbert, Alfred Carlton
Gilbert, Rufus Henry
Gillette, King Camp
Glidden, Joseph Farwell
Goddard, Calvin Luther
Goddu, Louis
Godfrey, Thomas
Goldmark, Peter Carl
Good, John
Goodwin, Hannibal Williston
Goodyear, Charles
Gordon, George Phineas
Grant, George Barnard
Gray, Elisha
Grinnell, Frederick

Haish, Jacob
Hall, Thomas
Hall, Thomas Seavey
Hallidie, Andrew Smith
Hamlin, Emmons
Hammerstein, Oscar
Hammond, James Bartlett
Hammond, Laurens
Hansburg, George Bernard
Harvey, Hayward Augustus
Haupt, Herman
Hayden, Hiram Washington
Hayden, Joseph Shepard
Hayward, Nathaniel Manley
Herdic, Peter
Herreshoff, James Brown
Hewitt, Peter Cooper
Heywood, Levi
Hoe, Richard March
Hogan, John Vincent Lawless
Holland, John Philip
Hollerith, Herman
Hotchkiss, Benjamin Berkeley
Houdry, Eugene Jules
House, Henry Alonzo
House, Royal Earl
Howe, Elias
Howe, Frederick Webster
Howe, John Ireland
Howe, William
Howell, Albert Summers
Howell, John Adams
Howey, Walter Crawford
Hoxie, William Dixie
Hubbard, Henry Griswold
Hubert, Conrad
Hudson, William Smith
Hughes, David Edward
Hughes, Howard Robard
Hussey, Obed
Hyatt, John Wesley
Ingersoll, Simon
Ives, Frederic Eugene
Janney, Eli Hamilton
Jarves, Deming
Jenkins, Nathaniel
Jenks, Joseph
Jenney, William Le Baron
Jerome, Chauncey
Johnson, Eldridge Reeves
Johnson, Tom Loftin
Johnston, Samuel
Jones, Amanda Theodosia
Jones, Evan William
Jones, Samuel Milton
Judson, Egbert Putnam
Kalmus, Herbert Thomas
Kalmus, Natalie Mabelle Dunfee
Keely, John Ernst Worrell
Keen, Morris Longstreth
Kelly, William
Kent, Arthur Atwater
Kettering, Charles Franklin
Kingsford, Thomas
Knight, Edward Collings
Knowles, Lucius James
Knox, Thomas Wallace
Kraft, James Lewis
Kruesi, John
Lake, Simon
Lamb, Isaac Wixom
Lamme, Benjamin Garver
Lanston, Tolbert
Larned, Joseph Gay Eaton
Latrobe, John Hazlehurst Boneval
Latta, Alexander Bonner
Lawrence, Richard Smith
Lay, John Louis
Leavitt, Frank McDowell
Leffel, James
Leonard, Harry Ward
Levy, Louis Edward
Levy, Max
Lewis, Isaac Newton
Leyner, John George
Lloyd, Marshall Burns
Locke, John
Lockheed, Malcolm
Longstreet, William
Lowe, Thaddeus Sobieski Coulincourt
Lucas, Jonathan, 1775–1832
Lundie, John
Lyall, James
McCarroll, James
McCormick, Cyrus Hall
McCormick, Robert
McCormick, Stephen
McCoy, Elijah
McCulloch, Robert Paxton
McDougall, Alexander
McKay, Gordon
McTammany, John
Manly, Charles Matthews
Mannes, Leopold Damrosch
Marks, Amasa Abraham
Marsh, Charles Wesley
Marsh, Sylvester
Marsh, William Wallace
Mason, Arthur John
Mason, William
Mast, Phineas Price
Masury, John Wesley
Matthews, John
Matzeliger, Jan Ernst
Maxim, Hiram Percy
Maxim, Hiram Stevens
Maxim, Hudson
Maynard, Edward
Melville, David
Mendelsohn, Samuel
Mercer, Henry Chapman
Mergenthaler, Ottmar
Merritt, Israel John
Midgley, Thomas
Miller, Ezra
Miller, Lewis
Mills, Anson
Moody, Paul
Morehead, John Motley
Morey, Samuel
Morgan, Charles Hill
Morse, Samuel Finley Breese
Morse, Sidney Edwards
Mowbray, George Mordey
Munger, Robert Sylvester
Murray, Thomas Edward
Nesmith, John
Nessler, Karl Ludwig
Newcomb, Charles Leonard
Newton, Henry Jotham
Nicholson, William Thomas
Niles, Nathaniel, 1741–1828
Norden, Carl Lukas
Nott, Eliphalet
Noyes, La Verne
Olds, Ransom Eli
Oliver, James
Oliver, Paul Ambrose
Orr, Hugh
Otis, Charles Rollin
Otis, Elisha Graves
Owens, Michael Joseph
Packard, James Ward
Painter, William
Parr, Samuel Wilson
Parrott, Robert Parker
Patterson, Rufus Lenoir
Paul, William Darwin ("Shorty")
Perkins, Jacob
Perry, Stuart
Pidgin, Charles Felton
Pitts, Hiram Avery
Pope, Franklin Leonard
Porter, Rufus
Potter, William Bancroft
Pratt, Francis Ashbury
Pratt, John
Pratt, Thomas Willis
Prince, Frederick Henry
Pullman, George Mortimer
Rains, George Washington
Ramsay, Erskine
Rand, James Henry
Read, Nathan
Rees, James
Reese, Abram
Reese, Isaac
Reese, Jacob
Renwick, Edward Sabine
Reynolds, Edwin
Reynolds, Samuel Godfrey
Rice, Richard Henry
Riddell, John Leonard
Roberts, Benjamin Stone
Robinson, Stillman Williams
Robinson, William
Rodman, Thomas Jackson
Rogers, Henry J.
Rogers, James Harris
Rogers, John Raphael
Rogers, Thomas
Roosevelt, Hilborne Lewis
Roosevelt, Nicholas J.
Root, Elisha King
Rowland, Thomas Fitch
Rumsey, James
Rust, John Daniel
Sargent, James
Saunders, William Lawrence
Sawyer, Sylvanus
Saxton, Joseph
Schieren, Charles Adolph
Schneller, George Otto
See, Horace
Seiberling, Frank Augustus
Selden, George Baldwin
Sellers, Coleman
Sellers, William
Sergeant, Henry Clark
Sessions, Henry Howard
Shaw, Thomas
Sholes, Christopher Latham
Short, Sidney Howe

Sickles, Frederick Ellsworth
Silver, Thomas
Simpson, Michael Hodge
Sims, Winfield Scott
Singer, Isaac Merrit
Skinner, Halcyon
Slocum, Samuel
Smith, Horace
Spencer, Christopher Miner
Sperry, Elmer Ambrose
Sprague, Frank Julian
Stanley, Francis Edgar
Stanley, William
Starrett, Laroy S.
Stearns, Frank Ballou
Stetefeldt, Carl August
Stevens, Edwin Augustus
Stevens, John
Stevens, Robert Livingston
Stewart, Philo Penfield
Stoddard, Joshua C.
Stoddard, William Osborn
Sturtevant, Benjamin Franklin
Tagliabue, Giuseppe
Taylor, Frederick Winslow
Terry, Eli
Tesla, Nikola
Thomson, Elihu
Thomson, John
Thornton, William
Thorp, John
Thurber, Charles
Timby, Theodore Ruggles
Timken, Henry
Treadwell, Daniel
Troland, Leonard Thompson
Tucker, Stephen Davis
Turner, Walter Victor
Twining, Alexander Catlin
Tytus, John Butler
Van de Graaff, Robert Jemison
Van Depoele, Charles Joseph
Van Dyke, John Wesley
Vauclain, Samuel Matthews
Verbeck, William
Wait, William Bell
Wallace, William
Waller, Frederic
Warren, Cyrus Moors
Warren, Henry Ellis
Warren, Josiah
Washburn, Nathan
Waterman, Lewis Edson
Webb, John Burkitt
Wellman, Samuel Thomas
Wesson, Daniel Baird
Westinghouse, George
Wetherill, Samuel
Wheeler, Nathaniel
Wheeler, Schuyler Skaats
Whipple, Squire
Whitney, Asa
Whitney, Eli
Whittemore, Amos
Wilcox, Stephen
Wilkinson, David
Wilkinson, Jeremiah
Wilson, Allen Benjamin
Wilson, George Francis
Winans, Ross
Winans, Thomas De Kay
Wood, Henry Alexander Wise
Wood, James J.
Wood, Jethro
Wood, Walter Abbott
Woodruff, Theodore Tuttle
Worthington, Henry Rossiter
Wright, Orville
Wyman, Horace
Yale, Linus
Zachos, John Celivergos
Zentmayer, Joseph

INVESTMENT COUNSELOR
Whitney, Richard

INVESTMENT EXECUTIVE
Erpf, Armand Grover
Levy, Gustave Lehmann
Paul, Josephine Bay

INVESTOR
Ball, George Alexander

IRONFOUNDER (See also TYPEFOUNDER)
Ames, Nathan Peabody
Foxall, Henry
Leach, Shepherd
Meneely, Andrew
Ogden, Samuel

IRONMASTER (See MANUFACTURER)

IRRIGATION ENGINEER (See ENGINEER, IRRIGATION)

ITALIAN CULTURE PROMOTER
Da Ponte, Lorenzo

JAYHAWKER (See also OUTLAW, VIGILANTE)
Montgomery, James

JAZZ BAND LEADER
Celestin, Oscar ("Papa")
Ellington, Edward Kennedy ("Duke")
Oliver, Joseph

JAZZ CORNET PLAYER
Celestin, Oscar ("Papa")
Hackett, Robert Leo ("Bobby")

JAZZ CRITIC
Gleason, Ralph Joseph

JAZZ DRUMMER
Catlett, Sidney

JAZZ GUITARIST
Condon, Albert Edwin ("Eddie")

JAZZ MUSICIAN
Armstrong, Louis ("Satchmo")
Ellington, Edward Kennedy ("Duke")
Jordan, Louis
Mingus, Charles, Jr.
Morton, Ferdinand Joseph ("Jelly Roll")
Parker, Charlie ("Bird")
Webster, Benjamin ("Ben") Francis

JAZZ PIANIST
Ellington, Edward Kennedy ("Duke")
Evans, William John ("Bill")
Garner, Erroll Louis
Tatum, Art
Tristano, Leonard Joseph ("Lennie")
Waller, Thomas Wright

JAZZ SINGER
Bailey, Mildred
Boswell, Connie (Connee)
Holiday, Billie

JAZZ TROMBONIST
Ory, Edward ("Kid")

JAZZ TRUMPET PLAYER
Celestin, Oscar ("Papa")
Prima, Luigi ("Louis")

JAZZ VIOLINIST
Venuti, Giuseppe ("Joe")

JEWELER (See also CRAFTSMAN, GOLDSMITH, SILVERSMITH)
Belden, Josiah
Ross, Alexander Coffman
Tiffany, Charles Lewis
Winston, Harry

JEWISH LEADER (See also CLERGYMAN, ZIONIST LEADER)
Lehman, Irving
Mack, Julian William
Monsky, Henry
Philipson, David
Vladeck, Baruch Charney

JOCKEY (See also ATHLETE, HORSEMAN, TURFMAN)
McCreary, Conn
Sande, Earl
Sloan, James Forman

JOURNALIST (See also FOREIGN CORRESPONDENT, NEWSPAPER CORRESPONDENT, NEWSPAPER REPORTER)
Abbot, Willis John
Abbott, Joseph Carter
Abell, Arunah Shepherdson
Adamic, Louis
Adams, Abijah
Adams, Franklin Pierce
Adams, Samuel Hopkins
Agee, James Rufus
Agnus, Felix
Alden, Cynthia May Westover
Alden, William Livingston
Alsop, Stewart Johonnot Oliver
Anderson, Paul Y.
Andrews, Sidney
Angell, James Burrill
Anthony, Henry Bowen
Astor, William Waldorf
Atkinson, Wilmer
Avery, Benjamin Parke
Avery, Isaac Wheeler
Bache, Benjamin Franklin
Bacon, Edwin Munroe
Bailey, Francis
Bailey, Gamaliel
Bailey, James Montgomery
Baker, James Heaton
Baker, Ray Stannard
Baldwin, John Denison
Ballou, Maturin Murray
Barrows, David Prescott
Barth, Alan
Bartlett, John Sherren
Basso, (Joseph) Hamilton
Beach, Moses Yale
Belo, Alfred Horatio
Bent, Silas
Benton, Joel
Berger, Victor Louis
Bernstein, Herman
Bernstein, Theodore Menline

Bierce, Ambrose Gwinett
Binns, John
Birchall, Frederick Thomas
Blair, Francis Preston
Bliss, George William
Bliss, Porter Cornelius
Bliven, Bruce Ormsby
Bonsal, Stephen
Boutelle, Charles Addison
Bowers, Claude Gernade
Boyle, Harold Vincent ("Hal")
Bradford, Joseph
Bradford, Roark Whitney Wickliffe
Brentano, Lorenz
Briggs, Charles Frederick
Bromley, Isaac Hill
Brooks, Erastus
Brooks, James
Brooks, Noah
Bross, William
Brown, Charles Brockden
Browne, Junius Henri
Bryan, Mary Edwards
Bundy, Jonas Mills
Burleigh, William Henry
Butterworth, Hezekiah
Cahan, Abraham
Cain, James Mallahan
Callimachos, Panos Demetrios
Campbell, Bartley
Campbell, John
Canonge, Louis Placide
Carpenter, Edmund Janes
Carpenter, Frank George
Carpenter, Stephen Cullen
Carr, Dabney Smith
Carter, Boake
Case, Francis Higbee
Cash, Wilbur Joseph
Cassidy, William
Cesare, Oscar Edward
Chamberlain, Henry Richardson
Chambers, James Julius
Chambers, Whittaker
Chandler, Joseph Ripley
Chapman, John Arthur
Cheetham, James
Child, David Lee
Clapp, William Warland
Clarke, Joseph Ignatius Constantine
Clement, Edward Henry
Cobbett, William
Cockerill, John Albert
Coffin, Charles Carleton
Coggeshall, William Turner
Colcord, Lincoln Ross
Coleman, William
Colton, Calvin
Colton, Walter
Conant, Charles Arthur
Conrad, Robert Taylor
Cook, Clarence Chatham
Cooke, Henry David
Cooper, Kent
Cortambert, Louis Richard
Cowles, Edwin
Craig, Daniel H.
Crane, Frank
Creel, George
Creelman, James
Croly, David Goodman
Croly, Jane Cunningham
Croswell, Edwin
Croy, Homer
Cummings, Amos Jay
Curtis, William Eleroy
Daniel, John Moncure
Davidson, James Wood
Davis, Matthew Livingston
Davis, Oscar King
Davis, Richard Harding
Dawson, Francis Warrington
Day, Benjamin Henry
Day, Holman Francis
De Fontaine, Felix Gregory
DeVoto, Bernard Augustine
Devoy, John
Dickinson, Charles Monroe
Dimitry, Charles Patton
Dodge, Jacob Richards
Dorsheimer, William Edward
Douglass, Frederick
Draper, John
Dromgoole, William Allen
Duane, William
Duranty, Walter
Durivage, Francis Alexander
Eastman, Charles Gamage
Eaton, Charles Aubrey
Edes, Benjamin
Eggleston, George Cary
Everett, David
Farago, Ladislas
Farson, Negley
Fessenden, Thomas Green
Field, Joseph M.
Field, Mary Katherine Kemble
Fischer, Louis
Fiske, Harrison Grey
Fiske, Stephen Ryder
Flynn, John Thomas
Ford, Patrick
Forney, John Wien
Foss, Sam Walter
Foster, Thomas Jefferson
Fowler, Gene
Fox, Richard Kyle
Franklin, Fabian
Frederic, Harold
Freeman, Joseph
Frick, Ford Christopher
Fry, William Henry
Fuller, Hiram
Fuller, Sarah Margaret
Gaillard, Edwin Samuel
Gaillardet, Théodore Frédéric
Gales, Joseph, 1761–1841
Gales, Joseph, 1786–1860
Gallico, Paul William
Gannett, Frank Ernest
Gardner, Charles Kitchell
Gardner, Gilson
Garis, Howard Roger
Gaston, Herbert Earle
Gay, Sydney Howard
George, Henry
Gilder, Jeannette Leonard
Gilder, William Henry
Gill, John
Gipson, Frederick Benjamin
Gleason, Ralph Joseph
Goddard, William
Gold, Michael
Goodall, Harvey L.
Goodrich, Frank Boott
Grady, Henry Woodfin
Graham, Philip Leslie
Grant, Jane Cole
Graves, John Temple
Gray, Joseph W.
Greathouse, Clarence Ridgeby
Green, Bartholomew
Green, Duff
Green, Jonas
Greenleaf, Thomas
Grieve, Miller
Griffin, Martin Ignatius Joseph
Griswold, Rufus Wilmot
Grosvenor, William Mason
Grund, Francis Joseph
Gue, Benjamin F.
Guild, Curtis, 1827–1911
Gunther, John
Hale, Charles
Hale, David
Hale, Nathan
Hale, William Bayard
Hall, Abraham Oakey
Hallock, Charles
Hallock, Gerard
Halpine, Charles Graham
Halstead, Murat
Hammond, Charles
Hapgood, Isabel Florence
Harby, Isaac
Hard, William
Hardy, William Harris
Harper, Ida Husted
Harris, Joel Chandler
Harris, Julian La Rose
Harrison, Henry Sydnor
Harvey, George Brinton McClellan
Haskell, Henry Jospeh
Hassard, John Rose Greene
Hassaurek, Friedrich
Hatton, Frank
Hay, John Milton
Hazertine, Mayo Williamson
Heath, Perry Sanford
Heatter, Gabriel
Hecht, Ben
Heinzen, Karl Peter
Hendrick, Burton Jesse
Herbst, Josephine Frey
Hewitt, John Hill
Hibben, Paxton Pattison
Higgins, Marguerite
Hill, Edwin Conger
Hirth, William Andrew
Hitchcock, James Ripley Wellman
Hittell, John Shertzer
Hodgins, Eric Francis
Holbrook, Stewart Hall
Holden, Liberty Emery
Holden, William Woods
Holt, John
Hooper, Lucy Hamilton
Hough, Emerson
House, Edward Howard
Howe, Quincy
Howell, James Bruen
Howey, Walter Crawford

Hudson, Charles
Hudson, Frederic
Hunt, William Gibbes
Hurlbert, William Henry
Ickes, Harold Le Clair
Inman, John
Irwin, William Henry
Isaacs, Samuel Myer
Jackson, Charles Douglas
Jacobs, Paul
James, Edwin Leland
Janvier, Thomas Allibone
Jemison, Alice Mae Lee
Jenks, George Charles
Johnson, Malcolm Malone
Johnston, William Andrew
Jones, Alexander
Jones, Herschel Vespasian
Jones, John Beauchamp
Jones, John Price
Jordan, Thomas
Josephson, Matthew
Keating, John McLeod
Keeler, Ralph Olmstead
Kendall, Amos
Kendall, George Wilkins
Kennan, George
Kester, Vaughan
Keys, Clement Melville
King, Edward Smith
King, Henry
Kinney, William Burnet
Kintner, Robert Edmonds
Kiplinger, Willard Monroe
Kirchwey, Freda
Knapp, George
Knox, Frank
Knox, Thomas Wallace
Koenigsberg, Moses
Kollock, Shepard
Krock, Arthur
Kroeger, Adolph Ernst
Laffan, William Mackay
Lamoureux, Andrew Jackson
Lanigan, George Thomas
Lapham, William Berry
Lardner, John Abbott
Lardner, Ringgold Wilmer
Lawson, Victor Freemont
Leggett, William
Leupp, Francis Ellington
Lewis, Alfred Henry
Lewis, Lloyd Downs
Liebling, Abbott Joseph
Link, Theodore Carl
Lippmann, Walter
Lisagor, Peer Irvin
List, Georg Friedrich
Littledale, Clara Savage
Lloyd, Henry Demarest
Locke, David Ross
Locke, Richard Adams
Loeb, Sophie Irene Simon
Logan, Olive
Lomax, Louis Emanuel
Loring, Frederick Wadsworth
Love, Robertus Donnell
Lunt, George
McAnally, David Rice
MacArthur, Charles Gordon
McBride, Henry
McBride, Mary Margaret
McCann, Alfred Watterson
McCarroll, James
McCormick, Anne Elizabeth O'Hare
McCormick, Joseph Medill
McCormick, Richard Cunningham
McCullagh, Joseph Burbridge
MacGahan, Januarius Aloysius
McGeehan, William O'Connell
McGill, Ralph Emerson
McGovern, John
Mackenzie, Robert Shelton
McKinley, Carlyle
McMaster, James Alphonsus
McNulty, John Augustine
Mailly, William
Manley, Joseph Homan
Marcosson, Isaac Frederick
Marden, Orison Swett
Marling, John Leake
Marshall, Samuel Lyman Atwood ("Slam")
Martin, John Alexander
Mathews, William
Matthews, Franklin
Medill, Joseph
Meeker, Nathan Cook
Mencken, Henry Louis
Meredith, Edwin Thomas
Meyer, Agnes Elizabeth Ernst
Meyer, Eugene Isaac
Michelson, Charles
Milton, George Fort
Mitchel, John
Moffett, Cleveland Langston
Moley, Raymond Charles
Moody, (Arthur Edson) Blair
Moore, Charles
Moore, Frederick Randolph
Moore, Jacob Bailey
Moore, John Trotwood
Morford, Henry
Morris, George Pope
Mott, Frank Luther
Mowrer, Edgar Ansel
Mulford, Prentice
Murdock, Victor
Neal, Joseph Clay
Nelson, William Rockhill
Nettleton, Alvred Bayard
Nevin, Robert Peebles
New, Harry Stewart
Newell, Robert Henry
Nixon, William Penn
Noah, Mordecai Manuel
Nordhoff, Charles
Norris, Benjamin Franklin
Noyes, Alexander Dana
Noyes, Crosby Stuart
Nye, Edgar Wilson
Oberholtzer, Ellis Paxson
O'Brien, Fitz-James
O'Brien, Frederick
O'Brien, Robert Lincoln
O'Connor, William Douglas
O'Hara, Theodore
O'Higgins, Harvey Jerrold
O'Mahoney, Joseph Christopher
Osborn, Chase Salmon
Osborn, Selleck
O'Sullivan, John Louis
Otis, Harrison Gray
Ottley, Roi
Page, Walter Hines
Paine, Ralph Delahaye
Parker, Henry Taylor
Parker, James
Parsons, Louella Rose Oettinger
Paschal, George Washington
Paul, Elliot Harold
Pearson, Drew
Peck, George Washington
Peck, George Wilbur
Peffer, William Alfred
Pegler, Westbrook
Peixotto, Benjamin Franklin
Pelham, Robert A.
Penfield, Frederic Courtland
Perry, Nora
Perry, Rufus Lewis
Phelan, David Samuel
Phillips, David Graham
Phillips, Harry Irving
Phillips, Walter Polk
Piatt, Donn
Piatt, John James
Picton, Thomas
Pike, James Shepherd
Pleasants, John Hampden
Plumb, Preston B.
Pollard, Edward Alfred
Pond, George Edward
Poole, Ernest Cook
Poole, Fitch
Poor, Henry Varnum
Poore, Benjamin Perley
Porter, Robert Percival
Porter, William Trotter
Posey, Alexander Lawrence
Powell, Thomas
Pratt, John
Pratt, Sereno Stansbury
Pray, Isaac Clark
Preetorius, Emil
Prentice, George Dennison
Prime, William Cowper
Pringle, Henry Fowles
Pulitzer, Joseph
Quigg, Lemuel Ely
Ralph, Julian
Randall, James Ryder
Randall, Samuel
Rapp, Wilhelm
Ray, Charles Bennett
Redpath, James
Reed, John, 1887–1920
Reedy, William Marion
Reick, William Charles
Reid, Whitelaw
Revell, Nellie MacAleney
Rice, Charles Allen Thorndike
Richardson, Albert Deane
Richardson, Willard
Riis, Jacob August
Ritchie, Thomas
Rives, John Cook
Rivington, James
Robb, Inez Early Callaway
Robertson, James, b. 1740
Robinson, Charles Mulford
Robinson, William Erigena
Robinson, William Stevens
Roche, James Jeffrey

Rorty, James Hancock
Rosewater, Edward
Rosewater, Victor
Ross, Edmund Gibson
Round, William Marshall Fitts
Rovere, Richard Halworth
Rowell, Chester Harvey
Ruark, Robert Chester
Ruhl, Arthur Brown
Runyon, Damon
Russell, Benjamin
Russell, Charles Edward
Ryan, Cornelius John ("Connie")
Sanborn, Franklin Benjamin
Sandburg, Carl August
Sands, Robert Charles
Sargent, Epes
Sargent, George Henry
Sargent, John Osborne
Sargent, Nathan
Savage, John
Schneider, George
Schuyler, Montgomery
Scott, James Wilmot
Scovel, Henry Sylvester
Scoville, Joseph Alfred
Scripps, Ellen Browning
Seaman, Elizabeth Cochrane
Searing, Laura Catherine Redden
Seaton, William Winston
Sedgwick, Arthur George
Seibold, Louis
Seitz, Don Carlos
Seldes, Gilbert Vivian
Selikovitsch, Goetzel
Seward, Frederick William
Shaw, Albert
Sheean, James Vincent
Shillaber, Benjamin Penhallow
Sholes, Christopher Latham
Short, Joseph Hudson, Jr.
Shrady, George Frederick
Sikes, William Wirt
Simmons, Roscoe Conkling Murray
Simonds, Frank Herbert
Simons, Algie Martin
Simonton, James William
Sinclair, Upton Beall, Jr.
Smalley, Eugene Virgil
Smalley, George Washburn
Smedley, Agnes
Smith, Albert Merriman
Smith, Charles Emory
Smith, Charles Henry ("Bill Arp"), 1826–1903
Smith, George Henry
Smith, Harry Allen
Smith, Samuel Harrison
Smith, William Henry, 1833–1896
Snelling, William Joseph
Snow, Edgar Parkes
Sonnichsen, Albert
Southall, James Cocke
Southwick, Solomon
Spencer, Anna Garlin
Spewack, Samuel
Squier, Ephraim George
Stanton, Frank Lebby
Stanton, Henry Brewster
Stearns, Harold Edmund
Steffens, Lincoln
Stevens, John Leavitt
Stillman, William James
Stokes, Thomas Lunsford, Jr.
Stolberg, Benjamin
Stone, Melville Elijah
Stone, William Leete, 1792–1844
Stone, William Leete, 1835–1908
Stromme, Peer Olsen
Strong, Anna Louise
Strong, Walter Ansel
Strunsky, Simeon
Sullivan, Mark
Swain, James Barrett
Swinton, John
Swinton, William
Switzler, William Franklin
Swope, Herbert Bayard
Taylor, Benjamin Franklin
Taylor, Bert Leston
Taylor, Charles Henry
Taylor, James Wickes
Testut, Charles
Thomas, Frederick William
Thompson, Dorothy
Thompson, Slason
Tibbles, Thomas Henry
Tierney, Richard Henry
Todd, Sereno Edwards
Towle, George Makepeace
Towne, Benjamin
Townsend, George Alfred
Tresca, Carlo
Truman, Benjamin Cummings
Turner, George Kibbe
Upton, George Putnam
Utley, Freda
Vallentine, Benjamin Bennaton
Van Anda, Carr Vattel
Vandenberg, Arthur Hendrick
Vanderbilt, Cornelius, Jr. ("Cornelius IV," "Neil")
Van Horn, Robert Thompson
Vedder, Henry Clay
Vignaud, Henry
Villard, Henry
Visscher, William Lightfoot
Vorse, Mary Heaton
Walker, Alexander
Walsh, Robert
Walton, Lester Aglar
Wardman, Ervin
Warman, Cy
Waymack, William Wesley
Webb, James Watson
Webber, Charles Wilkins
Weed, Thurlow
Weeks, Joseph Dame
Welch, Philip Henry
Welling, James Clarke
Wellman, Walter
Westcott, Thompson
Wheeler, Andrew Carpenter
White, Horace
Whiting, Charles Goodrich
Wilkes, George
Wilkie, Franc Bangs
Will, Allen Sinclair
Williams, Edwin
Williams, James
Williams, Talcott
Williams, Walter
Willis, Nathaniel
Willis, Nathaniel Parker
Wilson, Edmund, Jr.
Winchell, Walter
Woodworth, Samuel
Wright, William
Young, John Russell
Zenger, John Peter
Zollicoffer, Felix Kirk

JUDGE (See also CHIEF JUSTICE [STATE], JURIST, LAWYER, MAGISTRATE, SUPREME COURT JUSTICE)

Adams, Annette Abbott
Baker, Harvey Humphrey
Beardsley, Samuel
Biddle, Francis Beverley
Bouvier, John
Bowler, Metcalf
Boyle, John
Brantley, Theodore
Brawley, William Hiram
Brooks, George Washington
Brown, George William
Browne, William
Camp, John Lafayette
Cilley, Joseph
Clark, Bennett Champ
Clark, James
Clayton, Henry De Lamar
Clements, Judson Claudius
Cline, Genevieve Rose
Cobb, David
Collamer, Jacob
Conkling, Alfred
Connor, Henry Groves
Cox, Edward Eugene
Crane, Frederick Evan
Crawford, Martin Jenkins
Davis, George Breckenridge
Derbigny, Pierre Auguste Charles Bourguignon
Dole, Sanford Ballard
Duffy, Francis Ryan
Dunn, William McKee
Early, Peter
Fell, John
Fine, John Sydney
Foster, Lafayette Sabine
Frank, Jerome
Fuller, Thomas Charles
Gamble, Hamilton Rowan
Gansevoort, Leonard
Garrett, Finis James
George, Walter Franklin
Goldsborough, Thomas Alan
Goodman, Louis Earl
Grant, Robert
Grose, William
Hager, John Sharpenstein
Halderman, John A.
Hall, Domimck Augustin
Hamtramck, John Francis
Hand, Augustus Noble
Hand, Learned
Hardy, William Harris
Harper, William
Harris, Wiley Pope

Hatch, Carl A.
Hays, Paul R.
Hedding, Elijah
Hemphill, Joseph
Hill, Richard
Hiscock, Frank Harris
Hise, Elijah
Hobart, John Sloss
Holman, Jesse Lynch
Holmes, Nathaniel
Holt, Joseph
Hopkins, James Campbell
Hornblower, Josiah
Horner, Henry
Hosmer, Hezekiah Lord
Hough, Warwick
Hudson, Manley Ottmer
Huger, Daniel Elliott
Hughes, James
Innes, Harry
Jay, William
Jenkins, James Graham
Jones, John Marvin
Kerner, Otto, Jr.
Key, David McKendree
King, Austin Augustus
Larrabee, Charles Hathaway
Laurance, John
Law, John
Leibowitz, Samuel Simon
Lenroot, Irvine Luther
Lindsey, Benjamin Barr
McGranery, James Patrick
McPherson, Smith
McReynolds, Samuel Davis
Miller, Nathan Lewis
Mitchell, William, 1852–1900
Moore, George Fleming
Morris, Robert, 1745–1815
Musmanno, Michael Angelo
Nash, Simeon
Newman, William Truslow
Niblack, William Ellis
Nisbet, Eugenius Aristides
Ogden, David
Okey, John Waterman
O'Neill, C. William ("Bill")
Paine, Byron
Parker, Isaac Charles
Patterson, Robert Porter
Peckham, Rufus Wheeler
Penhallow, Samuel
Pennypacker, Samuel Whitaker
Perkins, Samuel Elliott
Peters, Richard, 1744–1828
Pickering, John
Pitkin, William, 1635–1694
Pitkin, William, 1694–1769
Pitney, Mahlon
Pritchard, Jeter Connelly
Randall, Samuel
Raulston, John Tate
Redfield, Isaac Fletcher
Rellstab, John
Richardson, William Merchant
Ross, Erskine Mayo
Ruggles, Timothy
Sanborn, Walter Henry
Saypol, Irving Howard
Sharswood, George
Shepley, George Foster
Sloan, Richard Elihu
Smith, William Nathan Harrell
Sobeloff, Simon E.
Taft, Alphonso
Taylor, Creed
Tazewell, Henry
Thacher, Thomas Day
Thomas, Jesse Burgess
Toulmin, Harry
Tyler, John, 1747–1813
Van Devanter, Willis
Wales, Leonard Eugene
Waring, Julius Waties
Weinberger, Jacob
Youngdahl, Luther Wallace
JURIST (See also CHIEF JUSTICE [STATE], JUDGE, LAWYER, MAGISTRATE, SUPREME COURT JUSTICE)
Adams, Andrew
Aldrich, Edgar
Allen, Charles
Allen, Florence Ellinwood
Allen, John James
Allen, William
Allen, William Joshua
Alvey, Richard Henry
Ames, Samuel
Amidon, Charles Fremont
Anderson, Joseph
Andrews, Charles
Andrews, Charles Bartlett
Andrews, George Pierce
Archer, Stevenson
Ashe, Samuel
Atkinson, George Wesley
Auchmuty, Robert, d. 1750
Auchmuty, Robert, d. 1788
Axtell, Samuel Beach
Badger, George Edmund
Baldwin, Joseph Glover
Baldwin, Simeon
Baldwin, Simeon Eben
Barbour, Philip Pendleton
Bassett, Richard
Bates, Daniel Moore
Battle, Burrell Bunn
Battle, William Horn
Batts, Robert Lynn
Baxter, Elisha
Bayard, Samuel
Baylor, Robert Emmet Bledsoe
Bayly, Thomas Henry
Beasley, Mercer
Beatty, William Henry
Bennett, Edmund Hatch
Bennett, Nathaniel
Benning, Henry Lewis
Bermudez, Edouard Edmond
Betts, Samuel Rossiter
Biddle, Horace P.
Biggs, Asa
Bishop, Robert Roberts
Blair, John
Blatchford, Samuel
Bleckley, Logan Edwin
Bliss, Jonathan
Bliss, Philemon
Blount, Willie
Blowers, Sampson Salter
Boise, Reuben Patrick
Bond, Hugh Lennox
Bourne, Benjamin
Brackenridge, Hugh Henry
Bradbury, Theophilus
Bradford, Edward Green
Bradford, William
Bradley, Stephen Row
Brannon, Henry
Brearly, David
Breaux, Joseph Arsenne
Breese, Sidney
Brennan, Francis James
Brewer, David Josiah
Brewster, Frederick Carroll
Brickell, Robert Coman
Brinkerhoff, Jacob
Brooke, Francis Taliaferro
Brown, Addison
Brown, Henry Billings
Bruce, Andrew Alexander
Bryan, George
Buchanan, John
Bullard, Henry Adams
Burke, Aedanus
Butler, Thomas Belden
Bynum, William Preston
Cadwalader, John
Cady, Daniel
Caldwell, Henry Clay
Campbell, James Valentine
Campbell, John Wilson
Campbell, Josiah A. Patterson
Campbell, William W.
Cardozo, Benjamin Nathan
Carleton, Henry
Carr, Dabney
Carrington, Paul
Case, William Scoville
Casey, Joseph
Cassoday, John Bolivar
Caton, John Dean
Catron, John
Chambers, Ezekiel Forman
Champlin, John Wayne
Charlton, Thomas Usher Pulaski
Chew, Benjamin
Chilton, William Paris
Chipman, Nathaniel
Clark, Daniel
Clark, Greenleaf
Clark, Walter
Clay, Joseph
Clayton, Thomas
Clifford, Nathan
Clopton, David
Cobb, Andrew Jackson
Cofer, Martin Hardin
Coffey, James Vincent
Cole, Chester Cicero
Collens, Thomas Wharton
Collier, Henry Watkins
Colt, Le Baron Bradford
Comstock, George Franklin
Conrad, Robert Taylor
Cooley, Thomas McIntyre
Cooper, William
Cranch, William
Cross, Edward
Crounse, Lorenzo
Crump, William Wood
Curtis, Benjamin Robbins
Cushing, Luther Stearns
Cushing, William
Daly, Charles Patrick

Dana, Francis
Daniel, Peter Vivian
Dargan, Edmund Strother
Davis, David
Davis, John
Davis, Noah
Day, James Gamble
Day, Luther
Deady, Matthew Paul
Deemer, Horace Emerson
Devaney, John Patrick
Devens, Charles
Dick, Robert Paine
Dickerson, Philemon
Dickey, Theophilus Lyle
Dickinson, John
Dill, James Brooks
Dillon, John Forrest
Dixon, Luther Swift
Doe, Charles
Doggett, David
Drake, Charles Daniel
Drayton, John
Drayton, William
Duane, James
Dudley, Paul
Duer, John
Dunn, Charles
Durell, Edward Henry
Durfee, Job
Durfee, Thomas
Dutton, Henry
Dyer, Eliphalet
Edmonds, John Worth
Edwards, Pierpont
Elliott, Charles Burke
Ellis, Powhatan
Elmer, Jonathan
Elmer, Lucius Quintus Cincinnatus
Emery, Lucilius Alonzo
Emott, James, 1771–1850
Emott, James, 1823–1884
Endicott, William Crowninshield
Erskine, John
Eustis, George
Evans, Walter
Ewing, Charles
Fahy, Charles
Farman, Elbert Eli
Farrar, Timothy
Fenner, Charles Erasmus
Field, Fred Tarbell
Field, Richard Stockton
Field, Walbridge Abner
Finch, Francis Miles
Fisher, George Purnell
Flandrau, Charles Eugene
Fleming, Aretas Brooks
Fletcher, Richard
Fletcher, William Asa
Folger, Charles James
Force, Manning Ferguson
Gaston, William
Gaynor, William Jay
George, James Zachariah
Gholson, Samuel Jameson
Gholson, Thomas Saunders
Gholson, William Yates
Gibson, John Bannister
Gilpin, Edward Woodward
Goddard, Luther Marcellus
Goff, John William
Goldthwaite, George
Goldthwaite, Henry Barnes
Goodenow, John Milton
Gould, James
Gould, Robert Simonton
Grant, Claudius Buchanan
Gray, George
Gray, Horace
Green, Henry Woodhull
Greene, Albert Gorton
Gresham, Walter Quintin
Griffin, Cyrus
Grimké, John Faucheraud
Griswold, Matthew
Groesbeck, William Slocum
Grosscup, Peter Stenger
Grundy, Felix
Gummere, William Stryker
Haines, Daniel
Hall, Hiland
Hall, James, 1793–1868
Hall, Nathan Kelsey
Hall, Willard
Hallett, Moses
Hamilton, Walton Hale
Handy, Alexander Hamilton
Hanson, Alexander Contee, 1749–1806
Hare, John Innes Clark
Harlan, John Marshall
Harmon, Judson
Harrington, Samuel Maxwell
Harris, Ira
Harris, William Littleton
Haselton, Seneca
Hastings, Serranus Clinton
Hay, George
Haywood, John
Hemphill, John
Henderson, Leonard
Heyward, Thomas
Hill, Robert Andrews
Hinman, Joel
Hitchcock, Peter
Hoadly, George
Hoar, Ebenezer Rockwood
Hoffman, David Murray
Hopkinson, Joseph
Hornblower, Joseph Coerten
Hornblower, William Butler
Hough, Charles Merrill
Hovey, Alvin Peterson
Howard, Timothy Edward
Howe, Samuel
Howe, William Wirt
Howell, David
Howry, Charles Bowen
Hughes, Robert William
Humphreys, West Hughes
Hunt, William Henry
Hutson, Richard
Iredell, James
Iverson, Alfred
Jackson, Howell Edmunds
Jackson, James, 1819–1887
Jackson, John George
Jackson, Mortimer Melville
Jackson, Robert Houghwout
Jameson, John Alexander
Jenckes, Thomas Allen
Jenkins, Charles Jones
Johns, Kensey, 1759–1848
Johns, Kensey, 1791–1857
Johnson, Alexander Smith
Johnson, Herschel Vespasian
Johnson, William
Johnson, William Samuel
Johnston, Job
Johnston, Peter
Jones, Joseph
Jones, Leonard Augustus
Jones, Samuel
Jones, Thomas
Jones, Thomas Goode
Kalisch, Samuel
Kane, John Kintzing
Keith, James
Kent, Edward
Kent, James
Kenyon, William Squire
Kephart, John William
Kershaw, Joseph Brevard
Kilty, William
Kinkead, Edgar Benton
Kinne, La Vega George
Kinsey, John
Kirkpatrick, Andrew
Knapp, Martin Augustine
Knowlton, Marcus Perrin
Körner, Gustav Philip
Lamar, Joseph Rucker
Lander, Edward
Landis, Kenesaw Mountain
Lansing, John
Larrazolo, Octaviano Ambrosio
Law, Richard
Lawrence, William, 1819–1899
Leavitt, Humphrey Howe
Lee, Charles, 1758–1815
Lee, Thomas
Lee, William Little
Lehman, Irving
Lewis, Ellis
Lewis, Joseph Horace
Lewis, Morgan
Lindley, Curtis Holbrook
Lindsay, William
Lipscomb, Abner Smith
Livermore, Samuel, 1732–1803
Livingston, Henry Brockholst
Livingston, Robert R., 1718–1775
Lockwood, Samuel Drake
Logan, James Harvey
Logan, Stephen Trigg
Lomax, John Tayloe
Longstreet, Augustus Baldwin
Loomis, Dwight
Lord, Otis Phillips
Lord, William Paine
Lowell, John, 1743–1802
Lowell, John, 1824–1897
Lucas, Daniel Bedinger
Lucas, John Baptiste Charles
Ludeling, John Theodore
Ludlow, George Duncan
Lurton, Horace Harmon
Lynde, Benjamin
Lyon, William Penn
Lyons, Peter
McAllister, Matthew Hall
McCaleb, Theodore Howard
McCarran, Patrick Anthony

McCay, Henry Kent
McComas, Louis Emory
McCrary, George Washington
McDonald, Charles James
McEnery, Samuel Douglas
McFarland, Thomas Bard
McGowan, Samuel
Mack, Julian William
McKean, Joseph Borden
McKenna, Joseph
McKinstry, Elisha Williams
McLean, John
McMaster, Guy Humphreys
Magie, William Jay
Magrath, Andrew Gordon
Malone, Walter
Manning, Thomas Courtland
Marchant, Henry
Marshall, Thomas Alexander
Martin, François-Xavier
Mason, Charles
Mason, John Young
Matthews, Stanley
Maxwell, Augustus Emmett
Maxwell, Samuel
Mercur, Ulysses
Merrick, Edwin Thomas
Merrick, Pliny
Merrimon, Augustus Summerfield
Metcalf, Theron
Miller, Oliver
Mills, Benjamin
Minot, George Richards
Mitchell, James Tyndale
Mitchell, Nahum
Mitchell, Stephen Mix
Mitchell, William, 1801–1886
Moncure, Richard Cassius Lee
Moody, William Henry
Moore, John Bassett
Moore, Maurice
Moore, William, 1699–1783
Moore, William, 1735–1793
Moreau-Lislet, Louis Casimir Elisabeth
Morgan, Philip Hicky
Morris, Richard
Morrow, William W.
Morton, Marcus, 1784–1864
Murphey, Archibald De Bow
Napton, William Barclay
Nash, Frederick
Nelson, Hugh
Nelson, Rensselaer Russell
Nelson, Roger
Nelson, Samuel
Nicholas, Philip Norborne
Nicholson, Alfred Osborne Pope
Nicholson, Joseph Hopper
Nicolls, Matthias
Nixon, John Thompson
Norton, Elijah Hise
Nott, Abraham
Nott, Charles Cooper
Noyes, Walter Chadwick
Oakley, Thomas Jackson
O'Brien, Morgan Joseph
Oldham, Williamson Simpson
Oliver, Andrew
O'Neall, John Belton
Orton, Harlow South
Otis, Charles Eugene
Otto, William Tod
Overton, John
Owsley, William
Paca, William
Paine, Elijah
Paine, Robert Treat
Pardee, Don Albert
Parke, Benjamin
Parker, Alton Brooks
Parker, Amasa Junius
Parker, Edwin Brewington
Parker, Isaac
Parker, Joel, 1795–1875
Parker, Joel, 1816–1888
Parker, John Johnston
Parker, Richard Elliot
Parsons, Theophilus
Paschal, George Washington
Paterson, William
Pearson, Richmond Mumford
Pease, Calvin
Peck, James Hawkins
Pecora, Ferdinand
Pendleton, Edmund
Penfield, William Lawrence
Pennington, William Sandford
Perley, Ira
Pettit, Thomas McKean
Phelps, Charles Edward
Philips, John Finis
Pitkin, William, 1725–1789
Plumley, Frank
Poland, Luke Potter
Porter, Alexander
Porter, James Madison
Potter, Elisha Reynolds
Potter, Platt
Potts, Richard
Pound, Cuthbert Winfred
Pound, (Nathan) Roscoe
Preble, William Pitt
Prentice, Samuel Oscar
Prentiss, Samuel
Prince, Le Baron Bradford
Provosty, Olivier Otis
Pryor, Roger Atkinson
Putnam, William Le Baron
Raney, George Pettus
Ranney, Rufus Percival
Read, Edwin Godwin
Read, John Meredith, 1797–1874
Reeve, Tapping
Requier, Augustus Julian
Richards, John Kelvey
Richardson, William Adams
Ridgely, Nicholas
Roane, Spencer
Roberts, Oran Milo
Robertson, George
Robertson, John
Robinson, John Mitchell
Robinson, Moses
Rodney, Thomas
Rogers, Henry Wade
Root, Jesse
Rose, John Carter
Rose, Uriah Milton
Rosenman, Samuel Irving
Ross, George
Rowan, John
Ruffin, Thomas
Rugg, Arthur Prentice
Rumsey, William
Rutledge, John
Ryan, Edward George
Sanford, Edward Terry
Sanford, Nathan
Sawyer, Lorenzo
Scott, William
Seabury, Samuel
Sebastian, Benjamin
Sedgwick, Theodore, 1746–1813
Seevers, William Henry
Sergeant, Thomas
Settle, Thomas
Shauck, John Allen
Shaw, Lemuel
Sheldon, Henry Newton
Shepard, Seth
Shepley, Ether
Sherwood, Thomas Adiel
Shields, George Howell
Shields, John Knight
Shiras, George
Shiras, Oliver Perry
Shorter, John Gill
Simmons, Thomas Jefferson
Simonton, Charles Henry
Smith, Erasmus Darwin
Smith, Henry Augustus Middleton
Smith, James Francis
Smith, Jeremiah, 1759–1842
Smith, Jeremiah, 1837–1921
Smith, Nathan, 1770–1835
Smith, Nathaniel
Smith, Walter Inglewood
Smith, William, 1697–1769
Smith, William, 1728–1793
Soulé, Pierre
Southard, Samuel Lewis
Spear, William Thomas
Speer, Emory
Spencer, Ambrose
Sprague, Peleg
Stacy, Walter Parker
Stanton, Richard Henry
Staples, Waller Redd
Stayton, John William
Stephens, Linton
Stiness, John Henry
Stockbridge, Henry
Stone, George Washington
Stone, John Wesley
Stone, Wilbur Fisk
Story, Joseph
Stuart, Archibald
Sulzberger, Mayer
Sumner, Increase
Swan, Joseph Rockwell
Swayne, Noah Haynes
Swift, Zephaniah
Tait, Charles
Tappan, Benjamin
Taylor, John Louis
Ten Broeck, Abraham
Terry, David Smith
Thacher, George
Thayer, Amos Madden
Thompson, Seymour Dwight
Thompson, Smith

Throop, Enos Thompson
Throop, Montgomery Hunt
Tichenor, Isaac
Tilghman, William
Tod, George
Toulmin, Harry Theophilus
Treat, Samuel
Treat, Samuel Hubbel
Tree, Lambert
Trimble, Robert
Tripp, Bartlett
Trott, Nicholas
Troup, Robert
Trowbridge, Edmund
Trumbull, John, 1750–1831
Trumbull, Lyman
Tucker, Henry St. George, 1780–1848
Tucker, St. George
Turner, Edward
Turney, Peter
Tyler, Royall
Underwood, John Curtiss
Underwood, Joseph Rogers
Upshur, Abel Parker
Valliant, Leroy Branch
Vanderbilt, Arthur T.
Van Ness, William Peter
Van Santvoord, George
Von Moschzisker, Robert
Wade, Decius Spear
Wade, Martin Joseph
Walker, David, 1806–1879
Walker, David Shelby
Walker, Jonathan Hoge
Walker, Pinkney Houston
Walker, Robert Franklin
Walker, Timothy, 1802–1856
Wallace, William James
Walworth, Reuben Hyde
Wanamaker, Reuben Melville
Warden, Robert Bruce
Ware, Ashur
Warner, Hiram
Watkins, George Claiborne
Weare, Meshech
Welch, John
Wells, Robert William
Wheaton, Henry
Wheeler, George Wakeman
Wheeler, Royal Tyler
White, Albert Smith
White, Edward Douglass
White, Hugh Lawson
Whitman, Ezekiel
Wilbur, Curtis Dwight
Wilkins, Ross
Wilkins, William
Williams, Marshall Jay
Williams, Thomas Scott
Willie, Asa Hoxie
Wilson, Bird
Wilson, James
Wilson, William
Wingate, Paine
Winslow, John Bradley
Winthrop, James
Woerner, John Gabriel
Wood, Reuben
Woodbury, Levi
Woods, William Allen
Woods, William Burnham
Woodward, Augustus Brevoort
Woolsey, John Munro
Woolsey, Theodore Salisbury
Wright, George Grover
Wright, Jonathan Jasper
Yates, Robert
Yeates, Jaster
Yerger, William
Zane, Charles Shuster

KINDERGARTEN EDUCATOR (See also EDUCATOR, TEACHER)
Blow, Susan Elizabeth
Hailmann, William Nicholas
Harrison, Elizabeth
Marwedel, Emma Jacobina Christiana
Wheelock, Lucy
Wiggin, Kate Douglas

LABOR ACTIVIST
Bloor, Ella Reeve
Lang, Lucy Fox Robins
Mooney, Thomas Joseph
Vorse, Mary Heaton

LABOR ARBITRATOR (See also LABOR MEDIATOR)
Billikopf, Jacob
Millis, Harry Alvin
Stacy, Walter Parker

LABOR ECONOMIST (See also ECONOMIST)
Witte, Edwin Emil

LABOR EXPERT
Andrews, John Bertram
Silcox, Ferdinand Augustus

LABOR LEADER
Arthur, Peter M.
Bellanca, Dorothy Jacobs
Berry, George Leonard
Bloor, Ella Reeve
Boyle, Michael J.
Brophy, John
Buchanan, Joseph Ray
Budenz, Louis Francis
Cahan, Abraham
Cameron, Andrew Carr
Duncan, James
Durkin, Martin Patrick
Fitzpatrick, John
Frayne, Hugh
Frey, John Philip
Furuseth, Andrew
Garretson, Austin Bruce
Gillespie, Mabel
Gompers, Samuel
Green, William
Hall, Paul
Harnden, William Frederick
Hayes, John William
Haywood, Allan Shaw
Haywood, William Dudley
Henry, Alice
Hillman, Sidney
Hoffa, James Riddle ("Jimmy")
Howard, Charles Perry
Hutcheson, William Levi
Iglesias, Santiago
Johnston, William Hugh
Jones, Mary Harris
Kearney, Denis
Keefe, Daniel Joseph
Lee, William Granville
Lewis, John Llewellyn
London, Meyer
Lundeberg, Harry
Lynch, James Mathew
McDonald, David John
McNeill, George Edwin
McNulty, Frank Joseph
Maurer, James Hudson
Meany, William George
Mitchell, John, 1870–1919
Moore, Ely
Morrison, Frank
Murray, Philip
Muste, Abraham Johannes
Nestor, Agnes
Noonan, James Patrick
Oliver, Henry Kemble
Olson, Floyd Bjerstjerne
O'Sullivan, Mary Kenney
Parker, Carleton Hubbell
Post, Charles William
Potofsky, Jacob Samuel
Powderly, Terence Vincent
Quill, Michael Joseph
Randolph, Asa Philip
Reuther, Walter Philip
Robins, Margaret Dreier
Roche, Josephine Aspinwall
Rombro, Jacob
Rose, Alex
Sargent, Frank Pierce
Schiesinger, Benjamin
Sigman, Morris
Sorge, Friedrich Adolph
Stephens, Uriah Smith
Steward, Ira
Sylvis, William H.
Tobin, Daniel Joseph
Townsend, Willard Saxby, Jr.
Tresca, Carlo
Trevellick, Richard F.
Ward, Cyrenus Osborne
Whitney, Alexander Fell
Wilson, William Bauchop
Woll, Matthew
Wright, James Lendrew

LABOR MEDIATOR (See also LABOR ARBITRATOR)
Davis, William Hammatt
Leiserson, William Morris
McEntee, James Joseph

LABOR ORGANIZER
Ameringer, Oscar
Anderson, Mary
Crosswaith, Frank Rudolph
Dennis, Eugene
Flynn, Elizabeth Gurley
Foster, William Z.
Giovannitti, Arturo
Mahler, Herbert
Schneiderman, Rose

LABOR REFORMER
Perkins, Frances
Walling, William English

LAND AGENT
Case, Leonard
Ellicott, Joseph
Mappa, Adam Gerard

LANDOWNER
Cooper, William
Coxe, Daniel
Gardiner, Silvester
Herrman, Augustine
Read, Charles
Rutgers, Henry
Smith, Peter
Wood, Abraham
LAND PROMOTER (See also PROMOTER)
McNutt, Alexander
Nicholson, John
Ogden, Samuel
Phelps, Oliver
Vaughan, Charles
Williamson, Charles
LAND PROPRIETOR
Marshall, James Markham
Philipse, Frederick
LANDSCAPE ARCHITECT
Church, Thomas Dolliver
Cleveland, Horace William Shales
Downing, Andrew Jackson
Eliot, Charles
Farrand, Beatrix Cadwalader Jones
Hansen, George
Jensen, Jens
McLaren, John
Mitchell, Donald Grant
Nolen, John
Olmsted, Frederick Law
Olmsted, John Charles
Parmentier, Andrew
Parsons, Samuel Bowne
Pilat, Ignaz Anton
Platt, Charles Adams
Ramée, Joseph Jacques
Sargent, Henry Winthrop
Saunders, William
Underwood, Loring
Vaux, Calvert
Vitale, Ferruccio
Weidenmann, Jacob
LANDSCAPE DESIGNER
Wright, Henry
LAND SPECULATOR (See also SPECULATOR)
Croghan, George
Crowne, William
Low, Nicholas
McCulloch, Robert Paxton
Morgan, George
Scott, John
Trent, William
Wharton, Samuel
LARYNGOLOGIST (See also PHYSICIAN)
Asch, Morris Joseph
Bishop, Seth Scott
Bosworth, Francke Huntington
Coakley, Cornelius Godfrey
Elsberg, Louis
Green, Horace
Jarvis, William Chapman
Knight, Frederick Irving
Kyle, David Braden
Lefferts, George Morewood
Lincoln, Rufus Pratt
Mackenzie, John Noland
Mayer, Emil
Schadle, Jacob Evans
Seiler, Carl
Simpson, William Kelly
Skillern, Ross Hall
Wagner, Clinton
LAWYER (See also CHIEF JUSTICE [STATE], JUDGE, JURIST, MAGISTRATE, SUPREME COURT JUSTICE)
Abbett, Leon
Abbott, Austin
Abbott, Benjamin Vaughan
Absalom, Harris Chappelle
Acheson, Dean Gooderham
Adams, Annette Abbott
Adams, Daniel Weissiger
Adams, Robert
Akerman, Amos Tappan
Aldrich, Winthrop William
Alexander, James
Allen, George Edward
Allen, James Browning
Alston, Joseph
Amlie, Thomas Ryum
Andrews, Christopher Columbus
Andrews, Garnett
Andrews, Sherlock James
Angel, Benjamin Franklin
Anthon, John
Appleton, John
Arnold, Isaac Newton
Arnold, Thurman Wesley
Arrington, Alfred W.
Arvey, Jacob M.
Atchison, David Rice
Atherton, Charles Gordon
Atherton, Joshua
Auchincloss, Hugh Dudley, Jr.
Austin, James Trecothick
Avery, William Waigstill
Axtell, Samuel Beach
Bacon, Augustus Octavius
Baer, George Frederick
Baker, Jehu
Baker, Newton Diehl
Baldwin, John Brown
Baldwin, Loammi
Baldwin, Roger Sherman
Ballantine, Arthur Atwood
Ballinger, Richard Achilles
Bancroft, Edgar Addison
Bangs, Francis Nehemiah
Bankhead, John Hollis
Barbour, John Strode, Jr.
Barbour, Oliver Lorenzo
Barbour, Philip Pendleton
Barden, Graham Arthur
Barker, Jacob
Barlow, Samuel Latham Mitchill
Barnard, Daniel Dewey
Barradall, Edward
Barringer, Daniel Moreau
Barry, William Taylor
Bartlett, Ichabod
Bartlett, Joseph
Barton, Robert Thomas
Bassett, Edward Murray
Bates, George Handy
Battle, William Horn
Bayard, James Asheton
Bayard, Richard Henry
Beach, William Augustus
Beaman, Charles Cotesworth
Beatty, Adam
Beaty, Amos Leonidas
Beck, John Brodhead
Belknap, William Worth
Bell, Charles Henry
Bell, Clark
Bell, Samuel
Bemis, George
Benedict, Erastus Cornelius
Benjamin, George Hillard
Benjamin, Judah Philip
Benjamin, Park
Bennett, Nathaniel
Benton, Josiah Henry
Bermudez, Edouard Edmond
Bettman, Alfred
Bibb, George Mortimer
Bickel, Alexander Mordecai
Bickerdyke, Mary Ann Ball
Biddle, Francis Beverley
Bidwell, Barnabas
Bidwell, Marshall Spring
Billings, Frederick
Bingham, Harry
Bingham, John Armor
Binney, Horace
Birney, James
Birney, James Gillespie
Bishop, Joel Prentiss
Bishop, Robert Roberts
Bissell, Wilson Shannon
Black, Frank Swett
Black, Hugo Lafayette
Black, James
Black, John Charles
Blackford, Charles Minor
Blaikie, William
Blair, Montgomery
Blanchard, Newton Crane
Blatchford, Richard Milford
Blatchford, Samuel
Bliss, George
Blodgett, Henry Williams
Bloomfield, Joseph
Bloomfield, Meyer
Blount, James Henderson
Bogy, Lewis Vital
Bollan, William
Bonaparte, Charles Joseph
Bonney, Charles Carroll
Bordley, John Beale
Boston, Charles Anderson
Botts, John Minor
Boudin, Louis Boudinoff
Boudinot, Elias Cornelius
Boutell, Henry Sherman
Bowen, Thomas Meade
Bowers, Lloyd Wheaton
Boyd, Lynn
Boyden, Roland William
Bozman, John Leeds
Brackenrldge, Henry Marie
Bradbury, James Ware
Bradford, Alexander Warfield
Bradwell, James Bolesworth
Bradwell, Myra
Brady, James Topham
Bragg, Thomas
Branch, Lawrence O'Bryan
Brandeis, Louis Dembitz

Brandon, Gerard Chittocque
Brayman, Mason
Breckenridge, James
Breckinridge, Henry Skillman
Breckinridge, John
Breckinridge, Robert Jefferson
Breckinridge, William Campbell Preston
Brennan, Francis James
Brewster, Frederick Carroll
Brewster, Ralph Owen
Briggs, George Nixon
Brightly, Frederick Charles
Brinkerhoff, Roeliff
Bristow, Benjamin Helm
Brown, David Paul
Brown, George William
Brown, Joseph Emerson
Brown, Neill Smith
Brown, Walter Folger
Browning, Orville Hickman
Bruce, Edward Bright
Buck, Daniel
Buckland, Ralph Pomeroy
Buckner, Emory Roy
Bundy, Harvey Hollister
Burdick, Usher Lloyd
Burke, Stevenson
Burke, Thomas
Burlingham, Charles Culp
Burnet, Jacob
Burnett, Henry Lawrence
Burr, Aaron
Burrall, William Porter
Burrell, Alexander Mansfield
Burrill, James
Burton, Clarence Monroe
Butler, Andrew Pickens
Butler, Benjamin Franklin
Butler, Charles
Butler, Pierce
Butler, William Allen
Butler, William Orlando
Butterworth, Benjamin
Byran, Thomas Barbour
Cabell, William Lewis
Cahn, Edmond Nathaniel
Caines, George
Calhoun, Patrick
Calhoun, William Barron
Camp, John Lafayette
Campbell, John Archibald
Cardozo, Benjamin Nathan
Carlile, John Snyder
Carlisle, James Mandeville
Carlson, Chester Floyd
Carpenter, Matthew Hale
Carrington, Henry Beebee
Carson, Hampton Lawrence
Carter, James Coolidge
Case, Leonard
Case, William Scoville
Chalmers, James Ronald
Chamberlain, George Earle
Chamberlain, Joseph Perkins
Chambers, George
Chandler, Peleg Whitman
Chapman, Oscar Littleton
Chavez, Dennis
Chester, Colby Mitchell
Chestnut, James
Chipman, Daniel
Choate, Joseph Hodges
Choate, Rufus
Christiancy, Isaac Peckham
Clagett, Wyseman
Clark, Abraham
Clark, Horace Francis
Clark, Joshua Reuben, Jr.
Clarke, John Hessin
Clay, Crement Claiborne
Clay, Joseph
Clayton, Augustin Smith
Clayton, John Middleton
Cleveland, Chauncey Fitch
Clifford, John Henry
Cline, Genevieve Rose
Clough, William Pitt
Cobb, Jonathan Holmes
Cobb, Thomas Reade Rootes
Cochran, William Bourke
Cogdell, John Stevens
Cohen, Felix Solomon
Colby, Bainbridge
Colden, Cadwallader David
Colquitt, Walter Terry
Conboy, Martin
Connally, Thomas Terry ("Tom")
Conner, James
Conover, Obadiah Milton
Conrad, Charles Magill
Conrad, Holmes
Converse, Charles Crozat
Cook, Philip
Cooke, John Rogers
Cooper, Henry Ernest
Cooper, James
Cornwallis, Kinahan
Costigan, Edward Prentiss
Cotton, Joseph Potter
Coudert, Frederic René
Coudert, Frederic René, Jr.
Cowen, John Kissig
Cowles, Charles
Cox, Edward Eugene
Cox, Rowland
Crafts, William
Crane, Frederick Evan
Cravath, Paul Drennan
Creighton, William
Crittenden, John Jordan
Crittenden, Thomas Leonidas
Cromwell, William Nelson
Crowder, Enoch Herbert
Culberson, Charles Allen
Culberson, David Browning
Cullom, Shelby Moore
Cummins, Albert Baird
Curran, Thomas Jerome
Curtis, Charles Pelham
Curtis, George Ticknor
Curtis, Samuel Ryan
Cutler, Robert
Cuyler, Theodore
Daggett, David
Dallas, Alexander James
Dana, Charles Anderson
Dana, Richard
Dana, Richard Henry
Dana, Samuel Whittelsey
Dane, Nathan
Darrow, Clarence Seward
Dart, Henry Paluché
Daugherty, Harry Micajah
Daveis, Charles Stewart
Daveiss, Joseph Hamilton
D'Avezac, Auguste Geneviève Valentin
Davies, Joseph Edward
Davis, Cushman Kellogg
Davis, Garret
Davis, George
Davis, John
Davis, John William
Davis, Reuben
Davis, William Thomas
Davison, George Willets
Dayton, William Lewis
Dean, Amos
Dean, Gordon Evans
De Forest, Robert Weeks
Delmas, Delphin Michael
Deming, Henry Champion
Deming, Philander
Denby, Charles
Denver, James William
Depew, Chauncey Mitchell
Derby, Elias Hasket
De Saussure, Henry William
Devaney, John Patrick
Dexter, Franklin
Dexter, Samuel
Dexter, Wirt
Dickerson, Edward Nicoll
Dickinson, Daniel Stevens
Dickinson, Donald McDonald
Dickinson, Jacob McGavack
Dillingham, William Paul
Diven, Alexander Samuel
Dodd, Samuel Calvin Tate
Doddridge, Philip
Donelson, Andrew Jackson
Donnelly, Charles Francis
Donovan, James Britt
Donovan, William Joseph
Doolittle, James Rood
Dorsheimer, William Edward
Dos Passos, John Randolph
Douglas, Henry Kyd
Dow, Neal
Doyle, John Thomas
Drake, Benjamin
Drake, Charles Daniel
Drayton, William
Dropsie, Moses Aaron
Duane, William John
Duff, James Henderson
Duffy, Francis Ryan
Dulany, Daniel, 1685–1753
Dulany, Daniel, 1722–1797
Dulles, Allen Welsh
Dulles, John Foster
Dunlop, James
Dunn, Charles
Du Ponceau, Pierre Étienne
Durant, Henry Fowle
Durant, Thomas Jefferson
Durrett, Reuben Thomas
Duval, William Pope
Dwight, Francis
Dwight, Theodore
Dwight, Theodore William
Dyatt, Thomas Ben
Eames, Charles
Earle, Thomas

Eaton, Dorman Bridgman
Eaton, John Henry
Echols, John
Eckels, James Herron
Edmunds, George Franklin
Edwards, Charles
Edwards, Henry Waggaman
Edwards, Pierpont
Elder, Samuel James
Elliott, Benjamm
Elliott, Charles Burke
Ellis, George Washington
Ellsworth, Henry William
Ellsworth, William Wolcott
Elwell, John Johnson
Emmet, Thomas Addis
Ernst, Morris Leopold
Evans, George
Evans, Hugh Davey
Evans, Lawrence Boyd
Evarts, Jeremiah
Evarts, William Maxwell
Everett, David
Ewing, Oscar Ross
Ewing, Thomas
Fairfield, John
Fall, Albert Bacon
Farnham, Thomas Jefferson
Farrar, Edgar Howard
Fearn, John Walker
Featherston, Winfield Scott
Felch, Alpheus
Ferry, Elisha Peyre
Fessenden, Francis
Fessenden, James Deering
Fessenden, Samuel
Fessenden, William Pitt
Field, David Dudley
Field, Maunsell Bradhurst
Finletter, Thomas Knight
Fisher, George Purnell
Fisher, Sidney George
Fisher, Sydney George
Fisher, Walter Lowrie
Fisk, James
Fiske, Haley
Fitch, Samuel
Fitch, Thomas
Fitzhugh, George
Fitzhugh, William
Flanders, Henry
Fletcher, Calvin
Fletcher, Thomas Clement
Flexner, Bernard
Fly, James Lawrence
Fogg, George Gilman
Folger, Henry Clay
Folger, Walter
Folk, Joseph Wingate
Foot, Solomon
Foote, Lucius Harwood
Forbes, John Murray
Ford, Gordon Lester
Forney, William Henry
Fosdick, Raymond Blaine
Foster, John Watson
Foster, Judith Ellen Horton
Foster, Murphy James
Foster, Roger Sherman Baldwin
Foulke, William Dudley
Freeman, Nathaniel
Frelinghuysen, Frederick
Frelinghuysen, Theodore
Freund, Ernst
Fry, Birkett Davenport
Gaines, John Pollard
Gaither, Horace Rowan, Jr.
Gamble, Hamilton Rowan
Gansevoort, Leonard
Gardiner, John
Garfield, Harry Augustus
Garfield, James Rudolph
Garrison, Lindley Miller
Gartrell, Lucius Jeremiah
Gary, Elbert Henry
Gaut, John McReynolds
Gerard, James Watson
Gerry, Elbridge Thomas
Geyer, Henry Sheffie
Gibbes, William Hasell
Gibbons, Thomas
Gibbons, William
Gibson, Randall Lee
Gilbert, Seymour Parker
Gilchrist, Robert
Gilmer, Francis Walker
Gilpin, Henry Dilworth
Glover, Samuel Taylor
Goldman, Mayer C.
Goldsborough, Robert
Goldsborough, Thomas Alan
Goode, John
Goodhue, James Madison
Goodman, Charles
Goodrich, Chauncey
Goodrich, Elizur
Goodwin, John Noble
Gordon, George Washington
Gordon, Laura De Force
Gordon, William Fitzhugh
Gordon, William Washington
Gorman, Willis Arnold
Goudy, William Charles
Gowen, Franklin Benjamin
Graham, David
Graham, John Andrew
Graham, William Alexander
Granger, Gideon
Grant, Madison
Gray, John Chipman
Greathouse, Clarence Ridgeby
Green, Andrew Haswell
Green, Benjamin Edwards
Green, William
Greenbaum, Edward Samuel
Greener, Richard Theodore
Greenleaf, Simon
Greenup, Christopher
Gregory, Charles Noble
Gregory, Thomas Watt
Gridley, Jeremiah
Griffith, William
Griggs, John William
Grimes, James Wilson
Grimké, Archibald Henry
Griscom, Lloyd Carpenter
Griswold, Roger
Grosvenor, Edwin Prescott
Grover, La Fayette
Grundy, Felix
Gummere, Samuel René
Guthrie, George Wilkins
Guthrie, William Dameron
Hackett, Frank Warren
Hager, John Sharpenstein
Haggin, James Ben Ali
Haight, Henry Huntly
Haines, Charles Glidden
Hale, Eugene
Hale, John Parker
Hale, Robert Safford
Hall, Abraham Oakey
Hall, John Elihu
Hall, Willard Preble
Halleck, Henry Wager
Hamilton, Andrew, d. 1741
Hamilton, James, 1710–1783
Hamilton, James Alexander
Hamilton, John Daniel Miller, II
Hamilton, Peter
Hamlin, Charles
Hamlin, Charles Sumner
Hammond, Charles
Hammond, Nathaniel Job
Hammond, William Gardiner
Hancock, John, 1824–1893
Hardin, Ben
Hardin, Martin D.
Harding, George
Hardy, William Harris
Harlan, James
Harris, John Woods
Harris, Nathaniel Harrison
Harris, Wiley Pope
Harrison, Fairfax
Hart, Charles Henry
Hartley, Thomas
Hasbrouck, Abraham Bruyn
Hascall, Milo Smith
Haskell, Ella Louise Knowles
Havens, James Smith
Hawkins, Dexter Arnold
Hawley, Gideon, 1785–1870
Hawley, James Henry
Hawley, Joseph
Hayes, John Lord
Hayne, Robert Young
Hays, Arthur Garfield
Hays, Harry Thompson
Hays, Will H.
Hazelton, George Cochrane
Helmer, Bessie Bradwell
Hemphill, Joseph
Henderson, Archibald
Henderson, John
Heney, Francis Joseph
Henry, John, 1750–1798
Henry, William Wirt
Herndon, William Henry
Herrick, Myron Timothy
Hickenlooper, Bourke Blakemore
Hildreth, Richard
Hilgard, Theodor Erasmus
Hill, David Bennett
Hill, Frederick Trevor
Hill, Walter Barnard
Hillard, George Stillman
Hilliard, Henry Washington
Hillquit, Morris
Hillyer, Junius
Hindman, Thomas Carmichael
Hindman, William
Hines, Walker Downer
Hirst, Henry Beck
Hiscock, Frank Harris

Hise, Elijah
Hitchcock, Henry
Hittell, Theodore Henry
Hoadly, George
Hoar, George Frisbie
Hoar, Samuel
Hoffman, David
Hoffman, John Thompson
Hoffman, Josiah Ogden
Hoffman, Ogden
Hogan, Frank Smithwick
Holcomb, Silas Alexander
Holcombe, James Philemon
Holden, Hale
Hollister, Gideon Hiram
Holls, George Frederick William
Holmes, Daniel Henry
Holmes, John
Hopkins, Arthur Francis
Hoppin, William Warner
Hornblower, Joseph Coerten
Hosmer, Titus
Hough, Warwick
Hourwich, Isaac Aaronovich
Houston, Charles Hamilton
Howard, Benjamin Chew
Howard, Volney Erskine
Howe, Frederic Clemson
Howe, Samuel
Howe, William F.
Hoyt, Henry Martyn
Hubbard, Richard Bennett
Hubbard, Thomas Hamlin
Hughes, Charles Evans
Hughes, Henry
Hughes, James
Hummel, Abraham Henry
Humphrey, George Magoffin
Hunt, Carleton
Hunter, Robert Mercer Taliaferro
Hunton, Eppa
Hunton, George Kenneth
Hurley, Patrick Jay
Hutchins, Harry Burns
Hyde, Charles Cheney
Ickes, Harold Le Clair
Ide, Henry Clay
Ingersoll, Charles Jared
Ingersoll, Edward
Ingersoll, Jared, 1722–1781
Ingersoll, Jared, 1749–1822
Ingersoll, Robert Green
Ingraham, Edward Duffield
Innes, James
Ireland, Charles Thomas, Jr. ("Chick")
Ireland, John, 1827–1896
Irving, Pierre Munro
Ivins, William Mills
Jackson, Charles
Jackson, Henry Rootes
Jackson, Robert Houghwout
James, Edward Christopher
Jamison, David
Jay, John
Jay, Peter Augustus
Jenkins, James Graham
Jenkins, John Stilwell
Jerome, William Travers
Jewell, Harvey
Johnson, Chapman
Johnson, Edward Austin
Johnson, John Graver
Johnson, Louis Arthur
Johnson, Reverdy
Johnson, Robert Ward
Johnston, Augustus
Johnston, Josiah Stoddard
Johnston, William Preston
Joline, Adrian Hoffman
Jones, Gabriel
Jones, Joel
Jones, Samuel
Jones, Walter
Joy, James Frederick
Judah, Samuel
Judd, Norman Buel
Judson, Frederick Newton
Keating, Kenneth Barnard
Keener, William Albert
Kefauver, (Carey) Estes
Keifer, Joseph Warren
Kellogg, Frank Billings
Kelly, Edmond
Kennedy, Robert Patterson
Kent, Edward
Kernan, Francis
Key, David McKendree
Key, Francis Scott
Keyes, Elisha Williams
Kimball, Richard Burleigh
King, Carol Weiss
King, Horatio
King, John Pendleton
King, Thomas Butler
Kinsey, John
Kirby, Ephraim
Kneeland, Stillman Foster
Knickerbocker, Herman
Knight, Goodwin Jess ("Goodie")
Knott, Aloysius Leo
Knott, James Proctor
Knox, Philander Chase
Kohler, Max James
Lacey, John Fletcher
Lamon, Ward Hill
Landis, James McCauley
Langlie, Arthur Bernard
Lanham, Frederick Garland ("Fritz")
Larned, Joseph Gay Eaton
Larrabee, Charles Hathaway
Lathrop, George Parsons
Lathrop, John
Latrobe, John Hazlehurst Boneval
Law, Jonathan
Lawton, Alexander Robert
Leaming, Thomas
Lechford, Thomas
Leffingwell, Russell Cornell
Leffler, Isaac
Legaré, Hugh Swinton
Leggett, Mortimer Dormer
Lehmann, Frederick William
Leibowitz, Samuel Simon
Leigh, Benjamin Watkins
Leonard, Daniel
Levin, Lewis Charles
Levinson, Salmon Oliver
Levitt, Abraham
Lewis, Charlton Thomas
Lewis, James Hamilton
Lewis, Lawrence
Lewis, William
Lewis, William Draper
Lewis, William Henry
Lexow, Clarence
L'Hommedieu, Ezra
Lile, William Minor
Lincoln, Enoch
Lincoln, Levi, 1749–1820
Lincoln, Levi, 1782–1868
Lind, John
Lindabury, Richard Vliet
Lindley, Curtis Holbrook
Lipscomb, Abner Smith
Littell, William
Littleton, Martin Wiley
Livermore, Edward St. Loe
Livermore, Samuel, 1786–1833
Livingston, William
Lloyd, David
Lockwood, Belva Ann Bennett
Lockwood, Ralph Ingersoll
Loeb, Milton B.
Logan, Stephen Trigg
Long, Edward Vaughn
Long, Joseph Ragland
Longfellow, Stephen
Lord, Daniel
Loring, Ellis Gray
Lovejoy, Asa Lawrence
Lovett, Robert Scott
Lowden, Frank Orren
Lowell, John, 1769–1840
Lowery, Woodbury
Lowry, Robert
Lucas, Scott Wike
Ludlow, Thomas William
Lynch, John Roy
Mabie, Hamilton Wright
McAdoo, William Gibbs
McAllister, Hall
McCarran, Patrick Anthony
McCartney, Washington
McClain, Emlin
McClure, Alexander Kelly
McCord, David James
McCrady, Edward
McCreery, James Work
McCullough, John Griffith
McCumber, Porter James
McDaniel, Henry Dickerson
McDonald, Joseph Ewing
McDowell, John
Mack, Julian William
McKinstry, Alexander
McLane, Robert Milligan
Maclay, William
Maclay, William Brown
McLean, Angus Wilton
McMahon, Brien
McMahon, John Van Lear
McNutt, Paul Vories
McRae, Duncan Kirkland
McRae, Thomas Chipman
MacVeagh, Charles
MacVeagh, Isaac Wayne
Magoffin, Beriah
Magoon, Charles Edward
Malone, Dudley Field
Manderson, Charles Frederick
Maney, George Earl

Mann, James Robert
Marcy, William Learned
Marquett, Turner Mastin
Marsh, George Perkins
Marshall, Louis
Martin, John Hill
Martindale, John Henry
Mason, Jeremiah
Mather, Samuel Holmes
Matthews, Francis Patrick
Maxcy, Virgil
Maxwell, George Hebard
Maxwell, Hugh
Maxwell, William
Mayer, Brantz
Mazureau, Étienne
Meagher, Thomas Francis
Mechem, Floyd Russell
Meigs, Josiah
Meigs, Return Jonathan
Meigs, William Montgomery
Meredith, William Morris
Metcalf, Lee Warren
Miller, Nathan Lewis
Millikin, Eugene Donald
Mills, Elijah Hunt
Mills, Ogden Livingston
Minor, Benjamin Blake
Mitchel, John Purroy
Mitchell, John Hipple
Mitchell, Stephen Arnold
Mitchell, William DeWitt
Money, Hernando De Soto
Monsky, Henry
Montague, Gilbert Holland
Montefiore, Joshua
Moore, Bartholomew Figures
Moore, John Bassett
Morawetz, Victor
Morell, George Webb
Morgan, George Washington
Morgenthau, Henry
Morris, Luzon Burritt
Morrow, Dwight Whitney
Morrow, Edwin Porch
Morton, Ferdinand Quintin
Moseley, Edward Augustus
Mosessohn, David Nehemiah
Murphy, Henry Cruse
Murray, Joseph
Murray, William Henry David
Mussey, Ellen Spencer
Nelson, Thomas Henry
Nelson, William, 1847–1914
Nesmith, James Willis
Neumann, Franz Leopold
Newberry, John Stoughton
Newel, Stanford
Nicoll, De Lancey
Nicolls, William
Noah, Mordecai Manuel
Noble, John Willock
Noyes, William Curtis
O'Brian, John Lord
O'Brien, Morgan Joseph
O'Brien, Thomas James
O'Conor, Charles
O'Donnell, Thomas Jefferson
O'Dwyer, William
Ogden, Aaron
Ogden, David
Ogden, David Bayard
Ogden, Thomas Ludlow
Olds, Irving Sands
Olds, Robert Edwin
Oliver, George Tener
Olmsted, Marlin Edgar
Olney, Richard
Ordronaux, John
Orr, Jehu Amaziah
Orton, Harlow South
Osborn, Thomas Andrew
Osborn, Thomas Ogden
Osborne, James Walker
Owen, Thomas McAdory
Paine, Halbert Eleazer
Paine, Henry Warren
Palmer, Alexander Mitchell
Palmer, Henry Wilbur
Palmer, William Adams
Park, Trenor William
Parker, Amasa Junius
Parker, John Cortlandt
Parkinson, Thomas Ignatius
Parsons, John Edward
Parsons, Lewis Baldwin
Parvin, Theodore Sutton
Pastorius, Francis Daniel
Patterson, Robert Porter
Patterson, Thomas MacDonald
Pattison, Robert Emory
Patton, John Mercer
Paul, Alice
Payne, Christopher Harrison
Payne, John Barton
Peabody, Oliver William Bourn
Peck, George Record
Peckham, Wheeler Hazard
Pecora, Ferdinand
Pennypacker, Samuel Whitaker
Penrose, Boies
Penrose, Charles Bingham
Pepper, George Wharton
Perkins, James Breck
Perkins, Thomas Nelson
Perley, Ira
Perlman, Philip Benjamin
Peters, John Andrew
Peters, Richard, 1744–1828
Petigru, James Louis
Pettigrew, James Johnston
Phelps, Edward John
Phelps, William Walter
Phillips, Willard
Pickering, John
Pierce, Edward Lillie
Pierrepont, Edwards
Piexotto, Benjamin Franklin
Pike, Albert
Pinchot, Amos Richards Eno
Pinkney, William
Pitkin, Frederick Walker
Pitkin, William, 1635–1694
Plumb, Glenn Edward
Polk, Frank Lyon
Pollak, Walter Heilprin
Pomerene, Atlee
Pool, Joe Richard
Poor, John Alfred
Pope, James Pinckney
Post, Melville Davisson
Powell, Thomas Reed
Pressman, Lee
Price, Eli Kirk
Prouty, Charles Azro
Pruyn, John Van Schaik Lansing
Pruyn, Robert Hewson
Pujo, Arsène Paulin
Purnell, William Henry
Putnam, (George) Herbert
Putnam, James Osborne
Quick, John Herbert
Quincy, Josiah, 1744–1775
Quitman, John Anthony
Radcliff, Jacob
Radcliffe, George Lovic Pierce
Radin, Max
Raines, John
Ralston, Samuel Moffett
Randall, Alexander Williams
Randolph, Edmund, 1819–1861
Randolph, George Wythe
Rankine, William Birch
Raulston, John Tate
Rawle, Francis, 1846–1930
Rawle, William
Rawle, William Henry
Raymond, Daniel
Rayner, Isidor
Read, Charles
Read, George
Read, John, 1679/80–1749
Read, John, 1769–1854
Rector, Henry Massey
Redfield, Amasa Angell
Reed, David Aiken
Reed, James Hay
Reed, Joseph
Reed, Thomas Brackett
Reed, William Bradford
Rellstab, John
Rice, Isaac Leopold
Richberg, Donald Randall
Riddle, Albert Gallatin
Ritchie, Albert Cabell
Rives, George Lockhart
Roane, John Selden
Roberts, Oran Milo
Robertson, William Joseph
Robinson, Christopher
Robinson, Conway
Robinson, Henry Cornelius
Rodney, Caesar Augustus
Roe, Gilbert Ernstein
Rogers, John Ignatius
Root, Elihu
Root, Erastus
Rorer, David
Roselius, Christian
Rosenman, Samuel Irving
Ross, James
Rublee, George
Ruggles, Samuel Bulkley
Rush, Richard
Russell, Charles Wells
Rutherford, Joseph Franklin
Rutledge, Wiley Blount
Sackett, Henry Woodward
Sage, Bernard, Janin
Sampson, William
Sanders, Wilbur Fisk
Sanger, George Partridge
Sargent, John Osborne
Sayles, John
Saypol, Irving Howard
Scammon, Jonathan Young

Schell, Augustus
Schoeppel, Andrew Frank
Schouler, James
Scott, Gustavus
Scott, James Brown
Scott, John Morin
Scott, Samuel Parsons
Seabury, Samuel
Sedgwick, Arthur George
Sedgwick, Theodore, 1780–1839
Sedgwick, Theodore, 1811–1859
Semmes, Thomas Jenkins
Sergeant, John, 1779–1852
Sergeant, Jonathan Dickinson
Sewall, Jonathan
Sewall, Jonathan Mitchell
Shannon, Wilson
Shearman, Thomas Gaskell
Shepard, Edward Morse
Shipman, Andrew Jackson
Shuster, W(illiam) Morgan
Simms, William Elliott
Smith, Buckingham
Smith, Caleb Blood
Smith, Chauncey
Smith, Israel
Smith, James Francis
Smith, Jeremiah
Smith, Junius
Smith, Melancton, 1744–1798
Smith, Oliver Hampton
Smith, Ralph Tyler
Smith, Richard
Smith, Richard Penn
Smith, Robert Hardy
Smith, Roswell
Smith, Truman
Smith, William, 1762–1840
Smith, William Russell
Smyth, John Henry
Snowden, James Ross
Sobeloff, Simon E.
Soley, James Russell
Southmayd, Charles Ferdinand
Sparks, William Andrew Jackson
Speed, James
Spencer, John Canfield
Spingarn, Arthur Barnett
Spooner, Lysander
Springer, Charles
Springer, Frank
Springer, William McKendree
Stallo, Johann Bernhard
Stanbery, Henry
Stanchfield, John Barry
Stanley, Augustus Owsley
Stanton, Henry Brewster
Starr, Merritt
Stearns, Asahel
Steinhardt, Laurence Adolph
Sterling, John William
Sterne, Simon
Stetson, Francis Lynde
Steuer, Max David
Stevens, Hiram Fairchild
Stevens, Thaddeus
Stewart, Alvan
Stewart, Arthur Thomas ("Tom")
Stewart, William Morris
Stickney, Alpheus Beede
Stillman, Thomas Edgar
Stilwell, Silas Moore
Stimson, Frederic Jesup
Stockbridge, Henry Smith
Stockton, Richard, 1730–1781
Stockton, Richard, 1764–1828
Stoddard, Amos
Stone, John Wesley
Storey, Moorfield
Storrow, James Jackson
Stoughton, Edwin Wallace
Straus, Oscar Solomon
Strawn, Silas Hardy
Street, Alfred Billings
Strong, Caleb
Strong, Moses McCure
Stryker, Lloyd Paul
Stuart, John Todd
Sullivan, George
Sullivan, William
Sumners, Hatton William
Swayne, Wager
Sweeney, Martin Leonard
Swift, John Franklin
Swift, Lucius Burrie
Taber, John
Taft, Charles Phelps
Taft, Henry Waters
Taft, Robert Alphonso
Tallmadge, James
Taylor, Hannis
Tazewell, Henry
Tazewell, Littleton Waller
Teller, Henry Moore
Temple, Oliver Perry
Tench, Francis
Terrell, Edwin Holland
Thatcher, Benjamin Bussey
Thayer, John Milton
Thomas, Charles Spalding
Thomas, William Widgery
Thompson, Daniel Pierce
Thompson, Richard Wigginton
Thompson, Robert Means
Thurston, Lorrin Andrews
Tichenor, Isaac
Tilden, Samuel Jones
Tilghman, Edward
Tilson, John Quillin
Todd, Charles Stewart
Toole, Edwin Warren
Towne, Charles Arnette
Tracy, Benjamin Franklin
Train, Arthur Cheney
Tremain, Henry Edwin
Trude, Alfred Samuel
Tucker, Henry St. George, 1853–1932
Tucker, John Randolph, 1823–1897
Turner, George
Tuttle, Charles Wesley
Tweed, Harrison
Tydings, Millard Evelyn
Tyler, Robert
Tyler, Samuel
Tyson, Job Roberts
Underwood, Francis Henry
Untermyer, Samuel
Usher, John Palmer
Van Buren, John
Vandenhoff, George
Vanderbilt, Arthur T.
Van Der Donck, Adriaen
Van Devanter, Willis
Van Dyke, Nicholas, 1770–1826
Van Schaack, Peter
Van Vechten, Abraham
Van Winkle, Peter Godwin
Van Wyck, Charles Henry
Varnum, James Mitchell
Vaux, Richard
Vilas, William Freeman
Vinton, Samuel Finley
Vroom, Peter Dumont
Wait, William
Walker, Frank Comerford
Wallace, Lewis
Waller, Thomas Macdonald
Wallis, Severn Teackle
Waln, Nicholas
Walsh, Francis Patrick
Walter, Francis Eugene
Ward, John Elliott
Waring, Julius Waties
Warmoth, Henry Clay
Warner, William
Washburn, Albert Henry
Washburn, Israel
Waterman, Thomas Whitney
Watson, David Thompson
Watson, John William Clark
Wayland, Francis, 1826–1904
Wehle, Louis Brandeis
Weinberger, Jacob
Welch, Joseph Nye
Welker, Herman
Wells, John
West, James Edward
Westcott, Thompson
Wharton, Francis
Wharton, Thomas Isaac
Wheeler, Everett Pepperrell
Wheeler, John Hill
Wheeler, Wayne Bidwell
Wherry, Kenneth Spicer
Whipple, Sherman Leland
White, Albert Smith
White, Alexander
White, John Blake
White, Samuel
White, Stephen Mallory
Whiting, William
Whyte, William Pinkney
Wickersham, George Woodward
Wickham, John
Wiley, Alexander
Wilkins, Ross
Willard, Joseph
Willard, Joseph Edward
Williams, Elisha
Williamson, Isaac Halstead
Williston, Samuel
Willkie, Wendell Lewis
Wilson, James Falconer
Wilson, John Lockwood
Wilson, Samuel Mountford
Winder, William Henry
Wise, John Sergeant
Wolf, Simon
Wood, Charles Erskine Scott
Wood, Frederick Hill
Wood, George

Work, Milton Cooper
Worthington, John
Wright, Robert William
Yates, John Van Ness
Yeadon, Richard
Yeates, Jasper
Yerger, William
Young, Clarence Marshall
Young, Owen D.
Youngdahl, Luther Wallace
Zeisler, Sigmund

League of Nations Official
Tyler, Royall

Lecture Promoter (See also Promoter)
Pond, James Burton
Redpath, James

Lecturer (See also Orator)
Antin, Mary
Atkinson, George Wesley
Bacon, Alice Mabel
Bangs, John Kendrick
Bell, James Madison
Bragdon, Claude Fayette
Brough, Charles Hillman
Brown, John Mason, Jr.
Burton, Richard Eugene
Buttrick, George Arthur
Chase, Mary Ellen
Coffin, Robert Peter Tristram
Colman, Lucy Newhall
Cook, Flavius Josephus
Cooke, George Willis
Dinwiddie, Edwin Courtland
Dixon, Thomas
Dyer, Louis
Elson, Louis Charles
Erskine, John
Farmer, Fannie Merritt
Field, Mary Katherine Kemble
Fletcher, Horace
Gibbons, Herbert Adams
Gilman, Charlotte Perkins Stetson
Goldman, Emma
Gronlund, Laurence
Hall, Florence Marion Howe
Herron, George Davis
Holmes, Elias Burton
Hubbard, Bernard Rosecrans
Ingersoll, Robert Green
James, George Wharton
James, Henry, 1811–1882
Johnson, John Albert
Keller, Helen Adams
King, Thomas Starr
Krebbiel, Henry Edward
Lease, Mary Elizabeth Clyens
Leipziger, Henry Marcus
Lockwood, Belva Ann Bennett
Logan, Olive
Lord, John
Morris, Robert, 1818–1888
Moulton, Richard Green
Murdoch, James Edward
Nason, Elias
Ng Poon Chew
Nicholson, Meredith
Ogilvie, James
Pattison, James William
Perry, Edward Baxter
Peters, Madison Clinton
Phelps, William Lyon
Pollock, Channing
Rossiter, Clinton Lawrence, III
Salter, William Mackintire
Sanborn, Katherine Abbott
Savage, Minot Judson
Schaeffer, Nathan Christ
Seton, Ernest Thompson
Slocum, Joshua
Slosson, Edwin Emery
Smith, Elizabeth Oakes Prince
Soulé, George
Starr, Eliza Allen
Stoddard, John Lawson
Stone, Ellen Maria
Strong, Anna Louise
Sunderland, Eliza Jane Read
Talmage, Thomas De Witt
Taylor, Benjamin Franklin
Taylor, Robert Love
Towle, George Makepeace
Underwood, Benjamin Franklin
Utley, Freda
Vasiliev, Alexander Alexandrovich
Warde, Frederick Barkham
Whipple, Edwin Percy
Wiley, Harvey Washington
Williams, Fannie Barrier
Winnemucca, Sarah
Winship, Albert Edward
Woolson, Abba Louisa Goold

Legal Annotator
Kirby, Ephraim
Lowery, Woodbury
Rose, Walter Malins

Legal Philosopher
Cahn, Edmond Nathaniel
Llewellyn, Karl Nickerson

Legislator (See also Congressman, Senator)
Adams, Robert
Anderson, William
Applegate, Jesse
Ashe, Thomas Samuel
Bacon, John
Beatty, John
Bingham, William
Bouligny, Dominique
Brinkerhoff, Jacob
Brown, John
Buck, Daniel
Clay, Green
Cocke, William
Curtis, Newton Martin
Edwards, Weldon Nathaniel
Elmer, Ebenezer
Elmer, Jonathan
Elmer, Lucius Quintius Cincinnatus
Fell, John
Garnett, James Mercer, 1770–1845
Garvin, Lucius Fayette Clark
Goebel, William
Green, Norvin
Grimes, James Wilson
Grose, William
Halderman, John A.
Hale, Eugene
Hamer, Thomas Lyon
Harlan, James
Hart, John
Hill, James
Hill, Richard
Holman, Jesse Lynch
Holmes, Ezekiel
Hooper, Samuel
Hoppin, William Warner
Hornblower, Josiah
Huntington, Jabez
Jenckes, Thomas Allen
Johnson, Chapman
Johnston, Peter
Jones, George Wallace
Lane, Joseph
Leffler, Isaac
Leffler, Shepherd
L'Hommedieu, Ezra
Lord, Otis Phillips
Low, Nicholas
Lowell, John, 1743–1802
Lyon, William Penn
McClure, Alexander Kelly
McCreery, James Work
Maclay, William Brown
Marshall, Thomas
Mason, Thomson
Maxcy, Virgil
Maxwell, David Hervey
Maxwell, George Troup
Memminger, Christopher Gustavus
Mills, Benjamin
Morris, Edward Joy
Munford, William
Nesmith, James Willis
Nisbet, Eugenius Aristides
Northen, William Jonathan
Orr, Jehu Amaziah
Osgood, Samuel
Parker, James
Pendleton, John Strother
Pitney, Mahlon
Pruyn, Robert Hewson
Purviance, David
Raines, John
Raney, George Pettus
Ridgely, Nicholas
Robinson, Henry Cornelius
Rodman, Isaac Peace
Rollins, Edward Henry
Sanford, Nathan
Sedgwick, Theodore, 1746–1813
Seevers, William Henry
Silver, Gray
Spalding, Thomas
Stephens, Linton
Strong, Moses McCure
Stuart, Archibald
Van Wyck, Charles Henry
White, James
Wingate, Paine
Wofford, William Tatum

Lettering Artist
Goudy, Frederic William

Lexicographer (See also Philologist)
Allibone, Samuel Austin
Foster, Frank Pierce
Funk, Wilfred John
Goodrich, Chauncey Allen
Jastrow, Marcus

Kohut, Alexander
McFarland, George Bradley
March, Francis Andrew
Sheldon, Edward Stevens
Thomas, Joseph
Vizetelly, Frank Horace
Webster, Noah
Wheeler, William Adolphus
Worcester, Joseph Emerson

LIBRARIAN
Adams, Randolph Greenfield
Allibone, Samuel Austin
Anderson, Edwin Hatfield
Beals, Ralph Albert
Beer, William
Billings, John Shaw
Binkley, Robert Cedric
Bjerregaard, Carl Henrik Andreas
Bostwick, Arthur Elmore
Boyd, Julian Parks
Brett, William Howard
Burr, George Lincoln
Canfield, James Hulme
Chadwick, James Read
Cheney, John Vance
Cobb, William Henry
Cogswell, Joseph Green
Cole, George Watson
Crunden, Frederick Morgan
Cutter, Charles Ammi
Dana, John Cotton
Davis, Raymond Cazallis
Dewey, Melvil
Draper, Lyman Copeland
Durrie, Daniel Steele
Eames, Wilberforce
Eastman, William Reed
Edmonds, John
Evans, Charles
Fairchild, Mary Salome Cutler
Farrand, Max
Fiske, Daniel Willard
Flexner, Jennie Maas
Flint, Weston
Folsom, Charles
Foss, Sam Walter
Galbreath, Charles Burleigh
Green, Samuel Abbott
Green, Samuel Swett
Greene, Belle Da Costa
Griffin, Appleton Prentiss Clark
Guild, Reuben Aldridge
Hamlin, Talbot Faulkner
Hanson, James Christian Meinich
Harris, Thaddeus William
Herrick, Edward Claudius
Holden, Edward Singleton
Homes, Henry Augustus
Hosmer, James Kendall
Isom, Mary Frances
Jackson, William Alexander
Jewett, Charles Coffin
Jordan, John Woolf
Klingelsmith, Margaret Center
Lamoureux, Andrew Jackson
Larned, Josephus Nelson
Legler, Henry Eduard
Lydenberg, Harry Miller
Martel, Charles
Moore, Anne Carroll
Moore, George Henry
Moore, Nathaniel Fish
Nelson, Charles Alexander
Parvin, Theodore Sutton
Pearson, Edmund Lester
Peckham, George Williams
Perkins, Frederic Beecher
Plummer, Mary Wright
Poole, Fitch
Poole, William Frederick
Putnam, (George) Herbert
Robertson, James Alexander
Rosenthal, Herman
Saunders, Frederick
Schwab, John Christopher
Sharp, Katharine Lucinda
Shaw, William Smith
Sibley, John Langdon
Skinner, Charles Rufus
Smith, John T.
Smith, Lloyd Pearsall
Sonneck, Oscar George Theodore
Spofford, Ainsworth Rand
Steiner, Bernard Christian
Steiner, Lewis Henry
Street, Alfred Billings
Tauber, Maurice Falcolm
Thwaites, Reuben Gold
Uhler, Philip Reese
Utley, George Burwell
Vail, Robert William Glenroie
Van Dyke, John Charles
Van Name, Addison
Vinton, Frederic
Ward, James Warner
Watterston, George
Whitney, James Lyman
Williams, John Fletcher
Winship, George Parker
Winsor, Justin
Winthrop, James
Wood, Mary Elizabeth

LIBRARY PROMOTER
Bowker, Richard Rogers

LIBRETTIST (See also LYRICIST)
Auden, Wystan Hugh
Da Ponte, Lorenzo
Fields, Dorothy
Hammerstein, Oscar, II
Smith, Harry Bache

LIEUTENANT GOVERNOR
Bull, William (S.C.)
Bullitt, Alexander Scott (Ky.)
Carlisle, John Griffin (Ky.)
Colden, Cadwallader (N.Y.)
De Lancey, James (N.Y.)
Eastman, Enoch Worthen (Iowa)
Gray, William (Mass.)
Gue, Benjamin F. (Iowa)
Hamilton, James, 1710–1783 (Pa.)
Hoffmann, Francis Arnold (Ill.)
Leisler, Jacob (N.Y.)
McKinstry, Alexander (Ala.)
Moultrie, John (East Fla.)
Oliver, Andrew (Mass.)
Penn, John (Pa.)
Penn, Richard (Pa.)
Phillips, William (Mass.)
Spotswood, Alexander (Va.)
Van Cortlandt, Pierre (N.Y.)
Woodruff, Timothy Lester (N.Y.)

LIGHTHOUSE BUILDER
Lewis, Winslow

LIMNOLOGIST (See also BIOLOGIST, HYDROGRAPHER, HYDROLOGIST)
Birge, Edward Asahel
Juday, Chancey

LINGUIST (See also INTERPRETER)
André, Louis
Avery, John
Bloomfield, Leonard
Bouvet, Marie Marguerite
Burritt, Elihu
Curtin, Jeremiah
Gatschet, Albert Samuel
Greenhow, Robert
McFarland, George Bradley
Pei, Mario Andrew
Radin, Paul
Riggs, Elias
Robeson, Paul Leroy
Sapir, Edward
Speiser, Ephraim Avigdor
Verwyst, Chrysostom Adrian
Whitney, William Dwight
Whorf, Benjamin Lee

LITERARY CRITIC (See also CRITIC, SCHOLAR)
Arvin, Newton
Blackmur, Richard Palmer
Burton, Richard Eugene
Canby, Henry Seidel
Cuppy, William Jacob ("Will")
Geismar, Maxwell David
Goldman, Emma
Hackett, Francis
Hazeltine, Mayo Williamson
Jackson, Joseph Henry
Kirkus, Virginia
Lewisohn, Ludwig
Lowes, John Livingston
Macy, John Albert
Matthiessen, Francis Otto
More, Paul Elmer
Payne, William Morton
Peck, Harry Thurston
Phelps, William Lyon
Pollard, Joseph Percival
Ransom, John Crowe
Ripley, George
Rosenfeld, Paul Leopold
Sherman, Stuart Pratt
Spingarn, Joel Elias
Tate, John Orley Allen
Van Doren, Carl Clinton
Van Doren, Mark Albert
Wallace, Horace Binney
Wilson, Edmund, Jr.
Wimsatt, William Kurtz

LITERARY HISTORIAN (See also HISTORIAN)
Brooks, Van Wyck
Lancaster, Henry Carrington

LITHOGRAPHER (See also ARTIST, ENGRAVER, ENGRAVER OF WOOD, ETCHER)
Alexander, Francis
Bellows, George Wesley
Bien, Julius

Haskell, Ernest
Hoen, August
Imbert, Antoine
Ives, James Merritt
Johnston, David Claypoole
Newsam, Albert
Otis, Bass
Pendleton, John B.
Prang, Louis
Rosenthal, Max
Rowse, Samuel Worcester
LITHOTOMIST (See also PHYSICIAN)
Spencer, Pitman Clemens
LITTERATEUR (See also AUTHOR, WRITER)
Biddle, Nicholas
Eliot, Samuel Atkins
Evans, Edward Payson
Hassard, John Rose Greene
Hillard, George Stillman
Lowell, James Russell
Matthews, James Brander
Norton, Andrews
Page, Thomas Nelson
Palmer, George Herbert
Peabody, Oliver William Bourn
Rae, John
Rattermann, Heinrich Armin
Reed, Henry Hope
Ricord, Frederick William
Simms, William Gilmore
Taylor, Bayard
Walsh, Robert
Wendell, Barrett
White, Richard Grant
LOBBYIST (See also POLITICIAN)
Tanner, James
Ward, Samuel, 1814–1884
LOCK EXPERT (See MANUFACTURER)
LOCOMOTIVE BUILDER (see MANUFACTURER)
LOGICIAN (See also MATHEMATICIAN, PHILOSOPHER, SCHOLAR)
Gödel, Kurt Friedrich
Ladd-Franklin, Christine
Peirce, Charles Sanders
Reichenbach, Hans
LOYALIST (See also PATRIOT)
Allen, Andrew
Atherton, Joshua
Auchmuty, Robert
Auchmuty, Samuel
Bailey, Jacob
Barclay, Thomas
Bates, Walter
Boucher, Jonathan
Browne, William
Butler, John
Butler, Walter N.
Chandler, Thomas Bradbury
Chipman, Ward
Clarke, Richard
Coffin, John
Colden, Cadwallader
Connolly, John
Coombe, Thomas
Cooper, Myles
Curwen, Samuel
De Lancy, James
Duché, Jacob
Eddis, William
Fanning, David
Fanning, Edmund
Fitch, Samuel
Fleming, John
Galloway, Joseph
Graham, John
Green, Francis
Hewat, Alexander
Inglis, Charles
Johnson, Guy
Johnson, Sir John
Jones, Thomas
Leonard, Daniel
Leonard, George
Loring, Joshua, 1716–1781
Loring, Joshua, 1744–1789
Low, Isaac
Ludlow, Gabriel George
Morris, Roger
Moultrie, John
Munro, Henry
Odell, Jonathan
Ogden, David
Oliver, Peter
Peters, Samuel Andrew
Randolph, John, 1727 or 1728–1784
Robinson, Beverley
Ruggles, Timothy
Sewall, Jonathan
Smith, William, 1728–1793
Sower, Christopher, 1754–1799
Stansbury, Joseph
Wentworth, John, 1737 N.S.–1820
White, Henry
Williams, Israel
Wragg, William
LUMBERMAN (See also MANUFACTURER)
Ayer, Edward Everett
Bell, Frederic Somers
Blodgett, John Wood
Donovan, John Joseph
Edgar, Charles
Fleming, Arthur Henry
Fordney, Joseph Warren
Griggs, Everett Gallup
Hackley, Charles Henry
Herdic, Peter
Jones, Jesse Holman
Sawyer, Philetus
Stephenson, Isaac
Sullivan, William Henry
Walker, Thomas Barlow
Weyerhaeuser, Frederick Edward
LYRICIST (See also BALLADIST, COMPOSOR, SONGWRITER)
Adams, Frank Ramsay
Cohan, George Michael
De Sylva, George Gard ("Buddy")
Fields, Dorothy
Freed, Athur
Hammerstein, Oscar, II
Hart, Lorenz Milton
Kahn, Gustav Gerson
Loesser, Frank
Mercer, John Herndon ("Johnny")
Porter, Cole
Razaf, Andy
Sissle, Noble Lee
White, George
White, Joseph Malachy

MACHINE DESIGNER
De Leeuw, Adolph Lodewyk
Norton, Charles Hotchkiss
MADAM
Adler, Polly
Everleigh, Ada
Everleigh, Minna
MAGAZINE PUBLISHER (See also PUBLISHER)
Armstrong, Hamilton Fish
Davis, Bernard George
Lane, Gertrude Battles
Nast, Condé Montrose
Phillips, John Sanburn
Sedgwick, Ellery
Smart, David Archibald
MAGICIAN
Blackstone, Harry
Goldin, Horace
Herrmann, Alexander
Houdini, Harry
Leipzig, Nate
Thurston, Howard
MAGISTRATE (See also JUDGE)
Boise, Reuben Patrick
Bridges, Robert
Browne, John
Dummer, Jeremiah
Forbes, John
Freeman, Nathaniel
Gookin, Daniel
Ludlow, Roger
Mason, John
Masterson, William Barclay
Pynchon, William
Sewall, Samuel
Stilwell, Simpson Everett
Stoughton, William
Tilghman, William Matthew
Underhill, John
Woodbridge, John
MAGNETICIAN (See also PHYSICIST)
Schott, Charles Anthony
MAIL RUNNER (See also TRANSPORTER)
Grimes, Absalom Carlisle
MALACOLOGIST (See also ZOOLOGIST)
Lea, Isaac
MAMMALOGIST (See also ZOOLOGIST)
Miller, Gerrit Smith, Jr.
Tate, George Henry Hamilton
MANAGEMENT CONSULTANT
Gilbreth, Lillian Evelyn Moller
MANHATTAN PROJECT DIRECTOR
Groves, Leslie Richard, Jr.
MAN OF AFFAIRS
Barker, James Nelson
Neal, John
Noailles, Louis Marie, Viscomte de
Peck, John James
MANUFACTURER (GENERAL)
Acker, Charles Ernest
Allen, Anthony Benezet
Allen, Philip

Allen, Richard Lamb
Allis, Edward Phelps
Ames, James Tyler
Ames, Nathan Peabody
Ames, Oakes
Ames, Oliver, 1779–1863
Ames, Oliver, 1807–1877
Anderson, Joseph Reid
Andrews, Chauncey Hummason
Appleton, Nathan
Atwood, Lewis John
Babbitt, Benjamin Talbot
Bachelder, John
Baldwin, Matthias William
Ball, Ephraim
Barber, Ohio Columbus
Batchelder, Samuel
Bent, Josiah
Bettendorf, William Peter
Billings, Charles Ethan
Blake, Eli Whitney
Bliss, Eliphalet Williams
Boott, Kirk
Borden, Richard
Boyden, Seth
Bradley, Milton
Bridgers, Robert Rufus
Brooker, Charles Frederick
Brown, Alexander Ephraim
Brown, Fayette
Brown, James Salisbury
Brown, Joseph
Brown, Joseph Rogers
Brown, Moses
Bullock, William A.
Burrowes, Edward Thomas
Burson, William Worth
Campbell, Andrew
Candler, Asa Griggs
Carnegie, Andrew
Case, Jerome Increase
Cheney, Person Colby
Coates, George Henry
Cochran, Alexander Smith
Coker, James Lide
Colburn, Irving Wightman
Colt, Samuel
Combs, Moses Newell
Conant, Hezekiah
Cone, Moses Herman
Cooper, Edward
Cooper, Peter
Corliss, George Henry
Cottrell, Calvert Byron
Crane, Winthrop Murray
Crocker, Alvah
Crompton, George
Crompton, William
Crozer, John Price
Cuppler, Samuel
Danforth, Charles
Davis, Horace
Deere, John
Deering, William
Dennison, Henry Sturgis
De Pauw, Washington Charles
De Wolf, James
Disston, Henry
Dixon, Joseph
Douglas, Benjamin
Downer, Samuel
Draper, Eben Sumner
Draper, Ira
Draper, William Franklin
Du Pont, Eleuthère Irénée
Du Pont, Henry
Du Pont, Victor Marie
Durfee, Zoheth Sherman
Dwight, Edmund
Dwight, William
Eickemeyer, Rudolf
Emerson, Ralph
Ensley, George
Esterbrook, Richard
Esterby, George
Ewbank, Thomas
Fairbanks, Henry
Fitler, Edwin Henry
Flagler, John Haldane
Fleischmann, Charles Louis
Ford, John Baptiste
Francis, Joseph
Fries, Francis
Fuller, Levi Knight
Gammon, Elijah Hedding
Gary, James Albert
Good, John
Goodall, Thomas
Griffin, Eugene
Grinnell, Joseph
Griswold, John Augustus
Grover, La Fayette
Haish, Jacob
Hall, Charles Martin
Hall, Thomas Seavey
Hamlin, Emmons
Hammond, James Bartlett
Hammond, Laurens
Harvey, Hayward Augustus
Hayden, Joseph Shepard
Hayward, Nathaniel Manley
Hazard, Augustus George
Hazard, Rowland Gibson
Hazard, Thomas Robinson
Heywood, Levi
Hoadley, John Chipman
Hobbs, Alfred Charles
Hoe, Richard March
Hoe, Robert, 1784–1833
Hoe, Robert, 1839–1909
Hogg, George
Hoover, Herbert William
Hotchkiss, Benjamin Berkeley
House, Henry Alonzo
Howe, John Ireland
Hubbard, Henry Griswold
Hughes, Howard Robard
Hunt, Charles Wallace
Hussey, Curtis Grubb
Ingersoll, Robert Hawley
Ingham, Samuel Delucenna
Jeffrey, Joseph Andrew
Jenkins, Nathaniel
Jewell, Marshall
Johnston, Samuel
Kemble, Gouverneur
Kingsford, Thomas
Knowles, Lucius James
Latta, Alexander Bonner
Lawrence, Abbott
Leffel, James
Leymer, John George
Lindsey, William
Lippitt, Henry
Lloyd, Marshall Burns
Loeb, Milton B.
Lyall, James
McArthur, John, 1826–1906
McCormick, Cyrus Hall
McCormick, Leander James
McCormick, Stephen
Mapes, Charles Victor
Marks, Amasa Abraham
Marsh, Charles Wesley
Marsh, William Wallace
Marshall, Benjamin
Mason, William
Mast, Phineas Price
Masury, John Wesley
Matthews, John
Matthiessen, Frederick William
Merrick, Samuel Vaughan
Miller, Lewis
Munger, Robert Sylvester
Murphy, Franklin
Nelson, Nelson Olsen
Nesmith, John
Newberry, John Stoughton
Newton, Henry Jotham
Nicholson, William Thomas
Niedringhaus, Frederick Gottlieb
Noyes, La Verne
O'Hara, James
Oliver, James
Oliver, Paul Ambrose
Otis, Charles Rollin
Otis, Elisha Graves
Packard, James Ward
Paine, Charles
Paine, Elijah
Palmer, Joseph
Parrott, Robert Parker
Phipps, Henry
Pingree, Hazen Stuart
Pitcairn, John
Pitkin, William, 1725–1789
Post, George Adams
Pratt, Zadock
Rand, Edward Sprague
Redfield, William Cox
Reese, Abram
Remington, Eliphalet
Remington, Philo
Rice, Alexander Hamilton
Richardson, Edmund
Roebling, John Augustus
Rowland, Thomas Fitch
Schieren, Charles Adolph
Schneller, George Otto
Scullin, John
Seed, Miles Ainscough
Seiberling, Frank Augustus
Simpson, Michael Hodge
Slater, John Fox
Slocum, Samuel
Smith, Horace
Smith, James Youngs
Spencer, Christopher Miner
Sproul, William Cameron
Stanley, Francis Edgar
Starrett, Laroy S.
Stearns, Frank Ballou
Sturtevant, Benjamin Franklin
Sweet, John Edson
Thomson, John

Thurber, Charles
Timken, Henry
Tompkins, Daniel Augustus
Towne, Henry Robinson
Tucker, Stephen Davis
Vought, Chance Milton
Wallace, William
Waller, Frederic
Waln, Robert, 1765–1836
Warner, Worcester Reed
Warren, Cyrus Moors
Washburn, Charles Grenfill
Washburn, Ichabod
Washburn, Nathan
Waterman, Lewis Edson
Weeden, William Babcock
Weightman, William
Wesson, Daniel Baird
Westinghouse, George
Wetherill, Samuel
Wharton, Joseph
Wheeler, Nathaniel
White, Samuel Stockton
Whitney, Asa
Wilkinson, David
Williams, David Rogerson
Wilson, George Francis
Winchester, Oliver Fisher
Winslow, Sidney Wilmot
Woodruff, Theodore Tuttle
Wright, John Stephen
Wright, William
Yale, Linus
Ziegler, William
MANUFACTURER (SPECIFIC)
Adding Machines
Burroughs, William Seward
Agricultural Equipment
Legge, Alexander
Agricultural Machinery
Wood, Walter Abbott
Aircraft
Martin, Glenn Luther ("Cy")
Airplanes
Bellanca, Giuseppe Mario
Burgess, W(illiam) Starling
Lockheed, Allan Haines
Lockheed, Malcolm
Piper, William Thomas
Automobiles
Chapin, Roy Dikeman
Chrysler, Walter Percy
Couzens, James
Durant, William Crapo
Duryea, Charles Edgar
Duryea, James Frank
Fisher, Frederic John
Ford, Edsel Bryant
Ford, Henry
Hupp, Louis Gorham
Knudsen, William S.
Nash, Charles Williams
Olds, Ransom Eli
Pope, Albert Augustus
Stutz, Harry Clayton
Wills, Childe Harold
Winton, Alexander
Automobile Bodies
Fisher, Alfred J.
Fisher, Charles T.
Baby Food
Gerber, (Daniel) Frank
Gerber, Daniel (Frank)
Brass
Coe, Israel
Hayden, Hiram Washington
Holmes, Israel
Bricks
Reese, Isaac
Business Machines
Watson, Thomas John
Candy
Gunther, Charles Frederick
Cash Registers
Patterson, John Henry
Cereal
Kellogg, John Harvey
Kellogg, Will Keith
Chemicals
Dow, Herbert Henry
Mallinckrodt, Edward
Merck, George Wilhelm
Pfister, Alfred
Chewing Gum
Wrigley, William
Chocolate
Hershey, Milton Snavely
Cigarettes
Hill, George Washington
Cocoa
Pierce, Henry Lillie
Collars (Detachable)
Brown, Ebenezer
Conveying Equipment
Piez, Charles
Cosmetics
Arden, Elizabeth
Revson, Charles Haskell
Rubinstein, Helena
Cotton
Fry, Birkett Davenport
Gray, George Alexander
Gregg, William
Hammett, Henry Pinckney
Holt, Edwin Michael
Lowell, Francis Cabot
Oliver, Henry Kamble
Sprague, William, 1773–1836
Weaver, Philip
Cotton Machinery
Earle, Pliny
Drugs
Lloyd, John Uri
Electronics Kits
Tandy, Charles David
Explosives
Du Pont, Irénée
Everendon, Walter
Judson, Egbert Putnam
Farm Machinery
McCormick, Cyrus Hall
Firearms
Eastman, Arthur MacArthur
North, Simeon, 1765–1852
Wisner, Henry
Flashbulbs
Mendelsohn, Samuel
Flour
Bell, James Stroud
Pillsbury, Charles Alfred
Pillsbury, John Sargent
Washburn, William Drew
Food (Prepared)
Heinz, Henry John
Horlick, William
Post, Charles William
Forging Machinery and Tools
Purtell, William Arthur
Games
Parker, Edward Pickering
Gelatin
Knox, Rose Markward
Glass
Biggers, John David
Dyott, Thomas W.
Houghton, Alanson Bigelow
Lyon, James Benjamin
Owens, Michael Joseph
Wistar, Caspar
Glass Jars
Ball, George Alexander
Gloves
Edwards, Talmage
Littauer, Lucius Nathan
Grindstones
Baldwin, John
Gunpowder
Du Pont, Alfred Irénée
Hats
Genin, John Nicholas
Stetson, John Batterson
Iron
Abbott, Horace
Alger, Cyrus
Benner, Philip
Berkeley, John
Bridges, Robert
Burden, Henry
Faesch, John Jacob
Fritz, John
Greenwood, Miles
Harrison, James
Hasenclever, Peter
Hewitt, Abram Stevens
Hill, William
Huston, Charles
Jenckes, Joseph
Lukens, Rebecca Webb Pennock
Meason, Isaac
Noble, Samuel
Oliver, Henry William
Porter, David Rittenhouse
Poulson, Niels
Read, Charles
Read, Nathan
Scranton, George Whitfield
Stiegel, Henry William
Taylor, George
Thomas, David
Torrence, Joseph Thatcher
Lighting Equipment
Thomson, Elihu
Locks
Hobbs, Alfred Charles
Locomotives
Baird, Matthew
Converse, John Heman
Norris, William
Parry, Charles Thomas
Rogers, Thomas
Vauclain, Samuel Matthews
Lumber (See also Lumberman)
Sage, Henry Williams
Washburn, William Drew
Machinery
Chalmers, William James

Marine Engines
Quintard, George William
Meat Packing
Cudahy, Edward Aloysius, Jr.
Hormel, George Albert
Nautical Instruments
King, Samuel
Newspaper Printing Machinery
Wood, Henry Alexander Wise
Oil Well Equipment
Jones, Samuel Milton
Organs
Audsley, George Ashdown
Estey, Jacob
Goodrich, William Marcellus
Hesselius, Gustavus
Roosevelt, Hilborne Lewis
Tanneberger, David
Paint
Callahan, Patrick Henry
Paper
Chisholm, Hugh Joseph
Fry, Richard
Miller, Warner
Pittock, Henry Lewis
Rittenhouse, William
West, George
Patent Medicine
Ayer, James Cook
Pinkham, Lydia Estes
Pencils
Faber, John Eberhard
Pharmaceuticals
Kiss, Max
Lilly, Josiah Kirby
Photographic Equipment
Eastman, George
Pianos
Bradbury, William Batchelder
Chickering, Jonas
Knabe, Valentine Wilhelm Ludwig
Mason, Henry
Steck, George
Steinway, Christian Friedrich Theodore
Steinway, Henry Engelhard
Steinway, William
Tremaine, Henry Barnes
Weber, Albert
Plumbing Fixtures
Kohler, Walter Jodok
Precision Instruments
Swasey, Ambrose
Prefabricated Housing
Gunnison, Foster
Radios
Crosley, Powel, Jr.
Kent, Arthur Atwater
Railroad Equipment
French, Aaron
Wagner, Webster
Razors/Razor Blades
Gillette, King Camp
Recording Instruments
Bristol, William Henry
Rubber
Candee, Leverett
Day, Horace H.
Firestone, Harvey Samuel
Litchfield Paul Weeks
Saddles and Harnesses
Redfield, William C.
Safes
Herring, Silas Clark
Scientific Instruments
Zentmayer, Joseph
Screws
Angell, William Gorham
Shoes
Douglas, William Lewis
Johnson, George Francis
McElwain, William Howe
Silk
Cheney, Ward
Cobb, Jonathan Holmes
Skinner, William
Soap
Colgate, William
Fels, Joseph
Fels, Samuel Simeon
Proctor, William Cooper
Soft Drinks
Hires, Charles Elmer
Sound Reproduction Equipment
Jensen, Peter Laurits
Sporting Goods
Reach, Alfred James
Spalding, Albert Goodwill
Starch
Perry, William
Steam Engines
Thurston, Robert Lawton
Steel
Carnegie, Andrew
Corey, William Ellis
Fairless, Benjamin F.
Frick, Henry Clay
Leishman, John G. A.
Metcalf, William
Moxham, Arthur James
Oliver, George Tener
Park, James
Verity, George Matthew
Weir, Ernest Tener
Sugar
Spreckels, Claus
Spreckels, Rudolph
Tabulating Machines
Hollerith, Herman
Telescopes
Fitz, Henry
Holcomb, Amasa
Lundin, Carl Axel Robert
Rittenhouse, David
Warner, Worcester Reed
Television Receivers
Dumont, Allen Balcom
Thermometers
Tagliabue, Giuseppe
Tobacco
Reynolds, William Neal
Tools
Billings, Charles Ethan
Howe, Frederick Webster
Lawrence, Richard Smith
Pratt, Francis Ashbury
Rand, Addison Crittenden
Sellers, William
Toys
Gilbert, Alfred Carlton
Toy Trains
Cowen, Joshua Lionel
Typewriters
Underwood, John Thomas
Violins
Gemdünder, August Martin Ludwig
Wagons
Studebaker, Clement
Washing Machines
Maytag, Frederick Louis
Watches
Dennison, Aaron Lufkin
Harland, Thomas

MAPMAKER (See also CARTOGRAPHER)
Bien, Julius
Bonner, John
Greenleaf, Moses
Hoen, August
Holme, Thomas
Mitchell, John, d. 1768
Osborn, Henry Stafford
Wood, John

MARINE ALGAE AUTHORITY (See also ZOOLOGIST)
Setchell, William Albert

MARINE BIOLOGIST (See also BIOLOGIST, ZOOLOGIST)
Carson, Rachel Louise

MARINE CORPS OFFICER
Butler, Smedley Darlington
Geiger, Roy Stanley
Lejeune, John Archer
McCawley, Charles Laurie
Puller, Lewis Burwell ("Chesty")
Smith, Holland McTyeire
Vandegrift, Alexander Archer

MARINER (See also NAVIGATOR, SEA CAPTAIN, STEAMBOAT OPERATOR)
Bickel, Luke Washington
Bonner, John
Clapp, Asa
Clark, Arthur Hamilton
Coxetter, Louis Mitchell
Douglas, William
Feke, Robert
Freneau, Philip Morin
Levy, Uriah Phillips
Lewis, Winslow
Newport, Christopher
O'Brien, Richard
Peabody, Joseph
Peirce, William
Samuels, Samuel
Slocum, Joshua
Thorndike, Israel

MARKETING EXPERT
Cort, Stewart Shaw

MARKETING RESEARCH ENGINEER
Nielsen, Arthur Charles

MARKSWOMAN
Oakley, Annie

MARTIAL ARTS EXPERT
Lee, Bruce

MARXIST THEORIST
Corey, Lewis

MATHEMATICIAN
Adrain, Robert
Bartlett, William Holmes Chambers
Bateman, Harry

Bayma, Joseph
Becker, George Ferdinand
Bell, Eric Temple
Birkhoff, George David
Blichfeldt, Hans Frederik
Bliss, Gilbert Ames
Bôcher, Maxime
Bolza, Oskar
Bowditch, Nathaniel
Brown, Ernest William
Byerly, William Elwood
Cain, William
Caldwell, Joseph
Chauvenet, William
Coffin, James Henry
Colburn, Zerah
Cole, Frank Nelson
Coolidge, Julian Lowell
Courant, Richard
Craig, Thomas
De Forest, Erastus Lyman
Dickson, Leonard Eugene
Eddy, Henry Turner
Eisenhart, Luther Pfahler
Ellicott, Andrew
Farrar, John
Fine, Henry Burchard
Frank, Philipp G.
Franklin, Fabian
Gibbs, Josiah Willard
Gödel, Kurt Friedrich
Godfrey, Thomas
Green, Gabriel Marcus
Greenwood, Isaac
Grew, Theophilus
Gummere, John
Halsted, George Bruce
Hardy, Arthur Sherburne
Harris, Rollin Arthur
Hassler, Ferdinand Rudolph
Hill, George William
Hull, Clark Leonard
Huntington, Edward Vermilye
Jackson, Dunham
Johnson, William Woolsey
Jones, Hugh
Kármán, Theodore (Todor) Von
Leavitt, Dudley
Leeds, John
Lewis, Enoch
Loomis, Elias
McCartney, Washington
McCay, Charles Francis
McClintock, Emory
Martin, Artemas
Maschke, Heinrich
Mason, Max
Miller, George Abram
Minto, Walter
Moore, Clarence Lemuel Elisha
Moore, Eliakim Hastings
Morley, Frank
Moulton, Forest Ray
Newton, Hubert Anson
Nicollet, Joseph Nicolas
Osgood, William Fogg
Patterson, Robert
Peirce, Benjamin
Peirce, Benjamin Osgood
Peirce, James Mills
Pike, Nicolas
Rademacher, Hans
Rittenhouse, David
Rogers, William Augustus
Runkle, John Daniel
Safford, Truman Henry
Sestini, Benedict
Sherman, Frank Dempster
Sherman, John, 1613–1685
Soulé, George
Steinmetz, Charles Proteus
Story, William Edward
Stringham, Washington Irving
Strong, Theodore
Sylvester, James Joseph
Tamarkin, Jacob David
Thompson, Zadock
Van Vleck, Edward Burr
Vaughan, Daniel
Veblen, Oswald
Venable, Charles Scott
Von Neumann, John
Walker, Sears Cook
Weaver, Warren
Weyl, Hermann
Wiener, Norbert
Wilczynski, Ernest Julius
Winlock, Joseph
Winthrop, John
Young, John Wesley

MAYOR
Baker, Newton Diehl (Cleveland)
Blankenburg, Rudolph (Philadelphia)
Cermak, Anton Joseph (Chicago)
Cobo, Albert Eugene (Detroit)
Colden, Cadwallader David (New York)
Couzens, James (Detroit)
Cruger, John (New York)
Crump, Edward Hull (Memphis)
Curtis, Edwin Upton (Boston)
Daley, Richard Joseph (Chicago)
Dilworth, Richardson (Philadelphia)
Fagan, Mark Matthew (Jersey City)
Gaynor, William Jay (New York)
Harrison, Carter Henry (Chicago)
Harrison, Carter Henry, Jr. (Chicago)
Hartsfield, William Berry (Atlanta)
Havemeyer, William Frederick (New York)
Hoffman, John Thompson (New York)
Hylan, John Francis (New York)
Johnson, Tom Loftin (Cleveland)
Kelly, Edward Joseph (Chicago)
La Guardia, Fiorello Henry (New York)
Lawrence, David Leo (Pittsburgh)
Lunn, George Richard (Schenectady)
Lyman, Theodore, 1792–1849 (Boston)
McKeldin, Theodore Roosevelt (Baltimore)
McMichael, Morton (Philadelphia)
Maverick, (Fontaine) Maury (San Antonio)
Mitchel, John Purroy (New York)
Moscone, George Richard (San Francisco)
Murphy, Frank (Detroit)
Norris, Isaac, 1671–1735 (Philadelphia)
O'Dwyer, William (New York)
Phelan, James Duval (San Francisco)
Pierce, Henry Lillie (Boston)
Pinckney, Henry Laurens (Charleston)
Pingree, Hazen Stuart (Detroit)
Radcliff, Jacob (New York)
Seidel, George Lukas Emil (Milwaukee)
Shippen, Edward, 1639–1712 (Philadelphia)
Shurtleff, Nathaniel Bradstreet (Boston)
Strong, William Lafayette (New York)
Swann, Thomas (Baltimore)
Thompson, William Hale (Chicago)
Tobin, Maurice Joseph (Boston)
Walker, James John (New York)
Wentworth, John, 1815–1888 (Chicago)
Westervelt, Jacob Aaron (New York)
Wharton, Robert (Philadelphia)
Whitlock, Brand (Toledo)
Wood, Fernando (New York)

MEAT PACKER (See also INDUSTRIALIST, MANUFACTURER)
Armour, Philip Danforth
Cudahy, Michael
Dold, Jacob
Eastman, Timothy Corser
Hammond, George Henry
Hormel, Jay Catherwood
Hubbard, Gurdon Saltonstall
Hutchinson, Benjamin Peters
Mayer, Oscar Gottfried
Morris, Nelson
Swift, Gustavus Franklin
Swift, Louis Franklin
Wilson, Samuel

MECHANIC
Allaire, James Peter
Ames, James Tyler
Borden, Simeon
Cox, Lemuel
Emerson, James Ezekiel
Knight, Edward Henry
Kruesi, John
Peale, Titian Ramsay
Root, Elisha King
Winans, Ross

MEDALIST (See also CRAFTSMAN, GOLDSMITH, JEWELER, SILVERSMITH)
Brenner, Victor David

MEDIATOR
Graham, Frank Porter
MEDICAL ADMINISTRATOR
Weed, Lewis Hill
MEDICAL CHARLATAN
Brinkley, John Richard
MEDICAL EDUCATOR (See also EDUCATOR)
Cabot, Hugh
Edsall, David Linn
Teuber, Hans-Lukas ("Luke")
Vaughan, Victor Clarence
Wiener, Alexander Solomon
Wilson, Louis Blanchard
MEDICAL HISTORIAN (See also HISTORIAN, PHYSICIAN)
Alden, Ebenezer
Buck, Albert Henry
Handerson, Henry Ebenezer
Sigerist, Henry Ernest
Williams, Stephen West
MEDICAL ILLUSTRATOR (See also ILLUSTRATOR)
Brödel, Max
MEDICAL INSTRUMENT MAKER
Schwidetzky, Oscar Otto Rudolf
MEDICAL REFORMER
Cabot, Hugh
MEDICAL RESEARCH WORKER (See also PHYSICIAN)
Agramonte y Simoni, Aristides
Ashford, Bailey Kelly
Goldberger, Joseph
Rous, Francis Peyton
Sawyer, Wilbur Augustus
Trask, James Dowling
Weil, Richard
MEDICAL SCIENTIST (See also BACTERIOLOCIST, PATHOLOGIST)
MacLeod, Colin Munro
Smith, Theobald
MEDICAL STATISTICIAN (See also STATISTICIAN)
Dorn, Harold Fred
MEDIEVALIST (See also HISTORIAN)
Beeson, Charles Henry
Rand, Edward Kennard
Stephenson, Carl
Tatlock, John Strong Perry
Thorndike, Lynn
Young, Karl
MEDIUM (See SPIRITUALIST)
MENTAL HYGIENIST (See also PHYSICIAN)
Burnham, William Henry
Salmon, Thomas William
MERCANTILE AGENT (See also MERCHANT)
Dun, Robert Graham
MERCENARY
Boyd, John Parker
Burgevine, Henry Andrea
MERCHANT (See also BUSINESSMAN, DEPARTMENT STORE EXECUTIVE, EXECUTIVE, FACTOR, MERCANTILE AGENT)
Abernethy, George
Allen, William
Altman, Benjamin
Amory, Thomas
Appleton, Samuel
Arbuckle, John
Archer, Samuel
Aspinwall, William Henry
Austin, Jonathan Loring
Austin, Moses
Bache, Richard
Bache, Theophylact
Bain, George Luke Scobie
Baker, Lorenzo Dow
Bamberger, Louis
Barker, Jacob
Barker, James William
Bartlet, William
Bayard, John Bubenheim
Bayard, William
Belcher, Jonathan
Bell, Isaac
Benner, Philip
Bertram, John
Biddle, Clement
Bliss, Cornelius Newton
Bliss, George
Blodget, Samuel
Blount, Thomas
Boorman, James
Borie, Adolph Edward
Bowdoin, James, 1726–1790
Bowdoin, James, 1752–1811
Bowen, Henry Chandler
Brattle, Thomas
Brewer, Charles
Bromfield, John
Brooks, Peter Chardon
Brown, John
Brown, Moses
Brown, Nicholas
Brown, Nicolas
Brown, Obadiah
Buchanan, Thomas
Byrd, William
Cabot, George
Calef, Robert
Capen, Samuel Billings
Carter, Henry Alpheus Peirce
Cerré, Jean Gabriel
Chalkley, Thomas
Chittenden, Simeon Baldwin
Chouteau, Pierre
Claflin, Horace Brigham
Claflin, John
Clapp, Asa
Clark, Daniel
Clarke, Richard
Clay, Joseph
Cleveland, Richard Jeffry
Coates, Samuel
Colby, Gardner
Coleman, William Tell
Colman, John
Cone, Moses Herman
Cook, Isaac
Coolidge, Thomas Jefferson
Cope, Thomas Pym
Coram, Thomas
Corbett, Henry Winslow
Corson, Robert Rodgers
Cozzens, Frederick Swartwout
Cresson, Elliott
Crocker, Charles
Crowninshield, Benjamin Williams
Crowninshield, George
Crowninshield, Jacob
Cruger, Henry
Cupples, Samuel
Cushing, John Perkins
Cushing, Thomas
Deane, Charles
Deas, Zachariah Cantey
De Forest, David Curtis
Delafield, John
De Peyster, Abraham
Derby, Elias Hasket, 1739–1799
Derby, Elias Hasket, 1766–1826
Derby, Richard
De Vries, David Pietersen
Dexter, Samuel
Dexter, Timothy
Dibrell, George Gibbs
Dodge, David Low
Dodge, William Earl
Duer, William
Duncan, Donald Franklin
Dunwoody, William Hood
Duryée, Abram
Dwight, Edmund
Eaton, Theophilus
Espejo, Antonio de
Faneuil, Peter
Fell, John
Field, Cyrus West
Field, Marshall
Filene, Edward Albert
Finlay, Hugh
Fish, Preserved
Forbes, John
Forbes, Robert Bennet
Foster, Charles
Fraley, Frederick
Francis, David Rowland
Gadsden, Christopher
Gaines, George Strother
Gardner, Caleb
Garrett, Robert
Genin, John Nicholas
Gillon, Alexander
Gimbel, Bernard Feustman
Girard, Stephen
Glenn, Hugh
Godfrey, Benjamin
Goodhue, Beniamin
Goodwin, Ichabod
Gorham, Jabez
Gould, Benjamin Apthorp
Grace, William Russell
Grant, William Thomas, Jr.
Gratz, Barnard
Gratz, Michael
Gray, William
Green, John Cleve
Green, Joseph
Grim, David
Grinnell, Henry
Grinnell, Joseph
Grinnell, Moses Hicks
Habersham, Alexander Wylly
Habersham, James
Hack, George
Hallowell, Richard Price
Hancock, John, 1736–1793
Hancock, Thomas
Hand, Daniel
Harris, Caleb Fiske
Harris, Townsend

Harrison, James
Haven, Henry Philemon
Hazard, Augustus George
Heard, Augustine
Heathcote, Caleb
Henchman, Daniel
Henderson, Peter
Herrman, Augustine
Hiester, Joseph
Higginson, Nathaniel
Higginson, Stephen
Higinbotham, Harlow Niles
Hill, Richard
Hillegas, Michael
Hogg, George
Hooper, Samuel
Hopkins, Johns
Howland, Gardiner Greene
Hubbard, Gurdon Saltonstall
Hull, John
Hunnewell, James
Hunter, William C.
Huntington, Jabez
Hutchinson, Charles Lawrence
Ingersoll, Robert Hawley
Inman, John Hamilton
Inman, Samuel Martin
Irving, William
James, Daniel Willis
Jarvis, William
Jones, George Wallace
Jordon, Eben Dyer
Juilliard, Augustus D.
Jumel, Stephen
Kemp, Robert H.
Kilby, Christopher
King, Charles
King, Charles William
Kirstein, Louis Edward
Kresge, Sebastian Spering
Kress, Samuel Henry
Ladd, William Sargent
Lamar, Gazaway Bugg
Lampson, Sir Curtis Miranda
Landreth, David
Langdon, John
Langdon, Woodbury
Larkin, Thomas Oliver
Laurens, Henry
Lawrence, Abbott
Lawrence, Amos
Lawrence, Amos Adams
Lawrence, William, 1783–1848
Leaming, Thomas
Lee, Henry, 1782–1867
Lee, William
Leiper, Thomas
Leiter, Levi Zeigler
Lewis, Francis
Lewis, William David
Livingston, Peter Van Brugh
Livingston, Philip
Lopez, Aaron
Lord, David Nevins
Lorillard, Pierre
Loudon, Samuel
Loveland, William Austin Hamilton
Low, Abiel Abbot
Low, Isaac
Low, Nicholas
Low, Seth
Ludlow, Daniel
Lumbrozo, Jacob
Macalester, Charles, 1765–1832
McClintock, Oliver
McDonogh, John
Mackenzie, Kenneth
McKim, Isaac
Macy, Josiah
Malcolm, Daniel
Manigault, Gabriel
Manigault, Pierre
Marshall, Benjamin
Marshall, James Fowle Baldwin
Mather, Samuel
May, Morton Jay
Mazzei, Philip
Meade, George
Meade, Richard Worsam
Melish, John
Menard, Pierre
Merry, William Lawrence
Mifflin, Thomas
Mills, Darius Ogden
Mills, Robert, 1809–1888
Minturn, Robert Bowne
Moore, William, 1735–1793
Mordecai, Moses Cohen
Morgan, Edwin Barber
Morgan, James Dada
Morris, Anthony, 1766–1860
Morris, Cadwalader
Morrison, William
Murray, John, 1737–1808
Murray, Robert
Nash, Arthur
Nelson, Thomas
Nelson, William, 1711–1772
Nesbitt, John Maxwell
Nesmith, John
Newberry, Oliver
Newberry, Walter Loomis
Nicola, Lewis
Nixon, John, 1733–1808
Norris, Isaac, 1671–1735
Norris, Isaac, 1701–1766
O'Brien, Edward Charles
Ochs, Julius
O'Fallon, John
Offley, David
Ogden, Robert Curtis
Olyphant, David Washington Cincinnatus
Olyphant, Robert Morrison
Opdyke, George
Orr, Alexander Ector
Orthwein, Charles F.
Outerbridge, Eugenius Harvey
Palmer, Potter
Partridge, Richard
Patten, James A.
Patterson, Morris
Patterson, William
Peabody, George
Peabody, Joseph
Peirce, Henry Augustus
Pemberton, Israel
Pemberton, James
Penhallow, Samuel
Penington, Edward
Pepperrell, Sir William
Perkins, Thomas Handasyd
Pettit, Charles
Phelan, James, 1824–1892
Phelps, Anson Greene
Phelps, Oliver
Phillips, William
Phinizy, Ferdinand
Pintard, John
Pintard, Lewis
Pinto, Isaac
Pratt, Charles
Pratte, Bernard
Price, Theodore Hazeltine
Purdue, John
Rand, Edward Sprague
Randall, Robert Richard
Randolph, William
Rawle, Francis, 1662–1726/27
Raymond, Benjamin Wright
Redwood, Abraham
Reed, Luman
Reed, Simeon Gannett
Reisinger, Hugo
Rhind, Charles
Rice, William Marsh
Rich, Isaac
Roberdeau, Daniel
Robert, Christopher Rhinelander
Roberts, Edmund
Robinson, Edward Mott
Rochester, Nathaniel
Roddey, Philip Dale
Ropes, Joseph
Rosenberg, Henry
Rosenwald, Julius
Rotch, William
Russell, Joseph
Sage, Henry Williams
St. Vrain, Ceran de Hault de Lassus de
Salomon, Haym
Sands, Comfort
Saunders, Clarence
Sayre, Stephen
Searle, James
Sears, Richard Warren
Seligman, Arthur
Servoss, Thomas Lowery
Sewall, Samuel
Shaw, Nathaniel
Shedd, John Graves
Sheedy, Dennis
Sheffield, Joseph Earl
Shelekhov, Grigorii Ivanovich
Silsbee, Nathaniel
Sleeper, Jacob
Smith, John, 1735–1824
Smith, Jonathan Bayard
Smith, Junius
Smith, Melancton, 1744–1798
Spalding, Albert Goodwill
Spreckels, John Diedrich
Stearns, Frank Waterman
Steenwyck, Cornelis
Stewart, Alexander Turney
Stokes, Anson Phelps
Straus, Isidor
Straus, Jesse Isidor
Strong, William Lafayette
Sturgis, William
Sublette, William Lewis
Sulzberger, Cyrus Lindauer
Swartwout, Samuel

Tappan, Lewis
Taylor, Joseph Wright
Telfair, Edward
Thatcher, Mahlon Daniel
Thompson, Jeremiah
Thorndike, Israel
Ticknor, Elisha
Tileston, Thomas
Tobey, Edward Silas
Tome, Jacob
Tracy, Nathaniel
Train, Enoch
Train, George Francis
Tulane, Paur
Tyndale, Hector
Upton, George Bruce
Van Cortlandt, Oloff Stevenszen
Van Cortlandt, Stephanus
Van Dam, Rip
Vassar, Matthew
Vaughan, Charles
Vernon, William
Vigo, Joseph Maria Francesco
Wagner, William
Wardo, Samuel
Waln, Robert, 1765–1836
Walters, William Thompson
Wanamaker, John
Wanamaker, Lewis Rodman
Ward, Aaron Montgomery
Ward, Samuel, 1756–1832
Ward, Thomas Wren
Watson, Elkanah
Weston, Thomas
Wharton, Richard
Wharton, Robert
Wharton, Samuel
Wharton, Thomas
White, Alexander
Whitney, Asa
Wilbur, Samuel
Wilder, Marshall Pinckney
Williams, Jonathan
Wolfe, John David
Wood, Robert Elkington
Woodruff, Timothy Lester
Woolworth, Frank Winfield

MESSENGER (See also TRANSPORTER)
Bailey, Ann

METAL DESIGNER
Yellin, Samuel

METALLOGRAPHER
Sauveur, Albert

METALLURGIST (See also CHEMIST, GEOLOGIST, MINERALOGIST)
Arents, Albert
Argall, Philip
Balback, Edward
Becket, Frederick Mark
Campbell, William
Church, John Adams
Daggett, Ellsworth
Daniels, Fred Harris
De Forest, Alfred Victor
Douglas, James
Eilers, Frederic Anton
Gayley, James
Gillett, Horace Wadsworth
Goetz, George Washington
Grant, James Benton
Hill, Nathaniel Peter
Hofman, Heinrich Oscar
Holley, Alexander Lyman
Howe, Henry Marion
Hunt, Alfred Ephraim
Hunt, Robert Woolston
Jackling, Daniel Cowan
Johnston, John
Mathews, John Alexander
Mathewson, Edward Payson
Matthiessen, Frederick William
Metcalf, William
Moldenke, Richard George Gottlob
Outerbridge, Alexander Ewing
Overman, Frederick
Pearce, Richard
Pearse, John Barnard Swett
Raht, August Wilhelm
Reese, Jacob
Richards, Joseph William
Sauveur, Albert
Spilsbury, Edmund Gybbon
Stanley, Robert Crooks
Stetefeldt, Carl August
Wahl, William Henry
Wills, Childe Harold

METAPHYSICIAN (See also PHILOSOPHER, RELIGIOUS LEADER)
Coomaraswamy, Ananda Kentish
Upham, Thomas Cogswell

METEOROLOGIST (See also CLIMATOLOGIST)
Abbe, Cleveland
Bentley, Wilson Alwyn
Bigelow, Frank Hagar
Coffin, James Henry
De Brahm, William Gerard
Engelmann, George
Espy, James Pollard
Ferrel, William
Gregg, Willis Ray
Harrington, Mark Walrod
Hayden, Edward Everett
Hazen, Henry Allen
Humphreys, Wiliam Jackson
Lippincott, James Starr
Lowe, Thaddeus Sobieski Coulincourt
McAdie, Alexander George
Marvin, Charles Frederick
Odenbach, Frederick Louis
Redfield, William C.
Rotch, Abbott Lawrence
Upton, Winslow

MICROBIOLOGIST
Gifford, Sanford Robinson
Henrici, Arthur Trautwein
Kelser, Raymond Alexander
Novy, Frederick George
Waksman, Selman Abraham

MICROPALEONTOLOGIST (See also PALEONTOLOGIST)
Cushman, Joseph Augustine

MICROSCOPIST (See also PHYSICIAN)
Ward, Richard Halsted

MIDGET
Stratton, Charles Sherwood

MILITARY ENGINEER (See ENGINEER, MILITARY)

MILITARY HISTORIAN
Marshall, Samuel Lyman Atwood ("Slam")

MILLER (see MANUFACTURER)

MILLWRIGHT (See also ENGINEER)
Brown, Sylvanus
Coney, Jabez
Dalzell, Robert M.
Lucas, Jonathan, 1754–1821
Lucas, Jonathan, 1775–1832

MINE OPERATOR (See also MINE OWNER, MINER)
Dern, George Henry
Harvey, William Hope
Mondell, Frank Wheeler
Penrose, Spencer

MINE OWNER (See also MINER)
Guggenheim, Solomon Robert
Heckscher, August
Scott, Walter Edward

MINER (See also INDUSTRIALIST, METALLURGIST, MINE OPERATOR, MINE OWNER, PROSPECTOR)
Agassiz, Alexander
Andrews, Chauncey Hummason
Austin, Moses
Bowen, Thomas Meade
Braden, Spruille
Cist, Jacob
Daly, Marcus
Fleming, Aretas Brooks
Godbe, William Samuel
Goold, William A.
Greene, William Cornell
Hauser, Samuel Thomas
Hearst, George
Henry, Andrew
Hussey, Curtis Grubb
Hutton, Levi William
Imboden, John Daniel
Jones, George Wallace
Mackay, John William
McKnight, Robert
Meeker, Moses
Newhouse, Samuel
Nicholson, Samuel Danford
O'Brien, William Shoney
Reed, John, 1757–1845
Ryan, John Dennis
Tabor, Horace Austin Warner
Thompson, William Boyce
Welch, Charles Clark

MINERALOGIST (See also GEOLOGIST)
Bruce, Archibald
Brush, George Jarvis
Dana, Edward Salisbury
Eggleston, Thomas
Koenig, George Augustus
Seybert, Henry
Shepard, Charles Upham
Smith, John Lawrence
Williams, George Huntington

MINIATURIST (See PAINTER)

MINING ENGINEER (See ENGINEER, [MINING])

MINING PROMOTER (See MINER)

MINSTREL (See also BALLADIST, FOLKLORIST, SINGER)
Christy, Edwin P.
Dockstader, Lew

Heath, Thomas Kurton
McIntyre, James
Rice, Thomas Dartmouth
MISSIONARY (See also CLERGYMAN, RELIGIOUS LEADER)
Abeel, David
Agnew, Eliza
Aremany, José Sadoc
Allen, David Oliver
Allen, Young John
Allonez, Claude Jean
Altham, John
Anderson, David Lawrence
André, Louis
Andrews, Lorrin
Apes, William
Appenzeller, Henry Gerhard
Ashmore, William
Bacon, David
Badger, Joseph
Badin, Stephen Theodore
Bailey, Jacob
Baldwin, Theron
Bapst, John
Baraga, Frederic
Barton, James Levi
Bashford, James Whitford
Bassett, James
Beach, Harlan Page
Belcourt, George Antoine
Benjamin, Nathan
Biard, Pierre
Bickel, Luke Washington
Bingham, Hiram, 1789–1869
Bingham, Hiram, 1831–1908
Blackburn, Gideon
Blanchet, François Norbert
Bliss, Daniel
Bliss, Edwin Elisha
Bliss, Edwin Munsell
Bliss, Howard Sweetser
Bowen, George
Brainerd, David
Brainerd, John
Bridgman, Elijah Coleman
Brondel, John Baptist
Brown, Samuel Robbins
Buck, Philo Melvin
Butler, John Wesley
Butler, William
Byington, Cyrus
Cammerhoff, John Christopher Frederick
Campanius, John
Cary, Lott
Cataldo, Joseph Maria
Chamberlain, Jacob
Chandler, John Scudder
Clough, John Everett
Coan, Titus
Copley, Thomas
Copway, George
Cort, Edwin Charles
Crespi, Juan
Cushing, Josiah Nelson
Dablon, Claude
Daeger, Albert Thomas
David, John Baptist Mary
Davis, Jerome Dean
Day, David Alexander
Dearing, John Lincoln
De Forest, John Kinne Hyde
Dennis, James Shepard
De Smet, Pierre-Jean
Doty, Elihu
Dougherty, Raymond Philip
Doyle, Alexander Patrick
Druillettes, Gabriel
Dwight, Harrison Gray Otis
Dwight, Henry Otis
Eliot, John
Elliott, Walter Hackett Robert
Engelhardt, Zephyrin
Ewing, James Caruthers Rhea
Farmer, Ferdinand
Ferguson, John Calvin
Filton, James
Fiske, Fidelia
Fleming, John
Fletcher, James Cooley
Flint, Timothy
Fout, Pedro
Frame, Alice Seymour Browne
Gallitzin, Demetrius Augustine
Garcés, Francisco Tomás Hermenegildo
Garry, Spokane
Gates, Caleb Frank
Gibault, Pierre
Going, Jonathan
Good, Adolphus Clemens
Goodell, William
Goodrich, Chauncey
Gordon, Andrew
Goupil, René
Graessl, Lawrence
Grant, Asahel
Graves, Rosewell Hobart
Greaton, Joseph
Greene, Daniel Crosby
Grube, Bernhard Adam
Guignas, Michel
Gulick, John Thomas
Gulick, Luther Halsey, 1828–1891
Gulick, Sidney Lewis
Hall, Sherman
Hamlin, Cyrus
Happer, Andrew Patton
Harding, Robert
Harpster, John Henry
Hart, Virgil Chittenden
Hawley, Gideon, 1727–1807
Haygood, Laura Askew
Heckewelder, John Gottlieb Ernestus
Heiss, Michael
Helbron, Peter
Hepburn, James Curtis
Heyer, John Christian Frederick
Hill, John Henry
Hoecken, Christian
Hoisington, Henry Richard
Holcombe, Chester
Homes, Henry Augustus
Hoover, James Matthews
Hume, Robert Allen
Ingalls, Marilla Baker
Innokentii
Jackson, Sheldon
Jacoby, Ludwig Sigmund
Jessup, Henry Harris
Jogues, Isaac
Jones, George Heber
Jones, John Peter
Jones, John Taylor
Judge, Thomas Augustine
Judson, Adoniram
Judson, Ann Hasseltine
Judson, Emily Chubbuck
Judson, Sarah Hall Boardman
Keith, George
Kellogg, Samuel Henry
King, Jonas
Kino, Eusebio Francisco
Kirkland, Samuel
Kohlmann, Anthony
Lambuth, James William
Lambuth, Walter Russell
Lane, Horace M.
Lansing, Gulian
Lee, Jason
Lefevere, Peter Paul
Lemke, Peter Henry
Lindley, Daniel
Loewenthal, Isidor
Loughridge, Robert McGill
Lowrie, James Walter
Lowrie, Walter
Lowry, Hiram Harrison
Luce, Henry Winters
McCartee, Divie Bethune
MacCauley, Clay
McCord, James Bennett
McCoy, Isaac
McElroy, John
McFarland, Samuel Gamble
McGilvary, Daniel
McKay, David Oman
McKean, James William
McKenna, Charles Hyacinth
Maclay, Robert Samuel
MacSparran, James
Mansell, William Albert
Marquette, Jacques
Martin, William Alexander Parsons
Marty, Martin
Mason, Francis
Mateer, Calvin Wilson
Mayhew, Experience
Mayhew, Thomas, 1593–1682
Mayhew, Thomas, 1621–1657
Mazzuchelli, Samuel Charles
Meeker, Jotham
Meerschaert, Théophile
Membré, Zenobius
Ménard, René
Menetrey, Joseph
Mengarini, Gregory
Mills, Cyrus Taggart
Mills, Susan Lincoln Tolman
Morrison, William McCutchan
Mott, John R.
Mudge, James
Murrow, Joseph Samuel
Nash, Daniel
Nassau, Robert Hamill
Nevins, John Livingston
Niza, Marcos de
O'Brien, Matthew Anthony
Occom, Samson
Padilla, Juan de
Palladino, Lawrence Benedict
Palóu, Francisco

Parker, Alvin Pierson
Parker, Edwin Wallace
Parker, Peter
Parker, Samuel
Perkins, Justin
Perry, Rufus Lewis
Pierre, Joseph Marie Chaumonot
Pierson, Arthur Tappan
Pierz, Franz
Pond, Samuel William
Poor, Daniel
Post, Christian Frederick
Post, George Edward
Pott, Francis Lister Hawks
Price, Thomas Frederick
Pye, Watts Orson
Raffeimer, John Stephen
Râle, Sébastien
Ravalli, Antonio
Ravoux, Augustin
Rawlinson, Frank Joseph
Reed, Mary
Reid, Gilbert
Reid, John Morrison
Rice, Luther
Richard, Gabriel
Richards, William
Riggs, Elias
Riggs, Stephen Return
Roberts, Issachar Jacob
Robot, Isidore
Ruter, Martin
Ryan, Arthur Clayton
Saenderl, Simon
Savage, Thomas Staughton
Schauffler, Henry Albert
Schauffler, William Gottlieb
Schereschewsky, Samuel Isaac Joseph
Schneider, Benjamin
Schneider, Theodore
Scudder, John
Seagrave, Gordon Stifler
Seghers, Charles Jean
Sergeant, John, 1710–1749
Serra, Junípero
Shedd, William Ambrose
Sheffield, Devello Zelotes
Shelton, Albert Leroy
Shepard, Fred Douglas
Shipherd, John Jay
Shuck, Jehu Lewis
Smith, Arthur Henderson
Smith, Azariah
Smith, Eli
Smith, Judson
Spaulding, Levi
Speer, William
Stewart, Philo Penfield
Stewart, Robert
Stoddard, David Tappan
Stone, Ellen Maria
Stuart, John Leighton
Swain, Clara A.
Talbot, John
Talcott, Eliza
Talmage, John Van Nest
Taylor, George Boardman
Taylor, William
Tenney, Charles Daniel
Thayer, John
Thoburn, Isabella
Thomson, William McClure
Tichenor, Isaac Taylor
Tou, Erik Hansen
Trumbull, Henry Clay
Tupper, Henry Allen
Turner, Fennell Parrish
Unangst, Erias
Underwood, Horace Grant
Van Allen, Frank
Van Dyck, Cornelius Van Alen
Van Lennep, Henry John
Van Quickenborne, Charles Felix
Verbeck, Guido Herman Fridolin
Verwyst, Chrysostom Adrian
Walworth, Clarence Augustus
Wanless, William James
Washburn, George
Watson, Andrew
Watson, Charles Roger
West, Henry Sergeant
Wharton, Greene Lawrence
Wherry, Elwood Morris
White, Andrew
Whitman, Marcus
Williams, Channing Moore
Williams, Edward Thomas
Williams, Eleazar
Williams, John Elias
Williams, Samuel Wells
Willingham, Robert Josiah
Williston, Seth
Wilson, John Leighton
Wilson, Samuel Graham
Winslow, Miron
Wood, Thomas Bond
Worcester, Samuel Austin
Yates, Matthew Tyson
Yergan, Max
Young, Samuel Hall
Zeisberger, David

MODELER (See also ARTIST, CRAFTSMAN, SCULPTOR)
Wright, Patience Lovell

MONOLOGUIST
Draper, Ruth

MORALIST
Atlas, Charles S.
Fisher, Dorothea Frances Canfield

MORMON LEADER
Smith, Joseph Fielding

MOTION PICTURE CAMERAMAN
Bitzer, George William

MOTION PICTURE DIRECTOR (See also DIRECTOR, FILMMAKER)
Arzner, Dorothy Emma
Berkeley, Busby
Borzage, Frank
Browning, Tod
Curtiz, Michael
Del Ruth, Roy
Fejos, Paul
Ford, John
Hawks, Howard Winchester
Hitchcock, Alfred Joseph
Johnson, Nunnally Hunter
Lang, Fritz
Pal, George
Sennett, Mack
Stevens, George Cooper
Sturges, Preston
Ulmer, Edgar Georg
Von Stroheim, Erich
Walsh, Raoul
Wellman, William Augustus

MOTION PICTURE DISTRIBUTOR
Laemmle, Carl

MOTION PICTURE EXECUTIVE
Balaban, Barney
Disney, Roy Oliver
Johnston, Eric Allen
Mayer, Louis Burt
Skouras, Spyros Panagiotes
Warner, Harry Morris
Warner, Jack Leonard
Zukor, Adolph

MOTION PICTURE EXHIBITOR
Balaban, Barney

MOTION PICTURE PIONEER
Blackton, James Stuart
Lasky, Jesse Louis

MOTION PICTURE PRODUCER
Borzage, Frank
Chaplin, Charles Spencer ("Charlie")
Fox, William
Freed, Arthur
Goldwyn, Samuel
Hawks, Howard Winchester
Hayward, Leland
Johnson, Nunnally Hunter
Pal, George
Schary, Dore
Selznick, David O.
Sennett, Mack
Stevens, George Cooper
Sturges, Preston
Todd, Mike
Ulmer, Edgar Georg
Waller, Frederic
Yates, Herbert John
Zanuck, Darryl Francis

MOTORIST (See also TRANSPORTER)
Glidden, Charles Jasper

MUCKRAKER (See AUTHOR, JOURNALIST, WRITER)

MUNICIPAL GOVERNMENT AUTHORITY
Sayre, Wallace Stanley

MURALIST (See also ARTIST, PAINTER)
Christy, Howard Chandler
Lebrun, Federico ("Rico")
Meière, Marie Hildreth
Sterne, Maurice

MURDERER
Leopold, Nathan Freudenthal, Jr.

MURDERESS (ALLEGED)
Borden, Lizzie Andrew

MUSEUM DIRECTOR (See also CURATOR)
Barbour, Thomas
Cesnola, Luigi Palma di
Clarke, Sir Caspar Purdon
Dana, John Cotton
D'Harnoncourt, René
Force, Juliana Rieser
French, William Merchant Richardson

Harshe, Robert Bartholow
Heye, George Gustav
Ives, Halsey Cooley
Johnston, John Taylor
Lodge, John Ellerton
Lucas, Frederic Augustus
Mather, Frank Jewett, Jr.
Miller, Gerrit Smith, Jr.
Morse, Edward Sylvester
Osborn, Henry Fairfield
Parker, Arthur Caswell
Putnam, Frederic Ward
Rathbun, Richard
Robinson, Edward, 1858–1931
Rorimer, James Joseph
Seitz, William Chapin
Spargo, John
Steichen, Edward Jean
Stevens, George Washington
Taylor, Francis Henry
Vaillant, George Clapp
Winlock, Herbert Eustis
MUSEUM FOUNDER
Guggenheim, Solomon Robert
MUSICAL SATIRIST
Templeton, Alec Andrew
MUSIC ARRANGER
Faith, Percy
Grofé, Ferde
Hathaway, Donny
Henderson, Fletcher Hamilton
Winterhalter, Hugo
MUSIC CRITIC (See also CRITIC)
Aldrich, Richard
Apthorp, William Foster
Chotzinoff, Samuel
Downes, (Edwin) Olin
Dwight, John Sullivan
Elson, Louis Charles
Finck, Henry Theophilus
Fry, William Henry
Gilman, Lawrence
Gleason, Frederic Grant
Hale, Philip
Henderson, William James
Krehbiel, Henry Edward
Parker, Henry Taylor
Peck, George Washington
Rosenfeld, Paul Leopold
Singleton, Esther
Taylor, Joseph Deems
Thompson, Oscar Lee
Upton, George Putnam
Van Vechten, Carl
Watson, Henry Cood
Woolf, Benjamin Edward
MUSIC EDUCATOR (See also EDUCATOR)
Bauer, Harold Victor
Casadesus, Robert Marcel
Damrosch, Frank Heino
Farwell, Arthur
Goldmark, Rubin
Mannes, Leopold Damrosch
White, Clarence Cameron
MUSICIAN (See also SPECIFIC INSTRUMENTS)
Adderley, Julian Edwin ("Cannonball")
Adgate, Andrew
Allen, Nathan H.
Baker, Benjamin Franklin
Bechet, Sidney
Brown, Gertrude Foster
Burnett, Chester Arthur ("Howlin' Wolf")
Clarke, Helen Archibald
Coltrane, John William
Cook, Will Marion
Duchin, Edward Frank ("Eddy")
Elman, Harry ("Ziggy")
Elman, Mischa
Erskine, John
Fiedler, Arthur
Fillmore, John Comfort
Flagg, Joslah
Gericke, Wilhelm
Gleason, Frederic Grant
Graupner, Johann Christian Gottlieb
Grierson, Francis
Hale, Philip
Haynes, Henry Doyle ("Homer")
Herbert, Victor
Hewitt, John Hill
Holden, Oliver
Holly, Charles Hardin ("Buddy")
Holmes, Daniel Henry
Hopkinson, Francis
Horst, Louis
House, Edward Howard
Humiston, William Henry
Huneker, James Gibbons
Koemmenich, Louis
Kroeger, Ernest Richard
Lanier, Sidney
Mason, Frank Stuart
Mathews, William Smythe Babcock
Merz, Karl
Moore, Annie Aubertine Woodward
Neuendorff, Adolph Heinrich Anton Magnus
Oberhoffer, Emil Johann
Oehmler, Leo Carl Martin
Oliver, Henry Kemble
Parsons, Albert Ross
Pearce, Stephen Austen
Peter, John Frederick
Peters, William Cumming
Pryor, Arthur W.
Read, Daniel, 1757–1836
Reinagle, Alexander
Rushing, James Andrew
Russell, Charles Ellsworth ("Pee Wee")
Scheve, Edward Benjamin
Schindler, Kurt
Seidl, Anton
Selby, William
Seward, Theodore Frelinghuysen
Shaw, Oliver
Sonneck, Oscar George Theodore
Southard, Lucien H.
Spicker, Max
Taylor, Raynor
Thomas, Christian Friedrich Theodore
Timm, Henry Christian
Tourjée, Eben
Trajetta, Philip
Ward, Thomas
Webb, George James
Weber, Max
Weld, Arthur Cyril Gordon
Wight, Frederick Coit
Wolfsohn, Carl
Yancey, James Edward ("Jimmy")
Young, Alfred
Zerralin, Carl
Ziehn, Bernhard
MUSICOLOGIST
Engel, Carl
Landowska, Wanda Aleksandra
Pratt, Waldo Selden
Spaeth, Sigmund
MUSIC PATRON (See also PHILANTHROPIST)
Coolidge, Elizabeth Penn Sprague
De Coppet, Edward J.
Frieze, Henry Simmons
Jordan, Eben Dyer
Juilliard, Augustus D.
Koussevitzky, Olga Naumoff
Nichols, George Ward
Robinson-Smith, Gertrude
Scherman, Harry
Sloan, George Arthur
Stoeckel, Carl
Thurber, Jeannette Meyer
Webb, Thomas Smith
Zellerbach, Harold Lionel
MUSIC PUBLISHER (See also EDITOR, PUBLISHER)
Bloom, Sol
Ditson, Oliver
Dreyfus, Max
Fisher, William Arms
Handy, William Christopher
Harris, Charles Kassell
Peters, William Cumming
Presser, Theodore
Schirmer, Gustav
Schirmer, Rudolph Edward
Schmidt, Arthur Paul
Stern, Joseph William
Witmark, Isidore
MUSIC THEORIST
Goetschius, Percy
Schillinger, Joseph
MYCOLOGIST (See also BOTANIST)
Ellis, Job Bicknell
Peck, Charles Horton
Schweinitz, Lewis David von
Whetzel, Herbert Hice
MYSTIC (See also RELIGIOUS LEADER)
Alcott, Amos Bronson
Blood, Benjamin Paul
Harris, Thomas Lake
Kelpius, Johann
Very, Jones

NATIONAL CELEBRITY
Mitchell, Martha Elizabeth Beall
NATIONAL ENDOWMENT FOR THE HUMANITIES CHAIR
Keeney, Barnaby Conrad

NATIONAL FOOTBALL LEAGUE COMMISSIONER
Bell, De Benneville ("Bert")
NATIONAL LABOR RELATIONS BOARD CHAIRMAN
Leedom, Boyd Stewart
NATURALIST (See also BIOLOGIST, BOTANIST, ECOLOGIST, ZOOLOGIST)
Abbott, Charles Conrad
Adams, Charles Baker
Agassiz, Jean Louis Rodolphe
Akeley, Carl Ethan
Allen, Glover Morrill
Bachman, John
Barbour, Thomas
Barton, Benjamin Smith
Bartram, William
Beebe, (Charles) William
Bland, Thomas
Boll, Jacob
Buckley, Samuel Botsford
Catesby, Mark
Cist, Jacob
Cockerell, Theodore Dru Alison
Cooper, James Graham
Dall, William Healey
De Brahm, William Gerard
De Kay, James Ellsworth
Doubleday, Neltje de Graff
Du Simitière, Pierre Eugène
Eiseley, Loren Corey
Emerton, James Henry
Flagg, Thomas Wilson
Forbes, Stephen Alfred
Garden, Alexander
Gibson, William Hamilton
Godman, John Davidson
Good, Adolphus Clemens
Goode, George Brown
Grant, Madison
Green, Jacob
Grinnell, George Bird
Grosvenor, Gilbert Hovey
Gulick, John Thomas
Harlan, Richard
Harshberger, John William
Henshall, James Alexander
Henshaw, Henry Wetherbee
Hildreth, Samuel Prescott
Holder, Charles Frederick
Holder, Joseph Bassett
Holland, Winiam Jacob
Hornaday, William Temple
Horsfield, Thomas
Hubbard, Wynant Davis
James, Edwin
Jordan, David Starr
Kennicott, Robert
Kirtland, Jared Potter
Kunze, Richard Ernest
Leidy, Joseph
Lesueur, Charles Alexandre
Lincecum, Gideon
Lucas, Frederick Augustus
McCook, Henry Christopher
Maynard, Charles Johnson
Mearns, Edgar Alexander
Merriam, Clinton Hart
Miles, Manly
Miller, Harriet Mann
Mills, Enos Abijah
Morton, Samuel George
Muir, John
Nelson, Edward William
Osborn, Henry Fairfield
Pavy, Octave
Peale, Charles Willson
Peale, Titian Ramsay
Peck, William Dandridge
Pickering, Charles
Pitcher, Zina
Putnam, Frederic Ward
Rafinesque, Constantine Samuel
Ravenel, Edmund
Ritter, William Emerson
Romans, Bernard
Samuels, Edward Augustus
Saugraïn de Vigni, Antoine François
Savage, Thomas Staughton
Seton, Ernest Thompson
Sharp, Dallas Lore
Snow, Francis Huntington
Stearns, Robert Edwards Carter
Stimpson, William
Stone, Witmer
Storer, David Humphreys
Thompson, Zadock
Tuckerman, Frederick
Verrill, Alpheus Hyatt
Ward, Henry Augustus
Webber, Charles Wilkins
White, Charles Abiathar
NATURAL SCIENTIST
Bateson, Gregory
NAVAL ARCHITECT (See also ARCHITECT)
Babcock, Washington Irving
Burgess, W(illiam) Starling
Eckford, Henry
Fairburn, William Armstrong
Forman, Cheesman
Griffiths, John Willis
Herreshoff, Nathanael Greene
Hovgaard, William
Humphreys, Joshua
Isherwood, Benjamin Franklin
Lenthall, John
McKay, Donald
Newton, Isaac, 1794–1858
Porter, John Luke
See, Horace
Steers, George
Stevens, Robert Livingston
Ward, Charles Alfred
Wilson, Theodore Delavan
NAVAL AVIATOR
Towers, John Henry
NAVAL CONSTRUCTOR
Taylor, David Watson
NAVAL ENGINEER (See ENGINEER, NAVAL)
NAVAL OFFICER
Abbot, Joel
Alden, James
Allen, William Henry
Almy, John Jay
Ammen, Daniel
Astor, William Vincent
Aylwin, John Cushing
Badger, Charles Johnston
Badger, Oscar Charles
Bailey, Frank Harvey
Bailey, Theodorus
Bainbridge, William
Balch, George Beall
Barbey, Daniel Edward
Barker, Albert Smith
Barney, Joshua
Barron, James
Barron, Samuel
Barry, John
Beary, Donald Bradford
Beaumont, John Colt
Belknap, George Eugene
Bell, Henry Haywood
Benson, William Shepherd
Bent, Silas
Biddle, James
Biddle, Nicholas
Blake, Homer Crane
Blakely, Johnston
Blandy, William Henry Purnell
Bloch, Claude Charles
Blue, Victor
Boggs, Charles Stuart
Bourne, Nehemiah
Boutelle, Charles Addison
Breese, Kidder Randolph
Bristol, Mark Lambert
Brooke, John Mercer
Brownson, Willard Herbert
Buchanan, Franklin
Bullard, William Hannum Grubb
Bulloch, James Dunwody
Burrows, William
Caldwell, Charles Henry Bromedge
Capps, Washington Lee
Carter, Samuel Powhatan
Chadwick, French Ensor
Chaffee, Roger Bruce
Champlin, Stephen
Chauncey, Isaac
Chester, Colby Mitchell
Clark, Charles Edgar
Clark, Joseph James ("Jocko")
Coffin, Sir Isaac
Collins, Napoleon
Colvocoresses, George Musalas
Cone, Hutchinson Ingham
Conner, David
Conyngham, Gustavus
Coontz, Robert Edward
Crane, William Montgomery
Craven, Thomas Tingey
Craven, Tunis Augustus MacDonough
Crosby, Peirce
Cushing, William Baker
Dahlgren, John Adolphus Bernard
Dale, Richard
Dale, Sir Thomas
Davis, Charles Henry, 1807–1877
Davis, Charles Henry, 1845–1921
Davis, John Lee
Davison, Gregory Caldwell
Decatur, Stephen
Decatur, Stephen (son of Stephen)
De Haven, Edwin Jesse

Delano, Amassa
Denfield, Louis Emil
Dewey, George
Dornin, Thomas Aloysius
Downes, John
Drayton, Percival
Du Pont, Samuel Francis
Dyer, Nehemiah Mayo
Earle, Ralph
Eberle, Edward Walter
Edwards, Richard Stanislaus
Elliott, Jesse Duncan
Emmons, George Foster
Evans, Robley Dunglison
Fairfax, Donald McNeill
Fanning, Nathaniel
Farragut, David Glasgow
Farragut, George
Fiske, Bradley Allen
Fiske, John
Foote, Andrew Hull
Forrest, French
Foulk, George Clayton
Frost, Holloway Halstead
Gherardi, Bancroft
Gillon, Alexander
Gleaves, Albert
Glynn, James
Goldsborough, Louis Malesherbes
Gorringe, Henry Honeychurch
Grant, Albert Weston
Greene, Samuel Dana
Greer, James Augustin
Gridley, Charles Vernon
Griffin, Robert Stanislaus
Grinnell, Henry Walton
Habersham, Alexander Wylly
Halsey, William Frederick ("Bull"), Jr.
Haraden, Jonathan
Harding, Seth
Hayden, Edward Everett
Hazelwood, John
Henley, Robert
Herndon, William Lewis
Hewitt, Henry Kent
Hichborn, Philip
Hinman, Elisha
Hobson, Richmond Pearson
Hollins, George Nichols
Hopkins, Esek
Hopkins, John Burroughs
Howell, John Adams
Hudde, Andries
Hughes, Charles Frederick
Hull, Isaac
Ingersoll, Royal Eason
Ingersoll, Royal Rodney
Ingraham, Duncan Nathaniel
Ingram, Jonas Howard
Jeffers, William Nicholson
Jenkins, Thornton Alexander
Jewett, David
Jones, Catesby Ap Roger
Jones, Hilary Pollard
Jones, Jacob
Jones, John Paul
Jones, Thomas Ap Catesby
Jouett, James Edward
Joy, Charles Turner
Kane, Elisha Kent
Kearney, Lawrence
Kelley, James Douglas Jerrold
Kempff, Louis
Kimball, William Wirt
Kimmel, Husband Edward
Kincaid, Thomas Cassin
King, Ernest Joseph
Kirk, Alan Goodrich
Knight, Austin Melvin
Knox, Dudley Wright
Lamberton, Benjamin Peffer
Landais, Pierre
Lanman, Joseph
Lardner, James Lawrence
La Ronde, Louis Denis, Sieur de
Lawrence, James
Leahy, William Daniel
Lee, Samuel Phillips
Lee, Willis Augustus
Little, George
Livingston, John William
Loring, Charles Harding
Loring, Joshua, 1716–1781
Luce, Stephen Bleecker
Lull, Edward Phelps
Lynch, William Francis
McArthur, William Pope
McCall, Edward Rutledge
McCalla, Bowman Hendry
McCann, William Penn
McCauley, Charles Stewart
McCauley, Edward Yorke
McCormick, Lynde Dupuy
Macdonough, Thomas
McDougal, David Stockton
McGiffin, Philo Norton
McKean, William Wister
Mackenzie, Alexander Slidell
McLean, Walter
McNair, Frederick Vallette
McNeill, Daniel
McNeill, Hector
Maffitt, John Newland
Mahan, Alfred Thayer
Manley, John
Marchand, John Bonnett
Mattice, Asa Martines
Maury, Matthew Fontaine
Mayo, Henry Thomas
Mayo, William Kennon
Meade, Richard Worsam
Melville, George Wallace
Mervine, William
Milligan, Robert Wiley
Mitscher, Marc Andrew
Moffett, William Adger
Montgomery, John Berrien
Moore, Edwin Ward
Morgan, James Morris
Morris, Charles
Morris, Richard Valentine
Mullany, James Robert Madison
Murdock, Joseph Ballard
Murray, Alexander
Nelson, William, 1824–1862
Niblack, Albert Parker
Nicholson, James
Nicholson, James William Augustus
Nicholson, Samuel
Nimitz, Chester William
O'Brien, Jeremiah
Page, Richard Lucian
Page, Thomas Jefferson
Parmer, James Shedden
Parker, Foxhall Alexander
Parker, William Harwar
Parrott, Enoch Greenleafe
Patterson, Daniel Todd
Patterson, Thomas Harman
Pattison, Thomas
Paulding, Hiram
Paulding, James Kirke
Pennock, Alexander Mosely
Percival, John
Perkins, George Hamilton
Perry, Christopher Raymond
Perry, Matthew Calbraith
Perry, Oliver Hazard
Phelps, Thomas Stowell
Philip, John Woodward
Pillsbury, John Elliott
Plunkett, Charles Peshall
Poor, Charles Henry
Porter, David
Porter, David Dixon
Pound, Thomas
Pratt, William Veazie
Preble, Edward
Preble, George Henry
Price, Rodman McCamley
Pring, Martin
Pringle, Joel Robert Poinsett
Quackenbush, Stephen Platt
Queen, Walter W.
Raby, James Joseph
Radford, Arthur William
Radford, William
Ramsay, Francis Munroe
Read, Charles William
Read, George Campbell
Read, Thomas
Reeves, Joseph Mason
Remey, George Collier
Revere, Joseph Warren
Reynolds, William
Rhind, Alexander Colden
Ribaut, Jean
Ricketts, Claude Vernon
Ridgely, Charles Goodwin
Ridgely, Daniel Bowly
Ringgold, Cadwalader
Robertson, Ashley Herman
Rodgers, Christopher Raymond Perry
Rodgers, George Washington, 1787–1832
Rodgers, George Washington, 1822–1863
Rodgers, John, 1773–1838
Rodgers, John, 1812–1882
Rodgers, John, 1881–1926
Roe, Francis Asbury
Rousseau, Harry Harwood
Rowan, Stephen Clegg
Russell, John Henry
Saltonstall, Dudley
Sampson, William Thomas
Sands, Benjamin Franklin
Sands, Joshua Ratoon
Schenck, James Findlay
Schley, Winfield Scott
Schroeder, Seaton
Selfridge, Thomas Oliver

Semmes, Raphael
Shaw, John, 1773–1823
Shaw, Nathaniel
Sherman, Forrest Percival
Sherman, Frederick Carl
Shubrick, John Templer
Shubrick, William Branford
Shufeldt, Robert Wilson
Sicard, Montgomery
Sigsbee, Charles Dwight
Simpson, Edward
Sims, William Sowden
Sloat, John Drake
Smith, Joseph, 1790–1877
Smith, Melancton, 1810–1893
Snowden, Thomas
Somers, Richard
Spruance, Raymond Ames
Standley, William Harrison
Stark, Harold Raynsford
Steedman, Charles
Sterett, Andrew
Stevens, Thomas Holdup, 1795–1841
Stevens, Thomas Holdup, 1819–1896
Stewart, Edwin
Stockton, Charles Herbert
Stockton, Robert Field
Strain, Isaac G.
Stringham, Silas Horton
Strong, James Hooker
Tabot, Silas
Tarbell, Joseph
Tattnall, Josiah
Taussig, Joseph Knefler
Taylor, David Watson
Taylor, William Rogers
Taylor, William Vigneron
Temple, William Grenville
Thatcher, Henry Knox
Theobald, Robert Alfred
Thompson, Egbert
Tingey, Thomas
Towers, John Henry
Townsend, Robert
Trenchard, Stephen Decatur
Trippe, John
Trott, Nicholas
Truxtun, Thomas
Truxtun, William Talbot
Tucker, John Randolph, 1812–1883
Tucker, Samuel
Turner, Daniel
Turner, Richmond Kelly
Tyng, Edward
Upshur, John Henry
Usher, Nathaniel Reilly
Vickery, Howard Leroy
Voorhees, Philip Falkerson
Waddell, James Iredell
Wainwright, Jonathan Mayhew, 1821–1863
Wainwright, Richard, 1817–1862
Wainwright, Richard, 1849–1926
Walke, Henry
Walker, Asa
Walker, John Grimes
Ward, James Harmon
Warren, Sir Peter
Warrington, Lewis
Waters, Daniel
Watson, John Crittenden
Weaver, Aaron Ward
Welles, Roger
Werder, Reed
Whipples Abraham
Wickes, Lambert
Wilde, George Francis Faxon
Wilkes, Charles
Wilkinson, John
Wilkinson, Theodore Stark
Williams, John Foster
Winslow, Cameron McRae
Winslow, John Ancrum
Wise, Henry Augustus
Wood, John Taylor
Woolsey, Melancthon Taylor
Wooster, Charles Whiting
Worden, John Lorimer
Wyman, Robert Harris
Zacharias, Ellis Mark
Ziegemeier, Henry Joseph

NAVIGATOR (See also MARINER, STEAMBOAT OPERATOR)
Allefonsce, Jean
Amadas, Phllip
Ayala, Juan Manuel de
De Brahm, William Gerard
Gosnold, Bartholomew
Gray, Robert
Hudson, Henry
Ingraham, Joseph
Kendrick, John
Waymouth, George

NAVY BUREAU OF YARDS AND DOCKS (U.S.) CHIEF
Moreell, Ben

NAVY SURGEON GENERAL
McIntire, Ross

NAZI PARTY (AMERICAN) LEADER
Rockwell, George Lincoln

NEMATOLOGIST (See also ANATOMIST)
Cobb, Nathan Augustus

NERO WOLFE CREATOR
Stout, Rex Todhunter

NEUROANATOMIST (See also ANATOMIST)
Hoerr, Normand Louis

NEUROBIOLOGIST
Loewi, Otto

NEUROLOGIST (See also PHYSICIAN)
Coriat, Isador Henry
Dana, Charles Loomis
Donaldson, Henry Herbert
Hammond, William Alexander
Jelliffe, Smith Ely
Kennedy, Robert Foster
Knapp, Philip Coombs
McCarthy, Daniel Joseph
Mills, Charles Karsner
Mitchell, Silas Weir
Morton, William James
Patrick, Hugh Talbot
Potts, Charres Sower
Putnam, James Jackson
Ranson, Stephen Walter
Sachs, Bernard
Seguin, Edward Constant
Spitzka, Edward Charles
Starr, Moses Allen
Tilney, Frederick
Timme, Walter
Weisenburg, Theodore Herman

NEUROPATHOLOGIST (See also PATHOLOGIST)
Barrett, Albert Moore
Southard, Elmer Ernest

NEUROPHARMACOLOGIST (See also PHARMACOLOGIST)
Loewi, Otto

NEUROPHYSIOLOGIST (See also PHYSIOLOGIST)
Fulton, John Farquhar

NEUROPSYCHIATRIST (See also PSYCHIATRIST)
Myerson, Abraham

NEUROPSYCHOLOGIST
Teuber, Hans-Lukas ("Luke")

NEUROSURGEON (See also SURGEON)
Craig, Winchell McKendree
Davidoff, Leo Max

NEWSAGENT (See also PUBLICIST)
Topliff, Samuel
Tousey, Sinclair

NEWS COMMENTATOR
Swing, Raymond Edwards (Gram)

NEWSPAPER COLUMNIST
Berger, Meyer
Broun, Heywood Campbell
Clapper, Raymond Lewis
Considine, Robert ("Bob") Bernard
Crouse, Russel McKinley
Franzblau, Rose Nadler
Gilmer, Elizabeth Meriwether ("Dorothy Dix")
Guest, Edgar Albert
Hopper, Hedda
Kilgallen, Dorothy Mae
Lewis, Fulton, Jr.
Lyons, Leonard
McIntyre, Oscar Odd
Morehouse, Ward
Patri, Angelo
Pyle, Ernest Taylor
Reese, Heloise Bowles
Stevens, Ashton
Sullivan, Edward Vicent ("Ed")
Vanderbilt, Amy

NEWSPAPER CORRESPONDENT (See also FOREIGN CORRESPONDENT, JOURNALIST, NEWSPAPER REPORTER)
Andrews, Bert
Ross, Charles Griffith
Stark, Louis

NEWSPAPER EXECUTIVE
Carvalho, Solomon Solis
Dryfoos, Orvil E.
Grant, Harry Johnston
Howard, Roy Wilson
Laffan, William Mackay
McCormack, Buren Herbert ("Mac")

NEWSPAPERMAN (See also JOURNALIST)
Asbury, Herbert

Cobb, Irvin Shrewsbury
Early, Stephen Tyree
Farrington, Wallace Rider
Hapgood, Hutchins
Mankiewicz, Herman Jacob
Neuberger, Richard Lewis
Wilson, J(ames) Finley
NEWSPAPER OWNER
Bingham, Robert Worth
Chandler, Harry
Farrington, Joseph Rider
Grasty, Charles Henry
Knutson, Harold
Lea, Luke
Livingstone, William
McCormick, Robert Rutherford
Nicholson, Eliza Jane Poitevent Holbrook
Patterson, Alicia
Pulitzer, Joseph, Jr.
Scripps, William Edmund
NEWSPAPER PUBLISHER (See also PUBLISHER)
Abbott, Robert Sengstacke
Annenberg, Moses Louis
Block, Paul
Bryan, John Stewart
Chandler, Norman
Copley, Ira Clifton
Cowles, Gardner
Cox, James Middleton
Dealey, George Bannerman
Fitzgerald, John Francis
Fleisher, Benjamin Wilfrid
Gaylord, Edward King
Glass, Carter
Knowland, William Fife
McClatchy, Charles Kenny
McLean, Edward Beale
McLean, Robert
Murphy, Frederick E.
Noyes, Frank Brett
Patterson, Eleanor Medill
Patterson, Joseph Medill
Pulitzer, Ralph
Reid, Ogden Mills
Ridder, Bernard Herman
Scripps, Robert Paine
Sulzberger, Arthur Hays
NEWSPAPER REPORTER (See also FOREIGN CORRESPONDENT, JOURNALIST, NEWSPAPER CORRESPONDENT)
Berger, Meyer
Kilgallen, Dorothy Mae
Laurence, William Leonard
Manning, Marie
Powell, John Benjamin
Stark, Louis
NEWSPAPER SYNDICATOR
Dille, John Flint
NEW YORK STOCK EXCHANGE CHAIRMAN
Coleman, John Aloysius
NIGHTCLUB OWNER
Billingsley, John Sherman
Livingstone, Belle
Rose, Billy
NOBEL LAUREATE
DuVigneaud, Vincent
Mayer, Maria Goeppert
Richards, Dickinson Woodruff
Sutherland, Earl Wilbur, Jr.
Van Vleck, John Hasbrouck
Waksman, Selman Abraham
Woodward, Robert Burns
NONGOVERNMENTAL ORGANIZATIONS DIRECTOR
Eichelberger, Clark Mell
NOVELIST (See also AUTHOR, WRITER)
Abbott, Eleanor Hallowell
Adamic, Louis
Adams, Frank Ramsay
Agee, James Rufus
Aldrich, Bess Genevra Streeter
Allen, Hervey
Allen, James Lane
Arlen, Michael
Atherton, Gertrude Franklin (Horn)
Bacheller, Irving
Bailey, (Irene) Temple
Baker, Dorothy Dodds
Basso, (Joseph) Hamilton
Baum, Hedwig ("Vicki")
Beach, Rex
Beer, Thomas
Benét, Stephen Vincent
Bennett, Emerson
Biggers, Earl Derr
Bird, Robert Montgomery
Boyd, James
Boyd, Thomas Alexander
Bradford, Roark Whitney Wickliffe
Brown, Charles Brockden
Buntline, Ned (See Judson, Edward Zane Carroll)
Burgess, Frank Gelett
Cabell, James Branch
Cahan, Abraham
Campbell, William Edward March
Catherwood, Mary Hartwell
Chambers, Robert William
Chase, Ilke
Chatterton, Ruth
Churchill, Winston
Clark, Walter Van Tilburg
Cleghorn, Sarah Norcliffe
Clemens, Jeremiah
Clemens, Samuel Langhorne
Cobb, Sylvanus
Cohen, Octavus Roy
Colum, Padraic
Comfort, Will Levington
Cooke, John Esten
Cooper, James Fenimore
Costain, Thomas Bertram
Cozzens, James Gould
Crawford, Francis Marion
Croy, Homer
Cullen, Countée Porter
Curwood, James Oliver
Davis, Rebecca Blaine Harding
Day, Holman Francis
Dell, Floyd James
Donn-Byrne, Brian Oswald
Dos Passos, John Roderigo
Douglas, Lloyd Cassel
Dreiser, Theodore
Dupuy, Eliza Ann
Eggleston, Edward
Eggleston, George Cary
Farrell, James Thomas
Faulkner (Falkner), William Cuthbert
Fearing, Kenneth Flexner
Ferber, Edna Jessica
Fitzgerald, Francis Scott Key
Forbes, Esther
Ford, Paul Leicester
Forester, Cecil Scott
Fox, John William
Frederic, Harold
Freeman, Joseph
Fuller, Henry Blake
Garland, Hamlin
Garreau, Armand
Gipson, Frederick Benjamin
Glasgow, Ellen Anderson Gholson
Grant, Robert
Gunter, Archibald Clavering
Hackett, Francis
Hagedorn, Hermann Ludwig Gebhard
Harben, William Nathaniel
Hardy, Arthur Sherburne
Harris, Miriam Coles
Harrison, Constance Cary
Harrison, Henry Sydnor
Hawthorne, Nathaniel
Hazelton, George Cochrane
Hemingway, Ernest Miller
Herbert, Frederick Hugh
Herbst, Josephine Frey
Hergesheimer, Joseph
Herrick, Robert Welch
Heyward, DuBose
Hirschbein, Peretz
Hobart, Alice Nourse Tisdale
Hoffman, Charles Fenno
Holley, Marietta
Holmes, Mary Jane Hawes
Howells, William Dean
Hughes, James Langston
Huntington, Jedediah Vincent
Hurst, Fannie
Hurston, Zora Neale
Inge, William Motter
Jackson, Charles Reginald
Jackson, Helen Maria Fiske Hunt
Jackson, Shirley Hardie
James, Henry, 1843–1916
Janson, Kristofer Nagel
Johnson, Owen McMahon
Johnston, Mary
Jones, James Ramon
Jordan, Kate
Judson, Edward Zane Carroll ("Ned Buntline")
Kantor, MacKinlay
Kelland, Clarence Budington
Kerouac, Jack
Kerr, Sophie
Kester, Vaughan
King, William Benjamin Basil
Koch, Vivienne
La Farge, Christopher Grant
Lennox, Charlotte Ramsay
Lewis, Harry Sinclair
Lewisohn, Ludwig
Lincoln, Joseph Crosby

Lippard, George
Lloyd, John Uri
Lynde, Francis
McCullers, Carson
McCutcheon, George Barr
MacDowell, Katherine Sherwood Bonner
McHenry, James
McKay, Claude
Magruder, Julia
Major, Charles
Marquand, John Phillips
Masters, Edgar Lee
Melville, Herman
Miller, Henry Valentine
Mitchell, Isaac
Mitchell, John Ames
Mitchell, Margaret Munnerlyn
Mitchell, Silas Weir
Morley, Christopher Darlington
Motley, Willard Francis
Murfree, Mary Noailles
Nin, Anaïs
Norris, Benjamin Franklin
Norris, Charles Gilman Smith
Norris, Kathleen Thompson
O'Connor, Edwin Greene
O'Connor, Mary Flannery
O'Hara, John Henry
O'Higgins, Harvey Jerrold
Oppenheim, James
Patchen, Kenneth
Patten, Gilbert
Paul, Elliot Harold
Phillips, David Graham
Pike, Mary Hayden Green
Poole, Ernest Cook
Porter, Gene Stratton
Porter, Katherine Anne
Post, Melville Davisson
Rawlings, Marjorie Kinnan
Reid, Thomas Mayne
Rice, Elmer
Rinehart, Mary Roberts
Rives, Hallie Erminie
Roche, Arthur Somers
Rowson, Susanna Haswell
Ruark, Robert Chester
Saltus, Edgar Evertson
Sandoz, Mari
Scarborough, Dorothy
Schomer, Nahum Meir
Schorer, Mark
Scoville, Joseph Alfred
Sealsfield, Charles
Sedgwick, Anne Douglas
Sheean, James Vincent
Shellabarger, Samuel
Simms, William Gilmore
Sinclair, Upton Beall, Jr.
Singer, Israel Joshua
Smith, Betty
Smith, Harry James
Southworth, Emma Dorothy Eliza Nevitte
Stafford, Jean
Stockton, Frank Richard
Stoddard, Elizabeth Drew Barstow
Stribling, Thomas Sigismund
Strubberg, Friedrich Armand
Tarkington, Booth
Tenney, Tabitha Gilman
Thayer, Tiffany Ellsworth
Thomas, Frederick William
Tincher, Mary Agnes
Trumbo, James Dalton
Twain, Mark (See Clemens, Samuel Longhorne)
Tyler, Royall
Vance, Louis Joseph
Van Vechten, Carl
Warfield, Catherine Ann Ware
Warner, Anna Bartlett
Warner, Charles Dudley
Warner, Susan Bogert
Wharton, Edith Newbold Jones
Wilder, Thornton Niven
Williams, Ben Ames
Williams, Catharine Read Arnold
Wilson, Harry Leon
Wilson, Robert Burns
Wodehouse, Pelham Grenville
Wolfe, Thomas Clayton
Wright, Harold Bell
Wylie, Elinor Morton Hoyt
Young, Stark

NUCLEAR PHYSICIST
Graves, Alvin Cushman

NUCLEAR-PLANT WORKER
Silkwood, Karen Gay

NUMISMATIST (See also COLLECTOR)
Anthon, Charles Edward
Du Bois, William Ewing
Newell, Edward Theodore
Phillips, Henry
Snowden, James Ross
Storer, Horatio Robinson

NUN
Alphonsa, Mother
Angela, Mother
Ayres, Anne
Cabrini, Francis Xavier
Cannon, Harriet Starr
Clarke, Mary Francis
Connelly, Cornelia
Drexel, Katharine Mary
Guérin, Anne-Thérèse
Hardey, Mother Mary Aloysia
Rogers, Mary Josephine
Russell, Mother Mary Baptist
Schrieck, Sister Louise Van der
Seton, Elizabeth Ann Bayley
Spalding, Catherine
Teresa, Mother

NURSE
Anthony, Sister
Barton, Clara
Delano, Jane Armindo
Dock, Lavinia Lloyd
Fitzgerald, Alice Louise Florence
Goodrich, Annie Warburton
Haupt, Alma Cecelia
Hopkins, Juliet Ann Opie
Law, Sallie Chapman Gordon
Minnigerode, Lucy
Noyes, Clara Dutton
Nutting, Mary Adelaide
Stimson, Julia Catherine
Wald, Lillian D.

NURSERYMAN (See also AGRICULTURIST)
Kenrick, William
Luelling, Henderson
Parsons, Samuel Bowne
Prince, William, c. 1725–1802
Prince, William, 1766–1842
Prince, William Robert
Pyle, Robert
Rock, John
Roeding, George Christian
Stark, Lloyd Crow
Vick, James

NURSING EDUCATOR (See also EDUCATOR)
Stimson, Julia Catherine

NUTRITIONAL BIOCHEMIST (See also BIOCHEMIST, NUTRITIONIST)
Nelson, Marjorie Maxine

NUTRITIONIST (See also DIETICIAN)
Davis, Adele
Hart, Edwin Bret
Rose, Mary Davies Swartz

OARSMAN (See also ATHLETE, ROWING CHAMPION, ROWING COACH)
Cook, Robert Johnson
Courtney, Charles Edward

OBSTETRICIAN (See also PHYSICIAN)
Atkinson, William Biddle
DeLee, Joseph Bolivar
Dewees, William Potts
Engelmann, George Julius
Guttmacher, Alan Frank
Hirst, Barton Cooke
Hodge, Hugh Lenox
Lloyd, James
Lusk, William Thompson
Parry, John Stubbs
Parvin, Theophilus
Polak, John Osborn
Richardson, William Lambert
Smith, Albert Holmes
Storer, David Humphreys
Thomas, Theodore Gaillard
Williams, John Whitridge

OCCULTIST
Comfort, Will Levington

OCEANOGRAPHER (See also HYDROGRAPHER)
Agassiz, Alexander
Beebe, (Charles) William
Bent, Silas
Bigelow, Henry Bryant
Harris, Rollin Arthur
Heezen, Bruce Charles
Lindenkohl, Adolph
Maury, Matthew Fontaine
Pillsbury, John Elliott
Smith, Edward Hanson
Vaughan, Thomas Wayland

OCULIST (See also Physician)
Chisolm, John Julian

OFFICIAL GREETER
Whalen, Grover Aloysius

OIL COMPANY EXECUTIVE
Beaty, Amos Leonidas
Cullen, Hugh Roy

Cullinan, Joseph Stephen
Farish, William Stamps
Gallagher, Ralph W.
Getty, George Franklin, II
Getty, Jean Paul
Kerr, Robert Samuel
Rathbone, Monroe Jackson ("Jack")
Richardson, Sid Williams
Rockefeller, John Davison
Rockefeller, John Davison, Jr.
Van Dyke, John Wesley
OIL PRODUCER (See also INDUSTRIALIST)
Abbott, William Hawkins
Bissell, George Henry
Doheny, Edward Laurence
Donnell, James C.
Getty, Jean Paul
Gregory, Thomas Barger
Guffey, James McClurg
Hunt, Haroldson Lafayette
Lockhart, Charles
Marland, Ernest Whitworth
Mellon, William Larimer
Murchison, Clinton Williams
Phillips, Frank
Phillips, Thomas Wharton
Sinclair, Harry Ford
Sterling, Ross Shaw
Vandergrift, Jacob Jay
OIL REFINER (See also INDUSTRIALIST)
Kier, Samuel M.
Lockhart, Charles
Merrill, Joshua
Mowbray, George Mordey
Nevin, Robert Peebles
Rockefeller, John Davison
Rockefeller, John Davison, Jr.
Sibley, Joseph Crocker
OLYMPIC GOLD MEDALIST
Owens, James Cleveland ("Jesse")
OLYMPIC LEADER
Brundage, Avery
ONCOLOGIST (See also PHYSICIAN)
Papanicolaou, George Nicholas
OOLOGIST (See also NATURALIST)
Brewer, Thomas Mayo
OPERA COMMENTATOR
Cross, Milton John
OPERA MANAGER (See also IMPRESARIO, THEATRICIAL MANAGER)
Gatt-Casazza, Giulio
Johnson, Edward
OPERA SINGER (See SINGER)
OPHTHALMOLOGIST (See also OCULIST, PHYSICIAN)
Agnew, Cornelius Rea
Delafield, Edward
Dix, John Homer
Duane, Alexander
Friedenwald, Aaron
Gifford, Sanford Robinson
Gould, George Milbry
Green, John
Gruening, Emil
Hays, Isaac
Hotz, Ferdinand Carl
Howe, Lucien
Jackson, Edward
Knapp, Herman
Koller, Carl
Lewis, Francis Park
Loring, Edward Greely
Norris, William Fisher
Noyes, Henry Drury
Oliver, Charles Augustus
Pyle, Walter Lytle
Randall, Burton Alexander
Reuling, George
Schweinitz, George Edmund de
Theobald, Samuel
Weeks, John Elmer
Wheeler, John Martin
Williams, Elkanah
Williams, Henry Willard
Wilmer, William Holland
Wood, Casey Albert
OPTICAL EXPERT
Ritchey, George Willis
OPTICIAN (See also OCULIST, OPHTHALMOLOGIST, PHYSICIAN)
Lundin, Carl Axel Robert
Porter, Russell Williams
ORATOR (See also LECTURER)
Alderman, Edwin Anderson
Bancroft, Edgar Addison
Bowers, Claude Gernade
Curtis, George William
Dickinson, Anna Elizabeth
Douglass, Frederick
Gillis, James Martin
Grady, Henry Woodfin
Graves, John Temple
Henry, Patrick
Innes, James
Logan, James, 1725–1780
Phillips, Wendell
Prentiss, Seargent Smith
Preston, John Smith
Randolph, John, 1773–1833
Russell, Jonathan
Simmons, Roscoe Conkling Murray
Stuart, Isaac William
Thomson, John
ORCHESTRAL CONDUCTOR (See CONDUCTOR)
ORDNANCE EXPERT
Benton, James Gilchrist
ORGAN BUILDER (See MANUFACTURER)
ORGANIC CHEMIST (See also CHEMIST)
Bachmann, Werner Emmanuel
Julian, Percy Lavon
ORGANIST (See also MUSICIAN, PIANIST)
Archer, Frederic
Biggs, Edward George Power
Blodgett, Benjamin Colman
Buck, Dudley
Cadman, Charles Wakefield
Dunham, Henry Morton
Eddy, Clarence
Fairlamb, James Remington
Fox, Virgil Keel
Hale, Philip
Jackson, George K.
Marzo, Eduardo
Mees, Arthur
Paine, John Knowles
Parker, James Cutler Dunn
Root, Frederic Woodman
Stewart, Humphrey John
Thayer, Whitney Eugene
Tuckey, William
Warren, Richard Henry
Warren, Samuel Prowse
Whiting, George Elbridge
Wolle, John Frederick
Wood, David Duffle
Yon, Pietro Alessandro
Zeuner, Charles
ORGANIZATION EXECUTIVE
Breckinridge, Aida de Acosta
Watt, Donald Beates
ORGANIZED CRIME LEADER (See also CRIMINAL, GANGSTER)
Bruno, Angelo
Evola, Natale ("Joe Diamond")
Luchese, Thomas
Luciano, Charles ("Lucky")
Profaci, Joseph
ORGANIZER (See PROMOTER)
ORIENTALIST (See also SCHOLAR, SINOLOGUE)
Adler, Cyrus
Barton, George Aaron
Bigelow, William Sturgis
Bloomfield, Maurice
Brown, John Porter
Casanowicz, Immanuel Moses
Chiera, Edward
Clay, Albert Tobias
Davis, Charles Henry Stanley
Gibbs, Josiah Willard
Hall, Isaac Hollister
Hodgson, William Brown
Hopkins, Edward Washburn
Hyvernat, Henri
Jackson, Abraham Valentine Williams
Lanman, Charles Rockwell
Lewis, Tayler
Lyon, David Gordon
Moore, George Foot
Müller, Wilhelm Max
Newbold, William Romaine
Nordheimer, Isaac
Olmstead, Albert Ten Eyck
Orne, John
Rockhill, William Woodville
Rogers, Robert William
Salisbury, Edward Elbridge
Schmidt, Nathaniel
Smith, Eli
Toy, Crawford Howell
Ward, William Hayes
Warren, Henry Clarke
ORNITHOLOGIST (See also NATURALIST, ZOOLOGIST)
Allen, Arthur Augustus
Audubon, John James
Bailey, Florence Augusta Merriam
Brewer, Thomas Mayo
Brewster, William
Cassin, John
Chapin, James Paul
Chapman, Frank Michler
Cory, Charles Barney

Coues, Elliott
Eckstorm, Fannie Hardy
Eklund, Carl Robert
Forbush, Edward Howe
Griscom, Ludlow
Henshaw, Henry Wetherbee
Jones, Lynds
Lawrence, George Newbold
Nehrling, Henry
Nuttall, Thomas
Nutting, Charles Cleveland
Ober, Frederick Albion
Oberholser, Harry Church
Pearson, Thomas Gilbert
Richmond, Charles Wallace
Ridgway, Robert
Samuels, Edward Augustus
Sennett, George Burritt
Todd, Walter Edmond Clyde
Torrey, Bradford
Townsend, John Kirk
Wayne, Arthur Trezevant
Wilson, Alexander
Wood, Casey Albert
Xántus, János

OSTEOPATH
Allen, Forrest Clare ("Phog")

OTOLOGIST (See also PHYSICIAN)
Buck, Albert Henry
Burnett, Charles Henry
Gruening, Emil
Leland, George Adams
Randall, Burton Alexander

OUTLAW (See also BANDIT, JAY-HAWKER, VIGILANTE)
Laffite, Jean
Murrell, John A.

OYSTER CULTURIST
Nelson, Julius
Oemler, Arminius

PACIFIST (See also PEACE ADVOCATE)
Day, Dorothy

PAINTER (See also ARTIST, ILLUSTRATOR, MURALIST)
Abbey, Edwin Austin
Agate, Alfred T.
Agate, Frederick Styles
Albers, Josef
Alexander, Francis
Alexander, John White
Ames, Ezra
Ames, Joseph Alexander
Anshutz, Thomas Pollock
Archipenko, Alexander
Armstrong, David Maitland
Aronson, Boris Solomon
Badger, Joseph
Baker, George Augustus
Banvard, John
Beaux, Cecilia
Beckwith, James Carroll
Bellows, Albert Fitch
Bellows, George Wesley
Benbridge, Henry
Benjamin, Samuel Greene Wheeler
Benson, Eugene
Benson, Frank Weston
Bierstadt, Albert
Bingham, George Caleb
Birch, Thomas
Birch, William Russell
Blackburn, Joseph
Blakelock, Ralph Albert
Blashfield, Edwin Howland
Bluemner, Oscar Florians
Blum, Robert Frederick
Bohm, Max
Borglum, John Gutzon de la Mothe
Borie, Adolphe
Bouché, René Robert
Bounetheau, Henry Brintnell
Bradford, William
Breck, George William
Brevoort, James Renwick
Bridgman, Frederick Arthur
Bristol, John Bunyan
Brown, John Appleton
Brown, John George
Brown, Mather
Bruce, Edward Bright
Brumidi, Constantino
Brush, George de Forest
Bunce, William Gedney
Burchfield, Charles Ephraim
Calder, Alexander
Carpenter, Francis Bicknell
Casilear, John William
Champney, Benjamin
Champney, James Wells
Chapman, John Gadsby
Church, Frederick Edwin
Church, Frederick Stuart
Clarke, Thomas Shields
Closson, William Baxter
Coffin, William Anderson
Cogdell, John Stevens
Cole, Joseph Foxcroft
Coleman, Charles Caryl
Colman, Samuel
Copley, John Singleton
Cornoyer, Paul
Cox, Kenyon
Cranch, Christopher Pearse
Cropsey, Jaspar Francis
Crowninshield, Frederic
Cummings, Thomas Seir
Curry, John Steuart
Cushman, George Hewitt
Danforth, Moseley Isaac
Davies, Arthur Bowen
Daviess, Maria Thompson
Dearth, Henry Golden
De Camp, Joseph Rodefer
Dewing, Maria Richards Oakey
Dewing, Thomas Wilmer
Dickinson, Anson
Dickinson, Preston
Dielman, Frederick
Diller, Burgoyne
Doughty, Thomas
Dove, Arthur Garfield
Dummer, Jeremiah
Dunlap, William
Durand, Asher Brown
Duveneck, Frank
Eakins, Thomas
Earle, James
Earle, Ralph
Eaton, Joseph Oriel
Eaton, Wyatt
Eckstein, John
Edmonds, Francis William
Ehninger, John Whetten
Eichholtz, Jacob
Eilshemius, Louis Michel
Elliott, Charles Loring
Elliott, John
Ennecking, John Joseph
Farrer, Henry
Feininger, Lyonel (Charles Léonell Adrian)
Feke, Robert
Ferris, Jean Léon Gérôme
Field, Robert
Fisher, Alvan
Flagg, George Whiting
Flagg, Jared Bradley
Folwell, Samuel
Forbes, Edwin
Foster, Benjamin
Fowler, Frank
Fraser, Charles
Frazer, Oliver
Freeman, James Edwards
Frieseke, Frederick Carl
Fuller, George
Gabo, Naum
Ganso, Emil
Garrett, Edmund Henry
Gaul, William Gilbert
Gay, Winckworth Allan
Gifford, Robert Swain
Gifford, Sanford Robinson
Glackens, William James
Godefroy, Maximilian
Goodridge, Sarah
Gorky, Arshile
Gray, Henry Peters
Greenough, Henry
Gregory, Eliot
Gropper, William
Grosz, George
Guy, Seymour Joseph
Hale, Philip Leslie
Hall, George Henry
Hall, Henry Bryan
Harding, Chester
Harrison, Gabriel
Harrison, Lovell Birge
Harrison, Thomas Alexander
Hart, George Overbury
Hart, James MacDougal
Hart, William
Hartley, Marsden
Haskell, Ernest
Havell, Robert
Hawthorne, Charles Webster
Hayden, Charles Henry
Hays, William Jacob
Healy, George Peter Alexander
Hennessy, William John
Henri, Robert
Henry, Edward Lamson
Herring, James
Hesselius, Gustavus
Hesselius, John
Hicks, John, 1823–1890
Hill, Thomas
Hofmann, Hans
Homer, Winslow
Hopper, Edward
Hovenden, Thomas

Howe, William Henry
Hubbard, Richard William
Hubley, John
Hunt, William Morris
Huntington, Daniel
Ingham, Charles Cromwell
Inman, Henry
Inness, George
Irving, John Beaufain
Jackson, William Henry
Janvier, Catharine Ann
Jarvis, John Wesley
Jewett, William
Jocelyn, Nathaniel
Johnson, Jonathan Eastman
Johnston, Thomas
Jones, Hugh Bolton
Jouett, Matthew Harris
Kane, John
Karfiol, Bernard
Keith, William
Keller, Arthur Ignatius
Kensett, John Frederick
King, Samuel
Kingsley, Elbridge
Kline, Franz Josef
Knight, Daniel Ridgway
Koehler, Robert
Koopman, Augustus
Krimmel, John Lewis
Kuhn, Walt
Kuniyoshi, Yasuo
La Farge, John
Lambdin, James Reid
Lathrop, Francis Augustus
Lawrie, Alexander
Lawson, Ernest
Lebrun, Federico ("Rico")
Le Clear, Thomas
Lehman, Adele Lewisohn
Leigh, William Robinson
Leslie, Charles Robert
Leutze, Emanuel
Lewis, Edmund Darch
Lie, Jonas
Lockwood, Robert Wilton
Loeb, Louis
Longfellow, Ernest Wadsworth
Loop, Henry, Augustus
Low, John Gardner
Luks, George Benjamin
MacCameron, Robert
McEntee, Jervis
Mackubin, Florence
Macomber, Mary Lizzie
Malbone, Edward Greene
Marsh, Reginald
Marshall, William Edgar
Martin, Homer Dodge
Matteson, Tompkins Harrison
May, Edward Harrison
Mayer, Constant
Maynard, George Willoughby
Melchers, Gari
Merritt, Anna Lea
Metcalf, Willard Leroy
Mifflin, Lloyd
Mignot, Louis Remy
Miles, Edward
Miller, Charles Henry
Miller, Kenneth Hayes
Millet, Francis Davis
Minor, Robert Crannell
Moran, Edward
Moran, Peter
Moran, Thomas
Morgan, Matthew Somerville
Moses, Anna Mary Robertson ("Grandma")
Mosler, Henry
Mostel, Samuel Joel ("Zero")
Mount, William Sidney
Mowbray, Henry Siddons
Murphy, Gerald Clery
Murphy, John Francis
Myers, Jerome
Neagle, John
Neal, David Dalhoff
Newman, Barnett
Newman, Henry Roderick
Newman, Robert Loftin
Nicoll, James Craig
Norton, William Edward
O'Donovan, William Rudolf
Otis, Bass
Page, William
Palmer, Walter Launt
Paris, Walter
Parton, Arthur
Patchen, Kenneth
Pattison, James William
Peale, Anna Claypoole
Peale, Charles Willson
Peale, James
Peale, Raphael
Peale, Rembrandt
Peale, Sarah Miriam
Pearce, Charles Sprague
Pelham, Henry
Penfield, Edward
Perry, Enoch Wood
Picknell, William Lamb
Pine, Robert Edge
Platt, Charles Adams
Pollock, (Paul) Jackson
Porter, Benjamin Curtis
Powell, Lucien Whiting
Powell, William Henry
Pratt, Matthew
Prendergast, Maurice Brazil
Quartley, Arthur
Quidor, John
Quinn, Edmond Thomas
Ramage, John
Ranger, Henry Ward
Ranney, William Tylee
Read, Thomas Buchanan
Reid, Robert
Reinhardt, Ad
Reinhart, Benjamin Franklin
Reinhart, Charles Stanley
Remington, Frederic
Reuterdahl, Henry
Richards, Thomas Addison
Richards, William Trost
Ritchie, Alexander Hay
Rix, Julian Walbridge
Roberts, Elizabeth Wentworth
Robertson, Archibald
Rolshoven, Julius
Rosenthal, Toby Edward
Rossiter, Thomas Prichard
Rothko, Mark
Rowse, Samuel Worcester
Ryder, Albert Pinkham
Sandham, Henry
Sargent, Henry
Sargent, John Singer
Sartain, Emily
Sartain, William
Savage, Edward
Schussele, Christian
Seitz, William Chapin
Sellstedt, Lars Gustaf
Shahn, Benjamin ("Ben")
Sharples, James
Shattuck, Aaron Draper
Shinn, Everett
Shirlaw, Walter
Shurtleff, Roswell Morse
Simmons, Edward
Sloan, John French
Smedley, William Thomas
Smillie, George Henry
Smith, Archibald Cary
Smith, John Rowson
Smith, John Rubens
Smith, Russell
Smith, Xanthus Russell
Soyer, Moses
Spencer, Robert
Stanley, John Mix
Steichen, Edward Jean
Stella, Joseph
Sterne, Maurice
Stetson, Charles Walter
Still, Clyfford
Stone, William Oliver
Story, Julian Russell
Stuart, Gilbert
Sully, Thomas
Sylvester, Frederick Oakes
Symons, George Gardner
Szyk, Arthur
Tait, Arthur Fitzwilliam
Tanner, Henry Ossawa
Tarbell, Edmund Charles
Taylor, Frank Walter
Tchelitchew, Pavel
Thayer, Abbott Handerson
Theus, Jeremiah
Thompson, Alfred Wordsworth
Thompson, Cephas Giovanni
Thompson, Jerome B.
Thulstrup, Bror Thure
Tilton, John Rollin
Tomlin, Bradley Walker
Trott, Benjamin
Troye, Edward
Trumbull, John, 1756–1843
Tryon, Dwight William
Tucker, Allen
Turner, Charles Yardley
Turner, Ross Sterling
Twachtman, John Henry
Vanderlyn, John
Vedder, Elihu
Vinton, Frederic Porter
Vonnoh, Robert William
Waldo, Samuel Lovett
Walker, Henry Oliver
Waugh, Frederick Judd
Weeks, Edwin Lord
Weir, Julian Alden
Weir, Robert Walter
Wentworth, Cecile de

West, Benjamin
West, William Edward
Whistler, James Abbott McNeill
Whitteredge, Worthington
Wiggins, Carleton
Wilmarth, Lemuel Everett
Wilson, Robert Burns
Wimar, Carl
Wood, Grant
Wood, Joseph
Wright, Joseph
Wyant, Alexander Helwig
Wyeth, Newell Convers
Wylie, Robert
Yohn, Frederick Coffay
Young, Mahonri Mackintosh

PALEOBOTANIST (See also BOTANIST, GEOLOGIST)
Berry, Edward Wilber
Lesquereux, Leo

PALEOGRAPHER
Beeson, Charles Henry

PALEONTOLOGIST (See also GEOLOGIST)
Beecher, Charles Emerson
Clarke, John Mason
Cope, Edward Drinker
Gabb, William More
Gidley, James Williams
Grabau, Amadeus William
Granger, Walter
Hall, James, 1811–1898
Hay, Oliver Perry
Heilprin, Angelo
Hyatt, Alpheus
Knowlton, Frank Hall
Marsh, Othniel Charles
Matthew, William Diller
Meek, Fielding Bradford
Merriam, John Campbell
Newberry, John Strong
Osborn, Henry Fairfield
Patten, William
Romer, Alfred Sherwood ("Al")
Schuchert, Charles
Scott, William Berryman
Smith, James Perrin
Springer, Frank
Ulrich, Edward Oscar
Vaughan, Thomas Wayland
Wachsmuth, Charles
Walcott, Charles Doolittle
White, Charles Abiathar
Whitfield, Robert Parr
Wieland, George Reber
Williams, Henry Shaler
Williston, Samuel Wendell
Yandell, Lunsford Pitts

PAMPHLETEER (See also PUBLICIST)
Dove, David James
Heywood, Ezra Hervey
King, Dan
Paine, Thomas
Penington, Edward
Pickering, Timothy
Smith, William Loughton
Wood, John
Yates, Abraham
Zubly, John Joachim

PAPYROLOGIST
Westermann, William Linn

PARACHUTE DESIGNER
Scott, Allen Cecil

PARASITOLOGIST (See also ZOOLOGIST)
Noguchi, Hideyo
Ward, Henry Baldwin

PARLIAMENTARIAN
Dalzell, John
Hinds, Asher Crosby
Reed, Thomas Brackett
Robert, Henry Martyn

PASSPORT DIVISION CHIEF
Shipley, Ruth Bielaski

PATENT COMMISSIONER
Ellsworth, Henry Leavitt
Leggett, Mortimer Dormer
Paine, Halbert Eleazer

PATENT EXPERT
Benjamin, George Hillard
Halt, Thomas
Knight, Edward Henry
Langner, Lawrence
Renwick, Edward Sabine
Renwick, Henry Brevoort
Selden, George Baldwin

PATENT LAWYER
Davis, William Hammatt

"PATENT MEDICINE KING"
Dyott, Thomas W.

PATHOLOGIST (See also PHYSICIAN)
Biggs, Herman Michael
Bloodgood, Joseph Colt
Carroll, James
Councilman, William Thomas
Darling, Samuel Taylor
Delafield, Francis
Dyer, Rolla Eugene
Ewing, James
Fenger, Christian
Fitz, Reginald Heber
Flexner, Simon
Gardner, Leroy Upson
Hess, Alfred Fabian
Landsteiner, Karl
Libman, Emanuel
Loeb, Leo
MacCallum, William George
Mallory, Frank Burr
Moore, Veranus Alva
Murphy, James Bumgardner
Ohlmacher, Albert Philip
Pearce, Richard Mills
Prudden, Theophil Mitchell
Ricketts, Howard Taylor
Stengel, Alfred
Warren, Shields
Welch, William Henry
Wells, Harry Gideon
Wesbrook, Frank Fairchild
Wilson, Louis Blanchard

PATRIOT (See also LOYALIST, REVOLUTIONARY PATRIOT)
Alexander, James
Anagnos, Michael
Boker, George Henry
Clark, Jonas
Dawes, William
Emmet, Thomas Addis
Freeman, Nathaniel
Gurowski, Adam
Henry, William
Hitchcock, Enos
Hudson, Edward
Jackson, David
Kosciuszko, Tadeusz Andrzej Bonawentura
Law, Richard
Levy, Uriah Phillips
MacNeven, William James
Malcolm, Daniel
Markoe, Abraham
Mitchel, John
O'Reilly, John Boyle
Orr, Hugh
Peale, Charles Willson
Pinto, Isaac
Prescott, Samuel
Pulaski, Casimir
Quincy, Josiah, 1744–1775
Revere, Paul
Rush, Benjamin
Sampson, William
Scott, Gustavus
Thacher, James
Tracy, Nathaniel
Varela y Morales, Félix Francisco José Maria de la Concepción

PEACE ADVOCATE (See also PACIFIST, REFORMER)
Abbot, Willis John
Balch, Emily Greene
Bok, Edward William
Clark, Grenville
Culbertson, Ely
Dingman, Mary Agnes
Dutton, Samuel Train
Garry, Spokane
Hooper, Jessie Annette Jack
Jewett, William Cornell
Jordan, David Starr
Levermore, Charles Herbert
Levinson, Salmon Oliver
Love, Alfred Henry
Muste, Abraham Johannes
Scott, Winfield
Trueblood, Benjamin Franklin
Woolley, Mary Emma

PEDAGOGUE
Ganz, Rudolph

PEDDLER (See also MERCHANT)
Plummer, Jonathan

PEDIATRICIAN (See also PHYSICIAN)
Abt, Isaac Arthur
Aldrich, Charles Anderson
Blackfan, Kenneth Daniel
Brennemann, Joseph
Chapin, Henry Dwight
Cooley, Thomas Benton
Hess, Alfred Fabian
Holt, Luther Emmett
Howland, John
Jacobi, Abraham
Kenyon, Josephine Hemenway
Marriott, Williams McKim
Mitchell, Albert Graeme
Morse, John Lovett
Rachford, Benjamin Knox
Rotch, Thomas Morgan
Ruhräh, John
Trask, James Dowling

PENMAN (See also CALLIGRAPHER)
Spencer, Platt Rogers
PENOLOGIST (See also PRISON REFORMER, REFORMER)
Brinkerhoff, Roeliff
Brockway, Zebulon Reed
Hart, Hastings Hornell
Kirchwey, George Washington
Lewis, Orlando Faulkland
Lewisohn, Sam Adolph
Lynds, Elam
Pilsbury, Amos
Russ, John Dennison
Vaux, Richard
PENSION COMMISSIONER
Murphy, Dominic Ignatius
Tanner, James
PERSONNEL MANAGEMENT PIONEER
Bloomfield, Meyer
PETROLEUM GEOLOGIST (See also GEOLOGIST, PETROLOGIST)
Wrather, William Embry
PETROLOGIST (See also GEOLOGIST, PETROLEUM GEOLOGIST)
Bowen, Norman Levi
Cross, Charles Whitman
Daly, Reginald Aldworth
Iddings, Joseph Paxon
Washington, Henry Stephens
Williams, George Huntington
PEWTERER (See also CRAFTSMAN)
Boardman, Thomas Danforth
Danforth, Thomas
Melville, David
PHARMACEUTICAL CHEMIST (See also CHEMIST)
Kremers, Edward
PHARMACIST (See also APOTHECARY, DRUGGIST)
Durand, Élie Magloire
Frasch, Herman
Fuller, Robert Mason
Jacobs, Joseph, 1859–1929
Kiss, Max
Lloyd, John Uri
Maisch, John Michael
Marshall, Christopher
Parrish, Edward
Proctor, William
Remington, Joseph Price
Rice, Charles
Seabury, George John
Smith, Daniel B.
Squibb, Edward Robinson
Whelpley, Henry Milton
PHARMACOGNOSIST (See also PHARMACOLOGIST)
Rusby, Henry Hurd
PHARMACOLOGIST (See also PHARMACOGNOSIST, PHYSICIAN)
Abel, John Jacob
Auer, John
Barbour, Henry Gray
Edmunds, Charles Wallis
Hatcher, Robert Anthony
Hunt, Reid
Kraemer, Henry
Underhill, Franklin Pell
Weiss, Soma
PHILANTHROPIST
Adams, Charles Francis
Aiken, William
Alden, Cynthia May Westover
Alphonsa, Mother
Altman, Benjamin
Anderson, Elizabeth Milbank
Appleton, Samuel
Archer, Samuel
Auchmuty, Richard Tylden
Augustus, John
Avery, Samuel Putnam
Baker, George Fisher
Baldwin, Matthias William
Ball, Frank Clayton
Ball, George Alexander
Bamberger, Louis
Bancroft, Frederic
Barnard, Charles Francis
Barrett, Kate Waller
Barsotti, Charles
Bartlet, William
Barton, Clara
Bates, Joshua
Benezet, Anthony
Billings, Frederick
Bishop, Charles Reed
Bishop, Nathan
Blaine, Anita (Eugenie) McCormick
Blair, John Insley
Bliss, Cornelius Newton
Blodgett, John Wood
Bok, Edward William
Bowen, Louise De Koven
Brace, Charles Loring
Bradley, Lydia Moss
Breckinridge, Aida de Acosta
Bromfield, John
Brookings, Robert Somers
Brown, Moses, 1738–1836
Brown, Moses, 1742–1827
Brown, Nicholas
Brown, Obadiah
Buchtel, John Richards
Buck, Pearl Comfort Sydenstricker
Bucknell, William
Burrett, Joseph
Butler, Charles
Cabot, Godfrey Lowell
Camp, Hiram
Candler, Asa Griggs
Carnegie, Andrew
Case, Leonard
Childs, George William
Clark, Jonas Gilman
Clarkson, Matthew
Clinton, De Witt
Coates, Samuel
Coburn, Abner
Cochran, Alexander Smith
Coffin, Lorenzo S.
Coker, David Robert
Coker, James Lide
Colby, Gardner
Colgate, James Boorman
Combs, Moses Newell
Comstock, Elizabeth L.
Converse, Edmund Cogswell
Cooper, Peter
Cooper, Sarah Brown Ingersoll
Cope, Thomas Pym
Corcoran, William Wilson
Crane, Charles Richard
Creighton, Edward
Creighton, John Andrew
Crerar, John
Cresson, Elliott
Crozer, John Price
Cullen, Hugh Roy
Cupples, Samuel
Cushing, John Perkins
Cutting, Robert Fulton
Dana, Charles Anderson
Davis, Arthur Vining
De Forest, Robert Weeks
De Pauw, Washington Charles
Dodge, Grace Hoadley
Drake, Francis Marion
Dreier, Mary Elisabeth
Drexel, Anthony Joseph
Drexel, Joseph William
Duke, Benjamin Newton
Durant, Henry Fowle
Dwight, Edmund
Dyer, Isadore
Eastman, George
Eliot, Samuel
Eustis, Dorothy Leib Harrison Wood
Evans, Thomas Wiltberger
Evarts, Jeremiah
Fahnestock, Harris Charles
Falk, Maurice
Farmer, Hannah Tobey Shapleigh
Farnam, Henry
Farnam, Henry Walcott
Farnham, Eliza Woodson Burhans
Fels, Samuel Simeon
Field, Benjamin Hazard
Field, Marshall, III
Firestone, Harvey Samuel
Fleming, Arthur Henry
Flexner, Bernard
Flower, Lucy Louisa Coues
Folger, Henry Clay
Ford, Daniel Sharp
Franklin Benjamin
Gammon, Elijah Hedding
Gardiner, Robert Hallowell
George, William Reuben
Gerard, James Watson
Gerry, Elbridge Thomas
Gibbons, Abigail Hopper
Gilbert, Linda
Ginn, Edwin
Ginter, Lewis
Girard, Stephen
Gleason, Kate
Godfrey, Benjamin
Goucher, John Franklin
Graff, Everett Dwight
Graham, Isabella Marshall
Grasselli, Caesar Augustin
Gratz, Rebecca
Gray, Francis Calley
Green, Francis
Green, John Cleve
Griffith, Goldsborough Sappington
Grinnell, Henry

Griscom, John
Guggenheim, Daniel
Guggenheim, Simon
Gurley, Ralph Randolph
Hackley, Charles Henry
Hand, Daniel
Hardin, Charles Henry
Harkness, Edward Stephen
Hart, Abraham
Haughery, Margaret Gaffney
Hayden, Charles
Hearst, Phoebe Apperson
Heckscher, August
Heilprin, Michael
Hemenway, Mary Porter Tileston
Hepburn, Alonzo Barton
Hershey, Milton Snavely
Hewitt, Abram Stevens
Heye, George Gustav
Higinbotham, Harlow Niles
Hires, Charles Elmer, Jr.
Hopkins, Johns
Horlick, William
Hoyt, John Sherman
Hutton, Levi William
Inman, Samuel Martin
Irene, Sister
Jackson, Helen Maria Fiske Hunt
Jackson, Samuel Macauley
Jacobs, Joseph, 1859–1929
James, Arthur Curtiss
James, Daniel Willis
Janney, Oliver Edward
Jeanes, Anna T.
Jesup, Morris Ketchum
Kelly, Eugene
Kennedy, John Stewart
Knapp, Joseph Palmer
Kresge, Sebastian Spering
Kress, Samuel Henry
Ladd, Kate Macy
Lafon, Thomy
Lamont, Thomas William
Lasker, Albert Davis
Lawrence, Abbott
Lawrence, Amos
Lawrence, Amos Adams
Lawrence, William, 1783–1848
Lehman, Adele Lewisohn
Lenox, James
Letchworth, William Pryor
Lewisohn, Adolph
Lewisohn, Sam Adolph
Libbey, Edward Drummond
Lick, James
Lilly, Eli
Littauer, Lucius Nathan
Loeb, James
Lowell, Josephine Shaw
Ludwick, Christopher
Lunt, Orrington
Lyman, Theodore, 1792–1849
McCormick, Cyrus Hall
McCormick, Leander James
McDonogh, John
Mackay, Clarence Hungerford
McKinley, William Brown
McLean, William Lippard
Maclure, William
Macy, Valentine Everit
Magee, Christopher Lyman
Mallinckrodt, Edward
Mallinckrodt, Edward, Jr.
Maloney, Martin
Marquand, Henry Gurdon
Martin, Frederick Townsend
Mather, Samuel
Matheson, William John
Matthiessen, Frederick William
Mercer, Jesse
Meyer, Agnes Elizabeth Ernst
Miller, Lewis
Mills, Darius Ogden
Morehead, John Motley
Morgan, Edwin Barber
Mott, Charles Stewart
Newberry, Walter Loomis
Newcomb, Josephine Louise Le Monnier
Newman, Henry
O'Fallon, John
Oglethorpe, James Edward
Olyphant, David Washington Cincinnatus
Osborn, William Henry
Ottendorfer, Anna Behr Uhl
Ottendorfer, Oswald
Packer, Asa
Paine, Robert Treat
Pardee, Ario
Parrish, Anne
Passavant, William Alfred
Patten, James A.
Patterson, Morris
Peabody, George
Peabody, George Foster
Pearsons, Daniel Kimball
Pellew, Henry Edward
Pemberton, Israel
Pemberton, James
Penrose, Spencer
Pepper, George Seckel
Pepper, William
Perkins, Thomas Handasyd
Peter, Sarah Worthington King
Pew, John Howard
Phelps, Anson Greene
Phillips, Thomas Wharton
Phillips, William
Phipps, Henry
Pintard, John
Pitcairn, John
Post, Marjorie Merriweather
Poulson, Niels
Poulson, Zachariah
Poydras, Julien De Lelande
Pratt, Charles
Pratt, Enoch
Pratt, John Lee
Presser, Theodore
Proctor, William Cooper
Prouty, Olive Higgins
Purdue, John
Rachford, Benjamin Knox
Ramsay, Erskine
Randall, Robert Richard
Rawle, William
Redwood, Abraham
Reilly, Marion
Reisinger, Hugo
Reynolds, William Neal
Rhoades, James E.
Rich, Isaac
Richardson, Sid Williams
Rindge, Frederick Hastings
Robert, Christopher Rhinelander
Rockefeller, Abby Greene Aldrich
Rockefeller, John Davison
Rockefeller, John Davison, Jr.
Rockefeller, John Davison, 3d
Rockefeller, Martha Baird
Rockefeller, Nelson Aldrich
Rockefeller, Winthrop
Rose, Chauncey
Rosenberg, Henry
Rosenstiel, Lewis Solon
Rosenwald, Julius
Rosenwald, Lessing Julius
Rutgers, Henry
Ryerson, Martin Antoine
Sachs, Paul Joseph
Sage, Henry Williams
Sage, Margaret Olivia Slocum
Sanborn, Franklin Benjamin
Say, Benjamin
Schiff, Jacob Henry
Scripps, Ellen Browning
Seligman, Jesse
Seney, George Ingraham
Severance, Louis Henry
Seybert, Henry
Shattuck, George Cheyne, 1783–1854
Shattuck, George Cheyne, 1813–1893
Shaw, Pauline Agassiz
Shedd, John Graves
Sheffield, Joseph Earl
Skouras, Spyros Panagiotes
Slater, John Fox
Sleeper, Jacob
Sloan, Alfred Pritchard, Jr.
Sloss, Louis
Smith, Daniel B.
Smith, Gerrit
Smith, Oliver
Snow, John Ben
Solomons, Adolphus Simeon
Speyer, James Joseph
Springer, Reuben Runyan
Sprunt, James
Sterling, John William
Stetson, John Batterson
Stewart, William Rhinelander
Stoeckel, Carl
Stokes, Caroline Phelps
Stokes, Olivia Egleston Phelps
Stone, Amasa
Straus, Nathan
Straus, Roger W(illiams)
Street, Augustus Russell
Stuart, Robert Leighton
Sulzberger, Cyrus Lindauer
Swasey, Ambrose
Syms, Benjamin
Taft, Charles Phelps
Talbot, Emily Fairbanks
Tappan, Arthur
Taylor, Joseph Wright
Thaw, William
Thayer, Nathaniel
Thomas, George Clifford

Thompson, Benjamin
Thompson, William Boyce
Tiffany, Louis Comfort
Tome, Jacob
Tompkins, Sally Louisa ("Captain Sally")
Towne, John Henry
Townsend, Mira Sharpless
Tracy, Nathaniel
Tulane, Paul
Vanderbilt, Cornelius, 1843–1899
Vaux, Roberts
Wade, Jeptha Homer
Wadsworth, Eliot
Wagner, William
Walker, William Johnson
Warburg, Felix Moritz
Ward, Marcus Lawrence
Weddell, Alexander Wilbourne
Welsh, John
Wharton, Joseph
Widener, George Dunton
Widener, Peter Arrell Brown
Williston, Samuel
Wolfe, Catharine Lorillard
Wolfe, John David
Wormeley, Katherine Prescott
Yeatman, James Erwin
Zellerbach, Harold Lionel

PHILOLOGIST (See also SCHOLAR)
Adler, George J.
Alden, Raymond MacDonald
Armstrong, Edward Cooke
Bloomfield, Maurice
Bright, James Wilson
Brown, Carleton
Callaway, Morgan
Child, Francis James
Churchill, William
Conant, Thomas Jefferson
Davis, Charles Henry Stanley
Elliott, Aaron Marshall
Emerson, Oliver Farrar
Flügel, Ewald
Francke, Kuno
Garnett, James Mercer
Gibbs, Josiah Willard
Gildersleeve, Basil Lanneau
Grandgent, Charles Hall
Greenough, James Bradstreet
Gummere, Francis Barton
Hadley, James
Haldeman, Samuel Steman
Hall, Fitzedward
Harrison, James Albert
Hart, James Morgan
Haupt, Paul
Hempl, George
Hills, Elijah Clarence
Hopkins, Edward Washburn
Jackson, Abraham Valentine Williams
Klipstein, Louis Frederick
Lang, Henry Roseman
Learned, Marion Dexter
Lounsbury Thomas Raynesford
Manly, John Matthews
March, Francis Andrew
Marden, Charles Carroll
Merriam, Augustus Chapman
Ord, George
Parrington, Vernon Louis
Peck, Harry Thurston
Pei, Mario Andrew
Phillips, Henry
Pickering, John
Price, Thomas Randolph
Prokosch, Eduard
Radin, Max
Reeves, Arthur Middleton
Rice, Charles
Rickert, Martha Edith
Robinson, Edward, 1794–1863
Robinson, Thérèse Albertine Louise von Jakob
Rolfe, William James
Royster, James Finch
Safford, William Edwin
Schele de Vere, Maximilian
Schilling, Hugo Karl
Seidensticker, Oswald
Sheldon, Edward Stevens
Short, Charles
Smith, Byron Caldwell
Smith, Charles Forster
Smith, Lloyd Logan Pearsall
Todd, Henry Alfred
Trumbull, James Hammond
Van Name, Addison
Wiener, Leo
Wilson, Peter

PHILOMATH (See also SCHOLAR)
Daboll, Nathan

PHILOSOPHER (See also SCHOLAR)
Abbot, Francis Ellingwood
Albee, Ernest
Alexander, Hartley Burr
Ames, Edward Scribner
Andrews, Stephen Pearl
Bascom, John
Beasley, Frederick
Bentley, Arthur Fisher
Bjerregaard, Carl Henrik Andreas
Blood, Benjamin Paul
Bode, Boyd Henry
Bowen, Francis
Bowne, Borden Parker
Bridgman, Percy Williams
Brightman, Edgar Sheffield
Brokmeyer, Henry C.
Buchanan, Joseph
Buchanan, Scott Milross
Calhoun, John Caldwell
Calkins, Mary Whiton
Carnap, Rudolf
Carus, Paul
Cohen, Morris Raphael
Creighton, James Edwin
Davidson, Thomas
Dewey, John
Edwards, Jonathan
Fiske, John
Fite, Warner
Frank, Philipp G.
Fullerton, George Stuart
Gardiner, Harry Norman
Gordy, John Pancoast
Grimes, James Stanley
Gros, John Daniel
Hall, Granville Stanley
Hamilton, Edward John
Harris, William Torrey
Hedge, Levi
Hibben, John Grier
Hickok, Laurens Perseus
Hocking, William Ernest
Howison, George Holmes
Hyslop, James Hervey
James, William
Jones, Rufus Matthew
Kallen, Horace Meyer
Kroeger, Adolph Ernst
Ladd, George Trumbull
Laguna, Theodore de Leo de
Lewis, Clarence Irving
Lloyd, Alfred Henry
Locke, Alain Leroy
Longfellow, Samuel
Lovejoy, Arthur Oncken
Lyman, Eugene William
Macy, Jesse
Marcuse, Herbert
Marsh, James
Mead, George Herbert
Michel, Virgil George
Montague, William Pepperell
Montgomery, Edmund Duncan
Moore, Addison Webster
More, Paul Elmer
Morris, George Sylvester
Mulford, Prentice
Neumark, David
Newbold, William Romaine
Niebuhr, Karl Paul Reinhold ("Reinie")
Overstreet, Harry Allen
Pace, Edward Aloysius
Palmer, George Herbert
Peirce, Charles Sanders
Perry, Ralph Barton
Powell, John Wesley
Prall, David Wight
Pratt, James Bissett
Radin, Max
Rauch, Frederick Augustus
Reichenbach, Hans
Riley, Isaac Woodbridge
Royce, Josiah
Salter, William Mackintire
Santayana, George
Saugrain de Vigni, Antoine François
Schurman, Jacob Gould
Seth, James
Smith, Thomas Vernor
Spaulding, Edward Gleason
Sterrett, James Macbride
Strong, Charles Augustus
Swenson, David Ferdinand
Tappan, Henry Philip
Thilly, Frank
Tillich, Paul
Tufts, James Hayden
Wenley, Robert Mark
Whitehead, Alfred North
Wilder, Alexander
Woodbridge, Frederick James Eugene
Woodward, Augustus Brevoort
Wright, John Joseph
Wright, Chauncey
Znaniecki, Florian Witold

PHONETIC SPELLING PIONEER
Masquerier, Lewis

PHONOGRAPHER
Pitman, Benn
PHOTOENGRAVER (See also ENGRAVER)
Levy, Max
Moss, John Calvin
PHOTOGRAPHER
Austen, (Elizabeth) Alice
Bachrach, Louis Fabian
Bourke-White, Margaret
Brady, Mathew B.
Carbutt, John
Cunningham, Imogen
Curtis, Edward Sheriff
Evans, Walker
Genthe, Arnold
Goddard, Paul Beck
Halsman, Philippe
Hare, James H.
Hine, Lewis Wickes
Hubbard, Bernard Rosecrans
Jackson, William Henry
Johnston, Frances Benjamin
Kanaga, Consuelo Delesseps
Lange, Dorothea
Muybridge, Eadweard
Plumbe, John
Sheeler, Charles R., Jr.
Smith, William Eugene
Steichen, Edward Jean
Stieglitz, Alfred
Strand, Paul
Van Vechten, Carl
Weston, Edward Henry
White, Minor Martin
PHOTOGRAPHIC SCIENTIST
Mees, Charles Edward Kenneth
PHOTOJOURNALIST
Bourke-White, Margaret
Chapelle, Dickey
PHRENOLOGIST
Fowler, Orson Squire
Sizer, Nelson
Wells, Samuel Roberts
PHYLOBIOLOGIST
Burrow, Trigant
PHYSICAL CULTURIST
Atlas, Charles S.
Macfadden, Bernarr
PHYSICAL EDUCATION LEADER (See also PHYSICIAN)
Alcott, William Andrus
Berenson, Senda
Blaikie, William
Gulick, Luther Halsey, 1865–1918
Kiphuth, Robert John Herman
Lewis, Dioclesian
Naismith, James
Sargent, Dudley Allen
PHYSICAL TRAINER
Muldoon, William
PHYSICIAN (See also ALIENIST, ANESTHESIOLOGIST, ANATOMIST, APOTHECARY, BACTERIOLOGIST, BIOCHEMIST, BIOMETRICIAN, DENTIST, DERMATOLOGIST, DIETICIAN, DRUGGIST, ELECTRO-THERAPIST, EMBRYOLOGIST, EPIDEMIOLOGIST, GYNECOLOGIST, HOMEOPATHIST, HYDROTHERAPIST, HYGIENIST, IMMUNOLOGIST, LARYNGOLOGIST, LITHOTOMIST, MEDICAL HISTORIAN, MEDICAL RESEARCH WORKER, MENTAL HYGIENIST, MICROSCOPIST, NEUROLOGIST, NEUROPATHOLOGIST, NURSE, OBSTETRICIAN, OCULIST, OPHTHALMOLOGIST, OPTICIAN, OTOLOGIST, PATHOLOGIST, PEDIATRICIAN, PHARMACIST, PHARMACOLOGIST, PHYSICAL EDUCATION LEADER, PHYSIOLOGIST, PSYCHIATRIST, PHYCHOANALYST, PSYCHOPATHOLOGIST, PUBLIC HEALTH OFFICIAL, RADIOGRAPHER, RHINOLOGIST, ROENTGENOLOGIST, SANITARIAN, SURGEON, TOXICOLOGIST, UROLOGIST, VACCINATOR, VETERINARIAN)
Abbott, Samuel Warren
Abrams, Albert
Adams, Daniel
Adams, William Lysander
Allen, Harrison
Allen, Nathan
Allen, Timothy Field
Allison, Richard
Alter, David
Ames, Nathaniel
Anderson, Victor Vance
Apgar, Virginia
Appleton, Nathaniel Walker
Arnold, Richard Dennis
Aspinwall, William
Ayer, James Cook
Bache, Franklin
Baetjer, Frederick Henry
Baker, Sara Josephine
Baldwin, Edward Robinson
Baldwin, William
Bard, John
Bard, Samuel
Barker, Benjamin Fordyce
Barker, Jeremiah
Bartholow, Roberts
Bartlett, Elisha
Bartlett, John Sherren
Bartlett, Josiah
Barton, Benjamin Smith
Baruch, Simon
Batchelder, John Putnam
Bates, James
Battey, Robert
Baxley, Henry Willis
Bayley, Richard
Beach, Wooster
Beard, George Miller
Beck, John Brodhead
Beck, Lewis Caleb
Beck, Theodric Romeyn
Bell, Luther Vose
Bennet, Sanford Fillmore
Bigelow, Jacob
Bigelow, William Sturgis
Biggs, Hermann Michael
Billings, Frank
Bird, Robert Montgomery
Blackburn, Luke Pryor
Blackwell, Elizabeth
Blake, Francis Gilman
Blalock, Nelson Gales
Blunt, James Gillpatrick
Bohune, Lawrence
Bond, Thomas
Bowditch, Henry Ingersoll
Boylston, Zabdiel
Bozeman, Nathan
Bridges, Robert
Brigham, Amariah
Brill, Nathan Edwin
Brincklé, William Draper
Brockett, Linus Pierpont
Bronson, Henry
Brown, George
Brown, Lawrason
Brown, Percy
Brown, Samuel
Brown, William
Bruce, Archibald
Brühl, Gustav
Buchanan, Joseph Rodes
Buckler, Thomas Hepburn
Bulkley, Lucius Duncan
Bullitt, Henry Massie
Burnett, Swan Moses
Burrage, Walter Lincoln
Burton, William
Bushnell, George Ensign
Byrne, John
Cabell, James Lawrence
Cabot, Richard Clarke
Cadwalader, Thomas
Caldwell, Charles
Campbell, Henry Fraser
Carson, Joseph
Carson, Simeon Lewis
Chadwick, James Read
Channing, Walter
Chapman, Alvan Wentworth
Chapman, Henry Cadwalader
Chapman, Nathaniel
Child, Robert
Christian, Henry Asbury
Church, Benjamin
Clayton, Joshua
Cochran, John
Cohen, Jacob da Silva Solis
Cohn, Alfred Einstein
Coit, Henry Leber
Cook, Frederick Albert
Cooke, Elisha
Cooke, John Esten
Cooke, Robert Anderson
Copeland, Royal Samuel
Craik, James
Cranston, John
Craven, John Joseph
Crawford, John
Crawford, John Martin
Crumbine, Samuel Jay
Cullis, Charles
Cushny, Arthur Robertson
Cutler, Ephraim
Da Costa, Jacob Mendez
Dalcho, Frederick

Darling, Samuel Taylor
Davidoff, Leo Max
Davis, Charles Henry Stanley
Davis, Edwin Hamilton
Davis, Nathan Smith
Delafield, Francis
Deléry, Franéois Charles
Dercum, Francis Xavier
De Rosset, Moses John
Dewees, William Potts
Dick, Elisha Cullen
Dickson, Samuel Henry
Disbrow, William Stephen
Doddridge, Joseph
Dooley, Thomas Anthony, III
Dorsch, Eduard
Doughty, William Henry
Douglass, William
Drake, Daniel
Dwight, Nathaniel
Dyer, Isadore
Earle, Pliny
Eberle, John
Edder, William
Edes, Robert Thaxter
Edsall, David Linn
Eliot, Charles
Ellis, Calvin
Elmer, Ebenezer
Elmer, Jonathan
Elwell, John Johnson
Elwyn, Alfred Langdon
Emerson, Gouverneur
Emmet, Thomas Addis
Emmons, Ebenezer
Engelmann, George
Evans, George Alfred
Evans, John
Ewell, James
Ewell, Thomas
Faget, Jean Charles
Favill, Henry Baird
Fay, Jonas
Fayssoux, Peter
Finlay, Carlos Juan
Fisher, George Jackson
Fisher, John Dix
Fletcher, William Baldwin
Flick, Lawrence Francis
Flint, Austin, 1812–1886
Flint, Austin, 1836–1915
Foote, John Ambrose
Fordyce, John Addison
Forwood, William Henry
Foster, Frank Pierce
Foster, John Pierrepont Codrington
Francis, John Wakefield
Francis, Samuel Ward
Freeman, Nathaniel
Friedenwald, Aaron
Fuller, Robert Mason
Fussell, Bartholomew
Gale, Benjamin
Gallinger, Jacob Harold
Gallup, Joseph Adams
Garcelon, Alonzo
Garden, Alexander
Gardiner, Silvester
Garnett, Alexander Yelverton Peyton
Garvin, Lucius Fayette Clark
Gerhard, William Wood
Gibbes, Robert Wilson
Gibbons, William
Gilbert, Rufus Henry
Girard, Charles Frédéric
Goddard, Paul Beck
Goforth, William
Goldsmith, Middleton
Goldstein, Max Aaron
Goodrich, Benjamin Franklin
Gorham, John
Gorrie, John
Gould, Augustus Addison
Gould, George Milbry
Gradle, Henry
Grant, Asahel
Gray, John Purdue
Green, Asa
Green, Horace
Green, Norvin
Green, Samuel Abbott
Greenhow, Robert
Guernsey, Egbert
Guild, La Fayette
Guiteras, Juan
Guthrie, Samuel
Guttmacher, Alan Frank
Hack, George
Hale, Edwin Moses
Hale, Enoch
Hall, William Whitty
Hamilton, Alexander, 1712–1756
Hamilton, Alice
Hamilton, Allan McLane
Hand, Edward
Harlan, Richard
Harrington, Thomas Francis
Hartshorne, Henry
Haviland, Clarence Floyd
Hawley, Paul Ramsey
Hayes, Isaac Israel
Hays, Isaac
Hempel, Charles Julius
Hench, Philip Showalter
Henderson, Thomas
Henry, Morris Henry
Henshall, James Alexander
Hering, Constantine
Herter, Christian Archibald
Hewes, Robert
Hildreth, Samuel Prescott
Hoagland, Charles Lee
Hoff, John Van Rensselaer
Holcombe, William Henry
Holder, Joseph Bassett
Holten, Samuel
Holyoke, Edward Augustus
Hooker, Worthington
Hoover, Charles Franklin
Hopkins, Lemuel
Horn, George Henry
Horsfield, Thomas
Hosack, David
Hough, Franklin Benjamin
House, Samuel Reynolds
Hubbard, John
Huger, Francis Kinloch
Hunt, Harriot Kezia
Huntington, Elisha
Husk, Charles Ellsworth
Huston, Charles
Hutchinson, James
Hutchinson, Woods
Hyde, James Nevins
Ingals, Ephraim Fletcher
Ives, Eli
Jackson, Abraham Reeves
Jackson, Chevalier
Jackson, David
Jackson, Hall
Jackson, James, 1777–1867
Jackson, James Caleb
Jackson, John Davies
Jackson, Mercy Ruggles Bisbe
Jackson, Samuel
Jacobi, Abraham
Jacobi, Mary Corinna Putnam
James, Edwin
James, Thomas Chalkley
Jameson, Horatio Gates
Janeway, Edward Gamaliel
Janeway, Theodore Caldwell
Janney, Oliver Edward
Jarvis, Edward
Jarvis, Wiliam Chapman
Jay, Sir James
Jeffries, John
Johnson, Joseph
Jones, Alexander
Jones, Calvin
Jones, Joseph
Jones, William Palmer
Kane, Elisha Kent
Keagy, John Miller
Kearsley, John
Keating, John Marie
Kedzie, Robert Clark
Keeley, Leslie E.
Kellogg, Albert
Kelly, Aloysius Oliver Joseph
Kempster, Walter
Kerr, John Glasgow
Keyt, Alonzo Thrasher
King, Albert Freeman Africanus
King, Dan
King, John
King, Samuel Ward
Kirkbridge, Thomas Story
Kirkland, Jared Potter
Kneeland, Samuel
Knight, Frederick Irving
Knight, Jonathan
Knowles, John Hilton
Knowlton, Charles
Kober, George Martin
Kolb, Lawrence
Kolle, Frederick Strange
Krause, Allen Kramer
Kuhn, Adam
Kunze, Richard Ernest
La Borde, Maximilian
Ladd, Joseph Brown
Landis, Henry Robert Murray
Lane, William Carr
Lapham, William Berry
La Roche, René
Lattimore, William
Lawson, Leonidas Merion
Lazear, Jesse William
Leathers, Waller Smith
Le Conte, John Lawrence
Lee, Charles Alfred
Leib, Michael

Leland, George Adams
Le Moyne, Francis Julius
Leonard, Charles Lester
Letterman, Jonathan
Lincecum, Gideon
Lincoln, Rufus Pratt
Linde, Christian
Lindsley, John Berrien
Lining, John
Linn, Lewis Fields
Littell, Squier
Lloyd, Thomas
Locke, John
Logan, Cornelius Ambrose
Logan, George
Long, Perrin Hamilton
Longcope, Warfield Theobald
Loring, George Bailey
Lozier, Clemence Sophia Harned
Lumbrozo, Jacob
Lydston, George Frank
Lynch, Robert Clyde
Lyster, Henry Francis Le Hunte
McCaw, James Brown
McClellan, George, 1849–1913
McClurg, James
McCormack, Joseph Nathaniel
McCrae, Thomas
McCreery, Charles
McDowell, Ephraim
McFarland, George Bradley
McIntire, Ross
Mackenzie, John Noland
McKenzie, Robert Tait
MacNeven, William James
Magruder, George Lloyd
Mahoney, John Friend
Manson, Otis Frederick
Marks, Elias
Marshall, Clara
Marshall, Louis
Massey, George Betton
Matas, Rudolph
Maxwell, David Hervey
Maxwell, George Troup
Mayo, William Starbuck
Mayo, William Worrell
Mazzei, Philip
Mease, James
Meeker, Moses
Meigs, Arthur Vincent
Meigs, Charles Delucena
Meigs, James Aitken
Meigs, John Forsyth
Meltzer, Samuel James
Menninger, Charles Frederick
Mergler, Marie Josepha
Metcalfe, Samuel Lytler
Mettauer, John Peter
Michel, William Middleton
Michener, Ezra
Middleton, Peter
Miles, Manly
Miller, Edward
Miller, Henry
Miller, James Alexander
Minot, George Richards
Mitchell, George Edward
Mitchell, John, d. 1768
Mitchell, John Kearsley
Mitchell, Silas Weir
Mitchell, Thomas Duché
Mitchill, Samuel Latham
Monette, John Wesley
Moore, Joseph Earle
Morgan, John
Morril, David Lawrence
Morris, Caspar
Morrow, Prince Albert
Morrow, Thomas Vaughan
Morton, Samuel George
Morwitz, Edward
Mosher, Eliza Maria
Moultrie, John
Mundé, Paul Fortunatus
Neal, Josephine Bicknell
Neidhard, Charles
Newton, Robert Safford
Nichols, Charles Henry
Nichols, Charles Lemuel
Nichols, Mary Sargeant Neal Gove
Noeggerath, Emil Oscar Jacob Bruno
North, Elisha
Nott, Josiah Clark
O'Callaghan, Edmund Bailey
O'Dwyer, Joseph
Oemler, Arminius
O'Fallon, James
Ohlmacher, Albert Philip
Oliver, Fitch Edward
Ordronaux, John
Osler, William
Otis, Fessenden Nott
Ott, Isaac
Otto, John Conrad
Page, Charles Grafton
Paine, Martyn
Palmer, Alonzo Benjamin
Palmer, Walter Walker
Pancoast, Seth
Parrish, Joseph
Parsons, Usher
Pascalis-Ouvrière, Felix
Pavy, Octave
Peabody, Nathaniel
Pearsons, Daniel Kimball
Peaslee, Edmund Randolph
Pendleton, Edmund Monroe
Pepper, William, 1810–1864
Pepper, William, 1843–1898
Pepper, William, III
Perkins, Elisha
Perrine, Henry
Perry, William
Peter, Robert
Peters, John Charles
Pickering, Charles
Pitcher, Zina
Plotz, Harry
Plummer, Henry Stanley
Polk, William Mecklenburg
Porcher, Francis Peyre
Post, George Edward
Pott, John
Potter, Ellen Culver
Potter, Nathaniel
Potts, Charles Sower
Potts, Jonathan
Powell, William Byrd
Prescott, Oliver
Prescott, Samuel
Preston, Ann
Preston, Jonas
Price, George Moses
Price, Joseph
Prime, Benjamin Youngs
Prince, Morton
Pulte, Joseph Hippolyt
Purple, Samuel Smith
Putnam, Charles Pickering
Putnam, Helen Cordelia
Quine, William Edward
Quintard, Charles Todd
Ramsay, David
Ramsey, James Gettys McGready
Ranney, Ambrose Loomis
Rauch, John Henry
Raue, Charles Gottlieb
Ravenel, Edmund
Ravenel, St. Julien
Redman, John
Reed, Walter
Rhoads, Cornelius Packard
Richards, Dickinson Woodruff
Richardson, Charles Williamson
Richardson, Robert
Richmond, John Lambert
Richmond, John Wilkes
Ricord, Philippe
Riddell, John Leonard
Rivers, Thomas Milton
Robertson, Jerome Bonaparte
Robinson, George Canby
Romayne, Nicholas
Roosa, Daniel Bennett St. John
Root, Joseph Pomeroy
Rothrock, Joseph Trimble
Rous, Francis Peyton
Rovenstine, Emery Andrew
Rowland, Henry Cottrell
Rubinow, Isaac Max
Rush, Benjamin
Rush, James
Russ, John Dennison
Russell, Bartholomew
Sachs, Theodore Bernard
Sajous, Charles Euchariste de Médicis
Salisbury, James Henry
Salmon, Thomas William
Sappington, John
Sargent, Dudley Allen
Sargent, Fitzwilliam
Sartwell, Henry Parker
Saugrain de Vigni, Antoine François
Saulsbury, Gove
Savage, Thomas Staughton
Say, Benjamin
Schöpf, Johann David
Scudder, John Milton
Semmes, Alexander Jenkins
Seybert, Adam
Shattuck, Frederick Cheever
Shattuck, George Brune
Shattuck, George Cheyne, 1783–1854
Shattuck, George Cheyne, 1813–1893
Shaw, Anna Howard
Shaw, John, 1778–1809

Shecut, John Linnaeus Edward Whitridge
Shepard, Fred Douglas
Shippen, William
Short, Charles Wilkins
Sibley, John
Small, Alvan Edmond
Smith, Elihu Hubbard
Smith, James McCune
Smith, Job Lewis
Smith, John Augustine
Smith, Nathan, 1762–1829
Snyder, Howard McCrum
Snyder, John Francis
Spalding, Lyman
Speir, Samuel Fleet
Spivak, Charles David
Squibb, Edward Robinson
Starr, Louis
Stearns, Henry Putnam
Steiner, Lewis Henry
Stephenson, Benjamin Franklin
Stiles, Henry Reed
Stillé, Alfred
Stockton, Charles G.
Stone, Abraham
Stone, Richard French
Stone, Warren
Strong, Richard Pearson
Strudwick, Edmund Charles Fox
Talbot, Israel Tisdale
Taussig, William
Taylor, Joseph Wright
Taylor, Robert Tunstall
Tennent, John
Terry, Marshall Orlando
Testut, Charles
Thacher, James
Thayer, William Sydney
Thomas, Joseph
Thomas, Richard Henry
Thompson, William Gilman
Thomson, Samuel
Thornton, Matthew
Ticknor, Francis Orray
Timberlake, Gideon
Timme, Walter
Todd, Eli
Toner, Joseph Meredith
Townsend, Francis Everett
Trudeau, Edward Livingston
Tufts, Cotton
Tully, William
Turnbull, Andrew
Tyson, James
Van Allen, Frank
Van Beuren, Johannes
Van Buren, William Holme
Van Fleet, Walter
Vedder, Edward Bright
Von Ruck, Karl
Walcott, Henry Pickering
Waldo, David
Walker, Mary Edwards
Walker, Thomas
Walker, William Johnson
Ward, Richard Halsted
Warder, John Aston
Ware, John
Warren, Joseph
Warthin, Aldred Scott
Waterhouse, Benjamin
Weber, Gustav Carl Erich
Weil, Richard
Welch, William Wickham
Wells, William Charles
Werde, Grover William
Wesselhoeft, Conrad
West, Henry Sergeant
White, Charles Abiathar
White, Paul Dudley
Whitman, Marcus
Wickes, Stephen
Widney, Joseph Pomeroy
Wiener, Alexander Solomon
Wilbur, Ray Lyman
Wilcox, Reynold Webb
Wilder, Alexander
Wilder, Russell Morse
Willard, De Forest
Williams, Francis Henry
Williams, John Whitridge
Williams, Linsly Rudd
Williams, Nathanael
Williams, William Carlos
Wistar, Caspar
Witherspoon, John Alexander
Wood, Edward Stickney
Wood, George Bacon
Wood, Horatio Charles
Woodhouse, James
Woodruff, Charles Edward
Woodward, Joseph Janvier
Woodward, Samuel Bayard
Work, Hubert
Wormley, Theodore George
Wright, Joseph Jefferson Burr
Wyckoff, John Henry
Wyman, Morrill
Yandell, David Wendell
Yandell, Lunsford Pitts
Young, Thomas
Zakrgewska, Marie Elizabeth
Zinsser, Hans

PHYSICIST (See also SCIENTIST)
Allison, Samuel King
Alter, David
Ames, Joseph Sweetman
Anthony, William Arnold
Bache, Alexander Dallas
Barker, George Frederick
Barus, Carl
Bauer, Louis Agricola
Bayma, Joseph
Becker, George Ferdinand
Békésy, Georg von
Bell, Louis
Blair, William Richards
Blake, Francis
Blodgett, Katharine Burr
Boltwood, Bertram Borden
Bowen, Ira Sprague
Boyé, Martin Hans
Brace, Dewitt Bristol
Bridgman, Percy Williams
Briggs, Lyman James
Buckley, Oliver Ellsworth
Bumstead, Henry Andrews
Burgess, George Kimball
Cohen, Jacob da Silva Solis
Compton, Arthur Holly
Compton, Karl Taylor
Condon, Edward Uhler
Davis, Harvey Nathaniel
Davisson, Clinton Joseph
Debye, Peter Joseph William
Duane, William
Dunning, John Ray
Eddy, Henry Turner
Einstein, Albert
Farrar, John
Fermi, Enrico
Franck, James
Frank, Philipp G.
Gale, Henry Gordon
Gamow, George
Germer, Lester Halbert
Gibbs, Josiah Willard
Goddard, Robert Hutchings
Goudsmit, Samuel Abraham
Gunn, Ross
Guthe, Karl Eugen
Hall, Edwin Herbert
Hansen, William Webster
Harkins, William Draper
Hastings, Charles Sheldon
Haworth, Leland John
Henry, Joseph
Hess, Victor Franz
Humphreys, Wiliam Jackson
Kármán, Theodore (Todor) von
Langmuir, Irving
Lawrence, Ernest Orlando
Lewis, Exum Percival
Loomis, Elmer Howard
Lyman, Chester Smith
Lyman, Theodore
Maclaurin, Richard Cockburn
Mayer, Alfred Marshall
Mayer, Maria Goeppert
Mendenhall, Charles Elwood
Mendenhall, Thomas Corwin
Michelson, Albert Abraham
Miller, Dayton Clarence
Millikan, Clark Blanchard
Millikan, Robert Andrews
Morley, Edward Williams
Nichols, Edward Leamington
Nichols, Ernest Fox
Nipher, Francis Eugene
Oppenheimer, Julius Robert
Page, Leigh
Pegram, George Braxton
Peirce, Benjamin Osgood
Pfund, August Herman
Pupin, Michael Idvorsky
Richtmyer, Floyd Karker
Rogers, William Augustus
Rood, Ogden Nicholas
Rosa, Edward Bennett
Rowland, Henry Augustus
Sabine, Wallace Clement Ware
Slater, John Clarke
Stern, Otto
Szilard, Leo
Tate, John Torrence
Thompson, Benjamin
Tolman, Richard Chace
Troland, Leonard Thompson
Trowbridge, Augustus
Trowbridge, John
Van de Graaff, Robert Jemison
Van Vleck, John Hasbrouck
Von Neumann, John
Waidner, Charles William
Waterman, Alan Tower

Webster, Arthur Gordon
Wells, William Charles
Winthrop, John
Woodward, Robert Simpson
PHYSIOGRAPHER (See also GEOGRAPHER, NATURALIST)
Campbell, Marius Robinson
PHYSIOLOGICAL CHEMIST (See also CHEMIST, PHYSIOLOGIST)
Mendel, Lafayette Benedict
PHYSIOLOGIST (See also PHYSICIAN)
Allen, Edgar
Auer, John
Bazett, Henry Cuthbert
Békésky, Georg von
Bowditch, Henry Pickering
Cannon, Walter Bradford
Carlson, Anton Julius
Curtis, John Green
Dalton, John Call
Drinker, Cecil Kent
Dusser de Barenne, Joannes Gregorius
Erlanger, Joseph
Flint, Austin
Gasser, Herbert Spencer
Hecht, Selig
Hemmeter, John Conrad
Henderson, Lawrence Joseph
Henderson, Yandell
Hooker, Donald Russell
Hough, Theodore
Howell, William Henry
Keyt, Alonzo Thrasher
Knowles, John Hilton
Lee, Frederic Schiller
Lining, John
Loeb, Jacques
Lombard, Warren Plimpton
Lusk, Graham
Martin, Henry Newell
Meltzer, Samuel James
Mitchell, John Kearsley
Murphy, Gardner
Osterhout, Winthrop John Vanleuven
Porter, William Townsend
Rachford, Benjamin Knox
Rolf, Ida Pauline
Smith, Homer William
Stewart, George Neil
Troland, Leonard Thompson
Vaughan, Daniel
Weiss, Soma
PIANIST (See also JAZZ PIANIST, MUSICIAN)
Armstrong, Henry Worthington ("Harry")
Baermann, Carl
Bauer, Harold Victor
Beach, Amy Marcy Cheney
Blodgett, Benjamin Colman
Cadman, Charles Wakefield
Casadesus, Robert Marcel
Chotzinoff, Samuel
Cole, Nat ("King")
Dresel, Otto
Duchin, Edward Frank ("Eddy")
Friml, Charles Rudolf
Gabrilowitsch, Ossip
Ganz, Rudolph
Godowsky, Leopold
Goldbeck, Robert
Gottschalk, Louis Moreau
Grainger, George Percy
Griffes, Charles Tomlinson
Hanchett, Henry Granger
Henderson, Fletcher Hamilton
Hoffman, Richard
Hofmann, Josef Casimir
Iturbi, José
Jarvis, Charles H.
Joseffy, Rafael
Katchen, Julius
Kenton, Stanley Newcomb
Klein, Bruno Oscar
Landowska, Wanda Aleksandra
Lang, Benjamin Johnson
Levant, Oscar
Lhévinne, Josef
Lhévinne, Rosina
Liebling, Emil
Lopez, Vincent Joseph
Mannes, Clara Damrosch
Mannes, Leopold Damrosch
Mason, William
Mitropoulos, Dimitri
Pease, Alfred Humphreys
Perabo, Johann Ernst
Perry, Edward Baxter
Pratt, Silas Gamaliel
Rachmaninoff, Sergei Vasilyevich
Rockefeller, Martha Baird
Runcie, Constance Faunt Le Roy
Rybner, Martin Cornelius
Samaroff, Olga
Schelling, Ernest Henry
Schnabel, Artur
Sherwood, William Hall
Siloti, Alexander Ilyitch
Sternberg, Constantin Ivanovich, Edler von
Stravinsky, Igor Fyodorovich
Tapper, Bertha Feiring
Templeton, Alec Andrew
Tiomkin, Dimitri
Vogrich, Max Wilhelm Karl
Washington, Dinah
Whiting, Arthur Battelle
Zeisler, Fannie Bloomfield
PILGRIM
Alden, John
Allerton, Isaac
Brewster, William
Morton, George
Morton, Nathaniel
Standish, Myles
Winslow, Edward
PIONEER (See also FRONTIERSMAN, GUIDE, SCOUT)
Atwater, Caleb
Ballard, Bland Williams
Bedinger, George Michael
Belden, Josiah
Birkbeck, Morris
Boone, Daniel
Bozeman, John M.
Brannan, Samuel
Bryant, John Howard
Burnett, Peter Hardeman
Carter, John
Carter, Landon
Chapman, John
Clark, George Rogers
Cleaveland, Moses
Connor, Patrick Edward
Cresap, Thomas
Dale, Samuel
Doddridge, Joseph
Duchesne, Rose Philippine
Dunn, Williamson
Dupratz, Antoine Simon Le Page
Dustin, Hannah
Faribault, Jean Baptiste
Flower, George
Flower, Richard
Folger, Peter
Fry, Joshua
Gaines, George Strother
Gerstle, Lewis
Gibson, Paris
Goodnow, Isaac Tichenor
Gross, Samuel David
Haraszthy de Mokcsa, Agoston
Harrod, James
Henderson, David Bremner
Hillis, David
Hitchcock, Phineas Warrener
Jenkins, John, 1728–1785
Jenkins, John, 1751–1827
Langworthy, James Lyon
Lee, Jason
Logan, Benjamin
Lyon, Matthew
McLeod, Martin
Magoffin, James Wiley
Marsh, Grant Prince
Marsh, John
Mattson, Hans
Mears, Otto
Meeker, Ezra
Meigs, Return Jonathan
Neighbors, Robert Simpson
Nesmith, James Willis
Newell, Robert
Nicholas, George
Overton, John
Palmer, Joel
Peary, Josephine Diebitsch
Piggott, James
Potter, Robert
Pryor, Nathaniel
Putnam, Rufus
Renick, Felix
Rice, Henry Mower
Robertson, James, 1742–1814
Robinson, Charles
Robinson, Solon
Russell, Osborne
Russell, William Henry
Sargent, Winthrop, 1753–1820
Sawyer, Lorenzo
Scholte, Hendrik Peter
Sevier, John
Stearns, Abel
Stevens, John Harrington
Stone, Wilbur Fisk
Stuart, Granville
Symmes, John Cleves
Thornton, Jesse Quinn
Tupper, Benjamin

Walderne, Richard
Warner, Jonathan Trumbull
Warren, Francis Emroy
White, James
Whitman, Marcus
Wilkeson, Samuel
Williams, Samuel May
Wolfskill, William
Young, Ewing
Zane, Ebenezer
Ziegler, David

PIRATE (See also BUCCANEER)
Halsey, John
Ingle, Richard
Kidd, William
Laffite, Jean
Mason, Samuel
Pound, Thomas
Quelch, John

PISCICULTURIST (See also ICHTHYOLOGIST, ZOOLOGIST
Garlick, Theodatus
Green, Seth
Mather, Fred
Titcomb, John Wheelock

PLANT BREEDER (See also AGRICULTURIST, BOTANIST)
Burbank, Luther
Coker, David Robert
Perrine, Henry
Pringle, Cyrus Guernsey
Pritchard, Frederick John
Steichen, Edward Jean

PLANTER (See AGRICULTURIST, FARMER, SUGAR PLANTER)
Aiken, William
Aime, Valcour
Allston, Robert Francis Withers
Alston, Joseph
Baker, Lorenzo Dow
Baldwin, Henry Perrine
Brandon, Gerard Chittocque
Byrd, William, 1652–1704
Byrd, William, 1674–1744
Cary, Archibald
Chesnut, James
Cloud, Noah Bartlett
Cocke, John Hartwell
Cocke, Philip St. George
Couper, James Hamilton
Dabney, Thomas Smith Gregory
Dibrell, George Gibbs
Drayton, Thomas Fenwick
Dunbar, William
Dymond, John
Edwards, John
Edwards, Weldon Nathaniel
Ensley, Enoch
Fagan, James Fleming
Gaines, George Strother
Gibson, Randall Lee
Habersham, James
Hampton, Wade, 1751–1835
Kermer, Duncan Farrar
King, Thomas Butler
Kinloch, Cleland
Kolb, Reuben Francis
Laurens, Henry
Leflore, Greenwood
Lewis, William Berkeley
Lumbrozo, Jacob
Lynch, Charles
Lynch, Thomas 1727–1776
Manigault, Gabriel
Manigault, Peter
Marigny, Bernard
Mason, George
Matthews, Samuel
Mills, Robert, 1809–1888
Nelson, William, 1711–1772
Page, Mann
Philips, Martin Wilson
Pollock, Oliver
Porter, Alexander
Randolph, William
Ravenel, Edmund
Rector, Henry Massey
Richardson, Edmund
Roane, John Selden
Sibley, John
Spalding, Thomas
Syms, Benjamin
Wailes, Benjamin Leonard Covington
Winston, John Anthony
Wofford, William Tatum
Yeardley, Sir George

PLANT GENETICIST (See also BOTANIST, GENETICIST)
East, Edward Murray
Shull, George Harrison

PLANT PATHOLOGIST (See also BOTANIST, PATHOLOGIST)
Duggar, Benjamin Minge
Galloway, Beverly Thomas
Jones, Lewis Ralph
Whetzel, Herbert Hice

PLANT PHYSIOLOGIST (See also BOTANIST, PHYSIOLOGIST)
Crocker, William
Hoagland, Dennis Robert
Kellerman, Karl Frederic
Livingston, Burton Edward
Webber, Herbert John

PLAYWRIGHT (See DRAMATIST)

PLEBISCITE AUTHORITY
Wambaugh, Sarah

POET (See also AUTHOR, WRITER)
Abbey, Henry
Adams, Charles Follen
Agee, James Rufus
Aiken, Conrad Potter
Ainslie, Hew
Akins, Zoë
Aldrich, Thomas Bailey
Allen, Hervey
Allen, Paul
Alsop, Richard
Appleton, Thomas Gold
Arensberg, Walter Conrad
Arnold, George
Arrington, Alfred W.
Auden, Wystan Hugh
Bacon, Leonard
Barlow, Joel
Bates, Katharine Lee
Beers, Ethel Lynn
Bell, James Madison
Benét, Stephen Vincent
Benét, William Rose
Benjamin, Park
Bennett, Emerson
Benton, Joel
Berryman, John
Bishop, Elizabeth
Bleecker, Ann Eliza
Bloede, Gertrude
Blood, Benjamin Paul
Bogan, Louise Marie
Boker, George Henry
Bolton, Sarah Tittle Bartlett
Boner, John Henry
Bradford, Gamaliel
Bradford, Joseph
Bradstreet, Anne
Brainard, John Gardiner Calkins
Brooks, Charles Timothy
Brooks, James Gordon
Brooks, Maria Gowen
Brown, Sólyman
Brownell, Henry Howard
Bryant, William Cullen
Burgess, Frank Gelett
Burgess, W(illiam) Starling
Burleigh, George Shepard
Burton, Richard Eugene
Calvert, George Henry
Carleton, Will
Carrothers, James David
Cary, Alice
Cary, Phoebe
Cawein, Madison Julius
Channing, William Ellery
Chaplin, Ralph Hosea
Chapman, John Jay
Chivers, Thomas Holley
Church, Benjamin
Clark, Walter Van Tilburg
Clark, Willis Gaylord
Clarke, McDonald
Cleghorn, Sarah Norcliffe
Cliffton, William
Coates, Florence Earle
Coffin, Robert Peter Tristram
Cole, Thomas
Colum, Padriac
Congdon, Charles Taber
Cooke, Ebenezer
Cooke, Philip Pendleton
Cooke, Rose Terry
Coolbrith, Ina Donna
Coombe, Thomas
Cox, Henry Hamilton
Cranch, Christopher Pearse
Crandall, Charles Henry
Crane, Harold Hart
Crapsey, Adelaide
Crawford, John Wallace ("Captain Jack")
Cromwell, Gladys Louise Husted
Cullen, Countée Porter
Cullum, George Washington
Cummings, E. E.
Dabney, Richard
Dana, Richard Henry
Da Ponte, Lorenzo
Davidson, Lucretia Maria
Davidson, Margaret Miller
Day, Holman Francis
Dickinson, Emily Elizabeth
Dinsmoor, Robert
Drake, Joseph Rodman
Duganne, Augustine Joseph Hickey
Dugué, Charles Oscar
Dunbar, Paul Laurence

Eastman, Charles Gamage
Eliot, T(homas) S(tearns)
Emerson, Ralph Waldo
Evans, Nathaniel
Eve, Joseph
Fairfield, Sumner Lincoln
Faust, Frederick Shiller
Fearing, Kenneth Flexner
Fenollosa, Ernest Francisco
Ferguson, Elizabeth Graeme
Fessenden, Thomas Green
Field, Eugene
Finch, Francis Miles
Fletcher, John Gould
Foss, Sam Walter
Freeman, Joseph
Freneau, Philip Morin
Frost, Robert Lee
Gallagher, William Davis
Gilder, Richard Watson
Giovannitti, Arturo
Godfrey, Thomas
Gould, Hannah Flagg
Greene, Albert Gorton
Guiney, Louise Imogen
Guthrie, Ramon
Hagedorn, Hermann Ludwig Gebhard
Hall, Hazel
Halleck, Fitz-Greene
Halpine, Charles Graham
Hammon, Jupiter
Harris, Thomas Lake
Hartley, Marsden
Hay, John Milton
Hayden, Robert Earl
Hayne, Paul Hamilton
Henderson, Daniel McIntyre
Hewitt, John Hill
Heyward, DuBose
Hillhouse, James Abraham
Hillyer, Robert Silliman
Hirst, Henry Beck
Hoffman, Charles Fenno
Holley, Marietta
Holmes, Daniel Henry
Holmes, Oliver Wendell
Hope, James Barron
Hosmer, William Howe Cuyler
Hovey, Richard
Hubner, Charles William
Hughes, James Langston
Humphreys, David
Humphries, George Rolfe
Imber, Naphtali Herz
Irving, William
Jackson, Helen Maria Fiske Hunt
Janson, Kristofer Nagel
Jarrell, Randall
Jeffers, John Robinson
Jeffrey, Rosa Griffith Vertner Johnson
Johnson, Henry
Johnson, Robert Underwood
Kerouac, Jack
Kilmer, Alfred Joyce
Kinney, Elizabeth Clementine Dodge Stedman
Kreymborg, Alfred Francis
Krez, Konrad
Lacy, Ernest
Ladd, Joseph Brown
La Farge, Christopher Grant
Lander, Frederick West
Lanier, Sidney
Lathrop, John
Latil, Alexandre
Lazarus, Emma
Leonard, William Ellery
Lindsay, Nicholas Vachel
Linn, John Blair
Linton, William James
Lodge, George Cabot
Longfellow, Henry Wadsworth
Longfellow, Samuel
Lord, William Wilberforce
Lowell, Amy
Lowell, Robert Traill Spence, Jr.
Lucas, Daniel Bedinger
Lytle, William Haines
McCarroll, James
McGinley, Phyllis
McHenry, James
McKay, Claude
MacKaye, Percy Wallace
MacKellar, Thomas
McKinley, Carlyle
McLellan, Isaac
McMaster, Guy Humphreys
Macy, John
Malone, Walter
Markham, Edwin
Markoe, Peter
Marquis, Donald Robert Perry
Martin, Edward Sandford
Masters, Edgar Lee
Menken, Adah Isaacs
Merrill, Stuart FitzRandolph
Mifflin, Lloyd
Miles, George Henry
Millay, Edna St. Vincent
Miller, Cincinnatus Hiner
Mitchell, Langdon Elwyn
Mitchell, Silas Weir
Moïse, Penina
Monroe, Harriet
Moody, William Vaughn
Moore, (Austin) Merrill
Moore, Marianne Craig
Morris, George Pope
Morrison, Jim
Morton, Sarah Wentworth Apthorp
Munford, William
Muñoz-Rivera, Luis
Nack, James M.
Nash, Frederick Ogden
Newell, Robert Henry
Nicholson, Eliza Jane Poitevent Holbrook
Nies, Konrad
Niles, Nathaniel
Oakes, Urian
Oppenheim, James
O'Reilly, John Boyle
Osborn, Laughton
Osborn, Selleck
Osgood, Frances Sargent Locke
Paine, Robert Treat
Parke, John
Parker, Dorothy Rothschild
Parsons, Thomas William
Patchen, Kenneth
Peabody, Josephine Preston
Percival, James Gates
Perry, Nora
Peterson, Henry
Piatt, John James
Piatt, Sarah Morgan Bryan
Pierpont, John
Pinkney, Edward Coote
Plath, Sylvia
Plummer, Jonathan
Plummer, Mary Wright
Poe, Edgrar Allan
Posey, Alexander Lawrence
Pound, Ezra Loomis
Powell, Thomas
Poydras, Julien de Lelande
Preston, Margaret Junkin
Randall, James Ryder
Rankin, Jeremiah Eames
Ransom, John Crowe
Read, Thomas Buchanan
Realf, Richard
Reed, John, 1887–1920
Reese, Lizette Woodworth
Reitzel, Robert
Requier, Augustus Julian
Ricketson, Daniel
Riley, James Whitcomb
Rittenhouse, Jessie Belle
Robinson, Edwin Arlington
Roche, James Jeffrey
Roethke, Theodore Huebner
Rorty, James Hancock
Rose, Aquila
Rosenfeld, Morris
Rouquette, Adrien Emmanuel
Rouquette, François Dominique
Rukeyser, Muriel
Russell, Irwin
Ryan, Abram Joseph
Saltus, Edgar Evertson
Sandburg, Carl August
Sandys, George
Santayana, George
Sargent, Epes
Savage, Philip Henry
Saxe, John Godfrey
Schnauffer, Carl Heinrich
Scollard, Clinton
Searing, Laura Catherine Redden
Seeger, Alan
Service, Robert William
Sewall, Jonathan Mitchell
Sexton, Anne Gray Harvey
Shaw, John, 1778–1809
Sherman, Frank Dempster
Shillaber, Benjamin Penhallow
Sill, Edward Rowland
Smith, Samuel Francis
Snow, Eliza Roxey
Spingarn, Joel Elias
Sprague, Charles
Stanton, Frank Lebby
Stedman, Edmund Clarence
Steendam, Jacob
Stein, Evaleen
Sterling, George
Stevens, Wallace
Stoddard, Elizabeth Drew Barstow
Stoddard, Richard Henry

Story, Isaac
Story, William Wetmore
Strange, Michael
Street, Alfred Billings
Sylvester, Frederick Oakes
Tabb, John Banister
Taggard, Genevieve
Tate, John Orley Allen
Taylor, Benjamin Franklin
Taylor, Edward
Teasdale, Sara
Testut, Charles
Thaxter, Celia Laighton
Thierry, Camille
Thomas, Edith Matilda
Thompson, James Maurice
Thompson, John Reuben
Thomson, Edward William
Thoreau, Henry David
Thorpe, Rose Alnora Hartwick
Ticknor, Francis Orray
Timrod, Henry
Torrence, Frederick Ridgely
Townsend, Mary Ashley
Trumbull, John, 1750–1831
Tuckerman, Frederick Goddard
Tuckerman, Henry Theodore
Turell, Jane
Untermeyer, Louis
Van Doren, Mark Albert
Van Dyke, Henry
Villagrá, Gasper Pérez de
Wallace, William Ross
Walsh, Thomas
Ward, Thomas
Warfield, Catherine Ann Ware
Warren, Mercy Otis
Wheatley, Phillis
Wheelock, John Hall
Whitman, Albery Allson
Whitman, Sarah Ellen Power
Whitman, Walt
Whitney, Anne
Whittier, John Greenleaf
Wilcox, Ella Wheeler
Wilde, Richard Henry
Williams, Catharine Read Arnold
Williams, William Carlos
Willis, Nathaniel Parker
Wilson, Robert Burns
Wilson, William
Winchevsky, Morris
Winter, William
Woodberry, George Edward
Woodworth, Samuel
Wright, James Arlington
Wright, Philip Green
Wylie, Elinor Morton Hoyt
Young, David
Zukofsky, Louis
Zunser, Eliakum
POGO STICK INVENTOR
Hansburg, George Bernard
POLAR EXPERT
Balchen, Bernt
POLICE COMMISSIONER
Connor, Theophilus ("Bull") Eugene
POLICE CONSULTANT
Smith, Bruce
POLICE EXECUTIVE
Byrnes, Thomas F.
Curtis, Edwin Upton
POLICE OFFICER
Glassford, Pelham Davis
McGrath, Matthew J.
Ruditsky, Barney
POLITICAL ACTIVIST
Du Bois, William Edward Burghardt
Harriman, Florence Jaffray Hurst
Lowenstein, Allard Kenneth
Meyer, Frank Straus
Robeson, Paul Leroy
Whitney, Charlotte Anita
Wolfe, Bertram David
POLITICAL ADVISER
Bryan, Charles Wayland
Clay, Lucius DuBignon
Ewing, Oscar Ross
Rosenman, Samuel Irving
Tugwell, Rexford Guy
Young, Owen D.
POLITICAL AIDE
Hinshaw, David Schull
POLITICAL BOSS
Hague, Frank
Kelly, Edward Joseph
Kenny, John V.
Pendergast, Thomas Joseph
Tweed, William Marcy
POLITICAL CARTOONIST
Fischetti, John
Gropper, William
POLITICAL COMMENTATOR
Dunne, Finley Peter
Gillis, James Martin
POLITICAL CRITIC (See also CRITIC)
Howard, Joseph Kinsey
POLITICAL ECONOMIST (See also ECONOMIST)
Colwell, Stephen
Coxe, Tench
Rawle, Francis, 1662–1726/27
POLITICAL FIGURE
Coughlin, Charles Edward
POLITICAL HOSTESS
Mesta, Perle Reid Skirvin
POLITICAL JOURNALIST
Rovere, Richard Halworth
POLITICAL LEADER
Raskob, John Jakob
Rose, Alex
POLITICAL ORGANIZER
Kohlberg, Alfred
Smith, Gerald L. K.
POLITICAL PHILOSOPHER
Arendt, Hannah
MacIver, Robert Morrison
POLITICAL REFORMER (See also REFORMER)
Churchill, Winston
Hawkins, Dexter Arnold
Kelly, Edmond
Linton, William James
McClintock, Oliver
MacVeagh, Isaac Wayne
Mitchell, Stephen Arnold
Moskowitz, Belle Lindner Israels
Pinchot, Amos Richards Eno
Roosevelt, Robert Barnwell
Shepard, Edward Morse
U'Ren, William Simon
Welling, Richard Ward Greene
POLITICAL SCIENTIST
Ascoli, Max
Barrows, David Prescott
Beard, Charles Austin
Bentley, Arthur Fisher
Burgess, John William
Corwin, Edward Samuel
Eastman, Max Forrester
Fairlie, John Archibald
Garner, James Wilford
Goodnow, Frank Johnson
Key, Valdimer Orlando, Jr.
Lasswell, Harold Dwight
Lieber, Francis
McBain, Howard Lee
McCarthy, Charles
Macy, Jesse
Merriam, Charles Edward, Jr.
Moley, Raymond Charles
Morgenthau, Hans Joachim
Moses, Bernard
Ogg, Frederic Austin
Parsons, Frank
Reinsch, Paul Samuel
Rossiler, Clinton Lawrence, III
Rowe, Leo Stanton
Sayre, Wallace Stanley
Smith, James Allen
Smith, Thomas Vernor
Thomas, Elbert Duncan
White, Leonard Dupee
Willoughby, Westel Woodbury
POLITICAL STRATEGIST
Hamilton, John Daniel Miller, II
POLITICAL THEORIST
Burdick, Eugene Leonard
Neumann, Franz Leopold
POLITICAL WIFE
Mitchell, Martha Elizabeth Beall
POLITICIAN (See also CONGRESSMAN, CONGRESSWOMAN, DIPLOMAT, LOBBYIST, POLITICAL LEADER, SENATOR, STATESMAN)
Abbott, Joseph Carter
Adair, John
Addicks, John Edward O'Sullivan
Alexander, James
Allen, Ira
Allen, James Browning
Ames, Oakes
Anthony, Henry Bowen
Appleton, Nathan
Archer, Branch Tanner
Armstrong, John
Arnold, Richard Dennis
Arvey, Jacob M.
Ashe, John
Ashe, John Baptista
Atherton, Charles Gordon
Atwood, David
Austin, Benjamin
Austin, James Trecothick
Avery, Isaac Wheeler
Axtell, Samuel Beach
Baker, James Heaton
Baldwin, John Brown

Bartlett, Dewey Follett
Bartlett, Ichabod
Bartlett, Joseph
Battle, Cullen Andrews
Beale, Richard Lee Turberville
Beall, Samuel Wootton
Beatty, John
Bedford, Gunning
Behan, William James
Bell, Charles Henry
Bell, Isaac
Bell, Luther Vose
Bidwell, John
Bidwell, Marshall Spring
Biggs, Asa
Bingham, Harry
Bingham, John Armor
Binns, John
Bishop, Abraham
Blair, Emily Newell
Blair, Francis Preston
Bliss, Cornelius Newton
Bloodworth, Timothy
Blount, Thomas
Blunt, James Gillpatrick
Boutwell, George Sewall
Bowen, Thomas Meade
Bowie, Richard Johns
Brady, James Topham
Brandegee, Frank Bosworth
Brayton, Charles Ray
Breese, Sidney
Bright, Jesse David
Broderick, David Colbreth
Brooks, Erastus
Brown, Neill Smith
Brown, Walter Folger
Browning, Orville Hickman
Bryan, George
Bryan, William Jennings
Bryce, Lloyd Stephens
Burnet, David Gouverneur
Burrill, James
Burrowes, Thomas Henry
Butler, Benjamin Franklin
Butterworth, Benjamin
Byrnes, James Francis
Cain, Richard Harvey
Caldwell, Alexander
Calhoun, John
Calhoun, William Barron
Camp, John Lafayette
Capehart, Homer Earl
Carr, Joseph Bradford
Cassidy, William
Caswell, Richard
Cattell, Alexander Gilmore
Cavanagh, Jerome Patrick ("Jerry")
Chaffee, Jerome Bonaparte
Chandler, Zachariah
Christian, William
Cilley, Joseph
Clark, Daniel
Clarke, John Hessin
Clayton, Powell
Clingman, Thomas Lanier
Cloud, Noah Bartlett
Cobb, David
Cochrane, John
Collins, Patrick Andrew
Colton, Calvin
Combs, Leslie
Connor, Theophilus ("Bull") Eugene
Cook, Isaac
Cook, James Merrill
Cooke, Elisha
Cooper, Mark Anthony
Corbett, Henry Winslow
Cornell, Alonzo B.
Cox, George Barnsdale
Cox, James Middleton
Cox, William Ruffin
Coxe, Daniel
Crocker, Alvah
Croker, Richard
Croswell, Edwin
Crowninshield, Benjamin Williams
Cruger, Henry
Cruger, John
Crump, Edward Hull
Curley, James Michael
Curran, Thomas Jerome
Currier, Moody
Cushing, Thomas
Daggett, David
Daugherty, Harry Micajah
Davis, Henry Winter
Davis, Matthew Livingston
Davis, Pauline Morton Sabin
Dawson, William Levi
Dayton, William Lewis
Dearborn, Henry Alexander Scammell
De Lancey, James, 1703–1760
De Lancey, James, 1732–1800
De Lancey, Oliver
Deming, Henry Champion
Devaney, John Patrick
Dibrell, George Gibbs
Dickinson, Daniel Stevens
Doddridge, Philip
Dodge, Grenville Mellon
Donelson, Andrew Jackson
Donnelly, Ignatius
Dorr, Thomas Wilson
Dorsheimer, William Edward
Doty, James Duane
Douglas, Helen Gahagan
Douglas, Stephen Arnold
Draper, Andrew Sloan
Draper, Eben Sumner
Duane, William
Dudley, Charles Edward
Duffy, Francis Ryan
Duncan, Joseph
Durant, Thomas Jefferson
Early, Peter
Eastman, Charles Gamage
Eastman, Enoch Worthen
Eastman, Harvey Gridley
Eaton, John Henry
Edgerton, Alfred Peck
Edwards, Pierpont
Egan, Patrick
Elliot, James
Ellis, Seth Hockett
English, Thomas Dunn
Evans, George
Evans, Henry Clay
Fairfield, John
Faran, James John
Farley, James Aloysius
Farnsworth, John Franklin
Farwell, Charles Benjamin
Fay, Jonas
Felton, William Harrell
Fernós Isern, Antonio
Fessenden, William Pitt
Fine, John Sydney
Fisk, James
Fitzgerald, John Francis
Flagg, Azariah Cutting
Flanagan, Webster
Flynn, Edward Joseph
Folsom, Nathaniel
Foot, Solomon
Frazier, Lynn Joseph
Frémont, John Charles
Gallinger, Jacob Harold
Gansevoort, Leonard
Gartrell, Lucius Jeremiah
Gary, James Albert
Gibbons, Thomas
Gibson, Walter Murray
Gillet, Ransom Hooker
Gilman, John Taylor
Gilman, Nicholas
Gitlow, Benjamin
Goodloe, William Cassius
Goodrich, Elizur
Goodwin, Ichabod
Goodwin, John Noble
Gordon, George Washington
Granger, Francis
Granger, Gideon
Greeley, Horace
Green, Duff
Greene, Nathaniel
Gregg, Andrew
Gregg, Maxcy
Griswold, Roger
Griswold, Stanley
Grover, La Fayette
Grow, Galusha Aaron
Grund, Francis Joseph
Grundy, Felix
Gwin, William McKendree
Hague, Frank
Haines, Charles Glidden
Hale, Charles
Hale, Eugene
Hale, John Parker
Hall, Abraham Oakey
Hall, Leonard Wood
Hallett, Benjamin Franklin
Hamilton, James Alexander
Hammond, Jabez Delano
Hancock, John, 1736–1793
Hanna, Marcus Alonzo
Hannegan, Robert Emmet
Hanson, Ole
Harper, Robert Goodloe
Harris, Isham Green
Harris, Townsend
Harrison, Carter Henry, Jr.
Harrison, George Paul
Hartranft, John Frederick
Haskell, Dudley Chase
Haskell, Ella Louise Knowles
Hassaurek, Friedrich
Hays, Will H.
Hazard, Jonathan J.
Heath, Perry Sanford

Heney, Francis Joseph
Henshaw, David
Hickenlooper, Bourke Blakemore
Higgins, Frank Wayland
Hill, David Bennett
Hill, Isaac
Hines, James
Hitchcock, Phineas Warrener
Hoan, Daniel Webster
Hoey, Clyde Roark
Hoffman, John Thompson
Holcomb, Silas Alexander
Howard, Benjamin Chew
Howard, Edgar
Howard, William Alanson
Howell, Clark
Hoyt, Henry Martyn
Hubbard, David
Hughes, James
Hunter, Whiteside Godfrey
Husting, Paul Oscar
Imlay, Gilbert
Irving, William
Jackson, Robert R.
Jardine, William Marion
Johnson, Albert
Johnson, Bradley Tyler
Johnson, Edward Austin
Kelly, Edward Joseph
Kelly, John
Kelly, John Brendan
Kennedy, John Doby
Kerens, Richard C.
Kerman, Francis
Keyes, Elisha Williams
King, Preston
Kinsella, Thomas
Kinsey, John
Knott, Aloysius Leo
Knox, Frank
Kohler, Walter Jodok, Jr.
Lane, James Henry
Langdon, John
Lasker, Albert Davis
Lewis, William Berkeley
Lexow, Clarence
Lincoln, Enoch
Lincoln, Levi, 1749–1820
Lincoln, Levi, 1782–1868
Lloyd, David
Logan, Cornelius Ambrose
Lorimer, William
Loring, George Bailey
Loucks, Henry Langford
Lovell, James
Lunn, George Richard
Lyon, Caleb
Lyon, Matthew
McAfee, Robert Breckinridge
McCarren, Patrick Henry
McClellan, George Brinton
McCormick, Richard Cunningham
McCumber, Porter James
McDonald, Joseph Ewing
McDowell, Joseph
McKinney, Frank Edward, Sr.
McLaughlin, Hugh
McLevy, Jasper
McMahon, Brien
McManes, James
McNutt, Paul Vories
Maestri, Robert Sidney
Magee, Christopher Lyman
Maginnis, Martm
Manigault, Peter
Manley, Joseph Homan
Marcantonio, Vito Anthony
Massey, John Edward
Mather, Increase
Meagher, Thomas Francis
Merriam, William Rush
Milk, Harvey Bernard
Mills, Ogden Livingston
Minor, Robert
Moore, Andrew
Moreau-Lislet, Louis Casimir Elisabeth
Morrissey, John
Morton, Ferdinand Quintin
Moses, George Higgins
Muhlenberg, Frederick Augustus Conrad
Muhlenberg, Henry Augustus Philip
Muhlenberg, John Peter Gabriel
Muñoz-Rivera, Luis
Murphy, Charles Francis
Murphy, Henry Cruse
Nairne, Thomas
Nelson, Hugh
New, Harry Stewart
Nicholas, George
Nicholas, Philip Norborne
Nicolls, William
Niles, David K.
Niles, Nathaniel
Norris, Isaac, 1701–1766
O'Dwyer, William
O'Fallon, James
Orth, Godlove Stein
Osgood, Samuel
Otis, James
Overton, John
Packer, William Fisher
Palmer, William Adams
Parker, John Milliken
Parker, Josiah
Partridge, James Rudolph
Patterson, James Willis
Payne, Sereno Elisha
Pecora, Ferdinand
Pelham, Robert A.
Penrose, Boies
Penrose, Charles Bingham
Perez, Leander Henry
Petigru, James Louis
Pew, Joseph Newton, Jr.
Pickering, Timothy
Pinchback, Pinckney Benton Stewart
Platt, Thomas Collier
Pleasants, John Hampden
Pomeroy, Marcus Mills
Porter, James Madison
Pringle, John Julius
Pusey, Caleb
Quay, Matthew Stanley
Quick, John Herbert
Quincy, Josiah, 1772–1864
Ramsay, Nathaniel
Randall, Alexander Williams
Randolph, John, 1728–1784
Ranney, Rufus Percival
Raum, Green Berry
Raymond, Henry Jarvis
Requa, Mark Lawrence
Reynolds, Julian Sargeant
Richmond, Dean
Ritchie, Thomas
Rives, William Cabell
Roberts, William Randall
Robertson, Absalom Willis
Robertson, William Henry
Robins, Raymond
Robinson, William Erigena
Rockefeller, Winthrop
Rollins, Edward Henry
Rollins, Frank West
Root, Erastus
Rosewater, Edward
Rosewater, Victor
Rowell, Chester Harvey
Ruef, Abraham
Russell, William Henry
Schell, Augustus
Schoeppel, Andrew Frank
Seidel, George Lukas Emil
Settle, Thomas
Sewell, William Joyce
Shannon, Wilson
Shields, George Howell
Shippen, Edward, 1639–1712
Sibley, John
Simmons, Roscoe Conkling Murray
Simons, Algie Martin
Skinner, Charles Rufus
Slidell, John
Smith, Buckingham
Smith, Charles Perrin
Smith, Frank Leslie
Smith, Israel
Smith, James, 1851–1927
Smith, Nathan, 1770–1835
Smith, Ralph Tyler
Smith, Thomas Vernor
Springer, Charles
Steedman, James Blair
Stevens, Thaddeus
Stevenson, Adlai Ewing, II
Stockton, Richard
Sullivan, Timothy Daniel
Swartwout, Samuel
Sweeny, Peter Barr
Swensson, Carl Aaron
Switzler, William Franklin
Taggart, Thomas
Terry, David Smith
Thayer, John Milton
Thomas, David
Thomas, Elbert Duncan
Thomas, (John William) Elmer
Thomas, William Widgery
Thompson, Richard Wigginton
Thornton, Daniel I. J.
Tichenor, Isaac
Tipton, John
Tumulty, Joseph Patrick
Tweed, William Marcy
Tyler, Robert
Upshaw, William David
Vallandigham, Clement Laird
Van Buren, John
Van Dam, Rip

Van Ness, WIlliam Peter
Vare, William Scott
Wagner, Robert Ferdinand
Walcott, Edward Oliver
Waldo, Samuel
Walker, Frank Comerford
Wallace, Hugh Campbell
Waln, Robert, 1765–1836
Walsh, Michael
Ward, John Elliott
Warren, Fuller
Warren, James
Watson, Thomas Edward
Weed, Thurlow
West, Roy Owen
White, Edward Douglass
Williams, Elisha
Wilson, J(ames) Finley
Wise, John Sergeant

POLO PLAYER
Rumsey, Charles Cary

POMOLOGIST (See also AGRICULTURIST)
Brincklé, William Draper
Coxe, William
Downing, Charles
Gideon, Peter Miller
Lyon, Theodatus Timothy
Manning, Robert
Thomas, John Jacobs

POPULATION-CONTROL ADVOCATE
Moore, Hugh Everett

PORTRAITIST (See also PAINTER, PHOTOGRAPHER)
Bachrach, Louis Fabian
Christy, Howard Chandler

POSTAL PIONEER
Bates, Barnabas
Chorpenning, George
Davis, William Augustine
Holt, John
Majors, Alexander

POSTMASTER GENERAL (CONFEDERATE)
Reagan, John Henninger

POSTMASTER GENERAL (See also POSTAL PIONEER)
Brown, Walter Folger
Burleson, Albert Sidney
Campbell, James
Collamer, Jacob
Cortelyou, George Bruce
Creswell, John Angel James
Dickinson, Donald McDonald
Donaldson, Jesse Monroe
Farley, James Aloysius
Gary, James Albert
Habersham, Joseph
Hatton, Frank
Hazard, Ebenezer
Hitchcock, Frank Harris
Holt, Joseph
Howe, Timothy Otis
James, Thomas Lemuel
Jewell, Marshall
Johnson, Cave
Kendall, Amos
King, Horatio
McLean, John
Meigs, Return Jonathan
Meyer, George von Lengerke
Niles, John Milton
Payne, Henry Clay
Randall, Alexander Williams
Smith, Charles Emory
Summerfield, Arthur Ellsworth
Vilas, William Freeman
Walker, Frank Comerford
Wickliffe, Charles Anderson
Wilson, William Lyne

POTTER (See also CRAFTSMAN)
Low, John Gardner
Martinez, Maria
Rellstab, John

POWDER MAKER (See also MANUFACTURER, *Explosives*)
Keppel, Frederlck

POWERBOAT-RACING ENTHUSIAST
Wood, Garfield Arthur ("Gar")

PREACHER
Kuhlman, Kathryn
Sheen, Fulton John

PRESIDENT, COLLEGE (See COLLEGE PRESIDENT)

PRESIDENT (COMMONWEALTH OF THE PHILIPPINES)
Quezon, Manuel Luis

PRESIDENT (CONFEDERATE STATES)
Davis, Jefferson

PRESIDENTIAL ADVISER
House, Edward Mandell
Howe, Louis McHenry
Moley, Raymond Charles
O'Donnell, Kenneth Patrick

PRESIDENTIAL CANDIDATE
Adams, Samuel
Babson, Roger Ward
Bell, John
Bidwell, John
Birney, James Gillespie
Blaine, James Gillespie
Brenckinridge, John Cabell
Brown, Benjamin Gratz
Bryan, Wilham Jennings
Burr, Aaron
Butler, Benjamin Franklin
Cass, Lewis
Chafin, Eugene Wilder
Clay, Henry
Clinton, De Witt
Clinton, George, 1739–1812
Cooper, Peter
Cox, James Middleton
Crawford, William Harris
Davis, David
Davis, John William
Debs, Eugene Victor
Dewey, Thomas Edward
Douglas, Stephen Arnold
Dow, Neal
Ellsworth, Oliver
Ferguson, James Edward
Fisk, Clinton Bowen
Floyd, John
Foster, William Z.
Frémont, John Charles
Greeley, Horace
Hale, John Parker
Hancock, Winfield Scott
Harvey, William Hope
Hendricks, Thomas Andres
Hughes, Charles Evans
Iredell, James
Jay, John
Jenkins, Charles Jones
King, Rufus, 1755–1827
La Follette, Robert Marion
Lemke, William Frederick
MacArthur, Douglas
Magnum, Willie Person
O'Connor, Charles
Palmer, John McAuley
Parker, Atlon Brooks
Pinckney, Charles Cotesworth
Pinckney, Thomas
St. John, John Pierce
Scott, Winfield
Seymour, Haratio, 1810–1886
Smith, Alfred Emanuel
Stevenson, Adlai Ewing, II
Swallow, Silas Comfort
Taft, Robert Alphonso
Thomas, Norman Mattoon
Tilden, Samuel Jones
Upshaw, William David
Wallace, Henry Agard
Watson, Thomas Edward
Weaver, James Baird
Webster, Daniel
White, Hugh Lawson
Willkie, Wendell Lewis
Wirt, William

PRESIDENT OF UNITED STATES
Adams, John
Adams, John Quincy
Arthur, Chester Alan
Buchanan, James
Cleveland, Stephen Grover
Coolidge, Calvin
Eisenhower, Dwight David
Fillmore, Millard
Garfield, James Abram
Grant, Ulysses Simpson
Harding, Warren Gamaliel
Harrison, Benjamin, 1833–1901
Harrison, William Henry
Hayes, Rutherford Birchard
Hoover, Herbert Clark
Jackson, Andrew
Jefferson, Thomas
Johnson, Andrew
Johnson, Lyndon Baines
Kennedy, John Fitzgerald
Lincoln, Abraham
McKinley, William
Madison, James
Monroe, James
Pierce, Franklin
Polk, James Knox
Roosevelt, Franklin Delano
Roosevelt, Theodore
Taft, William Howard
Taylor, Zachary
Truman, Harry S.
Tyler, John, 1790–1862
Van Buren, Martin
Washington, George
Wilson, Woodrow

PRESS AGENT
Thompson, Slason

PRESS SECRETARY (PRESIDENTIAL)
Early, Stephen Tyree
Ross, Charles Griffith
Short, Joseph Hudson, Jr.

PRINTER (See also PUBLISHER)
Adler, Elmer
Aitken, Robert
Alvord, Corydon Alexis
Ashmead, Isaac
Bailey, Francis
Bailey, Lydia R.
Baker, Peter Carpenter
Beadle, Erastus Flavel
Black, Douglas MacRae
Bradford, Andrew
Bradford, John
Bradford, Thomas
Bradford, William
Brewster, Osmyn
Carter, John
Charless, Joseph
Cist, Charles
Crocker, Uriel
Currier, Nathaniel
Dana, John Cotton
Day, Benjamin Henry
Day, Stephen
De Vinne, Theodore Low
Draper, Richard
Dunlap, John
Fleet, Thomas
Fleming, John
Foster, John
Fowle, Daniel
Franklin, Benjamin
Franklin, James
Gaine, Hugh
Gilliss, Walter
Goddard, William
Gordon, George Phineas
Goudy, Frederic William
Green, Bartholomew
Green, Jonas
Green, Samuel
Green, Thomas
Greenleaf, Thomas
Hall, David
Hall, Samuel, 1740–1807
Harper, Fletcher
Harper, James
Haswell, Anthony
Holt, John
Humphreys, James
Jansen, Reinier
Johnson, Marmaduke
Keimer, Samuel
Kneeland, Samuel
Linton, William James
Loudon, Samuer
MacKellar, Thomas
Mecom, Benjamin
Meeker, Jotham
Miller, John Henry
Moore, Jacob Bailey
Munsell, Joel
Nancrède, Paul Joseph Guérard de
Nash, John Henry
Nuthead, William
Parker, James
Parks, William
Pickard, Samuel Thomas
Pomeroy, Marcus Mills
Rivington, James
Robertson, James, b. 1740
Roulstone, George
Rudge, William Edwin
Sholes, Christopher Latham
Sower, Christopher, 1693–1758
Sower, Christopher, 1721–1784
Thomas, Isaiah
Tileston, Thomas
Timothy, Lewis
Towne, Benjamin
Trow, John Fowler
Updike, Daniel Berkeley
White, Thomas Willis
Williams, William
Zamorano, Augustin Juan Vicente
Zenger, John Peter

PRINTMAKER (See also ARTIST, ENGRAVER, ETCHER, LITHOGRAPHER)
Albers, Josef
Calder, Alexander
Ganso, Emil
Sloan, John French

PRISON ADMINISTRATOR
Lawes, Lewis Edward
Lynds, Elam
Pilsbury, Amos

PRISON REFORMER See also PENOLOGIST, REFORMER)
Davis, Katharine Bement
Gibbons, Abigail Hopper
Johnson, Ellen Cheney
Older, Fremont
Osborne, Thomas Mott
Round, William Marshall Fitts
Spear, Charles
Wines, Enoch Cobb

PRIVATEER (See also ADVENTURER, NAVAL OFFICER, NAVIGATOR)
Burns, Otway
Chever, James W.
Fanning, Nathaniel
Green, Nathan
Haraden, Jonathan
McNeill, Daniel
McNeill, Hector
Maffitt, David
Olmsted, Gideon
Peabody, Joseph
Randall, Robert Richard
Ropes, Joseph
Southack, Cyprian

PROBATION OFFICER
Augustus, John

PRODUCER (See also DIRECTOR, FILMMAKER, MOTION PICTURE DIRECTOR, MOTION PICTURE PRODUCER, THEATRICAL MANAGER)
Ames, Winthrop
Belasco, David
Berg, Gertrude Edelstein
Bonstelle, Jessie
Brackett, Charles William
Brady, William Aloysius
Brenon, Herbert
Carroll, Earl
Cohan, George Michael
Cohn, Harry
Conried, Heinrich
Cornell, Katharine
Crouse, Russel McKinley
Daly, John Augustin
DeMille, Cecil Blount
De Sylva, George Gard ("Buddy")
Dillingham, Charles Bancroft
Disney, Walter Elias ("Walt")
Dixon, Thomas
Faversham, William Alfred
Fiske, Harrison Grey
Frohman, Daniel
Gest, Morris
Golden, John
Hampden, Walter
Harrigan, Edward
Harris, Jed
Harris, Sam Henry
Helburn, Theresa
Hurok, Solomon Isaievitch
Janney, Russell Dixon
Johnson, Nunnally Hunter
Klaw, Marc
Laemmle, Carl
Langner, Lawrence
Leiber, Fritz
Liveright, Horace Brisbin
Loew, Marcus
MacArthur, Charles Gordon
McClintic, Guthrie
Mayer, Louis Burt
Miller, Gilbert Heron
Nichols, Dudley
Pemberton, Brock
Pickford, Mary
Rice, Elmer
Ritchard, Cyril
Rose, Billy
Rossen, Robert
Savage, Henry Wilson
Schary, Dore
Schwartz, Maurice
Selig, William Nicholas
Shubert, Lee
Shumlin, Herman Elliott
Taylor, Charles Alonzo
Thalberg, Irving Grant
Tyler, George Crouse
Walker, Stuart Armstrong
Wanger, Walter
White, George
Youmans, Vincent Millie
Ziegfeld, Florenz

PROFESSOR (See also EDUCATOR, SCHOLAR, TEACHER)
Abel-Henderson, Annie Heloise
Adams, George Burton
Adams, Herbert Baxter
Adams, Thomas Sewall
Allinson, Francis Greenleaf
Babbitt, Irving
Bachmann, Werner Emmanuel
Baker, Carl Lotus
Baker, George Pierce
Barus, Carl
Beach, Harlan Page
Beale, Joseph Henry
Bleyer, Willard Grosvenor
Borchard, Edwin Montefiore
Boring, Edwin Garrigues
Briggs, Charles Augustus
Brigham, Albert Perry
Brinton, Clarence Crane
Bristol, William Henry
Brown, Carleton

Brown, Francis
Bruce, Andrew Alexander
Burgess, John William
Cain, William
Calkins, Mary Whiton
Capps, Edward
Case, Shirley Jackson
Chafee, Zechariah, Jr.
Chamberlain, Joseph Perkins
Chase, George
Child, Charles Manning
Christian, Henry Asbury
Clarke, Frank Wigglesworth
Cook, Walter Wheeler
Cooper, Jacob
Cooper, Thomas
Copeland, Charles Townsend
Costigan, George Purcell
Crafts, James Mason
Crawford, James Pyle Wickersham
Cross, Arthur Lyon
Cross, Samuel Hazzard
Cross, Wilbur Lucius
Curme, George Oliver
Daggett, Naphtali
Da Ponte, Lorenzo
Dargan, Edwin Preston
Davls, William Morris
Dickinson, Edwin De Witt
Dod, Albert Baldwin
Dowling, Noel Thomas
Dubbs, Joseph Henry
Edman, Irwin
Elvehjem, Conrad Arnold
Evans, Bergen Baldwin
Fish, Carl Russell
Flather, John Joseph
Fleming, Walter Lynwood
Foresti, Elentario Felice
Forsyth, John
Franklin, Edward Curtis
Freund, Ernst
Friedlaender, Walter Ferdinand
Frieze, Henry Simmons
Frisbie, Levi
Fry, Joshua
Genung, John Franklin
Gildersleeve, Basil Lanneau
Gilmore, Joseph Henry
Glueck, Sheldon ("Sol")
Greenlaw, Edwin Almiron
Gregory, Charles Noble
Hamilton, Alice
Hanson, James Christian Meinich
Haring, Clarence
Hart, Albert Bushnell
Herrick, Robert Welch
Hitchcock, Edward, 1828–1911
Hohfeld, Wesley Newcomb
Hovgaard, William
Hudson, Manley Ottmer
Hulbert, Archer Butler
Hunt, Theodore Whitefield
Hyvernat, Henri
Johnson, Samuel William
Jones, Lynds
Jones, Rufus Matthew
Kelsey, Rayner Wickersham
Kemp, John
Kilpatrick, William Heard
Kittredge, George Lyman
Koch, Frederick Henry
Ladd, Carl Edwin
Lake, Kirsopp
Landis, James McCauley
Langdell, Chrisopher Columbus
Latané, John Holladay
Leonard, William Ellery
Lile, William Minor
Lincoln, John Larkin
Long, Joseph Ragland
Lovering, Joseph
Lowell, Abbott Lawrence
Lyman, Eugene William
Lyon, David Gordon
McCarthy, Daniel Joseph
McClellan, George Brinton
McGlothlin, William Joseph
Marquand, Allan
Marsh, Frank Burr
Mason, Daniel Gregory
Matthews, James Brander
Mead, George Herbert
Mendenhall, Thomas Corwin
Meyer, Adolf
Miller, George Abram
Mitchell, Edwin Knox
Mitchell, Langdon Elwyn
Moley, Raymond Charles
Moore, Eliakim Hastings
Moore, Nathaniel Fish
Morse, Harmon Northrop
Moulton, Richard Green
Muller, Hermann Joseph
Naismith, James
Neilson, William Allan
Noyes, George Rapall
Ogg, Frederic Austin
Oldfather, William Abbott
Osgood, William Fogg
Owsley, Frank Lawrence
Packard, Alpheus Spring
Panofsky, Erwin
Parker, George Howard
Parsons, Theophilus
Parvin, Theodore Sutton
Peabody, Andrew Preston
Peabody, Francis Greenwood
Perrin, Bernadotte
Perry, Bliss
Phelps, Austin
Phelps, William Lyon
Phillips, Ulrich Bonnell
Pirsson, Louis Valentine
Pond, Enoch
Pound, (Nathan) Roscoe
Prime, William Cowper
Putnam, Frederic Ward
Quine, William Edward
Rand, Edward Kennard
Randall, James Garfield
Rauschenbusch, Walter
Ravenel, Edmund
Read, Conyers
Reed, Richard Clark
Richardson, Robert
Rister, Carl Coke
Ritter, Frédéric Louis
Robertson, William Spence
Robinson, Edward, 1794–1863
Rostovtzeff, Michael Ivanovitch
Rupp, William
Russell, James Earl
Rutledge, Wiley Blount
Sampson, Martin Wright
Schelling, Felix Emanuel
Schevill, Rudolph
Schinz, Albert
Schlesinger, Arthur Meier
Schmidt, Nathaniel
Scott, Walter Dill
Scudder, (Julia) Vida Dutton
Searle, John Preston
Shannon, Fred Albert
Sherman, Henry Clapp
Shields, Charles Woodruff
Silliman, Benjamin, 1779–1864
Smith, Charles Forster
Smith, David Eugene
Smith, Edgar Fahs
Smith, Edmund Munroe
Smith, Henry Louis
Smith, Horatio Elwin
Smith, Nathan, 1762–1829
Smyth, Egbert Coffin
Smyth, Herbert Weir
Smyth, William
Sprague, Oliver Mitchell Wentworth
Spring, Leverett Wilson
Stephenson, Carl
Sumner, James Batcheller
Tansill, Charles Callan
Tatlock, John Strong Perry
Thacher, Thomas Anthony
Thayer, Ezra Ripley
Thayer, James Bradley
Thorndike, Lynn
Thurstone, Louis Leon
Tiedeman, Christopher Gustavus
Tigert, John James, IV
Timberlake, Gideon
Towler, John
Treadwell, Daniel
Trent, William Peterfield
Tucker, Nathaniel Beverley, 1784–1851
Tuttle, Herbert
Tyler, Charles Mellen
Tyler, William Seymour
Van Amringe, John Howard
Vasiliev, Alexander Alexandrovich
Venable, Francis Preston
Vincent, Marvin Richardson
Ward, Robert De Courcy
Ware, Henry, 1764–1845
Warner, Langdon
Webb, John Burkitt
Webster, John White
Weed, Lewis Hill
Weiss, Soma
Wertenbaker, Thomas Jefferson
West, Allen Brown
West, Andrew Fleming
Weyl, Hermann
Wheeler, Arthur Leslie
Willard, James Field
Williams, Edward Thomas
Willis, Henry Parker
Wilson, Bird
Wilson, George Grafton
Wilson, Peter

Wimsatt, William Kurtz
Woodbridge, Samuel Merrill
Woods, James Haughton
Woods, Leonard
Young, Karl
PROHIBITION ADMINISTRATOR
Yellowley, Edward Clements
PROHIBITIONIST (See also REFORMER, TEMPERANCE REFORMER)
Carmack, Edward Ward
Fisk, Clinton Bowen
Poling, Daniel Alfred
St. John, John Pierce
Wheeler, Wayne Bidwell
Wilson, Clarence True
Woolley, John Granville
PROMOTER (See also LAND PROMOTER, LECTURE PROMOTER, PRODUCER, SHOWMAN)
Addicks, John Edward O'Sullivan
Agnew, Cornelius Rea
Andrews, Israel DeWolf
Brady, Anthony Nicholas
Brown, Charlotte Emerson
Collier, Barron Gift
Durant, Henry
Fanning, Edmund
Flagler, Henry Morrison
Gates, John Warne ("Bet-you-a-million")
Goerz, David
Goldschmidt, Jakob
Green, Benjamin Edwards
Harrah, Charles Jefferson
Harvey, William Hope
Hatch, Rufus
Holladay, Ben
Holliday, Cyrus Kurtz
Hopkins, Edward Augustus
Hotchkiss, Horace Leslie
Hubbard, Gardiner Greene
Kearns, Jack
Law, Sallie Chapman Gordon
Lawrance, Uriah Marion
Moore, William Henry
Morgan, Anne
Morse, Charles Wyman
Patterson, John Henry
Paul, Alice
Penrose, Spencer
Perkins, Charles Callahan
Rankine, William Birch
Reed, James Hay
Rickard, George Lewis
Ryan, Thomas Fortune
Sanders, George Nicholas
Seiberling, Frank Augustus
Sheedy, Dennis
Sibley, Hiram
Smart, David Archibald
Smith, Junius
Smith, Robert Alexander C.
Thompson, Benjamin
Train, George Francis
Whalen, Grover Aloysius
Wharton, Richard
Wright, John Stephen
PROPAGANDIST (See also AGITATOR, REFORMER)
Bergh, Henry
Goldman, Emma
Kelley, Hall Jackson
Lovejoy, Owen Reed
Pomeroy, Marcus Mills
Viereck, George Sylvester
PROSECUTOR
Dewey, Thomas Edward
Hogan, Frank Smithwick
PROSPECTOR (See also MINER)
Broderick, David Colbreth
Fair, James Graham
Goold, William A.
La Ronde, Louis Denis, Sieur de
Marshall, James Wilson
Merritt, Leonidas
Osborn, Chase Salmon
Scott, Walter Edward
PROTESTANT MINISTER
Buttrick, George Arthur
PROTESTANT SPOKESMAN
Lyman, Eugene William
PSYCHIATRIC HISTORIAN (See also HISTORIAN, PSYCHIATRIST)
Zilboorg, Gregory
PSYCHIATRIST (See also PSYCHOANALYST, PSYCHOLOGIST, PHYSICIAN)
Anderson, Victor Vance
Babcock, James Woods
Barrett, Albert Moore
Briggs, Lloyd Vernon
Brush, Edward Nathaniel
Burrow, Trigant
Campbell, Charles Macfie
Clevenger, Shobal Vail
Dewey, Richard Smith
Earle, Pliny
Fisher, Theodore Willis
Fromm-Reichmann, Frieda
Gregory, Menas Sarkas Boulgourjian
Haviland, Clarence Floyd
Hinkle, Beatrice Moses
Hoch, August
Jones, William Parker
Kempster, Walter
Kerlin, Isaac Newton
Kirby, George Hughes
Little, Charles Sherman
Menninger, William Claire
Meyer, Adolf
Moore, (Austin) Merrill
Nichols, Charles Henry
Ray, Isaac
Rohé, George Henry
Sakel, Manfred Joshua
Salmon, Thomas William
Seguin, Edouard
Southard, Elmer Ernest
Spitzka, Edward Charles
White, William Alanson
PSYCHOANALYST (See also ALIENIST, PHYSICIAN, PSYCHIATRIST, PSYCHOLOGIST)
Alexander, Franz Gabriel
Brill, Abraham Arden
Brunswick, Ruth Mack
Coriat, Isador Henry
Dunbar, (Helen) Flanders
Fenichel, Otto
Franzblau, Rose Nadler
Fromm, Erich
Fromm-Reichmann, Frieda
Hinkle, Beatrice Moses
Horney, Karen Danielssen
Jelliffe, Smith Ely
Oberndorf, Clarence Paul
Rapaport, David
Reik, Theodor
Roheim, Geza
Sachs, Hanns
Zilboorg, Gregory
PSYCHOLOGIST (See also ALIENIST, EDUCATOR, PHYSICIAN, PSYCHIATRIST, PSYCHOANALYST, PSYCHOPATHOLOGIST, PROFESSOR, SCHOLAR)
Allport, Gordon Willard
Angell, James Rowland
Baldwin, James Mark
Bingham, Walter Van Dyke
Boisen, Anton Theophilus
Boring, Edwin Garrigues
Burnham, William Henry
Cattell, James McKeen
Dodge, Raymond
Downey, June Etta
Farrand, Livingston
Franz, Shepherd Ivory
Fryer, Douglas Henry
Gesell, Arnold Lucius
Goddard, Henry Herbert
Guthrie, Edwin Ray, Jr.
Haggerty, Melvin Everett
Hall, Granville Stanley
Hollingworth, Leta Stetter
Holt, Edwin Bissell
Hull, Clark Leonard
Hyslop, James Hervey
James, William
Jastrow, Joseph
Johnson, Wendell Andrew Leroy
Judd, Charles Hubbard
Kagan, Henry Enoch
Koffka, Kurt
Köhler, Wolfgang
Ladd, George Trumbull
Ladd-Franklin, Christine
Lashley, Karl Spencer
Lewin, Kurt
McDougall, William
McHale, Kathryn
Marshall, Henry Rutgers
Maslow, Abraham H.
Münsterberg, Hugo
Newbold, William Romaine
Norsworthy, Naomi
Otis, Arthur Sinton
Pace, Edward Aloysius
Prince, Morton
Rhine, Joseph Banks
Robinson, Edward Stevens
Rush, James
Sandford, Edmund Clark
Scott, Colin Alexander
Scott, Walter Dill
Seashore, Carl Emil
Sheldon, William Herbert
Smith, Theodate Louise
Starbuck, Edwin Diller
Strong, Charles Augustus

Terman, Lewis Madison
Thorndike, Edward Lee
Thurstone, Louis Leon
Titchener, Edward Bradford
Tolman, Edward Chace
Troland, Leonard Thompson
Warren, Howard Crosby
Washburn, Margaret Floy
Watson, John Broadus
Wertheimer, Max
Wolfe, Harry Kirke
PSYCHOPATHOLOGIST (See also ALIENIST, PHYSICIAN, PSYCHIATRIST, PSYCHOANALYST, PSYCHOLOGIST)
Sidis, Boris
PSYCHOSOMATIC MOVEMENT LEADER
Dunbar, (Helen) Flanders
PUBLIC ADMINISTRATOR
Abbott, Grace
Eastman, Joseph Bartlett
Hoover, Herbert Clark
Taylor, George William
PUBLIC ADVISER
Baruch, Bernard Mannes
PUBLIC AFFAIRS BROADCASTER
Murrow, Edward (Egbert) Roscoe
PUBLIC DEFENDER ADVOCATE
Goldman, Mayer C.
PUBLIC HEALTH ADMINISTRATOR
Baker, Sara Josephine
Dyer, Rolla Eugene
PUBLIC HEALTH EXPERT
Winslow, Charles-Edward Amory
PUBLIC HEALTH LEADER
Abbott, Samuel Warren
Beard, Mary
Emerson, Haven
Mahoney, John Friend
Price, George Moses
Ravenel, Mazyck Porcher
Rosenau, Milton Joseph
Smith, Stephen
Stiles, Charles Wardell
Strong, Richard Pearson
Walcott, Henry Pickering
PUBLIC HEALTH OFFICIAL (See also PHYSICIAN)
Banks, Charles Edward
Chapin, Charles Value
Copeland, Royal Samuel
Crumbine, Samuel Jay
Fernós Isern, Antonio
Goldwater, Sigismund Schulz
Gunn, Selskar Michael
Park, William Hallock
Rose, Wickliffe
Sawyer, Wilbur Augustus
Snow, William Freeman
Wende, Ernest
PUBLICIST (See also EDITOR, NEWSAGENT, PAMPHLETEER)
Alford, Leon Pratt
Ames, Fisher
Applegate, Jesse
Batch, Thomas Willing
Barker, Wharton
Barrett, John
Bates, George Handy
Beck, James Montgomery
Beer, George Louis
Bement, Caleb N.
Bemis, George
Birkbeck, Morris
Bradford, Gamaliel
Carnegie, Andrew
Clark, Willis Gaylord
Cobbett, William
Cocke, John Hartwell
Cohn, Alfred A.
Cunliffe-Owen, Philip Frederick
Curtis, William Eleroy
Elliot, Jonathan
Fisher, Joshua Francis
Ford, Henry Jones
Francis, John Morgan
Frank, Glenn
Franklin, Fabian
Freeman, Joseph
Gilman, Daniel Colt
Gmeiner, John
Grimké, Archibald Henry
Grosvenor, William Mason
Haines, Lynn
Hannagan, Stephen Jerome
Hapgood, Norman
Harvey, William Hope
Hinman, George Wheeler
Holls, George Frederick William
House, Edward Howard
Hurd, John Codman
Ives, Levi Silliman
Jewett, William Cornell
Kapp, Friedrich
Knox, Dudley Wright
Kohler, Max James
Lea, Henry Charles
Lee, Henry, 1782–1867
Lee, Ivy Ledbetter
Lewis, Charlton Thomas
Lewis, Enoch
McCarthy, Charles
MacCauley, Clay
McElroy, Robert McNutt
Manly, Basil Maxwell
Marburg, Theodore
Marshall, Louis
Mason, Lucy Randolph
Michelson, Charles
Minor, Raleigh Colston
Murphy, Edgar Gardner
Myrick, Herbert
Nichols, Clarina Irene Howard
Opdyke, George
Otis, James
Pallen, Condé Benoist
Parker, Theodore
Peixotto, Benjamin Franklin
Pinchot, Amos Richards Eno
Plumbe, John
Preetorius, Emil
Puryear, Bennet
Rauch, John Henry
Revell, Nellie MacAleney
Richmond, John Wilkes
Ruml, Beardsley
Scott, Emmett Jay
Seelye, Julius Hawley
Spink, John George Taylor
Stoddard, Theodore Lothrop
Stokes, Anson Phelps
Storey, Moorfield
Straight, Willard Dickerman
Struve, Gustav
Sumner, William Graham
Trueblood, Benjamin Franklin
Tucker, Gilbert Milligan
Turnbull, Robert James
Upshur, Abel Parker
Van Hise, Charles Richard
Ward, Herbert Dickinson
Ward, William Hayes
Waterhouse, Sylvester
Wolf, Simon
Wood, Henry Alexander Wise
Woolsey, Theodore Salisbury
Wright, John Stephen
PUBLIC OFFICIAL
Akerman, Amos Tappan
Allen, George Venable
Anderson, Mary
Beall, Samuel Wootton
Berle, Adolf Augustus, Jr.
Bulfinch, Charles
Carter, Landon
Cotton, Joseph Potter
Crosby, John Schuyler
Davis, Dwight Filley
De Peyster, Abraham
Dickinson, John
Dimitry, Alexander
Dykstra, Clarence Addison
Earle, Edward Mead
Fagan, James Fleming
Fairlie, John Archibald
Gallagher, William Davis
Garfield, Harry Augustus
Graham, James
Greenleaf, Halbert Stevens
Hawley, Joseph
Henderson, Thomas
Hoan, Daniel Webster
Holten, Samuel
Huntington, Elisha
Ingersoll, Jared, 1722–1781
Jennings, John
Jones, Jesse Holman
Kirtland, Jared Potter
Lacey, John
Latrobe, John Hazlehurst Boneval
Lawrence, William Beach
Levitt, Arthur
Lewis, William Henry
Lowell, James Russell
Macy, Valentine Everit
Meigs, Josiah
Morrison, Delesseps Story
Moseley, Edward Augustus
Murray, Thomas Edward
Newberry, Truman Handy
Nicola, Lewis
O'Brian, John Lord
Olds, Leland
Page, Thomas Walker
Paterson, John
Poydras, Julien de Lelande
Pynchon, John
Ricord, Frederick William
Roane, John Selden
Rockefeller, Nelson Aldrich
Rolph, James

Roosevelt, Theodore
Smith, George Otis
Smith, Harord Dewey
Thacher, John Boyd
Thompson, David P.
Thornton, William
Vaux, Richard
Waite, Henry Matson
Walsh, Francis Patrick
Ware, Nathaniel A.
Wehle, Louis Brandeis
Whiting, William
Williams, John Skelton
Winston, Joseph
Woytinsky, Wladimir Savelievich
Wright, Carroll Davidson

PUBLIC OPINION RESEARCH SPECIALIST
Robinson, Claude Everett
Roper, Elmo Burns, Jr.

PUBLIC POLICY ANALYST
Baroody, William Joseph

PUBLIC RELATIONS COUNSEL
Byoir, Carl Robert
Hill, John Wiley
Hinshaw, David Schull
Ross, Thomas Joseph

PUBLIC SERVANT
Folsom, Marion Bayard
Nourse, Edwin Griswold

PUBLIC SPEAKING EXPERT
Carnegie, Dale

PUBLIC UTILITIES EXPERT
Cooley, Mortimer Elwyn
Couch, Harvey Crowley
Dow, Alex
Mitchell, Sidney Zollicoffer
Sloan, Matthew Scott

PUBLIC UTILITY EXECUTIVE
Carlisle, Floyd Leslie
Cortelyou, George Bruce
Doherty, Henry Latham
Insull, Samuel

PUBLIC WELFARE LEADER
Rumsey, Mary Harriman

PUBLISHER (See also EDITOR, MAGAZINE PUBLISHER, NEWSPAPER PUBLISHER)
Adler, Elmer
Aiken, Andrew Jackson
Aitkin, Robert
Allen, Henry Justin
Anderson, Margaret Carolyn
Appleton, Daniel
Appleton, William Henry
Appleton, William Worthen
Armstrong, Samuel Turell
Ascoli, Max
Baird, Henry Carey
Baker, Peter Carpenter
Balestier, Charles Wolcott
Bancroft, Hubert Howe
Bardeen, Charles William
Barron, Clarence Walker
Barsotti, Charles
Bartlett, John
Beach, Sylvia Woodbridge
Beadle, Erastus Flavel
Bell, Robert
Benton, William Burnett
Bidwell, Walter Hilliard
Bladen, William
Bonfils, Frederick Gilmer
Bonner, Robert
Bowen, Abel
Bowen, Henry Chandler
Bowker, Richard Rogers
Brace, Donald Clifford
Bradford, Andrew
Bradford, Thomas
Bradford, William
Breckinridge, Desha
Brett, George Platt
Brewster, Osmyn
Bridgman, Herbert Lawrence
Brown, James
Bunce, Oliver Bell
Butler, Burridge Davenal
Butler, Simeon
Cameron, Andrew Carr
Capper, Arthur
Carey, Henry Charles
Carey, Mathew
Carter, William Hodding, Jr.
Cerf, Bennett Alfred
Charless, Joseph
Childs, Aphas Grier
Childs, George William
Cist, Charles
Clarke, Robert
Collier, Peter Fenelon
Cook, Robert Johnson
Covici, Pascal ("Pat")
Cox, James Middleton, Jr.
Crocker, Uriel
Currier, Nathaniel
Curtis, Cyrus Hermann Kotzschmar
Day, George Parmly
Delavan, Edward Cornelius
De Young, Michel Harry
Dodd, Frank Howard
Doran, George Henry
Doubleday, Frank Nelson
Doubleday, Nelson
Draper, Margaret Green
Dworshak, Henry Clarence
Ellmaker, (Emmett) Lee
Estes, Dana
Everett, Robert
Farrar, John Chipman
Field, Marshall, III
Field, Marshall, IV
Fields, James Thomas
Fitzgerald, Thomas
Ford, Daniel Sharp
Francis, Charles Stephen
Funk, Isaac Kauffman
Funk, Wilfred John
Gannett, Frank Ernest
Gernsback, Hugo
Ginn, Edwin
Gitt, Josiah Williams ("Jess")
Glass, Franklin Potts
Godey, Louis Antoine
Gonzales, Ambrose Elliott
Goodrich, Samuel Griswold
Gowans, William
Graham, George Rex
Graham, Philip Leslie
Grasty, Charles Henry
Greenslet, Ferris
Griscom, Lloyd Carpenter
Grosset, Alexander
Guggenheim, Harry Frank
Guinzburg, Harold Kleinert
Gunter, Archibald Clavering
Haldeman-Julius, Emanuel
Harcourt, Alfred
Harding, Jesper
Harding, William White
Harper, Fletcher
Harper, James
Harris, Benjamin
Harris, Julian La Rose
Hart, Abraham
Haynes, Williams
Heard, Dwight Bancroft
Hearst, William Randolph
Helmer, Bessie Bradwell
Hill, David Jayne
Hitchcock, Gilbert Monell
Hobby, William Pettus
Holt, Henry
Houghton, Henry Oscar
Huebsch, Benjamin W.
Humphreys, James
Hunt, Freeman
Jackson, Charles Samuel
Jewett, John Punchard
Jones, George
Judd, Orange
Kenedy, Patrick John
Kiplinger, Willard Monroe
Kirchwey, Freda
Kline, George
Klopch, Louis
Knapp, Joseph Palmer
Kneeland, Samuel
Knopf, Blanche Wolf
Kohlberg, Alfred
Kollock, Shepard
Lange, Louis
Langlie, Arthur Bernard
Lawrence, David
Lea, Henry Charles
Lea, Isaac
Leslie, Frank
Leslie, Miriam Florence Folline
Leypoldt, Frederick
Lippincott, Joseph Wharton
Lippincott, Joshua Ballinger
Littell, Eliakim
Little, Charles Coffin
Liveright, Horace Brisbin
Longley, Alcander
Lothrop, Daniel
Loudon, Samuel
Luce, Henry Robinson
McClurg, Alexander Caldwell
McCook, Anson George
McElrath, Thomas
Macfadden, Bernarr
McGraw, Donald Cushing
McGraw, James Herbert
McIntyre, Alfred Robert
McLean, William Lippard
Macrae, John
McRae, Milton Alexander
Marble, Manton Malone
Marquis, Albert Nelson
Mattson, Hans
Maxwell, William
Melcher, Frederic Gershom
Meredith, Edna C. Elliott

Meredith, Edwin Thomas
Merriam, Charles
Miller, John Henry
Mitchell, Samuel Augustus
Moody, John
Moreau de Saint-Méry, Médéric-Louis-Élie
Morwitz, Edward
Mosher, Thomas Bird
Munn, Orson Desaix
Munro, George
Munsey, Frank Andrew
Murphy, John
Myrick, Herbert
Nieman, Lucius William
Norman, John
Norton, William Warder
Oliver, George Tener
Parks, William
Patterson, Alicia
Peterson, Charles Jacobs
Pittock, Henry Lewis
Plimpton, George Arthur
Polock, Moses
Pomeroy, Marcus Mills
Poulson, Zachariah
Prang, Louis
Pulitzer, Joseph, Jr.
Putnam, Eben
Putnam, George Haven
Putnam, George Palmer
Redfield, Justus Starr
Revell, Fleming Hewitt
Rice, Edwin Wilbur
Ridder, Bernard Herman
Ridder, Herman
Rinehart, Stanley Marshall, Jr.
Root, Frank Albert
Rossiter, William Sidney
Roth, Samuel
Rowell, George Presbury
Rudge, William Edwin
Ruffin, Edmund
Sadlier, Denis
Sartain, John
Saxton, Eugene Francis
Scherman, Harry
Schocken, Theodore
Schuster, Max Lincoln
Scribner, Charles, 1821–1871
Scribner, Charles, 1854–1930
Scribner, Charles, 1890–1952
Scripps, Edward Wyllis
Scripps, James Edmund
Sears, Robert
Shuster, W(illiam) Morgan
Silverman, Sime
Simon, Richard Leo
Singerly, William Miskey
Smith, Gerald L. K.
Smith, Lloyd Pearsall
Smith, Ormond Gerald
Smith, Roswell
Sower, Christopher, 1693–1758
Sower, Christopher, 1721–1784
Sower, Christopher, 1754–1799
Stahlman, Edward Bushrod
Stephens, Edwin William
Stoddart, Joseph Marshall
Stokes, Frederick Abbot
Stone, David Marvin
Strong, Walter Ansel
Taft, Charles Phelps
Tammen, Harry Heye
Thomas, Robert Bailey
Thompson, John
Ticknor, William Davis
Trow, John Fowler
Tyson, Lawrence Davis
Vanderbilt, Cornelius, Jr. ("Cornelius IV," "Neil")
Van Nostrand, David
Vick, James
Victor, Orville James
Walker, John Brisben
Watson, John Fanning
Watts, Franklin Mowry
Williams, William
Wilson, Halsey William
Wilson, John Lockwood
Wilson, William
Wolff, Kurt August Paul
Wood, Samuel
Woodruff, William Edward
Wyeth, John
Yeager, Joseph
Young, Lafayette
Ziff, William Bernard

PUGILIST (See also ATHLETE, BOXER)
Corbett, James John
Fitzsimmons, Robert Prometheus
Heenan, John Carmel
Morrissey, John
Sullivan, John Lawrence

PUPPETEER
Sarg, Tony

PUZZLEMAKER
Kingsley, Elizabeth Seelman

QUAKER HISTORIAN (See also CLERGYMAN, *Quaker*)
Jones, Rufus Matthew

RABBI
Belkin, Samuel

RACEHORSE OWNER
Sloane, Isabel Cleves Dodge

RACE RELATIONS EXPERT
Alexander, Will Winton
Haynes, George Edmund

RACING CAR DRIVER
De Palma, Ralph

RACING-NEWS ENTREPRENEUR
Annenberg, Moses Louis

RACING OFFICIAL
Cassidy, Marshall Whiting

RACKETEER (See also BOOTLEGGER, CRIMINAL, GANGSTER, ORGANIZED CRIME LEADER)
Adonis, Joe
Cohen, Meyer Harris ("Mickey")
Colombo, Joseph Anthony
Costello, Frank
Gambino, Carlo
Giancana, Sam ("Mooney")
Luciano, Charles ("Lucky")
Madden, Owen Victor ("Owney")
Ricca, Paul
Valachi, Joseph Michael

RACONTEUR (See also HUMORIST, LECTURER, READER, WIT)
Beckwourth, James P.
King, Alexander
Levant, Oscar

RADICAL (See also AGITATOR, INSURGENT, REVOLUTIONIST, SOCIALIST ADVOCATE)
Alinsky, Saul David
Chaplin, Ralph Hosea
Gurowski, Adam
Mahler, Herbert
Steuben, John
Stokes, Rose Harriet Pastor

RADIO ANNOUNCER
Brokenshire, Norman Ernest
Cross, Milton John
Grauer, Benjamin Franklin ("Ben")
Husing, Edward Britt ("Ted")
McNamee, Graham

RADIO BROADCASTER
Bryson, Lyman Lloyd
Denny, George Vernon, Jr.
Murrow, Edward (Egbert) Roscoe

RADIO BROADCASTING EXECUTIVE
Trammell, Niles

RADIO COMMENTATOR
Carter, Boake
Davis, Elmer Holmes
Gibbons, Floyd
Grauer, Benjamin Franklin ("Ben")
Heatter, Gabriel
Hill, Edwin Conger
Kaltenborn, Hans Von
Lewis, Fulton, Jr.
Woollcott, Alexander Humphreys

RADIO COMMUNICATIONS PIONEER
Fessenden, Reginald Aubrey

RADIOGRAPHER (See also PHYSICIAN, RADIOLOGIST, ROENTGENOLOGIST)
Kolle, Frederick Strange

RADIO JOURNALIST
Huntley, Chester ("Chet") Robert

RADIOLOGIST (See also PHYSICIAN, ROENTGENOLOGIST)
Coutard, Henri
Hirsch, Isaac Seth
Pancoast, Henry Khunrath
Pfahler, George Edward

RADIO PERSONALITY
Ace, Jane
Adams, Franklin Pierce
Allen, Fred
Allen, Gracie
Arquette, Clifford
Burns, Bob
Considine, Robert ("Bob") Bernard
Correll, Charles James
Kilgallen, Dorothy Mae
McBride, Mary Margaret
Marx, Julius Henry ("Groucho")
Nelson, Oswald George ("Ozzie")

Revell, Nellie MacAleney
Sheen, Fulton John
Woollcott, Alexander Humphreys
Radio Sportscaster
McCarthy, Charles Louis ("Clem")
Railroad Builder
Allen, Thomas
Andrews, Chauncey Hummason
Barnum, Zenus
Brice, Calvin Stewart
Crocker, Alvah
Crocker, Charles
Davis, Henry Gassaway
Dillon, Sidney
Donovan, John Joseph
Drake, Francis Marion
Durant, Thomas Clark
Evans, John
Farnam, Henry
Grant, John Thomas
Holdrege, George Ward
Holliday, Cyrus Kurtz
Joy, James Frederick
Judah, Theodore Dehone
Keith, Minor Cooper
Kerens, Richard C.
Litchfield, Electus Backus
McCoy, George Braidwood
McDonald, John Bartholomew
Martin, William Thompson
Mason, Claibourne Rice
Meiggs, Henry
Mitchell, Alexander
Packer, Asa
Price, Thomas Lawson
Robinson, Albert Alonzo
Rose, Chauncey
Scullin, John
Stanford, Leland
Stickney, Alpheus Beede
Stone, Amasa
Welch, Charles Clark
Winslow, Edward Francis
Railroad Engineer
Cohen, Mendes
Fink, Albert
Pearson, Edward Jones
Schuyler, James Dix
Spencer, Samuel
Railroad Executive
Ashe, William Shepperd
Atterbury, William Wallace
Baer, George Frederick
Baldwin, William Henry
Bernet, John Joseph
Billings, Frederick
Bishop, William Darius
Boorman, James
Borden, Richard
Bridgers, Robert Rufus
Brown, William Carlos
Budd, Ralph
Burrall, William Porter
Callaway, Samuel Rodger
Cameron, James Donald
Cass, George Washington
Cassatt, Alexander Johnston
Clark, Horace Francis
Clement, Martin Withington
Clifford, John Henry
Clough, William Pitt
Colby, Gardner
Corbin, Austin
Corbin, Daniel Chase
Cowen, John Kissig
Depew, Chauncey Mitchell
Devereux, John Henry
Drayton, Thomas Fenwick
Dudley, Edward Bishop
Echols, John
Fink, Albert
Fish, Stuyvesant
Gadsden, James
Garrett, John Work
Gordon, William Washington
Gould, George Jay
Gowen, Franklin Benjamin
Gray, Carl Raymond
Harahan, James Theodore
Harahan, William Johnson
Harriman, Edward Henry
Harrington, Samuel Maxwell
Harrison, Fairfax
Hayne, Robert Young
Hill, James Jerome
Hine, Charles de Lano
Holden, Hale
Houston, Henry Howard
Hubbard, Thomas Hamlin
Huntington, Collis Potter
Huntington, Henry Edwards
Ingalls, Melville Ezra
Jeffers, William Martin
Jeffrey, Edward Turner
Jewett, Hugh Judge
Johnston, John Taylor
Jones, Frank
King, John Pendleton
Kirkman, Marshall Monroe
Kneass, Strickland
Lord, Eleazar
Loree, Leonor Fresnel
Lovett, Robert Scott
Lucas, James H.
McCullough, John Griffith
McKennan, Thomas McKean Thompson
Mahone, William
Markham, Charles Henry
Mellen, Charles Sanger
Merrick, Samuel Vaughan
Messler, Thomas Doremus
Minty, Robert Horatio George
Negley, James Scott
Newman, William H.
Oakes, Thomas Fletcher
Ogden, William Butler
Olyphant, Robert Morrison
Osborn, William Henry
Palmer, William Jackson
Parsons, Lewis Baldwin
Payne, Henry Clay
Pearson, Edward Jones
Perham, Josiah
Perkins, Charles Elliott
Peters, Richard, 1810–1889
Plumbe, John
Poor, John Alfred
Porter, Horace
Preble, William Pitt
Randolph, Epes
Rea, Samuel
Rice, Edmund
Ripley, Edward Payson
Robb, James
Roberts, George Brooke
Sayre, Robert Heysham
Scott, Thomas Alexander
Scott, William Lawrence
Sewell, William Joyce
Shonts, Theodore Perry
Sloan, Samuel
Smith, Alfred Holland
Smith, John Gregory
Smith, Milton Hannibal
Spencer, Samuel
Sproule, William
Stahlman, Edward Bushrod
Stephens, John Lloyd
Stevens, John Frank
Stewart, Robert Marcellus
Strong, William Barstow
Symes, James Miller
Thomas, John Wilson
Thompson, Arthur Webster
Thomson, Frank
Thomson, John Edgar
Thornton, Henry Worth
Underwood, Frederick Douglas
Vanderbilt, William Henry
Van Horne, William Cornelius
Van Sweringen, Mantis James
Vibbard, Chauncey
Wallace, John Findley
Walters, William Thompson
Willard, Daniel
Worcester, Edwin Dean
Wright, Charles Barston
Yeager, Joseph
Yoakum, Benjamm Franklin
Young, Robert Ralph
Zimmerman, Eugene
Railroad Expert
Adams, Charles Francis
Allen, William Frederick
Reagan, John Henninger
Railroad Owner
James, Arthur Curtiss
Morgan, Charles
Starin, John Henry
Railroad Promoter (See also Promoter)
Ames, Oliver
Andrews, Alexander Boyd
Brewster, James
Brown, George
Burke, Stevenson
Chapin, Chester William
Corbett, Henry Winslow
Diven, Alexander Samuel
Guthrie, James
Hardy, William Harris
Jackson, William, 1783–1855
Law, George
Le Duc, William Gates
Loveland, William Austin Hamilton
Paine, Charles
Rice, Edmund
Thomas, Philip Evan
Vanderbilt, Cornelius, 1794–1877
Villard, Henry
Whitney, Asa
Yulee, David Levy

RANCHER (See also COWBOY, CATTLEMAN, RANGER, STOCK BREEDER)
Ammons, Elias Milton
Bartlett, Dewey Follett
Haggin, James Ben Ali
Jardine, William Marion
Kendrick, John Benjamin
King, Richard, Jr.
Kleberg, Robert Justus, Jr.
Maxwell, Lucien Bonaparte
Thornton, Daniel I. J.
RANGER (See also RANCHER)
McNeill, John Hanson
Mosby, John Singleton
Rogers, Robert
Wallace, William Alexander Anderson
RARE BOOK DEALER (See also BIBLIOPHILE)
Rosenbach, Abraham Simon Wolf
Rosenbach, Philip Hyman
READER (See also LECTURER, RACONTEUR)
Kemble, Frances Anne
Riddle, George Peabody
READING DEVELOPMENT EXPERT
Gray, William Scott, Jr.
REAL ESTATE DEVELOPER
Chandler, Harry
Tishman, David
Zeckendorf, William
REAL-ESTATE OPERATOR (See also LAND AGENT)
Binga, Jesse
Bloom, Sol
Bowes, Edward J.
Hanson, Ole
Heckscher, August
MacArthur, John Donald
Marling, Alfred Erskine
Morgenthau, Henry
Palmer, Potter
Savage, Henry Wilson
Wright, John Stephen
REALTOR
De Priest, Oscar Stanton
REBEL (See also AGITATOR, INSURGENT, RADICAL, REVOLUTIONIST)
Ingle, Richard
Vesey, Denmark
REFORMER (See also AGITATOR, FEMINIST, HUMANITARIAN, PEACE ADVOCATE, POLITICAL REFORMER, PRISON REFORMER, PROHIBITIONIST, PROPAGANDIST, SOCIAL REFORMER, TEMPERANCE REFORMER)
Allen, Zachariah
Andrews, Stephen Pearl
Angell, George Thorndike
Anthony, Susan Brownell
Appleton, James
Ballou, Adin
Barrows, Samuel June
Beecher, Catharine Esther
Bishop, Robert Hamilton
Blackwell, Antoinette Louisa Brown
Blake, Lillie Devereux
Bloomer, Amelia Jenks
Boissevain, Inez Milholland
Bolton, Sarah Knowles
Bonney, Charles Carroll
Bright Eyes
Brooks, John Graham
Brown, William Wells
Bruce, William Cabell
Burleigh, George Shepard
Burleigh, William Henry
Burritt, Elihu
Cabet, Étienne
Cannon, Ida Maud
Chapman, Maria Weston
Cheever, George Barrell
Cheney, Ednah Dow Littlehale
Childs, Richard Spencer
Cleghorn, Sarah Norcliffe
Collier, John
Colver, Nathaniel
Comstock, Anthony
Coxey, Jacob Sechter
Crandall, Prudence
Dall, Caroline Wells Healey
Delavan, Edward Cornelius
Dewey, Melvil
Dike, Samuel Warren
Dinwiddie, Edwin Courtland
Donnelly, Ignatius
Dorr, Thomas Wilson
Easley, Ralph Montgomery
Eastman, Joseph Bartlett
Eddy, Thomas
Ely, Richard Theodore
Evans, Frederick William
Evans, George Henry
Farnam, Henry Walcott
Ferguson, William Porter Frisbee
Field, David Dudley
Filene, Edward Albert
Flower, Benjamin Orange
Fussell, Bartholomew
Gage, Frances Dana Barker
Gales, Joseph
Garrison, William Lloyd
George, Henry
Giesler-Anneke, Mathilde Franziska
Goodell, William
Gould, Elgin Ralston Lovell
Graham, Sylvester
Green, Beriah
Green, Frances Harriet Whipple
Griffing, Josephine Sophie White
Grimké, Thomas Smith
Hall, Bolton
Hapgood, Norman
Harriman, Florence Jaffray Hurst
Hastings, Samuel Dexter
Hepburn, William Peters
Higginson, Thomas Wentworth
Himes, Joshua Vaughan
Holbrook, Josiah
Hooker, Isabella Beecher
Howe, Frederic Clemson
Howe, Julia Ward
Howland, Emily
Hunt, Harriot Kezia
Ivins, William Mills
Jay, William
Johnson, Magnus
Jones, Samuel Milton
Kellor, Frances (Alice)
Kynett, Alpha Jefferson
Lay, Benjamin
Leavitt, Joshua
Lewelling, Lorenzo Dow
Livermore, Mary Ashton Rice
Loomis, Arphaxed
Lowell, Josephine Shaw
Luther, Seth
McCann, Alfred Watterson
Marsh, John
Masquerier, Lewis
Matthews, Joseph Brown
Matthews, Nathan
Mattison, Hiram
May, Samuel Joseph
Mead, Edwin Doak
Mifflin, Warner
Moss, Frank
Mott, James
Mott, Lucretia Coffin
Murphey, Archibald de Bow
Myers, Gustavus
Nichols, Clarina Irene Howard
Nichols, Mary Sargeant Neal Gove
Noyes, John Humphrey
Opdyke, George
O'Sullivan, Mary Kenney
Parkhurst, Charles Henry
Pennypacker, Elijah Funk
Philips, Martin Wilson
Phillips, Wendell
Pierpont, John
Pillsbury, Parker
Polk, Frank Lyon
Post, Louis Freeland
Poznanski, Gustavus
Price, Eli Kirk
Quincy, Edmund
Quincy, Josiah, 1772–1864
Rambaut, Mary Lucinda Bonney
Rantoul, Robert, 1778–1858
Rantoul, Robert, 1805–1852
Riis, Jacob August
Ripley, George
Rose, Ernestine Louise Siismondi Potowski
Rose, John Carter
Russell, Charles Edward
Sanders, Elizabeth Elkins
Saunders, Prince
Scott, Colin Alexander
Scott, Walter
Seidel, George Lukas Emil
Shaw, Albert
Shaw, Anna Howard
Sherwood, Katharine Margaret Brownlee
Sims, William Sowden
Smith, Elizabeth Oakes Prince
Smith, Fred Burton
Smith, Gerrit
Smith, Hannah Whitall
Spargo, John
Spencer, Anna Garlin
Spingarn, Joel Elias
Spreckels, Rudolph

Stanton, Elizabeth Cady
Stanton, Henry Brewster
Steffens, Lincoln
Sterne, Simon
Still, William
Stone, Lucy
Straton, John Roach
Sunderland, Eliza Jane Read
Swallow, Silas Comfort
Swisshelm, Jane Grey Cannon
Sylvis, William H.
Thomas, Norman Mattoon
Tutwiler, Julia Strudwick
Villard, Helen Frances Garrison
Villard, Oswald Garrison
Ward, Henry Dana
Warren, Josiah
Weber, Henry Adam
Whipple, Henry Benjamin
White, Alfred Tredway
Wiley, Harvey Washington
Willard, Frances Elizabeth Caroline
Woodhull, Victoria Claflin
Woods, Robert Archey
Wright, Elizur
Wright, Frances

REGICIDE
Dixwell, John
Goffe, William
Whalley, Edward

REGIONAL PLANNER
Behrendt, Walter Curt
MacKaye, Benton

REHABILITATION MEDICINE PIONEER
Paul, William Darwin ("Shorty")

RELIEF ORGANIZER
Morgan, Anne

RELIGIOUS ACTIVIST
Robins, Raymond

RELIGIOUS LEADER (See also ARCHABBOT, ARCHBISHOP, BISHOP, CABALIST, CHAPLAIN, CHRISTIAN SCIENCE LEADER, CLERGYMAN, EVANGELIST, INDIAN PROPHET, METAPHYSICIAN, MISSIONARY, MYSTIC, REVIVALIST, SPIRITUALIST, THEOLOGIAN, THEOSOPHIST, TRANSCENDENTALIST
Abbott, Benjamin
Adler, Cyrus
Adler, Felix
Albright, Jacob
Antes, Henry
Backus, Isaac
Bowne, John
Coe, George Albert
Coffin, Henry Sloane
Cox, Henry Hamilton
Dittemore, John Valentine
Divine, Father
Drexel, Katharine Mary
Eddy, Mary Morse Baker
Haven, Henry Philemon
Hodur, Francis
Hutchinson, Anne
Ivins, Anthony Woodward
Jones, Abner
McKay, David Oman
Metz, Christian
Middleton, Arthur
Mills, Benjamin Fay
Morris, Anthony, 1654–1721
Norris, Isaac, 1701–1766
Osgood, Jacob
Poznanski, Gustavus
Pratt, Orson
Rapp, George
Russell, Charles Taze
Rutherford, Joseph Franklin
Sharpless, Isaac
Skaniadariio
Smith, George Albert
Smith, Uriah
Thomas, Richard Henry
Tobias, Channing Heggie
Wilkinson, Jemima
Wood, James
Woolman, John

REMONSTRANT
Child, Robert

REPUBLICAN PARTY NATIONAL CHAIRMAN
Hamilton, John Daniel Miller, II

RESEARCH INSTITUTE EXECUTIVE
Baroody, William Joseph

RESETTLEMENT EXPERT
Rosen, Joseph A.

RESORT OWNER
Grossinger, Jennie

RESTAURANT CRITIC
Hines, Duncan

RESTAURATEUR
Delmonico, Lorenzo
Kohlsaat, Herman Henry
Romanoff, Michael ("Prince Mike")
Sanders, Harland David ("Colonel")
Sardi, Melchiorre Pio Vencenzo ("Vincent")
Sherry, Louis
Stevens, Frank Mozley
Stouffer, Vernon Bigelow

RETAILER
Cushman, Austin Thomas ("Joe")
Hughes, Albert William
Ohrbach, Nathan M. ("N.M.")

REVIVALIST (See also EVANGELIST, RELIGIOUS LEADER)
Alline, Henry
Finney, Charles Grandison
Kirk, Edward Norris
Wormley, James

REVOLUTIONARY HEROINE (See HEROINE)

REVOLUTIONARY LEADER (See also PATRIOT, REVOLUTIONARY PATRIOT, SOLDIER, STATESMAN)
Benson, Egbert
Carroll, Charles
Chase, Samuel
Drayton, William Henry
Gadsden, Christopher
Hanson, John
Hindman, William
Hobart, John Sloss
Houston, William Churchill
Houstoun, John
Huger, Isaac
Huger, John
Johnston, Samuel
Jones, Willie
Person, Thomas
Scott, John Morin
Sears, Isaac
Tilghman, Matthew

REVOLUTIONARY PATRIOT (See also PATRIOT, REVOLUTIONARY LEADER, SOLDIER)
Alexander, Abraham
Arnold, Benedict
Arnold, Jonathan
Banister, John
Bartlett, Josiah
Cabell, William
Frelinghuysen, Frederick
Habersham, Joseph
Harvie, John
Howell, Richard
Howley, Richard
Izard, Ralph
Jones, Noble Wymberley
Jouett, John
Lamb, John
Leaming, Thomas
Lewis, Andrew
Lewis, Fielding
Livingston, Robert R., 1718–1775
Marshall, Christopher
Mason, Thomson
Matlock, Timothy
Mercer, James
Milledge, John
Moore, Maurice
Moore, William, 1735–1793
Nicholas, Robert Carter
Nixon, John, 1733–1808
Page, John
Parsons, Samuel Holden
Peabody, Nathaniel
Pendleton, Edmund
Peters, Richard, 1744–1828
Pettit, Charles
Roberdeau, Daniel
Sands, Comfort
Smith, Robert, 1732–1801
Thornton, Matthew
Tyler, John, 1747–1813
Warren, Joseph
Weare, Meshech
Whipple, William
Yates, Abraham
Yates, Robert
Young, Thomas

REVOLUTIONIST (See also AGITATOR, INSURGENT, RADICAL)
Hecker, Friedrich Karl Franz
Heinzen, Karl Peter
Lee, Francis Lightfoot
Rapp, Wilhelm
Reed, John, 1887–1920
Sanders, George Nicholas
Wharton, William H.

RHEUMATOLOGIST (See also PHYSICIAN)
Hench, Philip Showalter

RHINOLOGIST (See also PHYSICIAN)
Jarvis, William Chapman
RHYTHM-AND-BLUES MUSICIAN
Jordan, Louis
ROAD BUILDER
Mears, Otto
Mullan, John
ROCKET PIONEER
Goddard, Robert Hutchings
ROCKET SCIENTIST
Braun, Wernher von
Ley, Willy
ROENTGENOLOGIST (See also PHYSICIAN, RADIOGRAPHER, RADIOLOGIST)
Baetjer, Frederick Henry
Brown, Percy
Caldwell, Eugene Wilson
Williams, Francis Henry
ROWING CHAMPION (See also OARSMAN)
Kelly, John Brendan
ROWING COACH (See also ATHLETE, OARSMAN)
Cook, Robert Johnson
Courtney, Charles Edward

SAILMAKER
Forten, James
SAILOR (see MARINER)
SALOONKEEPER
Shor, Bernard ("Toots")
SALVAGE EXPERT
Merritt, Israel John
SALVATION ARMY GENERAL
Booth, Evangeline Cory
SANITARIAN (See also ENGINEER (SANITARY)
Carter, Henry Rose
Freeman, Allen Weir
Gorgas, William Crawford
Harrington, Charles
Harris, Elisha
Jones, Joseph
Jordan, Edwin Oakes
Kedzie, Robert Clark
Logan, Thomas Muldrup, 1808–1876
McCormack, Joseph Nathaniel
Magruder, George Lloyd
Richards, Ellen Henrietta Swallow
Souchon, Edmond
SATIRIST (See also HUMORIST, WIT)
Alsop, Richard
Hopkins, Lemuel
Locke, David Ross
Smith, Seba
Snelling, William Joseph
Wright, Robert William
SAXOPHONIST
Adderley, Julian Edwin ("Cannonball")
Gray, Glen
SCENARIST
Beach, Rex
SCHOLAR (See also ARCHAEOLOGIST, ASSYRIOLOGIST, CLASSICIST, EGYPTOLOGIST, GENEALOGIST, GRAMMARIAN, HEBRAIST, HELLENIST, LOGICIAN, ORIENTALIST, PHILOLOGIST, PHILOSOPHER, SEMITIST, SINOLOGUE)
Abbot, Ezra
Abbott, Frank Frost
Adams, Jasper
Allen, Frederic de Forest
Allen, William Francis
Anderson, Henry Tompkins
Anthon, Charles
Baylies, Francis
Beck, Charles
Beeson, Charles Henry
Bennett, Charles Edwin
Biddle, Nicholas
Bliss, Tasker Howard
Botta, Vincenzo
Bunche, Ralph Johnson
Carter, Jesse Benedict
Chase, Thomas
Clinton, DeWitt
Coe, George Albert
Cook, Albert Stanburrough
Crane, Thomas Frederick
Cross, Wilbur Lucius
Curme, George Oliver
Currier, Charles Warren
Curtin, Jeremiah
Dargan, Edwin Preston
Davidson, Thomas
Dennison, Walter
D'Ooge, Martin Luther
Dowling, Noel Thomas
Dunbar, (Helen) Flanders
Dyer, Louis
Edgren, August Hjalmar
Eliot, Samuel
Fay, Edwin Whitefield
Felton, Cornelius Conway
Fenollosa, Ernest Francisco
Fletcher, Robert
Frothingham, Arthur Lincoln
Furness, Horace Howard, 1833–1912
Furness, Horace Howard, 1865–1930
Grandgent, Charles Hall
Green, William Henry
Griswold, Alfred Whitney
Gruening, Emil
Hale, William Gardner
Harkness, Albert
Haven, Joseph
Heilprin, Michael
Hirsch, Emil Gustav
Hohfeld, Wesley Newcomb
Holmes, George Frederick
Hudson, Henry Norman
Humphreys, Milton Wylie
Humphries, George Rolfe
Isaacs, Abram Samuel
Jastrow, Morris
Kaufmann, Walter Arnold
Kaye, Frederick Benjamin
Kendrick, Asahel Clark
Knapp, William Ireland
Kohut, George Alexander
Lewis, William Draper
Lincoln, John Larkin
Logan, James, 1674–1751
MacLean, George Edwin
Malter, Henry
Margolis, Max Leopold
Marsh, George Perkins
Mather, Cotton
Matthiessen, Francis Otto
Merrill, Elmer Truesdell
Miller, Perry Gilbert Eddy
Millett, Fred Benjamin
Mills, Lawrence Heyworth
Mitchell, Hinckley Gilbert Thomas
Monis, Judah
Moore, Clement Clarke
Murphy, Henry Cruse
Newell, William Wells
O'Brien, Justin
Perrin, Bernadotte
Perry, Thomas Sergeant
Pinto, Isaac
Platner, Samuel Ball
Prince, Thomas
Richardson, Rufus Byam
Rorimer, James Joseph
Schinz, Atbert
Schofield, William Henry
Schuyler, Eugene
Scott, Samuel Parsons
Shipman, Andrew Jackson
Soldan, Frank Louis
Solger, Reinhold
Sprecher, Samuel
Stiles, Ezra
Sulzberger, Mayer
Tait, Charles
Taylor, Hannis
Thomas, Calvin
Thorndike, Ashley Horace
Tolman, Herbert Cushing
Torrey, Charles Cutler
Trent, William Peterfield
Updike, Daniel Berkeley
Van der Kemp, Francis Adrian
Van Dyck, Cornelius van Alen
Viel, François Étienne Bernard Alexandre
Wallace, Charles William
Wallace, John William
Warren, Minton
Wiener, Leo
Wigmore, John Henry
Wilde, Richard Henry
Woolsey, Theodore Dwight
SCHOLAR (BIBLICAL)
Cone, Orello
Gregory, Caspar René
Hackett, Horatio Balch
Kent, Charles Foster
Mead, Charles Marsh
Mitchell, Edward Cushing
Moorehead, William Gallogly
Morgan, Abel
Norton, Andrews
Packard, Joseph
Paton, Lewis Boyles
Riddle, Matthew Brown
Ropes, James Hardy
Rosenberg, Abraham Hayyim
Sanders, Frank Knight
Sawyer, Leicester Ambrose
Smith, Henry Preserved

Smith, John Merlin Powis
Stevens, William Arnold
Strong, James
Stuart, Moses
Thayer, Joseph Henry

SCHOLAR (LAW)
Cook, Walter Wheeler

SCHOOL BUILDING SPECIALIST
Barrows, Alice Prentice

SCHOOLMASTER (See also EDUCATOR, TEACHER)
Coit, Henry Augustus
Dock, Christopher
Gould, Benjamin Apthorp
Gummere, John
Gunn, Frederick William
Keith, George
Ladd, Catherine
Lovell, James
Lovell, John
McCabe, William Gordon
Mazzuchelli, Samuel Charles
Morton, Charles
Nason, Elias
Peter, John Frederick
Pormort, Philemon
Truteau, Jean Baptiste
Williams, Nathanael

SCIENCE ADMINISTRATOR
Merriam, John Campbell
Ritter, William Emerson

SCIENCE HISTORIAN (See also HISTORIAN)
Thorndike, Lynn

SCIENCE REPORTER
Laurence, William Leonard

SCIENTIFIC MANAGEMENT CONSULTANT
Cooke, Morris Llewellyn

SCIENTIST (See also SPECIFIC SCIENCES)
Agassiz, Jean Louis Rodolphe
Alexander, John Henry
Alexander, William Dewitt
Allen, Zachariah
Arnold, Harold DeForest
Birdseye, Clarence
Brashear, John Alfred
Braun, Wernher von
Brewer, William Henry
Bronk, Detlev Wulf
Brooke, John Mercer
Caswell, Alexis
Clark, William Smith
Cleaveland, Parker
Conant, James Bryant
Cooper, Thomas
Dewey, Chester
Drake, Daniel
Dunbar, William
Durant, Charles Ferson
Eaton, Amos
Emerson, Rollins Adams
Eve, Joseph
Farnsworth, Philo Taylor
Ferguson, Thomas Barker
Ferree, Clarence Errol
Folger, Walter
Franklin, Benjamin
Frazer, John Fries
Frazer, Persifor
Gibbes, Robert Wilson
Gillman, Henry
Greely, Adolphus Washington
Greenhow, Robert
Haldeman, Samuel Steman
Hallock, Charles
Hayes, John Lord
Herrick, Edward Claudius
Hewitt, Peter Cooper
Hill, Thomas
Himes, Charles Francis
Humphreys, Andrew Atkinson
Hyer, Robert Stewart
Jefferson, Thomas
Jeffries, John
Lapham, Increase Allen
LeConte, John
Lee, Charles Alfred
Locke, John
Mease, James
Mell, Patrick Hues
Michaelis, Leonor
Minot, George Richards
Mitchill, Samuel Latham
Morton, Henry
Oliver, Andrew
Olmsted, Denison
Palmer, Walter Walker
Peirce, Charles Sanders
Pliny, Earle Chase
Potamian, Brother
Priestley, Joseph
Rhoads, Cornelius Packard
Saugrain de Vigni, Antoine François
Schöpf, Johann David
Seybert, Adam
Sheppard, Samuel Edward
Simpson, Charles Torrey
Spillman, William Jasper
Squier, George Owen
Stallo, Johann Bernhard
Thompson, Samuel Rankin
Thomson, Elihu
Totten, Joseph Gilbert
Trowbridge, William Petit
Van Depoele, Charles Joseph
Wailes, Benjamin Leonard Covington
Westergaard, Harald Malcolm
Wilder, Russell Morse
Williamson, Hugh
Wright, Hamilton Kemp

SCOUT (See also GUIDE, FRONTIERSMAN, PIONEER)
Bailey, Ann
Bridger, James
Burnham, Frederick Russell
Cody, William Frederick
Dixon, William
Grouard, Frank
Hamilton, William Thomas
Hickok, James Butler
Horn, Tom
Kelly, Luther Sage
McClellan, Robert
Navarre, Pierre
North, Frank Joshua
Reynolds, Charles Alexander
Sieber, Al
Stilwell, Simpson Everett
Stringfellow, Franklin

SCREENWRITER (See AUTHOR, DRAMATIST, WRITER)

SCULPTOR (See also ARTIST, MODELER)
Adams, Herbert Samuel
Akers, Benjamin Paul
Amateis, Louis
Archipenko, Alexander
Aronson, Boris Solomon
Augur, Hezekiah
Bailly, Joseph Alexis
Ball, Thomas
Barnard, George Grey
Bartholomew, Edward Sheffield
Bartlett, Paul Wayland
Bissell, George Edwin
Bitter, Karl Theodore Francis
Borglum, John Gutzon de la Mothe
Borglum, Solon Hannibal
Boyle, John J.
Brackett, Edward Augustus
Brenner, Victor David
Brooks, Richard Edwin
Browere, John Henri Isaac
Brown, Henry Kirke
Bush-Brown, Henry Kirke
Calder, Alexander
Calder, Alexander Stirling
Calverley, Charles
Clarke, Thomas Shields
Clevenger, Shobal Vail
Cogdell, John Stevens
Connelly, Pierce Francis
Crawford, Thomas
Dallin, Cyrus Edwin
Davidson, Jo
Dexter, Henry
Diller, Burgoyne
Donoghue, John
Doyle, Alexander
Duveneck, Frank
Eakins, Thomas
Eckstein, John
Edmondson, William
Elwell, Frank Edwin
Epstein, Jacob
Ezekiel, Moses Jacob
Flannagan, John Bernard
Fraser, James Earle
Frazee, John
French, Daniel Chester
Gabo, Naum
Garlick, Theodatus
Goldberg, Reuben Lucius ("Rube")
Gould, Thomas Ridgeway
Grafly, Charles
Greenough, Horatio
Greenough, Richard Saltonstall
Hart, Joel Tanner
Hartley, Jonathan Scott
Haseltine, James Henry
Hosmer, Harriet Goodhue
Hoxie, Vinnie Ream
Hughes, Robert Ball
Ives, Chauncey Bradley
Jackson, John Adams
Kemeys, Edward
Kingsley, Norman William
Lachaise, Gaston

Launitz, Robert Eberhard Schmidt von der
Lebrun, Federico ("Rico")
Lipchitz, Jacques
Lukeman, Henry Augustus
MacDonald, James Wilson Alexander
McKenzie, Robert Tait
MacMonnies, Frederick William
MacNeil, Hermon Atkins
Magonigle, Harold Van Buren
Manship, Paul Howard
Martiny, Philip
Mead, Larkin Goldsmith
Mears, Helen Farnsworth
Mestrovic, Ivan
Mills, Clark
Milmore, Martin
Mozier, Joseph
Mulligan, Charles J.
Nadelman, Elie
Newman, Barnett
Ney, Elisabet
Niehaus, Charles Henry
O'Donovan, William Rudolf
Palmer, Erastus Dow
Partridge, William Ordway
Perkins, Marion
Potter, Edward Clark
Potter, Louis McClellan
Powers, Hiram
Pratt, Bela Lyon
Putnam, Arthur
Quinn, Edmond Thomas
Remington, Frederic
Rimmer, William
Rinehart, William Henry
Roberts, Howard
Rogers, John, 1829–1904
Rogers, Randolph
Ruckstull, Frederick Wellington
Rumsey, Charles Cary
Rush, William
Saint-Gaudens, Augustus
Shrady, Henry Merwin
Simmons, Franklin
Smith, David Roland
Sterne, Maurice
Stone, Horatio
Story, William Wetmore
Taft, Lorado Zadoc
Thompson, Launt
Valentin, Edward Virginius
Volk, Leonard Wells
Ward, John Quincy Adams
Warner, Olin Levi
Whitney, Gertrude Vanderbilt
Whitney, Anne
Willard, Solomon
Young, Mahonri Mackintosh
Zorach, William

SEA CAPTAIN (See also MARINER, WHALING CAPTAIN)

Baker, Lorenzo Dow
Bertram, John
Boyle, Thomas
Brewer, Charles
Chever, James W.
Cobb, Elijah
Codman, John
Coggeshell, George
Creesy, Josiah Perkins
Crowninshield, George
Crowninshield, Jacob
Endicott, Charles Moses
Fanning, Edmund
Forbes, Robert Bennet
Godfrey, Benjamin
Harvey, Sir John
Heard, Augustine
Hunnewell, James
Malcolm, Daniel
Marshall, Charles Henry
Merry, William Lawrence
Morrell, Benjamin
Olmsted, Gideon
Palmer, Nathaniel Brown
Reid, Samuel Chester
Rogers, William Crowninshield
Shaler, William
Tompkins, Sally Louisa
Waterman, Robert H.

SECESSIONIST

Edwards, Weldon Nathaniel
Yancey, William Lowndes

SECRETARY

Thompson, Malvina Cynthia

SECRETARY OF AGRICULTURE (See also AGRICULTURIST)

Anderson, Clinton Presba
Colman, Norman Jay
Houston, David Franklin
Hyde, Arthur Mastick
Jardine, William Marion
Meredith, Edwin Thomas
Morton, Julius Sterling
Rusk, Jeremiah McClain
Wallace, Henry Agard
Wallace, Henry Cantwell
Wickard, Claude Raymond
Wilson, James

SECRETARY OF ARMY

Brucker, Wilber Marion

SECRETARY OF COMMERCE

Chapin, Roy Dikeman
Morton, Rogers Clark Ballard
Redfield, William Cox
Roper, Daniel Calhoun
Wallace, Henry Agard
Weeks, Sinclair

SECRETARY OF DEFENSE (See also SECRETARY OF WAR)

Forrestal, James Vincent
Johnson, Louis Arthur
McElroy, Neil Hosler
Wilson, Charles Erwin

SECRETARY OF LABOR

Davis, James John
Mitchell, James Paul
Perkins, Frances
Schwellenbach, Lewis Baxter
Tobin, Maurice Joseph
Wilson, William Bauchop

SECRETARY OF NAVY

Badger, George Edmund
Chandler, William Eaton
Daniels, Josephus
Denby, Edwin
Dickerson, Mahlon
Dobbin, James Cochran
Edison, Charles
Forrestal, James Vincent
Hamilton, Paul
Henshaw, David
Herbert, Hilary Abner
Hunt, William Henry
Jones, William, 1760–1831
Kimball, Dan Able
Knox, Frank
Long, John Davis
Meyer, George von Lengerke
Morton, Paul
Preston, William Ballard
Robeson, George Maxwell
Smith, Robert, 1757–1842
Southard, Samuel Lewis
Stoddert, Benjamin
Swanson, Claude Augustus
Tracy, Benjamin Franklin
Upshur, Abel Parker
Welles, Gideon
Whitney, William Collins
Wilbur, Curtis Dwight

SECRETARY OF NAVY (CONFEDERATE)

Mallory, Stephen Russell

SECRETARY OF STATE

Adams, John Quincy
Bacon, Robert
Bayard, Thomas Francis
Black, Jeremiah Sullivan
Blaine, James Gillespie
Bryan, William Jennings
Buchanan, James
Calhoun, John Caldwell
Cass, Lewis
Clay, Henry
Clayton, John Middleton
Colby, Bainbridge
Day, William Rufus
Dulles, John Foster
Evarts, William Maxwell
Everett, Edward
Fish, Hamilton
Forsyth, John
Foster, John Watson
Frelinghuysen, Frederick Theodore
Gresham, Walter Quintin
Hay, John Milton
Herter, Christian Archibald
Hughes, Charles Evans
Hull, Cordell
Jay, John
Jefferson, Thomas
Kellogg, Frank Billings
Knox, Philander Chase
Lansing, Robert
Legaré, Hugh Swinton
Livingston, Edward
McLane, Louis
Madison, James
Marcy, William Learned
Marshall, John
Monroe, James
Olney, Richard
Pickering, Timothy
Randolph, Edmund, 1753–1813
Root, Elihu
Seward, William Henry
Sherman, John
Smith, Robert, 1757–1842
Stettinius, Edward Reilly
Stimson, Henry Lewis
Upshur, Abel Parker
Van Buren, Martin

Washburne, Elihu Benjamin
Webster, Daniel

SECRETARY OF STATE (CONFEDERATE)
Benjamin, Judah Philip
Hunter, Robert Mercer Taliaferro

SECRETARY OF THE INTERIOR
Ballinger, Richard Achilles
Bliss, Cornelius Newton
Browning, Orville Hickman
Chandler, Zachariah
Cox, Jacob Dolson
Delano, Columbus
Ewing, Thomas
Fall, Albert Bacon
Fisher, Walter Lowrie
Francis, David Rowland
Garfield, James Rudolph
Harlan, James
Hitchcock, Ethan Allen, 1835–1909
Ickes, Harold Le Clair
Kirkwood, Samuel Jordan
Lamar, Lucius Quintus Cincinatus
Lane, Franklin Knight
McClelland, Robert
McKay, (James) Douglas
McKennan, Thomas McKean Thompson
Noble, John Willock
Payne, John Barton
Schurz, Carl
Smith, Caleb Blood
Smith, Hoke
Stuart, Alexander Hugh Holmes
Teller, Henry Moore
Thompson, Jacob
Usher, John Palmer
Vilas, William Freeman
West, Roy Owen
Wilbur, Ray Lyman
Work, Hubert

SECRETARY OF TREASURY
Campbell, George Washington
Carlisle, John Griffin
Chase, Salmon Portland
Corwin, Thomas
Dallas, Alexander James
Dix, John Adams
Ewing, Thomas
Fairchild, Charles Stebbins
Folger, Charles James
Forward, Walter
Gage, Lyman Judson
Gallatin, Abraham Alfonse Albert
Glass, Carter
Guthrie, James
Hamilton, Alexander
Humphrey, George Magoffin
Ingham, Samuel Delucenna
McAdoo, William Gibbs
McCulloch, Hugh
MacVeagh, Franklin
Manning, Daniel
Mellon, Andrew William
Meredith, William Morris
Mills, Ogden Livingston
Morgenthau, Henry, Jr.
Morrill, Lot Myrick
Richardson, William Adams
Shaw, Leslie Mortier
Spencer, John Canfield
Taney, Roger Brooke
Thomas, Philip Francis
Vinson, Fred(erick) Moore
Walker, Robert John
Wolcott, Oliver
Woodbury, Levi
Woodin, William Hartman

SECRETARY OF TREASURY (CONFEDERATE)
Trenholm, George Alfred

SECRETARY OF WAR (See also SECRETARY OF DEFENSE)
Alger, Russell Alexander
Baker, Newton Diehl
Belknap, William Worth
Calhoun, John Caldwell
Cameron, James Donald
Cameron, Simon
Crawford, William Harris
Davis, Dwight Filley
Dearborn, Henry
Dern, George Henry
Dickinson, Jacob McGavack
Elkins, Stephen Benton
Endicott, William Crowninshield
Floyd, John Buchanan
Garrison, Lindley Miller
Holt, Joseph
Knox, Henry
Lamont, Daniel Scott
Lincoln, Robert Todd
McHenry, James
Patterson, Robert Porter
Porter, Peter Buell
Proctor, Redfield
Ramsey, Alexander
Spencer, John Canfield
Stanton, Edwin McMasters
Stimson, Henry Lewis
Taft, Alphonso
Weeks, John Wingate
Wilkins, William
Woodring, Harry Hines
Wright, Luke Edward

SECRETARY OF WAR (CONFEDERATE)
Benjamin, Judah Philip

SECURITIES EXPERT
Stanley, Harold

SECURITY INDUSTRY EXECUTIVE
Burns, Raymond Joseph

SEEDSMAN (See also AGRICULTURIST)
Burpee, David
Thorburn, Grant
Vick, James

SEGREGATIONIST LEADER
Perez, Leander Henry

SEISMOLOGIST
Tondorf, Francis Anthony

SELECTIVE SERVICE SYSTEM DIRECTOR
Hershey, Lewis Blaine

SEMITIST (See also SCHOLAR)
Friedlaender, Israel
Gottheil, Richard James Horatio
Meyer, Martin Abraham
Torrey, Charles Cutler

SENATOR
Alcorn, James Lusk
Allen, Philip
Allen, William Vincent
Anderson, Clinton Presba
Anderson, Joseph
Ashurst, Henry Fountain
Atchison, David Rice
Austin, Warren Robinson
Bacon, Augustus Octavius
Badger, George Edwin
Bagby, Arthur Pendleton
Bailey, Joseph Weldon
Bailey, Josiah William
Baker, Edward Dickinson
Baldwin, Henry Porter
Baldwin, Roger Sherman
Bankhead, John Hollis
Barkley, Alben William
Barrett, Frank Aloysius
Bartlett, Edward Lewis ("Bob")
Barton, David
Bayard, James Asheton
Bayard, Richard Henry
Beall, James Glenn
Bender, George Harrison
Benton, William Burnett
Berry, George Leonard
Berry, James Henderson
Beveridge, Albert Jeremiah
Bibb, Georze Mortimer
Bigler, William
Bilbo, Theodore Gilmore
Bingham, Hiram
Black, Hugo Lafayette
Blackburn, Joseph Clay Styles
Blaine, John James
Blease, Coleman Livingston
Blount, William
Bogy, Lewis Vital
Booth, Newton
Borah, William Edgar
Boreman, Arthur Ingram
Borland, Solon
Bourne, Jonathan
Bradbury, James Ware
Bradley, Stephen Row
Bradley, William O'Connell
Brainerd, Lawrence
Brewster, Ralph Owen
Brice, Calvin Stewart
Bridges, (Henry) Styles
Bristow, Joseph Little
Brookhart, Smith Wildman
Brown, Bedford
Brown, Benjamin Gratz
Brown, James
Brown, John
Brown, Prentiss Marsh
Bruce, Blanche K.
Bruce, William Cabell
Buckalew, Charles Rollin
Buckingham, William Alfred
Bulkeley, Morgan Gardner
Burnet, Jacob
Burr, Aaron
Burrows, Julius Caesar
Burton, Theodore Elijah
Bush, Prescott Sheldon
Butler, Marion
Butler, Matthew Calbraith
Butler, Pierce

Butler, William Pickens
Byrd, Harry Flood
Cabat, George
Caffery, Donelson
Cain, Harry Pulliam
Camden, Johnson Newlon
Cameron, James Donald
Cameron, Simon
Campbell, George Washington
Capper, Arthur
Caraway, Hattie Ophelia Wyatt
Caraway, Thaddeus Horatius
Carlile, John Snyder
Carlisle, John Griffin
Carpenter, Matthew Hale
Carter, Thomas Henry
Case, Francis Higbee
Chamberlain, George Earle
Chandler, John
Chandler, William Eaton
Chandler, Zachariah
Chavez, Dennis
Chesnut, James
Christiancy, Isaac Peckham
Clark, Bennett Champ
Clark, William Andrews
Clarke, James Paul
Clay, Clement Claiborne
Clay, Clement Comer
Clay, Henry
Clemens, Jeremiah
Cobb, Howell
Cockrell, Francis Marion
Cohen, John Sanford
Coke, Richard
Collamer, Jacob
Colt, Le Baron Bradford
Conkling, Roscoe
Connally, Thomas Terry ("Tom")
Cooper, James
Copeland, Royal Samuel
Cordon, Guy
Corwin, Thomas
Costigan, Edward Prentiss
Couzens, James
Crane, Winthrop Murray
Crawford, William Harris
Curtis, Charles
Cutting, Bronson Murray
Daniel, John Warwick
Davis, Cushman Kellogg
Davis, Garret
Davis, Henry Gassaway
Davis, James John
Davis, Jeff
Dawes, Henry Laurens
Dawson, William Crosby
Depew, Chauncey Mitchell
De Wolf, James
Dickerson, Mahlon
Dill, Clarence Cleveland
Dirksen, Everett McKinley
Dodd, Thomas Joseph
Dodge, Augustus Caesar
Dodge, Henry
Dolph, Joseph Norton
Donnell, Forrest C.
Dorsey, Stephen Wallace
Douglas, Paul Howard
Douglas, Stephen Arnold
Downey, Sheridan
Drake, Charles Daniel
Dryden, John Fairfield
Duff, James Henderson
Du Pont, Henry Algernon
Dworshak, Henry Clarence
Edge, Walter Evans
Edmunds, George Franklin
Edwards, John
Edwards, Ninian
Elkins, Stephen Benton
Ellender, Allen Joseph
Ellis, Powhatan
Elmore, Franklin Harper
Engle, Clair William Walter
Eppes, John Wayles
Ewing, Thomas
Fairbanks, Charles Warren
Fall, Albert Bacon
Felch, Alpheus
Felton, Rebecca Latimer
Fenton, Reuben Eaton
Ferris, Woodbridge Nathan
Ferry, Orris Sanford
Ferry, Thomas White
Fess, Simeon Davidson
Field, Richard Stockton
Fitzpatrick, Benjamin
Flanders, Ralph Edward
Fletcher, Duncan Upshaw
Foot, Samuel Augustus
Foote, Henry Stuart
Foraker, Joseph Benson
Foster, Ephraim Hubbard
Foster, Lafayette Sabine
Foster, Theodore
Fowler, Joseph Smith
Francis, John Brown
Franklin, Jesse
Frazier, Lynn Joseph
Frelinghuysen, Frederick
Frelinghuysen, Theodore
Frye, William Pierce
Gaillard, John
Gear, John Henry
George, James Zachariah
George, Walter Franklin
Geyer, Henry Sheffie
Gibson, Paris
Gillett, Frederick Huntington
Gillette, Guy Mark
Glass, Carter
Goldthwaite, George
Goodhue, Benjamin
Goodrich, Chauncey
Gordon, James
Gore, Thomas Pryor
Gorman, Arthur Pue
Graham, Frank Porter
Grayson, William
Green, James Stephens
Green, Theodore Francis
Grimes, James Wilson
Gruening, Ernest
Grundy, Joseph Ridgway
Guffey, Joseph F.
Guggenheim, Simon
Hager, John Sharpenstein
Hale, Frederick
Hamilton, William Thomas
Hamlin, Hannibal
Hammond, James Henry
Hampton, Wade, 1818–1902
Hanna, Marcus Alonzo
Hannegan, Edward Allen
Hanson, Alexander Contee, 1786–1819
Hardin, Martin D.
Hardwick, Thomas William
Harlan, James
Harris, William Alexander
Harrison, Byron Patton
Hart, Philip Aloysius
Hastings, Daniel Oren
Hatch, Carl A.
Hawkins, Benjamin
Hawley, Joseph Roswell
Hayden, Carl Trumbull
Hayne, Robert Young
Hearst, George
Heflin, James Thomas
Henderson, John
Henderson, John Brooks
Hendricks, Thomas Andrews
Henry, John, 1750–1798
Hill, Joshua
Hill, Nathaniel Peter
Hindman, William
Hoar, George Frisbie
Holland, Spessard Lindsey
Holmes, John
Hopkins, Samuel, 1753–1819
Houston, George Smith
Howard, Jacob Merritt
Howe, Timothy Otis
Hull, Cordell
Humphrey, Hubert Horatio, Jr.
Hunt, Lester Callaway
Hunter, William
Hunton, Eppa
Ingalls, John James
Iverson, Alfred
Ives, Irving McNeil
Izard, Ralph
Jackson, Howell Edmunds
Jackson, James, 1757–1806
James, Charles Tillinghast
James, Ollie Murray
Johnson, Edwin Carl
Johnson, Hiram Warren
Johnson, Magnus
Johnston, Joseph Forney
Johnston, Olin DeWitt Talmadge
Jones, James Chamberlayne
Jones, James Kimbrough
Jones, John Percival
Jones, Wesley Livsey
Jordan, Benjamin Everett
Keating, Kenneth Barnard
Kefauver, (Carey) Estes
Kellogg, Frank Billings
Kellogg, William Pitt
Kendrick, John Benjamin
Kenna, John Edward
Kennedy, John Fitzgerald
Kennedy, Robert Francis
Kent, Joseph
Kenyon, William Squire
Kerr, Robert Samuel
Key, David McKendree
Kilgore, Harley Martin
King, John Pendleton
Kirkwood, Samuel Jordan
Knowland, William Fife

Knox, Philander Chase
Kyle, James Henderson
Lacock, Abner
Lad, Edwin Fremont
La Follette, Robert Marion
La Follette, Robert Marion, Jr.
Lamar, Lucius Quintus Cincinnatus
Lane, Henry Smith
Langer, William
Larrazolo, Octaviano Ambrosio
Latham, Milton Slocum
Laurence, John
Lea, Luke
Lehman, Herbert Henry
Leib, Michael
Lenroot, Irvine Luther
Lewis, Dixon Hall
Lewis, John Francis
Lindsay, William
Linn, Lewis Fields
Livermore, Samuel, 1732–1803
Lodge, Henry Cabot
Logan, George
Logan, John Alexander
Long, Edward Vaughn
Long, Huey Pierce
Lorimer, William
Lowrie, Walter
Lucas, Scott Wike
Lundeen, Ernest
McCarran, Patrick Anthony
McCarthy, Joseph Raymond
McClellan, John Little
McComas, Louis Emory
McCormick, Joseph Medill
McCreary, James Bennett
McDill, James Wilson
McDuffie, George
McEnery, Samuel Douglas
McGrath, James Howard
McKean, Samuel
McKellar, Kenneth Douglas
McKinley, John
McKinley, William Brown
McLauren, Anselm Joseph
Maclay, Samuel
Maclay, William
McMillan, James
McNary, Charles Linza
Macon, Nathaniel
Manderson, Charles Frederick
Mangum, Willie Person
Marshall, Humphrey
Martin, Alexander
Martin, Thomas Staples
Mason, James Murray
Mason, Jonathan
Mason, Stevens Thomson
Mason, William Ernest
Maxey, Samuel Bell
Maybank, Burnet Rhett
Mead, James Michael
Meigs, Return Jonathan
Mellen, Prentiss
Metcalf, Lee Warren
Metcalfe, Thomas
Milledge, John
Miller, John Franklin
Miller, Stephen Decatur
Miller, Warner
Mills, Roger Quarles
Minton, Sherman
Mitchell, John Hipple
Mitchell, Samuel Latham
Money, Hernando De Soto
Monroney, Almer Stillwell
Montoya, Joseph Manuel
Moody, (Arthur Edson) Blair
Moore, Andrew
Moore, Gabriel
Morehead, James Turner
Morgan, Edwin Denison
Morgan, John Tyler
Morril, David Lawrence
Morrill, Justin Smith
Morrill, Lot Myrick
Morris, Thomas
Morrow, Jeremiah
Morse, Wayne Lyman
Morton, Oliver Perry
Mouton, Alexander
Mundt, Karl Earl
Murray, James Edward
Neely, Matthew Mansfield
Nelson, Knute
Neuberger, Richard Lewis
Newberry, Truman Handy
Newlands, Francis Griffith
Nicholas, Wilson Cary
Nicholson, Alfred Osborne Pope
Nicholson, Samuel Danford
Niles, John Milton
Noble, James
Norbeck, Peter
Norris, George William
Nugent, John Frost
Nye, Gerald Prentice
Nye, James Warren
O'Daniel, Wilbert Lee ("Pappy")
Ogden, Aaron
Oglesby, Richard James
Oliver, George Tener
O'Mahoney, Joseph Christopher
Overman, Lee Slater
Owen, Robert Latham
Paddock, Algernon Sidney
Palmer, John McAuley
Palmer, Thomas Witherell
Parris, Albion Keith
Pasco, Samuel
Patterson, Thomas MacDonald
Payne, Henry B.
Pearce, James Alfred
Peffer, William Alfred
Pendleton, George Hunt
Penrose, Boies
Pepper, George Wharton
Perkins, George Clement
Pettigrew, Richard Franklin
Pettus, Edmund Winston
Phelan, James Duval
Phipps, Lawrence Cowle
Pierce, Gilbert Ashville
Pinckney, Charles
Pittman, Key
Platt, Orville Hitchcock
Plumb, Preston B.
Plumer, William
Poindexter, George
Poindexter, Miles
Poland, Luke Potter
Polk, Trusten
Pomerene, Atlee
Pomeroy, Samuel Clarke
Pool, John
Pope, James Pinckney
Porter, Alexander
Potter, Charles Edward
Potts, Richard
Prentiss, Samuel
Preston, William Campbell
Pritchard, Jeter Connelly
Pugh, George Ellis
Purtell, William Arthur
Radcliffe, George Lovic Pierce
Ralston, Samuel Moffett
Ramsey, Alexander
Randolph, Theodore Fitz
Ransom, Matt Whitaker
Rayner, Isidor
Read, George
Read, Jacob
Reagan, John Henninger
Reed, David Aiken
Reed, James Alexander
Revels, Hiram Rhoades
Reynolds, Robert Rice
Rice, Henry Mower
Roberts, Jonathan
Robinson, Joseph Taylor
Ross, Edmund Gibson
Ross, James
Rowan, John
Rusk, Thomas Jefferson
Russell, Richard Brevard, Jr. ("Dick")
Saltonstall, Leverett
Sanders, Wilbur Fisk
Sargent, Aaron Augustus
Saulsbury, Eli
Saulsbury, Willard, 1820–1892
Saulsbury, Willard, 1861–1927
Saunders, Alvin
Sawyer, Philetus
Schall, Thomas David
Schurz, Carl
Schwellenbach, Lewis Baxter
Scott, W(illiam) Kerr
Sevier, Ambrose Hundley
Shafroth, John Franklin
Shepley, Ether
Sheppard, John Morris
Shields, James
Shields, John Knight
Shipstead, Henrik
Simmons, Furnifold McLendel
Smith, Ellison DuRant
Smith, Hoke
Smith, James, 1851–1927
Smith, John, 1735–1824
Smith, Nathan, 1770–1835
Smith, Oliver Hampton
Smith, William, 1762–1840
Smoot, Reed Owen
Southard, Samuel Lewis
Spooner, John Coit
Sprague, William, 1830–1915
Squire, Watson Carvosso
Stanford, Leland
Stanley, Augustus Owsley
Stephenson, Isaac
Stevenson, John White
Stewart, Arthur Thomas ("Tom")

Stewart, William Morris
Stockton, John Potter
Stokes, Montfort
Stone, David
Stone, William Joel
Sumner, Charles
Sumter, Thomas
Sutherland, George
Swanson, Claude Augustus
Taft, Robert Alphonso
Tait, Charles
Tappan, Benjamin
Tazewell, Littleton Waller
Taylor, Robert Love
Tazewell, Henry
Teller, Henry Moore
Thomas, Charles Spalding
Thomas, Elbert Duncan
Thomas, Jesse Burgess
Thurman, Allen Granberry
Thye, Edward John
Tillman, Benjamin Ryan
Tipton, John
Tobey, Charles William
Toombs, Robert Augustus
Toucey, Isaac
Tracy, Uriah
Troup, George Michael
Trumbull, Jonathan, 1740–1809
Trumbull, Lyman
Turner, George
Tydings, Millard Evelyn
Tyson, Lawrence Davis
Underwood, Joseph Rogers
Underwood, Oscar Wilder
Vance, Zebulon Baird
Vandenberg, Arthur Hendrick
Van Dyke, Nicholas, 1770–1826
Van Winkle, Peter Godwin
Vardaman, James Kimble
Varnum, Joseph Bradley
Vest, George Graham
Vilas, William Freeman
Voorhees, Daniel Wolsey
Wade, Benjamin Franklin
Wadsworth, James Wolcott, Jr.
Wagner, Robert Ferdinand
Walker, Robert John
Wallgren, Mon(rad) C(harles)
Walsh, David Ignatius
Walsh, Thomas James
Walthall, Edward Cary
Walton, George
Warner, William
Warren, Francis Emroy
Washburn, William Drew
Watkins, Arthur Vivian
Watson, James Eli
Webb, William Robert
Weeks, John Wingate
Welker, Herman
Weller, John B.
Wheeler, Burton Kendall
Wherry, Kenneth Spicer
Whitcomb, James
White, Albert Smith
White, Hugh Lawson
White, Samuel
White, Stephen Mallary
Whyte, William Pinkney
Wigfall, Louis Frezevant
Wiley, Alexander
Wilkins, William
Willey, Waitman Thomas
Williams, George Henry
Williams, John
Williams, John Sharp
Williams, Reuel
Wilson, Henry
Wilson, James Falconer
Wilson, John Lockwood
Windom, William
Winthrop, Robert Charles
Wolcott, Edward Oliver
Woodbury, Levi
Worthington, Thomas
Wright, George Grover
Wright, Robert
Wright, Silas
Wright, William
Yulee, David Levy

SENATOR (CONFEDERATE)
Johnson, Herschel Vespasian
Maxwell, Augustus Emmett
Oldham, Williamson Simpson
Orr, James Lawrence
Semmes, Thomas Jenkins
Simms, William Elliott
Thomson, Charles
Vest, George Graham
Watson, John William Clark

SETTLEMENT HOUSE FOUNDER
Addams, Jane
Taylor, Graham
Wald, Lillian D.

SETTLEMENT WORKER
Simkhovitch, Mary Melinda Kingsbury
Woods, Robert Archey
Woolley, Celia Parker

SETTLER (See also PIONEER)
Baker, James
Clyman, James
Conant, Roger
Dubuque, Julien
Otto, Bodo
Whitfield, Henry
Woodward, Henry
Wootton, Richens Lacy

SHAKESPEAREAN SCHOLAR
Adams, Joseph Quincy
Brooke, Charles Frederick Tucker
Prouty, Charles Tyler

SHIPBUILDER
Bourne, Nehemiah
Burns, Otway
Cheesman, Forman
Claghorn, George
Cramp, Charles Henry
Cramp, William
Dickie, George William
Eckford, Henry
Englis, John
Hague, Robert Lincoln
Hall, Samuel, 1800–1870
Herreshoff, John Brown
Herreshoff, Nathanael Greene
Higgins, Andrew Jackson
Hill, James
Humphreys, Joshua
Johnson, Levi
Johnson, Seth Whitmore
McDougall, Alexander
McKay, Donald
Newberry, Oliver
Roach, John
Scott, Irving Murray
Sewall, Arthur
Vickery, Howard Leroy
Watson, Thomas Augustus
Webb, William Henry
Westervelt, Jacob Aaron

SHIPMASTER (see MARINER)

SHIP MODELER
Boucher, Horace Edward

SHIPOWNER
Collins, Edward Knight
Derby, Elias Hasket
Derby, Richard
Dollar, Robert
Fish, Preserved
Forbes, Robert Bennet
Grinnell, Moses Hicks
Griscom, Clement Acton
King, William
Lamar, Gazaway Bugg
Livingstone, William, 1844–1925
Moredecai, Moses Cohen
Morgan, Charles
Munson, Walter David
Perkins, George Clement
Russell, Joseph
Servoss, Thomas Lowery
Thompson, Jeremiah
Tileston, Thomas
Train, Enoch
Ward, James Edward

SHIPPING EXECUTIVE
Franklin, Philip Albright Small
Isbrandtsen, Hans Jeppesen
Luckenbach, J(ohn) Lewis
Mallory, Clifford Day
Moran, Eugene Francis

SHIPPING OFFICIAL
Boas, Emil Leopold
Borden, Richard
Cone, Hutchinson Ingham
McAllister, Charles Albert
Munson, Walter David
Raymond, Harry Howard
Roosevelt, Kermit
Smith, Robert Alexander C.

SHORTHAND INVENTOR
Gregg, John Robert

SHOWMAN (See also CONCESSIONAIRE, IMPRESARIO, PROMOTER, THEATRICAL MANAGER)
Bailey, James Anthony
Barnum, Phineas Taylor
Beatty, Clyde Raymond
Bowes, Edward J.
Buck, Franklyn Howard
Cody, William Frederick ("Buffalo Bill")
Forepaugh, Adam
Lillie, Gordon William
Perham, Josiah
Rice, Dan
Ringling, Charles
Rothafel, Samuel Lionel

SIGNER OF DECLARATION OF INDEPENDENCE
Adams, John

Adams, Samuel
Bartlett, Josiah
Braxton, Carter
Carroll, Charles
Chase, Samuel
Clark, Abraham
Clymer, George
Ellery, William
Floyd, William
Franklin, Benjamin
Gerry, Elbridge
Gwinnett, Button
Hall, Lyman
Hancock, John
Harrison, Benjamin
Hart, John
Hewes, Joseph
Heyward, Thomas
Hooper, William
Hopkins, Stephen
Hopkinson, Francis
Huntington, Samuel, 1731–1796
Jefferson, Thomas
Lee, Francis Lightfoot
Lee, Richard Henry
Lewis, Francis
Livingston, Philip
Lynch, Thomas, 1749–1779
McKean, Thomas
Middleton, Arthur
Morris, Lewis, 1726–1798
Morris, Robert, 1734–1806
Morton, John
Nelson, Thomas
Paca, William
Paine, Robert Treat
Penn, John
Read, George
Rodney, Caesar
Ross, George
Rush, Benjamin
Rutledge, Edward
Sherman, Roger
Smith, James, 1719–1806
Stockton, Richard
Stone, Thomas
Taylor, George
Thornton, Matthew
Walton, George
Whipple, William
Williams, William
Wilson, James, 1742–1798
Witherspoon, John
Wolcott, Oliver
Wythe, George

SILVERSMITH (See also CRAFTSMAN, JEWELER, GOLDSMITH)
Boelen, Jacob
Buell, Abel
Dummer, Jeremiah
Edward, John
Gorham, Jabez
Harland, Thomas
Hull, John
Hurd, Nathaniel
Le Roux, Bartholomew
Le Roux, Charles
Richardson, Joseph
Sanderson, Robert
Syng, Philip
Verhaegen, Peter Joseph
Winslow, Edward

SILVICULTURIST (See also AGRICULTURIST, FORESTER)
Michaux, André
Michaux, François André

SINGER (See also CANTOR, MINSTREL)
Abbott, Emma
Adams, Charles R.
Baccaloni, Salvatore
Barnabee, Henry Clay
Barton, James Edward
Bispham, David Scull
Bori, Lucrezia
Braslau, Sophie
Brice, Fanny
Burleigh, Henry Thacker
Callas, Maria
Caruso, Enrico
Cary, Annie Louise
Cole, Nat ("King")
Crosby, Harry Lillis ("Bing")
Dailey, Dan, Jr.
Daley, Cass
Dandridge, Dorothy Jean
Darin, Bobby
De Luca, Giuseppe
De Paolis, Alessio
Dunn, Michael
Eddy, Nelson
Elliot, Cass ("Mama")
Etting, Ruth
Farrar, Geraldine
Fischer, Emil Friedrich August
Fisher, Clara
Ford, Mary
Fox, Gilbert
Froman, Ellen Jane
Galli-Curci, Amelita
Garden, Mary
Garland, Judy
Gluck, Alma
Guthrie, Woody
Hall, Juanita Armethea
Hathaway, Donny
Hauk, Minnie
Haymes, Richard Benjamin ("Dick")
Heinrich, Max
Hendrix, Jimi
Homer, Louise Dilworth Beatty
Hunter, Ivory Joe
Jackson, Mahalia
Johnson, Edward
Jolson, Al
Joplin, Janis Lyn
Kane, Helen
Kellogg, Clara Louise
Lawrence, Gertrude
Ledbetter, Huddie ("Leadbelly")
Lehmann, Lotte
Lennon, John Winston Ono
Liebling, Estelle
Lynn, Diana ("Dolly")
McCormack, John Francis
McCracken, Joan
McDaniel, Hattie
MacDonald, Jeanette Anna
Martinelli, Giovanni
Maxwell, Marvel Marilyn
Melchior, Lauritz Lebrecht Hommel
Melton, James
Mercer, John Herndon ("Johnny")
Miranda, Carmen
Monroe, Vaughn Wilton
Moore, Grace
Morgan, Helen
Morrison, Jim
Muse, Clarence
Nevada, Emma
Nielsen, Alice
Nolan, Bob
Nordica, Lillian
Ochs, Phil
Olcott, Chauncey
Osgood, George Laurie
Page, Oran Thaddeus ("Lips")
Pinza, Ezio
Pons, Lily
Powell, Alma Webster
Presley, Elvis Aron
Prima, Luigi ("Louis")
Rainey, Gertrude Malissa Nix Pridgett
Ritter, Woodward Maurice ("Tex")
Robeson, Paul Leroy
Rogers, Clara Kathleen Barnett
Rosenblatt, Joseph
Roth, Lillian
Rushing, James Andrew
Russell, Lillian
Sanderson, Sibyl
Schumann-Heink, Ernestine
Sembrich, Marcella
Sherman, Allan
Sissle, Noble Lee
Smith, Bessie
Tanguay, Eva
Taylor, Theodore Roosevelt ("Hound Dog")
Thomas, John Charles
Thursby, Emma Cecilia
Tibbett, Lawrence Mervil
Tourel, Jennie
Traubel, Helen
Tucker, Richard
Tucker, Sophie
Warren, Leonard
Washington, Dinah
Waters, Ethel
Weede, Robert
Webb, Clifton
White, Joseph Malachy
White, Josh
Whitehill, Clarence Eugene
Whitney, Myron William
Williams, (Hiram) Hank
Witherspoon, Herbert

SINGING EVANGELIST
Bliss, Philip Paul
Phillips, Philip
Sankey, Ira David

SINGLE TAX ADVOCATE (See AGITATOR, REFORMER)
Fels, Joseph

SINOLOGUE (See also ORIENTALIST, SCHOLAR)
Bradley, Charles William

Laufer, Berthold
Williams, Samuel Wells
SISTER, RELIGIOUS (see NUN)
SLAVE
Burns, Anthony
Henson, Josiah
Scott, Dred
Tubman, Harriet
Turner, Nat
SLAVE TRADER
De Wolf, James
SLAVIC LANGUAGE SCHOLAR
Cross, Samuel Hazzard
SOCIAL ACTIVIST
Kent, Rockwell
Michaux, Lightfoot Solomon
Rukeyser, Muriel
SOCIAL ANALYST
Arnold, Thurman Wesley
SOCIAL COMMENTATOR
Dunne, Finley Peter
SOCIAL CRITIC (See also CRITIC)
Blanshard, Paul
Capp, Al
Dell, Floyd James
Howard, Joseph Kinsey
McWilliams, Carey
Martin, Anne Henrietta
Mills, Charles Wright
Stearns, Harold Edmund
Ward, Harry Frederick
Wilson, Edmund, Jr.
SOCIAL ECONOMIST (See also ECONOMIST)
Dugdale, Richard Louis
Sydenstricker, Edgar
Veblen, Thorstein Bunde
Wright, Carroll Davidson
SOCIAL ETHICS SPECIALIST
Holt, Arthur Erastus
SOCIAL INSURANCE EXPERT
Epstein, Abraham
SOCIALIST
Berger, Victor Louis
Bliss, William Dwight Porter
Bloor, Ella Reeve
Corey, Lewis
Debs, Eugene Victor
DeLeon, Daniel
Ghent, William James
Gronlund, Laurence
Hayes, Max Sebastian
Hillquit, Morris
Hoan, Daniel Webster
Hunter, Robert
London, Meyer
McLevy, Jasper
Mailly, William
Maurer, James Hudson
Mooney, Thomas Joseph
O'Hare, Kate (Richards) Cunningham
Russell, Charles Edward
Seidel, George Lukas Emil
Sorge, Friedrich Adolph
Spargo, John
Thomas, Norman Mattoon
Vladeck, Baruch Charney
Walling, William English
Young, Art
SOCIALITE
Belmont, Alva Ertskin Smith Vanderbilt
Bingham, Anne Willing
Gardner, Isabella Stewart
Harriman, Florence Jaffray Hurst
Longworth, Alice Lee Roosevelt
McAllister, Samuel Ward
Mackay, Clarence Hungerford
Manville, Thomas Franklyn ("Tommy"), Jr.
Paley, Barbara Cushing ("Babe")
Palmer, Bertha Honore
Rublee, George
Smith, Margaret Bayard
Thaw, Harry Kendall
Vanderbilt, Gloria Morgan
Vanderbilt, Grace Graham Wilson
SOCIAL PHILOSOPHER (See also PHILOSOPHER)
Fromm, Erich
Herberg, Will
Lindeman, Eduard Christian
SOCIAL PSYCHOLOGIST (See also PSYCHOLOGIST)
Cantril, Albert Hadley
Martin, Everett Dean
Overstreet, Harry Allen
SOCIAL REFORMER (See also REFORMER)
Addams, Jane
Andrews, John Bertram
Bellanca, Dorothy Jacobs
Blanshard, Paul
Blatch, Harriot Eaton Stanton
Brisbane, Albert
Chapin, Henry Dwight
Collins, John Anderson
Crosby, Ernest Howard
Darrow, Clarence Seward
Dennison, Henry Sturgis
Dietz, Peter Ernest
Dock, Lavinia Lloyd
Dreier, Mary Elisabeth
Fuller, Sarah Margaret
Gillette, King Camp
Gilman, Charlotte Perkins Stetson
Hamilton, Alice
Hazard, Thomas Robinson
Holmes, John Haynes
Jemison, Alice Mae Lee
Jones, Rufus Matthew
Kellogg, Paul Underwood
Lindsey, Benjamin Barr
Longley, Alcander
McBride, F(rancis) Scott
McClure, Samuel Sidney
Mussey, Ellen Spencer
Nathan, Maud
O'Hare, Kate (Richards) Cunningham
Owen, Robert Dale
Oxnam, Garfield Bromley
Peck, Lillie
Pinchot, Cornelia Elizabeth Bryce
Poling, Daniel Alfred
Regan, Agnes Gertrude
Robins, Margaret Dreier
Robins, Raymond
Roosevelt, (Anna) Eleanor
Ryan, John Augustine
Simkhovitch, Mary Melinda Kingsbury
Strong, Josiah
Swinton, John
Taylor, Graham
Tibbles, Thomas Henry
Tiffany, Katrina Brandes Ely
Voris, John Ralph
SOCIAL RESEARCHER
Bryant, Louise Frances Stevens
SOCIAL SCIENTIST (See also SPECIFIC SOCIAL SCIENCES)
Bateson, Gregory
Frank, Lawrence Kelso
Kracauer, Siegfried
Mayo, George Elton
Merriam, Charles Edward, Jr.
Mitchell, Wesley Clair
Sullivan, Harry Stack
Sumner, William Graham
SOCIAL SERVICES ADMINISTRATOR
Switzer, Mary Elizabeth
SOCIAL WELFARE LEADER
Brackett, Jeffrey Richardson
Mack, Julian William
Swift, Linton Bishop
SOCIAL WORKER (See also SETTLEMENT WORKER)
Abbott, Edith
Abbott, Grace
Adie, David Craig
Antin, Mary
Balch, Emily Greene
Barrett, Janie Porter
Billikopf, Jacob
Binford, Jessie Florence
Blaustein, David
Bloomfield, Meyer
Bowen, Louise De Koven
Brace, Charles Loring
Breckenridge, Sophonisba Preston
Cabot, Richard Clarke
Cannon, Ida Maud
Carr, Charlotte Elizabeth
Coyle, Grace Longwell
Cratty, Mabel
Devine, Edward Thomas
Dinwiddie, Courtenay
Dodge, Grace Hoadley
Doremus, Sarah Platt Haines
Dyott, Thomas W.
Elliott, John Lovejoy
Glueck, Eleanor Touroff
Hart, Hastings Hornell
Hersey, Evelyn Weeks
Hopkins, Harry Lloyd
Hunter, Robert
Johnson, Alexander
Kelley, Florence
Kober, George Martin
Lathrop, Alice Louise Higgins
Lathrop, Julia Clifford
Lee, Joseph
Lee, Porter Raymond
Lewis, Orlando Faulkland
Loeb, Sophie Irene Simon
Lovejoy, Owen Reed

McDowell, Mary Eliza
McHugh, Rose John
Mason, Lucy Randolph
Park, Maud Wood
Peirce, Bradford Kinney
Perkins, James Handasyd
Perry, Clarence Arthur
Potter, Ellen Culver
Richmond, Mary Ellen
Robertson, Alice Mary
Rubinow, Isaac Max
Schuyler, Louisa Lee
Shuey, Edwin Longstreet
Thurber, Christopher Carson
Veiller, Lawrence Turnure
West, James Edward
Willard, Mary Hatch
Williams, Aubrey Willis
SOCIAL WORK LEADER
Glenn, John Mark
SOCIOLOGIST
Bentley, Arthur Fisher
Brooks, John Graham
Butterfield, Kenyon Leech
Cayton, Horace Roscoe
Davis, Katharine Bement
Dawley, Almena
Dike, Samuel Warren
Du Bois, William Edward Burghardt
Ellis, George Washington
Fitzhugh, George
Frazier, Edward Franklin
Galpin, Charles Josiah
Giddings, Franklin Henry
Hayes, Edward Carey
Haynes, George Edmund
Henderson, Charles Richmond
Johnson, Charles Spurgeon
Kellor, Frances (Alice)
Kelly, Edmond
Kerby, William Joseph
Lazarsfeld, Paul Felix
Lynd, Robert Staughton
MacIver, Robert Morrison
Mills, Charles Wright
Morón, Alonzo Graseano
Morrow, Prince Albert
Odum, Howard Washington
Ogburn, William Fielding
Park, Robert Ezra
Parsons, Elsie Worthington Clews
Parsons, Talcott
Reid, Ira De Augustine
Ross, Edward Alsworth
Sanderson, Ezra Dwight
Small, Albion Woodbury
Stouffer, Samuel Andrew
Stuckenberg, John Henry Wilbrandt
Sutherland, Edwin Hardin
Teggart, Frederick John
Thomas, William Isaac
Vincent, George Edgar
Waller, Willard Walter
Warbasse, James Peter
Ward, Lester Frank
Warner, Amos Griswold
Wilson, Warren Hugh
Wing, John Joseph
Woods, Robert Archey
Wyckoff, Walter Augustus
Znaniecki, Florian Witold
SOIL CHEMIST (See also CHEMIST)
Hoagland, Dennis Robert
SOIL CONSERVATIONIST
Bennett, Hugh Hammond
SOIL EXPERT (See also AGRICULTURIST)
Hilgard, Eugene Woldemar
Marbut, Curtis Fletcher
SOIL SCIENTIST (See also AGRICULTURIST)
Lipman, Jacob Goodale
SOLAR ENERGY PROPONENT
Daniels, Farrington
SOLDIER OF FORTUNE (See also ADVENTURER)
Burnham, Frederick Russell
Lee, Charles, 1731–1782
Littlepage, Lewis
Picton, Thomas
SOLDIER (See also ARMY OFFICER, GENERAL, INDIAN CHIEF, JAYHAWKER)
Adair, John
Adams, Charles
Adams, Daniel Weissiger
Adams, John
Adams, William Wirt
Agnus, Felix
Alden, Ichabod
Alexander, Barton Stone
Alexander, Edward Porter
Alexander, William
Alger, Russell Alexander
Allan, John
Allen, Ethan
Allen, Henry Tureman
Allen, Henry Watkins
Allen, Robert
Allison, Richard
Alvord, Benjamin
Amherst, Jeffery
Ammen, Jacob
Anderson, George Thomas
Anderson, James Patton
Anderson, Joseph Reid
Anderson, Richard Clough
Anderson, Richard Heron
Anderson, Robert
Anderson, William
Andrews, Garnett
Andrews, George Leonard
Angell, Israel
Archer, James J.
Armistead, George
Armistead, Lewis Addison
Armstrong, Frank C.
Armstrong, John, 1717–1795
Armstrong, John, 1755–1816
Armstrong, John, 1758–1843
Armstrong, Robert
Arnold, Richard
Asboth, Alexander Sandor
Asch, Morris Joseph
Ashby, Turner
Ashe, John
Ashe, John Baptista
Atkinson, Henry
Augur, Christopher Columbus
Austin, Jonathan Loring
Averell, William Woods
Avery, Isaac Wheeler
Ayres, Romeyn Beck
Babcock, Orville E.
Bacon, Robert
Badeau, Adam
Bailey, Joseph
Baird, Absalom
Baker, Edward Dickinson
Baker, James Heaton
Baker, Laurence Simmons
Baker, Remember
Baldwin, Loammi
Banks, Nathaniel Prentiss
Barber, Francis
Barksdale, William
Barlow, Francis Channing
Barnard, John Gross
Barnes, James
Barnum, Henry A.
Barnwell, John
Barringer, Rufus
Barry, William Farquhar
Barry, William Taylor Sullivan
Barton, Seth Maxwell
Barton, William
Batcheller, George Sherman
Bate, William Brimage
Bates, John Coalter
Battle, Cullen Andrews
Baxter, Henry
Baylor, George
Beale, Richard Lee Turberville
Beall, John Yates
Beatty, John
Beauregard, Pierre Gustave Toutant
Beaver, James Addams
Bedford, Gunning
Bedinger, George Michael
Bee, Barnard Elliott
Bee, Hamilton Prioleau
Bell, Peter Hansborough
Belo, Alfred Horatio
Bemis, Harold Edward
Benham, Henry Washington
Bennett, Caleb Prew
Benning, Henry Lewis
Berry, Hiram Gregory
Biddle, Clement
Birge, Henry Warner
Birney, David Bell
Birney, William
Black, John Charles
Blackburn, Joseph Clay Styles
Blair, Francis Preston
Bland, Theodorick
Bliss, Tasker Howard
Bloomfield, Joseph
Blount, Thomas
Blunt, James Gillpatrick
Bomford, George
Bonaparte, Jerome Napoleon
Bonham, Milledge Luke
Bonneville, Benjamin Louis Eulalie de
Borland, Solon
Boteler, Alexander Robinson
Bouquet, Henry
Bourke, John Gregory
Bourne, Benjamin
Bowers, Theodore Shelton

Bowie, James
Boyle, Jeremiah Tilford
Boynton, Edward Carlisle
Bradstreet, John
Bragg, Braxton
Bragg, Edward Stuyvesant
Branch, Lawrence O'Bryan
Brannan, John Milton
Bratton, John
Brayman, Mason
Breckenridge, James
Breckinridge, John Cabell
Brodhead, Daniel
Brooke, Francis Taliaferro
Brooke, John Rutter
Brooks, John
Brooks, William Thomas Harbaugh
Brown, Jacob Jennings
Brown, John
Browne, Thomas
Buchanan, Robert Christie
Bucher, John Conrad
Buckland, Ralph Pomeroy
Buckner, Simon Bolivar
Buell, Don Carlos
Buford, Abraham, 1749–1833
Buford, Abraham, 1820–1884
Buford, John
Buford, Napoleon Bonaparte
Burbridge, Stephen Gano
Burleson, Edward
Burnett, Henry Lawrence
Burnside, Ambrose Everett
Burr, Aaron
Bussey, Cyrus
Butler, Benjamin Franklin
Butler, John
Butler, Matthew Calbraith
Butler, Richard
Butler, Walter N.
Butler, William
Butler, William Orlando
Butler, Zebulon
Butterfield, Daniel
Cabell, Samuel Jordan
Cabell, William Lewis
Cadwalader, John
Cadwalader, Lambert
Cameron, Robert Alexander
Camp, John Lafayette
Campbell, William
Canby, Edward Richard Sprigg
Capers, Ellison
Carlson, Evans Fordyce
Carr, Eugene Asa
Carr, Joseph Bradford
Carroll, Samuel Sprigg
Carson, Christopher
Casey, Silas
Cass, Lewis
Caswell, Richard
Cesnola, Luigi Palma di
Chaffee, Adna Romanza
Chalmers, James Ronald
Chamberlain, Joshua Lawrence
Chandler, John
Cheatham, Benjamin Franklin
Chesnut, James
Chetlain, Augustus Louis
Childs, Thomas
Chisolm, Alexander Robert
Christian, William
Church, Benjamin
Churchill, Thomas James
Cilley, Joseph
Cist, Henry Martin
Claghorn, George
Clark, Charles
Clark, William Smith
Clark, William Thomas
Clarke, Elijah
Clarkson, Matthew
Clay, Green
Clay, Joseph
Cleburne, Patrick Ronayne
Clemens, Jeremiah
Cleveland, Benjamin
Clinton, George
Clinton, James
Cobb, David
Cobb, Thomas Reade Rootes
Cochrane, Henry Clay
Cocke, Philip St. George
Cocke, William
Cockrell, Francis Marion
Cofer, Martin Hardin
Colquitt, Alfred Holt
Combs, Leslie
Conger, Edwin Hurd
Conner, James
Connor, Patrick Edward
Cook, Philip
Cooke, Philip St. George
Cooper, Joseph Alexander
Coppée, Henry
Corbin, Henry Clark
Cornell, Ezekiel
Cox, William Ruffin
Crane, John
Crawford, Martin Jenkins
Crawford, Samuel Johnson
Crawford, William
Cresap, Michael
Crittenden, George Bibb
Crittenden, Thomas Leonidas
Croghan, George
Croix, Teodore de
Crook, George
Crosby, John Schuyler
Crozet, Claude
Cullum, George Washington
Curtis, Newton Martin
Curtis, Samuel Ryan
Custer, George Armstrong
Dale, Samuel
Dale, Sir Thomas
Dana, Napoleon Jackson Tecumseh
Darke, William
Davenport, George
Davidson, John Wynn
Davidson, William Lee
Davie, William Richardson
Davies, Henry Eugene
Davis, George Breckenridge
Davis, George Whitefield
Davis, Jefferson Columbus
Davis, Joseph Robert
Dayton, Elias
Dayton, Jonathan
Dearborn, Henry
Deas, Zachariah Cantey
De Haas, John Philip
De Lacy, Walter Washington
De Lancey, James
De Lancey, Oliver
Delany, Martin Robinson
De Mézières y Clugny, Athanase
Dent, Frederick Tracy
Denver, James William
De Peyster, John Watts
De Trobriand, Régis Denis de Keredern
Devens, Charles
Devin, Thomas Casimer
Dibrell, George Gibbs
Dickey, Theophilus Lyle
Dickinson, Philemon
Dickman, Joseph Theodore
Diven, Alexander Samuel
Dix, John Adams
Dodge, Henry
Donelson, Andrew Jackson
Dongan, Thomas
Doniphan, Alexander William
Donovan, William Joseph
Doubleday, Abner
Douglas, Henry Kyd
Douglas, William
Douglass, David Bates
Dow, Henry
Draper, William Franklin
Drayton, Thomas Fenwick
Drayton, William
Duke, Basil Wilson
Du Pont, Henry Algernon
Durkee, John
Duryée, Abram
Dutton, Clarence Edward
Dwight, William
Dye, William McEntyre
Dyer, Alexander Brydie
Early, Jubal Anderson
Eaton, William
Echols, John
Edgren, August Hjalmar
Edwards, Oliver
Elbert, Samuel
Elliott, Washington Lafayette
Ellsworth, Elmer Ephraim
Elmer, Ebenezer
Elzey, Arnold
Emory, William Hensley
Ernst, Oswald Herbert
Eustis, Henry Lawrence
Ewell, Benjamin Stoddert
Ewell, Richard Stoddert
Ewing, Hugh Boyle
Ewing, James
Ewing, Thomas
Fagan, James Fleming
Fairchird, Lucius
Falk, Otto Herbert
Fannin, James Walker
Fanning, Alexander Campbell Wilder
Farnsworth, Elon John
Farnsworth, John Franklin
Farragut, George
Featherston, Winfield Scott
Febiger, Christian
Fenner, Charles Erasmus
Ferguson, Thomas Barker
Ferrero, Edward
Fersen, Hans Axel

Fessenden, Francis
Fessenden, James Deering
Fetterman, William Judd
Few, William
Field, Charles William
Findlay, James
Fish, Nicholas
Fiske, John
Flandrau, Charles Eugene
Fleming, William
Fleming, William Maybury
Fletcher, Benjamin
Fletcher, Thomas Clement
Folsom, Nathaniel
Forbes, John
Force, Manning Ferguson
Ford, Jacob
Forman, David
Forney, William Henry
Foster, John Gray
Foster, John Watson
Foster, Robert Sanford
Franklin, William Buel
Frazer, Persifor
Frémont, John Charles
French, William Henry
Fry, Birkett Davenport
Fry, James Barnet
Frye, Joseph
Fuller, John Wallace
Funston, Frederick
Furnas, Robert Wilkinson
Gaillard, David Du Bose
Gaines, Edmund Pendleton
Gaines, John Pollard
Gálvez, Bernardo de
Gansevoort, Peter
Garden, Alexander
Gardner, Charles Kitchell
Gardner, John Lane
Garfield, James Abram
Garnett, Robert Selden
Garrard, Kenner
Gary, Martin Witherspoon
Gates, Horatio
Geary, John White
Geddes, James Loraine
George, James Zachariah
Getty, George Washington
Gholson, Samuel Jameson
Gibbon, John
Gibson, George
Gibson, John
Gibson, Randall Lee
Gillem, Alvan Cullem
Gillmore, Quincy Adams
Gilmor, Harry
Gist, Christopher
Gist, Mordecai
Gladwin, Henry
Glover, John
Goethals, George Washington
Gookin, Daniel
Gordon, George Henry
Gordon, George Washington
Gordon, John Brown
Gorgas, Josiah
Gorman, Willis Arnold
Govan, Daniel Chevilette
Gracie, Archibald
Graham, Charles Kinnaird
Graham, James Duncan
Graham, Joseph
Graham, William Montrose
Granger, Gordon
Grant, Frederick Dent
Grant, Lewis Addison
Gray, Isaac Pusey
Grayson, William
Greaton, John
Greely, Adolphus Washington
Greene, Christopher
Greene, Francis Vinton
Greene, George Sears
Gregg, David McMurtrie
Gregg, Maxcy
Gresham, Walter Quintin
Gridley, Richard
Grierson, Benjamin Henry
Griffin, Charles
Griffin, Eugene
Griffin, Simon Goodell
Grose, William
Grosvenor, Charles Henry
Grover, Cuvier
Guild, Curtis, 1860–1915
Haan, William George
Hagood, Johnson
Halderman, John A.
Hall, Willard Preble
Halleck, Henry Wager
Hamblin, Joseph Eldridge
Hamer, Thomas Lyon
Hamilton, Charles Smith
Hamilton, Schuyler
Hamlin, Charles
Hammond, Samuel
Hampton, Wade, 1751–1835
Hampton, Wade, 1818–1902
Hamtramck, John Francis
Hancock, Winfield Scott
Hand, Edward
Hardee, William Joseph
Hardie, James Allen
Hardin, John
Hardin, John J.
Hardin, Martin D.
Harding, Abner Clark
Harlan, Josiah
Harmar, Josiah
Harney, William Selby
Harriman, Walter
Harris, Nathaniel Harrison
Harrison, George Paul
Harrod, James
Hartley, Thomas
Hartranft, John Frederick
Hartsuff, George Lucas
Hascall, Milo Smith
Hatch, Edward
Hatch, John Porter
Hawkins, Rush Christopher
Hawley, Joseph Roswell
Hayne, Isaac
Hays, Alexander
Hays, Harry Thompson
Hays, John Coffee
Hazen, Moses
Hazen, William Babcock
Heath, William
Hébert, Louis
Hébert, Paul Octave
Hecker, Friedrich Karl Franz
Heintzelman, Samuel Peter
Henderson, David Bremner
Henderson, Thomas
Henningsen, Charles Frederick
Herbert, Hilary Abner
Herkimer, Nicholas
Heth, Henry
Heyward, Thomas
Hibben, Paxton Pattison
Hickenlooper, Andrew
Hickok, James Butler
Hiester, Joseph
Higginson, Henry Lee
Higginson, Thomas Wentworth
Hill, Ambrose Powell
Hill, Daniel Harvey
Hill, James
Hill, William
Hindman, Thomas Carmichael
Hitchcock, Ethan Allen, 1798–1870
Hitchcock, Henry
Hobson, Edward Henry
Hodes, Henry Irving
Hodges, Courtney Hicks
Hoffman, Wickham
Hogun, James
Hoke, Robert Frederick
Holmes, Julius Cecil
Holmes, Theophilus Hunter
Hood, John Bell
Hooker, Joseph
Hopkins, Samuel, 1753–1819
Hough, Warwick
Houston, Samuel
Hovey, Alvin Peterson
Hovey, Charles Edward
Howard, Benjamin
Howard, John Eager
Howard, Oliver Otis
Howe, Albion Parris
Howe, Robert
Howe, William Wirt
Howze, Robert Lee
Hubbard, Lucius Frederick
Hubbard, Richard Bennett
Hubbard, Thomas Hamlin
Huger, Benjamin
Huger, Francis Kinloch
Hughes, George Wurtz
Hull, William
Humbert, Jean Joseph Amable
Humphreys, Andrew Atkinson
Humphreys, Benjamin Grubb
Humphreys, David
Hunt, Henry Jackson
Hunter, David
Huntington, Jedediah
Hunton, Eppa
Hurlburt, Stephen Augustus
Huse, Caleb
Hyrne, Edmund Massingberd
Imboden, John Daniel
Ingraham, Prentiss
Inman, George
Inman, Henry
Ireland, John, 1827–1896
Irvine, James
Irvine, William
Irwin, George Le Roy
Ives, Joseph Christmas
Izard, George
Jackson, Henry Rootes

Jackson, Thomas Jonathan
Jackson, William, 1759–1828
Jacob, Richard Taylor
Jadwin, Edgar
Jaquess, James Frazier
Jasper, William
Jenkins, Albert Gallatin
Jenkins, John
Jenkins, Micah
Jennings, John
Jesup, Thomas Sidney
Johnson, Bradley Tyler
Johnson, Bushrod Rust
Johnson, Edward
Johnson, James
Johnson, Richard W.
Johnston, Albert Sidney
Johnston, Joseph Eggleston
Johnston, Peter
Johnston, William Preston
Johnston, Zachariah
Jones, Allen
Jones, David Rumph
Jones, John B.
Jones, William
Jordan, Thomas
Kane, Thomas Leiper
Kautz, August Valentine
Kearney, Philip
Kearney, Stephen Watts
Keifer, Joseph Warren
Keitt, Lawrence Massillon
Kelton, John Cunningham
Kemper, James Lawson
Kennedy, John Doby
Kennedy, Robert Patterson
Kershaw, Joseph Brevard
Key, David McKendree
Keyes, Erasmus Darwin
Kilmer, Alfred Joyce
Kilpatrick, Hugh Judson
Kimball, Nathan
King, Rufus
Kirby-Smith, Edmund
Knowlton, Thomas
Kosciuszko, Tadeusz Andrzej Bonawentura
Lacey, John
Lacey, John Fletcher
Lafayette, Marie Joseph Paul Yves Roch Gilbert du Motier, Marquis de
Lamb, John
Lander, Frederick West
Lane, James Henry, 1814–1866
Lane, James Henry, 1833–1907
Lane, Joseph
Lane, Walter Paye
Larrabee, Charles Hathaway
Laurance, John
Laurens, John
Law, Evander McIvor
Lawton, Alexander Robert
Lawton, Henry Ware
Lea, Homer
Leaming, Thomas
Learned, Ebenezer
Leavenworth, Henry
Le Duc, William Gates
Ledyard, William
Lee, Fitzhugh
Lee, George Washington Custis
Lee, Henry ("Light-Horse Harry"), 1756–1818
Lee, Henry, 1787–1837
Lee, Robert Edward
Lee, Stephen Dill
Lee, William Henry Fitzhugh
Le Gendre, Charles William
Leggett, Mortimer Dormer
L'Enfant, Pierre Charles
Lewis, Andrew
Lewis, Isaac Newton
Lewis, Joseph Horace
Lewis, Morgan
Lewis, William Gaston
Liggett, Hunter
Lightburn, Joseph Andrew Jackson
Lincoln, Benjamin
Livingston, James
Locke, Matthew
Lockwood, James Booth
Logan, John Alexander
Lomax, Lunsford Lindsay
Longstreet, James
Lorimier, Pierre Louis
Loring, William Wing
Lovell, Mansfield
Lowrey, Mark Perrin
Lowry, Robert
Lubbock, Francis Richard
Ludlow, William
Lynch, Charles
Lynch, James Daniel
Lyon, Matthew
Lyon, Nathaniel
Lytle, William Haines
McArthur, John, 1826–1906
McCausland, John
McCawley, Charles Grymes
McCay, Henry Kent
McClellan, George Brinton
McClellan, Henry Brainerd
McClernand, John Alexander
McClintock, James Harvey
McClure, George
McClurg, Alexander Caldwell
McClurg, James
McCook, Alexander McDowell
McCook, Anson George
McCook, Edward Moody
McCrady, Edward
McCulloch, Ben
McCullough, Ernest
McDaniel, Henry Dickerson
McDougall, Alexander
McDowell, Charles
McDowell, Irvin
McDowell, Joseph
McElroy, John
McGowan, Samuel
McHenry, James
McIntosh, John Baillie
McIntosh, Lachlan
Mackenzie, Ronald Slidell
McKinstry, Alexander
McLane, Allan
McLaws, Lafayette
McLeod, Hugh
McMillan, James Winning
Macomb, Alexander
Macon, Nathaniel
McPherson, James Birdseye
McRae, Duncan Kirkland
Maginnis, Martin
Magruder, John Bankhead
Mahan, Dennis Hart
Mahone, William
Mallery, Garrick
Manderson, Charles Frederick
Maney, George Earl
Mappa, Adam Gerard
March, Peyton Conway
Marcy, Randolph Barnes
Marmaduke, John Sappington
Marshall, George Catlett, Jr.
Marshall, Humphrey
Marshall, Samuel Lyman Atwood ("Slam")
Marshall, Thomas
Marshall, William Louis
Marshall, William Rainey
Martin, Alexander
Martin, James Green
Martin, John Alexander
Martin, William Thompson
Martindale, John Henry
Mason, John
Mason, Richard Barnes
Matthews, George
Maury, Dabney Herndon
Maus, Marion Perry
Maxwell, William
Meade, George Gordon
Meade, Richard Kidder
Meade, Robert Leamy
Meagher, Thomas Francis
Meigs, Montgomery Cunningham
Meigs, Return Jonathan
Menoher, Charles Thomas
Mercer, Hugh
Mercer, John Francis
Merriam, Henry Clay
Merrill, Frank Dow
Merrill, William Emery
Merritt, Wesley
Meserve, Nathaniel
Michie, Peter Smith
Miles, Nelson Appleton
Mills, Anson
Milroy, Robert Huston
Minty, Robert Horatio George
Mitchel, Ormsby MacKnight
Mitchell, David Dawson
Mitchell, George Edward
Mitchell, Nathaniel
Mitchell, Robert Byington
Montefiore, Joshua
Montgomery, James
Montgomery, Richard
Moore, Alfred
Moore, James, 1737–1777
Mordecai, Alfred
Morell, George Webb
Morgan, Daniel
Morgan, George Washington
Morgan, James Dada
Morgan, James Morris
Morgan, John Hunt
Morgan, Thomas Jefferson
Morris, Roger
Morris, William Hopkins
Morton, James St. Clair
Mott, Gershom

Mower, Joseph Anthony
Moylan, Stephen
Muhlenberg, John Peter Gabriel
Mulholland, St. Clair Augustin
Munford, Robert
Myer, Albert James
Myers, Abraham Charles
Nancrède, Paul Joseph Guérard de
Narváez, Pánfilo de
Nash, Francis
Negley, James Scott
Neill, Thomas Hewson
Neilson, John
Nelson, Roger
Nelson, Thomas
Nelson, William, 1824–1862
Nesmith, James Willis
Nettleton, Alvred Bayard
Neville, John
Neville, Wendell Cushing
Newton, John
Nicholson, William Jones
Nicola, Lewis
Nixon, John, 1727–1815
Noailles, Louis Marie, Vicomte de
Noble, John Willock
North, William
Northen, William Jonathan
Northrop, Lucius Bellringer
Noyan, Gilles-Augustin Payen de
Noyen, Pierre-Jacques Payen de
Oates, William Calvin
O'Fallon, James
O'Fallon, John
Ogden, Aaron
Oglethorpe, James Edward
O'Hara, James
O'Hara, Theodore
Oliver, Paul Ambrose
O'Neal, Edward Asbury
O'Neill, John
Ord, Edward Otho Cresap
O'Reilly, Alexander
Osborn, Thomas Ogden
Osceola
Osgood, Samuel
Osterhaus, Peter Joseph
Otis, Elwell Stephen
Otis, Harrison Gray
Page, Richard Lucian
Paine, Charles Jackson
Paine, Halbert Eleazer
Painter, Gamaliel
Palfrey, John Carver
Palmer, Innis Newton
Palmer, John McAuley
Palmer, Joseph
Palmer, William Jackson
Pardee, Don Albert
Parke, Benjamin
Parke, John
Parke, John Grubb
Parker, Ely Samuel
Parker, John
Parker, Josiah
Parker, Richard Elliot
Parsons, Lewis Baldwin
Parsons, Samuel Holden
Paterson, John
Patrick, Marsena Rudolph
Patterson, Robert
Peck, John James
Pelham, John
Pemberton, John Clifford
Peñalosa Briceño, Diego Dionisio
Pender, William Dorsey
Pendleton, William Nelson
Pennypacker, Galusha
Pepperrell, Sir William
Perry, Edward Aylesworth
Pettigrew, James Johnston
Pettus, Edmund Winston
Phelps, Charles Edward
Philips, John Finis
Phillips, William Addison
Phisterer, Frederick
Pickens, Andrew
Pickering, Timothy
Pickett, George Edward
Pierce, William Leigh
Pike, Albert
Pike, Zebulon Montgomery
Pillow, Gideon Johnson
Pinckney, Charles Cotesworth
Pinckney, Thomas
Pitcairn, John
Plaisted, Harris Merrill
Pleasonton, Alfred
Plumb, Preston B.
Poe, Orlando Metcalfe
Polk, Lucius Eugene
Polk, Thomas
Polk, William
Pomeroy, Seth
Pond, Peter
Poor, Enoch
Pope, John
Porter, Andrew
Porter, Fitz-John
Porter, Horace
Posey, Thomas
Potter, James
Potter, Robert Brown
Potts, Benjamin Franklin
Powel, John Hare
Pratt, Richard Henry
Prentiss, Benjamin Mayberry
Prescott, Oliver
Prescott, William
Preston, John Smith
Preston, William
Price, Sterling
Pryor, Nathaniel
Pryor, Roger Atkinson
Pulaski, Casimir
Putnam, Eben
Putnam, George Haven
Putnam, Israel
Putnam, Rufus
Quesnay, Alexandre-Marie
Quimby, Isaac Ferdinand
Quitman, John Anthony
Rains, Gabriel James
Rains, George Washington
Ramsay, George Douglas
Ramsay, Nathaniel
Ramseur, Stephen Dodson
Ransom, Matt Whitaker
Ransom, Thomas Edward Greenfield
Raum, Green Berry
Rawlins, John Aaron
Read, Jacob
Reed, James, 1772–1807
Reed, John, 1757–1845
Reed, Joseph
Reno, Jesse Lee
Revere, Joseph Warren
Reynolds, Alexander Welch
Reynolds, John Fulton
Reynolds, Joseph Jones
Richardson, Israel Bush
Richardson, Wilds Preston
Ricketts, James Brewerton
Riley, Bennet
Ripley, Edward Hastings
Ripley, Eleazar Wheelock
Ripley, James Wolfe
Ripley, Roswell Sabine
Roane, John Selden
Roberts, Benjamin Stone
Roberts, Oran Milo
Robertson, Jerome Bonaparte
Robinson, John Cleveland
Robinson, Moses
Rochambeau, Jean Baptiste Donatien Vimeur, Comte de
Rockwell, Kiffin Yates
Roddey, Philip Dale
Rodenbough, Theophilus Francis
Rodes, Robert Emmett
Rodman, Isaac Peace
Rodman, Thomas Jackson
Rodney, Thomas
Romans, Bernard
Rosecrans, William Starke
Ross, Lawrence Sullivan
Rosser, Thomas Lafayette
Rousseau, Lovell Harrison
Ruger, Thomas Howard
Ruggles, Timothy
Rusk, Thomas Jefferson
Russell, David Allen
Rutgers, Henry
St. Ange Bellerive, Louis de
St. Clair, Arthur
St. Denis (Denys), Louis Juchereau de
St. Lusson, Simon François Daumont, Sieur de
St. Vrain, Ceran de Hault de Lassus de
Sargent, Henry
Sargent, Winthrop, 1753–1820
Scammell, Alexander
Scharf, John Thomas
Schenck, Robert Cumming
Schnauffer, Carl Heinrich
Schofield, John McAllister
Schriver, Edmund
Schurz, Carl
Schuyler, Peter
Schuyler, Philip John
Scott, Charles
Scott, Robert Kingston
Scott, Winfield
Scudder, Nathaniel
Sedgwick, John
Sedgwick, Robert
Seeger, Alan
Sevier, John
Sewell, William Joyce

Seymour, Truman
Shafter, William Rufus
Shaw, Samuel
Shays, Daniel
Shelby, Evan
Shelby, Isaac
Shelby, Joseph Orville
Shepard, William
Shepley, George Foster
Sheridan, Philip Henry
Sherman, Thomas West
Sherman, William Tecumseh
Sherwood, Isaac Ruth
Shields, James
Shipp, Scott
Shoup, Francis Asbury
Sickles, Daniel Edgar
Sidell, William Henry
Sigel, Franz
Simmons, Thomas Jefferson
Simms, William Elliott
Simonton, Charles Henry
Simpson, James Hervey
Smallwood, William
Smith, Andrew Jackson
Smith, Charles Ferguson
Smith, Charles Henry, 1827–1902
Smith, Daniel
Smith, Francis Henney
Smith, Giles Alexander
Smith, Gustavus Woodson
Smith, James, 1737–1814
Smith, James Francis
Smith, John Eugene
Smith, Martin Luther
Smith, Morgan Lewis
Smith, Persifor Frazer
Smith, Richard Somers
Smith, Samuel
Smith, Thomas Adams
Smith, Walter Bedell
Smith, William, 1797–1887
Smith, William Farrar
Smith, William Sooy
Smith, William Stephens
Smyth, Alexander
Snead, Thomas Lowndes
Snelling, Josiah
Snyder, John Francis
Spaulding, Oliver Lyman
Spencer, Joseph
Squier, George Owen
Squiers, Herbert Goldsmith
Stahel, Julius
Standish, Myles
Stanley, David Sloane
Stansbury, Howard
Stark, John
Steedman, James Blair
Steele, Frederick
Stephens, Linton
Steuben, Friedrich Wilhelm Ludolf Gerhard Augustin, Baron von
Stevens, Clement Hoffman
Stevens, Isaac Ingalls
Stevens, Walter Husted
Stewart, Alexander Peter
Stobo, Robert
Stoddard, Amos
Stone, Charles Pomeroy
Stoneman, George
Strother, David Hunter
Struve, Gustav
Stuart, Archibald
Stuart, James Ewell Brown
Sturgis, Samuel Davis
Summerall, Charles Pelot
Sumner, Edwin Vose
Sumner, Jethro
Sumter, Thomas
Swartwout, Samuel
Swayne, Wager
Sweeny, Thomas William
Swift, Joseph Gardner
Swift, William Henry
Sykes, George
Talcott, Andrew
Taliaferro, William Booth
Tallmadge, Benjamin
Taylor, Harry
Taylor, Richard
Taylor, Zachary
Ten Broeck, Abraham
Terry, Alfred Howe
Terry, David Smith
Thayer, John Milton
Thomas, Allen
Thomas, David
Thomas, George Henry
Thomas, John
Thomas, Lorenzo
Thompson, William
Thomson, William
Tidball, John Caldwell
Tilghman, Tench
Timberlake, Henry
Tipton, John, 1730–1813
Tipton, John, 1786–1839
Todd, Charles Stewart
Torbert, Alfred Thomas Archimedes
Totten, Joseph Gilbert
Toulmin, Harry Theophilus
Tousard, Anne Louis de
Tower, Zealous Bates
Townsend, Edward Davis
Tracy, Benjamin Franklin
Travis, William Barret
Tremain, Henry Edwin
Trimble, Isaac Ridgeway
Troup, Robert
Trumbull, Jonathan, 1740–1809
Tupper, Benjamin
Turnbull, William
Turner, John Wesley
Turney, Peter
Twiggs, David Emanuel
Tyler, Daniel
Tyler, Robert Ogden
Tyndale, Hector
Tyson, Lawrence Davis
Underhill, John
Upton, Emory
Vallejo, Mariano Guadalupe
Van Cortlandt, Philip
Van Rensselaer, Solomon
Van Rensselaer, Stephen
Van Schaick, Goose
Van Wyck, Charles Henry
Varick, Richard
Varnum, James Mitchell
Varnum, Joseph Bradley
Venable, Charles Scott
Vetch, Samuel
Vigo, Joseph Maria Francesco
Villagrá, Gasper Pérez de
Vincennes, Jean Baptiste Bissot, Sieur de
Vinton, Francis
Vinton, Francis Laurens
Waddell, Hugh
Wadsworth, James Samuel
Wadsworth, Jeremiah
Walderne, Richard
Walker, Reuben Lindsay
Walker, Thomas
Walker, William Henry Talbot
Wallace, Lewis
Ward, Samuel, 1756–1832
Warmoth, Henry Clay
Warner, Adoniram Judson
Warner, Seth
Warner, William
Warren, Gouverneur Kemble
Washburn, Cadwallader Colden
Washington, John Macrae
Wayne, Anthony
Weaver, James Baird
Webb, Alexander Stewart
Webb, Thomas
Webber, Charles Wilkins
Webster, Joseph Dana
Weitzel, Godfrey
Wetherill, Samuel
Wheaton, Frank
Wheeler, Joseph
Whipple, Amiel Weeks
Whistler, George Washington
White, James
Whiting, William Henry Chase
Wilcox, Cadmus Marcellus
Wilder, John Thomas
Wilkinson, James
Willcox, Orlando Bolivar
Willett, Marinus
Williams, Alpheus Starkey
Williams, Ephraim
Williams, George Washington
Williams, Jonathan
Williams, Otho Holland
Williamson, Andrew
Wilson, James Grant
Wilson, James Harrison
Winchester, James
Winder, John Henry
Winder, Levin
Winder, William Henry
Winn, Richard
Winslow, Edward Francis
Winslow, John
Winston, Joseph
Winthrop, John
Wofford, William Tatum
Wood, Leonard
Wood, Thomas John
Woodbury, Daniel Phineas
Woodford, Stewart Lyndon
Woodford, William
Woods, Charles Robert
Wool, John Ellis
Worth, William Jenkins
Wraxall, Peter

Wright, Horatio Gouveneur
Wright, Marcus Joseph
Wyatt, Aiken David
Yell, Archibald
York, Alvin Cullum
Young, Pierce Manning Butler
Youngs, John
Zeilin, Jacob
Ziegler, David
Zolticoffer, Felix Kirk
SONGWRITER (See also COMPOSER, HYMNOLOGIST, LYRICIST, MUSICIAN)
Bennet, Sanford Fillmore
Chaplin, Ralph Hosea
Emmett, Daniel Decatur
Golden, John
Guthrie, Woody
Hanby, Benjamin Russel
Handy, William Christopher
Harris, Charles Kassell
Hendrix, Jimi
Hopkinson, Joseph
Key, Francis Scott
Lennon, John Winston Ono
Lopez, Vincent Joseph
Maxwell, Elsa
Morrison, Jim
Ochs, Phil
Randall, James Ryder
Rooney, Pat
Rose, Billy
Ross, Alexander Coffman
Speaks, Oley
Stern, Joseph William
Wilder, Alexander Lafayette Chew ("Alec")
Williams, Bert
Williams, (Hiram) Hank
Work, Henry Clay
SONNETEER (See also BALLADIST, POET)
Very, Jones
SOPRANO (see SINGER)
SOVIET AGENT (See also SPY)
Abel, Rudolf Ivanovich
Bentley, Elizabeth Terrill
Chambers, Whittaker
SOVIETOLOGIST
Mosely, Philip Edward
SPACE PIONEER
Goddard, Robert Hutchings
SPEAKER OF HOUSE OF BURGESSES
Randolph, Sir John
Randolph, Peyton
Robinson, John
SPEAKER OF HOUSE OF REPRESENTATIVES
Bankhead, William Brockman
Byrns, Joseph Wellington
Clark, Champ
Henderson, David Bremner
Longworth, Nicholas, 1869–1931
McCormick, John William
Macon, Nathaniel
Martin, Joseph William, Jr.
Muhlenberg, Frederick Augustus Conrad
Orr, James Lawrence
Rainey, Henry Thomas
Randall, Samuel Jackson
Rayburn, Samuel Taliaferro ("Sam")
Reed, Thomas Brackett
Stevenson, Andrew
Varnum, Joseph Bradley
SPECULATOR (See also LAND SPECULATOR, REAL-ESTATE OPERATOR)
Craigie, Andrew
Doty, James Duane
Drew, Daniel
Fisk, James
Gates, John Warne ("Bet-you-a-million")
Hutchinson, Benjamin Peters
Keene, James Robert
Morse, Charles Wyman
Sully, Daniel John
Swartwout, Samuel
Wilson, James
SPIRITUALIST (See also RELIGIOUS LEADER)
Colby, Luther
Davenport, Ira Erastus
Davis, Andrew Jackson
Dods, John Bovee
Fox, Margaret
King, William Benjamin Basil
Post, Isaac
Sargent, Epes
Sprague, Achsa W.
SPORTS BROADCASTER
Stern, Bill
SPORTS CARTOONIST
Mullin, Willard Harlan
SPORTS CONCESSIONAIRE
Stevens, Frank Mozley
SPORTS ENTHUSIAST
Biddle, Anthony Joseph Drexel, Jr.
SPORTS ENTREPRENEUR
Reeves, Daniel F.
SPORTS EXECUTIVE
Kilpatrick, John Reed
SPORTS JOURNALIST
Rice, (Henry) Grantland
SPORTSMAN (See also ATHLETE, SPECIFIC SPORTS)
Astor, William Vincent
Chadwick, Henry
Cochran, Alexander Smith
Davis, Dwight Filley
Duryea, Hermanes Barkulo
Greenslet, Ferris
Hitchcock, Thomas
Holder, Charles Frederick
Lasker, Albert Davis
Lippincott, Joseph Wharton
Lorillard, Pierre
McLellan, Isaac
Reynolds, William Neal
Riddle, Samuel Doyle
Ruppert, Jacob
Samuels, Edward Augustus
Spalding, Albert Goodwill
Thompson, Robert Means
Vanderbilt, William Kissam
Wharton, Robert
Whitney, Harry Payne
Whitney, William Collins
Widener, George Dunton
SPORTS MEDICINE PIONEER
Paul, William Darwin ("Shorty")
SPORTS PROMOTER
Fox, Richard Kyle
Jacobs, Michael Strauss
Rickard, George Lewis ("Tex")
Sullivan, James Edward
Ward, Arch Burdette
SPORTS WRITER (See also JOURNALIST, SPORTS JOURNALIST)
Daley, Arthur John
Dorgan, Thomas Aloysius
Elliott, William
Fleischer, Nathaniel Stanley ("Nat")
Masterson, William Barclay
Ward, Arch Burdette
SPY (See also SOVIET AGENT)
Boyd, Belle
Cushman, Pauline
Eisler, Gerhart
Gold, Harry ("Raymond")
Hale, Nathan
Heron, William
Moody, James
Rosenberg, Ethel
Rosenberg, Julius
Scott, John
Vardill, John
Wentworth, Paul
Wright, Patience Lovell
SPY (ALLEGED)
Coe, Virginius ("Frank")
STAGE DESIGNER (See THEATRICAL DESIGNER)
STAGE DIRECTOR (See THEATRICAL DIRECTOR)
STAINED GLASS ARTIST
Connick, Charles Jay
STATE OFFICIAL
De Saussure, Henry William
Heath, James Ewell
Lloyd, Edward, 1744–1796
Matlack, Timothy
Mazureau, Étienne
Murphy, William Sumter
Robertson, Jerome Bonaparte
Schuyler, George Washington
Whitehill, Robert
Wickliffe, Charles Anderson
Wyllys, George
Yates, John Van Ness
STATESMAN (See also DIPLOMAT)
Acheson, Dean Gooderham
Adams, Charles Francis
Adams, Samuel
Aiken, William
Aldrich, Nelson Wilmarth
Alexander, James
Alston, Joseph
Ames, Fisher
Anderson, Richard Clough
Armstrong, Samuel Turell
Baldwin, Abraham
Barbour, James
Barbour, Philip Pendleton
Barker, Josiah
Barlow, Joel
Barnard, Daniel Dewey
Barnwell, Robert Woodward
Barry, William Taylor

Barry, William Taylor Sullivan
Barton, David
Bassett, Richard
Batcheller, George Sherman
Bates, Edward
Baxter, Henry
Bayard, James Ash(e)ton
Bayard, John Bubenheim
Bayard, Thomas Francis
Baylies, Francis
Bedford, Gunning
Belknap, William Worth
Bell, Jacob
Bell, John
Benjamin, Judah Philip
Benning, Henry Lewis
Benton, Thomas Hart
Bergh, Christian
Bergh, Henry
Biddle, Nicholas
Blaine, James Gillespie
Blair, Francis Preston
Blair, Montgomery
Bland, Richard
Boudinot, Elias
Bowdoin, James
Boyden, Roland William
Bradish, Luther
Bradstreet, Simon
Bragg, Thomas
Braxton, Carter
Brearly, David
Breckenridge, John
Breckinridge, John Cabell
Brentano, Lorenz
Briggs, George Nixon
Bristow, Benjamin Helm
Brown, Joseph Emerson
Bruce, David Kirkpatrick Este
Cary, Archibald
Cass, Lewis
Chase, Salmon Portland
Choate, Rufus
Clarke, John
Clayton, John Middleton
Clinton, De Witt
Clinton, George
Colquitt, Alfred Holt
Colquitt, Walter Terry
Conrad, Charles Magill
Cooke, Elisha
Crittenden, John Jordan
Culberson, Charles Allen
Culberson, David Browning
Cullom, Shelby Moore
Cummings, Albert Baird
Curry, Jabez Lamar Monroe
Cushing, Caleb
Dana, Samuel Whittelsey
Dane, Nathan
Davis, Henry Winter
Davis, John
Dawson, John
Dickinson, John
Dillingham, William Paul
Dolliver, Jonathan Prentiss
Doniphan, Alexander William
Doolittle, James Rood
Dow, Henry
Eaton, Charles Aubrey
Eliot, Samuel Atkins
Ellsworth, Oliver
Emerson, Haven
Eustis, George
Eustis, James Biddle
Evarts, William Maxwell
Everett, Edward
Fersen, Hans Axel
Few, William
Fish, Hamilton
Fleming, William
Forsyth, John
Franklin, Benjamin
Frelinghuysen, Frederick Theodore
Galloway, Joseph
Garnett, Muscoe Russell Hunter
Gerry, Elbridge
Gholson, Thomas Saunders
Gibson, Randall Lee
Giles, William Branch
Gillette, Francis
Gilmer, Thomas Walker
Goode, John
Gordon, John Brown
Gordon, William Fitzhugh
Gorham, Nathaniel
Graham, William Alexander
Gresham, Walter Quintin
Griffin, Cyrus
Griggs, John William
Hall, Lyman
Hamilton, Alexander, 1757–1804
Hardy, Samuel
Harnett, Cornelius
Harpur, Robert
Harrison, Benjamin, 1726–1791
Harvie, John
Heathcote, Caleb
Henry, Patrick
Hewitt, Abram Stevens
Hill, Benjamin Harvey
Hindman, Thomas Carmichael
Hopkinson, Francis
Hosmer, Titus
Houston, Samuel
Humphreys, David
Hunter, Robert Mercer Taliaferro
Ide, Henry Clay
Iredell, James
Jay, John
Jefferson, Thomas
Jenifer, Daniel of St. Thomas
Johnson, William Samuel
Johnston, Josiah Stoddard
Johnston, Zachariah
Jones, Joseph
Judd, Gerrit Parmele
Kennedy, John Pendleton
Kern, John Worth
Körner, Gustav Philip
Lafayette, Marie Joseph Paul Yves Roch Gilbert du Motier Marquis de
Lamar, Lucius Quintus Cincinnatus
Laurens, Henry
Lawrence, Abbott
Lee, Francis Lightfoot
Lee, Henry, 1756–1818
Lee, Richard
Lee, Richard Bland
Lee, Richard Henry
Leigh, Benjamin Watkins
Livingston, Edward
Livingston, Robert R., 1746–1813
Logan, James, 1674–1751
Lovejoy, Owen
Lumpkin, Wilson
McKean, Thomas
Marcy, William Learned
Marshall, George Catlett, Jr.
Mason, George
Menard, Pierre
Mitchell, Stephen Mix
Morris, Gouverneur
Morris, Lewis Richard
Nelson, John
Osborn, Thomas Andrew
Otis, Harrison Gray
Parker, Joel
Parker, Richard Elliot
Pattison, Robert Emory
Patton, John Mercer
Pinckney, Charles Cotesworth
Pinkney, William
Pitkin, Timothy
Poinsett, Joel Roberts
Porter, David Rittenhouse
Powel, John Hare
Randolph, John, 1773–1833
Reed, Joseph
Rhett, Robert Barnwell
Richardson, James Daniel
Roberts, Oran Milo
Robinson, Moses
Rodney, Caesar
Rodney, Caesar Augustus
Rublee, George
Rush, Richard
Rutledge, John
Schuyler, Philip John
Seward, William Henry
Sherman, John, 1823–1900
Sherman, Roger
Silsbee, Nathaniel
Slade, William
Smith, Meriwether
Smith, Samuel
Strong, Caleb
Sullivan, James
Sullivan, John
Tallmadge, James
Vane, Sir Henry
Watterson, Henry
Webster, Daniel
Williamson, Hugh

STATES RIGHTS ADVOCATE (See also AGITATOR, REFORMER)
Paine, Byron
Quitman, John Anthony

STATISTICIAN (See also INSURANCE EXPERT)
Abbott, Samuel Warren
Adams, Henry Carter
Ayres, Leonard Porter
Babson, Roger Ward
Day, David Talbot
De Bow, James Dunwoody Brownson
Dennis, James Shepard
Dodge, Jacob Richards
Dorchester, Daniel

Falkner, Roland Post
Hill, Joseph Adna
Hittell, John Shertzer
Hoffman, Frederick Ludwig
Hourwich, Isaac Aaronovich
Jarvis, Edward
Kennedy, Joseph Camp Griffith
Koren, John
McPherson, Logan Grant
Mayo-Smith, Richmond
North, Simon Newton Dexter
Ogburn, William Fielding
Pearl, Raymond
Persons, Warren Milton
Pidgin, Charles Felton
Rossiter, William Sidney
Rubinow, Isaac Max
Schem, Alexander Jacob
Shattuck, Lemuel
Stouffer, Samuel Andrew
Swank, James Moore
Sydenstricker, Edgar
Walker, Francis Amasa
Weeks, Joseph Dame
Wilbur, Cressy Livingston
Woytinsky, Wladimir Savelievich
Wright, Carroll Davidson

STEAMBOAT BUILDER
Rees, James

STEAMBOAT CAPTAIN (See also SHIP CAPTAIN)
Bixby, Horace Ezra
Ford, John Baptiste
King, Richard
Marsh, Grant Prince
Rogers, Moses
Sellers, Isaiah
Shreve, Henry Miller
Vandergrift, Jacob Jay

STEAMBOAT OPERATOR
Gibbons, Thomas
La Barge, Joseph
Ogden, Aaron
Reed, Simeon Gannett

STEAMSHIP OWNER (See also SHIPOWNER)
Grace, William Russell
Hallett, Benjamin
Newton, Isaac, 1794–1858
Ralston, William Chapman

STEEL COMPANY EXECUTIVE
Cort, Stewart Shaw
Farrell, James Augustine
Graff, Everett Dwight
Hood, Clifford Firoved

STOCK BREEDER (See also CATTLEMAN)
Allen, Lewis Falley
Buford, Abraham
Hammond, Edwin
Harris, William Alexander
Jackson, William Hicks
McNeill, John Hanson
Matthews, Claude
Morris, Nelson
Sheedy, Dennis

STOCKBROKER (See also BANKER, CAPITALIST, FINANCIER)
Auchincloss, Hugh Dudley, Jr.
Coleman, John Aloysius
Colgate, James Boorman
Cuppia, Jerome Chester
Du Pont, Francis Irénée
Hendrick, Ellwood
Hutton, Edward Francis
Lawson, Thomas William
Merrill, Charles Edward
Ouimet, Francis Desales
Riis, Mary Phillips

STONEMASON
Edmondson, William

STREET RAILWAY BUILDER
Stephenson, John
Wells, Erastus

STREET RAILWAY OPERATOR
Johnson, Tom Loftin
Mitten, Thomas Eugene
Scullin, John

SUBMARINE PIONEER
Lake, Simon

SUFFRAGIST (See also FEMINIST)
Belmont, Alva Ertskin Smith Vanderbilt
Blackwell, Alice Stone
Brown, Gertrude Foster
Catt, Carrie Clinton Lane Chapman
Flynn, Elizabeth Gurley
Hooper, Jessie Annette Jack
Stevens, Doris
Wells, Harriet Sheldon
Whitney, Charlotte Anita
Younger, Maud

SUGAR PLANTER (See also AGRICULTURIST, FARMER, PLANTER)
Behan, William James
Boré, Jean Étienne

SUGAR REFINER
Havemeyer, Henry Osborne
Havemeyer, William Frederick
Stuart, Robert Leighton

SUGAR TECHNOLOGIST
Hooker, Samuel Cox

SUPERINTENDENT OF INDIAN AFFAIRS
Johnson, Guy
Johnson, Sir John
Johnson, Sir William
Mitchell, David Dawson
Pilcher, Joshua
Stuart, John

SUPREME COURT CHIEF JUSTICE
Chase, Salmon Portland
Ellsworth, Oliver
Fuller, Melville Weston
Hughes, Charles Evans
Jay, John
Marshall, John
Stone, Harlan Fiske
Taft, William Howard
Taney, Roger Brooke
Vinson, Fred(erick) Moore
Warren, Earl
Waite, Morrison Remick
White, Edward Douglass

SUPREME COURT JUSTICE
Baldwin, Henry
Barbour, Philip Pendleton
Black, Hugo Lafayette
Blair, John
Blatchford, Samuel
Bradley, Joseph P.
Brandeis, Louis Dembitz
Brewer, David Josiah
Brown, Henry Billings
Burton, Harold Hitz
Butler, Pierce
Byrnes, James Francis
Campbell, John Archibald
Cardozo, Benjamin Nathan
Catron, John
Chase, Samuel
Clark, Tom Campbell
Clarke, John Hessin
Clifford, Nathan
Curtis, Benjamin Robbins
Cushing, William
Daniel, Peter Vivian
Davis, David
Day, William Rufus
Douglas, William Orville
Duvall, Gabriel
Field, Stephen Johnson
Frankfurter, Felix
Gray, Horace
Grier, Robert Cooper
Harlan, John Marshall (1833–1911)
Harlan, John Marshall (1899–1971)
Holmes, Oliver Wendell
Hughes, Charles Evans
Hunt, Ward
Iredell, James
Jackson, Howell Edmunds
Jackson, Robert Houghwout
Johnson, Thomas
Johnson, William
Lamar, Lucius Quintus Cincinnatus
Livingston, Henry Brockholst
Lurton, Horace Harmon
McKenna, Joseph
McKinley, John
McLean, John
McReynolds, James Clark
Matthews, Stanley
Miller, Samuel Freeman
Minton, Sherman
Moody, William Henry
Moore, Alfred
Murphy, Frank
Nelson, Samuel
Peckham, Rufus Wheeler
Pitney, Mahlon
Reed, Stanley Forman
Roberts, Owen Josephus
Rutledge, John
Rutledge, Wiley Blount
Sanford, Edward Terry
Shiras, George
Stone, Harlan Fiske
Story, Joseph
Strong, William
Sutherland, George
Swayne, Noah Haynes
Thompson, Smith
Todd, Thomas
Trimble, Robert
Van Devanter, Willis
Washington, Bushrod
Wayne, James Moore
White, Edward Douglass
Whittaker, Charles Evans
Wilson, James

Woodbury, Levi
Woods, William Burnham
SURGEON (See also PHYSICIAN)
Agnew, David Hayes
Allison, Nathaniel
Ambler, James Markham Marshall
Ashhurst, John
Atlee, John Light
Atlee, Washington Lemuel
Baer, William Stevenson
Barnes, Joseph K.
Barton, John Rhea
Barton, William Paul Crillon
Batchelder, John Putnam
Battey, Robert
Baxley, Henry Willis
Beaumont, William
Beck, Carl
Bernays, Augustus Charles
Bevan, Arthur Dean
Bigelow, Henry Jacob
Billings, John Shaw
Blackburn, Luke Pryor
Blalock, Alfred
Bloodgood, Joseph Colt
Bradford, Edward Hickling
Brainard, Daniel
Brinton, John Hill
Brophy, Truman William
Brown, Frederic Tilden
Bryant, Joseph Decatur
Buck, Gurdon
Bull, William Tillinghast
Bumstead, Freeman Josiah
Burnet, William
Cabot, Arthur Tracy
Cabot, Hugh
Carnochan, John Murray
Carrel, Alexls
Carson, Simeon Lewis
Chisolm, John Julian
Chovet, Abraham
Condit, John
Cooper, Elias Samuel
Crile, George Washington
Cushing, Harvey Williams
Cutler, Elliott Carr
Da Costa, John Chalmers
Dandy, Walter Edward
Davidge, John Beale
Davis, Henry Gassett
Davis, John Staige
Deaver, John Blair
Delafield, Edward
Dennis, Frederic Shepard
Dorsey, John Syng
Dowell, Greensville
Downer, Eliphalet
Drew, Charles Richard
Dudley, Benjamin Winslow
Edebohls, George Michael
Elman, Robert
Elsberg, Charles Albert
Eve, Paul Fitzsimons
Fayssoux, Peter
Fenger, Christian
Ferguson, Alexander High
Finney, John Miller Turpin
Floyd, John
Fowler, George Ryerson
Fowler, Russell Story
Frazier, Charles Harrison
Gaillard, Edwin Samuel
Garlick, Theodatus
Garretson, James
Gaston, James McFadden
Gerrish, Frederic Henry
Gerster, Arpad Geyza Charles
Gibson, William
Gihon, Albert Leary
Gilliam, David Tod
Goldsmith, Middleton
Gorgas, William Crawford
Graham, Evarts Ambrose
Gross, Samuel David
Gross, Samuel Weissell
Halsted, William Stewart
Hamilton, Frank Hastings
Hammond, William Alexander
Hartley, Frank
Hays, John Coffee
Hayward, George
Heap, Samuel Davies
Helmuth, William Tod
Henrotin, Fernand
Hodgen, John Thompson
Holmes, Bayard Taylor
Hosack, Alexander Eddy
Howe, Andrew Jackson
Hullihen, Simon P.
Jackson, Edward
Jackson, Hall
Jameson, Horatio Gates
Jeffries, Benjamin Joy
Johnston, George Ben
Jones, John
Judd, Edward Starr
Judson, Adoniram Brown
Kean, Jefferson Randolph
Keen, William Williams
Kellogg, John Harvey
Kelly, Howard Atwood
Keyes, Edward Lawrence
Kilty, William
Kimball, Gilman
Kinloch, Robert Alexander
Kirk, Norman Thomas
Kolle, Frederick Strange
Lahey, Frank Howard
Lane, Levi Cooper
Lawson, Thomas
Lefferts, George Morewood
Lewis, Dean De Witt
Lincoln, Rufus Pratt
Lloyd, James
Lockrey, Sarah Hunt
Long, Crawford Williamson
Lovell, Joseph
Lovett, Robert Williamson
Lower, William Edgar
McBurney, Charles
McClellan, George, 1796–1847
McCosh, Andrew James
McDowell, Ephraim
McGuire, Hunter Holmes
Mann, James
March, Alden
Marcy, Henry Orlando
Martin, Franklin Henry
Martin, Henry Austin
Mastin, Claudius Henry
Matas, Rudolph
Maury, Francis Fontaine
Maynard, Edward
Mayo, Charles Horace
Mayo, William James
Mayo, William Worrell
Mearns, Edgar Alexander
Merrill, James Cushing
Mettauer, John Peter
Mixter, Samuel Jason
Moore, Edward Mott
Moore, James Edward
Moore, Samuel Preston
Mott, Valentine
Mumford, James Gregory
Murphy, John Benjamin
Mussey, Reuben Dimond
Nancrède, Charles Beylard Guérard de
Neill, John
Norris, George Washington
Ochsner, Albert John
O'Reilly, Robert Maitland
Otto, Bodo
Owen, Griffith
Packard, John Hooker
Palmer, James Croxall
Pancoast, Joseph
Park, Roswell
Parker, Willard
Parsons, Usher
Peck, Charles Howard
Physick, Philip Syng
Pilcher, Lewis Stephen
Pilcher, Paul Monroe
Pinkney, Ninian
Post, Wright
Prevost, François Marie
Price, Joseph
Randolph, Jacob
Ransohoff, Joseph
Reid, Mont Rogers
Reid, William Wharry
Richardson, Maurice Howe
Richardson, Tobias Gibson
Robinson, Frederick Byron
Rogers, Stephen
Satterlee, Richard Sherwood
Sayre, Lewis Albert
Sayre, Reginald Hall
Senn, Nicholas
Shrady, George Frederick
Smith, Ashbel
Smith, Nathan, 1762–1829
Smith, Nathan Ryno
Smith, Stephen
Souchon, Edmond
Spalding, Lyman
Spencer, Pitman Clemens
Sternberg, George Miller
Stevens, Alexander Hodgdon
Stimson, Lewis Atterbury
Stitt, Edward Rhodes
Stone, Warren
Taylor, Charles Fayette
Teusler, Rudolf Bolling
Thorek, Max
Tiffany, Louis McLane
Tilton, James
Toland, Hugh Huger
Twitchell, Amos
Van Buren, William Holme
Vance, Ap Morgan

Vander Veer, Albert
Van Hook, Weller
Van Lennep, William Bird
Walter, Albert G.
Warbasse, James Peter
Warren, John
Warren, John Collins, 1778–1856
Warren, John Collins, 1842–1927
Weir, Robert Fulton
White, James William
Whitman, Royal
Willard, De Forest
Williams, Daniel Hale
Wilson, Henry Parke Custis
Wood, James Rushmore
Wood, Thomas
Woodhull, Alfred Alexander
Woodward, Henry
Wyeth, John Allan

SURVEYOR (See also GEODESIST, HYDROGRAPHER)
Applegate, Jesse
Borden, Gail
Burt, William Austin
Clark, Abraham
De Brahm, William Gerard
De Witt, Simeon
Ellicott, Andrew
Fry, Joshua
Holme, Thomas
Hooker, Philip
Hudde, Andries
Hulbert, Edwin James
Jenkins, John, 1728–1785
Jenkins, John, 1751 O.S.–1827
Kilbourne, James
Leeds, Damel
Marshall, Thomas
Mayo, William
Penington, Edward
Porter, Andrew
Strong, Moses McCure

SWIMMING COACH
Kiphuth, Robert John Herman

SWINDLER (See also CRIMINAL)
Means, Gaston Bullock
Musica, Philip Mariano Fausto
Scott, John

SYPHILOLOGIST (See also PHYSICIAN)
Pusey, William Allen

TANK (MILITARY) DESIGNER
Christie, John Walter

TANNER
Cummings, John
Easton, Nicholas
Edwards, William

TARIFF EXPERT
O'Brien, Robert Lincoln

TAVERN KEEPER (See HOTELMAN)

TAX COMMISSIONER
Haugen, Nils Pederson

TAX EXPERT (See also ACCOUNTANT)
Lasser, Jacob Kay
Purdy, Lawson

TAXIDERMIST
Akeley, Carl Ethan
Maynard, Charles Johnson

TAXONOMIST (See also Botanist, ZOOLOGIST)
Gill, Theodore Nicholas
Merrill, Elmer Drew

TEACHER (See also EDUCATOR, PROFESSOR, SCHOLAR)

General
Agnew, David Hayes
Allen, Hervey
Archer, John
Arvin, Newton
Bache, Franklin
Bacon, Alice Mabel
Baermann, Carl
Bailey, Florence Augusta Merriam
Baker, Benjamin Franklin
Barrows, Alice Prentice
Bartlett, Elisha
Barton, William Paul Crillon
Beal, William James
Beck, Johann Heinrich
Blackmur, Richard Palmer
Blodgett, Benjamin Colman
Bradbury, William Batchelder
Brooks, Byron Alden
Brown, Solyman
Bumstead, Harry Andrews
Cobb, Andrew Jackson
Coerne, Louis Adolphe
Coffin, Robert Peter Tristram
Cogswell, Joseph Green
Cole, Chester Cicero
Cooke, Josiah Parsons
Corson, Hiram
Crafts, James Mason
Crane, Thomas Frederick
Dabney, Robert Lewis
Dabney, Virginius
Dannreuther, Gustav
Davis, Noah Knowles
Delano, Jane Arminda
Dennison, Walter
Douglass, David Bates
Doyle, Sarah Elizabeth
Duchesne, Rose Philippine
Dunglison, Robley
Dunning, William Archibald
Durant, Henry
Duveneck, Frank
Eakins, Thomas
Edman, Irwin
Eichbery, Julius
Elson, Louis Charles
Emery, Henry Crosby
Emery, Stephen Albert
Emmons, Ebenezer
Erskine, John
Estabrook, Joseph
Eustis, Henry Lawrence
Everett, Edward
Eytinge, Rose
Fauset, Jessie Redmon
Fay, Edwin Whitefield
Fernald, Charles Henry
Fernow, Bernhard Eduard
Flint, Austin
Folsom, Charles
Francke, Kuno
Frazer, John Fries
Frothingham, Arthur Lincoln
Fulton, Robert Burwell
Gallaudet, Edward Miner
Garman, Charles Edward
Garry, Spokane
Gaston, James McFadden
Gibbs, Josiah Willard
Goessmann, Charles Anthony
Goodrich, Alfred John
Gorgas, Josiah
Gould, Nathaniel Duren
Gould, Robert Simonton
Green, Jacob
Griffes, Charles Tomlinson
Griscom, John
Gross, Samuel David
Gross, Samuel Weissell
Gruening, Emil
Guthrie, Ramon
Hale, Philip Leslie
Hamilton, Edith
Hamlin, Alfred Dwight Foster
Hanchett, Henry Granger
Harrison, Gessner
Harshberger, John William
Haven, Joseph
Henri, Robert
Herbermann, Charles George
Hodge, Archibald Alexander
Hoffman, David
Hoffman, Richard
Holmes, Nathaniel
Holmes, Oliver Wendell
Holyoke, Samuel
Hoppin, James Mason
Houston, William Churchill
Howard, George Elliott
Humphreys, Milton Wylie
Hyde, Charles Cheney
Inglis, Alexander James
Ives, Halsey Cooley
Jackson, George K.
James, Thomas Chalkley
Jameson, Horatio Gates
Jarrell, Randall
Jarvis, Charles H.
Jenks, Jeremiah Whipple
Johnson, Allen
Johnson, Henry
Jordan, David Starr
Joseffy, Rafael
Kaufmann, Walter Arnold
Kay, Edgar Boyd
Kearsley, John
Kelly, Aloysius Oliver Joseph
Kinnersley, Ebenezer
Kirkwood, Daniel
Klein, Bruno Oscar
Klein, Joseph Frederic
Knapp, Seaman Asabel
Knapp, William Ireland
Kneisel, Franz
Knight, Sarah Kemble
Larcom, Lucy
Law, Andrew
Leavenworth, Francis Preserved
Leavitt, Dudley
LeConte, John
Lee, James Melvin
Le Jan, Francis
Lewisohn, Ludwig
Liebling, Emil
Lincoln, John Larkin
Lincoln, Mary Johnson Bailey

Lockwood, Belva Ann Bennett
Locy, William Albert
Lomax, John Taylor
Longfellow, Samuel
Lowell, James Russell
Lowell, Robert Traill Spence, Jr.
McCaw, James Brown
McLain, Emlin
MacDonald, Ronald
Magill, Edward Hicks
Malin, Patrick Murphy
Malter, Henry
Mansfield, Jared
Margolis, Max Leopold
Marshall, Louis
Marzo, Eduardo
Mason, Lowell
Mason, Luther Whiting
Mason, William
Mathews, William
Mathews, William Smythe Babcock
Mechem, Floyd Russell
Mees, Arthur
Meigs, James Aitken
Mell, Patrick Hues
Mielziner, Moses
Miles, George Henry
Miller, Kenneth Hayes
Millington, John
Minor, John Barbee
Minor, Raleigh Colston
Mitchell, Maria
Montgomery, Thomas Harrison
Moore, Charles Herbert
Mortimer, Mary
Muhlenberg, Frederick Augustus
Mulford, Elisha
Nancrède, Paul Joseph Guérard de
Nash, Henry Sylvester
Nelson, Henry Loomis
Newman, Samuel Phillips
Nichols, Ernest Fox
Niemeyer, John Henry
Northen, William Jonathan
Norton, Charles Eliot
Ogilvie, James
Oliver, Henry Kemble
Olmsted, Denison
Onderdonk, Henry
Osgood, George Laurie
Osgood, Howard
Packard, Alpheus Spring
Paine, John Knowles
Palmer, Alonzo Benjamin
Palmer, George Herbert
Parker, James Cutler Dunn
Parker, Richard Green
Parr, Samuel Wilson
Parrington, Vernon Louis
Parrish, Edward
Parrish, Joseph
Parsons, Albert Ross
Paul, Henry Martyn
Payne, William Morton
Peck, Thomas Ephraim
Peck, Tracy
Peckham, George Williams
Pennington, James W. C.
Pepper, William
Perabo, Johann Ernst
Pickett, Albert
Pike, Nicolas
Pitkin, Walter Boughton
Platner, Samuel Ball
Plummer, Mary Wright
Pomeroy, John Norton
Porter, Andrew
Porter, Sarah
Powell, Alma Webster
Powell, Edward Payson
Prang, Mary Amelia Dana Hicks
Prentiss, George Lewis
Price, William Thompson
Proctor, William
Pyle, Howard
Randolph, Sarah Nicholas
Reeve, Tapping
Renwick, James, 1792–1863
Rice, Fenelon Bird
Rice, Nathan Lewis
Richards, Joseph William
Richards, Thomas Addison
Richardson, Charles Francis
Riddle, Matthew Brown
Rivers, William James
Roethke, Theodore Huebner
Rolfe, William James
Root, Frederic Woodman
Root, George Frederick
Royce, Josiah
Rybner, Martin Cornelius
Sadtler, Samuel Philip
Safford, Truman Henry
Salisbury, Edward Elbridge
Sanborn, Katherine Abbott
Sanderson, John
Schofield, Henry
Schradieck, Henry
Schussele, Christian
Sedgwick, William Thompson
Shawn, Edwin Meyers ("Ted")
Sherwood, William Hall
Shippen, William
Short, Charles Wilkins
Sill, Edward Rowland
Small, Albion Woodbury
Smith, James Perrin
Smith, Jeremiah, 1837–1921
Smith, John Augustine
Smith, Lucy Harth
Smith, Nathan Ryno
Soley, James Russell
Southard, Elmer Ernest
Spiering, Theodore
Sprague, Charles Ezra
Sproull, Thomas
Stanford, John
Steele, Daniel
Steiner, Bernard Christian
Sternberg, Constantin Ivanovich, Edler von
Stoddard, John Tappan
Suzzallo, Henry
Tapper, Bertha Feiring
Tarr, Ralph Stockman
Taylor, Creed
Thayer, Amos Madden
Thomas, Amos Russell
Thurber, Charles
Thursby, Emma Cecilia
Tomlins, William Lawrence
Toumey, James William
Toy, Crawford Howell
Treat, Samuel
Tucker, John Randolph, 1823–1897
Turner, Ross Sterling
Tyson, James
Upham, Thomas Cogswell
Van Dyke, Henry
Venable, William Henry
Vethake, Henry
Waddel, Moses
Walker, Timothy, 1802–1856
Warren, Minton
Washburn, Emory
Weidig, Adolf
Weir, John Ferguson
Weir, Robert Walter
Wendell, Barrett
Wentworth, George Albert
Wharton, Francis
Whedon, Daniel Denison
Whelpley, Henry Milton
Whitcomb, Selden Lincoln
White, George
White, Henry Clay
Whitney, Mary Watson
Wiley, Harvey Washington
Williams, Frederick Wells
Williams, George Huntington
Wilmarth, Lemuel Everett
Winchell, Alexander
Winchester, Caleb Thomas
Winship, Albert Edward
Winslow, Hubbard
Wood, Horatio Charles
Woodberry, George Edward
Woolson, Abba Louisa Goold
Wright, Philip Green
Wright, Theodore Lyman
Young, David
Zehn, Bernhard

Of American Literature
Miller, Perry Gilbert Eddy

Of Art
Gardner, Helen
McBride, Henry
Tarbell, Edmund Charles

Of Blind
Allen, Edward Ellis
Anagnos, Michael
Campbell, Francis Joseph
Churchman, William Henry
Holt, Winifred
Russ, John Dennison
Smith, Joel West
Wait, William Bell

Of Cooking
Carson, Juliet

Of Deaf
Clarke, Francis Devereux
Clerc, Laurent
Crouter, Albert Louis Edgerton
Fay, Edward Allen
Fisher, John Dix
Gallaudet, Edward Miner
Gallaudet, Thomas
Gallaudet, Thomas Hopkins
Hubbard, Gardiner Greene
Nitchie, Edward Bartlett
Peet, Harvey Prindle
Peet, Isaac Lewis

Porter, Samuel
Rogers, Harriet Burbank
Of Elocution
Murdock, James Edward
Of Insurance
Huebner, Solomon Stephen
Of Law
Llewellyn, Karl Nickerson
Oliphant, Herman
Of Music
Piston, Walter Hamor
Of Navigation
Daboll, Nathan
Of Piano
Lhévinne, Josef
Samaroff, Olga
Of Theater
Hamilton, Clayton
Of Voice
Liebling, Estelle
TELEGRAPHER (INCLUDING TELEPHONE)
Creighton, Edward
Eckert, Thomas Thompson
Glidden, Charles Jasper
Lefferts, Marshall
Phillips, Walter Polk
Stager, Anson
Vail, Alfred
Watson, Thomas Augustus
TELEPHONE EXECUTIVE
Barnard, Chester Irving
Craig, Cleo Frank
TELESCOPE MAKER
Porter, Russell Williams
TELEVISION ANNOUNCER
Grauer, Benjamin Franklin ("Ben")
TELEVISION BROADCASTING EXECUTIVE
Trammell, Niles
TELEVISION COMMENTATOR
Murrow, Edward (Egbert) Roscoe
TELEVISION JOURNALIST
Huntley, Chester ("Chet") Robert
TELEVISION NARRATOR
Serling, Rodman Edward ("Rod")
TELEVISION PERSONALITY
Arquette, Clifford
Considine, Robert ("Bob") Bernard
Evans, Bergen Baldwin
Kilgallen, Dorothy Mae
Kovacs, Ernie
Marx, Julius Henry ("Groucho")
Nelson, Oswald George ("Ozzie")
Sheen, Fulton John
Sullivan, Edward Vincent ("Ed")
Susann, Jacqueline
TELEVISION PRODUCER
Serling, Rodman Edward ("Rod")
Sherman, Allan
Todman, William Selden ("Bill")
TELEVISION WRITER
Serling, Rodman Edward ("Rod")
TEMPERANCE REFORMER (See also PROHIBITIONIST, REFORMER)
Boole, Ella Alexander
Cannon, James
Chafin, Eugene Wilder
Cherrington, Ernest Hurst
Dow, Neal
Dyott, Thomas W.
Foster, Judith Ellen Horton
Gough, John Bartholomew
Hunt, Mary Hannah Hanchett
Leavitt, Mary Greenleaf Clement
Lewis, Dioclesian
Minor, Lucian
Murphy, Francis
Nation, Carry Amelia Moore
Sargent, Lucius Manlius
Stearns, John Newton
Stewart, Eliza Daniel
TENNIS PLAYER (See also ATHLETE)
Connolly, Maureen Catherine
Larned, William Augustus
McLoughlin, Maurice Evans
Mallory, Anna Margrethe ("Molla") Bjurstedt
Richards, Vincent
Sears, Richard Dudley
Shields, Francis Xavier ("Frank")
Tilden, William Tatem ("Big Bill")
Wightman, Hazel Virginia Hotchkiss
TERRITORIAL DELEGATE (See also CONGRESSMAN, SENATOR)
Clark, Daniel
Kalanianaole, Jonah Kuhio
Pettigrew, Richard Franklin
Poindexter, George
Pope, Nathaniel
Poston, Charles Debrill
Sibley, Henry Hastings
TERRITORIAL GOVERNOR (see GOVERNOR, TERRITORIAL)
TEST PILOT
Royce, Ralph
TEXTILE EXECUTIVE
Hodges, Luther Hartwell
Jordan, Benjamin Everett
THEATER ANNALIST
Mantle, (Robert) Burns
THEATER CRITIC
Clurman, Harold Edgar
THEATER EXECUTIVE
Skouras, George Panagiotes
THEATER OPERATOR
Rothafel, Samuel Lionel
THEATER OWNER
Keith, Benjamin Franklin
Loew, Marcus
Proctor, Frederick Francis
THEATRE GUILD DIRECTOR
Helburn, Theresa
THEATRICAL AGENT
Marbury, Elisabeth
Marx, Herbert ("Zeppo")
Marx, Milton ("Gummo")
THEATRICAL DESIGNER
Geddes, Norman Bel
Jones, Robert Edmond
Mielziner, Jo
Tchelitchew, Pavel
Ulmer, Edgar Georg
Urban, Joseph
THEATRICAL DIRECTOR (See also DIRECTOR)
Carroll, Earl
Cowl, Jane
De Sylva, George Gard "Buddy"
Digges, Dudley
Fiske, Harrison Grey
Guthrie, Sir Tyrone
Harris, Jed
Howard, Leslie
Jones, Robert Edmond
Kaufman, George S.
Lunt, Alfred David, Jr.
McClintic, Guthrie
Seymour, William
Shumlin, Herman Elliott
Smith, Winchell
Webster, Margaret ("Peggy")
Woolley, Edgar Montillion ("Monty")
THEATRICAL MANAGER (See also IMPRESARIO)
Abbey, Henry Eugene
Albee, Edward Franklin
Ames, Winthrop
Arden, Edwin Hunter Pendleton
Baker, Benjamin A.
Bateman, Sidney Frances Cowell
Beck, Martin
Bernard, John
Blake, William Rufus
Brady, William Aloysius
Buchanan, William Insco
Campbell, Bartley
Clarke, John Sleeper
Cooper, Thomas Abthorpe
Cornell, Katharine
Davis, John
Dunlap, William
Erlanger, Abraham Lincoln
Fiske, Stephen Ryder
Fleming, William Maybury
Ford, John Thomson
Fox, George Washington Lafayette
Frohman, Charles
Frohman, Daniel
Hallam, Lewis
Hamblin, Thomas Sowerby
Hammerstein, Oscar
Harrison, Gabriel
Haverly, Christopher
Henry, John, 1746–1794
Hodgkinson, John
Hurok, Solomon Isaievitch
Keith, Benjamin Franklin
Klaw, Marc
Lewis, Arthur
Logan, Cornelius Ambrosius
Ludlow, Noah Miller
McVicker, James Hubert
Merry, Ann Brunton
Miller, Henry
Mitchell, William, 1798–1856
Niblo, William
Palmer, Albert Marshman

Pastor, Antonio
Powell, Snelling
Pray, Isaac Clark
Presbrey, Eugene Wiley
Price, Stephen
Proctor, Frederick Francis
Proctor, Joseph
Rankin, McKee
Richings, Peter
Seymour, William
Simpson, Edmund Shaw
Smith, Solomon Franklin
Thorne, Charles Robert
Tyler, George Crouse
Warren, William, 1767–1832
Wemyss, Francis Courtney
Wheatley, William
Wignell, Thomas
Wikoff, Henry
Wood, William Burke
THEATRICAL PRODUCER (See also PRODUCER)
Bloomgarden, Kermit
Harris, Jed
Hayward, Leland
Todd, Mike
THEOLOGIAN (See also RELIGIOUS LEADER)
Apple, Thomas Gilmore
Appleton, Jesse
Beckwith, Clarence Augustine
Bellamy, Joseph
Boisen, Anton Theophilus
Bouquillon, Thomas Joseph
Brown, William Adams
Bruté de Rémur, Simon William Gabriel
Bushnell, Horace
Chambers, Talbot Wilson
Cheever, Henry Theodore
Clarke, William Newton
Coit, Thomas Winthrop
Colton, Walter
Corcoran, James Andrew
Curtis, Olin Alfred
Curtiss, Samuel Ives
Dabney, Robert Lewis
David, John Baptist Mary
Dempster, John
Dodge, Ebenezer
Du Bose, William Porcher
Edwards, Jonathan, 1703–1758
Edwards, Jonathan, 1745–1801
Emmons, Nathanael
Erdman, Charles Rosenbury
Evans, Hugh Davey
Everett, Charles Carroll
Fenn, William Wallace
Foster, Frank Hugh
Fritschel, Conrad Sigmund
Fritschel, Gottfried Leonhard Wilhelm
Gerhart, Emanuel Vogel
Gillis, James Martin
Girardeau, John Lafayette
Gräbner, August Lawrence
Hall, Charles Cuthbert
Harris, Samuel
Hart, Samuel
Herberg, Will
Heschel, Abraham Joshua
Hodge, Charles
Hoenecke, Gustav Adolf Felix Theodor
Hopkins, Mark
Hopkins, Samuel, 1721–1803
Hoye, Elling
Huidekoper, Frederic
Huidekoper, Harm Jan
Jacobs, Henry Eyster
Johnson, Elias Henry
Johnson, Erik Kristian
King, Henry Churchill
Knox, George William
Krauth, Charles Porterfield
Ladd, George Trumbull
Little, Charles Joseph
Lord, David Nevins
McCaffrey, John
Machen, John Gresham
Macintosh, Douglas Clyde
Mathews, Shailer
Monis, Judah
Moore, George Foot
Nevin, John Williamson
Niebuhr, Helmut Richard
Niebuhr, Karl Paul Reinhold ("Reinie")
Niles, Nathaniel, 1741–1828
Oftedal, Sven
Park, Edwards Amasa
Parker, Theodore
Patton, Francis Landey
Pieper, Franz August Otto
Prince, Thomas
Raymond, Miner
Richard, James William
Ridgaway, Henry Bascom
Ropes, James Hardy
Schmidt, Friedrich August
Schmucker, Samuel Simon
Seyffarth, Gustavus
Shedd, William Greenough Thayer
Smith, Gerald Birney
Smith, Henry Boynton
Smyth, Newman
Sperry, Willard Learoyd
Stearns, Oliver
Stevens, George Barker
Strong, Augustus Hopkins
Stuckenberg, John Henry Wilbrandt
Sverdrup, Georg
Talmage, James Edward
Taylor, Nathaniel William
Thacher, Peter
Thacher, Samuel Cooper
Tillich, Paul
Tyler, Bennet
Valentine, Milton
Walther, Carl Ferdinand Wilhelm
Watson, Charles Roger
Weidner, Revere Franklin
Weigel, Gustave
Wigglesworth, Edward, 1693–1765
Wigglesworth, Edward, 1732–1794
Woodbridge, Samuel Merrill
THEOSOPHIST (See also RELIGIOUS LEADER)
Judge, William Quan
Tingley, Katherine Augusta Westcott
Warrington, Albert Powell
TOBACCONIST
Ginter, Lewis
TOOL BUILDER
Hartness, James
TOPOGRAPHER (See also CARTOGRAPHER, MAPMAKER)
Ogden, Herbert Gouverneur
TOPOGRAPHICAL ENGINEER (See ENGINEER, TOPOGRAPHICAL)
TOXICOLOGIST (See also PHYSICIAN)
Henderson, Yandell
Reese, John James
Underhill, Franklin Pell
Witthaus, Rudolph August
Wormley, Theodore George
TRACK AND FIELD COACH
Cromwell, Dean Bartlett
TRACK ATHLETE
Prefontaine, Steve Roland ("Pre")
TRADER (See also FUR TRADER, TRAPPER)
Allerton, Isaac
Becknell, William
Campau, Joseph
Chouteau, René Auguste
Davenport, George
Glenn, Hugh
Gratiot, Charles
Gregg, Josiah
Hamilton, William Thomas
Harrison, James
Hayes, William Henry
Hubbell, John Lorenzo
Ingraham, Joseph
James, Thomas
Johnson, Levi
Kendrick, John
Laclede, Pierre
Le Sueur, Pierre
Magoffin, James Wiley
Morton, Thomas
Nelson, John
Nolan, Philip
O'Fallon, Benjamin
Oldham, John
Pollock, Oliver
Pryor, Nathaniel
Pynchon, William
Robidou, Antoine
St. Vrain, Ceran de Hault de Lassus de
Smith, Jedediah Strong
Vetch, Samuel
Waldo, David
Wyeth, Nathaniel Jarvis
TRADER (GRAIN) (See also SPECULATOR)
Armour, Philip Danforth
Bacon, Edward Payson
Hutchinson, Benjamin Peters
TRADER (INDIAN)
Adair, James
Byrd, William
Croghan, George
Harris, John
Lorimier, Pierre Louis
McClellan, Robert

Menard, Michel Branamour
Panton, William
Rice, Henry Mower
Trent, William
Truteau, Jean Baptiste
TRADE UNIONIST
Sullivan, James William
Younger, Maud
TRADE UNION LEADER
Hoffa, James Riddle ("Jimmy")
TRAFFIC REGULATION EXPERT
Eno, William Phelps
TRAITOR
Arnold, Benedict
Church, Benjamin
TRANSCENDENTALIST (See also RELIGIOUS LEADER)
Hedge, Frederic Henry
Thoreau, Henry David
Very, Jones
TRANSLATOR (See also LINGUIST)
Anderson, Henry Tompkins
Bingham, Hiram
Booth, Mary Louise
Conant, Hannah O'Brien Chaplin
Conant, Thomas Jefferson
Cook, Martha Elizabeth Duncan Walker
Crawford, John Martin
Dole, Nathan Haskell
Ferguson, Elizabeth Graeme
George, Grace
Greene, Nathaniel
Hadas, Moses
Hapgood, Isabel Florence
Hedge, Frederic Henry
Hempel, Charles Julius
Humphries, George Rolfe
Johnson, Henry
Kaufmann, Walter Arnold
Kroeger, Adolph Ernst
Lenker, John Nicholas
Lennox, Charlotte Ramsay
Leonard, William Ellery
Mayhew, Experience
Montgomery, George Washington
Moore, Annie Aubertine Woodward
O'Brien, Justin
Parsons, Thomas William
Payne, William Morton
Phillips, Henry
Preston, Harriet Waters
Robinson, Thérèse Albertine Louise von Jakob
Rupp, Israel Daniel
Schereschewsky, Samuel Isaac Joseph
Taylor, Bayard
Worcester, Samuel Austin
TRANSPORTATION EXECUTIVE
Hertz, John Daniel
Hill, Arthur Middleton
TRANSPORTER (See EXPRESSMAN, MESSENGER, MAIL-RUNNER)
TRAPPER (See also FUR TRADER, TRADER)
Baker, James
Carson, Christopher ("Kit")
Clyman, James
Colter, John
Fitzpatrick, Thomas
Glass, Hugh
Hamilton, William Thomas
James, Thomas
Laramie, Jacques
Leonard, Zenas
Meek, Joseph L.
Newell, Robert
Pattie, James Ohio
Robidou, Antoine
Russell, Osborne
Walker, Joseph Reddeford
Williams, William Sherley
Wolfskill, William
Wootton, Richens Lacy
Young, Ewing
TRAVELER (See also ADVENTURER, EXPLORER)
Ballou, Maturin Murray
Bartram, William
Browne, John Ross
Carpenter, Frank George
Carver, Jonathan
Catesby, Mark
Cuming, Fortescue
Curtis, William Eleroy
Estes, Dana
Farnham, Thomas Jefferson
Flandrau, Charles Macomb
Josselyn, John
Knox, Thomas Wallace
Lahontan, Louis-Armand de Lom D'Arce, Baron de
Lawson, John
Lederer, John
Melish, John
Michaux, François André
Möllhausen, Heinrich Baldwin
Pory, John
Rowland, Henry Cottrell
Royall, Anne Newport
Scattergood, Thomas
Schöpf, Johann David
Scidmore, Eliza Ruhamah
Stephens, John Lloyd
Taylor, Bayard
Vincent, Frank
Wislizenus, Frederick Adolph
TREASURER OF UNITED STATES (See also COMPTROLLER OF CURRENCY, SECRETARY OF TREASURY)
Hillegas, Michael
Priest, Ivy Maude Baker
Spinner, Francis Elias
TREE-CARE EXPERT
Bartlett, Francis Alonzo
TREE SURGEON
Davey, John
TROMBONIST
Dorsey, Thomas Francis ("Tommy")
Teagarden, Weldon Leo ("Jack")
TRUMPETER
Elman, Harry ("Ziggy")
Monroe, Vaughn Wilton
Page, Oran Thaddeus ("Lips")
TUBERCULOSIS RESEARCHER
Baldwin, Edward Robinson
TURFMAN (See also ATHLETE, BREEDER OF RACEHORSES, HORSE BREEDER, HORSE TRAINER, HORSEMAN, RACE HORSE OWNER)
Bonner, Robert
De Lancey, James, 1732–1800
Geers, Edward Franklin
Hildreth, Samuel Clay
Johnson, William Ransom
Keene, James Robert
TYPE DESIGNER
Dwiggins, William Addison
Goudy, Frederic William
TYPEFOUNDER (See also IRONFOUNDER)
Bruce, George
Buell, Abel
Mappa, Adam Gerard
TYPOGRAPHER
McMurtrie, Douglas Crawford
TYPOGRAPHIC DESIGNER
Cooper, Oswald Bruce

UNDERWORLD FIGURE (See also CRIMINAL, GANGSTER, ORGANIZED CRIME LEADER, RACKETEER)
Genovese, Vito
Guzik, Jack
Luchese, Thomas
UNION ACTIVIST
Silkwood, Karen Gay
UNION OFFICIAL
Besse, Arthur Lyman
Carter, William Samuel
Stone, Warren Sanford
UNION ORGANIZER
Martin, Warren Homer
Steuben, John
Thomas, Roland Jay
Whitfield, Owen
UNION REPRESENTATIVE
Dodd, Bella Visono
UNITED NATIONS AMBASSADOR
Austin, Warren Robinson
Stevenson, Adlai Ewing, II
UNITED NATIONS DIPLOMAT
Roosevelt, (Anna) Eleanor
UNITED NATIONS OFFICIAL
Pate, Maurice
UNITED PRESS ASSOCIATIONS (UP) PRESIDENT
Bickel, Karl August
UNIVERSITY ADMINISTRATOR
Birge, Edward Asahel
Case, Shirley Jackson
Day, George Parmly
Simmons, James Stevens
Sydnor, Charles Sackett
UNIVERSITY PRESIDENT (See COLLEGE PRESIDENT)
UROLOGIST (See also PHYSICIAN)
Pilcher, Paul Monroe
Timberlake, Gideon
Young, Hugh Hampton
UTILITIES EXECUTIVE
McKinley, William Brown
Williams, Harrison Charles

VACCINATOR (See also PHYSICIAN)
Martin, Henry Austin
Waterhouse, Benjamin
VAGRANT
Pratt, Daniel, 1809–1887
VAUDEVILLE PERFORMER
Dale, Charles Marks
Marx, Herbert ("Zeppo")
Marx, Julius Henry ("Groucho")
Marx, Milton ("Gummo")
VENTRILOQUIST (See also ENTERTAINER)
Bergen, Edgar
Vattemare, Nicholas Marie Alexandre
VETERINARIAN (See also PHYSICIAN)
Bemis, Harold Edward
Kelser, Raymond Alexander
Moore, Veranus Alva
Pearson, Leonard
Salmon, Daniel Elmer
VICE-PRESIDENT OF CONFEDERACY
Stephens, Alexander Hamilton
VICE-PRESIDENT OF UNITED STATES
Adams, John
Arthur, Chester Alan
Barkley, Alben William
Breckinridge, John Cabell
Burr, Aaron
Calhoun, John Caldwell
Clinton, George
Colfax, Schuyler
Coolidge, Calvin
Curtis, Charles
Dallas, George Mifflin
Dawes, Charles Gates
Fairbanks, Charles Warren
Fillmore, Millard
Garner, John Nance
Gerry, Elbridge
Hamlin, Hannibal
Hendricks, Thomas Andrews
Hobart, Garret Augustus
Humphrey, Hubert Horatio, Jr.
Jefferson, Thomas
Johnson, Andrew
Johnson, Richard Mentor
King, William Rufus Devane
Marshall, Thomas Riley
Morton, Levi Parsons
Rockefeller, Nelson Aldrich
Roosevelt, Theodore
Sherman, James Schoolcraft
Stevenson, Adlai Ewing
Tompkins, Daniel D.
Tyler, John
Van Buren, Martin
Wallace, Henry Agard
Wheeler, William Almon
Wilson, Henry
VIGILANTE (See also JAYHAWKER, OUTLAW)
Langford, Nathaniel Pitt
VINTNER
Petri, Angelo
VIOLINCELLIST
Piatigorsky, Gregor
VIOLINIST
Beck, Johann Heinrich
Bristow, George Frederick
Damrosch, Leopold
Dannreuther, Gustav
Eichburg, Julius
Elman, Mischa
Hill, Ureli Corelli
Kneisel, Franz
Kreisler, Fritz
Listemann, Bernhard
Loeffler, Charles Martin
Lombardo, Gaetano Albert ("Guy")
Mannes, David
Mollenhauer, Emil
Musin, Ovide
Powell, Maud
Saslavsky, Alexander
Scheel, Fritz
Schradieck, Henry
Spalding, Albert
Spiering, Theodore
Stoessel, Albert Frederic
Urso, Camilla
Verbrugghen, Henri
White, Clarence Cameron
VIROLOGIST
Rivers, Thomas Milton
Stanley, Wendell Meredith
VITICULTURIST (See also AGRICULTURIST)
Adlum, John
Dufour, John James
Husmann, George
Munson, Thomas Volney
VOCATIONAL GUIDANCE PIONEER
Hatcher, Orie Latham
VOICE TEACHER
Tourel, Jennie
VOLCANOLOGIST
Jaggar, Thomas Augustus, Jr.

WALKER (See also ATHLETE)
O'Leary, Daniel
Weston, Edward Payson
WAR CORRESPONDENT (See also FOREIGN CORRESPONDENT, JOURNALIST, NEWSPAPER CORRESPONDENT, NEWSPAPER REPORTER, PHOTOJOURNALIST)
Chapelle, Dickey
Comfort, Will Levington
Fall, Bernard B.
Gibbons, Floyd
Hare, James H.
Higgins, Marguerite
Pyle, Ernest Taylor
Reynolds, Quentin James
Whitney, Caspar
WAR HERO (See also SOLDIER)
Murphy, Audie Leon
York, Alvin Cullum
WARTIME AIDE TO GENERAL EISENHOWER
Summersby, Kathleen Helen ("Kay")
WARTIME ADMINISTRATOR
Jones, John Marvin
WELFARE ADMINISTRATOR
Hodson, William
WELFARE PLANNER
Dennison, Henry Sturgis
WELFARE WORKER (See also SOCIAL WORKER)
Billikopf, Jacob
Folks, Homer
Moskowitz, Belle Lindner Israels
WESTERN MOVIE ACTOR
Brown, Johnny Mack
Ritter, Woodward Maurice ("Tex")
WHALING CAPTAIN (See also SEA CAPTAIN)
Tyson, George Emory
WILD ANIMAL TRAINER
Beatty, Clyde Raymond
WILDLIFE CONSERVATIONIST
Hornaday, William Temple
WIT (See also COMEDIAN, COMEDIENNE, HUMORIST, SATIRIST)
Depew, Chauncey Mitchell
Herford, Oliver Brooke
Hughes, Christopher
WITCHCRAFT VICTIM
Hibbins, Ann
WOMEN'S EDUCATOR
Bieber, Margarete
WOMEN'S FOREIGN MISSIONS LEADER
Peabody, Lucy Whitehead
WOMEN'S RIGHTS ACTIVIST
Paul, Alice
Schneiderman, Rose
WOOD CARVER (See also CRAFTSMAN)
Kirchmayer, John
McIntire, Samuel
Morse, Freeman Harlow
WRESTLER
Leavitt, Frank Simmons ("Man Mountain Dean")
Lewis, Ed ("Strangler")
Muldoon, William
WRITER (NOTE: *THE FOLLOWING ARE CLASSIFIED UNDER WRITERS BECAUSE THE SPECIFIC FIELD IN WHICH THEY WROTE WAS SO DESIGNATED AT HEAD OF THE ARTICLE. FOR COMPLETE LIST OF WRITERS SEE, IN ADDITION, AUTHOR, BIOGRAPHER, DIARIST, DRAMATIST, ESSAYIST, HISTORIAN, JOURNALIST, LITERATEUR*)
Abbott, Eleanor Hallowell (short story)
Adamic, Louis
Adams, Abigail (letter)
Adams, Cyrus Cornelius (geographical)
Adams, Frank Ramsay (screen)
Adams, Hannah (history)
Adams, William Taylor (juvenile)
Affleck, Thomas (agricultural)
Agee, James Rufus (screen)
Akins, Zoë (screen)
Aldrich, Bess Genevra Streeter (short story)
Aldrich, Thomas Bailey (story)
Alger, Horatio (juvenile)
Allen, James Lane (short story)
Allen, Lewis Falley (agricultural)
Allinson, Anne Crosby Emery

Ames, James Barr (legal)
Ammen, Daniel (naval)
Anderson, Margaret Carolyn (magazine)
Angell, Joseph Kinnicutt (legal)
Anthony, Katharine Susan
Arlen, Michael (short story)
Armstrong, George Dod (controversial)
Ascoli, Max
Bailey, Florence Augusta Merriam
Bailey, (Irene) Temple (short story)
Baird, Henry Carey (economics)
Bard, Samuel (midwifery)
Barrett, Benjamin Fiske (religious)
Beatty, Adam (agricultural)
Beer, Thomas (short story)
Bemelmans, Ludwig
Benchley, Robert Charles
Benét, Stephen Vincent (short story)
Bennett, Edmund Hatch (legal)
Benson, Sally (short story)
Bigelow, Melville Madison (legal)
Bingham, Caleb (textbook)
Blair, Emily Newell
Blakeslee, Howard Walter (science)
Blatch, Harriot Eaton Stanton (woman suffrage, peace)
Bogan, Louise Marie (short story)
Bolles, Frank (nature)
Bouvier, John (legal)
Bowles, Jane Auer
Bradford, Roark Whitney Wickliffe (short story)
Brickell, Henry Herschel
Brisbane, Arthur
Brown, John Mason, Jr.
Browne, Daniel Jay (agricultural)
Browne, Irving (legal)
Browning, Tod
Buck, Pearl Comfort Sydenstricker
Burdick, Eugene Leonard
Burdick, Francis Marion (legal)
Burgess, Thornton Waldo (juvenile)
Buttrick, George Arthur (religious)
Cabell, James Branch (essayist)
Callender, James Thomson (political)
Calverton, Victor Francis
Campbell, William Edward March (short story)
Cannon, James Thomas (columnist)
Capp, Al
Carr, John Dickson (mystery fiction)
Carrington, Elaine Stern (magazine, radio script)
Carson, Rachel Louise (nature)
Catchings, Waddill
Cayton, Horace Roscoe
Chambers, Whittaker
Chaplin, Charles Spencer ("Charlie")
Chapman, John Jay (essayist)
Checkley, John (controversial)
Clark, Walter Van Tilburg (short story)
Clarke, Rebecca Sophia (juvenile)
Cocke, Philip St. George (agricultural)
Cohen, Octavus Roy (screen)
Cohn, Alfred A. (magazine, screen)
Colburn, Dana Pond (textbook)
Coleman, Lyman (religious)
Colman, Henry (agricultural)
Colum, Padraic (children's books)
Considine, Robert ("Bob") Bernard (columnist)
Cooke, Philip Pendleton (story)
Cooke, Rose Terry (story)
Cozzens, James Gould
Cullen, Countée Porter (essayist)
Da Ponte, Lorenzo (librettist)
Davenport, Russell Wheeler
Davis, Elmer Holmes (magazine)
Davis, Watson (science)
Deane, Samuel (agricultural)
Dercum, Francis Xavier (medical)
Dickson, David (agricultural)
Dobie, J(ames) Frank
Drinkwater, Jennie Maria (juvenile)
Dunglison, Robley (medical)
Eastman, Max Forrester
Edman, Irwin (philosophy)
Elliott, Charles Burke (legal)
Epstein, Philip G. (screen)
Faulkner (Falkner), William Cuthbert (short story)
Fauset, Jessie Redmon
Ferguson, Elizabeth Graeme (letter)
Fischer, Louis
Fischer, Ruth
Flandrau, Charles Macomb (essayist)
Flanner, Janet
Fletcher, Alice Cunningham (Indian music)
Fletcher, Horace (nutrition)
Frank, Waldo David
Gág, Wanda (Hazel) (juvenile)
Gale, Benjamin (political)
Gardner, Erle Stanley (detective fiction)
Gaylord, Willis (agricultural)
Genung, John Franklin (religious)
Gilman, Charlotte Perkins Stetson
Gold, Michael
Goldbeck, Robert (music)
Gonzales, Ambrose Elliott (Negro dialect story)
Gouge, William M. (financial)
Grant, Jane Cole (free-lance)
Greene, Samuel Stillman (textbook)
Greenleaf, Benjamin (mathematical textbook)
Guest, Edgar Albert (popular verse)
Gulick, John Thomas (evolution)
Hall, Bolton
Halsman, Philippe
Hammett, Samuel Dashiell (detective fiction)
Hawes, Charles Boardman (adventure)
Hawks, Howard Winchester
Hazard, Rowland Gibson (philosophy)
Headley, Phineas Camp (biography)
Heard, Franklin Fiske (legal)
Heaton, John Langdon (editorial)
Hecht, Ben (screen)
Held, John, Jr.
Hemingway, Ernest Miller (short story)
Hening, William Waller (legal)
Henshall, James Alexander (angling)
Herbert, Frederick Hugh (screen)
Hergesheimer, Joseph (short story)
High, Stanley Hoflund (magazine)
Hilliard, Francis (legal)
Hindus, Maurice Gerschon
Hobart, Alice Nourse Tisdale
Hoffman, Frederick Ludwig
Hoffmann, Francis Arnold (agricultural)
Horner, William Edmonds (medical)
Huebner, Solomon Stephen
Hunter, Robert
Hutchinson, Paul (religious subjects)
Huxley, Aldous Leonard
Jackson, Charles Reginald (short story)
Jackson, Joseph Henry
Jackson, Shirley Hardie (short story)
James, George Wharton (Southwest)
James, Henry, 1811–1882 (religious)
Jarrell, Randall (essayist)
Jenks, George Charles (dime novel)
Johnson, Joseph French (financial)
Johnson, Nunnally Hunter (screen)
Johnson, Owen McMahon (short story)
Johnston, Annie Fellows (juvenile)
Jones, Leonard Augustus (legal)
Judson, Frederick Newton (legal)

Kaufman, George S. (screen)
Kellogg, Edward (commercial reform)
Kent, James (legal)
Kerouac, Jack (essayist)
Kerr, Sophie (short story)
Keyes, Frances Parkinson
Klippart, John Hancock (agricultural)
Kracauer, Siegfried
Kronenberger, Louis, Jr.
Krutch, Joseph Wood
Lahontan, Louis-Armand de Lom D'Arce, Baron de (travel)
Laimbeer, Nathalie Schenck (financial)
Lait, Jacquin Leonard Jack) (newspaper)
Langdell, Christopher Columbus (legal)
Lathrop, Harriett Mulford Stone (juvenile)
Lawrence, William Beach (legal)
Lawson, John Howard (screen)
Leaf, Wilbur Munro (children's books)
Lease, Mary Elizabeth Clyens
Lee, Gypsy Rose
Lee, Manfred B.
Ley, Willy
Liggett, Walter William
Linton, Ralph (popular)
Livermore, Samuel, 1786–1833 (legal)
Long, Joseph Ragland (legal)
Lowell, John, 1769–1840 (political)
Lowell, Robert Traill Spence, Jr.
McClintock, James Harvey (historical)
McCord, Louisa Susanna Cheves (Antebellum South)
McCullers, Carson (short story)
MacDowell, Katherine Sherwood Bonner (short story)
McFee, William (essayist, novelist)
MacKaye, Percy Wallace (essayist)
Mackey, Albert Gallatin (Masonic)
McNulty, John Augustine (short story)
McWilliams, Carey
Magruder, Julia (short story)
Mankiewicz, Herman Jacob (screen)
Martin, Edward Sandford (essayist)
Mathews, William Smythe Babcock (music)
Merton, Thomas (religious)
Metalious, Grace
Meyer, Agnes Elizabeth Ernst
Meyer, Annie Nathan
Meyer, Frank Straus
Millay, Edna St. Vincent (poetry)
Millington, John (scientific)
Millis, Walter
Minor, John Barbee (legal)
Montgomery, David Henry (textbook)
Moore, Charles Herbert (fine arts)
Moore, John Weeks (music)
Morley, Christopher Darlington (essayist)
Morris, Edmund (agricultural)
Morris, Robert, 1818–1888 (Masonic)
Morton, James St. Clair (engineering)
Moulton, Ellen Louise Chandler (juvenile)
Mulford, Clarence Edward (magazine)
Murfree, Mary Noailles (short story)
Musmanno, Michael Angelo
Nabokov, Nicolas
Nabokov, Vladimir Vladimirovich
Nichols, Dudley (screen)
Nin, Anasïs
Nitchie, Edward Bartlett (lip-reading)
O'Connor, Mary Flannery (short story)
Odets, Clifford (screen)
O'Hara, John Henry (short story)
Olney, Jesse (textbook)
Oursler, (Charles) Fulton
Paine, Albert Bigelow (light fiction)
Palmer, Alonzo Benjamin (medical)
Parker, Dorothy Rothschild (short story)
Parker, Henry Taylor (essayist)
Parker, Richard Green (textbook)
Peabody, Francis Greenwood (religious thought)
Pearson, Edmund Lester (crime stories)
Peary, Josephine Diebitsch
Peattie, Donald Culross (magazine)
Periam, Jonathan (agricultural)
Perkins, Samuel Elliott (legal)
Perry, Nora (juvenile)
Peterkin, Julia Mood (short story)
Peters, John Charles (medical)
Philips, Martin Wilson (agricultural)
Phillips, Thomas Wharton (religious)
Pitkin, Walter Boughton
Poe, Edgar Allan (short story)
Pomeroy, John Norton (legal)
Porter, Gene Stratton (nature)
Porter, Katherine Anne (short story)
Porter, William Sydney (short story)
Post, Augustus
Post, Melville Davisson (short story)
Powell, John Benjamin
Pratt, Eliza Anna Farman (juvenile)
Prentiss, Elizabeth Payson (juvenile)
Priestley, Joseph (religious)
Prince, William Robert (agricultural)
Proctor, Lucien Brock (legal)
Prouty, Olive Higgins
Pulitzer, Margaret Leech
Pusey, Caleb (Quaker controversial)
Quinan, John Russell (medical)
Ralph, James (political)
Rauschenbusch, Walter (religious)
Ravenel, Henry William (agricultural)
Rawle, William Henry (legal)
Redfield, Amasa Angell (legal)
Reed, Elizabeth Armstrong (Oriental literature)
Reed, Sampson (Swedenborgian)
Reeve, Tapping (legal)
Reid, Thomas Mayne (juvenile)
Reik, Theodor (psychology)
Repplier, Agnes
Richter, Conrad Michael
Rinehart, Mary Roberts (mystery story)
Ritter, Frédéric Louis (music)
Roane, Spencer (political)
Rohlfs, Anna Katharine Green (detective stories)
Rombauer, Irma Louise (cookbook)
Rorer, David
Rossen, Robert (screen)
Roulston, Marjorie Hillis
Rumsey, William (legal)
Runyon, Damon (short story)
Sayles, John (legal)
Schary, Dore (screen)
Schofield, Henry (legal)
Schorer, Mark
Schwartz, Delmore David (poetry)
Schwimmer, Rosika
Scudder, (Julia) Vida Dutton
Sergeant, Thomas (legal)
Seton, Ernest Thompson (nature)
Shawn, Edwin Meyers ("Ted")
Sherman, Allan (comedy)
Sherwood, Robert Emmet (dramatist)
Short, Luke (novelist)
Shub, Abraham David (Yiddish)
Smith, George Henry (juvenile)
Smith, Lillian Eugenia
Smith, Lloyd Logan Pearsall (essayist)
Soley, James Russell (naval)
Spewack, Samuel (screen)
Spooner, Lysander (political)
Sprague, Charles Ezra (accountancy)
Stafford, Jean (short story)
Stallings, Laurence Tucker
Stanton, Richard Henry (legal)
Stark, Louis (editorial)

Steele, Joel Dorman (textbook)
Steele, Wilbur Daniel
Steinbeck, John Ernst, Jr.
Stewart, Donald Ogden (screen)
Stilwell, Silas Moore (financial)
Stockton, Frank Richard (story)
Stoddard, John Fair (textbook)
Stratemeyer, Edward (juvenile)
Stribling, Thomas Sigismund (short story)
Strunsky, Simeon (essayist)
Swan, Joseph Rockwell (legal)
Talbot, Francis Xavier
Tanner, Edward Everett, III ("Patrick Dennis") (humor)
Tappan, Eva March (juvenile)
Tarbell, Ida Minerva
Taylor, Charles Alonzo
Taylor, John (political)
Terhune, Mary Virginia Hawes (household management)
Thomson, John (political)
Thurber, James Grover (humor)
Tiedeman, Christopher Gustavus (legal)
Toklas, Alice Babette
Towler, John (photography)
Trumbo, Dalton (screen)
Tyler, Ransom Hubert (legal)
Ulmer, Edgar Georg (screen)
Upshaw, William David
Viereck, George Sylvester (magazine, newspaper)
Wahl, William Henry (science)
Wait, William (legal)
Walker, James Barr (religious)
Walker, Timothy, 1802–1856 (legal)
Wallace, Henry (agricultural)
Ward, Charles Henshaw
Warner, Anna Bartlett (juvenile)
Warner, Anne Richmond (fiction)
Watson, Henry Clay (editorial, historical, juvenile)
Watson, James Madison (textbook)
Wentworth, George Albert (mathematics textbooks)
Will, Allen Sinclair (biography)
Willard, Josiah Flint (vagrancy, criminology)
Williams, Ben Ames (short story)
Williams, Catharine Read Arnold (biography)
Wood, Peggy
Wood, Sarah Sayward Barrell Keating (fiction)
Wright, Willard Huntington (detective fiction)
Youmans, William Jay (scientific)
Zanuck, Darryl Francis (screen)
Zevin, Israel Joseph (story)

YACHT DESIGNER (See also SHIPBUILDER)
Burgess, Edward
Herreshoff, John Brown
Lawley, George Frederick
Smith, Archibald Cary
Steers, George

YACHTSMAN (See also ATHLETE)
Adams, Charles Francis
Barr, Charles
Crowninshield, George
Paine, Charles Jackson

YMCA OFFICIAL
Mott, John R.
Tobias, Channing Heggie

YOUTH LEADER
Beard, Daniel Carter
Smith, George Albert

YWCA OFFICIAL
Cushman, Vera Charlotte Scott
Speer, Emma Bailey

ZEN BUDDHIST PHILOSOPHER
Watts, Alan Wilson

ZIONIST LEADER
Flexner, Bernard
Haas, Jacob Judah Aaron de
Lewisohn, Ludwig
Masliansky, Zvi Hirsch
Rosenblatt, Bernard Abraham
Silver, Abba Hillel
Szold, Henrietta
Wise, Stephen Samuel

ZONING EXPERT
Purdy, Lawson

ZOOLOGIST (See also APIARIST, ARACHNOLOGIST, CONCHOLOGIST, ENTOMOLOGIST, HERPETOLOGIST, ICHTHYOLOGIST, MALACOLOGIST, MAMMALOGIST, MARINE ALGAE AUTHORITY, MARINE BIOLOGIST, MICROBIOLOGIST, NATURALIST, ORNITHOLOGIST, PARASITOLOGIST, PISCICULTURIST, TAXONOMIST, VIROLOGIST)
Agassiz, Alexander
Agassiz, Jean Louis Rodolphe
Allen, Joel Asaph
Andrews, Roy Chapman
Anthony, John Gould
Baird, Spencer Fullerton
Binney, Amos
Brooks, William Keith
Calkins, Gary Nathan
Child, Charles Manning
Clark, Henry James
Cope, Edward Drinker
Dana, James Dwight
Dean, Bashford
Dubzhansky, Theodosius Grigorievich
Eigenmann, Carl H.
Elliot, Daniel Giraud
Field, Herbert Haviland
Garmon, Samuel
Gilbert, Charles Henry
Gill, Theodore Nicholas
Girard, Charles Frédéric
Holbrook, John Edwards
Hyatt, Alpheus
Just, Ernest Everett
Kinsey, Alfred Charles
Kneeland, Samuel
Kofoid, Charles Atwood
Locy, William Albert
Lyman, Theodore, 1833–1897
Montgomery, Thomas Harrison
Morgan, Thomas Hunt
Morse, Edward Sylvester
Nutting, Charles Cleveland
Orton, James
Parker, George Howard
Patten, William
Pourtalès, Louis François de
Rathbun, Richard
Stejneger, Leonhard Hess
Stiles, Charles Wardell
Sumner, Francis Bertody
True, Frederick William
Verrill, Addison Emery
Ward, Henry Baldwin
Wheeler, William Morton
Wilder, Harris Hawthorne

TOPICS

Under this heading have been included distinctive topics about which there are definite statements and discussions and not merely the mention of the topic.

A

"A" (poem), **Supp. 10**, 869, 870
AA. *See* Alcoholics Anonymous
AAA. *See* Agricultural Adjustment Administration
Aandahl, Sam, reference to, **Supp. 8**, 1
A&P. *See* Great Atlantic and Pacific Tea Co.
AARP. *See* American Association of Retired Persons
AAU. *See* Amateur Athletic Union
Abbe, Dorothy, reference to, **Supp. 6**, 186
Abbey Road Studios (London), **Supp. 10**, 449
Abbot, Willis J., reference to, **Supp. 3**, 851
Abbott, A. A. (Samuel Spewack pseudonym), **Supp. 10**, 749
Abbott, Edith, reference to, **Supp. 4**, 106, 107
Abbott, George, reference to, **Supp. 10**, 100
Abbott, Grace, reference to, **Supp. 6**, 1
Abbott, Lyman, reference to, **Vol. 6, Part 1**, 541
Abbott, Robert S., reference to, **Supp. 5**, 633; **Supp. 6**, 490
Abbott and Costello (comedy team), **Supp. 6**, 12; **Supp. 10**, 1–2
ABC. *See* American Broadcasting Co.
ABC Conference (1914), **Vol. 2, Part 1**, 195; **Vol. 10, Part 2**, 357
Abdullah, Achmed, reference to, **Supp. 10**, 21
Abel, Rudolf, reference to, **Supp. 8**, 135; **Supp. 10**, 1–2
Abele, Julian, reference to, **Supp. 2**, 668
Abelson, Phillip H., reference to, **Supp. 8**, 232
Abernathy, Ralph David, references to, **Supp. 10**, 424, 425
Abingdon, Va., skirmish at, **Vol. 7, Part 1**, 174
Abolition movement: **Vol. 1, Part 1**, 200, 205, 279, 297, 481, 496, 542, 568, 628; **Vol. 1, Part 2**, 292 f., 375, 382, 399, 485, 493; **Vol. 2, Part 1**, 43, 49, 105, 118, 132, 146, 161, 241, 284 f., 584; **Vol. 2, Part 2**, 19, 28, 68, 280, 296 f., 308, 313, 324, 407, 474 f.; **Vol. 3, Part 1**, 124 f., 406 f., 569 f., 597; **Vol. 3, Part 2**, 20, 65, 68, 82, 95, 106, 113, 118, 124, 168, 216, 227, 247, 278, 284, 297, 298, 310, 346, 360, 381, 416, 478, 481, 491 f., 514, 542, 551, 558, 561; **Vol. 4, Part 1**, 80 f., 85, 115, 118, 154, 165, 169 f., 195, 238, 260 f., 529, 539, 542, 622, 634; **Vol. 4, Part 2**, 34, 51, 56, 105, 160, 196 f., 386, 407, 421, 473, 564, 569; **Vol. 5, Part 1**, 17, 19, 150, 217, 292, 297, 328, 384, 547; **Vol. 5, Part 2**, 74, 112, 245 f., 399; **Vol. 6, Part 1**, 84 f., 163, 189, 237, 368, 416, 435 f., 459 f., 506 f.; **Vol. 6, Part 2**, 103, 363, 545, 633; **Vol. 7, Part 1**, 22 f., 227, 228 f., 413, 415, 447, 521 f.; **Vol. 7, Part 2**, 160, 546; **Vol. 8, Part 1**, 117, 306, 499; **Vol. 8, Part 2**, 44, 58, 84, 103, 120, 150, 175, 253, 343, 497 f., 551, 616 f.; **Vol. 9, Part 1**, 271, 466, 486, 525, 621; **Vol. 9, Part 2**, 5, 116 f., 298 f., 300, 303, 335, 493 f., 495, 595; **Vol. 10, Part 1**, 27, 112, 440, 625 f.; **Vol. 10, Part 2**, 174, 323, 548; **Supp. 1**, 83, 244; American Anti-Slavery Society, **Vol. 1, Part 2**, 292; **Vol. 2, Part 1**, 284; **Vol. 4, Part 1**, 169 f., 539, 634; **Vol. 7, Part 1**, 289, 415; **Vol. 7, Part 2**, 546; **Vol. 9, Part 1**, 525; **Vol. 9, Part 2**, 5, 299, 303; **Vol. 10, Part 1**, 625 f.; "Beecher Bible and Rifle Colony," **Vol. 8, Part 2**, 150; California, **Vol. 2, Part 1**, 62; District of Columbia, **Vol. 5, Part 2**, 12; foreign interest in, **Vol. 1, Part 2**, 350; **Vol. 4, Part 2**, 384, 502, 02, 509, 564; **Vol. 5, Part 2**, 496; **Vol. 8, Part 2**, 87; hymns, **Vol. 4, Part 2**, 396; Illinois, **Vol. 1, Part 2**, 128; **Vol. 6, Part 1**, 435; Kansas, **Vol. 5, Part 2**, 576; manuscript material on, **Vol. 10, Part 1**, 42; Massachusetts, **Vol. 2, Part 2**, 308; **Vol. 3, Part 1**, 407; **Vol. 5, Part 1**, 86 f., 89; **Vol. 6, Part 1**, 263; **Vol. 8, Part 2**, 326; Missouri, **Vol. 2, Part 1**, 105; Nat Turner insurrection, **Vol. 10, Part 1**, 70; national movement, disruption of, 1840, **Vol. 9, Part 2**, 5; New Jersey, **Vol. 1, Part 2**, 386; Ohio, **Vol. 6, Part 1**, 224; Pennsylvania, **Vol. 7, Part 2**, 413; **Vol. 8, Part 1**, 452; **Vol. 10, Part 2**, 517; press support, **Vol. 4, Part 1**, 195, 390; **Vol. 5, Part 2**, 112, 410; State Society, first, **Vol. 1, Part 2**, 128; Tennessee, **Vol. 5, Part 2**, 83; Texas, **Vol. 1, Part 1**, 298; "Underground Railroad," **Vol. 2, Part 2**, 268 f.; **Vol. 3, Part 2**, 247; **Vol. 4, Part 1**, 195, 622; **Vol. 5, Part 1**, 224, 576; **Vol. 5, Part 2**, 258; **Vol. 6, Part 1**, 163, 368; **Vol. 8, Part 1**, 403; **Vol. 8, Part 2**, 84, 315; **Vol. 9, Part 1**, 288, 379; **Vol. 9, Part 2**, 23, 304; **Vol. 10, Part 1**, 27; Webster's speech on, **Vol. 4, Part 1**, 170; writings on, **Vol. 1, Part 1**, 496; **Vol. 2, Part 1**, 285, 613; **Vol. 2, Part 2**, 68, 97, 364 f.; **Vol. 3, Part 1**, 407; **Vol. 4, Part 1**, 169, 310, 385, 390, 632, 634 f.; **Vol. 4, Part 2**, 572; **Vol. 5, Part 1**, 213; **Vol. 5, Part 2**, 112, 410; **Vol. 6, Part 1**, 85, 225, 434 f., 507; **Vol. 8, Part 1**, 499 f.; **Vol. 8, Part 2**, 58, 228; **Vol. 9, Part 2**, 5, 117 f., 595; **Vol. 10, Part 1**, 42, 625 f.
Abortion: liberalization of abortion laws advocated, **Supp. 9**, 352–53; therapeutic advocacy, **Supp. 3**, 763; writings on, **Vol. 9, Part 2**, 96
Abraham, Karl, reference to, **Supp. 5**, 315
Abraham Lincoln High School (Los Angeles), **Supp. 8**, 7–8
Abrams, Jacob, reference to, **Supp. 6**, 105
Absalom, Absalom!, **Supp. 7**, 233
Absentee Voting Act (1944), **Supp. 8**, 223
Abstract of the Suffering of the People Called Quakers, An, **Vol. 8, Part 1**, 399
Abyssinian Baptist Church (New York City), **Supp. 5**, 548; **Supp. 9**, 123
Academic freedom: **Supp. 9**, 429; **Supp. 10**, 137; Clark University, **Supp. 4**, 32; Columbia University, **Supp. 3**, 151; **Supp. 4**, 62, 135; Cornell University, **Supp. 3**, 698; Harvard University, **Supp. 3**, 471; **Supp. 10**, 143; Howard University, **Supp. 10**, 386; Johns Hopkins University, **Supp. 5**, 410; Kentucky, University of, **Supp. 5**, 461; loyalty issues, **Supp. 7**, 542; Scopes trial, **Supp. 8**, 582–84; **Supp. 9**, 769; Stanford University, **Supp. 7**, 481; University of Wisconsin, **Supp. 3**, 249; **Supp. 7**, 450; writings on, **Supp. 7**, 264, 481; **Supp. 8**, 272
Academician, educational periodical, one of first, **Vol. 7, Part 2**, 568
Academy Awards: **Supp. 7**, 32; first actor to win three Oscars, **Supp. 9**, 123; first black winner, **Supp. 5**, 451
Academy of Motion Picture Arts and Sciences: **Supp. 6**, 476; **Supp. 8**, 46, 678; founding of, **Supp. 7**, 32; **Supp. 8**, 459, 460
Academy of Music (Boston), **Vol. 3, Part 2**, 81
Academy of Natural Sciences (Philadelphia), **Vol. 6, Part 2**, 136; **Vol. 7, Part 2**, 351
Academy of Political and Social Science, **Vol. 5, Part l**, 574

Academy of the U.S.A., project for an, **Vol. 8, Part 1**, 300 f.
Acadians: **Vol. 5, Part 2**, 370; arrival of, **Vol. 4, Part 2**, 221; befriended by Quakers, **Vol. 1, Part 2**, 178; in South Carolina, **Vol. 6, Part 1**, 538 f.
Accardo, Tony, reference to, **Supp. 6**, 264
Accounting: modernization of, **Vol. 7, Part 2**, 478; professional organizations, **Supp. 6**, 397–98; tax forms, **Supp. 5**, 412
Ace, Goodman, reference to, **Supp. 9**, 5–6
Ace bandage, **Supp. 7**, 678
Acetylcholine, **Supp. 3**, 136; **Supp. 4**, 411; **Supp. 7**, 476
Acetylene gas, **Supp. 7**, 553–54
ACF Industries, predecessor, **Supp. 5**, 324
Acheson, Dean, references to, **Supp. 5**, 455, 705; **Supp. 6**, 556, 557; **Supp. 7**, 24, 423; **Supp. 8**, 303; **Supp. 9**, 814, 831
Acheson-Lilienthal atomic control plan, **Supp. 8**, 484
Acidosis, theories of, **Supp. 3**, 353
Acini, islets of, **Supp. 6**, 53
Ackerman, Frederick L., reference to, **Supp. 5**, 558, 559
ACLU. *See* American Civil Liberties Union
Acoustics, **Vol. 8, Part 2**, 277; **Vol. 10, Part 1**, 73; **Supp. 3**, 524; research in, **Supp. 1**, 32
ACS. *See* American Cancer Society
ACTH hormone, **Supp. 7**, 341; first pure sample obtained, **Supp. 9**, 266
Acting (for names of actors, playwrights, etc., *see* Occupations Index): **Supp. 3**, 713–14; **Supp. 4**, 414–15, 503–4, 821–23; **Supp. 5**, 237–38, 240, 726–27; **Supp. 7**, 32; 50–51, 107–8, 120–21, 237–38, 281–82, 321–23, 460–61, 544–45; **Supp. 8**, 31–32, 65, 66, 187–88, 368–69; acerbic roles, **Supp. 8**, 690–91; barnstorming tours, **Vol. 4, Part 1**, 266; Barrymore family, **Supp. 3**, 35–36; **Supp. 5**, 44–45; **Supp. 6**, 38–39; "Big Four," **Vol. 4, Part 1**, 266; blacks, **Vol. 1, Part 1**, 160; **Supp. 9**, 698–99; **Vol. 4, Part 1**, 314; blacks, controversial portrayals by, **Supp. 5**, 418–19; **Supp. 10**, 95, 147; black stereotypes, **Supp. 7**, 43–44; **Supp. 10**, 576, 661–62; character roles, **Supp. 3**, 640, 811; **Supp. 4**, 24–27; **Supp. 7**, 63; **Supp. 8**, 117, 452–53, 515–26, 711; **Supp. 9**, 123, 473, 536, 560, 577; **Supp. 10**, 33, 77, 85–86, 101, 178–79, 273, 488, 845; clowns, **Supp. 10**, 407; comedy, **Supp. 7**, 354–55; **Supp. 8**, 214–15; **Supp. 9**, 508–9, 514, 791–92, 879–80; **Supp. 10**, 560, 561, 739, 803–4; cowboys, **Supp. 10**, 489; Cushman School of, **Vol. 3, Part 1**, 2; deadpan comedy, **Supp. 8**, 284, 314–15; dowager roles, **Supp. 7**, 208; **Supp. 9**, 481; dramatic leads, **Supp. 10**, 63; drunk roles, **Supp. 7**, 34; eccentric, **Vol. 3, Part 2**, 393; female impersonations, **Vol. 2, Part 1**, 276; *femme fatale* roles, **Supp. 5**, 37–38; **Supp. 9**, 480, 540; floozy roles, **Supp. 10**, 828–30; French New Wave, **Supp. 10**, 725; gangster roles, **Supp. 9**, 665, 666; grande dame roles, **Supp. 10**, 515; grotesque roles, **Supp. 1**, 165; **Supp. 9**, 169; ingénues, **Supp. 5**, 7–8; **Supp. 9**, 409; "It Girl," **Supp. 7**, 68; leading ladies, **Supp. 9**, 376–77; 479–80; **Supp. 10**, 157–58, 599–600, 634–36; 807–8; 850–51; leading men, **Supp. 10**, 473–74; mimicry, **Vol. 2, Part 2**, 1; minstrelsy, **Vol. 2, Part 2**, 98; musical comedy, **Supp. 7**, 197–98; **Supp. 10**, 165–66; naturalistic, **Supp. 8**, 96; "other women" roles, **Supp. 10**, 712; pantomime, **Vol. 3, Part 2**, 566 f.; patriarchal roles, **Supp. 10**, 131; politician roles, **Supp. 7**, 551–52; residual payments, **Supp. 8**, 712; Revolutionary War period, **Vol. 4, Part 2**, 548; romantic leads, **Supp. 8**, 474; **Supp. 9**, 371; **Supp. 10**, 62, 68–69; 668; seriocomic, **Supp. 8**, 355–56; Shakespearean, **Supp. 4**, 477–79, 552–54; **Supp. 5**, 124, 268–69; **Supp. 9**, 692; **Supp. 10** 677, 678; Shaw's plays, **Supp. 4**, 369; sinister roles, **Supp. 9** 792–93; slapstick comedy, **Supp. 9**, 535–36; **Supp. 10**, 513, 514–15, 517; "smart-aleck" roles, **Supp. 10**, 105; sophisticated comedies, **Supp. 5**, 414–15; straight men, **Supp. 10**, 513, 517; suave and sophisticated roles, **Supp. 9**, 697; supporting roles, **Supp. 10**, 53–54, 100; tough guy roles, **Supp. 6**, 65; **Supp. 9**, 189–90, 242, 486–87, 692; **Supp. 10**, 500–501, 655, 656, 822, 823; training in, **Supp. 2**, 11; **Supp. 9**, 538; **Supp. 10**, 23–24, 131, 674, 822; unconventional roles, **Supp. 9**, 195; underplaying, **Supp. 8**, 659–60; **Supp. 10**, 380; unionization, **Supp. 4**, 234; **Supp. 8**, 459; villains, **Supp. 4**, 66; **Supp. 5**, 257–58; **Supp. 7**, 478–79; **Supp. 8**, 311–12, 518, 519; **Supp. 9**, 692; **Supp. 10**, 106, 131; war movies, **Supp. 10**, 823; Westerns, **Supp. 10**, 252–53; Yiddish theater, **Supp. 5**, 10–11
Active, case of the sloop, **Vol. 8, Part 2**, 177
Actors. For complete list, *see* Occupations Index
Actors' Equity Association, **Vol. 10, Part 2**, 430; administration, **Supp. 1**, 711; founding of, **Supp. 1**, 318; movie producers' relationship with, **Supp. 8**, 459; strike, **Supp. 3**, 174, 333; Theatre Guild support of, **Supp. 4**, 234
Actors' Fund of America: **Vol. 1, Part 1**, 151; **Vol. 7, Part 2**, 173; founding of, **Supp. 3**, 276
Actors' Home (Staten Island, N. Y.), **Vol. 1, Part 1**, 151
Actors Studio, founding of, **Supp. 10**, 129
Actuarial Society of America, **Vol. 3, Part 2**, 242; **Vol. 6, Part 1**, 588
Actuarial studies, **Supp. 4**, 384–85
ACWA. *See* Amalgamated Clothing Workers of America
ADA. *See* Americans for Democratic Action
Ada, **Supp. 10**, 583
Adairsville, Ga., engagement at, **Vol. 7, Part 1**, 473
Adams, Abigail, reference to, **Vol. 9, Part 1**, 49
Adams, Ansel, references to, **Supp. 10**, 162, 834
Adams, Charles Kendall, reference to, **Supp. 3**, 698
Adams, Edie, reference to, **Supp. 7**, 443
Adams, Franklin P., references to, **Supp. 5**, 568; **Supp. 6**, 113, 366; **Supp. 7**, 412, 413; **Supp. 8**, 217, 491, 492, 622
Adams, George Burton, reference to, **Supp. 8**, 580
Adams, Henry: editor of, **Supp. 6**, 251; references to, **Vol. 6, Part 1**, 347; **Supp. 7**, 55
Adams, Herbert Baxter, reference to, **Supp. 3**, 15
Adams, John: biography of, **Supp. 9**, 113; "Hot Water War," **Vol. 4, Part 1**, 34; references to, **Vol. 6, Part 1**, 316; **Vol. 7, Part 1**, 31, 369; **Vol. 8, Part 2**, 590, 607; **Vol. 10, Part 1**, 484
Adams, John Quincy: portrait of, **Vol. 4, Part 1**, 586; quarrel with, on floor of House, **Vol. 8, Part 1**, 417; references to, **Vol. 1, Part 1**, 591; **Vol. 5, Part 1**, 347, 474; **Vol. 6, Part 1**, 518; **Vol. 9, Part 2**, 304; **Supp. 5**, 5
Adams, Maude, references to, **Vol. 4, Part 1**, 41; **Supp. 3**, 713
Adams, N. I., Jr., **Supp. 5**, 528–29
Adams, Samuel: psychobiography of, **Supp. 6**, 279; references to, **Vol. 5, Part 1**, 440 f.; **Vol. 7, Part 2**, 104
Adams, Sherman, reference to, **Supp. 8**, 159, 219–20, 497
Adams, Walter S., reference to, **Supp. 3**, 291
Adams family, archives of, **Supp. 3**, 286
Adams Female Academy, **Vol. 1, Part 1**, 576
Adams House (Boston), **Vol. 1, Part 1**, 102
Adamson Act (1916), **Supp. 4**, 537; **Supp. 6**, 132
Addams, Jane, references to, **Vol. 8, Part 1**, 57 f.; **Supp. 3**, 355, 576; **Supp. 4**, 86, 106, 137, 157, 725; **Supp.**

5, 84; **Supp. 6**, 97, 102, 103; **Supp. 7**, 28, 29; **Supp. 8**, 442
Adderley, Julian E. ("Cannonball"), reference to, **Supp. 10**, 225
Adderley, Nat, reference to, **Supp. 9**, 454
Addes, George, reference to, **Supp. 8**, 527, 652
Addiction. *See* Alcoholism; Narcotics
Adding machines: development of, **Supp. 1**, 138–39; invention of, **Vol. 1, Part 1**, 533; **Vol. 10, Part 1**, 572 f.; voting applications, **Supp. 1**, 415
Addison's disease, research studies, **Supp. 9**, 454
Adee, Alvey A., references to, **Supp. 3**, 139; **Supp. 8**, 590
Adelphi Academy, presidency of, **Vol. 9, Part 1**, 472
Adelphi College, presidency of, **Vol. 6, Part 1**, 199 f.
Adenauer, Konrad, reference to, **Supp. 10**, 437
Adenosine triphosphate, **Supp. 5**, 489
Adhesive bandages, **Supp. 7**, 183
Adirondack Cottage Sanitarium, founding of, **Supp. 2**, 70
Adirondack Mountains: Adirondack Club, **Vol. 9, Part 2**, 29; geology of, **Vol. 5, Part 2**, 319; reservations in, **Vol. 5, Part 2**, 62; **Vol. 7, Part 1**, 412; short stories about, **Vol. 3, Part 1**, 231
Adkins v. *Children's Hospital*, **Supp. 4**, 537; **Supp. 5**, 572
Adler, Alfred, reference to, **Supp. 10**, 437
Adler, Felix, references to, **Vol. 8, Part 2**, 316; **Supp. 3**, 97, 246
Adler, Jacob Pavlovitch, reference to, **Supp. 5**, 10–11
Adler, Mortimer, references to, **Supp. 5**, 212; **Supp. 10**, 364–65
Adler, Paul, reference to, **Supp. 10**, 139
Adler, Stella, references to, **Supp. 10**, 129, 130, 131
Adler, Coleman and Co. (brokerage firm), **Supp. 10**, 139
Administrative law, education in, **Supp. 2**, 250
Admiralty law, **Vol. 1, Part 1**, 90; **Vol. 1, Part 2**, 177, 231; **Vol. 2, Part 1**, 99, 370, 399; **Vol. 3, Part 1**, 60, 79 f., 592 f.; **Vol. 3, Part 2**, 454; **Vol. 5, Part 2**, 64, 79; **Vol. 9, Part 2**, 28, 105
Adobe Walls, second battle of, **Vol. 3, Part 1**, 331
Adolescents: black, studies on, **Supp. 8**, 522; fiction about, **Supp. 4**, 816–17; **Supp. 5**, 372; organizations for, **Supp. 2**, 226–27; **Supp. 5**, 324; psychological studies of, **Supp. 4**, 805; science popularization programs for, **Supp. 8**, 119–20; studies of, **Supp. 2**, 313; work-relief, programs for, **Supp. 7**, 787–88
Adoption: foster care, **Supp. 2**, 57, 58; **Supp. 3**, 28, 160; **Supp. 4**, 871; reform legislation, **Supp. 6**, 515–16; Spence-Chapin service, **Supp. 3**, 160. *See also* Motherhood, unwed
Adrenal cortex, **Supp. 7**, 341
Adrenal glands, study of, **Vol. 9, Part 2**, 9
Adrenaline: **Supp. 3**, 134–36; discovery of, **Supp. 2**, 4; isolation of, **Vol. 9, Part 2**, 275; synthesis of, **Supp. 5**, 149
Adrian, Edgar Douglas, reference to, **Supp. 9**, 124
Adult education: **Vol. 5, Part 1**, 130; **Vol. 6, Part 1**, 155, 178; **Vol. 10, Part 2**, 640; **Supp. 2**, 45; **Supp. 3**, 64–65, 417, 677; **Supp. 4**, 833; **Supp. 6**, 83, 160, 203, 412; Carnegie Foundation grants, **Supp. 3**, 416; Chautauqua movement, **Supp. 3**, 64–65, 792–93; for immigrants, **Supp. 8**, 9; Great Books programs, **Supp. 8**, 58; New School for Social Research, **Supp. 2**, 563; People's Institute, **Supp. 3**, 511, 563; radio and television, **Supp. 6**, 83, 160; teaching programs, **Supp. 8**, 488; women, **Supp. 6**, 203, 412; writings on, **Supp. 5**, 431–32. *See also* Education
Adult Education Association, **Supp. 6**, 203
Ad valorem tax, **Supp. 1**, 385
Advance (brig), North Pole, **Vol. 5, Part 2**, 256
Advance, The, editing of, **Vol. 7, Part 1**, 538
Adventist movement, **Vol. 1, Part 1**, 432; **Vol. 5, Part 1**, 60; **Vol. 7, Part 1**, 589; **Vol. 9, Part 1**, 350; **Vol. 10, Part 1**, 422 f.; **Vol. 10, Part 2**, 98; founding and doctrines of, **Vol. 6, Part 2**, 642. *See also* Seventh-Day Adventists
Adventists. *See* Adventist movement; Seventh-Day Adventists
Advent Review, founding of, **Vol. 9, Part 1**, 350
Adventure Galley, Kidd's ship, **Vol. 5, Part 2**, 368
Adventures of Ellery Queen, The, **Supp. 9**, 488
Adventures of Ideas, **Supp. 4**, 883
Adventures of Ozzie and Harriet, The, **Supp. 9**, 580–81
Advertising and marketing: **Vol. 1, Part 1**, 413, 449; **Vol. 3, Part 1**, 405; **Vol. 4, Part 1**, 209, 318; **Vol. 4, Part 2**, 591; **Vol. 7, Part 2**, 251; **Vol. 8, Part 2**, 197; **Vol. 9, Part 1**, 138; agencies, **Supp. 7**, 101, 211–12, 641–42; **Supp. 8**, 27; "Arrow Collar Man," **Supp. 5**, 428, 429; art illustration, **Supp. 8**, 494; automobiles, **Supp. 8**, 599; chewing gum, **Supp. 1**, 715; Chicago school, **Supp. 9**, 140; cigarettes, **Supp. 4**, 371; **Supp. 5**, 411; **Supp. 10**, 145; Clairol, **Supp. 10**, 146; copywriting, **Supp. 1**, 287–88; **Supp. 5**, 411; **Supp. 6**, 627; **Supp. 10**, 145–46, 708; cosmetics, **Supp. 8**, 13; cotton and tobacco cooperatives, **Supp. 2**, 39, 79; Dial soap, **Supp. 10**, 146; Ex-Lax, **Supp. 8**, 339; farmers' cooperatives, **Supp. 2**, 307; flour products, **Supp. 7**, 47; frozen foods, **Supp. 10**, 555; General Foods, **Supp. 9**, 308–9; "Gerber Baby," **Supp. 9**, 303; illustration, **Supp. 5**, 428–29; **Supp. 7**, 66–67; Hallmark, **Supp. 10**, 146; image school, **Supp. 10**, 708; industrial, **Supp. 6**, 519; insurance, **Supp. 9**, 327; "Jolly Green Giant," **Supp. 9**, 139; layout and design, **Supp. 6**, 186; limitation on advertising parodies, **Supp. 9**, 139; "List system," **Vol. 8, Part 2**, 197; Lucky Strike "L.S./M.F.T." slogan developed, **Supp. 10**, 145; market research, **Supp. 10**, 708–9; "Marlboro Man," **Supp. 9**, 139; Maypo, **Supp. 10**, 352; newspaper, **Supp. 3**, 80; Pepsodent, **Supp. 10**, 145; pioneers in, **Supp. 6**, 519, 614; pipe tobacco, **Supp. 5**, 565, 567; poster, **Supp. 2**, 112; product distribution, **Supp. 2**, 333; product obsolescence strategy introduced, **Supp. 9**, 649; product promotion, innovations in, **Supp. 9**, 521; psychology of, **Supp. 5**, 433, 611–12; **Supp. 6**, 672–73; radio, **Supp. 3**, 103–4; **Supp. 8**, 52; **Supp. 10**, 555, 708; radio vs. newspaper, **Supp. 9**, 90; Raid, **Supp. 10**, 146; retail trades, **Supp. 2**, 105; Revlon, **Supp. 9**, 649; Reynolds Wrap, **Supp. 5**, 566; Sanka coffee, **Supp. 10**, 555; sign painting, **Vol. 7, Part 1**, 576; television commercials, **Supp. 9**, 66–67, 803; **Supp. 10**, 352; tobacco advertising ban, **Supp. 9**, 139, 316; trade books, **Supp. 8**, 536; truth in, early advocacy of, **Vol. 8, Part 2**, 197; "unique selling proposition" technique, **Supp. 9**, 67
Advise and Consent, **Supp. 10**, 239
Advocate of Peace, editing of, **Vol. 10, Part 1**, 6
AEC. *See* Atomic Energy Commission
AEF. *See* American Expeditionary Force
AEI. *See* American Enterprise Institute for Public Policy Research
Aeolian Co., **Vol. 9, Part 2**, 637; **Supp. 6**, 297
Aerial Experiment Association, **Vol. 1, Part 2**, 152; founding of, **Supp. 1**, 214
Aerial Navigation Co., **Vol. 4, Part 1**, 330
Aerial photography. *See* Photography, aerial
Aero Club of America, founding of, **Supp. 5**, 547
Aerodynamics, **Vol. 5, Part 2**, 596 f.; **Vol. 8, Part 2**, 576; first academic courses in, **Supp. 8**, 439–40
Aerojet General Corporation, founding of, **Supp. 7**, 411; **Supp. 8**, 440
Aeronautical engineering: air-cooled engine research, **Supp. 4**, 473–74; 486–87; balloon research, **Supp.**

7, 619–20; short-takeoff-and-landing (STOL) airplane, **Supp. 8**, 709
Aeronautics, **Vol. 6, Part 1**, 452; **Vol. 8, Part 2**, 79; balloon, **Vol. 5, Part 2**, 565; kites, **Vol. 8, Part 2**, 184. *See also* Aviation
Aeronautics, **Supp. 5**, 760–61
Aesthetics: **Vol. 4, Part 1**, 588; **Vol. 8, Part 1**, 408; **Vol. 8, Part 2**, 36; in conservation movement, **Supp. 4**, 522–23; order of merit rating scale, **Supp. 3**, 149; quantitative bases for, **Supp. 3**, 71; standards, **Supp. 2**, 540; writings on, **Supp. 5**, 39, 601–2; **Supp. 9**, 447–48
Aetna Explosives Co., **Vol. 7, Part 1**, 301
Aetna Life Insurance Co., **Vol. 2, Part 1**, 248
AFL. *See* American Federation of Labor
AFL-CIO. *See* American Federation of Labor-Congress of Industrial Organizations
Africa: colonization, **Vol. 6, Part 1**, 28; **Vol. 8, Part 2**, 349; "Dark Continent," first called the, **Vol. 9, Part 1**, 511; education, **Supp. 1**, 14; experts on, **Supp. 7**, 372; exploration, **Vol. 2, Part 1**, 591; **Vol. 6, Part 1**, 28; **Vol. 8, Part 2**, 142, 349; **Vol. 9, Part l**, 509 f.; **Supp. 5**, 370–71; missions in, **Vol. 4, Part 1**, 375; **Vol. 4, Part 2**, 371; **Vol. 5, Part 2**, 561; **Vol. 7, Part 1**, 231, 390 f.; **Vol. 8, Part 1**, 243 f.; **Vol. 8, Part 2**, 391; **Vol. 10, Part 2**, 338; **Supp. 1**, 499; music, **Supp. 5**, 436; ornithology, **Supp. 7**, 117; scouting, **Supp. 4**, 126–27; slave-trading, investigation of, **Vol. 3, Part 1**, 220; U.S. blacks' relationship with, **Supp. 2**, 222; **Supp. 6**, 716–17; **Supp. 7**, 509; writings on, **Supp. 4**, 878
African-Americans. *See* Blacks
African Methodist Episcopal Zion Church, **Vol. 1, Part l**, 204 f.; **Vol. 2, Part 2**, 229; **Vol. 4, Part 1**, 96; **Vol. 5, Part 1**, 192 f.; **Vol. 6, Part 1**, 368; **Vol. 7, Part 2**, 324; **Vol. 9, Part 2**, 296; **Vol. 10, Part 1**, 65 f., 398 f.; leadership, **Supp. 5**, 258–59; **Supp. 8**, 94; **Supp. 9**, 750, 751
African Protestant Episcopal Church, **Vol. 1, Part 1**, 204
Afro-American League, **Vol. 10, Part 1**, 398 f.; founding of, **Supp. 3**, 596
Afro-American Realty Co., **Supp. 3**, 535
After Dark, **Supp. 4**, 103
"After the Ball" (song), **Vol. 4, Part 2**, 306
Aftermath: Martin Bormann and the Fourth Reich, **Supp. 10**, 232
AFTRA. *See* American Federation of Television and Radio Artists
Agassiz, Alexander: biography of, **Vol. 1, Part 1**, 114; Garman, Samuel, **Vol. 4, Part 1**, 154; Le Conte, Joseph, **Vol. 6, Part 1**, 90; Lesquereux, **Vol. 6, Part 1**, 188; references to, **Vol. 1, Part 1**, 318, 514; **Vol. 3, Part 2**, 352; **Vol. 4, Part 2**, 63; **Vol. 5, Part 1**, 12, 141, 446, 591; **Vol. 5, Part 2**, 212; **Vol. 7, Part 1**, 606; **Vol. 9, Part 1**, 18
Agassiz, Louis, reference to, **Supp. 4**, 52
Agassiz Museum (Cambridge, Mass.), **Supp. 4**, 51–52
Age, founding of, **Supp. 1**, 363
Age of Anxiety, The, **Supp. 9**, 54
Age of Mammals in Europe, Asia and North America, The, **Supp. 1**, 586
Age of Reason, **Vol. 7, Part 2**, 162 f.
Age of Reform: From Bryan to F. D. R., The, **Supp. 8**, 271, 272, 273
Age of the Reformation, The, **Supp. 3**, 726
Agee, James, reference to, **Supp. 7**, 114; Evans association, **Supp. 9**, 268
Agency for International Development (AID), **Supp. 10**, 129
Aging and aged: advocacy organizations, **Supp. 8**, 10; group activities, **Supp. 7**, 151; social work, **Supp. 5**, 454; Townsend Plan, **Supp. 6**, 646–47. *See also* Social Security
Aglipayanism, **Supp. 5**, 178–79
Agnes Scott College, **Vol. 5, Part 1**, 485
Agnon, S. Y., references to, **Supp. 9**, 707, 708
Agora excavations, **Supp. 3**, 705
Agrarianism, **Supp. 3**, 363; literary movement, **Supp. 9**, 643; **Supp. 10**, 776
Agricultural Adjustment Acts (1933 and 1938), **Supp. 3**, 100, 319; **Supp. 4**, 50, 407, 795; **Supp. 5**, 358 572–73; **Supp. 7**, 760; **Supp. 8**, 277, 508
Agricultural Adjustment Administration, **Supp. 6**, 215–16, 487, 638; **Supp. 7**, 36; **Supp. 8**, 699–700; founding of, **Supp. 3**, 594, 650, 651–52; tenant farming under, **Supp. 7**, 781
Agricultural Credit Corporation, founding of, **Supp. 2**, 480
Agricultural Credits Act (1923), **Supp. 4**, 482
Agricultural Development Council, **Supp. 10**, 684
Agricultural Economics, Bureau of, **Vol. 10, Part 1**, 370; research, **Supp. 6**, 638
Agricultural History, founding of, **Supp. 5**, 201
Agricultural Marketing Act (1929), passage of, **Supp. 7**, 360–61
Agricultural Trade Development and Assistance Act (1954), **Supp. 7**, 678; **Supp. 8**, 278
Agriculture (general): **Vol. 1, Part 1**, 110, 316, 392, 408; **Vol. 1, Part 2**, 172, 283, 460; **Vol. 2, Part 1**, 25, 43; **Vol. 2, Part 2**, 185, 250; **Vol. 3, Part 1**, 304; **Vol. 3, Part 2**, 45, 128, 268, 424, 479; **Vol. 4, Part 1**, 200, 379, 595; **Vol. 4, Part 2**, 204, 207 f., 473 f.; **Vol. 5, Part 1**, 90, 128, 207, 348, 624; **Vol. 5, Part 2**, 45, 90, 142 f., 231 f., 446, 452 f.; **Vol. 6, Part 1**, 134, 163 418, 465, 481 f., 501, 516, 554 f.; **Vol. 7, Part 1**, 170, 205, 257, 629, f.; **Vol. 7, Part 2**, 464; **Vol. 8, Part 1**, 239; **Vol. 8, Part 2**, 15, 335; **Vol. 9, Part 1**, 69, 146, 148, 180, 200; **Vol. 9, Part 2**, 134, 333, 396, 574, 641; **Vol. 10, Part 1**, 68, 174, 180, 370, 444, 617; **Vol. 10, Part 2**, 460; aerial crop-dusting, **Supp. 8**, 707–8; agrarian movement, **Vol. 4, Part 1**, 529; **Vol. 5, Part 2**, 28; alfalfa, introduction of, **Vol. 10, Part 2**, 387; apple-raising, **Vol. 6, Part 1**, 535 f.; **Vol. 7, Part 1**, 197; biochemical research, **Supp. 3**, 145–46, 315; **Supp. 4**, 114; "Bloomsdale Farm," **Vol. 5, Part 2**, 571–72; boll weevil, Mexican, **Vol. 5, Part 2**, 453; chemistry, as applied to, **Vol. 1, Part 1**, 109, 349, 417; **Vol. 2, Part 1**, 238, 484; **Vol. 2, Part 2**, 304; **Vol. 3, Part 1**, 61, 210; **Vol. 4, Part 1**, 5; **Vol. 5, Part 1**, 22, 207; **Vol. 5, Part 2**, 45, 120, 231 f., 388 f.; **Vol. 6, Part 2**, 223, 263 f.; **Vol. 7, Part 1**, 574 f.; **Vol. 7, Part 2**, 388, 509; **Vol. 8, Part 1**, 96 f., 154 f., 257 f., 272 f., 397; **Vol. 8, Part 2**, 512; **Vol. 9, Part 2**, 37, 395, 514; **Vol. 10, Part 2**, 22, 104, 491; cold-resistant crop development, **Supp. 4**, 357; colonial, **Vol. 8, Part 1**, 419; colonies of Russian Jews, **Vol. 8, Part 2**, 168; cooperatives, **Vol. 7, Part 1**, 377; **Supp. 2**, 39, 79, 307, 426; **Supp. 4**, 36–37, 853; **Supp. 5**, 365; **Supp. 7**, 361; corn culture, **Vol. 1, Part 1**, 533; **Vol. 6, Part 1**, 74; **Vol. 8, Part 1**, 477 f.; correspondence course in, **Vol. 1, Part 1**, 236; cotton, **Vol. 3, Part 1**, 304; **Vol. 3, Part 2**, 482; **Vol. 8, Part 1**, 565 f.; **Vol. 9, Part 1**, 427; credit, **Supp. 4**, 406, 482; crop breeding, **Supp. 4**: 252–53, 862–63; **Supp. 5**, 629; crop quota system, **Supp. 6**, 639; dairy, **Supp. 1**, 37, 444; diversification, **Vol. 3, Part 2**, 411; **Supp. 2**, 480; domestic allotment, **Supp. 6**, 559; drainage, **Vol. 5, Part 2**, 143; economic relief legislation, **Supp. 2**, 492; economics, **Supp. 1**, 152, 384, 491; **Supp. 2**, 696; **Supp. 4**, 45; **Supp. 6**, 459, 638–39; education, **Vol. 1, Part 1**, 236, 592; **Vol. 1, Part 2**, 321, 568; **Vol. 2, Part 1**, 378, 428; **Vol. 2, Part 2**, 147, 165, 201; **Vol. 3, Part 1**, 242; **Vol. 3, Part 2**, 252, 351, 473; **Vol.**

4, Part 1, 139, 379, 383, 395; **Vol. 4, Part 2**, 34; **Vol. 5, Part 1**, 163; **Vol. 5, Part 2**, 453, 501, 525; **Vol. 6, Part 1**, 555; **Vol. 6, Part 2**, 613; **Vol. 7, Part 2**, 197, 282; **Vol. 8, Part 1**, 143 f., 175 f., 257 f.; **Vol. 8, Part 2**, 180, 512 f.; **Vol. 9, Part 2**, 78; **Vol. 10, Part 1**, 4, 139, 370, 617 f.; electrification, **Supp. 3**, 1 92–93; experimental, **Supp. 1**, 444; **Supp. 2**, 387; **Supp. 6**, 77–78; experiment stations established, **Vol. 1, Part 1**, 238, 417; **Vol. 2, Part 1**, 25; **Vol. 5, Part 2**, 120; **Vol. 9, Part 2**, 39; **Vol. 10, Part 1**, 4; extension service, **Supp. 1**, 144; **Supp. 2**, 217, 364; **Supp. 3**, 145–46; Federal Farm Loan Board, **Supp. 6**, 453; fertilizers, **Vol. 7, Part 2**, 419; **Vol. 8, Part 1**, 397; **Vol. 9, Part 2**, 39; 4-H clubs, **Supp. 5**, 51; geography, **Supp. 4**, 45; government aid, recognition of principle of, **Vol. 3, Part 2**, 110; **Vol. 4, Part 2**, 394; government assistance, attitudes on, **Supp. 1**, 197; Grange movement, **Vol. 5, Part 2**, 299; **Supp. 4**, 340–41; historical writings on, **Supp. 5**, 201–2; **Supp. 7**, 685; hybrid corn, **Supp. 10**, 271; insects, injuries to crops by, **Vol. 8, Part 1**, 609 f.; international organizations, **Supp. 4**, 341; journalism on, **Supp. 3**, 319; **Supp. 6**, 676–77; legislation, **Supp. 2**, 321, 380, 492; **Supp. 4**, 309, 479–80; **Supp. 8**, 277–78; machinery, invention and development of, **Vol. 1, Part 1**, 130, 178, 185, 406; **Vol. 1, Part 2**, 172, 230; **Vol. 2, Part 1**, 337, 557; **Vol. 3, Part 1**, 193 f., 195; **Vol. 3, Part 2**, 110, 188, 251; **Vol. 4, Part 1**, 98; **Vol. 4, Part 2**, 94; **Vol. 5, Part 2**, 53; **Vol. 6, Part 1**, 607 f., 614; **Vol. 6, Part 2**, 296, 303 f., 383, 635; **Vol. 7, Part 1**, 177, 590; **Vol. 7, Part 2**, 21, 471, 493, 537, 644; **Vol. 8, Part 1**, 101 f., 496, 498 f., 505; **Vol. 8, Part 2**, 9; **Vol. 9, Part 2**, 439; **Vol. 10, Part 2**, 464, 475; **Supp. 2**, 402; migrant workers, **Supp. 8**, 301; New Deal policies, **Supp. 3**, 434, 651–52; **Supp. 6**, 12, 638–39; **Supp. 7**, 760–61; **Supp. 8**, 445, 700; North Carolina programs, **Supp. 6**, 569; organizations, **Supp. 1**, 51, 645, 660; **Supp. 2**, 307, 426, 552; **Supp. 8**, 468; personal writings on, **Supp. 6**, 409; pest control, **Supp. 4**, 399, 601; physics application, **Supp. 7**, 76; political activity, **Supp. 3**, 108, 468, 723–24; **Supp. 6**, 86–87; price supports, **Supp. 6**, 487–88, 639; **Supp. 8**, 277–78; **Supp. 9**, 130, 257; publications, **Supp. 1**, 461–62; **Supp. 4**, 132; **Supp. 7**, 527; radio programs, **Supp. 4**, 132; regulation of, early attempts at, **Vol. 5, Part 2**, 120; relief programs, Depression-era, **Supp. 10**, 795; research in, **Supp. 1**, 183, 395; rice growing, **Vol. 1, Part 1**, 128, 224; **Vol. 5, Part 2**, 453; rotation of crops, **Vol. 1, Part 2**, 460; seed production, **Vol. 6, Part 1**, 74; socialist view of, **Supp. 4**, 746, 747; soil bacteriology, **Supp. 1**, 461; soil conservation, **Supp. 3**, 656; **Supp. 6**, 52–53, 639; soil erosion, **Vol. 8, Part 1**, 146 f.; Southern interests, **Supp. 4**, 50; Soviet Jewish resettlement, **Supp. 4**, 699–700; statistical information, early collection of, **Vol. 3, Part 1**, 349 f.; sugar, **Vol. 9, Part 1**, 427; sugar beet experimentation, **Vol. 8, Part 1**, 239 f.; surplus sales, **Supp. 1**, 384; **Supp. 3**, 496, 594; **Supp. 4**, 51; **Supp. 8**, 278; teaching of, **Supp. 3**, 216–17, 433–34; **Supp. 5**, 31; tenant farming, **Supp. 4**, 50, 251; **Supp. 5**, 511; **Supp. 7**, 781–82; voluntary allotment plant, **Supp. 7**, 760–61; wheat, **Vol. 6, Part 1**, 92; writings on, **Vol. 1, Part 1**, 185, 205, 413; **Vol. 1, Part 2**, 100, 172, 460; **Vol. 2, Part 1**, 155, 164, 238, 388, **Vol. 2, Part 2**, 254 f., 312, 314; **Vol. 3, Part 1**, 172 f., 304, 57 f.; **Vol. 3, Part 2**, 347; **Vol. 4, Part 1**, 200; **Vol. 4, Part 2**, 315; **Vol. 5, Part 1**, 118, 163; **Vol. 5, Part 2**, 90, 231, 445 f. 453, 501; **Vol. 6, Part 1**, 284, 377, 426, 516; **Vol. 7, Part 1**, 376 f.; **Vol. 7, Part 2**, 464, 537; **Vol. 8, Part 1**, 40 f; 143 f., 145 f., 347 f., 419; **Vol. 8, Part 2**, 9, 51, 215; **Vol. 9, Part 1**, 199 f., 201, 427; **Vol. 9, Part 2**, 38 f., 309, 396, 439, 514, 574; **Vol. 10, Part 1**, 4, 35 f., 369 f., 456 f.; **Vol. 10, Part 2**, 214, 387, 617. *See also* Agriculture, Department of (U.S.); Agriculture (by state); Farming; Food; Horticulture

Agriculture (by state): Alabama, **Vol. 2, Part 2**, 232; **Vol. 9, Part 2**, 524; Arizona, **Vol. 4, Part 2**, 483; **Vol. 6, Part 1**, 611; **Vol. 8, Part 1**, 121 f.; Colorado, **Vol. 3, Part 1**, 606; Connecticut, **Vol. 5, Part 2**, 45; Florida, **Vol. 9, Part 2**, 38; Georgia, **Vol. 5, Part 1**, 348; **Vol. 7, Part 1**, 564; Illinois, **Vol. 1, Part 2**, 289; Indiana, **Vol. 3, Part 1**, 419 f.; **Vol. 5, Part 1**, 55; Iowa, **Vol. 1, Part 2**, 96; **Vol. 2, Part 2**, 165; **Vol. 4, Part 2**, 34; **Vol. 7, Part 2**, 197; **Vol. 10, Part 1**, 617 f.; Kansas, **Vol. 1, Part 1**, 267, 316; **Vol. 3, Part 2**, 252; **Vol. 5, Part 2**, 504; **Vol. 7, Part 2**, 393; Kentucky, **Vol. 3, Part 1**, 491 f.; **Vol. 9, Part 1**, 18; Louisiana, **Vol. 3, Part 1**, 585 f.; Maine, **Vol. 4, Part 1**, 379; **Vol. 5, Part 1**, 163; Massachusetts, **Vol. 4, Part 1**, 383; **Vol. 10, Part 1**, 541 f.; Michigan, **Vol. 6, Part 2**, 613; Mississippi, **Vol. 7, Part 1**, 100; **Vol. 9, Part 2**, 78; Nebraska, **Vol. 4, Part 1**, 77; New England, **Vol. 3, Part 2**, 473; **Vol. 6, Part 1**, 418; **Vol. 7, Part 2**, 567; **Vol. 10, Part 2**, 210; New Hampshire, **Vol. 8, Part 2**, 120; New York, **Vol. 3, Part 1**, 210, 605 f.; **Vol. 5, Part 2**, 90; **Vol. 6, Part 1**, 232; **Vol. 7, Part 2**, 297; **Vol. 8, Part 1**, 347 f.; **Vol. 10, Part 2**, 460; North Carolina, **Vol. 8, Part 1**, 40 f.; North Dakota, **Vol. 5, Part 2**, 525; **Vol. 9, Part 2**, 38; Ohio, **Vol. 2, Part 1**, 600; **Vol. 3, Part 1**, 242; **Vol. 5, Part 2**, 445 f.; **Vol. 7, Part 2**, 62 f.; **Vol. 9, Part 2**, 641; **Vol. 10, Part 1**, 444 f.; Pennsylvania, **Vol. 8, Part 1**, 143 f.; **Vol. 8, Part 2**, 9; **Vol. 10, Part 1**, 556 f.; South Carolina, **Vol. 4, Part 2**, 85, 609; **Vol. 8, Part 1**, 397; Tennessee, **Vol. 8, Part 1**, 93 f.; **Vol. 9, Part 2**, 364; Virginia, **Vol. 4, Part 1**, 156; **Vol. 6, Part 1**, 555, **Vol. 8, Part 2**, 215; Wisconsin, **Vol. 2, Part 1**, 557; **Vol. 9, Part 1**, 280. *See also* Agriculture

Agriculture, Department of (U.S.), **Vol. 1, Part 1**, 238, 267; **Vol. 2, Part 1**, 164, 428; **Vol. 2, Part 2**, 314; **Vol. 3, Part 1**, 349 f.; **Vol. 4, Part 2**, 394; **Vol. 5, Part 1**, 328, 406; **Vol. 5, Part 2**, 453; **Vol. 6, Part 1**, 92; **Vol. 7, Part 1**, 183, 257, 406, 434, 460, 472; **Vol. 7, Part 2**, 262; **Vol. 8, Part 1**, 154 f., 610; **Vol. 8, Part 2**, 64, 236, 383, 481; **Vol. 9, Part 1**, 263, 298, 458; **Vol. 10, Part 1**, 370, 556; **Vol. 10, Part 2**, 331; **Supp. 9**, 31; administration, **Supp. 4**, 416; **Supp. 5**, 365; **Supp. 7**, 760–61; **Supp. 8**, 699–700; agrostology, **Supp. 7**, 119–20; biological survey, **Supp. 6**, 453; economics programs, **Supp. 6**, 638–39; forestry, **Supp. 4**, 664; ornithological survey, **Supp. 3**, 517; pest control, **Supp. 4**, 399; plant breeding, **Supp. 5**, 213–14; reorganization, **Supp. 2**, 217, 322; research, **Supp. 4**, 45, 838, 862–63; Soil Conservation Service, **Supp. 6**, 53

Agrostology. *See* Grasses

Aguinaldo Campaign (Philippines), **Vol. 3, Part 1**, 271; **Vol. 6, Part 1**, 62

Ahiman Rezon, Masonic Work, **Vol. 3, Part 1**, 32

AID. *See* Agency for International Development

Aiken, Howard, reference to, **Supp. 6**, 675

Aileron, **Supp. 1**, 214

Aimwell School, founding of, **Vol. 7, Part 2**, 256

Ainslee's, founding of, **Supp. 1**, 664

Air Commerce Act (1926), **Supp. 9**, 899

Airborne Symphony, **Supp. 7**, 61

Airbrakes, **Vol. 10, Part 1**, 72; **Supp. 1**, 397, 605

Air compressors, early manufacture of, **Vol. 8, Part 1**, 343

Air conditioning, development of, **Supp. 4**, 148–49

Air Corps Act (1926), **Supp. 3**, 585

Aircraft. *See* Aviation

Air currents, study of, **Vol. 6, Part 2**, 148

Air Force, Department of the (U.S.), administration, **Supp. 6**, 618; **Supp. 8**, 322
Air Force, United States: **Supp. 4**, 459; **Supp. 5**, 444, 706; **Supp. 7**, 664; circumnavigation flight of South America, **Supp. 4**, 259; defense policies, cold war era, **Supp. 9**, 227; establishment, **Supp. 3**, 314, 585; **Supp. 9**, 747; **Supp. 4**, 27–30; **Supp. 8**, 185; GHQ centralization, **Supp. 3**, 17; Mitchell court-martial issue, **Supp. 1**, 461; **Supp. 3**, 218; **Supp. 8**, 47; **Supp. 9**, 746; Norden bombsight development, **Supp. 7**, 577; plane designs, **Supp. 6**, 40, 50, 64, 145, 182, 221; **Supp. 9**, 255–56; segregation "test case," **Supp. 10**, 378; strategic air power concept, **Supp. 9**, 229; strategic defense command, **Supp. 10**, 379; tactical bombing concept, **Supp. 4**, 259; **Supp. 8**, 185; team combat tactics, **Supp. 6**, 109; Tuskegee Airmen, **Supp. 10**, 378. *See also* Aviation; *specific wars*
Airlines. *See* Aviation; *specific airlines*
Airmail: Air Force service, **Supp. 8**, 185; contracts, **Supp. 2**, 487; **Supp. 3**, 157; **Supp. 5**, 86; **Supp. 6**, 221; **Supp. 7**, 86; **Supp. 8**, 707–8; legislation, **Supp. 5**, 385; **Supp. 6**, 64; night, **Supp. 5**, 294; **Supp. 9**, 658
Air Mail Act (1934), **Supp. 5**, 385; **Supp. 6**, 64
Air Policy Commission, report of, **Supp. 10**, 243
Air pollution, **Supp. 7**, 368; control studies, **Supp. 10**, 297–98. *See also* Pollution
Airports: architectural design, **Supp. 7**, 671, 672; New York City, **Supp. 4**, 50, 466; Weather Bureau stations, **Supp. 3**, 512
Air Service, United States, development of, **Vol. 6, Part 2**, 538
Air Transport Association of America, founding of, **Supp. 3**, 314
Air University, first commanding general, **Supp. 4**, 259
Akeley, Carl, reference to, **Supp. 5**, 420; **Supp. 8**, 3
Akeley, Lewis, reference to, **Supp. 6**, 369
Akerman, John D., reference to, **Supp. 7**, 619
Akron, Ohio, development of, **Vol. 1, Part 1**, 590; **Vol. 2, Part 1**, 221; **Vol. 6, Part 2**, 635
Alabama: agriculture, **Vol. 2, Part 2**, 232; **Vol. 9, Part 2**, 524; banking, **Vol. 3, Part 1**, 178; border, enlargement of, **Vol. 10, Part 1**, 72; carpetbagging, **Vol. 10, Part 1**, 94; civil rights demonstrations, **Supp. 8**, 333–34; **Supp. 9**, 384; Civil War period, **Vol. 9, Part 1**, 130; **Vol. 10, Part 2**, 594 f.; coal, **Vol. 3, Part 1**, 179; **Vol. 4, Part 1**, 4 1 8; **Vol. 8, Part 1**, 170; constitution, first, **Vol. 7, Part 2**, 561; education, public, **Vol. 2, Part 2**, 329 f.; **Vol. 6, Part 2**, 238, 493; **Vol. 7, Part 2**, 494 f.; **Vol. 10, Part 1**, 76 f., 506 f.; Episcopal church, post–Civil War period, **Vol. 10, Part 2**, 315; Freedmen's Bureau, **Vol. 9, Part 2**, 240 f.; geology, **Vol. 9, Part 1**, 263 f.; governors, **Vol. 1, Part 1**, 491 f.; **Vol. 1, Part 2**, 235 f.; **Vol. 2, Part 2**, 20 f., 171 f., 302 f., 329 f.; **Vol. 3, Part 2**, 439 f.; **Vol. 4, Part 1**, 197 f.; **Vol. 5, Part 1**, 261 f.; **Vol. 5, Part 2**, 146 f., 202; **Vol. 7, Part 1**, 122 f., 605; **Vol. 7, Part 2**, 41, 561 f.; **Vol. 9, Part 1**, 129 f.; **Vol. 10, Part 1**, 557; **Vol. 10, Part 2**, 404 f.; **Supp. 3**, 317–18; **Supp. 8**, 676–77; **Supp. 10**, 4; historical preservation, **Supp. 1**, 591; history of, **Vol. 6, Part 2**, 493; **Vol. 8, Part 1**, 608; **Vol. 10, Part 1**, 557, 567; Indian relations, **Vol. 6, Part 2**, 535; industrial growth, **Vol. 3, Part 1**, 179; **Vol. 8, Part 1**, 170; iron, **Vol. 8, Part 1**, 170; **Vol. 10, Part 1**, 87; journalism of, **Vol. 8, Part 2**, 515; jury desegregation, **Supp. 10**, 447; legal reforms, **Vol. 4, Part 1**, 368; **Vol. 9, Part 2**, 74 f., 602; legal service, **Vol. 2, Part 2**, 71; **Vol. 3, Part 1**, 74; **Vol. 4, Part 2**, 190; **Vol. 5, Part 2**, 202; **Vol. 6, Part 1**, 528; **Vol. 7, Part 2**, 519; **Vol. 8, Part 1**, 509; **Vol. 9, Part 2**, 602; Methodism, **Vol. 6, Part 2**, 169; normal schools, established, **Vol. 7, Part 2**, 41; nullification, rejection of, by, **Vol. 4, Part 1**, 197; pioneering, **Vol. 4, Part 1**, 93 f.; plant life, **Vol. 7, Part 1**, 77 f.; plantations, **Vol. 5, Part 1**, 206; political service, **Vol. 1, Part 1**, 491, 577; **Vol. 1, Part 2**, 236, 291; **Vol. 2, Part 2**, 20, 170, 230; **Vol. 3, Part 1**, 34; **Vol. 3, Part 2**, 439; **Vol. 4, Part 1**, 197; **Vol. 5, Part 1**, 261, 322; **Vol. 5, Part 2**, 202, 492; **Vol. 6, Part 1**, 210; **Vol. 6, Part 2**, 110; **Vol. 7, Part 1**, 123, 605; **Vol. 7, Part 2**, 41, 269, 561; **Vol. 8, Part 1**, 170; **Vol. 9, Part 1**, 129, 130, 339; **Vol. 10, Part 1**, 65, 94, 117, 557; **Vol. 10, Part 2**, 51; politics, **Supp. 3**, 729–30; **Supp. 4**, 49–51; **Supp. 5**, 290–91; **Supp. 10**, 4; politics, pre–Civil War, **Vol. 5, Part 1**, 54; **Vol. 10, Part 2**, 404; preaching, pioneer, **Vol. 3, Part 1**, 367, 410; public service, **Vol. 1, Part 1**, 538; **Vol. 4, Part 2**, 340; **Vol. 5, Part 1**, 206, 262; **Vol. 6, Part 1**, 210; **Vol. 6, Part 2**, 515; **Vol. 7, Part 1**, 123, 605; Reconstruction, **Vol. 2, Part 1**, 33; reforms, **Vol. 2, Part 2**, 302 f.; secession agitation, **Vol. 10, Part 2**, 593; state bank, collapse of, **Vol. 3, Part 1**, 178; steel manufacture, **Vol. 3, Part 1**, 179; Whig party, **Vol. 5, Part 1**, 54
Alabama Anthropological Society, founding of, **Supp. 1**, 591
Alabama Claim Case, **Vol. 1, Part 1**, 47, 461, 535; **Vol. 1, Part 2**, 342; **Vol. 2, Part 2**, 627; **Vol. 3, Part 1**, 135; **Vol. 3, Part 2**, 217, 398; **Vol. 4, Part 1**, 499; **Vol. 4, Part 2**, 71; **Vol. 5, Part 1**, 86; **Vol. 5, Part 2**, 64, 114; **Vol. 7, Part 1**, 286, 423; **Vol. 8, Part 2**, 428; **Vol. 9, Part 2**, 212; **Vol. 10, Part 1**, 323
Alamance, battle of (May 16, 1771), **Vol. 2, Part 1**, 571; **Vol. 3, Part 2**, 265; **Vol. 4, Part 2**, 531; **Vol. 10, Part 1**, 26, 302
Alamo, Texas, massacre at (March 6, 1836), **Vol. 1, Part 2**, 510; **Vol. 2, Part 1**, 293; **Vol. 2, Part 2**, 555; **Vol. 5, Part 1**, 265; **Vol. 9, Part 2**, 630
Alaska: birds, **Supp. 1**, 572; bishopric of, **Vol. 5, Part 1**, 491; boundary surveys, **Vol. 3, Part 1**, 35 f., 92, 298, 315; **Vol. 5, Part 2**, 167; **Vol. 6, Part 1**, 348; **Vol. 7, Part 1**, 640; **Vol. 9, Part 1**, 492; **Vol. 10, Part 1**, 540 f.; cataloging of names in, **Vol. 7, Part 1**, 640; coal lands controversy, **Supp. 1**, 300; **Supp. 3**, 96, 321; **Supp. 4**, 665; **Supp. 5**, 666, 699; **Supp. 7**, 606; development of, **Vol. 3, Part 1**, 35 f.; **Vol. 9, Part 1**, 220; **Supp. 1**, 108; education, **Vol. 5, Part 1**, 555; ethnology, **Supp. 1**, 572; exploration, **Vol. 8, Part 2**, 481; **Supp. 4**, 674; **Supp. 7**, 371; flora of, **Vol. 8, Part 2**, 188; fur trade, **Vol. 6, Part 2**, 631; geography of, **Vol. 2, Part 1**, 73; geological expeditions, **Vol. 2, Part 1**, 73; **Vol. 8, Part 2**, 243; gold rush, **Supp. 5**, 578; governmental code, **Vol. 7, Part 2**, 31; governors, **Supp. 1**, 108; Harriman expedition, **Supp. 10**, 309–10; history, early, **Vol. 5, Part 1**, 489; Indian policy, **Vol. 5, Part 2**, 573; missions in, **Vol. 5, Part 1**, 489; **Vol. 8, Part 2**, 559; **Vol. 10, Part 2**, 634; mountain climbing in, **Vol. 8, Part 2**, 243; novels about, **Supp. 4**, 60; politics, **Supp. 8**, 25–26; **Supp. 9**, 346; purchase of, 1867, **Vol. 5, Part 2**, 88; **Vol. 8, Part 2**, 620; Roads Commission, U.S., **Vol. 8, Part 1**, 576; Russian colonization, **Vol. 5, Part 2**, 515; **Vol. 8, Part 1**, 523 f.; statehood, **Supp. 7**, 50, 590; **Supp. 8**, 26; **Supp. 9**, 346; **Supp. 10**, 748; trade with, **Vol. 4, Part 1**, 229; **Vol. 9, Part 1**, 67; **Vol. 10, Part 1**, 532 f.; World War II operations, **Supp. 3**, 118; Yukon, first steam vessel to go up, **Vol. 8, Part 1**, 406. *See also* Eskimos
Alaska-Canadian boundary arbitration (1903), **Vol. 3, Part 2**, 552; **Vol. 4, Part 2**, 435; **Vol. 6, Part 1**, 348; **Vol. 8, Part 2**, 139
Alaska Statehood Act (1958), passage of, **Supp. 8**, 25–26
Albany, Ga., civil rights demonstrations, **Supp. 8**, 334
Albany, N.Y.: Buffalo, connection of, by railroad, **Vol.**

8, Part 1, 582; capitol, construction of, **Vol. 9, Part 2**, 657; early history of, **Vol. 7, Part 1**, 333; education, **Vol. 1, Part 2**, 571; Episcopal diocese of, **Vol. 3, Part 1**, 334 f.; public service, **Vol. 4, Part 2**, 310; **Vol. 5, Part 1**, 198; **Vol. 9, Part 2**, 388
Albany Congress (1754), **Vol. 5, Part 2**, 125
Albany Free Academy (N.Y.), **Vol. 1, Part 2**, 570
Albany Institute, **Vol. 7, Part 1**, 333
Albany Law Journal, **Vol. 2, Part 1**, 166
Albany Law School, founding of, **Vol. 7, Part 2**, 215
Albany Medical College, **Vol. 3, Part 1**, 169
Albany Patriot, **Vol. 9, Part 2**, 596
"Albany Regency," **Vol. 10, Part 1**, 153
Albee, Edward Franklin, reference to, **Supp. 9**, 731
Albee, Ernest F., reference to, **Supp. 3**, 697
Albemarle and *Sassacus*, **Vol. 1, Part 2**, 487
Albemarle Sound, N. C., battle of, **Vol. 6, Part 2**, 393; **Vol. 8, Part 2**, 85; **Vol. 9, Part 1**, 321
Albert, Heinrich, reference to, **Supp. 7**, 757
Albino, famous, **Vol. 4, Part 2**, 388
Albion village, social experiment of, **Vol. 3, Part 2**, 478
Albright, William Foxwell, references to, **Supp. 4**, 595; **Supp. 9**, 319
Alchemy, **Supp. 1**, 174
Alcoa. *See* Aluminum Co. of America
Alcohol: addictive quality, **Supp. 3**, 354; liquor industry, **Supp. 7**, 780; **Supp. 10**, 41–42, 700; 701–2; physiologic effects, **Supp. 3**, 163. *See also* Prohibition
Alcoholics Anonymous (AA): **Supp. 10**, 731; founding of, **Supp. 9**, 883; organizing efforts, **Supp. 10**, 705
Alcoholism: cure for, **Vol. 5, Part 2**, 280; fictional writings on, **Supp. 8**, 298; liver involvement, **Supp. 3**, 503; psychiatric view of, **Supp. 3**, 320; recovery from, **Supp. 10**, 705, 706; support groups, **Supp. 9**, 883; writings on, **Supp. 9**, 883
Alcorn University, presidency of, **Vol. 8, Part 1**, 513
Alderman, Myrl, reference to, **Supp. 10**, 223
Aldrich, Chester Holmes, reference to, **Supp. 6**, 157, 158
Aldrich, Mary M., reference to, **Supp. 4**, 8
Aldrich, Nelson W., references to, **Vol. 7, Part 1**, 463; **Vol. 10, Part 1**, 412 f.; **Supp. 5**, 745; **Supp. 9**, 16; **Supp. 10**, 685
Aldrich Currency Bill, **Vol. 1, Part 1**, 157; **Vol. 2, Part 2**, 154
Aldrich Plan, formulation of, **Supp. 2**, 15, 544, 555
Alec Wilder Octet, **Supp. 10**, 838
Aleichem, Sholom, reference to, **Supp. 6**, 567
Alert, capture of, in War of 1812, **Vol. 8, Part 1**, 83 f.
Aleutian Islands, **Supp. 6**, 629; survey of, **Vol. 3, Part 1**, 36
Alexander, Annie M., reference to, **Supp. 3**, 519
Alexander, Archibald, reference to, **Vol. 7, Part 1**, 439
Alexander, Grover Cleveland, reference to, **Supp. 9**, 368
Alexander, Samuel T., reference to, **Supp. 1**, 48
Alexander, William C., reference to, **Vol. 5, Part 1**, 450
Alexandria, La., operation at, **Vol. 1, Part 1**, 579
Alexandria, Va., skirmish at, **Vol. 3, Part 2**, 110
Alfalfa: hybridization, **Supp. 4**, 357; introduction of, **Vol. 10, Part 2**, 387
Alfred, first to fly Continental flag, **Vol. 5, Part 2**, 184
"Alfred Hitchcock Presents," **Supp. 10**, 340
Alfred University, **Vol. 8, Part 2**, 114
Alfred Observatory, **Vol. 8, Part 2**, 114
Algae, marine, **Supp. 3**, 703–4
Alger, Horatio, books, **Vol. 1, Part 1**, 178 f.
Algiers: naval attack on, **Vol. 5, Part 1**, 152; **Vol. 8, Part 2**, 73; **Vol. 9, Part 1**, 19; **Vol. 9, Part 2**, 310; treaty with (1796), **Vol. 1, Part 1**, 611; **Vol. 5, Part 1**, 374. *See also* Tripoli, war with
Algonquian Indians, **Supp. 4**, 179
Algonquin Round Table, **Supp. 3**, 54, 841–42; **Supp. 5**, 464, 623; **Supp. 7**, 413, 516; **Supp. 8**, 491, 622; **Supp. 9**, 335; **Supp. 10**, 147
Ali, Muhammad, Liston heavyweight championship bouts, **Supp. 9**, 507
Alice Adams, **Supp. 9**, 766, 767
Alice in Wonderland: illustrations for, **Vol. 7, Part 1**, 458; original manuscript, **Supp. 5**, 587
Alien and Sedition Acts, **Vol. 1, Part 1**, 78; **Vol. 3, Part 1**, 54; **Vol. 4, Part 2**, 177; **Vol. 5, Part 2**, 27, 148; **Vol. 6, Part 2**, 33, 188, 319
Aliens. *See* Immigration
Alimony, **Supp. 8**, 10. *See also* Divorce
Alinsky, Saul, reference to, **Supp. 8**, 589
All About Eve, **Supp. 9**, 697
Allaire, James P., reference to, **Vol. 9, Part 2**, 520
All-American Conference (football), **Supp. 6**, 48
Allatoona, Ga., battle of, **Vol. 2, Part 2**, 453; **Vol. 9, Part 1**, 95
Alleghany Corporation: **Supp. 6**, 721; investment holdings, **Supp. 9**, 462; management, **Supp. 9**, 422–23, 462–63; proxy fight, **Supp. 9**, 463; railroad holdings, **Supp. 9**, 423, 462; takeover bid, **Supp. 10**, 568
Allegheny River, traffic on, **Vol. 8, Part 1**, 464
Allen, Ethan, references to, **Vol. 1, Part 1**, 526 f.; **Vol. 8, Part 2**, 49; **Vol. 10, Part 1**, 468
Allen, Fred, reference to, **Supp. 8**, 477; Benny "feud," **Supp. 9**, 646
Allen, Frederick Lewis, reference to, **Supp. 6**, 571
Allen, George, reference to, **Supp. 9**, 646
Allen, Hervey, reference to, **Supp. 8**, 536
Allen, Maryon, reference to, **Supp. 10**, 5
Allen, Moses, references to, **Supp. 4**, 510, 511
Allen, Richard Day, reference to, **Supp. 3**, 6
Allen, Robert S., reference to, **Supp. 8**, 496
Allen, Walter H., reference to, **Supp. 9**, 249
Allergies: anaphylactic shock from, **Supp. 4**, 701; first clinic, **Supp. 6**, 123; first recorded observation of, **Supp. 1**, 666; studies of, **Supp. 5**, 438
Alliance Book Corporation, **Supp. 5**, 761
Alliance College (Ohio), presidency of, **Vol. 1, Part 2**, 208
Alliance for Labor Action, founding of, **Supp. 8**, 528
Alliance for Progress, **Supp. 7**, 421
Alliance for the Guidance of Rural Youth, founding of, **Supp. 4**, 365–66
"Alliancemen," **Vol. 5, Part 2**, 492
Allied Chemical Co., **Supp. 6**, 452
Allied Jewish Appeal, founding of, **Supp. 4**, 262
Allied Relief Fund, **Supp. 9**, 17
Alliluyeva, Svetlana, reference to, **Supp. 8**, 224
Allis-Chalmers Manufacturing Co., **Supp. 5**, 597
Allison, Jerry, reference to, **Supp. 6**, 301
Allison Engineering Co., **Supp. 7**, 793
"Allison" letters, **Vol. 9, Part 2**, 351 f.
All My Sons, **Supp. 8**, 31
Alloys: experiments with, **Vol. 1, Part 1**, 456; property requirements, **Supp. 2**, 91
Almanacs: **Vol. 1, Part 1**, 250, 413; **Vol. 3, Part 1**, 23; **Vol. 3, Part 2**, 89, 489, 549, 587; **Vol. 4, Part 1**, 609; **Vol. 4, Part 2**, 43, 123, 390; **Vol. 5, Part 1**, 131; **Vol. 6, Part 1**, 16, 81, 135; **Vol. 9, Part 1**, 88, 416; **Vol. 9, Part 2**, 444, 480; **Vol. 10, Part 2**, 5, 625; computations of, **Vol. 8, Part 2**, 287; first in America, **Vol. 7, Part 2**, 406; nautical, **Vol. 7, Part 1**, 452; *New England, The*, **Vol. 3, Part 1**, 23; **Vol. 4, Part 2**, 390; phrenological, **Vol. 3, Part 2**, 565; *Poor Richard's*, **Vol. 1, Part 1**, 413; **Vol. 3, Part 2**, 587; **Vol. 4, Part 2**, 123; revolving, **Vol. 8, Part 1**, 101 f.; *Solomon Thrifty's*, **Vol. 4, Part 2**, 43
Alone, **Supp. 6**, 93
ALP. *See* American Labor party

Alpine Club, founding of, **Vol. 4, Part 2**, 501
Al Serena scandal, **Supp. 6**, 416
Alsop, Joseph W., Jr., reference to, **Supp. 9**, 26–27
Alsop, Stewart, reference to, **Supp. 7**, 724
Alston, Walter, reference to, **Supp. 10**, 606
Alternating current, **Supp. 3**, 231, 251
Altgeld, John P., references to, **Supp. 2**, 142; **Supp. 3**, 852
Althouse, Paul, reference to, **Supp. 9**, 816
Altmann, Richard, reference to, **Supp. 6**, 53, 54
Alton Observer, abolitionist paper, **Vol. 6, Part 1**, 434 f.
Altoona Conference, **Vol. 1, Part 1**, 280
Altruist, **Vol. 6, Part 1**, 389
Alum, first manufacture of, **Vol. 9, Part 2**, 648
Aluminum: **Vol. 5, Part 1**, 382; automobile industry use of, **Supp. 8**, 309; electrolytic refining process studies, **Supp. 8**, 193–94; foil wrap, **Supp. 5**, 565–66; manufacturing, **Vol. 4, Part 2**, 122; **Supp. 7**, 166; solder, first successful, **Vol. 8, Part 1**, 555; World War II production, **Supp. 5**, 566; **Supp. 7**, 92
Aluminum Co. of America: founding of, **Supp. 2**, 446; **Supp. 7**, 166; product diversification, **Supp. 5**, 565–66; research, **Supp. 8**, 193–94
Alvarez, Luis, reference to, **Supp. 7**, 275
Alvey Resolution, **Vol. 1, Part 1**, 235
Alvord, C. A., reference to, **Vol. 7, Part 1**, 613
AMA. *See* American Medical Association
Amahl and the Night Visitors, **Supp. 7**, 124
Amalgamated Clothing Workers of America: **Supp. 4**, 69, 279; **Supp. 7**, 801; founding of, **Supp. 4**, 375–76; **Supp. 10**, 643
Amalgamated Copper Co., **Vol. 6, Part 1**, 60; **Vol. 8, Part 2**, 95, 263; **Vol. 9, Part 2**, 589 f.
Amalgamated Textile Workers Union, **Supp. 8**, 457
Amana Society, founding of, **Vol. 6, Part 2**, 586
Amateur Athletic Union (AAU): **Supp. 9**, 624; Owens ban, **Supp. 10**, 611
Amateur Cinema League, founding of, **Supp. 2**, 436
"Amateur Hour." *See* "Major Bowes Amateur Hour"
Amateur Telescope Making, **Supp. 4**, 675
Amazing Stories, founding of, **Supp. 8**, 209
Amazon River, exploration, **Vol. 4, Part 1**, 481; **Vol. 4, Part 2**, 580
Ambassador Bridge (Detroit-Windsor), **Supp. 7**, 136
AMC. *See* American Motors Co.; Associated Merchandising Corporation, 176
Amdahl, Gene, reference to, **Supp. 9**, 844
Amelia Court House, Va., in Civil War, **Vol. 6, Part 1**, 127
Amerasian children, adoption agency for, **Supp. 9**, 133
America, attempted transatlantic flight in, **Vol. 10, Part 1**, 635 f.
America, Jesuit publication, **Vol. 9, Part 2**, 532; **Supp. 5**, 677; **Supp. 7**, 448
America (ship), presented to French government, **Vol. 5, Part 2**, 186
America (aircraft), **Supp. 5**, 3
America First Committee, **Supp. 4**, 303, 480; **Supp. 5**, 339–40, 674–77, 689–90; **Supp. 7**, 249, 451; **Supp. 8**, 410, 650, 705; **Supp. 9**, 133; founding of, **Supp. 3**, 605
America-Japan Society of Tokyo, **Supp. 4**, 284
American, **Supp. 3**, 556, 816
American Academy in Rome: **Vol. 2, Part 1**, 306, 539; **Vol. 6, Part 2**, 101; architecture, **Supp. 1**, 322; founding of, **Supp. 2**, 402. *See also* American School of Classical Studies (Rome)
American Academy of Allergy: founding of, **Supp. 5**, 438; predecessor, **Supp. 6**, 123
American Academy of Arts and Letters, founding of, **Supp. 2**, 349
American Academy of Arts and Sciences: **Vol. 1, Part 2**, 492, 501; **Vol. 2, Part 2**, 633; **Vol. 5, Part 1**, 185; **Vol. 6, Part 1**, 465; **Vol. 7, Part 2**, 156–57; Faulkner Farm, **Supp. 4**, 115
American Academy of Christian Democracy, founding of, **Supp. 4**, 232, 233
American Academy of Fine Arts, **Vol. 6, Part 1**, 325; **Vol. 7, Part 2**, 82, 350; **Vol. 8, Part 2**, 21
American Academy of Medicine, **Vol. 9, Part 1**, 563;
American Academy of Pediatrics: founding of, **Supp. 4**, 8; predecessors, **Supp. 5**, 553
American Academy of Political and Social Science, founding of, **Supp. 2**, 175
American Academy of Teachers of Singing, founding of, **Supp. 1**, 712
American Action, **Supp. 6**, 679
American Agriculturist, **Vol. 1, Part 1**, 185; **Vol. 5, Part 2**, 231; **Vol. 9, Part 2**, 514; **Supp. 3**, 434; **Supp. 8**, 445
American Airlines: **Supp. 6**, 145; predecessor, **Supp. 8**, 367
American Alliance for Labor and Democracy, founding of, **Supp. 8**, 611
American and Foreign Bible Society, **Vol. 2, Part 2**, 342
American Anthropological Association, founding of, **Supp. 3**, 84, 85; **Supp. 6**, 534
American Antiquarian and Oriental Journal, **Vol. 7, Part 2**, 392
American Antiquarian Society, **Vol. 5, Part 2**, 54; **Vol. 7, Part 2**, 384; **Vol. 9, Part 2**, 436; **Supp. 8**, 664
American Anti-Slavery Society, **Vol. 1, Part 2**, 292; **Vol. 2, Part 1**, 284; **Vol. 4, Part 1**, 169 f., 539, 634; **Vol. 7, Part 1**, 289, 415; **Vol. 7, Part 2**, 546; **Vol. 9, Part 1**, 525; **Vol. 9, Part 2**, 5, 299, 303; **Vol. 10, Part 1**, 625 f.
American Anti-Slavery Standard, **Vol. 4, Part 1**, 195
American Appeal, **Vol. 3, Part 1**, 184
American Architect, The, **Vol. 6, Part 1**, 389
American Archives, **Vol. 3, Part 2**, 513
American Artists' Congress, founding of, **Supp. 7**, 171
American Art Review, **Vol. 5, Part 2**, 485
American Association for Adult Education: first black president, **Supp. 5**, 437; founding of, **Supp. 3**, 677
American Association for Cancer Research, founding of, **Supp. 3**, 258, 503
American Association for Labor Legislation, founding of, **Supp. 3**, 18, 178
American Association for Old Age Security, founding of, **Supp. 3**, 255
American Association for Social Security, **Supp. 3**, 255
American Association for the Advancement of Science, **Vol. 1, Part 2**, 530; **Vol. 7, Part 2**, 207, 471; **Vol. 8, Part 1**, 442; **Supp. 3**, 150; **Supp. 5**, 509
American Association for the Study and Prevention of Infant Mortality, founding of, **Supp. 5**, 553
American Association of Advertising Agencies, **Supp. 8**, 53
American Association of Anatomists, **Supp. 6**, 296; first woman president, **Supp. 5**, 600
American Association of Cartoonists and Caricaturists, founding of, **Supp. 1**, 718
American Association of Collegiate Alumnae, **Vol. 4, Part 2**, 514; **Vol. 7, Part 2**, 174; **Vol. 8, Part 1**, 554; **Vol. 9, Part 2**, 276
American Association of Economic Entomologists, founding of, **Supp. 4**, 400
American Association of Hospital Social Workers, **Supp. 6**, 98
American Association of Labor Legislation, **Supp. 1**, 294
American Association of Marriage Counselors, founding of, **Supp. 6**, 602

American Association of Museums, founding of, **Supp. 1**, 415
American Association of Pathologists and Bacteriologists, founding of, **Supp. 3**, 503
American Association of Petroleum Geologists, founding of, **Supp. 7**, 804
American Association of Physical Anthropologists, founding of, **Supp. 3**, 372
American Association of Plastic Surgery, founding of, **Supp. 4**, 221
American Association of Retired Persons, founding of, **Supp. 8**, 9–10
American Association of Social Workers, founding of, **Supp. 2**, 376
American Association of Teachers of Italian, founding of, **Supp. 2**, 254
American Association of Teachers of Journalism, **Supp. 1**, 87
American Association of University Professors, founding of, **Supp. 1**, 683; **Supp. 3**, 151; **Supp. 6**, 467; **Supp. 7**, 481
American Association of University Women, **Vol. 4, Part 2**, 514; **Vol. 7, Part 2**, 174; **Vol. 9, Part 2**, 276; **Supp. 6**, 412, 413
American Association to Promote the Teaching of Speech to the Deaf, **Vol. 2, Part 2**, 574
American Astronomical Society, **Vol. 7, Part 2**, 563; **Supp. 1**, 187; first woman officer, **Supp. 3**, 131
American Automobile Association, **Vol. 4, Part 1**, 330
American Ballet Theatre, productions, **Supp. 10**, 206
American Bandmasters Association, **Supp. 6**, 242
American Bank Note Co., **Vol. 3, Part 2**, 22
American Baptist Education Society, **Vol. 4, Part 1**, 182
American Baptist Home Mission Society, **Vol. 4, Part 1**, 603; **Vol. 7, Part 1**, 160; **Vol. 8, Part 1**, 543
American Baptist Missionary Union, **Vol. 9, Part 2**, 143
American Bar Association: **Vol. 1, Part 1**, 544; **Vol. 5, Part 1**, 383; **Vol. 8, Part 1**, 400; **Vol. 8, Part 2**, 177; **Vol. 9, Part 1**, 612; **Supp. 6**, 651; **Supp. 8**, 662; blacks' membership in, **Supp. 4**, 493; first woman committee chairman, **Supp. 7**, 785
American Bar Association Journal, founding of, **Supp. 2**, 500
American Battle Monuments Commission, **Supp. 3**, 199
American Bell Telephone Co. *See* American Telephone & Telegraph Co.
American Bible League, **Vol. 4, Part 1**, 602
American Bible Society, **Vol. 1, Part 1**, 512; **Vol. 1, Part 2**, 136, 568; **Vol. 2, Part 2**, 299; **Vol. 3, Part 2**, 215; **Vol. 4, Part 1**, 619; **Vol. 5, Part 2**, 9, 12; **Vol. 7, Part 1**, 2, 16, 245 f., 411; **Vol. 7, Part 2**, 591; **Vol. 8, Part 1**, 542; **Vol. 8, Part 2**, 261; **Vol. 9, Part 1**, 204, 300; **Vol. 9, Part 2**, 11, 303
American Bibliography, **Supp. 1**, 290
American Bimetallic League, **Vol. 10, Part 1**, 459 f.
American Birth Control League, founding of, **Supp. 8**, 569
American Board of Anesthesia, founding of, **Supp. 6**, 554
American Board of Foreign Missions, **Vol. 2, Part 2**, 13; **Vol. 3, Part 1**, 573 f.; **Vol. 3, Part 2**, 215; **Vol. 5, Part 2**, 234
American Board of Obstetrics and Gynecology, founding of, **Supp. 6**, 555
American Board of Plastic Surgery, founding of, **Supp. 2**, 707
American Board of Psychiatry and Neurology, founding of, **Supp. 4**, 572
American Board of Radiology, founding of, **Supp. 2**, 512
American Board of Surgery, founding of, **Supp. 6**, 246
American Book Co., **Vol. 4, Part 2**, 503
American Book Publishers Council, censorship fight, **Supp. 10**, 47
American Booksellers Association, **Supp. 7**, 524, 525
American Bridge Co., **Supp. 3**, 367
American-British Mixed Claims Commission, **Vol. 4, Part 2**, 111
American Broadcasting Co.: film studios' bid to purchase, **Supp. 9**, 733; founding of, **Supp. 8**, 179; management, **Supp. 10**, 415; news commentary, **Supp. 6**, 148
American Bureau of Shipping, **Vol. 9, Part 2**, 344; **Supp. 5**, 440
American Cancer Society: **Supp. 4**, 617; national crusade, **Supp. 10**, 30; predecessor, **Supp. 3**, 258; **Supp. 4**, 385
American Can Co., **Vol. 7, Part 1**, 144; merger with Dixie Cup Corp., **Supp. 9**, 556
American Car and Foundry Co., founding of, **Supp. 5**, 324
American Catholic Historical Association, founding of, **Supp. 4**, 353
American Catholic Historical Society of Philadelphia, founding of, **Vol. 6, Part 2**, 604; **Supp. 2**, 197
American Catholic Philosophical Association, founding of, **Supp. 2**, 506
American Chemical Journal, **Vol. 8, Part 1**, 501 f.
American Chemical Society, **Vol. 1, Part 2**, 34; **Vol. 7, Part 2**, 540; founding of, **Supp. 1**, 178; history division, **Supp. 4**, 114; publications, **Supp. 3**, 566; **Supp. 10**, 594
American Child Health Association, publications and promotion, **Supp. 7**, 70
American China Policy Association, founding of, **Supp. 6**, 350
American Citizen, **Vol. 2, Part 2**, 47
American Citizenship Foundation, founding of, **Supp. 2**, 637
American Civil Liberties Union: **Supp. 4**, 539, 542, 837; **Supp. 6**, 392; **Supp. 7**, 262, 356; Academic Freedom Committee, **Supp. 10**, 137; administration, **Supp. 7**, 510; expulsion of Communists from, **Supp. 7**, 248–49; FBI informant, **Supp. 10**, 221; founding of, **Supp. 3**, 246; **Supp. 4**, 904; **Supp. 6**, 330; **Supp. 7**, 248, 375; involvement in politics, **Supp. 9**, 36–37; Jehovah's Witnesses, case, **Supp. 3**, 679; legal counsel, **Supp. 5**, 280; literary censorship cases, **Supp. 10**, 221; national board, **Supp. 8**, 35, 681; predecessor, **Supp. 3**, 604; **Supp. 8**, 649; Scopes trial, **Supp. 6**, 528; **Supp. 8**, 583–84
American Classical League, founding of, **Supp. 3**, 810
American Climatological Society, **Vol. 7, Part 2**, 454
American Clipper (airplane), **Supp. 9**, 725
American College for Girls at Constantinople, founding of, **Supp. 2**, 517
American College of Physicians, reorganization, **Supp. 2**, 628
American College of Surgeons: criticism of, **Supp. 6**, 246, 632; directorship, **Supp. 7**, 329; founding of, **Supp. 1**, 408, 542; **Supp. 2**, 722; **Supp. 3**, 67, 202; **Supp. 6**, 215
American Colonization Society, **Vol. 2, Part 2**, 540; **Vol. 4, Part 2**, 56, 286, 524; **Vol. 5, Part 2**, 204; **Vol. 6, Part 1**, 163; **Vol. 8, Part 2**, 10; **Vol. 9, Part 1**, 288, 330; **Vol. 9, Part 2**, 506, 623; **Vol. 10, Part 1**, 508 f.; **Vol. 10, Part 2**, 509
American Committee for Cultural Freedom, **Supp. 9**, 679
American Committee for Democracy and Intellectual Freedom, **Supp. 3**, 85

American Committee for Relief in Ireland, founding of, **Supp. 2**, 497
American Committee for the Outlawry of War, founding of, **Supp. 3**, 457
American Committee for the Revision of the Bible, **Vol. 2, Part 2**, 38
American Commonwealth Political Federation, **Supp. 9**, 29, 30
American Congress on Tuberculosis, **Vol. 1, Part 2**, 154
American Conservatory (Fontainebleau, France), **Supp. 9**, 161, 162
American Cotton Growers Exchange, founding of, **Supp. 1**, 566
American Council of Learned Societies: **Vol. 7, Part 1**, 331; **Supp. 3**, 22; founding of, **Supp. 2**, 186, 342; **Supp. 8**, 369, 370
American Council on Education, **Supp. 5**, 761
American Country Life Association, **Supp. 1**, 145; founding of, **Supp. 3**, 684
American Cyanamid Co., **Supp. 3**, 439–40
American Cyclopaedia, **Vol. 4, Part 2**, 503
American Dance Festival, Connecticut College, **Supp. 6**, 313
American De Forest Wireless Telegraph Co., founding of, **Supp. 7**, 175
American Dialect Society, **Vol. 9, Part 1**, 64
American Dilemma, An: The Negro Problem and Modern Democracy, **Supp. 9**, 137
American Dispensatory, **Vol. 5, Part 2**, 394
American Documentation Institute, founding of, **Supp. 8**, 120
American Drawing Book, **Vol. 2, Part 2**, 18
American Economic Association, **Vol. 5, Part 1**, 574; **Vol. 7, Part 2**, 300; **Supp. 3**, 248; founding of, **Supp. 2**, 106, 608
American Electric Co., founding of, **Supp. 2**, 658
American Electric Power, **Supp. 10**, 751
American Electro-Chemical Society, **Vol. 10, Part 1**, 570 f.
American Electrotherapeutic Association, **Vol. 6, Part 2**, 381
American Engineering Council, waste-inefficiency studies, **Supp. 3**, 189
American Enterprise Institute for Public Policy Research (AEI), influence of, **Supp. 10**, 22–23
American Equal Rights Association, **Vol. 7, Part 2**, 609
American Ethnological Society, **Vol. 1, Part 2**, 7; **Vol. 2, Part 2**, 540 f.; **Vol. 3, Part 2**, 228; **Vol. 4, Part 2**, 417
American Ethnology, Bureau of, **Vol. 4, Part 1**, 192; **Vol. 7, Part 2**, 603
American Eugenics Society, **Supp. 4**, 413
American Expeditionary Force, **Vol. 5, Part 1**, 571; **Vol. 9, Part 2**, 327; **Supp. 2**, 460; **Supp. 4**, 123, 656–57, 702; **Supp. 5**, 160, 186, 468–69; 530–31; 668–69; **Supp. 8**, 262, 705
American Export Lines, **Supp. 7**, 604
American Express Co., **Vol. 2, Part 2**, 50; **Vol. 3, Part 2**, 271; **Vol. 10, Part 1**, 639 f.
American Farm Book, **Vol. 1, Part 1**, 205
American Farm Bureau Federation, founding of, **Supp. 1**, 660; **Supp. 3**, 319; **Supp. 4**, 37
American Farmer, **Vol. 9, Part 1**, 200
American Farm Foundation, founding of, **Supp. 1**, 645
American Federation of Catholic Societies, Social Service Commission, **Supp. 4**, 232
American Federation of Labor (AFL): **Vol. 2, Part 2**, 338, 612; **Vol. 3, Part 1**, 510; **Vol. 4, Part 1**, 370 f.; **Vol. 5, Part 2**, 278; **Vol. 6, Part 1**, 170, 521; **Vol. 6, Part 2**, 150; **Vol. 7, Part 1**, 545; **Vol. 8, Part 1**, 142 f.; administration, **Supp. 2**, 218–19; **Supp. 3**, 347; **Supp. 4**, 606–7; **Supp. 5**, 253–54, 339–40, 691; **Supp. 6**, 706, 707; auto industry unions, **Supp. 8**, 418, 419, 526; blacks and, **Supp. 6**, 648; **Supp. 10**, 659; CIO v., **Supp. 6**, 219, 379, 707; conservatism, **Supp. 6**, 218–19; **Supp. 7**, 455; corrupt unions expelled from, **Supp. 10**, 525; craft v. industrial union issue, **Supp. 2**, 325; **Supp. 5**, 254–55, 339–40, 510, 654, 691; **Supp. 6**, 218–19; **Supp. 7**, 255; first woman organizers, **Supp. 3**, 576; **Supp. 7**, 455; founding of, **Supp. 1**, 317; leadership of, **Supp. 10**, 524–25; mass production workers' unionization, **Supp. 4**, 279–80; Metal Trade Department, **Supp. 6**, 218–19; organizers, **Supp. 8**, 374, 375; presidential endorsements by, **Supp. 5**, 255; socialist movement and, **Supp. 3**, 347–48, 373; theory behind, **Supp. 6**, 503
American Federation of Labor-Congress of Industrial Organizations (AFL-CIO): awards, **Supp. 8**, 309; blacks and, **Supp. 10**, 661; founding of, **Supp. 8**, 528; **Supp. 10**, 525; leadership, **Supp. 10**, 303–4; political influence, **Supp. 10**, 525; Teamsters Union expelled from, **Supp. 9**, 396
American Federation of Radio Artists, **Supp. 6**, 159–60
American Federation of Teachers, **Supp. 8**, 132
American Federation of Television and Radio Artists (AFTRA), black stereotyping resolution, **Supp. 10**, 662
American Field Service, organization of, **Supp. 2**, 15
American Fisheries Society, **Vol. 4, Part 2**, 562
American Folklore Society, **Vol. 1, Part 2**, 423; **Vol. 7, Part 1**, 460; **Supp. 3**, 83
American Forestry Association, **Vol. 10, Part 1**, 444 f.
American Foundation for the Blind: founding of, **Supp. 5**, 347; fund-raising, **Supp. 8**, 318
American Foundation, Inc., **Supp. 1**, 93
American Freedom and Catholic Power, **Supp. 10**, 48
American Friends of France, founding of, **Supp. 5**, 506
American Friends of the Middle East, **Supp. 7**, 740
American Friends' Peace Association, **Vol. 5, Part 2**, 4
American Friends Service Committee, founding of, **Supp. 4**, 442
American Fur Co., **Vol. 1, Part 1**, 397, 401; **Vol. 2, Part 2**, 565; **Vol. 5, Part 1**, 326; **Vol. 8, Part 2**, 117; **Vol. 9, Part 1**, 144
American Game Association, founding of, **Supp. 2**, 265
American Gas and Electric Co., founding of, **Supp. 5**, 750
American Geographical Society, **Vol. 4, Part 2**, 2, 417, 445; **Supp. 4**, 99; Arctic expeditions sponsored, **Supp. 9**, 117, 118
American Geologists and Naturalists Association, **Vol. 8, Part 2**, 94
American Geophysical Union, **Supp. 6**, 206
American Gothic (painting), **Supp. 3**, 841
American Greek War Relief Association, founding of, **Supp. 7**, 692
American Guild of Musical Artists, **Supp. 6**, 633
American Guild of Organists, **Vol. 10, Part 1**, 480; founding of, **Supp. 2**, 198
American Gynecological Society, **Vol. 9, Part 2**, 446; founding of, **Supp. 1**, 437
American Heart Association, **Supp. 9**, 862
American Hebrew, **Vol. 6, Part 2**, 532; founding of, **Supp. 2**, 453
American Heritage (magazine), editorship, **Supp. 10**, 108; predecessor, **Supp. 8**, 328
American Heritage Foundation, founding of, **Supp. 8**, 53
American Heritage Picture History of the Civil War, The, **Supp. 10**, 108
American Historical Association, **Vol. 1, Part 1**, 309; **Vol. 3, Part 1**, 523 f.; **Vol. 7, Part 1**, 331; **Vol. 8, Part**

2, 312; **Vol. 10, Part 1**, 93; **Supp. 4**, 162–63; **Supp. 6**, 531; **Supp. 7**, 253; **Supp. 8**, 369, 370; **Supp. 9**, 331; founding of, **Supp. 2**, 340
American Historical Review, **Supp. 6**, 310; **Supp. 7**, 253; **Supp. 8**, 169; **Supp. 10**, 137; founding of, **Supp. 2**, 341
American history. *See* Colonial Period; History; *specific events*
American History Told by Contemporaries, **Supp. 3**, 336
American Home Economics Association: **Vol. 7, Part 1**, 576; **Vol. 8, Part 1**, 554; founding of, **Supp. 3**, 507; predecessor, **Supp. 3**, 68
American Home Missionary Society, **Vol. 7, Part 2**, 318, 502
American Homes, **Vol. 9, Part 2**, 319, 329
American Hospital. *See* Thorek Hospital and Medical Center
American Humane Educational Society, **Vol. 1, Part 1**, 303
American Humor, **Supp. 3**, 672
American Ice Co., **Vol. 7, Part 1**, 240
American Imago, The, founding of, **Supp. 4**, 717
American Indian Day, **Supp. 5**, 662
American Indian Federation, **Supp. 7**, 393
American Indians. *See* Indians, American (general); Indians, American (by state); Indians, American (by tribe)
American Individualism, **Supp. 7**, 359
American Institute for Social Service, **Vol. 9, Part 2**, 150 f.
American Institute of Aeronautics and Astronautics, predecessor, **Supp. 6**, 666
American Institute of Architects, **Vol. 3, Part 1**, 104; **Vol. 4, Part 2**, 413; **Vol. 7, Part 2**, 342; **Vol. 10, Part 1**, 125 f., 397 f.; first woman member, **Supp. 6**, 463
American Institute of Christian Philosophy, **Vol. 3, Part 1**, 193
American Institute of Christian Sociology, **Supp. 3**, 177
American Institute of Civics, **Vol. 6, Part 1**, 424
American Institute of Electrical Engineers, **Vol. 3, Part 1**, 221; **Vol. 8, Part 1**, 75 f.; **Vol. 10, Part 1**, 570 f.
American Institute of Graphic Arts, **Vol. 8, Part 2**, 214
American Institute of Homeopathy, **Vol. 4, Part 2**, 516; **Vol. 8, Part 1**, 264
American Institute of Instruction, **Vol. 5, Part 2**, 408 f.; **Vol. 7, Part 2**, 18 f.; **Vol. 8, Part 2**, 250; **Vol. 10, Part 1**, 558 f.
American Institute of International Law: first woman elected to, **Supp. 7**, 718; founding of, **Supp. 3**, 700
American Institute of Mining and Metallurgical Engineers, **Supp. 7**, 804
American Institute of Mining Engineers, **Vol. 2, Part 2**, 486; **Vol. 3, Part 1**, 460 f.; **Vol. 7, Part 2**, 354; **Vol. 8, Part 1**, 415; **Vol. 8, Part 2**, 189
American Institute of Physics, founding of, **Supp. 4**, 818; **Supp. 5**, 126; **Supp. 6**, 500
American Institute of Planners, predecessors, **Supp. 4**, 56
American Institute of Public Opinion, **Supp. 7**, 649
American Iron and Steel Association, **Vol. 7, Part 2**, 206
"Americanism," coining of the term, **Vol. 10, Part 2**, 438
American Issue Publishing Co., **Supp. 4**, 161
"Americanizers," **Vol. 8, Part 2**, 124
American Jewish Committee, **Supp. 2**, 6; **Supp. 3**, 85; **Supp. 4**, 603; **Supp. 10**, 375; founding of, **Supp. 4**, 539; Joint Distribution Committee, **Supp. 4**, 699–700
American Jewish Conference, founding of, **Supp. 4**,
American Jewish Congress, **Supp. 4**, 905, 906; first, **Supp. 2**, 266; founding of, **Supp. 3**, 488
American Jewish Historical Society, **Vol. 9, Part 2**, 131.; **Supp. 1**, 473; **Supp. 5**, 587
American-Jewish Joint Distribution Committee, founding of, **Supp. 4**, 539
American Jewish League Against Communism, **Supp. 6**, 350
American Joint Agricultural Society, **Supp. 4**, 699
American Journal of Dental Science, pioneer dental periodical, **Vol. 7, Part 2**, 251
American Journal of Education, **Vol. 1, Part 1**, 624
American Journal of International Law, **Vol. 5, Part 2**, 609; founding of, **Supp. 1**, 358; **Supp. 5**, 751–52
American Journal of Mathematics, **Vol. 9, Part 2**, 109, 257
American Journal of Mining, **Vol. 8, Part 1**, 415
American Journal of Nursing, **Supp. 6**, 1 67; founding of, **Supp. 4**, 632
American Journal of Obstetrics, **Vol. 7, Part 1**, 325
American Journal of Philology, **Vol. 4, Part 1**, 281
American Journal of Physical Anthropology, founding of, **Supp. 3**, 372
American Journal of Physiology: editing of, **Supp. 4**, 390; founding of, **Supp. 4**, 676
American Journal of Police Science, founding of, **Supp. 5**, 245
American Journal of Psychology, **Vol. 4, Part 2**, 128; **Vol. 8, Part 2**, 346; **Supp. 8**, 44
American Journal of Public Health, **Supp. 3**, 324; **Supp. 4**, 684; **Supp. 6**, 703
American Journal of Science and Arts, **Vol. 4, Part 1**, 245; **Vol. 9, Part 1**, 161 f., 163 f.
American Journal of Sociology, **Vol. 9, Part 1**, 222; **Supp. 6**, 482–83
American Labor Legislation Review, **Supp. 3**, 18
American Labor party: **Supp. 5**, 466–67; **Supp. 7**, 156; **Supp. 8**, 512; **Supp. 9**, 458–59; founding of, **Supp. 2**, 684; **Supp. 4**, 69–70; **Supp. 10**, 697
American Laboratory Theater, **Supp. 8**, 54
American Language, The, **Supp. 6**, 445, 446
American Laryngological Association, **Vol. 1, Part 1**, 191; **Vol. 5, Part 2**, 465
American Law Institute: **Supp. 8**, 662; founding of, **Supp. 2**, 471; **Supp. 4**, 491–92; **Supp. 6**, 87; **Supp. 7**, 317; presidency, **Supp. 8**, 662
American Law Journal, **Vol. 4, Part 2**, 138
American Law Magazine, **Vol. 9, Part 1**, 29
American Law Register, **Vol. 7, Part 1**, 49
American Law Review, **Vol. 4, Part 1**, 520
American League Against War and Fascism, founding of, **Supp. 8**, 425, 681
American League (baseball), founding and development of, **Supp. 5**, 261; **Supp. 6**, 415; **Supp. 7**, 139
American Legal History Society, founding of, **Supp. 3**, 43
American Legion: **Supp. 5**, 363, 459; **Supp. 7**, 744; founding of, **Supp. 2**, 15; **Supp. 3**, 449, 668; **Supp. 5**, 113, 177; **Supp. 7**, 808; **Supp. 8**, 495; national commander, **Supp. 8**, 302; organization of, **Vol. 8, Part 1**, 276; state commander, **Supp. 8**, 410; subversives, investigation of, **Supp. 8**, 426
American Leprosy Foundation, **Supp. 7**, 195
American Liberty League: **Supp. 3**, 653, 720; **Supp. 8**, 593; founding of, **Supp. 4**, 171, 683; **Supp. 5**, 156, 494, 715
American Liberty Oil Co., founding of, **Supp. 8**, 454, 455
American Library Association: **Vol. 2, Part 1**, 20; **Vol. 2, Part 2**, 583; **Vol. 3, Part 1**, 15; **Vol. 3, Part 2**, 22; **Vol. 4, Part 1**, 557; **Vol. 4, Part 2**, 42; **Vol. 8, Part 1**, 66 f.; **Vol. 9, Part 1**, 24; **Vol. 10, Part 1**, 426; administration, **Supp. 4**, 846; **Supp. 5**, 554; founding of, **Supp. 1**, 101, 242, 290; uniform catalog code, **Supp. 3**, 326–27; **Supp. 6**, 554

American Literary, Scientific and Military Society, Scientific and Military Society. *See* Norwich University
American literature: **Supp. 2**, 189–90, 703–5, 730–33, **Supp. 3**, 234–38; **Supp. 7**, 334–39; **Supp. 8**, 491–93, 563–64, 581–82, 625–26; beat generation, **Supp. 8**, 326–27; **Supp. 9**, 846; bibliography, **Supp. 8**, 663–64; Buddhist influence, **Supp. 8**, 327; **Supp. 9**, 846; Chicago Renaissance, **Supp. 8**, 124; comprehensive library of, **Supp. 7**, 797; fiction, **Supp. 10**, 153–54; 235–36; first novel, **Supp. 1**, 125; Golden Age of Indiana, **Supp. 4**, 629–30; grotesque tradition, **Supp. 7**, 231–35, 582–83; "hard-boiled" realism, **Supp. 10**, 88–89; "Lost Generation," **Supp. 10**, 395; modern, **Supp. 10**, 538–41, 582, 583, 754–55; novel of manners, **Supp. 8**, 480–82; realism, **Supp. 10**, 235; scholarship in, **Supp. 7**, short stories, **Supp. 10**, 641–42; teaching of, **Supp. 5**, 542; **Supp. 9**, 807–8; writings on, **Supp. 3**, 72; **Supp. 6**, 6, 445, 523. *See also* English literature and language; *specific genres, works, and writers*
American Locomotive Co., **Vol. 2, Part 1**, 424
American Longshoremen's Union, founding of, **Supp. 2**, 272
American Machine and Foundry Co., **Supp. 3**, 587
American Machinist, **Supp. 3**, 5
American Magazine: **Vol. 9, Part 1**, 354; **Supp. 3**, 762; **Supp. 4**, 47; founding of, **Supp. 4**, 518, 662
American Mathematical Society, **Vol. 5, Part 2**, 134; **Vol. 10, Part 1**, 149; **Vol. 10, Part 2**, 632
American Mechanic, first scientific newspaper in U.S., **Vol. 8, Part 1**, 101 f.
American Medical Association: **Vol. 2, Part 2**, 20; **Vol. 3, Part 1**, 139 f., 595 f.; **Vol. 4, Part 2**, 20; **Vol. 5, Part 2**, 468; **Vol. 6, Part 1**, 606; **Vol. 7, Part 2**, 276, 286; antitrust action against, **Supp. 3**, 122; birth control sanction, **Supp. 8**, 569; on medical care costs, **Supp. 6**, 702–3; on medical quackery, **Supp. 3**, 104; opposition to universal health care, **Supp. 10**, 682; political influence, **Supp. 10**, 419; *See also Journal of the American Medical Association*
American Medical Biography, **Vol. 9, Part 2**, 388
American Medical Missionary College, **Supp. 3**,
American Medical Recorder, **Vol. 3, Part 1**, 615 f.
American Medical Weekly, **Vol. 4, Part 1**, 90
American Medico-Psychological Association, **Vol. 3, Part 1**, 595 f.
American Men of Science, **Supp. 3**, 150
American Mercury: contributors, **Supp. 3**, 147; **Supp. 5**, 4; **Supp. 7**, 20; **Supp. 8**, 426; covers, **Supp. 7**, 3; founding of, **Supp. 6**, 445, 470, 471, 571
American Messenger, **Vol. 4, Part 2**, 159
American Metal Co., **Supp. 3**, 214
American Methodist Conference, **Vol. 9, Part 2**, 133
American Metropolis, **Vol. 7, Part 1**, 280
American Microscopical Society, **Vol. 10, Part 1**, 435 f.; **Supp. 3**, 40
American Midland Naturalist, founding of, **Supp. 2**, 488
American Mining Co., **Vol. 7, Part 2**, 461
American Missionary Association, **Vol. 4, Part 2**, 223; **Vol. 8, Part 2**, 103; **Supp. 6**, 321
American Missionary Society, **Vol. 1, Part 2**, 552; **Vol. 9, Part 2**, 299
American Motors Co. (AMC): "Big Three" competition, **Supp. 10**, 2; founding of, **Supp. 10**, 1; management, **Supp. 10**, 1–2
American Museum of Natural History (New York City): **Vol. 1, Part 1**, 198; **Vol. 1, Part 2**, 239; **Vol. 2, Part 2**, 84; **Vol. 3, Part 2**, 356; **Vol. 4, Part 1**, 341; **Vol. 4, Part 2**, 437; **Vol. 5, Part 2**, 62; **Vol. 6, Part 1**, 484; **Vol. 6, Part 2**, 412; **Vol. 10, Part 2**, 135; administration, **Supp. 8**, 485; African Hall, **Supp. 5**, 420; **Supp. 8**, 3–4; anthropology division, **Supp. 3**, 83, 84; **Supp. 4**, 867, 907–8; **Supp. 6**, 392–93; archaeological halls, **Supp. 7**, 570; architecture of, **Supp. 5**, 300; arctic expeditions, **Supp. 7**, 716; exhibit design, **Supp. 1**, 585–86; fieldwork sponsored by, **Supp. 10**, 522; insects and spiders collections, **Supp. 3**, 478; **Supp. 6**, 341; mammals curation, **Supp. 5**, 678; Mexican archaeology collection, **Supp. 3**, 786; ornithology division, **Supp. 3**, 161; **Supp. 6**, 255; **Supp. 7**, 116–17; paleontology division, **Supp. 3**, 316–17; public health exhibits, **Supp. 6**, 701; sculptures of Indians, **Supp. 6**, 720; whale collection, **Supp. 6**, 17–18
American Musical Fund Association, **Vol. 10, Part 1**, 543
American Musical Magazine, **Vol. 8, Part 1**, 421
American Musicological Society, founding of, **Supp. 3**, 253
American Naturalist, **Vol. 5, Part 1**, 447; **Vol. 7, Part 1**, 242; **Vol. 7, Part 2**, 126
American Nazi party, founding of, **Supp. 8**, 540–41
American Neurological Association, **Vol. 8, Part 1**, 282 f.
American News Co., **Vol. 3, Part 1**, 278 f.; **Vol. 7, Part 1**, 332; **Vol. 9, Part 2**, 606 f.
American Newspaper Guild: founding of, **Supp. 2**, 14, 67; Hearst organization opposition to, **Supp. 5**, 287; Newhouse opposition to, **Supp. 10**, 586
American Newspaper Publishers Association, **Vol. 2, Part 1**, 37
American Newspapers, Inc., founding of, **Supp. 5**, 287
American Normal School Association, **Vol. 7, Part 2**, 532
American Nurses Association, founding of, **Supp. 1**, 556
American Olympic Association, **Supp. 9**, 131
American Opera Company, **Vol. 9, Part 2**, 425; **Supp. 4**, 834
American Ophthalmological Society, **Vol. 3, Part l**, 207; **Vol. 5, Part 2**, 38
American Oriental Society, **Vol. 1, Part 2**, 387; **Vol. 2, Part 2**, 168 f.; **Vol. 5, Part 2**, 54; **Vol. 7, Part 2**, 56, 476; **Vol. 8, Part 2**, 308
American Ornithologists' Union, **Vol. 2, Part 1**, 31; **Vol. 2, Part 2**, 459, 465; **Vol. 8, Part 1**, 598
American Orthopaedic Association, **Vol. 1, Part 2**, 556; **Vol. 5, Part 2**, 236
American Orthopsychiatric Association, founding of, **Supp. 6**, 17
American Otological Society, **Vol. 8, Part 2**, 132
American Oxonian, **Supp. 6**, 30
American Palestine Exploration Society, **Vol. 7, Part 2**, 150
American Park Association, **Vol. 8, Part 2**, 37
American Patriot, **Vol. 5, Part 1**, 34
American Peace Award, **Supp. 1**, 93
American Peace Society, **Vol. 3, Part 1**, 345; **Vol. 4, Part 1**, 170; **Vol. 5, Part 2**, 527; **Vol. 9, Part 1**, 271, 635
American Peace Society of Japan, **Supp. 3**, 322
American Pediatric Society, founding of, **Supp. 3**, 160
American Pharmaceutical Association, **Vol. 7, Part 2**, 259; **Vol. 8, Part 1**, 242, 259
American Philological Association, **Vol. 2, Part 2**, 535; **Vol. 3, Part 1**, 372
American Philosophical Association, founding of, **Supp. 1**, 332
American Philosophical Society, **Vol. 1, Part 2**, 434; **Vol. 4, Part 2**, 385, 561; **Vol. 5, Part l**, 220; **Vol. 5, Part 2**, 205; **Vol. 7, Part 1**, 510; **Vol. 7, Part 2**, 306; **Vol. 9, Part 1**, 355 f.; **Vol. 10, Part 1**, 433
American Photocopy, **Supp. 9**, 877, 878
American Physical Society, **Vol. 7, Part 2**, 397; **Vol. 10,**

Part 1, 584 f.; founding of, **Supp. 2**, 488; **Supp. 3**, 511
American Physiological Society, **Vol. 1, Part 2**, 496; **Vol. 2, Part 2**, 617; founding of, **Supp. 2**, 391
American Place, An (New York City gallery), **Supp. 4**, 781
American Political Parties, **Supp. 7**, 54
American Political Science Association, **Vol. 8, Part 1**, 491; founding of, **Supp. 2**, 250; **Supp. 3**, 831; **Supp. 4**, 260; **Supp. 5**, 485
American Political Science Review, **Supp. 3**, 831; **Supp. 5**, 522
American Political Tradition and the Men Who Made It, The, **Supp. 8**, 271, 272
American Pomological Society, **Vol. 4, Part 2**, 356; **Vol. 9, Part 2**, 439
American Presidency, The, **Supp. 8**, 552
American President Line, **Supp. 6**, 244
American Press Association, **Vol. 3, Part 1**, 220, 278; **Vol. 7, Part 1**, 332; **Vol. 9, Part 2**, 606 f.
American Psychiatric Association, **Vol. 4, Part 2**, 411
American Psychoanalytic Association: **Supp. 4**, 572; founding of, **Supp. 4**, 131; reorganization, **Supp. 5**, 518
American Psychological Association: **Vol. 5, Part 2**, 526; **Supp. 8**, 8; presidency, **Supp. 6**, 672, 718
American Public Health Association: **Vol. 1, Part 2**, 268; **Vol. 4, Part 2**, 369; **Vol. 8, Part 1**, 390; Committee on Control of Communicable Diseases, **Supp. 6**, 193; Municipal Health Dept., **Supp. 6**, 702
American Public Welfare Association, **Supp. 7**, 787
American Publishers Association, founding of, **Supp. 2**, 59
American Publishers' Copyright League, **Vol. 8, Part 1**, 278 f.
American Quarterly Review, **Vol. 10, Part 1**, 391 f.
American Radium Society, founding of, **Supp. 2**, 512
American Railway Union, **Vol. 3, Part 1**, 183; **Vol. 5, Part 2**, 196
American Red Cross: **Vol. 1, Part 2**, 20; **Vol. 3, Part 1**, 148 f., 203, 218 f.; **Vol. 3, Part 2**, 553; **Vol. 7, Part 1**, 238 f.; **Vol. 8, Part 2**, 432; **Vol. 9, Part 1**, 394; **Vol. 9, Part 2**, 636; administration, **Supp. 1**, 582, 583, 595; **Supp. 2**, 177; **Supp. 4**, 91–93; Allied prisoners of war, **Supp. 7**, 599; blood program, **Supp. 6**, 414, 547; disaster relief, **Supp. 4**, 228; Greek relief, **Supp. 4**, 143; nursing service, **Supp. 2**, 495; **Supp. 4**, 65, 789; presidency, **Supp. 3**, 219; Serbian relief, **Supp. 5**, 336; Volunteer Special Services, **Supp. 4**, 93
American Red Cross Building (Washington, D. C.), **Supp. 4**, 92
American Relief Administration, **Supp. 7**, 359; predecessor, **Supp. 6**, 37
American Repertory Theatre, **Supp. 9**, 848
American Review of History and Politics, first American quarterly, **Vol. 10, Part 1**, 391 f.
American Revolution. *See* Revolutionary War
American Rolling Mill Co., **Supp. 3**, 781–82, 792
American Rose Society, **Supp. 5**, 555
American Sanatorium Association, founding of, **Supp. 2**, 71
American-Scandinavian Foundation, **Vol. 8, Part 1**, 138 f.; founding of, **Supp. 5**, 308
American School for the Deaf, **Vol. 2, Part 2**, 201 f.; **Vol. 8, Part 1**, 102 f.
American School of Archaeology (Jerusalem), **Supp. 6**, 641
American School of Classical Studies (Athens), **Supp. 4**, 143–44
American School of Classical Studies (Rome), **Vol. 7, Part 2**, 648; **Vol. 10, Part 1**, 485. *See also* American Academy in Rome
American School of Landscape, **Vol. 3, Part 1**, 535 f.
American School of Oriental Research (Baghdad), **Supp. 3**, 37
American School of Oriental Research (Jerusalem), **Supp. 3**, 272; **Supp. 9**, 15, 16, 319, 320
American School of Playwriting, pioneer work of, **Vol. 8, Part 1**, 221
American School of Prehistoric Research (France), predecessor, **Supp. 4**, 521
American Shakespeare Festival Theater and Academy, (Stratford, Conn.), founding of, **Supp. 7**, 458
American Shipping and Industrial League, **Vol. 10, Part 1**, 424 f.
American Singing Book, The (1785), **Vol. 8, Part 1**, 421
American Sisters of Charity, **Vol. 8, Part 2**, 596
American Smelting and Refining Co., **Vol. 4, Part 2**, 37, 39; **Supp. 3**, 321; **Supp. 4**, 351–52, 557; **Supp. 6**, 606–7; founding of, **Supp. 4**, 245
American Social Hygiene Association, **Vol. 3, Part 1**, 347; founding of, **Supp. 4**, 758, 759
American Society for Metals, founding of, **Supp. 2**, 595
American Society for Pharmacology and Experimental Therapeutics, founding of, **Supp. 3**, 343
American Society for the Control of Cancer: **Supp. 4**, 617; founding of, **Supp. 3**, 729
American Society for the Judicial Settlement of International Disputes, founding of, **Supp. 2**, 276; **Supp. 4**, 550
American Society for the Prevention of Cruelty to Animals, **Vol. 1, Part 2**, 215
American Society for the Prevention of Cruelty to Children, **Vol. 1, Part 2**, 215
American Society for Thrift, **Vol. 9, Part 2**, 132
American Society of Biological Chemists, founding of, **Supp. 2**, 4; **Supp. 3**, 164
American Society of Church History, **Supp. 4**, 151
American Society of Civil Engineers, **Vol. 6, Part 1**, 36
American Society of Composers, Authors, and Publishers, founding of, **Supp. 3**, 834; **Supp. 7**, 198–99
American Society of Dental Surgeons, **Vol. 2, Part 1**, 156; **Vol. 4, Part 2**, 441; **Vol. 7, Part 2**, 251
American Society of International Law: **Vol. 3, Part 1**, 298; **Vol. 5, Part 2**, 609; founding of, **Supp. 1**, 358; **Supp. 3**, 700; **Supp. 5**, 341, 751
American Society of Landscape Architects, **Vol. 7, Part 2**, 30; founding of, **Supp. 6**, 196
American Society of Mammalogists, founding of, **Supp. 2**, 634
American Society of Mechanical Engineers: **Vol. 8, Part 1**, 172 f.; **Vol. 9, Part 2**, 243; **Vol. 10, Part 1**, 470 f.; founding of, **Supp. 2**, 643
American Society of Naval Architects, **Vol. 3, Part 1**, 292
American Society of Newspaper Editors, founding of, **Supp. 3**, 850
American Society of Parasitologists, founding of, **Supp. 3**, 803
American Society of Park Superintendents, **Vol. 7, Part 2**, 30
American Society of Pharmacology and Experimental Therapeutics, founding of, **Supp. 4**, 34
American Society of Water-Colorists, **Vol. 1, Part 2**, 167; **Vol. 2, Part 2**, 314, 566; **Vol. 4, Part 2**, 362; **Vol. 5, Part 2**, 159
American Sociological Society, founding of, **Supp. 1**, 388
American Speaking Telephone Co., founding of, **Vol. 8, Part 1**, 193 f.
American Spectator, **Supp. 6**, 471
American Standards Association, **Vol. 8, Part 2**, 154
American State Papers, **Vol. 8, Part 2**, 542

American Statistical Association, **Vol. 5, Part 2**, 495, **Vol. 9, Part 1**, 33
American Steam Music Co., **Vol. 9, Part 2**, 57
American Steel and Wire Co., **Vol. 4, Part 1**, 188; management, **Supp. 10**, 344–45
American Steel Hoop Co., **Vol. 7, Part 1**, 143
American Stock Exchange, illegal practices, **Supp. 8**, 113–14; predecessor, **Supp. 10**, 138–39
American Sugar Refining Co., **Vol. 7, Part 2**, 267
American Sunday School Union, **Vol. 5, Part 1**, 56, 132; **Vol. 7, Part 2**, 127 f.; **Vol. 8, Part 1**, 539
American Surgical Association, **Vol. 5, Part 1**, 100; **Vol. 7, Part 2**, 208; **Vol. 8, Part 1**, 575
American Telephone and Telegraph Co. (AT&T): **Vol. 5, Part 1**, 347; **Vol. 7, Part 2**, 65; **Vol. 8, Part 1**, 193 f.; **Vol. 10, Part 1**, 138 f.; **Supp. 3**, 299; **Supp. 6**, 43; **Supp. 7**, 29–30, 176; amplifier research, **Supp. 9**, 524, 676–77; **Supp. 10**, 154–55; engineering, **Supp. 4**, 173–74, 430; growth as monopoly, **Supp. 8**, 211–12; equal employment opportunities in, **Supp. 9**, 676; management, **Supp. 9**, 524, 676–77; **Supp. 10**, 154–55; patents, **Supp. 5**, 22; regulatory battles, **Supp. 9**, 676; **Supp. 10**, 155. *See also* Bell Telephone Laboratories
American Temperance Union, **Vol. 2, Part 1**, 42; **Vol. 3, Part 1**, 221; **Vol. 3, Part 2**, 40
American Testament: A Narrative of Rebels and Romantics An, **Supp. 7**, 269
American Theatre Wing, "Tony" awards, **Supp. 4**, 653
American Theological Society, founding of, **Supp. 3**, 111
American Tin Plate Co., **Vol. 7, Part 1**, 143
American Tobacco Co.: **Vol. 3, Part 1**, 496 f.; **Vol. 4, Part 1**, 318; **Vol. 7, Part 1**, 591; **Vol. 7, Part 2**, 330; **Vol. 8, Part 2**, 266; advertising, **Supp. 5**, 411; antitrust case, **Supp. 3**, 587; Lucky Strike cigarettes, **Supp. 4**, 371; Reynolds' competition with, **Supp. 5**, 565, 566–67
American Tobacco Co. v. *United States*, **Supp. 7**, 96
American Tract Society, **Vol. 2, Part 2**, 378 f.; **Vol. 4, Part 2**, 158; **Vol. 6, Part 1**, 183; **Vol. 8, Part 1**, 89 f.; **Vol. 8, Part 2**, 43
American Tragedy, An, **Supp. 3**, 235, 237
American Tree Association, founding of, **Supp. 2**, 507
American Trotting Register, **Vol. 10, Part 1**, 373 f.
American Union Against Militarism, **Supp. 7**, 356; **Supp. 8**, 649; founding of, **Supp. 6**, 664
American Unitarian Association, **Vol. 1, Part 1**, 561; **Vol. 9, Part l**, 551; **Vol. 10, Part l**, 448 f.; **Supp. 7**, 356
American University (Beirut, Lebanon), **Vol. 1, Part 2**, 370, 372; **Vol. 8, Part 1**, 116 f.
American University (Cairo, Egypt), predecessor, **Supp. 4**, 860
American University (Washington, D. C.): **Vol. 5, Part 1**, 426; **Vol. 6, Part 1**, 558; history studies, **Supp. 7**, 735; physics studies, **Supp. 8**, 231; reorganization of, **Supp. 9**, 483
American Vindicator, **Supp. 7**, 644
American Volunteer Group. *See* Flying Tigers
American Watchman, **Vol. 2, Part 2**, 47
American Weekly, circulation, **Supp. 2**, 242
American Weekly Mercury, **Vol. 1, Part 2**, 553
American Wine Co., **Vol. 2, Part 2**, 374 f.
American Woman Suffrage Association, **Vol. 1, Part 1**, 320; **Vol. 1, Part 2**, 581; **Supp. 4**, 85
American Women's Association, predecessor, **Supp. 5**, 506
American Wood Paper Co., **Vol. 5, Part 2**, 281 f.
American Woolen Co., **Supp. 3**, 577
American Youth Congress, **Supp. 7**, 660
American Zionist Emergency Council, **Supp. 7**, 689
America's Coming of Age, **Supp. 7**, 79–80
America's Cup, **Supp. 4**, 124, **Supp. 5**, 6; **Supp. 9**, 18
"America's Town Meeting of the Air" (radio program), **Supp. 6**, 160–61, **Supp. 8**, 488
"America the Beautiful" (song), **Supp. 1**, 59
Americana, **Supp. 7**, 436
Americana: art, **Supp. 7**, 556–57; bibliographies, **Supp. 1**, 375; **Supp. 2**, 111; 162–63; collections of, **Vol. 3, Part 2**, 514; **Vol. 6, Part 1**, 157; **Vol. 8, Part 1**, 51 f., 549; **Vol. 8, Part 2**, 275, 420; **Vol. 9, Part 1**, 432; **Vol. 9, Part 2**, 499; **Vol. 10, Part 1**, 443; **Supp. 1**, 139–40, 154, 180; Ford museum and restorations, **Supp. 4**, 302
Americans for Democratic Action: **Supp. 8**, 5; founding of, **Supp. 8**, 527; **Supp. 10**, 360; influence of, **Supp. 9**, 586; predecessor, **Supp. 5**, 135
Ames, Adelbert, Jr., reference to, **Supp. 8**, 69–70
Ames, Blanche, reference to, **Supp. 4**, 17
Ames, James Barr, reference to, **Vol. 9, Part 2**, 404
Ames, Winthrop, references to, **Supp. 3**, 685; **Supp. 7**, 495, 496
Amherst, General, reference to, **Vol. 6, Part 1**, 517; **Vol. 7, Part 1**, 647
Amherst College: **Vol. 4, Part 1**, 210; **Vol. 4, Part 2**, 308; **Vol. 5, Part 1**, 70 f., 369; **Vol. 8, Part 2**, 556; **Vol. 9, Part 1**, 549; **Vol. 10, Part 1**, 99; economics studies, **Supp. 6**, 271; founding of, **Vol. 7, Part 1**, 146; **Vol. 10, Part 1**, 594 f.; presidency, **Supp. 5**, 390–91; **Supp. 7**, 523; **Supp. 10**, 137–38
Amiel, Jack, reference to, **Supp. 10**, 490
Amino acids: chain synthesis, **Supp. 3**, 441–42; chemistry of, **Supp. 3**, 61; cystine as, **Supp. 5**, 623; definition and preparation of, **Supp. 4**, 720; nutrition research on, **Supp. 6**, 190; **Supp. 7**, 476; research on, **Supp. 5**, 122, 149
Amistad case, **Vol. 1, Part 1**, 542; **Vol. 8, Part 2**, 383
Ammann, Othmar H., reference to, **Supp. 6**, 594
Ammann and Whitney, founding of, **Supp. 7**, 12
Ammonia, isolation of, **Vol. 8, Part 1**, 223 f.
"Amnesty oath," Texas, **Vol. 1, Part 1**, 111
"Amos 'n' Andy": controversy over, **Supp. 9**, 197; radio program created, **Supp. 9**, 196, 802
Amoskeag Manufacturing Co., **Supp. 5**, 190
AMP. *See* Cyclic adenosine monophosphate
Amplification. *See* Audio systems
Amsterdam News, **Supp. 6**, 490
Amundsen, Roald: rescue of, **Supp. 9**, 63; references to, **Supp. 2**, 115; **Supp. 5**, 206; search for, **Supp. 9**, 117
Amusement parks, **Vol. 9, Part 2**, 553; first in U.S., **Vol. 10, Part 1**, 48
Amy Vanderbilt's Complete Book of Etiquette, **Supp. 9**, 824–25
Amyotrophic lateral sclerosis (Gehrig's disease), **Supp. 3**, 294–96
Anaconda Copper Co., **Vol. 8, Part 2**, 263; **Supp. 4**, 556–57; **Supp. 5**, 273; **Supp. 9**, 641, 859
Anagnos, Michael, reference to, **Supp. 8**, 316
Analog Science Fact–Science Fiction, **Supp. 9**, 155, 156
Analysts. *See* Psychoanalysis
Anaphylaxis, **Supp. 4**, 34, 701; **Supp. 6**, 481
Anarchist movement, **Supp. 2**, 37, 246, 670; **Supp. 7**, 254, 454–55
Anastasia, Albert, references to, **Supp. 7**, 585; **Supp. 8**, 208, 397; **Supp. 10**, 269
Anatomy: comparative and functional, **Supp. 6**, 704; embryological studies, **Supp. 5**, 600; endocrinology and reproduction hormones studies, **Supp. 3**, 6; neuroanatomy, **Supp. 1**, 439, 584; **Supp. 6**, 295–98; plant, **Supp. 2**, 488; research in, **Supp. 4**, 419–20; **Supp. 6**, 53–54; skeletal development, **Supp. 2**, 665–66; teaching of, **Supp. 2**, 422; **Supp. 3**, 619; tech-

niques of study, **Supp. 6**, 53–54; writings on, **Supp. 2**, 423. *See also* Medicine; Physiology
Anatomy of an Illness, **Supp. 10**, 370
Anatomy of Revolution, The, **Supp. 8**, 50–51
Anatomy of the Nervous System, **Supp. 3**, 620
ANC. *See* Army Nurse Corps
Anders, Gunther, reference to, **Supp. 9**, 40
Anderson, Carl D., references to, **Supp. 5**, 496; **Supp. 7**, 344
Anderson, Clinton P., reference to, **Supp. 9**, 774
Anderson, D. C., reference to, **Vol. 1, Part 2**, 445
Anderson, Eddie (actor), reference to, **Supp. 9**, 76
Anderson, Eddie (football coach), reference to, **Supp. 9**, 817
Anderson, Ernest, reference to, **Supp. 9**, 183
Anderson, Ernest G., reference to, **Supp. 3**, 540
Anderson, George W., reference to, **Supp. 3**, 98
Anderson, Henry W., reference to, **Supp. 3**, 304
Anderson, Jack, references to, **Supp. 8**, 497; **Supp. 9**, 241, 845
Anderson, John F., reference to, **Supp. 4**, 701
Anderson, John W., reference to, **Supp. 4**, 294
Anderson, Margaret, reference to, **Supp. 10**, 246
Anderson, Marian, references to, **Supp. 5**, 343; **Supp. 8**, 328; **Supp. 9**, 418; **Supp. 10**, 119
Anderson, Maxwell, references to, **Supp. 5**, 100; **Supp. 8**, 255, 529, 622
Anderson, Olaf, reference to, **Supp. 6**, 71
Anderson, Paul Y., reference to, **Supp. 3**, 92
Anderson, Robert B., reference to, **Supp. 6**, 540
Anderson, Sherwood, references to, **Supp. 4**, 131; **Supp. 7**, 231, 306, 334, 335
Anderson, Clayton, and Co., founding of, **Supp. 8**, 89
Anderson School (Staatsburg, N. Y.), **Supp. 6**, 17
Andersonville, **Supp. 10**, 400
Andersonville prison, **Vol. 5, Part 1**, 194; **Vol. 6, Part 1**, 162; **Vol. 7, Part 1**, 567; **Vol. 10, Part 2**, 381
Andover Academy. *See* Phillips Academy, Andover
Andover Review, founding of, **Vol. 9, Part 1**, 374
Andover Theological Seminary: **Vol. 1, Part 2**, 31; **Vol. 3, Part 1**, 573 f.; **Vol. 3, Part 2**, 40; **Vol. 7, Part 2**, 204 f., 548; controversy concerning, **Vol. 4, Part 2**, 308; **Vol. 7, Part 2**, 526; **Vol. 8, Part 2**, 46; **Vol. 9, Part 1**, 374, 377; **Vol. 10, Part 1**, 41; founding of, **Vol. 2, Part 1**, 147; **Vol. 7, Part 1**, 245; **Vol. 7, Part 2**, 358; **Vol. 9, Part 1**, 481; heterodoxy, charges of, **Vol. 3, Part 1**, 571 f.; **Supp. 5**, 649
Andr, John, references to, **Vol. 5, Part 1**, 295, 417; **Vol. 6, Part 1**, 31, 314; **Vol. 8, Part 2**, 34, 239, 407; **Vol. 9, Part 2**, 387
André Eglevsky Ballet Company (Massapequa, N.Y.), students at, **Supp. 10**, 207
Andrews, Charles McLean, reference to, **Supp. 9**, 314
Andrews, John, **Vol. 1, Part 1**, 245, 294
Andrews, John B., references to, **Supp. 3**, 178, 255, 256
Andrews, Roy Chapman, reference to, **Supp. 3**, 316
Andrews, Yvette, reference to, **Supp. 6**, 18
Andromeda, nebula, **Supp. 6**, 31
Andros, Sir Edmund, references to, **Vol. 1, Part 2**, 336; **Vol. 3, Part 1**, 481 f.; **Vol. 7, Part 1**, 500
Androscoggin River, power development, **Vol. 8, Part 2**, 399
Androsterone, **Supp. 4**, 460
Anemia: childhood, **Supp. 3**, 190; hypoplastic, **Supp. 3**, 75; iron treatment for, **Supp. 5**, 276; liver extract for pernicious, **Supp. 5**, 122, 149; nutritional deficiency and, **Supp. 4**, 580–82; treatment of, **Supp. 3**, 242; tropical, **Supp. 1**, 32
Anesthesia: childbirth, **Supp. 3**, 223; cocaine as, **Supp. 3**, 430–31; cyclopropane, **Supp. 6**, 334; ether production and packaging, **Supp. 8**, 411; ethylene, **Supp. 3**, 458; first ethylene-oxygen use, **Supp. 3**, 67; local and regional, **Supp. 6**, 435; shockless, **Supp. 3**, 201–2; side-effect counteraction, **Supp. 4**, 34; spinal, **Supp. 4**, 507; **Supp. 7**, 679; training in, **Supp. 6**, 553–54. *See also* Medicine
Angell, James Burrill, reference to, **Supp. 4**, 20
Angell, James Rowland, references to, **Supp. 6**, 559, 600, 671
Angelus Temple (Los Angeles), **Supp. 3**, 498
Anger (emotion), hypothalamus relationship, **Supp. 3**, 135
Anglican church. *See* Church of England; Protestant Episcopal church
Anglo-American Telegraph Co., **Vol. 3, Part 1**, 600
Anglo-Catholicism, **Supp. 3**, 195; **Supp. 6**, 45–46; **Supp. 7**, 220
Anglo-Chinese College, **Vol. 1, Part 1**, 263; **Vol. 7, Part 2**, 214
Anglo-Roman Union, founding of, **Supp. 2**, 201–2
Anheuser, Eberhard, reference to, **Supp. 1**, 142
Anhydremia syndrome, **Supp. 2**, 432
Animal Industry, Bureau of, **Vol. 6, Part 1**, 92; **Vol. 8, Part 2**, 311
Animals: antivivisectionism, **Supp. 6**, 113; behavior studies, **Supp. 2**, 489, 699; biochemical studies, **Supp. 5**, 275, 276; coloration, **Vol. 9, Part 2**, 400; diseases, research in, **Supp. 1**, 258; diseases of, **Vol. 7, Part 1**, 140; **Vol. 8, Part 2**, 311; game surveys, **Supp. 4**, 483; geographic distribution of, **Supp. 4**, 52; husbandry, **Vol. 4, Part 1**, 380; **Vol. 6, Part 1**, 163; **Vol. 7, Part 2**, 510 f.; **Vol. 8, Part 2**, 335 f.; locomotion, photography of, **Vol. 7, Part 1**, 373; Mexican survey, **Supp. 1**, 572; movie use of, **Supp. 4**, 735; nutrition, **Vol. 1, Part 1**, 349 f.; **Supp. 1**, 37; paintings of, **Vol. 1, Part 2**, 95; **Vol. 4, Part 2**, 463 f.; **Vol. 5, Part 1**, 299 f.; **Vol. 7, Part 1**, 152; **Vol. 9, Part 2**, 399 f.; **Vol. 10, Part 2**, 191; psychological studies, **Supp. 8**, 343; sculpture of, **Vol. 1, Part 2**, 11; **Vol. 5, Part 2**, 317 f.; **Vol. 8, Part 1**, 125 f.; seeing-eye dogs, **Supp. 4**, 253–55; shelters, **Supp. 8**, 78; stories about, **Supp. 3**, 767; **Supp. 4**, 736; use in research studies, **Supp. 2**, 157; **Supp. 4**, 832; welfare of, **Vol. 1, Part 1**, 303; **Vol. 1, Part 2**, 215, 424. *See also* Livestock; Psychology, comparative; Veterinary medicine; Wild animals; Zoology; *specific kinds*
Animal World, **Vol. 1, Part 1**, 304
Animated cartoons: animators and artists, **Supp. 9**, 797–98; **Supp. 10**, 351–53; Disney Studio, **Supp. 9**, 237; **Supp. 10**, 351, 441; first, **Supp. 3**, 76; Warner brothers, **Supp. 10**, 813
Anna Christie, **Supp. 4**, 503
Annal of the New York Stage, **Supp. 4**, 634
Annals of Mathematics, founding of, **Supp. 1**, 675
Annals of Surgery, editing of, **Supp. 1**, 599
Annals of the American Academy of Political and Social Science, founding of, **Supp. 2**, 175
Annapolis. *See* United States Naval Academy
Annapolis Convention (1786), **Vol. 1, Part 2**, 204
Anne (ship), **Vol. 7, Part 1**, 43
Anne Frank: The Diary of a Young Girl, **Supp. 10**, 47
Annenberg, Max, reference to, **Supp. 3**, 19
Annenberg, Moses, references to, **Supp. 4**, 613; **Supp. 6**, 232
Annenberg, Walter, reference to, **Supp. 3**, 21
Annie Get Your Gun, **Supp. 9**, 281
Anniston, Ala., founding of, **Vol. 7, Part 1**, 540
Annual Cyclopaedia, **Vol. 3, Part 2**, 416
Anson, Mortimer L., reference to, **Supp. 9**, 549
Ansonia, Conn., history of, **Vol. 7, Part 2**, 526
Antarctica: birds, **Supp. 7**, 217; exploration, **Supp. 2**, 115; **Supp. 6**, 92–93; first flight over South Pole, **Supp. 9**, 64; Ford, Edsel, commemoration, **Supp. 3**,

284; mapping, **Supp. 7**, 217; Palmer Peninsula exploration, **Supp. 5**, 206–7. *See also* Exploration
Antarctican Society, founding of, **Supp. 7**, 217
Antaya, Maurice, reference to, **Supp. 9**, 465
Anthologies, **Vol. 2, Part 1**, 263; **Vol. 3, Part 1**, 224; **Vol. 4, Part 2**, 11; **Vol. 5, Part 2**, 337, 361, 614; **Vol. 9, Part 1**, 259; **Vol. 9, Part 2**, 374; **Supp. 10**, 799
Anthology Club, founding of, **Vol. 6, Part 2**, 138
Anthony, Katharine, reference to, **Supp. 3**, 376
Anthony, Susan B., references to, **Vol. 5, Part 1**, 150, 195, 196, 312; **Vol. 9, Part 1**, 36; **Supp. 4**, 85, 86; **Supp. 5**, 532; **Supp. 6**, 1
Anthony Adverse, **Supp. 4**, 13–14; **Supp. 8**, 536
Anthrascosis, research in, **Supp. 2**, 371
Anthropogeography, **Vol. 8, Part 2**, 583
Anthropologists. For complete list, *see* Occupations Index
Anthropology: **Vol. 1, Part 1**, 537, 571; **Vol. 2, Part 1**, 51, 594; **Vol. 3, Part 1**, 384 f.; **Vol. 4, Part 1**, 421; **Vol. 4, Part 2**, 105; **Vol. 5, Part 2**, 205 f.; **Vol. 6, Part 2**, 47, 60, 373; **Vol. 7, Part 1**, 242, 265 f.; **Vol. 7, Part 2**, 392; **Vol. 8, Part 1**, 276 f., 388 f.; **Vol. 8, Part 2**, 391; **Vol. 9, Part 1**, 197, 532 f., academic, **Supp. 7**, 710–11; American community studies, **Supp. 8**, 684–85; American Indians, **Supp. 2**, 9, 176, 593; **Supp. 10**, 27; black folklore, **Supp. 6**, 313–14; cranial indices, **Supp. 1**, 252; cultural, **Supp. 5**, 435; cultural age-area theory, **Supp. 4**, 907–8; cultural reconstruction, **Supp. 6**, 524–25; cultural relativity, **Supp. 3**, 82–86; **Supp. 4**, 71–72; dean of American, **Supp. 6**, 352–53; education in, **Supp. 4**, 521; ethnographic films, **Supp. 7**, 241; field research, **Supp. 1**, 259, 436; **Supp. 10**, 27; fieldwork by women, **Supp. 8**, 509–10; **Supp. 10**, 521, 522; first American Ph.D., **Supp. 3**, 83; folk cultures, **Supp. 6**, 532–34, 611–13; geological relationship to, **Supp. 4**, 119; historical reconstruction, **Supp. 4**, 179; Mead findings controversy, **Supp. 10**, 523; Mexican Tepoztlán study, **Supp. 8**, 378; museum collections, **Supp. 1**, 435–36; Navajo Indian museum, **Supp. 6**, 688; North American Indian, **Supp. 2**, 9, 176, 593; **Supp. 6**, 611–13; physical, **Supp. 3**, 371–72; **Supp. 4**, 866–67; physical human types, **Supp. 5**, 312; primitive religious symbolism, **Supp. 6**, 688; professional master plan, **Supp. 3**, 83; psychoanalytic theory in, **Supp. 5**, 583–84; psychological, writings on, **Supp. 8**, 345; social, **Supp. 8**, 683–85; worker fatigue, **Supp. 8**, 684; writings on, **Supp. 3**, 632
Antibiotics: aureomycin, **Supp. 6**, 176; streptomycin, **Supp. 9**, 834
Antibodies, **Supp. 3**, 440–42
Antietam, battle of, **Vol. 2, Part 1**, 310; **Vol. 2, Part 2**, 476, 563; **Vol. 5, Part 1**, 25, 193, 197, 371, 559; **Vol. 6, Part 1**, 124, 253–54, 392, 583; **Vol. 6, Part 2**, 257; **Vol. 7, Part 2**, 408; **Vol. 8, Part 1**, 570; **Vol. 8, Part 2**, 72, 548; **Vol. 9, Part 1**, 224; **Vol. 9, Part 2**, 215, 591
Antifederalism, **Vol. 2, Part 1**, 189; **Vol. 3, Part 2**, 385; **Vol. 9, Part 2**, 320, 356; **Vol. 10, Part 2**, 598, 601
Antigens, **Supp. 3**, 440–42
Anti-Imperialist League, **Vol. 1, Part 2**, 490
Anti-Intellectualism in American Life, **Supp. 8**, 271, 272–73
Anti-Liturgical party, **Vol. 1, Part 2**, 426
Anti-Masonic movement, **Vol. 2, Part 2**, 177, 224; **Vol. 4, Part 1**, 482; **Vol. 4, Part 2**, 155; **Vol. 5, Part 2**, 158; **Vol. 6, Part 2**, 128; **Vol. 7, Part 1**, 188–89; **Vol. 8, Part 2**, 233, 615; **Vol. 9, Part 1**, 621; **Vol. 9, Part 2**, 89, 454; **Vol. 10, Part 1**, 422, 598; **Vol. 10, Part 2**, 420
Antin, Mary, reference to, **Supp. 4**, 343
Anti-Nazi League, founding of, **Supp. 8**, 492
Antinomians, **Vol. 7, Part 1**, 573; **Vol. 10, Part 1**, 627 f.
Antioch College, Ohio: **Vol. 1, Part 2**, 169; **Vol. 5, Part 1**, 46; presidency, **Supp. 9**, 561
Antiquarian studies, **Vol. 1, Part 1**, 149, 379; **Vol. 3, Part 1**, 172, 276 f., 433 f.; **Vol. 3, Part 2**, 157, 316, 494, 559; **Vol. 4, Part 1**, 356, 556, 629; **Vol. 4, Part 2**, 472, 562; **Vol. 5, Part 1**, 320; **Vol. 6, Part 1**, 305 f.; **Vol. 7, Part 1**, 333; **Vol. 8, Part 2**, 367, 387 f.; **Vol. 9, Part 1**, 142, 243, 607; **Vol. 10, Part 1**, 74, 546; **Vol. 10, Part 2**, 154
Antiques: books on, **Vol. 9, Part 1**, 190; Metropolitan Museum American Wing, **Supp. 6**, 562; reproductions, **Supp. 3**, 567. *See also* Americana; Rare books and manuscripts
Anti-Race-Track Gambling League, **Vol. 6, Part 1**, 269
Anti-Saloon League of America: **Vol. 4, Part 2**, 253; **Vol. 6, Part 1**, 171, 276; **Vol. 6, Part 2**, 483; **Vol. 10, Part 2**, 55; factions in, **Supp. 5**, 442; founding of, **Vol. 5, Part 2**, 517; Ohio, **Supp. 4**, 161; Virginia, **Supp. 3**, 132
Anti-Semitism. *See* Holocaust; Judaism and Jews, anti-Semitism
Antiseptics: Argyrol, **Supp. 5**, 39; for childbirth, **Supp. 3**, 223; Dakin's solution, **Supp. 5**, 149; mercurochrome development, **Supp. 3**, 854; research in, **Supp. 4**, 435; wound cleansing technique, **Supp. 3**, 141. *See also* Surgery
Antislavery movement. *See* Abolition movement
Antitrust actions: aluminum manufacturing, **Supp. 7**, 167; Associated Press, **Supp. 10**, 499; AT&T, **Supp. 9**, 676; **Supp. 10**, 155; Brandeis views, **Supp. 3**, 95, 97; chain stores, **Supp. 5**, 278; federal regulation advocacy, **Supp. 4**, 317; inequities, allegations of, **Supp. 4**, 268; International Business Machines, **Supp. 6**, 675; investment banking, **Supp. 7**, 715; Justice Dept. litigation, **Supp. 10**, 125, 126; legal experts, **Supp. 5**, 174; **Supp. 9**, 593; legislation, **Vol. 1, Part 2**, 428; **Vol. 3, Part 1**, 342; **Vol. 4, Part 1**, 217; **Vol. 4, Part 2**, 25; **Vol. 7, Part 2**, 32; **Vol. 8, Part 2**, 65; **Supp. 1**, 179; **Supp. 5**, 27, 174; **Supp. 6**, 556; **Supp. 7**, 547; motion pictures, **Supp. 6**, 668; New Deal policy, **Supp. 3**, 168; **Supp. 8**, 17; New York state prosecution, **Supp. 4**, 536, 785; organized medicine, **Supp. 3**, 122; radio networks, **Supp. 8**, 179; Senate committee on, **Supp. 7**, 416; Standard Oil case, **Supp. 2**, 355, 573, 714; **Supp. 4**, 317; steel industry, **Supp. 3**, 263; **Supp. 6**, 591; temporary National Economic Committee, **Supp. 7**, 590; theaters, **Supp. 3**, 276–77; **Supp. 5**, 628; tobacco industry, **Supp. 3**, 587; **Supp. 4**, 536; **Supp. 5**, 567; **Supp. 7**, 96; trade unions, **Supp. 5**, 340; Wilson v. Roosevelt, T., views, **Supp. 3**, 97. *See also* Federal Trade Commission; Sherman Antitrust Act
Antivivisectionism, **Supp. 6**, 113
Ants, study of, **Vol. 6, Part 1**, 242, 603; **Supp. 2**, 708
Anything Goes, **Supp. 8**, 108, 383
Apache Indians, **Vol. 2, Part 2**, 563; **Supp. 1**, 660; **Supp. 6**, 720
Apalachin, N.Y., organized-crime conference, **Supp. 9**, 269, 270, 306; **Supp. 10**, 269
Apartment houses: first in U.S., **Vol. 3, Part 1**, 327. *See also* Tenements
Aperture, founding of, **Supp. 10**, 834
Apgar Score System, development of, **Supp. 9**, 39
Aphasia: rehabilitation methods, **Supp. 1**, 317; studies on, **Supp. 4**, 570
Apollo Club, **Vol. 5, Part 2**, 584; **Vol. 8, Part 1**, 177 f.; **Vol. 9, Part 2**, 579
Apollo project, **Supp. 8**, 81, 225, 694; **Supp. 9**, 476; **Supp. 10**, 67

Appalachian Mountain Club, founding of, **Vol. 5, Part 1**, 447; **Vol. 7, Part 2**, 563
Appalachian Mountains: **Supp. 3**, 407–8; geology of, **Vol. 6, Part 1**, 189; **Vol. 8, Part 2**, 94, 115
Appalachian Trail, construction of, **Supp. 9**, 526
Apparel. *See* Clothing manufacture; Fashion
Apparel Arts, **Supp. 5**, 637
Appeal to Reason (Socialist weekly), **Vol. 3, Part 1**, 184; **Supp. 5**, 264
Appendectomy, procedures, **Supp. 1**, 236. *See also* Surgery
Appia, Dr. Louis, reference to, **Vol. 1, Part 2**, 20
Apples, Golden Delicious variety discovery, **Supp. 9**, 756
Appleton & Co., founding of, **Vol. 2, Part 2**, 554
Appleton-Century-Crofts (publishing), **Supp. 6**, 580
Appleton's Annual Cyclopaedia, **Vol. 9, Part 2**, 375
Appliances. *See* Home appliances; *specific types*
Applied Social Research, Bureau of, **Supp. 10**, 438
Appointment in Samarra, **Supp. 8**, 480
Appomattox Court House, surrender at, **Vol. 4, Part 1**, 424, 497; **Vol. 5, Part 2**, 202; **Vol. 6, Part 1**, 104, 127, 392; **Vol. 7, Part 2**, 49
Apprentice system, **Vol. 4, Part 2**, 275; **Vol. 8, Part 2**, 238 f.
"April in Paris" (song), **Supp. 8**, 145
"April Showers" (song), **Supp. 5**, 630
Aptheker, Herbert, reference to, **Supp. 10**, 699
Aptitude tests: correlation machine for, **Supp. 5**, 329; for learning, **Supp. 4**, 833; for music, **Supp. 4**, 731
Aquacade, **Supp. 8**, 547
Aquariums, New York, **Supp. 8**, 485–86
Aqueducts: Potomac River, **Vol. 9, Part 2**, 260; **Vol. 10, Part 1**, 57; Rochester, **Vol. 8, Part 2**, 13
Arab-Israeli conflict. *See* Palestine; Zionism
Arachnology. *See* Spiders
Arbeiter Zeitung, **Supp. 5**, 95; **Supp. 9**, 724
Arbor Day, origin of, **Vol. 4, Part 1**, 78; **Vol. 7, Part 1**, 258, 565 f.
Arboriculture, **Vol. 8, Part 2**, 354
Arbuckle, Roscoe ("Fatty"), reference to, **Supp. 8**, 314
Arcadia Conference (1941–42), **Supp. 6**, 339–40
Arcaro, Eddie, reference to, **Supp. 7**, 400
Arc de Triomphe (Paris), one-way traffic, **Supp. 3**, 254
Archaeological Institute of America, **Vol. 4, Part 2**, 460; **Vol. 7, Part 2**, 249; **Vol. 10, Part 2**, 113
Archaeologists. For complete list, *see* Occupations Index
Archaeology: **Vol. 1, Part 1**, 571, 588; **Vol. 1, Part 2**, 492, **Vol. 2, Part 1**, 361, 556, 583; **Vol. 3, Part 1**, 113, 240, 594 f.; **Vol. 3, Part 2**, 161; **Vol. 4, Part 1**, 42 f., 416, 421; **Vol. 4, Part 2**, 460, 519; **Vol. 5, Part 1**, 226; **Vol. 5, Part 2**, 313 f.; **Vol. 6, Part 2**, 292, 551, 564, 601; **Vol. 7, Part 1**, 56, 366, 519; **Vol. 7, Part 2**, 506; **Vol. 8, Part 1**, 388 f., 574; **Vol. 9, Part 1**, 4, 10 f., 482, 489, 594, 635; **Vol. 9, Part 2**, 306; **Vol. 10, Part 1**, 442 f.; **Vol. 10, Part 2**, 49, 132, 402; American Indian artifacts, **Supp. 6**, 289–90; Asia, **Supp. 6**, 18; biblical period, **Supp. 9**, 319–20; ceramic chronology, **Supp. 2**, 44; Crete, **Supp. 3**, 343–44; Egypt, **Supp. 1**, 111; **Supp. 3**, 272, 375, 626–28; **Supp. 4**, 901–2; first system of scientific excavation, **Supp. 3**, 626; geological relationship, **Supp. 4**, 119; Greece, **Supp. 3**, 705; Latin America, **Supp. 1**, 648; **Supp. 5**, 711; medieval, **Supp. 1**, 601; Mesopotamia (Iraq), **Supp. 7**, 709; Mexico, **Supp. 4**, 605–6; Middle East, **Supp. 3**, 37; Palestine, **Supp. 3**, 272; pre-Columbian Mexico, **Supp. 3**, 786; prehistoric, **Supp. 4**, 520–21; research in, **Supp. 1**, 428; Sidon excavation, **Supp. 6**, 641; southern Russia, **Supp. 5**, 595; Southwestern U.S., **Supp. 7**, 432; stratigraphic method of excavation, **Supp. 7**, 570; United States, **Vol. 1, Part 1**, 588; **Vol. 2, Part 1**, 50, 97; **Vol. 3, Part 1**, 113, 553 f.; **Vol. 3, Part 2**, 353; **Vol. 6, Part 1**, 193 f.; **Vol. 7, Part 1**, 366; **Vol. 7, Part 2**, 392; **Vol. 8, Part 1**, 276 f.; **Vol. 9, Part 1**, 389; **Vol. 10, Part 2**, 376; writings on, **Vol. 2, Part 1**, 51, 183, 361; **Vol. 3, Part 1**, 113, 226, 240 f.; **Vol. 4, Part l**, 42, 421; **Vol. 7, Part 1**, 519; **Vol. 8, Part 1**, 161 f., 229 f., 252 f., 389, 574; **Vol. 8, Part 2**, 41, 280; **Vol. 10, Part 1**, 124; **Supp. 1**, 316
Archbold, John D., reference to, **Supp. 5**, 286
"Archer, Corliss" (fictional character), **Supp. 6**, 288
Archery, writings on, **Vol. 9, Part 2**, 460
Architects. For complete list, *see* Occupations Index
Architectural Forum, **Supp. 7**, 384; founding of, **Supp. 8**, 393
Architectural Record, founding of, **Vol. 8, Part 2**, 476
Architectural Research Group, founding of, **Supp. 9**, 445
Architecture: **Vol. 1, Part 1**, 137, 208, 401, 418, 432 f., 478, 580, 587; **Vol. 2, Part 1**, 519; **Vol. 2, Part 2**, 379, 422 f., 566, 594; **Vol. 3, Part 1**, 103 f., 157 f., 417 f.; **Vol. 3, Part 2**, 60, 323; **Vol. 4, Part 1**, 585; **Vol. 4, Part 2**, 89, 153, 182, 389, 412; **Vol. 5, Part 1**, 91, 127, 198, 389 f.; **Vol. 5, Part 2**, 55, 225, 274, 454 f.; **Vol. 6, Part 1**, 8, 21, 86, 166, 388, 457, 550 f., 599 f.; **Vol. 6, Part 2**, 473, 489; **Vol. 7, Part 1**, 10 f., 545; **Vol. 7, Part 2**, 341 f., 411 f.; **Vol. 8, Part 1**, 45 f., 210 f., 366 f.; **Vol. 8, Part 2**, 98 f.; **Vol. 10, Part l**, 397 f., 452 f.; **Vol. 10, Part 2**, 117 f., 196, 435, 452 f.; aboriginal, **Vol. 7, Part 1**, 185; acoustics, **Vol. 8, Part 2**, 277; **Supp. 3**, 524; Adam style, **Vol. 2, Part 1**, 246; arts and crafts influence, **Supp. 5**, 207–8; bank, **Vol. 1, Part 2**, 380; Bauhaus, **Supp. 8**, 226–27, 436; Beaux-Arts, **Supp. 1**, 341; **Supp. 4**, 281–82; **Supp. 5**, 133–34; books, collection of, on, **Vol. 9, Part 2**, 611; Boston, **Vol. 2, Part 1**, 394; building and plumbing supplies, **Vol. 7, Part 1**, 419–20; bungalow style, **Supp. 5**, 256–57; California style, **Vol. 4, Part 1**, 388; **Vol. 8, Part 1**, 145 f.; **Supp. 5**, 256–57, 606–7; **Supp. 6**, 438–39, 463–64; **Supp. 8**, 463–64; Capitol, Washington, D. C., **Vol. 2, Part 1**, 246, 519; **Vol. 4, Part 2**, 77; **Vol. 6, Part 1**, 599; **Vol. 10, Part 1**, 397 f.; Chicago school, **Vol. 2, Part 1**, 303; **Vol. 8, Part 2**, 149 f.; **Supp. 2**, 537; **Supp. 3**, 598–99; churches, **Vol. 2, Part 2**, 609; **Vol. 4, Part 1**, 387 f.; **Vol. 8, Part 1**, 507 f., 553, 567 f.; **Supp. 3**, 195–97; city planning, **Vol. 8, Part 1**, 45 f.; **Supp. 9**, 445, 447, 526; classical revival, **Vol. 4, Part 1**, 388 f.; **Vol. 5, Part 2**, 33–34; college, **Vol. 9, Part 1**, 335; colonial, **Vol. 2, Part 1**, 552; **Vol. 4, Part 2**, 347, 417; **Vol. 5, Part 1**, 83, 91; **Vol. 6, Part 1**, 91; **Vol. 6, Part 2**, 66 f.; **Vol. 9, Part 1**, 335; **Vol. 10, Part 2**, 61, 241; colonial revival, **Supp. 4**, 115; commemorative, **Supp. 3**, 199; commercial, **Supp. 2**, 253; **Supp. 7**, 690–91; concrete and steel, use of, **Vol. 6, Part 2**, 8; "corn-cob capitals," **Vol. 6, Part 1**, 22; court houses, **Supp. 1**, 716; criticism, **Supp. 2**, 708–9; **Supp. 3**, 52–53; customs houses, **Supp. 1**, 716; decorative design, **Supp. 2**, 742; **Supp. 7**, 522–23; design spareness ("less is more"), **Supp. 8**, 437; design theories, **Supp. 9**, 445, 446; development of, as profession, **Vol. 6, Part 1**, 25; eclecticism in, **Vol. 10, Part 1**, 73, 150 f.; Faneuil Hall, **Vol. 9, Part 1**, 229; Finnish, **Supp. 4**, 714; functionalism, **Supp. 4**, 105; Georgian, **Vol. 4, Part 2**, 417; **Vol. 10, Part 2**, 61; Georgian/Regency style, **Supp. 2**, 7; Georgian-style modifications, **Supp. 6**, 157–58; Gothic, **Supp. 1**, 480; **Supp. 3**, 195–97; Gothic, collegiate, **Supp. 4**, 697–98; Gothic revival, **Vol. 1, Part 1**, 422 f.; **Vol. 4, Part 1**, 298, 343; **Vol. 9, Part 2**, 2; government buildings, **Supp. 1**, 341, 716; **Supp. 8**, 629–30; Greek revival, **Vol. 6, Part 1**, 20 f.; **Vol. 9, Part 2**, 137 f.; **Vol. 10, Part 1**, 487 f.; Grillage foun-

dations, **Vol. 8, Part 2**, 149; group association practice, **Supp. 2**, 117; history of, **Vol. 8, Part 2**, 476; **Supp. 3**, 52–53; hotel, **Vol. 4, Part 2**, 240, 389; **Vol. 8, Part 2**, 99; industrial, **Supp. 3**, 404–5; international style, **Supp. 8**, 226–27; iron, early use of, **Vol. 1, Part 2**, 407; **Vol. 8, Part 1**, 138 f.; landscape, **Vol. 2, Part 2**, 204; **Vol. 3, Part 2**, 70; **Vol. 4, Part 2**, 230; **Vol. 6, Part 1**, 457; **Vol. 7, Part 2**, 24 f., 29 f.; **Vol. 8, Part 1**, 336 f.; late Victorian eclectic, **Supp. 5**, 462–63; libraries, **Vol. 3, Part 1**, 604; **Vol. 6, Part 2**, 100; **Vol. 9, Part 2**, 549; light, use of, **Supp. 9**, 446, 447; Lincoln Memorial, **Vol. 1, Part 1**, 478; **Vol. 2, Part 1**, 306; **Vol. 6, Part 1**, 563; materials, innovations in use of, **Vol. 8, Part 1**, 45 f.; **Supp. 9**, 446; medieval, **Vol. 7, Part 1**, 117; **Supp. 1**, 600; modern innovative, **Supp. 7**, 670–72; **Supp. 9**, 893; monuments, **Vol. 4, Part 2**, 389; museums, **Supp. 9**, 445–46; naval, **Vol. 1, Part 1**, 461; **Vol. 2, Part 2**, 500 f.; **Vol. 3, Part 1**, 211, 292; **Vol. 3, Part 2**, 164; **Vol. 4, Part 1**, 626; **Vol. 4, Part 2**, 9; **Vol. 5, Part 1**, 3, 376 f., 515; **Vol. 6, Part 1**, 173; **Vol. 8, Part 1**, 83 f., 464 f.; **Vol. 8, Part 2**, 200, 553; **Vol. 9, Part 1**, 237 f., 310, 559, 619; **Vol. 9, Part 2**, 7, 48; **Vol. 10, Part 2**, 346; New Orleans, **Vol. 6, Part 1**, 24; New York City, **Vol. 1, Part 1**, 587; **Vol. 2, Part 1**, 519; **Vol. 3, Part 1**, 104; **Vol. 4, Part 2**, 240; **Vol. 6, Part 1**, 599 f.; **Vol. 6, Part 2**, 232; **Vol. 8, Part 1**, 507 f.; **Vol. 8, Part 2**, 98; **Vol. 10, Part 1**, 73; **Supp. 5**, 408–9; organic, **Supp. 6**, 711; **Supp. 9**, 894; Philadelphia, **Vol. 5, Part 2**, 274; **Vol. 6, Part 1**, 21, 551; **Vol. 9, Part 1**, 336 f.; **Supp. 9**, 445; photographs of, **Supp. 7**, 686–87; photographs of early American, **Supp. 5**, 373; Prairie school, **Supp. 3**, 599; **Supp. 6**, 712; **Supp. 9**, 893, 894; preservation and restoration, **Supp. 4**, 24; **Supp. 5**, 388; public buildings, **Supp. 2**, 117, 537, 539; **Supp. 5**, 300–1; **Supp. 10**, 199, 764, 765; Renaissance, **Vol. 10, Part 2**, 117; residential, **Supp. 2**, 538; Richardsonian, **Vol. 8, Part 1**, 566 f.; romantic, **Supp. 5**, 483; Salem, **Vol. 6, Part 2**, 66; school buildings, **Supp. 3**, 599; sculpture, **Supp. 3**, 2, 123–25; skeleton construction, **Vol. 5, Part 1**, 127; **Vol. 5, Part 2**, 55; skyscraper, **Vol. 2, Part 1**, 303; **Vol. 4, Part 1**, 389; **Vol. 6, Part 1**, 86; **Vol. 8, Part 1**, 115 f.; space, use of, **Supp. 9**, 446; **Supp. 10**, 765; Spanish renaissance, **Vol. 2, Part 1**, 518; stage, **Vol. 10, Part 1**, 133; steel construction, early use of, **Vol. 6, Part 1**, 86; teaching of, **Vol. 4, Part 2**, 193; **Vol. 8, Part 2**, 185; **Vol. 9, Part 1**, 82; **Vol. 10, Part 1**, 452 f.; **Supp. 1**, 699; **Supp. 4**, 714–15; **Supp. 8**, 226–27, 436; tenement housing, **Supp. 3**, 743–44; twentieth-century classicism, **Supp. 3**, 199–200; university and college buildings, **Supp. 2**, 118, 362; **Supp. 4**, 697–98; **Supp. 5**, 388; ventilation problems in, **Vol. 8, Part 1**, 475; Washington, D. C., **Vol. 2, Part 1**, 305; **Vol. 4, Part 2**, 153; **Vol. 6, Part 1**, 23, 167; **Vol. 6, Part 2**, 101; **Vol. 9, Part 2**, 506; World's Fair, Chicago, **Vol. 8, Part 2**, 150; writings on, **Vol. 1, Part 1**, 423, **Vol. 1, Part 2**, 180; **Vol. 2, Part 2**, 250; **Vol. 3, Part 1**, 104, 158; **Vol. 3, Part 2**, 566; **Vol. 4, Part 1**, 585; **Vol. 4, Part 2**, 193 f.; **Vol. 5, Part 2**, 55; **Vol. 6, Part 1**, 389; **Vol. 6, Part 2**, 8; **Vol. 7, Part 2**, 342; **Vol. 8, Part 1**, l f., 45 f., 210 f., 336 f.; **Vol. 9, Part 2**, 243, 611; **Vol. 10, Part 1**, 74, 151, 397 f., 452 f., 605 f.; **Supp. 1**, 480, 537; **Supp. 6**, 272. *See also* Buildings; City planning; Landscape architecture; Model communities; School buildings

Archives: access to Soviet, **Supp. 9**, 691; American folk songs, **Supp. 4**, 502; early U.S. archivists, **Supp. 1**, 29; **Supp. 4**, 176; federal, **Supp. 2**, 342; **Supp. 8**, 369, 370; historical research, **Supp. 10**, 60–61; keeping of, **Vol. 3, Part 2**, 337, 513; **Vol. 9, Part 2**, 90; Louisiana, **Supp. 1**, 223; Mormon church, **Supp. 9**, 737; presidential, **Supp. 3**, 285–86; states' departments, **Supp. 1**, 591; War Department, **Supp. 1**, 17. *See also* Bibliographies; Collections; Libraries and library work

Archives of Dermatology and Syphilology, founding of, **Supp. 2**, 547

Arc lighting, research in, **Supp. 2**, 658. *See also* Lighting

Arch Street Theatre, **Vol. 7, Part 1**, 341

Arctic, shipwreck of, **Vol. 8, Part 1**, 447

Arctic Club, organization of, **Vol. 10, Part 1**, 390

Arctic regions: exploration, **Supp. 1**, 47, 353; **Supp. 2**, 115–16; **Supp. 4**, 674; **Supp. 5**, 206–7, 295, 539–40; **Supp. 6**, 92, 93; **Supp. 7**, 716–17; oceanography, **Supp. 7**, 698; **Supp. 9**, 63; 117–18. *See also* Antarctica; Exploration

Area Redevelopment Act (1961), **Supp. 7**, 424

Arevalo, Juan Jos, reference to, **Supp. 8**, 495

Argentina: astronomy in, **Supp. 5**, 541; diplomacy with U.S., **Vol. 3, Part 1**, 197; **Vol. 7, Part 2**, 283; **Vol. 8, Part 2**, 83; **Supp. 3**, 740; **Supp. 4**, 864; **Supp. 5**, 332; **Supp. 6**, 451–52; **Supp. 7**, 60; missions in, **Vol. 9, Part 2**, 76; protection of American interests in, **Vol. 7, Part 2**, 71 f.; sea fighting in service of, **Vol. 3, Part 1**, 202 f.; Treaty of Friendship, Commerce and Navigation, **Vol. 7, Part 2**, 422; writings on, **Vol. 9, Part 2**, 122

Argentine National Observatory, **Supp. 5**, 541

Arginase, **Supp. 5**, 149

Argon (rare gas), **Supp. 3**, 439

Argonne National Laboratory, **Supp. 9**, 542

Argus, naval exploits of, **Vol. 1, Part 1**, 212

Argyrol, **Supp. 5**, 39

Arizona: agriculture, **Vol. 4, Part 2**, 483; **Vol. 6, Part 1**, 611; **Vol. 8, Part 1**, 121 f.; botany, **Vol. 6, Part 1**, 162; constitutional convention, **Supp. 1**, 445; **Supp. 9**, 853; cowpunching, **Vol. 4, Part 1**, 577; first representative to Congress, **Supp. 9**, 372; governors, **Supp. 1**, 144; historical writings on, **Supp. 1**, 524; history of, **Vol. 9, Part 1**, 213; Indians, **Vol. 8, Part 1**, 121 f.; irrigation, **Vol. 8, Part 1**, 121 f.; land claims, **Vol. 9, Part 2**, 87; legal service, **Vol. 9, Part 1**, 212; political service, **Vol. 4, Part 1**, 409; **Vol. 6, Part 1**, 611; **Vol. 8, Part 1**, 121; politics, **Supp. 7**, 21–22; **Supp. 9**, 372–73; railroad development, **Vol. 8, Part 1**, 357 f.; statehood, admission into, **Vol. 9, Part 1**, 213; **Vol. 9, Part 2**, 270; **Supp. 9**, 853; Taliesin West, **Supp. 6**, 714; territorial, **Vol. 8, Part 1**, 121 f.

Arizona, **Supp. 9**, 461

Arkansas: carpetbagging in, **Vol. 8, Part 1**, 33 f.; Civil War period, **Vol. 3, Part 2**, 454; **Vol. 5, Part 1**, 60; "criminal intruders," **Vol. 7, Part 2**, 225; exploration, **Vol. 3, Part 1**, 507 f.; first Republican governor since Reconstruction, **Supp. 9**, 672; frontier justice, **Vol. 8, Part 2**, 161; governors, **Vol. 1, Part 2**, 226 f.; **Vol. 2, Part 2**, 105 f., 154, 187 f., 363; **Vol. 3, Part 1**, 122 f.; **Vol. 3, Part 2**, 403, 454; **Vol. 6, Part 2**, 166 f.; **Vol. 7, Part 1**, 352; **Vol. 8, Part 1**, 436; **Vol. 10, Part 2**, 607 f.; **Supp. 1**, 124; **Supp. 9**, 672; "Johnson Family," **Vol. 5, Part 2**, 118; land claims in, **Vol. 2, Part 2**, 363; **Vol. 8, Part 1**, 436; legal service, **Vol. 1, Part 2**, 56, 506; **Vol. 7, Part 2**, 225, 594; **Vol. 8, Part 1**, 436; **Vol. 8, Part 2**, 161; **Vol. 10, Part 1**, 538 f.; missions in, **Vol. 7, Part 1**, 625; pioneer days in, **Vol. 10, Part 2**, 500, 607; political service, **Vol. 1, Part 2**, 227, 465, 479, 506; **Vol. 2, Part 2**, 154; **Vol. 3, Part 1**, 122, 389; **Vol. 3, Part 2**, 403, 454; **Vol. 4, Part 1**, 150; **Vol. 5, Part 1**, 523; **Vol. 6, Part 2**, 167; **Vol. 7, Part 1**, 352; **Vol. 7, Part 2**, 12; **Vol. 8, Part 1**, 436, 641; **Vol. 10, Part 2**, 608; politics, **Supp. 9**, 672; **Supp. 10**, 218; 481–82; public service, **Vol. 2, Part 2**, 362, 570; railroad scandal in, **Vol. 3, Part 1**, 387; Reconstruction, **Vol. 1, Part 2**, 61; **Vol. 2, Part 1**,

408; **Vol. 2, Part 2**, 187; **Vol. 4, Part 1**, 150; **Vol. 8, Part 1**, 33 f., 436; Republican party, **Supp. 9**, 672; roads, state system of, in, **Vol. 8, Part 1**, 641; school desegregation, **Supp. 8**, 57–58, 157; stories of, **Vol. 9, Part 2**, 509; Territory, organizing of, **Vol. 9, Part 2**, 335; writings on, **Supp. 4**, 286
Arkansas College, **Vol. 1, Part 2**, 63
Arkansas Folklore Society, founding of, **Supp. 4**, 286
Arkansas Institute for the Deaf, **Vol. 2, Part 2**, 151
Arkansas Light & Power Co., **Supp. 3**, 192–93
Arkansas Post, battle of, **Vol. 2, Part 2**, 105; **Vol. 6, Part 1**, 588; **Vol. 9, Part 1**, 95, 237, 556; **Vol. 10, Part 1**, 458
Arkansas Traveler, founding of, **Supp. 2**, 550
Arlen, Harold, reference to, **Supp. 10**, 527
Arlington, Va., **Vol. 3, Part 1**, 9; **Vol. 4, Part 2**, 77; **Vol. 6, Part 1**, 127
Arlington Memorial Bridge (Washington, D.C.–Va.), **Supp. 3**, 534
Arliss, George, references to, **Vol. 3, Part 1**, 590; **Supp. 3**, 277
ARMCO. *See* American Rolling Mill Co.
Armed forces and defense: aircraft development, **Supp. 3**, 314; **Supp. 6**, 182–83, 618; **Supp. 9**, 255–56; Air Force reorganization, post–World War II, **Supp. 9**, 747; air power advocacy, **Supp. 10**, 243; budget reduction, **Supp. 9**, 477; Army Corps of Engineers, **Supp. 6**, 508–9; Army War College, founding of, **Supp. 1**, 89; aviation, **Supp. 2**, 460–61; **Supp. 3**, 314; black, first four-star general, **Supp. 10**, 379; black, first general, **Supp. 8**, 118–19; budget reduction, **Supp. 7**, 795; **Supp. 8**, 157; chaplains, **Supp. 8**, 505–6; civilian v. military authority, **Supp. 6**, 432; communications systems, **Supp. 9**, 728; congressional interests, **Supp. 8**, 538; contracts investigations, **Supp. 6**, 618; **Supp. 7**, 764; conventional weapons v. nuclear, **Supp. 7**, 277; **Supp. 8**, 157–58; counterinsurgency, **Supp. 7**, 422; draft, **Supp. 1**, 211; **Supp. 5**, 482–531; gun carriage design, **Supp. 3**, 204; Joint Chiefs of Staff, **Supp. 5**, 706; **Supp. 6**, 374; **Supp. 8**, 156; **Supp. 9**, 636, 862; **Supp. 10**, 72–73; "military-industrial complex" warning, **Supp. 8**, 159; preparedness and mobilization issues, **Supp. 2**, 18; **Supp. 6**, 335; prison reform, **Supp. 1**, 211; procurement issues, **Supp. 9**, 477; segregation and desegregation, **Supp. 3**, 661; **Supp. 5**, 741; **Supp. 8**, 118–19; **Supp. 10**, 100; **Supp. 10**, 230, 378; tactical bombing, **Supp. 8**, 185; tanks and armored vehicles, **Supp. 3**, 165–66; **Supp. 10**, 177; training, **Supp. 1**, 211, 392; unification of branches, **Supp. 4**, 305–6; **Supp. 5**, 478; **Supp. 8**, 303; universal military training advocacy, **Supp. 5**, 531, 715; **Supp. 7**, 78; vertical envelopment strategy, **Supp. 9**, 823; writings on strategy, **Supp. 5**, 196. *See also* biological and chemical warfare; Nuclear weapons and energy; *specific branches of the armed forces; names of specific wars*
Armenia: language, **Vol. 3, Part 1**, 565 f.; literature, cataloguing, of, **Vol. 3, Part 1**, 565 f.; missions in, **Vol. 1, Part 2**, 187, 270; Turkish massacre in, **Supp. 4**, 604
Armor: bibliography of, **Vol. 3, Part 1**, 170; collections of, **Vol. 3, Part 1**, 170; **Vol. 8, Part 1**, 606; Indian wars, use of in, **Vol. 4, Part 2**, 560; plate, Harvey process, **Vol. 4, Part 2**, 374; ships, use of for, **Vol. 9, Part 1**, 608, 620
Armory Show (1913), **Supp. 2**, 239, 372, 483; **Supp. 4**, 463, 464, 774; **Supp. 5**, 20, 184, 376, 635; **Supp. 7**, 15, 486, 494, 686, 754; **Supp. 8**, 279, 714; **Supp. 9**, 759
Armour, Charles, reference to, **Supp. 9**, 586
Armour and Co., reorganization, **Supp. 5**, 551
Armour Institute, founding of, **Vol. 4, Part 2**, 53; presidency of, **Supp. 9**, 378
Armour Institute of Technology. *See* Illinois Institute of Technology
Arms. *See* Firearms; *specific types*
Arms control and disarmament: Baruch Plan, **Supp. 9**, 8; civil disobedience to promote, **Supp. 8**, 458; federal agency for, **Supp. 8**, 680; Geneva Conference (1927), **Supp. 4**, 685; Geneva Conference (1932), **Supp. 3**, 219; **Supp. 7**, 186, 362; Geneva Protocol (1925), **Supp. 7**, 537; Kellogg-Briand Pact, **Supp. 2**, 52, 356; **Supp. 3**, 219; **Supp. 4**, 137; **Supp. 7**, 112, 113, 688; mutual security agreement advocacy, **Supp. 3**, 219; naval limitation, **Supp. 3**, 219, 397, 668; **Supp. 4**, 405–6, 786; **Supp. 6**, 518, 519; nuclear inspection advocacy, **Supp. 7**, 750–51; nuclear scientists' advocacy, **Supp. 8**, 483–84; nuclear test-ban treaty, **Supp. 7**, 424; nuclear weapons' control plan, **Supp. 7**, 37; Pugwash Conferences on Sciences and World Affairs, **Supp. 7**, 732; reduction moves (1950s), **Supp. 5**, 455; women's organizations advocating, **Supp. 7**, 186. *See also* Peace, international
Armstrong, Edwin Howard, reference to, **Supp. 9**, 700
Armstrong, F. Wallis, reference to, **Supp. 10**, 708
Armstrong, John, reference to, **Vol. 5, Part 1**, 523
Armstrong, Louis, references to, **Supp. 5**, 105, 293, 529; **Supp. 10**, 159, 160, 298, 299, 543
Armstrong, Samuel C., reference to, **Vol. 7, Part 1**, 641
Armstrong Cork Co., **Supp. 6**, 519–20
Armstrong Transfer Co., **Vol. 1, Part 1**, 353
Army, Department of the, administration, **Supp. 8**, 57–58
Army, United States: Air Corps segregation "test case," **Supp. 10**, 378; armored force development, **Supp. 3**, 152; ballistic missile program, post–World War II, **Supp. 10**, 66; cavalry, **Supp. 3**, 152; chaplains, **Supp. 1**, 268; chiefs of staff, **Supp. 6**, 429–30; **Supp. 7**, 703–4; **Supp. 8**, 156, 262; **Supp. 9**, 861–62; control division, **Supp. 5**, 643; courts-martial, **Supp. 1**, 211; **Supp. 4**, 903; cryptologic program, **Supp. 8**, 196; enlargement proposal, **Supp. 1**, 336; European command, **Supp. 7**, 351; first black general, **Supp. 8**, 118–19; first woman commissioned, **Supp. 9**, 100; living conditions, **Supp. 1**, 67; loyalty issues, **Supp. 8**, 57; McCarthy charges, **Supp. 6**, 405, 432, 680; medical service, **Vol. 1, Part 1**, 631; **Vol. 1, Part 2**, 106–8; **Vol. 3, Part 2**, 538; **Vol. 4, Part 1**, 430–31; **Vol. 4, Part 2**, 210; **Vol. 6, Part 1**, 58, 441; **Vol. 7, Part 1**, 138; **Vol. 7, Part 2**, 54; **Vol. 8, Part 1**, 460–61; **Vol. 9, Part 1**, 591; **Supp. 1**, 26; **Supp. 3**, 202; **Supp. 4**, 448; **Supp. 5**, 335–36, 710; **Supp. 6**, 344–45; **Supp. 7**, 328–29; mobilization plans, **Supp. 8**, 706; modernization, **Supp. 3**, 194; **Supp. 5**, 715; nursing, **Supp. 4**, 789; **Supp. 5**, 251–52; Officers' Reserve Corps, **Supp. 1**, 627; ordnance, **Supp. 3**, 165, 204–5; peacetime strength, **Supp. 5**, 531; post–World War I reorganization, **Supp. 2**, 579; **Supp. 5**, 531; Quartermaster Corps, **Supp. 5**, 642; racial integration, **Supp. 9**, 100; **Supp. 10**, 230; reduction, **Supp. 8**, 157; reserves, **Supp. 7**, 78; Signal Intelligence Service, **Supp. 8**, 196; social psychological study of soldiers, **Supp. 6**, 605; staff administration, **Supp. 5**, 186–87, 468–69; **Supp. 9**, 861; tactical organization, **Supp. 4**, 657, 785; testing programs, **Supp. 3**, 718; **Supp. 6**, 626. *See also* American Expeditionary Force; United States Military Academy; *names of specific wars*
Army Air Corps. *See* Air Force, United States
Army Appropriation Act (1867), **Vol. 5, Part 2**, 87
Army Industrial College, **Supp. 3**, 218
Army Medical School, establishment of, **Vol. 9, Part l**, 592
Army Nurse Corps (ANC), **Supp. 9**, 99–100

Army War College: commandants, **Supp. 3**, 194, 204; first Marine officer admitted to, **Supp. 3**, 452–53; founding of, **Supp. 1**, 89; **Supp. 2**, 580
Arnall, Ellis G., reference to, **Supp. 4**, 814
Arnaz, Desi, references to, **Supp. 10**, 803, 804
Arnold, Benedict, references to, **Vol. 3, Part 1**, 200; **Vol. 4, Part 2**, 478; **Vol. 5, Part 1**, 124, 468, 499; **Vol. 7, Part 1**, 166, 624; **Vol. 8, Part 1**, 452; **Vol. 9, Part 1**, 517
Arnold, Henry H. ("Hap"), references to, **Supp. 3**, 194; **Supp. 6**, 109, 110, 145, 339; **Supp. 9**, 255, 746, 747
Arnold, Matthew, references to, **Supp. 7**, 380; **Supp. 9**, 807
Arnold, Samuel, reference to, **Vol. 1, Part 2**, 449
Arnold, Thomas, reference to, **Supp. 3**, 591
Arnold, Thurman, references to, **Supp. 3**, 656; **Supp. 6**, 271
Arnold Arboretum (Cambridge, Mass.), **Supp. 4**, 16
Arnold, Fortas, and Porter, **Supp. 8**, 18
Arnold, Porter, and Fortas, **Supp. 6**, 271
Aroostook War, **Vol. 8, Part 2**, 508; **Vol. 10, Part 1**, 155, 590
Arreta, Tony, reference to, **Supp. 10**, 408
"Arrow Collar Man," **Supp. 5**, 428, 429
Arrowsmith, **Supp. 9**, 225
Arsenic, effects of, **Vol. 8, Part 2**, 350
Arsenic and Old Lace, **Supp. 8**, 109, 383
Art: abstract, **Supp. 4**, 240–41; **Supp. 5**, 185; **Supp. 7**, 183–84; **Supp. 9**, 92; **Supp. 10**, 3, 263, 759, 787; abstract expressionism, **Supp. 4**, 339; **Supp. 7**, 39, 439–40; **Supp. 8**, 270–71, 524–25, 553–54; **Supp. 10**, 294–95; American folk, **Supp. 6**, 96; American Gothic, **Supp. 3**, 840–41; American Indian, **Supp. 8**, 126; American Indian subjects, **Supp. 3**, 113; anatomy in, **Vol. 3, Part 2**, 450; **Vol. 4, Part 2**, 366; **Vol. 8, Part 1**, 613 f.; Ashcan school (*see also* Urban realism), **Supp. 1**, 516; **Supp. 4**, 463–64; auctions, **Supp. 1**, 178; automatism, **Supp. 5**, 693; **Supp. 8**, 467–68; avant-garde, **Supp. 10**, 219; avant-garde forerunner, **Supp. 3**, 245; Bauhaus, **Supp. 6**, 199–200; **Supp. 8**, 226–27; **Supp. 10**, 3; black, **Supp. 5**, 436; **Supp. 10**, 832; Byzantine, **Supp. 4**, 890–91; **Supp. 5**, 699–700; **Supp. 5**, 708–9; **Supp. 7**, 60; catalogs, **Supp. 6**, 552; Chinese, **Supp. 3**, 268–69, 465; **Supp. 5**, 729; chromatics in, **Vol. 8, Part 2**, 131; classical, **Supp. 10**, 38–39; collages, **Supp. 4**, 774; collections, **Vol. 1, Part 1**, 232, 445; **Vol. 1, Part 2**, 170; **Vol. 3, Part 2**, 85, 354; **Vol. 4, Part 1**, 14, 143; **Vol. 4, Part 2**, 53, 55; **Vol. 5, Part 1**, 618 f.; **Vol. 5, Part 2**, 106 f., 143, 411; **Vol. 6, Part 1**, 210 f., 233; **Vol. 8, Part 1**, 157 f.; **Vol. 10, Part 1**, 399 f.; **Supp. 1**, 337; **Supp. 3**, 24; **Supp. 4**, 174–75, 351–52, 696; **Supp. 5**, 20, 39, 150–51, 401, 699–700; **Supp. 6**, 549; **Supp. 7**, 161–62, 294, 466; **Supp. 8**, 240, 367–68; collections, historical writings on, **Supp. 6**, 21; color reproduction of, in books, **Supp. 6**, 583; commercial, **Vol. 4, Part 2**, 503; **Vol. 6, Part 1**, 159; **Vol. 6, Part 2**, 634; **Vol. 7, Part 2**, 424; commissions, **Supp. 3**, 284; constructivism, **Supp. 10**, 263; criticism, **Supp. 2**, 99, 740; **Supp. 3**, 341–42; **Supp. 4**, 182–83, 702; **Supp. 5**, 478–79; **Supp. 7**, 260, 493–94; **Supp. 8**, 489–90; "Crucifixion cycle," **Supp. 7**, 465; cubism, **Supp. 4**, 771; **Supp. 7**, 170–71, 773, 789; **Supp. 9**, 501; **Supp. 10**, 263, 503, 786, 832; dadaism, **Supp. 5**, 20; **Supp. 6**, 256; **Supp. 10**, 219, 504, 505; dealers, **Supp. 6**, 552–53; **Supp. 8**, 239–40; decoration, **Supp. 1**, 514; dynamic symmetry, **Vol. 4, Part 2**, 166; education of women, **Vol. 8, Part 1**, 559; Egyptian, **Supp. 4**, 901, 902; "Eight, The," **Supp. 2**, 238; **Supp. 3**, 818; **Supp. 5**, 635–36; etchings, **Supp. 5**, 50; exhibitions, cooperative, **Supp. 1**, 177; **Supp. 2**, 239, 288, 647; experimental, **Supp. 10**, 220; expressionism, **Supp. 5**, 402, 402–3; figure, **Supp. 2**, 149; first European modern seen in U.S., **Supp. 4**, 780–81; first government-supported program, **Supp. 3**, 112; folk, **Supp. 4**, 289, 696; **Supp. 6**, 96; **Supp. 7**, 556–57; **Supp. 8**, 126, 240; "Four Doctors," **Supp. 3**, 413; French, collections of, **Supp. 5**, 150–51; French influence in, **Vol. 5, Part 1**, 514; frottage technique, **Supp. 10**, 220; futurism, **Supp. 4**, 774; **Supp. 6**, 256; German Autumn Salon, **Supp. 6**, 256; graphic, **Supp. 6**, 185–86; Harlem Renaissance, **Supp. 10**, 182, 832; historical studies of, **Supp. 8**, 194–95, 490; history, teaching of, **Supp. 4**, 313; **Supp. 10**, 38–39; illumination, **Vol. 9, Part 1**, 561; illustration, **Supp. 3**, 573–74; **Supp. 10**, 182; impressionism, **Vol. 3, Part 2**, 54; **Supp. 1**, 382; **Supp. 2**, 210; India, scholarship on, **Supp. 4**, 177; Indian, **Vol. 1, Part 1**, 588; **Supp. 10**, 511–12; Italian mannerism studies, **Supp. 8**, 194; Italian Renaissance studies, **Supp. 6**, 56–57; Japanese, **Supp. 3**, 341, 465; **Supp. 5**, 729–30; jazz influence, **Supp. 7**, 170, 171; landscape, **Supp. 1**, 227, 458; **Supp. 3**, 112; marine, **Supp. 2**, 700; medieval studies, **Supp. 2**, 22; **Supp. 8**, 545; miniatures, **Supp. 5**, 672–73; modern, **Vol. 3, Part 1**, 558 f.; **Supp. 2**, 740; **Supp. 4**, 590–91; **Supp. 5**, 376–77; modern, collections of, **Supp. 4**, 351–52, 697; **Supp. 5**, 20, 427; **Supp. 7**, 294; modern, leading American exponents, **Supp. 7**, 773; modern, promotion of, **Supp. 4**, 768–71, 780–81; **Supp. 5**, 184; modern American, exclusive galleries, **Supp. 8**, 240; modern German, first exhibition of, in U.S., **Vol. 8, Part 1**, 493; mother and child subjects, **Supp. 3**, 113; movable, **Supp. 10**, 90–92; museums, *see specific names*; naive style, **Supp. 4**, 667; **Supp. 5**, 200; nature scenes, **Supp. 7**, 25; neoplasticism, **Supp. 7**, 183; nontraditional media, **Supp. 10**, 92; 504; Old Masters, collections of, **Supp. 3**, 24; open-air school, **Supp. 1**, 514; Oregon Trail watercolors, **Supp. 3**, 380; Oriental, collections of, **Vol. 3, Part 2**, 325; **Supp. 1**, 641; patronage, **Vol. 1, Part 1**, 445; **Vol. 3, Part 2**, 214; **Vol. 4, Part 2**, 357; **Vol. 6, Part 1**, 527 f.; **Vol. 8, Part 1**, 453, 493; **Vol. 8, Part 2**, 5; **Vol. 10, Part 1**, 609 f.; **Supp. 1**, 457, 695; **Supp. 3**, 819; **Supp. 4**, 289–90, 696–97, 768, 771; **Supp. 7**, 486; **Supp. 10**, 423, 868; "Philadelphia Four," **Supp. 5**, 624–25; philanthropy, **Supp. 4**, 87; philosophy of, **Supp. 5**, 199; photography as, **Supp. 4**, 779–81; **Supp. 9**, 759–60; **Supp. 10**, 504, 505, 767; pop-art movement, **Supp. 8**, 494; popular American, **Supp. 5**, 112–13; popular color prints, **Supp. 8**, 494; portraits, **Supp. 1**, 98, 178; **Supp. 2**, 149, 650; **Supp. 5**, 50, 112; **Supp. 7**, 67; precisionism, **Supp. 7**, 686–87; preservation, **Supp. 8**, 545; realism, **Supp. 4**, 463–664; **Supp. 6**, 720; **Supp. 8**, 63–64, 280–81; regionalism, **Supp. 3**, 340, 40–41; **Supp. 4**, 204–5; **Supp. 5**, 580; religious, **Supp. 2**, 649; representational, **Supp. 6**, 625; "Rural," **Vol. 3, Part 1**, 418; school, oldest in America, **Vol. 3, Part 1**, 590 f.; selling, **Vol. 5, Part 2**, 143, 352; **Vol. 9, Part 1**, 229; semiabstract, **Supp. 7**, 560, 561; "Signing the Constitution," **Supp. 5**, 112; social realism, **Supp. 5**, 580; **Supp. 8**, 586–87; stained glass, **Supp. 3**, 183–84; still-life, **Supp. 1**, 238; surrealism, **Supp. 5**, 184–85; **Supp. 6**, 512–13; **Supp. 8**, 467–68; **Supp. 10**, 90–91, 220, 505; teaching of, **Vol. 3, Part 1**, 558 f., 590 f.; **Vol. 4, Part 2**, 110; **Vol. 5, Part 1**, 225 f.; **Vol. 5, Part 2**, 287, 485; **Vol. 7, Part 1**, 488; **Vol. 8, Part 1**, 166; **Vol. 9, Part 1**, 532; **Vol. 10, Part 1**, 70; **Supp. 1**, 596, 641; **Supp. 2**, 288, 647; **Supp. 3**, 292; **Supp. 4**, 591; **Supp. 5**, 39, 50, 492–93; **Supp. 7**, 15, 39, 773; **Supp. 8**, 271; technical bases of, **Vol. 4, Part 2**, 166; **Vol. 8, Part 1**, 408; **Vol. 9, Part 2**, 29; "Ten,

The," **Supp. 1**, 382; **Supp. 2**, 149, 649; **Supp. 8**, 553; urban realism, **Supp. 1**, 516; **Supp. 4**, 463–64; **Supp. 5**, 472–73, 492–93, 624–25, 635–36; **Supp. 7**, 170; "Veils" technique, **Supp. 7**, 480; Western themes, **Supp. 3**, 382–83; **Supp. 5**, 420; Whistlerian, **Supp. 5**, 470–71; writings on, **Vol. 1, Part 1**, 423; **Vol. 2, Part 1**, 37, 403; **Vol. 2, Part 2**, 371, 479; **Vol. 3, Part 1**, 169, 274; **Vol. 3, Part 2**, 563; **Vol. 4, Part 1**, 11, 65; **Vol. 5, Part 2**, 352, 485 f., 534, 539; **Vol. 6, Part 1**, 185; **Vol. 6, Part 2**, 292; **Vol. 7, Part 1**, 56; **Vol. 7, Part 2**, 285; **Vol. 8, Part 1**, 165 f., 408; **Vol. 9, Part 1**, 307, 532; **Vol. 9, Part 2**, 29; **Supp. 1**, 641; **Supp. 4**, 290; **Supp. 5**, 427; **Supp. 6**, 96. *See also* Armory Show (1913); Illustrations; Landscape painting; Mural painting; Museums; Oriental painting; Portrait painting; Sculpture; *specific museum names*
Art and Freedom, **Supp. 9**, 448
Art deco, **Supp. 5**, 134; **Supp. 7**, 308
Arthritis, cortisone treatment, **Supp. 7**, 340–41; **Supp. 9**, 444, 454–55
Arthur, Chester A., references to, **Vol. 2, Part 1**, 26; **Vol. 5, Part 1**, 589; **Vol. 7, Part 1**, 169
Articles of Confederation, **Vol. 3, Part 1**, 465 f.; **Vol. 4, Part 2**, 330 f., 375; **Vol. 5, Part 1**, 220, 245; **Vol. 5, Part 2**, 398; **Vol. 6, Part 1**, 119 f.; **Vol. 7, Part 1**, 221, 257; **Vol. 8, Part 1**, 423; **Vol. 8, Part 2**, 49
Artificial insemination, **Supp. 8**, 502–3
Artificial organ transplants, **Supp. 3**, 140–41
Art Institute of Chicago: **Vol. 4, Part 1**, 26; **Vol. 7, Part 1**, 321 f.; architecture, **Supp. 2**, 117; development of, **Supp. 2**, 288; lecture course, **Supp. 4**, 313; sculpture instruction, **Supp. 2**, 647
Artistry in Rhythm Orchestra, **Supp. 10**, 409
Artists. For complete list, *see* Occupations Index
Artists' Union, founding of, **Supp. 7**, 171
Art News, **Supp. 7**, 260
Art of Loving, The, **Supp. 10**, 261
Art of This Century gallery (New York City), **Supp. 6**, 512, 513
Art Students League (New York City), **Vol. 1, Part 2**, 121; **Vol. 2, Part 2**, 102; **Vol. 4, Part 2**, 366, 423; **Vol. 8, Part 2**, 54; **Supp. 3**, 113; **Supp. 5**, 492; **Supp. 6**, 257, 511–12
Art Through the Ages, **Supp. 4**, 313
Aruch, rabbinical dictionary, **Vol. 5, Part 2**, 490 f.
Arundel, **Supp. 6**, 545
Arvey, Jacob M., reference to, **Supp. 7**, 721
Asbury, Francis, references to, **Vol. 2, Part 2**, 280; **Vol. 5, Part 1**, 617; **Vol. 6, Part 1**, 560; **Vol. 7, Part 2**, 7; **Vol. 9, Part 1**, 382
ASCAP. *See* American Society of Composers, Authors, and Publishers
Ashburton Treaty, **Vol. 3, Part 1**, 79 f. *See also* Webster-Ashburton Treaty
Asher, Daniel, reference to, **Supp. 9**, 71
Asia: Christianity studies, **Supp. 8**, 360; diplomacy with U.S., **Vol. 8, Part 2**, 4; **Supp. 6**, 269–70; diplomatic history studies, **Supp. 4**, 224, 225; English language journals in, **Supp. 4**, 679; forerunner of journal *Asia*, **Vol. 9, Part 2**, 121; historical studies, **Supp. 4**, 532–33; missions, **Supp. 3**, 323; religions of, **Supp. 8**, 431; scientific expeditions, **Supp. 6**, 18; secret American agency in, **Vol. 8, Part 2**, 4; studies programs in U.S. universities, **Supp. 8**, 360; trade with U.S., **Vol. 8, Part 2**, 4; **Supp. 1**, 257. *See also individual country names*
Asia Minor, exploration in, **Vol. 9, Part 1**, 594
Asia Society, **Supp. 10**, 684
Asimov, Isaac, reference to, **Supp. 9**, 156
Asphalt, early use of, **Vol. 1, Part 1**, 586; **Vol. 10, Part 1**, 471
Asphyxia, theories of, **Supp. 3**, 353
Assassination attempts on: Congress, **Supp. 8**, 300; Frick, H. C., **Supp. 2**, 37; Mitchel, J. P., **Supp. 3**, 605; Roosevelt, F. D., **Supp. 1**, 160; **Supp. 3**, 648; **Supp. 6**, 23
Assassination of: Bernadotte, Count Folke, **Supp. 9**, 137–38; Evers, Medgar, **Supp. 7**, 227; Kennedy, J. F., **Supp. 7**, 227, 425, 593–94; **Supp. 8**, 323, 557–58, 607; **Supp. 9**, 413, 434, 715–16; Kennedy, R. F., **Supp. 8**, 324; **Supp. 9**, 437; King, M. L., Jr., **Supp. 8**, 324, 335; **Supp. 10**, 169; McKinley, W., **Supp. 5**, 285, 286; Malcolm X, **Supp. 7**, 509; **Supp. 9**, 571; Oswald, L. H., **Supp. 8**, 557–58; Rockwell, G. L., **Supp. 8**, 541; Tresca, C., **Supp. 3**, 778; underworld leaders, **Supp. 8**, 208
Assay Office, establishment of, **Vol. 9, Part 2**, 597
Assembly line, moving, **Supp. 4**, 296, 456; **Supp. 8**, 609
Associated Catholic Charities, founding of, **Supp. 2**, 478
Associated Dress Industries, **Vol. 7, Part 1**, 276 f.
Associated Dry Goods Corporation, **Supp. 7**, 440–41
Associated Gas and Electric Co. of New York, **Supp. 4**, 394–95
Associated Hospital Service Corporation, **Supp. 3**, 122, 313
Associated Merchandising Corporation (AMC), largest buying office in U.S., **Supp. 9**, 484
Associated Negro Press, **Supp. 5**, 544
Associated Press (AP): **Vol. 1, Part 2**, 84; **Vol. 3, Part 1**, 294; **Vol. 4, Part 2**, 158; **Vol. 5, Part 1**, 347; **Vol. 5, Part 2**, 331; **Vol. 6, Part 1**, 61; **Vol. 7, Part 1**, 428; **Vol. 7, Part 2**, 545; **Vol. 8, Part 2**, 518; **Vol. 9, Part 1**, 176 f., 364 f.; **Vol. 9, Part 2**, 74, 82, 592; **Supp. 5**, 65, 286, 626; **Supp. 6**, 202; **Supp. 9**, 484; administration, **Supp. 4**, 630–31; **Supp. 10**, 498–99; first executive committee, **Supp. 1**, 441; growth of, **Supp. 7**, 145; libel suit, **Supp. 3**, 852
Associated Refugees, **Vol. 3, Part 2**, 265
Association for Defense of the Constitution, **Supp. 6**, 75
Association for Prevention of Heart Disease, **Supp. 6**, 117
Association for Research in Nervous and Mental Disease, founding of, **Supp. 2**, 665
Association for the Advancement of Psychoanalysis, founding of, **Supp. 5**, 316
Association for the Improvement of Colored People, **Vol. 1, Part 2**, 432
Association for the Protection of Industry and for the Promotion of National Education, **Vol. 7, Part 2**, 119
Association for the Study of Negro Life and History, **Supp. 6**, 313; founding of, **Supp. 4**, 911
Association of All Classes of All Nations, **Vol. 8, Part 2**, 158
Association of American Geographers, **Supp. 1**, 119
Association of American Geologists and Naturalists, **Vol. 8, Part 2**, 94
Association of American Law Schools, founding of, **Supp. 1**, 358
Association of American Painters and Sculptors, founding of, **Supp. 4**, 463
Association of American Physicians, **Vol. 3, Part 1**, 208; **Vol. 8, Part 1**, 79
Association of American Publishers, **Supp. 10**, 47
Association of American Railroads, **Supp. 10**, 771; founding of, **Supp. 2**, 260
Association of American University Presses, founding of, **Supp. 6**, 155
Association of Bank Women, **Vol. 5, Part 2**, 549
Association of Collegiate Alumnae. *See* American Association of University Women

Association of Freemen of Maryland, **Vol. 5, Part 2**, 121
Association of History Teachers of the Middle States, founding of, **Supp. 2**, 419
Association of Licensed Automobile Manufacturers: Ford suit against, **Supp. 4**, 295–96; founding of, **Supp. 2**, 354
Association of Medical Superintendents of American Institutions for the Insane, **Vol. 5, Part 2**, 429
Association of Military Surgeons, **Vol. 8, Part 2**, 585
Association of Official Agricultural Chemists, **Vol. 5, Part 2**, 45
Association of Presidents of Women's Colleges in the South, **Vol. 2, Part 2**, 214
Association of Professional Baseball Players of America, **Supp. 8**, 107
Association of Schools and Departments of Journalism, **Supp. 1**, 87
Association of the Bar of the City of New York, **Vol. 7, Part 2**, 387; **Supp. 6**, 88
Association of the Customs Bar: duties, **Vol. 2, Part 2**, 322; **Vol. 4, Part 2**, 426 f.; law, **Vol. 9, Part 1**, 438; **Vol. 10, Part 1**, 495, f.
Association of the Historical Manuscripts Commission, founding of, **Supp. 2**, 341
Association on American Indian Affairs, **Supp. 7**, 449, 505
Association to Abolish War, **Vol. 3, Part 1**, 357
Assumption bill, **Vol. 5, Part 2**, 23 f.
Assyriology, **Vol. 4, Part 2**, 284, 401; **Vol. 5, Part 1**, 58 f.; **Supp. 1**, 172, 261, 519; **Supp. 3**, 572–73
Astaire, Fred, reference to, **Supp. 7**, 682
Asthma: causes of, **Supp. 4**, 34; **Supp. 6**, 123. *See also* Medicine
Astor, John Jacob, reference to, **Vol. 2, Part 2**, 273
Astor, John Jacob, IV, reference to, **Supp. 6**, 23, 24
Astor, Mary, reference to, **Supp. 7**, 413
Astor, William Waldorf, reference to, **Vol. 1, Part 2**, 418
Astor Fur Co., **Vol. 8, Part 2**, 173
Astoria, historical background of Irving's, **Vol. 3, Part 1**, 379 f.
Astoria Expedition, **Vol. 5, Part 1**, 398 f.
Astor Library. *See* New York Public Library
Astor Place riots (New York City), **Vol. 3, Part 1**, 41, 553
Astor Plaza, **Supp. 6**, 24
Astounding Stories (magazine), **Supp. 9**, 155–56
Astronautics. *See* Astrophysics; Space exploration
Astronomers. For complete list, *see* Occupations Index
Astronomical observatories: Alfred, **Vol. 8, Part 2**, 114; Allegheny, **Supp. 3**, 208, 692; Astrophysical, **Vol. 5, Part 2**, 595; Blue Hill, **Vol. 8, Part 2**, 183 f.; **Supp. 3**, 479; Chamberlin, **Vol. 5, Part 1**, 290; Córdoba, **Vol. 4, Part 1**, 448; Dearborn, **Vol. 5, Part 1**, 252; Dudley, **Vol. 5, Part 1**, 252; **Vol. 7, Part 1**, 39; Harvard, **Vol. 1, Part 2**, 431, 435; **Vol. 7, Part 1**, 39; **Vol. 7, Part 2**, 394; **Vol. 8, Part 1**, 308 f.; **Vol. 8, Part 2**, 114, 535; **Vol. 10, Part 2**, 390; **Supp. 3**, 130–31; **Supp. 9**, 713–14; **Supp. 10**, 625, 626; Inter-American Observatory, **Supp. 10**, 840; Kitt Peak National Observatory, **Supp. 10**, 840; Lick, **Vol. 3, Part 1**, 292; **Vol. 5, Part 1**, 136, 432; **Vol. 5, Part 2**, 279; **Vol. 6, Part 1**, 234; **Vol. 7, Part 1**, 6, 454; **Vol. 8, Part 2**, 412; **Supp. 2**, 92; **Supp. 3**, 207; **Supp. 4**, 600; **Supp. 5**, 513, 540, 541; **Supp. 9**, 713; Lowell, **Vol. 6, Part 1**, 458; **Supp. 7**, 193; **Supp. 8**, 597–98; Mars Hill, **Vol. 6, Part 1**, 469; McCormick, **Supp. 1**, 674–75; McDonald, **Supp. 7**, 726; McMath-Hulbert, **Supp. 3**, 208; Mount Palomar, **Supp. 7**, 517; **Supp. 9**, 114, 902, 903; Mount Wilson, **Supp. 2**, 271; **Supp. 3**, 291, 634; **Supp. 5**, 325; **Supp. 6**, 7, 30–31; **Supp. 7**, 573; **Supp. 9**, 114, 714, 902, 903; **Supp. 10**, 840; National, **Vol. 1, Part 1**, 91; **Vol. 5, Part 2**, 403; **Vol. 10, Part 1**, 91; National Radio, **Supp. 4**, 423; **Supp. 7**, 727; Naval, **Vol. 1, Part 1**, 1; **Vol. 4, Part 1**, 266; **Vol. 6, Part 1**, 39, 337, 452 f.; **Vol. 7, Part 2**, 319; **Vol. 8, Part 2**, 78, 341; **Vol. 9, Part 1**, 196; **Vol. 10, Part 1**, 359; site selection, **Supp. 1**, 43; Smithsonian, **Vol. 1, Part 2**, 152; Steward, **Supp. 7**, 193; Vassar, **Vol. 10, Part 2**, 164; Yerkes, **Vol. 7, Part 2**, 246; **Supp. 2**, 270–71; **Supp. 3**, 634, 692; **Supp. 6**, 7; **Supp. 7**, 726; **Supp. 9**, 475, 476
Astronomy: **Vol. 1, Part 1**, 174 f., 617 f,; **Vol. 1, Part 2**, 431, 434, 465, 497; **Vol. 2, Part 1**, 141, 307, 321, 409; **Vol. 2, Part 2**, 119 f,; **Vol. 3, Part 1**, 92 f., 274, 373 f., 435 f., 602 f.; **Vol. 3, Part 2**, 292 f., 470 f.; **Vol. 4, Part 1**, 13, 292, 400, 609; **Vol. 4, Part 2**, 118, 266, 301, 586; **Vol. 5, Part 1**, 32, 136, 252, 290, 329, 432; **Vol. 5, Part 2**, 170, 278 f., 387, 436, 595; **Vol. 6, Part 1**, 79, 83, 398, 406 f., 468 f., 515 f.; **Vol. 6, Part 2**, 581; **Vol. 7, Part 1**, 32, 38, 58, 67, 452 f.; **Vol. 7, Part 2**, 138, 246, 502 f., 563; **Vol. 8, Part 1**, 95 f., 465, 602, 630 f.; **Vol. 8, Part 2**, 114, 288, 412, 534 f., 594 f.; **Vol. 9, Part 1**, 28, 196; **Vol. 9, Part 2**, 50 f., 247 f.; **Vol. 10, Part 1**, 74, 84, 359, 543 f.; **Vol. 10, Part 2**, 6, 624; America, first astronomer in, **Vol. 10, Part 2**, 415; "American method" in, **Vol. 10, Part 1**, 359; Andromeda nebula, **Supp. 1**, 324; aurora borealis, **Vol. 4, Part 1**, 400; **Vol. 6, Part 1**, 398 f.; **Vol. 8, Part 1**, 193 f.; cataloguing, **Vol. 4, Part 1**, 448; Cepheid variables, **Supp. 9**, 713; comets, **Vol. 1, Part 1**, 618; **Vol. 2, Part 1**, 91; **Vol. 5, Part 1**, 329; **Vol. 5, Part 2**, 436; **Vol. 6, Part 1**, 469; **Vol. 9, Part 2**, 18, 248; dark matter theory, **Supp. 9**, 902; double-star studies, **Vol. 2, Part 1**, 307; **Vol. 3, Part 1**, 374; **Supp. 1**, 674; **Supp. 5**, 13–14; **Supp. 9**, 713; eclipses, **Vol. 3, Part 1**, 92 f., 274, 602 f.; **Vol. 8, Part 2**, 412; **Vol. 9, Part 2**, 50; galaxy classification system, **Supp. 5**, 325–26; galaxy motion studies, **Supp. 9**, 902; Hubble's law, **Supp. 5**, 326; instruments, **Supp. 1**, 383–84; **Supp. 2**, 642; **Supp. 4**, 674–75; **Supp. 7**, 517; Jovian planets, **Supp. 10**, 839, 840; Jupiter, discovery of satellites of, **Supp. 5**, 540; Jupiter, study of, **Vol. 5, Part 1**, 252; lunar studies, **Supp. 9**, 475–76; lunar theory, **Vol. 7, Part 1**, 453; magazine, first, **Vol. 7, Part 1**, 39; Mars studies, **Supp. 7**, 193; Mayan knowledge of, **Vol. 1, Part 2**, 492; meteors, **Vol. 5, Part 2**, 436; **Vol. 10, Part 1**, 84; moon, **Vol. 7, Part 1**, 453 f.; **Vol. 9, Part 2**, 50; **Supp. 2**, 69; "Neighbors" association, **Supp. 3**, 692; observatories, *see* Astronomical observatories; photography, **Vol. 1, Part 2**, 431; **Vol. 3, Part 1**, 435 f.; **Vol. 3, Part 2**, 462; **Vol. 5, Part 2**, 279, 387; **Vol. 6, Part 1**, 83; **Vol. 8, Part 1**, 472; **Vol. 8, Part 2**, 256; **Supp. 3**, 634, 692; **Supp. 6**, 31; **Supp. 9**, 476; planetarium, **Vol. 1, Part 1**, 487; planetary research, **Supp. 9**, 475, 476; planetesimal hypothesis of solar system, **Supp. 5**, 508–9; radio wave emissions from space, **Supp. 4**, 422–23; solar compass, **Vol. 2, Part 1**, 340; solar eclipse, **Supp. 2**, 92; solar radiation, **Vol. 5, Part 2**, 594 f.; solar research, **Supp. 7**, 573; spectroscopy, **Vol. 1, Part 1**, 230; **Vol. 1, Part 2**, 606; **Vol. 3, Part 1**, 436; **Vol. 6, Part 1**, 213, 406 f.; **Vol. 7, Part 1**, 492; **Vol. 8, Part 1**, 264; **Vol. 8, Part 2**, 198, 256; **Vol. 9, Part 2**, 655; spiral nebulae studies, **Supp. 3**, 208; **Supp. 8**, 597; **Supp. 9**, 713; stellar atmospheres, **Supp. 10**, 625; stellar classification, **Supp. 3**, 130–31; stellar distances, **Supp. 1**, 283; **Supp. 9**, 713, 714, 902; stellar motions, **Supp. 1**, 324; stellar radial velocity, **Supp. 4**, 600; stellar studies, **Supp. 6**, 7, 31, 560–62; Stevens Expedition, **Vol. 4, Part 1**, 481; sun's atmosphere, **Supp. 6**, 561; sunspots, **Vol. 10, Part 2**, 415; **Supp. 2**, 271; supernovas, **Supp. 9**, 902; T Coronae Borealis, discovery of,

Supp. 1, 229; telescopes, **Vol. 1, Part 2**, 605; **Vol. 2, Part 2**, 119 f.; **Vol. 3, Part 1**, 436; **Vol. 3, Part 2**, 433; **Vol. 5, Part 1**, 131, 432; **Vol. 5, Part 2**, 593; **Vol. 6, Part 1**, 234, 505; **Vol. 8, Part 1**, 30 f., 630 f.; **Vol. 8, Part 2**, 341, 412; **Vol. 10, Part 1**, 470 f.; time observations by, **Vol. 5, Part 2**, 594; variable stars, **Vol. 2, Part 1**, 616; **Supp. 10**, 625, 626; Venus, **Vol. 3, Part 1**, 602 f.; **Vol. 6, Part 1**, 516; **Vol. 7, Part 1**, 454; **Vol. 8, Part 1**, 630; **Vol. 9, Part 2**, 18; writings on, **Supp. 9**, 903; **Supp. 10**, 626. *See also* Astrophysics

Astrophysical Journal, **Supp. 7**, 726; founding of, **Supp. 2**, 271

Astrophysics: **Supp. 9**, 113–14; foundations for, **Supp. 2**, 92; periodic table analysis, **Supp. 9**, 114; research in, **Supp. 2**, 271; **Supp. 10**, 840; spectroscopic, **Supp. 3**, 291; **Supp. 7**, 726–27; universe origin theories, **Supp. 8**, 199. *See also* Astronomy

Aswan Dam, **Supp. 8**, 276

Atalanta and *Wasp*, naval engagement, **Vol. 1, Part 2**, 348

AT&T. *See* American Telephone & Telegraph Co.

Ataturk, Mustapha Kemal, reference to, **Supp. 5**, 562–63

Atchison Daily Globe, founding of, **Supp. 2**, 325

Atchison, Topeka & Santa Fe Railroad, **Vol. 5, Part 1**, 151; **Vol. 7, Part 2**, 375

"At Dawning" (song), **Supp. 4**, 138, 139

Atherton, Gertrude, reference to, **Supp. 6**, 309

Athletes. For complete list, *see* Occupations Index

Athletics: coaching, **Vol. 2, Part 1**, 444; **Vol. 4, Part 2**, 398; **Vol. 7, Part 1**, 355 f.; **Vol. 8, Part 2**, 68; colleges, athletic policy, **Vol. 3, Part 2**, 74; **Vol. 8, Part 2**, 67; Olympic Games, **Vol. 7, Part 1**, 356; writings on, **Vol. 2, Part 1**, 587; **Vol. 3, Part 2**, 545, 572; **Vol. 4, Part 2**, 570; **Vol. 7, Part 2**, 573; **Vol. 8, Part 1**, 58 f., 107 f.; **Vol. 10, Part 2**, 218. *See also specific sports*

Atkins, Garden (Cuba), **Supp. 4**, 16, 52

Atkins, Max, reference to, **Supp. 10**, 239

Atkinson, George F., reference to, **Supp. 6**, 175, 176

Atkinson, Henry, reference to, **Vol. 5, Part 2**, 273

Atlanta, naval prize, Civil War, **Vol. 3, Part 1**, 529 f.

Atlanta, Ga.: battles about, **Vol. 1, Part 1**, 267; **Vol. 4, Part 2**, 240; **Vol. 5, Part 1**, 193–94, 197; **Vol. 5, Part 2**, 145–46; **Vol. 6, Part 1**, 364; **Vol. 6, Part 2**, 160; **Vol. 8, Part 2**, 453; **Vol. 9, Part 1**, 95, 217; **Vol. 9, Part 2**, 434; first black education board member, **Supp. 8**, 95; infrastructure improvements, post-World War II, **Supp. 9**, 370; library service, **Vol. 5, Part 1**, 335; mayors, **Supp. 9**, 369–71; progressive racial policies, **Supp. 9**, 370; public service, **Vol. 5, Part 1**, 302; **Vol. 7, Part 2**, 511; **Vol. 9, Part 1**, 282

Atlanta Constitution: **Vol. 5, Part 1**, 302, 485; **Vol. 9, Part 1**, 249; editorial policy, **Supp. 8**, 404–5

Atlanta Journal, **Vol. 9, Part 1**, 281; **Supp. 1**, 184

Atlanta Municipal Airport, **Supp. 9**, 370

Atlanta University: founding of, **Vol. 2, Part 2**, 516; **Vol. 10, Part 1**, 446 f.; presidency, **Supp. 2**, 315; **Supp. 8**, 94–95; social work program, reform of, **Supp. 9**, 900–901; sociological studies of blacks, **Supp. 7**, 202, 203, 204; **Supp. 8**, 522

Atlantic & St. Lawrence Railroad Co., **Vol. 8, Part 1**, 71 f., 184 f.

Atlantic Charter (1941), **Supp. 3**, 660; **Supp. 7**, 778

Atlantic City, N.J.: casinos, organized crime involvement in, **Supp. 10**, 75; Monopoly street names controversy, **Supp. 9**, 601–2

Atlantic Coast Line Railroad Co., **Vol. 10, Part 1**, 199 f.

Atlantic, Gulf & West Indies Steamship Lines, **Supp. 3**, 501

Atlantic Improvement Co., founding of, **Vol. 10, Part 1**, 399 f.

Atlantic Monthly: **Vol. 1, Part 1**, 159, 335; **Vol. 3, Part 2**, 379; **Vol. 5, Part 1**, 173 f., 307, 580; **Vol. 6, Part 1**, 15, 461; **Vol. 7, Part 1**, 570; **Vol. 7, Part 2**, 143; **Vol. 8, Part 2**, 522; **Vol. 9, Part 2**, 529; **Supp. 3**, 719; **Supp. 6**, 252, 306, 571–72; **Supp. 8**, 476; **Supp. 9**, 37; editing of, **Supp. 5**, 16, 542; **Supp. 8**, 447–48; founding of, **Vol. 10, Part 1**, 112; Little, Brown association, **Supp. 4**, 526–27

Atlantic Ocean: early map of, **Vol. 3, Part 1**, 183; deepest recorded spot, **Supp. 2**, 239; first steam vessel to cross, **Vol. 3, Part 1**, 339; **Vol. 8, Part 1**, 214 f.; **Vol. 8, Part 2**, 106

Atlantic Refining Co., management, **Supp. 2**, 679

Atlantic Union, **Supp. 8**, 90

Atomic bomb: development of, **Supp. 3**, 664; **Supp. 4**, 453–54; **Supp. 5**, 204, 220–21, 663; **Supp. 6**, 166, 371, 501, 656; **Supp. 7**, 10–11, 76, 91, 135, 732; **Supp. 8**, 229–31, 411, 483–84; **Supp. 9**, 185, 218; **Supp. 10**, 102, 144; first explosion, **Supp. 8**, 230; German World War II research, **Supp. 10**, 289; radiation fallout studies, **Supp. 10**, 816; Roosevelt convinced of need for, **Supp. 9**, 696; scientists' concerns on use of, **Supp. 7**, 732, 733; **Supp. 9**, 696; Soviet espionage, **Supp. 9**, 321–22; test of first, **Supp. 7**, 10–11; testing, **Supp. 7**, 136, 300; Uranium Committee formed, **Supp. 9**, 696. *See also* Arms control and disarmament; Nuclear weapons and energy

Atomic Energy Act (1946), passage of, **Supp. 5**, 455

Atomic Energy Commission: **Supp. 10**, 320; civilian v. military control of, **Supp. 5**, 455; **Supp. 8**, 230, 484; first chemist appointed to, **Supp. 10**, 457; first commissioners, **Supp. 6**, 676–77; **Supp. 9**, 774; first engineer appointed to, **Supp. 7**, 565; first weapons' test series, **Supp. 7**, 300; hydrogen bomb development, **Supp. 6**, 156; Lilienthal appointment, **Supp. 6**, 419; mathematicians, **Supp. 6**, 656; nuclear power advocates, **Supp. 6**, 650

Atoms: electron chemical bond theory, **Supp. 4**, 488; far-ultraviolet spectra of, **Supp. 5**, 496; motion of suspended objects research, **Supp. 5**, 202; "octet" structure theory, **Supp. 6**, 365; particle accelerator, **Supp. 8**, 665–66; research technique, **Supp. 8**, 627–28; statistical model, **Supp. 5**, 219; weights, **Supp. 1**, 178

Attica state prison (New York), riot, **Supp. 10**, 688

"Atticus," letter of, **Vol. 7, Part 1**, 134

Attitude testing. *See* Public opinion

Attorney generals. For complete list, *see* Occupations Index

Attorneys. For complete list, *see* Occupations Index

Attucks, Crispus, erection of monument to memory of, **Vol. 7, Part 1**, 413

Atwater, W. O., reference to, **Supp. 5**, 622

Atwater Kent Manufacturing Works, founding of, **Supp. 4**, 452

Atzerodt, George A., reference to, **Vol. 1, Part 2**, 449

Auburn, N.Y., **Vol. 7, Part 2**, 330

Auburn Declaration, **Vol. 6, Part 1**, 554

Auburn Theological Seminary, founding of, **Vol. 6, Part 1**, 406; **Vol. 9, Part 2**, 299

Auction bridge, history of, **Vol. 10, Part 2**, 130, 533

Auden, W. H., reference to, **Supp. 10**, 321

Audiology, **Supp. 7**, 395–96. *See also* Deaf and deafness

Audion tube, **Supp. 5**, 21

Audio systems: high-fidelity reproduction, **Supp. 5**, 324; microphone invention, **Supp. 1**, 75; speaker development, **Supp. 7**, 395; tape recorder, **Supp. 9**, 274

Audubon, John James, references to, **Vol. 1, Part 1**, 467, 513; **Vol. 2, Part 1**, 24; **Vol. 5, Part 2**, 300, 517; **Vol. 6, Part 1**, 49; **Vol. 10, Part 1**, 580 f.

Audubon movement, **Supp. 3**, 592–93

Audubon Society, **Vol. 5, Part 2**, 62; founding of, **Supp. 2**, 265
Auer, Leopold, reference to, **Supp. 8**, 164
Auerbach, Artie, reference to, **Supp. 9**, 76
Augsburg Seminary (Minneapolis), controversy at, **Vol. 7, Part 1**, 635
Augusta, **Supp. 9**, 630
Augusta, Ga., attack on, **Vol. 6, Part 1**, 107; **Vol. 10, Part 1**, 83
Augusta College (Ky.), **Vol. 3, Part 1**, 544 f.
Augusta National golf course (Atlanta, Ga.), **Supp. 9**, 439
Auk (publication), **Supp. 3**, 9
"Auld Lang Syne" (song), **Supp. 10**, 463
Auntie Mame, **Supp. 10**, 713, 775
Aural surgery. *See* Surgery
Aurelio, Thomas A., reference to, **Supp. 9**, 198
Aureomycin, **Supp. 6**, 176
Auriol, Vincent, reference to, **Supp. 5**, 589
Aurora, Jeffersonian organ, **Vol. 1, Part 1**, 462; **Vol. 3, Part 1**, 467 f.
Aurora borealis. *See* Astronomy
Austin College (Tex.), **Vol. 1, Part 1**, 501, 517
Austin Riggs Center (Stockbridge), **Supp. 6**, 527
Australia, water reclamation, **Supp. 2**, 444
Australian ballot system, **Vol. 4, Part 1**, 215
Austria, diplomacy, **Vol. 5, Part 2**, 353; **Vol. 6, Part 1**, 613; **Vol. 7, Part 1**, 285, 309; **Vol. 9, Part 2**, 401; **Supp. 9**, 799
Austria-Hungary, diplomacy, **Vol. 7, Part 2**, 425, 533; **Vol. 9, Part 2**, 93, 607, 644
Author! Author! (radio program), **Supp. 9**, 488
Authors. For complete list, *see* Occupations Index
Authors' Club, founding of, **Vol. 4, Part 1**, 276
Authors' League of America, **Vol. 7, Part 2**, 6, founding of, **Supp. 3**, 773
Autobiographical writings, **Vol. 2, Part 1**, 52; **Vol. 3, Part 1**, 217, 245, 272, 403, 407, 426, 469, 472, 495, 508, 513, 598; **Vol. 3, Part 2**, 598; **Vol. 4, Part 1**, 501; **Vol. 4, Part 2**, 306, 338, 474; **Vol. 5, Part 1**, 74, 245, 257, 281, 386, 622; **Vol. 5, Part 2**, 213, 248, 301, 316, 321, 366; **Vol. 6, Part 1**, 185, 392, 433; **Vol. 7, Part 1**, 1, 172, 296, 314, 368, 451, 498; **Vol. 8, Part 1**, 4, 60, 151, 175, 228, 243, 278, 281, 301, 322, 430, 520; **Vol. 8, Part 2**, 113, 341, 352, 615; **Vol. 9, Part 1**, 18, 35, 57, 64, 75, 144, 156, 165, 168, 188, 251, 259, 261, 275, 279, 347, 377, 378, 380, 402, 508, 513, 630; **Vol. 9, Part 2**, 254, 377; **Vol. 10, Part 1**, 4, 15, 42, 71, 100, 119, 156, 180, 363, 440, 506, 541, 548, 552, 598, 647, 651; **Supp. 9**, 13, 14, 498, 575; **Supp. 10**, 6
Autobiography of Alice B. Toklas, The, **Supp. 4**, 769
Autographs, collecting of, **Vol. 3, Part 2**, 147; **Vol. 5, Part 1**, 445; **Vol. 5, Part 2**, 156; **Vol. 9, Part 1**, 476; **Vol. 9, Part 2**, 432
Automation, retail stores, **Supp. 5**, 604
Automobile Manufacturers Association, founding of, **Supp. 2**, 354
Automobile racing: **Supp. 2**, 525; **Supp. 5**, 618–19; **Supp. 6**, 163–64; Ford's "999," **Supp. 4**, 293, 636–37; Indianapolis 500, **Supp. 9**, 657
Automobiles: all-steel body, **Supp. 4**, 121; catalytic converter, **Supp. 7**, 368; compacts, **Supp. 10**, 1, 2; closed-body design, **Supp. 3**, 273–74; **Supp. 7**, 245–46; compacts, **Supp. 7**, 154–55; **Supp. 8**, 309; dealers, **Supp. 4**, 682; **Supp. 8**, 600; design and styling, **Supp. 2**, 721; **Supp. 3**, 284; Detroit as industry's center, **Supp. 3**, 550; **Supp. 4**, 293–94; diesel engine, **Supp. 5**, 654; Duco lacquer paint, **Supp. 5**, 235; electric, **Supp. 1**, 670; **Supp. 2**, 436; electrical system, **Supp. 3**, 184; **Supp. 4**, 452; **Supp. 6**, 332; engine power, **Supp. 3**, 247; engineering, **Supp. 2**, 108; executives, **Supp. 9**, 290; first gasoline-powered in U.S., **Supp. 8**, 148; first public garage, **Supp. 5**, 547; first starting motor, **Supp. 7**, 793; first successful American, **Supp. 2**, 160; first using gasoline, **Supp. 4**, 292; Fords' influence, **Supp. 3**, 283–84; four-wheel brakes, **Supp. 3**, 55; **Supp. 6**, 164; front-wheel drive, **Supp. 3**, 165; industry sit-down strikes, **Supp. 4**, 612–13; industry unionization, **Supp. 3**, 284; **Supp. 8**, 418–19; **Supp. 8**, 526–28, 600, 610, 651–53; internal combustion engine, **Supp. 5**, 654; labor benefits, **Supp. 7**, 794; luxury, **Supp. 8**, 149; manufacturing, **Vol. 5, Part 2**, 281; **Vol. 7, Part 2**, 128; **Vol. 8, Part 1**, 74 f.; **Vol. 8, Part 2**, 568; **Vol. 10, Part 2**, 418; **Supp. 1**, 709; **Supp. 2**, 102, 103; **Supp. 4**, 243–45, 291–304, 456–57, 620–21, 638, 682; **Supp. 5**, 193–94; **Supp. 7**, 154–55, 375–76, 793–94; **Supp. 8**, 318–19, 598–600; marketing, **Supp. 8**, 599; Model T, **Supp. 4**, 295–97, 300–3, 456, 457; motor design, **Supp. 10**, 285–86; moving assembly line, **Supp. 4**, 296, 456; **Supp. 8**, 609; paint for, **Supp. 3**, 247; **Supp. 5**, 235; **Supp. 6**, 333; parts manufacturing, **Supp. 6**, 67; **Supp. 9**, 568; **Supp. 10**, 691, 692; precision grinding tools, **Supp. 3**, 562; radios, **Supp. 10**, 442; speed records, **Supp. 9**, 657; starter link, **Supp. 3**, 55, 332; steam, **Vol. 9, Part 1**, 508; steel industry, **Supp. 6**, 678–79; taxicabs, **Supp. 7**, 343; tires, **Supp. 5**, 617–18. *See also* Gasoline; Traffic regulation
Auto-Strop Safety Razor Co.: Gillette merger, **Supp. 9**, 298; single-edge blade designed, **Supp. 9**, 297
Autry, Gene, reference to, **Supp. 8**, 712
Auzias, Nina, reference to, **Supp. 4**, 771
Ave Maria, editorship, **Supp. 1**, 440
Avery, Clarence W., reference to, **Supp. 3**, 283
Avery, Milton, reference to, **Supp. 8**, 553
Avery, Sewell, reference to, **Supp. 8**, 35
Aviation: **Vol. 1, Part 2**, 152, 195; **Vol. 3, Part 1**, 540; **Vol. 4, Part 1**, 180, 330; **Vol. 4, Part 2**, 38, 590; **Vol. 5, Part 2**, 153, 380, 401 f., 564 f., 595 f.; **Vol. 6, Part l**, 83, 452, 499; **Vol. 6, Part 2**, 239, 437, 568 f.; **Vol. 7, Part 1**, 235; **Vol. 7, Part 2**, 11; **Vol. 8, Part 2**, 79, 184; **Vol. 9, Part 1**, 490; **Vol. 10, Part 1**, 635 f.; aeronautical schools, **Supp. 9**, 348; air-coach travel, **Supp. 6**, 146; air-cooled engine, **Supp. 4**, 473–86; aircraft design and production, **Supp. 3**, 89; **Supp. 6**, 50–52; **Supp. 6**, 221; **Supp. 8**, 709; **Supp. 9**, 228–29, 273, 416–17, 498, 725–26; 757–58; **Supp. 10**, 355–56, 443–44, 494–96, 621; airlines, **Supp. 3**, 314; **Supp. 5**, 86, 384–85, 611; **Supp. 6**, 617–18; **Supp. 7**, 16; **Supp. 8**, 292–93, 707–8; **Supp. 9**, 337–38, 658, 659; **Supp. 10**, 620, 621; airmail, **Supp. 2**, 487; **Supp. 3**, 157; **Supp. 5**, 86, 294, 385; **Supp. 6**, 64, 221; **Supp. 7**, 86; **Supp. 8**, 185, 707–8; air power, **Supp. 9**, 229, 498; air races, **Supp. 3**, 56; **Supp. 6**, 168; **Supp. 10**, 132, 214; Air Service, U.S., **Vol. 6, Part 2**, 538; autogiro, **Supp. 5**, 377; automatic pilot, **Supp. 7**, 577; **Supp. 10**, 443; balloons, **Vol. 3, Part 1**, 540; **Vol. 4, Part 1**, 330, **Vol. 5, Part 2**, 38 f., 401 f., 565; **Vol. 6, Part l**, 452; **Vol. 8, Part 2**, 184; **Vol. 10, Part 2**, 428; **Supp. 1**, 214, 561; **Supp. 5**, 547; **Supp. 7**, 619; barnstorming, **Supp. 5**, 2; **Supp. 6**, 492–93; **Supp. 9**, 496; bomber development, **Supp. 5**, 475–76; **Supp. 6**, 40, 64, **Supp. 9**, 255–56; commercial, regulatory structure established for, **Supp. 9**, 899; components manufacture, **Supp. 3**, 55; **Supp. 9**, 416; **Supp. 10**, 442–43; congressional support, **Supp. 5**, 444; crop-dusting, **Supp. 8**, 707–8; decompression studies, **Supp. 6**, 224; direction finder, **Supp. 10**, 442; engine and fuel development, **Supp. 6**, 332; engineering, **Supp. 6**, 665–66; federal safety regulations, **Supp. 5**, 610–11; first automatic-tracking bombsight, **Supp. 5**, 229; first heavy

bomber, **Supp. 9**, 725; first mass flight of heavy bombers to cross western Pacific, **Supp. 9**, 595; first person to solo nonstop across Atlantic, **Supp. 9**, 496; first reconnaissance plane, **Supp. 9**, 725; first stainless steel plane, **Supp. 4**, 121; first time-of-flight clock, **Supp. 5**, 229; first transatlantic west-to-east, **Supp. 7**, 16; first transpacific, **Supp. 7**, 16; flight records, **Supp. 6**, 51–52, 493; **Supp. 10**, 149; Flying Tigers, **Supp. 6**, 109–10; gliders, **Vol. 4, Part 2**, 590; "Great Circle Route," **Supp. 8**, 292–93; helicopters, **Supp. 1**, 76; **Supp. 9**, 725, 726; hydroplane, **Vol. 4, Part 2**, 608; **Supp. 1**, 214; **Supp. 4**, 124; industry unionization, **Supp. 8**, 513; international, **Supp. 6**, 145–46, 666; **Supp. 8**, 292–93; investments in, **Supp. 8**, 367; jet propulsion, **Supp. 6**, 183; **Supp. 8**, 439–40; **Supp. 9**, 417, 902; **Supp. 10**, 495; manufacturing, **Supp. 8**, 384–85; medical research, **Supp. 2**, 722; military, **Supp. 8**, 185; military potential, **Supp. 2**, 460–61; organizations, **Supp. 2**, 109; parachutes, **Supp. 7**, 679; physiological studies, **Supp. 3**, 353; pioneer work in, **Supp. 4**, 913–14; **Supp. 5**, 475, 547; private plane industry, **Supp. 8**, 504–5; **Supp. 10**, 148–49; propeller development, **Supp. 6**, 182; propulsion research, **Supp. 4**, 486–87; **Supp. 6**, 183; radios, **Supp. 10**, 442; research in, **Supp. 3**, 12; **Supp. 7**, 381–82, 411; **Supp. 8**, 439–40; speed records, **Supp. 10**, 355; "Spruce Goose," **Supp. 10**, 356; supersonic, **Supp. 8**, 440; teaching of, **Supp. 8**, 439–40; transatlantic flights, **Supp. 2**, 164; **Supp. 5**, 2–3, 547; **Supp. 6**, 92; **Supp. 7**, 16; transoceanic flights, **Vol. 8, Part 2**, 79; **Vol. 10, Part 1**, 409 f., 635 f.; **Supp. 10**, 149, 213–14; transpacific flights, **Supp. 2**, 164; **Supp. 7**, 16; transport service, **Supp. 6**, 64; turbosuperchargers, **Supp. 4**, 609; VTOL designs, **Supp. 6**, 50; weather services, **Supp. 2**, 261; wind tunnels, **Supp. 4**, 486; **Supp. 8**, 439, 440; women in, **Supp. 6**, 477–78; **Supp. 10**, 132–33, 213–14; world circumnavigation, **Supp. 1**, 603; World War I, **Vol. 2, Part 2**, 21; **Vol. 3, Part 1**, 614 f.; **Vol. 6, Part 1**, 83, 499; **Vol. 8, Part 2**, 69, 263, 277; **Supp. 10**, 670; writings on, **Vol. 10, Part 1**, 72, 635 f.; **Supp. 6**, 666; **Supp. 7**, 115; zeppelin flights, **Supp. 7**, 759. *See also* Air Force, United States; Airports; Armed forces and defense; Navy, United States
Aviation Corporation, founding of, **Supp. 8**, 367
Aviators. For complete list, *see* Occupations Index
Avon and *Wasp*, naval engagement, **Vol. 1, Part 2**, 348
Avon Comedy Four (vaudeville team), **Supp. 9**, 213
Axel's Castle, **Supp. 9**, 875, 876
"Axe to grind," origin of phrase, **Vol. 7, Part 1**, 23
Axes, manufacture of, **Vol. 8, Part 2**, 144
Aydelotte, Frank, reference to, **Supp. 3**, 321–22
Ayllón, Lucus Vásquez de, reference to, **Vol. 3, Part 1**, 257
Azana, Manuel, reference to, **Supp. 6**, 72–73

B

Baade, Fritz, reference to, **Supp. 6**, 708–9
Baade, Walter, reference to, **Supp. 9**, 902
Babbitt, Frank L., Jr., reference to, **Supp. 6**, 665
Babbitt, Irving, references to, **Supp. 7**, 218, 624
Babcock, H. W., reference to, **Supp. 7**, 176
Babcock, John, reference to, **Vol. 9, Part 2**, 521
Babes in Arms, **Supp. 9**, 291
Babies. *See* Children; Pediatrics
Babies Hospital (New York City), **Supp. 7**, 427
Babson College, predecessor, **Supp. 8**, 19
Babson Statistical Organization, Inc., founding of, **Supp. 8**, 18–19
"Baby, It's Cold Outside" (song), **Supp. 5**, 529
Babylonia, archaeological research, **Vol. 7, Part 2**, 506; **Vol. 10, Part 1**, 442 f.; tablets, **Supp. 1**, 261; Yale Collection, **Vol. 2, Part 2**, 168
"Baby Snooks" (fictional character), **Supp. 5**, 88
Bacall, Lauren, reference to, **Supp. 6**, 66
Bach, Johann Sebastian, harpsichord works, **Supp. 6**, 357–58; reference to, **Supp. 10**, 762
Bache, J. S., & Co., **Supp. 3**, 24
Bachrach, David, Jr., references to, **Supp. 7**, 25, 26
Back of the Yards Council: **Supp. 9**, 18; founding of, **Supp. 8**, 589
Back Stage Club, **Supp. 8**, 546
Backus, Jim, reference to; **Supp. 10**, 352
BAC. *See* Business Advisory Council
Bacon, Augustus O., reference to, **Supp. 3**, 330
Bacon, Francis, Foundation, **Supp. 5**, 20
Bacon, Nathaniel, reference to, **Vol. 1, Part 2**, 218; **Vol. 6, Part 1**, 496; writings on, **Supp. 8**, 692, 693
Bacon, Roger, manuscript, decipherment of, **Vol. 7, Part 1**, 448
Bacone College, foundation of, **Vol. 7, Part 1**, 371
Baconian theory, Shakespeare, **Vol. 1, Part 1**, 475; **Vol. 5, Part 1**, 169, 244; **Vol. 7, Part 1**, 620
Bacon's Rebellion, **Vol. 1, Part 1**, 482; **Vol. 1, Part 2**, 218; **Vol. 6, Part 2**, 361
Bacq, Z. M., reference to, **Supp. 3**, 136
Bacteria: as animal disease carriers, **Supp. 5**, 383; conjunctivitis-causing, **Supp. 4**, 865; food preservation and spoilage, **Supp. 7**, 629–31; gangrene antitoxin developed, **Supp. 9**, 225; tuberculosis-causing, **Supp. 4**, 435, 684; typhus-causing, **Supp. 4**, 468; syphilis treatment research, **Supp. 9**, 226; writings on, **Supp. 10**, 699
Bacteriology: **Vol. 3, Part 1**, 478 f.; **Vol. 3, Part 2**, 177 f.; **Vol. 6, Part 1**, 66; **Vol. 7, Part 1**, 140, 542; **Vol. 8, Part 1**, 252 f., 391, 460 f.; **Vol. 8, Part 2**, 445, 483; **Vol. 9, Part 1**, 263, 591 f.; **Vol. 10, Part 1**, 621 f.; communicable diseases, **Supp. 6**, 481; development as discipline, **Supp. 2**, 513; disease relationship, **Supp. 4**, 287, 494; microscope use for, **Supp. 4**, 790; ophthalmic, **Supp. 3**, 302; plant pathology, **Supp. 3**, 400–401; preventive medicine, **Supp. 5**, 632; public health, **Supp. 6**, 701; research in, **Supp. 3**, 832; **Supp. 5**, 25–26; sanitary science, **Supp. 3**, 158; soil, **Supp. 1**, 461; surgery laboratory, **Supp. 6**, 664; teaching of, **Supp. 1**, 665; **Supp. 2**, 225, 353, 744; variation and order in, **Supp. 3**, 354; veterinary, **Supp. 5**, 382–89. *See also* Bacteria; Microbiology
Bad Axe, battle of. *See* Black Hawk War
Badlands National Monument, establishment of, **Supp. 2**, 492
Bad Seed, The, **Supp. 5**, 99, 100
Baehr, George, reference to, **Supp. 4**, 468
Baekeland, Leo, reference to, **Supp. 3**, 247
Baer, Max: Braddock heavyweight championship bout, **Supp. 9**, 121; reference to, **Supp. 10**, 699
Baffin Land, Eskimo studies, **Supp. 3**, 82
Baha'i, art influence, **Supp. 10**, 787
Bahamas: governorship of, **Vol. 4, Part 1**, 296; **Vol. 4, Part 2**, 382; zoölogical expedition, **Vol. 7, Part 1**, 598
Bailey, Mildred, reference to, **Supp. 8**, 697
Bailey, Pearce, reference to, **Supp. 4**, 249
Bailey, Pearl, references to, **Supp. 5**, 529; **Supp. 9**, 517; **Supp. 10**, 20
Bailey, Thomas, reference to, **Supp. 6**, 710
Bailey, Vernon, reference to, **Supp. 4**, 41
Bain, Alexander, reference to, **Supp. 3**, 149
"Baines, Scattergood" (fictional character), **Supp. 7**, 417
Baird, Bil, reference to, **Supp. 3**, 685

Baked goods: manufacturing and marketing, **Supp. 8**, 560–61; nutrient enriched, **Supp. 7**, 223
Bakelite (plastic), **Supp. 3**, 26–27
Baker, Georg Barr, reference to, **Supp. 6**, 514
Baker, George Pierce, references to, **Supp. 3**, 426, 448, 454, 471; **Supp. 4**, 54; **Supp. 6**, 286, 622; **Supp. 7**, 803; **Supp. 8**, 53; **Supp. 9**, 70
Baker, Helen Cody, reference to, **Supp. 6**, 1
Baker, Howard, Jr., reference to, **Supp. 8**, 92
Baker, James P., reference to, **Supp. 3**, 805
Baker, Newton D., references to, **Vol. 9, Part 1**, 601; **Supp. 3**, 168; **Supp. 5**, 468; **Supp. 7**, 370
Baker, Ray Stannard, reference to, **Supp. 3**, 762, 816; **Supp. 4**, 518, 662
Baker, Robert, references to, **Supp. 9**, 433, 440
Baker's Creek, battle of, **Vol. 4, Part 1**, 495; **Vol. 5, Part 1**, 271; **Vol. 6, Part 1**, 130, 420; **Vol. 8, Part 2**, 631; **Vol. 9, Part 1**, 631
Baker Street Irregulars, **Supp. 6**, 465
Baker University, **Vol. 1, Part 1**, 536; **Vol. 8, Part 1**, 298
Baker v. *Carr*, **Supp. 9**, 866; **Supp. 10**, 122, 126
Baking Powder, manufacture of, **Vol. 10, Part 2**, 655
Balanchine, George, references to, **Supp. 8**, 670; **Supp. 10**, 207
Balch, Emily Greene, reference to, **Supp. 5**, 508
Balchen, Bernt, reference to, **Supp. 5**, 3
Baldwin, E. J. ("Lucky"), reference to, **Supp. 3**, 155
Baldwin, Edward R., reference to, **Supp. 3**, 431
Baldwin, James, reference to, **Supp. 7**, 719
Baldwin, Raymond, reference to, **Supp. 9**, 58
Baldwin, Roger, references to, **Supp. 3**, 532; **Supp. 6**, 664; **Supp. 9**, 36
Baldwin, Ruth Standish, reference to, **Supp. 6**, 284
"Baldwin's Rules," **Vol. 1, Part 1**, 536
Baldwin University, founding of, **Vol. 1, Part 1**, 535 f.
Baldwin-Wallace College, **Vol. 7, Part 1**, 393
Balfour Declaration (1917), **Supp. 3**, 97; **Supp. 4**, 660
Ball, Joseph, reference to, **Supp. 10**, 360
Ball, Lucille, reference to, **Supp. 10**, 804
Ball, Thomas, references to, **Vol. 7, Part 1**, 18; **Supp. 3**, 266
Ballad of the Sad Cafe, The, **Supp. 9**, 247
Ballads, **Vol. 2, Part 1**, 492; **Vol. 4, Part 2**, 48, 390, 432, 464; **Vol. 6, Part 1**, 159; **Vol. 7, Part 1**, 23; **Vol. 8, Part 2**, 608; **Vol. 9, Part 1**, 245 f.; study of, **Supp. 3**, 423
Ball Brothers Co., **Supp. 3**, 29
Ball Grain Explosives Co., **Supp. 3**, 239
Ballet: **Vol. 4, Part 1**, 59 f.; **Supp. 5**, 74–76; **Supp. 7**, 173–74, 548, 560; **Supp. 8**, 669–70; American Jazz, **Supp. 5**, 103–4; choreography, **Supp. 3**, 281–82; **Supp. 9**, 776; **Supp. 10**, 207; companies, **Supp. 10**, 206–7; music, **Supp. 8**, 145, 146; **Supp. 9**, 775–76; musical composition for, **Supp. 10**, 580; teaching of, **Supp. 10**, 207
Ballet International, **Supp. 7**, 173
Ballet Intime, **Supp. 5**, 75
Ballet Russe (Diaghilev company), **Supp. 5**, 75; **Supp. 7**, 173, 548, 560; **Supp. 10**, 206
Ballet Russe de Monte Carlo (de Basil company), **Supp. 7**, 173
Ballinger, Richard A., references to, **Supp. 1**, 300; **Supp. 3**, 96, 321, 605, 724–25; **Supp. 4**, 664–66; **Supp. 5**, 666, 699; **Supp. 6**, 556; **Supp. 7**, 606
Ballinger-Pinchot controversy, **Vol. 1, Part 1**, 555; **Vol. 9, Part 2**, 269
Ballistics, **Vol. 10, Part 1**, 584 f. *See also* Firearms
Balloons: flights, **Supp. 5**, 547; motors for, **Supp. 1**, 214; naval experimentation, **Supp. 1**, 561; scientific research with, **Supp. 7**, 619. *See also* Aviation
Ballpoint pen, **Supp. 10**, 670
Ballroom dancing, **Supp. 7**, 563; **Supp. 8**, 77–78; **Supp. 8**, 690
Ball's Bluff, Va., engagement at, **Vol. 1, Part 1**, 518; **Vol. 3, Part 1**, 207; **Vol. 9, Part 2**, 72
Balsas, Andre, reference to, **Supp. 6**, 363
Baltimore, Md.: art, **Vol. 10, Part 1**, 399 f.; art collections, **Supp. 4**, 768; black education, **Vol. 1, Part 2**, 432; Catholic church, **Vol. 3, Part 1**, 473 f.; **Vol. 4, Part 1**, 240; charity organizations, **Supp. 4**, 100; Christian Association, **Vol. 4, Part 1**, 625; city planning, **Supp. 4**, 550–51; commercial life, **Vol. 6, Part 2**, 102; election violence (1857), **Vol. 6, Part 1**, 240; Gilman School, **Vol. 4, Part 1**, 303; Hospital for Crippled Children, **Vol. 9, Part 2**, 343; mayors, **Supp. 9**, 528; mob violence, **Vol. 6, Part 1**, 582; park construction, **Vol. 6, Part 1**, 27; Peabody Institute, founding of, **Vol. 7, Part 2**, 337; politics, **Supp. 9**, 527, 528; public service, **Vol. 1, Part 2**, 427; **Vol. 2, Part 2**, 521; **Vol. 4, Part 1**, 163; **Vol. 6, Part 2**, 102; **Vol. 7, Part 2**, 282, 310, 527; **Vol. 8, Part 1**, 171 f.; **Vol. 9, Part 1**, 342; **Vol. 9, Part 2**, 238; Reform League of, **Vol. 1, Part 2**, 427; **Vol. 8, Part 2**, 159; sewage disposal, **Vol. 8, Part 1**, 502; social hygiene movement, **Supp. 4**, 391; social work, **Supp. 4**, 333; Washington Monument in, **Vol. 9, Part 2**, 443; yellow-fever epidemic in, **Vol. 3, Part 1**, 91
Baltimore American, publication of "The Star-Spangled Banner" in, **Vol. 5, Part 2**, 362
Baltimore & Ohio Railroad: growth of, **Vol. 2, Part 2**, 471 f.; **Vol. 3, Part 2**, 319; **Vol. 4, Part 1**, 163; **Vol. 5, Part 1**, 214, 275; **Vol. 5, Part 2**, 348; **Vol. 6, Part 1**, 27, 380; **Vol. 9, Part 1**, 453; **Supp. 3**, 823–24; development of, **Vol. 2, Part 1**, 117; **Vol. 9, Part 2**, 237, 442, 449; engineering plans for, **Vol. 5, Part 2**, 467
Baltimore & Potomac Railroad, **Vol. 1, Part 2**, 510
Baltimore Central Railroad, **Vol. 1, Part 1**, 639
Baltimore College of Dental Surgery, founding of, **Vol. 1, Part 2**, 61
Baltimore Gynecological Society, founding of, **Supp. 1**, 437
Baltimore incident (1891). *See* Valparaiso affair (1891)
Baltimore Museum of Art, **Supp. 4**, 175, 768, 771; founding of, **Supp. 4**, 551
Baltimore Orioles (baseball), **Supp. 9**, 390
Baltimore Reform League, **Vol. 8, Part 2**, 159; **Supp. 4**, 116
Baltimore Sun, **Vol. 1, Part 1**, 374; **Supp. 6**, 443–46, 502; editorial cartoons, **Supp. 7**, 205–6
Balzac, Honoré de, studies on, **Supp. 2**, 141
Bamberger, Louis, reference to, **Supp. 6**, 208
Bamberger and Co., **Supp. 3**, 30
Banana: industry, **Supp. 9**, 94; introduction to U.S., **Vol. 1, Part 1**, 524; trade in, **Vol. 5, Part 2**, 291 f.
Bancitaly Corporation, organization of, **Supp. 4**, 326
Bancroft, Edward, reference to, **Vol. 10, Part 1**, 659
Bancroft, George, reference to, **Vol. 8, Part 2**, 486
Bandages: adhesive, **Supp. 7**, 183; elastic, **Supp. 7**, 678
Band-Aid, invention of, **Supp. 7**, 183
Banditry, **Vol. 3, Part 1**, 40 f.; **Vol. 8, Part 1**, 15 f.
Bandler, Bernard, reference to, **Supp. 7**, 55
Band music, **Supp. 3**, 610–11; **Supp. 5**, 106; **Supp. 6**, 241–42, 274–75; **Supp. 10**, 173–74
Bandsaw, invention of, **Vol. 8, Part 1**, 304 f.
Banga, Henry, reference to, **Supp. 6**, 632
Bangor Theological Seminary, founding of, **Vol. 8, Part 1**, 58
Banjo, **Supp. 5**, 657
Bank Convention of the Confederate States (1861), **Vol. 5, Part 2**, 550
Bankers. For complete list *see* Occupations Index
Banker's Life and Casualty, **Supp. 10**, 477

Bank for International Settlements: founding of, **Supp. 3**, 290; **Supp. 4**, 470; **Supp. 6**, 599; **Supp. 7**, 810; Morgan & Co., **Supp. 3**, 537
Bankhead, John H., Jr., references to, **Supp. 5**, 290–91; **Supp. 9**, 151
Bankhead, Tallulah, reference to, **Supp. 9**, 691
Bankhead-Jones Farm Tenant Act (1937), **Supp. 4**, 50
Banking: **Vol. 1, Part 1**, 90, 330; **Vol. 1, Part 2**, 170, 211, 244 f., 278, 359, 372, 443; **Vol. 2, Part 1**, 102, 126, 139; **Vol. 2, Part 2**, 30, 111, 144, 148, 183, 261, 359, 375, 383 f., 395, 436, 440, 522, 535, 613; **Vol. 3, Part 1**, 178, 283, 455 f., 514 f.; **Vol. 3, Part 2**, 48, 297, 343, 520; **Vol. 4, Part 1**, 8, 85 f., 109, 164, 242, 273; **Vol. 4, Part 2**, 257 f., 537, 545, 566; **Vol. 5, Part 1**, 13, 466, 532; **Vol. 5, Part 2**, 24, 78, 115, 308, 334; **Vol. 6, Part 1**, 51 f., 84, 131, 152, 409, 490; **Vol. 6, Part 2**, 22, 114, 397; **Vol. 7, Part 1**, 6, 39 f.,111, 175 f., 259, 360, 430, 645; **Vol. 7, Part 2**, 309, 522; **Vol. 8, Part 1**, 34 f., 322 f., 325 f., 333 f., 603 f., 636, 644; **Vol. 8, Part 2**, 274, 342, 569 f., 583; **Vol. 9, Part 1**, 268, 696; **Vol. 9, Part 2**, 66, 132, 304, 577, 631; **Vol. 10, Part 1**, 89, 438; **Vol. 10, Part 2**, 120, 212, 488; Aldrich Plan, **Supp. 2**, 15, 544, 555; black-owned, **Supp. 4**, 83, 916; branch, **Supp. 2**, 410; **Supp. 4**, 325–26; central system, **Supp. 2**, 123; **Supp. 3**, 414, 480; **Supp. 5**, 247; **Supp. 6**, 599; clearinghouse methods, **Vol. 2, Part 1**, 476; **Vol. 3, Part 2**, 524; commercial, **Supp. 4**, 470; **Supp. 7**, 782–83; crisis (1930s), **Supp. 1**, 84; **Supp. 3**, 648–49; **Supp. 5**, 158, 469–70; **Supp. 6**, 33–34; **Supp. 7**, 362; **Supp 8**, 112; development of, **Supp. 2**, 719; ethics issues, **Supp. 5**, 470, 745; executives, **Supp. 5**, 159–60; **Supp. 7**, 189–90; experiments in Massachusetts Colony, **Vol. 3, Part 1**, 106; federal deposit insurance, **Supp. 3**, 650, 730; first multibank holding company in U.S., **Supp. 10**, 205; Germany, **Supp. 5**, 249–50; guarantee funds, origin of, **Vol. 3, Part 2**, 525; Houston (Tex.), **Supp. 6**, 324; interest, time discount theory of, **Vol. 8, Part 1**, 321 f.; international banking house, early attempts to establish, **Vol. 3, Part 1**, 486 f.; investment, **Vol. 1, Part 1**, 607; **Vol. 2, Part 2**, 215; **Supp. 3**, 537–38; **Supp. 4**, 320, 470; **Supp. 7**, 715; **Supp. 8**, 78–79, 367–68; investment separation from commercial, **Supp. 4**, 470; Jekyll Island report, **Vol. 3, Part 1**, 148; land banks, **Vol. 2, Part 2**, 313; **Vol. 10, Part 2**, 482; legislation, **Vol. 3, Part 1**, 388 f.; **Supp. 3**, 730; **Supp. 4**, 331, 332, 470; **Supp. 5**, 158; **Supp. 9**, 208; mergers, **Supp. 2**, 411; **Supp. 5**, 744; Missouri paper money dispute, **Vol. 8, Part 1**, 43; money markets, **Supp. 9**, 661; Morris Plan, **Vol. 4, Part 1**, 450; Postal Saving system, **Vol. 6, Part 1**, 61; **Vol. 9, Part 2**, 269; record-keeping, **Supp. 3**, 618; reforms, **Vol. 5, Part 2**, 302; **Vol. 9, Part 1**, 471; **Vol. 9, Part 2**, 30; **Vol. 10, Part 1**, 412 f.; **Vol. 10, Part 2**, 279; regulation of, **Vol. 3, Part 1**, 37 f.; **Vol. 6, Part 1**, 528 f.; **Vol. 7, Part 1**, 2; Revolutionary War period, **Vol. 10, Part 2**, 303; savings banks, **Vol. 7, Part 2**, 630; **Vol. 8, Part 2**, 388; savings-bank workers' insurance, **Supp. 3**, 95; state banking systems, **Vol. 3, Part 1**, 468 f.; **Vol. 3, Part 2**, 99, 439, 464; studies in, **Supp. 2**, 555; unit v. branch banking, **Supp. 5**, 158; "wild cat" money, origin of the phrase, **Vol. 7, Part 1**, 447; **Vol. 9, Part 2**, 84; writings on, **Supp. 8**, 243; youngest president of financial institution, **Supp. 9**, 529. *See also* Credit; Finance; International banking and finance; *specific bank names*
Banking Act (1933). *See* Glass-Steagall Act
Banking Act (1935), **Supp. 9**, 208
Bank notes: engraving, **Vol. 2, Part 1**, 560; **Vol. 2, Part 2**, 434; **Vol. 3, Part 1**, 501 f., 535 f., 538; **Vol. 4, Part 1**, 322 f.; **Vol. 5, Part 1**, 165; **Vol. 5, Part 2**, 74, 159; **Vol. 7, Part 2**, 55, 370, 472; **Vol. 8, Part 1**, 253; **Vol. 8, Part 2**, 122, 451; **Vol. 9, Part 1**, 232; **Vol. 9, Part 2**, 295; gold certificates, **Vol. 7, Part 2**, 41; printing, **Vol. 8, Part 1**, 515
Bank of America: **Supp. 8**, 308–9; founding of, **Supp. 4**, 326–27
Bank of England, **Supp. 5**, 650
Bank of Italy, founding of, **Supp. 4**, 325–26
Bank of North Dakota, **Supp. 4**, 480
Bank of the United States: **Vol. 2, Part 2**, 63; **Supp. 5**, 469–70; formed, **Vol. 3, Part 1**, 514 f.; proposed transfer of money from, to state banks, **Vol. 3, Part 1**, 468 f.; rechartering of, **Vol. 2, Part 2**, 175, 181; second, established, **Vol. 1, Part 2**, 244 f.; war upon, during Andrew Jackson's administration, **Vol. 1, Part 2**, 211
Bank robbery, **Supp. 10**, 770, 771
Bankruptcy: biggest in retailing history, **Supp. 9**, 337; legislation, **Supp. 4**, 825; Penn Central Railroad, **Supp. 10**, 772; reorganization policies, **Supp. 4**, 193; **Supp. 5**, 190–91
Bankruptcy Act, **Vol. 6, Part 1**, 467
Banks (specific): Bank of America, **Vol. 7, Part 1**, 430; Bank of California, **Vol. 7, Part 1**, 6; **Vol. 8, Part 1**, 333 f.; Bank of Commerce, **Vol. 1, Part 2**, 443; **Vol. 9, Part 1**, 616; **Vol. 10, Part 1**, 438; Bank of England, **Vol. 1, Part 2**, 359; Bank for International Settlements, **Vol. 9, Part 2**, 631; Bank of the Manhattan Co., **Vol. 6, Part 1**, 490; Bank of Maryland, **Vol. 7, Part 2**, 309 f.; Bank of New York, **Vol. 3, Part 1**, 486 f.; **Vol. 6, Part 2**, 22; **Vol. 7, Part 1**, 360; Bank of North America, **Vol. 1, Part 2**, 278; **Vol. 3, Part 2**, 444; **Vol. 7, Part 1**, 201, 222, 531; Bank of South Carolina, **Vol. 6, Part 1**, 131; Bank of the State of Missouri, **Vol. 1, Part 2**, 409; Bank of the United States, **Vol. 1, Part 1**, 331; **Vol. 1, Part 2**, 359, 380; **Vol. 2, Part 2**, 183; **Vol. 3, Part 1**, 38, 468 f.; **Vol. 5, Part 1**, 466, 532; **Vol. 5, Part 2**, 24, 115; **Vol. 6, Part 1**, 84, 152; **Vol. 6, Part 2**, 114; **Vol. 7, Part 1**, 11; **Vol. 8, Part 1**, 34 f., 636; **Vol. 10, Part 1**, 89; **Vol. 10, Part 2**, 488; Bankers' Trust Co., **Vol. 3, Part 1**, 148; State Bank of Iowa, **Vol. 8, Part 1**, 212 f.; United States Trust Co., **Vol. 9, Part 2**, 11
Banks, Ernie, reference to, **Supp. 10**, 346
Banks and Politics in America from the Revolution to the Civil War, **Supp. 8**, 243
Bank Street College of Education, founding of, **Supp. 8**, 443
Banky, Vilma, reference to, **Supp. 6**, 120
Banner of Light, **Vol. 2, Part 2**, 285
Banner of the Cross, **Vol. 6, Part 1**, 296
Bannock Indian Campaign, **Vol. 6, Part 2**, 615
Baptism, debate on meaning and mode of, **Vol. 8, Part 1**, 544
Baptist church: "Association Book," **Vol. 4, Part 1**, 624; black branches, **Vol. 1, Part 2**, 528; **Vol. 7, Part 2**, 323 f., 492; "Circular" letters, **Vol. 8, Part 2**, 180; clergymen, *see under* Clergyman for specific names by specific denomination in Occupations Index; colleges, **Vol. 3, Part 1**, 141; evangelism, **Supp. 4**, 691–92; **Supp. 5**, 198; factions in, **Vol. 2, Part 1**, 139, 448; **Vol. 4, Part 1**, 62, 508; **Vol. 6, Part 1**, 160; "Freewill" Baptists, **Vol. 8, Part 1**, 345 f.; fundamentalism, **Supp. 4**, 691–92; **Supp. 5**, 516–17; Georgia, **Vol. 6, Part 2**, 543; **Vol. 8, Part 2**, 330; "Great Awakening," **Vol. 1, Part 1**, 469; history of, **Vol. 2, Part 1**, 44, 573; **Vol. 3, Part 2**, 41; **Vol. 4, Part 1**, 624; **Vol. 8, Part 1**, 608; **Vol. 10, Part 1**, 383 f.; **Vol. 10, Part 2**, 170; **Supp. 1**, 529, 694; Kentucky, **Vol. 10, Part 1**, 383 f.; largest in the world, **Vol. 6, Part 1**, 432; leadership, **Supp. 1**, 625; missionary activity, **Vol. 1, Part 1**, 392; **Vol. 2, Part 2**, 130; **Vol. 5, Part 1**, 463; **Vol.**

5, Part 2, 234; **Vol. 7, Part 1**, 160; **Vol. 8, Part 1**, 543; **Vol. 9, Part 1**, 137, 603; **Vol. 9, Part 2**, 143, 579; **Supp. 7**, 679–81; North Carolina, **Vol. 8, Part 2**, 180; organizations, **Vol. 7, Part 1**, 281; **Vol. 8, Part 2**, 180; **Vol. 9, Part 1**, 23; political affiliation, **Vol. 6, Part 1**, 160 f.; **Vol. 8, Part 2**, 273; Quakers, relations with, **Vol. 8, Part 2**, 101; Sabbath, observance of, **Vol. 8, Part 2**, 114; Seventh-Day Baptists of Ephrata, **Vol. 8, Part 2**, 282; slavery, attitude toward, **Vol. 4, Part 1**, 62, 68; **Vol. 8, Part 2**, 273; South Carolina, **Vol. 5, Part 2**, 130; Southern Convention, **Supp. 5**, 176; southern convention of 1845, **Vol. 5, Part 2**, 130; southern evangelism, **Supp. 3**, 687–88, 778–79; Tennessee, **Vol. 5, Part 2**, 582; theological writings, **Supp. 4**, 524–26; University of Chicago, raising of funds for, **Vol. 4, Part 1**, 406; Virginia, **Vol. 4, Part 2**, 395; **Vol. 8, Part 2**, 273; **Vol. 9, Part 2**, 331; writings on, **Vol. 4, Part 1**, 508; **Vol. 5, Part 2**, 64, 97; **Vol. 8, Part 2**, 273; **Supp. 1**, 693
Baquet, George, reference to, **Supp. 6**, 41
Baratarians, service of, in battle of New Orleans, **Vol. 5, Part 2**, 540
Barbara, Joseph, reference to, **Supp. 8**, 397
Barbary pirates, **Vol. 1, Part 1**, 504; **Vol. 5, Part 2**, 7, 22, 30; **Vol. 6, Part 1**, 77
Barbary states, diplomacy, **Vol. 6, Part 1**, 76
Barbed wire, **Vol. 4, Part 1**, 331; **Vol. 4, Part 2**, 94
Barber, Samuel, reference to, **Supp. 6**, 457
Barbiturates, **Supp. 8**, 102
Barbizon school, influence of, **Vol. 7, Part 1**, 466
Barcelona Pavilion, **Supp. 8**, 436
Barclay, Robert, reference to, **Vol. 5, Part 2**, 290
Barcroft, Joseph, reference to, **Supp. 3**, 353
Bard College, predecessor, **Supp. 6**, 45
"Bargain" of President Hayes, **Vol. 4, Part 2**, 450
Bargain basements, **Supp. 2**, 183
Barges, original use of, **Vol. 8, Part 1**, 442
Baring Brothers & Co., **Vol. 1, Part 2**, 52; **Vol. 10, Part 1**, 441
Barium X-ray diagnosis, **Supp. 3**, 133
Barkla, C. G., reference to, **Supp. 7**, 10, 133
Barkley, Alben W., references to, **Supp. 3**, 335; **Supp. 6**, 601; **Supp. 8**, 36
Barlow, Joel, reference to, **Vol. 5, Part 1**, 245; **Vol. 7, Part 1**, 583
Barlow, William, reference to, **Supp. 6**, 71
Barnard, Ernest S., reference to, **Supp. 9**, 365
Barnard, Frederick A. P., reference to, **Supp. 4**, 133
Barnard, George G., references to, **Supp. 4**, 902; **Supp. 6**, 193
Barnard, Henry, references to, **Vol. 6, Part 1**, 404; **Vol. 10, Part 1**, 645 f.
Barnard, John, Associates, **Supp. 5**, 756
Barnard College, **Vol. 1, Part 1**, 263, 621; **Vol. 3, Part 1**, 594 f.; **Vol. 4, Part 1**, 285; **Vol. 8, Part 1**, 278 f.; administration, **Supp. 7**, 288–89; founding of, **Supp. 2**, 532; **Supp. 5**, 488
"Barnburners" and "Hunkers" (1848), **Vol. 1, Part 2**, 332; **Vol. 2, Part 1**, 204; **Vol. 3, Part 1**, 326; **Vol. 3, Part 2**, 447; **Vol. 6, Part 2**, 276; **Vol. 7, Part 1**, 600; **Vol. 9, Part 2**, 538; **Vol. 10, Part 1**, 151, 156; **Vol. 10, Part 2**, 567
Barnes, Alfred, reference to, **Supp. 9**, 502
Barnes, Charles R., reference to, **Supp. 3**, 164
Barnes, Harry Elmer, reference to, **Supp. 4**, 62
Barnes, Mildred (Bliss), references to, **Supp. 5**, 699, 700; **Supp. 6**, 197
Barnes Foundation, founding of, **Supp. 5**, 39
Barnes of New York, great success of, **Vol. 4, Part 2**, 54
Barnett, George E., references to, **Supp. 2**, 311
Barney, Ida, reference to, **Supp. 3**, 692
Barney, Natalie, reference to, **Supp. 10**, 246
Barnsdall, Aline, reference to, **Supp. 6**, 713
Barnstorming, **Vol. 6, Part 1**, 216, 493; **Supp. 9**, 496
Barnum, P. T.: references to, **Vol. 5, Part 1**, 117; **Vol. 5, Part 2**, 289; **Vol. 9, Part 2**, 126; writings on, **Supp. 3**, 672
Barnum and Bailey Circus, **Supp. 6**, 8
Barometer, new type invented, **Supp. 9**, 357; portable, **Vol. 3, Part 1**, 540
Baroudi, Sam, reference to, **Supp. 9**, 171
Barr, Alfred H., Jr., references to, **Supp. 8**, 126–27; **Supp. 9**, 502, 708
Barr, Stringfellow, reference to, **Supp. 8**, 59
Barren Ground, **Supp. 3**, 304–5
Barrère Little Symphony, **Supp. 3**, 33
Barret, Clifton Waller, Library, **Supp. 7**, 797
Barrett, Lawrence, references to, **Vol. 5, Part 1**, 586; **Supp. 3**, 713
Barrie, Sir James, references to, **Vol. 4, Part 1**, 41; **Supp. 5**, 8
Barriger, John W., reference to, **Supp. 5**, 551
Barron, Captain James, court-martial of, **Vol. 3, Part 1**, 188 f.
Barron's Weekly, **Supp. 1**, 52
Barrows, John, reference to, **Supp. 10**, 838
Barry, Joan, Chaplin paternity suit, **Supp. 10**, 117
Barrymore, Ethel, references to, **Supp. 3**, 34; **Supp. 5**, 44
Barrymore, John: biography of, **Supp. 6**, 214; references to, **Supp. 3**, 341, 342; **Supp. 4**, 798; **Supp. 5**, 44; **Supp. 8**, 461
Barrymore, Lionel, references to, **Supp. 3**, 34, 35
Bartelmez, George William, reference to, **Supp. 6**, 295, 296
Barth, Karl, reference to, **Supp. 7**, 746
Barth, Theodore H., reference to, **Supp. 7**, 577
Barthel, Oliver E., references to, **Supp. 4**, 292, 293
Barthes, Roland, reference to, **Supp. 9**, 884
Bartlett, Captain "Bob," reference to, **Vol. 7, Part 2**, 365 f.
Bartlett, Charles L., reference to, **Supp. 7**, 724
Bartlett, Robert Abram, reference to, **Supp. 9**, 118
Bartlett, Truman H., reference to, **Supp. 3**, 210–11
Bartlett's Familiar Quotations, **Supp. 6**, 465
Bartlett Shade Tree Experts Co., founding of, **Supp. 7**, 33
Bartol Research Foundation, **Supp. 7**, 619; founding of, **Supp. 1**, 523
Barton, Bruce, reference to, **Supp. 7**, 211
Barton, Clara, reference to, **Supp. 4**, 91; **Supp. 6**, 167
Barton, Otis, reference to, **Supp. 7**, 45
"Barton's Bandage," **Vol. 1, Part 2**, 22
Bartram, John, reference to, **Vol. 6, Part 1**, 362
Baruch, Bernard, references to, **Supp. 3**, 293, 335, 399; **Supp. 6**, 616, 617; **Supp. 8**, 546; **Supp. 9**, 8
Barzun, Jacques, reference to, **Supp. 9**, 808
Baseball: **Vol. 1, Part 1**, 311; **Vol. 2, Part 2**, 165; **Vol. 3, Part 2**, 177; **Vol. 4, Part 1**, 8; **Vol. 4, Part 2**, 399; **Vol. 5, Part 1**, 345 f.; **Vol. 5, Part 2**, 92, 309 f.; **Vol. 6, Part 2**, 408; **Vol. 8, Part 1**, 418; **Vol. 8, Part 2**, 104; **Vol. 9, Part 1**, 420, 499; **Vol. 10, Part 2**, 554; batting, **Supp. 3**, 294–95; **Supp. 5**, 291–92, 716; **Supp. 6**, 347, 488, 582, 589; **Supp. 7**, 27–28, 128–29, 365, 513–14, 763; **Supp. 8**, 105–7, 186–87, 497; American League Championship Series, **Supp. 10**, 567; base stealing, **Supp. 10**, 99; batting, **Supp. 9**, 178–79, 294–95, 369, 390, 543–44, 729, 730; batting records, **Supp. 9**, 857–58; "Black Sox" scandal, **Supp. 3**, 438; **Supp. 8**, 85–86, 574–75; "bonehead" play, **Supp. 8**, 713; "Boys of Summer," **Supp. 9**, 390; brawls, **Supp. 10**, 532; broadcasting, **Supp. 9**, 224, 295, 533; "Bronx Bombers," **Supp. 10**, 141; "called-shot" home run, **Supp. 4**, 711; catching, **Supp. 7**,

130; **Supp. 8**, 574–75; **Supp. 9**, 82, 368–69; **Supp. 10**, 566–67; collegiate, **Supp. 9**, 294, 729; **Supp. 10**, 14–15; collegiate coaching, **Supp. 8**, 107; commissioners, **Supp. 3**, 438; **Supp. 5**, 411; **Supp. 10**, 256–57, 606; deadball era, **Supp. 9**, 857–58; ethics issues, **Supp. 3**, 438; **Supp. 6**, 589; **Supp. 8**, 85–86, 574–75, 713–14; executives, **Supp. 5**, 40–41; farm system, **Supp. 5**, 41; **Supp. 7**, 646; **Supp. 9**, 365–66, 529, 531–33, 854–55; **Supp. 10**, 278; fielding, **Supp. 5**, 465–66; fielding records, **Supp. 9**, 289, 294, 404, 806; first All-Star game, **Supp. 5**, 724; **Supp. 9**, 366; first black American Leaague coach, **Supp. 10**, 347; first black major league player, **Supp. 9**, 668–69; **Supp. 10**, 256; first black MVP American League, **Supp. 10**, 346; first black umpire, **Supp. 10**, 15; first commissioner, **Supp. 3**, 438; first game televised, **Supp. 9**, 765; food concessions, **Supp. 7**, 718–19; franchise expansion, **Supp. 7**, 647; **Supp. 10**, 257, 278; franchise ownership, **Supp. 2**, 589–90; **Supp. 7**, 155, 646–47; **Supp. 10**, 605–6, 857, 859–61; franchise shifts, **Supp. 9**, 366; **Supp. 10**, 257, 278, 606; "Gashouse Gang," **Supp. 9**, 224, 294, 543; "Green Monster," **Supp. 10**, 860; "Heavenly Twins" outfielding, **Supp. 5**, 189; Hispanic players, highest salary paid to, **Supp. 9**, 178; Hispanic players, treatment of, **Supp. 9**, 179; home-run record, single season, **Supp. 10**, 257; home-run records, **Supp. 2**, 737; **Supp. 4**, 327–28, 710; **Supp. 8**, 187; infielders, **Supp. 9**, 289, 294–95, 668–69, 729–30, 806; in Japan, **Supp. 8**, 479; integration of, **Supp. 10**, 278; International League, **Supp. 9**, 344; knuckle ball, **Supp. 8**, 543–44; Lajoie-Cobb competition, **Supp. 6**, 356–57; league presidents, **Supp. 10**, 256, 278; magazines, **Supp. 7**, 711–12; malapropisms, **Supp. 9**, 224, 764; managers, **Supp. 5**, 261; **Supp. 6**, 415–16; **Supp. 7**, 501–2; **Supp. 9**, 295, 390, 763–64; **Supp. 10**, 100, 574–75; "Murders' Row," **Supp. 10**, 142, 532–33; Negro American League, **Supp. 3**, 378; **Supp. 9**, 668; Negro League, **Supp. 4**, 327–28; **Supp. 9**, 840; **Supp. 10**, 201, 279, 346; night games inaugurated, **Supp. 9**, 532; **Supp. 10**, 256; origin of, **Vol. 3, Part 1**, 391; **Vol. 4, Part 2**, 47; outfielders, **Supp. 6**, 589; **Supp. 9**, 328–29; 403–4; 543–44, 653–54, 857–58; **Supp. 10**, 99–100, 141–42; Pacific Coast League, **Supp. 10**, 202; pitching, **Supp. 10**, 508–9; pitching records, **Supp. 4**, 8–9, 435–36, 710; **Supp. 5**, 48, 759–60; **Supp. 6**, 663; **Supp. 7**, 663; **Supp. 8**, 49–50, 85, 543–44, 558–59; **Supp. 9**, 224, 344–45; player-coaches, **Supp. 8**, 141–42; **Supp. 9**, 369; **Supp. 10**, 202; player-managers, **Supp. 1**, 530; **Supp. 5**, 124–25, 189; **Supp. 7**, 129, 130, 365–66; **Supp. 8**, 542–43; **Supp. 9**, 368, 729, 806; **Supp. 10**, 314; pranks, **Supp. 9**, 763; protective cap for batters, **Supp. 4**, 214; racism in, **Supp. 9**, 668–69; **Supp. 10**, 347, 860–61; Sally League, **Supp. 9** 328; scouting, **Supp. 9**, 730; "Stengelese," **Supp. 9**, 764; team symbols, **Supp. 10**, 564; Triple Crown, last National League player to win, **Supp. 9**, 543; umpires, **Supp. 5**, 393; **Supp. 7**, 139; **Supp. 8**, 544; **Supp. 10**, 14–16, 351; unionization of umpires thwarted, **Supp. 9**, 366; "Who's on first," comedy routine, **Supp. 6**, 128; **Supp. 9**, 2; winding of ball by machine, **Vol. 8, Part 1**, 419; World Series, **Supp. 9**, 179, 294–95, 368, 403, 543, 763, 764; **Supp. 10**, 10, 99, 314, 480, 532, 533, 567, 574, 575, 860, 861; writings on, **Supp. 9**, 215. *See also* American League; Continental League; National League; *specific teams*

Baseball Anonymous, founding of, **Supp. 8**, 575

Baseball Hall of Fame (Cooperstown, N. Y.), first inductees, **Supp. 5**, 717, 129

Bashford, Coles, reference to, **Vol. 1, Part 2**, 1

Basic History of the United States, The, **Supp. 6**, 41

Basic Writings of Sigmund Freud, The, **Supp. 4**, 109

Basie, Count, Orchestra, **Supp. 6**, 300; **Supp. 9**, 687

Basketball: **Supp. 8**, 358–59, 630–31; coaching, **Supp. 9**, 20–21; **Supp. 10**, 711; fast-break, **Supp. 10**, 711; invention of, **Supp. 2**, 484; tournament established, **Supp. 9**, 20; racism in, **Supp. 10**, 711; women's, **Supp. 5**, 52

BASR. *See* Applied Social Research, Bureau of

Bassler, Ray S., reference to, **Supp. 3**, 783

Batchelder, Alice L., reference to, **Supp. 7**, 64

Bates College, founding of, **Vol. 2, Part 2**, 54

Bateson, Mary Catherine, reference to, **Supp. 10**, 522

Bateson, William, reference to, **Supp. 3**, 215

Bates Treaty, **Vol. 1, Part 2**, 52

Bathing suits, design and manufacture of, **Supp. 10**, 667–68

Baths: medicinal, **Vol. 9, Part 2**, 488; public, **Vol. 1, Part 2**, 29

Batista, Fulgencio, reference to, **Supp. 6**, 451

Bats, study of, **Vol. 1, Part 1**, 191; **Supp. 6**, 453, 454

Battelle Memorial Institute, **Supp. 8**, 71–72; metallurgical research, **Supp. 4**, 328–29

Batten, Barton, Durstine and Osborn, founding of, **Supp. 7**, 211; **Supp. 8**, 27

Battery, the revolving, **Vol. 9, Part 2**, 554

Battle Creek Food Co., **Supp. 3**, 411

Battle Creek Sanitarium (Mich.), **Supp. 5**, 378

Battle Creek Toasted Corn Flake Co., founding of, **Supp. 5**, 379

Battle Cry of Peace, The (movie), **Supp. 3**, 76; **Supp. 6**, 619

"Battle Hymn of the Republic, The" (song), **Vol. 5, Part 1**, 292

Battle of the Century, **Supp. 7**, 463

"Battle of the Kegs, The," **Vol. 5, Part 1**, 222

Battles, Heye, and Harrison, **Supp. 6**, 289

Battleships, design of, **Supp. 1**, 151

"Batture Case," **Vol. 6, Part 1**, 310; **Vol. 8, Part 1**, 163 f.

Bauer, Louis A., reference to, **Supp. 6**, 205

Baugh, Sammy, reference to, **Supp. 10**, 600

Bauhaus, **Supp. 4**, 591; **Supp. 6**, 199–200; **Supp. 8**, 226–27, 436; **Supp. 10**, 3

Baum, Vicki, reference to, **Supp. 10**, 733

Bausch & Lomb Optical Co., **Supp. 3**, 40

Bauxite, discovery of, **Vol. 7, Part 1**, 413

"Baxter Blues," New York regiment, **Vol. 9, Part 2**, 242

Bayard, Thomas F., references to, **Supp. 3**, 285; **Supp. 6**, 253

Bayh, Birch Evan, Jr., reference to, **Supp. 10**, 29

Baylor Hospital and Medical Center, predecessor, **Supp. 3**, 779

Baylor University, founding of, **Vol. 1, Part 2**, 78; **Vol. 2, Part 1**, 287

Bayne, Beverly, reference to, **Supp. 6**, 440; **Supp. 8**, 65, 66

Bay of Pigs (1961), **Supp. 7**, 421–22, 723–24; **Supp. 8**, 135, 147

Bay Psalm Book, **Supp. 5**, 587

Baziotes, William, reference to, **Supp. 6**, 512

BBC. *See* British Broadcasting Corporation

Beach, Charles, reference to, **Supp. 5**, 429

Beach Haven, N. J., founding of, **Vol. 7, Part 2**, 263

Beach, Sylvia, reference to, **Supp. 10**, 246, 776

Beacon Biographies, **Supp. 6**, 306

Beadle, George W., references to, **Supp. 4**, 252–53; **Supp. 9**, 793–94

Beadle and Adams, **Supp. 3**, 585–86

Beadle's Home Monthly, **Supp. 1**, 63

Beal, William James, reference to, **Supp. 4**, 46–47

"Beale Street Blues" (song), **Supp. 6**, 275
Beall, J. Glenn, Sr., reference to, **Supp. 9**, 528
Bean, L. L., Inc., founding of, **Supp. 8**, 28–29
Beans, breeding of garden, **Supp. 4**, 252
Beard, Charles A., references to, **Supp. 3**, 151; **Supp. 4**, 135, 587; **Supp. 5**, 429–30, 638; **Supp. 6**, 40, 41; **Supp. 9**, 428
Beard, Daniel Carter, reference to, **Supp. 4**, 872
Beard, Mary R., reference to, **Supp. 4**, 63
Bearden, J. A., reference to, **Supp. 7**, 134
Beards, **Supp. 6**, 636
Beardsley, Monroe C., reference to, **Supp. 9**, 884
Bear Flag Revolt, **Vol. 4, Part 1**, 21; **Vol. 9, Part 2**, 49
Bearings, roller, **Vol. 5, Part 1**, 448; **Vol. 9, Part 2**, 555; tilting-pad thrust, **Supp. 3**, 419
Bear Mountain Bridge, construction of, **Vol. 8, Part 2**, 90; financing of, **Supp. 10**, 310
Beat generation, **Supp. 7**, 239; **Supp. 8**, 56, 326–27; **Supp. 9**, 605
Beatles (music group): member, **Supp. 10**, 448–50; Sullivan show appearance, **Supp. 9**, 780
Beaufort, S. C., attack on, **Vol. 2, Part 1**, 310; **Vol. 7, Part 1**, 293
Beaumarchais, Caron de, munitions for Revolutionary War supplied by, **Vol. 3, Part 1**, 174
Beaumont Enterprise, **Supp. 7**, 349, 350
Beauregard, General Pierre, reference to, **Vol. 6, Part 1**, 127 f.
Beauty products. *See* Cosmetics
Beaux-arts Apartments (New York City), architecture, **Supp. 1**, 430
Beaux-arts architecture, **Supp. 1**, 341; **Supp. 4**, 281–82; **Supp. 5**, 133–34
Beaver: study of the, **Vol. 7, Part 1**, 185; trade, **Vol. 8, Part 1**, 320 f.
Beaver Club, founding of, **Supp. 1**, 394
Beaver Dam Creek, Va., **Vol. 5, Part 1**, 558; **Vol. 6, Part 1**, 123. *See also*. Peninsular campaign
Bebop (jazz style), **Supp. 5**, 534
Bechet, Sidney, reference to, **Supp. 3**, 188
Bechtel Corporation, founding of, **Supp. 8**, 308–9
Beck, Dave, references to, **Supp. 7**, 119; **Supp. 9**, 395; **Supp. 10**, 482
Beck, Marshall, reference to, **Supp. 6**, 67
Becker, Carl L., reference to, **Supp. 4**, 63
Becker, Charles, reference to, **Supp. 4**, 885–86
Becker, G. F., reference to, **Vol. 5, Part 1**, 457
Becker, Marion Rombauer, references to, **Supp. 7**, 656, 657
Beckham, John C., reference to, **Supp. 6**, 591
Becky Sharp (movie), **Supp. 7**, 407
Becton, Dickinson and Co., **Supp. 7**, 678
Bedford, N. Y., public service, **Vol. 7, Part 2**, 410
Bedloe's Island, purchase of, **Vol. 1, Part 1**, 597
Bed springs, manufacture of, **Vol. 6, Part 1**, 334
Beebe, William, reference to, **Supp. 3**, 835
Beech, importation of purple tree, **Vol. 5, Part 2**, 341
Beech, Walter, reference to, **Supp. 9**, 757
Beecham, Sir Thomas, reference to, **Supp. 6**, 324
Beecher, Catharine, reference to, **Vol. 7, Part 1**, 252
Beecher, Charles Emerson, reference to, **Supp. 3**, 695
Beecher, Henry Ward, references to, **Vol. 1, Part 1**, 336, 641; **Vol. 1, Part 2**, 505; **Vol. 7, Part 1**, 36; **Vol. 8, Part 1**, 60 f.; **Vol. 8, Part 2**, 290, 398; **Vol. 9, Part 1**, 52, 588; **Vol. 9, Part 2**, 551 f., 622
Beecher, Lyman: reference to, **Vol. 1, Part 2**, 129; writings on, **Supp. 3**, 672
Beecher Bible and Rifle Colony (Kans.), **Vol. 8, Part 2**, 150
Beef, shipping methods revolutionized, **Vol. 1, Part 1**, 111; **Vol. 3, Part 1**, 603
Beef Steak Club, **Vol. 5, Part 2**, 456
Beef Trust case, **Vol. 7, Part 1**, 108
Beer: legalization, **Supp. 3**, 649; pasteurization of, **Supp. 1**, 142
Beers, Clifford, reference to, **Supp. 4**, 571
Beery, Wallace, reference to, **Supp. 9**, 535
Bees, **Vol. 3, Part 1**, 17, 343; **Vol. 5, Part 2**, 598; **Vol. 8, Part 2**, 144; **Supp. 4**, 167
Beeson, Mabel Banta, reference to, **Supp. 4**, 67–68
Beethoven, Ludwig van: biographer of, **Vol. 9, Part 2**, 401; piano interpretation of, **Supp. 5**, 607
Beethoven Association, founding of, **Supp. 5**, 45–46
Beethoven Society, **Vol. 5, Part 2**, 486
Beet sugar industry, **Vol. 2, Part 2**, 66; **Vol. 5, Part 2**, 277; **Supp. 1**, 431
Beginnings of Christianity, The, **Supp. 4**, 468
Begich, Nick, reference to, **Supp. 9**, 104–5
Begin, Menachem, reference to, **Supp. 10**, 135
Behavior and behaviorism: animal studies, **Supp. 2**, 699; conditioned reflex, application to education, **Supp. 3**, 119; conditioned-reflex studies, **Supp. 5**, 329–30; criminology theory, **Supp. 4**, 809; goal-directed, **Supp. 6**, 640; habit inventory for kindergartens, **Supp. 4**, 374; lower organisms, **Supp. 4**, 425; modification studies, **Supp. 6**, 17, 262, 528; neurological research, **Supp. 2**, 664; physiology of, **Supp. 3**, 172; **Supp. 6**, 367–68; political science studies, **Supp. 5**, 485–86; **Supp. 7**, 430, 431; stimulus and response studies, **Supp. 4**, 832–33; **Supp. 6**, 262, 672; synthesis with Freudian theory, **Supp. 4**, 387; writings on, **Supp. 8**, 489
Behemoth, **Supp. 5**, 514
Behn Brothers, **Supp. 6**, 43
Behrens, Peter, references to, **Supp. 8**, 226, 435
Behrman, S. N., reference to, **Supp. 8**, 529
Beiderbecke, Leon ("Bix"), references to, **Supp. 8**, 20; **Supp. 10**, 299
Beirne, Michael J., reference to, **Supp. 3**, 181
Bekker, Paul, reference to, **Supp. 6**, 351
Belasco, David, references to, **Vol. 6, Part 1**, 379; **Supp. 3**, 39, 40, 297; **Supp. 5**, 726–27; **Supp. 6**, 305, 306, 369
Belcher, Marjorie Celeste ("Marge"). *See* Champion, Marge
Belding, Don, reference to, **Supp. 10**, 145
Bel Geddes, Norman, & Co., **Supp. 6**, 233
Belgium: Confederate relations with, **Vol. 6, Part 2**, 240; diplomacy with, **Vol. 1, Part 2**, 464; **Vol. 6, Part 1**, 145; **Vol. 8, Part 2**, 349; **Vol. 9, Part 2**, 93, 377, 635; **Supp. 7**, 438; World War II, **Supp. 9**, 519
Belknap, Jeremy, reference to, **Vol. 9, Part 2**, 391
Bell, Alexander Graham, references to, **Vol. 5, Part 1**, 325; **Vol. 8, Part 2**, 534; **Vol. 10, Part 1**, 548 f.; **Supp. 8**, 228, 316
Bell, Don J., reference to, **Supp. 5**, 321
Bell, John, reference to, **Vol. 9, Part 2**, 363
Bell, Theodore, reference to, **Supp. 3**, 394
Bell Aircraft Corporation, **Supp. 6**, 50
Bellanca, August, reference to, **Supp. 4**, 69; **Supp. 6**, 51
Bell and Howell Co., founding of, **Supp. 5**, 321–22
Bellefonte, Pa., founding of, **Vol. 1, Part 2**, 190
Belleville, N. Y., sociological study of, **Supp. 4**, 312
Bellevue Hospital (New York City): **Vol. 5, Part 1**, 240; **Vol. 10, Part 1**, 150; **Vol. 10, Part 2**, 463; anesthesia program, **Supp. 6**, 553, 554; first nurses' training school in America, **Vol. 8, Part 2**, 474; forensic pathology, **Supp. 10**, 328–29; Medical College, **Vol. 8, Part 2**, 403 f.; psychiatric facilities, **Supp. 3**, 320; tuberculosis clinic, **Supp. 4**, 578; X-ray department, **Supp. 3**, 360
Bell for Adano, A, **Supp. 9**, 189, 375
Bell Jar, The, **Supp. 9**, 628

Bellringer, Clarence, reference to, **Supp. 4**, 808
Bell-making, **Vol. 6, Part 2**, 533
Bellows, George: reference to, **Supp. 5**, 636; sculpture, **Supp. 3**, 124
Bellows, Henry W., reference to, **Vol. 1, Part 2**, 20
Bell System. *See* American Telephone & Telegraph Co.
Bell Telephone Co., **Vol. 1, Part 2**, 151; **Vol. 9, Part 1**, 253; patent litigations, **Vol. 9, Part 2**, 99
Bell Telephone Laboratories: **Supp. 6**, 84, 152; electron diffraction research, **Supp. 9**, 304; founding of, **Supp. 4**, 430; management, **Supp. 9**, 676. *See also* American Telephone & Telegraph Co.
Belluschi, Pietro, reference to, **Supp. 7**, 800
Belmont, Mo., engagement at, **Vol. 4, Part 1**, 493; **Vol. 6, Part 1**, 587; **Vol. 7, Part 2**, 604; **Vol. 8, Part 1**, 40; **Vol. 9, Part 2**, 3
Belmont, Mrs. O. H. P., references to, **Supp. 7**, 717, 718
Beloit College, founding of, **Vol. 2, Part 2**, 12
Beltrami, Eugenio, reference to, **Supp. 7**, 216
Bemis Heights, N. Y., battle of, **Vol. 1, Part 1**, 365; **Vol. 4, Part 1**, 185; **Vol. 7, Part 1**, 166
Ben Ami, Jacob, reference to, **Supp. 6**, 566
Benbrook Reservoir (Tex.), **Supp. 6**, 540
Benchley, Robert, references to, **Supp. 7**, 413; **Supp. 8**, 491, 492
Bendix Corporation, founding of, **Supp. 3**, 55–56
Benedict, Ruth, references to, **Supp. 8**, 378; **Supp. 9**, 276
Benedictine Order, **Vol. 4, Part 2**, 88; **Vol. 6, Part 1**, 162; **Vol. 7, Part 1**, 149; **Vol. 8, Part 2**, 59; **Vol. 10, Part 2**, 370
Benedum, Michael L., reference to, **Supp. 7**, 804
Bene Israel congregation (Cincinnati), **Supp. 4**, 659
Beneke, Tex, reference to, **Supp. 3**, 525
Benét, Stephen Vincent, references to, **Supp. 9**, 276
Bent, Laura, reference to, **Supp. 3**, 56
Bent, Stephen Vincent, reference to, **Supp. 4**, 73
Bent, William Rose, references to, **Supp. 3**, 56; **Supp. 5**, 439; **Supp. 7**, 103
Ben-Gurion, David, reference to, **Supp. 7**, 689
Ben Hur: influence of book, **Vol. 9, Part 1**, 69; movie, **Supp. 6**, 440–41
Benjamin, Asher, reference to, **Vol. 9, Part 2**, 610
Benjamin, Walter, reference to, **Supp. 9**, 41
Benjamin, ship out of Salem, **Vol. 9, Part 1**, 165
Bennett, Arnold, reference to, **Supp. 6**, 171
Bennett, Floyd, references to, **Supp. 6**, 92, 93; **Supp. 9**, 63
Bennett, Glenda Heller, reference to, **Supp. 3**, 59
Bennett, Harry H., Ford relationship, **Supp. 3**, 284; **Supp. 4**, 302–3; **Supp. 8**, 610
Bennett, James Gordon, references to, **Vol. 5, Part 1**, 106, 354; **Vol. 8, Part 1**, 474 f.; **Vol. 8, Part 2**, 513; **Vol. 9, Part 1**, 510; **Vol. 9, Part 2**, 334; **Supp. 5**, 78
Bennett, Joan, references to, **Supp. 3**, 59; **Supp. 8**, 678
Bennett, Richard, reference to, **Supp. 7**, 50
Bennett, Wallace, reference to, **Supp. 7**, 562
Bennett Law, **Vol. 5, Part 2**, 262, 506; **Vol. 7, Part 2**, 377
Bennington, Vt., **Vol. 7, Part 2**, 209; **Vol. 8, Part 2**, 49; Battle of, **Vol. 6, Part 1**, 260; **Vol. 9, Part 1**, 531; **Vol. 10, Part 1**, 468
Bennington College: dance studies, **Supp. 6**, 312, 313; founding of, **Supp. 5**, 427, 435; poetry studies, **Supp. 7**, 654
Bennington Historical Museum, founding of, **Supp. 8**, 611–12
Benny, Jack, references to, **Supp. 6**, 13; **Supp. 7**, 282; **Supp. 10**, 178; "Rochester" character developed, **Supp. 10**, 7,8
Benny Goodman Quartet, **Supp. 9**, 475
Bensley, Robert Russell, references to, **Supp. 6**, 295, 296
Bentley, Elizabeth, references to, **Supp. 5**, 564; **Supp. 7**, 114, 291
Benton, Rube, reference to, **Supp. 8**, 713
Benton, Thomas Hart (1782–1858), references to, **Vol. 5, Part 1**, 243, 538; **Vol. 5, Part 2**, 382; **Vol. 8, Part 2**, 503; **Supp. 9**, 78
Benton, Thomas Hart (1889–1975), **Supp. 9**, 78; references to, **Supp. 3**, 841; **Supp. 6**, 511–12; **Supp. 10**, 244
Benton, William B.: opposition to McCarthyism, **Supp. 9**, 311–12; reference to, **Supp. 10**, 652
Bentonville, N. C., battle of, **Vol. 5, Part 1**, 27, 126; **Vol. 9, Part 2**, 284
Bent's Fort (Nebr.), **Vol. 1, Part 2**, 205; **Vol. 2, Part 1**, 531; **Vol. 3, Part 1**, 365; **Vol. 3, Part 2**, 442; **Vol. 4, Part 1**, 21; **Vol. 10, Part 1**, 356
Berber language, studies in, **Supp. 1**, 412
Berea, Ohio, early history, **Vol. 1, Part 1**, 535
Berea College, founding of, **Vol. 3, Part 2**, 311; **Vol. 8, Part 2**, 103 f.
Berenson, Bernard, references to, **Supp. 4**, 345, 755
Berenson, Mary Smith Costelloe, references to, **Supp. 6**, 57
Bergen, Candice, reference to, **Supp. 10**, 33
Berger, Meyer, reference to, **Supp. 7**, 473
Berger, Victor, references to, **Supp. 3**, 10, 298, 438; **Supp. 7**, 348
Bergman, Ingrid, reference to, **Supp. 7**, 682
Beriberi, studies on, **Supp. 5**, 710; **Supp. 8**, 197–98. *See also* Medicine
Bering Sea arbitration, **Vol. 1, Part 2**, 71; **Vol. 4, Part 2**, 271; **Vol. 7, Part 1**, 181; **Vol. 8, Part 1**, 285 f.; **Vol. 9, Part 2**, 623
Berkeley, Busby, references to, **Supp. 10**, 53, 813
Berkeley Divinity School, **Vol. 4, Part 2**, 360
Berkeley Women's City Club, **Supp. 6**, 463, 464
Berkman, Alexander, reference to, **Supp. 3**, 329
Berkshire Chamber Music Festival, founding of, **Supp. 5**, 128
Berkshire Music Center (Mass.), **Supp. 7**, 652; **Supp. 8**, 451; **Supp. 10**, 423
Berkshire Music Festival. *See* Tanglewood Music Festival
Berkshire Playhouse (Mass.), founding of, **Supp. 1**, 177
Berkshire Symphonic Festival, founding of, **Supp. 2**, 267. *See also* Tanglewood Music Festlval
Berlin, Germany: airlift, **Supp. 6**, 431; **Supp. 10**, 128; Berlin Wall crisis, **Supp. 10**, 128; Olympic Games (1936), **Supp. 10**, 610–11; Russian émigré community, **Supp. 10**, 581; school system, **Supp. 10**, 145; U.S. occupation of, **Supp. 10**, 127–28; World War II action, **Supp. 8**, 155
Berlin, Irving, references to, **Supp. 4**, 374; **Supp. 6**, 9; **Supp. 9**, 281; **Supp. 10**, 818
Berlin Academy, founding of, **Vol. 7, Part 1**, 561
Berliner's Improved Gramophone Co., **Supp. 3**, 392
Berlin Philharmonic, **Supp. 6**, 456
Berman, Harry, reference to, **Supp. 6**, 212
Bermuda Hundred, Va., operations at, **Vol. 1, Part 2**, 112; **Vol. 2, Part 1**, 358; **Vol. 4, Part 1**, 295; **Vol. 7, Part 2**, 570
Bermudiana, collections of, **Supp. 2**, 111
Bernard, Claude, reference to, **Supp. 3**, 136, 137
Bernardes, Arthur, reference to, **Supp. 5**, 215
Bernadotte, Count Folke, assasination of, **Supp. 9**, 137–38
Bernard Geis Associates, Susann novels, marketing of, **Supp. 9**, 785
Bernstein, Aline, reference to, **Supp. 2**, 731

Bernstein, Henry, references to, **Supp. 10**, 62, 63
Bernstein, Leonard: Koussevitzky relationship, **Supp. 10**, 423; references to, **Supp. 6**, 457; **Supp. 7**, 354; **Supp. 9**, 800–801; **Supp. 10**, 722
Berra, Yogi, reference to, **Supp. 9**, 764
Berry, George P., reference to, **Supp. 7**, 648
Berryman, Jim, reference to, **Supp. 4**, 76
Berryman, John, reference to, **Supp. 9**, 15
Bertoia, Harry, reference to, **Supp. 4**, 715
Bertrand, Clay (Clay L. Shaw alleged alias), **Supp. 9**, 715
Beryllium, **Supp. 7**, 10
Besant, Annie, reference to, **Supp. 4**, 105, 106
Bessemer, Sir Henry, reference to, **Vol. 7, Part 2**, 206
Bessemer process, steel, **Vol. 3, Part 1**, 549 f.; **Vol. 4, Part 1**, 39; **Vol. 4, Part 2**, 8; **Vol. 5, Part 1**, 148, 392; **Vol. 5, Part 2**, 209, 311
Besser, Joe, reference to, **Supp. 9**, 282
Bessey, Charles E., reference to, **Supp. 3**, 23
Best, Marshall A., reference to, **Supp. 7**, 374
Best, Pete, reference to, **Supp. 10**, 449
Best Years of Our Lives, The (movie), **Supp. 5**, 624; **Supp. 9**, 324; **Supp. 10**, 400
Bethany, Ga., founding of, **Vol. 3, Part 1**, 182
Bethany College, **Vol. 2, Part 1**, 448; **Vol. 7, Part 2**, 423; **Vol. 8, Part 1**, 573; **Vol. 9, Part 2**, 243 f.
Bethel movement, **Vol. 4, Part 2**, 154
Bethel Regiment, **Vol. 5, Part 2**, 578
Bethesda Church, Va., **Vol. 4, Part 1**, 497; **Vol. 6, Part 1**, 127. *See also* Cold Harbor, Va.
Beth Israel Hospital (New York City), X-ray department, **Supp. 3**, 360
Bethlehem, Pa., **Vol. 7, Part 2**, 498 f.; **Vol. 10, Part 2**, 24
Bethlehem Choir, founding of, **Vol. 10, Part 2**, 453
Bethlehem Steel Corporation: **Vol. 5, Part 2**, 312; **Vol. 9, Part 2**, 324; **Supp. 3**, 77; **Supp. 6**, 243–44; **Supp. 9**, 402–3; discriminatory labor practices, **Supp. 10**, 150; founding of, **Supp. 2**, 600; management, **Supp. 10**, 149–50; price rigging, accused of, **Supp. 10**, 150
Beth Shemesh, excavation of, **Supp. 3**, 272
Bethune, Mary McLeod, reference to, **Supp. 7**, 787
Bethune-Cookman College, presidency, **Supp. 5**, 56
Better Government Association (Chicago, Ill.), investigations, **Supp. 10**, 49
Better Homes and Gardens, founding of, **Supp. 7**, 527, 528
Betting, legislation against, **Vol. 3, Part 1**, 552 f.
Beulah, ship controversy, **Vol. 7, Part 1**, 360, 367
Beverages, soft drinks, **Supp. 2**, 306; **Supp. 10**, 338, 339
Beverley, Mass., public service, **Vol. 8, Part 1**, 381
Beverly, W. Va., engagement at, **Vol. 1, Part 1**, 442
Beverly Ford, Va., engagement at, **Vol. 5, Part 2**, 375
Bevier, Isabel, reference to, **Supp. 3**, 217
Beyond the Horizon, **Supp. 4**, 355
Bianchi, John, reference to, **Supp. 3**, 784
Bianchi, Luigi, reference to, **Supp. 7**, 216
Bibelot, publishing of, **Vol. 7, Part 1**, 278
Bible: Aitken, the, **Vol. 1, Part 1**, 132; American and Foreign Bible Society, **Vol. 2, Part 2**, 342; American Bible League, **Vol. 4, Part 1**, 602; American Bible Society, **Vol. 1, Part 1**, 512; **Vol. 1, Part 2**, 136, 568; **Vol. 2, Part 2**, 299, 342; **Vol. 3, Part 2**, 215; **Vol. 4, Part 1**, 619; **Vol. 5, Part 2**, 12; **Vol. 7, Part 1**, 2, 16, 245 f., 411; **Vol. 7, Part 2**, 591; **Vol. 8, Part 1**, 542; **Vol. 8, Part 2**, 261; **Vol. 9, Part 1**, 204, 300; **Vol. 9, Part 2**, 11, 303; archaeological studies related to, **Supp. 9**, 319–20; Catholic revision, **Supp. 7**, 533; collecting of, **Vol. 6, Part 1**, 172, 305; **Vol. 8, Part 1**, 298; Collins' Quarto, **Vol. 6, Part 1**, 165; compulsory use of in schools, **Vol. 3, Part 1**, 541 f.; **Vol. 6, Part 1**, 241; critical analysis, **Supp. 2**, 597; distribution of, **Vol. 3, Part 2**, 52; **Vol. 4, Part 2**, 46; English translation of Hebrew, **Supp. 4**, 659; figures in sculpture, **Vol. 7, Part 1**, 304; first printing of, in English in U.S., **Vol. 5, Part 2**, 458; **Vol. 9, Part 2**, 435; Gilbertese translation of, **Vol. 1, Part 2**, 277; Gutenberg, **Supp. 5**, 554, 587; Hebrew scholarship, **Supp. 1**, 408; "higher-criticism" scholarship, **Supp. 1**, 38; illustrations for, **Vol. 8, Part 2**, 372; **Vol. 9, Part 2**, 346; Jefferson, **Supp. 2**, 5; liberal scholarship popularization, **Supp. 3**, 825; literal acceptance of, **Supp. 4**, 691; Marathi, the, **Vol. 1, Part 1**, 187; model critical edition of *Acts*, **Vol. 8, Part 2**, 151; Polychrome, **Vol. 4, Part 2**, 401; publishing of, **Vol. 6, Part 1**, 287; Revised Standard Version, **Supp. 3**, 529–30; **Supp. 5**, 649; revision of, **Vol. 2, Part 2**, 38, 337; **Vol. 3, Part 1**, 577 f.; **Vol. 6, Part 2**, 471; scholarship, **Vol. 1, Part 1**, 558; **Vol. 2, Part 1**, 110, 115; **Vol. 2, Part 2**, 370; **Vol. 3, Part 1**, 573 f., 577 f.; **Vol. 3, Part 2**, 57; **Vol. 4, Part 1**, 211, 247, 560 f., 601 f.; **Vol. 4, Part 2**, 72, 132; **Vol. 5, Part 2**, 54, 343, 501; **Vol. 6, Part 1**, 303, 405; **Vol. 7, Part 1**, 43, 48, 124 f., 147, 292, 475; **Vol. 8, Part 1**, 322 f., 451, 568 f., 588, 593; **Vol. 8, Part 2**, 110, 151, 333, 394; **Vol. 9, Part 1**, 278 f., 305, 628; **Vol. 9, Part 2**, 148, 622; **Vol. 10, Part 1**, 71, 105; **Supp. 3**, 37, 529–30; **Supp. 4**, 467–68, 595–96; **Supp. 6**, 641; **Supp. 7**, 313; uniform lesson system for Sunday schools, **Vol. 10, Part 1**, 9; university curriculum studies, **Supp. 4**, 468; "White Man's Book of God," **Vol. 4, Part 1**, 173
Bible Looking Glass, **Vol. 1, Part 1**, 589
Bible translations: **Vol. 1, Part 1**, 265 f., 296; **Vol. 1, Part 2**, 277, 388; **Vol. 4, Part 1**, 564; **Vol. 6, Part 1**, 356, 594; **Vol. 7, Part 1**, 82 f., 342, 391, 588; **Vol. 8, Part 1**, 602 f.; **Vol. 9, Part 2**, 482; **Vol. 10, Part 1**, 108; **Supp. 7**, 710; Arabic, **Vol. 9, Part 1**, 258; Armeno-Turkish, **Vol. 4, Part 1**, 384; Chinese, **Vol. 4, Part 1**, 399; **Vol. 7, Part 2**, 214; **Vol. 8, Part 2**, 428 f.; **Vol. 9, Part 1**, 58; German, **Vol. 9, Part 1**, 416; Hawaiian, **Vol. 1, Part 1**, 296; **Vol. 8, Part 1**, 561; Hebrew, **Vol. 5, Part 2**, 2; Indian, **Vol. 1, Part 2**, 478; **Vol. 3, Part 2**, 80; **Vol. 4, Part 1**, 8; **Vol. 5, Part 2**, 110; **Vol. 8, Part 1**, 61, 605; Korean, **Vol. 5, Part 2**, 172; **Vol. 10, Part 1**, 113; Norwegian, **Vol. 5, Part 2**, 78; Siamese, **Vol. 5, Part 2**, 190
Bibliographers. For complete list, *see* Occupations Index
Bibliographical Society of America, founding of, **Supp. 2**, 112
Bibliographies: **Vol. 3, Part 1**, 551 f.; **Vol. 3, Part 2**, 365, 467; **Vol. 4, Part 1**, 617; **Vol. 4, Part 2**, 13, 437; **Vol. 5, Part 2**, 65 f.; **Vol. 7, Part 1**, 413 f., 490; **Vol. 7, Part 2**, 603; **Vol. 8, Part 1**, 122 f.; **Vol. 8, Part 2**, 275, 360; **Vol. 9, Part 1**, 464, 611; **Vol. 9, Part 2**, 109, 388; **Vol. 10, Part 1**, 603 f.; American Indians, **Supp. 2**, 163; American literature and history, **Supp. 8**, 663–64; Americana, **Supp. 2**, 111, 162; books and periodicals, **Supp. 5**, 752–53; Division of, in Library of Congress, **Vol. 4, Part 1**, 617; early voyages to America, **Supp. 5**, 755–56; English literature, **Supp. 7**, 387; entomology, **Vol. 4, Part 2**, 82; federal and state documents, **Supp. 1**, 101; geological, **Supp. 4**, 218; historical, **Supp. 1**, 375; mathematics, **Vol. 9, Part 2**, 109; medicine, **Vol. 6, Part 2**, 561; microfilm and microfiche, **Supp. 8**, 120; printing examples, **Supp. 1**, 290; **Supp. 3**, 492–93
Bibliography of Fishes, **Vol. 3, Part 1**, 170
Bibliography of the History of Agriculture in the United States, **Supp. 5**, 201
Biblioteca Benjamin Franklin (Mexico City), **Supp. 6**, 399
Biblioteca Feminina, **Supp. 6**, 576

Bibliotheca Americana, **Vol. 8, Part 2**, 275,; **Supp. 8**, 664
Bicycles: coaster brake, invention of, **Vol. 8, Part 2**, 56; manufacture of, **Vol. 1, Part 1**, 248; **Vol. 8, Part 1**, 74 f.; **Vol. 10, Part 2**, 418; promotion of riding, **Vol. 8, Part 1**, 74 f.
Biddle, Francis, references to, **Supp. 6**, 28; **Supp. 10**, 229
Biddle, Jayne, **Supp. 8**, 34
Biddle, Nicholas, reference to, **Vol. 8, Part 2**, 588 f.
Biddle, Paul, **Supp. 8**, 34
Bierce, Ambrose: influence of, **Vol. 9, Part 1**, 586; references to, **Supp. 5**, 283, 285; **Supp. 10**, 502
Bifocal lenses, **Vol. 4, Part 1**, 451
Big bands. *See* Dance bands; Swing bands
Big Bethel, Va., **Vol. 2, Part 1**, 338; **Vol. 5, Part 1**, 27; **Vol. 6, Part 2**, 205.
Big Brother and the Holding Company (rock group), **Supp. 8**, 305–6
Big Brothers of America, founding of, **Supp. 5**, 138
Big Creek transmission system, **Supp. 3**, 746
Bigelow, Henry Jacob, reference to, **Vol. 7, Part 1**, 269
Bigelow, John, biography of, **Supp. 9**, 174
Bigelow-Sanford (carpet manufacturer), **Supp. 10**, 826–27
Biggs, Edward Power, reference to, **Supp. 10**, 254
Biggs, Herman M., reference to, **Supp. 6**, 701
Bighorn Expedition (1876), **Vol. 3, Part 1**, 8; **Vol. 4, Part 1**, 237; **Vol. 6, Part 2**, 614; **Vol. 9, Part 2**, 379
Big Laudy region, W. Va., operations in, **Vol. 3, Part 2**, 483
Biglow Papers, **Vol. 6, Part 1**, 460
"Big stick," origin of phrase, **Vol. 8, Part 2**, 139
Bilbo, Theodore, references to, **Supp. 6**, 710; **Supp. 9**, 160
Bilby, Kenneth, reference to, **Supp. 9**, 702
Bilingual education, **Supp. 7**, 43
Billiard balls, manufacture of, **Vol. 5, Part 1**, 448
Billiards, world champion, **Supp. 6**, 303–4
Billings, Warren K., reference to, **Supp. 3**, 532–33; **Supp. 7**, 248
Billings, Mont., public service, **Vol. 1, Part 2**, 266
Billroth, Theodor, reference to, **Supp. 6**, 664
Bimetallism, **Vol. 4, Part 2**, 14; **Vol. 5, Part 1**, 238; **Vol. 8, Part 2**, 189, 220; **Vol. 10, Part 1**, 459 f.
BINAC (computer), **Supp. 10**, 520
Binet, Alfred, references to, **Supp. 6**, 240–41, 626
Binet-Simon intelligence test, **Supp. 4**, 439
Bing, Rudolph, references to, **Supp. 9**, 805, 816
Binga State Bank (Chicago), **Supp. 4**, 83
Bing Crosby Pro-Amateur Golf Tournament (Pebble Beach, Calif.), **Supp. 10**, 161
Bingham, Alfred M., reference to, **Supp. 9**, 29
Bingham, Robert W., reference to, **Supp. 9**, 471
Binghamton, N. Y., founding of, **Vol. 1, Part 2**, 278
Biochemistry: **Vol. 8, Part 2**, 483; agricultural, **Supp. 3**, 315; **Supp. 4**, 114; carbonic acid buffer system, **Supp. 3**, 350; cholesterol research, **Supp. 3**, 693; colloidal systems, **Supp. 3**, 315; education and research facilities, **Supp. 4**, 720; enzyme studies, **Supp. 5**, 149, 669; **Supp. 6**, 126–27, 595–96; **Supp. 10**, 427; eyes studies, **Supp. 3**, 302; hormone studies, **Supp. 10**, 198; immunological studies, **Supp. 4**, 380–81; laboratory equipment, **Supp. 4**, 460; medical research use of, **Supp. 3**, 243; muscle contraction studies, **Supp. 5**, 489; nutrition studies, **Supp. 5**, 275–76, 622–23; **Supp. 7**, 223, 568–69; physiological, **Supp. 3**, 163–64; plant hormone studies, **Supp. 10**, 297; protein research, **Supp. 2**, 379; **Supp. 3**, 60–61; **Supp. 10**, 427; **Supp. 5**, 122–23, 149; sex hormones, **Supp. 4**, 460; sex hormone synthesis, **Supp. 9**, 444; sulfur compounds, research on, **Supp. 10**, 197–98; synthesis studies, **Supp. 10**, 852–53; teaching of, **Supp. 3**, 315, 350; urine analysis, **Supp. 2**, 35–36; vitamin research, **Supp. 8**, 197–98. *See also* Biology
Biographers. For complete list, *see* Occupations Index
Biograph Studios: **Supp. 4**, 349–50; **Supp. 6**, 573; **Supp. 8**, 214; productions, **Supp. 10**, 634
Biography: **Supp. 2**, 475, 509, 266; **Supp. 8**, 181; business figures, **Supp. 9**, 582; City Beautiful movement, **Supp. 3**, 534; historical, **Supp. 4**, 489–90, 556, 848; **Supp. 5**, 364; **Supp. 9**, 112–13, 582, 583, 629; **Supp. 10**, 846, 847; juvenile, **Supp. 3**, 630; literary, **Supp. 4**, 13, 14; **Supp. 10**, 395; of women, **Supp. 7**, 13; popular, **Supp. 4**, 368; psychobiography, **Supp. 1**, 106; **Supp. 7**, 80; **Supp. 8**, 61; theatrical, **Supp. 8**, 54. *See also* Autobiographical writings
Biography (play), **Supp. 9**, 70
Biological Abstracts, **Supp. 4**, 516
Biological and chemical warfare: development of, **Supp. 6**, 448; gas mask design, **Supp. 3**, 353; napalm, **Supp. 7**, 617; poison gas studies, **Supp. 5**, 710; U.S. research in, **Supp. 10**, 698; World War I studies, **Supp. 4**, 838; World War II studies, **Supp. 4**, 6
Biological Experiment Station (Woods Hole, Mass.). *See* Marine Biological Laboratory
Biology: animal form, **Supp. 6**, 281; cell lineage, **Supp. 2**, 723; engineering, **Supp. 8**, 502–3; experimental, **Supp. 3**, 540; **Supp. 4**, 425–27; first use of laboratory methods in high-school teaching of, **Vol. 7, Part 2**, 384; historical writings on, **Supp. 4**, 910; marine, **Vol. 6, Part 2**, 468; **Vol. 8, Part 1**, 387; molecular, **Supp. 8**, 450; **Supp. 9**, 550; philosophy of, **Supp. 4**, 427; protozoa immortality study, **Supp. 4**, 910; psychological problems arising from, **Supp. 3**, 172; reproductive cycle, **Supp. 2**, 632; research, **Supp. 4**, 515–16; statistical methodology, **Supp. 2**, 521; **Supp. 3**, 214–15; **Supp. 3**, 477; teaching of, **Supp. 4**, 253; tissue culture experiments, **Supp. 6**, 282. *See also* Biochemistry; Botany; Natural history; Zoology. For complete list of biologists, *see* Occupations Index
Biometry, **Vol. 4, Part 2**, 312. *See also* Biostatistics
Biophysics, development of, **Supp. 6**, 69–70; photoreception studies, **Supp. 4**, 367
Biostatistics, **Supp. 2**, 251; **Supp. 3**, 214–15, 477
Bird, William, reference to, **Supp. 7**, 335
"Bird in a Gilded Cage, A" (song), **Supp. 4**, 835
Bird-Lore, **Supp. 7**, 8
Birds: Alaskan studies, **Supp. 1**, 572; Antarctica, **Supp. 7**, 217; Audubon movement, **Supp. 3**, 592–93; children's books on, **Vol. 6, Part 2**, 625; collections, **Vol. 1, Part 1**, 513; **Vol. 3, Part 2**, 91; **Vol. 4, Part 2**, 564; **Vol. 9, Part 1**, 385; colored engravings, **Vol. 6, Part 1**, 56; clubs, **Vol. 3, Part 2**, 511; counts, **Supp. 5**, 374; distribution survey, **Supp. 3**, 517; **Supp. 8**, 655; drawings of, **Vol. 1, Part 1**, 427; eyes, studies of, **Supp. 3**, 835; field identification, **Supp. 6**, 255–56; identification and classification of, **Vol. 8, Part 1**, 598; **Supp. 7**, 578; illustrations of, **Supp. 4**, 736; 737; Maine, writings on, **Supp. 4**, 248–49; museum displays, **Supp. 3**, 161; song recordings, **Supp. 7**, 8; studies of, **Vol. 6, Part 1**, 49; **Vol. 7, Part 1**, 406; **Vol. 9, Part 2**, 617–18; Texas and Louisiana, **Supp. 7**, 578–79; western, writings on, **Supp. 4**, 41; writings on, **Vol. 1, Part 1**, 426; **Vol. 3, Part 2**, 511; **Vol. 4, Part 1**, 367; **Vol. 8, Part 2**, 324; **Vol. 9, Part 1**, 32; **Vol. 9, Part 2**, 595; **Supp. 3**, 162. *See also* Ornithology
Birdseye, Clarence, reference to, **Supp. 10**, 555
Birds of the Belgian Congo, **Supp. 7**, 117
Birmingham, Ala.: civil rights demonstrations, **Supp. 8**, 334; **Supp. 9**, 186; development of, **Vol. 3, Part 1**, 179; **Vol. 5, Part 1**, 57; **Vol. 8, Part 1**, 170; **Vol. 9, Part 1**, 125, 219

Birney, J. G., reference to, **Vol. 2, Part 2**, 28
Biro, László, reference to, **Supp. 10**, 670
Birth control. *See* Family planning
Birth control pills. *See* Oral contraceptives
Birth Control Review, founding of, **Supp. 8**, 568
Birth defects: nutrition linked, **Supp. 7**, 569; pathology of, **Supp. 4**, 801, 802; research, **Supp. 9**, 39–40; Rh-negative blood type, **Supp. 3**, 441
Birth of a Nation, The: **Supp. 3**, 73, 535, 708; **Supp. 4**, 235, 350, 351; **Supp. 6**, 657; **Supp. 9**, 205; production of, **Supp. 2**, 693
Birthrate, **Supp. 4**, 45
Births, first English, in America, **Vol. 3, Part 1**, 73 f.; first registration of, **Vol. 9, Part 1**, 33
BIS. *See* Bank for International Settlements
Bishop, Bernice P., Museum, **Supp. 1**, 82
Bishop, Isabel, reference to, **Supp. 5**, 493
Bishop, James W., reference to, **Supp. 4**, 292
Bishop, John Peale, references to, **Supp. 9**, 874, 876
Bishop, William Sutton, reference to, **Supp. 3**, 170
Bixby, Mrs., Lincoln's letter to, **Vol. 6, Part 1**, 256
Blaauw, Gerrit, reference to, **Supp. 9**, 844
Black, Harry S., reference to, **Supp. 6**, 593
Black, Hugo L.: Ku Klux Klan membership, **Supp. 9**, 95; references to, **Supp. 3**, 80; **Supp. 5**, 294, 358, 574, 575, 576, 713; **Supp. 7**, 541; **Supp. 9**, 657, 835; **Supp. 10**, 188
Black, Newton Henry, reference to, **Supp. 5**, 154
"Black and Blue," first black racial protest song, **Supp. 9**, 644
Black and Decker Manufacturing Co., **Supp. 10**, 491, 492
Blackberries, raising of, **Vol. 6, Part 1**, 363
"Black-birding," in South Seas, **Vol. 4, Part 2**, 451
Blackboards in school, first use of, **Vol. 4, Part 2**, 142
Black Boy, **Supp. 6**, 716
Blackburn, Jack, reference to, **Supp. 9**, 493
Black Cat, The, **Supp. 9**, 819–20
Black Cat Minstrels, **Supp. 6**, 89
"Black Cockade" forces in Pennsylvania, **Vol. 6, Part l**, 154
Black Code. *See* Blacks
Black Crook, production of, **Vol. 7, Part 1**, 482
Blackfan, Kenneth D., references to, **Supp. 3**, 244; **Supp. 4**, 213
Blackfoot Indians, **Supp. 2**, 265; **Supp. 4**, 907
"Black Friday" (1869), **Vol. 1, Part 1**, 489; **Vol. 3, Part 2**, 415; **Vol. 4, Part 1**, 454, 499; **Vol. 9, Part 2**, 304; **Vol. 10, Part 1**, 81
"Black Hawk": locomotive, **Vol. 7, Part 1**, 556; references to, **Vol. 1, Part 2**, 314; **Vol. 5, Part 2**, 350
Black Hawk War: Lincoln's service in, **Vol. 6, Part 1**, 244; service in: **Vol. 1, Part 1**, 410; **Vol. 1, Part 2**, 314; **Vol. 2, Part 2**, 389; **Vol. 3, Part 1**, 123, 349, 510, 520; **Vol. 3, Part 2**, 497; **Vol. 4, Part 1**, 93; **Vol. 5, Part 2**, 135, 172, 350, 583, 600; **Vol. 6, Part 1**, 114, 587; **Vol. 6, Part 2**, 373; **Vol. 8, Part 1**, 609; **Vol. 8, Part 2**, 251, 507; **Vol. 9, Part 2**, 350, 437
Black Kettle's Village, Okla., attack on, **Vol. 3, Part 1**, 8
Black Like Me, **Supp. 10**, 292
Blacklisting. *See* Loyalty issues; Motion pictures
Black literature: **Supp. 5**, 490; **Supp. 6**, 715–17; **Supp. 8**, 286–89; **Supp. 9**, 107–10; biographies, **Supp. 10**, 193; collections of; **Supp. 1**, 717; *Crisis* influence on, **Supp. 7**, 203–4; middle-class society depiction, **Supp. 7**, 236; playwriting, **Supp. 7**, 319; **Supp. 10**, 193; poetry, **Supp. 10**, 321–22; slave narratives, **Supp. 9**, 109. *See also* Harlem Renaissance
Black markets, **Supp. 5**, 737
Blackmer, Harry M., reference to, **Supp. 6**, 455
Black Metropolis, **Supp. 8**, 81
Black Mountain College, founding of, **Supp. 8**, 530–31; **Supp. 10**, 3
Black Muslims: **Supp. 7**, 507–9; **Supp. 8**, 388; creed, **Supp. 9**, 570; economic base broadened, **Supp. 9**, 571; founding of, **Supp. 9**, 569; Malcolm X, assasination of, **Supp. 9**, 571; membership growth, **Supp. 9**, 570; power struggles, **Supp. 9**, 570, 571
Black Power, **Supp. 6**, 716
Black Power movement: **Supp. 8**, 335, 383; black criticism of, **Supp. 9**, 751; **Supp. 10**, 612; Olympic games demonstration (1968), **Supp. 10**, 612
"Black Republicanism," **Vol. 6, Part 1**, 200
"Black-Robe" Fathers, **Vol. 8, Part 2**, 192
Blacks: **Vol. 1, Part 1**, 23, 549, 562; **Vol. 1, Part 2**, 554; **Vol. 2, Part 1**, 161; **Vol. 3, Part 2**, 536; **Vol. 4, Part 1**, 578 f.; **Vol. 5, Part 2**, 546; **Vol. 7, Part 2**, 324; **Vol. 8, Part 2**, 212, 382, 409; **Vol. 9, Part 1**, 225; acting, **Vol. 1, Part 1**, 160; **Vol. 4, Part 1**, 314; advancement of, **Vol. 2, Part 1**, 180; **Vol. 4, Part 1**, 633; **Vol. 8, Part 1**, 171 f.; **Vol. 10, Part 2**, 264; agriculture, **Supp. 3**, 145–46; anti-Communism by, **Supp. 7**, 156; art, major survey exhibit of, **Supp. 8**, 240; arts participation, **Supp. 5**, 436–37; awards, **Supp. 2**, 623; "Back to Africa" movement, **Supp. 2**, 222; baseball, **Supp. 8**, 142; baseball, Negro League, **Supp. 3**, 378; **Supp. 4**, 327–28; biological sciences, **Supp. 3**, 403; "Black Code," **Vol. 1, Part 1**, 297; **Vol. 5, Part 1**, 373; boxing, **Supp. 5**, 368–69; **Supp. 6**, 362–63, 699–700; caste system among, **Supp. 5**, 544; Catholic church, **Supp. 8**, 293–94; Catholic mission schools for, **Supp. 5**, 185–86; choral music, **Supp. 3**, 225–26; civil rights, **Vol. 8, Part 1**, 327 f.; Civil War, regiments in, **Vol. 3, Part 1**, 322, 407; **Vol. 3, Part 2**, 508; **Vol. 5, Part 2**, 577, 597 f.; **Vol. 6, Part 1**, 306; classical music, **Supp. 4**, 125–26; colonization of, **Vol. 6, Part 1**, 507; **Vol. 9, Part 1**, 207; Corps d'Afrique, **Vol. 1, Part 1**, 292; Democratic party, **Supp. 4**, 607–8; **Supp. 6**, 260; **Supp. 7**, 767; **Supp. 8**, 121; dialect, use of, in literature, **Vol. 3, Part 1**, 138; **Vol. 4, Part 1**, 373; **Vol. 8, Part 2**, 242 f.; disfranchisement of, Rhode Island, **Vol. 3, Part 1**, 407; economic self-sufficiency advocacy, **Supp. 5**, 741; education, **Vol. 1, Part 1**, 360, 473; **Vol. 1, Part 2**, 367, 432; **Vol. 2, Part 1**, 138, 262; **Vol. 2, Part 2**, 504 f., 516; **Vol. 3, Part 2**, 132, 391, **Vol. 4, Part 1**, 36, 96; **Vol. 4, Part 2**, 223, 453, 543; **Vol. 5, Part 1**, 177, 312; **Vol. 5, Part 2**, 578, 598; **Vol. 7, Part 1**, 23 f., 43; **Vol. 7, Part 2**, 324, 442, 492; **Vol. 8, Part 1**, 374, 513; **Vol. 8, Part 2**, 171; **Vol. 9, Part 2**, 12, 19; **Vol. 10, Part 1**, 66 f., 506 f.; **Vol. 10, Part 2**, 229, 253, 558, 641; **Supp. 2**, 150–51, 315, 456, 476–77; **Supp. 5**, 55–56, 642; **Supp. 7**, 83; **Supp. 10**, 172; emancipation of, **Vol. 1, Part 1**, 280; **Vol. 1, Part 2**, 554; entrepreneurs, **Supp. 2**, 221; **Supp. 4**, 82–83, 916; **Supp. 5**, 548, 647–48, 741; first Academy Award winner, **Supp. 5**, 451; first Army general, **Supp. 8**, 118–19; first college graduate, **Vol. 8, Part 2**, 253; first congressman from North, **Supp. 5**, 166; first Democratic National Committee vice-chairman, **Supp. 8**, 121; first in federal service, **Vol. 7, Part 1**, 413; first heavyweight boxing champion, **Supp. 4**, 432–34; first importation of to New England, **Vol. 7, Part 2**, 406; first institutional church for in South, **Vol. 8, Part 1**, 243 f.; first Ivy League football player, **Supp. 4**, 492; first mainstream artist, **Supp. 4**, 667; first major league baseball player, **Supp. 7**, 646; **Supp. 9**, 668–69; first official cabinet adviser, **Supp. 5**, 343; first professor of African-American studies on major U.S. college campus, **Supp. 9**, 898; first serious theatrical depiction of, **Supp. 4**, 841; first social work school graduate, **Supp. 6**, 284; first state-supported liberal arts college for, **Supp. 4**, 742; first television newsman,

Supp. 8, 387–88; folklore, **Vol. 4, Part 2**, 312 f.; **Supp. 2**, 346; **Supp. 6**, 313–14; folk songs, **Supp. 4**, 476–77, 502; **Supp. 8**, 695–96; football, **Supp. 7**, 167–68; **Supp. 9**, 646, 817–18, 840–41; **Supp. 10**, 727; foreign service, **Vol. 4, Part 1**, 579; fraternal orders, **Supp. 5**, 754–55; Free African Society, **Vol. 1, Part 1**, 204; freedmen, organization of as, **Vol. 3, Part 1**, 608 f.; government service, **Supp. 5**, 163–64; Harvard policies toward, **Supp. 3**, 472; history, **Supp. 4**, 911; **Supp. 5**, 642; hospital for Charleston, **Vol. 8, Part 1**, 79; hotel kept by, in Washington, D. C., **Vol. 10, Part 2**, 535; housing, **Supp. 3**, 744; Howard University, law teaching at, **Vol. 5, Part 2**, 598; inventions by, **Vol. 6, Part 1**, 617; jazz, **Supp. 2**, 502; **Supp. 4**, 510; journalism, **Vol. 8, Part 1**, 403 f.; labor movement, **Supp. 5**, 511; **Supp. 6**, 647–48; **Supp. 7**, 155–56, 781; **Supp. 10**, 659–61; law cases involving, **Vol. 9, Part 1**, 315; **Vol. 9, Part 2**, 37; leadership, **Vol. 4, Part 1**, 579; **Vol. 9, Part 2**, 22; **Supp. 3**, 378, 390–91; **Supp. 6**, 567–68; **Supp. 7**, 200–205; **Supp. 7**, 748; **Supp. 8**, 332–35; legal practice, **Vol.4, Part 1**, 181, 578 f.; **Vol. 5, Part 2**, 598; **Vol. 9, Part 1**, 375; **Supp. 2**, 345; libraries for, **Supp. 3**, 280, 281; literary treatment of, **Supp. 2**, 303; **Supp. 6**, 116; Massachusetts, legal rights in, **Vol. 2, Part 2**, 585; medicine, **Supp. 5**, 104–5; migration westward, **Vol. 4, Part 1**, 579; militancy, **Supp. 8**, 383; minstrels, **Vol. 4, Part 2**, 411; mission work among, **Vol. 1, Part 2**, 528; music, **Vol. 2, Part 1**, 288; **Supp. 5**, 758; **Supp. 6**, 275, 690; musicals, **Supp. 3**, 187–88; music education for, **Supp. 4**, 834; **Supp. 6**, 427; Myrdal study of, **Supp. 6**, 605; "Negro Plot" (1741), **Vol. 5, Part 1**, 237; **Vol. 6, Part 1**, 182; New Deal measures for, **Supp. 3**, 656, 661; **Supp. 5**, 56; newspapers and magazines, **Supp. 2**, 3; **Supp. 3**, 596; **Supp. 5**, 567–68; **Supp. 7**, 202–4; North Carolina, **Vol. 1, Part 2**, 39; novel hero, first use of, as, **Vol. 9, Part 2**, 118; organizations for betterment of, **Supp. 2**, 221–22, 346; poetry, **Vol. 3, Part 1**, 505 f.; **Vol. 4, Part 2**, 201; polar exploration, **Supp. 5**, 295; in politics, **Vol. 4, Part 1**, 578 f.; **Vol. 5, Part 2**, 597 f.; **Vol. 8, Part 1**, 327 f.; private southern schools for, **Supp. 7**, 83; Prudence Crandall case, **Vol. 3, Part 1**, 27; race pride promotion, **Supp. 3**, 535; race relations, **Supp. 3**, 577–79, 827–28; **Supp. 5**, 544, 633, 740–41; **Supp. 6**, 11–12, 321–22, 600, **Supp. 7**, 203, 266, 319, 448; **Supp. 8**, 434–35; racial prejudice, crusade against, **Vol. 4, Part 1**, 632; **Supp. 10**, 95; Reconstruction, **Vol. 4, Part 1**, 623; **Vol. 5, Part 1**, 280; **Vol. 10, Part 1**, 457; regiment, first, in Civil War, **Vol. 1, Part 1**, 280; religion, **Vol. 1, Part 1**, 411, 484; **Vol. 5, Part 1**, 177, 193; **Vol. 7, Part 2**, 410; **Vol. 8, Part 1**, 243 f., 455; **Supp. 1**, 645; **Supp. 5**, 258–59, 548; **Supp. 7**, 186–88; **Supp. 8**, 434–435; Republican party, **Supp. 3**, 378–79, 596; **Supp. 5**, 632–33; Rosenwald Fund aid to, **Supp. 4**, 251; Schurz, Carl, report of, on, **Vol. 8, Part 2**, 468; sculpture by, **Supp. 7**, 610–11; separatism v. assimilation, **Supp. 7**, 508; **Supp. 8**, 335, 388; **Supp. 10**, 321–22; Slater fund, **Vol. 9, Part 1**, 205; social work, **Supp. 4**, 53–54; sociological studies of, **Supp. 5**, 520; **Supp. 7**, 202–4, 266; **Supp. 8**, 81, 521–22; songwriting, **Supp. 9**, 644–45; spirituals, **Vol. 8, Part 2**, 614; stereotypical depiction of, **Supp. 4**, 102–3; **Supp. 5**, 451; **Supp. 7**, 43–44, 163, 237; **Supp. 10**, 7–8; 676; 661–62, 678; streetcars and right to use, **Vol. 9, Part 2**, 23; suffrage, **Vol. 1, Part 2**, 324, **Vol. 3, Part 1**, 597; **Vol. 4, Part 1**, 273, 633; **Vol. 5, Part 2**, 114; **Vol. 8, Part 2**, 176; Sunday school for, **Vol. 8, Part 1**, 39 f.; theater, **Supp. 5**, 418–20; **Supp. 8**, 547; universities and colleges, **Supp. 2**, 315, 456, 477; **Supp. 4**, 742, 916; **Supp. 5**, 56, 436; **Supp. 6**, 11–12; **Supp. 8**, 86–87, 94–95; vaudeville, **Supp. 4**, 695; Virginia, work among, **Vol. 8, Part 2**, 273; voting rights, **Supp. 4**, 331, 384–85; **Supp. 8**, 682; welfare work for, **Vol. 3, Part 1**, 597 f.; **Vol. 4, Part 2**, 160; **Vol. 7, Part 1**, 232; **Vol. 8, Part 1**, 243 f.; **Vol. 10, Part 1**, 398 f.; women's organizations, **Supp. 5**, 680; writings on, **Supp. 3**, 391; **Supp. 4**, 841; **Supp. 6**, 490; **Supp. 8**, 388. *See also* Black literature; Civil rights movement; Harlem Renaissance; Racism; School desegregation; Segregation

"Black Sox" scandal (baseball), **Supp. 3**, 438; **Supp. 8**, 85–86, 383, 574–75

Blackstone Female Institute (Va.), **Supp. 3**, 132

Black Thunder, **Supp. 9**, 108

Blackwell, Alice Stone, reference to, **Supp. 5**, 532

Blackwell, Elizabeth, reference to, **Supp. 4**, 85

Bladensburg, Md., battle of, **Vol. 1, Part 1**, 357; **Vol. 7, Part 1**, 90; **Vol. 10, Part 2**, 382

Blaffer, Robert Lee, reference to, **Supp. 3**, 260–61

Blaik, Earl H. ("Red"), reference to, **Supp. 8**, 389

Blaine, James G., references to, **Vol. 2, Part 2**, 206 f., 346 f.; **Vol. 4, Part 2**, 333 f.; **Vol. 5, Part 1**, 159; **Vol. 6, Part 1**, 283; **Vol. 6, Part 2**, 236; **Vol. 7, Part 2**, 533; **Vol. 9, Part 1**, 87, 526, 618; **Supp. 7**, 568

Blaine-Cleveland election, news reports of, **Vol. 6, Part 1**, 283

Blair, Francis P., reference to, **Vol. 5, Part 2**, 326

Blair, James, reference to, **Vol. 7, Part 1**, 500

Blake, Clarence J., reference to, **Vol. 1, Part 2**, 149

Blake, Eubie, references to, **Supp. 9**, 60, 644, 645, 730, 731, 732

Blake, Francis G., references to, **Supp. 3**, 774, 775

Blake, Tiffany, reference to, **Supp. 7**, 309

Blanc, Mel, reference to, **Supp. 9**, 76

Bland-Allison Act, **Vol. 1, Part 2**, 355; **Vol. 9, Part 1**, 86 f.

Blanshard, Paul, reference to, **Supp. 8**, 614

Blants, breeding of, **Supp. 10**, 10, 80, 81

Blashfield, E. H., reference to, **Vol. 7, Part 1**, 299

Blass, Bill, reference to, **Supp. 9**, 465

Blast furnaces, **Vol. 8, Part 1**, 517, 544; **Vol. 9, Part 1**, 428; **Vol. 10, Part 1**, 465 f., 602 f.; feat, reduction of, **Vol. 8, Part 1**, 326; turboblower for, **Vol. 8, Part l**, 544

Blasting powder, manufacture of, **Vol. 3, Part 1**, 528

Blatchford, Thomas W., reference to, **Vol. 10, Part 1**, 435 f.

Blavatsky, Mme., references to, **Vol. 5, Part 2**, 233; **Vol. 7, Part 2**, 10 f.

Blease, Cole L., reference to, **Supp. 9**, 150

Bledsoe, Jules, reference to, **Supp. 3**, 418

"Bleeding Kansas," **Vol. 6, Part 1**, 534; **Vol. 9, Part 2**, 13

Blegen, Carl, reference to, **Supp. 4**, 144

Blennerhasset Papers, **Vol. 8, Part 2**, 288

Bleuler, Eugen, references to, **Supp. 4**, 107, 108

Blind and blindness: **Supp. 10**, 245; books and magazines for, **Vol. 3, Part 1**, 512 f.; **Vol. 5, Part 2**, 288; **Vol. 9, Part 1**, 294; care of, **Vol. 2, Part 2**, 107; **Vol. 5, Part 1**, 296; **Vol. 6, Part 1**, 296, 404; **Vol. 7, Part 2**, 305; **Vol. 8, Part 2**, 238; **Supp. 1**, 19; dog guides, **Supp. 4**, 253–55; education, **Vol. 1, Part 1**, 261; **Vol. 2, Part 1**, 38, 451; **Vol. 2, Part 2**, 106 f.; **Vol. 3, Part 2**, 409 f.; **Vol. 9, Part 1**, 294; **Vol. 10, Part 2**, 455; **Supp. 4**, 10–11; **Supp. 5**, 347–48; **Supp. 8**, 316–17; eye banks, **Supp. 7**, 70; federal aid programs, **Supp. 5**, 347; first blind U.S. senator, **Supp. 4**, 338; Lighthouse organization, **Supp. 3**, 364–65; prevention, **Supp. 2**, 381; **Supp. 3**, 364–65, 377. *See also* Color blindness; Vision

Bliss, Eleanor, reference to, **Supp. 7**, 477

Bliss, George, reference to, **Vol. 10, Part 1**, 637 f.

Bliss, Gilbert A., reference to, **Supp. 3**, 87
Bliss, Mildred Barnes. *See* Barnes, Mildred
Bliss, Robert Woods, reference to, **Supp. 5**, 700
Blizzard of 1888, **Vol. 8, Part 1**, 393
Bloch, Felix, reference to, **Supp. 4**, 358
Bloch, Louis, reference to, **Supp. 8**, 586
Bloch, Suzanne, reference to, **Supp. 6**, 62
Block, Herbert, reference to, **Supp. 10**, 245
Block, Paul, & Associates, **Supp. 3**, 80
Blockade-running in Civil War, **Vol. 3, Part 1**, 60; **Vol. 5, Part 2**, 550; **Vol. 8, Part 1**, 47 f.; **Vol. 8, Part 2**, 149, 341
Block Island, discovery of, **Vol. 1, Part 2**, 378
Block signals. *See* Railroads
Blondell, Joan, reference to, **Supp. 6**, 637
Blood: abnormalities, **Supp. 3**, 75; clotting, **Supp. 3**, 369–70; coagulation, **Supp. 9**, 862; component interaction, **Supp. 3**, 350–51; Cooley's anemia, **Supp. 3**, 190; culture studies, **Supp. 4**, 494; embryological cell studies, **Supp. 5**, 600; exsanguination, process, **Supp. 10**, 837; hemolytic transfusion, reactions, **Supp. 10**, 837; hypoplastic anemia, **Supp. 3**, 75; physiology of circulation, **Supp. 3**, 352–53; plasma, **Supp. 5**, 122–23; plasma preservation, **Supp. 4**, 242–43; research on, **Supp. 4**, 580–81; RH factor, **Supp. 10**, 837–38; Rh-negative factor, **Supp. 3**, 441; writings on, **Supp. 4**, 866; **Supp. 10**, 836, 837, 838. *See also* Anemia
Blood cells: hemoglobin determination, **Supp. 4**, 643; role of white, **Supp. 4**, 616
Blood pressure: choline relationship to lowering, **Supp. 4**, 411; measurement, **Supp. 2**, 137; **Supp. 7**, 226; monitoring in surgery, **Supp. 3**, 201
Blood transfusions: blood banks, **Supp. 4**, 242; **Supp. 6**, 547; **Supp. 8**, 556; blood type, **Supp. 3**, 440; donor program, **Supp. 6**, 547; first blood bank, **Supp. 4**, 242; first clinical studies, **Supp. 4**, 494; heparin use, **Supp. 3**, 370; plasma development, **Supp. 5**, 122–23; plasma for burn patients, **Supp. 6**, 190; regional donor centers, **Supp. 6**, 414; surgical use of, **Supp. 3**, 201; **Supp. 7**, 59
Blood vessels: clots and heparin, **Supp. 3**, 370; surgery of, **Supp. 3**, 140; 626; temperature effect on, **Supp. 4**, 59. *See also* Cardiovascular system; Circulatory system
"Bloody Angle," **Vol. 3, Part 2**, 230; **Vol. 5, Part 2**, 96; **Vol. 6, Part 1**, 126; **Vol. 10, Part 1**, 129
"Bloody Monday," **Vol. 7, Part 1**, 158
"Bloody Shirt," **Vol. 9, Part 2**, 540
Bloomer costume, **Vol. 1, Part 1**, 319; **Vol. 4, Part 2**, 376
Bloomfield, N.J., early history of, **Vol. 1, Part 2**, 385
Bloomingdale's department store, **Supp. 9**, 483
Bloomsbury group, **Supp. 7**, 219
Blough, Roy, reference to, **Supp. 9**, 589
Blount, William, references to, **Vol. 1, Part 2**, 64, 390; **Vol. 3, Part 1**, 613; **Vol. 5, Part 1**, 527 f.; **Vol. 8, Part 2**, 128
Blount conspiracy. *See* Conspiracy, Blount (1797)
Blow, Henry T., case of Dred Scott, **Vol. 8, Part 2**, 488 f.
"Blue and the Gray," **Vol. 3, Part 2**, 383
Blue Angel, The, **Supp. 8**, 672, 688
Bluecher, Heinrich, reference to, **Supp. 9**, 41
Blue Cross and Blue Shield: development of, **Supp. 4**, 251; predecessors, **Supp. 3**, 122
Blue Dahlia, The, **Supp. 9**, 480
Blue Devils (blues group), **Supp. 9**, 687
"Blue Eagle." *See* National Recovery Administration
Blue Hill Observatory, **Vol. 8, Part 2**, 183 f.
Bluemont Central College, founding of, **Vol. 4, Part 1**, 395
Blue Mountain College, founding of, **Vol. 6, Part 1**, 475
Blue Mountain Valley, capture of, **Vol. 1, Part 1**, 175
Blue Sky Boys (musical-comedy team), **Supp. 9**, 373–74
Blues music: **Supp. 2**, 547, 616; **Supp. 6**, 275; boogie-woogie, **Supp. 5**, 758; **Supp. 9**, 644, 645; **Supp. 10**, 77–78; bands, **Supp. 9**, 687–88; influence on rock and roll, **Supp. 10**, 78; urban, **Supp. 9**, 413–14, 796
Bluffton movement, **Vol. 7, Part 2**, 59
Blum, Ren, reference to, **Supp. 3**, 283
Blumenfeld, Kurt, reference to, **Supp. 9**, 40
Blumenthal, George, reference to, **Supp. 3**, 24
Blunt, E. M., reference to, **Vol. 5, Part 1**, 201
Bly, Robert, reference to, **Supp. 10**, 854
B'nai B'rith, **Supp. 4**, 593–94
Boag, Gil, reference to, **Supp. 6**, 247
Board of Jewish Ministers (New York City), founding of, **Supp. 2**, 453
Board of Missionary Preparation, **Vol. 10, Part 1**, 62
Board of Missions, for Freedmen, **Vol. 8, Part 2**, 332
Board of Navy Commissioners, **Vol. 7, Part 2**, 321
Board of Regents of New York, **Vol. 4, Part 2**, 419
Board of Temperance, Prohibition and Public Morals, **Vol. 5, Part 2**, 517
Boas, Franz, references to, **Supp. 4**, 71, 72, 907; **Supp. 5**, 435; **Supp. 6**, 314, 352, 353, 393, 524, 611; **Supp. 7**, 710, 711; **Supp. 10**, 521, 522
Boas, Sophie Meyer, reference to, **Supp. 3**, 81
Boat building: **Vol. 3, Part 2**, 582; **Vol. 4, Part 2**, 585; **Vol. 5, Part 1**, 155; first iron boat, **Vol. 3, Part 1**, 211; PT boat prototype, **Supp. 9**, 892
Bob Jones University, founding of, **Supp. 8**, 304
Boccia, Ferdinand ("The Shadow"), reference to, **Supp. 8**, 208
Bôcher, Maxime, reference to, **Supp. 3**, 70, 575
Boddy, Manchester, reference to, **Supp. 10**, 184
Bodleian Library, **Vol. 7, Part 2**, 86
Body, human: anthropological study of types, **Supp. 5**, 312; heat and temperature, **Supp. 3**, 32; **Supp. 4**, 58–59. *See also* Anatomy; Physiology
Body and Soul, **Supp. 10**, 348
Body building, **Supp. 9**, 51–52
Boeing Aircraft: bomber development, **Supp. 9**, 255–56; founding of, **Supp. 6**, 63–64; management, **Supp. 10**, 620–21
Boer War, **Supp. 4**, 126–27
Bogalusa Paper Co., **Supp. 7**, 293
Bogan, Louise, references to, **Supp. 7**, 654, 655; **Supp. 10**, 831
Bogardus, Emory S., reference to, **Supp. 3**, 578
Bogart, Humphrey, reference to, **Supp. 10**, 656
Boggs, Corinne ("Lindy"), references to, **Supp. 9**, 103, 105
Boggs, Hale, reference to, **Supp. 7**, 555
Bohemian church, first in U.S., **Vol. 4, Part 2**, 599
Bohemian Roman Catholic Union, **Vol. 4, Part 2**, 600
Bohemians, The: activities of, **Vol. 10, Part 2**, 406; founding of, **Supp. 2**, 250
Bohlen, Charles E., references to, **Supp. 7**, 212; **Supp. 8**, 90
Bohr, Niels, references to, **Supp. 6**, 501; **Supp. 7**, 133, 134, 258; **Supp. 8**, 199, 483; **Supp. 10**, 288, 741
BOI. *See* Investigation, Bureau of (U.S.)
Boilers: inventions relating to, **Vol. 1, Part 1**, 457; **Vol. 8, Part 1**, 429; **Vol. 10, Part 2**, 205; plate manufacture, **Vol. 5, Part 1**, 434; for steamers and battleships, **Vol. 5, Part 1**, 318
Bok, Edward W., peace prize, **Vol. 6, Part 1**, 199; reference to, **Supp. 3**, 573
Bolack, Tom, references to, **Supp. 10**, 548, 549
Bolden, Buddy, reference to, **Supp. 9**, 598

Boldini, Giovanni (portraitist), reference to, **Supp. 6**, 552
Bolero, **Supp. 10**, 655–56
Bolger, Ray, reference to, **Supp. 10**, 301
Bolick, Bill, reference to, **Supp. 9**, 373–74
Bolick, Earl, reference to, **Supp. 9**, 373–74
Bolivia, diplomatic relations with, **Vol. 1, Part 1**, 329
Boll weevil, **Vol. 5, Part 1**, 406; **Vol. 5, Part 2**, 453; **Supp. 4**, 601
Bolles, H. Eugene, reference to, **Supp. 6**, 562
Bolshevik Bureau of Information, founding of, **Supp. 5**, 135
Bolshevik Revolution. *See* Russian Revolution (1917)
Bolshevism. *See* Communism; Communist party; Loyalty issues
Bolton, Guy, reference to, **Supp. 3**, 417
Bolton, Herbert Eugene, reference to, **Supp. 4**, 824
Bolts, invention and manufacture of, **Vol. 4, Part 2**, 374
Boltzius, I. M., reference to, **Vol. 7, Part 1**, 310
Boltzmann, Ludwig, reference to, **Supp. 8**, 190
Bombings and terrorism: *Los Angeles Times* unionization issue, **Supp. 3**, 156; San Francisco Preparedness Day (1916), **Supp. 3**, 532–33; St. Valentine's Day massacre, **Supp. 4**, 141
Bonanno, Joseph: crime syndicate organized, **Supp. 9**, 269; deposed as syndicate boss, **Supp. 9**, 270; **Supp. 10**, 266, 269; reference to, **Supp. 9**, 821; **Supp. 10**, 140
"Bonanza," **Supp. 9**, 101–2
Bonaparte, Napoleon, biography of, **Vol. 9, Part 1**, 214
Bonar, Ronald E., reference to, **Supp. 3**, 289
Bond, Dr. Thomas E., Jr., reference to, **Vol. 1, Part 2**, 61
Bonds, coupon, **Vol. 8, Part 1**, 322 f.; government, **Vol. 2, Part 2**, 383 f.
Bone surgery. *See* Surgery
Bonfils, Frederick G., reference to, **Supp. 3**, 851
Bonhomme Richard, and the *Serapis*, naval engagement, **Vol. 5, Part 2**, 185
Boni, Albert, reference to, **Supp. 8**, 577
Boni, Charles, reference to, **Supp. 8**, 577
Boni Brothers Bookshop, **Supp. 8**, 349
Bonsack Machines, perfection of, **Vol. 3, Part 1**, 497 f.
Bonstelle, Jessie, references to, **Supp. 3**, 796; **Supp. 6**, 311; **Supp. 9**, 194; 481
Bonus army (1932), **Supp. 5**, 502; **Supp. 6**, 239–40; **Supp. 7**, 363, 377, 488; **Supp. 8**, 497
Boogie-woogie (musical style), **Supp. 5**, 758
Book clubs. *See* Book-of-the-Month Club; Literary Guild
Bookman, The, **Vol. 3, Part 1**, 341; **Vol. 7, Part 2**, 378; **Vol. 9, Part 1**, 607; **Supp. 6**, 172
Book of Common Prayer, **Vol. 1, Part 2**, 564; **Vol. 5, Part 1**, 421; **Vol. 9, Part 1**, 207, 359; **Supp. 3**, 785
Book of Daniel (Old Testament), **Supp. 4**, 595–96
Book of Mormon, The: **Vol. 9, Part 1**, 310 f.; authorship of, **Vol. 8, Part 1**, 600 f.; translations of, **Vol. 9, Part 2**, 334
Book-of-the-Month Club: editorial board, **Supp. 5**, 439; founding of, **Supp. 8**, 577–78; judges, **Supp. 6**, 203, 465; **Supp. 7**, 104; lawsuit, **Supp. 3**, 500
Book reviews. *See* Criticism, literature
Books: anitwar novels, **Supp. 10**, 793; art reproduction, **Supp. 6**, 583; auctioneering, **Vol. 1, Part 2**, 161; authors' agents, **Supp. 1**, 539; baby-care, **Supp. 7**, 528; binding, **Vol. 1, Part 1**, 131; **Vol. 4, Part 1**, 445; **Vol. 6, Part 2**, 421; **Vol. 7, Part 1**, 503; blind, for the use of, **Vol. 3, Part 1**, 512 f.; **Vol. 5, Part 2**, 288; **Vol. 9, Part 1**, 294; braille, **Supp. 5**, 347; cataloguing, **Vol. 4, Part 1**, 460; **Vol. 6, Part l**, 231; **Vol. 8, Part 2**, 275; censorship, **Supp. 7**, 98, 149, 292, 293; **Supp. 8**, 605; **Supp. 10**, 47, 221, 539, 540; child guidance, **Supp. 7**, 601; child-care, **Supp. 4**, 8; children's, *see* Children's literature; collecting, **Vol. 1, Part 2**, 173; **Vol. 2, Part 1**, 137; **Vol. 3, Part 2**, 158, 363, 407, 417; **Vol. 4, Part 1**, 561; **Vol. 4, Part 2**, 305; **Vol. 5, Part 1**, 445; **Vol. 5, Part 2**, 155 f., 174 f.; **Vol. 6, Part 1**, 110, 308; **Vol. 6, Part 2**, 97; **Vol. 8, Part 1**, 51 f., 232 f.; **Vol. 9, Part 1**, 256; **Vol. 9, Part 2**, 586; **Vol. 10, Part 1**, 443; **Vol. 10, Part 2**, 185; collections, *see* Collections; Rare books and manuscripts; cooking, **Supp. 7**, 528, 656–57; Copyright Act of 1909, **Vol. 8, Part 1**, 279 f.; design, *see* Typographical design; detective stories, **Supp. 9**, 487–88; 772–73; dime novel, **Supp. 3**, 586; editing, **Supp. 3**, 686; **Supp. 4**, 651-52; erotica, **Supp. 10**, 592; first movie-rights contract clause, **Supp. 4**, 60; folk music collections, **Supp. 10**, 589, 590; historical fiction, **Supp. 10**, 518, 519; hoax, **Supp. 7**, 643; household hints, **Supp. 10**, 666; humor, **Supp. 10**, 631, 746–47; illustrations, **Vol. 5, Part 2**, 139; **Supp. 10**, 688, 690, *see also* Illustration; indexes to, **Supp. 5**, 752–53; "inside"genre, **Supp. 8**, 232–33; inspirational novels, **Supp. 5**, 182; limited editions, **Supp. 4**, 622; literary fiction, **Supp. 9**, 870, 871; litigation, **Supp. 8**, 224; muckraking, **Supp. 8**, 594–95; mystery fiction, **Supp. 10**, 103–4, 518, 519; novels about emancipated women, **Supp. 4**, 31; paperback, **Supp. 5**, 264–65; **Supp. 6**, 583; **Supp. 7**, 307; **Supp. 8**, 579; plates, **Vol. 5, Part 1**, 424; **Vol. 8, Part 1**, 361 f.; photography, **Supp. 10**, 766, 767; political commentary, **Supp. 10**, 707; popular adventure, **Supp. 4**, 60; popular culture, **Supp. 3**, 846–47; popular fiction, **Supp. 4**, 372; **Supp. 9**, 735–36, 785–86, 895; popular psychology, **Supp. 3**, 384; **Supp. 4**, 495–96; popular romance, **Supp. 5**, 33; popular sensations, **Supp. 7**, 531–32; preservation of, **Supp. 2**, 40; **Supp. 6**, 399; pulp fiction, **Supp. 3**, 264; **Supp. 9**, 722; religious, **Supp. 10**, 729; reviews of, **Supp. 9**, 738, *see also* Criticism, literature; self-improvement, **Supp. 5**, 102; technical, **Supp. 4**, 523–24; social issues, **Supp. 10**, 375; trade, **Vol. 1, Part 2**, 161; **Vol. 2, Part 1**, 367; **Vol. 2, Part 2**, 162; **Vol. 3, Part 2**, 188, 576; **Vol. 4, Part 1**, 91 f., 398, 460, 536; **Vol. 4, Part 2**, 303, 525; **Vol. 5, Part 2**, 66 f., 444; **Vol. 6, Part 1**, 565 f.; **Vol. 7, Part 1**, 156, 278, 352 f., 508; **Vol. 8, Part 1**, 279 f.; **Vol. 9, Part 2**, 652; **Vol. 10, Part 1**, 604 f.; travel narratives, **Supp. 9**, 457; *Tropic of Cancer* censorship, **Supp. 10**, 539, 540; *Ulyses* censorship, **Supp. 3**, 844; vocabulary-building, **Supp. 7**, 275; Westerns, **Supp. 2**, 262–63, 729; **Supp. 3**, 382–83; **Supp. 9**, 312–13, 722–23; World War II novels, **Supp. 10**, 390. *See also* Bibliographies; Biography; Detective stories; Dictionaries; Illustration; Libraries and library work; Literature; Publishing; Rare books and manuscripts; Textbooks; *types of literature and genre;* Typographical design
Bookstores: associations, **Supp. 7**, 524–25; English language in Paris, **Supp. 7**, 40–41; inventory control, **Supp. 10**, 46; small retail v. discount, **Supp. 3**, 499–500
Boone, Daniel: first account of, **Vol. 3, Part 2**, 382; references to, **Vol. 3, Part 2**, 475; **Vol. 5, Part 1**, 482; **Vol. 5, Part 2**, 349
Boone and Crockett Club, founding of, **Supp. 2**, 265
Booneville, Mo., engagement at, **Vol. 6, Part 2**, 290
Booth, Bramwell, reference to, **Supp. 4**, 95, 96
Booth, Edwin, references to, **Vol. 1, Part 1**, 647; **Vol. 2, Part 2**, 157; **Vol. 4, Part 2**, 542; **Vol. 5, Part 1**, 605; **Supp. 3**, 713
Booth, George Gough, reference to, **Supp. 7**, 670
Booth, Henry S., reference to, **Supp. 4**, 714, 715
Booth, John Wilkes: **Vol. 5, Part 1**, 182; assassination

of Lincoln, **Vol. 6, Part 1**, 257; capture of, **Vol. 1, Part 1**, 523; false accusation of association with, **Vol. 3, Part 1**, 396
Booth, Maud Ballington, reference to, **Supp. 2**, 48–49
Booth, Sherman M., reference to, **Vol. 7, Part 2**, 145 f.
Booth, Shirley, reference to, **Supp. 9**, 98
Bootlegging. *See* Prohibition
Boott, Kirk, reference to, **Vol. 5, Part 1**, 553
Borah, William E., references to, **Supp. 3**, 457, 561; **Supp. 5**, 579; **Supp. 9**, 504, 590
Borax, discovery of, **Vol. 9, Part 1**, 267
Bordeaux mixture, **Supp. 3**, 400–401
Bordello. *See* Prostitution
Borden, Lizzie, murder case, **Vol. 7, Part 1**, 107
Border City During the Civil War, **Vol. 1, Part 1**, 264
Borderline personality, **Supp. 6**, 724
Bordes, Charles, reference to, **Supp. 6**, 357
Bordin, Michael, reference to, **Supp. 8**, 564
Boré, Étienne de, reference to, **Vol. 1, Part 1**, 130
Borg, Max, reference to, **Supp. 8**, 482
Borgana (synthetic fabric), **Supp. 6**, 67
Borglum, Lincoln, reference to, **Supp. 3**, 89
Borglum, Solon, reference to, **Supp. 8**, 414
Borg-Warner Corporation, **Supp. 6**, 67
Bori, Lucrezia, references to, **Supp. 6**, 323, 324
Boris Godunov, **Supp. 10**, 722–23
Bormann, Martin, World War II survival reports, **Supp. 10**, 232
Born, Gustav, reference to, **Supp. 6**, 282
Born, Max, references to, **Supp. 7**, 258–59, 411; **Supp. 9**, 541
Borneo, missions in, **Vol. 3, Part 1**, 389
Born Yesterday, **Supp. 7**, 355
Borodin, Mikhail, reference to. **Supp. 8**, 635
Borrow, George, biography of, **Vol. 5, Part 2**, 454
Bosis, Lauro de, reference to, **Supp. 6**, 174
Boston, Mass.: Academy of Music, **Vol. 3, Part 2**, 81; Adams House, **Vol. 1, Part 1**, 102; apartment house, site of first in U.S., **Vol. 3, Part 1**, 327; architectural firms, **Supp. 3**, 195–97; Arnold Arboretum, **Vol. 8, Part 2**, 355; Associated Charities, **Vol. 6, Part 1**, 423; **Vol. 7, Part 2**, 158 f.; **Vol. 8, Part 1**, 275 f.; Beacon Hill, development of, **Vol. 6, Part 2**, 371; book publishing, **Supp. 4**, 526–27; Boylston Club, **Vol. 7, Part 2**, 78; Brattle Street Church, **Vol. 2, Part 2**, 311, 410 f.; British evacuation of, **Vol. 6, Part 1**, 77; Castle Square Theatre, **Vol. 8, Part 2**, 386; Catholic church, **Vol. 3, Part 1**, 361; **Vol. 6, Part 2**, 37, 408; **Vol. 8, Part 2**, 63; **Vol. 10, Part 2**, 277; censorship, **Supp. 7**, 20; **Supp. 8**, 605; Chamber of Commerce, **Supp. 2**, 183; charter for, **Vol. 8, Part 1**, 230 f.; **Vol. 9, Part 1**, 42; **Supp. 5**, 730; Church of the Advent, founding of, in Boston, **Vol. 9, Part 1**, 33; Church of the Disciples, **Vol. 2, Part 2**, 153; Church of the New Jerusalem, **Vol. 8, Part 1**, 448 f.; city form of government, adoption of, **Vol. 8, Part 1**, 308 f.; city ordinances, digest of, **Vol. 2, Part 1**, 615; city planning, 1855, **Vol. 4, Part 2**, 523; civic service, **Vol. 1, Part 1**, 361; **Vol. 3, Part 1**, 501 f.; **Vol. 3, Part 2**, 81; **Vol. 7, Part 2**, 582; **Vol. 8, Part 1**, 308 f., 534; **Vol. 9, Part 1**, 31, 33, 142; **Vol. 10, Part 2**, 395; commerce, **Vol. 5, Part 1**, 16; **Vol. 5, Part 2**, 370; Common, movement for perservation of, **Vol. 4, Part 2**, 41; Directory of Nurses, **Vol. 8, Part 1**, 275 f.; education, public, **Vol. 1, Part 2**, 274, 297; **Vol. 2, Part 1**, 482; **Vol. 7, Part 2**, 221; **Vol. 8, Part 1**, 80; **Vol. 9, Part 2**, 276, 524; Emmanuel Church, **Vol. 6, Part 1**, 278; engineering, **Vol. 1, Part 1**, 540; engraved map of harbor, first, **Vol. 8, Part 1**, 140 f.; engravings, **Vol. 2, Part 1**, 278; Eye & Ear Infirmary, founding of, **Vol. 3, Part 1**, 207; faith-cure movement, **Vol. 2, Part 2**, 588; Faneuil Hall, **Vol. 3, Part 2**, 263; **Vol. 6, Part 1**, 439; **Vol. 8, Part 1**, 308 f.; **Vol. 9, Part 1**, 229; Faneuil Hall Market built, **Vol. 8, Part 1**, 308 f.; fire alarm, first electric, **Vol. 2, Part 2**, 265; fire department, first organized, **Vol. 8, Part 1**, 308 f.; fish horn, first, **Vol. 8, Part 1**, 548; Franklin Park, **Vol. 7, Part 2**, 26 f.; Franklin Square House, **Vol. 1, Part 1**, 560; Free Bridges party, **Vol. 4, Part 2**, 563; Gardner Museum, **Vol. 4, Part 1**, 143; Handel and Haydn Society, **Vol. 5, Part 2**, 584; **Vol. 10, Part 1**, 577 f.; Hide and Leather National Bank, **Vol. 2, Part 2**, 111; hotel building, **Vol. 8, Part 2**, 98; housing, improvements in, **Vol. 6, Part 1**, 45 f.; Howard Athenaeum, **Vol. 6, Part 1**, 164; ice, exportation, **Vol. 10, Part 1**, 47 f.; journalism, **Vol. 4, Part 2**, 41; **Vol. 5, Part 2**, 458; **Vol. 9, Part 2**, 609; **Vol. 10, Part 2**, 306; King's Chapel, **Vol. 4, Part 1**, 10; **Vol. 5, Part 1**, 414; letter boxes, introduction of, **Vol. 2, Part 1**, 482; library, public, **Vol. 1, Part 2**, 24, 53; **Vol. 4, Part 1**, 617; **Vol. 5, Part 2**, 66; **Vol. 6, Part 2**, 100; **Vol. 7, Part 2**, 241; **Vol. 9, Part 2**, 405, 528; **Vol. 10, Part 2**, 161, 403; life in early nineteenth century, **Vol. 4, Part 2**, 603; literary fame of, in the nineteenth century, **Vol. 1, Part 2**, 17; **Vol. 7, Part 1**, 283; magazines, **Vol. 8, Part 2**, 203; Manufacturer's Mutual Insurance Co., **Vol. 1, Part 1**, 406; mayors, **Supp. 6**, 139–41; municipal improvements, **Supp. 2**, 183; music, **Vol. 3, Part 1**, 513; **Vol. 8, Part 2**, 567; newspapers, early, **Vol. 3, Part 2**, 458; Old Corner Bookstore, **Vol. 9, Part 2**, 529; Old South Church, **Vol. 5, Part 1**, 88; **Vol. 9, Part 2**, 390, 392; Opera House, **Vol. 5, Part 2**, 264; Park Commission, **Supp. 6**, 485; parks, **Vol. 3, Part 2**, 70; Park Street Church, **Vol. 1, Part 1**, 581; philanthropy in, **Vol. 3, Part 1**, 321, 368; **Vol. 7, Part 2**, 158 f.; **Vol. 9, Part 2**, 393; **Vol. 10, Part 1**, 46; pirates, hanging of, in, **Vol. 8, Part 1**, 299 f.; police strike, **Supp. 1**, 194–95; **Supp. 3**, 471; political irregularities, **Supp. 8**, 219; political service, **Vol. 2, Part 2**, 612; **Vol. 7, Part 2**, 101 f.; politics, **Supp. 4**, 277–78; **Supp. 6**, 139–41; **Supp. 9**, 210; pre-Revolutionary War agitation, **Vol. 4, Part 1**, 87 f.; **Vol. 6, Part 2**, 455; printing, **Vol. 3, Part 2**, 460; **Vol. 5, Part 2**, 110; **Vol. 9, Part 2**, 435; psychoanalysis in, **Supp. 4**, 717; Public Franchise League, **Vol. 8, Part 1**, 230 f.; **Supp. 3**, 240; public health, **Vol. 4, Part 2**, 303; **Vol. 9, Part 1**, 543; public service, **Vol. 2, Part 2**, 52 f.; **Vol. 3, Part 1**, 361; **Vol. 6, Part 2**, 370, 418, 587; real estate, **Vol. 2, Part 2**, 136; reforms, **Vol. 2, Part 2**, 595; **Vol. 8, Part 1**, 308 f.; Republican mayor, first, **Vol. 8, Part 1**, 534; Revolutionary War period, **Vol. 2, Part 1**, 381, 395; **Vol. 9, Part 2**, 476; Roman Catholic diocese, **Supp. 3**, 568–71; **Supp. 8**, 114–16, 612–13; rural free delivery, introduction of, **Vol. 2, Part 1**, 482; Saturday Club, **Vol. 5, Part 1**, 86, 173; settlement houses in, **Vol. 10, Part 1**, 41; sewer systems, **Vol. 8, Part 1**, 308 f.; shipbuilding, **Vol. 4, Part 2**, 142; siege of, **Vol. 4, Part 1**, 184, 569; **Vol. 4, Part 2**, 490; **Vol. 10, Part 1**, 415, 514; **Vol. 10, Part 2**, 222; social service, **Vol. 8, Part 1**, 275 f.; south, development of, **Vol. 1, Part 1**, 177; South End House founded, **Vol. 10, Part 1**, 41; street cleaning, **Vol. 8, Part 1**, 308 f.; town hall, first, **Vol. 5, Part 2**, 225; trade, colonial period, **Vol. 4, Part 2**, 220; Tremont Temple, **Vol. 6, Part 1**, 412; Trinity Church, **Vol. 2, Part 1**, 85 f.; **Vol. 4, Part 1**, 137; **Vol. 7, Part 2**, 223, 228; water system, **Vol. 4, Part 2**, 109; **Vol. 8, Part 1**, 308 f.; **Vol. 9, Part 1**, 543; welfare organizations, **Supp. 9**, 210; West Church, **Vol. 1, Part 2**, 17; Wintergreen Club, **Vol. 8, Part 2**, 45; Women's Educational and Industrial Union, **Vol. 5, Part 2**, 287; writings about, **Vol. 1, Part 1**, 477; **Vol. 3, Part 1**, 433; **Vol. 10, Part 2**, 403; **Supp. 6**, 307

Boston & Lowell Railroad, **Vol. 5, Part 1**, 552; **Vol. 9, Part 2**, 98
Boston & Maine Railroad, **Vol. 5, Part 2**, 169; N. Y. Central merger, **Supp. 3**, 95
Boston & Westchester Railroad, **Vol. 8, Part 1**, 71 f.
Boston Adventure, **Supp. 10**, 754
Boston Art Club, **Vol. 8, Part 2**, 339
Boston Athenaeum, **Vol. 2, Part 1**, 233; **Vol. 3, Part 1**, 15 f.; **Vol. 5, Part 2**, 431; **Vol. 7, Part 2**, 272; **Vol. 8, Part 2**, 388; **Vol. 9, Part 1**, 49; **Supp. 6**, 307; architecture of, **Vol. 2, Part 1**, 394
Boston Braves (baseball), **Supp. 5**, 465; **Supp. 9**, 729, 763; **Supp. 10**, 573
Boston Children's Hospital, **Supp. 3**, 75
Boston City Club, founding of, **Supp. 2**, 626
Boston City Hospital: as teaching center, **Supp. 10**, 369; first clinical research laboratory, **Supp. 4**, 581–82; pathology laboratory, **Supp. 3**, 502–3, 805
Boston College, **Vol. 1, Part 1**, 584; **Vol. 4, Part 1**, 179; financial support, **Supp. 3**, 569; football team, **Supp. 9**, 484, 485
Boston Cook Book, **Vol. 6, Part 1**, 265
Boston Cooking School, **Vol. 3, Part 2**, 276; **Vol. 6, Part 1**, 265
Boston Daily Advertiser, **Vol. 4, Part 2**, 109; **Vol. 6, Part 1**, 563
Boston Daily Courier, **Vol. 5, Part 2**, 361; **Vol. 6, Part 1**, 508
Boston Daily Globe, **Vol. 9, Part 2**, 319
Boston Directory, **Vol. 7, Part 1**, 550
Boston Episcopal Charitable Society, **Vol. 2, Part 2**, 46
Boston Equal Suffrage Association for Good Government, founding of, **Supp. 5**, 532
Boston Evening American, **Supp. 5**, 323
Boston Evening Transcript, **Vol. 2, Part 2**, 198 f.; **Vol. 9, Part 2**, 483; **Supp. 5**, 518; **Supp. 8**, 447, 448; art criticism, **Supp. 3**, 195; arts pages, **Supp. 1**, 593
Boston Farm School, **Vol. 6, Part 1**, 518
Boston Gazette, **Vol. 3, Part 2**, 17; **Vol. 5, Part 2**, 458
Boston Herald-Traveler, **Supp. 5**, 518
Boston *Index*, **Vol. 10, Part 1**, 111
Boston Industrial School for Crippled and Deformed Children, **Vol. 1, Part 2**, 556
Boston Investigator, first rationalist journal in U.S., **Vol. 5, Part 2**, 457
Boston Journal, **Vol. 2, Part 2**, 118
Boston Latin School, **Vol. 1, Part 2**, 256; **Vol. 2, Part 2**, 48; **Vol. 4, Part 1**, 447; **Vol. 8, Part 1**, 80
Boston Lyceum Bureau, **Vol. 8, Part 1**, 444
Boston Massacre: **Vol. 1, Part 1**, 73, 97, 415, 421; **Vol. 4, Part 2**, 218; **Vol. 5, Part 1**, 441; **Vol. 7, Part 2**, 156; **Vol. 8, Part 1**, 307; **Vol. 10, Part 1**, 482; investigation of, **Vol. 3, Part 1**, 59; trial, **Vol. 7, Part 2**, 156; **Vol. 9, Part 2**, 654
Boston Medical Library, **Vol. 8, Part 1**, 275 f.; **Vol. 9, Part 2**, 94
Boston Medical Society, **Vol. 10, Part 1**, 479 f.
Boston Museum of Fine Arts: **Vol. 1, Part 2**, 261; **Vol. 3, Part 2**, 325; **Vol. 5, Part 2**, 485; **Vol. 7, Part 1**, 242; **Vol. 7, Part 2**, 465; **Vol. 8, Part 2**, 41; administration, **Supp. 6**, 124; Egyptology collection, **Supp. 3**, 627; **Supp. 4**, 902; Indian and Muhammadan Art collection, **Supp. 4**, 177; Oriental collection, **Supp. 1**, 641; **Supp. 3**, 465; teaching program, **Supp. 5**, 50
Boston Musical Review, **Vol. 7, Part 2**, 376
Boston Music Co., **Supp. 3**, 252
Boston News-Letter, first established paper in America, **Vol. 2, Part 1**, 456; **Vol. 3, Part 1**, 437 f.
Boston Patriot, **Vol. 3, Part 2**, 222
Boston Pilot, **Vol. 8, Part 2**, 63; **Supp. 3**, 569
Boston Pops Orchestra, directorship, **Supp. 10**, 237–38
Boston Port Act, John Adams's condemnation of, **Vol. 1, Part 1**, 73
Boston Post, **Supp. 8**, 219; music criticism, **Supp. 5**, 183
Boston Psychoanalytic Institute, **Supp. 3**, 191
Boston Psychopathic Hospital, **Supp. 3**, 102, 128
Boston Public Library, **Supp. 5**, 554; documents and statistics department, **Supp. 3**, 285–86
Boston Recorder, early religious weekly, **Vol. 4, Part 2**, 157
Boston Red Sox (baseball): **Supp. 4**, 710; **Supp. 5**, 125, 189; **Supp. 6**, 588–89; **Supp. 8**, 186; **Supp. 9**, 345, 403–4, 806; **Supp. 10**, 315, 346, 859–61; first black player, **Supp. 10**, 861
"Boston Report," concerning tariff, **Vol. 6, Part 1**, 108 f.
Boston School of Social Work, **Supp. 6**, 98; predecessor, **Supp. 4**, 101
Boston Settlement Council, **Supp. 6**, 499
Boston Sinfonietta (orchestral group), **Supp. 10**, 237
Boston Singers' Society, **Vol. 7, Part 2**, 78
Boston Society of Architects, **Vol. 8, Part 2**, 342
Boston Society of Civil Engineers, **Vol. 6, Part 1**, 36
Boston Society of Landscape Architects, **Vol. 7, Part 2**, 30
Boston Society of Natural History, **Vol. 1, Part 2**, 279; **Supp. 3**, 8–9
Boston Society of Printers, founding of, **Supp. 3**, 785
Boston Society for Medical Improvement, **Vol. 10, Part 1**, 449 f.
Boston Society for the Relief of Destitute Mothers and Infants, **Vol. 8, Part 1**, 275
Boston Symphony Orchestra, **Vol. 3, Part 1**, 71; **Vol. 4, Part 1**, 220; **Vol. 5, Part 1**, 12; **Vol. 6, Part 1**, 293; **Supp. 5**, 398–99; **Supp. 6**, 456; **Supp. 7**, 548–49, 652; **Supp. 8**, 451; **Supp. 10**, 236, 237, 423
Boston Tea Party, **Vol. 1, Part 1**, 73, 78, 98; **Vol. 4, Part 1**, 88; **Vol. 4, Part 2**, 390; **Vol. 5, Part 1**, 442; **Vol. 8, Part 1**, 308, 515; **Vol. 8, Part 2**, 539; **Vol. 9, Part 2**, 234; **Vol. 10, Part 2**, 635
Boston Theatre, **Vol. 8, Part 1**, 150 f.
Boston Transcript, **Vol. 8, Part 2**, 359
Boston University: **Vol. 1, Part 2**, 260, 522; **Vol. 5, Part 1**, 420; **Vol. 9, Part 1**, 208; **Vol. 10, Part 1**, 490 f.; **Vol. 10, Part 2**, 4; expansion, **Supp. 5**, 90; founding of, **Vol. 10, Part 1**, 490 f.; gastroenterology studies, **Supp. 10**, 369
Boston Young Men's Congress, **Vol. 2, Part 2**, 367
Boswell, James, manuscripts, **Supp. 5**, 349–50
Botanical Gazette, **Vol. 1, Part 1**, 629; **Vol. 2, Part 2**, 468
Boswell Sisters (music group), **Supp. 10**, 59
Botanical Society of America, founding of, **Supp. 1**, 121
Botany: **Vol. 1, Part 1**, 208, 229, 236, 407 f., 498, 513 f., 546, 548, 575, 593, 599, 629; **Vol. 2, Part 1**, 25, 232; **Vol. 2, Part 2**, 16, 288 f., 306 f., 467f.; **Vol. 3, Part 2**, 99, 105, 274; **Vol. 4, Part 1**, 378, 511 f., 564 f.; **Vol. 4, Part 2**, 312, 354; **Vol. 5, Part 1**, 590; **Vol. 5, Part 2**, 262 f., 300, 472 f., 499, 511, 612; **Vol. 6, Part 1**, 68, 162, 274; **Vol. 6, Part 2**, 312; **Vol. 7, Part 1**, 17, 308, 596 f.; **Vol. 8, Part 1**, 104 f., 236 f., 396, 589 f., 598; **Vol. 8, Part 2**, 159 f., 188, 269, 374, 609; **Vol. 9, Part 1**, 39; **Vol. 9, Part 2**, 598; **Vol. 10, Part 1**, 396 f., 547 f.; Alabama, **Vol. 7, Part 1**, 77 f.; Arizona, **Vol. 6, Part 1**, 162; book collections, **Supp. 2**, 390; botanic gardens, **Vol. 2, Part 1**, 100; **Vol. 6, Part 1**, 465; **Vol. 7, Part 2**, 480; **Vol. 8, Part 1**, 445; **Vol. 8, Part 2**, 269; **Vol. 9, Part 1**, 38; **Vol. 9, Part 2**, 597; **Supp. 4**, 16–17; **Supp. 6**, 450; botanic gardens, first instructional, **Supp. 3**, 775–76; California, **Vol. 6, Part 1**, 162; **Supp. 4**, 428–29; Canadian Northwest, **Supp. 8**, 3; classification systems, **Vol. 8, Part 1**, 322 f.; **Supp. 3**, 23; **Supp. 7**, 625; Colorado, **Vol. 7**,

Part 2, 262; cryptogams (lower plants), Supp. 5, 98; cycads, Supp. 3, 153–54; ecology, Supp. 3, 168–70; economic, Supp. 4, 17; edible wild plants, Supp. 4, 266; Supp. 9, 307, 308; experimental, Supp. 2, 374; explorations, Vol. 8, Part 2, 632; Vol. 8, Part 1, 236 f., 271; genetic studies, Supp. 2, 113; Supp. 8, 596; glass models, Vol. 4, Part 1, 378; government survey, Vol. 8, Part 2, 269, 288; grasses studies, Supp. 7, 119–20; herbariums, Supp. 1, 632; Supp. 4, 16–17; hybridization, Supp. 10, 80, 81, 271; plant hormone studies, Supp. 10, 297; Illinois, Vol. 2, Part 1, 327; Maine, Vol. 10, Part 2, 617; marine algae, Supp. 3, 703–4; medical, Vol. 1, Part 2, 258; Vol. 8, Part 1, 79; Vol. 9, Part 2, 488; Vol. 10, Part 2, 208; medieval, Supp. 7, 742; morphological emphasis, Supp. 8, 596; Mexico, Vol. 5, Part 2, 425; Vol. 8, Part 1, 236 f.; mulberry, cultivation of, Vol. 3, Part 1, 595; museum, Vol. 4, Part 1, 378; mycology, Vol. 5, Part 2, 262; Vol. 7, Part 2, 373; Nevada, Vol. 6, Part 1, 162; New York, Vol. 7, Part 2, 373; Vol. 9, Part 2, 597; nomenclature, Supp. 1, 122, 632; North Carolina, Vol. 7, Part 1, 45; northeastern American, Supp. 4, 266; organizations, Supp. 1, 121; paleobotany, Supp. 1, 416, 702; Supp. 3, 62; plant anatomy, Supp. 2, 488; plant collections, Supp. 2, 591; plant pathology, Supp. 3, 814–15; popularization of, Vol. 3, Part 1, 78 f.; Vol. 10, Part 1, 116; professorship, first in U.S., Vol. 5, Part 2, 511, publication of U.S. flora, first complete, Vol. 8, Part 1, 271; South Carolina, Vol. 10, Part 1, 396 f.; southern states, Vol. 3, Part 1, 72; teaching of, Vol. 4, Part 1, 98, Vol. 5, Part 1, 240, 305; Vol. 5, Part 2, 262; Vol. 7, Part 1, 17; Vol. 9, Part 1, 127, 427; Vol. 9, Part 2, 398, 514, 603; Texas, Vol. 6, Part 1, 274; Vol. 10, Part 2, 546; Vermont, Vol. 1, Part 2, 593; West, American, Vol. 7, Part 2, 262; writings on, Vol. 1, Part 2, 18, 229; Vol. 2, Part 1, 100, 232; Vol. 3, Part 1, 268, 417, 485, 538, 605 f., 615 f.; Vol. 4, Part 1, 378, 511, 565; Vol. 5, Part 2, 263, 472, 499; Vol. 7, Part 1, 18, 50, 72, 309; Vol. 8, Part 1, 104, 116, 239 f., 249, 271, 396; Vol. 8, Part 2, 270, 288; Vol. 9, Part 1, 53; Vol. 9, Part 2, 398, 488; Vol. 10, Part 1, 43, 52, 116, 396 f., 435, 547 f.; Supp. 3, 776; Supp. 6, 450. *See also* Horticulture

Bothe, Walter, reference to, Supp. 7, 134

Bottles, manufacture of, Vol. 7, Part 2, 122

Bottle-stopper, invention of, Vol. 7, Part 2, 167

Boudinot, Elias, reference to, Vol. 6, Part 1, 419

Bouillon, Jo-Baker, J., relationship, Supp. 9, 61

Boulanger, Nadia, reference to, Supp. 10, 312

Boulder Dam. *See* Hoover Dam

Boulware, Lemuel, reference to, Supp. 9, 874

Boundary questions: Vol. 5, Part 2, 344; Vol. 6, Part 1, 261; Vol. 7, Part 1, 51; Vol. 8, Part 1, 426; Alaska, Vol. 3, Part 1, 35 f., 92, 298, 315; Vol. 5, Part 2, 167; Vol. 6, Part 1, 348; Vol. 7, Part 1, 640; Vol. 9, Part 1, 492; Vol. 10, Part 1, 540 f.; British Guiana, Vol. 1, Part 1, 235; Canada, Vol. 1, Part 2, 576; Vol. 5, Part 2, 167, 455; Vol. 8, Part 1, 506; Vol. 8, Part 2, 507 f.; Vol. 9, Part 2, 455; Connecticut, Vol. 5, Part 2, 41; Vol. 8, Part 1, 290 f., 426; Vol. 9, Part 2, 633; Vol. 10, Part 1, 121; Delaware, Vol. 1, Part 2, 460; Vol. 5, Part 2, 42; Florida, Vol. 3, Part 1, 557 f.; Illinois, Vol. 8, Part 1, 77 f.; Iowa, Vol. 3, Part 1, 601 f.; Kentucky, Vol. 4, Part 2, 513; Maine, Vol. 3, Part 1, 79, 515 f.; Vol. 3, Part 2, 258 f.; Vol. 8, Part 1, 71 f., 100, 505; Massachusetts, Vol. 1, Part 2, 460; Vol. 5, Part 2, 41, 150, 608; Vol. 8, Part 1, 290 f., 422, 423, 426; Vol. 10, Part 1, 121; Mexico, Vol. 1, Part 2, 7; Vol. 8, Part 1, 353 f.; Vol. 9, Part 2, 260; Michigan, Vol. 2, Part 2, 185; Mississippi, Vol. 6, Part 1, 29; New Brunswick, Vol. 3, Part 1, 515 f.; Vol. 8, Part 1, 71 f., 100, 505; New Hampshire, Vol. 5, Part 1, 439; Vol. 8, Part 1, 426; New Jersey, Vol. 5, Part 2, 6, 11; Vol. 7, Part 1, 363; Vol. 7, Part 2, 228; New York, Vol. 5, Part 2, 6, 11, 150, 608; Vol. 8, Part 1, 426, 633; North Carolina, Vol. 5, Part 1, 449; Vol. 5, Part 2, 140; Vol. 8, Part 1, 42; Ohio, Vol. 2, Part 2, 185; Oregon, Vol. 7, Part 2, 119; Vol. 8, Part 1, 34 f.; Pennsylvania, Vol. 1, Part 2, 17; Vol. 5, Part 2, 42, 47; Vol. 8, Part 1, 82 f.; Rhode Island, Vol. 1, Part 2, 460; Vol. 8, Part 1, 426; Vol. 10, Part 1, 121; South Carolina, Vol. 5, Part 2, 140; Vol. 8, Part 1, 42; Spain, Vol. 3, Part 1, 507 f.; Vol. 5, Part 2, 423; territorial, Vol. 8, Part 1, 78; Texas, Vol. 1, Part 2, 125; Vol. 8, Part 2, 237; Vermont, Vol. 5, Part 2, 608; Virginia, Vol. 3, Part 2, 298

Bounties, military, Vol. 8, Part 1, 281 f., 284 f.

Bounty, Mutiny on the, Vol. 9, Part 2, 592; Supp. 5, 266–67

"Bounty jumping," Vol. 6, Part 1, 252

Bourke-White, Margaret, reference to, Supp. 4, 806

Bourne, Jonathan, reference to, Supp. 4, 844

Bourne, Randolph, references to, Supp. 4, 702; Supp. 6, 557, 572

Bovard, Oliver K., reference to, Supp. 5, 552

Boveri, Theodore, reference to, Supp. 4, 516

Bovine tuberculosis, Supp. 4, 684

Bow, Clara: first sound film, Supp. 10, 11; reference to, Supp. 8, 678; Supp. 9, 538

Bowditch, Henry Pickering, references to, Vol. 10, Part 1, 481 f.; Supp. 3, 133; Supp. 4, 676

Bowditch, Nathaniel, reference to, Vol. 7, Part 2, 394

Bowdoin College: Vol. 1, Part 1, 328; Vol. 3, Part 1, 515 f.; Vol. 4, Part 2, 319; Vol. 5, Part 1, 332, 452; Vol. 7, Part 1, 586; Vol. 7, Part 2, 125; Vol. 9, Part 1, 78, 379; Vol. 10, Part 2, 503; English literature and language studies, Supp. 5, 118; founding of, Vol. 1, Part 2, 501; growth of, Vol. 1, Part 1, 209; Vol. 6, Part 2, 83; influence of Newman, Vol. 7, Part 1, 466; "Phi Chi" Song, Vol. 7, Part 1, 43

Bowdoin Scientific Review, Vol. 4, Part 1, 378

Bowen, Ira S., reference to, Supp. 5, 496

Bowen, Norman L., reference to, Supp. 6, 144

"Bowery Boys" (fictional characters), Supp. 8, 220

Bowie, James, reference to, Vol. 9, Part 2, 630

Bowie knife, origin of, Vol. 1, Part 2, 510

Bowker, R. R., Co., Supp. 7, 525; Supp. 9, 738, 739

Bowles, Chester, references to, Supp. 7, 723; Supp. 9, 58, 80, 81

Bowles, Paul: Bowles, J., relationship, Supp. 9, 115, 116; homosexuality, Supp. 9, 115

Bowles, Samuel, reference to, Vol. 5, Part 1, 147

Bowling Green, Ky., operation about (1861–62), Vol. 2, Part 1, 235, 240; Vol. 4, Part 1, 494; Vol. 5, Part 2, 136

Bowne, Borden Parker, references to, Supp. 5, 90, 91

Bowron, Fletcher, reference to, Supp. 3, 156

Boxer Rebellion (1900): Vol. 1, Part 1, 106, 241, 263; Vol. 2, Part 1, 589–90; Vol. 3, Part 1, 110; Vol. 4, Part 2, 434; Vol. 5, Part 2, 324; Vol. 6, Part 1, 475; Vol. 6, Part 2, 108; Vol. 9, Part 1, 238; Vol. 9, Part 2, 372; Vol. 10, Part 2, 335; Supp. 7, 358

Boxing: Vol. 8, Part 2, 222; black heavyweights, Supp. 6, 362–63, 699–700; Supp. 9, 493–94, 507; cartoons, Vol. 3, Part 1, 378 f.; featherweight, Supp. 7, 209; first black heavyweight champion, Supp. 4, 432–34; first white heavyweight champion since 1937, Supp. 8, 417–18; Golden Gloves, Supp. 9, 506; Supp. 10, 268, 736; "Great White Hope," Supp. 5, 368–69; heavyweight championship bouts, Supp. 9, 121–22, 172, 493, 507; Supp. 10, 797–98; left hook, Supp. 1, 201; light-heavyweight bouts, Supp. 9, 122, 171; Supp. 10, 797; "long-count"

bout, **Supp. 10**, 798; middleweight, **Supp. 5**, 418; promotion, **Vol. 8, Part 1**, 585 f.; **Supp. 5**, 359–60; **Supp. 7**, 414–15; radio broadcasts, **Supp. 7**, 494–95; rating system developed, **Supp. 9**, 285; reform campaign, **Supp. 9**, 285; training sites, **Supp. 9**, 343
Boyce Thompson Institute, founding of, **Supp. 4**, 191
Boyd, Ernest, reference to, **Supp. 6**, 471
Boyd, William, reference to, **Supp. 6**, 466
Boyden, Allen, reference to, **Supp. 4**, 420
Boyle, Kay, references to, **Supp. 10**, 247, 294
Boyle, William, Jr., reference to, **Supp. 9**, 500
Boylston Medical School, founding of, **Vol. 5, Part 2**, 459
Boy Meets Girl, **Supp. 9**, 748
Boys Brotherhood Republic, founding of, **Supp. 4**, 870
Boy Scouts of America: **Vol. 8, Part 2**, 432; administration, **Supp. 4**, 871–72; founding of, **Supp. 4**, 737; **Supp. 5**, 138, 325; rural services, **Supp. 5**, 51; uniform design, **Supp. 3**, 44–45
Boys, Inc., **Supp. 6**, 541
Boy's King Arthur, **Vol. 5, Part 2**, 604
Boys' Life: **Supp. 3**, 45; illustration, **Supp. 10**, 689
Boys Town (Nebr.), **Supp. 4**, 594; founding of, **Supp. 4**, 282–83
Boy's Will, The, **Supp. 7**, 271, 272
Bozeman Trail, **Vol. 1, Part 2**, 538; **Vol. 8, Part 1**, 437
Brach Candy Co., **Supp. 9**, 245
Brachiopods, **Supp. 3**, 696
Brackenridge, H. H., reference to, **Vol. 8, Part 2**, 526
Bradbury, Ray, reference to, **Supp. 6**, 166
Bradbury, William B., reference to, **Vol. 7, Part 1**, 470
Braddock, James, Lewis heavyweight bout, **Supp. 9**, 493
Braddock Expedition, **Vol. 1, Part 2**, 550; **Vol. 3, Part 1**, 317; **Vol. 4, Part 1**, 87, 184, 327; **Vol. 6, Part 2**, 183; **Vol. 7, Part 1**, 100, 226; **Vol. 9, Part 1**, 59, 121; **Vol. 10, Part 1**, 525
Bradford, William, references to, **Vol. 7, Part 1**, 254; **Vol. 9, Part 2**, 503; writings of, **Supp. 3**, 286
Bradley, F. H., reference to, **Vol. 5, Part 1**, 594 f.
Bradley, Omar N., reference to, **Supp. 8**, 267–68
Bradley Polytechnic Institute, **Vol. 1, Part 2**, 574
Brady, James B. ("Diamond Jim"), reference to, **Supp. 3**, 854; **Supp. 6**, 22
Brady, William A., reference to, **Supp. 6**, 65
Bragan, Bobby, references to, **Supp. 10**, 574
Bragg, Braxton, reference to, **Vol. 1, Part 1**, 266
Brahms, Johannes, reference to, **Supp. 7**, 444
Braille, **Supp. 3**, 365; **Supp. 4**, 11; **Supp. 5**, 347
Brain: behavior relationship, **Supp. 2**, 664; damage, rehabilitation for, **Supp. 1**, 316–17; damage studies, **Supp. 10**, 779, 780; embryological development of, **Supp. 4**, 801, 802; functional organization studies, **Supp. 2**, 162; growth studies, **Supp. 2**, 156; metabolism studies, **Supp. 4**, 618; prefrontal lobotomy, **Supp. 6**, 223; research in, **Supp. 2**, 406; studies of, **Vol. 5, Part 2**, 325; **Vol. 9, Part 1**, 461; surgery, **Supp. 6**, 70, 130–31, 223–24; tumor diagnosis, **Supp. 4**, 214, 250; **Supp. 5**, 384. *See also* Intelligence; Nervous system
Brain Trust: **Supp. 3**, 399–400; **Supp. 4**, 136; **Supp. 8**, 679; **Supp. 9**, 84, 85, 553; concept established, **Supp. 9**, 680; formation, **Supp. 3**, 647; labor board representative, **Supp. 9**, 706
Brakes: bicycle, **Vol. 8, Part 2**, 56; elevator, **Vol. 7, Part 2**, 93
Branch Will Not Break, The, **Supp. 10**, 854
Brancusi, Constantin, reference to, **Supp. 6**, 194
Brandegee, Frank, reference to, **Supp. 6**, 59
Brandeis, Louis D.: Public Franchise League, **Supp. 3**, 240; railroad rate-setting, **Supp. 3**, 212; references to, **Supp. 2**, 266; **Supp. 3**, 472; **Supp. 5**, 571, 573, 574; **Supp. 6**, 35, 271, 556, 591, 677; **Supp. 7**, 261, 262, 263, 264; Zionism, **Supp. 3**, 279–80, 489; **Supp. 9**, 7
Brandeis University: original faculty, **Supp. 5**, 425, 426; psychology studies, **Supp. 8**, 423
Brandenburg v. *Ohio*, **Supp. 7**, 317
Brandt, Carl, reference to, **Supp. 3**, 57
Brandt, Raymond P., reference to, **Supp. 3**, 92
Brandy Station, Va., operation at (1863), **Vol. 6, Part 1**, 134; **Vol. 8, Part 1**, 8; **Vol. 9, Part 2**, 171
Brandywine, battle of, **Vol. 1, Part 1**, 176; **Vol. 1, Part 2**, 356; **Vol. 5, Part 2**, 536; **Vol. 8, Part 1**, 259; **Vol. 9, Part 2**, 193; **Vol. 10, Part 1**, 517, 563
Branford, Conn., early land grant, **Vol. 3, Part 1**, 611
Braniff Airways: Calder design for flagship, **Supp. 10**, 92; founding of, **Supp. 5**, 86
Braque, Georges, references to, **Supp. 6**, 552, 553
Brass manufacture, **Vol. 2, Part 1**, 72; **Vol. 2, Part 2**, 261 f.; **Vol. 3, Part 2**, 425; **Vol. 4, Part 2**, 440; **Vol. 5, Part 1**, 166; **Vol. 8, Part 2**, 448; **Supp. 1**, 58
Braunell Ltd., **Supp. 8**, 397
Braut, Bessie, reference to, **Supp. 9**, 705
Brave New World, **Supp. 7**, 380
Bray, John Randolph, reference to, **Supp. 9**, 797
Brazil: Caffery ambassadorship, **Supp. 9**, 154; diplomacy, **Vol. 1, Part 1**, 285; **Vol. 1, Part 2**, 392; **Vol. 9, Part 2**, 473, 567; **Vol. 10, Part 1**, 49; diplomacy with U.S., **Supp. 1**, 563; **Supp. 5**, 345; **Supp. 6**, 254; education, **Vol. 5, Part 2**, 575; geological survey, **Vol. 1, Part 2**, 603; **Vol. 8, Part 1**, 387; hydroelectric power, **Supp. 4**, 80–81; missions, **Vol. 5, Part 2**, 561, 575; Navy, **Vol. 5, Part 2**, 67 f.; Presbyterian church, **Vol. 5, Part 2**, 575; railroad development, **Vol. 4, Part 2**, 294; **Vol. 8, Part 2**, 19; transit systems, **Supp. 5**, 215; writings on, **Vol. 1, Part 1**, 114; **Vol. 4, Part 1**, 180; **Vol. 5, Part 2**, 565 f.
Brazilian Traction, Light and Power Co., **Supp. 4**, 81–82
Bread, regulations concerning, **Vol. 4, Part 1**, 480
"Bread Crust" papers, **Vol. 6, Part 1**, 285
Bread Loaf School of English, **Supp. 7**, 797
Bread Loaf Writers' Conference (Middlebury, Vt.), **Supp. 4**, 13; **Supp. 9**, 277
Bread-Winners' College, **Vol. 3, Part 1**, 96 f.; **Vol. 7, Part 2**, 266
Brearley School (New York City), **Supp. 4**, 847
Breast: cancer education, **Supp. 10**, 30; cancer treatment, **Supp. 6**, 70; reconstruction of, **Supp. 6**, 631–32
Breasted, James Henry, reference to, **Supp. 4**, 902
Breast-feeding, maternal milk collection stations, **Supp. 3**, 159
Breathitt County, Ky., demonstration school, **Supp. 4**, 365
Brecht, Bertolt, references to, **Supp. 4**, 868; **Supp. 7**, 61
Breckinridge, Sophonisba, reference to, **Supp. 6**, 1
Breed's Hill (Boston). *See* Bunker Hill (Boston)
Breitmann Ballads, **Vol. 6, Part 1**, 159
Brennan, Walter, reference to, **Supp. 9**, 282
Brennan, William, **Supp. 9**, 837; reference to, **Supp. 10**, 189
Brent, Charles H., reference to, **Supp. 3**, 111
Brero, Vittorio, references to, **Supp. 7**, 511, 512
Bresnahan, Lawrence J., reference to, **Supp. 8**, 421
Breton, André, reference to, **Supp. 6**, 512
Bretton Woods Agreements Act (1945), **Supp. 8**, 616
Brewing, **Vol. 5, Part 2**, 168 f.
Brewster, William, references to, **Vol. 7, Part 1**, 254; **Vol. 9, Part 1**, 500
Brice, Fanny, references to, **Supp. 8**, 546, 547

Brice's Crossroads, Miss., engagement at, **Vol. 3, Part 2**, 532; **Vol. 9, Part 2**, 183
Brick, manufacture of, **Vol. 4, Part 2**, 77, 506; **Vol. 8, Part 1**, 395, 466 f.
Bricker, John W., reference to, **Supp. 7**, 84; **Supp. 8**, 157
Bricker Amendment, **Supp. 6**, 336, 361
Bridge: auction, **Vol. 5, Part 2**, 153; **Vol. 10, Part 2**, 130, 533; contract, **Supp. 5**, 146; **Supp. 6**, 134, 380
Bridge, The, **Supp. 1**, 207
Bridge of San Luis Rey, The, **Supp. 9**, 870, 871; **Supp. 10**, 668
Bridge on the River Kwai, The, **Supp. 9**, 372
Bridgeport, Conn., Socialist mayor, **Supp. 7**, 503
Bridges, Calvin B., references to, **Supp. 3**, 539–40; **Supp. 8**, 448
Bridges, Harry, references to, **Supp. 6**, 396; **Supp. 7**, 73, 96, 119, 292, 609
Bridges, Robert, reference to, **Supp. 4**, 755–56
Bridges, Styles, references to, **Supp. 5**, 338, 690
Bridges: bascule, **Supp. 2**, 637; caissons, **Vol. 8, Part 2**, 90; collapse of, **Vol. 9, Part 2**, 70; covered, etchings of, **Vol. 8, Part 1**, 9; design and construction, **Vol. 1, Part 1**, 147, 194; **Vol. 1, Part 2**, 421, 441; **Vol. 2, Part 1**, 227; **Vol. 2, Part 2**, 110, 413 f., 497; **Vol. 3, Part l**, 459 f., 587 f., 602; **Vol. 3, Part 2**, 387, 445, 539; **Vol. 4, Part 2**, 307; **Vol. 5, Part 1**, 298; **Vol. 5, Part 2**, 59, 261, 455; **Vol. 6, Part 1**, 27, 549, 565 f.; **Vol. 7, Part 1**, 191, 351, 355; **Vol. 8, Part 1**, 179; **Vol. 8, Part 2**, 19, 48, 52, 88 f., 577, 592 f.; **Vol. 9, Part 1**, 251, 368, 538; **Vol. 9, Part 2**, 70, 385, 611; **Vol. 10, Part 1**, 372 f.; **Vol. 10, Part 2**, 2, 71, 339; **Supp. 1**, 136, 498; **Supp. 2**, 29, 463; **Supp. 3**, 77, 530–31; **Supp. 6**, 331–32, 367, 594; **Supp. 7**, 11–12; foundation work, **Supp. 2**, 469–70; Hell-Gate Bridge, **Vol. 8, Part 1**, 418; "Latrobe's Folly," **Vol. 6, Part 2**, 26; navigable streams, **Vol. 8, Part 1**, 253 f.; Newburyport, Mass., **Vol. 8, Part 1**, 179; railroad, **Supp. 2**, 638; St. Louis, **Vol. 3, Part 1**, 587 f.; Schuylkill River, **Vol. 3, Part 1**, 549 f.; subaqueous foundations, **Vol. 9, Part 1**, 397; suspension, **Vol. 3, Part 2**, 87; **Vol. 4, Part 2**, 156; **Vol. 8, Part 2**, 88; **Supp. 7**, 135–36; turntable for swing, **Supp. 3**, 367; truss, **Vol. 3, Part 2**, 387; **Vol. 8, Part 1**, 179; **Vol. 9, Part 2**, 70; **Vol. 10, Part 1**, 487 f.; vertical lift, **Supp. 2**, 686; **Supp. 3**, 332. *See also* Tunnels; *specific bridge names*
Bridges v. *California*, **Supp. 9**, 96
Bridge Too Far, A, **Supp. 9**, 691
Bridgewater, Canada. *See* Lundy's Lane
Bridgewater Collection, **Vol. 7, Part 1**, 59
Bridge World, founding of, **Supp. 5**, 146; **Supp. 6**, 134, 135
Bridgman, Laura, reference to, **Vol. 5, Part 1**, 296; **Supp. 8**, 316
Bridgman, Percy W., references to, **Supp. 4**, 807; **Supp. 8**, 482
Brieux, Eugene, reference to, **Supp. 3**, 58
Brigandage, **Vol. 7, Part 1**, 370; **Vol. 9, Part 2**, 74; **Vol. 10, Part 2**, 636
Briggs, Charles A., reference to, **Supp. 3**, 110
Briggs, John, reference to, **Supp. 10**, 537
Briggs, Le Baron R., reference to, **Supp. 3**, 470
Briggs, Walter O., reference to, **Supp. 10**, 316
Briggs v. *Elliot*, **Supp. 8**, 682
Brighton, Mass., early history of, **Vol. 3, Part 1**, 430
Brill, Abraham A., references to, **Supp. 3**, 236, 386; **Supp. 5**, 517
Brillo Manufacturing Co., **Supp. 9**, 510–11
Brillo Pads, **Supp. 9**, 510, 511
Brill's disease, **Supp. 4**, 667
Brine, electrolysis of, **Supp. 2**, 314
Brines, commercial processing of, **Supp. 1**, 261
Brinkley, David, reference to, **Supp. 9**, 415
Brinkley, John, reference to, **Supp. 8**, 706
Brisbane, Arthur, references to, **Supp. 3**, 504; **Supp. 5**, 284; **Supp. 6**, 232
Brisbane, Walter, reference to, **Supp. 3**, 19–20
Brissot, scheme to seize Louisiana, **Vol. 5, Part 1**, 461 f.
Bristol, R. I., **Vol. 3, Part 1**, 275, 312
Bristol Itinerant Society, founding of, **Supp. 1**, 332
Bristol-Myers Co., **Supp. 10**, 624
British: captive seamen, **Vol. 8, Part 2**, 175; colonial policy, **Vol. 1, Part 2**, 137; Indian support, **Vol. 9, Part 2**, 359 f.; severity to Continentals, **Vol. 4, Part 2**, 454; spies, **Vol. 7, Part 1**, 106; war with, averted, **Vol. 8, Part 2**, 508
British Broadcasting Corporation (BBC), radio programs, **Supp. 10**, 85, 103
British Museum, mammalogy collection, **Supp. 6**, 454
Britten, Benjamin, reference to, **Supp. 9**, 55
Broadcasting. *See* Radio; Television
Broadhurst, George, reference to, **Supp. 3**, 198
Broad Seal War, **Vol. 7, Part 2**, 443
Broadus, John, reference to, **Supp. 6**, 671
Broadway. *See* Theater
Brobeck, William, reference to, **Supp. 6**, 370
Brödel, Max, reference to, **Supp. 3**, 412; **Supp. 5**, 147
Broderick, David, reference to, **Vol. 9, Part 2**, 380
Broderick, Johnny, reference to, **Supp. 7**, 667
Brokerage houses. *See* Stock market
Bromine, Dow process, **Supp. 1**, 261
Bromley, Dorothy Dunbar, reference to, **Supp. 8**, 520
Bronchoscope, development of, **Supp. 6**, 317
Broneer, Oscar, reference to, **Supp. 4**, 144
Brontosaurus skeleton, **Supp. 3**, 316
Bronx (New York City), politics, **Supp. 5**, 227–28
Bronx House (New York City), founding of, **Supp. 4**, 603
Bronxville (N. Y.), individualized education system, **Supp. 7**, 42
Bronx-Whitestone Bridge (New York City), **Supp. 3**, 531; **Supp. 7**, 12
Bronx Zoo. *See* New York Zoological Park
Bronze casting, **Vol. 7, Part 1**, 5; **Vol. 8, Part 1**, 274 f.
Brooke, John R., reference to, **Supp. 2**, 332
Brookes, Norman, reference to, **Supp. 6**, 421
Brook Farm: **Vol. 3, Part 1**, 49, 284, 567 f.; **Vol. 3, Part 2**, 137; **Vol. 4, Part 1**, 351; **Vol. 5, Part 1**, 578; **Vol. 8, Part 1**, 623 f.; Hawthorne at, **Vol. 4, Part 2**, 426; journal of, **Vol. 3, Part 1**, 567 f., 624
Brookhaven National Laboratory (N.Y.): **Supp. 6**, 501; nuclear reactor construction, **Supp. 10**, 320; physics studies, **Supp. 10**, 289
Brookings, Robert S., references to, **Supp. 6**, 250, 271
Brookings Institution: **Vol. 10, Part 2**, 563; **Supp. 5**, 537, 538; **Supp. 6**, 271, 586, 600; **Supp. 10**, 287; founding of, **Supp. 1**, 123; Indian affairs survey, **Supp. 4**, 165–66
Brooklyn, N. Y.: battle of, **Vol. 1, Part 1**, 175–76; **Vol. 4, Part 1**, 332; **Vol. 7, Part 2**, 270; **Vol. 8, Part 1**, 281–82; **Vol. 9, Part 2**, 192; **Vol. 10, Part 1**, 515; civic service, **Vol. 1, Part 2**, 372; **Vol. 4, Part 2**, 121, 537; **Vol. 7, Part 1**, 351; **Vol. 8, Part 2**, 430; **Vol. 9, Part 2**, 123; **Vol. 10, Part 2**, 87; "common school revival" in, **Vol. 2, Part 1**, 250; consolidation of, with New York City, **Vol. 9, Part 2**, 123; drama, **Vol. 4, Part 2**, 339 f.; Gothic churches, **Supp. 1**, 480; Greenwood Cemetery, **Vol. 3, Part 1**, 406; medical service, **Vol. 9, Part 1**, 443; modern paving introduced, **Vol. 8, Part 1**, 442; Plymouth Institute, **Vol. 5, Part 1**, 56; Prospect Park, **Vol. 6, Part 1**, 294; **Vol. 7, Part 2**, 26 f.; **Vol. 9, Part 2**, 123; religious service, **Vol. 3, Part 1**, 19; **Vol. 8, Part 1**, 322; **Vol. 8, Part 2**, 240; street

railways, **Vol. 3, Part 2**, 480; **Vol. 6, Part 1**, 294; **Vol. 7, Part 2**, 358
Brooklyn Academy of Design, **Vol. 4, Part 2**, 361 f.
Brooklyn Anatomical and Surgical Society, founding of, **Supp. 1**, 599
Brooklyn-Battery Tunnel, **Supp. 6**, 587
Brooklyn Bridge: **Vol. 1, Part 1**, 194; **Vol. 7, Part 1**, 351; **Vol. 8, Part 2**, 88 f., 577; modernization, **Supp. 6**, 594
Brooklyn City Planning Committee, founding of **Supp. 4**, 56
Brooklyn College, psychology studies, **Supp. 8**, 423
Brooklyn Collegiate and Polytechnic Institute, **Vol. 4, Part 1**, 416; **Vol. 6, Part 1**, 484; **Vol. 8, Part 1**, 412, **Vol. 10, Part 2**, 462
Brooklyn Daily Eagle: founding of, **Vol. 7, Part 1**, growth of, **Vol. 6, Part 2**, 85; **Vol. 7, Part 1**, 351
Brooklyn Daily Times, founding of, **Vol. 4, Part 2**, 35
Brooklyn Dodgers (baseball): **Supp. 8**, 142, 558–59; **Supp. 9**, 178, 389–90, 532, 543–44, 668–69; 730, 763, 857–58; **Supp. 10**, 99–100, 279, 605–6; black players, **Supp. 8**, 142; "Boys of Summer," **Supp. 9**, 390; predecessor, **Supp. 7**, 751–52
Brooklyn Eagle, **Supp. 7**, 409
Brooklyn Edison Co., **Supp. 3**, 716
Brooklyn Ethical Association, **Vol. 5, Part 1**, 606
Brooklyn Museum, Exposition of Indian Tribal Arts, **Supp. 3**, 55
Brooklyn Robins (baseball), **Supp. 7**, 751–52
Brooklyn Philharmonic Society, **Vol. 9, Part 2**, 424
"Brooklyn Ring," **Vol. 5, Part 1**, 522
"Brooklyn Tabernacle," **Vol. 8, Part 2**, 240
Brooklyn *Union*, **Vol. 9, Part 2**, 552
Brookmeade Stable, **Supp. 7**, 695–96
Brooks, Alexander, reference to, **Supp. 3**, 278
Brooks, Cleanth, reference to, **Supp. 9**, 885
Brooks, Joseph, reference to, **Vol. 1, Part 2**, 62
Brooks, Phillips: biography of, **Supp. 6**, 306; references to, **Vol. 5, Part 1**, 12; **Supp. 3**, 221, 591
Brooks, Van Wyck, references to, **Supp. 4**, 702; **Supp. 6**, 557; **Supp. 7**, 18
Brooks, William K., reference to, **Supp. 6**, 281
Brooks and Baxter War (1868), **Vol. 1, Part 2**, 62; **Vol. 2, Part 2**, 187; **Vol. 3, Part 2**, 244
Brookwood Labor College (Katonah, N. Y.), founding of, **Supp. 8**, 458
Broom: An International Magazine of the Arts, **Supp. 8**, 350
Brothels. *See* Prostitution
Brotherhood of Locomotive Engineers, **Vol. 9, Part 2**, 86
Brotherhood of Locomotive Firemen, **Vol. 2, Part 1**, 545; **Vol. 3, Part 1**, 183
Brotherhood of Railroad Trainmen, **Vol. 6, Part 1**, 133; leadership, **Supp. 4**, 889–90
Brotherhood of Railway Trainmen, dispute arbitration, **Supp. 5**, 651
Brotherhood of Sleeping Car Porters, **Supp. 6**, 648; **Supp. 7**, 155; organizing of, **Supp. 10**, 659
Brotherhood of the Kingdom, **Vol. 8, Part 1**, 393
Brotherhood of the Union, **Vol. 6, Part 1**, 286
Brothers of the Christian Schools, **Vol. 1, Part 1**, 454
Broun, Heywood, references to, **Supp. 7**, 369, 370, 413; **Supp. 8**, 622; **Supp. 10**, 183, 383
Browder, Earl, references to, **Supp. 5**, 70, 500; **Supp. 7**, 255, 751; **Supp. 8**, 192; **Supp. 10**, 265, 266
Brown, A. Page, reference to, **Supp. 6**, 438
"Brown, Buster" (fictional character), **Vol. 7, Part 2**, 112
Brown, Charles Brockden, reference to, **Vol. 9, Part 1**, 259
Brown, Edmund G., references to, **Supp. 6**, 111; **Supp. 9**, 468
Brown, F. Donaldson, reference to, **Supp. 4**, 682
Brown, Gould, influence of, **Vol. 8, Part 1**, 412
Brown, Harry Fletcher, reference to, **Supp. 5**, 235
Brown, Henry Kirke, reference to, **Vol. 10, Part 1**, 427 f.
Brown, Ignacio ("Nacio") Herb, reference to, **Supp. 9**, 291
Brown, Joe L., reference to, **Supp. 10**, 574
Brown, John: **Vol. 1, Part 1**, 280, 384; **Vol. 1, Part 2**, 399; **Vol. 4, Part 2**, 4; **Vol. 5, Part 1**, 297; **Vol. 6, Part 1**, 48; **Vol. 7, Part 1**, 97, 570; **Vol. 8, Part 2**, 104; **Vol. 9, Part 1**, 480; **Vol. 9, Part 2**, 403; association with, **Vol. 8, Part 1**, 434; defended by Thoreau, **Vol. 9, Part 2**, 495; execution of, **Vol. 5, Part 1**, 556; **Vol. 6, Part 1**, 575, **Vol. 9, Part 1**, 265; in Kansas, **Vol. 9, Part 1**, 544; **Vol. 9, Part 2**, 522; New England agent for, **Vol. 8, Part 2**, 326; picture of, **Vol. 5, Part 1**, 269; protection of widow of, **Vol. 10, Part 1**, 100; raid, **Vol. 2, Part 1**, 133–34; **Vol. 4, Part 2**, 163; **Vol. 6, Part 1**, 122; **Vol. 9, Part 1**, 291
Brown, John Carter, references to, **Vol. 1, Part 2**, 7; **Supp. 5**, 755
Brown, John Nicholas, reference to, **Supp. 3**, 196, 197
Brown, Lawrason, references to, **Supp. 3**, 431; **Supp. 4**, 49
Brown, Lew, reference to, **Supp. 8**, 250–51
Brown, Norris, reference to, **Supp. 3**, 558
Brown, Walter F., reference to, **Supp. 6**, 648
Brown & Sharpe Manufacturing Co., **Supp. 3**, 561–62
Brown Brothers Harriman (investment bankers), founding and growth of, **Supp. 10**, 310
Browne, Carl, reference to, **Supp. 5**, 140
Browne, Charles Farrar, reference to, **Vol. 6, Part 1**, 491; **Vol. 9, Part 1**, 39
Browne, E. Martin, reference to, **Supp. 7**, 221
Browne, Francis E., reference to, **Supp. 9**, 33
Browne, George E., reference to, **Supp. 3**, 181
Brownell, Herbert, Jr., reference to, **Supp. 9**, 743–44
Brownell, William E., reference to, **Supp. 7**, 79
Brownies' Book, The, **Supp. 7**, 236
Browning, Jim, reference to, **Supp. 8**, 372
Brown's Ferry, Tenn., **Vol. 9, Part 1**, 363
Brownsville, Ark., operation at (1864), **Vol. 1, Part 1**, 579
Brownsville riots (1906), **Vol. 3, Part 2**, 503; **Vol. 8, Part 2**, 140
Brown University: **Vol. 2, Part 1**, 69, 129; **Vol. 3, Part 2**, 41, 299; **Vol. 4, Part 2**, 42; **Vol. 5, Part 1**, 220, 301; **Vol. 5, Part 2**, 564, 586; **Vol. 6, Part 1**, 262; **Vol. 6, Part 2**, 250; **Vol. 8, Part 2**, 43, 537; **Vol. 9, Part 1**, 279; **Vol. 9, Part 2**, 19, 27; **Vol. 10, Part 1**, 437; development of, **Vol. 1, Part 1**, 287 f.; **Vol. 2, Part 1**, 150, 570; **Vol. 6, Part 2**, 528; **Vol. 10, Part 1**, 558 f.; "New System," endowments raised for, **Vol. 5, Part 2**, 409; freedom of speech, **Vol. 1, Part 1**, 288 f.; establishment of Women's College, **Vol. 3, Part 1**, 423; minority enrollment, **Supp. 10**, 403; physical chemistry studies, **Supp. 10**, 608–9; presidency, **Supp. 10**, 403; Romance languages studies, **Supp. 4**, 754
Brown v. *Board of Education of Topeka*, **Supp. 5**, 156, 359; **Supp. 7**, 264, 501; **Supp. 8**, 25, 157; **Supp. 9**, 104, 364, 391, 401, 433, 743, 836; **Supp. 10**, 127, 189
Bruccoli, Matthew J., reference to, **Supp. 6**, 329
Bruce, Alexander, reference to, **Supp. 3**, 127
Bruce, Lenny, reference to, **Supp. 9**, 399
Brugler, Frank, reference to, **Supp. 9**, 402
Bruenn, Howard, reference to, **Supp. 6**, 414
Brunini, John, reference to, **Supp. 5**, 564; **Supp. 7**, 52

Bruno crime family (Philadelphia, Pa.), **Supp. 10**, 75–76
Brussels Conference (1937), **Supp. 3**, 219; **Supp. 6**, 270
Bryan, Anna, reference to, **Supp. 4**, 373
Bryan, William Jennings: **Vol. 6, Part 1**, 616; **Vol. 7, Part 2**, 520; family of, **Supp. 3**, 114; **Supp. 5**, 582; monetary views, **Supp. 3**, 97; presidential bids, **Supp. 4**, 216; **Supp. 6**, 132, 137; religious beliefs, **Supp. 6**, 195; Scopes trial, **Supp. 4**, 85, 692; **Supp. 5**, 461; **Supp. 6**, 528–29; **Supp. 7**, 624, 631; **Supp. 8**, 583; **Supp. 9**, 769; state secretaryship, **Supp. 3**, 139, 658; **Supp. 6**, 687; Wilson, relations with, **Vol. 10, Part 2**, 356; writings on, **Supp. 1**, 327
Bryant, Paul ("Bear"), reference to, **Supp. 9**, 148
Bryant, William Cullen, reference to, **Vol. 6, Part 1**, 147
Bryn Athyn, Pa., cathedral at, **Vol. 7, Part 2**, 636
Bryn Mawr College: **Vol. 8, Part 1**, 488 f., 530 f.; **Vol. 9, Part 2**, 336 f.; English literature and language studies, **Supp. 3**, 109; geology department, founding of, **Supp. 3**, 38; presidency, **Supp. 1**, 684; Semitic studies, **Supp. 3**, 37
Bryozoa fossils, **Supp. 3**, 782–83
Buber, Martin, reference to, **Supp. 9**, 384
Buccaneering, **Vol. 10, Part 2**, 615
Buchalter, Louis Lepke, references to, **Supp. 4**, 613; **Supp. 9**, 886
Buchanan, James, references to, **Vol. 1, Part 2**, 312; **Vol. 3, Part 1**, 401; **Vol. 3, Part 2**, 482 f.; **Vol. 5, Part 1**, 182; **Vol. 7, Part 1**, 150; **Vol. 7, Part 2**, 578 f.; **Vol. 9, Part 1**, 210, 518
Buchanan, Patrick, *Nation* article, **Supp. 10**, 503
Buchanan v. *Warley*, **Supp. 9**, 749
Buchner, Eduard, reference to, **Supp. 5**, 489
Buckley, William F., Jr., reference to, **Supp. 7**, 115
Buckminister, Joseph S., reference to, **Vol. 9, Part 2**, 391
Bucknell University, **Vol. 2, Part 1**, 234; presidency, **Supp. 1**, 401
Buckner, Emory R., reference to, **Supp. 9**, 364
Buckner, H. F., reference to, **Vol. 7, Part 1**, 371
Buckner, Simon Bolivar, Jr., reference to, **Supp. 6**, 629
Buck Privates, **Supp. 9**, 1–2
Bucks County Historical Society, **Vol. 6, Part 2**, 540
Bucks County Playhouse (New Hope, Pa.), **Supp. 3**, 59
Buck Shot War, **Vol. 5, Part 2**, 257; **Vol. 8, Part 1**, 94 f., 629
"Budd, Lanny" (fictional character), **Supp. 8**, 595
Budd Co., founding of, **Supp. 4**, 121–22
Buddhism: first major infusion into American fiction, **Supp. 8**, 327; **Supp. 9**, 846; studies in, **Supp. 1**, 713; **Supp. 9**, 845, 846; writings on, **Supp. 3**, 445
Budenz, Louis, references to, **Supp. 7**, 291; **Supp. 8**, 162, 511
Budget, Bureau of the, **Supp. 4**, 753; **Supp. 5**, 160; **Supp. 7**, 190; **Supp. 10**, 287; first budget director appointed, **Supp. 9**, 243
Budget and Accounting Act (1921), **Supp. 1**, 344; **Supp. 6**, 187
Budget (U.S.), **Vol. 6, Part 1**, 407 f.; **Vol. 9, Part 2**, 270; balanced, **Supp. 8**, 290; congressional cuts, **Supp. 7**, 734; defense cuts, **Supp. 7**, 795; Eisenhower administration cuts, **Supp. 8**, 157; legislation, **Supp. 1**, 344; presidential control of, **Supp. 4**, 753
Budweiser beer, **Supp. 1**, 42
Buena Vista, Mexico, battle of, **Vol. 1, Part 2**, 586; **Vol. 3, Part 1**, 17, 125; **Vol. 9, Part 2**, 351; **Vol. 10, Part 2**, 514
Buenos Aires Conference (1936), **Supp. 5**, 332
Buffalo, N. Y.: connection with Albany by railroad, **Vol. 8, Part 1**, 582; development of, **Vol. 4, Part 2**, 141; **Vol. 6, Part 1**, 2; **Vol. 8, Part 1**, 283; **Vol. 8, Part 2**, 578; **Vol. 9, Part 1**, 209, 436; **Vol. 10, Part 2**, 219; exposition, **Vol. 4, Part 1**, 221; Eye and Ear Infirmary, founded, **Vol. 5, Part 1**, 293; in 1812, **Vol. 3, Part 1**, 388; Fine Arts Academy, **Vol. 8, Part 2**, 578; grain market, growth of, as, **Vol. 3, Part 1**, 506 f.; Historical Society of, **Vol. 8, Part 1**, 283; library service, **Vol. 10, Part 1**, 426; public health, **Vol. 10, Part 1**, 648 f.; Wright's architecture, **Supp. 6**, 712
"Buffalo Bill." *See* Cody, "Buffalo Bill"
Buffalo Museum of Fine Arts, modern art collection, **Supp. 7**, 294
"Bugs Bunny" (fictional character), **Supp. 10**, 813
Bühler, Charlotte, references to, **Supp. 10**, 437, 438
Bühler, Karl, reference to, **Supp. 10**, 437
Buick Motor Car Co., **Supp. 4**, 243
Building: concrete, use of, **Vol. 9, Part 2**, 386, 545 f.; financing of, **Vol. 9, Part 2**, 132; inventions relating to, **Vol. 1, Part 2**, 407
Building and loan associations, early, **Vol. 4, Part 2**, 194
Building industry. *See* Construction industry
Buildings: acoustics, **Supp. 3**, 524; air-conditioning, **Supp. 4**, 149; art deco, **Supp. 7**, 308; art works for public, **Supp. 3**, 112; beaux-arts, **Supp. 4**, 281–82; door ornamentation, **Supp. 3**, 2; federal government, **Supp. 3**, 199; first multiclassroom one-story school, **Supp. 3**, 599; height restrictions, **Supp. 4**, 56; interior design, **Supp. 8**, 140–41; New York City, **Supp. 6**, 593; **Supp. 7**, 691, 799–800; public, **Supp. 3**, 656; public works projects, **Supp. 5**, 342–43; skyscrapers, *see* Skyscrapers; steel-framed, **Supp. 3**, 611–12; steel sections, **Supp. 3**, 77; steel structural beam, **Supp. 6**, 243; Supreme Court, **Supp. 3**, 99; theater, **Supp. 1**, 18. *See also* Architecture
Bukharin, Nikolai, reference to, **Supp. 8**, 162
Bulfinch, Charles, reference to, **Vol. 7, Part 1**, 10
Bulgaria: diplomacy, **Vol. 3, Part 1**, 294; missions, **Vol. 9, Part 2**, 74
Bullard, Dexter, reference to, **Supp. 6**, 220
Bullitt, William C., references to, **Supp. 7**, 536; **Supp. 9**, 105
Bull Moose party, **Vol. 1, Part 2**, 232; **Vol. 8, Part 2**, 142; **Vol. 9, Part 2**, 270
Bull Run: first battle of, **Vol. 1, Part 2**, 111, 124; **Vol. 4, Part 2**, 214; **Vol. 5, Part 1**, 556; **Vol. 5, Part 2**, 144, 216, 425; **Vol. 6, Part 1**, 253, 391; **Vol. 6, Part 2**, 29; **Vol. 8, Part 1**, 77, 91; **Vol. 9, Part 1**, 94; **Vol. 9, Part 2**, 255; **Vol. 10, Part 1**, 87; second battle of, **Vol. 2, Part 1**, 244; **Vol. 4, Part 2**, 214; **Vol. 5, Part 1**, 558; **Vol. 6, Part 1**, 124, 253, 391; **Vol. 6, Part 2**, 29; **Vol. 7, Part 2**, 307; **Vol. 8, Part 1**, 204
Bumpers, Dale, reference to, **Supp. 9**, 672
Bunche, Ralph, reference to, **Supp. 10**, 245
Bundy, McGeorge, reference to, **Supp. 7**, 91
Bunker, George M., reference to, **Supp. 5**, 476
Bunker Hill, battle of: **Vol. 4, Part 2**, 490; **Vol. 6, Part 1**, 44; **Vol. 7, Part 2**, 635; **Vol. 8, Part 1**, 195 f., 282; **Vol. 10, Part 1**, 415, 483; munitions, source of, **Vol. 8, Part 1**, 515
Bunker Hill Monument: **Vol. 1, Part 1**, 540 f.; **Vol. 6, Part 1**, 145; **Vol. 10, Part 2**, 242; designing of, **Vol. 7, Part 1**, 12
Bunts, Frank E., reference to, **Supp. 4**, 507
Burbank, Luther, reference to, **Supp. 7**, 592
Burch, George E., reference to, **Supp. 6**, 117
Burdick, Quentin, references to, **Supp. 6**, 85, 86, 87
Burger, Warren E., reference to, **Supp. 9**, 838
Burgess, Charles Paine, reference to, **Supp. 4**, 124
Burgess, Ernest W., reference to, **Supp. 3**, 578
Burgess, John W., reference to, **Supp. 4**, 133
Burgess-Dunne seaplane, **Supp. 4**, 124

Burglar on the Roof, The (first "posed" movie), **Supp. 3,** 75
Burgoyne, General John, references to, **Vol. 1, Part 1,** 365; **Vol. 9, Part 2,** 365
Burial alive, escape from, **Vol. 9, Part 2,** 371
Burk, Frederic, reference to, **Supp. 7,** 42
Burke, John J., references to, **Supp. 3,** 325; **Supp. 6,** 85
Burke, Kenneth, reference to, **Supp. 7,** 654
Burke-Wadsworth Act. *See* Selective Service Act
Burleigh, Harry T., reference to, **Supp. 4,** 834
Burlesque: **Vol. 6, Part 1,** 217; **Vol. 8, Part 2,** 247; comedy, **Supp. 3,** 803–4; **Supp. 4,** 739; **Supp. 5,** 726; **Supp. 6,** 112; **Supp. 8,** 355; dance acts, **Supp. 10,** 657; dance teams, **Supp. 8,** 694; dialect, **Supp. 3,** 803–4; **Supp. 5,** 726; striptease, **Supp. 8,** 363–65
Burley (Idaho) *Bulletin,* **Supp. 7,** 212
Burley Tobacco Growers Cooperative Association, organization of, **Supp. 2,** 39
Burlingame Treaty (1868), **Vol. 2, Part 1,** 289–90; **Vol. 4, Part 2,** 450
Burlington, N.J.: founding of, **Vol. 7, Part 2,** 434; founding of St. Mary's Hall for girls at, **Vol. 3, Part 1,** 333; political service, **Vol. 1, Part 2,** 386
Burlington College (N.J.), **Vol. 3, Part 1,** 333
Burlington Railroad, **Vol. 5, Part 1,** 38 f.
Burma: medical missions, **Supp. 7,** 680–81; missions in, **Vol. 2, Part 2,** 631; **Vol. 5, Part 2,** 236, 242 f.; **Vol. 6, Part 2,** 359; World War II action, **Supp. 4,** 782–83; **Supp. 6,** 508
Burnelli Co., **Supp. 6,** 493
Burnett, Frances Hodgson, reference to, **Supp. 3,** 69
Burney, Leroy E., reference to, **Supp. 7,** 192
Burnham, Daniel H., references to, **Vol. 8, Part 1,** 45 f.; **Supp. 3,** 533, 534, 771–72; **Supp. 6,** 593
Burns, Allen, reference to, **Supp. 4,** 810
Burns, Anthony, case of, **Vol. 5, Part 1,** 17
Burns, Arthur, reference to, **Supp. 10,** 376
Burns, Arthur F., reference to, **Supp. 4,** 587
Burns, George, references to, **Supp. 7,** 9; **Supp. 9,** 219
Burns, Kenneth, reference to, **Supp. 9,** 373–74
Burns, Lucy, reference to, **Supp. 7,** 717
Burns, Robert E., reference to, **Supp. 9,** 689
Burns, Tommy, reference to, **Supp. 4,** 433
Burns, William, reference to, **Supp. 9,** 405
Burns, W. Sherman, reference to, **Supp. 10,** 79
Burns, blood plasma for, **Supp. 6,** 190
Burns, collecting of works on, **Vol. 5, Part 1,** 567
Burns and Allen (comedy team), **Supp. 7,** 9
Burns Detective Agency, founding and growth of, **Supp. 10,** 79–80
Burns Mantle Yearbook of the Theatre, The, **Supp. 4,** 549
Burnt Coat Islands, purchase of, **Vol. 9, Part 2,** 234
Burr, Aaron: **Vol. 1, Part 2,** 386, 422; **Vol. 2, Part 2,** 47; **Vol. 3, Part 1,** 138; **Vol. 5, Part 1,** 486, 504; **Vol. 7, Part 1,** 636; **Vol. 8, Part 2,** 544, 604; **Vol. 9, Part 1,** 41, 297; **Vol. 9, Part 2,** 536, 601, 651; Burr, Theodosia, relations with, **Vol. 1, Part 1,** 229; **Vol. 2, Part 1,** 322; Clay, relations with, **Vol. 2, Part 2,** 174; conspiracy, *see* Conspiracy, Burr; duel with Hamilton, **Vol. 4, Part 2,** 178; **Vol. 5, Part 1,** 240; Latrobe, relations with, **Vol. 6, Part 1,** 23; Livingston, relations with, **Vol. 6, Part 1,** 309 f.; Martin, relations with, **Vol. 6, Part 2,** 344; Ohio expedition, **Vol. 3, Part 1,** 166; presidential election disputed, **Vol. 1, Part 2,** 64; "Spanish Conspiracy," **Vol. 1, Part 1,** 229; **Vol. 3, Part 1,** 80; trial of, **Vol. 1, Part 2,** 368; **Vol. 2, Part 1,** 317; **Vol. 3, Part 1,** 166, 613; **Vol. 4, Part 2,** 430; **Vol. 5, Part 1,** 507, 528; **Vol. 5, Part 2,** 30; **Vol. 6, Part 2,** 324, 345; **Vol. 8, Part 1,** 353 f.; **Vol. 8, Part 2,** 505; **Vol. 9, Part 2,** 238; **Vol. 10, Part 2,** 182, 225, 420; Wickham, relations with, **Vol. 10, Part 2,** 181; Wilkinson, relations with, **Vol. 10, Part 2,** 224; Wood, relations with, **Vol. 10, Part 2,** 464
Burrage, Walter, reference to, **Supp. 3,** 412
Burrill, Thomas J., reference to, **Supp. 3,** 400
Burroughs, John, references to, **Vol. 5, Part 2,** 293; **Supp. 4,** 737
Burroughs, William, references to, **Supp. 8,** 325, 326
Burroughs Adding Machine Co., **Supp. 6,** 114–15
Busch, Adolf, reference to, **Supp. 9,** 140
Busch, Fritz, reference to, **Supp. 6,** 324
Busch Quartet, **Supp. 9,** 140–41
Bush, George, parents of, **Supp. 9,** 141, 142–43
Bush, Prescott, reference to, **Supp. 9,** 81
Bush, Vannevar, references to, **Supp. 5,** 355; **Supp. 7,** 275; **Supp. 8,** 229; **Supp. 10,** 144
"Bush-lopers," **Vol. 7, Part 1,** 417
Bushman, Francis X., reference to, **Supp. 6,** 440
Bushnell, Horace, references to, **Vol. 10, Part 1,** 605 f.; **Supp. 4,** 512
Bushwick, N. Y. *See* Brooklyn, N. Y., battle of
Bushy Run, battle of, **Vol. 1, Part 2,** 481
Bus industry, **Supp. 9,** 388, 389
Business: bankruptcy, biggest in retailing history, **Supp. 9,** 337; black-owned, **Supp. 3,** 535; **Supp. 4,** 82–83; **Supp. 5,** 548, 647–48, 741; businessmen, studies of, **Supp. 2,** 651; capitalization of, **Supp. 2,** 446; civic affairs and, **Supp. 9,** 484; company towns, **Supp. 2,** 366; competition and economy, **Supp. 8,** 82; consolidation of, **Supp. 1,** 306; corporate finance methods, **Supp. 4,** 681–82; corporate investment, **Supp. 8,** 78–79, 367–68; Cromwell salvage plan, **Supp. 4,** 193; cycles studies, **Vol. 8, Part 1,** 325 f.; **Supp. 4,** 585–86, 587, 722, 723; financial reorganization, **Supp. 3,** 456–57; forecasting, **Supp. 8,** 18–19; franchises, **Supp. 9,** 429–30; **Supp. 10,** 718; franchising concept introduced, **Supp. 9,** 246; government regulation, **Supp. 2,** 31, 553; high school, first in U.S., **Vol. 8, Part 1,** 152; influence on society, **Supp. 8,** 685; interlocking directorates, **Vol. 3, Part 1,** 356; law, **Supp. 1,** 223; **Supp. 4,** 192–93; **Supp. 7,** 792; merchandising, **Supp. 9,** 483–84; mergers, **Supp. 2,** 674; modern methods, introduction of, **Vol. 3, Part 2,** 367; **Vol. 6, Part 1,** 608; National Survey Conference (1929–31), **Supp. 6,** 37; New Deal relationship, **Supp. 6,** 520, 615, 675; organized-crime fronts, **Supp. 7,** 632; **Supp. 8,** 208, 397, 546; politics and, **Supp. 1,** 168; public opinion research, **Supp. 7,** 650; public relations, **Supp. 5,** 303; regulation of, **Vol. 2, Part 1,** 16, 249; **Vol. 4, Part 2,** 104; religious faith and success in, **Supp. 8,** 27; reports of business conditions, **Vol. 3, Part 1,** 503; Rotary Clubs, founding of, **Supp. 4,** 362; seasonal influences, **Supp. 2,** 530; Swope plan, **Supp. 6,** 615; taxes favoring, **Supp. 2,** 448–49; trade association movement, **Supp. 5,** 54–55; **Supp. 7,** 359, 360; trade associations, **Supp. 5,** 54–55; training, first attempt to supply in academic institution, **Vol. 7, Part 2,** 299. *See also* Antitrust actions; Economics; Finance; Management; Multinational corporations; Stock Market; *types and names of businesses*
Business Advisory Council (BAC), **Supp. 9,** 392
Business and Professional Women's Clubs. *See* National Federation of Business and Professional Women's Clubs
Business Bulletin, **Supp. 4,** 36
Business Cycles, **Supp. 4,** 585, 586
Business Week, founding of, **Supp. 4,** 524
Bus Stop, **Supp. 9,** 421–22
But for Whom Charlie, **Supp. 9,** 71
Butler, Benjamin Franklin, references to, **Vol. 3, Part 1,** 368; **Vol. 5, Part 1,** 341; **Vol. 8, Part 2,** 461; **Vol. 9, Part 1,** 79; **Vol. 9, Part 2,** 364, 378

Butler, Burridge D., reference to, **Supp. 3**, 319
Butler, Frank E., assistant to Annie Oakley, **Vol. 7, Part 1**, 603–4
Butler, Howard Crosby, reference to, **Supp. 3**, 705
Butler, John, reference to, **Supp. 5**, 251
Butler, John Marshall, references to, **Supp. 5**, 633; **Supp. 7**, 751
Butler, Jonathan F., reference to, **Supp. 4**, 697
Butler, Nicholas Murray, references to, **Supp. 3**, 151, 677; **Supp. 4**, 62, 793, 794; **Supp. 5**, 558; **Supp. 6**, 675; **Supp. 7**, 288; **Supp. 10**, 333
Butler, Pierce, references to, **Supp. 4**, 537; **Supp. 5**, 502, 571, 574
Butler, William O., reference to, **Supp. 6**, 629
Butler University, **Vol. 1, Part 2**, 208; **Vol. 4, Part 1**, 407; **Vol. 5, Part 1**, 241
Butte, Mont., discovery of copper near, **Vol. 3, Part 1**, 45
Butterfield, John, reference to, **Vol. 10, Part 1**, 639 f.
Butterflies, collections of, **Vol. 3, Part 2**, 46 f.; **Vol. 8, Part 2**, 525 f.
Buttons, manufacture of, **Vol. 4, Part 2**, 442
Buttree, Julia M., reference to, **Supp. 4**, 737
Buttrick, Wallace, reference to, **Supp. 4**, 346
Buzzard Roost, Ga., operation at, **Vol. 9, Part 1**, 95
By Love Possessed, **Supp. 10**, 153
Byoir, Carl, and Associates, **Supp. 6**, 90–91
Byrd, Harry F., references to, **Supp. 6**, 75, 235; **Supp. 8**, 68; **Supp. 9**, 664
Byrd, Richard Evelyn: Balchen relationship, **Supp. 9**, 63, 64; described, **Supp. 9**, 220; expeditions, **Supp. 9**, 63–64, 220; first polar flights, **Supp. 9**, 63, 64; references to, **Vol. 1, Part 2**, 194; **Supp. 3**, 284; **Supp. 5**, 3; **Supp. 6**, 478; **Supp. 10**, 213
Byrnes, James F., references to, **Supp. 3**, 660; **Supp. 5**, 332; **Supp. 7**, 24; **Supp. 9**, 7
Byzantine art, **Supp. 4**, 890–91; **Supp. 5**, 699–700, 708–9; **Supp. 7**, 60
Byzantine studies, **Supp. 5**, 708–9

C

CAB. *See* Civil Aeronautics Board
Cabals, in Congress, **Vol. 9, Part 1**, 342
Cabaret, **Supp. 4**, 867–88; **Supp. 7**, 563
Cabell, James Branch, references to, **Supp. 3**, 303; **Supp. 6**, 445, 471
Cabinetmaking, **Vol. 3, Part 2**, 129; **Vol. 4, Part 1**, 338, 440; **Vol. 7, Part 2**, 553 f.; **Vol. 8, Part 2**, 392
Cabin in the Sky, **Supp. 8**, 145; **Supp. 10**, 7, 8
Cable, George W., references to, **Vol. 5, Part 2**, 388; **Vol. 7, Part 1**, 295
Cables, Atlantic: **Vol. 3, Part 1**, 221, 336, 600; **Vol. 3, Part 2**, 358; **Vol. 5, Part 2**, 566; **Vol. 6, Part 1**, 141, 445; **Vol. 6, Part 2**, 430; **Vol. 8, Part 2**, 343, 521; **Vol. 9, Part 2, Vol. 2, Part 1**, 122, 338, 533, **Vol. 10, Part 1**, 421; insulation of, **Vol. 2, Part 2**, 517; street cars, use of, **Vol. 3, Part 1**, 394; **Vol. 4, Part 2**, 156; wire, early use of, **Vol. 8, Part 2**, 88
Cabot, Philip, reference to, **Supp. 3**, 121
Cabot, Richard Clarke, references to, **Supp. 6**, 97, 98; **Supp. 9**, 318
Cabot Corporation, **Supp. 7**, 98
Cabot voyages, research into, **Vol. 3, Part 1**, 172
Cadillac Motor Car Co., founding of, **Supp. 4**, 293
Cadman, Charles W., reference to, **Vol. 7, Part 1**, 629
Cadwalader, Wickersham & Taft, **Supp. 3**, 758
Caesar, Arthur, reference to, **Supp. 6**, 516
Caesarian section, **Supp. 3**, 412. *See also* Surgery
Café des Artistes (New York City), **Supp. 5**, 113
Café society, **Supp. 4**, 199–200; **Supp. 8**, 38–39
Cagney, James, references to, **Supp. 8**, 220; **Supp. 10**, 53
Cahan, Abraham, reference to, **Supp. 3**, 329
Cahenslyism, **Vol. 4, Part 1**, 336
Cairo Christian University. *See* American University (Cairo)
Cairo manuscripts, discovery of, **Vol. 8, Part 2**, 422
Cakewalk, **Supp. 3**, 187
Calcium, dietary, **Supp. 5**, 623
Calcium carbide, **Supp. 7**, 553–54
Calculating machine, invention of, **Vol. 1, Part 1**, 533; **Vol. 4, Part 1**, 488
Calculators, first automatic, **Supp. 6**, 675
Calculus, **Supp. 5**, 67–68; of variations, **Supp. 3**, 86–87
Calder, Alexander, references to, **Supp. 3**, 124; **Supp. 9**, 60
"Caldonia," **Supp. 9**, 442
Caldor, Louis J., reference to, **Supp. 7**, 556
Caldwell, Erskine, reference to, **Supp. 9**, 111
Caldwell, Rogers, reference to, **Supp. 3**, 449
Caledonia, capture of, **Vol. 3, Part 2**, 96
Calendars: advertising, first use for, **Vol. 9, Part 2**, 491; perpetual, **Vol. 1, Part 2**, 573; quotation, **Vol. 8, Part 2**, 327
Calhoun, John C., **Vol. 4, Part 2**, 187 f.; **Vol. 5, Part 1**, 531; **Vol. 6, Part 1**, 473; **Vol. 8, Part 2**, 237, 513; **Vol. 10, Part 1**, 585 f.; life of, **Vol. 5, Part 1**, 385; nullification, advocacy of, **Vol. 10, Part 1**, 585 f.; successor to, **Vol. 8, Part 1**, 526 f.
Calhoun, Patrick, reference to, **Supp. 3**, 394
California: anti-gay legislative proposals, **Supp. 10**, 537; art, history of, in, **Vol. 8, Part 1**, 274 f.; annexation, **Vol. 3, Part 2**, 263; **Vol. 6, Part 2**, 373; **Vol. 8, Part 1**, 34 f.; **Vol. 9, Part 2**, 49; **Vol. 10, Part 2**, 643; architecture, **Supp. 5**, 256–57, 606; **Supp. 6**, 438–39, 462–64, 714, 715; **Supp. 8**, 463–64; "back to the land" movement, in, **Vol. 8, Part 2**, 327; banking in, **Vol. 3, Part 1**, 283; **Vol. 7, Part 1**, 6; **Vol. 7, Part 2**, 522; **Vol. 8, Part 1**, 333 f.; banking law, **Supp. 4**, 325; Bear Flag Revolt, **Vol. 4, Part 1**, 21; botanical studies, **Supp. 4**, 428–29; botany, **Vol. 6, Part 1**, 162; business, **Vol. 6, Part 1**, 445; **Vol. 9, Part 2**, 385; capital punishment, **Supp. 6**, 111; Catholic church, **Vol. 3, Part 1**, 421; **Vol. 4, Part 1**, 102; **Vol. 8, Part 1**, 619; **Vol. 8, Part 2**, 248; **Supp. 3**, 325–26; civil code, **Vol. 6, Part 1**, 274; **Vol. 8, Part 1**, 52 f.; Civil War issues, **Vol. 5, Part 2**, 136; **Vol. 6, Part 1**, 13; coast survey, **Vol. 8, Part 1**, 617; colonization of Lower, **Vol. 10, Part 1**, 363 f.; Communist party in, **Supp. 5**, 742; conquest of, **Vol. 1, Part 2**, 88; **Vol. 2, Part 1**, 531; **Vol. 3, Part 1**, 125, 365; **Vol. 4, Part 1**, 21–22, 203; **Vol. 4, Part 2**, 151; **Vol. 5, Part 2**, 273–74, 617; **Vol. 6, Part 2**, 373–74, 576; **Vol. 8, Part 1**, 37–38, 609; **Vol. 9, Part 1**, 210, 215; **Vol. 9, Part 2**, 49, 379; constitution, formation of, **Vol. 6, Part 2**, 42; dam construction, **Supp. 2**, 305; development of, **Vol. 4, Part 2**, 487 f.; **Vol. 5, Part 1**, 415 f.; **Vol. 7, Part 2**, 100; **Vol. 8, Part 1**, 333 f.; education, **Vol. 5, Part 2**, 591; **Vol. 8, Part 1**, 52 f.; **Vol. 9, Part 1**, 388; **Vol. 9, Part 2**, 244; environmentalism, **Supp. 6**, 486; EPIC campaign (1934), **Supp. 8**, 595; Episcopal church, **Vol. 5, Part 2**, 422 f.; exploration, **Vol. 1, Part 1**, 322; **Vol. 2, Part 1**, 396; **Vol. 3, Part 1**, 252; **Vol. 3, Part 2**, 244; **Vol. 4, Part 1**, 132; **Vol. 5, Part 2**, 419; **Vol. 6, Part 1**, 180; **Vol. 7, Part 2**, 310; **Vol. 8, Part 1**, 109 f.; **Vol. 8, Part 2**, 32; **Vol. 9, Part 1**, 290 f.; financial history of, **Vol. 8, Part 1**, 333 f.; first woman high school principal, **Supp. 8**, 9; first woman treasurer of, **Supp. 9**, 625; forest preservation, **Vol. 3, Part 1**, 485; **Vol. 6, Part 1**, 162; Franciscan Order, **Vol. 7, Part 2**, 197; Frémont regime, **Vol. 8, Part 2**, 252; fruit growing, **Vol. 6, Part 1**, 481;

Vol. 8, Part 1, 145 f.; geology of, **Vol. 2, Part 1**, 25; **Supp. 4**, 896–97; **Supp. 5**, 416; Gold Rush, **Vol. 1, Part 1**, 396, 446; **Vol. 1, Part 2**,228; **Vol. 2, Part 1**, 62, 300; **Vol. 4, Part 1**, 22, 168; **Vol. 4, Part 2**, 363, 387; **Vol. 5, Part 1**, 81; **Vol. 5, Part 2**, 188, 407; **Vol. 6, Part 1**, 516; **Vol. 6, Part 2**, 314; **Vol. 7, Part 1**, 6, 612; **Vol. 8, Part 2**, 11, 35, 205, 248; **Vol. 9, Part 2**, 315, 384; governors, **Vol. 1, Part 2**, 263 f., 455 f.; **Vol. 3, Part 2**, 244; **Vol. 4, Part 2**, 90; **Vol. 6, Part 1**, 445 f.; **Vol. 6, Part 2**, 373 f.; **Vol. 7, Part 2**, 124 f., 468 f.; **Vol. 9, Part 1**, 501 f.; **Vol. 9, Part 2**, 92 f.; **Vol. 10, Part 1**, 628 f.; **Supp. 1**, 639; **Supp. 3**, 393–96; **Supp. 8**, 340–41; **Supp. 9**, 835; history of, **Vol. 3, Part 1**, 40 f.; **Vol. 6, Part 1**, 82; **Vol. 6, Part 2**, 372; **Vol. 8, Part 1**, 109 f., 214 f., 355 f.; **Vol. 10, Part 1**, 146; **Vol. 10, Part 2**, 246; horticulture, **Vol. 1, Part 2**, 599; **Vol. 4, Part 2**, 229; **Vol. 5, Part 2**, 300; **Vol. 6, Part 1**, 162, 498; **Vol. 8, Part 2**, 90; **Vol 9, Part 1**, 548; Indian insurrections, **Vol. 2, Part 1**, 485; iron foundries, **Vol. 3, Part 1**, 362; Japanese-Americans, internment of, **Supp. 10**, 502; Japanese current, **Vol. 3, Part 1**, 394; Jesuit activities, **Vol. 3, Part 1**, 422; **Vol. 5, Part 2**, 420; **Vol. 8, Part 1**, 109 f.; journalism in, **Vol. 1, Part 1**, 443 f.; **Vol. 2, Part 2**, 323; **Vol. 5, Part 1**, 81 f.; **Vol. 9, Part 1**, 175; judiciary, **Supp. 7**, 292–93; **Supp. 9**, 853; kindergarten movement, **Vol. 6, Part 2**, 355; Know-Nothing party, **Vol. 8, Part 2**, 248; land titles, **Vol. 6, Part 1**, 547; legal service, **Vol. 1, Part 2**, 102, 202, 265, 472; **Vol. 3, Part 1**, 226, 422; **Vol. 3, Part 2**, 373; **Vol. 4, Part 2**, 387; **Vol. 6, Part 1**, 546; **Vol. 6, Part 2**, 11, 42, 110; **Vol. 8, Part 1**, 52, 214, 355; **Vol. 8, Part 2**, 176; **Vol. 10, Part 2**, 344; library, first public, **Vol. 3, Part 1**, 121; meteorology, **Supp. 3**, 479; mission preservation, **Supp. 3**, 88; missions in, **Vol. 1, Part 1**, 161, 322; **Vol. 3, Part 1**, 422; **Vol. 3, Part 2**, 497; **Vol. 5, Part 1**, 577; **Vol. 7, Part 1**, 536; **Vol. 8, Part 1**, 109 f.; **Vol. 8, Part 2**, 591 f.; National Guard, **Supp. 5**, 43; newspaper, first in, **Vol. 2, Part 2**, 323; newspapers, **Supp. 4**, 283–84; normal schools, **Vol. 2, Part 1**, 279; **Vol. 7, Part 1**, 578; oil, **Vol. 7, Part 2**, 386; packet boats, **Vol. 8, Part 2**, 42; painting, **Vol. 5, Part 1**, 46; **Vol. 5, Part 2**, 293; **Vol. 9, Part 1**, 597; penal reform, **Supp. 4**, 636; pioneer life, **Vol. 1, Part 2**, 247, 602; **Vol. 4, Part 1**, 229; **Vol. 6, Part 2**, 301, 621; **Vol. 8, Part 2**, 395; **Vol. 9, Part 1**, 540 f.; **Vol. 10, Part 2**, 245, 452, 637; political service, **Vol. 1, Part 1**, 234, 263, 455; **Vol. 1, Part 2**, 247, 410; **Vol. 3, Part 1**, 121, 243; **Vol. 4, Part 2**, 90, 487; **Vol. 6, Part 1**, 13, 445; **Vol. 6, Part 2**, 631; **Vol. 7, Part 2**, 124, 468, 524; **Vol. 8, Part 1**, 109, 355; **Vol. 9, Part 1**, 502, 505; **Vol. 9, Part 2**, 92; **Vol. 10, Part 1**, 466, 628; **Vol. 10, Part 2**, 119; politics, **Supp. 3**, 394–96; **Supp. 4**, 446–47; **Supp. 7**, 224–25; **Supp. 8**, 595; **Supp. 9**, 467, 468–69, 625; **Supp. 10**, 183–84, 558; printing, pioneer, **Vol. 10, Part 2**, 643; probate administration, **Vol. 2, Part 2**, 264; progressive movement, **Supp. 4**, 707; public health, **Supp. 5**, 604; public service, **Vol. 1, Part 2**, 602; **Vol. 2, Part 2**, 552; **Vol. 3, Part 1**, 121 f.; **Vol. 4, Part 2**, 64 f., 83, 463; **Vol. 5, Part 1**, 81 f.; **Vol. 5, Part 2**, 250, 405; **Vol. 7, Part 1**, 238; **Vol. 7, Part 2**, 100 f., 124 f., 522, 523 f.; **Vol. 9, Part 1**, 550; **Vol. 9, Part 2**, 147, 379, 473; public utilities, development of, **Vol. 3, Part 1**, 362; railroad development, **Vol. 5, Part 1**, 408 f.; **Vol. 9, Part 2**, 92; real estate operations, **Vol. 6, Part 1**, 234; redwoods conservation, **Supp. 3**, 520; **Supp. 4**, 429; **Supp. 10**, 191, 192; relics, collection of, **Vol. 6, Part 1**, 502; Republican party, **Supp. 9**, 467, 468–69; Royce, Josiah, influence on, **Vol. 8, Part 2**, 206; Russian settlements, **Vol. 5, Part 2**, 514 f.; slavery question, **Vol. 2, Part 1**, 62; **Vol. 3, Part 1**, 125; southern, development of, **Supp. 3**, 154–56; **Supp. 5**, 309–10; Spanish enterprise in, **Vol. 8, Part l**, 109 f.; state forests, **Supp. 3**, 7; statehood, admission to, **Vol. 8, Part 1**, 609; **Vol. 9, Part 2**, 353; teacher training, **Vol. 7, Part 1**, 578; Un-American Activities Committee, state senate, **Supp. 9**, 753 venereal disease prevention, **Supp. 4**, 758; vigilantes, **Vol. 6, Part 1**, 282*;* vineyards, **Vol. 4, Part 2**, 236; water supply, **Supp. 3**, 155; **Supp. 6**, 3–4; **Supp. 7**, 224; wheat exportation, **Vol. 7, Part 2**, 522; wineries, **Supp. 7**, 613–14; woman suffrage, **Supp. 5**, 742; wool exportation, **Vol. 7, Part 2**, 522; writings on, **Vol. 4, Part 1**, 425; **Vol. 5, Part 1**, 81 f.; **Vol. 9, Part 2**, 473

California Botanical Garden (Los Angeles), **Supp. 6**, 450

California Club, **Vol. 8, Part 2**, 177

California Institute of Technology: aerodynamics studies, **Supp. 8**, 439–40; astrophysical laboratory, **Supp. 4**, 675; astrophysical studies, **Supp. 9**, 113–14, 902–3; cancer therapy research, financing of, **Supp. 9**, 773; development of, **Supp. 2**, 271, 494; **Supp. 3**, 157; experimental biology studies, **Supp. 3**, 540; financing of, **Supp. 2**, 193; Guggenheim Aeronautical Laboratory, **Supp. 7**, 411; mathematics studies, **Supp. 6**, 49; Observatory Council, **Supp. 7**, 516–17; photography innovations, **Supp. 9**, 114; physical chemistry studies, **Supp. 4**, 838–39; physics studies, **Supp. 4**, 57–58; **Supp. 5**, 496–97; **Supp. 8**, 482–84; predecessor, **Supp. 3**, 157; theoretical physics studies, **Supp. 8**, 482–84; World War II research, **Supp. 5**, 497

California School of Fine Arts (San Francisco), **Supp. 10**, 758, 759

California Star, **Vol. 1, Part 2**, 602

Calkins, Richard W., reference to, **Supp. 6**, 166

Calkins and Holden, founding of, **Supp. 7**, 101

Callahan, James, reference to, **Supp. 8**, 109

Calligraphy, **Supp. 5**, 693; **Supp. 6**, 185–86

Calliope, invention of, **Vol. 9, Part 2**, 57

Call Northside 777, **Supp. 9**, 189

Call of the Wild, The, **Vol. 6, Part 1**, 371

Calloway, Cab, reference to, **Supp. 9**, 442; **Supp. 10**, 298

Calorimetry, **Vol. 1, Part 1**, 417; **Vol. 2, Part 1**, 144; **Vol. 7, Part 2**, 252; **Supp. 1**, 517–18

Caltech. *See* California Institute of Technology

Calumet Farm (Lexington, Ky.), **Supp. 7**, 399–400

Calumet-Hecla Co., **Vol. 5, Part 1**, 360

Calvinism, **Vol. 2, Part 1**, 354; **Vol. 3, Part 2**, 130; **Vol. 4, Part 2**, 560; **Vol. 7, Part 1**, 339, 390

Cambria Iron Works, **Vol. 5, Part 2**, 312

Cambridge, Mass.: college, committee to consider establishment of, **Vol. 3, Part 1**, 484 f.; Congregational church, **Vol. 6, Part 2**, 90; founding of, **Vol. 8, Part 1**, 66 f.; Germanic Museum, **Vol. 8, Part 1**, 493; printing in, **Vol. 5, Part 2**, 110; printing press, first in America, **Vol. 3, Part 1**, 163; public service, **Vol. 1, Part 2**, 258; social life, **Vol. 5, Part 1**, 307; Washington Elm, **Vol. 6, Part 1**, 381

Cambridge History of American Literature, **Supp. 4**, 847

Cambridge Platform, **Vol. 7, Part 1**, 573

Cambridge School of Drama, founding of, **Supp. 2**, 11

Cambridge Theological School, **Vol. 5, Part 1**, 101

Cambridge University (England), first woman awarded physics Ph.D. by, **Supp. 10**, 52

Camden, S.C., battle of, **Vol. 2, Part 1**, 571; **Vol. 4, Part 1**, 187, 324, 571; **Vol. 5, Part 2**, 254; **Vol. 7, Part 1**, 421; **Vol. 9, Part 1**, 226, 603

Camel cigarettes, **Supp. 5**, 567; **Supp. 7**, 267

Camel experiment (1858), **Vol. 1, Part 2**, 88; **Vol. 3, Part 1**, 126

Cameo cutting, **Vol. 8, Part 2**, 296

Camera: Akeley, **Vol. 1, Part 1**, 133; manufacture, early, **Vol. 5, Part 1**, 131; obscura, **Vol. 8, Part 1**, 101 f.
Camera Club of New York, **Vol. 1, Part 2**, 81
Cameras. *See* Photography
Camera Work, founding of, **Supp. 4**, 779–80
Cameron, Andrew C., references to, **Vol. 6, Part 1**, 249 f.; **Vol. 9, Part 2**, 640
Camouflage devices, **Vol. 9, Part 2**, 400
Campaign for World Government, founding of, **Supp. 4**, 727
Campanella, Roy, reference to, **Supp. 8**, 142
Campbell, Alan, reference to, **Supp. 8**, 492
Campbell, Alexander, references to, **Vol. 6, Part 1**, 401; **Vol. 7, Part 2**, 422 f.; **Vol. 8, Part 2**, 502
Campbell, C. Macfie, reference to, **Supp. 7**, 64
Campbell, George A., reference to, **Supp. 4**, 430
Campbell, William Wallace, reference to, **Supp. 3**, 207
Campbellism, **Vol. 1, Part 1**, 102; **Vol. 2, Part 2**, 532 f.; **Vol. 4, Part 1**, 407, 440; **Vol. 5, Part 2**, 615; **Vol. 9, Part 2**, 71
Campbellite church. *See* Disciples of Christ
Campbell Soup Co., **Supp. 8**, 560
Camp Fire Club, **Vol. 9, Part 1**, 106
Camp Fire Girls, **Vol. 4, Part 2**, 47
Camp Meetings, **Vol. 3, Part 1**, 410; **Vol. 9, Part 1**, 176
Camp Mystic (Conn.), **Supp. 8**, 3
Cam pump, invention of, **Vol. 8, Part 2**, 145
Camus, Albert: reference to, **Supp. 8**, 342; translation of, **Supp. 8**, 475–76
Cana Conference, establishment of, **Supp. 6**, 608
Canada: botany studies, **Supp. 8**, 3; boundary with U.S., **Vol. 1, Part 2**, 576; **Vol. 8, Part 2**, 507 f.; ceding of, **Vol. 5, Part 2**, 7; civil war, negotiations with England, involving, **Vol. 3, Part 2**, 398; conquest of, **Vol. 6, Part 1**, 428; consular service, **Vol. 9, Part 2**, 330; diplomacy with U.S., **Supp. 8**, 410; discovery of, **Vol. 2, Part 1**, 605; explorations, **Vol. 2, Part 1**, 183; **Vol. 4, Part 2**, 17; **Vol. 5, Part 1**, 456; **Vol. 9, Part 2**, 455; **Supp. 5**, 225; **Supp. 8**, 3; Fenian raid, **Vol. 7, Part 2**, 45; **Vol. 9, Part 2**, 242; French colonial service, **Vol. 7, Part 1**, 585; frontier disturbance of 1838–39, *see* Aroostook War, fugitive slaves in, **Vol. 4, Part 2**, 564; geological studies, **Supp. 5**, 415–16; hydroelectric development, **Vol. 1, Part 2**, 408; invasion of (1775), **Vol. 1, Part 1**, 363; **Vol. 2, Part 1**, 314; **Vol. 3, Part 1**, 175; **Vol. 4, Part 1**, 127; **Vol. 7, Part 1**, 99; Joint High Commission with U.S., **Vol. 4, Part 1**, 516; Methodist church, **Vol. 1, Part 1**, 574 f.; northwest, **Vol. 9, Part 2**, 330; Northwest Coast Indian studies, **Supp. 3**, 82–84; proposed invasion of, **Vol. 2, Part 2**, 366; **Vol. 4, Part 1**, 186; **Vol. 5, Part 2**, 253, 537; railroad building in, **Vol. 1, Part 2**, 594; **Vol. 9, Part 2**, 501; reciprocal trade treaty with U.S., **Supp. 1**, 29–30; travel, early, **Vol. 5, Part 2**, 548; writings on, **Vol. 5, Part 2**, 548
Canadian National Railways, **Vol. 9, Part 2**, 501
Canals (general): building, **Vol. 1, Part 1**, 540; **Vol. 1, Part 2**, 266, 380; **Vol. 2, Part 1**, 113, 338; **Vol. 3, Part 1**, 116, 421 f.; **Vol. 3, Part 2**, 117, 281; **Vol. 4, Part 1**, 89, 205, 355 f.; **Vol. 5, Part 1**, 69, 102, 247; **Vol. 5, Part 2**, 59, 96, 296, 455, 521; **Vol. 6, Part 1**, 39; **Vol. 6, Part 2**, 332, 537, 569, 575; **Vol. 7, Part 1**, 148, 227; **Vol. 7, Part 2**, 227; **Vol. 8, Part 1**, 359 f., 506; **Vol. 8, Part 2**, 15, 18, 30, 48, 87; **Vol. 9, Part 2**, 138, 598; **Vol. 10, Part 1**, 372 f., 616 f.; **Vol. 10, Part 2**, 21, 93, 260, 268, 350, 544; inventions concerning, **Vol. 4, Part 1**, 69 f.; irrigation, use of, for, **Vol. 2, Part 1**, 96; lock designs, **Supp. 3**, 310–11; locks, **Vol. 3, Part 1**, 406; **Vol. 5, Part 2**, 97; **Vol. 6, Part 1**, 327; **Vol. 8, Part 1**, 28 f.; **Vol. 10, Part 1**, 616 f., 618 f.; machinery, **Vol. 10, Part 2**, 539; policies, state and national; **Vol. 8, Part 2**, 220; promotion, **Vol. 3, Part 2**, 525; **Vol. 9, Part 1**, 7; **Vol. 9, Part 2**, 651; **Vol. 10, Part 1**, 541 f.; railroads, comparison with, **Vol. 9, Part 2**, 442; trade, effect on, **Vol. 9, Part 2**, 396
Canals (specific): Cape Cod, **Vol. 7, Part 2**, 277; Chenango, **Vol. 5, Part 2**, 59; Chesapeake and Ohio, **Vol. 5, Part 2**, 348; **Vol. 9, Part 2**, 249; Delaware and Hudson, **Vol. 3, Part 1**, 306 f.; **Vol. 5, Part 2**, 59; **Vol. 7, Part 2**, 35; Erie, **Vol. 3, Part 2**, 15, 90, 195, 525; **Vol. 5, Part 1**, 83, 150 f., 395; **Vol. 5, Part 2**, 59, 120, 320; **Vol. 6, Part 1**, 323; **Vol. 7, Part 1**, 212, 355, 563, 604; **Vol. 7, Part 2**, 52; **Vol. 8, Part 2**, 12, 21; **Vol. 9, Part 1**, 7; **Vol. 9, Part 2**, 651; **Vol. 10, Part 2**, 93, 544; James River, **Vol. 2, Part 2**, 580; **Vol. 8, Part 2**, 30; Morris, **Vol. 8, Part 1**, 506; Nicaragua, **Vol. 1, Part 2**, 266; **Vol. 3, Part 1**, 116, 421 f.; **Vol. 5, Part 1**, 69, 247; **Vol. 6, Part 2**, 537, 575; Panama, *see* Panama Canal; Sault Ste. Marie, **Vol. 2, Part 1**, 338; **Vol. 5, Part 2**, 225
Canals (by state): Florida, **Vol. 9, Part 2**, 249; Illinois, **Vol. 6, Part 2**, 332; Michigan, **Vol. 10, Part 1**, 616 f.; New York, **Vol. 3, Part 1**, 274; **Vol. 8, Part 1**, 324 f.; **Vol. 9, Part 2**, 260; **Vol. 10, Part 1**, 541 f.; Ohio, **Vol. 2, Part 1**, 113; **Vol. 5, Part 2**, 296, 521; **Vol. 6, Part 2**, 569; Pennsylvania, **Vol. 5, Part 2**, 521; **Vol. 9, Part 2**, 486
Canal Zone. *See* Panama Canal
Canby, Henry Seidel, reference to, **Supp. 5**, 439
Cancer: **Vol. 1, Part 1**, 227; **Vol. 4, Part 2**, 20 f.; **Vol. 7, Part 1**, 475 f.; **Vol. 8, Part 1**, 449; **Vol. 8, Part 2**, 385; **Vol. 10, Part 1**, 608; breast, **Supp. 6**, 70; breast cancer education, **Supp. 10**, 30; carcinogens, **Supp. 10**, 769; cervical, **Supp. 6**, 554; cervical smear, **Supp. 10**, 817; chemotherapy research, **Supp. 10**, 769; classification, **Supp. 3**, 503; detection, Pap test, **Supp. 2**, 632; diagnosis, **Supp. 7**, 598–99; diet-link studies, **Supp. 3**, 141; early detection of, **Supp. 2**, 632; **Supp. 4**, 616–17; electrosurgical knife treatment, **Supp. 6**, 69–70; genetic relationship, **Supp. 3**, 807; larynx, **Supp. 4**, 185–86; lung surgery, **Supp. 6**, 246; nonsurgical treatment of, **Vol. 2, Part 1**, 251; pathology, **Supp. 3**, 257–58; public education on, **Supp. 5**, 147; radiation-induced, **Supp. 4**, 112; radiation treatment for, **Supp. 3**, 412; **Supp. 4**, 185–86; **Supp. 10**, 769, 816–17; research, **Supp. 2**, 36; **Supp. 4**, 615–17; **Supp. 6**, 537–38; sex hormones relationship to, **Supp. 3**, 6; Sloan-Kettering research institute, **Supp. 6**, 333; smoking link, **Supp. 8**, 7; statistical studies, **Supp. 4**, 385; **Supp. 7**, 192; surgery, **Supp. 1**, 91; uterine, **Supp. 3**, 106; virus, **Supp. 8**, 556; vulval, **Supp. 3**, 763; writings on, **Supp. 7**, 513
Candlemaking, **Vol. 2, Part 1**, 148; **Vol. 8, Part 2**, 246
Candy manufacture, **Vol. 4, Part 2**, 54; Hershey chocolate bars, **Supp. 3**, 358
Canfield, Cass, reference to, **Supp. 3**, 686
Canfield, Dorothy. *See* Fisher, Dorothy Canfield
Cannibals, **Vol. 3, Part 1**, 475 f.
Canning and canned goods: bacteria-killing process, **Supp. 7**, 630–31; cold-pack method, **Supp. 5**, 51; fruit, **Vol. 5, Part 1**, 568; glass jars, **Supp. 5**, 343; meat products, **Supp. 4**, 395–96; **Supp. 5**, 314–15; salmon, **Vol. 5, Part 1**, 366; **Vol. 9, Part 1**, 220; strained baby food, **Supp. 5**, 242–43
Cannon, James J., Jr., Tinkham libel suit, **Supp. 6**, 636
Cannon, Joseph G., references to, **Supp. 3**, 464, 544, 558; **Supp. 4**, 481; **Supp. 5**, 666
Cannon, Poppy, reference to, **Supp. 5**, 741
Cannon, Walter B., references to, **Supp. 3**, 134; **Supp. 4**, 676
Cannon: inventions, **Vol. 1, Part 1**, 248; **Vol. 3, Part 1**, 600; **Vol. 8, Part 2**, 80, 397; **Vol. 9, Part 1**, 188; manufacture, **Vol. 3, Part 1**, 237; **Vol. 5, Part 1**, 246;

Vol. 5, Part 2, 164, 317; **Vol. 7, Part 2**, 58; **Vol. 8, Part 1**, 172 f.; **Vol. 9, Part 2**, 632 f.; wrought iron, first use of, **Vol. 3, Part 1**, 237
Cannonball Adderley Quintet, **Supp. 9**, 11
Canon law, **Vol. 3, Part 1**, 368
Cantalupo, Joseph, reference to, **Supp. 10**, 140
Cantatas, composition of, **Vol. 5, Part 2**, 251; **Vol. 7, Part 1**, 441
Cantellops, Nelson, reference to, **Supp. 9**, 269
Cantor, Eddie, references to, **Supp. 3**, 406; **Supp. 9**, 343; **Supp. 10**, 59
Cantors, **Vol. 8, Part 2**, 167; **Vol. 9, Part 1**, 530
Cantos, The, **Supp. 9**, 617, 618
Canyons, paintings of, **Vol. 7, Part 1**, 153
Cape Cod ballads, **Supp. 3**, 461
Cape Girardeau, settlement of, **Vol. 6, Part 1**, 413
Capital Airlines, **Supp. 10**, 621
Capitalism: "enlightened," **Supp. 6**, 615; Nazism related to, **Supp. 5**, 514; new, **Supp. 7**, 809; welfare, **Supp. 3**, 762–63, 792; writings on, **Supp. 3**, 179, 180
Capitalism, Socialism, and Democracy, **Supp. 4**, 722, 723
Capital punishment: **Vol. 2, Part 1**, 285; **Vol. 3, Part 2**, 166; **Vol. 4, Part 1**, 529; arguments against, **Supp. 3**, 103; **Supp. 4**, 472; biblical authority for, **Vol. 3, Part 1**, 339; Chessman case, **Supp. 6**, 111; **Supp. 7**, 292–93; electric chair, first use of, **Vol. 8, Part 2**, 69; in Kansas, **Supp. 7**, 678; Massachusetts, early move toward abolition of, in, **Vol. 8, Part 1**, 381; state opposition, **Supp. 8**, 92
Capital Transit Co. (Washington, D. C.), **Supp. 4**, 397
Capital University, **Vol. 4, Part l**, 590–91; **Vol. 6, Part l**, 479
Capitol, Washington, D. C.: **Vol. 1, Part 2**, 380; **Vol. 6, Part 1**, 86; architecture of, **Vol. 6, Part 1**, 599; **Supp. 8**, 629–30; burning of, by British (1814), **Vol. 6, Part 1**, 23; cane-fight in corridors of, **Vol. 8, Part 2**, 195; "Columbus Doors," **Vol. 8, Part 2**, 107; erection of, **Vol. 6, Part 1**, 22; extensions to, **Vol. 10, Part 1**, 397 f.; landscape gardening, **Vol. 7, Part 2**, 26; plans for, **Vol. 9, Part 2**, 505; restoration of (1815), **Vol. 6, Part 1**, 23
Capitol Magazine, collapse of, **Vol. 4, Part 2**, 364
Capitol Records Co., **Supp. 7**, 131; founding of, **Supp. 4**, 226
Capitol Theatre (New York City), **Supp. 4**, 97
Capone, Al, references to, **Supp. 3**, 772; **Supp. 6**, 58, 263, 264; **Supp. 7**, 806; **Supp. 9**, 651
Capp, Al, reference to, **Supp. 5**, 223
Capper, Arthur, reference to, **Supp. 3**, 106
Capper-Ketchum Act (1928), **Supp. 5**, 101
Capper-Volstead Cooperative Marketing Act (1922), **Supp. 4**, 853; **Supp. 5**, 101
Capps, Richard B., reference to, **Supp. 3**, 806
Capra, Frank, references to, **Supp. 3**, 443–44; **Supp. 6**, 118, 119; **Supp. 9**, 767
Captain from Castile, **Supp. 5**, 620
"Captain Video" (fictional character), **Supp. 10**, 343–44
Capuchin Order, **Vol. 1, Part 1**, 321
Carbines, manufacture of, **Vol. 3, Part 1**, 600; **Vol. 7, Part 1**, 228
Carbobenzoxy method, **Supp. 3**, 61
Carbohydrates: chemistry of, **Supp. 3**, 61; research in, **Supp. 2**, 379
Carbon black, **Supp. 7**, 98
Carbon dioxide, plant interaction, **Supp. 4**, 192
Carbonic acid, **Supp. 3**, 350
Carbon monoxide, isolation of, **Vol. 8, Part 1**, 223 f.
Carbon-ratio hypothesis, **Supp. 1**, 703
Carborundum. *See* Silicon carbide
Carcinoma. *See* Cancer
Cardiology. *See* Heart; Heart disease
Cardiovascular system, **Supp. 6**, 117
Cardozo, Benjamin, references to, **Supp. 5**, 572, 573, 574; **Supp. 6**, 88
CARE (Cooperative for American Remittances to Everywhere), **Supp. 6**, 217–18
Carey, Hugh, reference to, **Supp. 10**, 698
Carey, William F., reference to, **Supp. 6**, 337
Carhart, Arthur, reference to, **Supp. 4**, 483
Caricatures. *See* Cartoons and caricatures
Caricography, writings on, **Vol. 3, Part 1**, 268
Carlen, Robert, reference to, **Supp. 4**, 667
Carles, Arthur B., reference to, **Supp. 5**, 470
Carleton College, **Vol. 9, Part 2**, 149 f.
Carleton Opera Company, **Vol. 5, Part 1**, 78
Carlisle, F. L., and Co., founding of, **Supp. 3**, 138
Carlisle, Kitty, reference to, **Supp. 7**, 325
Carlisle Indian School: **Vol. 8, Part 1**, 176; football team, **Supp. 5**, 683, 727–28
Carlson, Chester, reference to, **Supp. 9**, 877
Carlson, George A., reference to, **Supp. 6**, 455
Carlson's Raiders, **Supp. 4**, 147
Carlyle, Thomas, references to, **Vol. 1, Part 1**, 140, 475; **Vol. 7, Part 1**, 570
Carmack, Edward W., references to, **Supp. 1**, 656; **Supp. 3**, 449
Carman, Bliss, reference to, **Vol. 5, Part 1**, 273
Carmen Jones, **Supp. 7**, 162–63; **Supp. 8**, 547
Carmichael, Hoagy, reference to, **Supp. 9**, 474
Carmody, John M., references to, **Supp. 6**, 122, 437
Carnap, Rudolf, reference to, **Supp. 5**, 563
Carnation Co., founding of, **Supp. 3**, 750
Carnegie, Andrew: biography of, **Supp. 4**, 368; references to, **Vol. 4, Part 1**, 30, 189; **Vol. 6, Part 1**, 155; **Vol. 7, Part 1**, 143; **Vol. 7, Part 2**, 171, 550; **Vol. 9, Part 2**, 237, 386; **Supp. 3**, 90, 129; **Supp. 6**, 25, 506–7
Carnegie, Hattie, reference to, **Supp. 9**, 587
Carnegie Corporation: **Supp. 6**, 559; administration philosophy, **Supp. 3**, 416–17
Carnegie Endowment for International Peace: **Supp. 1**, 123; **Supp. 3**, 366; **Supp. 7**, 91, 114, 688; founding of, **Supp. 3**, 700; **Supp. 4**, 136–37; funding for, **Supp. 5**, 308
Carnegie Foundation for the Advancement of Teaching, **Supp. 1**, 327; **Supp. 3**, 387; **Supp. 6**, 208; **Supp. 8**, 72; founding of, **Supp. 2**, 542
Carnegie Hall (New York City): architecture of, **Vol. 10, Part 1**, 73; founding of, **Supp. 4**, 211; jazz concert (1938), **Supp. 8**, 163; Ochs concerts, **Supp. 10**, 602, 603; organ design, **Supp. 3**, 850
Carnegie-Illinois Steel Corporation, **Supp. 5**, 510; **Supp. 10**, 345
Carnegie Institute of Technology: library school, **Supp. 4**, 19; psychology studies, **Supp. 5**, 58
Carnegie Institution: **Vol. 4, Part 1**, 302; **Vol. 4, Part 2**, 606; **Vol. 8, Part 2**, 98; **Vol. 10, Part 2**, 92; archaeological studies, **Supp. 4**, 605–6; **Supp. 7**, 432; archives, **Supp. 8**, 369; ecology studies, **Supp. 3**, 169; embryology studies, **Supp. 4**, 801–2; genetics department, **Supp. 3**, 215–16; 445–46; geophysical laboratory, **Supp. 6**, 70–71, 153, 154; historical research department, **Supp. 2**, 341; **Supp. 4**, 530–31; presidency, **Supp. 3**, 519; **Supp. 9**, 145; terrestrial magnetism department, **Supp. 6**, 205, 206; trustees, **Supp. 6**, 211; war technology research, **Supp. 9**, 144
Carnegie Laboratory of Medical Research, **Supp. 1**, 240
Carnegie Museum (Pittsburgh, Pa.): curator of birds, **Supp. 8**, 654; growth of, **Supp. 1**, 414
Carnegie Steel Co., **Supp. 1**, 203
Carney, Robert B., reference to, **Supp. 8**, 157–58
Carnochan, J. M., reference to, **Vol. 9, Part 2**, 318

Carolina Playmakers, **Supp. 3**, 426–27; **Supp. 5**, 109
Carolinas, the: colonial government, **Vol. 5, Part 2**, 111, 116 f.; **Vol. 6, Part 1**, 496; division of, into North and South, **Vol. 5, Part 2**, 117; Sherman's campaign in, **Vol. 1, Part 2**, 587; **Vol. 5, Part 2**, 146; **Vol. 8, Part 2**, 453; **Vol. 9, Part 1**, 96; writings on, **Vol. 5, Part 2**, 484
Carothers, Wallace Hume, reference to, **Supp. 5**, 663
Carpenter, Rhys, reference to, **Supp. 4**, 144
Carpet-Bag, **Vol. 9, Part 1**, 110
Carpetbagging: **Vol. 1, Part 1**, 133, 138; **Vol. 2, Part 2**, 148; **Vol. 3, Part 2**, 403; **Vol. 5, Part 1**, 624; **Vol. 5, Part 2**, 305 f., 492; **Vol. 9, Part l**, 110; **Vol. 9, Part 2**, 592, 603 f.; **Vol. 10, Part 1**, 94; Arkansas, **Vol. 8, Part 1**, 33 f.; Florida, **Vol. 8, Part 1**, 372 f.; Louisiana, **Vol. 3, Part 2**, 554; Mississippi, **Vol. 9, Part 2**, 78; North Carolina, **Vol. 10, Part 1**, 69; South Carolina, **Vol. 1, Part 1**, 127
Carpet manufacture, **Vol. 2, Part 2**, 250; **Vol. 9, Part 2**, 183, 198
Carr, Harvey, reference to, **Supp. 4**, 21
Carr, Julian S., reference to, **Supp. 3**, 587
Carr, Ralph A., reference to, **Supp. 6**, 455
Carrel, Alexis, references to, **Supp. 4**, 287, 288; **Supp. 6**, 386; **Supp. 9**, 497
Carriage manufacturing, **Vol. 2, Part 1**, 28; **Vol. 8, Part 2**, 9; **Vol. 9, Part 2**, 555; **Supp. 7**, 245
Carrick's Ford, W. Va., engagement at, **Vol. 4, Part 1**, 159; **Vol. 7, Part 1**, 228
Carrier Corporation, founding of, **Supp. 4**, 149
Carrillo, Leo, reference to, **Supp. 10**, 669
Carroll, B. H., references to, **Supp. 3**, 687, 688
Carroll, Coleman F., reference to, **Supp. 8**, 295
Carroll, John, references to, **Vol. 7, Part 1**, 400, 429; **Vol. 9, Part 2**, 376
Carroll, Lewis, reference to, **Supp. 5**, 587
Carson, Christopher, references to, **Vol. 4, Part 1**, 20; **Vol. 7, Part 1**, 560; **Vol. 7, Part 2**, 111
Carson's Private Hospital (Washington, D.C.), **Supp. 5**, 104
Carswell, G. Harold, reference to, **Supp. 9**, 681
Cartan, Elie Joseph, reference to, **Supp. 7**, 216
Cartography: **Vol. 1, Part 2**, 250; **Vol. 3, Part 2**, 497; **Vol. 4, Part 2**, 592; **Vol. 5, Part 1**, 107; **Vol. 5, Part 2**, 157, 419 f.; **Vol. 6, Part l**, 272; **Vol. 7, Part 1**, 61; **Vol. 8, Part 2**, 39; **Vol. 9, Part 1**, 409; **Vol. 9, Part 2**, 296 f.; **Vol. 10, Part 2**, 404; agricultural regions, **Supp. 4**, 45; Antarctic, **Supp. 7**, 217; commercial maps, **Supp. 1**, 350; geological, **Supp. 3**, 407–8, 696; **Supp. 4**, 896; Indian trails, **Supp. 1**, 443; topographical of West, **Supp. 4**, 558; writings on, **Supp. 2**, 56. *See also* Maps; Topography
Cartoons and caricatures: **Vol. 2, Part 2**, 22; **Vol. 5, Part 1**, 324; **Vol. 5, Part 2**, 352 f.; **Vol. 7, Part 1**, 186, 391 f.; **Vol. 8, Part 2**, 113; animated, **Supp. 3**, 76; **Supp. 8**, 129–30; **Supp. 9**, 237, 797–98; **Supp. 10**, 351–53, 441, 813; boxing, **Vol. 3, Part 1**, 378 f.; cell animation, **Supp. 9**, 797; Civil War, **Vol. 7, Part 1**, 186; comic strips, **Vol. 3, Part 1**, 378 f.; **Vol. 7, Part 2**, 112; **Supp. 9**, 452–53; **Supp. 10**, 98–99, 353; correspondence school, **Supp. 1**, 718; editorial, **Supp. 1**, 707; **Supp. 4**, 76; **Supp. 7**, 205–6; **Supp. 8**, 173–74; **Supp. 10**, 244–45; first animated, **Supp. 3**, 76; "flapper," **Supp. 6**, 278–88; German political, **Supp. 6**, 256; Gibson Girl, **Supp. 3**, 300–301; Goldberg, Rube, inventions, **Supp. 8**, 217; "hot dog," **Supp. 7**, 719; humorous, **Supp. 5**, 732; legislation against, attempted, **Vol. 3, Part 1**, 83; *New Yorker*, **Supp. 7**, 743; **Supp. 8**, 15–16; one-line caption, **Supp. 8**, 15; painting style, **Supp. 6**, 199–200; political, **Vol. 3, Part 1**, 83 f., 378 f.; **Vol. 4, Part 1**, 286 f.; **Vol. 5, Part 2**, 139; **Vol. 7, Part 1**, 392; **Vol. 8, Part 1**, 514; **Vol. 8, Part 2**, 113; **Supp. 1**, 718; **Supp. 3**, 852; **Supp. 4**, 159–60; **Supp. 5**, 391–92, 499, 580, 672; **Supp. 7**, 164; **Supp. 8**, 218; **Supp. 10**, 292–93; *Puck*, in, **Vol. 8, Part 2**, 31; "Ripley's Believe It or Not!," **Supp. 4**, 693; Sardi's dlsplay of, **Supp. 8**, 571; satiric, **Supp. 4**, 386; **Supp. 10**, 832; social and political commentary, **Supp. 9**, 453; sports, **Supp. 10**, 563–64; syndicate, first, **Vol. 8, Part 2**, 113; "Terrytoons," **Supp. 9**, 797–98. *See also* Comic strips
Cartridge belt, invention of, **Vol. 7, Part 1**, l
Carty, John J., references to, **Supp. 3**, 299; **Supp. 4**, 430
Caruso, Dorothy, reference to, **Supp. 9**, 34
Caruso, Enrico, references to, **Supp. 3**, 742; **Supp. 6**, 323
Carvalho, S. S., references to, **Supp. 3**, 427; **Supp. 5**, 284
Casablanca, **Supp. 5**, 209; **Supp. 7**, 160
Casablanca Conference (1942), **Supp. 3**, 662; **Supp. 5**, 334
Casa del Libro, La (Puerto Rico), **Supp. 7**, 3
Casa Loma Orchestra, **Supp. 7**, 300–301
Cascade Tunnel, **Supp. 3**, 735, 737
Casella, Alfredo, reference to, **Supp. 10**, 237
Case School of Applied Science: **Vol. 2, Part 1**, 558; **Vol. 3, Part 1**, 262; **Vol. 9, Part 1**, 495; **Vol. 9, Part 2**, 50; physics studies, **Supp. 3**, 523
"Case system" of law, **Vol. 3, Part 1**, 571 f.; **Vol. 3, Part 2**, 75; **Vol. 5, Part 2**, 285
Cash, Johnny, reference to, **Supp. 10**, 105
Cash, June Carter, reference to, **Supp. 10**, 105
Cash registers, manufacture of, **Vol. 7, Part 2**, 304; **Vol. 9, Part 1**, 138; electrification of, **Supp. 6**, 332
Cassady, Neal, reference to, **Supp. 8**, 326
"Cassidy, Hopalong" (fictional character), **Supp. 6**, 466; **Supp. 8**, 248
Castellammare war (organized crime), **Supp. 7**, 632; **Supp. 8**, 396–7
Castellano, Paul, reference to, **Supp. 10**, 267
Castle, Vernon, reference to, **Supp. 8**, 77
Castle, William B., reference to, **Supp. 4**, 582
Castro, Fidel, references to, **Supp. 7**, 116, 421, 422; **Supp. 8**, 135, 323; **Supp. 9**, 780
CAT. *See* Civil Air Transport
Catalases (enzymes), **Supp. 6**, 595
Catalogs: library, **Supp. 1**, 242; **Supp. 3**, 326–27, 375, 510, 664; of rare books, **Supp. 7**, 387. *See also* Bibliographies
Catalogue of Incipits of Mediaeval Scientific Writings in Latin, **Supp. 7**, 742
Catalogue sales. *See* Mail order houses
Cataloguing, **Vol. 1, Part 1**, 218; **Vol. 3, Part 1**, 15 f.; **Vol. 7, Part 1**, 414; **Vol. 8, Part 2**, 114, 275; **Vol. 10, Part 1**, 107
Catamarans, design of, **Supp. 2**, 298
Cataract, pioneer operations for removal of, **Vol. 3, Part 1**, 478 f.; **Vol. 5, Part 1**, 541
Catchings, Waddill, reference to, **Supp. 4**, 307
Catechism of Money, **Vol. 8, Part 2**, 150
Catena, Gerardo (Jerry), **Supp. 8**, 208, 209
Catering industry, sporting events, **Supp. 7**, 719
Cathcart, James, reference to, **Vol. 3, Part 1**, 613
Cathedral: administration, **Vol. 3, Part 1**, 335; Episcopal, first, **Vol. 5, Part 2**, 422
Cathedral College, **Vol. 8, Part 1**, 303 f.; establishment of, **Supp. 2**, 293
Cathedral of St. John the Divine (New York City): **Vol. 3, Part 2**, 354; **Vol. 4, Part 2**, 389; **Vol. 5, Part 1**, 421; architecture, **Supp. 2**, 369; **Supp. 3**, 196–97; design and building, **Supp. 4**, 547; sculpture, **Supp. 3**, 88; stained-glass windows, **Supp. 3**, 183

Cather, Willa, references to, **Supp. 4**, 518; **Supp. 6**, 251
Cathode ray: oscilloscope, **Supp. 7**, 226, 280; tubes, **Supp. 1**, 646; **Supp. 7**, 206
Catholic Action, **Supp. 6**, 607, 608
Catholic Association for International Peace, founding of, **Supp. 2**, 87
Catholic Book Exchange, **Vol. 3, Part 1**, 421
Catholic Charities, founding of, **Supp. 2**, 294; **Supp. 6**, 608
Catholic Charities Review, founding of, **Supp. 2**, 360; **Supp. 3**, 680
Catholic church (general); for specific priests, bishops, etc., *see* Occupations Index: Anglican reunification issue, **Supp. 2**, 201; Anglo-Catholicism, **Supp. 3**, 195; **Supp. 6**, 46; apologetical journalism, **Supp. 6**, 478–79; appointments in, early, **Vol. 8, Part 2**, 155; as presidential campaign issue, **Supp. 3**, 719–20; **Supp. 6**, 572; **Supp. 7**, 361; **Supp. 8**, 115–16; beatification, **Supp. 1**, 147–48; bishop, first in United States, **Vol. 2, Part 1**, 527; bookselling, **Vol. 5, Part 2**, 329 f.; Cahensly movement, **Vol. 4, Part 1**, 241; California, **Vol. 3, Part 1**, 421; **Vol. 4, Part 1**, 102; **Vol. 8, Part 1**, 619; **Vol. 8, Part 2**, 248; **Supp. 10**, 497–98; civil rights support by, **Supp. 1**, 159; **Supp. 7**, 448, 533; **Supp. 8**, 293–94, 500, 537; Communism, **Supp. 9**, 135; controversies, **Vol. 5, Part 1**, 352 f.; **Vol. 6, Part 1**, 201; **Vol. 8, Part 2**, 265; **Supp. 10**, 151–52; conversions to, **Vol. 5, Part 1**, 417; **Vol. 9, Part 2**, 374; **Vol. 10, Part 1**, 98; **Supp. 10**, 467, 777; coordination of activities, **Supp. 2**, 73; Curia, **Supp. 8**, 46–47; dogma, defense of, **Supp. 10**, 498; dogma relativism, **Supp. 3**, 325; ecumenism, **Supp. 8**, 115; education, **Vol. 1, Part 1**, 302 f.; **Vol. 2, Part 2**, 337 f.; **Vol. 3, Part 2**, 393, 440; **Vol. 4, Part 2**, 541; **Vol. 7, Part 1**, 74; **Vol. 7, Part 2**, 3; **Vol. 8, Part 2**, 265; **Vol. 9, Part 1**, 108; establishment of, in U.S., **Vol. 2, Part 1**, 383; first English mass, **Supp. 8**, 537; excommunication and return, **Supp. 9**, 134, 135; first U.S. president, **Supp. 7**, 420; foreign missions, **Supp. 5**, 178–79, 581; "Friar Lands," **Vol. 4, Part 1**, 241; Greek Orthodox church reconciliation, **Supp. 9**, 50–51; history in U.S., **Supp. 1**, 360; **Supp. 4**, 353; immigrants, **Vol. 9, Part 1**, 113; Iowa, **Vol. 4, Part 1**, 167; **Vol. 4, Part 2**, 541; Jewish relations, **Supp. 8**, 307, 537, 589; **Supp. 9**, 384; Kentucky, **Vol. 3, Part 2**, 329; **Vol. 6, Part 2**, 194, 616; **Vol. 10, Part 2**, 346; labor movement support by, **Supp. 2**, 135; **Supp. 5**, 263; lay organizations, **Supp. 1**, 456; **Supp. 3**, 180, 569, 694; Legion of Decency censorship, **Supp. 5**, 419, 677; **Supp. 7**, 71; liturgical movement, **Supp. 2**, 455; Maryland, **Vol. 4, Part 1**, 240; **Vol. 5, Part 2**, 470; Massachusetts, **Vol. 3, Part 1**, 361; **Vol. 6, Part 2**, 408; **Vol. 10, Part 2**, 277; Middle West, **Vol. 6, Part 1**, 138; Michigan, **Vol. 6, Part 1**, 139; military chaplains, **Supp. 7**, 581; missions, **Vol. 1, Part 1**, 161, 231 f., 276 f., 383 f.; **Vol. 2, Part 1**, 67; **Vol. 3, Part 1**, 477 f.; **Vol. 3, Part 2**, 100, 161, 355, 432, 435, 497; **Vol. 4, Part 1**, 113, 128, 235, 466; **Vol. 4, Part 2**, 34, 495, 510, 542; **Vol. 5, Part 1**, 106; **Vol. 5, Part 2**, 267, 419 f., 567; **Vol. 6, Part 1**, 161, 231, 403; **Vol. 6, Part 2**, 61, 87; **Vol. 7, Part 1**, 148 f., 428 f., 533, 536, 610 f., 625; **Vol. 7, Part 2**, 170 f., 202 f., 591; **Vol. 8, Part 1**, 217 f., 330 f., 394; **Vol. 8, Part 2**, 59, 155, 263 f., 447; **Vol. 10, Part 1**, 405; **Supp. 1**, 158; **Supp. 2**, 692; **Supp. 7**, 447; **Supp. 10**, 404–5; missions for American Indians, **Supp. 1**, 158–59, 218–19, 289–90; Mississippi, **Vol. 2, Part 1**, 611; modernist controversy, **Supp. 3**, 325; **Supp. 10**, 497; monasticism, **Supp. 8**, 430–31; music, **Vol. 7, Part 2**, 512; musicians in, **Supp. 3**, 849–50; Nebraska, **Vol. 7, Part 1**, 618; New England, **Vol. 6, Part 2**, 408; New Jersey, **Vol. 6, Part 2**, 44; **Vol. 10, Part 2**, 189; New York, **Vol. 1, Part 2**, 373; **Vol. 3, Part 1**, 470 f.; **Vol. 6, Part 2**, 226; **Supp. 10**, 497; North Carolina, **Vol. 4, Part 1**, 239; **Vol. 8, Part 1**, 217 f.; Ohio, **Vol. 8, Part 1**, 266 f.; organizations, **Supp. 2**, 87; Pacific Coast, **Vol. 1, Part 1**, 161; pacifism, **Supp. 10**, 175–76; parochial school policies, **Supp. 3**, 393; **Supp. 4**, 334; **Supp. 5**, 179, 358; **Supp. 7**, 533; **Supp. 8**, 25, 115–16, 537; Paulist Fathers, **Supp. 6**, 237–38; Pennsylvania, **Vol. 4, Part 1**, 527; **Vol. 6, Part 1**, 161; **Vol. 6, Part 2**, 59; **Vol. 7, Part 1**, 619; **Vol. 10, Part 2**, 461, 632; philanthropy, **Vol. 8, Part 2**, 248; **Vol. 9, Part 1**, 483; Philippines, **Vol. 4, Part 1**, 241; political influence critcized, **Supp. 10**, 48; Polish National church founding, **Supp. 5**, 304–6; prelates, **Supp. 1**, 263; **Supp. 2**, 293–94, 477–78; **Supp. 3**, 325–26, 568–70, 694–95; **Supp. 4**, 334–35, 535–36; **Supp. 5**, 179, 722–23; **Supp. 7**, 532–34, 668–69; **Supp. 8**, 114–16, 294–95, 536–37, 588–89, 612–15; publications, **Supp. 5**, 677–78; **Supp. 7**, 448, *see also* Catholic church, publications; religious orders, **Supp. 1**, 158–59; **Supp. 5**, 185–86; **Supp. 6**, 237–38; **Supp. 7**, 447–48, *see also names of specific orders*; Revolutionary War, growth following, **Vol. 2, Part 1**, 527; schisms within, **Supp. 5**, 178–79, 305; Second Vatican Council, **Supp. 7**, 534, 776; **Supp. 8**, 46, 115, 307, 537, 614–15; **Supp. 10**, 498; seal of the confessional, court decision on, **Vol. 5, Part 2**, 488 f.; seminaries, **Supp. 3**, 325–26; **Supp. 10**, 404; sisterhoods, formation of, **Vol. 2, Part 1**, 475; social reform, **Supp. 2**, 359, 478; **Supp. 3**, 624–25, 679–81; **Supp. 4**, 232–33, 282–83, 562; **Supp. 6**, 607–8; **Supp. 8**, 588–89; societies, **Supp. 1**, 360; South Dakota, **Vol. 7, Part 2**, 3; Soviet Union, **Supp. 6**, 662; Texas, **Vol. 7, Part 1**, 625 f.; theology, **Supp. 7**, 775–76; **Supp. 10**, 855–56; universities and colleges, **Supp. 1**, 159; **Supp. 6**, 662; **Supp. 8**, 115; Vatican declaration on non-Christian religions, **Supp. 9**, 384; Vatican Library reorganization, **Supp. 3**, 327; Virginia, **Vol. 8, Part 1**, 123 f.; West, **Vol. 3, Part 2**, 312; writings on, **Vol. 3, Part 1**, 361; **Vol. 4, Part 1**, 114, 129, 239, 242, 313, 336; **Vol. 4, Part 2**, 383, 510, 604; **Vol. 5, Part 2**, 340, 437, 558, 559; **Vol. 6, Part 1**, 68, 540; **Vol. 7, Part 1**, 24, 190; **Vol. 8, Part 2**, 283 f.; **Vol. 9, Part 1**, 16 f., 51, 108, 425; **Vol. 9, Part 2**, 76 f.; **Vol. 10, Part 2**, 614; **Supp. 6**, 46; **Supp. 10**, 729, 735. *See also* Vatican
Catholic church (publications): **Vol. 3, Part 2**, 162, 329, 396; **Vol. 5, Part 1**, 418; **Vol. 5, Part 2**, 329 f., 339 f., 589; **Vol. 6, Part 1**, 201; **Vol. 7, Part 1**, 353; **Vol. 8, Part 2**, 260, 265; *Catholic Educational Review,* **Vol. 9, Part 1**, 108, founding of, **Supp. 2**, 506; *Catholic Encyclopedia,* **Vol. 3, Part 2**, 274; **Vol. 4, Part 2**, 570; **Vol. 7, Part 2**, 171; **Vol. 9, Part 1**, 17; *Catholic Herald,* **Vol. 5, Part 2**, 339 f.; *Catholic Historical Review,* founding of, **Supp. 4**, 353; *Catholic Mind,* **Supp. 5**, 677; *Catholic News,* **Vol. 8, Part 1**, 590; *Catholic Telegraph,* **Vol. 3, Part 2**, 329; *Catholic Times,* **Vol. 5, Part 2**, 558; **Vol. 8, Part 2**, 265; *Catholic Worker,* **Supp. 10**, 175–76; *Catholic World,* **Vol. 3, Part 1**, 421; **Vol. 4, Part 2**, 495; **Supp. 4**, 689; **Supp. 6**, 237, 298; *Pilot,* **Vol. 8, Part 2**, 63
Catholic Church Extension Society, **Vol. 8, Part 1**, 303 f.
Catholic Foreign Mission Bureau, founding of, **Supp. 2**, 602
Catholic Foreign Mission Society of America, **Vol. 8, Part 1**, 217 f. *See also* Maryknoll
Catholic Interracial Council: founding of, **Supp. 8**, 293; New York, **Supp. 7**, 448
Catholic Laymen's Association of Georgia, founding of, **Supp. 2**, 87

Catholic Laymen's Union of New York, founding of, **Supp. 7**, 448
Catholic literature, **Supp. 5**, 677–78; **Supp. 7**, 582–83
Catholic Missionary Union, **Vol. 3, Part 1**, 421; **Vol. 3, Part 2**, 100; **Vol. 8, Part 2**, 265
Catholic Near East Welfare Association, founding of, **Supp. 2**, 202
Catholic Press Association, founding of, **Supp. 2**, 72
Catholic Principles of Politics, **Supp. 3**, 681
Catholic Summer School of America, **Vol. 2, Part 2**, 338; **Vol. 6, Part 1**, 15
Catholic Total Abstinence Union of America, **Supp. 2**, 135
Catholic University of America (Washington, D.C.): **Vol. 1, Part 2**, 482; **Vol. 4, Part 1**, 240; **Vol. 5, Part 1**, 495; **Vol. 5, Part 2**, 268; **Vol. 8, Part 2**, 57; anthropology studies, **Supp. 4**, 179; church history studies, **Supp. 4**, 353; development of, **Supp. 2**, 506; education studies, **Supp. 3**, 393; Semitic and Egyptian studies, **Supp. 3**, 374–75; trustees, **Supp. 4**, 335
Catholic University of Chile, **Supp. 7**, 775
Catholic University of St. Louis, **Vol. 3, Part 1**, 255
Catholic Worker movement, **Supp. 4**, 562
Catholic Youth Organization, founding of, **Supp. 8**, 588–89
Catledge, Turner, reference to, **Supp. 7**, 200
Catskill Mountains (N.Y.), resort business in, **Supp. 9**, 341–43
Catt, Carrie Chapman, references to, **Supp. 1**, 17; **Supp. 5**, 532; **Supp. 6**, 79; **Supp. 7**, 778, 779; **Supp. 9**, 641
Cattell, James McKeen, references to, **Supp. 4**, 62, 135; **Supp. 6**, 671–72
Cattle: **Vol. 1, Part 1**, 238, 260, 326; **Vol. 2, Part 2**, 77; **Vol. 3, Part 2**, 302, 393, 453; **Vol. 4, Part 2**, 326, 494; **Vol. 6, Part 1**, 12, 301, 618 f.; **Vol. 9, Part 1**, 57; **Vol. 9, Part 2**, 134; auction sale, **Vol. 8, Part 1**, 503 f.; breeding, **Supp. 9**, 463–64; **Supp. 10**, 782; diseases of, **Vol. 7, Part 1**, 418; **Vol. 7, Part 2**, 359; **Vol. 8, Part 1**, 396; importation, **Vol. 8, Part 1**, 503 f.; raising, **Vol. 1, Part 1**, 326; **Vol. 4, Part 2**, 326; **Vol. 6, Part 1**, 618 f.; **Vol. 7, Part 1**, 100; **Vol. 8, Part 1**, 456; **Vol. 10, Part 1**, 472 f. *See also* Live-stock
Cato Letters, **Vol. 3, Part 1**, 28
"Caucus Club," **Vol. 1, Part 1**, 96
Causality concept, **Supp. 8**, 190
Caustic Labeling Act (1927), **Supp. 6**, 317
Cavalry: Civil War raids, **Vol. 3, Part 1**, 600; **Vol. 3, Part 2**, 100, 532; **Vol. 6, Part 1**, 104; **Vol. 8, Part 2**, 70; equipment, **Vol. 3, Part 1**, 600. *See also* Army, United States
Cayley, Arthur, reference to, **Supp. 5**, 491
CBS. *See* Columbia Broadcasting System
CBS Building (New York City), architectural design, **Supp. 7**, 672
CBS Symphony, **Supp. 9**, 382
CCC. *See* Civilian Conservation Corps
CEA. *See* Council of Economic Advisors
CED. *See* Committe on Economic Development
Cecilia Society (Cincinnati, Ohio), **Vol. 8, Part 1**, 633
Cedar Creek, Va., battle of, **Vol. 3, Part 1**, 598; **Vol. 8, Part 1**, 341; **Vol. 9, Part 1**, 80; **Vol. 10, Part 2**, 555
Cedar Mountain, Va., battle of, **Vol. 1, Part 1**, 579; **Vol. 5, Part 1**, 25, 558; **Vol. 8, Part 1**, 77; **Vol. 9, Part 2**, 284
Cedar Rapids, Iowa, **Vol. 7, Part 2**, 285
Celler, Emmanuel, reference to, **Supp. 5**, 348
Celluloid, manufacture of, **Vol. 5, Part 1**, 448; **Vol. 7, Part 1**, 298
Cemeteries, landscaping of, **Vol. 3, Part 1**, 406; **Vol. 10, Part 1**, 605 f.
Cemetery Ridge, Gettysburg. *See* Gettysburg, battle of
Censorship: books, **Supp. 7**, 98, 149, 292, 293; **Supp. 8**, 605; **Supp. 9**, 165, 782; **Supp. 10**, 47, 221, 539, 540; Boston Watch and Ward Society, **Supp. 7**, 98; comic strips, **Supp. 9**, 453; Legion of Decency, **Supp. 5**, 419, 617; **Supp. 7**, 71; legislation advocates, **Supp. 3**, 181; literary, **Supp. 3**, 844; **Supp. 5**, 270; **Supp. 6**, 94–95, 445; magazine, **Supp. 5**, 638; motion pictures, **Supp. 4**, 535; **Supp. 5**, 281–82, 677; **Supp. 6**, 288–89, 479; **Supp. 7**, 71; **Supp. 10**, 324; organizations opposed to, **Supp. 10**, 47; radio, **Supp. 10**, 463; postal service, **Supp. 6**, 661; radio, **Supp. 6**, 631; textbooks, **Supp. 6**, 528, 558; **Supp. 7**, 330
Census, Bureau of the (U.S.): **Vol. 3, Part 1**, 181; **Vol. 5, Part 1**, 251, 622; **Vol. 5, Part 2**, 335, 495; **Vol. 6, Part 2**, 554; **Vol. 7, Part 1**, 562; **Vol. 8, Part 1**, 100 f.; **Vol. 8, Part 2**, 182; **Vol. 9, Part 1**, 34; **Vol. 10, Part 2**, 198; establishment of, **Supp. 2**, 175; statistical research division, **Supp. 2**, 303; tabulating and tallying machines, **Supp. 3**, 596
Centenarian, **Vol. 5, Part 1**, 185
Centenary College (La.), **Vol. 5, Part 2**, 579; **Vol. 6, Part 1**, 390; football team, **Supp. 5**, 458
Centennial Exposition (Philadelphia, Pa.), **Vol. 6, Part 1**, 187; **Vol. 7, Part 1**, 413; **Vol. 8, Part 2**, 197; **Vol. 10, Part 1**, 647
Centennial History of the Civil War, The, **Supp. 10**, 108
"Centennial Law Suit," **Vol. 6, Part 1**, 41
Center for Blood Research, founding of, **Supp. 5**, 123
Center for the Study of Democratic Institutions: founding of, **Supp. 8**, 59; **Supp. 10**, 366; writings on military, **Supp. 8**, 441–42
Centinel, first issue of, in Boston, **Vol. 8, Part 2**, 239
Central America: authority on, **Vol. 9, Part 1**, 489; birds of, **Vol. 6, Part 1**, 49; diplomacy with, **Vol. 3, Part 1**, 39; **Vol. 5, Part 1**, 69; railroad building, **Vol. 5, Part 2**, 292; writings on, **Vol. 9, Part 1**, 579
Central Bank and Trust Co. (Asheville, N.C.), **Supp. 3**, 449
Central City College, **Vol. 6, Part 1**, 432
Central College (Mo.), **Vol. 6, Part 1**, 549; **Vol. 9, Part 1**, 362
Central College (Ohio), **Vol. 8, Part 2**, 394
Central Committee for the United Study of Missions, founding of, **Supp. 4**, 647–48
Central Conference of American Rabbis, **Vol. 1, Part 2**, 220; founding of, **Supp. 4**, 659
Central Hanover Bank and Trust Co., founding of, **Supp. 5**, 158, 756
Central High School (Philadelphia, Pa.), **Vol. 5, Part 1**, 261
Central Institute for the Deaf, founding of, **Supp. 3**, 311
Central Intelligence Agency (CIA): administration, **Supp. 7**, 703; Cuban policies, **Supp. 7**, 421–22; **Supp. 8**, 323; Far Eastern operations, **Supp. 6**, 110; **Supp. 7**, 191; first civilian director, **Supp. 8**, 147; founding of, **Supp. 6**, 170; Kennedy, J. F., assassination of, **Supp. 8**, 558; predecessor, **Supp. 5**, 706; research and analysis, **Supp. 10**, 432; U-2 reconnaissance flights over Soviet Union, **Supp. 10**, 646
Central lighting plants, **Vol. 6, Part 1**, 235
Central Pacific Railroad, **Vol. 2, Part 2**, 552; **Vol. 5, Part 1**, 409 f.; **Vol. 5, Part 2**, 229; **Vol. 9, Part 1**, 502 f.
Central Railroad of Georgia, **Vol. 4, Part 1**, 427 f.
Central Railroad of New Jersey, **Vol. 5, Part 2**, 143
Central Republic Bank and Trust Co., **Supp. 5**, 160
Central States Electric Corporation, founding of, **Supp. 5**, 750
Central Trust Co. of Illinois, **Supp. 5**, 159
Centre College (Ky.), **Vol. 1, Part 2**, 315; **Vol. 9, Part**

1, 62; **Vol. 10, Part 2**, 629; football team, **Supp. 5**, 458
Centrifugation technique, **Supp. 6**, 54
Century, **Supp. 6**, 580; founding of, **Supp. 2**, 348
Century Association, **Vol. 5, Part 2**, 159; **Vol. 7, Part 1**, 299
Century Club (New York City), **Vol. 1, Part 2**, 169; **Vol. 3, Part 1**, 535 f.
Century Dictionary, **Vol. 9, Part 1**, 241, 340; **Vol. 9, Part 2**, 357
Century Magazine, **Vol. 4, Part 1**, 276; **Vol. 5, Part 1**, 147, 308; **Vol. 6, Part 1**, 526; **Vol. 9, Part 1**, 340; art department, **Vol. 3, Part 1**, 423 f.
Century of Progress Exposition. *See* Chicago Century of Progress Exposition
Century Theater (New York City), **Supp. 3**, 296
Cepheids, **Supp. 5**, 326
Ceramics: **Vol. 1, Part 1**, 588; **Vol. 8, Part 1**, 228 f.; **Vol. 10, Part 1**, 100; archaeological chronology, **Supp. 2**, 44
Ceraunograph, invention of, **Supp. 1**, 579
Cereal, flaked, **Supp. 3**, 411; **Supp. 5**, 378–79
Cerf, Bennett, references to, **Supp. 7**, 3; **Supp. 10**, 221
Cerf, Phyllis, references to, **Supp. 9**, 165, 166
Cermak, Anton J., references to, **Supp. 3**, 772; **Supp. 4**, 450; **Supp. 6**, 23
Cerro Gordo, Mexico, battle of, **Vol. 4, Part 2**, 280; **Vol. 6, Part 1**, 121; **Vol. 8, Part 1**, 607; **Vol. 8, Part 2**, 509; **Vol. 9, Part 1**, 331; **Vol. 10, Part 2**, 537
Cervantes, Miguel de, writings on, **Supp. 4**, 719
Cervix, cancer of, **Supp. 6**, 554
Cesàro, Ernesto, reference to, **Supp. 7**, 216
Cessna, Clyde, reference to, **Supp. 9**, 757
Ceylon, missions in, **Vol. 1, Part 1**, 125; **Vol. 8, Part 1**, 68 f.
Ceylon Social Reform Society, founding of, **Supp. 4**, 177
Cézanne, Paul, references to, **Supp. 4**, 771, 780; **Supp. 6**, 552
Chaco Peace Conference, **Supp. 10**, 64
Chaco War (1936), **Supp. 7**, 778
Chadds Ford, Pa. *See* Brandywine, Pa.
Chadeloid Chemical Co., **Supp. 3**, 247
Chadwick, James, reference to, **Supp. 5**, 220
Chafee, Zechariah, reference to, **Supp. 3**, 471
Chaffee, Roger, reference to, **Supp. 8**, 225
Chain stores: **Vol. 1, Part 2**, 582; **Vol. 5, Part 1**, 122; **Vol. 7, Part 1**, 334; first long-lasting, **Supp. 5**, 277–78. *See also* Retail trades; *specific types and names*
Chairs, making of, **Vol. 4, Part 2**, 611; **Vol. 8, Part 2**, 392
Chalasinski, Joseph, reference to, **Supp. 6**, 726
Chaliapin, Fyodor, references to, **Supp. 10**, 112, 783
Chalmers, T. A., reference to, **Supp. 7**, 731
Chamberlain, J. Austen, reference to, **Supp. 5**, 160
Chamberlain, Joseph P., references to, **Supp. 3**, 19; **Supp. 6**, 101–2
Chamberlain, Neville, reference to, **Supp. 6**, 101; **Supp. 7**, 89
Chamberlin, Clarence D., reference to, **Supp. 6**, 51
Chamberlin, Thomas C., reference to, **Vol. 5, Part 2**, 389 f.; **Supp. 3**, 265; **Supp. 3**, 455
Chamberlin Observatory, **Vol. 5, Part 1**, 290
Chamber music: **Vol. 3, Part 1**, 70 f.; **Vol. 5, Part 2**, 460 f.; **Vol. 8, Part 1**, 149 f.; **Vol. 9, Part 2**, 305, 424; **Supp. 4**, 545; **Supp. 7**, 511–12; Library of Congress concerts, **Supp. 3**, 252; **Supp. 5**, 555; promotion of, **Supp. 5**, 128–29; **Supp. 9**, 141; woodwind, **Supp. 3**, 33
Chambers, J. J., reference to, **Vol. 8, Part 2**, 533
Chambers, Whittaker: references to, **Supp. 5**, 19, 665; **Supp. 7**, 269–70, 291; **Supp. 8**, 176, 511; **Supp. 9**, 84, 549; **Supp. 10**, 719; *Witness* published, **Supp. 9**, 166
Chambersburg, Pa., burning of, **Vol. 6, Part 1**, 575
Chambers of Commerce: development of, **Supp. 2**, 184; International, **Supp. 5**, 634, 675; Los Angeles, **Vol. 7, Part 2**, 100; New York, **Vol. 2, Part 2**, 582; **Vol. 6, Part 1**, 445, 450; **Vol. 7, Part 2**, 56; **Vol. 8, Part 1**, 348 f.; U.S., **Supp. 2**, 184; **Supp. 5**, 479; **Supp. 6**, 37, 660; **Supp. 7**, 397
Chambers v. *Florida*, **Supp. 9**, 96
Champion, Albert, reference to, **Supp. 4**, 244
Champion, Marge, references to, **Supp. 10**, 113, 114
Champion's Hill. *See* Baker's Creek, battle of
Championship Football, **Supp. 10**, 38
"Chan, Charlie" (fictional character), **Supp. 1**, 79
Chancellorsville, Va., battle of, **Vol. 2, Part 2**, 463; **Vol. 3, Part 2**, 230; **Vol. 5, Part 1**, 25, 197, 279, 559; **Vol. 6, Part 1**, 125; **Vol. 6, Part 2**, 475; **Vol. 8, Part 1**, 520; **Vol. 8, Part 2**, 72; **Vol. 9, Part 1**, 150; **Vol. 9, Part 2**, 171
Chandler, A. B. ("Happy"), references to, **Supp. 6**, 35; **Supp. 8**, 352; **Supp. 9**, 594; **Supp. 10**, 606
Chandler, Charles Frederick, reference to, **Supp. 3**, 26
Chandler, Thomas B., reference to, **Vol. 8, Part 2**, 528
Chandler, William E., reference to, **Supp. 3**, 543
Chandlery, **Vol. 4, Part 1**, 463; **Vol. 5, Part 1**, 561
Chanel, Coco, reference to, **Supp. 9**, 465
Chaney, Lon, Sr., references to, **Supp. 7**, 87; **Supp. 9**, 168
Changing Times, founding of, **Supp. 8**, 338
Channing, Carol, reference to, **Supp. 10**, 113
Channing, Edward, reference to, **Supp. 3**, 336
Channing, William Ellery, references to, **Vol. 3, Part 1**, 323 f.; **Vol. 5, Part 1**, 217; **Vol. 9, Part 2**, 298, 303, 391
Chantilly (or Ox Hill), Va., battle of, **Vol. 2, Part 2**, 147; **Vol. 5, Part 2**, 272; **Vol. 6, Part 1**, 124; **Vol. 9, Part 1**, 613
Chapin, Alfred Clark, reference to, **Supp. 7**, 387
Chapin, Charles V., reference to, **Supp. 3**, 324
Chaplin, Charlie, references to, **Supp. 3**, 238; **Supp. 4**, 350; **Supp. 5**, 523; **Supp. 6**, 573; **Supp. 7**, 462; **Supp. 8**, 282; **Supp. 9**, 508; **Supp. 10**, 598
Chaplin, Geraldine, reference to, **Supp. 10**, 118
Chaplins' Aid Association, founding of, **Supp. 2**, 73
Chapman, Frank M., references to, **Supp. 6**, 255; **Supp. 7**, 7
Chapman, Mark David, reference to, **Supp. 10**, 451
Chapman, Oscar, reference to, **Supp. 10**, 192
Chappell and Co., **Supp. 7**, 199
Chapple, John B., reference to, **Supp. 10**, 192
Chapultepec, Mexico, battle of; **Vol. 2, Part 1**, 560; **Vol. 6, Part 1**, 121; **Vol. 7, Part 2**, 604; **Vol. 8, Part 2**, 509; **Vol. 9, Part 1**, 331; **Vol. 10, Part 2**, 537
Character education. *See* Ethics
Charcoal Sketches, **Vol. 7, Part 1**, 400
Charitable organizations: **Supp. 1**, 237; financing of, **Supp. 1**, 695; Jewish, **Supp. 3**, 488; **Supp. 4**, 79–80; relief aid, **Supp. 4**, 87, 100–101. *See also* Philanthropy; Welfare; *names of specific organizations*
Charities. *See* Survey
Charity Hospital (New Orleans, La.), **Supp. 3**, 313
Charity organization, first state, **Vol. 5, Part 1**, 297
Charity Organization Society of Baltimore, **Supp. 4**, 333
Charity Organization Society of Buffalo, **Supp. 3**, 4
Charity Organization Society of New York, **Vol. 6, Part 1**, 468; **Vol. 7, Part 2**, 410; **Supp. 1**, 237; **Supp. 3**, 743–44; **Supp. 6**, 654
Charles V, contract for conquest of Florida, **Vol. 3, Part 1**, 256
Charles Scribner's Sons. *See* Scribner's, Charles, Sons

Charleston, S. C.: antebellum history of, **Vol. 4, Part 2**, 455; **Vol. 8, Part 1**, 395; black education, **Vol. 7, Part 2**, 324; civic service, **Vol. 5, Part 1**, 444; **Vol. 6, Part 2**, 234; **Vol. 7, Part 1**, 154; **Vol. 7, Part 2**, 617; **Vol. 9, Part 1**, 53, 173 f., 365; **Vol. 10, Part 2**, 602; commerce, **Vol. 2, Part 1**, 487; **Vol. 5, Part 1**, 345; **Vol. 6, Part 1**, 32; defense installations, **Supp. 8**, 538; defense of, **Vol. 4, Part 2**, 455; **Vol. 8, Part 1**, 626; Democratic Convention (1860), **Vol. 5, Part 2**, 552; earthquake (1886), **Vol. 8, Part 1**, 395; first Museum of Natural History in U.S., **Vol. 3, Part 2**, 307; Jackson at, **Vol. 5, Part 1**, 526; Jacobinism, **Vol. 4, Part 2**, 285; Medical College, **Vol. 3, Part 1**, 305; piracy near, **Vol. 5, Part 2**, 116 f.; political reform, **Supp. 5**, 481–82; Reconstruction, **Vol. 6, Part 2**, 602; Reform Judaism, birthplace of, in America, **Vol. 8, Part 1**, 164 f.; siege of (1780), **Vol. 4, Part 1**, 572; **Vol. 4, Part 2**, 454; **Vol. 5, Part 1**, 454; **Vol. 6, Part 1**, 260, 280; **Vol. 6, Part 2**, 405, 600; **Vol. 7, Part 1**, 293; **Vol. 8, Part 2**, 259; **Vol. 9, Part 1**, 61; **Vol. 10, Part 2**, 297, 299; siege of (1863), **Vol. 1, Part 1**, 274; **Vol. 1, Part 2**, 111; **Vol. 3, Part 1**, 31, 532; **Vol. 4, Part 1**, 295; **Vol. 4, Part 2**, 240; **Vol. 7, Part 2**, 560; **Vol. 9, Part 1**, 12; **Vol. 9, Part 2**, 378; Scots Church, **Vol. 4, Part 2**, 601; site of, **Vol. 10, Part 2**, 604; water supply of, **Vol. 8, Part 1**, 397
Charleston College, **Vol. 1, Part 1**, 72
Charleston Mercury, **Vol. 7, Part 2**, 617; **Vol. 8, Part 1**, 527
Charlotte, a Tale of Truth, **Vol. 8, Part 2**, 203
Charlotte, N. C.: branch mint established at, **Vol. 8, Part 1**, 450; founding of, **Vol. 8, Part 1**, 42
Charlotte, raising of, **Vol. 3, Part 1**, 210
Charlotte Daily Observer, **Vol. 9, Part 2**, 582
Charlotte News, **Supp. 3**, 148
Charm Magazine, founding of, **Supp. 3**, 30
Chase, Edna Woolman, reference to, **Supp. 3**, 547
Chase, Ilka, reference to, **Supp. 6**, 108
Chase, Mary Coyle, references to, **Supp. 4**, 649, 653
Chase, Mary Ellen, reference to, **Supp. 6**, 311
Chase, Salmon P., references to, **Vol. 6, Part 1**, 249 f.; **Vol. 8, Part 1**, 54 f.
Chase, Samuel, references to, **Vol. 3, Part 1**, 599; **Vol. 7, Part 2**, 123 f., 599, 626 f.
Chase, William Merritt, reference to, **Supp. 7**, 685–86
Chase Economic Bulletin, **Supp. 4**, 18
Chase Manhattan Bank, **Supp. 9**, 17
Chase National Bank, **Supp. 5**, 744–45; founding of, **Vol. 9, Part 2**, 463
Chasins, Abram, reference to, **Supp. 6**, 297
Chatham House Conference (1935), **Supp. 4**, 137
Chattahoochee River, Ga., operations on. *See* Atlanta campaign
Chattanooga, Tenn., **Vol. 3, Part 2**, 202
Chattanooga Daily Times, **Vol. 7, Part 1**, 601
Chattanooga News, **Supp. 5**, 497–98
Chattanooga Ringgold campaign, **Vol. 1, Part 2**, 587; **Vol. 2, Part 2**, 190; **Vol. 3, Part 1**, 50–51; **Vol. 3, Part 2**, 532; **Vol. 4, Part 1**, 484, 496; **Vol. 4, Part 2**, 240; **Vol. 5, Part 1**, 193, 197, 280; **Vol. 8, Part 2**, 631; **Vol. 9, Part 1**, 80, 95, 363; **Vol. 9, Part 2**, 433
Chatterton, Ruth, reference to, **Supp. 7**, 591
Chattopadhyaya, Virendraneth, reference to, **Supp. 4**, 749
Chaucer, Geoffrey: scholarship on, **Supp. 2**, 558; **Supp. 3**, 474–75, 855; **Supp. 4**, 819–20; studies in, **Vol. 2, Part 2**, 66; **Vol. 3, Part 2**, 485; **Vol. 6, Part l**, 430
Chauncy-Hall School, **Vol. 9, Part 2**, 405
Chautauqua Institution and Movement: **Vol. 4, Part 1**, 288; **Vol. 5, Part 1**, 425; **Vol. 6, Part 1**, 14; **Vol. 6, Part 2**, 635; **Vol. 7, Part 2**, 184; **Vol. 9, Part 1**, 104; **Supp. 3**, 64–65, 249; lecture circuit, **Supp. 8**, 317; Music Festival, **Supp. 3**, 742; presidency, **Supp. 3**, 792–93
Chayefsky, Paddy, references to, **Supp. 9**, 666, 667
Checkley, John, reference to, **Vol. 10, Part 1**, 395 f.
Cheek, Jim, reference to, **Supp. 6**, 135
Cheese, processing of, **Supp. 5**, 399–400
Cheetham, James, reference to, **Vol. 10, Part 1**, 642 f.
Chefs. *See* Cooking
Chemical Abstracts, founding of, **Supp. 2**, 494
Chemical engineering. *See* Engineering, chemical
Chemical industry: diversification, **Supp. 5**, 191–94; **Supp. 6**, 447–48; **Supp. 7**, 210; drug manufacturing, **Supp. 6**, 447; dyes, **Supp. 7**, 616; explosives manufacture, **Supp. 1**, 271; historical writings on, **Supp. 8**, 249–50; manufacturing, **Supp. 8**, 411; **Supp. 10**, 42; plant design and construction, **Supp. 1**, 682; sulfuric acid production, **Supp. 5**, 319–20
Chemical Pathology, **Supp. 3**, 807
Chemical Society of Philadelphia, **Vol. 10, Part 2**, 491
Chemical transmitters. *See* Neurotransmitter
Chemicals, manufacture of, **Vol. 2, Part 1**, 299; **Vol. 6, Part 2**, 224; **Vol. 7, Part 1**, 495; **Vol. 9, Part 1**, 488; **Vol. 10, Part 2**, 23;
Chemical warfare. *See* Biological and chemical warfare
Chemical Who's Who, founding of, **Supp. 8**, 249
Chemistry: For complete list of chemists, *see* Occupations Index; agricultural, **Vol. 1, Part 1**, 349, 417; **Vol. 2, Part 2**, 304; **Vol. 5, Part 2**, 45, 120, 231 f.; **Vol. 6, Part 2**, 223, 263; **Vol. 7, Part 1**, 574 f.; **Vol. 8, Part 1**, 96 f., 154 f., 239 f, 257 f, 272 f., 397; **Vol. 9, Part 2**, 395; **Vol. 10, Part 2**, 22, 104, 491; **Supp. 3**, 145–46; alloys, experiments with, **Vol. 1, Part 1**, 456; ammonia, isolation of, **Vol. 8, Part 1**, 223 f.; ammonia-cobalt bases, **Vol. 4, Part 1**, 210; analytical, **Vol. 3, Part 1**, 376; **Vol. 4, Part 1**, 210; **Vol. 9, Part 2**, 27; atomic weights, **Vol. 8, Part 1**, 556 f.; **Supp. 1**, 178; book collections on, **Supp. 1**, 431; carbon monoxide, isolation of, **Vol. 8, Part 1**, 223 f.; catalytic reactions, **Supp. 4**, 6; colloids, **Supp. 4**, 743–44; crystals, artificial, **Vol. 5, Part 2**, 487; cyanamide process of nitrogen fixation, **Supp. 3**, 439–40; dyes, synthetic, **Vol. 6, Part 2**, 401; elements, search for rare, **Vol. 5, Part 1**, 572; fluorine, discovery of, **Vol. 9, Part 1**, 3; food, application to, **Vol. 1, Part 1**, 457; **Vol. 1, Part 2**, 448; **Vol. 5, Part 1**, 237; **Vol. 5, Part 2**, 524; **Vol. 8, Part 1**, 192 f., 553 f.; **Vol. 9, Part 2**, 28; free-radical, **Supp. 6**, 334–35; genetic code, **Supp. 9**, 753–54; Gomberg-Bachmann reaction, **Supp. 5**, 28; historical studies, **Supp. 4**, 114; home economics and, **Supp. 3**, 68; hydrogen bond characteristics, **Supp. 5**, 413; hydrochloric acid, isolation of, **Vol. 8, Part 1**, 223 f.; hydrocyanic acid gas, **Vol. 2, Part 2**, 434; hydrolysis, **Vol. 9, Part 2**, 544; industrial, **Vol. 2, Part 1**, 612; **Vol. 3, Part 1**, 70, 157, 479 f.; **Vol. 4, Part 1**, 502; **Vol. 4, Part 2**, 344, 443; **Vol. 6, Part 2**, 147; **Vol. 7, Part 1**, 162; **Vol. 8, Part 2**, 110; **Vol. 10, Part 1**, 607 f.; **Vol. 10, Part 2**, 572; **Supp. 3**, 25–26, 239, 247, 521–22; **Supp. 4**, 184–85; **Supp. 5**, 235, 319–20; **Supp. 6**, 623–24; ionization, **Supp. 2**, 631; medical, **Vol. 10, Part 2**, 455; mineralogical, **Vol. 5, Part 2**, 276; mohawkite, discovery of, **Vol. 5, Part 2**, 487; nitric oxide, isolation of, **Vol. 8, Part 1**, 223 f.; nitrogen, discovery of, **Vol. 5, Part 1**, 50; nitrogen fixation, **Supp. 9**, 217, 218; nitrogen peroxide, isolation of, **Vol. 8, Part 1**, 233 f.; nitrogen system of compounds, **Supp. 2**, 205–6; nitroglycerine, **Vol. 7, Part 1**, 297; nitrous oxide, isolation of, **Vol. 8, Part 1**, 223 f.; Nobel Prize, **Supp. 5**, 670; **Supp. 8**, 123; of nutrition, **Supp. 5**, 622–23; organic, *see* Organic chemistry; organic compound identification, **Supp. 1**, 571; oxygen, discovery of, **Vol. 8, Part 1**, 223 f.; oxygen, experiments with, **Vol. 3, Part**

1, 376; **Vol. 7, Part 1**, 192; patent litigation, **Vol. 6, Part 1**, 143; **Vol. 8, Part 2**, 285; **Vol. 9, Part 2**, 28; pharmaceutical, **Vol. 8, Part 1**, 154 f.; photo, **Vol. 6, Part 1**, 71; physical, **Vol. 5, Part 2**, 173 f.; **Vol. 6, Part 1**, 353 f.; *see also* Physical Chemistry; physiological, **Supp. 1**, 549; plant, **Vol. 8, Part 1**, 154 f.; proteins, **Vol. 7, Part 2**, 74; **Supp. 6**, 346; research techniques, **Supp. 6**, 695; silicon fluoride, isolation of, **Vol. 8, Part 1**, 223 f.; structural, **Supp. 4**, 488–89; sugar, **Supp. 5**, 327–28; sulphur, researches in, **Vol. 8, Part 1**, 223 f.; **Vol. 9, Part 1**, 235; surface, **Supp. 6**, 365; teaching of, **Vol. 3, Part 1**, 10; **Vol. 4, Part 2**, 7, 96; **Vol. 5, Part 1**, 33, 236, 394, 438, 527; **Vol. 5, Part 2**, 277, 418, 486, 593; **Vol. 6, Part 1**, 143, 378, 540, 576; **Vol. 6, Part 2**, 126; **Vol. 7, Part 1**, 66, 69 f., 136, 162, 192, 243, 404; **Vol. 8, Part 2**, 99 f., 350; **Vol. 9, Part 1**, 74, 160, 163, 235, 255 f., 304, 562; **Vol. 9, Part 2**, 56, 278, 596 f.; textbooks on, **Vol. 3, Part l**, 10; **Vol. 9, Part 1**, 256; **Supp. 1**, 376; theoretical physical, **Supp. 6**, 345–46; thermodynamics, **Supp. 4**, 488–89; Wisconsin process developed, **Supp. 9**, 218; Woodward-Hoffman Rules, **Supp. 10**, 853; writings on, **Supp. 3**, 565–66; **Supp. 5**, 407. *See also* Biochemistry; Organic chemistry; Petrochemistry; Pharmacology; Physical chemistry

Chemistry of Paper Making, The, **Supp. 1**, 500

Chemists' Club of New York, **Vol. 6, Part 1**, 353

Chenault, Anna Chan, reference to, **Supp. 10**, 362

Cheney, Russell, references to, **Supp. 4**, 559, 560, 561

Cherkassky, Shura, reference to, **Supp. 6**, 297

Cherington, Paul T., reference to, **Supp. 9**, 677

Cherokee Indians: **Vol. 7, Part 1**, 401, 622; **Vol. 10, Part 1**, 67; appropriations to, **Vol. 10, Part 1**, 67; Bible translation, **Vol. 1, Part 2**, 478; Confederacy, relations with, **Vol. 8, Part 2**, 179; England, visit to, **Vol. 9, Part 2**, 554; government relations, **Supp. 2**, 291; land, ceding of, **Vol. 8, Part 1**, 595; language, syllabary of, **Vol. 8, Part 2**, 586; negotiations with, **Vol. 2, Part 2**, 96; **Vol. 8, Part 2**, 508; removal of, **Vol. 6, Part 1**, 504; **Vol. 8, Part 2**, 179; **Vol. 9, Part 2**, 615; Revolutionary War, leader among, during, **Vol. 10, Part 1**, 433

Cherokee Phoenix, **Vol. 1, Part 2**, 478

Cherrington, Ernest H., reference to, **Supp. 5**, 442

Cherry Valley (Pa.) Massacre (1779), **Vol. 1, Part 2**, 604; **Vol. 2, Part 1**, 362, 368, 372

Chesapeake: engagements, **Vol. 1, Part 1**, 650; **Vol. 5, Part 2**, 30; **Vol. 6, Part 1**, 50; **Vol. 7, Part 1**, 477, 486; surrender, **Vol. 3, Part 2**, 96; writings on, **Vol. 1, Part 1**, 80

Chesapeake & Ohio Canal, **Vol. 5, Part 2**, 348; **Vol. 9, Part 2**, 249

Chesapeake & Ohio Railroad: **Vol. 3, Part 2**, 1; **Vol. 5, Part 1**, 411, 464; **Vol. 6, Part 1**, 445; **Supp. 6**, 721; **Supp. 9**, 462; **Supp. 10**, 203; management, **Supp. 2**, 282

Chesney, Alan M., reference to, **Supp. 6**, 460–61

Chesnut, Mary Boykin, reference to, **Supp. 10**, 842

Chess, **Vol. 1, Part 1**, 190; **Vol. 3, Part 2**, 417; **Vol. 6, Part 1**, 479; **Vol. 6, Part 2**, 92; **Vol. 7, Part 1**, 193 f.; **Vol. 7, Part 2**, 606; **Vol. 8, Part 1**, 541; **Vol. 9, Part 1**, 564; **Supp. 3**, 509; **Supp. 5**, 20

Chessman, Caryl, reference to, **Supp. 7**, 292

Chester, Colby M., reference to, **Supp. 7**, 379

"Chesterfield Hour" (radio program), **Supp. 10**, 421

Chevrolet, Louis, reference to, **Supp. 4**, 244

Chevrolet car, **Supp. 4**, 301, 302, 457

Chevrolet Motor Car Co., founding of, **Supp. 4**, 244

Chewing gum, manufacture of, **Supp. 1**, 715

Cheyenne Indians: revolt of (1879), **Vol. 2, Part 2**, 530, 563; **Vol. 7, Part 1**, 1; **Vol. 8, Part 1**, 520; **Vol. 9, Part 2**, 379; studies on, **Supp. 2**, 265

Chiang Kai-shek, references to, **Supp. 4**, 147, 750, 782–83; **Supp. 6**, 109, 110, 230–31, 350; **Supp. 7**, 377, 761; **Supp. 8**, 395, 506; **Supp. 9**, 830; **Supp. 10**, 528

Chiaotung University, forerunner, **Supp. 3**, 268

Chicago, Ill.: architecture, **Vol. 8, Part 2**, 149 f.; **Supp. 2**, 117, 537–38, 598–99; **Supp. 6**, 712–13; **Supp. 8**, 463; art, **Vol. 1, Part 1**, 448 f.; **Vol. 9, Part 1**, 53; **Vol. 10, Part 2**, 86; Bauhaus school, **Supp. 4**, 591; banking, **Vol. 1, Part 1**, 217; **Vol. 5, Part 1**, 118; **Vol. 7, Part 1**, 645; **Vol. 9, Part 2**, 631; **Vol. 10, Part 2**, 611; baseball, White Stockings, **Vol. 5, Part 2**, 310; black art projects, **Supp. 7**, 611; black community, studies of, **Supp. 8**, 81; black entrepreneurs, **Supp. 4**, 82–83; black politicians, **Supp. 3**, 378; **Supp. 5**, 166; **Supp. 8**, 121; blues scene, **Supp. 9**, 796; **Supp. 10**, 78; business development, **Vol. 3, Part 2**, 295, 366 f.; **Vol. 5, Part 1**, 326; **Vol. 6, Part 1**, 157, 508 f.; **Vol. 7, Part 1**, 447; **Vol. 10, Part 1**, 414; Catholic church, **Vol. 8, Part 1**, 295; **Supp. 7**, 533; Century of Progress Exposition, **Vol. 10, Part 1**, 133; charter, first, **Vol. 5, Part 2**, 230; civic corruption, **Supp. 10**, 49–50; 169; civil rights movement, **Supp. 8**, 335; commercial growth of, **Vol. 8, Part 1**, 405; Debs, Eugene V., demonstration for, **Vol. 3, Part 1**, 184; Democratic National Convention (1968), **Supp. 10**, 168, 362; Democratic political machine, **Supp. 10**, 9–10, 167, 185; detective, first on police force in, **Vol. 7, Part 2**, 622; development of, **Vol. 1, Part 1**, 217; **Vol. 1, Part 2**, 486; **Vol. 2, Part 1**, 360, 575; **Vol. 2, Part 2**, 537; **Vol. 3, Part l**, 431; **Vol. 3, Part 2**, 262 f., 302; **Vol. 4, Part 2**, 53, 55, 336, 545; **Vol. 5, Part 1**, 438, 452; **Vol. 6, Part 1**, 61, 157, 612; **Vol. 6, Part 2**, 244; **Vol. 7, Part 2**, 191, 362; **Vol. 8, Part l**, 405, 435 f.; **Vol. 8, Part 2**, 171, 272; **Vol. 10, Part 1**, 131, 414; **Vol. 10, Part 2**, 86, 557; drainage canal, **Vol. 8, Part 1**, 359 f.; drama movement, **Vol. 4, Part 1**, 393; education, **Vol. 1, Part 1**, 289; **Vol. 7, Part 2**, 221; **Vol. 8, Part 2**, 408; **Vol. 10, Part 1**, 645 f.; **Supp. 1**, 191; **Supp. 4**, 451; Field Museum of Natural History, **Vol. 1, Part 1**, 448 f.; fire, **Vol. 3, Part 1**, 283; **Vol. 8, Part 1**, 390; **Vol. 8, Part 2**, 84; **Vol. 9, Part 2**, 82, 98, Fire Department, **Vol. 10, Part 1**, 657 f.; Gas Trust, **Vol. 1, Part 1**, 104; Haymarket riot, **Vol. 1, Part 1**, 231; **Vol. 7, Part 2**, 264 f.; **Vol. 10, Part 2**, 648; **Supp. 2**, 142; hospital, first general, **Vol. 1, Part 2**, 589; hotel management, **Vol. 3, Part 1**, 431; Immanuel Hall, **Vol. 7, Part 2**, 207; jazz, **Supp. 3**, 541–42; **Supp. 8**, 561; **Supp. 9**, 598; Jewish community, **Supp. 3**, 488; juvenile social work, **Supp. 8**, 40; labor movement, **Supp. 4**, 279–80, 606; **Supp. 6**, 73–74; **Supp. 7**, 254; lake front, litigation over, **Vol. 4, Part 1**, 605; law, **Vol. 4, Part 1**, 61; libraries, **Vol. 1, Part 1**, 448; **Vol. 6, Part 1**, 148; **Supp. 4**, 846; Marshall Fields', **Vol. 6, Part 1**, 157; mayors, **Vol. 7, Part 1**, 644; **Supp. 3**, 771–72; **Supp. 4**, 450–51; **Supp. 5**, 274–75, 323; **Supp. 10**, 10, 11, 167–69; Methodist church, **Supp. 4**, 837; music, **Vol. 4, Part 1**, 328; **Vol. 6, Part 1**, 512; **Vol. 8, Part 1**, 177 f.; **Vol. 8, Part 2**, 146 f.; **Vol. 9, Part 2**, 579; **Vol. 10, Part 1**, 131; newspapers, **Vol. 5, Part 2**, 489; **Vol. 6, Part 1**, 60 f.; **Supp. 5**, 285–86, 323, 449; **Supp. 6**, 400; Norton, as idealized by, **Vol. 7, Part 1**, 571; organized crime, **Supp. 4**, 140–42; **Supp. 6**, 263–64; **Supp. 9**, 306–7, 651–52; **Supp. 10**, 49, 134, 135; parks, **Vol. 2, Part 1**, 306; **Vol. 8, Part 1**, 405; **Supp. 5**, 369–70; pediatrics practice, **Supp. 5**, 1–2; philanthropy, **Vol. 3, Part 2**, 295; **Vol. 5, Part 1**, 18; **Vol. 6, Part 1**, 508 f.; **Vol. 7, Part 1**, 218; **Vol. 7, Part 2**, 72; **Vol. 8, Part 2**, 272; **Vol. 9, Part 1**, 55; pioneer days in, **Vol. 10, Part 2**, 557; playground system, **Supp. 1**, 595; police corruption scandal, **Supp. 9**, 881; police reform,

Supp. 9, 882; political machines (1890–1900), **Vol. 6, Part 2**, 180; politics, **Supp. 5**, 448, 450, 598; **Supp. 6**, 683–84; **Supp. 8**, 121; **Supp. 10**, 9–10, 11, 167–68, 185, 186; Prohibition enforcement, **Supp. 7**, 805–6; prostitution, **Supp. 4**, 255–56; **Supp. 5**, 274–75; public health, **Vol. 3, Part 1**, 139; **Vol. 7, Part 2**, 175; **Vol. 8, Part 2**, 281; race riots, **Supp. 6**, 321; **Supp. 10**, 169; railway development, **Vol. 3, Part 1**, 399; **Vol. 7, Part 1**, 594, 645; **Vol. 8, Part 1**, 405; real estate, **Vol. 7, Part 1**, 644; **Vol. 7, Part 2**, 191; reform politics, **Supp. 2**, 166; **Supp. 5**, 485, 579, 698, 699; restaurant business, **Vol. 5, Part 2**, 489; Roman Catholic diocese, **Supp. 6**, 607–8; **Supp. 8**, 588–89; sanitation, **Vol. 4, Part 1**, 605; **Vol. 6, Part 1**, 378; **Vol. 8, Part 1**, 390; settlement houses, **Supp. 2**, 655–56; skyscrapers in, **Vol. 9, Part 1**, 368; **Supp. 3**, 611–12; social life, **Vol. 7, Part 2**, 176 f.; social service, **Vol. 8, Part 1**, 57 f.; steel-strike massacre, **Supp. 5**, 510; stockyards, **Supp. 4**, 279–80; **Supp. 5**, 70; surveying of, **Vol. 3, Part 1**, 520 f.; theater, **Supp. 7**, 1; topographical reconstruction, **Vol. 3, Part 2**, 569; "Traction Tangle," **Vol. 10, Part 2**, 610; transit systems, **Supp. 8**, 112; Tuberculosis Institute, **Vol. 7, Part 2**, 298; World's Fair, *see* World's Columbian Exposition; vote fraud investigation, **Supp. 10**, 50

Chicago Academy of Sciences, **Vol. 5, Part 2**, 338; **Vol. 9, Part 2**, 32

Chicago Agricultural and Horticultural Society, **Vol. 7, Part 2**, 464

Chicago American, **Supp. 3**, 427–28; **Supp. 5**, 285

Chicago & Alton Railroad, **Vol. 7, Part 1**, 144 f.

Chicago & Calumet Railroad, **Vol. 9, Part 2**, 594

Chicago & Northwestern Railroad, **Vol. 1, Part 2**, 382; **Vol. 7, Part 1**, 645

Chicago & Rock Island Railroad, **Vol. 3, Part 2**, 281; **Vol. 5, Part 2**, 60

Chicago Art Institute, **Vol. 5, Part 1**, 438; **Vol. 8, Part 2**, 272

Chicago Bears (football), **Supp. 10**, 585

Chicago Bible Institute, **Vol. 7, Part 1**, 104

Chicago Board of Trade, **Vol. 7, Part 2**, 297

Chicago, Burlington & Quincy Railroad, **Vol. 7, Part 2**, 466; **Supp. 3**, 381, 823; **Supp. 7**, 90

Chicago Cardinals (football), **Supp. 9**, 841; **Supp. 10**, 585

Chicago Century of Progress Exposition (1933): **Vol. 10, Part 1**, 133; administration, **Supp. 2**, 147; All-Star baseball game, **Supp. 5**, 724; architectural commission, **Supp. 5**, 134; art exhibition, **Supp. 2**, 288; design, **Supp. 7**, 690; Hall of Science, **Supp. 3**, 199; structural design, **Supp. 3**, 531

Chicago City Mission Society, **Vol. 2, Part 2**, 621

Chicago Civic Opera Company, predecessor, **Supp. 8**, 201

Chicago Civic Shakespeare Society, founding of, **Supp. 4**, 478

Chicago College of Pharmacy, **Vol. 8, Part 1**, 390

Chicago College of Physicians and Surgeons, **Vol. 5, Part 1**, 526

Chicago Commons, founding of, **Supp. 2**, 655–56

Chicago Cubs (baseball), **Supp. 5**, 411; **Supp. 6**, 347; **Supp. 9**, 368; **Supp. 10**, 480, 857

Chicago Daily News: **Supp. 2**, 620; **Supp. 3**, 425; **Supp. 4**, 489–90; **Supp. 6**, 197–98, 202; **Supp. 7**, 243, 244, 331; **Supp. 8**, 563–64; **Supp. 10**, 562; cartoons, editorial, **Supp. 10**, 245; first penny newspaper, **Vol. 6, Part 1**, 60; **Vol. 9, Part 2**, 82; investigative reporting, **Supp. 10**, 461; political reporting, **Supp. 10**, 461–62; Watergate scandal, **Supp. 10**, 462

Chicago Daily Times, **Vol. 2, Part 2**, 374

Chicago Daily Tribune, **Vol. 10, Part 1**, 131

Chicago Defender, **Supp. 5**, 633; **Supp. 8**, 287–88, 605; founding of, **Supp. 2**, 3

Chicago Dial, **Vol. 7, Part 2**, 332 f.

Chicago Evening Journal, **Vol. 10, Part 1**, 131

Chicago Evening Post, **Supp. 8**, 124; literary editor, **Supp. 7**, 309–10

Chicago Examiner, drama criticism, **Supp. 5**, 658

Chicago Federation of Churches, founding of, **Supp. 3**, 825

Chicago Federation of Labor, **Supp. 4**, 279

Chicago Fresh Air Hospital, **Vol. 7, Part 2**, 298

Chicago Great Western Railroad, **Vol. 9, Part 2**, 16

Chicago Herald, **Vol. 8, Part 2**, 492

Chicago Herald-Examiner, **Supp. 5**, 323

Chicago Historical Society, **Vol. 1, Part 2**, 612; **Vol. 7, Part 1**, 447; **Supp. 9**, 300

Chicago Institute for Psychoanalysis, founding of, **Supp. 7**, 6

Chicago Institute of Social Science, founding of, **Supp. 1**, 485

Chicago Inter-Ocean, **Vol. 7, Part 1**, 532

Chicago Legal News, **Vol. 1, Part 2**, 580, 581

Chicago Lutheran Theological Seminary, **Vol. 7, Part 2**, 289; **Vol. 10, Part 1**, 606 f.

Chicago Lying-in Dispensary, **Supp. 2**, 222–23

Chicago Medical College, **Vol. 10, Part 2**, 253

Chicago Medical Journal, **Vol. 1, Part 2**, 589

Chicago, Milwaukee & St. Paul Railroad, **Vol. 5, Part 2**, 498; **Vol. 8, Part 2**, 263; **Vol. 9, Part 2**, 70; **Supp. 3**, 783

Chicago Municipal Tuberculosis Sanitarium, **Vol. 8, Part 2**, 281

Chicago Musical College, **Vol. 6, Part 1**, 293; **Supp. 9**, 300

Chicago Neurological Society, founding of, **Supp. 2**, 516

Chicago Normal School, **Vol. 9, Part 2**, 581

Chicago Opera Company, **Supp. 6**, 323, 630, 670

Chicago Poems, **Supp. 8**, 563

Chicago Public Library, architecture, **Supp. 2**, 117; White mural, **Supp. 10**, 832

Chicago Record-Herald, **Vol. 5, Part 2**, 489

Chicago Relief and Aid Society, **Vol. 3, Part 1**, 283

Chicago Renaissance, **Supp. 7**, 331; **Supp. 8**, 124

Chicago, St. Louis & New Orleans Railroad, **Vol. 7, Part 2**, 72

Chicago Society of Etchers, **Vol. 8, Part 1**, 446

Chicago Sun-Times, **Supp. 6**, 202; **Supp. 7**, 243, 244

Chicago Symphony Orchestra, **Vol. 9, Part 2**, 425; **Supp. 3**, 740–41; **Supp. 6**, 550; **Supp. 7**, 640

Chicago Theatre Society, organized, **Vol. 4, Part 1**, 393

Chicago Theological Seminary, **Vol. 1, Part 2**, 15; **Supp. 3**, 363

Chicago Times, **Vol. 9, Part 2**, 97 f.

Chicago Times-Herald, **Supp. 6**, 54

Chicago Tribune: **Vol. 2, Part 1**, 94; **Vol. 5, Part 2**, 109; **Vol. 6, Part 1**, 609 f.; **Vol. 9, Part 2**, 317; **Supp. 4**, 644, 645; **Supp. 6**, 490, 698, 699; **Supp. 8**, 128; circulation war, **Supp. 5**, 286; columnists, **Supp. 5**, 633; drama criticism, **Supp. 4**, 548–49; editorial policy, **Supp. 5**, 449, 450; Ford libel suit against, **Supp. 4**, 299, 302; investigative reporting, **Supp. 10**, 49, 50; sports column, **Supp. 5**, 724

Chicago White Sox (baseball), **Supp. 3**, 438; **Supp. 5**, 125; **Supp. 6**, 120–21, 663; **Supp. 8**, 85–86, 574–75; **Supp. 9**, 289

Chicago Woman's Club, only black member of, **Supp. 3**, 827

Chicago World's Fair of 1893. *See* World's Columbian Exposition (1893)

Chickamauga Campaign: **Vol. 1, Part 2**, 287, 601; **Vol.**

2, Part 1, 10, 236; Vol. 2, Part 2, 190, 549; Vol. 3, Part 2, 532; Vol. 4, Part 1, 146, 484, 496; Vol. 5, Part 1, 27, 193; Vol. 6, Part 1, 392, 601; Vol. 6, Part 2, 348; Vol. 8, Part 1, 40; Vol. 8, Part 2, 164; Vol. 9, Part 1, 80; Vol. 9, Part 2, 433; Vol. 10, Part 2, 475; National Military Park, Vol. 9, Part 2, 3
Chickasaw Baptist Association, Vol. 7, Part 1, 371
Chickasaw Indians, Supp. 6, 468–69
Chicken, fast-food chains, Supp. 10, 717–18
Chicken raising, brooders, invention of, Vol. 8, Part 1, 505; incubators, Vol. 8, Part 1, 505; Perdue industry, Supp. 10, 629–30
"Chico and the Man," Supp. 10, 651, 652
Chihuahua, Mexico, expedition to, Vol. 8, Part 1, 216; Vol. 10, Part 2, 513–14
Child, Abbie B., reference to, Supp. 4, 647
Child, Francis James, references to, Vol. 9, Part 1, 434; Supp. 3, 422, 423
Child, Lydia Maria, reference to, Vol. 5, Part 1, 384
Childbirth. *See* Obstetrics
Child Guidance Clinic (Philadelphia) Supp. 6, 152
Child Health Bulletin, predecessor, Supp. 5, 553
Child Health Day, Supp. 7, 70
Child Health Organization, Supp. 5, 553
Child labor: Vol. 1, Part 2, 232; Vol. 5, Part 2, 196; Vol. 6, Part 1, 511; Vol. 7, Part 1, 348; Supp. 2, 408; Supp. 7, 483, 484; legislation, Supp. 1, 463; Supp. 2, 1, 43; Supp. 3, 655–56, 852; New Deal reforms, Supp. 3, 228; psychology, Vol. 7, Part 1, 558; show business, Supp. 8, 314, 354–55, 363; study impetus given to, in U.S., Vol. 6, Part 1, 276; Vol. 9, Part 2, 276; welfare, Vol. 3, Part 1, 108; Vol. 6, Part 1, 355; writings on, Supp. 5, 141; Supp. 6, 113
Child Labor Act (1918), political cartoon about, Supp. 3, 852
Children: anemia, Supp. 3, 190; blind, care of, Supp. 1, 19; blind, education, Supp. 5, 347–48; blue-baby surgery, Supp. 7, 59; care of, Vol. 5, Part 2, 354 f.; Vol. 6, Part 1, 194; collections of sayings of, Vol. 8, Part 1, 183 f.; concerts for, Supp. 4, 212; custody cases, Supp. 7, 753; development studies, Supp. 3, 119; Supp. 4, 7–8, 805, 807; Supp. 6, 203; Supp. 7, 284; diseases of, Vol. 5, Part 1, 183 f., 313 f., 563; Vol. 9, Part 1, 294; fiction about, Supp. 4, 816–17; first mental hygiene clinic for, Supp. 1, 485; foster care, Supp. 2, 57–58; Supp. 3, 28, 160; Supp. 4, 871; growth studies, Supp. 2, 665–66; guidance clinics, Supp. 6, 17, 152, 636; home education, Supp. 5, 437–38; infant feeding, Supp. 2, 432; juvenile paresis studies, Supp. 8, 429; legal protection, Supp. 3, 279, 462–63, 463; nutrition, Supp. 1, 398; orthopedics, Supp. 1, 40–41; psychological development of, Supp. 5, 316–17; publications for, Vol. 9, Part 2, 436; Vol. 10, Part 2, 603; Supp. 3, 44–45; rearing theories, Supp. 4, 7–8; Supp. 6, 673; Supp. 7, 428, 528, 600–1; Supp. 8, 189; refugee settlements in Palestine, Supp. 3, 757; rights protection, Supp. 5, 138; scouting movement, Supp. 3, 44–45; sermons to, Vol. 7, Part 1, 478; settlement farms, Supp. 2, 226–27; social welfare reform, Supp. 2, 1, 57, 110, 126; Supp. 3, 28, 159, 228, 361–62; Supp. 4, 282–83, 871; Supp. 5, 454; Supp. 6, 1–2, 81, 103, 202, 515–16; Supp. 7, 251, 483–84; Supp. 8, 40, 611, 673–74; strained baby food, Supp. 5, 242–43; UNICEF relief work, Supp. 7, 599–600; writings on, Supp. 6, 382. *See also* Adolescents; Child labor; Children's literature; Education; Juvenile delinquency; Pediatrics; Preschool education; Prodigies
Children's Aid Society, Vol. 1, Part 2, 540; Vol. 4, Part 1, 625; Vol. 5, Part 1, 573; Supp. 2, 57–58
Children's Book Week, Supp. 7, 525
Children's Bureau, Vol. 10, Part 2, 487
Children's Bureau (U.S.), Supp. 1, 1–2, 687; Supp. 3, 28; Supp. 7, 251; establishment of, Supp. 1, 485
Children's Fund of Michigan, founding of, Supp. 2, 126
Children's Hospital (Mich.), Supp. 3, 189–90
Children's Hospital School, Supp. 1, 40
Children's Hour, The, Supp. 10, 733
Children's Library Association, founding of, Supp. 1, 242
Children's literature: Supp. 2, 660; Supp. 3, 44, 69, 629–30; Supp. 6, 372–73, 603, 696–97; Supp. 8, 564; animal stories, Supp. 7, 94–95; Supp. 10, 268, 440–41, 460; awards, Supp. 7, 525; Bobbsey Twins series, Supp. 9, 787; Bret King series, Supp. 9, 788; collections, Supp. 5, 587; dog stories, Supp. 3, 767; First Books series, Supp. 10, 821; game books, Supp. 10, 418; Happy Hollisters series, Supp. 9, 787, 788; Hardy Boys series, Supp. 9, 787; here-and-now technique, Supp. 5, 92–93; historical novels, Supp. 8, 181; history, Supp. 10, 400; horse stories, Supp. 10, 6; illustrations, Supp. 3, 44, 69, 848; Supp. 5, 93; Supp. 6, 372; Supp. 7, 17; Supp. 8, 494; Supp. 9, 829; Supp. 10, 688, 690; Landmark Books, Supp. 10, 400; library programs, Supp. 7, 550; light verse, Supp. 9, 579; *Millions of* Cats, Supp. 4, 310; mysteries, Supp. 5, 526; Pansy books, Supp. 1, 20; publishing of, Supp. 2, 59; Supp. 7, 307; Supp. 9, 166; space stories, Supp. 8, 380; Tolliver Family series, Supp. 9, 787–88; Uncle Wiggily stories, Supp. 7, 279
Children's Medical and Surgical Center (Baltimore, Md.), Supp. 7, 59
Children's Memorial Hospital (Chicago, Ill.), Supp. 3, 101
Childrens' Museum (Brooklyn, N. Y.), Vol. 4, Part 1, 416
Children's Television Workshop, productions, Supp. 10, 352
Childs, Cephas G., reference to, Vol. 7, Part 1, 469
Childs, Marquis W., reference to, Supp. 3, 92
Chile: diplomacy, Vol. 5, Part 2, 375; Vol. 6, Part 1, 358; Vol. 7, Part 1, 425; Vol. 8, Part 2, 150; Vol. 9, Part 2, 141; Supp. 6, 73, 207; independence, agitation for, Vol. 8, Part 1, 30 f.; Patagonian dispute, Vol. 7, Part 2, 71 f.; public service, Vol. 8, Part 2, 150; writings on, Vol. 9, Part 2, 122
"Chillicotte Junto," Vol. 9, Part 2, 536, 568
Chilton Press, Supp. 7, 615
China: air force, Supp. 6, 109; American mission universities, Supp. 4, 677–78; American University, Vol. 5, Part 2, 208; anthropological studies, Supp. 4, 867; armed landing force, first U.S., Vol. 8, Part 1, 183 f.; art, Supp. 3, 268–69, 465; art history, Supp. 5, 729; Bible translation, Vol. 4, Part 1, 399; Vol. 7, Part 2, 214; Vol. 8, Part 2, 428 f.; Vol. 9, Part 1, 58; Boxer Rebellion, Vol. 1, Part 1, 106, 241, 263; Vol. 2, Part 1, 589 f.; Vol. 3, Part 1, 110; Vol. 4, Part 2, 434; Vol. 5, Part 2, 324; Vol. 6, Part 1, 475; Vol. 6, Part 2, 108; Vol. 9, Part 1, 238; Vol. 9, Part 2, 372; Vol. 10, Part 2, 335; Supp. 7, 358; Catholic University, Vol. 9, Part 1, 560; Communist, journalism on, Supp. 8, 635; Supp. 9, 740–41; Communist movement in, Supp. 4, 749–51; Supp. 6, 110, 270, 350; Communist-Nationalist split, Supp. 4, 147; Supp. 5, 544, 705; Supp. 6, 230–31, 350; Supp. 7, 728; Supp. 8, 158; Communist victory, Supp. 9, 8; cultural studies, Supp. 1, 486; diplomacy, Vol. 1, Part 1, 308, 443; Vol. 1, Part 2, 241; Vol. 3, Part 1, 234; Vol. 5, Part 1, 133; Vol. 5, Part 2, 324; Vol. 6, Part 1, 146, 446; Vol. 6, Part 2, 348; Vol. 7, Part 2, 34, 235; Vol. 8, Part 1, 121 f., 477, 491 f.; Vol. 8, Part 2, 66, 613; Vol. 9, Part 1, 140, 491, 493; Vol. 9, Part 2, 310, 371, 640; Vol. 10, Part 1, 426 f., 437 f., 585 f.; Supp.

2, 129; **Supp. 3**, 699, 826; **Supp. 6**, 229–31; **Supp. 7**, 377, 728; **Supp. 9**, 845; **Supp. 10**, 528; education, **Vol. 9, Part 1**, 58; **Vol. 9, Part 2**, 372; education modernization, **Supp. 4**, 592; English-language journals, **Supp. 4**, 679; Exclusion Act, constitutionality of, **Vol. 9, Part 2**, 246; explorations, **Vol. 8, Part 2**, 244; first American exchange professor, **Supp. 6**, 410; Formosa defense, **Supp. 6**, 235; geological expeditions, **Supp. 4**, 344, 896; government advisers, **Supp. 3**, 831; historical writings on, **Supp. 8**, 360; history studies, **Supp. 4**, 532; immigration from, **Vol. 1, Part 1**, 308; **Vol. 5, Part 2**, 269; **Vol. 9, Part 2**, 642; insane, care of, **Vol. 5, Part 2**, 357; Korean War, **Supp. 6**, 327; **Supp. 9**, 9; loan, negotiations for international, **Vol. 9, Part 2**, 121; medical education, **Supp. 4**, 346–47; medicine and public health, **Supp. 3**, 324; metallurgical operations, **Vol. 2, Part 2**, 103 f.; Methodist church, **Vol. 7, Part 2**, 214; **Supp. 6**, 315; military adviser, unofficial, **Vol. 6, Part 1**, 70; missions in, **Vol. 1, Part 1**, 215, 263, 392; **Vol. 1, Part 2**, 34; **Vol. 2, Part 1**, 36, 154; **Vol. 4, Part 1**, 399, 509 f.; **Vol. 4, Part 2**, 234, 361, 453 f.; **Vol. 5, Part 1**, 132; **Vol. 5, Part 2**, 357, 560 f.; **Vol. 6, Part 1**, 475 f., 570; **Vol. 6, Part 2**, 122, 347, 385; **Vol. 7, Part 1**, 444; **Vol. 7, Part 2**, 34 f., 214, 235; **Vol. 8, Part 1**, 286 f., 476 f.; **Vol. 8, Part 2**, 8, 428 f.; **Vol. 9, Part 1**, 57 f., 68 f., 137, 238, 314, 442; **Vol. 10, Part 2**, 250, 274, 290, 469, 599; **Supp. 1**, 433; **Supp. 2**, 548; **Supp. 3**, 268–69, 288–89, 476–77; **Supp. 4**, 514–15; **Supp. 9**, 132; **Supp. 10**, 636–37; motion pictures, **Supp. 8**, 495; newspaper, first, **Vol. 7, Part 1**, 480; "Open Door" policy, **Vol. 4, Part 2**, 434; Protestant Christianity, introduction of, **Vol. 8, Part 1**, 286 f.; public libraries, **Supp. 3**, 91; Quemoy and Matsu defense, **Supp. 8**, 223; students from, in U.S., **Vol. 10, Part 2**, 639; Taiping rebellion, **Vol. 10, Part 1**, 419 f.; tariff conferences (1925), **Supp. 4**, 800; trade, **Vol. 2, Part 1**, 66, 129, 149, 289 f.; **Vol. 3, Part 2**, 507 f.; **Vol. 4, Part 1**, 523, 551; **Vol. 4, Part 2**, 324, 482; **Vol. 5, Part 1**, 408; **Vol. 5, Part 2**, 271, 383 f.; **Vol. 6, Part 1**, 444 f.; **Vol. 7, Part 2**, 34; **Vol. 9, Part 2**, 499; **Vol. 10, Part 1**, 585 f.; translations, **Vol. 1, Part 1**, 215; **Vol. 7, Part 1**, 444; treaty, first with, 1846, **Vol. 1, Part 2**, 241; Treaty of Tientsin (1858), **Vol. 2, Part 1**, 289; **Vol. 4, Part 2**, 324; **Vol. 8, Part 1**, 462; U.S. China lobby, **Supp. 8**, 506; **Supp. 9**, 830–31; U.S. military in, **Supp. 4**, 782–83; **Supp. 6**, 429; **Supp. 9**, 630, 822, 830–31; writings on, **Vol. 3, Part 1**, 234; **Vol. 5, Part 1**, 133; **Vol. 8, Part 1**, 477; **Vol. 9, Part 1**, 58, 138, 238 f.; **Vol. 10, Part 1**, 387 f.; **Vol. 10, Part 2**, 261; **Supp. 8**, 264–65; **Supp. 9**, 133, 134, 740–41. *See also* Sino-Japanese War

China Christian Advocate, **Supp. 6**, 214

China Clipper (airplane), **Supp. 9**, 899

China Medical Board, founding of, **Supp. 4**, 346–47

China Weekly Review, founding of, **Supp. 4**, 679

Chinese-Americans: movie depictions of, **Supp. 7**, 802; San Francisco Chinatown photographs, **Supp. 3**, 295

Chinese Christian Advocate, **Vol. 7, Part 2**, 214

Chinese Recorder, founding of, **Supp. 2**, 549

Chippewa Indians: **Supp. 6**, 162; language of, **Vol. 1, Part 1**, 585; missionary work, **Vol. 1, Part 2**, 145; Sioux, peace with, **Vol. 3, Part 1**, 500 f.

Chiropractic, founding and development of, **Vol. 7, Part 2**, 177

Chisholm v. *Georgia,* **Vol. 5, Part 2**, 8

Chivington Massacre, **Vol. 2, Part 2**, 620; **Vol. 3, Part 2**, 205

Chlorine: **Supp. 3**, 26; commercial production of, **Supp. 1**, 262; use as disinfectant, **Vol. 3, Part 1**, 377

Chloroform, **Vol. 4, Part 2**, 59, 62

Choate, Joseph H., reference to, **Vol. 6, Part 1**, 270

Choate, Hall and Stewart, **Supp. 7**, 91

Chocolates, **Supp. 3**, 357–58

Choctaw Academy, **Vol. 5, Part 2**, 115

Choctaw Indians, **Vol. 5, Part 2**, 115; **Vol. 7, Part 2**, 638; **Supp. 7**, 376

Chocura, **Vol. 7, Part 2**, 308

Cholera: **Vol. 1, Part 1**, 383, 413; **Vol. 2, Part 1**, 68, 231; **Vol. 3, Part 1**, 204; **Vol. 5, Part 1**, 234, 546, 553; **Vol. 5, Part 2**, 517; **Vol. 6, Part 1**, 59, 282; **Vol. 7, Part 1**, 628; **Vol. 7, Part 2**, 110; **Vol. 9, Part 1**, 606; **Vol. 9, Part 2**, 311; chlorine, use of as disinfectant, **Vol. 3, Part 1**, 377; Cincinnati, **Vol. 3, Part 1**, 615 f.; epidemic of 1830, **Vol. 8, Part 2**, 238; investigation by *New York Times,* **Vol. 4, Part 1**, 7; Jacksonville, Ill., **Vol. 8, Part 1**, 120 f.; New Orleans, La., **Vol. 9, Part 2**, 85; Pittsburgh, Pa., **Vol. 3, Part 1**, 220

Cholesterol, **Supp. 3**, 693

Choral music: black, **Supp. 3**, 225–26; conducting, **Vol. 10, Part 2**, 453; New York Choral Society, **Vol. 4, Part 2**, 505; singing, **Vol. 7, Part 2**, 78; **Vol. 10, Part 1**, 46 f.

Choreographers. For complete list, *see* Occupations Index

Chorus line, first, **Supp. 6**, 305

Chotiner, Murray, "Pink Sheet," produced in Nixon-Douglas Senate campaign, **Supp. 10**, 184

Christ and Culture, **Supp. 7**, 575

Christensen, Parley, reference to, **Supp. 3**, 347

Christian Advocate, **Vol. 2, Part 1**, 231; **Vol. 3, Part 2**, 436; **Vol. 9, Part 1**, 605; **Vol. 9, Part 2**, 482

Christian and Missionary Alliance, **Vol. 9, Part 1**, 176

Christian Catholic Apostolic Church in Zion, **Vol. 3, Part 1**, 413 f.

Christian Century, **Supp. 6**, 315

Christian church: **Vol. 1, Part 1**, 207; **Vol. 4, Part 1**, 407, 440; **Vol. 7, Part 2**, 7; **Vol. 8, Part 1**, 271 f.; **Vol. 9, Part 2**, 71; administration, **Vol. 3, Part 1**, 335; architecture, **Vol. 4, Part 1**, 387 f.; **Vol. 8, Part 1**, 507, 553, 567 f.; fraud, "Miracle Wheat," **Vol. 8, Part 2**, 240; history, **Vol. 2, Part 1**, 60; **Vol. 3, Part 1**, 469 f.; **Vol. 4, Part 1**, 376; **Vol. 5, Part 1**, 554; **Vol. 5, Part 2**, 470; **Vol. 6, Part 2**, 210; **Vol. 7, Part 1**, 205; **Vol. 8, Part 1**, 393; **Vol. 8, Part 2**, 417 f.; **Vol. 9, Part 2**, 618; "Institutional," movement, **Vol. 1, Part 2**, 137; law, **Vol. 4, Part 1**, 194; **Vol. 7, Part 1**, 625; music, **Vol. 4, Part 2**, 388; **Vol. 8, Part 1**, 421; **Vol. 10, Part 1**, 50 f.; social responsibilities, **Vol. 9, Part 2**, 150 f.; unity, **Vol. 1, Part 2**, 133; **Vol. 2, Part 1**, 40, 179; **Vol. 5, Part 1**, 453; **Vol. 7, Part 1**, 386; **Vol. 8, Part 2**, 18. *See also* Bible; Christianity; Jesus Christ; Religion; *specific denominations*

Christian College, **Vol. 9, Part 2**, 254

Christian Conference, **Vol. 5, Part 2**, 158

Christian Connection, **Vol. 9, Part 1**, 37 f., 258; **Vol. 10, Part 1**, 636 f.

Christian Endeavor Society, **Vol. 2, Part 2**, 126 f.; **Supp. 8**, 505

Christian Endeavor Union (South India), **Vol. 5, Part 2**, 190

Christian Endeavor World, **Vol. 2, Part 2**, 127

Christian Era, **Vol. 1, Part 2**, 351

Christian Female College, **Vol. 1, Part 1**, 207

Christian Front, founding of, **Supp. 10**, 152

Christian Herald, **Vol. 5, Part 2**, 447; **Vol. 9, Part 2**, 377; **Supp. 7**, 345; **Supp. 8**, 505

Christian Index, **Vol. 10, Part 1**, 31 f.

Christian Intelligencer, The, **Vol. 3, Part 1**, 463

Christianity: apologetics, **Supp. 4**, 525–26; Asian, studies in, **Supp. 8**, 360; crucifixion and anti-Semitism, **Supp. 8**, 307, 537; historical writings on, **Supp. 8**, 359–60; history of, **Supp. 4**, 151–52; modernism, **Supp. 3**, 514–16; practical, **Supp. 4**, 271–72; Social-

ist movements and, **Supp. 5**, 616–17; **Supp. 7**, 746; "social gospel" school, **Supp. 9**, 585. *See also* Bible; Christian church; Jesus Christ; Religion; *specific denominations*
Christianity and Crisis (journal), **Supp. 9**, 586
Christian Literature Society for China, **Vol. 7, Part 2**, 214
Christian Messenger, **Vol. 9, Part 2**, 71
"Christian Quakers," **Vol. 5, Part 2**, 289
Christian Quarterly, **Vol. 7, Part 1**, 146
Christian Register, **Vol. 1, Part 2**, 169; **Vol. 8, Part 1**, 445, 623, 645
Christian Science: **Vol. 2, Part 1**, 302; **Vol. 3, Part 2**, 7 f.; **Vol. 4, Part 1**, 7; **Vol. 5, Part 1**, 342; **Vol. 9, Part 1**, 595, f.; beginnings of, **Vol. 3, Part 2**, 10 f., 213; **Vol. 8, Part 1**, 304; "Christian Science," first use of term, **Vol. 8, Part 1**, 304 f.; First Church of Christ, Scientist, leadership, **Supp. 2**, 151; writings on, **Vol. 8, Part 1**, 611
Christian Science Monitor, **Vol. 3, Part 2**, 14; **Vol. 8, Part 1**, 542; **Supp. 1**, 1
Christian Socialist Society, **Vol. 1, Part 2**, 377
Christian Social Union, **Supp. 3**, 249
Christian Soldier, establishment of, to oppose Universalist church, **Vol. 5, Part 2**, 112
Christian Spectator, **Vol. 9, Part 2**, 339
Christian's Secret of a Happy Life, **Vol. 9, Part 1**, 274
Christian Standard, **Vol. 3, Part 2**, 179; **Vol. 5, Part 1**, 66
Christian Union, **Vol. 6, Part 1**, 541
Christian Union Quarterly, **Supp. 1**, 16
Christian unity, advocacy of, **Vol. 5, Part 1**, 421. *See also* Ecumenism
Christian World, **Vol. 4, Part 1**, 376
Christmas: American Catholics' gift to pope, **Supp. 4**, 535; antituberculosis seal sales, **Supp. 4**, 92; decorations, **Supp. 3**, 685; radio programs commemorating, **Supp. 5**, 44
Christmas cards, decoration of, **Vol. 8, Part 1**, 165 f.
Christoffel, Elwin Bruno, reference to, **Supp. 7**, 216
Christopher House (New York City), **Supp. 5**, 325
Christopher movement, founding of, **Supp. 10**, 405
Chromosomes: mapping, **Supp. 2**, 61; **Supp. 8**, 448, 449; **Supp. 9**, 550; sex-linked, **Supp. 2**, 725; **Supp. 4**, 515–16
Chronicles of America, **Vol. 5, Part 2**, 80
Chronograph, invention of, **Vol. 6, Part 1**, 337
Chronometry, **Vol. 1, Part 2**, 434; **Vol. 5, Part 2**, 487
Chrysanthemum and the Sword, The, **Supp. 4**, 72
Chrysler, Walter P., references to, **Supp. 4**, 244; **Supp. 6**, 337; **Supp. 8**, 319; **Supp. 9**, 290
Chrysler Corporation: acquisitions, **Supp. 9**, 290; labor relations, **Supp. 8**, 652; management, **Supp. 8**, 319
Chrysler Institute for Engineering, founding of, **Supp. 2**, 104
Chrysler's Field, battle of, **Vol. 1, Part 2**, 527; **Vol. 4, Part 1**, 93; **Vol. 10, Part 2**, 225
Church, Frank, reference to, **Supp. 6**, 681
Church and State in the United States, **Supp. 6**, 600
Church Choral Union, **Vol. 7, Part 2**, 184
Church Divinity School of the Pacific, **Vol. 7, Part 1**, 497
Churches, Federal Council of. *See* Federal Council of Churches
Churches, World Council of. *See* World Council of Churches
Churches (buildings): architecture, **Supp. 3**, 195–97; stained-glass windows, **Supp. 3**, 183–84. *See also names of specific edifices and denominations*
Churchill, Winston: Marshall, G. C., relationship, **Supp. 6**, 430, 431; references to, **Supp. 5**, 5; **Supp. 6**, 147, 361; **Supp. 7**, 778; **Supp. 9**, 783; Roosevelt, F. D., relationship, **Supp. 3**, 660, 662, 663, 664; sculpture of, **Supp. 3**, 125; World War I, **Supp. 3**, 204
Church Journal, **Vol. 4, Part 2**, 416
Church League of America, **Supp. 8**, 426
Churchman, **Vol. 8, Part 2**, 530; **Vol. 9, Part 1**, 301
Church music, **Supp. 4**, 125
Church of Christ. *See* Federal Council of Churches of Christ in America
Church of England: **Vol. 5, Part 2**, 118; **Vol. 7, Part 1**, 131, 646 f.; **Vol. 9, Part 2**, 19; **Supp. 3**, 175; **Supp. 6**, 102; Anglo-Catholicism, **Supp. 2**, 201–2; **Supp. 3**, 195; **Supp. 6**, 45–46; **Supp. 7**, 220; Carolinas, **Vol. 5, Part 2**, 111; Maryland, **Vol. 1, Part 2**, 610; missionary work, **Vol. 1, Part 1**, 497; **Vol. 3, Part 2**, 505; New York, establishment of, in, **Vol. 6, Part 1**, 326; ordination, first recipients of, in America, **Vol. 10, Part 1**, 604 f.; Revolutionary War period, **Vol. 1, Part 1**, 422; **Vol. 2, Part 1**, 616. See also Protestant Episcopal church
Church of Jesus Christ of Latter-Day Saints (LDS). *See* Mormon church
Church of St. Francis Xavier (New York City), **Supp. 3**, 849
Church of the Holy Communion, **Vol. 7, Part 1**, 313
Church of the New Jerusalem, **Vol. 4, Part 1**, 282; **Vol. 8, Part 1**, 448 f.; **Vol. 9, Part 1**, 376
Church of the Transfiguration (New York City), **Vol. 5, Part 1**, 255
Church of the United Brethren in Christ, **Vol. 1, Part 2**, 405; **Vol. 7, Part 2**, 108
Church Peace Union, Carnegie Foundation, **Vol. 8, Part 2**, 98; founding of, **Supp. 6**, 25
Church-state separation: advocacy, **Supp. 6**, 636; Catholic-as-president issue, **Supp. 3**, 681, 719–20, 361; **Supp. 8**, 115–16, 614; evolution, teaching of, **Supp. 5**, 461; **Supp. 8**, 582–84; flag salute case, **Supp. 5**, 358; Mormons in political office, **Supp. 3**, 727; opposition to, **Supp. 1**, 217; parochial school aid, **Supp. 8**, 25, 115–16; Supreme Court decisions on, **Supp. 4**, 713, 796; **Supp. 5**, 358
Church Temperance Society, **Vol. 3, Part 1**, 191
CIA. *See* Central Intelligence Agency
Cicero, Ill., organized crime in, **Supp. 4**, 141–42; **Supp. 6**, 263–64
Cicognani, Amleto, reference to, **Supp. 8**, 46
Cicotte, Ed, references to, **Supp. 8**, 574, 575
Cigarettes: advertising and promotion of, **Supp. 4**, 371; **Supp. 5**, 411, 567; cancer link, **Supp. 6**, 246; **Supp. 8**, 7; manufacture of, **Vol. 3, Part 1**, 496 f.; **Vol. 4, Part 1**, 318
Cigars, **Supp. 7**, 614; selling of, **Vol. 3, Part 1**, 497 f.
Cimarron, **Supp. 9**, 762
Cinaudagraph Corporation, founding of, **Supp. 5**, 324
Cincinnati, Ohio: "Bibles in the schools" case, **Vol. 6, Part 1**, 241; cholera outbreak, **Vol. 3, Part 1**, 615 f.; civic service, **Vol. 3, Part 1**, 426 f.; **Vol. 3, Part 2**, 458; **Vol. 5, Part 1**, 464; **Vol. 6, Part 1**, 241; **Vol. 6, Part 2**, 255, 419; **Vol. 7, Part 2**, 475; **Vol. 8, Part 1**, 317 f.; **Vol. 8, Part 2**, 462; **Vol. 9, Part 1**, 135; educational service, **Vol. 9, Part 1**, 496; fire prevention, early, **Vol. 4, Part 1**, 593; German singing societies, **Vol. 8, Part 1**, 388; history of, **Vol. 2, Part 2**, 108; **Vol. 3, Part 1**, 424, 426 f.; **Vol. 3, Part 2**, 382; **Vol. 9, Part 2**, 259; **Vol. 10, Part 2**, 655; legal service, **Vol. 9, Part 1**, 498; municipal management of, **Supp. 4**, 246–47; music in, **Vol. 7, Part 1**, 494; **Vol. 8, Part 1**, 633; **Vol. 9, Part 1**, 483; **Vol. 9, Part 2**, 265, 424, Phonography Institute, **Vol. 7, Part 2**, 642; planning of, **Supp. 1**, 311; political reform, **Supp. 5**, 674; public library, **Vol. 8, Part 1**, 66 f.; real estate, **Vol. 6, Part 1**, 394; railroad development, **Vol. 5, Part 1**, 464; Roman Catholic diocese, **Supp. 4**, 535–36; Sun-

day school, first in, **Vol. 2, Part 2**, 108; university, bequest for free, **Vol. 9, Part 2**, 264
Cincinnati, Society of the. *See* Society of the Cincinnati
Cincinnati Chronicle, **Vol. 3, Part 1**, 424
Cincinnati Convention, **Vol. 1, Part 2**, 517
Cincinnati Enquirer, **Vol. 2, Part 1**, 94; **Vol. 3, Part 2**, 270; **Vol. 4, Part 2**, 163; **Vol. 7, Part 2**, 557; **Supp. 3**, 491
Cincinnati Gazette, **Vol. 8, Part 1**, 482
Cincinnati General Hospital, surgery training, **Supp. 3**, 626
Cincinnati, Hamilton, and Dayton Railroad, **Supp. 5**, 550
Cincinnati Medical College, **Vol. 7, Part 1**, 237
Cincinnati Post, cartoons, **Supp. 5**, 732
Cincinnati Reds (baseball): **Supp. 7**, 155, 502; **Supp. 8**, 141; **Supp. 10**, 278; night games inaugurated, **Supp. 9**, 532
Cincinnati Repertory Company, **Supp. 3**, 797
Cincinnati Social Unit, **Supp. 3**, 227
Cincinnati Times, **Vol. 7, Part 1**, 532
Cincinnati Union Terminal Co., **Supp. 3**, 795
Cinema. *See* Motion pictures
CinemaScope, **Supp. 7**, 692, 693
Cinematography: **Supp. 3**, 73–74; first mass-market inexpensive camera, **Supp. 5**, 322; innovations in, **Supp. 10**, 347–48
Cinerama, **Supp. 5**, 721–22; **Supp. 6**, 638
CIO. *See* Congress of Industrial Organizations
"Cipher Despatches," **Vol. 8, Part 1**, 457, 484; **Vol. 9, Part 2**, 541
Circle of Russian Culture, founding of, **Supp. 2**, 505
Circuit riding, **Vol. 1, Part 1**, 574 f.; **Vol. 1, Part 2**, 31; **Vol. 4, Part 2**, 497; **Vol. 5, Part 2**, 169, 226, 579; **Vol. 6, Part 1**, 113; **Vol. 6, Part 2**, 86; **Vol. 8, Part 2**, 13, 15, 315; **Vol. 9, Part 1**, 4, 382
Circulating libraries, **Vol. 4, Part 2**, 591; **Vol. 6, Part 1**, 427; **Vol. 7, Part 1**, 510; **Vol. 9, Part 2**, 445
Circulatory system, writings on, **Supp. 4**, 390. *See also* Blood vessels; Heart; Lungs
Circumstantial evidence, famous definitions of, **Vol. 10, Part 1**, 592 f.
Circus: **Vol. 1, Part 1**, 498, 636 f.; **Vol. 3, Part 2**, 522; **Vol. 8, Part 1**,536 f., 618 f.; art depicting, **Supp. 4**, 289, 463–64; **Supp. 10**, 90; calliope, invention of, **Vol. 9, Part 2**, 57; clowns, **Supp. 6**, 8, 112; **Supp. 10**, 406, 407; high-wire acts, **Supp. 10**, 809–10; Madison Square Garden, **Vol. 1, Part 1**, 638; management, **Vol. 1, Part 1**, 499; publicity for, **Supp. 6**, 536; Tom Thumb, **Vol. 9, Part 2**, 126; tragedies, **Supp. 10**, 810; trapeze acts, **Supp. 10**, 406; wild animal collections, **Supp. 4**, 120; **Supp. 7**, 41–42
"Cisco Kid" (fictional character), **Supp. 10**, 669
Citadel, The (S.C.), presidency, **Supp. 5**, 669
Cities: architecture, **Supp. 6**, 593; Cincinnati model, **Supp. 4**, 247; City Beautiful movement, **Supp. 3**, 533–34; community organization, **Supp. 9**, 19; engineering projects, **Supp. 4**, 756; first major social survey of, **Supp. 6**, 329–30; geography studies, **Supp. 4**, 424; historical writings on, **Supp. 7**, 676; housing, **Supp. 5**, 630, 631; medieval, studies of, **Supp. 5**, 655–56; neighborhood unit concept, **Supp. 3**, 601; planning studies, *see* City planning; political reform, **Supp. 6**, 467–68; quality of life in, **Supp. 2**, 374; recreation planning, **Supp. 2**, 375; slum clearance, **Supp. 2**, 684; sociological studies, **Supp. 3**, 578; **Supp. 8**, 398–99; urban renewal, **Supp. 10**, 168. *See also* City planning; Model communities; Municipal government; Zoning; *specific city names*
Cities of the Interior, **Supp. 10**, 591
Cities Service, management of, **Supp. 2**, 154
Citizen Kane, **Supp. 3**, 93; **Supp. 5**, 287–88, 464; **Supp. 6**, 441; **Supp. 7**, 166; **Supp. 9**, 382, 560
Citizens and Southern Bank and Trust Co., founding of, **Supp. 4**, 916
Citizens' Association of Chicago, founding of, **Supp. 1**, 535
Citizens' Federal Research Bureau, founding of, **Supp. 2**, 678
Citizenship: diplomatic protection for aliens, **Supp. 5**, 81; dual, **Vol. 8, Part 2**, 124; for Indians, **Vol. 8, Part 1**, 175 f., 335 f.; literacy tests, **Vol. 5, Part 2**, 32; passport issuance, **Supp. 8**, 590–91; Supreme Court decisions, **Supp. 4**, 727; woman's right of choice, **Supp. 5**, 532
Citizens' Industrial Alliance, **Vol. 8, Part 1**, 112 f.
Citizens Union, founding of, **Supp. 1**, 216
Citizen Training Corps, founding of, **Supp. 2**, 637
Citric acid, first manufacture of, **Vol. 10, Part 1**, 607 f.
Citrus fruit industry, **Vol. 4, Part 1**, 144; **Vol. 8, Part 1**, 145 f.; canker disease, **Supp. 1**, 462; diseases, **Supp. 4**, 862–63
City charters, model for, **Vol. 3, Part 1**, 168
City College. *See* College of the City of New York
City Hall (Philadelphia, Pa.), sculpture, **Supp. 3**, 123
City Lights, **Supp. 10**, 116
City Missionary Society, **Vol. 5, Part 2**, 54
City of New York, airship, **Vol. 6, Part 1**, 452
City planning: **Vol. 3, Part 1**, 168; **Vol. 3, Part 2**, 323; **Vol. 4, Part 2**, 389; **Vol. 5, Part 1**, 56, 108; **Vol. 6, Part 1**, 167; **Vol. 7, Part 2**, 435; **Vol. 8, Part 1**, 45 f.; **Vol. 8, Part 2**, 36; **Supp. 1**, 311; **Supp. 2**, 158, 490, 738; **Supp. 3**, 51–52, 66, 533–34; **Supp. 6**, 486, 522; Baltimore, **Supp. 4**, 550–51; beltway proposal, **Supp. 9**, 526; Boston, 1855, **Vol. 4, Part 2**, 523; first national conference on, **Supp. 5**, 631; New York, **Supp. 4**, 56; Philadelphia, **Supp. 9**, 445, 447; Washington, D. C., **Vol. 2, Part 1**, 305,; **Vol. 6, Part 1**, 167; **Vol. 8, Part 1**, 647. *See also* Model communities; Zoning
City Planning, founding of, **Supp. 1**, 311
City Temple (London), **Supp. 4**, 628
Civic design, first chair of, **Vol. 8, Part 2**, 37
Civic Federation of Chicago, organization of, **Supp. 2**, 166
Civics. *See* Municipal government; Political science
Civil Aeronautics Administration (U.S.), administration of, **Supp. 8**, 709
Civil Aeronautics Board (CAB), **Supp. 6**, 666; chairmanship, **Supp. 7**, 453, 454; predecessor, **Supp. 5**, 444
Civil Air Transport (CAT), **Supp. 6**, 1 10
Civil defense, World War II, **Supp. 4**, 466; **Supp. 7**, 453, 780
Civil engineering. *See* Engineering, civil
Civil Engineering, founding of, **Supp. 2**, 170
Civilian Conservation Corps (CCC): camps, **Supp. 6**, 429–30; founding of, **Supp. 3**, 652; **Supp. 6**, 411–12
Civilization and Its Discontents, **Supp. 10**, 506
Civil liberties: academic freedom, **Supp. 9**, 429, 769; **Supp. 10**, 137, 143, 386; "clear and present danger" test, **Supp. 3**, 99, 168; **Supp. 6**, 495; **Supp. 7**, 317; **Supp. 9**, 593; cold war-era threats to, **Supp. 10**, 502–3; congressional support for, **Supp. 5**, 480–81; **Supp. 9**, 511–12; defendants' rights decisions, **Supp. 3**, 755; FBI abuses of, **Supp. 9**, 407–8; free speech issues, **Supp. 6**, 104–5, 651; Jehovah's Witnesses cases, **Supp. 3**, 679; judicial decisions, **Supp. 9**, 865; judicial support, **Supp. 7**, 317; **Supp. 10**, 863; law enforcement issues, **Supp. 9**, 95; legal defense, **Supp. 2**, 534; **Supp. 5**, 280; **Supp. 8**, 18, 35; legislation, **Supp. 4**, 407; National Civil Liberties Bureau, founding of, **Supp. 3**, 604; New Deal policies, **Supp. 5**, 343; New York State judicial decisions, **Supp. 3**,

451; organizations, **Supp. 7**, 510–11; preferred freedoms concept, **Supp. 4**, 796–97; press freedom landmark decision (1941), **Supp. 3**, 157; Scopes trial, **Supp. 6**, 528–29; Supreme Court decisions, **Supp. 4**, 537, 614, 713, 796; **Supp. 5**, 358, 389, 574–75, 714; **Supp. 7**, 96, 263–64, 291, 541–42; **Supp. 9**, 96, 97, 364–65, 593, 837, 865; **Supp. 10**, 126, 188, 665; World War I issues, **Supp. 4**, 62, 542, 613, 636; **Supp. 7**, 248, 356; World War II issues, **Supp. 3**, 93; **Supp. 4**, 614; writings on, **Supp. 4**, 851; **Supp. 8**, 408; **Supp. 10**, 24–25

Civil Rights Act (1865), **Vol. 5, Part 2**, 86

Civil Rights Act (1964), **Supp. 8**, 323, 334; **Supp. 9**, 434, 620; **Supp. 10**, 127, 748

Civil Rights Commission, **Supp. 9**, 68

Civil Rights Congress, **Supp. 7**, 315

Civil rights movement: American Indian advocacy, **Supp. 5**, 119–20; antilynching law campaign, **Supp. 9**, 749, 750; black criticism of, **Supp. 8**, 435; **Supp. 9**, 138–39; **Supp. 10**, 612; black indifference to, **Supp. 6**, 314; **Supp. 8**, 121; black leadership, **Supp. 8**, 332–35; black organizations, **Supp. 8**, 539–40; "black power" advocacy, **Supp. 8**, 335; black professional race-relations training, **Supp. 6**, 284–85; black women in, **Supp. 3**, 827–28; **Supp. 10**, 307–8; Catholic church involvement, **Supp. 7**, 533; **Supp. 8**, 293–4; Communist support for, **Supp. 5**, 499, 500; congressional opposition, **Supp. 9**, 401; congressional support, **Supp. 6**, 636; **Supp. 9**, 69–70; Democratic 1948 proposals, **Supp. 6**, 710–11; demonstrations, **Supp. 9**, 384, 425, 619, 901; **Supp. 10**, 171; early activism, **Supp. 2**, 315, 346; **Supp. 7**, 155, 201–5; early leadership, **Supp. 5**, 680, 740–41; **Supp. 9**, 619; 620; editorial support, **Supp. 8**, 404–5; FBI policies toward, **Supp. 9**, 407; federal support, **Supp. 8**, 406; financial support, **Supp. 8**, 88; Jewish support for, **Supp. 9**, 384; labor involvement, **Supp. 6**, 648; legal action, **Supp. 4**, 397–98; **Supp. 8**, 285; legislation, **Supp. 4**, 407, 493; **Supp. 7**, 425; **Supp. 8**, 323, 333–34; **Supp. 10**, 659, 660, 661; legislation, **Supp. 9**, 433, 434, 435, 620; **Supp. 10**, 361, 362; legislation opposition, **Supp. 8**, 68; local organizations, **Supp. 9**, 900, 901; March on Washington, **Supp. 9**, 425, 901; **Supp. 10**, 341, 661; martyrs, **Supp. 7**, 227; **Supp. 8**, 335–36; **Supp. 9**, 152, 689; mid-1960s intensification, **Supp. 7**, 319, 425; **Supp. 8**, 333–35; militancy, **Supp. 7**, 508–9; military segregation, **Supp. 10**, 230, 378; New York City, **Supp. 9**, 619; New York State legislation, **Supp. 3**, 391; nonviolence tactics, **Supp. 7**, 781; **Supp. 8**, 86, 332, 333–35, 458, 606; **Supp. 10**, 386; performers supporting, **Supp. 9**, 425; pioneer work in, **Supp. 4**, 493, 850–51; progressive policies toward, **Supp. 9**, 370; real estate restrictive covenants, **Supp. 6**, 502; religious support, **Supp. 6**, 649; school desegregation, **Supp. 5**, 156; **Supp. 9**, 68, 190–91, 258; Selma (Ala.) march, **Supp. 9**, 384; "separate but equal" doctrine, **Supp. 6**, 495, 502; southern, 1930s, **Supp. 6**, 11–12; southern activism, **Supp. 8**, 322–23, 333–35; southern resistance to, **Supp. 8**, 500; **Supp. 9**, 150, 152, 161, 186–87, 190–91, 391–92, 393; southern white advocacy, **Supp. 7**, 235, 788; **Supp. 8**, 682–83; **Supp. 9**, 650–51; student sit-ins, **Supp. 8**, 86; Supreme Court decisons, **Supp. 4**, 796; **Supp. 5**, 713–14; **Supp. 7**, 96; **Supp. 8**, 406; **Supp. 9**, 749; **Supp. 10**, 126–27, 665; Truman policies, **Supp. 5**, 479; **Supp. 5**, 515, 741; **Supp. 7**, 748; urban North activism, **Supp. 8**, 335; voter registration drives, **Supp. 10**, 171; white establishment support for, **Supp. 9**, 901; writings on, **Supp. 8**, 387–88. *See also* Racism; School desegregation; Segregation

Civil service: **Vol. 1, Part 1**, 375; **Vol. 1, Part 2**, 169, 427; **Vol. 2, Part 2**, 616; **Vol. 3, Part 1**, 607 f.; **Vol. 3, Part 2**, 26; **Vol. 4, Part 1**, 401; **Vol. 4, Part 2**, 192, 333 f., 397, 450; **Vol. 5, Part 1**, 81; **Vol. 5, Part 2**, 41 f.; **Vol. 6, Part 1**, 67; **Vol. 7, Part 2**, 420; **Vol. 8, Part 1**, 241 f.; **Vol. 8, Part 2**, 136, 468 f.; **Vol. 9, Part 2**, 248 f.; **Vol. 10, Part 2**, 46; legislation benefiting federal employees, **Supp. 9**, 639; New York City system, reform of, **Supp. 9**, 704; women in, **Vol. 9, Part 1**, 460; writings on, **Vol. 9, Part 2**, 249

Civil Service Chronicle, **Vol. 9, Part 2**, 249

Civil Service Commission, United States: **Vol. 2, Part 2**, 208; **Vol. 3, Part 2**, 475; **Vol. 4, Part 1**, 135, 604; Loyalty Review Board, **Supp. 6**, 60; **Supp. 9**, 639; professional exams, **Supp. 6**, 692; reforms in, **Supp. 1**, 101, 294, 315. *See also* Government employees

Civil Service Reform Association, **Supp. 1**, 101

Civil service reform (1883), **Vol. 2, Part 2**, 208, 616; **Vol. 3, Part 1**, 607; **Vol. 4, Part 2**, 833; **Vol. 5, Part 1**, 81; **Vol. 5, Part 2**, 41, 260; **Vol. 7, Part 2**, 420, 533; **Vol. 8, Part 2**, 137, 469

Civil War, Spanish. *See* Spanish Civil War

Civil War (U.S.; general): allegiance, divided, **Vol. 3, Part 2**, 403, 410; arbitration, international, resulting from, **Vol. 3, Part 1**, 135; biographical writings on, **Supp. 4**, 490; British, diplomacy, **Vol. 1, Part 1**, 43 f.; **Vol. 7, Part 2**, 520; **Supp. 1**, 9; cartoons, **Vol. 7, Part 1**, 186; chaplain, first black, **Vol. 10, Part 1**, 65; Confederate financial agents, **Supp. 1**, 690; conscientious objectors, **Vol. 8, Part 1**, 236 f.; cotton, **Vol. 1, Part 1**, 45; **Vol. 3, Part 1**, 182, 592 f.; Cuba, **Vol. 4, Part 2**, 513; *De Bow's Review*, **Vol. 3, Part 1**, 181; draft methods, **Vol. 3, Part 2**, 580; **Vol. 5, Part 1**, 129; **Vol. 8, Part 1**, 202 f., 358 f.; events leading to, **Vol. 2, Part 1**, 78; **Vol. 3, Part 1**, 399 f.; **Vol. 8, Part 1**, 34 f.; financing of, **Vol. 2, Part 2**, 383; **Vol. 3, Part 1**, 326; **Vol. 5, Part 1**, 129; **Vol. 8, Part 2**, 572; fort construction, **Supp. 1**, 157; France, diplomacy, **Vol. 1, Part 2**, 259; **Vol. 3, Part 1**, 167; "Frank Leslie's" artists, **Vol. 6, Part 1**, 186; historical writings on, **Supp. 1**, 303; **Supp. 5**, 234–35; **Supp. 5**, 498; **Supp. 10**, 107–8; Indians, part played by, **Vol. 5, Part 1**, 322; **Vol. 10, Part 1**, 537 f.; journalism, **Vol. 1, Part 2**, 199; **Vol. 4, Part 2**, 259; **Vol. 6, Part 2**, 5, 267; **Vol. 8, Part 1**, 482; **Vol. 9, Part 1**, 409 f.; **Vol. 9, Part 2**, 253; **Vol. 10, Part 1**, 6; **Supp. 1**, 441; Kentucky, early neutrality of, **Vol. 2, Part 1**, 235; **Vol. 8, Part 1**, 39 f., 148 f.; laundries, military, **Vol. 1, Part 2**, 238; legal issues, **Vol. 4, Part 1**, 121; Lincolniana collection, **Supp. 7**, 529–30; Lincoln's Cabinet, **Vol. 3, Part 2**, 568; lithographic sketches, **Vol. 8, Part 2**, 169; Louisiana's attempt to organize as free state, **Vol. 3, Part 1**, 543 f.; "Loyal League," **Vol. 4, Part 1**, 623; Lutheran attitude toward, **Vol. 4, Part 2**, 529; medical care, **Vol. 1, Part 1**, 124, 318, 389, 631; **Vol. 4, Part 1**, 238, 319; **Vol. 5, Part 2**, 439; **Vol. 6, Part 1**, 42, 194, 576; **Vol. 9, Part 1**, 426; **Vol. 10, Part 2**, 492, 509, 607; **Supp. 1**, 364; munitions, **Vol. 1, Part 1**, 248, 269; **Vol. 2, Part 2**, 56; **Vol. 4, Part 1**, 593; **Vol. 7, Part 2**, 45 f.; **Vol. 8, Part 1**, 328 f., 496, 625; **Vol. 8, Part 2**, 303; novels about, **Supp. 4**, 583; **Supp. 5**, 747–48; **Supp. 10**, 399, 400; official records of, **Supp. 1**, 17; Ohio steamboat service during, **Vol. 3, Part 2**, 516; peace, efforts toward, **Vol. 5, Part 2**, 73; **Vol. 9, Part 1**, 191; personal writings on, **Supp. 1**, 418; Peru, diplomatic relations during, **Vol. 8, Part 2**, 38; photographic records of, **Vol. 1, Part 2**, 585; play, first based on, **Vol. 6, Part 1**, 483; political issues, **Vol. 3, Part 1**, 119 f.; **Vol. 4, Part 2**, 534; **Vol. 6, Part 1**, 238; prisons, **Vol. 1, Part 1**, 214; **Vol. 2, Part 1**, 168; **Vol. 5, Part 2**, 603; profiteering, **Vol. 8, Part 2**, 11; Quakers, **Vol. 8, Part 1**, 236 f.; religious movement among Confederate soldiers, **Vol. 7, Part**

2, 424; revisionist historical studies of, **Supp. 5**, 557; sanitation, **Vol. 9, Part 2**, 4; **Vol. 10, Part 2**, 607; songs, **Vol. 8, Part 2**, 148; Spanish sympathy for Union, **Vol. 5, Part 2**, 496; Stone Mountain (Ga.) memorial, **Supp. 3**, 88–89; supplies, **Vol. 9, Part 2**, 8; **Vol. 10, Part 1**, 38; Supreme Court during, **Vol. 4, Part 1**, 613; uniforms, **Vol. 7, Part 2**, 45 f.; **Vol. 10, Part 1**, 509 f.; women, contributions of, **Vol. 1, Part 2**, 237; Women's National Loyal League, **Vol. 8, Part 2**, 158; writings on, **Vol. 1, Part 1**, 264; **Vol. 3, Part 1**, 224, 259 f., 394, 396 f; **Vol. 3, Part 2**, 411, 569; **Vol. 4, Part 1**, 48, 58, 276, 402, 422, 424, 425, 596, 615; **Vol. 5, Part 1**, 461; **Vol. 5, Part 2**, 116, 191, 216, 426, 432; **Vol. 6, Part 1**, 53; **Vol. 7, Part 1**, 580, 605; **Vol. 8, Part 1**, 313 f.; **Vol. 8, Part 2**, 169, 582; **Vol. 9, Part 2**, 253, 525

Civil War (U.S.; military aspects with, specific battles listed elsewhere): Army of Northern Virginia, **Vol. 1, Part 2**, 111; Army of the Cumberland, **Vol. 8, Part 2**, 163, **Vol. 9, Part 2**, 434; Army of the Potomac, **Vol. 1, Part 1**, 656; **Vol. 1, Part 2**, 583; Army of the Tennessee, **Vol. 5, Part 2**, 145 f.; artillery, horse, **Vol. 7, Part 2**, 408; Atlanta campaign, **Vol. 9, Part 2**, 434; balloons, **Vol. 6, Part 1**, 452; black regiments in, **Vol. 1, Part 1**, 280; **Vol. 3, Part 1**, 322, 407; **Vol. 3, Part 2**, 508; **Vol. 5, Part 2**, 577, 597 f.; **Vol. 6, Part 1**, 306; **Vol. 8, Part 1**, 499 f.; **Vol. 9, Part 2**, 441 f.; campaigns, detailed account of early, **Vol. 1, Part 2**, 587; **Vol. 4, Part 2**, 506; cavalry, **Vol. 3, Part 1**, 600; **Vol. 9, Part 2**, 232; Confederate secret agent, **Vol. 9, Part 2**, 459 f.; disbanding of federal army, **Vol. 5, Part 2**, 84; East Tennessee campaign, **Vol. 2, Part 1**, 312; flags, capture of battle, **Vol. 8, Part 2**, 242; German officers, **Vol. 8, Part 2**, 310; Grand Army of the Republic, **Vol. 1, Part 1**, 180; **Vol. 3, Part 2**, 254, 556; **Vol. 5, Part 1**, 426; **Vol. 6, Part 1**, 364; **Vol. 8, Part 2**, 47; **Vol. 9, Part 1**, 582; "Iron Brigade," **Vol. 4, Part 1**, 237; **Vol. 5, Part 2**, 400; Kansas Brigade, **Vol. 5, Part 2**, 577; military maps, **Vol. 5, Part 2**, 456; mines, use of, **Vol. 8, Part 1**, 328 f.; mobilization of troops, **Vol. 1, Part 1**, 280; Morgan's raid, **Vol. 5, Part 1**, 96; "Orphan Brigade," **Vol. 6, Part 1**, 218; service in, military, **Vol. 1, Part 1**, 55, 82, 103, 125, 127, 138, 163, 165, 179, 191, 206, 235 f., 259, 265, 266, 268, 272 f., 274 f., 282, 284, 286, 291, 295, 316, 340, 347, 351, 368, 370, 371, 372, 374, 379, 383, 384, 399, 404, 420, 427, 441 f., 444, 446, 448, 453, 460, 467, 473, 485, 489, 499, 500, 508, 518, 521, 523, 528, 536, 573, 577, 578, 607, 608 f., 626, 630 f., 636, 647, 649, 656; **Vol. 1, Part 2**, 2, 19, 23, 41, 42, 56, 62, 89, 91, 101, 111, 112, 124, 125, 148, 170, 179, 203, 220, 226, 227, 237, 288, 290, 294, 313, 316, 318, 320, 332, 334, 348, 349, 364, 368, 373, 388, 399, 436, 465, 466, 467, 506, 509, 524, 525, 532, 547, 586, 587, 595, 598, 600, 608, 609, 611; **Vol. 2, Part 1**, 92, 217, 230, 236, 241, 243, 244, 245, 270, 298, 309, 310, 355, 358, 363, 372, 391, 406, 436, 443, 469, 483, 517, 529, 531, 560, 593, 598; **Vol. 2, Part 2**, 45, 57 f., 60, 75, 102, 104 f., 105, 109, 122, 140, 147, 148, 150 f., 187, 190, 243, 247, 252, 253, 254, 257, 263 f., 265 f., 279, 281, 315, 317, 344, 350 f., 352 f., 355, 377, 385 f., 389, 400, 407, 411 f., 452 f., 463 f., 476 f., 480, 483, 523 f., 554 f., 546, 549 f., 563, 568, 590, 618, 635 f.; **Vol. 3, Part 1**, 4, 7, 22, 50 f., 58, 68, 93, 94, 101 f., 109, 112, 114, 115, 116, 123 f., 131, 131 f., 137, 156, 160, 178, 179, 190, 196, 198, 199, 202, 210, 220, 224, 230 f., 234, 241, 242, 243, 248, 253, 259, 261, 262, 263, 286, 291, 314, 322 f., 324, 325 f., 348, 351 f., 373, 387, 388, 391 f., 393, 395 f., 405, 411, 412, 429, 430, 433, 436, 466 f., 472 f., 479 f., 492 f., 494 f., 495 f., 521 f., 528 f., 549, 553, 555, 566 f., 578, 579 f., 580 f., 584 f., 595 f., 598 f., 604, 606 f., 608 f.; **Vol. 3, Part 2**, 1, 4, 20 f., 43, 54, 55, 69, 83, 85, 87 f., 100, 101, 123, 150, 153 f., 178, 179, 188, 192, 193, 196, 202, 207, 212, 219, 225, 228, 229, 234, 283, 243, 254, 261, 267, 277, 284 f., 299, 308, 319, 323, 332 f., 335, 337, 338, 342, 343, 345 f., 350, 356, 413, 445, 456, 462, 468, 483, 496, 509, 511, 528, 533, 550, 551, 555 f., 601; **Vol. 4, Part 1**, 4, 9, 26, 46, 47, 58 f., 77, 95, 100, 121, 131, 144, 145, 155, 158, 160, 165, 173, 177, 179, 204, 205, 216, 230, 232, 237, 257, 264, 2772, 273, 275, 278, 280, 287, 295, 309, 317, 322, 367, 380, 382, 383, 396, 422, 423–24, 429, 436, 451, 456, 458, 459, 464, 471, 481, 484, 486, 490, 519, 520, 550, 564, 567, 582, 596, 597, 598, 608, 613, 617, 618, 621; **Vol. 4, Part 2**, 5, 16, 20, 24, 26, 28, 32, 35, 85, 89, 95, 100, 151, 161, 167, 168, 183, 184, 191, 194, 213 f., 221, 224, 232, 235, 239 f., 242, 247, 261, 272 f., 300, 316, 318, 326, 331 f., 340, 353, 368, 369, 377, 378, 380, 391, 392 f.; 394, 397, 401, 415, 421, 445, 447 f., 461, 478, 492 f., 494, 506, 525 f., 568, 572, 593, 600; **Vol. 5, Part 1**, 3, 4, 12, 16, 25, 27, 55, 61, 74, 76, 96, 117, 126, 130, 176, 193, 196–97, 214, 244, 253–54, 256, 270, 271–72, 279, 281, 283, 287 f., 299, 302, 315, 319–20, 321, 330, 331, 332, 335, 343, 355, 371, 372, 377, 382, 400, 404, 406, 422, 425, 428, 461, 469, 483, 485, 493, 494, 520–21, 539, 543, 546, 556 f., 561 f., 562, 575, 609, 616, 623; **Vol. 5, Part 2**, 43, 45, 48, 49, 55, 91–92, 95 f., 106, 116, 136, 137, 142, 144 f., 146, 153, 165, 166 f., 170, 178, 179, 182, 191, 193, 202, 209, 216, 263, 272, 294, 314, 317, 322, 324–25, 330, 332, 336, 359–60, 361, 366, 375, 378, 390, 414–15, 424, 425, 459, 481, 492, 505, 520, 552, 557, 562, 565, 569, 571, 577, 582, 602 f., 613; **Vol. 6, Part 1**, 5, 27, 39, 42, 52, 54, 61, 62, 90, 92, 98, 102, 104, 105 f., 121 f., 130, 134, 141, 145, 146, 151, 162, 164, 190, 194, 207, 218, 227, 239, 268, 272, 277, 300 f., 363, 367, 369, 391–92, 411, 420, 429–30, 441, 474, 477, 483, 509, 519, 520, 534, 536, 537, 538, 551, 554, 557–58, 572, 575–76, 578, 581 f. 585, 587–88, 595–96, 597, 600–601, 602, 603, 604, 605; **Vol. 6, Part 2**, 29, 55, 59, 69, 95, 110, 120, 145, 152, 160, 165, 205, 211, 233, 290, 311, 341, 348, 349, 426, 435, 475, 482, 508, 569, 597, 614; **Vol. 7, Part 1**, 1, 14, 20, 21, 29, 33, 39, 60, 62, 86, 102, 123, 139, 160–61, 170–71, 171, 174, 180, 188, 197, 228, 232, 256, 272, 287, 299, 301, 318–19, 325, 336, 349, 350, 352, 374, 375, 404, 408, 410, 418, 419–20, 426, 431–32, 466, 467, 473, 487, 494, 536–37, 539, 545, 564, 567–68, 579–80, 587, 605, 608–9, 616, 617, 627, 629, 634, 648; **Vol. 7, Part 2**, 21, 36, 41, 44 f., 48 f., 60, 71, 88, 94, 97, 100, 129, 139, 140, 147, 149, 169, 184, 195, 196, 201, 211 f., 219, 221, 243, 288, 296 f., 306 f., 308, 330, 375, 380 f., 386, 408, 415, 416, 424, 446 f., 484 f., 495, 501, 516, 519, 527, 536, 549, 552, 556, 570 f., 581, 594, 604, 621, 623, 645 f.; **Vol. 8, Part 1**, 8, 10 f., 28 f., 39 f., 40 f., 41 f., 43, 44 f., 59 f., 60 f., 74 f., 76 f., 79, 90 f., 92 f., 93 f., 115 f., 116 f., 126, 134 f., 135 f., 146 f., 149, 170, 172 f., 175 f., 185, 188, 200 f., 202 f., 205 f., 216 f., 219 f., 220, 234 f., 241 f., 245 f., 255 f., 260 f., 268 f., 278 f., 294 f., 296 f., 306, 313 f., 326 f., 328 f., 329 f., 340, 341, 350 f., 352 f., 358 f., 379, 380, 390, 392, 397, 402 f., 406, 428, 431 f., 434, 435, 468, 490, 499 f., 504, 513, 514, 516, 520, 521 f., 570, 574, 575, 587, 609, 620, 625, 626, 641; **Vol. 8, Part 2**, 2, 13, 26, 31, 47, 64, 68, 70, 71 f., 79, 80, 84, 89, 97, 132, 150, 163, 172, 175, 179, 181, 188, 194, 215, 219, 223 f., 236, 242, 249, 289, 303, 307, 337, 341, 374, 376, 384, 388, 403, 419 f., 428, 453, 459 463, 467, 498, 505, 514, 521, 528, 548, 578, 592,

598; **Vol. 9, Part 1**, 12, 15, 18, 62, 71, 77, 79 f., 92, 93, 100, 114, 130, 131, 142, 150, 152, 153, 169 f., 170, 174, 179, 184, 216, 223 f., 237, 240, 247, 249, 251, 271, 273, 301, 319, 323, 334, 361, 362, 367 f., 369, 376, 379, 383, 389, 404, 411, 438, 453, 465, 471, 472, 491, 492, 493, 507, 526, 540, 544, 554, 555, 580, 582, 591, 607 f., 613, 627, 631; **Vol. 9, Part 2**, 3, 39, 60, 62, 71, 72, 75, 76, 78, 85, 92, 138 f., 232, 233, 240, 242, 247, 248, 255, 262, 298, 325, 340, 378, 379–80, 385, 402, 423, 433 f., 441, 459, 471, 483, 484, 509, 524, 529, 588, 593, 594, 602, 604, 607, 608, 615–16, 621–22, 636, 642; **Vol. 10, Part 1**, 6, 8, 53, 67, 69, 72, 83, 86, 87, 95, 100, 103, 111, 129, 147, 150, 159, 365, 375 f., 401 f., 430 f., 456 f., 457 f., 459 f., 469 f., 472 f., 473 f., 495 f., 537 f., 540 f., 552 f., 557, 568 f., 571 f., 579 f., 593 f., 600 f., 611 f., 616 f., 635, 651 f.; **Vol. 10, Part 2**, 39, 51, 67, 136, 201, 209, 228, 243, 247, 334, 381, 395, 424, 475, 486, 501, 555, 560, 562, 633; Texas Rangers, **Vol. 4, Part 1**, 393; transportation of troops, **Vol. 7, Part 2**, 268; **Vol. 9, Part 2**, 440; troops, first offer of, **Vol. 8, Part 1**, 341 f.

Civil War (U.S.; naval aspects): battles, specific, **Vol. 1, Part 1**, 146; **Vol. 3, Part 1**, 107, 136; **Vol. 4, Part 1**, 574, 595; **Vol. 6, Part 1**, 173; **Vol. 8, Part 1**, 420; **Vol. 8, Part 2**, 244; **Vol. 9, Part 2**, 139, 149; blockades, **Vol. 1, Part 1**, 226; **Vol. 3, Part 1**, 60; **Vol. 5, Part 2**, 550; **Vol. 8, Part 1**, 47 f.; **Vol. 8, Part 2**, 149, 341; **Vol. 9, Part 2**, 139 f.; Confederate navy, **Vol. 2, Part 1**, 258; England, naval activities of, **Vol. 3, Part 1**, 135; gunboats, **Vol. 8, Part 2**, 85; hospital ships, **Vol. 4, Part 1**, 556; ironclad vessels in, **Vol. 3, Part 1**, 211, 295; **Vol. 8, Part 1**, 97; **Vol. 8, Part 2**, 78, 85; legal aspects of blockade, **Vol. 3, Part 1**, 60; Mississippi Fleet, **Vol. 8, Part 2**, 78; "Mosquito Fleet," **Vol. 5, Part 1**, 152; Naval Academy during, **Vol. 8, Part 2**, 72, 74; naval service (Confederate and Union), **Vol. 1, Part 1**, 258, 452, 488, 502, 650 f.; **Vol. 1, Part 2**, 104, 146, 154, 342, 409, 487; **Vol. 2, Part 1**, 543; **Vol. 2, Part 2**, 123, 308 f., 518, 569, 635; **Vol. 3, Part 1**, 29 f., 31, 107, 136, 186 f., 269, 488, 529 f. 584 f., 587 f., 592f., 614 f.; **Vol. 3, Part 2**, 170, 210, 255, 286, 334, 405, 499, 509, 531, 539, 568; **Vol. 4, Part 1**, 232, 265, 366, 437, 594; **Vol. 4, Part 2**, 2, 68, 71, 554; **Vol. 5, Part 1**, 152, 247; **Vol. 5, Part 2**, 14, 50, 221, 323, 593, 615; **Vol. 6, Part 1**, 64, 81, 129, 315, 500, 524, 525, 568, 572, 573 f.; **Vol. 6, Part 2**, 21, 49, 82, 91, 149, 196, 271, 429, 465, 479, 480; **Vol. 7, Part 1**, 97 f., 172, 320, 503, 504; **Vol. 7, Part 2**, 185 f., 220, 314, 444, 470, 531 f., 534, 626; **Vol. 8, Part 1**, 17 f., 67 f., 85 f., 97, 182 f., 214 f., 293 f., 298 f., 314 f., 319 f., 327 f., 339, 420, 495, 522 f., 529, 535, 597, 617 f.; **Vol. 8, Part 2**, 22, 72 f., 74, 78, 85, 114, 116, 196, 244, 322, 325, 426 f., 437 f., 568, 579, 580 f.; **Vol. 9, Part 1**, 139, 148, 156, 178, 320, 553 f., 626; **Vol. 9, Part 2**, 7 f., 42, 139 f., 149, 457, 620 f.; **Vol. 10, Part 1**, 23, 34, 101, 128, 425, 545 f., 568; **Vol. 10, Part 2**, 1, 206, 217, 398, 425, 466, 531, 585; "Porter Mortar Fleet," **Vol. 8, Part 2**, 200; privateering, **Vol. 8, Part 2**, 73; prize cases, **Vol. 3, Part 1**, 186, 592 f.; vessels, listing of, **Vol. 6, Part 1**, 129

Civil War and Reconstruction, The, **Supp. 5**, 557

Civil War period (by state): Alabama, **Vol. 10, Part 2**, 594 f.; Arkansas, **Vol. 5, Part 1**, 60; California, **Vol. 5, Part 2**, 136; **Vol. 6, Part 1**, 13; Connecticut, **Vol. 2, Part 1**, 228; Delaware, **Vol. 2, Part 1**, 345, 478; Georgia, **Vol. 6, Part 1**, 578; Illinois, **Vol. 10, Part 2**, 600; Indiana, **Vol. 5, Part 2**, 601; **Vol. 7, Part 1**, 263; Iowa, **Vol. 10, Part 2**, 395; Kansas, **Vol. 5, Part 2**, 577; **Vol. 7, Part 2**, 579; Kentucky, **Vol. 2, Part 1**, 235; **Vol. 3, Part 1**, 114; **Vol. 4, Part 2**, 243 f., 269; **Vol. 5, Part 1**, 562; **Vol. 6, Part 2**, 200; **Vol. 8, Part 1**, 39 f., 148 f.; **Vol. 8, Part 2**, 53; Louisiana, **Vol. 3, Part 1**, 543 f.; Maryland, **Vol. 2, Part 1**, 528; Massachusetts, **Vol. 1, Part 1**, 280; **Vol. 10, Part 2**, 324; Mississippi, **Vol. 10, Part 2**, 609; Missouri, **Vol. 5, Part 1**, 253; **Vol. 6, Part 1**, 55; New Jersey, **Vol. 2, Part 1**, 577; North Carolina, **Vol. 6, Part 2**, 570; Ohio, **Vol. 2, Part 1**, 95, 521; **Vol. 3, Part 2**, 516; **Vol. 8, Part 1**, 483; **Vol. 10, Part 2**, 505; Rhode Island, **Vol. 8, Part 2**, 38; South Carolina, **Vol. 6, Part 2**, 203; **Vol. 10, Part 2**, 602; Tennessee, **Vol. 4, Part 2**, 311; **Vol. 10, Part 2**, 660; Texas, **Vol. 4, Part 1**, 393; Virginia, **Vol. 10, Part 2**, 424

Civil Works Administration: **Supp. 7**, 787; art proect, **Supp. 3**, 112; development of, **Supp. 4**, 392; founding of, **Supp. 3**, 653

Cladocera, **Supp. 4**, 84

Claflin, Lee, reference to, **Vol. 10, Part 1**, 490 f.

"Claiborne Beds," **Vol. 9, Part 2**, 275

Clair, René, reference to, **Supp. 9**, 479

Clairvoyancy: **Supp. 10**, 672; medical use of, **Vol. 3, Part 1**, 105

Clan-na-Gael, **Vol. 3, Part 1**, 265

Clansman, The, **Supp. 4**, 235, 350

Claremont Graduate School, presidency, **Supp. 10**, 404

Clarendon Dictionary, **Supp. 5**, 711

Clarendon Press, **Supp. 3**, 855

Clark, Alfred, reference to, **Supp. 3**, 392

Clark, Alonzo, reference to, **Vol. 5, Part 1**, 607

Clark, Bobby, reference to, **Supp. 6**, 637

Clark, Champ, references to, **Supp. 3**, 621; **Supp. 5**, 113, 114; **Supp. 9**, 810

Clark, Charles Hopkins, reference to, **Supp. 6**, 232

Clark, D. Worth, references to, **Supp. 6**, 681; **Supp. 8**, 508

Clark, Daniel, reference to, **Vol. 5, Part 2**, 323

Clark, George Rogers, reference to, **Vol. 1, Part 1**, 554; **Vol. 4, Part 1**, 235; **Vol. 4, Part 2**, 354; **Vol. 7, Part 1**, 632; **Vol. 9, Part 2**, 461

Clark, Grenville, reference to, **Supp. 3**, 117

Clark, Harold W., reference to, **Supp. 7**, 631

Clark, John Bates, references to, **Supp. 6**, 271, 458, 459; **Supp. 7**, 124

Clark, Kenneth B., reference to, **Supp. 9**, 251

Clark, Ramsey, reference to, **Supp. 10**, 127

Clark, Tom, references to, **Supp. 6**, 502; **Supp. 8**, 35; **Supp. 9**, 652

Clark, William, reference to, **Vol. 7, Part 1**, 631

Clark, William Bullock, reference to, **Supp. 3**, 62

Clarke, Edward Young, reference to, **Supp. 3**, 709

Clarke, James F., reference to, **Vol. 5, Part 1**, 358

Clarke, John M., reference to, **Supp. 3**, 695

Clarke, Thomas B., reference to, **Vol. 5, Part 1**, 488

Clarke-McNary Act (1924), **Supp. 3**, 7

Clark School for the Deaf, **Vol. 8, Part 2**, 93

Clark University, **Vol. 2, Part 2**, 136; **Vol. 4, Part 2**, 128; child-study program, **Supp. 3**, 119; first American Ph.D. in anthropology, **Supp. 3**, 83; Freud's lectures, **Supp. 3**, 191; geography studies, **Supp. 4**, 32–33; physics studies, **Supp. 3**, 306; presidency, **Supp. 4**, 32–33; psychiatry studies, **Supp. 4**, 571, 572

Classical Conference, **Vol. 5, Part 2**, 314

Classical literature: Great Books courses, **Supp. 5**, 212; **Supp. 8**, 59; in translation, teaching of, **Supp. 8**, 236; translations, **Supp. 8**, 291

Classical music. *See* Music; Opera; for complete list of composers and performers, *see* Occupations Index

Classical Philology, **Vol. 9, Part 1**, 248

Classical studies: **Supp. 7**, 313–14, 388; Loeb Library, **Supp. 1**, 503; teaching of, **Supp. 10**, 333, 334. *See also* Greece, classical studies; Latin literature and language; Roman Empire, classical studies

Clay, Cassius. *See* Ali, Muhammad
Clay, Henry: biography of, **Vol. 8, Part 2**, 470; **Supp. 2**, 495; references to, **Vol. 2, Part 2**, 169 f., 185, 547 f., 624, 629; **Vol. 3, Part 2**, 381; **Vol. 5, Part 1**, 192, 206, 347, 531; **Vol. 5, Part 2**, 325, 348; **Vol. 6, Part 1**, 193, 561; **Vol. 7, Part 1**, 91, 158 f., 521; **Vol. 7, Part 2**, 421; **Vol. 8, Part 1**, 99 f., 636; **Vol. 8, Part 2**, 616; **Vol. 9, Part l**, 328, 342; **Vol. 9, Part 2**, 351, 363, 645 f.; **Vol. 10, Part 1**, 89 f., 585 f.; statue of, **Vol. 4, Part 2**, 358
Clay, Jakob, reference to, **Supp. 7**, 134
Clay, Lucius, reference to, **Supp. 6**, 431
Clay, Virginia, reference to, **Supp. 10**, 842
Clayton, Buck, reference to, **Supp. 6**, 300
Clayton, Henry D., reference to, **Supp. 3**, 729
Clayton, John M., reference to, **Vol. 9, Part 2**, 352 f.
Clayton, Lou, Durante relationship, **Supp. 10**, 195, 196
Clayton, William L., reference to, **Supp. 7**, 36
Clayton Antitrust Act (1914), **Supp. 2**, 213; **Supp. 5**, 27; **Supp. 6**, 591
Clayton-Bulwer Treaty, **Vol. 1, Part 2**, 328; **Vol. 2, Part 1**, 211, 564; **Vol. 2, Part 2**, 186; **Vol. 3, Part 1**, 39; **Vol. 7, Part 2**, 578; **Vol. 9, Part 2**, 353
Clearing, the, founding of, **Supp. 5**, 370
Clemens, Samuel L. *See* Twain, Mark
Clement, Frank Goad, reference to, **Supp. 9**, 258
Clement, Martin W., references to, **Supp. 10**, 771, 772
Clemente, Roberto, references to, **Supp. 10**, 574, 575
Clements Library of American History, **Supp. 5**, 9–10
Clemson, Thomas Green, reference to, **Vol. 9, Part 2**, 547
Clemson College, **Vol. 2, Part 2**, 201; **Vol. 9, Part 2**, 548
Cleopatra, **Supp. 8**, 678; **Supp. 9**, 734; **Supp. 10**, 865
"Cleopatra's Needle" (N.Y.), **Vol. 3, Part 1**, 377; **Vol. 3, Part 2**, 276; **Vol. 4, Part 1**, 437
Clergue, Francis H., reference to, **Supp. 3**, 534
Clergy. For complete list, *see* Occupations Index
Clermont, **Vol. 4, Part 1**, 71; **Vol. 8, Part 2**, 106
"C" Letters, **Vol. 9, Part 2**, 604
Cleveland, Frank E., reference to, **Supp. 3**, 196
Cleveland, Grover: biography of, **Supp. 6**, 410; references to, **Vol. 2, Part 1**, 199, 495; **Vol. 5, Part 1**, 28, 85; **Vol. 6, Part 2**, 249; **Vol. 7, Part 1**, 176; **Vol. 7, Part 2**, 32 f.; **Vol. 8, Part 2**, 450, 520; **Vol. 9, Part 1**, 281, 598, 629; **Vol. 9, Part 2**, 548; **Supp. 1**, 459; **Supp. 5**, 518; election, news reports of, **Vol. 6, Part 1**, 283; Hawaii, opposition to annexation of, **Vol. 3, Part 1**, 358 f.; monetary adviser to, **Vol. 9, Part 2**, 129; nomination of, **Vol. 3, Part 1**, 388
Cleveland, Ohio: financial history, **Vol. 6, Part 2**, 397; founding of, **Vol. 5, Part 2**, 296; history and growth, **Vol. 2, Part 1**, 557; industrial history, **Vol. 5, Part 2**, 297; **Vol. 6, Part 2**, 398; medical college, **Vol. 5, Part 2**, 438; municipal facilities improvements, **Supp. 2**, 17; municipal government, **Supp. 7**, 95; Museum of Natural History, **Vol. 5, Part 2**, 439; orphanage, **Vol. 7, Part 2**, 407; philanthropy, **Vol. 2, Part 1**, 558; politics, **Supp. 3**, 167–68; public service, **Vol. 5, Part 1**, 137; **Vol. 5, Part 2**, 123 f.; **Vol. 7, Part 2**, 325 f.; railroads, financing of, by city, **Vol. 3, Part 1**, 262; Roman Catholic diocese, **Supp. 3**, 694–95
Cleveland Blues (baseball), **Supp. 6**, 356
Cleveland Browns (football), **Supp. 10**, 727
Cleveland Citizen, **Supp. 3**, 347
Cleveland Clinic Foundation, founding of, **Supp. 4**, 508
Cleveland Heights, Ohio, **Supp. 3**, 126
Cleveland Indians (baseball), **Supp. 6**, 589; **Supp. 10**, 202
Cleveland Institute of Music, **Supp. 6**, 62
Cleveland Municipal Association, **Supp. 3**, 292
Cleveland Museum of Art, founding of, **Supp. 1**, 695
Cleveland Naps (baseball), **Supp. 6**, 356–57
Cleveland Orchestra, **Supp. 6**, 550; **Supp. 8**, 642
Cleveland Plain Dealer, **Vol. 5, Part 1**, 137
Cleveland Rams (football), **Supp. 9**, 645–46; franchise move to Los Angeles, **Supp. 9**, 646
Cliburn, Van, reference to, **Supp. 7**, 512
Cliff-dwelling materials, collecting of, **Vol. 8, Part 1**, 252 f.
Clifford, Clark, references to, **Supp. 5**, 515; **Supp. 10**, 227, 372
Clifton Springs Sanitarium, **Vol. 7, Part 1**, 324
Climatology: **Vol. 1, Part 2**, 379; **Vol. 2, Part 2**, 27, 267; **Vol. 3, Part 1**, 394, 427, 507 f.; **Vol. 3, Part 2**, 160, 185, 338; **Vol. 4, Part 2**, 64, 301, 477; **Vol. 6, Part 1**, 287, 367, 452; **Vol. 7, Part 2**, 454; **Vol. 8, Part 1**, 441 f., 573; **Vol. 8, Part 2**, 184; **Vol. 10, Part 1**, 594 f.; hurricanes, study of, **Vol. 8, Part 1**, 441 f.; professorship, first in U.S., **Vol. 10, Part 1**, 436; rainmaking, experiments in, **Vol. 8, Part 1**, 112 f.; Weather Bureau, U.S., establishment of, **Vol. 3, Part 1**, 149; wind measurement, **Vol. 5, Part 1**, 252; **Vol. 7, Part 1**, 526; writings on, **Vol. 2, Part 1**, 367; **Vol. 10, Part 1**, 436. *See also* Meteorology; Weather
Clinton, DeWitt: references to, **Vol. 5, Part 1**, 356; **Vol. 9, Part 1**, 444; writings on, **Supp. 2**, 399
Clinton, George, references to, **Vol. 7, Part 1**, 210, 364; **Vol. 9, Part 1**, 320
Clinton, Henry, reference to, **Vol. 7, Part 1**, 106
Clinton, Mass., development of, **Vol. 1, Part 2**, 255
Clinton, N. Y., **Vol. 3, Part 1**, 563
Clipper ships. *See* Ships, clipper
Clocks and watches: astronomic, **Vol. 3, Part 2**, 489; "grandfather," **Vol. 9, Part 2**, 394; manufacture of, **Vol. 1, Part 2**, 407; **Vol. 2, Part 1**, 144, 442; **Vol. 3, Part 2**, 166, 489; **Vol. 4, Part 1**, 272; **Vol. 4, Part 2**, 275; **Vol. 5, Part 2**, 58; **Vol. 8, Part l**, 101 f., 631; **Vol. 9, Part 2**, 380 f., 445; **Vol. 10, Part 2**, 240; synchronous electrical clock, **Vol. 9, Part 2**, 394; **Supp. 6**, 668–69; writings on, **Vol. 5, Part 2**, 58
Cloete, Stuart, reference to, **Supp. 6**, 251
Cloisters (New York City): landscape architecture for, **Supp. 6**, 486; medieval art collection, **Supp. 6**, 549; opening of, **Supp. 4**, 902; planning and building of, **Supp. 2**, 22; **Supp. 8**, 545
Clorindy: The Origin of the Cakewalk (musical), **Supp. 3**, 834
"Closed shop," 1810, **Vol. 8, Part 2**, 321
Clothing manufacture: **Vol. 6, Part 1**, 513; **Vol. 7, Part 1**, 384 f.; **Vol. 7, Part 2**, 45; **Vol. 9, Part 1**, 208; gloves, **Supp. 3**, 463–44; health and sanitation, **Supp. 3**, 609–10; high fashion ready-to-wear, **Supp. 10**, 699–700; innovations, **Supp. 9**, 465; sport shoes, **Supp. 8**, 28; strike (1910), **Supp. 3**, 96; Triangle Shirtwaist fire, **Supp. 5**, 718; unionization, **Supp. 1**, 403; **Supp. 4**, 69, 375–76; **Supp. 5**, 95; **Supp. 7**, 801; **Supp. 10**, 643, 644, 696–97; women's apparel, **Supp. 9**, 587. *See also* Fashion
Cloud seeding, **Supp. 6**, 364, 365
Clover Leaf Newspapers, **Supp. 4**, 132
Clowes, George Henry Alexander, reference to, **Supp. 10**, 458
Clowns, circus: **Vol. 3, Part 2**, 522; **Vol. 8, Part 1**, 536 f.; **Supp. 6**, 8, 112; **Supp. 10**, 406, 407; paintings of, **Supp. 4**, 463–64
Club Durant, opening of, **Supp. 10**, 195
Clubs, group process concept, **Supp. 7**, 151
Cluett, Peabody and Co., **Supp. 5**, 428; **Supp. 8**, 97
Clurman, Harold, reference to, **Supp. 5**, 10
Clutch, automotive, **Supp. 6**, 67
CMA. *See* Country Music Association

Coal: anthracite, use of, **Vol. 7, Part 1**, 23; by-products, **Supp. 5**, 556; classification of, **Supp. 1**, 703; coke, use of, **Vol. 4, Part 1**, 29 f.; **Vol. 9, Part 1**, 124 f.; **Vol. 10, Part 1**, 400 f.; gas, first use of, for illumination, **Vol. 6, Part 2**, 520; mapping of, **Supp. 2**, 90; stove, invention of, **Vol. 2, Part 2**, 110
Coal Conservation Act, unconstitutionality of, **Supp. 5**, 573
Coal industry: **Vol, 8, Part 1**, 170; **Vol. 10, Part 1**, 465 f.; conveyors in, **Vol. 2, Part 1**, 103; distribution, **Vol. 7, Part 2**, 20; economic studies of, **Supp. 10**, 471; Ludlow massacre, **Supp. 2**, 124; mine ownership, **Supp. 2**, 38; mining, **Vol. 1, Part 2**, 338; **Vol. 2, Part 1**, 160; **Vol. 2, Part 2**, 108, 110; **Vol. 3, Part 1**, 179, 306; **Vol. 3, Part 2**, 47, 84, 459; **Vol. 4, Part 1**, 9, 136, 418; **Vol. 4, Part 2**, 226; **Vol. 5, Part 1**, 238, 383; **Vol. 6, Part 1**, 79, 189; **Vol. 7, Part 2**, 305, 330; **Vol. 8, Part 1**, 170; **Vol. 8, Part 2**, 48, 189, 504; **Vol. 9, Part 1**, 124 f., 273; mining machinery, manufacture of, **Vol. 5, Part 2**, 36; mining safety, **Supp. 4**, 690; mining technology, **Supp. 5**, 556; strikes, **Vol. 1, Part 1**, 260; surveys, **Vol. 6, Part 1**, 189; **Vol. 9, Part 2**, 341; unionization, **Supp. 5**, 282–83; **Supp. 7**, 81–82; **Supp. 8**, 374–77; **Supp. 10**, 681
Coast and Geodetic Survey, United States: **Vol. 1. Part 1**, 1, 119, 169, 461 f.; **Vol. 1, Part 2**, 342; **Vol. 3, Part 2**, 64; **Vol. 4, Part 1**, 481; **Vol. 4, Part 2**, 385, 452; **Vol. 5, Part 1**, 23, 303; **Vol. 5, Part 2**, 167, 256; **Vol. 6, Part 1**, 272, 553; **Vol. 6, Part 2**, 531; **Vol. 7, Part 1**, 47, 640; **Vol. 7, Part 2**, 395, 399 f.; **Vol. 8, Part 1**, 617; **Vol. 8, Part 2**, 400, 459; **Vol. 9, Part 1**, 156; **Vol. 9, Part 2**, 656; nonmagnetic observatories, **Supp. 6**, 205
Coast defenses, **Vol. 1, Part 2**, 223; **Vol. 2, Part 2**, 222; **Vol. 3, Part 1**, 210; **Vol. 3, Part 2**, 159; **Vol. 6, Part 2**, 169; **Vol. 7, Part 2**, 169, 619; **Vol. 9, Part 2**, 608
Coast Guard, United States: **Vol. 6, Part 1**, 545; arctic oceanographic studies, **Supp. 7**, 698–99; establishment of, **Vol. 5, Part 2**, 379; **Supp. 2**, 123; **Supp. 4**, 854; *Tars and Spars* revue, **Supp. 8**, 145–46
Cobb, Ty, references to, **Supp. 3**, 438; **Supp. 5**, 291–92; **Supp. 6**, 356–57, 589; **Supp. 7**, 139; **Supp. 8**, 106; **Supp. 10**, 859
Cobbett, William, references to, **Vol. 1, Part 2**, 559; **Vol. 7, Part 1**, 614
Cobbling, **Vol. 9, Part 1**, 88
Coca-Cola, manufacture of, **Vol. 2, Part 1**, 471
Coca-Cola Export Co., management, **Supp. 10**, 234
Cocaine: **Vol. 4, Part 2**, 165; **Vol. 5, Part 1**, 625; abuse of, **Supp. 9**, 564; as anesthetic, **Supp. 3**, 430–31
Cochran, Welker, reference to, **Supp. 6**, 304
Cochran, William F., reference to, **Supp. 3**, 734
"Cockrell's Brigade," **Vol. 2, Part 2**, 257
Cockcroft, John D., reference to, **Supp. 8**, 199
Cockran, Bourke, reference to, **Supp. 3**, 532
Cocktail Party, The, **Supp. 7**, 222
Cocoa, manufacture of, **Vol. 7, Part 2**, 582
Cocoanuts, The, **Supp. 7**, 515
Codes and ciphers. *See* Cryptology
Cody, "Buffalo Bill": origin of nickname, **Vol. 5, Part 2**, 238; references to, **Vol. 2, Part 2**, 260 f., 522 f.; **Vol. 5, Part 1**, 480, 483; **Vol. 5, Part 2**, 238; **Vol. 7, Part 1**, 603 f.; **Supp. 3**, 460
Coe, George, reference to, **Supp. 4**, 766
Coe College (Iowa), **Vol. 6, Part 1**, 613; **Vol. 6, Part 2**, 295
Coeducation. *See* Education
Coffin, Charles, reference to, **Supp. 3**, 527
Coffin, Howard E., reference to, **Supp. 2**, 102
"Coggins, Birdie Lee" (fictional character), **Supp. 10**, 662
Coghill, Chester, reference to, **Supp. 9**, 53
Cognitive psychology. *See* Learning, theory
Cohan, George M., references to, **Supp. 3**, 333; **Supp. 5**, 524
Cohen, Benjmain V., reference to, **Supp. 7**, 263
Cohen, Felix S., reference to, **Supp. 8**, 99
Cohen, Wilbur J., reference to, **Supp. 9**, 29
Cohen v. *California,* **Supp. 9**, 365
Cohens v. *Virginia,* **Vol. 7, Part 1**, 638 f.
Cohn, Edwin J., references to, **Supp. 3**, 350; **Supp. 4**, 581
Cohn, Roy: McCarthy hearings, **Supp. 6**, 405, 680; references to, **Supp. 10**, 719, 720
Coils, electric, **Vol. 4, Part 2**, 551
Coinage: **Vol. 3, Part 1**, 533 f.; **Vol. 6, Part 1**, 273; **Vol. 8, Part 1**, 49 f.; **Vol. 9, Part 2**, 94; buffalo nickel design, **Supp. 5**, 231; changes in, **Vol. 8, Part 2**, 301; collecting of coins, **Vol. 1, Part 2**, 173; collections of Greek and Roman, **Supp. 3**, 551; designs on early, **Vol. 6, Part 1**, 381; free, **Vol. 1, Part 2**, 355; free silver, **Supp. 2**, 289; **Supp. 5**, 381; gold, first, **Vol. 3, Part l**, 254; Liberty head dime, **Supp. 5**, 659; Liberty quarter design, **Supp. 4**, 534; pine tree shilling, **Vol. 6, Part 1**, 363; writings on, **Supp. 3**, 551, 564
"Coin's Financial School," **Vol. 7, Part 1**, 533
Coit, Margaret L., reference to, **Supp. 7**, 37
Coke, Sir Edward, biography of, **Supp. 9**, 113
Coke, use of, **Vol. 4, Part 1**, 29 f.; **Vol. 9, Part 1**, 124 f.; **Vol. 10, Part 1**, 400 f.
Coker College, **Vol. 3, Part 1**, 281
Cokesbury College, **Vol. 3, Part 1**, 293
Colbert, Claudette, reference to, **Supp. 6**, 225
Colby College, **Vol. 2, Part 2**, 15, 285; **Vol. 6, Part 2**, 558; **Vol. 8, Part 2**, 32, 114; **Vol. 9, Part 1**, 221
Cold Harbor, Va., attack at, **Vol. 1, Part 1**, 273; **Vol. 4, Part 1**, 496 f.; **Vol. 6, Part 1**, 127; **Vol. 6, Part 2**, 349
Cold storage, **Vol. 8, Part 1**, 145 f.
Cold Spring Harbor (Long Island, N. Y.), **Supp. 3**, 215–16; **Supp. 3**, 445–46, 477–78
Cold war: Berlin airlift, **Supp. 10**, 128; China policy, **Supp. 6**, 231; containment policy, **Supp. 4**, 306; Cuban missile crisis, **Supp. 9**, 106–7, 449–50, 799; Eisenhower administration policies, **Supp. 8**, 157–60; hard-line policy, **Supp. 6**, 178–79; journalism, **Supp. 10**, 231–32; McCarthyism, *see* Loyalty issues; nuclear policies, **Supp. 7**, 565; **Supp. 8**, 230–31; Powers, F. G., capture, **Supp. 10**, 646–47; propaganda, **Supp. 7**, 438; **Supp. 8**, 6–7; term coined, **Supp. 6**, 617; Truman administration policies, **Supp. 6**, 374, 431–32; **Supp. 9**, 7–9, 152; Truman-Wallace split over, **Supp. 7**, 762–63; U.S. intelligence activities, **Supp. 8**, 147; U.S. policies, opposition to, **Supp. 4**, 147; **Supp. 5**, 675, 677; U.S.-Soviet confrontations, **Supp. 7**, 423–44, 426; **Supp. 10**, 128. *See also* Korean War; Loyalty issues; Soviet Union
Colds, cause studies, **Supp. 7**, 194
Cole, Frank N., references to, **Vol. 10, Part 1**, 655 f. **Supp. 5**, 491
Cole, Rufus, reference to, **Supp. 6**, 546
Cole, Thomas, reference to, **Vol. 2, Part 2**, 101
Coleman, A. P., reference to, **Supp. 6**, 143
Coleman, Charles Caryl, reference to, **Supp. 3**, 573
Coleman, George W., reference to, **Supp. 5**, 515
Coleman, John, reference to, **Supp. 9**, 213
Coleman, William, reference to, **Vol. 10, Part 1**, 642 f.
Coleoptera, collection of, **Vol. 4, Part 1**, 54; **Vol. 5, Part 1**, 329; **Vol. 8, Part 2**, 481
Coleridge, Samuel Taylor, scholarship on, **Supp. 3**, 475
Colette, reference to, **Supp. 9**, 60
Colfax, Schuyler, reference to, **Vol. 9, Part 2**, 334

Colgate University, **Vol. 2, Part 2**, 299; **Vol. 6, Part 2**, 559; **Vol. 8, Part 1**, 412
Coll, Vincent ("Mad Dog"), reference to, **Supp. 7**, 5
Collages, **Supp. 4**, 774
Collars, detachable, **Vol. 2, Part 1**, 112
Collections: Acadians, material on, **Vol. 5, Part 2**, 370; American antiques, **Supp. 3**, 567; **Supp. 6**, 562; American Indian artifacts, **Supp. 6**, 289–90; Americana, **Vol. 3, Part 2**, 514; **Vol. 6, Part 1**, 157; **Supp. 1**, 139, 154, 180; archaeological specimens, **Vol. 2, Part 2**, 168; architectural writings, **Supp. 4**, 116; armor, **Vol. 8, Part 1**, 606; art, **Vol. 1, Part 1**, 232; **Vol. 1, Part 2**, 170; **Vol. 3, Part 2**, 84, 354; **Vol. 4, Part 1**, 14, 143; **Vol. 4, Part 2**, 53, 55; **Vol. 5, Part 1**, 618 f.; **Vol. 5, Part 2**, 106 f., 142 f., 411; **Vol. 6, Part 1**, 210 f., 233; **Vol. 8, Part 1**, 157 f.; **Vol. 10, Part 1**, 399 f.; **Supp. 1**, 337; **Supp. 3**, 24; **Supp. 4**, 174–75, 696–97; **Supp. 5**, 39, 401; **Supp. 7**, 161–62, 466; **Supp. 8**, 367–68; art, American, **Supp. 4**, 290; art, Byzantine, **Supp. 5**, 700; **Supp. 7**, 60; art, French, **Supp. 5**, 150–51; art, Indian and Islamic, **Supp. 4**, 177; art, modern, **Supp. 4**, 351–52, 768, 771; **Supp. 5**, 20, 184–85, 427; **Supp. 7**, 294; art, portrait paintings, **Supp. 1**, 178; as a hobby, discussion of, **Vol. 2, Part 1**, 318; autographs, **Vol. 3, Part 2**, 147; **Vol. 5, Part 1**, 445; **Vol. 5, Part 2**, 156; **Vol. 9, Part 1**, 476; **Vol. 9, Part 2**, 432; ballads, **Vol. 9, Part 1**, 245 f.; Bermudiana, **Supp. 2**, 111; Bibles, **Vol. 6, Part 1**, 172, 305; **Vol. 8, Part 1**, 298; birds, **Vol. 1, Part 1**, 513; **Vol. 3, Part 2**, 91; **Vol. 4, Part 2**, 564; **Vol. 4, Part 1**, 385; black folk songs, **Supp. 4**, 476–77, 502; black literature, **Supp. 1**, 717; **Supp. 9**, 109–10, 750; books, **Vol. 1, Part 2**, 173; **Vol. 2, Part 1**, 137; **Vol. 3, Part 2**, 158, 363, 407, 419; **Vol. 4, Part 1**, 561; **Vol. 4, Part 2**, 305; **Vol. 5, Part 1**, 445; **Vol. 5, Part 2**, 155 f., 174 f.; **Vol. 6, Part 1**, 110, 308; **Vol. 6, Part 2**, 97; **Vol. 8, Part 1**, 232 f.; **Vol. 9, Part 1**, 256; **Vol. 9, Part 2**, 586; **Vol. 10, Part 1**, 443; **Vol. 10, Part 2**, 185; botanical specimens, **Vol. 8, Part 1**, 104 f., 236 f.; botany writings, **Supp. 2**, 390; butterflies, **Vol. 3, Part 2**, 46 f.; **Vol. 3, Part 2**, 525 f.; **Supp. 1**, 414; **Supp. 10**, 580, 582; Catholic publications, **Vol. 3, Part 2**, 396; Chaliapin paintings, **Supp. 10**, 113; chemistry books, **Supp. 1**, 431; children's books, **Vol. 8, Part 1**, 51 f.; children's sayings, **Vol. 8, Part 1**, 183 f.; cliff-dwelling materials, **Vol. 8, Part 1**, 252 f.; coins, **Vol. 1, Part 2**, 173; coins, ancient Greek and Roman, **Supp. 3**, 551; coleoptera, **Vol. 4, Part 1**, 54; **Vol. 5, Part 1**, 329; **Vol. 8, Part 2**, 481; criminology writings, **Supp. 2**, 522–23; economic writings, **Supp. 2**, 607; educational historical writings, **Supp. 2**, 532; Egyptology, **Supp. 4**, 900–901; electricity writings, **Supp. 2**, 38; elements, specimens of, **Supp. 1**, 477; English common law, **Supp. 1**, 154; engravings, **Vol. 9, Part 1**, 538; fishes, **Vol. 9, Part 2**, 94; flints, **Vol. 3, Part 2**, 161; flutes, **Supp. 3**, 524; folk songs, **Supp. 1**, 651; **Supp. 8**, 564; French Revolution, publications on, **Vol. 10, Part 1**, 570 f.; fungi, **Vol. 3, Part 2**, 105; **Vol. 8, Part 1**, 396; **Supp. 3**, 815; furniture, period, **Vol. 6, Part 1**, 210 f.; gall wasp, **Supp. 6**, 342; glass flowers, **Vol. 4, Part 1**, 378; glassware, Stiegel, **Vol. 9, Part 2**, 17; historical source material, **Vol. 10, Part 1**, 566 f.; human crania, **Vol. 8, Part 1**, 152, f.; hymns, **Vol. 4, Part 2**, 387; **Vol. 5, Part 1**, 186; **Vol. 6, Part 1**, 530; illustrated works, **Vol. 5, Part 1**, 445; **Vol. 8, Part 1**, 228 f.; incunabula, **Vol. 4, Part 2**, 415; legal decision, **Vol. 8, Part 1**, 439; Lincolniana, **Supp. 2**, 318; **Supp. 7**, 529, 530; **Supp. 9**, 37; magic, apparatus relating to, **Vol. 5, Part 1**, 249; manuscripts, **Vol. 3, Part 2**, 519; **Supp. 4**, 5, 345; **Supp. 5**, 349–50; maps, **Vol. 6, Part 1**, 471; Marshall's legal writings, **Vol. 3, Part 1**, 311; masks, portrait, **Vol. 5, Part 1**, 445; Masonry, **Vol. 9, Part 2**, 389; mathematical writings, **Supp. 3**, 722; medical journals, **Vol. 8, Part 1**, 269 f.; medicinal plants, **Supp. 2**, 591; medieval armor, **Supp. 2**, 415; meteorites, **Vol. 9, Part 1**, 71, 304; **Vol. 10, Part 1**, 421 f.; minerals, **Vol. 1, Part 1**, 248; **Vol. 1, Part 2**, 173; **Vol. 4, Part 1**, 245; **Vol. 6, Part 1**, 71; **Vol. 8, Part 2**, 90; **Vol. 9, Part 1**, 262; **Vol. 9, Part 2**, 629; modern art, **Supp. 10**, 568; mollusks, **Vol. 6, Part 1**, 71; Morrisiana, **Vol. 7, Part 1**, 213 f., 218 f., 224, f.; movie memorabilia, **Supp. 10**, 101; music, **Supp. 2**, 8; music, black, **Vol. 2, Part 1**, 288; **Vol. 5, Part 2**, 505; music, Indian, **Vol. 2, Part 1**, 288, 342; musical instruments, **Vol. 9, Part 1**, 563; natural science, in field of, **Vol. 6, Part 1**, 71; newspapers and pamphlets, Revolutionary period, **Vol. 3, Part 1**, 553 f.; **Vol. 3, Part 2**, 519; orchids, **Supp. 4**, 16–17; paintings, **Vol. 3, Part 2**, 158, 407, 535, 437; **Vol. 8, Part 1**, 493; periodicals, early, **Vol. 6, Part 1**, 110; petrographic, **Supp. 4**, 194; pharmacological writings, **Supp. 2**, 390; phonograph records, **Vol. 7, Part 1**, 136 f.; photograph, **Supp. 10**, 306; plants, **Vol. 8, Part 2**, 484; poetry, American, **Vol. 4, Part 1**, 561; **Vol. 4, Part 2**, 305; porcelain, **Vol. 3, Part 2**, 435; **Vol. 6, Part 1**, 210; **Vol. 8, Part 1**, 228 f.; postcards, **Supp. 2**, 112; pottery, **Vol. 3, Part 2**, 161, 435; **Vol. 6, Part 1**, 210; prints, **Vol. 3, Part 2**, 147, 519; **Vol. 9, Part 1**, 256; Quakeriana, **Supp. 1**, 463; rare books, **Supp. 4**, 5; **Supp. 5**, 586–87; **Supp. 7**, 2–3, 295, 387, 547; **Supp. 10**, 702–3; rare books on ophthalmology, **Supp. 3**, 836; relics, **Vol. 6, Part 1**, 502; Russian Imperial art, **Supp. 9**, 615; scientific materials, **Vol. 10, Part 1**, 421 f.; sermons, **Vol. 1, Part 1**, 501; Shakespeariana, **Vol. 3, Part 2**, 487; **Vol. 9, Part 1**, 372; **Vol. 9, Part 2**, 432; shells, **Vol. 3, Part 2**, 269; **Vol. 6, Part 1**, 71; **Vol. 8, Part 1**, 192, 394 f.; **Vol. 9, Part 2**, 94; silver, old, **Vol. 6, Part 1**, 210; songs, **Vol. 5, Part 2**, 101; synagogic music, **Vol. 5, Part 2**, 251; **Vol. 6, Part 1**, 210; theatrical, **Supp. 9**, 376; tracts, historical, **Vol. 3, Part 2**, 512; transportation, early models, **Vol 10, Part 1**,539; tree specimens, **Supp. 3**, 621; Washingtonia, **Vol. 8, Part 1**, 51 f.; wild animals, **Supp. 4**, 120; Wisconsin, historical material concerning, **Vol. 3, Part 1**, 551 f.; women writers' works, **Supp. 6**, 576; woodcuts, **Vol. 8, Part 1**, 228 f.; zoological specimens, **Vol. 6, Part 1**, 190; **Supp. 3**, 667–69. *See also* Archives; Art; Libraries and library work; Museums; *specific museums*
College: administration, **Vol. 3, Part 2**, 71, 300, 317, 386, 496, 540; **Vol. 4, Part 2**, 96, 288 f., 376, 384 f., 406 f., 409, 453; **Vol. 5, Part 1**, 153; **Vol. 6, Part 1**, 106, 278, 280, 290, 303, 328; **Vol. 8, Part 2**, 17, 32, 43, 97, 346; **Vol. 9, Part 2**, 392, 479; admission, **Vol. 3, Part 2**, 74; **Vol. 10, Part 1**, 537; architecture, **Vol. 9, Part 1**, 335; black graduate, first, **Vol. 8, Part 2**, 253; coeducational, first woman to head in U.S., **Supp. 9**, 299; fraternity, first national, **Vol. 8, Part 2**, 176; municipal, first in U.S., **Vol. 7, Part 2**, 617. *See also* Universities and colleges
College Association of Pennsylvania, **Vol. 7, Part 2**, 455
College Entrance Examination Board, founding of, **Supp. 4**, 134
College Equal Suffrage League, founding of, **Supp. 5**, 532
College of Agriculture and Mechanics (Ohio), **Vol. 7, Part 2**, 62 f.
College of California, **Vol. 3, Part 1**, 540 f.
College of Charleston, **Vol. 6, Part 2**, 602; **Vol. 9, Part 1**, 336
College of Medicine of Maryland, **Vol. 3, Part 1**, 91
College of Music, Cincinnati (Ohio), **Vol. 7, Part 1**, 494; **Vol. 9, Part 1**, 483

College of New Jersey. *See* Princeton University
College of New Rochelle (N.Y.), architecture of, **Supp. 6**, 272
College of Pharmacy of the City of New York, **Vol. 6, Part 1**, 49
College of Philadelphia, **Vol. 5, Part 1**, 220; **Vol. 5, Part 2**, 4; **Vol. 9, Part 1**, 354 f.
College of Physicians (Philadelphia), **Vol. 2, Part 2**, 96; **Vol. 8, Part 1**, 443
College of Physicians and Surgeons (New York City), **Vol. 3, Part 2**, 581; **Vol. 7, Part 2**, 242; **Vol. 8, Part 1**, 121; **Vol. 8, Part 2**, 127; **Vol. 9, Part 1**, 606
College of St. Francis Xavier, **Vol. 5, Part 2**, 616
College of St. James, **Vol. 5, Part 2**, 354
College of the City of New York: **Vol. 1, Part 2**, 177; **Vol. 6, Part 2**, 589; **Vol. 8, Part 1**, 500; **Vol. 9, Part 1**, 72; founded with free tuition, **Vol. 4, Part 2**, 324; Museum of, **Vol. 5, Part 2**, 142; Negro history chair, **Supp. 9**, 898; philosophy and psychology studies, **Supp. 8**, 488; philosophy studies, **Supp. 4**, 168; psychology studies, **Supp. 10**, 570; presidency, **Supp. 2**, 185
College of the Fathers of the Precious Blood, **Vol. 8, Part 1**, 266 f.
College of the Pacific (Stockton, Calif.), football team, **Supp. 7**, 713
College of William and Mary: **Vol. 2, Part 1**, 440; **Vol. 3, Part 1**, 266; **Vol. 8, Part 1**, 371 f.; **Vol. 9, Part 2**, 34; founding of, **Vol. 1, Part 2**, 335; **Vol. 7, Part 1**, 500; presidency, **Vol. 1, Part 2**, 335; **Vol. 3, Part 2**, 228 f.; **Vol. 5, Part 1**, 235; **Vol. 5, Part 2**, 75; **Vol. 9, Part 1**, 297; **Supp. 1**, 164; **Supp. 3**, 115–16; reorganization after Revolutionary War, **Vol. 6, Part 2**, 183; restoration of, **Supp. 1**, 164; Thomas Jefferson and, **Vol. 5, Part 2**, 32
College Settlements Association, founding of, **Supp. 5**, 616
Colleges and universities. *See* Universities and colleges; *specific institutions*
Collegiate Institute (New York City), **Vol. 3, Part 1**, 268
Collentine, Thomas, reference to, **Supp. 10**, 384
Collier, John, references to, **Supp. 4**, 238; **Supp. 5**, 342; **Supp. 7**, 122, 393, 486
Collier, Robert J., reference to, **Supp. 5**, 666–67
Collier's, **Supp. 7**, 643; cartoons, **Supp. 3**, 300–301; cover art, **Supp. 5**, 428
Collier's Weekly, **Vol. 2, Part 2**, 305; **Supp. 3**, 96; **Supp. 5**, 666–67
Colliery Engineer, founding of, **Supp. 2**, 200
Collins, Eddie, references to, **Supp. 8**, 713; **Supp. 10**, 859
Collins, Frank S., reference to, **Supp. 3**, 703
Collins, Joseph, reference to, **Supp. 4**, 249
Collinson, Peter, celebrated correspondence with, **Vol. 1, Part 2**, 26
Collodion, making of, **Vol. 3, Part 1**, 329
Colloids, **Supp. 4**, 743–44; **Supp. 5**, 36
Collyer, Robert, **Vol. 6, Part 1**, 573
Colman, Samuel, **Vol. 9, Part 2**, 534
Colombia: cultural exchange, **Supp. 5**, 89; diplomacy with U.S., **Vol. 1, Part 1**, 271; **Vol. 8, Part 2**, 520; **Vol. 9, Part 2**, 570; **Supp. 6**, 556, 557
Colombo, Joseph, reference to, **Supp. 10**, 269
Colonel Carter of Cartersville, **Vol. 9, Part 1**, 266
Colonel Crockett's Exploits and Adventures in Texas, authorship of, **Vol. 9, Part 1**, 334
Colonel Saunders Kentucky Fried Chicken (fast-food franchise), **Supp. 10**, 718
Colonial period: administration, **Vol. 2, Part 2**, 419; **Vol. 3, Part 1**, 316 f.; **Vol. 3, Part 2**, 16, 204, 301, 329 f., 438, 506, 584; **Vol. 4, Part 1**, 119 f., 138; **Vol. 5, Part 1**, 604; **Vol. 5, Part 2**, 111, 116 f.; **Vol. 7, Part 1**, 573; **Vol. 8, Part 1**, 356 f.; **Vol. 8, Part 2**, 549, 611; **Vol. 9, Part 1**, 587, agents, **Supp. 1**, 467–68; architectural preservation and restoration, **Supp. 4**, 24, 115, 696; **Supp. 5**, 388; chronicles, **Vol. 5, Part 2**, 95; church, **Vol. 6, Part 2**, 167; **Vol. 8, Part 2**, 75; **Vol. 10, Part 2**, 237; commerce, **Vol. 4, Part 2**, 379; **Vol. 6, Part 1**, 215; **Vol. 8, Part 2**, 406; **Vol. 10, Part 2**, 30; furniture reproduction, **Supp. 3**, 567; governors, **Supp. 1**, 304, 380; historical bibliographies, **Supp. 1**, 375; historical view of, **Supp. 3**, 15–16; historical writings on, **Supp. 4**, 848; **Supp. 8**, 552; **Supp. 9**, 314–15; **Supp. 10**, 429, 846, 847; Jewish commerce in, **Supp. 1**, 473; land patents, **Vol. 5, Part 1**, 80; lawmaking, **Vol. 4, Part 2**, 549; **Vol. 6, Part 1**, 493; poetry, **Vol. 7, Part 1**, 602 f.; population of, estimate of, **Vol. 3, Part 1**, 277; pre-Revolutionary activities, **Vol. 1, Part 2**, 468; **Vol. 3, Part 1**, 173 f., 299 f.; **Vol. 4, Part 1**, 438; **Vol. 7, Part 1**, 267; press, political importance of, in, **Vol. 3, Part 1**, 212; Puritanism studies, **Supp. 7**, 538; reports on, **Vol. 8, Part 1**, 356 f.; social historical writings on, **Supp. 8**, 692, 693; writings on, **Vol. 8, Part 2**, 126 f; **Vol. 10, Part 1**, 93, 104; **Vol. 10, Part 2**, 476
Colonization (general): American Colonization Society, **Vol. 2, Part 2**, 540; **Vol. 4, Part 2**, 56, 286, 524; **Vol. 5, Part 2**, 98, 204; **Vol. 6, Part 1**, 163; **Vol. 8, Part 2**, 10; **Vol. 9, Part 1**, 288, 330; **Vol. 9, Part 2**, 506, 623; **Vol. 10, Part 1**, 508 f.; blacks, **Vol. 4, Part 2**, 56; **Vol. 5, Part 2**, 12; **Vol. 6, Part 1**, 28; **Vol. 6, Part 2**, 545; **Vol. 7, Part 2**, 487; **Vol. 8, Part 2**, 349; **Vol. 9, Part 2**, 393; French, **Vol. 8, Part 1**, 533 f.; London Co., **Vol. 3, Part 1**, 34; "military adventurers," **Vol. 6, Part 1**, 517; Swiss exiles, **Vol. 4, Part 1**, 468; **Vol. 5, Part 2**, 117, 491; writings on, **Vol. 8, Part 1**, 270 f.
Colonization (by state): Florida, **Vol. 10, Part 1**, 55; Louisiana, **Vol. 5, Part 2**, 453; Maine, **Vol. 10, Part 2**, 397; New Jersey, **Vol. 9, Part 2**, 48; New Mexico, **Vol. 5, Part 2**, 554; New York, **Vol. 3, Part 1**, 265; North Carolina, **Vol. 1, Part 1**, 239; **Vol. 4, Part 1**, 468; **Vol. 10, Part 2**, 110; Pennsylvania, **Vol. 5, Part 2**, 47; **Vol. 10, Part 2**, 32; South Carolina, **Vol. 2, Part 1**, 252; **Vol. 10, Part 2**, 11; Utah, **Vol. 6, Part 1**, 115; **Vol. 9, Part 1**, 386; **Vol. 10, Part 2**, 621; Vermont, **Vol. 7, Part 2**, 148; Virginia, **Vol. 3, Part 1**, 34; **Vol. 4, Part 1**, 190; **Vol. 5, Part 2**, 581; **Vol. 8, Part 2**, 117; **Vol. 10, Part 2**, 9, 80, 110, 388, 574
Colony Club (New York City), **Supp. 4**, 229; founding of, **Supp. 5**, 505; **Supp. 8**, 243
Colophon: A Book Collector's Quarterly, founding of, **Supp. 1**, 288; **Supp. 7**, 3
Color, nomenclature for, established, **Vol. 8, Part 1**, 598; photography, **Vol. 9, Part 2**, 647; reproduction of, **Vol. 8, Part 1**, 287 f.
Colorado: agriculture, **Vol. 3, Part 1**, 606; botany in, **Vol. 7, Part 2**, 262; business, **Vol. 9, Part 1**, 57; cattle ranching, **Supp. 10**, 782; coal strikes, **Vol. 1, Part 1**, 260; **Vol. 5, Part 2**, 196; education, **Vol. 4, Part 1**, 459; **Vol. 10, Part 1**, 619 f.; finance, **Vol. 9, Part 2**, 395; first woman gubernatorial candidate, **Supp. 10**, 681; gold mining, **Vol. 3, Part 1**, 210; **Vol. 4, Part 1**, 316; **Vol. 9, Part 2**, 87; governors of, **Vol. 1, Part 1**, 36 f., 259 f.; **Vol. 4, Part 1**, 488 f.; **Vol. 7, Part 2**, 638 f.; **Vol. 9, Part 1**, 14 f.; **Supp. 8**, 301; **Supp. 10**, 782; health, **Vol. 9, Part 1**, 462; historical writings on, **Supp. 1**, 705; history of, **Vol. 1, Part 1**, 522; **Vol. 1, Part 2**, 207; **Vol. 2, Part 1**, 437, 590; **Vol. 6, Part 2**, 61, 383, 485; **Vol. 7, Part 2**, 638; **Vol. 10, Part 1**, 619 f.; **Vol. 10, Part 2**, 525; Indians, Ute, **Vol. 7, Part 2**, 111, 638; irrigation, **Vol. 3, Part 1**, 605; **Vol. 7, Part 1**, 434; **Vol. 10, Part 1**, 619 f.; judiciary, **Supp. 3**,

462–63; Kansas, separation from, **Vol. 3, Part 1**, 243; law, mining, **Vol. 9, Part 2**, 423; legal service, **Vol. 1, Part 2**, 507; **Vol. 4, Part 2**, 155; **Vol. 7, Part 1**, 626; **Vol. 7, Part 2**, 308; mining, **Vol. 2, Part 1**, 186, 511, 590; **Vol. 3, Part 1**, 210; **Vol. 5, Part 1**, 619 f.; missions, **Vol. 6, Part 2**, 61; **Vol. 8, Part 1**, 349 f.; paleontology, **Vol. 10, Part 2**, 310; political service, **Vol. 1, Part 1**, 259; **Vol. 1, Part 2**, 507; **Vol. 3, Part 1**, 606; **Vol. 3, Part 2**, 205; **Vol. 4, Part 1**, 316, 489; **Vol. 6, Part 1**, 602; **Vol. 7, Part 2**, 309, 638; **Vol. 9, Part 1**, 14; **Vol. 9, Part 2**, 362, 373, 423; **Vol. 10, Part 1**, 619 f.; **Vol. 10, Part 2**, 441; politics, **Supp. 3**, 321; **Supp. 6**, 455, 507; **Supp. 10**, 119, 782; public health committee, **Supp. 5**, 601; railroad promotion, **Vol. 6, Part 1**, 437 f.; **Vol. 10, Part 1**, 619 f.; Republican party, **Vol. 1, Part 1**, 260; **Vol. 10, Part 2**, 441; **Supp. 10**, 782; road building, **Vol. 6, Part 2**, 484; Supreme Court of, **Vol. 4, Part 1**, 339; University of, **Vol. 8, Part 2**, 609
Colorado, **Supp. 9**, 461
Colorado Biological Association, founding of, **Supp. 4**, 167
Colorado Coal and Iron Co., **Vol. 7, Part 2**, 196
Colorado Colleges, **Vol. 7, Part 1**, 434; **Vol. 7, Part 2**, 196; **Vol. 9, Part 2**, 373
Colorado Fuel and Iron Co., **Supp. 6**, 548
Colorado River, **Supp. 6**, 182; **Supp. 7**, 22, 360; conservation of flood waters, **Vol. 9, Part 2**, 147; exploration of, **Vol. 5, Part 1**, 521; **Vol. 7, Part 1**, 445; **Vol. 8, Part 1**, 146 f.; levees, **Vol. 7, Part 1**, 617
Colorado River Aqueduct, **Supp. 3**, 814
Colorado River Land Co., **Supp. 3**, 155
Colorado Springs, Colo., **Vol. 7, Part 2**, 196; development of, **Supp. 2**, 525
Colorado State School of Mines, **Vol. 10, Part 1**, 619 f.
Color blindness, **Supp. 3**, 270
Colored American, second black weekly in U.S., **Vol. 8, Part 1**, 403
Colored Methodist Episcopal Church in America, **Vol. 6, Part 2**, 170; **Vol. 7, Part 2**, 155; founding of, **Vol. 6, Part 2**, 170
Colored Presbyterian Church, **Vol. 8, Part 2**, 332
Colored Woman in a White World, A, **Supp. 5**, 680
Colorimeter, invention of, **Supp. 2**, 36
Color photography, **Supp. 3**, 296
Color television, standards, **Supp. 6**, 32–33
Colosimo, James ("Big Jim"), references to, **Supp. 4**, 140, 142; **Supp. 6**, 263
Colt, Samuel, **Vol. 8, Part 1**, 101 f.
Colton, D. D., **Vol. 5, Part 1**, 410 f.
Colt Patent Fire Arms Co., **Vol. 4, Part 1**, 191; **Vol. 8, Part 2**, 145,
Coltrane, John, reference to, **Supp. 10**, 225
Columbia, and *Shamrock*, **Vol. 1, Part 1**, 641
Columbia, S. C., invasion of, during Civil War, **Vol. 8, Part 1**, 395,
Columbia Athenaeum, **Vol. 5, Part 2**, 518
Columbia Broadcasting System (CBS): education programs, **Supp. 6**, 83; executives, **Supp. 9**, 423; game shows, **Supp. 10**, 790; Lindbergh kidnapping coverage, **Supp. 3**, 142; news and special affairs commentary, **Supp. 6**, 148; **Supp. 7**, 566–67; **Supp. 10**, 349–50; sports broadcasting, **Supp. 7**, 378; symphony orchestra, **Supp. 10**, 421
Columbia Dictionary of Modern European Literature, **Supp. 4**, 744
Columbia Gas and Electric Corporation, founding of, **Supp. 5**, 260
Columbia Historical Society, **Vol. 9, Part 2**, 587
Columbian College. *See* George Washington University
Columbian Star, **Vol. 8, Part 1**, 543
Columbia Pictures, **Supp. 6**, 118–19; productions, **Supp. 10**, 436–37
Columbia-Presbyterian Medical Center (New York City): building architecture, **Supp. 4**, 698; founding of, **Supp. 5**, 325; heart disease reserach, **Supp. 9**, 654; ophthalmology institute, **Supp. 2**, 706
Columbia River: discovery of, **Vol. 4, Part 1**, 522 f.; survey of, **Vol. 9, Part 2**, 260, 455
Columbia Springs plantation, **Vol. 1, Part 2**, 600
Columbia Telescope, nullification paper, **Vol. 6, Part 1**, 604
Columbia Theological Seminary, **Vol. 8, Part 1**, 454
Columbia University: **Vol. 1, Part 1**, 620 f.; **Vol. 2, Part 2**, 408; **Vol. 4, Part 2**, 293; **Vol. 5, Part 2**, 4; **Vol. 6, Part 1**, 492; **Vol. 7, Part 1**, 364; **Vol. 8, Part 2**, 220, 528; academic freedom, **Supp. 4**, 135; administration, **Supp. 1**, 133; **Supp. 2**, 734; **Supp. 6**, 675; **Supp. 9**, 192; anthropology studies, **Supp. 3**, 83–84; **Supp. 4**, 907–8; **Supp. 5**, 435; **Supp. 6**, 393; architecture studies, **Supp. 5**, 133; **Supp. 6**, 272; Barnard College, **Supp. 2**, 532, 488; **Supp. 7**, 288–89; baseball team, **Supp. 3**, 294; biochemistry studies, **Supp. 3**, 693; biophyphysics studies, **Supp. 4**, 367; charter of 1787, **Vol. 8, Part 2**, 127; chemistry studies, **Supp. 5**, 622–23; classical studies, **Supp. 5**, 736; **Supp. 8**, 236; **Supp. 10**, 333, 334; Columbia College administration, **Supp. 3**, 416; contemporary drama courses, **Supp. 4**, 354; dean, first, **Vol. 3, Part 1**, 458 f.; curriculum reform, **Supp. 9**, 192; economic studies, **Supp. 10**, 794, 795; **Supp. 4**, 586–87; **Supp. 6**, 459; **Supp. 7**, 801; embryology studies, **Supp. 3**, 539–40; engineering department, **Vol. 2, Part 2**, 553; English literature and language studies, **Supp. 4**, 634, 847; **Supp. 5**, 211–12; **Supp. 9**, 828; faculty, **Supp. 9**, 427, 428; first black doctorate recipient, **Supp. 6**, 284; first cyclotron, **Supp. 9**, 248; first industrial engineering department, **Supp. 5**, 558; first protozoology course, **Supp. 3**, 126–27; first Zionist society, **Supp. 8**, 549; football abolishment, **Supp. 4**, 135; founding of, **Vol. 5, Part 2**, 118 f.; **Vol. 6, Part 1**, 317, 326; French literature and language studies, **Supp. 4**, 754–55; **Supp. 8**, 475–76; geomorphology studies, **Supp. 3**, 389–90; geophysics program established, **Supp. 9**, 271; gifts to, **Supp. 3**, 32; growth of, **Vol. 1, Part 1**, 620; **Vol. 6, Part 2**, 369; **Vol. 7, Part 2**, 377; **Vol. 8, Part 1**, 506, 634; **Vol. 10, Part 1**, 149; **Vol. 10, Part 2**, 479; history studies, **Supp. 2**, 563, 564; **Supp. 3**, 287; **Supp. 4**, 61–62; **Supp. 6**, 40–41; **Supp. 7**, 329–30, 518, 567–68; **Supp. 8**, 271–73, 580–81; **Supp. 9**, 582; Institute of Arts and Sciences, **Supp. 6**, 160; Institute of Social Research, **Supp. 5**, 514; international law studies, **Supp. 5**, 341; Journalism, School of, **Vol. 8, Part 1**, 260 f.; **Supp. 1**, 391; **Supp. 10**, 35; Law School, **Vol. 3, Part 1**, 571 f.; **Vol. 5, Part 2**, 486; **Supp. 3**, 185–86, 700; **Supp. 4**, 598, 793, 794; **Supp. 7**, 474–75; **Supp. 8**, 139; law school case-study method, **Supp. 3**, 420; library school, **Supp. 1**, 242; **Supp. 4**, 19; **Supp. 10**, 778; Medicine, School of, **Vol. 6, Part 2**, 603; **Supp. 4**, 643; **Supp. 5**, 438, 512; Medicine, School of, Teaching Hospital, **Supp. 2**, 284; medieval studies, **Supp. 7**, 741–42; Mines, School of, **Vol. 2, Part 1**, 612; **Vol. 3, Part 2**, 56; **Vol. 7, Part 1**, 446; music studies, **Vol. 6, Part 2**, 26; **Supp. 5**, 477; nuclear research, **Supp. 5**, 220–21; **Supp. 6**, 501; obstetrics and gynecology, **Supp. 6**, 555; oral history program founded, **Supp. 9**, 582; pathology studies, **Supp. 3**, 483; philosophy studies, **Supp. 2**, 734; **Supp. 5**, 171–72, 198–99, 503; **Supp. 6**, 45; physics studies, **Supp. 6**, 500–501; **Supp. 9**, 248, 249, 541–42; political science studies, **Supp. 1**, 132–33; **Supp. 5**, 107; presidency, **Vol. 1, Part 1**, 620 f.; **Vol. 4, Part 2**, 325 f.; **Vol. 5, Part 2**,

118 f., 133, 382 f.; **Vol. 6, Part 1**, 449 f.; **Vol. 7, Part 1**, 115, 134; **Supp. 4**, 133–37; **Supp. 8**, 156; psychology studies, **Supp. 3**, 149; **Supp. 9**, 567; psychosomatic medicine studies, **Supp. 6**, 180–81; public health school, **Supp. 6**, 193; research institutes, **Supp. 2**, 60; rhetoric department, **Vol. 2, Part 1**, 511; "Riot of 1811," **Vol. 6, Part 2**, 441; Russian studies, **Supp. 9**, 567; social work school, **Supp. 4**, 227; sociology, first professorship, **Supp. 1**, 339–40; sociology studies, **Supp. 6**, 482–83, 726–27, 539; **Supp. 8**, 399, 407; **Supp. 10**, 438–39; student unrest, **Supp. 9**, 192, 808; Teachers College, **Vol. 3, Part 1**, 346 f.; **Supp. 3**, 206, 552, 671, 677, 721–22, 729; **Supp. 4**, 40, 134, 139, 373–74, 832; **Supp. 5**, 171–72, 251; **Supp. 6**, 83, 208, 557; **Supp. 7**, 427, 435; Teachers College nursing education, **Supp. 4**, 632–33

Colum, Mary, reference to, **Supp. 9**, 182

Columbus, Christopher: biography of, **Vol. 5, Part 1**, 509; landing place, location of, claimed, **Vol. 10, Part 1**, 635 f.; references to, **Supp. 8**, 457; **Supp. 10**, 554; tomb, discovery of, **Vol. 7, Part 1**, 156

Columbus, Ga., *Enquirer-Sun*, **Supp. 7**, 324

Columbus, Ky., seizure of, **Vol. 2, Part 1**, 235; **Vol. 4, Part 1**, 493; **Vol. 8, Part 1**, 40

Columbus, Ohio, **Vol. 6, Part 1**, 404

Columbus Circle (New York City), one-way traffic, **Supp. 3**, 254

Columbus College (S. Dak.), **Vol. 7, Part 2**, 3

Columbus Dispatch, **Supp. 6**, 422

Columbus Doors of Capitol, Washington, D. C., **Vol. 8, Part 2**, 107

Columbus Savings and Loan Society, **Supp. 4**, 324–25

Columnist, one of first in U.S., **Vol. 5, Part 1**, 320

Colver Institute, **Vol. 2, Part 2**, 324

Comanche, **Supp. 9**, 728

Comanduras, Peter, reference to, **Supp. 7**, 191

Comden, Betty, reference to, **Supp. 7**, 354

Come Back, Little Sheba, **Supp. 9**, 98, 421

Comedians. For complete list, *see* Occupations Index

Comedy: acting, **Vol. 1, Part 1**, 645; **Vol. 4, Part 2**, 73; **Vol. 5, Part 1**, 143 f., 146; eccentric, **Vol. 3, Part 2**, 393; Irish-American, **Vol. 3, Part 2**, 476 f.; musical, **Vol. 3, Part 2**, 573; **Supp. 9**, 374; **Supp. 10**, 195; of manners, **Vol. 3, Part 1**, 516 f.; slapstick, **Supp. 10**, 115; stand-up, **Supp. 9**, 517–18; **Supp. 10**, 95, 560, 651. *See also* Burlesque; Humor; Motion pictures; Radio; Satire; Television; Theater; Vaudeville

"Come-outism," **Vol. 7, Part 1**, 22

Comer, Braxton Bragg, reference to, **Supp. 3**, 729

Comets: **Vol. 1, Part 1**, 618; **Vol. 5, Part 1**, 329; **Vol. 5, Part 2**, 419; **Vol. 9, Part 2**, 248; **Supp. 5**, 540; discovery of, **Vol. 2, Part 1**, 91; **Vol. 9, Part 2**, 18; writings on, **Vol. 5, Part 2**, 419, 436

Comic opera: acting, **Vol. 8, Part 2**, 246; composition, **Vol. 4, Part 2**, 573; **Vol. 9, Part 1**, 408

Comic strips: **Vol. 3, Part 1**, 378 f.; "Bringing Up Father," **Supp. 5**, 456–57; "Buck Rogers," **Supp. 6**, 165–66; color press, **Supp. 2**, 242; "Doonesbury," **Supp. 10**, 353; "Flash Gordon," **Supp. 6**, 530; "Gumps," **Supp. 1**, 665; "Happy Hooligan," **Supp. 2**, 504; "Joe Palooka," **Supp. 5**, 222; **Supp. 10**, 98; "Jungle Jim," **Supp. 6**, 530, 531; "Krazy Kat," **Supp. 3**, 356–57; "Krazy Kat and Ignatz," **Supp. 3**, 356–57; "Lala Palooza," **Supp. 8**, 218; "Li'l Abner," **Supp. 10**, 98, 99; "Little Orphan Annie," **Supp. 8**, 221–22; "Moon Mullins," **Supp. 6**, 698–99; "Mutt and Jeff," **Supp. 5**, 223–24; "Nize Baby," **Supp. 5**, 262; origin of, **Vol. 7, Part 2**, 112; "Pogo," **Supp. 9**, 452–53; science fiction, **Supp. 6**, 530–31; "Skippy," **Supp. 7**, 153, 154; syndication, **Supp. 3**, 428; **Supp. 10**, 98; tabloids, **Supp. 4**, 646; "Tarzan," **Supp. 4**, 129; "They'll Do It Every Time," **Supp. 7**, 327–28; "Timid Soul," **Supp. 5**, 732; "Toonerville Folks," **Supp. 7**, 257–58; "Uncle Walt," **Supp. 2**, 435

Coming Battle of Germany, The, **Supp. 5**, 761

Coming of Age in Samoa, **Supp. 10**, 521

Coming Victory of Democracy, The, **Supp. 8**, 433

Comique Film Corporation, **Supp. 8**, 314

Comiskey, Charles, references to, **Supp. 6**, 121, 663; **Supp. 8**, 85, 575

Comiskey, J. Louis, reference to, **Supp. 6**, 120–21

Commerce: Charleston, colonial, **Vol. 6, Part 1**, 32; colonial, **Vol. 6, Part 1**, 215; development of, **Vol. 1, Part 1**, 503; **Vol. 1, Part 2**, 182; **Vol. 3, Part 1**, 249 f.; **Vol. 7, Part 1**, 635; **Vol. 8, Part 2**, 268; education in, **Vol. 3, Part 1**, 602; **Vol. 7, Part 2**, 130 f.; **Vol. 9, Part 1**, 404; magazine of early, **Vol. 5, Part 1**, 384; treaty with Holland, **Vol. 6, Part 1**, 113; wartime, **Vol. 3, Part 2**, 314; **Vol. 8, Part 1**, 442 f.; **Vol. 10, Part 1**, 130 f. *See also* Interstate commerce; Tariff; Trade

Commerce, Bureau of Foreign and Domestic, **Vol. 8, Part 1**, 443

Commerce, Department of (U.S.): **Vol. 7, Part 1**, 419, 591; **Vol. 8, Part 1**, 442 f.; administration, **Supp. 2**, 122; **Supp. 3**, 670; **Supp. 4**, 393; **Supp. 5**, 174; **Supp. 7**, 76, 360; **Supp. 8**, 89; **Supp. 9**, 392, 852, 899; air commerce regulations established, **Supp. 9**, 899; loyalty issues, **Supp. 5**, 564

Commerce and Finance, **Supp. 1**, 609

Commerce and Labor, Department of (U.S.), **Vol. 7, Part 1**, 419, 591

Commerce of the Prairies, **Vol. 4, Part 1**, 597 f.

Commercial Cable Co., **Vol. 1, Part 2**, 200

Commercial law. *See* Law, commercial

Commercial Review of the South and Southwest, publication of, **Vol. 3, Part 1**, 181

Commercial Telegraph Co., **Vol. 3, Part 2**, 372

Commercial Wireless and Development Co., **Supp. 7**, 394

Commins, Saxe, reference to, **Supp. 9**, 165

Commission of Fish and Fisheries, **Vol. 1, Part 1**, 514

Commission on Interracial Cooperation, founding of, **Supp. 6**, 11–12

Committee for Economic Development, founding of, **Supp. 9**, 81

Committee for Industrial Organization. *See* Congress of Industrial Organizations

Committee for Nonviolent Action, **Supp. 8**, 458

Committee of Fifty, antitemperance movement, **Supp. 3**, 164

Committee of Five for the Betterment of Radio, **Supp. 10**, 463

Committee of Forty-Eight, founding of, **Supp. 3**, 604

Committee of Historians to Analyze and Appraise Current Conditions and Prospective Developments in Germany. *See under* World War II

Committee of One Hundred (N.Y.), **Vol. 5, Part 2**, 197; **Vol. 7, Part 2**, 631

Committee of Safety (N.Y.), **Vol. 7, Part 2**, 340, 417 f.; **Vol. 8, Part 2**, 341 f.; **Vol. 9, Part 2**, 365

Committee of Seventy, **Vol. 9, Part 2**, 539

Committee of the Pay-Table, **Vol. 3, Part 2**, 112

Committee of Thirteen, **Vol. 2, Part 2**, 400

Committee of Vigilance, 1851, **Vol. 2, Part 2**, 295

Committee on Appropriations, **Vol. 7, Part 2**, 31

Committee on Christian Literature for Women and Children, founding of, **Supp. 4**, 467

Committee on Civil Rights, **Supp. 9**, 334

Committee on Dispensary Development, **Supp. 6**, 81

Committee on Economic Development, administration, **Supp. 10**, 250

Committee on Foreign Affairs, **Vol. 5, Part 1**, 81

Committee on Insular Affairs, **Vol. 7, Part 2**, 31

Committee on Technocracy, founding of, **Supp. 5**, 558–59
Committee on Urban Conditions Among Negroes, **Supp. 6**, 284
Committees of correspondence, **Vol. 6, Part 1**, 119, 330; **Vol. 7, Part 1**, 530; **Vol. 9, Part 2**, 325
Committee to Defend America by Aiding the Allies. *See under* World War II
Committee to Uphold Constitutional Government, founding of, **Supp. 6**, 227
Commodity Credit Corporation, founding of, **Supp. 4**, 50
Common law. *See* Law, common
Common Law, The, **Supp. 1**, 420–21
Common Law Tradition: Deciding Appeals, **Supp. 7**, 475
Commoner, **Supp. 3**, 114
Commons, John R.: economic theories, **Vol. 5, Part 1**, 125; **Vol. 6, Part 1**, 571; **Supp. 3**, 18; **Supp. 6**, 705; influence of, **Supp. 9**, 29, 362; references to, **Supp. 3**, 248; **Supp. 4**, 394, 733; **Supp. 6**, 255, 324, 378, 503, 585–86; **Supp. 9**, 28
Commons (publication). *See* Survey
Common Sense, influence of, **Vol. 1, Part 1**, 74; **Vol. 7, Part 2**, 160 f.; **Supp. 1**, 74; **Supp. 4**, 160 f.
Common Sense in the Household, **Vol. 9, Part 2**, 377
Commonwealth, Fall River boat, **Vol. 9, Part 2**, 344
Commonwealth Edison Co., **Supp. 2**, 333
Commonwealth Fund: Child Health Demonstration Committee, **Supp. 3**, 228, 262; founding of, **Supp. 2**, 283
Communication: deaf, **Supp. 3**, 322; electrical, **Supp. 1**, 613; research, **Supp. 10**, 28; satellite networks, **Supp. 10**, 828; social activity, **Supp. 1**, 548. *See also* Radio; Speech; Telegraphy; Television
Communications Satellite Corporation (COMSAT), **Supp. 10**, 828
Communications Workers of America, founding of, **Supp. 5**, 282
Communism: **Vol. 6, Part 1**, 389; anti-Stalinism, **Supp. 7**, 244–45; **Supp. 8**, 150; **Supp. 10**, 849; congressional opposition to, **Supp. 7**, 74; **Supp. 9**, 69, 468; Dies crusade against, **Supp. 9**, 233–34; journalism, **Supp. 8**, 634–35; organizations opposing, **Supp. 5**, 702; **Supp. 9**, 413; Palmer raids, **Supp. 9**, 404–5; propaganda against, **Supp. 6**, 410; social causes, **Supp. 3**, 237–38; U.S. Socialist opposition to, **Supp. 3**, 298; writings on, **Supp. 2**, 89; **Supp. 5**, 134–36; **Supp. 7**, 268–69; **Supp. 8**, 552; **Supp. 10**, 800, 801, 849, 850. *See also* China; Cold war; Communist party (U.S.); Loyalty issues; Maxism; Soviet Union
Communist Control Act (1954), **Supp. 8**, 457
Communist Front Organizations with Special Reference to the National Citizens Political Action Committee, **Supp. 8**, 426
Communistic experiments, **Vol. 1, Part 2**, 272; **Vol. 4, Part 2**, 323; **Vol. 5, Part 1**, 130; **Vol. 6, Part 1**, 389; **Vol. 6, Part 2**, 586; **Vol. 8, Part 1**, 383; **Vol. 10, Part 2**, 449
Communist Labor party, founding of, **Supp. 7**, 290
Communist party, **Vol. 8, Part 1**, 451; **Vol. 9, Part 1**, 399; **Vol. 9, Part 2**, 69
Communist party (U.S.): ACLU disassociation from, **Supp. 7**, 248; anti-Stalin wing, expulsion of, **Supp. 10**, 330, 849; black involvement with, **Supp. 7**, 204–5; **Supp. 7**, 611–12; black opposition to, **Supp. 7**, 156; California, **Supp. 5**, 742; civil liberties issues, **Supp. 5**, 481; Comintern liaison, **Supp. 8**, 162; congressional investigations, **Supp. 9**, 233–34, *see also* Loyalty issues; defection and expulsion from, **Supp. 3**, 14; **Supp. 6**, 598, 716; **Supp. 7**, 113–14, 118, 269, 291, 583–84; **Supp. 8**, 133; espionage for Soviet Union, *see* Espionage; founding of, **Supp. 5**, 135; **Supp. 8**, 458; FBI campaign against, **Supp. 9**, 406; founding of, **Supp. 10**, 849; front organizations, **Supp. 8**, 132, 425; **Supp. 9**, 458; labor involvement with, **Supp. 5**, 511, 664; **Supp. 6**, 597–98, 648, 707; **Supp. 7**, 255–56; **Supp. 8**, 375, 458, 511–13, 527; labor opposition to, **Supp. 5**, 664; **Supp. 7**, 82, 156; leadership, **Supp. 7**, 179–81, 248–49, 255–56, 611–12; **Supp. 9**, 127; leadership, prosecution of, **Supp. 5**, 389, 500, 714; **Supp. 7**, 96, 180–81, 256, 290–91, 317, 389–90, 612; leadership trial, **Supp. 10**, 718–19; left-wing opposition to, **Supp. 9**, 679; link to New York City schools investigated, **Supp. 9**, 199–200; march on Washington, D.C., **Supp. 6**, 239; membership, **Supp. 9**, 127; motion-picture industry, **Supp. 8**, 550–51; **Supp. 9**, 602–3; organizers for, **Supp. 5**, 70; passport policy toward, **Supp. 8**, 590–91; political candidates, **Supp. 5**, 499–500; **Supp. 8**, 192; Progressive party (1948) alleged links with, **Supp. 6**, 681; **Supp. 7**, 763; publications, **Supp. 7**, 268–69; **Supp. 8**, 216; **Supp. 9**, 134; relations with Soviet Union, **Supp. 9**, 127; trials, **Supp. 9**, 135; World War II position, **Supp. 5**, 500. *See also* Espionage; Loyalty issues
Communist Political Association, founding of, **Supp. 7**, 256
Community center movement, **Supp. 3**, 600–601
Community Church of New York: marriage consultation center, **Supp. 6**, 602; name change, **Supp. 7**, 356
Community of True Inspiration, **Vol. 6, Part 2**, 586
Como, Perry, reference to, **Supp. 7**, 774
Comparative literature, scholarship and studies, **Supp. 10**, 388
Comparative Literature Society, **Vol. 9, Part 1**, 252
Compass: earth inductor, **Supp. 7**, 76; solar, **Vol. 2, Part 1**, 340
Compass Books, founding of, **Supp. 7**, 307
Compilations, **Vol. 3, Part 1**, 549 f.; **Vol. 7, Part 1**, 333; **Vol. 8, Part 2**, 541; **Vol. 10, Part 1**, 637 f.
Complete Angler, first American edition of, **Vol. 1, Part 2**, 230
Composers. For complete list, *see* Occupations Index
Compressed air, early use of, **Vol. 3, Part 1**, 334
Compromise of 1850, **Vol. 1, Part 1**, 403; **Vol. 1, Part 2**, 158, 212; **Vol. 2, Part 1**, 418; **Vol. 2, Part 2**, 179, 242; **Vol. 3, Part 1**, 399; **Vol. 3, Part 2**, 381; **Vol. 8, Part 2**, 617; **Vol. 9, Part 1**, 570; **Vol. 9, Part 2**, 209, 353, 590; **Vol. 10, Part 1**, 591
Compton, Arthur H., references to, **Supp. 7**, 10; **Supp. 8**, 122, 411
Compton, Karl, references to, **Supp. 4**, 818, **Supp. 7**, 275; **Supp. 8**, 665, 686, 687; **Supp. 9**, 144
Compton's Pictured Encyclopedia, **Supp. 7**, 253
Compulsion, **Supp. 9**, 490
Computation, mechanical development of present methods in, **Vol. 7, Part 2**, 574
Computers: development of, **Supp. 10**, 10, 520; first commercial, **Supp. 6**, 675; first electronic digital, **Supp. 9**, 184; **Supp. 10**, 519–21; forerunner, **Supp. 5**, 329; information theories as basis for, **Supp. 7**, 731, 785; MANIAC development, **Supp. 6**, 656
Computing-Tabulating-Recording Co., **Supp. 6**, 674
COMSAT. *See* Communications Satellite Corporation
Comstock, Anthony, references to, **Vol. 9, Part 2**, 626; **Supp. 5**, 453
Comstock, F. Ray, references to, **Supp. 3**, 296, 297
Comstock, William A., reference to, **Supp. 6**, 34
Comstock lode, **Vol. 2, Part 2**, 333; **Vol. 3, Part 2**, 246; **Vol. 5, Part 2**, 283; **Vol. 7, Part 1**, 612; **Vol. 9, Part 2**, 146
Conant, James B.: National Defense Research Commit-

tee, **Supp. 9**, 144; references to, **Supp. 8**, 687; **Supp. 10**, 240, 467
Conant Thread Co., **Vol. 2, Part 2**, 336
Concentration camps. *See* Holocaust; War crimes
Concert band. *See* Band music
Concertgebouw Orchestra, **Supp. 7**, 549
Concert playing, **Vol. 5, Part 1**, 368; **Vol. 5, Part 2**, 217 f., 320 f.
Condé Nast Publications, Inc., **Supp. 3**, 547; **Supp. 10**, 586
Concessions and Agreements of 1677, **Vol. 7, Part 2**, 434
Conchology, **Vol. 4, Part 1**, 446; **Vol. 6, Part 1**, 67, 70; **Vol. 8, Part 1**, 394 f.; **Vol. 8, Part 2**, 401 f.; **Vol. 9, Part 1**, 548, 585; **Vol. 9, Part 2**, 599; **Vol. 10, Part l**, 25
Concilium Bibliographicum, **Vol. 3, Part 2**, 365
Concord, Mass.: "Concord Group," **Vol. 4, Part 2**, 329, 426; **Vol. 8, Part 2**, 326; **Vol. 9, Part 1**, 383; **Vol. 9, Part 2**, 492 f.; history of, **Vol. 2, Part 2**, 250; **Vol. 3, Part 1**, 150; **Vol. 7, Part 2**, 635; **Vol. 9, Part 1**, 33; religious service, **Vol. 8, Part 1**, 622
Concord, N. H., **Vol. 7, Part 2**, 577
Concord Antiquarian Society, **Vol. 8, Part 2**, 5
Concord Art Association, **Vol. 8, Part 2**, 5
Concordia Seminary, **Vol. 7, Part 2**, 574
Concrete construction, **Vol. 6, Part 2**, 8; **Vol. 9, Part 2**, 386, 545 f.
Condensation, **Supp. 1**, 58
Conditioned response. *See* Behaviorism; Learning, theory
Condon, Eddie, references to, **Supp. 8**, 562; **Supp. 10**, 299
Condon, Edward U., references to, **Supp. 7**, 259; **Supp. 8**, 199, 649
"Condor" towboats, **Vol. 5, Part 1**, 238 f.
Conductors. For complete list, *see* Occupations Index
Cone, Claribel, reference to, **Supp. 4**, 768
Cone, Etta, reference to, **Supp. 4**, 768
Cone, Lee H., reference to, **Supp. 4**, 336
Cone Export & Commission Co., **Vol. 2, Part 2**, 340 f.
Conestoga wagon, **Vol. 6, Part 1**, 590; **Vol. 9, Part 1**, 303
Coney Island (N.Y.), **Vol. 2, Part 2**, 436; **Vol. 9, Part 2**, 553
Confederacy of New England (1650), **Vol. 4, Part 2**, 396
Confederate States: **Vol. 1, Part 1**, 640; **Vol. 4, Part 1**, 560; **Vol. 5, Part 1**, 26; **Vol. 5, Part 2**, 102, 337, 552, 591 f.; **Vol. 9, Part 1**, 130; attorney general of, **Vol. 1, Part 2**, 182; banking, **Vol. 5, Part 2**, 550; battle flags, **Vol. 8, Part 2**, 242; battle flags, proposed return of, **Vol. 2, Part 2**, 209; **Vol. 3, Part 2**, 503; "Bethel Regiment," **Vol. 5, Part 2**, 578; cabinet, **Vol. 2, Part 1**, 10; cavalry raids, **Vol. 8, Part 2**, 70; Congress, **Vol. 1, Part 2**, 204, 467; **Vol. 2, Part 1**, 34; **Vol. 7, Part 1**, 87; **Vol. 9, Part 1**, 339, 528; Constitution, **Vol. 9, Part 1**, 130; *Diary, Confederate Girl's*, **Vol. 3, Part 1**, 152; dissension, **Vol. 3, Part 2**, 501; financial agents of, **Supp. 1**, 690; financing of, **Vol. 6, Part 2**, 527; flag, design for, **Vol. 5, Part 2**, 524; flag of truce, surrender of, **Vol. 3, Part 1**, 7; food supplies, **Vol. 7, Part 2**, 580; foreign relations, **Vol. 1, Part 1**, 43; **Vol. 3, Part 2**, 308; **Vol. 4, Part 2**, 513; **Vol. 5, Part 1**, 134, 428; **Vol. 5, Part 2**, 337; **Vol. 6, Part 2**, 240, 365; **Vol. 8, Part 2**, 335; **Vol. 10, Part 2**, 267; formation of, **Vol. 10, Part 2**, 593; history of, **Vol. 1, Part 2**, 183 f.; **Vol. 3, Part 1**, 128 f.; Ladies' Relief Association, **Vol. 5, Part 2**, 524; mail carrying, **Vol. 4, Part 1**, 630; major-general, last, **Vol. 6, Part 1**, 39; *Messages and Papers of the Confederacy*, **Vol. 8, Part 1**, 571; "Mosquito Fleet," **Vol. 5, Part 1**, 152; Napoleon III, **Vol. 9, Part 1**, 210 f.; naval engagements, **Vol. 1, Part 1**, 226; **Vol. 2, Part 1**, 70, 207, 258; **Vol. 5, Part 1**, 152; **Vol. 5, Part 2**, 164; **Vol. 6, Part 2**, 225, 430; *see also* Civil War, naval service; "Pacific Republic," **Vol. 5, Part 2**, 580; postmaster general, **Vol. 8, Part 1**, 433; privateers, **Vol. 3, Part 1**, 42; quartermaster-generals, **Vol. 6, Part 1**, 62; **Vol. 7, Part 1**, 375; Rangers, **Vol. 6, Part 1**, 104; records, capture of, during the war, **Vol. 6, Part 1**, 238; secretary of state, **Vol. 1, Part 2**, 183; **Vol. 9, Part 2**, 590 f.; secretary of treasury, **Vol. 8, Part 1**, 433; secretary of war, **Vol. 1, Part 2**, 183; **Vol. 8, Part 2**, 545; Senate, **Vol. 4, Part 1**, 481; **Vol. 8, Part 2**, 582; support of, **Vol. 4, Part 1**, 429, 541; **Vol. 5, Part 2**, 102, 155, 550; surgeon general of, **Vol. 7, Part 1**, 138; treasonable correspondence with Davis, charged, **Vol. 5, Part 2**, 173; vice-president, **Vol. 9, Part 1**, 569 f.; war office, criticism of, **Vol. 1, Part 2**, 183; writings on, **Vol. 3, Part 1**, 130; **Vol. 4, Part 1**, 459, 541; **Vol. 5, Part 2**, 183; **Vol. 10, Part 2**, 562
Conference for Education in the South, **Supp. 3**, 209
Conference for Progressive Political Action, founding of, **Supp. 2**, 351
Conference of Mayors (U.S.), founding of, **Supp. 4**, 611–12
Conference on Jewish Relations, founding of, **Supp. 4**, 168
Conference on Progressive Labor Action, **Supp. 8**, 458
Confessional, affirmation of inviolacy by court, **Vol. 5, Part 2**, 488 f.
Confessional History of the Lutheran Church, The, **Vol. 8, Part 1**, 551
Confessional poetry, **Supp. 9**, 85–87; **Supp. 10**, 469
Confiscation: Louisiana policy, **Vol. 3, Part 1**, 545 f.; Loyalists' property, **Vol. 8, Part 2**, 342
Conflict of Laws, **Vol. 7, Part 1**, 28
Congo Free State: **Vol. 8, Part 2**, 267; language of, **Vol. 7, Part 1**, 231; organization of, **Vol. 9, Part 1**, 512 f.
Congregational church: **Vol. 1, Part 1**, 93 f., 328, 408, 467, 474, 479 f., 481, 625, 651 f.; **Vol. 2, Part 1**, 341, 344; **Vol. 2, Part 2**, 116, 135, f.; **Vol. 3, Part 2**, 31 f., 34 f., 44, 129, 227, 250, 360, 407; **Vol. 4, Part 1**, 325, 420, 619; **Vol. 4, Part 2**, 4, 53, 140, 326; **Vol. 5, Part 1**, 125, 160, 199, 217, 333, 365, 369; **Vol. 5, Part 2**, 302 f.; **Vol. 6, Part 1**, 409, 514; **Vol. 7, Part 1**, 146, 245, 253, 302, 327, 342, 385 f., 389 f., 432, 450 f., 537, 552, 583; **Vol. 7, Part 2**, 191, 204, 217 f., 237, 333 f., 343, 393, 404, 410, 583, 585, 589; **Vol. 8, Part 2**, 331, 348, 420, 544 f.; **Vol. 9, Part 1**, 376, 481, 549; **Vol. 9, Part 2**, 59 f., 149 f., 302, 307, 349, 373, 390, 572, 595, 623; **Vol. 10, Part 1**, 82, 85 f.; **Supp. 5**, 648–49; Andover controversy, **Vol. 10, Part 1**, 41; "Congregational Way," **Vol. 5, Part 2**, 118; Council for Social Action, **Supp. 3**, 363; half-way covenant, **Vol. 3, Part 1**, 86 f.; **Vol. 7, Part 1**, 55 f.; **Vol. 9, Part 2**, 59; heresy, **Vol. 2, Part 1**, 351; history of, **Vol. 8, Part 2**, 172; Illinois, **Vol. 10, Part 1**, 58; library, Boston, **Vol. 2, Part 2**, 137, 247; Middle West, establishment of, in, **Vol. 10, Part 1**, 58, 429; missionary work, **Vol. 1, Part 1**, 149, 186, 295; **Vol. 4, Part 2**, 144; **Vol. 8, Part 1**, 286 f.; **Vol. 9, Part 1**, 238; **Vol. 9, Part 2**, 101; **Supp. 2**, 28; **Supp. 3**, 322–23; Mississippi, advancement of, west of the, **Vol. 8, Part 1**, 120 f.; New England, establishment in, **Vol. 1, Part 1**, 479 f.; **Vol. 1, Part 2**, 129; **Vol. 2, Part 1**, 381; **Vol. 6, Part 2**, 391 f., 396; **Vol. 8, Part 2**, 317; **Vol. 9, Part 2**, 100 f.; **Vol. 10, Part 1**, 362 f.; "Plan of Union," **Vol. 1, Part 1**, 480, 628; schisms in, **Vol. 3, Part 2**, 565; **Vol. 4, Part 1**, 194, 397; **Vol. 7, Part 1**, 245; **Vol. 8, Part 2**, 331; **Vol. 9, Part 2**, 84; **Vol. 10, Part 1**, 447 f.; **Vol. 10, Part 2**, 502; social action, **Supp. 4**, 111, 741; **Supp. 6**, 25; Stoddardean-

ism, **Vol. 9, Part 2**, 59; Winslow Covenant, **Vol. 3, Part 1**, 3; "Wood'n ware" controversy, **Vol. 10, Part 1**, 447 f.; writings on, **Vol. 3, Part 1**, 279; **Vol. 5, Part 1**, 72; **Vol. 5, Part 2**, 588; **Vol. 8, Part 2**, 173
Congregational Church Building Society, **Vol. 1, Part 2**, 505; **Vol. 7, Part 2**, 191
Congregationalist, **Vol. 8, Part 1**, 562
Congregation Quarterly, **Vol. 3, Part 1**, 279
Congress, United States: air-conditioning of chambers, **Supp. 4**, 149; Alaska Statehood, **Supp. 8**, 25–26; *Annals of Congress*, **Vol. 4, Part 1**, 101; bearded members, **Supp. 6**, 636; cabals in, **Vol. 9, Part 1**, 342; Capitol buildings, **Supp. 8**, 630; dean of, **Supp. 5**, 598; election of senators, regulation of, **Vol. 9, Part 2**, 45; ethics issues, **Supp. 7**, 111; **Supp. 8**, 497; filibustering, regulation of, **Vol. 8, Part 1**, 457 f.; historical studies of, **Supp. 5**, 429; Joint Budget Committee, **Supp. 7**, 734; Joint Committee on the Organization of Congress, **Supp. 10**, 530, 547; Joint Economic Committee, **Supp. 7**, 590; "lame duck" sessions, **Vol. 9, Part 1**, 15; librarian of, first, **Vol. 10, Part 1**, 555 f.; New Deal legislation, **Supp. 3**, 650; oldest member, **Supp. 8**, 223; presidential relations, **Supp. 3**, 661; priest, election of, to, **Vol. 8, Part 1**, 550; radio news coverage, **Supp. 8**, 373; reforms of, **Supp. 7**, 415; reports of proceedings, **Vol. 3, Part 2**, 93; **Vol. 4, Part 1**, 100; representational apportionment, **Supp. 5**, 338; salary of members, **Vol. 1, Part 2**, 236; **Vol. 5, Part 2**, 115; televised press conferences, **Supp. 8**, 128; women in, **Supp. 6**, 551–52; youngest member, **Supp. 8**, 245. *See also* House of Representatives, United States; Lobbying; Senate, United States
Congressional Directory, first issue of, **Vol. 8, Part 1**, 73 f.
Congressional investigations, Roosevelt and, **Vol. 8, Part 2**, 141
Congressional Record, forerunner of, **Vol. 8, Part 1**, 635
Congressional Union, founding of, **Supp. 6**, 41
Congress of Industrial Organizations (CIO): AFL v., **Supp. 5**, 339–40, 691; **Supp. 6**, 219, 379, 707; **Supp. 10**, 524; auto industry unions, **Supp. 8**, 419, 526, 652; black rights and, **Supp. 5**, 511; **Supp. 6**, 648; Committee to Abolish Racial Discrimination, **Supp. 6**, 648; Communist relations, **Supp. 5**, 664; **Supp. 7**, 118–19, 290; **Supp. 8**, 511–12, 527; founding of; **Supp. 2**, 323; **Supp. 4**, 376; **Supp. 5**, 254–55, 282–83, 510, 654; **Supp. 8**, 375–77; leadership, **Supp. 5**, 282–83, 510–11; **Supp. 8**, 512–13; **Supp. 10**, 493, 643; organizing drives, **Supp. 7**, 82; political action committee, **Supp. 5**, 511; **Supp. 6**, 679; southern representation, **Supp. 6**, 433–34; steel industry, **Supp. 6**, 622. *See also* American Federation of Labor-Congress of Industrial Organizations
Congress of Racial Equality (CORE): **Supp. 8**, 335, 388, 605, 606; founding of, **Supp. 8**, 458; leadership, **Supp. 10**, 341
Conjunctivitis, **Supp. 4**, 865
Conkling, Roscoe, references to, **Vol. 1, Part 2**, 324 f.; **Vol. 3, Part 2**, 326; **Vol. 8, Part 1**, 4 f.; **Vol. 8, Part 2**, 6; **Vol. 9, Part 2**, 511
Conkling, Wallace E., reference to, **Supp. 6**, 45
Connally, John B., reference to, **Supp. 7**, 594
Connecticut: Agricultural Experiment Station, **Vol. 5, Part 2**, 45; architecture, colonial, **Vol. 5, Part 1**, 83; boundary disputes, **Vol. 5, Part 2**, 41; **Vol. 8, Part 1**, 290 f., 426; **Vol. 9, Part 2**, 633; brick house, first, **Vol. 8, Part 1**, 290 f.; charter, suspension of, **Vol. 10, Part 2**, 414; child welfare, **Vol. 3, Part 1**, 108; Civil War period, **Vol. 2, Part 1**, 228; colonial public records, **Vol. 10, Part 1**, 9; Committee of the Pay Table, **Vol. 3, Part 2**, 112; Constitutional Convention, **Vol. 3, Part 2**, 44; Council of Safety, 1776, **Vol. 6, Part 1**, 42; deadlocked legislature under Bulkeley, **Vol. 2, Part 1**, 248; Democratic party, **Supp. 9**, 57–58, 59; Dutch in New York, early relations with, **Vol. 10, Part 2**, 637; education, **Vol. 1, Part 1**, 537; **Vol. 2, Part 1**, 402, 442; **Vol. 3, Part 1**, 502 f.; **Vol. 7, Part 1**, 565; **Vol. 8, Part 1**, 102 f.; "equivalent lands" given by Massachusetts, **Vol. 8, Part 1**, 426; finance services, **Vol. 10, Part 1**, 629 f.; first Jewish governor of, **Supp. 9**, 59; first woman governor of, **Supp. 9**, 59; Fish Commission, **Vol. 9, Part 2**, 566; flora of, **Vol. 1, Part 2**, 599; Fundamental Orders of, **Vol. 6, Part 1**, 494; geology of, **Vol. 1, Part 2**, 54; **Vol. 7, Part 2**, 460; **Vol. 8, Part 1**, 548; glass monopoly, **Vol. 7, Part 2**, 641; Governor's Foot Guards, **Vol. 3, Part 1**, 372 f.; governors of, **Vol. 1, Part 1**, 542 f., 544 f.; **Vol. 2, Part 1**, 228 f., 248 f.; **Vol. 2, Part 2**, 203; **Vol. 3, Part 2**, 28 f., 115 f., 498; **Vol. 4, Part 2**, 9 f., 341 f., 459 f.; **Vol. 5, Part 1**, 207 f., 395 f.; **Vol. 5, Part 2**, 65; **Vol. 7, Part 1**, 216 f.; **Vol. 7, Part 2**, 640 f.; **Vol. 9, Part 1**, 11 f., 300; **Vol. 9, Part 2**, 600 f.; **Vol. 10, Part 1**, 15, 17, 384 f.; **Vol. 10, Part 2**, 443, 445; **Supp. 4**, 197; **Supp. 6**, 59; Hartford *Times*, influence of, **Vol. 2, Part 1**, 321; historical writings on, **Supp. 9**, 339; history of, **Vol. 3, Part 1**, 550; **Vol. 3, Part 2**, 427; **Vol. 5, Part 1**, 154, 200; **Vol. 5, Part 2**, 412; **Vol. 6, Part 2**, 367; **Vol. 7, Part 2**, 640; **Vol. 9, Part 2**, 90; **Vol. 10, Part 1**, 7; **Vol. 10, Part 2**, 134, 256, 412, 636; humorous characters, **Vol. 6, Part 1**, 397; Indians, **Vol. 3, Part 1**, 199; **Vol. 10, Part 1**, 9 f.; industrial service, **Vol. 3, Part 1**, 395, 563 f.; **Vol. 8, Part 1**, 172 f.; **Vol. 9, Part 1**, 45; **Vol. 10, Part 1**, 376 f.; insane, treatment of, **Vol. 3, Part 1**, 568 f.; journalism, **Vol. 10, Part 2**, 565; land grants, **Vol. 3, Part 1**, 581 f.; land titles, Indian, **Vol. 8, Part 1**, 426; laws of, codification, **Vol. 1, Part 1**, 545; **Vol. 6, Part 1**, 42; **Vol. 9, Part 1**, 90; **Vol. 9, Part 2**, 250; legal cases, **Supp. 6**, 137; legal service, **Vol. 1, Part 1**, 543; **Vol. 2, Part 1**, 559; **Vol. 3, Part 1**, 230, 555, 581; **Vol. 5, Part 1**, 66, 154; **Vol. 6, Part l**, 39 f., 41 f.; **Vol. 7, Part 1**, 65; **Vol. 7, Part 2**, 639, 641; **Vol. 8, Part 1**, 187, 426, 468; **Vol. 8, Part 2**, 45, 148; **Vol. 10, Part 1**, 11, 384 f., 560 f.; **Vol. 10, Part 2**, 48; Loyalists, **Vol. 1, Part 2**, 54; medical service, **Vol. 10, Part 1**, 52; **Vol. 10, Part 2**, 511; military expeditions of 1745–47, **Vol. 6, Part 1**, 41; missions, **Vol. 3, Part 1**, 573 f.; **Vol. 8, Part 1**, 645; money, engraving of, **Vol. 3, Part 1**, 501 f.; Pennsylvania, relations with, **Vol. 1, Part 2**, 566; political service, **Vol. 1, Part 1**, 542, 544; **Vol. 1, Part 2**, 295, 298, 569, 598; **Vol. 2, Part 1**, 228; **Vol. 3, Part 1**, 26, 62, 171, 173, 230, 328, 395, 555, 569, 581; **Vol. 3, Part 2**, 343, 427, 498, 538, 553; **Vol. 4, Part 2**, 9, 341, 459; **Vol. 5, Part 1**, 207, 418; **Vol. 5, Part 2**, 132; **Vol. 6, Part 1**, 41, 138; **Vol. 7, Part 1**, 216, 522; **Vol. 7, Part 2**, 32, 639, 641; **Vol. 8, Part 1**, 2, 187; **Vol. 8, Part 2**, 45, 145, 317; **Vol. 9, Part 1**, 11, 300; **Vol. 9, Part 2**, 600 f., 633; **Vol. 10, Part 1**, 8, 11, 16, 18, 384, 624, 629; **Vol. 10, Part 2**, 414, 443, 445, 582; politics, **Supp. 5**, 70, 455–56; **Supp. 9**, 57–58, 59, 81, 142, 240; **Supp. 10**, 652, 653; powder-mill, first, **Vol. 7, Part 2**, 641; printing, 18th century, **Vol. 10, Part 1**, 10; public health department, **Supp. 6**, 702; public service, **Vol. 2, Part 2**, 139; **Vol. 3, Part 1**, 108, 502 f.; **Vol. 3, Part 2**, 498; **Vol. 4, Part 2**, 9 f., 341, 421; **Vol. 5, Part 1**, 52, 207 f., 245, 416, 419; **Vol. 7, Part 2**, 69; **Vol. 8, Part 2**, 148; **Vol. 9, Part 1**, 300, 327; **Vol. 10, Part 1**, 560 f.; **Vol. 10, Part 2**, 293; **Supp. 10**, 654; railway building and consolidation, **Vol. 1, Part 2**, 298; **Vol. 2, Part 1**, 324; religious history, **Vol. 3, Part 1**, 54 f., 84 f.; **Vol. 5, Part 1**, 620; **Vol. 8, Part 2**, 101; **Vol. 10, Part 1**, 85, 632; **Vol. 10, Part 2**, 42; Republican party, organization of, **Vol. 4, Part 2**, 421; Republican-

Tolerationist, revolution in, **Vol. 9, Part 2**, 250; Revolutionary War period, **Vol. 3, Part 2**, 112; **Vol. 5, Part 1**, 416; **Vol. 10, Part 2**, 293, 442; separation of Springfield from, **Vol. 8, Part 1**, 292 f.; Sons of Liberty, **Vol. 3, Part 1**, 550; theocratic government, **Vol. 3, Part 1**, 611; verse, first volume written in, **Vol. 10, Part 2**, 446; woman suffrage, **Supp. 5**, 296, 297, 742
Connecticut Academy of Sciences, **Vol. 1, Part 2**, 341
Connecticut Birth Control Movement, founding of, **Supp. 5**, 297
Connecticut Civil Service Reform Association, **Vol. 7, Part 2**, 69
Connecticut College for Women, **Vol. 7, Part 2**, 647
Connecticut Compromise, **Vol. 3, Part 1**, 98
Connecticut Forestry Association, **Vol. 5, Part 2**, 45
Connecticut Gazette, **Vol. 5, Part 1**, 180
Connecticut Historical Society, **Vol. 8, Part 1**, 646
Connecticut Land Co., **Vol. 2, Part 2**, 189
Connecticut Medical College, **Vol. 7, Part 2**, 466
Connecticut Medical Society, **Vol. 5, Part 2**, 468
Connecticut Mutual Life Insurance Co., **Vol. 7, Part 2**, 529
Connecticut Nutmeg, founding of, **Supp. 2**, 68
Connecticut Society for Mental Hygiene, **Supp. 3**, 51
Connecticut Society of the Cincinnati, **Vol. 5, Part 2**, 423
Connecticut Sound Money League, **Vol. 7, Part 2**, 69
Connelly, Marc, references to, **Supp. 4**, 102; **Supp. 7**, 412–13
Conner, Fox, reference to, **Supp. 8**, 154
Connolly, Maurice E., prosecution of, **Supp. 3**, 117
Connor, Eugene ("Bull"), reference to, **Supp. 8**, 334
Conover, Harry, Modeling Agency, **Supp. 7**, 140–41
Conrad, Johannes, references to, **Vol. 7, Part 2**, 298; **Supp. 3**, 248
Conrad and Jones Co., **Supp. 5**, 555
Conscientious objectors, **Supp. 4**, 441, 526, 794; **Supp. 6**, 217; **Supp. 7**, 597; Civil War, **Vol. 8, Part 1**, 236 f.; Revolutionary War, **Vol. 8, Part 1**, 139 f.
Conscription: draft riots, **Vol. 3, Part 2**, 580; **Vol. 4, Part 1**, 238; Civil War, **Vol. 3, Part 2**, 580; **Vol. 5, Part 1**, 129; **Vol. 8, Part 1**, 202 f., 358 f.; World War I, **Vol. 5, Part 2**, 251. *See also* Draft
Conservation: **Vol. 1, Part 1**, 555; **Vol. 3, Part 2**, 403; **Vol. 4, Part 2**, 157, 354; **Vol. 5, Part 1**, 74 f., 167, 250, 433; **Vol. 5, Part 2**, 520, 573; **Vol. 7, Part 1**, 315 f., 457; **Vol. 8, Part 2**, 45, 134; **Vol. 9, Part 1**, 106; **Vol. 9, Part 2**, 565; aesthetic approach to, **Supp. 4**, 522–23; Alaska, **Supp. 3**, 96; Audubon movement, **Supp. 3**, 592–93; Benbrook Reservoir (Tex.), **Supp. 6**, 540; California redwoods, **Supp. 3**, 520; **Supp. 4**, 429; **Supp. 6**, 486; **Supp. 10**, 191, 192; congressional advocacy, **Supp. 6**, 475; **Supp. 7**, 212, 224–25; ecology, terminology established, **Supp. 3**, 168–70; ecology, writings on, **Supp. 7**, 109–10; federal policies, **Supp. 1**, 300; **Supp. 2**, 553; **Supp. 5**, 342; **Supp. 6**, 416–17; **Supp. 10**, 191–92; forest preserves, **Supp. 1**, 555; **Supp. 2**, 128, 264, 507, 610; **Supp. 3**, 78; **Supp. 4**, 663–66; **Supp. 6**, 486; fossil sites, **Supp. 5**, 743–44; legal decisions, **Supp. 10**, 324; legislation, **Supp. 4**, 666; **Supp. 7**, 225; **Supp. 9**, 663; Oregon, **Supp. 6**, 682; organizations, **Supp. 7**, 164–65; **Supp. 9**, 608; petroleum, **Supp. 7**, 771–72, 804; popular writings on, **Supp. 8**, 486; Prairie Club, **Supp. 3**, 599; public lands, **Supp. 4**, 317–18; Rockefeller preserves, **Supp. 6**, 549; Roosevelt, Teddy, efforts toward, **Vol. 2, Part 2**, 145; **Vol. 7, Part 1**, 316; shade trees, **Supp. 7**, 33; Washington (state), **Supp. 7**, 353; water supply, **Supp. 4**, 563–64; wilderness areas, **Supp. 6**, 486; **Supp. 7**, 164, 225, 813–14; wildlife, **Supp. 2**, 265; **Supp. 8**, 3–4; **Supp. 10**, 264–66; writings on, **Supp. 5**, 169; **Vol. 8, Part 2**, 134 f. *See also* Natural history
Conservation Foundation, founding of, **Supp. 8**, 486
Conservatism: public policy influence of, **Supp. 10**, 22–23; writings on, **Supp. 8**, 552; **Supp. 9**, 547–48
Conservator, **Vol. 9, Part 2**, 628
Consolidated Edison Co.: founding of, **Supp. 3**, 138; management, **Supp. 2**, 123; predecessors, **Supp. 3**, 716
Consolidated Film Industries, founding of, **Supp. 8**, 712
Consolidated Gas Co., **Vol. 8, Part 2**, 95
Consolidated Press Association (CPA), **Supp. 9**, 482
Consolidated Shipping Co., **Vol. 7, Part 1**, 240
Consolidated Virginia Mine, **Vol. 3, Part 2**, 246
Conspiracies: Blount (1797), **Vol. 1, Part 1**, 78; **Vol. 1, Part 2**, 390; **Vol. 5, Part 1**, 469; **Vol. 6, Part 2**, 82, 403; **Vol. 8, Part 2**, 604; Burr (1806–7), **Vol. 1, Part 1**, 34; **Vol. 1, Part 2**, 369; **Vol. 2, Part 1**, 317–19; **Vol. 2, Part 2**, 116, 125, 174; **Vol. 3, Part 1**, 80, 166, 613; **Vol. 5, Part 1**, 528; **Vol. 5, Part 2**, 30; **Vol. 6, Part 2**, 310; **Vol. 8, Part 2**, 84; **Vol. 9, Part 2**, 238, 536; **Vol. 10, Part 1**, 22; **Vol. 10, Part 2**, 225, 298; Grey (1755), **Vol. 8, Part 1**, 518; Pontiac (1763), **Vol. 1, Part 2**, 481, 579, 604; **Vol. 2, Part 2**, 556; **Vol. 4, Part 1**, 253, 327; **Vol. 8, Part 1**, 63, 578; **Vol. 9, Part 1**, 59; **Vol. 10, Part 2**, 103, 126
Constantinople, foreign missions in, **Vol. 8, Part 2**, 261
Constantinople Woman's College. *See* American College for Girls at Constantinople
Constellation (airplane), **Supp. 6**, 221
Constellation, refractory officers on, **Vol. 8, Part 1**, 424
Constitution ("Old Ironsides"), **Vol. 1, Part 1**, 506 f., 606; **Vol. 5, Part 1**, 360 f.; **Vol. 6, Part 1**, 500; **Vol. 7, Part 1**, 506; **Vol. 8, Part 1**, 424; **Vol. 8, Part 2**, 74; **Vol. 9, Part 1**, 135; **Vol. 9, Part 2**, 7, 306
Constitution (Confederate), **Vol. 9, Part 1**, 130
Constitution (U.S.): **Vol. 1, Part 1**, 91, 405; **Vol. 1, Part 2**, 501; **Vol. 3, Part 1**, 153; **Vol. 3, Part 2**, 374; **Vol. 4, Part 1**, 104, 224 f., 304 f., 479; **Vol. 4, Part 2**, 330 f., 366; **Vol. 5, Part 1**, 492 f.; **Vol. 5, Part 2**, 24, 88; **Vol. 7, Part 1**, 215, 218, 222, 412; **Vol. 9, Part 1**, 322; **Vol. 10, Part 1**, 35; Adams, John Quincy, views of, on, **Vol. 1, Part 1**, 91; amendments, *see* Constitutional amendments; antifederalism, **Vol. 2, Part 1**, 189; **Vol. 3, Part 2**, 385; **Vol. 9, Part 2**, 320, 356; **Vol. 10, Part 2**, 598, 601; bearer of, in procession of July 23, 1788, **Vol. 6, Part 1**, 32; Bible and, **Vol. 4, Part 2**, 272; Delaware, prompt ratification by, **Vol. 1, Part 2**, 39; **Vol. 8, Part 1**, 423; drafting of, **Vol. 1, Part 2**, 338, 499; **Vol. 5, Part 1**, 94 f.; **Vol. 10, Part 1**, 597 f.; interpretation of, **Vol. 4, Part 2**, 270 f.; **Vol. 6, Part 2**, 322 f.; **Vol. 7, Part 2**, 628; Jefferson's approval of, **Vol. 5, Part 2**, 23; Louisiana Purchase and, **Vol. 5, Part 2**, 29; making of, **Vol. 10, Part 2**, 329; nationalistic theory refuted, **Vol. 10, Part 1**, 127; opposition to, **Vol. 2, Part 2**, 227; **Vol. 6, Part 1**, 472 f.; Pinckney draft, **Vol. 7, Part 2**, 612; ratification of, **Vol. 1, Part 2**, 39, 483; **Vol. 2, Part 1**, 280; **Vol. 4, Part 2**, 230; **Vol. 6, Part 2**, 187; **Vol. 8, Part 1**, 138, 237 f., 312, 423; **Vol. 8, Part 2**, 49; **Vol. 9, Part 1**, 320; **Vol. 10, Part 1**, 509 f.; scholarship on, **Supp. 8**, 139; sesquicentennial, **Supp. 4**, 88; signing of, **Vol. 2, Part 2**, 235; **Vol. 9, Part 1**, 90; Webster's theory concerning, **Vol. 10, Part 1**, 585 f.; writings on, **Vol. 5, Part 2**, 8, 260; **Vol. 8, Part 1**, 401; **Supp. 1**, 154, 424–26; **Supp. 2**, 399; **Supp. 4**, 64; 530–31, 680; **Supp. 5**, 429, 549; **Supp. 7**, 146–47
Constitutional amendments: equal rights proposal, **Supp. 5**, 474, 532, 543; First, preferred freedoms of, **Supp. 4**, 796–97, *see also* Civil liberties; Fifth, **Supp.**

6, 105; Sixth, **Supp. 3**, 755; Tenth, **Supp. 5**, 573; Twelfth, **Vol. 9, Part 2**, 332; Thirteenth, **Vol. 10, Part 1**, 19 f.; Fourteenth, **Vol. 1, Part 2**, 489; **Vol. 4, Part 1**, 499; **Vol. 5, Part 1**, 139; **Vol. 5, Part 2**, 86, 88; **Vol. 7, Part 2**, 209; **Vol. 9, Part 1**, 624; **Supp. 3**, 415; Fifteenth, **Vol. 1, Part 2**, 489; **Vol. 5, Part 2**, 86; **Vol. 9, Part 1**, 624; **Vol. 9, Part 2**, 14; Seventeenth, **Supp. 3**, 105; Eighteenth, **Vol. 4, Part 1**, 112; **Vol. 7, Part 1**, 235; **Supp. 3**, 132, 181, 706; **Supp. 4**, 136, 161; **Supp. 6**, 3, 480, 548; Nineteenth, **Vol. 4, Part 1**, 112; **Vol. 6, Part 1**, 341; **Supp. 4**, 158, 861–62; **Supp. 7**, 779; **Supp. 10**, 622, 623; Twentieth, **Supp. 3**, 559, **Supp. 7**, 363; Twenty-Fifth, **Supp. 10**, 486; Twenty-Second, **Supp. 8**, 421; Twenty-Fourth, **Supp. 7**, 416; **Supp. 9**, 401; Twenty-Third, **Supp. 9**, 449
Constitutional Convention (1787), **Vol. 1, Part 2**, 123, 390; **Vol. 2, Part 1**, 1; **Vol. 3, Part 1**, 166; **Vol. 3, Part 2**, 113; **Vol. 4, Part 1**, 479; **Vol. 5, Part 2**, 133, 398; **Vol. 6, Part 1**, 308; **Vol. 6, Part 2**, 186; **Vol. 7, Part 2**, 584; **Vol. 8, Part 1**, 354; **Vol. 10, Part 2**, 601; Hamilton's part in, **Vol. 4, Part 2**, 174; history of its proceedings, **Vol. 5, Part 1**, 602; record of, **Vol. 5, Part 1**, 560; South Carolina's part in, **Vol. 2, Part 1**, 365
Constitutional History of the United States, **Supp. 4**, 530–31
Constitutional Jeffersonian Democratic party, founding of, **Supp. 4**, 813
Constitutional Union party, **Vol. 1, Part 2**, 158; **Vol. 9, Part 2**, 590
Constitution and What It Means Today, The, **Supp. 7**, 146
Constitution Hall (Washington, D. C.): architecture, **Supp. 5**, 300; racial policy, **Supp. 5**, 343; **Supp. 8**, 328
Constitutions (state). *See* specific states
Construction industry: first multinational firm, **Supp. 8**, 308–9; government-funded works projects, **Supp. 8**, 308; **Supp. 10**, 413, 414; mass construction techniques, **Supp. 1**, 349; New York City, **Supp. 6**, 337, 593; Philadelphia, **Supp. 6**, 331; skyscrapers, **Supp. 6**, 593; **Supp. 7**, 799–800; unionization, **Supp. 5**, 339; **Supp. 6**, 73–74
Consular Service, United States, merit system, **Supp. 3**, 139, 467
Consular system, regulation of, **Vol. 3, Part 1**, 294; **Vol. 8, Part 1**, 634
Consumer Distribution Corporation, organization of, **Supp. 2**, 184
Consumerism: boycotts, **Supp. 4**, 623–24; cooperatives, **Supp. 2**, 184; economic theory and, **Supp. 4**, 585; **Supp. 8**, 79; public education in, **Supp. 4**, 307–8; writings on, **Supp. 4**, 267–68; **Supp. 7**, 69; **Supp. 8**, 425
Consumer price index, **Supp. 7**, 794
Consumer Reports, **Supp. 7**, 69
Consumers' cooperatives, **Vol. 9, Part 1**, 396
Consumers' League of Ohio, founding of, **Supp. 3**, 347
Consumers' League of the City of New York, **Supp. 4**, 623–24
Consumers' research, **Supp. 8**, 425
Consumers Union, **Supp. 7**, 69
Contact, **Supp. 7**, 790
Contact dermititis, **Supp. 3**, 442
Containers: for tobacco, **Supp. 5**, 565; glass canning jars, **Supp. 3**, 29; **Supp. 5**, 343. *See also* Canning and canned goods; Packaging
Contemporary Psychology, **Supp. 8**, 44
Continental Association, **Vol. 6, Part 1**, 119
Continental Bank Note Co., **Vol. 7, Part 2**, 55
Continental Bank of New York, **Vol. 2, Part 2**, 613
Continental Congress: **Vol. 1, Part 1**, 73 f.; **Vol. 1, Part 2**, 354, 477; **Vol. 2, Part 1**, 296, 523; **Vol. 3, Part 1**, 174, 581 f.; **Vol. 3, Part 2**, 352; **Vol. 4, Part 1**, 366, 525, 618; **Vol. 4, Part 2**, 219, 232, 260, 279; **Vol. 5, Part 1**, 204, 220 f., 245, 267 f., 301, 314, 385, 418, 469, 539; **Vol. 5, Part 2**, 6, 42, 121 f., 159, 192, 587, 590, 599; **Vol. 6, Part 1**, 34, 105, 108, 132, 215, 232, 307, 318, 321, 438, 446, 464, 472, 523; **Vol. 6, Part 2**, 405, 600; **Vol. 7, Part 1**, 128 f., 210, 220, 307, 383, 411 f., 424; **Vol. 7, Part 2**, 417; **Vol. 8, Part 1**, 138, 338, 340 f., 533 f.; **Vol. 8, Part 2**, 257, 524, 535; **Vol. 9, Part 1**, 89, 307, 319, 322, 333, 451; **Vol. 9, Part 2**, 46, 84, 258, 361, 386, 481, 504, 543, 545; **Vol. 10, Part 1**, 17 f.; **Vol. 10, Part 2**, 327, 431, 442; "Americanus" articles, **Vol. 5, Part 2**, 599; comptroller of treasury under, **Vol. 10, Part l**, 17 f.; diary of, **Vol. 9, Part 1**, 333; journals of, **Vol. 5, Part 1**, 385; negotiations with France, **Vol. 3, Part 1**, 174; political factions, **Vol. 6, Part 1**, 34; **Vol. 8, Part 2**, 257; president of, **Vol. 4, Part 1**, 618; **Vol. 5, Part l**, 418
Continental currency, **Vol. 3, Part 1**, 281 f.
Continental drift, **Supp. 2**, 654
Continental League (baseball), **Supp. 7**, 646–47
Continental Oil Co., Marland merger, **Supp. 3**, 505
Continental shelf, **Supp. 5**, 656–57
Contraband, trade in, **Vol. 7, Part 1**, 543
Contraceptives. *See* Family planning; *specific types*
Contract bridge, authorities on, **Supp. 5**, 146; **Supp. 6**, 134–35, 380
Convent of St. Elizabeth, **Vol. 8, Part 2**, 597
Convent of the Sisters of Notre Dame de Nemours, **Vol. 8, Part 1**, 266 f.
Convention of 1787. *See* Constitutional Convention
"Convention of Slaveholders," **Vol. 9, Part 2**, 596
Converse, Harriet Maxwell, reference to, **Supp. 5**, 533
Convulsions, **Supp. 1**, 241
Conway cabal, **Vol. 1, Part 1**, 176; **Vol. 2, Part 1**, 315, 398; **Vol. 2, Part 2**, 498; **Vol. 3, Part 1**, 486 f.; **Vol. 4, Part 1**, 186, 570; **Vol. 5, Part 2**, 100, 537; **Vol. 6, Part 1**, 34, 36, 439; **Vol. 6, Part 2**, 120, 607; **Vol. 8, Part 2**, 228; **Vol. 10, Part 1**, 509, 517–18; **Vol. 10, Part 2**, 223
Cook, Frederick A.: **Vol. 6, Part 1**, 529; **Vol. 7, Part 2**, 366; **Vol. 10, Part 1**, 390; reference to, **Supp. 4**, 674
Cook, George Cram, reference to, **Supp. 4**, 330
Cook, Nancy, references to, **Supp. 7**, 659, 660
Cook, Will Marion, reference to, **Supp. 3**, 834
Cookbooks: **Vol. 6, Part 1**, 185; **Vol. 9, Part 2**, 377; **Supp. 4**, 455; **Supp. 7**, 528, 656–57; **Supp. 8**, 656
Cook County (Ill.), Democratic party machine, **Supp. 10**, 167, 411
Cooke, Jay, **Vol. 7, Part 1**, 176, 436
Cooking: cake mixes, **Supp. 6**, 292; Pyrex ovenware, **Supp. 6**, 624; recipe innovation, **Supp. 6**, 165; teaching of, **Vol. 2, Part 2**, 454; **Vol. 3, Part 2**, 276; **Vol. 6, Part 1**, 265. *See also* Diet and nutrition; Restaurants
Cooley, Charles H., reference to, **Supp. 3**, 601
Cooley's anemia, **Supp. 3**, 190
Coolidge, Archibald Cary, reference to, **Supp. 5**, 130
Coolidge, Calvin: biography of, **Supp. 3**, 817; references to, **Vol. 5, Part 2**, 546; **Vol. 7, Part 1**, 234; **Supp. 1**, 636; **Supp. 6**, 507; **Supp. 7**, 211; **Supp. 8**, 420; **Supp. 9**, 496; Stearns relationship, **Supp. 2**, 624; Teapot Dome scandal, **Supp. 3**, 715; **Supp. 9**, 859; West, R. O., relationship, **Supp. 6**, 684
Coolidge, Elizabeth Sprague: chamber-music concerts, **Supp. 3**, 252; radio concerts sponsorship, **Supp. 10**, 43; references to, **Supp. 5**, 76, 554; **Supp. 8**, 443; **Supp. 10**, 312
Coolidge, Elizabeth Sprague, Foundation, founding of, **Supp. 5**, 129

Coolidge, Ellen W., reference to, **Supp. 6**, 499
Coolidge, Shepley, Bulfinch & Abbott, **Supp. 2**, 117
"Coon songs," **Supp. 3**, 187
Cooper, Gary, reference to, **Supp. 8**, 649
Cooper, James Fenimore, references to, **Vol. 7, Part 1**, 423; **Vol. 9, Part 1**, 136, 261
Cooper, Kent, reference to, **Supp. 4**, 631
Cooper, Merian C., reference to, **Supp. 7**, 580
Cooper, Peter, references to, **Vol. 5, Part 1**, 347; **Vol. 9, Part 2**, 640
Cooper, Tom, reference to, **Supp. 4**, 293
Cooperative Communities, **Vol. 6, Part 2**, 136, 497
Cooperative Education Association of Virginia, founding of, **Supp. 3**, 115
Cooperative for American Remittances to Everywhere. See CARE
Cooperative Grange League Federation Exchange, founding of, **Supp. 4**, 37
Cooperative League of America, **Supp. 6**, 664
Cooperative Marketing Act (1926), **Supp. 5**, 365
Cooperatives: agricultural, **Supp. 2**, 307, 426; **Supp. 4**, 36–37, 340–41, 853; **Supp. 5**, 365; **Supp. 7**, 361; consumer, **Supp. 2**, 184; housing, **Supp. 6**, 615; organizations, **Supp. 6**, 664; tobacco, **Supp. 2**, 39, 79; utopian, **Supp. 1**, 345
Cooperative School for Teachers, founding of, **Supp. 8**, 443
Cooper Medical College, **Vol. 5, Part 2**, 580
Coopers and Lybrand, **Supp. 6**, 397
Cooperstown (N. Y.), baseball, origin of, at, **Vol. 3, Part 1**, 391
Cooper Union (New York City), **Vol. 2, Part 2**, 410; **Vol. 4, Part 2**, 605; **Vol. 6, Part 1**, 248; **Vol. 7, Part 1**, 579; **Vol. 8, Part 2**, 467; **Vol. 9, Part 1**, 252
Cooper Union Forum, **Supp. 3**, 511, 563
Coote, Richard, reference to, **Vol. 7, Part 1**, 517
Copacabana (nightclub, New York City), **Supp. 5**, 501
Copland, Aaron, references to, **Supp. 5**, 398; **Supp. 10**, 312
Copper: engraving, **Vol. 3, Part 1**, 272 f.; **Vol. 5, Part 1**, 424; exploitation, **Vol. 4, Part 2**, 507; extraction, **Vol. 3, Part 1**, 396; in electrical conduction, **Supp. 2**, 383; mining, *see* Mining, copper; porphyry deposits development, **Supp. 6**, 315–16; processing, **Supp. 1**, 58; rolling, **Vol. 6, Part 1**, 60; **Vol. 8, Part 2**, 95, 263; selling, **Vol. 3, Part 1**, 353; stock trading, **Supp. 2**, 292
"Copperheads," **Vol. 5, Part 2**, 437; **Vol. 6, Part 1**, 251, 336; **Vol. 7, Part 1**, 263; **Vol. 10, Part 1**, 144
Copper House, **Supp. 1**, 31
Coppolino, Carl, reference to, **Supp. 10**, 329
Coptic studies, **Supp. 3**, 374–75
Copy editing, **Supp. 6**, 236; **Supp. 10**, 35
Copying machines: **Supp. 8**, 71–72; Xerox products, **Supp. 9**, 878
Copyright: Act of 1891, **Vol. 1, Part 1**, 335; Act of 1909, **Vol. 8, Part 1**, 279 f.; American Authors' Authority plan debated, **Supp. 10**, 89; book publishing reform, **Supp. 3**, 773; Copyright League, American Publishers', **Vol. 1, Part 1**, 334; infringement test case, **Supp. 9**, 682–83; international, **Vol. 1, Part 1**, 537; **Vol. 1, Part 2**, 329; **Vol. 2, Part 2**, 149; **Vol. 3, Part 2**, 189; **Vol. 4, Part 1**, 73; **Vol. 5, Part 1**, 417; **Vol. 6, Part 1**, 15; **Vol. 8, Part 1**, 2 f., 19 f., 278 f.; **Vol. 8, Part 2**, 381; **Vol. 10, Part 1**, 594 f.; **Supp. 2**, 348; laws governing, authority on, **Vol. 3, Part 2**, 66; **Supp. 1**, 101; music publishing, **Supp. 3**, 834; news syndicate suit, **Supp. 5**, 223; songwriting, **Supp. 8**, 546; theatrical, **Supp. 6**, 150; writings on, **Vol. 8, Part 1**, 278 f.
Coquelin, Benoît-Constant, reference to, **Supp. 5**, 124
Coral: reefs, **Supp. 3**, 704; **Supp. 6**, 144; study of, **Vol. 1, Part 1**, 113
Corals, **Supp. 5**, 709
Coral Sea, battle of the (1942), **Supp. 6**, 577
Corcoran, Thomas G., references to, **Supp. 7**, 72, 263
Corcoran, W. W., reference to, **Vol. 10, Part 1**, 633 f.
Corcoran Gallery of Art, **Vol. 2, Part 2**, 440; **Vol. 3, Part 2**, 214
Cordmaking machine, invention of, **Vol. 8, Part 1**, 101 f.
Córdoba Observatory, **Vol. 4, Part 1**, 448
CORE. *See* Congress of Racial Equality
Corea, Chick, reference to, **Supp. 10**, 226
Corfu, **Supp. 9**, 49–50
Cori cycle, **Supp. 6**, 126
Corinth, Miss.: operation about (1862–63), **Vol. 1, Part 2**, 112; **Vol. 4, Part 1**, 495s; **Vol. 4, Part 2**, 151; **Vol. 6, Part 2**, 160, 427; **Vol. 7, Part 1**, 76; **Vol. 7, Part 2**, 48; **Vol. 8, Part 1**, 216; **Vol. 8, Part 2**, 163; **Vol. 9, Part 1**, 94; **Vol. 10, Part 1**, 185
Corinth excavations, **Supp. 3**, 705
Corliss engines, **Vol. 7, Part 1**, 546–47
Corn: culture, **Vol. 6, Part 1**, 74; **Vol. 8, Part 1**, 477 f.; first hybrid commercial, **Supp. 7**, 760; genetic studies, **Supp. 2**, 114; growing, **Vol. 6, Part 1**, 74; hybridization, **Supp. 2**, 167; **Supp. 4**, 252–53; **Supp. 5**, 629; **Supp. 7**, 760; milling, **Vol. 8, Part 1**, 273 f.; planting machine, **Vol. 1, Part 1**, 533
"Corn-cob capitals," style of architecture, **Vol. 6, Part 1**, 22
Corneal tissue transplants, **Supp. 7**, 70
Cornell, Katharine, references to, **Supp. 6**, 286, 517; **Supp. 7**, 496
Cornell Greenland Expedition, **Vol. 9, Part 2**, 308
Cornell-Guggenheim Aviation Safety Center, **Supp. 8**, 709
Cornell Medical College (New York City), biochemistry studies, **Supp. 10**, 197–98
Cornell University: **Vol. 1, Part 1**, 53; **Vol. 1, Part 2**, 419; **Vol. 8, Part 2**, 320; **Vol. 10, Part 2**, 349; agricultural extension service, **Supp. 3**, 433–34; **Supp. 4**, 36–37; agricultural studies, **Supp. 4**, 252–53; **Supp. 5**, 31; biochemistry studies, **Supp. 5**, 670; biology studies, **Supp. 4**, 253; botany studies, **Supp. 3**, 815; **Supp. 6**, 176; chemistry studies, **Supp. 5**, 35–36; engineering studies, **Vol. 4, Part 1**, 52; **Vol. 9, Part 2**, 519; **Supp. 1**, 31, 175; **Supp. 5**, 387; English drama studies, **Supp. 4**, 4–5; first black woman admitted, **Supp. 7**, 236; football team, **Supp. 4**, 236; **Supp. 5**, 727–28; founding of, **Vol. 3, Part 1**, 445 f.; **Vol. 3, Part 2**, 326, 383; **Vol. 7, Part 2**, 296; **Vol. 9, Part 1**, 146; **Vol. 10, Part 2**, 89; gifts to, **Vol. 8, Part 2**, 283, 290; **Supp. 6**, 623; historical library, **Supp. 2**, 75; history studies, **Supp. 3**, 47–48, 726; horticultural studies, **Supp. 5**, 30–31; laboratory courses, **Supp. 1**, 30; "Masterpieces of European Fiction" courses, **Supp. 10**, 582–83; mechanical engineering studies, **Supp. 6**, 182; medical school, **Vol. 7, Part 2**, 330; **Vol. 8, Part 1**, 44 f.; **Vol. 9, Part 2**, 33; **Supp. 2**, 177; **Supp. 6**, 123, 537, 546–47; nutrition school, **Supp. 4**, 37; ornithology studies, **Supp. 7**, 7; pathology studies, **Supp. 3**, 257–58; pharmacology studies, **Supp. 3**, 342–43; philosophy studies, **Supp. 3**, 697–98; plant pathology herbarium, **Supp. 3**, 815; political science studies, **Supp. 8**, 551–52; presidency, **Supp. 2**, 177; **Supp. 3**, 698; **Supp. 5**, 161; veterinary college, **Vol. 7, Part 1**, 140
Corn flakes, **Supp. 3**, 411; **Supp. 5**, 379
Corning Glass Works: defense research, **Supp. 9**, 185; founding, **Supp. 3**, 365; research, **Supp. 6**, 153, 623–24

Cornish, N. H., artists' colony, **Supp. 3**, 1, 2; **Supp. 8**, 493
Cornstalk, Shawnee chief, reference to, **Vol. 3, Part 1**, 519 f.
Cornwallis, Lord, references to, **Vol. 5, Part 1**, 474 f.; **Vol. 6, Part 1**, 36, 107; **Vol. 9, Part 2**, 387, 545
Coronado, Francisco Vázquez de, reference to, **Vol. 7, Part 2**, 135
Coronation hymn, composition of, **Vol. 5, Part 1**, 138
Coronet, founding of, **Supp. 5**, 637–38
Corporal punishment, abandonment of, **Vol. 3, Part 1**, 409; **Vol. 8, Part 1**, 412
Corporations, Bureau of, **Vol. 7, Part 2**, 544
Corporations: laws relating to, **Vol. 2, Part 1**, 281; **Vol. 3, Part 2**, 155; **Vol. 5, Part 2**, 241; **Vol. 6, Part 1**, 269 f.; **Vol. 8, Part 2**, 29, 424; **Vol. 9, Part 2**, 28; management, **Vol. 3, Part 2**, 452 f.; **Vol. 4, Part 1**, 529; **Vol. 4, Part 2**, 52; **Vol. 8, Part 1**, 449; special privileges of, attacked, **Vol. 8, Part 1**, 382; taxation of, important American decisions, **Vol. 7, Part 2**, 30 f. *See also* Antitrust actions; Business; Multinational corporations; *specific company and industry names*
Correspondence courses, early, **Vol. 8, Part 1**, 126
Corriden, John ("Red"), reference to, **Supp. 6**, 357
Corrupt Practices Act (1925), **Supp. 3**, 550
Cort, Edwin C., reference to, **Supp. 4**, 530
Cortisone: **Supp. 10**, 435; as arthritis treatment, **Supp. 9**, 444, 454–55; mass-production of, **Supp. 9**, 444; synthesis of, **Supp. 9**, 454
Corts, Hernando, reference to, **Vol. 7, Part 1**, 382
Corticosteroids, discovery of, **Supp. 6**, 447
Cortisone, **Supp. 6**, 447; **Supp. 7**, 341
Cosa Nostra. *See* Organized crime
Cosio y Cisneros, Evangelina, reference to, **Supp. 5**, 284
Cosmetics: "kissproof lipstick," **Supp. 6**, 609; manufacturing and promoting, **Supp. 7**, 666–67; **Supp. 8**, 12–14; **Supp. 9**, 648–49; **Supp. 10**, 133
Cosmic rays, studies of, **Supp. 5**, 496, 497; **Supp. 7**, 134, 344, 619; **Supp. 8**, 483
Cosmopolitan, founding of, **Supp. 5**, 286
Cosmopolitan Book Co., **Supp. 8**, 535–36
Cosmopolitan University (N.Y.), **Vol. 8, Part 1**, 126
Cosmos Club, **Vol. 3, Part 2**, 65
Coss, John, reference to, **Supp. 6**, 557
Costa Rica, diplomacy, **Vol. 3, Part 1**, 314
Costello, Dolores, references to, **Supp. 3**, 35, 36
Costello, Frank, references to, **Supp. 6**, 56; **Supp. 7**, 586; **Supp. 8**, 208, 397; **Supp. 9**, 399
Costello, Lou, reference to, **Supp. 9**, 1–2
Costello, Maurice, reference to, **Supp. 6**, 619
Costello, Paul V., reference to, **Supp. 6**, 331
Costigan, Edward P., reference to, **Supp. 10**, 119
Costume design. *See* Fashion; Theater
Cotner College, founding of, **Vol. 8, Part 2**, 381
Cotton, John, references to, **Vol. 5, Part 1**, 199, 436
Cotton, Joseph, reference to, **Supp. 9**, 559
Cotton (general): boll weevil, **Vol. 5, Part 1**, 406; breeding studies, **Supp. 2**, 110; **Supp. 4**, 862, 863; brokerage firms, **Supp. 1**, 609; Civil War period, **Vol. 1, Part 1**, 45; **Vol. 3, Part 1**, 182, 592 f.; cooperatives, **Supp. 1**, 566; economics of, **Vol. 4, Part 2**, 208; Exchange, New York, **Vol. 5, Part 1**, 484; exchanges, reform of, **Supp. 1**, 152; growers' organization, **Supp. 3**, 723; insects affecting, **Vol. 5, Part 1**, 406; legislation, **Supp. 4**, 50; marketing, **Supp. 2**, 79; **Supp. 8**, 89; Panic, **Vol. 8, Part 2**, 593; paper money based on, **Vol. 10, Part 1**, 451; picking machine, **Supp. 5**, 596–97; planting, **Vol. 3, Part 1**, 304; **Vol. 3, Part 2**, 482; **Vol. 5, Part 1**, 562; **Vol. 8, Part 1**, 565 f.; **Vol. 9, Part 1**, 427; tariff, "40 bale" theory, **Vol. 6, Part 2**, 35; trade, **Vol. 3, Part 1**, 178; **Vol. 3, Part 2**, 456; **Vol. 5, Part 1**, 485; **Vol. 7, Part 2**, 549; **Vol. 8, Part 2**, 593; **Vol. 9, Part 1**, 58, 486; **Vol. 9, Part 2**, 461
Cotton and Finance, founding of, **Supp. 1**, 609
Cotton and Tobacco Cooperative Marketing Association of the South, organization of, **Supp. 2**, 79
Cotton Club (Harlem): **Supp. 7**, 504; **Supp. 9**, 280; "jungle" style (jazz) developed at, **Supp. 9**, 260
Cotton Control Act (1934), passage of, **Supp. 4**, 50
Cotton Textile Institute, founding of, **Supp. 5**, 252
Cotton manufacture: **Vol. 1, Part 1**, 203, 330, 465; **Vol. 1, Part 2**, 457, 459; **Vol. 2, Part 1**, 146, 150; **Vol. 2, Part 2**, 329, 340; **Vol. 3, Part 1**, 275, 435, 507 f.; **Vol. 3, Part 2**, 579; **Vol. 4, Part 1**, 46 f., 176, 516 f., 599 f.; **Vol. 4, Part 1**, 200; **Vol. 5, Part 1**, 179, 522; **Vol. 6, Part 1**, 289, 456 f.; **Vol. 7, Part 1**, 107; **Vol. 8, Part 1**, 565 f.; **Vol. 9, Part 1**, 53, 205, 290, 475; **Vol. 9, Part 2**, 582; **Vol. 10, Part 1**, 570; bleaching process, **Vol. 3, Part 1**, 61; gin, invention of, **Vol. 10, Part 2**, 158; gin, electrification of, **Supp. 3**, 192; machinery, improvements in, **Vol. 1, Part 1**, 361; **Vol. 1, Part 2**, 40, 407; **Vol. 2, Part 1**, 128; **Vol. 3, Part 1**, 65, 435, 437, 507 f., 595; **Vol. 3, Part 2**, 218; **Vol. 7, Part 1**, 327; **Vol. 10, Part 2**, 158; spinning, first use of machinery for, **Vol. 3, Part 1**, 595
Cottonseed oil, manufacture of, early, **Vol. 3, Part 1**, 507 f.
Coty Award, first designer to win three times, **Supp. 9**, 587
Coudert, Frederic Ren, Sr., reference to, **Supp. 5**, 136
Coughlin, Charles, references to, **Supp. 3**, 653, 681; **Supp. 4**, 480; **Supp. 6**, 613, 647; **Supp. 10**, 745
Coughlin, John ("Bathhouse"), reference to, **Supp. 6**, 263
Coulter, John M., reference to, **Supp. 3**, 153
Council Against Communist Aggression, founding of, **Supp. 6**, 350
Council for Financial Aid to Education, founding of, **Supp. 7**, 587
Council of Appointment (N.Y.), **Vol. 2, Part 2**, 228; **Vol. 9, Part 1**, 444; **Vol. 10, Part 1**, 153
Council of Colonial Virginia, **Vol. 1, Part 2**, 336
Council of Economic Advisers, founding of, **Supp. 7**, 590; **Supp. 10**, 376; **Supp. 9**, 589
Council of Safety, **Vol. 5, Part 1**, 345; **Vol. 5, Part 2**, 197; **Vol. 8, Part 2**, 148
Council of Young Men's Hebrew and Kindred Associations, organization of, **Supp. 2**, 6
Council on African Affairs, founding of, **Supp. 9**, 898
Council on Foreign Relations, founding of, **Supp. 3**, 219
Council on Library Resources, **Supp. 7**, 276
Counterattack, **Supp. 6**, 350
Counterculture: beat generation, **Supp. 7**, 239; **Supp. 9**, 605; **Supp. 8**, 56, 326–27; Buddhist influence on, **Supp. 9**, 846; humor, **Supp. 8**, 56; liberation theory, **Supp. 10**, 506–7; 508; movie hero, **Supp. 5**, 162–63; music, **Supp. 8**, 305–6
Counterfeiting, **Vol. 3, Part 1**, 151, 273, 535 f.
Country and Western music, **Supp. 5**, 748–49; **Supp. 9**, 414, 662–63; **Supp. 10**, 104–5
"Country Gardens" (song), **Supp. 7**, 297
Country Gentleman, **Vol. 6, Part 1**, 284; **Vol. 10, Part 1**, 30 f., 36
Country Girl, The, **Supp. 7**, 583; **Supp. 10**, 160
Country life. *See* Rural areas
Country Music Association (CMA), founding of, **Supp. 9**, 663
Coupon bonds, first use of, **Vol. 8, Part 1**, 322 f.
Courant Institute (New York University), **Supp. 9**, 201
Cournand, André, references to, **Supp. 9**, 654, 655
Courthouse, architecture, **Supp. 1**, 716

Court martials, military manual revision, **Supp. 1**, 211
Court of Claims, United States, **Vol. 1, Part 1**, 409; **Vol. 2, Part 1**, 559; **Vol. 6, Part 1**, 219; **Vol. 7, Part l**, 580
Courts, coercion of, **Vol. 3, Part 1**, 160. *See also* Judicial system; Judiciary; Supreme Court
Court stories, **Supp. 3**, 773–74
Cousins, Norman, reference to, **Supp. 10**, 370
Couzens, James, references to, **Supp. 4**, 293, 294, 295, 297, 298
Coventry, R.I., site of one of earliest cotton mills in U.S., **Vol. 3, Part 1**, 275
Covered Wagon, **Vol. 5, Part 1**, 250
Covici, Pascal, reference to, **Supp. 7**, 307
Covici-Friede, **Supp. 7**, 307; founding of, **Supp. 7**, 148–49
Covington, Burling, Rublee, Acheson and Shorb, **Supp. 6**, 556, 557
Covode investigations (1857), **Vol. 2, Part 1**, 212
Cowboy Songs and Other Frontier Ballads, **Supp. 4**, 502
Cowan, Ruth, reference to, **Supp. 10**, 675
Coward, Nöel, reference to, **Supp. 10**, 851
Cowboys: fiction on, **Supp. 2**, 729–30; **Supp. 3**, 383; movie, **Supp. 4**, 363–64, 734–35; **Supp. 7**, 286–87; songs of, **Supp. 4**, 502. *See also* West (U.S.)
Cowles, Henry C., reference to, **Supp. 3**, 169
Cowles Foundation, predecessors, **Supp. 4**, 275
Cowley Fathers (Society of St. John the Evangelist), establishment of, **Vol. 4, Part 1**, 470
Cowpens, battle of, **Vol. 4, Part 1**, 572; **Vol. 7, Part 1**, 167; **Vol. 7, Part 2**, 559
Cowpox vaccination, first demonstration of, in U.S., **Vol. 10, Part 1**, 479 f., 529
Cox, Archibald, reference to, **Supp. 8**, 322
Cox, Eugene, reference to, **Supp. 7**, 276
Cox, George B., reference to, **Vol. 6, Part 1**, 394
Cox, James M., references to, **Supp. 3**, 21, 643; **Supp. 5**, 697; **Supp. 8**, 404
Cox Broadcasting Corporation, **Supp. 9**, 202–3
CPA. *See* Consolidated Press Association
Crackers, water, first manufacturing of, **Vol. 1, Part 2**, 205
Craddock, Charles Egbert, reference to, **Vol. 7, Part l**, 344
Cradle, Will Rock, The, **Supp. 7**, 61, 62
Craft, Robert, Stravinsky relationship, **Supp. 9**, 777, 778
Crafts, Charley, reference to, **Supp. 10**, 300
Crafts: American Indian, **Supp. 1**, 437–38; **Supp. 8**, 126; museum interest in, **Supp. 6**, 96–97; youth training in, **Supp. 3**, 44. *See also specific crafts*
Craig, Samuel, reierence to, **Supp. 7**, 306
Craig headrest, **Supp. 6**, 131
Craig's Wife, **Supp. 9**, 451
Cram, Ralph Adams, references to, **Supp. 3**, 183, 183–84; **Supp. 4**, 547
Cram and Ferguson (architects), **Supp. 3**, 183
Cram and Goodhue (architects), **Supp. 3**, 195–97
Cramer, Stuart W., reference to, **Supp. 4**, 148
Crampton, Henry E., reference to, **Supp. 3**, 478
Cranbrook Foundation, **Supp. 4**, 714–15; **Supp. 7**, 670
Crandall, Eddie, reference to, **Supp. 6**, 301
Crandall, Prudence, case, **Vol. 3, Part 1**, 27
Crandon, Margery, reference to, **Supp. 8**, 44
Crane, Hart, reference to, **Supp. 9**, 267; **Supp. 10**, 776
Crane, Stephen, reference to, **Supp. 4**, 38
Cranes, bullding of, **Vol. 9, Part 2**, 613
Cravath, de Gersdorff, Swaine, and Wood, **Supp. 3**, 839
Craven, Avery, reference to, **Supp. 7**, 685
Craven, Thomas, reference to, **Supp. 9**, 79
Crawford, Cheryl, references to, **Supp. 10**, 129, 130
Crawford, Christina, reference to, **Supp. 10**, 158
Crawford, Harry J., reference to, **Supp. 5**, 260
Crawford, Jimmy, reference to, **Supp. 4**, 510, 511
Crawford, William H., reference to, **Vol. 5, Part 1**, 531
Crawfordsville, Ind., **Vol. 3, Part 1**, 522
Crayon, publication of, **Vol. 9, Part 2**, 29
Crayon portraits, **Vol. 6, Part 1**, 54; **Vol. 8, Part 2**, 54, 202
Crazy Horse, Indian chief, references to, **Vol. 2, Part 2**, 530 f.; **Vol. 4, Part 2**, 28; **Vol. 7, Part 1**, 560
Credit: for securities purchases, **Supp. 1**, 84; automobile industry–related, **Supp. 4**, 682; economy, relationship to, **Supp. 6**, 599; farm, **Supp. 4**, 341, 480, 482; interest-rate theory, **Supp. 4**, 272–73; ratings, **Supp. 6**, 693–94; rediscount rates, **Supp. 3**, 730; World War I loans, **Supp. 4**, 469–70
Credit Mobilier scandal (1867), **Vol. 1, Part 1**, 251, 580; **Vol. 1, Part 2**, 78, 148; **Vol. 2, Part 1**, 78, 298; **Vol. 4, Part 1**, 146, 500, 539; **Vol. 5, Part 1**, 87; **Vol. 5, Part 2**, 42; **Vol. 8, Part 1**, 33–34
Credit Union Act (1934), **Supp. 3**, 706
Credit unions, **Supp. 2**, 184
Creek Indians: **Vol. 1, Part 2**, 520; **Vol. 7, Part 2**, 569; **Vol. 9, Part 2**, 580, 650; disturbances (1836–37), **Vol. 2, Part 1**, 423; **Vol. 4, Part 1**, 93; **Vol. 5, Part 1**, 73; **Vol. 5, Part 2**, 63; **Vol. 9, Part 2**, 350; treaty with Carolina, **Vol. 5, Part 2**, 111; war (1813–14), **Vol. 1, Part 2**, 391; **Vol. 2, Part 2**, 253; **Vol. 4, Part 2**, 414; **Vol. 5, Part 1**, 263, 529; **Vol. 6, Part 2**, 70, 538; **Vol. 8, Part 1**, 274; **Vol. 10, Part 1**, 567; **Vol. 10, Part 2**, 106, 108
Creel, George, references to, **Supp. 3**, 39, 396
Creighton, James Edwin, reference to, **Supp. 3**, 697
Creighton University, **Vol. 2, Part 2**, 535 f.; **Vol. 7, Part 1**, 618
Cremation, **Vol. 6, Part 1**, 163 f.; **Vol. 7, Part 1**, 470
Crenshaw, Daniel, reference to, **Vol. 7, Part 1**, 369
Creole: case of, **Vol. 1, Part 1**, 90; **Vol. 4, Part 2**, 446 creole Indians, **Vol. 2, Part 1**, 480; **Vol. 6, Part 2**, 283; **Vol. 8, Part 2**, 192 f.
Creole Jazz Band, **Supp. 9**, 45, 599
Crescent City Democratic Association, **Supp. 7**, 555, 556
Cressman, Luther, Sheeleigh, references to, **Supp. 10**, 521, 522
Crete: archaeology in, **Supp. 3**, 343–44; diplomacy, **Vol. 9, Part 2**, 29
Crichton, Kyle, reference to, **Supp. 7**, 52
Crickets, chirps as temperature measurement, **Supp. 1**, 325
Crickets (singing group), **Supp. 6**, 301
Criger, Lou, reference to, **Supp. 5**, 759
Crile, George, references to, **Supp. 4**, 507, 508
Crime: bank robbery, **Supp. 10**, 770, 771, body traits of criminals, **Supp. 5**, 312; criminal administration methodology, **Supp. 3**, 65–66; federal campaigns against, **Supp. 4**, 613; **Supp. 9**, 405–7; first U.S. government officer convicted of, **Supp. 3**, 259–60; forensic pathology, **Supp. 10**, 328–29; investigative techniques, **Supp. 5**, 245; **Supp. 9**, 405, 406; Lindbergh law, **Supp. 9**, 497; prevention, **Supp. 1**, 173; psychiatric evaluation of defendants, **Supp. 3**, 102; **Supp. 9**, 490; sociological theory of, **Supp. 4**, 808–9; statistical survey, **Supp. 5**, 639; tax evasion, **Supp. 3**, 21; white collar, **Supp. 4**, 809. *See also* Assassinations; Bombings and terrorism; Capital punishment; Judicial system; Kidnapping; Law; Murders; Organized crime; Prisons
Crimean War, **Vol. 6, Part 1**, 611; **Vol. 7, Part 2**, 578 f.
Criminal justice: model parole system developed, **Supp. 9**, 553; prison reforms, **Supp. 9**, 490–91; Supreme Court decisions, **Supp. 9**, 837; **Supp. 10**, 665; writings on, **Supp. 9**, 552. *See also* Prison

Criminal law. *See* Law, criminal
Criminology: **Vol. 2, Part 1**, 386; early studies in, **Vol. 3, Part 1**, 493; research, **Supp. 9**, 318–19; **Supp. 10**, 280; statistics, **Vol. 5, Part 2**, 495; writings on, **Vol. 3, Part 1**, 493; **Vol. 7, Part 1**, 389; **Supp. 10**, 280, 281
Cripple Creek, **Vol. 7, Part 1**, 75
Crisis, **Supp. 5**, 741; **Supp. 7**, 202, 203, 236
Crisis, **Supp. 9**, 108; 749–50
Criterion, **Supp. 7**, 219
Criticism: architecture, **Supp. 2**, 708–9; **Supp. 3**, 52–53; art, **Supp. 2**, 99, 740; **Supp. 3**, 341–42; **Supp. 4**, 182–83, 702; **Supp. 5**, 478–79; **Supp. 7**, 260, 493–94; **Supp. 8**, 489–90; botany, **Supp. 4**, 267; dramatic, **Vol. 8, Part 1**, 132; **Vol. 10, Part 2**, 44, 406; literary, **Vol. 2, Part 1**, 173; **Vol. 4, Part 2**, 11 f.; **Vol. 5, Part 1**, 310, 379; **Vol. 6, Part 1**, 459 f., 540 f.; **Vol. 7, Part 1**, 359, 398; **Vol. 8, Part 1**, 19 f., 46 f., 48 f., 623f.; **Vol. 9, Part 1**, 91; **Vol. 10, Part 1**, 45, 387 f., 392 f., **Vol. 10, Part 2**, 480; **Supp. 2**, 100, 471, 623; **Supp. 3**, 72; **Supp. 4**, 559–61, 702, 847; **Supp. 5**, 89–90, 168–69, 356, 425, 542; **Supp. 7**, 18, 55–56, 79–80, 103–4, 219–22, 309–10, 638, 754; **Supp. 8**, 124, 353–54, 492, 493, 584–85, 667–68; **Supp. 9**, 637–38, 642–43, 785, 807, 829, 875–76, 884–85; **Supp. 10**, 274–75, 418, 707, 724, 776–77; Marxist literary, **Supp. 7**, 268; motion picture, **Supp. 5**, 12, 623; **Supp. 8**, 491, 584–85; music, **Vol. 4, Part 1**, 50; **Vol. 5, Part 1**, 379; **Supp. 1**, 369, 592; **Supp. 2**, 237, 295; **Supp. 3**, 770–71; **Supp. 4**, 702; **Supp. 5**, 183; **Supp. 7**, 124, 754; **Supp. 9**, 316–17; New Criticism, **Supp. 7**, 55, 219, 347, 442; **Supp. 8**, 325–27; of press, **Supp. 3**, 59–60; **Supp. 7**, 473; poetry, **Supp. 3**, 475; **Supp. 4**, 694, 812; **Supp. 7**, 391; **Supp. 8**, 42, 43; popular entertainment, **Supp. 8**, 584–85; restaurant, **Supp. 6**, 291–92; social, **Supp. 6**, 445–47, 557–58; **Supp. 7**, 80–81; 539–40; **Supp. 9**, 325–26, 827, 875, 876; **Supp. 10**, 98–99, 117–18, 235, 293, 375–76, 502, 507–8, 539, 832–33; television, **Supp. 6**, 366; theater, **Supp. 1**, 369, 592, 643; **Supp. 2**, 76, 277; **Supp. 3**, 53–54, 841–42; **Supp. 4**, 354, 548–49; **Supp. 5**, 17–18, 425, 463–64, 657–58; **Supp. 6**, 237, 470–71; **Supp. 7**, 412, 811–12; **Supp. 8**, 53–55, 353, 444–45, 491, 492, 584–85; **Supp. 9**, 170–71, 885–86; **Supp. 10**, 130, 146, 424–25
Crittenden Compromise (1860), **Vol. 2, Part 1**, 9; **Vol. 2, Part 2**, 548; **Vol. 3, Part 1**, 403; **Vol. 6, Part 2**, 249; **Vol. 7, Part 2**, 420; **Vol. 8, Part 1**, 485; **Vol. 8, Part 2**, 618; **Vol. 10, Part 1**, 304
Crittenton Mission for Wayward Girls, **Vol. 1, Part 1**, 646
"Croaker & Co.," secret authorship of, **Vol. 3, Part 1**, 203
"Crocker, Betty" (fictional character), **Supp. 7**, 47; **Supp. 8**, 27
Crockett, David, reference to, **Vol. 2, Part 2**, 555 f.
"Croghan Hall" (Pittsburgh), **Vol. 2, Part 2**, 556
Croker, Richard, references to, **Vol. 5, Part 2**, 309; **Supp. 3**, 717; **Supp. 6**, 294
Croly, Herbert, reference to, **Supp. 7**, 310, 316
Cromwell, John, references to, **Supp. 9**, 538, 539
Cronin, Joe, reference to, **Supp. 10**, 15
Crop Improvement Bureau (Chicago), founding of, **Supp. 1**, 142
Crops, rotation of, **Vol. 1, Part 2**, 460; insect injuries, **Vol. 8, Part 1**, 609 f.
Crosby, Bing, references to, **Supp. 5**, 32–33; **Supp. 10**, 323
Crosby, Maunsell, reference to, **Supp. 6**, 255
Crosley Radio Corporation, founding of, **Supp. 7**, 154
Cross, Wilbur, reference to, **Supp. 7**, 103
Cross country. *See* Track and field, long-distance running
Crossfire, **Supp. 9**, 692; **Supp. 10**, 720
Cross Keys, Va., battle of, **Vol. 4, Part 1**, 23; **Vol. 5, Part 1**, 557–58
Crossley, Archibald M., reference to, **Supp. 5**, 311
Crossword puzzles, **Supp. 6**, 583
Crothers, Samuel McChord, reference to, **Vol. 6, Part 1**, 423
Croup, treatment of, **Vol. 1, Part 2**, 74
Crouse, Russel, reference to, **Supp. 8**, 383
Crow Indians, **Supp. 6**, 392–93
Crowe, Pat, reference to, **Supp. 8**, 109
Crowell-Collier Publishing Co.: **Supp. 5**, 394; acquisitions, **Supp. 9**, 264–65
Crowell Publishing Co., **Supp. 3**, 442–43
Crowley, Jim, references to, **Supp. 7**, 451, 729; **Supp. 9**, 485
Crown Cork & Seal Co., **Vol. 7, Part 2**, 168
Crowninshield, Frank, reference to, **Supp. 3**, 547; **Supp. 8**, 491
Crown Point, N.Y., operation at (1775–77), **Vol. 1, Part 1**, 257, 363–64; **Vol. 3, Part 2**, 185; **Vol. 8, Part 2**, 477–78; **Vol. 9, Part 1**, 531
Crown Zellerbach Corporation, organization of, **Supp. 7**, 814; **Supp. 10**, 868
Crowther, Bosley, reference to, **Supp. 9**, 540
Crozier, William, references to, **Supp. 8**, 502, 503
Crudhup, Arthur, reference to, **Supp. 10**, 648
Cruickshank, Bobby, reference to, **Supp. 8**, 14
Crump, Edward Hull ("Boss"), references to, **Supp. 6**, 419; **Supp. 7**, 415; **Supp. 9**, 769, 770
Cruse, Poncé, reference to, **Supp. 10**, 667
Cryptograms, **Vol. 3, Part 1**, 370; **Vol. 8, Part 1**, 19 f.
Cryptography, literary, **Supp. 5**, 20
Cryptology, **Supp. 8**, 195–96
Crystallography, **Supp. 3**, 38
Crystals, artificial, **Vol. 5, Part 2**, 487
Cry, the Beloved Country, **Supp. 5**, 419
CTR. See Computing-Tabulating-Recording Co.,
Cuba: **Vol. 4, Part 2**, 527; **Vol. 8, Part 1**, 315 f.; **Vol. 8, Part 2**, 511; **Vol. 9, Part 2**, 326; annexation of, **Vol. 2, Part 1**, 212 f.; **Vol. 3, Part 1**, 329; **Vol. 9, Part 1**, 406; Bay of Pigs, **Supp. 7**, 421–22, 723–24; **Supp. 8**, 135, 147; Civil administration following Spanish-American War, **Vol. 6, Part 2**, 201; conditions in, famous speech on, **Vol. 8, Part 1**, 245 f.; diplomatic relations with U.S., **Vol. 1, Part 1**, 485; **Vol. 3, Part 2**, 224; **Vol. 4, Part 2**, 513; **Vol. 6, Part 1**, 104; **Vol. 8, Part 1**, 2 f.; **Vol. 9, Part 1**, 491; **Vol. 10, Part 2**, 467 f.; **Supp. 1**, 89; **Supp. 6**, 451; explorations, **Vol. 7, Part 1**, 382 f.; filibustering expeditions, **Vol. 2, Part 1**, 96; **Vol. 4, Part 1**, 233; **Vol. 4, Part 2**, 527; **Vol. 9, Part 2**, 510; Guggenheim ambassadorship, **Supp. 9**, 348; independence of, **Vol. 4, Part 2**, 527, 543; **Vol. 9, Part 2**, 363; intervention in, **Vol. 3, Part 1**, 110; **Vol. 6, Part 2**, 108; **Vol. 8, Part 1**, 302 f.; insurrection, **Vol. 2, Part 2**, 211; **Vol. 3, Part 2**, 399; **Vol. 7, Part 2**, 154; Isle of Pines ceded to, **Vol. 8, Part 1**, 333; photographic study, **Supp. 9**, 268; Platt Amendment, **Vol. 6, Part 2**, 108; prisoner exhange with U.S., **Supp. 8**, 135; public relations, **Supp. 6**, 90; revolution (1959), **Supp. 7**, 116; soil conservation, **Supp. 6**, 52; Soviet missiles in, **Supp. 7**, 423, 724; **Supp. 8**, 323; **Supp. 9**, 106–7, 449–50, 799; Spanish-American War, **Vol. 1, Part 1**, 154, 180; **Vol. 2, Part 2**, 145; **Vol. 6, Part 1**, 377; **Vol. 6, Part 2**, 107; **Vol. 8, Part 2**, 136–37; **Vol. 9, Part 1**, 16; **Vol. 10, Part 2**, 467; sugar plantations, **Vol. 9, Part 2**, 338; trade, **Vol. 7, Part 1**, 336; **Vol. 9, Part 1**, 338, **Vol. 10, Part 1**, 424 f.; transportation systems, **Supp. 5**, 215; U.S. intervention in, **Supp. 7**, 777; U.S. presence in, **Supp. 2**, 579; **Supp. 6**, 206
Cuban Telephone Co., **Supp. 6**, 43

Cudahy, Edward, Sr., reference to, **Supp. 8**, 109
Cudahy Packing Co., **Supp. 8**, 109–10
Culbertson, Ely, references to, **Supp. 6**, 134–35, 380
Cullen, Countée, reference to, **Supp. 6**, 321; **Supp. 9**, 109
Cullen, Thomas S., reference to, **Supp. 3**, 106
Cullen Foundation, **Supp. 6**, 136
Cults, Peoples Temple, **Supp. 10**, 391–92
Cultural history. *See* Ethnology
Cultural relativity, **Supp. 4**, 71–72
Culture and Democracy in the United States, **Supp. 9**, 448
Cultures. *See* Anthropology; Ethnology; Sociology
Cumberland, command of, **Vol. 9, Part 1**, 310
Cumberland College, **Vol. 7, Part 2**, 591
"Cumberland Compact," **Vol. 8, Part 2**, 24 f.
Cumberland Gap, Tenn., capture of, **Vol. 7, Part 1**, 171
Cumberland Road, **Vol. 7, Part 1**, 90
Cumberland University, **Vol. 3, Part 1**, 368
Cummings, Homer S., references to, **Supp. 6**, 4, 156
Cummings Act (1896), **Supp. 3**, 276
Cummings and Lockwood, **Supp. 6**, 137
Cummins, Albert B., references to, **Supp. 3**, 107; **Supp. 6**, 256
Cumulative Book Index, **Supp. 5**, 752
Cuneiform, studies in, **Supp. 1**, 171, 261
Cuney, Norris, reference to, **Supp. 6**, 567
Cunow, John G., reference to, **Vol. 6, Part 1**, 421
Curators. For complete list, *see* Occupations Index
Curie, Marie, reference to, **Vol. 3, Part 1**, 511 f.
Curie, Pierre, reference to, **Vol. 3, Part 1**, 511 f.
Curley, James M.: gubernatorial campaign (1936), **Supp. 10**, 715; references to, **Supp. 5**, 692; **Supp. 8**, 219; **Supp. 9**, 210; **Supp. 10**, 486
Curran, Charles, reference to, **Supp. 10**, 856
Curran, Pearl Lenore Pollard, reference to, **Supp. 3**, 851
Currency: **Vol. 1, Part 1**, 510; **Vol. 3, Part 1**, 553 f.; **Vol. 3, Part 2**, 3, 188; **Vol. 5, Part 1**, 203; **Vol. 6, Part 1**, 273, 406; **Vol. 8, Part 1**, 49 f., 325 f.; **Vol. 8, Part 2**, 301; **Vol. 9, Part 1**, 89; Aldrich Plan v. Federal Reserve Act, **Vol. 4, Part 2**, 567; Bland-Allison Act, **Vol. 1, Part 2**, 355; coinage, free, **Vol. 1, Part 2**, 355; counterfeiting, **Vol. 3, Part 1**, 151, 273, 535 f.; designing and printing of first issue, **Vol. 8, Part 1**, 515; engraving of, **Vol. 2, Part 2**, 343; **Vol. 5, Part 2**, 456; Massachusetts experiments with, **Vol. 3, Part 1**, 106; minting of, **Vol. 1, Part 2**, 478; **Vol. 3, Part 1**, 254; **Vol. 5, Part 1**, 362; **Vol. 5, Part 2**, 456; **Vol. 6, Part 1**, 90, 273; **Vol. 8, Part 1**, 49 f., 450, 631; **Vol. 8, Part 2**, 100, 110, 400; **Vol. 9, Part 1**, 387; paper, **Vol. 1, Part 2**, 564; **Vol. 9, Part 2**, 84; paper money based on cotton, **Vol. 10, Part 1**, 451; publication of valuation of, **Vol. 9, Part 2**, 462; speculation in continental, **Vol. 3, Part 1**, 281 f. *See also* Coinage; Monetary system
Current Anthropology, founding of, **Supp. 7**, 241
Current Events, **Vol. 7, Part 1**, 377
Current History, **Supp. 6**, 410
Currier and Ives (lithographers), **Vol. 2, Part 2**, 604; **Vol. 5, Part 1**, 520
Curry, John Steuart, references to, **Supp. 3**, 841; **Supp. 9**, 79
Curtain manufacture, **Vol. 3, Part 2**, 279
Curtis, Charles, references to, **Supp. 3**, 106, 251; **Supp. 7**, 361
Curtis, Edward S., reference to, **Supp. 10**, 161
Curtis, George William, references to, **Vol. 7, Part 1**, 33, 569
Curtis, Heber D., reference to, **Supp. 9**, 713
Curtis, King, reference to, **Supp. 10**, 317
Curtis, Richard Cary, reference to, **Supp. 6**, 143
Curtis, S. R., reference to, **Vol. 7, Part 1**, 560
Curtis Institute, directors, **Supp. 6**, 297
Curtis Publishing Co., **Supp. 1**, 212–13; **Supp. 7**, 602
Curtiss, Glen, reference to, **Supp. 5**, 2
Curtiss Aeroplane and Motor Co., **Supp. 6**, 145
Curtiss-Wright Corporation: founding of, **Supp. 5**, 384–85; management, **Supp. 9**, 416–17; project-engineer system, **Supp. 8**, 709
Curtiz, Michael, reference to, **Supp. 10**, 813
Cushing, Caleb, reference to, **Vol. 5, Part 2**, 256
Cushing, Harvey, references to, **Supp. 3**, 201; **Supp. 4**, 208, 209, 213; **Supp. 6**, 70, 223, 224
Cushing's disease, studies of, **Supp. 2**, 139
Cushman, Charlotte, reference to, **Vol. 5, Part 1**, 242
Custer, George A., references to, **Vol. 8, Part 2**, 181; **Vol. 9, Part 1**, 192
Custer Hill, battle of, **Vol. 3, Part 1**, 8; **Vol. 9, Part 2**, 379
Custis, John Parker, reference to, **Vol. 1, Part 2**, 474
Custody, child, **Supp. 7**, 753
Customs Court, United States, **Supp. 6**, 114
Customs houses, architecture, **Supp. 1**, 716
Cutlery, manufacturing of, **Vol. 1, Part 1**, 248
Cutting, Bronson F., reference to, **Supp. 7**, 121
Cvetic, Matthew, reference to, **Supp. 6**, 681
CWA. See Civil Works Administration
Cyanamide, **Supp. 3**, 438–39
Cybernetics, **Supp. 3**, 137; **Supp. 7**, 785; **Supp. 10**, 28
Cycads, **Supp. 3**, 153–54
Cyclic adenosine monophosphate (AMP), discovery of, **Supp. 9**, 786
Cyclooctatetraene, **Supp. 8**, 103
Cyclopedia of Education, **Supp. 4**, 592
Cyclopropane, **Supp. 6**, 334
Cyclotron, **Supp. 5**, 273, 274; invention of, **Supp. 6**, 370–771
Cygnus A (galaxy), **Supp. 6**, 31
"Cy-près," doctrine of: **Vol. 10, Part 1**, 620
Cystoscope, **Supp. 3**, 854
Cytochemistry, term coined, **Supp. 6**, 295–96
Cytology, **Supp. 6**, 53–54; chromosome behavior, **Supp. 4**, 515–16
Cytosine, synthesis of, **Supp. 4**, 434
Czechoslovakia, diplomacy with U.S., **Supp. 4**, 773
Czolgosz, Leon, reference to, **Supp. 5**, 285, 286

D

Dabney, Virginius, reference to, **Supp. 3**, 115
Dacron, **Supp. 5**, 191
Dadaism, **Supp. 5**, 20; **Supp. 6**, 256
Daddario, Emilio, reference to, **Supp. 9**, 59
Daddy Long Legs, **Supp. 10**, 635
Daguerreotype, **Vol. 1, Part 2**, 529; **Vol. 7, Part 1**, 280 f.; **Vol. 8, Part 2**, 174, 362; **Vol. 9, Part 1**, 514
Dahl, Francis, reference to, **Supp. 8**, 448
Dahl, Nikolai, reference to, **Supp. 3**, 616
Dahlberg, Mae, reference to, **Supp. 7**, 462
Dahl-Wolfe, Louise, reference to, **Supp. 5**, 200
Daily Chicago Herald, **Vol. 2, Part 2**, 374
Daily Chronicle, Minneapolis, **Vol. 2, Part 2**, 367
"Daily dozen" exercises, origin of, **Vol. 2, Part 1**, 445
Daily Evening Bulletin, San Francisco, **Vol. 5, Part 2**, 408
Daily Graphic, first illustrated daily paper in U.S., **Vol. 8, Part 1**, 332 f.
Daily News. *See* New York *Daily News*
Daily News Building, architecture, **Supp. 1**, 430
Daily Pioneer Press, St. Paul, **Vol. 10, Part 2**, 60
Daily Racing Form, **Supp. 3**, 20
Daily Southern Carolinian, **Vol. 3, Part 1**, 196

Daily Times, Louisville, first newspaper of its kind west of Alleghenies, **Vol. 9, Part 2**, 607
Daily Worker: **Supp. 7**, 113, 256; columnists, **Supp. 8**, 216, 217; **Supp. 10**, 436; editing of, **Supp. 5**, 499–500; Harlem editor, **Supp. 6**, 715
Dairy, farming, **Vol. 1, Part 1**, 238, 370; **Vol. 8, Part 2**, 512; **Vol. 9, Part 1**, 280; **Supp. 1**, 37, 444; herd improvement, **Supp. 3**, 750; school, first in U.S., **Vol. 9, Part 1**, 280; promotion, Wisconsin, **Vol. 5, Part 1**, 90. *See also* Milk
Dairy industry: cheese processing, **Supp. 5**, 399–400; chemistry of production, **Supp. 5**, 275–76. *See also* Milk
Dairymen's Associations of the West, **Vol. 5, Part 1**, 90
Dakin, Henry B., reference to, **Supp. 3**, 141
Dakota language, readers in the, **Vol. 8, Part 1**, 61 f., 605
Dakota Playhouse, **Supp. 3**, 426
Dakota Territory: division of, **Vol. 7, Part 2**, 517; governorship of, **Vol. 3, Part 2**, 297; **Vol. 5, Part 1**, 283; **Vol. 7, Part 2**, 581; surveying of, **Vol. 1, Part 2**, 86
Dakota Ruralist, **Vol. 6, Part 1**, 426
Dale, Chester, references to, **Supp. 5**, 150, 151
Dale, Henry H., references to, **Supp. 3**, 134, 136, 137
Dale, Maud, reference to, **Supp. 7**, 161
Dale, Sir Thomas, reference to, **Vol. 7, Part 1**, 468
Daley, Richard, references to, **Supp. 8**, 121; **Supp. 9**, 740, 881; **Supp. 10**, 10, 11, 411
Daley, Richard M. (son), reference to, **Supp. 10**, 169
Dalhousie University, **Vol. 7, Part 1**, 332
Dallas-Clarendon Treaty, **Vol. 3, Part 1**, 39; **Vol. 7, Part 2**, 579
Dallas Cowboys (football), founding of, **Supp. 10**, 568
Dallas Morning News, **Supp. 4**, 222
Dallas News, **Vol. 1, Part 2**, 171
Dallas *Times-Herald*, **Supp. 7**, 434
Dalton, Ga., operation at (1863–64), **Vol. 1, Part 2**, 487; **Vol. 4, Part 2**, 240; **Vol. 5, Part 1**, 193; **Vol. 9, Part 1**, 95; **Vol. 9, Part 2**, 3
Daly, Augustin, references to, **Vol. 5, Part 1**, 586, 605; **Vol. 8, Part 1**, 471 f.
Daly, Marcus, reference to, **Vol. 2, Part 2**, 145
Daly, Maurice, reference to, **Supp. 6**, 303
Daly, William M., reference to, **Supp. 8**, 465
Damaged Goods, **Supp. 3**, 58
Damone, Vic, reference to, **Supp. 9**, 35
Damrosch, Clara, reference to, **Supp. 6**, 426
Damrosch, Frank, reference to, **Supp. 3**, 309
Damrosch, Leopold, references to, **Vol. 8, Part 2**, 562; **Supp. 4**, 210, 213, 544, 545
Damrosch, Walter, references to, **Supp. 3**, 33, 742; **Supp. 5**, 646; **Supp. 6**, 20, 426; **Supp. 9**, 804
Damrosch Opera Company, founding of, **Supp. 4**, 210–11
Damrosch Park (New York City), **Supp. 4**, 213
Dams: collapse, **Supp. 1**, 570; design and construction of, **Vol. 2, Part 2**, 570; **Vol. 8, Part 1**, 359 f.; **Vol. 8, Part 2**, 474; **Supp. 1**, 225, 393, 700; **Supp. 2**, 304–5; **Supp. 3**, 814; **Supp. 4**, 198–99; **Supp. 6**, 182; **Supp. 8**, 572–73; federal, **Supp. 2**, 119; **Supp. 3**, 397; flood control, **Supp. 9**, 561; geological determination of sites, **Supp. 4**, 119; Hetch Hetchy Valley, **Supp. 4**, 522. *See also* Tennessee Valley Authority
Dana, Charles A., references to, **Vol. 2, Part 1**, 99; **Vol. 5, Part 1**, 65; **Vol. 7, Part 1**, 44; **Supp. 1**, 509–10
Dana, Charles R., reference to, **Supp. 5**, 301
Dana, Henry W. L., references to, **Supp. 4**, 62, 135
Dana, John Cotton, references to, **Supp. 3**, 30; **Supp. 6**, 96
Dana, R. H., reference to, **Vol. 7, Part 1**, 107
Dana Foundation, founding of, **Supp. 9**, 217
Danbury, Conn.: *Danbury News Man*, **Vol. 1, Part 1**, 499; "Sandemanians," Scotch religious sect, **Vol. 8, Part 2**, 329; writings on, **Vol. 1, Part 1**, 499
Dance: ballet, **Vol. 4, Part 1**, 59 f.; **Supp. 5**, 74–76; **Supp. 8**, 669–70; **Supp. 9**, 418, 494; **Supp. 10**, 207; ballet companies, **Supp. 7**, 173–74; **Supp. 10**, 206–7; ballet scores, **Supp. 8**, 145, 146; **Supp. 9**, 775–76; ballet sets and costumes, **Supp. 6**, 625; ballroom, **Vol. 2, Part 1**, 569; **Supp. 7**, 563; **Supp. 8**, 77–78, 690; black bottom, **Supp. 8**, 694, 695; burlesque, **Supp. 8**, 694; cakewalk, **Supp. 3**, 187; Charleston, **Supp. 8**, 695; choreography, **Supp. 6**, 312–13; **Supp. 9**, 494, 495, 717; **Supp. 10**, 113–14, 802; companies, **Supp. 9**, 494, 495, 716; creative art, as a, **Vol. 3, Part 1**, 508 f.; ethnic, **Supp. 9**, 717; fan, **Supp. 10**, 657; first chorus line, **Supp. 6**, 305; "Hootchy Kootchy," **Supp. 4**, 88; modern, **Supp. 5**, 129; **Supp. 6**, 312–13; **Supp. 8**, 620–21, 643–44; **Supp. 9**, 494, 495; modern ballet choreography, **Supp. 3**, 281–82; modern, teaching of, **Supp. 7**, 366–67; "moonwalk" step invented, **Supp. 10**, 20; musical revues, **Supp. 8**, 694–95; **Supp. 10**, 300; photographs, **Supp. 3**, 296; set designs, **Supp. 7**, 560; shimmy popularization, **Supp. 6**, 247; tap, **Supp. 4**, 695; **Supp. 10**, 19–20; teaching of, **Vol. 4, Part 1**, 60; **Supp. 9**, 716, 717; **Supp. 10**, 207; theatrical musicals and revues, **Supp. 7**, 34, 497, 563; **Supp. 10**, 33, 113–14, 802; turkey trot, **Supp. 8**, 694, 695; waltz clog, **Supp. 7**, 657–58; writings on, **Vol. 4, Part 1**, 60
Dance bands, **Supp. 3**, 524–25; **Supp. 5**, 187–88; **Supp. 7**, 300–1, 774; **Supp. 8**, 697–98. *See also* Swing bands
Dance Girl, Dance, **Supp. 10**, 12
Dance Observer, founding of, **Supp. 7**, 367
Dance Repertory Theatre, **Supp. 6**, 312; **Supp. 8**, 643
Dancing Rabbit Creek, Treaty of (1830), **Vol. 6, Part 2**, 82
Daniels, Josephus, references to, **Supp. 3**, 275, 642, 643; **Supp. 5**, 332
Danielson, Jacques, reference to, **Supp. 8**, 296
Dannay, Frederic, references to, **Supp. 9**, 487, 488
Dante, translations and studies of, **Vol. 3, Part 1**, 72; **Vol. 3, Part 2**, 303; **Vol. 6, Part 1**, 383; **Vol. 7, Part 1**, 570; **Vol. 7, Part 2**, 274 f.; **Supp. 2**, 254; **Supp. 5**, 19, 20
Danville, Ky., political club at (1789), **Vol. 5, Part 1**, 486; **Vol. 8, Part 2**, 543
DAR. *See* Daughters of the American Revolution
Darboux, Gaston, reference to, **Supp. 7**, 216
Dargan, E. Preston, reference to, **Supp. 3**, 22
Dark at the Top of the Stairs, The, **Supp. 9**, 422
"Dark Continent," first use of name, **Vol. 9, Part 1**, 511
"Dark horse," use of term, in politics, **Vol. 8, Part 1**, 34 f.
Darlan, François, reference to, **Supp. 8**, 274–75
Darling, Jay Norwood ("Ding"), reference to, **Supp. 10**, 264–65
Darling Nelly Gray, **Vol. 4, Part 2**, 217
Darmstädter und Nationalbank (Danatbank), founding of, **Supp. 5**, 249–50
Darrow, Clarence: references to, **Vol. 8, Part 1**, 9 f.; **Supp. 3**, 156, 822; **Supp. 4**, 542; **Supp. 6**, 528, 529; **Supp. 7**, 624, 631; **Supp. 8**, 583, 660; **Supp. 9**, 490, 749; Scopes trial, **Supp. 9**, 769
Dartmouth College: **Vol. 1, Part 1**, 56, 126; **Vol. 3, Part 1**, 180; **Vol. 4, Part 1**, 304; **Vol. 5, Part 1**, 166; **Vol. 7, Part 2**, 301, 303, 478; **Vol. 8, Part 2**, 325; **Vol. 10, Part 1**, 585 f., 656; **Vol. 10, Part 2**, 59, 81; architectural studies, **Supp. 3**, 52–53; engineering school, **Supp. 2**, 195; gifts to, **Supp. 6**, 549; French department, **Supp. 9**, 349; graduates, sketches of early, **Vol. 3, Part 2**, 278; "Laureate" of, **Vol. 5, Part 1**, 273; master plan, **Supp. 2**, 539; medical school,

founding of, **Vol. 9, Part 1**, 324; presidency of, **Vol. 1, Part 2**, 15; **Vol. 2, Part 1**, 114; **Vol. 6, Part 1**, 409; **Vol. 7, Part 1**, 493; **Vol. 9, Part 1**, 239; **Vol. 10, Part 1**, 41, 85
Darwin, Charles, references to, **Vol. 1, Part 1**, 112, 120; **Vol. 4, Part 1**, 513; **Vol. 8, Part 1**, 624; **Vol. 10, Part 1**, 644 f.; **Supp. 3**, 697, 704; **Supp. 4**, 691; **Supp. 9**, 239
Darwinism. *See* Evolutionism
Dashiell, Alfred Sheppard, reference to, **Supp. 5**, 614
Daugherty, Harry M., references to, **Supp. 3**, 117, 489; **Supp. 9**, 859
Daughter of Earth, **Supp. 4**, 749, 750
Daughters of the American Revolution (DAR): Constitution Hall, **Supp. 5**, 300, 343; **Supp. 8**, 328; founding of, **Vol. 3, Part 1**, 76
Daughters of the United States of the War of 1812, founding of, **Vol. 3, Part 1**, 76
Davenport, Charles B., references to, **Supp. 3**, 133, 477–78; **Supp. 6**, 241
Davenport, Frances G., reference to, **Supp. 3**, 16
Davenport, James, reference to, **Vol. 7, Part 1**, 614
Davenport, John, reference to, **Vol. 5, Part 1**, 200
Davenport, Russell, reference to, **Supp. 8**, 394
Davenport, Iowa, founding of, **Vol. 3, Part 1**, 83
David, Donald K., reference to, **Supp. 7**, 276
David Harum, writing of, **Vol. 10, Part 2**, 13
Davidson, Donald, reference to, **Supp. 9**, 642
Davidson, Thomas, reference to, **Supp. 4**, 168
Davies, A. Powell, reference to, **Supp. 4**, 712
Davies, Arthur B., references to, **Supp. 3**, 278, 340; **Supp. 5**, 635
Davies, John Paton, references to, **Supp. 6**, 230, 231; **Supp. 9**, 831; **Supp. 10**, 801
Davies, Joseph E., reference to, **Supp. 6**, 184
Davies, Marion, references to, **Supp. 5**, 286–88; **Supp. 6**, 440; **Supp. 7**, 759
Davis, Arthur Powell, references to, **Supp. 3**, 813–14, 845–46
Davis, Arthur V., reference to, **Supp. 5**, 565–66
Davis, Benjamin O., Jr., reference to, **Supp. 10**, 379
Davis, Bergen, reference to, **Supp. 7**, 10
Davis, Bernard G., reference to, **Supp. 5**, 760
Davis, Bette: feud with Joan Crawford, **Supp. 10**, 158; references to, **Supp. 7**, 591; **Supp. 9**, 409
Davis, Chester C., references to, **Supp. 6**, 638, 639
Davis, Donald, reference to, **Supp. 6**, 149
Davis, Dwight F., reference to, **Supp. 3**, 152
Davis, Glenn R., reference to, **Supp. 8**, 701
Davis, Harry Phillips, reference to, **Supp. 3**, 184–85
Davis, James J., reference to, **Supp. 7**, 305
Davis, Jefferson: **Vol. 1, Part 1**, 523; **Vol. 1, Part 2**, 82 f.; **Vol. 3, Part 2**, 483; **Vol. 5, Part 1**, 176, 183, 193, 404; **Vol. 5, Part 2**, 210; **Vol. 6, Part 1**, 106, 122, 481, 522, 581; **Vol. 7, Part 1**, 375, 567 f., 620; **Vol. 8, Part 2**, 545; **Vol. 9, Part 1**, 130, 573; **Vol. 9, Part 2**, 351 f.; amanuensis for, **Vol. 3, Part 1**, 386; biography of, **Vol. 8, Part 2**, 420; **Supp. 6**, 410; capture of, **Vol. 7, Part 1**, 33; trial of, **Vol. 8, Part 2**, 290; **Vol. 10, Part 1**, 114
Davis, Jefferson Columbus, reference to, **Vol. 7, Part 1**, 426
Davis, John W., references to, **Supp. 3**, 114, 481, 606, 644
Davis, Mildred, reference to, **Supp. 9**, 509
Davis, Miles, references to, **Supp. 8**, 100; **Supp. 9**, 11; **Supp. 10**, 225
Davis, Mrs. Jefferson, references to, **Vol. 5, Part 1**, 85; **Supp. 10**, 842
Davis, Owen, reference to, **Supp. 9**, 70
Davis, Richard Harding, references to, **Supp. 3**, 300–301; **Supp. 6**, 253
Davis, Varina Howell. *See* Davis, Mrs. Jefferson
Davis, William Morris, references to, **Supp. 3**, 389–90; **Supp. 4**, 98, 423–24, 765, 766; **Supp. 9**, 525
Davis-Bacon Act (1930), **Supp. 4**, 220
Davis, Hoxie, Faithfull and Hapgood, founding of, **Supp. 7**, 172
Davis Publications, founding of, **Supp. 9**, 223
Davison, Henry P., references to, **Supp. 4**, 469; **Supp. 6**, 27
Davisson, Clinton J., references to, **Supp. 9**, 303, 304
Davy Crockett (drama), **Vol. 7, Part 1**, 340
Dawes, Charles, reference to, **Supp. 7**, 809
Dawes Act (1887), status of Indians under, **Vol. 8, Part 1**, 335 f.
Dawes Plan (1924), **Supp. 2**, 356; **Supp. 6**, 177–78; **Supp. 7**, 809–10
Day, Arthur L., reference to, **Supp. 6**, 70
Day, Clarence, references to, **Supp. 6**, 154, 155; **Supp. 8**, 383
Day, Dennis, reference to, **Supp. 9**, 76
Day, Dorothy, reference to, **Supp. 4**, 562
Day, Edmund Ezra, reference to, **Supp. 6**, 599
Day, William A., reference to, **Supp. 6**, 497
Day-Lewis, Cecil, reference to, **Supp. 9**, 53
Day, The, **Supp. 1**, 78
Daylight saving time, first laws concerning, **Vol. 9, Part 2**, 477
Day Missions Library (New Haven, Conn.), **Supp. 1**, 63
Day the Earth Stood Still, The, **Supp. 9**, 647
Dayton, Ohio, naming of, **Vol. 3, Part 1**, 166
Dayton *Daily News*, **Supp. 6**, 129
Dayton "Empire," **Vol. 10, Part 1**, 143
Dayton Engineering Laboratories Co. (Delco), **Supp. 3**, 520–23; **Supp. 6**, 332
Dayton Metal Products Co., **Supp. 6**, 617
Daytona Normal and Industrial Institute, founding of, **Supp. 5**, 55
"Day with the Cow" column, **Vol. 1, Part 1**, 326
DDT, **Supp. 7**, 109
De Abatino, Pepito, reference to, **Supp. 9**, 60
Dead End, **Supp. 10**, 24
"Dead End Kids" (fictional characters), **Supp. 8**, 220–21
Dead Sea Scrolls, **Supp. 7**, 624; **Supp. 9**, 16
Deadwood, S. D., engagement near (1890), **Vol. 6, Part 2**, 615
Deaf and deafness: education for the deaf, **Vol. 1, Part 2**, 139, 149 f.; **Vol. 2, Part 1**, 38; **Vol. 2, Part 2**, 131, 150 f., 201 f., 574; **Vol. 3, Part 2**, 303; **Vol. 4, Part 1**, 110 f., 543; **Vol. 5, Part 1**, 325; **Vol. 7, Part 1**, 528; **Vol. 7, Part 2**, 391 f.; **Vol. 8, Part 1**, 102 f.; **Vol. 8, Part 2**, 93 f.; **Vol. 9, Part 2**, 324 f.; **Vol. 10, Part 2**, 590; education in speaking, **Supp. 3**, 311–12; **Supp. 8**, 316–17; hearing aids, **Supp. 8**, 209; philanthropies, **Vol. 4, Part 1**, 543; physical causes of, first survey concerning, **Vol. 8, Part 1**, 565; research, **Supp. 9**, 72; writings on, **Vol. 4, Part 1**, 111, 543
Dean, Francis Winthrop, reference to, **Supp. 3**, 500
Dean, James, reference to, **Supp. 9**, 35
Dean, Jay Hanna ("Dizzy"), references to, **Supp. 9**, 368, 369
Dean, Paul Dee ("Daffy"), references to, **Supp. 9**, 223, 224
Deane, Silas, references to, **Vol. 5, Part 2**, 253; **Vol. 6, Part 1**, 120, 439; **Vol. 7, Part 1**, 220 f.
Dearborn, Michigan, **Supp. 4**, 291–92, 300, 302, 303
Dearborn Independent, editorial on anti-Semitism, **Supp. 4**, 299
Dearborn Observatory, **Vol. 5, Part 1**, 252
"Death, I have a rendezvous with," **Vol. 8, Part 2**, 555
Death at the stake, **Vol. 7, Part 1**, 379

Death in the Family, A, **Supp. 5**, 11, 12, 13
Death of a President, The, **Supp. 8**, 224; **Supp. 10**, 462
Death of a Salesman, **Supp. 10**, 131–32, 535
Debating: in public schools, **Vol. 5, Part 2**, 523; writings on, **Vol. 3, Part 2**, 93
De Beers Co., **Supp. 10**, 847–48
De Bois, W. E. B., reference to, **Supp. 9**, 749–50
De Bow's Review, part played by, in bringing on Civil War, **Vol. 3, Part 1**, 181
Debs, Eugene V., references to, **Vol. 4, Part 2**, 21; **Vol. 9, Part 2**, 267; **Supp. 3**, 347; **Supp. 4**, 733; **Supp. 5**, 69–70; **Supp. 7**, 455
Debts: imprisonment for, **Vol. 3, Part 1**, 599; **Vol. 5, Part 2**, 460; **Vol. 6, Part 1**, 211, 568; **Vol. 9, Part 2**, 30, 491; Shays's Rebellion, **Vol. 9, Part 1**, 50; state, Hamilton's attitude on, **Vol. 4, Part 2**, 175; staylaw for relief of debtors, **Vol. 3, Part 1**, 599 f.; Stilwell Act (1831), **Vol. 9, Part 2**, 30
Debussy, Claude, references to, **Supp. 8**, 200–1; **Supp. 9**, 775, 776
Debye, Peter, references to, **Supp. 7**, 133, 411; **Supp. 10**, 608
Decatur, Stephen, references to, **Vol. 5, Part 1**, 115; **Vol. 9, Part 2**, 310
Decca Records, **Supp. 6**, 301; **Supp. 10**, 463
Decimal system, **Vol. 8, Part 1**, 631; **Vol. 8, Part 2**, 145
"Decius" letters, **Vol. 8, Part 1**, 363 f.
Decker, Howell and Co., **Supp. 4**, 193
Declaration of Independence: **Vol. 6, Part 1**, 119; **Vol. 7, Part 1**, 220, 485; **Vol. 9, Part 1**, 89; **Vol. 10, Part 2**, 294; Jefferson and, **Vol. 3, Part 1**, 514 f.; **Vol. 5, Part 2**, 19; **Vol. 10, Part 2**, 437; New York, attitude of, **Vol. 6, Part 1**, 321; political import of, **Vol. 8, Part 2**, 257; ratifying of, **Vol. 5, Part 2**, 6; reading of, **Vol. 7, Part 1**, 531; signers of, *see* Occupations Index for complete list
"Declaration of the Causes of Taking Up Arms," drafting of, **Vol. 3, Part 1**, 300
Decline of American Capitalism, The, **Supp. 5**, 135
Declos, Jacques, reference to, **Supp. 7**, 256
Dedham, Mass., settling of, **Vol. 3, Part 1**, 578
Dee, Sandra, reference to, **Supp. 9**, 219
"Deep Purple" (song), **Supp. 5**, 167
Deep-sea exploration, **Vol. 2, Part 1**, 70; **Vol. 8, Part 1**, 141 f.
Deerfield massacre, **Vol. 10, Part 2**, 270
Deering, Milliken, and Co., **Supp. 7**, 529
Deerslayer, The, **Vol. 2, Part 2**, 404
Defender, **Supp. 6**, 490
"Defender of the Faith," Mormon, **Vol. 8, Part 2**, 4
Defense. *See* Armed forces and defense; Nuclear weapons; *specific branches of service*
Defense, Department of (U.S.): administration, **Supp. 4**, 306; **Supp. 6**, 431–32; **Supp. 7**, 794; **Supp. 8**, 57–58; **Supp. 10**, 72; administration controversy, **Supp. 8**, 303; first secretary of, **Supp. 4**, 306; "missile gap" issue, **Supp. 9**, 522; press relations, **Supp. 5**, 197
Defense, The, **Supp. 10**, 581
Defense contracts. *See* Armed forces and defense; *war names*
De Forest, Lee, references to, **Supp. 5**, 21, 22; **Supp. 6**, 298
De Forest, Robert W., reference to, **Supp. 6**, 26
De Franco, Buddy, reference to, **Supp. 3**, 525
De Galindez, Jésus, reference to, **Supp. 10**, 222
De Gaulle, Charles, references to, **Supp. 3**, 662, 663; **Supp. 5**, 334
De Graff, Robert Fair, reference to, **Supp. 8**, 579
De Gaulle, Charles, references to, **Supp. 9**, 107; **Supp. 10**, 63
De Haas, Jacob, reference to, **Supp. 3**, 96
Deism, **Vol. 7, Part 1**, 414 f.; **Vol. 7, Part 2**, 178
De la Beckwith, Byron, reference to, **Supp. 7**, 227
De la Renta, Oscar, reference to, **Supp. 8**, 14
De Lamar, Joseph R., reference to, **Supp. 6**, 316
Delaunay, Robert, reference to, **Supp. 6**, 199
Delaware: boundaries, determination of, **Vol. 1, Part 2**, 460; **Vol. 5, Part 2**, 42, 76; Civil War period, **Vol. 2, Part 1**, 345, 478; Constitution, first state to accept, **Vol. 1, Part 2**, 39; **Vol. 8, Part 1**, 423; Constitutional Convention, **Vol. 1, Part 2**, 66; **Vol. 8, Part 1**, 422 f.; education, **Vol. 8, Part 1**, 268 f.; governors, **Vol. 2, Part 1**, 190 f., 345 f., 478 f.; **Vol. 2, Part 2**, 186 f.; **Vol. 7, Part 1**, 59; **Vol. 8, Part 2**, 378 f.; history of, **Vol. 3, Part 1**, 265; **Vol. 6, Part 2**, 109; **Vol. 8, Part 1**, 422 f.; industrial growth, **Vol. 3, Part 1**, 526 f.; legal service, **Vol. 1, Part 2**, 70, 555; **Vol. 4, Part 2**, 146, 302; **Vol. 5, Part 2**, 76; **Vol. 8, Part 1**, 422, 597; **Vol. 8, Part 2**, 81, 83 f.; political service, **Vol. 1, Part 2**, 39, 47, 50, 64, 69, 122, 190, 555; **Vol. 2, Part 2**, 188; **Vol. 3, Part 1**, 180, 300, 303, 528; **Vol. 5, Part 2**, 292; **Vol. 6, Part 2**, 79; **Vol. 7, Part l**, 59; **Vol. 8, Part 1**, 422, 597; **Vol. 8, Part 2**, 81 f., 83 f., 378; **Vol. 9, Part 2**, 431; **Vol. 10, Part 2**, 115; politics, **Supp. 8**, 246–47; Republican party, organizing of, **Vol. 1, Part 2**, 555; Revolutionary War period, **Vol. 1, Part 2**, 191; **Vol. 6, Part 2**, 79; **Vol. 8, Part 2**, 81 f.; road construction, **Supp. 1**, 272; statutes, codifying of, **Vol. 1, Part 2**, 47; Swedish colonists, **Vol. 4, Part 2**, 25; **Vol. 7, Part 1**, 34; **Vol. 8, Part 1**, 627
Delaware & Hudson Canal Co., **Vol. 3, Part 1**, 306 f.; **Vol. 5, Part 2**, 59; **Vol. 7, Part 2**, 35
Delaware Chemical Engineering Co., **Supp. 3**, 239
Delaware College, **Vol. 1, Part 1**, 181; **Vol. 5, Part 2**, 436; **Vol. 8, Part 1**, 268 f.
Delaware Indians, **Vol. 9, Part 2**, 360 f., 431
Delaware, Lackawanna & Western Railroad, **Vol. 1, Part 2**, 338; **Vol. 9, Part 1**, 213; **Vol. 9, Part 2**, 338
Delaware, Lehigh, Schuylkill & Susquehanna Railroad, **Vol. 8, Part 1**, 94 f.
Delaware River Bridge, **Supp. 3**, 531; **Supp. 7**, 135
Delaware, Wilmington & Baltimore Railroad, development of, **Vol. 4, Part 2**, 302
De Leon, Daniel, references to, **Supp. 3**, 297–98, 346, 347
Delbrck, Max, reference to, **Supp. 3**, 540
Delco. *See* Dayton Engineering Laboratories Co.
Delhi Oil Corporation, founding of, **Supp. 8**, 454–55
Delineator, **Supp. 7**, 320
Delirium tremens, early study of, **Vol. 10, Part 1**, 449 f.
Dell, Floyd, references to, **Supp. 7**, 309; **Supp. 9**, 33
De Long, George Washington, Arctic expedition, **Vol. 1, Part 2**, 200
Delta Air Lines, founding of, **Supp. 8**, 707–8
Deluge Geology Society, founding of, **Supp. 7**, 631
Dembitz, Lewis, reference to, **Supp. 3**, 94
Demerec, Milislav, reference to, **Supp. 4**, 253
DeMille, Agnes, reference to, **Supp. 5**, 75–76
DeMille, Cecil B.: first film directed, **Supp. 9**, 323; references to, **Supp. 6**, 159, 368–69; **Supp. 7**, 143; **Supp. 9**, 819; **Supp. 10**, 347, 348, 657, 872
Democracy: theory of defense of, **Supp. 5**, 485–86; writings on, **Supp. 7**, 702
Democracy and Education, **Supp. 5**, 172
Democratic party (general): **Vol. 1, Part 1**, 204, 329, 566, 648; **Vol. 1, Part 2**, 170; **Vol. 2, Part 1**, 192 f., 208 f.; **Vol. 3, Part 1**, 402 f.; **Vol. 3, Part 2**, 193, 439, 476; **Vol. 4, Part 1**, 61, 174, 289, 435, 540, 549; **Vol. 4, Part 2**, 14; **Vol. 5, Part 1**, 533; **Vol. 5, Part 2**, 552; **Vol. 7, Part 2**, 60, 577; **Vol. 8, Part 2**, 98, 570; **Vol. 9, Part 1**, 8, 72, 102, 199, 217, 281, 499; **Vol. 9, Part 2**, 88; Advisory Council, **Supp. 7**, 636, 723; blacks in,

Supp. 6, 260; **Supp. 7**, 767; **Supp. 9**, 152; Dixiecrat ranks depleted in, **Supp. 10**, 4; donkey symbol, invented by Nast, **Vol. 7, Part 1**, 392; Equal Rights Amendment first supported, **Supp. 9**, 546; finances, **Supp. 6**, 324; first Democratic governor of Maine, **Vol. 4, Part 1**, 131; first success in North Dakota, **Supp. 6**, 87; fund-raising, **Supp. 5**, 242; **Supp. 9**, 547; Illinois delegation refused seats at National Convention (1972), **Supp. 10**, 169; Jacksonian Democrats, **Vol. 3, Part 1**, 600 f.; **Vol. 5, Part 2**, 82; labor relations, **Supp. 8**, 527; **Supp. 10**, 643, 644, 697; leadership, **Supp. 6**, 34–36; **Supp. 7**, 634–37, 662; liberal wing, **Supp. 10**, 315, 316, 326, 470, 486, 530; loyalty oath, **Supp. 9**, 68; national chairmen, **Supp. 9**, 530, 551; **Supp. 10**, 233; National Committee, **Supp. 4**, 216, 356, 682–83; **Supp. 5**, 62, 227, 331; **Supp. 6**, 137, 388, 660, 661; **Supp. 7**, 428, 467, 590; **Supp. 8**, 121, 405–6, 592; **Supp. 9**, 58–59, 440, 530; **Supp. 10**, 605, 703–4; National Committee, social service bureau, **Supp. 2**, 690; National Committee, treasurer, **Supp. 8**, 112; National Committee, women's division, **Supp. 8**, 244; National Convention (1932), **Supp. 10**, 233; National Convention (1940), **Supp. 10**, 234; National Convention (1944), **Supp. 9**, 546; **Supp. 10**, 234; National Convention (1948), **Supp. 10**, 360; National Convention (1964), **Supp. 10**, 307; National Convention (1968), **Supp. 10**, 168, 307, 362; National Convention (1972), **Supp. 10**, 169; National Convention parliamentarian, **Supp. 7**, 105; newspaper, first in West, **Vol. 3, Part 2**, 231; New York City, **Supp. 6**, 294–95; nomination policy, **Supp. 5**, 114; orators, **Supp. 6**, 72; pioneer, **Vol. 9, Part 1**, 203; publicist for, **Supp. 4**, 575; states' rights and, **Vol. 4, Part 1**, 427; women in, **Supp. 10**, 29, 183–84. *See also* Democratic party (by state); New Deal; *presidential election headings*

Democratic party (by state): Alabama, **Supp. 3**, 729–30; **Supp. 5**, 290–91; **Supp. 8**, 676–77; Alaska, **Supp. 8**, 25–26; Arizona, **Supp. 7**, 21–22; California, **Supp. 7**, 224–25; Colorado, **Supp. 8**, 300–301; Connecticut, **Supp. 4**, 197; **Supp. 5**, 455–56; **Supp. 9**, 57–58; Florida, **Supp. 5**, 582; Georgia, **Supp. 4**, 813–14; **Supp. 5**, 139; **Supp. 8**, 703; Idaho, **Supp. 8**, 508; Illinois, **Vol. 3, Part 1**, 398 f.; **Supp. 4**, 450–51; **Supp. 5**, 274–75, 598; **Supp. 7**, 702, 721–22; **Supp. 8**, 121, 391–92; **Supp. 10**, 9–11, 167, 168, 169, 185, 186, 411; Indiana, **Vol. 6, Part 2**, 18, **Supp. 5**, 459; **Supp. 7**, 541; **Supp. 8**, 699; **Supp. 9**, 529; Iowa, **Supp. 7**, 527; **Supp. 9**, 312; Kansas, **Supp. 8**, 591–92, 706; Kentucky, **Supp. 5**, 712; **Supp. 8**, 615–16; Louisiana, **Supp. 7**, 78–79, 555; **Supp. 9**, 533–34; **Supp. 10**, 325; Maine, **Vol. 4, Part 1**, 131; Maryland, **Supp. 5**, 248; **Supp. 7**, 750–51; **Supp. 9**, 633–34; Massachusetts, **Supp. 3**, 740; **Supp. 4**, 277–7, 58–59; **Supp. 5**, 692; **Supp. 6**, 139–41; **Supp. 7**, 419; **Supp. 10**, 484, 486; Michigan, **Supp. 10**, 109, 315; Minnesota, **Supp. 3**, 227; **Supp. 10**, 359, 360; Mississippi, **Vol. 2, Part 1**, 101; **Supp. 3**, 334–35; **Supp. 4**, 78–79; **Supp. 6**, 710–11; **Supp. 10**, 307; Missouri, **Supp. 3**, 596–97; 621–23; **Supp. 4**, 355–6; **Supp. 9**, 756–57, 809–11; Montana, **Supp. 7**, 561–62; Nebraska, **Supp. 3**, 114; **Supp. 5**, 318–19, 479–80; New Jersey, **Vol. 9, Part 1**, 285 f.; **Supp. 5**, 696; **Supp. 6**, 265–66, 479–80; **Supp. 8**, 152–53; **Supp. 9**, 263; New Mexico, **Supp. 7**, 121–22, 326; **Supp. 10**, 549; New York, **Supp. 3**, 641–46, 717–21, 751; **Supp. 4**, 88, 512, 542, 607–8, 855–56; **Supp. 5**, 227–28, 242, 285–86, 357, 717–19; **Supp. 7**, 467, 521, 585–86, 659–60; **Supp. 8**, 323; **Supp. 10**, 232–33, 234, 453; North Carolina, **Supp. 4**, 42–43, 216, 315–16; **Supp. 5**, 306–7; **Supp. 7**, 644; **Supp. 9**, 190–91, 440; **Supp. 10**, 814–15; North Dakota, **Supp. 6**, 87; Ohio, **Vol. 1, Part 1**, 210; Oklahoma, **Supp. 5**, 662; **Supp. 7**, 738–39; Pennsylvania, **Vol. 6, Part 1**, 226; **Vol. 8, Part 2**, 104; **Vol. 9, Part 1**, 189; **Supp. 6**, 260, 331; **Supp. 7**, 302, 766; **Supp. 8**, 360–61; **Supp. 9**, 253; Rhode Island, **Supp. 8**, 222–23, 405–6; South Carolina, **Vol. 7, Part 2**, 59; **Supp. 5**, 481–82; **Supp. 7**, 398; **Supp. 8**, 538, 682; Tennessee, **Supp. 3**, 449; **Supp. 4**, 75; **Supp. 5**, 144–45, 497–98; **Supp. 7**, 415; **Supp. 8**, 91–92; **Supp. 9**, 258, 259; Texas, **Supp. 3**, 266–67; **Supp. 4**, 776; **Supp. 7**, 137–38, 242, 349–50, 459–60, 634–35, 730–31; **Supp. 8**, 205–6, 478, 506–7; **Supp. 9**, 431, 432; Utah, **Supp. 5**, 681; Vermont, **Vol. 3, Part 1**, 600 f.; Virginia, **Supp. 4**, 331–332; **Supp. 8**, 67–68; **Supp. 9**, 68, 650; Washington, **Supp. 4**, 723–24; **Supp. 7**, 764; West Virginia, **Supp. 6**, 335; Wisconsin, **Supp. 7**, 349; **Supp. 10**, 194; Wyoming, **Supp. 5**, 337; **Supp. 7**, 590; **Supp. 10**, 703, 704

Demography. *See* Population

Dempsey, Jack: references to, **Supp. 6**, 700; **Supp. 7**, 414–14; Tunney championship bouts, **Supp. 10**, 797–98

Denby, Edwin, reference to, **Supp. 3**, 259

Dendrochronology, **Supp. 7**, 193–94

Deneen, Charles S., references to, **Supp. 3**, 710; **Supp. 6**, 683–84

Denfield, Louis E., references to, **Supp. 5**, 66, 478; **Supp. 8**, 329

Denim mills, **Vol. 2, Part 2**, 341

Denishawn School and Dance Company, **Supp. 6**, 312; **Supp. 7**, 366; **Supp. 8**, 620; **Supp. 9**, 716

Denis, Patrick (Edward Tanner pseudonym), **Supp. 10**, 774, 775

Denison House (Boston, Mass.), founding of, **Vol. 5, Part 2**, 288; **Supp. 5**, 616; **Supp. 7**, 28

Denison University, presidency of, **Vol. 1, Part 1**, 287; **Vol. 4, Part 1**, 362

Denmark: Butterfield claims, **Vol. 4, Part 2**, 513; diplomatic relations, **Vol. 4, Part 1**, 616; **Supp. 5**, 582–83

Dennett, Tyler, reference to, **Supp. 3**, 293

Denney, Joseph Villiers, reference to, **Supp. 7**, 742

Dennie, Joseph, reference to, **Vol. 1, Part 2**, 243

Dennis, Eugene, reference to, **Supp. 7**, 256

Dennis, Lawrence, reference to, **Supp. 6**, 161

Dennis v. *United States*, **Supp. 10**, 189

Dennison Manufacturing Co., **Supp. 5**, 165

Denny, Jim, reference to, **Supp. 6**, 301

Densmore, John, references to, **Supp. 9**, 563, 564

Dentistry: **Vol. 1, Part 2**, 308; **Vol. 2, Part 1**, 156; **Vol. 3, Part 2**, 379, 450; **Vol. 4, Part 1**, 592; **Vol. 4, Part 2**, 441; **Vol. 5, Part 1**, 337, 364; **Vol. 5, Part 2**, 412; **Vol. 6, Part 2**, 644; **Vol. 7, Part 1**, 268 f.; **Vol. 7, Part 2**, 251; **Vol. 9, Part 1**, 467; **Vol. 10, Part 2**, 112; amalgam fillings, **Vol. 1, Part 2**, 440; anesthetics, pioneer use of, **Vol. 10, Part 1**, 640 f.; artificial teeth, manufacture of, **Vol. 10, Part 2**, 115; dental college, first, **Vol. 1, Part 2**, 61; education in, **Supp. 1**, 276, 591; **Supp. 4**, 402; gold fillings, first use of, **Vol. 3, Part 2**, 211; **Vol. 6, Part 2**, 458; inventions relating to, **Vol. 1, Part 1**, 19; **Vol. 1, Part 2**, 309, 440; **Vol. 5, Part 2**, 412; laughing gas, first use of, **Vol. 8, Part 1**, 604; machinery, use of, **Vol. 4, Part 1**, 161; nitrous oxide, use of, **Vol. 10, Part 1**, 640 f.; oral surgery, first to make specialty of, **Vol. 4, Part 1**, 161; orthodontics, **Supp. 2**, 666; profession, founding of, **Vol. 2, Part 1**, 155; **Vol. 4, Part 2**, 305, **Vol. 7, Part 2**, 251; pyorrhea, early treatment of, **Vol. 8, Part 1**, 604; research in, **Supp. 4**, 401–3; teaching of, **Vol. 1, Part 2**, 61; **Vol. 3, Part 2**, 212; **Vol. 4, Part 2**, 441; **Vol. 6, Part 2**, 164; Washington, George, **Vol. 4, Part**

1, 592; writings on, **Vol. 1, Part 2**, 309; **Vol. 2, Part 1**, 156; **Vol. 4, Part 1**, 161; **Vol. 4, Part 2**, 306; **Vol. 5, Part 1**, 541; **Vol. 5, Part 2**, 412; **Vol. 7, Part 2**, 251; **Vol. 8, Part 1**, 604; **Vol. 10, Part 1**, 640
Denver, Colo.: growth of, **Vol. 9, Part 2**, 263; life in 1860s, **Vol. 2, Part 1**, 121; Moffat, service of, **Vol. 7, Part 1**, 75; naming of, **Vol. 3, Part 1**, 243; public education, **Supp. 2**, 140
Denver & Rio Grande Railroad, **Vol. 5, Part 2**, 36; **Vol. 7, Part 2**, 195
Denver Post, **Supp. 1**, 94
De Palma Manufacturing Co., **Supp. 6**, 164
Department stores: advertising, **Supp. 5**, 433; air-conditioning of, **Supp. 4**, 149; Bamberger's, **Supp. 3**, 30; Christmas window decoration, **Supp. 3**, 685; discount, **Supp. 8**, 348–49; executives, **Supp. 7**, 440–41; Federated, **Supp. 3**, 421–22; Filene's, **Supp. 2**, 183; Gimbel's, **Supp. 8**, 212–13; Lazarus, **Supp. 9**, 483–84; Macy's, **Supp. 2**, 636; **Supp. 3**, 748–49; management, **Vol. 9, Part 2**, 129 f.; **Vol. 10, Part 1**, 407 f.; May's, **Supp. 8**, 427–28; Penney, J. C., **Supp. 9**, 609–10; **Supp. 10**, 353–54; Sears, Roebuck, **Supp. 8**, 705; **Supp. 9**, 163–64; women's working conditions, **Supp. 4**, 623–24
DePauw University: **Vol. 1, Part 2**, 521; **Vol. 3, Part 1**, 244; **Vol. 9, Part 1**, 181; chemistry studies, **Supp. 9**, 443; presidency, **Supp. 4**, 408; **Supp. 7**, 597
Depew Memorial Fountain (Indianapolis), **Supp. 3**, 124
Deportation. *See* Immigration; Loyalty issues
Depression, economic. See Economics; Great Depression; Welfare
Deputy, The, **Supp. 10**, 734
Dermatology: **Vol. 2, Part 1**, 251; **Vol. 3, Part 1**, 494 f.; **Vol. 3, Part 2**, 521; **Vol. 5, Part 1**, 451, 540 f.; **Vol. 5, Part 2**, 364; **Vol. 7, Part 1**, 237; **Vol. 8, Part 2**, 418 f.; **Vol. 10, Part 1**, 648 f.; **Vol. 10, Part 2**, 193; first school of, in U.S., **Vol. 10, Part 2**, 109. *See also* Skin
DeRita, Joe, reference to, **Supp. 9**, 282
Derleth, August, references to, **Supp. 10**, 723, 724
De Sapio, Carmine, reference to, **Supp. 6**, 142
Desch, Cecil H., reference to, **Supp. 6**, 70
Desegregation. *See* Civil rights movement; School desegregation
Deseret, state of, **Vol. 5, Part 2**, 377; **Vol. 8, Part 1**, 175
Desert, description of early crossing, **Vol. 8, Part 2**, 251; plants, study of, **Vol. 9, Part 1**, 427
De Sica, Vittorio, reference to, **Supp. 9**, 35
Design. *See subject areas*, e.g, Art; Fashion
Des Moines *Register and Leader*, **Supp. 4**, 189; **Supp. 6**, 676; **Supp. 7**, 164
Desperadoes of the South West, **Vol. 1, Part 1**, 373
Dessauer, John, reference to, **Supp. 9**, 877
De Sylva, Buddy, reference to, **Supp. 8**, 250–51
Detective agency, private, first in U.S., **Vol. 7, Part 2**, 622 f.
Detective stories: **Vol. 5, Part 2**, 153; **Vol. 8, Part 1**, 119 f.; **Supp. 1**, 80, 635, 637, 692; **Supp. 2**, 740; **Supp. 6**, 106–7, 116; **Supp. 7**, 314, 315; **Supp. 8**, 202–3; Carr novels, **Supp. 10**, 103–4; "Ellery Queen" series, **Supp. 9**, 487–88; "locked-room mystery," **Supp. 9**, 104; Mason novels, **Supp. 10**, 518, 519; "Nero Wolfe" series, **Supp. 9**, 772–73
Detective work, **Supp. 7**, 667–68
Detour, **Supp. 9**, 820
Detroit, Mich.: auto industry, **Supp. 3**, 550; **Supp. 4**, 291–304; 293–94; capture of, **Vol. 2, Part 1**, 563; **Vol. 3, Part 1**, 175; **Vol. 5, Part 1**, 363; **Vol. 6, Part 1**, 550; Catholic bishop, first, **Vol. 8, Part 1**, 510; civic and public service, **Vol. 3, Part 1**, 490 f.; **Vol. 6, Part 1**, 396; **Vol. 6, Part 2**, 144; **Vol. 7, Part 1**, 445; **Vol. 7, Part 2**, 192, 621, 637; **Vol. 8, Part 2**, 519 f.; civil distrubance (1967), **Supp. 10**, 109; commercial and industrial architecture, **Supp. 3**, 404–5; electric plant, **Supp. 3**, 231; founding of, **Vol. 2, Part 1**, 397; French colony of Father Constantin, **Vol. 6, Part 1**, 231; history, of early, **Vol. 10, Part 2**, 507; Hull's army at, surrender of, **Vol. 3, Part 1**, 175; Indians, trading with, **Vol. 2, Part 1**, 446; international vehicular tunnel, **Vol. 7, Part 2**, 278; living conditions of auto workers, **Supp. 9**, 584; mayors, **Supp. 2**, 126; **Supp. 4**, 611–12; **Supp. 6**, 115; **Supp. 10**, 109; Museum of Art, founding of, **Vol. 7, Part 2**, 192; newspaper, first to be printed in, **Vol. 8, Part 1**, 550; pediatrics; **Supp. 3**, 189–90; Polish immigrants, **Vol. 3, Part 1**, 24; politics, **Supp. 10**, 109; public schools, first free, **Vol. 7, Part 2**, 637; urban renewal and economic redevelopment programs in, **Supp. 10**, 109
Detroit, the, capture of, **Vol. 3, Part 2**, 96
Detroit Aircraft Corporation, founding of, **Supp. 8**, 385
Detroit Automobile Co., founding of, **Supp. 4**, 292–93
Detroit Bank and Trust Co., **Supp. 7**, 189, 190
Detroit Edison Co., **Supp. 3**, 231
Detroit Evening News, **Supp. 5**, 615
Detroit Free Press, **Vol. 9, Part 2**, 97; **Supp. 5**, 58; **Supp. 6**, 258
Detroit Lions (football), **Supp. 5**, 458
Detroit News, **Supp. 5**, 55–56, 504; **Supp. 10**, 510
Detroit River, Indian council at mouth of, **Vol. 8, Part 1**, 437
Detroit Symphony Orchestra, development of, **Supp. 2**, 214
Detroit Tigers (baseball), **Supp. 5**, 291–92; **Supp. 7**, 128, 130, 139, 663; **Supp. 8**, 49–50, 106–7, 142, 542–43; **Supp. 9**, 328–29; **Supp. 10**, 314, 315, 316, 532, 859
Deuterium, **Supp. 3**, 693; **Supp. 4**, 488–89
Deutsche Pionier, **Vol. 8, Part 1**, 388
Deutscher Werkbund, **Supp. 8**, 226
De Veaux College, founding of, **Vol. 3, Part 1**, 216
Development theory, **Supp. 4**, 805, 807–8
Dever, Paul A., reference to, **Supp. 8**, 219
De Voto, Bernard, references to, **Supp. 7**, 517, 518
De Vries, Hugo, reference to, **Supp. 3**, 539
Dewey, Admiral George: biography of, **Supp. 2**, 25; relations with Gridley, **Vol. 4, Part 1**, 610
Dewey, John, references to, **Supp. 1**, 548; **Supp. 2**, 728; **Supp. 3**, 363, 457, 555, 577, 677, 780; **Supp. 4**, 20, 21, 374, 584, 585, 809; **Supp. 5**, 39, 71, 199, 549, 630, 664; **Supp. 6**, 46, 54, 55, 96, 261, 671; **Supp. 7**, 435; **Supp. 9**, 29
Dewey, Thomas E.: biography of, **Supp. 6**, 310; civic corruption fought by, **Supp. 9**, 229–30; Curran relationship, **Supp. 6**, 141, 142; law practice, **Supp. 6**, 34; organized crime indictments by, **Supp. 5**, 665; **Supp. 6**, 295; **Supp. 7**, 485; presidential bids, **Supp. 3**, 664, 830; **Supp. 8**, 143, 144; **Supp. 9**, 230–31, 814; references to, **Supp. 5**, 343; **Supp. 9**, 399; Straus relationship, **Supp. 6**, 607; Talbott relationship, **Supp. 6**, 618
Dewey, Ballantine, Bushby, Palmer and Wood, **Supp. 6**, 33
Dewing, Thomas, reference to, **Vol. 9, Part 2**, 400
DeWitt, John L., reference to, **Supp. 6**, 629
De Wolfe, Elsie, reference to, **Supp. 1**, 539
Dewson, Mary Williams, reference to, **Supp. 6**, 4
Diabetes: research, **Supp. 10**, 815–16; treatment of, **Supp. 6**, 698; **Supp. 10**, 458; urine analysis for, **Supp. 2**, 36
Diaghilev, Sergei: references to, **Supp. 3**, 282; **Supp. 5**, 75; **Supp. 7**, 548, 549, 560; **Supp. 8**, 145, 669–70; Stravinsky collaboration, **Supp. 9**, 775–76

Dial, The, founding of, **Vol. 2, Part 1**, 165; **Vol. 3, Part 1**, 567 f.; **Vol. 8, Part 1**, 596; **Vol. 8, Part 1**, 623; **Supp. 7**, 158, 219, 494; **Supp. 8**, 584; **Supp. 9**, 33, 558
Dialect: American Dialect Society, **Vol. 9, Part 1**, 64; American, pioneer scientific study of, **Vol. 4, Part 2**, 522; black, use of, in literature, **Vol. 4, Part 1**, 373; Indian, **Vol. 4, Part 2**, 94; Pennsylvania-German, **Vol. 6, Part 1**, 78; use of, in writing, **Vol. 4, Part 2**, 314
"Diamond Dick" ("dime" novel character), **Vol. 5, Part 2**, 51
Diamond Horseshoe (New York City nightclub), **Supp. 8**, 547
Diamond Lil, **Supp. 10**, 829
Diamond Match Co., **Vol. 1, Part 1**, 590; **Vol. 7, Part 1**, 143; **Vol. 9, Part 1**, 600; safety matches, **Supp. 4**, 257–58
Diamonds: cutting, **Vol. 7, Part 1**, 244; **Supp. 10**, 848; discovered in meteoric iron, **Vol. 5, Part 2**, 487; Dewey diamond, **Vol. 7, Part 1**, 244; Hope, **Supp. 10**, 848; mining, **Vol. 10, Part 2**, 261; **Supp. 2**, 701; Star of the East, **Supp. 10**, 848
Dianetics, **Supp. 9**, 155, 156
Diaries: **Vol. 1, Part 1**, 513; **Vol. 2, Part 1**, 5, 64; **Vol. 3, Part 1**, 135, 152, 229; **Vol. 3, Part 2**, 92, 131; **Vol. 4, Part 1**, 116, 130, 133, 183, 378, 424, 461, 470, 497; **Vol. 4, Part 2**, 34 f., 248, 276, 538, 612; **Vol. 5, Part 1**, 192; **Vol. 5, Part 2**, 459, 468 f.; **Vol. 6, Part 1**, 182, 468; **Vol. 7, Part 1**, 150 f.; **Vol. 8, Part 1**, 12 f.; **Vol. 9, Part 1**, 147, 501; **Vol. 9, Part 2**, 20; **Vol. 10, Part 1**, 97, 99, 509 f., 629 f.; Adams, John Quincy, **Vol. 1, Part 1**, 84; Bentley, William, **Vol. 1, Part 2**, 207; Civil War, military diary, **Vol. 10, Part l**, 95; colonial life, **Vol. 10, Part 1**, 362 f.; Continental Congress, **Vol. 9, Part 1**, 333; Ferguson, E. G., **Vol. 3, Part 2**, 331; Leaming, Aaron, **Vol. 8, Part 1**, 420; Lickford, Thomas, **Vol. 6, Part 1**, 87; McClure, David, **Vol. 3, Part 1**, 277; Ravenel, H. W., **Vol. 8, Part 1**, 396; Read, Daniel, **Vol. 8, Part 1**, 421; Reeder, Andrew Horatio, **Vol. 8, Part 1**, 463; Revolutionary War period, **Vol. 10, Part 2**, 434; Riddle, George Peabody, **Vol. 8, Part 1**, 592; Rieger, Joseph, **Vol. 8, Part 1**, 600; Robbins, Thomas, **Vol. 8, Part 1**, 646; Roebling, J. A., **Vol. 8, Part 2**, 87; Rogers, Robert, **Vol. 8, Part 2**, 109; Root, F. A., **Vol. 8, Part 2**, 146; Royce, Sarah Eleanor, **Vol. 8, Part 2**, 205; Rupp, Israel D., **Vol. 8, Part 2**, 226; Russell, Jonathan, **Vol. 8, Part 2**, 245; Russell, Osborne, trapper, **Vol. 8, Part 2**, 248; Sewall, **Vol. 8, Part 2**, 610 f.; Seybert, **Vol. 9, Part 1**, 4; Spanish expedition into California, **Vol. 8, Part 1**, 109 f.; Stiles, Ezra, **Vol. 3, Part 1**, 277; trip by ox team from Connecticut to Ohio, **Vol. 8, Part 1**, 441; Tudor, Frederic, **Vol. 10, Part 1**, 48; Welles, Gideon, **Vol. 8, Part 1**, 618. *See also* Journals and memoirs
Diarrhea: causes of, **Supp. 4**, 494; infant treatment, **Supp. 5**, 1
Diary of Anaïs Nin, The, **Supp. 10**, 591
Diary of Anne Frank, The (film), **Supp. 9**, 768
"Diary of a Public Man," **Vol. 5, Part 2**, 327
"Dick and Jane" reading textbooks, **Supp. 6**, 248
Dickens, Charles, references to, **Vol. 7, Part 1**, 400; **Vol. 8, Part 1**, 19 f.
Dickerman, Marion, references to, **Supp. 7**, 659, 660
Dickey, Bill, reference to, **Supp. 7**, 130
Dickinson, Emily: references to, **Vol. 5, Part 1**, 542; **Vol. 9, Part 2**, 573; **Supp. 7**, 547; **Supp. 9**, 14; writings on, **Supp. 4**, 812
Dickinson, Robert L., references to, **Supp. 6**, 81–82; **Supp. 8**, 569
Dickinson College: founding of, **Vol. 3, Part 1**, 544 f.; **Vol. 7, Part 1**, 526; **Vol. 8, Part 2**, 228; first elective laboratory courses, **Vol. 5, Part l**, 59; presidency of, **Vol. 7, Part 1**, 411
Dickmann, Bernard F., reference to, **Supp. 4**, 355
Dickstein, Samuel, reference to, **Supp. 10**, 484
Dictionaries: Century, **Vol. 9, Part 1**, 241; English-German, **Vol. 7, Part 1**, 272; making of, **Vol. 3, Part 2**, 484 f.; **Vol. 10, Part 2**, 527; modern European literature, **Supp. 4**, 755; music, of, **Vol. 6, Part 1**, 239; *New Standard Dictionary,* **Supp. 2**, 682; publication, **Vol. 6, Part 1**, 287; Thai-English, **Supp. 3**, 486; "War of the Dictionaries," **Vol. 10, Part 1**, 594 f.; Webster's, first edition of, **Vol. 5, Part 1**, 288; *Webster's New International,* **Supp. 4**, 624
Dictionary of American Biography, **Vol. 3, Part 1**, 430; **Vol. 5, Part 2**, 80 f.; **Vol. 8, Part 2**, 517; **Supp. 5**, 614; **Supp. 8**, 370, 580; planning of, **Supp. 2**, 186, 342
Dictionary of American Medical Biography, **Supp. 3**, 413
Dictionary of Philosophy and Psychology, **Supp. 1**, 50
Dictionary of the United States Congress, **Vol. 5, Part 2**, 606
Didrikson, Mildren ("Babe"), reference to, **Supp. 9**, 131
"Die Hard" Republicanism, **Vol. 3, Part 2**, 581
Dielectric constants, **Supp. 6**, 346
Diem, Ngo Dinh, reference to, **Supp. 7**, 422
Dies, Martin, Committee, **Supp. 6**, 392; reference to, **Supp. 5**, 544
Diesel power, development of, **Supp. 6**, 333
Die-sinking, **Vol. 5, Part 2**, 456
Diet and nutrition: animal, **Supp. 1**, 37; baby food, **Supp. 5**, 242–43; **Supp. 9**, 302–3; biochemical studies, **Supp. 3**, 243, 244; **Supp. 5**, 275–76, 622–23; calorimetry studies, **Supp. 1**, 517–18; cancer-link studies **Supp. 3**, 141; children, **Supp. 3**, 28, 159; **Supp. 6**, 81; dental disease relationship, **Supp. 4**, 402; disease relationship studies, **Supp. 1**, 398; **Supp. 4**, 580–82; **Supp. 5**, 710; **Supp. 8**, 197–98; economic aspects of, **Supp. 9**, 589; fetal development studies, **Supp. 7**, 568–69; growth relationship, **Supp. 4**, 420; health foods, **Supp. 5**, 378–79, 452–53; **Supp. 9**, 221–22; infants', **Vol. 3, Part 2**, 464; **Vol. 8, Part 2**, 186; **Supp. 2**, 432; infant's appestat, **Supp. 4**, 7–8; low-protein diets, **Supp. 3**, 163; natural products, **Supp. 3**, 409–10; nutrient deficiency research, **Supp. 7**, 223; protein studies, **Supp. 6**, 190; **Supp. 7**, 476; spas, **Supp. 8**, 13; study of, **Vol. 10, Part 2**, 630; teaching of, **Supp. 3**, 671; **Supp. 4**, 37; UNICEF program, **Supp. 7**, 600; vegetarianism, **Supp. 6**, 113, 409–10; vitamin E deficiency, **Supp. 9**, 222; vitamin E discovery, **Supp. 9**, 266; vitamins, **Supp. 1**, 398, 560; wild edibles, **Supp. 9**, 307, 308; writings on, **Supp. 3**, 68; **Supp. 9**, 221–22. *See also* Cookbooks; Cooking; Food
Die tote Stadt (opera), **Supp. 6**, 351–52
Dietrich, Marlene, reference to, **Supp. 8**, 672
Dietrich, Noah, reference to, **Supp. 10**, 356–57
Diffraction gratings, **Supp. 3**, 291
Digestion, contributions to study of, **Vol. 1, Part 2**, 106; **Supp. 10**, 369
Dighton Rock, inscriptions on, **Vol. 1, Part 2**, 7
Digitalis, **Supp. 2**, 741; **Supp. 3**, 343; first experimental analysis, **Vol. 3, Part 1**, 6
Dillard University, founding of, **Supp. 6**, 11
Diller, Burgoyne, reference to, **Supp. 6**, 512
Dillingham, Charles B., reference to, **Supp. 6**, 318
Dillingham, William P., reference to, **Supp. 6**, 320
Dillon, C. Douglas, reference to, **Supp. 7**, 421
Dillon, Read and Co., **Supp. 4**, 305
Dilworth, Dewees, reference to, **Supp. 6**, 337
Di Maggio, Joe, references to, **Supp. 7**, 546, 668; **Supp. 8**, 479; **Supp. 9**, 855; **Supp. 10**, 142, 481
"Dime" novels, **Vol. 3, Part 2**, 102; **Vol. 5, Part 1**, 480;

Vol. 5, Part 2, 51, 238; **Vol. 7, Part 1**, 331 f.; **Supp. 3**, 585–86
Dime stores. *See* Five and dime stores
Dingley Act, tariff, **Vol. 3, Part 1**, 315; **Vol. 8, Part 1**, 2 f.
Dinkeloo, John, reference to, **Supp. 7**, 671
Dinkins, David N., first black mayor of New York City, **Supp. 9**, 251
Dinner at Antoine's, **Supp. 8**, 328
Dinner at the White House, **Supp. 5**, 5
Dinosaur National Monument: **Supp. 7**, 814; **Supp. 8**, 412; **Supp. 10**, 120; dam proposal opposition, **Supp. 10**, 192
Dinosaurs: egg findings, **Supp. 3**, 316; **Supp. 6**, 18; North American, **Supp. 3**, 316–17
Dior, Christian, reference to, **Supp. 10**, 248
Diphtheria: antitoxin, **Supp. 2**, 353; epidemiology of, **Supp. 7**, 194; research in, **Supp. 2**, 513; Schick test for determining, **Supp. 4**, 701; vaccine, **Supp. 5**, 1; treatment of, **Vol. 1, Part 2**, 263; **Vol. 7, Part 1**, 628; **Vol. 8, Part 1**, 252 f., 460, 565
Diplomacy: **Vol. 1, Part 1**, 84 f., 106 f., 302, 356, 483, 545, 562 f., 591 f.; **Vol. 1, Part 2**, 38, 241, 389, 417, 464 f.; **Vol. 2, Part 1**, 210, 219, 309, 420, 535; **Vol. 2, Part 2**, 83 f., 173 f., 205 f., 221 f., 625; **Vol. 3, Part 1**, 38, 153 f., 294, 510, 592 f.; **Vol. 3, Part 2**, 49, 52, 111, 114, 144, 165, 181, 192 f., 212, 220, 224, 254, 275, 298, 305, 307 f., 332, 344, 368, 398 f., 417, 448, 485, 490, 502, 506 f., 515, 533, 535, 538, 551, 569, 572, 576, 581, 592 f.; **Vol. 4, Part 1**, 107 f., 109, 202, 477 f., 538; **Vol. 4, Part 2**, 95, 97, 101, 106, 162, 260, 350, 378, 384, 428, 432 f., 460, 481, 545, 588; **Vol. 5, Part 1**, 1, 8, 54 f., 81, 117 f., 156, 346, 374, 397, 407, 458, 543 f.; **Vol. 5, Part 2**, 207, 260, 264, 418, 617; **Vol. 6, Part 1**, 35, 53, 86, 97, 132, 155, 189, 267, 269, 292, 302, 322; **Vol. 6, Part 2**, 18, 114, 248; **Vol. 7, Part 1**, 122, 210, 347, 351, 369, 417, 607 f., 634 f.; S0600; **Vol. 8, Part 1**, 2 f., 30 f., 83 f., 92 f., 184 f., 205 f., 254 f., 283, 285 f., 344 f., 363 f.; **Vol. 8, Part 2**, 63, 66, 213, 247, 252, 348, 406, 428, 471, 520 f., 522, 588, 606 f., 613 f., 619; **Vol. 9, Part 1**, 42, 128, 140, 209 f., 243, 489, 618; **Vol. 9, Part 2**, 93, 141, 246, 377, 401, 474, 607, 639, 644; **Vol. 10, Part 1**, 443, 551 f., 574 f., 585 f., 628 f., 647; **Vol. 10, Part 2**, 102, 267, 325, 357, 467 f., 561; *Alabama* case, **Vol. 3, Part 1**, 135; Argentina, **Vol. 3, Part 1**, 197; **Vol. 7, Part 2**, 283; **Vol. 8, Part 2**, 83; **Supp. 3**, 740; **Supp. 4**, 864; **Supp. 5**, 332; **Supp. 7**, 60; Austria, **Supp. 9**, 799; Austria-Hungary, **Vol. 5, Part 2**, 353; **Vol. 6, Part 1**, 613; **Vol. 7, Part 1**, 285, 309; **Vol. 7, Part 2**, 5, 33, 425; **Vol. 9, Part 2**, 93, 401, 607, 644; Barbary States, **Vol. 6, Part 1**, 76; **Vol. 8, Part 2**, 349; Belgium, **Vol. 1, Part 2**, 464; **Vol. 6, Part 1**, 145; **Vol. 8, Part 2**, 349; **Vol. 9, Part 2**, 93, 377, 635; **Supp. 7**, 438; Brazil, **Vol. 5, Part 1**, 392; **Vol. 9, Part 2**, 473, 567; **Vol. 10, Part 1**, 49; **Supp. 1**, 563; **Supp. 5**, 345; *Brazil*, **Supp. 9**, 154; Bulgaria, **Vol. 3, Part 1**, 294; Canada, **Supp. 8**, 410; **Supp. 10**, 529; Central America, **Vol. 3, Part 1**, 39; **Vol. 5, Part 1**, 69; Chile, **Vol. 5, Part 2**, 375; **Vol. 6, Part 1**, 358; **Vol. 7, Part 1**, 425; **Vol. 8, Part 2**, 510; **Vol. 9, Part 2**, 141; China, **Vol. 1, Part 1**, 308, 443; **Vol. 1, Part 2**, 241; **Vol. 3, Part 1**, 234; **Vol. 4, Part 2**, 434; **Vol. 5, Part 1**, 133; **Vol. 6, Part 1**, 146, 446; **Vol. 6, Part 2**, 248; **Vol. 7, Part 2**, 34, 235; **Vol. 8, Part 1**, 462, 477, 491 f.; **Vol. 8, Part 2**, 66; **Vol. 9, Part 1**, 140, 491, 493; **Vol. 9, Part 2**, 310, 371, 640; **Vol. 10, Part 1**, 426 f., 585; **Supp. 2**, 129; **Supp. 3**, 699, 826; **Supp. 7**, 377, 728; **Supp. 9**, 830–31; **Supp. 10**, 528; Clayton-Bulwer Treaty, **Vol. 3, Part 1**, 39; Colombia, **Vol. 1, Part 1**, 271; **Vol. 8, Part 2**, 520; **Vol. 9, Part 2**, 570; Consular Service, **Supp. 3**, 138–39; **Supp. 3**, 467; Costa Rica, **Vol. 3, Part 1**, 314; Crete, **Vol. 9, Part 2**, 29; Cuba, **Vol. 1, Part 1**, 485; **Vol. 3, Part 2**, 224; **Vol. 4, Part 2**, 513; **Vol. 6, Part 1**, 104; **Vol. 8, Part 1**, 2 f.; **Vol. 9, Part 1**, 491; **Vol. 10, Part 2**, 467 f.; **Supp. 1**, 89; Czechoslovakia, **Supp. 4**, 773; Dallas-Clarendon Convention, **Vol. 7, Part 2**, 579; Denmark, **Vol. 4, Part 1**, 616; **Supp. 5**, 582–83; dollar, **Supp. 6**, 206; Dominican Republic, **Vol. 4, Part 1**, 499, 538; Ecuador, **Vol. 9, Part 2**, 141; education in, **Supp. 1**, 401; **Supp. 4**, 598; Egypt, **Vol. 3, Part 2**, 275 f.; **Supp. 9**, 154; England, **Vol. 1, Part 1**, 85, 567, **Vol. 1, Part 2**, 327; **Vol. 3, Part 1**, 39, 134; **Vol. 5, Part 2**, 7, 403; **Vol. 6, Part 1**, 463; **Vol. 7, Part 1**, 150, 286; **Vol. 7, Part 2**, 520, 627; **Vol. 8, Part 1**, 485; **Vol. 8, Part 2**, 232; **Vol. 10, Part 1**, 136, 154; **Vol. 10, Part 2**, 102, 267; **Supp. 1**, 9; **Supp. 3**, 366; **Supp. 4**, 900; **Supp. 5**, 155, 160; **Supp. 8**, 320–21; Far East, studies of, **Supp. 4**, 224, 225; first American to represent united colonies abroad, **Vol. 3, Part 1**, 173 f.; France, **Vol. 1, Part 1**, 75 f., 78, 356; **Vol. 1, Part 2**, 259; **Vol. 3, Part 1**, 127, 104, 164, 167, 173, 174; **Vol. 5, Part 2**, 21 f., 204, 406 f.; **Vol. 6, Part 1**, 4, 312, 323; **Vol. 6, Part 2**, 114; **Vol. 7, Part 1**, 88, 259, 369, 524, 534, 587; **Vol. 7, Part 2**, 615; **Vol. 8, Part 1**, 428, 484 f., 626; **Vol. 8, Part 2**, 4; **Vol. 9, Part 1**, 25; **Vol. 9, Part 2**, 234; **Supp. 6**, 187; **Supp. 8**, 61–62; **Supp. 9**, 154; Germany, **Vol. 3, Part 1**, 363; **Vol. 5, Part 1**, 548 f.; **Vol. 7, Part 2**, 88 f.; **Supp. 3**, 699; **Supp. 4**, 898; **Supp. 5**, 241; **Supp. 10**, 144, 571; Greece, **Vol. 5, Part 1**, 548 f.; **Vol. 8, Part 1**, 428 f.; **Vol. 8, Part 2**, 77; **Supp. 6**, 245; Guatemala, **Supp. 8**, 495; Haiti, **Vol. 5, Part 2**, 597; Hawaii, **Vol. 1, Part 1**, 77, 187; **Vol. 1, Part 2**, 389; **Vol. 2, Part 1**, 535; **Vol. 3, Part 1**, 592 f.; **Vol. 4, Part 1**, 609; **Vol. 7, Part 2**, 405; Iceland, **Supp. 5**, 582–83; India, **Vol. 4, Part 1**, 578 f.; **Supp. 8**, 501; **Supp. 9**, 450; international law, **Supp. 5**, 136–37; Iran (Persia), **Vol. 1, Part 2**, 38, 187, 506; **Vol. 8, Part 2**, 241; **Supp. 6**, 388–89; **Supp. 8**, 5–6, 275; Ireland, **Vol. 7, Part 2**, 557; Israel, **Supp. 7**, 498; **Supp. 9**, 450; Italy, **Vol. 5, Part 2**, 400; **Vol. 7, Part 2**, 141; **Vol. 9, Part 1**, 497; **Supp. 6**, 388–89; **Supp. 7**, 815; Japan, **Vol. 1, Part 1**, 563; **Vol. 1, Part 2**, 277; **Vol. 3, Part 1**, 245; **Vol. 4, Part 2**, 60, 324; **Vol. 6, Part 1**, 570, 573; **Vol. 6, Part 2**, 18; **Vol. 8, Part 1**, 244, 254 f.; **Vol. 9, Part 2**, 423; **Vol. 10, Part 2**, 561; **Supp. 2**, 580; **Supp. 3**, 323; **Supp. 5**, 333; **Supp. 6**, 211; **Supp. 7**, 112–13, 303; journal, diplomatic and consular, first example of, **Vol. 3, Part 2**, 572; Korea, **Vol. 3, Part 2**, 560; **Vol. 4, Part 1**, 526; **Vol. 4, Part 2**, 613; Latin America, **Vol. 1, Part 2**, 327; **Vol. 2, Part 1**, 219, 420; **Vol. 3, Part 1**, 153 f.; **Vol. 10, Part 2**, 325, 357; **Supp. 2**, 25, 580; **Supp. 7**, 777–78; **Supp. 9**, 153; **Supp. 10**, 13–14, 64; Liberia, **Vol. 4, Part 1**, 155; **Vol. 8, Part 2**, 10 f.; **Vol. 9, Part 1**, 375; **Vol. 10, Part 1**, 66 f.; **Supp. 7**, 767–68; Luxembourg, **Supp. 9**, 547; Mexico, **Vol. 1, Part 2**, 225, 377; **Vol. 2, Part 1**, 309, 461; **Vol. 3, Part 2**, 108; **Vol. 4, Part 1**, 84, 538; **Vol. 5, Part 2**, 617; **Vol. 6, Part 1**, 193; **Vol. 7, Part 1**, 234 f.; **Vol. 8, Part 1**, 30 f., 379; **Vol. 8, Part 2**, 85; **Vol. 9, Part 1**, 20, 210; **Vol. 9, Part 2**, 474; **Supp. 1**, 589; **Supp. 4**, 217; **Supp. 5**, 332; Monroe Doctrine, **Vol. 1, Part 1**, 86 f.; **Vol. 2, Part 1**, 210; **Vol. 3, Part 2**, 507; **Vol. 6, Part 2**, 192; **Vol. 7, Part 1**, 92; **Vol. 8, Part 1**, 34 f.; **Vol. 8, Part 2**, 139 f.; Morocco, **Vol. 4, Part 2**, 50; Netherlands, the, **Vol. 1, Part 1**, 76; **Vol. 3, Part 1**, 89; **Vol. 5, Part 1**, 346; Nicaragua, **Vol. 1, Part 2**, 465; **Vol. 3, Part 1**, 314; **Vol. 5, Part 1**, 152; **Vol. 5, Part 2**, 554; **Vol. 10, Part 1**, 363 f.; Norway, **Vol. 1, Part 1**, 285; **Supp. 8**, 244; Orient, **Vol. 3, Part 2**, 560; **Vol. 8, Part 2**, 4; Paraguay, **Vol. 7, Part 1**, 608; **Vol. 7, Part 2**, 422; **Vol. 9, Part 1**, 136 f.; Peru, **Vol. 7, Part 2**, 571; **Vol. 8, Part**

2, 38; **Vol. 10, Part 1**, 49; **Supp. 4**, 670; Philippines, the, **Vol. 10, Part 2**, 561; Poland, **Supp. 7**, 53; Portugal, **Vol. 1, Part 2**, 41; **Vol. 3, Part 1**, 176; **Vol. 7, Part 2**, 582; professionalization of, **Supp. 6**, 207, 686–87; Revolutionary War period, **Vol. 1, Part 1**, 435; **Vol. 2, Part 1**, 497; **Vol. 3, Part 1**, 52 f.; **Vol. 6, Part 1**, 36; Salvador, **Vol. 3, Part 1**, 296; Santo Domingo, **Vol. 5, Part 2**, 598; **Vol. 6, Part 1**, 76; Sardinia, **Vol. 5, Part 2**, 418; **Vol. 7, Part 1**, 524; Siam, **Vol. 1, Part 2**, 569; Sicily, **Vol. 3, Part 1**, 89; South America, **Vol. 1, Part 1**, 271; **Vol. 3, Part 2**, 507; **Vol. 4, Part 2**, 162; **Vol. 7, Part 1**, 139; **Vol. 8, Part 2**, 83; Soviet Union, **Vol. 1, Part 1**, 85, 329; **Vol. 1, Part 2**, 417; **Vol. 3, Part 1**, 38, 510; **Vol. 3, Part 2**, 578; **Vol. 6, Part 1**, 424, 613; **Vol. 7, Part 2**, 560, 628; **Vol. 9, Part 1**, 11; **Vol. 9, Part 2**, 607, 635; **Supp. 4**, 772; **Supp. 6**, 147; **Supp. 7**, 438, 703, 714; **Supp. 8**, 61; **Supp. 9**, 798–99; Spain, **Vol. 1, Part 1**, 75, 105, 648; **Vol. 1, Part 2**, 502; **Vol. 2, Part 1**, 498; **Vol. 3, Part 1**, 164, 344, 507, 609; **Vol. 3, Part 2**, 399; **Vol. 4, Part 1**, 478; **Vol. 5, Part 1**, 510; **Vol. 5, Part 2**, 6 f.; **Vol. 6, Part 1**, 463; **Vol. 7, Part 1**, 96; **Vol. 7, Part 2**, 613; **Vol. 8, Part 2**, 383, 543; **Vol. 9, Part 1**, 406; **Vol. 9, Part 2**, 93; **Vol. 10, Part 2**, 490; **Supp. 4**, 864; **Supp. 7**, 53, 330–31; Sweden, **Vol. 1, Part 1**, 285; Switzerland, **Vol. 1, Part 2**, 487; **Supp. 1**, 675; **Supp. 4**, 898; Tripoli, **Vol. 1, Part 2**, 241; **Vol. 3, Part 1**, 613; Tunis, **Vol. 3, Part 1**, 613; **Vol. 4, Part 2**, 481 f.; **Vol. 7, Part 2**, 329; Turkey, **Vol. 1, Part 1**, 309; **Vol. 1, Part 2**, 417, 567; **Vol. 2, Part 1**, 139; **Vol. 3, Part 1**, 294; **Vol. 7, Part 1**, 206; **Vol. 8, Part 1**, 529; **Vol. 8, Part 2**, 77; **Vol. 9, Part 2**, 131; **Supp. 2**, 65; **Supp. 4**, 603–4; **Supp. 4**, 772; **Supp. 7**, 303, 384; Tuscarora Treaty, **Vol. 3, Part 1**, 99; Uruguay, **Vol. 7, Part 1**, 608; Vatican, the, **Supp. 8**, 613, 614; Venezuela, **Vol. 1, Part 2**, 392, 506; **Vol. 7, Part 2**, 283; **Vol. 8, Part 1**, 14 f.; **Vol. 8, Part 2**, 520; **Vol. 9, Part 2**, 608; Webster-Ashburton Treaty, **Vol. 3, Part 1**, 79 f.; **Vol. 3, Part 2**, 258; **Vol. 10, Part 1**, 91; West Indies, **Vol. 4, Part 1**, 538; **Vol. 7, Part 2**, 324; women in, **Supp. 5**, 582; World War II, events leading to, **Supp. 3**, 528–29; writings on, **Supp. 1**, 239, 338; Yugoslavia, **Supp. 6**, 359; **Supp. 8**, 6, 495. *See also* Foreign relations; Foreign service; World War I; World War II

Diplomats. For complete list, *see* Occupations Index

Dirac, P. A. M., reference to, **Supp. 5**, 219, 221

Directors. For complete list, *see* Occupations Index

Directory of Worship, **Vol. 1, Part 1**, 324

Direct primary, **Vol. 8, Part 2**, 86

Dirigibles. *See* Balloons

Dirksen, Everett M., references to, **Supp. 6**, 12; **Supp. 9**, 434, 739; **Supp. 10**, 81, 361

Disarmament. *See* Arms control and disarmament; Peace, international

Disaster relief, **Supp. 4**, 228

Disasters. *See* Fires; Floods; Shipping disasters; *specific incidents*

Disc jockeys, **Supp. 7**, 267, 378

Disciples of Christ (for complete list of clergymen, *see* Occupations Index): **Vol. 1, Part 1**, 207; **Vol. 3, Part 2**, 179, 268, 598; **Vol. 4, Part 1**, 407, 440; **Vol. 4, Part 2**, 437 f., 442 f.; **Vol. 5, Part 1**, 241; **Vol. 6, Part 1**, 401; **Vol. 6, Part 2**, 46, 646; **Vol. 7, Part 1**, 145; **Vol. 7, Part 2**, 423; **Vol. 8, Part 1**, 155 f.; **Supp. 3**, 824, 846; **Supp. 6**, 14; doctrinal development of, **Vol. 8, Part 1**, 573; founding of, **Vol. 2, Part l**, 447, 463; **Vol. 8, Part 2**, 502 f.; growth, **Vol. 6, Part 2**, 125; **Vol. 7, Part 2**, 623 f.; missions, **Vol. 9, Part 1**, 68 f.

Discount stores, **Supp. 2**, 183; **Supp. 8**, 348–49; **Supp. 9**, 336–37, 597

Discovery: Canada, **Vol. 2, Part 1**, 605; Florida, **Vol. 8, Part 1**, 56 f.; Maine, **Vol. 10, Part 1**, 562 f.; Mississippi River, **Vol. 3, Part 1**, 20, 256 f. *See also* Exploration

Discovery, Hudson's bark, **Vol. 5, Part 1**, 339

Discrimination. *See* Civil rights movement; Racism; Segregation; *specific groups and subjects*

Diseases: bacteria and, **Supp. 6**, 481; carriers, **Supp. 5**, 382; children's, **Supp. 1**, 437; **Supp. 3**, 28; **Supp. 3**, 774–75; **Supp. 5**, 1; diagnosis, studies in, **Supp. 1**, 307; **Supp. 2**, 35; diet and nutrition relationship, **Supp. 4**, 580–82; **Supp. 7**, 223; **Supp. 8**, 197–98; emotional-psychological factors, **Supp. 8**, 429; epidemics, **Supp. 2**, 212; eye, **Supp. 4**, 865; insects as carriers, **Supp. 1**, 666; **Supp. 4**, 400; **Supp. 5**, 143; **Supp. 9**, 249–50; kidney, **Supp. 5**, 111; livestock-related, **Supp. 3**, 737–38; metabolic, **Supp. 2**, 35; **Supp. 6**, 698; nervous system, **Supp. 8**, 429; origin and transmission studies, **Supp. 4**, 287–88; research on, **Supp. 5**, 512; sanitary preventive measures, **Supp. 5**, 143–44; social and psychic factors, **Supp. 2**, 84; transmission studies, **Supp. 3**, 158; virus-causing, **Supp. 7**, 648–49. *See also* Preventive medicine; Public health; Tropical diseases; *specific diseases*

Dismal Swamp, drainage of, **Vol. 7, Part 1**, 426

Disney, Roy, reference to, **Supp. 8**, 130

Disney, Walt, references to, **Supp. 7**, 407; **Supp. 9**, 237, 238. *See also* Walt Disney Studios

Disneyland (Anaheim, Calif.), founding of, **Supp. 8**, 131; **Supp. 9**, 237–38

Dispensary, first free in U.S., **Vol. 8, Part 2**, 228

Displaced Persons Act (1950), **Supp. 6**, 336, 472

Disposable products, **Supp. 5**, 144

Disraeli, **Supp. 4**, 26–27

District of Columbia. *See* Washington, D. C.

District of Columbia Medical Society, antitrust action against, **Supp. 3**, 122

Disutopian communities, Jonestown (Guyana), **Supp. 10**, 391–92

Ditson, Oliver, Co., **Supp. 4**, 276–77

Diving, **Vol. 7, Part 2**, 291 f.

Diving bell, invention of, **Vol. 3, Part 1**, 587 f.

Divorce: alimony, **Supp. 8**, 10; Episcopal church and, **Vol. 4, Part 1**, 491; facts as to divorce in New England, **Vol. 3, Part 1**, 308; Forrest divorce case, **Vol. 7, Part 1**, 621; laws, **Vol. 3, Part 1**, 308; **Vol. 3, Part 2**, 486; liberalization of, **Supp. 3**, 463; National Divorce Reform League, **Vol. 3, Part 1**, 308; religion and, **Supp. 4**, 547; study of, **Supp. 3**, 799 Dix,

Dixie Cup Corporation, founding and growth of, **Supp. 9**, 556

"Dixie Duo, The" (musical team), **Supp. 9**, 731

Dix, Dorothea, reference to, **Vol. 5, Part 1**, 297

Dix, J. A., reference to, **Vol. 7, Part 1**, 645

Dixie, **Vol. 3, Part 2**, 148; **Vol. 4, Part 2**, 464

Dixiecrat party, **Supp. 6**, 470, 710; **Supp. 7**, 398; **Supp. 8**, 24–25; founding of, **Supp. 8**, 500

Dixon, George S., reference to, **Supp. 4**, 865

Dixon, Maynard, reference to, **Supp. 7**, 456

Dixon, Roland, reference to, **Supp. 6**, 611

Dixon, Thomas, reference to, **Supp. 4**, 350

Djerassi, Carl, reference to, **Supp. 8**, 503

DNA (deoxyribonucleic acid), **Supp. 4**, 426; **Supp. 5**, 26; **Supp. 8**, 200 Doan, R. f., reference to, **Supp. 7**, 134; research, **Supp. 9**, 530, 550

Doane College, founding of, **Vol. 3, Part 1**, 334

Dobbs Fort, building of (1757), **Vol. 3, Part 1**, 337; **Vol. 10, Part 1**, 301

Dobzhansky, Theodosius, reference to, **Supp. 3**, 540

Doctors. For complete list, *see* Occupations Index

"Doctors' Mob," anatomical riots, **Vol. 8, Part 1**, 121
Documentary photography, **Supp. 3**, 295–96 **Supp.** 9, 267–68
Documents Relating to Reconstruction, **Supp. 1**, 303
Dodd, Christopher J., reference to, **Supp. 9**, 240
Dodd, Thomas J., reference to, **Supp. 8**, 497
Dodd, William E., references to, **Supp. 3**, 528; **Supp. 6**, 491
Dodge, Edwin S., reference to, **Supp. 7**, 486
Dodge, Grace H., reference to, **Supp. 3**, 677 Dodge, Horace E., references to, **Supp. 4**, 293, 294, 298
Dodge, John F., references to, **Supp. 4**, 293, 294, 298
Dodge, Mabel. *See* Luhan, Mabel Dodge
Dodge, Mary Mapes, reference to, **Vol. 9, Part 1**, 340
Dodge, William, reference to, **Vol. 7, Part 1**, 105; **Supp. 5**, 544
Doeg, Johnny, reference to, **Supp. 9**, 721
"Dogpatch" (fictional locale), **Supp. 10**, 98
Dog racing, organized crime investments, **Supp. 6**, 263–65
Dogs: breeding, **Supp. 7**, 695; seeing-eye, **Supp. 4**, 253–55; stories about, **Supp. 3**, 767
Doheny, Edward L., references to, **Supp. 3**, 259, 260, 481; **Supp. 6**, 584, 713
Doherty, Denny, reference to, **Supp. 9**, 262
Dohnányi, Ernő, reference to, **Supp. 10**, 236
Doisy, Edward A., reference to, **Supp. 3**, 6
DOJ. *See* Justice, Department of (U.S.)
Doll, speaking, invention of, **Vol. 4, Part 1**, 336
Dollar, Robert, reference to, **Supp. 6**, 354
Dollard, John, reference to, **Supp. 8**, 509
Dollar Diplomacy: A Study in American Imperialism, **Supp. 7**, 268
Domestic science, pioneer teaching in, **Vol. 6, Part 1**, 265
Dominican Republic: diplomatic relations, **Vol. 4, Part 1**, 499, 538; financial reorganization, **Supp. 2**, 311; U.S. presence in, **Supp. 7**, 777
Dominican Order, **Vol. 3, Part 2**, 328, f.; **Vol. 7, Part 1**, 611
"Dominion" movement, in Massachusetts Colony, **Vol. 1, Part 1**, 301; **Vol. 10, Part 2**, 31
Donahey, James H., reference to, **Supp. 6**, 233
Donahue's Magazine, **Vol. 3, Part 1**, 361
Donaldson, H. H., reference to, **Supp. 6**, 671
Donaldson, Walter, reference to, **Supp. 3**, 406
Donen, Stanley, reference to, **Supp. 9**, 291
Don Giovanni, **Supp. 10**, 763
Donham, Wallace, reference to, **Supp. 4**, 565
Doniphan's Expedition, **Vol. 3, Part 1**, 365
"Don Juan in Hell," **Supp. 9**, 560
Donkey, origin of, as Democratic symbol, **Vol. 7, Part l**, 392
Doolittle, Hilda, reference to, **Supp. 9**, 616; **Supp. 10**, 869
Doolittle, William, reference to, **Supp. 9**, 568
"Doonesbury" (comic strip), **Supp. 10**, 353
Doors (music group), **Supp. 9**, 563–64
Donovan, William J., reference to, **Supp. 6**, 531
"Don't give up the ship," **Vol. 6, Part 1**, 50; **Vol. 7, Part 2**, 491
Doolittle, James, references to, **Supp. 4**, 589; **Supp. 6**, 267–68
Doors, architectural design, **Supp. 3**, 2
Doran, George H., reference to, **Supp. 4**, 239–40
Doran, George H., Co., reference to, **Supp. 8**, 535
Dorchester, Mass., founding of, **Vol. 6, Part 1**, 494
Dorchester Heights, attack on, **Vol. 9, Part 2**, 438
Dorgan, Thomas A. ("Tad"), references to, **Supp. 5**, 262; **Supp. 7**, 719
Dorin, Phoebe, reference to, **Supp. 9**, 247
Dorland Advertising Co., **Supp. 6**, 187
Dorman-Smith, Eric, reference to, **Supp. 7**, 335
Dornberger, Walter, reference to, **Supp. 6**, 50
"Dorothy Dix Talks" (column), **Supp. 5**, 244
Dorr, Thomas W., reference to, **Vol. 5, Part 2**, 402
Dorr Rebellion, **Vol. 3, Part 1**, 176, 382, 546; **Vol. 3, Part 2**, 324; **Vol. 5, Part 2**, 386, 402; **Vol. 8, Part 1**, 126 f.; **Vol. 10, Part 1**, 91
Dorrellites, Massachusetts, **Vol. 3, Part 1**, 382 f.
Dorsey, Jimmy, references to, **Supp. 3**, 524–25, **Supp. 6**, 172–73
Dorsey, Thomas A. (gospel songwriter), reference to, **Supp. 9**, 424
Dorsey, Tommy, references to, **Supp. 3**, 524–25; **Supp. 8**, 163; **Supp. 9**, 474–75; **Supp. 10**, 322
Dos Passos, John, references to, **Supp. 7**, 335, 560
Double Agent, The, **Supp. 7**, 55
Double-crostic puzzle, **Supp. 6**, 342
Doubleday, Frank, references to, **Supp. 3**, 234; **Supp. 4**, 239; **Supp. 6**, 465
Doubleday, Nelson, references to, **Supp. 7**, 307; **Supp. 8**, 535; **Supp. 10**, 46
Doubleday and Co.: Anchor books introduced, **Supp. 10**, 46; bookseller inventory levels, **Supp. 10**, 46; management and expansion, **Supp. 10**, 46–47
Doubleday, Doran and Co., **Supp. 4**, 239–40; founding of, **Supp. 6**, 172; **Supp. 8**, 535
Doubleday, Page & Co.: **Vol. 7, Part 2**, 143; **Supp. 8**, 594; Pennsylvania Station bookshop, **Supp. 10**, 46
Double Man, The, **Supp. 9**, 54
Doubrovska, Felia, reference to, **Supp. 8**, 670
Dougherty, Denis Cardinal, reference to, **Supp. 7**, 71
Douglas, Aaron, reference to, **Supp. 6**, 321
Douglas, Donald W., references to, **Supp. 3**, 157; **Supp. 6**, 221
Douglas, Helen Gahagan: Nixon campaign charges against, **Supp. 10**, 184; references to, **Supp. 8**, 282; **Supp. 10**, 57
Douglas, James, reference to, **Vol. 7, Part 1**, 641; **Supp. 3**, 258
Douglas, John, reference to, **Supp. 6**, 426
Douglas, Melvyn, reference to, **Supp. 10**, 183
Douglas, Paul H., references to, **Supp. 3**, 255; **Supp. 7**, 814; **Supp. 10**, 10, 411
Douglas, Stephen A., **Vol. 2, Part 1**, 15, 175; **Vol. 4, Part 2**, 528; **Vol. 8, Part 2**, 467; **Vol. 9, Part 1**, 570; Lincoln's debates with, **Vol. 6, Part 1**, 247 f.; Pendleton's support of, **Vol. 7, Part 2**, 420; nomination of, **Vol. 8, Part 1**, 582; relations with Henry B. Payne, **Vol. 7, Part 2**, 325
Douglas, William O.: Black, H. L., relationship, **Supp. 9**, 96; references to, **Supp. 5**, 575, 576, 589, 714; **Supp. 6**, 216; **Supp. 7**, 453; **Supp. 8**, 36; **Supp. 9**, 835–36
Douglas, Ariz., naming of, **Vol. 3, Part 1**, 396
Douglas Aircraft Co., **Supp. 6**, 666; **Supp. 10**, 495
Douglas DC airplane design, **Supp. 6**, 64, 221
Douglass, Frederick, references to, **Vol. 7, Part 1**, 24, 180, 413; **Supp. 3**, 827–28
Dow, Ada, reference to, **Supp. 4**, 551
Dow, Willard, **Supp. 9**, 75
Dow Chemical Co.: **Supp. 9**, 74–75; antiknock gasoline, **Supp. 3**, 522
Down Argentine Way, **Supp. 5**, 501
Downes, Edward, reference to, **Supp. 5**, 183
Downey, E. H., reference to, **Supp. 6**, 598
Downey, Hal, reference to, **Supp. 4**, 420
Downey, Sheridan, reference to, **Supp. 10**, 183
Downing Street, London, origin of name, **Vol. 3, Part l**, 419
Downtown Gallery (New York City), **Supp. 8**, 239–40
Doyle, Arthur Conan, references to, **Supp. 6**, 465; **Supp. 10**, 103, 104

Doyle, Thomas, J., Co., **Supp. 7**, 189
D'Oyly Carte, Richard, reference to, **Vol. 9, Part 2**, 62
Dracula (play and movie), **Supp. 6**, 395
Draft: boards, establishment of, **Supp. 1**, 211; "genderless" proposal, **Supp. 10**, 57; legal basis, **Supp. 3**, 399; legislation, **Supp. 5**, 715; nurses, **Supp. 9**, 100; post–World War II, **Supp. 7**, 78; universal military training proposals, **Supp. 5**, 531; Vietnam War, **Supp. 10**, 332; World War II, **Supp. 4**, 247; **Supp. 5**, 482, 531; **Supp. 10**, 332. *See also* Conscription
Dragon in the Dust, **Supp. 6**, 686
Drainage: **Vol. 3, Part 1**, 210; **Vol. 5, Part 2**, 143; **Vol. 6, Part 1**, 505; Dismal Swamp, **Vol. 7, Part 1**, 426; Florida Everglades, **Vol. 2, Part 1**, 96; **Vol. 8, Part 1**, 359 f.; house, **Vol. 3, Part 1**, 549; New Orleans, **Vol. 1, Part 2**, 111; Philadelphia, **Vol. 5, Part 2**, 456; Chicago canal, **Vol. 8, Part 1**, 359 f. *See also* Irrigation
Drake, Alexander Wilson, reference to, **Vol. 9, Part 1**, 340
Drake, Charles D., reference to, **Vol. 6, Part 1**, 598
Drake, Edwin L., first oil well drilled by, **Vol. 7, Part 1**, 297, 443
Drake, Joseph, references to, **Vol. 3, Part 1**, 203; **Vol. 4, Part 2**, 159
Drake University, early history of, **Vol. 3, Part 1**, 429
Drama. *See* Theater; *specific play titles*
Drama League of America, founding of, **Supp. 2**, 76
Drama of the Medieval Church, The, **Supp. 3**, 855
Dramatic Technique, **Supp. 1**, 45
Dramatists. For complete list, *see* Occupations Index
Dranesville, Va., action at, **Vol. 7, Part 2**, 48
Draper, Andrew S., reference to, **Supp. 3**, 216
Draper, Dorothy, and Co., founding of, **Supp. 8**, 140–41
Draper, Lyman C., reference to, **Vol. 9, Part 2**, 521
Draper, Paul, reference to, **Supp. 6**, 174
Draper, William Henry, reference to, **Vol. 8, Part 2**, 560
Drawing: birds, **Vol. 1, Part 1**, 427; **Vol. 4, Part 1**, 259; caricatures, **Supp. 10**, 423; comic, **Vol. 2, Part 2**, 480; Booth, Edwin, **Vol. 4, Part 2**, 542; pen, **Vol. 1, Part 2**, 396; teaching of, **Vol. 7, Part 1**, 518; **Vol. 8, Part 1**, 165 f.; writings on, **Vol. 2, Part 2**, 18. *See also* Cartoons; Comic strips; Illustration
Dream We Lost, The: Soviet Russia Then and Now, **Supp. 10**, 800
Dreamer religion, **Vol. 9, Part 1**, 342, 372
Dredging, steam, **Vol. 3, Part 2**, 569; **Vol. 9, Part 1**, 156
Dreier, Margaret, reference to, **Supp. 5**, 578–79
Dreier, Mary, reference to, **Supp. 3**, 639; **Supp. 5**, 380
Dreiser, Theodore, references to, **Vol. 6, Part 1**, 529; **Supp. 6**, 444, 445, 471; **Supp. 7**, 198
"Dress Circular" (1856), **Vol. 6, Part 2**, 277
Dress patterns: paper, **Vol. 2, Part 1**, 375; reform for women, **Vol. 1, Part 2**, 385; **Vol. 4, Part 2**, 376; **Vol. 10, Part 2**, 521; of United States envoys, **Vol. 8, Part 2**, 348; Vogue Pattern Co., **Supp. 3**, 547. *See also* Clothing; Fashion
Dresser, Paul, references to, **Supp. 3**, 233–35; **Supp. 7**, 197, 198
Drew, Daniel, reference to, **Vol. 7, Part 1**, 471
Drew, John, reference to, **Supp. 6**, 38
Drew, Louisa Lane, reference to, **Supp. 3**, 34
Drew Theological Seminary, **Vol. 2, Part 1**, 379; **Vol. 5, Part 1**, 426; **Vol. 6, Part 1**, 590
Drexel and Co., **Supp. 4**, 320
Drexel Institute, **Vol. 3, Part 1**, 455 f.; **Vol. 6, Part 1**, 544
Dreyfus, Louis, reference to, **Supp. 7**, 199
Drills: manufacture of, **Vol. 6, Part 1**, 230; steam, **Vol. 2, Part 2**, 544
Drinking cups, disposable, **Supp. 5**, 144
Dr. Jekyll and Mr. Hyde (movie), **Supp. 3**, 35
"Dr. Kildare" series (movies), **Supp. 3**, 264
"Dr. Kronkhite" (comedy act), **Supp. 9**, 213
Drop hammer, invention of, **Vol. 8, Part 2**, 145
Dropsie College for Hebrew and Cognate Learning, **Vol. 3, Part 1**, 459 f.
Drosophila. *See* Fruit-fly studies
Dr. Seuss. *See* Geisel, Theodor
Drug addiction. *See* Narcotics
Drug Addiction: A Medical Problem, **Supp. 9**, 470
Drug Merchants of America, founding of, **Supp. 4**, 496
Drugs: antibacterial sulfonamide, **Supp. 7**, 477; barbiturates, **Supp. 8**, 102; bioassay methods for standardization of, **Supp. 3**, 242; body temperature relationship, **Supp. 3**, 32; cold-still extraction, **Supp. 2**, 389; custom inspection, **Vol. 8, Part 1**, 242; digitalis, **Supp. 3**, 343; government supervision of, **Vol. 8, Part 1**, 103 f.; laxatives, **Supp. 8**, 339; opium trade, **Vol. 1, Part 1**, 308; **Vol. 3, Part 2**, 508 f.; **Vol. 4, Part 2**, 369; **Vol. 5, Part 2**, 270, 384; **Vol. 6, Part 1**, 491; **Vol. 8, Part 1**, 103 f.; **Vol. 10, Part 2**, 553; patent medicines, **Supp. 5**, 143, 666; penicillin synthetic, **Supp. 10**, 197; pharmacology, **Supp. 3**, 805–6; physiological action of, **Vol. 3, Part 1**, 6; **Vol. 8, Part 1**, 317 f.; plant extracts, **Supp. 2**, 591; prescription, manufacture of, **Supp. 4**, 499–500; research and development, **Supp. 3**, 343; **Supp. 6**, 447–48; **Supp. 9**, 443–44; venereal disease therapy, **Supp. 3**, 854; **Supp. 6**, 424, 460. *See also* Narcotics; Pharmacology; *specific kinds*
Drugstore (painting), **Supp. 8**, 339
Drugstores: chain founding, **Supp. 4**, 496–97; father of modern, **Supp. 2**, 688
Drug traffic. *See* Narcotics
Drummond, Henry, reference to, **Vol. 7, Part 1**, 105
Drury College, presidency of, **Vol. 7, Part 1**, 230
Dry-goods trade, **Vol. 1, Part 2**, 372; **Vol. 2, Part 2**, 110, 285; **Vol. 5, Part 2**, 214; **Vol. 7, Part 2**, 191; **Vol. 9, Part 1**, 135
Dual citizenship, **Vol. 8, Part 2**, 124
Duane, William, references to, **Vol. 6, Part 2**, 81; **Supp. 6**, 69; **Supp. 7**, 10, 134
Duanesburg, N. Y., founding of, **Vol. 3, Part 1**, 465 f.
DuBois, Eugene F., reference to, **Supp. 3**, 805
Du Bois, W. E. B.: biography of, **Supp. 10**, 193; references to, **Supp. 3**, 828; **Supp. 4**, 200–201; **Supp. 5**, 467, 544, 741; **Supp. 6**, 284, 285, 322, 567–68; **Supp. 8**, 95, 522; **Supp. 10**, 137, 192, 193
DuBose, William P., reference to, **Supp. 4**, 546
DuBridge, Lee, reference to, **Supp. 7**, 275
Duchamp, Marcel, references to, **Supp. 3**, 245; **Supp. 5**, 20, 184, 185; **Supp. 10**, 90, 294, 504
Duchin Orchestra, **Supp. 5**, 187–88
Dudley, Dorothy, reference to, **Supp. 3**, 236
Dudley, H. W., reference to, **Supp. 5**, 149
Dudley, Pendleton, reference to, **Supp. 9**, 682
Dudley Observatory, **Vol. 5, Part 1**, 252; **Vol. 7, Part 1**, 39
Duelling, laws against, **Vol. 3, Part 1**, 152; **Vol. 7, Part 1**, 40; **Vol. 8, Part 1**, 190 f.
Duels: **Vol. 1, Part 1**, 650; **Vol. 1, Part 2**, 210; **Vol. 2, Part 1**, 62, 316; **Vol. 2, Part 2**, 116, 125, 177; **Vol. 3, Part 1**, 131; **Vol. 3, Part 2**, 96 f., 373, 448, 501, 529, 533, 571; **Vol. 4, Part 1**, 186; **Vol. 4, Part 2**, 66, 178, 188, 232, 260; **Vol. 5, Part 2**, 526; **Vol. 6, Part 1**, 33, 36, 200, 204, 227, 266; **Vol. 6, Part 2**, 35; **Vol. 7, Part 1**, 426; **Vol. 8, Part 1**, 34 f., 37 f., 220, 365, 425, 526; **Vol. 8, Part 2**, 233, 343; **Vol. 9, Part 1**, 153, 170, 395, 420; **Vol. 9, Part 2**, 48, 366, 380; Barron,

James, v. the secretary to the governor of Malta, **Vol. 3, Part 1**, 187; Broderick v. Terry, **Vol. 10, Part 1**, 628 f.; Brown v. Reynolds, **Vol. 7, Part 1**, 41; Burr v. Hamilton, **Vol. 3, Part 1**, 573 f.; **Vol. 5, Part 1**, 240; Cadwalader v. Conway, **Vol. 3, Part 1**, 303; Cilley v. Graves, **Vol. 5, Part 2**, 172; Clay v. Randolph, **Vol. 5, Part 2**, 63; Decatur v. Barron, **Vol. 3, Part 1**, 187 f.; Denver v. Gilbert, **Vol. 3, Part 1**, 243; De Trobriand, **Vol. 3, Part 1**, 258; Dickinson v. Jackson, **Vol. 5, Part 1**, 528; Dudley v. Richardson, **Vol. 3, Part 1**, 478 f.; Du Pont v. rival suitor, **Vol. 3, Part 1**, 526 f.; Durrett v. Prentice, **Vol. 3, Part 1**, 550 f.; Gadsden v. Howe, **Vol. 5, Part 1**, 295; Hughes v. Cameron, **Vol. 5, Part 1**, 357; Jackson v. Avery, **Vol. 5, Part 1**, 527; Jackson v. Wells, **Vol. 5, Part 1**, 545; Laurens v. Lee, C., **Vol. 6, Part 1**, 100; Leggett v. Banks, **Vol. 6, Part 1**, 147; McIntosh v. Gwinnett, **Vol. 10, Part 1**, 403 f.; Perry v. marine officer, **Vol. 3, Part 1**, 189; Pleasants v. Ritchie, **Vol. 8, Part 1**, 7 f.; Poe v. Daniel, **Vol. 8, Part 1**, 19 f.; Poindexter v. Hunt, **Vol. 8, Part 1**, 29 f.; Poor v. junior officer, **Vol. 8, Part 1**, 69; Porter v. fellow officer, **Vol. 8, Part 1**, 82 f.; Porter v. Smyth, **Vol. 8, Part 1**, 99 f.; Price v. Thomas, **Vol. 9, Part 2**, 429; Pryor, Roger Atkinson, **Vol. 8, Part 1**, 255 f.; Queen v. Byrd, **Vol. 8, Part 1**, 298 f.; Randolph v. Clay, **Vol. 8, Part 1**, 363 f.; Randolph v. Taylor, **Vol. 8, Part 1**, 363 f.; slidell, **Vol. 9, Part 1**, 210; Snipes v. Simons, **Vol. 8, Part 1**, 425; Tattnall, **Vol. 9, Part 2**, 310; Van Allen v. Crawford, **Vol. 9, Part 2**, 274; Walker, William, **Vol. 10, Part 1**, 363 f.; Webb, James Watson, **Vol. 10, Part 1**, 574 f.; Webb v. fellow officers, **Vol. 10, Part 1**, 574 f.; Wilkinson v. Gates, **Vol. 4, Part 1**, 186
Duff, James H., references to, **Supp. 7**, 305; **Supp. 10**, 241, 242
Duffey, Joseph, reference to, **Supp. 9**, 59
Duffy, Richard, reference to, **Supp. 6**, 514
Dugan, Raymond Smith, reference to, **Supp. 6**, 560
Duke, James B., references to, **Supp. 3**, 587; **Supp. 4**, 370, 371; **Supp. 5**, 566–67
Duke University: **Vol. 1, Part 2**, 38; **Vol. 2, Part 2**, 516 f.; **Vol. 3, Part 1**, 496 f.; endowment and establishment of, **Supp. 2**, 181, 668; **Supp. 5**, 567; parapsychology studies, **Supp. 10**, 672
Duke's Laws, legal code, **Vol. 7, Part 1**, 515 f.
Dulles, Allen W., references to, **Supp. 6**, 170; **Supp. 8**, 159; **Supp. 9**, 3
Dulles, John Foster, references to, **Supp. 6**, 235; **Supp. 7**, 35, 420, 467; **Supp. 8**, 147, 157, 160, 223, 276; **Supp. 9**, 10, 106, 230, 831; **Supp. 10**, 144
Dulles International Airport (Va.), architectural design, **Supp. 7**, 671, 672
Duluth Eskimos (football), **Supp. 10**, 585
Dumbarton Oaks (Washington, D.C.): Byzantine art collection, **Supp. 5**, 700, 708; **Supp. 7**, 60, 673; gardens, **Supp. 6**, 197; UN conference (1944), **Supp. 5**, 537
Dumont, Margaret, reference to, **Supp. 10**, 515
Dumont Laboratories, **Supp. 7**, 206
Dumont Television Network, **Supp. 10**, 343–44
Dun and Bradstreet, Inc., founding of, **Supp. 6**, 693–94
Dunbar, Paul Laurence, references to, **Supp. 3**, 187, 834
Duncan, Isadora, photographs of, **Supp. 3**, 296
Duncan, Otis Dudley, reference to, **Supp. 6**, 483
Duncan Hines cake mixes, **Supp. 6**, 292
Duncker, Karl, reference to, **Supp. 3**, 808
Dunglison, Robley, reference to, **Vol. 1, Part 2**, 108
Dunkers, leadership of, **Vol. 9, Part 1**, 416
Dunlap, William, references to, **Vol. 5, Part 1**, 103, 498; **Vol. 8, Part 2**, 386; **Vol. 9, Part 1**, 260
Dunmore's War (1774–75), **Vol. 4, Part 2**, 353; **Vol. 5, Part 2**, 433; **Vol. 6, Part 1**, 206, 357, 362 f.; **Vol. 9, Part 2**, 563; **Supp. 1**, 189. *See also* Indians, American (by tribe); Oneida; Point Pleasant, battle of
Dunn, Jack, reference to, **Supp. 9**, 343
Dunne, Edward F., reference to, **Supp. 3**, 599
Dunne, Finley Peter, reference to, **Supp. 3**, 762
Dunning, John R., reference to, **Supp. 6**, 501
Dunning, William A., reference to, **Supp. 5**, 498
Dun's Review, inaugurated, **Vol. 3, Part 1**, 503
Dunster, Henry, reference to, **Vol. 7, Part 1**, 55
Dunster House Book Shop (Cambridge, Mass.), **Supp. 7**, 55
Du Pont, Alfred I., references to, **Supp. 5**, 192, 193
Du Pont, Coleman, reference to, **Supp. 5**, 192–93
Du Pont, Ernest, reference to, **Supp. 3**, 239
Du Pont, Pierre S., references to, **Supp. 1**, 270–71; **Supp. 4**, 244, 681, 682, 683, 684; **Supp. 5**, 191, 192; **Supp. 7**, 169, 210; **Supp. 8**, 598–600
Du Pont, E. I., de Nemours & Co.: **Supp. 1**, 270–71; **Supp. 4**, 681; **Supp. 5**, 191–92, 235, 662–63; **Supp. 7**, 11, 169, 210; antiknock gasoline, **Supp. 3**, 522; management, **Supp. 10**, 102; munitions manufacture, **Supp. 9**, 622; research laboratories, **Supp. 2**, 551; **Supp. 3**, 239
Du Pont Powder Co., **Vol. 7, Part 1**, 301; **Supp. 1**, 270
DuPre, George, reference to, **Supp. 7**, 643
Duran, Carolus, reference to, **Vol. 1, Part 2**, 120
Durant, Henry F., references to, **Vol. 5, Part 1**, 274; **Vol. 7, Part 1**, 104
Durant, Will, reference to, **Supp. 8**, 579
Durant, William C., references to, **Supp. 3**, 273–74; **Supp. 4**, 295, 620, 681–82; **Supp. 5**, 193; **Supp. 7**, 246; **Supp. 8**, 598; **Supp. 9**, 568
Durant-Dort Carriage Co., **Supp. 4**, 620
Durante, Jimmy, references to, **Supp. 8**, 547; **Supp. 9**, 513
Durham, N. C., development of, **Vol. 3, Part 1**, 496 f., 549 f.
Durkin, Martin P., reference to, **Supp. 8**, 156
Durocher, Leo, reference to, **Supp. 6**, 489
Durrell, Lawrence, reference to, **Supp. 10**, 539
Durstine, Roy, reference to, **Supp. 8**, 27
Durstine, Roy S., Inc., **Supp. 7**, 211
Duryea, Charles, references to, **Supp. 4**, 292; **Supp. 8**, 148
Duryea, J. Frank, reference to, **Supp. 4**, 292
Duse, Eleanora, reference to, **Supp. 3**, 297
Dutch East India Co., **Vol. 5, Part 1**, 339
Dutch elm disease, **Supp. 7**, 33
Dutch Reformed church, **Vol. 4, Part 2**, 241, 367, 376; **Vol. 6, Part 1**, 314; **Vol. 6, Part 2**, 591; **Vol. 8, Part 2**, 572 f.; **Vol. 9, Part 2**, 366 f.; **Supp. 8**, 457
Dutch settlements in America, **Vol. 5, Part 1**, 503; **Vol. 6, Part 1**, 156; **Vol. 7, Part 1**, 284, 613; **Vol. 8, Part 2**, 455
Dutton, E. P., & Co., Everyman's Library, **Supp. 3**, 499
Duveen, Joseph, references to, **Supp. 3**, 24; **Supp. 5**, 401
Duveen brothers (art dealers), **Supp. 6**, 56
Duxbury, Mass., founding of, **Vol. 9, Part 1**, 500
Dvořák, Antonín, references to, **Supp. 4**, 125, 276, 834, 835; **Supp. 5**, 218
Dvorak, Frank, reference to, **Supp. 6**, 27
Dwight, James, reference to, **Supp. 3**, 701
Dwight, Timothy, references to, **Vol. 9, Part 2**, 338, 392
Dwight and Lloyd Metallurgical Co., founding of, **Supp. 4**, 246
Dworshak, Henry, reference to, **Supp. 6**, 681
Dyes, **Vol. 1, Part 1**, 563; **Vol. 6, Part 2**, 43, 401, 417;

Vol. 7, Part 1, 404; **Vol. 7, Part 2**, 616; industry development, **Supp. 2**, 301, 631
Dylan, Bob, references to, **Supp. 8**, 235; **Supp. 9**, 317; **Supp. 10**, 602, 603
Dynamite, first use of, **Vol. 5, Part 2**, 239; **Vol. 7, Part 2**, 22
Dynamos, electric, **Vol. 5, Part 2**, 509; **Vol. 8, Part 2**, 198; **Vol. 10, Part 1**, 376 f.; **Vol. 10, Part 2**, 462
Dynel (synthetic fabric), **Supp. 6**, 67
Dysentery, bacillus discovery, **Supp. 4**, 287

E

Eads, James Buchanan, references to, **Vol. 7, Part 1**, 617; **Vol. 9, Part 2**, 311
Eads Bridge (St. Louis), **Vol. 3, Part 2**, 445; **Vol. 6, Part 1**, 549; **Vol. 8, Part 2**, 19
Eagels, Jeanne, references to, **Supp. 8**, 444; **Supp. 10**, 237
Eagleton, Thomas, reference to, **Supp. 9**, 512
Eaker, Ira, reference to, **Supp. 9**, 746, 747
Eakins, Thomas, reference to, **Vol. 7, Part 1**, 627
Eames, Charles, references to, **Supp. 4**, 715; **Supp. 7**, 670, 671
Eames, Emma, reference to, **Supp. 3**, 42
Eames, Wilberforce, references to, **Supp. 8**, 663, 664
Ear, study of, **Supp. 9**, 72
Earhart, Amelia: Cochran relationship, **Supp. 10**, 133; references to, **Supp. 6**, 477, 478
Earle, Ellis B., reference to, **Supp. 6**, 187
Earle, George H., references to, **Supp. 3**, 20; **Supp. 8**, 360
Earle, George Howard, III, reference to, **Supp. 9**, 426
Early childhood education. *See* Preschool education; Kindergartens
Early Elizabethan Playhouse, An, **Supp. 9**, 627
Earthquakes: **Vol. 8, Part 1**, 395; **Vol. 9, Part 2**, 308, 586; research on, **Supp. 4**, 897; **Supp. 6**, 154; San Andreas Fault map, **Supp. 4**, 558; San Francisco, **Supp. 1**, 638; **Supp. 4**, 325, 417; **Supp. 5**, 416; San Francisco photographs, **Supp. 3**, 295; seismological observatories, **Supp. 1**, 579–80
East, Edward M., reference to, **Supp. 4**, 252
Eastern Airlines: **Supp. 7**, 16; management, **Supp. 9**, 658, 659
Eastern Air Transport. *See* Eastern Airlines
Eastern Livestock Cooperative Marketing Association, founding of, **Supp. 1**, 644
Eastern Railroads Presidents Conference, **Supp. 6**, 91
Eastern religions, **Supp. 8**, 431
East India: exploration, **Vol. 5, Part 1**, 236; trade, **Vol. 2, Part 1**, 83, 149; **Vol. 4, Part 1**, 523; **Vol. 4, Part 2**, 482; **Vol. 6, Part 1**, 108
East India Co., **Vol. 3, Part 1**, 467 f.; **Vol. 10, Part 2**, 591
East India Marine Society, founding of, **Vol. 8, Part 2**, 153
Eastman, Crystal, reference to, **Supp. 5**, 631
Eastman, Edward R., reference to, **Supp. 3**, 434
Eastman, George, references to, **Supp. 3**, 26, 41; **Supp. 4**, 105; **Supp. 10**, 249
Eastman, Max, references to, **Supp. 3**, 852; **Supp. 6**, 664; **Supp. 7**, 269
Eastman Kodak Co.: **Vol. 4, Part 2**, 410; **Vol. 8, Part 2**, 554; Nepera Chemical Co. acquisition, **Supp. 3**, 26; business operations, **Supp. 10**, 249; research laboratory, **Supp. 4**, 743–44; **Supp. 6**, 442; **Supp. 7**, 511, 512
Eastman School of Music, founding of, **Supp. 1**, 276
Eastman's National Business College, **Vol. 3, Part 1**, 602
East River (New York City), bridges, **Supp. 3**, 530–31
Eastwood, Clint, **Supp. 10**, 239
"Easy Aces" (radio program), **Supp. 9**, 6
Easy Chair, **Vol. 5, Part 1**, 310
Eaton, Cyrus, reference to, **Supp. 7**, 289
Eaton, John H., references to, **Vol. 5, Part 1**, 532; **Vol. 7, Part 2**, 41 f.
Eaton, Theophilus, reference to, **Vol. 5, Part 1**, 207
Ebbetts, Charles, references to, **Supp. 7**, 752; **Supp. 9**, 858
Eben Holden, **Supp. 4**, 38
Eberhard Faber Company, **Supp. 10**, 670
Eberhardt, Ernest G., reference to, **Supp. 4**, 499
Eberhart, Nelle Richmond, reference to, **Supp. 4**, 138
Ebsen, Buddy, reference to, **Supp. 10**, 301
Eccles, Marriner, reference to, **Supp. 8**, 446
Echo Park (Colo.), **Supp. 7**, 31
Eckert, John Presper, references to, **Supp. 10**, 519, 520, 521
Eckhart, Percy B., reference to, **Supp. 6**, 683
Eckstine, Billy, Orchestra, **Supp. 5**, 534
Eclectic Medical College, founding of, **Vol. 7, Part 1**, 476; **Vol. 8, Part 2**, 524
Eclectic Medical Journal, founding of, **Vol. 1, Part 2**, 86; **Vol. 8, Part 2**, 524
Eclectic medicine, **Supp. 2**, 389; pioneer works in, **Vol. 5, Part 2**, 393; **Vol. 7, Part 1**, 237, 475 f.; **Vol. 8, Part 2**, 524
Eclipse, study of, **Vol. 3, Part 1**, 92 f., 274, 602; **Vol. 8, Part 2**, 412; **Vol. 9, Part 2**, 50
École des Beaux Arts, first woman at, **Supp. 6**, 463
Ecological Society of America, founding of, **Supp. 2**, 128
Ecology: **Vol. 9, Part 1**, 427; first college department of, **Supp. 5**, 374; founding as science, **Supp. 2**, 127–28; pesticides and herbicides, writings on, **Supp. 7**, 109–10; plant, **Supp. 4**, 501; pollution control advocacy, **Supp. 10**, 297–98; popular writings on, **Supp. 8**, 486; terminology development, **Supp. 3**, 168–170; wildlife, **Supp. 4**, 482–84. *See also* Conservation; Environment; Pollution
Econometrics, **Supp. 6**, 459, 656
Econometric Society, founding of, **Supp. 2**, 599; **Supp. 4**, 275
Economic Advisory Council, Truman political dispute with, **Supp. 9**, 589
Economic and Social History of the World War, **Supp. 7**, 688
Economic Consequences of the Peace, The, **Supp. 5**, 85, 272
Economic Geography, founding of, **Supp. 4**, 33
Economic Geology, founding of, **Vol. 5, Part 1**, 502
Economic Interpretation of the Constitution of the United States, An, **Supp. 4**, 62
Economics: **Vol. 1, Part 1**, 67 f.; **Vol. 3, Part 1**, 503; **Vol. 4, Part 1**, 211 f., 213; **Vol. 5, Part 1**, 238, 574; **Vol. 5, Part 2**, 52; **Vol. 6, Part 1**, 292; **Vol. 8, Part 2**, 42; **Vol. 9, Part 1**, 183, 419; **Vol. 10, Part 2**, 212; academics' impact on institutions, **Supp. 6**, 585–86; agricultural, **Supp. 4**, 45; **Supp. 6**, 638–39; **Supp. 9**, 588–89; base pricing, **Supp. 4**, 268; business cycles, **Supp. 4**, 722, 723; business fluctuations, **Supp. 2**, 529; business studies, **Supp. 7**, 124–25, 440, 441; Chicago school, **Supp. 4**, 748–49; **Supp. 9**, 466; **Supp. 10**, 382; credit relationship to, **Supp. 6**, 599; culture of poverty theory, **Supp. 8**, 335; demand-side, **Supp. 8**, 79; fiscal and monetary policy, **Supp. 10**, 205; forecasting, **Supp. 4**, 36; foreign development and technical aid, **Supp. 10**, 472; government planning v. free theories, **Supp. 6**, 494–95; **Supp. 9**, 466; **Supp. 10**, 22, 287, 382–83, 752; historical analysis of, **Supp. 4**, 322, 721–23; **Supp. 8**, 669; historical writings on, **Supp. 8**, 243, 669; home, **Vol. 7**,

Part 1, 575; **Vol. 8, Part 1**, 554, 563 f.; in government policy making, **Supp. 5**, 247; **Supp. 10**, 376–77, 471; institutional, **Supp. 3**, 176–80; **Supp. 6**, 705; institutional forerunners, **Supp. 3**, 248–49; journals, **Supp. 1**, 487; Keynesian, **Supp. 3**, 656; **Supp. 8**, 446; **Supp. 9**, 362–63, 366; **Supp. 10**, 382; labor, **Supp. 4**, 579–80; **Supp. 6**, 503–4, 705–6, 801; laissez-faire, **Supp. 1**, 197; legal research and, **Supp. 6**, 271; marginal utility principle of value, **Supp. 2**, 106–7; medical care, **Supp. 6**, 702–3; **Supp. 9**, 366–67; microeconomics, **Supp. 8**, 82–83; monetary theory, **Supp. 2**, 577; **Supp. 3**, 413–14, 307, 585–88; monopolistic competition theory, **Supp. 8**, 82–83; National Industrial Conference Board, **Supp. 7**, 404–5; organizations, **Supp. 2**, 106; post-World War I study, **Supp. 5**, 85, 272, 537; prices, **Supp. 2**, 175; production functions, **Supp. 10**, 185; quantitative, **Supp. 4**, 584–88; socialist, **Supp. 5**, 134–36; societal change and, **Supp. 3**, 248; statistical application to, **Supp. 6**, 459, 656; **Supp. 9**, 661; study of immigration and census, **Vol. 6, Part 2**, 467; supply and demand, **Supp. 2**, 599; teaching of, **Vol. 5, Part 1**, 316; **Vol. 5, Part 2**, 52; **Vol. 8, Part 2**, 480, 531; **Vol. 9, Part 2**, 323; **Vol. 10, Part 2**, 19, 619; **Supp. 2**, 650; **Supp. 5**, 161; **Supp. 8**, 165–66; **Supp. 9**, 362, 466–67; theory and analysis, **Supp. 9**, 362–63; transactions as units in, **Supp. 3**, 179; value theories; **Supp. 4**, 18, 267–68, 272–73; wealth distribution, **Supp. 3**, 545–46; World War I study, **Supp. 2**, 108; writings on, **Vol. 2, Part 1**, 379, 425; **Vol. 2, Part 2**, 335; **Vol. 3, Part 1**, 266, 408, 463 f., 503 f.; **Vol. 4, Part 1**, 214, 216, 541 f.; **Vol. 5, Part 2**, 52; **Vol. 6, Part 2**, 43, 173; **Vol. 7, Part 1**, 548; **Vol. 7, Part 2**, 639; **Vol. 8, Part 1**, 70 f., 100 f., 118 f., 161 f., 176 f., 229 f., 248 f., 301 f., 321 f., 325 f.; **Vol. 8, Part 2**, 531; **Vol. 9, Part 1**, 593; **Vol. 10, Part 1**, 29, 594, 637; **Vol. 10, Part 2**, 564, 620; **Supp. 1**, 487; **Supp. 2**, 607, 651; **Supp. 4**, 18; **Supp. 8**, 165–66; **Supp. 9**, 362, 363, 366–67, 466, 589; **Supp. 10**, 185, 186, 377, 383. *See also* Great Depression

Economics of Collective Action, The, **Supp. 3**, 179

Economics of Labor, **Supp. 4**, 577

Economics of Recovery, The, **Supp. 4**, 36

Economists. For complete list, *see* Occupations Index

Economists' National Committee on Monetary Policy, founding of, **Supp. 4**, 18

Economy, Pa., Harmony Society of, **Vol. 8, Part 1**, 383 f.

Ecstasy (movie), censorship of, **Supp. 3**, 181

Ectomorphic personality, **Supp. 10**, 731

Ectopic pregnancy, **Supp. 6**, 555

Ecuador, diplomacy, **Vol. 9, Part 2**, 141

Ecumenism: **Supp. 2**, 86; **Supp. 3**, 110–11; **Supp. 6**, 315, 548, 600, 607; **Supp. 7**, 597; Catholic church, **Supp. 8**, 115, 537; Christian religions in China, **Supp. 2**, 549; conferences, **Vol. 5, Part 2**, 561; **Supp. 1**, 116; **Supp. 4**, 547–48; organizations, **Supp. 3**, 514–16; **Supp. 10**, 111, 405; Polish Catholic church, **Supp. 5**, 305; theological advocacy, **Supp. 3**, 825; **Supp. 7**, 775–76; **Supp. 10**, 111

Eddington, A. S., reference to, **Supp. 6**, 8

Eddy, Mary Baker, references to, **Vol. 9, Part 1**, 596; **Vol. 10, Part 2**, 189; biography of, **Supp. 2**, 152

Eddy, Nelson, reference to, **Supp. 7**, 499

Eddy, Sherwood, reference to, **Supp. 3**, 476

Eddy, Thomas, reference to, **Vol. 7, Part l**, 360

Edelbaum, Maurice, reference to, **Supp. 9**, 269

Edison, Charles, references to, **Supp. 6**, 265, 266, 339

Edison, Thomas A., references to, **Vol. 5, Part 2**, 562; **Vol. 6, Part 1**, 176, 235; **Vol. 7, Part 1**, 368; **Vol. 8, Part 1**, 75 f.; **Supp. 1**, 669; **Supp. 2**, 333; **Supp. 3**, 75, 527, 768, 769; **Supp. 4**, 216; **Supp. 5**, 229; **Supp. 8**, 151, 152

Edison Co., **Supp. 3**, 607; **Supp. 7**, 579

Edison Electric Illuminating Co., **Vol. 6, Part 1**, 235; **Supp. 3**, 746; **Supp. 8**, 152

Edison Electric Institute, **Supp. 3**, 138; **Supp. 4**, 302

Edison General Electric Co., **Vol. 8, Part 2**, 359. *See also* General Electric Co.

Editing, historical texts, **Supp. 10**, 429–30

Editors. For complete list, *see* Occupations Index

Edmonds, Walter D., reference to, **Supp. 5**, 132

Edson, Theodore, reference to, **Vol. 1, Part 2**, 457

"Ed Sullivan Show, The": Beatles appearance on, **Supp. 10**, 449; influence on television, **Supp. 9**, 780; Presley appearance on, **Supp. 10**, 648

Education (general; for educators, teachers, professors, college presidents, etc., *see* Occupations Index), **Vol. 1, Part 1**, 289, 293, 295, 388, 408, 447 f., 522, 600; **Vol. 2, Part 1**, 2, 118, 250, 288, 335, 378, 402, 409, 442, 482; **Vol. 2, Part 2**, 370 f., 418; **Vol. 3, Part 1**, 459 f., 563 f.; **Vol. 3, Part 2**, 127, 202, 391, 418, 561; **Vol. 4, Part 1**, 115, 165, 183, 219, 280 f., 299 f., 459, 602 f.; **Vol. 4, Part 2**, 43, 76, 129; **Vol. 5, Part 1**, 66, 133, 260; **Vol. 5, Part 2**, 32, 94, 130, 266, 411 f., 575; **Vol. 6, Part 1**, 16, 39, 72, 177 f., 203 f., 223 f., 278 f., 404, 544, 555; **Vol. 6, Part 2**, 58, 71, 124, 171, 238, 241 f., 266, 445; **Vol. 7, Part 1**, 641; **Vol. 7, Part 2**, 18 f., 404, 598; **Vol. 8, Part 1**, 126 f., 223 f., 381, 546; **Vol. 8, Part 2**, 122, 218, 250, 253 f., 255, 280, 330, 371; **Vol. 9, Part 1**, 58, 98 f., 184, 204; **Vol. 9, Part 2**, 244, 301, 479; **Vol. 10, Part 1**, 490 f., 558, 645; **Vol. 10, Part 2**, 179, 213, 484, 495, 625; academic freedom, **Vol. 8, Part 1**, 118 f.; **Supp. 8**, 582–84; **Supp. 9**, 429, 769; **Supp. 10**, 137, 143, 386; administration, **Supp. 3**, 205–6; **Supp. 6**, 97–98; **Supp. 8**, 9; **Supp. 10**, 31–32; adult, **Vol. 5, Part 1**, 130; **Vol. 6, Part 1**, 155, 178; **Vol. 10, Part 2**, 640; **Supp. 2**, 45, 455; **Supp. 4**, 833; **Supp. 5**, 431–32; **Supp. 8**, 58, 488; **Supp. 9**, 447; Bennett Law, compulsory English, **Vol. 5, Part 2**, 506; bilingual, **Supp. 7**, 43; black, **Vol. 1, Part 1**, 360; **Vol. 1, Part 2**, 432; **Vol. 2, Part 1**, 138; **Vol. 2, Part 2**, 504 f.; **Vol. 4, Part 1**, 36, 96; **Vol. 4, Part 2**, 453; **Vol. 5, Part 2**, 598; **Vol. 7, Part 1**, 43; **Vol. 7, Part 2**, 324; **Vol. 8, Part 1**, 513; **Vol. 10, Part 1**, 66, 506 f.; **Vol. 10, Part 2**, 229, 253, 641; **Supp. 2**, 150, 315, 476; **Supp. 4**, 915; **Supp. 5**, 55–56, 642; **Supp. 7**, 83; **Supp. 9**, 108, 562; **Supp. 10**, 172; blind, for the, **Vol. 1, Part 1**, 261; **Vol. 2, Part 1**, 38, 451; **Vol. 2, Part 2**, 106 f,; **Vol. 3, Part 2**, 409 f.; **Vol. 9, Part 1**, 29 f.; **Vol. 10, Part 2**, 455; **Supp. 3**, 364; **Supp. 4**, 10–11; **Supp. 5**, 347–48; boards, **Supp. 5**, 432; Catholic, **Vol. 1, Part 1**, 302; **Vol. 2, Part 2**, 337 f.; **Vol. 3, Part 2**, 440; **Vol. 4, Part 2**, 541; **Vol. 6, Part 2**, 163; **Vol. 7, Part 1**, 74; **Vol. 8, Part 2**, 265; **Supp. 3**, 325–26, 393; character development, **Supp. 4**, 767; child-oriented, **Supp. 7**, 600–601; child-study, early, **Vol. 6, Part 1**, 276; church-state separation issues, **Supp. 4**, 796; **Supp. 5**, 358, 461; classical approach to, **Supp. 3**, 810; **Supp. 6**, 46; coeducation, **Vol. 1, Part 2**, 430; **Vol. 3, Part 1**, 423; **Vol. 3, Part 2**, 95; commercial, **Vol. 3, Part 1**, 602; **Vol. 7, Part 2**, 130 f.; Committee of Ten of the National Education Association, **Vol. 5, Part 2**, 60; corporal punishment, abandonment of, **Vol. 3, Part 1**, 409; **Vol. 8, Part 1**, 412; correspondence courses, **Vol. 8, Part 1**, 126; **Supp. 2**, 199; curriculum determination, **Supp. 3**, 552; curriculum reform, **Supp. 10**, 138; day nurseries, **Vol. 1, Part 2**, 471; deaf, of the, **Vol. 1, Part 2**, 139, 149 f.; **Vol. 2, Part 1**, 38; **Vol.2, Part 2**, 150 f., 201 f.; **Vol. 4, Part l**, 110 f.; **Vol. 8, Part 2**, 94; **Supp. 3**, 311–12; Eaton's system, **Vol. 3, Part 1**, 608 f.; endowments, **Supp. 9**, 623; elective

system, **Vol. 3, Part 2**, 73; **Vol. 7, Part 2**, 405; **Vol. 8, Part 1**, 308 f.; elementary, **Vol. 1, Part 1**, 621 f.; **Vol. 4, Part 1**, 574 f.; **Vol. 4, Part 2**, 91; **Vol. 9, Part 1**, 141; evening classes, **Supp. 2**, 45; federal involvement, **Supp. 9**, 25–26; field schools, **Vol. 5, Part 2**, 149; films, **Supp. 9**, 80–81; financial gifts to, **Supp. 9**, 743; financing of, **Supp. 8**, 166; **Supp. 10**, 250–51; first business course in academic institution, **Vol. 7, Part 2**, 299; first business high school in U.S., **Vol. 8, Part 1**, 152; first college to offer graduate work to women, **Vol. 8, Part 1**, 531; first free school west of the Mississippi, **Vol. 3, Part 1**, 477 f.; first institution designed primarily for research, **Vol. 8, Part 1**, 501; first primary school, **Vol. 8, Part 1**, 80; **Vol. 9, Part 2**, 524; first public school nursing, **Supp. 2**, 687; first state charter to be granted for girls' education in U.S., **Vol. 8, Part 1**, 71; first survey of U.S. theological, **Supp. 3**, 111; first university to have school of education, **Vol. 9, Part 1**, 37; first university to open all its professional schools to women, **Vol. 10, Part 1**, 490 f.; first work-study plan, **Supp. 3**, 63; first women's school in South, **Vol. 6, Part 2**, 289; food programs, **Supp. 3**, 28; **Supp. 6**, 81; foreign exchange students, **Supp. 4**, 592–93; free schools, **Vol. 2, Part 2**, 108; **Vol. 3, Part 2**, 99; **Vol. 4, Part 2**, 314, 415; **Vol. 9, Part 1**, 63; **Vol. 9, Part 2**, 261; for freedmen, **Vol. 9, Part 2**, 11; **Vol. 10, Part 1**, 27; general science courses, **Supp. 4**, 139–40; German system, **Supp. 3**, 676; gifted students, **Supp. 2**, 110; **Supp. 4**, 732; health standards in schools, **Supp. 5**, 553; Herbartian method, **Supp. 2**, 424; higher education, public support of, **Vol. 2, Part 1**, 462; **Vol. 3, Part 2**, 319; **Vol. 10, Part 1**, 558 f.; high school administration, **Vol. 9, Part 1**, 37; historical studies on, **Supp. 2**, 532, 663; **Supp. 4**, 592; **Supp. 10**, 136; home, **Supp. 5**, 437–38; honor system, **Vol. 5, Part 2**, 148; **Vol. 10, Part 1**, 32; Indian, **Vol. 1, Part 1**, 238; **Vol. 1, Part 2**, 478 f.; **Vol. 2, Part 1**, 446; **Vol. 3, Part 1**, 376; **Vol. 4, Part l**, 101; **Vol. 4, Part 2**, 332, 380, 414; **Vol. 5, Part 2**, 115, 176, 428, 504; **Vol. 6, Part 1**, 428 f.; **Vol. 6, Part 2**, 453, 471, 496; **Vol. 7, Part 2**, 336; **Vol. 8, Part 1**, 111, 175; **Vol. 8, Part 2**, 30; **Vol. 10, Part 2**, 58; individualism in, **Vol. 6, Part 2**, 325; industrial, **Vol. 1, Part 1**, 421; **Vol. 3, Part 1**, 319, 455 f.; **Vol. 3, Part 2**, 479; **Vol. 4, Part 2**, 518; **Vol. 5, Part 1**, 130; **Vol. 6, Part 1**, 178; **Vol. 7, Part 2**, 398; **Vol. 9, Part 2**, 282; **Vol. 10, Part 1**, 68, 407 f., 617 f.; inspection of private schools, **Vol. 3, Part 1**, 369; international meetings on, **Supp. 4**, 449; intuitive-thinking emphasis, **Supp. 3**, 429, journals, **Supp. 1**, 103; junior high school and junior college movements, **Vol. 1, Part 1**, 522; **Vol. 5, Part 2**, 591; **Vol. 8, Part 2**, 42; kindergartens, **Vol. 1, Part 2**, 392, 393, 575; **Vol. 2, Part 2**, 412; **Vol. 4, Part 2**, 90, 338; **Vol. 5, Part 2**, 499 f.; **Vol. 6, Part 2**, 355; **Vol. 7, Part 2**, 336; **Vol. 8, Part 2**, 560; **Vol. 9, Part 1**, 47; **Vol. 10, Part 2**, 180; **Supp. 1**, 13, 407; **Supp. 4**, 373–74; **Supp. 4**, 874–75; **Supp. 5**, 437–38; laboratory courses, **Supp. 1**, 30; Lancastrian system, **Vol. 2, Part 2**, 224; **Vol. 6, Part 1**, 440; land grants for, **Vol. 9, Part 2**, 261; law school, first in America, **Vol. 8, Part 1**, 469; legal issues, **Supp. 2**, 143; liberal arts curriculum, **Supp. 10**, 364–65; liberal undergraduate studies, **Supp. 10**, 542; libraries, popularizing, **Supp. 3**, 90–91; Little Red School House, **Supp. 3**, 376; Lyceum system, **Vol. 5, Part 2**, 149; McGuffey Readers, effect of, **Vol. 6, Part 2**, 58; mentally retarded, **Vol. 2, Part 1**, 117; **Vol. 10, Part 2**, 199; **Supp. 3**, 389; **Supp. 4**, 438–39; **Supp. 6**, 241; **Supp. 7**, 284; military, **Vol. 2, Part 2**, 581; **Vol. 4, Part 1**, 206; **Vol. 5, Part 2**, 49, 91, 115; **Vol. 6, Part 1**, 39; **Vol. 7, Part 2**, 281 f.; **Vol. 8, Part 1**, 49 f.; **Vol. 9, Part 1**, 115, 264, 600; mission schools, **Supp. 3**, 476–77; **Supp. 5**, 185–86; "modern methods" in eighteenth century, **Vol. 3, Part 1**, 332 f.; Montessori method, **Vol. 9, Part 1**, 349; national department of, **Vol. 4, Part 2**, 415; **Vol. 8, Part 1**, 562; naval, **Supp. 3**, 275; New York centralization, **Supp. 4**, 134; "object teaching," **Vol. 5, Part 2**, 510; parent-teacher associations, **Vol. 2, Part 1**, 345; Peabody Fund, for promotion of Southern, **Vol. 2, Part 2**, 606; **Vol. 7, Part 2**, 57, 337; **Vol. 8, Part 2**, 537 f.; pedagogy, first chair of, **Vol. 7, Part 2**, 332; Pestalozzian principles, **Vol. 5, Part 2**, 510; philanthropic gifts for, **Supp. 2**, 375; **Supp. 5**, 61; philosophical approaches to, **Supp. 5**, 71–72; physical, **Vol. 1, Part 2**, 322; **Vol. 4, Part 2**, 47; **Vol. 5, Part 1**, 71; **Vol. 6, Part 1**, 160, 209, 353; **Vol. 7, Part 1**, 277; **Vol. 8, Part 2**, 355; **Vol. 10, Part 1**, 92; **Supp. 5**, 553; physical, introduction to Japan, **Vol. 6, Part 1**, 160; physical, teaching of, **Vol. 7, Part 1**, 277–78; physical, for women, **Supp. 5**, 51–52; platoon (work-study-play) system, **Supp. 2**, 728; popular, **Vol. 4, Part 1**, 217; preceptorial system, Princeton, **Vol. 10, Part 2**, 354; private schools, **Vol. 6, Part 2**, 93; **Supp. 3**, 591–92; **Supp. 9**, 173, 174–75; progressive, **Vol. 1, Part 1**, 139, 142; **Vol. 2, Part 1**, 538; **Vol. 3, Part 1**, 337 f.; **Vol. 3, Part 2**, 468; **Vol. 8, Part 1**, 97 f., 152; **Vol. 8, Part 2**, 42; **Vol. 9, Part 1**, 64, 67, 600; **Vol. 10, Part 2**, 626; **Supp. 3**, 375–76, 552, 677; **Supp. 4**, 139, 373–74; **Supp. 5**, 71–72.; **Supp. 6**, 208, 558; **Supp. 8**, 443; progressive, criticism of, **Supp. 3**, 555; **Supp. 4**, 40; progressive, Gary system, **Supp. 2**, 728; progressive, individualized, **Supp. 7**, 42–43, 435; progressive, opposition to, **Supp. 4**, 40; progressive, Lincoln school, **Supp. 3**, 552; **Supp. 4**, 139; progressive, training in, **Supp. 8**, 443; project method, **Vol. 8, Part 2**, 312; psychology and, **Supp. 3**, 119; **Supp. 4**, 832–33; **Supp. 6**, 17; public, pioneering in, **Vol. 1, Part 1**, 621 f.; **Vol. 1, Part 2**, 335, 570; **Vol. 2, Part 1**, 538; **Vol. 3, Part 1**, 314, 416 f., 556, 597 f., 608 f.; **Vol. 4, Part 1**, 117 f.; **Vol. 7, Part 2**, 332; **Vol. 8, Part 2**, 217; **Vol. 9, Part 1**, 353; **Vol. 10, Part 2**, 392; public school system, **Vol. 4, Part 2**, 43, 146, 315; **Vol. 5, Part 1**, 353 f.; **Vol. 8, Part 2**, 388, 616; Quaker, **Vol. 5, Part 2**, 4; Quincy system, **Vol. 1, Part 1**, 50; reading, **Supp. 6**, 248; reform proposals, **Supp. 1**, 200; refugee scholars, contributions of, **Supp. 10**, 39; religious, **Vol. 2, Part 2**, 26, 98 f., 611; **Vol. 3, Part 1**, 522 f.; **Vol. 4, Part 1**, 99; **Vol. 6, Part 2**, 40, 242, 461; **Vol. 10, Part 1**, 653; research in, **Supp. 3**, 677; Rockefeller Foundation, **Vol. 2, Part 1**, 378; rural schools, **Vol. 7, Part 2**, 257; school desegregation, **Supp. 9**, 68, 251, 258, 391–92; school keeping, earliest treatise on, **Vol. 3, Part 1**, 337; school libraries, **Vol. 8, Part 1**, 17; school readers, **Vol. 8, Part 2**, 357; school survey, **Supp. 3**, 328; science popularization programs, **Supp. 8**, 119–20; secondary schools, **Vol. 2, Part 1**, 377; **Vol. 3, Part 1**, 563; **Vol. 7, Part 2**, 83; **Vol. 8, Part 1**, 223 f.; **Vol. 8, Part 2**, 118; **Vol. 9, Part 1**, 37; sectarian schools, legal status of, **Vol. 3, Part 1**, 368; self-, **Vol. 3, Part 2**, 489; **Vol. 5, Part 1**, 131; **Vol. 8, Part 2**, 254; sex, **Supp. 3**, 463; social reconstructionists, **Supp. 6**, 558; social work, **Vol. 5, Part 1**, 128; **Vol. 8, Part 2**, 488; **Supp. 3**, 4; **Supp. 6**, 1–2; sociological aspects, **Supp. 6**, 726–27; South, promotion of universal, **Supp. 3**, 209; specialized facilities, **Supp. 3**, 206; spoils system in, **Vol. 9, Part 2**, 244; standards, **Supp. 2**, 542; state university, position of, **Vol. 3, Part 1**, 168; **Vol. 6, Part 1**, 55; "subscription school," **Vol. 3, Part 1**, 397; summer school, first, **Vol. 7, Part 1**, 300; **Vol. 9, Part 1**, 472; teacher-training, **Vol. 1, Part 2**, 546; **Vol. 2, Part 1**, 74, 279, 420; **Vol. 3, Part 1**, 347; **Vol. 4, Part 2**, 143; **Vol. 6, Part 2**, 242; **Vol.**

8, Part 1, 152; **Vol. 8, Part 2**, 307; **Vol. 9, Part 1**, 542; **Vol. 10, Part 1**, 645 f.; teaching materials, **Supp. 2**, 419; teaching of, **Vol. 5, Part 1**, 475, 525; **Vol. 7, Part 2**, 238; **Vol. 8, Part 2**, 310; **Supp. 2**, 268; **Supp. 3**, 205–6, 327–28; **Supp. 4**, 444–45; **Supp. 5**, 171–72; **Supp. 7**, 435; technological, **Vol. 8, Part 2**, 225; temperance activities in, **Vol. 5, Part 1**, 388; theories of, **Supp. 2**, 424; topical method of teaching, **Vol. 1, Part 1**, 211; university extension courses, **Vol. 7, Part 1**, 292; U.S. commissioners, **Supp. 1**, 200; visual aids, **Supp. 3**, 223; vocational, **Supp. 2**, 45, 398, 728; vocational guidance, **Vol. 5, Part 1**, 348; **Vol. 6, Part 1**, 178; **Vol. 9, Part 1**, 388; Western, in China, **Supp. 3**, 268; women, **Vol. 1, Part 1**, 125, 494, 576; **Vol. 1, Part 2**, 19, 125 f.; **Vol. 2, Part 1**, 44, 402; **Vol. 2, Part 2**, 321; **Vol. 3, Part 1**, 408, 423, 541 f.; **Vol. 3, Part 2**, 125, 129 f.; **Vol. 4, Part 1**, 64 f., 156 f., 636; **Vol. 4, Part 2**, 111 f.; **Vol. 5, Part 2**, 408; **Vol. 6, Part 1**, 306, 531; **Vol. 6, Part 2**, 71, 289; **Vol. 8, Part 1**, 71, 285, 531; **Vol. 9, Part 2**, 136; **Vol. 10, Part 1**, 78, 490 f., 617 f.; **Vol. 10, Part 2**, 231; **Supp. 1**, 170, 684; **Supp. 2**, 79, 398; **Supp. 10**, 38–39; women's studies, **Supp. 6**, 41; work/study programs, **Supp. 2**, 598, 728; writings on, **Vol. 1, Part 1**, 53 f., 148, 416, 600, 621; **Vol. 2, Part 1**, 118, 279, 422; **Vol. 3, Part 1**, 158, 225, 301, 368, 434, 488, 556 f., 563, 570 f., 605 f., 608; **Vol. 4, Part 1**, 303, 428, 443, 575, 603; **Vol. 5, Part 2**, 266, 481 f., 510, 591; **Vol. 7, Part 2**, 48, 83; **Vol. 8, Part 1**, 97 f., 124 f., 126 f., 223 f., 257 f., 272 f., 311 f., 347 f., 351, 382, 562, 588, 644; **Vol. 8, Part 2**, 250, 307; **Vol. 9, Part 1**, 242; **Vol. 9, Part 2**, 115, 244, 453, 581; **Vol. 10, Part 1**, 537; **Vol. 10, Part 2**, 392, 508, 641; **Supp. 3**, 555. *See also* Adult education; Parochial schools; Preschool education; School buildings; School desegregation; Teachers; Textbooks; Universities and colleges; *specific subjects and institutions*

Education (by locality): Boston, **Vol. 1, Part 2**, 256, 274, 297; **Vol. 2, Part 2**, 48; **Vol. 4, Part 1**, 447; **Vol. 7, Part 2**, 221; **Vol. 9, Part 2**, 276, 524; Chicago, **Vol. 7, Part 2**, 221; **Vol. 8, Part 2**, 408; **Vol. 10, Part 1**, 645 f.; China, **Vol. 9, Part 1**, 58; **Vol. 9, Part 2**, 372; Chinese students in U.S., **Vol. 10, Part 2**, 639; Cincinnati, **Vol. 9, Part 1**, 496; District of Columbia, **Vol. 8, Part 1**, 152, 562; Japan, **Vol. 7, Part 1**, 242, 358; Philadelphia, **Vol. 3, Part 1**, 408, 459; **Vol. 6, Part 1**, 544; **Vol. 9, Part 1**, 635; Philippines, the, **Vol. 8, Part 1**, 152; Puerto Rico, **Vol. 3, Part 1**, 608 f.; South, the, **Vol. 2, Part 1**, 378; **Vol. 2, Part 2**, 606; **Vol. 5, Part 2**, 227; **Vol. 7, Part 1**, 348; **Vol. 10, Part 2**, 495. *See also specific states*

Education, Bureau of (U.S.), **Vol. 1, Part 2**, 45; **Vol. 3, Part 1**, 608 f.; **Vol. 5, Part 1**, 272; **Vol. 7, Part 2**, 48; **Supp. 7**, 744

Education of Henry Adams, **Vol. 1, Part 1**, 66 f.

Educational Review, founding of, **Supp. 4**, 134

Educational television, **Supp. 6**, 33

Educators. For complete lists *see* Occupations Index

EDVAC (computer), **Supp. 10**, 520

Edward VIII (King of Great Britain). *See* Windsor, Duke and Duchess of

Edward Waters College, presidency, **Supp. 5**, 259

Edwards, Douglas, reference to, **Supp. 10**, 350

Edwards, E. I., reference to, **Supp. 6**, 265

Edwards, Gus, references to, **Supp. 5**, 629; **Supp. 9**, 885

Edwards, Harry, reference to, **Supp. 3**, 443

Edwards, Jonathan, references to, **Vol. 1, Part 2**, 165; **Vol. 5, Part 1**, 217; **Vol. 7, Part 1**, 583; **Vol. 9, Part 1**, 375; **Vol. 9, Part 2**, 36, 302, 339, 369; **Supp. 1**, 332

Edwards, Richard S., reference to, **Supp. 6**, 341

Efficiency engineering. *See* Engineering efficiency

Efficiency management, **Supp. 2**, 26–27

Egg and I, The, **Supp. 9**, 535

Eggers, Frank Hague, reference to, **Supp. 6**, 266

Eggers, Otto R., reference to, **Supp. 5**, 300

Eggers and Higgins, founding of, **Supp. 5**, 300–1

Egg Harbor, battle of, **Vol. 8, Part 1**, 259

Eggleston, Cary, reference to, **Supp. 3**, 343

Eggleston, Edward, reference to, **Vol. 6, Part 1**, 541

Egypt: archaeology, **Vol. 6, Part 1**, 573 f.; **Vol. 7, Part 1**, 320 f.; **Vol. 8, Part 2**, 573 f.; **Vol. 9, Part 1**, 5; **Supp. 1**, 112; **Supp. 3**, 272; **Supp. 3**, 374–75, 626–28; **Supp. 4**, 901–902; culture and language studies, **Supp. 1**, 111; gentlemen adventurers in, following civil war, **Vol. 8, Part 1**, 516; international tribunal for the legal administration of, **Vol. 1, Part 2**, 41; missions, **Supp. 4**, 860; missions to, **Vol. 5, Part 2**, 607 f.; **Vol. 10, Part 1**, 539 f.; relations with, **Vol. 3, Part 2**, 275 f.; Suez Canal compromise (1954), **Supp. 9**, 154; universities and colleges, **Supp. 4**, 860. *See also* Suez Crisis (1956)

Ehrenberg, Wilhelm, reference to, **Supp. 9**, 304

Ehrenfest, Paul, reference to, **Supp. 10**, 288

Eichmann, Adolf: reference to, **Supp. 8**, 456; trial of, **Supp. 9**, 42

Eichmann in Jerusalem, **Supp. 9**, 42

Eight-hour day, **Vol. 6, Part 2**, 500

Einhorn, Max, reference to, **Supp. 6**, 318

Einstein, Albert: biography of, **Supp. 8**, 191; Godel relationship, **Supp. 10**, 282; references to, **Supp. 3**, 31, 664; **Supp. 4**, 839, 880; **Supp. 5**, 326, 495, 528, 562, 589, 738; **Supp. 6**, 209; **Supp. 7**, 75, 133, 216, 731, 732; **Supp. 8**, 627; **Supp. 9**, 162, 696; **Supp. 10**, 305

Einthoven, Willem, reference to, **Supp. 6**, 117

Eisenhower, David, reference to, **Supp. 9**, 783; **Supp. 10**, 213

Eisenhower, Dwight D.: Allen, G. E., relationship, **Supp. 9**, 23, 24; atomic energy adviser, **Supp. 9**, 774; cabinet, **Supp. 6**, 416–17; China policy, **Supp. 6**, 235; cold war policy, **Supp. 8**, 147; **Supp. 9**, 799; Columbia University presidency, **Supp. 6**, 675; **Supp. 10**, 211–12; congressional relations, **Supp. 7**, 50; **Supp. 8**, 422; criticism of, **Supp. 6**, 472–73; defense policy advisers, **Supp. 9**, 522, 636; Donovan relationship, **Supp. 6**, 170–71; Duff relationship, **Supp. 8**, 144; economic advisers, **Supp. 10**, 376–77; foreign policy, **Supp. 6**, 179; **Supp. 9**, 211; **Supp. 10**, 529, 686; Humphrey, G., relationship, **Supp. 8**, 290; influence-peddling scandal, **Supp. 8**, 219–20; Jackson, C., relationship, **Supp. 7**, 384; labor relations, **Supp. 10**, 494; Luce relationship, **Supp. 8**, 395; McCarthyism and, **Supp. 6**, 405, 406; **Supp. 10**, 421; marriage, **Supp. 9**, 783; **Supp. 10**, 211–13; Marshall, G. C., relationship, **Supp. 6**, 430, 432; military cutbacks, **Supp. 9**, 477, 478; Murphy, R. D., relationship, **Supp. 10**, 572; nuclear policies, **Supp. 8**, 157–58; personal physician, **Supp. 8**, 608–9; **Supp. 9**, 862; presidency, **Supp. 9**, 81, 211, 231, 625, 852; **Supp. 10**, 212, 421; presidential candidacy, **Supp. 5**, 450, 676; **Supp. 6**, 136, 618; **Supp. 8**, 144; press relations, **Supp. 8**, 498; reelection campaign, **Supp. 10**, 213, 302; references to, **Supp. 9**, 9, 10; Richardson relationship, **Supp. 6**, 540–41; Summersby relationship, **Supp. 9**, 783–84; **Supp. 10**, 211; tax policies, **Supp. 6**, 535; World War II, **Supp. 7**, 703, 704; **Supp. 8**, 274–75; **Supp. 10**, 177

Eisenhower, Edgar, reference to, **Supp. 8**, 153

Eisenhower, Julie Nixon, reference to, **Supp. 10**, 213

Eisenhower, Mamie Doud, reference to, **Supp. 9**, 783

Eisenhower, Milton, reference to, **Supp. 8**, 153

Eisler, Gerhart, reference to, **Supp. 7**, 244–45

Ekern, Herman, reference to, **Supp. 9**, 30
Elasticity, mathematical theory of, **Supp. 4**, 873–74
El Caney, battle of, **Vol. 6, Part 1**, 62; **Vol. 8, Part 2**, 137; **Vol. 9, Part 1**, 16; **Vol. 10, Part 2**, 51, 467. *See also* San Juan Hill
Elderly. *See* Aging and aged; Pensions and retirement
Eldridge, Florence, references to, **Supp. 9**, 538, 539
Eldridge, Roy, reference to, **Supp. 10**, 791
Eldridge Reaves Johnson Foundation for Medical Physics (University of Pennsylvania), **Supp. 9**, 125
Elections: contested, **Supp. 5**, 290–91; direct primary, **Vol. 8, Part 2**, 86; **Supp. 4**, 844; disputed presidential, **Vol. 1, Part 2**, 64; financing of, **Supp. 4**, 752; initiative and referendum, **Supp. 2**, 640; **Supp. 4**, 844–45; militia marched to polls, **Vol. 5, Part 2**, 519; presidential primary, **Supp. 2**, 55; primaries, **Supp. 5**, 575; public opinion surveys, **Supp. 8**, 70; Ross election bill, **Vol. 3, Part 1**, 467 f.; senatorial primaries, **Supp. 2**, 54; violence in Baltimore (1857), **Vol. 6, Part 1**, 240; voting tabulating machines, **Supp. 1**, 415. *See also presidential election headings*; Voting rights; Woman suffrage
Electoral commission, **Vol. 1, Part 2**, 572; **Vol. 4, Part 1**, 449
Electoral Court Act, **Vol. 3, Part 2**, 25
Electrical engineering. *See* Engineering, electrical
Electrical industry: Bakelite uses in, **Supp. 3**, 27; chemical research techniques, **Supp. 6**, 695; labor movement, **Supp. 6**, 73–74
Electric Boat Co., **Supp. 3**, 120
Electric Bond & Share Co., **Supp. 3**, 192, 527
Electricity: agricultural use, **Supp. 3**, 192–93; alternating current, **Supp. 1**, 292; **Supp. 3**, 231, 768–69; arc light, early demonstration of, **Vol. 3, Part 1**, 376; arc lighting, **Supp. 1**, 129; **Supp. 2**, 658; authority on, **Vol. 4, Part 2**, 58; automobile, **Supp. 2**, 436; automobile ignition and starter, **Supp. 6**, 332; book collections on, **Supp. 2**, 38; bulb improvement, **Supp. 6**, 624, 695; **Supp. 10**, 52; cash register, **Supp. 6**, 332; chair, first use of electric, **Vol. 8, Part 2**, 69; circuit theory, **Supp. 2**, 98, 358; coils, early investigation with, **Vol. 4, Part 2**, 551; communication, **Supp. 1**, 613–14; copper conduction, **Supp. 2**, 383; development of, **Vol. 3, Part 2**, 372; **Vol. 4, Part 2**, 550; **Vol. 7, Part 1**, 388; **Vol. 9, Part 2**, 644; dielectric constants, **Supp. 6**, 396; dynamos, **Vol. 10, Part 2**, 462; economics of, **Supp. 2**, 333; electrostatic doublet theory, **Supp. 1**, 297; elevators, **Vol. 4, Part 1**, 75; energy, studies in, **Vol. 7, Part 1**, 268; equipment, making of, **Vol. 5, Part 2**, 509; **Vol. 10, Part 2**, 54, 462; experiments with (1750), **Vol. 6, Part 1**, 280; **Vol. 7, Part 2**, 136; first indoor lighted movie, **Supp. 3**, 73; furnace, **Vol. 4, Part 2**, 575; gas lighter, **Vol. 5, Part 1**, 335; high-frequency transmission, **Supp. 2**, 98; high-power transmission, **Supp. 2**, 199; high-tension transmission, **Supp. 1**, 292; high voltage, **Supp. 1**, 646; high-voltage measurement, **Supp. 2**, 199; hydroelectric power, **Supp. 2**, 118, 583; illumination, science of, **Vol. 8, Part 2**, 268; incandescent lamp, **Supp. 1**, 270; inventions, **Vol. 1, Part 1**, 443; **Vol. 3, Part 1**, 220; **Vol. 3, Part 2**, 59, 279; **Vol. 5, Part 1**, 259; **Vol. 5, Part 2**, 562; **Vol. 6, Part 1**, 176, 400; **Vol. 10, Part 1**, 168 f.; lamps, **Vol. 3, Part 2**, 280; **Vol. 7, Part 2**, 128; **Vol. 9, Part 1**, 514; lighting fixtures, **Supp. 7**, 308; lighting plant, first municipal, **Vol. 7, Part 1**, 450; lighting studies, **Supp. 3**, 269–70; long-distance transmission, **Supp. 1**, 614, 646; magnetic reaction, **Supp. 2**, 273; motor, invention of, **Vol. 3, Part 1**, 87 f.; motors, **Supp. 1**, 669–70; naval use of, **Supp. 3**, 275; Niagara Falls as source of, **Vol. 8, Part 1**, 375 f.; open-hearth charging machine, **Vol. 10, Part 1**, 635; organ, electric, **Vol. 8, Part 2**, 133; pioneer work with, **Vol. 3, Part 1**, 25; plant financing and operating, **Supp. 3**, 745–47; power, first underground conduit for electrical, **Vol. 9, Part 2**, 485; power plants, **Vol. 3, Part 1**, 355; **Vol. 5, Part 1**, 415; **Vol. 7, Part 1**, 367 f.; **Vol. 8, Part 2**, 359; public utility uniformity, **Supp. 3**, 716; railroads, **Vol. 6, Part 1**, 176; **Vol. 7, Part 2**, 358; **Vol. 9, Part 1**, 128; **Supp. 1**, 34, 351; **Supp. 4**, 370; **Supp. 8**, 93; research in, **Vol. 6, Part 1**, 235; **Supp. 2**, 658; "round-type" meter, **Supp. 3**, 184; rural, **Supp. 3**, 193, 560; **Supp. 6**, 122; **Supp. 8**, 700; science of, **Vol. 4, Part 2**, 550 f.; smelting, **Vol. 2, Part 2**, 472; stage lighting, **Supp. 6**, 233; steam turbine use for, **Supp. 4**, 383–84; synchronous clock, **Supp. 6**, 668–69; tests in, **Vol. 7, Part 1**, 342 f.; textbooks, **Vol. 5, Part 1**, 261; thermo, **Supp. 2**, 273; tractor, **Vol. 6, Part 1**, 505; traffic lights, **Supp. 3**, 254; transmission lines, lighting protection, **Supp. 2**, 199; turbine generation, **Supp. 3**, 251; units and standards, **Vol. 8, Part 2**, 154; **Supp. 2**, 358, 702; use of, in medicine, **Vol. 9, Part 1**, 53; valve, **Vol. 8, Part 2**, 133; writings on, **Vol. 8, Part 1**, 73 f., 122 f., 193 f., 223. *See also* Public utilities
Electrocardiography, **Supp. 6**, 117
Electrochemistry, **Vol. 8, Part 1**, 558 f.; **Vol. 10, Part 1**, 570; commercial applications, **Supp. 1**, 262; **Supp. 2**, 314
Electrodynamical theory, **Supp. 4**, 58
Electrodynamics, **Supp. 5**, 529
Electrolytes, physical chemistry of, **Supp. 8**, 123
Electromagnetic field: emission theory, **Supp. 5**, 528–29; infrared, **Supp. 4**, 658; separation, **Supp. 4**, 453–54
Electromagnets, **Vol. 9, Part 1**, 188; **Vol. 10, Part 1**, 635
Electro Metallurgical Co., **Supp. 3**, 48
Electronic music: **Supp. 3**, 690; **Supp. 9**, 341; organ, **Supp. 10**, 43
Electronics: circuit inventions, **Supp. 5**, 21–22; computational devices, **Supp. 10**, 519–20; device patents, **Supp. 8**, 209; instruments, **Supp. 7**, 756; microwave development, **Supp. 4**, 358–59; retail stores, **Supp. 10**, 773–74; transistors, **Supp. 6**, 85; **Supp. 7**, 175
Electrons: change measurement, **Supp. 5**, 495; photoelectrons, **Supp. 6**, 370; "spinning" concept, **Supp. 5**, 496; temperature concept, **Supp. 6**, 365; wave nature of, **Supp. 6**, 151–52; **Supp. 9**, 304
Electron spin, **Supp. 10**, 288–89
Electrophysiology, **Supp. 7**, 281
Electroplating, dynamos, **Supp. 2**, 702
Electrostatics, **Vol. 8, Part 1**, 223 f.
Electrosurgical knife, **Supp. 6**, 69–70
Electrotherapeutics, **Vol. 1, Part 2**, 93; **Vol. 3, Part 1**, 354; **Vol. 6, Part 2**, 381; **Vol. 8, Part 2**, 68
Electrothermal processes, **Supp. 1**, 5
Electrotyping, **Vol. 1, Part 1**, 93; **Vol. 9, Part 2**, 652
Elementary Economics, **Supp. 8**, 165
Elementary School Teacher, **Vol. 5, Part 1**, 525
Elements: chemical analysis, **Supp. 2**, 493; rare, researches in, **Vol. 5, Part 1**, 572; specimen collections, **Supp. 1**, 477
Elements of Analytical Mechanics, **Supp. 1**, 53
Elements of Logick, **Vol. 4, Part 2**, 499
Elevated railways, **Vol. 2, Part 2**, 544; **Vol. 4, Part 1**, 172, 272
Elevators: building of, **Vol. 7, Part 2**, 93 f., 371; **Vol. 8, Part 1**, 115 f.; first electric control of, **Vol. 6, Part 1**, 176; first safety appliance for, **Vol. 7, Part 2**, 93 f.; manufacture of, **Supp. 1**, 669
Elgar, Edward, reference to, **Supp. 5**, 103
Eliot, Charles W., references to, **Vol. 4, Part 2**, 57; **Vol.**

5, Part 1, 169, 591; Vol. 7, Part 1, 570; Supp. 3, 327–28, 336, 422–23, 457, 470; Supp. 6, 208, 249, 485
Eliot, John, references to, Vol. 5, Part 1, 199; Vol. 7, Part 1, 328; Vol. 10, Part 1, 627 f.
Eliot, T. S.: Aiken relationship, Supp. 9, 14; critical analysis of, Supp. 4, 559, 560; references to, Supp. 7, 339, 347, 790; Supp. 8, 176, 584; Supp. 9, 53, 558
Eliot School case, Vol. 3, Part 1, 541 f.
Elitcher, Max, reference to, Supp. 5, 589
Elizabeth, early boat to America (1634), Vol. 6, Part 1, 531
Elizabeth and Mary, seventeenth-century ship, Vol. 9, Part 2, 542, 543
Elizabethan history studies, Supp. 6, 531–32
Elk Hills, Calif., oil scandal of, Vol. 8, Part 2, 194; Vol. 10, Part 1, 393 f. *See also* Teapot Dome scandal
Elkhorn Tavern (or Pea Ridge), Ark., Vol. 2, Part 2, 620; Vol. 6, Part 2, 6, 427; Vol. 10, Part 1, 185
Elkins, William M., reference to, Supp. 5, 586
Elkins, W. Va., founding of, Vol. 3, Part 2, 84
Elks (fraternal order), Supp. 5, 754
Ellender, Allen J., reference to, Supp. 5, 719
Ellery Queen's Mystery Magazine, Supp. 9, 488
Ellicott, Andrew, reference to, Vol. 7, Part 1, 544
Ellington, Duke, references to, Supp. 3, 188; Supp. 6, 42, 43; Supp. 9, 317, 847
Elliott, A. Marshall, reference to, Supp. 3, 22
Elliott, John Lovejoy, reference to, Supp. 3, 175
Elliott, Maud Howe, reference to, Supp. 3, 630
Elliott, Thomas Renton, reference to, Supp. 3, 134
Elliott Monograph, Supp. 3, 22
Ellis, Emory, reference to, Supp. 3, 540
Ellis, Havelock, reference to, Supp. 8, 568
Ellis, John Tracy, reference to, Supp. 6, 600
Ellis-Foster Co., founding of, Supp. 3, 247
Ellis Island, Vol. 7, Part 1, 432; Vol. 8, Part 2, 169, 313; Vol. 9, Part 2, 549; Supp. 9, 469
Ellison, Ralph, reference to, Supp. 5, 529
Ellsworth, Oliver, reference to, Vol. 7, Part 1, 369
Elmer's Digest, Vol. 7, Part 1, 531
Elmhurst College, presidency, Supp. 7, 574
Elmira, N. Y., battle of, Vol. 2, Part 1, 362; Vol. 2, Part 2, 229; Vol. 4, Part 2, 223; Vol. 8, Part 1, 69; Vol. 9, Part 2, 193
Elm Street Politics, Supp. 9, 552
Elm trees. *See* Dutch elm disease
El Salvador, diplomatic relations, Vol. 3, Part 1, 296
Elsie series, Vol. 3, Part 2, 390
Elwyn Institution, Vol. 5, Part 2, 355
Ely, Richard T., references to, Supp. 3, 18, 175–78, 176–77, 514, 680; Supp. 4, 738, 746, 747; Supp. 5, 591
Emancipation of slaves. *See* Slavery
Emancipator, founding of, Vol. 5, Part 2, 12; Vol. 9, Part 2, 299
Emanuel, Victor, reference to, Supp. 10, 335
"Embalmed beef" scandals, Vol. 1, Part 1, 348
Embargo Act (1807), Vol. 4, Part 1, 107; Vol. 5, Part 2, 30, 405; Vol. 7, Part 2, 89; Vol. 8, Part 1, 365; Vol. 8, Part 2, 76
Embryo. *See* Fetus
Embryology: Vol. 6, Part 2, 221; Vol. 7, Part 1, 30; blood cell and lymph vessel studies, Supp. 5, 600; cell lineage, Supp. 2, 723; cytoplasm studies, Supp. 5, 127; descriptive, Supp. 4, 801–802; experimental, Supp. 3, 403, 539–40; fertilization studies, Supp. 4, 497–98; marine organisms, Supp. 3, 403; nervous system development, Supp. 6, 282–83; nutritional studies, Supp. 7, 569; textbooks, Supp. 4, 573; uriniferous tubule, Supp. 1, 439
Emergency Banking Relief Act (1933), Supp. 4, 810; Supp. 5, 158
Emergency Fleet Corporation, World War, Vol. 8, Part 2, 194
Emergency Relief Administration, founding of, Supp. 3, 652
Emerson, John, owner of Dred Scott, Vol. 8, Part 2, 488 f.; reference to, Supp. 6, 657
Emerson, John (playwright), Supp. 9, 791
Emerson, Joseph, reference to, Vol. 6, Part 1, 531
Emerson, Ralph Waldo: references to, Vol. 1, Part 1, 139 f., 475; Vol. 4, Part 1, 43; Vol. 5, Part 1, 606; Vol. 6, Part 1, 65; Vol. 8, Part 1, 455 f.; Vol. 9, Part 2, 492 f.; bust of, Supp. 1, 321; works editing, Supp. 5, 542; writings on, Supp. 7, 18–19
Emerson Radio and Phonograph Co., Supp. 7, 207
Emery, discovery of deposits of, Vol. 9, Part 1, 304
Emigrants' Guide to New Mexico, California, and Oregon, Vol. 3, Part 1, 319
Emigrant wagon train, first, Vol. 8, Part 2, 32
Emmanuel movement, Vol. 7, Part 1, 324; Supp. 2, 736; Supp. 3, 190–91
Emma Willard School, founding and history of, Vol. 10, Part 2, 232
Emmett, Burton, reference to, Supp. 3, 14
Emmet conspiracy, Vol. 5, Part 1, 337
Emmons, Samuel F., references to, Supp. 4, 765, 766
Emory and Henry College, history of, Vol. 10, Part 2, 214
Emory College, Vol. 2, Part 1, 471; Vol. 5, Part 1, 210; Vol. 6, Part 1, 390
Emory University: admissions standards controversy, Supp. 10, 842; founding of, Supp. 3, 129; history studies, Supp. 10, 841, 842
Emotions, studies of, Supp. 3, 134–37; Supp. 6, 527
Emperor Jones, The, Supp. 10, 677
Empire Athletic Association, founding of, Vol. 7, Part 2, 602
Empire State Building (New York City): architectural design, Supp. 5, 408; construction, Supp. 6, 593; construction photographs, Supp. 2, 306; corporation, Supp. 3, 720–21; investors in, Supp. 4, 682
Empire Theater (New York City), Supp. 6, 306
Empiricism, theological, Supp. 4, 525–26
Employees and employers. *See* Labor and labor movement; Management
Employment. *See* Labor and labor movement; Management; Occupational safety and health; Public works; Trade unions; Unemployment; Wages and hours
Employment Act (1946), Supp. 7, 562, 590
Employment Managers' Association, founding of, Supp. 2, 45
Emporia Gazette, Supp. 3, 816–17
Empyema, Supp. 6, 246
Emulsions: photographic, Supp. 4, 744; synthetic rubber, Supp. 5, 273
Encephalitis, research on, Supp. 5, 512
Encyclopaedia Americana, Vol. 6, Part 1, 236
Encyclopaedia Britannica: editorship, Supp. 10, 365; expansion of business interests, Supp. 9, 81; first American on editorial board, Supp. 5, 245; first edition, Vol. 6, Part 1, 56
Encyclopedia of Materia Medica, Vol. 1, Part 1, 208
Encyclopedia of the Social Sciences, Supp. 2, 244; Supp. 9, 428
Enders, John, reference to, Supp. 4, 468
Endicott-Johnson Corporation, founding of, Supp. 4, 431–32
Endocarditis, subacute bacterial, Supp. 4, 494
Endocrine glands: cancer-resistance research, Supp. 4, 616; emotions study, Supp. 3, 134–37; pharmacological research, Supp. 2, 4; research on, Supp. 3, 6;

Supp. 6, 100, 186, 386; sex hormone research, **Supp. 4**, 498. *See also* Hormones
Endocrinology, **Vol. 8, Part 2**, 306
End of Summer, **Supp. 9**, 70
"End of the Trail" (sculpture), **Supp. 5**, 231
Endomorph personality, **Supp. 10**, 731
Engineering (for complete list of engineers, *see* Occupations Index): **Vol. 1, Part 1**, 344, 457, 630, 642 f.; **Vol. 2, Part 2**, 460 f., 580 f.; **Vol. 3, Part 1**, 587 f.; **Vol. 3, Part 2**, 7, 178, 192; **Vol. 4, Part 1**, 75, 129, 136, 178, 565 f.; **Vol. 4, Part 2**, 492; **Vol. 5, Part 1**, 3, 371, 570, 572; **Vol. 5, Part 2**, 59, 208, 229, 249 f., 358; **Vol. 6, Part 1**, 23, 414; **Vol. 6, Part 2**, 9; **Vol. 8, Part 1**, 415; **Vol. 8, Part 2**, 12 f., 15 f., 359, 385, 398 f., 574; **Vol. 9, Part 1**, 179, 265, 363; **Vol. 9, Part 2**, 628 f., 656; **Vol. 10, Part 1**, 487 f., 539, 551; applications research, **Supp. 1**, 627; architectural, **Vol. 6, Part 1**, 166; bridge, **Vol. 1, Part 1**, 147; **Vol. 2, Part 2**, 110; **Vol. 3, Part 1**, 587 f.; **Vol. 4, Part 2**, 156, 400; **Vol. 5, Part 2**, 59; **Vol. 8, Part 1**, 418; **Vol. 8, Part 2**, 90, 592; **Vol. 9, Part 1**, 251; chemical, **Vol. 3, Part 2**, 603; **Vol. 9, Part 2**, 28; **Supp. 8**, 193–94; chemical (calcium carbide), **Supp. 7**, 553–54; civil, **Vol. 1, Part 1**, 193 f., 539 f.; **Vol. 1, Part 2**, 421, 441; **Vol. 2, Part 1**, 227; **Vol. 2, Part 2**, 69, 102, 187, 391, 413 f., 456 f., 479 f.; **Vol. 3, Part 1**, 258, 262, 334, 406, 459, 602; **Vol. 3, Part 2**, 339, 357, 387, 445, 569; **Vol. 4, Part 1**, 13, 52, 68, 205, 289, 471, 562, 567; **Vol. 4, Part 2**, 307, 452; **Vol. 5, Part 1**, 142, 298, 349; **Vol. 5, Part 2**, 91, 96, 106, 261, 454 f., 467, 498, 569; **Vol. 6, Part 1**, 27, 36, 380, 441, 505, 548, 549, 565; **Vol. 6, Part 2**, 142, 647; **Vol. 7, Part 1**, 255, 433, 456, 473, 536, 617; **Vol. 8, Part 1**, 19, 52, 179, 406, 417 f., 647; **Vol. 8, Part 2**, 48, 71, 88 f., 577, 592; **Vol. 9, Part 1**, 151, 165, 251, 272, 307, 319, 334, 368, 538, 543; **Vol. 9, Part 2**, 70, 98 f., 249, 309, 385, 519, 598, 611, 614; **Vol. 10, Part 1**, 2, 364, 372 f., 618 f., 634; **Vol. 10, Part 2**, 71, 260, 268, 339, 350, 538; civil (Army Corps of Engineers), **Supp. 6**, 508–9; civil (bridges and tunnels), **Supp. 1**, 135–36; **Supp. 3**, 331–32, 367; **Supp. 4**, 756–57; **Supp. 6**, 587; **Supp. 7**, 11–12; civil (canals), **Supp. 3**, 310–11; civil (dams), **Supp. 4**, 198–99; **Supp. 8**, 572–73; **Supp. 9**, 561; civil (foundations), **Supp. 2**, 469–70; civil (public works), **Supp. 3**, 795; civil (railroads), **Supp. 3**, 735–37, 759; civil (stress analysis), **Supp. 4**, 873–74; civil (structural), **Supp. 1**, 680; **Supp. 2**, 77; civil (teaching of), **Vol. 4, Part 1**, 52; **Vol. 5, Part 2**, 91; **Supp. 2**, 598; civil (textbooks on), **Supp. 1**, 148; civil (TVA project), **Supp. 3**, 580–81; civil (writings on), **Vol. 4, Part 1**, 289, 562; **Vol. 5, Part 2**, 106; **Vol. 6, Part 2**, 647; efficiency, **Vol. 9, Part 2**, 324; electrical, **Vol. 2, Part 2**, 553; **Vol. 3, Part 1**, 87, 220 f.; **Vol. 4, Part 1**, 620; **Vol. 4, Part 2**, 574; **Vol. 5, Part 1**, 261; **Vol. 6, Part 1**, 176; **Vol. 7, Part 1**, 526; **Vol. 7, Part 2**, 358, 480; **Vol. 8, Part 1**, 75, 221; **Vol. 8, Part 2**, 56, 154; **Vol. 9, Part 1**, 128, 275, 454, 490, 504, 514; **Vol. 9, Part 2**, 111; **Vol. 10, Part 1**, 57, 570; **Supp. 3**, 120, 184–85, 251–52, 744–47, 768–70; **Supp. 4**, 81–82; electrical (radio), **Supp. 4**, 422; **Supp. 5**, 21–22; electrical (railroads), **Supp. 4**, 369–70; electrical (studies, in), **Supp. 2**, 357; electrical (teaching of), **Supp. 1**, 31, 630; **Supp. 5**, 354–55; electrical (telephones), **Supp. 4**, 430; hydraulic, **Vol. 1, Part 2**, 529; **Vol. 3, Part 1**, 585 f., 587; **Vol. 3, Part 2**, 2, 228, 267, 434, 579; **Vol. 7, Part 1**, 39, 40, 467; **Vol. 4, Part 2**, 59, 283 f., 595 f.; **Vol. 5, Part 1**, 349 f., 371; **Vol. 8, Part 1**, 324 f., 375 f.; **Vol. 8, Part 2**, 398 f., 473; **Vol. 9, Part 1**, 54, 273; illuminating, **Vol. 8, Part 2**, 268; insurance covering, **Supp. 1**, 319; journals, **Supp. 1**, 552; marine, **Vol. 1, Part 1**, 193 f.; **Vol. 2, Part 1**, 468; **Vol. 2, Part 2**, 500; **Vol. 3, Part 1**, 211, 288, 292; **Vol. 3, Part 2**, 143; **Vol. 5, Part 1**, 318; **Vol. 6, Part 1**, 545; **Vol. 8, Part 1**, 314, 639; **Vol. 9, Part 2**, 344; mechanical, **Vol. 3, Part 1**, 142, 288; **Vol. 3, Part 2**, 456; **Vol. 4, Part 1**, 38, 488; **Vol. 4, Part 2**, 345; **Vol. 5, Part 1**, 84, 127, 153, 155, 342, 370, 383, 444, 515; **Vol. 5, Part 2**, 168, 348, 443; **Vol. 6, Part 1**, 81, 235; **Vol. 6, Part 2**, 422; **Vol. 7, Part 1**, 449, 546; **Vol. 8, Part 1**, 172 f., 517, 551; **Vol. 8, Part 2**, 52; **Vol. 9, Part 1**, 429; **Vol. 9, Part 2**, 243, 518, 581; **Vol. 10, Part 1**, 470 f., 575; mechanical (air conditioning), **Supp. 4**, 148–49; mechanical (bridge design), **Supp. 3**, 331–32; mechanical (hydroelectric power plants), **Supp. 3**, 500; mechanical (inspection and testing), **Supp. 3**, 220; mechanical (lubrication and bearing design), **Supp. 3**, 419; mechanical (machine design), **Supp. 5**, 386–87; mechanical (machine tools), **Supp. 3**, 561–62; mechanical (Manhattan Project plant), **Supp. 4**, 453–54; mechanical (steam tables for), **Supp. 5**, 154; mechanical (teaching of), **Supp. 3**, 188, 331–32; **Supp. 6**, 181–82; mechanical (turbines), **Supp. 4**, 383–84; mechanical (turbosuper-charger engine), **Supp. 4**, 609; metallurgical, **Vol. 7, Part 2**, 504; military, **Vol. 1, Part 1**, 163, 500, 626; **Vol. 2, Part 2**, 78; **Vol. 3, Part 1**, 210; **Vol. 3, Part 2**, 153 f., 550; **Vol. 4, Part 1**, 138, 343, 612; **Vol. 4, Part 2**, 52, 151; **Vol. 5, Part l**, 101 f.; **Vol. 6, Part 1**, 182, 495, 496; **Vol. 6, Part 2**, 257; **Vol. 7, Part 1**, 100 f., 154; **Vol. 8, Part 1**, 406, 647; **Vol. 9, Part 2**, 247, 260, 327; mining, **Vol. 2, Part 1**, 511; **Vol. 2, Part 2**, 200, 274, 485 f.; **Vol. 3, Part 1**, 27, 225 f., 396 f., 460; **Vol. 3, Part 2**, 2; **Vol. 4, Part 2**, 87; **Vol. 6, Part 1**, 167, 360, 608 f.; **Vol. 5, Part 2**, 55, 319; **Vol. 6, Part 1**, 482 f., 515; **Vol. 6, Part 2**, 458; **Vol. 7, Part 1**, 135, 412; **Vol. 7, Part 2**, 9 f., 354; **Vol. 8, Part 1**, 412, 414; **Vol. 8, Part 2**, 189; **Vol. 9, Part 1**, 273, 459, 545; **Vol. 9, Part 2**, 64, 146; **Vol. 10, Part 2**, 261; municipal, **Vol. 8, Part 1**, 415; naval, **Vol. 1, Part 1**, 495; **Vol. 2, Part 2**, 423; **Vol. 3, Part 2**, 158, 170, 405; **Vol. 4, Part 2**, 391; **Vol. 5, Part 1**, 153; **Vol. 7, Part 1**, 639; **Vol. 7, Part 2**, 487; **Vol. 8, Part 1**, 640; **Vol. 8, Part 2**, 194; **Vol. 9, Part 2**, 613; railway, **Vol. 2, Part 1**, 562; **Vol. 2, Part 2**, 275 f.; **Vol. 3, Part 1**, 348; **Vol. 5, Part 2**, 292; **Vol. 8, Part 1**, 417 f.; **Vol. 8, Part 2**, 19, 33; **Vol. 9, Part 2**, 642; **Vol. 10, Part l**, 372; research, **Supp. 2**, 104; rocket, **Supp. 10**, 65–67; sanitary, **Vol. 1, Part 1**, 597; **Vol. 3, Part 1**, 78; **Vol. 4, Part 1**, 433; **Vol. 4, Part 2**, 576 f.; **Vol. 5, Part 2**, 193, 265, 275, 277, 418 f.; **Vol. 8, Part 1**, 390 f., 475, 553 f.; **Vol. 8, Part 2**, 553, 606; **Vol. 9, Part 1**, 495; **Vol. 10, Part 1**, 456 f.; structural, **Supp. 3**, 611–12; structural steel, **Supp. 3**, 77; teaching of, **Supp. 1**, 175, 629, 680; **Supp. 3**, 188; **Supp. 5**, 154; telephone, **Supp. 3**, 298–99; topographical, **Vol. 3, Part 1**, 251 f.; **Vol. 4, Part 1**, 476; **Vol. 5, Part 1**, 348; **Vol. 10, Part 1**, 473 f.; writings on, **Vol. 1, Part 1**, 627; **Vol. 3, Part 1**, 292, 470, 547 f., 587 f.; **Vol. 4, Part 1**, 295; **Vol. 5, Part 1**, 444; **Vol. 5, Part 2**, 60, 106, 443 f.; **Vol. 8, Part 1**, 28 f., 91 f., 329 f., 552; **Vol. 9, Part 1**, 495; **Vol. 9, Part 2**, 520; **Vol. 10, Part 1**, 539, 618 f., 634. *See also specific types of engineering*
Engineering and Mining Journal, **Vol. 8, Part 2**, 189
Engineering Foundation, founding of, **Supp. 2**, 643
Engineering Record, founding of, **Supp. 1**, 552
Engineering Researches, **Vol. 5, Part 1**, 516
Engineers. For complete list, *see* Occupations Index
"Engineers' Bible," **Vol. 4, Part 2**, 391
Engineers' Club (New York City), **Vol. 8, Part 1**, 343
Engineers Group, Inc., **Supp. 6**, 140
Engineers' Pocket Book, **Vol. 9, Part 2**, 629
Engineers Public Service Corporation, founding of, **Supp. 3**, 747

Engines: air-cooled, **Supp. 4**, 473–74, 486; diesel for automobiles, **Supp. 5**, 654; internal-combustion, **Supp. 6**, 332; train, **Supp. 1**, 397; turbine, **Supp. 1**, 65; **Supp. 4**, 383–84; turbosupercharger, **Supp. 4**, 609
England. *See* Great Britain
English literature and language: Chaucer studies, **Supp. 3**, 475, 855; **Supp. 4**, 819–20; Coleridge scholarship, **Supp. 3**, 475; Elizabethan studies, **Supp. 4**, 4–5, 110, 624, 634; grammar, writing on, **Supp. 4**, 203; Jewish immigrants' adaptation, **Supp. 5**, 95–96; manuscript collections, **Supp. 5**, 349–50; Middle English studies, **Supp. 3**, 109; Old English syntax, **Supp. 2**, 88; popularization of, **Supp. 3**, 601–3; rare book catalogs, **Supp. 7**, 387; scholarship, seventeenth- and eighteenth-century, **Supp. 7**, 402–3, 798; **Supp. 9**, 884–885; Shakespearean scholarship, **Supp. 3**, 423; Society for Pure English, founding of, **Supp. 4**, 755–56; "Stengelese," **Supp. 9**, 764; Sterne and Fielding scholarship, **Supp. 4**, 197; studies, **Supp. 1**, 474; teaching of, **Supp. 1**, 356; **Supp. 3**, 422–23, 454–55, 624; **Supp. 5**, 131–32, 211–12, 645–46; **Supp. 7**, 56, 797, 798; **Supp. 9**, 828; textbooks on, **Supp. 1**, 697; usage, writings on, **Supp. 2**, 683; words coined, **Supp. 5**, 94, 480, 481; writings on, **Supp. 3**, 689; **Supp. 4**, 559–61; **Supp. 9**, 807, 829; **Supp. 10**, 224, 388, 389, 424–25, 723–24, 735. *See also* American literature; Criticism; Poetry; Reading
English-Speaking Union, founding of American branch, **Vol. 8, Part 1**, 278 f.
English, Thomas Dunn, reference to, **Vol. 9, Part 2**, 314
Engraving: **Vol. 1, Part 1**, 131, 589; **Vol. 1, Part 2**, 284; **Vol. 2, Part 1**, 278; **Vol. 2, Part 2**, 55, 172, 231; **Vol. 3, Part 1**, 3, 66, 150 f., 272, 372 f., 535 f., 538; **Vol. 3, Part 2**, 5, 47 f., 370, 495, 567; **Vol. 4, Part 1**, 286, 336, 432; **Vol. 4, Part 2**, 131, 198; **Vol. 5, Part 1**, 41, 157, 200 f.; **Vol. 5, Part 2**, 73 f., 139, 152, 159, 293 f., 342, 411, 456; **Vol. 6, Part 1**, 56, 165, 186, 285, 381; **Vol. 6, Part 2**, 219, 432; **Vol. 7, Part 1**, 550; **Vol. 8, Part 1**, 140 f., 253, 514, 627; **Vol. 8, Part 2**, 305, 370 f., 386, 451; **Vol. 9, Part 1**, 119 f., 232 f., 307; **Vol. 9, Part 2**, 137, 295, 530; **Vol. 10, Part 1**, 12 f.; **Supp. 3**, 292; aquatint, **Vol. 4, Part 2**, 403; **Vol. 5, Part 2**, 269 f., 456; bank notes, **Vol. 1, Part 2**, 502; **Vol. 2, Part 1**, 56; **Vol. 2, Part 2**, 343; **Vol. 3, Part 1**, 501, 535, 538; **Vol. 4, Part 1**, 322 f.; **Vol. 5, Part 1**, 165; **Vol. 5, Part 2**, 74, 159, 243, 456; **Vol. 6, Part 1**, 284, 422; **Vol. 7, Part 2**, 55, 370, 472; **Vol. 8, Part 1**, 253, 515; **Vol. 8, Part 2**, 122, 451; **Vol. 9, Part 1**, 232; **Vol. 9, Part 2**, 43, 295; book-plates, **Vol. 5, Part 1**, 424; **Vol. 8, Part 1**, 361 f.; Boston, pictorial plates of early, **Vol. 2, Part 1**, 278; colored, **Vol. 6, Part 1**, 56; collecting, **Vol. 9, Part 1**, 538; copper, **Vol. 3, Part 1**, 272 f.; **Vol. 5, Part 1**, 424; first U.S. coins, **Vol. 6, Part 1**, 381; "golden age of American reproductive engraving," **Vol. 4, Part 2**, 503; line, **Vol. 2, Part 2**, 52; **Vol. 4, Part 1**, 392; **Vol. 5, Part 2**, 269 f., 456; **Vol. 6, Part 1**, 56; **Vol. 7, Part 2**, 369 f., 592; **Vol. 8, Part 2**, 122; lithographic, **Vol. 3, Part 1**, 170; **Vol. 7, Part 2**, 421; machines, invention of, **Vol. 1, Part 2**, 407; magazines, early use of, in, **Vol. 3, Part 1**, 613 f.; maps, **Vol. 5, Part 2**, 152; **Vol. 8, Part 1**, 140 f.; **Vol. 9, Part 2**, 295; mezzotint, **Vol. 7, Part 2**, 409; **Vol. 8, Part 2**, 169; miniatures, **Vol. 8, Part 2**, 305; photo-engraving, **Vol. 6, Part 1**, 203; portraits, **Vol. 3, Part 1**, 535 f.; **Vol. 5, Part 2**, 509; **Vol. 6, Part 1**, 165; **Vol. 6, Part 2**, 331; **Vol. 10, Part 2**, 603; postage stamps, **Vol. 5, Part 2**, 159; stipple, **Vol. 5, Part 2**, 456; wood, **Vol. 1, Part 1**, 93, 262, 315; **Vol. 3, Part 1**, 423 f.; **Vol. 3, Part 2**, 549; **Vol. 4, Part 2**, 321; **Vol. 6, Part 1**, 56; **Vol. 9, Part 2**, 43; **Vol. 10, Part 2**, 447; **Supp. 1**, 185
Engraving and Printing, Bureau of, **Vol. 3, Part 1**, 535 f., 538
ENIAC computer, **Supp. 6**, 675; **Supp. 10**, 520
Enormous Room, The, **Supp. 7**, 157, 158
Entailed Hat, **Vol. 9, Part 2**, 617
Enterprise, **Supp. 9**, 461
Enterprise (schooner), **Vol. 5, Part 2**, 541; **Vol. 9, Part l**, 41
Enterprise (steamboat), **Vol. 5, Part 2**, 110; **Vol. 9, Part l**, 134
Enterprise (yacht), **Supp. 4**, 124
Entertainers. For complete list, *see* Occupations Index
Entertaining, social, **Supp. 7**, 519, 527; **Supp. 9**, 547
Enter the Dragon, **Supp. 9**, 486
Entomological Commisslon, United States, **Vol. 8, Part 1**, 610
Entomological Society of America, founding of, **Supp. 3**, 478
Entomologists. For complete list, *see* Occupations Index
Entomology: **Vol. 1, Part 1**, 392, 575; **Vol. 2, Part 2**, 433, 541; **Vol. 3, Part 1**, 578 f.; **Vol. 3, Part 2**, 334, 424, 510; **Vol. 4, Part 1**, 333; **Vol. 4, Part 2**, 27, 82, 586; **Vol. 5, Part 1**, 229, 327, 406; **Vol. 5, Part 2**, 448; **Vol. 6, Part 1**, 89, 283; **Vol. 6, Part 2**, 519; **Vol. 7, Part 2**, 87 f., 384; **Vol. 8, Part 1**, 610; **Vol. 8, Part 2**, 401 f., 525; **Vol. 9, Part 1**, 298, 385; **Vol. 9, Part 2**, 319, 426; **Vol. 10, Part 1**, 106 f., 388 f.; agricultural, **Supp. 4**, 601; "agricultural" ants, **Vol. 6, Part 1**, 241 f.; bees, taxonomy of, **Supp. 4**, 167; economic, **Vol. 8, Part 1**, 609 f.; popularization of, **Supp. 4**, 399–400; practical use of first, **Vol. 4, Part 2**, 321; research in, **Supp. 1**, 187, 414; writings on, **Supp. 3**, 683. *See also* Insects
Entwhistle, Frederick I., reference to, **Supp. 7**, 577
Environment: health relationship, **Supp. 2**, 646; pioneer in protection movement, **Supp. 4**, 484; radiation-level control, **Supp. 8**, 26. *See also* Conservation; Ecology; Natural history; Pollution
Environment v. heredity. *See* Genetics
Enzymes: biochemical studies of; **Supp. 5**, 26, 149, 489, 622, 623, 670–71; **Supp. 6**, 127, 295–96, 595; **Supp. 10**, 427; "one gene, one enzyme theory," **Supp. 9**, 793–94
Ephemeris, computation of the, **Vol. 7, Part 1**, 453
Ephron, Nora, reference to, **Supp. 9**, 785
Epic Mythology, **Supp. 1**, 434
Epidemics: American aid in European, **Vol. 3, Part 2**, 572; cholera, *see* Cholera; control of, **Supp. 2**, 212; **Supp. 4**, 700–1; meningitis, **Supp. 4**, 287; pneumonia, **Supp. 3**, 483; poliomyelitis, **Supp. 4**, 287–88; **Supp. 6**, 192; study of, **Vol. 3, Part 2**, 128; **Vol. 5, Part 2**, 325; **Vol. 8, Part 1**, 131 f.; **Vol. 8, Part 2**, 552 f.; **Vol. 9, Part 1**, 190 f., 590 f.; typhus, **Supp. 4**, 668, 803; **Supp. 5**, 336; yellow fever, *see* Yellow fever
Epidemiology: family concept of, **Supp. 3**, 775; infectious disease studies, **Supp. 7**, 194; preventive measures, **Supp. 3**, 158; **Supp. 5**, 143–44; rickettsial disease studies, **Supp. 9**, 249–50; statistics used in, **Supp. 7**, 192. *See also* Public health; *specific disease names*
Epigraphy, writings on, **Vol. 9, Part 1**, 594
Epileptics, care of, **Vol. 3, Part 1**, 478 f.; **Vol. 6, Part 1**, 194; **Vol. 7, Part 2**, 6
Epinephrine; surgical shock, **Supp. 3**, 201; synthesis of, **Supp. 9**, 454
Episcopal Academy of Connecticut, founding of, **Vol. 1, Part 2**, 491
Episcopal church. *See* Protestant Episcopal church
Epstein, Abraham, reference to, **Supp. 3**, 19, 517

Epstein, Brian, reference to, **Supp. 10**, 449
Epstein, Jacob, reference to, **Supp. 3**, 329
Epstein, Julius J., reference to, **Supp. 5**, 209
Epworth League: adoption of, in India, **Vol. 7, Part 2**, 219; organized in China, **Supp. 6**, 315
Equality League of Self-Supporting Women, founding of, **Supp. 2**, 43
Equal rights: **Vol. 1, Part 2**, 581; **Vol. 2, Part 1**, 19, 151; **Vol. 6, Part 1**, 480; **Vol. 9, Part 2**, 253 f.; Amendment, **Supp. 5**, 474, 532, 543; cosponsor, **Supp. 4**, 145; initiation of, **Supp. 7**, 717
Equal Rights Amendment (ERA): first introduction into Congress, **Supp. 10**, 622, 623; opposition to, **Supp. 9**, 706; support for, **Supp. 9**, 546
Equal Rights Association, American, **Vol. 7, Part 2**, 609
Equal Rights Society, organization of, in Oregon, **Vol. 3, Part 1**, 513 f.
Equations: differential, **Supp. 3**, 70; linear difference, **Supp. 3**, 70; linear integral, **Supp. 3**, 87
Equilenin, synthesis of, **Supp. 5**, 28
Equilibrium, studies in, **Supp. 2**, 373
Equitable Life Assurance Society, **Vol. 5, Part 1**, 450; **Vol. 7, Part 1**, 265; **Supp. 6**, 497
"Equivalent Lands," **Vol. 8, Part 1**, 426
Equus, **Supp. 10**, 55
ERA. *See* Equal Rights Amendment
Erasmus, writings on, **Supp. 3**, 726
Erdmann, Benno, references to, **Supp. 3**, 81, 229
Erector Set (toy), **Supp. 7**, 287–88
Ergodic theorem (1931), **Supp. 3**, 70–71
Ergotocin, **Supp. 6**, 334
Ericsson, John, use of revolving battery, **Vol. 9, Part 2**, 554; **Vol. 10, Part 1**, 618 f.
Ericsson, Leif: reference to, **Supp. 8**, 457; sculpture of, **Supp. 3**, 124
Erie Canal: **Vol. 3, Part 2**, 15, 90, 195, 525; **Vol. 5, Part 1**, 83, 150, 395; **Vol. 5, Part 2**, 59, 120, 320; **Vol. 6, Part 1**, 323; **Vol. 7, Part 1**, 212, 355, 563, 604; **Vol. 8, Part 2**, 12; **Vol. 9, Part 1**, 7; **Vol. 9, Part 2**, 651; **Vol. 10, Part 2**, 40, 93; opening (1825), **Vol. 8, Part 2**, 21; writings on, **Vol. 9, Part 2**, 89
Erie Railroad, **Vol. 1, Part 1**, 614; **Vol. 3, Part 1**, 322; **Vol. 3, Part 2**, 361, 415; **Vol. 4, Part 1**, 454; **Vol. 5, Part 2**, 68, 229; **Vol. 6, Part 2**, 11; **Vol. 7, Part 1**, 191; **Vol. 9, Part 1**, 262; **Vol. 9, Part 2**, 241; **Vol. 10, Part 1**, 81; **Supp. 3**, 783–84, 823
Erikson, Erik H., reference to, **Supp. 6**, 528
Erlanger, Joseph, references to, **Supp. 3**, 243, 370; **Supp. 7**, 280, 281
Erman, Adolf, reference to, **Supp. 3**, 626
Ernst, Max, reference to, **Supp. 10**, 294
Ernst, Morris, reference to, **Supp. 9**, 165
Eros and Civilization, **Supp. 10**, 506
Erosion: first use of term "base-level," **Vol. 8, Part 1**, 147; studies of, **Supp. 4**, 119; **Supp. 6**, 52–53
Erskine, Albert, reference to, **Supp. 9**, 166
Erskine, Albert R., reference to, **Supp. 6**, 650
Ervin, Sam, Jr., reference to, **Supp. 9**, 440
Esalen Institute (Calif.): **Supp. 8**, 424; rolfing, **Supp. 10**, 696
Escape from Freedom, **Supp. 10**, 260–61
Escapist literature, **Supp. 10**, 20–21
Esch-Cummins Act, **Vol. 2, Part 2**, 598
Escoffier, Auguste, reference to, **Supp. 6**, 164
Eskimos: anthropological studies, **Supp. 3**, 82; **Supp. 6**, 353; dialects, writing on, **Vol. 10, Part 1**, 632 f.; documentary films on, **Supp. 5**, 225–26; ethnology, **Supp. 1**, 572; language studies, **Supp. 3**, 84; **Supp. 7**, 371
Esmond, Henry V., reference to, **Supp. 5**, 123
Esophagoscope, development of, **Supp. 6**, 318
ESP. *See* Extrasensory perception
Esperanto (language), **Vol. 4, Part 1**, 25; **Supp. 4**, 185, 348
Espionage: FBI investigations, **Supp. 9**, 406; ITT in Hungary, **Supp. 6**, 45; Soviet, in U.S., **Supp. 5**, 564, 588–90, 714; **Supp. 7**, 51–52, 113–14, 244; **Supp. 8**, 135, 162, 230; **Supp. 9**, 3–4; trials, **Supp. 9**, 321–22; U-2 overflights of Soviet Union, **Supp. 8**, 135, 147, 159, 258; **Supp. 10**, 646–47; World War I countermeasures, **Supp. 1**, 359; writings on, **Supp. 10**, 232. *See also* Spies
Espionage Act, sentence under, **Vol. 9, Part 2**, 69
Esquire: censorship, **Supp. 6**, 661; founding of, **Supp. 5**, 637–38
"Essay on the Mule," **Vol. 9, Part 1**, 39
Essayists. For complete list of essayists, *see* Occupations Index
Essay writing, **Supp. 4**, 689, 804–5
Essex, first U.S. naval vessel in Pacific, **Vol. 8, Part 1**, 83f.
Essex Junto, **Vol. 6, Part 1**, 518
Estates. For specific names, *see* Homesteads
Estermann, Immanuel, reference to, **Supp. 8**, 628
Estes, Billie Sol: references to, **Supp. 9**, 433, 573; reference to, **Supp. 10**, 483
Estradiol, **Supp. 3**, 6
Estrogen, first isolation of, **Supp. 7**, 598
Esty, William, and Co., **Supp. 6**, 673
Etching: **Vol. 1, Part 1**, 465 f.; **Vol. 2, Part 2**, 18, 22, 172; **Vol. 3, Part 1**, 558 f.; **Vol. 3, Part 2**, 294, 504, 568; **Vol. 4, Part 1**, 162, 263; **Vol. 4, Part 2**, 381; **Vol. 5, Part 1**, 157 f.; **Vol. 5, Part 2**, 494; **Vol. 6, Part 2**, 604, 620; **Vol. 7, Part 1**, 513; Vol. 7, Part 2. 437 f.; **Vol. 8, Part 1**, 9, 446, 627, 639; **Vol. 9, Part 1**, 233; **Vol. 10, Part 2**, 77 f.; **Supp. 1**, 377; **Supp. 5**, 50, 635; inventions concerning, **Vol. 6, Part 1**, 202; writings on, **Vol. 8, Part 1**, 446
Ether, **Vol. 2, Part 2**, 4; **Vol. 4, Part 2**, 464 f.; **Vol. 5, Part 1**, 239, 537; **Vol. 6, Part 1**, 374 f.; **Vol. 7, Part 1**, 269 f.; **Vol. 10, Part 1**, 480 f.; **Supp. 8**, 411
Ether-drift experiments, **Supp. 3**, 523–24
Ethical culture movement: **Vol. 8, Part 2**, 316; **Vol. 9, Part 1**, 66; **Supp. 1**, 13; **Supp. 3**, 246; **Supp. 7**, 567–68; in Great Britain, **Supp. 3**, 175–76
Ethics: **Supp. 3**, 780; philosophical studies, **Supp. 10**, 261
Ethics: economics and, **Supp. 3**, 179, 249; land, **Supp. 4**, 483–84; legal and judicial standards, **Supp. 1**, 99, 204; medical, **Supp. 2**, 85; Navaho Indian, **Supp. 5**, 644–45; personal, **Supp. 4**, 767; philosophical studies, **Supp. 6**, 505; **Supp. 7**, 472; religious pragmatism, **Supp. 3**, 363; social, **Supp. 2**, 85, 518; writings on, **Supp. 3**, 697, 780. *See also* Philosophy
Ethnic groups: marginal man theory, **Supp. 3**, 579; Massachusetts politics, **Supp. 4**, 858–59; sociological studies of, **Supp. 4**, 828, 829–30, 831; World War II policies toward, **Supp. 3**, 661. *See also* Immigration; *specific groups*
Ethnobotany, South Seas, **Vol. 8, Part 2**, 289
Ethnography: American Indians, **Supp. 4**, 907–8; documentary films, **Supp. 7**, 241. *See also* Anthropology; Ethnology
Ethnology: **Vol. 2, Part 1**, 183; **Vol. 3, Part 1**, 77, 288, 496; **Vol. 3, Part 2**, 269 f., 353; **Vol. 4, Part 1**, 192, 245, 340 f.; **Vol. 4, Part 2**, 104, 519; **Vol. 6, Part 2**, 270; **Vol. 7, Part 1**, 110, 183, 582; **Vol. 8, Part 1**, 146 f., 389; **Vol. 8, Part 2**, 288, 457; **Vol. 9, Part 1**, 197, 262, 631, 634; **Vol. 9, Part 2**, 426; age and area, **Supp. 7**, 570; American culture, **Supp. 3**, 672–73; American Indian, **Vol. 3, Part 1**, 553 f.; **Vol. 3, Part 2**, 126, 463; **Vol. 5, Part 2**, 205, f.; **Vol. 7, Part 1**, 138 f., 512; **Vol. 7, Part 2**, 602; **Vol. 8, Part 2**, 55, 278; **Supp. 3**, 582; **Supp. 4**, 761–62; **Supp. 6**, 611–13;

Supp. 7, 710–11; Eskimos, **Supp. 1**, 572; Latin American, **Supp. 1**, 648; Pueblo Indians, **Supp. 3**, 582; writings on, **Supp. 4**, 179; **Supp. 6**, 393–94
Ethnology, Bureau of, **Vol. 4, Part 1**, 192; **Supp. 3**, 83, 84; **Supp. 6**, 162
Ethnomusicology, pioneer work in, **Supp. 4**, 762
Ethylene, anesthesia, **Supp. 3**, 458
Ethyl gasoline, **Supp. 3**, 521–22
Etiquette: **Supp. 6**, 514–15; writings on, **Vol. 2, Part 1**, 263; **Vol. 9, Part 1**, 102; **Supp. 9**, 824–25
Ettor, Joseph J., reference to, **Supp. 6**, 238
Etymology, **Vol. 4, Part 2**, 522; **Vol. 9, Part 2**, 441
Eubie, **Supp. 9**, 732
Eucalyptus trees, introduction of seeds, **Vol. 9, Part 2**, 345
Eugene, Oreg., early history, **Vol. 6, Part 2**, 621
Eugenics: **Vol. 1, Part 2**, 151; **Vol. 3, Part 2**, 566; **Vol. 4, Part 2**, 412; **Vol. 9, Part 2**, 69; as birth control argument, **Supp. 8**, 569; movement, **Supp. 3**, 215–16; 445–46, 632; **Supp. 4**, 413, 618, 792, **Supp. 6**, 320; positive philosophy of germinal choice, **Supp. 8**, 449; research in, **Supp. 1**, 130
Eureka College, presidency of, **Vol. 6, Part 1**, 401
Eureka Springs Railway, **Vol. 2, Part 2**, 187
Europe, James Reese, reference to, **Supp. 9**, 731
Europe: historical writings on, **Supp. 2**, 469, 564; modern architecture, **Supp. 8**, 436
European & North American Railway Co., **Vol. 8, Part 1**, 71 f.
European Coal Council, **Supp. 7**, 359
European Recovery Program. *See* Marshall Plan
European Times, **Vol. 1, Part 2**, 8
Eutaw Springs, S.C., battle of, **Vol. 4, Part 1**, 572; **Vol. 4, Part 2**, 212; **Vol. 6, Part 1**, 107; **Vol. 6, Part 2**, 284; **Vol. 7, Part 2**, 584; **Vol. 9, Part 2**, 216
Euthanasia Society of America, founding of, **Supp. 7**, 624
Evangelical Alliance, **Vol. 1, Part 1**, 101; **Vol. 5, Part 2**, 428; **Vol. 7, Part 2**, 14
Evangelical Association, **Vol. 3, Part 2**, 184; **Vol. 6, Part 2**, 625; **Vol. 9, Part 1**, 4
Evangelical Review, **Vol. 5, Part 2**, 502 f.
Evangeline, **Vol. 6, Part 1**, 386
Evangelische Synode von Nord-Amerika, founding of, **Vol. 8, Part 1**, 600
Evangelism: **Vol. 1, Part 2**, 376; **Vol. 2, Part 2**, 19; **Vol. 3, Part 1**, 84 f., 410, 413 f.; **Vol. 3, Part 2**, 390; **Vol. 4, Part 2**, 203; **Vol. 5, Part 2**, 199; **Vol. 7, Part 1**, 2, 103, 529; **Vol. 8, Part 1**, 599 f.; **Vol. 8, Part 2**, 18, 74 f., 352; **Vol. 9, Part 2**, 345, **Vol. 10, Part 1**, 625; **Vol. 10, Part 2**, 125 f.; charismatic conservative, **Supp. 1**, 679; fundamentalism, **Supp. 4**, 691–92; **Supp. 5**, 346; **Supp. 8**, 303–4; labor movement, **Supp. 3**, 734; Men and Religion Forward Movement, **Supp. 2**, 20, 617–18; **Supp. 5**, 579; missions, **Supp. 10**, 636–37; nondenominational, **Supp. 2**, 48–49; Oxford Group, **Supp. 7**, 88–89; radio, **Supp. 4**, 541; **Supp. 8**, 434; Social Gospel movement, **Supp. 7**, 185, 624; Southern Baptist, **Supp. 3**, 497–98, 778–79; student-oriented, **Supp. 5**, 506–8; teaching of, **Supp. 3**, 687–88
Evangelist, **Vol. 3, Part 2**, 364
Evans, Arthur J., reference to, **Supp. 3**, 343
Evans, Donald, reference to, **Supp. 5**, 659
Evans, Hiram W., reference to, **Supp. 3**, 709
Evans, Robley D., reference to, **Vol. 5, Part 1**, 471–72
Evans, Wainwright, reference to, **Supp. 3**, 462
Evans, Walker, references to, **Supp. 5**, 512; **Supp. 9**, 760
Evanston, Ill., **Vol. 3, Part 2**, 205; **Vol. 6, Part 1**, 509; **Vol. 7, Part 2**, 298
Evening Post (New York City), **Vol. 8, Part 2**, 546
Evening Telegram (New York City), founding of, **Vol. 1, Part 2**, 200
Eveready Flashlight Co., founding of, **Supp. 7**, 150
Everett, Edward, references to, **Vol. 9, Part 1**, 431; **Vol. 9, Part 2**, 526
Evers, Charles, reference to, **Supp. 7**, 227
Evers, Johnny, reference to, **Supp. 5**, 465
Evers, Medgar, **Supp. 10**, 307
Eversharp, Inc., **Supp. 10**, 670
Everson, George, reference to, **Supp. 9**, 275
Everybody's Magazine, **Supp. 7**, 320
Everyman's Library, **Supp. 3**, 499
Evolution: **Vol. 1, Part 2**, 134 f.; **Vol. 3, Part 1**, 268; **Vol. 3, Part 2**, 421 f.; **Vol. 4, Part 2**, 46; **Vol. 5, Part 1**, 342; **Vol. 6, Part 1**, 616; **Vol. 8, Part 1**, 144 f.; **Vol. 8, Part 2**, 389; **Vol. 9, Part 1**, 547; **Vol. 10, Part 1**, 111; acquired characteristics, theory of, **Supp. 1**, 50; anthropological study of human, **Supp. 3**, 82–84; **Supp. 4**, 866–67; **Supp. 8**, 85–86; botanical, **Supp. 8**, 596; conflict concerning, **Vol. 8, Part 2**, 56; economic theory, **Supp. 3**, 170; fossil studies relationship to, **Supp. 4**, 206, 730; fundamentalist opposition to, **Supp. 4**, 691, 692; history of, **Supp. 7**, 481; in historical scholarship, **Supp. 4**, 152; interpretation of, in the South, **Vol. 10, Part 2**, 496; Mendelian genetics, **Supp. 3**, 539–40; mind studies, **Supp. 6**, 718–19; natural selection, studies defending, **Supp. 8**, 499; **Supp. 9**, 239–40; paleontological studies, **Supp. 5**, 743; popularization of, **Vol. 8, Part 2**, 599; psychology, **Supp. 3**, 149–50; religious defense of, **Supp. 4**, 85; research in, **Supp. 1**, 586; teaching of, **Supp. 4**, 692, 542; **Supp. 5**, 461; **Supp. 6**, 528–29; **Supp. 7**, 624, 631; **Supp. 8**, 582–84; "teleological order," **Supp. 3**, 350; textbook on organic, **Supp. 1**, 697; theory conflicts, **Supp. 6**, 393; writings against, **Supp. 7**, 631; writings on, general, **Supp. 10**, 210; writings on human, **Supp. 5**, 127. *See also* Scopes trial
Ewald, P. P., reference to, **Supp. 7**, 10
Ewell, R. S., reference to, **Vol. 6, Part 1**, 125
Ewing, William, reference to, **Supp. 7**, 715
Excavation, steam drills, use of, in, **Vol. 2, Part 2**, 544; **Vol. 3, Part 2**, 569
Excise Act, **Vol. 3, Part 2**, 560
Excursion trips, early, **Vol. 7, Part 2**, 463
Execution, death at stake, **Vol. 7, Part 1**, 379
Executive. *See* Presidency (U.S.)
Exercise. *See* Physical fitness; Sports; *specific sports*
Exeter Academy. *See* Phillips-Exeter Academy
Exhibition of Independent Arts, **Supp. 5**, 635
Existentialism, **Supp. 6**, 716, 725; **Supp. 7**, 746, 747; **Supp. 9**, 40; writings on, **Supp. 10**, 401, 402
Ex-Lax, **Supp. 8**, 339
Exner, Judith Campbell, reference to, **Supp. 9**, 307
"Experiment," railroad train, **Vol. 5, Part 2**, 59
Experimental Theatre, founding of, **Supp. 9**, 849
Experiment in International Living, **Supp. 10**, 819
Exploration: **Vol. 2, Part 2**, 23; **Vol. 3, Part 2**, 266, 309; **Vol. 4, Part 1**, 323, 439; **Vol. 5, Part 2**, 156 f., 569; **Vol. 7, Part 1**, 514; **Vol. 10, Part 1**, 635 f.; Africa, **Vol. 2, Part 1**, 591; **Vol. 4, Part 2**, 2, 415, 417, 439, 540; **Vol. 6, Part 1**, 28; **Vol. 8, Part 1**, 320 f.; **Vol. 8, Part 2**, 142, 349; **Vol. 9, Part 1**, 509 f.; **Supp. 4**, 127–28; **Supp. 5**, 370–71; **Supp. 8**, 3–4; Alaska, **Vol. 7, Part 1**, 315; **Vol. 8, Part 2**, 481; **Supp. 7**, 371; Amazon, **Vol. 4, Part 1**, 481; **Vol. 4, Part 2**, 580; America, discoverer controversy, **Supp. 8**, 457; Antarctica, **Vol. 7, Part 1**, 195; **Vol. 7, Part 2**, 189 f.; **Vol. 10, Part 2**, 217; **Supp. 2**, 115; **Supp. 5**, 206–7; **Supp. 6**, 17–18; **Supp. 9**, 64; archaeological, **Supp. 6**, 17–18; Arctic, **Vol. 1, Part 1**, 240, 529; **Vol. 1, Part 2**, 200; **Vol. 2, Part 1**, 38; **Vol. 3, Part 1**, 64 f., 200 f.,

228; **Vol. 4, Part 2**, 2, 120, 445f.; **Vol. 5, Part 2**, 62, 256; **Vol. 6, Part 1**, 341 f.; **Vol. 6, Part 2**, 521; **Vol. 7, Part 2**, 323, 362, 366; **Vol. 8, Part 2**, 31, 481; **Vol. 10, Part 1**, 102, 390, 635 f.; **Supp. 4**, 674; **Supp. 5**, 206–7, 295, 539–40; **Supp. 6**, 17–18; **Supp. 7**, 716–17; **Supp. 9**, 63, 117–18, 220; Arkansas, **Vol. 3, Part 1**, 507 f.; Asia Minor, **Vol. 9, Part 1**, 594; Cabot's voyages, **Vol. 3, Part 1**, 172; California, **Vol. 1, Part 1**, 322; **Vol. 2, Part 1**, 396; **Vol. 3, Part 1**, 252; **Vol. 3, Part 2**, 244; **Vol. 4, Part 1**, 132; **Vol. 5, Part 2**, 419; **Vol. 6, Part 1**, 180; **Vol. 7, Part 2**, 310; **Vol. 8, Part 1**, 109 f.; **Vol. 8, Part 2**, 32; **Vol. 9, Part 1**, 290 f.; Canada, **Vol. 2 Part 1**, 183; **Vol. 4, Part 2**, 17; **Vol. 5, Part 1**, 456; **Vol. 9, Part 2**, 455; **Supp. 8**, 3; **Supp. 5**, 225; China, **Vol. 8, Part 2**, 244; Colorado River, **Vol. 5, Part 1**, 521; **Vol. 7, Part 1**, 445; **Vol. 8, Part 1**, 146 f.; Columbia River, **Vol. 4, Part 1**, 522 f.; Cuba, **Vol. 7, Part 1**, 382 f.; Dunbar, **Vol. 3, Part 1**, 507; East Indies, **Vol. 5, Part 1**, 236; Fanning's Islands, **Vol. 9, Part 2**, 266; Florida, **Vol. 6, Part 2**, 533; **Vol. 7, Part 1**, 382, 593; **Vol. 8, Part 1**, 281 f., 284 f.; Fremont, **Vol. 2, Part 1**, 531; **Vol. 4, Part 1**, 20, 316; French, **Vol. 1, Part 1**, 183; **Vol. 3, Part 1**, 500 f.; **Vol. 6, Part 1**, 4, 10, 37, 182; **Vol. 6, Part 2**, 511 f.; **Vol. 8, Part 2**, 293, 295, 304; Georgia, **Vol. 1, Part 1**, 451; Grand Canyon, **Vol. 2, Part 1**, 486; **Vol. 7, Part 2**, 603; **Vol. 8, Part 1**, 146; Great Lake Region, **Vol. 2, Part 1**, 183; **Vol. 3, Part 1**, 500 f.; **Vol. 5, Part 2**, 156; **Vol. 6, Part 2**, 295; Greenland, **Vol. 9, Part 2**, 308; Grinnell Land, **Vol. 3, Part 1**, 200 f.; Gunnison, **Vol. 4, Part 2**, 52; **Vol. 9, Part 2**, 40, 49; Hakluyt's voyages, **Vol. 2, Part 1**, 39; Hudson River, **Vol. 5, Part 1**, 338 f.; Isthmus of Darien (Panama), **Vol. 9, Part 2**, 122; Jessup Expedition, **Vol. 8, Part 1**, 276 f.; Kentucky, **Vol. 3, Part 2**, 382; **Vol. 10, Part 1**, 360 f.; Latin America, **Supp. 6**, 59; Lederer, **Vol. 6, Part 1**, 91; Lewis and Clark expeditions, **Vol. 2, Part 2**, 142 f., 319, 435; **Vol. 4, Part 1**, 178; **Vol. 4, Part 2**, 354; **Vol. 5, Part 2**, 29; **Vol. 6, Part 1**, 221, 291; **Vol. 7, Part 1**, 631; **Vol. 7, Part 2**, 51; **Vol. 8, Part 1**, 255; **Vol. 8, Part 2**, 278; Long, **Vol. 5, Part 2**, 276; **Vol. 6, Part 1**, 380; Lumholtz expedition, **Vol. 5, Part 2**, 62; Maine, **Vol. 2, Part 1**, 606; **Vol. 8, Part 1**, 78; **Vol. 10, Part 1**, 562 f.; Michigan, **Vol. 2, Part 1**, 582; **Vol. 6, Part 1**, 395; Minnesota, **Vol. 3, Part 1**, 500 f.; Mississippi River, **Vol. 1, Part 2**, 251; **Vol. 2, Part 1**, 97; **Vol. 3, Part 1**, 257; **Vol. 5, Part 2**, 157, 223 f.; **Vol. 6, Part 2**, 526; **Vol. 7, Part 1**, **Vol. 8, Part 2**, 295, 457; **Vol. 9, Part 2**, 587; Missouri River, **Vol. 1, Part 1**, 354; **Vol. 1, Part 2**, 482; **Vol. 2, Part 1**, 397; **Vol. 2, Part 2**, 143; Montana, **Vol. 6, Part 2**, 299; Mount Washington, **Vol. 3, Part 1**, 13; National Geographic Society–sponsored, **Supp. 8**, 228; New England coast, **Vol. 1, Part 2**, 378; **Vol. 10, Part 1**, 562 f.; New Mexico, **Vol. 1, Part 1**, 571; **Vol. 2, Part 1**, 486; **Vol. 3, Part 2**, 184; **Vol. 7, Part 1**, 533; Nicaragua, **Vol. 6, Part 1**, 500; North Carolina, **Vol. 2, Part 1**, 328; North Pacific expedition of U.S. Navy, **Vol. 5, Part 2**, 62; **Vol. 8, Part 2**, 244; **Vol. 9, Part 2**, 32; Northwest, **Vol. 2, Part 2**, 127 f, 319; **Vol. 4, Part 2**, 276; **Vol. 6, Part 1**, 191; **Vol. 6, Part 2**, 74; **Vol. 7, Part 2**, 186 f.; **Vol. 8, Part 1**, 320; **Vol. 8, Part 2**, 457; Ohio River, **Vol. 2, Part 1**, 582; Oregon Trail, **Vol. 4, Part 1**, 19; Orient, **Vol. 5, Part 1**, 58; Orinoco River, **Vol. 10, Part 1**, 632 f.; Palestine, **Vol. 5, Part 1**, 80; **Vol. 7, Part 2**, 150; Pikes Peak, **Vol. 5, Part 1**, 576; **Vol. 7, Part 2**, 599; **Vol. 10, Part 2**, 224; Red River, **Vol. 1, Part 1**, 579; **Vol. 5, Part 2**, 441; Rocky Mountains, **Vol. 5, Part 1**, 576; **Vol. 7, Part 1**, 81, 319; **Vol. 8, Part 1**, 250; South America, **Vol. 2, Part 2**, 103; **Vol. 3, Part 2**, 465 f.; **Vol. 7, Part 1**, 594; **Vol. 7, Part 2**, 140; South Carolina, **Vol. 10, Part 2**, 509; South Seas, **Vol. 7, Part 2**, 562; Southwest, **Vol. 2, Part 2**, 449 f.; space, **Supp. 7**, 424, 429; Spanish, **Vol. 1, Part 1**, 135, 322, 451; **Vol. 2, Part 2**, 449 f.; **Vol. 6, Part 1**, 504; Syria, **Vol. 9, Part 1**, 258; Virginia, **Vol. 10, Part 2**, 154; West, **Vol. 2, Part 2**, 234; **Vol. 3, Part 2**, 496; **Vol. 4, Part 1**, 13, 132, 327, 329; **Vol. 6, Part 1**, 180, 380; **Vol. 6, Part 2**, 332; **Vol. 7, Part 1**, 315, 641; **Vol. 7, Part 2**, 481, 599; **Vol. 9, Part 1**, 516, 631 f.; Wilkes expedition, **Vol. 3, Part 1**, 55, 200; **Vol. 7, Part 2**, 185; **Vol. 9, Part 2**, 457; Wisconsin, **Vol. 3, Part 1**, 500 f.; writings on, **Vol. 3, Part 1**, 475 f., 507 f.; **Vol. 4, Part 1**, 18, 20; **Vol. 5, Part 2**, 606; **Vol. 6, Part 1**, 91; Yosemite Valley, **Vol. 6, Part 1**, 180; zoological collections, **Supp. 3**, 667–69. *See also specific states, regions*

Explorations, Journal of, **Vol. 6, Part 1**, 221

Explorers. For complete list, *see* Occupations Index

Explorers' Club of New York, **Vol. 10, Part 1**, 390; founding of, **Supp. 1**, 238

Explosives: **Vol. 3, Part 1**, 528; **Vol. 5, Part 2**, 239; **Vol. 6, Part 2**, 438; **Vol. 7, Part 2**, 22; dynamite, use of, **Vol. 5, Part 2**, 239; **Vol. 7, Part 2**, 22; industry research, **Supp. 2**, 479; manufacturing, **Supp. 1**, 271; **Supp. 2**, 551; **Supp. 3**, 239; **Supp. 4**, 681; **Supp. 5**, 191–93; **Supp. 7**, 169, 210; RDX (cyclonite), **Supp. 5**, 28; safe transportation of, **Vol. 3, Part 1**, 479 f.; smokeless powder, **Supp. 5**, 235

Export-Import Bank, **Supp. 6**, 229, 231, 325; **Supp. 8**, 66

Export trade, **Vol. 3, Part 1**, 429; **Vol. 7, Part 2**, 62

Express business: **Vol. 1, Part 1**, 37, 354; **Vol. 2, Part 1**, 375; **Vol. 2, Part 2**, 50; **Vol. 3, Part 2**, 271; **Vol. 4, Part 2**, 278; **Vol. 9, Part 2**, 385; Post Office and, **Vol. 10, Part 1**, 639 f.; writings on, **Vol. 9, Part 2**, 32, 385

Expressways. *See* Road building

Exter, Alexandra, reference to, **Supp. 6**, 624

Extragalactic nebulae, **Supp. 5**, 326

Extrasensory perception, **Supp. 2**, 407; **Supp. 6**, 612; **Supp. 10**, 672

Eye-Bank for Sight Restoration, founding of, **Supp. 7**, 70

Eyes: astigmatism, **Supp. 3**, 377; belladonna, use of, **Vol. 10, Part 1**, 644 f.; bird and reptile studies, **Supp. 3**, 835; color blindness, **Supp. 3**, 270; color heredity, **Supp. 3**, 215; diseases of, **Vol. 3, Part 1**, 207, 253, 327; **Vol. 5, Part 1**, 293; **Vol. 5, Part 2**, 38; **Vol. 8, Part 1**, 510, 565; **Supp. 2**, 604; **Supp. 3**, 835; **Supp. 4**, 865; dispensary, first in U.S., **Vol. 7, Part 1**, 559; glaucoma drug, **Supp. 9**, 443; operations on, **Vol. 3, Part 1**, 478 f.; **Vol. 5, Part 1**, 248, 541; **Vol. 7, Part 1**, 557; reading movement of, **Supp. 3**, 229–30; surgery, **Supp. 3**, 301–2; surgery anesthetic, **Supp. 3**, 430–31; visual acuity testing, **Supp. 3**, 269–70. *See also* Blind and blindness; Ophthalmology; Vision

Ezra Church, battle of, **Vol. 1, Part 1**, 266; **Vol. 5, Part 1**, 280; **Vol. 6, Part 1**, 130; **Vol. 9, Part 2**, 3

F

Faber and Faber (publishers), **Supp. 7**, 220

Fabian Society, **Vol. 3, Part 1**, 96

Fabrics. *See* Textiles; specific types

Fabulist, The, **Supp. 6**, 185

Factorage, Indian, **Vol. 2, Part 2**, 565; **Vol. 4, Part 1**, 94; **Vol. 6, Part 2**, 89; **Vol. 7, Part 1**, 633

Factories in the Field, **Supp. 10**, 502

Facts Forum (foundation), **Supp. 9**, 413

Fagan, Mark, reference to, **Supp. 6**, 265

Fagan, Ruth, reference to, **Supp. 5**, 74

Fail-Safe, **Supp. 7**, 93, 94

Fair, James G., reference to, **Vol. 7, Part 1**, 612

Fairbanks, Douglas, Jr., reference to, **Supp. 10**, 158
Fairbanks, Douglas, Sr., references to, **Supp. 4**, 350; **Supp. 10**, 635, 636
Fairchild, George Winthrop, reference to, **Supp. 9**, 273
Fairchild Tropical Garden (Fla.), **Supp. 5**, 214
Fair Employment Practices Commission, **Supp. 7**, 122; founding of, **Supp. 5**, 120
Fairfax, Beatrice, column of, **Supp. 3**, 504
Fairfax, Sally, reference to, **Supp. 6**, 310
Fairfax Court-House, Va., capture of, **Vol. 7, Part 1**, 272
Fairfax proprietary, **Vol. 3, Part 2**, 256
Fairfield, Calif., founding of, **Vol. 10, Part 1**, 534 f.
Fairfield, Conn., **Vol. 2, Part 2**, 67; settlement of, **Vol. 6, Part 1**, 494
"Fair Harvard," **Vol. 4, Part 1**, 305
Fair Housing Act (1968), **Supp. 10**, 316
Fair Labor Standards Act (1938), **Supp. 3**, 228; Supp. 46, 376, 614; **Supp. 5**, 358; **Supp. 6**, 480; **Supp. 7**, 609; passage of, Supp. 3, 655–56
Fairless, Benjamin, reference to, **Supp. 7**, 587
Fairmount College, presidency of, **Vol. 7, Part 1**, 230
Fair Oaks, Va., battle of. *See* Seven Pines, battle of
Fairs, county, beginning of American, **Vol. 10, Part 1**, 542; state, **Vol. 8, Part 1**, 347; **Vol. 10, Part 1**, 36
Faith-cure movement, **Vol. 2, Part 2**, 588; **Supp. 4**, 271–72; **Supp. 10**, 426
Falk, Stanley L., reference to, **Supp. 6**, 268
Falk Foundation, founding of, **Supp. 4**, 261–62
Fall, Albert B., references to, **Supp. 3**, 491, 715; **Supp. 6**, 584; **Supp. 9**, 590
Falla, Manuel de, reference to, **Supp. 6**, 358
Fallingwater (Mill Run, Pa.), **Supp. 6**, 714
Fallopian tubes, **Supp. 6**, 555
Fallout shelters, legislation mandating construction of, **Supp. 9**, 524
Fall River, Mass., **Vol. 1, Part 2**, 459
Fall River Line, **Vol. 1, Part 2**, 459; **Vol. 9, Part 2**, 344
Fallen Timbers, battle of, **Vol. 2, Part 2**, 142; **Vol. 4, Part 2**, 216, 348; **Vol. 5, Part 2**, 8–9; **Vol. 6, Part 1**, 300; **Vol. 8, Part 2**, 487; **Vol. 10, Part 1**, 210, 524, 564
Falls, Mildred, reference to, **Supp. 9**, 424
Families: anthropological study of, **Supp. 8**, 378; pioneer in study of, **Vol. 3, Part 1**, 308; popular writings on, **Supp. 8**, 189; situation comedies, **Supp. 7**, 9; social work, **Supp. 4**, 810–11; sociology of black, **Supp. 7**, 266
"Family Affair" (television program), **Supp. 10**, 86
Family Circle, **Supp. 6**, 449
Family Digest, **Supp. 6**, 478–79
Family Magazine, founding of, **Vol. 8, Part 1**, 440
Family planning: abortion advocacy, **Supp. 9**, 353; birth control advocacy, **Supp. 5**, 297; **Supp. 6**, 602; **Supp. 9**, 352, 556–57; **Supp. 10**, 683, 684; first birth control clinic in U.S., **Supp. 8**, 568; oral contraceptive development, **Supp. 8**, 503; Planned Parenthood associations, **Supp. 4**, 391; **Supp. 9**, 352; religious objections to contraception, **Supp. 8**, 116; social research in, **Supp. 6**, 82
Family School for Young Ladies, **Vol. 9, Part 2**, 621
Family Service Association of America, predecessors, **Supp. 4**, 810
Famous-Barr Co., **Supp. 8**, 427
Famous Players Film Co., **Supp. 3**, 607; **Supp. 6**, 369; **Supp. 10**, 339; founding of, **Supp. 10**, 871; productions, **Supp. 10**, 635, 871–72
Famous Players-Lasky (film production), **Supp. 10**, 872
Faneuil Hall (Boston), **Vol. 3, Part 2**, 263; **Vol. 6, Part 1**, 439; building of, **Vol. 8, Part 1**, 308 f.; designs for, **Vol. 9, Part 1**, 229
Fanning's Islands, discovery of, **Vol. 3, Part 2**, 266
Fanny, fastest merchant vessel of the time, **Vol. 6, Part 1**, 543
Fanny (musical), **Supp. 9**, 71
Fantasia (movie), **Supp. 9**, 237; **Supp. 10**, 351, 763
FAO. *See* Food and Agriculture Organization
Fard, W. D., reference to, **Supp. 9**, 569
Far Eastern Commission, **Supp. 6**, 270
Fargo, William G., reference to, **Vol. 10, Part 1**, 639 f.
Farish, William S., reference to, **Supp. 4**, 775–76
Farley, James A., references to, **Supp. 3**, 560, 646, 647, 659
Farley, Thomas M., reference to, **Supp. 6**, 570
Farlow, William G., reference to, **Vol. 9, Part 2**, 398
Farm, The, **Supp. 6**, 78
Farm and Home, **Vol. 7, Part 1**, 377
Farm Bankruptcy Act (1934), Frazier-Lemke amendment, **Supp. 4**, 309
Farm Bureau Federation. *See* American Farm Bureau Federation
Farm Bureau system, **Supp. 4**, 36–37
Farm Credit Act (1953), **Supp. 8**, 278
Farm Credit Administration: **Supp. 8**, 445–46; **Supp. 10**, 393; land banks, **Supp. 4**, 341
Farmer, Moses G., references to, **Vol. 2, Part 2**, 9; **Vol. 10, Part 1**, 376 f.
"Farmer Al Falfa" (fictional character), **Supp. 9**, 797
Farmer-Labor party: **Supp. 3**, 347; **Supp. 6**, 572, 645; **Supp. 9**, 30; Democratic party fusion, **Supp. 3**, 227; founding of, **Supp. 4**, 280, 542
Farmer-Labor Political Federation. *See* American Commonwealth Political Federation
Farmer-Labor Reconstruction League, founding of, **Supp. 3**, 10
Farmers' Alliance, **Vol. 1, Part 1**, 522; **Vol. 9, Part 1**, 199; **Supp. 6**, 468
Farmers' Alliance Exchange of Texas, founding of, **Supp. 2**, 426
Farmers' Almanack, founding of, **Vol. 9, Part 2**, 444 f.
Farmers' Club of Pennsylvania, **Vol. 5, Part 2**, 572
Farmers' Educational and Cooperative Union (Farmers' Union), **Supp. 1**, 51; **Supp. 2**, 426; **Supp. 6**, 86, 645
Farmers' Institutes, plan for, **Vol. 10, Part 1**, 617 f.
Farmers' Museum, publication of, **Vol. 3, Part 1**, 236
Farmers' Political League, **Vol. 7, Part 1**, 377
Farmers' Protective Association, Vol. 29 Part 2, 165
Farmers' Register, publication of, **Vol. 8, Part 2**, 215
Farmers' Tribune, **Supp. 7**, 527
Farmer's Union, **Vol. 9, Part 1**, 180. *See also* Farmers' Educational and Cooperative Union
Farmer's Wife, **Supp. 7**, 615
Farm Foundation, founding of, **Supp. 1**, 491
Farm Holiday Association, **Supp. 4**, 480; **Supp. 6**, 86, 645; founding of, **Supp. 2**, 552
Farming: **Vol. 1, Part 1**, 316; **Vol. 1, Part 2**, 183; **Vol. 2, Part 1**, 25; **Vol. 2, Part 2**, 185; **Vol. 4, Part 1**, 595; **Vol. 4, Part 2**, 207 f.; **Vol. 6, Part 1**, 482; **Vol. 7, Part 2**, 148; **Vol. 9, Part 1**, 458; **Vol. 9, Part 2**, 134; **Vol. 10, Part 2**, 460; colonial, **Vol. 8, Part 1**, 419; cooperative, **Vol. 7, Part 1**, 377; dairy, **Vol. 1, Part 1**, 370; **Vol. 5, Part 1**, 90; **Vol. 8, Part 2**, 512; **Vol. 9, Part 1**, 280; drainage, **Vol. 3, Part 1**, 210; "dry," **Vol. 1, Part 1**, 408; fertilizers, **Vol. 7, Part 2**, 419; **Vol. 8, Part 1**, 397; **Vol. 9, Part 2**, 37; machinery, **Vol. 1, Part 1**, 178, 185, 284, 551; **Vol. 1, Part 2**, 172, 230; **Vol. 2, Part 1**, 337; **Vol. 3, Part 1**, 437; **Vol. 3, Part 2**, 110, 132; **Vol. 4, Part 1**, 122; **Vol. 5, Part 2**, 53, 151 f.; **Vol. 6, Part 1**, 230, 505, 607, 610 f.; **Vol. 6, Part 2**, 304, 383; **Vol. 7, Part 1**, 590; **Vol. 7, Part 2**, 644; **Vol. 8, Part 1**, 101 f.; **Vol. 9, Part 2**, 439; **Vol. 10, Part 2**, 464, 475; rotation of crops, **Vol. 1, Part**

2, 460; schools, **Vol. 1, Part 2**, 568; **Vol. 3, Part 2**, 351; **Vol. 4, Part 1**, 379; soil analysis, **Vol. 3, Part 1**, 210; writings on, **Vol. 1, Part 1**, 110 f., 205; **Vol. 6, Part 2**, 547; **Vol. 9, Part 1**, 200; **Vol. 9, Part 2**, 388. *See also* Agriculture
Farmington, Conn., early history of, **Vol. 8, Part 1**, 97 f., 102 f.
Farm Journal, **Vol. 1, Part 1**, 413; **Supp. 7**, 615
Farm Mortgage Moratorium Act (1935), **Supp. 4**, 480
Farm Security Administration: **Supp. 4**, 50; **Supp. 6**, 12; **Supp. 7**, 456; founding of, **Supp. 4**, 251; photographs, **Supp. 8**, 586; **Supp. 9**, 268
Farragut, David Glasgow, references to, **Vol. 1, Part 1**, 146, 502; **Vol. 5, Part 2**, 221; **Vol. 7, Part 1**, 320, 402; **Vol. 9, Part 1**, 321
Farragut, Loyall, reference to, **Vol. 7, Part 2**, 186
Farrar, John, reference to, **Supp. 8**, 535–36
Farrar, Margaret, reference to, **Supp. 9**, 277
Farrar and Rinehart, **Supp. 6**, 543; founding of, **Supp. 8**, 535; **Supp. 9**, 276
Farrell, Charles, reference to, **Supp. 7**, 65
Farrell, Edelmiro, reference to, **Supp. 5**, 332
Farrell, James T., reference to, **Supp. 6**, 663
Farwell, J. V., reference to, **Vol. 7, Part 1**, 103
Fascism: Anti-Fascist Alliance, **Supp. 6**, 239; Italian-American opposition to, **Supp. 3**, 777–78; journalism opposing, **Supp. 5**, 447; **Supp. 9**, 618–19; opposition, **Supp. 6**, 237, 359, 643; sympathy with, **Supp. 3**, 50; Supp-4, 518. *See also* Nazism
Fashion: best dressed list, **Supp. 10**, 616; design, **Supp. 5**, 385–86; **Supp. 6**, 9, 100–101, 402; **Supp. 7**, 591; **Supp. 8**, 14; **Supp. 9**, 465, 586–88, 587; entertainers' influence on, **Supp. 5**, 501; haute couture, **Supp. 9**, 587; illustration, **Supp. 7**, 66–67; jeans, **Supp. 5**, 386; liberated women's, **Supp. 4**, 231; **Supp. 7**, 634; **Supp. 8**, 77; Little Lord Fauntleroy style, **Supp. 3**, 69; magazines, **Supp. 3**, 547; **Supp. 6**, 107–8; **Supp. 7**, 704–5; Metropolitan Museum Costume Institute, **Supp. 6**, 621; photography, **Supp. 9**, 760; **Supp. 10**, 305; ready-to-wear, **Supp. 10**, 699; swimwear, **Supp. 10**, 667–68; theatrical costume design, **Supp. 5**, 52–53; women's trendsetting,**Supp. 8**, 77; **Supp. 9**, 465. *See also* Clothing; Dress
Fashion; or, Life in New York, **Vol. 7, Part 1**, 296
Fassett Committee, **Vol. 3, Part 2**, 297
Fast Day Proclamation (N.H., 1899), **Vol. 8, Part 2**, 121
Fast food, fried-chicken franchises, **Supp. 10**, 717–18
Fatigue: muscular, **Supp. 2**, 391; physiological studies in, **Supp. 3**, 351; studies, **Supp. 2**, 373–74; **Supp. 4**, 565; **Supp. 8**, 684
Faubus, Orval E., references to, **Supp. 8**, 157; **Supp. 9**, 672
Faucets, invention of, **Vol. 5, Part 2**, 49 f.
Faulconer, Robert C., reference to, **Supp. 3**, 562
Faulkner, William, references to, **Supp. 3**, 14; **Supp. 6**, 106; **Supp. 9**, 165, 166; **Supp. 10**, 274
Faulkner Farm (Brookline, Mass.), **Supp. 4**, 115
Fauna, history of American, **Vol. 5, Part 1**, 141; deep sea, **Vol. 8, Part 1**, 141 f.
Faust, Clarence, reference to, **Supp. 7**, 276
FBI. *See* Federal Bureau of Investigation
FCA. *See* Farm Credit Administration
FCC. *See* Federal Communications Commission
FDIC. *See* Federal Deposit Insurance Corporation
Fechner, Robert, reference to, **Supp. 6**, 411
Federal Art Commission, **Vol. 4, Part 2**, 389
Federal Art Project, **Supp. 6**, 96, 97
Federal Bureau of Investigation (FBI): **Supp. 7**, 52; **Supp. 8**, 322, 323, 335, 489; administration, **Supp. 4**, 794; civil liberties abuses by, **Supp. 9**, 407–8; civil rights investigations, **Supp. 9**, 407; congressional support, **Supp. 4**, 446; crime laboratory, **Supp. 5**, 245; **Supp. 9**, 405; Crime Records Division, **Supp. 9**, 405; espionage investigations by, **Supp. 9**, 406; loyalty investigations by, **Supp. 10**, 221; National Police Academy, **Supp. 9**, 405; organized crime investigation by, **Supp. 9**, 821; political use of, **Supp. 9**, 406; public image of, **Supp. 9**, 405, 408; Seberg pregnancy fabrication by, **Supp. 10**, 726; Special Intelligence Service, **Supp. 9**, 406; subversive groups, investigations of, **Supp. 9**, 404, 406; World War I growth, **Supp. 1**, 359
"Federal City," designs for Washington, D.C., **Vol. 6, Part 1**, 167
Federal Communications Commission (FCC): AT&T regulatory battles with, **Supp. 9**, 676; "blue book," **Supp. 9**, 803; chairmanship, **Supp. 8**, 179–80
Federal Convention. *See* Constitutional Convention
Federal Council of Churches, **Vol. 7, Part 1**, 160
Federal Council of the Churches of Christ in America: **Vol. 2, Part 2**, 229; **Vol. 4, Part 2**, 536; **Vol. 8, Part 2**, 348; **Vol. 9, Part 2**, 151; **Vol. 10, Part 1**, 653; **Supp. 5**, 446; interchurch cooperation, **Supp. 10**, 110; Oriental race relations, **Supp. 3**, 322, 323; peace commission, **Supp. 6**, 178; presidency, **Supp. 6**, 649; race relations commission, **Supp. 6**, 285; religion and medicine committee, **Supp. 6**, 180–81; World War I activities, **Supp. 3**, 110
Federal Deposit Insurance Act, **Supp. 8**, 616
Federal Deposit Insurance Corporation (FDIC): **Supp. 3**, 730; first chairman, **Supp. 8**, 112; founding of, **Supp. 3**, 650; **Supp. 4**, 332; **Supp. 8**, 207; legislation creating, **Supp. 5**, 248; **Supp. 9**, 208
Federal Emergency Relief Act (1933), **Supp. 2**, 170
Federal Emergency Relief Administration, **Supp. 5**, 515; **Supp. 8**, 301
Federal Farm Loan Act (1916), **Vol. 7, Part 1**, 377; **Supp. 8**, 592
Federal Farm Loan Board, **Supp. 6**, 453; **Supp. 7**, 361
Federal Gazette, **Vol. 5, Part 2**, 24
Federalism, attitudes on, **Supp. 1**, 210
Federalist papers, **Vol. 4, Part 2**, 174 f.; **Vol. 5, Part 2**, 8
Federalist party: **Vol. 1, Part 1**, 77 f., 245; **Vol. 1, Part 2**, 64; **Vol. 2, Part 1**, 395; **Vol. 3, Part 1**, 569 f.; **Vol. 4, Part 1**, 208, 225, 365, 397 f.; **Vol. 4, Part 2**, 10, 202, 224, 524; **Vol. 6, Part 1**, 101; **Vol. 7, Part 1**, 7; **Vol. 9, Part 1**, 365, 444; **Vol. 9, Part 2**, 144 f.; abuse of, **Vol. 4, Part 2**, 231; Adams, J. Q., and, **Vol. 1, Part 1**, 87 f.; "Indian summer" of, **Vol. 2, Part 1**, 80; Jefferson, T., and, **Vol. 5, Part 2**, 26 f.; New Hampshire, **Vol. 7, Part 2**, 575; North Carolina, **Vol. 4, Part 2**, 414; passing of, **Vol. 7, Part 2**, 99; Pennsylvania, **Vol. 4, Part 2**, 521; **Vol. 8, Part 2**, 178; publications, **Vol. 1, Part 1**, 87, 244; **Vol. 7, Part 2**, 566 f.; **Vol. 9, Part 2**, 136 f.; South Carolina, **Vol. 4, Part 2**, 286; states' rights, attitude toward, **Vol. 4, Part 2**, 458; Virginia, **Vol. 4, Part 2**, 557 f.; **Vol. 6, Part 1**, 117; **Vol. 6, Part 2**, 318
Federal League (baseball), **Supp. 8**, 106
Federal Loan Agency, **Supp. 6**, 325
Federal Orrery, founding of, **Vol. 7, Part 2**, 157
Federal Power Commission (FPC), **Supp. 4**, 544; forming of, **Supp. 6**, 484; private ownership advocacy **Supp. 3**, 725
Federal Radio Commission, license renewal denial, **Supp. 3**, 104
Federal Reserve Act (1913): **Vol. 1, Part 1**, 157; **Vol. 4, Part 2**, 567; **Supp. 3**, 480; preliminaries to, **Vol. 2, Part 1**, 336
Federal Reserve Act (1933), sponsorship of, **Supp. 4**, 641; writing of, **Supp. 2**, 719
Federal Reserve Bank of New York: **Supp. 3**, 290; **Supp.**

6, 559; growth of, **Vol. 9, Part 2**, 143 f.; presidency, **Supp. 10**, 752
Federal Reserve Bank of Philadelphia, architecture, **Supp. 3**, 199
Federal Reserve Board, **Vol. 4, Part 2**, 258; analytical and statistical reports, **Supp. 6**, 599; **Supp. 9**, 661; governors, **Supp. 3**, 203; **Supp. 6**, 453
Federal Reserve Board Building, architecture, **Supp. 3**, 199
Federal Reserve System: credit control, **Supp. 6**, 599; discussion of, **Vol. 9, Part 2**, 144; economic research and analysis, **Supp. 5**, 247–48; events leading to creation of, **Vol. 3, Part 1**, 148; federal government control of, **Supp. 3**, 97; founding of, **Vol. 10, Part 1**, 412 f.; **Supp. 2**, 274, 719; **Supp. 4**, 331, 332; governorship, **Supp. 10**, 205; monetary policy, **Supp. 10**, 752, 753; precursor to, **Vol. 8, Part 1**, 34 f.; publications, **Supp. 8**, 242; role limitation, **Supp. 8**, 79; state bank membership, **Supp. 3**, 730
Federal Security Agency, **Supp. 5**, 459–60; **Supp. 9**, 789
Federal Telegraph Co., **Supp. 7**, 394
Federal Theatre Project, **Supp. 8**, 176–77; **Supp. 10**, 272
Federal Trade Commission (FTC): **Vol. 2, Part 2**, 325; **Supp. 1**, 446; **Supp. 3**, 97; **Supp. 5**, 27; **Supp. 7**, 521; **Supp. 8**, 219–20; administration, **Supp. 1**, 446; first chairman, **Supp. 6**, 146; powers, **Supp. 6**, 556; price-fixing actions, **Supp. 4**, 268
Federal Trade Commission Act (1914), **Supp. 3**, 97
Federated Department Stores; founding of, **Supp. 3**, 421–22; growth of, **Supp. 9**, 483–84
Federated Organization of Colored People, **Supp. 5**, 755
Federation for Jewish Philanthropies, **Supp. 7**, 466
Federation for the Support of Jewish Philanthropic Societies, founding of, **Supp. 2**, 695
Federation of American Zionists, **Supp. 2**, 252; **Supp. 3**, 756–57; founding of, **Supp. 4**, 905
Federation of Children's Agencies (New York City), **Supp. 3**, 28
Federation of Jewish Charities, **Vol. 8, Part 2**, 171; **Supp. 4**, 80; founding of, **Supp. 4**, 262
Federation of Organized Trades and Labor Unions, dissolution of, **Vol. 3, Part 1**, 510
Federation of Palestinian Jews in America, founding of, **Supp. 1**, 407
Feeney, Leonard, reference to, **Supp. 8**, 115
Feeney, T. L., reference to, **Vol. 7, Part 2**, 238
Feet, treatment for flat, **Supp. 4**, 887
Feldman, Charles, reference to, **Supp. 10**, 62
Feldspar, measurement, **Supp. 6**, 153
Felker, Clay, reference to, **Supp. 9**, 265
Fellenberg Manual Labor Institution, **Vol. 2, Part 2**, 267
Fellini, Federico, reference to, **Supp. 9**, 66
Fellowship of Reconciliation, **Supp. 7**, 356; **Supp. 8**, 425, 458, 649; **Supp. 9**, 585
Fels Fund, founding of, **Supp. 4**, 262–63
Fels Naptha soap, **Supp. 4**, 262
Felton, Rebecca Latimer, reference to, **Supp. 4**, 144–45
Female Medical College of Pennsylvania, earliest medical college for women, **Vol. 4, Part 1**, 81; **Vol. 8, Part 1**, 201
Female Medical Education Society, **Vol. 4, Part 1**, 604
Feminism: **Vol. 2, Part 1**, 19, 151; **Vol. 6, Part 1**, 480; **Vol. 9, Part 2**, 253 f.; film theory icon, **Supp. 10**, 11–12. *See also* Woman suffrage; Women's rights
Feminist fiction, **Supp. 7**, 386
"Fencibles," use of the term, **Vol. 8, Part 1**, 315 f.
Fenian Brotherhood: **Vol. 3, Part 1**, 264 f.; **Vol. 5, Part 2**, 88; **Vol. 8, Part 2**, 389; **Vol. 9, Part 2**, 242; founding of, **Vol. 7, Part 2**, 36; militant character of, **Vol. 8, Part 2**, 19 f.; organization of, in Tennessee, **Vol. 7, Part 2**, 45; raids, **Vol. 7, Part 2**, 45; **Vol. 9, Part 2**, 242
Fenway Park (Boston, Mass.), **Supp. 10**, 860
Ferber, Edna, references to, **Supp. 3**, 418; **Supp. 7**, 413; **Supp. 9**, 464
Ferguson, Bob, reference to, **Supp. 7**, 168
Ferguson, Frank W., reference to, **Supp. 3**, 195–96
Ferguson, Homer, reference to, **Supp. 7**, 72
Ferguson, James E., references to, **Supp. 4**, 776; **Supp. 7**, 242, 349
Ferguson, Miriam A. ("Ma"), reference to, **Supp. 4**, 776
Fermi, Enrico, references to, **Supp. 6**, 501; **Supp. 7**, 10, 11, 135, 732; **Supp. 8**, 627; **Supp. 9**, 541, 696
Fermi-Dirac statistics, **Supp. 5**, 219, 221
Fernald, Walter E., reference to, **Vol. 5, Part 1**, 296
Fernow, Bernhard E., reference to, **Supp. 4**, 43
Ferns, study of, **Vol. 3, Part 1**, 606 f.; **Vol. 10, Part 1**, 116
Ferrer, José, reference to, **Supp. 9**, 849
Ferrie, David, reference to, **Supp. 9**, 715
Ferris, Eugene B., Jr., reference to, **Supp. 3**, 805–6
Ferris wheel, designing of, **Vol. 3, Part 2**, 339
Ferryboats; early, **Vol. 9, Part 1**, 615, 619; horsepower, New York Harbor (1814), **Vol. 8, Part 2**, 106; Mississippi River, **Vol. 3, Part 1**, 249; St. Louis, **Vol. 7, Part 2**, 593; steam, first on Mississippi River, **Vol. 3, Part 1**, 249; *Susquehanna* (1748), **Vol. 4, Part 2**, 314; Weehawken, N.J., to New York City, **Vol. 8, Part 1**, 214 f.
Fertility. *See* Gynecology; Infertility; Obstetrics; Reproductive system
Fertilization: artificial insemination, **Supp. 8**, 502; studies in, **Supp. 4**, 498
Fertilizer: **Vol. 9, Part 2**, 39; ammoniated, discovery and manufacturing of, **Vol. 8, Part 1**, 397; first use of cotton seed in manufacture of, **Vol. 7, Part 2**, 419
Fessenden, Reginald A., reference to, **Supp. 7**, 175
Fetterman Massacre (Wyo., 1866), **Vol. 2, Part 1**, 521; **Vol. 3, Part 2**, 350; **Vol. 8, Part 1**, 437
Fetus: development studies, **Supp. 4**, 801, 802; maternal nutrition impact on, **Supp. 7**, 259. *See also* Embryology
Feuds: Horrell-Higgins, **Vol. 5, Part 2**, 182; Lane-Robinson, **Vol. 5, Part 2**, 577
Feustel, Louis, reference to, **Supp. 5**, 569
Fevers: first to abandon heroic treatments for, **Vol. 3, Part 1**, 306; treatment of, **Vol. 8, Part 2**, 353; writings on, **Vol. 7, Part 1**, 66
Fibers, synthetic, **Supp. 2**, 97
Fibrillation, cardiac, **Supp. 4**, 390
Fickert, Charles M., reference to, **Supp. 3**, 532
Fiction. *See* Historical fiction
Fiction writers. For complete list, *See* Occupations Index
Fiedler, Emanuel, reference to, **Supp. 10**, 236
Field, Betty, reference to, **Supp. 8**, 529
Field, Crosby, **Supp. 10**, **Supp. 9**, 510
Field, Cyrus W., references to, **Vol. 5, Part 1**, 347; **Vol. 8, Part 2**, 521; **Vol. 9, Part 2**, 338
Field, David Dudley, references to, **Vol. 6, Part 1**, 396; **Vol. 7, Part 1**, 621
Field, Eugene, reference to, **Vol. 6, Part 1**, 596
Field, Marshall, reference to, **Vol. 6, Part 1**, 157
Field, Stephen J., references to, **Vol. 7, Part 1**, 462; **Vol. 9, Part 2**, 380
Field Afar, The, founding of, **Supp. 2**, 692
Field Enterprises, **Supp. 7**, 243; **Supp. 8**, 579
Field Foundation, founding of, **Supp. 6**, 202

Field Museum of Natural History (Chicago), **Vol. 1, Part 1**, 448 f.; **Vol. 2, Part 2**, 459; **Vol. 3, Part 2**, 367; **Vol. 7, Part 1**, 17; **Vol. 8, Part 1**, 276 f.; **Vol. 8, Part 2**, 272; **Supp. 1**, 259
Fielding, Henry, scholarship on, **Supp. 4**, 197
Fielding, Mildred, reference to, **Supp. 3**, 233
Fields, Herbert, references to, **Supp. 9**, 280, 281
Fields, James T., reference to, **Vol. 9, Part 2**, 529
Fields, Joseph, reference to, **Supp. 9**, 280
Fields, Lew M., reference to, **Supp. 9**, 280
Fields, W. C., references to, **Supp. 10**, 32, 830
"Fifty-four-forty," **Vol. 3, Part 1**, 398
Figs, introduction of, to California, **Vol. 8, Part 2**, 90 f.
Figureheads, for prows of ships, **Vol. 8, Part 2**, 234 f.
Figure painting, **Supp. 2**, 149
Figure skating. *See* Ice skating
Filene, Lincoln, reference to, **Supp. 5**, 165
Filene's department store, **Supp. 2**, 183; **Supp. 3**, 421–22; **Supp. 9**, 483
Files, manufacture of, **Vol. 7, Part 1**, 509
Filibustering, regulation of, **Vol. 8, Part 1**, 457 f.
Filibustering expeditions: Cuba, **Vol. 2, Part 1**, 96; **Vol. 4, Part 1**, 233; **Vol. 4, Part 2**, 527; **Vol. 9, Part 2**, 510; Nicaragua, **Vol. 8, Part 2**, 343
Films. *See* Motion pictures
Filson Club, founding of, **Vol. 3, Part 1**, 550 f.
Finance: **Vol. 1, Part 1**, 430, 606 f.; **Vol. 3, Part 1**, 455 f.; **Vol. 3, Part 2**, 349 f.; **Vol. 4, Part 1**, 146, 164, 167 f., 172, 175, 189, 345, 444; **Vol. 5, Part 2**, 109, 286, 392 f., 478, 563; **Vol. 6, Part 1**, 60, 407 f., 494 f., 543; **Vol. 10, Part 1**, 175 f.; Aldrich currency bill, **Vol. 2, Part 2**, 154; Astor family dealings, **Supp. 6**, 23–24; Budget Act (1921), **Supp. 1**, 344; building projects, financing of, **Vol. 9, Part 2**, 132; Civil War, monetary policies following, **Vol. 6, Part 2**, 7; collapse (1873), **Vol. 4, Part 1**, 499; Colorado, **Vol. 9, Part 2**, 395; corporate investment, **Supp. 8**, 78–79, 367–68, 679; federal, restructuring, **Supp. 2**, 448; federal budget, **Vol. 6, Part 1**, 407 f.; **Vol. 9, Part 2**, 270; **Supp. 4**, 753; **Supp. 7**, 190, 734; **Supp. 8**, 290; First Savings Bank, **Vol. 8, Part 2**, 388; first treasurer of the U.S., **Vol. 6, Part 2**, 548; foreign, **Supp. 2**, 678; Gallatin and, **Vol. 4, Part 1**, 105 f.; Gold Standard Act, **Vol. 1, Part 1**, 221; government bonds, **Vol. 2, Part 2**, 838 f.; Hamilton and, **Vol. 4, Part 2**, 175; history of, in U.S., **Vol. 8, Part 2**, 480; holding companies, New Jersey, **Vol. 3, Part 1**, 309; holding company, first in U.S., **Vol. 8, Part 2**, 266; industrial reorganizations, **Supp. 5**, 190–91, 550–51; inflation, **Vol. 8, Part 1**, 578; **Vol. 9, Part 1**, 86; international, **Vol. 3, Part 1**, 148 f.; International Monetary Conference, **Vol. 9, Part 2**, 378; Irish Free State, floating of first bonds in U.S., **Vol. 3, Part 1**, 265; investment banking, **Vol. 1, Part 1**, 607; **Vol. 2, Part 2**, 215; **Supp. 7**, 715; **Supp. 9**, 264–65; **Supp. 10**, 203, 533–34, 568; journalism, **Supp. 1**, 52, 609; **Supp. 3**, 564–65; Legal Tender Acts, **Vol. 3, Part 2**, 166; **Vol. 7, Part 1**, 423; Liberty Loans, **Vol. 4, Part 1**, 241; **Vol. 5, Part 1**, 56; modern cooperate methods, **Supp. 4**, 681–82; Monetary Commission of 1876, **Vol. 5, Part 2**, 189; monometalism, **Vol. 9, Part 2**, 636; Morgan, J. P., and, **Vol. 4, Part 2**, 372; **Vol. 7, Part 1**, 175, 234; **Vol. 9, Part 1**, 453; "Morris Plan," **Vol. 9, Part 2**, 614; National Monetary Commission, **Vol. 9, Part 2**, 363; Pennsylvania Academy of, **Vol. 8, Part 2**, 187; Pennsylvania Province, credit of, **Vol. 8, Part 1**, 400; personal, courses on, **Supp. 8**, 534; personal, writings on, **Supp. 8**, 338; "pooled" credit, **Vol. 9, Part 2**, 305; public, **Supp. 2**, 607; "Ryan Crowd," **Vol. 8, Part 2**, 266; state debts, **Vol. 4, Part 2**, 175; "uncurrent money," **Vol. 3, Part 1**, 456 f.; Virginia, **Vol. 5, Part 2**, 91; Wall Street operations, **Vol. 4, Part 2**, 394; **Vol. 7, Part 1**, 143, 144, 240, 258; **Vol. 8, Part 1**, 176 f.; **Vol. 8, Part 2**, 266, 292; **Vol. 10, Part 2**, 120; "Wildcat banking," **Vol. 9, Part 2**, 84; Wilson and, **Vol. 4, Part 2**, 372; writings on, **Vol. 1, Part 1**, 407, 510; **Vol. 2, Part 2**, 215; **Vol. 3, Part 1**, 225 f., 468 f.; **Vol. 4, Part 1**, 242, 444, 541 f.; **Vol. 5, Part 2**, 109, 302, 434, 478, 549; **Vol. 8, Part 1**, 176 f.; **Vol. 8, Part 2**, 150; **Vol. 9, Part 2**, 30, 66, 234, 462 f.; **Vol. 10, Part 1**, 412; **Supp. 5**, 650–51; **Supp. 8**, 79, 166. *See also* Banking; Credit; International banking and finance; Stock market; *specific companies, industries, and wars*
Financial and Mining Record, **Vol. 2, Part 2**, 76
Financial panics. *See* Panics
Finch, Robert H., references to, **Supp. 9**, 25, 26; **Supp. 10**, 419
Fine, Larry, reference to, **Supp. 9**, 410
Fine arts; **Vol. 7, Part 1**, 116 f., 570; Vol. 7, Part 2 312; **Vol. 8, Part 1**, 453; **Vol. 8, Part 2**, 7, 372; American Academy of, **Vol. 6, Part 1**, 325; **Vol. 7, Part 2**, 82, 350; **Vol. 8, Part 2**, 21; Minneapolis School of, **Vol. 5, Part 2**, 485; Minneapolis Society of, **Vol. 10, Part 1**, 361; Museum of, Boston, **Vol. 7, Part 2**, 465; Pennsylvania Academy of, **Vol. 3, Part 1**, 590 f.; Vol. 7, Part 2. 346, 349; **Vol. 8, Part 1**, 401; **Vol. 8, Part 2**, 235; Yale University, **Vol. 5, Part 2**, 74; **Vol. 9, Part 2**, 136; **Vol. 10, Part 1**, 108 f. *See also* Museum; *specific arts*
Fine Arts Commission, United States, **Supp. 6**, 486
Finland, architecture of, **Supp. 4**, 714
Finlay, Carlos Juan, reference to, **Vol. 9, Part 1**, 591; **Supp. 6**, 434
Finletter, Thomas K., reference to, **Supp. 8**, 303
Finley, John Stuart, reference to, **Vol. 1, Part 2**, 442
Finnegan's Wake, serialization of, **Supp. 9**, 682
Finney, Charles Grandison, references to, **Vol. 7, Part 1**, 433; **Vol. 10, Part 1**, 625 f.
Finney, Ronald, reference to, **Supp. 7**, 678
Firearms; **Vol. 1, Part 1**, 178, 325, 550; **Vol. 1, Part 2**, 209, 265, 341, 352; **Vol. 2, Part 1**, 229; **Vol. 2, Part 2**, 318; **Vol. 5, Part 1**, 247, 286, 573; **Vol. 5, Part 2**, 460; **Vol. 6, Part 1**, 51; **Vol. 6, Part 2**, 458; **Vol. 7, Part 1**, 509, 561; **Vol. 7, Part 2**, 58; **Vol. 8, Part 1**, 101 f., 496; **Vol. 8, Part 2**, 2, 145; **Vol. 9, Part 1**, 447; **Vol. 10, Part 1**, 572 f.; **Vol. 10, Part 2**, 5, 379; ballistic effects on tissues study, **Supp. 3**, 832; ballistic identification techniques, **Supp. 5**, 244–45; design of, **Supp. 1**, 231; foreign trade in, **Supp. 1**, 305; large-caliber wire-wrapped gun, **Supp. 3**, 204; sights, **Supp. 1**, 232; silencer, **Supp. 2**, 436. *See also* Guns
Firebird, The, **Supp. 9**, 775
Firebrick, manufacture of, **Vol. 5, Part 2**, 372; **Vol. 8, Part 1**, 466 f.
Fire insurance company, first in America, **Vol. 8, Part 1**, 1, 139 f.
Fire Island, N.Y., **Supp. 6**, 236, 237
Fire prevention: alarm systems, **Vol. 2, Part 2**, 9, 265; **Vol. 3, Part 2**, 280; **Vol. 8, Part 1**, 101 f.; **Supp. 1**, 554; Baltimore, **Vol. 9, Part 2**, 238; Boston, **Vol. 8, Part 1**, 308 f.; Cincinnati, **Vol. 4, Part 1**, 593; fire engines, **Vol. 1, Part 1**, 540; **Vol. 3, Part 1**, 211; **Vol. 4, Part 1**, 593; **Vol. 4, Part 2**, 1, 275; **Vol. 5, Part 2**, 53; **Vol. 6, Part 1**, 1, 29; fire extinguishers, **Vol. 3, Part 1**, 377; fire nozzles, **Vol. 7, Part 1**, 450; fireproof stairs, **Vol. 8, Part 1**, 138 f.; libraries, **Vol. 8, Part 1**, 138 f.; New York, **Vol. 3, Part 1**, 248; study of, **Vol. 3, Part 1**, 248
Fires: Apollo spacecraft, **Supp. 8**, 694; San Francisco, **Supp. 4**, 325, 417; Triangle Shirtwaist Co., **Supp. 3**, 355–56, 717–18; **Supp. 5**, 718; **Supp. 7**, 608
Fireside Companion, **Vol. 7, Part 1**, 331
Firestone, Harvey S., Sr., reference to, **Supp. 9**, 283

Firestone Tire and Rubber Co.: establishment of, **Supp. 2**, 187; rubber production, **Supp. 9**, 283, 284
Firpo, Luis Angel, reference to, **Supp. 6**, 700
First aid, introduction into class work, of, **Vol. 3, Part 2**, 563
First American, The, **Supp. 7**, 393, 394
First Baptist Church of Dallas (Tex.), **Supp. 3**, 778–79
First Baptist Church of Fort Worth (Tex., **Supp. 5**, 516
First Century Christian Fellowship. *See* Oxford Group
First Church of Christ Scientist (Berkeley, Calif.), **Supp. 6**, 438
First Humanist Society (N.Y.), founding of, **Supp. 7**, 624
"First in war, first in peace," etc., origin of phrase, **Vol. 6, Part 1**, 108
First National Bank of New York, **Supp. 3**, 290; founding of, **Supp. 1**, 44
First National City Bank (New York City), **Supp. 6**, 24
First National Corporation, **Supp. 3**, 443–44
First National Exhibitors' Circuit, comedies, **Supp. 10**, 115–16
First National Pictures. *See* Warner Brothers
First Presbyterian Church (New York City), **Supp. 8**, 183
First Presbyterian Church (Princeton, N.J.), **Supp. 6**, 195
First Security Corporation, founding of, **Supp. 10**, 205
Firuski, Maurice, reference to, **Supp. 7**, 55
Fischer, Carl, reference to, **Supp. 6**, 242
Fischer, Emil, reference to, **Supp. 3**, 60–61
Fish, Hamilton, references to, **Vol. 7, Part 1**, 286–87; **Supp. 1**, 327
Fish: Birdseye quick-frozen, **Supp. 6**, 61; colored plates of, **Vol. 5, Part 1**, 129; culture, **Vol. 4, Part 1**, 558; **Vol. 4, Part 2**, 562; **Vol. 6, Part 2**, 390; **Vol. 9, Part 2**, 565; osteology research, **Supp. 1**, 672–73; preservation of, **Vol. 1, Part 2**, 92; protective coloration and pigmentation, **Supp. 3**, 753; studies of, **Vol. 1, Part 1**, 515; **Vol. 3, Part 1**, 170; **Vol. 3, Part 2**, 63; **Vol. 6, Part 1**, 101; **Vol. 7, Part 1**, 70
Fish and Wildlife Service, administration, **Supp. 10**, 265
Fisher, Albert, reference to, **Supp. 7**, 245,
Fisher, Alfred, reference to, **Supp. 7**, 246
Fisher, Charles, reference to, **Supp. 3**, 273–74
Fisher, Dorothy (Canfield), references to, **Supp. 5**, 439; **Supp. 6**, 113, 114
Fisher, Eddie, reference to, **Supp. 9**, 343
Fisher, Edward F., reference to, **Supp. 7**, 246
Fisher, Frederick G., Jr., reference to, **Supp. 6**, 680
Fisher, Ham, reference to, **Supp. 10**, 98
Fisher, Irving, references to, **Supp. 4**, 18, 550
Fisher, John S., reference to, **Supp. 7**, 305
Fisher, Lawrence, reference to, **Supp. 3**, 273–74
Fisher, William, reference to, **Supp. 3**, 273–74
Fisher Body Corporation: founding of, **Supp. 3**, 273–74; **Supp. 7**, 245–46; General Motors' acquisition of, **Supp. 4**, 244
Fisheries: **Vol. 1, Part 1**, 309; **Vol. 3, Part 2**, 333; **Vol. 4, Part 2**, 562; **Vol. 8, Part 1**, 387; Connecticut River, **Vol. 8, Part 2**, 45; reports on (1853), **Vol. 8, Part 2**, 276
Fish horn, first recorded use of, in U.S., **Vol. 8, Part 1**, 548
Fishing equipment, sport, **Supp. 8**, 28–29
Fishing rights: **Vol. 1, Part 1**, 309; negotiations with Great Britain concerning, **Vol. 1, Part 2**, 71; **Vol. 3, Part 1**, 251; **Vol. 8, Part 1**, 285 f.; U.S. coastline extension, **Supp. 8**, 25–26
Fisk, Carlton, reference to, **Supp. 10**, 567
Fisk, James, reference to, **Vol. 7, Part 1**, 175 f.
Fiske, John, reference to, **Supp. 3**, 160
Fisk University: **Vol. 4, Part 1**, 184; founding of, **Vol. 2, Part 2**, 516; **Vol. 3, Part 2**, 413; growth of, **Vol. 6, Part 2**, 561; Jubilee singers, **Vol. 10, Part 2**, 100; Langston Hughes collection, **Supp. 9**, 108; race relations studies, **Supp. 6**, 321, 322
Fitch, John, reference to, **Vol. 8, Part 2**, 401; **Vol. 9, Part 1**, 614; **Vol. 9, Part 2**, 594
Fitchburg Railroad, **Vol. 2, Part 2**, 551
Fitz, Reginald Heber, reference to, **Supp. 5**, 111
Fitzgerald, F. Scott, references to, **Supp. 3**, 72; **Supp. 4**, 651; **Supp. 5**, 614; **Supp. 6**, 21, 287; **Supp. 7**, 335, 336, 339, 560; **Supp. 9**, 874, 876
Fitzgerald, John Francis ("Honey Fitz"), references to, **Supp. 5**, 23, 730; **Supp. 6**, 139; **Supp. 8**, 320
Fitzpatrick, Daniel R., reference to, **Supp. 5**, 552
Fitzsimmons, Bob, reference to, **Supp. 5**, 368
Fitzsimmons, Frank, reference to, **Supp. 9**, 397
Fitzsimmons, James ("Sunny"), reference to, **Supp. 5**, 757
Five and dime stores, **Supp. 5**, 400–401; **Supp. 8**, 347–49
Five Forks, battle of, **Vol. 1, Part 1**, 454; Vol. 4, Part, 597, 618; **Vol. 5, Part 1**, 25; **Vol. 6, Part 1**, 104, 134; **Vol. 7, Part 2**, 570; **Vol. 9, Part 1**, 80; **Vol. 10, Part 1**, 474
Five Little Peppers and How They Grew, **Vol. 6, Part 1**, 425
Flack, Marjorie, reference to, **Supp. 4**, 74
Flack, Roberta, reference to, **Supp. 10**, 317
Flag, American: compulsory salute issue, **Supp. 3**, 451; **Supp. 4**, 796; **Supp. 5**, 358, 575; **Supp. 7**, 264; design of, **Vol. 5, Part 1**, 222; **Vol. 8, Part 1**, 481 f.; **Vol. 8, Part 2**, 174; first appearance of, in British port, **Vol. 8, Part 2**, 186; first use of, in battle, **Vol. 9, Part 1**, 128; first use of thirteen stripes, **Vol. 6, Part 2**, 287
Flagler, Henry M., references to, **Vol. 7, Part 1**, 132; **Supp. 2**, 569, 572, 573; **Supp. 4**, 211
Flagstad, Kirsten Malfrid, reference to, **Supp. 9**, 804
Flanagan, Edward J., references to, **Supp. 4**, 594; **Supp. 8**, 659
Flanders, Ralph, McCarthy censure resolution, **Supp. 6**, 405
Flanders, Walter E., reference to, **Supp. 4**, 294
Flanner, Janet, reference to, **Supp. 9**, 60
"Flapper" (term), **Supp. 5**, 372; **Supp. 6**, 287
Flashlights, battery-powered, **Supp. 7**, 149–50
Flatiron Building (New York City), steel framing, **Supp. 3**, 611
Flaxseed, exporting to Ireland, following Revolution, **Vol. 7, Part 2**, 631
Fleetwood, battle of. *See* Brandy Station, Va.
Flegenheimer, Arthur. *See* Schultz, Dutch
Fleischer, Andrew W., reference to, **Supp. 7**, 678
Fleischmann, Raoul, reference to, **Supp. 5**, 593–94
Fleming, Erin, references to, **Supp. 10**, 513, 516
Fleming, Ian, reference to, **Supp. 9**, 263
Fleming, John Ambrose, reference to, **Supp. 7**, 176
Fletcher, Alice, reference to, **Supp. 6**, 162
Fletcher, Henry P., reference to, **Supp. 9**, 356
Fletcher, Horace, reference to, **Supp. 3**, 163, 410
"Fletcherism," **Vol. 3, Part 2**, 465
Flexner, Abraham, references to, **Supp. 2**, 574–75; **Supp. 3**, 31, 67, 279, 280, 555, 676; **Supp. 4**, 139 286; **Supp. 6**, 30
Flexner, Bernard, references to, **Supp. 3**, 280; **Supp. 4**, 286
Flexner, James T., reference to, **Supp. 6**, 310
Flexner, Simon, references to, **Vol. 10, Part 1**, 621 f.; **Supp. 3**, 141, 279, 441; **Supp. 6**, 537; **Supp. 8**, 556
Flight. *See* Aviation; Balloons
Flikke, Julia, reference to, **Supp. 9**, 99

Flint, Austin, reference to, **Vol. 9, Part 1**, 293
Flint glass, manufacture, **Vol. 5, Part 1**, 618
Flint, Mich., civic improvement projects, **Supp. 9**, 569
Flint River, Indian agency, **Vol. 4, Part 2**, 414
Flints, collecting of, **Vol. 3, Part 2**, 161
Flogging, abolition of, from navy, **Vol. 6, Part 1**, 204
Flonzaley Quartet, **Vol. 3, Part 1**, 190
Flood control: **Supp. 4**, 563–64; **Supp. 5**, 394–96; **Supp. 6**, 435–36, 508; early advocacy of, **Vol. 4, Part 2**, 353; **Vol. 9, Part 2**, 147; Colorado River, **Vol. 7, Part 1**, 617; **Vol. 9, Part 2**, 147; dam building, **Supp. 9**, 560–61; Mississippi, **Vol. 3, Part 2**, 403; **Vol. 4, Part 2**, 353; New Orleans, **Vol. 8, Part 1**, 589; Pennsylvania, **Vol. 8, Part 2**, 188
Flood Control Act (1944), **Supp. 6**, 508
Floodlighting, pioneer use of, **Vol. 8, Part 2**, 268
Floods: Mississippi River relief, **Supp. 7**, 360; Ohio River (1937), **Supp. 4**, 247
Floor beams, iron, pioneer use of, **Vol. 8, Part 1**, 115 f.
Flora, catalog of: **Vol. 5, Part 1**, 305; Mexico, **Vol. 8, Part 2**, 160; North America, **Vol. 9, Part 2**, 597; Virginia, **Vol. 2, Part 2**, 184
Flora of California, A, **Supp. 4**, 428
Florey, Howard, reference to, **Supp. 6**, 224
Florianopóis Bridge (Brazil), **Supp. 6**, 594
Florida: acquisition, efforts toward, **Vol. 7, Part 1**, 90; admission to statehood, **Vol. 2, Part 1**, 423; annexation, **Vol. 6, Part 2**, 403; border controversy, **Vol. 5, Part 2**, 323; boundary disputes, **Vol. 3, Part 1**, 557 f.; carpetbagging, **Vol. 8, Part 1**, 372 f.; cession (1819), **Vol. 1, Part 1**, 86; **Vol. 2, Part 1**, 414; **Vol. 5, Part 1**, 529; **Vol. 7, Part 1**, 91; citrus industry, **Vol. 4, Part 2**, 356; colonization, **Vol. 10, Part 1**, 55; "conquest" of, **Vol. 3, Part 1**, 256; **Vol. 7, Part 1**, 273; Creek country, **Vol. 1, Part 2**, 520; development of, as a "playground," **Vol. 3, Part 2**, 452; **Supp. 2**, 112; discovery of, **Vol. 8, Part 1**, 56 f.; education, **Vol. 3, Part 1**, 557 f.; **Vol. 6, Part 1**, 39; electoral machinery, **Vol. 3, Part 1**, 557 f.; Everglades, drainage of, **Vol. 2, Part 1**, 96; **Vol. 8, Part 1**, 359 f.; expeditions, **Vol. 7, Part 1**, 593; exploration, **Vol. 6, Part 2**, 533; **Vol. 7, Part 1**, 382 f.; **Vol. 8, Part 2**, 126; fiber plants, raising of, **Vol. 7, Part 2**, 480 f.; financial history, **Vol. 1, Part 2**, 394; first board of education created in, **Vol. 3, Part 1**, 557 f.; formation of bicameral legislature in, **Vol. 3, Part 1**, 557 f.; fossils, **Supp. 4**, 52; governorship of, **Vol. 1, Part 2**, 394 f.; **Vol. 2, Part 1**, 96 f., 422 f.; **Vol. 3, Part 1**, 557 f., 609; **Vol. 7, Part 1**, 21; **Vol. 7, Part 2**, 484 f.; **Vol. 10, Part 1**, 341 f.; **Vol. 10, Part 2**, 638; **Supp. 9**, 400, 839–40; history of, **Vol. 3, Part 1**, 182, 557 f.; **Vol. 7, Part 2**, 647; **Vol. 8, Part 1**, 56 f., 372 f.; **Vol. 9, Part 1**, 243; horticulture, **Vol. 4, Part 2**, 356; hotels, **Vol. 4, Part 2**, 389; Huguenot settlement, **Vol. 6, Part 1**, 30; Indians, **Vol. 2, Part 1**, 423; **Vol. 3, Part 1**, 557 f.; **Vol. 4, Part 1**, 83; **Vol. 9, Part 2**, 475; insects, study of, **Vol. 5, Part 1**, 328; land development, **Supp. 10**, 478; land development of west coast, **Vol. 8, Part 1**, 618; landowning in, **Vol. 7, Part 1**, 292–93; legal service, **Vol. 1, Part 2**, 544; **Vol. 3, Part 1**, 557; **Vol. 6, Part 2**, 439; **Vol. 8, Part 1**, 372; maps, **Vol. 8, Part 2**, 126; military bounties, **Vol. 8, Part 1**, 281 f., 284 f.; military governorship of, **Vol. 6, Part 1**, 602; New France, expedition for the founding of, **Vol. 8, Part 1**, 533; oceanography, **Vol. 8, Part 1**, 141 f.; organized crime in, **Supp. 6**, 263, 264; plant introduction garden, **Supp. 5**, 214; political scandals, **Supp. 9**, 839–40; politics, **Supp. 9**, 400–401, 840; political service, **Vol. 3, Part 1**, 609; **Vol. 6, Part 2**, 440; **Vol. 7, Part 1**, 21; **Vol. 7, Part 2**, 288, 485; **Vol. 8, Part 1**, 372; politics, **Supp. 5**, 582; public service, **Vol. 7, Part 1**, 339; **Vol. 8, Part 2**, 348; purchase of, **Vol. 7, Part 1**, 201; racism in, **Supp. 9**, 840; railroad promotion, **Vol. 10, Part 2**, 638; resort architecture of, **Supp. 1**, 559; Roman Catholic diocese, **Supp. 8**, 295; secession in Civil War, **Vol. 10, Part 2**, 638; sounding and mapping of coast, **Vol. 3, Part 1**, 182; Spanish colony proposed in, **Vol. 7, Part 1**, 632; survey for projected canal across, **Vol. 9, Part 2**, 249; surveyor-generalship of, **Vol. 1, Part 2**, 394; World War II impact on, **Supp. 9**, 400
Florida Agricultural College and Experiment Station, **Vol. 9, Part 2**, 38
"Floridian Freedom," **Vol. 5, Part 2**, 323
Flour mills, **Vol. 1, Part 1**, 503; **Vol. 3, Part 1**, 524 f.; **Vol. 3, Part 2**, 90, 209, 525; **Vol. 7, Part 2**, 604 f., 607; **Vol. 10, Part 1**, 495 f.; **Supp. 7**, 46–47
Flowering of New England, The, **Supp. 7**, 80
Flowers. *See* Horticulture
Fluorine, discovery of, **Vol. 9, Part 1**, 3
Flushing, N.Y., public service, **Vol. 7, Part 2**, 269
Flute, playing of, **Vol. 5, Part 2**, 603
Fly, as disease carrier, **Supp. 5**, 143
Flye, James Harold, reference to, **Supp. 5**, 11–12
Flying, founding of, **Supp. 2**, 733
Flying Cloud, **Vol. 9, Part 2**, 626
Flying Dutchman, packet boat, **Vol. 8, Part 2**, 324
Flying Fish, clipper ship, **Vol. 4, Part 2**, 142
Flying Tigers (American Volunteer Group), **Supp. 6**, 109–10
Flynn, Edward J., reference to, **Supp. 3**, 227
Flynn, Elizabeth Gurley, references to, **Supp. 3**, 777; **Supp. 7**, 356, 612
Fly shuttle, first use in America, **Vol. 7, Part 2**, 58
FM (frequency modulation), **Supp. 5**, 22
Foam rubber, **Supp. 7**, 169
Fodor, Marcel, reference to, **Supp. 7**, 739
Foerster, Norman, reference to, **Vol. 6, Part 1**, 462 f.
Fog chamber, **Supp. 1**, 58
Fogg Museum (Cambridge, Mass.), **Supp. 1**, 641; **Supp. 2**, 118; **Supp. 7**, 673–74
Fokina, Vera, reference to, **Supp. 3**, 282
Fokine, Michel, references to, **Supp. 3**, 297; **Supp. 10**, 206, 207
Fokker, Anthony, reference to, **Supp. 6**, 92
Foley, Tom, reference to, **Supp. 3**, 717
Folger, Henry C., reference to, **Supp. 5**, 586
Folger, Peter, reference to, **Vol. 7, Part 1**, 209
Folger Shakespeare Library (Washington, D.C.): **Supp. 4**, 4–5; **Supp. 5**, 586–87; **Supp. 9**, 626, 627; architecture, **Supp. 3**, 199
Folic acid, **Supp. 7**, 223
Folk art. *See* Art, folk
Folk ballads, **Vol. 2, Part 1**, 492
Folk culture, **Supp. 5**, 520–21
Folklore: **Vol. 4, Part 2**, 312 f.; American, **Supp. 3**, 672–73; American Indian, **Vol. 5, Part 2**, 206; **Vol. 8, Part 1**, 301 f.; **Supp. 3**, 582; **Supp. 6**, 612; Arkansas, writings on, **Supp. 4**, 286; black, **Vol. 4, Part 2**, 312 f.; **Supp. 6**, 313–14; Canadian Indian, **Supp. 3**, 83–84; Creole, **Vol. 3, Part 2**, 537; folk plays, **Supp. 3**, 426–27; southern, **Supp. 1**, 649; southwestern, **Supp. 7**, 188–89; studies in, **Vol. 5, Part 1**, 566; **Vol. 7, Part 1**, 460 f.; **Supp. 10**, 781
Folk music: **Vol. 3, Part 2**, 120, 558; **Supp. 1**, 651; Appalachian, **Supp. 10**, 589; social protest, **Supp. 10**, 602, 603
"Folk opera," experiment in, **Vol. 3, Part 1**, 205
Folk songs, **Supp. 8**, 695–96; black, **Supp. 4**, 476–77, 502; writings on, **Supp. 4**, 249
Folly, Guilt and Mischief of Duelling, **Vol. 3, Part 1**, 573 f.
Fonck, René, reference to, **Supp. 9**, 725

Fonda, Henry, reference to, **Supp. 9**, 375
Fontaine, Joan, reference to, **Supp. 7**, 682
Fontanne, Lynn, references to, **Supp. 5**, 525; **Supp. 6**, 286; **Supp. 8**, 444; **Supp. 9**, 70; **Supp. 10**, 473, 474
Food: additives and contamination, **Supp. 5**, 143–44; business, youthful prodigy in, **Vol. 4, Part 2**, 506; chemistry of, **Vol. 1, Part 1**, 457; **Vol. 1, Part 2**, 448; **Vol. 5, Part 1**, 237; **Vol. 5, Part 2**, 524; **Vol. 8, Part 1**, 192 f., 553 f.; **Vol. 9, Part 2**, 28; chicken industry, **Supp. 10**, 629–30; concentrated, **Vol. 1, Part 2**, 458; Delmonico, influence of, on, **Vol. 3, Part 1**, 227; edible wild plants, **Supp. 4**, 266; **Supp. 9**, 307, 308; frozen, **Supp. 6**, 61; health, **Supp. 5**, 378–79; **Supp. 5**, 452–53; **Supp. 9**, 770; **Supp. 10**, 555, 556; health, **Supp. 9**, 222; hunger studies, **Supp. 3**, 133–34, **Supp. 6**, 100; intravenous feeding, **Supp. 6**, 190; irradiation of, **Supp. 1**, 398; Kentucky fried-chicken franchise, **Supp. 10**, 718; pineapple industry, **Supp. 6**, 168–69; poisoning, research on, **Supp. 2**, 353; preservation and additives, **Supp. 3**, 164; **Supp. 7**, 629–30; strained canned, for babies, **Supp. 5**, 242–43; **Supp. 9**, 302–3. *See also* Canning and canned goods; Cooking; Diet and nutrition; Grocery industry; Restaurants; *specific foods and products*
Food administration: Confederate army, **Vol. 7, Part 2**, 580; World War I, **Vol. 6, Part 1**, 12, 275; Vol. 85, Part 1, 145 f.
Food Administration, United States, **Vol. 6, Part 1**, 12; **Supp. 7**, 358–59
Food aid: CARE, **Supp. 6**, 217–18; India, **Supp. 8**, 468; underdeveloped countries, **Supp. 7**, 421; World War I and aftermath, **Supp. 6**, 36–37; **Supp. 7**, 358–59; World War II and aftermath, **Supp. 7**, 492; **Supp. 8**, 90
Food and Agriculture Act (1965), **Supp. 8**, 468
Food and Agriculture Organization (FAO), founding of, **Supp. 6**, 639
Fool, The, **Supp. 4**, 671
Fool's Errand, A, **Vol. 9, Part 2**, 604
Football; **Vol. 2, Part 1**, 444; **Vol. 4, Part 2**, 398; **Vol. 8, Part 2**, 68; A-formation offense, **Supp. 10**, 444; All-American Conference founding, **Supp. 5**, 725; All-American team, **Supp. 1**, 704; black players, **Supp. 7**, 167–68; **Supp. 9**, 646, 817–18, 840–41; **Supp. 10**, 727; coaching, **Supp. 5**, 458, 727–28; **Supp. 6**, 728; **Supp. 8**, 389–91, 587–88; **Supp. 9**, 484–85; **Supp. 10**, 37–38, 40–41, 585, 727–28; collegiate, **Supp. 4**, 492, 893, 917; **Supp. 5**, 288–89, 568, 683–84; **Supp. 6**, 66; **Supp. 7**, 167–68; **Supp. 9**, 484–85, 817; **Supp. 10**, 37–38, 40–41, 350, 444, 584, 600–601, 676, 726, 727, 728, 767; collegiate coaching, **Supp. 4**, 236–37; **Supp. 7**, 571–72, 712–13; Cotton Bowl, **Supp. 10**, 38; headgear, **Supp. 2**, 484; Heisman Trophy, **Supp. 10**, 600; huddle origination, **Supp. 7**, 712; intercollegiate abolishment, **Supp. 4**, 135; management, **Supp. 7**, 451–52; "Notre Dame shift," **Supp. 7**, 729; **Supp. 9**, 485; "point-a-minute" teams, **Supp. 4**, 917; professional leagues, **Supp. 5**, 684; **Supp. 6**, 47–48; **Supp. 10**, 676, 727–28; professional player-coaches, **Supp. 7**, 595–96; quarterbacks, **Supp. 10**, 600–601; Rose Bowl, **Supp. 10**, 584; "Seven Blocks of Granite," **Supp. 9**, 485; single-wing formation, **Supp. 5**, 289; **Supp. 7**, 571, 572; spiral forward pass, **Supp. 6**, 336; Sugar Bowl, **Supp. 10**, 600, 727; televised games, **Supp. 6**, 48; T formation, **Supp. 8**, 588; **Supp. 9**, 485; trick plays, **Supp. 9**, 485; umbrella defense, **Supp. 9**, 818. *See also* National Football League
Foote, Emerson, reference to, **Supp. 10**, 145
Foote, Cone, and Belding: founding and growth of, **Supp. 10**, 145–46; predecessor, **Supp. 5**, 411
Foraker, Joseph B., reference to, **Supp. 5**, 286
Foraker Act (1900), **Vol. 7, Part 2**, 31
Foraminifera, **Supp. 4**, 205–6; **Supp. 5**, 710
Forbes, J. M., and Co., **Supp. 6**, 210
Forbes, Malcolm S., New Jersey state senate race, **Supp. 9**, 263
Forbes, Stephen A., reference to, **Supp. 3**, 802
"Forbes Purchase," **Vol. 3, Part 2**, 506
Force, Juliana, reference to, **Supp. 3**, 818
"Forces bill": **Vol. 2, Part 1**, 415; **Vol. 2, Part 2**, 177, 185; **Vol. 3, Part 2**, 534; **Vol. 5, Part 1**, 533; **Vol. 6, Part 1**, 347; **Vol. 6, Part 2**, 233; **Vol. 10, Part 1**, 90, 589; **Vol. 10, Part 2**, 221; only vote recorded against, **Vol. 10, Part 1**, 90
Ford, Charles-Henri, reference to, **Supp. 6**, 625
Ford, Edsel, references to, **Supp. 3**, 550; **Supp. 4**, 292, 298, 301, 303; **Supp. 6**, 92; **Supp. 8**, 610
Ford, Francis, reference to, **Supp. 9**, 286–87
Ford, Franklin, reference to, **Supp. 3**, 577
Ford, Gerald R.: economic advisers, **Supp. 10**, 558; references to, **Supp. 7**, 140; **Supp. 10**, 22, 23, 190; Rockefeller, N., appointed as vice-president, **Supp. 10**, 688
Ford, Henry: anti-Semitism, **Supp. 10**, 745; automobile manufacture, **Supp. 4**, 243; museum, **Supp. 4**, 302; peace expedition, **Supp. 4**, 725–26; politics, **Supp. 3**, 550; references to, **Supp. 1**, 78, 280; **Supp. 3**, 63, 283–84, 555, 559, 562, 762; **Supp. 4**, 518, 637; **Supp. 5**, 450; **Supp. 6**, 148, 562, 614; **Supp. 7**, 29; **Supp. 8**, 419, 609–10
Ford, Henry, II, references to, **Supp. 3**, 284; **Supp. 4**, 303; **Supp. 7**, 275, 276; **Supp. 8**, 610; **Supp. 9**, 252
Ford, John, references to, **Supp. 6**, 420, 421, 476; **Supp. 7**, 286; **Supp. 8**, 117; **Supp. 10**, 387, 822, 823, 824
Ford, Nathan, reference to, **Vol. 7, Part 1**, 643
Ford, Paul, reference to, **Supp. 3**, 285
Ford, Worthington C., reference to, **Supp. 9**, 73
Ford Foundation: **Supp. 6**, 639; civil liberties projects, **Supp. 10**, 365; directorship and policy; **Supp. 7**, 275–76; **Supp. 9**, 378, 398; finances of, **Supp. 4**, 303; founding, **Supp. 3**, 284; right-wing attacks on, **Supp. 10**, 365–66
Ford Hall Forum, **Supp. 5**, 515
Fordham University: **Vol. 7, Part 2**, 171; baseball team, **Supp. 9**, 294; football team, **Supp. 9**, 484, 485
Ford Instrument Co., founding of, **Supp. 5**, 228–29
Ford Motor Co.: founding and growth of, **Supp. 2**, 125; **Supp. 4**, 294–304; General Motors' competition, **Supp. 4**, 301–2, 456–57; **Supp. 8**, 599; management, **Supp. 9**, 252; modernization and expansion, **Supp. 3**, 283–84; plant architecture, **Supp. 3**, 404; **Supp. 6**, 405, predecessors, **Supp. 4**, 293; quality control, **Supp. 9**, 252; social criticism of, **Supp. 9**, 584–85; unionization, **Supp. 8**, 419, 652; Willow Run aviation plant, **Supp. 8**, 610
Ford Peace Ship Mission, **Vol. 5, Part 2**, 180
Ford stock valuation tax case (1927–28), **Supp. 6**, 146
Forecasting the Yield and Price of Cotton, **Supp. 6**, 459
Foreign Affairs: **Supp. 3**, 219; founding of, **Supp. 4**, 322; growth of, **Supp. 9**, 44
Foreign aid. *See* Food aid; Marshall Plan; Truman Doctrine
Foreign and Domestic Commerce, Bureau of, **Vol. 8, Part 1**, 443
Foreign Christian Missionary Society, formed, **Vol. 7, Part 1**, 145 f.
Foreign correspondents. For complete list, *see* Occupations Index
Foreign Intelligence Advisory Board, **Supp. 10**, 432
Foreign Missions Conference of North America, **Vol. 8, Part 2**, 333

Foreign Policy Association, founding of, **Supp. 6**, 330; **Supp. 7**, 498
Foreign relations: academic seminars on, **Supp. 5**, 195; antifascism, **Supp. 5**, 343; bipartisan, **Supp. 5**, 505, 704–5; **Supp. 6**, 235; **Supp. 7**, 138, 326; **Supp. 8**, 701; Bricker amendment, **Supp. 6**, 336; China lobby, **Supp. 6**, 350; China policy, **Supp. 6**, 230–31; containment policy, **Supp. 6**, 178–79, 406; Council on Foreign Relations, **Supp. 6**, 377; Cuban missile crisis, **Supp. 8**, 323; "domino theory," **Supp. 7**, 422; economic aid, Sup. 8, 89–90; economic sanctions policy, **Supp. 4**, 786–87; Eisenhower administration policies, **Supp. 8**, 157–58; Good Neighbor policy, **Supp. 4**, 706; **Supp. 7**, 777; internationalism, **Supp. 1**, 483–84; **Supp. 3**, 219, 829–30; **Supp. 4**, 136, 332, 550–51, 598–99; **Supp. 5**, 198; **Supp. 7**, 23–24, 687–88, 761–63; **Supp. 8**, 508; isolationism, **Supp. 3**, 396–98; **Supp. 5**, 396–97, 450, 674–77, 689–90, 739; **Supp. 6**, 87, 361, 455, 578, 613–14, 436; **Supp. 8**, 268–69, 373; **Supp. 9**, 498, 572, 591; Japanese expansionism, **Supp. 3**, 657–59; **Supp. 6**, 269–70; Marshall Plan, **Supp. 6**, 431, 432; Migratory Bird Treaty (1916), **Supp. 3**, 593; "military-industrial complex" warning, **Supp. 8**, 159; neutrality advocacy, **Supp. 4**, 63; **Supp. 5**, 81–82, 114; New Deal policies, **Supp. 3**, 657–59; nonrecognition policy, **Supp. 4**, 898; **Supp. 7**, 112–13; particularism, **Supp. 2**, 51–52; Persian-Russian-British dispute, **Supp. 6**, 579; political geography studies, **Supp. 4**, 99; professional organizations, **Supp. 7**, 498; psychological studies of, **Supp. 8**, 70; realist school, **Supp. 10**, 551–52; study of, **Supp. 6**, 662; teaching of, **Supp. 4**, 224; transitional policy, **Supp. 7**, 421; Truman Doctrine, **Supp. 6**, 431, 432; **Supp. 8**, 680; writings on, **Supp. 1**, 173; **Supp. 10**, 231–32, 551, 552. *See also* Arms control and disarmament; Cold war; Diplomacy; Foreign Service; Peace, international; *specific countries, organizations, and wars*
Foreign Service Act (1946), **Supp. 3**, 139
Foreign Service Institute, **Supp. 8**, 7
Foreign Service, United States: career officers, **Supp. 7**, 60; **Supp. 10**, 528–29, 571–72; China, **Supp. 9**, 830–31; first career diplomat, **Supp. 6**, 686–87; first woman diplomat, **Supp. 5**, 582; founding of, **Supp. 3**, 138–39; **Supp. 4**, 898; graduate program for, **Supp. 6**, 622; merit system, **Supp. 3**, 138–39; **Supp. 3**, 467; patronage in, **Supp. 6**, 254; restructuring of, **Supp. 7**, 303; social welfare attach, **Supp. 7**, 342; writings on, **Supp. 6**, 452
Foreign trade. *See* Tariff; Trade
Forerunner, founding of, **Supp. 1**, 346
Forest and Stream, founding of, **Vol. 4, Part 2**, 157
Forest Hills Gardens (Queens, N.Y.), **Supp. 3**, 601; **Supp. 4**, 333; **Supp. 6**, 26
Forestier, Auber, reference to, **Vol. 7, Part 1**, 114
Forest Management Act (1897), **Supp. 4**, 663–66
Forestry: **Vol. 1, Part 1**, 285; **Vol. 1, Part 2**, 87; **Vol. 3, Part 1**, 485; **Vol. 3, Part 2**, 336, 578; **Vol. 5, Part 1**, 251; **Vol. 5, Part 2**, 45, 62; **Vol. 6, Part 1**, 162; **Vol. 7, Part 1**, 316, 539; **Vol. 7, Part 2**, 517; **Vol. 8, Part 2**, 121, 188; **Vol. 9, Part 1**, 427; **Vol. 9, Part 2**, 603; **Vol. 10, Part 1**, 174, 444; California, **Vol. 3, Part 1**, 485; **Vol. 6, Part 1**, 162; conservation, **Supp. 1**, 555; **Supp. 2**, 128, 264, 507, 610; **Supp. 4**, 429, 663–66; first class in, **Supp. 2**, 72; identification of woods, **Supp. 3**, 621; management, **Supp. 2**, 507; Michigan, **Vol. 1, Part 2**, 87; Minnesota, **Vol. 1, Part 1**, 285; national and state programs, **Supp. 3**, 7–8; New Hampshire, **Vol. 8, Part 2**, 121; Oregon, **Supp. 8**, 104; Pennsylvania, **Vol. 8, Part 2**, 188; preservation and recreation, **Supp. 9**, 526; redwoods conservation, **Supp. 3**, 520; reforestation, **Supp. 2**, 264; taxation report, **Supp. 8**, 166; teaching of, **Vol. 9, Part 2**, 603; **Supp. 2**, 72; **Supp. 4**, 43–44; writings on, **Vol. 3, Part 2**, 366; **Vol. 10, Part 1**, 444 f.; **Supp. 7**, 353, 354. *See also* Lumber industry; Trees
Forestry News Digest, founding of, **Supp. 2**, 507
Forest Service, United States, **Supp. 3**, 7; founding of, **Supp. 4**, 664; wildlife and wilderness protection, **Supp. 4**, 482–83; **Supp. 9**, 525–26
Forges, early importance of, **Vol. 3, Part 2**, 516
Forgotten First Citizen, **Supp. 9**, 174
Formosa Resolution (1955), **Supp. 6**, 235
Forrest's expedition, **Vol. 3, Part 2**, 532; **Vol. 9, Part 1**, 237; **Vol. 9, Part 2**, 183
Forssman, Werner, references to, **Supp. 9**, 654, 655
Forsyth Dental Infirmary for Children (Boston, Mass.), **Supp. 4**, 402
Fort, Charles, reference to, **Supp. 6**, 628
Fort Adams, construction of, **Vol. 7, Part 2**, 207
Fortas, Abe, references to, **Supp. 9**, 432, 837, 838
Fort Atkinson, building of, **Vol. 1, Part 1**, 391, 410; **Vol. 5, Part 2**, 273; **Vol. 6, Part 1**, 80
Fort Benning (Ga.), infantry school, **Supp. 6**, 429
Fort Blakely (Ala.), attack on, **Vol. 2, Part 1**, 469; **Vol. 4, Part 1**, 160, 484; **Vol. 6, Part 2**, 427; **Vol. 9, Part 1**, 237, 556
Fort Bridger, **Vol. 2, Part 1**, 33; **Vol. 10, Part 1**, 350, 494
Fort Clinch, first fort upon which the flag of the Union was restored, in Civil War, **Vol. 3, Part 1**, 529 f.
Fort Crèvecoeur, building of, **Vol. 9, Part 2**, 587
Fort Dearborn, massacre at, **Vol. 5, Part 2**, 422
Fort Donelson (Tenn.), capture of, **Vol. 2, Part 1**, 235–36; **Vol. 3, Part 2**, 483; **Vol. 4, Part 1**, 494, 597; **Vol. 5, Part 2**, 136; **Vol. 6, Part 1**, 587; **Vol. 7, Part 2**, 604; **Vol. 8, Part 1**, 380; **Vol. 9, Part 1**, 247; **Vol. 10, Part 1**, 375
Fort Dunmore, **Vol. 3, Part 1**, 317, 519 f.
Fort Duquesne: building of, **Vol. 9, Part 2**, 638; expedition against (1758), **Vol. 1, Part 2**, 480; 551; **Vol. 2, Part 2**, 556; **Vol. 3, Part 2**, 505; **Vol. 4, Part 2**, 353; **Vol. 9, Part 1**, 59; **Vol. 10, Part 1**, 301, 512; journey made by Washington to, **Vol. 4, Part 1**, 324. *See also* Fort Pitt
Fort Durkee, settlement at, **Vol. 3, Part 1**, 550
Fortean Society, **Supp. 6**, 628
Fort Erie, attack on, **Vol. 2, Part 1**, 125; **Vol. 4, Part 1**, 93; **Vol. 8, Part 1**, 621; **Vol. 8, Part 2**, 374, 506
Fort Fisher: battle of, **Vol. 7, Part 2**, 447; capture of, **Vol. 2, Part 2**, 637; **Vol. 3, Part 1**, 598; **Vol. 8, Part 1**, 87–88; **Vol. 8, Part 2**, 453; **Vol. 9, Part 2**, 378; **Vol. 10, Part 2**, 137
Fort Frontenac, Bradstreet's expedition to, **Vol. 1, Part 2**, 578
Fort Gaines (Ala.), attack on, **Vol. 3, Part 2**, 289; **Vol. 4, Part 1**, 484
Fort George, in War of 1812, **Vol. 1, Part 2**, 527; **Vol. 6, Part 2**, 595; **Vol. 8, Part 2**, 506
Fort Halifax, built (1752), **Vol. 4, Part 1**, 612
Fort Hamilton Relief Society, **Vol. 7, Part 2**, 21
Fort Henry (Wheeling, W. Va.): capture of, **Vol. 2, Part 1**, 240; **Vol. 3, Part 2**, 500; **Vol. 4, Part 1**, 494; **Vol. 5, Part 2**, 136; **Vol. 6, Part 1**, 587; **Vol. 9, Part 1**, 247; engagement at, **Vol. 4, Part 2**, 223; **Vol. 10, Part 2**, 644
Fort Hill (S.C.), home of J. C. Calhoun, **Vol. 2, Part 1**, 412
Fortifications, on Atlantic coast, **Vol. 3, Part 2**, 159; French, **Vol. 6, Part 1**, 182
Fort Jackson (La.), attack on (1862). *See* New Orleans (1862)
Fort Jefferson, **Vol. 1, Part 1**, 370
Fort Johnson. *See* Charleston, S.C.

Fort Kearney, Nebr., **Vol. 2, Part 1**, 521; **Vol. 3, Part 2**, 33, 351
Fort Keogh, Mont., army post at, **Vol. 5, Part 2**, 219
Fort Laramie, Wyo., **Vol. 6, Part 1**, 613; **Vol. 8, Part 1**, 437; **Vol. 9, Part 1**, 469; council at (1866), **Vol. 8, Part 1**, 437
Fort Leavenworth, Kans., **Vol. 1, Part 1**, 410; **Vol. 6, Part 1**, 80; **Vol. 8, Part 1**, 95
Fort Le Boeuf, **Vol. 10, Part 1**, 511
Fort Lee, building of, **Vol. 1, Part 1**, 175, 493
Fort Lincoln, Ariz., post at, **Vol. 9, Part 2**, 379
Fort McHenry, bombardment of, **Vol. 1, Part 1**, 346; **Vol. 5, Part 2**, 362; **Vol. 9, Part 1**, 341
Fort McIntosh, Treaty of (1785), **Vol. 2, Part 1**, 366; **Vol. 2, Part 2**, 142; **Vol. 5, Part 1**, 276; **Vol. 6, Part 1**, 98
Fort Mackenzie, **Vol. 7, Part 1**, 41
Fort Mackinac, **Vol. 1, Part 2**, 105; **Vol. 5, Part 1**, 363; **Vol. 6, Part 1**, 11; **Vol. 7, Part 2**, 63
Fort Meigs, **Vol. 2, Part 2**, 173, 557; **Vol. 4, Part 2**, 350; **Vol. 6, Part 1**, 550; **Vol. 7, Part 2**, 491; **Vol. 9, Part 2**, 51
Fort Michelemackinac, surrender of, **Vol. 5, Part 1**, 363
Fort Mifflin, **Vol. 6, Part 1**, 168; **Vol. 9, Part 1**, 341
Fort Mimms, Ala., massacre at, **Vol. 1, Part 2**, 391; **Vol. 5, Part 1**, 263, 529
Fort Monmouth, N.J., **Supp. 6**, 680
Fort Morgan, Ala., operations at (1864). *See* Mobile, Ala.
Fort Moultrie, S.C. (1780), **Vol. 1, Part 1**, 274; **Vol. 1, Part 2**, 111; **Vol. 6, Part 1**, 99; **Vol. 10, Part 2**, 188
Fort Myer, **Vol. 7, Part 1**, 375
Fort Necessity, Pa., battle of, **Vol. 10, Part 1**, 511
Fort Niagara, **Vol. 1, Part 2**, 106; **Vol. 3, Part 1**, 175; **Vol. 3, Part 2**, 89
Fort Orange, **Vol. 5, Part 2**, 508
Fort Orlans, **Vol. 1, Part 2**, 482
Fort Phil Kearney, Wyo., **Vol. 2, Part 1**, 521; **Vol. 3, Part 2**, 350
Fort Pillow, massacre at, **Vol. 3, Part 2**, 532; **Vol. 9, Part 1**, 237; **Vol. 9, Part 2**, 183
Fort Pitt, **Vol. 1, Part 2**, 481, 550; **Vol. 3, Part 2**, 505; **Vol. 5, Part 2**, 125; **Vol. 9, Part 2**, 638; **Vol. 10, Part 1**, 512
Fort Recovery, Ohio, fighting at (1791–94), **Vol. 6, Part 1**, 300; **Vol. 8, Part 2**, 294, 487; **Vol. 10, Part 1**, 564; **Vol. 10, Part 2**, 223
Fortress Monroe, **Vol. 6, Part 1**, 582 f.
Fort Robinson, Nebr., **Vol. 2, Part 2**, 530
Fort Ross, Russian settlement, **Vol. 5, Part 2**, 514–15
Fort St. Louis, building of, **Vol. 9, Part 2**, 587
Fort Sanders, assault of. *See* Knoxville campaign (1863)
Fort Schuyler, siege of, **Vol. 4, Part 1**, 127–28
Fort Smith, **Vol. 1, Part 2**, 538; **Vol. 8, Part 1**, 437
Fort Snelling, **Vol. 5, Part 2**, 273; **Vol. 9, Part 1**, 381
Fort Stanwix, **Vol. 1, Part 1**, 364; **Vol. 1, Part 2**, 604; **Vol. 2, Part 1**, 362; **Vol. 4, Part 1**, 104, 127; **Vol. 8, Part 2**, 478; **Vol. 10, Part 2**, 244
Fort Stanwix, Treaty of (1768), **Vol. 5, Part 2**, 126–27; **Vol. 7, Part 2**, 430; **Vol. 10, Part 2**, 644; of 1784, **Vol. 6, Part 1**, 98
Fort Stephenson, siege of, **Vol. 2, Part 2**, 557; **Vol. 4, Part 2**, 350; **Vol. 7, Part 2**, 491; **Vol. 9, Part 2**, 51
Fort Sumter: **Vol. 1, Part 1**, 274–75; **Vol. 2, Part 2**, 57; **Vol. 3, Part 2**, 483, 550, 568; **Vol. 5, Part 2**, 333; **Vol. 6, Part 1**, 130, 250–51; **Vol. 6, Part 2**, 617; **Vol. 7, Part 1**, 275, 352, 409, 504; **Vol. 7, Part 2**, 560; **Vol. 8, Part 2**, 216, 618; **Vol. 10, Part 2**, 188; Beauregard at, **Vol. 1, Part 2**, 111; first shot fired from, **Vol. 3, Part 1**, 391; **Vol. 8, Part 2**, 216; Lincoln's actions concerning, **Vol. 6, Part 1**, 250 f.; plans for relief of, **Vol. 4, Part 2**, 139
Fort Ticonderoga, **Vol. 1, Part 1**, 29, 188, 257; 362–64; **Vol. 3, Part 2**, 185; **Vol. 4, Part 1**, 87; **Vol. 7, Part 2**, 270; **Vol. 8, Part 2**, 477–78; **Vol. 9, Part 1**, 531; **Vol. 10, Part 2**, 259
Fortune, Reo Franklin, references to, **Supp. 10**, 521, 522
Fortune (magazine): **Supp. 5**, 11–12, 152–53; **Supp. 7**, 17, 383–84; Bourke-White photographs, **Supp. 9**, 111; editorial development, **Supp. 9**, 394; Evans photographs, **Supp. 9**, 268; founding of, **Supp. 8**, 393, 394, 395; public opinion surveys, **Supp. 9**, 677, 678
Fortune, from Plymouth, **Vol. 6, Part 2**, 254
Fort Vancouver, **Vol. 7, Part 1**, 641
Fort Vincennes, **Vol. 8, Part 2**, 293
Fort Washakie, Wyo., **Vol. 10, Part 1**, 494
Fort Wayne, Ind., Roman Catholic diocese, **Supp. 6**, 478–79
Fort Wayne, Mich. *See* Detroit, Mich., surrender of
Fort Western, building of, **Vol. 4, Part 1**, 612
Fort William and Mary, seizure of munitions from, by colonists, **Vol. 8, Part 1**, 515
Fort William Henry: attack on, **Vol. 1, Part 1**, 258; **Vol. 4, Part 2**, 533; **Vol. 5, Part 2**, 125; **Vol. 6, Part 1**, 428; **Vol. 8, Part 1**, 161; **Vol. 9, Part 1**, 530; **Vol. 10, Part 2**, 259; building of, **Vol. 4, Part 1**, 612; **Vol. 5, Part 2**, 125
Fort Worth, Tex., Baptist church in, **Supp. 5**, 516–17
Fort Worth & Rio Grande Railroad in Texas, building of, **Vol. 7, Part 2**, 277
"Forty-day" proclamation of Davis, Jefferson, **Vol. 3, Part 2**, 564
"Forty-Niners." *See* Gold rush
42nd Street, **Supp. 10**, 34, 114
47 Workshop (Harvard), **Supp. 1**, 45
Forum, **Vol. 7, Part 2**, 143; **Vol. 8, Part 1**, 541
Forum exhibition of modern American painters (1916), **Supp. 2**, 740
For Whom the Bell Tolls, **Supp. 7**, 337; **Supp. 10**, 669
Fosdick, Harry Emerson, references to, **Supp. 5**, 117; **Supp. 6**, 548
Fossil Cycad National Monument, **Supp. 5**, 743–44
Fossils: **Vol. 5, Part 1**, 446; **Vol. 6, Part 1**, 337; **Vol. 7, Part 1**, 446; **Vol. 9, Part 1**, 482; **Vol. 10, Part 2**, 134; colored plates, **Vol. 8, Part 2**, 91 f.; vertebrate studies, **Supp. 9**, 674–75; writings on, **Vol. 4, Part 2**, 437; **Vol. 8, Part 2**, 91 f. *See also* Dinosaurs; Paleobotany; Paleontology
Foster, Nathaniel L., reference to, **Supp. 3**, 247
Foster, Stephen C., references to, **Vol. 8, Part 2**, 533; **Supp. 4**, 500
Foster, William Trufant, reference to, **Supp. 8**, 79
Foster, William Z., references to, **Supp. 4**, 279–80; **Supp. 7**, 291, 612
Foster care, **Supp. 2**, 57, 58; **Supp. 3**, 28, 160; **Supp. 4**, 871
Foster Parents' Plan, **Supp. 9**, 824
Foundation for Population Research, founding of, **Supp. 3**, 635–36
Founding of American Civilization series, **Supp. 8**, 693
Foundlings. *See* Adoption
Foundry work, **Vol. 6, Part 1**, 73, 139; **Vol. 7, Part 2**, 20 f.
Fountain pens, **Vol. 10, Part 1**, 533 f.
Four Freedoms, **Supp. 3**, 660, 665
4-H Clubs, **Supp. 5**, 101; founding of, **Supp. 5**, 51
Fourierism, **Vol. 2, Part 2**, 357 f.; **Vol. 4, Part 1**, 529; **Vol. 5, Part 1**, 578
Four Quartets, **Supp. 7**, 221
Four Star Productions, founding of, **Supp. 10**, 63

Foursquare Gospel movement, **Supp. 3**, 498
"Fourteen Points" of Wilson's peace proposal, **Vol. 10, Part 2**, 362
Fowler, Gene, reference to, **Supp. 3**, 342
Fowler, George Ryerson, reference to, **Supp. 6**, 214–15
Fowler, William A., reference to, **Supp. 8**, 483
Fox, Austen, G., reference to, **Supp. 6**, 105
Fox, William, references to, **Supp. 6**, 76, 440; **Supp. 8**, 576
Fox and Sac Indian troubles, **Vol. 2, Part 1**, 563; **Vol. 5, Part 2**, 350; **Vol. 8, Part 1**, 438. *See also* Black Hawk War
Fox Film Corporation: founding of, **Supp. 5**, 230; newsreels, **Supp. 6**, 291
Fox Indians, studies of, **Vol. 5, Part 2**, 206
Fox Movietone News, **Supp. 5**, 230
Fox River settlement, **Vol. 3, Part 2**, 62
Fox sisters, attempted exposure of methods of, **Vol. 3, Part 1**, 540
Foy, Fred C., reference to, **Supp. 5**, 643
FPC. *See* Federal Power Commission
Fraenkel, Joseph, reference to, **Supp. 4**, 249
France: architecture of, **Supp. 5**, 388; art collections, **Supp. 5**, 150–51; Caffery ambassadorship, **Supp. 9**, 154; colonial negotiations with, **Vol. 3, Part 1**, 173 f.; Confederate relations with, **Vol. 6, Part 2**, 240; diplomacy with, **Vol. 1, Part 1**, 75 f., 356; **Vol. 2, Part 1**, 259; **Vol. 3, Part 1**, 167, 173 f., 614; **Vol. 5, Part 2**, 21 f., 406 f.; **Vol. 6, Part 1**, 4, 97, 312, 323, 360; **Vol. 6, Part 2**, 114; **Vol. 7, Part 1**, 88, 259, 369, 524, 587; **Vol. 7, Part 2**, 88, 616; **Vol. 8, Part 1**, 428, 484 f., 636; **Vol. 8, Part 2**, 232; **Vol. 9, Part 1**, 25; **Vol. 9, Part 2**, 234; **Supp. 6**, 187–88; **Supp. 8**, 61–62; expatriates in, **Supp. 4**, 768–70, 771; **Supp. 7**, 40–41, 334–36, 560; **Supp. 8**, 656; first stronghold of, in North America, **Vol. 8, Part 1**, 533; foreign correspondents in, **Supp. 6**, 183–84; government-in-exile, World War II, **Supp. 10**, 63; historical writings on, **Supp. 9**, 329–30; **Supp. 10**, 138; indemnity treaty (1831), **Vol. 8, Part 1**, 636; in Indochina, **Supp. 9**, 9; opera, **Supp. 8**, 200–201; peace with (1800), **Vol. 3, Part 1**, 98; **Vol. 3, Part 2**, 114; **Vol. 7, Part 1**, 369; privateers in American ports, **Vol. 4, Part 1**, 208; reconstruction post-World War I, **Supp. 5**, 506; relations with Siam, **Vol. 9, Part 2**, 141; treaty messenger, **Vol. 5, Part 2**, 204; tuberculosis prevention, **Supp. 3**, 324; Vichy government, **Supp. 3**, 50, 141–42; **Supp. 6**, 376; **Supp. 10**, 571–72; war with, **Vol. 1, Part 1**, 78–79, 505, 650, 654; **Vol. 3, Part 1**, 33, 187; **Vol. 4, Part 1**, 225–26; **Vol. 4, Part 2**, 177; **Vol. 5, Part 2**, 27, 477; **Vol. 6, Part 2**, 63; **Vol. 7, Part 1**, 369; **Vol. 7, Part 2**, 567, 615; **Vol. 8, Part 1**, 182; **Vol. 8, Part 2**, 76; **Vol. 9, Part 1**, 394; **Vol. 9, Part 2**, 280, **Vol. 10, Part 1**, 22, 525. *See also* French, alliance, etc.; Paris; World War I; World War II; *city and institution names*
France-American Society of New York, founding of, **Supp. 1**, 368
Franchises: Colonel Sanders Kentucky Fried Chicken, **Supp. 10**, 718; concept introduced, **Supp. 9**, 246; Howard Johnson, **Supp. 9**, 429–30
Francis, Kay, reference to, **Supp. 7**, 591
Franciscan Order, **Vol. 7, Part 2**, 197; **Vol. 8, Part 1**, 511; missionary work, **Supp. 1**, 218–19, 289–90
"Francis the Talking Mule" (fictional character), **Supp. 10**, 845
Franco, Francisco, references to, **Supp. 5**, 544; **Supp. 6**, 572; **Supp. 7**, 330–31
Franco-Prussian War, **Vol. 7, Part 2**, 323
Frank, Glenn, references to, **Supp. 7**, 450, 523
Frank, James, reference to, **Supp. 7**, 732
Frank, Jerome, reference to, **Supp. 7**, 99, 475
Frank, Lawrence, reference to, **Supp. 8**, 399
Frank, Leo Max, reference to, **Supp. 7**, 550
Frank, Morris S., reference to, **Supp. 4**, 254
Frank, Waldo, references to, **Supp. 4**, 702; **Supp. 6**, 557
Frank, William O., reference to, **Supp. 2**, 668
Frankenstein, **Supp. 6**, 395; **Supp. 8**, 312
Frankfort, Ky., secession government at (1862), **Vol. 1, Part 2**, 586
Frankfurter, Felix: Black, H. L., relationship, **Supp. 9**, 96; Buckner relationship, **Supp. 3**, 116, 117; references to, **Supp. 3**, 97, 822; **Supp. 4**, 796; **Supp. 5**, 515, 574; **Supp. 6**, 105, 117; **Supp. 7**, 453 541, 542; **Supp. 9**, 318, 835, 836, 865; Sacco-Vanzetti case, **Supp. 3**, 473; **Supp. 10**, 126
Franklin, Benjamin: **Vol. 1, Part 1**, 563, 597; **Vol. 5, Part 1**, 220, 467, 524; **Vol. 5, Part 2**, 288; **Vol. 6, Part 1**, 97 f., 280; **Vol. 7, Part 1**, 225, 555; **Vol. 8, Part 1**, 161 f.; **Vol. 9, Part 1**, 602; **Vol. 9, Part 2**, 261, 557 f.; **Vol. 10, Part 1**, 594 f., 659; as practical joker, **Vol. 6, Part 1**, 136; biography of, **Supp. 4**, 116, 848; daughter of, **Vol. 1, Part 1**, 464; influence of, **Vol. 6, Part 1**, 360; monument to, erected in Mount Auburn Cemetery by admirer, **Vol. 3, Part 1**, 420; papers of, **Supp. 10**, 430; relations with Bond, Thomas, **Vol. 1, Part 2**, 433; relations with Bradford, Andrew, **Vol. 1, Part 2**, 553; relations with Jefferson, Thomas, **Vol. 5, Part 2**, 22; relations with Parker, James, **Vol. 7, Part 2**, 226 f.; relations with Williams, Jonathan, **Vol. 10, Part 2**, 281; works of, **Vol. 9, Part 1**, 373, 432
Franklin, John, reference to, **Vol. 8, Part 2**, 481
Franklin, Sir John: **Vol. 5, Part 2**, 256; rescue expedition to Arctic, in search of, **Vol. 3, Part 1**, 200 f.
Franklin, "State" of, later Tennessee, **Vol. 1, Part 2**, 390; **Vol. 2, Part 2**, 255; **Vol. 3, Part 1**, 332; **Vol. 8, Part 2**, 603; **Vol. 9, Part 1**, 60; **Vol. 9, Part 2**, 563
Franklin (aircraft carrier), **Supp. 7**, 581
Franklin and Marshall College: beginnings of, **Vol. 8, Part 1**, 389 f.; formation of by combining Marshall College and Franklin College, **Vol. 8, Part 1**, 104 f.; presidency of, **Vol. 4, Part 1**, 219; **Vol. 7, Part 1**, 442 f.; **Vol. 9, Part 1**, 494
Franklin College (Ohio), presidency of, **Vol. 7, Part 1**, 439
Franklin College (Pa.), first president, **Vol. 7, Part 1**, 308
Franklin College (Tenn.), opening of, **Vol. 3, Part 2**, 268
Frankliniana, authority on, **Vol. 8, Part 1**, 51 f.
Franklin Inn, founding of, **Vol. 7, Part 1**, 65
Franklin Institute, **Supp. 4**, 452; **Supp. 7**, 619; founding of, **Vol. 1, Part 1**, 542; **Vol. 4, Part 2**, 462; **Vol. 5, Part 2**, 202 f., 276, 456; **Vol. 8, Part 2**, 373, 577; administration, **Supp. 1**, 523; journal, **Vol. 5, Part 2**, 203
Franklin, Tenn., battle of, **Vol. 2, Part 1**, 136; **Vol. 2, Part 2**, 45, 190; **Vol. 5, Part 1**, 194; **Vol. 8, Part 2**, 453; **Vol. 9, Part 1**, 508; **Vol. 9, Part 2**, 434; **Vol. 10, Part 2**, 335
Franklin Watts, Inc., **Supp. 10**, 820, 821
Franko, Nahan, reference to, **Supp. 6**, 242
Franks, Robert ("Bobby"), reference to, **Supp. 9**, 490
Franz Josef Archipelago, **Supp. 4**, 674
Fraser, Allan G., reference to, **Supp. 4**, 252–53
Fraser, John, reference to, **Vol. 10, Part 1**, 396 f.
Fraser, Leon, reference to, **Supp. 4**, 62
Fraternal orders, **Supp. 4**, 219; **Supp. 5**, 754–55
Fraternity, first national, **Vol. 8, Part 2**, 176
Frawley, T. Daniel, reference to, **Supp. 3**, 39
Frawley, William, reference to, **Supp. 10**, 804
Frazer, Joseph W., reference to, **Supp. 8**, 309

Frazier, E. Franklin, reference to, **Supp. 6**, 322
Frazier, Lynn J., references to, **Supp. 4**, 479, 80; **Supp. 6**, 361
Frazier-Lemke Farm Bankruptcy Act (1934), **Supp. 4**, 480
Frazier's farm (Va.), battle of, **Vol. 5, Part 1**, 25; **Vol. 6, Part 1**, 123, 391. *See also* Peninsular Campaign
"Fred Allen Show, The" (radio program), **Supp. 6**, 13
Frederick, Md., occupation of, **Vol. 6, Part 1**, 583; **Vol. 8, Part 1**, 504; **Vol. 9, Part 2**, 290
Fredericksburg, Va., battle of, **Vol. 1, Part 1**, 608; **Vol. 2, Part 1**, 311; **Vol. 2, Part 2**, 247; **Vol. 3, Part 2**, 602; **Vol. 5, Part 1**, 197, 559; **Vol. 6, Part 1**, 124, 392; **Vol. 6, Part 2**, 475; **Vol. 8, Part 1**, 548; **Vol. 9, Part 1**, 363; **Vol. 9, Part 2**, 215
Free Acres (Summit, N.J.), founding of, **Supp. 2**, 272
Free-Bridges party (Boston), **Vol. 4, Part 2**, 563
Free Company of Players, **Supp. 3**, 93
Freedman's Village, **Vol. 5, Part 1**, 312
Freedmen: Board of Missions for, **Vol. 8, Part 2**, 332; Organization of, in the department of the Tennessee, **Vol. 3, Part 1**, 608 f.; schools for, **Vol. 9, Part 2**, 11; **Vol. 10, Part 1**, 27. *See also* Abolition
Freedmen, Bureau of, **Vol. 5, Part 1**, 280, 283; **Vol. 8, Part 2**, 47
Freedmen's Aid Society, **Vol. 6, Part 1**, 451; **Vol. 8, Part 2**, 254
Freedmen's Association, **Vol. 6, Part 1**, 468
Freedmen's Bureau, **Vol. 1, Part 1**, 360, 508; **Vol. 3, Part 1**, 98, 608 f.; **Vol. 3, Part 2**, 413; **Vol. 4, Part 1**, 623; Vol. 5, Part 1, 280, 283; **Vol. 5, Part 2**, 86, 114, 598; **Vol. 8, Part 2**, 47, 463, 600; **Vol. 9, Part 1**, 520, 624; **Vol. 9, Part 2**, 240 f.; **Vol. 10, Part 1**, 20; **Vol. 10, Part 2**, 324
Freedmen's Hospital (Washington, D.C.), **Supp. 5**, 104
Freedom, **Supp. 7**, 319
Freedom and Union, founding of, **Supp. 5**, 576
Freedom House, founding of, **Supp. 7**, 740
Freedom of speech, Brown University, and, **Vol. 1, Part 1**, 288 f.
Freedom of the press, first victory of, in colonial America, **Vol. 10, Part 2**, 649
Freedom of the seas, **Vol. 4, Part 1**, 70
Freedom riders (1960s), **Supp. 7**, 425; **Supp. 8**, 322, 323, 388, 539
Freedoms Foundation (Valley Forge, Pa.), founding of, **Supp. 7**, 379
"Freedom's Lyre," antislavery hymns, **Vol. 4, Part 2**, 396
Free French Movement, **Supp. 10**, 63
Freehold Court-House, battle of. *See* Monmouth, battle of
Free love, advocacy of, **Vol. 7, Part 1**, 589–90
Free Love League, **Vol. 4, Part 2**, 610
Freeman, Alice E., reference to, **Vol. 7, Part 1**, 277
Freeman, Derek, reference to, **Supp. 10**, 523
Freeman, Douglas Southall, references to, **Supp. 3**, 115; **Supp. 6**, 310
Freeman, founding of, **Supp. 3**, 554; **Supp. 7**, 374
Freeman's farm, battle of. *See* Bemis Heights
Freeman's Journal, **Vol. 1, Part 1**, 495
Freemasons. *See* Masons
Free Methodist Church, organization of, **Vol. 8, Part 2**, 3
Free Public Library of Louisville, Ky., **Supp. 3**, 280
Freer, Charles L., references to, **Supp. 3**, 465; **Supp. 8**, 432
Free-radical chemistry, **Supp. 4**, 336–37, 573–74; **Supp. 6**, 334–35
Free Religious Association, **Vol. 8, Part 1**, 135; **Vol. 10, Part 1**, 615 f.
Freer Gallery of Art (Washington, D.C.): **Vol. 4, Part 1**, 14; concerts, **Supp. 3**, 252; Oriental art collection, **Supp. 3**, 465
Free Silver movement, **Vol. 1, Part 1**, 221; **Vol. 1, Part 2**, 355–56; **Vol. 2, Part 1**, 192, 495; **Vol. 2, Part 2**, 211; **Vol. 3, Part 1**, 69; **Vol. 3, Part 2**, 578; **Vol. 4, Part 2**, 334; **Vol. 5, Part 1**, 93, 182; **Vol. 5, Part 2**, 146, 189, 552, 571; **Vol. 6, Part 1**, 268; **Vol. 6, Part 2**, 106; **Vol. 7, Part 1**, 15; **Vol. 8, Part 2**, 87, 251; **Vol. 9, Part 1**, 148, 180; **Vol. 9, Part 2**, 14, 612; **Vol. 10, Part 2**, 441
Free Soil movement: **Vol. 1, Part 1**, 279, 368, 537; **Vol. 1, Part 2**, 48, 258, 489; **Vol. 2, Part 1**, 204; **Vol. 2, Part 2**, 29; **Vol. 3, Part 1**, 375; **Vol. 3, Part 2**, 227, 485, 565, 580; **Vol. 4, Part 1**, 394, 530 f.; **Vol. 4, Part 2**, 106; **Vol. 5, Part 2**, 356; **Vol. 6, Part 1**, 1; **Vol. 7, Part 1**, 645; **Vol. 9, Part 1**, 271, 544; **Vol. 10, Part 1**, 151, 156; **Vol. 10, Part 2**, 323; convention of 1848, **Vol. 8, Part 2**, 58; Iowa, **Vol. 4, Part 2**, 268; Kansas, **Vol. 3, Part 1**, 570 f.; **Vol. 4, Part 1**, 394; Massachusetts, **Vol. 2, Part 2**, 111; **Vol. 5, Part 1**, 86 f., 89; Missouri, **Vol. 1, Part 2**, 332; **Vol. 2, Part 1**, 105; Ohio, **Vol. 8, Part 1**, 591
Free speech. *See* Censorship; Civil liberties; Libel
Free State movement, **Vol. 3, Part 1**, 202; **Vol. 3, Part 2**, 69; **Vol. 5, Part 2**, 576; **Vol. 8, Part 2**, 36, 175
Free Synagogue (New York City), founding of, **Supp. 4**, 603, 904
Freethinkers, writers, **Supp. 3**, 329–30, 341–42, 454–55, 554–55
Freethinkers Colony, Iowa, **Vol. 5, Part 2**, 457 f.
Free trade, **Vol. 1, Part 2**, 134; **Vol. 2, Part 1**, 488; **Vol. 3, Part 1**, 289; **Vol. 6, Part 1**, 109, 292, 609; **Vol. 8, Part 1**, 325 f.; **Vol. 8, Part 2**, 450 f.; **Vol. 10, Part 1**, 387, 637 f
Free-Will Baptists, origin of, **Vol. 8, Part 1**, 345 f.
Freeze-drying technique, **Supp. 6**, 54
Frege, Gottlob, reference to, **Supp. 8**, 74
Freight: carrying of, **Vol. 9, Part 2**, 396; Atlantic seaboard, **Vol. 7, Part 1**, 336; Great Lakes, **Vol. 6, Part 1**, 327; **Vol. 6, Part 2**, 23; ox and wagon, **Vol. 2, Part 1**, 405; **Vol. 6, Part 2**, 214; stagecoach, **Vol. 8, Part 2**, 252; **Vol. 9, Part 1**, 203
Freiheit, anarchist paper, **Vol. 7, Part 1**, 282
Frelinghuysen, T. J., reference to, **Vol. 7, Part 1**, 366
Frémont, Jessie Benton, reference to, **Supp. 3**, 87–88
Frémont, John, references to, **Vol. 1, Part 1**, 206; **Vol. 1, Part 2**, 333; **Vol. 5, Part 2**, 273
Fremont Canning Co., **Supp. 9**, 302
French, Daniel Chester, references to, **Vol. 1, Part 1**, 478; **Vol. 7, Part 1**, 19; **Supp. 3**, 1
French: alliance with U.S., **Vol. 1, Part 1**, 74–75; **Vol. 3, Part 1**, 174; **Vol. 3, Part 2**, 593–94; **Vol. 5, Part 2**, 536; **Vol. 6, Part 1**, 98; **Vol. 7, Part 1**, 210, 221; **Vol. 10, Part 1**, 518; biographies, translation of, **Vol. 8, Part 1**, 217 f.; colonization, **Vol. 8, Part 1**, 533 f.; exploration, **Vol. 1, Part 1**, 183; **Vol. 6, Part 1**, 4, 10, 37, 182; **Vol. 7, Part 1**, 511 f.; **Vol. 8, Part 2**, 293, 304; Huguenot colonies, **Vol. 6, Part 1**, 30; influence of Isham's art, **Vol. 5, Part 1**, 514; Jesuits, political influence of, **Vol. 3, Part 1**, 364; Louisiana, political affairs of, **Vol. 6, Part 1**, 19; Ohio Valley, **Vol. 3, Part 1**, 317; **Vol. 8, Part 2**, 293; painting, influence on American, **Vol. 7, Part 1**, 29; spoliation claims, **Vol. 1, Part 2**, 23; **Vol. 8, Part 2**, 241; translations, **Vol. 6, Part 1**, 171; Treaty of 1801, **Vol. 8, Part 2**, 77; voyageurs, **Vol. 8, Part 2**, 117; withdrawal of, from Mexico, **Vol. 5, Part 2**, 88. *See also* France; French literature and language
French and Indian War: **Vol. 1, Part 2**, 550; **Vol. 7, Part 2**, 457; **Vol. 8, Part 1**, 62 f.; **Vol. 8, Part 2**, 34; **Vol. 9, Part 1**, 26; **Vol. 10, Part 2**, 543; history of,

Vol. 8, Part 2, 369; *Niagara*, capture of, **Vol. 5, Part 2**, 126; North Carolina's support in, **Vol. 3, Part 1**, 337; Rhode Island and, **Vol. 4, Part 1**, 575 f.; service in, **Vol. 1, Part 2**, 379; **Vol. 2, Part 2**, 251; **Vol. 3, Part 1**, 74, 216, 550, 581 f.; Vol. 3, Part 2. 505; **Vol. 4, Part 2**, 420, 478; **Vol. 5, Part 2**, 100, 181; **Vol. 6, Part 1**, 77, 98; **Vol. 8, Part 1**, 55, 61, 62 f., 69 f., 129 f., 161 f., 195 f., 281 f., 284 f., 419, 448; **Vol. 8, Part 2**, 108 f., 221; **Vol. 9, Part 2**, 476, 553 f.; **Vol. 10, Part 1**, 52, 360 f., 415 f., 509 f., 614 f.; **Vol. 10, Part 2**, 397; writings on, **Vol. 9, Part 2**, 35
French-Indian alliances (1670), **Vol. 8, Part 2**, 304
French literature and language: Alexander corpus, **Supp. 3**, 22; classical drama scholarship, **Supp. 5**, 409–10; modern fiction, **Supp. 10**, 590–91; Rousseau scholarship, **Supp. 3**, 691; studies in, **Supp. 1**, 36; **Supp. 2**, 141; **Supp. 3**, 22; teaching of, **Supp. 4**, 754–55; translations, **Supp. 8**, 474–76; writings on, **Supp. 10**, 394, 395
French Revolution: collections on, **Supp. 2**, 75; effect of, on American politics, **Vol. 1, Part 1**, 245; historical writings on, **Supp. 9**, 330; neutrality toward, **Vol. 5, Part 2**, 25; Paine, Thomas, **Vol. 7, Part 2**, 162 f.; studies of, **Supp. 3**, 47
Frenzied Finance, **Vol. 6, Part 1**, 60; **Vol. 8, Part 2**, 65
Freon, development of, **Supp. 3**, 522; **Supp. 6**, 333
Fresco art, **Supp. 5**, 473
Freshman, The, **Supp. 9**, 509
Fresno Republican (Calif.), **Supp. 4**, 707
Freud, Sigmund: Clark University lectures, **Supp. 3**, 190–91; cocaine studies, **Supp. 3**, 430; collaboration with, **Supp. 4**, 117–18; influence of, **Supp. 4**, 130; psychoanalytic theory, **Supp. 6**, 527–28, 724–25; references to, **Supp. 3**, 151, 385; relationships with, **Supp. 4**, 716–17; **Supp. 8**, 7, 61, 523; theories of, **Supp. 4**, 387, 572; **Supp. 5**, 301, 315–17, 583; **Supp. 7**, 6, 7; training by, **Supp. 5**, 517; translations of, **Supp. 4**, 108, 109; **Supp. 5**, 108
Freudian Wish and Its Place in Ethics, The, **Supp. 4**, 387
Freund, John Cristian, reference to, **Supp. 8**, 465
"Friar lands," Catholic church, **Vol. 4, Part 1**,
Friars Club, **Supp. 5**, 629
Frick, Henry Clay, assassination attempt, **Supp. 2**, 37; references to, **Vol. 2, Part 1**, 502 f.; **Vol. 7, Part 1**, 143; **Supp. 6**, 507
Frick Collection (New York City), building architecture, **Supp. 5**, 301
Friday Literary Review, **Supp. 8**, 124
Friede, Donald, reference to, **Supp. 7**, 148–49
Friedman, Milton, references to, **Supp. 10**, 383, 753
Fridenwald, Harry, reference to, **Supp. 4**, 905
Fridman, Alexander Alexandrovich, reference to, **Supp. 3**, 760
Friedman, Elizabeth Smith, reference to, **Supp. 8**, 195–96
Friedman, Hugo, reference to, **Supp. 6**, 491
Friend, colonial ship, **Vol. 7, Part 1**, 369
Friendly, Fred W., reference to, **Supp. 7**, 566
Friendly Sons of St. Patrick, **Vol. 7, Part 1**, 430
Friends. *See* Society of Friends
Friends' Expositor, **Vol. 10, Part 1**, 120
Friends' Historical Association, founding of, **Vol. 9, Part 1**, 28
Friends of Music in the Library of Congress, founding of, **Supp. 3**, 252
Friends of Negro Freedom, **Supp. 7**, 155
Friends of the Young Artists, founding of, **Supp. 4**, 289–90
Friends' Review, **Vol. 6, Part 1**, 212; **Vol. 8, Part 1**, 531,
Fries's Rebellion (1799), **Vol. 1, Part 1**, 79; **Vol. 4, Part 1**, 34
Frigates. For complete list of frigates, *see* Ships
Frigidaire Co., **Supp. 4**, 244
Friml, Rudolf, references to, **Supp. 7**, 198, 389
Frisian Societies, **Vol. 4, Part 2**, 604
Fritchie, Barbara, references to, **Vol. 8, Part 1**, 504; **Vol. 10, Part 2**, 175
Froebel, Friedrich, references to, **Supp. 4**, 373–74; **Supp. 6**, 711
Frohman, Charles, references to, **Vol. 5, Part 1**, 146; **Vol. 9, Part 1**, 401 f.; **Supp. 3**, 58, 276; **Supp. 5**, 7–8; **Supp. 6**, 19, 305; **Supp. 7**, 197
Frolic, building of, **Vol. 1, Part 1**, 606
From Here to Eternity, **Supp. 10**, 390
From Jordan's Delight, **Supp. 7**, 55
Fromm, Erich, references to, **Supp. 6**, 220; **Supp. 7**, 747; **Supp. 10**, 507
From the Forecastle to the Cabin, **Vol. 8, Part 2**, 324
"From the Land of the Sky-Blue Water" (song), **Supp. 4**, 138
From the Stone Age to Christianity, **Supp. 9**, 16
Frontenac, reference to, **Vol. 6, Part 1**, 10
Frontier: defense of, **Vol. 1, Part 1**, 354 f.; **Vol. 3, Part 2**, 455; **Vol. 4, Part 2**, 463; **Vol. 5, Part 2**, 272 f.; **Vol. 6, Part 1**, 80; **Vol. 8, Part 2**, 293 f.; **Vol. 9, Part 2**, 546; **Vol. 10, Part 1**, 146; life, **Vol. 1, Part 2**, 88, 471; **Vol. 2, Part 1**, 121; **Vol. 3, Part 1**, 331; **Vol. 3, Part 2**, 386, 496, 536; **Vol. 4, Part 1**, 145, 323; **Vol. 4, Part 2**, 30; **Vol. 5, Part 2**, 349; **Vol. 6, Part 1**, 534; **Vol. 8, Part 2**, 108, 153, 157, 603; **Vol. 9, Part 1**, 59, 468; **Vol. 9, Part 2**, 247, 563; medical care, **Vol. 6, Part 1**, 241; religious service, **Vol. 3, Part 2**, 542; **Vol. 9, Part 2**, 71, 331; sculpture depicting life on the, **Vol. 1, Part 2**, 463; significance in American history, **Supp. 7**, 771–72; writings on, **Vol. 3, Part 2**, 456; **Vol. 4, Part 1**, 389 f.; **Vol. 5, Part 2**, 182 f., 430; **Vol. 8, Part 2**, 51, 173; **Vol. 10, Part 1**, 63 f., 580 f. *See also* Cowboys; Pioneering
Frontiers Films, **Supp. 10**, 766
Front Page, The, **Supp. 5**, 323; **Supp. 7**, 148, 331, 413, 526
Front Royal, operation at, **Vol. 1, Part 1**, 578; **Vol. 5, Part 1**, 557
Frost, Robert, references to, **Supp. 5**, 272; **Supp. 6**, 572; **Supp. 7**, 339, 425; **Supp. 9**, 828–29; **Supp. 10**, 799, 800
Frost, Wade Hampton, reference to, **Supp. 7**, 194
Frozen food, **Supp. 6**, 61; **Supp. 9**, 770; **Supp. 10**, 555, 556. *See also* Freeze-drying technique
Fruit: canning, early experiments with, **Vol. 5, Part 1**, 568; citrus diseases, **Supp. 4**, 862–63; culture, **Vol. 2, Part 2**, 489; **Vol. 3, Part 2**, 376; **Vol. 4, Part 1**, 144; **Vol. 4, Part 2**, 356; **Vol. 5, Part 1**, 328; **Vol. 5, Part 2**, 341; **Vol. 6, Part 1**, 363, 481, 498, 535 f.; **Vol. 7, Part 1**, 197; **Vol. 8, Part 1**, 145 f., 233; **Vol. 8, Part 2**, 91; **Vol. 9, Part 2**, 439; diseases, **Supp. 1**, 462; hybridization of, **Supp. 4**, 357; merchandising of, **Vol. 5, Part 2**, 291 f.; preserving of, **Vol. 5, Part 2**, 160; use of cold storage, **Vol. 8, Part 1**, 145 f.; writings on, **Vol. 9, Part 2**, 439
Fruit fly studies, **Supp. 3**, 539–40; **Supp. 5**, 357; **Supp. 8**, 448, 449
Fruton, John S., reference to, **Supp. 3**, 61
Fry, Joshua, reference to, **Vol. 6, Part 1**, 193
Fry, Vernon C., reference to, **Supp. 4**, 294
Frye, Jack, reference to, **Supp. 6**, 146
Frying Pan Co., organization of, **Vol. 7, Part 2**, 139
FSA. *See* Farm Security Administration
FTC. *See* Federal Trade Commission
Fuchs, Klaus, references to, **Supp. 5**, 588; **Supp. 8**, 230; **Supp. 9**, 321, 322
Fuert, Woody, reference to, **Supp. 6**, 9
Fuertes, Louis Agassiz, reference to, **Supp. 3**, 162
Fugitive, The: (publication), **Supp. 6**, 461; **Supp. 10**,

776; literary and critical movements introduced by, **Supp. 9**, 643
Fugitive, The (television show and movie), **Supp. 10**, 380
Fugitive Slave Law: **Vol. 1, Part 2**, 133; **Vol. 2, Part 1**, 49, 132–33, 564; **Vol. 2, Part 2**, 179, 242; **Vol. 3, Part 1**, 399; **Vol. 3, Part 2**, 216, 381; **Vol. 6, Part 2**, 419; **Vol. 7, Part 2**, 67, 145, 214; **Vol. 8, Part 2**, 35; **Vol. 9, Part 1**, 271, 570; **Vol. 9, Part 2**, 209, 293; constitutionality of, **Vol. 3, Part 1**, 330; **Vol. 6, Part 1**, 84; **Vol. 8, Part 2**, 153; defense of, **Vol. 3, Part 1**, 399; opposition to, **Vol. 2, Part 2**, 203
Fugitive slaves, **Vol. 10, Part 1**, 440; Iowa, **Vol. 8, Part 2**, 153
Fugitives (literary group): **Supp. 10**, 776; founding of, **Supp. 9**, 642; mythology of Old South disdained by, **Supp. 10**, 215
Fulbright, J. William, reference to, **Supp. 6**, 661
Fuld, Carrie, references to, **Supp. 3**, 30, 31; **Supp. 6**, 208
Fuld, Felix, reference to, **Supp. 3**, 30
Fuller, Alvan T., reference to, **Supp. 3**, 473
Fuller, George A., references to, **Supp. 3**, 611–12; **Supp. 6**, 337
Fuller, Margaret, reference to, **Vol. 6, Part 1**, 460 f.
Fulton, Fred, reference to, **Supp. 6**, 363
Fulton, Robert, references to, **Vol. 3, Part 1**, 339; **Vol. 3, Part 2**, 5; **Vol. 6, Part 1**, 324; **Vol. 7, Part 1**, 161; **Vol. 9, Part 2**, 309
Fulton-Livingston steamboat monopoly, **Vol. 5, Part 2**, 608
Functions of the Executive, The, **Supp. 7**, 30
Fundamentalism: **Vol. 3, Part 2**, 257; Vol. 9, Part 2 126; **Supp. 3**, 129; **Supp. 4**, 691–92; **Supp. 5**, 176, 345–46, 516–17; **Supp. 6**, 195; Methodist organizations, **Supp. 7**, 694; scientific argument for, **Supp. 7**, 631–32; Scopes trial issue, **Supp. 8**, 583–84
Fundamental Orders of Connecticut, **Vol. 5, Part 1**, 200; **Vol. 6, Part 1**, 494
Fund for the Advancement of Education, **Supp. 7**, 276
Fund-raising, **Supp. 7**, 401–2
Fungi: collections of, **Vol. 3, Part 2**, 105; **Vol. 8, Part 1**, 396; **Supp. 3**, 815; Michigan, **Vol. 5, Part 2**, 263; North Carolina, **Vol. 8, Part 2**, 484; rust, **Supp. 3**, 23
Fungicides, **Supp. 3**, 400–401, 815
Funk, Wilfred, Inc., **Supp. 7**, 274
Funk and Wagnalls, **Supp. 2**, 682–83; **Supp. 7**, 274
Funny Thing Happened on the Way to the Forum, A, **Supp. 10**, 561
Furnace, Elizabeth, reference to, **Vol. 9, Part 2**, 17
Furnaces: blast, early development, **Vol. 10, Part 1**, 465 f.; electric, **Vol. 4, Part 2**, 575; first use of gas in a puddling, **Vol. 10, Part 1**, 602 f.; gas, **Vol. 7, Part 2**, 206; open hearth, **Vol. 5, Part 1**, 382
Furness, Thelma Morgan, reference to, **Supp. 7**, 752,
Furniture: Barcelona chair, **Supp. 8**, 436; colonial period, collecting of, **Vol. 6, Part 1**, 210 f.; design, **Vol. 6, Part 2**, 68; **Vol. 7, Part 2**, 553 f.; **Supp. 4**, 715; **Supp. 10**, 200; making of, **Vol. 7, Part 2**, 553 f.; **Vol. 8, Part 2**, 392; reproductions of early American, **Supp. 3**, 567; "womb" chair, **Supp. 7**, 670
Fur-trading: **Vol. 1, Part 1**, 391, 397 f., 585 f.; **Vol. 1, Part 2**, 438; **Vol. 2, Part 1**, 33, 383, 462; **Vol. 2, Part 2**, 92 f., 565; **Vol. 3, Part 1**, 305, 612; **Vol. 3, Part 2**, 282 f., 382, 442, 575; **Vol. 4, Part 1**, 504, 523; **Vol. 4, Part 2**, 17, 192 f., 276; **Vol. 5, Part 1**, 326, 478; **Vol. 5, Part 2**, 329, 422, 441, 517; **Vol. 6, Part 1**, 4, 37, 180, 191, 291; **Vol. 6, Part 2**, 91, 94, 133 f., 529; **Vol. 7, Part 1**, 41, 231, 395 f., 417, 585, 640; **Vol. 7, Part 2**, 601; **Vol. 8, Part 1**, 61, 180 f., 250 f., 290 f., 292 f., 320 f.; **Vol. 8, Part 2**, 32, 117, 157, 173, 305 f., 370; **Vol. 9, Part 1**, 19, 59, 67, 124, 133, 144; **Vol. 9, Part 2**, 455; **Vol. 10, Part 1**, 20 f., 177 f.; **Vol. 10, Part 2**, 240; **Supp. 1**, 394; Alaska, control of, in, **Vol. 6, Part 2**, 631; French patents of La Salle, **Vol. 6, Part 1**, 11; fur-seal arbitration, Great Britain, Russia, and U.S., **Vol. 3, Part 2**, 551; Illinois, **Vol. 2, Part 1**, 582; Massachusetts, **Vol. 10, Part 2**, 240; merchandising of, **Vol. 8, Part 2**, 173; Missouri, **Vol. 6, Part 1**, 5; **Vol. 8, Part 1**, 180 f.; **Vol. 10, Part 1**, 20 f.; Missouri River, **Vol. 6, Part 1**, 291; "Overland Brigade," **Vol. 3, Part 2**, 575; St. Louis, **Vol. 2, Part 2**, 92 f.; **Vol. 4, Part 1**, 504; **Vol. 4, Part 2**, 546; Virginia, **Vol. 2, Part 1**, 383; writings on, **Vol. 3, Part 2**, 575
Fur-trapping: **Vol. 1, Part 1**, 520; **Vol. 2, Part 1**, 531; **Vol. 4, Part 1**, 328; **Vol. 4, Part 2**, 546; **Vol. 5, Part 1**, 587; **Vol. 5, Part 2**, 613; **Vol. 6, Part 1**, 180, **Vol. 7, Part 1**, 458; **Vol. 8, Part 2**, 248; **Vol. 9, Part 1**, 381; **Vol. 10, Part 2**, 296, 452; diary of, **Vol. 8, Part 2**, 248; Indian attacks on trappers, **Vol. 4, Part 2**, 546; Missouri, **Vol. 4, Part 2**, 439; Oregon, **Vol. 8, Part 2**, 248
Furman University, **Vol. 4, Part 1**, 77; **Vol. 5, Part 2**, 130
Furuseth, Andrew, reference to, **Supp. 6**, 707
Fury, **Supp. 10**, 431
Fusion party in New York City, **Vol. 7, Part 1**, 37 f.

G

Gable, Clark, references to, **Supp. 3**, 466; **Supp. 9**, 128; **Supp. 10**, 158
Gabo, Naum, reference to, **Supp. 10**, 91
Gabor, Zsa Zsa, reference to, **Supp. 9**, 697; **Supp. 10**, 337
Gadsden Purchase (1854), **Vol. 3, Part 1**, 126; **Vol. 4, Part 1**, 84; **Vol. 5, Part 2**, 567; **Vol. 6, Part 2**, 276; **Vol. 7, Part 2**, 578
Gaelic American, founding of, **Vol. 3, Part 1**, 265
Gage, Lyman J., reference to, **Vol. 9, Part 2**, 127
Gage, Thomas (British general), reference to, **Vol. 6, Part 1**, 419 f.
Gager, William, reference to, **Supp. 4**, 110
Gages, establishment of standard system of, **Vol. 8, Part 1**, 172 f.
Gagliano, Gaetano, reference to, **Supp. 8**, 396–97
"Gag resolutions," **Vol. 1, Part 1**, 404
Gaines, Charlie, reference to, **Supp. 9**, 441
Gaines's Mill, Va., battle of, **Vol. 5, Part 1**, 343, 558; **Vol. 6, Part 1**, 123, 583, **Vol. 8, Part 1**, 90; **Vol. 10, Part 1**, 473; **Vol. 10, Part 2**, 137. *See also* Peninsular campaign
Gainesville, Va. *See* Bull Run, second battle of
Galbraith, John Kenneth, reference to, **Supp. 5**, 165
Gale, Henry, reference to, **Supp. 6**, 7
Gale, Leonard D., reference to, **Vol. 7, Part 1**, 248 f.
Gale, Zona, reference to, **Supp. 5**, 631
Galerie Druet (Paris), **Supp. 6**, 625
Gallagher, Ed, reference to, **Supp. 4**, 739
Gallagher, Helen, reference to, **Supp. 10**, 802
Gallagher, Walter E., reference to, **Supp. 6**, 156
Gallatin, Albert, references to, **Vol. 8, Part 1**, 184 f.; **Vol. 9, Part 1**, 337
Gallaudet, Thomas Hopkins, reference to, **Vol. 2, Part 2**, 201
Gallaudet College, founding of, **Vol. 5, Part 2**, 327
Gallbladder: function studies, **Supp. 8**, 556; one of first operations on, **Vol. 8, Part 1**, 378; surgery, **Supp. 6**, 632
Gallery Secession (New York City), **Supp. 8**, 553
Galli-Curci, Amelita, reference to, **Supp. 8**, 381
Gallinger, Jacob H., reference to, **Supp. 6**, 556

Gallo, Joey, references to, **Supp. 10**, 140, 141
Gallup, George: public opinion poll, **Supp. 4**, 189; **Supp. 7**, 649, 650; **Supp. 8**, 69; references to, **Supp. 10**, 708–9
Gallup and Robinson, founding of, **Supp. 7**, 650
Gall wasp, **Supp. 6**, 342, 343
"Galphin Claim," **Vol. 9, Part 2**, 353
Galton, Francis, references to, **Supp. 3**, 149; **Supp. 6**, 725
Galvanized iron, **Vol. 6, Part 1**, 141
Galveston, Tex.: **Vol. 1, Part 2**, 458; **Vol. 8, Part 2**, 166; capture of, **Vol. 5, Part 2**, 540; **Vol. 6, Part 1**, 376; **Vol. 6, Part 2**, 205; commission form of government, **Supp. 5**, 698; founding of, **Vol. 6, Part 2**, 528
Galveston News, **Vol. 8, Part 1**, 576 f.
Gambino, Carlo, references to, **Supp. 9**, 270; **Supp. 10**, 140, 141, 266
Gamble, James L., references to, **Supp. 3**, 75, 244
Gamble House (Pasadena, Calif.), **Supp. 5**, 257
Gambling: **Vol. 7, Part 1**, 233; Anti Race-Track League, **Vol. 6, Part 1**, 269; antiracing legislation, **Vol. 3, Part 1**, 552; Atlantic City casinos, **Supp. 10**, 75; "Dick" Canfield, **Vol. 2, Part 1**, 472; lotteries, **Vol. 3, Part 1**, 408; **Vol. 4, Part 1**, 268; **Vol. 4, Part 2**, 591; **Vol. 7, Part 1**, 581; **Vol. 8, Part 1**, 637; Nevada casinos, **Supp. 10**, 308–9, 357; New Orleans, licensed gambling in, **Vol. 8, Part 2**, 28; New York City raids, **Supp. 4**, 885; organized crime involvement, **Supp. 4**, 141–42; **Supp. 6**, 263–64; pari-mutuel betting, **Supp. 1**, 114; racing forms, **Supp. 3**, 20; reform activities, **Vol. 6, Part 1**, 269
Game Management, **Supp. 4**, 483
Game preservation, **Vol. 4, Part 2**, 157; **Vol. 8, Part 2**, 134; **Vol. 9, Part 2**, 565
Games: inventions of, **Vol. 6, Part 1**, 479; manufacture of, **Vol. 1, Part 2**, 574; **Supp. 9**, 601, 602
Gametophyte, **Supp. 5**, 98
Gamio, Manuel, reference to, **Supp. 6**, 532
Gamma globulin, **Supp. 5**, 123
Gandhi, Mohandas: biography of, **Supp. 9**, 718–19; references to, **Supp. 7**, 356, 748; **Supp. 8**, 172, 332
Gandhi Peace Prize, **Supp. 8**, 680
Gandil, Chick, reference to, **Supp. 8**, 574, 575
Gangemi, Thomas, reference to, **Supp. 9**, 456
Gangsters. *See* Organized crime
Gannett, William Channing, reference to, **Vol. 5, Part 1**, 242
Gannett Co., founding of, **Supp. 6**, 227
Gans, Joe, reference to, **Supp. 6**, 362
Gantt, Henry L., reference to, **Supp. 5**, 558
Gantt chart, for visual control of work, **Vol. 4, Part 1**, 129
Garabedian, Carl, reference to, **Supp. 3**, 71
Garbage. *See* Sewerage
Garbo, Greta, references to, **Supp. 3**, 296; **Supp. 6**, 440–41
García Lorca, Federico, translations of, **Supp. 8**, 291
Gard, Alex, reference to, **Supp. 8**, 571
Garden and Forest, **Vol. 7, Part 2**, 27 f.
Garden City, Long Island, built as "model town," **Vol. 9, Part 2**, 4
Garden Club of America, founding of, **Supp. 1**, 541
Gardenia, origin of name, **Vol. 4, Part 1**, 133
Gardening: first book in the American colonies on, **Vol. 8, Part 1**, 362 f.; first notable exponent of, **Vol. 3, Part 1**, 417 f.; landscape, **Vol. 3, Part 1**, 417 f.; **Vol. 7, Part 2**, 269, 600; **Vol. 8, Part 1**, 1; **Vol. 8, Part 2**, 355, 361, 383; mail-order seeds, **Supp. 10**, 80–81; writings on, **Vol. 8, Part 1**, 144 f., 362 f.; **Vol. 10, Part 1**, 116. *See also* Horticulture; Pesticides and herbicides
Gardens. *See* Botanic gardens; Horticulture; *specific garden names*
Gardiner, J. Stanley, reference to, **Supp. 3**, 704
Gardiner Lyceum, establishment of, **Vol. 4, Part 1**, 139
Gardiners Island (N.Y.), **Vol. 4, Part 1**, 138
Gardner, Burleigh, reference to, **Supp. 8**, 684, 685
Gardner, Erle Stanley, reference to, **Supp. 9**, 491
Gardner, Isabella Stewart, reference to, **Supp. 6**, 56
Gardner, John W., reference to, **Supp. 9**, 790
Gardner, L. U., reference to, **Supp. 4**, 49
Gardner, Mary, reference to, **Supp. 8**, 684, 685
Gardner, Nathaniel L., reference to, **Supp. 3**, 703–4
Gardner, Orville, reference to, **Vol. 6, Part 1**, 553
Gardner Mine fraud, **Vol. 3, Part 1**, 391
Garfield, James A.: campaign biography of, **Vol. 2, Part 1**, 264; references to, **Vol. 1, Part 2**, 325; **Vol. 4, Part 2**, 478; **Vol. 5, Part 1**, 66, 216; **Vol. 7, Part 2**, 544, **Vol. 8, Part 2**, 113; **Vol. 9, Part 1**, 132; **Supp. 3**, 292; **Supp. 4**, 316
Garland, Judy, reference to, **Supp. 9**, 291; **Supp. 10**, 301
Garman, Charles Edward, reference to, **Supp. 4**, 512–13
Garment industry. *See* Clothing manufacture; International Ladies' Garment Workers' Union
Garner, James, reference to, **Supp. 9**, 486
Garner, John Nance, references to, **Supp. 3**, 646, 659; **Supp. 5**, 287, 318–19; **Supp. 7**, 635; **Supp. 10**, 233, 484, 619
Garrett, John W., reference to, **Vol. 5, Part 1**, 214
Garrett Biblical Institute, **Vol. 3, Part 1**, 233; **Vol. 6, Part 1**, 298
Garrison, Fielding H., reference to, **Supp. 3**, 835
Garrison, Jim, Kennedy assasination conspiracy theory, **Supp. 9**, 715–16
Garrison, Lindley M., reference to, **Supp. 6**, 75
Garrison, William Lloyd, **Vol. 5, Part 2**, 112; **Vol. 6, Part 1**, 431, 436; **Vol. 9, Part 1**, 271; **Vol. 9, Part 2**, 299, 303, 393, 595; Phillips Wendell and, **Vol. 7, Part 2**, 546
Garsson, Henry M., reference to, **Supp. 6**, 437
Garst, Robert E., reference to, **Supp. 10**, 35
Garst and Thomas Hi-Bred Corn Company, **Supp. 10**, 271, 272
Garvey, Marcus, references to, **Supp. 3**, 489; **Supp. 5**, 544; **Supp. 7**, 203; **Supp. 9**, 423, 570, 571; **Supp. 10**, 658
Gar Wood Industries, Inc., **Supp. 9**, 892
Gary, Elbert H., reference to, **Vol. 7, Part 1**, 177
Gary, Romain, references to, **Supp. 10**, 725, 726
"Gary dinners," **Vol. 4, Part 1**, 175
Gas: companies, promotion of, **Vol. 1, Part 1**, 104; **Vol. 8, Part 2**, 66; development, **Vol. 4, Part 2**, 36; engine, invention of, **Vol. 7, Part 2**, 492 f.; incandescent lamp, **Supp. 6**, 365; laughing, first use of, as anesthetic, **Vol. 8, Part 1**, 604; lighting, pioneer in, **Vol. 6, Part 2**, 227; manufacture of, **Vol. 6, Part 1**, 452; **Vol. 9, Part 2**, 614; meters, **Vol. 1, Part 2**, 407; **Vol. 8, Part 2**, 115; **Vol. 9, Part 1**, 48; natural, pioneer use of, **Vol. 3, Part 2**, 517; **Vol. 6, Part 1**, 233; **Vol. 7, Part 2**, 635 f.; **Vol. 10, Part 1**, 179; *see also* Natural gas; plants building of, **Vol. 5, Part 1**, 370; Trust, Chicago, **Vol. 1, Part 1**, 104; use of, as anesthetic, **Vol. 10, Part 1**, 640 f. *See also* Gasoline
Gases, theoretical constitution of, **Supp. 6**, 346
"Gas Fight of 1905" (Philadelphia), **Vol. 3, Part 1**, 356
Gas lighter, electric, **Vol. 5, Part 1**, 335
Gasoline: catalytic cracking process, **Supp. 7**, 368; ethyl, **Supp. 3**, 521–22; first automobile design using, **Supp. 4**, 292; **Supp. 8**, 148; first drive-in service station, **Supp. 4**, 568; first synthetic high-test, **Supp.**

6, 332; high-octane, **Supp. 3**, 247; no-knock, **Supp. 3**, 521–22; octane ratings, **Supp. 7**, 615; polymerization process, **Supp. 4**, 661; tax for road building, **Supp. 1**, 671
Gasser, Herbert, reference to, **Supp. 7**, 226
Gastonia, N.C., labor violence, **Supp. 9**, 334
Gastric digestion, pioneer work in, **Vol. 1, Part 2**, 106
Gastroenterology, **Vol. 4, Part 2**, 519; **Vol. 9, Part 1**, 463; **Supp. 10**, 369–70
Gastrointestinal system: hunger and thirst studies, **Supp. 3**, 133–34; surgery, **Supp. 3**, 271
Gates, John, reference to, **Supp. 7**, 256
Gates, Sir Thomas, reference to, **Vol. 7, Part 1**, 468
Gates, Thomas S., reference to, **Supp. 10**, 72
Gateway Arch (St. Louis, Mo.), **Supp. 7**, 671–72
"Gathering Shells from the Seashore," popular song, (1872), **Vol. 9, Part 2**, 475
GATT. *See* General Agreement on Tariffs and Trade
Gatty, Harold, reference to, **Supp. 6**, 493
Gaudier-Brzeska, Henri, reference to, **Supp. 6**, 194
Gauntlet scandal, **Supp. 3**, 464
Gauss, Karl Friedrich, reference to, **Supp. 7**, 216
Gavin, James A., reference to, **Supp. 7**, 795
Gay, Maria, references to, **Supp. 10**, 639, 640
Gaylord Container Corporation, **Supp. 7**, 293
Gaynor, Janet, reference to, **Supp. 5**, 230; **Supp. 7**, 65
Gaynor, William J., reference to, **Vol. 7, Part 1**, 346; **Supp. 5**, 286
Gazette and Daily (York, Pa.), **Supp. 9**, 315
Gazette of the United States, **Vol. 3, Part 2**, 325; **Vol. 5, Part 2**, 25
GE. *See* General Electric Co.
Gears, mechanics of, **Supp. 1**, 492
Gebhard, Paul H., reference to, **Supp. 6**, 343
Geddes, Patrick, reference to, **Supp. 9**, 526
Gehrig's disease. *See* Amyotrophic lateral sclerosis
Geiger, Hans, reference to, **Supp. 7**, 134
Geisel, Theodor (Dr. Seuss), references to, **Supp. 9**, 166; **Supp. 10**, 441
Gelatin: manufacture of, **Supp. 4**, 455; photographic development use of, **Supp. 4**, 744
Geldner, Karl, reference to, **Supp. 3**, 445
Gellhorn, Martha, references to, **Supp. 7**, 337, 339
Gelsthorpe, Edward, reference to, **Supp. 9**, 94
Gemini project, **Supp. 8**, 225, 694; **Supp. 10**, 491
Gemmell, Robert C., reference to, **Supp. 6**, 316
Gems, **Supp. 1**, 477; **Supp. 2**, 701; historic, of early Tiffany, **Vol. 9, Part 2**, 533
Gender: chromosomes determining, **Supp. 2**, 725; **Supp. 4**, 515–16; masculinity-femininity measurement, **Supp. 6**, 626, 627; psychological differences, study of, **Supp. 5**, 316; sex hormone research, **Supp. 4**, 460, 498; sex hormones and cancer, **Supp. 3**, 6; sex-linked recessive traits, **Supp. 3**, 539–40
Genealogy, **Vol. 1, Part 1**, 144, 529; **Vol. 2, Part 2**, 59; **Vol. 3, Part 1**, 472, 551, 563, 595 f., 602 f., 606 f.; **Vol. 3, Part 2**, 278, 489; **Vol. 4, Part 2**, 322, 477; **Vol. 5, Part 2**, 54, 460, 612 f.; **Vol. 6, Part 1**, 2, 399; **Vol. 8, Part 1**, 183, 269, 276; **Vol. 8, Part 2**, 276, 308; **Vol. 9, Part 1**, 33 f., 82, 204, 250; **Vol. 9, Part 2**, 21, 307, 503; **Vol. 10, Part 1**, 44, 117, 406, 657 f.; **Vol. 10, Part 2**, 154; **Supp. 1**, 51; **Supp. 6**, 94
Geneen, Harold, reference to, **Supp. 9**, 423
General Accounting Office, administration, **Supp. 10**, 815
General Agreement on Tariffs and Trade (GATT), forerunner of, **Supp. 5**, 333
General Association of Kentucky Baptists, **Vol. 10, Part 1**, 384 f.
General Association of the Members of the Pierian Sodality, **Vol. 3, Part 1**, 567 f.
General Convention of the Christian Church, South, **Vol. 10, Part 1**, 636 f.
General Dynamics Corporation, **Supp. 6**, 156
General Education Board: **Vol. 7, Part 1**, 642; founding of, **Supp. 2**, 574; presidency, **Supp. 9**, 288
General Eldership of Churches of God in North America, **Vol. 10, Part 2**, 384
General Electric Co.: **Vol. 2, Part 2**, 264 f.; **Vol. 5, Part 1**, 261; **Vol. 7, Part 2**, 388; **Vol. 8, Part 2**, 268; **Vol. 9, Part 1**, 566; clock development, **Supp. 6**, 669; computer venture, **Supp. 9**, 194; electrical dlstribution research, **Supp. 3**, 251–52; employee programs, **Supp. 6**, 615; founding of, **Supp. 1**, 279; **Supp. 2**, 333, 659; growth, **Supp. 1**, 627; holding companies, **Supp. 3**, 527; international subsidiary, **Supp. 6**, 614; management, **Supp. 7**, 808–10; **Supp. 9**, 193–94, 873, 874; postwar growth of, **Supp. 9**, 874; postwar restructuring, **Supp. 9**, 193; research laboratory, **Supp. 4**, 609; **Supp. 6**, 32, 364–65; 695–96; **Supp. 10**, 52; unethical business practices, **Supp. 9**, 194; wireless communications venture, **Supp. 9**, 700
General Equipment Corporation, **Supp. 6**, 140
General Federation of Women's Clubs, **Vol. 2, Part 1**, 111
General Foods Corporation: **Supp. 7**, 739; executives, **Supp. 6**, 80; **Supp. 10**, 555–56; first president, **Supp. 7**, 123; founding of, **Supp. 9**, 615; frozen foods, **Supp. 6**, 61; **Supp. 10**, 555, 556; television advertising, **Supp. 9**, 308–9
General Mills Co.: founding of, **Supp. 7**, 46–47; purchase of Parker Bros., **Supp. 9**, 601
General Motors Acceptance Corporation, founding of, **Supp. 4**, 244, 682; **Supp. 9**, 290
General Motors Corporation: automotive glass, **Supp. 9**, 92; aviation interests, **Supp. 9**, 658; design complex, **Supp. 7**, 671; development and growth, **Supp. 7**, 793–95; du Pont interests, **Supp. 7**, 169, 210; **Supp. 9**, 622; finances, **Supp. 4**, 681–82; Fisher Body Division, **Supp. 3**, 273–74; **Supp. 7**, 246; Ford competition, **Supp. 4**, 301–2, 456–57; **Supp. 8**, 599; founding and growth, **Supp. 4**, 244, 457–59; **Supp. 8**, 598–600; **Supp. 9**, 568–69; Futurama exhibit, **Supp. 6**, 234; management, **Supp. 4**, 620–21; **Supp. 5**, 191, 193–4; **Supp. 8**, 318; **Supp. 9**, 290, 477, 622; **Supp. 10**, 285–86; military production, **Supp. 9**, 477; parts manufacture, **Supp. 3**, 55; plant architecture, **Supp. 3**, 405; research laboratories, **Supp. 3**, 522; **Supp. 6**, 332, 333; sit-down strike, **Supp. 4**, 612; unionization and contracts, **Supp. 8**, 375, 419, 526–27, 652; war production, **Supp. 10**, 285
General, The, **Supp. 8**, 314
General Shoe Co. *See* Genesco
General staff, U.S., beginning of, **Vol. 4, Part 2**, 151 f.; **Vol. 8, Part 2**, 139; **Vol. 10, Part 1**, 129
General Theological Seminary, **Vol. 5, Part 1**, 113; **Vol. 7, Part 1**, 118; **Vol. 10, Part 2**, 321
Generators: alternating-current, **Supp. 1**, 292; steam, **Supp. 1**, 232; turbine, **Supp. 3**, 251–52
Genesco (holding company), founding and growth of, **Supp. 10**, 381
Genesee Farmer, **Vol. 10, Part 1**, 35 f.
Genesis of Social Conscience, **Vol. 7, Part 1**, 388
Genetics: adaptive characteristics study, **Supp. 3**, 752–53; anemia, **Supp. 3**, 190; cancer relationship, **Supp. 3**, 807; **Supp. 6**, 383; chromosome mapping, **Supp. 2**, 61; **Supp. 8**, 448; **Supp. 9**, 550; code chemistry, **Supp. 5**, 413; **Supp. 8**, 200; **Supp. 9**, 753–54; Darwinian selectionism, **Supp. 9**, 238–39; DNA research, **Supp. 9**, 530, 550; environment and, **Supp. 3**, 84; **Supp. 6**, 368, 626–27, 672, 673; learning studies, **Supp. 4**, 832–33; mental disorder inheritance, **Supp. 4**, 618; mental retardation studies, **Supp. 6**,

241; modes theory, **Supp. 1**, 50; mutation theory, **Supp. 5**, 367–68; **Supp. 8**, 449; "one gene, one enzyme theory," **Supp. 9**, 793–94; petrography, pioneer in, **Vol. 5, Part 1**, 505; plant breeding, **Supp. 2**, 113, 167–68; **Supp. 4**, 252–53; **Supp. 5**, 628–29; **Supp. 8**, 596; psychology, **Vol. 9, Part 1**, 349; research in, **Supp. 2**, 60, 632; RNA discovered in viruses, **Supp. 9**, 754; sex chromosomes, **Supp. 2**, 725; **Supp. 4**, 515–16; sex-linked recessive traits, **Supp. 3**, 539–40; statistical analysis, **Supp. 3**, 215–16; Tay-Sachs disease, **Supp. 3**, 682; unicellular clone constancy, **Supp. 4**, 425–26. *See also* Eugenics

Genetics, founding of, **Supp. 5**, 629

Genêt (pseudonym of Janet Flanner), **Supp. 10**, 246

Genêt's mission, **Vol. 2, Part 2**, 150; **Vol. 4, Part 1**, 208; **Vol. 4, Part 2**, 177; **Vol. 5, Part 2**, 25 f.; **Vol. 6, Part 2**, 592; **Vol. 7, Part 1**, 212, 632; **Vol. 8, Part 1**, 355; **Vol. 10, Part 1**, 524

Geneva College (Pa.): football, **Supp. 5**, 458; founding of, **Vol. 8, Part 1**, 124 f.

Geneva Conference (1955), **Supp. 8**, 158

Geneva Disarmament Conference (1927), **Supp. 4**, 685

Geneva General Disarmament Conference (1932), **Supp. 3**, 219; **Supp. 7**, 186, 362

Geneva Protocol (1925), **Supp. 7**, 537

Geneva Tribunal of Arbitration, **Vol. 1, Part 2**, 91

Genitourinary system, **Supp. 5**, 688; surgery, **Supp. 4**, 507, 508

Genovese, Vito, references to, **Supp. 9**, 198, 269, 820, 821; **Supp. 10**, 266, 269

Gentlemen's Quarterly, founding of, **Supp. 5**, 637

Geodesy: **Vol. 3, Part 1**, 92 f.; **Vol. 4, Part 2**, 452; **Vol. 5, Part 1**, 23; **Vol. 8, Part 1**, 465; **Vol. 8, Part 2**, 459; first scientific bureau of, in America, **Vol. 4, Part 2**, 384

Geodetic surveys. *See* Surveys

Geographical Distribution of the Vote of the Thirteen States on the Federal Constitution, The, **Supp. 5**, 429, 430

Geographic Board, United States, organization of, **Vol. 4, Part 1**, 124

Geography: **Vol. 1, Part 1**, 525; **Vol. 3, Part 1**, 73, 92 f.; **Vol. 4, Part 1**, 123 f.; **Vol. 8, Part 2**, 39, 244; **Vol. 9, Part 2**, 296 f., 308, 309; agricultural, **Supp. 4**, 45; cultural, **Supp. 9**, 703; doctoral program, **Supp. 4**, 33; father of, **Vol. 7, Part 1**, 245; influences on history, **Supp. 1**, 119; **Supp. 4**, 113; "man in geography" manifesto, **Supp. 4**, 424; political boundary-setting, **Supp. 4**, 99, 113; popularization of, **Supp. 4**, 33; shoreline evolution, **Supp. 3**, 389–90; teaching of, **Supp. 4**, 98–99, 423–24; textbooks, **Supp. 1**, 7; **Supp. 4**, 33, 412–13, 423–24; U.S. regional boundaries, **Supp. 3**, 265–66; urban studies, **Supp. 4**, 424; writings on, **Vol. 2, Part 1**, 97; **Vol. 3, Part 1**, 565 f., 568 f.; **Vol. 4, Part 1**, 124; **Vol. 4, Part 2**, 63f.; **Vol. 7, Part 1**, 61; **Vol. 8, Part 1**, 473; **Vol. 8, Part 2**, 42, 583; **Vol. 9, Part 2**, 308; **Vol. 10, Part 1**, 124; **Vol. 10, Part 2**, 484; **Supp. 9**, 703–4. *See also* Cartography; Topography

Geography III, **Supp. 10**, 45

Geological Society of America, **Supp. 6**, 154; founding of, **Vol. 8, Part 1**, 247

Geological Survey, United States: **Vol. 1, Part 1**, 525; **Vol. 4, Part 2**, 439, 444; **Vol. 5, Part 1**, 50, 167, 457, 502, 505; **Vol. 5, Part 2**, 385; **Vol. 8, Part 2**, 525; **Vol. 9, Part 1**, 18, 289; administration, **Supp. 7**, 804–5; bibliographical project, **Supp. 4**, 218; coastal plain investigations, **Supp. 5**, 709–10; establishment of, **Vol. 8, Part 1**, 146 f.; fieldwork, **Supp. 3**, 265; **Supp. 9**, 685–86; first woman assistant in, **Supp. 3**, 38, 39; geological mining, **Supp. 4**, 765; geophysical laboratory, **Supp. 6**, 153; glacial geology division, **Supp. 3**, 455; groundwater studies, **Supp. 4**, 567; mapping program, **Supp. 3**, 407; midcontinent and Great Plains region, **Supp. 9**, 685–86; Pacific Northwest studies, **Supp. 4**, 896; petrography, **Supp. 3**, 724–25; petrology, **Supp. 6**, 70; photography, **Supp. 3**, 380; power supply survey, **Supp. 3**, 725; Rocky Mountain division, **Supp. 4**, 194; stratigraphy, **Supp. 3**, 782–83; topography, **Supp. 4**, 557–58; volcanology section, **Supp. 5**, 361

Geological Survey of Canada, **Supp. 5**, 415–16; **Supp. 6**, 144

Geology: **Vol. 1, Part 1**, 643; **Vol. 1, Part 2**, 118, 345, 570, 602; **Vol. 2, Part 2**, 97 f.; **Vol. 3, Part 1**, 55, 156 f., 396 f., 555; **Vol. 3, Part 2**, 56, 149; **Vol. 4, Part 1**, 4 f., 268 f.; **Vol. 4, Part 2**, 85, 136, 444, 446; **Vol. 5, Part 1**, 22, 69 f., 254, 457; **Vol. 5, Part 2**, 319, 358 f., 384 f.; **Vol. 6, Part 1**, 90, 183, 190, 482 f., 515; **Vol. 6, Part 2**, 136, 272, 400; **Vol. 7, Part 1**, 445 f.; **Vol. 8, Part 1**, 247, 264 f., 415; **Vol. 8, Part 2**, 91 f., 94, 287, 309 f.; **Vol. 9, Part 1**, 17, 161, 262, 289; **Vol. 9, Part 2**, 308, 341, 647 f.; **Vol. 10, Part 2**, 94, 375; Adirondack Mountains, **Vol. 5, Part 2**, 319; Alabama, **Vol. 9, Part 1**, 263 f.; Alaska, **Vol. 2, Part 1**, 73; **Vol. 8, Part 2**, 243; Appalachian chain, **Vol. 8, Part 2**, 94, 115; **Supp. 3**, 407–8; Atlantic coastal plain, **Vol. 6, Part 2**, 47; Brazil, **Vol. 1, Part 2**, 603; **Vol. 8, Part 1**, 387; building stones, **Vol. 6, Part 2**, 560; California, **Vol. 2, Part 1**, 25; Chinese studies, **Supp. 4**, 344, 896; climates, **Vol. 2, Part 1**, 601; coal mapping, **Supp. 2**, 90; Connecticut, **Vol. 1, Part 2**, 54; **Vol. 7, Part 2**, 460; **Vol. 8, Part 1**, 548; continental drift, **Supp. 2**, 654; **Supp. 9**, 675; Coon Butte Crater, **Vol. 4, Part 1**, 269; crystallography, **Supp. 3**, 38; cycle of erosion, **Supp. 1**, 230; discovery of emery deposits, **Vol. 9, Part 1**, 304; earth, theory of origin of, **Vol. 2, Part 1**, 601; earth's crust, **Supp. 1**, 177; **Supp. 9**, 271; explorations, **Vol. 8, Part 1**, 264 f.; field courses, **Supp. 5**, 416; geography relationship, **Supp. 3**, 265, 389–90; glacial, **Supp. 2**, 654; **Supp. 3**, 455–56; glacial period, **Vol. 2, Part 1**, 600; **Vol. 10, Part 2**, 512, 551; groundwater studies, **Supp. 4**, 567; igneous rocks, **Vol. 5, Part 1**, 457; **Vol. 10, Part 1**, 527 f.; **Supp. 4**, 194; **Supp. 6**, 70–71; Illinois, **Vol. 10, Part 2**, 538; Indiana, **Vol. 7, Part 2**, 116; isostasy, **Vol. 1, Part 1**, 643; **Vol. 3, Part 1**, 555; **Vol. 4, Part 2**, 452; **Supp. 2**, 56; Japan, **Vol. 6, Part 1**, 515; Kansas, **Vol. 8, Part 1**, 247; Kentucky, **Vol. 7, Part 2**, 499; land-formation theories, **Supp. 4**, 118–19; landforms classification, **Supp. 1**, 231; Maine, **Vol. 5, Part 1**, 536 f.; **Vol. 3, Part 1**, 515 f.; marine, **Supp. 5**, 656–57; Maryland, **Vol. 2, Part 2**, 146; **Vol. 8, Part 1**, 247; **Supp. 3**, 62; Massachusetts, **Vol. 5, Part 1**, 69 f.; measurement and structure, **Supp. 6**, 143–45; meteorites, **Vol. 6, Part 2**, 560; Michigan, **Vol. 2, Part 1**, 90; **Vol. 5, Part 1**, 254; **Vol. 8, Part 1**, 264 f.; **Vol. 10, Part 2**, 162; mineral collections, **Supp. 6**, 212; mining, **Supp. 4**, 765–66; Minnesota, **Vol. 10, Part 2**, 375; Mississippi, **Vol. 5, Part 1**, 22; Mississippi Valley, **Vol. 2, Part 1**, 432; Missouri, **Vol. 9, Part 2**, 232; Montana survey, **Supp. 1**, 176; New England, effect of glaciers on, **Vol. 10, Part 2**, 512; New Hampshire, **Vol. 5, Part 1**, 70; New Jersey, **Vol. 2, Part 2**, 373 f.; **Vol. 8, Part 1**, 214 f.; New York, **Vol. 3, Part 1**, 605 f.; **Vol. 8, Part 1**, 247; Noachian flood as basis theory, **Supp. 7**, 631; North American bibliography, **Supp. 4**, 218; North Carolina, **Vol. 5, Part 1**, 167; **Vol. 5, Part 2**, 359; Ohio, **Vol. 7, Part 2**, 62; **Vol. 8, Part 1**, 247; oil fields, **Vol. 2, Part 1**, 496; **Vol. 4, Part 2**, 444; **Vol. 10, Part 2**, 107; Outer Mongolia, **Supp. 6**, 18; paleontology, **Vol. 1, Part 2**, 127; **Vol. 3, Part 1**, 36; **Vol. 4, Part 1**, 81 f.; **Vol. 4, Part 2**, 136, 273 f., 436 f., 501, **Vol. 5, Part 2**, 472; **Vol. 6, Part 1**,

151; **Vol. 6, Part 2**, 302, 412, 494; **Vol. 7, Part 1**, 445 f., 597; **Vol. 8, Part 1**, 247, 386 f.; **Vol. 9, Part 1**, 289, 482; **Vol. 10, Part 2**, 134, 265, 310, 597; Pennsylvania, **Vol. 1, Part 2**, 448; **Vol. 6, Part 1**, 184; Permian rocks, **Vol. 9, Part 2**, 233; petrography, **Supp. 1**, 247; petroleum, **Supp. 2**, 681; **Supp. 7**, 803–5; physiographic terminology, **Supp. 2**, 90; physiography, **Vol. 4, Part 2**, 444; **Vol. 8, Part 1**, 146 f.; **Vol. 8, Part 2**, 243; **Vol. 10, Part 1**, 124; **Supp. 4**, 32; Precambrian, **Supp. 5**, 415–16; pulsation hypothesis, **Supp. 4**, 344; reference works in, **Supp. 4**, 896; seismic activity, continental, **Supp. 9**, 272; seismograph, use of, in, **Vol. 9, Part 2**, 585 f.; **Vol. 10, Part 1**, 106; soils, **Supp. 1**, 540; specimen collections, **Supp. 1**, 477; stratigraphy, **Supp. 3**, 782–83; **Supp. 9**, 686; studies in, **Supp. 1**, 177, 247; survey, **Vol. 1, Part 1**, 525; **Vol. 3, Part 2**, 151; **Vol. 4, Part 2**, 439, 444; **Vol. 5, Part 1**, 50, 167, 457, 502, 505; **Vol. 5, Part 2**, 385; **Vol. 7, Part 2**, 116, 450 f.; **Vol. 8, Part 2**, 94, 243, 525; **Vol. 9, Part 1**, 18, 289, **Vol. 10, Part 2**, 510; teaching of, **Vol. 2, Part 2**, 182; **Vol. 5, Part 1**, 502, 505; **Vol. 5, Part 2**, 319, 358 f.; **Vol. 7, Part 2**, 633; **Vol. 8, Part 1**, 247; **Vol. 8, Part 2**, 287, 310; **Vol. 9, Part 1**, 632; **Vol. 10, Part 2**, 163, 374, 512; **Supp. 1**, 285, **Supp. 4**, 730; Tennessee, **Vol. 8, Part 2**, 287; **Vol. 9, Part 2**, 648; terms, first use of, in, **Vol. 8, Part 1**, 147 f.; Texas, **Vol. 1, Part 2**, 419; **Vol. 8, Part 2**, 91 f.; topography, **Vol. 1, Part 1**, 384; **Supp. 9**, 685; Vermont, **Vol. 5, Part 1**, 71; **Vol. 7, Part 2**, 471; Virginia, **Vol. 8, Part 2**, 115; volcanoes, study of, **Vol. 4, Part 2**, 502; **Vol. 5, Part 1**, 70; **Supp. 1**, 247; western topographical origin, **Supp. 4**, 558; Wisconsin, **Vol. 7, Part 2**, 460; writings on, **Vol. 2, Part 1**, 73, 167; **Vol. 2, Part 2**, 374, 570; **Vol. 3, Part 1**, 268, 555, 605 f.; **Vol. 4, Part 2**, 441; **Vol. 5, Part 2**, 319, 472 f.; **Vol. 6, Part 1**, 515; **Vol. 6, Part 2**, 272; **Vol. 8, Part 1**, 146 f., 241 f., 247, 264 f.; **Vol. 8, Part 2**, 243, 310, 458; **Vol. 9, Part 1**, 289, 632; **Vol. 10, Part 1**, 106; **Vol. 10, Part 2**, 374; **Supp. 3**, 696; **Supp. 4**, 343–44; **Supp. 4**, 897; **Supp. 5**, 361–62. *See also* Cartography

Geometry: **Supp. 2**, 473; **Supp. 3**, 79; **Supp. 6**, 653–54; new differential, **Supp. 7**, 216; study of, **Vol. 2, Part 2**, 580; **Vol. 4, Part 2**, 164; **Vol. 7, Part 1**, 118

Geomorphology, **Supp. 1**, 230; **Supp. 3**, 389–90. *See also* Physiography

Geophysics: **Supp. 1**, 58, 61; **Supp. 6**, 153–54; earth tides, **Supp. 10**, 742; electrical conductivity of earth, **Supp. 10** 743; magnetic measurement, **Supp. 6**, 205–6; seismic profiles, **Supp. 9**, 271; temperature and pressure studies, **Supp. 10**, 407

George, Grace, reference to, **Supp. 4**, 104

George, Henry, references to, **Vol. 2, Part 1**, 82; **Vol. 9, Part 1**, 52, 286; **Supp. 3**, 44; **Supp. 6**, 522, 570

George, Walter F., reference to, **Supp. 4**, 316

George Peabody College for Teachers (Nashville, Tenn.), **Vol. 8, Part 1**, 222

George VI (King of Great Britain), U.S. visit (1939), **Supp. 6**, 614, 636

George Washington (frigate), **Vol. 1, Part 1**, 505

George Washington (locomotive), **Vol. 7, Part 1**, 556

George Washington Bridge (N.Y.-N.J.), design, **Supp. 3**, 530–31; **Supp. 6**, 594; **Supp. 7**, 11

George Washington University: **Vol. 8, Part 1**, 543; **Vol. 8, Part 2**, 483; **Vol. 9, Part 1**, 539; **Vol. 9, Part 2**, 42; **Vol. 10, Part 1**, 633 f.; bacteriology studies, **Supp. 1**, 665; founding of, **Vol. 5, Part 2**, 115; physics studies, **Supp. 8**, 199

Georgetown University: **Vol. 2, Part 1**, 527; **Vol. 5, Part 2**, 115, 489; **Vol. 7, Part 1**, 400; **Vol. 9, Part 2**, 376; foreign service studies, **Supp. 6**, 662

Georgia: African Methodist Episcopal church in, **Vol. 10, Part 1**, 66; agriculture, promotion of, **Vol. 5, Part 1**, 348; **Vol. 7, Part 1**, 564; Baptist denomination, **Vol. 6, Part 2**, 543; **Vol. 8, Part 2**, 330; Bermuda grass in, **Vol. 2, Part 2**, 468; blacks' influence in, **Supp. 4**, 915–16; Burns extradition controversy, **Supp. 9**, 689; business, first, in, **Vol. 4, Part 2**, 69; Cherokee Indians, **Vol. 2, Part 2**, 182 f.; civil rights demonstrations, **Supp. 8**, 334; Civil War, **Vol. 6, Part 1**, 578; colonial history of, **Vol. 3, Part 1**, 182; **Vol. 7, Part 1**, 463; **Vol. 8, Part 1**, 518; constitution, revision of, **Vol. 2, Part 2**, 180; court decisions, **Vol. 2, Part 2**, 24; Department of Health, **Vol. 3, Part 1**, 394; diplomatic service, **Vol. 10, Part 1**, 537 f.; economic development of, **Vol. 5, Part 1**, 58; educational work in, **Vol. 1, Part 1**, 5; **Vol. 4, Part 2**, 208 f.; **Vol. 5, Part 1**, 58, 348; **Vol. 6, Part 2**, 543; **Vol. 7, Part 2**, 57; **Vol. 9, Part 1**, 282; **Vol. 9, Part 2**, 615; **Vol. 10, Part 1**, 403 f., 446 f.; explorations, **Vol. 1, Part 1**, 451; **Vol. 8, Part 2**, 126; founding of colony, **Vol. 7, Part 2**, 1; gold, discovered, **Vol. 2, Part 2**, 183; governors of, **Vol. 1, Part 1**, 412; **Vol. 2, Part 1**, 258 f., 470; **Vol. 2, Part 2**, 134 f., 520 f.; **Vol. 3, Part 2**, 65, f.; **Vol. 4, Part 1**, 306 f.; **Vol. 5, Part 1**, 268, 544 f.; **Vol. 5, Part 2**, 44; **Vol. 6, Part 2**, 13 f., 15, 617 f.; **Vol. 7, Part 1**, 40 f., 564; **Vol. 9, Part 1**, 280 f.; **Vol. 9, Part 2**, 361 f., 615; **Supp. 3**, 331; **Supp. 4**, 813–14; **Supp. 9**, 688–89; Greenback party convention (1880), **Vol. 4, Part 1**, 539; Grey's conspiracy in, **Vol. 8, Part 1**, 518; history of, **Vol. 1, Part 1**, 444; **Vol. 1, Part 2**, 611; **Vol. 3, Part 1**, 182; **Vol. 9, Part 1**, 628; **Vol. 10, Part 2**, 100; **Supp. 1**, 472; Indians, **Vol. 1, Part 2**, 478; **Vol. 2, Part 2**, 182 f.; **Vol. 5, Part 2**, 165; **Vol. 6, Part 1**, 503 f.; **Vol. 6, Part 2**, 51, 70; laws, compilation of, **Vol. 3, Part 1**, 154; legal service, **Vol. 1, Part 2**, 203, 224, 364; **Vol. 2, Part 2**, 24, 239; **Vol. 3, Part 1**, 154, 599; **Vol. 4, Part 2**, 208, 327; **Vol. 5, Part 1**, 48, 546; **Vol. 6, Part 1**, 502, 546; **Vol. 7, Part 1**, 467, 527; **Vol. 9, Part 1**, 170, 441; **Vol. 9, Part 2**, 274; **Vol. 10, Part 1**, 403 f., 426 f., 464 f., 565; Loyalists, **Vol. 4, Part 1**, 476; maps, **Vol. 3, Part 1**, 182; **Vol. 8, Part 2**, 126; medicine in, **Vol. 7, Part 2**, 419; Methodist church in, **Supp. 3**, 129–30; oyster industry in, **Vol. 7, Part 1**, 629; panic of 1907 in, **Vol. 2, Part 1**, 471; Peabody Fund in, **Vol. 7, Part 2**, 57; penal code, **Vol. 6, Part 1**, 502–3; periodicals, early, **Vol. 9, Part 2**, 479; plantations in, **Vol. 4, Part 1**, 489; political service, **Vol. 1, Part 1**, 412; **Vol. 1, Part 2**, 203, 225, 388; **Vol. 2, Part 2**, 134, 199, 241, 315, 520, 523, 545; **Vol. 3, Part 1**, 154, 599; **Vol. 3, Part 2**, 534 f.; **Vol. 4, Part 1**, 307, 425; **Vol. 4, Part 2**, 66, 140; **Vol. 5, Part 1**, 268, 544; **Vol. 5, Part 2**, 44, 102; **Vol. 6, Part 2**, 13, 15; **Vol. 7, Part 1**, 40, 564; **Vol. 7, Part 2**, 584; **Vol. 8, Part 1**, 518; **Vol. 9, Part 1**, 280, 569; **Vol. 9, Part 2**, 361, 474, 615, 650; **Vol. 10, Part 1**, 66, 403 f., 426, 464, 549, 565 f.; **Vol. 10, Part 2**, 207, 440, 634; politics, **Vol. 2, Part 1**, 470; **Vol. 6, Part 1**, 62; **Supp. 4**, 813–14, 915; **Supp. 5**, 139; **Supp. 6**, 234–35; **Supp. 8**, 703; **Supp. 9**, 369, 639, 688–89; post-Civil War politics of, **Vol. 6, Part 1**, 62; Provincial Congress, **Vol. 2, Part 1**, 257; public service, **Vol. 1, Part 1**, 531; **Vol. 2, Part 2**, 22, 377; **Vol. 3, Part 2**, 456; **Vol. 4, Part 1**, 425; **Vol. 4, Part 2**, 65, 140; **Vol. 5, Part 1**, 26, 42 f., 517; **Vol. 6, Part 1**, 61; **Vol. 6, Part 2**, 514, 618; **Vol. 8, Part 2**, 330; **Vol. 9, Part 1**, 281, 426, 580; **Vol. 9, Part 2**, 479, 590 f.; **Vol. 10, Part 1**, 403 f., 565 f.; railroads, **Vol. 4, Part 1**, 489; Reconstruction, **Vol. 1, Part 1**, 133, 430; **Vol. 2, Part 1**, 143, 258; **Vol. 4, Part 1**, 424; **Vol. 5, Part 2**, 44; **Vol. 6, Part 2**, 13; religious service, **Vol. 9, Part 1**, 99; resources developed, **Vol. 2, Part 2**, 408; Revolutionary War period, **Vol. 4, Part 2**, 70; **Vol. 5, Part 1**, 314; Salzburgers, colony of, **Vol. 1,**

Part 2, 425; school of technology, **Vol. 5, Part 1**, 210; scientific, **Vol. 2, Part 2**, 468 f.; secession, **Vol. 2, Part 2**, 246 f.; **Vol. 5, Part 2**, 165; **Vol. 6, Part 1**, 61; slaves, **Vol. 4, Part 2**, 69; South Carolina's help in founding, **Vol. 5, Part 2**, 117; state university recommended, **Vol. 4, Part 2**, 140; Troup and Clark parties in, **Vol. 2, Part 2**, 134; war with Spain, **Vol. 7, Part 2**, 2; work-study schools, **Supp. 3**, 63; writings on, **Vol. 4, Part 1**, 307; **Vol. 4, Part 2**, 238; **Vol. 5, Part 2**, 165; **Vol. 6, Part 1**, 390; **Vol. 9, Part 1**, 249; **Vol. 9, Part 2**, 479 f.
Georgia Female College. *See* Wesleyan College
"Georgia platform," **Vol. 9, Part 2**, 615
Georgia Railroad, surveying and building of, **Vol. 7, Part 2**, 510
Georgia School of Technology, **Vol. 5, Part 1**, 210
Georgia State Industrial College, founding of, **Supp. 4**, 916
Georgia Warm Springs Foundation, founding of, **Supp. 3**, 644
Gerber, Daniel F., reference to, **Supp. 5**, 242–43
Gerber Products Co., founding of, **Supp. 5**, 242–43; **Supp. 9**, 302–3
Gerlach, Walther, reference to, **Supp. 8**, 628
German American Annals, **Vol. 6, Part 1**, 78
German-American Bund, **Supp. 9**, 131
German-American Reform Union, one of the founders of, **Vol. 8, Part 1**, 46 f.
German-Americans: California, **Vol. 8, Part 2**, 90; Illinois, **Vol. 5, Part 2**, 496; "Latin farmer" community, Belleville, Ill., **Vol. 6, Part 1**, 274; Missouri, **Vol. 5, Part 2**, 496; organizations, **Vol. 8, Part 1**, 46 f.; **Vol. 8, Part 2**, 91; **Supp. 1**, 696; pioneers, information concerning, **Vol. 8, Part 1**, 388; Pennsylvania, **Vol. 6, Part 1**, 292; **Vol. 7, Part 1**, 309, 529; **Vol. 7, Part 2**, 108 f.; **Vol. 8, Part 1**, 113 f.; **Vol. 8, Part 2**, 225, f., 282, 447; political influences, **Supp. 1**, 363; political journalism, **Supp. 7**, 757–58; priest, first in Northwest, **Vol. 8, Part 1**, 509; Texas, communist colony, **Vol. 6, Part 1**, 274; World War I policies, **Supp. 5**, 279; writers, **Supp. 3**, 232–33; **Supp. 6**, 443, 444
German Evangelical church, **Supp. 7**, 574
German Reformed church: **Vol. 4, Part 1**, 219, 375 f.; **Vol. 4, Part 2**, 15, 237, 523; **Vol. 7, Part 2**, 107 f.; **Vol. 8, Part 1**, 389 f.; **Vol. 8, Part 2**, 435; Pennsylvania, **Vol. 1, Part 2**, 404; **Vol. 2, Part 1**, 220; **Vol. 4, Part 2**, 578; **Vol. 8, Part 2**, 227, 436
Germantown, Pa.: battle of, **Vol. 4, Part 1**, 570; **Vol. 7, Part 1**, 87; **Vol. 8, Part 1**, 259; **Vol. 10, Part 1**, 517, 564; settlement of, **Vol. 3, Part 2**, 260; **Vol. 7, Part 2**, 291; **Vol. 8, Part 1**, 632
Germany: abstract art movement, **Supp. 8**, 270; architectural design, **Supp. 5**, 483; **Supp. 8**, 226, 435–36; art, modern, first exhibition of, in U.S., **Vol. 8, Part 1**, 493; atomic bomb research, World War II era, **Supp. 10**, 289; banking, **Supp. 5**, 249–50; Berlin airlift, **Supp. 6**, 431; **Supp. 10**, 128; Berlin Wall, **Supp. 7**, 423; **Supp. 10**, 128; book publishing, **Supp. 7**, 799; Catholic church, **Vol. 4, Part 2**, 515, 542; Catholic newspaper in U.S. (1837), **Vol. 4, Part 2**, 542; Communist party, **Supp. 7**, 244; **Supp. 8**, 162; culture, devotion to, **Vol. 5, Part 2**, 506; de-Nazification, **Supp. 6**, 407; diplomacy with U.S., **Vol. 5, Part 1**, 548 f.; **Vol. 7, Part 2**, 88, 420, 533; **Vol. 9, Part 2**, 316, 608; **Supp. 3**, 366, 699; **Supp. 4**, 898; **Supp. 5**, 241; education, **Supp. 3**, 676; **Supp. 6**, 207, 208; emigration, **Vol. 5, Part 2**, 484, 491; **Vol. 8, Part 2**, 87; **Supp. 10**, 431, 840; ethnological study of, **Supp. 6**, 394; Federal Republic, U.S. recognition of, **Supp. 10**, 144; food relief, **Supp. 7**, 359; Great Depression in, **Supp. 6**, 708–9; housing programs (1920s), **Supp. 3**, 52; immigration, **Vol. 3, Part 2**, 260; **Vol. 4, Part 2**, 383; **Vol. 5, Part 2**, 496; **Vol. 8, Part 1**, 392; **Vol. 8, Part 2**, 87; *Lied*, **Vol. 4, Part 2**, 505; literature and language, grammar studies, **Supp. 4**, 203; Methodism, **Vol. 7, Part 1**, 393; newspapers, German-language, **Vol. 2, Part 1**, 19; **Vol. 4, Part 1**, 262; **Vol. 4, Part 2**, 509, 542; **Vol. 5, Part 2**, 259, 592; **Vol. 6, Part 1**, 274; **Vol. 8, Part 2**, 446 f.; philosophy, conveyed into fashionable English, **Vol. 5, Part 2**, 507; political cartoons, **Supp. 6**, 256; post-World War II occupation of, **Supp. 4**, 900; **Supp. 8**, 275, 446; **Supp. 10**, 127–28; press in America, **Vol. 7, Part 1**, 271 f.; radicalism, **Vol. 4, Part 2**, 508 f.; refugees, **Vol. 4, Part 2**, 383; **Vol. 6, Part 1**, 237, 292; **Vol. 8, Part 2**, 444; reparations payments, **Supp. 2**, 234, 356; **Supp. 7**, 809–10; rocket development, **Supp. 3**, 306, 307–8; satirical cabaret, **Supp. 4**, 867–68; scholarship, **Vol. 3, Part 2**, 491 f., 584 f.; **Vol. 8, Part 2**, 55; sentiment, **Vol. 9, Part 1**, 153; study, influence of, **Vol. 1, Part 1**, 564; teaching of German, **Vol. 5, Part 1**, 244, 513; **Vol. 5, Part 2**, 227; Third Humanism, **Supp. 7**, 388; translations, **Vol. 4, Part 2**, 520; **Vol. 6, Part 1**, 103; **Vol. 8, Part 1**, 188 f.; **Vol. 8, Part 2**, 362 f.; universities, **Vol. 9, Part 2**, 526; writings on, **Supp. 4**, 851. *See also* German-Americans; Nazism; War crimes; World War I; World War II
Germer, Lester H., reference to, **Supp. 6**, 151
Germicides. *See* Antiseptics
Germ theory of disease, **Vol. 4, Part 1**, 464; **Vol. 8, Part 2**, 309
Geronimo, reference to, **Vol. 6, Part 1**, 62
Gerontological Society, founding of, **Supp. 5**, 454
Gerrymandering: **Vol. 4, Part 1**, 226; Illinois, **Vol. 3, Part 1**, 398; Massachusetts, **Vol. 9, Part 2**, 145; origin of the word, **Vol. 8, Part 2**, 239; **Vol. 9, Part 2**, 499
Gerry Society, **Vol. 4, Part 1**, 228; **Supp. 8**, 314
Gersh, Isidore, reference to, **Supp. 6**, 54
Gershwin, George, references to, **Supp. 2**, 303; **Supp. 3**, 690; **Supp. 4**, 211, 226; **Supp. 7**, 199; **Supp. 8**, 697, 698; **Supp. 9**, 340, 491, 492; **Supp. 10**, 421
Gershwin, Ira, reference to, **Supp. 5**, 415
Gerstenfeld, Norman, reference to, **Supp. 6**, 600
Gesell, Arnold, reference to, **Supp. 6**, 626
Gesell Institute of Child Development, **Supp. 7**, 284
Gestalt psychology: **Supp. 3**, 428–30; **Supp. 4**, 485; **Supp. 8**, 343–45; **Supp. 9**, 325; **Supp. 10**, 696; founding of, **Supp. 3**, 808–9
Get Rich Quick Wallingford (stories), **Vol. 2, Part 2**, 58
Getty, George F., reference to, **Supp. 10**, 275
Getty, J. Paul, reference to, **Supp. 9**, 305
Getty, J. Paul, Museum, **Supp. 10**, 277
Getty Oil company: development of, **Supp. 9**, 305–6; management, **Supp. 10**, 275–76; predecessor, **Supp. 10**, 275–76
Gettysburg, Pa.: **Vol. 1, Part 1**, 165, 524; **Vol. 2, Part 1**, 71, 373; **Vol. 3, Part 2**, 230, 254, 284; **Vol. 4, Part 2**, 152, 168, 194, 214, 222, 235, 243, 600; **Vol. 5, Part 1**, 25, 193, 279 f., 283, 372, 386 f., 422; **Vol. 5, Part 2**, 209, 258, 359, 375; **Vol. 6, Part 1**, 39, 125, 159, 370, 392, 430; **Vol. 6, Part 2**, 193, 476; **Vol. 7, Part 1**, 20, 228, 350, 410, 473, 552, 605; **Vol. 7, Part 2**, 8, 516, 570; **Vol. 8, Part 1**, 520; **Vol. 8, Part 2**, 47, 71, 72, 152, 219, 285, 463, 468, 548; **Vol. 9, Part 1**, 115, 150, 216, 249, 471; **Vol. 9, Part 2**, 66, 171, 255, 530, 593, 621, 636, 642; **Vol. 10, Part 1**, 571; address, Everett, **Vol. 3, Part 2**, 225; address, Lincoln, **Vol. 6, Part 1**, 256; history of, **Vol. 5, Part 1**, 371; **Vol. 10, Part 2**, 628; monuments, **Vol. 4, Part 1**, 471; painting of, battle, **Vol. 8, Part 2**, 187; Pickett's charge, **Vol. 5, Part 2**, 322; religious service in con-

nection with dedication, **Vol. 9, Part 2**, 50; sculpture on battlefield, **Vol. 8, Part 1**, 125 f.
Gettysburg College (formerly Pennsylvania College), **Vol. 1, Part 2**, 59; **Vol. 5, Part 2**, 502; **Vol. 8, Part 2**, 443
Gewandhaus Orchestra of Leipzig, **Supp. 8**, 450
Ghana, **Supp. 7**, 205
Ghent, Treaty of, **Vol. 1, Part 1**, 85; **Vol. 1, Part 2**, 66; **Vol. 2, Part 2**, 175; **Vol. 4, Part 1**, 106; **Vol. 5, Part 1**, 346, 529; **Vol. 6, Part 2**, 192; **Vol. 7, Part 1**, 90; **Vol. 8, Part 2**, 245
"Ghetto" (New York City), **Vol. 8, Part 2**, 165, 168
"Ghost Dance," origin of, **Vol. 10, Part 2**, 541
Ghostwriting, **Supp. 10**, 774–75
Giancana, Sam, references to, **Supp. 9**, 651, 652
Giannini Foundation for Agricultural Economics, founding of, **Supp. 6**, 638
Giant, **Supp. 9**, 464, 768
Giant Powder Co., **Vol. 5, Part 2**, 239
Giants in the Earth, **Supp. 4**, 172
Giauque, William, reference to, **Supp. 8**, 122
Gibbons, Thomas, reference to, **Vol. 7, Part 1**, 637
Gibbs, George, reference to, **Vol. 9, Part 1**, 161
Gibbs, Josiah Willard, references to, **Supp. 4**, 272, 273; **Supp. 6**, 153
Gibbs, Wolcott, reference to, **Supp. 5**, 594
Gibbs and Cox, predecessor, **Supp. 5**, 725
Gibbs & Hill, **Supp. 4**, 370
GI Bill of Rights, passage of, **Supp. 3**, 661; **Supp. 6**, 526, 551
Gibson, Charles Dana, reference to, **Supp. 4**, 826
Gibson, Edmund Richard ("Hoot"), reference to, **Supp. 9**, 286
Gibson, William, reference to, **Supp. 8**, 318
Gibson Girl, **Supp. 3**, 300
Giddings, Franklin H., reference to, **Supp. 4**, 227
Gide, André, scholarship on, **Supp. 8**, 475
Gideon v. *Wainwright*, **Supp. 9**, 837
Gielgud, John, reference to, **Supp. 10**, 673
Gifford, Walter S., reference to, **Supp. 7**, 362
Gifted children. *See* Prodigies
Gift of God, vessel in Popham's colonizing attempt, **Vol. 8, Part 1**, 78
Gilbert, Grove K., references to, **Supp. 4**, 765, 766; **Supp. 5**, 416
Gilbert, A. C., Co., **Supp. 7**, 287
Gilbert Academy and Industrial College, **Vol. 4, Part 1**, 273
Gilbert and Sullivan operas: American rights for publishing of scores, **Vol. 9, Part 2**, 62; presentation of, in New York, **Vol. 3, Part 1**, 91; **Vol. 8, Part 2**, 246
Gilbert Islands, World War II action, **Supp. 4**, 147; **Supp. 8**, 619
Gilbreth, Frank, references to, **Supp. 9**, 309, 310
Gilder, Richard Watson, references to, **Vol. 8, Part 2**, 516; **Vol. 9, Part 1**, 340
Gilder, William Henry, reference to, **Vol. 8, Part 2**, 481
Gillette, King Camp, reference to, **Supp. 9**, 297
Gillette Safety Raxor Co.: Auto-Strop merger, **Supp. 9**, 298; double-edged blade invented, **Supp. 9**, 297
Gillman, Daniel Coit, references to, **Vol. 5, Part 1**, 179; **Vol. 5, Part 2**, 304; **Vol. 9, Part 1**, 159
Gilman, Lawrence, reference to, **Supp. 5**, 183
Gilmore, Patrick S., reference to, **Vol. 9, Part 2**, 516
Gimbel, Bernard F., reference to, **Supp. 6**, 337
Gimbel, Isaac, reference to, **Supp. 8**, 212, 213
Gimbel Brothers, **Supp. 8**, 512–13
Gimpel, Bronislav, reference to, **Supp. 7**, 511–12
Gingrich, Arnold, reference to, **Supp. 5**, 637
Ginn, Edwin, reference to, **Vol. 10, Part 1**, 655 f.
Ginn and Co., **Supp. 6**, 558
Ginsberg, Allen, references to, **Supp. 8**, 325, 326
Ginzberg, Eli, reference to, **Supp. 8**, 608
Ginzberg, Louis, reference to, **Supp. 3**, 756
Girard, Alice, reference to, **Supp. 6**, 284
Girard, Stephen, reference to, **Vol. 7, Part 2**, 554
Girard College, **Vol. 1, Part 1**, 213; **Vol. 4, Part 1**, 321; **Vol. 5, Part 2**, 180; **Vol. 9, Part 1**, 335
Giraud, Henri H., reference to, **Supp. 3**, 662
Girl Scouts of America: **Supp. 6**, 81; **Supp. 8**, 83–84; founding of, **Vol. 6, Part 1**, 447–48
Girls' Friendly Society, **Vol. 2, Part 2**, 413
Girty's Town, Ohio, **Vol. 2, Part 2**, 527; **Vol. 4, Part 1**, 323; **Vol. 5, Part 2**, 349
Gish, Dorothy, reference to, **Supp. 7**, 32
Gish, Lillian, reference to, **Supp. 8**, 213–14
Gitlow, Benjamin, reference to, **Supp. 3**, 718
Gitlow, Kate, reference to, **Supp. 7**, 290
Gitlow v. *New York*, **Supp. 7**, 291
"Give Peace a Chance," **Supp. 10**, 450
Gizycki, Georg von, reference to, **Supp. 3**, 175–76
Glacial period, study of, **Vol. 2, Part 1**, 600; **Vol. 10, Part 2**, 512, 551
Glacier National Park, **Supp. 4**, 558, 896; establishment of, **Supp. 2**, 265
Glaciers, research and writings on, **Supp. 2**, 654; **Supp. 3**, 455–56, 558
Glackens, William, references to, **Supp. 5**, 624, 635, 636
Glamour, founding of, **Supp. 3**, 547
Glancy, A. Estelle, reference to, **Supp. 5**, 541
Glaser, Joe, reference to, **Supp. 9**, 47
Glasgow, Ellen, references to, **Supp. 6**, 95; **Supp. 7**, 797
Glass, Carter, references to, **Supp. 3**, 97, 132; **Supp. 4**, 641; **Supp. 7**, 362; **Supp. 8**, 592
Glass: as sun filter, **Supp. 6**, 69; automotive, **Supp. 9**, 92; canning jars, **Supp. 3**, 29; **Supp. 5**, 34; Favrile, **Vol. 9, Part 2**, 534; heat-resistant, **Supp. 3**, 365; **Supp. 6**, 624; industry growth, **Supp. 9**, 92–93; lead-flint, **Vol. 5, Part 1**, 618; **Vol. 6, Part 1**, 153; machinery, invention of, **Vol. 2, Part 2**, 282; **Vol. 7, Part 2**, 122; making of, **Vol. 2, Part 2**, 282; **Vol. 3, Part 1**, 586 f.; **Vol. 4, Part 1**, 345; **Vol. 4, Part 2**, 602; **Vol. 5, Part 1**, 122, 617; **Vol. 6, Part 1**, 153, 233, 530 f.; **Vol. 7, Part 2**, 4, 122, 189, 638; **Vol. 9, Part 2**, 17, 534 f.; **Vol. 10, Part 2**, 432 f.; **Supp. 9**, 92; monopoly in Connecticut, **Vol. 7, Part 2**, 641; opaline, **Vol. 5, Part 2**, 533; optical, **Supp. 3**, 40–41; **Supp. 6**, 153; plate, **Vol. 3, Part 2**, 517; **Vol. 5, Part 1**, 74; **Vol. 7, Part 2**, 636; sandwich, **Vol. 5, Part 1**, 95, 618; **Vol. 6, Part 1**, 530; stained, **Vol. 1, Part 1**, 350; **Vol. 4, Part 2**, 423, 438; **Vol. 5, Part 2**, 533 f.; **Vol. 6, Part 1**, 153; **Vol. 10, Part 2**, 244; Stiegel, **Vol. 9, Part 2**, 17. *See also* Stained glass
Glass flowers, collection of, **Vol. 4, Part 1**, 378
"Glassites," religious sect, **Vol. 8, Part 2**, 329
Glass Menagerie, The, **Supp. 4**, 823; **Supp. 8**, 444
Glass-Steagall Act (1933), **Supp. 3**, 730; **Supp. 4**, 332, 470; **Supp. 5**, 158, 159; **Supp. 9**, 208, 607
Glaucoma, treatment for, **Supp. 9**, 443
Glavis, Louis R., references to, **Supp. 3**, 96; **Supp. 4**, 665
Glazunov, Alexander, reference to, **Supp. 10**, 783
Gleason's Pictorial, one of earliest illustrated papers, **Vol. 1, Part 1**, 560; **Vol. 6, Part 1**, 186
Glebe, founding of, **Supp. 8**, 349
Glenwood Ladies' Seminary, establishment of, **Vol. 7, Part 2**, 47
Glidden Paint Co., **Supp. 9**, 444
Gliding, experiments in, **Vol. 2, Part 2**, 10; **Vol. 4, Part 2**, 590
Globe Theatre (New York City), founding of, **Supp. 1**, 249

Globeville, Colo., founding of, **Vol. 9, Part 1**, 57
Glory of Their Times, The, **Supp. 10**, 509
Gloucester, Mass., **Vol. 7, Part 1**, 361 f.; artists' colony, **Supp. 7**, 24, 25
Glover, Jim, reference to, **Supp. 10**, 602
Gloves: manufacture of, **Vol. 3, Part 2**, 45; **Vol. 5, Part 2**, 555; **Supp. 9**, 322; tariffs, **Supp. 3**, 463–64; traveling salesman, **Supp. 9**, 322; union organizing, **Supp. 4**, 625–26
Glucose: metabolism, **Supp. 6**, 595; research in, **Supp. 5**, 489
Glue, manufacture of, **Vol. 2, Part 2**, 409 f.
Glueck, Sheldon, reference to, **Supp. 9**, 318
Gluecks, Eleanor Touroff, references to, **Supp. 10**, 280, 281
"Glycerine tonic," invention of, **Vol. 7, Part 2**, 51
Glycogen, conversion studies, **Supp. 6**, 126–27
Glyoxalase, **Supp. 5**, 149
GM. *See* General Motors Corporation
"Gobbledygook," term coined, **Supp. 5**, 480, 481
Gobi Desert: archaeology, **Supp. 6**, 18; paleontology, **Supp. 3**, 316
Godard, Jean-Luc, reference to, **Supp. 10**, 725
Godbeite movement, **Vol. 4, Part 1**, 337
Goddard, Benjamin, reference to, **Vol. 10, Part 1**, 501 f.
Goddard, Henry H., reference to, **Supp. 7**, 284
Goddard, Morrill, reference to, **Supp. 5**, 284
Goddard, Robert H., reference to, **Supp. 9**, 497
Gödel, Kurt, reference to, **Supp. 6**, 655
Godey's Lady's Book, **Vol. 4, Part 1**, 344; **Vol. 5, Part 2**, 159; **Vol. 9, Part 1**, 319
Godfather, The, **Supp. 10**, 140
Godfrey, Chester N., reference to, **Supp. 3**, 196
Godkin, Edwin Lawrence: biography, **Supp. 2**, 499; references to, **Vol. 5, Part 1**, 596; **Vol. 8, Part 2**, 469, 515; **Supp. 3**, 249
Godowsky, Leopold, references to, **Supp. 6**, 297; **Supp. 7**, 511
Godsol, Frank Joseph, reference to, **Supp. 9**, 323
Godsy, John L., reference to, **Supp. 6**, 528
God That Failed, The, **Supp. 8**, 172
Godwin, Frank, reference to, **Supp. 3**, 685
Godwin, William, reference to, **Vol. 2, Part 1**, 107 f.
Goebbels, Joseph, references to, **Supp. 10**, 430, 562
Goebel, William, reference to, **Vol. 5, Part 1**, 586
Goering, Hermann, references to, **Supp. 5**, 359; **Supp. 9**, 498
Goethals, George W., reference to, **Supp. 3**, 310
Goethe, Johann Wolfgang von, reference to, **Supp. 10**, 402
Goetz, William, reference to, **Supp. 10**, 864
Going My Way, **Supp. 10**, 160
"Goin' Home" (song), **Supp. 4**, 276
Goiter: iodine to prevent, **Supp. 5**, 275; treatment of, **Vol. 4, Part 2**, 7
Gold, Harry, references to, **Supp. 3**, 343; **Supp. 5**, 588, 589; **Supp. 7**, 500; **Supp. 9**, 357; **Supp. 10**, 719
Gold, Michael, reference to, **Supp. 7**, 268
Gold: certificates, adopted by national government, **Vol. 7, Part 2**, 46; dentistry, use of, in, **Vol. 3, Part 2**, 211; **Vol. 6, Part 2**, 458; discovery of, in California, *see* Gold rush; discovery of, in Georgia, **Vol. 2, Part 2**, 183; Exchange, New York, **Vol. 2, Part 2**, 298; first coinage of, **Vol. 3, Part 1**, 254; mining, **Supp. 2**, 701, *see also* Mining, gold; prices, **Supp. 8**, 445–46; prospecting, **Vol. 1, Part 1**, 443; search for, by De Soto, **Vol. 3, Part 1**, 256 f.; standard, *see* Gold standard; supply and commodity price fluctuation, **Supp. 2**, 696; vigilante methods, among miners, **Vol. 5, Part 2**, 592
Goldberg, Arthur, references to, **Supp. 7**, 421; **Supp. 9**, 837
"Goldberg, Molly" (fictional character), **Supp. 8**, 33
Goldberg, Rube, contrivance, **Supp. 8**, 217
Goldberger, Joseph, reference to, **Supp. 4**, 701
"Goldbergs, The," **Supp. 8**, 32–33
"Gold" Democrats, **Vol. 2, Part 1**, 403; **Vol. 3, Part 2**, 292, 480
Gold Diggers of 1933, **Supp. 10**, 34
Golden Age, founding of, **Supp. 5**, 701
Golden Age Clubs, founding of, **Supp. 7**, 151
Golden Argosy, magazine for boys and girls, **Vol. 7, Part 1**, 334
Golden Boy, **Supp. 7**, 583, 584
Golden Gate Bridge (San Francisco, Calif.), **Supp. 3**, 531; **Supp. 4**, 897; design, **Supp. 2**, 637
Golden Gate International Exposition (1939): American Indian art exhibition, **Supp. 8**, 126; aquacade, **Supp. 8**, 547; Pacific Cultures exhibition, **Supp. 5**, 729
Golden Gate Park (San Francisco, Calif.), **Supp. 3**, 490–91
Golden Rule Stores, **Supp. 9**, 609; **Supp. 10**, 353
Goldenson, Leonard, reference to, **Supp. 10**, 415
Goldenweiser, Alexander, reference to, **Supp. 4**, 71
Goldfine, Bernard, reference to, **Supp. 8**, 497
Goldfinger, **Supp. 9**, 263
Goldfish, Samuel. *See* Goldwyn, Samuel
Goldin, Harrison J., reference to, **Supp. 10**, 453
Goldman, J. J., reference to, **Vol. 7, Part 1**, 276
Goldman Band, **Supp. 6**, 242
Goldman, Sachs and Co., **Supp. 8**, 78; **Supp. 10**, 454
Goldman Sachs Trading Corporation, **Supp. 6**, 61
Gold rush: **Vol. 1, Part 1**, 396, 446; **Vol. 1, Part 2**, 228; **Vol. 2, Part 1**, 62, 300; **Vol. 4, Part 1**, 22, 168; **Vol. 4, Part 2**, 363, 387; **Vol. 5, Part 1**, 81; **Vol. 5, Part 2**, 188, 407; **Vol. 6, Part 1**, 516; **Vol. 6, Part 2**, 314; **Vol. 7, Part 1**, 6, 612; **Vol. 8, Part 2**, 11, 35, 205, 248; **Vol. 9, Part 1**, 20; **Vol. 9, Part 2**, 225, 263, 315, 345, 384; Alaska, **Supp. 5**, 578; Nevada, **Supp. 5**, 613
Gold Rush, The, **Supp. 10**, 116
Goldsborough, N.C., operation at, **Vol. 8, Part 2**, 453; **Vol. 9, Part 1**, 96; **Vol. 9, Part 2**, 378
Goldsmith, Alfred N., reference to, **Supp. 6**, 298
Gold standard, **Supp. 3**, 414, 649, 652, 839; **Supp. 5**, 651; advocacy of, **Supp. 4**, 18; compensated dollar theory, **Supp. 4**, 274
Gold Standard Act, **Vol. 1, Part 1**, 221
Goldstein, Jonah J., reference to, **Supp. 6**, 142
Goldstein, Kurt, reference to, **Supp. 6**, 220
Goldwater, Barry: campaign slogan, **Supp. 9**, 140; presidential candidacy, **Supp. 9**, 435; reference to, **Supp. 10**, 687
Goldwater, Peggy Warner, reference to, **Supp. 6**, 68
Goldwater, Sigismund S., references to, **Supp. 3**, 320; **Supp. 6**, 192
Goldwater Memorial Hospital (New York City), **Supp. 3**, 313
Goldwyn, Samuel, references to, **Supp. 6**, 158, 368, 439, 440; **Supp. 8**, 465; **Supp. 10**, 34, 599
Golf: **Supp. 5**, 695–96; **Supp. 6**, 722–23; **Supp. 7**, 700–1; **Supp. 8**, 14–15, 384, 486–87, 702; course design, **Vol. 7, Part 2**, 633; **Supp. 2**, 678; **Supp. 9**, 439; first superstar, **Supp. 8**, 237–38; playing, **Vol. 9, Part 2**, 629–30; **Supp. 9**, 537; popularity of, **Supp. 9**, 438; promotion of, **Vol. 5, Part 1**, 247; **Supp. 9**, 439; Ryder Cup, **Supp. 9**, 537; tournaments, **Supp. 9**, 438, 439, 536, 537; **Supp. 10**, 161
Golf—A New Approach, **Supp. 9**, 537
Goliad expedition, **Vol. 3, Part 2**, 263
Golos, Jacob, reference to, **Supp. 7**, 51, 52

Gomberg, Moses, reference to, **Supp. 5**, 28; **Supp. 6**, 334
Gompers, Samuel: political parties defined by, **Vol. 4, Part 1**, 372; references to, **Vol. 3, Part 1**, 510; **Vol. 8, Part 2**, 358; **Supp. 2**, 213; **Supp. 3**, 179, 517, 532, 576; **Supp. 4**, 75; **Supp. 5**, 253, 254, 255; **Supp. 6**, 218, 219, 677, 706; **Supp. 7**, 455; **Supp. 8**, 374, 375
Gonadal transplant, **Supp. 6**, 632
Gone with the Wind, **Supp. 3**, 368; **Supp. 4**, 583–84; **Supp. 5**, 451; **Supp. 6**, 225; **Supp. 7**, 407, 545, 682; **Supp. 8**, 368, 369; **Supp. 9**, 370, 762; **Supp. 10**, 231, 283
Gonzaga University, founding of, **Supp. 1**, 159
Gonzales, Pancho, reference to, **Supp. 9**, 722
Gonzales, attack on, **Vol. 5, Part 1**, 265
Goodale, George Lincoln, reference to, **Supp. 4**, 16
Good Earth, The, **Supp. 9**, 133, 134
Good Health, **Supp. 3**, 410
Good Housekeeping: **Supp. 5**, 286; columns, **Supp. 7**, 427–28; **Supp. 8**, 328; founding of, **Vol. 7, Part 1**, 377
Goodhue, Bertram, references to, **Supp. 3**, 195–97; **Supp. 7**, 522
Good Humor company, **Supp. 9**, 246
Goodman, Benny, references to, **Supp. 3**, 690; **Supp. 5**, 293; **Supp. 8**, 163; **Supp. 9**, 474; **Supp. 10**, 299, 300, 373, 526
Goodman, Percival, reference to, **Supp. 9**, 326
Good Neighbor Committee, **Supp. 3**, 246
Goodnow, Frank J., reference to, **Supp. 3**, 11
Goodson, Mark, references to, **Supp. 9**, 719; **Supp. 10**, 789, 790
Goodson-Todman Productions, **Supp. 9**, 719, 720; **Supp. 10**, 789–90
Good Templars. *See* International Order of Good Templars
Good Will Fund, Inc., organization of, **Supp. 2**, 184
Goodwin, William A. R., reference to, **Supp. 6**, 549
"Goodwin, Archie" (fictional character), **Supp. 9**, 772, 773
Goodyear, Charles, reference to, **Vol. 4, Part 2**, 466
Goodyear Tire and Rubber Co., **Supp. 6**, 380–81; founding of, **Supp. 5**, 617–18
Gordin, Jacob, reference to, **Supp. 6**, 566
"Gordon, Flash" (fictional character), **Supp. 6**, 530, 531
Gordon, Max, reference to, **Supp. 9**, 203
Gordon, Ruth, reference to, **Supp. 10**, 311
Gordon Rest, established for working women, **Vol. 1, Part 2**, 471
Gore, Albert, reference to, **Supp. 6**, 419
Gore, Robert, reference to, **Supp. 10**, 565
Gorgas, William C., references to, **Vol. 9, Part 1**, 124; **Supp. 1**, 543; **Supp. 3**, 736
Gorgas Memorial Institute of Tropical and Preventive Medicine, founding of, **Supp. 1**, 543
Gorham, Nathaniel, reference to, **Vol. 7, Part 2**, 531
Gorillas: first brought to America, **Vol. 3, Part 1**, 475 f.; first moving pictures of, **Vol. 1, Part 1**, 133; study of, **Vol. 8, Part 2**, 391
Gorrell, Leslie, reference to, **Supp. 9**, 275
"Gortonites," **Vol. 4, Part 1**, 439
Gosden, Freeman, "Amos 'n' Andy" program, **Supp. 9**, 197–98
Goslin, Leon ("Goose"), reference to, **Supp. 9**, 653
Gosnold, Bartholomew, reference to, **Vol. 2, Part 1**, 39
Gospel Singers Convention, **Supp. 7**, 769
Gospel-Spreading Association, **Supp. 8**, 434
Gospel Visitant, founding of, **Vol. 1, Part 1**, 558
Goss and De Leeuw Machine Co., **Supp. 3**, 224
Gothic architecture, **Supp. 1**, 480; **Supp. 3**, 195–97
Gottheil, Richard, reference to, **Supp. 4**, 905
Göttingen, University of, physics studies, **Supp. 7**, 258–59
Gottlieb, Adolph, reference to, **Supp. 5**, 693; **Supp. 8**, 467, 553
Goucher College: **Vol. 4, Part 1**, 443; English literature studies, **Supp. 10**, 846
Goudsmit, Samuel A., reference to, **Supp. 5**, 496
Goudy, Frederic W., reference to, **Supp. 6**, 185
Gould, Jay, references to, **Vol. 1, Part 1**, 50, 255; **Vol. 3, Part 1**, 348; **Vol. 3, Part 2**, 4; **Vol. 5, Part 2**, 283; **Vol. 7, Part 1**, 175 f.; **Vol. 9, Part 1**, 52, 588; **Vol. 10, Part 1**, 81
Gourmet, **Supp. 6**, 165
Gournia, discovery of, **Supp. 3**, 344
Goursat, Edouard, reference to, **Supp. 3**, 86
Gout, diagnosis and treatment, **Supp. 7**, 340
Gouzenko, Igor, references to, **Supp. 7**, 114; **Supp. 8**, 497
Government: business, regulation of, **Vol. 2, Part 1**, 16, 249; **Vol. 4, Part 2**, 104; business relationship, **Supp. 2**, 31; centralization of, opposed, **Vol. 3, Part 1**, 289; contracts for army supplies (1755), **Vol. 6, Part 1**, 316; contracts for cannon and shot (1812), **Vol. 3, Part 2**, 573; council-manager plan, **Supp. 10**, 122; credit and Revolutionary paper securities, **Vol. 8, Part 2**, 314; economics as tool in, **Supp. 5**, 247; executive branch reorganization, **Supp. 6**, 692; finances, **Vol. 8, Part 2**, 6; **Supp. 10**, 215; first woman cabinet member, **Supp. 7**, 609–10; influence-peddling investigation, **Supp. 5**, 307; insurance investigations, **Vol. 8, Part 2**, 96; land office, **Vol. 9, Part 1**, 435; lands, development of, **Vol. 3, Part 2**, 110 f.; legislative malapportionment, reform of, **Supp. 10**, 122; municipal, **Supp. 6**, 467–68; municipal, writings on, **Supp. 6**, 467–68; **Supp. 9**, 705; philosophy of, **Vol. 2, Part 1**, 418; planned v. free economy theories, **Supp. 6**, 494–95; pressure groups, **Supp. 6**, 54; progressive movement view of, **Supp. 6**, 541–42; public administration and public policy, **Supp. 3**, 178; **Supp. 6**, 692–93; "pure" scientific research sponsorship, **Supp. 8**, 687; regulatory agencies, **Supp. 6**, 484; theocratic in New Haven colony, **Vol. 3, Part 1**, 612; women in, **Supp. 9**, 625, 789–90. *See also* Government employees; Municipal government; Political science; Politics; World-government movements
Government and religion. *See* Church-state separation
Government employees: black equal opportunity, **Supp. 4**, 493; **Supp. 5**, 343; bureaucratic jargon reform, **Supp. 5**, 481; cutbacks, **Supp. 8**, 300; diplomatic service merit system, **Supp. 3**, 139; first career postmaster general, **Supp. 8**, 134; first U.S. officer convicted, **Supp. 3**, 259–60; historical study of, **Supp. 6**, 693; loyalty issues, **Supp. 5**, 410, 479, 564, 665, 676; **Supp. 7**, 52, 114; **Supp. 8**, 57; patronage, **Supp. 2**, 399; political activity restraints, **Supp. 3**, 707; **Supp. 6**, 602; **Supp. 7**, 326–27; status improvement, **Supp. 6**, 692–93; studies on administration, **Supp. 2**, 251; unionization, **Supp. 6**, 586
Governors. *See state names;* for complete list, *see* Occupations Index
Governors Island (New York City), fortifications on, **Vol. 2, Part 2**, 222
Gower and Bell (dance team), **Supp. 10**, 113
"Go west, young man," origin of phrase, **Vol. 4, Part 1**, 531
Grabiner, Harry, references to, **Supp. 6**, 120, 121
Grace (Princess of Monaco). *See* Kelly, Grace (Princess of Monaco)
Grace, Eugene, reference to, **Supp. 9**, 402
Grace, W. R., Co., **Supp. 9**, 874
Grace Institute, founding of, **Vol. 4, Part 1**, 463

Graduate Education: A Critique and a Program, **Supp. 8**, 73
Graceland (Memphis, Tenn.), **Supp. 10**, 649, 650
Grady, Henry W., reference to, **Vol. 5, Part 1**, 302
Graham, Bessie, reference to, **Supp. 9**, 738
Graham, Billy: biography of, **Supp. 7**, 346; reference to, **Supp. 6**, 541; **Supp. 10**, 818
Graham, Evarts A., references to, **Supp. 6**, 189, 190
Graham, Frank P., reference to, **Supp. 6**, 569
Graham, Isabella Marshall, reference to, **Vol. 8, Part 2**, 596
Graham, John, reference to, **Supp. 6**, 512
Graham, Katharine Meyer, references to, **Supp. 6**, 452; **Supp. 7**, 295, 296; **Supp. 8**, 433
Graham, Martha, references to, **Supp. 6**, 312; **Supp. 7**, 366
Graham, Philip L., reference to, **Supp. 6**, 453; **Supp. 10**, 25
Graham, Sylvester, reference to, **Supp. 5**,
"Grahamism." **Vol. 4, Part 1**, 480
Graham's Lady's and Gentlewoman's Magazine, **Vol. 5, Part 2**, 159; **Vol. 8, Part 1**, 19 f.
Grain: binder, invention of, **Vol. 1, Part 1**, 325; center, St. Louis as, **Vol. 7, Part 2**, 62; Corporation, United States, **Vol. 6, Part 1**, 275; **Supp. 6**, 36–37; elevators, **Vol. 3, Part 1**, 48, 506 f.; export, **Vol. 3, Part 1**, 429; **Vol. 7, Part 2**, 62; market, Buffalo, N.Y., as a, **Vol. 3, Part 1**, 506 f.; milling, **Vol. 3, Part 2**, 51; reaper, **Vol. 5, Part 1**, 431; rust, **Vol. 8, Part 1**, 239 f.; speculation, **Vol. 1, Part 1**, 347, 476; **Vol. 7, Part 2**, 297 f., 605; **Vol. 8, Part 1**, 435; strain breeding, **Supp. 4**, 699
Grammar: scholarship in, **Supp. 4**, 202; study of, **Vol. 1, Part 2**, 274; **Vol. 2, Part 1**, 237; **Vol. 5, Part 2**, 175; **Vol. 7, Part 1**, 365; **Vol. 7, Part 2**, 117; **Supp. 10**, 35–37
"Grammatical mirror," invention of, **Vol. 3, Part 1**, 538
Gramophone. *See* Phonograph
Grand Army of the Republic: **Vol. 1, Part 1**, 180; **Vol. 3, Part 1**, 348; **Vol. 3, Part 2**, 254; **Vol. 6, Part 1**, 364; **Vol. 8, Part 2**, 47; first commander, **Vol. 5, Part 1**, 426; founding of, **Vol. 3, Part 2**, 556; **Vol. 9, Part 1**, 582; organization of, **Vol. 6, Part 1**, 364
Grand Canyon: **Supp. 4**, 218, 558; books on, **Vol. 5, Part 1**, 577; discovery of, **Vol. 2, Part 1**, 486; exploration of, **Vol. 7, Part 2**, 603; **Vol. 8, Part 1**, 146 f.
Grand Canyon Suite, **Supp. 9**, 340
Grand Central Terminal (New York City): electric lines, **Supp. 2**, 232; reconstruction, **Supp. 1**, 574
Grand Coulee Dam (Washington State), **Supp. 10**, 180
"Grand Depot," name applied to Wanamaker's N.Y. store, **Vol. 10, Part 1**, 407 f.
Grand Hotel, **Supp. 10**, 733
Grandma's Boy, **Supp. 9**, 509
"Grand Ole Opry," **Supp. 5**, 749
Grand Rapids Herald, **Supp. 5**, 702, 705
Grand Teton National Park, **Supp. 10**, 120
Grand Trunk Railway of Canada, **Vol. 8, Part 1**, 71 f.
Grange, Harold ("Red"), reference to, **Supp. 6**, 728; **Supp. 10**, 585
Granger cases, **Vol. 3, Part 1**, 330
Granger movement, **Vol. 1, Part 1**, 56; **Vol. 2, Part 1**, 43; **Vol. 3, Part 1**, 109; **Vol. 3, Part 2**, 108; **Vol. 5, Part 2**, 298 f.; **Vol. 6, Part 2**, 463; **Supp. 4**, 340–41; **Supp. 8**, 468
Granite City, Ill., founding of, **Vol. 7, Part 1**, 518
Grant, Cary, references to, **Supp. 10**, 367, 829
Grant, Elihu, reference to, **Supp. 3**, 272
Grant, Madison, references to, **Supp. 3**, 520, 632
Grant, Robert, reference to, **Supp. 3**, 473
Grant, Ulysses S.: **Vol. 1, Part 1**, 134; **Vol. 1, Part 2**, 464; **Vol. 2, Part 2**, 477; **Vol. 3, Part 2**, 998 f.; **Vol. 4, Part 1**, 493 f.; **Vol. 4, Part 2**, 221 f.; **Vol. 5, Part 1**, 126; **Vol. 6, Part 1**, 126 f., 253 f., 597 f.; **Vol. 7, Part 2**, 219; **Vol. 8, Part 2**, 571; **Vol. 9, Part 1**, 94, 132, 323, 363; **Vol. 9, Part 2**, 253; **Vol. 10, Part 1**, 504 f.; appointments, of, **Vol. 3, Part 1**, 609; **Vol. 5, Part 1**, 86; biography of, **Supp. 10**, 108; election of, **Vol. 9, Part 1**, 9; Hamer's service to, **Vol. 4, Part 2**, 170; memorial to, **Vol. 4, Part 1**, 501; **Vol. 8, Part 1**, 92 f.; **Vol. 9, Part 1**, 133; **Vol. 9, Part 2**, 15; most influential adviser to, during Civil War, **Vol. 8, Part 1**, 402 f.; *Personal Memoirs*, **Vol. 4, Part 1**, 501; reference to, **Supp. 4**, 490; reports on competence of, **Vol. 3, Part 1**, 50 f.; Sherman, relations with, **Vol. 9, Part 1**, 96 f.
Grant, W. T., Co., **Supp. 9**, 336–37
Grant, Zilpah, reference to, **Vol. 6, Part 1**, 531
"Grant Guard," **Vol. 3, Part 2**, 453
Granz, Norman, reference to, **Supp. 6**, 620
Grape culture, **Vol. 1, Part 1**, 109; **Vol. 2, Part 1**, 251, 453; **Vol. 3, Part 1**, 491 f.; **Vol. 5, Part 1**, 430; **Vol. 5, Part 2**, 111; **Vol. 6, Part 1**, 394; **Vol. 7, Part 1**, 335; **Vol. 8, Part 1**, 233 f.; **Vol. 8, Part 2**, 93
Grapes of Wrath, The, **Supp. 8**, 117, 625, 626; **Supp. 10**, 244
Graphic arts. *See* Illustration; Typographical design
Graphite, discovery of uses for, **Vol. 3, Part 1**, 329
Grasselli Chemical Co., **Vol. 4, Part 1**, 502
Grasses, study of, **Supp. 7**, 119–20
Grasso, Ella T., reference to, **Supp. 9**, 59
Grattan, C. Hartley, reference to, **Supp. 8**, 441
Gratz College, first Jewish teachers college in America, **Vol. 3, Part 1**, 459 f.
Graves, Robert, reference to, **Supp. 9**, 643
Gravity: studies on, **Supp. 1**, 130; theory of, **Supp. 5**, 203
Gray, Asa, references to, **Vol. 3, Part 2**, 274 f.; **Vol. 6, Part 1**, 162; **Vol. 8, Part 2**, 354; **Vol. 9, Part 2**, 597; **Vol. 10, Part 1**, 547 f.
Gray, Horace, reference to, **Supp. 3**, 94
Gray, John S., reference to, **Supp. 4**, 294
Gray, L. C., reference to, **Supp. 4**, 45
Gray, William, reference to, **Vol. 1, Part 2**, 52
Graybar Electric Co., **Supp. 8**, 211
Gray-Bell controversy, vol. 4, Part 1, 514
Gray Herbarium, **Supp. 1**, 632; **Supp. 4**, 266
Gray Ladies, founding of, **Supp. 4**, 93
Graymoor. *See* Society of the Atonement
Gray's Manual of Botany, **Supp. 4**, 266
Grayson, Cary, reference to, **Supp. 6**, 413
Grayson, David (pseudonym), **Supp. 4**, 47
Great Atlantic and Pacific Tea Co.: **Supp. 6**, 90–91; **Supp. 10**, 738; founding of, **Supp. 5**, 277–78
"Great Awakening," **Vol. 3, Part 2**, 391; **Vol. 4, Part 1**, 17; **Vol. 7, Part 1**, 614; **Vol. 8, Part 2**, 545; **Vol. 9, Part 2**, 367
Great Books studies, **Supp. 5**, 211–12; **Supp. 8**, 59
Great Britain: *Alabama* and, **Vol. 5, Part 2**, 114; American cataloguing code, **Supp. 3**, 327; American distrust of, **Supp. 6**, 361, 614; American fishermen in Canadian waters, **Vol. 8, Part 1**, 285 f.; American Revolution studies, **Supp. 3**, 15–16; **Supp. 9**, 315; antislavery interests, **Vol. 4, Part 2**, 564; armed forces and defense, **Supp. 3**, 166; atomic bomb project, **Supp. 8**, 230; Confederate relations with, **Vol. 1, Part 1**, 43; **Vol. 6, Part 2**, 240, 365; **Vol. 10, Part 2**, 267; controversy with, on Civil War commerce, **Vol. 3, Part 2**, 398; diplomacy during U.S. Civil War, **Supp. 1**, 9; diplomacy with, **Vol. 1, Part 1**, 85, 567; **Vol. 1, Part 2**, 327; **Vol. 3, Part 1**, 39, 134; **Vol. 5, Part 2**, 7 f., 8 f., 398, 403, 566; **Vol. 6, Part 1**, 4, 463; **Vol. 6, Part 2**, 114; **Vol. 7, Part 1**, 150, 286; **Vol. 7, Part 2**, 143, 528, 587, 618; 627; **Vol. 8, Part**

1, 353 f., 485; **Vol. 8, Part 2**, 232; 245; **Vol. 9, Part 2**, 484; **Vol. 10, Part 1**, 136, 154; **Vol. 10, Part 2**, 102; **Supp. 3**, 366; **Supp. 4**, 900; **Supp. 5**, 155, 160; **Supp. 7**, 437–38; **Supp. 8**, 320–21; **Supp. 9**, 244; educational system, **Supp. 4**, 880; Elizabethan history, **Supp. 6**, 531–32; **Supp. 9**, 627; ethical culture movement in, **Supp. 3**, 175–76; expatriates in, **Supp. 4**, 755–56; **Supp. 6**, 101–2; historical writings on, **Supp. 8**, 472–73; law, collections of, **Supp. 1**, 154; Massachusetts Colony, relations with, **Vol. 6, Part 2**, 391 f.; **Vol. 10, Part 2**, 412; Mohawk Indians, relations with, **Vol. 4, Part 2**, 532; printing of first penny postage stamps in, **Vol. 7, Part 2**, 472; oil dispute with Iran, **Supp. 8**, 276; Russian agreement on Persia, **Supp. 6**, 579; theater, **Supp. 8**, 21–22; trade with U.S., **Supp. 2**, 39; **Supp. 8**, 90; woman suffrage movement, **Supp. 5**, 473. *See also* Suez crisis (1956); World War I; World War II

Great Chain of Being, The, **Supp. 7**, 482

Great Depression: art reflecting, **Supp. 5**, 580; banking crisis, **Supp. 5**, 158, 469–70; **Supp. 6**, 33–34; bonus army, **Supp. 5**, 502; **Supp. 6**, 239–40; **Supp. 7**, 488; Detroit relief measures, **Supp. 4**, 611–12; economic program to end, **Supp. 10**, 795; economic views of, **Supp. 4**, 36; **Supp. 9**, 466; federal intervention advocacy, **Supp. 5**, 403; Glass-Steagall Act, **Supp. 3**, 730; Hoover policies, **Supp. 7**, 362–63; impact on agriculture, **Supp. 7**, 361, 760–61; journalistic analysis of, **Supp. 4**, 704; National Business Survey Conference, **Supp. 6**, 37; photographic documentation of, **Supp. 7**, 456; **Supp. 8**, 586; **Supp. 9**, 268; public relations to counter, **Supp. 5**, 304; **Supp. 6**, 90; relief programs, **Supp. 6**, 103; religious interpretation of, **Supp. 7**, 761; Roosevelt, F. D., policies, **Supp. 3**, 647–58; social legislation, **Supp. 6**, 378–79; sociological surveys in, **Supp. 6**, 605; Stage Relief Fund, **Supp. 6**, 133; unemployment economics, **Supp. 6**, 708–9; wealth during, **Supp. 5**, 550. *See also* New Deal; Welfare

Great Dictator, The, **Supp. 10**, 117

Great Eastern: laying of cable by, **Vol. 5, Part 2**, 566; repairing of, while afloat, **Vol. 8, Part 1**, 505

Great Escape, The, **Supp. 10**, 501

Greater New York Racing Association, **Supp. 8**, 76

Greatest Show on Earth, The, **Supp. 10**, 407

Greatest Story Ever Told, The, **Supp. 5**, 528

Great Frontier, The, **Supp. 7**, 771

Great Gatsby, The, **Supp. 2**, 189, 190

Great Kanawa, battle of. *See* Point Pleasant, battle of

Great Lakes: exploration of, **Vol. 2, Part 1**, 183, 606; **Vol. 5, Part 2**, 156 f.; **Vol. 6, Part 2**, 295; glacial history, **Supp. 2**, 654; lunar tides on, **Vol. 4, Part 1**, 476; report on projected opening of, to ocean shipping, **Vol. 9, Part 2**, 260; shipbuilding, **Vol. 5, Part 2**, 110, 120; shipping on, **Vol. 6, Part 1**, 327; **Vol. 6, Part 2**, 23; **Vol. 7, Part 1**, 472; strategic importance of, for the British against the French, **Vol. 8, Part 1**, 161 f.; survey of, **Vol. 8, Part 2**, 52

Great Lakes Steel Corporation, **Supp. 6**, 678

Great London Circus, **Supp. 10**, 406

Great Northern Railroad: **Vol. 3, Part 1**, 183; **Vol. 5, Part 1**, 37 f.; **Vol. 5, Part 2**, 498; **Supp. 7**, 89–90; Pacific extension construction, **Supp. 3**, 735, 736

Great Plains, The, **Supp. 7**, 771

Great Salt Lake: steamboat, first on, **Vol. 2, Part 2**, 353; white man, first to visit, **Vol. 8, Part 1**, 250 f.

"Great Seal War" (New Jersey), **Vol. 3, Part 1**, 290

Great Southern Lumber Co., **Supp. 7**, 293

Great Train Robbery, The, **Supp. 3**, 607

Great Wallendas (circus act), **Supp. 10**, 809, 810

Great Western, early steamship, **Vol. 9, Part 1**, 315

Greco-Turkish War, refugee resettlement, **Supp. 4**, 604

Greece: ancient coins collection, **Supp. 3**, 551; ancient slave system, **Supp. 5**, 736; archaeology in, **Vol. 3, Part 1**, 594 f.; **Vol. 8, Part 1**, 574; **Supp. 3**, 705; classical studies, **Supp. 1**, 24, 657, 701; **Supp. 2**, 621, 701; **Supp. 7**, 313–14, 388; **Supp. 10**, 334; classical studies, American School, **Supp. 4**, 143–44; classical studies, Loeb Classical Library, **Supp. 1**, 503; diplomatic relations with, **Vol. 5, Part 1**, 548; **Vol. 5, Part 2**, 396; **Vol. 8, Part 1**, 428 f.; **Vol. 8, Part 2**, 77; **Supp. 6**, 245; expeditions to aid Greek patriots, **Vol. 8, Part 2**, 238; historical writings on, **Supp. 5**, 595–96; independence from Turkey, **Vol. 5, Part 1**, 296, 312; Kallinean Free Schools, **Vol. 1, Part 1**, 261; Marshall Plan, **Supp. 6**, 431; missions in, **Vol. 1, Part 2**, 187; **Vol. 5, Part 1**, 41 f. *See also* Greco-Turkish War; Greek

Greed, **Supp. 6**, 657

Greek: art, **Vol. 4, Part 2**, 166; drama studies, **Supp. 4**, 143; Homeric studies, **Supp. 4**, 728–29; music, **Vol. 1, Part 1**, 189; plays, production of, **Vol. 8, Part 1**, 592; scholarship, **Vol. 3, Part 1**, 372; **Vol. 5, Part 2**, 328; **Vol. 9, Part 2**, 576 f.; teaching of, **Vol. 6, Part 1**, 72; **Vol. 7, Part 1**, 584; **Vol. 9, Part 1**, 398, 449, 594; **Vol. 10, Part 1**, 99; **Vol. 10, Part 2**, 556, 567; translations, **Vol. 5, Part 2**, 287; **Vol. 6, Part 1**, 229; **Vol. 10, Part 2**, 519; **Supp. 8**, 236; vases, **Vol. 5, Part 1**, 227; writings on, **Vol. 4, Part 1**, 412; **Vol. 9, Part 1**, 398; **Vol. 10, Part 2**, 113, 556

Greek-Americans, Panhellenism, **Supp. 7**, 702

Greek Catholics, protection in the U.S., **Vol. 7, Part 2**, 66

Greek Orthodox Church in America, **Supp. 7**, 102; **Supp. 9**, 50–51

Greek Revival architecture, **Vol. 6, Part 1**, 20 f.; **Vol. 8, Part 2**, 99; **Vol. 9, Part 2**, 137 f.; **Vol. 10, Part 1**, 487 f.; **Supp. 6**, 272

Greek Way, The, **Supp. 7**, 313

Greeley, A. W., references to, **Vol. 1, Part 2**, 256; **Vol. 7, Part 2**, 323; **Vol. 8, Part 2**, 438

Greeley, Horace: **Vol. 4, Part 2**, 4; **Vol. 5, Part 2**, 112, 260; **Vol. 6, Part 2**, 36; **Vol. 7, Part 1**, 205; **Vol. 8, Part 1**, 408 f., 483; **Vol. 8, Part 2**, 468 f.; **Vol. 9, Part 2**, 314, 403; Lincoln's letter to, **Vol. 6, Part 1**, 256; political influence of, **Vol. 8, Part 1**, 408 f.; writings on, **Supp. 3**, 672

Greeley, William B., reference to, **Supp. 3**, 7

Greeley arctic expedition. *See* Exploration, arctic

Green, Adolph, reference to, **Supp. 7**, 354

Green, Hetty, father of, **Vol. 8, Part 2**, 41 f.

Green, Paul, references to, **Supp. 3**, 427; **Supp. 5**, 419; **Supp. 6**, 716

Green, William, references to, **Vol. 3, Part 1**, 510; **Supp. 5**, 654; **Supp. 6**, 615, 706

Greenback controversy: **Vol. 1, Part 1**, 510; **Vol. 1, Part 2**, 358; **Vol. 2, Part 1**, 359; **Vol. 2, Part 2**, 410; **Vol. 3, Part 2**, 129, 239, 518; **Vol. 4, Part 1**, 539; **Vol. 4, Part 2**, 103; **Vol. 7, Part 2**, 420; **Vol. 8, Part 1**, 53 f.; **Vol. 8, Part 2**, 36, 105, 150; **Vol. 9, Part 1**, 85; **Vol. 9, Part 2**, 640; **Supp. 4**, 585; **Supp. 5**, 138–40; "Father" of, **Vol. 5, Part 2**, 302

Green Bay Packers (football team), **Supp. 8**, 389–90; **Supp. 9**, 818; **Supp. 10**, 351, 728; founding of, **Supp. 7**, 451–52

Green Berets, **Supp. 7**, 422

Green Berets, The, (movie), **Supp. 10**, 823

Greenberg, Clement, references to, **Supp. 6**, 512–13; **Supp. 7**, 480

Greenberg, Joanne, reference to, **Supp. 6**, 220

Greene, Edward L., reference to, **Supp. 4**, 428

Greene, John Morton, reference to, **Vol. 9, Part 1**, 347

Greene, Nathaniel, references to, **Vol. 4, Part 1**, 568; **Vol. 7, Part 2**, 518

Greene, William, references to, **Supp. 3**, 259; **Supp. 8**, 420
Greeneville, Tenn., **Vol. 1, Part 2**, 63; **Vol. 4, Part 1**, 287
Greenfield Village (Mich.), **Supp. 4**, 302
Greenglass, David: references to, **Supp. 5**, 588–90; **Supp. 10**, 10, 719; trial of, **Supp. 9**, 321
Greenglass, Ruth, reference to, **Supp. 5**, 589
Green Hat, The, **Supp. 6**, 20
"Green Hornet, The" (radio program), **Supp. 10**, 343
"Green Hornet, The" (television program), **Supp. 9**, 486, 487
Greenland exploration, **Vol. 1, Part 2**, 194; **Vol. 6, Part 1**, 342; **Vol. 9, Part 2**, 308; **Supp. 5**, 539, 540; **Supp. 6**, 92, 93
Greenlee, Gus, reference to, **Supp. 9**, 493
Greenman, Milton J., reference to, **Supp. 3**, 172
Green Mountain Boys, **Vol. 1, Part 1**, 523; **Vol. 9, Part 2**, 454
Green Mountains, geological researches in, **Vol. 8, Part 1**, 264 f.
Greenough, James B., reference to, **Supp. 3**, 424
Green Pastures, The, **Supp. 4**, 102; **Supp. 10**, 147
Green River, exploration of, **Vol. 8, Part 1**, 146 f.
Greenspan, Solomon, reference to, **Supp. 6**, 632
Greenstreet, Sidney, reference to, **Supp. 7**, 479
Greenville, Treaty of, **Vol. 6, Part 1**, 300; **Vol. 10, Part 1**, 565; **Vol. 10, Part 2**, 22, 644
Greenville College, presidency of, **Vol. 5, Part 1**, 123
Green Wall, The, **Supp. 10**, 854
Greenwich House (New York City), **Supp. 5**, 630–31
Greenwich Village (New York City): folk music scene, **Supp. 10**, 602; migration of New York artists to, **Vol. 1, Part 2**, 396; origin of, **Vol. 10, Part 1**, 485 f.
Gregg, John Robert, reference to, **Supp. 8**, 546
Gregory, Clifford V., reference to, **Supp. 4**, 132
Gregory, Elinor, reference to, **Supp. 6**, 307
Gregory, Paul, reference to, **Supp. 7**, 461
Gregory of Nyssa, reference to, **Supp. 7**, 388
Grenfell, W. T., reference to, **Vol. 7, Part 1**, 104
Gresham, Walter Q., reference to, **Supp. 3**, 346
Greve, William M., reference to, **Supp. 6**, 337
Grew, Joseph C., references to, **Supp. 6**, 269, 358
Greyhound Corporation, **Supp. 9**, 388, 389
Grey's conspiracy (Ga.), **Vol. 8, Part 1**, 518
"Gridley, you may fire when you are ready," origin of phrase, **Vol. 4, Part 1**, 610
Griffin, Chris, reference to, **Supp. 8**, 163
Griffin, Winthrop's arrival at Boston on, **Vol. 6, Part 1**, 425
Griffith, Clark, references to, **Supp. 9**, 653, 654; **Supp. 10**, 314
Griffith, D. W., references to, **Supp. 3**, 73–74, 76; **Supp. 4**, 235; **Supp. 5**, 44, 630; **Supp. 6**, 619, 657, 659; **Supp. 7**, 32; **Supp. 8**, 214; **Supp. 9**, 205, 286, 791; **Supp. 10**, 634, 635, 810, 811, 871
Griffith Stadium (Washington, D.C.), **Supp. 8**, 434
Griffon, LaSalle's ship, **Vol. 6, Part 1**, 11; **Vol. 9, Part 2**, 587
Griggs, Edward Howard, reference to, **Supp. 7**, 374
Griggs, Baldwin & Baldwin, **Supp. 3**, 180
Grindstone, manufacturing of, **Vol. 1, Part 1**, 535
Grinnell, George Bird, reference to, **Supp. 5**, 148
Grinnell, Henry, reference to, **Vol. 3, Part 1**, 201
Grinnell College (Iowa), **Vol. 4, Part 2**, 4; **Vol. 6, Part 2**, 176, 202; presidency, **Supp. 1**, 538
Grinnell Land, discovery of, **Vol. 3, Part 1**, 200 f.
Griswold, Erwin, reference to, **Supp. 9**, 594
Griswold, Roger, reference to, **Vol. 6, Part 1**, 533
Griswold, Rufus W., references to, **Vol. 7, Part 2**, 77; **Vol. 9, Part 2**, 314
Griswold v. *Connecticut,* **Supp. 9**, 97, 837
Groat, Dick, reference to, **Supp. 10**, 574
Grocery industry: automated, **Supp. 5**, 604; chains, **Supp. 2**, 367; **Supp. 5**, 277–78, 603–4; **Supp. 10**, 738; financing of, **Supp. 6**, 448–49; supermarket chains, **Supp. 7**, 141–42
Groddeck, Georg, reference to, **Supp. 6**, 220
Grofé, Ferde, reference to, **Supp. 8**, 697–98
Grolier Club: **Vol. 1, Part 1**, 299; **Vol. 4, Part 1**, 294; **Vol. 5, Part 2**, 411; founding of, **Vol. 3, Part 1**, 264; **Vol. 5, Part 1**, 106
Grolier Enterprises, Inc., **Supp. 10**, 821
Gropius, Walter, references to, **Supp. 6**, 199; **Supp. 7**, 800
Gross, Harry, reference to, **Supp. 7**, 586
Gross, Robert, reference to, **Supp. 9**, 758
Gross, Robert E., reference to, **Supp. 6**, 221
Gross, Samuel D., sculpture of, **Supp. 3**, 123
Grossett & Dunlap, founding of, **Supp. 1**, 362
Grossinger's Hotel and Country Club, **Supp. 9**, 342–44
Gross national product (GNP), theory of, **Supp. 4**, 585
Grosz, Georg, reference to, **Supp. 6**, 552; **Supp. 7**, 436
Groton, Mass., **Vol. 1, Part 2**, 489; **Vol. 4, Part 1**, 556
Groton Academy, **Vol. 6, Part 1**, 44 f., 52; **Vol. 8, Part 1**, 194 f.
Groton School, founding of, **Supp. 3**, 591–92
Group: analysis and therapy, **Supp. 4**, 130–31; behavior studies, **Supp. 4**, 565; dynamics studies, **Supp. 4**, 485, 831–32; encounter psychotherapy, **Supp. 8**, 424; social work theory on, **Supp. 7**, 151–52; therapy to combat anti-Semitism, **Supp. 8**, 307
Group for the Advancement of Psychiatry, founding of, **Supp. 8**, 430
Group f64 (photography), **Supp. 6**, 685; **Supp. 10**, 398; founding of, **Supp. 10**, 162
Group Health Association of Washington, **Supp. 3**, 122
Group Theatre (New York City), **Supp. 5**, 237; founding of, **Supp. 7**, 583; **Supp. 10**, 129; influence of, **Supp. 9**, 188–89; leftist sympathies of, **Supp. 10**, 131
Grove, Robert ("Lefty"), reference to, **Supp. 6**, 415
Groves, Leslie R., references to, **Supp. 4**, 453–54; **Supp. 7**, 732; **Supp. 10**, 144
Groveton, Va., battle of. *See* Bull Run, second battle of
Growing Up Absurd, **Supp. 9**, 325
Growth: human heredity v. environment, **Supp. 3**, 84; human malnutrition studies, **Supp. 4**, 420; studies of child, **Supp. 2**, 665–66
Growth of the American Republic, The, **Supp. 10**, 553
Gruening, Ernest L., reference to, **Supp. 8**, 26
Grundy, Joseph R., references to, **Supp. 7**, 607; **Supp. 8**, 143
Grunewald, Henry W., reference to, **Supp. 7**, 73
Guadalcanal, World War II action, **Supp. 3**, 450; **Supp. 4**, 147, 323; **Supp. 5**, 621; **Supp. 6**, 267–68; **Supp. 7**, 352, 750
Guadalcanal Diary, **Supp. 9**, 189
Guadalupe Hidalgo, Treaty of (1848), **Vol. 2, Part 1**, 417; **Vol. 2, Part 2**, 217; **Vol. 8, Part 1**, 38; **Vol. 8, Part 2**, 509, 602; **Vol. 9, Part 2**, 646
Guaranty Trust Co., **Vol. 7, Part 1**, 259; **Supp. 7**, 715, 783
Guardian Society for Preventing Drunkenness, **Vol. 6, Part 2**, 597
Guard of Honor, **Supp. 10**, 153
Guatemala: diplomacy with U.S., **Supp. 8**, 495; ornithology study, **Supp. 6**, 255
Guequier, Jules, reference to, **Supp. 3**, 25
Guernica (painting), **Supp. 6**, 512
Guernsey cattle, raising of, **Vol. 7, Part 1**, 72
Guerrière, **Vol. 5, Part 1**, 361; **Vol. 9, Part 1**, 136
"Guerrillas," in Kansas and Missouri, **Vol. 8, Part 1**, 294 f.

Guffey, Joseph F., references to, **Supp. 3**, 20; **Supp. 9**, 253, 254
Guffey-Vincent Act (1937), **Supp. 6**, 260
Guggenheim, Daniel: Foundation for the Promotion of Aeronautics, founding of, **Supp. 8**, 439; **Supp. 9**, 348; references to, **Supp. 3**, 307, 321; **Supp. 6**, 182, 183, 242, 606
Guggenheim, Edmond, references to, **Supp. 6**, 606, 607
Guggenheim, Gladys Eleanor, reference to, **Supp. 6**, 606
Guggenheim, Harry, references to, **Supp. 3**, 307; **Supp. 6**, 182, 606; **Supp. 7**, 603
Guggenheim, Murray, reference to, **Supp. 6**, 242
Guggenheim, Peggy: art gallery, **Supp. 6**, 512; **Supp. 10**, 294–95, 758; reference to, **Supp. 10**, 220
Guggenheim, Simon, reference to, **Supp. 6**, 606
Guggenheim, Solomon R., reference to, **Supp. 6**, 715
Guggenheim, Solomon R., Foundation: art collection, **Supp. 10**, 295; founding of, **Supp. 4**, 352; presidency of, **Supp. 9**, 348
Guggenheim fellowships, **Supp. 3**, 322
Guggenheim Memorial Foundation, founding of, **Supp. 3**, 321–22
Guggenheim Museum (New York City): design and building of, **Supp. 4**, 352; **Supp. 9**, 348; Wright design, **Supp. 6**, 715
Guidebooks, travel, **Supp. 6**, 291–92
Guideposts, **Supp. 5**, 527
Guide to the Archives of the Government of the United States in Washington, **Supp. 8**, 369
Guiler, Hugh Parker, references to, **Supp. 10**, 590, 591
Guilford, Conn., colony at, **Vol. 6, Part 1**, 138
Guilford College, founding of, **Vol. 5, Part 1**, 389
Guilford Court House, battle of, **Vol. 2, Part 1**, 465; **Vol. 4, Part 1**, 572; **Vol. 5, Part 2**, 107; **Vol. 7, Part 1**, 422
Guilmant, Alexandre, reference to, **Supp. 6**, 357
Guinzburg, Harold K., reference to, **Supp. 7**, 374
Guiteau, Charles J.: brain of, discussed, **Vol. 7, Part 1**, 268; trial of, for assassination of Garfield, **Vol. 3, Part 1**, 596
Guiterus, Juan, reference to, **Vol. 9, Part 1**, 591
Gulf Coast Oil Producers Association, **Supp. 3**, 260–61
Gulf of California, efforts to obtain a port on, **Vol. 8, Part 1**, 121 f.
Gulf of Tonkin Resolution. *See* Tonkin Gulf Resolution
Gulf Oil Corporation, founding of, **Supp. 4**, 568–69
Gulf Stream, opinions on course of, **Vol. 3, Part 1**, 394
Gulick, Luther Halsey, reference to, **Supp. 4**, 35
Gunboat fleet, construction of, **Vol. 3, Part 1**, 587 f.; **Vol. 3, Part 2**, 164; **Vol. 9, Part 2**, 7
Gun control, editorials for, **Supp. 10**, 25
Guncotton, discovery of, **Vol. 5, Part 1**, 536
"Gung ho!" (slogan), **Supp. 4**, 147
Gunnison Housing Corporation, **Supp. 7**, 308
Gunpowder: experiments with, **Vol. 3, Part 1**, 377; manufacture of, **Vol. 3, Part 1**, 526 f., 528; **Vol. 3, Part 2**, 220, 231; **Vol. 8, Part 1**, 329 f.
Guns: identification of, **Vol. 10, Part 1**, 584 f.; Gatling, **Vol. 4, Part 1**, 191; manufacture, **Vol. 4, Part 2**, 560; **Vol. 6, Part 1**, 51; **Vol. 7, Part 2**, 261; **Vol. 9, Part 1**, 282; **Vol. 10, Part 2**, 379; Maxim, **Vol. 6, Part 2**, 437; rapid-fire, **Vol. 8, Part 1**, 172 f.; repeating rifles, **Vol. 6, Part 1**, 51. *See also* Firearms
Gunther, John, reference to, **Supp. 9**, 718
Günzberg, Ilya, reference to, **Supp. 9**, 501
Gurdjieff, George I., references to, **Supp. 9**, 33, 34
Gurney, Elizabeth, reference to, **Vol. 8, Part 2**, 393
Gurney, Ronald W., reference to, **Supp. 8**, 199
Gurney, Samuel, reference to, **Vol. 5, Part 1**, 389
Gustavus Adolphus College, founding of, **Vol. 7, Part 1**, 550
Guston, Philip, reference to, **Supp. 6**, 511
Gutenberg Bible, **Supp. 5**, 554, 587
Guthrie, Arlo, references to, **Supp. 8**, 234, 235
Guthrie, George W., reference to, **Vol. 6, Part 1**, 590
Guthrie Theatre (Minneapolis, Minn.), founding of, **Supp. 9**, 351
Guttmacher, Manfred, reference to, **Supp. 9**, 351–52
Guttman, Louis, reference to, **Supp. 6**, 605
Guyana, **Supp. 10**, 392
Guys and Dolls, **Supp. 4**, 708, 709; **Supp. 7**, 413, 658; **Supp. 8**, 386
Gymnastics. *See* Physical education
Gynecology: **Vol. 1, Part 2**, 55, 538; **Vol. 2, Part 1**, 380, 385; **Vol. 2, Part 2**, 14; **Vol. 3, Part 2**, 16, 160, 547; **Vol. 4, Part 1**, 291; **Vol. 4, Part 2**, 545; **Vol. 5, Part 2**, 276, 376, 580; **Vol. 6, Part 1**, 510, 615; **Vol. 6, Part 2**, 273, 551; **Vol. 7, Part 1**, 541; **Vol. 7, Part 2**, 96; **Vol. 8, Part 1**, 32, 44, 213 f.; **Vol. 8, Part 2**, 44; **Vol. 9, Part 1**, 186, 234; **Vol. 9, Part 2**, 95, 446; **Vol. 10, Part 2**, 280; birth control advocacy, **Supp. 4**, 231; **Supp. 9**, 352; cancer education, **Supp. 5**, 147; fallopian tube studies, **Supp. 6**, 555; infertility, **Supp. 6**, 555; instruments, **Supp. 1**, 437; journals, **Supp. 1**, 542; obstetrics as interdependent discipline, **Supp. 1**, 408; ovarian hormones, **Supp. 2**, 632; Pap test, **Supp. 7**, 598–99; pioneer work in, **Vol. 2, Part 1**, 380; **Vol. 3, Part 2**, 147; **Vol. 9, Part 1**, 195; surgery, **Supp. 1**, 542; teaching of, **Vol. 5, Part 1**, 526; **Vol. 7, Part 1**, 325; **Supp. 4**, 230–31; textbooks, **Supp. 1**, 352; writings on, **Supp. 3**, 763. *See also* Obstetrics; Reproductive system
Gynescope, **Vol. 9, Part 1**, 455; **Vol. 9, Part 1**, 455
Gypsy moth, study of, **Vol. 3, Part 2**, 335, 511
Gyroscope, **Supp. 5**, 228–29; **Supp. 7**, 576–77, 615

H

Haas, Robert, reference to, **Supp. 9**, 165
Habeas corpus, writ of, **Vol. 1, Part 2**, 422; **Vol. 5, Part 1**, 467
Haber, Joyce, reference to, **Supp. 10**, 726
Hackett, James K., reference to, **Vol. 10, Part 1**, 625; **Supp. 3**, 607
Hackley, E. Azalia, reference to, **Supp. 3**, 225
Hadassah, women's Zionist organization, **Supp. 3**, 756–57; founding of, **Supp. 8**, 549
Hadden, Briton, reference to, **Supp. 8**, 393
Haddonfield, N.J., founding of, **Vol. 3, Part 2**, 186
Hadley, Henry Kimball, reference to, **Supp. 7**, 651
Hagenow, C. F., reference to, **Supp. 7**, 134
Haggard, Howard Wilcox, reference to, **Supp. 3**, 353
Haggard, Wallace C., reference to, **Supp. 6**, 528
Hagia Sophia (Constantinople), **Supp. 4**, 890–91
Hague, Arnold, reference to, **Vol. 5, Part 1**, 457
Hague, Frank, references to, **Supp. 5**, 213; **Supp. 6**, 188, 479–80, 651; **Supp. 8**, 152–53; **Supp. 9**, 245, 455
Hague Congress of Women (1915), **Supp. 4**, 725
Hague Peace Conference, **Vol. 2, Part 2**, 85; **Vol. 7, Part 1**, 456; **Vol. 10, Part 2**, 91
Haida Indians, **Supp. 6**, 611
Hail Columbia, **Vol. 3, Part 2**, 568; **Vol. 5, Part 1**, 223
Hair: clipper, invention of, **Vol. 2, Part 2**, 238; color heredity, **Supp. 3**, 215; permanent wave development, **Supp. 5**, 512–13
Haiti: blacks, advocated as an asylum for southern, **Vol. 8, Part 1**, 444; diplomatic relations with, **Vol. 5, Part 2**, 597; Gendarmerie d'Haiti, **Supp. 9**, 630; historical opera, **Supp. 6**, 690; Holy See, relations with,

Vol. 8, Part 2, 156; Hoover Commission on conditions in, **Supp. 6**, 211; independence, U.S. recognition of, **Vol. 8, Part 1**, 444; missions, **Vol. 6, Part 1**, 95; public service, **Vol. 8, Part 2**, 382; U.S. presence in, **Supp. 2**, 81
Hakluyt, account of early voyages, **Vol. 2, Part 1**, 39
Halas, George, reference to, **Supp. 9**, 840
Haldane, J. S., reference to, **Supp. 3**, 353
Haldeman, Walter N., reference to, **Vol. 10, Part 1**, 552 f.
Hale, Edward Everett, reference to, **Vol. 7, Part 1**, 2
Hale, George Ellery, references to, **Supp. 3**, 262, 290–91, 634; **Supp. 4**, 675; **Supp. 5**, 495, 496; **Supp. 6**, 7, 8
Hale, Horatio, reference to, **Supp. 3**, 83
Hale, James W., reference to, **Vol. 10, Part 1**, 639 f.
Hale, Nathan, execution of, **Vol. 7, Part 1**, 102
Hale, Philip, reference to, **Supp. 5**, 353
Hale, William Gardner, reference to, **Supp. 4**, 67
Hale and Dorr, **Supp. 6**, 680
Hale Observatories (California), **Supp. 9**, 114
Hale telescope, **Supp. 9**, 114
Haley, Bill, references to, **Supp. 6**, 301; **Supp. 9**, 443
Haley and Crafts (song-and-dance team), **Supp. 10**, 300
"Half-breed," use of term, in politics, **Vol. 1, Part 2**, 324 f.; **Vol. 8, Part 1**, 4 f.; **Vol. 8, Part 2**, 6
Half Moon, **Vol. 5, Part 1**, 339
Half-tone screens for photoengraving, **Vol. 6, Part 1**, 203
Half-Way Covenant, **Vol. 3, Part 1**, 86 f.; **Vol. 7, Part 1**, 5 f.; **Vol. 9, Part 2**, 59
Halifax, Nova Scotia: consular service at, **Vol. 5, Part 1**, 551; explosion at, **Vol. 6, Part 1**, 423
Hall, Adelaide, reference to, **Supp. 6**, 619–20
Hall, Arthur C. A., reference to, **Supp. 3**, 195
Hall, Charles F., reference to, **Vol. 5, Part 2**, 256
Hall, Charles Martin, references to, **Vol. 5, Part 1**, 382; **Supp. 7**, 166
Hall, Franklin Herbert, reference to, **Supp. 10**, 302
Hall, G. Stanley, references to, **Vol. 5, Part 1**, 592; **Supp. 3**, 199; **Supp. 5**, 170
Hall, Helen, references to, **Supp. 6**, 330, 499
Hall, Huntz, reference to, **Supp. 8**, 220
Hall, James, reference to, **Supp. 3**, 695
Hall, Mortimer, reference to, **Supp. 9**, 515
Hall, Radclyffe, reference to, **Supp. 7**, 149
Hall, William, reference to, **Vol. 1, Part 2**, 148
Halleck, Charles, references to, **Supp. 8**, 128, 422
Halleck, Fitz-Greene, references to, **Vol. 3, Part 1**, 203; **Vol. 9, Part 1**, 470
Halleck, Henry Wager, reference to, **Vol. 6, Part 1**, 583
Hallet, Étienne Sulpice, reference to, **Vol. 9, Part 2**, 505
Hall Johnson Choir, **Supp. 8**, 238
Hall of Fame (New York University), **Vol. 4, Part 1**, 470; **Vol. 7, Part 1**, 58
Haloid Co., **Supp. 8**, 71–72; **Supp. 9**, 877
Halsey, William F., Jr., references to, **Supp. 4**, 895; **Supp. 6**, 577; **Supp. 7**, 489; **Supp. 8**, 618–19
Halsted, William S., references to, **Vol. 10, Part 1**, 621 f.; **Supp. 3**, 270, 271, 412–13, 483, 625, 853
Halston, career boosted, **Supp. 9**, 588
Hambletonian Stakes, founding of, **Supp. 5**, 567
Hamburg-American Steamship Line, **Vol. 1, Part 2**, 400
Hamburg Landing, Tenn. *See* Shiloh, Tenn.
"Hamilcar speech," **Vol. 9, Part 2**, 590
Hamilton, Alexander, **Vol. 3, Part 2**, 325; **Vol. 5, Part 1**, 206, 469; **Vol. 5, Part 2**, 24; **Vol. 6, Part 1**, 117, 281, 347; **Vol. 7, Part 1**, 88, 312, 43; **Vol. 8, Part 2**, 474, 529; **Vol. 9, Part 1**, 320, 604; relations with Fisher Ames, **Vol. 1, Part 1**, 244; relations with Aaron Burr, **Vol. 2, Part 1**, 315 f.; relations with Nicholas Fish, **Vol. 3, Part 2**, 401; relations with Thomas Jefferson, **Vol. 5, Part 2**, 25; relations with Oliver Wolcott, **Vol. 10, Part 2**, 443
Hamilton, Alice, references to, **Supp. 3**, 244; **Supp. 8**, 40
Hamilton, Edith, reference to, **Supp. 8**, 241
Hamilton, James, reference to, **Vol. 7, Part 2**, 514
Hamilton, William F., reference to, **Supp. 3**, 32
Hamilton College, **Vol. 1, Part 1**, 468; **Vol. 2, Part 1**, 15, 3; **Vol. 3, Part 1**, 77, 117, 569; **Vol. 7, Part 1**, 558, 561 f.; charter for, **Vol. 5, Part 2**, 434; Law School, **Vol. 3, Part 1**, 571 f.; **Vol. 7, Part 1**, 592
Hamlet: **Supp. 9**, 350, 351; Barrymore, J., in, **Supp. 3**, 35; Todd's military version of, **Supp. 6**, 637
Hamline University, **Vol. 4, Part 2**, 199
Hammarskjöld, Dag: references to, **Supp. 10**, 245; special envoy for, **Supp. 9**, 192
Hammerstein, Arthur, references to, **Supp. 6**, 273; **Supp. 9**, 293
Hammerstein, James, reference to, **Supp. 6**, 273
Hammerstein, Oscar, references to, **Supp. 3**, 296; **Supp. 8**, 164, 201
Hammerstein, Oscar II, references to, **Supp. 3**, 418; **Supp. 8**, 238–39, 547; **Supp. 9**, 281
Hammer throw, **Supp. 3**, 487
Hammett, Dashiell, references to, **Supp. 6**, 65, 530
Hammond, Dean, reference to, **Supp. 9**, 758
Hammond, John, reference to, **Supp. 6**, 299
Hammond, John Hays, reference to, **Supp. 4**, 127
Hammond, William A., reference to, **Supp. 3**, 697
Hammond organ, **Supp. 9**, 341; invention of, **Supp. 9**, 358
Hampden, Walter, reference to, **Supp. 4**, 106
Hampden-Sydney College, **Vol. 1, Part 2**, 402; **Vol. 4, Part 1**, 554; **Vol. 5, Part 1**, 120; **Vol. 5, Part 2**, 522, **Vol. 6, Part 2**, 65; **Vol. 8, Part 1**, 486; founding of, **Vol. 9, Part 1**, 344; Theological School, **Vol. 8, Part 1**, 542
Hampshire House (New York City), interior design, **Supp. 8**, 140
Hampton, Lionel, references to, **Supp. 7**, 131, 764
Hampton, Wade, references to, **Vol. 6, Part 1**, 585; **Vol. 9, Part 2**, 547, 549, 593
Hampton Institute: **Vol. 4, Part 1**, 36; **Vol. 7, Part 1**, 641; experimental programs, **Supp. 9**, 562; music studies, **Supp. 3**, 225–26; presidency, **Supp. 9**, 562; survey of, **Supp. 3**, 328
Hampton, N.H., early history of, **Vol. 3, Part 1**, 409
Hampton Normal and Agricultural Institute (Va.), **Vol. 1, Part 1**, 360; **Vol. 8, Part 1**, 175 f.
Hampton Roads, fortifications at, **Vol. 9, Part 2**, 608
Hampton Roads Peace Conference (1865), **Vol. 1, Part 2**, 185, 332; **Vol. 2, Part 1**, 458; **Vol. 2, Part 2**, 482; **Vol. 5, Part 1**, 404; **Vol. 6, Part 1**, 257; **Vol. 9, Part 1**, 574
Hancock, Herbie, reference to, **Supp. 10**, 226
Hand, Daniel, reference to, **Vol. 7, Part 1**, 566
Hand, Learned, references to, **Supp. 6**, 88; **Supp. 9**, 323
Handbook of American Indian Languages, **Supp. 3**, 84
Handbook of Birds of the Western United States, **Supp. 4**, 41
Handbook of Latin American Studies, **Supp. 8**, 370
Handicapped, **Supp. 8**, 316–18; apparatus for, **Vol. 10, Part 1**, 158; employment of, **Supp. 6**, 414; kitchen developed for, **Supp. 9**, 310. *See also* Mentally retarded; *types of handicap*
Handicrafts. *See* Crafts
Hand-in-Hand, colonial brig, **Vol. 7, Part 1**, 361
"Hand in Hand," Jewish synagogue, **Vol. 4, Part 2**, 316

Handy, Harry, reference to, **Supp. 10**, 390
Handy, Lowney, references, **Supp. 10**, 390, 391
Handy, W. C., references to, **Supp. 10**, 760, 761
Handy, W. C., Music Co., **Supp. 6**, 275
Handy Artist Group, founding of, **Supp. 10**, 390
Hanford Engineering Works, **Supp. 10**, 102
Hanford, Wash., plutonium production, **Supp. 6**, 371; **Supp. 7**, 11; **Supp. 8**, 230; **Supp. 10**, 102
Hanks, Nancy, mother of A. Lincoln, **Vol. 6, Part 1**, 242 f.
Hanna, Mark, references to, **Vol. 6, Part 2**, 106 f.; **Vol. 8, Part 1**, 296 f.
Hanna Co., **Supp. 6**, 678; **Supp. 8**, 289–90
Hanna house (Palo Alto, Calif.), **Supp. 6**, 714
Hannegan, Robert E., reference to, **Supp. 10**, 226
Hannibal & St. Joseph Railroad, **Vol. 9, Part 2**, 13
Hanover Bank. *See* Central Hanover Bank and Trust Co.
Hanover College, founding of, **Vol. 3, Part 1**, 522; **Vol. 3, Part 2**, 405
Hansberry, Carl Augustus, reference to, **Supp. 7**, 318
Hansberry, Lorraine, reference to, **Supp. 8**, 287
Hans Brinker, events leading to writing of, **Vol. 3, Part 1**, 351
Hansen, Alvin H., reference to, **Supp. 6**, 586
Hanson, J. C. M., reference to, **Supp. 3**, 510
Hapgood, Norman, references to, **Supp. 3**, 96, 329; **Supp. 5**, 666–67
Happiest Millionaire, The, **Supp. 7**, 52
"Happy Birthday to You" (song), **Supp. 4**, 374
Hapten, **Supp. 3**, 441–42
Harbach, Otto, reference to, **Supp. 3**, 418
Harbinger, Brook Farm periodical, **Vol. 3, Part 1**, 567 f., 624
Harbor Association, **Vol. 1, Part 2**, 84
Harbors: engineering, **Supp. 1**, 157; improvements, **Vol. 8, Part 1**, 406; **Vol. 9, Part 1**, 179; surveying of, **Vol. 3, Part 1**, 92; **Vol. 9, Part 2**, 247
Harcourt, Alfred, reference to, **Supp. 5**, 85
Harcourt, Brace and Co., founding of, **Supp. 5**, 85, 272
Hard Day's Night, A, **Supp. 10**, 449
Hardin College for Women, **Vol. 4, Part 2**, 245
Hardin, Lillian, reference to, **Supp. 9**, 46
Harding, Warren G.: Daugherty relationship, **Supp. 3**, 213–14; Fall relationship, **Supp. 3**, 259–60; League of Nations, **Supp. 3**, 472–73; presidential candidacy, **Supp. 3**, 643, 129; **Supp. 7**, 86, 305; references to, **Supp. 1**, 173; **Supp. 3**, 203; **Supp. 6**, 114, 291; **Supp. 9**, 590; Sutherland relationship, **Supp. 3**, 754; writings on, **Supp. 6**, 6. *See also* Teapot Dome scandal
"Harding Bible," **Vol. 4, Part 2**, 259
Hard Lines, **Supp. 9**, 578
Hardware, manufacture of, **Vol. 1, Part 2**, 341
Hardwick, Elizabeth, reference to, **Supp. 10**, 468
Hardy, Oliver, references to, **Supp. 7**, 462, 463–64
Hare-Hawes-Cutting Act (1933), **Supp. 3**, 614; **Supp. 4**, 612
Harinck, early Dutch boat, **Vol. 5, Part 2**, 371
Harkins, W. D., reference to, **Supp. 7**, 10
Harkness, Edward S., references to, **Supp. 3**, 262, 471; **Supp. 4**, 22
Harlan, John Marshall, references to, **Supp. 3**, 15, 117; **Supp. 9**, 837
Harlan, Richard, reference to, **Vol. 7, Part 1**, 265
Harlem (New York City): development as community, **Supp. 3**, 535; jazz, **Supp. 3**, 798; libraries, **Supp. 3**, 281; political leadership, **Supp. 5**, 548; Protestant Episcopal churches in, **Supp. 4**, 547
Harlem Hospital (New York City), founding of, **Supp. 1**, 240
Harlem Renaissance, **Supp. 4**, 200–201; **Supp. 4**, 527–28, 436; **Supp. 6**, 314, 321, 489; **Supp. 7**, 203, 236, 754; **Supp. 8**, 286; **Supp. 9**, 108, 109; **Supp. 10**, 321, 832
Harlem River Drive (New York City), construction of, **Supp. 1**, 136
Harlem River–155th Street Bridge (New York City), **Supp. 3**, 77
Harlow, Jean, reference to, **Supp. 10**, 355
Harmar's defeat (1790), **Vol. 2, Part 1**, 366; **Vol. 4, Part 2**, 276; **Vol. 6, Part 1**, 300; **Vol. 8, Part 2**, 294; **Vol. 10, Part 1**, 523
Harmonium, **Supp. 5**, 660
Harmony Society, **Vol. 8, Part 1**, 383
Harms, T. B., reference to, **Supp. 3**, 417
Harms, T. B., Inc., **Supp. 7**, 198
Harmsworth, Alfred C. W. (viscount of Northcliffe), **Supp. 9**, 826
Harmsworth, Sir Leicester, reference to, **Supp. 4**, 5
Harnack, Adolf, reference to, **Supp. 3**, 110
Harness making, **Vol. 10, Part 2**, 571
Harness racing, **Supp. 5**, 567; **Supp. 6**, 688–89
Harper, William Rainey, references to, **Vol. 5, Part 1**, 67; **Vol. 5, Part 2**, 241 f.; **Vol. 10, Part 1**, 606 f.; **Supp. 3**, 64, 153, 793, 824; **Supp. 5**, 171; **Supp. 7**, 712
Harper & Bros., publishing house, **Vol. 4, Part 2**, 281 f.; **Vol. 5, Part 1**, 76, 187, 308; **Supp. 3**, 686; **Supp. 10**, 418
Harper and Row, **Supp. 8**, 224
Harper's Bazaar, **Vol. 8, Part 2**, 352; **Supp. 4**, 842; **Supp. 5**, 286; **Supp. 7**, 704
Harper's Dictionary of Classical Literature and Antiquities, **Vol. 7, Part 2**, 378
Harper's Ferry, W.Va., **Vol. 1, Part 2**, 339; **Vol. 2, Part 1**, 133; **Vol. 4, Part 2**, 163; **Vol. 5, Part 1**, 386, 460, 556; **Vol. 6, Part 1**, 122; **Vol. 6, Part 2**, 120; **Vol. 9, Part 1**, 153; **Vol. 10, Part 1**, 144
Harper's magazine, **Vol. 1, Part 1**, 144 f.; **Vol. 4, Part 2**, 283, 486; **Vol. 5, Part 1**, 445; **Vol. 7, Part 1**, 457, 608; **Supp. 5**, 16–17, 168, 169
Harper's Monthly, **Vol. 5, Part 1**, 308
Harper's New Monthly Magazine, **Vol. 8, Part 1**, 409, 624
Harper's Weekly, **Vol. 1, Part 1**, 3, 573 f.; **Vol. 4, Part 2**, 372; **Vol. 5, Part 1**, 187, 201; **Vol. 7, Part 1**, 392, 416; **Vol. 8, Part 2**, 469; **Vol. 9, Part 1**, 227; **Vol. 10, Part 1**, 81
Harpsichord, revival of, **Supp. 6**, 357–58
Harriet Lane Home (Baltimore, Md.), **Supp. 3**, 74
Harriman, Edward H., references to, **Vol. 5, Part 1**, 38; **Vol. 7, Part 1**, 177; **Supp. 1**, 457; **Supp. 3**, 728, 736; **Supp. 10**, 309, 768, 769
Harriman, Job, reference to, **Supp. 3**, 347
Harriman, Mary Williamson, reference to, **Supp. 3**, 215
Harriman, W. Averell, references to, **Supp. 8**, 69–70; **Supp. 9**, 812; **Supp. 10**, 309, 310, 453, 472, 686–87
Harriman Alaska expedition, **Supp. 1**, 237
Harriman State Park (N.Y.), nature trail, **Supp. 3**, 478
Harrington, Mark R., reference to, **Supp. 5**, 533
Harrington, Michael, reference to, **Supp. 3**, 373
Harris, Bucky, reference to, **Supp. 8**, 49
Harris, James Arthur, reference to, **Supp. 3**, 315
Harris, Joel Chandler, references to, **Vol. 5, Part 1**, 302; **Vol. 9, Part 1**, 523; **Supp. 7**, 323, 324
Harris, Phil, reference to, **Supp. 9**, 76
Harris, Roy, reference to, **Supp. 3**, 359
Harris, Sam H., reference to, **Supp. 3**, 173–74
Harris, Theodore H., reference to, **Supp. 9**, 133
Harris, Townsend, reference to, **Vol. 5, Part 1**, 613
Harris, William B., reference to, **Supp. 9**, 335
Harris, William J., reference to, **Supp. 3**, 331

Harris, W. T., references to, **Vol. 5, Part 1**, 311; **Vol. 9, Part 1**, 66, 383, 391, 593
Harrison, Benjamin, **Vol. 8, Part 1**, 296 f.; **Vol. 10, Part 1**, 88; nomination of, **Vol. 3, Part 1**, 246; **Vol. 8, Part 1**, 80 f.
Harrison, Carter H., references to, **Supp. 4**, 256; **Supp. 5**, 273
Harrison, Francis Burton, reference to, **Supp. 3**, 614
Harrison, George, reference to, **Supp. 10**, 449
Harrison, Marie L., reference to, **Supp. 6**, 107
Harrison, Pat, reference to, **Supp. 6**, 35
Harrison, Richard, reference to, **Supp. 8**, 444
Harrison, Richard B., reference to, **Supp. 10**, 147
Harrison, Ross G., references to, **Supp. 3**, 140; **Supp. 6**, 386
Harrison, Samuel, reference to, **Supp. 6**, 281
Harrison, Wallace K., reference to, **Supp. 5**, 133
Harrison, William Henry, references to, **Vol. 5, Part 1**, 158; **Vol. 7, Part 1**, 633; **Vol. 9, Part 2**, 359, 375 f., 570
Harrison Act (1914), **Supp. 5**, 138
Harrison Narcotics Act (1914), **Supp. 6**, 280
Harrison's Landing, Va., operation at, **Vol. 6, Part 1**, 583. *See also* Peninsular Campaign
Harrod's Fort, **Vol. 1, Part 2**, 442; **Vol. 4, Part 2**, 353, 531; **Vol. 6, Part 1**, 357
Harshbarger, Dema, reference to, **Supp. 8**, 282
Har Sinai Temple (Baltimore, Md.), **Supp. 4**, 659
Hart, Jane, reference to, **Supp. 10**, 316
Hart, Lorenz, references to, **Supp. 8**, 481, 547; **Supp. 10**, 693–94
Hart, Moss, references to, **Supp. 3**, 333, 842; **Supp. 4**, 374; **Supp. 5**, 415; **Supp. 6**, 311; **Supp. 7**, 413, 803; **Supp. 10**, 720
Hart, Philip, reference to, **Supp. 10**, 645
Hart, William S., references to, **Supp. 4**, 240
Hartford, Conn.: civic service, **Vol. 4, Part 2**, 600 f.; **Vol. 6, Part 1**, 604; **Vol. 7, Part 2**, 217 f., 529, 641; **Vol. 8, Part 1**, 187 f.; **Vol. 10, Part 1**, 82; deaf, school for, in, **Vol. 1, Part 2**, 139; **Vol. 2, Part 1**, 201 f.; **Vol. 8, Part 1**, 102 f.; industrial development, **Vol. 8, Part 1**, 74 f., 172 f.; newspapers, **Vol. 7, Part 1**, 522; philanthropy, **Vol. 7, Part 1**, 182; politics, **Supp. 9**, 57; settlement of, **Vol. 5, Part 1**, 200; **Vol. 8, Part 1**, 175; social reform in, **Supp. 5**, 296–97; "Wits," *see* "Hartford Wits"
Hartford Accident and Indemnity Co., **Supp. 5**, 659–61
Hartford Convention (1814–15), **Vol. 4, Part 1**, 304; **Vol. 7, Part 1**, 212, 523; **Vol. 7, Part 2**, 99; **Vol. 8, Part 1**, 310; **Vol. 9, Part 1**, 300, 329; **Vol. 9, Part 2**, 145
Hartford Courant, **Supp. 6**, 231–32
Hartford Electric Co. (HELCO), **Supp. 4**, 265
Hartford Female Seminary, **Vol. 1, Part 2**, 541
Hartford Theological Foundation, **Supp. 3**, 477
Hartford Theological Seminary, **Vol. 4, Part 2**, 367; **Vol. 7, Part 1**, 433; **Vol. 7, Part 2**, 295 f.; forerunner of, **Vol. 10, Part 1**, 85
"Hartford Wits," **Vol. 1, Part 1**, 228, 610; **Vol. 3, Part 1**, 236, 573 f.; **Vol. 7, Part 1**, 559; **Vol. 9, Part 1**, 259; **Vol. 10, Part 1**, 11
Hartley, Frank, reference to, **Vol. 9, Part 2**, 535
Hartley, Marsden, reference to, **Supp. 6**, 552
Hartmann, Heinz, reference to, **Supp. 6**, 528
Hart, Shaffner and Marx, strike (1910), **Supp. 4**, 375; **Supp. 10**, 643
Harvard Advertising Awards, establishment of, **Supp. 1**, 93
Harvard Alumni Association, **Supp. 6**, 659
Harvard Alumni Bulletin, **Supp. 6**, 249, 306
Harvard Apparatus Co., founding of, **Supp. 4**, 676
Harvard Classics, **Vol. 3, Part 2**, 78
Harvard Club, **Vol. 1, Part 2**, 169
"Harvard Commemoration Ode," **Vol. 6, Part 1**, 462
Harvard Cooperative Society, **Vol. 1, Part 2**, 421
Harvard Corporation, **Supp. 3**, 448; **Supp. 6**, 249, 250; youngest elected to, **Supp. 6**, 143
Harvard Crimson, founding of, **Vol. 9, Part 1**, 168; **Supp. 6**, 249, 677
Harvard Endowment Fund, **Supp. 6**, 659
Harvard Lampoon, **Supp. 5**, 283; founding of, **Supp. 2**, 434
Harvard Law Review: Brandeis article, **Supp. 3**, 94, 95; founding of, **Vol. 1, Part 1**, 247; **Supp. 3**, 43, 821
Harvard Law School, youngest graduate, **Supp. 9**, 83
Harvard Monthly, founding of, **Supp. 1**, 592
Harvard Philosophical Club, founding of, **Supp. 2**, 639
Harvard Research in International Law, **Supp. 6**, 308
Harvard Theological Review, **Vol. 7, Part 1**, 124; **Vol. 8, Part 2**, 151
Harvard Trade Union Fellowship, **Supp. 6**, 586
Harvard University: **Vol. 1, Part 1**, 51; **Vol. 1, Part 2**, 421; **Vol. 2, Part 2**, 42; **Vol. 3, Part 1**, 611; **Vol. 3, Part 2**, 72 f.; **Vol. 4, Part 1**, 411; **Vol. 4, Part 2**, 57, 499; **Vol. 5, Part 1**, 333, 535, 592; **Vol. 5, Part 2**, 431; **Vol. 6, Part 1**, 198, 383 f., 461 f.; **Vol. 6, Part 2**, 387, 391; **Vol. 7, Part 1**, 119, 124, 253; **Vol. 7, Part 2**, 335; **Vol. 8, Part 2**, 355 f.; **Vol. 9, Part 2**, 526 f.; **Vol. 10, Part 1**, 649 f.; **Vol. 10, Part 2**, 192 f., 235, 238, 415; administration, **Supp. 5**, 5, 6; **Supp. 10**, 143–44; alumni dlrectory, **Supp. 6**, 249; American literature and language studies, **Supp. 5**, 542; **Supp. 7**, 538; "Annex," *see* Radcliffe College; anthropology, first chair of, **Vol. 8, Part 1**, 276 f.; anthropology studies, **Supp. 5**, 312; **Supp. 8**, 684; anti-Semitism at, **Supp. 9**, 503; Appleton Chapel, **Vol. 1, Part 1**, 332 f.; architecture studies, **Supp. 8**, 227; astronomical observatories, **Supp. 1**, 43; **Supp. 3**, 130–31; **Supp. 9**, 713–14; **Supp. 10**, 625, 626; astronomy, **Vol. 7, Part 2**, 563; "Augustan Age," **Vol. 5, Part 2**, 431; biological chemistry studies, **Supp. 3**, 350; biological laboratories, **Supp. 4**, 16; black, first degree awarded to, **Vol. 4, Part 1**, 578; Boston School for Social Workers, **Supp. 4**, 101; botanical facilities, **Supp. 4**, 16; botanical garden, **Vol. 7, Part 1**, 597; botany, first professorship of, **Vol. 4, Part 1**, 512; business school, **Supp. 1**, 45; business school, business economics, **Supp. 6**, 585; business school, fatigue laboratory, **Supp. 3**, 351; business school, founding of, **Supp. 3**, 448, 471; business school, Kresge Hall, **Supp. 8**, 349; Cancer Commission, **Supp. 6**, 69; Center for Italian Renaissance Studies, **Supp. 6**, 57; chemical engineering studies, **Supp. 2**, 479; chemistry studies, **Vol. 2, Part 2**, 387; **Supp. 5**, 407; climatology, first professorship in, **Vol. 7, Part 2**, 436; curriculum reform, **Supp. 3**, 328, 470–74; **Supp. 10**, 144; Dante course, **Supp. 2**, 254; dean, first, **Vol. 3, Part 1**, 503 f.; dental school, founding of, **Supp. 4**, 402; department of social relations, **Supp. 10**, 616; divinity school, **Vol. 1, Part 2**, 306; **Vol. 3, Part 2**, 75, 221; **Vol. 7, Part 1**, 588; **Vol. 8, Part 2**, 151; **Vol. 10, Part 1**, 447 f.; **Supp. 5**, 649; **Supp. 7**, 747; Dumbarton Oaks Research Library and Collection, **Supp. 5**, 700, 708; **Supp. 7**, 60, 673; ecclesiastical history studies, **Supp. 4**, 467–68; economic history studies, **Supp. 4**, 321, 322; economics studies, **Supp. 4**, 721–23; **Supp. 6**, 585–86; **Supp. 8**, 82–83; **Supp. 9**, 362; education graduate studies, **Supp. 3**, 327–28, 471; Egyptology collection, **Supp. 4**, 902; elective system, **Vol. 7, Part 2**, 405; **Vol. 8, Part 1**, 308 f.; endowment fund, **Supp. 7**, 401; engineering school, **Vol. 5, Part 1**, 349; engineering studies, **Supp. 4**, 873; English literature and lan-

guage studies, **Supp. 3**, 422, 423, 474–76; **Supp. 4**, 560; **Supp. 5**, 131–32; **Supp. 10**, 389; English 12 course, **Supp. 5**, 131–32; exchange professorships inaugurated, **Vol. 10, Part 1**, 649 f.; fatigue laboratory, **Supp. 3**, 551; **Supp. 5**, 565; first woman professor, **Supp. 8**, 242; first woman to achieve full professorship, **Supp. 10**, 626; Five-Foot Bookshelf classics series, **Supp. 4**, 624; Fogg Museum, **Vol. 7, Part 1**, 116; **Supp. 1**, 641; **Supp. 5**, 729; **Supp. 7**, 673–74; football team, **Supp. 4**, 492; founding of, **Vol. 1, Part 2**, 166; **Vol. 3, Part 1**, 419, 484 f., 524; **Vol. 4, Part 2**, 372; French literature and language studies, **Supp. 1**, 36; geology studies, **Supp. 6**, 144; gifts to, **Vol. 4, Part 1**, 515; **Vol. 5, Part 1**, 13; **Vol. 9, Part 2**, 113; **Supp. 3**, 464, 471; Gore Hall, **Vol. 9, Part 2**, 632; government studies, **Supp. 3**, 337, 469–70; **Supp. 10**, 215, 217; graduate of, first class, **Vol. 1, Part 2**, 166; graduates, biographical sketches of, **Vol. 3, Part 1**, 277; Gray Herbarium, **Supp. 1**, 632; **Supp. 4**, 266, 428; **Supp. 6**, 450; Gray's Hall, **Vol. 4, Part 1**, 515; "Great Rebellion" of 1823, **Vol. 5, Part 2**, 431; Hasty Pudding Club, **Vol. 7, Part 2**, 247; **Vol. 10, Part 1**, 480 f.; **Supp. 5**, 629; Hebrew literature and language studies, **Supp. 9**, 891; history, **Vol. 9, Part 1**, 147, 433; **Supp. 10**, 432–33; history of science studies, **Supp. 3**, 351; **Supp. 6**, 564–65; history studies, **Supp. 3**, 336–37; **Supp. 7**, 676; **Supp. 8**, 50, 169–70; Holyoke Center mural, **Supp. 8**, 554; Houghton Library, **Supp. 7**, 387; house plan, **Supp. 2**, 284, **Supp. 3**, 471; **Supp. 5**, 130; international law studies, **Supp. 5**, 751; international relations studies, **Supp. 8**, 167; I Tatti Foundation, **Supp. 7**, 673; Jefferson Laboratory, **Vol. 9, Part 2**, 655; Jew, first, to receive degree, **Vol. 7, Part 1**, 87; John Harvard sculpture, **Supp. 1**, 321; landscape architecture studies, **Supp. 6**, 485; Latin American studies, **Supp. 6**, 277; Latin studies, **Supp. 3**, 617–18; Lawrence Scientific School, **Vol. 3, Part 2**, 192; **Vol. 5, Part 1**, 237; **Vol. 8, Part 1**, 74 f.; **Vol. 9, Part 1**, 18; law school, **Vol. 1, Part 1**, 247; **Vol. 3, Part 2**, 75; **Vol. 4, Part 1**, 520, 584; **Vol. 5, Part 1**, 169; **Vol. 5, Part 2**, 585 f.; **Vol. 7, Part 2**, 225; **Vol. 8, Part 1**, 308 f.; **Vol. 9, Part 1**, 541; **Vol. 9, Part 2**, 106, 404, 406; **Supp. 3**, 43, 94; **Supp. 5**, 549; **Supp. 6**, 104–6; **Supp. 7**, 261, 453, 626–27, 792; **Supp. 8**, 285; liberal traditions challenged, **Vol. 8, Part 1**, 308 f.; libraries, **Vol. 2, Part 2**, 273; **Vol. 4, Part 2**, 321; **Vol. 7, Part 1**, 463, 568; **Vol. 8, Part 1**, 308 f.; **Vol. 9, Part 1**, 147; **Vol. 9, Part 2**, 391; **Vol. 10, Part 2**, 403; **Supp. 5**, 756, mammalogy studies, **Supp. 3**, 9; Mark I automatic calculator, **Supp. 6**, 675; Massachusetts Hall, building of, **Vol. 6, Part 1**, 198; mathematics studies, **Vol. 4, Part 1**, 591; **Vol. 7, Part 2**, 394, 405; **Supp. 3**, 70, 575; **Supp. 5**, 130–31, 338; medical school, **Vol. 1, Part 2**, 556; **Vol. 3, Part 2**, 76, 102, 178, 434; **Vol. 4, Part 2**, 303, 465; **Vol. 5, Part 1**, 172, 546; **Vol. 7, Part 1**, 324; **Vol. 8, Part 2**, 186; **Vol. 9, Part 1**, 33; **Vol. 10, Part 1**, 474, 479 f., 529 f.; **Supp. 1**, 206; **Supp. 3**, 121, 502, 806; **Supp. 4**, 208–9, 582, 676; **Supp. 5**, 122; **Supp. 6**, 175; **Supp. 8**, 241–42; medical school, pediatrics, **Supp. 3**, 75; medical school, psychiatry studies, **Supp. 3**, 128; **Supp. 4**, 617–18, 717; medical school, research, **Supp. 3**, 243–44; medical school, teaching hospital, **Supp. 2**, 138; meteorology studies, **Supp. 3**, 479; Museum of Comparative Zoology, **Vol. 1, Part 1**, 119, 198; **Vol. 8, Part 1**, 141 f.; **Supp. 4**, 51–52; **Supp. 5**, 656; **Supp. 6**, 255; music, **Vol. 3, Part 1**, 567 f.; **Vol. 7, Part 2**, 151; neuropsychology studies, **Supp. 6**, 367; observatory, **Vol. 1, Part 2**, 431, 435; **Vol. 7, Part 1**, 39; **Vol. 7, Part 2**, 394; **Vol. 8, Part 1**, 308 f.; **Vol. 8, Part 2**, 535; **Vol. 10, Part 2**, 390; oceanography studies, **Supp. 8**, 37; organic chemistry studies, **Supp. 3**, 520–21; **Supp. 10**, 240; Oriental series, **Supp. 3**, 445; overseers, **Supp. 3**, 448; **Supp. 6**, 125, 250, 659; Peabody Museum, **Vol. 1, Part 2**, 492; **Vol. 7, Part 1**, 242; **Vol. 7, Part 2**, 337; **Vol. 8, Part 1**, 276 f., 583; pharmacology studies, **Supp. 4**, 411; Philharmonic Society, **Vol. 3, Part 1**, 567 f.; Phillips Brooks House, **Vol. 7, Part 2**, 159; philosophy studies, **Vol. 7, Part 1**, 338; **Vol. 7, Part 2**, 181; **Supp. 1**, 713–14; **Supp. 4**, 880–81, 883; **Supp. 5**, 601–2; **Supp. 6**, 504–5; **Supp. 7**, 471; **Supp. 8**, 266; physics studies, **Vol. 9, Part 2**, 654; **Vol. 10, Part 1**, 529 f.; **Supp. 5**, 441–42; **Supp. 7**, 74–75; **Supp. 8**, 191; **Supp. 10**, 805; physiography studies, **Supp. 4**, 32; physiology studies, **Supp. 3**, 133; **Supp. 4**, 676; political economy, **Vol. 3, Part 1**, 503 f.; presidency, **Vol. 3, Part 1**, 524; **Vol. 3, Part 2**, 71, 317; **Vol. 5, Part 1**, 46, 87 f.; **Vol. 5, Part 2**, 431, 588 f.; **Vol. 6, Part 1**, 197 f.; **Vol. 7, Part 1**, 343, 603; **Vol. 8, Part 1**, 308 f.; **Vol. 9, Part 1**, 433; **Vol. 9, Part 2**, 391; **Supp. 3**, 468–74; president, first, **Vol. 3, Part 1**, 524; press sold to, **Vol. 4, Part 1**, 555; promotion and tenure, **Supp. 10**, 143; psychology studies, **Supp. 6**, 718–19; **Supp. 8**, 7, 44; public administration school, **Supp. 3**, 464; public health school, **Supp. 3**, 244; **Supp. 4**, 701; **Supp. 5**, 632; quota system, **Supp. 3**, 472, 489; **Supp. 6**, 250; Radcliffe College, **Supp. 1**, 146; Robbins Philosophical Library, **Supp. 1**, 619; Sanskrit studies, **Supp. 3**, 444–45; Saunders Theatre, **Vol. 8, Part 2**, 332; scholarship fund, first, **Vol. 10, Part 1**, 627 f.; Semitic Museum, founding of, **Supp. 1**, 519; Slavic language studies, **Supp. 2**, 717; **Supp. 4**, 195–96; social relations laboratory, **Supp. 6**, 605; Society of Fellows, **Supp. 3**, 351, 352, 473, 476; **Supp. 4**, 884; Soldiers Field, **Vol. 5, Part 1**, 153; stadium, first, in U.S., **Vol. 5, Part 1**, 143; theater studies, **Supp. 1**, 45; tropical medicine studies, **Supp. 4**, 803; tutorial and reading period, **Supp. 3**, 470; Widener collection, **Supp. 5**, 756; Yard, use of, by Revolutionary soldiers, **Vol. 8, Part 2**, 239; zoology studies, **Supp. 5**, 536; **Supp. 9**, 674–75

Harvard University Press, **Vol. 3, Part 2**, 493

Harvesting machinery, **Vol. 3, Part 1**, 195; **Vol. 3, Part 2**, 188; **Vol. 6, Part 2**, 296; **Vol. 8, Part 1**, 505

Harvey, A. McGehee, reference to, **Supp. 7**, 59

Harvey, C. B. H., reference to, **Supp. 6**, 632

Harvey, Sir John, deposed as governor of Virginia, **Vol. 8, Part 1**, 123 f.

Harvey, William H., reference to, **Supp. 3**, 564

Harvey, **Supp. 4**, 649, 653; **Supp. 6**, 311; **Supp. 7**, 238

Harvey Cushing, **Supp. 6**, 224

Harvey Society of New York, founding of, **Supp. 1**, 518

Hasheesh Eater, **Vol. 6, Part 1**, 491

Hastings, Sue, reference to, **Supp. 3**, 685

Hasty Pudding Club (Harvard), **Vol. 7, Part 2**, 247; **Vol. 10, Part 1**, 480 f.; **Supp. 5**, 629

Hatch, Carl, reference to, **Supp. 9**, 31

Hatch Act (1887), **Vol. 2, Part 2**, 314; **Vol. 4, Part 2**, 394

Hatch Acts (1939 and 1940), **Supp. 3**, 707; **Supp. 6**, 602; **Supp. 7**, 326–27

Hatcher, Robert A., reference to, **Supp. 3**, 805

Hatcher's Run, Va., battle of, **Vol. 4, Part 1**, 237

Hatfield, Mark, reference to, **Supp. 9**, 566

Hat manufacture, **Vol. 3, Part 2**, 59; **Vol. 4, Part 1**, 209; **Vol. 9, Part 1**, 599. *See also* Clothing manufacture

Hats, **Supp. 5**, 501

Hatteras, and *Alabama*, naval battle, **Vol. 1, Part 2**, 342

Hatteras Inlet, N.C., operation at, **Vol. 2, Part 1**, 310; **Vol. 4, Part 1**, 366

Hauer, Joseph Mathias, reference to, **Supp. 5**, 609

Haugen, Gilbert N., reference to, **Supp. 3**, 496
Hauptmann, Bruno, references to, **Supp. 3**, 142; **Supp. 9**, 379, 497
Hauser, Gayelord, reference to, **Supp. 8**, 13
Hauss, Rosetta V., reference to, **Supp. 4**, 294, 298
Havana Conference (1947), **Supp. 8**, 90
Havemeyer, Henry O., reference to, **Supp. 6**, 26
Haverford College: **Vol. 4, Part 2**, 48; **Vol. 9, Part 1**, 27; philosophy studies, **Supp. 4**, 441–42; sociology studies, **Supp. 8**, 522
Haverford School, **Vol. 4, Part 2**, 49
Haverhill, Mass., Indian attack on, **Vol. 3, Part 1**, 544
Havoc, June, reference to, **Supp. 8**, 363
Hawaii: annexation of (1896), **Vol. 1, Part 2**, 329, 389; **Vol. 2, Part 2**, 211; **Vol. 3, Part 1**, 109, 358; **Vol. 3, Part 2**, 551; **Vol. 4, Part 1**, 609; **Vol. 4, Part 2**, 333; **Vol. 5, Part 1**, 81; **Vol. 6, Part 2**, 108, 312; **Vol. 8, Part 1**, 458; **Vol. 9, Part 1**, 618 f.; **Vol. 10, Part 2**, 305; Bible translated into Hawaiian, **Vol. 1, Part 1**, 296; **Vol. 8, Part 1**, 561; diplomatic relations with, **Vol. 1, Part 1**, 187; **Vol. 1, Part 2**, 329, 388 f.; **Vol. 2, Part 1**, 535; **Vol. 3, Part 1**, 592 f.; **Vol.4, Part 1**, 609; **Vol. 7, Part 2**, 405; economic and political system in, **Vol. 8, Part 1**, 560; education, **Vol. 1, Part 1**, 295; flight to, **Vol. 8, Part 2**, 79; governors, **Supp. 1**, 295; "Hawaii for the Hawaliians," **Vol. 4, Part 1**, 258; historical writings on, **Vol. 1, Part 1**, 176 f.; **Supp. 7**, 445–46; Home Rule party, **Vol. 5, Part 2**, 252; Homes Commission Act (1921), **Vol. 5, Part 2**, 252; missions, **Vol. 1, Part 1**, 295; Vol. 2 Part 2, 236 f.; **Vol. 3, Part 1**, 357; **Vol. 5, Part 2**, 229 f.; **Vol. 8, Part 1**, 560; newspaper, first in, **Vol. 1, Part 1**, 295; **Vol. 5, Part 1**, 618; pineapple industry, **Supp. 6**, 168; public service, **Vol. 3, Part 1**, 358; **Vol. 4, Part 1**, 258; **Vol. 5, Part 2**, 229 f., 252; **Vol. 6, Part 1**, 135; **Vol. 8, Part 1**, 560; **Vol. 8, Part 2**, 607; **Vol. 9, Part 2**, 517; revolution in, **Vol. 2, Part 2**, 398 f.; songs, **Vol. 1, Part 1**, 296; statehood, **Supp. 5**, 216–17; **Supp. 7**, 590; **Supp. 8**, 104; sugar industry, **Vol. 2, Part 1**, 535; **Vol. 9, Part 1**, 478 f.; sugar plantation, **Supp. 1**, 48; trade with, **Vol. 3, Part 2**, 400; **Vol. 5, Part 1**, 381; volcanoes, study of, **Vol. 5, Part 1**, 70; **Supp. 5**, 361; warship, first American, to visit, **Vol. 7, Part 2**, 461
Hawaiian Dredging and Construction Co., founding of, **Supp. 7**, 184–84
Hawaiian Pineapple Co., **Supp. 6**, 168–69
Hawaiian Volcano Observatory, **Supp. 5**, 361
Hawikuh Pueblo, N.Mex., excavation of, **Supp. 6**, 290
"Hawkeyes," origin of term, **Vol. 8, Part 2**, 153
Hawkins, Norval A., reference to, **Supp. 4**, 300
Hawkins Zouaves, **Vol. 4, Part 2**, 415
Hawks, Howard, **Supp. 7**, 234, 235; reference to, **Supp. 9**, 123
Hawks, Nancy ("Slim"), reference to, **Supp. 9**, 375
Hawley, Joseph R., reference to, **Vol. 10, Part 1**, 462 f.
Hawthorne, Nathaniel: **Vol. 5, Part 1**, 50, 242, 580; literary studies on, **Supp. 1**, 386; relations with Bacon, **Vol. 1, Part 1**, 475; relations with Longfellow, **Vol. 6, Part 1**, 383 f.; relations with Ticknor, **Vol. 9, Part 2**, 529; satirical portrait of, **Vol. 10, Part 1**, 122; witchcraft trial, **Vol. 4, Part 2**, 424; writings on, **Supp. 7**, 18
Hay, John, references to, **Vol. 1, Part 1**, 106; **Vol. 4, Part 2**, 432; **Vol. 7, Part 1**, 511; **Supp. 6**, 254
Hayakawa, Sessue, reference to, **Supp. 10**, 808
Hayden, Carl, reference to, **Supp. 7**, 105
Hayden, Ferdinand V., reference to, **Supp. 3**, 380
Hayden, Horace H., reference to, **Vol. 1, Part 2**, 61
Hayden Planetarium (New York City): building design for, **Supp. 6**, 234; establishment of, **Supp. 2**, 293
Hayden's Forge, first ironworks, **Vol. 7, Part 1**, 505
Hayes, Helen, references to, **Supp. 4**, 104; **Supp. 5**, 525; **Supp. 6**, 401
Hayes, Max, reference to, **Supp. 3**, 347
Hayes, Roland, reference to, **Supp. 7**, 549
Hayes, Rutherford B.: **Vol. 9, Part 1**, 365; "bargain" of, **Vol. 4, Part 2**, 450; election, *see* Hayes-Tilden election; nomination of, **Vol. 7, Part 1**, 587; relations with Blaine, **Vol. 1, Part 2**, 325; relations with Blair, **Vol. 1, Part 2**, 340
Hayes, Samuel P., reference to, **Supp. 4**, 11
Hayes, William C., reference to, **Supp. 4**, 901
Hayes-Binet Intelligence Tests, **Supp. 4**, 11
Hayes-Tilden election, **Vol. 3, Part 2**, 218, 344, 361; **Vol. 4, Part 2**, 29; **Vol. 5, Part 1**, 87; **Vol. 9, Part 2**, 112 f., 540
Hay fever, first desensitizing treatment of, **Supp. 6**, 123; study of, **Vol. 8, Part 2**, 411
Haygood, Atticus Green, reference to, **Supp. 3**, 129
Hayhanen, Reino, reference to, **Supp. 9**, 3
Hay-Herrán Treaty (1903), **Vol. 1, Part 2**, 110; Vol. 49 Part 2, 4; **Vol. 8, Part 2**, 138
Hayman, Al, reference to, **Supp. 3**, 276
Haymarket Riot (Chicago, 1886), **Vol. 1, Part 1**, 231; **Supp. 2**, 142
Haymes, Joe, reference to, **Supp. 6**, 172
Hayne, Paul Hamilton, reference to, **Vol. 9, Part 2**, 558 f.
Hayne, Robert Y., reference to, **Vol. 10, Part 1**, 585 f.
Hay-Pauncefote Treaty (1900), **Vol. 1, Part 2**, 110; **Vol. 4, Part 2**, 435; **Vol. 6, Part 1**, 348; **Vol. 8, Part 2**, 138; **Vol. 10, Part 2**, 102; **Supp. 4**, 599
Hays, Arthur Garfield, reference to, **Supp. 8**, 853
Hays, Will, reference to, **Supp. 7**, 71
Hayward, Brooke, reference to, **Supp. 9**, 375
Hayward, John, reference to, **Supp. 7**, 221
Hayward, William, reference to, **Supp. 9**, 375
Haywire, **Supp. 9**, 375
Haywood, William D. ("Big Bill"): references to, **Supp. 3**, 298, 438; **Supp. 5**, 699; **Supp. 7**, 118; trial of, **Vol. 7, Part 1**, 593; **Supp. 2**, 50, 142
Hazeltine Corporation, **Supp. 4**, 452
H. D. *See* Doolittle, Hilda
Head's Spring Temperance Society, **Vol. 7, Part 2**, 43
Health, Clark W., reference to, **Supp. 4**, 582
Health. *See* Diet and nutrition; Hospitals; International Board of Health; Medicine; Occupational health and safety; Physical fitness; Public health; *specific medical disciplines*
Health and Human Services, Department of (U.S.): administration, **Supp. 10**, 226, 227; government health insurance advocated, **Supp. 10**, 227
Health, public: **Vol. 1, Part 2**, 493; **Vol. 4, Part 2**, 45; **Vol. 8, Part 1**, 390 f.; **Vol. 8, Part 2**, 356; appointment of national secretary of, urged, **Vol. 8, Part 1**, 575; code of laws, **Vol. 9, Part 1**, 403; conservation of, **Vol. 3, Part 2**, 419; writings on, Vol. 4, Part 2 147 f.; **Vol. 5, Part 1**, 443; **Vol. 7, Part 1**, 277 f., 495 f
Health, Education, and Welfare, Department of (HEW): **Supp. 6**, 130; administration, **Supp. 10**, 250–51; creation of, **Supp. 10**, 686; welfare reduction measures, **Supp. 9**, 790
Health food, **Supp. 5**, 378–79, 452–53; **Supp. 9**, 221–22. *See also* Diet and nutrition
Health insurance: legislation, **Supp. 9**, 449; national advocates, **Supp. 3**, 18; **Supp. 6**, 703; prepayment plans, **Supp. 3**, 122, 313; private, **Supp. 4**, 747; retired people, **Supp. 8**, 10; universal access advocacy, **Supp. 10**, 682. *See also* Blue Cross and Blue Shield; Insurance
Health-maintenance organizations (HMOs), Kaiser Permanente founding, **Supp. 8**, 309
Health Services, Inc., **Supp. 3**, 122

Healthy Babies Are Happy Babies, **Supp. 7**, 428
Heap, Jane, reference to, **Supp. 9**, 33
Hearing. *See* Audiology; Deaf and deafness
Hearing aids, **Supp. 8**, 209
Hearst, Patricia, kidnapping of, **Supp. 10**, 135
Hearst, Phoebe Apperson, references to, **Supp. 3**, 144, 626; **Supp. 5**, 283, 284, 287; **Supp. 6**, 353, 438, 463
Hearst, William Randolph: Annenberg relationship, **Supp. 3**, 19–20; Block association, **Supp. 3**, 80; building commissions by, **Supp. 6**, 463, 464; Chandler relationship, **Supp. 3**, 156; circulation war, **Supp. 3**, 19, 144; **Supp. 6**, 686; *Citizen Kane*, **Supp. 3**, 80; **Supp. 5**, 464; critical writings on, **Supp. 4**, 481–82; Davies relationship, **Supp. 7**, 165–66; foreign policy, **Supp. 3**, 397; Fowler relationship, **Supp. 6**, 214; motion-picture industry, **Supp. 6**, 440–41; newspaper interests, **Supp. 3**, 425, 427–28; **Supp. 5**, 456, 657, 658; New York gubernatorial bid, **Supp. 10**, 233; political interests, **Supp. 8**, 207, 320; Pulitzer rivalry, **Supp. 5**, 551; references to, **Supp. 3**, 718; **Supp. 4**, 62, 404, 644, 872; **Supp. 5**, 244, 323; **Supp. 9**, 246, 604, 826; von Wiegand relationship, **Supp. 7**, 758–59
Heart: electrocardiography, **Supp. 6**, 117; first surgery on valve, **Supp. 4**, 209; inorganic salts to maintain beat of, **Supp. 3**, 369; research on, **Supp. 3**, 806; studies of the, **Vol. 5, Part 2**, 366; **Vol. 7, Part 1**, 120; surgery, **Supp. 7**, 59; ventricular fibrillation, **Supp. 4**, 390
Heartbreak Hotel, **Supp. 10**, 648
Heart disease: diagnosis and treatment of, **Supp. 2**, 84; **Supp. 4**, 494; **Supp. 9**, 654–55; lifestyle factor, **Supp. 9**, 862; prevention of, **Supp. 9**, 862; smoking link, **Supp. 7**, 192
Hearth and Home, **Vol. 8, Part 2**, 352
Heart Is a Lonely Hunter, The, **Supp. 8**, 400, 401
Heat: body studies, **Supp. 3**, 32; cramps, **Supp. 3**, 243; hot-air, **Vol. 3, Part 1**, 549; steam, **Vol. 7, Part 1**, 581; **Vol. 8, Part 1**, 115 f.
"Heathen Chinee," **Vol. 4, Part 2**, 363
Heatter, Maida, reference to, **Supp. 9**, 379
Heavenly Discourse, **Supp. 3**, 837
Heavy water, **Supp. 4**, 488–89
Hebras Zion, founding of, **Supp. 3**, 756
Hebrew: Bible, translated into English, **Vol. 5, Part 2**, 2; *Cyclopedia of Biblical Literature*, **Vol. 8, Part 2**, 165; dictionary, **Vol. 4, Part 1**, 247; language, grammar of, **Vol. 4, Part 1**, 247; **Vol. 7, Part 1**, 87, 547 f.; literature, dictionary of, **Vol. 5, Part 2**, 2; **Vol. 8, Part 2**, 574; literature and language, revival as a spoken language, **Supp. 1**, 407; literature and language, studies in, **Supp. 2**, 145; printing in Philadelphia, **Vol. 6, Part 1**, 137; study of, **Vol. 3, Part 1**, 459 f.; **Vol. 4, Part 2**, 262, 287; **Vol. 7, Part 1**, 118; **Vol. 8, Part 2**, 422, 612; teaching of, **Vol. 4, Part 1**, 560; **Vol. 6, Part 2**, 282; **Vol. 7, Part 1**, 48, 86, 547, 584; technical institute established, **Vol. 6, Part 1**, 155
Hebrew Immigrant Aid Society, founding of, **Supp. 4**, 262
Hebrew Union College (Cincinnati, Ohio), **Vol. 3, Part 1**, 259; **Vol. 5, Part 2**, 488; **Vol. 10, Part 2**, 426; **Supp. 4**, 659, 905; **Supp. 9**, 384
Hebrew University of Jerusalem, first president, **Supp. 4**, 539
Hecht, Ben: MacArthur collaboration, **Supp. 6**, 400–401; references to, **Supp. 5**, 73, 74, 323; **Supp. 6**, 628; **Supp. 7**, 148, 413; **Supp. 8**, 547
"Heckle and Jeckle" (fictional characters), **Supp. 9**, 798
Hecla Architectural Iron Works, **Vol. 8, Part 1**, 138 f.
Hedding, Elijah, reference to, **Vol. 9, Part 2**, 321
Heflin, Thomas, reference to, **Supp. 4**, 50
Hegel, Georg Wilhelm Friedrich, reference to, **Supp. 10**, 402
Hegel: A Reinterpretation, **Supp. 10**, 402
Heidegger, Martin, reference to, **Supp. 9**, 40
Heidelberg College, founding of, **Vol. 4, Part 1**, 376
Heifetz, Jascha, references to, **Supp. 6**, 352; **Supp. 7**, 124
Heinlein, Robert A., reference to, **Supp. 9**, 156
Heins, George Lewis, reference to, **Supp. 3**, 197
Heins, John, reference to, **Supp. 6**, 397
Heinz Memorial Chapel (Pittsburgh, Pa.), stained-glass windows, **Supp. 3**, 183
Heinze, F. A., reference to, **Vol. 9, Part 2**, 589 f.
Heinze-Morse banks, **Vol. 7, Part 1**, 240
Heisenberg, Werner, references to, **Supp. 7**, 133, 784; **Supp. 10**, 289
Heisman Trophy, first black awarded, **Supp. 7**, 167–68
Helburn, Theresa, reference to, **Supp. 3**, 811
HELCO. *See* Hartford Electric Co.
Helena, Ark., battle of (1863), **Vol. 5, Part 1**, 176; **Vol. 6, Part 2**, 291; **Vol. 8, Part 1**, 188, 216; **Vol. 9, Part 1**, 63
Helena, Mont., state capitol at, **Vol. 9, Part 2**, 589
Helen's Babies, **Vol. 4, Part 2**, 67 f.
Helft, Jacques, reference to, **Supp. 6**, 552
Helical measuring instrument, invention of, **Supp. 1**, 120
Helicon Hall (Englewood, N.J.), **Supp. 6**, 328; **Supp. 8**, 594
Helicopter: development of, **Supp. 5**, 377, 378; first commercial license, **Supp. 6**, 50; invention of, **Vol. 2, Part 2**, 553; **Supp. 1**, 76
Helium, **Supp. 4**, 184; production of, **Vol. 7, Part 1**, 136
Heller, Walter W., reference to, **Supp. 10**, 287
Hell Gate, **Vol. 6, Part 1**, 442, 473 f.
Hell Gate Bridge (New York City), **Supp. 6**, 594; **Supp. 7**, 11
Heller, Louis B., reference to, **Supp. 6**, 344
Hellman, Lillian, references to, **Supp. 3**, 315; **Supp. 7**, 314; **Supp. 8**, 704; **Supp. 10**, 54, 55
"Hello Muddah, Hello Faddah," **Supp. 9**, 720
Hell's Canyon (Idaho), **Supp. 7**, 213, 562
Hellzapoppin, **Supp. 7**, 588–89; **Supp. 9**, 886
Helmholtz, Hermann von, reference to, **Supp. 9**, 72
Helmle, Frank J., reference to, **Supp. 5**, 133
Helmle and Corbett, **Supp. 5**, 133–34
Helms, Jesse, reference to, **Supp. 9**, 441
Help!, **Supp. 10**, 449
Helsinki railroad station (Finland), **Supp. 4**, 714
Hematology. *See* Blood
Hemingway, Ernest: first story published, **Supp. 6**, 571; references to, **Supp. 4**, 769; **Supp. 6**, 21; **Supp. 7**, 560; **Supp. 9**, 34, 157; **Supp. 10**, 510, 756
Hemoglobin, **Supp. 4**, 643
Hempstead, Charles S., reference to, **Vol. 10, Part 1**, 504 f.
Hench, Philip, reference to, **Supp. 9**, 454–55
Henderson, Fletcher, reference to, **Supp. 9**, 46
Henderson, Joseph L., reference to, **Supp. 6**, 512
Henderson, Lawrence J., references to, **Supp. 3**, 137; **Supp. 4**, 565; **Supp. 5**, 122; **Supp. 8**, 50
Henderson, Leon, references to, **Supp. 3**, 660; **Supp. 4**, 458; **Supp. 5**, 558, 559
Henderson, Lightner, reference to, **Supp. 3**, 611–12
Henderson, Richard, reference to, **Vol. 6, Part 1**, 357
Henderson, Yandell, reference to, **Supp. 3**, 163
Heney, Francis J., references to, **Supp. 3**, 394; **Supp. 6**, 590
Henley Royal Regatta (Great Britain), **Supp. 6**, 331
Henri, Robert, references to, **Supp. 2**, 238; **Supp. 3**,

818; **Supp. 5**, 472, 625; **Supp. 7**, 170; **Supp. 8**, 279; **Supp. 9**, 456, 745
Henry, Alexander, reference to, **Vol. 8, Part 1**, 61
Henry, Arthur, reference to, **Supp. 3**, 233–34
Henry, Joseph, references to, **Vol. 1, Part 2**, 150; **Vol. 7, Part 1**, 248 f., 452 f.; **Vol. 10, Part 1**, 618 f.
Henry, O., references to, **Vol. 9, Part 1**, 245; **Supp. 6**, 5
Henry, Patrick, references to, **Vol. 2, Part 2**, 96; **Vol. 5, Part 1**, 118, 537, 597; **Vol. 7, Part 1**, 369, 424, 483; **Vol. 7, Part 2**, 417 f.; **Vol. 9, Part 2**, 332; **Vol. 10, Part 1**, 87 f.
Henry J (automobile), **Supp. 8**, 309
Henry Street Settlement House (New York City), **Supp. 2**, 687; **Supp. 6**, 499; **Supp. 7**, 466; visiting nurse service, **Supp. 6**, 167
Henson, Matthew, reference to, **Supp. 5**, 539
Heparin, **Supp. 3**, 370
Hepburn, Katharine, references to, **Supp. 4**, 55; **Supp. 5**, 296; **Supp. 7**, 682; **Supp. 8**, 659, 660; **Supp. 9**, 380, 692; **Supp. 10**, 12
Hepburn, Katharine Houghton (actress's mother), reference to, **Supp. 5**, 742
Hepburn Act, **Vol. 2, Part 2**, 145, 154; Vol. 4, Part 2 566; **Vol. 8, Part 1**, 248 f.
Hepburn Rate Act (1906), passage of, **Supp. 1**, 42
Herald of Gospel Liberty, earliest religious newspaper, **Vol. 9, Part 1**, 38, 259
Herbariums, **Vol. 1, Part 2**, 546; **Vol. 3, Part 1**, 538 f., 606 f.; **Vol. 7, Part 1**, 17; **Vol. 8, Part 1**, 104 f.; **Vol. 9, Part 1**, 127; **Supp. 1**, 632; **Supp. 3**, 23, 815; **Supp. 4**, 16–17, 266
Herbart, Johann Friedrich, references to, **Supp. 2**, 424
Herbert, Victor, references to, **Supp. 1**, 222; **Supp. 3**, 553; **Supp. 9**, 293
Herbicides. *See* Pesticides and herbicides
Herblock. *See* Block, Herbert
Her Cardboard Lover, **Supp. 3**, 368
Hercules mine, **Vol. 5, Part 1**, 446
Heredity. *See* Genetics
Heresy, **Vol. 8, Part 1**, 127 f., 292 f.; Congregational church, **Vol. 2, Part 1**, 351; Episcopal church, **Vol. 9, Part 2**, 34
Herman Melville, **Supp. 7**, 18
Hermaphroditism, **Supp. 3**, 854
Herndon, Hugh, references to, **Supp. 6**, 52, 493
Herndon, William H., references to, **Vol. 6, Part 1**, 246 f.; **Supp. 9**, 38
Herne, James A., reference to, **Supp. 4**, 369
Hernia, strangulated, first operation in U.S., **Vol. 10, Part 1**, 480 f.
Heroin, **Supp. 7**, 485
Herold, David E., reference to, **Vol. 1, Part 2**, 449
Herpetology. *See* Reptiles
Herreshoff Motor Co., **Supp. 7**, 245
Herrick, Clarence L., reference to, **Supp. 3**, 172
Herrmann, Bernard, reference to, **Supp. 10**, 239
Herrmann, John, reference to, **Supp. 8**, 255
Herron, George D., reference to, **Vol. 7, Part 1**, 2
Hersey, John, reference to, **Supp. 7**, 114; **Supp. 9**, 375
Hershey, Lewis, reference to, **Supp. 9**, 36
Hershey, Pa., founding of, **Supp. 3**, 358
Hershfield, Harry, reference to, **Supp. 5**, 18
Herter, Christian, reference to, **Supp. 6**, 350
Hertig, Arthur T., reference to, **Supp. 4**, 802
Hertz, Gustav, reference to, **Supp. 7**, 258
Hertzfeld, Karl, reference to, **Supp. 4**, 337
Hertzsprung, Ejnar, reference to, **Supp. 6**, 561
Herzl, Theodor, references to, **Supp. 2**, 265; **Supp. 4**, 905
Hess, Thomas B., reference to, **Supp. 7**, 260
Hess, V. F., reference to, **Supp. 7**, 134
Hess, Willy, references to, **Supp. 10**, 236, 237
Hetch Hetchy Valley dam project, **Supp. 4**, 522, 664; **Supp. 5**, 395
Heuer, George J., reference to, **Supp. 3**, 625
HEW. *See* Health, Education, and Welfare, Department of
Hexaphenylethane, **Supp. 4**, 336
Hey, D. H., reference to, **Supp. 6**, 334
Heye Foundation, **Supp. 6**, 289–90
Heyl, Paul, reference to, **Supp. 7**, 76
Heyward, DuBose, reference to, **Supp. 4**, 13
Hiawatha, **Vol. 6, Part 1**, 385; **Vol. 8, Part 1**, 104 f.
Hibbard, Hall L., reference to, **Supp. 9**, 758
Hi-Bred Corn Co., founding of, **Supp. 7**, 760
Hickman, Clarence N., reference to, **Supp. 3**, 306
Hickok, Lorena, references to, **Supp. 7**, 660, 664
Hicks, Elias, reference to, **Vol. 7, Part 1**, 288 f.
Hicks, Sue K., reference to, **Supp. 6**, 528
Hicksite movement, **Vol. 7, Part 1**, 288 f.
Hidatsa Indians, **Supp. 5**, 430
Hieroglyphics, Mayan, **Vol. 1, Part 2**, 492
Higgins, Aldus C., reference to, **Supp. 6**, 27
Higgins, Andrew Jackson, reference to, **Supp. 8**, 603
Higgins, Marguerite, reference to, **Supp. 8**, 520
Higgins Industries, **Supp. 5**, 299
Higginson, T. W., references to, **Vol. 5, Part 1**, 606; **Vol. 8, Part 2**, 522; **Vol. 9, Part 1**, 464
Higher education. *See* Education; Universities and colleges; *specific institutions*
High-fidelity sound, **Supp. 5**, 324. *See also* Audio systems
High-frequency transmission, **Supp. 3**, 748, 768–69
High Noon, **Supp. 7**, 143–44; **Supp. 10**, 784
High Society, **Supp. 10**, 160
High Voltage Engineering Corporation, **Supp. 8**, 666
Highways. *See* Road building
Hilbert, David, reference to, **Supp. 9**, 201; **Supp. 10**, 282
Hildebrand, George, reference to, **Supp. 6**, 663
Hilgard, J. E., reference to, **Vol. 7, Part 1**, 452 f.
Hill, A. P., reference to, **Vol. 6, Part 1**, 125 f.
Hill, Archibald V., references to, **Supp. 5**, 489; **Supp. 9**, 124
Hill, Adams Sherman, reference to, **Vol. 10, Part 1**, 649f.
Hill, B. H., reference to, **Supp. 4**, 144
Hill, Cumorah, reference to, **Vol. 9, Part 1**, 310
Hill, D. H., reference to, **Vol. 6, Part 1**, 124
Hill, David B., reference to, **Vol. 7, Part 2**, 213
Hill, James J., references to, **Vol. 2, Part 2**, 233; **Vol. 7, Part 1**, 177, 299; **Vol. 9, Part 1**, 52; **Supp. 3**, 381, 735, 736, 823; **Supp. 7**, 89
Hill, Joe, reference to, **Supp. 7**, 248
Hill, John Alexander, reference to, **Supp. 4**, 523
Hill, John W., reference to, **Supp. 9**, 682
Hill, Percival, reference to, **Supp. 4**, 370, 371
Hill, Ployer ("Pete"), reference to, **Supp. 9**, 255
Hill, Virginia, reference to, **Supp. 9**, 12
Hill and Knowlton, **Supp. 5**, 271; **Supp. 10**, 334–35
Hillman, Sidney, references to, **Supp. 4**, 75, 356, 458; **Supp. 6**, 378; **Supp. 7**, 172; **Supp. 10**, 643
Hillsborough, battle of, **Vol. 4, Part 1**, 571
Hillsboro Mob (N.C.), **Vol. 10, Part 1**, 26
Hill School, history of, **Vol. 6, Part 2**, 505
Hillsdale College, presidency of, **Vol. 3, Part 2**, 257
Hilton, Barron, references to, **Supp. 10**, 337, 338
Hilton Hotels, **Supp. 10**, 337
Himes, Norman E., reference to, **Supp. 6**, 602
Hine, Lewis W., reference to, **Supp. 10**, 765
Hines, Duncan, Foundation, **Supp. 6**, 292
Hines, James J., reference to, **Supp. 5**, 665
Hinks, Arthur Robert, reference to, **Supp. 6**, 560

"Hints from Heloise" column, **Supp. 10**, 666, 667
Hiram College, **Vol. 5, Part 1**, 66; **Vol. 4, Part 2**, 438
Hires, Charles E., Co., management, **Supp. 10**, 338, 339
Hires Root Beer, **Supp. 10**, 339
Hiroshima and Nagasaki: atomic bombing of, **Supp. 8**, 230, 231; **Supp. 9**, 747, 812; medical effects of atomic bombing, **Supp. 10**, 816
Hirschfeld, Al, references to, **Supp. 10**, 630, 631
His Girl Friday, **Supp. 10**, 713
Hispanic American Historical Review, founding of, **Supp. 5**, 577
Hispanic Americans, historical writings on, **Supp. 5**, 77, 577
Hispanic Review, founding of, **Supp. 2**, 132
Hiss, Alger: perjury trial, **Supp. 10**, 665, 719; references to, **Supp. 5**, 19, 665; **Supp. 7**, 114; **Supp. 9**, 572, 814
Histology, **Vol. 3, Part 2**, 201; research in, **Supp. 6**, 295–96
Historical fiction: **Supp. 3**, 93; **Supp. 4**, 13–14, 163–65, 583; **Supp. 5**, 266–67, 297–98, 620, 747–48; **Supp. 6**, 544, 544–46; **Supp. 7**, 148; **Supp. 8**, 180–82; Douglass, Frederick, **Supp. 10**, 193; Kantor novels, **Supp. 10**, 399–400; Mason novels, **Supp. 10**, 518, 519
Historical Geography in the United States, **Supp. 4**, 113
Historical materials, collections of, **Vol. 3, Part 2**, 559; **Vol. 7, Part 1**, 351; **Vol. 9, Part 1**, 538
Historical Outlook, founding of, **Supp. 2**, 419
Historical Records Survey, **Supp. 2**, 40
Historical societies: Georgia, **Supp. 1**, 472; Jewish, **Supp. 1**, 473
Historical Society of Pennsylvania, **Vol. 8, Part 1**, 401; **Vol. 10, Part 1**, 546; as center for historical research, **Supp. 10**, 60
Historic sites and buildings: Alabama, **Supp. 1**, 591; California missions, **Supp. 3**, 88; Conner homestead (Ind.), **Supp. 10**, 459; Dearborn, Mich., museums, **Supp. 4**, 302; Death Valley, **Supp. 5**, 613; Fossil Cycad National Monument, **Supp. 5**, 743–44; Japanese preservation, **Supp. 5**, 730; Jefferson Memorial, **Supp. 4**, 448; La Villita (San Antonio, Tex.), restoration, **Supp. 5**, 481; Lincoln Memorial, **Supp. 1**, 322; New England preservations and restorations, **Supp. 3**, 567; **Supp. 4**, 24; photography of, **Supp. 5**, 373; Rockefeller endowments, **Supp. 6**, 549; Roosevelt, Theodore, homes, **Supp. 7**, 311; Washington, D.C., restorations, **Supp. 7**, 425; Washington Monument, **Supp. 1**, 157; Williamsburg restoration, **Supp. 1**, 165; **Supp. 4**, 696; **Supp. 5**, 388
Historiography, **Supp. 5**, 557
History *(see also specific subjects)*: American business, writings on, **Supp. 10**, 395; American, ancient, **Supp. 6**, 612, American, colonial, **Supp. 3**, 55–16; **Supp. 9**, 314–15; **Supp. 10**, 429, 846, 847; American, writings on, **Supp. 1**, 166, 673; **Supp. 2**, 495; **Supp. 4**, 3–4; **Supp. 5**, 234–35; **Supp. 8**, 552, 580; **Supp. 9**, 581, 582, 583, 584, 629; **Supp. 10**, 107–8, 136–37, 432–33, 553, 554; American banking and politics study, **Supp. 8**, 243; American bibliography, **Supp. 8**, 663–64; American cultural, **Supp. 3**, 672–73; **Supp. 10**, 389; American diplomatic studies, **Supp. 7**, 683–84; American frontier, writings on, **Supp. 7**, 771–72; **Supp. 8**, 60; American intellectual, writings on, **Supp. 8**, 271–74; American political and constitutional, **Supp. 3**, 336–37; **Supp. 9**, 629; American regional, **Supp. 5**, 320–21; American social, **Supp. 3**, 287; **Supp. 6**, 696–97; American social, writings on, **Supp. 7**, 79–80, 741–42; **Supp. 8**, 692, 693; American studies, **Supp. 5**, 5–10, 667; American West, writings on, **Supp. 5**, 169; ancient civilizations studies, **Supp. 5**, 595–96; **Supp. 10**, 38–39; ancient slave systems, **Supp. 5**, 736; black, **Supp. 4**, 911; **Supp. 5**, 642; **Supp. 6**, 490; British, writings on, **Supp. 8**, 472–73, 580; Civil War and Reconstruction era, writings on, **Supp. 5**, 498; **Supp. 9**, 629; **Supp. 10**, 107–8, 136, 841, 842, 843–44; comparative, **Supp. 4**, 824; constitutional, **Supp. 4**, 530–31; cycles in, **Supp. 7**, 627; economic, teaching of, **Supp. 4**, 322; economic interpretation of, **Supp. 4**, 61–64; editing of, **Supp. 3**, 262, 285–86, 287, 337; **Supp. 7**, 253; Elizabethan English, **Supp. 6**, 531–32; **Supp. 9**, 627; European, **Supp. 4**, 162; European, writings on, **Supp. 2**, 564; **Supp. 7**, 517–18; **Supp. 8**, 50; French, writings on, **Supp. 9**, 329–30; geographic interpretation of, **Supp. 1**, 119; "great man" theory of, **Supp. 6**, 279; Hawaiian studies, **Supp. 7**, 445–46; intellectual, **Supp. 3**, 47; **Supp. 7**, 482; **Supp. 8**, 51; interdisciplinary studies, **Supp. 8**, 271–73; Jefferson papers, editing of, **Supp. 10**, 61; Latin American studies, **Supp. 5**, 577; **Supp. 6**, 277–78; medieval studies, **Supp. 1**, 285, 705; **Supp. 3**, 765–66; **Supp. 7**, 741–42; military, writings on, **Supp. 10**, 510, 511; modern nationalism studies, **Supp. 7**, 329–30; multiple causation of human progress theory, **Supp. 4**, 413; naval, writings on, **Supp. 10**, 553–54; new approach to, **Vol. 10, Part 1**, 63 f.; new social sciences approach to, **Supp. 2**, 564–66; **Supp. 4**, 62, 152, 162, 824; **Supp. 8**, 50; oral, **Supp. 9**, 582; original documents, **Supp. 2**, 40; **Supp. 4**, 1–2; pageants about, **Supp. 3**, 427; popular writings on, **Supp. 3**, 790; **Supp. 4**, 116, 368; pre-Islamic civilization, **Supp. 3**, 572–73; Quaker, **Supp. 4**, 441–42; quantitative approach to, **Supp. 5**, 429–30; relativism in, **Supp. 3**, 47–48; research in field of, **Vol.2, Part 1**, 63; **Vol. 6, Part 1**, 68; **Vol. 8, Part 2**, 137 f., 276; **Vol. 10, Part 1**, 603 f.; revisionism, **Supp. 3**, 555; revisionist Civil War, **Supp. 5**, 557–58; revisionist World War I, **Supp. 7**, 735; **Supp. 8**, 169; socialist interpretation of, **Supp. 4**, 746–47; source material, early use of, **Vol. 10, Part 1**, 603 f.; source standards, **Supp. 3**, 285–86; South (U.S.), **Supp. 3**, 31–32; **Supp. 5**, 671–72; **Supp. 6**, 491–92; Spanish-American, **Supp. 5**, 77, 570; Spanish influence on American, **Supp. 2**, 561; state commissions, **Supp. 4**, 176; teaching of, **Vol. 1, Part 1**, 70, 314; **Vol. 4, Part 1**, 568 f.; **Vol. 4, Part 2**, 18, 57, 116; **Vol. 5, Part 1**, 178, 244, 277; **Vol. 5, Part 2**, 241; **Vol. 7, Part 1**, 239, 274 f., 330 f.; **Vol. 8, Part 2**, 486; **Vol. 9, Part 1**, 214, 221, 314, 316, 430, 578; **Vol. 10, Part 1**, 92 f.; **Vol. 10, Part 2**, 2; **Supp. 2**, 563; **Supp. 3**, 287; **Supp. 6**, 491; **Supp. 7**, 329–30, 684–85, 770; **Supp. 9**, 330, 582; **Supp. 10**, 844; textbooks, **Supp. 1**, 484; **Supp. 2**, 564; **Supp. 6**, 278; **Supp. 7**, 568; urban, **Supp. 9**, 339; women's studies programs, **Supp. 6**, 41; writings on, **Vol. 1, Part 1**, 18, 20, 33, 38, 51 f., 65, 70, 81, 92 f., 164, 176 f., 236, 369, 372, 444, 566, 583; **Vol. 1, Part 2**, 7, 22, 38 f., 103, 137, 147, 153, 232, 377, 469, 483 f., 485, 537, 539 f., 551; **Vol. 2, Part 1**, 60, 97, 103, 159, 161, 324, 451, 599; **Vol. 2, Part 2**, 21 f., 109, 113, 385 f., 393 f., 431 f., 433, 448 f., 453 f., 473, 477 f., 603, 628; **Vol. 3, Part 1**, 106, 130, 147 f., 152, 169, 172, 180, 190 f., 199, 226, 248, 259 f., 266, 352, 394, 396 f., 408, 424, 433 f., 492 f., 495 f., 502., 516 f., 518 f., 523 f., 525, 534, 545 f., 550 f., 561 f., 569 f., 593 f., 602 f., 604; **Vol. 3, Part 2**, 53, 88, 197, 278, 410 f., 422, 519; **Vol. 4, Part 1**, 7, 46, 134, 166, 195 f., 235, 237, 261, 297, 364, 397, 525, 565 f., 568 f., 580, 583, 617, 628 f.; **Vol. 4, Part 2**, 18, 135, 163, 429, 470, 561 f.; **Vol. 5, Part 1**, 18 f., 31, 160, 178, 244, 251, 281, 288, 337, 385, 442, 467, 503, 560, 604; **Vol. 5, Part 2**, 8, 45 f., 48, 80,

124, 137, 142, 149 f., 219, 242, 259, 559, 598, 606; **Vol. 6, Part 1**, 2, 18, 40, 67, 131, 148, 172, 200, 219, 279, 296, 306, 347, 408; **Vol. 6, Part 2**, 1, 138, 141, 214, 385, 449, 481; **Vol. 7, Part 1**, 94, 125, 283 f., 300; **Vol. 7, Part 2**, 17, 78 f., 154, 169 f., 246 f., 253, 321 f., 392, 422, 427, 448, 456, 459 f., 474, 495 f., 519 f., 553, 568, 596, 639; **Vol. 8, Part 1**, 8, 11 f., 28 f., 58 f., 61 f., 66 f., 71 f., 75 f., 92 f., 100 f., 120 f., 126 f., 144 f., 161 f., 183 f., 189 f., 193 f., 196 f., 202, 211 f., 229 f., 232 f., 245 f., 276, 279 f., 285, 308 f., 311 f., 325 f., 331 f., 338, 341 f., 351 f., 368 f., 388, 400, 429, 443, 462, 474, 503, 519 f., 531 f., 599, 625, 633 f., 645 f.; **Vol. 8, Part 2**, 276, 312, 472; **Vol. 9, Part 1**, 296, 316, 379, 395, 430 f., 527, 617; **Vol. 9, Part 2**, 21, 25, 89 f., 326 f., 387, 503; **Vol. 10, Part 1**, 29, 43, 61 f., 76, 140, 146, 161, 178 f., 374 f., 466, 484, 497 f., 499 f., 502 f., 504 f., 533, 541 f., 546, 549 f., 571, f., 600 f., 603 f., 629 f.; **Vol. 10, Part 2**, 2, 26, 255, 404; **Supp. 3**, 947–48; **Supp. 5**, 364; **Supp. 6**, 41, 95, 409–10; **Supp. 9**, 277–78. *See also* Archives; *specific subjects, e.g.,* Art

History of American Life series, **Supp. 7**, 676; **Supp. 8**, 692; **Supp. 10**, 136

History of American Literature, **Vol. 2, Part 1**, 69

History of American Magazines, **Supp. 7**, 559

History of American Painting, **Vol. 5, Part 1**, 515

History of Brown University, **Vol. 2, Part 1**, 69

History of Carolina (North), **Vol. 6, Part 1**, 57

History of Colorado, **Vol. 9, Part 2**, 87

History of Economic Analysis, **Supp. 4**, 723

History of Economic Doctrines, **Supp. 4**, 722, 723

History of Labor in the United States, **Supp. 3**, 178–79, **Supp. 6**, 503

History of Magic and Experimental Science, A, **Supp. 7**, 741–42

History of New Hampshire, by Jeremy Belknap, **Vol. 1, Part 2**, 147

History of New Hampshire, by Edwin David Sanborn, **Vol. 8, Part 2**, 325

History of New York, **Vol. 5, Part 1**, 507

History of New York During the Revolution, **Vol. 5, Part 2**, 200

History of Oregon and California, **Vol. 4, Part 1**, 580

History of Plimmoth [Plymouth] Plantation, **Vol. 1, Part 2**, 562; **Vol. 3, Part 1**, 172

History of Rhode Island and Providence Plantation, **Vol. 1, Part 1**, 372

History of Science Society, founding of, **Supp. 3**, 722

History of the Ancient World, A, **Supp. 5**, 595

History of the Colony of Massachusetts Bay, **Vol. 5, Part 1**, 440 f.

History of the Expedition Under the Command of Captains Lewis and Clark, **Vol. 1, Part 1**, 203

History of the Great American Fortunes, **Supp. 3**, 545–46

History of the Standard Oil Co., The, **Supp. 3**, 762

History of the United States, by H. B. Adams, **Vol. 1, Part 1**, 65

History of the United States, by G. Bancroft, **Vol. 1, Part 1**, 566

History of the United States of America Under the Constitution, **Vol. 8, Part 2**, 460

History of Vermont, Natural, Civil and Statistical, **Vol. 9, Part 2**, 480

History of Wallingford, Conn., **Vol. 3, Part 1**, 108

History Teacher's Magazine, founding of, **Supp. 2**, 419

Hitchcock, Albert S., references to, **Supp. 7**, 119, 120

Hitchcock, Alfred: Carroll roles in films of, **Supp. 9**, 158; Herrmann relationship, **Supp. 9**, 383; references to, **Supp. 7**, 682

Hitchcock, Dal, reference to, **Supp. 5**, 558, 559

Hitchcock, Gilbert, reference to, **Supp. 3**, 114

Hitchcock, Henry, reference to, **Vol. 9, Part 2**, 634

Hitchcock, Henry-Russell, Wright architectural study, **Supp. 6**, 714

"Hitching Post," applied to Philippines, **Vol. 3, Part 1**, 164

Hitler, Adolf, references to, **Supp. 3**, 658, 8, 659, 661; **Supp. 4**, 898; **Supp. 5**, 60; **Supp. 6**, 636, 675, **Supp. 7**, 740, 757, 759; **Supp. 8**, 456; **Supp. 9**, 44, 131; **Supp. 10**, 246, 432, 533, 562, 571. *See also* Nazism

HMOs. *See* Health-maintenance organizations

Hoagland, Hudson, reference to, **Supp. 8**, 503

Hoax, literary, **Supp. 7**, 643; **Supp. 10**, 358

Hoban, James, reference to, **Vol. 7, Part 1**, 10

Hobart College: **Vol. 3, Part 1**, 561 f.; **Vol. 4, Part 2**, 96; **Vol. 7, Part 1**, 5, 74; **Vol. 8, Part 1**, 124 f., 126; **Vol. 9, Part 2**, 76; founding of, **Vol. 9, Part 2**, 652

Hobby, Oveta Culp, references to, **Supp. 7**, 350; **Supp. 9**, 784

Hobo, adventures of a, **Vol. 6, Part 1**, 371

Hobson, John A., reference to, **Supp. 3**, 680, 681

Hodges, Johnny, references to, **Supp. 6**, 43; **Supp. 9**, 847

Hodges, Luther Hartwell, reference to, **Supp. 9**, 440

Hodgins, Frederic Brinkley, **Supp. 9**, 393

Hodgkin, Alan, reference to, **Supp. 6**, 100

Hodgson, Richard, reference to, **Vol. 5, Part 1**, 455

Hodson, William, reference to, **Supp. 4**, 810

Hoffa, James R., references to, **Supp. 7**, 50; **Supp. 8**, 322; **Supp. 9**, 512

Hoffa, Portland, reference to, **Supp. 6**, 13

Hoffman, Elizabeth, reference to, **Supp. 8**, 683

Hoffman, Paul G., reference to, **Supp. 6**, 650; **Supp. 7**, 276

Hoffman, Roald, reference to, **Supp. 10**, 853

Hogan, Ernest, reference to, **Supp. 3**, 187

"Hogan's Heroes" (television program), **Supp. 10**, 156

Hogarth, David G., reference to, **Supp. 3**, 343

Hogarth, Jr., (Rockwell Kent pseudonym), **Supp. 9**, 458

Hogate, Kenneth Craven ("Casey"), reference to, **Supp. 9**, 520

Hogg, James S., references to, **Supp. 2**, 319; **Supp. 6**, 468

Hogs, keeping of, on roof of a N.Y. hotel, **Vol. 9, Part 2**, 69

Hohfeld, Wesley Newcomb, reference to, **Supp. 3**, 186

Hoke, Helen, reference to, **Supp. 10**, 820–21

Holden, Charles, reference to, **Supp. 6**, 194

Holden, Isaac, reference to, **Supp. 3**, 703

Holden, Ralph, reference to, **Supp. 7**, 101

Holden, William W., reference to, **Vol. 10, Part 1**, 69

Hole, The, **Supp. 10**, 353

Holderness community (N.H.), **Supp. 8**, 189, 399

Holding companies: first in U.S., **Vol. 8, Part 2**, 266; legislation regulating, **Supp. 4**, 395; New Jersey, **Vol. 3, Part 1**, 309

Holiday, Ensor R., reference to, **Supp. 6**, 595

Holiday, **Supp. 7**, 602

Holiness movement, **Vol. 5, Part 1**, 490

Holistic medicine, **Supp. 6**, 181

Holke, Walter, reference to, **Supp. 8**, 713

Holland, George, reference to, **Vol. 5, Part 1**, 255

Holland, John P., references to, **Vol. 5, Part 2**, 380; **Supp. 3**, 436–37

Holland, Josiah Gilbert, references to, Vol. 5, Part 2. 388; **Vol. 8, Part 2**, 516; **Vol. 9, Part 1**, 340

Holland, diplomatic relations with, **Vol. 1, Part 1**, 76 f.

Hollander, Jacob H., reference to, **Supp. 2**, 24

Holland Land Co., **Vol. 2, Part 1**, 315, 581; **Vol. 3, Part 2**, 90; **Vol. 10, Part 2**, 297

Holland Tunnel (N.Y.-N.J.), **Vol. 5, Part 1**, 142; **Supp. 3**, 353; **Supp. 4**, 690, 757; **Supp. 6**, 187, 587

Hollerith, Herman, reference to, **Supp. 6**, 674
Holley, Alexander L., reference to, **Vol. 9, Part 2**, 581
Holly Springs, Miss., raid on (1863), **Vol. 3, Part 2**, 495; **Vol. 10, Part 1**, 185
Hollywood. *See* Motion pictures
Hollywood Bowl (Calif.), concerts, **Supp. 3**, 359; **Supp. 4**, 139; construction of, **Supp. 2**, 697
Hollywood Production Code Administration, **Supp. 6**, 288
"Hollywood Ten," **Supp. 9**, 602; **Supp. 10**, 437, 793
Holm, Eleanor, reference to, **Supp. 8**, 547
Holman, Libby, reference to, **Supp. 9**, 115
Holmes, John Hayes, reference to, **Supp. 6**, 664
Holmes, Oliver Wendell: Bausch & Lomb microscope endorsement, **Supp. 3**, 40; biography of, **Supp. 9**, 112, 113; references to, **Vol. 5, Part 1**, 141, 160; **Supp. 9**, 593
Holmes, Oliver Wendell, Jr.: biography of, **Supp. 8**, 285; Brandeis relationship, **Supp. 3**, 94, 98–99; legal realism, **Supp. 3**, 185, 186; references to, **Supp. 4**, 727; **Supp. 5**, 571, 574; **Supp. 6**, 271; **Supp. 7**, 261, 317, 475; **Supp. 8**, 34
"Holmes, Sherlock" (fictional character), **Supp. 8**, 519; **Supp. 10**, 104
Holmes, William H., reference to, **Supp. 3**, 372
"Holmes' arithmetic," phrase applied to vote counting, **Vol. 8, Part 1**, 184 f.
Holocaust, **Supp. 3**, 661; **Supp. 4**, 593–94; **Supp. 5**, 177, 552; **Supp. 7**, 498; first American to document Dachau, **Supp. 9**, 767; study of, **Supp. 9**, 42; Zionism as reaction to, **Supp. 4**, 906. *See also* Refugees, Jewish; War crimes; Zionism
Holt, Edwin B., reference to, **Supp. 5**, 503
Holt, Hamilton, references to, **Supp. 1**, 340; **Supp. 4**, 550; **Supp. 6**, 25
Holt, Henry, reference to, **Supp. 5**, 85
Holt, Henry, and Co., **Supp. 5**, 271
Holt, Luther Emmett, references to, **Vol. 5, Part 1**, 313; **Supp. 3**, 370; **Supp. 7**, 427
Holt, Robert, reference to, **Supp. 6**, 527
Holt, Rinehart and Winston, founding of, **Supp. 8**, 536
Holtz, Lou, reference to, **Supp. 7**, 282
Holy Cross College, founding of, **Vol. 3, Part 2**, 432
Holy Name Journal, founding of, **Supp. 4**, 535
Holyoke, E. A., reference to, **Vol. 5, Part 1**, 545
Holyoke, Mass.: civic service, **Vol. 9, Part 1**, 202; as manufacturing center, **Vol. 3, Part 1**, 563 f.
Holy Rosary Cathedral (Toledo, Ohio), **Supp. 6**, 607
Homages to the Square, **Supp. 10**, 3–4
"Homage to Mistress Bradstreet" (poem), **Supp. 9**, 86
Homart Development (Sears subsidiary), **Supp. 10**, 164
Home appliances: manufacturing, **Supp. 7**, 809; refrigerators, **Supp. 4**, 244; **Supp. 7**, 154; vacuum cleaner, **Supp. 5**, 313–14; washing machine, **Supp. 2**, 441; **Supp. 3**, 56
Home economics: **Vol. 7, Part 1**, 575; **Vol. 8, Part 1**, 554, 563 f.; **Vol. 10, Part 1**, 617 f.; cleaning products, **Supp. 9**, 510; "Hints from Heloise" column, **Supp. 10**, 666, 667; household efficiency studies, **Supp. 9**, 309–10; professionalization of, **Supp. 3**, 67–68; teaching of, **Supp. 3**, 507
Home Economics, Bureau of, **Vol. 10, Part 1**, 370
Homecroft living, **Supp. 4**, 564
Home furnishings, design, **Supp. 4**, 715; **Supp. 7**, 670; **Supp. 8**, 435, 436
Homeless: children, **Supp. 2**, 57; in Great Depression, **Supp. 6**, 516; tramps, writings on, **Supp. 1**, 706–7; youth facilities, **Supp. 4**, 282–83
Home Missionary Society. *See* Missions
Homeopathy: **Vol. 1, Part 1**, 208; **Vol. 3, Part 2**, 450; **Vol. 4, Part 2**, 35, 101, 576; **Vol. 5, Part 1**, 135, 551; **Vol. 6, Part 1**, 209, 480; **Vol. 7, Part 1**, 406 f.; **Vol. 8, Part 1**, 264, 391; **Vol. 9, Part 1**, 222; **Vol. 9, Part 2**, 278; **Vol. 10, Part 2**, 4; first school of, **Vol. 4, Part 2**, 575; yellow fever, application of, to, **Vol. 5, Part 1**, 135; writings on, **Vol. 4, Part 2**, 520; **Vol. 8, Part 1**, 391
Homeostasis, term coined, **Supp. 3**, 136, 137
Homer, scholarship on, **Supp. 4**, 728–29
Homer and Jethro (comedy team), **Supp. 9**, 374–75
Homer G. Phillips Hospital (St. Louis), **Supp. 6**, 190
Homestead Act (1862), **Vol. 2, Part 2**, 362; **Vol. 4, Part 2**, 30 f.; **Vol. 5, Part 2**, 82, 246; **Vol. 10, Part 1**, 134
Homesteader, The, **Supp. 5**, 490
Homestead (Pa.) Grays (baseball), **Supp. 4**, 327
Homesteads: Acton, **Vol. 5, Part 2**, 414; Alta Vista, **Vol. 8, Part 1**, 47; Anchorage, **Vol. 5, Part 2**, 221; Andalusia, **Vol. 10, Part 1**, 397 f.; Arden, **Vol. 4, Part 2**, 300; Arlington, **Vol. 6, Part 1**, 121, 134; Ashland, **Vol. 5, Part 2**, 337 f.; **Vol. 10, Part 1**, 156; Aspet, **Vol. 8, Part 2**, 302; Barrington, **Vol. 5, Part 2**, 162; Bayside, **Vol. 9, Part 2**, 544; Bayside Farm, **Vol. 6, Part 1**, 547; Beauvoir, **Vol. 3, Part 1**, 146; **Vol. 9, Part 2**, 375; Beech Grove, **Vol. 10, Part 1**, 551 f.; Beechmoor, **Vol. 10, Part 1**, 454; Bel Air, **Vol. 10, Part 1**, 604 f.; Belair, **Vol. 7, Part 1**, 648; **Vol. 8, Part 2**, 348; Bella Vista, **Vol. 7, Part 1**, 292; Belle Grove, **Vol. 5, Part 2**, 272; Belleville, **Vol. 1, Part 2**, 539; **Vol. 9, Part 2**, 650; Bellevue, **Vol. 7, Part 1**, 365; Bellwood, **Vol. 5, Part 2**, 191; Belvidere, **Vol. 7, Part 1**, 431; Belvoir, **Vol. 5, Part 2**, 362; **Vol. 6, Part 2**, 416; **Vol. 10, Part 1**, 509 f.; Berkeley, **Vol. 8, Part 1**, 568; Bermuda Hundred, **Vol. 8, Part 1**, 372; Bethphage, **Vol. 8, Part 1**, 573; Biltmore, **Vol. 7, Part 2**, 27; **Vol. 10, Part 1**, 174; Birchbrow, **Vol. 8, Part 2**, 336; Bizarre, **Vol. 8, Part 1**, 364; **Vol. 9, Part 2**, 320; Bluff Cottage, **Vol. 5, Part 2**, 101; Bois des Fosss, **Vol. 3, Part 1**, 526, 533; Bonaventure, **Vol. 9, Part 2**, 310; Bouwery, **Vol. 8, Part 2**, 256; Brandon, **Vol. 8, Part 1**, 628; Bremo, **Vol. 8, Part 1**, 372; Brick House, **Vol. 5, Part 2**, 49; Brierfield, **Vol. 3, Part 1**, 130; Brier Hill, **Vol. 9, Part 2**, 567 f.; Brooklawn, **Vol. 8, Part 1**, 586; Buchoi, **Vol. 7, Part 1**, 112; Buena Vista, **Vol. 5, Part 2**, 524; Bush Hill, **Vol. 4, Part 2**, 182, 186; Calverton, **Vol. 8, Part 1**, 336; Canonchet, home of Spragues, **Vol. 9, Part 1**, 473; Cassada Garden, **Vol. 8, Part 1**, 445; Castle Hill, **Vol. 8, Part 1**, 636 f.; **Vol. 10, Part 1**, 360 f.; Cedarcroft, **Vol. 9, Part 2**, 315; Cedar Grove, **Vol. 5, Part 2**, 550; Chantilly, **Vol. 6, Part 1**, 118; Chase House, **Vol. 5, Part 2**, 362; Chatsworth, **Vol. 8, Part 1**, 372; Cherry Grove, **Vol. 5, Part 2**, 144; Cherry Lawn, **Vol. 5, Part 2**, 383; China Grove, **Vol. 5, Part 2**, 136; Clermont, **Vol. 6, Part 1**, 309, 319 f.; **Vol. 7, Part 1**, 84; Clifton Hall, **Vol. 5, Part 2**, 515; Cockloft Hall, **Vol. 5, Part 1**, 512; **Vol. 5, Part 2**, 316 f.; College Hill, **Vol. 10, Part 1**, 403 f.; Contention, **Vol. 8, Part 1**, 7; Coolfont, **Vol. 8, Part 1**, 302; Craigie House, **Vol. 2, Part 2**, 497; **Vol. 6, Part 1**, 381 f.; Curles, **Vol. 8, Part 1**, 372; Dungeness, **Vol. 8, Part 1**, 372; Edgehill, **Vol. 8, Part 1**, 359, 368, 370 f.; Edgewood, **Vol. 7, Part 1**, 42; **Vol. 8, Part 1**, 272; Elmwood, **Vol. 6, Part 1**, 458; Epping Forest, **Vol. 10, Part 1**, 509 f.; Fair Hill, **Vol. 7, Part 1**, 554 f.; Fairview, **Vol. 1, Part 2**, 510; Fansley, **Vol. 9, Part 2**, 545; Fashion, **Vol. 9, Part 2**, 340; Federal Hill, **Vol. 8, Part 2**, 196; Ferry Farm, **Vol. 10, Part 1**, 509 f.; Fieldhead, **Vol. 8, Part 1**, 223 f.; Firleigh Hall, **Vol. 5, Part 2**, 134; Fort Hill, **Vol. 2, Part 1**, 412; Fountain Rock, **Vol. 8, Part 1**, 617; Fox Chase, **Vol. 5, Part 2**, 13; Fox Hill, **Vol. 10, Part 1**, 471 f.; Gamble House, **Vol. 4, Part 2**, 375; Gapland, **Vol. 9, Part 2**, 617; Georgian Court, **Vol. 4, Part 1**,

450; **Vol. 8, Part 1**, 210 f.; Glen Iris, **Vol. 6, Part 1**, 193; Glenview, **Vol. 1, Part 2**, 511; Goat Hill, **Vol. 9, Part 2**, 403; Good Luck, **Vol. 7, Part 1**, 361; Governor Wentworth House, **Vol. 3, Part 1**, 545 f.; Grantlands, **Vol. 7, Part 1**, 344; Grapevine Cottage, **Vol. 6, Part 1**, 425; Grasmere, **Vol. 8, Part 1**, 470; Gravelly Ridge, **Vol. 5, Part 2**, 169; Great House, **Vol. 9, Part 1**, 115; Greenaway Court, **Vol. 3, Part 2**, 256; Greenbank, **Vol. 8, Part 1**, 84; Green Bottom, **Vol. 5, Part 2**, 43; Greenfield, **Vol. 8, Part 1**, 237; Green Hill, **Vol. 8, Part 1**, 604; Greenway, **Vol. 6, Part 1**, 88; Greenwich House, **Vol. 10, Part 1**, 485 f.; Greystone, **Vol. 9, Part 2**, 541; Grove, The (N.C.), **Vol. 5, Part 2**, 210; Grove, The (N.Y.), **Vol. 10, Part 1**, 421 f.; Gunston Hall, **Vol. 5, Part 2**, 360; Habrede-Venture, **Vol. 9, Part 2**, 84; Hampden Place, **Vol. 8, Part 1**, 644; Hampton Plantation, **Vol. 8, Part 1**, 395; Hare Forest, **Vol. 9, Part 2**, 349; Hayes, **Vol. 5, Part 2**, 150; Hayfield, **Vol. 5, Part 2**, 203; **Vol. 9, Part 1**, 127; Hazelfield, **Vol. 10, Part 1**, 37; Hazelwood, **Vol. 9, Part 2**, 331; Hermitage, **Vol. 5, Part 1**, 527 f.; **Vol. 8, Part 1**, 36; **Vol. 9, Part 2**, 366, 564; **Vol. 10, Part 1**, 156; Highland Grove, **Vol. 5, Part 2**, 282; Hill Crest, **Vol. 9, Part 2**, 395; Hill of the Painted Men, **Vol. 8, Part 1**, 120; Hobcaw, **Vol. 8, Part 1**, 425; Homus, **Vol. 8, Part 1**, 202; Hope, **Vol. 9, Part 2**, 72; Indian Hill Farm, **Vol. 8, Part 1**, 73; Jessamine Hill, **Vol. 10, Part 1**, 641 f.; Johnson Hall, **Vol. 5, Part 2**, 104, 127; Kalorama, **Vol. 1, Part 2**, 427; Kenmore, **Vol. 6, Part 1**, 214; King's Bend, **Vol. 5, Part 2**, 407; La Belle Knoll, **Vol. 10, Part 1**, 414; Lang Syne, **Vol. 6, Part 1**, 605; Landsdowne, **Vol. 5, Part 2**, 68; Laudamus Farm, **Vol. 8, Part 1**, 614; Leesylvania, **Vol. 6, Part 1**, 107, 117; Levinworth Manor, **Vol. 8, Part 1**, 149; Liberty Hall, **Vol. 5, Part 2**, 11, 326; Liendo, **Vol. 7, Part 1**, 95, 479; Lindenhurst, **Vol. 10, Part 1**, 407 f.; Lindenshade, **Vol. 5, Part 2**, 13; Lindenwald, **Vol. 10, Part 1**, 156; Lipona, **Vol. 7, Part 1**, 339; Little Versailles, **Vol. 1, Part 1**, 130; Longwood, **Vol. 8, Part 1**, 192; Low Foxton, **Vol. 8, Part 1**, 247; Magnolia Plantation, **Vol. 10, Part 1**, 457 f.; Malmaison, **Vol. 6, Part 1**, 144; Mansfield, **Vol. 10, Part 1**, 552 f.; Mansion House, **Vol. 8, Part 2**, 186; Maplewood, **Vol. 3, Part 1**, 522; Marshes Seat, **Vol. 10, Part 1**, 604 f., Matoax, **Vol. 8, Part 1**, 363; **Vol. 10, Part 1**, 32, 36, 38; Mattaponi, **Vol. 1, Part 2**, 511; Meadow Farm, **Vol. 9, Part 2**, 349; Meadow Garden, **Vol. 10, Part 1**, 403 f.; Menokin, **Vol. 6, Part 1**, 105; Meridian Hill, **Vol. 8, Part 1**, 84; Millwood, **Vol. 4, Part 2**, 213; Monmouth Plantation, **Vol. 8, Part 1**, 316; Montgomery Place, **Vol. 6, Part 1**, 312; Monticello, **Vol. 5, Part 2**, 18, 26, 34, 222; **Vol. 6, Part 1**, 52, 204; **Vol. 7, Part 1**, 10, 88, 487; **Vol. 8, Part 1**, 358, 369, 371; **Vol. 9, Part 2**, 526; Montpelier, **Vol. 9, Part 2**, 343; Morven, **Vol. 9, Part 2**, 46 f.; Morven Park, **Vol. 9, Part 2**, 238; Mount Airy, **Vol. 9, Part 1**, 171; Mount Lowe, **Vol. 6, Part 1**, 453; Mount Pitt, **Vol. 5, Part 2**, 200; Mount Radnor, **Vol. 9, Part 2**, 442; Mount Vernon, **Vol. 2, Part 2**, 601; **Vol. 3, Part 2**, 225; **Vol. 7, Part 1**, 297; **Vol. 8, Part 1**, 604; **Vol. 8, Part 2**, 292; **Vol. 10, Part 1**, 508 f.; Mount Welcome, **Vol. 5, Part 2**, 146; Needham, **Vol. 9, Part 2**, 320; Needwood, **Vol. 6, Part 1**, 132; New Hope, **Vol. 10, Part 1**, 641 f.; Oak Grove, **Vol. 5, Part 2**, 148; Oak Lawn, **Vol. 8, Part 1**, 82; Ogontz, **Vol. 7, Part 1**, 432; Old Ironsides, **Vol. 9, Part 2**, 7; Old Place, **Vol. 8, Part 1**, 256; Ophir Farm, **Vol. 8, Part 1**, 484; Ophir Place, **Vol. 5, Part 1**, 142; Pembroke, **Vol. 7, Part 1**, 384; Pine Grove, **Vol. 10, Part 1**, 406 f.; Pines, The, **Vol. 9, Part 2**, 514; Plantation, **Vol. 5, Part 2**, 421; Polk Place, **Vol. 8, Part 1**, 38; Pontine, **Vol. 5, Part 2**, 163; Pooshee, **Vol. 8, Part 1**, 396; Poplar Grove, **Vol. 9, Part 2**, 584; Poplar Mount, **Vol. 3, Part 2**, 45; Popodickon, **Vol. 8, Part 1**, 137; Port Tobago, **Vol. 6, Part 1**, 369; Poynton Manor, **Vol. 9, Part 2**, 84; Ravenhill, **Vol. 10, Part 1**, 607 f.; Retreat, **Vol. 5, Part 2**, 403; **Vol. 9, Part 2**, 138; Rion Hall, **Vol. 6, Part 1**, 483; Rippon Lodge, **Vol. 10, Part 1**, 508 f.; Roanoke, **Vol. 8, Part 1**, 366; Rock Castle, **Vol. 9, Part 1**, 254; Rosemount, **Vol. 5, Part 2**, 348; **Vol. 9, Part 2**, 395; Rosewell, **Vol. 7, Part 2**, 138 f.; Rosmont, **Vol. 9, Part 2**, 651; Runnymede, **Vol. 8, Part 1**, 238; Sabot Hill, **Vol. 8, Part 2**, 545; Sevenels, **Vol. 6, Part 1**, 453; Shad, The, **Vol. 7, Part 1**, 624; Shadwell, **Vol. 7, Part 1**, 10; Shady Hill, **Vol. 7, Part 1**, 569; Sherwood Forest, **Vol. 10, Part 1**, 91; Sidney, **Vol. 9, Part 1**, 344; Silk Hope, **Vol. 5, Part 2**, 111; Slate-roof House, **Vol. 7, Part 1**, 554 f.; Smithfield, **Vol. 8, Part 1**, 206 f.; Soldier's Retreat, **Vol. 1, Part 1**, 271; Springfields, **Vol. 9, Part 2**, 340; Spring Garden, **Vol. 8, Part 1**, 643; Spring Hill, **Vol. 10, Part 1**, 552 f.; Stenton, **Vol. 6, Part 1**, 359, 362; Stepney, **Vol. 5, Part 2**, 42; Stratford, **Vol. 6, Part 1**, 96, 105, 108 f., 116 f., 120, 132; Summerton Plantation, **Vol. 8, Part 1**, 395; Sunnyside, **Vol. 5, Part 1**, 504, 511; Tazewell Hall, **Vol. 8, Part 1**, 353, 362, 367, 372; Terra Rubra, **Vol. 5, Part 2**, 362; Torch Hill, **Vol. 9, Part 2**, 525; Town Head, **Vol. 9, Part 2**, 361; Trotwood, **Vol. 7, Part 1**, 132; Tuckahoe, **Vol. 8, Part 1**, 370, 372; Turkey Island, **Vol. 8, Part 1**, 361, 371 f.; Turrets, **Vol. 8, Part 1**, 210 f.; Turtle Bay, **Vol. 8, Part 1**, 19 f.; Vernon House, **Vol. 1, Part 2**, 512; Wakefield, **Vol. 9, Part 2**, 139; **Vol. 10, Part 1**, 509 f.; Waln-Grove, **Vol. 10, Part 1**, 387 f.; Walnut Grove, **Vol. 6, Part 1**, 607, 610 f.; Wantoot, **Vol. 8, Part 1**, 394; Warner Hall, **Vol. 6, Part 1**, 214; Wayside, **Vol. 6, Part 1**, 425; Wehaw, **Vol. 5, Part 2**, 414; Wellston, **Vol. 10, Part 1**, 638 f.; Westover, **Vol. 6, Part 1**, 558; Whitehall, **Vol. 9, Part 1**, 26; White House (Boston), **Vol. 1, Part 1**, 73; White House of Confederacy, **Vol. 7, Part 1**, 11; Willington, **Vol. 8, Part 1**, 542; Willowbrook, **Vol. 9, Part 2**, 511; Wilson Park, **Vol. 10, Part 1**, 470 f.; Windsor Forest, **Vol. 10, Part 1**, 528 f.; Wood End, **Vol. 8, Part 1**, 247; Wormsloe, **Vol. 5, Part 2**, 197; Wye House, **Vol. 6, Part 1**, 331; **Vol. 7, Part 1**, 505 f.

Homestead strike (1892), **Vol. 4, Part 2**, 27; **Supp. 3**, 94

"Home, Sweet Home," writing of, **Vol. 7, Part 2**, 328

Homiletics, **Vol. 8, Part 1**, 89 f.; teaching of, **Vol. 9, Part 1**, 201; writings on, **Vol. 6, Part 1**, 552; **Vol. 8, Part 1**, 13 f., 89 f., 374

Homosexuality: Milk and Moscone murders (San Francisco), **Supp. 10**, 558, 536–37; 559; psychiatric view of, **Supp. 4**, 808

Honduras, **Vol. 1, Part 2**, 62; "interoceanic railway," survey for, **Vol. 5, Part 2**, 14

Hone, Philip, **Vol. 5, Part 1**, 503; diary of, **Vol. 5, Part 2**, 393

Honolulu, education in, **Vol. 7, Part 1**, 5

Honolulu Advertiser, **Vol. 9, Part 2**, 517

Honolulu Star Bulletin, **Supp. 5**, 216

"Honor system," in education, **Vol. 5, Part 2**, 148; **Vol. 10, Part 1**, 32

Hook, Charles R., reference to, **Supp. 3**, 781

Hooker, Joseph, references to, **Vol. 5, Part 1**, 559; **Vol. 6, Part 1**, 125; **Vol. 9, Part 1**, 217

Hooker Electrochemical Co., **Supp. 3**, 26

Hookworm: **Supp. 3**, 738; **Supp. 5**, 232, 605; eradication of, **Supp. 1**, 639; pathogenicity of, **Supp. 1**, 33; study of, **Vol. 4, Part 2**, 45

Hooper, Ben W., reference to, **Supp. 3**, 449

Hooper, C. E., reference to, **Supp. 10**, 587–88

Hooper, Frederic, reference to, **Supp. 10**, 835

Hooperating, **Supp. 5**, 310–11
Hoor, G. F., reference to, **Vol. 7, Part 1**, 571
Hoosac Tunnel (Mass.), **Vol. 3, Part 1**, 251, 334; **Vol. 4, Part 2**, 400; **Vol. 6, Part 1**, 37; **Vol. 7, Part 1**, 297; **Vol. 7, Part 2**, 329; **Vol. 8, Part 2**, 592; **Vol. 9, Part 2**, 99
Hoosiers, The, **Supp. 4**, 629
"Hootchy Kootchy" dance, **Supp. 4**, 88
Hoover, Herbert C.: **Vol. 5, Part 1**, 609; **Vol. 9, Part 2**, 372; Barnes, J. H., relationship, **Supp. 6**, 36–37; Belgian relief, **Vol. 9, Part 2**, 477; bonus marchers, **Supp. 6**, 240; family, **Supp. 8**, 275; food relief administration, **Supp. 3**, 622; **Supp. 4**, 699; foreign relations, **Supp. 6**, 187; **Supp. 7**, 112; German reparations moratorium, **Supp. 6**, 188; Haiti, commission on, **Supp. 6**, 211; Herter relationship, **Supp. 8**, 257; Hinshaw relationship, **Supp. 5**, 304; presidential candidacy, **Supp. 3**, 720; **Supp. 5**, 442; **Supp. 7**, 86; presidential policies, **Supp. 3**, 646–47; references to, **Supp. 7**, 85, 488; **Supp. 9**, 553; **Supp. 10**, 619; Sullivan, M., relationship, **Supp. 5**, 667; Wilbur relationship, **Supp. 4**, 892, 893, 894; writings on, **Supp. 6**, 601
Hoover, J. Edgar: anti-Communist views, **Supp. 9**, 406; civil rights views, **Supp. 9**, 407; criminal justice theories, **Supp. 9**, 405; Ernst relationship, **Supp. 10**, 221; King, M. L., vendetta against, **Supp. 9**, 407; Palmer raids, **Supp. 9**, 404; presidential relations, **Supp. 9**, 406, 407; public image of, **Supp. 9**, 405, 408; references to, **Supp. 4**, 794; **Supp. 5**, 590; **Supp. 8**, 322, 323, 335; **Supp. 9**, 593; Winchell relationship, **Supp. 9**, 886
Hoover Commissions on the Organization of the Executive Branch of the Government, **Supp. 6**, 692
Hoover Dam (Boulder Dam): **Supp. 3**, 397, 814; **Supp. 4**, 198; **Supp. 6**, 182, 507; **Supp. 7**, 360, construction, **Supp. 8**, 308; design and engineering, **Supp. 8**, 573
Hoover International Corporation, predecessor, **Supp. 5**, 313–14
Hoover Library, development of, **Supp. 2**, 40
Hoover's Gap, Tenn., operations at (June 1863), **Vol. 8, Part 1**, 521
Hoover War Library, **Supp. 1**, 9
Hope, Bob, reference to, **Supp. 9**, 540; **Supp. 10**, 159
Hope-Aiken Watershed Act (1953), **Supp. 8**, 278
Hopedale Community, Mass., **Vol. 1, Part 1**, 556 f.; **Vol. 3, Part 1**, 435
Hope Institute, **Vol. 3, Part 2**, 269
Hopewell, Hudson's ship, **Vol. 5, Part 1**, 338
Hopi Indians, **Supp. 6**, 720; linguistic studies of, **Supp. 3**, 820
Hopkins, Arthur, references to, **Supp. 5**, 375; **Supp. 6**, 65
Hopkins, Harry: references to, **Supp. 3**, 646, 652, 653, 654; **Supp. 4**, 578; **Supp. 5**, 515, 642; **Supp. 6**, 601, 660, 661; **Supp. 7**, 787; **Supp. 8**, 176, 301; **Supp. 9**, 105, 106; writings on, **Supp. 5**, 624
Hopkins, Johns, references to, **Vol. 1, Part 2**, 267; **Vol. 7, Part 1**, 24
Hopkins, Lemuel, reference to, **Vol. 7, Part 1**, 559
Hopkins, Mark, references to, **Vol. 3, Part 2**, 372; **Vol. 7, Part 1**, 5
"Hopkinsianism," **Vol. 5, Part 1**, 217
Hopkinson, Joseph, reference to, **Vol. 8, Part 2**, 588
Hopkins plan (Johns Hopkins University), **Supp. 9**, 125
Hopper, DeWolf, reference to, **Supp. 6**, 305
Hopper, Edward, references to, **Supp. 5**, 493, 636; **Supp. 8**, 339
Hopper, Hedda, reference to, **Supp. 7**, 143
Hopson, Howard, reference to, **Supp. 3**, 138
Hopwood, Avery, reference to, **Supp. 6**, 543
Horgan, Paul, reference to, **Supp. 3**, 848
"Horizontal Bill," **Vol. 7, Part 1**, 233
Hormel, Jay Catherwood, reference to, **Supp. 4**, 396
Hormel and Co., **Supp. 4**, 395–96; **Supp. 5**, 314–15
Hormones: adrenal cortex study, **Supp. 9**, 454; adrenalin synthesis, **Supp. 5**, 149; discovery of, in pure form, **Vol. 9, Part 2**, 275; oral contraceptives, **Supp. 8**, 503; ovarian, **Supp. 2**, 51; oxytocin synthesis, **Supp. 10**, 198; plant studies, **Supp. 10**, 297; sex hormone syntheses, **Supp. 9**, 444; sex-related, **Supp. 4**, 460, 498; steroids, **Supp. 5**, 28; **Supp. 10**, 240; vasopressin synthesis, **Supp. 10**, 198. *See also* Endocrine glands; *specific hormones*
Hornaday, William Temple, reference to, **Supp. 3**, 229
Hornbeck, Stanley K., references to, **Supp. 6**, 269, 270; **Supp. 7**, 112, 303
"Hornblower, Horatio" (fictional character), **Supp. 8**, 182
Horne, F. J., reference to, **Supp. 6**, 339
Horne, Herbert P., reference to, **Supp. 3**, 785
Horne, Lena, references to, **Supp. 10**, 7, 8
Horner, Henry, references to, **Supp. 4**, 451; **Supp. 10**, 10
Hornet, **Vol. 9, Part 2**, 7; **Supp. 9**, 461
Horney, Karen, reference to, **Supp. 7**, 6
Horney, Karen, Clinic (New York City), founding of, **Supp. 5**, 317
Hornsby, Rogers, **Supp. 9**, 294
Horowitz, David, reference to, **Supp. 3**, 143
Horowitz, Vladimir, reference to, **Supp. 10**, 632
Horse-car lines, New York City, **Vol. 6, Part 1**, 40
Horse racing: associations, **Supp. 9**, 866, 867; gambling circuits, **Supp. 3**, 20; horse breeding and training, **Supp. 5**, 567, 569, 757; Supp 7, 399–401, 695–96; **Supp. 8**, 174–75, 263–64, 299, 367, 566; **Supp. 9**, 264, 464, 866; **Supp. 10**, 491; jockeys, **Supp. 8**, 565, 566; **Supp. 10**, 490–91; modernization, **Supp. 8**, 76; officials, **Supp. 8**, 75–76; **Supp. 10**, 311; pari-mutuel betting, **Supp. 1**, 114; radio broadcasts, **Supp. 7**, 494–95; stable ownership, **Supp. 8**, 13; **Supp. 9**, 264, 866; tracks, **Supp. 9**, 866. *See also* Harness racing
Horses: blankets, manufacture of, **Vol. 4, Part 1**, 380; breeding of, **Vol. 3, Part 2**, 459; **Vol. 4, Part 2**, 84, 454; **Vol. 5, Part 1**, 562; **Vol. 5, Part 2**, 441; **Vol. 7, Part 1**, 145, 182 f., 425 f.; **Vol. 8, Part 1**, 456; **Vol. 8, Part 2**, 335 f.; **Vol. 9, Part 1**, 200; **Vol. 10, Part 1**, 373 f.; paintings of, **Vol. 7, Part 1**, 373; **Vol. 8, Part 1**, 497; **Vol. 10, Part 1**, 1 f.; Percheron, introduction of, **Vol. 10, Part 1**, 400 f.; railroads, early use of as motive power, **Vol. 3, Part 1**, 258; statues of, **Vol. 8, Part 2**, 222; trotting, **Vol. 10, Part 1**, 373 f.; wild, taming of, **Vol. 8, Part 1**, 385; writings on, **Vol. 7, Part 1**, 132; **Vol. 8, Part 1**, 385; **Vol. 10, Part 1**, 2, 373 f.
Horses, race: **Vol. 3, Part 1**, 213; **Vol. 3, Part 2**, 545; **Vol. 4, Part 1**, 206; **Vol. 5, Part 1**, 20; **Vol. 5, Part 2**, 130 f., 283; **Vol. 8, Part 1**, 107 f.; **Vol. 8, Part 2**, 505; **Vol. 9, Part 1**, 211 f.; **Vol. 9, Part 2**, 365 f.; **Vol. 10, Part 1**, 373 f.; American horses in English and French races, **Vol. 3, Part 1**, 552 f.; antibetting legislation, **Vol. 3, Part 1**, 552 f.; breeding for racing in Kentucky, **Vol. 6, Part 1**, 411 f.; **Vol. 6, Part 2**, 180; JJJ, 866; importation from England, drug-detection tests for, **Supp. 8**, 76; evolutionary studies of, **Supp. 1**, 340; **Vol. 3, Part 1**, 213; **Vol. 9, Part 2**, 641; quarterhorses, **Supp. 9**, 464; training of, **Supp. 8**, 174–75. *See also* Horse racing
Horse Shoe Bend, battle of. *See* Creek war in Alabama, 1813
Horseshoe nails, manufacture of, **Vol. 3, Part 1**, 547 f.

Horsley, Victor, reference to, **Supp. 3**, 201
Horticulture (general): **Vol. 1, Part 1**, 56, 246, 655; **Vol. 2, Part 1**, 237, 251, 327, 453; **Vol. 2, Part 2**, 184, 380; **Vol. 3, Part 1**, 177, 417 f., 419; **Vol. 4, Part 1**, 53 f., 98, 144, 359, 398, 557; **Vol. 4, Part 2**, 229, 236, 312, 356, 530; **Vol. 5, Part 1**, 24, 272, 305, 380 f.; **Vol. 5, Part 2**, 341; **Vol. 6, Part 1**, 287, 363, 393 f.; **Vol. 6, Part 2**, 137, 492, 637; **Vol. 7, Part 1**, 315, 335 f., 405 f.; **Vol. 7, Part 2**, 248, 464; **Vol. 8, Part 1**, 145 f:, 229 f., 233 f.; **Vol. 8, Part 2**, 64, 90, 92, 144, 160, 354, 355, 361, 383 f., 401; **Vol. 9, Part 2**, 147, 514, 596, 597; **Vol. 10, Part 1**, 68, 444 f.; **Vol. 10, Part 2**, 123; blackberry raising, **Vol. 6, Part 1**, 363; chemical solutions, **Supp. 3**, 247; citrus fruits, **Vol. 4, Part 2**, 356; commercial nurseries, **Supp. 1**, 594; desert plants, study of, **Vol. 9, Part 1**, 427; development as science, **Supp. 5**, 30–31; ferns, **Vol. 3, Part 1**, 606 f.; **Vol. 10, Part 1**, 116; fig growing, **Vol. 8, Part 2**, 91; fruit growing, Oregon, **Vol. 6, Part 1**, 498; grape culture, **Vol. 3, Part 1**, 491; **Vol. 8, Part 2**, 93; home-gardening promotion, **Supp. 4**, 564; hybridization, **Vol. 1, Part 2**, 26; **Vol. 8, Part 2**, 93; **Supp. 4**, 357; **Supp. 5**, 629; **Supp. 10**, 80, 81, 271; Jalap plant, introduction of, **Vol. 2, Part 2**, 487; landscape gardening, **Supp. 6**, 196; lemon, **Vol. 4, Part 1**, 145; medicinal plants, **Supp. 3**, 433; nurseries, **Vol. 1, Part 2**, 192; **Vol. 5, Part 2**, 341; **Vol. 8, Part 1**, 233; **Vol. 9, Part 1**, 146; **Supp. 9**, 756; orchids, **Vol. 4, Part 2**, 229; organizations, **Supp. 1**, 541; pathology studies, **Supp. 3**, 400–401; photographic studies, **Supp. 10**, 162; plant breeding, **Supp. 4**, 862–63; plant diseases, **Supp. 1**, 462; **Supp. 2**, 215; plant growth measurement, **Supp. 6**, 69; plant illustrations, **Supp. 1**, 121; plant introduction gardens, **Supp. 5**, 214; plant physiology, **Supp. 4**, 192, 500–501; **Supp. 6**, 176; plants, scientific study of, **Vol. 3, Part 1**, 606 f.; **Vol. 7, Part 1**, 266 f.; **Vol. 7, Part 2**, 480 f.; **Vol. 8, Part 1**, 154 f., 233, 236 f., 239 f.; **Vol. 8, Part 2**, 309; **Vol. 9, Part 1**, 263, 458; **Vol. 9, Part 2**, 477, 596; **Vol. 10, Part 2**, 321; poinsettia, **Vol. 8, Part 1**, 30 f.; pomology, **Vol. 2, Part 1**, 48; **Vol. 2, Part 2**, 489; **Vol. 3, Part 1**, 418 f.; **Vol. 4, Part 1**, 261; **Vol. 6, Part 1**, 535; **Vol. 6, Part 2**, 252; **Vol. 8, Part 1**, 145; **Vol. 9, Part 2**, 439; rose growing, **Supp. 4**, 194–95; **Supp. 5**, 555; seeds, **Supp. 10**, 80–81; strawberry cultivation, **Vol. 5, Part 1**, 272; **Vol. 6, Part 1**, 394; tomatoes, disease-resistant, **Vol. 8, Part 1**, 239 f.; water culture, **Supp. 4**, 382; writings on, **Vol. 2, Part 1**, 49, 236, 266 f.; **Vol. 2, Part 2**, 489; **Vol. 3, Part 1**, 177, 418, 419; **Vol. 4, Part 1**, 53, 144, 398, 557; **Vol. 4, Part 2**, 530; **Vol. 5, Part 1**, 272; **Vol. 5, Part 2**, 341, 572; **Vol. 8, Part 1**, 233 f.; **Vol. 8, Part 2**, 84; **Vol. 10, Part 1**, 36, 444 f.; **Vol. 10, Part 2**, 123. *See also* Botanic gardens; Herbariums; *specific garden names*
Horticulture (by state): California, **Vol. 1, Part 2**, 599; **Vol. 4, Part 2**, 229; **Vol. 5, Part 2**, 300; **Vol. 6, Part 1**, 162, 481, 498; **Vol. 8, Part 1**, 145; **Vol. 8, Part 2**, 90, **Vol. 9, Part 1**, 548; **Vol. 10, Part 2**, 184; Connecticut, **Vol. 1, Part 2**, 599; Florida, **Vol. 4, Part, 2**, 356; Louisiana, **Vol. 8, Part 1**, 589; Massachusetts, **Vol. 1, Part 2**, 319; **Vol. 10, Part 2**, 210; Michigan, **Vol. 6, Part 1**, 535 f.; New Mexico, **Vol. 8, Part 1**, 229 f.; New York, **Vol. 9, Part 2**, 439; Pennsylvania, **Vol. 7, Part 2**, 452; Texas, **Vol. 6, Part 2**, 482; **Vol. 7, Part 1**, 335 f.
Horton, George Plant, reference to, **Supp. 6**, 262
Horton, Henry H., reference to, **Supp. 3**, 449
Hospital for the Ruptured and Crippled (New York City), **Supp. 4**, 887
Hospital for the Women of Maryland, founding of, **Supp. 1**, 437
Hospitals: **Vol. 4, Part 1**, 301; **Vol. 8, Part 1**, 213 f.; **Vol. 9, Part 2**, 85; blacks', **Supp. 5**, 104; building architecture, **Supp. 5**, 301; children's wards, **Vol. 8, Part 1**, 317 f.; design and services, **Supp. 3**, 312; in Thailand, **Supp. 3**, 486; medically trained administrators, **Supp. 3**, 312; mental, **Supp. 1**, 243; **Supp. 2**, 711–12; **Supp. 3**, 50–51, 102; **Supp. 4**, 571; milltary, **Vol. 2, Part 2**, 251 f.; **Vol. 5, Part 1**, 109; **Vol. 7, Part 1**, 409; **Vol. 9, Part 2**, 550, 584; nurses aides, **Supp. 4**, 93; patients' records, **Supp. 5**, 111; pediatric, **Supp. 3**, 74–75; **Supp. 5**, 1–2; philanthropy, **Supp. 3**, 435; social work, **Supp. 6**, 97–98; tuberculosis, **Supp. 7**, 251; women's, **Supp. 1**, 437. *See also specific hospital names*
Hospital ship, for fishermen at sea, **Vol. 8, Part 2**, 313
Hotchkiss School, **Vol. 2, Part 1**, 237
Hot dog, baseball concession fare, **Supp. 7**, 719
Hotel management: **Vol. 1, Part 1**, 102, 639; **Vol. 1, Part 2**, 418; **Vol. 3, Part 1**, 431; **Vol. 3, Part 2**, 452; **Vol. 4, Part 1**, 318, 331; **Vol. 5, Part 2**, 169, 528; **Vol. 6, Part 2**, 279; **Vol. 7, Part 1**, 7, 482; **Vol. 7, Part 2**, 191; **Vol. 8, Part 1**, 115 f.; **Vol. 8, Part 2**, 98; **Vol. 9, Part 1**, 537, 596 f.; chains, **Supp. 10**, 336–38; Chicago, **Vol. 3, Part 1**, 431; New York, **Vol. 1, Part 1**, 400 f.; **Vol. 1, Part 2**, 149
Hotels: architecture, **Vol. 8, Part 2**, 99; building of, **Vol. 4, Part 2**, 240; **Vol. 8, Part 2**, 98; development of, **Supp. 1**, 272; labor movement, **Supp. 6**, 598; modern, **Vol. 1, Part 2**, 419; nature resorts, **Supp. 1**, 554; Wright design, **Supp. 6**, 713
Hot Fives (jazz ensemble), **Supp. 9**, 46
"Hot oil." *See* Oil, production quotas
Hot Oil: The Problem of Petroleum, **Supp. 9**, 611
Hot Springs, Ark., first scientific analysis of water, **Vol. 3, Part 1**, 507 f.
"Hot Water War," **Vol. 4, Part 1**, 34
Houdini, Harry, reference to, **Supp. 8**, 314
Houdry Process Corporation, founding of, **Supp. 7**, 368
Hough, Will M., reference to, **Supp. 7**, 1
Houghton, Arthur Amory, Jr., reference to, **Supp. 5**, 756
Houghton, Henry O., reference to, **Vol. 8, Part 2**, 522
Houghton Library (Cambridge, Mass.), **Supp. 7**, 387
Houghton Mifflin Co., **Supp. 5**, 542; growth of, **Supp. 6**, 251; Riverside textbooks, **Supp. 3**, 206
Hound and Horn, **Supp. 7**, 55
Houqua, clipper ship, **Vol. 6, Part 1**, 444
Hours of work. *See* Wages and hours
House, Edward M.: Page, Walter Hines, and, **Vol. 7, Part 2**, 144; references to, **Supp. 3**, 532; **Supp. 4**, 171, 725; **Supp. 5**, 79, 697; **Supp. 6**, 207; **Supp. 7**, 536, 683–84, 796; **Supp. 9**, 504; Wilson, Woodrow, and, **Vol. 10, Part 2**, 355 f.
House and Garden, **Supp. 3**, 547
House and Home, **Supp. 7**, 384
House Divided, **Supp. 5**, 747–48
Houseman, John, reference to, **Supp. 5**, 464; **Supp. 7**, 61; **Supp. 9**, 692
House of David (cult), founding of, **Supp. 1**, 615–16
House of Governors, **Vol. 5, Part 2**, 217
House of Mirth, The, **Supp. 2**, 704, 705
House of Morgan. *See* Morgan and Co.
House of Representatives, United States: agricultural interests, **Supp. 4**, 480; **Supp. 6**, 86–87; **Supp. 10**, 393–94; Agriculture Committee, **Supp. 8**, 277–78; Appropriations Committee, **Supp. 7**, 105, 110–11, 733–34; **Supp. 8**, 2, 300; Armed Services Committee, **Supp. 7**, 78; **Supp. 10**, 326; assassination attempt in, **Supp. 8**, 300; Banking and Currency Committee, **Supp. 3**, 178, 730; **Supp. 4**, 331; **Supp. 5**, 248; **Supp. 8**, 615–16; **Supp. 10**, 619; big business, opposition to, **Supp. 10**, 619; civil liberties,

free speech issues, **Supp. 10**, 748; civil rights legislation opposition, **Supp. 10**, 748; civil service legislation, **Supp. 9**, 639; conservation committee, **Supp. 9**, 663; conservatives, **Supp. 5**, 715–16; **Supp. 6**, 588; **Supp. 7**, 84–85; **Supp. 7**, 212, 639, 733–34; **Supp. 8**, 268–69, 703; **Supp. 10**, 557, 653, 748; dean of, **Supp. 5**, 598; declaration of war against Japan, lone vote against, **Supp. 9**, 641; Democratic Committee on Committees, **Supp. 8**, 206; Democratic leadership in, **Supp. 5**, 318–19; **Supp. 9**, 639; **Supp. 10**, 484–87; Democratic Steering Committee, **Supp. 6**, 132; Democratic Study Group, **Supp. 10**, 530, 531; District Affairs Committee, **Supp. 10**, 325; Education and Labor Committee, **Supp. 9**, 620; environmental issues, **Supp. 10**, 557; ethics issues, **Supp. 6**, 437; **Supp. 8**, 649; first black member from North, **Supp. 5**, 166; first black member from Northeast, **Supp. 9**, 619; first black standing committee head, **Supp. 8**, 121; first congresswoman from Deep South, **Supp. 5**, 582; first congresswoman to have child serving simultaneously, **Supp. 10**, 57; first compact set of rules, **Vol. 8, Part 1**, 350 f.; first woman in, **Supp. 9**, 640; first woman to lead congressional mission abroad, **Supp. 10**, 57; fist fights in, **Supp. 5**, 139; Foreign Affairs Committee, **Supp. 4**, 88; **Supp. 5**, 198; **Supp. 10**, 56–57; Foreign Aid Committee, **Supp. 8**, 257; Government Operations Committee, **Supp. 8**, 269; Hawaiian representation, **Supp. 5**, 217; Hiss investigation, **Supp. 9**, 572; Immigration and Naturalization Committee, **Supp. 5**, 598; **Supp. 6**, 320; Indian concerns, **Supp. 5**, 662; insurgents, **Supp. 3**, 558; **Supp. 4**, 481, 669; **Supp. 5**, 666; Interstate and Foreign Commerce Committee, **Supp. 3**, 256–57; **Supp. 6**, 132; **Supp. 9**, 611; interventionism, **Supp. 10**, 485; isolationists, **Supp. 5**, 396–97; **Supp. 6**, 613–14, 636; Judiciary Committee, **Supp. 7**, 730; Labor Committee, **Supp. 6**, 480; labor interests, **Supp. 7**, 302; labor legislation, **Supp. 8**, 245–46; **Supp. 10**, 653; lend-lease passage, **Supp. 10**, 485; liberals, **Supp. 4**, 465; **Supp. 10**, 183, 486, 487, 530; majority rule, **Vol. 8, Part 1**, 457 f.; Maverick bloc, **Supp. 5**, 480–81; Military Affairs Committee, **Supp. 4**, 446; **Supp. 6**, 436–37; military interests, **Supp. 8**, 538; **Supp. 10**, 325–26; minority leaders, **Supp. 6**, 636; Mother's Day resolution, **Supp. 5**, 290; New Deal opposition, **Supp. 5**, 715; **Supp. 8**, 27, 532; New Deal support, **Supp. 10**, 814; oldest member, **Supp. 8**, 615; Old Guard, **Supp. 4**, 861; oratory, **Supp. 7**, 459; party responsibility, principle of, established, **Vol. 8, Part 1**, 457 f.; personal encounters, **Vol. 6, Part 1**, 533; **Supp. 6**, 614; "Powell Amendment," **Supp. 9**, 620; Powell exclusion, **Supp. 9**, 621, 838; procedure of, **Vol. 5, Part 1**, 63; prohibitionism, **Supp. 4**, 853; **Supp. 5**, 701; proportional representation, **Supp. 1**, 461; public flogging of members, **Supp. 1**, 667; radicalism, **Supp. 5**, 466–67; reform of rules, **Vol. 8, Part 1**, 456 f.; regional interests, **Supp. 7**, 31, 224; Republican leadership, **Supp. 8**, 128, 420–21, 422; Rules Committee, **Supp. 3**, 544, 558; **Supp. 4**, 481; **Supp. 5**, 139, 598–99, **Supp. 6**, 588; **Supp. 7**, 636, 637; **Supp. 10**, 748; "Southern Manifesto" on school desegregation, **Supp. 8**, 25; space program, **Supp. 7**, 79; speakership, **Vol. 2, Part 1**, 477, 495; **Vol. 2, Part 2**, 121; **Vol. 6, Part 1**, 394 f.; **Vol. 7, Part 1**, 307; **Supp. 1**, 344, 617; **Supp. 2**, 19, 82; **Supp. 7**, 634–37; **Supp. 8**, 207, 421; **Supp. 10**, 465, 484–87; Special Committee on Un-American Activities, **Supp. 10**, 484; Steering Committee, **Supp. 10**, 531; subversive groups, investigations of, **Supp. 10**, 484; taxation measures, **Supp. 5**, 712; trade measures, **Supp. 6**, 280; Un-American Activities Committee, **Supp. 5**, 139; **Supp. 6**, 219, 392, 526; **Supp. 7**, 52, 244–45, 397, 597, 609, 766–67; **Supp. 8**, 162, 425–26, 492, 506–7, 511, 551, 648, 705–4; **Supp. 9**, 135, 185, 233–34, 324, 458, 539, 572, 602–3, 666, 849; **Supp. 10**, 25, 134, 239, 273, 325, 437, 560, 720, 757, 793; Un-American Activities Committee, founding, **Supp. 5**, 599; Vietnam War policies, **Supp. 8**, 507; Ways and Means Committee, **Supp. 3**, 345; **Supp. 5**, 180–81; **Supp. 6**, 125–26, 535; **Supp. 8**, 206; **Supp. 10**, 484, 530; women elected to, **Supp. 4**, 446–47; **Supp. 6**, 479–81; **Supp. 9**, 640; **Supp. 10**, 57, 183. *See also* Congress, United States; Lobbying; Senate, United States

House of the Holy Family, **Vol. 8, Part 1**, 205

House of Truth, **Supp. 7**, 261

Housewares: cleaning products, **Supp. 9**, 510; cooking utensils, **Supp. 6**, 624

Housing: apartment houses, **Vol. 3, Part 1**, 327; bungalow style, **Supp. 5**, 256–57; colonial, **Vol. 5, Part 1**, 91; comprehensive planning, Supp. 25 738; cooperative, **Supp. 6**, 615; development, **Vol. 3, Part 2**, 419; low-income, design of, **Supp. 4**, 282; model, **Vol. 9, Part 1**, 301; prefabricated, **Supp. 6**, 26; **Supp. 7**, 308; public, **Supp. 3**, 656; **Supp. 5**, 631, 675, 719; public, federally subsidized, **Supp. 3**, 730, 838; public health relationship, **Supp. 6**, 702; reform, **Vol. 10, Part 2**, 86; **Supp. 3**, 52–53, 837–38; **Supp. 6**, 654–55; restrictive covenants, **Supp. 4**, 397; **Supp. 7**, 318, 319; suburban developments, **Supp. 7**, 469–70; tenement, **Supp. 3**, 743–44; Supp.6, 23, 26, 522; urban, **Supp. 5**, 630, 631; Usonian designs, **Supp. 6**, 714. *See also* Architecture; Model communities

Housing Study Guild, founding of, **Supp. 2**, 739

Housman, A. A., and Co., largest wire-service brokerage firm in U.S., **Supp. 9**, 613

Houston, David F., reference to, **Supp. 8**, 84

Houston, Sam: biography of, **Supp. 5**, 364; references to, **Vol. 5, Part 1**, 264; **Vol. 5, Part 2**, 161; **Vol. 8, Part 1**, 89; **Vol. 8, Part 2**, 237

Houston, Tex.: business ventures, **Supp. 6**, 324, 325; early history of, **Vol. 8, Part 1**, 546 f.; port development, **Supp. 6**, 135

Houston Chronicle, **Supp. 6**, 325

Houston Post, **Supp. 7**, 349, 350

Howard, Cy, reference to, **Supp. 9**, 880

Howard, Eugene, reference to, **Supp. 4**, 400–401

Howard, Jerome ("Curly"), references to, **Supp. 9**, 281, 282, 410

Howard, John Galen, reference to, **Supp. 6**, 463

Howard, Maxwell, reference to, **Supp. 8**, 566

Howard, Moe, references to, **Supp. 9**, 281, 282

Howard, O. O., reference to, **Supp. 3**, 836

Howard, Roy, UP presidency, **Supp. 9**, 89

Howard, Samuel ("Shemp"), references to, **Supp. 9**, 282, 410

Howard, Sidney, reference to, **Supp. 8**, 529

Howard Johnson (restaurant chain), **Supp. 9**, 429–30

Howard University: administration, **Supp. 2**, 456; **Supp. 6**, 568; **Supp. 9**, 385–86; as intellectual center for black activists, **Supp. 9**, 137; black literature collection, **Supp. 9**, 750; financing of, **Supp. 10**, 386; first black president, **Supp. 10**, 385; founding of, **Vol. 5, Part 1**, 280; history studies, **Supp. 4**, 911; law school, **Supp. 4**, 397, 398; patrons, **Supp. 5**, 343; Phi Beta Kappa chapter, **Supp. 5**, 437; philosophy studies, **Supp. 5**, 436; political science department established, **Supp. 9**, 136; sociology studies, **Supp. 7**, 266; zoology studies, **Supp. 3**, 402–3

Howe, Elias, references to, **Vol. 5, Part 1**, 95; **Vol. 9, Part 1**, 189

Howe, Julia Ward, biography of, **Supp. 3**, 630

Howe, Louis: references to, **Supp. 5**, 682; **Supp. 7**,

659; Roosevelt, F. D., relationship, **Supp. 3**, 642, 644–47
Howe, Samuel Gridley, reference to, **Vol. 2, Part 1**, 38; **Supp. 8**, 316
Howe, Will, reference to, **Supp. 5**, 272
Howe, Sir William, reference to, **Vol. 5, Part 1**, 481
Howe, William F., reference to, **Vol. 5, Part 1**, 368
Howell, Harry, reference to, **Supp. 6**, 357
Howell, William H., reference to, **Vol. 10, Part 1**, 621 f.; **Supp. 6**, 671
Howells, John Mead, reference to, **Supp. 3**, 743
Howells, William Dean, references to, **Vol. 5, Part 1**, 579; **Vol. 5, Part 2**, 360; **Vol. 7, Part 2**, 556; **Supp. 4**, 816, 817; **Supp. 5**, 95–96
Howes, Wright, reference to, **Supp. 7**, 295
How Green Was My Valley, **Supp. 9**, 206
Howland, John, reference to, **Supp. 3**, 74, 243
Howland, Silas W., reference to, **Supp. 3**, 116–17
How to Win Friends and Influence People, **Supp. 5**, 102
Hoyle, Alexander E., reference to, **Supp. 3**, 196
Huancayo Magnetic Observatory (Lima, Peru), **Supp. 6**, 205
Hubbard, Gardiner H., reference to, **Vol. 1, Part 2**, 149, 151
Hubbard, L. Ron, references to, **Supp. 9**, 155, 156
Hubbard, Robert ("Cal"), reference to, **Supp. 5**, 458
Hubbert, Marion King, reference to, **Supp. 5**, 558
Hubble, Edwin, references to, **Supp. 3**, 208; **Supp. 8**, 597; **Supp. 9**, 714
Huber, G. Carl, reference to, **Supp. 3**, 369
Hubert, Conrad, reference to, **Supp. 7**, 150
Hückel, Erich, reference to, **Supp. 8**, 123
Huckleberry Finn, **Vol. 2, Part 2**, 192, 195
Hudson, Henry, reference to, **Vol. 5, Part 1**, 338
Hudson Bay, early explorations near, **Vol. 8, Part 1**, 320 f.
Hudson County, N.J., political machine, **Supp. 6**, 265
Hudson Guild, **Supp. 3**, 175, 246
Hudson Motor Car Co., **Supp. 10**, 1; establishment of, **Supp. 2**, 102
Hudson River: blockade of, during Revolution, **Vol. 10, Part 2**, 432; boats *(see also* Hudson River Day Line), **Vol. 3, Part 2**, 164; **Vol. 7, Part 1**, 471; bridges, **Supp. 7**, 11; exploration, **Vol. 5, Part 1**, 338 f.; law granting Livingston and Fulton navigation rights, **Vol. 3, Part 1**, 488; paintings of, **Vol. 5, Part 2**, 72; tunnels under, **Vol. 1, Part 2**, 408; **Vol. 4, Part 2**, 446; **Vol. 5, Part 1**, 142; **Vol. 8, Part 1**, 406; **Supp. 2**, 146, 559; **Supp. 4**, 690, 757
Hudson River Day Line, **Vol. 7, Part 2**, 9 f.
Hudson River Railroad, **Vol. 1, Part 2**, 443; **Vol. 5, Part 1**, 313; **Vol. 5, Part 2**, 60
Hudson River school, **Vol. 5, Part 1**, 488
Hudson's Bay Co., **Vol. 1, Part 2**, 145; **Vol. 3, Part 1**, 336 f.; **Vol. 4, Part 2**, 17; **Vol. 5, Part 2**, 441; **Vol. 7, Part 1**, 640; **Vol. 8, Part 1**, 320 f.
Hudson Tunnel, for Pennsylvania Railroad, plans for, **Vol. 8, Part 1**, 406
Huebsch, Benjamin W., references to, **Supp. 3**, 13; **Supp. 7**, 306
Huggins, Miller, references to, **Supp. 5**, 40–41; **Supp. 10**, 141
Hughes, Charles Evans: insurance investigation, **Vol. 6, Part 1**, 562; references to, **Supp. 3**, 99, 100, 396, 559, 668, 717; **Supp. 5**, 286, 342, 571, 572, 573, 574, 575; **Supp. 7**, 361; **Supp. 10**, 226
Hughes, Howard, references to, **Supp. 6**, 145, 146, 221, 308; **Supp. 7**, 71, 587; **Supp. 10**, 670
Hughes, John, reference to, **Vol. 6, Part 1**, 591
Hughes, Langston, references to, **Supp. 6**, 314, 321; **Supp. 9**, 108, 109
Hughes, Ted, reference to, **Supp. 7**, 621–22
Hughes Aircraft Co., **Supp. 7**, 73
Hughes Tool Co., **Supp. 10**, 355, 356, 358
Hugh Selwyn Mauberly, **Supp. 9**, 618
Hugo, Ian. *See* Guiler, Hugh Parker
Huguenots: settlements of, **Vol. 1, Part 1**, 509; **Vol. 3, Part 1**, 534 f.; **Vol. 4, Part 2**, 375 f.; **Vol. 6, Part 1**, 30; writings on, **Vol. 1, Part 1**, 510 f.
Hull, Cordell, references to, **Supp. 3**, 449, 647, 657; **Supp. 5**, 519, 537; **Supp. 6**, 230; **Supp. 7**, 303, 777; **Supp. 9**, 553; **Supp. 10**, 243
Hull, Susanna E., reference to, **Vol. 1, Part 2**, 149
Hull House (Chicago): **Supp. 1**, 11–12; **Supp. 4**, 106; **Supp. 5**, 84; **Supp. 6**, 1, 102, 103, 392, 614; **Supp. 8**, 40, 241; erection of, **Vol. 8, Part 1**, 57 f.
Hull Laboratory of Anatomy (Chicago), **Supp. 6**, 53
Hulme, T. E., reference to, **Supp. 9**, 617
"Hulsemann Letter," **Vol. 10, Part 1**, 585
Human Biology, founding of, **Supp. 2**, 522
Humanism: neohumamsm, **Supp. 1**, 36; political science, **Supp. 8**, 407; psychoanalysis and, **Supp. 6**, 724–25; psychology, **Supp. 8**, 423–24; scientific, **Supp. 6**, 83, 596; **Supp. 7**, 624; **Supp. 8**, 596
Humanist's Library, The, **Supp. 3**, 785
Human relations, **Supp. 4**, 805–8
Human rights, advocacy, **Supp. 8**, 5; Four Freedoms, **Supp. 3**, 660, 665. *See also* Civil liberties; Civil rights movement; Racism
Humble Oil & Refining Co.: **Supp. 9**, 464; **Supp. 10**, 663; founding of, **Supp. 3**, 260–61; **Supp. 4**, 775–76
Humidity, control of environmental, **Supp. 4**, 148–49
Humor: **Vol. 1, Part 1**, 499, 573 f.; **Vol. 2, Part 1**, 162, 264; **Vol. 2, Part 2**, 491; **Vol. 3, Part 1**, 417; **Vol. 3, Part 2**, 166, 541; **Vol. 4, Part 2**, 309; **Vol. 5, Part 1**, 150, 202; **Vol. 5, Part 2**, 139, 153; **Vol. 6, Part 1**, 207, 336, 390, 397; **Vol. 6, Part 2**, 402; **Vol. 7, Part 1**, 399 f., 598 f.; **Vol. 7, Part 2**, 37, 377; **Vol. 9, Part 1**, 39, 70, 109, 248 f., 269, 345; **Vol. 9, Part 2**, 487; **Vol. 10, Part 1**, 620 f.; **Vol. 10, Part 2**, 82; Abbott and Costello, **Supp. 9**, 1; adlibbing, **Supp. 10**, 159; black, **Supp. 8**, 55–56; blackface, **Supp. 2**, 412; burlesque, **Supp. 3**, 803–5; **Supp. 5**, 87–88, 726; **Supp. 9**, 213–14; cartoons, **Supp. 5**, 732; deadpan, **Supp. 8**, 314–15; essays and sketches, **Supp. 4**, 202, 804–5; **Supp. 7**, 743; ethnic, **Supp. 9**, 720–21; **Supp. 10**, 651; first situation comedies, **Supp. 7**, 9; folk, **Supp. 10**, 452; hillbilly, **Supp. 6**, 89; literary, **Supp. 10**, 630–31; malapropisms, **Supp. 9**, 6; Marx Brothers, **Supp. 7**, 514–15; musical, **Supp. 7**, 403–4; parody, **Supp. 10**, 755; political, **Supp. 10**, 465–66; "screwball" comedies, **Supp. 3**, 466; slapstick, **Supp. 2**, 672; **Supp. 5**, 210–11; **Supp. 6**, 573; **Supp. 7**, 208, 238, 462–64; **Supp. 7**, 588–89; **Supp. 9**, 282, 410, 508–9, 535–36; **Supp. 10**, 756; "Western," **Vol. 3, Part 1**, 252; **Vol. 6, Part 1**, 208; **Vol. 9, Part 2**, 509; writings, **Supp. 1**, 544–45, 635–37; **Supp. 3**, 53–54, 170–71; **Supp. 10**, 746–47; writings on, **Supp. 3**, 672; zany comedians, **Supp. 7**, 514–15; **Supp. 8**, 710–11. *See also* Comedy; Motion pictures, comedy; Radio, comedy programs; Television, comedy programs
Humphrey, Doris, references to, **Supp. 9**, 494, 495
Humphrey, George, references to, **Supp. 8**, 276; **Supp. 10**, 376
Humphrey, Hubert H.: references to, **Supp. 6**, 235; **Supp. 7**, 420, 814; anti-Communism, **Supp. 10**, 360–61; civil rights record, **Supp. 10**, 360, 361; majority whip, **Supp. 10**, 361; mayoral campaign, **Supp. 10**, 359, 360; presidential bid (1960), **Supp. 10**, 361; presidential candidacy, **Supp. 10**, 168–69, 362–63; references to, **Supp. 10**, 186; senatorial campaign (1948), **Supp. 10**, 360; vice presidency, **Supp. 10**, 362; vice-presidential candidacy, **Supp. 10**, 361; Vietnam War, support for, **Supp. 10**, 362

Humphrey, Maud, reference to, **Supp. 6**, 65
Humphrey-Weidman Co. (dance), **Supp. 9**, 494, 495
Hungarian Feminist Association, founding of, **Supp. 4**, 724–25
Hungary: ITT in, **Supp. 6**, 44–45; post–World War I reorganization, **Supp. 1**, 662; uprising (1956), **Supp. 7**, 116; women's rights activism, **Supp. 4**, 724–25
Hunger, physiology of, **Supp. 3**, 133–34; **Supp. 6**, 100. *See also* Food aid
Hungry i (club), **Supp. 8**, 56
"Hunkers." *See* "Barnburners" and "Hunkers"
Hunnewell, H. H., reference to, **Vol. 8, Part 2**, 361
Hunt, Leigh, father of, **Vol. 5, Part 1**, 388
Hunt, Richard M., reference to, **Vol. 1, Part 2**, 303
Hunt, W. M., reference to, **Vol. 5, Part 1**, 591
Hunter, Allan, reference to, **Supp. 3**, 238
Hunter, John, reference to, **Vol. 7, Part 2**, 554 f.
Hunter, Kermit, reference to, **Supp. 3**, 427
Hunter, Robert, reference to, **Supp. 5**, 531
Hunter, William, reference to, **Supp. 3**, 139
Hunter College: founding of, **Vol. 5, Part 1**, 405; master plan, **Supp. 2**, 539; presidency, **Supp. 10**, 735–36
Hunter-Gault, Charlayne, reference to, **Supp. 8**, 540
Hunterian Laboratory of Experimental Medicine, **Supp. 4**, 213
Hunting (sport); big-game, **Supp. 10**, 460; equipment, **Supp. 8**, 28–29;
Huntington, Archer, reference to, **Supp. 6**, 280
Huntington, Collis P.: references to, **Vol. 5, Part 1**, 415; **Vol. 9, Part 1**, 502 f., 505; Fund, **Supp. 3**, 257–58
Huntington, George S., reference to, **Supp. 3**, 371
Huntington, Helen, reference to, **Supp. 6**, 306
Huntington, Henry E., references to, **Supp. 2**, 112, 271; **Supp. 3**, 262; **Supp. 5**, 586
Huntington, Samuel, reference to, **Vol. 9, Part 2**, 568
Huntington Library and Art Gallery (San Marino, Calif.), **Vol. 5, Part 1**, 415; planning and development, **Supp. 2**, 271; **Supp. 3**, 262
"Huntley-Brinkley Report," **Supp. 9**, 415–16
Hunton, Alphaeus, reference to, **Supp. 7**, 204
Hupmobile car, **Supp. 7**, 375
Hupp, Robert Craig, reference to, **Supp. 7**, 375–76
Hupp Motor Car Corporation, founding of, **Supp. 7**, 375–76
Hurd, Peter, references to, **Supp. 3**, 848, 849
Hurley, Edgar, reference to, **Supp. 7**, 462
Hurley, Patrick, references to, **Supp. 6**, 231; **Supp. 7**, 488
Huron College, presidency of, **Vol. 1, Part 2**, 318
Hurricanes: early study of, **Vol. 8, Part 1**, 441 f.; research on, **Supp. 1**, 387
Hurst, Sir Cecil, reference to, **Supp. 7**, 536
Hurst, Fannie, reference to, **Supp. 6**, 314
Hurst, Frank, reference to, **Supp. 10**, 408
Hurston, Zora Neale, reference to, **Supp. 6**, 321
Husch, Richard Gerard, reference to, **Supp. 5**, 23
Hussar, Austrian brig, **Vol. 5, Part 1**, 477
Hussey, Obed, reference to, **Vol. 6, Part 1**, 607–8
Hussey, W. J., reference to, **Supp. 5**, 13–14
Hutcheson, William L., references to, **Supp. 5**, 654; **Supp. 6**, 218
Hutchins, Robert M., references to, **Supp. 3**, 555; **Supp. 6**, 533, 559, 693; **Supp. 7**, 276; **Supp. 8**, 59; **Supp. 9**, 80, 870; **Supp. 10**, 542, 796
Hutchinson, Thomas, references to, **Vol. 7, Part 2**, 14 f., 23, 101 f.
"Hutchinson Letters," **Vol. 1, Part 1**, 98
Hutton, Betty, reference to, **Supp. 10**, 239
Hutton, Edward Francis, reference to, **Supp. 9**, 615
Hutton, E. F., and Co., **Supp. 7**, 379; **Supp. 10**, 366
Hutton, Frankyn Laws, references to, **Supp. 10**, 366, 367
Hutton, Marjorie Merriweather Post, reference to, **Supp. 6**, 147
Huxley, Fielding, reference to, **Supp. 6**, 100
Huxley, Julian, reference to, **Supp. 7**, 380
Huxley, Thomas Henry, references to, **Supp. 6**, 443, 444; **Supp. 7**, 380
Hyatt Roller Bearing Co., **Supp. 8**, 598
Hyde, Donald F., reference to, **Supp. 5**, 350
Hydraulic engineering: **Vol. 1, Part 2**, 529; **Vol. 3, Part 1**, 585 f., 587 f.; **Vol. 3, Part 2**, 2, 228, 267, 434, 579; **Vol. 4, Part 1**, 39, 40, 467; **Vol. 4, Part 2**, 59, 576 f., 595 f.; **Vol. 5, Part 1**, 349 f., 371; **Vol. 8, Part 1**, 324 f., 375 f.; **Vol. 8, Part 2**, 398 f., 473; **Vol. 9, Part 1**, 54, 273; **Supp. 1**, 524, 588; **Supp. 5**, 395–96; **Supp. 6**, 182, 435–36; fire-stream hydraulics, **Supp. 1**, 319; reclamation, **Supp. 3**, 813–14; writings on, **Vol. 4, Part 2**, 5, 96; **Vol. 7, Part 1**, 8. *See also* Dams; Engineering; Flood control; Irrigation; Water supply
Hydrocarbons, **Supp. 4**, 336–37
Hydrocephalus, **Supp. 4**, 213
Hydrochloric acid: isolation of, **Vol. 8, Part 1**, 223 f.; secretion of, **Supp. 6**, 296
Hydrocyanic-acid gas, perfection of, **Vol. 2, Part 2**, 434
Hydrodynamics, **Vol. 4, Part 2**, 318 f.
Hydrodynamics, **Supp. 4**, 58
Hydroelectric development, **Vol. 1, Part 2**, 408
Hydroelectric power: Brazilian project, **Supp. 4**, 81–82; construction and financing, **Supp. 3**, 745–47; development of, **Supp. 2**, 118, 583; Dixon-Yates syndicate, **Supp. 8**, 157; **Supp. 9**, 774; Niagara Falls, **Supp. 3**, 769; plant design, **Supp. 3**, 500, 745–47; public ownership, **Supp. 3**, 559; turbine bearings, **Supp. 3**, 419. *See also* Dams; Tennessee Valley Authority
Hydrogen: characteristics, **Supp. 5**, 413; discovery in atomic form, **Supp. 6**, 364; in solar atmosphere, **Supp. 6**, 561
Hydrogen bomb, **Supp. 5**, 455; **Supp. 7**, 565; **Supp. 8**, 200, 484; Public opposition to, **Supp. 8**, 301. *See also* Atomic bomb
Hydrographic Office, United States, **Vol. 1, Part 2**, 397 f.
Hydrography, **Vol. 1, Part 2**, 397 f.; **Vol. 3, Part 2**, 157; **Vol. 4, Part 1**, 543 f.; **Vol. 6, Part 1**, 552–53; **Vol. 7, Part 1**, 47, 457; **Vol. 9, Part 1**, 156
Hydrology, **Supp. 4**, 567; writings on, **Vol. 8, Part 1**, 324 f.
Hydrolosis, studies in, **Vol. 9, Part 2**, 544
Hydrometallurgy, **Vol. 3, Part 1**, 27
Hydrometers, perfection of, **Vol. 9, Part 2**, 273
Hydrophobia, study of, **Vol. 6, Part 2**, 486; **Vol. 9, Part 2**, 388
Hydroplanes, **Supp. 1**, 214; **Supp. 4**, 124. *See also* Aviation
Hydrotherapy, **Vol. 1, Part 2**, 29; **Vol. 5, Part 2**, 459
Hydrothermal theory, **Supp. 2**, 386
Hygeia, **Supp. 3**, 104
Hylan, John F., references to, **Supp. 3**, 718; **Supp. 5**, 286; **Supp. 6**, 88; **Supp. 7**, 779
Hyman, Stanley Edgar, reference to, **Supp. 7**, 385
Hymnal, Methodist, **Vol. 4, Part 1**, 405
Hymn books, editing of, **Vol. 4, Part 1**, 462; **Vol. 4, Part 2**, 387, 438; **Vol. 6, Part 1**, 38
Hymns, writing of, **Vol. 1, Part 2**, 142; **Vol. 2, Part 1**, 152; **Vol. 2, Part 2**, 531, 567; **Vol. 3, Part 1**, 333 f., 335, 337, 491; **Vol. 3, Part 2**, 481; **Vol. 4, Part 1**, 311; **Vol. 4, Part 2**, 203, 388, 395 f.; **Vol. 5, Part 1**, 138, 242; **Vol. 5, Part 2**, 119, 295 f.; **Vol. 6, Part 1**, 14, 479; **Vol. 7, Part 1**, 314, 569, 595, 605 f.; **Vol. 7, Part 2**, 192; **Vol. 8, Part 1**, 175, 374, 645; **Vol. 8,**

Part 2, 37, 352 f., 539, 606; **Vol. 9, Part 1**, 343; **Vol. 9, Part 2**, 444, 475; **Vol. 10, Part 1**, 108, 651 f.; **Vol. 10, Part 2**, 239
Hyperinsulinism, **Supp. 6**, 698
Hypnosis, **Supp. 5**, 329, 330; for birth delivery, **Supp. 6**, 555
Hypodermic needle, **Supp. 7**, 678, 679
Hypoglycemia, insulin-produced, **Supp. 6**, 563–64
Hypoplastic anemia, **Supp. 3**, 75
Hypothalamus, **Supp. 3**, 620; rage and, **Supp. 3**, 135

I

"I Almost Lost My Mind," **Supp. 9**, 414
I Am a Fugitive from a Georgia Chain Gang, **Supp. 9**, 689
I Am Curious—Yellow, **Supp. 10**, 324
Iannelli, Alfonso, references to, **Supp. 9**, 893, 894
Iba, Hank, reference to, **Supp. 9**, 21
IBM Corp. *See* International Business Machines Corporation
IBRD. *See* International Bank for Reconstruction and Development
Ibsen, first presentation of, in America, **Vol. 7, Part 1**, 73
ICAO. *See* International Civil Aviation Organization
Icarian colonies (Ill.), **Vol. 2, Part 1**, 391; **Vol. 6, Part 1**, 389
ICC. *See* Interstate Commerce Commission
Ice: artificial, first in U.S., **Vol. 6, Part 1**, 452; exportation, **Vol. 10, Part 1**, 47 f.; manufacture, **Vol. 10, Part 1**, 84; shipping, **Vol. 7, Part 1**, 240; **Vol. 10, Part 1**, 47 f.
Icelandic, first teaching of, in America, **Vol. 9, Part 1**, 252
Icelandic Literary Societies, **Vol. 3, Part 2**, 417
Iceman Cometh, The, **Supp. 7**, 34
Ice skating, **Supp. 7**, 528; **Supp. 8**, 253–54
Ichthyology: **Vol. 3, Part 1**, 169 f.; **Vol. 3, Part 2**, 63; **Vol. 5, Part 2**, 213; **Vol. 6, Part 1**, 191; writings on, **Vol. 5, Part 1**, 130; **Vol. 8, Part 1**, 322 f.
Ickes, Harold, L., references to, **Supp. 3**, 647, 651, 795, 796; **Supp. 4**, 392–93, 666; **Supp. 5**, 485; **Supp. 6**, 392, 451, 660, 661, 671, 692; **Supp. 10**, 119, 191, 795
I Confess: The Truth About American Communism, **Supp. 7**, 291
Iconoclast, **Supp. 1**, 100
Idaho: governorship, **Vol. 1, Part 2**, 611; **Vol. 4, Part 2**, 419 f.; labor riots, **Vol. 4, Part 2**, 419, 468; legal service, **Vol. 7, Part 2**, 592; mining, **Vol. 4, Part 2**, 419; **Vol. 8, Part 1**, 456; political service, **Vol. 1, Part 2**, 611; **Vol. 3, Part 1**, 210; **Vol. 4, Part 2**, 419; **Vol. 6, Part 1**, 528; **Vol. 9, Part 1**, 131; politics, **Supp. 6**, 681; **Supp. 7**, 212–13; **Supp. 8**, 508; public service, **Vol. 4, Part 2**, 419; **Vol. 9, Part 1**, 131; Sun Valley resort, **Supp. 5**, 270–71; territorial governorship, **Vol. 9, Part 1**, 131 f.; **Vol. 9, Part 2**, 456; woman suffrage, adoption of, **Vol. 3, Part 1**, 513 f.
Iddings, Joseph P., reference to, **Supp. 4**, 194
Idealism, absolute, **Supp. 6**, 505
Idlewild Airport (New York City). *See* Kennedy International Airport
Igneous rocks, **Supp. 4**, 194; **Supp. 6**, 145, 153
"I Led Three Lives" (television program), **Supp. 10**, 101
ILGWU. *See* International Ladies' Garment Workers' Union
Iliad, translation of, **Vol. 7, Part 1**, 326–27
Ilion, N.Y., history of, **Vol. 8, Part 1**, 496
I'll Cry Tomorrow, **Supp. 10**, 705
Illinois: agricultural libraries in schools, introduction of, **Vol. 1, Part 2**, 321; agricultural society, first in, **Vol. 1, Part 2**, 289; antislavery movement in, **Vol. 1, Part 2**, 128; **Vol. 6, Part 1**, 435; archaeology, **Vol. 9, Part 1**, 389; architecture, **Supp. 5**, 208; botany, **Vol. 2, Part 1**, 327; boundary disputes, **Vol. 8, Part 1**, 77 f.; canal building, **Vol. 6, Part 2**, 332; Civil War period, **Vol. 10, Part 2**, 600; coal survey in, **Vol. 6, Part 1**, 189; Congregational church, **Vol. 10, Part 1**, 58; Democratic party, **Vol. 3, Part 1**, 398 f.; **Supp. 10**, 167, 168, 169, 185, 186, 411; education in, **Vol. 1, Part 2**, 439; **Vol. 3, Part 1**, 510 f.; **Vol. 5, Part 1**, 271; **Vol. 8, Part 1**, 77 f., 120 f., 152; **Vol. 10, Part 1**, 645 f., 657 f.; entomology, **Vol. 10, Part 1**, 388 f.; Episcopal church in, **Vol. 6, Part 2**, 116; **Vol. 9, Part 1**, 6; ethics issues, **Supp. 6**, 74; frontier church activities, **Vol. 2, Part 1**, 547; fur trading, **Vol. 2, Part 1**, 582; geology of, **Vol. 10, Part 2**, 538; "George Smith's money," **Vol. 9, Part 1**, 268; German immigration to, **Vol. 5, Part 2**, 496; gerrymandering in, **Vol. 3, Part 1**, 398; governors, **Vol. 1, Part 1**, 231; **Vol. 1, Part 2**, 302, 432 f.; **Vol. 2, Part 2**, 296 f.; **Vol. 3, Part 1**, 510 f.; **Vol. 3, Part 2**, 41 f., 520 f.; **Vol. 6, Part 2**, 410 f.; **Vol. 7, Part 1**, 648 f.; **Vol. 7, Part 2**, 187 f.; **Vol. 8, Part 1**, 519 f.; **Vol. 10, Part 2**, 599 f.; **Supp. 2**, 182, 318; **Supp. 3**, 467–68; **Supp. 7**, 721–22; **Supp. 9**, 551, 552; **Supp. 10**, 168, 169, 411; history of, **Vol. 1, Part 1**, 236; **Vol. 8, Part 1**, 77 f.; **Vol. 10, Part 1**, 657 f.; Icarian colonies, **Vol. 2, Part 1**, 391; **Vol. 6, Part 1**, 389; Indian mounds, **Vol. 9, Part 1**, 389; Indians in, **Vol. 4, Part 1**, 510; industrial history of, **Vol. 8, Part 1**, 9 f., 263 f.; jurisprudence in, **Vol. 2, Part 1**, 575; Kerner corruption scandal, **Supp. 10**, 413; land claims, **Vol. 1, Part 2**, 432; land speculation, **Vol. 4, Part 2**, 247; "Latin settlement," **Vol. 5, Part 2**, 496; laws, digest of, **Vol. 8, Part 1**, 77 f.; lead mining, **Vol. 6, Part 2**, 496; legal service, **Vol. 1, Part 2**, 313, 382, 439, 580, 611; **Vol. 3, Part 1**, 110, 282, 291, 397; **Vol. 4, Part 1**, 605; **Vol. 6, Part 1**, 267, 344; **Vol. 8, Part 1**, 77, 519; **Vol. 9, Part 1**, 534; **Vol. 9, Part 2**, 634–35; **Vol. 10, Part 1**, 2, 19; **Vol. 10, Part 2**, 347, 469 f.; library, first, **Vol. 3, Part 2**, 479; Lincoln's life in, **Vol. 6, Part 1**, 243 f.; liquor control, **Vol. 8, Part 1**, 392; Lutheran church, **Vol. 4, Part 2**, 594; market gardening in, **Vol. 7, Part 2**, 464; Medical Practice Act, importance of, **Vol. 8, Part 1**, 390; missionary work in, **Vol. 1, Part 1**, 547; **Vol. 4, Part 1**, 235, 510; **Vol. 6, Part 2**, 280; **Vol. 10, Part 1**, 58; natural history of, **Vol. 5, Part 2**, 338; pioneer life in, **Vol. 1, Part 2**, 432; **Vol. 2, Part 1**, 198; **Vol. 3, Part 2**, 478; **Vol. 6, Part 2**, 280, 529, 610; **Vol. 7, Part 2**, 593; **Vol. 8, Part 1**, 519 f.; political parties, midcentury, **Vol. 4, Part 2**, 247; political service, **Vol. 1, Part 1**, 231; **Vol. 1, Part 2**, 110, 302, 313, 382, 432, 439, 580; **Vol. 3, Part 1**, 111 f., 398, 510, 520; **Vol. 3, Part 2**, 41; **Vol. 5, Part 2**, 496; **Vol. 6, Part 2**, 181, 244, 410, 491; **Vol. 7, Part 1**, 648; **Vol. 7, Part 2**, 187; **Vol. 8, Part 1**, 392, 519; **Vol. 9, Part 1**, 106, 191, 629; **Vol. 10, Part 1**, 19, 504 f., 657 f.; **Vol. 10, Part 2**, 600; politics, **Supp. 3**, 710–11; **Supp. 4**, 180, 280, 751–52; **Supp. 5**, 450, 598; **Supp. 6**, 683–84; **Supp. 7**, 702; **Supp. 8**, 121, 127–29, 391–92; **Supp. 9**, 551, 552, 739, 740; **Supp. 10**, 10, 167, 168, 169, 411, 531; progressive movement in, **Supp. 5**, 579; public service, **Vol. 1, Part 2**, 44; **Vol. 3, Part 1**, 510 f.; **Vol. 4, Part 2**, 134 f.; **Vol. 6, Part 2**, 379; **Vol. 7, Part 2**, 252; **Vol. 8, Part 1**, 263 f., 359 f.; **Vol. 9, Part 1**, 483 f.; **Vol. 10, Part 1**, 657 f.; public utilities in, **Vol. 8, Part 1**, 9 f.; railroad development in, **Vol. 4, Part 2**, 247; **Vol. 8, Part 1**, 359 f., 392; Republican party in, **Vol. 1, Part 2**, 382; **Vol. 7, Part 2**, 187; **Vol. 8, Part 1**, 392; **Supp. 9**, 739, 740; school system, organization of, **Vol. 10, Part 1**,

68; scientific services, **Vol. 10, Part 1**, 582; social reform, **Vol. 10, Part 2**, 386; statehood, admission to, **Vol. 8, Part 1**, 77 f.; Swedenborgian church in, **Vol. 6, Part 2**, 544; territory, organization of, **Vol. 8, Part 1**, 77 f.; urban violence, **Supp. 10**, 411; Whigs in pre-Civil War politics, **Vol. 4, Part 2**, 246; wool manufacture, **Vol. 8, Part 1**, 405. *See also city and institution names*
Illinois Agricultural Association, **Supp. 3**, 319
Illinois & Rock River Railroad, **Vol. 8, Part 1**, 9 f.
Illinois Association, organization of, at Yale, **Vol. 10, Part 1**, 58
Illinois Central Railroad Co., **Vol. 1, Part 2**, 182; **Vol. 3, Part 2**, 402; **Vol. 4, Part 2**, 297; **Vol. 25, Part 2**, 35; **Vol. 6, Part 1**, 495; **Vol. 7, Part 2**, 72; **Supp. 4**, 193
Illinois College: **Vol. 1, Part 1**, 547; **Vol. 1, Part 2**, 128, 571; founding of, **Vol. 10, Part 1**, 58
Illinois Farmers' Institute, **Supp. 3**, 68, 216
Illinois Female College, **Vol. 5, Part 1**, 616
Illinois Industrial University. *See* University of Illinois
Illinois Institute of Technology: architecture, **Supp. 8**, 436; design institute, **Supp. 4**, 591; expansion, **Supp. 9**, 378
Illinois Miner, **Supp. 3**, 10
Illinois Miners and Mechanics' Institute, **Vol. 9, Part 2**, 65
Illinois Monthly Magazine, **Vol. 4, Part 2**, 135
Illinois Municipal League, founding of, **Supp. 4**, 260
Illinois Natural History Society, **Vol. 9, Part 2**, 426; **Vol. 10, Part 1**, 68
Illinois Pipe-line Co., **Vol. 3, Part 1**, 367
Illinois Staats-Zeitung, **Vol. 8, Part 1**, 384
Illionis State Historical Society, Lincoln collection at, **Supp. 9**, 37
Illinois State Normal School, **Vol. 1, Part 2**, 44; **Vol. 2, Part 2**, 376; **Vol. 9, Part 2**, 581
Illinois Wesleyan University, **Vol. 3, Part 2**, 262
Illinois Women Suffrage Association, **Vol. 1, Part 2**, 581
Illuminism, **Vol. 7, Part 1**, 246
Illustrated Flora of the Northern United states, Canada, and the British Possessions, An, **Supp. 1**, 121
Illustrated Graphic News, **Vol. 10, Part 1**, 111
Illustrating, **Vol. 1, Part 1**, 465 f.; **Vol. 1, Part 2**, 93, 95, 168, 396; **Vol. 2, Part 1**, 17, 610; **Vol. 2, Part 2**, 480; **Vol. 3, Part 1**, 75 f.; **Vol. 3, Part 2**, 56; **Vol. 4, Part 1**, 41 f., 162, 193, 263; **Vol. 4, Part 2**, 542; **Vol. 5, Part 1**, 225; **Vol. 5, Part 2**, 294 f.; **Vol. 6, Part 1**, 284, 353; **Vol. 7, Part 1**, 53; **Vol. 7, Part 2**, 424 f., 438f.; **Vol. 8, Part 1**, 287 f., 490 f., 497, 511 f; **Vol. 8, Part 2**, 113, 202, 339, 371; **Vol. 9, Part 1**, 227, 575; **Vol. 9, Part 2**, 322, 346, 512
Illustration: **Supp. 1**, 298; **Supp. 6**, 204, 287; advertising, **Supp. 5**, 428–29; book, **Supp. 3**, 44, 69, 300, 848; **Supp. 5**, 580, 672–73; **Supp. 7**, 17, 48, 436; **Supp. 8**, 493, 494; botanic, **Supp. 1**, 121; **Supp. 4**, 17; brush drawing, **Supp. 5**, 473; children's books, **Supp. 3**, 69; **Supp. 4**, 310; **Supp. 5**, 93; **Supp. 6**, 372–73; **Supp. 10**, 688, 690; Christy Girl, **Supp. 5**, 112, 113; decoration, **Supp. 1**, 514; Gibson Girl, **Supp. 3**, 300–301; **Supp. 4**, 826; magazine, **Supp. 3**, 573–74; **Supp. 5**, 625; **Supp. 8**, 493; magazine covers, **Supp. 5**, 428, 429, 594; **Supp. 10**, 689, 690, 691; medical, **Supp. 3**, 106–7, 412; military, **Supp. 5**, 112; natural history, **Supp. 4**, 736–37; Petty Girl, **Supp. 5**, 637; scientific subjects, **Supp. 1**, 428
Illustrations of Masonry, **Vol. 7, Part 1**, 189
Illustrative art, development of, **Vol. 3, Part 1**, 423 f.
Illustrators. For complete list, *see* Occupations Index
ILO. *See* International Labor Office
"I Love Lucy" (television program), **Supp. 10**, 803–4
Il Progresso, Italian daily, first in U.S., **Vol. 1, Part 2**, 1
ILWU. *See* International Longshoremen's and Warehousemen's Union
Imagists: French, influence on Amy Lowell, **Vol. 6, Part 1**, 454; **Supp. 4**, 285–86; Pound's concept of, **Supp. 9**, 617
Imago, **Supp. 4**, 716
I Married Adventure, **Supp. 5**, 371
I Married a Witch, **Supp. 9**, 479
IMF. *See* International Monetary Fund
Immigrants' Protective League, **Supp. 2**, 1; **Supp. 4**, 107
Immigration: **Vol. 1, Part 1**, 646; **Vol. 5, Part 1**, 257; **Vol. 6, Part 2**, 326 f., 467; **Vol. 7, Part 1**, 33; **Vol. 8, Part 1**, 142 f.; **Vol. 8, Part 2**, 35 f.; adult education programs, **Supp. 8**, 9; anthropological study, **Supp. 3**, 84; assimilation advocacy, **Supp. 5**, 380–81; Catholic, **Vol. 9, Part 1**, 113; Catholic immigrants' resettlement, **Supp. 4**, 335; Chinese, **Vol. 1, Part 1**, 308; **Vol. 5, Part 2**, 269; **Vol. 9, Part 2**, 640; deportation cases, **Supp. 5**, 389; Ellis Island, **Vol. 7, Part 1**, 432; **Vol. 8, Part 2**, 169, 313; **Vol. 9, Part 2**, 549; examination at point of emigration, **Vol. 8, Part 1**, 142 f.; first authentic novel about, **Supp. 5**, 96; German, **Vol. 8, Part 2**, 87; histories of, **Supp. 7**, 28; Irish, **Vol. 3, Part 2**, 440; **Vol. 9, Part 2**, 4; Jewish Americanization, **Supp. 3**, 513; Jewish writings on, **Supp. 5**, 95–96; labor, European, first attempt at importation, **Vol. 4, Part 2**, 279; legislation, **Supp. 1**, 472; **Supp. 2**, 46; liberalization efforts, **Supp. 6**, 472; Massachusetts Colony, exclusion of immigrants from, **Vol. 10, Part 2**, 410, "melting pot" concept, **Supp. 4**, 23; national-origin restrictions, **Supp. 3**, 215, 346, 389, 502, 632; **Supp. 5**, 444–45, 561; **Supp. 6**, 320; **Supp. 7**, 644, 766, 767; National Research Council studies, **Supp. 6**, 718; nonrestrictive advocacy, **Supp. 5**, 598; Norwegian, **Vol. 3, Part 2**, 478; **Vol. 5, Part 1**, 612; **Vol. 6, Part 1**, 9; **Vol. 7, Part 1**, 419; **Vol. 7, Part 2**, 390; **Vol. 8, Part 1**, 487 f.; **Vol. 8, Part 2**, 124, 274; personal writings on, **Supp. 5**, 4–5; quota principle, **Vol. 3, Part 1**, 310; **Vol. 8, Part 2**, 183; racially nonrestrictive quota system, **Supp. 3**, 322, 323; regulation of, **Vol. 8, Part 1**, 142 f.; restrictive, eugenic basis for, **Supp. 4**, 413; restrictive legislation, **Supp. 4**, 792; Roman Catholic aid, **Supp. 5**, 722; social work, **Vol. 8, Part 1**, 295; **Supp. 6**, 1–2; **Supp. 7**, 341–42; sociological study of, **Supp. 6**, 726; studies on, **Supp. 2**, 278–79; survey of, **Vol. 3, Part 1**, 310; textbook on, **Vol. 5, Part 2**, 52; United States Bureau of, **Vol. 7, Part 1**, 432; war brides, **Supp. 7**, 541–42; World War I aliens, **Supp. 3**, 65; Zionist organizations, **Supp. 3**, 756. *See also* Refugees; *specific national and racial groups*
Immigration and Nationality Act (1952), passage of, **Supp. 5**, 445; **Supp. 7**, 766
Immigration and Naturalization Service, United States, **Supp. 8**, 35; Chaplin case, **Supp. 10**, 118
Immigration Commission (1907), **Vol. 5, Part 2**, 52
Immigration Restriction League, **Vol. 10, Part 1**, 436
Immunology: allergy, **Supp. 5**, 438; **Supp. 6**, 123–24; antigen-antibody reaction, **Supp. 3**, 441–42; development of, **Supp. 2**, 745; fertilization studies, **Supp. 4**, 497–98; pneumococci, **Supp. 5**, 26; public health and, **Supp. 1**, 667–67; research, **Supp. 1**, 628–29; viral research, **Supp. 4**, 287–88, 380–81, 615–16; yellow fever, **Supp. 5**, 605
Impeachment: **Vol. 4, Part 1**, 236; **Vol. 3, Part 1**, 89, 118 f.; Chase, Samuel, **Vol. 3, Part 1**, 363 f., 599 f.; **Vol. 8, Part 2**, 83; Jefferson's views on, **Vol. 5, Part 2**, 29; Johnson, Andrew, **Vol. 3, Part 2**, 564; **Vol. 4, Part 1**, 632; **Vol. 5, Part 2**, 87 f.; New York judges, removal by, **Vol. 8, Part 1**, 229 f.; New York gover-

nor, **Supp. 3**, 751; trial, first in America, **Vol. 7, Part 1**, 155
Impelliteri, Vincent R., references to, **Supp. 8**, 397; **Supp. 9**, 251, 607; **Supp. 10**, 453
Impending Crisis, The, **Vol. 4, Part 2**, 517; **Vol. 5, Part 1**, 266; **Vol. 9, Part 1**, 85
Imperial Chinese University, **Vol. 9, Part 2**, 372
Imperial College of Architecture (Japan), **Vol. 2, Part 2**, 147
Imperial Research Institute, **Vol. 9, Part 2**, 275
Imperial Tobacco Co., **Vol. 3, Part 1**, 497 f.
Imperial Valley (Calif.), **Supp. 5**, 309
Impressionist movement, in art, **Vol. 8, Part 2**, 54
Impressment of seamen, **Vol. 1, Part 1**, 80; **Vol. 3, Part 1**, 128; **Vol. 5, Part 2**, 30; **Vol. 9, Part 2**, 47
Improved Benevolent and Protective Order of Elks of the World, **Supp. 5**, 754
Inca Indians, **Supp. 4**, 670; **Supp. 6**, 59; **Supp. 7**, 241
Incandescent lighting, invention of, **Supp. 1**, 279; **Supp. 2**, 702
Ince, Thomas H., references to, **Supp. 4**, 363; **Supp. 9**, 807, 808
Incinerator, invention of, **Vol. 5, Part 2**, 265
Income, national, studies in, **Supp. 4**, 585
Income tax: **Supp. 1**, 385, 533; constitutionality of, **Vol. 3, Part 2**, 24; **Vol. 9, Part 1**, 413, exemptions, **Supp. 8**, 166; law, **Vol. 2, Part 2**, 85; **Vol. 3, Part 2**, 375; preparation guide, **Supp. 5**, 412; state, **Supp. 2**, 148; theory development, **Supp. 4**, 748; withholding, **Supp. 5**, 180; writings on, **Vol. 3, Part 2**, 556. *See also* Taxation
Income Tax Revision Act (1954), **Supp. 10**, 250
Incubators, invention of, **Vol. 8, Part 1**, 505
Incunabula, collection of, **Vol. 4, Part 2**, 415
In Defense of Freedom: A Conservative Credo, **Supp. 9**, 548
Independence, battleship, **Vol. 1, Part 1**, 507, 606
Independence Hall, erection of, **Vol. 1, Part 1**, 208; **Vol. 4, Part 2**, 182
Independence Mall (Philadelphia, Pa.), **Supp. 9**, 445
Independent, **Vol. 9, Part 1**, 220; **Vol. 9, Part 2**, 552, 622; **Supp. 5**, 308
Independent Air Transport Operator's Association, founding of, **Supp. 5**, 86
Independent Board for Presbyterian Foreign Missions, founding of, **Supp. 2**, 412
Independent League (N.Y.), **Supp. 5**, 286
Independent Woman, founding of, **Supp. 5**, 543
Indexes, **Supp. 5**, 752; medical literature, **Supp. 1**, 334–35
Indexing (economic), **Supp. 4**, 274–75; **Supp. 6**, 586
Index making, books and magazines, **Vol. 4, Part 2**, 13; **Vol. 7, Part 1**, 414; **Vol. 8, Part 1**, 66 f.; manuscripts on American, **Vol. 9, Part 1**, 607; medical writings, **Vol. 3, Part 2**, 467
Index Medicus, **Supp. 1**, 335; founding of, **Supp. 2**, 613
Index to North American Geology, **Supp. 4**, 218
Index to the Stratigraphy of North America, **Supp. 4**, 896
"In God We Trust," motto for coins, **Vol. 8, Part 1**, 49 f.
In His Steps, **Supp. 4**, 741
India: adventures in, **Vol. 4, Part 2**, 272; art-historical scholarship, **Supp. 4**, 177; diplomacy with U.S., **Vol. 4, Part 1**, 578 f.; **Supp. 8**, 501; Epworth League, **Vol. 7, Part 2**, 219; first U.S. ambassador to, **Supp. 6**, 245; food aid, **Supp. 8**, 468; grammar of language, **Vol. 5, Part 2**, 304; Keating ambassadorship, **Supp. 9**, 450; leper colony, **Supp. 3**, 623–24; literary heritage, **Supp. 1**, 434; medical school, first missionary, in, **Vol. 10, Part 1**, 411; missionary work, **Vol. 1, Part 1**, 186; **Vol. 1, Part 2**, 504; **Vol. 2, Part 1**, 225, 597; **Vol. 3, Part 2**, 235; **Vol. 4, Part 1**, 354, 419; **Vol. 4, Part 2**, 608; **Vol. 5, Part 1**, 125 f., 365, 463; **Vol. 5, Part 2**, 189 f., 236, 240, 242 f., 304 f.; **Vol. 6, Part 1**, 356; **Vol. 6, Part 2**, 255; **Vol. 7, Part 1**, 5, 305; **Vol. 7, Part 2**, 218; **Vol. 8, Part 1**, 68 f.; **Vol. 8, Part 2**, 523; **Vol. 9, Part 1**, 437; **Vol. 9, Part 2**, 12; **Vol. 10, Part 1**, 108, 148, 411; **Vol. 10, Part 2**, 29, 65, 401; social work in, **Supp. 7**, 342; steel plant, **Supp. 2**, 526; trade with, **Vol. 5, Part 1**, 552; World War II defense of, **Supp. 4**, 782–83; writings on, **Vol. 5, Part 1**, 366; **Vol. 5, Part 2**, 190
Indiana: agriculture, **Vol. 3, Part 1**, 491 f.; Civil War period in, **Vol. 5, Part 2**, 601; **Vol. 7, Part 1**, 263; coal survey in, **Vol. 6, Part 1**, 189; constitution of, **Vol. 3, Part 1**, 521 f.; Democratic party in, **Vol. 6, Part 2**, 18; **Supp. 9**, 529; education, **Vol. 2, Part 1**, 118; **Vol. 3, Part 1**, 521 f.; **Vol. 5, Part 1**, 241; **Vol. 6, Part 1**, 7; **Vol. 7, Part 1**, 229; **Vol. 7, Part 2**, 210; **Vol. 8, Part 1**, 421; farm life, early, **Vol. 5, Part 1**, 55; finance in, **Vol. 5, Part 2**, 600 f.; geology, **Vol. 7, Part 2**, 116; governors, **Vol. 4, Part 1**, 519 f.; **Vol. 4, Part 2**, 534 f., 535 f.; **Vol. 5, Part 1**, 270 f.; **Vol. 5, Part 2**, 57 f.; **Vol. 6, Part 2**, 330 f., 412 f.; **Vol. 7, Part 1**, 262 f.; **Vol. 8, Part 1**, 80 f., 333; **Vol. 10, Part 1**, 368 f.; **Vol. 10, Part 2**, 82 f., 267 f., 559 f.; **Supp. 5**, 459; **Supp. 9**, 359–60; history of, **Vol. 3, Part 1**, 521 f.; **Vol. 5, Part 1**, 55, 281; **Vol. 9, Part 1**, 331; Indian trade, **Vol. 6, Part 2**, 529; insane, first hospital for care of, in, **Vol. 3, Part 2**, 205; land speculation, **Vol. 8, Part 2**, 51; legal service, **Vol. 1, Part 2**, 240; **Vol. 3, Part 1**, 522; **Vol. 5, Part 1**, 158, 352; **Vol. 6, Part 1**, 40; **Vol. 6, Part 2**, 330; **Vol. 7, Part 1**, 538; **Vol. 7, Part 2**, 110, 210, 426, 476; **Vol. 8, Part 2**, 194; **Vol. 10, Part 1**, 134, 368 f.; **Vol. 10, Part 2**, 84, 505; Lincoln's life in, **Vol. 6, Part 1**, 243; literature, **Supp. 4**, 629–30; Log Cabin convention (1840), **Vol. 8, Part 2**, 51; missions in, **Vol. 2, Part 1**, 189; orphan asylums in, **Vol. 3, Part 1**, 562 f.; panic of 1867; **Vol. 5, Part 2**, 601; philanthropy, **Vol. 3, Part 1**, 244; **Vol. 8, Part 1**, 268; **Vol. 8, Part 2**, 156 f.; pioneer days, **Vol. 6, Part 2**, 563; **Vol. 10, Part 2**, 268; political service, **Vol. 1, Part 2**, 231, 240; **Vol. 2, Part 2**, 266; **Vol. 3, Part 1**, 136, 183, 521; **Vol. 4, Part 1**, 520; **Vol. 4, Part 2**, 228, 331; **Vol. 5, Part 1**, 270; **Vol. 5, Part 2**, 57, 227; **Vol. 6, Part 2**, 17, 413; **Vol. 7, Part 1**, 262; **Vol. 7, Part 2**, 60; **Vol. 8, Part 1**, 80, 111, 333; **Vol. 8, Part 2**, 194, 610; **Vol. 9, Part 1**, 330; **Vol. 9, Part 1**, 245; **Vol. 9, Part 2**, 272; **Vol. 10, Part 1**, 134, 368 f, 375 f.; **Vol. 10, Part 2**, 83, 268, 478, 560; politics, **Supp. 4**, 861–62; **Supp. 5**, 281; **Supp. 7**, 541; **Supp. 8**, 699; **Supp. 9**, 359–60, 529; **Supp. 10**, 97; Presbyterian church in, **Vol. 4, Part 2**, 119; public service, **Vol. 1, Part 2**, 424; **Vol. 2, Part 2**, 39; **Vol. 4, Part 2**, 16, 535; **Vol. 5, Part 1**, 158 f., 281, 352; **Vol. 5, Part 2**, 355 f.; **Vol. 7, Part 1**, 481 f.; **Vol. 7, Part 2**, 116 f., 119; railroad promotion and building, **Vol. 5, Part 2**, 601; **Vol. 7, Part 1**, 228; **Vol. 8, Part 2**, 157; Republican party in, **Vol. 2, Part 2**, 297; **Vol. 7, Part 2**, 61; **Supp. 9**, 360 **Supp. 10**, 97; Riley, J. W., tribute of state to, **Vol. 8, Part 1**, 612; Robinson's Prairie, pioneer settlement, **Vol. 8, Part 2**, 51; Squatter's Union against speculators, **Vol. 8, Part 2**, 51; statehood, admission to, **Vol. 3, Part 1**, 522; **Vol. 6, Part 2**, 439; **Vol. 8, Part 1**, 111 f.; Swiss settlement in, **Vol. 3, Part 1**, 491 f.; territory, **Vol. 4, Part 1**, 254; **Vol. 9, Part 2**, 437; women, first academy for young, **Vol. 4, Part 2**, 34; writers, **Supp. 4**, 816–17
"Indiana," land enterprise, **Vol. 9, Part 2**, 638
Indian Affairs, Bureau of, **Vol. 6, Part 2**, 89; **Supp. 3**, 846; **Supp. 7**, 43, 393–94, 505, 506
Indiana Asbury University. *See* De Pauw University
Indiana Christian Home Missionary Society, **Vol. 4, Part 1**, 407
Indiana Civil Service Reform Association, **Vol. 9, Part 2**, 248

Indiana Civil Service Reform Organization, **Supp. 1**, 15
Indiana Historical Society, **Vol. 7, Part 2**, 210
Indiana Hospital for the Insane, **Vol. 9, Part 2**, 249
Indiana Institution for the Education of the Blind, **Vol. 2, Part 2**, 107
Indiana Medical College, **Vol. 3, Part 2**, 469
Indiana Medical Society, **Vol. 7, Part 2**, 286
Indianapolis, **Supp. 9**, 461
Indianapolis, Ind.: public service, **Vol. 6, Part 2**, 8, 563; Roman Catholic diocese, **Supp. 8**, 537
Indianapolis 500. *See* Automobile racing
Indianapolis News, **Vol. 5, Part 1**, 324
Indianapolis Repertory Company, **Supp. 3**, 797
Indianapolis Speedway, **Supp. 9**, 658
Indiana Sentinel, **Vol. 9, Part 1**, 244
Indianapolis Star: "Comments on the Screen" column, **Supp. 10**, 246; "Impressions in the Field of Art" column, **Supp. 10**, 246
Indiana State Board of Charities, **Supp. 3**, 388
Indiana University: **Vol. 4, Part 2**, 119; **Vol. 5, Part 1**, 158; **Vol. 5, Part 2**, 212; **Vol. 6, Part 2**, 440; **Vol. 7, Part 1**, 281; **Vol. 10, Part 2**, 578; folklore studies, **Supp. 10**, 781; football team, **Supp. 5**, 458; genetics studies, **Supp. 8**, 449, 450; history studies, **Supp. 8**, 60; human sexuality studies, **Supp. 6**, 342–44; sociology studies, **Supp. 4**, 808–9
Indian Defense League of America, **Supp. 9**, 656
Indian Reorganization Act (1934), **Supp. 5**, 119, 319; **Supp. 7**, 393; **Supp. 8**, 99
Indians, American (general): agents for, **Vol. 3, Part 2**, 443, 455, 536; **Vol. 4, Part 2**, 215; **Vol. 5, Part 1**, 355 f.; **Vol. 6, Part 1**, 617; **Vol. 7, Part 1**, 379, 407; **Vol. 9, Part 1**, 144, 146; **Vol. 9, Part 2**, 31, 137; Albany Conference (1745), **Vol. 9, Part 2**, 431; alphabet, Dakota, **Vol. 8, Part 1**, 61 f.; anthropological studies, **Supp. 2**, 9, 176, 593; **Supp. 3**, 82–84; **Supp. 4**, 179; **Supp. 6**, 353; 612–13; archaeological studies, **Supp. 5**, 533–34; archaeological studies in Mexico, **Supp. 4**, 605–6; art, research in, **Vol. 1, Part 1**, 588; art exhibitions, **Supp. 8**, 126; artifact collection, **Supp. 6**, 289–90; autobiography of Indian chief, **Vol. 1, Part 2**, 314; Bacon's Rebellion, **Vol. 6, Part 2**, 361; Bering Strait migration theory, **Supp. 3**, 372; Bethlehem, Pa., raids on, **Vol. 8, Part 1**, 113 f.; Bible translations, **Vol. 1, Part 1**, 478; **Vol. 5, Part 2**, 110; **Vol. 8, Part 1**, 61 f.; bibliographies, **Supp. 2**, 163; books, translation of, **Vol. 4, Part 2**, 144; books for, **Vol. 5, Part 1**, 576; boundary disputes with, **Vol. 5, Part 2**, 126; captives, **Vol. 4, Part 1**, 501; **Vol. 5, Part 2**, 39, 47; **Vol. 8, Part 2**, 201; **Vol. 9, Part 1**, 216, 285; Catholic mission schools for, **Supp. 5**, 185–86; chiefs, **Vol. 1, Part 2**, 314; **Vol. 4, Part 1**, 101; **Vol. 4, Part 2**, 28; **Vol. 5, Part 2**, 115, 218 f., 255, 350, 367, 583; **Vol. 6, Part 1**, 182, 299 f., 362 f.; **Vol. 7, Part 1**, 560, 621; **Vol. 8, Part 1**, 294; **Vol. 8, Part 2**, 178, 375 f., 542; **Vol. 9, Part 1**, 13, 109, 192, 194, 469; **Vol. 9, Part 2**, 375 f., 474 f., 580; **Vol. 10, Part 1**, 409 f.; Cienequeilla, battle of, **Vol. 3, Part 1**, 93 f.; citizenship for, **Vol. 8, Part 1**, 175 f., 335 f.; civil government for, **Vol. 7, Part 2**, 225; Civil War, Cherokees' part in, **Vol. 10, Part 1**, 537 f.; contemporary, writings on, **Supp. 7**, 449; conversion of, **Vol. 4, Part 2**, 611; **Vol. 8, Part 1**, 294; **Vol. 9, Part 1**, 75 f.; Court of Indian Offenses, **Vol. 4, Part 1**, 502; crafts, **Supp. 1**, 437; **Supp. 10**, 511–12; cultural anthropological studies, **Supp. 4**, 71–72; culture, **Supp. 1**, 651; Dawes, status of; under, **Vol. 8, Part 1**, 335 f.; dialects, **Vol. 4, Part 2**, 94; Easton, Pa., Treaty of, **Vol. 9, Part 2**, 481; education, **Vol. 1, Part 1**, 216, 238; **Vol. 1, Part 2**, 478 f.; **Vol. 2, Part 1**, 4, 46; **Vol. 3, Part 1**, 376, 477 f.; **Vol. 4, Part 1**, 101; **Vol. 4, Part 2**, 332, 380, 414; **Vol. 5, Part 2**, 115, 504; **Vol. 6, Part 1**, 176, 428 f.; **Vol. 6, Part 2**, 453, 471, 496; **Vol. 7, Part 2**, 336; **Vol. 8, Part 1**, 111, 175 f.; **Vol. 8, Part 2**, 30; **Vol. 10, Part 2**, 58; **Supp. 4**, 165–66; **Supp. 7**, 43; equestrian sculpture of,**Supp. 3**, 210–11; ethnographic studies, **Supp. 1**, 252; **Supp. 4**, 907–8; **Supp. 6**, 524–25; ethnological studies, **Vol. 3, Part 1**, 553 f.; **Vol. 3, Part 2**, 126; **Vol. 5, Part 2**, 205 f., 208; **Vol. 7, Part 1**, 183 f., 512; **Vol. 7, Part 2**, 603; **Vol. 8, Part 2**, 55, 278; **Supp. 3**, 582; **Supp. 4**, 761–62; **Supp. 6**, 392–93; **Supp. 7**, 710–11; evangelism, **Vol. 7, Part 1**, 529; folklore, **Vol. 5, Part 1**, 566; **Vol. 5, Part 2**, 206; **Vol. 7, Part 1**, 460 f.; **Vol. 8, Part 1**, 301 f.; **Supp. 3**, 582; **Supp. 6**, 612; French alliance, breakup of, **Vol. 8, Part 1**, 113 f.; French and Indian War, plight of Abnakis during, **Vol. 8, Part 1**, 330 f.; fur trappers, attack on, Vol. 4, Part 2 546; "ghost dance," **Vol. 10, Part 2**, 541; governmental supervision of, **Vol. 1, Part 1**, 33 f., 39; **Vol. 1, Part 2**, 390; **Vol. 3, Part 1**, 149 f., 243, 349; **Vol. 3, Part 2**, 41, 66, 483; **Vol. 4, Part 1**, 31, 171; **Vol. 4, Part 2**, 186, 414; **Vol. 5, Part 1**, 263 f., 363, 449, 500, 523, 577; **Vol. 5, Part 2**, 100, 103, 124 f., 126 f., 247, 293, 573; **Vol. 6, Part 1**, 195, 260 f., 291 318, 362, 550, 587, 611; **Vol. 6, Part 2**, 89; **Vol. 7, Part 1**, 40, 126, 246, 379, 407, 437, 594; **Vol. 7, Part 2**, 225, 601; **Vol. 8, Part 1**, 99 f., 121 f., 146 f., 175 f., 335f.; **Vol. 8, Part 2**, 475, 611; **Vol. 9, Part 1**, 109, 121, 145, 231, 468; **Vol. 9, Part 2**, 359 f., 375 f.; **Vol. 10, Part 2**, 69, 255, 391; government policies, **Supp. 2**, 291; **Supp. 5**, 319, 342, 662; **Supp. 7**, 122; government policy reforms, **Supp. 8**, 98–99; government relations, **Supp. 3**, 846; **Supp. 4**, 165–66; Great Britain, relations with, **Vol. 6, Part 1**, 300; **Vol. 8, Part 1**, 18 f.; **Vol. 9, Part 2**, 359 f.; **Vol. 10, Part 1**, 109; Greenville, Treaty of, **Vol. 3, Part 1**, 255; guiding immigrants through Indian lands, **Vol. 3, Part 1**, 34; historical writings on, **Supp. 5**, 430; history of, **Supp. 6**, 612; idealization of, **Supp. 4**, 737; Inca civilization, **Supp. 4**, 670; **Supp. 6**, 59; interpreting, **Vol. 4, Part 1**, 323; **Vol. 9, Part 1**, 487; **Supp. 4**, 237; inventions by, **Vol. 8, Part 2**, 586; King Philip's War, **Vol. 4, Part 1**, 360; **Vol. 8, Part 1**, 290 f.; land, matters relating to, **Vol. 3, Part 1**, 176; **Vol. 4, Part 1**, 502; **Vol. 4, Part 2**, 531; **Vol. 5, Part 2**, 40; **Vol. 7, Part 1**, 642; **Vol. 8, Part 1**, 274, 341 f., 426, 595; **Vol. 10, Part 1**, 26; languages, study of, **Vol. 1, Part 1**, 585; **Vol. 3, Part 1**, 277, 385, 507; **Vol. 3, Part 2**, 460; **Vol. 4, Part 1**, 192; **Vol. 4, Part 2**, 104; **Vol. 5, Part 2**, 33; **Vol. 6, Part 1**, 561 f.; **Vol. 7, Part 1**, 559; **Vol. 8, Part 1**, 61 f., 605; **Vol. 8, Part 2**, 586; **Vol. 9, Part 1**, 51; **Vol. 9, Part 2**, 389; **Vol. 10, Part 1**, 9 f.; law codification, **Supp. 8**, 99; leadership, **Supp. 8**, 647; **Supp. 9**, 656–57; legal rights of, **Supp. 9**, 656–57; linguistics studies, **Supp. 3**, 819–20; Logstown, Treaty of, **Vol. 4, Part 1**, 48; Lost Valley, battle of, **Vol. 5, Part 2**, 182; Loyalists, relations with, **Vol. 5, Part 2**, 100; Maine, writings, **Supp. 4**, 248–49; massacres, **Vol. 1, Part 1**, 145; **Vol. 1, Part 2**, 217; **Vol. 3, Part 1**, 554 f.; **Vol. 3, Part 2**, 350; **Vol. 4, Part 2**, 362; **Vol. 5, Part 1**, 437; **Vol. 5, Part 2**, 47, 100, 371; medical practice among, **Vol. 6, Part 1**, 272; Medicine Lodge Treaty, **Vol. 8, Part 1**, 294; medicine men, **Vol. 9, Part 1**, 193, 371; missionary work among, *see* Missions, Indian; missions, **Supp. 1**, 134, 158–59, 218–19, 289–90; mixed marriages, **Vol. 1, Part 1**, 345, 521; **Vol. 4, Part 2**, 276; **Vol. 6, Part 1**, 98; **Vol. 7, Part 1**, 458; **Vol. 8, Part 1**, 18 f.; **Vol. 8, Part 2**, 118, 173; mound building, **Vol. 2, Part 1**, 51; **Vol. 5, Part 2**, 612; **Vol. 9, Part 1**, 389; **Vol. 9, Part 2**, 426; Mount Dexter Treaty, **Vol. 8, Part 1**, 274; murdered by, **Vol. 7, Part 1**, 401; museum exhibits, **Supp. 6**, 355; music, **Vol. 1, Part 1**,

276; **Vol. 2, Part 1**, 288, 342; **Vol. 3, Part 2**, 379, 463; **Vol. 5, Part 2**, 505; **Supp. 4**, 138; **Supp. 5**, 218; **Supp. 6**, 162–63; Oklahoma Territory, **Supp. 4**, 641; paintings of, **Vol. 2, Part 1**, 574; **Vol. 8, Part 2**, 123; **Vol. 9, Part 1**, 513 f.; **Vol. 10, Part 2**, 369; **Supp. 3**, 113; Penn, William, attitude toward, **Vol. 7, Part 2**, 435 f.; philosophy and ethics, **Supp. 5**, 644–45; photography depicting, **Supp. 3**, 295; **Supp. 5**, 148; physical anthropology studies of, **Supp. 3**, 372; Pilgrims, relations with, **Vol. 6, Part 2**, 380; plays, vogue of, **Vol. 9, Part 2**, 77; protection of property, **Vol. 10, Part 1**, 142; records, **Vol. 9, Part 2**, 545; relics, **Vol. 3, Part 1**, 113, 553 f.; **Vol. 6, Part 1**, 193 f.; **Vol. 7, Part 1**, 366; religion of, **Vol. 9, Part 1**, 372; **Vol. 10, Part 2**, 541; reservations, removal to, **Vol. 3, Part 1**, 557 f.; **Vol. 3, Part 2**, 110; **Vol. 4, Part 1**, 83; **Vol. 6, Part 2**, 89; **Vol. 7, Part 1**, 408; **Vol. 8, Part 1**, 111, 210, 419; **Vol. 8, Part 2**, 59; **Vol. 9, Part 2**, 475; **Vol. 10, Part 1**, 537 f.; **Supp. 1**, 3; Revolution, participation in, **Vol. 10, Part 2**, 123; rights, **Vol. 2, Part 1**, 46; **Vol. 8, Part 1**, 530 f.; rights activism, **Supp. 1**, 463; **Supp. 5**, 119–20; **Supp. 7**, 393–94, 449–50, 486–87; 505–6; **Supp. 8**, 98–99; scouts, **Supp. 1**, 660; sculpture depicting, **Supp. 4**, 533, 534; **Supp. 5**, 231–32; **Supp. 6**, 720; Seminole War, **Vol. 1, Part 1**, 359; **Vol. 1, Part 2**, 436, 586, 597; **Vol. 3, Part 1**, 363, 580 f., 598; **Vol. 3, Part 2**, 264; **Vol. 4, Part 1**, 83, 144, 230, 237, 287, 481; **Vol. 5, Part 2**, 63, 91, 144; **Vol. 6, Part 1**, 130; **Vol. 7, Part 2**, 296, 414; **Vol. 8, Part 1**, 8, 328, 570, 609; **Vol. 8, Part 2**, 196; **Vol. 9, Part 1**, 331; **Vol. 9, Part 2**, 255, 350, 432, **Vol. 10, Part 1**, 365, 571; Sheridan's operations against, **Vol. 9, Part 1**, 81; Sioux confederacy, **Vol. 2, Part 2**, 530 f.; Sioux uprising of 1862, **Vol. 6, Part 1**, 300; **Vol. 8, Part 1**, 605; Six Nations, **Vol. 5, Part 2**, 125; **Vol. 7, Part 1**, 642; slavery, introduction of, **Vol. 10, Part 1**, 433; Spanish allegiance, winning of, **Vol. 3, Part 1**, 229; Spanish frontier, **Vol. 7, Part 2**, 199 f.; squaw, famous, **Vol. 8, Part 2**, 278; Standish, Myles, and, **Vol. 9, Part 1**, 500; stereotypical depictions of, **Supp. 10**, 736; studies of, **Vol. 1, Part 1**, 571; **Vol. 1, Part 2**, 483; **Vol. 3, Part 1**, 384 f.; **Vol. 3, Part 2**, 269, 353 f.; **Vol. 5, Part 1**, 245; **Vol. 5, Part 2**, 205 f.; **Vol. 6, Part 1**, 262; **Vol. 6, Part 2**, 420; **Vol. 7, Part 1**, 13, 110, 184 f., 461; **Vol. 8, Part 2**, 457; **Vol. 9, Part 1**, 197, 262, 632, 634; **Supp. 2**, 265; teaching of Christian songs, to, **Vol. 1, Part 1**, 276; trade with, **Vol. 2, Part 1**, 295, 446, 487; **Vol. 3, Part 1**, 83, 229, 305; **Vol. 3, Part 2**, 442, 506; **Vol. 4, Part 2**, 192 f., 314; **Vol. 5, Part 1**, 587 f.; **Vol. 5, Part 2**, 111; **Vol. 6, Part 1**, 191, 413, 586; **Vol. 6, Part 2**, 111, 528 f.; **Vol. 7, Part 1**, 631, 641; **Vol. 7, Part 2**, 4, 12; **Vol. 8, Part 2**, 108; **Vol. 9, Part 1**, 59, 332; **Vol. 9, Part 2**, 489, 638; trails, tracing of, **Supp. 1**, 443; treachery of, **Vol. 4, Part 2**, 245; treaties with, **Vol. 1, Part 2**, 314; **Vol. 2, Part 1**, 366; **Vol. 3, Part 1**, 83, 255 f., 500; **Vol. 3, Part 2**, 600; **Vol. 4, Part 1**, 48; **Vol. 4, Part 2**, 459; **Vol. 5, Part 1**, 160, 208, 280; **Vol. 5, Part 2**, 255 f.; **Vol. 6, Part 1**, 206, 299 f.; **Vol. 8, Part 1**, 274, 284 f., 294, 341 f., 437; **Vol. 8, Part 2**, 24, 157, 393; **Vol. 9, Part 1**, 61, 143; **Vol. 9, Part 2**, 481, 564, 580; **Vol. 10, Part 1**, 614 f.; treatment of, **Vol. 3, Part 2**, 215; trial of, **Vol. 6, Part 1**, 182; tribal leadership, **Supp. 4**, 237–38; vernacular, satirical sketches in, **Vol. 8, Part 1**, 111; Vincennes, Treaty of, **Vol. 8, Part 1**, 284 f.; vote, first, **Vol. 9, Part 1**, 228; War of 1812, part played in, **Vol. 3, Part 1**, 305; "White Man's Book of God," search for, **Vol. 4, Part 1**, 173; "White Woman of the Genesee," **Vol. 5, Part 2**, 39; Wild West shows, **Supp. 3**, 460; Wounded Knee, siege at, **Supp. 10**, 557; writings on, **Supp. 2**, 163; **Supp. 5**, 533, 534; Yakima outbreak of 1856, **Vol. 8, Part 1**, 394. *See also* Indians, American (by tribe); *specific tribes*

Indians, American (by state): Alabama, **Vol. 3, Part 1**, 528; **Vol. 6, Part 2**, 535; Arizona, **Vol. 8, Part 1**, 121 f.; California, **Vol. 2, Part 1**, 485; Connecticut, **Vol. 3, Part 1**, 199; **Vol. 8, Part 1**, 426; Delaware, **Vol. 9, Part 2**, 431; Florida, *see* Indians, American (by tribe), Seminole; Georgia, **Vol. 1, Part 2**, 478; **Vol. 2, Part 2**, 182 f.; **Vol. 6, Part 1**, 503 f.; **Vol. 10, Part 1**, 537 f.; Illinois, **Vol. 4, Part 1**, 510; **Vol. 9, Part 1**, 387; Indiana, **Vol. 5, Part 1**, 55; **Vol. 6, Part 2**, 529; Kentucky, **Vol. 4, Part 2**, 531; Louisiana, **Vol. 1, Part 2**, 251; **Vol. 10, Part 1**, 107; Massachusetts **Vol. 2, Part 1**, 480; **Vol. 3, Part 1**, 176; **Vol. 6, Part 2**, 590; **Vol. 10, Part 2**, 287; Minnesota, **Vol. 6, Part 1**, 300; **Vol. 8, Part 1**, 341 f., 540; **Vol. 10, Part 2**, 383; Mississippi, **Vol. 6, Part 1**, 144; Missouri, **Vol. 10, Part 1**, 20 f.; Montana, **Vol. 8, Part 1**, 135 f.; New Jersey, **Vol. 8, Part 1**, 419; New Mexico, **Vol. 3, Part 1**, 93 f.; **Vol. 7, Part 2**, 90; **Supp. 10**, 511–12; New York, **Vol. 2, Part 1**, 295; **Vol. 7, Part 1**, 646 f.; **Supp. 9**, 655–57; Ohio, **Vol. 1, Part 2**, 481; **Vol. 3, Part 1**, 75; **Vol. 10, Part 1**, 563 f.; Oregon, **Vol. 1, Part 1**, 236; **Vol. 5, Part 2**, 579; **Vol. 7, Part 2**, 237; Pennsylvania, **Vol. 4, Part 2**, 366; **Vol. 8, Part 1**, 113 f., 129 f.; **Vol. 8, Part 2**, 177; **Vol. 10, Part 1**, 614 f., *see also* Wyoming Massacre; Rhode Island, **Vol. 6, Part 2**, 590; South Carolina, **Vol. 6, Part 1**, 158; **Vol. 9, Part 2**, 489; South Dakota, **Vol. 4, Part 1**, 502; Tennessee, **Vol. 6, Part 2**, 146; Texas, **Vol. 6, Part 1**, 104; **Vol. 8, Part 2**, 179; Virginia, **Vol. 4, Part 2**, 375; **Vol. 8, Part 1**, 111 f.; **Vol. 8, Part 2**, 118, 293 f.; **Vol. 9, Part 2**, 121

Indians, American (by tribe): Abnaki, **Vol. 8, Part 1**, 330 f.; Algonquian, **Vol. 5, Part 2**, 205–6; Apache, **Vol. 5, Part 1**, 609; Arapaho, **Vol. 4, Part 1**, 31; Cherokee, **Vol. 1, Part 2**, 478; **Vol. 2, Part 2**, 182 f.; **Vol. 6, Part 1**, 504, 539; **Vol. 6, Part 2**, 82, 453; **Vol. 7, Part 1**, 401, 622; **Vol. 8, Part 2**, 179; **Vol. 9, Part 1**, 61; **Vol. 9, Part 2**, 615; **Vol. 10, Part 1**, 537 f.; Chickasaw, **Vol. 6, Part 1**, 241; Chippewa, **Vol. 3, Part 1**, 500 f.; **Vol. 7, Part 2**, 591; **Vol. 8, Part 1**, 540; Choctaw, **Vol. 5, Part 2**, 115; **Vol. 6, Part 1**, 144, 241; **Vol. 6, Part 2**, 82; **Vol. 7, Part 2**, 638; **Vol. 8, Part 1**, 274; **Vol. 8, Part 2**, 191; Comanche, **Vol. 3, Part 1**, 331; **Vol. 8, Part 1**, 294; Creek, **Vol. 1, Part 2**, 520; **Vol. 3, Part 2**, 308; **Vol. 4, Part 1**, 307; **Vol. 4, Part 2**, 414; **Vol. 5, Part 2**, 92, 111; **Vol. 6, Part 1**, 428 f.; **Vol. 6, Part 2**, 51, 70; **Vol. 7, Part 1**, 371; **Vol. 7, Part 2**, 569; **Vol. 8, Part 2**, 30; **Vol. 9, Part 2**, 580, 650; Creole, **Vol. 1, Part 2**, 479; **Vol. 2, Part 1**, 480; **Vol. 3, Part 2**, 537; **Vol. 6, Part 2**, 283; **Vol. 8, Part 2**, 192; Delaware, **Vol. 2, Part 1**, 445; **Vol. 9, Part 2**, 360 f.; Fox, **Vol. 1, Part 2**, 314, **Vol. 5, Part 2**, 206; Hopi, **Vol. 3, Part 2**, 353; **Vol. 5, Part 1**, 577; Iroquois, **Vol. 1, Part 2**, 103, 604; **Vol. 3, Part 1**, 19, 364, 462; **Vol. 4, Part 1**, 130; **Vol. 5, Part 2**, 548; **Vol. 9, Part 1**, 194; **Vol. 9, Part 2**, 90, 184, 431; **Supp. 9**, 655–57; Kiowa, **Vol. 5, Part 2**, 367; Miami, **Vol. 3, Part 1**, 75; **Vol. 6, Part 1**, 300; **Vol. 8, Part 2**, 294; Mohawk, **Vol. 1, Part 2**, 604; **Vol. 4, Part 2**, 370, 532; **Vol. 7, Part 1**, 646 f.; **Vol. 8, Part 1**, 290 f.; **Supp. 10**, 736; Mohegan, **Vol. 10, Part 1**, 108; Natchez, **Vol. 1 Part 2**, 251; **Vol. 6, Part 1**, 144, 226; Narragansett, **Vol. 2, Part 1**, 479; Omaha, **Vol. 9, Part 2**, 522; Oneida, **Vol. 5, Part 2**, 432 f.; Ottawa, **Vol. 8, Part 1**, 330 f.; Pawnee, **Vol. 7, Part 1**, 560; Pequot, **Vol. 1, Part 1**, 323; **Vol. 3, Part 2**, 156; **Vol. 10, Part 1**, 110; Pueblo, **Vol. 3, Part 1**, 260; **Vol. 3, Part 2**, 185, 353; **Vol. 6, Part 1**, 501, **Vol. 7, Part 1**, 185, 594; **Vol. 9, Part 2**, 394 f.; **Supp. 10**, 511–12; Sauk, **Vol. 5, Part 2**, 350; Seminole, **Vol. 3, Part 1**, 557 f.; **Vol. 3, Part 2**, 264; **Vol. 4, Part 1**, 83, 230,

237, 287, 481; **Vol. 5, Part 2,** 63, 91; **Vol. 6, Part 1,** 573; **Vol. 9, Part 1,** 331; **Vol. 9, Part 2,** 350, 474 f.; Seneca, **Vol. 8, Part 1,** 437 f.; Shawnee, **Vol. 2, Part 1,** 366; **Vol. 3, Part 1,** 519 f., 549 f.; **Vol. 9, Part 2,** 358 f., 375; Sioux, **Vol. 2, Part 2,** 530 f.; **Vol. 3, Part 1,** 500 f.; **Vol. 4, Part 1,** 501; **Vol. 5, Part 2,** 309; **Vol. 6, Part 1,** 299 f.; **Vol. 6, Part 2,** 117; **Vol. 8, Part 1,** 341 f., 437 f., 605; **Vol. 9, Part 1,** 192; Spokane, **Vol. 4, Part 1,** 173; Ute, **Vol. 7, Part 2,** 111, 638; Wabash, **Vol. 8, Part 1,** 284 f.

Indian Tribes of North America, The, **Supp. 6,** 612

Indigo, culture of, **Vol. 7, Part 2,** 616

Indiscretions, **Supp. 9,** 616

Indochina, **Supp. 5,** 334. *See also* Laos; Vietnam; Vietnam War

Industrial: arts, **Vol. 6, Part 1,** 159; **Vol. 6, Part 2,** 634; chemistry, **Vol. 2, Part 1,** 612; **Vol. 3, Part 1,** 70, 157, 479 f.; **Vol. 4, Part 1,** 502; **Vol. 4, Part 2,** 344, 443; **Vol. 6, Part 2,** 147; **Vol. 8, Part 2,** 110; **Vol. 10, Part 1,** 607 f.; **Vol. 10, Part 2,** 572; **Supp. 3,** 239; counselor, founding of profession, **Vol. 10, Part 1,** 143; design, **Supp. 6,** 233; engineering, **Vol. 3, Part 2,** 456; **Vol. 4, Part 2,** 51; **Vol. 9, Part 2,** 324; **Vol. 10, Part 2,** 485, *see also* Management; hygiene, *see* Occupational health and safety; imperialism, **Vol. 4, Part 2,** 37; insurance, **Vol. 3, Part 1,** 463 f.; management, *see* Management; planning, Gantt chart, **Vol. 4, Part 1,** 129; relations, **Vol. 3, Part 1,** 511 f.; **Vol. 4, Part 2,** 38; **Vol. 7, Part 1,** 419; **Vol. 8, Part 1,** 91 f.; **Vol. 9, Part 2,** 477; **Vol. 10, Part 1,** 602 f.; **Vol. 10, Part 2,** 273; **Supp. 9,** 795–96; research, pioneer in, **Vol. 3, Part 1,** 511 f.; writings, **Vol. 3, Part 1,** 586 f.; **Vol. 4, Part 1,** 129 f.; **Vol. 8, Part 1,** 9 f., 91 f.

Industrial Areas Foundation, founding of, **Supp. 8,** 589; **Supp. 9,** 18, 19

Industrial Brotherhood, **Vol. 8, Part 1,** 142 f.

Industrial Commission, United States, **Vol. 7, Part 1,** 563; **Vol. 7, Part 2,** 554

Industrial Congress, **Vol. 5, Part 2,** 82

Industrial Education Association, **Vol. 3, Part 1,** 346 f.

Industrialists. For complete list, *See* Occupations Index

Industrial research: **Supp. 1,** 31, 132, 274, 500, 627, 682; **Supp. 2,** 551; air conditioning, **Supp. 4,** 148–49; aluminum metallurgy, **Supp. 8,** 193–94; aviation turbosuperchargers, **Supp. 4,** 609; Bell Telephone Laboratories, founding of, **Supp. 4,** 430; chemical, **Supp. 5,** 191, 235, 319–20, 662–63; **Supp. 8,** 411–12; chemical emissions' reduction, **Supp. 4,** 184–85; drugs, **Supp. 6,** 447–48; electrical generators, **Supp. 3,** 251–52; fatigue, **Supp. 3,** 351; financing, **Supp. 2,** 447; first laboratories, **Supp. 3,** 365; forerunner of, **Supp. 1,** 278; gelatin manufacturing, **Supp. 4,** 455; marketing, **Supp. 6,** 614; metallurgy, **Supp. 4,** 556–57; petroleum products, **Supp. 3,** 247; **Supp. 4,** 661; pharmacological, **Supp. 8,** 102; photography, **Supp. 3,** 26; photography-related, **Supp. 4,** 743–44; plastics, **Supp. 3,** 26; railroads, **Supp. 2,** 282; safety match, **Supp. 4,** 257–58; steel industry, **Supp. 4,** 437–38; synthetics, **Supp. 3,** 239; **Supp. 7,** 169; working conditions, **Supp. 4,** 565–66; writings on, **Supp. 6,** 442. *See also specific industries*

Industrial Socialism, **Vol. 4, Part 2,** 468

Industrial Workers of the World (IWW): **Vol. 3, Part 1,** 184, 223; **Vol. 4, Part 1,** 468; **Vol. 4, Part 2,** 468; **Supp. 3,** 438, 777; **Supp. 7,** 118, 248, 254, 486, 506–7; **Supp. 8,** 317, 634; Anaconda Copper conflict, **Supp. 9,** 641; criticism of, **Supp. 3,** 373; Lawrence (Mass.) textile strike, **Supp. 6,** 238; lumber strike, **Supp. 6,** 320

Industries for Small Communities, **Supp. 9,** 561

Industry: apprentice system, **Vol. 4, Part 2,** 275; **Vol. 8, Part 2,** 238 f.; colonial, **Vol. 4, Part 2,** 592; efficiency studies, **Supp. 9,** 309–10; twelve-month operating schedule, **Vol. 3, Part 1,** 586 f.; training of men for, **Vol. 9, Part 2,** 128. *See also specific industries*

Infantile paralysis. *See* Poliomyelitis

Infant mortality, **Supp. 3,** 28; **Supp. 5,** 553

Infant Nutrition, founding of, **Supp. 2,** 432

Infertility, research in, **Supp. 6,** 555

Inflation, discussion of, **Vol. 9, Part 1,** 86

Influence peddling, **Supp. 8,** 219–20

Influenza, epidemic of 1891, **Vol. 5, Part 2,** 415; study of, **Vol. 9, Part 1,** 31; war-gas poisoning, and, **Vol. 10, Part 1,** 109 f.

Information Agency, United States (USIA), **Supp. 7,** 567; **Supp. 8,** 6–7, 640

Information Please Almanac, **Supp. 7,** 269

"Information Please" (radio program), **Supp. 6,** 5; **Supp. 9,** 492; **Supp. 10,** 739

Information Service, United States, predecessor, **Supp. 6,** 399

Informer, The, **Supp. 6,** 420, 476

Infrared radiation, **Supp. 4,** 658

Ingalls, Albert G., reference to, **Supp. 4,** 675

Ingersoll, Ralph, reference to, **Supp. 9,** 394

Ingersoll, Robert, reference to, **Supp. 3,** 246

Ingersoll, Robert G., reference to, **Vol. 3, Part 2,** 365

Ingersoll-Rand Co., **Vol. 8, Part 2,** 385

Ingham, Harvey, reference to, **Supp. 6,** 603

Ingres, influence of, **Vol. 7, Part 1,** 518

Inherit the Wind, **Supp. 8,** 31–32

Initiative and referendum, **Supp. 2,** 640; **Supp. 4,** 844–45; first use of, **Vol. 3, Part 2,** 109

Ink: for secret correspondence, **Vol. 5, Part 2,** 4; printers', making of, from coal, **Vol. 2, Part 2,** 110

"Inka Dinka Doo" (song), **Supp. 10,** 195

Inland Steel Co., **Supp. 8,** 517

Inland waterway system, **Supp. 2,** 195

Inman, Henry, reference to, **Vol. 5, Part 1,** 623

Inness, George, references to, **Vol. 5, Part 1,** 332; **Vol. 5, Part 2,** 293; **Vol. 9, Part 2,** 534

Innocent Eyes, **Supp. 10,** 157

Innocents Abroad, **Vol. 2, Part 2,** 194; **Vol. 5, Part 1,** 526

Innovations in Modern Music Orchestra, **Supp. 10,** 409

Inoculation. *See* Smallpox

Inquiry (social work organization), **Supp. 7,** 151; **Supp. 10,** 819

Inquiry (World War I peace-planning group), **Supp. 2,** 290, 320; **Supp. 7,** 536, 683, 687

INS. *See* International News Service

Insanity: treatment of, **Vol. 1, Part 1,** 201; **Vol. 2, Part 2,** 415; **Vol. 3, Part 1,** 323 f., 515 f., 568 f., 595 f.; **Vol. 3, Part 2,** 205, 412, 469, 473; **Vol. 4, Part 1,** 180, 521 f.; **Vol. 4, Part 2,** 412; **Vol. 5, Part 1,** 297, 622; **Vol. 5, Part 2,** 207, 325, 357, 429; **Vol. 6, Part 1,** 194, 468; **Vol. 7, Part 1,** 13, 489 f.; **Vol. 8, Part 1,** 132 f., 369, 404; **Vol. 8, Part 2,** 2, 116, 474, 559; **Vol. 9, Part 1,** 545; **Vol. 9, Part 2,** 249, 571; **Vol. 10, Part 1,** 643; "Kirkbride plan," **Vol. 5, Part 2,** 429; laws relating to, **Vol. 7, Part 2,** 50; **Vol. 8, Part 1,** 404; Maine, first asylum in, **Vol. 3, Part 1,** 515 f.; Massachusetts, in, **Vol. 3, Part 1,** 232 f.; **Vol. 8, Part 1,** 275 f., 404; writings on, **Vol. 2, Part 1,** 43; **Vol. 3, Part 1,** 595 f.; **Vol. 5, Part 1,** 161; **Vol. 5, Part 2,** 429; **Vol. 8, Part 1,** 404; **Vol. 8, Part 2,** 116 f.; **Vol. 9, Part 1,** 462. *See also* Mental health and illness

Inscoe, James, reference to, **Supp. 4,** 806

Insecticlde Act (11910), **Supp. 3,** 683

Insects: affecting cotton, **Vol. 5, Part 1,** 406; biological control of, **Supp. 4,** 400; boll weevils, **Supp. 4,** 601; disease-carrying, **Supp. 4,** 400; **Supp. 9,** 249–50; Florida, **Vol. 5, Part 1,** 328; gall wasp studies, **Supp. 6,** 342–43; museum collections and displays, **Supp.**

3, 478; social, **Supp. 2**, 708; studies of, **Vol. 5, Part 1**, 328; **Vol. 9, Part 2**, 319 f.; writings on, **Vol. 4, Part 2**, 321. *See also* Pesticides and herbicides
Inside Europe, **Supp. 8**, 232–33
Institute for Advanced Study (Princeton): **Supp. 3**, 31; **Supp. 6**, 30, 208–9, 653–54, 656; administration, **Supp. 8**, 484; art history studies, **Supp. 8**, 490; astronomy studies, **Supp. 10**, 840; economics studies, **Supp. 9**, 661; mathematical physics studies, **Supp. 5**, 738; mathematics studies, **Supp. 10**, 282; military and foreign policy seminar, **Supp. 5**, 195; physics studies, **Supp. 5**, 204
Institute for Government Research, founding of, **Supp. 6**, 250
Institute for International Social Research, **Supp. 8**, 69, 70
Institute for Jewish Studies, founding of, **Supp. 2**, 695
Institute for Religious and Social Studies, **Supp. 8**, 398, 408
Institute for Research in Land Economics, founding of, **Supp. 3**, 250
Institute for Sex Research, founding of, **Supp. 6**, 343
Institute for the Study of Law, founding of, **Supp. 2**, 501
Institute of American Meat Packers, **Vol. 3, Part 1**, 357
Institute of Child Welfare Research, founding of, **Supp. 3**, 677
Institute of Current World Affairs, establishment of, **Supp. 2**, 130
Institute of Design (Chicago), forerunner, **Supp. 4**, 591
Institute of Educational Research, founding of, **Supp. 3**, 677
Institute of Ethnic Affairs, founding of, **Supp. 8**, 99
Institute of Federal Taxation, founding of, **Supp. 5**, 412
Institute of Human Relations, **Supp. 5**, 330; founding of, **Supp. 2**, 562
Institute of Management, founding of, **Supp. 3**, 5
Institute of Medicine of Chicago, founding of, **Vol. 5, Part 1**, 465; **Supp. 1**, 616
Institute of Musical Art, **Vol. 5, Part 2**, 461; founding of, **Supp. 2**, 140
Institute of Pacific Relations, **Supp. 6**, 250, 350, 615
Institute of Phrenology, **Vol. 10, Part 1**, 643 f.
Institute of Public Administration, **Supp. 5**, 639
Institute of Radio Engineers, founding of, **Supp. 6**, 298
Institute of Scientific Research, founding of, **Supp. 2**, 598
Institute of the Missionary Sisters of the Sacred Heart, **Supp. 1**, 147
Institute of Tropical Medicine and Hygiene, **Supp. 1**, 33
Institutional Church, **Vol. 5, Part 2**, 237
Institut Pasteur, **Supp. 4**, 468
Insulation, research in, **Supp. 1**, 296
Insulin: crystallization of, **Supp. 2**, 4; first commercially produced in U.S., **Supp. 4**, 499; **Supp. 10**, 458; groundwork for discovery of, **Supp. 6**, 53; hyperinsulinism, **Supp. 6**, 698; overdose and hunger, **Supp. 6**, 100; shock treatment using, **Supp. 6**, 563–64
Insull, Martin, reference to, **Supp. 3**, 279
Insull, Samuel, references to, **Supp. 5**, 270; **Supp. 6**, 684; **Supp. 9**, 207, 346
Insurance: **Vol. 1, Part 1**, 599; **Vol. 2, Part 2**, 380; **Vol. 3, Part 1**, 209, 463 f.; **Vol. 3, Part 2**, 242; **Vol. 4, Part 2**, 168; **Vol. 6, Part 1**, 562, 577; **Vol. 7, Part 1**, 39; **Vol. 10, Part 1**, 119; accident, **Vol. 1, Part 2**, 54; employee groups, **Supp. 2**, 87; executives, **Supp. 6**, 497; fire, **Vol. 1, Part 1**, 216; **Vol. 6, Part 1**, 405; **Vol. 8, Part 1**, 139 f.; **Supp. 10**, 477–78; industrial, **Vol. 3, Part 1**, 463 f.; industrial accident, **Supp. 2**, 404; investigation, **Vol. 3, Part 1**, 246; **Vol. 5, Part 1**, 451; **Vol. 6, Part 1**, 60; laws, **Vol. 3, Part 1**, 485; **Vol. 6, Part 1**, 208; **Vol. 10, Part 2**, 549; liability, first sold through newspaper subscriptions, **Supp. 9**, 327; life, **Vol. 3, Part 1**, 463 f.; **Vol. 3, Part 2**, 419; **Vol. 4, Part 2**, 500; **Vol. 6, Part 1**, 588; **Vol. 6, Part 2**, 12; **Vol. 7, Part 1**, 323; **Vol. 7, Part 2**, 313, 547; marine, **Vol. 3, Part 1**, 485 f.; **Vol. 9, Part 2**, 105; mutual system of, **Vol. 7, Part 2**, 529; premium system, **Supp. 2**, 586; savings-bank, for workers, **Supp. 3**, 95; social, **Supp. 2**, 586; teaching of, **Supp. 7**, 373; traveler's, **Vol. 1, Part 2**, 54; unemployment, **Supp. 7**, 543, 764; workmen's compensation, **Vol. 8, Part 2**, 531. *See also* Blue Cross and Blue Shield; Health insurance; Life insurance; Social Security
Insurance Co. of North America, **Vol. 7, Part 2**, 518
Intelligence, hereditary origins, **Supp. 2**, 406
Intelligence operations. *See* Central Intelligence Agency; Espionage; *names of specific wars*
Intelligence tests: **Supp. 5**, 59; **Supp. 6**, 240–41, 626–27, 718; Binet-Simon, **Supp. 4**, 439; children, **Supp. 2**, 269; for blind, **Supp. 4**, 11; for blind children, **Supp. 5**, 347; for World War I draftees, **Supp. 8**, 44; multiple correlation, **Supp. 5**, 685; Otis group measurement, **Supp. 7**, 594. *See also* Tests and measurements
INTELSAT. *See* International Telecommunications Satellite Consortium
Inter-American Bar Association, founding of, **Supp. 3**, 821
Inter-American Commission of Women, **Supp. 7**, 718
Interborough Co., **Vol. 9, Part 1**, 124
Inter-American Observatory, **Supp. 10**, 840
Inter-Catalog of Medical and Veterinary Zoology, **Supp. 3**, 738
Interchurch World Movement, **Vol. 7, Part 1**, 403; **Supp. 6**, 548
Intercollegiate Socialist Society, founding of, **Supp. 8**, 593–94
Interdenominational Christian Temperance Alliance of Ohio, **Vol. 5, Part 2**, 517
Interdenominational Conference of Woman's Boards of Foreign Missions, **Supp. 4**, 467
Interest rates, prices and, **Supp. 4**, 272–73
Interferometer, **Supp. 1**, 58
Interior, Department of the (U.S.): **Vol. 1, Part 1**, 555; **Vol. 3, Part 2**, 238; **Vol. 5, Part 1**, 74; **Vol. 5, Part 2**, 552, 573; **Vol. 6, Part 1**, 586–87; **Vol. 7, Part 1**, 539; **Vol. 8, Part 2**, 469; **Vol. 9, Part 1**, 281; **Vol. 9, Part 2**, 362, 459; administration, **Supp. 1**, 300; **Supp. 3**, 845–46; **Supp. 4**, 317–18, 893–94; **Supp. 5**, 342–43; **Supp. 6**, 684; **Supp. 8**, 2, 352; **Supp. 10**, 119–20, 558; conservation policy controversy, **Supp. 1**, 300; **Supp. 4**, 664–65; **Supp. 6**, 416–17; development of public lands, **Supp. 10**, 120; Indian affairs, **Supp. 5**, 119; **Supp. 8**, 126; murals, **Supp. 3**, 380; Soil Erosion Service, **Supp. 6**, 53. *See also* Natural resources; Teapot Dome scandal
Interior decoration: **Vol. 2, Part 1**, 186; **Vol. 4, Part 2**, 596; first woman decorator, **Supp. 4**, 229; institutional, **Supp. 8**, 140–41; Victorian revival, **Supp. 4**, 290
Intermolecular forces, **Supp. 6**, 346
Internal-combustion engine, **Supp. 6**, 332
Internal Revenue Service (IRS): administration, **Supp. 4**, 356; corruption exposed in, **Supp. 9**, 500; counsel, **Supp. 5**, 357; organized crime and, **Supp. 6**, 264; Prohibition enforcement, **Supp. 7**, 805–6
Internal Security Act (1950). *See* McCarran Act (1950)
International Association of Chiefs of Police, **Supp. 5**, 639

International Association of Colored People of the World, **Supp. 5**, 755
International Association of Machinists, **Supp. 6**, 411
International Astronomical Union, founding of, **Supp. 2**, 271
International Bank for Reconstruction and Development (IBRD): **Supp. 8**, 616; **Supp. 10**, 753; first president, **Supp. 6**, 453; **Supp. 7**, 295–96; founding of, **Supp. 5**, 247, 713; **Supp. 8**, 446
International banking and finance: **Supp. 3**, 219; **Supp. 5**, 247; Dawes Plan, **Supp. 7**, 809–10; investments in U.S., **Supp. 4**, 193; Morgan & Co., **Supp. 3**, 537; **Supp. 4**, 469–70; **Supp. 7**, 782–83; promotion of, **Supp. 2**, 678; **Supp. 8**, 616; Speyer & Co., **Supp. 3**, 728–29; Tripartite Stabilization Pact (1936), **Supp. 8**, 446; World War II era, **Supp. 5**, 713; Young Plan, **Supp. 7**, 810. *See also* Bank for International Settlements; International Bank for Reconstruction and Development
International Board of Health, **Vol. 3, Part 1**, 78
International Boundary Commission, **Vol. 5, Part 2**, 167; **Vol. 7, Part 1**, 1
International Brotherhood of Electrical Workers, **Supp. 6**, 73–74
International Brotherhood of Red Caps, founding of, **Supp. 6**, 647–48
International Brotherhood of Teamsters, Chauffeurs, Warehousemen and Helpers of America. *See* Teamsters Union
International Bureau of American Republics, **Vol. 3, Part 2**, 572; **Vol. 8, Part 2**, 67
International Business Machines Corporation: employment policies, **Supp. 4**, 432; founding of, **Supp. 1**, 416; **Supp. 6**, 674–75; management, **Supp. 9**, 843–44
International Civil Aviation Organization, **Supp. 6**, 666
International College of Surgeons, founding of, **Supp. 6**, 632
International Committee for Bird Preservation, **Supp. 3**, 593
International Committee for Mental Hygiene, founding of, **Supp. 3**, 51
International Committee for Standards of Analysis of Iron and Steel, **Vol. 5, Part 2**, 593
International Committee of Historical Sciences, founding of, **Supp. 8**, 370
International Committee on Electrical Units and Standards, **Vol. 8, Part 2**, 154
International Composers' Guild, founding of, **Supp. 7**, 755
International Confederation of Free Trade Unions (1949), founding of, **Supp. 5**, 255; **Supp. 8**, 527, 652; **Supp. 10**, 524
International Confederation of Trade Unions (1937), founding of, **Supp. 6**, 707
International Congregational Council, **Vol. 8, Part 2**, 173
International Congress for Testing Materials, **Vol. 8, Part 1**, 91 f.
International Congress of Women, **Supp. 7**, 28
International Congress of Working Women, first, **Supp. 3**, 639
International Congress on Tuberculosis (1908), **Supp. 4**, 684
International Cooperation Administration, **Supp. 7**, 342
International Correspondence Schools, founding of, **Supp. 2**, 199
International Court of Justice, **Vol. 5, Part 1**, 156; **Supp. 5**, 537
International Cyclopedia of Music and Musicians, The, **Supp. 3**, 770–71
International Education Board, **Supp. 1**, 640
International Encyclopedia of Unified Science, founding of, **Supp. 8**, 74–75
International Exhibition of Modern Art. *See* Armory Show (1913)
International Federation of Settlements, **Supp. 6**, 499–500
International Federation of University Women, founding of, **Supp. 7**, 288
International General Electric, **Supp. 6**, 614
International Geodetic Association, founding of, **Supp. 2**, 56
International Geophysical year (1957–58), **Supp. 7**, 217
International Glove Workers Union, founding of, **Supp. 4**, 626
International Harvester Co., **Vol. 7, Part 1**, 177; **Vol. 7, Part 2**, 471; founding of, **Supp. 2**, 403
International Herald Tribune, **Supp. 4**, 687
International Institute, founding of, **Supp. 3**, 677
International Institute of China, **Vol. 8, Part 1**, 477
International Institute of Education, founding of, **Supp. 4**, 592–93
International Iron Workers, **Supp. 3**, 156
International Juridical Association Bulletin, founding of, **Supp. 5**, 389
International Kindergarten Union, founding of, **Supp. 4**, 875
International Labor Organization, **Supp. 6**, 707, 709
International Labor Union, **Vol. 9, Part 2**, 1
International Ladies' Garment Workers' Union: **Vol. 8, Part 2**, 437; organizing for, **Supp. 6**, 239; **Supp. 7**, 155; **Supp. 9**, 706; **Supp. 10**, 375; Sanitary Control Board, **Supp. 3**, 609–10; strike settlement (1910–11), **Supp. 4**, 375
International law: advocacy, **Supp. 2**, 52; codification, **Supp. 3**, 457; consultant on, **Supp. 5**, 107; diplomatic issues, **Supp. 5**, 136–37; judicial system, **Supp. 2**, 276; organizations, **Supp. 1**, 358; **Supp. 4**, 599; outer space, **Supp. 8**, 5; plebiscites, **Supp. 5**, 723; teaching of, **Supp. 4**, 598; **Supp. 5**, 81–82, 751–52; theories of, **Supp. 3**, 700; World Law Fund, **Supp. 8**, 88; writings on, **Supp. 2**, 220–21; **Supp. 3**, 821; **Supp. 5**, 340–41; **Supp. 5**, 730–31; **Supp. 6**, 307–8; **Supp. 7**, 182. *See also* Law
International Law and Order League, **Vol. 1, Part 2**, 439
International Law, Chiefly as Interpreted and Applied by the United States, **Supp. 5**, 340, 341
International Longshoremen's and Warehousemen's Union, **Supp. 6**, 396
International Mercantile Marine Co., **Vol. 7, Part 2**, 471; predecessor, **Supp. 3**, 667
International Missionary Council, **Supp. 5**, 507–8
International Molders and Foundry Workers Union, **Supp. 6**, 218
International Monetary Conference, **Vol. 9, Part 2**, 378
International Monetary Fund: first secretary of, **Supp. 10**, 134; founding of, **Supp. 5**, 247, 713; **Supp. 8**, 446, 616
International Navigation Co., **Vol. 4, Part 2**, 6
International News Service, **Supp. 3**, 428; **Supp. 5**, 286; **Supp. 9**, 187
International Nickel Co. of Canada, Ltd., **Supp. 5**, 652–53
International Olympic Committee (IOC), **Supp. 9**, 131. *See also* Olympic games
International Order of Good Templars, **Vol. 4, Part 2**, 386
International Order of King's Daughters and Sons, **Vol. 1, Part 2**, 471

International Paper Co., **Vol. 2, Part 2**, 75
International Photo-Engravers Union of North America, **Supp. 6**, 706
International Photographers of the Motion Picture Industry, founding of, **Supp. 3**, 74
International Postal Union, **Vol. 5, Part 2**, 260
International Printing Pressmen and Assistants' Union, **Supp. 4**, 74
International Public Health Nursing Course, founding of, in Great Britain, **Supp. 7**, 247
International Radio and Telegraph Co., **Supp. 6**, 298
International Railway Congress, **Vol. 8, Part 1**, 114 f.
International Red Cross of Geneva, **Vol. 1, Part 2**, 19 f.; presidency, **Supp. 3**, 219
International relations. *See* Diplomacy; Foreign relations; *country names*
International Slave Trade Conference, **Vol. 9, Part 2**, 377
International Smokeless Powder and Chemical Co., **Supp. 5**, 235
International Sunday School activities, **Vol. 4, Part 2**, 409; **Vol. 6, Part 1**, 44
International Teamster, **Supp. 5**, 691
International Telecommunications Satellite Consortium (INTELSAT), **Supp. 10**, 828
International Telephone and Telegraph Corporation: **Supp. 9**, 423; acquisitions, **Supp. 10**, 534; foundation of, **Supp. 6**, 43–44
International Tennis Hall of Fame (Newport, R.I.), founding of, **Supp. 7**, 127
International trade. *See* Tariff; Trade
International Trade Mart (ITM): CIA link uncovered, **Supp. 9**, 716; founding of, **Supp. 9**, 715
International Trade Organization, founding of, **Supp. 8**, 90
International Typographical Union, **Vol. 6, Part 1**, 521; **Supp. 2**, 323; **Supp. 3**, 297, 346–47; **Supp. 4**, 606
International Union Against the Venereal Diseases, founding of, **Supp. 4**, 759
International Union of Geodesy and Geophysics, organization of, **Supp. 2**, 56
International Union of Physiological Sciences, founding of, **Supp. 4**, 59
International Woman Suffrage Alliance, **Supp. 4**, 725; founding of, **Supp. 4**, 157
Inter Ocean, **Vol. 5, Part 1**, 65; **Vol. 8, Part 2**, 408
Interparliamentary Union (1912), **Vol. 8, Part 1**, 14 f.
Interparliamentary Union for the Promotion of International Arbitration, **Supp. 1**, 53
Interpersonal relations. *See* Human relations
Interpleader Act (1936), **Supp. 6**, 106
Interracial Commission, **Vol. 2, Part 2**, 229; **Vol. 8, Part 1**, 243 f.
Interracial Review, **Supp. 8**, 293–94
Interstate commerce: court decisions on, **Supp. 4**, 404–5; quotas theory, **Supp. 2**, 30
Interstate Commerce Act, **Vol. 2, Part 2**, 199, 545
Interstate Commerce Commission (ICC): **Vol. 4, Part 2**, 295 f.; **Vol. 5, Part 1**, 64; **Vol. 5, Part 2**, 572; **Vol. 7, Part 1**, 232, 274; organization of, **Vol. 2, Part 2**, 393, 589; **Vol. 6, Part 2**, 15; **Vol. 7, Part 1**, 591; **Vol. 8, Part 1**, 434; railroad rate-setting, **Supp. 3**, 212, 241, 256–57; regulatory powers of, **Vol. 3, Part 1**, 479 f.; valuation reports of, **Vol. 8, Part 1**, 248 f.
Interstellar absorption, **Supp. 6**, 7
In the Days of McKinley, **Supp. 9**, 629
In the Summer House, **Supp. 9**, 116
Intimate Gallery (New York City), **Supp. 4**, 781
Intolerance, **Supp. 3**, 73; **Supp. 4**, 350, 351; **Supp. 6**, 619; **Supp. 9**, 791
Intravenous feeding, **Supp. 6**, 190
Intrepid, exploits of, at Tripoli, **Vol. 3, Part 1**, 187
Introduction to Social Anthropology, **Supp. 4**, 908–9
Introduction to the History of Medicine, An, **Supp. 1**, 335
Introduction to the Literature of the New Testament, **Supp. 3**, 530
Intruder in the Dust, **Supp. 7**, 234
Inventions: **Vol. 1, Part 1**, 19, 31, 71, 178, 198 f., 216, 230, 248, 258, 310, 325, 361, 400, 406 f., 420, 443, 455 f., 457, 465, 511, 533, 551, 563; **Vol. 1, Part 2**, 83, 254, 429, 528, 529; **Vol. 2, Part 1**, 103, 128, 144, 175, 187, 198, 229, 259, 272, 334, 337, 340, 349, 375, 407, 449; **Vol. 2, Part 2**, 110, 236, 238, 282, 286, 301 f., 318, 336, 359, 441, 463, 561, 575; **Vol. 3, Part 1**, 237, 239, f., 547 f., 580 f.; **Vol. 3, Part 2**, 16, 59, 129, 142, 219, 251, 347, 372, 405, 432, 445, 458, 583, 588; **Vol. 4, Part 1**, 59, 70 f., 75, 119, 152, 178, 191, 199, 246, 331, 336, 338, 342, 345, 377, 408, 413, 422, 457, 488, 514, 606; **Vol. 4, Part 2**, 1, 62, 145, 196, 199, 263, 283, 373, 401, 440, 442, 462, 561, 575, 584, 607; **Vol. 5, Part 1**, 104, 130, 145 f., 207, 246, 252, 259, 285 f., 290, 298, 327, 334 f., 347, 351, 448, 609 f., 617; **Vol. 5, Part 2**, 239, 280 f., 282, 509; **Vol. 6, Part 1**, 51, 176, 203, 228, 230, 333 f., 337, 392, 452, 487, 505, 513, 569; **Vol. 6, Part 2**, 23, 77, 168, 239, 288, 296, 303 f., 377, 383, 385, 426, 436 f., 438, 458, 520, 550, 571, 624, 635; **Vol. 7, Part 1**, 106 f., 161, 251, 314, 368, 431, 469 f., 495, 509, 523, 581, 590; **Vol. 7, Part 2**, 24, 93 f., 122, 167, 252, 261, 472 f., 492 f., 644; **Vol. 8, Part 1**, 75 f., 101 f., 158 f., 165 f., 172 f., 179, 304 f., 321 f., 329 f., 369, 429 f., 505; **Vol. 8, Part 2**, 9, 27, 52, 56, 80, 88, 95, 97, 99 f., 105, 133, 145, 189, 223 256, 361 f., 385, 397, 400, 448, 553 f., 567, 574, 586; **Vol. 9, Part 1**, 48, 123, 128, 188, 198, 282, 351, 454 f., 515; **Vol. 9, Part 2**, 324, 380 f., 485, 513, 553, 632; **Vol. 10, Part 1**, 40; **Vol. 10, Part 2**, 23, 371, 379, 497; aerial camera linkage, **Supp. 9**, 273; baby products, **Supp. 9**, 361; ballpoint pen, **Supp. 10**, 670; barometer, **Supp. 9**, 357; buffered aspirin, **Supp. 10**, 623–24; color television, **Supp. 10**, 283–84; disposable drinking cup, **Supp. 9**, 556; double-edged razor blade, **Supp. 9**, 297; electronic video recording, **Supp. 10**, 284; *Encyclopedia of Inventions*, **Vol. 5, Part 2**, 464 f.; Freon, **Supp. 9**, 622; Hammond organ, **Supp. 9**, 358; hydraulic hoist, **Supp. 9**, 891; long-playing record, **Supp. 10**, 284; perfusion pump, **Supp. 9**, 497; pogo stick, **Supp. 9**, 361; portable chainsaw, **Supp. 10**, 491; radar jammer, **Supp. 10**, 283; radio and television audience monitoring devices, **Supp. 10**, 587, 588; recording devices, **Supp. 9**, 274; rotary drill bit, **Supp. 10**, 355; scouring pad, steel wool, **Supp. 9**, 510; single-edge razor blade, **Supp. 9**, 197; step gauge, **Supp. 10**, 52; synchronous motor, **Supp. 9**, 357; television camera tube, **Supp. 9**, 275; three-dimensional movie device, **Supp. 9**, 357; toys, **Supp. 9**, 361; writings on patentable, **Vol. 8, Part 1**, 505. For complete list of inventors, *see* Occupations Index; *see also specific fields and names*
Inventors Foundation, **Supp. 9**, 298
Inventors' Guild, **Vol. 6, Part 1**, 177
Investigation, Bureau of (U.S.), **Supp. 9**, 404–5
Investment banking: **Supp. 3**, 537–38; **Supp. 4**, 320, 470; **Supp. 9**, 264–65; **Supp. 10**, 533–34; Murchison interests, **Supp. 10**, 568; railroads, **Supp. 10**, 203. *See also* Banking; Finance; Stock market
Investors Diversified Services, **Supp. 9**, 462–63
Invisible Man, The, **Supp. 8**, 516
Invitation to a Beheading, **Supp. 10**, 582, 583
In vitro fertilization, **Supp. 8**, 502
IOC. *See* International Olympic Committee
Iodine, **Supp. 5**, 275

Ionization: manometer, **Supp. 6**, 84; mercury potential, **Supp. 6**, 370; theory of, **Supp. 2**, 631; **Supp. 8**, 123

Iowa: agricultural education, **Vol. 2, Part 2**, 165; banking, **Vol. 8, Part 1**, 212 f.; Black Hawk War, **Vol. 5, Part 2**, 600; boundary disputes, **Vol. 3, Part 1**, 601 f.; Catholic church, **Vol. 4, Part 1**, 167; **Vol. 4, Part 2**, 541; Civil War, furnishing of troops for, **Vol. 10, Part 2**, 395; "Copperheads," **Vol. 5, Part 2**, 437; Democratic party, **Supp. 9**, 312; education, **Vol. 1, Part 2**, 213; **Vol. 6, Part 1**, 613; **Vol. 6, Part 2**, 295; **Vol. 10, Part 1**, 617 f.; Free Soil party in, **Vol. 4, Part 2**, 268; Freethinkers colony in, **Vol. 5, Part 2**, 457 f.; fugitive slaves, **Vol. 8, Part 2**, 153; governors, **Vol. 1, Part 2**, 413 f.; **Vol. 2, Part 1**, 508 f., 603 f.; **Vol. 3, Part 1**, 429 f.; Vol. 4, **Part 1**, 202 f., 631 f.; **Vol. 5, Part 2**, 436 f.; **Vol. 6, Part 1**, 6 f., 451 f.; **Supp. 9**, 387; history of, **Vol. 3, Part 1**, 83; **Vol. 4, Part 2**, 34; **Vol. 5, Part 2**, 600; **Vol. 8, Part 1**, 212 f.; journalism in, **Vol. 5, Part 1**, 302; **Vol. 7, Part 2**, 469; lead mining, **Vol. 3, Part 1**, 475; **Vol. 5, Part 2**, 600; legal service, **Vol. 3, Part 1**, 153, 160, 191, 311, 430; **Vol. 4, Part 2**, 212; **Vol. 6, Part 1**, 149, 578 f.; **Vol. 6, Part 2**, 162, 357; **Vol. 7, Part 2**, 285; **Vol. 8, Part 2**, 153, 558; **Vol. 9, Part 1**, 119; **Vol. 10, Part 1**, 568 f.; **Vol. 10, Part 2**, 552; Lutheran church, **Vol. 4, Part 1**, 37; **Vol. 4, Part 2**, 23; mining, **Vol. 3, Part 1**, 475; missions, **Vol. 8, Part 2**, 315; newspapers, **Supp. 4**, 189; **Supp. 6**, 676–77; parks, state, **Vol. 7, Part 2**, 197; political service, **Vol. 1, Part 2**, 148, 213, 413; **Vol. 2, Part 2**, 597, 620; **Vol. 3, Part 1**, 344, 359, 429, 601 f.; **Vol. 4, Part 1**, 202, 632; **Vol. 4, Part 2**, 387, 568; **Vol. 5, Part 2**, 436 f.; **Vol. 6, Part 1**, 6, 142, 487–88; **Vol. 6, Part 2**, 451; **Vol. 7, Part 2**, 469; **Vol. 8, Part 1**, 212, 301; **Vol. 9, Part 1**, 43, 351; **Vol. 10, Part 1**, 568 f.; **Vol. 10, Part 2**, 331, 332, 552; politics, **Vol. 2, Part 1**, 509; **Supp. 3**, 107–9; **Supp. 8**, 300; **Supp. 9**, 310–11, 387; Prohibition, **Vol. 8, Part 1**, 212 f.; public service, **Vol. 2, Part 2**, 289; **Vol. 4, Part 2**, 34, 268; **Vol. 5, Part 2**, 260; **Vol. 6, Part 2**, 14; **Vol. 8, Part 1**, 212 f.; **Vol. 8, Part 2**, 380 f.; railroad development, **Vol. 6, Part 1**, 6; **Vol. 8, Part 1**, 212 f.; Republican party, **Vol. 1, Part 2**, 413; **Vol. 6, Part 2**, 638; **Vol. 10, Part 2**, 633; statehood, admission to, **Vol. 6, Part 1**, 142; territory, **Vol. 2, Part 1**, 604; **Vol. 4, Part 2**, 387; **Vol. 5, Part 2**, 172; **Vol. 6, Part 1**, 487 f.

Iowa City, **Vol. 5, Part 2**, 600

Iowa College, **Vol. 10, Part 1**, 58

Iowa Improved Stock Breeders' Association, **Vol. 5, Part 2**, 453

Iowa Law School, **Vol. 2, Part 2**, 289

Iowa State Agricultural College, **Vol. 4, Part 2**, 34; **Vol. 5, Part 2**, 453; **Vol. 10, Part 1**, 617 f.

Iowa State College of Agriculture and Mechanic Arts, **Vol. 1, Part 2**, 96; **Vol. 7, Part 2**, 197

Iowa State Teachers' Association, **Vol. 7, Part 2**, 285

Iowa State University: expansion, **Supp. 3**, 387; presidency, **Supp. 2**, 419

"Ioway Outfit," **Vol. 7, Part 1**, 41

IQ tests. *See* Intelligence tests

Iran: Anglo-Russian agreement, **Supp. 6**, 579; diplomacy with U.S., **Supp. 6**, 245; **Supp. 8**, 5–6, 275; oil dispute with Great Britain, **Supp. 8**, 276; scholarship on, **Supp. 2**, 338–39; Teheran Conference declaration on, **Supp. 7**, 377

Ireland, Charles Thomas, Jr. ("Chick"), reference to, **Supp. 9**, 423

Ireland, John, references to, **Vol. 5, Part 1**, 496 f.; **Supp. 3**, 568, 680

Ireland: diplomacy with, **Vol. 7, Part 2**, 557; emigration from, to United States, **Vol. 3, Part 2**, 440; **Vol. 5, Part 1**, 353; **Vol. 8, Part 2**, 57 f., 63, 248, 321; **Vol. 9, Part 2**, 4; **Vol. 10, Part 2**, 615; freedom, cause of, **Vol. 5, Part 1**, 405; **Vol. 7, Part 1**, 36; **Vol. 8, Part 1**, 156 f.

Irish-Americans: novels about, **Supp. 8**, 477; physical type survey, **Supp. 5**, 312; political activity, **Supp. 4**, 277–78, 858–59; **Supp. 6**, 139, 142, 66

Irish Citizen, **Vol. 7, Part 1**, 36

Irish Emigrant Society, **Vol. 8, Part 1**, 156 f.

Irish Free State, **Vol. 3, Part 1**, 265; **Vol. 4, Part 1**, 335; **Vol. 9, Part 2**, 242

Irish Land League, **Vol. 3, Part 2**, 518

Irish Republican Brotherhood, **Vol. 3, Part 1**, 265

"Irish Rescue Party," **Vol. 4, Part 1**, 359

Irish Societies of New York, **Vol. 8, Part 2**, 19

Irish World, **Vol. 3, Part 2**, 518

Iron (nutrient): anemia relationship, **Supp. 4**, 581–82, 276; average human requirement, **Supp. 5**, 623

Iron and Steel Magazine, founding of, **Supp. 2**, 595

"Iron Brigade," **Vol. 5, Part 2**, 400

"Ironclad oath," **Vol. 4, Part 1**, 150

Ironclad vessels, **Vol. 3, Part 1**, 211, 529 f.; **Vol. 8, Part 1**, 97; **Vol. 8, Part 2**, 78–85

Iron Horse, The, **Supp. 9**, 286

Iron industry: Bessemer process, **Vol. 7, Part 2**, 356; brokerage, **Vol. 6, Part 1**, 155; building, early use, in, **Vol. 1, Part 2**, 407; **Vol. 3, Part 1**, 211, 529 f.; **Vol. 8, Part 1**, 138 f., 639 f.; conveyors in, **Vol. 2, Part 1**, 103; factory conditions, **Vol. 4, Part 2**, 605; galvanizing process, **Vol. 6, Part 1**, 141; manufacturing, **Vol. 1, Part 1**, 219, 268 f.; **Vol. 1, Part 2**, 127, 217; **Vol. 2, Part 1**, 35, 114, 149, 272, 338; **Vol. 2, Part 2**, 327, 396, 409; **Vol. 3, Part 1**, 362, 395; **Vol. 3, Part 2**, 124, 243, 251, 405, 452, 573; **Vol. 4, Part 1**, 4, 38 f., 199, 593; **Vol. 4, Part 2**, 9, 343, 379, 605; **Vol. 5, Part 1**, 48, 57, 433 f.; **Vol. 5, Part 2**, 40, 54, 156, 162, 426; **Vol. 6, Part 1**, 73, 139, 174, 395, 500, 551; **Vol. 6, Part 2**, 398; **Vol. 7, Part 1**, 79, 505, 540, 642 f.; **Vol. 7, Part 2**, 20 f., 206, 330, 550; **Vol. 8, Part 1**, 89, 115 f., 138 f., 149, 314 f.; **Vol. 8, Part 2**, 504 f., 513 f.; **Vol. 9, Part 1**, 25, 48, 125, 621; **Vol. 9, Part 2**, 17, 236 f., 258, 325, 427 f., 568; **Vol. 10, Part 1**, 400 f., 635; **Vol. 10, Part 2**, 399, 412; mining, **Vol. 2, Part 1**, 90; **Vol. 3, Part 1**, 90; **Vol. 3, Part 2**, 79, 118; **Vol. 4, Part 1**, 183; **Vol. 5, Part 1**, 505; **Vol. 6, Part 2**, 397, 487, 572; **Vol. 7, Part 1**, 20, 135; Vol. 8, Part, t 1, 264 f.; **Vol. 10, Part 2**, 375; pig iron, **Vol. 3, Part 1**, 548 f.; **Vol. 9, Part 1**, 219; smelting, first, **Vol. 1, Part 2**, 217; wages, sliding scale of, **Vol. 5, Part 2**, 162; woman, first, in, **Vol. 6, Part 1**, 500

Iroquois Confederacy, **Supp. 8**, 647

Irradiation. *See* Radiation

Irrepressible Conflict, 1850–1865, The, **Supp. 10**, 136

Irrigation: **Vol. 3, Part 1**, 606; **Vol. 4, Part 2**, 84; **Vol. 6, Part 1**, 505; **Vol. 7, Part 1**, 433, 457; **Vol. 8, Part 1**, 121 f.; **Vol. 10, Part 2**, 212; Colorado, **Vol. 3, Part 1**, 605; **Vol. 7, Part 1**, 434; ditching machines, **Vol. 8, Part 1**, 369; electric-powered, **Supp. 3**, 192; first Hawaiian, **Supp. 1**, 48; Florida Everglades, **Vol. 2, Part 1**, 96; laws relating to, **Vol. 6, Part 2**, 4; litigation, **Supp. 1**, 620; national program, **Supp. 4**, 563–64; project design, **Supp. 2**, 304; New Mexico, **Vol. 3, Part 1**, 606; Southern California, **Supp. 5**, 310; western development, **Supp. 2**, 443; **Supp. 4**, 567. *See also* Dams; Drainage

IRS. *See* Internal Revenue Service

Irvin, Rea, reference to, **Supp. 5**, 594

Irving, Clifford, literary hoax, **Supp. 10**, 358

Irving, Washington: biography of, **Vol. 5, Part 1**, 505; influence of, **Vol. 9, Part 1**, 70; printing of works, **Vol. 1, Part 1**, 526; references to, **Vol. 4, Part 1**, 505; **Vol. 5, Part 1**, 503 f., 512; **Vol. 5, Part 2**, 316 f.; **Vol. 7, Part 1**, 96, 643; **Vol. 7, Part 2**, 321, 328 f.

Irvingites, Catholic Apostolic church, **Vol. 1, Part 1,** 299
Irwin, Amelia, reference to, **Supp. 6,** 8
Irwin, Inez Hayes, reference to, **Supp. 5,** 532
Isaak Walton League, **Vol. 3, Part 1,** 299
Isbrandtsen Lines, founding of, **Supp. 5,** 348
Isherwood, Christopher, references to, **Supp. 9,** 53, 54
Isis, **Supp. 6,** 564, 565
Island No. 10, capture of (1862), **Vol. 3, Part 1,** 107; **Vol. 3, Part 2,** 500; **Vol. 8, Part 1,** 76
Isle of Pines, ceding of, to Cuba, **Vol. 8, Part 1,** 333
Isles of Shoals, **Vol. 9, Part 2,** 397
Isolationism. *See* Foreign relations; World War I; World War II
Isomorphism, **Supp. 8,** 344
Isostasy: doctrine of, **Vol. 3, Part 1,** 555; **Vol. 4, Part 2,** 452; mathematical formulation of, **Supp. 2,** 56; writings on, **Vol. 1, Part 1,** 643
Isotopic tracers, **Supp. 3,** 693–94
Israel, Harold, reference to, **Supp. 6,** 137
Israel: American Zionist relations, **Supp. 7,** 690; diplomacy with U.S., **Supp. 7,** 498; Eichmann trial, **Supp. 8,** 456; independence, **Supp. 5,** 599; **Supp. 6,** 431; Keating ambassadorship, **Supp. 9,** 450; U.S. recognition of, **Supp. 5,** 515; **Supp. 10,** 227. *See also* Middle East; Palestine; Suez Crisis (1956); Zionism
Israel Philharmonic, predecessor, **Supp. 6,** 643–44
Israfel: The Life and Times of Edgar Allan Poe, **Supp. 4,** 13, 14
Isthmian Canal Commission, **Vol. 1, Part 1,** 258; **Vol. 7, Part 1,** 191, 347, 537; **Vol. 7, Part 2,** 288; **Vol. 8, Part 2,** 193. *See also* Panama Canal
Isthmian Canal project, early history of, **Vol. 1, Part 1,** 258; **Vol. 1, Part 2,** 327–28; **Vol. 2, Part 2,** 186; **Vol. 4, Part 1,** 16; **Vol. 4, Part 2,** 439; **Vol. 6, Part 2,** 108, 201; **Vol. 7, Part 1,** 181, 191, 347, 537; **Vol. 7, Part 2,** 288; **Vol. 8, Part 2,** 193. *See also* Panama canal
Isthmus of Tehuantepec, projected railway across, **Vol. 3, Part 1,** 587 f.
Italian-American Civil Rights league, founding of, **Supp. 10,** 140
Italian-Americans: banks for, **Supp. 4,** 325–26; labor movement, **Supp. 3,** 777–78; **Supp. 6,** 238; political activity, **Supp. 4,** 464; writings on, **Supp. 8,** 457
Italian Villas and Their Gardens, **Supp. 8,** 494
Italy: anti-Fascism, **Supp. 6,** 237; art history, **Supp. 6,** 56–57; culture, spread of, **Vol. 3, Part 1,** 71 f.; diplomacy with U.S., **Supp. 6,** 254, 388–89; **Supp. 7,** 815; **Supp. 8,** 395; diplomatic service, **Vol. 5, Part 2,** 400; **Vol. 7, Part 2,** 141; **Vol. 9, Part 1,** 497; historical writings on, **Supp. 2,** 402; influence on Sargent, **Vol. 8, Part 2,** 363 f.; mannerism art studies, **Supp. 8,** 194; missions, **Vol. 9, Part 2,** 326; opera, Italian, introduction of, **Vol. 9, Part 1,** 177; Trieste dispute, **Supp. 9,** 799; *See also* Vatican; World War I; World War II
I Tatti, **Supp. 6,** 57; **Supp. 7,** 673
ITM. *See* International Trade Mart
It's a Mad Mad Mad Mad World, **Supp. 9,** 103
It's a Wonderful Life, **Supp. 9,** 767
ITT. *See* International Telephone and Telegraph Corporation
Iuka, Miss., battle of, **Vol. 5, Part 1,** 442; **Vol. 7, Part 2,** 48; **Vol. 8, Part 1,** 216; **Vol. 8, Part 2,** 163; **Vol. 10, Part 1,** 185
"I've Got a Secret" (television program), **Supp. 9,** 719, 720
Ives, Charles, reference to, **Supp. 9,** 382
Ives, J. C., reference to, **Vol. 7, Part 1,** 445
Ives and Myrick Insurance Co., founding of, **Supp. 5,** 351
Ives Co., **Supp. 7,** 150
Ivory soap, **Supp. 1,** 610
"I Want to Hold Your Hand" (song), **Supp. 10,** 449
"I Want to Live, **Supp. 9,** 377
Iwerks, Ub, references to, **Supp. 8,** 129–30, 131
Iwo Jima, World War II action, **Supp. 5,** 66; **Supp. 8,** 603
IWW. *See* Industrial Workers of the World
Izaak Walton League of America, service in, **Supp. 9,** 608

J

Jaboulay, Mathieu, reference to, **Supp. 3,** 140
Jacchia, Agide, reference to, **Supp. 10,** 237
Jackson, Andrew: bas-relief of, **Vol. 4, Part 1,** 152; biography of, **Vol. 6, Part 1,** 226; **Supp. 5,** 364; campaign of, **Vol. 6, Part 1,** 109; close friendship with, **Vol. 3, Part 1,** 363 f.; Creek Indians and, **Vol. 4, Part 2,** 414; dissolution of cabinet as result of Peggy O'Neale stir, **Vol. 3, Part 1,** 610; Felix Grundy, and, **Vol. 4, Part 2,** 33; Florida, **Vol. 7, Part 1,** 414; Hall case, **Vol. 4, Part 2,** 124; opposition to policies of, **Vol. 3, Part 1,** 510 f.; references to, **Vol. 1, Part 1,** 87; **Vol. 1, Part 2,** 157, 211; **Vol. 2, Part 1,** 104; **Vol. 5, Part 1,** 263, 365, 474, 526f.; **Vol. 5, Part 2,** 257, 264, 325 f.; **Vol. 6, Part 1,** 226, 310, 518; **Vol. 7, Part 1,** 91; **Vol. 7, Part 2,** 115 f.; **Vol. 8, Part 1,** 34 f.; **Vol. 8, Part 2,** 9 f., 507, 604; **Vol. 9, Part 1,** 319, 412; **Vol. 9, Part 2,** 645 f.; **Vol. 10, Part 1,** 89 f.; relations with Clay, **Vol. 2, Part 2,** 176 f.; re-formation of cabinet, **Vol. 10, Part 2,** 106; war against national bank, **Vol. 1, Part 2,** 157
Jackson, Charles T., reference to, **Vol. 7, Part 1,** 269
Jackson, Chevalier Lawrence, reference to, **Supp. 6,** 318
Jackson, Eddie, Durante relationship, **Supp. 10,** 195
Jackson, F. J. Foakes, reference to, **Supp. 4,** 468
Jackson, James, reference to, **Vol. 10, Part 1,** 480 f.
Jackson, Joe, references to, **Supp. 8,** 574, 575
Jackson, Robert H., references to, **Supp. 6,** 156, 662
Jackson, Robert Tracy, references to, **Supp. 4,** 205, 206
Jackson, "Stonewall": nickname, origin of, **Vol. 1, Part 2,** 124; **Vol. 9, Part 2,** 642; references to, **Vol. 5, Part 1,** 556; **Vol. 6, Part 1,** 123 f., 391, 420; **Vol. 8, Part 2,** 71 f.; statue of, **Vol. 7, Part 1,** 4
Jackson, Tony, reference to, **Supp. 3,** 541
Jackson Hole National Monument, **Supp. 10,** 120
Jackson Hole Wildlife Park (Wyo.), founding of, **Supp. 7,** 31; **Supp. 8,** 486
Jacksonians, The, **Supp. 6,** 693
"Jacksonis Americus," pseudonym for Tilden, **Vol. 9, Part 2,** 538
Jackson-Monroe correspondence, **Vol. 6, Part 1,** 26
Jacobi, Abraham, references to, **Vol. 7, Part 1,** 628; **Supp. 3,** 159
Jacobi, Leonard, reference to, **Supp. 3,** 26
Jacobin Club, Charleston, S.C., **Vol. 4, Part 2,** 285
"Jacobinism," **Vol. 1, Part 1,** 245
Jacobs, Mike, reference to, **Supp. 9,** 493
Jacobs, Randall, reference to, **Supp. 8,** 23
Jacobson, Paul, references to, **Supp. 4,** 336, 337
Jacob's Pillow Dance Festival (Becket, Mass.), **Supp. 9,** 717
Jacob Tome Institute, founding of, **Vol. 9, Part 2,** 578
Jacoby, Oswald, reference to, **Supp. 6,** 380
Jadassohn, Salomon, reference to, **Supp. 1,** 16
Jails. *See* Prisons
James, Arthur H., references to, **Supp. 3,** 20; **Supp. 7,** 615–16

James, Edmund J., references to, **Vol. 7, Part 2**, 298 f.; **Supp. 4**, 40, 227
James, Harry, references to, **Supp. 8**, 163; **Supp. 9**, 332; **Supp. 10**, 322
James, Henry: references to, **Vol. 5, Part 1**, 310; **Supp. 6**, 174; **Supp. 7**, 55; **Supp. 10**, 274; Wharton relationship, **Supp. 2**, 703, 704, 705; writings on, **Supp. 4**, 560
James, Jesse, references to, **Vol. 6, Part 1**, 433; **Vol. 9, Part 2**, 634
James, Walter B., reference to, **Supp. 4**, 49
James, William, references to, **Vol. 5, Part 1**, 311; **Vol. 7, Part 2**, 400 f.; **Vol. 8, Part 2**, 152, 207 f.; **Vol. 9, Part 1**, 410; **Supp. 3**, 51, 577, 578, 608, 682; **Supp. 4**, 20, 21, 387, 766, 767, 832, 833; **Supp. 6**, 454, 504, 505; **Supp. 7**, 201, 481; **Supp. 9**, 447
James Foundation, founding of, **Supp. 3**, 381–82
Jameson, J. Franklin, references to, **Supp. 3**, 15–16; **Supp. 8**, 369, 370
James River Canal, **Vol. 2, Part 2**, 580; **Vol. 8, Part 2**, 30
Jamestown, Va.: **Vol. 4, Part 1**, 190, 439; **Vol. 5, Part 1**, 391; **Vol. 7, Part 1**, 468; **Vol. 9, Part 1**, 295; first legislative assembly in America, **Vol. 8, Part 1**, 110; first printing press south of Massachusetts, **Vol. 7, Part 1**, 596; removal of capital from, **Vol. 7, Part 1**, 500
Janet, Pierre, reference to, **Supp. 3**, 190–91
Japan: anthropological cultural study of, **Supp. 4**, 72; art, **Vol. 5, Part 1**, 450; art and culture studies, **Supp. 3**, 341, 465; **Supp. 5**, 729–30; atomic bombing of, **Supp. 8**, 230, 231; baseball in, **Supp. 8**, 479; Bible translated into Japanese, **Vol. 3, Part 2**, 80; **Vol. 4, Part 1**, 8, 564; diplomatic relations with U.S., **Vol. 1, Part 1**, 563; **Vol. 1, Part 2**, 277; **Vol. 3, Part 1**, 245; **Vol. 4, Part 2**, 60, 324; **Vol. 6, Part 1**, 570, 573; **Vol. 6, Part 2**, 18; **Vol. 7, Part 2**, 488; **Vol. 8, Part 1**, 254 f.; **Vol. 9, Part 2**, 423; **Vol. 10, Part 2**, 561; **Supp. 2**, 580; **Supp. 3**, 323; **Supp. 5**, 333; **Supp. 6**, 211; **Supp. 7**, 112–13, 303; education in, **Vol. 7, Part 1**, 242, 358; English-language newspapers, **Supp. 4**, 284–85; General Le Gendre in, **Vol. 6, Part 1**, 146; geological surveys for, **Vol. 6, Part 1**, 515; historical writings on, **Supp. 8**, 360; Imperial College of Agriculture and Engineering, **Vol. 9, Part 2**, 38; Imperial Research Institute, **Vol. 9, Part 2**, 275; labor movement, **Supp. 6**, 648; medicine, **Vol. 9, Part 2**, 384; Methodist church in, **Supp. 1**, 208; missionary activities, **Vol. 1, Part 2**, 236; **Vol. 2, Part 1**, 154; **Vol. 3, Part 1**, 132, 177, 198; **Vol. 4, Part 1**, 563f.; **Vol. 4, Part 2**, 317; **Vol. 5, Part 2**, 560 f.; **Vol. 6, Part 2**, 122; **Vol. 10, Part 2**, 250; missions in, **Supp. 3**, 322–23; **Supp. 5**, 681; **Supp. 6**, 649; peace treaty, **Supp. 6**, 176; Perry's misslon to (1853), **Vol. 4, Part 1**, 334, 481; **Vol. 4, Part 2**, 324; **Vol. 7, Part 2**, 488; **Vol. 8, Part 1**, 462; physical education, **Vol. 6, Part 1**, 160; postwar industrial rehabilitation, **Supp. 7**, 190; post–World War II occupation of, **Supp. 5**, 730; pre–World War II expansionism, **Supp. 3**, 657–59; **Supp. 4**, 171, 679, 786; **Supp. 5**, 333; **Supp. 6**, 269–70; **Supp. 7**, 362; **Supp. 8**, 617; publicity, **Vol. 5, Part 1**, 258; scientific school, first, **Vol. 1, Part 2**, 345; service to, **Vol. 4, Part 2**, 567; **Vol. 7, Part 1**, 358; students from, in U.S., **Vol. 7, Part 1**, 566; studies of, **Vol. 9, Part 1**, 533; surrender conditions, **Supp. 7**, 813; tea, first, from, **Vol. 4, Part 2**, 68; trade relations with, **Vol. 2, Part 2**, 186; **Vol. 4, Part 2**, 324; U.S. minister to, first, **Vol. 3, Part 1**, 245; U.S. occupation policies, **Supp. 7**, 490–92, 493; **Supp. 8**, 699; U.S. restrictions on immigration, **Supp. 3**, 323; **Supp. 6**, 320; war with China, **Supp. 4**, 750–51; **Supp. 6**, 230; Wright's architecture in, **Supp. 6**, 712, 713; writings on, **Vol. 1, Part 1**, 473; **Vol. 4, Part 1**, 623; **Vol. 4, Part 2**, 486 f.; **Vol. 5, Part 2**, 475, 534, 606; **Vol. 6, Part 1**, 468 f., 573; **Vol. 8, Part 2**, 485. *See also* Pearl Harbor attack; World War II
Japan Advertiser, **Supp. 4**, 284
Japanese-Americans: cancer research, **Supp. 10**, 769; immigration policies toward, **Supp. 3**, 323; **Supp. 6**, 230; internment during World War II, **Supp. 3**, 661; **Supp. 4**, 286, 787; **Supp. 5**, 43, 343, 358, 574–75; **Supp. 7**, 292, 457; **Supp. 8**, 650; **Supp. 9**, 96, 835; **Supp. 10**, 502, 769; internment during World War II, Supreme Court decision on, **Supp. 10**, 229
Japanese current, first study of, **Vol. 3, Part 1**, 394
Japanese Exclusion Treaty (1905), **Vol. 4, Part 2**, 434; **Vol. 8, Part 2**, 139
Japanese Sculpture of the Suiko Period, **Supp. 5**, 729
Japanning, **Vol. 5, Part 2**, 152
Japan Society, **Supp. 10**, 684; founding of, **Supp. 5**, 308
Jarman, Franklin Maxey, reference to, **Supp. 10**, 381
Jarrell, Randall, reference to, **Supp. 9**, 41
Jarrett, Keith, reference to, **Supp. 10**, 226
Jarvis, J. W., reference to, **Vol. 5, Part 1**, 48
Jaspers, Karl, references to, **Supp. 9**, 40, 42
Jaundice, **Supp. 7**, 340
Java, missions, **Supp. 8**, 425
Jay, John: Carmichael, William, relations with, **Vol. 2, Part 1**, 497; Gardoqui negotiations, **Vol. 7, Part 1**, 87 f.; probably first portrait engraved, **Vol. 9, Part 2**, 530; Spain, **Vol. 6, Part 1**, 302. *See also* Jay Treaty
Jay Treaty, **Vol. 1, Part 1**, 78; **Vol. 2, Part 2**, 135; **Vol. 4, Part 1**, 106; **Vol. 4, Part 2**, 176; **Vol. 8, Part 2**, 7, 9, 12, 26, 398; **Vol. 6, Part 1**, 312; **Vol. 7, Part 1**, 88, 210; **Vol. 8, Part 1**, 355; **Vol. 8, Part 2**, 49; **Vol. 9, Part 2**, 651; **Vol. 10, Part 1**, 524, 565; Jefferson's opinion of, **Vol. 5, Part 2**, 26
Jayhawking, **Vol. 7, Part 1**, 97
Jazz: bands, **Supp. 2**, 502; **Supp. 4**, 510; **Supp. 5**, 106; **Supp. 8**, 163, 697–98; **Supp. 9**, 11, 45, 46, 183, 260–61, 441, 474–75, 598–99, 846, 847; **Supp. 10**, 298, 299, 408, 409, 543, 806; bebop style, **Supp. 5**, 534; **Supp. 9**, 47, 847; **Supp. 10**, 791; blues trumpet, **Supp. 5**, 529–30; Chicago style, **Supp. 8**, 561; **Supp. 9**, 183, 474; clarinet, **Supp. 6**, 42–43; composition, **Supp. 10**, 225–26, 543–44, 791–92; "Condon mob," **Supp. 8**, 562; **Supp. 10**, 299; "cool" jazz movement, **Supp. 10**, 792; cornet, **Supp. 9**, 45–46; criticism, **Supp. 9**, 316–17; drummers, **Supp. 5**, 105–6; **Supp. 9**, 474–75; festivals, **Supp. 10**, 807; first composer, **Supp. 3**, 541–42; first in Soviet Union, **Supp. 3**, 690; fusion, **Supp. 10**, 410; groups, **Supp. 10**, 225; guitar, **Supp. 9**, 183–84; "hot," **Supp. 5**, 293; improvisation, **Supp. 10**, 225–26, 543–44, 791–92; influence on art, **Supp. 7**, 170, 171; introduced in Europe, **Supp. 3**, 187; introduced in London, **Supp. 9**, 513; "jungle" style, **Supp. 9**, 260; King Creole band, **Supp. 2**, 502; "Krazy Kat" pantomime, **Supp. 3**, 357; modal scales in, **Supp. 8**, 100; nightclubs, **Supp. 9**, 183, 260, 280, 442; **Supp. 10**, 270; novel about, **Supp. 8**, 20; orchestral compositions, **Supp. 5**, 103–4; organ, **Supp. 3**, 798; piano, **Supp. 3**, 797–99; **Supp. 6**, 619–20; **Supp. 7**, 131; **Supp. 9**, 259–61; **Supp. 10**, 225–26, 791–92; poetry readings accompanying, **Supp. 9**, 605–6; ragtime influence on, **Supp. 9**, 259; saxophone, **Supp. 8**, 100; **Supp. 9**, 10–11; 441–43, 847–48; singing, **Supp. 5**, 32–33; **Supp. 6**, 299–300; **Supp. 10**, 58–60; solo, **Supp. 9**, 46, 474; swing, **Supp. 5**, 534–35; **Supp. 9**, 46, 317; "symphonic" style, **Supp. 9**, 340; trombone, **Supp. 7**, 735–36; **Supp. 9**, 598–99; trumpet, **Supp. 9**, 46–47; **Supp. 10**, 650; writings on, **Supp. 10**, 479. *See also* Recordings, jazz

Jazz Age, **Supp. 6**, 287–88
Jazz Information (magazine), **Supp. 9**, 316
Jazz Records, **Supp. 10**, 792
Jazz Singer, The, **Supp. 4**, 440; **Supp. 5**, 121, 630; **Supp. 8**, 459
J. C. Penney. *See* Penney, J. C.
Jeanes Fund. *See* Negro Rural School Fund
Jean Goldkette Orchestra (jazz), **Supp. 10**, 806
Jeannette, Arctic voyage of the, **Vol. 1, Part 1**, 240; **Vol. 3, Part 1**, 228
Jeans, fashion of, **Supp. 5**, 386
"Jeeves" (fictional character), **Supp. 9**, 888, 889
Jeffers, Robinson, reference to, **Supp. 5**, 4
Jefferson, Blind Lemon, references to, **Supp. 8**, 695, 696
Jefferson, Joseph, references to, **Vol. 5, Part 1**, 143 f., 255
Jefferson, Mark S. W., reference to, **Supp. 4**, 98
Jefferson, Thomas: **Vol. 1, Part 1**, 246; **Vol. 3, Part 1**, 512 f.; **Vol. 4, Part 2**, 176; **Vol. 5, Part 1**, 206; **Vol. 5, Part 2**, 210; **Vol. 6, Part 1**, 360; **Vol. 7, Part 1**, 10, 88 f., 483, 484, 502, 505, 645; **Vol. 7, Part 2**, 137 f.; **Vol. 8, Part 2**, 395; **Vol. 9, Part 1**, 129, 343, 400; **Vol. 9, Part 2**, 309, 332, 526, 575, 645; **Vol. 10, Part 2**, 224; biographies of, **Vol. 8, Part 1**, 347; **Supp. 6**, 72, 73; critics, one of most outspoken, **Vol. 8, Part 1**, 363 f.; descendant of, **Supp. 6**, 124–25; election of, **Vol. 1, Part 2**, 64; **Vol. 7, Part 1**, 216; first published collection of the works of, **Vol. 8, Part 1**, 369 f.; guardian of, **Vol. 4, Part 2**, 375; Jouett, famous ride of, **Vol. 5, Part 2**, 222; Lewis-Clark expedition, plan for, **Vol. 6, Part 1**, 221; Madison, James, relations with, **Vol. 6, Part 2**, 189 f.; Marshall, John, relations with, **Vol. 6, Part 2**, 320 f.; papers, definitive edition published, **Supp. 10**, 61; personal Bible, **Supp. 2**, 5; political pamphleteering, **Vol. 2, Part 1**, 425; private secretary to, **Vol. 6, Part 1**, 220; sculpture depicting, **Supp. 3**, 89; sourcebook on, **Vol. 8, Part 1**, 368 f.; writings of, **Supp. 3**, 285; **Supp. 5**, 388; writings on, **Supp. 3**, 555; **Supp. 5**, 681
Jefferson Barracks, Mo., **Vol. 1, Part 1**, 410; **Vol. 6, Part 1**, 80
Jefferson College, **Vol. 1, Part 2**, 366; **Vol. 3, Part 1**, 340; **Vol. 8, Part 2**, 125
Jeffersonians, The, **Supp. 6**, 693
Jefferson Medical College **Vol. 1, Part 2**, 25; **Vol. 7, Part 2**, 198, 311; founding of, **Vol. 3, Part 1**, 615 f.; **Vol. 6, Part 1**, 579–80; **Vol. 9, Part 1**, 328
Jefferson Memorial (Washington, D.C.): architecture of, **Supp. 2**, 539; **Supp. 5**, 300; creation of, **Supp. 4**, 448; inscription selection, **Supp. 4**, 448; **Supp. 5**, 681
Jefferson School of Social Science, founding of, **Supp. 8**, 132
Jefferson: The Forgotten Man, **Supp. 9**, 611
Jeffries, James J. ("Jim"), reference to, **Supp. 4**, 433
Jehovah's Witnesses: flag salute issue, **Supp. 3**, 451; **Supp. 4**, 796; **Supp. 5**, 358, 575; **Supp. 7**, 264; leadership, **Supp. 3**, 678–79
Jekyll, Gertrude, reference to, **Supp. 6**, 196
Jelliffe, Smith Ely, reference to, **Supp. 4**, 108
"Jelly Roll Blues," **Supp. 3**, 541
Jencks v. *United States,* **Supp. 10**, 126
Jenkins' Ferry, battle of, **Vol. 1, Part 1**, 579; **Vol. 2, Part 2**, 105; **Vol. 5, Part 2**, 425; **Vol. 9, Part 1**, 556; **Vol. 9, Part 2**, 340
Jenner, William E., references to, **Supp. 5**, 554; **Supp. 9**, 359, 360
Jennings, Hughie, reference to, **Supp. 8**, 106
Jensen Industries, **Supp. 7**, 395
Jeritza, Maria, references to, **Supp. 10**, 445, 446
Jerome, Albert, reference to, **Supp. 9**, 340
Jerome, Jerome K., reference to, **Vol. 6, Part 1**, 397
Jerome, William T., reference to, **Supp. 4**, 827
Jersey City, N.J.: corruption investigation, **Supp. 9**, 456; founding of, **Vol. 8, Part 1**, 318 f.; mayors, **Supp. 9**, 455, 456; patronage, **Supp. 9**, 455, 456; politics, **Supp. 5**, 212–13; **Supp. 6**, 265–66, 479–80, 651; **Supp. 9**, 455–56
Jerseys, the, governorship of, **Vol. 4, Part 2**, 180
"Jersey Settlement," **Vol. 3, Part 2**, 106
Jervis, John B., reference to, **Vol. 6, Part 1**, 548
Jessel, George, references to, **Supp. 6**, 619; **Supp. 7**, 106
Jessup expedition, **Vol. 8, Part 1**, 276 f.
Jesuit Order: **Vol. 1, Part 2**, 141 f.; **Vol. 3, Part 2**, 392, 396; **Vol. 4, Part 1**, 458, 527; **Supp. 7**, 444–48; California, **Vol. 3, Part 1**, 422; **Vol. 5, Part 2**, 420; **Vol. 8, Part 1**, 109 f.; conversion of Iroquois chief by, **Vol. 4, Part 1**, 130–31; education, **Vol. 2, Part 2**, 432 f.; establishment, **Vol. 1, Part 1**, 222; Indian attacks on, **Vol. 5, Part 2**, 75; history of, **Vol. 2, Part 1**, 464; Maryland, **Vol. 4, Part 2**, 250; missions, **Vol. 3, Part 2**, 276 f.; **Vol. 5, Part 2**, 419; **Vol. 6, Part 1**, 10 f.; **Supp. 1**, 158–59; **Supp. 7**, 447; publications, **Supp. 7**, 448; recollect priests, relations with, **Vol. 6, Part 1**, 231; seismological service, **Supp. 1**, 579–80; universities, **Supp. 1**, 159
Jesus Christ: black sculpture of: **Supp. 7**, 610; novels about, **Supp. 5**, 182; **Supp. 7**, 235; paintings of martyrdom, **Supp. 7**, 465; philosophical writings on, **Supp. 5**, 225; popular writings on, **Supp. 4**, 741; **Supp. 5**, 527–28; **Supp. 8**, 27; scholarship on, **Supp. 4**, 152; **Supp. 7**, 624; theological writings on, **Supp. 7**, 575. *See also* Christianity
Jet propulsion: development of, **Supp. 6**, 183; engine design pioneering, **Supp. 9**, 902; first academic course in, **Supp. 8**, 439–440; plane production, **Supp. 9**, 417; research and development, **Supp. 10**, 495
Jet Propulsion Laboratory, **Supp. 7**, 411
Jewell Ridge case, **Supp. 5**, 358
Jewelry, ancient, **Supp. 1**, 477
Jewelry trade, **Vol. 9, Part 2**, 533
Jewett, Frank B.: National Defense Research Committee, **Supp. 9**, 144; reference to, **Supp. 6**, 84
Jewish Agency for Palestine, founding of, **Supp. 3**, 280
Jewish Daily Forward: **Supp. 10**, 475; editing for, **Supp. 5**, 96; founding of, **Supp. 2**, 684; writing for, **Supp. 9**, 724
Jewish Encyclopedia, **Supp. 2**, 6
Jewish Hospital of Brooklyn, blood studies, **Supp. 10**, 836–37
Jewish Institute of Religion, founding of, **Vol. 4, Part 2**, 316; **Supp. 2**, 252; **Supp. 4**, 905
Jewish Publication Society of America: editing for, **Supp. 3**, 756; translation of Hebrew Bible, **Supp. 4**, 659
Jewish Theological Seminary (New York City), first professor of Jewish ethics and mysticism, **Supp. 9**, 384
Jewish Welfare Board, **Supp. 2**, 6; **Supp. 3**, 452
Jewish World, The, **Supp. 3**, 513
Jew Suess, **Supp. 6**, 200, 201
Jews Without Money, **Supp. 8**, 216, 217
"Jiggs and Maggie" (fictional characters), **Supp. 5**, 456–57
Jim Crow laws, **Supp. 3**, 391. *See also* Civil rights movement; Racism; Segregation
Jimi Hendrix Experience (group), **Supp. 8**, 252–53
Jimmy Fund (Boston, Mass.), cancer research funded by, **Supp. 10**, 861
Jobling, J. W., reference to, **Supp. 4**, 288
Jockey Club (New York City), **Supp. 8**, 75–76

Johannsen, Wilhelm, reference to, **Supp. 5**, 629
John Adams and the American Revolution, **Supp. 9**, 113
John Barnard Associates. *See* Barnard, John, Associates
John B. Stetson University, founding of, **Vol. 9, Part 1**, 599
John Bull, first locomotive in New Jersey, **Vol. 9, Part 1**, 620
John Carroll University: founding of, **Vol. 1, Part 2**, 142; meteorological observatory, **Supp. 1**, 579
John Carter Brown Catalogue, **Vol. 1, Part 2**, 7
John Hancock Mutual Life Insurance Co., organized, **Vol. 8, Part 2**, 351
Johnny Eager, **Supp. 9**, 381
Johnny Got His Gun, **Supp. 10**, 239, 793
Johnny Tremain: A Novel for Young and Old, **Supp. 8**, 181
Johnny, We Hardly Knew Ye, **Supp. 10**, 605
John Randolph, first American iron steamship, **Vol. 5, Part 2**, 549
Johns Hopkins Hospital: Brady Urological Institute, **Supp. 3**, 854; gynecology department, **Supp. 3**, 412–13; obstetrics, **Supp. 9**, 352; resident program, **Supp. 6**, 546; surgery, **Supp. 3**, 270–71
Johns Hopkins University: **Vol. 4, Part 1**, 280, 300 f.; **Vol. 5, Part 1**, 214, 314; **Vol. 5, Part 2**, 173, 529; **Vol. 6, Part 2**, 338; **Vol. 7, Part 1**, 243; **Vol. 8, Part 1**, 501 f.; **Vol. 10, Part 1**, 621 f.; academic freedom, **Supp. 5**, 410; **Supp. 9**, 125; administration, **Supp. 3**, 11; art as applied to medicine department, **Supp. 3**, 106; economic studies; **Supp. 3**, 248; first woman doctorate recipient, **Supp. 3**, 38; first woman full professor, **Supp. 5**, 600; French literature and language studies, **Supp. 5**, 409; geology studies, **Supp. 3**, 62; German educational model for, **Supp. 6**, 207; growth, **Supp. 2**, 250; history studies, **Supp. 2**, 340; **Supp. 3**, 16; "Hopkins plan" formulated, **Supp. 9**, 125; hygiene and public health school, **Supp. 2**, 212; **Supp. 3**, 371; Institute of the History of Medicine, **Supp. 6**, 580–81; international studies school, **Supp. 8**, 258; Law Institute, **Supp. 3**, 186; master plan, **Supp. 2**, 539; medical illustration, **Supp. 3**, 106; medical school, **Vol. 1, Part 2**, 267; **Vol. 3, Part 2**, 76; **Vol. 4, Part 1**, 301; **Vol. 7, Part 1**, 202; **Vol. 7, Part 2**, 85, 551; **Vol. 10, Part 1**, 621 f.; **Supp. 3**, 853–54; **Supp. 4**, 213–14, 221, 287, 801–2; **Supp. 5**, 147, 438, 600, 733; **Supp. 6**, 460–61, 547; **Supp. 7**, 59, 477; medical school, gynecology studies, **Supp. 3**, 412–13; medical school, pediatrics, **Supp. 3**, 74; medical school, physiology studies, **Supp. 3**, 370; **Supp. 7**, 225–26; medical school, psychiatry studies, **Supp. 3**, 128; **Supp. 4**, 572; medical school, surgery studies, **Supp. 3**, 271, 458; nursing curriculum, **Supp. 4**, 632–33; ophthalmology studies, **Supp. 2**, 722; philosophy studies, **Supp. 5**, 170; **Supp. 7**, 481; physics studies, **Supp. 4**, 658; **Supp. 9**, 541; physiology studies, **Supp. 3**, 370; **Supp. 7**, 225–26; plant physiology studies, **Supp. 4**, 500 1; political science studies, **Supp. 3**, 831; presidency, **Supp. 4**, 99; psychology studies, **Supp. 6**, 671–72; public health studies, **Supp. 5**, 233; **Supp. 7**, 194; Romance languages studies, **Supp. 3**, 22; surgery studies, **Supp. 3**, 271, 458; tuberculosis laboratories, **Supp. 3**, 431; zoology studies, **Supp. 5**, 425–26
Johnson, Albert, references to, **Supp. 3**, 446; **Supp. 5**, 613
Johnson, Alexander, references to, **Supp. 3**, 211; **Supp. 4**, 438, 439
Johnson, Alvanley, reference to, **Supp. 4**, 890
Johnson, Alvin S., reference to, **Supp. 4**, 63
Johnson, Andrew: **Vol. 1, Part 2**, 489; **Vol. 7, Part 1**, 200, 286; **Vol. 8, Part 2**, 599, 620; **Vol. 9, Part 1**, 519, 441, 574, 624; **Vol. 9, Part 2**, 363; biographies of, **Supp. 6**, 72; change in attitude toward South, **Vol. 8, Part 1**, 433; impeachment of, **Vol. 1, Part 2**, 278; **Vol. 3, Part 2**, 350, 564; **Vol. 4, Part 1**, 632; **Vol. 6, Part 1**, 52; **Vol. 8, Part 2**, 175; **Vol. 9, Part 1**, 498; **Vol. 9, Part 2**, 14; **Vol. 10, Part 1**, 19 f.; nomination for vice-president, **Vol. 8, Part 1**, 410; *Reconstructionist* attack on, **Vol. 9, Part 2**, 254
Johnson, Arno J., reference to, **Supp. 7**, 642
Johnson, Arnold M., reference to, **Supp. 6**, 415
Johnson, Ban, references to, **Supp. 3**, 438; **Supp. 6**, 357
Johnson, Charles S., reference to, **Supp. 8**, 521
Johnson, Ed, reference to, **Supp. 6**, 455
Johnson, Enoch L., reference to, **Supp. 4**, 613
Johnson, Ferd, reference to, **Supp. 6**, 699
Johnson, Hiram, references to, **Supp. 3**, 156, 559, 650; **Supp. 4**, 707; **Supp. 5**, 579
Johnson, Hugh S., references to, **Supp. 3**, 594, 651, 670; **Supp. 5**, 343; **Supp. 7**, 36
Johnson, Jack, references to, **Supp. 5**, 369; **Supp. 6**, 362, 700
Johnson, James P., reference to, **Supp. 3**, 798
Johnson, James Weldon, reference to, **Supp. 6**, 321
Johnson, Jerome A., reference to, **Supp. 10**, 141
Johnson, Joseph French, reference to, **Vol. 7, Part 2**, 298 f.
Johnson, Ladybird. *See* Taylor, Claudia Alta ("Lady Bird")
Johnson, Louis, references to, **Supp. 5**, 197, 479; **Supp. 8**, 329, 807; **Supp. 9**, 227, 228
Johnson, Lyndon B.: Baker relationship, **Supp. 9**, 433, 440; civil rights legislation, **Supp. 9**, 432, 433, 434, 435; **Supp. 10**, 361, 362; Estes relationship, **Supp. 9**, 433; first black appointed to Supreme Court by, **Supp. 9**, 436; Great Society programs, **Supp. 9**, 434, 435, 437; **Supp. 10**, 361–62; gubernatorial candidacy, **Supp. 9**, 431; House services, **Supp. 9**, 431; Humphrey, H. H., relationship, **Supp. 9**, 435; **Supp. 10**, 361–62; Kennedy family relationship, **Supp. 7**, 420, 425; **Supp. 8**, 323–24; **Supp. 9**, 433–34; Kennedy, R. F., rejected as running mate, **Supp. 9**, 435; Knowland relationship, **Supp. 9**, 468; labor relations, **Supp. 10**, 494; life saved, **Supp. 10**, 133; Lippman relationship, **Supp. 9**, 506; McCarthyism, strategy regarding, **Supp. 9**, 433; McCormack relationship, **Supp. 10**, 486; marriage, **Supp. 9**, 431; National Youth Administration service, **Supp. 9**, 431; O'Donnell relationship, **Supp. 10**, 604, 605; Olds, L., relationship, **Supp. 6**, 484–85; presidency, **Supp. 5**, 343; Presidential bids, **Supp. 9**, 433, 435; presidential election (1968), **Supp. 9**, 436–37; **Supp. 10**, 362; Presidential Library, **Supp. 6**, 541; racial views, **Supp. 9**, 433; radio station ownership, **Supp. 9**, 431–32; Rayburn relationship, **Supp. 7**, 635, 636; **Supp. 9**, 431; references to, **Supp. 9**, 862; **Supp. 10**, 186, 469, 618; Senate majority leadership, **Supp. 9**, 433; Senate service, **Supp. 9**, 432–33; senatorial campaign (1948), **Supp. 9**, 97, 432; social legislation passage, **Supp. 10**, 486; special assistants to, **Supp. 10**, 416; urban policy, **Supp. 10**, 109; U.S.-Soviet summit meeting, **Supp. 9**, 799; vice-presidency, **Supp. 9**, 9, 433–34; vice-presidential candidacy, **Supp. 7**, 296, 723; **Supp. 8**, 361; **Supp. 9**, 433; Vietnam War policies, **Supp. 7**, 724; **Supp. 9**, 4, 5, 10, 434, 435, 436, 437, 862; **Supp. 10**, 462; war on poverty, **Supp. 9**, 434, 435; World War II service, **Supp. 9**, 431
Johnson, Martin, reference to, **Supp. 5**, 370–71
Johnson, Mordecai, reference to, **Supp. 6**, 568
Johnson, Robert Underwood, reference to, **Supp. 3**, 769
Johnson, Roy, reference to, **Supp. 6**, 469
Johnson, Dam Ealy, reference to, **Supp. 10**, 618

Johnson, Samuel, manuscripts, **Supp. 5**, 349–50
Johnson, Tom L., references to, **Supp. 2**, 17; **Supp. 3**, 167; **Supp. 6**, 132; **Supp. 9**, 553
Johnson, Walter, references to, **Supp. 8**, 544; **Supp. 10**, 99
Johnson, William, reference to, **Vol. 9, Part 1**, 122
Johnson and Johnson Co., **Supp. 7**, 182–83
Johnson-Clarendon Convention (1869), **Vol. 5, Part 2**, 88; **Vol. 9, Part 2**, 212
Johnson Female University, establishment of, **Vol. 5, Part 2**, 130
Johnson-Reed Act (1924), **Supp. 6**, 320
Johnson's Cyclopaedia, **Vol. 1, Part 1**, 270
Johnson's Island plot, **Vol. 1, Part 2**, 90
Johnson's Wax, administrative center design, **Supp. 6**, 714
Johnston, Alva, reference to, **Supp. 7**, 473
Johnston, Douglas H., reference to, **Supp. 6**, 468
Johnston, Joseph, reference to, **Vol. 6, Part 1**, 576
Johnston, Joseph E., references to, **Vol. 6, Part 1**, 123 f.; **Vol. 8, Part 2**, 546
Johnston, Samuel, reference to, **Vol. 5, Part 2**, 210
Johnston, William H., reference to, **Supp. 9**, 839
Johnston, William M. reference to, **Supp. 6**, 538
Johnstone, Edward R., reference to, **Supp. 4**, 11
Johnstown flood, **Vol. 5, Part 2**, 123, 135, 209; **Vol. 7, Part 1**, 301
Joiner, C. M. ("Dad"), reference to, **Supp. 9**, 411
Joint Chiefs of Staff. *See under* Armed Forces and defense
Joint Committee Against Communism, **Supp. 6**, 350
Joint Committee on Conduct of War (1862–64), **Vol. 2, Part 1**, 618; **Vol. 2, Part 2**, 470; **Vol. 5, Part 2**, 246; **Vol. 9, Part 1**, 623; **Vol. 10, Part 1**, 304
Joint Palestine Survey Commission, founding of, **Supp. 2**, 695
Jolson, Al, references to, **Supp. 4**, 225; **Supp. 5**, 121, 629, 630; **Supp. 6**, 536; **Supp. 8**, 251
Jolson Story, The, **Supp. 9**, 602
Jones, Bassett, references to, **Supp. 5**, 558, 559
Jones, Ernest, references to, **Supp. 4**, 108, 109, 716, 717
Jones, Eugene Kinckle, reference to, **Supp. 6**, 285
Jones, Faith, reference to, **Supp. 6**, 103
Jones, George, refusal of bribe by, **Vol. 10, Part 1**, 81
Jones, Isham, reference to, **Supp. 3**, 406
Jones, Jacob, reference to, **Vol. 1, Part 2**, 241
Jones, Jennifer, reference to, **Supp. 7**, 682
Jones, Jesse H., references to, **Supp. 6**, 135, 136; **Supp. 7**, 761; **Supp. 8**, 89
Jones, Jim, references to, **Supp. 10**, 558, 559
"Jones, Jingles B." (fictional character), **Supp. 10**, 178
Jones, John Paul, references to, **Vol. 3, Part 2**, 268; **Vol. 5, Part 1**, 210; **Vol. 8, Part 1**, 92 f.; **Vol. 9, Part 1**, 156
Jones, John Price, Corporation, **Supp. 7**, 401–2
Jones, Mary, reference to, **Supp. 6**, 196
Jones, Robert Edmond, reference to, **Supp. 3**, 35
Jones, Samuel ("Golden Rule"), references to, **Supp. 3**, 298; **Supp. 7**, 85
Jones, Shirley, references to, **Supp. 10**, 106, 107
Jones, Spike, and His City Slickers, **Supp. 7**, 403–4
Jones, William Atkinson, reference to, **Supp. 3**, 614
Jonesborough, Ga., capture of, **Vol. 1, Part 1**, 266; **Vol. 5, Part 1**, 194; **Vol. 9, Part 1**, 95; **Vol. 8, Part 1**, 380
Jonestown massacre, **Supp. 10**, 392, 558
Jordan, Camille, reference to, **Supp. 5**, 491
Jordan, David Starr, references to, **Vol. 3, Part 2**, 62; **Vol. 5, Part 1**, 277; **Vol. 7, Part 1**, 598; **Supp. 3**, 205–6, 262, 602
Jordan, Sara Murray, reference to, **Supp. 5**, 405
Joseph, Chief, reference to, **Supp. 3**, 836
Joseph in Egypt, **Supp. 8**, 433
Joss, Addie, reference to, **Supp. 6**, 663
Joshua Tree National Monument, **Supp. 10**, 120
Jouett, Captain John, famous ride of, **Vol. 5, Part 2**, 222
Journal General of Physiology, founding of, **Supp. 7**, 592
Journalism (for complete list of journalists, *see* Occupations Index): agricultural, **Vol. 8, Part 1**, 40 f.; **Supp. 3**, 319; Asian affairs, **Supp. 4**, 679, 749–51; black, early, Vol. 8, Parts, 253; black-related, **Supp. 7**, 767; Boston, **Vol. 2, Part 1**, 456; **Vol. 2, Part 2**, 118, 198; **Vol. 3, Part 2**, 458; **Vol. 4, Part 2**, 41, 109; **Vol. 5, Part 2**, 361, 457, 458; **Vol. 6, Part 1**, 285, 508, 563; **Vol. 8, Part 2**, 239, 359; **Vol. 9, Part 2**, 319, 609; business forecasting, **Supp. 8**, 19; California, **Vol. 1, Part 1**, 443 f.; **Vol. 1, Part 2**, 602; **Vol. 2, Part 2**, 323; **Vol. 5, Part 2**, 408; **Vol. 9, Part 1**, 195; cartoons, **Supp. 10**, 244–45, *see also* Cartoons and caricatures; Catholic, **Supp. 6**, 478–79, 448; Chicago, **Vol. 2, Part 1**, 94; **Vol. 2, Part 2**, 374; **Vol. 5, Part 2**, 109, 489; **Vol. 6, Part 1**, 60, 609 f.; **Vol. 8, Part 2**, 492; **Vol. 9, Part 2**, 82, 317; child-care advice, **Supp. 6**, 382; child-oriented, **Supp. 3**, 44–45; civic-minded, **Supp. 4**, 222, 738; Civil War, **Vol. 9, Part 1**, 409 f.; Cleveland election, **Vol. 6, Part 1**, 283; college, **Vol. 8, Part 2**, 57; colonial, **Vol. 3, Part 1**, 347 f.; columnist, one of first in America, **Vol. 3, Part 2**, 364; **Vol. 5, Part 1**, 320; **Vol. 9, Part 2**, 317; columns, "About New York," **Supp. 6**, 58; columns, advice, **Supp. 5**, 244; columns, "Amy Vanderbilt's Etiquette," **Supp. 9**, 825; columns, "As Pegler Sees It," **Supp. 8**, 498–99; columns, "Assignment: America," **Supp. 10**, 675; "Backstairs at the White House," **Supp. 8**, 607; columns, "Between You and Me," **Supp. 3**, 166; columns, black-oriented, **Supp. 8**, 287–88; columns, book, **Supp. 1**, 92; columns, "Broadway After Dark," **Supp. 8**, 444; columns, "Capital Parade," **Supp. 10**, 414, 415; columns, "Comments on the Screen," **Supp. 10**, 246; columns, "Conning Tower," **Supp. 6**, 4, 5; columns, daily, **Supp. 2**, 431; columns, "Easy Chair," **Supp. 5**, 168, 169; columns, etiquette, **Supp. 6**, 514; **Supp. 9**, 825; columns, "Fair Enough," **Supp. 8**, 498; columns, gossip, **Supp. 7**, 433, 444; **Supp. 8**, 282; **Supp. 9**, 604–4, 885; **Supp. 10**, 475; columns, "Hints from Heloise," **Supp. 10**, 666, 667; columns, "Human Relations," **Supp. 10**, 255; columns, humor, **Supp. 9**, 166; columns, "Impressions in the Field of Art," **Supp. 10**, 246; columns, "In the Nation," **Supp. 9**, 471, 472; columns, "Jots and Tittles," **Supp. 10**, 146; columns, "Leaves from a Senator's Wife," **Supp. 8**, 328; columns, "Leaves from a War Correspondent's Notebook," **Supp. 9**, 120; columns, "Letter from Paris," **Supp. 10**, 246; columns, "Letter from Washington," **Supp. 10**, 707; columns, "lovelorn," **Supp. 3**, 504; columns, "Lyon's Den," **Supp. 10**, 475; columns, "Mainly about Manhattan," **Supp. 9**, 170; columns, "Matter of Fact," **Supp. 9**, 26–27; columns, "My Day," **Supp. 7**, 660; columns, "Notes of a Biology Watcher," **Supp. 10**, 370; columns, oldest continuous on sports, **Supp. 5**, 724; columns, "On the Line," **Supp. 9**, 187; columns, opinion, **Supp. 10**, 675–76; columns, "Pitching Horsehoes," **Supp. 8**, 547; columns, "Principles and Heresies," **Supp. 9**, 549; columns, "Seeing Things," **Supp. 8**, 54; columns, show business, **Supp. 8**, 547; **Supp. 9**, 604, 779; columns, society, **Supp. 10**, 674–75; columns, sports, **Supp. 9**, 157, 215, 779; columns, "Sports of the Times," **Supp. 9**, 215; columns, "Stories of the Streets and of the Towns," **Supp. 3**, 3; columns, "Sun Dial," **Supp. 7**, 617–18; columns, syndicated, **Supp. 2**, 69; **Supp. 7**, 665;

Supp. 9, 604; columns, "Today and Tomorrow," **Supp. 9**, 505; columns, "Totem Pole, The," **Supp. 10**, 747; columns, "Washington Merry-Go-Round," **Supp. 8**, 496; columns, "What's News," **Supp. 9**, 520; columns, "Your Broadway and Mine," **Supp. 9**, 885; columns, "Your Family and You," **Supp. 10**, 255; Communist China affairs, **Supp. 8**, 635; Communist-oriented, **Supp. 7**, 268–69; Connecticut, **Vol. 10, Part 2**, 565; consumer protection, **Supp. 7**, 69; criticism, *see* Criticism; Democratic newspaper, first in West, **Vol. 3, Part 2**, 231; documentary, **Supp. 5**, 511; early attempt at unbiased presentation, **Vol. 8, Part 1**, 409 f.; editorials, *see* Newspapers, editorials; effect of *New York Sun's* style, **Vol. 3, Part 1**, 51; ethics issues, **Supp. 3**, 851; **Supp. 4**, 668; ethics of, **Vol. 7, Part 1**, 335; exposé, *see subhead* muckraking; "family type," **Vol. 1, Part 2**, 437; feature writing, **Supp. 2**, 415; financial, **Supp. 3**, 564–65; **Supp. 6**, 457–58; **Supp. 8**, 338; **Supp. 9**, 482, 520–21; first American newspaper in Paris, **Vol. 3, Part 2**, 212; first astronomical magazine, **Vol. 7, Part 1**, 39; first "comic strips," **Vol. 7, Part 2**, 112; first daily in U.S., **Vol. 3, Part 1**, 514 f.; **Vol. 8, Part 1**, 139 f., 638; first "extra," **Vol. 8, Part 1**, 299 f.; first illustrated dailies in U.S., **Vol. 6, Part 1**, 186; **Vol. 8, Part 1**, 332 f., 440; first illustrated weekly, **Vol. 3, Part 1**, 155; first Italian paper, **Vol. 1, Part 2**, 1; first newspaper chain, **Vol. 8, Part 2**, 518; first newspaper in German, **Vol. 9, Part 2**, 557; first newspaper in Hawaii, **Vol. 1, Part 1**, 295; **Vol. 5, Part 1**, 618; first newspaper in Middle Colonies, **Vol. 1, Part 2**, 553; first newspaper in New Jersey, **Vol. 7, Part 2**, 227; first newspaper in New York, **Vol. 1, Part 2**, 564; first newspaper in Pennsylvania, **Vol. 1, Part 2**, 553; first newspaper in South Carolina, **Vol. 10, Part 1**, 644 f.; first newspaper in Utah, **Vol. 2, Part 2**, 353; first newspapers in U.S., **Vol. 2, Part 1**, 456; **Vol. 4, Part 2**, 304; **Vol. 8, Part 1**, 139 f.; first newspaper syndicate, **Vol. 8, Part 2**, 518; first newspaper to have literary supplement, **Vol. 1, Part 2**, 559; first paper devoted to woman's rights, **Vol. 3, Part 1**, 141; first papers published by a woman, **Vol. 1, Part 2**, 385, 581; first religious newspaper, **Vol. 7, Part 1**, 251; first successful penny paper, **Vol. 3, Part 1**, 155; first syndicated dispatches carried nationally by wire, **Supp. 9**, 482; first woman Pulitzer Prize winner, **Supp. 5**, 447; foreign correspondents, **Supp. 3**, 612–13; **Supp. 5**, 60, 78–79, 362–63, 446–47; **Supp. 6**, 183–84, 197–98, 366, 543; **Supp. 7**, 115–16, 643, 758–59; **Supp. 8**, 172, 232–33, 259–60, 498, 639, 675; **Supp. 9**, 120, 187–88, 690, 718–19, 740–41; **Supp. 10**, 231, 349, 510–11, 519, 562–63, 800–801; freedom of the press, **Vol. 3, Part 2**, 560; **Vol. 10, Part 2**, 649; free-lance, **Supp. 9**, 876; **Supp. 10**, 479; "Harding Bible, The," **Vol. 4, Part 2**, 259, headlines, startling use of, **Vol. 9, Part 1**, 10; historical writings on, **Supp. 1**, 441; **Supp. 7**, 559; humorous, **Supp. 3**, 53–54; **Supp. 9**, 166; interviews, **Supp. 7**, 512–13; investigative reporting, **Supp. 3**, 80, 91–92; **Supp. 6**, 616–17; **Supp. 9**, 499–500; **Supp. 10**, 49–50, 384, 461; "journalist's creed," **Supp. 1**, 709; Kentucky, **Vol. 9, Part 2**, 607; labor issues, **Supp. 3**, 10, 347, 355–56; **Supp. 5**, 653–54, 663–64, 484; **Supp. 8**, 675; left-wing, **Supp. 8**, 216, 255–56; liberal, **Supp. 4**, 850–51; **Supp. 6**, 202; liberal southern, **Supp. 7**, 323–24; literary syndicalism, **Vol. 9, Part 2**, 125; livestock publication, **Vol. 4, Part 1**, 380; Louisiana, **Vol. 9, Part 2**, 509; Massachusetts, **Vol. 3, Part 1**, 437 f.; **Vol. 8, Part 1**, 73 f.; **Vol. 8, Part 2**, 461; medical, **Vol. 9, Part 1**, 132; Minnesota, **Vol. 2, Part 2**, 367; *Moon Hoax*, **Vol. 3, Part 1**, 155; muckraking, **Supp. 2**, 14, 626; **Supp. 3**, 675, 762; **Supp. 4**, 46–47, 518, 662, 707; **Supp. 5**, 141, 286, 406, 666–67, 698–99; **Supp. 6**, 6; **Supp. 8**, 496–97; **Supp. 8**, 498–99, 594–95; **Supp. 9**, 679; natural history, **Supp. 3**, 8–9; news agencies, **Supp. 4**, 630–31; newspaper editing, **Vol. 3, Part 2**, 476, 486 f., 515; **Vol. 4, Part 1**, 425; **Vol. 4, Part 2**, 11; **Vol. 5, Part 1**, 396; **Vol. 5, Part 2**, 45, 48, 160, 417 f., 444, 452; **Vol. 6, Part 2**, 159, 166, 267, 297, 568; **Vol. 7, Part 1**, 48, 204 f.; **Vol. 7, Part 2**, 475; **Vol. 8, Part 2**, 468, 491, 514; **Vol. 8, Part 2**, 526; **Vol. 9, Part 1**, 577; **Vol. 9, Part 2**, 98; **Vol. 10, Part 2**, 292, 617, 633; newspaper illustrating, **Vol. 8, Part 2**, 113; "newspaper of record" concept, **Supp. 3**, 787–88; newspaper publishing, **Vol. 1, Part 2**, 437, 565; **Vol. 5, Part 1**, 535; **Vol. 6, Part 2**, 130; **Vol. 7, Part 1**, 271; **Vol. 7, Part 2**, 376 f., 643; **Vol. 8, Part 2**, 517, 519 f.; **Vol. 10, Part 2**, 500; New York, **Vol. 6, Part 1**, 354 f.; North Carolina, **Vol. 9, Part 2**, 582; organizations, *see specific names*; Philadelphia, **Vol. 1, Part 2**, 417; **Vol. 5, Part 1**, 203; photography, **Vol. 9, Part 1**, 380; **Supp. 4**, 361; **Supp. 7**, 115–16, 535–36; **Supp. 9**, 111; **Supp. 10**, 397–98, 749–50; pioneer women in field of, **Vol. 1, Part 2**, 513 f., 581; **Vol. 4, Part 2**, 281 f., 303; **Vol. 6, Part 1**, 288; **Vol. 8, Part 2**, 518; political, **Supp. 3**, 702, 816; **Supp. 4**, 574–75; **Supp. 5**, 19, 152–53, 205, 497–98, 518–19, 626, 504–5; **Supp. 6**, 601–2; **Supp. 7**, 249–50, 320–21, 706, 739–40; **Supp. 8**, 149–50, 173–74, 394–95, 496–97; **Supp. 9**, 159–61, 471–72, 482–83; 503–6; 826; **Supp. 10**, 13, 14, 51, 247, 375, 414–15, 416, 417, 461–62; 706, 707; political attacks on, **Supp. 9**, 415; presidential relations, **Supp. 3**, 649–50; **Supp. 4**, 704; **Supp. 5**, 196–97; **Supp. 8**, 160, 607; press freedom landmark decision (1941), **Supp. 3**, 157; pro-German, **Supp. 7**, 756–57, 759; Quaker, **Vol. 6, Part 1**, 212; racing news, **Supp. 3**, 20; radio, *see* Radio, news commentary; reform criticism of, **Supp. 3**, 59–60; religious, **Vol. 3, Part 2**, 53; **Vol. 7, Part 1**, 439; **Vol. 8, Part 2**, 348; **Supp. 6**, 315–16; **Supp. 7**, 345–46; religious weekly, one of first in U.S., **Vol. 4, Part 2**, 157; reprint periodicals, **Vol. 6, Part 1**, 295; San Francisco earthquake and fire coverage, **Supp. 4**, 417; satiric essays, **Supp. 4**, 804; science, **Supp. 5**, 65; **Supp. 6**, 327–28; **Supp. 8**, 119–20; **Supp. 10**, 435; scientific newspapers, first in U.S., **Vol. 8, Part 1**, 101 f.; second black weekly in U.S., **Vol. 8, Part 1**, 403; second newspaper in U.S., **Vol. 5, Part 2**, 458; sensationalism, *see subhead* yellow; social criticism by, **Supp. 6**, 330, 571–72; **Supp. 8**, 433, *see also subhead* muckraking; socialist-oriented, **Supp. 5**, 264; Soviet Union affairs, **Supp. 8**, 635; sports, **Supp. 1**, 527, 704; **Supp. 4**, 708–9; **Supp. 5**, 568, 724; **Supp. 6**, 366; **Supp. 8**, 498; **Supp. 9**, 157, 215; **Supp. 10**, 267–68; Swedish newspapers, **Vol. 7, Part 1**, 550; syndicated columns, *see subhead* columns, syndicated; syndication, **Supp. 4**, 38; teaching of, **Vol. 5, Part 2**, 60, 391; **Vol. 6, Part 1**, 110; **Vol. 8, Part 1**, 260 f.; **Vol. 9, Part 1**, 578; **Vol. 10, Part 2**, 292; **Supp. 1**, 87, 391, 708; **Supp. 2**, 610; television, *see* Television, news commentary; Tennessee, **Vol. 7, Part 1**, 601; tennis, **Supp. 6**, 538; theatrical, **Supp. 3**, 276–77; **Supp. 9**, 170–71, 885–86; third newspaper in U.S., **Vol. 1, Part 2**, 553; war correspondence, **Vol. 7, Part 2**, 154; **Vol. 8, Part 1**, 451; war correspondents, *see subhead* foreign correspondents; "War of the News Giants," **Vol. 7, Part 2**, 545; Washington correspondents, *see subheads* political; presidential relations; wire services, **Supp. 7**, 144–45; women in, **Supp. 10**, 666, 675–76; women's interests, **Supp. 1**, 91; **Supp. 8**, 471; women's rights, **Supp. 3**, 355–56; writings on, **Supp. 4**, 704; yellow, **Vol. 5, Part 2**, 156; **Vol. 10, Part 1**, 445; **Supp. 1**, 94; **Supp. 2**, 63, 242; **Supp. 3**, 427; **Supp. 5**,

284–85, 453; **Supp. 6**, 686; Yiddish-language, **Supp. 9**, 724. *See also* Magazines; Newspapers; Publishing (*for publication ownership and management*); Radio; Television
Journalists. For complete list, *see* Occupations Index
Journal of Agricultural Research, founding of, **Supp. 1**, 461–62
Journal of Albion Moonlight, The, **Supp. 9**, 605
Journal of American Ethnology and Archaeology, **Vol. 4, Part 2**, 519
Journal of American History, predecessor, **Supp. 10**, 137
Journal of Applied Physics, predecessor, **Supp. 4**, 818
Journal of a Residence in America, **Vol. 5, Part 2**, 315
Journal of Biological Chemistry, editing of, **Supp. 2**, 36; founding of, **Supp. 2**, 4
Journal of Cancer Research, **Vol. 10, Part 1**, 608
Journal of Chronic Diseases, predecessor, **Supp. 6**, 461
Journal of Clinical Investigation, founding of, **Supp. 6**, 547
Journal of Commerce, **Vol. 4, Part 2**, 157 f.; **Vol. 9, Part 2**, 73 f.
Journal of Education, **Vol. 9, Part 1**, 67
Journal of Experimental Medicine: editing, **Supp. 8**, 556; founding of, **Supp. 2**, 4
Journal of Forestry, **Vol. 3, Part 2**, 336
Journal of Geology, **Vol. 8, Part 2**, 310
Journal of Geomorphology, founding of, **Supp. 3**, 390
Journal of Health, **Vol. 4, Part 2**, 148
Journal of Home Economics, **Supp. 3**, 68
Journal of Humanistic Psychology, founding of, **Supp. 8**, 424
Journal of Negro History, founding of, **Supp. 4**, 911
Journal of Nervous and Mental Disease, **Supp. 3**, 386
Journal of Neurophysiology, editing, **Supp. 2**, 162
Journal of Parapsychology, **Supp. 10**, 672
Journal of Parasitology, founding of, **Supp. 3**, 802
Journal of Pharmacology and Experimental Therapeutics, founding of, **Supp. 2**, 4
Journal of Philosophy, Psychology, and Scientific Method, founding of, **Supp. 2**, 734
Journal of Physical Chemistry, founding of, **Supp. 5**, 36
Journal of Political Economy: editing, **Supp. 8**, 668; founding of, **Supp. 1**, 487
Journal of Religion, **Vol. 9, Part 1**, 270
Journal of Social Forces, founding of, **Supp. 5**, 520
Journal of Speculative Philosophy, **Vol. 4, Part 2**, 329
Journal of the American Chemical Society, **Supp. 5**, 407
Journal of the American Folklore Society, **Supp. 3**, 83
Journal of the American Institute of Architects, editing, **Supp. 2**, 709
Journal of the American Medical Association, socialized medicine article, **Supp. 6**, 664
Journal of the Franklin Institute, **Vol. 5, Part 2**, 203
Journal of the Outdoor Life, founding of, **Supp. 2**, 71
Journal of Transpersonal Psychology, founding of, **Supp. 8**, 424
Journal of Travels over the Rocky Mountains, **Vol. 7, Part 2**, 186
Journal of Urology, founding of, **Supp. 3**, 854
Journals: **Vol. 6, Part 1**, 221; **Vol. 8, Part 1**, 55, 61, 68 f., 307 f.; **Vol. 10, Part 1**, 20 f., 537; collection of, **Vol. 3, Part 2**, 512; Continental Congress, of, **Vol. 5, Part 1**, 385; De Long's ill-fated polar expedition, **Vol. 3, Part 1**, 228; fur trader, of a, **Vol. 6, Part 1**, 5; livestock, **Vol. 8, Part 2**, 335; Reeves, Arthur Middleton, **Vol. 8, Part 1**, 470; technical editing of, **Vol. 5, Part 2**, 426. *See also* Diaries and memoirs
Journeyman Tailors' Union of America, **Vol. 6, Part 1**, 170
Joyce, James: Colum relationship, **Supp. 9**, 181, 182; *Finnegan's Wake* serialized, **Supp. 9**, 682; references to, **Supp. 3**, 844; **Supp. 5**, 270, 587; **Supp. 6**, 497; **Supp. 7**, 40, 306, 374; *Ulysses* banned, **Supp. 9**, 33, 165, 683; **Supp. 10**, 221; unauthorized use of works, **Supp. 9**, 682
Joy of Cooking, The, **Supp. 7**, 656–57
Juanita Hall Choir, **Supp. 8**, 238
Judah, T. O., reference to, **Vol. 5, Part 1**, 409
Judaism and Jews: **Vol. 3, Part 2**, 65; **Vol. 7, Part 1**, 125, 150; **Vol. 8, Part 2**, 433; anti-Communist organizations, **Supp. 6**, 350; anti-Semitism, **Supp. 1**, 78–79; **Supp. 4**, 299; **Supp. 6**, 526; **Supp. 8**, 541; **Supp. 9**, 40, 591, 618; **Supp. 10**, 152, 438, 745; "Biblical Hebrew" movement, **Supp. 3**, 143; books about, **Supp. 9**, 707–8; Catholic relations, **Supp. 2**, 87; **Supp. 8**, 307, 537, 589; **Supp. 9**, 384; community activism, **Supp. 3**, 452; Conservative branch, **Supp. 2**, 6; controversies concerning, **Vol. 5, Part 2**, 2, 490 f.; **Vol. 8, Part 1**, 161 f.; early American Judaica collection, **Supp. 5**, 587; emigration of, from Russia, **Vol. 5, Part 2**, 501; first Jewish college in America, **Vol. 3, Part 1**, 459 f.; garment industry unionization, **Supp. 1**, 403; **Supp. 5**, 95–96; "Goldbergs" radio series, **Supp. 8**, 32–33; Harvard policies toward, **Supp. 3**, 472; Hebrew language popularization, **Supp. 1**, 407; historical writings on, **Supp. 1**, 473, 474; humor, **Supp. 9**, 720–21; immigrant assimilation, **Supp. 4**, 23; Jewish Institute of Religion, *see separate entry;* journalism, **Vol. 5, Part 1**, 513 f.; **Vol. 7, Part 1**, 277; **Vol. 7, Part 2**, 168; leadership, **Vol. 1, Part 1**, 33, 108, 388; **Vol. 3, Part 1**, 259 f.; **Vol. 4, Part 1**, 7, 32 f., 441, 504 f.; **Vol. 4, Part 2**, 512; **Vol. 5, Part 1**, 67 f., 334, 514; **Vol. 5, Part 2**, 2, 254, 487 f., 490 f.; **Vol. 6, Part 1**, 137 f., 241; **Vol. 7, Part 1**, 149; **Vol. 8, Part 2**, 128 f., 165, 168, 432 f., 436 f., 456, 565; **Vol. 9, Part 1**, 166, 394, 463; literature, **Supp. 6**, 200–201; music, **Supp. 5**, 609; **Supp. 6**, 62–63; musical compositions, **Vol. 5, Part 2**, 25 f.; **Vol. 9, Part 1**, 530; Nazi persecution, *see* Holocaust; Refugees; newspapers, **Supp. 3**, 513; **Supp. 9**, 724; organizations, *see specific names;* orthodoxy defended, **Vol. 5, Part 1**, 514; **Vol. 8, Part 1**, 383; philanthropy, **Vol. 1, Part 2**, 361; **Vol. 8, Part 2**, 171; **Vol. 9, Part 2**, 131; **Supp. 3**, 31; **Supp. 4**, 261–62; "Pittsburgh Platform" (1885), **Vol. 5, Part 2**, 487; **Supp. 4**, 659; Prayer Book, **Vol. 7, Part 2**, 631; propaganda in behalf of, **Vol. 10, Part 2**, 449; rabbinical training, **Supp. 4**, 905; reform, **Vol. 3, Part 2**, 315; **Vol. 5, Part 2**, 254, 487 f., 490 f.; **Vol. 6, Part 1**, 65, 201; **Vol. 8, Part 1**, 164; Reform branch, **Supp. 1**, 288; **Supp. 3**, 488; **Supp. 4**, 603, 903–6; **Supp. 7**, 689; **Supp. 9**, 320; religion v. nationality issue, **Supp. 4**, 659–60; right to vote, **Vol. 7, Part 1**, 364; secularism, **Supp. 9**, 448; social work, Supp. 29 694; Soviet collective farming by, **Supp. 4**, 699–70; *Spirit of the Ghetto, The*, **Supp. 3**, 329, 330; studies and scholarship, **Supp. 2**, 554, 695; **Supp. 3**, 464; **Supp. 9**, 384, 890, 891; **Supp. 10**, 31; Sunday services, instituted, **Vol. 5, Part 2**, 487; synagogue, first use of organ in a, **Vol. 8, Part 1**, 164; synagogue architecture, **Supp. 5**, 483; theatrical portrayal of, **Supp. 4**, 26–27; Theological Seminary of America, **Vol. 1, Part 1**, 388; **Vol. 5, Part 2**, 487, 490; **Vol. 7, Part 1**, 150; **Vol. 8, Part 2**, 422; theological writings on, **Supp. 4**, 494–95; **Supp. 9**, 384; **Supp. 10**, 31, 330; theology, **Vol. 1, Part 1**, 108 f., 388; **Vol. 3, Part 2**, 65; **Vol. 4, Part 1**, 29; **Vol. 4, Part 2**, 23; **Vol. 8, Part 2**, 565; unity advocacy, **Vol. 10, Part 2**, 426; **Supp. 4**, 593–94; *Year Book*, **Vol. 5, Part 1**, 567. *See also* Holocaust; Immigration; Israel; Refugees; Yiddish literature and language; Zionism
Juday, Chauncey, references to, **Supp. 4**, 84, 85
Judd, Charles H., reference to, **Supp. 6**, 557
Judge, William Quon, reference to, **Vol. 9, Part 2**, 562
Judges. For complete list, *See* Occupations Index

Judges, popular election of, **Vol. 3, Part 1**, 110
"Judicial review" first enunciation of principle, **Vol. 10, Part 2**, 588
Judicial system: "Brandeis brief," **Supp. 3**, 96; capital punishment, **Supp. 6**, 111, Civil procedure rules revision, **Supp. 5**, 502; criminal law practice, **Supp. 5**, 665; defendants' rights, **Supp. 1**, 451; **Supp. 3**, 755; **Supp. 4**, 614; **Supp. 5**, 358–59; **Supp. 7**, 264; economics analysis, **Supp. 3**, 180; ethical standards, **Supp. 1**, 99, 204; expert witness, **Supp. 3**, 320, 385; **Supp. 6**, 403; fact-skepticism approach, **Supp. 7**, 99–100; fictional stories about, **Supp. 3**, 773–74; free press–free trial issues, **Supp. 10**, 608; international, **Supp. 2**, 276, *see also* World Court; jury selection, **Supp. 2**, 385; juvenile court, first, **Supp. 1**, 485; juvenile court movement, **Supp. 3**, 279, 462–63; **Supp. 5**, 84, 746; **Supp. 7**, 251; legal process reforms, **Supp. 3**, 227; military, **Supp. 6**, 34; model statutes and published opinions, **Supp. 7**, 317–18; procedure, writings on, **Supp. 7**, 261; psychiatric testimony, **Supp. 2**, 143; **Supp. 3**, 320; public defender, **Supp. 2**, 248; realism school, **Supp. 7**, 475; reform, **Supp. 1**, 179; **Supp. 2**, 12; **Supp. 6**, 651; self-incrimination laws, **Supp. 1**, 451; sociological jurisprudence, **Supp. 3**, 185–86, 451–52; **Supp. 7**, 625–26, 627, 628; studies in, **Supp. 2**, 501; **Supp. 4**, 491–92; writings on, **Supp. 2**, 94–96; **Supp. 3**, 821–22. *See also* Judciary; Law; Prisons; Supreme Court
Judiciary: appeals court, federal, **Supp. 9**, 744; **Supp. 10**, 324, 394; California, **Supp. 6**, 4; **Supp. 7**, 292–93; **Supp. 9**, 853; champion of the independence of, **Vol. 8, Part 1**, 132 f.; Colorado, **Supp. 3**, 462–63; district court, federal, **Supp. 9**, 865; **Supp. 10**, 863; early development of, **Vol. 3, Part 2**, 112 f.; ethics issues, **Supp. 1**, 99; Federal Court of Customs and Patent Appeals, **Supp. 6**, 228; labor rulings, **Supp. 5**, 248–49; Louisiana, **Supp. 8**, 499; Maryland, **Supp. 9**, 743; Massachusetts, **Supp. 1**, 421–22; **Supp. 4**, 269; "midnight judges," **Vol. 1, Part 1**, 80; **Vol. 5, Part 2**, 28 f.; **Vol. 6, Part 1**, 101; **Vol. 6, Part 2**, 319 f.; Minnesota, **Supp. 10**, 862; New Jersey, **Supp. 1**, 365; **Supp. 6**, 651; New York, **Supp. 3**, 451–52, 190–91, 379–80, 825, 826; **Supp. 5**, 269–70, 357, 493; **Supp. 6**, 88; **Supp. 7**, 316–18; **Supp. 10**, 718–20; North Carolina, **Supp. 5**, 651; Ohio, **Supp. 8**, 4; **Supp. 10**, 607–8; Pennsylvania, **Supp. 3**, 415; **Supp. 10**, 241; **Supp. 7**, 500; **Supp. 8**, 456; Roman Catholic, **Supp. 8**, 46–47; self-restraint doctrine, **Supp. 3**, 94; South Carolina, **Supp. 8**, 682; Wisconsin, **Supp. 10**, 194; women in, **Supp. 6**, 4, 114. *See also* World Court
Judiciary Act: of 1789, **Vol. 7, Part 2**, 294; **Supp. 5**, 731; of 1801, **Vol. 4, Part 2**, 524; **Vol. 5, Part 2**, 29
Judson, Arthur, reference to, **Supp. 6**, 550
Judson Female Institute, **Vol. 3, Part 1**, 141; **Vol. 5, Part 2**, 70
Juilliard Foundation, **Vol. 5, Part 2**, 244
Juilliard Graduate School, **Supp. 10**, 456
Juilliard School of Music: **Supp. 3**, 708, 742; **Supp. 5**, 212; dance department, **Supp. 6**, 313; forerunner, **Supp. 3**, 309; founding of, **Supp. 2**, 140
Julian, Rupert, reference to, **Supp. 6**, 657
Jukebox, manufacture of, **Supp. 10**, 96
Jukes family, sociological studies of, **Vol. 3, Part 1**, 493
Juliana, first ferryboat, **Vol. 9, Part 1**, 615, 619
Jumbo, **Supp. 8**, 547
June, Harold, reference to, **Supp. 6**, 92
Jung, Carl: references to, **Supp. 4**, 108, 130; **Supp. 7**, 347; theories of, **Supp. 4**, 572; **Supp. 5**, 301–2
Jungle, The, **Supp. 8**, 594
"Jungle Jim" (fictional character), **Supp. 6**, 530, 531
Junior Achievement organizations, **Supp. 5**, 51
Junior college movement, **Vol. 1, Part 1**, 522
Junior high school movement, **Vol. 8, Part 2**, 42
Junior League, founding of, **Supp. 1**, 644
Junior Miss, **Supp. 9**, 78
Junior Republic, founding of, **Supp. 2**, 226–27
"Junius Americanus" letters, **Vol. 6, Part 1**, 97
Jupiter (planet), satellites, discovery of, **Supp. 5**, 540; **Supp. 7**, 573
Juries, selection of, **Supp. 2**, 385
"Just from Georgia," column, **Vol. 9, Part 1**, 523
Justice, Department of (U.S.): attorneys general, **Supp. 1**, 359; **Supp. 4**, 536–37, 613, 794; **Supp. 5**, 357, 502; **Supp. 7**, 500–501; **Supp. 8**, 34–35, 322–23, 406; **Supp. 10**, 125–26; Biddle mural criticized, **Supp. 9**, 91; creation of, **Vol. 6, Part 1**, 52; criminal division, **Supp. 5**, 455; ethics issues, **Supp. 3**, 213–14; **Supp. 8**, 406; Hoover service in, **Supp. 9**, 404–5; mural, **Supp. 6**, 597; Prohibition enforcement, **Supp. 7**, 786; prosecutors, **Supp. 6**, 3, 502; reforms, **Supp. 4**, 794; **Supp. 6**, 137–38, 156; **Supp. 10**, 125; U.S. attorneys, **Supp. 3**, 116–17; World War I legal issues, **Supp. 5**, 730
Juvenile books, first collection of, in U.S., **Vol. 8, Part 1**, 51 f.
Juvenile courts, **Supp. 1**, 485; **Supp. 3**, 279, 462–63; **Supp. 5**, 84, 746; **Supp. 7**, 251
Juvenile delinquency: **Vol. 1, Part 1**, 520; **Vol. 4, Part 1**, 217; **Vol. 7, Part 1**, 389; adult responsibility, **Supp. 3**, 462; factors in determining, **Supp. 9**, 318; **Supp. 10**, 280; prevention, **Supp. 4**, 870; **Supp. 5**, 137–38; reformatories, **Supp. 4**, 471–72; social work, **Supp. 7**, 28; **Supp. 8**, 40; Virginia Industrial School for Colored Girls, **Supp. 4**, 53–54; writings on, **Supp. 10**, 280
Juvenile Protective Association, **Supp. 8**, 40
Juvenile Psychopathic Institute, founding of, **Supp. 1**, 485
Juvenile Rambler, probably first magazine for children, **Vol. 1, Part 1**, 143
J. Walter Thompson Co., **Supp. 6**, 672; **Supp. 7**, 641–42

K

Kafka, Franz: first published work, **Supp. 7**, 798; interpretation of, **Supp. 9**, 637; references to, **Supp. 9**, 41, 707, 708
Kahn, Otto, references to, **Supp. 1**, 4; **Supp. 6**, 233
Kahn, Roger, reference to, **Supp. 6**, 366
Kairos Circle, founding of, **Supp. 7**, 746
Kaiser, Georg, reference to, **Supp. 4**, 868
Kaiser, Henry J., reference to, **Supp. 10**, 355
Kaiser Aluminum Corporation, **Supp. 8**, 309
Kaiser-Frazer Corporation: **Supp. 9**, 290–91; founding of, **Supp. 8**, 309
Kaiser Permanente organization, **Supp. 8**, 309
Kalamazoo College, **Vol. 4, Part 1**, 603
Kalich, Bertha, reference to, **Supp. 3**, 277
Kallen, Horace, reference to, **Supp. 6**, 96
Kallikak Family: A Study in the Heredity of Feeblemindedness, The, **Supp. 6**, 241
Kallir, Otto, references to, **Supp. 7**, 566, 557
Kallman, Chester, Auden relationship, **Supp. 9**, 54, 55
Kamen, M. C., reference to, **Supp. 5**, 273
Kane, Elias Kent, references to, **Vol. 1, Part 2**, 433; **Vol. 2, Part 1**, 14
Kanin, Garson, reference to, **Supp. 7**, 355
Kansas: admission to statehood, **Vol. 8, Part 2**, 618; Agricultural College, **Vol. 1, Part 1**, 267; **Vol. 3, Part 2**, 252; agriculture, **Vol. 1, Part 1**, 316; **Vol. 5, Part 2**, 504; Beecher Bible and Rifle Colony, **Vol. 8, Part**

2, 150; "border ruffians," **Vol. 5, Part 2**, 576–77; Brown, John, **Vol. 9, Part 1**, 544; **Vol. 9, Part 2**, 522; business service, **Vol. 6, Part 1**, 618–9; cattle breeding, **Vol. 4, Part 2**, 326; cattle shipping, **Vol. 6, Part 1**, 618 f.; civil war in, **Vol. 7, Part 2**, 579; Emigrant Aid Association, **Vol. 4, Part 2**, 380; first constitutional prohibitory amendment, **Vol. 8, Part 2**, 304; first radio station, **Supp. 3**, 103–4; fraudulent elections in 1871, **Vol. 2, Part 1**, 405; Free-Soil movement, **Vol. 3, Part 1**, 570 f.; **Vol. 4, Part 1**, 394; Free-State movement, **Vol. 3, Part 1**, 202; **Vol. 5, Part 2**, 576; **Vol. 8, Part 2**, 36, 175; Frontier Guard, **Vol. 5, Part 2**, 576; geological researches, **Vol. 8, Part 1**, 247; governors, **Vol. 1, Part 1**, 315 f.; **Vol. 2, Part 1**, 506; **Vol. 2, Part 2**, 523 f.; **Vol. 6, Part 1**, 204 f.; **Vol. 6, Part 2**, 341 f.; **Vol. 7, Part 1**, 197 f.; **Vol. 8, Part 2**, 303; **Supp. 4**, 12; **Supp. 5**, 101; **Supp. 7**, 677–78; **Supp. 8**, 706; growth of, **Vol. 6, Part 2**, 342; **Supp. 9**, 355, 356; guerrillas, **Vol. 8, Part 1**, 294 f.; history of, **Vol. 1, Part 2**, 482; **Vol. 2, Part 1**, 506; **Vol. 8, Part 1**, 54 f.; **Vol. 8, Part 1**, 294 f.; **Vol. 9, Part 1**, 480; **Vol. 9, Part 2**, 403–4; Indian schools, **Vol. 4, Part 2**, 380; Lane's Army of the North, **Vol. 5, Part 2**, 576; "law and order," **Vol. 9, Part 1**, 20; Lecompton Constitution, **Vol. 2, Part 1**, 411; **Vol. 3, Part 1**, 401; legal service, **Vol. 3, Part 1**, 410; Mennonite settlements, **Vol. 5, Part 2**, 504; Montgomery, James, **Vol. 7, Part 1**, 97; Mormon church in, **Vol. 4, Part 2**, 380; newspapers, **Vol. 8, Part 1**, 10 f.; **Vol. 8, Part 2**, 146; **Supp. 3**, 816–17; **Supp. 4**, 12; paintings of, **Supp. 4**, 204; paleontology, **Vol. 10, Part 2**, 310; "Peace now reigns in Kansas," **Vol. 4, Part 1**, 203; political service, **Vol. 1, Part 1**, 315; **Vol. 2, Part 2**, 524; **Vol. 3, Part 1**, 202, 243; **Vol. 4, Part 1**, 203; **Vol. 4, Part 2**, 380; **Vol. 6, Part 1**, 204; **Vol. 7, Part 2**, 70, 393, 549; **Vol. 8, Part 1**, 10, 54, 463; **Vol. 8, Part 2**, 35, 175, 303; **Vol. 9, Part 1**, 20, 524; politics, **Vol. 1, Part 2**, 399; **Vol. 8, Part 2**, 36; **Vol. 4, Part 2**, 326; **Vol. 5, Part 2**, 576–77; **Vol. 8, Part 2**, 150; **Supp. 1**, 677; **Supp. 3**, 105–6, 544–45, **Supp. 5**, 101; **Supp. 8**, 277, 591–92; **Supp. 9**, 355; Populist party, **Vol. 6, Part 1**, 205; Prohibition, **Vol. 6, Part 2**, 342; public service, **Vol. 2, Part 2**, 250; **Vol. 5, Part 1**, 462; raids, **Vol. 1, Part 1**, 403; Republican party, **Supp. 9**, 355–56; sanitation, **Vol. 6, Part 1**, 357–8; science, **Vol. 8, Part 1**, 247; separation of, from Colorado, **Vol. 3, Part 1**, 243; settlement of, **Vol. 7, Part 2**, 71; slavery, **Vol. 3, Part 1**, 202, 400 f.; **Vol. 3, Part 2**, 69; **Vol. 4, Part 1**, 204; **Vol. 5, Part 2**, 576; **Vol. 8, Part 2**, 35; "squatter sovereignty," **Vol. 4, Part 1**, 550; temperance, **Vol. 7, Part 1**, 394; Wakarusa War, **Vol. 3, Part 1**, 202

Kansas City, Mo.: first bureau of charities in, **Vol. 1, Part 2**, 220; jazz style, **Supp. 5**, 534; **Supp. 9**, 847; Jewish charities, **Supp. 4**, 79; Pendergast machine, **Supp. 3**, 596–97, 621

Kansas City Athletics (baseball), **Supp. 6**, 415

Kansas City Blues (baseball), **Supp. 9**, 855

Kansas City Monarchs (baseball), **Supp. 9**, 668; **Supp. 10**, 346

Kansas City Royals (baseball), **Supp. 10**, 567

Kansas City Star (Mo.), **Vol. 7, Part 1**, 428; editorial page, **Supp. 5**, 279

Kansas Commoner, **Vol. 8, Part 2**, 105

Kansas Farmer, **Vol. 1, Part 1**, 316; **Vol. 7, Part 2**, 393

Kansas Industrial Act (1920), **Supp. 4**, 12

Kansas-Nebraska Act (1854): **Vol. 1, Part 1**, 403; **Vol. 1, Part 2**, 158; **Vol. 2, Part 1**, 88, 132, 211; **Vol. 2, Part 2**, 548; **Vol. 3, Part 1**, 344, 400–402; **Vol. 3, Part 2**, 224, 348 f.; **Vol. 4, Part 1**, 203, 607–8; **Vol. 5, Part 1**, 17, 187; **Vol. 5, Part 2**, 576–77; **Vol. 7, Part 2**, 187, 241, 578–79; **Vol. 8, Part 1**, 463, 570; **Vol. 8, Part 2**, 35, 617; **Vol. 9, Part 1**, 20, 331; **Vol. 9, Part 2**, 210, 214, 590, 601; **Vol. 10, Part 1**, 19 f., 122, 357, 599; Branch's speeches on, **Vol. 1, Part 2**, 598; events leading up to, **Vol. 3, Part 1**, 400; newspaper comment, **Vol. 1, Part 2**, 515; passage of, **Vol. 7, Part 2**, 578

Kansas News, **Vol. 8, Part 1**, 10 f.

Kansas State Agricultural College, **Vol. 4, Part 1**, 395; presidency, **Supp. 5**, 364–65

Kansas State University, football team, **Supp. 5**, 458

Kansas Tribune, **Vol. 3, Part 1**, 410

Kant, Immanuel, reference to, **Supp. 3**, 697

Karan, Donna, reference to, **Supp. 9**, 465

Kariton, Mickel, reference to, **Supp. 10**, 783–84

Karloff, Boris, reference to, **Supp. 9**, 820

Karno, Fred, reference to, **Supp. 7**, 462

Károlyi, Count Michael, reference to, **Supp. 4**, 62

Kaskaskia, capture of, Vol. 29 Part 2, 128; **Vol. 8, Part 1**, 51

Kast, Ludwig, reference to, **Supp. 3**, 435

"Kato" (fictional character), **Supp. 9**, 486, 487

Katz, Milton, reference to, **Supp. 7**, 276

Katz, Sam, reference to, **Supp. 9**, 62

Katzenbach, Nicholas, reference to, **Supp. 8**, 322

Kauffmann, John, reference to, **Supp. 8**, 335

Kaufman, George S., references to, **Supp. 3**, 333, 842; **Supp. 6**, 311; **Supp. 7**, 325, 803; **Supp. 8**, 170–71; **Supp. 10**, 146, 311

Kaufman, Irving R., references to, **Supp. 5**, 589; **Supp. 9**, 270; **Supp. 10**, 718

Kazan, Elia: directorial debut, **Supp. 9**, 735; references to, **Supp. 10**, 129, 131

KDKA (radio station), founding of, **Supp. 3**, 184–85

Kean, Charles, reference to, **Vol. 1, Part 2**, 453

Kearsarge, fight with *Alabama*, **Vol. 8, Part 2**, 58

Keaton, Buster, references to, **Supp. 9**, 508; **Supp. 10**, 118

Keedoozle automated store, **Supp. 5**, 604

Keeler, James E., reference to, **Supp. 5**, 540

Keeler, Ruby, reference to, **Supp. 4**, 440

Keeley movement, **Vol. 5, Part 2**, 280

Keene, Laura, reference to, **Vol. 1, Part 2**, 444

Keep American Out of War Committee, **Supp. 8**, 650

Kefauver, Estes; organized-crime hearings, **Supp. 9**, 13, 198, 269, 839; references to, **Supp. 6**, 264, 618; **Supp. 7**, 420, 586, 723; **Supp. 8**, 406; **Supp. 9**, 500, 507; **Supp. 10**, 135, 361

Kefauver-Harris Drug Safety Act (1962), **Supp. 7**, 416

"Kegs, battle of the," **Vol. 5, Part 1**, 222

Kehillah (New York City), founding of, **Supp. 4**, 539

Keith, B. F., references to, **Supp. 1**, 18

Keith-Albee-Orpheum Theaters Corporation, **Supp. 8**, 320

Keitt, Lawrence M., reference to, **Vol. 5, Part 1**, 604

Kellams, Vivian, reference to, **Supp. 7**, 503

Kellar, Harry, reference to, **Supp. 2**, 662

Keller, Allen D., reference to, **Supp. 6**, 223

Kellett, William Wallace, reference to, **Supp. 9**, 228–29

Kelley, Florence, reference to, **Supp. 3**, 576

Kellogg, Arthur, reference to, **Supp. 6**, 330

Kellogg, Frank B., references to, **Supp. 1**, 582; **Supp. 7**, 112, 303

Kellogg, John Harvey, reference to, **Supp. 9**, 614

Kellogg-Briand Peace Pact (1928), **Supp. 2**, 52, 356; **Supp. 3**, 457; **Supp. 4**, 137; **Supp. 7**, 112, 113, 688

Kellogg Sanitorium. *See* Percy Jones Hospital

Kellstadt, Charles, reference to, **Supp. 10**, 163

Kelly, Charles, reference to, **Supp. 6**, 331

Kelly, Edward J., reference to, **Supp. 5**, 448

Kelly, Gene, reference to, **Supp. 10**, 165

Kelly, George, reference to, **Supp. 6**, 331

Kelly, Grace (Princess of Monaco), references to, **Supp. 6**, 331; **Supp. 9**, 61, 451; **Supp. 10**, 160
Kelly, Howard A., reference to, **Supp. 3**, 106; **Supp. 5**, 147
Kelly, John, reference to, **Vol. 8, Part 2**, 425
Kelly, John B., reference to, **Supp. 9**, 451
Kelly, John W., reference to, **Vol. 10, Part 1**, 632 f.
Kelly, Walter, reference to, **Supp. 6**, 331
Kelly's Ford, Va., battle of (Mar. 1, 1863), **Vol. 1, Part 1**, 442; **Vol. 1, Part 2**, 104; **Vol. 7, Part 2**, 408
Kelvinator Co., **Supp. 4**, 621
Kemble, Fanny, reference to, **Vol. 5, Part 1**, 242
Kemper, Reuben, reference to, **Vol. 9, Part 2**, 602
Kemper College, **Vol. 5, Part 2**, 321
Kemper's Insurrection (1810), **Vol. 5, Part 1**, 162; **Vol. 5, Part 2**, 323; **Vol. 9, Part 2**, 602
Kendall, Amos, reference to, **Vol. 7, Part 1**, 250
Kendall, Edward C., references to, **Supp. 3**, 832; **Supp. 7**, 340
Kendrick, John B., reference to, **Supp. 7**, 590
Kenesaw Mountain, battle of, **Vol. 5, Part 2**, 145; **Vol. 6, Part 2**, 160; **Vol. 8, Part 1**, 40–41; **Vol. 9, Part 1**, 95; **Vol. 9, Part 2**, 3,
Kenna, Michael ("Hinky Dink"), reference to, **Supp. 6**, 263
Kennan, George F., references to, **Supp. 4**, 306; **Supp. 8**, 90; **Supp. 9**, 10, 44, 831
Kennard, Margaret, reference to, **Supp. 6**, 223
Kennecott Copper Corporation, **Supp. 6**, 606, 607
Kennedy, Albert J., reference to, **Supp. 6**, 499
Kennedy, Edward M., presidential nomination (1968), draft movement for, **Supp. 10**, 168
Kennedy, Jacqueline, references to, **Supp. 8**, 224; **Supp. 10**, 16, 17, 94, 174, 534
Kennedy, John F.: assassination of, **Supp. 7**, 425, 593–94; **Supp. 8**, 607; **Supp. 9**, 413; 434; assassination of, conspiracy theory regarding, **Supp. 9**, 715–16; assassination of, only suspect brought to trial for, **Supp. 9**, 716; Bay of Pigs policy, **Supp. 8**, 147; Berlin Wall crisis, **Supp. 9**, 799; **Supp. 10**, 128–29; church-state separation statement, **Supp. 8**, 614; civil rights movement, **Supp. 8**, 333; Cuban missile crisis, **Supp. 9**, 106–7, 449–50, 799; Cushing relationship, **Supp. 8**, 115–16; economic advisers, **Supp. 10**, 287; foreign aid programs, **Supp. 10**, 129; foreign relations, **Supp. 10**, 529; grandfather, **Supp. 4**, 277, 278; Hoffa hatred for, **Supp. 9**, 397; "Irish Mafia" advisory group, **Supp. 10**, 604; Johnson, L. B., chosen as running mate, **Supp. 10**, 604; Johnson, L. B., relationship, **Supp. 9**, 433–34; Kennedy, Robert, relationship, **Supp. 8**, 321–22; labor relations, **Supp. 10**, 494; McCormack relationship, **Supp. 10**, 486; Nixon Senate campaign, contribution to, **Supp. 10**, 184; O'Donnell relationship, **Supp. 10**, 604; presidency, **Supp. 7**, 273, 296, 454, 723, 724; presidential candidacy, **Supp. 8**, 321, 361; **Supp. 9**, 58, 433; **Supp. 10**, 168; press relations, **Supp. 8**, 396; references to, **Supp. 9**, 3, 10, 187, 751; **Supp. 10**, 17, 469; Senate, **Supp. 7**, 383; senatorial campaign (1952), **Supp. 10**, 604; steel industry showdown, **Supp. 9**, 403; urban policy, **Supp. 10**, 109; vice-presidential bid, **Supp. 7**, 416; **Supp. 9**, 58; *Why England Slept*, **Supp. 7**, 274; writings on, **Supp. 8**, 224
Kennedy, Joseph P.: family, **Supp. 4**, 277–78; **Supp. 7**, 418, 419; **Supp. 8**, 321; film interests, **Supp. 6**, 658; **Supp. 10**, 872; politics, **Supp. 6**, 660; **Supp. 7**, 454; references to, **Supp. 9**, 62, 607, 700, 747; Spellman relationship, **Supp. 8**, 613, 614
Kennedy, Patrick J., reference to, **Supp. 6**, 139
Kennedy, Richard, associate of Mary Baker Eddy, **Vol. 3, Part 2**, 9
Kennedy, Robert F.: as attorney general, **Supp. 7**, 421, 423, 425; assassination of, **Supp. 9**, 437; civil rights movement, **Supp. 8**, 333, 334, 335; attorney general appointment, **Supp. 9**, 88; defense contracts investigation, **Supp. 6**, 618; Democratic National Committee role, **Supp. 9**, 59; Hoffa hatred for, **Supp. 9**, 397; Johnson, L. B., relationship, **Supp. 9**, 433; McClellan Committee counsel, **Supp. 10**, 482; O'Donnell relationship, **Supp. 10**, 604, 605; organized-crime investigation, **Supp. 9**, 307; presidential bid, **Supp. 9**, 450; Teamsters Union investigations, **Supp. 9**, 396
Kennedy Center for the Performing Arts (Washington, D.C.), design of, **Supp. 10**, 765
Kennedy International Airport (New York City): predecessor, **Supp. 4**, 466; Trans World Airlines Terminal, **Supp. 7**, 672
Kennelly, Martin H., reference to, **Supp. 10**, 167
Kenney, George C., reference to, **Supp. 7**, 490
Kenny, John V., reference to, **Supp. 6**, 266
Kent, Robert H., reference to, **Supp. 6**, 656
Kent, Rockwell, references to, **Supp. 7**, 306; **Supp. 8**, 590
Kent State University, student deaths at, **Supp. 10**, 98–99
Kentucke Almanac, pioneer pamphlet of the West, **Vol. 1, Part 2**, 557
Kentucky: admission to statehood, **Vol. 2, Part 1**, 131; **Vol. 5, Part 2**, 222; **Vol. 6, Part 2**, 313; agriculture, **Vol. 3, Part 1**, 491 f.; **Vol. 9, Part 1**, 18; Baptist church in, **Vol. 10, Part 1**, 383 f.; barnstorming in, **Vol. 6, Part 1**, 493; Bell-Everett party, **Vol. 4, Part 2**, 269; black education in, **Supp. 5**, 642; boundary disputes, **Vol. 4, Part 2**, 513; bridge engineering, **Vol. 9, Part 1**, 251; Catholic church, **Vol. 3, Part 1**, 90; **Vol. 3, Part 2**, 329; **Vol. 6, Part 2**, 50, 194, 616; **Vol. 10, Part 2**, 346; Catholic missions, **Vol. 1, Part 1**, 448 f.; church-state separation issues, **Supp. 5**, 461; Civil War agitation, **Vol. 2, Part 1**, 235; **Vol. 3, Part 1**, 114; **Vol. 4, Part 2**, 243 f., 269; **Vol. 5, Part 1**, 562; **Vol. 6, Part 2**, 200; **Vol. 8, Part 2**, 53; Clay's influence, **Vol. 2, Part 2**, 173 f.; coal survey, **Vol. 6, Part 1**, 189; Committee of 13, **Vol. 8, Part 1**, 148 f.; Democratic party before Civil War, **Vol. 2, Part 1**, 371; Disciples of Christ, established, **Vol. 1, Part 1**, 207; dramatic presentations, **Vol. 3, Part 1**, 432; education, **Vol. 7, Part 2**, 302 f., 389; **Vol. 8, Part 1**, 643 f.; exploration, **Vol. 3, Part 2**, 382; first recorded expedition to, by white man, **Vol. 10, Part 1**, 360 f.; first woman admitted to bar, **Supp. 4**, 106–7; framing of constitution, **Vol. 8, Part 1**, 537 f.; geological survey of 1854, **Vol. 7, Part 2**, 499; governors, **Vol. 1, Part 2**, 317, 576 f., 595 f.; **Vol. 2, Part 1**, 140 f.; **Vol. 2, Part 2**, 133 f.; **Vol. 3, Part 1**, 254 f.; **Vol. 4, Part 1**, 159 f., 352, 589 f.; **Vol. 4, Part 2**, 513 f.; **Vol. 5, Part 2**, 470; **Vol. 6, Part 1**, 193; **Vol. 6, Part 2**, 3, 199 f., 584 f.; **Vol. 7, Part 1**, 157 f., 158 f.; **Vol. 7, Part 2**, 122 f.; **Vol. 8, Part 2**, 487; **Vol. 9, Part 1**, 60 f., 633 f.; **Vol. 10, Part 2**, 312; **Supp. 1**, 564; **Supp. 6**, 591–92; history, **Vol. 1, Part 2**, 442; **Vol. 2, Part 1**, 256, 546; **Vol. 3, Part 1**, 491 f., 555 f.; **Vol. 3, Part 2**, 382, 461; **Vol. 4, Part 2**, 246, 353; **Vol. 5, Part 1**, 218; **Vol. 6, Part 2**, 329; **Vol. 8, Part 1**, 148 f., 186 f.; **Vol. 9, Part 1**, 18; Indian land rights in, **Vol. 4, Part 2**, 531; land claims, **Vol. 3, Part 2**, 425; **Vol. 9, Part 2**, 575; land speculation, **Vol. 5, Part 1**, 461; laws, **Vol. 6, Part 1**, 296; **Vol. 7, Part 1**, 157; legal service, **Vol. 1, Part 2**, 235, 533, 595; **Vol. 3, Part 1**, 495; **Vol. 4, Part 2**, 243 f.; **Vol. 5, Part 1**, 485; **Vol. 6, Part 1**, 218, 277; **Vol. 7, Part 2**, 123; **Vol. 9, Part 2**, 601, 643; **Vol. 10, Part 1**, 115; "Lincoln guns," **Vol. 4, Part 2**, 267; Lincoln's life in, **Vol. 6, Part 1**, 243; Mammoth Cave, **Vol. 5, Part 1**, 328; missions in, **Vol. 1, Part 1**, 448 f.;

Vol. 8, Part 1, 537 f.; neutrality in Civil War, **Vol. 2, Part 1**, 235; **Vol. 8, Part 1**, 39 f., 148 f.; normal schools in, **Vol. 8, Part 1**, 643; novels about, **Supp. 3**, 637–38; "old" and "new" court, **Vol. 8, Part 2**, 23; pioneering, **Vol. 1, Part 1**, 554; **Vol. 2, Part 1**, 256; **Vol. 6, Part 1**, 357 f., 365, 533; **Vol. 7, Part 1**, 483; **Vol. 9, Part 1**, 61; pioneer medicine men, **Vol. 6, Part 2**, 4; police force, Fox's, **Vol. 3, Part 2**, 570; political service, **Vol. 1, Part 1**, 124, 527, 533; **Vol. 1, Part 2**, 235, 316, 317, 442, 557, 576, 595; **Vol. 2, Part 2**, 133, 328, 546, 571; **Vol. 3, Part 1**, 113, 254, 557; **Vol. 3, Part 2**, 29; **Vol. 4, Part 1**, 159, 353, 590; **Vol. 4, Part 2**, 243 f.; **Vol. 5, Part 1**, 69, 587; **Vol. 5, Part 2**, 470; **Vol. 6, Part 1**, 193, 218, 277, 542; **Vol. 6, Part 2**, 3, 104, 200, 310, 584; **Vol. 7, Part 1**, 158; **Vol. 8, Part 1**, 111, 148, 205, 271; **Vol. 8, Part 2**, 195, 487; **Vol. 9, Part 1**, 60, 170, 526, 633; **Vol. 10, Part 1**, 115, 552 f.; **Vol. 10, Part 2**, 182, 304, 312; politics, **Vol. 2, Part 1**, 495; **Vol. 4, Part 2**, 513; **Vol. 8, Part 2**, 23; **Supp. 5**, 712; **Supp. 6**, 436, 591–92; **Supp. 8**, 615–16; Presbyterian church in, **Vol. 2, Part 1**, 435; **Vol. 6, Part 2**, 57; **Vol. 8, Part 1**, 271 f.; printing, **Vol. 1, Part 2**, 557; public health, **Vol. 6, Part 1**, 606; public schools, **Vol. 2, Part 1**, 11; public service, **Vol. 7, Part 1**, 2; **Vol. 4, Part 2**, 32, 61; **Vol. 7, Part 2**, 123, 500; **Vol. 8, Part 2**, 23, 195; **Vol. 9, Part 1**, 285, 440 f.; race-horse breeding in, **Vol. 6, Part 2**, 180; **Supp. 9**, 866; railroad development in, **Vol. 8, Part 1**, 357 f.; Reconstruction, **Vol. 2, Part 1**, 55; **Vol. 3, Part 1**, 114; religious revival of 1800, **Vol. 6, Part 2**, 57; rise of the Republican party in, **Vol. 4, Part 1**, 391; sculpture, **Vol. 4, Part 2**, 358; secession, opposition to, **Vol. 8, Part 1**, 148 f., 186 f.; separation from Virginia, **Vol. 10, Part 2**, 223; slavery, **Vol. 1, Part 2**, 292; **Vol. 29, Part 1**, 371; Spanish plots, **Vol. 7, Part 1**, 483; **Vol. 8, Part 2**, 195; **Vol. 9, Part 2**, 326; stock breeding in, **Vol. 6, Part 2**, 412; surveying, **Vol. 2, Part 2**, 173; **Vol. 9, Part 1**, 60; Swiss settlement in, **Vol. 3, Part 1**, 491 f.; Transylvania Co., **Vol. 4, Part 2**, 354; Trappist monastery in, **Vol. 8, Part 2**, 286; union cause, **Vol. 3, Part 1**, 114; Virginia and Kentucky Resolutions, **Vol. 1, Part 1**, 36; Whig party, **Vol. 4, Part 2**, 267; WPA political investigation, **Supp. 6**, 601–2; writings, **Vol. 6, Part 1**, 296; **Vol. 10, Part 1**, 383 f.

Kentucky Resolutions. *See* Virginia and Kentucky Resolutions

Kentucky University, **Vol. 1, Part 2**, 520; **Vol. 8, Part 1**, 643

Kent v. *Dulles*, **Supp. 9**, 458

Kenyon, W. Johnson, reference to, **Supp. 7**, 183

Kenyon and Eckhardt, **Supp. 8**, 52–53

Kenyon College: **Vol. 2, Part 2**, 66; **Vol. 3, Part 1**, 406; **Vol. 9, Part 1**, 126, 436; **Vol. 9, Part 2**, 299, 301; literature studies, **Supp. 9**, 643

Kenyon Review, founding of, **Supp. 9**, 643

Kern, Jerome, references to, **Supp. 4**, 226; **Supp. 6**, 273; **Supp. 7**, 198; **Supp. 9**, 280, 281

Kerner, Otto, references to, **Supp. 9**, 551, 552; **Supp. 10**, 168

Kerner Commission. *See* National Advisory Commission on Civil Disorders

Kerosene oil, early use of, for illumination, **Vol. 3, Part 1**, 415

Kerouac, Jack, reference to, **Supp. 9**, 846

Kerr, Robert, reference to, **Supp. 6**, 484

Kerr, Russell, reference to, **Supp. 6**, 309

Kerr, William H., reference to, **Supp. 3**, 587

Kerr-McGee Nuclear Corporation, health and safety hazards at, **Supp. 9**, 726–27

Kerr-McGee Oil Industries, **Supp. 7**, 428

Kerr natural gas deregulation bill (1949), **Supp. 7**, 636

Kershaw's Brigade, **Vol. 5, Part 2**, 359

Kesselring, Joseph, reference to, **Supp. 6**, 311

Kessler, David, reference to, **Supp. 6**, 566

Kettering, Charles F., references to, **Supp. 3**, 522; **Supp. 4**, 244

Kewpie doll, **Supp. 3**, 573

Key, Francis Scott, reference to, **Vol. 1, Part 1**, 347

Keyes, Frederick G., reference to, **Supp. 6**, 345

Keyes, Henry Wilder, reference to, **Supp. 8**, 328

Keynes, John Maynard: references to, **Supp. 3**, 656; **Supp. 5**, 85, 272; **Supp. 8**, 446; economic theory, **Supp. 9**, 362–63, 366; **Supp. 10**, 382

Keyseling, Leon, reference to, **Supp. 9**, 589

Keystone Bridge Co., **Vol. 9, Part 2**, 385

Keystone Film Co., **Supp. 2**, 672; **Supp. 6**, 573; **Supp. 7**, 177, 238

Keystone Studios, comedies, **Supp. 10**, 115

Key West, Fla., **Supp. 7**, 336

Kharasch, Morris, reference to, **Supp. 4**, 337

Khirbet Nahas (ruin), **Supp. 9**, 320

Khrushchev, Nikita: interview with, **Supp. 9**, 188; references to, **Supp. 7**, 421, 422, 423–24; **Supp. 8**, 6, 158, 159, 258, 323, 497; **Supp. 9**, 106, 506; **Supp. 10**, 271, 462; U-2 overflights espionage evidence, **Supp. 10**, 647

Kidd, Captain, **Vol. 5, Part 2**, 367 f.

Kidder, A. M., & Co., **Supp. 7**, 604

Kidnapping: "crime of the century" (Franks), **Supp. 9**, 490; legislation against, **Vol. 4, Part 1**, 482; of Cudahy, **Supp. 8**, 109–10; of Getty, J. P., III, **Supp. 10**, 276–77; of Hearst, P., **Supp. 10**, 135; of Lindbergh baby, **Supp. 3**, 142; **Supp. 9**, 405; of Urschel, **Supp. 5**, 381–82

Kidneys: disease research, **Supp. 5**, 111, 438; function studies, **Supp. 7**, 699–700; one of first operations on, **Vol. 8, Part 1**, 378

Kierkegaard, Soren, reference to, **Supp. 2**, 643

Kilauea, **Supp. 5**, 361

Kilbane, Johnny, reference to, **Supp. 7**, 209

Kilbride, Percy, references to, **Supp. 9**, 535, 536

Kilgore, Bernard ("Barney"), reference to, **Supp. 9**, 520

Killian, James, reference to, **Supp. 7**, 275

Kill Van Kull Bridge (N.J.), **Supp. 7**, 11

Kilpatrick, William H., reference to, **Supp. 3**, 677

Kimball, Helen C., reference to, **Vol. 9, Part 2**, 333 f.

Kimball Art Museum (Fort Worth, Tex.), design of, **Supp. 9**, 446

"Kimble, Richard" (fictional character), **Supp. 10**, 380

Kimmel, Husband E., references to, **Supp. 4**, 686, 745; **Supp. 6**, 629; **Supp. 7**, 813; **Supp. 8**, 42

Kincheloe, Samuel C., reference to, **Supp. 3**, 363

Kindergarten Guide, **Vol. 5, Part 2**, 500

Kindergartens: **Vol. 1, Part 2**, 392, 393, 575; **Vol. 2, Part 2**, 412; Vol. 4, Part 2 90, 338; **Vol. 5, Part 2**, 499 f.; **Vol. 6, Part 2**, 355; **Vol. 7, Part 2**, 336; **Vol. 8, Part 2**, 560; **Vol. 9, Part 1**, 47; **Vol. 10, Part 2**, 190; first free, **Supp. 1**, 13; first Hebrew in U.S., **Supp. 1**, 407; manufacture of materials for, **Vol. 1, Part 2**, 574; progressive methods, **Supp. 4**, 373–74; public school, **Supp. 5**, 437–38; teacher training, **Supp. 4**, 874–75; writings on, **Vol. 5, Part 2**, 499. *See also* Preschool education

King, Alexander, reference to, **Supp. 6**, 257

King, Charles B., reference to, **Supp. 4**, 292

King, Clarence, references to, **Vol. 5, Part 1**, 457; **Vol. 10, Part 1**, 547 f.

King, Dexter, reference to, **Vol. 1, Part 2**, 149

King, Edward, references to, **Supp. 3**, 175; **Supp. 5**, 720
King, Ernest J., references to, **Supp. 3**, 662; **Supp. 4**, 305; **Supp. 5**, 695; **Supp. 6**, 188; **Supp. 7**, 749
King, Harold, references to, **Supp. 5**, 558, 559
King, Henrietta M., references to, **Supp. 9**, 459, 463
King, Martin Luther, Jr.: assassination of, **Supp. 10**, 169; Hoover vendetta against, **Supp. 9**, 407; March on Washington role, **Supp. 10**, 661; references to, **Supp. 7**, 425; **Supp. 8**, 116, 323, 435, 458; **Supp. 9**, 138, 424, 425, 750, 882; **Supp. 10**, 386; Southern Christian Leadership Council, founding of, **Supp. 10**, 170–71
King, Richard, references to, **Supp. 9**, 459, 463
King, Thomas, reference to, **Supp. 3**, 516
King, Thomas Starr, references to, **Vol. 9, Part 1**, 550; **Vol. 10, Part 1**, 651 f.
King, William H., reference to, **Supp. 6**, 114
King Cole Trio, **Supp. 7**, 131
King Features Syndicate, **Supp. 3**, 428; **Supp. 5**, 286; **Supp. 6**, 530, 538
King George's War, **Vol. 8, Part 1**, 195 f.
King Kong, **Supp. 7**, 580; **Supp. 9**, 459, 463–64
King Oliver's Creole Jazz Band, **Supp. 2**, 502
King Philip's War, **Vol. 2, Part 2**, 99; **Vol. 3, Part 1**, 481 f.; **Vol. 4, Part 1**, 360; **Vol. 4, Part 2**, 396; **Vol. 6, Part 1**, 97; **Vol. 7, Part 2**, 1534; **Vol. 8, Part 1**, 290 f.; **Vol. 8, Part 2**, 201
King Ranch, **Supp. 9**, 459, 463–64; largest beef producer in U.S., **Supp. 9**, 464
King's College. *See* Columbia Univeristy
King's Henchman, The (opera), **Supp. 4**, 576; **Supp. 8**, 645
Kings Mountain, battle of (Oct. 7, 1780), **Vol. 2, Part 1**, 465; **Vol. 6, Part 2**, 33; **Vol. 8, Part 2**, 603; **Vol. 9, Part 1**, 61
King's Mountain Military School, establishment of, **Vol. 5, Part 2**, 49
Kingston, N.H., incorporation of, **Vol. 8, Part 1**, 193 f.
Kinsey, Alfred, references to, **Supp. 6**, 252, 718
Kiowa Indians, **Vol. 5, Part 2**, 367
Kipling, Rudyard, reference to, **Supp. 1**, 260
Kiplinger Washington Letter, founding of, **Supp. 8**, 338
Kips Bay Boys Club (New York City), design of, **Supp. 2**, 7
Kirby, Allan P., references to, **Supp. 6**, 721; **Supp. 10**, 568
"Kirby, Rip" (fictional character), **Supp. 6**, 530, 531
Kirby, Rollin, references to, **Supp. 7**, 369, 370
Kirchwey, Freda, references to, **Supp. 3**, 420; **Supp. 10**, 502, 503
Kirk, Russell, references to, **Supp. 9**, 548, 549
Kirk-Holden War, **Vol. 7, Part 2**, 361; **Vol. 8, Part 1**, 379
Kirkland, James H., reference to, **Supp. 3**, 129
Kirstein, Lincoln, references to, **Supp. 7**, 55; **Supp. 9**, 267, 268
Kirtland Society of Natural Science, **Vol. 5, Part 2**, 439
Kiss and Tell, **Supp. 9**, 481
Kissinger, Henry: Elliott relationship, **Supp. 10**, 217; reference to, **Supp. 9**, 10
Kiss Me Kate, **Supp. 9**, 748
"Kitchen Cabinet," **Vol. 3, Part 1**, 610; **Vol. 4, Part 1**, 540; **Vol. 5, Part 1**, 532; **Vol. 5, Part 2**, 326; **Vol. 6, Part 1**, 226; **Vol. 10, Part 1**, 154
Kites: aeronautical experiments with, **Vol. 8, Part 2**, 184; high-altitude exploration, **Supp. 3**, 479
Kittredge, George Lyman, references to, **Supp. 3**, 454; **Supp. 4**, 502
Kitty Foyle, **Supp. 6**, 465
Klauber, Adolph E., reference to, **Supp. 4**, 187
Kleberg, Richard, reference to, **Supp. 9**, 430–31
Kleberg, Robert Justus, Jr., reference to, **Supp. 9**, 459
Kleiber, Erich, reference to, **Supp. 6**, 456
Klein, Arthur L., reference to, **Supp. 8**, 439
Klein, Ben, reference to, **Supp. 9**, 465
Klein, Felix, references to, **Supp. 3**, 574, 575, 791
Klem, Bill, reference to, **Supp. 9**, 329
Klingensmith, Frank L., reference to, **Supp. 4**, 300
Klondike, verse about, **Supp. 6**, 574
Klopfer, Donald, references to, **Supp. 7**, 3; **Supp. 9**, 164, 165
Klystron device, **Supp. 4**, 358
K-Mart stores, founding of, **Supp. 8**, 348
Knapp, Charles, reference to, **Supp. 8**, 236
Knapp, Joseph Palmer, reference to, **Supp. 3**, 442–43
Knappen Engineering, founding of, **Supp. 5**, 396
Knaths, Karl, reference to, **Supp. 6**, 552
Knauff, Ellen, reference to, **Supp. 7**, 542
Kneisel Quartet, **Vol. 5, Part 2**, 460 f.; **Vol. 9, Part 2**, 305
Knepper, Jimmy, reference to, **Supp. 10**, 544
Knickerbocker Magazine, **Vol. 2, Part 2**, 137, 149
Knickerbocker School, **Vol. 7, Part 1**, 207
Knickerbocker Whist Club (New York City), **Supp. 6**, 134
Knight, Charles Y., reference to, **Supp. 5**, 654
Knight, Robert, reference to, **Supp. 6**, 527
Knight Errant, **Supp. 3**, 196
Knight-Ridder Newspapers, founding of, **Supp. 9**, 660
Knights of Columbus, founding of, **Vol. 6, Part 2**, 53
Knights of Labor, **Vol. 1, Part 1**, 231; **Vol. 4, Part 1**, 215, 240; **Vol. 5, Part 2**, 195; **Vol. 8, Part 1**, 142; **Vol. 9, Part 1**, 581; **Vol. 9, Part 2**, 640; **Supp. 3**, 249, 346, 516. *See also* Haymarket Riot
Knights of Pythias. *See* Order of the Knights of Pythias
Knights of Pythias Band, **Supp. 6**, 275
Knights of the Golden Circle, **Vol. 3, Part 2**, 168; **Vol. 5, Part 1**, 271; **Vol. 5, Part 2**, 378; **Vol. 7, Part 1**, 263.
Knitting machinery, **Vol. 3, Part 2**, 132; **Vol. 5, Part 2**, 54; **Vol. 9, Part 1**, 190
Knoblauch (Knoblock), Edward, reference to, **Supp. 3**, 277
Knock on Any Door, **Supp. 7**, 558
Knoll Associates, **Supp. 4**, 715; **Supp. 7**, 670
Knopf, Alfred A., references to, **Supp. 6**, 445, 471; **Supp. 7**, 2; **Supp. 8**, 341–421 **Supp. 10**, 424
Knopf, Alfred A., Co., **Supp. 8**, 341–43; book design, **Supp. 6**, 186
Knowland, Joseph Russell, reference to, **Supp. 9**, 467
Knowland, William F., reference to, **Supp. 8**, 341
Knowledge: philosophical theory of, **Supp. 2**, 639; **Supp. 7**, 471; vital symbolism concept, **Supp. 2**, 9–10. *See also* Learning
Know-Nothing party, **Vol. 1, Part 1**, 578, 605; **Vol. 1, Part 2**, 350, 515; **Vol. 3, Part 2**, 6, 381; **Vol. 4, Part 1**, 307, 142; **Vol. 5, Part 1**, 26; **Vol. 5, Part 2**, 238; **Vol. 6, Part 1**, 40, 240; **Vol. 7, Part 1**, 528; **Vol. 7, Part 2**, 59; **Vol. 8, Part 2**, 58, 248, 617; **Vol. 9, Part 2**, 379; **Vol. 10, Part 2**, 323
Knox, Frank, references to, **Supp. 3**, 543; **Supp. 6**, 339, 340; **Supp. 7**, 720; **Supp. 9**, 356
Knox, Seymour, reference to, **Supp. 6**, 689
Knox College, **Vol. 1, Part 2**, 351; **Vol. 4, Part 1**, 99
Knoxville, Tenn., public service to, **Vol. 6, Part 2**, 48
Knoxville campaign (1863), **Vol. 1, Part 2**, 586; **Vol. 2, Part 1**, 177, 236, 311; **Vol. 5, Part 1**, 392; **Vol. 5, Part 2**, 425; **Vol. 6, Part 2**, 121
Knoxville Gazette, **Vol. 8, Part 2**, 190
Knudsen, William S., references to, **Supp. 4**, 300, 301; **Supp. 7**, 794; **Supp. 8**, 610
Kobe College, founding of, **Vol. 3, Part 1**, 132
Koch, Robert, references to, **Vol. 7, Part 1**, 541; **Supp. 3**, 400; **Supp. 4**, 48, 684, 865; **Supp. 6**, 481

Kocourek, Albert, reference to, **Supp. 3**, 186
Kodachrome, invention of, **Supp. 7**, 511, 512
Kodak Co. *See* Eastman Kodak Co.
Koffka, Kurt, references to, **Supp. 3**, 808; **Supp. 8**, 343
Köhler, Wolfgang, references to, **Supp. 3**, 429, 808
Kohler Co. management, **Supp. 2**, 366
Kohut Foundation, establishment of, **Vol. 5, Part 2**, 491
Kolhörster, Werner, reference to, **Supp. 7**, 134
Kollmar, Richard Tompkins, reference to, **Supp. 7**, 433
Kolster Radio Corporation, **Supp. 6**, 591
Konitz, Lee, reference to, **Supp. 10**, 791
Konoye, Fumumaro, reference to, **Supp. 7**, 303
Koppers Co., **Supp. 5**, 643
Korda, Alexander, references to, **Supp. 7**, 461; **Supp. 10**, 23, 599, 600
Korea: **Vol. 1, Part 1**, 324; **Vol. 3, Part 1**, 579 f.; **Vol. 4, Part 1**, 526; **Vol. 6, Part 1**, 146, 468; **Vol. 8, Part 2**, 78; Bible translations into Korean, **Vol. 5, Part 2**, 172; **Vol. 10, Part 1**, 113; diplomatic relations with, **Vol. 3, Part 2**, 560; **Vol. 4, Part 1**, 526; **Vol. 9, Part 2**, 613; emigration from, to Hawaiian Islands, **Vol. 5, Part 2**, 172; laws, **Vol. 4, Part 1**, 526; missions, **Vol. 1, Part 1**, 224, 324; **Vol. 5, Part 2**, 171 f.; **Vol. 6, Part 2**, 122; newspapers, **Vol. 5, Part 2**, 172; writings on, **Vol. 5, Part 2**, 172
Korean Commission, **Vol. 9, Part 2**, 423
Korean War: American ground forces command, **Supp. 4**, 857; army engineers, **Supp. 6**, 509; aviation in, **Supp. 8**, 292, 633; **Supp. 9**, 596; **Supp. 10**, 378; cease-fire, **Supp. 6**, 326–27; **Supp. 8**, 158; Chinese intervention, **Supp. 9**, 813, 814; congressional opposition to, **Supp. 5**, 467; defense production, **Supp. 5**, 482; **Supp. 7**, 587; entertainment of troops, **Supp. 9**, 540; expansion advocacy, **Supp. 5**, 478; **Supp. 10**, 87; foreign correspondents, **Supp. 8**, 259–60; integration of combat units, **Supp. 9**, 519; MacArthur recall, **Supp. 5**, 676, 706; **Supp. 6**, 432; **Supp. 7**, 74, 492–93; **Supp. 8**, 421–22; **Supp. 9**, 9, 596, 813; military action, **Supp. 7**, 351–52; **Supp. 9**, 630; mobilization, **Supp. 9**, 874; naval fleet, **Supp. 5**, 622; **Supp. 6**, 326; political issues over, **Supp. 5**, 676; **Supp. 9**, 596; support for, **Supp. 7**, 763; United Nations Command, **Supp. 8**, 699; U.S. policy in, **Supp. 9**, 9
Korematsu v. *United States*, **Supp. 9**, 96
Kornei, Otto, reference to, **Supp. 8**, 71
Kossel, Albrecht, reference to, **Supp. 5**, 149
Kossuth's cause, **Vol. 5, Part 2**, 418
Kostelanetz, André, reference to, **Supp. 10**, 640
Koszta affair, **Vol. 5, Part 1**, 477
Koussevitzky, Serge, references to, **Supp. 4**, 715; **Supp. 6**, 456; **Supp. 7**, 652; **Supp. 8**, 145; **Supp. 10**, 312, 422, 638
Koussevitzky Music Foundation, **Supp. 10**, 423
Koverman, Ida, references to, **Supp. 6**, 440; **Supp. 8**, 281–82
Kowal, Charles T., reference to, **Supp. 5**, 540
Kozelugh, Karel, reference to, **Supp. 6**, 539
Kozlowski, Anthony, reference to, **Supp. 5**, 305
Kraft Foods Co., founding of, **Supp. 5**, 399–400
"Kraft Music Hall, The" (radio program), **Supp. 5**, 188, 400; **Supp. 6**, 83; **Supp. 7**, 403; **Supp. 10**, 159
Kramer, Stanley, reference to, **Supp. 8**, 660
Kramers, H. A., reference to, **Supp. 7**, 134
Krasner, Lee, reference to, **Supp. 6**, 512, 513
Krause, Allen K., reference to, **Supp. 4**, 49
Krause, Charles A., reference to, **Supp. 9**, 218
Krauth, Charles Porterfield, reference to, **Vol. 8, Part 2**, 441
Krazy Kat (jazz pantomime), **Supp. 5**, 103, 104
Kresge, S. S., Co., founding of, **Supp. 8**, 347–49
Kresge Foundation, founding of, **Supp. 8**, 348–49
Kress, S. H., Co., founding of, **Supp. 5**, 401
Kreuger, Ivar, references to, **Supp. 4**, 258; **Supp. 6**, 250, 287
Kreutzberg, Harald, reference to, **Supp. 9**, 494
Krey, Laura, reference to, **Supp. 6**, 251
Krieger, Robby, references to, **Supp. 9**, 563, 564
Kristol, Irving, reference to, **Supp. 10**, 25
Kroeber, A. L., reference to, **Supp. 6**, 524
Kroger Grocery and Baking Co., founding of, **Supp. 2**, 367–68
Kronprinzessin Cecilie, decision in case of, **Vol. 8, Part 1**, 285 f.
Kubelik, reference to, **Supp. 9**, 292
Kubrick, Stanley, reference to, **Supp. 10**, 583
Krueger, Louise, reference to, **Supp. 6**, 557
Kuhn, Loeb & Co., **Supp. 1**, 457; **Supp. 9**, 773
Kühne, Wilhelm, reference to, **Supp. 3**, 163
Ku Klux Klan: **Vol. 1, Part 2**, 432; **Vol. 2, Part 1**, 595; **Vol. 2, Part 2**, 187; **Vol. 3, Part 2**, 533; **Vol. 4, Part 1**, 424; **Vol. 4, Part 2**, 215; **Vol. 5, Part 1**, 81; **Vol. 5, Part 2**, 114; **Vol. 8, Part 1**, 33 f., 64 f., 118 f.; **Vol. 8, Part 2**, 384, 499; **Vol. 10, Part 1**, 118; editorial opposition to, **Supp. 3**, 816–17; **Supp. 6**, 11; **Supp. 7**, 324; judicial opposition to, **Supp. 8**, 24; legislation against, **Supp. 3**, 718–19; membership in, **Supp. 9**, 95, 840; membership expos, **Supp. 3**, 80; political opposition to, **Supp. 3**, 267, 331; **Supp. 7**, 242; **Supp. 10**, 618; political support for, **Supp. 5**, 701; political support from, **Supp. 3**, 317–18; **Supp. 5**, 290; **Supp. 6**, 507; resurgence of, **Supp. 3**, 708–9; **Supp. 4**, 235; **Supp. 7**, 361; targets of, **Supp. 3**, 463; writings supporting, **Supp. 4**, 876
Kullback, Solomon, reference to, **Supp. 8**, 196
Kunsman, Charles H., references to, **Supp. 6**, 151; **Supp. 9**, 303, 304
Kwakiutl Indians, **Supp. 3**, 83
Kyser, Kay, reference to, **Supp. 10**, 239

L

Labor, Department of (U.S.): **Vol. 6, Part 1**, 171; administration, **Supp. 2**, 122; **Supp. 4**, 219–20, 724; **Supp. 5**, 194–95, 692; **Supp. 7**, 543–44, 609–10; black issues, **Supp. 6**, 285; established, **Vol. 1, Part 2**, 335; **Vol. 10, Part 2**, 545; Industries and Immigration Bureau, **Supp. 5**, 381; Women's Bureau, **Supp. 2**, 408; **Supp. 7**, 12–13
Labor and Aid Society, **Vol. 4, Part 1**, 238
Labor and labor movement: **Vol. 4, Part 1**, 288; **Vol. 4, Part 2**, 38, 468; **Vol. 5, Part 2**, 82, 195 f., 268 f., 277 f.; **Vol. 6, Part 1**, 52, 133, 373, 511; **Vol. 6, Part 2**, 150, 154, 212; **Vol. 7, Part 1**, 51 f., 121 f., 276 f., 544 f.; **Vol. 8, Part 1**, 142 f.; **Vol. 8, Part 2**, 128, 358, 436 f.; **Vol. 9, Part 1**, 154, 399, 581; **Vol. 9, Part 2**, 257 f., 267, 640; **Vol. 10, Part 2**, 402, 487, 556; American Federation of Labor, **Vol. 2, Part 2**, 338, 612; **Vol. 3, Part 1**, 510; **Vol. 4, Part 1**, 370; **Vol. 5, Part 2**, 278; **Vol. 6, Part 1**, 170, 521; **Vol. 6, Part 2**, 150; **Vol. 7, Part 1**, 545; **Vol. 8, Part 1**, 142 f.; arbitration and mediation system, **Supp. 5**, 263, 651; **Supp. 6**, 74, 411, 706; Bedaux unit incentive system, opposition to, **Supp. 3**, 49–50; black leaders, **Supp. 6**, 648; **Supp. 10**, 659–61; "Boulwarism," **Supp. 9**, 874; bureaus, establishment of, by states, **Vol. 8, Part 1**, 142 f., 545; "business unionism," **Supp. 4**, 75; Catholic reform programs, **Supp. 2**, 135; **Supp. 3**, 680–81; **Supp. 4**, 232–33; **Supp. 8**, 589; collective bargaining, **Supp. 2**, 73, 166; **Supp. 9**, 395, 396, 795, 796; company towns, **Supp. 2**, 366; conciliation, World War I period, **Vol. 7, Part 2**, 216; corruption charges

against, **Supp. 10**, 304; Department of Labor, creation of, **Vol. 1, Part 2**, 335; **Vol. 6, Part 1**, 171; **Vol. 7, Part 1**, 419, 591; economics, **Supp. 6**, 503–4; **Supp. 6**, 705–6; eight-hour day, **Vol. 6, Part 2**, 150; **Vol. 9, Part 2**, 1 f.; employer relations, **Supp. 2**, 66; **Supp. 9**, 561; employment benefits, **Supp. 8**, 348; **Supp. 10**, 249, 250; equal employment opportunity, **Supp. 4**, 397; **Supp. 7**, 382, 425; fair employment practices, **Supp. 5**, 692; **Supp. 6**, 480; **Supp. 7**, 122, 382, 425, 459, 543; fatigue studies, **Supp. 8**, 684; federal policies, **Supp. 8**, 366; garment industry, **Supp. 10**, 643, 644, 696–97; Golden Rule reforms, **Supp. 1**, 453; grievances bill, **Supp. 2**, 213; group insurance, **Supp. 2**, 87; handicapped, employment of, **Supp. 6**, 414; history of, **Supp. 3**, 178–79; human needs in employment, **Supp. 8**, 424; importation of European, **Vol. 4, Part 2**, 279; incentive system, **Supp. 3**, 49–50; industrial accident insurance, **Supp. 2**, 404; international, **Supp. 5**, 511; **Supp. 6**, 707; Italian-American workers, **Supp. 3**, 777–78; Italian Socialist Federation, **Supp. 6**, 238; journalism, **Supp. 3**, 347, 355–56; **Supp. 5**, 653–54, 663–64; **Supp. 6**, 484; Knights of Labor, **Vol. 5, Part 2**, 195; **Vol. 8, Part 1**, 142 f.; **Vol. 9, Part 1**, 581; **Vol. 9, Part 2**, 640; **Supp. 3**, 249, 346; Labor Day, first observance of, **Vol. 8, Part 1**, 118 f.; Labor Reform Convention (1872), **Vol. 3, Part 1**, 111; legal counsel, **Supp. 2**, 142, 691; **Supp. 6**, 541; legislation experts, **Supp. 1**, 294, 567; **Supp. 3**, 18; legislation protecting, **Supp. 2**, 50; **Supp. 3**, 654, 655–56, 717–18; **Supp. 4**, 407, 607, 614; **Supp. 5**, 718–19; **Supp. 6**, 480; **Supp. 7**, 543; legislation restricting, **Supp. 4**, 12, 724; **Supp. 7**, 110–11, 801; **Supp. 8**, 25, 245–46, 269; management relations, **Supp. 3**, 96; **Supp. 6**, 136, 548; **Supp. 10**, 493–94; Manly report on, **Supp. 4**, 543; migrant workers, **Supp. 8**, 301; **Supp. 10**, 502; minority groups in, **Supp. 10**, 644; New Unionism, **Supp. 4**, 375–76; NRA policies, **Supp. 3**, 651; organized crime links to, **Supp. 9**, 395–96, 397; organizing efforts, **Supp. 10**, 47; organizing tactics, **Supp. 9**, 395, 396; party, opposition to formation of, **Vol. 8, Part 1**, 142 f.; pension systems, **Supp. 2**, 404, 542–43, 645; **Supp. 10**, 269; piecework system, introduction of, **Vol. 7, Part 2**, 263; productivity and working conditions, **Supp. 4**, 565–66; profit-sharing benefits, **Supp. 1**, 275, 370–71; **Supp. 2**, 87; **Supp. 4**, 432; **Supp. 5**, 165; publications, **Vol. 4, Part 2**, 55; reform, **Supp. 7**, 360, 607–9; religious leaders' involvement with, **Supp. 3**, 733–34; **Supp. 4**, 111, 904; **Supp. 5**, 445–46; **Supp. 6**, 25; **Supp. 8**, 680–81; riots of 1877, Vol. 4, Part 2 419, 450; **Vol. 5, Part 2**, 196; savings-bank life insurance, **Supp. 3**, 95; schools, **Supp. 8**, 458; seamen, **Supp. 10**, 303–4; Socialist party, **Supp. 3**, 10, 297–98, 347, 373, 516–17, 532–33; "Solidarity Forever," **Supp. 7**, 118; stock purchase options, **Supp. 5**, 315; strike, Homestead, Pa. (1892), **Vol. 4, Part 1**, 30; strikebreaking, **Supp. 10**, 79; Supreme Court decisions, **Supp. 4**, 407, 537; **Supp. 5**, 358, 714; ten-hour day, early experiment with, **Vol. 8, Part 1**, 465; trade unionism, **Supp. 9**, 705–6; unions, **Vol. 1, Part 1**, 376 f.; **Vol. 2, Part 1**, 216, 434, 545; **Vol. 3, Part 1**, 183; **Vol. 3, Part 2**, 323; **Vol. 4, Part 1**, 369 f.; **Vol. 4, Part 2**, 228, 468; **Vol. 8, Part 1**, 112 f., 142; **Vol. 9, Part 2**, 1; **Vol. 10, Part 1**, 416 f.; **Vol. 10, Part 2**, 273, 349; **Supp. 9**, 237; violence, **Supp. 9**, 334; wages and hours, *see* Wages and hours; "Wisconsin school" writings on, **Supp. 3**, 178; women's activism in, **Supp. 1**, 346, 463; **Supp. 2**, 408; **Supp. 3**, 355–56, 576–77, 639; **Supp. 5**, 69–70; **Supp. 10**, 681; women's working conditions, **Supp. 4**, 623–26; workers' benefits, **Supp. 6**, 381, 615; workers' living conditions, **Supp. 9**, 584–85; working conditions' improvement, **Supp. 1**, 610; **Supp. 2**, 184; World War II disputes, **Supp. 3**, 660; **Supp. 6**, 28; writings on, **Supp. 3**, 249; **Supp. 6**, 597. *See also* Child labor; Government employees; Management; Occupational health and safety; Strikes; Trade unions; Unemployment; Wages and hours

Labor Management Relations Act (1947). *See* Taft-Hartley Act

Labor Reform Act (1959), **Supp. 8**, 322

Labor's League for Political Education, founding of, **Supp. 5**, 255

Labor Statistics, Bureau of, **Supp. 10**, 471

Labor Temple, **Supp. 3**, 110; founding of, **Supp. 3**, 734

Labrador, first mission to, **Vol. 8, Part 1**, 113 f.

Lachman, Charles, references to, **Supp. 9**, 648, 649

Lackawanna Coal & Iron Co., **Vol. 1, Part 2**, 338

Laconia State School, founding of, **Supp. 2**, 388

La Crosse and Milwaukee Railroad, **Vol. 1, Part 2**, 33

Lactic acid, **Supp. 5**, 489

Lacy, Joseph N., reference to, **Supp. 7**, 671

Ladd, Alan, reference to, **Supp. 9**, 480

Ladd, William, reference to, **Vol. 6, Part 1**, 408

Ladies' Clay Association (Richmond, Va.), **Vol. 4, Part 2**, 358

Ladies' Garment Workers' Union. *See* International Ladies' Garment Workers Union

Ladies' Home Journal: **Vol. 9, Part 2**, 346; **Supp. 1**, 92, 212, 213; **Supp. 10**, 441; "Beautiful America" column, **Supp. 4**, 522; illustrations, **Supp. 3**, 573; music column, **Supp. 6**, 297; travel articles, **Supp. 6**, 302

Ladies' Magazine, **Vol. 4, Part 2**, 111; **Vol. 5, Part 1**, 384

Ladies' Repository, **Vol. 6, Part 1**, 7; **Vol. 9, Part 2**, 482, 621

Lady Chatterley's Lover, Postal Service ban on, **Supp. 9**, 782

Lady Doak School (Madras, India), **Supp. 9**, 175

Lady Franklin Bay expedition, **Vol. 7, Part 2**, 323

Lady in the Dark, **Supp. 4**, 869; **Supp. 5**, 415; **Supp. 7**, 325

"Lady or the Tiger?, The," **Vol. 9, Part 2**, 44

Lady's Home Magazine, **Vol. 9, Part 2**, 621

Laemmle, Carl, reference to, **Supp. 6**, 657

La Farge, C. Grant, reference to, **Supp. 3**, 197

La Farge, John, references to, **Vol. 1, Part 1**, 66; **Vol. 5, Part 1**, 591; **Supp. 8**, 293–94

La Farge, Oliver, references to, **Supp. 6**, 355; **Supp. 7**, 505

Lafayette, Marquis de: **Vol. 1, Part 2**, 275 f.; **Vol. 3, Part 2**, 401; **Vol. 5, Part 1**, 344; **Vol. 5, Part 2**, 253; **Vol. 7, Part 1**, 46, 60; **Vol. 9, Part 1**, 200; biography of, **Supp. 9**, 330; Bollman, Justus Erich, **Vol. 1, Part 2**, 422; bust of, **Vol. 4, Part 1**, 587; Jefferson, Thomas, **Vol. 5, Part 2**, 22; List, Georg, **Vol. 6, Part 1**, 292; portrait of, **Vol. 5, Part 1**, 473, 482; relations with Barton, William, **Vol. 1, Part 2**, 24; welcoming of, by New York, **Vol. 8, Part 1**, 529 Lafayette College, **Vol. 2, Part 1**, 578; **Vol. 5, Part 2**, 249; **Vol. 6, Part 2**, 270; **Vol. 7, Part 2**, 201; **Vol. 8, Part 1**, 94 f.; **Vol. 10, Part 2**, 608; poetry studies, **Supp. 7**, 653

Lafayette Escadrille, **Vol. 2, Part 2**, 21; **Vol. 6, Part 1**, 499; **Vol. 8, Part 2**, 69 f.

Lafayette Motor Co., **Supp. 4**, 621

Lafayette Players (New York City), **Supp. 10**, 576

Laffite, Jean, reference to, **Vol. 6, Part 1**, 376

La Follette, Philip Fox, references to, **Supp. 5**, 404; **Supp. 9**, 29, 30

La Follette, Robert M.: references to, **Vol. 1, Part 1**, 156 f.; **Vol. 8, Part 2**, 396; **Supp. 9**, 29, 565; Commons relationship, **Supp. 3**, 177–78; Ely relationship, **Supp. 3**, 249–50; family of, **Supp. 5**, 403;

Lenroot relationship, **Supp. 4**, 480, 482; Manly relationship, **Supp. 4**, 543–44; references to, **Supp. 3**, 95, 105, 256–57, 395–97, 558, 559, 561, 604, 650, 816; **Supp. 4**, 47; **Supp. 5**, 392; **Supp. 6**, 404; **Supp. 7**, 450

La Follette, Robert M., Jr., references to, **Supp. 7**, 450–51; **Supp. 9**, 29, 30; **Supp. 10**, 334

La Grange College, first president of, **Vol. 7, Part 2**, 155

La Guardia, Fiorello H.: mayoral campaigns, **Supp. 9**, 84; references to, **Supp. 4**, 485, 547, 825, 826, 870; **Supp. 5**, 227, 466; **Supp. 6**, 51, 88, 142, 363, 571; **Supp. 10**, 48

La Guardia Airport (New York City), opening of, **Supp. 4**, 466

Lahey Clinic (Boston, Mass.), **Supp. 5**, 404–5

Lahr, Bert, reference to, **Supp. 10**, 301

Laird Rams (1862), **Vol. 1, Part 1**, 46; **Vol. 6, Part 2**, 365; **Vol. 8, Part 2**, 619

Laissez-faire, **Vol. 8, Part 2**, 532

Laity's Directory, **Vol. 8, Part 1**, 156 f.

Lake Carriers' Association, **Vol. 6, Part 1**, 327

Lake Champlain, battle on (1813), **Vol. 4, Part 1**, 523; **Vol. 6, Part 2**, 20, 156

Lake Champlain, operation on (1776), **Vol. 1, Part 1**, 363; **Vol. 4, Part 1**, 185; **Vol. 8, Part 2**, 294, 478; **Vol. 9, Part 1**, 531; **Vol. 10, Part 1**, 468

Lake Erie, battle of, **Vol. 2, Part 1**, 609; **Vol. 3, Part 2**, 97; **Vol. 7, Part 2**, 490 f.; **Vol. 9, Part 2**, 348 f.

Lake Forest University, **Vol. 3, Part 2**, 295; **Vol. 4, Part 1**, 602

Lake George, battle of, **Vol. 5, Part 2**, 125

Lake Mohonk Conference, **Vol. 9, Part 1**, 231

Lake navigation, beginning of, **Vol. 5, Part 2**, 110

Lake Placid Conferences on Home Economics, **Supp. 3**, 507

Lake Superior region, exploration, **Vol. 3, Part 1**, 500 f.

Lake Tahoe, Nev., gambling in, **Supp. 10**, 309

Lakewood, N.J., first tuberculosis preventorium for children established at, **Vol. 9, Part 2**, 130

Lalique, René, reference to, **Supp. 1**, 478

Lambert, Gerard, reference to, **Supp. 9**, 298

Lame-duck session of Congress, **Vol. 9, Part 1**, 15

Lamont, Corliss, reference to, **Supp. 9**, 36

Lamont, Thomas W., references to, **Supp. 3**, 208; **Supp. 7**, 782

Lamont-Doherty Geological Observatory (Columbia University), **Supp. 9**, 271; **Supp. 10**, 326

Lamont, Corliss and Co., founding of, **Supp. 4**, 469

Lamp. *See* Light

Lamp, The, founding of, **Supp. 2**, 201, 202

Lancaster, H. Carrington, reference to, **Supp. 3**, 22

Lancaster, Mass.: early settlement, **Vol. 8, Part 1**, 192 f.; state industrial school, **Vol. 7, Part 2**, 398

Lancaster Lodge of Good Templars, founding of, **Vol. 1, Part 2**, 310

Lancastrian system of instruction, **Vol. 2, Part 2**, 224; **Vol. 6, Part 1**, 440

Lanchester, Elsa, references to, **Supp. 7**, 460, 461

Land, Edwin H., reference to, **Supp. 8**, 679

Land and land use: agents, **Vol. 4, Part 2**, 531; **Vol. 5, Part 1**, 359; **Vol. 7, Part 1**, 357; agricultural, **Supp. 4**, 45; banks, **Vol. 2, Part 2**, 313; **Vol. 10, Part 2**, 482; cases, **Vol. 4, Part 2**, 220; ceding of Indian, **Vol. 4, Part 2**, 531; **Vol. 8, Part 1**, 393, 595; claims, **Vol. 1, Part 2**, 432; **Vol. 2, Part 2**, 363; **Vol. 3, Part 1**, 317; **Vol. 3, Part 2**, 425; **Vol. 4, Part 1**, 523; **Vol. 8, Part 1**, 436; **Vol. 9, Part 2**, 87, 575; classification, **Supp. 2**, 696; controversies, **Vol. 3, Part 1**, 465 f.; **Vol. 4, Part 2**, 30; **Vol. 8, Part 2**, 396; **Vol. 10, Part 1**, 653; development, **Vol. 2, Part 2**, 189; **Vol. 3, Part 1**, 238, 465; **Vol. 8, Part 1**, 618; **Vol. 10, Part 1**, 360, 495 f.; ecological principles, **Supp. 3**, 169; ethics of, **Supp. 2**, 296; **Supp. 4**, 483–84; federal policy-making, **Supp. 8**, 104; frauds, **Vol. 8, Part 2**, 363 f.; **Vol. 9, Part 2**, 274; geological formation studies, **Supp. 4**, 119; grants, **Vol. 2, Part 1**, 100; **Vol. 3, Part 1**, 182, 316, 422, 606, 611; **Vol. 3, Part 2**, 110 f., 154; **Vol. 5, Part 1**, 359; **Vol. 6, Part 1**, 307; **Vol. 8, Part 1**, 421, 540, 595; **Vol. 8, Part 2**, 49, 306; **Vol. 9, Part 1**, 333, 350; **Vol. 9, Part 2**, 63, 259, 261; **Vol. 10, Part 1**, 26; **Supp. 1**, 380; Indian claims, **Supp. 4**, 641; **Supp. 8**, 99; laws relating to, **Vol. 1, Part 1**, 555; **Vol. 2, Part 1**, 294; **Vol. 8, Part 1**, 10 f.; office, general, **Vol. 9, Part 1**, 435; Oregon federal timber receipts, **Supp. 8**, 104; Oregon legislation, **Supp. 6**, 682; patents, colonial, **Vol. 5, Part 1**, 80; policy, **Vol. 4, Part 1**, 140; **Vol. 4, Part 2**, 380; **Vol. 8, Part 2**, 479; **Vol. 9, Part 1**, 332; **Vol. 10, Part 1**, 362 f.; promotion, **Vol. 3, Part 1**, 465 f.; **Vol. 3, Part 2**, 518, 525; **Vol. 4, Part 2**, 517; **Vol. 6, Part 2**, 155; public, **Vol. 1, Part 2**, 211; **Vol. 3, Part 2**, 110; **Vol. 6, Part 1**, 587; **Vol. 9, Part 1**, 331; public land conservation, **Supp. 4**, 317, 318; reclamation, **Vol. 8, Part 1**, 359 f.; **Vol. 9, Part 1**, 427 f.; **Supp. 2**, 444; reform, **Vol. 3, Part 2**, 201; **Vol. 5, Part 2**, 82; "ripening costs" appreciation, **Supp. 3**, 250; sales, **Vol. 7, Part 1**, 223; **Vol. 8, Part 2**, 544; speculation, **Vol. 2, Part 1**, 581; **Vol. 3, Part 1**, 390, 465, 486 f., 609; **Vol. 4, Part 2**, 247; **Vol. 5, Part 1**, 461, 527; **Vol. 6, Part 1**, 168, 448; **Vol. 7, Part 1**, 170; **Vol. 7, Part 2**, 531; **Vol. 8, Part 1**, 129, 419, 601; **Vol. 8, Part 2**, 51, 178, 494; **Vol. 9, Part 2**, 651, 604; **Vol. 10, Part 1**, 495; surveying, *see* Boundaries; titles, **Vol. 1, Part 1**, 642; **Vol. 3, Part 2**, 105, 525; **Vol. 6, Part 1**, 547, **Vol. 7, Part 1**, 642; **Vol. 8, Part 1**, 426; Western grazing interests, **Supp. 7**, 31

Land-Grant College Endowment Act, **Vol. 1, Part 1**, 238; **Vol. 7, Part 1**, 199

Land-grant colleges, **Supp. 3**, 209; **Supp. 5**, 49

Landis, James M., reference to, **Supp. 7**, 263

Landis, Kenesaw Mountain, references to, **Supp. 1**, 74; **Supp. 6**, 74, 589; **Supp. 7**, 118, 129, 646; **Supp. 8**, 85–86, 575; **Supp. 9**, 653

Landon, Alfred M.: elected Kansas governor, **Supp. 9**, 355; presidential candidacy, **Supp. 9**, 356; references to, **Supp. 3**, 425, 655; **Supp. 7**, 274; **Supp. 8**, 421; **Supp. 10**, 233, 611

Landrum-Griffin Labor Management Act (1959), **Supp. 7**, 543; **Supp. 8**, 25, 366; **Supp. 10**, 482

Landry, Tom, reference to, **Supp. 9**, 818

Landscape architecture: **Vol. 2, Part 2**, 204; **Vol. 3, Part 2**, 70; **Vol. 4, Part 2**, 230; **Vol. 6, Part 1**, 457; **Vol. 7, Part 2**, 24, 29, 30; **Vol. 8, Part 1**, 336 f.; **Vol. 10, Part 1**, 605; **Supp. 1**, 594; **Supp. 3**, 490-91; **Supp. 5**, 359–70; **Supp. 6**, 196, 485–86; gardening, **Vol. 3, Part 1**, 417; **Vol. 7, Part 2**, 26 f., 269, 417, 600; **Vol. 8, Part 1**, 1; **Vol. 8, Part 2**, 355, 361, 383 f.; public prjects, **Supp. 10**, 124; residential garden design, **Supp. 10**, 123–24; writings on, **Supp. 10**, 124

Landscape painting, **Supp. 1**, 227, 458; **Supp. 3**, 112. *See also* Painting

Landsteiner, Karl, reference to, **Supp. 10**, 837

Lane, Chester, references to, **Supp. 6**, 155, 186

"Lane, Drury" (fictional character), **Supp. 9**, 487

Lane, Franklin K., references to, **Supp. 4**, 216; **Supp. 6**, 121

Lane, Harry, reference to, **Supp. 4**, 904

Lane College, founding of, **Vol. 5, Part 1**, 177

Lane Theological Seminary, **Vol. 1, Part 2**, 136; **Vol. 9, Part 2**, 299

Laney, Al, reference to, **Supp. 6**, 363

Lang, Eddie, reference to, **Supp. 10**, 806

Lang, Fritz, references to, **Supp. 7**, 478; **Supp. 9**, 819
Lang, Jennings, reference to, **Supp. 8**, 678
Lange, Dorothea, reference to, **Supp. 10**, 834
Langerhans, islets of, **Supp. 3**, 483; **Supp. 6**, 53
Langley, Samuel P., references to, **Vol. 6, Part 2**, 239; **Vol. 9, Part 2**, 397
Langley (ship), **Supp. 4**, 685
Langmuir, Irving, references to, **Supp. 4**, 488; **Supp. 5**, 273.; **Supp. 6**, 695
Langmuir isotherm and probe, **Supp. 6**, 365
Langner, Lawrence, references to, **Supp. 3**, 811, 812; **Supp. 6**, 285
Language, **Supp. 4**, 90
Language as Gesture, **Supp. 7**, 56
Language. *See* Dictionaries; Philology; Speech; *specific languages*
Lanham Defense Housing Act (1940), **Supp. 7**, 459
Lanier, Sidney, references to, **Vol. 9, Part 2**, 262, 559; **Vol. 10, Part 1**, 442 f.
Lanman, Charles R., reference to, **Vol. 10, Part 1**, 474 f.
Lansing, Robert, references to, **Supp. 3**, 139, 605, 606; **Supp. 5**, 137; **Supp. 6**, 177
Lansing-Ishii agreement, **Vol. 5, Part 2**, 610
Lansky, Meyer, references to, **Supp. 9**, 12, 198
Lanterns on the Levee: Recollections of a Planter's Son, **Supp. 3**, 598
Laos: medical relief work in, **Supp. 7**, 190–91; neutralization of, **Supp. 7**, 422
Lap robes, manufacture of, **Vol. 4, Part 1**, 380
Lard-burning lamp, invention, **Vol. 10, Part 1**, 483 f.
Lardner, David, reference to, **Supp. 6**, 366
Lardner, James, reference to, **Supp. 6**, 366
Lardner, Ring, references to, **Supp. 6**, 365, 366–67; **Supp. 7**, 413; **Supp. 8**, 649
Lark, The, founding of, **Supp. 5**, 94
Larkin, Jim, reference to, **Supp. 3**, 718
Larkin Building (Buffalo, N. Y.), **Supp. 6**, 712
Laryngectomy, first successful total, **Supp. 3**, 202
Laryngology: **Vol. 1, Part 1**, 191, 383; **Vol. 1, Part 2**, 467; **Vol. 3, Part 2**, 119; **Vol. 4, Part 1**, 547; **Vol. 5, Part 1**, 625; **Vol. 5, Part 2**, 465, 515; **Vol. 6, Part 1**, 140, 160, 268; **Vol. 6, Part 2**, 94, 450; **Vol. 8, Part 2**, 306, 411, 562; **Vol. 9, Part 1**, 185, 195; research in, **Supp. 1**, 181; **Supp. 6**, 317–18
Laryngoscope, founding of, **Supp. 3**, 311
Laryngoscope, use of, **Vol. 2, Part 2**, 275
Larynx, cancer diagnosis and treatment, **Supp. 4**, 185–86
La Salle, Robert Cavelier, Sieur de, references to, **Vol. 5, Part 2**, 223; **Vol. 6, Part 2**, 526; **Vol. 9, Part 2**, 587
La Salle, Ill., public service to, **Vol. 6, Part 2**, 422
La Scala Opera Company (Milan, Italy): management of, **Supp. 2**, 222–23; Toscanini association, **Supp. 6**, 323, 642–43, 644; **Supp. 8**, 19
Lascher, Andrew, reference to, **Supp. 6**, 318
Las Guasimas, Cuba, battle of, **Vol. 8, Part 2**, 137; **Vol. 9, Part 1**, 16; **Vol. 10, Part 2**, 51, 467
Lasker, Albert D., reference to, **Supp. 10**, 145
Laski, Harold J., references to, **Supp. 3**, 471, 473; **Supp. 6**, 271; **Supp. 8**, 50
Lasky, Blanche, references to, **Supp. 6**, 368, 370
Lasky, Jesse L., references to, **Supp. 6**, 158–59, 439; **Supp. 8**, 677–78; **Supp. 9**, 322, 323; **Supp. 10**, 347, 872
Lassen Peak, eruption of, **Supp. 1**, 247
Lasser, J. K., and Co., founding of, **Supp. 5**, 412
La Starza, Roland, reference to, **Supp. 8**, 417
Last Battle, The, **Supp. 9**, 691
Lastex, **Supp. 7**, 169
Last Hurrah, The, **Supp. 8**, 477, 660
Last of the Mohicans, The, **Vol. 2, Part 2**, 402, f.
Las Vegas, Nev.: casino shows, **Supp. 10**, 649; gambling in, **Supp. 10**, 308–9; organized crime in, **Supp. 6**, 264; **Supp. 9**, 198
Late George Apley, The, **Supp. 6**, 428
Lathe, flat-turret, invention of, **Supp. 1**, 378
Lathrop, Barbour, reference to, **Supp. 5**, 213–14
Lathrop, John E, reference to, **Supp. 5**, 699
Lathrop, Julia, biography of, **Supp. 1**, 12
Latin America: Alliance for Progress, **Supp. 7**, 421; archaeological expeditions, **Supp. 5**, 711; diplomacy during World War II, **Supp. 7**, 778; diplomacy with U.S., **Vol. 1, Part 2**, 327; **Vol. 2, Part 1**, 219, 420; **Vol. 10, Part 2**, 325, 357; **Supp. 2**, 25, 580; **Supp. 7**, 777–78; ethnology studies, **Supp. 1**, 648; exploration, **Supp. 6**, 59; Good Neighbor policy, **Supp. 4**, 171, 706; **Supp. 5**, 89, 332; Good Neighbor policy forerunner, **Supp. 4**, 406; historical studies of, **Supp. 1**, 655; **Supp. 5**, 77; **Supp. 6**, 277–78; longest suspension bridge, **Supp. 6**, 594; mammology expeditions to, **Supp. 5**, 678; missions, **Supp. 2**, 500; **Supp. 8**, 537; paleobotany, **Supp. 3**, 62; retail stores, **Supp. 8**, 705; Rockefeller, N., interest in, **Supp. 10**, 685–86; U.S. experts on, **Supp. 4**, 705–6; U.S. mutual security agreements, **Supp. 3**, 657. *See also specific countries*
Latin literature and language: classical studies, **Supp. 2**, 204; **Supp. 10**, 333, 334; medieval, **Supp. 4**, 68; poetry, **Supp. 1**, 701; scholarship on, **Supp. 1**, 657; sixteenth-century poems and plays, **Supp. 4**, 110; teaching of, **Supp. 2**, 454; translations, **Supp. 7**, 742; **Supp. 8**, 236
Latitude, determination of the variation of, **Vol. 3, Part 1**, 373; **Vol. 8, Part 1**, 95 f., 465
La Tour, Charles de, reference to, **Vol. 8, Part 2**, 318
La Tour, Le Blond de, reference to, **Vol. 7, Part 2**, 318 f.
"La Tour, Marie" (fictional character), **Supp. 7**, 633
Latrobe, Benjamin Henry: biography of, **Supp. 6**, 272; references to, **Vol. 6, Part 1**, 24; **Vol. 7, Part 1**, 10; **Vol. 9, Part 2**, 505
"Latrobe's Folly," **Vol. 6, Part 1**, 26
Latter-Day Saints (LDS). *See* Mormon church
Lattimore, Owen: loyalty investigation of, **Supp. 10**, 801; perjury indictment dismissal, **Supp. 10**, 863; reference to, **Supp. 5**, 410; **Supp. 9**, 1351 **Supp. 8**, 133
Laughing Boy, **Supp. 7**, 449
Laughing gas, use of, in dentistry, **Vol. 8, Part 1**, 604
Laughlin, Clara E., references to, **Supp. 9**, 32, 33
Laughlin, Harry H., reference to, **Supp. 3**, 215
Laughlin, J. Laurence, reference to, **Supp. 4**, 584
Laundries, Civil War, **Vol. 1, Part 2**, 238
Laurel, Stan, reference to, **Supp. 6**, 276
Laurel and Hardy (comedy team), **Supp. 6**, 276; **Supp. 7**, 463–64
Laurel Falls Camp for Girls (Ga.), **Supp. 8**, 605, 606
Lauritsen, Charles C., reference to, **Supp. 8**, 483
Lausanne Conference on Near Eastern Affairs (1922–23), **Supp. 7**, 303
Lausche, Frank J., reference to, **Supp. 6**, 614
Lautner, John, references to, **Supp. 6**, 681; **Supp. 7**, 291
Lavender Mist (painting), **Supp. 6**, 513
La Victoire, ship which brought Lafayette to America, **Vol. 5, Part 2**, 536
L'Avvenire, **Supp. 3**, 777
Law, Vernon, reference to, **Supp. 10**, 574
Law (for complete list of lawyers jurists, etc., *see* Occupations Index): **Vol. 1, Part 1**, 94, 329, 342, 368, 386, 445, 617; **Vol. 2, Part 1**, 401; **Vol. 2, Part 2**, 83 f.; **Vol. 3, Part 1**, 311, 619; **Vol. 3, Part 2**, 486; **Vol. 4, Part 1**, 12, 15, 126, 175, 182, 306, 315, 369, 382,

487, 518, 578 f.; **Vol. 5, Part 1**, 211, **Vol. 5, Part 2**, 106, 114, 128, 180, 345 f.; **Vol. 6, Part 1**, 341; **Vol. 7, Part 1**, 69, 466, 638; **Vol. 7, Part 2**, 627; **Vol. 9, Part 2**, 79, 96, 239; **Vol. 10, Part 1**, 406; administrative, **Supp. 2**, 250; admiralty, **Vol. 1, Part 2**, 177, 231; **Vol. 2, Part 1**, 99, 370, 399; **Vol. 3, Part 1**, 60, 79 f., 592 f.; **Vol. 3, Part 2**, 454; **Vol. 5, Part 2**, 64; **Vol. 9, Part 2**, 28, 105; agricultural, **Supp. 4**, 50; American Indian, **Supp. 5**, 119–20; American Indian codification; **Supp. 8**, 99; antitrust, **Supp. 5**, 27, 174; **Supp. 7**, 547; **Supp. 9**, 593; **Supp. 10**, 125, 126, 155, 499; appellate, **Supp. 5**, 155, 156; arbitration and mediation, **Supp. 9**, 565; associations, **Supp. 8**, 662–63; attorneys general, U.S., **Vol. 7, Part 1**, 108; **Vol. 7, Part 2**, 587, 627; **Vol. 8, Part 1**, 353 f.; **Vol. 8, Part 2**, 347; **Vol. 9, Part 1**, 518; banking, **Vol. 3, Part 1**, 388 f.; **Supp. 4**, 325–26, 331, 332; bankruptcy, **Supp. 4**, 825; bar admission standards, **Supp. 2**, 685; bar associations, **Supp. 1**, 223; British common, historical writings collection, **Supp. 1**, 154; business, **Supp. 4**, 192–93; **Supp. 7**, 792; canon, **Vol. 3, Part 1**, 368; case method of teaching, **Supp. 3**, 820; **Supp. 4**, 77; cases, *see also* Law cases; church, **Vol. 4, Part 1**, 194; **Vol. 7, Part 1**, 625; censorship, **Supp. 10**, 221; circuit riding, **Vol. 4, Part 2**, 497; **Vol. 5, Part 2**, 169, 226; **Vol. 8, Part 2**, 15; **Vol. 9, Part 1**, 382; circumstantial evidence defined, **Vol. 10, Part 1**, 592 f.; civil, **Vol. 5, Part 2**, 569; civil liberties issues, **Supp. 5**, 280; **Supp. 6**, 104–6; **Supp. 10**, 229; civil rights issues, **Supp. 4**, 397–98; **Supp. 8**, 323, 333–34; **Supp. 10**, 230, 378; codification, **Vol. 2, Part 2**, 587; **Vol. 8, Part 1**, 29 f., 33 f., 52 f., 426; colonial, **Vol. 1, Part 1**, 421; **Vol. 6, Part 1**, 525; **Vol. 8, Part 1**, 426; commercial, **Vol. 3, Part 1**, 388 f.; **Vol. 5, Part 2**, 460; **Vol. 9, Part 2**, 96 f.; **Supp. 2**, 93, 501; **Supp. 7**, 792; common, **Supp. 1**, 420–21; **Supp. 2**, 94; **Supp. 7**, 475; common, codification of, **Vol. 4, Part 1**, 385, 583; **Vol. 4, Part 2**, 212; **Vol. 8, Part 2**, 321; comparative studies, **Supp. 3**, 821; compendium of, **Vol. 3, Part 1**, 64; conservation, **Supp. 4**, 481–82, 666; constitutional, **Vol. 4, Part 1**, 273; **Vol. 5, Part 2**, 572, 573; **Vol. 6, Part 2**, 318 f.; **Vol. 9, Part 2**, 406; **Supp. 1**, 367, 422–23; **Supp. 8**, 139; **Supp. 9**, 593; **Supp. 10**, 229; corporation, **Vol. 2, Part 2**, 131; **Vol. 2, Part 1**, 281; **Vol. 3, Part 1**, 47, 291, 309, 311, 341, 388 f.; **Vol. 5, Part 2**, 241; **Vol. 6, Part 1**, 269; **Vol. 7, Part 1**, 591; **Vol. 7, Part 2**, 30 f.; **Vol. 8, Part 1**, 449, 634; **Vol. 8, Part 2**, 29, 424; **Supp. 1**, 223; **Supp. 2**, 131, 470; **Supp. 3**, 117; courts, coercion of, by popular feeling, **Vol. 3, Part 1**, 160; criminal, **Vol. 2, Part 2**, 174; **Vol. 4, Part 1**, 66, 231, 360, 472; **Vol. 5, Part 1**, 116; **Supp. 2**, 142; **Supp. 3**, 65–66; **Supp. 5**, 665; **Supp. 10**, 281, 447–48; criminal, deterrence theory of, **Supp. 3**, 822; debtors, for relief of, **Vol. 3, Part 1**, 599 f.; demurrage, **Vol. 5, Part 2**, 573; economics and, **Supp. 6**, 271; editorial work, **Vol. 6, Part 1**, 471; **Vol. 9, Part 1**, 253; enforcement of, **Vol. 6, Part 2**, 643; **Supp. 2**, 535, 715; environmental, **Supp. 10**, 324; equal employment, **Supp. 7**, 382; equity, **Vol. 8, Part 1**, 440; **Vol. 9, Part 2**, 103, f.; ethical standards in, **Supp. 1**, 99, 204; ethics, **Vol. 6, Part 1**, 149; evidence, **Vol. 9, Part 2**, 406; federal v. state, **Supp. 3**, 99; fees, large, **Vol. 3, Part 1**, 309; habeas corpus, **Vol. 1, 2**, 422; **Vol. 5, Part 1**, 467; historical studies, **Supp. 2**, 133; homestead, **Vol. 5, Part 2**, 82; immigration, **Supp. 1**, 472; **Supp. 2**, 46; impeachment, **Vol. 4, Part 1**, 236; intemperance, statutes to prevent, **Vol. 5, Part 2**, 79; international, **Vol. 2, Part 1**, 494; **Vol. 2, Part 2**, 464; **Vol. 3, Part 1**, 61, 296, 592; **Vol. 5, Part 2**, 609; **Vol. 6, Part 1**, 53, 238; **Vol. 8, Part 2**, 241; **Vol. 9, Part 1**, 43, 392; **Vol. 9, Part 2**, 42; irrigation, **Vol. 6, Part 2**, 4; journals, **Vol. 9, Part 1**, 65; judges, popular election of, **Vol. 5, Part 1**, 77; judicial review, **Vol. 2, Part 2**, 536 f.; **Vol. 10, Part 2**, 588; jurisprudence, **Vol. 8, Part 1**, 440; Korean, **Vol. 4, Part 1**, 526; law, Indians, regarding, **Vol. 3, Part 1**, 149 f.; **Vol. 4, Part 1**, 502; law, insurance, **Vol. 3, Part 1**, 485 f.; **Vol. 6, Part 1**, 208; legislative power, **Vol. 4, Part 1**, 255; libraries, **Vol. 5, Part 2**, 445; maritime, **Vol. 1, Part 2**, 360; **Vol. 3, Part 1**, 60; **Vol. 3, Part 2**, 454; **Vol. 10, Part 1**, 446; martial, **Vol. 5, Part 2**, 569; "midnight judges," **Vol. 5, Part 2**, 28; **Vol. 6, Part 1**, 101; military, **Vol. 3, Part 1**, 111, 115; mining, **Vol. 3, Part 1**, 238; **Vol. 6, Part 1**, 275; **Vol. 8, Part 1**, 415; **Vol. 9, Part 2**, 13, 589; patent, **Vol. 1, Part 2**, 360; **Vol. 2, Part 2**, 481, 613; **Vol. 3, Part 1**, 288; **Vol. 4, Part 2**, 249, 590; **Vol. 5, Part 2**, 41, 464 f.; **Vol. 6, Part 1**, 27; **Vol. 8, Part 1**, 75 f., 504 f.; **Vol. 8, Part 2**, 567; **Vol. 9, Part 1**, 614; **Vol. 9, Part 2**, 99; philosophies of, **Supp. 3**, 185–86; **Supp. 6**, 216; **Supp. 7**, 99–100; precedent, sanctity of, **Vol. 3, Part 1**, 355, Prohibition, **Supp. 3**, 706; **Supp. 4**, 853; Prohibition enforcement, **Supp. 7**, 786, 805–6; property, **Vol. 4, Part 1**, 255, 444, 456, 559; **Vol. 5, Part 2**, 195, 197 f.; public relief, **Supp. 4**, 810; railroad, **Vol. 3, Part 1**, 245 f.; **Vol. 4, Part 1**, 609; **Vol. 5, Part 2**, 450; **Vol. 7, Part 2**, 375; **Vol. 8, Part 1**, 440, 541; **Vol. 9, Part 2**, 28; **Supp. 3**, 167–68; railroad labor representation, **Supp. 6**, 542; reform, **Vol. 1, Part 1**, 431; **Vol. 3, Part 2**, 360, 373; **Vol. 4, Part 2**, 81; **Vol. 6, Part 1**, 396; **Vol. 8, Part 1**, 211 f.; reporting, **Vol. 5, Part 2**, 128, 424; **Vol. 8, Part 1**, 10 f.; reports, first complete, **Vol. 5, Part 2**, 424; riots, **Vol. 4, Part 1**, 255; school, first in America, **Vol. 8, Part 1**, 496; securities, **Vol. 5, Part 2**, 195; slavery, **Vol. 4, Part 1**, 121, 315, 607; **Vol. 9, Part 2**, 37; social, **Supp. 1**, 323; social psychology of, **Supp. 2**, 562; special pleading, **Vol. 8, Part 1**, 426; state uniformity, **Supp. 3**, 737; **Supp. 7**, 792; statute improvement, **Supp. 5**, 107–8; strikes, **Vol. 3, Part 2**, 556; studies in, **Supp. 1**, 420; **Supp. 2**, 501; teaching of, **Vol. 1, Part 1**, 246, 247, 614; **Vol. 1, Part 2**, 375; **Vol. 2, Part 2**, 239, 289; **Vol. 3, Part 1**, 571; **Vol. 3, Part 2**, 75; **Vol. 4, Part 1**, 453, 456, 520 f.; **Vol. 4, Part 2**, 212, 529; **Vol. 5, Part 1**, 111, 124, 134, 382; **Vol. 5, Part 2**, 285, 435, 585; **Vol. 6, Part 1**, 369; **Vol. 7, Part 1**, 26 f.; **Vol. 8, Part 1**, 52 f., 469; **Vol. 8, Part 2**, 57, 451, 459; **Vol. 9, Part 1**, 29, 35, 250, 292, 531; **Vol. 9, Part 2**, 141, 320, 402, 404, 405, 406; **Vol. 10, Part 1**, 363, 499; **Supp. 1**, 323, 358, 497; **Supp. 2**, 482; **Supp. 3**, 43, 185–86, 700; **Supp. 4**, 490–91, 680, 793–94; **Supp. 7**, 474–75, 627, 792; **Supp. 8**, 17, 138–39, 285; textbooks, **Vol. 2, Part 1**, 166; **Vol. 5, Part 1**, 53; trial, **Supp. 2**, 629, 674; "Twinkie Defense," **Supp. 10**, 537; veterans, **Supp. 3**, 661; voting rights, **Supp. 8**, 334, 335; women in, **Vol. 1, Part 2**, 581; writings on, **Vol. 1, Part 1**, 73; 81, 309, 329, 546, 593; **Vol. 1, Part 2**, 193, 260, 296, 491; **Vol. 2, Part 1**, 16, 20, 27, 47, 54, 99, 120, 166, 274, 325, 356, 370, 404; **Vol. 2, Part 2**, 25, 264, 350, 393, 614; **Vol. 3, Part 1**, 38, 42, 64, 110, 115, 135, 168, 192, 226, 309, 311, 342, 389, 459, 468, 485, 488, 498, 518, 525, 546, 555, 566, 571, 597; **Vol. 3, Part 2**, 203, 455, 556; **Vol. 4, Part 1**, 151, 234, 255, 315, 385, 478, 521, 560, 584, 634; **Vol. 4, Part 2**, 92, 138, 263, 484, 537; **Vol. 5, Part 1**, 111, 134, 467, 478; **Vol. 5, Part 2**, 91, 128, 195, 240, 285, 413, 415, 421, 424, 445, 460, 585; **Vol. 6, Part 1**, 219, 296, 308, 579; **Vol. 6, Part 2**, 443, 488, 511; **Vol. 7, Part 1**, 27, 94, 353; **Vol. 7, Part 2**, 8, 231, 274, 287, 476, 527; **Vol. 8, Part 1**, 29, 33, 52, 77, 132, 211, 229, 245, 307, 392, 400, 428, 432, 439, 469, 578, 591, 634, 642; **Vol. 8, Part 2**, 39, 57, 86, 98, 161, 162, 224, 402, 547, 552, 591; **Vol. 9, Part 1**, 29, 525; **Vol. 9,**

Part 2, 45, 103, 110, 135, 235, 250, 272, 326, 335, 406, 531, 557; **Vol. 10, Part 1**, 32, 33, 37, 39, 93, 98, 148, 363, 370, 374, 446, 494, 499, 508, 535, 560, 620, 643; **Vol. 10, Part 2**, 27, 33, 40, 440; **Supp. 1**, 509; **Supp. 3**, 739–40, 820–22; **Supp. 4**, 491; **Supp. 5**, 549, 731; zoning, **Supp. 3**, 66; **Supp. 4**, 56; **Supp. 6**, 522. *See also* American Bar Association; International law; Judicial system; Judiciary; Supreme Court; *specific types and acts*
Law (by state): Delaware, **Vol. 5, Part 2**, 76; Georgia, **Vol. 2, Part 2**, 24; Maryland, **Vol. 2, Part 1**, 214; **Vol. 10, Part 1**, 987 f.; Maine, **Vol. 4, Part 1**, 583; Massachusetts, **Vol. 1, Part 2**, 174; New Jersey, **Vol. 4, Part 1**, 626; New York, **Vol. 4, Part 1**, 217; Ohio, **Vol. 3, Part 1**, 241; South Carolina, **Vol. 4, Part 1**, 634; **Vol. 5, Part 2**, 155; Texas, **Vol. 4, Part 1**, 96; Virginia, **Vol. 4, Part 1**, 460; **Vol. 5, Part 2**, 94
Law Academy of Philadelphia, **Vol. 3, Part 1**, 525 f.
Law and Peace, **Supp. 7**, 182
Law cases: *Amistad* captives, **Vol. 1, Part 1**, 90; barbed-wire trust, **Vol. 2, Part 2**, 597; bribery cases, **Vol. 5, Part 2**, 414; Chicago Traction cases, **Vol. 4, Part 1**, 605; *Cohens* v. *Virginia,* **Vol. 7, Part 1**, 638 f.; *Commonwealth* v. *Green,* **Vol. 4, Part 1**, 255; Daly's cases, **Vol. 3, Part 1**, 42; Dartmouth College case, **Vol. 1, Part 1**, 57; **Vol. 2, Part 1**, 114; **Vol. 4, Part 1**, 304; **Vol. 5, Part 1**, 166; **Vol. 9, Part 1**, 292; **Vol. 10, Part 1**, 585 f.; *De Chastellux* v. *Fairchield,* **Vol. 4, Part 1**, 255; *Donoghue* v. *County,* **Vol. 4, Part 1**, 255; Dred Scott, **Vol. 4, Part 1**, 121, 231; **Vol. 5, Part 2**, 113; *Ex parte* Bushnell, **Vol. 9, Part 2**, 234; *Farmers Loan & Trust Co.* v. *Northern Pacific Railway Co.,* **Vol. 5, Part 2**, 46; *Gibbons* v. *Ogden,* **Vol. 4, Part 1**, 242–43; *Goodyear* v. *Day,* **Vol. 3, Part 1**, 288; Granger cases, **Vol. 3, Part 1**, 283, 330; *Hendrickson* v. *Decow,* **Vol. 4, Part 1**, 17; Homestead, **Vol. 3, Part 1**, 296; insular cases, **Vol. 4, Part 1**, 628; *Mason and Slidell,* **Vol. 3, Part 1**, 42; *Mason* v. *Wilson,* **Vol. 3, Part 1**, 80; *Milligan* case, **Vol. 3, Part 2**, 360 f.; Ninety-Nine Year case, **Vol. 8, Part 1**, 9 f.; *Osborn* v. *Nicholson,* **Vol. 4, Part 1**, 150; *Pillsbury* v. *Pillsbury Washburn Co., Ltd.,* **Vol. 5, Part 2**, 46; *Prudence Crandall* case, **Vol. 3, Part 1**, 27; "Slaymaker" case, **Vol. 5, Part 2**, 413 f.; *Strother* v. *Lucas,* **Vol. 4, Part 1**, 231; Telephone Appeals case, **Vol. 3, Part 1**, 296; *Vanderbilt* v. *Aspinwall,* **Vol. 1, Part 1**, 614; Wabash case, **Vol. 4, Part 1**, 609; *Webster* v. *Harwinton,* **Vol. 1, Part 1**, 283; *Wynehamer* v. *People,* **Vol. 5, Part 2**, 78
Lawn tennis: Larned, W. A., **Vol. 6, Part 1**, 3; steel-framed racket, invention of, **Vol. 6, Part 1**, 3. *See also* Tennis
Law of Freedom and Bondage in the United States, **Vol. 5, Part 1**, 423
Lawrance Aeronautical Corporation, founding of, **Supp. 4**, 473, 474
Lawrence, David L., references to, **Supp. 9**, 253, 254
Lawrence, D. H.: biography of, **Supp. 10**, 724; references to, **Supp. 4**, 131; **Supp. 7**, 306, 380, 487; **Supp. 9**, 782; **Supp. 10**, 539, 540
Lawrence, Ernest O., references to, **Supp. 4**, 483; **Supp. 5**, 529; **Supp. 7**, 275; **Supp. 8**, 229–30
Lawrence, Gertrude, reference to, **Supp. 9**, 587
Lawrence, Pauline, reference to, **Supp. 6**, 312
Lawrence, Mass., textile strike. *See* Textile industry
Lawrence Academy, founding of, **Vol. 5, Part 1**, 186
Lawrence Scientific School. *See* Harvard University
Lawrenceville School, founding of, **Vol. 4, Part 1**, 124, 552; **Vol. 6, Part 2**, 193
Lawrenceville stories, **Supp. 5**, 372
Laws of the Province of South-Carolina, **Vol. 9, Part 2**, 557
Lawson, Ernest, reference to, **Supp. 5**, 635
Lawson, John Howard, reference to, **Supp. 3**, 238
Lawson, Ted W., reference to, **Supp. 9**, 188
"Lawson panic," **Vol. 4, Part 1**, 578
Lawyers. For complete list, *see* Occupations Index
Lawyers' Constitutional Defense Committee, founding of, **Supp. 8**, 285
Lawyers Guild Review, predecessor, **Supp. 5**, 389
Laxalt, Paul D., reference to, **Supp. 10**, 357
Laxatives, **Supp. 8**, 339
Lay analysis, **Supp. 3**, 385
Layden, Elmer, reference to, **Supp. 7**, 729
Laymen's Foreign Missions Inquiry: Fact-Finders' Reports, **Vol. 10, Part 1**, 62
Lazard, Paul D., reference to, **Supp. 10**, 357
Lazard Frères (banking), **Supp. 10** 533, 534
Lazarists, in Louisiana, Vol. 3, Pan 1, 437 f.
Lazarsfeld, Paul F., reference to, **Supp. 6**, 605
Lazarus, F. & R., Co., founding of, **Supp. 9**, 483
Lazarus, Hyman, **Supp. 10**, 586
Lazovich, Olga, references to, **Supp. 6**, 713, 714
LDS. *See* Mormon church
Lea, Henry C., reference to, **Vol. 7, Part 1**, 330
Lead mining: **Vol. 1, Part 1**, 435; **Vol. 1, Part 2**, 392; **Vol. 3, Part 1**, 475; **Vol. 4, Part 2**, 546; **Vol. 5, Part 2**, 600; **Vol. 6, Part 2**, 496, 497; pencils, first use of graphite in, **Vol. 3, Part 1**, 329; refining, **Vol. 1, Part 1**, 528; smelting, **Vol. 8, Part 1**, 326.
Leadville mine, **Vol. 7, Part 1**, 461, 507; **Vol. 9, Part 2**, 263
Leaf, Munro, references to, **Supp. 6**, 372; **Supp. 7**, 307
League for Crippled Children (Md.), **Supp. 1**, 40
League for Industrial Democracy, **Supp. 5**, 664; **Supp. 6**, 392; **Supp. 8**, 649
League for Peace and Democracy. *See* American League Against War and Fascism
League for Political Education, **Supp. 6**, 160
League of Catholic Unity, **Vol. 5, Part 2**, 590
League of Liberty, **Vol. 6, Part 1**, 368
League of Nations: **Vol. 2, Part 1**, 196; Vol. 3, Part 1. 265; **Vol. 4, Part 1**, 45; **Vol. 4, Part 2**, 354; **Vol. 5, Part 2**, 217, 267, 610; **Vol. 6, Part 1**, 348; **Vol. 7, Part 1**, 44; **Vol. 8, Part 1**, 92 f.; **Vol. 10, Part 2**, 103, 364; covenant drafting, **Supp. 5**, 308; **Supp. 7**, 536–37; economic reorganization of Europe, **Supp. 1**, 662; Financial Committee, **Supp. 5**, 700–701; health issues, **Supp. 6**, 703; first undersecretary, **Supp. 9**, 288; labor movement, **Supp. 6**, 707; opposition to, **Supp. 3**, 396–97; philanthropic support for, **Supp. 5**, 61; refugee commission, **Supp. 7**, 498; resettlement commission, **Supp. 4**, 604; Saar plebiscite, **Supp. 5**, 723; Senate opposition to, **Supp. 3**, 622; **Supp. 9**, 504; support for, **Supp. 3**, 472–73; **Supp. 6**, 556; **Supp. 7**, 360; **Supp. 9**, 556; **Supp. 10**, 208; Wilson administration advocacy, **Supp. 4**, 170–71; women's organized support for, **Supp. 4**, 158
League of Nations Association: **Supp. 7**, 688; directorship, **Supp. 10**, 208; predecessor, **Supp. 5**, 308
League of Nations Non-Partisan Association, **Supp. 3**, 168
League of Red Cross Societies, **Supp. 6**, 703
League of Universal Brotherhood, founding of, **Vol. 2, Part 1**, 329
League of Women Voters: founding of, **Supp. 1**, 432; **Supp. 4**, 158; **Supp. 5**, 532–33; Massachusetts, **Supp. 4**, 86; nonpartisanship, **Supp. 5**, 62; predecessors, **Supp. 6**, 79
League to Enforce Peace, **Supp. 3**, 472–74; **Supp. 6**, 25; founding of, **Supp. 4**, 550; **Supp. 5**, 308
Leahy, William D., references to, **Supp. 6**, 339–40, 430
Lear Jet Corporation, **Supp. 10**, 442–43
"Learned the case," use of the phrase in printer's trade, **Vol. 8, Part 1**, 60 f.
Learning: by problem-solving, **Supp. 5**, 72; research,

Supp. 10, 28; theory, **Supp. 4**, 485, 832–33; **Supp. 5**, 328–30; **Supp. 6**, 261–62, 527–28; **Supp. 6**, 640. *See also* Textbooks
Learson, Vincent, reference to, **Supp. 9**, 844
Leather industry, **Vol. 1, Part 1**, 299; Vol. 2, Part a2, 595 f.; **Vol. 3, Part 2**, 46, 306; **Vol. 4, Part 1**, 229; **Vol. 5, Part 2**, 65; **Vol. 8, Part 2**, 430; **Supp. 10**, 773
Leaves of Grass, **Vol. 6, Part 1**, 145 f.
Leavitt, Dorris Dean, reference to, **Supp. 5**, 417
Leavitt, Henrietta S., references to, **Supp. 5**, 326; **Supp. 10**, 625
Lebanon crisis (1958), **Supp. 8**, 158
Lebanon University, founding of, **Vol. 5, Part 1**, 128
Leblanc, Georgette: Anderson, M. C., relationship, **Supp. 9**, 33–34
Leclaire, model village of, **Vol. 7, Part 1**, 420
Lecompton (Kans.) Constitution, **Vol. 2, Part 1**, 411; **Vol. 3, Part 1**, 401
Le Conte, Joseph, teacher of Royce, **Vol. 8, Part 2**, 206
Lecturing: **Vol. 1, Part 1**, 409, 574; **Vol. 2, Part 2**, 371 f.; **Vol. 3, Part 2**, 135 f., 145, 368, 422; **Vol. 4, Part 1**, 480; **Vol. 4, Part 2**, 53, 79, 364; **Vol. 5, Part 1**, 67; **Vol. 5, Part 2**, 69 f., 105, 172, 416, 525, 571, 595, 604; **Vol. 6, Part 1**, 102, 140, 155, 286, 408; **Vol. 6, Part 2**, 416; **Vol. 6, Part 2**, 341, 599 f., 646; **Vol. 7, Part 2**, 493; **Vol. 8, Part 2**, 110, 327, 389; **Vol. 9, Part 1**, 39, 126, 161, 221, 260 f., 266 f.; **Vol. 9, Part 2**, 55 f., 74, 492 f., 609; bookings, organized, **Vol. 8, Part 1**, 444; Chautauqua circuit, **Supp. 8**, 317; Chautauqua lyceum bureau, **Vol. 5, Part 2**, 105; first $1000 fee for, **Vol. 8, Part 1**, 60 f.; internationalism advocacy, **Supp. 7**, 498; music appreciation, **Supp. 5**, 183; **Supp. 7**, 707; musical readings, **Supp. 4**, 798–99; on Alaskan exploration, **Supp. 7**, 371; on American literature, **Supp. 5**, 542; on Bible, **Supp. 3**, 825; on birds, **Supp. 7**, 8; on socialism, **Supp. 4**, 635–36; on theater, **Supp. 8**, 54; prohibition advocacy, **Supp. 4**, 741; **Supp. 5**, 701, 702; **Supp. 8**, 505; public-speaking education, **Supp. 5**, 102; race relations improvement, **Supp. 3**, 827–28
Ledbetter, Huddie ("Leadbelly"), references to, **Supp. 4**, 502; **Supp. 8**, 696
Lederberg, Joshua, reference to, **Supp. 9**, 794
Lederer, William J., reference to, **Supp. 7**, 93
Lederle Laboratories, **Supp. 6**, 176
Ledo Road, **Supp. 6**, 508
Lee, Arthur, colonial negotiations with France, **Vol. 3, Part 1**, 174; **Vol. 6, Part 1**, 133
Lee, Brandon, reference to, **Supp. 9**, 486
Lee, Charles, trial of, **Vol. 5, Part 1**, 500; **Vol. 8, Part 2**, 407
Lee, Doc, reference to, **Supp. 9**, 653
Lee, Gypsy Rose, reference to, **Supp. 6**, 637
Lee, Henry ("Light-Horse Harry"), references to, **Vol. 6, Part 1**, 121; **Vol. 7, Part 1**, 636
Lee, Hugh J., reference to, **Supp. 5**, 539
Lee, Ivy, biography of, **Supp. 6**, 520; reference to, **Supp. 9**, 681; **Supp. 10**, 335
Lee, John, reference to, **Vol. 7, Part 1**, 304
Lee, John R., reference to, **Supp. 4**, 300
Lee, Richard Henry, references to, **Vol. 6, Part 1**, 597; **Vol. 8, Part 2**,; 536; **Vol. 9, Part 1**, 322
Lee, Robert E.: **Vol. 3, Part 2**, 9, 357; **Vol. 5, Part 1**, 126, 197, 557; **Vol. 6, Part 1**, 106, 391 f.; **Vol. 8, Part 2**, 26; **Vol. 9, Part 1**, 80, 170; biographies of, **Vol. 5, Part 2**, 191; **Vol. 6, Part 1**, 374; **Supp. 1**, 105; military secretary of, **Vol. 6, Part 1**, 374; Richmond operations, **Vol. 3, Part 1**, 598; sculpture of, **Supp. 3**, 88; surrender of, **Vol. 3, Part 1**, 395; **Vol. 6, Part 1**, 519; **Vol. 7, Part 2**, 219; West Point, **Vol. 5, Part 1**, 428; writings on, **Supp. 5**, 234
Lee, Roger I., reference to, **Supp. 9**, 862
Lee and Gordon's Mills, Ga., operation at. *See* Chickamauga campaign
Leech, John, reference to, **Supp. 5**, 636
Leeds, William B., reference to, **Vol. 7, Part 1**, 143
Leedy, Harry, reference to, **Supp. 10**, 59
Lee, Harris and Lee. *See* Ross, T. J., and Associates
Lee's Lieutenants, **Supp. 5**, 234
Leg, artificial, **Vol. 1, Part 1**, 428
Legal Aid Society of New York, **Supp. 8**, 662
Le Gallienne, Eva, references to, **Supp. 9**, 848, 849
Legal profession. *See* American Bar Association; Judiciary; Law
Legal realism, **Supp. 3**, 185–86
Legal Tender Acts, **Vol. 3, Part 2**, 166; **Vol. 7, Part 1**, 423
Legends, Indian, **Vol. 5, Part 2**, 208
Léger, Fernand, reference to, **Supp. 6**, 552, 553
Legion of Decency, **Supp. 5**, 419; **Supp. 6**, 288, 479
Legion of Honor, **Vol. 5, Part 2**, 533
Legislative assembly, first in America, **Vol. 8, Part 1**, 110
Legislative Drafting Research Fund, founding of, **Supp. 5**, 107
Legislative Reorganization Act (1946), **Supp. 8**, 128; **Supp. 10**, 547
Legislative Reorganization Act (1970), **Supp. 10**, 530
Lehigh Coal Mine Co., **Vol. 2, Part 2**, 108, 110
Lehigh Crane Iron Co., **Vol. 9, Part 2**, 427 f.
Lehigh University, **Vol. 3, Part 1**, 460 f.; **Vol. 5, Part 2**, 443; **Vol. 7, Part 2**, 129, 132; **Vol. 8, Part 1**, 126; **Vol. 9, Part 1**, 629; **Supp. 9**, 314
Lehigh Valley Railroad, **Vol. 7, Part 1**, 355; **Vol. 7, Part 2**, 131; **Vol. 8, Part 1**, 94; **Vol. 8, Part 2**, 405
Lehigh Zinc & Iron Co., reference to, **Supp. 3**, 348
Lehman, Herbert H., references to, **Supp. 3**, 280; **Supp. 9**, 230
Lehman, Mrs. Herbert, reference to, **Supp. 10**, 172
Lehman, Irving, reference to, **Supp. 7**, 467
Lehman, Philip, reference to, **Supp. 3**, 24
Lehman Brothers, **Supp. 8**, 367; establishment of, **Supp. 2**, 377
Leipziger, Henry, reference to, **Supp. 3**, 600
Leipzig Institute, history of medicine, **Supp. 6**, 580
Leisler, Jacob, references to, **Vol. 5, Part 1**, 603; **Vol. 7, Part 1**, 476, 516 f.; **Vol. 8, Part 2**, 476
Leisler Rebellion (N.Y.), **Vol. 3, Part 1**, 247; **Vol. 6, Part 1**, 181, 319
Leland, Henry M., references to, **Supp. 3**, 562; **Supp. 4**, 244, 293; **Supp. 8**, 609
Leland, Faulconer & Norton Co., **Supp. 3**, 562
Leland Stanford University, **Vol. 1, Part 1**, 632; **Vol. 1, Part 2**, 603; **Vol. 5, Part 2**, 211; **Vol. 7, Part 1**, 43; **Vol. 7, Part 2**, 480; **Vol. 9, Part 1**, 504
LeMay, Curtis, reference to, **Supp. 9**, 255; **Supp. 10**, 400
Lemke, William J., references to, **Supp. 6**, 613; **Supp. 9**, 30; **Supp. 10**, 152, 745
Lemons, culture of, **Vol. 4, Part 1**, 145
Lend-a-Hand movement, **Vol. 4, Part 2**, 100; **Vol. 8, Part 2**, 191
Lend-Lease Act (1941), **Supp. 3**, 659; **Supp. 4**, 88; **Supp. 6**, 437; **Supp. 8**, 446
L'Enfant, Pierre L., reference to, **Supp. 3**, 533
Lenglen, Suzanne, reference to, **Supp. 6**, 425
Lenin, Vladimir I.: biography of, **Supp. 9**, 724; references to, **Supp. 5**, 135, 499, 579; **Supp. 8**, 61, 564
Lenroot, Irvine L, reference to, **Supp. 6**, 146
Lenses: achromatic, **Supp. 1**, 383; development of, **Supp. 3**, 40–41; manufacture of, **Vol. 6, Part 1**, 506
Lenya, Lotte, reference to, **Supp. 4**, 868–69
Lenz, Sidney, reference to, **Supp. 5**, 146
Leonard, Benny, reference to, **Supp. 7**, 209

Leonard, Dutch, reference to, **Supp. 7**, 129
Leonard, John William, reference to, **Supp. 3**, 508
Leonard, Robert Z., reference to, **Supp. 7**, 563
Leonard, Sheldon, reference to, **Supp. 9**, 76
Leopard, firing of, on the *Chesapeake*, **Vol. 5, Part 2**, 30
Leopold, Aldo, reference to, **Supp. 9**, 526
Leopold-Loeb murder trial, **Supp. 2**, 142; **Supp. 3**, 822
Lepidoptera, collections of, **Supp. 1**, 414
Leprosy, **Vol. 3, Part 1**, 582; **Vol. 6, Part 1**, 17; **Vol. 8, Part 1**, 154 f.; **Vol. 8, Part 2**, 8; missions, **Supp. 3**, 623–24; treatment of, **Supp. 4**, 529–30; **Supp. 7**, 195
L'Esaminatore, official Catholic organ, **Vol. 5, Part 2**, 589
Lescohier, Don D., reference to, **Supp. 3**, 178
Leslie, Frank, references to, **Vol. 7, Part 1**, 186, 392
Leslie, Miriam Florence Folline (Mrs. Frank), reference to, **Supp. 4**, 158; **Supp. 7**, 779
Lester, Will, reference to, **Supp. 9**, 213
Letchworth Village (N.Y.), **Vol. 6, Part 1**, 194; administration, **Supp. 2**, 388
"Letheon," early name for ether, **Vol. 7, Part 1**, 269
Let It Be, **Supp. 10**, 450
"Letter from Birmingham Jail," **Supp. 8**, 334
Lettering. *See* Calligraphy; Typographical design
Letts, F. Dickenson, reference to, **Supp. 9**, 395
Let Us Now Praise Famous Men, **Supp. 5**, 511; **Supp. 9**, 268
Leuba, James, reference to, **Supp. 4**, 766, 767
Leukemia: "Auer bodies," **Supp. 4**, 34; X-ray treatment, **Supp. 4**, 581
Levant, Oscar, reference to, **Supp. 3**, 690
Levees, construction of, along Mississippi, **Vol. 3, Part 2**, 403; **Vol. 4, Part 2**, 353
Levene, P. A. T., reference to, **Supp. 4**, 287
Lever House (New York City), design, **Supp. 7**, 691
Levi-Civita, Tullio, reference to, **Supp. 7**, 216
Levin, Hymie, reference to, **Supp. 6**, 263, 264
Levin, Meyer, reference to, **Supp. 9**, 490
Levine, Charles A., reference to, **Supp. 6**, 51
Levine, Philip, reference to, **Supp. 3**, 441–42
Levitt, Alfred S., reference to, **Supp. 7**, 469–70
Levitt, William J., reference to, **Supp. 7**, 469–70
Levitt and Sons, **Supp. 7**, 469–70
Levittown, N.Y., **Supp. 7**, 470
Levy, Jules, reference to, **Supp. 6**, 241
Lew, Henri, references to, **Supp. 6**, 357, 358
Lewis, George Edward ("Duffy"), reference to, **Supp. 9**, 403
Lewis, Gilbert N., reference to, **Supp. 4**, 839
Lewis, Jerry, telethons, **Supp. 9**, 99
Lewis, J. Hamilton, references to, **Supp. 3**, 710; **Supp. 6**, 636
Lewis, John L., references to, **Supp. 3**, 656, 660; **Supp. 4**, 75, 376; **Supp. 5**, 248–49; **Supp. 5**, 254, 282, 339–40, 509–10, 654, 691, 714; **Supp. 7**, 81–82, 172; **Supp. 8**, 207, 290, 510–11, 652; **Supp. 9**, 565; **Supp. 10**, 203, 524, 643, 682
Lewis, Oscar, references to, **Supp. 3**, 373; **Supp. 6**, 533
Lewis, Paul A., references to, **Supp. 3**, 441; **Supp. 4**, 34, 287
Lewis, Robert, reference to, **Supp. 5**, 53
Lewis, Ruth Maslow, references to, **Supp. 8**, 377, 378
Lewis, Sinclair: biography of, **Supp. 10**, 724; de Kruif relationship, **Supp. 9**, 225; Kelley relationship, **Supp. 6**, 328, 329; references to, **Supp. 5**, 85, 272; **Supp. 6**, 95; **Supp. 7**, 740; **Supp. 9**, 349
Lewis, Thomas, reference to, **Supp. 6**, 117
Lewis and Clark expedition, **Vol. 2, Part 2**, 143, 319, 435; **Vol. 4, Part 1**, 178; **Vol. 5, Part 2**, 29; **Vol. 6, Part 1**, 221, 291; **Vol. 7, Part 2**, 51; **Vol. 8, Part 1**, 255; **Vol. 8, Part 2**, 278; history of, **Vol. 1, Part 1**, 203
Lewisohn, Adolph, reference to, **Supp. 5**, 426–27
Lewisohn, Ludwig, reference to, **Supp. 5**, 673
Lewisohn, Margaret Seligman, reference to, **Supp. 5**, 427
Lewisohn Brothers, establishment of, **Supp. 2**, 383
Lexer, Erich, reference to, **Supp. 3**, 67
Lexicography, **Vol. 1, Part 1**, 218; **Vol. 3, Part 1**, 458, 464, 512, 567, 570, 597, 606; **Vol. 4, Part 1**, 399 f.; **Vol. 5, Part 2**, 2, 490 f.; **Vol. 8, Part 1**, 59 f., 95 f., 116 f., 122 f., 305, 330; **Vol. 9, Part 1**, 64; **Vol. 9, Part 2**, 440; **Vol. 10, Part 1**, 594 f.; **Vol. 10, Part 2**, 56. *See also* Dictionaries; Words
Lexington, Mass.: battle at, **Vol. 3, Part 1**, 150; **Vol. 7, Part 1**, 530; **Vol. 7, Part 2**, 233; **Vol. 8, Part 1**, 515; **Vol. 9, Part 1**, 531; **Vol. 10, Part 1**, 415; civic service, **Vol. 5, Part 1**, 337; normal school, first, state, **Vol. 7, Part 2**, 404
Lexington, Mo., battle of, **Vol. 8, Part 1**, 216
Lexington, race horse, **Vol. 9, Part 2**, 366
Lexington Morning Herald, **Supp. 1**, 114
"Lexington of the Seas," **Vol. 7, Part 1**, 610
Lexow investigation, **Vol. 7, Part 1**, 280; **Vol. 7, Part 2**, 245
Leyte, World War II action, **Supp. 4**, 589; **Supp. 6**, 268
Lhévinne, Josef, reference to, **Supp. 10**, 455
Lhévinne, Rosina, reference to, **Supp. 3**, 459
Liability, legal writings on, **Supp. 3**, 43
Libbey, Edward Drummond, references to, **Vol. 7, Part 2**, 122; **Vol. 9, Part 1**, 611; **Supp. 9**, 92
Libbey-Owens-Ford Glass Co., **Supp. 9**, 92, 93
Libby Prison, **Vol. 1, Part 1**, 636; **Vol. 6, Part 1**, 557 f.; **Vol. 9, Part 2**, 636
Libel law and suits: **Vol. 3, Part 1**, 276; **Vol. 3, Part 2**, 167; **Vol. 4, Part 2**, 182; **Vol. 8, Part 1**, 112, f., 118 f.; **Vol. 8, Part 2**, 282 f.; AP political cartoon suit, **Supp. 3**, 852; *Confidential* series suits, **Supp. 5**, 406; Ford-Hearst suit, **Supp. 4**, 288, 302; **Supp. 5**, 450; Hiss-Chambers suit, **Supp. 5**, 665; **Supp. 7**, 114; Reynolds-Pegler suit, **Supp. 7**, 643; **Supp. 8**, 498; suits against Pearson, **Supp. 8**, 497; Tinkham-Cannon suit, **Supp. 6**, 636; wartime, **Supp. 6**, 105
Liberal Christian League, **Vol. 2, Part 2**, 310
Liberalism: Democratic party, Truman era, **Supp. 10**, 226–27; journalistic voice of, **Supp. 4**, 850–51; non-Communist left, **Supp. 3**, 777; theological, **Supp. 4**, 512–13, 525–26; writings on, **Supp. 3**, 731; **Supp. 4**, 804
Liberal party, founding of, **Supp. 7**, 156
Liberal party (New York State), founding of, **Supp. 10**, 324, 697
Liberal Republican movement, **Vol. 2, Part 1**, 106; **Vol. 5, Part 2**, 421; **Vol. 8, Part 2**, 122, 473
Liberator: **Supp. 7**, 268; abolition paper, **Vol. 4, Part 1**, 169; **Vol. 5, Part 2**, 112; **Vol. 9, Part 2**, 299; **Supp. 7**, 268; founding of, **Supp. 3**, 852; **Supp. 4**, 528; **Supp. 8**, 149
Liberia: **Vol. 1, Part 1**, 394 f.; **Vol. 3, Part 2**, 104; **Vol. 4, Part 2**, 56, 371; **Vol. 5, Part 2**, 97 f.; **Vol. 7, Part 1**, 16; **Vol. 8, Part 2**, 11, 212, 253; botany of, **Supp. 2**, 113; colonization of, **Vol. 6, Part 2**, 545; development of, **Supp. 2**, 188; diplomatic relations with U.S., **Vol. 8, Part 2**, 10; **Vol. 9, Part 1**, 155, 375; **Vol. 10, Part 1**, 66 f.; **Supp. 7**, 767–68; Firestone operations in, **Supp. 9**, 283; first president of, **Vol. 8, Part 2**, 10; missions, **Vol. 2, Part 1**, 555; **Vol. 3, Part 1**, 156; **Vol. 7, Part 2**, 428
Liberia College, founding of, **Vol. 9, Part 2**, 623
Liberia Co., founding of, **Supp. 4**, 778
Liberty, **Supp. 5**, 527; founding of, **Supp. 2**, 670; **Supp. 5**, 453

Liberty, Hancock's sloop, **Vol. 4, Part 2**, 218
Liberty Bell, **Vol. 7, Part 1**, 554
"Liberty Boys," **Vol. 9, Part 2**, 361
Liberty Films, **Supp. 9**, 767–68
Liberty Hall Academy, forerunner of Washington and Lee University, **Vol. 8, Part 1**, 222
Liberty League, **Supp. 6**, 679; founding of, **Vol. 4, Part 1**, 385; **Vol. 6, Part 1**, 368
Liberty loans, **Vol. 4, Part 1**, 241; **Vol. 5, Part 1**, 56; **Supp. 3**, 480; **Supp. 4**, 469; **Supp. 6**, 376
Liberty Memorial (Kansas City, Mo.), **Supp. 1**, 537
Liberty party, **Vol. 1, Part 2**, 293; **Vol. 2, Part 2**, 28; **Vol. 5, Part 1**, 151; **Vol. 6, Part 1**, 116; **Vol. 9, Part 1**, 271
Libman-Sacks disease, **Supp. 4**, 494
Libraries and library work: administration, **Supp. 4**, 845–46; Americana, **Supp. 5**, 9, 10; as popular education tool, **Supp. 3**, 90–91, 416; Australia survey, **Supp. 10**, 778; bookstacks, fire-proof, **Vol. 8, Part 1**, 138 f.; branch, early experiments in, **Vol. 8, Part 1**, 171 f.; branch for blacks, **Supp. 3**, 280–81; branch system, **Supp. 3**, 90–91; **Supp. 4**, 19; building and equipment of, **Vol. 3, Part 1**, 604; catalog cards, **Supp. 3**, 510; **Supp. 5**, 753; catalogs for, **Vol. 1, Part 1**, 218; **Vol. 3, Part 1**, 15 f.; **Vol. 5, Part 2**, 666; **Vol. 10, Part 1**, 107; catalog uniformity, **Supp. 3**, 326–27; circulating, **Vol. 1, Part 1**, 335; **Vol. 1, Part 2**, 162; **Vol. 3, Part 2**, 356; **Vol. 4, Part 2**, 591; **Vol. 6, Part 1**, 427; **Vol. 7, Part 1**, 510; **Vol. 9, Part 2**, 445; classification systems, **Supp. 5**, 554; **Supp. 10**, 778; contributions to development of, **Vol. 1, Part 1**, 640; **Vol. 1, Part 2**, 557, 610; **Vol. 3, Part 1**, 121, 143, 192, 277, 550; **Vol. 3, Part 2**, 55, 206, 254 f., 475, 479, 487, 493, 519, 541; **Vol. 4, Part 1**, 21, 557, 617; **Vol. 4, Part 2**, 42, 51, 321, 483; **Vol. 5, Part 1**, 137, 191, 244, 335, 516; **Vol. 5, Part 2**, 206, 215, 606; **Vol. 6, Part 1**, 148, 172, 231, 570; **Vol. 7, Part 1**, 127, 134, 172, 413 f., 447; **Vol. 8, Part 1**, 65, 229; **Vol. 8, Part 2**, 382, 525; **Vol. 9, Part 1**, 24, 49, 147, 198, 229, 303, 317, 463 f., 562; **Vol. 9, Part 2**, 135, 330, 521, 587; **Vol. 10, Part 1**, 558 f.; **Vol. 10, Part 2**, 403; decimal classification, **Supp. 1**, 242; first conference of librarians, **Vol. 4, Part 1**, 557; **Vol. 8, Part 1**, 66 f.; first in county jail, **Vol. 4, Part 1**, 271; first free in New York City, **Vol. 8, Part 1**, 168 f.; history research center, **Supp. 3**, 262; journals, **Supp. 1**, 101; **Supp. 5**, 753; Lippincott Award, **Supp. 10**, 461; mercantile, **Vol. 10, Part 2**, 471; microfilm and microfiche, **Supp. 8**, 120; naval, **Supp. 6**, 348; New York Conference of Librarians, **Vol. 5, Part 2**, 66; organization of, **Vol. 2, Part 1**, 20; **Vol. 3, Part 1**, 57, 143; **Vol. 6, Part 1**, 2; **Vol. 8, Part 1**, 66 f.; organizations, *see specific names;* physiology, **Supp. 6**, 223, 224; presidential, **Supp. 4**, 176; **Supp. 6**, 541; public libraries, **Vol. 1, Part 2**, 610; **Vol. 2, Part 2**, 583; **Vol. 5, Part 2**, 66, 445; **Vol. 8, Part 1**, 66 f.; **Vol. 9, Part 2**, 549; **Vol. 10, Part 1**, 558 f.; publications for, **Supp. 10**, 418; reference library, first official, **Vol. 6, Part 1**, 570; research and scholarly, **Supp. 6**, 398–99; schools for library work, **Vol. 6, Part 1**, 148; **Vol. 8, Part 1**, 17; standards, **Supp. 1**, 101; teaching of, **Supp. 1**, 242; **Supp. 3**, 280; **Supp. 4**, 19; **Supp. 5**, 47; technical services, **Supp. 10**, 777, 778; traveling, establishment of, **Vol. 3, Part 1**, 192; women writers' collection, **Supp. 6**, 576; World's Congress of Librarians, **Vol. 4, Part 1**, 558; writings on, **Vol. 3, Part 1**, 604; **Vol. 4, Part 1**, 558; **Vol. 5, Part 2**, 66; **Vol. 7, Part 2**, 467; **Vol. 8, Part 1**, 17, 66. *See also* American Library Association; Archives; Bibliographies; Libraries (specific); *names of specific libraries*
Libraries (specific): Astor, *see* New York Public Library; Avery Architectural Library, **Supp. 6**, 272; Baltimore, **Vol. 8, Part 1**, 171 f.; Boston Medical, **Vol. 8, Part 1**, 275; **Vol. 9, Part 2**, 94; Boston Public, **Vol. 1, Part 2**, 24, 53; **Vol. 4, Part 1**, 617; **Vol. 6, Part 2**, 100; **Vol. 7, Part 2**, 241; **Vol. 9, Part 2**, 405, 528; **Vol. 10, Part 2**, 161, 403; Buffalo, N.Y., **Vol. 10, Part 1**, 426; California, **Vol. 3, Part 1**, 121; Chicago, **Vol. 1, Part 1**, 448; Galveston, Tex., **Vol. 8, Part 2**, 166; Harvard University, **Vol. 8, Part 1**, 308 f.; Lenox Library, New York City, **Vol. 6, Part 1**, 172; **Vol. 7, Part 1**, 126; New York Academy of Medicine, **Vol. 8, Part 1**, 269 f.; New York Public, **Vol. 1, Part 1**, 335, 445; **Vol. 1, Part 2**, 268; **Vol. 7, Part 2**, 107; **Vol. 8, Part 1**, 17, 125 f., 634 f.; **Vol. 8, Part 2**, 382; Tilden, New York City, **Vol. 9, Part 2**, 541; University of Pennsylvania, **Vol. 7, Part 2**, 441; University of Pennsylvania Law School, **Vol. 5, Part 2**, 445; Wisconsin State Historical Society, **Vol. 3, Part 1**, 551 f.; Yale University, **Vol. 3, Part 1**, 277; **Vol. 3, Part 2**, 79; **Vol. 8, Part 2**, 480
Library Journal, founding of, **Vol. 6, Part 1**, 231; **Supp. 1**, 101
Library of American Biography, **Vol. 7, Part 2**, 341, 343
Library of Congress: **Vol. 4, Part 1**, 285; **Vol. 5, Part 1**, 385; **Vol. 5, Part 2**, 31; **Vol. 9, Part 1**, 463; **Vol. 9, Part 2**, 587; administration, **Supp. 5**, 554–55; annex construction, **Supp. 5**, 554; Bibliography, Division of, **Vol. 4, Part 1**, 617; Bollingen Prize in Poetry, **Supp. 7**, 347; Catalog Division, **Supp. 3**, 326; chamber music auditorium, **Supp. 5**, 129, 554; classification system, **Supp. 5**, 664; **Supp. 10**, 778; collection improvement, **Supp. 9**, 73; collections, **Supp. 5**, 586; designing of, **Vol. 7, Part 2**, 411; folk-song archives, **Supp. 4**, 502; foreign copying program, **Supp. 8**, 369; Manuscripts Division, **Supp. 1**, 343; **Supp. 2**, 191–92; **Supp. 3**, 285–86; **Supp. 3**, 534; mosaics in, **Supp. 1**, 247; murals in, **Vol. 7, Part 2**, 352; Music Division, **Supp. 3**, 252; **Vol. 9, Part 1**, 395; rare books, donation of, **Supp. 10**, 702; reclassification, **Supp. 3**, 510; statues in, **Vol. 1, Part 2**, 12
Library of Education, **Vol. 1, Part 1**, 624
Library of Southern Literature, **Vol. 9, Part 1**, 245
Lichenology, **Vol. 10, Part 1**, 43
Lick Observatory, **Vol. 3, Part 1**, 292; **Vol. 5, Part 1**, 136, 432; **Vol. 5, Part 2**, 279; **Vol. 6, Part 1**, 234; **Vol. 7, Part 1**, 6, 454; **Vol. 8, Part 2**, 412; **Supp. 9**, 713
Lie, Trygve, reference to, **Supp. 9**, 192
Liebig, Justus von, reference to, **Vol. 8, Part 1**, 96
Liebler, Theodore A., reference to, **Supp. 4**, 842–43
Liebling, A. J., reference to, **Supp. 10**, 754–55
Liebold, Ernest G., reference to, **Supp. 4**, 300
Lie-detector, introduction of, **Vol. 8, Part 2**, 445
Life (general-interest magazine): **Vol. 1, Part 1**, 573; **Vol. 7, Part 1**, 53; **Supp. 7**, 382, 383, 384, 436, 437; Bourke-White photographs, **Supp. 9**, 111; cover photographs, **Supp. 10**, 305; drama criticism, **Supp. 3**, 53–54; editorial writing, **Supp. 5**, 152–53; founding of, **Supp. 8**, 394–96; illustrations, **Supp. 3**, 300–301; **Supp. 7**, 17; movie reviews, **Supp. 5**, 623
Life (humor magazine), editing, **Supp. 1**, 544–45
Life Begins at Forty, **Supp. 5**, 546
Lifeboats, **Vol. 3, Part 2**, 582
Life Extension Institute, **Supp. 4**, 275
Life in a Mexican Village: Tepoztlan Restudied, **Supp. 8**, 378
Life insurance: **Vol. 1, Part 1**, 599; **Vol. 3, Part 1**, 463; **Vol. 3, Part 2**, 419; **Vol. 4, Part 2**, 500; **Vol. 5, Part 1**, 450; **Vol. 6, Part 1**, 495, 562, 588; **Vol. 6, Part 2**, 12; **Vol. 7, Part 1**, 248, 265, 323; **Vol. 7, Part 2**, 56, 313, 381, 471, 547; **Vol. 8, Part 2**, 351; actuarial studies, **Supp. 4**, 384–85; investigations of, **Vol. 8, Part 2**, 96; mail-order marketing of, **Supp. 10**, 478; mortality, first table of, **Vol. 6, Part 1**, 577 f.; orga-

nization of companies, **Vol. 6, Part 1**, 588; **Vol. 8, Part 2**, 267; pioneer work in, **Vol. 3, Part 1**, 463 f.; reform, **Vol. 3, Part 2**, 402; **Vol. 4, Part 2**, 501; **Vol. 6, Part 2**, 12
Life Line (organization), **Supp. 9**, 413
Life masks, **Vol. 2, Part 1**, 97
Life of Johnny Reb, the Common Soldier of the Confederacy, The, **Supp. 10**, 841, 842
Life of Michelangelo Buonarroti, The, **Supp. 3**, 785
Life of Reason: Of the Phases of Human Progress, The, **Supp. 5**, 602
Life of the Mind, The, **Supp. 9**, 43
Life Plus 99 Years, **Supp. 9**, 491
Lifesaving service, **Vol. 2, Part 2**, 483; **Vol. 3, Part 2**, 582; **Vol. 5, Part 2**, 379 f.; **Vol. 7, Part 1**, 460; **Vol. 8, Part 1**, 214 f.
Life Studies, **Supp. 10**, 468
Life with Father, **Supp. 8**, 108–9, 383
Liggett, Hunter, reference to, **Supp. 6**, 429
Liggett and Myers Tobacco Co., **Supp. 5**, 567
Light: and visual acuity, **Supp. 3**, 269–70; arc lamp, **Supp. 2**, 658; earth's effect on circuit time, **Supp. 3**, 291; gas-filled incandescent lamp, **Supp. 6**, 365; growth-related studies, **Supp. 6**, 69; incandescent lamp, **Supp. 1**, 279, 373; **Supp. 2**, 702; infrared, **Supp. 4**, 658; refraction of, **Supp. 1**, 187; study of, **Vol. 4, Part 1**, 249; **Vol. 6, Part 2**, 594 f.; ultraviolet research, **Supp. 5**, 441, 496; **Supp. 6**, 69; vision stimulation studies, **Supp. 4**, 367. velocity of, **Vol. 6, Part 1**, 442–3, **Vol. 7, Part 1**, 453. *See also* Electricity and electrification
Light, The. *See* Brazilian Traction, Light and Power Co.
Light Crust Doughboys (Western swing band), **Supp. 9**, 872
Light Horse of the City of Philadelphia, **Vol. 6, Part 1**, 75
Lighthouse Board: establishment of, **Vol. 9, Part 2**, 599; building, **Vol. 1, Part 1**, 163; **Vol. 3, Part 1**, 529 f.; **Vol. 4, Part 2**, 353; **Vol. 5, Part 1**, 515; **Vol. 5, Part 2**, 110; **Vol. 6, Part 1**, 228; **Vol. 8, Part 1**, 28 f.; **Vol. 9, Part 1**, 265; **Vol. 9, Part 2**, 249, 397, 599; **Vol. 10, Part 1**, 616 f.; first skeleton iron tower, in U.S., **Vol. 9, Part 2**, 249; government contracts, **Vol. 6, Part 1**, 228; reflectors, **Vol. 6, Part 1**, 228; service, **Vol. 5, Part 2**, 50
Lighthouse for the Blind, **Supp. 3**, 364–65
Lighting: arc, **Vol. 3, Part 1**, 376; **Vol. 5, Part 1**, 261; **Vol. 10, Part 1**, 376 f.; electric lamps, **Vol. 6, Part 2**, 436; **Vol. 7, Part 2**, 128; **Vol. 8, Part 2**, 268; flood, **Vol. 8, Part 2**, 268; gas, **Vol. 6, Part 2**, 227; kerosene, **Vol. 3, Part 1**, 415; oil, **Vol. 3, Part 1**, 415; **Vol. 4, Part 2**, 440
"Light My Fire," **Supp. 9**, 563
Lightner, Theodore, reference to, **Supp. 6**, 134
Lightnin' (play), **Vol. 1, Part 1**, 477
Lightning: investigation of, **Vol. 7, Part 2**, 388; protection from, **Supp. 2**, 199
Light quanta, **Supp. 5**, 202–3
Lights of New York, **Supp. 10**, 812
Lilienthal, David E., references to, **Supp. 4**, 601; **Supp. 6**, 419, 437; **Supp. 7**, 18; **Supp. 8**, 179; **Supp. 9**, 8, 387
Lilienthal, Gustav, reference to, **Vol. 2, Part 2**, 10
Lilienthal, Joseph L., reference to, **Supp. 7**, 59
Lilienthal, Otto, reference to, **Vol. 2, Part 2**, 10
Lilith, **Supp. 10**, 725, 726
Lilly, Eli, and Co.: founding and growth of, **Supp. 4**, 499–500; management, **Supp. 10**, 458–59
Lily, possibly first paper published by a woman, **Vol. 1, Part 2**, 385
Lily-White movement, **Vol. 3, Part 1**, 585 f.; **Vol. 3, Part 2**, 554
Limited Test Ban Treaty (1963), **Supp. 10**, 320
Limnology, **Supp. 3**, 402; **Supp. 4**, 84
Límon, José, reference to, **Supp. 6**, 313
Límon Co. (dance), **Supp. 9**, 495
Lincoln, Abraham: **Vol. 1, Part 1**, 518; **Vol. 3, Part 1**, 110 f.; **Vol. 4, Part 1**, 310; **Vol. 5, Part 1**, 80, 182, 197, 283, 302, 307, 355, 401, 404; **Vol. 5, Part 2**, 224, 305, 390; **Vol. 6, Part 1**, 204, 306, 336, 435 f., 593; **Vol. 7, Part 1**, 352, 392, 425, 579, 586, 600; **Vol. 8, Part 2**, 368; **Vol. 9, Part 1**, 106 f., 191, 310, 440, 518, 572, 623; **Vol. 9, Part 2**, 60 f.; and his son, **Vol. 6, Part 1**, 267; assassination of, **Vol. 1, Part 2**, 449; **Vol. 3, Part 2**, 333; **Vol. 4, Part 2**, 194; **Vol. 5, Part 2**, 263 f., 284; **Vol. 8, Part 2**, 335; **Vol. 9, Part 2**, 298, 460, 616, 635; assassins, trial of, **Vol. 1, Part 2**, 277; **Vol. 5, Part 2**, 84; at Harrisburg, **Vol. 6, Part 1**, 572; biographies of, **Vol. 4, Part 2**, 433, 579; **Vol. 5, Part 2**, 563, **Vol. 7, Part 1**, 511; **Supp. 1**, 56; **Supp. 2**, 495; **Supp. 8**, 564; campaign of, **Vol. 2, Part 1**, 176; candidacy, one of first editors to propose, **Vol. 9, Part 2**, 60; collections of writings on, **Supp. 2**, 318; Cooper Institute speech, **Vol. 6, Part 1**, 248; **Vol. 7, Part 1**, 579; debates with Douglas, **Vol. 3, Part 1**, 402; **Vol. 6, Part 1**, 247 f.; election of, **Vol. 8, Part 2**, 618; father of, **Vol. 6, Part 1**, 242 f.; "Hardin County" cartoon on, **Supp. 5**, 732; inauguration, **Vol. 8, Part 2**, 196; in Black Hawk War, **Vol. 6, Part 1**, 244; Vaquess mission, failure of, **Vol. 4, Part 1**, 310; last days of, **Vol. 8, Part 2**, 613; law partner of, **Vol. 4, Part 2**, 579; letters and papers, **Supp. 9**, 37, 38; marital relations, **Vol. 4, Part 2**, 268; **Vol. 6, Part 1**, 265 f.; Memorial, **Vol. 1, Part 1**, 478; **Vol. 2, Part 1**, 306; **Vol. 6, Part 1**, 563; mother of, **Vol. 6, Part 1**, 242 f.; nomination of, **Vol. 3, Part 1**, 110; **Vol. 3, Part 2**, 360; **Vol. 8, Part 2**, 447, 456; opposition to policies of, **Vol. 3, Part 1**, 120 f.; partnership with, **Vol. 6, Part 1**, 366; photographs of, **Supp. 7**, 529–30; political manager, **Vol. 5, Part 2**, 231; political rise, **Vol. 3, Part 1**, 402 f.; political rivals of, **Vol. 4, Part 2**, 246; reference to, **Supp. 10**, 313; relations with C. F. Adams, **Vol. 1, Part 1**, 42; relations with J. A. Andrew, **Vol. 1, Part 1**, 280; relations with Bancroft, **Vol. 1, Part 1**, 568; relations with J. Calhoun, **Vol. 2, Part 1**, 410; relations with S. P. Chase, **Vol. 2, Part 2**, 29; relations with S. Douglas, **Vol. 1, Part 1**, 394; relations with N. W. Edwards, **Vol. 3, Part 2**, 42; relations with W. P. Fessenden, **Vol. 3, Part 2**, 349; relations with H. Greeley, **Vol. 4, Part 1**, 532; relations with H. Hamlin, **Vol. 4, Part 2**, 197 f.; relations with G. B. McClellan, **Vol. 6, Part 1**, 582 f.; relations with J. Medill, **Vol. 6, Part 2**, 491; relations with C. Schurz, **Vol. 8, Part 2**, 467; relations with E. D. Townsend, **Vol. 9, Part 2**, 615 f.; relations with S. H. Tree, **Vol. 9, Part 2**, 635 f.; sculpture of, **Supp. 1**, 322; **Supp. 3**, 88, 89; **Supp. 8**, 414; secretary of, **Vol. 4, Part 2**, 431; **Vol. 7, Part 1**, 510 f.; **Vol. 9, Part 2**, 60; statue of, **Vol. 5, Part 1**, 317; Washington, route to, **Vol. 8, Part 2**, 500; writings on, **Supp. 5**, 557; **Supp. 10**, 843
Lincoln, Mary Todd, reference to, **Vol. 6, Part 1**, 245 f.
Lincoln, Robert, reference to, **Vol. 7, Part 1**, 511
Lincoln and His Generals, **Supp. 10**, 843
Lincoln Centennial Association (Springfield, Ill.), **Supp. 9**, 37, 38
Lincoln Center (New York City), creation, **Supp. 10**, 684
Lincon Center Repertory Company, **Supp. 9**, 71
Lincoln County War, **Vol. 2, Part 2**, 77
"Lincoln Guns," **Vol. 4, Part 2**, 267
Lincoln League of America, founding of, **Supp. 5**, 633
Lincoln Memorial (Washington, D.C.): Anderson concert at, **Supp. 5**, 343; Lincoln statue, **Supp. 1**, 322

Lincoln Motor Co., executives, **Supp. 8**, 609–10
Lincoln, Nebr., development of, **Vol. 3, Part 2**, 51
Lincoln-Roosevelt League, **Supp. 3**, 394; founding of, **Supp. 4**, 707
Lincoln School (Teachers College, New York City), **Supp. 3**, 552, 667; **Supp. 4**, 139; **Supp. 6**, 208
Lincoln Tunnel (N.Y.-N.J.), **Supp. 6**, 587
Lincoln University, **Vol. 10, Part 1**, 66
Lincoln-Zephyr automobile, **Supp. 3**, 284
Lind, Jenny, references to, **Vol. 1, Part 1**, 638; **Vol. 4, Part 1**, 209; **Vol. 5, Part 1**, 117
Lindbergh, Anne Morrow, reference to, **Supp. 9**, 497
Lindbergh, Charles A.: barnstorming, **Supp. 9**, 496; Breckinridge relationship, **Supp. 6**, 75; environmental views, **Supp. 9**, 499; isolationist views, **Supp. 9**, 498; kidnapping case, **Supp. 3**, 142; laboratory pump design, **Supp. 3**, 141; Nazism, views of, **Supp. 9**, 498; references to, **Supp. 4**, 303; **Supp. 5**, 547; **Supp. 6**, 51, 470; **Supp. 7**, 504, 779; **Supp. 8**, 373, 650, 679; **Supp. 9**, 725; **Supp. 10**, 148, 213; rocket development, **Supp. 3**, 306–7; Roosevelt, F. D., relationship, **Supp. 9**, 498; transatlantic solo flight, first nonstop, **Supp. 9**, 496; transcontinental speed record, **Supp. 9**, 496
Lindenthal, Gustav, reference to, **Supp. 6**, 594
Lindgren, Carl C., reference to, **Supp. 3**, 540
Lindgren, Waldemar, reference to, **Supp. 4**, 765
Lindsay, Howard, reference to, **Supp. 8**, 108–9
Lindsay, John V., reference to, **Supp. 10**, 697
"Line o' Type or Two, A," **Vol. 9, Part 2**, 317
Lingg, Claire, reference to, **Supp. 6**, 117
Ling-Temco-Vought, Inc., **Supp. 8**, 367
Linguistics. *See* Philology; *specific language*
Linguistic Society of America, **Vol. 1, Part 2**, 387
Linnaean Society of New York, founding of, **Supp. 3**, 518
Linotype machine, inventions relating to, **Vol. 6, Part 2**, 550; **Vol. 8, Part 1**, 484; **Vol. 8, Part 2**, 106
Lionel Corporation, **Supp. 7**, 150
Lipids, chemistry of, **Supp. 3**, 61
Lipman, Jacob G., reference to, **Supp. 9**, 833
Lippincott, J. B., Co., management, **Supp. 10**, 460–61
Lippincott, Joshua B., reference to, **Supp. 10**, 460
Lippincott's Magazine, **Vol. 5, Part 1**, 202; **Vol. 5, Part 2**, 429; **Vol. 9, Part 1**, 317
Lippmann, Walter: Johnson, L. B., presidency, assessment of, **Supp. 9**, 506; League of Nations, position on, **Supp. 9**, 504; *New Republic*, **Supp. 9**, 504; *New York Herald Tribune*, **Supp. 9**, 505–6; Pulitzer Prizes, **Supp. 9**, 505; references to, **Supp. 3**, 852; **Supp. 4**, 510; **Supp. 5**, 85, 272; **Supp. 7**, 310, 316; **Supp. 8**, 520; **Supp. 9**, 581; Roosevelt presidency, opinions of, **Supp. 9**, 505; Truman presidency, criticism of, **Supp. 9**, 505; Vietnam War, position on, **Supp. 9**, 506; World War I peace commission, **Supp. 9**, 504;
Lip-reading, **Vol. 7, Part 1**, 528
Lipschultz, Louis, reference to, **Supp. 6**, 264
Liquor: control, local option, **Vol. 3, Part 2**, 166; **Vol. 6, Part 2**, 330; 1896 excise bill, **Vol. 8, Part 1**, 326 f.; legal distilleries in Illinois, **Vol. 8, Part 1**, 392; "legal suppressionism," **Vol. 3, Part 1**, 19; "Raines Law," **Vol. 8, Part 1**, 326 f.; writings on the question, **Vol. 3, Part 1**, 376; **Vol. 4, Part 1**, 449; **Vol. 5, Part 2**, 494 f. *See also* Alcohol; Prohibition
Lissák, Kalman, reference to, **Supp. 3**, 136
Lister, Joseph, reference to, **Supp. 1**, 240
Lister, antiseptic system of, **Vol. 2, Part 1**, 393;
Litchfield, Conn., first law school in U.S., founded in, **Vol. 8, Part 1**, 469
Literacy test for citizenship, **Vol. 5, Part 2**, 32
Literary and Philosophical Society, **Vol. 2, Part 2**, 224
"Literary Confederacy," **Vol. 8, Part 2**, 344
Literary criticism. *See* Criticism, literary
Literary Digest, **Supp. 7**, 274, 649–50; founding of, **Vol. 4, Part 1**, 73; lexicography column, **Supp. 2**, 683; science editor, **Supp. 3**, 90
Literary Guild of America, **Supp. 4**, 239; **Supp. 6**, 628; founding of, **Supp. 7**, 306
Literary History of America, A, **Vol. 10, Part 1**, 649 f.
Literary Review, **Supp. 7**, 103; founding of, **Supp. 4**, 73; **Supp. 5**, 439
Literary World, **Vol. 3, Part 1**, 561 f.
Literati: Hartford, *see* "Hartford Wits"; New York City, nineteenth century, **Vol. 4, Part 1**, 276; **Vol. 5, Part 2**, 206; **Vol. 6, Part 1**, 56 f., 491; **Vol. 8, Part 2**, 344
Literature: anthologies, **Supp. 10**, 799; biographical approach to criticism, **Supp. 9**, 884; classical works in translation courses, **Supp. 8**, 236; criticism, **Supp. 4**, 702, 847; **Supp. 5**, 89–90, 168–69, 356, 425, 542; **Supp. 7**, 18, 55–56, 79–81, 103–4, 219–22, 309–10, 638, 754; **Supp. 8**, 124, 353–54, 492, 493, 584–85, 667–68; Great Books courses, **Supp. 5**, 211–12; **Supp. 8**, 59; historical writings on, **Supp. 4**, 819–20; **Supp. 6**, 523–24; Irish, **Supp. 9**, 181–82; Little Masterpieces series, **Supp. 5**, 541–42; McClure's syndicate, **Supp. 4**, 517; Marxist criticism, **Supp. 7**, 268; neohumanism, **Supp. 1**, 36; Nobel Prize, **Supp. 5**, 423, 524; **Supp. 7**, 222, 234, 338; **Supp. 8**, 626; religious, **Supp. 8**, 431; teaching of, **Supp. 5**, 239. *See also* American literature; Black literature; Books; Children's literature; Classical literature; Criticism; English literature and language; Historical fiction; Poetry; Romance novels; Theater; *specific genres and languages*
Lithography: **Vol. 1, Part 1**, 166; **Vol. 1, Part 2**, 168; **Vol. 2, Part 2**, 69, 604; **Vol. 3, Part 1**, 170, 329; **Vol. 5, Part 1**, 107, 460, 520; **Vol. 5, Part 2**, 139; **Vol. 7, Part 1**, 469; **Vol. 7, Part 2**, 421, 439; **Vol. 8, Part 1**, 165 f.; **Vol. 8, Part 2**, 202, 470; **Supp. 7**, 15, 153; architectural, **Vol. 3, Part 1**, 103; chromolithography, **Vol. 8, Part 2**, 169; Civil War sketches, **Vol. 8, Part 2**, 169; colored, **Vol. 8, Part 1**, 165 f.; first in America, **Vol. 7, Part 2**, 92; inventions concerning, **Vol. 8, Part 1**, 165 f.; portraits of distinguished Americans, **Vol. 8, Part 2**, 169; "silver points," **Vol. 4, Part 2**, 38
Lithotomy, **Vol. 5, Part 2**, 181; **Vol. 9, Part 1**, 451
Littauer Brothers, **Supp. 3**, 463–64
Little, Clarence Cook, reference to, **Supp. 3**, 121
Little and Browne, founding of, **Supp. 4**, 115
Little Bighorn, battle of, **Vol. 2, Part 2**, 530; **Vol. 3, Part 1**, 8; **Vol. 4, Part 1**, 101, 237; **Vol. 9, Part 2**, 379; **Supp. 5**, 430
Little Blue Books, **Supp. 5**, 264–65
Little, Brown and Co., growth of, **Supp. 4**, 526–27
"Little Cabinet," **Vol. 9, Part 2**, 599; **Supp. 10**, 119
Little Caesar, **Supp. 9**, 666
"Little Church Around the Corner" (Church of the Transfiguration, New York City), **Vol. 5, Part 1**, 255
Little Citizens, **Vol. 5, Part 2**, 310
Little Colonel series, **Vol. 5, Part 2**, 138
"Little Giffen," **Vol. 9, Part 2**, 525
Little Galleries of the Photo-Secession ("291"), founding of, **Supp. 4**, 780, 781; **Supp. 5**, 471
Little House books, **Supp. 6**, 696
"Little Longfellow War," **Vol. 8, Part 1**, 19 f.
Little Orchestra Society of New York, **Supp. 8**, 578
"Little Orphan Annie" (comic strip), **Supp. 8**, 221–22
Little Red School House (New York City), **Supp. 3**, 376
Little Review (journal), founding of, **Supp. 9**, 33
Little Rock, Ark.: battle of (1863), Vol. 29 Part 1, 391; **Vol. 2, Part 2**, 105, 187; **Vol. 4, Part 1**, 237; **Vol. 5,**

Part 1, 176; **Vol. 5, Part 2**, 425; **Vol. 6, Part 2**, 291; **Vol. 9, Part 1**, 556; school desegregation, **Supp. 8**, 57–58, 157
Little Theatre of St. Louis, founding of, **Supp. 1**, 519
Littleton, Jesse T., reference to, **Supp. 6**, 624
"Little Turtle," reference to, **Vol. 1, Part 1**, 34
Little Women, **Vol. 1, Part 1**, 141
Litton Industries, Inc., **Supp. 8**, 367
Liturgiology, **Vol. 5, Part 1**, 229
Liver: alcoholic cirrhosis, **Supp. 3**, 503; extract for anemia, **Supp. 4**, 581–82; **Supp. 5**, 122, 149
Liveright, Horace, references to, **Supp. 3**, 14; **Supp. 7**, 335, 436; **Supp. 9**, 164
Livestock: bovine tuberculosis, **Supp. 4**, 684; breeding, **Vol. 1, Part 2**, 172; **Vol. 4, Part 2**, 483; **Supp. 2**, 416; cooperatives, **Supp. 1**, 644; disease control, **Supp. 1**, 444; **Supp. 3**, 737–38; feeding research, **Supp. 1**, 395; nutritional studies, **Supp. 5**, 276
Live Stock Journal, founding of, **Vol. 7, Part 1**, 100
Living Age, **Vol. 6, Part 1**, 295
Livingston, M. Stanley, cyclotron research, **Supp. 6**, 370
Livingston, Robert R., references to, **Vol. 5, Part 2**, 367; **Vol. 7, Part 1**, 88 f., 210; **Vol. 9, Part 1**, 614
Livingston College, administration, **Supp. 8**, 94
Livingstone, David, reference to, **Vol. 9, Part 1**, 510
Livingstone, Mary, references to, **Supp. 9**, 75, 76
Livingstons and De Lanceys, political quarrels of (N.Y.), **Vol. 6, Part 1**, 317
Livius, Peter, reference to, **Vol. 10, Part 1**, 656 f.
Llewellyn, Karl N., reference to, **Supp. 3**, 186
Lloyd, David, reference to, **Vol. 6, Part 1**, 361
Lloyd, Wray, reference to, **Supp. 5**, 605
Lloyd Library of Botany and Pharmacy (St. Louis), **Supp. 2**, 390
Lobbying: agricultural, **Supp. 8**, 468; **Supp. 10**, 271–72; American Indian Federation, **Supp. 7**, 393; conservationist, **Supp. 4**, 665–66; corporate, **Supp. 4**, 316; labor, **Supp. 4**, 376, 607; **Supp. 10**, 394; Prohibition, **Supp. 2**, 723; protective tariff, **Supp. 7**, 305; retired persons, **Supp. 8**, 10; trade unions, **Supp. 5**, 254; woman suffrage amendment, **Supp. 5**, 533; women's rights, **Supp. 5**, 532
Lobotomy, prefrontal, **Supp. 6**, 223
"Local option," **Vol. 3, Part 2**, 166; **Vol. 6, Part 2**, 330
Locke, Alain, references to, **Supp. 6**, 313, 314
Lockheed Aircraft Co.: founding of, **Supp. 8**, 385; management, **Supp. 9**, 758; predecessor, **Supp. 6**, 385
Locks, canal, **Vol. 3, Part 1**, 406; **Vol. 5, Part 2**, 97; **Vol. 6, Part 1**, 327; **Vol. 8, Part 1**, 28, 324; **Vol. 10, Part 1**, 616 f.
Locks: manufacture of, **Vol. 4, Part 1**, 582; **Vol. 5, Part 1**, 95; **Vol. 7, Part 2**, 493; **Vol. 8, Part 2**, 362; **Vol. 9, Part 2**, 613; **Vol. 10, Part 2**, 592
Lockwood, Charles D., reference to, **Supp. 6**, 137
"Locofoco," use of the term in politics, **Vol. 8, Part 1**, 94 f.
Locomotives, railroad: construction, **Vol. 1, Part 1**, 511, 541; **Vol. 1, Part 2**, 457, 529; **Vol. 2, Part 1**, 424; **Vol. 2, Part 2**, 361; **Vol. 3, Part 1**, 65, 458; **Vol. 3, Part 2**, 527, 579; **Vol. 4, Part 2**, 1, 345; **Vol. 5, Part 1**, 84, 148, 342; **Vol. 6, Part 2**, 378, 412; **Vol. 7, Part 1**, 556; **Vol. 7, Part 2**, 263, 361; **Vol. 8, Part 2**, 112; **Vol. 9, Part 1**, 620; **Vol. 9, Part 2**, 484; braking device, invention of, **Vol. 6, Part 2**, 303; "experiment," **Vol. 5, Part 2**, 59; first, **Vol. 2, Part 2**, 410; **Vol. 9, Part 1**, 616; inventions, concerning, **Vol. 5, Part 2**, 59, 97; "Star," **Vol. 7, Part 1**, 556; "Stourbridge Lion," **Vol. 5, Part 2**, 59
Locust Street Social Settlement (Hampton, Va.), **Supp. 4**, 53
Lodge, Henry Cabot: children of, **Supp. 3**, 464; Lawrence, W., relationship, **Supp. 3**, 448; League of Nations, **Supp. 3**, 472–73; references to, **Vol. 1, Part 1**, 494 f.; **Supp. 3**, 396; **Supp. 9**, 504
Lodge, John Davis, reference to, **Supp. 10**, 652
Loeb, Jacques, references to, **Supp. 3**, 236; **Supp. 4**, 287; **Supp. 6**, 671; **Supp. 7**, 592; **Supp. 8**, 502; **Supp. 10**, 426, 427
Loeb Classical Library (Harvard), **Supp. 1**, 503
Loew, Arthur, reference to, **Supp. 8**, 577
Loew, Marcus, references to, **Supp. 6**, 440; **Supp. 8**, 576; **Supp. 10**, 871, 872
Loewi, Otto, references to, **Supp. 3**, 135, 136
Loew's Incorporated, **Supp. 5**, 726; **Supp. 8**, 576; **Supp. 9**, 323
"Log Cabin and Hard Cider Campaign," **Vol. 8, Part 2**, 174
Log Cabin Convention (Ind.), **Vol. 8, Part 2**, 51
"Log College," **Vol. 3, Part 1**, 302; **Vol. 9, Part 2**, 366 f., 369 f., 371
Logan, James, reference to, **Vol. 9, Part 2**, 370
Loganberry, first production of, **Vol. 6, Part 1**, 363
Logan Historical Society, founding of, **Vol. 8, Part 1**, 503
Logan's Crossroads, battle of, **Vol. 2, Part 2**, 546; **Vol. 5, Part 2**, 136; **Vol. 9, Part 2**, 433; **Vol. 10, Part 2**, 660
Logic: conceptual pragmatism in, **Supp. 7**, 471; mathematical, **Supp. 4**, 169–70; philosophical, **Supp. 2**, 644; **Supp. 4**, 168–70, 879–80; **Supp. 8**, 74–75; physics, **Supp. 7**, 75; positivism, **Supp. 5**, 562–63; symbolic, **Supp. 5**, 563
Lolita, **Supp. 10**, 583
Lomax, Alan, references to, **Supp. 4**, 476, 502; **Supp. 8**, 234
Lomax, John, reference to, **Supp. 4**, 476
Lomb, Henry, reference to, **Supp. 3**, 40
Lombard, Carole, reference to, **Supp. 6**, 225
Lombard Governor Co., **Supp. 6**, 668–69
Lombardi, Vincenzo, references to, **Supp. 6**, 323; **Supp. 9**, 485, 818; **Supp. 10**, 728
Lombardo, Guy, reference to, **Supp. 7**, 9
London, Frank, reference to, **Supp. 5**, 693
London, Jack, reference to, **Supp. 8**, 593
London: donation for workingmen's tenements in, **Vol. 7, Part 2**, 337; influence on Henry James, **Vol. 5, Part 1**, 581
London Bridge, **Supp. 10**, 492
London Co. (Va.), **Vol. 1, Part 2**, 412; **Vol. 3, Part 1**, 34
London Conference (1924), **Supp. 7**, 809
London Economic Conference (1933), **Supp. 3**, 648, 657; **Supp. 5**, 332
London Naval Conference (1930), **Vol. 7, Part 1**, 235; **Supp. 3**, 397; **Supp. 4**, 786; **Supp. 6**, 518
London Naval Conference (1935–36), **Supp. 3**, 219
London Philharmonic, **Supp. 5**, 398
London Symphony, **Supp. 7**, 549
London Temperance League, **Vol. 4, Part 1**, 445
Lone Cowboy, **Supp. 3**, 382, 383
"Lone Ranger, The" (television program), **Supp. 10**, 737
"Lonesome Luke" (fictional character), **Supp. 9**, 508
Lone Star Gas Co., **Supp. 5**, 260
Long, Breckinridge, reference to, **Supp. 3**, 622
Long, Crawford W., reference to, **Vol. 5, Part 1**, 567
Long, Earl, references to, **Supp. 7**, 556; **Supp. 9**, 534
Long, Henry, reference to, **Supp. 3**, 347
Long, Huey P.: biography of, **Supp. 10**, 844; opposition to, **Supp. 9**, 159–60; political machine, **Supp. 9**, 533; **Supp. 10**, 325, 744; references to, **Supp. 3**, 653, 654; **Supp. 4**, 145, 613; **Supp. 5**, 343; **Supp. 6**,

390, 647; **Supp. 7**, 22, 555; **Supp. 8**, 36, 499; **Supp. 9**, 30, 256
Long, Russell, reference to, **Supp. 7**, 556
Long, Stephen H., references to, **Vol. 5, Part 1**, 576; **Vol. 5, Part 2**, 276; **Vol. 7, Part 1**, 556, 631; **Vol. 8, Part 2**, 401
Long Day's Journey into Night, **Supp. 5**, 523, 525
Longest Day, The, **Supp. 9**, 690, 691
Longfellow, H. W., references to, **Vol. 1, Part 1**, 120; **Vol. 5, Part 1**, 603; **Vol. 6, Part 1**, 384
Long Island, battle of. *See* Brooklyn, N.Y.
Long Island College of Medicine, **Supp. 6**, 665
Long Island Railroad, **Vol. 1, Part 1**, 549; **Vol. 2, Part 2**, 436
Longitude, determination of, **Vol. 3, Part 1**, 107 f., 507 f., 602 f.
Long Remember, **Supp. 10**, 399
Longshoremen's Union. *See* International Longshoremen's and Warehousemen's Union
Longstreet, James, reference to **Vol. 6, Part 1**, 124
Longworth, Alice Roosevelt, references to, **Supp. 9**, 26, 98
Longworth, Nicholas, references to, **Vol. 5, Part 1**, 430; **Supp. 6**, 588; **Supp. 8**, 420; **Supp. 10**, 465
"Lonigan, Studs" (fictional character), **Supp. 10**, 235
Look, **Supp. 7**, 535; founding of, **Supp. 4**, 189
Look Homeward, Angel, **Supp. 2**, 730, 733; **Supp. 4**, 651
Looking Forward, **Vol. 8, Part 2**, 105
Lookout Mountain, battle on. *See* Chattanooga-Ringgold campaign
Loom, improvement of, **Vol. 2, Part 2**, 561; **Vol. 3, Part 1**, 437; **Vol. 5, Part 2**, 471; **Vol. 8, Part 2**, 112; **Vol. 9, Part 1**, 198; **Vol. 10, Part 2**, 582
Loomis, Alfred, reference to, **Supp. 7**, 275
Loomis Laboratory, first institute of experimental medicine, **Vol. 9, Part 2**, 478
Loos, Anita, reference to, **Supp. 9**, 791
Lopez, Vincent, reference to, **Supp. 5**, 417
LoPezzi, Anna, reference to, **Supp. 6**, 238
Lopokova, Lydia, reference to, **Supp. 3**, 277
"Loramie's" Post, **Vol. 6, Part 1**, 413
Lord, Chester S., reference to, **Supp. 6**, 290
Lord, Daniel, reference to, **Supp. 7**, 71
Lord and Taylor, **Supp. 5**, 433
Lord and Thomas (advertising), **Supp. 5**, 270, 410–11; **Supp. 10**, 145
Lorgnette, **Vol. 7, Part 1**, 42
Lorimer, George Horace, references to, **Supp. 10**, 689, 690
Lorimer, William: references to, **Supp. 3**, 771; **Supp. 5**, 450; **Supp. 6**, 683; trial of, **Vol. 5, Part 2**, 356
Lorraine, William, reference to, **Supp. 7**, 9
Los Alamos, N.Mex.: atomic bomb project, **Supp. 5**, 221, 590; **Supp. 6**, 656; **Supp. 7**, 11, 300; **Supp. 8**, 230, 483; **Supp. 9**, 185; **Supp. 10**, 144; hydrogen bomb project, **Supp. 8**, 200
Los Angeles, Calif.: Catholic church, **Supp. 10**, 497–98; Chamber of Commerce, **Vol. 7, Part 2**, 100; Chamber of Commerce, founding of, **Supp. 2**, 716; day nursery, **Vol. 1, Part 2**, 471; expansion and development of, **Supp. 3**, 155–56; public health, **Supp. 2**, 716; smog control ordinances, **Supp. 10**, 297; water supply, **Supp. 1**, 570; **Supp. 3**, 814; Watts riots, **Supp. 8**, 335
Los Angeles Dodgers (baseball), **Supp. 9**, 390; **Supp. 10**, 279, 567, 606
Los Angeles Philharmonic Orchestra, **Supp. 6**, 550; **Supp. 10**, 760
Los Angeles Rams (football), **Supp. 9**, 646, 841
Los Angeles Times: **Supp. 3**, 154–56; **Supp. 8**, 282; bombing of, **Supp. 1**, 135; **Supp. 2**, 142, 626; **Supp. 10**, 79; emergence as national newspaper, **Supp. 9**, 167–68
Lost-Found Nation of Islam. *See* Black Muslims
Lost Horizon, **Supp. 10**, 784
Lost Son and Other Poems, The, **Supp. 7**, 654
Lost Weekend, The, **Supp. 8**, 298
Lotos Club, founding of, **Supp. 1**, 510
Lotteries, **Vol. 3, Part 1**, 408; **Vol. 4, Part 1**, 268; **Vol. 4, Part 2**, 591; **Vol. 7, Part 1**, 58–1; Louisiana, **Vol. 3, Part 1**, 585 f., 598 f.; **Vol. 3, Part 2**, 554; **Vol. 4, Part 1**, 608 f.; **Vol. 4, Part 2**, 512; **Vol. 7, Part 1**, 488; **Vol. 7, Part 2**, 176; **Vol. 8, Part 1**, 251, 637
"Lottery, The," **Supp. 7**, 385
Lotus Club, founding of, **Vol. 1, Part 1**, 150
Loudown School (Va.), founding of, **Vol. 3, Part 1**, 22
Loudspeakers, development of, **Supp. 7**, 394–95
Loughran, Tommy, Braddock light-heavyweight bout, **Supp. 9**, 121
Louis, Joe: heavyweight championship bouts, **Supp. 9**, 122, 172, 493; references to, **Supp. 5**, 360; **Supp. 7**, 494; **Supp. 9**, 668; **Supp. 10**, 610
Louis, P. C. A., reference to, **Vol. 9, Part 1**, 32
Louisburg campaign, **Vol. 6, Part 1**, 257; **Vol. 6, Part 1**, 428; **Vol. 7, Part 2**, 457; **Vol. 9, Part 1**, 121
Louisiana: admission to statehood, **Vol. 2, Part**, 126; **Vol. 3, Part 1**, 249; agriculture, **Vol. 3, Part 1**, 586 f.; bird study, **Supp. 7**, 578; black education, **Vol. 7, Part 1**, 43; capitol building, **Supp. 1**, 220; carpetbagging, **Vol. 3, Part 2**, 554; civil code, revision of, **Vol. 3, Part 1**, 249; confiscation in, **Vol. 3, Part 1**, 545 f.; court procedure, **Vol. 3, Part 2**, 191; Creole uprising, **Vol. 10, Part 1**, 107; Democratic party, **Supp. 9**, 533–34; **Supp. 10**, 325; education, **Vol. 1, Part 2**, 525; **Vol. 3, Part 1**, 314; **Vol. 3, Part 2**, 191; Episcopal church, following Civil War, **Vol. 10, Part 2**, 314; first civil and military commander of upper, **Vol. 9, Part 2**, 51; first governorship of, **Vol. 6, Part 1**, 221; free state, movement to organize as, **Vol. 3, Part 1**, 543 f.; French colony of, **Vol. 6, Part 1**, 19; **Vol. 7, Part 2**, 319; governors, **Vol. 1, Part 1**, 191; **Vol. 1, Part 2**, 250, 351; **Vol. 29, Part 1**, 397, 507; **Vol. 2, Part 2**, 115 f.; **Vol. 3, Part 1**, 248; **Vol. 3, Part 2**, 554; **Vol. 4, Part 2**, 87, 139, 492, **Vol. 5, Part 2**, 305; **Vol. 6, Part 2**, 39; **Vol. 7, Part 1**, 138, 295, 487; **Vol. 8, Part 2**, 28, 125 f.; **Vol. 10, Part 1**, 457, 641; **Vol. 100, Part 2**, 183, 368; **Supp. 1**, 506; **Supp. 2**, 514; **Supp. 6**, 391; **Supp. 9**, 534; history of, **Vol. 2, Part 1**, 508; **Vol. 3, Part 1**, 380, 534, 543 f., 585; **Vol. 3, Part 2**, 537; **Vol. 4, Part 1**, 196, 202, 257; **Vol. 6, Part 2**, 282; **Vol. 8, Part 1**, 81 f., 251, 503; **Vol. 9, Part 1**, 146; **Vol. 9, Part 2**, 51, 383; Indians, **Vol. 1, Part 2**, 251; Lazarists, **Vol. 3, Part 1**, 473 f.; legal and political service, **Vol. 1, Part 1**, 192; **Vol. 1, Part 2**, 140, 182, 220, 351, 479, 553; **Vol. 2, Part 1**, 485, 507; **Vol. 2, Part 2**, 115 f.; **Vol. 3, Part 1**, 89, 248, 543, 585; **Vol. 3, Part 2**, 292, 554; **Vol. 4, Part 2**, 87, 124, 139, 492; **Vol. 5, Part 1**, 383, 397, 492; **Vol. 5, Part 2**, 305, 337; **Vol. 6, Part 1**, 311, 490, 561; **Vol. 6, Part 2**, 39, 253, 335, 469, 555; **Vol. 7, Part 1**, 139, 187, 295, 487, 584; **Vol. 7, Part 2**, 201, 611; **Vol. 8, Part 1**, 81, 111, 163, 251, 622, 644; **Vol. 8, Part 2**, 28, 125, 164, 582; **Vol. 9, Part 1**, 79, 210, 405; **Vol. 10, Part 1**, 107, 457; **Vol. 10, Part 2**, 95, 183, 369; legal code, **Vol. 7, Part 1**, 157; legal history studies, **Supp. 1**, 223; lottery, **Vol. 3, Part 1**, 585 f., 598 f.; **Vol. 3, Part 2**, 554; **Vol. 4, Part 1**, 608 f.; **Vol. 4, Part 2**, 512; **Vol. 7, Part 1**, 488; **Vol. 7, Part 2**, 176; **Vol. 8, Part 1**, 251, 637; Louisiana Historical Society, **Vol. 2, Part 1**, 254; **Vol. 3, Part 1**, 181; Louisiana Leper Home, **Vol. 3, Part 1**, 582; Louisiana Scientific Agricultural Association, **Vol. 3, Part 1**, 585 f.; Louisiana State University, *see* Tulane University;

mammoth bones, discovery of, **Vol. 3, Part 1**, 507 f.; maps, early, **Vol. 3, Part 1**, 73; mercantile ventures, early, **Vol. 6, Part 2**, 19; Mexican War, activities during, **Vol. 2, Part 1**, 491; "midnight order," **Vol. 3, Part 1**, 545 f.; missions, **Vol. 1, Part 1**, 277; named for King Louis XIV, **Vol. 6, Part 1**, 11; newspapers, **Vol. 9, Part 2**, 509; oil industry, **Supp. 6**, 540–41; philanthropy, **Vol. 8, Part 1**, 163 f.; plants, **Vol. 8, Part 1**, 589; politics, **Supp. 6**, 390–91; **Supp. 7**, 78–79; **Supp. 7**, 555–56; **Supp. 8**, 499–500; **Supp. 9**, 103–5, 256, 257, 533–34; **Supp. 10**, 325; purchase of, **Vol. 4, Part 1**, 557; **Vol. 5, Part 2**, 29; **Vol. 6, Part 1**, 221, 323, 324; **Vol. 6, Part 2**, 189; **Vol. 7, Part 1**, 89; **Vol. 10, Part 2**, 224; railroad development, **Vol. 7, Part 1**, 295; Reconstruction, **Vol. 1, Part 1**, 192 f.; **Vol. 2, Part 1**, 218, 402, 459; **Vol. 3, Part 1**, 545 f.; **Vol. 6, Part 2**, 555; secession of, **Vol. 1, Part 2**, 182; **Vol. 8, Part 1**, 251; seizure of, attempted, **Vol. 5, Part 1**, 461 f.; Spanish rule, **Vol. 3, Part 1**, 229; state constitutions of, **Vol. 3, Part 1**, 543 f.; sugar industry, **Vol. 1, Part 2**, 461; **Vol. 3, Part 1**, 585 f.; **Vol. 10, Part 1**, 457
Louisiana Bar Association, founding of, **Supp. 1**, 223
Louisiana Educator, founding of, **Supp. 1**, 103
Louisiana School Review, founding of, **Supp. 1**, 103
Louisiana State University, history studies, **Supp. 10**, 843
Louisiana Story, **Supp. 5**, 226
Louisiana Sugar Planters' Association, **Vol. 3, Part 1**, 585 f.
Louisville, Ky.: civic leadership, **Vol. 4, Part 2**, 61; **Vol. 9, Part 1**, 135; medical service, **Vol. 10, Part 2**, 596; public library, establishment, **Vol. 3, Part 1**, 550 f.
Louisville and Nashville Railroad, **Vol. 3, Part 2**, 387; **Vol. 4, Part 2**, 61; **Vol. 9, Part 1**, 251, 322 f.
Louisville City Railway Co., **Vol. 1, Part 2**, 532
Louisville Courier Journal, **Vol. 8, Part 1**, 186 f.; **Vol. 10, Part 1**, 552 f.; **Supp. 9**, 471; ownership of, **Supp. 2**, 39
Louisville Municipal College for Negroes, administration, **Supp. 8**, 94
Louisville Times, **Supp. 9**, 471
Louisville Training School for Kindergarten and Primary Teachers, **Supp. 4**, 373
Love, Harry S., captor of Murrieta, **Vol. 7, Part 1**, 370
Lovejoy, Elijah P., reference to, **Vol. 7, Part 1**, 415
Lovejoy's Station, operation at (October 1864), **Vol. 10, Part 2**, 475
Lovell (Health) House (Hollywood), **Supp. 8**, 463
Lovell's Progessive Readers, **Vol. 6, Part 1**, 440
Love Machine, The, **Supp. 9**, 785
Loveman, Amy, references to, **Supp. 6**, 342; **Supp. 7**, 103
Love Me or Leave Me, **Supp. 10**, 223
Lovestone, Jay, references to, **Supp. 7**, 291; **Supp. 8**, 419; **Supp. 10**, 330
Lovett, Edgar O., reference to, **Supp. 6**, 560
"Lovewell's Fight," **Vol. 6, Part 1**, 444
Low, Juliette Gordon, references to, **Supp. 8**, 83, 84
Low, Seth, references to, **Supp. 3**, 677; **Supp. 4**, 133, 134
Lowden, Frank O., reference to, **Supp. 6**, 683–84
Lowe, Thaddeus, reference to, **Vol. 9, Part 2**, 248
Lowell, A. Lawrence, references to, **Supp. 3**, 328, 351, 476, 489, 822; **Supp. 4**, 32; **Supp. 5**, 130; **Supp. 6**, 105; **Supp. 6**, 249, 250
Lowell, Amy, references to, **Supp. 3**, 253; **Supp. 4**, 285
Lowell, James Russell, references to, **Vol. 1, Part 2**, 6, 41; **Vol. 5, Part 1**, 173; **Vol. 7, Part 1**, 570; **Vol. 8, Part 1**, 59 f.
Lowell, Percival, references to, **Supp. 7**, 192; **Supp. 8**, 597
Lowell, Robert: Bishop relationship, **Supp. 10**, 45; references to, **Supp. 9**, 711; **Supp. 10**, 754, 776
Lowell, Mass., **Vol. 1, Part 2**, 4, 457; **Vol. 3, Part 2**, 272; **Vol. 5, Part 1**, 413, 552; **Vol. 6, Part 2**, 613; **Vol. 7, Part 1**, 107; **Vol. 9, Part 2**, 98
Lowell Courier, **Vol. 8, Part 2**, 461
Lowell Institute, **Vol. 3, Part 2**, 103; **Vol. 6, Part 1**, 457, 466; **Vol. 9, Part 1**, 161
Lowell Observatory, **Vol. 6, Part 1**, 458
Lowell Offering, **Vol. 5, Part 2**, 614; **Vol. 8, Part 2**, 44
Lowell School of Practical Design, **Vol. 8, Part 2**, 225
Lower Colorado River Basin bill, **Supp. 9**, 373
Lower East Side (New York City): Jewish life in, **Supp. 3**, 329, 330; Neighborhood Guilds, **Supp. 3**, 175
Lowie, Robert H., references to, **Supp. 6**, 524, 613
Low-protein diets, **Supp. 3**, 163
"Loyal America Associators," **Vol. 8, Part 2**, 221
Loyalists: **Vol. 1, Part 1**, 185, 293, 405, 421 f., 464, 497, 596; **Vol. 1, Part 2**, 54, 393, 474; **Vol. 2, Part 1**, 280; **Vol. 3, Part 1**, 52, 215, 299f., 473; **Vol. 3, Part 2**, 6, 103, 190, 264 f., 426, 459, 506, 600 f.; **Vol. 4, Part 1**, 117, 133, 140, 243, 476 f., 543, 553; **Vol. 4, Part 2**, 230, 601; **Vol. 5, Part 1**, 376, 387, 468, 476, 480; **Vol. 5, Part 2**, 100, 103, 200, 257, 375; **Vol. 6, Part 1**, 136, 175 f., 418 f., 439, 446, 492; **Vol. 6, Part 2**, 50, 258; **Vol. 7, Part 1**, 226, 292, 332, 623, 637; **Vol. 8, Part 1**, 247 f., 334 f., 362 f.; **Vol. 8, Part 2**, 34, 221, 529, 607; **Vol. 9, Part 1**, 116, 358, 417, 517; **Vol. 9, Part 2**, 489; **Vol. 10, Part 1**, 644 f.; **Vol. 10, Part 2**, 101, 266, 542, 661; Anglican clergy, and, **Vol. 1, Part 1**, 422; activities during Revolution, **Vol. 2, Part 1**, 169; biographical sketches, **Vol. 8, Part 2**, 276; compensation for, **Vol. 3, Part 1**, 214; confiscation of, property, **Vol. 8, Part 2**, 342; England, attitude toward, **Vol. 8, Part 1**, 401; feuds with Whigs, **Vol. 4, Part 2**, 577; Indians, relation with, **Vol. 5, Part 2**, 100; treaty with, during Revolutionary War, **Vol. 7, Part 2**, 559; New England Club of, **Vol. 1, Part 2**, 393; New Hampshire's provincial governor, exile of; **Vol. 10, Part 1**, 656 f.; Rhode Island governor as a, **Vol. 10, Part 1**, 412; "Royal Greens," **Vol. 5, Part 2**, 104; satirical verse, **Vol. 7, Part 1**, 624; "Snow campaign," **Vol. 8, Part 1**, 42; **Vol. 9, Part 2**, 499; uprisings, suppression of, **Vol. 3, Part 2**, 524; treatment of, **Vol. 6, Part 1**, 75
Loyal National League (N.Y.), **Vol. 8, Part 2**, 134
Loyal Order of Moose, **Supp. 4**, 219
Loyalty issues: Army-McCarthy hearings, **Supp. 6**, 680; **Supp. 7**, 212–13; **Supp. 8**, 57; atomic bomb secrets, **Supp. 5**, 714, 588–90; **Supp. 8**, 230, 484, 649; black leftists, **Supp. 8**, 288; **Supp. 10**, 679–80; blacklisting, **Supp. 5**, 419; **Supp. 6**, 350; **Supp. 7**, 315, 367; **Supp. 8**, 492, 550–51; **Supp. 9**, 849; **Supp. 10**, 239, 273, 437, 560, 680, 794, 823; charges against China "hands," **Supp. 9**, 831; charges against government employees, **Supp. 5**, 479, 564, 676; **Supp. 7**, 751; charges against religious leaders, **Supp. 7**, 597; **Supp. 8**, 426; charges against teachers, **Supp. 7**, 132–33, 542; Civil Service Review Board, **Supp. 6**, 60; **Supp. 9**, 639; Communist China relations, **Supp. 4**, 750–51; Communist trials, **Supp. 5**, 389, 500, 564, 589–90, 714; **Supp. 7**, 52, 256, 389–90, 612; **Supp. 9**, 135; **Supp. 10**, 718–19; congressional investigations, **Supp. 8**, 648–49; **Supp. 9**, 135, 539; **Supp. 10** 134, 293, 801; deportation orders, **Supp. 5**, 136; deportation threat, **Supp. 10**, 323; ex-Communist witnesses, **Supp. 7**, 291; government appointments, **Supp. 6**, 143, 484–85, "guilt by association," **Supp. 8**, 426; Hiss case, **Supp. 5**, 19, 665; **Supp. 7**, 114–15; **Supp. 10**, 719; Idaho politics, **Supp. 6**, 681; Internal Security Act (1950), **Supp. 5**, 444–45; journalism on, **Supp. 5**, 19; judicial rulings,

Supp. 10, 863; labor movement, **Supp. 6**, 219, 598; **Supp. 8**, 511; left-wing front organizations, investigations of, **Supp. 8**, 425–42; **Supp. 10**, 239; legal defense, **Supp. 5**, 389; **Supp. 8**, 18; legislation, **Supp. 5**, 444–45; **Supp. 8**, 392; loyalty oaths, **Supp. 5**, 410, 480–81; **Supp. 9**, 753, 754; McCarthyism, **Supp. 6**, 148, 404–6; **Supp. 6**, 432, 606, 645, 680; McCarthyism, writings on, **Supp. 8**, 272; motion-picture industry, **Supp. 5**, 238; **Supp. 8**, 648–49, 704; **Supp. 9**, 539, 602–3, 666; **Supp. 10**, 63, 352, 720–21, 793, 823; Palmer raids, **Supp. 9**, 404–5; passport issuance, **Supp. 8**, 590–91; "Red raids," **Supp. 3**, 65; **Supp. 4**, 670; Rosenberg case, **Supp. 5**, 588–90, 714; **Supp. 9**, 321–22; **Supp. 10**, 719; security clearances, **Supp. 9**, 903; Subversive Activities Control Board, **Supp. 6**, 413; Supreme Court decisions, **Supp. 5**, 358, 714; **Supp. 7**, 96–97; Truman program, **Supp. 5**, 564; Un-American Activities Committee founding, **Supp. 5**, 599; Un-American Activities Committee hearings, **Supp. 5**, 139; **Supp. 6**, 526; **Supp. 7**, 244–45, 766–67; **Supp. 10**, 25, 134, 239; universities and colleges, **Supp. 6**, 640; World War I, **Supp. 7**, 506; **Supp. 8**, 488. See *also* Espionage
Loyalty of Free Men, The, **Supp. 10**, 24
Loy, Myrna, reference to, **Supp. 10**, 157
Lubitsch, Ernst, reference to, **Supp. 7**, 499
Lubrication, study of, **Vol. 3, Part 1**, 415; **Vol. 6, Part 1**, 617
Lucchese, Thomas, reference to, **Supp. 10**, 140
Luce, Clare Boothe, references to, **Supp. 8**, 394, 395–96; **Supp. 9**, 566
Luce, Harry Winters, reference to, **Supp. 7**, 727
Luce, Henry R., references to, **Supp. 5**, 734; **Supp. 7**, 114, 269–70, 383; **Supp. 9**, 869; **Supp. 10**, 424
Luciano, Charles ("Lucky"): prosecution of, **Supp. 9**, 230; references to, **Supp. 3**, 181; **Supp. 8**, 208; **Supp. 9**, 12, 198, 820–21
Luckhardt, Arno B., references to, **Supp. 3**, 458; **Supp. 6**, 100
Lucky Strike cigarettes, **Supp. 4**, 371; **Supp. 5**, 411
Lucy, Autherine, reference to, **Supp. 8**, 73
Lucy Cobb Institute, **Vol. 2, Part 2**, 247
"Lucy Show, The" (television), **Supp. 10**, 804
Ludlow massacre (1914), **Vol. 5, Part 2**, 196; **Supp. 2**, 124; **Supp. 6**, 548
"Ludlow's Code," **Vol. 6, Part 1**, 494
Luft, Lorna, reference to, **Supp. 8**, 205
Luger, Paul, reference to, **Supp. 7**, 344
Lugosi, Bela, reference to, **Supp. 9**, 820
Luhan, Mabel Dodge, reference to, **Supp. 4**, 109; **Supp. 7**, 754
Lujan, Antomo, references to, **Supp. 7**, 486, 487
Luks, George, references to, **Supp. 5**, 624, 635, 636
Lumbard, J. Edward, reference to, **Supp. 9**, 270
Lumber, exchange of, for rum and sugar, **Vol. 3, Part 1**, 252
Lumber industry: **Vol. 3, Part 1**, 318 f.; **Vol. 3, Part 2**, 19, 343; **Vol. 4, Part 2**, 75, 94; **Vol. 7, Part 1**, 240; **Vol. 8, Part 2**, 272, 290, 396; **Vol. 9, Part 1**, 583; **Vol. 10, Part 1**, 361; cooperative forestry policies, **Supp. 3**, 7; development of, **Supp. 2**, 158; logging and milling, **Supp. 5**, 68–69; mill pooling, **Supp. 2**, 34; reforestation, **Supp. 2**, 264; sales and marketing, **Supp. 3**, 812–13; standard grading, **Supp. 2**, 264; strike, **Supp. 6**, 320; Texas, **Supp. 6**, 324; writings on, **Supp. 7**, 353. *See also* Trees
Luminescence, research in, **Supp. 2**, 487
Lummis, Charles F., reference to, **Supp. 3**, 88
Lunar studies. *See* Moon
Lunar theory, **Vol. 7, Part 1**, 453
Lunar tide, Great Lakes, **Vol. 4, Part 1**, 476
Lunceford, Jimmie, reference to, **Supp. 3**, 525
"Luncheon at the Waldorf" (radio program), **Supp. 10**, 120
Lundin, Fred, reference to, **Supp. 3**, 771–72
Lundy's Lane, battle of, **Vol. 2, Part 1**, 125; **Vol. 5, Part 2**, 62; **Vol. 8, Part 1**, 100, 621; **Vol. 8, Part 2**, 506; **Vol. 10, Part 2**, 537
Lungs: cancer surgery, **Supp. 6**, 246; research on, **Supp. 2**, 458; smoking effects on, **Supp. 6**, 246; **Supp. 7**, 192
Lunn, George, reference to, **Supp. 9**, 503–4
Lunt, Alfred, references to, **Supp. 5**, 525; **Supp. 6**, 286; **Supp. 8**, 444; **Supp. 9**, 70
Lunt-Fontanne Theater (New York City), **Supp. 10**, 474
Lupino, Ida, reference to, **Supp. 10**, 63
Lusitania, **Vol. 4, Part 1**, 41; **Vol. 5, Part 1**, 324; **Vol. 5, Part 2**, 443; **Vol. 6, Part 1**, 278; **Supp. 5**, 241
Luther, Martin, writings on, **Supp. 3**, 726
Lutheran church: **Vol. 3, Part 1**, 29; **Vol. 3, Part 2**, 261; **Vol. 4, Part 1**, 38, 72; **Vol. 4, Part 2**, 429, 515; **Vol. 5, Part 2**, 503, 514; **Vol. 6, Part 1**, 270; **Vol. 7, Part 2**, 289; **Vol. 8, Part 2**, 441; **Vol. 9, Part 2**, 243 f.; **Vol. 10, Part 1**, 142, 402, 606 f., 653; activities of, **Vol. 4, Part 2**, 22 f.; Augustana Synod, **Vol. 6, Part 1**, 270; biographies of clergymen, **Vol. 9, Part 2**, 65; Civil War and, **Vol. 4, Part 2**, 429; clergy, **Vol. 1, Part 1**, 32, 466 f.; **Vol. 4, Part 1**, 461; **Vol. 4, Part 2**, 370, 538; **Vol. 5, Part 1**, 108, 118, 228, 268, 319, 422 f., 568; **Vol. 5, Part 2**, 373, 512; **Vol. 6, Part 1**, 335, 478 f.; **Vol. 7, Part 1**, 212 f., 306 f., 308 f., 549, 635; **Vol. 7, Part 2**, 289, 574; **Vol. 8, Part 2**, 284, 412 f., 439, 441 f., 449 f., 563; **Vol. 9, Part 1**, 418, 477; **Vol. 9, Part 2**, 40; colleges, **Vol. 8, Part 2**, 285; community, **Vol. 5, Part 2**, 313; dissension within, **Vol. 3, Part 1**, 201; **Vol. 4, Part 1**, 590 f., **Vol. 4, Part 2**, 370, 429; English, use of, in, **Vol. 5, Part 2**, 512; funds of, **Vol. 6, Part 1**, 169; Illinois, **Vol. 4, Part 2**, 384; Iowa, **Vol. 3, Part 1**, 201; **Vol. 4, Part 2**, 23; liturgy, **Supp. 1**, 449; Maryland, **Vol. 5, Part 2**, 502, 514; middle colonies, **Vol. 7, Part 1**, 311; missionary work, **Vol. 2, Part 1**, 445; **Vol. 3, Part 1**, 29; **Vol. 4, Part 2**, 292, 538, 608; **Vol. 5, Part 2**, 514; **Vol. 7, Part 1**, 78 f.; **Vol. 9, Part 2**, 599 f.; Missouri Synod, **Vol. 10, Part 1**, 402 f.; **Supp. 4**, 540–41; Moravian's and, **Vol. 4, Part 2**, 474; Norwegian branch of, **Vol. 3, Part 1**, 308; **Vol. 5, Part 1**, 269, 319; organization, **Vol. 3, Part 2**, 260; Palestine representative, **Supp. 3**, 272; Pennsylvania, **Vol. 3, Part 1**, 201, 232; **Vol. 4, Part 2**, 538; **Vol. 5, Part 2**, 502; **Vol. 6, Part 2**, 247, 452; **Vol. 7, Part 1**, 306 f.; publications, **Vol. 8, Part 2**, 439, 442; Swedish, **Vol. 3, Part 2**, 182; theology, **Vol. 5, Part 1**, 268–69, 423; **Vol. 7, Part 1**, 635; **Vol. 5, Part 2**, 77; **Vol. 8, Part 2**, 440 f.; writings on, **Vol. 4, Part 1**, 462, 591; **Vol. 4, Part 2**, 474; **Vol. 5, Part 2**, 77, 373; **Vol. 6, Part 1**, 170, 270; **Vol. 8, Part 1**, 551; **Vol. 8, Part 2**, 413, 441, 444, 450; **Vol. 9, Part 2**, 244; **Vol. 10, Part 1**, 606, 653
Lutheran Church Review, **Vol. 5, Part 2**, 503
Lutheran Historical Society, **Vol. 7, Part 1**, 213
"Lutheran Hour" (radio program), **Supp. 4**, 541
Lutheran Intelligencer, **Vol. 8, Part 2**, 414
Lutheran Observer, **Vol. 5, Part 2**, 503, 514
Lutheran Ouarterly, **Vol. 10, Part 1**, 142
Lutheran Seminary (Milwaukee, Wis.) **Vol. 5, Part 1**, 108
Lutheran Standard, first issue of, **Vol. 4, Part 1**, 590
Luther College (Iowa), founding of, **Vol. 5, Part 2**, 495; **Vol. 8, Part 1**, 208 f.
"Lux Radio Theater, The" (radio program), **Supp. 6**, 159–60
Luzerne County Agricultural Society, **Vol. 2, Part 2**, 110

Luzon, World War II action, **Supp. 7**, 490
Lyceum movement, **Vol. 5, Part 1**, 130; **Vol. 5, Part 2**, 404; **Vol. 6, Part 1**, 164; **Vol. 8, Part 1**, 60 f.; **Vol. 8, Part 2**, 226; **Vol. 9, Part 2**, 101
Lyceum of Natural History (New York City), establishment of, **Vol. 9, Part 2**, 596
Lyceum Theatre (New York City), **Supp. 3**, 333; founding of, **Supp. 2**, 211
"Lyceum" Village, **Vol. 5, Part 1**, 131
Lycoming Gazette, **Vol. 7, Part 2**, 132
Lye, labeling as poison, **Supp. 6**, 317
Lyles, Aubrey, reference to, **Supp. 9**, 731
Lymphocytes, **Supp. 4**, 616
Lymph system: embryological studies, **Supp. 5**, 600; writings on, **Supp. 4**, 866
Lynch, Edmund, references to, **Supp. 9**, 613, 614
Lynch, Edward, reference to, **Supp. 6**, 448
Lynch, Frederick, reference to, **Supp. 6**, 25
Lynch, John L., reference to, **Supp. 3**, 20
Lynchburg, Va., operation at (1864), **Vol. 5, Part 1**, 401; **Vol. 9, Part 1**, 361
Lynching: campaign against, **Supp. 9**, 749, 750; first law against, **Supp. 8**, 67; political debate over, **Supp. 9**, 150; writings on, **Supp. 5**, 740
"Lynch law," **Vol. 1, Part 1**, 373; **Vol. 6, Part 1**, 519 f.
Lynd, Helen, references to, **Supp. 3**, 30; **Supp. 4**, 908; **Supp. 5**, 35; **Supp. 8**, 398–99
Lynd, Robert S., references to, **Supp. 3**, 30; **Supp. 4**, 908; **Supp. 5**, 35; **Supp. 8**, 407; **Supp. 10**, 438
Lynd, Staughton, reference to, **Supp. 8**, 398
Lyndon School of Agriculture, **Vol. 10, Part 1**, 139
Lyon, Mary, reference to, **Vol. 7, Part 1**, 16
Lyon, Matthew, references to, **Vol. 4, Part 2**, 10; **Vol. 9, Part 2**, 386
Lyons Musical Academy, founding of, **Vol. 9, Part 1**, 103
Lysenko, Trofim D., reference to, **Supp. 8**, 449; **Supp. 9**, 239
Lythgoe, Albert M., reference to, **Supp. 3**, 627

M

M (movie), **Supp. 7**, 478
"Ma and Pa Kettle" (fictional characters), **Supp. 9**, 535–56
Macadam, use of in road construction, **Vol. 4, Part 2**, 61; **Vol. 8, Part 1**, 74 f.
McAdoo, William Gibbs: presidential bid, **Supp. 3**, 644, 670, 719; **Supp. 5**, 497; references to, **Vol. 9, Part 2**, 144; **Supp. 3**, 114, 772; **Supp. 4**, 537; **Supp. 7**, 512, 537, 796; **Supp. 8**, 592; West relationshlp, **Supp. 6**, 682–83
Macalaster College, **Vol. 6, Part 1**, 543; **Vol. 7, Part 1**, 408
McAndrew, William, reference to, **Supp. 3**, 772
MacArthur, Charles, references to, **Supp. 5**, 323; **Supp. 7**, 148, 331, 413; **Supp. 8**, 547; **Supp. 10**, 478
MacArthur, Douglas: bonus marchers, **Supp. 6**, 240; Eisenhower relationship, **Supp. 8**, 154; journalism on, **Supp. 8**, 497; Korean War, **Supp. 5**, 676, 706; **Supp. 6**, 432; **Supp. 8**, 421–22; 633; **Supp. 9**, 9, 813; Pacific Theater operations, **Supp. 9**, 461; Philippine command, **Supp. 8**, 637–38, 698; references to, **Supp. 7**, 74, 215, 363, 451; **Supp. 9**, 892; **Supp. 10**, 478; Whitney relationship, **Supp. 8**, 698–99; World War II, **Supp. 5**, 720; **Supp. 6**, 170, 268, 340; **Supp. 8**, 23–24, 48, 351
McCall's magazine, **Supp. 8**, 357
McCarran Act (1950), **Supp. 8**, 392, 590, 703; **Supp. 9**, 573; **Supp. 10**, 126; passage of, **Supp. 5**, 544
McCarran-Walter Act (1946), **Supp. 7**, 766
McCarran-Walter Act (1952). *See* Immigration and Nationality Act
"McCarthy, Charlie" (fictional character), **Supp. 10**, 32, 33
McCarthy, Eugene: presidential bid, **Supp. 9**, 59, 436; **Supp. 10**, 470; references to, **Supp. 8**, 324; **Supp. 10**, 362
McCarthy, Joe (baseball manager), reference to, **Supp. 10**, 613
McCarthy, Joseph R.: accusations against Bunche, **Supp. 9**, 138; anti-Tydings campaign, **Supp. 7**, 751; **Supp. 9**, 311; Army hearings, **Supp. 6**, 680; **Supp. 8**, 57; **Supp. 10**, 645; censure vote, **Supp. 6**, 681; **Supp. 7**, 31, 74, 213, 383, 419–20; **Supp. 8**, 178, 302, 322, 701; **Supp. 9**, 69, 312, 401, 433, 468; charges against Coe, **Supp. 10**, 134; charges against G. Marshall, **Supp. 6**, 432; **Supp. 10**, 421; charges against State Department employees, **Supp. 9**, 135, 813–14; condemnation of Carlson, **Supp. 4**, 147; congressional opposition to, **Supp. 5**, 690; **Supp. 8**, 654; **Supp. 9**, 81, 311–12; Eisenhower relationship, **Supp. 8**, 156; journalism exposés of, **Supp. 8**, 497; Kelly caricature of, **Supp. 9**, 453; Kohlberg relationship, **Supp. 6**, 350; Matthews relationship, **Supp. 8**, 426; media support, **Supp. 8**, 373, 498; Murrow TV program on, **Supp. 7**, 567; opposition to, **Supp. 7**, 468; **Supp. 8**, 272–73, 285, 392; **Supp. 9**, 27, 211; **Supp. 10**, 87–88; references to, **Supp. 5**, 343, 404, 410, 676; **Supp. 7**, 315, 451, 510, 511; **Supp. 8**, 288, 406, 492, 701; **Supp. 9**, 9, 458, 842; **Supp. 10**, 293, 801; support for, **Supp. 6**, 360, 441; **Supp. 7**, 212–13, 250; **Supp. 8**, 128, 150; **Supp. 9**, 387, 413, 573, 860, 887; **Supp. 10**, 653; survey of public reaction to, **Supp. 6**, 605–6. *See also* Loyalty issues, McCarthyism
McCarthy, Mary, references to, **Supp. 9**, 41, 43, 876
McCarthy, Tommy, reference to, **Supp. 5**, 189
Macartney, Clarence E., reference to, **Supp. 6**, 195
McCartney, Paul, reference to, **Supp. 10**, 448
Macbeth Gallery Show (1908), **Supp. 5**, 636
McClellan, G. B., references to, **Vol. 6, Part 1**, 123 f., 253 f.; **Vol. 9, Part 1**, 518 f., 613
McClellan, John L., references to, **Supp. 8**, 208; **Supp. 9**, 395, 821
McClennen, Edward F., reference to, **Supp. 3**, 98
McClintic, Guthrie, references to, **Supp. 6**, 517; **Supp. 7**, 283; **Supp. 9**, 195, 196
McCloy, John J., reference to, **Supp. 7**, 276
McClure, S. S., references to, **Supp. 3**, 762, 816; **Supp. 4**, 662; **Supp. 5**, 698
McClure's Magazine: **Vol. 7, Part 1**, 551; **Supp. 3**, 761, 816; **Supp. 4**, 46–47, 368, 417–18, 841–42; **Supp. 5**, 530, 666, 698; **Supp. 6**, 6; editing of, **Supp. 4**, 662; founding of, **Supp. 4**, 517–18
McCollum, E. V., reference to, **Supp. 4**, 381–82
McComb, Samuel, reference to, **Supp. 3**, 191
McCord Zulu Hospital (South Africa), founding of, **Supp. 4**, 519–20
McCormack, John, reference to, **Supp. 6**, 69
McCormick, Cyrus, reference to, **Vol. 5, Part 1**, 432
McCormick, Joseph Medill, references to, **Supp. 3**, 772; **Supp. 5**, 448, 633
McCormick, Katharine Dexter, reference to, **Supp. 8**, 503
McCormick, Robert R., references to, **Supp. 4**, 644, 645; **Supp. 7**, 296, 473, 603; **Supp. 9**, 80
McCormick, Robert Sanderson, reference to, **Supp. 5**, 449
McCormick Hospital (Thailand), founding of, **Supp. 4**, 529–30
McCormick Theological Seminary, **Vol. 6, Part 1**, 608
McCosh, Isabella Guthrie, reference to, **Vol. 6, Part 1**, 617

McCosh, James, reference to, **Vol. 7, Part 1**, 359
McCoy, John, reference to, **Supp. 3**, 848
McCracken, William P., Jr., civil aeronautics code development, **Supp. 9**, 899
McCrea, Joel, reference to, **Supp. 9**, 479
McCrory, J. G., reference to, **Supp. 8**, 347
McCulloch Corporation, **Supp. 10**, 491
McCulloch Oil Corporation, **Supp. 10**, 491–92
McCullough, Paul, reference to, **Supp. 6**, 112
McCully, Newton, reference to, **Supp. 7**, 749
McCutcheon, John T., reference to, **Supp. 3**, 3
McDaniel, Hattie, reference to, **Supp. 7**, 44
McDonald, David, reference to, **Supp. 7**, 229
MacDonald, Dwight, references to, **Supp. 7**, 80; **Supp. 9**, 41; **Supp. 10**, 153
MacDonald, Jeanette, reference to, **Supp. 8**, 151
McDonald Observatory, founding of, **Supp. 7**, 726
McDonnell-Douglas Aircraft Corporation, **Supp. 10**, 495
McDonough, John, reference to, **Vol. 6, Part 1**, 561
McDonough, Joseph P., reference to, **Supp. 10**, 167
McDougall, Alexander, reference to, **Vol. 8, Part 2**, 539
McDougall, William, references to, **Supp. 3**, 151; **Supp. 10**, 671, 672
McDougall Shipbuilding Co., **Supp. 6**, 36
MacDowell, Edward, reference to, **Vol. 5, Part 1**, 367; **Supp. 4**, 135
McDowell, Ephraim, reference to, **Vol. 5, Part 1**, 549
MacDowell, Frances Knapp, reference to, **Supp. 4**, 125
McDowell, John R., reference to, **Supp. 6**, 500
McDowell, Roddy, reference to, **Supp. 9**, 247
Macedonian, naval exploits of, **Vol. 1, Part 1**, 212; **Vol. 3, Part 1**, 188
MacFadden, Bernard, references to, **Supp. 5**, 205, 527, 528; **Supp. 9**, 51, 52
McFadden, Louis T., references to, **Supp. 6**, 509, 510
McFadden Act (1927), **Supp. 4**, 326
McFadden Publications, **Supp. 5**, 453
"M'Fingal," popularity of poem, **Vol. 10, Part 1**, 11
MacGahan, Aloysius, reference to, **Vol. 1, Part 2**, 200
McGee, Dean A., reference to, **Supp. 7**, 428
McGee, Lemuel C., reference to, **Supp. 4**, 460
McGovern, George S., references to, **Supp. 7**, 421; **Supp. 9**, 202, 573
McGovern, Terry, reference to, **Supp. 3**, 333
MacGowan, Kenneth, reference to, **Supp. 5**, 375
McGrath, J. Howard, reference to, **Supp. 7**, 500
McGraw, John J., references to, **Supp. 5**, 393; **Supp. 6**, 488; **Supp. 9**, 294; **Supp. 10**, 314, 508
McGraw-Hill Building, **Supp. 6**, 593
McGraw-Hill Publishing Co.: **Supp. 5**, 350; **Supp. 6**, 665; Hughes autobiography hoax, **Supp. 10**, 358; organization and growth of, **Supp. 4**, 523–24; **Supp. 9**, 522–23
"McGrew, Dan" (fictional character), **Supp. 6**, 574, 575
McGuire, Phyllis, reference to, **Supp. 9**, 306–7
Machado, Gerardo, reference to, **Supp. 6**, 90
Machen, John Gresham, reference to, **Supp. 6**, 195
Machias, **Supp. 9**, 461
"Machine Age," early exposition of nature and consequences of, **Vol. 10, Part 1**, 637 f.
Machine guns, invention of, **Vol. 5, Part 1**, 246; Browning, **Vol. 2, Part 1**, 175; Lewis, **Vol. 6, Part 1**, 215
Machinery: conveyance, **Supp. 1**, 598; cotton picker, **Supp. 5**, 596–97; design of, **Vol. 5, Part 1**, 84; **Vol. 7, Part 2**, 167; **Vol. 8, Part 1**, 517 f.; **Supp. 5**, 387; dynamo, electric, **Vol. 10, Part 1**, 376 f.; farm, **Supp. 2**, 402; fatigue testing, **Supp. 3**, 220; manufacture of, **Vol. 8, Part 1**, 442; **Vol. 9, Part 2**, 614; **Vol. 10, Part 1**, 470 f.; **Supp. 2**, 174; mining, **Supp. 2**, 101; rock-drilling, **Vol. 8, Part 1**, 343
Machine tools: **Vol. 8, Part 1**, 172 f.; **Vol. 8, Part 2**, 576–77; flat-turret lathe, **Supp. 1**, 378; gauging of, **Supp. 1**, 379; multiple rotary tooth cutter, **Supp. 3**, 224; pneumatic, **Supp. 1**, 446; precision grinding, **Supp. 3**, 561–62
Machinists, International Association of. *See* International Association of Machinists
McHugh, Jimmy, reference to, **Supp. 9**, 280
McIntire, Ross T., reference to, **Supp. 6**, 131
McIntosh, John, reference to, **Vol. 7, Part 1**, 371
McIntyre, James Francis, reference to, **Supp. 8**, 613
MacIntyre, Malcolm, reference to, **Supp. 9**, 659
McIntyre, Marvin, reference to, **Supp. 5**, 196–97
Mack, Connie, references to, **Supp. 5**, 48, 124–25; **Supp. 7**, 27, 129, 130; **Supp. 8**, 186, 543, 544; **Supp. 9**, 344, 345; **Supp. 10**, 314
Mack, Julian W., reference to, **Supp. 3**, 97
Mack, Max Jacob, reference to, **Supp. 3**, 488
Mack, Ruth, reference to, **Supp. 3**, 488
McKay, Claude, reference to, **Supp. 6**, 321
Mackay, John W., reference to, **Vol. 1, Part 2**, 200
MacKaye, Steele, references to, **Supp. 6**, 417, 418
McKeldin, Theodore, reference to, **Supp. 9**, 743
McKellar, Kenneth D., references to, **Supp. 3**, 449; **Supp. 6**, 228; **Supp. 7**, 415
Mackenzie, Alistair, reference to, **Supp. 9**, 439
Mackenzie, James, reference to, **Supp. 6**, 117
Mackenzie, Morrell, reference to, **Supp. 6**, 317
McKenzie, Red, reference to, **Supp. 9**, 183
Mackenzie King, William L., reference to, **Supp. 6**, 548
McKesson & Robbins, **Supp. 2**, 481
McKim, Charles F., references to, **Supp. 3**, 533, 534; **Vol. 7, Part 1**, 571
McKim, Mead, and White, **Supp. 6**, 355
Mackinac Bridge Authority, **Supp. 9**, 130
Mackinac Strait Bridge (Mich.), **Supp. 3**, 531; **Supp. 6**, 594; **Supp. 9**, 130
McKinley, Ray, reference to, **Supp. 3**, 525
McKinley, William: assassination of, **Supp. 5**, 285, 286; biography of, **Supp. 9**, 629; references to, **Vol. 4, Part 2**, 226, 490; **Vol. 5, Part 1**, 496 f.; **Vol. 8, Part 1**, 2 f.; **Vol. 9, Part 2**, 41
McKinley Publishing Co., founding of, **Supp. 2**, 419
McKinley Tariff of 1890, drafting of, **Vol. 7, Part 2**, 331
McKinly, Ashley, reference to, **Supp. 6**, 92
McKnight, Robert, trading party of (1812), **Vol. 5, Part 1**, 587
Mack Stadium (Philadelphia, Pa.), **Supp. 6**, 415
"Mack the Knife" (song), **Supp. 9**, 219
McLaughlin, Frances Howard, reference to, **Supp. 9**, 323
McLaughlin, Hugh, reference to, **Vol. 6, Part 1**, 568
McLaughlin, James, reference to, **Vol. 4, Part 1**, 101
McLawim, John L., reference to, **Vol. 9, Part 2**, 548
McLean, Edward B., references to, **Supp. 3**, 259, 715
McLean, Jay, reference to, **Supp. 3**, 370
McLean, William Lippard, reference to, **Supp. 10**, 498
MacLeish, Archibald, references to, **Supp. 3**, 72; **Supp. 7**, 339, 560, 561
McLoughlin, John, references to, **Vol. 5, Part 2**, 297; **Vol. 9, Part 1**, 291
Maclure, William, reference to, **Vol. 7, Part 1**, 402
McMahon, Brien, reference to, **Supp. 6**, 156
McMaster, J. B., reference to, **Vol. 8, Part 2**, 460
McMasters, Philip D., reference to, **Supp. 6**, 189
McMath, Robert R., reference to, **Supp. 3**, 208
McMillan, James, reference to, **Supp. 3**, 533
Macmillan Co., **Supp. 4**, 583; establishment of, **Supp. 2**, 59

McMillen Gallery (New York City), **Supp. 6**, 512
MacMurray, William H., reference to, **Supp. 5**, 134
McNamara, Robert, references to, **Supp. 7**, 421, 423; **Supp. 9**, 252; **Supp. 10**, 72
McNary, Charles L., references to, **Supp. 6**, 131, 683; **Supp. 8**, 104, 617; **Supp. 9**, 151, 356
McNary-Haugen bills, **Supp. 3**, 319, 399, 496, 559, 594; **Supp. 7**, 760
MacNeice, Louis, references to, **Supp. 9**, 53, 54
MacNeill, Charles M., reference to, **Supp. 6**, 316
McNutt, Maxwell, reference to, **Supp. 3**, 532
McNutt, Paul, reference to, **Supp. 9**, 789
McPeak, William, reference to, **Supp. 7**, 276
McQuaid, Bernard, reference to, **Supp. 3**, 325–26
McRae, Milton A., reference to, **Vol. 8, Part 2**, 518
McReynolds, James Clark, references to, **Supp. 3**, 168; **Supp. 5**, 571, 572, 574; **Supp. 6**, 138
Macromolecules, **Supp. 6**, 346
McWilliams, Carey, references to, **Supp. 4**, 326; **Supp. 5**, 4
Macy, John, references to, **Supp. 8**, 317, 318
Macy, Josiah, Jr., Foundation (New York City), **Supp. 3**, 435
Macy, V. Everit, reference to, **Supp. 3**, 677
Macy, R. H., and Co.: Bamberger Co. acquisition by, **Supp. 3**, 30; cash-time plan, **Supp. 6**, 559; development of, **Supp. 2**, 636; growth and innovations, **Supp. 3**, 748–49, 440; partnership in, **Vol. 9, Part 2**, 129; Thanksgiving Day parade, **Supp. 3**, 685
Madagascar, **Supp. 5**, 435; missions in, **Vol.9, Part 2**, 599 f.
Madame Butterfly, **Vol. 6, Part 1**, 379; Belasco production of, **Supp. 1**, 67
Maddox, Jack L., reference to, **Supp. 7**, 16
Madeira-Mamor Railway, **Supp. 5**, 215
Madison, James: edition of works of, **Vol. 5, Part 1**, 385; Monroe friendship of, **Vol. 7, Part 1**, 88 f.; references to, **Vol. 4, Part 2**, 175, 550; **Vol. 5, Part 1**, 162; **Vol. 6, Part 1**, 597; **Vol. 7, Part 1**, 113; **Vol. 9, Part 1**, 337; teacher of, **Vol. 9, Part 2**, 331
Madison, Wis., **Vol. 5, Part 2**, 365; **Vol. 7, Part 2**, 117
Madison Avenue Presbyterian Church (New York City), **Supp. 5**, 116
Madison College, **Vol. 1, Part 2**, 31
Madison Square Garden (New York City): **Vol. 1, Part 1**, 638; financial problems, **Supp. 6**, 337; fireworks explosion in, **Supp. 5**, 285; operation of, **Supp. 5**, 360; Thaw's shooting of White in, **Supp. 4**, 827; **Supp. 8**, 461–62
Madison University, **Vol. 3, Part 1**, 346; **Vol. 8, Part 1**, 412
Maestri, Robert S., reference to, **Supp. 7**, 555
Mafia riots, negotiations with Italy following, **Vol. 8, Part 1**, 80 f.
Magazines: advertising and circulation, **Vol. 5, Part 1**, 323; antisegregationist, **Supp. 8**, 605; baseball, **Supp. 7**, 711–12; black-oriented, **Supp. 7**, 202, 203; confession, **Supp. 5**, 453, 527; cover illustration, **Supp. 5**, 428, 429, 594; **Supp. 8**, 493; **Supp. 10**, 689, 690, 691; cover models, **Supp. 7**, 140–41; current events, **Supp. 4**, 739; **Supp. 9**, 482–83; **Supp. 10**, 14; Davis interests, **Supp. 9**, 223; editing, **Supp. 4**, 662, 841–42; **Supp. 7**, 535, 602; editorial development, **Supp. 5**, 16–17; **Supp. 9**, 394; fashion, **Supp. 3**, 547; **Supp. 6**, 107–8; **Supp. 7**, 704–5; financial, **Supp. 8**, 338; first American jazz publication, **Supp. 9**, 316; first movie fan publication, **Supp. 3**, 76; *Foreign Affairs*, growth of, **Supp. 9**, 44; Hearst interests, **Supp. 5**, 286; history of, **Supp. 7**, 559; humor, **Supp. 10**, 630; illustration, **Vol. 8, Part 1**, 287 f.; **Supp. 5**, 625; **Supp. 7**, 17; indexes to, **Supp. 5**, 752–53; jazz criticism, **Supp. 9**, 316–17; literary, **Supp. 4**, 517–18; **Supp. 5**, 94, 614; **Supp. 7**, 103–4; **Supp. 9**, 637; **Supp. 10**, 394–95; *Little Review*, **Supp. 9**, 33; *Look* founding, **Supp. 4**, 189; McGraw-Hill, **Supp. 9**, 522–23; male-oriented, **Supp. 5**, 637; medical, **Supp. 10**, 370; mystery, **Supp. 9**, 488; *National Geographic* growth, **Supp. 8**, 228; news, **Supp. 8**, 393–94; Newhouse publications, **Supp. 10**, 586; news, **Supp. 9**, 521; *New Yorker*, **Supp. 5**, 593–94; *New York* founding, **Supp. 9**, 265; on photography, **Supp. 4**, 779–80; **Supp. 8**, 394–96; **Supp. 10**, 834; pictures, first lavish use of, **Vol. 3, Part 2**, 572; poetry, **Supp. 8**, 349–50; political, **Supp. 8**, 149; **Supp. 9**, 504, 637; **Supp. 10**, 51; Postal Service censorship, **Supp. 6**, 661; publication, **Vol. 1, Part 1**, 573; **Vol. 3, Part 2**, 49, 54, 477; **Vol. 6, Part 1**, 110; **Vol. 7, Part 1**, 353; **Vol. 10, Part 2**, 80; publishing industry, **Supp. 9**, 738, 739; religious, **Supp. 9**, 586; science fiction, **Supp. 9**, 155–56; **Supp. 8**, 209–10; serialization, **Supp. 10**, 20–21; subscriptions, **Supp. 1**, 212; syndicated, **Supp. 5**, 394; technical, **Supp. 4**, 523–24; **Supp. 9**, 523; tinted paper, first use of, **Vol. 3, Part 2**, 572; women-oriented, **Vol. 4, Part 2**, 111; **Supp. 3**, 442–43; Ziff interests, **Supp. 9**, 222–23
Magdalen Society, **Vol. 4, Part 1**, 475
Magee, Christopher L., reference to, **Vol. 6, Part 1**, 590
"Maggie" (fictional character). *See* "Jiggs and Maggie"
Magic: **Vol. 4, Part 2**, 593; **Vol. 5, Part 1**, 248; **Vol. 7, Part 2**, 194; acts, **Supp. 2**, 245–46, 377–78, 661–62; **Supp. 7**, 56–57; materials relating to, collecting of, **Vol. 5, Part 1**, 249
Magical Mystery Tour, **Supp. 10**, 450
Magliocco, Joseph, reference to, **Supp. 10**, 140
Magmatic differentiation, **Supp. 6**, 71
Magnaflux Corporation, **Supp. 3**, 220
Magna Theatre Corporation, **Supp. 7**, 692–93
Magnesium industry, **Supp. 8**, 308
Magnesium sulphate, **Supp. 4**, 34
Magnetic observatories, design of, **Supp. 6**, 205
Magnetic Telegraph Co., **Vol. 1, Part 1**, 639
Magnetism: **Vol. 1, Part 1**, 461 f.; **Vol. 3, Part 1**, 87 f.; **Vol. 4, Part 1**, 3; airborne detector, **Supp. 6**, 501; crystal field theory, **Supp. 10**, 805; electrical reaction to, **Supp. 2**, 273; electromagnets, **Vol. 9, Part 1**, 188; electrons, theory of, **Vol. 8, Part 2**, 198; magnetic field, **Supp. 6**, 31; magnetic needle, table of variations, **Vol. 3, Part 1**, 274; measurement, **Supp. 6**, 205–6; observatories, **Supp. 6**, 205; of earth, **Supp. 1**, 61; of sun, **Supp. 2**, 271; resonance, **Supp. 10**, 805
Magnetohydrodynamics, development of, **Supp. 6**, 365
Magnificent Ambersons, The, **Supp. 9**, 560
Magnificent Obsession, **Supp. 5**, 182
Magnuson, Warren, reference to, **Supp. 10**, 87
Mahara's Minstrels, **Supp. 6**, 274–75
Maheu, Robert, references to, **Supp. 10**, 356, 357, 358
Mahidol (Prince of Thailand), **Supp. 4**, 181
Mahler, Alma Schindler, reference to, **Supp. 8**, 226
Mahler, Gustav, references to, **Supp. 2**, 47; **Supp. 6**, 351; **Supp. 7**, 764
Mahogonny (opera), **Supp. 4**, 868
Mahoney, Michael, reference to, **Supp. 3**, 605
Maid of Northumberland, first play on Civil War, **Vol. 6, Part 1**, 483
Mail-order houses, **Vol. 8, Part 2**, 170, 540; **Vol. 10, Part 1**, 414; **Supp. 8**, 28–29
Mail service: **Vol. 5, Part 2**, 93; **Vol. 9, Part 1**, 466; **Vol. 10, Part 1**, 138; chutes, patenting of, **Vol. 3, Part 1**, 11; coach, **Vol. 9, Part 1**, 361; express companies, competition between post office and, **Vol. 10, Part 1**, 639 f.; overland, **Vol. 2, Part 2**, 298; **Vol. 10, Part**

1, 639 f; post office cars, **Vol. 3, Part 1**, 147; **Vol. 5, Part 2**, 93; railway, **Vol. 1, Part 1**, 351 f.; stamps, introduction of, **Vol. 5, Part 2**, 93; steamships, subsidies for, **Vol. 8, Part 2**, 11; U.S. Mail Service, development of, **Vol. 4, Part 2**, 397. *See also* Postal Service, United States

Maimonides College of Philadelphia, first Jewish college in America, **Vol. 3, Part 1**, 459 f.

Maine: agriculture, **Vol. 4, Part 1**, 379; **Vol. 5, Part 1**, 163; Aroostook County, publicity for, **Vol. 8, Part 1**, 71 f.; boundary disputes, **Vol. 3, Part 1**, 515 f.; **Vol. 8, Part 1**, 71 f., 100, 505; **Vol. 10, Part 1**, 385 f.; botany, **Vol. 10, Part 2**, 617; colonization of, **Vol. 10, Part 2**, 397; discovery of, **Vol. 10, Part 1**, 562 f.; economic development, **Vol. 8, Part 1**, 71 f.; **Vol. 10, Part 2**, 285; education, **Vol. 2, Part 1**, 606; **Vol. 3, Part 1**, 515 f.; **Vol. 9, Part 1**, 600; exploration, **Vol. 8, Part 1**, 78; fictional writings on, **Supp. 5**, 747–48; **Supp. 9**, 173; fiction writer, first in, **Vol. 10, Part 2**, 472; first senator elected by popular vote, **Supp. 7**, 312; geology, **Vol. 3, Part 1**, 515 f.; **Vol. 5, Part 1**, 536 f.; governors, **Vol. 2, Part 1**, 597 f.; **Vol. 2, Part 2**, 249 f.; **Vol. 3, Part 1**, 314 f., 151 f.; **Vol. 4, Part 1**, 131; **Vol. 5, Part 1**, 328 f.; **Vol. 5, Part 2**, 264 f., 343 f., 405 f.; **Vol. 7, Part 1**, 196 f., 199 f.; **Vol. 7, Part 2**, 254, 645 f.; **Vol. 10, Part 1**, 502 f.; **Vol. 10, Part 2**, 301 f.; **Supp. 7**, 72; history of, **Vol. 3, Part 1**, 515 f.; **Vol. 4, Part 1**, 583; **Vol. 4, Part 2**, 194; **Vol. 8, Part 1**, 184 f., 330 f.; industry in, **Vol. 8, Part 2**, 398–99; insane, care of, **Vol. 3, Part 1**, 515 f.; land promotion, **Vol. 6, Part 2**, 155; legal service, **Vol. 1, Part 2**, 548 f.; **Vol. 3, Part 1**, 79; **Vol. 4, Part 1**, 583; **Vol. 6, Part 2**, 517; **Vol. 7, Part 2**, 505; **Vol. 8, Part 1**, 184, 184 f., 430, 457; **Vol. 9, Part 1**, 78; **Vol. 10, Part 1**, 446; Maine-Missouri question, **Vol. 8, Part 2**, 10; maps, **Vol. 4, Part 1**, 582 f.; Massachusetts, separation from, **Vol. 1, Part 1**, 337 f.; **Vol. 2, Part 1**, 614; **Vol. 5, Part 1**, 167; **Vol. 8, Part 1**, 184 f., 356 f.; **Vol. 10, Part 1**, 446; **Vol. 10, Part 2**, 141; medical service, **Vol. 5, Part 1**, 328–29; Methodist church, **Vol. 6, Part 1**, 1; missionary work, **Vol. 7, Part 2**, 334; newspaper, first in, **Vol. 9, Part 1**, 345; oceanography studies, **Supp. 8**, 37; poetry, **Supp. 5**, 118–19; political service, **Vol. 1, Part 2**, 323, 487, 548; **Vol. 3, Part 1**, 4, 79, 315, 515; **Vol. 3, Part 2**, 257; **Vol. 4, Part 2**, 103; **Vol. 5, Part 1**, 63, 328; **Vol. 5, Part 2**, 264, 343, 344, 405; **Vol. 6, Part 1**, 261; **Vol. 6, Part 2**, 237; **Vol. 7, Part 1**, 196–97, 199; **Vol. 7, Part 2**, 254, 505, 646; **Vol. 10, Part 1**, 40, 502; **Vol. 10, Part 2**, 141, 285, 301; **Vol. 10, Part 2**, 301; politics, **Supp. 7**, 72–73; public service, **Vol. 2, Part 2**, 249; **Vol. 3, Part 1**, 515 f.; **Vol. 4, Part 1**, 140; **Vol. 4, Part 2**, 103, 194, 196; **Vol. 5, Part 2**, 344; **Vol. 6, Part 1**, 388; **Vol. 7, Part 1**, 243; **Vol. 8, Part 2**, 276; railroad promotion, **Vol. 8, Part 1**, 184 f.; settlement of, **Vol. 8, Part 1**, 78; temperance movement in, **Vol. 3, Part 1**, 411; writings on, **Vol. 5, Part 2**, 71, 303; **Vol. 10, Part 2**, 301, 309; **Supp. 4**, 248–49

Maine, destruction of, **Vol. 6, Part 1**, 104, 377; **Vol. 6, Part 2**, 107; **Vol. 8, Part 2**, 322; **Vol. 9, Part 1**, 156

Maine Central Railroad, **Vol. 8, Part 1**, 71 f.

Maine Chance Farm, founding of, **Supp. 8**, 13

Maine Historical Society, **Vol. 7, Part 2**, 125; **Vol. 10, Part 1**, 446

Maine State Temperance Society, **Vol. 3, Part 1**, 411

Maine Temperance Union, **Vol. 3, Part 1**, 411

Main Street, **Supp. 5**, 272, 422, 423; **Supp. 6**, 95

Maitland, Frederic W., references to, **Supp. 3**, 15, **Supp. 6**, 271

Maize. *See* Corn

"Major Bowes' Amateur Hour" (radio program), **Supp. 4**, 97

Making of Americans, The, **Supp. 4**, 768–69

Malabar Farm (Ohio), **Supp. 6**, 78

Malacology, **Vol. 6, Part 1**, 70

Malapropisms, **Supp. 9**, 6, 224, 764

Malaria, study of, **Vol. 3, Part 1**, 78; **Vol. 3, Part 2**, 160; **Vol. 5, Part 2**, 381; **Vol. 6, Part 2**, 262; **Supp. 3**, 736

Malbone, Edward G., reference to, **Vol. 9, Part 2**, 649

Malcolm X: assassination of, **Supp. 9**, 571; reference to, **Supp. 8**, 388; role in Black Muslim growth, **Supp. 9**, 570

Malcomson, Alexander Y., references to, **Supp. 4**, 293, 294

Male Animal, The, **Supp. 7**, 742

Male sex hormones, **Supp. 4**, 460

Malina, Frank, reference to, **Supp. 8**, 439–40

Malinowski, Bronislaw, reference to, **Supp. 8**, 509

Mall, Franklin P., reference to, **Supp. 3**, 106

Mallinckrodt Chemical Works, **Supp. 8**, 411–12

Mallory, C. D., & Co., **Supp. 3**, 502

Malnutrition. *See* Diet and nutrition

Malone, Dudley Field, references to, **Supp. 6**, 528; **Supp. 7**, 717; **Supp. 8**, 853

Malotte, Albert Hay, reference to, **Supp. 6**, 630

Malpractice, medical, **Supp. 3**, 103–4

Malted milk, **Supp. 2**, 316, 688

Maltese Falcon, The, **Supp. 5**, 258; **Supp. 7**, 314, 479

Malvern Hill, Va., battle of, **Vol. 5, Part 1**, 558; **Vol. 6, Part 1**, 123, 583; **Vol. 6, Part 2**, 205. *See also* Peninsular campaign

"Mama" (television program), **Supp. 10**, 851

Mamas and the Papas, The (music group), **Supp. 9**, 262

Mammalogy, **Supp. 5**, 678–79. *See also* Animals; Embryology; Paleontology; Zoology

Mammoth, discovery of bones of, **Vol. 3, Part 1**, 507 f.

Mammoth Cave, **Vol. 5, Part 1**, 328

Man and His Changing Society (textbook series), **Supp. 6**, 557–58

Management: bonus system, **Supp. 6**, 243; controls checking, **Supp. 5**, 643; economics, **Supp. 6**, 586; efficiency theory, **Supp. 3**, 49–50; employee benefits, **Supp. 2**, 66; **Supp. 5**, 164–65, 315; **Supp. 8**, 348; executive training programs, **Supp. 5**, 314; Golden Rule of, **Supp. 1**, 453–54; labor relations, **Supp. 6**, 548; new capitalism, **Supp. 7**, 809; personnel practices, **Supp. 2**, 45; **Supp. 4**, 747; **Supp. 6**, 520; profit-sharing, **Supp. 1**, 370–71; psychology application, **Supp. 5**, 59, 612; **Supp. 6**, 17, 222; science of, **Supp. 2**, 26–27; **Supp. 6**, 122, 222; **Supp. 8**, 685; shared worker responsibility, **Supp. 3**, 96; statistical controls, **Supp. 8**, 599; theories of, **Supp. 1**, 308, 371; welfare capitalism, **Supp. 3**, 762–63, 792; **Supp. 4**, 431–32; worker productivity studies, **Supp. 4**, 565–66; work-motion studies, **Supp. 4**, 296; writings on, **Supp. 3**, 5–6; **Supp. 7**, 30. *See also* Labor and labor movement; Wages and hours

Manassas, Va., battle at. *See* Bull Run

Manchester, William: Kennedy family dispute, **Supp. 10**, 462; reference to, **Supp. 8**, 224

Manchester, N.H., public service, **Vol. 2, Part 2**, 126, 603; **Vol. 3, Part 2**, 267

Manchuria, Japanese invasion of, **Supp. 4**, 786; **Supp. 7**, 112, 362

Mancini, Henry, reference to, **Supp. 10**, 527

Mandan Indians, **Supp. 5**, 430

Mandolute, **Supp. 8**, 349

Man for Himself, **Supp. 10**, 261

"Man from U.N.C.L.E., The" (television program), **Supp. 9**, 159

Mangano, Vincent, reference to, **Supp. 10**, 269

Mangin, Joseph F., reference to, **Vol. 6, Part 1**, 599

Manhattan Beach Railway, **Vol. 2, Part 2**, 437

Manhattan Elevated Railway, electrification of, **Vol. 8, Part 1**, 221 f.
Manhattan Eye, Ear and Throat Hospital, **Supp. 7**, 70
Manhattan Fire Insurance Co., **Vol. 6, Part 1**, 405
Manhattan Opera House, **Supp. 3**, 296
Manhattan Project: **Supp. 3**, 664; **Supp. 4**, 453–54; **Supp. 5**, 220–21, 273; **Supp. 6**, 501; **Supp. 7**, 135, 259, 691, 732; **Supp. 8**, 411; administration, **Supp. 9**, 185; directorship, **Supp. 8**, 229–30; gaseous diffusion process, **Supp. 9**, 248, 542; **Supp. 10**, 456
Manhattan School of Music, founding of, **Supp. 5**, 44–46
Manhattan Symphony Orchestra, founding of, **Supp. 2**, 267
MANIAC computer, **Supp. 6**, 656
Manic-depression, genetic aspects of, **Supp. 4**, 618
"Manifest destiny," first use of phrase, **Vol. 7, Part 2**, 89
Manila Bay, battle of, **Vol. 3, Part 1**, 269 f., 271; **Vol. 4, Part 1**, 610; **Vol. 5, Part 2**, 559; **Vol. 6, Part 2**, 573
Manistique (Mich.) Pulp and Paper Co., **Supp. 7**, 243
Manly, Charles Matthews, reference to, **Supp. 4**, 543
Manly, John M., references to, **Supp. 2**, 557; **Supp. 3**, 855; **Supp. 4**, 543
Mann, Erika, reference to, **Supp. 9**, 54
Mann, Horace, references to, **Vol. 2, Part 2**, 605; **Vol. 5, Part 1**, 296; **Vol. 6, Part 1**, 549; **Vol. 7, Part 2**, 127
Mann, Thomas, reference to, **Supp. 8**, 433
Mann-Elkins Act (1910), **Supp. 5**, 698
Manners, John Hartley, references to, **Supp. 4**, 821, 822
Mannes, Clara, reference to, **Supp. 7**, 511
Mannes, David, references to, **Supp. 4**, 545; **Supp. 7**, 511
Mannes Quartet, **Supp. 6**, 426
Mannes School of Music, **Supp. 7**, 511; founding of, **Supp. 4**, 545–46; **Supp. 6**, 427
Man Nobody Knows, The, **Supp. 8**, 27
Man o' War (horse), **Supp. 5**, 569
Mansfield, Irving, references to, **Supp. 9**, 784, 785
Mansfield, Mike, reference to, **Supp. 8**, 26
Manton, Martin T., reference to, **Supp. 4**, 613
Manual of Parliamentary Practice, **Vol. 5, Part 2**, 26
Manual of the New York Society for the Prevention of Cruelty to Children, compiled 1902, **Vol. 4, Part 1**, 228
Manual of Tides, **Vol. 4, Part 2**, 318
Manual training, **Vol. 4, Part 1**, 636; **Vol. 9, Part 1**, 47; **Vol. 10, Part 2**, 507
Manufacturers' Club (Philadelphia), **Vol. 2, Part 2**, 124; **Vol. 3, Part 1**, 356
Manufacturers' Mutual Fire Insurance Co., **Vol. 1, Part 1**, 216
Manufacturing: by-products, **Supp. 2**, 572; efficiency studies, **Supp. 2**, 26; electric power, early use, **Vol. 3, Part 1**, 355; mass production, **Supp. 2**, 174; **Supp. 4**, 303–4; moving assembly line, **Supp. 4**, 296, 456; natural gas, first used in, **Vol. 7, Part 2**, 635 f.; New England, early, **Vol. 3, Part 1**, 563 f.; South Carolina, early, **Vol. 10, Part 2**, 254; Virginia colony, **Vol. 8, Part 2**, 345; writings on, **Vol. 4, Part 1**, 600. *See also specific industries*
Manumission societies, **Vol. 3, Part 2**, 124; death-blow to, **Vol. 10, Part 1**, 70; Tennessee, **Vol. 7, Part 2**, 67
Manuscripts, collecting of, **Vol. 3, Part 2**, 519. *See also* Rare books and manuscripts
Man Who Came to Dinner, The, **Supp. 3**, 482; **Supp. 7**, 325, 413, 803
Manzarek, Ray, reference to, **Supp. 9**, 563
Mao Tse-tung, references to, **Supp. 6**, 230; **Supp. 8**, 635; **Supp. 10**, 528
Mapp v. *Ohio*, **Supp. 9**, 837; **Supp. 10**, 126
Maps (general): **Vol. 3, Part 2**, 206 f., 278 f.; **Vol. 5, Part 1**, 107, 201; **Vol. 5, Part 2**, 612; **Vol. 6, Part 1**, 272; **Vol. 6, Part 2**, 513; **Vol. 7, Part 1**, 161; **Vol. 7, Part 2**, 68; **Vol. 8, Part 1**, 140 f.; **Vol. 8, Part 2**, 126; **Vol. 9, Part 1**, 409; **Vol. 9, Part 2**, 455; commercial, **Supp. 1**, 350; engraving, **Vol. 5, Part 2**, 152; **Vol. 9, Part 2**, 295; *Farmer's Almanack*, in, **Vol. 9, Part 2**, 445; geologic and topographic, **Vol. 8, Part 1**, 146 f; **Supp. 3**, 407–8, 696; **Supp. 4**, 194, 219, 557–58, 896; military, **Vol. 5, Part 2**, 456; printing, **Vol. 7, Part 1**, 251; Spanish collection of, **Vol. 6, Part 1**, 471. *See also* Cartography; Topography
Maps (by region): agricultural regions, **Supp. 4**, 45; Antarctica, **Supp. 7**, 217; Arctic regions, **Vol. 3, Part 1**, 228; Boston Harbor, first engraved map of, **Vol. 8, Part 1**, 140 f.; British dominions, **Vol. 7, Part 1**, 50–51; Florida, **Vol. 3, Part 1**, 182; Georgia, **Vol. 3, Part 1**, 182; **Vol. 8, Part 2**, 126; Louisiana, **Vol. 3, Part 1**, 73; Maine, **Vol. 9, Part 1**, 582 f.; Maryland, **Vol. 9, Part 2**, 592; Mexico, **Vol. 5, Part 1**, 348; Montana, **Vol. 3, Part 1**, 207; New England, **Vol. 1, Part 2**, 378; New Hampshire, **Vol. 5, Part 2**, 588; New Jersey, **Vol. 6, Part 1**, 135; New York, **Vol. 3, Part 1**, 274; Northwest, **Vol. 3, Part 2**, 425; **Vol. 8, Part 1**, 61; Oregon, **Vol. 5, Part 1**, 194 f.; Pennsylvania, **Vol. 5, Part 1**, 160; South Carolina, **Vol. 3, Part 1**, 182; Tennessee, **Vol. 9, Part 1**, 254; United States, **Vol. 3, Part 1**, 73; **Vol. 9, Part 2**, 296 f.; Virginia, **Vol. 4, Part 1**, 48; **Vol. 8, Part 1**, 235 f.; **Vol. 10, Part 2**, 465; Wisconsin, **Vol. 3, Part 1**, 390; **Vol. 5, Part 2**, 612
Maranzano, Salvatore, references to, **Supp. 7**, 632; **Supp. 8**, 208, 396–97
Marble carvings, **Vol. 6, Part 1**, 31; quarries, **Vol. 8, Part 1**, 245 f.
Marble Collegiate Reformed Church (New York City), pastorate, **Supp. 8**, 505
Marblehead, Mass., founding of, **Vol. 3, Part 1**, 262
Marble House (Newport, R.I.), **Supp. 1**, 68
Marbury, Elizabeth, reference to, **Supp. 5**, 505
Marc, Franz, reference to, **Supp. 6**, 199
Marcantonio, Vito, reference to, **Supp. 10**, 184
Marcel, Henri, reference to, **Supp. 5**, 512
March, Francis Andrew, reference to, **Supp. 3**, 148
March, Frederic, references to, **Supp. 5**, 525; **Supp. 10**, 11, 12
March, Juan, reference to, **Supp. 7**, 333
March, Peyton C., references to, **Supp. 5**, 531
Marchand, Clothilde, references to, **Supp. 7**, 393; **Supp. 9**, 656
March of Dimes, **Supp. 10**, 59–60
March of Dimes Foundation, directorship, **Supp. 9**, 39–40
March of Time, The, **Supp. 8**, 393–94
March on Washington for Jobs and Freedom (1963), **Supp. 9**, 425, 901; **Supp. 10**, 341, 661
Marciano, Rocky, heavyweight championship bouts, **Supp. 9**, 172
Marconi, Guglielmo, references to, **Supp. 9**, 699, 701
Marconi Co., **Supp. 7**, 175, 177
Marconi Wireless Telegraph Company of America, **Supp. 9**, 699–700
Marcuse, Herbert, reference to, **Supp. 5**, 514
Marcy, R. B., reference to, **Vol. 6, Part 1**, 581
Marcy, William L., references to, **Vol. 7, Part 2**, 577 f.; **Vol. 9, Part 1**, 406; **Vol. 9, Part 2**, 536 f.
Margarine, **Supp. 3**, 247; **Supp. 5**, 400
Marginal-man theory, **Supp. 3**, 579
Margiotti, Charles J., reference to, **Supp. 9**, 254
Mariana Islands, World War II action, **Supp. 7**, 352; **Supp. 8**, 619
Mariano, Nicky, reference to, **Supp. 6**, 57

Marietta, Ohio, founding of, **Vol. 3, Part 1**, 13; **Vol. 8, Part 1**, 284 f.
Marietta College, **Vol. 1, Part 1**, 293; **Vol. 3, Part 1**, 608 f.; **Vol. 5, Part 1**, 65
Marigolds, odorless, **Supp. 10**, 80–81
Marijuana, **Supp. 9**, 470
Marin, Roberto, references to, **Supp. 9**, 178, 179
Marine: architecture, *see* Naval vessels; Ships and shipbuilding; engineering, **Vol. 1, Part 1**, 193 f.; **Vol. 2, Part 2**, 500 f.; **Vol. 5, Part 1**, 318; **Vol. 6, Part 1**, 545; **Vol. 8, Part 1**, 314 f.; **Vol. 9, Part 2**, 344; expeditions, **Vol. 1, Part 2**, 436; exploration, **Vol. 2, Part 1**, 70; **Vol. 8, Part 1**, 141 f.; insurance, **Vol. 3, Part 1**, 485 f.; **Vol. 9, Part 2**, 105; inventions, **Vol. 4, Part 2**, 584; invertebrates, **Vol. 8, Part 1**, 387
Marine Biological Association of San Diego, founding of, **Supp. 3**, 635
Marine Biological Laboratory (Woods Hole, Mass.): **Vol. 10, Part 2**, 140; **Supp. 3**, 126, 403; **Supp. 4**, 516, 909–10; **Supp. 5**, 128, 536; administration, **Supp. 4**, 497–98. *See also* Woods Hole Oceanographic Institution
Marine Corps, United States: **Vol. 2, Part 2**, 252; **Vol. 7, Part 1**, 438; **Vol. 10, Part 2**, 645; **Supp. 4**, 306; Band, **Vol. 9, Part 1**, 407; Belleau Wood battle, **Supp. 4**, 359–60; Carlson's Raiders, **Supp. 4**, 147; China campaigns, **Supp. 9**, 630, 822; hospital service, **Vol. 3, Part 2**, 550; Korean War operations, **Supp. 9**, 630; landing craft, **Supp. 5**, 299; legislation protecting, **Supp. 8**, 269; modernization, **Supp. 3**, 452–53; operations, **Supp. 8**, 603–5; most decorated person in history of, **Supp. 9**, 286–87, 630; World War II Pacific operations, **Supp. 4**, 323–24; **Supp. 9**, 822–23
Marine geology. *See* Oceanography
Marine life: algae, **Supp. 3**, 703–4; embryology of, **Supp. 3**, 403; fertilization studies, **Supp. 4**, 497–98; fish osteology, **Supp. 1**, 672–73; lake studies, **Supp. 4**, 84; mollusks, **Supp. 1**, 661; plankton research, **Supp. 4**, 461, 462; studies of, **Supp. 5**, 656–57, 709; writings on, **Supp. 7**, 109. *See also* Fish
Marine painting, **Supp. 2**, 700
Marine Society in New York, **Vol. 8, Part 1**, 348 f.
Marion College, **Vol. 7, Part 1**, 415
Marionettes. *See* Puppetry
Marion Star, **Vol. 8, Part 1**, 509
Marital Relations Institute, founding of, **Supp. 8**, 10–11
Maritime Federation of the Pacific, **Supp. 6**, 396
Maritime history, **Supp. 4**, 172
Maritime law, **Vol. 1, Part 2**, 360; **Vol. 3, Part 1**, 60; **Vol. 3, Part 2**, 454; **Vol. 10, Part 1**, 446
Mark, Edward L., references to, **Supp. 3**, 214; **Supp. 6**, 223
Mark Cross Co., **Supp. 7**, 560, 561
Marketing. *See* Advertising and marketing
Market research: advertising use of, **Supp. 7**, 642; **Supp. 10**, 709; psychological studies for, **Supp. 5**, 433–34; radio audience survey, **Supp. 5**, 310–11; **Supp. 10**, 587–88; sociological studies for, **Supp. 10**, 439; television audience survey, **Supp. 10**, 588
Markovnikov, Vladimir, reference to, **Supp. 4**, 336
Marks, Lionel S., reference to, **Supp. 5**, 154
Marland, Ernest, reference to, **Supp. 6**, 469–70
Marland Oil Co., founding of, **Supp. 3**, 505
Marlboro School of Music (Marlboro, Vt.), founding of, **Supp. 9**, 141
Marlborough Galleries (New York City), **Supp. 8**, 554–55
Marlowe, Christopher, reference to, **Supp. 4**, 110
Marlowe, **Supp. 9**, 486
Marquesas Islands, **Supp. 5**, 435
Marquette University, **Vol. 1, Part 2**, 367
Marquis, Samuel S., references to, **Supp. 4**, 300, 301
Marriage: counseling, **Supp. 6**, 602; legal issues, **Supp. 89**, 10–11; Roman Catholic position on mixed, **Supp. 8**, 537; sociology of, **Supp. 3**, 799–800. *See also* Divorce
Marriott, Robert H., reference to, **Supp. 6**, 298
Mars (planet), **Supp. 6**, 8; **Supp. 7**, 193
Marsh, Herbie, reference to, **Supp. 10**, 298
Marsh, Othniel Charles, reference to, **Supp. 5**, 743
Marsh, Reginald, references to, **Supp. 5**, 493, 636
Marshall, Alfred, reference to, **Supp. 6**, 271
Marshall, Armina, reference to, **Supp. 7**, 458
Marshall, Burke, reference to, **Supp. 8**, 322
Marshall, Charles C., references to, **Supp. 3**, 719; **Supp. 6**, 572
Marshall, George C.: China mission, **Supp. 7**, 728; **Supp. 9**, 146; loyalty issue, **Supp. 10**, 421; references to, **Supp. 3**, 194; **Supp. 5**, 530, 531. 538–39; **Supp. 6**, 110, 339, 451; **Supp. 7**, 24; **Supp. 9**, 7, 8, 106, 783, 814; War Department reorganization, **Supp. 5**, 643; World War II command, **Supp. 3**, 494, 583, 662; **Supp. 8**, 154, 267; **Supp. 10**, 177
Marshall, George Preston, reference to, **Supp. 7**, 452
Marshall, Humphrey, reference to, **Vol. 2, Part 2**, 174
Marshall, J. Markham, reference to, **Supp. 6**, 677
Marshall, John, references to, **Vol. 3, Part 1**, 311; **Vol. 5, Part 1**, 487; **Vol. 9, Part 2**, 106, 472, 575
Marshall, Leon C., reference to, **Supp. 3**, 186
Marshall, Louis, references to, **Supp. 3**, 280; **Supp. 4**, 904
Marshall, Marty, reference to, **Supp. 9**, 506
Marshall, Thomas, reference to, **Vol. 6, Part 2**, 316
Marshall, Thurgood: reference to, **Supp. 9**, 837; **Supp. 10**, 378; Supreme Court appointment, **Supp. 9**, 436
Marshall, Verne, reference to, **Supp. 3**, 387
Marshall College, founding of, **Vol. 6, Part 2**, 451; **Vol. 8, Part 1**, 389
Marshall Field & Co., **Vol. 3, Part 2**, 295, 366 f.; **Vol. 5, Part 1**, 18; **Vol. 9, Part 1**, 54 f.; **Supp. 9**, 391
Marshall Islands, World War II action, **Supp. 8**, 619
Marshall Plan: **Supp. 5**, 307, 397, 704; **Supp. 6**, 361, 431; **Supp. 7**, 32, 419, 762, 766; **Supp. 8**, 68, 257; administration, **Supp. 9**, 398; criticism of, **Supp. 7**, 49; fund reduction, **Supp. 7**, 734; **Supp. 8**, 421; inception of, **Supp. 8**, 90
Mars Hill, observatory, **Vol. 6, Part 1**, 469
Martel, Charles, reference to, **Supp. 3**, 326
Martha's Vineyard, Mass.: early history, **Vol. 6, Part 2**, **455; Indian conversions on, Vol. 4, Part 2**, 611; Summer Institute, pioneer summer school, **Vol. 7, Part 1**, 300
Martial arts, movies, **Supp. 9**, 486–87
Martin, Clyde E., reference to, **Supp. 6**, 343
Martin, Glenn L., reference to, **Supp. 6**, 49
Martin, Henry George, reference to, **Supp. 10**, 670
Martin, Henry Newell, reference to, **Supp. 3**, 369
Martin, Homer, references to, **Supp. 8**, 526, 652
Martin, John S., reference to, **Supp. 8**, 393
Martin, Joseph W., reference to, **Supp. 7**, 637
Martin, Mary, reference to, **Supp. 9**, 748
Martin, Sallie, reference to, **Supp. 7**, 69
Martin, William McChesney, Jr., reference to, **Supp. 9**, 662; **Supp. 10**, 139
Martin Co., founding of, **Supp. 5**, 475–76
Martinez, Julian, references to, **Supp. 10**, 511, 512
Marvin, Walter T., reference to, **Supp. 5**, 503
Marx, Chico, references to, **Supp. 10**, 512, 513, 514, 515, 516, 517–18
Marx, Groucho, references to, **Supp. 7**, 514–15; **Supp. 10**, 239, 512, 513, 517–18, 631, 823, 845

Marx, Gummo, references to, **Supp. 7**, 514–15; **Supp. 10**, 512, 513, 514
Marx, Harpo, references to, **Supp. 9**, 720; **Supp. 10**, 512, 513, 514, 515, 516, 517–18
Marx, Karl: representative of, in America, **Vol. 9, Part 1**, 399; writings on, **Supp. 5**, 82–83; **Supp. 7**, 746
Marx, Zeppo, references to, **Supp. 7**, 514–15; **Supp. 10**, 24, 514, 515, 516, 517–18
Marx Brothers (comedy team), **Supp. 7**, 207, 208, 413, 514–16; **Supp. 10**, 512–13, 514–16; 517–18; 631
Marxism: psychoanalysis, application to, **Supp. 10**, 260; studies critical of orthodox, **Supp. 10**, 330, 506, 507. *See also* Communism
Mary and John, colonial ship, **Vol. 6, Part 1**, 493
Marye's Heights, battle of. *See* Fredericksburg, battle of
Maryinsky Ballet Company (Leningrad), **Supp. 5**, 74–75
Maryknoll, founding of, **Supp. 2**, 692; **Supp. 3**, 569; **Supp. 5**, 581
Maryknoll movement, **Vol. 8, Part 1**, 217 f.; **Supp. 10**, 404–5
Maryland: banking, **Vol. 4, Part 1**, 8; **Vol. 7, Part 2**, 309 f.; boundary with Delaware, **Vol. 1, Part 2**, 460; cartography of, **Vol. 4, Part 2**, 592; Catholic, first in, **Vol. 3, Part 1**, 470 f.; Church of England established in, **Vol. 1, Part 2**, 610; colonial period, **Vol. 1, Part 2**, 610; **Vol. 2, Part 1**, 427, 429 f.; **Vol. 3, Part 1**, 498 f.; **Vol. 5, Part 1**, 62; **Vol. 5, Part 2**, 121, 363; **Vol. 9, Part 2**, 87 f., 543; **Vol. 10, Part 2**, 87; Constitution, U.S., ratification of, **Vol. 8, Part 1**, 138; Democratic party, **Vol. 5, Part 2**, 469; education, **Vol. 6, Part 2**, 31; **Vol. 8, Part 1**, 171 f.; emancipation of blacks, **Vol. 1, Part 2**, 554; federal government, relations with, **Vol. 1, Part 2**, 554; geological survey, **Vol. 2, Part 2**, 146; **Vol. 8, Part 1**, 247; **Supp. 3**, 62; governors, **Vol. 1, Part 2**, 510 f., 511 f., 553 f.; **Vol. 2, Part 1**, 528; **Vol. 4, Part 1**, 365; **Vol. 4, Part 2**, 191 f., 549; **Vol. 5, Part 1**, 8 f.; **Vol. 5, Part 2**, 121 f., 347 f.; **Vol. 6, Part 1**, 132, 471 f.; **Vol. 6, Part 2**, 543 f.; **Vol. 7, Part 2**, 123 f., 647 f.; **Vol. 8, Part 1**, 178 f.; **Vol. 9, Part 1**, 225 f.; **Vol. 9, Part 2**, 238, 429 f., 443; **Vol. 10, Part 1**, 240 f.; **Vol. 10, Part 2**, 381 f., 564 f.; **Supp. 2**, 559; **Supp. 9**, 528, 633, 634; historic preservation in, **Supp. 9**, 635; interracial issues, state commission on, **Supp. 9**, 528; Jesuits, **Vol. 4, Part 2**, 250; Know-Nothing party, **Vol. 6, Part 1**, 240; legal service, **Vol. 1, Part 2**, 322, 431, 460, 511, 539; **Vol. 2, Part 1**, 214, 602; **Vol. 3, Part 1**, 396, 498; **Vol. 4, Part 2**, 230; **Vol. 5, Part 1**, 275; **Vol. 5, Part 2**, 375; **Vol. 6, Part 2**, 344, 434, 636; **Vol. 7, Part 2**, 626, 647; **Vol. 8, Part 1**, 138, 268, 416; **Vol. 8, Part 2**, 47, 159; **Vol. 10, Part 1**, 97, 385 f.; legal system in, **Supp. 6**, 502; lottery in, **Vol. 8, Part 1**, 637; loyalty oath law, **Supp. 5**, 410; Lutheran Synod of, **Vol. 5, Part 2**, 502, 514; missionary work in, **Vol. 1, Part 1**, 231; **Vol. 2, Part 2**, 430 f.; political service, **Vol. 1, Part 2**, 510, 511, 543, 553; **Vol. 3, Part 1**, 119, 498; **Vol. 3, Part 2**, 320; **Vol. 4, Part 1**, 365; **Vol. 4, Part 2**, 191, 231; **Vol. 5, Part 1**, 8, 279; **Vol. 5, Part 2**, 121, 122. 348; **Vol. 6, Part 1**, 132, 240, 331, 471; **Vol. 6, Part 2**, 62, 115, 138, 544; **Vol. 7, Part 1**, 500, 647; **Vol. 7, Part 2**, 123, 353, 527, 647; **Vol. 8, Part 1**, 138, 178, 416; **Vol. 8, Part 2**, 47 f., 490; **Vol. 9, Part 1**, 26, 225; **Vol. 9, Part 2**, 238, 429, 443; **Vol. 10, Part 1**, 455 f.; **Vol. 10, Part 2**, 381, 564; politics, **Supp. 5**, 248; **Supp. 7**, 750–51; **Supp. 9**, 69, 527–28, 633, 634; **Supp. 10**, 557; politics, after Civil War, **Vol. 2, Part 1**, 528; politics, during Revolution, **Vol. 2, Part 1**, 523; Presbyterian church, **Vol. 6, Part 2**, 216; printing, **Vol. 1, Part 2**, 322; **Vol. 7, Part 1**, 596; **Vol. 7, Part 2**, 250; public health, **Vol. 10, Part 1**, 621 f.; public service, **Vol. 1, Part 2**, 539; **Vol. 2, Part 1**, 427; **Vol. 2, Part 2**, 34 f., 541 f.; **Vol. 4, Part 1**, 367; **Vol. 4, Part 2**, 232; **Vol. 6, Part 1**, 136, 330, 598; **Vol. 7, Part 1**, 422, 505; **Vol. 7, Part 2**, 337; **Vol. 9, Part 1**, 226, 337, 562; **Vol. 9, Part 2**, 88, 545, f.; **Vol. 10, Part 2**, 178; religious freedom in, **Vol. 9, Part 2**, 87; Republican party, **Supp. 9**, 528; **Supp. 10**, 557; Revolutionary War period, **Vol. 4, Part 2**, 549; secession, **Vol. 2, Part 1**, 602; **Vol. 3, Part 1**, 119 f.; senators, first election of, **Vol. 4, Part 2**, 549; Union party, **Vol. 1, Part 2**, 554; **Vol. 5, Part 2**, 469; War of 1812, **Vol. 10, Part 2**, 382; writings about, **Vol. 1, Part 1**, 227, 484; **Vol. 6, Part 2**, 138, 449
Maryland Agricultural College, **Vol. 2, Part 1**, 428; **Vol. 2, Part 2**, 201
Maryland Almanack for the Year of Our Lord God 1733, **Vol. 4, Part 1**, 609
Maryland, Delaware, and D.C. Christian Missionary Society, **Vol. 8, Part 1**, 155 f.
Maryland Eye and Ear Infirmary, **Vol. 8, Part 1**, 510
Maryland Fidelity and Guarantee Co., **Vol. 4, Part 1**, 8
Maryland Heights, Md. *See* Harpers Ferry, capture of
Maryland Historical Society: **Vol. 2, Part 1**, 170; **Vol. 6, Part 2**, 449; **Vol. 10, Part 1**, 385, f.; presidency, **Supp. 9**, 635
"Maryland, My Maryland," writing of, **Vol. 8, Part 1**, 348
Maryland National Guard, **Vol. 7, Part 2**, 527
Maryland Ophthalmological Society, **Vol. 4, Part 1**, 32
Maryland Peace Society, founding of, **Supp. 4**, 550
Maryland Prisoners' Aid Association, founded, **Vol. 4, Part 1**, 625
Maryland Society for the Promotion of Useful Knowledge, **Vol. 8, Part 1**, 222
Mary Sharp College for Women, **Vol. 4, Part 1**, 508
"Mary's Lamb" (poem), **Vol. 4, Part 2**, 111
Maschke, Heinrich, reference to, **Supp. 3**, 86
Maslow, Abraham H., references to, **Supp. 7**, 747, **Supp. 8**, 378
Masochism in Modern Man, **Supp. 8**, 523–24
Mason, George, reference to, **Vol. 9, Part 2**, 332
Mason, John, reference to, **Vol. 8, Part 2**, 375
Mason, John L., reference to, **Supp. 5**, 34
Mason, Lowell, reference to, **Vol. 10, Part 1**, 574
"Mason, Perry" (fictional character), **Supp. 8**, 202–3
Mason and Slidell. *See* Trent affair
Mason-Dixon Line, **Vol. 3, Part 2**, 89; **Vol. 4, Part 1**, 476; **Vol. 6, Part 1**, 136; **Vol. 9, Part 1**, 26
Masonic College, **Vol. 7, Part 1**, 224
Mason jar, **Supp. 3**, 29
Masons (fraternal order): **Vol. 3, Part 1**, 515 f.; **Vol. 3, Part 2**, 165, 299, 371, 395, 561; **Vol. 4, Part 1**, 361; **Vol. 4, Part 2**, 60, 321; **Vol. 5, Part 1**, 243 f., 396; **Vol. 5, Part 2**, 161, 163, 423; **Vol. 6, Part 1**, 223; **Vol. 6, Part 2**, 98; **Vol. 7, Part 1**, 224 f.; **Vol. 7, Part 2**, 595; **Vol. 8, Part 1**, 571; **Vol. 8, Part 2**, 204, 328; **Vol. 9, Part 2**, 335, 436, 448; **Vol. 10, Part 1**, 577 f.; *Ahiman Rezon*, **Vol. 3, Part 1**, 32; collections, relating to, **Vol. 9, Part 2**, 389; Grand Master, first in America, **Vol. 2, Part 2**, 485; investigations, **Vol. 9, Part 1**, 449 f.; lodge, first in U. S., **Vol. 9, Part 2**, 261; opposition to, **Vol. 3, Part 2**, 224; **Vol. 4, Part 1**, 482; **Vol. 4, Part 2**, 155; **Vol. 5, Part 2**, 158; **Vol. 7, Part 2**, 194, 450; **Vol. 9, Part 1**, 475, 621; **Vol. 9, Part 2**, 89, 454; **Vol. 10, Part 1**, 422 f., 598 f.; painting for, **Vol. 4, Part 2**, 591; Pennsylvania, history of, in, **Vol. 8, Part 2**, 282; revelations of, alleged, **Vol. 7, Part 1**, 189; ritual writings on, **Vol. 10, Part 1**, 577 f.; vigilante method, **Vol. 5, Part 2**, 592; women in, **Vol. 2, Part 2**, 554; writings on, **Vol. 4, Part 1**, 584; **Vol. 6, Part 2**, 98; **Vol. 7, Part 1**, 189
Masques, **Supp. 6**, 417–18
Massachusetts: agriculture, **Vol. 4, Part 1**, 383; **Vol. 10**,

Part 1, 541 f.; banishment from, **Vol. 5, Part 1**, 436; **Vol. 8, Part 2**, 221; banking, **Vol. 3, Part 1**, 106; **Vol. 10, Part 2**, 482; bishop, first in, **Vol. 1, Part 2**, 35; blacks, legal rights of, **Vol. 2, Part 2**, 585; Blue Hill Observatory, **Vol. 8, Part 2**, 183 f.; "Body of Liberties," **Vol. 10, Part 1**, 433 f.; boundary disputes, **Vol. 1, Part 2**, 460; **Vol. 5, Part 2**, 41, 150, 608; **Vol. 7, Part 1**, 290 f.; **Vol. 8, Part 1**, 422, 426; **Vol. 10, Part 1**, 121; capital punishment, **Vol. 8, Part 1**, 381; Catholic church, **Vol. 10, Part 2**, 277; charities, state, first in America, **Vol. 5, Part 1**, 297; **Vol. 8, Part 2**, 326; charter, colonial, **Vol. 1, Part 2**, 579; **Vol. 3, Part 1**, 86; **Vol. 8, Part 1**, 356 f.; **Vol. 10, Part 2**, 408; Civil Service Commission, **Supp. 5**, 730; Civil War, supplying of troops for, **Vol. 1, Part 1**, 280; **Vol. 10, Part 2**, 324; colonial period, **Vol. 1, Part 2**, 319, 420, 436; **Vol. 2, Part 2**, 634 f.; **Vol. 3, Part 1**, 180, 484 f., 501 f.; **Vol. 3, Part 2**, 155; **Vol. 4, Part 1**, 611; **Vol. 4, Part 2**, 396, 420; **Vol. 5, Part 1**, 200, 333, 362; **Vol. 6, Part 1**, 97, 198, 262; **Vol. 6, Part 2**, 386, 391 f., 394, 433; **Vol. 7, Part 2**, 599; **Vol. 8, Part 1**, 161 f., 290 f., 292 f., 356 f.; **Vol. 8, Part 2**, 221, 318 f.; **Vol. 9, Part 2**, 113, 390; **Vol. 10, Part 1**, 627 f.; **Vol. 10, Part 2**, 20, 194, 259, 284, 288, 336, 394 f., 409 f.; **Supp. 1**, 174; Constitution, federal, **Vol. 1, Part 2**, 501; Constitution, state, framing of, **Vol. 1, Part 2**, 499; **Vol. 7, Part 2**, 271; counterfeiting, colonial period, **Vol. 3, Part 1**, 273; Democratic party, **Vol. 4, Part 2**, 563; **Supp. 10**, 484; dominion movement in, **Vol. 1, Part 1**, 301; **Vol. 10, Part 2**, 31; Dorrellites in, **Vol. 3, Part 1**, 382 f.; education, **Vol. 3, Part 1**, 301, 369, 503 f., 563 f.; **Vol. 5, Part 1**, 29; **Vol. 6, Part 1**, 72; **Vol. 6, Part 2**, 241 f., 266; **Vol. 7, Part 2**, 404; **Vol. 8, Part 1**, Z76 f., 307 f., 381, 646; **Vol. 8, Part 2**, 151; **Vol. 9, Part 1**, 33; **Vol. 10, Part 1**, 551, 645 f.; elections, **Vol. 1, Part 2**, 556; **Supp. 10**, 484; England, colonial relations with, **Vol. 6, Part 2**, 391 f.; **Vol. 10, Part 2**, 412; Episcopal church, **Vol. 6, Part 1**, 87; "equivalent lands," to Connecticut, **Vol. 8, Part 1**, 426; Federalist party, **Vol. 9, Part 2**, 144 f., 380, 395; Free Soil party, **Vol. 2, Part 2**, 111; **Vol. 5, Part 1**, 86, 89; fur trade, **Vol. 10, Part 2**, 240; geology of, **Vol. 5, Part 1**, 69 f.; gerrymandering in, **Vol. 9, Part 2**, 145; government, transition from provincial to commonwealth, **Vol. 1, Part 2**, 499; governors, **Vol. 1, Part 1**, 279 f., 577 f.; **Vol. 1, Part 2**, 221, 500, 579; **Vol. 2, Part 1**, 357 f.; **Vol. 2, Part 2**, 110 f., 510 f; **Vol. 3, Part 1**, 404 f., 484 f.; **Vol. 3, Part 2**, 155 f.; **Vol. 4, Part 1**, 142, 579 f.; **Vol. 4, Part 2**, 41 f.; **Vol. 6, Part 1**, 377 f., 562 f.; **Vol. 7, Part 1**, 259 f.; **Vol. 8, Part 1**, 534 f.; **Vol. 8, Part 2**, 250 f.; **Vol. 9, Part 2**, 145, 215 f.; **Vol. 10, Part 1**, 499 f.; **Vol. 10, Part 2**, 408; **Supp. 1**, 194; **Supp. 4**, 858–59; **Supp. 5**, 692; **Supp. 6**, 140; **Supp. 8**, 258; **Supp. 10**, 715–16; health, first state board of, **Vol. 1, Part 2**, 493; Hopedale Community, **Vol. 3, Part 1**, 435; Hutchinson, Anne, expulsion of, **Vol. 5, Part 1**, 436; immigrants, exclusion of, **Vol. 10, Part 2**, 410; Indians, relations with, **Vol. 2, Part 1**, 480; **Vol. 3, Part 1**, 176; **Vol. 6, Part 2**, 590; **Vol. 10, Part 2**, 287; Industrial Safety Division, **Supp. 3**, 577; industry, **Vol. 3, Part 1**, 435, 563 f.; **Vol. 7, Part 2**, 58; **Vol. 8, Part 1**, 344; **Vol. 10, Part 1**, 497 f., 501 f., 503; **Vol. 10, Part 2**, 310, 412; insane, care of, **Vol. 3, Part 1**, 323 f.; **Vol. 8, Part 1**, 275 f., 404; "Ipswich Group," **Vol. 8, Part 2**, 318; journalism in, **Vol. 3, Part 1**, 437 f.; **Vol. 8, Part 1**, 73 f.; **Vol. 8, Part 2**, 461; judiciary, **Supp. 1**, 421–22; **Supp. 4**, 269; lawyer, first professional in, **Vol. 6, Part 1**, 87; legal history of, **Vol. 1, Part 1**, 186; **Vol. 7, Part 2**, 272; **Vol. 8, Part 1**, 426, 577; **Vol. 10, Part 1**, 433 f.; legal service, **Vol. 1, Part 2**, 166, 174, 297, 549; **Vol. 2, Part 2**, 609, 634; **Vol. 3, Part 1**, 63, 132, 134, 251, 261, 276, 280, 483; **Vol. 5, Part 1**, 86, 89, 295, 535; **Vol. 6, Part 1**, 263, 464–65, 467; **Vol. 6, Part 2**, 557, 582; **Vol. 7, Part 1**, 260, 476; **Vol. 7, Part 2**, 22, 150, 156, 225, 546, 565, 576; **Vol. 8, Part 1**, 194, 381, 577; **Vol. 8, Part 2**, 380; **Vol. 9, Part 1**, 42, 65, 541; **Vol. 9, Part 2**, 51, 103, 110, 144 f., 386; **Vol. 10, Part 1**, 74, 415 f., 433 f., 494 f., 499 f.; **Vol. 10, Part 2**, 70, 235; libraries, free public, **Vol. 3, Part 2**, 206; **Vol. 10, Part 1**, 558 f.; Louisburg expedition, **Vol. 1, Part 2**, 420; Loyalists, **Vol. 6, Part 1**, 175 f.; **Vol. 8, Part 2**, 221; Maine and New Hampshire withdrawal of, from, **Vol. 8, Part 1**, 356 f.; Masons in, **Vol. 4, Part 2**, 321; militia, **Vol. 4, Part 1**, 611; **Vol. 6, Part 1**, 73; navy, **Vol. 10, Part 1**, 101; normal schools, **Vol. 3, Part 1**, 563 f.; **Vol. 6, Part 2**, 242; orchards, first in, **Vol. 1, Part 2**, 319; periodicals, **Vol. 10, Part 2**, 239; political history, **Vol. 2, Part 1**, 357, 396; **Vol. 4, Part 2**, 563; **Vol. 6, Part 1**, 108 f.; **Vol. 10, Part 2**, 416; political irregularities, **Supp. 8**, 219; political service, **Vol. 1, Part 1**, 254, 280, 578; **Vol. 1, Part 2**, 144, 160, 166, 205, 246, 297, 420, 498, 502, 549, 551, 556; **Vol. 2, Part 2**, 111, 310, 510, 577, 579, 623, 633; **Vol. 3, Part 1**, 4, 14, 52, 63, 66, 132, 134, 149, 176, 261, 276, 280, 405, 435, 481, 547, 563, 573, 613; **Vol. 4, Part 1**, 87, 142, 182, 579; **Vol. 4, Part 2**, 41, 219, 459; **Vol. 5, Part 1**, 439; **Vol. 6, Part 1**, 196, 264, 305, 347, 348, 377, 562; **Vol. 7, Part 1**, 259; **Vol. 7, Part 2**, 14, 98, 159, 254, 477, 531, 543, 548, 551, 567, 582; **Vol. 8, Part 1**, 161, 195, 308, 344, 281, 430, 534, 579, 621; **Vol. 8, Part 2**, 59, 251; **Vol. 9, Part 1**, 120, 143, 165; **Vol. 9, Part 2**, 104, 113, 144 f.; **Vol. 10, Part 1**, 40, 48, 53, 122, 130, 415 f., 478 f., 482 f., 497 f., 585 f., 601 f.; **Vol. 10, Part 2**, 323, 416; politics, **Supp. 3**, 740; **Supp. 4**, 277–78; **Supp. 6**, 551–52, 636; **Supp. 7**, 419; **Supp. 8**, 257, 420–21; **Supp. 9**, 210, 851; **Supp. 10**, 484, 486, 604, 605, 715; politics and Catholic church, **Supp. 3**, 569–70; Protestant Episcopal bishoprics, **Supp. 3**, 447–48; public service, **Vol. 1, Part 2**, 33, 551, 607; **Vol. 2, Part 2**, 380 f., 461 f., 473, 531, 624 f.; **Vol. 3, Part 1**, 58 f., 524; **Vol. 4, Part 2**, 3, 41 f., 97, 109, 307; **Vol. 5, Part 1**, 86, 185, 203, 336; **Vol. 6, Part 1**, 48, 228, 259, 263 f., 297, 417–18, 508; **Vol. 7, Part 1**, 7, 59; **Vol. 7, Part 2**, 477; **Vol. 8, Part 1**, 276, 290 f., 292 f., 307 f.; **Vol. 8, Part 2**, 239, 245, 277, 461, 556; **Vol. 10, Part 1**, 627 f.; Public Service Commission, **Supp. 3**, 240–41; punishment system of, **Vol. 1, Part 2**, 174; railroads, **Vol. 5, Part 1**, 561; reform movements in, **Vol. 7, Part 2**, 546 f.; **Vol. 8, Part 1**, 381 f.; **Vol. 8, Part 2**, 58; regicides in, **Vol. 8, Part 2**, 319; religious controveries, **Vol. 3, Part 1**, 584; **Vol. 6, Part 1**, 87; **Vol. 7, Part 2**, 541, 598; **Vol. 10, Part 2**, 62, 427, 481; representative government, beginnings of, **Vol. 7, Part 2**, 541; Republican party, **Vol. 1, Part 2**, 489; **Vol. 2, Part 1**, 289, 358 f., 542; Revolutionary War agitation, in, **Vol. 4, Part 2**, 420; **Vol. 6, Part 2**, 218; **Vol. 7, Part 2**, 565; **Vol. 9, Part 2**, 499; **Vol. 10, Part 2**, 540, 635; Sacco-Vanzetti trial, **Vol. 8, Part 2**, 279; state seal, designing of, **Vol. 8, Part 1**, 515; shipbuilding, **Vol. 10, Part 1**, 548 f.; silversmith, **Vol. 8, Part 2**, 338; slavery, agitation against, **Vol. 3, Part 1**, 268; **Vol. 5, Part 1**, 86 f., 89; **Vol. 6, Part 1**, 263; **Vol. 8, Part 1**, 499 f.; **Vol. 8, Part 2**, 326; Sons of Liberty, **Vol. 4, Part 2**, 420; state employee unionization, **Supp. 6**, 586; State House, mural paintings in, **Vol. 8, Part 1**, 479; trade unions, **Vol. 2, Part 2**, 473; taxes, colonial resistance to, **Vol. 10, Part 2**, 427; temperance movement, **Vol. 1, Part 1**, 255; **Vol. 8, Part 1**, 381; Unitarianism, **Vol. 8, Part 1**, 622, 645; Whig party, **Vol. 2, Part 2**, 87; War of 1812, refusal of, to furnish troops, **Vol. 9, Part 2**, 145; water supply, **Vol. 3, Part 1**, 460 f.; **Vol. 8, Part 1**, 553

Massachusetts, battleship, **Vol. 4, Part 1**, 485

Massachusetts Abolitionist, **Vol. 9, Part 2**, 595
Massachusetts Agricultural College, **Vol. 2, Part 2**, 147; **Vol. 3, Part 2**, 473; **Vol. 4, Part 1**, 383; **Vol. 9, Part 2**, 39, 396
Massachusetts Anti-Slavery Society, **Vol. 2, Part 2**, 308; **Vol. 3, Part 1**, 407
Massachusetts Bay Colony "Remonstrance and Humble Petition," **Supp. 1**, 174
Massachusetts Bay Co., **Vol. 8, Part 1**, 292 f.
Massachusetts Bureau of Statistics and Labor, **Vol. 7, Part 2**, 19; **Vol. 10, Part 2**, 546
Massachusetts Civic League, **Vol. 8, Part 1**, 275 f.; founding of, **Supp. 2**, 374
Massachusetts Co., **Vol. 3, Part 1**, 612
Massachusetts Department of Mental Health, **Supp. 3**, 102
Massachusetts Fish and Game Protective Association, **Vol. 8, Part 2**, 323
Massachusetts General Hospital: **Vol. 5, Part 1**, 546; **Vol. 6, Part 1**, 465; **Vol. 8, Part 1**, 282 f.; genitourinary surgery, **Supp. 3**, 121; research, **Supp. 3**, 243–44; social service department, **Supp. 4**, 101; **Supp. 6**, 97–98
Massachusetts Highway Commission, **Vol. 8, Part 1**, 74 f.
Massachusetts Historical Society, **Vol. 1, Part 2**, 147; **Vol. 3, Part 1**, 133, 419 f.; **Vol. 4, Part 1**, 10, 556; **Vol. 5, Part 2**, 54; **Vol. 7, Part 1**, 31; **Vol. 8, Part 1**, 196 f.; **Supp. 3**, 286; **Supp. 6**, 125
Massachusetts Homeopathic Medical Society, **Vol. 9, Part 2**, 278
Massachusetts Horticultural Society, **Vol. 3, Part 1**, 177; **Vol. 5, Part 2**, 341; **Vol. 7, Part 2**, 248
Massachusetts Humane Society, **Vol. 10, Part 1**, 479 f.
Massachusetts Institute of Technology (MIT): **Vol. 4, Part 2**, 523; **Vol. 6, Part 2**, 120; **Vol. 7, Part 1**, 493; **Vol. 7, Part 2**, 562; **Vol. 8, Part 1**, 74 f.; **Vol. 9, Part 2**, 128; aeronautical engineering studies, **Supp. 6**, 665; atom-smasher invention, **Supp. 8**, 665–66; Brandeis business law lectures, **Supp. 3**, 94; chemistry studies, **Supp. 8**, 103; electrical engineering studies, **Supp. 3**, 745–47; **Supp. 5**, 354–55; **Supp. 9**, 143–44; engineering studies, **Supp. 1**, 680; first woman admitted to, **Supp. 3**, 631; founding of, **Vol. 3, Part 2**, 473; **Vol. 8, Part 2**, 115, 225; **Vol. 9, Part 1**, 99; **Vol. 9, Part 2**, 567; **Vol. 10, Part 1**, 551; gifts to, **Supp. 8**, 600; group dynamics studies, **Supp. 4**, 485; Harvard engineering school merger, **Supp. 3**, 471; mathematics studies, **Supp. 7**, 784–85, mechanical engineering studies, **Supp. 3**, 220; mining engineering studies, **Supp. 3**, 631; physical chemistry studies, **Supp. 2**, 494; physics studies, **Supp. 10**, 741–42; presidency, **Supp. 5**, 126; radiation laboratory, **Supp. 4**, 358–59; **Supp. 7**, 275; sanitary biology, **Supp. 3**, 324; sewage experimental station, **Supp. 6**, 701
Massachusetts Law Quarterly, **Vol. 9, Part 1**, 65
Massachusetts Medical Society, **Vol. 1, Part 1**, 332; **Vol. 8, Part 1**, 194 f.; **Vol. 10, Part 1**, 50
Massachusetts Mental Hygiene Association, **Vol. 8, Part 1**, 275 f.
Massachusetts Naval Brigade, **Vol. 8, Part 1**, 276
Massachusetts Peace Society, **Vol. 8, Part 1**, 381
Massachusetts School of Art, **Vol. 7, Part 2**, 465
Massachusetts Society for the Prevention of Cruelty to Animals, **Vol. 1, Part 1**, 303
Massachusetts Society for the University Education of Women, **Vol. 9, Part 2**, 276
Massachusetts State Board of Education, **Vol. 8, Part 1**, 381
Massachusetts State College, presidency, **Supp. 4**, 44
Massachusetts State Society for Mental Hygiene, **Supp. 3**, 119
Massachusetts Teachers' Association, **Vol. 10, Part 1**, 645 f.
Massachusetts Tariff Reform League, **Vol. 7, Part 2**, 582
Massacres: **Vol. 1, Part 1**, 145; **Vol. 1, Part 2**, 217; **Vol. 49, Part 2**, 362; **Vol. 5, Part 1**, 437; **Vol. 5, Part 2**, 47, 100, 371; **Vol. 7, Part 1**, 401; Boston, **Vol. 1, Part 1**, 415; Deerfield, **Vol. 10, Part 2**, 270; Fetterman, **Vol. 8, Part 1**, 437; Fort Dearborn, **Vol. 5, Part 2**, 422; Fort Mimms, **Vol. 10, Part 1**, 135; Fort Pillow, **Vol. 3, Part 2**, 532; **Vol. 9, Part 1**, 237; **Vol. 9, Part 2**, 183; Haverhill, Mass., **Vol. 3, Part 1**, 554 f.; Meeker, **Vol. 7, Part 2**, 638; Mountain Meadows, **Vol. 6, Part 1**, 115; St. Francis, 175–77, **Vol. 8, Part 2**, 108; Whitman, **Vol. 1, Part 1**, 30; **Vol. 10, Part 2**, 142; Wyoming, Pa., **Vol. 2, Part 1**, 372; Yellow Creek, **Vol. 2, Part 2**, 538
Massee, May, reference to, **Supp. 7**, 307
Masseria, Joe (The Boss), references to, **Supp. 7**, 632, 784; **Supp. 8**, 208
Masses, The: **Supp. 3**, 852; **Supp. 5**, 635; **Supp. 7**, 268; editorial policy, **Supp. 8**, 149; editors' trial, **Supp. 8**, 124–25
Masses Publishing Co. v. *Patten,* **Supp. 7**, 317
Mass production, moving, **Supp. 4**, 303–4
Mass transit. *See* Transit systems
Massine, Leonide, references to, **Supp. 10**, 206, 207
Master Building (New York City), architecture of, **Supp. 5**, 133
Mastoid operation, first in Chicago, **Vol. 5, Part 1**, 248
Matabele rebellions (southern Africa), **Supp. 4**, 126–27
Matamoras, Mex., occupation of (1846), **Vol. 9, Part 2**, 250
Matches: manufacture of, **Vol. 1, Part 1**, 590; **Vol. 7, Part 1**, 143; **Vol. 9, Part 1**, 600; safety, **Supp. 4**, 257–58
Maternal health. *See* Motherhood; Obstetrics
Mathematical bibliography: **Vol. 9, Part 2**, 109; instruments, manufacture of, **Vol. 5, Part 1**, 130 f.; physics, **Vol. 7, Part 2**, 397; prodigies, **Vol. 2, Part 2**, 283; **Vol. 7, Part 1**, 514; **Vol. 8, Part 2**, 287; tables, **Vol. 8, Part 2**, 225
Mathematics (for complete list of mathematicians, *see* Occupations Index): application to economics, **Supp. 6**, 459, 656; application to sociology, **Supp. 6**, 482–83; Bateman functions and expansions, **Supp. 4**, 58; calculus of variations, **Supp. 3**, 86–87; **Supp. 5**, 67–68; colonial period, **Vol. 4, Part 1**, 591, 609; **Vol. 6, Part 1**, 136; demographic, **Supp. 4**, 505–6; elasticity, **Supp. 4**, 873–74; ergodic theorem, **Supp. 3**, 70–71; finite fields, **Supp. 5**, 175; functional analysis theory, **Supp. 3**, 761; functions theory, **Supp. 3**, 574–75; general analysis, **Supp. 1**, 562; geometry, **Supp. 2**, 473; **Supp. 6**, 653; geometry, new differential, **Supp. 7**, 216; geometry of numbers, **Supp. 3**, 79; Gödel's theorem, **Supp. 10**, 281–82; groups theory, **Supp. 3**, 79; **Supp. 5**, 491; harmonic analysis, **Supp. 7**, 784; harmonic curves, **Vol. 8, Part 1**, 602; historical writings on, **Supp. 1**, 149; **Supp. 5**, 491; journals, **Supp. 1**, 562, 675; logical foundations of, **Supp. 5**, 338; logic of, **Vol. 3, Part 2**, 386; musical composition, application to, **Supp. 3**, 690; number theory, **Supp. 5**, 175; **Supp. 6**, 49; **Supp. 8**, 514–15; partition function, **Supp. 8**, 514; physics application, **Supp. 5**, 528–29; **Supp. 9**, 201; probability and error in, **Vol. 3, Part 1**, 197; probability theory, **Supp. 10**, 825; relativity theory framework, **Supp. 5**, 738; Riemann mapping theorem, **Supp. 3**, 575; spectral theory of unbounded self-adjoint operators in

Hilbert space, **Supp. 6**, 655; teaching of, **Supp. 1**, 146; **Supp. 3**, 721–22, 760, 791; **Supp. 5**, 130–31, 338; textbooks, **Supp. 1**, 145–46; Weyl sum, **Supp. 5**, 738; writings on, **Supp. 2**, 27; **Supp. 3**, 722; **Supp. 4**, 421, 879–80. *See also* Statistics
Mather, Cotton, references to, **Vol. 2, Part 1**, 410; **Vol. 6, Part 1**, 198; **Vol. 9, Part 2**, 389; **Vol. 10, Part 1**, 122; **Vol. 10, Part 2**, 238
Mather, Increase, references to, **Vol. 7, Part 2**, 551 f.; **Vol. 10, Part 2**, 238, 427
Mather, Richard, reference to, **Vol. 10, Part 1**, 627 f.
Matheus, John Frederick, reference to, **Supp. 6**, 690
Mathews, Shailer, reference to, **Supp. 3**, 322; **Supp. 4**, 152
Mathewson, Christy, references to, **Supp. 1**, 530; **Supp. 10**, 509
Mathiesen Chemical Corporation, **Supp. 10**, 826
Matisse, Henri, references to, **Supp. 4**, 174, 175, 771, 780; **Supp. 6**, 552, 553; **Supp. 7**, 25
Matsu. *See* Quemoy and Matsu
Matthew, William Diller, reference to, **Supp. 3**, 316–17
Matthews, Francis P., references to, **Supp. 8**, 329; **Supp. 9**, 227, 228
Mattresses, manufacture of, **Vol. 6, Part 1**, 334
Mature, Victor, reference to, **Supp. 9**, 734
Mature Mind, The, **Supp. 8**, 489
Mauerer, Alfred, reference to, **Supp. 5**, 471
Maulbetsch, Johnny, reference to, **Supp. 7**, 595
Mauna Loa, **Supp. 5**, 361
Maurer, James H., reference to, **Supp. 3**, 255
Maurin, Peter, reference to, **Supp. 10**, 175
Maury, Antonia C., reference to, **Supp. 3**, 130
"Maverick," term coined, **Supp. 5**, 480
Maxim, Hiram, reference to, **Vol. 7, Part 1**, 298
Maxim gun, invention of, **Vol. 6, Part 2**, 437
Maximilian, effort to expel from Mexico, **Vol. 2, Part 1**, 461; **Vol. 8, Part 2**, 85
Maximum Security Ward, **Supp. 9**, 349
Max Planck Institute, naming of, **Supp. 8**, 122
Maxwell, James Clark, reference to, **Supp. 4**, 58
Maxwell, William Donald, reference to, **Supp. 10**, 49
Maxwell Land Grant, **Vol. 3, Part 1**, 606
Maxwell Street Settlement (Chicago), **Supp. 3**, 488
May, Rollo, reference to, **Supp. 7**, 747
Mayan civilization: archaeological studies, **Supp. 1**, 685; **Supp. 4**, 606–7; **Supp. 7**, 432; hieroglyphic writings, **Vol. 1, Part 2**, 492; writmgs on, **Vol. 9, Part 2**, 426
Maybank, Burnett, reference to, **Supp. 8**, 682
May Department Stores Co., **Supp. 8**, 427–28
Mayer, Joseph Edward, references to, **Supp. 9**, 541, 542
Mayer, Louis B., references to, **Supp. 6**, 657, 658; **Supp. 8**, 576–77, 646, 649, 659, 660; **Supp. 9**, 291, 322
Mayer, Louis B., Productions, **Supp. 9**, 323. *See also* Metro-Goldwyn-Mayer (MGM)
Mayfield, Earle B., reference to, **Supp. 7**, 137
Mayflower, **Vol. 2, Part 1**, 30; **Vol. 7, Part 1**, 525; **Vol. 10, Part 2**, 20; account of, **Vol. 7, Part 1**, 254; organizer of, **Vol. 3, Part 1**, 5
Maynard, Leonard A., reference to, **Supp. 4**, 37
Maynard, Robert C., reference to, **Supp. 9**, 316
Mayo, Frank, reference to, **Supp. 6**, 334
Mayo, George Elton, references to, **Supp. 3**, 351; **Supp. 8**, 684
Mayo, Henry T., reference to, **Supp. 6**, 338
Mayo, William James, reference to, **Vol. 7, Part 1**, 354; **Supp. 3**, 121
Mayo Clinic: **Supp. 3**, 121; **Supp. 6**, 130, 131, 697; founding of, **Supp. 2**, 438–40; laboratory research, **Supp. 3**, 832; **Supp. 9**, 454
Mayo Foundation for Medical Education and Research, founding of, **Supp. 2**, 440
Mayo Graduate School of Medicine, predecessor, **Supp. 3**, 832
Mayors. For complete list, *see* Occupations Index
Mayors, U.S. Conference of. *See* Conference of Mayors
Maytag Co., founding of, **Supp. 2**, 441
MDA. *See* Muscular Dystrophy Association
Mead, Elwood, reference to, **Supp. 3**, 846
Mead, George Herbert, references to, **Supp. 3**, 779; **Supp. 6**, 671; **Supp. 8**, 639
Mead, James M., reference to, **Supp. 6**, 437
Mead, Margaret, references to, **Supp. 4**, 71, 72; **Supp. 8**, 189; **Supp. 10**, 27–28
Mead, McKim and White, **Supp. 5**, 388
Meade, George G., references to, **Vol. 6, Part 1**, 126; **Vol. 9, Part 1**, 150 f.; **Vol. 9, Part 2**, 253, 255
Meadville Theological School, **Vol. 6, Part 1**, 303; **Vol. 9, Part 1**, 547, 551; founding of, **Vol. 5, Part 1**, 358 f.
Meaning and Truth of Religion, The, **Supp. 4**, 513
Meaning of Adult Education, The, **Supp. 5**, 431
Means, Gardiner C., reference to, **Supp. 9**, 84
Means, J. Howard, reference to, **Supp. 3**, 244
Means, Rice W., reference to, **Supp. 6**, 507
Meany, George, references to, **Supp. 8**, 528, 653; **Supp. 10**, 304, 697
Measurements: electrical, **Vol. 8, Part 2**, 154; physical devices for, **Vol. 8, Part 2**, 199
Meat chopper, invention of, **Vol. 9, Part 1**, 535
Meat-packing industry: **Vol. 1, Part 1**, 111, 347 f.; **Vol. 2, Part 2**, 584 f.; **Vol. 3, Part 1**, 356, 603; **Vol. 5, Part 1**, 326, 437; **Vol. 7, Part 1**, 217 f.; **Vol. 9, Part 2**, 16, 245 f.; **Vol. 10, Part 2**, 343; canning and processing, **Supp. 4**, 395–96; **Supp. 5**, 314–15; Chicago investigation, **Supp. 5**, 70; financial reorganization, **Supp. 5**, 550–51; inspection of, **Vol. 8, Part 2**, 236; **Supp. 1**, 258; management, **Supp. 2**, 644–45; **Supp. 8**, 109–11; manufacturing, **Supp. 7**, 519–20; muckraking on, **Supp. 3**, 675; novel about, **Supp. 8**, 594; price-fixing charges, **Supp. 8**, 110, 111; refrigerator cars, **Vol. 9, Part 2**, 245; scandals, **Vol. 1, Part 1**, 348; unionization, **Supp. 2**, 408; **Supp. 4**, 279–80; **Supp. 7**, 254, 255; **Supp. 8**, 589
Meat products, hot dog, **Supp. 7**, 719
Mechanical engineering. *See* Engineering, mechanical
Mechanical Engineers' Pocket-Book, **Vol. 5, Part 2**, 349
Mechanical inventions, encyclopedia of, **Vol. 5, Part 2**, 464 f.
Mechanical laboratory, first in country, **Vol. 9, Part 2**, 518
Mechanical power, development of, **Supp. 1**, 670
Mechanics' Institute Library, **Vol. 8, Part 1**, 65 f.
Mechanics' Line, shipping, **Vol. 5, Part 2**, 372
Mechanicsville, Va., battle of, **Vol. 6, Part 1**, 123, 583 *See also* Seven-Days' Battles
Mechanism of Mendelian Heredity, The, **Supp. 3**, 540
Mecklenberg Resolution (1775), **Vol. 2, Part 1**, 571; **Vol. 6, Part 2**, 343; **Vol. 8, Part 1**, 42
Medallions, **Vol. 1, Part 1**, 503; **Vol. 2, Part 1**, 427; **Vol. 4, Part 1**, 336
Medford, Mass., early history of, **Vol. 2, Part 1**, 75; **Vol. 8, Part 2**, 331
"Medford Crackers," **Vol. 3, Part 2**, 577
Mediaeval Academy of America, founding of, **Supp. 2**, 291; **Supp. 3**, 618
Mediaeval Mind, The, **Supp. 3**, 765–66
Mediaeval Sinhalese Art, **Supp. 4**, 177
Medical and Chirurgical Faculty of Maryland, **Vol. 1, Part 1**, 340
Medical and Surgical History of the War of the Rebellion, **Vol. 1, Part 1**, 631

Medical Bibliography, **Vol. 6, Part 2**, 561
Medical College of Maryland, **Vol. 8, Part 1**, 131 f.; **Vol. 9, Part 1**, 42
Medical College of South Carolina, **Vol. 3, Part 1**, 305
Medical Institute of Philadelphia, **Vol. 2, Part 2**, 20
Medical Library and Journal Society, **Vol. 7, Part 2**, 505
Medical Repository, first medical journal, **Vol. 9, Part 1**, 260
Medical Society of the State of California, **Vol. 2, Part 2**, 397
Medical Society of the State of New York, **Vol. 1, Part 1**, 598; **Vol. 7, Part 2**, 208
Medicare: **Supp. 10**, 419; first bill, **Supp. 7**, 562
Medicine (for list of physicians, *see* Occupations Index): administration, **Supp. 4**, 803; adrenaline, **Vol. 9, Part 2**, 275; alcohol, **Vol. 1, Part 1**, 144; **Vol. 5, Part 2**, 280; algoid vegetations, disease theory of, **Vol. 8, Part 2**, 309; anatomy, **Vol. 1, Part 1**, 191, 519; **Vol. 2, Part 2**, 95; **Vol. 3, Part 1**, 91, 385 f., 573; **Vol. 4, Part 1**, 221, 351; **Vol. 4, Part 2**, 19, 30; **Vol. 6, Part 1**, 151; **Vol. 6, Part 2**, 221; **Vol. 7, Part 2**, 311; **Vol. 8, Part 1**, 575; **Vol. 8, Part 2**, 44; anesthetics, **Vol. 1, Part 2**, 34; **Vol. 2, Part 2**, 76; **Vol. 5, Part 1**, 537; **Vol. 7, Part 1**, 290, 373, 589; **Vol. 9, Part 1**, 350; **Vol. 10, Part 1**, 640 f.; aneurism, **Vol. 8, Part 1**, 360 f.; antiseptics, early use of, **Vol. 1, Part 2**, 224; **Vol. 2, Part 1**, 393; apparatus for cripples, **Vol. 10, Part 1**, 158; arsenic, effect of, **Vol. 8, Part 2**, 350; asthma, **Vol. 8, Part 2**, 411; aviation, **Supp. 2**, 722; baths, therapeutic, **Vol. 1, Part 2**, 433; **Vol. 9, Part 2**, 488; beriberi, **Vol. 10, Part 2**, 552; blacks in, **Supp. 5**, 104; blood pressure, **Vol. 5, Part 1**, 608; bone fractures, **Vol. 7, Part 1**, 120; botanic, **Vol. 1, Part 2**, 25; **Vol. 9, Part 2**, 488; **Vol. 10, Part 2**, 208; brain, study of, **Vol. 5, Part 2**, 325; cancer, **Vol. 1, Part 1**, 227; **Vol. 2, Part 1**, 251; **Vol. 4, Part 2**, 20 f.; **Vol. 7, Part 1**, 475 f.; **Vol. 8, Part 1**, 449; **Vol. 8, Part 2**, 385; **Vol. 10, Part 1**, 608; care costs, **Supp. 6**, 702–3; cardiac catheterization technique, **Supp. 9**, 654; chemistry as applied to, **Vol. 10, Part 2**, 455; children's diseases, **Vol. 5, Part 1**, 183 f., 313 f., 563; **Vol. 9, Part 1**, 294; cholera, **Vol. 1, Part 1**, 383, 413; **Vol. 2, Part 1**, 68, 231; **Vol. 3, Part 1**, 204, 220, 615 f.; **Vol. 5, Part 1**, 234, 546, 553; **Vol. 5, Part 2**, 517; **Vol. 6, Part 1**, 59, 282; **Vol. 7, Part 1**, 628; **Vol. 7, Part 2**, 110; **Vol. 9, Part 1**, 606; **Vol. 9, Part 2**, 311; chloroform, first use of, **Vol. 4, Part 2**, 59; Civil War, **Vol. 1, Part 1**, 124, 389, 631; **Vol. 4, Part 1**, 319; **Vol. 6, Part 1**, 42; **Vol. 10, Part 2**, 509; clairvoyance, use of, **Vol. 3, Part 1**, 105; climate, relation of, to, **Vol. 3, Part 1**, 394; clinical, **Vol. 1, Part 2**, 434; **Vol. 3, Part 1**, 24 f.; **Vol. 7, Part 2**, 454; **Vol. 10, Part 1**, 493 f.; clinical observation-pathological findings correlation, **Supp. 5**, 438; cocaine, use of, **Vol. 4, Part 2**, 165; **Vol. 5, Part 1**, 625; college, earliest for women, **Vol. 8, Part 1**, 201; collodion, **Vol. 3, Part 1**, 329; convulsions, **Supp. 1**, 241; croup, **Vol. 1, Part 2**, 74; curative to preventive, shift in emphasis from, **Vol. 1, Part 2**, 268; cures, erratic, **Vol. 2, Part 1**, 217; *Cushing's Manual*, **Vol. 2, Part 2**, 632; deafness, physical causes of, **Vol. 8, Part 1**, 565; degree, first to be granted in colonies, **Vol. 2, Part 2**, 512; delirium tremens, **Vol. 10, Part 1**, 449 f.; dermatology, **Vol. 2, Part 1**, 251; diagnostic laboratories, **Supp. 2**, 513; diet and nutrition, **Vol. 10, Part 2**, 630; digestion, **Vol. 1, Part 2**, 106; digitalis, early experiments with, **Vol. 3, Part 1**, 6; diphtheria, **Vol. 1, Part 2**, 263; **Vol. 7, Part 1**, 628; **Vol. 8, Part 1**, 252 f., 460, 565; dislocations, treatment of, **Vol. 8, Part 1**, 486 f.; dispensary, first free in U.S., **Vol. 8, Part 2**, 228; dissection, first use of in teaching, **Vol. 1, Part 1**, 597; "Doctors' mob," **Vol. 8, Part 1**, 121; Duhreng's dlsease, **Vol. 3, Part 1**, 494 f.; eclectic, school of, **Vol. 5, Part 2**, 393; **Vol. 7, Part 1**, 237, 475 f.; **Vol. 8, Part 2**, 524; **Supp. 2**, 389; education, **Supp. 1**, 81, 276, 437; **Supp. 2**, 706; **Supp. 3**, 122, 243–44, 486; **Supp. 4**, 642–43, 650, 892; **Supp. 6**, 252–53, 296, 546–47, 553; educational advances, **Vol. 4, Part 2**, 554; **Vol. 6, Part 2**, 268; **Vol. 7, Part 2**, 454; **Vol. 8, Part 1**, 44 f.; **Vol. 8, Part 2**, 127; **Vol. 10, Part 1**, 621 f.; education funding, **Supp. 2**, 283; education in China, **Supp. 4**, 346–47; education standards, **Supp. 2**, 208, 542, 575; education survey, **Supp. 3**, 67; **Supp. 6**, 208; electrotherapy, **Vol. 1, Part 2**, 93; **Vol. 3, Part 1**, 354; **Vol. 6, Part 2**, 381; **Vol. 8, Part 2**, 68 f.; **Vol. 9, Part 1**, 53; embryology, **Vol. 6, Part 2**, 221; **Vol. 7, Part 1**, 30; epidemics, study of, **Vol. 3, Part 2**, 128, 572; **Vol. 5, Part 2**, 325; **Vol. 8, Part 1**, 131 f.; **Vol. 8, Part 2**, 552 f.; **Vol. 9, Part 1**, 590 f.; epilepsy, **Vol. 3, Part 1**, 78 f.; **Vol. 6, Part 1**, 19 f.; **Vol. 7, Part 2**, 6; ether, early use of, **Vol. 2, Part 2**, 4; **Vol. 4, Part 2**, 464 f.; **Vol. 5, Part 1**, 239, 537; **Vol. 6, Part 1**, 374; **Vol. 7, Part 1**, 269 f.; **Vol. 10, Part 1**, 480 f.; eugenics, **Vol. 1, Part 2**, 151; **Vol. 3, Part 2**, 566; **Vol. 4, Part 2**, 412; **Vol. 9, Part 2**, 69; experimental methods, introduction of, **Vol. 3, Part 1**, 40; **Vol. 9, Part 2**, 478; eye diseases, **Vol. 3, Part 1**, 253, 327; **Vol. 5, Part 1**, 293; **Vol. 8, Part 1**, 510, 565; faith healing, **Supp. 4**, 271–72; febrile diseases, **Vol. 3, Part 1**, 306; federal aid advocates, **Supp. 3**, 122; fevers, treatment of, **Vol. 3, Part 1**, 306; **Vol. 7, Part 1**, 66; **Vol. 8, Part 2**, 353; first aid, **Vol. 3, Part 2**, 563; first clinical research, **Supp. 6**, 117; foreign medicines, introduction of, to U.S., **Vol. 3, Part 1**, 538 f.; foreign missions, **Supp. 4**, 181–82, 529–30; **Supp. 7**, 680–81; free treatment, **Vol. 4, Part 1**, 118; gastric digestion, **Vol. 1, Part 2**, 106; **Vol. 7, Part 2**, 374; gas, use as anesthetic, **Vol. 10, Part 1**, 640 f.; germ theory, **Vol. 4, Part 1**, 464; **Vol. 8, Part 2**, 309; goiter, treatment of, **Vol. 4, Part 2**, 7; gynecology, **Vol. 1, Part 1**, 414; **Vol. 1, Part 2**, 538; **Vol. 3, Part 2**, 16, 160, 547; **Vol. 4, Part 1**, 291; **Vol. 4, Part 2**, 545; **Vol. 5, Part 2**, 276, 376, 580; **Vol. 6, Part 1**, 510, 615; **Vol. 6, Part 2**, 551; **Vol. 7, Part 1**, 541; **Vol. 7, Part 2**, 96, 263; **Vol. 8, Part 1**, 32 f., 44, 213 f.; **Vol. 8, Part 2**, 44; **Vol. 9, Part 1**, 186, 234; **Vol. 9, Part 2**, 95, 446; **Vol. 10, Part 2**, 280; hare lip, **Vol. 5, Part 2**, 580; hay fever, **Vol. 8, Part 2**, 411; health-maintenance organizations, **Supp. 8**, 309; hemophilia, original description of, **Vol. 7, Part 2**, 109; historical studies and writings on, **Supp. 1**, 335; **Supp. 2**, 458; **Supp. 5**, 733; **Supp. 6**, 580–81; history of, **Vol. 1, Part 1**, 143; **Vol. 3, Part 1**, 427; **Vol. 4, Part 2**, 224; **Vol. 9, Part 2**, 586; holistic, **Supp. 6**, 181; homeopathy, **Vol. 4, Part 2**, 576; **Vol. 10, Part 2**, 4; hormone of milk secretion, discovery of, **Vol. 7, Part 2**, 106; hydrophobia, **Vol. 6, Part 2**, 486; **Vol. 9, Part 2**, 388; hydrotherapy, **Vol. 1, Part 2**, 29; **Vol. 5, Part 2**, 459; hygiene, **Vol. 1, Part 1**, 25 f.; **Vol. 5, Part 1**, 253; illustration, **Supp. 3**, 106–7, 412; immunology, **Vol. 7, Part 1**, 542; **Vol. 10, Part 1**, 608; **Supp. 1**, 628; indexing of literature, **Supp. 1**, 334; Indians, practice by, **Vol. 6, Part 1**, 272; **Vol. 9, Part 1**, 193, 371; influenza, **Vol. 5, Part 2**, 415; **Vol. 9, Part 1**, 31; **Vol. 10, Part 1**, 109 f.; instruments, invention of, **Vol. 3, Part 2**, 16; **Vol. 4, Part 1**, 152; **Supp. 7**, 678–79; journals, **Vol. 8, Part 1**, 269 f.; **Vol. 9, Part 1**, 31, 132; jurisprudence, **Vol. 1, Part 2**, 154; **Vol. 3, Part 1**, 377; **Vol. 3, Part 2**, 122, 145, 467; kidney, early operation on, **Vol. 8, Part 1**, 378; laboratory, analytical, one of earliest, **Vol. 3, Part 1**, 376; laryngology, **Vol. 1, Part 1**, 191, 383; **Vol. 1, Part 2**, 467; **Vol. 2, Part 2**, 275; **Vol. 3, Part 2**, 119; **Vol. 4, Part 1**, 547; **Vol. 5, Part 1**, 625; **Vol.**

5, Part 2, 465, 515; Vol. 6, Part 1, 140, 160, 268; Vol. 6, Part 2, 94, 450; Vol. 8, Part 2, 306, 411 f., 562; Vol. 9, Part 1, 185, 195 f.; laughing gas, first use of, Vol. 8, Part 1, 604; leprosy, Vol. 3, Part 1, 582; Vol. 6, Part 1, 17; Vol. 8, Part 1, 154 f.; Vol. 8, Part 2, 8; libraries, founding of, Vol. 2, Part 1, 588; Vol. 8, Part 1, 269 f.; malaria, Vol. 3, Part 1, 78; Vol. 3, Part 2, 160; Vol. 5, Part 2, 381; Vol. 6, Part 2, 262; malpractice, Supp. 3, 103–4; mechanical aids, Supp. 2, 533; meningitis, Vol. 7, Part 1, 559; mental cure, Vol. 3, Part 2, 213; mental diseases, Vol. 1, Part 1, 446; Vol. 8, Part 1, 404; Vol. 10, Part 2, 511; mental healing, Vol. 4, Part 1, 691; Vol. 8, Part 1, 304 f.; "metallic tractors," Vol. 7, Part 2, 466; microscopy, Vol. 1, Part 1, 106; Vol. 2, Part 2, 132; Vol. 5, Part 2, 79; Vol. 6, Part 1, 151, 202; Vol. 7, Part 2, 370; Vol. 8, Part 1, 589; Vol. 8, Part 2, 562 f.; Vol. 10, Part 1, 435 f.; midwifery, Vol. 1, Part 1, 599; Vol. 3, Part 1, 267; Vol. 3, Part 2, 160; Vol. 6, Part 1, 333, 510; Vol. 6, Part 2, 503; Vol. 9, Part 1, 117; migraine, Vol. 8, Part 1, 317 f.; military, Supp. 4, 448; milk, "modifying" of, Vol. 6, Part 2, 502; mosquitoes, Vol. 3, Part 1, 578 f.; Vol. 3, Part 2, 388; Vol. 5, Part 2, 381; Vol. 9, Part 1, 298; moss, use of for surgical dressings, Vol. 9, Part 1, 276; Naval Bureau, Vol. 1, Part 2, 25; nephrolithotomy, first in America, Vol. 9, Part 2, 535; "new system" of Rush, Vol. 8, Part 2, 228, 229; nitrous oxide as anesthetic, Vol. 2, Part 2, 322; Nobel Prize, Supp. 4, 581; Supp. 5, 489; Supp. 7, 226, 281, 341, 476; Supp. 8, 556; nursing, Vol. 1, Part 2, 18; Vol. 3, Part 1, 219; Vol. 4, Part 1, 285; Vol. 5, Part 2, 570; nutrition, Vol. 1, Part 1, 349; obstetrics, Vol. 1, Part 1, 411, 599, 601; Vol. 3, Part 1, 267, 394; Vol. 3, Part 2, 160, 409, 581; Vol. 4, Part 1, 291; Vol. 5, Part 1, 99, 229 f., 588; Vol. 5, Part 2, 381; Vol. 6, Part 1, 333, 510; Vol. 6, Part 2, 504, 626; Vol. 7, Part 1, 541; Vol. 7, Part 2, 129, 263, 286; Vol. 8, Part 1, 32 f., 578 f.; Vol. 9, Part 1, 117, 234; Vol. 9, Part 2, 94, 446; Vol. 10, Part 2, 280; "old-school" doctor, description of, Vol. 5, Part 2, 511; ophthalmology, Vol. 1, Part 1, 123 f.; Vol. 2, Part 1, 301; Vol. 3, Part 1, 464 f.; Vol. 4, Part 1, 31 f., 451; organizations, Vol. 3, Part 1, 139; Supp. 2, 440; oroya fever, Vol. 7, Part 1, 543; osteopathy, Vol. 9, Part 2, 21 f.; otology, Vol. 2, Part 1, 297; paresthesia, Vol. 8, Part 1, 282 f.; patent, Vol. 1, Part 1, 413, 450; Vol. 3, Part 1, 586 f.; Vol. 7, Part 2, 624 f.; Vol. 8, Part 2, 197; pathology, Vol. 2, Part 1, 260; Vol. 3, Part 1, 77 f., 208, 306; Vol. 3, Part 2, 320 f., 433; Vol. 4, Part 2, 44 f.; Vol. 5, Part 2, 306; Vol. 7, Part 2, 208, 354 f.; Vol. 8, Part 1, 252 f., 391, 404; Vol. 9, Part 2, 23; Vol. 10, Part 1, 493 f., 621 f.; patient recordkeeping, Supp. 5, 111; patient-doctor relationship, Supp. 6, 547; pediatrics, Vol. 2, Part 2, 277; Vol. 5, Part 1, 185, 313, 563; Vol. 6, Part 2, 506; Vol. 8, Part 2, 185 f.; Vol. 9, Part 1, 294, 533; pharmacopeia, first in U.S., Vol. 2, Part 1, 757; philanthropy, Supp. 3, 435; Supp. 4, 261; Supp. 6, 549; photography in, Vol. 4, Part 1, 63; Vol. 7, Part 1, 557; physiology, Vol. 1, Part 2, 494 f.; Vol. 2, Part 2, 616 f.; Vol. 3, Part 1, 512 f; Vol. 3, Part 2, 472; Vol. 5, Part 1, 205, 252 f.; Vol. 5, Part 2, 366 f., 459; Vol. 6, Part 1, 349 f.; Vol. 6, Part 2, 338, 520; Vol. 7, Part 1, 558; Vol. 8, Part 1, 317 f.; Vol. 9, Part 1, 298; Vol. 9, Part 2, 9 f., 478; pleurisy, Vol. 10, Part 2, 585; pneumonia, Vol. 7, Part 1, 628; Pott's disease, Vol. 9, Part 2, 318; preventive, Supp. 3, 158, 409–10; Supp. 4, 684, 700–701; Supp. 5, 632; preventive, pioneer in, Vol. 1, Part 2, 262; professional ethics, improvement of standards, Vol. 4, Part 1, 155; protoplasm, study of, Vol. 7, Part 1, 95; psychiatry, Vol. 2, Part 2, 213; Vol. 3, Part 1, 595 f.; Vol. 3, Part 2, 412; Vol. 4, Part 2, 411; Vol. 5, Part 1, 97; Vol. 5, Part 2, 207, 324 f., 354 f.; Vol. 7, Part 1, 489 f.; Vol. 8, Part 1, 404; Vol. 8, Part 2, 116, 313, 559; Vol. 9, Part 1, 462; Supp. 4, 572; psychosomatic illness, Supp. 3, 128, 136, 385; Supp. 6, 181, 220; psychotherapy, Vol. 9, Part 1, 152; Vol. 9, Part 2, 318; purging, theory of, Vol. 8, Part 2, 229; quackery, Vol. 4, Part 2, 554; Vol. 9, Part 2, 369; quinine, Vol. 8, Part 2, 353; rattlesnake root, therapeutic use of, Vol. 9, Part 2, 369; religion and, Supp. 2, 736; Supp. 3, 190–91; research, funding of, Supp. 2, 283, 574; research, medical, first chair of, Vol. 7, Part 2, 355; research reporting in lay press, Supp. 4, 668; resuscitation methods, Supp. 3, 202; Revolutionary War, Vol. 5, Part 1, 185; Vol. 5, Part 2, 181; rickets, study of, Vol. 5, Part 1, 314; roentgenology, Vol. 6, Part 1, 174; scarlet fever, Vol. 3, Part 1, 408; skin diseases, Vol. 3, Part 1, 494 f., 582; Vol. 5, Part 1, 451; Vol. 7, Part 1, 236; Vol. 8, Part 1, 449; Vol. 8, Part 2, 419; sleeping sickness, Vol. 6, Part 2, 401; smallpox, Vol. 1, Part 1, 395; Vol. 1, Part 2, 535; Vol. 3, Part 1, 408; Vol. 4, Part 1, 97, 331; Vol. 5, Part 1, 185, 541, 546; Vol. 5, Part 2, 163; Vol. 6, Part 1, 333; Vol. 8, Part 1, 391; Vol. 8, Part 2, 377; Vol. 10, Part 1, 150, 529 f.; snake poisoning, Vol. 7, Part 1, 542; social ethics, Supp. 2, 85; social services, Supp. 2, 84, 209; Supp. 6, 81–82, 97–98; societies, Vol. 1, Part 1, 414; Vol. 6, Part 1, 4; Supp. 1, 518; sociology of, Supp. 6, 664–65; spotted fever, Vol. 7, Part 1, 559; stethoscope, use of Vol. 5, Part 1, 240; summer school, first, Vol. 2, Part 2, 76; surveys, Vol. 3, Part 1, 478 f.; teaching of, Vol. 1, Part 1, 340; Vol. 1, Part 2, 268; Vol. 2, Part 1, 256; Vol. 2, Part 2, 415; Vol. 3, Part 1, 24, 426 f., 582; Vol. 4, Part 2, 101, 554; Vol. 5, Part 1, 205, 240, 253, 465, 519, 553, 601, 608, 621; Vol. 5, Part 2, 305, 415, 580; Vol. 6, Part 1, 58, 337; Vol. 6, Part 2, 603; Vol. 7, Part 1, 30, 55, 130; Vol. 7, Part 2, 453; Vol. 8, Part 1, 264, 285, 443; Vol. 9, Part 1, 31, 33; Vol. 9, Part 2, 33; Vol. 10, Part 1, 449 f., 480 f., 581 f., 621 f.; Vol. 10, Part 2, 3, 433, 438; throat diseases, Vol. 4, Part 1, 547; Vol. 5, Part 2, 393; Vol. 7, Part 2, 153; Vol. 8, Part 2, 69; tropics, study of white men in the, Vol. 3, Part 1, 77 f.; Vol. 10, Part 2, 496; tuberculosis, Vol. 1, Part 2, 493; Vol. 2, Part 1, 349 f.; Vol. 3, Part 2, 102, 201, 301 f., 472, 550; Vol. 4, Part 2, 165, 501; Vol. 5, Part 1, 215; Vol. 5, Part 2, 483; Vol. 7, Part 2, 550 f., Vol. 8, Part 1, 245 f.; Vol. 8, Part 2, 188, 281; Vol. 9, Part 2, 130; Vol. 10, Part 1, 2 f.; Vol. 10, Part 2, 282; typhoid fever, Vol. 1, Part 2, 4, 29; Vol. 5, Part 2, 483; Vol. 8, Part 1, 317 f., 460; Vol. 8, Part 2, 553; Vol. 9, Part 1, 31; typhus fever, Vol. 4, Part 1, 218; Vol. 5, Part 1, 429; Vol. 9, Part 1, 32; U.S. Department of, Vol. 5, Part 1, 109; Vol. 9, Part 1, 117; urology, Vol. 5, Part 1, 239; Vol. 7, Part 2, 602; vaccination, Vol. 2, Part 2, 487; Vol. 3, Part 2, 229, 547; Vol. 4, Part 1, 361; Vol. 4, Part 2, 308; Vol. 6, Part 1, 33; Vol. 6, Part 2, 337; Vol. 7, Part 1, 559; Vol. 9, Part 1, 325; Vol. 10, Part 1, 479, 529; venereal diseases, Vol. 2, Part 1, 260; Vol. 5, Part 2, 364; Vol. 7, Part 1, 542; Vol. 8, Part 1, 588 f.; Vol. 8, Part 2, 419; veterans' services, Supp. 7, 328–29; vivisection, Vol. 3, Part 1, 40; War of 1812, Vol. 6, Part 2, 243; water cure, Vol. 7, Part 1, 496; weather theory, Vol. 1, Part 1, 606; women in, Vol. 1, Part 2, 320; Vol. 3, Part 1, 141; Vol. 4, Part 1, 604; Vol. 4, Part 2, 376; Vol. 5, Part 1, 385 f., 564 f.; Vol. 6, Part 2, 307, 550; Vol. 8, Part 1, 201; Vol. 9, Part 1, 234; Vol. 10, Part 2, 642; World War I, Vol. 7, Part 1, 409; Vol. 8, Part 2, 313; writings on, Supp. 1, 137, 525; X-ray, Vol. 1, Part 2, 113, 407; Vol. 2, Part 1, 407; Vol. 6, Part 1, 173 f.; Vol. 7, Part 1, 268; yellow fever, *see* Yellow fever. *See*

also American Medical Association; Diseases; Hospitals; Nursing; Public health; *specific fields and areas of specialization,* e.g., Pediatrics and Surgery
Medico-Chirurgical College, Philadelphia, founding of, **Vol. 7, Part 2**, 16
Medico-Legal Journal, **Vol. 1, Part 2**, 154
Medico-Legal Society of New York, **Vol. 1, Part 2**, 154; **Vol. 8, Part 2**, 111
MEDICO (Medical International Corporation Organization), founding of, **Supp. 7**, 191
Medieval Academy of America, founding of, **Supp. 3**, 197
Medieval history. *See* Middle Ages
Medill, Joseph, references to, **Supp. 5**, 448, 449
Medina, Harold, references to, **Supp. 7**, 180, 390
Mediterranean anemia. *See* Cooley's anemia
Mediums, controversy concerning, **Vol. 3, Part 1**, 84; **Vol. 3, Part 2**, 570
Meek, Joseph L., reference to, **Vol. 7, Part 1**, 458
Meeker massacre, **Vol. 7, Part 2**, 638
Meeropol, Michael and Robert, reference to, **Supp. 5**, 589–90
Mees, Charles E., reference to, **Supp. 4**, 743, 744
Meet Me in St. Louis, **Supp. 9**, 78
Megiddo, excavation of, **Supp. 3**, 272
Meiklejohn, Alexander, reference to, **Supp. 6**, 271
Meilland, Francis, reference to, **Supp. 5**, 555
Meir, Golda, reference to, **Supp. 9**, 451
Meisner, Sanford, references to, **Supp. 10**, 129, 130
Melcher, Frederic G., reference to, **Supp. 9**, 738
Mellon, Andrew, references to, **Supp. 5**, 357, 561; **Supp. 7**, 361; **Supp. 10**, 73, 619
Mellon, Richard K., reference to, **Supp. 8**, 361
Mellon Institute of Industrial Research, founding of, **Supp. 2**, 447
Melodeons, making of, **Vol. 4, Part 2**, 196
Meltzer, Samuel J., references to, **Supp. 4**, 34, 287
Melville, Herman, reference to, **Vol. 1, Part 1**, 108; scholarship on, **Supp. 5**, 587
Member of the Wedding, The, **Supp. 9**, 232; **Supp. 10**, 818
Memoirs: **Vol. 2, Part 1**, 227; **Vol. 3, Part 2**, 126, 212, 475; **Vol. 4, Part 2**, 31, 481; **Vol. 5, Part 1**, 117, 292, 467, 596, 611; **Vol. 5, Part 2**, 309; **Vol. 6, Part 1**, 359, 374, 378, 594; **Vol. 7, Part 1**, 273, 300, 372, 563, 634; **Vol. 8, Part 1**, 16, 73, 141 f., 208, 264, 284 f., 369 f.; **Vol. 8, Part 2**, 26 f., 241, 372, 411, 580 f., 596 f., 598; **Vol. 9, Part 1**, 81, 88, 97, 102, 162, 248, 304, 313, 367; **Vol. 10, Part 1**, 75, 168, 449 f., 504 f., 558 f. *See also* Diaries; Journals
Memoirs of a Superfluous Man, **Supp. 3**, 555
Memoirs of Hecate County, **Supp. 9**, 876; **Supp. 10**, 47
Memorial Day, establishment of, **Vol. 6, Part 1**, 364
Memorial Hospital (New York City): **Supp. 10**, 769; cancer research and treatment, **Supp. 3**, 258
Memorial Movement, **Vol. 7, Part 1**, 314
Memorial Sloan-Kettering Cancer Center (New York City), **Supp. 10**, 769
Memphis, Tenn.: Crump machine, **Supp. 5**, 144–45; De Soto's discovery of Mississippi near, **Vol. 3, Part 1**, 257; founding of, **Vol. 7, Part 2**, 115; medical care, **Vol. 7, Part 2**, 626; music scene, **Supp. 10**, 648; sanitation, **Vol. 10, Part 1**, 456 f.
Memphis Institute, **Vol. 8, Part 1**, 152 f.
Menace, anti-Catholic magazine, **Vol. 3, Part 2**, 478
Men and Religion Forward Movement: administration, **Supp. 2**, 20; **Supp. 5**, 579; founding of, **Supp. 2**, 617–18
Men and Steel, **Supp. 8**, 675
Mencken, H. L.: Dreiser relationship, **Supp. 3**, 232, 235, 236; references to, **Vol. 9, Part 1**, 91; **Supp. 3**, 107, 413; **Supp. 5**, 4; **Supp. 6**, 471, 571, 616; **Supp. 7**, 3, 19–20, 331; **Supp. 8**, 341–42, 364; **Supp. 9**, 225, 886
Mendel, Lafayette B., reference to, **Supp. 3**, 163
Mendel's laws of heredity, **Supp. 3**, 215, 539–40; **Supp. 4**, 252, 516
Mendelssohn, Louis, reference to, **Supp. 7**, 245
Mendelssohn Club, **Vol. 4, Part 1**, 274; **Vol. 5, Part 2**, 486
Meneghini, Giovanni Battista, references to, **Supp. 10**, 93, 94
Mengelberg, Willem, reference to, **Supp. 7**, 549
Ménière's disease, **Supp. 4**, 214
Meningitis, **Vol. 7, Part 1**, 559; serum for, **Supp. 4**, 287
Menninger, Charles Frederick, reference to, **Supp. 8**, 428
Menninger, Karl, references to, **Supp. 5**, 484; **Supp. 8**, 429
Menninger, William C., reference to, **Supp. 5**, 484
Menninger Clinic, **Supp. 6**, 527; **Supp. 8**, 429–30; founding of, **Supp. 5**, 484
Menninger School of Psychiatry, **Supp. 8**, 429
Mennonite church: **Vol. 1, Part 2**, 405; **Vol. 4, Part 1**, 353; **Vol. 5, Part 2**, 491, 503; bishop of, first in America, **Vol. 8, Part 1**, 632; Charite, organized 1908, **Vol. 5, Part 2**, 504; Kansas settlement, **Vol. 5, Part 2**, 504
Menotti, Gian-Carlo, references to, **Supp. 7**, 61, 124; **Supp. 10**, 722, 723
Menorah, founding of, **Vol. 7, Part 2**, 407
Men's League for Women Suffrage, **Vol. 1, Part 1**, 413
Mental: computations, prodigy, **Vol. 8, Part 2**, 287; cure, books on, **Vol. 3, Part 2**, 213; defectives, care of, **Vol. 6, Part 1**, 468; diseases, treatment of, **Vol. 1, Part 1**, 446; **Vol. 8, Part 1**, 404; **Vol. 10, Part 2**, 511; dissociation, **Vol. 8, Part 1**, 230 f.; healing, **Vol. 4, Part 1**, 631; **Vol. 8, Part 1, 304 f.; hygiene, Vol. 4, Part 2**, 412; **Vol. 8, Part 1**, 275 f., 404; **Vol. 8, Part 2**, 313
Mental health and illness: child development movement, **Supp. 3**, 119; clinics, **Supp. 2**, 388, 711–12; **Supp. 5**, 301, 484; community facilities, **Supp. 3**, 50–51, 128; **Supp. 6**, 17; counseling services, **Supp. 7**, 466; disease relationship, **Supp. 2**, 24; emotional adjustment, **Supp. 3**, 128; first children's clinic, **Supp. 1**, 485; heredity studies, **Supp. 4**, 618; hospitals, **Supp. 1**, 243–44; **Supp. 3**, 50–51, 320; insulin shock treatment, **Supp. 6**, 563–64; interpersonal relations, **Supp. 4**, 806–8; law and, **Supp. 3**, 102; **Supp. 6**, 403; legislation regarding, **Supp. 2**, 712; neurotic character structure origin, **Supp. 5**, 316–17; occupational therapy, **Supp. 1**, 131; personal development writings, **Supp. 8**, 488; physiologic basis, **Supp. 3**, 172; **Supp. 6**, 403–4; popular writings on, **Supp. 8**, 189; psychobiological concept of, **Supp. 4**, 570–72; psychotherapy, **Supp. 2**, 736; **Supp. 4**, 571; **Supp. 8**, 430; religion and, **Supp. 7**, 64–65; research in, **Supp. 2**, 665; self-help movement, **Supp. 5**, 434; state treatment of, **Supp. 3**, 102. *See also* Psychiatry; Psychoanalysis; *specific disorders*
Mental hygiene movement. *See* Mental health and illness
Mentally retarded: care of, **Vol. 6, Part 1**, 468; education of, **Vol. 2, Part 1**, 117; **Vol. 10, Part 2**, 199; **Supp. 4**, 438–39; **Supp. 7**, 284; genetic relationship, **Supp. 4**, 618; institutions for, **Supp. 2**, 388; **Supp. 3**, 388–89; research on, **Supp. 6**, 240–41
Mentor, first magazine for blind, **Vol. 9, Part 1**, 294
Men Without Faces, **Supp. 9**, 135
Mercantile Agency, **Vol. 3, Part 1**, 503; **Vol. 9, Part 2**, 303
Mercantile Library, founding of, **Vol. 10, Part 2**, 471

Mercer, Lucy, references to, **Supp. 3**, 643; **Supp. 7**, 659, 661
Mercersburg Academy, **Vol. 5, Part 1**, 501
Mercersburg College, **Vol. 1, Part 1**, 324
Mercersburg Seminary, **Vol. 8, Part 2**, 417–18
"Mercersburg theology," **Vol. 1, Part 1**, 324; **Vol. 8, Part 1**, 389
Mercer University: founding of, **Vol. 8, Part 2**, 330; **Vol. 9, Part 1**, 99; presidency of, **Vol. 10, Part 1**, 31; removal of, **Vol. 10, Part 1**, 31 f.
Merchandising: **Vol. 1, Part 1**, 332, 336, 341, 396, 464, 602; **Vol. 2, Part 1**, 102; **Vol. 2, Part 2**, 295 f., 491; **Vol. 4, Part 1**, 320; **Vol. 4, Part 2**, 218, 220; **Vol. 6, Part 1**, 132; **Vol. 7, Part 1**, 359 f.; **Vol. 7, Part 2**, 525, 630; **Vol. 8, Part 2**, 536; **Vol. 9, Part 1**, 45; **Vol. 9, Part 2**, 394 f., 567; chain stores, **Vol. 1, Part 2**, 582; **Vol. 5, Part 1**, 122; **Vol. 7, Part 1**, 334; dry goods, **Vol. 2, Part 2**, 110, 285; **Vol. 5, Part 2**, 214; **Vol. 7, Part 2**, 191; **Vol. 9, Part 1**, 135; mail-order houses, **Vol. 8, Part 2**, 170, 540; **Vol. 10, Part 1**, 414; New York, **Vol. 1, Part 1**, 232; pack peddlers, **Vol. 9, Part 2**, 445; "Palmer system," **Vol. 7, Part 2**, 191; specifications, emphasis on, **Vol. 3, Part 1**, 479 f.; wholesale, **Vol. 2, Part 2**, 144 f.; Woolworth stores, **Vol. 10, Part 2**, 523
Merchant marine: **Vol. 3, Part 2**, 401; **Vol. 4, Part 2**, 6, 251; **Vol. 6, Part 1**, 545; **Vol. 8, Part 1**, 17 f.; **Vol. 8, Part 1**, 17 f.; **Vol. 8, Part 2**, 76; **Vol. 10, Part 1**, 424 f.; **Supp. 1**, 447; **Supp. 3**, 501–2; **Supp. 4**, 848–49; **Supp. 5**, 440, 441; development of, **Supp. 2**, 208; expansion advocates, **Supp. 3**, 182; government-ownership, **Supp. 2**, 195
Merchant Marine Act (1936), **Supp. 9**, 634
Merchant Marine Act (1970), **Supp. 10**, 304
Merchants and Manufacturers Association, founding of, **Supp. 3**, 156
Merchants' Daily Advertiser, **Vol. 1, Part 2**, 559
Merchants' Exchange Building (New York City), architecture of, **Vol. 8, Part 2**, 98
Merchant ships, **Vol. 1, Part 1**, 260; **Vol. 3, Part 2**, 314, 401; **Vol. 4, Part 2**, 476; **Vol. 6, Part 1**, 227; **Vol. 8, Part 2**, 27
Merchants Loan & Trust Co. (Chicago), **Vol. 7, Part 1**, 645
"Merchant venturers," **Vol. 4, Part 1**, 504
Mercier, Cardinal, reference to, **Vol. 9, Part 1**, 242
Merck and Co., founding of, **Supp. 6**, 447
Mercurochrome, **Supp. 3**, 854
Mercury automobile, **Supp. 3**, 284
Mercury project, **Supp. 8**, 225; **Supp. 10**, 495
Mercury Theater, **Supp. 5**, 464; **Supp. 9**, 382, 560
Mercury vapor turbine, **Supp. 3**, 251–52
Meredith, Edwin T., reference to, **Supp. 7**, 527
Meredith, James, references to, **Supp. 7**, 227, 425; **Supp. 8**, 322
Meredith, Wendell, Jr., reference to, **Supp. 9**, 753
Meredith Publishing Co., **Supp. 7**, 527, 528
Meridian, Miss., operation at, **Vol. 6, Part 1**, 130; **Vol. 9, Part 1**, 95
Meridian Line, establishment of, at Albany, suggested, **Vol. 3, Part 1**, 274
Meritt, B. D., reference to, **Supp. 4**, 144
Merovitch, Alexander, references to, **Supp. 10**, 632, 633
Merriam, C. Hart, reference to, **Supp. 6**, 453
Merriam, Charles E., references to, **Supp. 6**, 692–93; **Supp. 7**, 430
Merrick, David, reference to, **Supp. 10**, 114
Merrick, John, reference to, **Supp. 5**, 647–48
Merril Aircraft Co., founding of, **Supp. 5**, 229
Merrill, Albert, reference to, **Supp. 8**, 439
Merrill, Charles, references to, **Supp. 9**, 613, 614
Merrill, Howard, reference to, **Supp. 9**, 719
Merrill, John O., reference to, **Supp. 7**, 691
Merrill Lynch, Pierce, Fenner, and Beane, founding of, **Supp. 6**, 448–49; **Supp. 9**, 613, 614
Merrimac: **Vol. 3, Part 1**, 529 f.; **Vol. 5, Part 1**, 343; **Vol. 8, Part 2**, 568; **Vol. 9, Part 2**, 567; burning of, **Vol. 9, Part 2**, 311; reconstruction of, as ironclad, **Vol. 8, Part 1**, 97. *See also Monitor*
Merrimac Chemical Co., **Supp. 5**, 319–20
Merriman, Roger Bigelow, reference to, **Supp. 7**, 517
"Merriwell, Frank" (fictional character), **Supp. 3**, 586
Merrymount Press, founding of, **Supp. 3**, 784–85
Merry Widow, The, **Vol. 8, Part 2**, 387
Merthiolate, **Supp. 6**, 334
Merton, Robert K., social psychology theory, **Supp. 6**, 605
"Mertz, Ethel and Fred" (fictional characters), **Supp. 10**, 803–4
Mescaline, **Supp. 7**, 381
Mesmerism, **Vol. 3, Part 1**, 353; **Vol. 3, Part 2**, 8; **Vol. 4, Part 1**, 631
Mesomorph personality, **Supp. 10**, 731
Meson, discovery of, **Supp. 5**, 496
Message to Garcia, A, **Vol. 5, Part 1**, 323
Messenger: **Vol. 5, Part 2**, 335; **Supp. 4**, 541
Messner, Kathryn, reference to, **Supp. 7**, 531–32
Metabolic pool, **Supp. 3**, 693
Metabolism: brain, **Supp. 4**, 618; diseases of, **Supp. 2**, 35; **Supp. 6**, 698; enzyme, **Supp. 6**, 127, 595; glucose, **Supp. 6**, 595; infant, **Supp. 2**, 433; measurement of, **Supp. 2**, 391; microorganisms, **Supp. 6**, 482; phosphorylated compounds in, **Supp. 5**, 276; protein, **Supp. 1**, 307; research in, **Supp. 1**, 517
Metallographist, founding of, **Supp. 2**, 595
Metallography, **Supp. 1**, 58; **Supp. 2**, 594; **Supp. 3**, 220
Metallurgy: **Vol. 1, Part 1**, 343 f., 528; **Vol. 1, Part 2**, 103 f.; **Vol. 3, Part 1**, 396 f., 460 f.; **Vol. 3, Part 2**, 56, 64; **Vol. 4, Part 1**, 199, 358, 488 f.; **Vol. 5, Part 1**, 43, 289, 381 f., 392; **Vol. 5, Part 2**, 483; **Vol. 7, Part 1**, 79 f.; **Vol. 7, Part 2**, 113 f., 354, 356, 504; **Vol. 8, Part 1**, 326, 467, 555 f.; **Vol. 9, Part 1**, 459, 595; aluminum research, **Supp. 8**, 193–94; automobile construction, **Supp. 2**, 721; industrial research, **Supp. 4**, 556–57; inspecting and testing, **Supp. 1**, 58; **Supp. 3**, 220; Monel production, **Supp. 5**, 652; Montana survey, **Supp. 1**, 176; physical, **Supp. 1**, 131; **Supp. 2**, 91; research in, **Supp. 4**, 328–29, 437–38; rocking arc electric furnace development, **Supp. 4**, 327; silicon reduction process, **Supp. 3**, 48–49; sintering process, **Supp. 4**, 245–46; teaching of, **Vol. 5, Part 1**, 119; writings on, **Vol. 3, Part 1**, 225 f.; **Vol. 5, Part 1**, 119; **Vol. 5, Part 2**, 593. *See also specific metals and ores*
Metals, rotary multiple-tooth cutter, **Supp. 3**, 224
Metals and Alloys, founding of, **Supp. 4**, 328, 329
Metal tubing manufacture, **Vol. 3, Part 2**, 227
Metaphysics, **Supp. 4**, 178, 525–26, 881–83
Metart Gallery (San Francisco), **Supp. 10**, 759
Meteorites, collection and study of, **Vol. 6, Part 2**, 560; **Vol. 9, Part 1**, 71, 304; **Vol. 10, Part 1**, 421 f.
Meteorology: **Vol. 1, Part 2**, 257; **Vol. 2, Part 2**, 27, 256, 267; **Vol. 3, Part 1**, 427, 507 f.; **Vol. 3, Part 2**, 160, 185, 338; **Vol. 4, Part 1**, 245; **Vol. 4, Part 2**, 64, 301, 477; **Vol. 5, Part 1**, 252; **Vol. 6, Part 1**, 280, 287, 367, 452; **Vol. 7, Part 1**, 526; **Vol. 8, Part 1**, 441 f., 573 f.; **Vol. 8, Part 2**, 184; **Supp. 3**, 478–79, 511–12; atmospheric physics research, **Supp. 4**, 410; hurricanes, **Supp. 1**, 387; measuring instruments, **Supp. 1**, 120–21; observations, beginnings of systematic, **Vol. 3, Part 1**, 274; observatories, **Supp. 1**, 579; thunderstorms, **Supp. 1**, 579; writings on, **Vol. 2, Part 1**, 367; **Vol. 3, Part 1**, 274; **Vol. 8, Part 1**, 441; **Vol. 8,**

Part 2, 184; **Vol. 10, Part 1**, 132; **Supp. 1**, 355; *See also* Weather
Meteors, cosmic origin of, **Vol. 10, Part 1**, 84
Methodist Book Concern, **Vol. 3, Part 1**, 293, 608; **Vol. 7, Part 1**, 421
Methodist church (general; for complete list of clergymen, bishops, etc., *see* Occupations Index): administration, **Vol. 4, Part 2**, 407; **Vol. 6, Part 1**, 111; bishops, **Supp. 7**, 597; Board of Education, **Vol. 3, Part 2**, 416; Board of Temperance, Prohibition and Public Morals, **Vol. 5, Part 2**, 517; Calvinism and, **Vol. 1, Part 1**, 16; **Vol. 8, Part 2**, 201; Church Extension Society, **Vol. 5, Part 2**, 517; circuit riding, **Vol. 1, Part 1**, 574 f.; **Vol. 1, Part 2**, 31; **Vol. 5, Part 2**, 579; **Vol. 6, Part 2**, 86; constitution of, **Vol. 9, Part 1**, 404; critics within, **Supp. 4**, 875–76; educational work, **Vol. 6, Part 1**, 7; **Vol. 8, Part 2**, 254; establishment and growth of, **Vol. 3, Part 1**, 292 f.; **Vol. 6, Part 1**, 114, 560; **Vol. 6, Part 2**, 565; **Vol. 7, Part 2**, 7; **Vol. 9, Part 1**, 110, 114, 382; **Vol. 9, Part 2**, 133; **Vol. 10, Part 1**, 576 f.; **Vol. 10, Part 2**, 36, 286; Evangelical Association, **Vol. 1, Part 1**, 136 f.; Freedman's Aid Society, **Vol. 8, Part 2**, 254; General Conference, admission of women, **Supp. 1**, 372; General Conference of, 1844, **Vol. 5, Part 2**, 579; historical records, **Vol. 10, Part 1**, 561 f.; hymnal, **Vol. 4, Part 1**, 405; **Vol. 4, Part 2**, 453; labor movement support, **Supp. 8**, 680–81; law of, **Vol. 1, Part 1**, 525; leadership, **Supp. 1**, 577; **Supp. 2**, 499; liberal wing, **Supp. 4**, 837; meeting house, first, **Vol. 9, Part 2**, 133; Methodist Episcopal Church, South, **Vol. 3, Part 1**, 597 f.; **Vol. 4, Part 2**, 265, 352, 453, 536; **Vol. 7, Part 2**, 155; **Supp. 3**, 129, 132; missionary work, **Vol. 1, Part 1**, 243, 263, 286, 324; **Vol. 1, Part 2**, 34, 504; **Vol. 2, Part 1**, 225, 369; **Vol. 3, Part 1**, 544 f.; **Vol. 3, Part 2**, 540; **Vol. 4, Part 1**, 115; **Vol. 4, Part 2**, 294, 316, 361, 453 f.; **Vol. 5, Part 1**, 569; **Vol. 6, Part 1**, 112, 476 f.; **Vol. 7, Part 2**, 218; **Vol. 8, Part 1**, 478; **Vol. 10, Part 1**, 53 f.; **Supp. 1**, 433; **Supp. 2**, 188; **Supp. 6**, 315; **Supp. 8**, 425; philanthropic service, **Vol. 9, Part 1**, 208; Prohibition stance, **Supp. 6**, 636; "promiscuous sitting," **Vol. 5, Part 1**, 490; "quarterly meeting," **Vol. 8, Part 2**, 254; racial amalgamation, **Vol. 4, Part 2**, 408; reunification issue, **Supp. 1**, 208, 372; **Supp. 2**, 409; **Supp. 3**, 129, 132; **Supp. 4**, 408–9, schism in, **Vol. 1, Part 2**, 31; **Vol. 3, Part 2**, 152; **Vol. 8, Part 2**, 3; slavery, disruption over, **Vol. 2, Part 1**, 484; **Vol. 3, Part 1**, 544 f.; **Vol. 4, Part 1**, 328, 407; **Vol. 6, Part 1**, 114 f., 116; **Vol. 6, Part 2**, 423; **Vol. 10, Part 2**, 422; social activism, **Supp. 5**, 445–46; **Supp. 7**, 596–97; theological seminary, first in U.S., **Vol. 3, Part 1**, 233; theology, **Supp. 7**, 693–94; Women's Foreign Missionary Society, **Supp. 3**, 623–24; writings on, **Vol. 1, Part 1**, 575; **Vol. 2, Part 1**, 232; **Vol. 4, Part 1**, 166 f.; **Vol. 4, Part 2**, 353; **Vol. 5, Part 2**, 517; **Vol. 6, Part 1**, 7, 560; **Vol. 9, Part 1**, 605
Methodist church (by location): Alabama, **Vol. 6, Part 2**, 169; Canada, **Vol. 1, Part 1**, 574 f.; China, **Vol. 1, Part 2**, 34; **Vol. 6, Part 1**, 476 f.; **Vol. 7, Part 2**, 214; India, **Vol. 1, Part 1**, 286; **Vol. 2, Part 1**, 369; Korea, **Vol. 1, Part 1**, 324; Maine, **Vol. 6, Part 1**, 7; Mexico, **Vol. 2, Part 1**, 363, 369; Mississippi, **Vol. 5, Part 2**, 579; **Vol. 10, Part 2**, 373; Mississippi Valley, **Vol. 6, Part 2**, 610; New England, **Vol. 6, Part 1**, 112 f.; Ohio, **Vol. 9, Part 2**, 482; South, the, **Vol. 2, Part 1**, 483; **Vol. 5, Part 2**, 579; Tennessee, **Vol. 6, Part 2**, 45; Texas, **Vol. 1, Part 2**, 234; Virginia, **Vol. 6, Part 1**, 113
Methodist Episcopal Hospital (Brooklyn, N.Y.), **Supp. 6**, 664
Methodist Federation for Social Action, founding of, **Supp. 8**, 681
Methodist League for Faith and Life, **Supp. 7**, 694
Methodist Missionary Society, **Vol. 3, Part 1**, 544 f.
Methodist Wesleyan Female College, **Vol. 1, Part 2**, 36
Metric system, **Vol. 7, Part 1**, 471; **Vol. 9, Part 2**, 128
Metro-Goldwyn-Mayer (MGM): **Supp. 4**, 66–67, 97; **Supp. 5**, 627; **Supp. 7**, 499, 515, 563, 681–82; **Supp. 8**, 151, 203–4, 315, 646, 659; **Supp. 9**, 473; costume design, **Supp. 6**, 9; directors, **Supp. 6**, 9, 657–58; *Dr. Kildare* series, **Supp. 3**, 264; founding of, **Supp. 6**, 440; **Supp. 8**, 576–77; **Supp. 9**, 323; 323; Freed unit, **Supp. 9**, 291–92; "MGM musical," **Supp. 9**, 291; motion-picture production halted, **Supp. 9**, 292; musicals, **Supp. 10**, 34–35; productions, **Supp. 10**, 195–96, 436, 515; stars, **Supp. 3**, 35; **Supp. 6**, 225–26; **Supp. 9**, 128
Metromedia, predecessors, **Supp. 7**, 207
Metropolis, **Supp. 9**, 819; **Supp. 10**, 430
Metropolitan Engineering Co., **Supp. 7**, 564, 565
Metropolitan Life Insurance Co.: **Vol. 3, Part 2**, 419; **Vol. 4, Part 2**, 500; **Supp. 5**, 394; home nursing bureau, **Supp. 6**, 283, 284; statistical bureau, **Supp. 4**, 506
Metropolitan magazine, political cartoons, **Supp. 3**, 852
Metropolitan Museum of Art (New York City): **Vol. 1, Part 1**, 233, 445; **Vol. 2, Part 1**, 583; **Vol. 2, Part 2**, 105, 149; **Vol. 4, Part 2**, 404; **Vol. 5, Part 1**, 619; **Vol. 5, Part 2**, 144, 540; **Vol. 7, Part 1**, 179; **Vol. 8, Part 2**, 40 f.; administration, **Supp. 8**, 545; American Wing, **Supp. 1**, 237; **Supp. 6**, 562; Bache collection, **Supp. 3**, 24; Chinese art, **Supp. 3**, 268–69; Cloisters, **Supp. 2**, 22; **Supp. 4**, 902; **Supp. 6**, 486, 549; **Supp. 8**, 545; collection development, **Supp. 1**, 138; **Supp. 7**, 466; **Supp. 8**, 368; concerts, **Supp. 6**, 426–27; Costume Institute, **Supp. 5**, 53; **Supp. 6**, 621; Egyptian collection, **Supp. 4**, 901, 902; expansion of, **Supp. 4**, 902; founding of, **Vol. 5, Part 1**, 106; **Vol. 6, Part 2**, 293; **Vol. 8, Part 1**, 228 f.; gifts to, **Supp. 6**, 623; international exhibitions, **Supp. 6**, 621; Whitney collection rejection, **Supp. 4**, 290
Metropolitan Opera Company (New York City): **Vol. 1, Part 1**, 9; **Vol. 2, Part 2**, 357; **Vol. 3, Part 2**, 396 f.; **Vol. 4, Part 1**, 506; **Vol. 5, Part 2**, 244, 584; **Vol. 7, Part 1**, 434, 549; **Vol. 7, Part 2**, 311; **Vol. 8, Part 2**, 562; ballet choreography **Supp. 5**, 75; Callas performances and firing by, **Supp. 10**, 93, 94; conducting, **Supp. 3**, 359; **Supp. 6**, 643; **Supp. 7**, 548, 640, 765; **Supp. 8**, 641; **Supp. 10**, 722; costumes and sets, **Supp. 6**, 233; *Die Tote Stadt*, **Supp. 6**, 351; first live radio broadcast, **Supp. 9**, 207; first national fund-raising, **Supp. 4**, 87; **Supp. 5**, 634; **Supp. 6**, 69; German opera productions, **Supp. 3**, 359; **Supp. 4**, 210–11; Hofmann recital, **Supp. 6**, 297, 298; management, **Supp. 2**, 223; **Supp. 6**, 323–24; orchestra, **Supp. 6**, 242; premieres, **Supp. 6**, 457; radio broadcasts, **Supp. 5**, 183; **Supp. 9**, 802; reorganization of, **Supp. 1**, 457; **Supp. 4**, 603; singing, **Supp. 3**, 553; **Supp. 4**, 388–89; **Supp. 6**, 510; **Supp. 7**, 179, 525–26; **Supp. 8**, 20, 422–23; **Supp. 9**, 544–55, 804, 816, 850; **Supp. 10**, 639–40
Metropolitan Street Railway Co. (New York City), **Vol. 7, Part 2**, 358 f.
Metropolitan Telephone & Telegraph Co. (New York City), **Vol. 8, Part 1**, 183 f.
Metropolitan Traction Co., first holding company in U.S., **Vol. 8, Part 2**, 266
Metropolitan Transit Co., charter for, **Vol. 9, Part 2**, 232
Metzger, Wolfgang, reference to, **Supp. 3**, 808
Mexican Power and Light Co., **Supp. 6**, 452
Mexican Revolution (1915–16), **Supp. 3**, 453, 606; **Supp. 4**, 656
Mexican War: **Vol. 2, Part 1**, 8; **Vol. 4, Part 1**, 203, 421;

Vol. 5, Part 1, 265; Vol. 6, Part 2, 201, 257, 276, 475; Vol. 8, Part 1, 609; Vol. 8, Part 2, 508 f.; Vol. 9, Part 2, 350; Buena Vista, battle of, Vol. 3, Part 1, 17; Buchanan's part in negotiations, Vol. 2, Part 1, 209; causes of, Vol. 8, Part 1, 34 f.; financing of, Vol. 8, Part 1, 603; Louisiana, Vol. 2, Part 1, 491; military service in, Vol. 1, Part 1, 271, 502, 518; Vol. 1, Part 2, 124, 125, 161, 179, 332, 436, 438, 465, 509 f., 537, 600; Vol. 2, Part 1, 92, 371; Vol. 2, Part 2, 71, 105, 122, 169, 191, 389, 431, 546, 619; Vol. 3, Part 1, 17, 58, 93, 124, 131, 144, 206, 242, 243, 251, 291, 365, 391, 580, 598; Vol. 3, Part 2, 149, 153, 528, 550, 568; Vol. 4, Part 1, 92, 94, 158, 316, 429, 435, 484; Vol. 4, Part 2, 147, 151, 169, 183, 191, 216, 221, 232, 239, 242, 24 f., 280, 392, 415, 461, 463, 492, 505, 527; Vol. 5, Part 1, 275 196, 283, 343; Vol. 5, Part 2, 63, 91, 95, 136, 144, 166, 21 f., 272, 425, 449, 574, 579, 582 f.; Vol. 6, Part 1, 121, 239, 391, 420, 441, 538, 576, 581, 600; Vol. 6, Part 2, 29, 205; Vol. 7, Part 1, 20, 41, 46, 60, 139, 160, 170, 171, 375, 410, 648; Vol. 7, Part 2, 4, 19, 184, 243, 306, 380, 414, 519, 570, 577, 594, 604; Vol. 8, Part 1, 8, 76, 90, 188, 205, 258, 306, 315, 329, 340, 377, 481, 504, 516, 520, 521, 538, 570, 587, 609, 625, 641; Vol. 8, Part 2, 2, 46, 194, 196, 236, 343, 376, 505, 548; Vol. 9, Part 1, 11, 12, 92, 107, 247, 272, 331, 555, 613, 617; Vol. 9, Part 2, 71 f., 242, 350, 379, 441, 608; Vol. 10, Part 1, 57, 83, 365, 375, 377, 528, 628, Vol. 10, Part 2, 513, 537; naval affairs, Vol. 9, Part 2, 364; naval service, Vol. 1, Part 1, 488, 528; Vol. 3, Part 1, 136, 200, 529 f.; Vol. 3, Part 2, 255, 531; Vol. 4, Part 2, 580; Vol. 5, Part 1, 152; Vol. 5, Part 2, 50, 256; Vol. 6, Part 1, 129, 315, 524; Vol. 6, Part 2, 82, 576; Vol. 7, Part 1, 120 f., 426; Vol. 7, Part 2, 185, 260, 314, 487; Vol. 8, Part 1, 85 f., 183 f., 293 f., 298 f., 319 f., 529 f., 596; Vol. 8, Part 2, 72, 196, 244, 341, 343, 426 f., 579; Vol. 9, Part 1, 136, 215, 320; Vol. 9, Part 2, 48 f., 620; Vol. 10, Part 1, 34, 128, 425; naval vessels listed, Vol. 6, Part 1, 129, 315; territorial acquisitions, Vol. 8, Part 1, 34 f.; Texas, Vol. 2, Part 1, 491

Mexico: American frontier in 1844, Vol. 8, Part 2, 306; animal surveys, Supp. 1, 572; anthropological studies, Supp. 8, 378; archaeological excavations, Pre-Columbian, Supp. 3, 786; botanical explorations, Vol. 5, Part 2, 425; Vol. 8, Part 1, 236 f.; Vol. 8, Part 2, 160; botanical studies, Supp. 3, 153; boundary survey of, Vol. 1, Part 2, 7; Vol. 9, Part 2, 260; California, acquisition from, by U.S., Vol. 3, Part 2, 263; Vol. 5, Part 2, 617; Vol. 6, Part 2, 373; Vol. 8, Part 1, 34 f.; diplomatic relations with, Vol. 1, Part 2, 225, 377; Vol. 3, Part 2, 108; Vol. 4, Part 1, 84, 538; Vol. 6, Part 1, 193, 269; Vol. 7, Part 1, 234 f.; Vol. 8, Part 1, 379; Vol. 8, Part 2, 85; Vol. 9, Part 1, 20, 210; Vol. 9, Part 2, 474; Vol. 10, Part 2, 643; Supp. 1, 589; Supp. 3, 156; Supp. 4, 217; Supp. 5, 332; Supp. 6, 207, 451, 452; folk art, Supp. 8, 126; French, retirement of, Vol. 5, Part 2, 88; maps, Vol. 5, Part 1, 348; Maximilian in, Vol. 2, Part 1, 461; Vol. 8, Part 2, 85; Maya civilization studies, Supp. 4, 605–6; medical work in, Vol. 5, Part 1, 429; Methodist church, Vol. 2, Part 1, 363; mineralogy, Supp. 6, 212, 213; mining promotion, Supp. 3, 259; minister to, first, Vol. 8, Part 1, 30 f.; missions in, Vol. 2, Part 1, 363, 369; Vol. 6, Part 1, 95; Vol. 10, Part 1, 54, national hymn, writing, Vol. 7, Part 1, 595; ornithology study, Supp. 6, 255; photographic study, Supp. 10, 766; photography of, Supp. 6, 685; Pious Fund, claim against, Vol. 7, Part 2, 426; railroad building in, Vol. 7, Part 2, 195; Vol. 8, Part 2, 527; real estate development, Supp. 3, 154–55; social anthropological studies, Supp. 6, 532–34; Treaty of 1828, Vol. 3, Part 2, 108; Trist, activities of, Vol. 9, Part 2, 646; typhus fever, Vol. 5, Part 1, 429; U.S. oil claims, Supp. 7, 377; Water Treaty, Supp. 6, 455; Wood, Leonard, expedition led by, Vol. 7, Part 2, 296; writings on, Vol. 8, Part 1, 30 f., 503, 634; Vol. 9, Part 1, 316; Supp. 9, 345–46

Mexico City: capture of (1847), Vol. 8, Part 2, 509; Vol. 9, Part 2, 646; Olympic Games (1968), Supp. 10, 612; paving of, Supp. 1, 255

Meyer, Adolf, references to, Supp. 3, 51, 127–28; Supp. 4, 107; Supp. 6, 367, 672

Meyer, Eugene, references to, Supp. 3, 492; Supp. 7, 295–96; Supp. 8, 432, 433

M (film), Supp. 10, 431

MGM. *See* Metro-Goldwyn-Mayer

Miami, Fla., gambling in, Supp. 3, 20

Miami Beach, Fla., tourism promotion, Supp. 5, 270

Miami Indians: disastrous expedition against, Vol. 8, Part 2, 294; Little Turtle, relations with, Vol. 6, Part 1, 300

Miami Tribune, founding of, Supp. 3, 20

Miami University (Ohio), Vol. 3, Part 1, 615 f.; Vol. 5, Part 2, 249; Vol. 8, Part 1, 271 f.; Foundation for Population Research, Supp. 3, 635

Michael Reese Hospital (Chicago, Ill.), pediatrics service, Supp. 5, 1

Michelson, Albert A., references to, Supp. 3, 291; Supp. 5, 495

Michigan: boundary disputes, Vol. 2, Part 2, 185; Catholic church, Vol. 1, Part 1, 448 f.; Vol. 6, Part 1, 139; canal building, Vol. 10, Part 1, 616 f.; deaf, state school for, Vol. 3, Part 2, 151; Democratic party, Supp. 10, 109; education, Vol. 7, Part 2, 583, 637; Vol. 10, Part 1, 617 f., 652 f.; exploration, Vol. 2, Part 1, 582; Vol. 6, Part 1, 395; forestry, Vol. 1, Part 2, 87; fruit growing in, Vol. 6, Part 1, 535 f.; fungi of, Vol. 5, Part 2, 263; geology, Vol. 2, Part 1, 90; Vol. 5, Part 1, 254; governors, Vol. 1, Part 1, 179 f., 534 f., 654 f.; Vol. 1, Part 2, 329 f., 368 f.; Vol. 3, Part 2, 313 f., 341 f.; Vol. 6, Part 1, 586 f.; Vol. 6, Part 2, 375 f.; Vol. 7, Part 2, 621 f.; Vol. 10, Part 1, 463 f.; Vol. 10, Part 2, 483 f.; Supp. 4, 640; Supp. 8, 57; iron, discovery of, Vol. 2, Part 1, 338; industrial development, Vol. 3, Part 1, 547 f.; jurisprudence in, Vol. 2, Part 1, 608; land surveys, Vol. 2, Part 1, 90; legal service, Vol. 2, Part 1, 456; Vol. 2, Part 2, 392; Vol. 3, Part 1, 390; Vol. 3, Part 2, 468; Vol. 6, Part 1, 424; Vol. 10, Part 2, 220, 507; library work, early, Vol. 3, Part 1, 143; missionary work, Vol. 1, Part 1, 585; Vol. 7, Part 2, 583; Vol. 8, Part 1, 550; mining, Vol. 2, Part 1, 338; Vol. 8, Part 1, 264 f., Vol. 10, Part 2, 162; Mormonism, opposition to, Vol. 9, Part 2, 124; pioneer days in, Vol. 2, Part 1, 340, 563; Vol. 10, Part 2, 483; political service, Vol. 1, Part 1, 179, 534, 655; Vol. 1, Part 2, 291, 329, 368; Vol. 2, Part 1, 336; Vol. 3, Part 1, 109, 234, 296; Vol. 3, Part 2, 313, 341; Vol. 5, Part 1, 282, 363; Vol. 6, Part 1, 141, 327, 586; Vol. 6, Part 2, 144; Vol. 7, Part 2, 583, 621; Vol. 9, Part 2, 124; Vol. 10, Part 1, 463 f.; Vol. 10, Part 2, 247, 483; politics, Supp. 3, 550, 596; Supp. 4, 299, 612–13; Supp. 5, 505, 702–5; Supp. 8, 268–69; Supp. 9, 129, 781; Supp. 10, 109, 315, 645; politics, Civil War period, Vol. 2, Part 1, 336; public service, Vol. 1, Part 2, 369; Vol. 5, Part 1, 278; reforms, Vol. 1, Part 1, 534; Republican party, Vol. 2, Part 1, 618; Vol. 6, Part 1, 327; Supp. 9, 781; Roman Catholic diocese, Supp. 5, 263–64; scientific services, Vol. 8, Part 1, 192 f.; shipping, Vol. 2, Part 1, 338; statehood, admission to, Vol. 6, Part 2, 376; Vol. 10, Part 2, 483; steel industry, Vol. 3, Part 1, 547 f.; Sunday school, first, Vol. 9, Part 1, 33; surgery, Vol. 6, Part 1, 537; territorial code, first, Vol. 1, Part 2, 50; territory, extent of, Vol. 3, Part 1, 349

Michigan Car Co., **Vol. 7, Part 1**, 445
Michigan Central Railroad, **Vol. 5, Part 2**, 224
Michigan Railroad Commission, **Supp. 3**, 188
Michigan Southern & Northern Indiana Railroad, **Vol. 5, Part 2**, 60
Michigan State Agricultural College, **Vol. 6, Part 2**, 613
Michigan State College, women, establishing courses for, **Vol. 6, Part 2**, 463
Michigan State Normal School: geography studies, **Supp. 4**, 423–24; at Ypsilanti, **Vol. 10, Part 1**, 617 f.
Michigan State Psychopathic Hospital, founding of, **Supp. 2**, 24
Michigan State Teachers' Association, **Vol. 10, Part 1**, 617 f.
Michigan State University: mechanical engineering studies, **Supp. 6**, 181; social research, **Supp. 8**, 685
Microbe Hunters, The, **Supp. 9**, 225
Microbiology: **Supp. 2**, 225; **Supp. 3**, 354; **Supp. 6**, 481–82; soil, **Supp. 2**, 387; actinomycetes, study of, **Supp. 9**, 833, 834; Virus bacteria differentiation, **Supp. 7**, 648. *See also* Bacteriology
Microfilm: early work with, **Supp. 6**, 70; library use of, **Supp. 6**, 399; **Supp. 8**, 120; Postal Service use of, **Supp. 6**, 661
Micropaleontology, **Supp. 4**, 205–6
Microphone, invention of, **Vol. 5, Part 1**, 347; **Supp. 1**, 75
Microscopes, for diagnosis, **Supp. 4**, 790; writings on, **Supp. 4**, 516
Microscopy, **Vol. 1, Part 1**, 106; **Vol. 2, Part 2**, 132; **Vol. 5, Part 2**, 79; **Vol. 6, Part 1**, 151, 202; **Vol. 7, Part 2**, 370; **Vol. 8, Part 1**, 589; **Vol. 8, Part 2**, 562 f.; **Vol. 10, Part 1**, 435 f.; **Vol. 10, Part 2**, 650; **Supp. 3**, 40; **Supp. 6**, 704
Microtome, **Vol. 7, Part 1**, 30
Microwaves: radar development, **Supp. 4**, 358–59; radio relay, **Supp. 6**, 85
Middle Ages: architecture, **Supp. 1**, 600; armor collection, **Supp. 2**, 415; art collection, **Supp. 2**, 22; art studies, **Supp. 8**, 545; Chaucer chronology, **Supp. 4**, 819–20; church drama studies, **Supp. 3**, 855; Cloisters collection, **Supp. 4**, 902; Hebrew literature, **Supp. 2**, 145; Latin literature and language studies, **Supp. 4**, 68; manuscripts, **Supp. 3**, 109; religious sensibility studies, **Supp. 3**, 765–66; scholarship on, **Supp. 2**, 290; **Supp. 7**, 741–42; stained glass, **Supp. 3**, 183–84; textbooks on, **Supp. 1**, 285; towns, studies of, **Supp. 5**, 655–56; writings on, **Supp. 1**, 705; **Supp. 3**, 617–18
Middlebury, Vt., **Vol. 7, Part 2**, 167
Middlebury College, **Vol. 1, Part 2**, 593; **Vol. 4, Part 2**, 195; **Vol. 7, Part 2**, 167; **Vol. 8, Part 1**, 280 f.
Middle East: archaeology, **Supp. 3**, 37; Byzantine studies, **Supp. 5**, 708–9; education, **Supp. 2**, 517; Lebanon crisis (1958), **Supp. 8**, 158; missionary work in, **Supp. 4**, 860; pre-Islamic civilizations, studies on, **Supp. 3**, 572–73; scholarship on, **Supp. 7**, 709–10; Suez crisis (1956), **Supp. 6**, 179; **Supp. 8**, 147, 158, 276. *See also* country and institution names
Middle English studies, **Supp. 3**, 109
Middle States Oil Corporation, **Supp. 1**, 381
Middletown, **Supp. 10**, 438
Middletown, Conn., **Vol. 3, Part 1**, 395
Middletown, **Supp. 4**, 408; **Supp. 5**, 35; **Supp. 8**, 398–*99*
Middletown in Transition, **Supp. 3**, 30
Middle West (U.S.): art reflecting, **Supp. 3**, 841, 204–5; fiction about, **Supp. 4**, 329; **Supp. 5**, 14–15, 422–24; literature associated with, **Supp. 4**, 629–30; progressive movement, **Supp. 6**, 578; sociological study, **Supp. 8**, 398–99; writings on, **Supp. 4**, 816–17. *See also specific states and city names*
Midget, **Vol. 9, Part 2**, 126 f.
"Midnight judges," **Vol. 1, Part 1**, 80; **Vol. 5, Part 2**, 28 f.; **Vol. 6, Part 1**, 101; **Vol. 6, Part 2**, 319 f.
"Midnight Order," **Vol. 3, Part 1**, 545 f.
Midway, World War II action, **Supp. 4**, 589; **Supp. 5**, 450; **Supp. 6**, 340; **Supp. 8**, 619
Midway Studios, **Supp. 2**, 647
Midwifery: **Vol. 1, Part 1**, 599; **Vol. 3, Part 1**, 267; **Vol. 6, Part 1**, 510; **Vol. 9, Part 1**, 117; first physician to practice, **Vol. 6, Part 1**, 333; School of, **Vol. 3, Part 2**, 160; training program, **Supp. 2**, 495; **Supp. 3**, 28
"Mighty Mouse" (fictional character), **Supp. 9**, 798
Migraine, cause of, **Vol. 8, Part 1**, 317 f.
Migrant labor, **Supp. 7**, 456; **Supp. 8**, 301, 625; **Supp. 10**, 502
Migratory Bird Law (1913), **Supp. 3**, 593
Milbank, Tweed, Hadley, and McCloy, **Supp. 8**, 662
Mildred series, **Vol. 3, Part 2**, 390
Miles, Robert E. J., reference to, **Supp. 4**, 551
Miles Davis Sextet, **Supp. 9**, 11; **Supp. 10**, 225
Military: "Adventurers," colonizers in the West, **Vol. 6, Part 1**, 517; commission, trial of civilians, by, **Vol. 3, Part 1**, 111; education, **Vol. 4, Part 1**, 206; **Vol. 6, Part 1**, 39; **Vol. 7, Part 2**, 282; engineering, **Vol. 1, Part 1**, 163, 500, 626; **Vol. 2, Part 2**, 78; **Vol. 3, Part 1**, 210; **Vol. 3, Part 2**, 550; **Vol. 4, Part 1**, 52, 138, 343, 612; **Vol. 4, Part 2**, 151; **Vol. 5, Part 1**, 101 f.; **Vol. 6, Part 1**, 69, 182, 495 f.; **Vol. 6, Part 2**, 257; **Vol. 7, Part 1**, 100 f., 154; **Vol. 8, Part 1**, 406, 647; **Vol. 8, Part 2**, 592; **Vol. 9, Part 2**, 247, 260, 363; history, **Vol. 2, Part 2**, 109; **Vol. 3, Part 1**, 352, 394, 396 f.; hospitals, **Vol. 7, Part 1**, 409; law, **Vol. 3, Part 1**, 115; manuals, **Vol. 7, Part 1**, 510; monuments, **Vol. 8, Part 2**, 107; prisons, **Vol. 9, Part 2**, 616; Quaker attitude regarding service, **Vol. 6, Part 1**, 70; service, selective, **Vol. 5, Part 2**, 251; Student Army Training Corps, **Vol. 6, Part 2**, 120; surgery, **Vol. 3, Part 2**, 538; **Vol. 8, Part 2**, 585; tactics, **Vol. 3, Part 1**, 579 f.; **Vol. 7, Part 1**, 229; **Vol. 8, Part 2**, 507; **Vol. 10, Part 1**, 130; writings, **Vol. 2, Part 1**, 50, 119; **Vol. 3, Part 1**, 210, 248, 467 f., 579 f.; **Vol. 4, Part 1**, 141, 144; **Vol. 5, Part 2**, 146, 150, 264, 315, 498; **Vol. 6, Part 2**, 210; **Vol. 7, Part 1**, 154; **Vol. 8, Part 1**, 514; **Vol. 8, Part 2**, 71, 152,; **Vol. 9, Part 2**, 530; **Vol. 10, Part 1**, 130. *See also* Armed forces and defense; *specific branches of the armed forces; specific war names*
Military Academy, U.S. *See* United States Military Academy
Military Historical Society of Massachusetts, **Vol. 8, Part 2**, 152
Militia of Christ for Social Service, founding of, **Supp. 4**, 232
Milk, Harvey, references to, **Supp. 10**, 558, 559
Milk: child nourishment, **Supp. 3**, 159; condensed and evaporated, **Supp. 2**, 306; **Supp. 3**, 750; fat-test, **Supp. 1**, 37; infant diarrhea treatment, **Supp. 5**, 1; malted, **Supp. 2**, 316, 688; modifying of, **Vol. 6, Part 2**, 502; nutrients in, **Supp. 5**, 276; pasteurization and sanitation, **Vol. 8, Part 2**, 553; **Vol. 9, Part 2**, 130; **Supp. 2**, 353, 514; **Supp. 4**, 701; **Supp. 5**, 144; school programs, **Supp. 8**, 468
Milk chocolate, **Supp. 3**, 358
Milky Way, **Supp. 6**, 30; **Supp. 9**, 713, 714
Millard's Review of the Far East, founding of, **Supp. 4**, 679
Millay, Edna St. Vincent, references to, **Supp. 8**, 124, 645; **Supp. 9**, 718, 875
Mill Creek Redevelopment Porject (Philadephia, Pa.), **Supp. 9**, 445
Millenarianism, **Supp. 1**, 615–16; **Supp. 3**, 678
Millenarian, The, **Vol. 8, Part 1**, 453

Millennial Dawn, tremendous sale of, **Vol. 8, Part 2**, 240
Millennial Harbinger, **Vol. 6, Part 1**, 401
Millennium, calculations on, **Vol. 1, Part 1**, 432; **Vol. 5, Part 2**, 313
Miller, Ann, reference to, **Supp. 10**, 802
Miller, Arthur, references to, **Supp. 7**, 546; **Supp. 8**, 31; **Supp. 10**, 54, 55, 131
Miller, Charles R., reference to, **Supp. 3**, 787
Miller, Dayton C., reference to, **Vol. 7, Part 1**, 192
Miller, Don, reference to, **Supp. 7**, 729
Miller, Earl, references to, **Supp. 7**, 660, 662, 664
Miller, Flournoy, reference to, **Supp. 9**, 731
Miller, Francis Pickens, reference to, **Supp. 9**, 67–68
Miller, Glenn, references to, **Supp. 3**, 690; **Supp. 10**, 299
Miller, Henry, references to, **Supp. 7**, 292, 293; **Supp. 10**, 590
Miller, Joaquin, reference to, **Vol. 6, Part 1**, 433
Miller, June Mansfield Smith, references to, **Supp. 10**, 538, 590
Miller, Kenneth Hayes, reference to, **Supp. 5**, 472
Miller, Mitchell ("Mitch"), reference to, **Supp. 10**, 838
Miller, Thomas W., prosecution of, **Supp. 3**, 117
Miller, William, reference to, **Vol. 5, Part 1**, 60
Miller, Zack, reference to, **Supp. 9**, 313
Millers' National Association, **Vol. 1, Part 1**, 504
Millet, Jean Francois, reference to, **Vol. 5, Part 1**, 397
Milligan, Lambdin P., reference to, **Vol. 5, Part 1**, 182
Milligan, Maurice M., reference to, **Supp. 3**, 597
Milligan case before Supreme Court, **Vol. 3, Part 2**, 360 f.
Millikan, Robert A., references to, **Supp. 2**, 494; **Supp. 3**, 291; **Supp. 5**, 202; **Supp. 6**, 150, 151; **Supp. 7**, 133, 134, 344, 619; **Supp. 8**, 439, 440; **Supp. 9**, 113, 901
Millinery. *See* Hats
Milling: industry, **Vol. 1, Part 2**, 157; flour, **Vol. 1, Part 1**, 503; **Vol. 3, Part 1**, 524 f.; **Vol. 3, Part 2**, 90, 209, 525; **Vol. 7, Part 2**, 604 f., 607; **Vol. 10, Part 1**, 495 f.; grain, **Vol. 3, Part 2**, 51; machinery, **Vol. 5, Part 1**, 286
Millions of Cats, **Supp. 4**, 310
Millis, Harry A., reference to, **Supp. 6**, 379
Mills, C. Wright, reference to, **Supp. 10**, 439
Mills College, **Vol. 7, Part 1**, 6, 16 f.; building program, **Supp. 6**, 463; presidency, **Supp. 4**, 687–88
"Mills money," **Vol. 7, Part 1**, 14
Mill Spring, Ky., battle of. *See* Logan's Cross Roads
Milne, Edward A., reference to, **Supp. 10**, 625
"Milquetoast, Caspar" (fictional character), **Supp. 5**, 732
Milstein, Nathan, reference to, **Supp. 10**, 632
Milton Academy (Pa.), **Vol. 5, Part 2**, 249
Milwaukee, Wis.: industrial development, **Vol. 1, Part 1**, 219; founding, **Vol. 5, Part 2**, 247 f.; German Catholicism, **Vol. 6, Part 2**, 580; library service, **Vol. 7, Part 2**, 384; Lutheran Seminary, **Vol. 5, Part 1**, 108; newspapers, **Supp. 3**, 19–20; public service, **Vol. 7, Part 2**, 326, 535; Roman Catholic diocese, **Supp. 6**, 607; **Supp. 7**, 533; Socialist politics in, **Supp. 4**, 733, 746; **Supp. 7**, 348
Milwaukee and St. Paul Railroad, **Vol. 7, Part 1**, 40
Milwaukee College, **Vol. 7, Part 1**, 252
Milwaukee-Downer College, **Vol. 5, Part 2**, 612
Milwaukee Journal, **Supp. 1**, 576; **Supp. 7**, 299
Milwaukee Leader, **Supp. 1**, 74; **Supp. 3**, 10; **Supp. 4**, 746; **Supp. 7**, 348
Milwaukee Sanitarium, **Supp. 1**, 244
Milwaukee Sentinel, **Vol. 5, Part 2**, 400
Milwaukee Töchter Institute, **Vol. 4, Part 1**, 262
Mind. *See* Intelligence tests; Learning; Psychology; Thinking
Mind and the World-Order, **Supp. 7**, 471–72
Mind in the Making, The, **Supp. 2**, 564
Mind of Primitive Man, The, **Supp. 3**, 84
Mind Reading. *See* Telepathy
Miner, Luella, reference to, **Supp. 3**, 288–89
Mineral Leasing Act (1920), **Supp. 4**, 481
Mineralogy: **Vol. 1, Part 2**, 570; **Vol. 2, Part 1**, 180, 184, 187; **Vol. 5, Part 1**, 50, 240; **Vol. 5, Part 2**, 276 f., 486 f.; **Vol. 6, Part 1**, 70; **Vol. 7, Part 2**, 114; **Vol. 9, Part 1**, 2 f., 71, 304; book on, first, **Vol. 2, Part 2**, 189; chemistry applied to, **Vol. 5, Part 2**, 276; classification studies, **Supp. 2**, 386; collections, **Vol. 1, Part 1**, 248; **Vol. 1, Part 2**, 173; **Vol. 4, Part 1**, 245; **Vol. 6, Part 1**, 71; **Vol. 8, Part 2**, 90; **Vol. 9, Part 1**, 262; **Vol. 9, Part 2**, 629; **Supp. 6**, 212; field studies, **Supp. 1**, 176; identification, **Supp. 1**, 177; silica particles causing tuberculosis, **Supp. 4**, 314; teaching of, **Vol. 5, Part 1**, 254; **Vol. 5, Part 2**, 486; **Vol. 10, Part 2**, 263; textbooks, **Supp. 1**, 221; writings on, **Vol. 3, Part 1**, 268; **Vol. 5, Part 2**, 487
Mineral water, first bottled in U.S., **Vol. 3, Part 1**, 538 f.
Minersville School District v. *Gobitis*, **Supp. 4**, 796
Mines, Bureau of, **Vol. 5, Part 1**, 167; **Vol. 6, Part 2**, 254; engineering, **Supp. 4**, 690
Mine-sweeping, origin of, **Vol. 10, Part 1**, 135
Mine Workers. *See* United Mine Workers
Mingus, Charles, reference to, **Supp. 10**, 225, 791
Minhag America, Jewish prayer book, **Vol. 5, Part 2**, 254
Miniatures: **Vol. 9, Part 2**, 649; engraving of, detail of process (1797), **Vol. 8, Part 2**, 305; ivory, **Vol. 7, Part 1**, 247; painting, **Vol. 3, Part 1**, 516 f.; **Vol. 3, Part 2**, 603; toy trains, Supp. 67, 150
Minimum wage, **Supp. 3**, 655–5; **Supp. 4**, 900
Minimum Wage Law for Women, District of Columbia, **Vol. 9, Part 2**, 271
Mining (general; for list of mining engineers, *see* Occupations Index): Alaskan conservation, **Supp. 3**, 96, 321; Alaskan copper, **Supp. 3**, 321; Alder Gulch, **Vol. 4, Part 2**, 402; "Apex Law," **Vol. 4, Part 2**, 507; **Vol. 9, Part 2**, 589; Assay Office, U.S., **Vol. 5, Part 2**, 135; **Vol. 9, Part 2**, 597; colonial period, **Vol. 4, Part 2**, 379; **Vol. 6, Part 1**, 4; Comstock lode, **Vol. 2, Part 2**, 333; **Vol. 3, Part 2**, 246; **Vol. 5, Part 2**, 283; **Vol. 7, Part 1**, 612; **Vol. 9, Part 2**, 146; development of, **Supp. 1**, 413; engineering, **Supp. 1**, 357; **Supp. 5**, 556; **Supp. 7**, 357–58; financing of, **Vol. 9, Part 1**, 27; Gardner Mine fraud, **Vol. 3, Part 1**, 391; geological, **Supp. 4**, 765–66; government supervision, **Vol. 8, Part 1**, 415; Hunt and Douglas process, **Vol. 3, Part 1**, 396; industrial development, **Supp. 6**, 606–7; inventions, **Vol. 1, Part 2**, 412; labor movement, **Supp. 6**, 548; labor unions, **Vol. 4, Part 2**, 468; laws relating to, **Vol. 3, Part 1**, 238; **Vol. 6, Part 1**, 275; **Vol. 8, Part 1**, 415; **Vol. 9, Part 2**, 13 f., 423, 589; Leadville Mine, **Vol. 7, Part 1**, 461, 507; **Vol. 9, Part 2**, 263; leases, **Supp. 2**, 148; Little Pittsburgh Mine, **Vol. 9, Part 2**, 263; locomotives, first underground, **Vol. 8, Part 2**, 189; machinery, **Vol. 1, Part 1**, 551; **Vol. 2, Part 1**, 187; **Vol. 5, Part 2**, 36, 38; **Vol. 6, Part 1**, 82, 230; **Vol. 8, Part 1**, 518; **Supp. 1**, 544; **Supp. 2**, 101; mass-production process; **Supp. 6**, 316–17; Mexico, **Supp. 3**, 259; ores, testing of, **Vol. 3, Part 1**, 547 f.; prospecting, **Supp. 5**, 613; rock drills, **Vol. 5, Part 1**, 472; **Vol. 6, Part 1**, 230; **Vol. 8, Part 1**, 343; **Vol. 8, Part 2**, 587; Russell process in, **Vol. 3, Part 1**, 27; safety measures, **Supp. 2**, 200; **Supp. 4**, 690; sintering process, **Supp. 4**, 245–46; statistics, **Vol. 8, Part 1**, 415; teaching of, **Vol. 2, Part 1**, 612; **Vol. 3,**

Part 2, 56; Vol. 9, Part 2, 64 f.; Vol. 10, Part 1, 619 f.; Supp. 3, 631; textbooks on, Supp. 2, 200; U.S. Bureau of Mines, Vol. 5, Part 1, 167; Vol. 6, Part 2, 254; water control, Supp. 1, 620; woman expert, Vol. 4, Part 2, 381; writings on, Vol. 1, Part 1, 643; Vol. 2, Part 1, 73, 186 f.; Vol. 4, Part 1, 199; Vol. 8, Part 1, 415; Vol. 9, Part 1, 460; Vol. 9, Part 2, 64 f.; Supp. 1, 714; Supp. 7, 358. *See also specific ores*

Mining (by location): Colorado, Vol. 2, Part 1, 186, 511; Vol. 2, Part 1, 590; Vol. 3, Part 1, 210; Vol. 5, Part 1, 43; Vol. 10, Part 1, 619 f.; Idaho, Vol. 4, Part 2, 419; Vol. 8, Part 1, 546; Iowa, Vol. 3, Part 1, 475; Kentucky, Vol. 6, Part 1, 189; Michigan, Vol. 2, Part 1, 338; Montana, Vol. 3, Part 1, 45; Vol. 9, Part 2, 589; Nevada, Vol. 6, Part 2, 76; Vol. 9, Part 2, 13 f., 146; Oregon, Vol. 8, Part 1, 456; Pennsylvania, Vol. 1, Part 2, 530; Peru, Vol. 7, Part 2, 9; Utah, Vol. 4, Part 1, 9; Vol. 7, Part 2, 209, 451; West, the, Vol. 2, Part 1, 187; Vol. 2, Part 2, 144 f.; Vol. 8, Part 2, 35

Mining (by product): coal, Vol. 1, Part 2, 338; Vol. 2, Part 2, 108, 110; Vol. 4, Part 1, 9; Vol. 6, Part 1, 189; Vol. 8, Part 2, 189; copper, Vol. 1, Part 1, 112; Vol. 3, Part 1, 45, 396 f.; Vol. 4, Part 1, 577; Vol. 4, Part 2, 37 f.; Vol. 5, Part 1, 289, 360, 431, 573; Vol. 6, Part 1, 4; Vol. 7, Part 1, 461; Vol. 8, Part 1, 264 f.; Vol. 8, Part 2, 263, 304; diamond, Vol. 10, Part 2, 261; gold, Vol. 1, Part 1, 396, 443, 446; Vol. 1, Part 2, 228; Vol. 2, Part 1, 62, 300; Vol. 3, Part 1, 210; Vol. 3, Part 2, 246; Vol. 4, Part 1, 22, 168, 316; Vol. 4, Part 2, 363, 387; Vol. 5, Part 1, 81; Vol. 5, Part 2, 55 f., 188, 407, 583; Vol. 6, Part 1, 516; Vol. 6, Part 2, 76, 314; Vol. 7, Part 1, 6, 612; Vol. 8, Part 1, 450; Vol. 8, Part 2, 11, 35, 205, 248; Vol. 9, Part 1, 273; Vol. 9, Part 2, 87, 315, 384; iron, Vol. 2, Part 1, 90; Vol. 3, Part 1, 90; Vol. 3, Part 2, 79, 118; Vol. 4, Part 1, 183; Vol. 5, Part 1, 505; Vol. 6, Part 1, 73; Vol. 6, Part 2, 397, 487, 572; Vol. 7, Part 1, 20, 135; Vol. 8, Part 1, 264 f., Vol. 10, Part 2, 375; lead, Vol. 1, Part 1, 435 f.; Vol. 1, Part 2, 392; Vol. 3, Part 1, 457, 475; Vol. 4, Part 2, 546; Vol. 5, Part 2, 600; Vol. 6, Part 2, 496 f.; niter, Vol. 8, Part, 329 f.; salt, Vol. 3, Part 2, 322; silver, Vol. 4, Part 1, 337; Vol. 5, Part 1, 137, 446, 609; Vol. 7, Part 1, 507, 612; Vol. 8, Part 1, 326; Vol. 8, Part 2, 336; Vol. 9, Part 2, 265

Mining Herald, founding of, Supp. 2, 200

Ministers' Institute (Unitarian), Vol. 1, Part 2, 169

Minkowski, Hermann, reference to, Supp. 9, 201

Minkowski, Rudolph, references to, Supp. 6, 31; Supp. 9, 902

Minneapolis, Minn.: art, Vol. 5, Part 2, 485; Vol. 10, Part 1, 361 f.; civic service, Vol. 6, Part 1, 414 f., 478; Vol. 7, Part 1, 636; mayors, Supp. 10, 359–60; milling industry, Vol. 3, Part 1, 524 f.; Vol. 7, Part 2, 605

Minneapolis Daily News, founding of, Supp. 4, 132

Minneapolis, St. Paul & Sault Ste. Marie Railway (Soo Line), Supp. 3, 783, 823

Minneapolis Society of Fine Arts, Vol. 5, Part 2, 485; Vol. 10, Part 1, 361 f.

Minneapolis Star, Supp. 6, 228

Minneapolis Symphony Orchestra: conductors, Supp. 6, 456; founding of, Supp. 1, 578

Minnehaha, Falls of, Vol. 2, Part 2, 204

Minnelli, Liza, reference to, Supp. 8, 204

Minnelli, Vincente, reference to, Supp. 9, 291

Minnesota: architecture, Supp. 5, 208; child welfare, Supp. 3, 361–62; criminal code revision, Supp. 3, 227; Democratic-Farmer-Labor fusion, Supp. 3, 227; Supp. 10, 359; education, Vol. 7, Part 1, 408–9; exploration, Vol. 3, Part 1, 500 f.; flour-milling, Vol. 10, Part 1, 495 f.; forestry, Vol. 1, Part 1, 285; geology, Vol. 10, Part 2, 375; governors, Vol. 3, Part 1, 109 f.; Vol. 5, Part 1, 330 f.; Vol. 5, Part 2, 104 f.; Vol. 6, Part 1, 268 f.; Vol. 6, Part 2, 333; Vol. 7, Part 1, 418 f.; Vol. 7, Part 2, 607 f.; Vol. 8, Part 1, 341 f.; Vol. 9, Part 1, 144 f.; Supp. 2, 503; Supp. 8, 653; Supp. 10, 862–63; history and development, Vol. 1, Part 1, 522; Vol. 3, Part 2, 456; Vol. 6, Part 2, 133, 333; Indian land cessions, Vol. 8, Part 1, 341 f., 540; Indians, relations with, Vol. 6, Part 1, 300; Vol. 8, Part 1, 341 f.; Vol. 10, Part 2, 383; industrial development, Vol. 3, Part 1, 524 f.; Vol. 8, Part 2, 42; Vol. 10, Part 1, 504; legal service, Vol. 2, Part 2, 131; Vol. 3, Part 1, 109; Vol. 7, Part 1, 69; Vol. 7, Part 2, 92; Vol. 8, Part 2, 328; Vol. 3, Part 2, 455; Vol. 9, Part 1, 175; Vol. 9, Part 1, 612; Supp. 10, 862, 863; lumber industry, Vol. 10, Part 1, 361 f.; mortgage moratorium case, Supp. 4, 406; Norwegian culture in, Vol. 8, Part 2, 124; political service, Vol. 1, Part 1, 242; Vol. 3, Part 1, 370; Vol. 4, Part 1, 435; Vol. 5, Part 1, 330; Vol. 5, Part 2, 105 f., 105; Vol. 6, Part 1, 268, 271; Vol. 6, Part 2, 554; Vol. 7, Part 1, 418, 514; Vol. 7, Part 2, 608; Vol. 8, Part 1, 341, 538; Vol. 9, Part 1, 145; Vol. 10, Part 1, 504; Vol. 10, Part 2, 383; politics, Supp. 4, 852–53; Supp. 5, 396–97; Supp. 6, 577, 645; Supp. 9, 30; Supp. 10, 359–60, 862; public service, Vol. 1, Part 1, 521; Vol. 3, Part 2, 496; Vol. 4, Part 2, 93; Vol. 5, Part 1, 330; Vol. 7, Part 1, 420 f.; Vol. 7, Part 1, 456; Vol. 7, Part 2, 608; Vol. 10, Part 2, 60; railroad promotion, Vol. 8, Part 1, 538; reform, Vol. 3, Part 1, 370 f.; Republican party, Vol. 1, Part 1, 242; Vol. 6, Part 2, 554; settlement of, Vol. 2, Part 1, 552; Vol. 3, Part 2, 455; Vol. 4, Part 1, 390; Vol. 6, Part 1, 92; Vol. 6, Part 2, 133, 425; Swedish immigration, Vol. 6, Part 2, 425; Tax Commission, Vol. 8, Part 2, 42; territory, establishment of, Vol. 8, Part 1, 540

Minnesota Art Society, Vol. 5, Part 2, 485

Minnesota Historical Society, Vol. 10, Part 2, 275

Minnesota Indian Outbreak (1862), Vol. 6, Part 1, 300; Vol. 9, Part 1, 144

Minnesota Pioneer, Vol. 4, Part 1, 390

Minor, Robert C., references to, Supp. 3, 245, 532

Minorities. *See* Ethnic groups; Immigration; *specific groups*

Minstrel shows: Vol. 2, Parl 2, 98; Vol. 3, Part 1, 338; Vol. 3, Part 2, 557, 574; Vol. 4, Part 2, 410 f.; Vol. 5, Part 2, 279; Vol. 8, Part 1, 545 f.; origin of, Vol. 3, Part 2, 148

Mint, United States: Vol. 1, Part 2, 478; Vol. 3, Part 1, 254; Vol. 5, Part 1, 362; Vol. 5, Part 2, 456; Vol. 6, Part 1, 90, 273; Vol. 8, Part 1, 49 f.; Vol. 8, Part 2, 100, 110, 400; Vol. 9, Part 1, 387; director of, first, Vol. 8, Part 1, 631; directorship, Supp. 10, 704; first gold coinage by, Vol. 3, Part 1, 254

Minter, Mary Miles, reference to, Supp. 10, 348

"Minute-Men," Vol. 9, Part 2, 435

Miracle at Philadelphia: The Story of the Constitutional Convention, Supp. 9, 113

Miracle of the Bells, Supp. 7, 389

"Miracle Wheat," spectacular church fraud, Vol. 8, Part 2, 240

Miracle Worker, The, Supp. 8, 318

Miranda, Francesco, reference to Vol. 8, Part 2, 406

Miranda v. *Arizona*, Supp. 9, 837; Supp. 10, 483

Miró, E. R., reference to, Vol. 7, Part 1, 632

Miró, Joan, reference to, Supp. 10, 90

Missiles: early guided, Supp. 6, 50, 332; gap with Soviet Union issue, Supp. 7, 795; medium-range ballistic research, U.S., Supp. 10, 66; Soviet in Cuba, Supp. 7, 423, 724

Missionaries. For complete list, *see* Occupations Index

Missionary, edition of, Vol. 3, Part 1, 421

Missionary Ridge, battle of, Vol. 1, Part 2, 586; Vol. 2,

Part 2, 190; **Vol. 4, Part 1**, 496; **Vol. 4, Part 2**, 240; **Vol. 9, Part 1**, 80, 95; **Vol. 9, Part 2**, 434
Missionary societies: American Board of Foreign Missions, **Vol. 5, Part 2**, 234; American Missionary Society, **Vol. 1, Part 2**, 552; **Vol. 9, Part 2**, 299; Christian Home Missionary Society, **Vol. 4, Part 1**, 407; Foreign Christian Missionary Society, **Vol. 7, Part 1**, 145 f.; Presbyterian Board of Foreign Missions, **Vol. 8, Part 1**, 542; Women's Foreign Missionary Society, **Vol. 7, Part 2**, 218; Women's Union Missionary Society, **Vol. 3, Part 1**, 378; **Vol. 8, Part 1**, 335 f.
Missionary work (foreign): administration of, **Supp. 4**, 763–64; Africa, **Vol. 4, Part 1**, 375; **Vol. 4, Part 2**, 371; **Vol. 5, Part 2**, 561; **Vol. 7, Part 1**, 231, 390 f.; **Vol. 7, Part 2**, 324; **Vol. 8, Part 2**, 391; **Vol. 9, Part 2**, 296; **Vol. 5, Part 1**, 65, 398; **Vol. 10, Part 2**,. 338; **Supp. 1**, 499; Alaska, **Vol. 5, Part 1**, 489; **Vol. 8, Part 2**, 559; **Vol. 10, Part 2**, 634; Argentina, **Vol. 9, Part 2**, 76; Armenia, **Vol. 1, Part 2**, 187, 370; Borneo, **Vol. 3, Part 1**, 389; Brazil, **Vol. 5, Part 2**, 561, 575; **Vol. 9, Part 2**, 74; Burma, **Vol. 2, Part 2**, 631; **Vol. 5, Part 2**, 236, 242 f.; **Vol. 6, Part 2**, 359; Ceylon, **Vol. 1, Part 1**, 125; **Vol. 8, Part 1**, 68 f.; Chandag Heights (India) leper colony, **Supp. 3**, 623–24; China, **Vol. 1, Part 1**, 215, 241, 263, 392; **Vol. 1, Part 2**, 34; **Vol. 2, Part 1**, 36, 154; **Vol. 3, Part 1**, 389; **Vol. 4, Part 1**, 399, 509 f.; **Vol. 4, Part 2**, 361, 234, 453 f.; **Vol. 5, Part 1**, 132; **Vol. 5, Part 2**, 357, 560 f.; **Vol. 6, Part 1**, 475 f., 570; **Vol. 6, Part 2**, 122, 347, 385; **Vol. 7, Part 1**, 444; **Vol. 7, Part 2**, 34 f., 214, 235; **Vol. 8, Part 1**, 286 f., 476 f.; **Vol. 8, Part 2**, 8, 428 f.; **Vol. 9, Part 1**, 57 f., 68 f., 137, 238, 314, 442; **Vol. 10, Part 2**, 250, 274, 290, 469, 599; **Supp. 1**, 433; **Supp. 2**, 258, 548; **Supp. 3**, 288–89, 476–77; **Supp. 4**, 514–15, 677–78; **Supp. 9**, 132; **Supp. 10**, 636–37; Egypt, **Vol. 5, Part 2**, 607 f.; **Vol. 10, Part 1**, 539 f.; Gilbert Islands, **Vol. 1, Part 2**, 277; Greece, **Vol. 1, Part 2**, 187; **Vol. 5, Part 1**, 41 f.; Haiti, **Vol. 6, Part 1**, 95; Hawaii, **Vol. 1, Part 1**, 295; **Vol. 1, Part 2**, 276; **Vol. 2, Part 2**, 236 f.; **Vol. 3, Part 1**, 357; **Vol. 5, Part 2**, 229 f.; **Vol. 8, Part 1**, 560; India, **Vol. 1, Part 1**, 186, 286, 504; **Vol. 2, Part 1**, 225, 369; **Vol. 3, Part 2**, 235; **Vol. 4, Part 1**, 354, 419; **Vol. 4, Part 2**, 608; **Vol. 5, Part 1**, 125 f., 365, 463; **Vol. 5, Part 2**, 189 f., 234 f., 236, 240, 242 f., 304 f.; **Vol. 6, Part 1**, 356; **Vol. 6, Part 2**, 255,; **Vol. 7, Part 1**, 5, 305; **Vol. 7, Part 2**, 218; **Vol. 8, Part 1**, 68 f.; **Vol. 8, Part 2**, 523; **Vol. 9, Part 2**, 12; **Vol. 10, Part 1**, 108, 148, 411; **Vol. 10, Part 2**, 29, 65, 401; **Supp. 2**, 188; Italy, **Vol. 9, Part 2**, 326; Japan, **Vol. 1, Part 2**, 236; **Vol. 2, Part 1**, 154; **Vol. 3, Part 1**, 132, 177, 198; **Vol. 4, Part 1**, 563 f.; **Vol. 4, Part 2**, 317; **Vol. 5, Part 2**, 560 f.; **Vol. 6, Part 2**, 122; **Vol. 10, Part 2**, 250; **Supp. 3**, 322–23; **Supp. 5**, 681; Java, **Supp. 8**, 425; Korea, **Vol. 1, Part 1**, 324; **Vol. 5, Part 2**, 171 f.; **Vol. 6, Part 2**, 122; Kenya, **Supp. 9**, 897; Labrador, **Vol. 8, Part 1**, 133 f.; Latin America, **Supp. 2**, 500; **Supp. 8**, 537; Madagascar, **Vol. 9, Part 2**, 599 f.; Maryknoll Sisters, **Supp. 3**, 569; **Supp. 5**, 581; medical, in Burma, **Supp. 7**, 680–81; medical, in Indochina, **Supp. 7**, 190–91; Mexico, **Vol. 2, Part 1**, 363, 369; **Vol. 6, Part 1**, 95; **Vol. 10, Part 1**, 54; Mormon, **Supp. 5**, 640; Near East, **Vol. 1, Part 2**, 371; Persia, **Vol. 1, Part 2**, 37; **Vol. 3, Part 1**, 565 f.; **Vol. 3, Part 2**, 418; **Vol. 4, Part 1**, 486; **Vol. 7, Part 2**, 475; **Vol. 9, Part 2**, 53; **Vol. 10, Part 2**, 344; Philippines, **Supp. 1**, 115–16; **Supp. 5**, 178–79; Portuguese West Africa, **Vol. 8, Part 1**, 243 f.; Siam, **Vol. 5, Part 1**, 260; **Vol. 5, Part 2**, 190; **Vol. 6, Part 2**, 41, 52, 424; Siberia, **Vol. 2, Part 1**, 555; **Vol. 3, Part 1**, 156; **Vol. 7, Part 2**, 428; South Africa, **Supp. 4**, 519–20; **Supp. 5**, 259; **Supp. 9**, 897–98; South America, **Vol. 10, Part 2**, 474; South Korea, **Supp. 10**, 637; student movements, **Supp. 5**, 506–8; Syria, **Vol. 1, Part 2**, 370; **Vol. 3, Part 1**, 238 f.; **Vol. 5, Part 2**, 61; **Vol. 9, Part 2**, 490; Thailand, **Supp. 4**, 181–82, 529–30; Turkey, **Vol. 3, Part 1**, 565 f.; **Vol. 5, Part 1**, 191; **Vol. 8, Part 2**, 261, 421, 446; **Vol. 9, Part 1**, 73, 241; **Vol. 10, Part 1**, 500; **Vol. 10, Part 2**, 11; West Indies, **Vol. 6, Part 1**, 158; women's leadership in, **Supp. 4**, 647–48; YWCA, **Supp. 7**, 185
Missionary work (general): **Vol. 1, Part 1**, 243, 263, 276, 295, 497, 517, 532, 547, 583 f.; **Vol. 1, Part 2**, 528, 552; **Vol. 2, Part 1**, 189, **Vol. 2, Part 2**, 130, 232 f., 280, 539; **Vol. 3, Part 1**, 90, 333, 421, 565 f.; **Vol. 3, Part 2**, 100, 161, 183, 185, 340, 355, 405, 432, 435, 465, 474, 497, 505, 540; **Vol. 4, Part 1**, 97, 131, 115, 128, 173, 337, 443, 466, 606 f.; **Vol. 4, Part 2**, 34, 144, 195, 292, 316 f., 453 f., 495 f., 510, 523, 538, 542, 567; **Vol. 5, Part 2**, 54, 234, 248, 267, 395 f., 419 f., 567; **Vol. 6, Part 1**, 64, 231, 278, 356, 476, 569 f.; **Vol. 6, Part 2**, 125, 167; **Vol. 7, Part 1**, 16, 105, 148, 78 f., 533, 536; **Vol. 7, Part 2**, 135, 590; **Vol. 8, Part 1**, 286 f., 599 f.; **Vol. 8, Part 2**, 1, 4, 59, 263 f., 286, 315; **Vol. 9, Part 1**, 55, 176, 238, 314; **Vol. 9, Part 2**, 74, 299; **Vol. 10, Part 1**, 62, 405 411; book collections on, **Supp. 1**, 63; cyclopaedia of, **Vol. 7, Part 1**, 451; enterprises, consolidation of, **Vol. 3, Part 1**, 177; fund-raising, **Supp. 10**, 404, 405; higher education in, **Supp. 2**, 28; histories of, **Vol. 9, Part 2**, 623; lectures on, **Vol. 5, Part 2**, 171; **Vol. 9, Part 2**, 74; reports on, **Vol. 3, Part 1**, 238; **Vol. 10, Part 1**, 62; societies, directory of, **Vol. 3, Part 1**, 239; statistics, **Vol. 3, Part 1**, 239; training, **Vol. 3, Part 1**, 421; World Conference (1910), **Vol. 5, Part 2**, 561; writings on, **Vol. 3, Part 1**, 293, 390, 565 f., 566 f.; **Vol. 8, Part 1**, 477 f.; **Vol. 8, Part 2**, 333; **Vol. 9, Part 2**, 12, 346; **Vol. 10, Part 1**, 54; **Supp. 1**, 289
Missionary work (U.S.): Arkansas, **Vol. 7, Part 1**, 625; California, **Vol. 1, Part 1**, 161, 322; **Vol. 3, Part 1**, 422; **Vol. 3, Part 2**, 497; **Vol. 5, Part 1**, 577; **Vol. 7, Part 1**, 536; **Vol. 8, Part 1**, 109 f.; **Vol. 8, Part 2**, 591 f.; Catholic schools for blacks and American Indians, **Supp. 5**, 185–86; cities, **Supp. 2**, 655; Colorado, **Vol. 6, Part 2**, 61; **Vol. 8, Part 1**, 349 f.; Connecticut, **Vol. 3, Part 1**, 573 f.; **Vol. 8, Part 1**, 645; Illinois, **Vol. 1, Part 1**, 547; **Vol. 4, Part 1**, 235, 510; **Vol. 6, Part 2**, 280; **Vol. 7, Part 1**, 103; **Vol. 10, Part 1**, 58; Indiana, **Vol. 4, Part 2**, 189; Indians, **Vol. 1, Part 1**, 149, 276, 323, 475; **Vol. 1, Part 2**, 145, 234, 315, 353, 591, 593; **Vol. 2, Part 1**, 380, 441, 445, 592; **Vol. 3, Part 1**, 19 f., 255 f., 462, 473 f., 477 f.; **Vol. 3, Part 2**, 79, 95, 460, 497; **Vol. 4, Part 1**, 128, 130 f., 173, 458; **Vol. 4, Part 2**, 31, 144, 264, 294, 418, 496; **Vol. 5, Part 1**, 555; **Vol. 5, Part 2**, 432 f.; **Vol. 6, Part 1**, 429, 618; **Vol. 6, Part 2**, 294, 352, 454, 456, 470, 496, 500, 530, 534 f.; **Vol. 7, Part 1**, 370 f., 529, 614 f., 646 f.; **Vol. 7, Part 2**, 591; **Vol. 8, Part 1**, 61 f., 113 f., 330 f., 394, 398 f., 510, 530 f., 605 f.; **Vol. 8, Part 2**, 20, 30, 59, 286, 559, 587, 591; **Vol. 9, Part 1**, 75 f., 447; **Vol. 10, Part 2**, 141, 530, 646; **Supp. 1**, 134, 158, 218, 289; Iowa, **Vol. 8, Part 2**, 315; Kentucky, **Vol. 8, Part 1**, 537 f.; labor movement, **Supp. 3**, 733–34; Louisiana, **Vol. 1, Part 1**, 277; Maine, **Vol. 7, Part 2**, 334; Maryland, **Vol. 1, Part 1**, 231 f.; Michigan, **Vol. 1, Part 1**, 585; **Vol. 7, Part 2**, 583; **Vol. 8, Part 1**, 550; Mississippi, **Vol. 9, Part 2**, 11; Missouri, **Vol. 1, Part 1**, 277; **Vol. 8, Part 2**, 155; Montana, **Vol. 2, Part 1**, 67; **Vol. 8, Part 1**, 394; New Mexico, **Vol. 1, Part 2**, 174; **Vol. 5, Part 2**, 567; **Vol. 6, Part 2**, 61; New York, **Vol. 10, Part 2**, 311; **Supp. 10**, 404; Northwest, **Vol. 5, Part 2**, 267, 321; **Vol. 8, Part 1**, 399, 509 f.; Ohio, **Vol. 1, Part 1**, 487; **Vol. 3, Part 1**, 343; **Vol. 5, Part 2**, 166; Oregon, **Vol. 1, Part 1**, 408;

Vol. 6, Part 1, 112; **Vol. 7, Part 2**, 237; Pennsylvania, **Vol. 2, Part 1**, 441; **Vol. 4, Part 2**, 510; **Vol. 5, Part 2**, 514; **Vol. 6, Part 1**, 161, 162; Presbyterian church, **Supp. 3**, 110; Southern Baptist evangelism, **Supp. 3**, 687–88; Tennessee, **Vol. 6, Part 2**, 498; Utah, **Vol. 8, Part 2**, 408 f.; **Vol. 9, Part 1**, 422; Virginia, **Vol. 8, Part 1**, 542, West, **Vol. 1, Part 2**, 583; **Vol. 6, Part 1**, 9

Mission of the Immaculate Virgin (New York City), **Vol. 3, Part 1**, 462 f.

Mission to Moscow, **Supp. 6**, 147

Missiquoi Railroad, **Vol. 1, Part 2**, 594

Mississippi: agriculture, **Vol. 7, Part 1**, 100; **Vol. 7, Part 2**, 537; anthropology studies in, **Supp. 8**, 509; boundary disputes, **Vol. 6, Part 1**, 29; Catholic church, **Vol. 2, Part 1**, 611; civil rights movement in, **Supp. 7**, 227; **Supp. 8**, 285, 322; Civil War period, **Vol. 10, Part 2**, 609; constitution, first, **Vol. 8, Part 1**, 29 f.; cotton, **Vol. 3, Part 1**, 507 f.; Democratic party, **Supp. 10**, 307; economic service, **Vol. 10, Part 1**, 451; fiction about, **Supp. 7**, 231; geology of, **Vol. 5, Part 1**, 22; governors, **Vol. 1, Part 1**, 137 f.; **Vol. 1, Part 2**, 600; **Vol. 2, Part 1**, 100 f.; **Vol. 2, Part 2**, 122; **Vol. 3, Part 2**, 500 f.; **Vol. 5, Part 1**, 162 f, 372; **Vol. 6, Part 1**, 477; **Vol. 6, Part 2**, 118 f.; **Vol. 9, Part 2**, 78 f.; **Vol. 10, Part 1**, 221 f.; **Supp. 1**, 27; **Supp. 4**, 78; **Supp. 6**, 710–11; historical writings on, **Supp. 5**, 671–72; history of, **Vol. 6, Part 1**, 477; **Vol. 8, Part 1**, 274, 547; Indians, **Vol. 6, Part 1**, 144; land reclamation, **Vol. 8, Part 1**, 359 f.; law, **Vol. 2, Part 1**, 460; **Vol. 6, Part 1**, 289; laws, codification of, **Vol. 8, Part 1**, 29 f.; legal service, **Vol. 3, Part 1**, 144; **Vol. 4, Part 2**, 225, 325, 327; **Vol. 6, Part 2**, 453; **Vol. 8, Part 1**, 29 f., 29, 417; **Vol. 9, Part 2**, 40; **Vol. 10, Part 1**, 60, 401 f., 547; **Vol. 10, Part 2**, 609; Methodism, **Vol. 5, Part 2**, 579; missions, **Vol. 9, Part 2**, 11; plantations, **Vol. 5, Part 1**, 206; political service, **Vol. 1, Part 1**, 137; **Vol. 1, Part 2**, 600; **Vol. 2, Part 2**, 122; **Vol. 3, Part 1**, 144; **Vol. 4, Part 2**, 325, 461; **Vol. 5, Part 1**, 162, 372; **Vol. 6, Part 1**, 29, 131, 147; **Vol. 6, Part 2**, 118; **Vol. 7, Part 2**, 60; **Vol. 8, Part 1**, 29 f., 29, 191, 315 f., 315, 513; **Vol. 8, Part 2**, 369; **Vol. 9, Part 1**, 21; **Vol. 9, Part 2**, 40, 78, 459, 602; **Vol. 10, Part 1**, 60, 401 f., 547; **Vol. 10, Part 2**, 278; politics, **Supp. 3**, 334; **Supp. 4**, 78–79; **Supp. 6**, 525–26; **Supp. 10**, 307; pre-Civil War policies in, **Vol. 2, Part 1**, 101; public service, **Vol. 1, Part 1**, 538; **Vol. 3, Part 1**, 507 f.; **Vol. 4, Part 1**, 217; **Vol. 5, Part 1**, 44 f., 315; **Vol. 5, Part 2**, 552; **Vol. 6, Part 1**, 30; **Vol. 7, Part 1**, 86; **Vol. 7, Part 2**, 537; **Vol. 9, Part 1**, 21; **Vol. 10, Part 1**, 451; re-admission to Union following Civil War, **Vol. 10, Part 2**, 609; Reconstruction, **Vol. 2, Part 1**, 593; **Vol. 4, Part 1**, 233; **Vol. 4, Part 2**, 327; **Vol. 5, Part 2**, 552; **Vol. 9, Part 2**, 78; secession, **Vol. 10, Part 1**, 547; slavery, **Vol. 4, Part 1**, 216 f.; temperance movement, **Vol. 10, Part 1**, 547; writings on, **Vol. 4, Part 1**, 115; yellow fever epidemic, **Vol. 8, Part 2**, 242

Mississippi, side-wheeler, Civil War, **Vol. 9, Part 1**, 321

Mississippi Agricultural and Mechanical College, **Vol. 9, Part 2**, 78

Mississippi Freedom Democratic party, **Supp. 10**, 307

Mississippi River: Civil War, during, **Vol. 8, Part 2**, 78, 85; commerce on, **Vol. 1, Part 2**, 306; **Vol. 3, Part 2**, 106; **Vol. 10, Part 1**, 509 f.; **Vol. 10, Part 2**, 224; Commission, **Vol. 5, Part 2**, 106; **Vol. 7, Part 1**, 47, 617; control of, **Vol. 5, Part 1**, 571; discovery of, **Vol. 3, Part 1**, 20, 256 f.; discovery of Upper, **Vol. 6, Part 2**, 295; explorations, **Vol. 1, Part 2**, 251; **Vol. 2, Part 1**, 97; **Vol. 5, Part 2**, 223 f.; **Vol. 6, Part 2**, 526; **Vol. 7, Part 1**, 514; **Vol. 8, Part 2**, 457; **Vol. 9, Part 2**, 587; flood control, **Supp. 4**, 563; **Supp. 5**, 395; **Supp. 6**, 436; flood relief, **Supp. 7**, 360; free navigation of assured, **Vol. 8, Part 1**, 353 f.; jetties at mouth, construction of, **Vol. 4, Part 1**, 257; levees, improvement of, **Vol. 1, Part 2**, 351; **Vol. 3, Part 2**, 403; **Vol. 4, Part 2**, 353; life on, **Vol. 8, Part 2**, 242; navigation, **Vol. 1, Part 1**, 582; **Vol. 4, Part 2**, 67; **Vol. 8, Part 2**, 575; **Vol. 9, Part 1**, 134; paintings of, **Vol. 1, Part 1**, 582; **Vol. 9, Part 2**, 256; piracy on, **Vol. 6, Part 2**, 374; Spain's title, **Vol. 5, Part 2**, 7 f.; steam ferry, first on, **Vol. 3, Part 1**, 249; survey of, **Vol. 5, Part 1**, 371

Mississippi Valley: Catholic church, **Vol. 1, Part 2**, 350; geology of, **Vol. 2, Part 1**, 432; history of, **Vol. 7, Part 1**, 85; Methodism, **Vol. 5, Part 2**, 579; **Vol. 6, Part 2**, 610; **Vol. 10, Part 2**, 373; missions, **Vol. 1, Part 2**, 350; **Vol. 6, Part 1**, 403; settlements in, first, **Vol. 9, Part 2**, 587; yellow fever epidemics, **Vol. 1, Part 2**, 317

Mississippi Valley Historical Association, founding of, **Supp. 5**, 430

Mississippi Valley Historical Review, **Supp. 10**, 137

Missouri: abolition movement in, **Vol. 2, Part 1**, 105; banking, **Vol. 1, Part 2**, 409; black school, first, **Vol. 10, Part 1**, 66; "Bleeding Kansas," **Vol. 9, Part 2**, 13; "boodling" exposures, **Vol. 9, Part 2**, 88; capitol building, **Vol. 1, Part 2**, 409; Civil War period, **Vol. 5, Part 1**, 253; **Vol. 6, Part 1**, 55; commercial enterprises, **Vol. 3, Part 1**, 77; **Vol. 6, Part 1**, 291; **Vol. 7, Part 2**, 601; **Vol. 8, Part 1**, 218 f.; Constitutional Convention, **Vol. 6, Part 2**, 147; Democratic party, **Vol. 1, Part 2**, 411; **Supp. 9**, 756–57; Disciples of Christ, established, **Vol. 1, Part 1**, 207; education, **Vol. 1, Part 1**, 538; **Vol. 1, Part 2**, 409; **Vol. 3, Part 1**, 477 f.; **Vol. 8, Part 1**, 43, 421; **Vol. 8, Part 2**, 121 f; **Vol. 9, Part 1**, 577 f.; entomology, **Vol. 8, Part 1**, 609; Evangelical Seminary, **Vol. 8, Part 1**, 600; exploration, **Vol. 2, Part 2**, 143; Free Soil party, **Vol. 1, Part 2**, 332; **Vol. 2, Part 1**, 105; fur trade, **Vol. 4, Part 2**, 439; **Vol. 6, Part 1**, 5; **Vol. 8, Part 1**, 180 f.; **Vol. 10, Part 1**, 20 f.; geological survey, **Vol. 9, Part 2**, 232; German immigration, **Vol. 5, Part 2**, 496; governors, **Vol. 1, Part 2**, 49 f., 409 f.; **Vol. 2, Part 1**, 105 f.; **Vol. 2, Part 2**, 550; **Vol. 3, Part 2**, 489 f., 577 f.; **Vol. 4, Part 1**, 120 f.; **Vol. 4, Part 2**, 80 f., 146 f., 244 f.; **Vol. 5, Part 1**, 538; **Vol. 5, Part 2**, 382; **Vol. 6, Part 1**, 239 f., 331, 597; **Vol. 6, Part 2**, 147 f., 290 f., 628 f.; **Vol. 7, Part 2**, 530; **Vol. 8, Part 1**, 216 f.; **Vol. 9, Part 2**, 13 f., 88 f., 237 f.; **Supp. 4**, 416; **Supp. 9**, 756–57; **Supp. 10**, 181; guerrillas, **Vol. 8, Part 1**, 294 f.; historical society, **Supp. 1**, 709; history of, **Vol. 8, Part 1**, 218 f.; **Vol. 10, Part 1**, 638 f., 643; insane, care of, **Vol. 10, Part 1**, 643; journalism, **Vol. 8, Part 1**, 185; land surveys, **Vol. 25, Part 1**, 58; lead mines, **Vol. 1, Part 2**, 392; legal journals, **Vol. 9, Part 2**, 471; legal service, **Vol. 1, Part 2**, 375, 339; **Vol. 3, Part 1**, 365, 425; **Vol. 5, Part 1**, 253; **Vol. 6, Part 1**, 149; **Vol. 7, Part 1**, 381, 539; **Vol. 7, Part 2**, 379, 536; **Vol. 8, Part 1**, 180, 220; **Vol. 8, Part 2**, 503; **Vol. 10, Part 1**, 147, 457 f., 643; **Vol. 10, Part 2**, 440, 469 f.; Lutheran church, **Vol. 7, Part 2**, 574; **Vol. 10, Part 1**, 402 f.; missions, **Vol. 1, Part 1**, 277; **Vol. 8, Part 2**, 155; Mormons, conflicts with, **Vol. 1, Part 2**, 409; **Vol. 3, Part 1**, 365; **Vol. 8, Part 1**, 175; "Norton Constitution," **Vol. 7, Part 1**, 572; paleontology, **Vol. 6, Part 2**, 494; panic of 1893, **Vol. 9, Part 2**, 88; paper-money dispute, **Vol. 8, Part 1**, 43; Pendergast machine, **Supp. 3**, 596–97; **Supp. 9**, 756, 809–10, 811; philanthropy, **Vol. 7, Part 1**, 633; pioneer life, **Vol. 1, Part 2**, 442; **Vol. 3, Part 1**, 477 f.; **Vol. 6, Part 1**, 282; political history of, **Vol. 3, Part 1**, 425 f.; political service, **Vol. 1, Part 2**, 48, 211, 275, 332, 355, 392, 409, 411; **Vol. 2, Part 2**, 121, 550; **Vol. 3, Part 1**, 425; **Vol. 3, Part 2**, 468, 490, 577 f.; **Vol. 4,**

Part 1, 121, 549; **Vol. 4, Part 2**, 80, 147, 209, 244, 286, 394; **Vol. 5, Part 1**, 275, 538; **Vol. 5, Part 2**, 353, 382; **Vol. 6, Part 1**, 282, 485, 597; **Vol. 6, Part 2**, 147, 291, 628; **Vol. 7, Part 2**, 530, 536; **Vol. 8, Part 1**, 43, 185, 216, 218, 220, 260; **Vol. 9, Part 1**, 105; **Vol. 9, Part 2**, 13, 88, 254; **Vol. 10, Part 1**, 469 f., 638 f., 643; politics, **Supp. 3**, 621–23; **Supp. 4**, 355–56; **Supp. 5**, 113–14; **Supp. 6**, 387–88; **Supp. 7**, 104; **Supp. 9**, 511, 512, 756–57, 809–11; **Supp. 10**, 181; postal service, **Vol. 8, Part 1**, 188; printing, first book in, **Vol. 1, Part 2**, 50; public service, **Vol. 4, Part 2**, 80 f., 147, 343; **Vol. 6, Part 1**, 149; **Vol. 7, Part 1**, 572; **Vol. 8, Part 1**, 43; **Vol. 8, Part 2**, 121; **Vol. 9, Part 1**, 153; **Vol. 9, Part 2**, 634; **Vol. 10, Part 1**, 533, 643; **Vol. 10, Part 2**, 65; publicity, **Vol. 10, Part 1**, 533; religious service, **Vol. 6, Part 1**, 549; **Vol. 8, Part 1**, 120 f.; railroad development, **Vol. 8, Part 1**, 218 f.; Republican party, **Vol. 1, Part 2**, 333 f., 392, 411; **Vol. 2, Part 1**, 105 f.; seal, designing of, **Vol. 10, Part 1**, 643; secession, question of, **Vol. 3, Part 1**, 365, 495 f.; **Vol. 4, Part 1**, 121; **Vol. 5, Part 2**, 470; **Vol. 6, Part 1**, 535; **Vol. 8, Part 1**, 120 f., 185; **Vol. 9, Part 2**, 13; slavery issues, **Vol. 4, Part 2**, 244; **Vol. 8, Part 2**, 122; "Solemn Public Act," **Vol. 4, Part 1**, 231; statehood, **Supp. 1**, 54; transportation, **Vol. 10, Part 1**, 638 f.; Union, admission to, **Vol. 9, Part 2**, 437; Union party, **Vol. 1, Part 2**, 332; woman suffrage in, **Vol. 7, Part 1**, 29

Missouri (battleship), **Supp. 6**, 268

Missouri, one of first steam warships to cross Atlantic, **Vol. 8, Part 1**, 214 f.

Missouri Botanical Gardens, **Vol. 9, Part 1**, 38; founding of, **Supp. 3**, 775–76

Missouri Compromise: **Vol. 2, Part 2**, 176; **Vol. 6, Part 1**, 474; **Vol. 9, Part 2**, 437; Adams, J. Q., attitude toward, **Vol. 1, Part 1**, 86; adopted, **Vol. 2, Part 2**, 176; **Vol. 3, Part 2**, 41; **Vol. 5, Part 2**, 399; **Vol. 7, Part 1**, 91; drafting of, **Vol. 9, Part 1**, 412; Pacific extension of line to, **Vol. 3, Part 1**, 125; repeal agitation for, **Vol. 8, Part 1**, 220; repeal of, **Vol. 1, Part 1**, 403; **Vol. 1, Part 2**, 212; **Vol. 4, Part 2**, 30; **Vol. 2, Part 2**, 242, 176; **Vol. 6, Part 2**, 247

Missouri Farmer and Breeder, founding of, **Supp. 2**, 307

Missouri Farmers' Association, founding of, **Supp. 2**, 307

Missouri Fur Co., **Vol. 6, Part 1**, 291; **Vol. 7, Part 2**, 601

Missouri Gazette, **Vol. 2, Part 2**, 23

Missouri Historical and Philosphical Society, **Vol. 10, Part 1**, 643

Missouri Republican ("Old 1808"), **Vol. 5, Part 2**, 449

Missouri River: boatmen, **Vol. 5, Part 2**, 518; exploration, **Vol. 1, Part 2**, 482; **Vol. 2, Part 1**, 97; **Vol. 6, Part 1**, 354; flood control, **Supp. 6**, 508; fur trade, **Vol. 6, Part 1**, 291; navigation, **Vol. 5, Part 2**, 517 f.; trade, **Vol. 1, Part 2**, 306; **Vol. 5, Part 2**, 517 f.

Missouri Synod, **Supp. 4**, 540–41

Mr. Blandings Builds His Dream House, **Supp. 9**, 394

"Mr. Dooley" (fictional character), **Supp. 2**, 159

Mr. Lincoln's Army, **Supp. 10**, 108

"Mr. Magoo" (fictional character), **Supp. 10**, 352

"Mr. Peepers" (television program), **Supp. 9**, 204

Mrs. Wiggs of the Cabbage Patch, **Supp. 3**, 628

MIT. *See* Massachusetts Institute of Technology

Mitchel, John Purroy, references to, **Supp. 3**, 117, 605, 751; **Supp. 4**, 542; **Supp. 5**, 286; **Supp. 6**, 88

Mitchell, Billy: biography of, **Supp. 6**, 232; references to, **Supp. 3**, 218, 585; **Supp. 4**, 28, 903; **Supp. 5**, 669, 760–61; **Supp. 6**, 182; **Supp. 8**, 47, 185; **Supp. 9**, 228, 657, 746

Mitchell, John Ames, reference to, **Supp. 3**, 300

Mitchell, John H., reference to, **Supp. 4**, 844

Mitchell, John N., references to, **Supp. 10**, 545, 546

Mitchell, Joseph, reference to, **Supp. 7**, 473

Mitchell, Margaret, references to, **Supp. 7**, 682; **Supp. 8**, 368

Mitchell, S. Weir, references to, **Vol. 7, Part 1**, 321, 542; **Vol. 8, Part 2**, 560; **Supp. 3**, 435

Mitchell, Sidney Z., reference to, **Supp. 3**, 192

Mitchell, Wesley C., references to, **Supp. 3**, 177, 248; **Supp. 5**, 485; **Supp. 6**, 599; **Supp. 8**, 443

Mitchell, William D., reference to, **Supp. 7**, 361

Mitchell Motor Car Co., **Supp. 4**, 621

Mitochondria, **Supp. 6**, 53, 54, 295–96

Mix, Tom, reference to, **Supp. 4**, 734–35

Mixed Claims Commission, **Vol. 7, Part 2**, 217

Mob behavior, **Supp. 3**, 511

Mobile, Ala.: capture of, **Vol. 2, Part 1**, 207, 469; **Vol. 3, Part 2**, 289; **Vol. 9, Part 1**, 95, 556; Catholic church, **Vol. 8, Part 1**, 108 f.; envisioned as commercial center of South, **Vol. 3, Part 1**, 178; founding of, **Vol. 1, Part 2**, 251

Mobile, as art form, **Supp. 10**, 90, 91

Mobile Act, passage of, **Vol. 7, Part 2**, 613

Mobile Bay, battle of, **Vol. 3, Part 2**, 289; **Vol. 5, Part 2**, 221

Mobile Institute, **Vol. 7, Part 2**, 629

Mobsters. See Organized crime

Moby Dick, evaluation of, **Vol. 6, Part 2**, 523

"Mockin' Bird Hill" (song), **Supp. 10**, 251–52

Model A car, **Supp. 3**, 284; **Supp. 4**, 301, 302, 457; **Supp. 8**, 610

Model communities: Disney World, **Supp. 8**, 131; Forest Hills Gardens (New York City), **Supp. 6**, 26; Free Acres (Summit, N.J.), **Supp. 2**, 272; Goodyear Heights Allotment Co. (Akron, Ohio), **Supp. 5**, 618; Hershey, Pa., **Supp. 3**, 358; Kohler Village (Sheboygan, Wis.), **Supp. 2**, 366; planning, **Supp. 2**, 738; Southern California, **Supp. 5**, 309. *See also* Utopian communities

Modeling; **Supp. 7**, 140–41; fashion, **Supp. 10**, 842–43; male, **Supp. 9**, 52

Modeling, wax, **Vol. 8, Part 1**, 158 f.; **Vol. 10, Part 2**, 562

Model T car, **Supp. 3**, 283, 284; **Supp. 4**, 295–97, 300–303, 456, 457; **Supp. 8**, 609–10

Modern dance, **Supp. 5**, 129; **Supp. 8**, 620–21, 643–44; **Supp. 9**, 494, 495

Modern History, **Supp. 7**, 330

Modern History of Warships, **Supp. 4**, 399

Modern Jazz Quartet, **Supp. 9**, 317

Modern Language Association of America, **Vol. 3, Part 2**, 93; **Vol. 4, Part 2**, 357; **Vol. 9, Part 2**, 423; **Supp. 3**, 22, 109

Modern Language News, **Supp. 5**, 409

Modern Language Notes, **Vol. 9, Part 2**, 571

Modern Library. *See* Random House

Modern Maturity, founding of, **Supp. 8**, 10

Modern Quarterly, founding of, **Supp. 2**, 89

Modern Times, **Supp. 10**, 115, 117

Modigliani, Amadeo, reference to, **Supp. 6**, 194

Modjeska, Helena, references to, **Vol. 1, Part 1**, 659, 660; **Supp. 3**, 713

Modoc Indian campaign (1873), **Vol. 2, Part 1**, 469; **Vol. 4, Part 1**, 287

Modotti, Tina, reference to, **Supp. 6**, 685

Moe, Henry Allen, reference to, **Supp. 3**, 321–22

Moguy, Leonide, reference to, **Supp. 9**, 34

Mohawk & Hudson Railway, **Vol. 5, Part 2**, 59

Mohawk Drama Festival, **Supp. 3**, 287

Mohawk Indians, **Vol. 1, Part 2**, 604; **Vol. 4, Part 2**, 370; Bible translation for, **Vol. 4, Part 1**, 8; English affiliation with, **Vol. 4, Part 2**, 532; ministry to, **Vol. 7, Part 1**, 646 f.

Mohawk Valley: history of, **Vol. 1, Part 2**, 604; land developments, **Vol. 3, Part 1**, 465 f.
Mohr, Otto L. reference to, **Supp. 3**, 540
Moisseiff, Leon S., reference to, **Supp. 6**, 594
Molasses Act, **Vol. 7, Part 2**, 283
Molders' Union. *See* International Molders and Foundry Workers Union
Molecules: biology, **Supp. 6**, 283; **Supp. 8**, 450; dipole moment measurement, **Supp. 8**, 122–23; Franck-Condon principle, **Supp. 7**, 259; interactions, **Supp. 6**, 346; macromolecules, **Supp. 6**, 346; physics, **Supp. 8**, 482, 627–28; valence and electromc structure of, **Supp. 4**, 488–89
Moley, Raymond, references to, **Supp. 3**, 647; **Supp. 6**, 23–24, 34, 161
Moline Plow Co., **Supp. 3**, 399
Molineaux, Tom, first black boxing champion in U.S., **Supp. 9**, 493
Molino Del Ray, battle of, **Vol. 8, Part 2**, 509
Mollusks: collecting of, **Vol. 6, Part 1**, 71; researches in, **Vol. 1, Part 2**, 357; **Vol. 1, Part 2**, 70; **Vol. 9, Part 1**, 585; **Supp. 1**, 661
Mommie Dearest, **Supp. 10**, 158
Mondrian, Piet, references to, **Supp. 7**, 183–84; **Supp. 10**, 90
Monel (alloy), **Supp. 5**, 652–53
Monetary system: circular flow, **Supp. 4**, 307; compensated dollar standard, **Supp. 4**, 274; easy-money policy, **Supp. 8**, 446; economic theory relationship to, **Supp. 4**, 585–88; federal regulation advocacy, **Supp. 4**, 748; free-silver movement, **Supp. 2**, 289; gold standard advocacy, **Supp. 5**, 651; greenback controversy, **Supp. 4**, 585; managed currency theory, **Supp. 2**, 696; non-metal-based advocacy, **Supp. 5**, 138–40; quantity theory, **Supp. 3**, 413–14; quantity theory, criticism of, **Supp. 1**, 487–88; removal from gold standard, **Supp. 3**, 649, 652, 839; supply and prices, **Supp. 8**, 79; writings on, **Supp. 2**, 577. *See also* Coinage; Gold standard; Silver
Money: books on, **Vol. 1, Part 1**, 510; "sound," **Vol. 3, Part 2**, 252; study of, **Vol. 3, Part 1**, 226; **Vol. 6, Part 1**, 273; **Vol. 9, Part 2**, 323
Money, **Supp. 8**, 79
Mongolia, paleontology in, **Supp. 3**, 316; **Supp. 6**, 18
Monism, **Vol. 7, Part 1**, 95–96
Monitor: battle with *Merrimac*, **Vol. 2, Part 1**, 207; **Vol. 3, Part 1**, 529 f.; **Vol. 3, Part 2**, 173, 532, 568; **Vol. 4, Part 1**, 366, 574; **Vol. 5, Part 1**, 343; **Vol. 5, Part 2**, 164, 278; **Vol. 6, Part 2**, 225; **Vol. 9, Part 2**, 554, 638; **Vol. 10, Part 1**, 630; **Vol. 10, Part 2**, 531; building of, **Vol. 1, Part 1**, 21; **Vol. 3, Part 1**, 211; **Vol. 4, Part 2**, 9; **Vol. 8, Part 2**, 200; **Vol. 9, Part 1**, 310; **Vol. 10, Part 2**, 400; report on, **Vol. 5, Part 2**, 14
"Monitor's letters" (1768), **Vol. 6, Part 1**, 96
Monkey trial. *See* Evolutionism; Scopes trial
Monmouth, battle of, **Vol. 1, Part 1**, 177; **Vol. 2, Part 1**, 315; **Vol. 2, Part 2**, 366; **Vol. 1, Part 2**, 570; **Vol. 5, Part 2**, 476, 537; **Vol. 6, Part 1**, 100; **Vol. 9, Part 1**, 603; **Vol. 10, Part 1**, 518, 564
Monmouth College, **Vol. 10, Part 1**, 372 f.
Monnier, Adrienne, reference to, **Supp. 7**, 40
Monocacy, battle of, **Vol. 3, Part 1**, 598; **Vol. 10, Part 1**, 375
Monologues, **Vol. 8, Part 2**, 249; **Supp. 6**, 174
Monometalism, **Vol. 9, Part 2**, 636
Monophone, invention of, **Vol. 9, Part 1**, 490
Monopolies: automobile industry suit, **Supp. 4**, 295–96; base pricing, **Supp. 4**, 268; economic theory, **Supp. 8**, 82; laws regulating, **Vol. 1, Part 2**, 428; telephone, **Supp. 8**, 211–12. *See also* Antitrust actions
Monopoly (game), **Supp. 9**, 601, 602
Monotype, invention of, **Vol. 5, Part 2**, 611
Monroe, Harriet, references to, **Supp. 8**, 563; **Supp. 10**, 869
Monroe, James, reference to, **Vol. 5, Part 1**, 529 f.; **Vol. 6, Part 2**, 192; **Vol. 7, Part 1**, 416, 534; **Vol. 9, Part 2**, 570
Monroe, Marilyn, reference to, **Supp. 7**, 668
Monroe, Paul, reference to, **Supp. 3**, 677
Monroe Doctrine: **Vol. 1, Part 1**, 86–87; **Vol. 3, Part 2**, 507; **Vol. 7, Part 1**, 90, 92; **Vol. 8, Part 1**, 37–38; **Vol. 8, Part 2**, 139, 232; Buchanan, J., and, **Vol. 2, Part 1**, 210, fundamental character, first change in, **Vol. 8, Part 1**, 34 f.; origins, **Vol. 6, Part 2**, 192; Roosevelt, T. R., and, **Vol. 8, Part 2**, 139 f.
Monsky, Henry, reference to, **Supp. 4**, 283
Montallegro font, **Supp. 3**, 785
Montana: banditry, **Vol. 8, Part 1**, 15 f.; constitution of, **Vol. 1, Part 2**, 605; copper, effect of, on state history, **Vol. 3, Part 1**, 45; copper mining, **Vol. 3, Part 1**, 45; **Vol. 4, Part 2**, 403, 507; **Vol. 8, Part 2**, 263; governor of, **Vol. 9, Part 2**, 589 f.; history of, **Vol. 1, Part 2**, 538; Indians, **Vol. 8, Part 1**, 135 f., 394; irrigation, **Vol. 4, Part 2**, 403; legal service, **Vol. 1, Part 2**, 605; **Vol. 5, Part 1**, 243; **Vol. 8, Part 2**, 336; **Supp. 10**, 529, 530; map of first, **Vol. 3, Part 1**, 207; mineral resources survey, **Supp. 1**, 176; mining laws, **Vol. 9, Part 2**, 589; missions, **Vol. 2, Part 1**, 67; **Vol. 8, Part 1**, 394; paleontology, **Vol. 10, Part 2**, 310; pioneering, **Vol. 4, Part 1**, 256; **Vol. 4, Part 2**, 193; **Vol. 6, Part 2**, 534; political parties, early, **Vol. 8, Part 2**, 337; political service, **Vol. 1, Part 2**, 605; **Vol. 2, Part 2**, 144; **Vol. 4, Part 2**, 403; **Vol. 6, Part 2**, 199; **Vol. 8, Part 1**, 135; **Vol. 4, Part 2**, 403; **Vol. 9, Part 2**, 589; **Vol. 10, Part 1**, 393 f.; politics, **Supp. 7**, 561–62; **Supp. 9**, 640, 641; **Supp. 10**, 529; public service, **Vol. 3, Part 2**, 20; **Vol. 4, Part 1**, 256; Republican party, **Vol. 8, Part 2**, 337; rivers, exploration of, **Vol. 6, Part 2**, 299; silver mining, **Vol. 4, Part 2**, 403; statehood, admission to, **Vol. 2, Part 1**, 544; **Vol. 2, Part 2**, 145; **Vol. 9, Part 2**, 589; writings on, **Supp. 5**, 320–21
Montana Power Co., **Vol. 8, Part 2**, 263
Montana State University, **Supp. 1**, 176
Montclair Art Gallery and Museum, **Vol. 3, Part 2**, 214
Monterey, Calif., **Vol. 8, Part 1**, 109 f.
Monterey, Mexico, battle of, **Vol. 8, Part 1**, 316, 625; **Vol. 9, Part 2**, 351; **Vol. 10, Part 1**, 83; **Vol. 10, Part 2**, 537
Montessori, Maria, reference to, **Supp. 6**, 90, 202
Montessori methods, **Vol. 9, Part 1**, 349
Montgomerie Charter, **Vol. 7, Part 1**, 363
Montgomery, Alan, reference to, **Supp. 3**, 37
Montgomery, Bernard, reference to, **Supp. 8**, 155
Montgomery, Bob, reference to, **Supp. 6**, 301
Montgomery, Helen Barrett, references to, **Supp. 4**, 647, 648
Montgomery, Ala.: civil rights movement in, **Supp. 8**, 333–34; civil rights opposition, **Supp. 9**, 68; first public library building, **Vol. 7, Part 1**, 348
Montgomery Advertiser, editorial leadership, **Supp. 1**, 347
Montgomery Ward and Co., **Supp. 6**, 27–28; **Supp. 8**, 35, 705; **Supp. 10**, 163
Monthly Anthology, **Vol. 5, Part 2**, 431
Monticello (Va.), restoration of, **Supp. 5**, 388
Montreal, expedition against, **Vol. 5, Part 2**, 126
Monumental City (steamship), **Vol. 4, Part 1**, 164
Monuments: architecture of, **Vol. 3, Part 1**, 420; **Vol. 4, Part 2**, 389; historical, **Vol. 8, Part 1**, 368 f.; military, **Vol. 8, Part 2**, 107
Moody, Dan, reference to, **Supp. 4**, 776
Moody, Dwight L.: biography of, **Supp. 6**, 195;

references to, **Vol. 1, Part 2**, 376; **Vol. 8, Part 1**, 512 f.; **Vol. 8, Part 2**, 352; **Vol. 10, Part 1**, 606 f.
Moody, Helen Wills, references to, **Supp. 6**, 425, 426; **Supp. 9**, 868
Moody, William Vaughn, references to, **Supp. 6**, 19, 391
Moody Memorial Church, **Supp. 5**, 346
Moody's Magazine, **Supp. 6**, 458
Moon, Parker T., reference to, **Supp. 7**, 330
Moon: motions of, **Vol. 7, Part 1**, 453 f.; **Vol. 9, Part 2**, 50; **Supp. 2**, 69; space program, **Supp. 7**, 424, 429; topography, writings on, **Supp. 4**, 766
Mooney, Edward, reference to, **Supp. 8**, 613
Mooney, Rena, reference to, **Supp. 3**, 532
Mooney, Thomas J. (Tom), references to, **Supp. 5**, 499; **Supp. 7**, 248, 455; **Supp. 8**, 586
"Moon Hoax," **Vol. 3, Part 1**, 155; **Vol. 6, Part 1**, 339
Moon Is Blue, The, **Supp. 6**, 288, 289; **Supp. 7**, 71
Moore, A. Harry, reference to, **Supp. 6**, 265
Moore, Aaron, reference to, **Supp. 5**, 647–48
Moore, Douglas, reference to, **Supp. 3**, 57
Moore, Eliakim, reference to, **Supp. 3**, 86
Moore, Garry, reference to, **Supp. 10**, 196
Moore, Gordon B., reference to, **Supp. 6**, 671
Moore, Harry T., reference to, **Supp. 9**, 840
Moore, Marianne: influence on Bishop's poetry, **Supp. 10**, 44; reference to, **Supp. 5**, 660
Moore, Mary Tyler, reference to, **Supp. 9**, 380
Moore, Oscar, reference to, **Supp. 7**, 131
Moore, Underhill, reference to, **Supp. 3**, 186
Moore, William, trial of, **Vol. 9, Part 1**, 355
Moore's Creek, battle of, **Vol. 2, Part 1**, 571
Moorland-Spingarn Research Center (Howard University), black literature collection, **Supp. 9**, 750
Moos, Malcolm, reference to, **Supp. 8**, 159
Moose, Loyal Order of. *See* Loyal Order of Moose
Moot, founding of, **Vol. 9, Part 1**, 357
Moral Decision, The, **Supp. 7**, 99
Moral development, **Supp. 4**, 767
Moral optimism, **Supp. 4**, 525–26
Moral Re-Armament movement, **Supp. 7**, 89
Moran, James J., reference to, **Supp. 7**, 585
Moran Towing and Transportation Co., **Supp. 7**, 552–53
Moravian church: **Vol. 1, Part 1**, 312; **Vol. 1, Part 2**, 402; **Vol. 2, Part 2**, 214; **Vol. 3, Part 2**, 190; **Vol. 4, Part 2**, 31; **Vol. 5, Part 1**, 569; **Vol. 6, Part 1**, 198 f., 421; **Vol. 8, Part 1**, 473 f.; **Vol. 8, Part 2**, 130, 465, 482 f.; **Vol. 9, Part 1**, 109, 428; **Vol. 10, Part 2**, 658; formation of, **Vol. 7, Part 1**, 529; history of, **Vol. 6, Part 1**, 199; **Vol. 8, Part 2**, 482; missions, **Vol. 2, Part 1**, 441; **Vol. 4, Part 2**, 495 f.; **Vol. 5, Part 2**, 248; **Vol. 8, Part 1**, 113 f.; **Vol. 10, Part 2**, 646; writings on, **Vol. 6, Part 1**, 421; **Vol. 8, Part 1**, 474; **Vol. 8, Part 2**, 130
Moravian College, **Vol. 5, Part 1**, 569; **Vol. 8, Part 2**, 456
More, Paul Elmer, references to, **Supp. 1**, 36; **Supp. 7**, 624
Morehead, John M., reference to, **Vol. 8, Part 2**, 383
Morehead Foundation, **Supp. 7**, 554
Morehouse, D. W., reference to, **Supp. 7**, 572
Morehouse College, administration, **Supp. 2**, 315
Morelli, Giovanni, reference to, **Supp. 6**, 56
"Morey" letter, libel indictment based on, **Vol. 8, Part 1**, 118 f.
Morgan, Arthur E., references to, **Supp. 4**, 601, 602
Morgan, Dennis, reference to, **Supp. 7**, 107
Morgan, Edwin B., reference to, **Vol. 10, Part 1**, 639 f.
Morgan, Helen, reference to, **Supp. 8**, 546
Morgan, Henry S., reference to, **Supp. 7**, 715
Morgan, J. Pierpont, references to, **Vol. 1, Part 1**, 483; **Vol. 5, Part 1**, 38; **Vol. 9, Part 1**, 598 f.; **Supp. 3**, 321, 375, 783, 785; **Supp. 4**, 345; **Supp. 5**, 148, 505, 550; **Supp. 6**, 622
Morgan, J. Pierpont, Jr., reference to, **Supp. 9**, 606–7
Morgan, J. P., & Co.: railroad investment banking, **Supp. 10**, 203; Senate investigation of, **Supp. 9**, 606–7
Morgan, Thomas Hunt, references to, **Supp. 2**, 60; **Supp. 5**, 367, 368; **Supp. 8**, 448, 499
Morgan, J. P., & Co.: **Vol. 4, Part 2**, 372; **Vol. 7, Part 1**, 234; **Vol. 9, Part 1**, 453; **Supp. 4**, 320, 469–70, 682; **Supp. 6**, 376–77; **Supp. 7**, 715, 782–83; international loans, **Supp. 3**, 537–38; oil interests, **Supp. 3**, 505; utility holding companies, **Supp. 3**, 138
Morgan, Stanley, and Co., **Supp. 7**, 715
Morgan Guaranty Trust Co. of New York, **Supp. 7**, 783
"Morgan Horse," **Vol. 7, Part 1**, 183
Morgan Library (New York City), **Supp. 3**, 375; **Supp. 4**, 345
Morgan's raid (U.S. Civil War), **Vol. 5, Part 1**, 96; **Vol. 9, Part 2**, 594
Morgenstern, Oskar, reference to, **Supp. 6**, 656
Morgenthau, Henry, Jr., references to, **Supp. 2**, 501; **Supp. 3**, 647, 653, 656; **Supp. 4**, 604; **Supp. 6**, 124, 229, 230; **Supp. 8**, 445; **Supp. 9**, 661; **Supp. 10**, 205
Morgenthau, Henry, Co., founding of, **Supp. 4**, 603
Morgenthau Plan, **Supp. 5**, 335
Morison, George S., reference to, **Supp. 3**, 367
Morison, Samuel Eliot, references to, **Supp. 6**, 268, 341; **Supp. 10**, 371
Morley, Christopher, reference to, **Supp. 5**, 439; **Supp. 7**, 103
Morley, Edward W., reference to, **Supp. 3**, 523–24
Mormon church: **Vol. 1, Part 1**, 446; **Vol. 1, Part 2**, 601, 611; **Vol. 3, Part 2**, 521; **Vol. 4, Part 1**, 258; **Vol. 5, Part 2**, 258, 377; **Vol. 6, Part 1**, 115; **Vol. 8, Part 2**, 3 f.; **Vol. 9, Part 1**, 311 f., 313, 384; **Vol. 9, Part 2**, 123 f., 333; **Vol. 10, Part 2**, 621; administration, **Supp. 5**, 640; archives, **Supp. 9**, 737; *Book of Mormon*, **Vol. 8, Part 1**, 600 f.; **Vol. 9, Part 1**, 310 f.; **Vol. 9, Part 2**, 334; church-state separation issues, **Supp. 3**, 727; colonization, **Vol. 6, Part 1**, 115; **Vol. 8, Part 1**, 175; **Vol. 9, Part 1**, 23; **Vol. 10, Part 2**, 499, 621; disturbances of 1857, **Vol. 2, Part 1**, 33, 290; **Vol. 2, Part 2**, 593; **Vol. 3, Part 1**, 256; **Vol. 5, Part 2**, 136; **Vol. 6, Part 1**, 134, 258; **Vol. 6, Part 2**, 274; **Vol. 8, Part 1**, 90; **Vol. 8, Part 2**, 510; **Vol. 9, Part 1**, 247, 331; **Vol. 10, Part 2**, 560, 622; government, U.S., conflict with, **Vol. 10, Part 2**, 622, 644; historian, **Supp. 9**, 737; history of, **Vol. 6, Part 1**, 283; **Vol. 8, Part 1**, 600 f.; hymns, **Vol. 9, Part 1**, 385; Kansas, **Vol. 4, Part 2**, 380; leadership, **Supp. 1**, 448, 607; **Supp. 7**, 126; **Supp. 8**, 408–9; *Lectures on Faith*, authorship of, **Vol. 8, Part 1**, 601; Michigan, opposition of, **Vol. 9, Part 2**, 124; military organization of, **Vol. 6, Part 1**, 115; missionary work, **Vol. 4, Part 1**, 337; **Vol. 8, Part 2**, 4; **Supp. 1**, 607; **Supp. 5**, 681; Missouri, conflict with, **Vol. 1, Part 2**, 409; **Vol. 3, Part 1**, 365; **Vol. 8, Part 1**, 175; monuments, **Supp. 6**, 720; *Mormonism Unveiled*, **Vol. 6, Part 1**, 115; persecutions, **Vol. 2, Part 1**, 474; polygamy, **Vol. 4, Part 2**, 334; **Vol. 6, Part 1**, 115; **Vol. 8, Part 1**, 341 f., 601; **Vol. 9, Part 2**, 334; presidency of, **Vol. 9, Part 1**, 386; **Vol. 9, Part 2**, 333 f.; **Supp. 9**, 736–37; prophet, **Vol. 9, Part 1**, 310 f.; **Supp. 9**, 737; psychological aspects of, **Vol. 8, Part 1**, 610; publications, **Vol. 8, Part 2**, 4; Salt Lake City, building of, **Vol. 10, Part 2**, 621 f.; spread of, **Vol. 10, Part 2**, 152, 499; theology, **Supp. 9**, 737; "Twelve Apostles," **Vol. 9, Part 2**, 333 f.; writings on, **Vol. 9, Part 2**, 124 f.; **Vol. 10, Part 1**, 68;

Vol. 10, Part 2, 610; Young, Brigham, **Vol. 10, Part 2**, 620 f.
Morning Courier and New York Enquirer, first issue of, **Vol. 1, Part 2**, 196
Morocco, diplomatic relations with, **Vol. 4, Part 2**, 50
"Moron," term coined, **Supp. 6**, 240
Morphine, addiction studies, **Supp. 3**, 242
Morrill Tariff Act, **Vol. 7, Part 1**, 198; **Vol. 7, Part 2**, 206
Morris, George Pope, reference to, **Vol. 7, Part 1**, 608
Morris, George Sylvester, reference to, **Supp. 5**, 170
Morris, Newbold, reference to, **Supp. 8**, 406
Morris, Robert: biography of, **Supp. 2**, 495; reference to, **Vol. 7, Part 1**, 142, 430, 504
Morris, Robert Hunter, reference to, **Vol. 7, Part 1**, 637
Morris, William, references to, **Vol. 5, Part 1**, 323; **Supp. 4**, 177
Morrisania, **Vol. 7, Part 1**, 213 f., 218 f., 224 f.
Morris Brown College, **Vol. 4, Part 1**, 96
Morris Canal, **Vol. 8, Part 1**, 506
Morrison, Charles Clayton, references to, **Supp. 3**, 457; **Supp. 6**, 315
Morris Plan Co., **Vol. 9, Part 2**, 614
Morristown, N.J., **Vol. 8, Part 1**, 369
Morrow, Dwight W., references to, **Supp. 3**, 218; **Supp. 6**, 182, 187
Morrow, Edwin, reference to, **Supp. 6**, 591
Morse, Barry, reference to, **Supp. 10**, 380
Morse, Samuel F. B., references to, **Vol. 5, Part 1**, 412, 536; **Vol. 5, Part 2**, 326; **Vol. 7, Part 1**, 248 f.; **Vol. 8, Part 1**, 49 f.; **Vol. 9, Part 2**, 611
Morse, Wayne, references to, **Supp. 6**, 618; **Supp. 8**, 395–96, 590; **Supp. 9**, 347
Mortality, infant. *See* Infant mortality
Mortgages, farm, **Supp. 4**, 406, 480
Mortimer, Lee, reference to, **Supp. 5**, 406
Mortimer, Stanley Grafton, Jr., reference to, **Supp. 10**, 616
Morton, Jelly Roll, reference to, **Supp. 9**, 687
Morton, Julius Sterling, reference to, **Supp. 3**, 209
Morton, Levi P., biography of, **Supp. 6**, 410
Morton, Oliver P., reference to, **Vol. 5, Part 1**, 241
Morton, Samuel George, reference to, **Vol. 7, Part 1**, 597
Morton, W. T. G., references to, **Vol. 5, Part 1**, 537; **Vol. 6, Part 1**, 375; **Vol. 10, Part 1**, 640 f.
Mosaics, **Supp. 1**, 247; **Supp. 4**, 890–91; **Supp. 7**, 522–23
Mosby, J. S., prosecution of, **Vol. 8, Part 2**, 29
Moscone, George, references to, **Supp. 10**, 536, 537
Moscow Art Theatre, **Supp. 3**, 297
Moscow Daily News, founding of, **Supp. 8**, 635
Moscow purge trials (1930s), **Supp. 6**, 184
Moses, George, reference to, **Supp. 3**, 559
Moses, Robert, references to, **Supp. 3**, 718; **Supp. 7**, 586; **Supp. 10**, 788
Moses Brown School, **Vol. 2, Part 1**, 150; **Vol. 4, Part 2**, 49
Moskowitz, Belle, references to, **Supp. 3**, 645, 718, 719
Mosler, Thomas Bird: reference to, **Vol. 5, Part 1**, 162
Mosley, Oswald, reference to, **Supp. 9**, 889
"Mosquito fleet," Confederate navy, **Vol. 5, Part 1**, 152; **Vol. 9, Part 2**, 394
Mosquitos: study of, **Vol. 3, Part 1**, 413, 578 f.; **Vol. 3, Part 2**, 388; **Vol. 5, Part 2**, 381, 448; **Vol. 9, Part 1**, 298; **Supp. 4**, 400; as virus host, **Supp. 5**, 383; yellow fever and, **Supp. 3**, 736; **Supp. 6**, 434
Moss, use of, for surgical dressings, **Vol. 9, Part 1**, 276
Most Happy Fella, The, **Supp. 8**, 386; **Supp. 9**, 850
Moten, Bennie, references to, **Supp. 9**, 687, 847
Mother Angela, reference to, **Vol. 9, Part 1**, 400
Mother Earth, founding of, **Supp. 2**, 247
Motherhood: maternal childbirth death prevention, **Supp. 3**, 222–23; unwed, services for, **Supp. 3**, 221. *See also* Obstetrics
"Mother Macree," **Vol. 7, Part 2**, 9
Mother's Day, **Supp. 5**, 290
Mother's Magazine, **Vol. 10, Part 2**, 171
Motherwell, Robert, reference to, **Supp. 6**, 512
Motion Picture Association of America, **Supp. 7**, 397
Motion Picture Magazine, **Supp. 3**, 76
Motion Picture Producers and Distributors of America, Inc., **Supp. 5**, 281–82
Motion pictures: **Vol. 3, Part 2**, 333; **Vol. 5, Part 1**, 78; **Vol. 6, Part 1**, 355 f.; **Vol. 7, Part 2**, 463; **Vol. 8, Part 2**, 16; **Vol. 9, Part 1**, 164; Academy of Motion Picture Arts and Sciences, **Supp. 7**, 32; **Supp. 8**, 678; action-adventure films, **Supp. 9**, 577; **Supp. 10**, 318; African exploration, **Supp. 5**, 371; agents, **Supp. 9**, 375; **Supp. 10**, 513, 515; animated cartoons, **Supp. 8**, 129–30; **Supp. 9**, 237, 797–98; **Supp. 10**, 351–53, 441, 813; animated puppets, **Supp. 10**, 614–15; anthropological study of, **Supp. 8**, 510; arcades, **Supp. 10**, 871; B films, **Supp. 8**, 712; **Supp. 10**, 822; biographical, **Supp. 10**, 223; black films, **Supp. 5**, 490; **Supp. 10**, 7–8; blacklisting, **Supp. 5**, 238, 419; **Supp. 7**, 315, 397; **Supp. 8**, 492, 550–51, 704; **Supp. 10**, 437, 793; blacks in, **Supp. 10**, 95; black stereotypes in, **Supp. 4**, 695; **Supp. 5**, 451; **Supp. 7**, 163; **Supp. 10**, 576, 662; boom microphone first used, **Supp. 10**, 11; boxing films, **Supp. 9**, 692, 697; box-office draw, top female, **Supp. 9**, 377; censorship, **Supp. 4**, 535; **Supp. 5**, 281–82, 677; **Supp. 6**, 288–89; **Supp. 7**, 71; **Supp. 10**, 324; chase scenes, **Supp. 10**, 501; China, **Supp. 8**, 495; choreography, **Supp. 10**, 34; CinemaScope, **Supp. 9**, 733; **Supp. 10**, 865; cinematography, **Supp. 3**, 73–74, **Supp. 10**, 347–48; Cinerama, **Supp. 5**, 721–22; close-up technique, **Supp. 3**, 73, 76; color, use of, **Vol. 9, Part 2**, 647; color film, **Supp. 2**, 338; **Supp. 7**, 406–8; comedy, **Supp. 1**, 636–37; **Supp. 4**, 270; **Supp. 6**, 13, 128, 276, 573, 609; **Supp. 7**, 107, 515–16; **Supp. 9**, 1–2, 77, 489, 514, 879, 880; **Supp. 10**, 115–17, 195, 597–98; 631, 705, 713, 829–30; Communist party members, **Supp. 9**, 602–3; **Supp. 10**, 436, 437; composers, **Supp. 6**, 352; **Supp. 9**, 492; costume design, **Supp. 5**, 386; **Supp. 6**, 9; **Supp. 7**, 591–92; **Supp. 9**, 587–88; counterculture, **Supp. 5**, 162–63; crime dramas, **Supp. 10**, 431; crime films, **Supp. 9**, 189–90, 480; criticism, **Supp. 5**, 12, 623; **Supp. 8**, 491, 584–85; Dead End Kids, **Supp. 8**, 220–21; dialogue writing, **Supp. 5**, 464; direction, **Supp. 6**, 76–77, 609–10, 657–58; **Supp. 7**, 65–66, 87, 160, 177–78, 240–41; **Supp. 8**, 671–72; **Supp. 9**, 766–68, 856; **Supp. 10**, 11–12, 34–35, 115–17, 318–19, 339–40, 387, 430–31, 615, 733–34, 811; directorial innovations, **Supp. 4**, 349–51; dissolve technique, **Supp. 3**, 607; distribution, **Supp. 7**, 692–93; *Dr. Kildare* series, **Supp. 5**, 44; documentaries, **Supp. 5**, 225–26; **Supp. 7**, 241; **Supp. 9**, 286; **Supp. 10**, 200–201, 319, 766; earliest talking, **Supp. 7**, 176–77; early developments in, **Supp. 3**, 75–76; early technology, **Supp. 1**, 121; Edison patents, **Supp. 1**, 280–81; edited for television, **Supp. 9**, 768; editing, **Supp. 10**, 11; exhibition business, **Supp. 9**, 62; **Supp. 10**, 812, 871; film noir, **Supp. 9**, 692; **Supp. 10**, 89, 387, 811; first Academy Award for best film, **Supp. 9**, 856; first all-black musical, **Supp. 10**, 576; first black Academy Award winner, **Supp. 5**, 451; first black star, **Supp. 7**, 44; first book contract movie rights clause, **Supp. 4**, 60; first fan magazine, **Supp. 3**, 76; first five-reel American film, **Supp. 3**, 607; first indoor lighted movie, **Supp. 3**, 73; first sound, **Supp. 4**, 440; **Supp. 5**, 121, 630;

Supp. 8, 459–60; **Supp. 10**, 812; first use of music under dialogue, **Supp. 9**, 762; first woman member of Directors Guild, **Supp. 10**, 12; French New Wave, **Supp. 10**, 725; gangster films, **Supp. 6**, 668; **Supp. 9**, 665, 666; **Supp. 10**, 318, 655, 811; German, **Supp. 10**, 430–31; German, psychological study of, **Supp. 8**, 346; Goldwyn as "voice of the industry," **Supp. 9**, 324; gossip columns about, **Supp. 8**, 282; **Supp. 9**, 603–4; Hearst interests, **Supp. 5**, 286–87; highest-paid woman, **Supp. 9**, 332; historical studies of, **Supp. 8**, 346–47; Hitchcock films, **Supp. 9**, 158; Hollywood social scene, **Supp. 9**, 673–74; horror films, **Supp. 6**, 395; **Supp. 8**, 312; **Supp. 9**, 169, 819, 820; indecency charges, **Supp. 10**, 829–30; industry leaders, **Supp. 6**, 118–19, 158–60, 368–69, 439–50, 667–68; industry standardization, **Supp. 1**, 279; "It" girl, **Supp. 8**, 678; **Supp. 9**, 538; loyalty investigation, **Supp. 8**, 648–49; **Supp. 9**, 539, 602–3, 666; **Supp. 10**, 63, 352, 720–21, 793, 823; makeup, **Supp. 1**, 165; martial arts films, **Supp. 9**, 486–87; movie themes, **Supp. 10**, 527; musicals, **Supp. 4**, 226; **Supp. 6**, 89, 273, 274, 663; **Supp. 7**, 178, 628–29; **Supp. 8**, 204–5; **Supp. 9**, 215–16, 280, 291–92, 331, 332–33; **Supp. 10**, 34, 35, 113, 165–66, 301, 318, 323, 373, 561, 649, 651, 694, 775, 802; musical scores, **Supp. 8**, 251–52, 688–89; **Supp. 9**, 382–83, 761–62; **Supp. 10**, 231, 239, 317, 784; musical Westerns, **Supp. 10**, 593; music direction, **Supp. 5**, 630; **Supp. 8**, 465–66, 688–89; newsreels, **Supp. 5**, 230, 286; **Supp. 6**, 291; **Supp. 8**, 393–94; **Supp. 9**, 765; operettas, **Supp. 7**, 499; **Supp. 8**, 151; Oriental roles, **Supp. 7**, 802; "patent war," **Supp. 4**, 734; penny arcades, **Supp. 5**, 726; pioneers in, **Supp. 4**, 734–35; **Supp. 9**, 62, 322–23; **Supp. 10**, 871–73; production, **Supp. 2**, 368, 657; **Supp. 5**, 229–30; **Supp. 6**, 431; **Supp. 7**, 681–82; **Supp. 8**, 677–78; **Supp. 9**, 375–76; **Supp. 10**, 355, 356, 387, 615, 720, 721, 812–13, 864–65, 871–73; production code, **Supp. 6**, 288–89; **Supp. 10**, 830; projection, **Supp. 5**, 321–22; racism in, **Supp. 10**, 677–78; rating system, **Supp. 6**, 479; "road" films, Hope and Crosby, **Supp. 10**, 159; Roaring Twenties, **Supp. 7**, 68; romances, **Supp. 8**, 66–67; **Supp. 9**, 371; science fiction, **Supp. 6**, 530; **Supp. 8**, 379; **Supp. 10**, 101, 615; screen credits establishment, **Supp. 5**, 229; screenwriting, **Supp. 3**, 264; **Supp. 5**, 12, 120–21, 209–10, 624; **Supp. 6**, 11, 106, 133, 214, 288–89, 476, 609, 628; **Supp. 7**, 232–33, 234, 331–32, 583–84; **Supp. 8**, 45, 108–9, 492, 622; **Supp. 9**, 71, 78, 188, 422, 488, 579, 691, 711, 723, 736, 748, 870; **Supp. 10**, 88, 268, 387, 430, 436–37, 576, 583, 631, 720, 756, 757, 793–94, 863–64; "screwball" comedies, **Supp. 3**, 466; **Supp. 10**, 318; serials, **Supp. 2**, 710; **Supp. 3**, 76; **Supp. 9**, 98; set design, **Supp. 10**, 200; sex goddesses, **Supp. 7**, 546; **Supp. 8**, 412–13; *Sherlock Holmes* series, **Supp. 8**, 519; short musical films, **Supp. 9**, 442; short subjects, **Supp. 3**, 54; silent era, **Supp. 3**, 443–44; **Supp. 6**, 76–77, 618–19; **Supp. 7**, 229–30, 462–63, 563; **Supp. 8**, 214; **Supp. 9**, 205, 371, 409, 791–92, 819; **Supp. 10**, 10, 11, 115–16, 430–31, 634–35, 656–57, 807–8, 810–11, 871–72; slapstick comedy, **Supp. 5**, 210–11; **Supp. 7**, 208, 238, 462–64; **Supp. 7**, 589; **Supp. 8**, 314–15; **Supp. 9**, 282, 410, 508–9, 535–36; **Supp. 10**, 513, 514–15, 517; social-consciousness films, **Supp. 8**, 453, 456, 550; song lyrics, **Supp. 3**, 406; sophisticated comedy, **Supp. 4**, 509; sound development, **Supp. 5**, 230; special effects, **Supp. 7**, 579–80; **Supp. 10**, 614, 615; star system, **Supp. 7**, 68, 142–44; **Supp. 10**, 115; studios, **Supp. 6**, 439–50, 667–68; **Supp. 8**, 576–77; **Supp. 9**, 322–24, 732–34; **Supp. 10**, 195, 812–13, 864–66, 872–73; studio system, **Supp. 9**, 206; suspense movies, **Supp. 10**, 339–40; "Tarzan" movies, **Supp. 4**, 129; **Supp. 9**, 65–66; Technicolor development, **Supp. 7**, 406–8; television threat to industry, **Supp. 9**, 733; theater chains, **Supp. 2**, 584; **Supp. 8**, 320, 576–77; **Supp. 9**, 62–63; **Supp. 10**, 871, 872; 3D fad, **Supp. 10**, 813; three-dimensional projection device, **Supp. 9**, 357; Todd-AO process, **Supp. 6**, 638; travelogues, **Supp. 6**, 302; unionization, **Supp. 8**, 459–60, 492; war movies, **Supp. 10**, 318, 823; Westerns, **Supp. 2**, 462; **Supp. 4**, 363–64; **Supp. 6**, 466; **Supp. 7**, 229, 286–87; **Supp. 8**, 248, 712; **Supp. 9**, 119, 123, 124, 128, 232, 286, 663, 692, 723, 768; **Supp. 10**, 178, 318, 489, 669, 736, 737, 811, 822, 823, 845, 846; wide-screen processes, **Supp. 5**, 721–22; **Supp. 7**, 692–93; wild-animal films, **Supp. 4**, 734; women, role of, **Supp. 9**, 767; "women's movies," **Supp. 8**, 188; World War II films, **Supp. 6**, 668; **Supp. 9**, 189, 372, 575, 691; World War II relief efforts, **Supp. 10**, 63. *See also* Acting

Motion theory, **Supp. 9**, 309, 310

Motivation. *See* Behaviorism

Motivation and Personality, **Supp. 8**, 423–24

Moton, Robert R., reference to, **Supp. 6**, 568

Motor, synchronous, **Supp. 9**, 357

Motor, founding of, **Supp. 5**, 286

Motor coach industry. *See* Bus industry

Motorcycles, manufacture of, **Supp. 1**, 213

Mott, John R., reference to, **Supp. 7**, 29

Mott, Lucretia, reference to, **Vol. 9, Part 1**, 521 f.

Mould, Adelaide Manola, reference to, **Supp. 6**, 309

Moulders' International Union, **Vol. 9, Part 2**, 258

Moulton, Elton J., reference to, **Supp. 5**, 508

Moulton, Harold G., references to, **Supp. 5**, 508, 537, 538; **Supp. 6**, 271

Mound builders, Indian, **Vol. 2, Part 1**, 51; **Vol. 3, Part 1**, 113; **Vol. 5, Part 2**, 612; **Vol. 9, Part 2**, 426

Mountain climbing, **Vol. 4, Part 2**, 502; **Vol. 8, Part 2**, 184; **Vol. 9, Part 2**, 448

Mountain Lion, The, **Supp. 10**, 754

Mountain Meadows massacre, **Vol. 6, Part 1**, 115

Mount Auburn Cemetery, founding of, **Vol. 1, Part 2**, 258

Mountbatten, Louis, reference to, **Supp. 9**, 386

Mount Berry School for Boys, **Supp. 3**, 63

Mount Carmel, Ill., **Vol. 1, Part 2**, 103

Mount Hermon School, **Vol. 7, Part 1**, 104

Mount Holyoke College: missionary work, **Supp. 3**, 288; presidency, **Supp. 4**, 912–13

Mount Holyoke Seminary, founding of, **Vol. 6, Part 1**, 532; **Vol. 9, Part 2**, 572

Mount McKinley, **Supp. 4**, 674

Mount Mitchell, **Vol. 7, Part 1**, 46

Mount Monadnock, **Vol. 9, Part 2**, 399

Mount Morris Park (N.Y.), **Vol. 7, Part 2**, 600

Mount Palomar Observatory (Calif.): astrophysical research, **Supp. 9**, 114; sky survey, **Supp. 9**, 902, 903

Mount Rainier, **Supp. 4**, 896

Mount Rushmore National Memorial (S.Dak.), carving of, **Supp. 2**, 492; **Supp. 3**, 89

Mount St. Mary's College, **Vol. 6, Part 1**, 559; **Vol. 8, Part 1**, 266 f.

Mount Sinai Hospital (New York City): electrocardiography, **Supp. 6**, 117; gynecology and obstetrics, **Supp. 6**, 554, 555; neurological bed service, **Supp. 3**, 682; pathology laboratory, **Supp. 4**, 493, 667–668; psychiatric outpatient clinic, **Supp. 5**, 517; social services and outpatient departments, **Supp. 3**, 312

Mount Vernon Ladies' Association of the Union, **Vol. 2, Part 2**, 601

Mount Washington, early exploration of, **Vol. 3, Part 1**, 13

Mount Wilson Observatory (Calif.): **Supp. 2**, 271; **Supp. 9**, 713, 714; **Supp. 10**, 840; research programs, **Supp. 9**, 114; sky survey, **Supp. 9**, 902, 903
"Mouse, Mickey" (fictional character), **Supp. 8**, 130, 131
"Movement Cure," **Vol. 9, Part 2**, 318
Movies. *See* Motion pictures
Movie stars. For complete list, *See* Occupations Index
Mowing machine, first use of, **Vol. 3, Part 2**, 110
Moynihan, Daniel P., reference to, **Supp. 9**, 751
Mozart, Wolfgang Amadeus, operas popularized, **Supp. 6**, 324
Muckraking, **Vol. 6, Part 1**, 332; **Vol. 8, Part 2**, 497. *See also* Journalism
Mudd, Samuel A., reference to, **Vol. 1, Part 2**, 450
Mugwump movement, **Supp. 1**, 101
Mugwumps (1884–89), **Vol. 1, Part 2**, 326; **Vol. 2, Part 2**, 207; **Vol. 7, Part 2**, 469; **Vol. 9, Part 1**, 97
Muhammad, Elijah, reference to, **Supp. 7**, 508
Muhammad Speaks, founding of, **Supp. 7**, 508
Muhlenberg College, presidency of, **Vol. 7, Part 1**, 306; **Vol. 8, Part 2**, 563
Muir, John, references to, **Vol. 5, Part 2**, 293; **Supp. 2**, 16; **Supp. 4**, 522
Mulberry, attempted cultivation of, **Vol. 3, Part 1**, 595
Mullen, William, Chicago vote fraud exposé, **Supp. 10**, 50
Muller, Hermann J., reference to, **Supp. 3**, 540
Muller, Richard, reference to, **Supp. 6**, 256
"Mulligan Letters" (1876), **Vol. 1, Part 2**, 324; **Vol. 2, Part 2**, 207; **Vol. 5, Part 2**, 422
Mulligan, P. B., and Co., **Supp. 6**, 618
"Mullins, Moon" (fictional character), **Supp. 6**, 699
Mullins, Paddy, reference to, **Supp. 6**, 700
Multinational corporations: General Electric, **Supp. 6**, 614; ITT, **Supp. 6**, 43–45
Mulvane, David W., reference to, **Supp. 9**, 355
Mumford, Lewis, reference to, **Supp. 9**, 526
Munch, Edvard, reference to, **Supp. 6**, 256
Muncie, Ind., sociological study of, **Supp. 3**, 29; **Supp. 5**, 35; **Supp. 8**, 398–99
Mundelein, George Cardinal, reference to, **Supp. 8**, 588
Mundt-Nixon Anti-Communist Bill (1948), **Supp. 9**, 572
Munfordville, Ky., capture of, **Vol. 1, Part 2**, 586; **Vol. 2, Part 1**, 240
Muni, Paul, references to, **Supp. 8**, 456; **Supp. 10**, 655
Munich crisis (1938), **Supp. 3**, 658; **Supp. 7**, 409
Munich Opera, **Supp. 7**, 765
Municipal Art Society, founding of, **Supp. 2**, 42
Municipal government: Boston reforms (1915), **Supp. 2**, 183; charters, **Vol. 3, Part 1**, 11; Chicago reforms, **Supp. 2**, 166; Cincinnati model, **Supp. 4**, 247; commission form, **Supp. 5**, 698; Crump machine, **Supp. 5**, 144–45; first electric-lighting plant in U.S., **Vol. 7, Part 1**, 450; first Socialist mayor, **Supp. 4**, 733; Golden Rule administration, **Supp. 1**, 453–54; Milwaukee model, **Supp. 7**, 348; Philadelphia city charter, **Supp. 4**, 262; Pittsburgh reforms, **Supp. 8**, 361; reform movements, **Vol. 3, Part 1**, 607 f.; **Vol. 5, Part 1**, 522; **Supp. 4**, 522, 738, 870; **Supp. 5**, 212–13; research in, **Supp. 2**, 608; Socialist party in, **Supp. 4**, 511–12, 733; writings on, **Supp. 2**, 251, 399; **Supp. 4**, 260; **Supp. 6**, 467–68
Munitions manufacture: **Vol. 1, Part 2**, 265; **Vol. 2, Part 1**, 229; **Vol. 2, Part 2**, 318; **Vol. 3, Part 1**, 377, 600; **Vol. 5, Part 1**, 247, 573; **Vol. 5, Part 2**, 239; **Vol. 6, Part 1**, 215; **Vol. 7, Part 1**, 301, 503, 509; **Vol. 7, Part 2**, 58; **Vol. 8, Part 1**, 91 f.; **Vol. 8, Part 2**, 145; **Vol. 10, Part 2**, 379; Civil War (U.S.), **Vol. 1, Part 1**, 248; **Vol. 4, Part 1**, 429; **Vol. 8, Part 1**, 496; **Vol. 8, Part 2**, 303; Revolutionary War, **Vol. 3, Part 1**, 173 f.; 250; **Vol. 4, Part 1**, 253; **Vol. 4, Part 2**, 454; **Vol. 5, Part 1**, 209; **Vol. 6, Part 1**, 214; **Vol. 7, Part 2**, 58; **Vol. 8, Part 1**, 515, 646; **Vol. 8, Part 2**, 63 f.; War of 1812, **Vol. 3, Part 2**, 573; World War I, **Supp. 9**, 622. *See also* Armed forces and defense; Firearms; Nuclear weapons and energy
Muñoz Marín, Luís, references to, **Supp. 5**, 545; **Supp. 10**, 795
Munsey, Frank A., references to, **Vol. 7, Part 1**, 44; **Vol. 10, Part 1**, 445; **Supp. 9**, 284
Munsey's Magazine, **Vol. 7, Part 1**, 334
Mnsterberg, Hugo, reference to, **Supp. 3**, 471
Mural painting. *See* Painting, mural
Murchison, Clinton Williams, references to, **Supp. 6**, 540, 541; **Supp. 9**, 462; **Supp. 10**, 568
Murchison, Clinton Williams, Jr., references to, **Supp. 9**, 462, 463; **Supp. 10**, 568, 569
Murchison, John (son of Clinton Williams Murchison), references to, **Supp. 9**, 462, 463
Murchison, John Dabney, Jr., reference to, **Supp. 10**, 569
Murchison Brothers (investment banking), **Supp. 10**, 568–69
"Murder, Inc.," **Supp. 7**, 585
Murder in the Cathedral, **Supp. 7**, 221; **Supp. 8**, 176
Murders: Marchand case, **Supp. 7**, 393; Rosenthal case (New York City), **Supp. 4**, 885–86; studies of, **Supp. 2**, 522–23; Thaw's shooting of White, **Supp. 3**, 170; **Supp. 4**, 826–27; **Supp. 8**, 460–62; writings on, **Supp. 2**, 522. *See also* Assassinations; Crime
Murdock, Abe, reference to, **Supp. 9**, 842
Murdock, Kenneth B., reference to, **Supp. 4**, 559
Murdock, Thomas Benton, reference to, **Supp. 3**, 544
Murdock, Victor, reference to, **Supp. 3**, 106
Murfin, Jane, reference to, **Supp. 9**, 206
Murfreesboro, battle of. *See* Stone River
Murphy, Charles F., references to, **Vol. 6, Part 1**, 568; **Supp. 3**, 717–19, 751; **Supp. 4**, 88, 608, 855; **Supp. 5**, 285–86, 717; **Supp. 6**, 294
Murphy, Frank, references to, **Supp. 5**, 575; **Supp. 6**, 86
Murphy, Paul Charles, **Vol. 6, Part 1**, 479
Murphy, William H., references to, **Supp. 4**, 292, 293
Murphy, William Parry, reference to, **Supp. 4**, 581
Murray, Jim, reference to, **Supp. 9**, 507
Murray, John Courtney, reference to, **Supp. 8**, 614–15
Murray, Natalia Danesi, reference to, **Supp. 10**, 247
Murray, Philip, references to, **Supp. 5**, 282, 283, 654; **Supp. 7**, 82, 587; **Supp. 8**, 511, 652, 653; **Supp. 10**, 493
Murray, Robert K., reference to, **Supp. 6**, 6
Murray, William B., references to, **Supp. 10**, 120, 121
Murray, William H. ("Alfalfa Bill"), reference to, **Supp. 9**, 301
Murray, William Vans, **Vol. 6, Part 1**, 360
Murray Manufacturing Co., **Supp. 7**, 564, 565
Murrow, Edward R., references to, **Supp. 8**, 373, 640; **Supp. 10**, 349, 350
Muscles: cerebral control of, **Supp. 6**, 223; contraction studies, **Supp. 5**, 489; fatigue research, **Supp. 2**, 391
Muscle Shoals, Ala.: **Vol. 5, Part 1**, 571; **Vol. 8, Part 2**, 603; **Vol. 9, Part 2**, 328; power facilities, **Supp. 3**, 559; **Supp. 4**, 465; **Supp. 5**, 290, 407
Muscular Dystrophy Association (MDA), **Supp. 9**, 99
Museum of Art (Philadelphia), growth of; **Supp. 5**, 388
Museum of French Art (New York City), founding of, **Supp. 5**, 151
Museum of Modern Art (New York City): administration, **Supp. 7**, 294; **Supp. 8**, 126–27; **Supp. 9**, 709; collection and space expansion, **Supp. 8**, 127; "Fam-

ily of Man" photography exhibition, **Supp. 7**, 457; **Supp. 9**, 760–61; **Supp. 10**, 398; first one-man show by black artist, **Supp. 5**, 200; founding of, **Supp. 4**, 199, 697; surrealism exhibit, **Supp. 5**, 184–85; Tchelitchew retrospective, **Supp. 6**, 625; Weston retrospective, **Supp. 6**, 686

Museum of Natural History (New York City). *See* American Museum of Natural History (New York City)

Museum of Navajo Ceremonial Art (Santa Fe), **Supp. 6**, 688

Museum of Science and Industry (Chicago), **Supp. 6**, 327

Museum of the American Indian (New York City), founding of, **Vol. 9, Part 1**, 197; **Supp. 6**, 289, 290

Museums: administration, **Vol. 4, Part 1**, 381; **Vol. 5, Part 2**, 485; **Vol. 6, Part 1**, 484; **Vol. 8, Part 1**, 276 f.; administration, teaching of, **Supp. 7**, 673–74; Americana collections, **Supp. 4**, 302; American art, **Supp. 4**, 289–90; architectural design of, **Supp. 9**, 445–46; associations of, **Supp. 1**, 415; directors, **Supp. 3**, 465; **Supp. 6**, 620–22; docent training, **Supp. 2**, 562; exhibit design, **Supp. 1**, 585; **Supp. 2**, 317; first in U.S., **Vol. 3, Part 1**, 553 f.; Guggenheim design, **Supp. 6**, 714–15. *See also specific museum names*

Mushrooms: culture methods, **Supp. 6**, 176; studies of, **Vol. 5, Part 2**, 263; **Vol. 8, Part 2**, 411

Music: **Vol. 1, Part 2**, 216; **Vol. 4, Part 1**, 270; **Vol. 4, Part 2**, 394, 606; **Vol. 5, Part 2**, 504 f., 584; **Vol. 6, Part 1**, 293; **Vol. 7, Part 2**, 224; **Vol. 8, Part 2**, 146 f., 149 f., 440; **Vol. 9, Part 1**, 103, 359, 457, 507; **Vol. 9, Part 2**, 424 f.; **Vol. 10, Part 1**, 181 f., 574, 577 f.; acoustic deslgn, **Supp. 3**, 524; African, **Supp. 5**, 436; American Indian, **Supp. 6**, 162–63; arrangement, **Supp. 9**, 887; **Supp. 10**, 408–9; atonal, **Supp. 7**, 647; **Supp. 8**, 100; band, **Supp. 3**, 610–11; **Supp. 5**, 106; **Supp. 6**, 241–42, 274–75; **Supp. 10**, 173–74; bebop, **Supp. 5**, 534; big bands, **Supp. 9**, 475–75; **Supp. 10**, 409, 463; black, **Supp. 5**, 436; black classical, **Supp. 6**, 690; blues, **Supp. 2**, 547, 616; **Supp. 6**, 275; **Supp. 8**, 695–96; **Supp. 9**, 413–14, 644, 645, 687–88; **Supp. 10**, 77–78; boogie-woogie, **Supp. 5**, 758; chamber, **Vol. 3, Part 1**, 70 f., 190; **Vol. 5, Part 2**, 460 f.; **Vol. 8, Part 1**, 149 f.; **Vol. 9, Part 2**, 305, 424; **Supp. 3**, 33; **Supp. 4**, 545; **Supp. 7**, 511–12; Chautauqua movement, **Supp. 3**, 65; children's concerts, **Supp. 2**, 596; **Supp. 4**, 212; choral, **Vol. 1, Part 1**, 202; **Vol. 5, Part 2**, 486; **Vol. 10, Part 1**, 46 f.; **Vol. 7, Part 2**, 184; **Vol. 8, Part 1**, 388; **Vol. 9, Part 2**, 244; **Supp. 1**, 650; **Supp. 3**, 225–26; church, **Vol. 1, Part 2**, 270; **Vol. 3, Part 1**, 328; **Vol. 4, Part 2**, 388; **Vol. 5, Part 2**, 251; **Vol. 6, Part 1**, 38; **Vol. 8, Part 1**, 421; **Vol. 9, Part 1**, 46, 530; **Vol. 9, Part 2**, 47 f.; **Vol. 10, Part 1**, 50 f., 487, 574; church organ, **Supp. 3**, 849–50; **Supp. 10**, 43, 254; classical instrumental, **Supp. 3**, 459; **Supp. 5**, 45–46, 607–8, 646–47; **Supp. 6**, 297–98; **Supp. 7**, 297–98, 443–45; **Supp. 8**, 164–65, 312–13; **Supp. 9**, 140–41, 162–63, 292, 300, 670, 777; **Supp. 10**, 43–44, 236, 237, 312–13, 372–73, 455, 456, 632–33, 638, 783; classical popularization, **Supp. 7**, 707; collections, **Supp. 2**, 8; composition, **Vol. 1, Part 1**, 340, 516; **Vol. 1, Part 2**, 5, 270; **Vol. 2, Part 1**, 57, 223, 514; **Vol. 2, Part 2**, 152, 262 f., 358 f.; **Vol. 3, Part 1**, 48 f., 205; **Vol. 3, Part 2**, 39, 58, 145, 259, 449, 557; **Vol. 4, Part 1**, 49 f., 128, 269 f., 274, 312, 328, 363, 395, 442, 616; **Vol. 4, Part 2**, 217 f., 306, 367, 464, 504, 519, 573, 606; **Vol. 5, Part 1**, 117, 186, 319, 367 f.; **Vol. 5, Part 2**, 251 f., 295 f., 442, 486, 584; **Vol. 6, Part 1**, 238; **Vol. 6, Part 2**, 25 f., 356, 360; **Vol. 7, Part 1**, 371 f., 440 f., 594 f., 628 f.; **Vol. 7, Part 2**, 78, 152, 184, 222 f., 228 f., 265, 356, 367, 458, 485, 498, 512, 542; **Vol. 8, Part 1**, 177 f., 421, 489; **Vol. 8, Part 2**, 92, 146 f., 148, 167, 224, 269, 339, 430, 496, 566 f.; **Vol. 9, Part 1**, 46, 390 f., 408, 411, 456, 530, 589 f.; **Vol. 9, Part 2**, 10, 236, 339, 556, 566, 627; **Vol. 10, Part 2**, 136, 195, 341, 487, 513, 532, 651; **Supp. 1**, 161, 451, 475, 504; **Supp. 2**, 114, 198, 227, 267–68; **Supp. 3**, 42, 187–88, 253, 408–9, 616–17, 689–90, 743; **Supp. 5**, 218, 351–54, 476–77, 608–9; **Supp. 6**, 62–63, 298, 351–52, 690; **Supp. 7**, 297–98; **Supp. 8**, 145–46, 641–45; **Supp. 9**, 491, 492, 580, 598–99, 644–45, 662, 730–32, 777–78, 887; **Supp. 10**, 6, 230–31, 239, 312–13, 409–10, 526–27, 579–80, 592, 638, 760–61, 762, 784, 838; composition, American vernacular, **Supp. 5**, 103–4; composition for ballet, **Supp. 9**, 775–76; composition for movies, **Supp. 8**, 251–52, 466, 688–89; **Supp. 9**, 382–83; **Supp. 10**, 576, 694, 784; conducting, **Vol. 3, Part 1**, 48 f., 205, 377, 504, 567 f.; **Vol. 4, Part 1**, 507, 220, 274, 455; **Vol. 4, Part 2**, 504, 606; **Vol. 5, Part 1**, 47, 367 f.; **Vol. 5, Part 2**, 486, 584; **Vol. 6, Part 1**, 238, 293, 512; **Vol. 6, Part 2**, 499; **Vol. 7, Part 1**, 80, 434, 549, 594 f.; **Vol. 8, Part 1**, 633; **Vol. 8, Part 2**, 423, 561 f.; **Vol. 9, Part 1**, 459; **Vol. 9, Part 2**, 424 f.; **Vol. 10, Part 1**, 543; **Vol. 10, Part 2**, 453, 640, 651; **Supp. 1**, 267, 578; **Supp. 2**, 47; **Supp. 3**, 358, 707, 740–41, 742–43; **Supp. 4**, 210–12; **Supp. 5**, 398–99; **Supp. 6**, 456, 549–50, 642–44; **Supp. 7**, 548–49, 640–41, 764–65; **Supp. 8**, 450–51, 465, 641; **Supp. 9**, 382, 887; **Supp. 10**, 237–38, 373, 421–22, 422–23, 722–23, 760, 761–63; country and western, **Supp. 5**, 748–49; **Supp. 9**, 414, 662–63; **Supp. 10**, 104–5; criticism, **Vol. 1, Part 1**, 335; **Supp. 9**, 316–17; **Vol. 3, Part 1**, 205, 567 f.; **Vol. 3, Part 2**, 120, 384 f.; **Vol. 5, Part 1**, 257; **Vol. 5, Part 2**, 482, 504; **Vol. 9, Part 2**, 401; **Vol. 10, Part 1**, 543; **Vol. 10, Part 2**, 514; **Supp. 1**, 369, 592; **Supp. 2**, 8, 237, 295; **Supp. 3**, 770–71; **Supp. 4**, 702; **Supp. 5**, 183; **Supp. 7**, 124, 754; **Supp. 9**, 316–17; dance bands, **Supp. 3**, 524–25, 187–88; **Supp. 7**, 300–301; **Supp. 7**, 774; **Supp. 8**, 163, 697–98; **Supp. 10**, 463; Dixieland, **Supp. 10**, 513; "easy listening" style, **Supp. 10**, 231; editing, **Supp. 3**, 708; **Supp. 4**, 276–77; ethnological studies of, **Supp. 4**, 762; film scores, **Supp. 9**, 382–83, 761–62; **Supp. 10**, 231; first black to conduct major orchestra, **Supp. 10**, 760; first pop crossover star, **Supp. 9**, 442; folk pop, **Supp. 9**, 262; folk songs, **Supp. 1**, 651; **Supp. 4**, 249, 502; **Supp. 8**, 695–96; **Supp. 10**, 589–90, 602–3; "free music," **Supp. 7**, 298; gospel, **Supp. 9**, 423–25; heavy metal, **Supp. 8**, 252–53; improvisation, **Supp. 7**, 737; inaugural balls, **Supp. 10**, 174; jazz, **Supp. 2**, 502; **Supp. 3**, 798–99; **Supp. 4**, 510; **Supp. 5**, 32–33, 103–4, 105–6, 292–93, 529–30, 534–35; **Supp. 6**, 42–43, 299–300, 619–20; **Supp. 7**, 131, 735–36; **Supp. 8**, 20, 100–101, 163, 561–62, 697–98; light classical, **Supp. 5**, 585; **Supp. 10**, 237–38; light opera, **Vol. 3, Part 1**, 205; **Vol. 5, Part 2**, 443; **Vol. 8, Part 2**, 246, 387; **Vol. 9, Part 2**, 62; **Vol. 10, Part 2**, 513; modern instrumental, **Supp. 10**, 760–61; museum and library concerts, **Supp. 3**, 252; New England group, **Supp. 6**, 161–62; Nickelodeon jukebox, **Supp. 9**, 442; nontraditional sounds, **Supp. 9**, 340–41; opera, **Vol. 2, Part 2**, 357; **Vol. 3, Part 1**, 48 f., 205; **Vol. 4, Part 1**, 50, 506; **Vol. 5, Part 1**, 78; **Vol. 5, Part 2**, 244, 301, 442; **Vol. 6, Part 1**, 379; **Vol. 6, Part 2**, 281; **Vol. 7, Part 1**, 434, 549; **Vol. 8, Part 1**, 144, 487 f.; **Vol. 8, Part 2**, 92, 562; **Vol. 9, Part 1**, 177; **Supp. 9**, 544–45; organizations, **Supp. 2**, 268; parody, **Supp. 7**, 737; patrons, **Supp. 4**, 834–35; **Supp. 5**, 128–29; philanthropy, **Supp. 4**, 87; photographic recording of sound waves, **Supp. 3**, 523; pitchless, **Supp. 7**, 755–56; plagiarism, **Supp. 7**, 707; publishing, **Vol. 1, Part 1**, 202; **Vol. 3,**

Part 1, 321 f.; **Vol. 4, Part 1**, 363; **Vol. 6, Part 1**, 38; **Vol. 7, Part 1**, 133; **Vol. 7, Part 2**, 512; **Vol. 8, Part 2**, 146 f., 323, 434 f., 440; **Vol. 9, Part 1**, 589; **Supp. 3**, 563; **Supp. 4**, 836; **Supp. 6**, 275; **Supp. 7**, 198–99; radio programs, **Supp. 3**, 359; **Supp. 4**, 452; **Supp. 6**, 691; **Supp. 9**, 207, 382, 662, 802, 804; **Supp. 10**, 43–44, 59, 105, 160, 223, 230, 239, 251, 421, 463, 593, 648, 789, 806; ragtime, **Supp. 2**, 286, 336; **Supp. 10**, 195; religious, **Supp. 2**, 49; **Supp. 4**, 125; **Supp. 5**, 117; rhythm and blues, **Supp. 9**, 414, 441–42; **Supp. 10**, 251–52; rock, **Supp. 8**, 252–53, 305–6; rock and roll, **Supp. 6**, 301–2; **Supp. 7**, 267; **Supp. 9**, 262, 317, 563–64; **Supp. 10**, 448–50, 648–50; satire, **Supp. 7**, 403–4; Schillinger system, **Supp. 3**, 690; Seashore talent measurement test, **Supp. 4**, 731; society balls, **Supp. 10**, 173–74; Spanish, **Supp. 1**, 651; swing, **Supp. 3**, 524–25; **Supp. 5**, 32–33, 293, 534–35; **Supp. 6**, 172–73; **Supp. 7**, 300–301; "symphonic" jazz, **Supp. 9**, 340; Tanglewood festival, **Supp. 4**, 715; teaching, **Vol. 1, Part 1**, 516; **Vol. 3, Part 1**, 513, 570 f.; **Vol. 3, Part 2**, 81, 379, 437; **Vol. 4, Part 1**, 35, 274, 328, 395, 455, 617; **Vol. 4, Part 2**, 217; **Vol. 5, Part 1**, 117, 621; **Vol. 5, Part 2**, 214, 442; **Vol. 6, Part 1**, 238, 512; **Vol. 6, Part 2**, 26, 360, 371 f., 378, 576; **Vol. 7, Part 1**, 114; **Vol. 7, Part 2**, 151 f., 184, 265; **Vol. 8, Part 1**, 144, 200 f., 539 f.; **Vol. 8, Part 2**, 146, 269, 331, 429 f., 614; **Vol. 9, Part 1**, 391, 457, 506 f., 590; **Vol. 9, Part 2**, 578 f., 605; **Vol. 10, Part 2**, 656; **Supp. 1**, 161, 276; **Supp. 2**, 140, 249, 541; **Supp. 3**, 309, 459, 741, 742; **Supp. 4**, 545–46, 718; **Supp. 5**, 45–46; **Supp. 6**, 426–27; **Supp. 7**, 511–12; **Supp. 9**, 300; **Supp. 10**, 456, 638; theory teaching, **Supp. 3**, 309; twelve-tone, **Supp. 5**, 609; **Supp. 7**, 647–48; **Supp. 8**, 100; "urban" blues, **Supp. 9**, 414, 796; vocal, **Vol. 1, Part 1**, 19, 54, 615; **Vol. 1, Part 2**, 299; **Vol. 2, Part 1**, 550, 553; **Vol. 3, Part 2**, 397; **Vol. 4, Part 2**, 399, 505, **Vol. 5, Part 2**, 251, 301; **Vol. 6, Part 1**, 74; **Vol. 7, Part 1**, 549; **Vol. 8, Part 1**, 144; **Vol. 8, Part 2**, 146, 167, 339 f.; **Vol. 9, Part 2**, 405, 516; **Vol. 10, Part 2**, 131, 164; **Supp. 10**, 159–60; western, **Supp. 10**, 592–93; western swing, **Supp. 9**, 872–73; writings on, **Vol. 1, Part 1**, 107, 336; **Vol. 1, Part 2**, 115, 285, 382; **Vol. 3, Part 1**, 513, 567 f.; **Vol. 4, Part 1**, 220, 363, 395, 455, 507; **Vol. 5, Part 1**, 540; **Vol. 5, Part 2**, 321, 482, 505, 604; **Vol. 6, Part 2**, 407; **Vol. 7, Part 2**, 19, 184, 376, 512; **Vol. 8, Part 1**, 144, 149 f., 177 f., 200 f., 541, 633; **Vol. 9, Part 1**, 190, 395, 411; **Vol. 9, Part 2**, 627; **Vol. 10, Part 1**, 25, 131, 488, 542 f., 574, 606, 625; **Vol. 10, Part 2**, 619, 656; **Supp. 5**, 476–77; **Supp. 8**, 644–45. *See also* Dance; Jazz; Motion pictures, music; Musicology; Opera; Singing; Songs and songwriting; Theater, musicals

Musical America, **Supp. 3**, 770

Musical Art Society, founding of, **Supp. 2**, 140

Musical comedy. *See* Motion pictures; Theater

Musical instruments: banjo, **Supp. 5**, 657; **Supp. 10**, 104; bass fiddle, **Supp. 10**, 592; cello, **Supp. 9**, 140–41, 163; **Supp. 10**, 632, 633; clarinet, **Supp. 6**, 41, 42; **Supp. 8**, 561; cornet, **Supp. 6**, 241, 242, 274, 368; **Supp. 10**, 298–300; double bass, **Supp. 5**, 397, 398; drum, **Supp. 5**, 105–6; dulcimer, **Supp. 10**, 589; electric guitar, **Supp. 10**, 448, 449–50; electronic, **Supp. 3**, 690; **Supp. 7**, 756; electronic keyboards, **Supp. 9**, 341; fiddle, **Supp. 9**, 872–73; flute, **Vol. 5, Part 2**, 603; **Supp. 3**, 33; flute collection, **Supp. 3**, 524; guitar, **Supp. 8**, 252–53; **Supp. 9**, 373–74, 563, 796; **Supp. 10**, 104–5, 251–52, 592, 648; Hammond organ, **Supp. 9**, 341, 358; harmonica, **Supp. 10**, 78; harpsichord, **Supp. 6**, 357–58; **Supp. 10**, 838; mandolin, **Supp. 9**, 373–74; mandolute, **Supp. 8**, 349; oboe, **Vol. 4, Part 1**, 207; **Supp. 10**, 838; organ, **Vol. 1, Part 1**, 339; **Vol. 2, Part 1**, 223; **Vol. 3, Part 1**, 513; **Vol. 5, Part 1**, 540; **Vol. 7, Part 2**, 151, 228 f., 355; **Vol. 8, Part 1**, 164 f.; **Vol. 9, Part 2**, 10, 339; **Vol. 10, Part 1**, 488; **Vol. 10, Part 2**, 136, 455; **Supp. 2**, 169; **Supp. 3**, 798; **Supp. 3**, 849–50; **Supp. 9**, 563; **Supp. 10**, 43–44, 254; piano, **Vol. 1, Part 1**, 491; **Vol. 3, Part 1**, 205; **Vol. 4, Part 1**, 442, 614, 616; **Vol. 5, Part 1**, 117, 621; **Vol. 5, Part 2**, 217 f., 442; **Vol. 6, Part 1**, 238; **Vol. 6, Part 2**, 378; **Vol. 7, Part 2**, 265; **Vol. 9, Part 1**, 103, 590; **Vol. 9, Part 2**, 305 f., 425, 556; **Vol. 10, Part 2**, 453, 647; **Supp. 3**, 42, 458–59, 615–17, 797–99; **Supp. 4**, 545, 717–18; **Supp. 5**, 45–46, 188, 607, 758; **Supp. 6**, 297, 619–20; **Supp. 7**, 123, 131, 297–98, 737–38; **Supp. 8**, 312–13; **Supp. 9**, 162–63, 259–61, 292–93, 299–300, 340, 491, 492, 512–13, 670, 887; **Supp. 10**, 6, 195, 225–26, 230, 270, 317, 372–73, 408, 455–56, 637, 638, 783–84, 839; saxophone, **Supp. 5**, 534; **Supp. 6**, 41, 42; **Supp. 8**, 100; **Supp. 9**, 10–11, 441–43, 847–48, 887; trombone, **Supp. 3**, 610; **Supp. 7**, 736; **Supp. 9**, 598–99; trumpet, **Supp. 5**, 529–30; **Supp. 6**, 41; **Supp. 8**, 163; **Supp. 9**, 46–47, 554; viol, **Vol. 1, Part 2**, 270; viola, **Supp. 9**, 340; violin, **Vol. 2, Part 1**, 57; **Vol. 4, Part 1**, 207, 269; **Vol. 4, Part 2**, 196; **Vol. 5, Part 1**, 47; **Vol. 5, Part 2**, 460, 295; **Vol. 7, Part 1**, 80, 371 f.; **Vol. 8, Part 1**, 149 f.; **Vol. 8, Part 2**, 374, 423, 461; **Vol. 9, Part 1**, 457; **Vol. 9, Part 2**, 566; **Supp. 5**, 646–47; **Supp. 7**, 443–45; **Supp. 8**, 164–65; **Supp. 9**, 887; **Supp. 10**, 236, 637, 638, 806–7

Musical Quarterly, **Supp. 3**, 253

Music Box Theatre (New York City), **Supp. 3**, 333

Music Lovers' Encylopedia, **Supp. 6**, 309

Music Man, The, **Supp. 10**, 55

Musicology: Bach works, **Supp. 6**, 357–58; teaching of, **Supp. 3**, 252–53

Music School Settlement (New York City), **Supp. 4**, 545; **Supp. 6**, 426, 427

Musket, manufacture for Revolution, **Vol. 7, Part 1**, 503

"Muskrat Ramble" (song), **Supp. 9**, 599

Muslim Mosque, Incorporated, founding of, **Supp. 7**, 508

Mussolini, Benito: biography of, **Supp. 1**, 173; references to, **Supp. 3**, 658, 659; **Supp. 4**, 518; **Supp. 5**, 447; **Supp. 6**, 140, 170, 237, 388–89; **Supp. 9**, 618; **Supp. 10**, 13, 266, 562; Toscanini opposition to, **Supp. 6**, 643

Muste, A. J., reference to, **Supp. 6**, 16

Mutiny of 1793, **Vol. 5, Part 2**, 568

"Mutt and Jeff" (fictional characters), **Supp. 5**, 223–24

Mutual Film Corporation, **Supp. 10**, 115

Mutual Life Insurance Co., **Vol. 6, Part 1**, 588; **Vol. 6, Part 2**, 12; **Vol. 7, Part 1**, 323

Mutual Welfare League, **Vol. 7, Part 2**, 75

Muzak Corporation, **Supp. 9**, 81

My America, **Supp. 5**, 4

Myasthenia gravis, **Supp. 7**, 59

Mycology: **Vol. 5, Part 2**, 262; **Vol. 7, Part 2**, 373; **Vol. 9, Part 2**, 398; plant pathology, **Supp. 3**, 400, 815; rust fungi studies, **Supp. 3**, 23

My Fair Lady, **Supp. 7**, 325

My Friend Flicka, **Supp. 10**, 6

"My Friend Irma" (radio program), **Supp. 9**, 880

My Life As a Small Boy, **Supp. 9**, 204

Myrdal, Gunnar: Bunche association, **Supp. 9**, 137; sociological studies, **Supp. 6**, 605

Myrick, Julian, reference to, **Supp. 5**, 351

Mystery fiction, **Supp. 6**, 543

Mystery of Hamlet, The, **Supp. 6**, 418

Mystery stories. *See* Detective stories

Mystery Writers of America, Edgar Award, **Supp. 10,** 104
Mysticism: **Vol. 4, Part 1,** 615; **Vol. 4, Part 2,** 323; **Vol. 5, Part 2,** 312 f.; **Vol. 7, Part 1,** 577 f.; study of, **Supp. 4,** 441–42; **Supp. 7,** 380–81
Mythology, writings on, **Supp. 1,** 434
"My Wild Irish Rose" (song), **Vol. 7, Part 2,** 9

N

NAACP. *See* National Association for the Advancement of Colored People
Nabokov, Vladimir, reference to, **Supp. 9,** 876
Nagasaki. *See* Hiroshima and Nagasaki
Nail manufacture: by hand, **Vol. 9, Part 2,** 491; by machinery, **Vol. 1, Part 1,** 254; **Vol. 8, Part 1,** 429, 522; **Vol. 9, Part 2,** 243
Naismith, James, references to, **Supp. 9,** 20, 21
NALC. *See* Negro American Labor Council
Nally, Edward J., reference to, **Supp. 9,** 700
NAM. *See* National Association of Manufacturers
Nanking University, founding of, **Supp. 3,** 268
Nanook of the North, **Supp. 5,** 225–26
Nantucket, Mass.: **Vol. 2, Part 2,** 267; Athenaeum, **Vol. 7, Part 1,** 67; colonial life in, **Vol. 3, Part 2,** 488; genealogy of, **Vol. 3, Part 2,** 489; history of, **Vol. 3, Part 2,** 488; **Vol. 6, Part 2,** 456; purchase of, **Vol. 7, Part 2,** 599; Revolutionary period, **Vol. 8, Part 2,** 186; topographical studies of, **Vol. 3, Part 2,** 489; War of 1812 period, **Vol. 6, Part 2,** 178; whaling, **Vol. 7, Part 1,** 67; **Vol. 8, Part 2,** 186; wives secured by labor purchase, **Vol. 3, Part 2,** 488
Napalm, **Supp. 7,** 617
Naphtha, separation of crude oil from, **Vol. 8, Part 2,** 95
Napoleonic wars, privateering, **Vol. 3, Part 1,** 250
Napoleon prints and cartoons, collection of, **Vol. 8, Part 1,** 489
Napoleon III and Confederacy, **Vol. 9, Part 1,** 210 f.
"Narcissus," music by Nevin, **Vol. 7, Part 1,** 441
Narcotics: abuse rehabilitation, **Supp. 8,** 424; **Supp. 9,** 470; alcohol as, **Supp. 3,** 354; consciousness-enhancing, **Supp. 7,** 381; detection in horse racing, **Supp. 8,** 76; government supervision of, **Vol. 8, Part 1,** 103 f.; heroin, **Supp. 7,** 485; juvenile use of, **Supp. 8,** 40; legislation, **Supp. 5,** 138; **Supp. 6,** 280; opium traffic control, **Supp. 1,** 116; safe use in medicine, **Supp. 3,** 242; traffic in, **Supp. 5,** 736–37; **Supp. 7,** 485; **Supp. 9,** 821
Narragansett, part played by, in battle of Manila Bay, **Vol. 3, Part 1,** 269 f.
NASA. *See* National Aeronautics and Space Administration
Nash car, **Supp. 4,** 6; **Supp. 10,** 1, 2
Nash-Kelvinator Corporation, **Supp. 4,** 621; **Supp. 10,** 1
Nash Motors Co., founding of, **Supp. 4,** 620
Nash's Magazine, **Supp. 4,** 286
Nashville, battle of, **Vol. 2, Part 2,** 45, 464, 476; **Vol. 3, Part 2,** 533; **Vol. 5, Part 1,** 194; **Vol. 6, Part 1,** 131; **Vol. 8, Part 2,** 453; **Vol. 9, Part 1,** 237, 508; **Vol. 9, Part 2,** 434; **Vol. 10, Part 1,** 401; **Vol. 10, Part 2,** 335
Nashville, Tenn., **Vol. 1, Part 2,** 157; **Vol. 9, Part 1,** 494
Nashville Banner, **Vol. 5, Part 1,** 396; **Vol. 9, Part 1,** 495
Nashville Convention (1850), **Vol. 2, Part 1,** 457; **Vol. 2, Part 2,** 242; **Vol. 3, Part 1,** 363; **Vol. 5, Part 1,** 403; **Vol. 5, Part 2,** 102; **Vol. 9, Part 1,** 21
Nashville Tennessean, **Supp. 3,** 449
Nassau Hall, building of, **Vol. 9, Part 1,** 335
Nasser, Gamal Abdel, references to, **Supp. 8,** 276; **Supp. 9,** 154
Nast, Condé, references to, **Supp. 4,** 199, 200; **Supp. 6,** 107–8
Nast, Thomas, campaign against Tweed, **Vol. 10, Part 1,** 81
Natchez, operation at. *See* Vicksburg campaign
Natchez Indians, **Vol. 1, Part 2,** 251; **Vol. 6, Part 1,** 226
Nathan, George Jean: relations with Mencken, **Supp. 6,** 444, 445; reference to, **Supp. 7,** 3
Nation, The: **Vol. 4, Part 1,** 347, 349; **Vol. 5, Part 1,** 307; **Vol. 5, Part 2,** 564; **Vol. 6, Part 1,** 195; **Vol. 7, Part 1,** 57; **Vol. 8, Part 2,** 546; **Vol. 10, Part 2,** 105; Catholic church attacked in, **Supp. 10,** 48; drama criticism, **Supp. 5,** 425; editing, **Supp. 2,** 498; **Supp. 4,** 487; **Supp. 9,** 345–46; **Supp. 10,** 416–17, 502, 503; foreign correspondent, **Supp. 8,** 172; movie reviews, **Supp. 5,** 12; women's issues series, **Supp. 10,** 417
National Academy of Design: **Vol. 1, Part 1,** 249, **Vol. 2, Part 2,** 596, **Vol. 7, Part 2,** 35; first exhibition by, **Vol. 3, Part 1,** 535 f.; founded, **Vol. 3, Part 1,** 516 f.; **Vol. 4, Part 1,** 2; **Vol. 9, Part 2,** 611; gifts to, **Vol. 1, Part 1,** 233
National Academy of Sciences: **Vol. 4, Part 1,** 252; **Vol. 7, Part 2,** 395; **Vol. 9, Part 1,** 163; first psychologist elected to, **Supp. 3,** 150; first woman Draper Medal recipient, **Supp. 3,** 131; first woman member, **Supp. 5,** 600; forest commission, **Supp. 4,** 663–66; gift to, **Supp. 6,** 154; Research Council, **Supp. 5,** 733; spiral nebulae debate (1920), **Supp. 3,** 208
National Advisory Commission on Civil Disorders, recommendations, **Supp. 10,** 411
National Advisory Committee for Aeronautics, **Supp. 3,** 12; **Supp. 4,** 486, 487; **Supp. 6,** 182, 183, 665–66; **Supp. 7,** 381–82
National Aeronautic Association, founding of, **Supp. 2,** 109
National Aeronautics and Space Administration: **Supp. 10,** 495; astronaut program, **Supp. 8,** 81, 225, 694; launch vehicle research program, **Supp. 10,** 66–67; unmanned probes, **Supp. 9,** 476
National Agricultural Convention, **Vol. 5, Part 2,** 446
National Air Transport, **Supp. 5,** 385; founding of, **Supp. 2,** 109; **Supp. 5,** 294
National American Woman Suffrage Association: **Supp. 5,** 532; **Supp. 10,** 622; field secretary, **Supp. 9,** 640; founding of, **Supp. 4,** 156–58; trade union liaison, **Supp. 9,** 706
National Anti-Slavery Standard, **Vol. 2, Part 2,** 68
National Archives, founding of, **Supp. 2,** 342; **Supp. 4,** 176; **Supp. 8,** 370
National Archives Building, **Supp. 2,** 342, 539
National Association for American Composers and Conductors, founding of, **Supp. 2,** 268
National Association for the Advancement of Colored People (NAACP): **Vol. 4, Part 1,** 633; **Supp. 3,** 828; **Supp. 5,** 548, 740, 741; **Supp. 6,** 494, 568; **Supp. 9,** 620; administration, **Supp. 2,** 346; **Supp. 5,** 544; antilynching law campaign, **Supp. 9,** 749, 750; *Birth of a Nation,* opposition by, **Supp. 4,** 235; black education, funding of, **Supp. 10,** 172; black militants' criticism of, **Supp. 8,** 388; black stereotypes in entertainment industry, protest against, **Supp. 10,** 662; field secretary, **Supp. 7,** 227; founding and policies, **Supp. 2,** 623, 689; **Supp. 3,** 674; **Supp. 4,** 850, 851, 904; **Supp. 5,** 308; **Supp. 7,** 202–3, 204, 356; leadership, **Supp. 9,** 751; **Supp. 10,** 341; legal counsel, **Supp. 4,** 397, 398; Legal Defense and Educational Fund activities, **Supp. 9,** 749–50; predecessor, **Supp. 2,** 315
National Association for the Study and Prevention of Tuberculosis, administration of, **Supp. 2,** 176; founding of, **Supp. 4,** 578

National Association of Audubon Societies, **Vol. 9, Part 2**, 400. *See also* Audubon movement
National Association of Book Publishers, founding of, **Supp. 1**, 362; **Supp. 7**, 375
National Association of Christians and Jews, founding of, **Supp. 7**, 330
National Association of Colored Women, **Supp. 5**, 56; founding of, **Supp. 5**, 680
National Association of Democratic Clubs, **Supp. 5**, 285
National Association of Manufacturers, **Supp. 6**, 520; **Supp. 7**, 123
National Association of Owners of Railroad Securities, **Vol. 10, Part 1**, 455 f.
National Association of Science Writers, **Supp. 6**, 327; founding of, **Supp. 8**, 119
National Association of Trotting Horse Breeders, **Vol. 10, Part 1**, 373 f.
National Association of Wool Manufacturers, **Supp. 5**, 54
National Bank Note Engraving Co., **Vol. 5, Part 2**, 74
National Baptist Publishing Board, **Vol. 1, Part 2**, 528
"National Barn Dance" (radio program), **Supp. 4**, 132
National Bell Telephone Co., **Vol. 8, Part 2**, 336
National Biscuit Co., **Vol. 7, Part 1**, 143
National Board for Historical Service, founding of, **Supp. 7**, 687
National Broadcasting Co. (NBC): "Bookman's Guide" program, **Supp. 5**, 356; classical music programs, **Supp. 7**, 124; **Supp. 9**, 802; founding of, **Supp. 7**, 809; management, **Supp. 10**, 415–16; monopoly hearings, **Supp. 8**, 179; **Supp. 9**, 803; music programs, **Supp. 4**, 212; **Supp. 6**, 550, 643, 644; news commentary, **Supp. 7**, 321; **Supp. 10**, 415; public affairs programs, **Supp. 6**, 161; **Supp. 9**, 802; **Supp. 10**, 415; soap operas, **Supp. 6**, 104; "White Paper" series, **Supp. 10**, 415
National Bureau of Economic Research, founding of, **Supp. 4**, 586–87; **Supp. 9**, 661
National Business Survey Conference (1929–31), **Supp. 6**, 37
National Cancer Act (1971), **Supp. 9**, 754
National Cash Register Co., **Vol. 7, Part 2**, 304; **Vol. 9, Part 1**, 138; **Supp. 6**, 332, 673–74
National Cathedral (Washington, D. C.), **Supp. 6**, 600
National Cathedral School, **Vol. 4, Part 2**, 488
National Catholic Beneficial Society, **Supp. 1**, 360
National Catholic School of Social Service: founding of, **Supp. 2**, 360; predecessor, **Supp. 3**, 625
National Catholic War Council, **Supp. 3**, 694; founding of, **Supp. 2**, 73, 359
National Catholic Welfare Conference, **Supp. 5**, 454; founding of, **Supp. 2**, 73; **Supp. 3**, 325, 570; **Supp. 4**, 232–33; predecessor, **Supp. 3**, 694; Social Action Department, **Supp. 3**, 681
National Child Labor Committee, **Supp. 7**, 483; founding of, **Supp. 7**, 251
National City Bank: Latin American operations, **Supp. 10**, 827; management, **Supp. 2**, 678
National Civic Federation, **Vol. 5, Part 2**, 278; organization of, **Supp. 2**, 166
National Civil Service Reform League, **Vol. 1, Part 2**, 427
National College Equal Suffrage Association, founding of, **Supp. 5**, 532
National Collegiate Athletic Association (NCAA), basketball tournament established, **Supp. 9**, 20
National Commission on Prison Labor, **Vol. 9, Part 1**, 209
National Commission on the Churches and the Moral Aims of the War, **Supp. 6**, 25
National Committee for Mental Hygiene, founding of, **Supp. 3**, 51
National Committee for the Defense of Political Prisoners, **Supp. 3**, 237
National Committee for the Prevention of Blindness, **Supp. 2**, 381
National Committee on Maternal Health, **Supp. 6**, 81–82; predecessor, **Supp. 4**, 231
National Conference of Catholic Charities, founding of, **Supp. 2**, 359
National Conference of Charities, **Vol. 7, Part 1**, 323, 508
National Conference of Christians and Jews, **Supp. 6**, 607; founding of, **Supp. 2**, 87
National Conference of Social Welfare, **Supp. 3**, 388
National Conference of Social Work, **Supp. 6**, 330; **Supp. 7**, 483–84
National Conference of Unitarian Churches, **Vol. 1, Part 2**, 129, 169; **Vol. 8, Part 1**, 135
National Conservation Association, founding of, **Supp. 2**, 507; **Supp. 4**, 665–66
National Conservation Commission, **Supp. 4**, 664
National Conservatory of Music (New York City), **Supp. 6**, 241; predecessor, **Supp. 4**, 834
National Consumers League, **Supp. 6**, 433
National Cooperative Council, founding of, **Supp. 1**, 566
National Council for the Social Studies, **Supp. 2**, 419
National Council of Catholic Men, founding of, **Supp. 3**, 694
National Council of Catholic Women, **Supp. 3**, 624, 625; founding of, **Supp. 3**, 694
National Council of Churches: **Supp. 5**, 305; founding of, **Supp. 10**, 111
National Council of Negro Women, **Supp. 5**, 56
National Council of the Teachers of English, **Vol. 6, Part 1**, 178
National Council on Religion in Higher Education, **Vol. 5, Part 2**, 343
National Credit Office, **Supp. 6**, 693–94
National Crime Commission, organization of, **Supp. 1**, 173; **Supp. 9**, 553
National Deaf-Mute College, **Vol. 8, Part 1**, 102 f.
National Defense Act, **Vol. 5, Part 2**, 251
National Defense Act (1920), **Supp. 5**, 531, 715
National Defense Advisory Committee, founding of, **Supp. 4**, 458–59
National Defense Education Act (1958), **Supp. 10**, 250
National Defense League, **Vol. 5, Part 2**, 251
National Defense Research Committee (NRDC), **Supp. 6**, 501; **Supp. 4**, 430. *See also under* World War II
National Dental Association, **Vol. 1, Part 2**, 309
National Department of Education, **Vol. 4, Part 2**, 415
National Distillers Products Corporation, management, **Supp. 10**, 41–42
National Divorce Reform League, **Vol. 3, Part 1**, 308
National Eclectic Medical Association, **Vol. 1, Part 2**, 86
National Education Association: Committee of Ten, **Vol. 5, Part 2**, 60; forerunner of, **Vol. 8, Part 1**, 562; geography curriculum, **Supp. 4**, 424; nationwide standard setting, **Supp. 4**, 134
National Electrical Manufacturers Association, **Supp. 6**, 615
National electric code, **Vol. 2, Part 2**, 553
National Electric Signaling Co., **Supp. 6**, 298
National Emergency Council, **Supp. 6**, 660
National Emigration Convention, **Vol. 5, Part 1**, 157
National Endowment for the Humanities, **Supp. 10**, 403

National Endowments for the Arts and for the Humanities, founding of, **Supp. 7**, 425
National Era: antislavery paper, **Vol. 1, Part 1**, 496; founded, **Vol. 4, Part 1**, 390; **Vol. 9, Part 2**, 299; *Uncle Tom's Cabin* in, **Vol. 5, Part 2**, 69; **Vol. 9, Part 2**, 177 f.
National Farm School, **Vol. 5, Part 2**, 501
National Federation of Business and Professional Women's Clubs, founding of, **Supp. 5**, 543
National Federation of Settlements, **Supp. 6**, 499–500
National Florence Crittenton Missions, **Vol. 2, Part 2**, 550 f.
National Football League: championship games, **Supp. 9**, 828; **Supp. 10**, 444, 728, 767, 768; commissioners, **Supp. 6**, 47–48; **Supp. 9**, 646; first black coach, **Supp. 9**, 818; franchise shifts, **Supp. 9**, 646; interceptions record, **Supp. 9**, 818; merger with American Football League, **Supp. 9**, 646–47; predecessor, **Supp. 5**, 684; racism in, **Supp. 9**, 817, 840–41; scouting network, **Supp. 9**, 646
National Foundry Association, **Vol. 7, Part 1**, 450
National Gallery of Art (Washington, D. C.): architecture of, **Supp. 5**, 300, 301; Dale Collection, **Supp. 7**, 161–62; design, **Supp. 2**, 539; founding of, **Supp. 2**, 451; French art collection, **Supp. 5**, 151; Gellatly Collection, **Supp. 1**, 337; Kress Collection, **Supp. 5**, 401; rare books, donation of, **Supp. 10**, 702
National Gazette and Literary Register, **Vol. 10, Part 1**, 391 f.
National Geographic Magazine, editing, **Supp. 8**, 228
National Geographic Society (Washington, D.C.): **Vol. 1, Part 1**, 525; **Vol. 1, Part 2**, 152; **Vol. 8, Part 2**, 484; **Supp. 7**, 76; **Supp. 8**, 228; founding of, **Vol. 4, Part 1**, 124; **Vol. 5, Part 1**, 325; **Vol. 8, Part 1**, 152; **Supp. 1**, 355; **Supp. 3**, 518; headquarters, **Supp. 10**, 765
National Grange. *See* Grange movement
National Guard: **Vol. 3, Part 2**, 576; **Vol. 4, Part 2**, 368; California, **Supp. 5**, 43; Fighting Sixty-Ninth Regiment, **Supp. 1**, 268; New York, **Supp. 6**, 337; Pennsylvania, **Supp. 7**, 53; training requirement, **Supp. 7**, 78–79; writings on, **Supp. 6**, 309
National Health and Welfare Retirement Association, **Supp. 6**, 615
National Health Council, founding of, **Supp. 2**, 177
National Herbarium, **Vol. 1, Part 2**, 546; **Vol. 8, Part 2**, 160
National Herbart Society, founding of, **Supp. 2**, 424
National Historical Magazine, founding of, **Supp. 8**, 328
National Housing Association, **Supp. 6**, 26, 654
National Industrial Commission, **Vol. 5, Part 2**, 516
National Industrial Conference Board, **Supp. 7**, 404–5
National Industrial Recovery Act (1933): **Supp. 3**, 399–400, 650; **Supp. 4**, 50, 432; **Supp. 5**, 54, 254, 510, 631; **Supp. 6**, 615; opposition to, **Supp. 7**, 249; unconstitutionality of, **Supp. 3**, 99, 839; **Supp. 4**, 406–7; **Supp. 6**, 679. *See also* National Recovery Administration
National Industrial Recovery Board, **Supp. 4**, 376
National Industries for the Blind, **Supp. 5**, 347–48
National Institute for the Promotion of Science and the Useful Arts, **Vol. 8, Part 1**, 30 f.
National Institute of Arts and Letters, **Vol. 7, Part 2**, 473 f.
National Institute of Mental Health, founding of, **Supp. 9**, 789
National Institute of Science, founding of, **Supp. 1**, 3
National Institutes of Health: drug addiction studies, **Supp. 9**, 470; founding of, **Supp. 9**, 789; medical statistics, **Supp. 7**, 192; predecessor, **Supp. 4**, 701
National Intelligencer, **Vol. 8, Part 2**, 542
Nationalism: **Vol. 1, Part 2**, 164; **Vol. 8, Part 1**, 491; studies in, **Supp. 7**, 330
National Jeffersonian Democrats, founding of, **Supp. 3**, 623
National Junior Republic (Washington, D. C.), **Vol. 1, Part 2**, 471
National Kindergarten Association, founding of, **Supp. 5**, 437
National Labor College, founding of, **Supp. 4**, 233
National Labor Relations Act (1935): **Supp. 5**, 254; **Supp. 7**, 609; constitutionality upheld, **Supp. 4**, 407; **Supp. 10**, 229; legal status, **Supp. 6**, 679; passage of, **Supp. 3**, 654–55; **Supp. 5**, 718–19. *See also* Taft-Hartley Act
National Labor Relations Board (NLRB): chairman, **Supp. 8**, 34; factions on, **Supp. 6**, 379; founding of, **Supp. 3**, 651; **Supp. 5**, 718–19; general counsel, **Supp. 10**, 229; McKinsey report on, **Supp. 8**, 366–67
National Labor Relations Boards, **Supp. 4**, 579–80
National Labor Relations Board v. *Jones and Laughlin Steel Corp.,* **Supp. 4**, 407; **Supp. 10**, 229
National Labor Union, **Vol. 9, Part 2**, 258, 640; founding of, **Vol. 2, Part 1**, 434
National Lawyers Guild, formation of, **Supp. 3**, 227
National League (baseball), **Supp. 5**, 393; early years of, **Vol. 8, Part 1**, 418
National League for the Protection of the Family, **Vol. 3, Part 1**, 308
National League of Decency, founding of, **Supp. 4**, 535
National League of Women Voters. *See* League of Women Voters
National Legislative League, **Vol. 1, Part 2**, 344
National Longshoremen's Association, **Vol. 5, Part 2**, 278 f.
National Mediation Board, **Supp. 6**, 379
National Medical Convention, **Vol. 5, Part 2**, 468
National Merit Scholarship Corporation, **Supp. 7**, 276
National Monetary Commission, **Vol. 5, Part 2**, 189; **Vol. 9, Part 2**, 363
National Municipal League; **Vol. 1, Part 2**, 428; **Supp. 6**, 468; ballet reform plan, **Supp. 10**, 121; founding of, **Supp. 4**, 870; presidency, **Supp. 10**, 122
National Museum: founding and growth of, **Vol. 6, Part 2**, 373; mound collections, **Vol. 9, Part 2**, 426
National Museum of Engineering and Industry, **Vol. 8, Part 1**, 91 f.
National Music Teachers' Association, **Vol. 8, Part 1**, 200 f.
National Negro Business League: **Supp. 3**, 535; **Supp. 5**, 648; founding of, **Supp. 3**, 391; **Supp. 6**, 568
National Negro Congress, **Supp. 6**, 285
National Negro Insurance Association, founding of, **Supp. 5**, 648
National Observatory, **Vol. 1, Part 1**, 91; **Vol. 5, Part 2**, 403; **Vol. 10, Part 1**, 91
National Observer, **Supp. 9**, 521
National Organization for Public Health Nursing, **Supp. 4**, 65; founding of, **Supp. 2**, 687
National parks. *See* Forestry; Parks
National Park Service: **Vol. 6, Part 2**, 399; administration, **Supp. 10**, 191–92; founding of, **Supp. 4**, 522; **Supp. 6**, 486
National People's party, **Vol. 6, Part 1**, 332
National Police Academy. *See under* Federal Bureau of Investigation (FBI)
National Popular Government League, **Supp. 4**, 641
National Portrait Gallery of Distinguished Americans, **Vol. 6, Part 1**, 381
National Prison Association of the United States, **Vol. 7, Part 2**, 610
National Progressive League, founding of, **Supp. 2**, 691; **Supp. 4**, 544
National Progressive Republican League: **Vol. 5, Part**

2, 545; founding of, **Supp. 2**, 55, 237; **Supp. 3**, 558, 604, 816; **Supp. 4**, 665
National Progressives of America (1938), founding of, **Supp. 7**, 440–51
National Prohibition party, **Vol. 1, Part 2**, 310
National Psychological Association for Psychoanalysis, founding of, **Supp. 8**, 523
National Radio Astronomy Observatory, **Supp. 7**, 727; founding of, **Supp. 4**, 423
National Railway Co., **Vol. 7, Part 2**, 62
National Reclamation Association, predecessor, **Supp. 4**, 563
National Recovery Administration (NRA): **Supp. 3**, 670; **Supp. 5**, 515, 654; **Supp. 7**, 36, 171–72; activities, **Supp. 3**, 399–400; child labor, **Supp. 3**, 228; codes, **Supp. 4**, 457; **Supp. 6**, 378, 448, 622; economic research and planning, **Supp. 9**, 695; Ford's relationship with, **Supp. 4**, 302; founding of, **Supp. 3**, 650–54; legal counsel, **Supp. 6**, 542; legal decisions on, **Supp. 4**, 406–7; New York, **Supp. 7**, 780; opposition to, **Supp. 9**, 590
National Recreation Association, founding of, **Supp. 2**, 375
National Refugee Service, **Supp. 3**, 281
National Republican party, **Vol. 9, Part 2**, 641
National Research Council: **Supp. 3**, 150–51; **Supp. 5**, 64; drug addiction studies, **Supp. 3**, 242; food and nutrition subcommittee, **Supp. 3**, 68; founding of, **Supp. 1**, 156; human sexuality studies, **Supp. 6**, 343, 344, 718; postdoctoral fellowships, **Supp. 5**, 495–96
National Resources Planning Board, **Supp. 5**, 485; dismantling of, **Supp. 5**, 661
National Retired Teachers Association, founding of, **Supp. 8**, 9–10
National Review, **Supp. 7**, 115; **Supp. 8**, 150, 426; **Supp. 9**, 548, 549
National Rifle Association: **Vol. 2, Part 2**, 105; journalism criticizing, **Supp. 10**, 25
National Road, extension of, **Vol. 5, Part 2**, 467
National Rural Electric Cooperative Association (NRECA): founding of, **Supp. 10**, 218; lobbying by, **Supp. 10**, 218, 219
National Science Foundation: **Supp. 10**, 320; first director, **Supp. 8**, 687; founding of, **Supp. 6**, 335–36
National Sculpture Society: **Vol. 1, Part 2**, 301, 304; **Vol. 8, Part 1**, 125 f.; **Vol. 10, Part 1**, 427 f.; founding of, **Supp. 3**, 2, 673
National Security Act (1947), **Supp. 4**, 306; **Supp. 8**, 147
National Security Council (NSC): Acheson memorandum, **Supp. 9**, 8; expanded role in foreign policy, **Supp. 9**, 211
National Security League, **Supp. 6**, 410
Naitonal Security Resources Board, **Supp. 9**, 389
National Self Government Committee, founding of, **Supp. 4**, 870
National Service Board for Religious Objectors, **Supp. 6**, 217
National Society for the Prevention of Blindness, **Supp. 3**, 364
National Society for the Study of Education, **Vol. 7, Part 2**, 238
National Society of Mural Painters, **Vol. 2, Part 2**, 578
National Society of Penal Information, **Vol. 7, Part 2**, 76
National Steel Corporation: **Vol. 7, Part 1**, 143; founding of, **Supp. 6**, 678–79; **Supp. 8**, 289
National Student Federation, **Supp. 7**, 566
National Television System Committee, **Supp. 6**, 32
National Temperance Advocate, **Vol. 9, Part 1**, 546
National Temperance Society, **Vol. 3, Part 1**, 19, 353
National Trades' and Workers' Association, **Vol. 8, Part 1**, 112 f.
National Trades Union, **Vol. 7, Part 1**, 121
National Tuberculosis Association, founding of, **Supp. 2**, 71, 197, 371
National Typographlcal Union, **Vol. 2, Part 2**, 364
National Union Convention, **Vol. 8, Part 1**, 410
National Union for Social Justice: **Supp. 6**, 613, 647; founding of, **Supp. 10**, 152
National Union Movement, **Vol. 8, Part 1**, 582
National University (Peking), paleontology studies, **Supp. 4**, 344
National Urban League. *See* Urban League
National Vocational Guidance Association, founding of, **Supp. 2**, 45
National War Labor Board, **Supp. 7**, 172
National Wildlife Federation, **Supp. 7**, 164
National Women's party: **Supp. 4**, 157, 576; **Supp. 5**, 474; **Supp. 10**, 622; founding of, **Supp. 7**, 717–18
National Women's Political Caucus, **Supp. 10**, 307
National Women's Trade Union League, **Supp. 3**, 355; **Supp. 4**, 626; **Supp. 7**, 196; founding of, **Supp. 2**, 689; **Supp. 3**, 576
National Youth Administration: **Supp. 5**, 56; founding of, **Supp. 7**, 787; Johnson, L. B., appointed to, **Supp. 9**, 431
Nation of Islam. *See* Black Muslims
"Nations of the North," winning of, to Spanish rule, **Vol. 3, Part 1**, 229
Nationwide News Service, **Supp. 3**, 20, 21
Native American movement, **Vol. 6, Part 1**, 200
Native Americans. *See* Indians, American; *specific groups*
Native Races, **Vol. 1, Part 1**, 570
Native Son, **Supp. 5**, 419; **Supp. 6**, 715, 716
Native's Return, The, **Supp. 5**, 4
Natural, The, **Supp. 9**, 219
Naval Advisory Board, **Vol. 8, Part 2**, 78
Naval Aeronautics, Bureau of, **Vol. 8, Part 2**, 79
Naval architecture. *See* Naval vessels; Ships and shipbuilding
Naval Institute, United States, **Vol. 7, Part 2**, 220; **Vol. 9, Part 1**, 178
Naval Lyceum, United States, **Vol. 7, Part 2**, 487
Naval Observatory, **Vol. 1, Part 1**, 1; **Vol. 4, Part 2**, 266; **Vol. 6, Part 1**, 39, 337, 452 f.; **Vol. 7, Part 1**, 39, 452 f.; **Vol. 7, Part 2**, 319; **Vol. 8, Part 2**, 78, 341; **Vol. 9, Part 1**, 196; **Vol. 10, Part 1**, 359
Naval oil reserves, **Vol. 3, Part 1**, 156, 234 f.; **Vol. 4, Part 2**, 255; **Vol. 5, Part 2**, 546; **Vol. 8, Part 2**, 194; **Vol. 10, Part 1**, 393 f.
Naval Operations Office, founding of, **Supp. 1**, 70
Naval Research Laboratory, **Supp. 8**, 231
Naval vessels: aircraft carriers, **Supp. 4**, 589, 685; **Supp. 9**, 635, 636; battleship design, **Supp. 1**, 151; construction and repair, **Supp. 1**, 361; design, **Supp. 2**, 652; **Supp. 3**, 275; **Supp. 4**, 398–99; Eureka landing craft, **Supp. 8**, 603; first flight-deck carrier, **Supp. 4**, 685; foreign sales of, **Supp. 1**, 305–6; Franklin, bombing of, **Supp. 7**, 58 landing craft, **Supp. 8**, 23, 603; *Lexington*, **Supp. 6**, 577; *Missouri*, **Supp. 6**, 268; nuclear-powered, **Supp. 8**, 330; PT boat introduction, **Supp. 8**, 152; refueling at sea, **Supp. 2**, 239; repair, **Supp. 1**, 361; *Saratoga*, **Supp. 6**, 577, torpedo boats, **Supp. 1**, 231–32, 298; warship design, **Supp. 4**, 398–99. *See also* Ships and shipbuilding; Submarines
Naval War College: **Supp. 6**, 348, 629; administration, **Supp. 4**, 820; first presidency of, **Vol. 6, Part 1**, 489; international law studies, **Supp. 5**, 751
Navigation: **Vol. 1, Part 2**, 436; **Vol. 2, Part 2**, 205; **Vol. 3, Part 1**, 274; **Vol. 5, Part 2**, 517; aerial, **Vol. 8, Part 1**, 101 f.; eighteenth century, **Vol. 5, Part 2**, 329;

Vol. 8, Part 2, 126; Mississippi River, **Vol. 1, Part 1**, 582; **Vol. 3, Part 1**, 249; **Vol. 3, Part 2**, 106; **Vol. 4, Part 1**, 257; **Vol. 4, Part 2**, 67; **Vol. 8, Part 1**, 353 f.; **Vol. 9, Part 1**, 134; Missouri River, **Vol. 1, Part 2**, 306; **Vol. 5, Part 2**, 518; quadrant, use of, in, **Vol. 4, Part 1**, 345; steam, early experiments, **Vol. 3, Part 1**, 339; **Vol. 8, Part 1**, 429, 442; teaching of, **Vol. 6, Part 1**, 79; triangulation, **Vol. 3, Part 1**, 29 f.; writings on, **Vol. 3, Part 1**, 23, 468 f.; **Vol. 5, Part 2**, 51; **Vol. 8, Part 2**, 126 f.

Navigation, Bureau of, **Vol. 1, Part 2**, 395

Navigation Act (1818), **Vol. 5, Part 2**, 399

Navin, Frank, reference to, **Supp. 9**, 365

"Navy, New," **Vol. 3, Part 1**, 270 f.

Navy, state, **Vol. 8, Part 1**, 276

Navy, Department of the (U.S.; for list of naval officers, *see* Occupations Index): **Vol. 1, Part 1**, 258, 502, 529, 634; **Vol. 1, Part 2**, 242; **Vol. 2, Part 1**, 70, 207; **Vol. 3, Part 1**, 189, 269 f., 336; **Vol. 3, Part 2**, 85; **Vol. 4, Part 2**, 103, 190, 391, 602; **Vol. 5, Part 1**, 115, 303, 360 f.; **Vol. 5, Part 2**, 67, 164, 607, 615; **Vol. 6, Part 1**, 173, 299, 413 f., 418 f., 488 f.; **Vol. 6, Part 2**, 225, 430; **Vol. 7, Part 2**, 260, 314, 321, 445, 470, 487, 532, 535; **Vol. 8, Part 1**, 430; **Vol. 8, Part 2**, 22, 72 f., 139, 244, 341; **Vol. 9, Part 1**, 412; **Vol. 9, Part 2**, 122, 306 f., 310, 347 f., 349, 364, 393, 637 f.; **Vol. 10, Part 2**, 276, 392, 653; administration, **Supp. 3**, 425–26, 642, 688; **Supp. 4**, 216–17, 305–6; **Supp. 5**, 6–7, 479–80, 746; **Supp. 8**, 23, 152–53, 329–30; aircraft, **Supp. 3**, 182; **Supp. 6**, 91–94, 267, 338, 576–77, 665–66; *Albemarle* and *Sassacus*, **Vol. 1, Part 2**, 487; Algiers, **Vol. 5, Part 1**, 152; **Vol. 8, Part 2**, 73; **Vol. 9, Part 1**, 19; **Vol. 9, Part 2**, 310; amphibious warfare, **Supp. 8**, 23, 603; **Supp. 9**, 385–86; architecture, **Vol. 1, Part 1**, 461; **Vol. 2, Part 1**, 468; **Vol. 3, Part 1**, 211, 292; **Vol. 4, Part 1**, 626; **Vol. 4, Part 2**, 9; **Vol. 5, Part 1**, 3, 376 f., 515; **Vol. 6, Part 1**, 173; **Vol. 8, Part 1**, 83 f.; **Vol. 8, Part 2**, 200, 553; **Vol. 9, Part 1**, 237 f., 310, 619; **Vol. 9, Part 2**, 7, 48, 345; **Vol. 10, Part 2**, 346; archives, **Supp. 6**, 348; armament, **Vol. 3, Part 1**, 30 f.; **Vol. 9, Part 1**, 149; Asiatic squadron, **Vol. 7, Part 2**, 308; *Atlanta* and *Wasp*, **Vol. 1, Part 2**, 348; Atlantic Fleet, **Supp. 6**, 188, 348; **Supp. 10**, 371; aviation, **Supp. 1**, 561; **Supp. 3**, 182; **Supp. 4**, 306, 588–90, 685; **Supp. 5**, 621–22, 694–95, 746; **Supp. 6**, 91–94, 267, 338, 576–77, 665–66; **Supp. 8**, 303; aviation training program and facilities, expansion of, **Supp. 9**, 635–36; "Board of Fifteen," **Vol. 6, Part 1**, 204; Board of Navy Commissioners, **Vol. 7, Part 2**, 321; bombsight development, **Supp. 7**, 577; Bureau of Construction, **Vol. 6, Part 1**, 173; Bureau of Detail, **Vol. 7, Part 2**, 321; Bureau of Medicine and Surgery, **Vol. 1, Part 2**, 25; Bureau of Supplies and Accounts, created, **Vol. 9, Part 2**, 8; Bureau of System investigated, **Vol. 8, Part 1**, 512; *Caledonia*, capture of, **Vol. 3, Part 2**, 96; chaplains, **Supp. 7**, 581; *Chesapeake*, **Vol. 1, Part 1**, 212; **Vol. 3, Part 1**, 188; **Vol. 3, Part 2**, 96; Chief of Operations, **Supp. 5**, 66, 621; **Supp. 9**, 755; *Chocura*, **Vol. 7, Part 2**, 308; civilian physicians, **Supp. 6**, 130; civilian v. military control issue, **Supp. 4**, 305; *Columbia* and *Shamrock*, **Vol. 1, Part 1**, 641; commander in chief (COMINCH), **Supp. 6**, 339–40; congressional investigation, **Vol. 8, Part 2**, 31; construction, **Vol. 3, Part 1**, 211; **Vol. 5, Part 1**, 3; **Vol. 8, Part 1**, 83 f.; **Vol. 9, Part 2**, 7; **Vol. 10, Part 2**, 346; **Supp. 10**, 550; continental, **Vol. 3, Part 1**, 173; **Vol. 5, Part 1**, 209; **Vol. 5, Part 2**, 184 f.; **Vol. 10, Part 1**, 251; convoy operations, **Supp. 9**, 385; court reform, **Supp. 6**, 34; created, **Vol. 1, Part 1**, 78; defense policies, cold war era, **Supp. 9**, 227–28; *Detroit*, **Vol. 3, Part 2**, 96; development of, **Vol. 2, Part 1**, 586, 617; **Vol. 3, Part 1**, 335 f.; **Vol. 4, Part 2**, 572; **Vol. 6, Part 1**, 489; **Vol. 6, Part 2**, 207, 522, 587; **Vol. 8, Part 1**, 83 f., 237; **Vol. 9, Part 2**, 63, 623; **Vol. 10, Part 1**, 629 f.; **Vol. 10, Part 2**, 165; diplomatic posts, **Supp. 7**, 437–38; discipline, **Vol. 3, Part 1**, 336; **Vol. 6, Part 1**, 204; education, **Supp. 3**, 275; engineering, **Vol. 1, Part 1**, 495; **Vol. 2, Part 2**, 423; **Vol. 3, Part 2**, 158, 170, 405; **Vol. 4, Part 2**, 391; **Vol. 5, Part 1**, 153; **Vol. 7, Part 2**, 487; **Vol. 8, Part 1**, 640; **Vol. 8, Part 2**, 194; **Vol. 9, Part 2**, 613; engineering modernization, **Supp. 3**, 182; expansion, **Supp. 1**, 361; **Supp. 2**, 641; first carrier-to-carrier battle, **Supp. 6**, 577; first engineer in, **Vol. 4, Part 2**, 391; first government vessels produced on Pacific coast, **Vol. 3, Part 1**, 362; first submarine, **Supp. 3**, 120; first warship to visit Hawaii, **Vol. 7, Part 2**, 461; Great White Fleet, **Supp. 8**, 330; **Supp. 9**, 755; **Supp. 10**, 370; gun-boat fleet, construction of, **Vol. 3, Part 1**, 587 f.; **Vol. 9, Part 2**, 7; gunfire control system, **Supp. 5**, 228–29; *Hatteras* and *Alabama*, **Vol. 1, Part 2**, 342; historical writings on, **Supp. 1**, 325; history, **Vol. 3, Part 1**, 107 f.; **Vol. 3, Part 2**, 149 f.; **Vol. 9, Part 1**, 392; impressment of seamen, **Vol. 1, Part 1**, 80; **Vol. 5, Part 2**, 30; **Vol. 9, Part 2**, 47; *Kearsarge* and *Alabama*, **Vol. 8, Part 2**, 581; landing craft, **Supp. 5**, 299; *Leopard* and *Chesapeake*, **Vol. 5, Part 2**, 30; limitation movement, **Supp. 4**, 405–6; **Supp. 5**, 746; **Supp. 6**, 518, 519; London Conference (1930), **Supp. 4**, 786; *Macedonian*, **Vol. 1, Part 1**, 212; *Maine*, destruction of, **Vol. 8, Part 2**, 322; **Vol. 9, Part 1**, 156; Manila Bay, **Vol. 4, Part 1**, 610; **Vol. 5, Part 2**, 559; Medical Corps, **Supp. 4**, 790; Mediterranean squadron, **Vol. 7, Part 2**, 302; merit system of promotion, **Vol. 3, Part 1**, 336; *Merrimac*, **Vol. 3, Part 1**, 529 f.; **Vol. 5, Part 1**, 343; **Vol. 5, Part 2**, 164, 278 f.; **Vol. 8, Part 1**, 97; **Vol. 8, Part 2**, 568; **Vol. 10, Part 2**, 531; mine-sweeping, **Vol. 10, Part 1**, 135; *Mississippi*, **Vol. 9, Part 1**, 321; *Missouri*, **Vol. 8, Part 1**, 214 f.; modernization efforts, **Supp. 7**, 714; *Monitor*, **Vol. 3, Part 1**, 529; **Vol. 5, Part 2**, 14, 164, 278 f.; **Vol. 10, Part 2**, 531; "Mosquito Fleet," **Vol. 5, Part 1**, 152; *Niagara*, capture of, **Vol. 5, Part 2**, 126; nursing, **Vol. 3, Part 1**, 217; operations office, **Supp. 1**, 70; **Supp. 6**, 373, 408; Orient, **Vol. 8, Part 1**, 424; Pacific Fleet, **Supp. 6**, 267–68; Pacific Plans Division, **Supp. 6**, 326; paintings, **Vol. 8, Part 1**, 511 f.; Pearl Harbor investigations, **Supp. 9**, 755; Pennsylvania, **Vol. 8, Part 1**, 430; periscope invented, **Vol. 8, Part 2**, 27; Portsmouth prison reform controversy, **Supp. 4**, 820; preparedness advocacy, **Supp. 8**, 41; *President* and *Little Belt*, **Vol. 3, Part 1**, 188; public works projects, **Supp. 5**, 343; *Randolph* and *True Briton*, **Vol. 1, Part 2**, 242; *Randolph* and *Yarmouth*, **Vol. 1, Part 2**, 242; reforms, **Vol. 4, Part 2**, 106; **Supp. 3**, 275; **Supp. 4**, 216–17; *Reindeer* and *Wasp*, **Vol. 1, Part 2**, 348; reorganization, **Supp. 2**, 614; **Supp. 8**, 152; research, **Vol. 7, Part 2**, 607; **Supp. 8**, 687; retired list of officers on half-pay created, **Vol. 3, Part 1**, 336; "revolt of the admirals," **Supp. 9**, 227; scientific progress of, **Vol. 3, Part 1**, 106 f.; Seabees, **Supp. 10**, 550; Secretary of the Navy, **Vol. 1, Part 1**, 486; **Vol. 4, Part 1**, 481; **Vol. 5, Part 2**, 205; **Vol. 6, Part 1**, 377; **Vol. 7, Part 1**, 108, 264; **Vol. 8, Part 1**, 206 f.; **Vol. 9, Part 2**, 63, 601, 622 f.; **Vol. 10, Part 1**, 629 f.; *Serapis*, **Vol. 3, Part 2**, 268; Siberia, **Vol. 3, Part 2**, 559; smoke screens, developed, **Vol. 3, Part 1**, 614 f.; South Seas, **Vol. 4, Part 2**, 451; **Vol. 8, Part 2**, 77 f., 289; space program, **Supp. 8**, 81; Spanish-American War, preparation, **Vol. 3, Part 1**, 270 f.; strategy, **Supp. 6**, 629; submarine flotilla of the Atlantic Fleet, **Vol. 4, Part 1**, 485; tactics, **Vol. 3, Part 1**, 614 f.; **Vol. 5, Part 1**, 152; telescope sight, **Supp. 3**, 275; *Tigress*, **Vol. 4, Part 1**,

95; *Trent,* **Vol. 4, Part 1,** 594; *True Briton and Randolph,* **Vol. 1, Part 2,** 242; "turret vessels," **Vol. 3, Part 2,** 568; underway replenishment support force, **Supp. 8,** 30; War of 1812, **Vol. 2, Part 1,** 337; **Vol. 6, Part 1,** 50; **Vol. 8, Part 2,** 77; war rules, **Vol. 5, Part 2,** 147; *Wasp* and *Atlanta, Wasp* and *Avon, Wasp* and *Reindeer,* **Vol. 1, Part 2,** 348; West India squadron, **Vol. 7, Part 2,** 186; wireless used, **Vol. 3, Part 1,** 614 f.; women's naval reserve (WAVES), **Supp. 7,** 289; wood and steel, **Vol. 10, Part 2,** 347; world tour of, **Vol. 8, Part 2,** 139; writings on, **Vol. 1, Part 2,** 188; **Vol. 5, Part 2,** 14, 170, 298, 462; **Vol. 6, Part 1,** 489; **Vol. 6, Part 2,** 91, 121, 207; **Vol. 7, Part 2,** 243 f.; **Vol. 8, Part 2,** 86, 543; **Vol. 9, Part 1,** 178, 196; **Vol. 10, Part 1,** 21 f., 425; **Vol. 10, Part 2,** 589; **Supp. 3,** 275; **Supp. 4,** 821; *Yarmouth* and *Randolph,* **Vol. 1, Part 2,** 242. *See also* United States Naval Academy; *names of specific wars*

Navy Athletic Association, founding of, **Supp. 1,** 687

Navy Day, **Supp. 6,** 75

Nazareth, Pa., history of academy at, **Vol. 8, Part 1,** 473

Nazareth Unitarian Society, organization of, **Vol. 5, Part 1,** 612

Nazism: American party, **Supp. 8,** 540–41; art, **Supp. 6,** 552; diplomacy with, **Supp. 4,** 898; ethnological study of, **Supp. 6,** 394; journalism on, **Supp. 10,** 246–47, 562; *Kristallnacht,* **Supp. 7,** 740; movies opposing, **Supp. 6,** 668; **Supp. 10,** 117; opposition to, **Supp. 3,** 85; **Supp. 6,** 25, 201, 451, 643; **Supp. 7,** 498; **Supp. 10,** 143; post-World War II denazification program, **Supp. 3,** 590; **Supp. 6,** 407; study of, **Supp. 5,** 514; **Supp. 9,** 42; support for, **Supp. 4,** 792–93; **Supp. 10,** 152; writings on, **Supp. 10,** 735. *See also* Fascism; Holocaust; War crimes; World War II

NBC Symphony Orchestra: Rodzinski association, **Supp. 6,** 550; Toscanini association, **Supp. 6,** 643, 644; **Supp. 7,** 124

NBER. *See* National Bureau of Economic Research

NCAA. *See* National Collegiate Athletic Association

NEA. *See* Newspaper Enterprise Association

Neal, John Randolph, reference to, **Supp. 6,** 528; **Supp. 8,** 853

Neale, Leonard, reference to, **Vol. 9, Part 2,** 376

Near East: missions, **Vol. 1, Part 2,** 371; relief, **Vol. 8, Part 2,** 261; **Vol. 9, Part 2,** 513 f. *See also* Middle East

Near East Relief, Inc.: organization of, **Supp. 2,** 28; predecessor, **Supp. 4,** 604

Nearing, Scott, references to, **Supp. 4,** 32; **Supp. 7,** 268; **Supp. 10,** 795

Nebraska: botanical survey, **Supp. 7,** 625; Catholic service, **Vol. 7, Part 1,** 618; editorial service, **Vol. 8, Part 2,** 172; first resident of, **Vol. 8, Part 2,** 370; governors, **Vol. 2, Part 2,** 573 f.; **Vol. 4, Part 1,** 77 f.; **Vol. 7, Part 1,** 257; **Supp. 3,** 114; legal service, **Vol. 5, Part 1,** 132; "little TVA," **Supp. 3,** 560; national bank, first in, **Vol. 2, Part 2,** 535; novels about, **Supp. 4,** 154–55; political servlce, **Vol. 2, Part 2,** 573; **Vol. 4, Part 1,** 77; **Vol. 5, Part 1,** 78, 132; **Vol. 6, Part 2,** 230; **Vol. 7, Part 1,** 257; **Vol. 8, Part 2,** 380; politics, **Supp. 3,** 556–61; **Supp. 5,** 318–19, 479, 739; public service, **Vol. 7, Part 2,** 133; railroad incorporation law in, **Vol. 6, Part 2,** 293; Republican party, formation of, **Vol. 5, Part 1,** 78; state capitol architectural design, **Supp. 3,** 196; state fair, **Vol. 4, Part 1,** 77; statehood admission, **Vol. 6, Part 2,** 293; Territory, organization of, as, **Vol. 3, Part 1,** 399 f.

Nebraska state capitol, interior design, **Supp. 7,** 522

Nebulae, **Supp. 5,** 325–26; photographs of, **Vol. 5, Part 2,** 279

Neely, Matthew, reference to, **Supp. 6,** 335

Neff, John M., reference to, **Supp. 7,** 111

Negri, Pola, references to, **Supp. 4,** 508, 509

Negrín, Juan, reference to, **Supp. 3,** 137

Negro American Labor Council (NALC), **Supp. 10,** 661

Negro American League (baseball), **Supp. 3,** 378

Negroes. *See* Blacks

Negro Factories Corporation, founding of, **Supp. 2,** 221

Negro Family in the United States, The, **Supp. 7,** 266

Negro History Week, **Supp. 4,** 911

Negro in American Civilization, The, **Supp. 8,** 521

Negro in Chicago, The (report), **Supp. 6,** 321

Negro Labor Committee, **Supp. 7,** 156

Negro League (baseball), **Supp. 4,** 327–28

Negro Rural School Fund: **Vol. 5, Part 2,** 13; organization of, **Supp. 2,** 150

"Negro" school of literature, **Vol. 6, Part 1,** 276

Negro World, founding of, **Supp. 2,** 221

NEH. *See* National Endowment for the Humanities

Neighborhood Guild, **Supp. 3,** 175

Neighborhood Playhouse (New York City), **Supp. 2,** 687; **Supp. 5,** 52–53; **Supp. 7,** 367

Neighborhoods: criteria, **Supp. 3,** 684; unit concept, **Supp. 3,** 601

Neilan, Marshall, references to, **Supp. 10,** 635, 636

Neilson, Francis, reference to, **Supp. 3,** 554

Nelson, David, reference to, **Supp. 9,** 581

Nelson, Donald M., references to, **Supp. 3,** 660; **Supp. 4,** 458

Nelson, Frank, reference to, **Supp. 9,** 76

Nelson, Gaylord, reference to, **Supp. 8,** 701

Nelson, Harriet, reference to, **Supp. 9,** 580–81

Nelson, Horatio, reference to, **Vol. 1, Part 2,** 242

Nelson, Ricky, reference to, **Supp. 9,** 581

Nematology, research in, **Supp. 1,** 182

Nemiroff, Robert, reference to, **Supp. 7,** 319

Nemours Foundation, **Supp. 1,** 271

Neohumanism, **Supp. 1,** 36

Neologisms, **Supp. 9,** 886

Neoprene, development of, **Supp. 2,** 97, 489

Nepera Chemical Co., **Supp. 3,** 26

Nephritis. *See* Kidneys

Nephrolithotomy, first in America, **Vol. 9, Part 2,** 535

Neptune, **Vol. 4, Part 2,** 162

Nernst, Walther, reference to, **Supp. 6,** 364

Nervous disorders. *See* Mental health and illness

Nervous system: behavior influenced by, **Supp. 3,** 172; convulsion, photographs of, **Supp. 1,** 241; development of, **Supp. 6,** 282–83; disease studies, **Supp. 4,** 249–50; **Supp. 8,** 429; fiber categorization, **Supp. 7,** 280; impulse conduction, **Supp. 6,** 100; **Supp. 7,** 226, 280; perception theory, **Supp. 8,** 344, 345; reflex actions, **Supp. 2,** 390; research on, **Supp. 3,** 805–6; research on origin of, **Supp. 5,** 536; synapse structure, **Supp. 6,** 296; transmitters, **Supp. 3,** 134–36. *See also* Neurology

Nesbitt, Evelyn, reference to, **Supp. 4,** 826–27

Ness, Eliot, reference to, **Supp. 7,** 806

Nestle-LeMur Co., founding of, **Supp. 5,** 512

Netherlands, **Vol. 7, Part 1,** 456; **Vol. 8, Part 1,** 285; diplomacy, **Vol. 3, Part 1,** 89; mission to, **Vol. 5, Part 1,** 346

Neuberger, Maurine Brown, reference to, **Supp. 6,** 475

Neuberger, Richard L., reference to, **Supp. 7,** 814

Neuralgla, facial, **Supp. 4,** 214

Neuroanatomy, studies in, **Supp. 1,** 439, 584; **Supp. 6,** 295–96

Neurological Institute of New York, founding of, **Supp. 4,** 249–50

Neurology: **Vol. 1, Part 2,** 93; **Vol. 3, Part 2,** 18, 469; **Vol. 4, Part 2,** 180, 210; **Vol. 5, Part 1,** 97; **Vol. 5, Part 2,** 451; **Vol. 7, Part 1,** 3, 267 f.; **Vol. 8, Part 1,**

136 f., 282 f.; **Vol. 8, Part 2**, 560; **Vol. 9, Part 1**, 461, 534; **Vol. 10, Part 1**, 613 f.; diagnostic procedures, **Supp. 4**, 214, 250; **Supp. 10**, 780; expert medical testimony, **Supp. 3**, 385; **Supp. 6**, 403; Kennedy syndrome, **Supp. 5**, 384; neuroanatomy, **Supp. 1**, 439, 584; **Supp. 6**, 295–96; neuropathology, **Supp. 1**, 241; **Supp. 2**, 24; organic, **Supp. 2**, 161; psychiatric relationship to, **Supp. 4**, 618; **Supp. 8**, 429–30; research in, **Supp. 1**, 220; **Supp. 2**, 516; **Supp. 9**, 125; sensory perception, **Supp. 2**, 156; shell-shock studies, **Supp. 5**, 383; strychnine studies, **Supp. 2**, 161; surgery, *see* Neurosurgery; teaching of, **Supp. 3**, 620; translation of writings on, **Supp. 3**, 386; writings on, **Vol. 5, Part 2**, 451; **Vol. 7, Part 1**, 62; **Vol. 9, Part 1**, 535; **Vol. 10, Part 1**, 613 f.; **Supp. 3**, 386, 682; **Supp. 4**, 250. *See also* Brain; Nervous system; Psychiatry; Psychoanalysis
Neuropathology, research in, **Supp. 1**, 241; **Supp. 2**, 24
Neurophysiology, **Supp. 7**, 226, 280–81, 476–77
Neuropsychiatry, **Vol. 9, Part 1**, 410; **Vol. 10, Part 1**, 613 f.
Neuropsychology, brain damage studies, **Supp. 10**, 779, 780
Neurosis, basis of, **Supp. 5**, 316–17
Neurosurgery, **Supp. 2**, 137, 209; **Supp. 6**, 130–31, 223–24; **Supp. 9**, 220–21
Neurotransmitters: early studies in, **Supp. 3**, 134–37; noradrenaline discovery, **Supp. 3**, 136
Neutra, Richard J., reference to, **Supp. 5**, 606
Neutral Ground Agreement (1806). *See* Sabine expedition, La. (1806)
Neutrality: "Freedom of the Seas," **Vol. 4, Part 1**, 70; legal aspects of, **Vol. 9, Part 2**, 105; Proclamation, 1793, **Vol. 5, Part 2**, 8
Neutrality Acts (1935, 1936, 1937), **Supp. 5**, 731; **Supp. 8**, 441
Neutrino, **Supp. 5**, 220
Neutrons: bombardment reactions, **Supp. 5**, 273; research in, **Supp. 5**, 220, 221; **Supp. 6**, 501
Nevada: botany in, **Vol. 6, Part 1**, 162; free-silver agitation, **Vol. 9, Part 2**, 14; frontier life, **Vol. 9, Part 2**, 247; gambling in, **Supp. 10**, 308–9; 357; gold rush, **Supp. 5**, 613; governors, **Vol. 1, Part 2**, 358 f.; legal service, **Vol. 1, Part 2**, 102; mining, **Vol. 6, Part 2**, 76; mining law in, **Vol. 9, Part 2**, 13 f.; political service, **Vol. 1, Part 2**, 358; **Vol. 7, Part 1**, 600; politics, **Supp. 5**, 443; public service, **Vol. 7, Part 1**, 462; woman suffrage, **Supp. 5**, 473–74, 742
Nevelska, Maria, reference to, **Supp. 10**, 206
Never-Ending Wrong, **Supp. 10**, 641
Nevins, Allan, reference to, **Supp. 3**, 32
Nevler, Leona, reference to, **Supp. 7**, 531–32
New America, **Supp. 8**, 681
New American Cyclopaedia, edition of, **Vol. 8, Part 1**, 624
New American Orchardist, The, **Vol. 5, Part 2**, 341
New Amsterdam: **Vol. 5, Part 2**, 371; **Vol. 6, Part 2**, 500, 591; **Vol. 7, Part 1**, 34; **Vol. 10, Part 1**, 162; commerce, **Vol. 4, Part 2**, 592; **Vol. 6, Part 1**, 156; first church edifice in, **Vol. 1, Part 2**, 406; surveying work, **Vol. 5, Part 1**, 336
Newark, N.J.: development, **Vol. 2, Part 1**, 296; **Vol. 10, Part 2**, 571; first bishop of, **Vol. 1, Part 2**, 74; philanthropic services, **Vol. 10, Part 1**, 432 f.; public service, **Vol. 2, Part 2**, 328 f.; street-paving fraud in, **Vol. 8, Part 1**, 588; water supply, **Supp. 1**, 663
Newark Bears (baseball), **Supp. 9**, 854
Newark College, **Vol. 4, Part 1**, 268
Newark Library, development of, **Vol. 3, Part 1**, 57
Newark Museum, **Vol. 3, Part 1**, 318; **Supp. 3**, 30–31; **Supp. 6**, 96
New Bedford, Mass.: founding and naming of, **Vol. 8, Part 2**, 246; history of, **Vol. 4, Part 2**, 4; **Vol. 8, Part 1**, 586 f.; raided by British (1778), **Vol. 8, Part 2**, 246; shipping industry, **Vol. 8, Part 2**, 246; whaling industry, **Vol. 8, Part 2**, 41, 246
New Bern, N.C.: colonial architecture of, **Vol. 4, Part 2**, 417; German Palatines there, **Vol. 6, Part 1**, 58
Newberry, Truman H., references to, **Supp. 3**, 559; **Supp. 4**, 299
Newberry Library (Chicago), **Vol. 7, Part 1**, 447; **Vol. 9, Part 2**, 587; **Supp. 4**, 846; **Supp. 7**, 295
Newbery Medal, **Supp. 7**, 525
New Brunswick, N.J.: Civic service, **Vol. 8, Part 2**, 486; legal service, **Vol. 1, Part 2**, 375; Presbytery of, **Vol. 1, Part 2**, 340
New Brunswick Theological Seminary, **Vol. 10, Part 2**, 482
Newburgh, N.Y., founding of, **Vol. 5, Part 2**, 484
Newburgh Letters (1783), **Vol. 1, Part 1**, 355; **Vol. 2, Part 1**, 80; **Vol. 4, Part 1**, 187; **Vol. 7, Part 1**, 510; **Vol. 8, Part 1**, 284 f.; **Vol. 10, Part 1**, 519
Newbury, Mass., **Vol. 7, Part 2**, 242
Newburyport, Mass.: **Vol. 3, Part 1**, 282; **Vol. 8, Part 1**, 179; **Supp. 6**, 427, 428; anthropological study of, **Supp. 8**, 684; legal service, **Vol. 1, Part 2**, 549; public service, **Vol. 7, Part 2**, 280, 597
New Caledonia, **Supp. 3**, 583
New capitalism, **Supp. 7**, 809
New Cascade Tunnel (Wash.), **Supp. 7**, 90
New Challenge, founding of, **Supp. 6**, 715
New Choral Society of New York, conducting of, **Vol. 5, Part 2**, 486
New Church, **Vol. 1, Part 1**, 644; **Vol. 8, Part 1**, 448 f. *See also* Swedenborgian church
New-Church Magazine for Children, **Vol. 8, Part 1**, 455
New Colophon, founding of, **Supp. 7**, 3
Newcomb, Simon, reference to, **Vol. 5, Part 1**, 136
Newcombe, Don, reference to, **Supp. 8**, 142
Newcomer, J. Sidney, reference to, **Supp. 7**, 280
New Criticism, **Supp. 7**, 55, 219, 347, 442; **Supp. 8**, 325–27; **Supp. 9**, 643
New Deal: **Vol. 10, Part 2**, 495; agricultural policies, **Supp. 3**, 319, 434; **Supp. 6**, 487, 559, 638–39; **Supp. 7**, 760–61; **Supp. 8**, 445, 700; American Indian organization opposing, **Supp. 7**, 393–94; antitrust actions, **Supp. 3**, 168; **Supp. 8**, 17; arts progects, **Supp. 8**, 176–77; black representation in, **Supp. 4**, 251; Brain Trust, **Supp. 3**, 399–400, 647; **Supp. 9**, 84, 85, 553; **Supp. 8**, 679; business relationship, **Supp. 5**, 165; **Supp. 6**, 520, 615, 675; child labor codes, **Supp. 3**, 228; congressional opposition, **Supp. 5**, 114, 139, 561–62, 674–75, 703, 715; **Supp. 7**, 312; **Supp. 8**, 27, 68, 247, 268–69, 532; **Supp. 9**, 151, 590, 610–11; congressional relations, **Supp. 5**, 180–81; **Supp. 7**, 467–68, 541; **Supp. 8**, 508; **Supp. 9**, 95, 150–51, 256, 373, 634, 689; **Supp. 10**, 484, 814; construction projects, **Supp. 8**, 308–9; criticism of, **Supp. 9**, 243, 426, 554, 695; economic policies, **Supp. 3**, 649–51; **Supp. 8**, 79; Farm Security Administration, **Supp. 6**, 12; Federal Arts Project, **Supp. 3**, 112; **Supp. 6**, 96, 97; federal patronage in, **Supp. 6**, 260, 419, 601; "first hundred days," **Supp. 3**, 650; **Supp. 9**, 554; first steel code, **Supp. 6**, 622; fiscal policies, **Supp. 6**, 33–34, 377; journalism criticizing, **Supp. 5**, 664; **Supp. 9**, 472, 482; labor legislation, **Supp. 5**, 718–19; labor relations, **Supp. 3**, 547; **Supp. 4**, 376; **Supp. 5**, 263; **Supp. 8**, 375–76; legal defense of, **Supp. 2**, 501; **Supp. 5**, 174, 572; legislation, **Supp. 7**, 635; **Supp. 9**, 95; National Emergency Council, **Supp. 6**, 542, 660; organizations opposing, **Supp. 8**, 592–93; **Supp. 10**,

22; political activity against, **Supp. 4**, 42, 480; public utilities policies, **Supp. 3**, 138; relief legislation, **Supp. 4**, 810; "second," **Supp. 3**, 654–56; social welfare policies, **Supp. 7**, 488, 787; social welfare programs, **Supp. 9**, 28; state programs, **Supp. 4**, 612–13; **Supp. 5**, 459; **Supp. 6**, 474–75; stock-market reform legislation, **Supp. 9**, 607; Supreme Court decisions on, **Supp. 3**, 99–100, 755, 789, 839; **Supp. 4**, 406–7, 537, 795–97; **Supp. 5**, 358, 572–75; **Supp. 6**, 137–38; **Supp. 7**, 263; **Supp. 8**, 35; *Survey*, **Supp. 6**, 330; tax legislation, **Supp. 5**, 180–81, 712; term coined, **Supp. 3**, 647; **Supp. 9**, 680; work-relief concept, **Supp. 4**, 391–92; writings on, **Supp. 10**, 796. *See also* Public works; *specific agencies and legislation*

New Delhi, India, U.S. embassy, **Supp. 10**, 764–65

"New Divinity," opposition to, **Vol. 10, Part 1**, 85

New Durham, N.H., birthplace of the Freewill Baptist denomination, **Vol. 8, Part 1**, 345 f.

New England: agriculture, **Vol. 3, Part 2**, 479; **Vol. 10, Part 2**, 210; "American System of Tariff," **Vol. 6, Part 1**, 45; architectural tradition, **Supp. 4**, 24, 115; birds of, **Vol. 8, Part 2**, 324; blacks imported to, **Vol. 7, Part 2**, 406; Cape Cod, writings on, **Supp. 3**, 461; Catholic church, **Supp. 3**, 568–71; coast survey, **Vol. 3, Part 1**, 106; composers, **Supp. 3**, 42; Confederacy of (1650), **Vol. 4, Part 2**, 396; discovery of, **Vol. 2, Part 1**, 39; Episcopal church, **Vol. 8, Part 2**, 529; exploration of, **Vol. 1, Part 2**, 378; **Vol. 10, Part 1**, 562 f.; federalism in, **Vol. 7, Part 2**, 566 f.; glaciers' effect on, **Vol. 10, Part 2**, 512; historic preservations and restorations, **Supp. 3**, 567; history and folklore studies, **Supp. 3**, 423–24; history of, **Vol. 2, Part 2**, 336; **Vol. 3, Part 1**, 612; **Vol. 5, Part 1**, 333; **Vol. 5, Part 2**, 370; **Vol. 7, Part 1**, 361, 476; **Vol. 8, Part 2**, 388; **Vol. 9, Part 1**, 142; **Vol. 9, Part 2**, 653; iron works in, **Vol. 6, Part 1**, 73; Indian wars in, **Vol. 10, Part 1**, 8; Loyalists, **Vol. 1, Part 2**, 54; **Vol. 6, Part 1**, 175; **Vol. 10, Part 2**, 266; map of, **Vol. 1, Part 2**, 378; Methodist church, **Vol. 6, Part 1**, 112; manufacturing in, **Vol. 3, Part 1**, 563 f.; piracy, **Vol. 3, Part 1**, 483; **Vol. 8, Part 1**, 140 f.; religious persecution, **Vol. 3, Part 2**, 488; tariff, **Vol. 6, Part 1**, 45, 108 f.; textile industry, **Vol. 1, Part 1**, 348; **Vol. 6, Part 1**, 45 f., 47, 51; War of 1812, opposed, **Vol. 9, Part 2**, 145; westward migration from, **Supp. 7**, 353–54; woolen manufacture, **Vol. 6, Part 1**, 51; **Vol. 8, Part 1**, 334; writers, **Supp. 6**, 252; writings on, **Vol. 1, Part 1**, 434; **Vol. 4, Part 1**, 12; **Vol. 5, Part 2**, 72. *See also specific state and city names*

New England Agricultural Society, **Vol. 6, Part 1**, 418

New England Almanack, The, **Vol. 3, Part 1**, 23; **Vol. 4, Part 2**, 390

New England Anti-Slavery Society, **Vol. 3, Part 1**, 407; **Vol. 4, Part 1**, 169; **Vol. 5, Part 2**, 112

New England Bureau of Education, **Vol. 7, Part 2**, 48

New England Club of Loyalists, **Vol. 1, Part 2**, 393

New England Confederation, **Vol. 1, Part 2**, 579

New England Conservatory of Music, **Vol. 3, Part 1**, 513; **Vol. 5, Part 2**, 214; **Vol. 9, Part 2**, 605; **Supp. 1**, 161, 162

New England Council, **Vol. 8, Part 2**, 183

New England Courant, **Vol. 3, Part 2**, 599

New England Divorce Reform League, **Vol. 3, Part 1**, 308

New England Emigrant Aid Co., **Vol. 3, Part 2**, 69; **Vol. 6, Part 1**, 48; **Vol. 8, Part 1**, 54 f.; **Vol. 8, Part 2**, 35; **Vol. 9, Part 2**, 402 f.

New England Farmer, **Vol. 3, Part 2**, 347

New England Female Medical College, **Vol. 4, Part 1**, 604

New England Galaxy, **Vol. 9, Part 2**, 592

New England Girlhood, A, **Vol. 5, Part 2**, 614

New England Historic Genealogical Society, **Vol. 5, Part 2**, 54; **Vol. 9, Part 2**, 503

New England Hospital for Women and Children, **Vol. 10, Part 2**, 642

New England Journal of Medicine, editorship, **Supp. 10**, 370

New England Mutual Life Insurance Co., **Vol. 7, Part 2**, 547

New England Primer, **Vol. 4, Part 2**, 304

New England Review, **Vol. 8, Part 1**, 186 f.

New-Englands Plantation, **Vol. 5, Part 1**, 12

New England Tract Society, **Vol. 7, Part 1**, 245

New England Trust Co., **Vol. 2, Part 2**, 111

New England's Rarities Discovered, **Vol. 5, Part 2**, 219–20

New France: downfall of, **Vol. 3, Part 1**, 317; founding of, in Florida, **Vol. 8, Part 1**, 533; martyrdom, **Vol. 5, Part 2**, 75; missions, **Vol. 5, Part 2**, 74 f.

New Granada, **Vol. 5, Part 2**, 173

New Guinea, anthropological studies, **Supp. 10**, 522

New Hampshire: agriculture, **Vol. 8, Part 2**, 120, boundary disputes with Connecticut, **Vol. 8, Part 1**, 426; codification of laws, **Vol. 8, Part 1**, 579 f.; education, **Vol. 4, Part 2**, 76; **Vol. 8, Part 1**, 12 f., 345 f.; exile of governor, **Vol. 10, Part 1**, 656 f.; federalists in, **Vol. 7, Part 2**, 575; geology of, **Vol. 5, Part 1**, 70; governors, **Vol. 1, Part 2**, 9 f., 162 f., 227 f.; **Vol. 2, Part 2**, 54 f.; **Vol. 4, Part 1**, 311; **Vol. 4, Part 2**, 300 f.; **Vol. 7, Part 1**, 195 f.; **Vol. 7, Part 2**, 575; **Vol. 8, Part 2**, 121; **Vol. 9, Part 1**, 291 f.; **Vol. 10, Part 1**, 653 f., 656 f.; **Supp. 4**, 899–900; **Supp. 5**, 689; **Supp. 7**, 73; historian, state, **Vol. 1, Part 2**, 488; history of, **Vol. 1, Part 2**, 153; **Vol. 2, Part 2**, 603; **Vol. 3, Part 2**, 304 f.; **Vol. 6, Part 2**, 581; **Vol. 7, Part 1**, 127; **Vol. 10, Part 1**, 653 f., 656 f.; land grants, **Vol. 6, Part 1**, 307; legal service, **Vol. 1, Part 2**, 210, 380; **Vol. 2, Part 2**, reference to; **Vol. 3, Part 1**, 354, 409; **Vol. 6, Part 1**, 304; **Vol. 6, Part 2**, 366; **Vol. 8, Part 1**, 230, 341, 427, 478, 564, 579; **Vol. 9, Part 1**, 291, 293; **Vol. 10, Part 1**, 566 f.; **Vol. 10, Part 2**, 388; maps of, **Vol. 5, Part 2**, 588; Massachusetts, withdrawal from, **Vol. 8, Part 1**, 356 f.; "Old Home Week," origin of, **Vol. 8, Part 2**, 121; political service, **Vol. 1, Part 2**, 11, 144, 153, 162, 227, 275, 334; **Vol. 2, Part 2**, 54; **Vol. 3, Part 1**, 600; **Vol. 3, Part 2**, 293; **Vol. 4, Part 1**, 304, 311, 409; **Vol. 4, Part 2**, 105, 300; **Vol. 5, Part 1**, 35; **Vol. 5, Part 2**, 587, 588; **Vol. 7, Part 1**, 196; **Vol. 7, Part 2**, 303, 575; **Vol. 7, Part 1**, 12; **Vol. 8, Part 1**, 12; **Vol. 8, Part 2**, 121; **Vol. 9, Part 1**, 291; **Vol. 10, Part 1**, 28, 566 f., 585 f., 653 f., 656 f.; **Vol. 10, Part 2**, 388, 488; politics, **Supp. 3**, 425, 543; **Supp. 4**, 164–65, 899–900; **Supp. 5**, 689–90; printer, first in, **Vol. 3, Part 2**, 561; public service, **Vol. 1, Part 2**, 5 f.; **Vol. 3, Part 2**, 494 f.; **Vol. 4, Part 1**, 304 f; **Vol. 4, Part 2**, 105, 446; **Vol. 5, Part 1**, 34, 5; **Vol. 5, Part 2**, 404 f.; **Vol. 6, Part 1**, 81, 304, 308; **Vol. 6, Part 2**, 580; **Vol. 7, Part 2**, 340; **Vol. 8, Part 1**, 12 f.; reforestation in, **Vol. 8, Part 2**, 121; Republican party, **Vol. 8, Part 2**, 120; Revolutionary War period, **Vol. 10, Part 2**, 71

New Hampshire Historical Society, **Vol. 1, Part 2**, 6; **Vol. 7, Part 1**, 127

New Hampshire Journal, **Vol. 7, Part 1**, 127

New Hampshire Medical Society, **Vol. 1, Part 2**, 11; founding of, **Vol. 7, Part 2**, 340

New Harmony, Ind., **Vol. 3, Part 2**, 479; **Vol. 6, Part 1**, 190; **Vol. 7, Part 1**, 402; **Vol. 7, Part 2**, 119; **Vol. 8, Part 2**, 224, 402; **Vol. 9, Part 2**, 648

New Haven, Conn.: **Vol. 3, Part 1**, 612, **Vol. 6, Part 1**, 138; business and civic service, **Vol. 9, Part 1**, 456; colonial architecture of, **Vol. 5, Part 1**, 83; dancing master, compelled to leave, **Vol. 9, Part 2**, 20; doc-

umentary history of, **Vol. 3, Part 1**, 227; first settlement of, **Vol. 3, Part 1**, 612; founding of, **Vol. 3, Part 1**, 86 f.; **Vol. 8, Part 1**, 252 f.; history of, **Vol. 3, Part 1**, 612; independence of, **Vol. 3, Part 1**, 86 f.; medal to commemorate founding of, **Vol. 9, Part 2**, 611; musical development of, **Vol. 9, Part 1**, 564; public affairs, **Vol. 1, Part 1**, 544 f.; theocratic government, **Vol. 3, Part 1**, 612

New Haven Colony Historical Society, formation of, **Vol. 1, Part 2**, 97

New Haven Railraod, **Supp. 5**, 190–91

New Hope Church, Ga., operation at. *See* Atlanta campaign

Newhouse, Samuel, **Supp. 10**, 414

New Humanism, The, **Supp. 7**, 374

New Jersey: boundary disputes, **Vol. 5, Part 2**, 6, 11; Calvinism in, **Vol. 3, Part 1**, 302; Catholic church, **Vol. 6, Part 2**, 44, 163; **Vol. 10, Part 2**, 189; Civil War period, **Vol. 2, Part 1**, 577; constitution, **Vol. 1, Part 2**, 478; **Vol. 4, Part 1**, 546; **Supp. 9**, 245; Democratic party, **Vol. 10, Part 2**, 355; **Supp. 9**, 263, 455–56; education, **Vol. 1, Part 1**, 511 f.; **Vol. 1, Part 2**, 19; **Vol. 3, Part 2**, 369; **Vol. 4, Part 2**, 92; **Vol. 7, Part 1**, 359; **Vol. 7, Part 2**, 228; **Vol. 8, Part 1**, 214 f.; Emancipation Act, **Vol. 1, Part 2**, 386; Episcopal church, **Vol. 8, Part 1**, 249 f.; geology, **Vol. 2, Part 2**, 373 f.; **Vol. 8, Part 1**, 214 f.; governors, **Vol. 1, Part 1**, 2 f.; **Vol. 1, Part 2**, 221, 386; **Vol. 2, Part 1**, 546; **Vol. 3, Part 1**, 289 f.; **Vol. 4, Part 2**, 92 f.; **Vol. 5, Part 1**, 304; **Vol. 7, Part 1**, 213 f., 350, 459 f., 636 f.; **Vol. 7, Part 2**, 11 f., 232, 442, 443 f.; **Vol. 8, Part 1**, 214 f., 369; **Vol. 9, Part 1**, 411 f.; **Vol. 10, Part 1**, 295 f., 432 f.; **Vol. 10, Part 2**, 300 f.; **Supp. 6**, 187–88, 265–66; **Supp. 8**, 152–53, **Supp. 9**, 244–45; "Great Seal War," **Vol. 3, Part 1**, 290; highway system modernized, **Supp. 9**, 245; history of, **Vol. 2, Part 1**, 546; **Vol. 3, Part 2**, 118; **Vol. 7, Part 1**, 427; holding companies legalized, **Vol. 3, Part 1**, 309; Indian reservation in, **Vol. 8, Part 1**, 419; insane, care of, **Vol. 8, Part 1**, 369; judicial reform, **Supp. 6**, 651–52; judiciary, **Supp. 1**, 365; land speculation, **Vol. 8, Part 1**, 419; legal reforms, **Vol. 1, Part 1**, 168; **Vol. 3, Part 1**, 289 f.; **Vol. 4, Part 1**, 626; **Vol. 5, Part 2**, 421; **Vol. 7, Part 1**, 531; legal service, **Vol. 1, Part 2**, 98, 386, 572; **Vol. 3, Part 1**, 167, 289, 309; **Vol. 4, Part 1**, 546, 626, 627; **Vol. 5, Part 1**, 230; **Vol. 5, Part 2**, 255; **Vol. 6, Part 1**, 270; **Vol. 6, Part 2**, 198; **Vol. 7, Part 1**, 224, **Vol. 7, Part 2**, 233, 234, 443, 517; **Vol. 8, Part 1**, 419, 494; **Vol. 9, Part 1**, 412; **Vol. 10, Part 2**, 301; lifesaving apparatus on coast, **Vol. 8, Part 1**, 214 f.; maps, **Vol. 6, Part 1**, 315; newspaper, first in, **Vol. 7, Part 2**, 227; organized crime, **Supp. 10**, 75; oyster culture, **Vol. 7, Part 1**, 418; paleobotanical systems, **Supp. 3**, 62; political service, **Vol. 1, Part 2**, 68, 101, 144, 221, 386, 477; **Vol. 3, Part 1**, 166, 289, 290, 302, 463, 540; **Vol. 3, Part 2**, 600; **Vol. 4, Part 2**, 92; **Vol. 5, Part 1**, 92, 304, 401; **Vol. 6, Part 1**, 325, 584; **Vol. 7, Part 1**, 168, 213 f., 350, 459, 636; **Vol. 7, Part 2**, 11, 232, 294, 442, 533, 642; **Vol. 8, Part 1**, 46, 214, 369, 494, 588; **Vol. 8, Part 2**, 31, 589; **Vol. 9, Part 1**, 1, 286; **Vol. 9, Part 2**, 45, 47, 49; **Vol. 10, Part 1**, 432 f.; **Vol. 10, Part 2**, 300; politics, **Supp. 5**, 198, 696; **Supp. 6**, 265–66, 479–80; **Supp. 8**, 245–46, 648; **Supp. 9**, 244–45, 263, 455–56; Port Authority, **Supp. 10**, 788–89; Presbyterian church, **Vol. 6, Part 2**, 32; pre-Revolutionary War Period, **Vol. 10, Part 2**, 437; printing, public, **Vol. 7, Part 2**, 227; proprietary rule, overthrow of, **Vol. 1, Part 2**, 36; public service, **Vol. 2, Part 2**, 442; **Vol. 4, Part 2**, 180 f.; **Vol. 5, Part 1**, 232, 267; **Vol. 6, Part 1**, 283; **Vol. 7, Part 1**, 350; **Vol. 7, Part 2**, 228, 233 f., 293 f.; **Vol. 8, Part 1**, 214 f., 369; **Vol. 9, Part 1**, 250, 333; **Vol. 10, Part 1**, 618 f.; public welfare, **Supp. 6**, 515–16; railroad consolidation in, **Vol. 10, Part 1**, 618 f.; Republican party, **Vol. 7, Part 2**, 233; retail business, **Supp. 3**, 30; Revolutionary War period, **Vol. 4, Part 2**, 241, 359; **Vol. 7, Part 2**, 631; **Vol. 10, Part 2**, 437; Riparian-Rights Act, **Vol. 4, Part 1**, 274; Roman Catholic dioceses, **Supp. 5**, 722–23; special education programs, **Supp. 4**, 438–39

New Jersey Colonization Society, founding of, **Vol. 9, Part 2**, 48

New Jersey Medical Society: **Vol. 2, Part 2**, 251; **Vol. 1, Part 2**, 385; first of its kind, **Vol. 4, Part 2**, 532

New Jersey Historical Society, **Vol. 3, Part 2**, 370

New Jersey State College. *See* Rutgers University

New Jersey State Normal School, **Vol. 4, Part 2**, 360

New Jersey Training School for Feeble-Minded Boys and Girls, **Supp. 6**, 240

New Jersey Woman's Press Club, **Vol. 3, Part 1**, 394

New Jersey Zinc & Iron Co., **Supp. 3**, 348

New Jerusalem Magazine, **Vol. 8, Part 1**, 448, 455

New Journal of Commerce, **Vol. 4, Part 2**, 98, 157 f.; **Vol. 8, Part 1**, 228 f.; **Vol. 9, Part 2**, 73 f., 299, 303

New Left: **Supp. 7**, 540; Marcuse influence, **Supp. 10**, 507

New Light movement, **Vol. 1, Part 1**, 219; **Vol. 1, Part 2**, 165; **Vol. 4, Part 2**, 554, **Vol. 6, Part 1**, 41; **Vol. 9, Part 2**, 71

New London, Conn.: civic services to, **Vol. 10, Part 1**, 384 f.; legal service, **Vol. 1, Part 2**, 598; submarine base, **Supp. 6**, 338

New Machine (organization), **Supp. 5**, 558

New Market, Va., battle of, **Vol. 2, Part 1**, 10; **Vol. 3, Part 2**, 1; **Vol. 5, Part 1**, 401

New Masses: **Supp. 7**, 113, 114, 239, 268; **Supp. 8**, 216; **Supp. 10**, 706

New Mexico: colonizing of, **Vol. 5, Part 2**, 554; education, **Vol. 8, Part 1**, 229 f.; *Emigrant's Guide to New Mexico, The*, published 1849, **Vol. 3, Part 1**, 319; exploration, **Vol. 1, Part 1**, 571; **Vol. 2, Part 1**, 486; **Vol. 3, Part 2**, 184; **Vol. 7, Part 1**, 533; founding of, **Vol. 7, Part 2**, 38 f.; governors, **Vol. 5, Part 2**, 583; **Vol. 6, Part 1**, 7 f.; **Vol. 7, Part 2**, 89 f., 415 f., 458 f.; **Vol. 8, Part 2**, 569 f.; **Vol. 10, Part 1**, 375 f.; history of, **Vol. 2, Part 2**, 584; **Vol. 8, Part 1**, 229 f.; horticulture, **Vol. 8, Part 1**, 229 f.; Indians, relations with, **Vol. 3, Part 1**, 93 f.; **Vol. 7, Part 2**, 90; irrigation, **Vol. 3, Part 1**, 606; insurance companies, **Supp. 9**, 31; legal service, **Vol. 1, Part 2**, 332; **Vol. 8, Part 1**, 229; **Vol. 9, Part 1**, 482; legislation, **Supp. 1**, 671; missions, **Vol. 1, Part 2**, 174; **Vol. 5, Part 2**, 567; **Vol. 6, Part 2**, 61; photographs of Indians, **Supp. 3**, 295; pioneer life, **Vol. 6, Part 2**, 442; political service, **Vol. 1, Part 1**, 446; **Vol. 2, Part 2**, 348; **Vol. 3, Part 1**, 260; **Vol. 5, Part 2**, 273, 583; **Vol. 6, Part 1**, 7 f.; **Vol. 7, Part 1**, 60; **Vol. 7, Part 2**, 415, 458; **Vol. 8, Part 1**, 229; **Vol. 8, Part 2**, 176, 569; **Vol. 10, Part 1**, 375 f., 528 f.; **Supp. 10**, 548; politics, **Supp. 3**, 258–60; **Supp. 7**, 121–22, 326; **Supp. 10**, 548, 549; public service, **Vol. 8, Part 1**, 229 f.; **Vol. 8, Part 2**, 306; reconquest of (1693), **Vol. 3, Part 1**, 260; researches in, **Vol. 1, Part 1**, 571; road building, **Supp. 1**, 671; rocket experiments, **Supp. 3**, 307; Spanish settlers in, **Vol. 7, Part 2**, 89 f.; statehood, admission to, **Vol. 3, Part 2**, 83; **Vol. 9, Part 2**, 270; territorial government, creation of, **Vol. 3, Part 1**, 399

New Monetary System, A, **Vol. 5, Part 2**, 302

New Music Recordings, **Supp. 5**, 353

New National Museum, **Vol. 1, Part 2**, 346

New Netherlands, history of, **Vol. 5, Part 2**, 370 f., 508; **Vol. 7, Part 1**, 613; **Vol. 10, Part 1**, 178

New Netherlands Bank, **Supp. 10**, 847

New Orleans, La.: **Vol. 6, Part 1**, 24; **Vol. 7, Part 1**, 35;

Vol. 7, Part 2, 459; Vol. 8, Part 2, 164 f., 289; architecture, Supp. 1, 219, 331; banking in, Vol. 8, Part 1, 644; battle of, Vol. 1, Part 1, 34; Vol. 5, Part 1, 365, 529, 589; Vol. 5, Part 2, 540; Vol. 6, Part 2, 192; Vol. 7, Part 1, 90; Vol. 7, Part 2, 301 f.; Cajun tradition, Supp. 4, 102; capture of, Vol. 1, Part 1, 34, 500, 502, 579–80; Vol. 2, Part 1, 358; Vol. 3, Part 2, 288; Vol. 6, Part 1, 288, 442; Vol. 8, Part 1, 87; Catholic church, Vol. 1, Part 1, 321; charities, Vol. 4, Part 2, 398; Vol. 5, Part 2, 547; cholera epidemic, Vol. 9, Part 2, 85; city charter of, Vol. 3, Part 1, 545 f.; civic service, Vol. 4, Part 2, 353; Vol. 5, Part 1, 300; civil rights movement in, Supp. 10, 170–71; Creole families of, Vol. 1, Part 2, 479; Delgado Museum of Art, Vol. 4, Part 2, 353; draining of, Vol. 1, Part 2, 111; Vol. 8, Part 2, 125; early settlement, Vol. 3, Part 1, 534; educational service, Vol. 3, Part 1, 493 f.; Vol. 9, Part 1, 404; first black city councilman, Supp. 10, 171; flood control, Vol. 8, Part 1, 589; founding, of, Vol. 1, Part 2, 251; Vol. 7, Part 2, 318 f.; French newspapers, Vol. 9, Part 2, 383; gambling licensed, Vol. 8, Part 2, 28; health service, Vol. 8, Part 1, 575; inner navigation canal, Supp. 3, 310; Jackson's defense of, in War of 1812, Vol. 8, Part 1, 480; jazz, Supp. 2, 502; Supp. 3, 541; Supp. 5, 106; Supp. 6, 41; Supp. 9, 45–46, 598; Supp. 10, 58; legal service, Vol. 5, Part 1, 300; mayors, Supp. 9, 533–34; medical development in, Vol. 9, Part 2, 85; *Picayune*, Vol. 5, Part 2, 327; Vol. 7, Part 1, 499; Supp. 5, 244; political patronage, Supp. 9, 533–34; political service, Vol. 1, Part 2, 140, 461; politics, Supp. 7, 555; reform, Vol. 3, Part 2, 292; religious services, Vol. 3, Part 1, 473 f.; riots in, Vol. 1, Part 2, 351; Vol. 5, Part 2, 305; Vol. 6, Part 2, 39; Vol. 7, Part 1, 487; Vol. 7, Part 2, 611; Vol. 10, Part 1, 458; Roman Catholic diocese, Supp. 7, 668–69; sanitation, Vol. 5, Part 2, 193; school desegregation, Supp. 8, 500; stones, Vol. 5, Part 2, 390; surgery in, Vol. 9, Part 2, 85; theater in, Vol. 3, Part 1, 133; Vol. 6, Part 1, 493; Vieux Carr, Vol. 6, Part 1, 19; White League, Vol. 4, Part 2, 353; yellow fever epidemic in, Vol. 9, Part 2, 85

New Orleans Canal Co., Supp. 4, 193

New Orleans Polyclinic, absorption by Tulane, Vol. 3, Part 1, 582

New Panama Canal Co., Supp. 4, 193

New Playwrights Theatre, Supp. 10, 436

Newport, R.I.: Vol. 6, Part 1, 547; Congregationalism, Vol. 9, Part 2, 18; founding of, Vol. 2, Part 2, 258; history of, Vol. 6, Part 2, 271; Vol. 8, Part 1, 445; influence of library at, Vol. 8, Part 1, 445; Naval Academy, removal to, during Civil War, Vol. 8, Part 2, 72; Philosophical Society of, Vol. 8, Part 1, 445; privateering from, Vol. 1, Part 2, 512; settlement of, Vol. 2, Part 2, 155; Vol. 3, Part 1, 604

Newport Jazz Festival, Supp. 10, 300, 807

New Purchase, The, Vol. 4, Part 2, 119

New Republic, The: Vol. 9, Part 2, 121; columns, Supp. 7, 249; Supp. 9, 467, 504; correspondents, Supp. 7, 261, 320; editing, Supp. 6, 15, 392; Supp. 10, 51; Supp. 7, 762, 811–12; founding of, Supp. 1, 210; Supp. 7, 10, 316; poetry editor, Supp. 4, 841

New Scholasticism, The, founding of, Supp. 2, 506

New School Association, founding of, Supp. 3, 563

New School for Social Research: Supp. 3, 809; Supp. 5, 431; Supp. 7, 801; Supp. 8, 488; adult education, Supp. 9, 447; Benton Mural, Supp. 9, 79; building constructed, Supp. 9, 428; faculty bill of rights, Supp. 9, 429; founding of, Supp. 2, 563; Supp. 4, 63, 586–87; Supp. 5, 172; German refugee scholars, Supp. 4, 80; scholar recruitment, Supp. 9, 428; Supp. 10, 13

New School Presbyterian Church, Vol. 1, Part 2, 595; Vol. 4, Part 2, 396

News collecting, early, Vol. 9, Part 2, 592

Newsday, founding of, Supp. 7, 603–4

"New Side," Vol. 9, Part 2, 370

Newspaper Enterprise Association (NEA), Supp. 10, 244–45

"New South," Vol. 5, Part 1, 57; Vol. 5, Part 2, 552

Newspaper Enterprise Association, Supp. 5, 499

Newspaper Feature Service, Supp. 3, 428

Newspaper Guild, founding of, Supp. 10, 383–84

"Newspaperman's newspaper," *(New York Sun)*, Vol. 3, Part 1, 52

Newspapers: Asian correspondents, Supp. 4, 679; association, Vol. 2, Part 1, 37; black, Supp. 2, 3; Supp. 3, 535, 596, 632–33; Supp. 7, 203, 204; broadcasting interests, Supp. 5, 615; cartoons and caricatures, *see* Cartoons and caricatures; censorship by, Supp. 9, 453; civic improvement, Supp. 4, 222; color press, Supp. 2, 242; columnist work, Vol. 3, Part 2, 364; Vol. 9, Part 2, 317; comic strips, *see* Comic strips; comic strips, origin of, Vol. 7, Part 2, 112; Cox family interests, Supp. 9, 202; dealers consolidated, Vol. 3, Part 1, 278 f.; Denver wars between, Supp. 1, 95; editing of, Vol. 3, Part 2, 476, 486 f., 515; Vol. 4, Part 1, 425; Vol. 4, Part 2, 11; Vol. 6, Part 1, 396; Vol. 5, Part 2, 45, 48, 160, 417, 444, 452; Vol. 6, Part 2, 159, 166, 267, 290, 568; Vol. 7, Part 1, 48, 204 f.; Vol. 7, Part 2, 475; Vol. 8, Part 2, 468, 491, 514, 526; Vol. 9, Part 1, 577; Vol. 9, Part 2, 98; Vol. 10, Part 2, 292, 617, 633; Supp. 10, 35–37; editorials, Supp. 1, 391; Supp. 3, 850–51; Supp. 5, 279, 391–92, 499; Supp. 6, 676–77; Supp. 10, 24–25; English-language in Europe, Supp. 4, 687; English-language in Japan, Supp. 4, 284–85; feature syndication, Supp. 3, 427–28; Supp. 4, 693; financial, Supp. 9, 520; first edition using computerized typesetting, Supp. 9, first illustrated daily in U.S., Vol. 8, Part 1, 332 f.; first in California, Vol. 2, Part 2, 323; first chain of, Vol. 8, Part 2, 518; first daily in U.S., Vol. 3, Part 1, 514 f.; Vol. 8, Part 1, 139 f., 638; first "extra," Vol. 8, Part 1, 299 f.; first in France, Vol. 4, Part 1, 91; first in Hawaii, Vol. 1, Part 1, 295; Vol. 5, Part 1, 618; first in New Jersey, Vol. 7, Part 2, 227; first in Pennsylvania, Vol. 1, Part 2, 553; first in South Carolina, Vol. 10, Part 1, 644 f.; first in the middle colonies, Vol. 1, Part 2, 553; 302; first in Utah, Vol. 2, Part 2, 353; first penny, Vol. 3, Part 1, 155; Vol. 6, Part 1, 60; Vol. 9, Part 2, 82; first-prize contests used, Vol. 3, Part 2, 572; first scientific, Vol. 8, Part 1, 101 f.; first syndicate, Vol. 8, Part 2, 518; first in U.S., Vol. 2, Part 1, 456; Vol. 4, Part 2, 304; Vol. 8, Part 1, 139 f.; first syndicated weekly jazz column, Supp. 9, 317; first with literary supplement, Vol. 1, Part 2, 559; Gaylord interests, Supp. 9, 301–2; German, Vol. 4, Part 1, 262; Vol. 5, Part 2, 259; Supp. 1, 72; Supp. 9, 659, 660; Greek-American, Supp. 7, 102–3; Hearst chain, Supp. 5, 283–84, 448–49; Hearst-Pulitzer competition, Supp. 3, 144; Supp. 5, 284; illustrated methods, Vol. 8, Part 2, 113; Jewish, Supp. 3, 513, 711–12; letters to the editor, Supp. 5, 488; management, Supp. 3, 144, 816–17; Supp. 4, 12, 189, 215–16, 217, 686–87; Supp. 5, 55–56; Supp. 7, 369–70; McLean interests, Supp. 10, 499; monopolies, Supp. 4, 180; Newhouse chain, Supp. 10, 586–87; New South, Supp. 8, 404–5; "newspaper of record" concept, Supp. 3, 787–88; Supp. 5, 362–63; period collection of, Vol. 3, Part 1, 553 f.; Vol. 3, Part 2, 519; political importance of in colonial period, Vol. 3, Part 1, 212; printing processes, Supp. 2, 733; public opinion column, syndicated, Supp. 9, 678; publishing, Vol. 1, Part 2,

437, 565; **Vol. 5, Part 1**, 535; **Vol. 6, Part 2**, 130; **Vol. 7, Part 1**, 271; **Vol. 7, Part 2**, 376 f., 643; **Vol. 8, Part 2**, 517, 519 f.; **Vol. 10, Part 2**, 500; rapid service developed; **Vol. 10, Part 1**, 574 f.; Ridder family interests, **Supp. 9**, 660; rotogravure picture sections, **Supp. 5**, 394, 551; Scripps-Howard chain, **Supp. 2**, 606; **Supp. 9**, 90; second in colonies, **Vol. 3, Part 2**, 17; **Vol. 5, Part 2**, 458; sketch artists, **Supp. 2**, 238; Snow-Speidel interests, **Supp. 9**, 742; Southern California boosting by, **Supp. 3**, 156; special sections, **Supp. 5**, 552; sports editing, **Vol. 5, Part 2**, 92; syndication, **Supp. 4**, 38; **Supp. 10**, 98; tabloids, **Supp. 4**, 645–46; **Supp. 5**, 205, 323, 449, 453; telegraph used by, **Vol. 1, Part 2**, 198; third in U.S., **Vol. 1, Part 2**, 553; Times-Mirror group, **Supp. 9**, 168; Vanderbilt interests, **Supp. 9**, 826; wirephotos, **Supp. 5**, 323–24; wire services, **Supp. 1**, 510; **Supp. 5**, 286; women connected with, **Vol. 1, Part 2**, 581; **Vol. 8, Part 2**, 518; women's page, **Supp. 1**, 91; writings on, **Supp. 4**, 481–82; **Supp. 7**, 473; Yiddish-language, **Supp. 5**, 95, 96, 597; **Supp. 9**, 724. *See also* Journalism; Publishing; *specific publications*
News service, foreign, promotion of, **Vol. 6, Part 1**, 61
New Sweden: history of, **Vol. 8, Part 1**, 238 f., 627; immigration to, **Vol. 9, Part 2**, 447
Newsweek, **Supp. 6**, 23–24, 366–67; **Supp. 7**, 296
New Testament, scholarship, **Supp. 4**, 467–68
New Theatre (New York City), founding of, **Supp. 2**, 10
New Theatre Group (Los Angeles), **Supp. 10**, 272
New thought, **Vol. 3, Part 2**, 464,; **Vol. 7, Part 1**, 318; **Vol. 8, Part 1**, 304 f.
Newton, Mass., **Vol. 7, Part 2**, 398, 495
Newton Theological Institution, **Vol. 5, Part 1**, 235, 270
Newtowne (Cambridge), Mass., founding of, **Vol. 8, Part 1**, 66 f.
New towns. *See* Model communities
New Universal Atlas, A, **Vol. 7, Part 1**, 61
New World (journal), **Vol. 3, Part 2**, 222
New World: Problems in Political Geography, The, **Supp. 4**, 99
New York (magazine), financing of, **Supp. 9**, 265
New York Academy of Medicine, **Vol. 8, Part 1**, 269 f.; **Vol. 9, Part 1**, 606; **Vol. 10, Part 2**, 282
New York Adult Education Council, founding of, **Supp. 2**, 186
New York Advocate, **Vol. 1, Part 1**, 575
New York Age, **Supp. 3**, 535; **Supp. 7**, 767
New York American, **Supp. 6**, 213–14; comic strips, **Supp. 5**, 456
New York & Erie Railroad, **Vol. 6, Part 1**, 405 f.
New York and New Jersey Telephone Co., **Supp. 3**, 299
New York & Ohio Co., **Vol. 7, Part 2**, 128
New York Anti-Slavery Society, **Vol. 5, Part 2**, 12; **Vol. 9, Part 2**, 5
New York Aquarium, **Supp. 8**, 485–86
New York Associated Press, **Vol. 1, Part 2**, 84; **Vol. 9, Part 2**, 74
New York Association for the Blind, **Supp. 3**, 364
New York Barge Canal, **Supp. 3**, 311
New York Bible Society, **Vol. 3, Part 1**, 345
New York Botanical Garden: **Vol. 2, Part 1**, 100; **Vol. 7, Part 2**, 480; **Vol. 8, Part 2**, 269; **Vol. 9, Part 2**, 597; administration, **Supp. 2**, 374; **Supp. 6**, 450; founding and development of, **Supp. 1**, 122; orchid collection, **Supp. 4**, 16–17
New York Building Trades Council, **Supp. 10**, 524
New York Bureau of Municipal Research, **Supp. 2**, 608
New York Canoe Club, **Vol. 1, Part 1**, 150
New York Celtics (basketball), **Supp. 8**, 358
New York Central Railroad: **Vol. 2, Part 1**, 158; **Vol. 2, Part 2**, 446; **Vol. 8, Part 1**, 253 f., 582; **Vol. 8, Part 2**, 424; **Vol. 9, Part 1**, 236; **Supp. 1**, 574; Alleghany takeover, **Supp. 9**, 423, 462; early history of, **Vol. 10, Part 1**, 172 f.; merger with Pennsylvania Railroad, **Supp. 10**, 772; Richardson-Young takeover, **Supp. 6**, 540, 721–22
New York Central Railroad Station (Rochester), architecture, **Supp. 4**, 105
New York Charity Organization Society, **Vol. 6, Part 1**, 468; **Vol. 7, Part 2**, 410; **Supp. 4**, 227, 546–47
New York Citizen, **Vol. 8, Part 2**, 134
New York City: acting in, **Vol. 4, Part 1**, 314; adult education, **Supp. 3**, 511; American Labor party, **Supp. 5**, 466–67; **Supp. 8**, 512; antinoise movement, **Vol. 8, Part 1**, 541; architecture, **Vol. 1, Part 1**, 587; **Vol. 3, Part 1**, 104; **Vol. 4, Part 2**, 240; **Vol. 6, Part 1**, 599 f.; **Vol. 6, Part 2**, 232; **Vol. 8, Part 1**, 507 f.; **Vol. 8, Part 2**, 98; **Supp. 4**, 281–82; **Supp. 5**, 133–34, 408; **Supp. 6**, 26; Armory Show (1913), **Supp. 9**, 759; assessment and taxation, **Supp. 6**, 522; Astor library, **Vol. 1, Part 1**, 39; Astor Place riots, **Vol. 3, Part 1**, 41, 553; banking, **Vol. 1, Part 2**, 443; **Vol. 2, Part 2**, 359, 613; **Vol. 3, Part 1**, 486 f.; **Vol. 6, Part 1**, 490; **Vol. 6, Part 2**, 22; **Vol. 7, Part 1**, 259, 360; **Vol. 9, Part 1**, 616; **Vol. 9, Part 2**, 132; **Vol. 10, Part 1**, 438; banking panics, **Vol. 2, Part 2**, 375; **Vol. 3, Part 1**, 484 f.; Bar Association, **Vol. 6, Part 2**, 327; Bedloe's Island, **Vol. 1, Part 1**, 592; Bellevue Hospital, **Vol. 6, Part 1**, 240; **Vol. 10, Part 1**, 150; **Vol. 10, Part 2**, 463; **Supp. 9**, 328–29; black leadership in, **Supp. 4**, 607–8; **Supp. 5**, 548; blizzard of 1888, **Vol. 8, Part 1**, 393; Booth's Theatre, **Vol. 1, Part 1**, 256; **Vol. 1, Part 2**, 446; Boston, first post road to, **Vol. 6, Part 1**, 437; Botanical Garden, *see* New York Botanical Garden; Brick Church, **Vol. 9, Part 1**, 480; bridges, **Supp. 3**, 530–31; Broadway Tabernacle, **Vol. 9, Part 2**, 299, 303; Brooklyn consolidated with, **Vol. 9, Part 2**, 123; building construction, **Supp. 1**, 342, 430; **Supp. 6**, 337, 593; **Supp. 7**, 800; Cathedral of St. John the Divine, **Vol. 3, Part 2**, 354; **Vol. 4, Part 1**, 594; **Vol. 4, Part 2**, 389; **Vol. 5, Part 1**, 421; Catholic archbishop, first, **Vol. 3, Part 1**, 470 f.; Catholic church, **Vol. 1, Part 2**, 373; **Vol. 6, Part 2**, 226; **Supp. 10**, 497; Catholic mayor of, first, **Vol. 4, Part 1**, 463; Central Park, **Vol. 4, Part 1**, 471; **Vol. 4, Part 2**, 5; **Vol. 7, Part 2**, 25 f., 600; **Vol. 8, Part 2**, 200, 464; **Vol. 9, Part 1**, 151; Century Club, **Vol. 1, Part 2**, 169; **Vol. 3, Part 1**, 535 f.; Chamber of Commerce, **Vol. 2, Part 2**, 582; **Vol. 6, Part 1**, 445 f., 450; **Vol. 8, Part 1**, 348 f.; Charity Organization Society, *see* New York Charity Organization Society; charter of 1873, **Vol. 1, Part 2**, 373; charter revision, **Supp. 2**, 250, 497; Child Hygiene Bureau, **Supp. 3**, 28; Children's Welfare Federation, **Supp. 3**, 159; cholera epidemic of 1830, **Vol. 8, Part 2**, 238; Choral Society, **Vol. 4, Part 2**, 505,; Church of the Ascension, **Vol. 4, Part 1**, 491; City Club, **Vol. 5, Part 2**, 307; **Supp. 10**, 121, 122; City Hall, **Vol. 6, Part 2**, 232; **Supp. 6**, 26; city seal of, **Vol. 6, Part 1**, 181; civic and philanthropic service, **Vol. 1, Part 1**, 549; **Vol. 1, Part 2**, 359; **Vol. 2, Part 2**, 166, 566; **Vol. 3, Part 1**, 279, 346 f., 378, 462 f., 493; **Vol. 4, Part 1**, 475, 535; **Vol. 4, Part 2**, 491 f.; **Vol. 5, Part 1**, 573 f.; **Vol. 5, Part 2**, 308, 334; **Vol. 6, Part 1**, 172, 181; **Vol. 6, Part 2**, 293; **Vol. 7, Part 1**, 37, 168 f., 615; **Vol. 7, Part 2**, 56, 72, 243, 410, 630; **Vol. 8, Part 1**, 106 f., 127 f., 278, 348 f.; **Vol. 8, Part 2**, 570, 572; **Vol. 9, Part 1**, 209; **Vol. 9, Part 2**, 129 f.; civil rights movement, **Supp. 9**, 619; "Cleopatra's Needle," **Vol. 3, Part 1**, 277; **Vol. 3, Part 2**, 276; **Vol. 4, Part 1**, 437; clothing factory, early, **Vol. 7, Part 2**, 45; clothing industry in, **Vol. 7, Part 2**, 45; commerce commis-

sion, **Supp. 5**, 634; Committee on Safety, **Supp. 4**, 603; **Supp. 7**, 608; Communist party, **Supp. 5**, 500; community councils, **Supp. 6**, 484; Conference of Charities and Corrections, founded, **Vol. 9, Part 2**, 15; consolidation plan for, **Vol. 9, Part 2**, 123; Consumers' League, **Supp. 7**, 608; Cooper Union, **Vol. 2, Part 2**, 410; **Vol. 4, Part 2**, 605; **Vol. 8, Part 2**, 467; corruption investigations, **Supp. 4**, 856; **Supp. 6**, 570; **Supp. 7**, 4–5, 585–86; **Supp. 9**, 230, 287, 400, 607, 680; **Supp. 10**, 48; Cotton Exchange, Vol. 5;, Part 1, 484; crime investigations, **Supp. 7**, 585–86; Crystal Palace, **Vol. 3, Part 1**, 258; defense, **Vol. 3, Part 1**, 210; **Vol. 9, Part 2**, 247, 599; directories of, **Vol. 9, Part 2**, 652; district attorney, **Supp. 9**, 399; docks, **Vol. 7, Part 1**, 607 f.; **Vol. 9, Part 1**, 338; draft riots in, **Vol. 4, Part 1**, 47; **Vol. 10, Part 1**, 145; early history of, **Vol. 1, Part 2**, 68; education, **Vol. 3, Part 1**, 346 f., 458 f.; **Vol. 4, Part 2**, 47; **Vol. 5, Part 1**, 405; **Vol. 8, Part 1**, 44 f., 351 f.; **Vol. 9, Part 1**, 353; education board, **Supp. 8**, 135; Emergency Relief Bureau, **Supp. 6**, 102; engineering, **Vol. 7, Part 1**, 473; engraving, "historical," of 1806, **Vol. 6, Part 1**, 165; epidemics, **Supp. 4**, 287; Exhibition of the Industries of All Nations, **Vol. 3, Part 1**, 258; Federal Art Project, **Supp. 7**, 184; Federal Hall, **Vol. 6, Part 1**, 166; financial management of, **Vol. 4, Part 1**, 535; fire-alarm system, **Supp. 1**, 554; firehouses, architecture of, **Vol. 6, Part 1**, 86; fire prevention, early advocacy of, **Vol. 3, Part 1**, 248; first black councilman elected, **Supp. 9**, 619; first black mayor, **Supp. 9**, 251; first comprehensive zoning, **Supp. 6**, 522; first municipal art exhibit, **Supp. 8**, 240; first omnibus in, **Vol. 9, Part 1**, 583; first savings bank in, **Vol. 7, Part 2**, 630; free circulating library, **Vol. 3, Part 2**, 356; fusion movements, **Supp. 4**, 825–26; **Supp. 5**, 285–86; Fusion party in, **Vol. 7, Part 1**, 37 f.; garment industry, **Supp. 3**, 609–10; *Gazette*, New York's first newspaper, **Vol. 1, Part 2**, 564; "ghetto," **Vol. 8, Part 2**, 165; Gold Exchange, **Vol. 2, Part 2**, 298; Grace Church, **Vol. 5, Part 1**, 421; **Vol. 8, Part 1**, 127 f.; Gramercy Park, **Vol. 8, Part 2**, 220; Greenwich Village, **Vol. 10, Part 1**, 485 f.; A *Guide to the City of New York*, published 1836, **Vol. 3, Part 1**, 319; handicapped education, **Supp. 3**, 365; harbor, **Supp. 7**, 552–53; Harlem River Bridge, **Vol. 5, Part 2**, 261; health department, **Supp. 3**, 312; **Supp. 6**, 424; Hearst newspapers in, **Supp. 5**, 284–85; Hell Gate Bridge, construction of, **Vol. 8, Part 1**, 418; home-rule issue, **Supp. 3**, 717, 718; hospital, **Vol. 1, Part 1**, 598; hospital commissioner, **Supp. 3**, 313, 320; hotels, **Vol. 1, Part 1**, 400 f.; **Vol. 1, Part 2**, 419; housing and parks, **Supp. 3**, 744; **Supp. 5**, 630–31; **Supp. 6**, 615; Irish Societies of, **Vol. 8, Part 2**, 19; jazz scene, **Supp. 9**, 847; **Supp. 10**, 791, 792; Jewish organizations, **Supp. 4**, 539; journalism, **Vol. 2, Part 2**, 455 f.; **Vol. 3, Part 2**, 576; **Vol. 5, Part 1**, 424, 483; **Vol. 6, Part 1**, 283; **Vol. 7, Part 1**, 534, **Vol. 7, Part 2**, 538 f.; **Vol. 8, Part 1**, 260 f., 409, 474 f.; **Vol. 8, Part 2**, 475; **Vol. 9, Part 2**, 551; judicial reform, **Supp. 6**, 87–88; judiciary, **Supp. 10**, 447–48; Kips Bay, **Vol. 7, Part 1**, 367; Knapp Commission, **Supp. 9**, 400; laws, codification of, **Vol. 1, Part 2**, 374; lighting system, electric, **Vol. 5, Part 2**, 509; literati of, **Vol. 1, Part 2**, 469; **Vol. 3, Part 2**, 305; lithograph of, **Vol. 5, Part 1**, 460; Little Church Around the Corner, **Vol. 5, Part 1**, 255; **Vol. 7, Part 1**, 204; Lower East Side, **Supp. 3**, 329, 330; Lyceum of Natural History, **Vol. 3, Part 1**, 204; Madison Square Presbyterian Church, **Vol. 7, Part 2**, 245; Manhattan elevated railway, **Vol. 8, Part 1**, 221; Manhattan Island, purchase of, **Vol. 7, Part 1**, 34; mass meetings, Civil War, **Vol. 4, Part 2**, 405; mayor, first native-born, **Vol. 10, Part 1**, 164; mayors, **Supp. 2**, 330; **Supp. 4**, 465–66, 855–56; **Supp. 5**, 227; **Supp. 7**, 585–86; **Supp. 9**, 251, 607; **Supp. 10**, 453, 697; medical and health reserarch group, **Supp. 9**, 531; medical examiners office, **Supp. 10**, 328–29; medical schools in, **Vol. 6, Part 2**, 268; medical services, **Supp. 6**, 81–82; Merchantile Agency, first of its kind, **Vol. 3, Part 1**, 503; **Vol. 9, Part 1**, 558 f.; **Vol. 10, Part 1**, 409; Metropolitan Museum of Art, **Vol. 5, Part 2**, 144; Metropolitan Street Railway Co., **Vol. 7, Part 2**, 358 f.; mob infiltration of Democratic party, **Supp. 9**, 198; Municipal Art Committee, **Supp. 7**, 70; Murray Hill, **Vol. 7, Part 1**, 367; National City Bank, **Vol. 9, Part 2**, 26; "Neutral Ground," around, during Revolution, **Vol. 3, Part 1**, 214; newspaper, first, **Vol. 1, Part 2**, 564; *New York Picayune*, **Vol. 9, Part 2**, 488; nightclubs, **Supp. 8**, 546, 547, 562; official greeters, **Supp. 7**, 779–80, 496; organized-crime activities, **Supp. 9**, 269–70, 399; **Supp. 10**, 140–41, 266–67, 268–69; organized crime in, **Supp. 7**, 484–85, 632–33; **Supp. 8**, 396–97; parades, **Supp. 7**, 779, 780; Park Avenue Hotel, **Vol. 9, Part 2**, 4; park planning, **Vol. 1, Part 2**, 408; **Vol. 8, Part 2**, 220; parks, **Supp. 4**, 213; Pathological Society, **Vol. 7, Part 2**, 505; Peace Society, **Vol. 3, Part 1**, 345; Pennsylvania Station, **Vol. 8, Part 1**, 406, 418; "People's University," **Vol. 6, Part 1**, 155; philanthropy, **Vol. 6, Part 1**, 172; **Supp. 6**, 24; Philharmonic Society, *see* New York Philharmonic; piano manufacture, **Vol. 10, Part 1**, 581; pilotage system in harbor, **Vol. 1, Part 2**, 398; Planning Commission, **Supp. 10**, 795; police, **Vol. 2, Part 1**, 386; **Vol. 6, Part 1**, 229; **Vol. 8, Part 2**, 136; **Supp. 3**, 116; **Supp. 7**, 779–80; police department corruption, **Supp. 9**, 400; political reform movements, **Supp. 3**, 605, 717–18; **Supp. 4**, 465–66, 547, 825–26, 870, 885–86, 904; **Supp. 8**, 467, *see also subhead:* fusion movements; politics, **Supp. 4**, 88, 464–66, 542–43; **Supp. 6**, 88, 141–42, 280, 294–95; **Supp. 8**, 27, 397; **Supp. 9**, 399–400, 607, 620, 621, 680; **Supp. 10** 121, 122, 697; Polyclinic Hospital, **Vol. 10, Part 2**, 576; Port Authority, **Supp. 1**, 589; Post-Graduate Medical School, **Vol. 8, Part 2**, 132; Presbyterian church, **Supp. 5**, 116–17; printing in colonial period, **Vol. 1, Part 2**, 564; **Vol. 7, Part 2**, 226; **Vol. 8, Part 1**, 637 f.; Prison Association, **Vol. 3, Part 1**, 493; prisons, **Supp. 8**, 495; progressive education, **Supp. 3**, 375–76; Prohibition enforcement, **Supp. 7**, 805; as prominent port, **Vol. 6, Part 2**, 306; prostitution reform efforts, **Supp. 5**, 698, 699; public health, **Vol. 1, Part 2**, 262 f.; **Vol. 3, Part 1**, 377; **Vol. 5, Part 1**, 607; **Vol. 8, Part 1**, 44 f.; **Vol. 9, Part 1**, 187, 348; **Supp. 2**, 121; **Supp. 6**, 192; public parks, **Vol. 7, Part 2**, 600; public schools, **Vol. 6, Part 1**, 155; **Vol. 6, Part 2**, 124, 445; **Vol. 9, Part 1**, 353; public utilities, **Supp. 3**, 138, 715–16; public welfare, **Vol. 6, Part 2**, 179; railroad development, **Vol. 2, Part 2**, 446 f.; Rapid Transit Commission, **Vol. 8, Part 1**, 634; real estate, **Vol. 1, Part 1**, 397; **Vol. 2, Part 2**, 136; **Vol. 5, Part 2**, 332; **Vol. 6, Part 1**, 448; **Vol. 9, Part 2**, 69 f., 132; **Supp. 2**, 64; **Supp. 6**, 23, 24; real estate, **Supp. 10**, 478, 785–86, 866–67; reform measures, **Vol. 4, Part 1**, 335; **Vol. 5, Part 1**, 523; **Vol. 6, Part 1**, 229; **Vol. 7, Part 2**, 56, 506; **Vol. 8, Part 1**, 607; **Vol. 9, Part 1**, 593; restaurant business, **Vol. 3, Part 1**, 227; **Vol. 9, Part 1**, 97 f.; Riverside Drive, construction of, **Vol. 6, Part 1**, 548; Roman Catholic diocese, **Supp. 8**, 613–15; St. Patrick's Cathedral, **Vol. 8, Part 1**, 507 f., St. Thomas Church, **Vol. 4, Part 1**, 388; saloon business, **Supp. 10**, 732–33; sanitation, **Vol. 8, Part 1**, 607; **Vol. 8, Part 2**, 404; **Vol. 10, Part 1**, 456 f.; **Supp. 4**, 855; savings bank, first, **Vol. 7, Part 2**, 630; school

buildings, **Supp. 5**, 301; School of Philanthropy, **Vol. 6, Part 1**, 223; school system centralization, **Supp. 4**, 134; **Supp. 9**, 25; school system integration, **Supp. 9**, 251; school system survey, **Supp. 3**, 328; Seabury corruption investigation, *see subhead:* corruption investigations; Seamen's Institute, **Vol. 7, Part 2**, 129; settlement work, **Supp. 3**, 175; shipbuilding, **Vol. 1, Part 2**, 156, 215; **Vol. 2, Part 2**, 46; **Vol. 8, Part 2**, 341 f.; shipyards, **Vol. 1, Part 2**, 156; silver-workers of, **Vol. 1, Part 2**, 406; **Vol. 6, Part 1**, 181; skyscrapers, **Supp. 3**, 611–12; slavery, **Vol. 1, Part 2**, 507; **Vol. 9, Part 2**, 583; slum clearance, **Vol. 8, Part 1**, 607; **Supp. 2**, 684; Socialist activity in, **Vol. 3, Part 1**, 223; **Vol. 8, Part 2**, 129; social leadership of McAllister, **Vol. 4, Part 2**, 357; **Vol. 6, Part 1**, 547 f.; Social Reform Club, **Vol. 2, Part 2**, 566; **Supp. 3**, 297–98, 545; social register, **Supp. 5**, 707–8; social work, **Supp. 4**, 391–92; **Supp. 6**, 102–3; Sons of Liberty, **Vol. 8, Part 2**, 495; "Stalwart" supremacy in, **Vol. 8, Part 1**, 484; steamship, launching of first oceanic, **Vol. 1, Part 2**, 156; Stock Exchange, **Vol. 2, Part 2**, 76, 133; **Vol. 4, Part 2**, 393 f.; **Vol. 5, Part 1**, 247; streetcar strike, **Vol. 5, Part 2**, 196; street railways, **Vol. 1, Part 2**, 408; **Vol. 2, Part 2**, 544; **Vol. 4, Part 2**, 605; **Vol. 6, Part 1**, 478; **Vol. 7, Part 2**, 56, 277; **Vol. 8, Part 2**, 265 f.; **Vol. 9, Part 1**, 124; **Vol. 9, Part 2**, 232, 241; subway system, **Vol. 1, Part 2**, 408; **Vol. 2, Part 2**, 544; **Vol. 4, Part 1**, 8; **Vol. 4, Part 2**, 605; **Vol. 7, Part 2**, 56, 277, 602; **Vol. 9, Part 1**, 124; **Supp. 2**, 559, 675; **Supp. 4**, 855; **Supp. 5**, 228, teachers' issues, **Supp. 8**, 132; teachers' training in, **Vol. 3, Part 1**, 347; temperance reform in, **Vol. 3, Part 1**, 221; tenements, supervision of, **Vol. 1, Part 2**, 373; **Vol. 7, Part 2**, 551; **Vol. 8, Part 1**, 607; theater, only one in 1796, **Vol. 3, Part 1**, 516 f.; theaters in, **Vol. 1, Part 1**, 256; **Vol. 1, Part 2**, 446; **Vol. 5, Part 2**, 284; **Vol. 8, Part 1**, 221; Tilden Library, **Vol. 9, Part 2**, 541; Tompkins Square labor demonstration, **Vol. 9, Part 2**, 252; traffic congestion in, **Vol. 8, Part 1**, 138 f.; traffic regulation, **Supp. 3**, 253–54; transit strike, **Supp. 8**, 513; transportation in, **Vol. 2, Part 2**, 544; **Vol. 5, Part 1**, 483; **Vol. 6, Part 2**, 17; **Vol. 7, Part 2**, 277, 602; **Vol. 8, Part 1**, 418; **Vol. 9, Part 1**, 529, 568, 583; **Vol. 9, Part 2**, 241; Trinity Church, **Vol. 2, Part 1**, 86; **Vol. 3, Part 1**, 327 f.; **Vol. 5, Part 1**, 93; tunnel engineering, **Supp. 4**, 690, 757; Union League Club, **Vol. 1, Part 2**, 169; **Vol. 7, Part 2**, 26; **Vol. 8, Part 2**, 134; universities and colleges, **Supp. 5**, 488; University Club, **Vol. 5, Part 1**, 180; Washington Square, **Vol. 3, Part 2**, 56; **Vol. 5, Part 1**, 615; **Vol. 5, Part 2**, 530; **Vol. 9, Part 2**, 15; water supply, **Vol. 3, Part 1**, 406; **Vol. 5, Part 2**, 59; **Vol. 6, Part 1**, 39; Vol. 8, Part 1, 324 f., 607; **Vol. 9, Part 1**, 307 f., **Vol. 10, Part 2**, 21; **Supp. 1**, 663, 700; **Supp. 2**, 558; Welfare Council, **Supp. 3**, 362; WPA construction projects, **Supp. 5**, 642–43; writings on, **Vol. 1, Part 1**, 188; **Vol. 3, Part 1**, 319; **Vol. 4, Part 1**, 629; **Vol. 5, Part 1**, 308, 615; **Vol. 5, Part 2**, 310, 383, 556; **Vol. 9, Part 1**, 338; yellow-fever epidemic, **Vol. 1, Part 2**, 75; **Vol. 6, Part 1**, 309; YMCA building, **Vol. 6, Part 1**, 556; zoning law, **Supp. 4**, 56. *See also specific sections, buildings, and attractions*

New York City Ballet, productions, **Supp. 10**, 207

New York City Opera, *Die tote Stadt* production, **Supp. 6**, 351–52

New York Clearing House, **Vol. 2, Part 1**, 476; **Vol. 2, Part 2**, 261, 613; **Vol. 3, Part 2**, 22, 524; **Vol. 9, Part 2**, 304, 542

New York College of Dentistry, **Vol. 7, Part, 2**, 252

New York College for the Training of Teachers, **Vol. 3, Part 1**, 347

New York Commercial Advertiser. See New York Globe

New York Commission of Charities, **Vol. 8, Part 1**, 253 f.

New York Committee of One Hundred, **Vol. 5, Part 2**, 197; **Vol. 7, Part 2**, 631

New York Committee of Safety: **Vol. 7, Part 2**, 340, 417 f.; **Vol. 8, Part 2**, 341 f.; **Vol. 9, Part 2**, 365; Committee of Sixty, **Vol. 6, Part 1**, 316 f.

New York Conference of Librarians (1853), **Vol. 5, Part 2**, 66

New York Confidential, **Supp. 5**, 406

New York Consolidated Gas Co. *See* Consolidated Edison Co.

New York Courier, **Vol. 1, Part 2**, 196

New York Court of Common Pleas, **Vol. 3, Part 1**, 41 f.

New York Cricket Club, **Vol. 8, Part 1**, 107 f.

New York Curb Exchange. *See* American Stock Exchange

New York Daily News: comic strip, **Supp. 6**, 699; drama criticism, **Supp. 4**, 548–49; **Supp. 9**, 170–71; founding of, **Supp. 4**, 646; **Supp. 5**, 449; society column, **Supp. 10**, 674–75

New York Daily Times, **Vol. 8, Part 1**, 409

New York Drama Critics' Circle Award, **Supp. 6**, 11, 15, 471

New York Dramatic Mirror, **Vol. 3, Part 2**, 423

New York Edison Co., **Vol. 6, Part 1**, 235; **Vol. 7, Part 1**, 368

New York Employment Club, founding of, **Vol. 3, Part 1**, 272

New York Enquirer, **Vol. 1, Part 2**, 196

New Yorker (magazine): articles and profiles, **Supp. 6**, 236–37, 422, 423; **Supp. 7**, 38, 473–74; **Supp. 8**, 447; book-review column, **Supp. 8**, 492; cartoons, **Supp. 4**, 386; **Supp. 8**, 15–16; drama criticism, **Supp. 5**, 464; fiction, **Supp. 8**, 480, 481; **Supp. 9**, 77–78; **Supp. 10**, 147, 754; first cover, **Supp. 5**, 594; founding of, **Supp. 5**, 593–94; **Supp. 9**, 335; humor, **Supp. 7**, 743; illustrations, **Supp. 6**, 287; "Letter from Paris" column, **Supp. 10**, 246, 247; Mencken autobiography, **Supp. 6**, 446; poetry, **Supp. 9**, 558, 578; poetry reviews, **Supp. 8**, 42, 43; television column, **Supp. 6**, 366; typography, **Supp. 7**, 2; "Wayward Press" column, **Supp. 3**, 54

New Yorker-Staats-Zeitung, **Vol. 7, Part 2**, 106 f.

New York Etching Club, **Vol. 9, Part 1**, 233

New York Evening Graphic, **Supp. 5**, 453

New York Evening Journal: drama criticism, **Supp. 5**, 658; yellow journalism, **Supp. 5**, 284, 285

New York Evening Mail, **Supp. 6**, 4

New York Evening Post: **Vol. 2, Part 1**, 202; **Vol. 3, Part 1**, 203; **Vol. 4, Part 1**, 347; **Vol. 4, Part 2**, 178; **Vol. 6, Part 1**, 147, 195, 208, 283; **Vol. 7, Part 1**, 378, 548; **Vol. 8, Part 2**, 469; **Vol. 10, Part 2**, 105; **Supp. 4**, 322, 850; **Supp. 7**, 103; book reviews, **Supp. 5**, 439; drama criticism, **Supp. 8**, 54; editing, **Supp. 2**, 498; editorial writing, **Supp. 4**, 804–5; music criticism, **Supp. 7**, 124

New York Evening World, **Vol. 6, Part 1**, 354 f.; **Vol. 8, Part 1**, 260 f.; **Supp. 3**, 144; **Supp. 5**, 552

New York Eye Infirmary, founding of, **Vol. 3, Part 1**, 207

New York Free Circulating Library. *See* New York Public Library

New York Gazeteer, **Vol. 8, Part 1**, 638

New York Giants (baseball): **Supp. 1**, 530; **Supp. 6**, 488–89; **Supp. 8**, 713; **Supp. 9**, 294, 369, 544, 763, 841; **Supp. 10**, 508–9, 606

New York Giants (football): **Supp. 7**, 595–96; **Supp. 8**, 389; **Supp. 10**, 351, 444, 767–68; first black player, **Supp. 9**, 817–18

New York Globe, **Supp. 3**, 329; **Supp. 8**, 108

New York Gold Exchange, **Vol. 2, Part 2**, 298

New York Heart Association, **Supp. 6**, 117; founding of, **Supp. 2**, 742
New York Herald: **Vol. 1, Part 2**, 199; **Vol. 5, Part 1**, 106; **Vol. 7, Part 1**, 548; **Vol. 8, Part 1**, 409, 474; **Supp. 3**, 841–42; **Supp. 5**, 78–79; Civil War coverage, **Supp. 1**, 441; foreign correspondents, **Supp. 8**, 639–40
New York Herald Tribune: **Vol. 4, Part 2**, 432 f.; **Vol. 8, Part 2**, 282; **Vol. 9, Part 1**, 92; "Capital Parade" collumn, **Supp. 10**, 414, 415; cartoons, **Supp. 5**, 732; cartoons, editorial, **Supp. 10**, 245; "Conning Tower" column, **Supp. 6**, 4, 5, 113; editorial policies, **Supp. 8**, 441, 520–21; foreign correspondents, **Supp. 8**, 259–60; formation of, **Supp. 4**, 686–87; literary editor, **Supp. 8**, 667–68; "On the Record" column, **Supp. 7**, 740; reporting, **Supp. 5**, 18–19; "Today and Tomorrow" column, **Supp. 9**, 505, 506
New York Historical Society, **Vol. 1, Part 2**, 70, 204, 568; **Vol. 2, Part 2**, 224; **Vol. 3, Part 1**, 279; **Vol. 3, Part 2**, 356; **Vol. 4, Part 2**, 417; **Vol. 5, Part 1**, 240; **Vol. 7, Part 1**, 125; **Vol. 7, Part 2**, 630; **Supp. 8**, 664
New York Home for Incurables, founding of, **Vol. 3, Part 2**, 356
New York Hospital, **Supp. 6**, 123, 546–47
New York Humane Society, **Vol. 7, Part 1**, 360
New York Institution for the Blind, **Vol. 2, Part 2**, 107; **Vol. 8, Part 2**, 238
New York Institution for the Instruction of the Deaf and Dumb, **Vol. 7, Part 2**, 391
New York Intercollegiate Bureau of Occupations, **Vol. 9, Part 2**, 534
New York Journal, **Vol. 8, Part 1**, 332 f.; editing, **Supp. 2**, 63
New York Journal American, founding of, **Supp. 5**, 285
New York Journal of Commerce, **Vol. 4, Part 2**, 98; **Vol. 8, Part 1**, 228 f.; **Vol. 9, Part 2**, 73 f., 299, 303
New York Juvenile Asylum, **Vol. 8, Part 2**, 238
New York Kindergarten Society, **Supp. 5**, 437
New York Knickerbockers (basketball), **Supp. 8**, 358
New York Laryngological Society, **Vol. 1, Part 2**, 467
New York Law Institute, founding of, **Vol. 1, Part 1**, 314
New York Law Journal, **Vol. 6, Part 1**, 602; **Vol. 9, Part 2**, 636
New York Law School, **Vol. 2, Part 2**, 25; **Vol. 3, Part 1**, 571 f.
New York Law Society, founding of, **Supp. 2**, 501
New York Ledger, **Vol. 1, Part 2**, 437; **Vol. 7, Part 2**, 281
New York Life Insurance Co., **Vol. 1, Part 1**, 599; **Vol. 6, Part 1**, 495, 562; **Vol. 7, Part 2**, 56, 381, 471; **Supp. 1**, 470
New York Life Insurance Co. Building, **Supp. 6**, 593
New York Mail, cartoons and caricatures, **Supp. 8**, 217
New York Medical College, **Vol. 1, Part 1**, 601; **Vol. 3, Part 1**, 376
New York Medical Journal, **Vol. 4, Part 2**, 211; **Supp. 3**, 385–86
New York Mets (baseball), **Supp. 9**, 390, 764, 855
New York Military Band, **Supp. 6**, 242
New York Mining and Stock Exchange, **Vol. 6, Part 1**, 13
New York Mirror, **Supp. 3**, 20; **Supp. 1**, 323, 406; **Supp. 6**, 232
New York Morning Journal, **Supp. 5**, 284
New York Morning News, **Vol. 7, Part 2**, 89; **Vol. 9, Part 2**, 538
New York Morning Sun, first woman reporter, **Supp. 8**, 432
New York Morning Telegraph, **Supp. 3**, 20; **Supp. 6**, 214
New York Museum of Science and Industry, **Vol. 9, Part 2**, 614; founding of, **Supp. 1**, 627
New York Music Critics' Circle Award, **Supp. 6**, 63
New York, New Haven & Hartford Railroad, **Vol. 7, Part 1**, 179; **Vol. 7, Part 2**, 357; **Vol. 8, Part 2**, 200
New York Observer, **Vol. 8, Part 1**, 228
New York Obstetrical Society, founding of, **Vol. 9, Part 2**, 446
New York Oratorio Society, **Vol. 5, Part 2**, 486; **Supp. 3**, 742; **Supp. 4**, 210
New York Orthopaedic Hospital, **Vol. 9, Part 2**, 318
New York Packet, **Vol. 6, Part 1**, 427
New York Philharmonic: **Vol. 3, Part 1**, 377; **Vol. 4, Part 2**, 504; **Vol. 10, Part 1**, 543; **Supp. 7**, 651, 652, 765; **Supp. 8**, 641–42; **Supp. 10**, 456; broadcasts, **Supp. 8**, 645; Central Park concerts, **Supp. 10**, 422; conductors, **Supp. 6**, 457, 550, 643; **Supp. 10**, 722; first flute, **Supp. 3**, 33; musical advisers, **Supp. 8**, 641–42; predecessors, *see* New York Symphony Orchestra; New York Symphony Society; Philharmonic Society of New York; Philharmonic-Symphony of New York; Promenade concerts, **Supp. 10**, 422; Young People's Concerts, **Supp. 2**, 596
New York Post: **Supp. 6**, 5; **Supp. 7**, 740; **Supp. 10**, 475; Winchell attacks on, **Supp. 9**, 887
New York Press, **Vol. 8, Part 1**, 100 f.; **Supp. 6**, 686
New York Press Syndicate, founding of, **Supp. 4**, 38
New York Printing Co., **Vol. 1, Part 1**, 237
New York Prison Association, **Vol. 3, Part 1**, 493
New York Psychoanalytic Society, founding of, **Supp. 4**, 108; **Supp. 5**, 517
New York Public Library: **Vol. 1, Part 1**, 335, 445; **Vol. 1, Part 2**, 12, 268; **Vol. 2, Part 1**, 519; **Vol. 7, Part 2**, 107; **Vol. 8, Part 1**, 17, 125 f., 634; **Vol. 8, Part 2**, 382; branch expansion, **Supp. 3**, 90–91; **Supp. 4**, 19; children's collections, **Supp. 7**, 550; establishment of, **Supp. 2**, 162; finances of, **Supp. 5**, 47; gifts to, **Supp. 3**, 90; **Supp. 6**, 24, 549; Readers' Adviser's Office, **Supp. 3**, 281; research collection, **Supp. 6**, 398–99
New York Review of Books, **Supp. 10**, 418
New York School of Philanthropy, **Vol. 6, Part 1**, 223; **Supp. 4**, 227
New York School of Social Work: **Supp. 1**, 237; **Supp. 3**, 420; **Supp. 5**, 431; **Supp. 6**, 284; founding of, **Supp. 2**, 376
New York Social Register, **Supp. 9**, 827
New York Society for the Suppression of Vice, **Supp. 6**, 94–95
New York Star, **Vol. 3, Part 1**, 388
New York State: agricultural extension program, **Supp. 4**, 36–37; agriculture, **Vol. 3, Part 1**, 605 f.; **Vol. 6, Part 1**, 232; **Vol. 8, Part 1**, 347 f.; **Supp. 3**, 433–34; archaeological museum, **Supp. 5**, 533; Bear Mountain Bridge, **Vol. 8, Part 2**, 90; betting legislation, **Vol. 3, Part 1**, 552 f.; Board of Regents, **Vol. 4, Part 2**, 419; botany, **Vol. 7, Part 2**, 373; boundary disputes, **Vol. 5, Part 2**, 6, 11, 150, 608; **Vol. 7, Part 2**, 228; **Vol. 8, Part 1**, 423, 426, 633; canals, **Vol. 3, Part 1**, 274; **Vol. 9, Part 2**, 260; **Vol. 10, Part 1**, 541 f.; Chamber of Commerce, **Vol. 7, Part 2**, 56; Charities Aid Association, **Supp. 7**, 251; Charter of Liberties, **Vol. 3, Part 1**, 564; civil code of, **Vol. 3, Part 2**, 361 f.; "clean book bill," **Supp. 3**, 181; Communist party, **Supp. 5**, 499–500; constitution, changes in, **Vol. 5, Part 2**, 6; **Vol. 8, Part 1**, 318 f.; constitution, drafting of, **Vol. 3, Part 1**, 486 f., **Vol. 8, Part 1**, 249 f.; constitution, printing of, **Vol. 6, Part 1**, 427; constitutional reform, **Supp. 9**, 593; Coudert subcommittee (Senate), **Supp. 9**, 199–200; currency, first, paper, **Vol. 1, Part 2**, 564; Democratic party, **Supp. 10**, 232–33, 234; discovery, tricentennial of, **Vol. 8, Part 1**, 590; education, **Vol. 3, Part 1**, 347, 434, 564 f., 570 f., 604; **Vol. 4, Part 2**, 419; **Vol. 7, Part 1**, 358; **Vol. 7, Part 2**, 137; **Vol. 8, Part 1**, 17, 126, 253 f., 347 f., 351 f., 546; **Vol. 10, Part 1**, 537;

educational system, **Supp. 4**, 134; **Supp. 9**, 25; entomology, first state to create office of, **Vol. 10, Part 1**, 388 f.; Episcopal diocese, division of original, **Vol. 3, Part 1**, 215; equal employment laws, **Supp. 7**, 382; fairs, state, **Vol. 8, Part 1**, 347 f.; **Vol. 10, Part 1**, 36; farming, **Vol. 10, Part 2**, 460; federal judgeship, first, **Vol. 3, Part 1**, 465 f.; first antidiscrimination law in U.S., **Supp. 9**, 429; first black elected to legislature, **Supp. 3**, 391; first black judge on Court of Appeals, **Supp. 9**, 251; first black-owned banking institution, **Supp. 9**, 251; Fishery Commission, **Vol. 8, Part 2**, 134; flora of, **Vol. 9, Part 2**, 597; fossils, **Vol. 10, Part 2**, 134; geological researches, **Vol. 3, Part 1**, 605 f.; **Vol. 8, Part 1**, 247; governors, **Vol. 1, Part 2**, 308, 476 f.; **Vol. 2, Part 2**, 138, 205, 212, 441 f., 442 f.; **Vol. 3, Part 1**, 325 f.; **Vol. 3, Part 2**, 326 f, 479 f.; **Vol. 4, Part 1**, 334; **Vol. 5, Part 1**, 113 f., 395 f.; **Vol. 5, Part 2**, 9, 394 f.; **Vol. 6, Part 1**, 156, 222 f.; **Vol. 7, Part 1**, 168 f., 258 f., 622 f.; **Vol. 9, Part 1**, 6 f.; **Vol. 9, Part 2**, 510 f., 537 f., 540 f., 583 f.; **Vol. 10, Part 2**, 565 f.; **Supp. 3**, 645–46, 668–69, 718–21, 751; **Supp. 4**, 404, 886; **Supp. 5**, 493–94; **Supp. 7**, 467, 659–60; **Supp. 9**, 230, 231, 524, 525, 680; **Supp. 10**, 232, 233, 686–88; history of, early, **Vol. 1, Part 2**, 406; **Vol. 2, Part 1**, 63 f.; **Vol. 2, Part 2**, 151 f.; **Vol. 3, Part 1**, 212 f., 247, 265, 364, 519 f.; **Vol. 5, Part 1**, 237; **Vol. 5, Part 2**, 332; **Vol. 6, Part 1**, 156, 309, 313, 316 f., 319, 322, 436; **Vol. 7, Part 1**, 613; **Vol. 7, Part 2**, 322; **Vol. 8, Part 2**, 473, 475 f.; **Vol. 9, Part 1**, 9, 357, 617; **Vol. 9, Part 2**, 365, 472; **Vol. 10, Part 1**, 163 f., 166 f.; **Vol. 10, Part 2**, 493, 542 f.; horse-racing, legislation against, **Vol. 3, Part 1**, 213, 552 f.; housing reform, **Supp. 6**, 522, 654; impeachment of governor, **Supp. 3**, 751; impeachment of judges, **Vol. 8, Part 1**, 229 f.; Indian massacres, **Vol. 2, Part 1**, 295; **Vol. 5, Part 2**, 371; **Vol. 7, Part 1**, 646 f.; industrial education, introduction of, **Vol. 3, Part 1**, 347; industrial relations, **Supp. 9**, 795–96; insane, care of, **Vol. 7, Part 1**, 489; **Vol. 8, Part 1**, 132 f.; iron manufacture and industry, **Vol. 10, Part 2**, 399; judicial reform, **Vol. 3, Part 2**, 486; **Vol. 6, Part 1**, 320; judiciary, **Supp. 3**, 451–52; **Supp. 4**, 190–91, 379–80; **Supp. 5**, 269–70, 357, 493; **Supp. 6**, 88; **Supp. 7**, 316–18; Juvenile courts, **Supp. 7**, 251; labor legislation, **Supp. 7**, 608; land speculation, **Vol. 2, Part 1**, 581; **Vol. 3, Part 1**, 465 f.; **Vol. 7, Part 2**, 531; laws, codification of, **Vol. 1, Part 1**, 593; Vol. 2, Part 1, 537; **Vol. 3, Part 2**, 23; **Vol. 8, Part 1**, 318 f.; **Vol. 9, Part 1**, 52, 357; legal service, **Vol. 1, Part 1**, 282, 572; **Vol. 1, Part 2**, 97, 154, 177, 204, 231, 248, 308, 322, 360, 373, 393, 552, 583; **Vol. 2, Part 1**, 356, 467, 537; **Vol. 3, Part 1**, 41, 140, 212, 231, 247, 288, 294, 375, 387, 465, 485, 488, 571; **Vol. 4, Part 1**, 360, 472; **Vol. 4, Part 2**, 410; **Vol. 5, Part 1**, 112, 115, 116, 232, 249, 299, 368, 575; **Vol. 5, Part 2**, 198, 345, 460; **Vol. 6, Part 1**, 222, 396; **Vol. 6, Part 2**, 326, 353; **Vol. 7, Part 1**, 68, 512, 517, 592, 604, 638; **Vol. 7, Part 2**, 73, 212, 267, 385, 387, 587; **Vol. 8, Part 1**, 132, 245, 253, 255, 318, 375, 439, 509, 634; **Vol. 8, Part 2**, 92, 224; **Vol. 9, Part 1**, 261, 352, 445, 449, 499, 598; **Vol. 10, Part 1**, 93, 152, 165, 378, 406 f., 642 f.; **Vol. 10, Part 2**, 46, 457; Leisler rebellion, **Vol. 3, Part 1**, 247; **Vol. 6, Part 1**, 181; Liberal party, **Supp. 10**, 324, 697; Loyalist affairs in, **Vol. 8, Part 2**, 34; lunacy laws, **Vol. 7, Part 2**, 50; map of, in 1802, **Vol. 3, Part 1**, 274; military artist, **Supp. 6**, 204; missions, **Vol. 10, Part 2**, 311; model parole system developed, **Supp. 9**, 553; municipal betterment, **Vol. 3, Part 1**, 11; National Guard, **Vol. 7, Part 2**, 553; nursing education, **Supp. 5**, 251; penal reform, **Supp. 3**, 420–21; **Supp. 9**, 553; planning, **Supp. 2**, 739; political service, **Vol. 1, Part 2**, 170, 204, 231, 259, 308, 369, 476, 568, 584; **Vol. 2, Part 2**, 99, 138, 225, 253, 558; **Vol. 3, Part 1**, 138, 212, 214, 245, 247, 294 f., 322, 325, 378, 387, 465, 480, 519, 602; **Vol. 3, Part 2**, 326, 397, 480, 486; **Vol. 4, Part 1**, 335; **Vol. 4, Part 2**, 405; **Vol. 5, Part 1**, 10, 28, 113, 395, 401; **Vol. 6, Part 1**, 227, 316, 319, 449, 528; **Vol. 6, Part 2**, 78, 124, 275, 641; **Vol. 7, Part 1**, 83, 126, 514 f., 622; **Vol. 7, Part 2**, 46, 82, 107, 215, 331, 474; **Vol. 8, Part 1**, 4 f., 132, 179, 229, 253, 283, 302, 318, 326, 347, 409, 442, 582; **Vol. 8, Part 2**, 6, 28, 137, 255, 615; **Vol. 9, Part 1**, 6, 444; **Vol. 9, Part 2**, 129, 427, 510 f., 537, 583; **Vol. 10, Part 1**, 80, 151, 154, 163, 166, 390, 406 f., 598 f.; **Vol. 10, Part 2**, 245, 257, 456, 490, 566, 598, 628; politics, **Supp. 3**, 641–46, 717–21, 751; **Supp. 4**, 511–12, 855–56; **Supp. 5**, 285–86, 493–94, 715–16, 717–19; **Supp. 6**, 535, 588, 660; **Supp. 7**, 382–83, 467, 468, 521, 659–60, 733–34; **Supp. 8**, 323; **Supp. 9**, 200, 230, 250–51, 399, 449, 450, 524–25, 594, 680; **Supp. 10**, 232–33, 453, 686–88, 697, 698; Port Authority, **Supp. 10**, 788–89; Power Authority, **Supp. 6**, 484; **Supp. 9**, 656; prison reform, **Vol. 3, Part 1**, 378; **Vol. 7, Part 2**, 75; **Supp. 4**, 471–72; **Supp. 5**, 427; Prohibition (1854), **Vol. 3, Part 1**, 353; public health, **Supp. 6**, 701; **Supp. 7**, 251–52; public service, **Vol. 1, Part 2**, 239; **Vol. 2, Part 2**, 410, 443, 618; **Vol. 3, Part 1**, 486, 488; **Vol. 3, Part 2**, 447, 484; **Vol. 4, Part 2**, 173 f., 205; **Vol. 5, Part 1**, 28; **Vol. 5, Part 2**, 399; **Vol. 6, Part 1**, 32, 215, 232, 313 f.; **Vol. 7, Part 1**, 422; **Vol. 7, Part 2**, 293, 472; **Vol. 8, Part 1**, 99 f., 138, 243, 253 f., 324, 634; **Vol. 8, Part 2**, 134, 220, 255, 292, 342, 349, 478 f.; **Vol. 9, Part 1**, 460; **Vol. 9, Part 2**, 130 f.; **Vol. 10, Part 1**, 598 f.; **Supp. 10**, 232–33, 453; "Quids" political party, **Vol. 6, Part 1**, 222; railroad development in, **Vol. 2, Part 2**, 446 f.; regional planning groups, **Supp. 9**, 526; Republican party, **Supp. 9**, 524–25; **Supp. 10**, 302–3, 686–88; Republican party, organization of, **Vol. 2, Part 2**, 138; Revolution period; **Vol. 3, Part 1**, 214 f., 404; **Vol. 8, Part 1**, 452; Revolution of 1689, **Vol. 6, Part 1**, 156; Roman Catholic diocese, **Supp. 8**, 613–15; sanitation, **Vol. 4, Part 2**, 308; settlement of, **Vol. 6, Part 2**, 265; **Vol. 10, Part 2**, 227, 297; Socialist party, **Supp. 3**, 853; **Supp. 5**, 635; **Supp. 8**, 649–50; Social Welfare Board, **Supp. 3**, 4; society, colonial, **Vol. 8, Part 2**, 475, 477; "Stalwarts," **Vol. 4, Part 2**, 450; **Vol. 5, Part 2**, 543 f.; **Vol. 8, Part 1**, 4 f.; **Vol. 8, Part 2**, 28 f.; statutes, revision of, **Vol. 9, Part 2**, 511; Supreme Court, youngest justice, **Supp. 2**, 496; Supreme Court of, **Vol. 4, Part 1**, 360; surveying, **Vol. 3, Part 1**, 274; Taylor Law, **Supp. 9**, 796; Tuscarora Reservation land seizure, **Supp. 9**, 656–57; unemployment insurance pooled-fund plan, **Supp. 3**, 19; Uniform Commercial Code, **Supp. 7**, 474; U.S. attorneys, **Supp. 3**, 117, 181; **Supp. 4**, 785; **Supp. 6**, 141; welfare, **Supp. 4**, 391–92; *Westchester County During the American Revolution*, **Vol. 3, Part 1**, 152; White Charter Commission, **Vol. 3, Part 1**, 11; woman suffrage, **Supp. 4**, 157; **Supp. 6**, 79; **Supp. 7**, 778–79; workmen's compensation law, **Vol. 4, Part 1**, 335

New York State Agricultural College. *See* Cornell University

New York State Agricultural Society, **Vol. 3, Part 1**, 210; **Vol. 5, Part 2**, 90; **Vol. 7, Part 2**, 297

New York State Charities Aid Association, **Vol. 8, Part 2**, 474

New York State Conference of Charities and Corrections, organized, **Vol. 9, Part 2**, 15

New York State Crime Commission, **Supp. 9**, 364

New York State Farm Bureau Federation, predecessors, **Supp. 4**, 37

New York State Federation of Labor, presidency of, **Supp. 10**, 524
New York State Historical Society, **Supp. 3**, 287
New York State Institute for the Study of Malignant Diseases (Buffalo), **Vol. 7, Part 2**, 208; **Supp. 6**, 126
New York State Library, director, **Supp. 8**, 664
New York State Ranger School, founding of, **Supp. 4**, 44
New York State Temperance Society, **Vol. 3, Part 1**, 221
New York State Woman's Suffrage Association, **Vol. 1, Part 2**, 344
New York Stock Exchange: **Vol. 2, Part 2**, 76, 133; **Vol. 4, Part 2**, 393 f.; **Vol. 5, Part 1**, 247; first gambling company listed, **Supp. 10**, 309; reform, **Supp. 9**, 864; reorganization, **Supp. 9**, 613–14; **Supp. 10**, 139; scandal, **Supp. 9**, 864; specialists, **Supp. 10**, 139
New York Sun: **Vol. 1, Part 2**, 80; **Vol. 3, Part 1**, 51 f., 155; **Vol. 4, Part 2**, 475; **Vol. 5, Part 1**, 65; **Vol. 5, Part 2**, 539; **Vol. 6, Part 1**, 339; **Vol. 6, Part 2**, 413; **Vol. 7, Part 1**, 44; **Vol. 9, Part 2**, 252; **Supp. 6**, 6, 290–91; art criticism, **Supp. 7**, 494; columns, **Supp. 8**, 444; editorship, **Supp. 1**, 510; news reporting, **Supp. 10**, 383–84; political cartoons, **Supp. 8**, 218; "Sun Dial" column, **Supp. 7**, 617–18
New York Sunday School Union, **Vol. 6, Part 1**, 406
New York Symphony Orchestra, predecessor of New York Philharmonic, **Supp. 3**, 33, 64–65; **Supp. 6**, 426
New York Symphony Society, predecessor of New York Philharmonic, **Supp. 4**, 210, 211, 212
New York Tax Reform Association, founding of, **Supp. 2**, 272
New York Teacher, **Vol. 9, Part 1**, 64
New York Telegram, **Supp. 7**, 369
New York Telephone Co., **Supp. 3**, 299
New York Theological Seminary, **Vol. 6, Part 1**, 554
New York Times: **Vol. 4, Part 1**, 7; **Vol. 5, Part 1**, 148, 424; **Vol. 5, Part 2**, 171, 231; **Vol. 6, Part 1**, 455; **Vol. 6, Part 2**, 620; **Vol. 7, Part 1**, 601; **Vol. 8, Part 1**, 408, 409; **Vol. 9, Part 1**, 175; **Vol. 9, Part 2**, 252, 539; authorized biographies, **Supp. 6**, 58, 148; *Current History*, **Vol. 7, Part 1**, 601; *Dictionary of American Biography* funding, **Supp. 2**, 186, 342; drama criticism, **Supp. 3**, 842; **Supp. 7**, 412, 811; editing of, **Supp. 10**, 35–37; editorial policies in 1870–1920, **Vol. 2, Part 1**, 554; financial column, **Supp. 3**, 564–65; first bridge column, **Supp. 6**, 380; first woman editorial board member, **Supp. 5**, 447; foreign correspondents, **Supp. 5**, 60; founding of, **Vol. 8, Part 1**, 408 f.; **Vol. 9, Part 1**, 175; labor correspondent, **Supp. 5**, 653–54; legal counsel, **Supp. 8**, 224; medical reporting, **Supp. 4**, 667–68; music criticism, **Supp. 2**, 8; **Supp. 5**, 183; "newspaper of record," **Supp. 3**, 787–88; **Supp. 5**, 362–63; opinion column, **Supp. 9**, 471, 472; Paris bureau, **Supp. 6**, 183–84; Pentagon Papers case, **Supp. 9**, 88, 97; **Supp. 10**, 324; political caricatures, **Supp. 4**, 159–60; publishing, **Supp. 7**, 199–200; **Supp. 8**, 636; science articles, **Supp. 6**, 327, 328; **Supp. 10**, 435; "Sports of the Times" column, **Supp. 9**, 215; "Topics of the Times," **Supp. 4**, 804; Tweed, attack on, **Vol. 10, Part 1**, 81; typography, **Supp. 7**, 2; Washington bureau, **Supp. 9**, 471–72; *Winners and Sinners*, in-house publication, **Supp. 10**, 36
New York Times Building, construction of, **Supp. 3**, 612
New York Times Index, **Supp. 3**, 788
New York Times Magazine, The: double-crostic puzzle, **Supp. 6**, 342; illustrated interviews in, **Supp. 4**, 160
New York Times v. *United States*, **Supp. 9**, 97
New York Tract Society, **Vol. 3, Part 1**, 345
New York Trade School, **Vol. 1, Part 1**, 421
New York Tribune: **Vol. 3, Part 1**, 50 f.; **Vol. 4, Part 1**, 529 f., 533; **Vol. 4, Part 2**, 383, 480; **Vol. 5, Part 1**, 104; **Vol. 5, Part 2**, 135; **Vol. 7, Part 2**, 188; **Vol. 8, Part 1**, 483, f., 624; **Vol. 8, Part 2**, 51, 57; **Vol. 9, Part 1**, 223, 261; **Vol. 9, Part 2**, 403, 487; art criticism, **Supp. 4**, 182–83; founding of, **Vol. 8, Part 1**, 408 f.; Fresh Air Fund, **Vol. 7, Part 2**, 209; Platt, T. C., attacks on, **Vol. 8, Part 1**, 485; "scoops" of Smalley, **Vol. 9, Part 1**, 224; sports column, **Supp. 5**, 568; syndicated column, **Supp. 5**, 667; under Horace Greeley, **Vol. 6, Part 2**, 36; union boycott of, **Vol. 8, Part 1**, 484
New York University: **Vol. 6, Part 1**, 619 f.; **Vol. 7, Part 2**, 311; **Vol. 9, Part 1**, 37, 471; administration, **Supp. 1**, 125; **Supp. 5**, 109; **Supp. 9**, 378; aeronautics school endowed, **Supp. 9**, 348; anesthesia program, **Supp. 6**, 553, 554; building architecture, **Supp. 5**, 388; English studies, **Supp. 3**, 109; football team, **Supp. 10**, 767; founding of, **Vol. 2, Part 2**, 481; Hall of Fame, **Vol. 6, Part 1**, 619–20; Institute of Fine Arts, **Supp. 8**, 195; law school, **Supp. 6**, 651; mathematics studies, **Supp. 9**, 201; Medical College, promotion of, **Vol. 7, Part 2**, 153; physiology studies, **Supp. 7**, 699; poetry center, **Supp. 7**, 442; psychology studies, **Supp. 6**, 222; **Supp. 10**, 780; State Museum, **Vol. 2, Part 2**, 156; tax studies, **Supp. 5**, 412
New York Woman Suffrage party, founding of, **Supp. 4**, 157
New York Women's Press Club, **Vol. 2, Part 2**, 561
New York World: **Vol. 2, Part 2**, 241, 256 f.; **Vol. 5, Part 1**, 106, 424; **Vol. 6, Part 2**, 267, 568; **Vol. 8, Part 1**, 253 f., 260 f.; **Vol. 8, Part 2**, 533; **Vol. 9, Part 2**, 616; **Supp. 3**, 170, 702, 842; **Supp. 4**, 885; **Supp. 6**, 5, 11, 15, 229, 536, 616–17; **Supp. 7**, 369, 370, 758, 767; comic strips, **Supp. 5**, 262; editorial cartoons, **Supp. 5**, 391–92, 499; editorial page, **Supp. 9**, 504–5; editorship, **Supp. 1**, 653; Hearst competition, **Supp. 5**, 284; music criticism, **Supp. 7**, 124; Washington correspondent, **Supp. 4**, 574–75
New York World's Fair (1939–40): aquacade, **Supp. 8**, 547; American Artists Today exhibit, **Supp. 6**, 97; Birth Series exhibit, **Supp. 4**, 230; design of, **Supp. 7**, 691; GM Futurama exhibit, **Supp. 6**, 234; in music director, **Supp. 5**, 183; organization of, **Supp. 7**, 780; sculpture, **Supp. 8**, 415; Todd attractions, **Supp. 6**, 637
New York World Telegram: **Supp. 6**, 601–2; **Supp. 7**, 368, 370, 472; sports cartoons, **Supp. 10**, 563
New York World Telegram and Sun: **Supp. 7**, 369; "Broadway After Dark" column, **Supp. 8**, 444
New York Yankees (baseball): **Vol. 5, Part 1**, 346; **Supp. 2**, 589; **Supp. 4**, 710–11; **Supp. 7**, 27; **Supp. 8**, 542; **Supp. 9**, 533, 764, 854–55; **Supp. 10**, 141–42, 314, 346, 347, 480, 566, 567, 574, 613–14; "Bronx Bombers," **Supp. 10**, 141; development of, **Supp. 5**, 40–41; first black player, **Supp. 10**, 346; "Murderers' Row," **Supp. 10**, 142, 532–33
New York Zoological Park: administration, **Supp. 2**, 317; **Supp. 8**, 485–86; architecture, **Supp. 2**, 369; gateway sculpture, **Supp. 8**, 414–15; reptile collection, **Supp. 3**, 228–29; specimen contributions, **Supp. 6**, 23
New York Zoological Society, **Supp. 7**, 45–46; administration, **Supp. 8**, 485–86
Neylan, John Francis, reference to, **Supp. 5**, 287
Nez Perc Indians, surrender of, **Vol. 4, Part 1**, 237; **Vol. 5, Part 1**, 280; **Vol. 5, Part 2**, 219; **Vol. 6, Part 2**, 614
NFL. *See* National Football League
Niacin, **Supp. 7**, 233
Niagara Falls, N. Y.: **Vol. 4, Part 1**, 136; bridge, **Vol. 8,**

Part 2, 592; electric power, source of, **Vol. 8, Part 1**, 375 f.; obelisk dam above, construction of, **Vol. 8, Part 1**, 359 f.; power canal utilized, **Vol. 3, Part 1**, 1, 59; power project, **Supp. 3**, 251, 769; waterpower development, **Vol. 8, Part 1**, 99 f.; **Vol. 8, Part 2**, 575

Niagara Falls Power Co., **Vol. 4, Part 2**, 283; **Vol. 8, Part 1**, 375 f.; **Vol. 8, Part 2**, 199

Niagara frontier, **Vol. 6, Part 1**, 595

Niagara Hudson Power Co., **Supp. 3**, 138

Niagara Movement, founding of, **Supp. 7**, 202

Niblo's Gardens, **Vol. 7, Part 1**, 542

Nicaragua: American retaliation against (1854), **Vol. 5, Part 1**, 152; canal proposal, **Supp. 4**, 193; diplomacy with U.S., **Vol. 1, Part 2**, 465; **Vol. 3, Part 1**, 314; **Vol. 5, Part 2**, 554; **Vol. 10, Part 1**, 363 f.; **Supp. 6**, 359; exploring expedition, **Vol. 6, Part 1**, 500; filibustering in, **Vol. 8, Part 2**, 343; inauguration of an American president, **Vol. 10, Part 1**, 363 f.; invasion of, by William Walker, **Vol. 7, Part 2**, 572; **Vol. 8, Part 1**, 356, 503; ornithology study, **Supp. 6**, 255

Nicaragua Canal Co., **Vol. 5, Part 1**, 247

Nicaragua canal project, **Vol. 1, Part 2**, 266; **Vol. 3, Part 1**, 116, 421 f.; **Vol. 5, Part 1**, 69; **Vol. 6, Part 2**, 537, 575

Nichols, Edward, reference to, **Vol. 7, Part 1**, 412

Nicholson, Alma Stotts, reference to, **Supp. 7**, 573

Nicholson, Francis, reference to, **Vol. 1, Part 2**, 336

Nicholson, J. Kenyon, reference to, **Supp. 9**, 70

Nicholson, Seth B., reference to, **Supp. 5**, 540

Nick Carter dime novels, **Vol. 5, Part 2**, 41

Nickel: mining, **Supp. 1**, 687; new uses for, **Supp. 5**, 652–53

Nickel and dime stores. *See* Five and dime stores

Nickelodeon, **Supp. 2**, 368

Nicknames and epithets: "Abe Martin," **Vol. 5, Part 1**, 324; "Admiral of the Lakes," **Vol. 7, Part 1**, 446; "Alfalfa Bill," **Supp. 9**, 301; "Ambassador of Heaven," **Vol. 3, Part 1**, 256; "American Addison," **Vol. 3, Part 1**, 236; "American Cicero," **Vol. 3, Part 2**, 534; "American Cruikshank," **Vol. 5, Part 2**, 139; "American Erskine," **Vol. 5, Part 1**, 115; "American Hogarth," **Vol. 5, Part 2**, 506; "American Joan of Arc," **Vol. 1, Part 2**, 415; "American Newman," **Vol. 5, Part 2**, 558; "American Tragedian," **Vol. 3, Part 1**, 81; "Angel of the Battlefield," **Vol. 1, Part 1**, 318; "Angel of the Stockyards," **Supp. 2**, 408; "Annalist of Yale," **Vol. 3, Part 1**, 276; "Antiquarian of Nassau Street," **Vol. 4, Part 1**, 460; "Apostle of Peace," **Vol. 5, Part 2**, 527; "Apostle to the Illinois Indians," **Vol. 4, Part 1**, 510; "Apostle to the Lost," **Vol. 6, Part 1**, 553; "Apostle to the Sioux," **Vol. 4, Part 2**, 264; "Apostle to the Slavs," **Vol. 8, Part 2**, 420; "archbishop of fundamentalism," **Supp. 5**, 345–46; "Art Jockey," **Vol. 1, Part 1**, 166; "Atomic Bill," **Supp. 10**, 435; "Atomic General," **Supp. 8**, 230; "Aunt Fanny," **Vol. 4, Part 1**, 84 f.; "B," **Supp. 7**, 315; "Babe," **Supp. 4**, 710–11; **Supp. 10**, 616; "Barley Jim," **Vol. 9, Part 2**, 312; "Baskerville of America," **Vol. 9, Part 2**, 436; "Bear, The," **Supp. 9**, 506; "Beau James," **Supp. 4**, 855; "Beau Jonathan," **Vol. 4, Part 2**, 470; "Beloved Man of the Four Nations," **Vol. 4, Part 2**, 414; "Beloved Woman," **Vol. 10, Part 1**, 433; "Bengal Tiger," **Vol. 10, Part 1**, 83; "Benicia Boy," **Vol. 4, Part 2**, 500; "Bet-You-a-Million Gates," **Vol. 4, Part 1**, 189; "Big Ban," **Vol. 5, Part 2**, 92; "Big Bill," **Supp. 5**, 340, 686; "Big Daddy of Little Dams," **Supp. 10**, 547; "Bigfoot," **Vol. 10, Part 1**, 377 f.; "Big Guts," **Vol. 8, Part 1**, 238 f.; "Big Poison," **Supp. 7**, 768; "Big Sid," **Supp. 5**, 105; "Bill W.," **Supp. 9**, 883; "Billy Sunday of the South," **Supp. 8**, 304; "Billy, the Flower-Hunter," **Vol. 1, Part 2**, 28; "Billy the Kid," **Vol. 9, Part 1**, 192; "Bing," **Supp. 10**, 158; "Bird," **Supp. 5**, 534; "Birdie," **Supp. 8**, 261; "Bishop Dan," **Vol. 10, Part 1**, 75; "Bishop of Hampshire County," **Vol. 10, Part 1**, 99; "Bismarck of Western Politics," **Vol. 5, Part 2**, 365; "Black Ben," **Vol. 3, Part 2**, 509; "Black Dan," **Vol. 10, Part 1**, 585 f.; "Black Daniel Webster," **Vol. 10, Part 1**, 440; "Black Hawk," **Vol. 8, Part 2**, 41 f.; "Black Jack," **Supp. 4**, 655; "Black Mike," **Supp. 7**, 130; "Blackrobe," **Vol. 3, Part 1**, 256; "Black Sam," **Vol. 4, Part 1**, 1; "Bloody Shirt," **Vol. 3, Part 2**, 503; "Bo," **Supp. 5**, 458; "Bobbin Boy of Massachusetts," **Vol. 1, Part 1**, 577; "Bojangles," **Supp. 4**, 695; "Bold Man of Bean Hill," **Vol. 3, Part 1**, 550; "Bonanza King," **Vol. 9, Part 2**, 263; "Boston Rebel," **Vol. 6, Part 1**, 453, 465; "Boswell of modern American science," **Supp. 10**, 435; "Boy Major," **Vol. 7, Part 2**, 408; "Boy Preacher," **Vol. 3, Part 2**, 554; "Boys of Summer," **Supp. 9**, 390; "Brazilian Bombshell," **Supp. 5**, 500; "Brick," **Vol. 8, Part 1**, 53 f.; "Bronx Bombers," **Supp. 10**, 141; "Brother Pourquoi," **Vol. 10, Part 1**, 405; "Brutal Friend," **Vol. 5, Part 2**, 490; "Brute," **Supp. 9**, 847; "Buck," **Supp. 9**, 857; "Buckskin Joe," **Supp. 2**, 133; "Bucky," **Supp. 10**, 313; "Buffalo Bill," **Vol. 2, Part 2**, 260 f., 522 f.; **Vol. 5, Part 1**, 480, 483; **Vol. 5, Part 2**, 238; **Vol. 7, Part 1**, 603 f.; "Bugsy," **Supp. 9**, 12; "Bula Matari," **Vol. 9, Part 1**, 512; "Bull," **Vol. 10, Part 1**, 655 f.; **Supp. 9**, 186; **Supp. 10**, 350; "Bull dog," **Supp. 4**, 857; "Buncombe Bob," **Supp. 7**, 644; "Burbank of the Range," **Vol. 4, Part 1**, 394; "Calico Charlie," **Vol. 3, Part 2**, 544; "California Humorist," **Vol. 10, Part 1**, 572 f.; "Camp-Meeting John," **Vol. 7, Part 1**, 548; "Cannonball," **Supp. 9**, 10; "Captain Nat," **Supp. 2**, 299; "Casey," **Supp. 9**, 762; "Cast-Iron Charlie," **Supp. 8**, 609; "Cattle King," **Vol. 9, Part 2**, 134; "Chairman," **Supp. 10**, 701; "Champion Crank," **Vol. 9, Part 2**, 626; "Chappie," **Supp. 10**, 377; "Chep," **Supp. 7**, 555; "Chesterdale," **Supp. 7**, 161; "Chesterfield of the House," **Vol. 8, Part 1**, 538; "Chesterfield of the Navy," **Vol. 10, Part 1**, 128; "Chesty," **Supp. 9**, 629; "Chick," **Supp. 9**, 422; "Chief," **Supp. 5**, 287; "Children's Statesman," **Supp. 7**, 483; "Chinese," **Vol. 10, Part 1**, 419 f.; "Christian Statesman," **Vol. 4, Part 1**, 17; "Cinderella Man," **Supp. 9**, 121; "Clem," **Supp. 7**, 494; "Clown Prince," **Supp. 7**, 49; "Cocky," **Supp. 5**, 125; "Coin," **Supp. 2**, 288; "Coke King," **Vol. 4, Part 1**, 30; "Colonel," **Supp. 2**, 319; **Supp. 5**, 449; **Supp. 10**, 453; "Colonel, The," **Supp. 10**, 691; "Colonel Bill," **Vol. 4, Part 1**, 577; "Colorado," **Vol. 5, Part 2**, 73; "Commodore," **Supp. 9**, 891; "Confederate Von Lückner," **Vol. 8, Part 1**, 420; "conscience of Chicago," **Supp. 8**, 40; "Conscience of the Senate," **Supp. 10**, 316; "Convertible Conn," **Supp. 10**, 491; "Cool Philosopher," **Vol. 9, Part 2**, 124; "Copey," **Supp. 5**, 131; "Copperhead," **Vol. 9, Part 1**, 8; "Corporal Tanner," **Vol. 9, Part 2**, 297; "Cotton King," **Vol. 8, Part 1**, 566; "Cotton Tom," **Supp. 5**, 290; "Count of the Holy Roman Empire," **Vol. 4, Part 1**, 378; "Cracker," **Supp. 8**, 574; "creator of American characters," **Vol. 8, Part 1**, 413; "Curly," **Supp. 9**, 281; "Daffy," **Supp. 9**, 223; "Dark Horse," **Vol. 8, Part 1**, 34 f.; "D'Artagnan of the AEF," **Supp. 7**, 488; "Daughter of the Confederacy," **Vol. 3, Part 1**, 146; "Dazzy," **Supp. 7**, 751; "Deacon Bill," **Supp. 7**, 501; "deaf and dumb poet," **Vol. 7, Part 1**, 377; "dean of American Baladeers," **Supp. 10**, 590; "Dean of American Folklore," **Supp. 10**, 781; "dean of American poets," **Supp. 2**, 430; "Dean of Black Lawyers," **Supp. 9**, 251; "dean of inconsistency," **Supp. 7**, 21; "dean of Negro publishers," **Supp. 2**, 3; "dean of the mining

and metallurgical professions," **Vol. 3, Part 1**, 396; "Death Valley Scotty," **Supp. 5**, 613; "Defender of the Constitution," **Vol. 10, Part 1**, 585 f.; "destiny's tot," **Supp. 10**, 311; "Detroit's Edison," **Vol. 10, Part 1**, 168; "Ding," **Supp. 7**, 163; "Diplomatic Corps," **Vol. 4, Part 1**, 135; "Diplomat of the Church," **Vol. 4, Part 2**, 371; "Dizzy," **Supp. 9**, 223; "Docile Don," **Supp. 10**, 75; "Doctor's Boys," **Vol. 3, Part 1**, 513; "Don Juan Largo," **Vol. 10, Part 1**, 466; "Duchess of Bubbly Creek," **Supp. 2**, 408; "Dude," **Supp. 5**, 475; "Duke," **Supp. 9**, 259; "Electric Charlie," **Supp. 7**, 794; "Elevator King," **Vol. 7, Part 2**, 371; "Elizabeth Fry of America," **Vol. 4, Part 1**, 238; "Emperor," **Vol. 9, Part 1**, 328; "Empress of the Blues," **Supp. 2**, 616; "Engine Charlie," **Supp. 7**, 794; "Farmer Smith," **Vol. 9, Part 1**, 269; "Father Murrow," **Vol. 7, Part 1**, 371; "father of the American anthracite-iron industry," **Vol. 9, Part 2**, 428; "father of American anthropology," **Vol. 7, Part 1**, 189; "father of American drama," **Vol. 3, Part 1**, 516 f.; "father of American history," **Vol. 1, Part 1**, 569; "father of American mapmaking," **Vol. 4, Part 1**, 124; "father of the American Medical Assocation," **Vol. 3, Part 1**, 139; "father of American playgrounds," **Supp. 2**, 374; "father of American radio," **Vol. 2, Part 1**, 255; "father of American surgery," **Vol. 7, Part 2**, 555; "father of American watchmaking," **Vol. 3, Part 1**, 240; "father of the Appalachian Trail," **Supp. 9**, 526; "father of architects," **Vol. 1, Part 1**, 433; "father of baseball," **Vol. 2, Part 1**, 587; "father of the cheap land system," **Vol. 1, Part 2**, 211; "father of Chinese geology," **Supp. 4**, 344; "father of Congregationalism in Dakota," **Vol. 10, Part 1**, 429 f.; "father of cotton manufacturing in the South," **Vol. 4, Part 1**, 600; "father of entomology in America," **Vol. 8, Part 2**, 40; "father of the Grand Coulee Dam," **Supp. 10**, 180; "father of Greater New York," **Vol. 4, Part 1**, 535; "father of greenbacks," **Vol. 9, Part 1**, 436; "father of iron shipbuilding in America," **Vol. 8, Part 1**, 640; "father of the Maine law," **Vol. 3, Part 1**, 411; "father of the Marshall Plan," **Supp. 8**, 90; "father of the Minnesota railroad system," **Vol. 8, Part 1**, 538; "father of missions," **Vol. 7, Part 1**, 15; "father of modern American blast furnace practice," **Vol. 4, Part 1**, 199; "father of modern American journalism," **Supp. 1**, 441; "father of modern photography," **Supp. 4**, 779, 781; "father of New York State Barge Canal," **Vol. 9, Part 2**, 260; "father of the New York turf," **Vol. 3, Part 1**, 213; "father of Niagara power," **Vol. 8, Part 1**, 376; "father of our national architecture," **Vol. 5, Part 2**, 34; "father of the nuclear submarine," **Supp. 8**, 231–32; "father of Presbyterianism in Kentucky," **Vol. 8, Part 1**, 537; "father of radio," **Supp. 7**, 177; "father of reclamation," **Vol. 10, Part 1**, 472 f.; "father of secession," **Vol. 8, Part 1**, 527; "father of the Senate," **Vol. 1, Part 1**, 317; "father of the skyscraper," **Vol. 5, Part 2**, 55; "father of tree surgery in America," **Vol. 3, Part 1**, 88; "father of trusts," **Supp. 1**, 306; "father of the United Nations," **Supp. 5**, 334; "father of the University of Georgia," **Vol. 1, Part 1**, 531; "father of Wisconsin," **Vol. 3, Part 1**, 216; "Father Ritchie," **Vol. 8, Part 1**, 628; "Father Welles," **Vol. 10, Part 1**, 629 f.; "Fatty," **Vol. 10, Part 1**, 389; "Fiery Star," **Vol. 1, Part 2**, 445; "Fighting Bob," **Vol. 3, Part 2**, 210; "Fighting Dick," **Vol. 8, Part 1**, 570; "Fighting Engineer," **Vol. 1, Part 1**, 496; "Fighting Joe," **Vol. 5, Part 1**, 196; "Fighting Parson," **Vol. 5, Part 2**, 191; **Vol. 9, Part 2**, 234; "Fighting Quaker," **Vol. 10, Part 1**, 539; **Supp. 2**, 511; "Fighting Surgeon of the Revolution," **Vol. 3, Part 1**, 414; "Finger, the," **Supp. 10**, 370; "Fire Alarm," **Vol. 3, Part 2**, 503; "first citizen of Atlanta," **Vol. 5, Part 1**, 485; "first citizen of Connecticut," **Vol. 1, Part 1**, 547; "first citizen of Minnesota," **Vol. 9, Part 1**, 618; "first citizen of Newark," **Vol. 3, Part 1**, 57; "first citizen of Richmond, Va." **Vol. 5, Part 1**, 121; "First Daughter," **Supp. 10**, 464; "first jester in California," **Vol. 3, Part 1**, 452; "First Lady of the American Theater," **Supp. 9**, 196; "first lady of the screen," **Supp. 10**, 807; "first lady of Yiddish theater," **Supp. 10**, 253; "Fitznoodle," **Vol. 10, Part 1**, 147; "Florence Nightingale of America," **Vol. 1, Part 1**, 318; "Flying Dutchman," **Vol. 10, Part 1**, 154; **Supp. 5**, 716; "flying grandfather," **Supp. 10**, 149; "Fordham Flash," **Supp. 9**, 293; "Forty-Eight Hours," **Vol. 3, Part 1**, 392; "Forty Thieves," **Vol. 10, Part 1**, 80; "founder of American architectural education," **Vol. 10, Part 1**, 452 f.; "Four Horsemen" (Notre Dame), **Supp. 7**, 729; "Four-String Joe," **Supp. 10**, 806; "Frank," **Supp. 10**, 133; "Free Trapper," **Vol. 8, Part 1**, 250 f.; "Fritz," **Supp. 7**, 459; "Fuss and Feathers," **Vol. 8, Part 2**, 511; "Gar," **Supp. 9**, 891; "Garbage Lady," **Supp. 2**, 408; "Gashouse Gang," **Supp. 7**, 514; "Gene," **Supp. 10**, 796; "Generous John," **Supp. 7**, 734; "Gentleman George," **Vol. 1, Part 1**, 645; "Gentle Producer," **Supp. 10**, 615; "geographer to the United States," **Vol. 5, Part 1**, 435; "Georgia Peach," **Supp. 7**, 128; "Gerald the Giant-Killer," **Supp. 9**, 590; "Girl with the Bee-Stung Lips," **Supp. 7**, 563; "Goddess in the Cloud," **Vol. 8, Part 1**, 472; "Godless Anne," **Vol. 8, Part 2**, 204; "Golden Rule Jones," **Supp. 1**, 454; "Golden Rule Nash," **Vol. 7, Part 1**, 384 f.; "Gold Dust Twins," **Supp. 9**, 840; "Gold-Plated Hart," **Supp. 7**, 325; "Good Gray Governor," **Vol. 3, Part 2**, 342; "Goody," **Supp. 8**, 502; "Goose," **Supp. 9**, 328; "Gorgeous George," **Supp. 9**, 729; "Grandma," **Supp. 7**, 556; "grandmother of American sentimental novel," **Supp. 8**, 471; "Gray Eagle," **Vol. 7, Part 1**, 20, 600; "gray eminence of the Republican party," **Supp. 7**, 73; "Gray Fox of algonac," **Supp. 9**, 892; "Great Agnostic," **Vol. 5, Part 1**, 469; "Great Commoner of medicine," **Vol. 9, Part 2**, 85; "Great Faffler," **Supp. 10**, 85; "Great Pacificator," **Vol. 8, Part 2**, 508 f.; "Great Renegade," **Vol. 4, Part 1**, 323; "Great Stone Face," **Supp. 9**, 780; "Grecian," **Vol. 3, Part 1**, 79; "Green Monster," **Supp. 10**, 860; "Groucho," **Supp. 10**, 514; "Gummo," **Supp. 10**, 517; "Gum-Shoe Bill," **Vol. 9, Part 2**, 88; "Guy," **Supp. 10**, 463; "Hammering Hank," **Supp. 7**, 351; "Handsome Jack," **Vol. 10, Part 1**, 33; "hero of Fort McHenry," **Vol. 1, Part 1**, 347; "Hell 'n Maria," **Supp. 5**, 160; "He-Who-Sees-in-the-Dark," **Supp. 4**, 128; "High Tax Harold," **Supp. 9**, 360; "Hoboken Bill," **Supp. 7**, 437; "Home Run," **Supp. 7**, 27; "Honest Harold," **Supp. 5**, 342–43; "Honest John," **Vol. 3, Part 1**, 134; "Honest lawyer," **Vol. 8, Part 1**, 422; "Honus," **Supp. 5**, 716; "Hoosier poet," **Vol. 8, Part 1**, 611; "Hoot," **Supp. 7**, 286; "Horace Mann of the South," **Vol. 8, Part 2**, 219; "Horse, The," **Vol. 10, Part 1**, 83; "Horse-Head," **Vol. 4, Part 1**, 253; "Hot Dog King," **Supp. 7**, 719; "Hound Dog," **Supp. 9**, 796; "Howlin' Mad," **Supp. 8**, 602; "Howlin' Wolf," **Supp. 10**, 77; "Hurry-up," **Supp. 4**, 917; "Ice King," **Vol. 7, Part 1**, 240; "I-Don't-Care Girl," **Supp. 4**, 815; "Ike," **Supp. 8**, 159; "Indian Man," **Supp. 7**, 450; "Inspired Declaimer," **Vol. 8, Part 1**, 207 f.; "Jack Dempsey of the Navy," **Supp. 8**, 41; "Jack Downing, Major," **Vol. 9, Part 1**, 345; "Jack the Liar," **Vol. 8, Part 1**, 451; "Jersey cow candidate," **Vol. 5, Part 1**, 90; "Jersey Slick," **Vol. 9, Part 2**, 523; "Johnny Appleseed," **Vol. 2, Part 2**, 17;

"John Taylor of Caroline," **Vol. 9, Part 2**, 331; "Jonker," **Vol. 10, Part 1**, 178; "Josiah Allen's wife," **Vol. 5, Part 1**, 150; "Judge," **Supp. 10**, 747; "Judge Wick," **Vol. 8, Part 1**, 611; "Julia of Julias," **Vol. 3, Part 1**, 170; "Junior," **Supp. 10**, 278; "Kentucky Colonel," **Supp. 10**, 141; "Kid," **Supp. 9**, 598; "King," **Supp. 7**, 131; "King of the Cherokees," **Vol. 2, Part 2**, 592; "King of Clowns," **Supp. 8**, 356; "King of Daredevil Comedy," **Supp. 9**, 508; "Kingfisher," **Supp. 5**, 707; "King Hendrick," **Vol. 4, Part 2**, 532; "King of Jazz," **Supp. 8**, 697, 698; **Supp. 9**, 340; "King Kelly," **Vol. 5, Part 2**, 310; "King Lincoln," **Vol. 10, Part 1**, 145; "King of the Lobby," **Vol. 10, Part 1**, 439; "King Rolette," **Vol. 8, Part 2**, 117; "King of the Slab," **Supp. 5**, 759; "King of the Southern Iron Word" **Vol. 3, Part 1**, 179; "King's Botanist," **Vol. 8, Part 2**, 126; "Lady Bird," **Supp. 9**, 431; "Lame Lion," **Vol. 3, Part 1**, 68; "Landlord of New York," **Vol. 1, Part 1**, 401; "Last Literary Cavalier," **Vol. 4, Part 2**, 456; "last of the muckrackers," **Supp. 9**, 678; "Leadbelly," **Supp. 4**, 475–77, 502; "Lean Jimmy," **Vol. 5, Part 2**, 177; "Leaping Parson," **Supp. 8**, 418; "Learned Blacksmith," **Vol. 2, Part 1**, 328; "Lefty," **Supp. 8**, 478–79; "Light-Horse Harry," **Vol. 10, Part 1**, 509 f.; "Lips," **Supp. 5**, 529; "Little Ellick," **Vol. 9, Part 1**, 569; "Little Flower," **Supp. 4**, 464; "Little General," **Vol. 5, Part 2**, 578; "Little Giant from Connecticut," **Vol. 10, Part 1**, 384 f.; "little guy," **Supp. 9**, 455; "Little Magician," **Vol. 10, Part 1**, 154; "Little Mo," **Supp. 8**, 101; "Little Mother of the Prisons," **Supp. 2**, 49; "Little Napoleon of Baseball," **Supp. 1**, 530; "Littte Poison," **Supp. 7**, 768; "Little Van," **Vol. 10, Part 1**, 155; "Little Villain," **Vol. 8, Part 1**, 409; "Logician of the West," **Vol. 3, Part 2**, 237; "Lone Eagle," **Supp. 9**, 496; "Lonesome Charley," **Vol. 8, Part 1**, 516; "Long John," **Vol. 10, Part 1**, 657 f.; "Lucky," **Supp. 7**, 484; "Lucky Lindy," **Supp. 9**, 496; "Ma," **Supp. 7**, 242; "Machine Gun," **Supp. 5**, 381; "Madam Knight," **Vol. 5, Part 2**, 468; "Mad Jack," **Vol. 8, Part 1**, 397; "Mad Poet," **Vol. 2, Part 2**, 160; "Mahatma of Music," **Supp. 9**, 418; "Maker of Champions," **Supp. 7**, 152; "Maker of Painters," **Vol. 1, Part 1**, 310; "Man on Horseback," **Vol. 10, Part 1**, 552 f.; "Man Who Always Comes Back," **Supp. 9**, 658; "Man with the Iron Hand," **Vol. 9, Part 1**, 587; "Man Mountain Dean," **Supp. 5**, 417; "Martyr Abolitionist," **Vol. 6, Part 1**, 434; "Martyr Spy," **Vol. 4, Part 2**, 107; "Master of Corn," **Vol. 8, Part 1**, 477; "Mayor Von O'Hall," **Vol. 4, Part 2**, 115; "Merry Mortician," **Supp. 5**, 739; "Meteor, the," **Supp. 10**, 311; "Mickey," **Supp. 10**, 134; "Mighty Mite," **Supp. 10**, 491, 600; "millionaire maestro," **Supp. 10**, 173; "Miracle Worker," **Supp. 8**, 316; "Missionary to the Armenians," **Vol. 3, Part 1**, 565 f.; "Moms," **Supp. 9**, 517; "Mooney," **Supp. 9**, 306; "Moses," **Vol. 10, Part 1**, 27; "Moses and Aaron," **Vol. 3, Part 1**, 85; "Moses of the Mormons," **Vol. 9, Part 2**, 123; "Mother Bailey," **Vol. 1, Part 1**, 494; "Mother Bloor," **Supp. 5**, 70; "Mother of the Confederacy," **Vol. 6, Part 1**, 42; "Mother Jones," **Vol. 5, Part 2**, 195; "Mother Margaret," **Vol. 4, Part 2**, 398; "mother of Methodism in America," **Vol. 4, Part 2**, 493; "Mother Stewart," **Vol. 9, Part 2**, 8; "mother of the FBI," **Supp. 4**, 446; "Mr. and Mrs. Swing," **Supp. 5**, 32; "Mr. Capitalist," **Supp. 5**, 551; "Mr. Conversation," **Supp. 10**, 265; "Mr. Five-by-Five," **Supp. 9**, 688; "Mr. Helicopter," **Supp. 9**, 726; "Mr. Moneybags of Morristown," **Vol. 8, Part 1**, 369; "Mr. National Defense," **Supp. 5**, 715; "Mr. Public Utility," **Supp. 10**, 751; "Mr. Republican," **Supp. 5**, 676; "Mr. Reserve," **Supp. 7**, 78; "Mr. Sam," **Supp. 7**, 636; "Mr. Social Security," **Supp. 9**, 28; "Mr. Willie," **Vol. 1, Part 1**, 334; "Mrs. Wightie," **Supp. 9**, 868; "Muley Bob," **Supp. 5**, 181; "Murderers' Row," **Supp. 10**, 142; "naïve sophisticate," **Supp. 9**, 827; "Nap," **Supp. 8**, 558–59; "Napoleon of the Drama," **Vol. 4, Part 1**, 40; "Napoleon of the Turf," **Vol. 5, Part 2**, 130; **Vol. 9, Part 2**, 365; "Napoleon of the West," **Vol. 8, Part 2**, 252; "Negro Debs," **Supp. 7**, 155; "Nestor of American literature," **Vol. 9, Part 2**, 58; "Nestor of the German-American journalists," **Vol. 8, Part 1**, 185; "Number-Two Wood," **Supp. 8**, 702; "Ohio Mower," **Vol. 1, Part 1**, 551; "Old Boy in Specs," **Vol. 3, Part 1**, 138; "Old Brains," **Vol. 4, Part 2**, 151; "Old Bullion," **Vol. 1, Part 2**, 211; "Old Captain Harris," **Vol. 9, Part 2**, 360; "Old Dander," **Vol. 9, Part 2**, 489; "Old Davy," **Vol. 10, Part 1**, 83; "Old Duck," **Vol. 3, Part 2**, 229; "Old Duckboard," **Supp. 2**, 81; "Old Duke," **Vol. 9, Part 2**, 47; "Old Dutch Cleanser," **Vol. 1, Part 2**, 358; "Old Figgers," **Vol. 4, Part 2**, 24; "Old Flintlock," **Vol. 4, Part 2**, 232 f.; "Old Gimlet Eye," **Supp. 2**, 81; "Old Hero," **Vol. 8, Part 1**, 34 f.; "Old Hickory," **Vol. 5, Part 1**, 531; **Vol. 8, Part 1**, 34 f.; "Old Professor," **Supp. 9**, 763; "Old Ranger," **Vol. 8, Part 1**, 519; "Old Roman," **Vol. 9, Part 1**, 202; **Vol. 9, Part 2**, 515; "Old Rosy," **Vol. 8, Part 2**, 164; "Old Rough and Ready," **Vol. 9, Part 2**, 353; "Old Sachem," **Vol. 5, Part 2**, 33; "Old Slackwater," **Vol. 7, Part 1**, 148; "Old Tom," **Vol. 9, Part 2**, 434; "Old War Horse," **Vol. 3, Part 1**, 263; "Old Whitey," **Vol. 8, Part 1**, 576; "Old Zach," **Vol. 6, Part 1**, 47; "Oliver Oldschool," **Vol. 8, Part 2**, 368; "Oliver Optic," **Vol. 1, Part 1**, 102; "Orphans' Friend," **Vol. 3, Part 1**, 562 f.; "our most delightful old lady," **Vol. 8, Part 2**, 332; "Our Patrick Henry," **Vol. 5, Part 2**, 492; "Outlaw of the Bronx," **Vol. 3, Part 1**, 214; "Owl," **Vol. 8, Part 2**, 252; "Pap," **Vol. 9, Part 2**, 434; "Papa," **Supp. 5**, 106; "Pappy," **Supp. 8**, 477; **Supp. 9**, 431; "Pathfinder of the Pacific," **Vol. 3, Part 2**, 266; "Patrick Henry of the West," **Vol. 7, Part 1**, 356; "Patriot Printer," **Vol. 10, Part 1**, 374 f.; "Patton of the Pacific," **Supp. 7**, 351; **Supp. 9**, 176; "Peace-Maker," **Vol. 5, Part 2**, 147; "Pee Wee," **Supp. 8**, 561; "Pepper," **Supp. 7**, 513; "Percy Bysshe Shelley Pinchback," **Vol. 7, Part 2**, 611; "Perfect Fool," **Supp. 8**, 710; "Peter of the Mills," **Vol. 3, Part 1**, 214; "Phog," **Supp. 9**, 20; "physician of Wall Street," **Supp. 4**, 193; "physician's physician," **Vol. 3, Part 1**, 25; "Pirate of Peru," **Vol. 4, Part 1**, 463; "Pitchfork Ben," **Vol. 9, Part 2**, 548; **Supp. 3**, 78; "Plumed Knight," **Vol. 5, Part 1**, 470; **Vol. 9, Part 2**, 147; "poet of the American Revolution," **Vol. 4, Part 1**, 27 f.; "poet of Charleston," **Vol. 4, Part 2**, 455; "poet of the Confederacy," **Vol. 8, Part 2**, 260; "poet of the Italian theatre," **Vol. 3, Part 1**, 71; "poet laureate of the Confederacy," **Vol. 9, Part 2**, 558; "poet laureate of Freemasonry," **Vol. 7, Part 1**, 225; "poet laureate of the Revolution," **Vol. 3, Part 1**, 508 f.; "poet of the Shenandoah Valley," **Vol. 6, Part 1**, 483; "Poor Man's Plato," **Supp. 9**, 119; "Pop," **Supp. 5**, 727; "Pope," **Vol. 9, Part 2**, 60; "Pope Dwight," **Vol. 3, Part 1**, 576 f.; "Pops," **Supp. 8**, 697; "Poughkeepsie Seer," **Vol. 3, Part 1**, 105; "Praying Student," **Vol. 8, Part 1**, 232 f.; "Priest of the Poor," **Vol. 3, Part 2**, 311; "Prince John," **Vol. 10, Part 1**, 151; "Prince Mike," **Supp. 9**, 673; "Prince of the Oyster Pirates," **Vol. 6, Part 1**, 370; "Prince of Schaghticoke," **Vol. 5, Part 2**, 461; "princess Alice," **Supp. 10**, 465; "Pudge," **Supp. 5**, 289; "purple cow man," **Supp. 5**, 94; "Queen of the Blues," **Supp. 7**, 769; "Rabbit," **Supp. 5**, 465; "Railroad Bishop," **Vol. 9, Part 1**, 23; "Rajah," **Supp. 7**,

365; "Raymond," **Supp. 9**, 320; "Red Fox of Kinderhook," **Vol. 10, Part 1**, 154; "Rico," **Supp. 7**, 464; "Rock of the Marne," **Supp. 2**, 397; "rowboat secretary," **Supp. 8**, 329; "Roxy," **Supp. 2**, 584; "Rosy," **Supp. 9**, 595; "Rube," **Supp. 8**, 217; **Supp. 10**, 508; "Run Forever," **Vol. 5, Part 2**, 492; "Russian Columbus," **Vol. 8, Part 1**, 523; "Rustic Bard," **Vol. 3, Part 1**, 315; "Sage of Nininger," **Vol. 3, Part 1**, 369; "Sage of Pittsfield," **Vol. 3, Part 1**, 149; "St. Thomas of Cantingbury," **Vol. 8, Part 1**, 363 f.; "Sam," **Supp. 9**, 652; "Sam Slick," **Vol. 7, Part 1**, 201; "Samson," **Vol. 3, Part 1**, 255; "Satchmo," **Supp. 9**, 45; "Savior of Georgia," **Vol. 10, Part 1**, 83; "Sawney," **Vol. 10, Part 1**, 579 f.; "Schnozzola," **Supp. 10**, 195; "Schoolboy," **Supp. 7**, 663; "Scoops," **Supp. 10**, 99; "Scotch Tom," **Vol. 7, Part 1**, 425; "Senator from Formosa," **Supp. 9**, 468; "Shag," **Supp. 8**, 587; "Shemp," **Supp. 9**, 282; "Shorty," **Supp. 10**, 623; "Silent Man from Tennessee," **Vol. 4, Part 1**, 207; "Silver Dick," **Vol. 1, Part 2**, 355; "Silver Fox of the Northland," **Supp. 10**, 40; "Silver-Masked Tenor," **Supp. 6**, 691; "Silver-Tongued Orator of the House of Bishops," **Vol. 8, Part 1**, 352 f.; "Silver-Tongued Spell-Binder of the Pacific Coast," **Vol. 3, Part 1**, 226; "Simon Suggs," **Vol. 5, Part 1**, 202; "Single-Speech," **Vol. 4, Part 2**, 521; "Sitting Bull," **Supp. 5**, 669; "Slam," **Supp. 10**, 509; "Slow Trot," **Vol. 9, Part 2**, 434; "Smiling Statesman," **Vol. 10, Part 1**, 601 f.; "Sockless Jerry," **Vol. 9, Part 1**, 180; "Spike," **Supp. 5**, 65; **Supp. 7**, 300, 403; "Spy of the Cumberland," **Vol. 3, Part 1**, 4; "Star-Giver General to the United States," **Vol. 8, Part 1**, 215 f.; "Star of the West," **Vol. 3, Part 1**, 428; "Steamboat," **Vol. 4, Part 1**, 338; "Stonewall," **Vol. 8, Part 1**, 44 f.; "Stonewall Jackson of the West," **Vol. 8, Part 1**, 41 f.; "Storm King," **Vol. 3, Part 2**, 185; "Stout Steve," **Supp. 7**, 596; "Strangler," **Supp. 8**, 371; "Sugartail," **Vol. 4, Part 2**, 309; "Sunny Jim," **Supp. 2**, 493; "Sunny Sol," **Supp. 7**, 373; "Swamp Fox of the Tennessee Valley," **Vol. 8, Part 2**, 70; "Tardy George," **Vol. 9, Part 2**, 255; "Tarheel Fuhrer," **Supp. 7**, 644; "Tariff Andy," **Vol. 9, Part 2**, 6; "Ten Thousand Dollar Beauty," **Vol. 5, Part 2**, 310; "Tex," **Supp. 9**, 662; "Three-Finger," **Supp. 8**, 396; "Tiger," **Supp. 9**, 566; "Tommy," **Supp. 5**, 682; "Tom-Tom," **Supp. 5**, 290; "Toots," **Supp. 10**, 731; "Tory Hunter," **Vol. 3, Part 2**, 314; "Tragedy Queen of the American Stage," **Vol. 3, Part 1**, 428; "Tricky Dick," **Supp. 10**, 184; "Trumpet King of the West," **Supp. 5**, 529; "Tuffy," **Supp. 10**, 444; "Tune Detective," **Supp. 7**, 707; "Uncle Ben," **Vol. 1, Part 1**, 516; "Uncle Billy," **Vol. 4, Part 1**, 418; "Uncle Frank," **Supp. 4**, 661; "Uncle Henry," Vol. 1, Part, 269; "Uncle of the Human Race," **Vol. 10, Part 1**, 439; "Uncle Jerry," **Vol. 8, Part 2**, 236; "Uncle John," **Vol. 8, Part 2**, 548; "Uncle Mike," **Supp. 5**, 360; "Van Am," **Vol. 10, Part 1**, 149; "Verbose Annie," **Supp. 5**, 447; "Vinegar Joe," **Supp. 4**, 782; "Virginian Saint Michael," **Vol. 8, Part 1**, 363 f.; "Vitagraph Tomboy," **Supp. 10**, 791; "voice of the industry," **Supp. 9**, 324; "Wahoo Sam," **Supp. 8**, 105; "Waiter," **Supp. 9**, 651; "Warwick of Massachusets Politics," **Vol. 8, Part 2**, 59; "Watchdog of the Treasury," **Vol. 5, Part 1**, 158; **Vol. 10, Part 1**, 504 f.; "Wee Charlie," **Vol. 1, Part 1**, 642; "Whirlwind," **Vol. 3, Part 2**, 562; "Whispering Charlie," **Supp. 10**, 229; "White Woman of the Genesee," **Vol. 5, Part 2**, 39; "Whitefield of Nova Scotia," **Vol. 1, Part 1**, 219; "Wild Bill," **Supp. 10**, 217; "Wild Horse of the Osage," **Supp. 7**, 513; "William the Silent," **Vol. 5, Part 2**, 286; "Wizard of Ooze," **Supp. 8**, 128; "wizard of the rule book," **Supp. 10**, 4–5; "Woman Who Always Prays," **Vol. 3, Part 1**, 477 f.; "Yellowstone," **Vol. 5, Part 2**, 309; "York's Tall Son," **Vol. 8, Part 1**, 107 f.; "Young Fox," **Vol. 10, Part 1**, 151; "Zeppo," **Supp. 10**, 559; "Zeus," **Vol. 8, Part 2**, 332; "Ziggy," **Supp. 8**, 163

Niebuhr, Reinhold, references to, **Supp. 7**, 574, 576; **Supp. 10**, 330

Nielsen, A. C., Co.: **Supp. 5**, 310–11; founding and growth of, **Supp. 10**, 587–88

Nieman, Lucius W., reference to, **Supp. 7**, 299

Nier, Alfred O., references to, **Supp. 4**, 818; **Supp. 6**, 371

Nietzsche, Friedrich Wilhelm, reference to, **Supp. 10**, 401–2

Nietzsche: Philospher, Psychologist, Antichrist, **Supp. 10**, 401

Nightclubs: **Supp. 3**, 536; **Supp. 5**, 501; **Supp. 8**, 38–39, 546, 547, 562; **Supp. 9**, 517, 563; acts, **Supp. 10**, 106, 107; comedy acts, **Supp. 10**, 452

Nighthawks, **Supp. 8**, 280

Night vision, studies in, **Supp. 4**, 357

Nijinsky, Vaslav F., reference to, **Supp. 9**, 776

Nimitz, Chester W., references to, **Supp. 5**, 621, 695; **Supp. 6**, 268, 339, 340, 629; **Supp. 7**, 490; **Supp. 8**, 42

Nin, Anaïs, reference to, **Supp. 10**, 539

"999" racing car, **Supp. 4**, 637

"Ninety-Nine-Year Case," **Vol. 8, Part 1**, 9 f.

Ninety-six, battle of, **Vol. 4, Part 1**, 572

Niter, mining of, **Vol. 8, Part 1**, 329 f.

Nitric oxide, isolation of, **Vol. 8, Part 1**, 223 f.

Nitrogen: **Supp. 4**, 838; cyanamide process, **Supp. 3**, 439–40; discovery of, **Vol. 5, Part 1**, 50

Nitrogen-15 isotope, **Supp. 3**, 693

NItrogen fixation, **Supp. 9**, 217, 218

Nitrogen peroxide, isolation of, **Vol. 8, Part 1**, 223 f.

Nitroglycerin, early use of, **Vol. 7, Part 1**, 297

Nitrous oxide: anesthetic, use of, **Vol. 2, Part 2**, 322; dentistry use of, **Vol. 10, Part 1**, 640 f.; isolation of, **Vol. 8, Part 1**, 223 f.

Nitti, Frank, references to, **Supp. 6**, 263, 264; **Supp. 9**, 651

Nitze, Paul, reference to, **Supp. 9**, 8

Nivison, Josephine Verstille, reference to, **Supp. 8**, 279–80

Nixon, Donald, reference to, **Supp. 10**, 357

Nixon, Richard M.: Acheson relationship, **Supp. 9**, 10; administration accused of racial bias, **Supp. 9**, 751; campaign contributions, **Supp. 10**, 357; "Checkers" speech, **Supp. 9**, 782; Cox newspapers endorsement of, **Supp. 9**, 202; Douglas, H. G., Senate campaign against, **Supp. 10**, 184; draft lottery, **Supp. 10**, 332; "Dump Nixon movement," (1952), **Supp. 9**, 781–82; **Supp. 10**, 302; education policies, **Supp. 9**, 25–26; Hiss case, **Supp. 10**, 719; Knowland opposition to, **Supp. 9**, 468, 469; Mitchell, J. N., relationship, **Supp. 10**, 545, 546; Pentagon Papers trial, **Supp. 9**, 88; "Pink Sheet" used in Senate campaign, **Supp. 10**, 184; presidential candidacy (1968), **Supp. 10**, 362–63; presidential reelection committee, **Supp. 10**, 345; references to, **Supp. 5**, 19, 343; **Supp. 7**, 73, 115, 420, 723; **Supp. 8**, 6, 282, 341; **Supp. 9**, 287, 838; **Supp. 10**, 212, 325; Supreme Court decisions, criticism of, **Supp. 9**, 96; Supreme Court nominations (unconfirmed), **Supp. 9**, 681, 739; **Supp. 10**, 316; "Tricky Dick" epithet, **Supp. 10**, 184; vice-presidential candidacy (1952), **Supp. 9**, 231, 781–82; **Supp. 10**, 716; Vietnam War policy, **Supp. 9**, 5; Watergate scandal, **Supp. 9**, 27; **Supp. 10**, 357, 462, 545–46

Nixon, Samuel, reference to, **Supp. 3**, 276

Nixon Foundation, **Supp. 9**, 284

"Nize Baby" (comic strip), **Supp. 5**, 262
Nizer, Louis, reference to, **Supp. 7**, 643
Nkrumah, Kwame, reference to, **Supp. 7**, 205
NLRB. *See* National Labor Relations Board
Nobel Prizes: chemistry, **Supp. 5**, 670; **Supp. 6**, 365; **Supp. 8**, 123; **Supp. 9**, 754; **Supp. 10**, 198, 427, 457, 609, 853; literature, **Supp. 5**, 423, 524; **Supp. 7**, 222, 234, 338; **Supp. 8**, 626; literature, first American woman to receive, **Supp. 9**, 133; peace, **Supp. 1**, 12; **Supp. 2**, 357, 580; **Supp. 4**, 137, 442; **Supp. 5**, 160, 335, 508; **Supp. 6**, 428; **Supp. 7**, 29; **Supp. 8**, 335; peace, first black to receive, **Supp. 9**, 138; physics, **Supp. 3**, 769; **Supp. 5**, 202, 220, 494, 496; **Supp. 6**, 151, 372; **Supp. 7**, 75, 133, 258, 344; **Supp. 8**, 628; **Supp. 9**, 542; **Supp. 10**, 805; physiology or medicine, **Supp. 3**, 136, 140–41, 440, 540; **Supp. 4**, 581; **Supp. 5**, 489; **Supp. 6**, 127, 223; **Supp. 7**, 226, 281, 341, 476; **Supp. 8**, 450, 556; **Supp. 9**, 72, 455, 655, 787, 794, 834
Noble, Ray, reference to, **Supp. 3**, 524
"Nocturne at Bethesda" (poem), **Supp. 9**, 108
Noel, Miriam, references to, **Supp. 6**, 713, 714
Noeldeke, Theodor, reference to, **Supp. 6**, 641
Noguchi, Hideyo, reference to, **Supp. 4**, 287
Noise, **Supp. 3**, 254
Noisy Book, **Supp. 5**, 92–93
Noland, Kenneth, reference to, **Supp. 7**, 479–80
Nolde, Emil, reference to, **Supp. 6**, 552
Nonimportation Act (1806), **Vol. 5, Part 2**, 30
Nonintercourse Act (1809), **Vol. 5, Part 2**, 30 f.
Nonpartisan Direct Legislation League (1897), founding of, **Supp. 4**, 844–45
Nonpartisan League (agricultural) (1915), **Vol. 6, Part 1**, 271; **Supp. 4**, 308–9, 479, 480; **Supp. 5**, 430; **Supp. 6**, 86–87, 360–61, 645; **Supp. 8**, 1
Nonpartisan League (labor) (1936), founding of, **Supp. 4**, 75, 376; **Supp. 8**, 376
Non-Resistance Society, formed, **Vol. 8, Part 1**, 306 f.
Non-Sectarian Anti-Nazi League, **Supp. 6**, 25
Nook Farm, **Vol. 5, Part 1**, 195
Noonan, Gregory, reference to, **Supp. 5**, 564
Noradrenaline, **Supp. 3**, 136
Norden Laboratories Corporation, **Supp. 7**, 577
Norfolk, Conn., musical festivals, at, **Vol. 9, Part 2**, 64
Norfolk (ship), **Vol. 1, Part 1**, 505
Norfolk, Va.: **Vol. 6, Part 2**, 445; **Vol. 7, Part 2**, 139 f.; as naval base, **Vol. 3, Part 1**, 189; **Vol. 6, Part 1**, 572; **Vol. 7, Part 2**, 576
Norma (opera), **Supp. 10**, 93
Normal schools: **Vol. 8, Part 2**, 250; Alabama, **Vol. 7, Part 2**, 41; California, **Vol. 7, Part 1**, 578; first state, **Vol. 7, Part 2**, 404; Illinois, **Vol. 1, Part 2**, 44; **Vol. 2, Part 2**, 376, 418; **Vol. 9, Part 2**, 581; Kentucky, **Vol. 8, Part 1**, 643; Massachusetts, **Vol. 2, Part 1**, 420; **Vol. 3, Part 1**, 563 f.; Michigan, **Vol. 10, Part 1**, 617 f.; Missouri, **Vol. 1, Part 1**, 538; modern type of, **Vol. 5, Part 1**, 128; New Jersey, **Vol. 4, Part 2**, 360; Wisconsin, **Vol. 8, Part 2**, 307
Normal Training Kindergarten (New York City), organized, **Vol. 5, Part 2**, 500
Normal University, establishment, **Vol. 5, Part 1**, 271
Norris, Charles, references to, **Supp. 8**, 471; **Supp. 10**, 328
Norris, Frank, references to, **Supp. 3**, 234, 555–56, 557; **Supp. 6**, 657
Norris, George W., references to, **Supp. 3**, 544, 645, 647, 650; **Supp. 4**, 185, 465, 536, 851; **Supp. 5**, 290; **Supp. 6**, 526, 684; **Supp. 9**, 590
Norris, James Flack, reference to, **Supp. 10**, 852
Norris, Kathleen, reference to, **Supp. 3**, 556
Norris Dam, **Supp. 3**, 560
Norris-Doxey Farm Forestry Act (1937), **Supp. 3**, 560
Norris-La Guardia Anti-Injunction Act (1932), **Supp. 3**, 559; **Supp. 4**, 465, 607; **Supp. 6**, 706
Norris-Rayburn Rural Electrification Act (1936), **Supp. 3**, 560
Norris v. *Alabama*, **Supp. 10**, 447
"North, Hugh" (fictional character), **Supp. 10**, 518
North Africa, World War II invasion, **Supp. 6**, 407
North American, **Vol. 2, Part 2**, 70, 185
North American Air Defense Command (NORAD), **Supp. 10**, 379
North American Aviation Co., **Supp. 5**, 229; **Supp. 6**, 618
North American Co., **Supp. 5**, 750
North American Datum, **Vol. 4, Part 2**, 452
North American Herpetology, publication of, **Vol. 5, Part 1**, 129
North American Index of Fossils, The, **Supp. 4**, 343
North American Indians, The, **Supp. 5**, 148
North American Magazine, **Vol. 9, Part 2**, 258
North American Newspaper Alliance, **Supp. 6**, 366
North American Review, **Vol. 2, Part 1**, 206; **Vol. 2, Part 2**, 3; **Vol. 3, Part 2**, 221, 223; **Vol. 4, Part 1**, 372; **Vol. 4, Part 2**, 57, 109; **Vol. 6, Part 1**, 347, 461 f.; **Vol. 7, Part 1**, 570; **Vol. 7, Part 2**, 169, 335, 341, 343; **Vol. 8, Part 1**, 444, 536; **Vol. 9, Part 1**, 431; **Vol. 10, Part 1**, 48
North American Telegraph Co., organization of, **Vol. 1, Part 1**, 639
Northampton School of Technology, **Vol. 9, Part 1**, 300
North and South (poetry collection), **Supp. 10**, 45
North Anna River, operation on. *See* Wilderness campaign
North Atlantic Treaty Organization (NATO): **Supp. 7**, 138, 214, 411; **Supp. 10**, 826; Senate opposition, **Supp. 10**, 842; strengthening of, **Supp. 10**, 9; supreme allied commander, **Supp. 6**, 408; **Supp. 8**, 156; treaties establishing, **Supp. 6**, 431; Vandenberg Resolution, **Supp. 5**, 704, 705
North Attleboro Evening Chronicle, **Supp. 8**, 420
North Carolina: agriculture, **Vol. 8, Part 1**, 40 f.; Audubon Society, **Supp. 3**, 592; Badger ordinance of revolution, **Vol. 3, Part 1**, 287; biographical history of, **Vol. 10, Part 1**, 603 f.; black education, **Supp. 7**, 83; botany, **Vol. 7, Part 1**, 45; boundary disputes, **Vol. 5, Part 2**, 140; **Vol. 6, Part 2**, 464; **Vol. 8, Part 1**, 42; carpetbagging, **Vol. 10, Part 1**, 69; Catholic church, **Vol. 4, Part 1**, 239; **Vol. 8, Part 1**, 217 f.; Civil War period, **Vol. 6, Part 2**, 570; **Vol. 10, Part 1**, 159 f.; colonial period, **Vol. 3, Part 1**, 337; **Vol. 2, Part 1**, 328; **Vol. 6, Part 2**, 343; **Vol. 9, Part 2**, 309; colonization of, **Vol. 4, Part 1**, 468; **Vol. 10, Part 2**, 110; constitution revision, **Supp. 5**, 652; Democratic party, **Supp. 9**, 440; **Supp. 10**, 814–15; education, **Vol. 2, Part 1**, 409; **Vol. 3, Part 1**, 480 f.; **Vol. 3, Part 1**, 496 f.; **Vol. 5, Part 1**, 193; **Vol. 6, Part 2**, 71; **Vol. 7, Part 1**, 345; **Vol. 8, Part 1**, 42, 43 f.; **Vol. 10, Part 2**, 213; Episcopal church, **Vol. 8, Part 1**, 398; **Supp. 1**, 169–70; exploration, **Vol. 2, Part 1**, 328; "Farmers' clubs," **Vol. 8, Part 1**, 40 f.; Federalists in, **Vol. 4, Part 2**, 414; "free suffrage," **Vol. 8, Part 1**, 476; freedmen, schools for, **Vol. 10, Part 1**, 27; French and Indian War, support of, **Vol. 3, Part 1**, 337; fungi of, **Vol. 8, Part 2**, 484; geology of, **Vol. 5, Part 1**, 167; **Vol. 5, Part 2**, 359; gold mining in, **Vol. 8, Part 1**, 450; governors, **Vol. 1, Part 1**, 386 f., 447 f.; **Vol. 1, Part 2**, 238, 596 f.; **Vol. 2, Part 1**, 282 f., 343, 516; **Vol. 3, Part 1**, 98 f., 480 f.; **Vol. 3, Part 2**, 16, 106, 108; **Vol. 5, Part 1**, 138, 140, 623 f.; **Vol. 5, Part 2**, 440 f.; **Vol. 6, Part 2**, 33 f.; **Vol. 7, Part 1**, 159, 383 f.; **Vol. 8, Part 1**, 476; **Vol. 9, Part 1**, 419 f.; **Vol. 9, Part 2**, 67 f., 73, 230 f.; **Vol. 10, Part 1**, 158 f.; **Vol.**

10, Part 2, 536 f.; **Supp. 1**, 532; **Supp. 4**, 315–16; **Supp. 5**, 306–7; **Supp. 6**, 568–69; **Supp. 9**, 391–92; Hillsboro mob, **Vol. 10, Part 1**, 26; historical commission, **Supp. 4**, 176; historical writings, **Supp. 1**, 310; **Supp. 2**, 57; history of, **Vol. 8, Part 2**, 385; **Vol. 8, Part 1**, 64 f., 603 f.; independence of western portion of, **Vol. 8, Part 1**, 640; industrial history of, **Vol. 3, Part 1**, 496 f.; judiciary, **Supp. 5**, 651; jurisprudence in, following Civil War, **Vol. 2, Part 1**, 382; Kirk-Holden War in, **Vol. 8, Part 1**, 379; Ku Klux Klan, laws against, **Vol. 8, Part 1**, 64 f.; law courts in 1803, **Vol. 4, Part 2**, 524; laws, codifying of, **Vol. 1, Part 2**, 262; legal service, **Vol. 1, Part 2**, 58, 238, 262, 588; **Vol. 2, Part 2**, 140; **Vol. 3, Part 1**, 98, 114, 287; **Vol. 4, Part 2**, 416, 466; **Vol. 6, Part 2**, 335; **Vol. 7, Part 1**, 112, 387; **Vol. 7, Part 2**, 360; **Vol. 8, Part 1**, 379, 432, 640; **Vol. 8, Part 2**, 216; **Vol. 9, Part 2**, 335; newspapers, **Supp. 4**, 215–16; **Supp. 4**, 217; political service, **Vol. 1, Part 1**, 386, 447; **Vol. 1, Part 2**, 238, 384, 389, 390, 435, 588, 597, 596; **Vol. 2, Part 1**, 516; **Vol. 2, Part 2**, 220, 483; **Vol. 3, Part 1**, 98, 114, 287, 335, 480; **Vol. 4, Part 1**, 480; **Vol. 4, Part 2**, 279, 417; **Vol. 5, Part 1**, 138, 449, 623; **Vol. 5, Part 2**, 140, 440; **Vol. 6, Part 1**, 338; **Vol. 6, Part 2**, 75, 158, 233, 570; **Vol. 7, Part 1**, 159, 383; **Vol. 7, Part 2**, 114, 431, 496, 561; **Vol. 8, Part 1**, 40, 42, 64, 133, 240, 379, 416, 432, 476, 524; **Vol. 9, Part 1**, 199, 515, 557; **Vol. 9, Part 2**, 67, 73, 231; **Vol. 10, Part 1**, 25, 69, 158; **Vol. 10, Part 2**, 405, 536; politics, **Supp. 4**, 42–43, 215–16; **Supp. 6**, 494; **Supp. 7**, 644; **Supp. 8**, 24–25; **Supp. 9**, 190, 191, 391–92, 440, 441; **Supp. 10**, 814; Post-Revolutionary War politics, **Vol. 2, Part 1**, 571; public service, **Vol. 1, Part 2**, 238; **Vol. 2, Part 2**, 220 f.; **Vol. 3, Part 1**, 480 f., 496 f.; **Vol. 4, Part 2**, 417; **Vol. 5, Part 1**, 204; **Vol. 6, Part 1**, 228; **Vol. 6, Part 2**, 71; **Vol. 7, Part 1**, 159, 345 f.; **Vol. 8, Part 1**, 42; **Vol. 8, Part 2**, 383, 395, 599; **Vol. 9, Part 1**, 420; **Vol. 10, Part 2**, 300; race relations, **Supp. 9**, 392; railroad promotion, **Vol. 3, Part 1**, 480 f.; **Vol. 7, Part 1**, 159; Raleigh's commanders, **Vol. 1, Part 1**, 239; Reconstruction, **Vol. 2, Part 1**, 77; **Vol. 3, Part 1**, 287 f.; **Vol. 6, Part 2**, 570; **Vol. 7, Part 1**, 115; **Vol. 8, Part 1**, 64 f.; **Vol. 10, Part 1**, 69; **Vol. 10, Part 2**, 536; Regulator movement, **Vol. 2, Part 1**, 571; **Vol. 3, Part 2**, 265, 352; **Vol. 4, Part 2**, 531; **Vol. 5, Part 1**, 427 f.; **Vol. 6, Part 2**, 334; **Vol. 7, Part 1**, 134, 383; **Vol. 9, Part 2**, 489; **Vol. 10, Part 1**, 26, 302; religious service, **Vol. 4, Part 2**, 88 f., 133; **Vol. 7, Part 2**, 515; Revolutionary War period, **Vol. 2, Part 1**, 407; **Vol. 5, Part 1**, 492; **Vol. 6, Part 2**, 334; **Vol. 8, Part 1**, 43 f.; Safety, State Council of, **Vol. 1, Part 1**, 386; secession, **Vol. 3, Part 2**, 107; **Vol. 8, Part 2**, 216; Secession, Ordinance of, **Vol. 3, Part 1**, 287; separation from South Carolina, **Vol. 5, Part 2**, 117; surveys, **Vol. 6, Part 1**, 58; **Vol. 9, Part 1**, 254; Swiss colonization, **Vol. 4, Part 1**, 468; writings on, **Vol. 2, Part 1**, 282; **Vol. 9, Part 2**, 231

North Carolina Central University, predecessors, **Supp. 4**, 742

North Carolina Council of Safety, **Vol. 1, Part 1**, 386

North Carolina Historical Review, founding of, **Supp. 2**, 57

North Carolina Historical Society, **Vol. 9, Part 2**, 231

North Carolina Medical Society, **Vol. 5, Part 2**, 163

North Carolina Mutual Life Insurance Co., predecessor, **Supp. 5**, 647

North Carolina State College, endowment, **Supp. 5**, 567

North China Union College for Women (Peking), **Supp. 3**, 288; **Supp. 7**, 727

North Dakota: agriculture, teaching of, **Vol. 4, Part 2**, 525; **Vol. 9, Part 2**, 38; first Republican Organizing Committee governor, **Supp. 8**, 2; governors, **Supp. 4**, 308–9; **Supp. 6**, 360; Indians, **Vol. 6, Part 2**, 117; political service, **Vol. 7, Part 2**, 582; politics, **Supp. 4**, 479–80; **Supp. 6**, 85–87, 360, 644, 645; **Supp. 8**, 1–2; **Supp. 9**, 590

North Dakota Agricultural College, **Vol. 4, Part 2**, 525; **Vol. 9, Part 2**, 38

North Dakota Historical Quarterly, founding of, **Supp. 5**, 430

North Dakota Mill and Elevator Association, **Supp. 4**, 308–9

North Dakota State Historical Society, **Supp. 5**, 429

Northeastern boundary dispute with Great Britain, **Vol. 4, Part 1**, 108 f.; **Vol. 5, Part 2**, 344; **Vol. 6, Part 1**, 261; **Vol. 7, Part 1**, 91

Northern Pacific Railroad, **Vol. 1, Part 2**, 265; **Vol. 3, Part 1**, 207; **Vol. 3, Part 2**, 246, **Vol. 5, Part 1**, 38; **Vol. 7, Part 1**, 602; **Vol. 7, Part 2**, 463; **Vol. 10, Part 2**, 547; **Supp. 6**, 360, 361; **Supp. 7**, 89–90

Northern Securities Co., **Vol. 5, Part 1**, 39; **Vol. 7, Part 1**, 178; **Vol. 7, Part 2**, 47

Northfield Seminary, **Vol. 7, Part 1**, 104

North of Boston, **Supp. 7**, 271, 272

North Pacific exploring expedition, **Vol. 9, Part 2**, 32; **Vol. 8, Part 2**, 244

North Pole: **Vol. 5, Part 2**, 62, 256; **Vol. 8, Part 2**, 31; first flight over, **Supp. 9**, 63; Peary's attainment of, **Vol. 7, Part 2**, 366. *See also* Arctic regions; Exploration

Northrop, John H., references to, **Supp. 9**, 753, 754; **Supp. 10**, 427

Northrop, John K., references to, **Supp. 5**, 670, 671; **Supp. 6**, 385; **Supp. 8**, 385

Northrup, W. P., reference to, **Vol. 7, Part 1**, 628

North Star, antislavery journal, **Vol. 3, Part 1**, 407

Northwest (U.S.; not to be confused with the Old Northwest or Northwest Territory): **Vol. 5, Part 1**, 40; **Vol. 7, Part 2**, 186 f.; exploration, **Vol. 2, Part 2**, 319; **Vol. 4, Part 2**, 276; **Vol. 8, Part 2**, 457; fur trade, **Vol. 2, Part 2**, 565; missions, **Vol. 5, Part 2**, 321; writings on, **Vol. 9, Part 1**, 223

North West Co., organization of, **Vol. 8, Part 1**, 61

Northwestern Bible Training School, founding of, **Supp. 4**, 691

Northwestern Christian Advocate, **Vol. 8, Part 1**, 478

Northwestern Indians, war with (1791–95), **Vol. 1, Part 1**, 34; **Vol. 2, Part 1**, 366; **Vol. 2, Part 2**, 129, 557; **Vol. 4, Part 2**, 276, 349; **Vol. 5, Part 2**, 349; **Vol. 6, Part 1**, 300; **Vol. 8, Part 2**, 294; **Vol. 9, Part 1**, 62; **Vol. 9, Part 2**, 359 f., 375; **Vol. 10, Part 1**, 564; **Vol. 10, Part 2**, 223 f.

"Northwestern pool," **Vol. 4, Part 2**, 393

Northwestern States Portland Cement Co., **Supp. 8**, 410

Northwestern University: **Vol. 2, Part 2**, 596; **Vol. 5, Part 1**, 574; **Vol. 5, Part 2**, 266; **Vol. 6, Part 2**, 624; **Vol. 7, Part 1**, 555; **Vol. 8, Part 2**, 97; Biblioteca Feminina, **Supp. 6**, 576; biophysics studies, **Supp. 6**, 70; building architecture, **Supp. 4**, 698; classical language studies, **Supp. 4**, 728–29; criminology studies, **Supp. 5**, 245; economic studies, **Supp. 3**, 250; founding of, **Vol. 3, Part 2**, 205; **Vol. 5, Part 2**, 208; international law studies, **Supp. 5**, 341; law school, **Supp. 5**, 820, 822; literature studies, **Supp. 10**, 224; neurology studies, **Supp. 3**, 620; ophthalmic clinic, **Supp. 3**, 302; presidency, **Supp. 5**, 612; psychology studies, **Supp. 5**, 611–12

Northwest Ordinance. *See* Northwest Territory

Northwest Orient Airlines, founding of, **Supp. 8**, 292–93

Northwest Passage, **Supp. 6**, 545

Northwest Territory: **Vol. 2, Part 2**, 127 f., 433; **Vol. 4**,

Part 2, 276, 348 f.; **Vol. 5, Part 2**, 267, 321; **Vol. 7, Part 2**, 271; **Vol. 8, Part 2**, 294, 369; **Vol. 10, Part 1**, 53; first survey of states, **Vol. 9, Part 2**, 598; map of, **Vol. 3, Part 2**, 425; Ordinance, **Vol. 3, Part 1**, 63; **Vol. 5, Part 2**, 398; **Vol. 6, Part 1**, 120; preserved to U.S., **Vol. 5, Part 2**, 192; slavery, **Vol. 2, Part 2**, 297; **Vol. 3, Part 1**, 63
Norton, Charles Eliot, references to, **Vol. 5, Part 1**, 579; **Vol. 6, Part 1**, 461; **Vol. 7, Part 1**, 116; **Vol. 8, Part 2**, 546–47; **Supp. 3**, 336; **Supp. 6**, 56
Norton, Mary, reference to, **Supp. 10**, 57
"Norton Constitution" of Missouri, **Vol. 7, Part 1**, 572
Norton, W. W., & Co., founding of, **Supp. 3**, 562–64
Norvo, Red, reference to, **Supp. 5**, 32–33
Norwalk, Conn., political history (1835–50), **Vol. 2, Part 1**, 367
Norway, diplomacy with U.S., **Supp. 8**, 244
Norwegian Lutheran Church of America, **Vol. 3, Part 2**, 62; **Vol. 5, Part 1**, 269; **Vol. 8, Part 1**, 208 f.
Norwegians: **Vol. 1, Part 1**, 285; **Vol. 8, Part 2**, 454; Bible translation into, **Vol. 5, Part 2**, 78; immigrant guide book for, **Vol. 8, Part 2**, 274; immigration to America, **Vol. 3, Part 2**, 478; **Vol. 5, Part 1**, 612; **Vol. 6, Part 1**, 9; **Vol. 7, Part 1**, 419; **Vol. 7, Part 2**, 390; **Vol. 8, Part 1**, 487 f.; **Vol. 8, Part 2**, 124, 274; in Minnesota, **Vol. 8, Part 2**, 124; in Texas, **Vol. 8, Part 1**, 488; translations, **Vol. 7, Part 1**, 114; in the West, **Vol. 7, Part 2**, 390; writings, **Vol. 5, Part 2**, 77 f.; **Vol. 9, Part 2**, 142
Norwegian Synod, **Vol. 2, Part 2**, 167; **Vol. 5, Part 2**, 495. f.
Norwich, Conn., grant of original site of, **Vol. 10, Part 1**, 109
Norwich Art School, **Vol. 5, Part 2**, 287
Norwich Free Academy, founding of, **Vol. 9, Part 1**, 205
Norwich University, **Vol. 7, Part 2**, 281
Nosferatu, **Supp. 9**, 819
Notes on the State of Virginia, **Vol. 5, Part 2**, 21
"Nottingham Sermon," **Vol. 9, Part 2**, 368
Nova Scotia, land promotion, **Vol. 6, Part 2**, 155
Novelists. For complete list, *see* Occupations Index
Nowlan, Philip, reference to, **Supp. 6**, 165
Noyes, Arthur Amos, reference to, **Supp. 4**, 838
Noyes, Frank B., reference to, **Vol. 10, Part 1**, 635 f.
Noyes, James, reference to, **Vol. 7, Part 2**, 242
Noyes, John Humphrey, reference to, **Supp. 5**, 492
Noyes, Theodore Williams, reference to, **Supp. 4**, 631
NRA. *See* National Recovery Administration
NRECA. *See* National Rural Electric Cooperative Association
NRTA. *See* National Retired Teachers Association
NSC. *See* National Security Council
NSF. *See* National Sciene Foundation
Nuclear beta decay, **Supp. 5**, 219–21
Nuclear energy. *See* Nuclear weapons and energy
Nuclear physics: **Supp. 7**, 10–11, 300, 731–32; **Supp. 8**, 627–28; atom-smasher invention, **Supp. 8**, 665–66; beta decay selection rule, **Supp. 8**, 199; constants in, **Supp. 5**, 495; cosmic-ray research, **Supp. 5**, 496, 497; electron research, **Supp. 10**, 319; first U.S. research in reactions, **Supp. 5**, 273; liquid-drop model of nucleus, **Supp. 8**, 199–200; molecular-beam method, **Supp. 8**, 627–28; neutron studies, **Supp. 5**, 220–21; radiocarbon dating, **Supp. 10**, 457; writings on, **Supp. 8**, 483
Nuclear Science and Engineering Corporation, **Supp. 6**, 156
Nuclear weapons and energy: as foreign policy tool, **Supp. 8**, 157–58; atmospheric testing concerns, **Supp. 8**, 449, 450; atomic bomb development, **Supp. 3**, 664; **Supp. 4**, 453–54; **Supp. 5**, 204, 220–21, 663; **Supp. 6**, 166, 371, 501, 656; **Supp. 7**, 10–11, 76, 91, 135, 732; **Supp. 8**, 229–30, 411, 483–84; **Supp. 9**, 185, 218, 696; **Supp. 10**, 102, 144, 289; atomic bomb testing, **Supp. 7**, 136, 300; Baruch plan, **Supp. 6**, 617; civilian control, **Supp. 9**, 185; cold war policies, **Supp. 8**, 230–31; defense emphasis on, **Supp. 8**, 290; deterrence, **Supp. 10**, 243; first atomic bomb explosion, **Supp. 8**, 230; first full-scale power plant, **Supp. 7**, 565; first nuclear fission reactor, **Supp. 7**, 300, 732; first self-sustaining chain reaction, **Supp. 5**, 221; fission research, **Supp. 8**, 199; government advisers, **Supp. 10**, 320; hydrogen bomb advocacy, **Supp. 5**, 455; **Supp. 9**, 774; hydrogen bomb development, **Supp. 6**, 156; **Supp. 8**, 200, 301, 484; international control proposals, **Supp. 7**, 30, 37, 259, 762; **Supp. 8**, 484; journalism on, **Supp. 10**, 375–76, 417, 435; labor relations, **Supp. 6**, 706; nuclear power advocacy, **Supp. 10**, 751; peacetime reactor use, **Supp. 9**, 218; radioactive fallout tests, **Supp. 7**, 344; **Supp. 10**, 457; scientists' concerns, **Supp. 7**, 732, 733; security issues, **Supp. 5**, 588–90, 714; **Supp. 8**, 230, 301, 484, 649; **Supp. 9**, 321–22, 387; Soviet-U.S. competition, **Supp. 7**, 423–24, 795; strong federal program advocacy, **Supp. 7**, 565; submarines, **Supp. 8**, 232, 330; test ban treaties, **Supp. 10**, 320. *See also* Atomic Energy Commission
Nucleoproteins, **Supp. 6**, 596
Nudity, photography, **Supp. 8**, 412
Nugent, Elliott, reference to, **Supp. 7**, 742
Nullification: **Vol. 1, Part 1**, 640; **Vol. 2, Part 1**, 414; **Vol. 3, Part 2**, 94, 118; **Vol. 4, Part 1**, 635; **Vol. 4, Part 2**, 187, 207, 286, 458; **Vol. 5, Part 2**, 147; **Vol. 9, Part 1**, 171; Alabama, **Vol. 4, Part 1**, 197; Calhoun's doctrine of, opposed, **Vol. 10, Part 1**, 585 f.; *Columbia Telescope*, **Vol. 6, Part 1**, 604; Convention of 1832, **Vol. 5, Part 2**, 155; debate on, **Vol. 10, Part 1**, 585 f.; in South Carolina (1832–33), **Vol. 1, Part 1**, 88; **Vol. 1, Part 2**, 331; **Vol. 2, Part 1**, 415, 563; **Vol. 2, Part 2**, 177; **Vol. 3, Part 2**, 101, 115; **Vol. 4, Part 2**, 187, 458; **Vol. 5, Part 1**, 532; **Vol. 6, Part 2**, 35, 251, 601, 640; **Vol. 8, Part 1**, 35; **Vol. 8, Part 2**, 507; **Vol. 10, Part 1**, 56 f., 154, 589; writings on, **Vol. 6, Part 1**, 604
Numbers, theory of. *See* Mathematics
Numerology, **Supp. 9**, 514
Numismatics: **Vol. 1, Part 1**, 314; **Vol. 1, Part 2**, 173; **Vol. 2, Part 1**, 18; **Vol. 3, Part 1**, 472; **Vol. 7, Part 1**, 224; **Vol. 8, Part 1**, 614; collections, **Supp. 3**, 551; writings on, **Vol. 7, Part 2**, 541; **Vol. 8, Part 1**, 228 f.; **Vol. 9, Part 1**, 387
Nuremberg trials (1945–46), **Supp. 5**, 359; Supp. 6 156, 496, 662; **Supp. 8**, 35, 135, 456; **Supp. 10**, 57
Nureyev, Rudolf, reference to, **Supp. 7**, 174
Nurseries, **Vol. 1, Part 2**, 192; **Vol. 5, Part 2**, 341; **Vol. 8, Part 1**, 233; **Vol. 9, Part 1**, 146
Nursery schools. *See* Preschool education
Nurses. For complete list, *see* Occupations Index
Nursing: **Vol. 1, Part 2**, 18; **Vol. 4, Part 1**, 285; **Vol. 5, Part 2**, 570; Army, **Vol. 1, Part 1**, 318; **Vol. 3, Part 1**, 219; international organizations, **Supp. 7**, 247; military, **Supp. 4**, 789–90; **Supp. 10**, 57; professional education, **Supp. 4**, 65, 632–33; **Supp. 5**, 251–52; **Supp. 6**, 166–67; public health, **Vol. 3, Part 1**, 219; **Vol. 8, Part 1**, 275 f.; **Supp. 4**, 64–66; **Supp. 6**, 283–84; public schools, **Supp. 2**, 687; Red Cross service, **Supp. 2**, 495; studies on, **Supp. 4**, 633; training school, first in America, **Vol. 8, Part 2**, 474; Navy, **Vol. 3, Part 1**, 219; visiting nurse service, **Supp. 2**, 687; volunteer aides, **Supp. 4**, 93; working conditions, improvement of, **Supp. 1**, 555
Nussbaum, Moritz, reference to, **Supp. 6**, 281
Nutrition. *See* Diet and nutrition

Nuttall, Thomas, reference to, **Vol. 9, Part 2**, 617
Nye, Bill, reference to, **Vol. 7, Part 1**, 599 f.
Nye, Gerald P., references to, **Supp. 3**, 538; **Supp. 5**, 192; **Supp. 6**, 4, 86, 351
Nylon, invention of, **Supp. 2**, 96; **Supp. 5**, 191, 663

O

Oabu College (Honolulu), **Vol. 7, Part 1**, 5
Oahspe: A New Bible, **Vol. 7, Part 1**, 449
Oak Hall, original name of Wanamaker store, **Vol. 10, Part 1**, 407 f.
Oakland, Calif.: **Vol. 3, Part 1**, 540 f.; **Vol. 9, Part 1**, 267; racial issues, **Supp. 9**, 469
Oakland Tribune, influence of, **Supp. 9**, 468–69
Oak Ridge, Tenn.: atomic bomb laboratories, **Supp. 8**, 230; atomic bomb plant design, **Supp. 4**, 454; Manhattan Project community design, **Supp. 7**, 691
O'Banion, Dion, reference to, **Supp. 6**, 263
Obelisks, Egyptian, **Vol. 4, Part 1**, 437
Oberlin College: **Vol. 1, Part 2**, 466; **Vol. 3, Part 2**, 253, 395; **Vol. 4, Part 2**, 122; **Vol. 6, Part 2**, 209; **Vol. 8, Part 1**, 539 f.; **Vol. 9, Part 1**, 111 f.; **Vol. 9, Part 2**, 11 f.; first ecology department, **Supp. 5**, 374; first ornithology course, **Supp. 5**, 374; presidency, **Supp. 1**, 469
Oberlin stove, invention of, **Vol. 9, Part 2**, 12
Oberth, Hermann, references to, **Supp. 3**, 306, 308
Oblate Sisters of Providence, **Vol. 5, Part 2**, 220
Oboe, playing of, **Vol. 4, Part 1**, 507
O'Brien, Brian, reference to, **Supp. 6**, 638
O'Brien, Joe, reference to, **Supp. 8**, 675
O'Brien, Lawrence, reference to, **Supp. 10**, 357
Obscenity. *See* Pornography
Observatories. *See* Astronomical observatories; Magnetic observatories; Meteorological observatories
Obstetrical Society of New York, **Vol. 9, Part 2**, 446
Obstetrical Society of Philadelphia, **Vol. 7, Part 2**, 129
Obstetrics: **Vol. 1, Part 1**, 411, 599, 601; **Vol. 3, Part 1**, 267, 394; **Vol. 3, Part 2**, 160, 409, 581; **Vol. 4, Part 1**, 291; **Vol. 5, Part 1**, 99, 229, 588; **Vol. 5, Part 2**, 381; **Vol. 6, Part 1**, 333, 510; **Vol. 7, Part 1**, 541; **Vol. 7, Part 2**, 263, 286; **Vol. 8, Part 1**, 32 f., 578; **Vol. 9, Part 1**, 117, 234; **Vol. 9, Part 2**, 94, 446; **Vol. 10, Part 2**, 280, 326; asepsis precautions, **Supp. 3**, 223; caesarian section, **Supp. 3**, 412; forceps use, **Supp. 3**, 223; gynecology as interdependent discipline, **Supp. 1**, 408; journals, **Supp. 1**, 542; local anesthesia use, **Supp. 3**, 223; maternal death prevention, **Supp. 3**, 222–23; maternal health, **Supp. 2**, 2; midwife training, **Supp. 2**, 495; **Supp. 3**, 28; septic-induced abortions, **Supp. 9**, 352; silver nitrate solution for newborn's eyes, **Supp. 3**, 364; teaching of, **Supp. 3**, 222–23; toxemia, **Supp. 3**, 257. *See also* Gynecology; Motherhood
OCAW. *See* Oil, Chemical and Atomic Workers International Union
Occultism, **Vol. 9, Part 2**, 561–2
Occupational health and safety: compensation laws, **Supp. 2**, 586; **Supp. 3**, 717–18; department store clerks, **Supp. 4**, 623–24; garment industry, **Supp. 3**, 609–10; heat cramps, **Supp. 3**, 243, 244; industrial accident insurance, **Supp. 2**, 404; industrial poisons, **Supp. 3**, 18; **Supp. 6**, 175; **Supp. 8**, 241; Massachusetts Industrial Safety Division, **Supp. 3**, 577; mining, **Supp. 4**, 690; New York City, **Supp. 5**, 718; nuclear energy industry, **Supp. 9**, 726–27; reform legislation, **Supp. 3**, 717–18; reform movement, **Supp. 4**, 603; **Supp. 7**, 608; silicosis and tuberculosis studies, **Supp. 4**, 314; social aspects, **Supp. 4**, 565–66. *See also* Labor and labor movement
Occupational surveys, **Vol. 6, Part 1**, 178
Occupational therapy, **Supp. 1**, 131, 485; **Supp. 4**, 570. 571
Ocean liners. *See* Ships and shipbuilding
Oceanography: **Vol. 4, Part 2**, 318; **Vol. 6, Part 1**, 129, 272; **Vol. 6, Part 2**, 429; **Vol. 8, Part 1**, 141 f.; **Vol. 8, Part 2**, 77; **Vol. 9, Part 2**, 656; **Supp. 10**, 327; arctic region, **Supp. 7**, 698–99; bathysphere use, **Supp. 7**, 45–46; continental shelf studies, **Supp. 5**, 656–57; early work in, **Supp. 4**, 498; glacial control theory of coral reefs, **Supp. 6**, 144; Gulf of Maine, **Supp. 8**, 37; magnetic measurement, **Supp. 6**, 205; pioneer work in, **Supp. 4**, 498; **Supp. 8**, 37–38; seafloor mapping, **Supp. 10**, 327; seafloor spreading, **Supp. 9**, 271–72; seismic studies, **Supp. 9**, 271; writings on, **Supp. 7**, 109. *See also* Flsh; Marine life; Woods Hole Oceanographic Institution
Ocean Pond, Fla., battle of. *See* Oduster, Fla., battle of
Ocean Steam Navigation Co., **Vol. 9, Part 1**, 580
Ochs, Adolph S., references to, **Supp. 3**, 787; **Supp. 4**, 222; **Supp. 6**, 327; **Supp. 7**, 199; **Supp. 8**, 636. *See also New York Times*
Ochs, Iphigene, reference to, **Supp. 7**, 199
O'Connell, Denis, reference to, **Supp. 3**, 568
O'Connell, William Henry, reference to, **Supp. 8**, 612
O'Connor, Basil, reference to, **Supp. 3**, 643
O'Connor, Edwin, reference to, **Supp. 6**, 141
O'Connor, Jack, reference to, **Supp. 6**, 357
O'Connor, Leslie M., reference to, **Supp. 3**, 438
O'Connor, Richard, reference to, **Supp. 7**, 394
O'Conor, Herbert R., references to, **Supp. 9**, 634, 839
O'Daniel, W. Lee ("Pappy"), references to, **Supp. 9**, 431, 432, 872
Odd Fellows, Order of, **Vol. 7, Part 1**, 503
Oden, Melita, reference to, **Supp. 6**, 626
Odets, Clifford, references to, **Supp. 5**, 237; **Supp. 10**, 129, 130, 131
O'Dwyer, William, references to, **Supp. 5**, 227; **Supp. 8**, 397, 512; **Supp. 9**, 607
Office of Foreign Economic Coordination. *See under* World War II
Office of Naval Records and Library, **Supp. 6**, 348
Office of Naval Research, **Supp. 8**, 687
Office of Price Administration. *See under* World War II
Office of Public Opinion Research, founding of, **Supp. 8**, 69
Office of Radio Research. *See* Applied Social Research, Bureau of
Office of Science and Technology, **Supp. 9**, 531
Office of Scientific Research and Development (OSRD). *See under* World War II
Office of Strategic Services (OSS). *See under* World War II
Office of the Foreign Economic Administration. *See under* World War II
Office of War Information (OWI). *See under* World War II
Officers' Training Corps. *See* Reserve Officers' Training Corps
Of Mice and Men, **Supp. 9**, 169
Of Stars and Men, **Supp. 10**, 353
Of Thee I Sing, **Supp. 7**, 551
Ogburn, William F., references to, **Supp. 5**, 520; **Supp. 6**, 604
Ogden, Marguerite, reference to, **Supp. 6**, 3
Ogden, Robert C, reference to, **Vol. 10, Part 1**, 407 f.
Ogden, Utah, founding of, **Vol. 7, Part 1**, 641
"Ogden movement," **Vol. 7, Part 1**, 642
Ogdensburg, founding of, **Vol. 7, Part 1**, 643
Oglethorpe, J. E., treaties with Indians, **Vol. 9, Part 1**, 580
Ogontz School for Young Ladies, **Vol. 8, Part 1**, 335 f.

O'Gorman, James A., references to, **Supp. 3**, 642, 643

O'Hara, John, references to, **Supp. 3**, 339; **Supp. 6**, 236; **Supp. 9**, 15, 409

O'Hara, Mary (pseudonym of Mary O'Hara Alsop), **Supp. 10**, 6

Ohio: admission to statehood, **Vol. 2, Part 1**, 294; **Vol. 8, Part 2**, 295; **Vol. 10, Part 2**, 540; agriculture, **Vol. 2, Part 1**, 600; **Vol. 5, Part 2**, 445 f.; **Vol. 7, Part 2**, 62 f.; **Vol. 9, Part 2**, 641; **Vol. 10, Part 1**, 444 f.; antislavery movement, **Vol. 6, Part 1**, 224; archaeology in, **Supp. 1**, 316; "black laws," repeal of, **Vol. 3, Part 1**, 241; boundary disputes, **Vol. 2, Part 2**, 185; canal building, **Vol. 2, Part 1**, 113; **Vol. 5, Part 2**, 296, 521; **Vol. 6, Part 2**, 569; Catholic church, **Vol. 8, Part 1**, 266 f.; **Vol. 10, Part 2**, 632; cattle importation, **Vol. 8, Part 1**, 503; city planning boards, **Supp. 3**, 66; Civil War period, **Vol. 2, Part 1**, 95; **Vol. 8, Part 1**, 483; **Vol. 10, Part 2**, 505; common law crimes, **Vol. 4, Part 1**, 385; constitution of 1845, **Vol. 5, Part 1**, 77; Episcopal church, **Vol. 3, Part 1**, 343; **Vol. 6, Part 1**, 179; expedition into, Burr's association with, **Vol. 3, Part 1**, 166; first woman to serve in Congress, **Supp. 10**, 56; Franklin County Agricultural Society, **Vol. 3, Part 1**, 242; Free Soil party, **Vol. 8, Part 1**, 591; French claims in, **Vol. 3, Part 1**, 317; **Vol. 8, Part 2**, 293; geological researches, **Vol. 7, Part 2**, 62; **Vol. 8, Part 1**, 247; governors, **Vol. 1, Part 1**, 210 f.; **Vol. 1, Part 2**, 16 f.; **Vol. 2, Part 1**, 94 f., 347 f.; **Vol. 2, Part 2**, 457 f., 476 f.; **Vol. 3, Part 1**, 241 f.; **Vol. 3, Part 2**, 502, 504, 544; **Vol. 4, Part 2**, 276, 278; **Vol. 1, Part 1**, 84 f., 419 f.; **Vol. 6, Part 1**, 487, 549; **Vol. 6, Part 2**, 509; **Vol. 7, Part 1**, 235, 287; **Vol. 7, Part 2**, 312; **Vol. 9, Part 2**, 535, 567, 641; **Vol. 10, Part 2**, 470, 540; **Supp. 6**, 129; **Supp. 10**, 607; historical writings on, **Supp. 1**, 330; history of, **Vol. 5, Part 1**, 21, 288; **Vol. 8, Part 1**, 258 f.; **Vol.9, Part 2**, 330; Indians, fights with, **Vol. 1, Part 2**, 481; **Vol. 3, Part 1**, 75; industrial service, **Vol. 6, Part 2**, 397; **Vol. 10, Part 1**, 635; judges, popular election of, **Vol. 5, Part 1**, 77; judicial review, **Vol. 2, Part 2**, 536 f.; judiciary, **Supp. 8**, 4; legal service, **Vol. 1, Part 2**, 375; **Vol. 2, Part 1**, 460; **Vol. 3, Part 1**, 162, 164; **Vol. 4, Part 1**, 234; **Vol. 4, Part 2**, 202; **Vol. 5, Part 1**, 77, 84, 544; **Vol, 6, Part 1**, 52, 84, 146; **Vol. 7, Part 1**, 388; **Vol. 7, Part 2**, 8; **Vol. 8, Part 1**, 258, 377, 544; **Vol. 9, Part 1**, 34, 440; **Vol. 9, Part 2**, 264–265, 300, 515; **Vol. 10, Part 1**, 363, 410, 444, 620; **Vol. 10, Part 2**, 283; library service, **Vol. 9, Part 2**, 330; manufacturing enterprises, **Vol. 3, Part 1**, 244; Methodism, **Vol. 9, Part 2**, 482; missions, **Vol. 1, Part 1**, 487; **Vol. 3, Part 1**, 343; **Vol. 5, Part 2**, 166; opening up of territory, **Vol. 3, Part 1**, 13 f.; paleontology, **Vol. 10, Part 2**, 597; Peace Democrats, **Vol. 10, Part 1**, 144 f.; pioneer days, **Vol. 2, Part 1**, 294; **Vol. 3, Part 2**, 390; **Vol. 6, Part 2**, 509; **Vol. 8, Part 1**, 284 f.; **Vol. 10, Part 2**, 470, 644, 646; politics, **Vol. 2, Part 1**, 348, 521; **Vol. 2, Part 2**, 473 f.; **Vol. 4, Part 2**, 448; **Vol. 5, Part 1**, 85; **Vol. 6, Part 2**, 105; **Supp. 3**, 213; **Supp. 4**, 317–18; **Supp. 5**, 674; **Supp. 6**, 132, 613–14; **Supp. 7**, 49–50, 84–86, 95–96; **Supp. 9**, 581; pre-Civil War agitation, **Vol. 6, Part 2**, 491; Presbyterianism, **Vol. 10, Part 2**, 340; progressive wave in 1910, **Vol. 4, Part 2**, 277; public schools, **Vol. 4, Part 2**, 43; **Vol. 5, Part 1**, 21; **Vol. 5, Part 2**, 70; **Vol. 6, Part 1**, 146, 224, 233 f.; **Vol. 6, Part 2**, 58; **Vol. 7, Part 2**, 569; **Vol. 9, Part 2**, 115, 641; **Vol. 10, Part 2**, 99; public service, **Vol. 1, Part 2**, 16, 102, 156, 277, 375; **Vol. 2, Part 2**, 476; **Vol. 3, Part 1**, 217, 241; **Vol. 3, Part 2**, 384, 544; **Vol. 4, Part 2**, 14, 24, 169, 277, 351, 448, 587; **Vol. 5, Part 1**, 419; **Vol. 5, Part 2**, 336; **Vol. 6, Part 2**, 127, 490, 510; **Vol. 7, Part 1**, 227, 235, 356, 587; **Vol. 7, Part 2**, 313, 368, 420, 556; **Vol. 8, Part 1**, 135, 258, 271, 377, 554, 591; **Vol. 9, Part 1**, 20, 84, 87, 100, 554; **Vol. 9, Part 2**, 93, 265, 535, 641; **Vol. 10, Part 1**, 143, 459, 620, 628; **Vol. 10, Part 2**, 470, 505, 540; **Supp. 10**, 607–8; Republican party, **Vol. 2, Part 1**, 376; Roman Catholic dioceses, **Supp. 3**, 694–95; school legislation, **Vol. 9, Part 2**, 301; social reform, **Vol. 10, Part 2**, 541; surveys of, **Vol. 5, Part 2**, 372; transportation, **Vol. 5, Part 2**, 296 f.; Washington's expedition into, **Vol. 3, Part 1**, 317; waterpower, early, **Vol. 6, Part 1**, 139; woman suffrage, **Supp. 8**, 4; Women's Temperance Crusade, **Vol. 1, Part 2**, 423

Ohio Archaeological Association, founding of, **Vol. 2, Part 1**, 50; **Vol. 7, Part 2**, 392

Ohio Automobile Co., **Vol. 7, Part 2**, 128

Ohio Co., **Vol. 3, Part 1**, 13, 316 f., 367; **Vol. 5, Part 2**, 127; **Vol. 7, Part 2**, 271, 293; **Vol. 8, Part 1**, 284 f.; **Vol. 10, Part 1**, 53

Ohio Fuel Corporation, predecessor, **Supp. 5**, 260

Ohio Medical College, **Vol. 3, Part 1**, 426 f.

Ohio Press (Columbus), **Vol. 9, Part 2**, 301

Ohio River: exploration, **Vol. 2, Part 1**, 582; flood control, **Supp. 4**, 564; flooding (1937), **Supp. 4**, 247

Ohio School Journal, **Vol. 6, Part 1**, 404

Ohio Society of New York, **Vol. 3, Part 2**, 239

Ohio State University, track and field team, **Supp. 10**, 610, 611

Ohio Wesleyan University, **Vol. 1, Part 2**, 34; **Vol. 6, Part 2**, 556; **Vol. 9, Part 2**, 482

Oil: Acme Oil Co., **Vol. 1, Part 1**, 337; by-product research, **Supp. 4**, 661; California, **Vol. 7, Part 2**, 386; companies, **Supp. 3**, 260–61; **Supp. 4**, 568–69, 660–61; **Supp. 6**, 584–85; company mergers, **Supp. 4**, 775–76; cone-type drills, **Vol. 5, Part 1**, 351; conservation advocacy, **Supp. 2**, 155, 553; **Supp. 7**, 771–72, 804; corporate executives, **Supp. 5**, 236; cotton seed used for, **Vol. 3, Part 1**, 507 f.; crude, separation of naphtha from, **Vol. 8, Part 2**, 95; discovery depletion allowance, **Supp. 4**, 338; documentary film on drilling, **Supp. 5**, 226; drilling, first driving of pipe to bedrock, **Vol. 3, Part 1**, 428; drilling methods, **Supp. 7**, 615; exporting of, **Supp. 2**, 572; first successful well, **Vol. 3, Part 1**, 427 f.; **Vol. 7, Part 1**, 297; geological studies, **Vol. 4, Part 2**, 444; geology of, **Supp. 2**, 681; **Supp. 7**, 803–5; Getty interests, **Supp. 9**, 305–6; industry, **Vol. 1, Part 2**, 301; **Vol. 3, Part 2**, 602; **Vol. 6, Part 1**, 540; **Vol. 8, Part 1**, 168 f.; **Vol. 8, Part 2**, 56, 65; industry reversionary interest concept, **Supp. 8**, 454; Iran's nationalization of, **Supp. 8**, 276; leases, Teapot Dome, **Vol. 3, Part 1**, 234 f.; **Vol. 4, Part 2**, 255; **Vol. 8, Part 2**, 86, 194; **Vol. 10, Part 1**, 393 f.; lighting, **Vol. 3, Part 1**, 415; **Vol. 4, Part 2**, 440; Mexican fields, **Supp. 6**, 451; **Supp. 7**, 377; monopoly, **Supp. 2**, 571–73; multinational companies, **Supp. 8**, 455; **Supp. 10**, 663; NRA code, **Supp. 2**, 30; offshore production, **Supp. 10**, 664; Oklahoma fields, **Supp. 3**, 505; **Supp. 6**, 469; **Supp. 10**, 275; paleontological research application to, **Supp. 4**, 205, 206; Pennsylvania, **Vol. 1, Part 1**, 26; **Vol. 2, Part 1**, 496; **Vol. 3, Part 1**, 427 f.; **Vol. 3, Part 2**, 85; **Vol. 6, Part 1**, 340; **Vol. 8, Part 12**, 95; **Vol. 10, Part 1**, 179; **Vol. 10, Part 2**, 107; Persian Gulf fields, **Supp. 10**, 276; pipelines, **Vol. 3, Part 1**, 367; **Vol. 3, Part 2**, 452; **Vol. 4, Part 2**, 401; **Vol. 8, Part 2**, 95; **Supp. 2**, 133; **Supp. 4**, 568–69, 661; production, **Vol. 3, Part 1**, 367; **Vol. 4, Part 2**, 36; **Vol. 5, Part 1**, 262; **Vol. 6, Part 1**, 339 f.; **Vol. 7, Part 2**, 544; **Vol. 8, Part 2**, 65; production quotas, **Supp. 9**, 411–12, 611; products, extension of uses for, **Vol. 3, Part 1**, 415; quotas in commerce, **Supp. 2**, 30; refineries, **Supp. 2**, 133, 568–69, 679; **Supp. 4**, 568–

69; refining, **Vol. 3, Part 1**, 415, 367; **Vol. 5, Part 2**, 371 f.; **Vol. 6, Part 2**, 562; **Vol. 7, Part 1**, 297 f., 443; **Vol. 7, Part 2**, 330; **Vol. 9, Part 1**, 148; reserves, leasing of, **Vol. 3, Part 1**, 156, 234 f.; shale industry, **Vol. 1, Part 2**, 34; **Vol. 3, Part 1**, 156 f.; sperm oil, efforts to find substitutes for, as lubricant, **Vol. 3, Part 1**, 415; **Vol. 3, Part 2**, 401; Standard Oil Co., **Vol. 1, Part 1**, 337; **Vol. 3, Part 1**, 341 f.; **Vol. 3, Part 2**, 85, 451, 487; **Vol. 4, Part 2**, 21, 81, 401; **Vol. 6, Part 1**, 60, 332, 340; **Vol. 8, Part 2**, 65, 95; studies in, **Vol. 6, Part 6**, 332–33; Texas, **Vol. 6, Part 1**, 483; **Supp. 4**, 775; **Supp. 6**, 135–36, 540–41; **Supp. 9**, 411, 412, 464; tidelands bill, **Supp. 8**, 104; transportation of by water, **Vol. 8, Part 1**, 464; tube and tank process for crude, **Supp. 3**, 247; well machinery, **Supp. 1**, 453; writings on, **Supp. 3**, 762. *See also* Gasoline; Natural gas; Petro-chemistry; Petrology; Teapot Dome scandal
Oil, Chemical and Atomic Workers International Union (OCAW), Kerr-McGee strike, **Supp. 9**, 726–27
Oils and fats, margarine development, **Supp. 3**, 247; **Supp. 5**, 400
Okakura, Kakuzo, reference to, **Supp. 3**, 465
Okeechobee Lake, battle of, **Vol. 9, Part 2**, 350
O'Keeffe, Georgia, reference to, **Supp. 4**, 781
Okeh Records, **Supp. 9**, 183
Okinawa, World War II action, **Supp. 3**, 118; **Supp. 4**, 323, 589; **Supp. 5**, 66; **Supp. 6**, 268; **Supp. 7**, 352
Oklahoma: banditry in early days, **Vol. 3, Part 1**, 40 f.; civil government for Indians, **Vol. 7, Part 2**, 225; early state history, **Vol. 9, Part 2**, 546; governors, **Supp. 1**, 380; **Supp. 3**, 506; **Supp. 6**, 468–70; **Supp. 7**, 429; **Supp. 10**, 26–27; oil wells, **Supp. 3**, 505; pioneering, **Vol. 10, Part 2**, 530; politics, **Supp. 3**, 10; **Supp. 4**, 338; **Supp. 5**, 662; **Supp. 7**, 738–39; **Supp. 10**, 26–27; public service, **Vol. 8, Part 1**, 111; **Vol. 8, Part 2**, 20 f.; statehood, **Supp. 4**, 641
Oklahoma! **Supp. 6**, 273–74, 286, 638; **Supp. 7**, 497, 692, 693; **Supp. 10**, 106, 107, 694, 802
Oklahoma Agricultural and Mechanical College, presidency, **Supp. 5**, 49
Oklahoma Leader, **Supp. 3**, 10
Oland, Warner, reference to, **Supp. 1**, 80
O'Laughlin, Michael, reference to, **Vol. 1, Part 2**, 449
Olcott, Henry Steel, reference to, **Vol. 1, Part 2**, 362
Old Age Revolving Pension Plan. *See* Townsend Plan
Old American Co., sole theatrical concern in New York City in 1796, **Vol. 3, Part 1**, 516 f.
"Old Cattleman" stories, **Vol. 6, Part 1**, 205
Old Colony Building (Chicago), steel framing, **Supp. 3**, 611
Old English, syntax studies in, **Supp. 2**, 88
Older, Fremont, references to, **Supp. 3**, 394, 532; **Supp. 6**, 590
Oldfield, Barney, references to, **Supp. 4**, 293; **Supp. 6**, 163
"Old Folks' Concerts," **Vol. 5, Part 2**, 320
"Old Home Week," origin of **Vol. 8, Part 2**,
Old Ironsides. See Constitution
Old Jules, **Supp. 8**, 566–67
Old Maid and the Thief, The, **Supp. 7**, 125
Old Man and the Sea, The, **Supp. 7**, 339
Old Northwest. *See* Northwest Territory
Old Northwest: Pioneer Period (1815–1840), The, **Supp. 8**, 60
Olds, Ransom E., reference to, **Supp. 4**, 243
Oldsmobile car, **Supp. 4**, 638
Old South Church (Boston), **Vol. 5, Part 1**, 88, **Vol. 9, Part 2**, 390, 392
Old Swamp Church, **Vol. 7, Part 1**, 307
Old Testament. *See* Bible
Old Yeller, **Supp. 9**, 313
O'Leary, Irwin, reference to, **Supp. 7**, 4
Oleomargarine, early use of, **Vol. 9, Part 2**, 245. *See also* Margarine
Oliphant, Herman, reference to, **Supp. 3**, 186
Oliphant, Lawrence, reference to, **Vol. 10, Part 1**, 421
Olive Branch Petition, **Vol. 7, Part 2**, 156
Oliver, Joseph ("King"), reference to, **Supp. 9**, 45
Oliver, Sy, reference to, **Supp. 4**, 510
"Oliver Optic," **Vol. 1, Part 1**, 103
Olivet College, founding of, **Vol. 7, Part 1**, 230; **Vol. 9, Part 1**, 112
Olivier, Laurence, reference to, **Supp. 8**, 368–69; **Supp. 10**, 600
Olmsted, Frederick Law, references to, **Vol. 10, Part 1**, 605 f.; **Supp. 3**, 533; **Supp. 6**, 26
Olmstead, John C., reference to, **Supp. 6**, 485
Olsen and Johnson (comedy team), **Supp. 7**, 588–89
Olson, Culbert L., references to, **Supp. 3**, 156, 533; **Supp. 10**, 502
Olson, Floyd B., reference to, **Supp. 3**, 226
Olustee, battle of, **Vol. 2, Part 2**, 315; **Vol. 4, Part 2**, 421; **Vol. 9, Part 1**, 12
Olvany, George W., reference to, **Supp. 6**, 141–42
Olympia, construction of, for Navy, **Vol. 3, Part 1**, 292
Olympic games: **Vol. 7, Part 1**, 356; amateurism defined, **Supp. 9**, 131; Brundage influence, **Supp. 9**, 131–32; Germany (1936), **Supp. 10**, 610–11; rowing, **Supp. 6**, 331; swimming, **Supp. 8**, 336–37; track and field, **Supp. 3**, 487; **Supp. 5**, 683–84, 722; **Supp. 7**, 152; **Supp. 10**, 531, 610–11, 612. *See also* International Olympic Committee (IOC)
Olympic National Park, **Supp. 7**, 764
Omaha, Nebr.: **Vol. 2, Part 2**, 536; **Vol. 7, Part 1**, 618; starting point of the Union Pacific Railroad, **Vol. 3, Part 1**, 542 f.; Trans-Mississippi Exposition, **Vol. 4, Part 1**, 221; **Vol. 8, Part 2**, 172
Omaha Daily Bee, **Vol. 8, Part 2**, 172
Omaha Indians, **Vol. 9, Part 2**, 522
Omaha World-Herald: **Vol. 9, Part 2**, 522; Newhouse takeover bid, **Supp. 10**, 414
O'Mahoney, Joseph C., reference to, **Supp. 7**, 31
Omnibus: first in New York, **Vol. 9, Part 1**, 583; first west of Mississippi, **Vol. 10, Part 1**, 638 f.
"Omnibus" (television program), **Supp. 6**, 680
Onassis, Aristotle, Callas relationship, **Supp. 10**, 93, 94
Onassis, Jacqueline. *See* Kennedy, Jacqueline
Oncology, **Supp. 3**, 258. *See also* Cancer
Onderdonk, Henry U., reference to, **Vol. 8, Part 2**, 530
O'Neal, Edward A., reference to, **Supp. 6**, 12
O'Neale, Margaret ("Peggy") references to, **Vol. 3, Part 1**, 610; **Vol. 5, Part 1**, 474, 532; **Vol. 7, Part 2**, 42; **Vol. 9, Part 1**, 319
One-Dimensional Man, **Supp. 10**, 507
Oneida Community, **Vol. 4, Part 1**, 99; **Vol. 4, Part 2**, 589; **Vol. 7, Part 1**, 590; **Supp. 5**, 492
Oneida Indians, **Vol. 5, Part 2**, 432 f.
"O'Neill, Danny" (fictional character), **Supp. 10**, 236
O'Neill, Eugene: Bennett relationship, **Supp. 3**, 58, 59; references to, **Supp. 4**, 330, 355, 503, 504, 843; **Supp. 5**, 375; **Supp. 6**, 471; **Supp. 9**, 165; **Supp. 10**, 117
O'Neill, James, references to, **Supp. 5**, 522, 523
O'Neill, Oona, references to, **Supp. 5**, 523; **Supp. 10**, 117
O'Neill; Rose, reference to, **Supp. 7**, 436
One Touch of Venus, **Supp. 9**, 579
One World, **Supp. 3**, 829; **Supp. 8**, 668
Only Yesterday, **Supp. 5**, 16
Ono, Yoko, references to, **Supp. 10**, 450, 451
Onondaga Indians, **Supp. 8**, 647

Onsager's reciprocal relations (thermal diffusion), **Supp. 10**, 609
On the Origin of Species, **Supp. 9**, 239
On the Road, **Supp. 8**, 326
On the Waterfront, **Supp. 10**, 384
Onyx Club (New York City), **Supp. 6**, 620
Oölogy, **Vol. 2, Part 1**, 24
OPA. *See* World War II, Office of Price Administration
OPEC. *See* Organization of Petroleum Exporting Countries
Open Court, **Vol. 10, Part 1**, 111
Open-Door policy in China, **Vol. 4, Part 2**, 434; **Vol. 6, Part 2**, 109; **Vol. 8, Part 2**, 67, 139
Open Letter, Workingmen's party organ, **Vol. 5, Part 2**, 269
Open-hearth furnace. *See* Steel
"Open shop," advocate of, **Vol. 8, Part 1**, 112 f.
Opequon Creek, battle of, **Vol. 3, Part 1**, 598; **Vol. 3, Part 2**, 153; **Vol. 4, Part 1**, 424; **Vol. 8, Part 1**, 341; **Vol. 8, Part 2**, 72, 242; **Vol. 9, Part 1**, 80; **Vol. 10, Part 2**, 334
Opera: American, **Supp. 6**, 633; American Opera Company, **Vol. 9, Part 2**, 425; bel canto, **Supp. 4**, 223; Boston, **Vol. 5, Part 2**, 214; broadcasts of, **Supp. 6**, 324; Chautauqua Company, **Supp. 3**, 65; comic, **Vol. 3, Part 1**, 204 f.; **Vol. 4, Part 2**, 573; **Vol. 9, Part 1**, 408; composition, **Vol. 3, Part 1**, 205; **Vol. 3, Part 2**, 39, 259; **Vol. 5, Part 1**, 78; **Vol. 8, Part 1**, 144; **Vol. 9, Part 1**, 390 f., 411; **Supp. 6**, 351–52, 690; **Supp. 8**, 645; comprimario roles, **Supp. 7**, 179; conducting, **Supp. 7**, 765; contemporary American, **Supp. 7**, 61–62, 124; early American, **Vol. 8, Part 1**, 489 f.; *El Capitan,* **Vol. 5, Part 2**, 443; *Faust,* **Vol. 5, Part 2**, 301; first composed for radio and television, **Supp. 7**, 124; first successful American, **Vol. 4, Part 1**, 50; first woman company director, **Supp. 8**, 201; folk, **Supp. 4**, 868–69; *Four Saints in Three Acts,* premiere of, **Supp. 4**, 769; French, **Supp. 8**, 200–1; Gilbert and Sullivan, **Vol. 8, Part 2**, 246, **Vol. 9, Part 2**, 62; Indian themes, **Supp. 4**, 138; introduction of Italian, **Vol. 9, Part 1**, 177; *Kenilworth,* **Vol. 5, Part 2**, 442; librettos for, **Vol. 8, Part 1**, 388; **Supp. 4**, 576; **Supp. 9**, 55; light, **Vol. 8, Part 2**, 387; **Vol. 10, Part 2**, 513; *Madame Butterfly,* **Vol. 6, Part 1**, 379; *Mahagonny,* **Supp. 4**, 868; management, **Vol. 4, Part 2**, 199 f.; Metropolitan, **Vol. 2, Part 2**, 357; **Vol. 3, Part 2**, 396; **Vol. 4, Part 1**, 506; **Vol. 5, Part 2**, 584; **Vol. 7, Part 2**, 311; **Supp. 9**, 544, 545; **Supp. 10**, 93, 94, 722; on radio, **Supp. 9**, 207, 802, 804; operetta singing, **Supp. 8**, 151; Parepa-Rosa Opera Company, **Vol. 8, Part 2**, 92; patrons, **Supp. 1**, 457; *Porgy and Bess,* **Supp. 2**, 303; recordings, **Supp. 9**, 545, 805, 851; **Supp. 10**, 94; *Red Feather,* **Vol. 5, Part 2**, 443; *Rigoletto,* **Supp. 9**, 851; singing of, **Vol. 1, Part 1**, 19, 54; **Vol. 1, Part 2**, 299; **Vol. 2, Part 1**, 550, 553, **Vol. 3, Part 2**, 397; **Vol. 4, Part 2**, 399; **Vol. 7, Part 1**, 549; **Vol. 8, Part 1**, 144; **Vol. 8, Part 2**, 339; **Vol. 10, Part 2**, 131; **Supp. 1**, 654–55; **Supp. 3**, 553–54; **Supp. 4**, 223, 388–89, 597; **Supp. 6**, 68–69, 322–23, 510–11, 630–31, 632–33, 669–70; **Supp. 7**, 277–78, 525–26; **Supp. 8**, 19–20, 168, 200–201, 422–23; **Supp. 9**, 544–55, 800–801, 804–5, 816, 850–51; **Supp. 10**, 92–94, 445–46, 639–40; sung in English, **Supp. 1**, 4; **Supp. 4**, 834; theater management, **Supp. 2**, 223; *Three-Penny Opera,* **Supp. 4**, 868, 869; Wagnerian introduced in U.S., **Supp. 3**, 359; **Supp. 4**, 210–11; **Supp. 6**, 643; *Walküre, Die,* **Vol. 7, Part 1**, 434; **Supp. 9**, 544, 545, 804–5. *See also* Metropolitan Opera Company
Opéra-Comique, **Supp. 8**, 200
Operettas, **Supp. 1**, 3–4; **Supp. 5**, 585, 627; **Supp. 8**, 151; writing of, **Vol. 4, Part 2**, 199 f.; **Vol. 10, Part 1**, 487
Ophthalmic and Aural Institute, **Vol. 5, Part 2**, 449 f.
Ophthalmological Society, **Vol. 3, Part 1**, 207; **Vol. 4, Part 1**, 32; **Vol. 5, Part 2**, 38
Ophthalmology: **Vol. 1, Part 1**, 123; **Vol. 2, Part 1**, 301; **Vol. 2, Part 2**, 76; **Vol. 3, Part 1**, 207, 253, 327, 464; **Vol. 3, Part 2**, 388; **Vol. 4, Part 1**, 31, 451, 550; **Vol. 4, Part 2**, 32, 462; **Vol. 5, Part 1**, 247, 293; **Vol. 5, Part 2**, 37, 38, 499; **Vol. 6, Part 1**, 296, 415; **Vol. 7, Part 1**, 556, 580; **Vol. 7, Part 2**, 16; **Vol. 8, Part 1**, 290, 346, 376, 510; **Vol. 8, Part 2**, 357; **Vol. 10, Part 2**, 258, 265; laboratory importance to, **Supp. 4**, 865; physiological response testing, **Supp. 3**, 269–70; refraction, **Supp. 3**, 377; surgery, **Supp. 2**, 706; writings on history of, **Supp. 3**, 835–36. *See also* Blind and blindness; Eyes; Vision
Ophthalmoscope, first practical, **Vol. 6, Part 1**, 415
Opie, Eugene L., references to, **Supp. 3**, 243; **Supp. 4**, 287
Opinion Research Corporation, founding of, **Supp. 7**, 650
Opium trade, **Vol. 1, Part 1**, 308; **Vol. 3, Part 2**, 508 f.; **Vol. 4, Part 2**, 369; **Vol. 5, Part 2**, 270, 384; **Vol. 6, Part 1**, 491; **Vol. 8, Part 1**, 103 f.; **Vol. 10, Part 2**, 553; **Supp. 1**, 116
Oppenheimer, George S., references to, **Supp. 7**, 306, 374
Oppenheimer, Harry, reference to, **Supp. 9**, 263
Oppenheimer, J. Robert: hydrogen bomb development, opposition to, **Supp. 9**, 774; references to, **Supp. 4**, 839; **Supp. 5**, 156, 221; **Supp. 6**, 143, 371; **Supp. 8**, 230; **Supp. 9**, 27; **Supp. 10**, 144; security clearance controversy, **Supp. 9**, 774
Opportunity, **Supp. 6**, 321; **Supp. 9**, 108
Optics: **Vol. 8, Part 1**, 630 f.; **Vol. 8, Part 2**, 131 achromatic lenses, **Supp. 1**, 383; astronomical instruments, **Supp. 1**, 383–84; glass, **Supp. 6**, 153 microscope design and production, **Supp. 3**, 40; teaching of, **Supp. 5**, 441
Optometry, bifocal lenses, cementing of, **Vol. 4, Part 1**, 451
Orage, Alfred Richard, reference to, **Supp. 9**, 33
Oral contraceptives, development of, **Supp. 8**, 503
Oral surgery, **Vol. 2, Part 1**, 93; **Vol. 4, Part 1**, 167
Orange Court House, operations at. *See* Wilderness campaign
Oranges, scientific breeding of, **Vol. 4, Part 1**, 144; **Vol. 4, Part 2**, 356; **Vol. 5, Part 1**, 328
Orate Fratres, founding of, **Supp. 2**, 455
Oratorio Society, Brooklyn, **Vol. 5, Part 2**, 486
Oratorio Society of New York. *See* New York Oratorio Society
Oratory: **Vol. 1, Part 1**, 518, 562; **Vol. 3, Part 2**, 223 f., 300, 562; **Vol. 4, Part 1**, 134, 465, 509; **Vol. 4, Part 2**, 555 f.; **Vol. 5, Part 1**, 463; **Vol. 7, Part 1**, 580; **Vol. 8, Part 2**, 195, 264; **Vol. 9, Part 1**, 36; **Vol. 10, Part 1**, 101, 585 f.; civil rights, **Supp. 8**, 333, 334; congressional, **Supp. 7**, 21–22; teaching of, **Vol. 8, Part 1**, 408. *See also* Evangelism
Orchard, Harry, reference to, **Supp. 5**, 699
Orchestras. *See specific orchestras*
Orchids: collections of, **Supp. 4**, 16–17; specialist in, **Vol. 4, Part 2**, 229
Ordeal of the Union, The, **Supp. 9**, 582, 583
Order of Spiritual Virgins and the Solitary Brethren, **Vol. 1, Part 2**, 142
Order of the Knights of Pythias, founding of, **Vol. 8, Part 1**, 386
Order of the Star-Spangled Banner, **Vol. 1, Part 1**, 605
Ordnance: **Vol. 1, Part 2**, 209, 427; **Vol. 3, Part 1**, 580, 587, 614 f.; **Vol. 3, Part 2**, 142; **Vol. 5, Part 1**, 471;

development of, **Vol. 3, Part 1**, 29 f.; manufacturing, **Vol. 5, Part 2**, 317; waterproof cartridge, invention of, **Vol. 3, Part 1**, 410
Ordnance, Bureau of, **Vol. 9, Part 1**, 149; **Supp. 9**, 773
Oread Collegiate Institute, **Vol. 9, Part 2**, 403
Oregon: boundary disputes, **Vol. 1, Part 1**, 566; **Vol. 1, Part 2**, 212; **Vol. 2, Part 1**, 209, 417, 563; **Vol. 6, Part 1**, 112; **Vol. 6, Part 2**, 134–35; **Vol. 7, Part 2**, 119; **Vol. 8, Part 1**, 37; **Vol. 10, Part 1**, 356; **Vol. 10, Part 2**, 142, 577; cattle raising in, **Vol. 1, Part 1**, 326; codification of laws, **Vol. 1, Part 2**, 414; compromise on Oregon question, **Vol. 3, Part 1**, 74, 180; constitution, **Vol. 1, Part 2**, 414; **Vol. 3, Part 1**, 162, 292; education, **Vol. 1, Part 1**, 408; Episcopal diocese, **Supp. 1**, 678; first archbishop of Oregon City, **Vol. 1, Part 2**, 352; fruit culture, **Vol. 6, Part 1**, 498; governors, **Vol. 2, Part 1**, 595 f.; **Vol. 6, Part 1**, 410 f.; **Vol. 7, Part 2**, 445 f.; **Supp. 6**, 416, 682–83; **Supp. 8**, 617; growth of, **Vol. 1, Part 1**, 326; history of, **Vol. 1, Part 1**, 518; **Vol. 1, Part 2**, 414; **Vol. 2, Part 2**, 604 f.; **Vol. 3, Part 1**, 513 f.; **Vol. 6, Part 2**, 135; **Vol. 7, Part 2**, 186 f.; **Vol. 8, Part 1**, 456; **Vol. 8, Part 2**, 491; **Vol. 10, Part 2**, 627; Indian affairs, **Vol. 1, Part 1**, 236; **Vol. 5, Part 2**, 579; Indian missions, **Vol. 7, Part 2**, 237; Kelley expedition to, **Vol. 5, Part 2**, 297; land claims, **Vol. 4, Part 1**, 523; land fraud, **Supp. 2**, 296; legal service, **Vol. 1, Part 2**, 414; **Vol. 3, Part 1**, 168; **Vol. 6, Part 1**, 410; maps, **Vol. 5, Part 1**, 194 f.; mining, **Vol. 8, Part 1**, 456; missions, **Vol. 1, Part 1**, 408; **Vol. 6, Part 1**, 112; Mitchell, leadership of, **Vol. 7, Part 1**, 54; newspaper service, **Vol. 1, Part 1**, 535; petition for territorial government, **Vol. 6, Part 1**, 112; philanthropy, **Vol. 5, Part 2**, 528; pioneer Catholic history of, **Vol. 1, Part 2**, 353; pioneer days, **Vol. 1, Part 1**, 102; **Vol. 2, Part 1**, 300; **Vol. 6, Part 2**, 92, 494 f.; **Vol. 7, Part 1**, 458; **Vol. 10, Part 2**, 577, 627; politics, **Vol. 2, Part 1**, 596; **Supp. 3**, 345, 496; **Supp. 4**, 844; **Supp. 6**, 474–75; **Supp. 8**, 104; **Supp. 9**, 565, 566; public service, **Vol. 1, Part 2**, 414; **Vol. 2, Part 2**, 435 f.; **Vol. 3, Part 1**, 168, 360; **Vol. 3, Part 2**, 481; **Vol. 4, Part 1**, 94; **Vol. 4, Part 2**, 29; **Vol. 5, Part 2**, 579; **Vol. 6, Part 1**, 410; **Vol. 9, Part 2**, 455; **Vol. 10, Part 2**, 262; reforms, **Vol. 5, Part 1**, 535–36, Republican party, "Salem Clique," **Vol. 1, Part 1**, 102; settlement, **Vol. 1, Part 1**, 29, 326; **Vol. 3, Part 1**, 379 f.; **Vol. 6, Part 2**, 134; **Vol. 10, Part 2**, 142, 577; slavery, **Vol. 3, Part 1**, 125; state printer, **Vol. 7, Part 2**, 643; treaty with Great Britain, **Vol. 8, Part 1**, 34 f.; trapping, **Vol. 8, Part 2**, 248; U.S. claim to, **Vol. 3, Part 1**, 398; wheat growing, **Vol. 1, Part 1**, 408; Whitman's ride, **Vol. 6, Part 1**, 433 f.; woman suffrage, **Vol. 3, Part 1**, 513; **Supp. 5**, 742. *See also* Oregon Trail
Oregon bill (Organic Act of July 5, 1843), **Vol. 6, Part 1**, 282
Oregon Free Press, **Vol. 2, Part 2**, 604
Oregon Statesman, **Supp. 8**, 616
Oregon State University, formative period of, **Vol. 3, Part 1**, 168
Oregon Steam Navigation Co., **Vol. 8, Part 1**, 456
Oregon Trail, **Vol. 3, Part 1**, 379 f.; **Vol. 4, Part 1**, 19; **Vol. 6, Part 2**, 495; **Vol. 7, Part 2**, 247; **Vol. 10, Part 2**, 142; watercolors, **Supp. 3**, 380
Oregon Trunk Railway Co., **Supp. 3**, 736
Oregon Woman Suffrage Association, **Vol. 3, Part 1**, 513 f.
Ore Magmas, The, **Supp. 4**, 765, 766
Organ: building of, **Vol. 3, Part 2**, 189; **Vol. 4, Part 1**, 403 f.; **Vol. 4, Part 2**, 196, 598; **Vol. 5, Part 2**, 152; **Vol. 6, Part 1**, 234; **Vol. 8, Part 2**, 133; **Vol. 9, Part 2**, 295; electric, **Vol. 8, Part 2**, 133; first use of in American synagogue, **Vol. 8, Part 1**, 164 f.; inventions concerning, **Vol. 4, Part 1**, 59; literature, library of, **Vol. 1, Part 1**, 423; **Vol. 3, Part 1**, 513; music for, **Vol. 1, Part 1**, 340; **Vol. 2, Part 1**, 223; **Vol. 7, Part 2**, 151, 228 f.; **Vol. 9, Part 2**, 10; **Vol. 10, Part 1**, 488; playing, **Vol. 1, Part 1**, 339; **Vol. 3, Part 1**, 513; **Vol. 5, Part 1**, 540; **Vol. 9, Part 2**, 339; **Vol. 10, Part 2**, 136, 455; Reed, invention of, **Vol. 4, Part 1**, 336
Organic chemistry: **Supp. 2**, 96, 379, 493, 631; **Supp. 3**, 520–21; **Supp. 6**, 333–35; analytic methods, **Supp. 3**, 565–46; carbon rearrangement studies, **Supp. 8**, 102; catalytic reactions, **Supp. 4**, 5–6; cyclooctatetraene synthesis, **Supp. 8**, 103; industrial, **Supp. 5**, 662–63; intramolecular rearrangement studies, **Supp. 4**, 888; naphthoquinones, **Supp. 10**, 240; pyrimidine, **Supp. 4**, 434–35; stable free radicals, **Supp. 4**, 336–37; steroid hormones, **Supp. 5**, 28; steroids, **Supp. 10**, 240; substance oxidation and reduction, **Supp. 4**, 573–74; teaching of, **Supp. 1**, 571; **Supp. 10**, 241
Organization of Afro-American Unity, founding of, **Supp. 7**, 509
Organization of American Historians, **Supp. 10**, 844; predecessor, **Supp. 5**, 430
Organization of Petroleum Exporting Countries (OPEC), **Supp. 10**, 663–64
Organized crime: Apalachin, N.Y., conference, **Supp. 9**, 269, 270, 306; **Supp. 10**, 269; Chicago politics, **Supp. 3**, 772; Chicago underworld, **Supp. 4**, 140–42; **Supp. 6**, 263–64, **Supp. 9**, 306–7; 651–52; **Supp. 10**, 49, 134, 135; "Cosa Nostra" term explained, **Supp. 9**, 821; drug trafficking, **Supp. 9**, 821; initiation rites, **Supp. 9**, 820; internal wars, **Supp. 7**, 632, 633; **Supp. 9**, 12, 198–99, 270; **Supp. 10**, 140–41, 266, 267, 269; investigations of, **Supp. 9**, 399, 499–500, 821; **Supp. 10**, 482–83; Israeli aid scheme, **Supp. 10**, 135; judicial efforts against, **Supp. 3**, 226–27; leadership, **Supp. 5**, 736–37; **Supp. 7**, 484–85, 504–5, 632–33; **Supp. 8**, 207–9, 396–98; **Supp. 10**, 135–36; legitimate businesses, **Supp. 8**, 208, 397, 546; movies about, **Supp. 6**, 668; **Supp. 10**, 140; New Jersey, **Supp. 10**, 75; New York City, **Supp. 6**, 295; **Supp. 7**, 585–86, 667; **Supp. 8**, 397; **Supp. 9**, 197–99, 269–70, 399, 820–21; **Supp. 10**, 266–68; "Outfit, The," **Supp. 9**, 306, 307, 651, 652; Philadelphia rackets, **Supp. 10**, 75–76; presidential election vote fraud (1960), **Supp. 9**, 307; public relations, **Supp. 10**, 140; secrecy vow, **Supp. 10**,140; Senate investigations of, **Supp. 7**, 416, 586; **Supp. 9**, 13, 198, 269, 500, 512, 652, 821; **Supp. 10**, 135; Teamsters Union infiltration, **Supp. 9**, 395–96, 397; trade union infiltration, **Supp. 8**, 322; Valachi testimony, **Supp. 9**, 821
Organized Crime Control Act (1970), **Supp. 10**, 483
Organized labor. *See* Trade unions; *specific union names*
Organ transplants. *See* Transplants
Orient, the: diplomacy with, **Vol. 3, Part 2**, 560; **Vol. 8, Part 2**, 4; excavations, **Vol. 4, Part 2**, 284; exploration, **Vol. 5, Part 1**, 58; **Vol. 8, Part 2**, 66; languages, study of, **Vol. 8, Part 2**, 308; literature of, **Vol. 3, Part 2**, 197; **Vol. 7, Part 1**, 448; **Vol. 8, Part 2**, 110; **Vol. 9, Part 1**, 242, 257 f.; naval expeditions, **Vol. 8, Part 1**, 424; scholarship, **Vol. 2, Part 2**, 169; **Vol. 4, Part 1**, 247; **Vol. 5, Part 2**, 3; **Vol. 6, Part 1**, 224; **Vol. 7, Part 1**, 547; **Vol. 9, Part 2**, 622; **Vol. 10, Part 1**, 474 f.; trade with, **Vol. 5, Part 1**, 39; **Vol. 7, Part 2**, 477; **Vol. 9, Part 1**, 48; **Vol. 9, Part 2**, 499; writings on, **Vol. 4, Part 2**, 132; **Vol. 5, Part 2**, 561; **Vol. 8, Part 1**, 446 f.; **Vol. 8, Part 2**, 67, 111, 308; **Vol. 10, Part 1**, 442 f., 474 f.
Oriental art: **Vol. 3, Part 2**, 325; collections, **Supp. 1**,

641; first history studies, **Supp. 5**, 729–30. *See also specific country*
Orientalism, **Vol. 8, Part 2**, 110
Orientalists. For complete list, *see* Occupations Index
Original Carter Family (country and western group): career of, **Supp. 10**, 104–5; influence on folk music, **Supp. 10**, 105
Origin of Species, influence of, **Vol. 5, Part 1**, 470
Origins of the World War, The, **Supp. 8**, 169, 170
Origins of Totalitarianism, The, **Supp. 9**, 41
Orinoco River, exploration, **Vol. 10, Part 1**, 632 f.
Oriskany, battle of, **Vol. 1, Part 1**, 364; **Vol. 1, Part 2**, 604; **Vol. 4, Part 2**, 578
Orlando, Fla., harness racing, **Supp. 6**, 689
Orleans, Territory of, **Vol. 8, Part 1**, 163 f., 308 f.
Orlenev, Paul, reference to, **Supp. 3**, 548
Orlon, **Supp. 5**, 191
Ormandy, Eugene, reference to, **Supp. 10**, 762
Ormiston, Kenneth G., reference to, **Supp. 3**, 498
Ornithology: **Vol. 1, Part 1**, 423 f., 514; **Vol. 2, Part 1**, 24, 30, 31, 75, 569; **Vol. 2, Part 2**, 458 f., 465 f.; **Vol. 3, Part 2**, 510 f.; **Vol. 6, Part 1**, 49, 56; **Vol. 6, Part 2**, 457, 561; **Vol. 7, Part 1**, 405 f., 597 f., 606; **Vol. 8, Part 1**, 581, 598 f.; **Vol. 8, Part 2**, 323, 585; **Vol. 9, Part 2**, 594, 617; **Vol. 10, Part 1**, 565; **Vol. 10. Part 2**, 318, 589; classification, **Supp. 3**, 517; **Supp. 8**, 654–55; conservation movement, **Supp. 3**, 593–94; popularization of, **Supp. 7**, 7–8; studies on Antarctica, **Supp. 7**, 217; teaching of, **Supp. 5**, 374–75; writings on, **Supp. 2**, 634; **Supp. 4**, 41, 248–49; writings on Texas and Louisiana, **Supp. 7**, 578–79. *See also* Birds
Ornstein, Leo, reference to, **Supp. 4**, 702
Oroya fever, study of, **Vol. 7, Part 1**, 543
Orozco, José Clemente, reference to, **Supp. 6**, 512
Orphanages, **Vol. 3, Part 1**, 562 f.; **Vol. 4, Part 2**, 398; **Vol. 5, Part 1**, 568; **Vol. 6, Part 1**, 60; **Vol. 8, Part 2**, 103; **Vol. 9, Part 2**, 586
Orphan Asylum Society, **Vol. 4, Part 1**, 475
"Orphan Brigade," Civil War, **Vol. 6, Part 1**, 218
Orpheum Vaudeville Circuit, establishment of, **Supp. 2**, 32
Orteig, Raymond, reference to, **Supp. 5**, 547; **Supp. 9**, 496
Orth bill, **Vol. 7, Part 2**, 61
Orthodontics, development of, **Supp. 2**, 666
Orthodox churches: Greek, **Supp. 7**, 102–3; Russian, **Supp. 7**, 468–69
Orthodox Presbyterian church, founding of, **Supp. 2**, 412
Orthography, **Vol. 10, Part 1**, 594 f.
Orthopedics: amputation treatment, **Supp. 6**, 344–45; children, **Supp. 1**, 40–41; hip fracture surgery, **Supp. 4**, 887; surgery, **Vol. 1, Part 2**, 22, 257; **Vol. 3, Part 1**, 118; **Vol. 6, Part 1**, 443; **Vol. 8, Part 2**, 404; **Vol. 9, Part 2**, 343; **Supp. 1**, 25, 40–41; **Supp. 4**, 887
Orthoptera, **Vol. 8, Part 2**, 526
Osborn, Alex F., references to, **Supp. 7**, 211; **Supp. 8**, 27
Osborn, Henry Fairfield, references to, **Supp. 3**, 160, 316, 520; **Supp. 6**, 18; **Supp. 8**, 485
Osborn Concession, link of Pan-American Railway, **Vol. 7, Part 2**, 72
Osborne, John, reference to, **Supp. 7**, 114
Osborne, Thomas B., references to, **Supp. 3**, 807; **Supp. 5**, 122
Osborne, Thomas Mott, references to, **Supp. 3**, 420–21; **Supp. 4**, 472
Osborne Association, **Vol. 7, Part 2**, 76
Oscar Mayer and Co., **Supp. 7**, 519–20
Oscar II (ship), **Supp. 4**, 726
Osgood, Herbert L., reference to, **Supp. 3**, 287
"Osgoodites," founding of, **Vol. 7, Part 2**, 80 f.;
Osiris (journal), **Supp. 6**, 565
Osler, William: biography of, **Supp. 2**, 138; references to, **Vol. 5, Part 1**, 97; **Supp. 1**, 525; **Supp. 3**, 243, 412, 413, 835; **Supp. 5**, 438; **Supp. 6**, 223
Osmeña, Sergio, references to, **Supp. 3**, 614; **Supp. 6**, 211
OSS. *See* World War II, Office of Strategic Services
Ossining, N.Y. *See* Sing Sing penitentiary
Ostend Manifesto (1854), **Vol. 2, Part 1**, 210–11; **Vol. 3, Part 1**, 126; **Vol. 6, Part 2**, 277, 370; **Vol. 7, Part 2**, 578–79; **Vol. 9, Part 1**, 406
Osteomyelitis, cure for, **Supp. 1**, 40
Osteopathy, **Vol. 9, Part 2**, 21 f.
Osteotomy, **Vol. 10, Part 1**, 158
Oswald, Lee Harvey: conspiracy theory about, **Supp. 9**, 715; references to, **Supp. 7**, 425, 434; **Supp. 8**, 557–58
Oswego Training School, first in U.S., **Vol. 2, Part 2**, 418; **Vol. 5, Part 2**, 510; **Vol. 9, Part 1**, 64
Otego Patent, land grant, **Vol. 9, Part 1**, 333
Others: A Magazine of New Verse, founding of, **Supp. 8**, 350
Othello, **Supp. 10**, 677, 678
Otis, Boss, influence of, **Vol. 7, Part 1**, 396
Otis, Harrison Gray, reference to, **Supp. 10**, 553
Otis, Harry Gray, references to, **Supp. 3**, 154, 155
Otis Elevator Co., predecessor, **Supp. 1**, 669–70
Otis Group Intelligence Scale, **Supp. 7**, 594
Otley, Jess, reference to, **Supp. 6**, 331
Otology, **Vol. 2, Part 1**, 221, 296 f.; **Vol. 3, Part 1**, 253; **Vol. 4, Part 2**, 32; **Vol. 6, Part 1**, 160; **Vol. 8, Part 1**, 364 f., 510. *See also* Deaf and deafness
Otterbein, William, reference to, **Vol. 1, Part 2**, 405
Ottley, William, reference to, **Vol. 8, Part 2**, 371
Ouanga (opera), **Supp. 6**, 690
Our American Cousin, **Vol. 5, Part 2**, 284
Our Danger and Our Duty, defense of South, **Vol. 9, Part 2**, 508
Our Hearts Were Young and Gay, **Supp. 10**, 740
Our Plundered Planet, **Supp. 8**, 486
Oursler, Fulton, reference to, **Supp. 5**, 453
Oursler, Grace Perkins, reference to, **Supp. 5**, 527
"Our Talisman" papers, **Vol. 6, Part 1**, 285
Our Times, **Supp. 5**, 667
Our Town, **Supp. 3**, 198; **Supp. 9**, 870, 871; **Supp. 10**, 311–12
Our Young Folks, **Vol. 3, Part 1**, 350; **Vol. 9, Part 2**, 656
Outcault, R. F., reference to, **Supp. 5**, 284
Outdoor Recreation Resources Review Commission, **Supp. 9**, 608
Outlaw, The, **Supp. 7**, 71; **Supp. 10**, 355
Outlaw Josie Wales, The, **Supp. 10**, 239
Outlaws, **Vol. 1, Part 2**, 271; **Vol. 5, Part 2**, 540 f.; **Vol. 7, Part 1**, 369 f.
Outline of Clinical Psychoanalysis, The, **Supp. 4**, 264
Outlook, The, **Vol. 1, Part 1**, 25; **Vol. 6, Part 1**, 541; **Vol. 9, Part 1**, 419
Outlook for the Blind, The, magazine for the blind, **Vol. 5, Part 2**, 288
Ovary, endocrinology of, **Supp. 3**, 6; **Supp. 6**, 186
Ovens, Florence Jane, reference to, **Supp. 5**, 437
Overberger, C. G., reference to, **Supp. 8**, 103
"Overland brigade," of fur traders, **Vol. 3, Part 2**, 575
Overland Monthly, **Vol. 4, Part 2**, 363
Overland stage line, St. Louis–San Francisco, **Vol. 2, Part 1**, 375
Overland Stage to California, **Vol. 8, Part 2, 146**
Overman Law, **Vol. 7, Part 2**, 115
Overstreet, Bonaro Wilkinson, reference to, **Supp. 8**, 488–89

Overstreet, Harry, reference to, **Supp. 3**, 65
"Over the Rainbow" (song), **Supp. 8**, 204
Over There Theatre League, **Supp. 2**, 11
Overton, John, friend of A. Jackson, **Vol. 5, Part 1**, 527 f.
Oviatt, Edwin, reference to, **Supp. 6**, 154
Owen, Chandler, reference to, **Supp. 10**, 658
Owen, Robert Dale, references to **Vol. 6, Part 1**, 190; **Vol. 7, Part 1**, 402; **Vol. 8, Part 2**, 402; **Vol. 9, Part 1**, 183, 306; **Vol. 9, Part 2**, 648
Owen, Steve, references to, **Supp. 9**, 817, 818; **Supp. 10**, 444
Owens, Jesse, reference to, **Supp. 9**, 131; **Supp. 10**, 531
OWI. *See* World War II, Office of War Information
Owings, Nathaniel A., reference to, **Supp. 7**, 690–91
Ox-Bow Incident, The, **Supp. 9**, 177
Oxford English Dictionary, **Vol. 4, Part 2**, 125; **Vol. 7, Part 2**, 541
Oxford Group, **Supp. 7**, 88. *See also* Moral Re-Armament
Oxford Movement, **Vol. 4, Part 2**, 604; **Vol. 10, Part 1**, 71; **Supp. 1**, 668
Oxford University: American history studies, **Supp. 6**, 410; first woman doctorate in science, **Supp. 3**, 131; Ruskin Hall, **Supp. 4**, 61–62
Ox Hill, battle of. *See* Chantilly, battle of
Oxides, system study, **Supp. 6**, 153
Oxman, Frank C., reference to, **Supp. 3**, 532
Oxygen: discovery of, **Vol. 8, Part 1**, 223 f.; experiments with, in connection with coal-gas flame, **Vol. 3, Part 1**, 376; **Vol. 7, Part 1**, 192; poisoning, **Supp. 6**, 175
Oxytocin, synthesis of, **Supp. 10**, 198
Oyrimidine chemistry, **Supp. 4**, 434–35
Oyster culture, **Vol. 7, Part 1**, 418, 629

P

Paar, Jack, references to, **Supp. 7**, 436; **Supp. 9**, 48, 780
Pace and Handy (music publishers), **Supp. 6**, 275
Pach, Walter, references to, **Supp. 5**, 20, 659
Pacific Air Transport, **Supp. 10**, 620
Pacific Coast: forests, first reports on, **Vol. 6, Part 1**, 162; medical college, first on, **Vol. 2, Part 2**, 397; missions, **Vol. 2, Part 2**, 539; survey of, **Vol. 3, Part 1**, 92
Pacific Coast Lumber Manufacturers Association, founding of, **Supp. 2**, 263
Pacific Electric Railway, **Vol. 8, Part 1**, 357 f.
Pacific Express Co., **Vol. 9, Part 2**, 385
Pacific Gas and Electric Co., **Supp. 6**, 591; strike, **Supp. 3**, 532
Pacific Grove, Calif., Spanish explorers at, **Vol. 8, Part 1**, 109 f.
Pacific Mail Steamship Lines, **Vol. 1, Part 1**, 396; **Vol. 7, Part 2**, 209
Pacific Northwest Development League, **Vol. 3, Part 1**, 238
Pacific-Panama International Exposition (1915): landscaping, **Supp. 3**, 490; sculpture, **Supp. 3**, 124
Pacific Railroad: development of, **Vol. 1, Part 2**, 333; **Vol. 6, Part 1**, 485; explorations for route for, **Vol. 1, Part 2**, 471
Pacific School of Religion, Palestine Institute, **Supp. 2**, 16
Pacific Theological Seminary, **Vol. 7, Part 1**, 385
Pacifism: **Vol. 3, Part 1**, 357; **Vol. 3, Part 2**, 558, 573; **Vol. 4, Part 2**, 547; **Vol. 6, Part 1**, 241, 271; **Vol. 10, Part 1**, 5 f.; ACLU support of, **Supp. 9**, 36; religious, **Supp. 10**, 82, 176. *See also* Conscientious objectors; Peace, international; *World War headings*
Packaging: meat products, **Supp. 7**, 520; standard sizes, **Supp. 7**, 358
Packard Motor Car Co.: **Supp. 3**, 550; **Supp. 6**, 164, 650; **Supp. 9**, 290; factory architecture, **Supp. 3**, 404
Packer Collegiate Institute of Brooklyn, **Vol. 1, Part 1**, 472 f.; **Vol. 9, Part 2**, 101
Packers and Stockyards Act (1921), **Supp. 3**, 839
Packet boats, **Vol. 2, Part 2**, 421; **Vol. 3, Part 2**, 401; **Vol. 4, Part 2**, 154; **Vol. 8, Part 2**, 42, 324, 593; building of, **Vol. 10, Part 2**, 15; first ocean line to run on definite schedule, **Vol. 9, Part 2**, 461
Pack peddlars, **Vol. 9, Part 2**, 445
PACs. *See* Political action committees
Paddleford, Clementine, reference to, **Supp. 8**, 520
Paderewski, Ignace, references to, **Vol. 9, Part 2**, 425; **Supp. 6**, 174; **Supp. 10**, 372–73
Padmore, George, reference to, **Supp. 6**, 716
Paducah, Ky., founding of, **Vol. 2, Part 2**, 144
Page, Oran ("Hot Lips"), reference to, **Supp. 9**, 687
Page, Ruth, reference to, **Supp. 5**, 75
Page, T. H., reference to, **Supp. 5**, 529
Page, Thomas Nelson, reference to, **Supp. 6**, 359
Page, Walter (bassist), reference to, **Supp. 9**, 687
Page, Walter Hines, references to, **Vol. 7, Part 1**, 316; **Supp. 4**, 239
Pageants, **Supp. 3**, 427; historical, one of earliest in U.S., **Vol. 5, Part 1**, 76
Page Communications Engineers, defense projects, **Supp. 9**, 728
Pagliacci, I, world premiere, **Supp. 6**, 642
Pahlavi, Shah Mohammed Reza, reference to, **Supp. 8**, 275
Paideia, **Supp. 7**, 388
Paine, Thomas, references to, **Vol. 2, Part 2**, 47; **Vol. 3, Part 2**, 201; **Vol. 5, Part 1**, 476
Paine College, **Vol. 5, Part 1**, 177; founding of, **Supp. 3**, 130
Paint: automobile lacquer, **Supp. 5**, 235; fast-drying automobile, **Supp. 6**, 333; manufacture of, **Vol. 2, Part 2**, 110; **Vol. 10, Part 2**, 23; remover compound, **Supp. 3**, 247; synthetic resins, **Supp. 3**, 247
Painters. For complete list, *see* Occupations Index
Painting (for complete list of artists, painters, etc., *see* Occupations Index): **Vol. 1, Part 1**, 3 f., 123, 224, 310, 582 f.; **Vol. 1, Part 2**, 412; **Vol. 2, Part 1**, 21, 37, 567; **Vol. 2, Part 2**, 231, 447; **Vol. 3, Part 1**, 103, 558 f., 590 f.; **Vol. 3, Part 2**, 56, 98, 168 f., 404, 543; **Vol. 4, Part 1**, 54 f., 69, 162, 193, 585; **Vol. 4, Part 2**, 59, 126, 381, 404, 423, 544; **Vol. 5, Part 1**, 186 f., 311, 331 f., 397 f., 514 f., 603, 613 f.; **Vol. 5, Part 2**, 72 f., 152, 159, 222 f., 293 f., 295, 411, 463, 484 f., 494, 530 f., 606; **Vol. 6, Part 1**, 87 f., 353, 382, 447; **Vol. 6, Part 2**, 570, 645; **Vol. 7, Part 1**, 116 f., 488, 630 f.; **Vol. 7, Part 2**, 193, 203, 312, 351; **Vol. 8, Part 1**, 149, 497, 627; **Vol. 8, Part 2**, 5, 54, 187, 271, 370, 373, 470; **Vol. 9, Part 1**, 230, 266, 307, 453, 513 f., 597; **Vol. 9, Part 2**, 322, 509, 534, 551; **Vol. 10, Part 1**, 70, 78 f., 180 f., 601, 608 f., 612; **Vol. 10, Part 2**, 74 f., 313, 342; abstract, **Supp. 9**, 92; **Supp. 10**, 3, 263, 759, 787; animals, **Vol. 1, Part 2**, 95; **Vol. 4, Part 2**, 463 f.; **Vol. 5, Part 1**, 299 f.; **Vol. 7, Part 1**, 152; **Vol. 9, Part 2**, 399 f.; **Vol. 10, Part 1**, 1 f.; **Vol. 10, Part 2**, 191; birds, **Vol. 4, Part 1**, 53; child life, **Vol. 3, Part 1**, 610; **Vol. 4, Part 2**, 63; child prodigy, **Vol. 6, Part 1**, 87; cubism, **Vol. 5, Part 1**, 100 f.; **Supp. 9**, 501; **Supp. 10**, 263, 503, 786, 832; exhibitions, **Supp. 10**, 758, 759; figure, **Vol. 3, Part 1**, 535 f., 590 f.; **Vol. 4, Part 2**, 110; **Vol. 5, Part 2**, 494; **Vol. 6, Part 2**, 459, 582; **Vol. 7, Part 1**, 465; **Vol. 8, Part 1**, 479 f.; **Vol. 9, Part 2**, 448; flowers, **Vol. 3, Part 1**,

273; **Vol. 5, Part 2**, 532; **Vol. 6, Part 1**, 344; **Vol. 7, Part 1**, 464; **Supp. 9**, 745; **Supp. 10**, 787, 832–33; French influence, **Vol. 5, Part 2**, 532; **Vol. 7, Part 1**, 29; genre, **Vol. 1, Part 2**, 275; **Vol. 2, Part 1**, 138; **Vol. 3, Part 2**, 448; **Vol. 4, Part 1**, 11, 517 f.; **Vol. 4, Part 2**, 62, 542; **Vol. 5, Part 1**, 269 f., 481, 501 f.; **Vol. 5, Part 2**, 107 f.; **Vol. 6, Part 1**, 185; **Vol. 6, Part 2**, 450; **Vol. 7, Part 1**, 279; **Vol. 8, Part 1**, 186, 377 f., 490 f.; **Vol. 8, Part 2**, 123, 170; **Vol. 9, Part 1**, 119; heraldic, **Vol. 5, Part 2**, 152; historical, **Vol. 2, Part 1**, 574; **Vol. 2, Part 2**, 428 f.; **Vol. 3, Part 1**, 596 f.; **Vol. 3, Part 2**, 340; **Vol. 4, Part 2**, 547; **Vol. 5, Part 1**, 269 f.; **Vol. 6, Part 1**, 196; **Vol. 6, Part 2**, 411, 446; **Vol. 7, Part 1**, 397; **Vol. 7, Part 2**, 349; **Vol. 8, Part 1**, 153 f., 377 f., 490; **Vol. 8, Part 2**, 182, 340; **Vol. 9, Part 2**, 448; **Vol. 10, Part 1**, 12; **Vol. 10, Part 2**, 7 f.; Hudson River school, **Vol. 4, Part 1**, 265; **Vol. 4, Part 2**, 361 f.; Indian, subjects, **Vol. 2, Part 1**, 574; **Vol. 8, Part 2**, 123; **Vol. 9, Part 1**, 513 f.; **Vol. 10, Part 2**, 369; landscape, **Vol. 1, Part 2**, 167, 253, 284, 347; **Vol. 2, Part 1**, 55, 135, 263, 561, 610; **Vol. 2, Part 2**, 18, 101, 270, 290 f., 292 f., 314 f., 327, 501, 566; **Vol. 3, Part 1**, 99 f., 177 f., 392 f., 535 f.; **Vol. 3, Part 2**, 59; **Vol. 4, Part 1**, 196, 264; **Vol. 4, Part 2**, 346, 356, 438; **Vol. 5, Part 1**, 46, 299 f., 487 f.; **Vol. 5, Part 2**, 72, 175 f., 342, 448, 506, 532 f.; **Vol. 6, Part 1**, 54, 210; **Vol. 6, Part 2**, 40, 339, 512, 582, 609, 619; **Vol. 7, Part 1**, 26, 152, 354, 627; **Vol. 7, Part 2**, 193, 278 f., 572, 597; **Vol. 8, Part 1**, 373 f., 559, 638 f.; **Vol. 8, Part 2**, 123, 270, 339, 373; **Vol. 9, Part 1**, 30, 142, 229 f., 306, 341; **Vol. 9, Part 2**, 259, 273 f., 448, 462, 551; **Vol. 10, Part 1**, 23 f.; **Vol. 5, Part 2**, 177, 191, 572, 580; **Supp. 1**, 227, 458; **Supp. 3**, 112; marine, **Vol. 1, Part 2**, 284, 566; **Vol. 4, Part 2**, 377; **Vol. 5, Part 1**, 188 f., 460; **Vol. 5, Part 2**, 494; **Vol. 7, Part 1**, 151 f., 513, 576 f.; **Vol. 8, Part 1**, 296, 472 f., 561; **Vol. 9, Part 1**, 237; military and naval scenes, **Vol. 3, Part 2**, 504; **Vol. 8, Part 1**, 511 f.; **Vol. 9, Part 1**, 371; **Vol. 9, Part 2**, 512 f.; **Vol. 10, Part 2**, 111, 658; miniature, **Vol. 1, Part 1**, 122, 243; **Vol. 1, Part 2**, 284, 479; **Vol. 2, Part 2**, 596 f.; **Vol. 3, Part 1**, 3, 293, 516 f.; **Vol. 3, Part 2**, 495, 603; **Vol. 4, Part 1**, 404; **Vol. 5, Part 1**, 623, **Vol. 5, Part 2**, 506, 557; **Vol. 6, Part 2**, 112, 217, 611; **Vol. 7, Part 2**, 345 f., 347 f., 407; **Vol. 8, Part 1**, 334 f.; **Vol. 8, Part 2**, 21, 305, 603; **Vol. 9, Part 2**, 649; **Vol. 10, Part 2**, 466; mural, **Vol. 2, Part 1**, 3, 185; **Vol. 2, Part 2**, 578; **Vol. 3, Part 2**, 98; **Vol. 4, Part 2**, 59; **Vol. 5, Part 1**, 398; **Vol. 5, Part 2**, 533; **Vol. 6, Part 1**, 14; **Vol. 7, Part 1**, 298; **Vol. 7, Part 2**, 352; **Vol. 8, Part 1**, 479 f.; **Vol. 8, Part 2**, 54, 365; **Vol. 9, Part 1**, 120, 168; **Vol. 10, Part 1**, 59; **Supp. 5**, 112–13, 625; **Supp. 6**, 597; **Supp. 7**, 465, 522–23; **Supp. 8**, 554; **Supp. 9**, 79–80, 91; **Supp. 10**, 182, 560, 832; mural, break wlth Beaux-Arts school, **Supp. 5**, 580; mural, Chicago World's Fair (1893) impetus, **Supp. 2**, 41–42; mural, hotels, **Supp. 8**, 494; mural, public buildings, **Supp. 1**, 254, 515; **Supp. 4**, 204–5, 339; **Supp. 8**, 586; mural, Rockefeller Center, **Supp. 8**, 586; National park subjects, **Vol. 10, Part 2**, 186; Oriental compositions, **Vol. 4, Part 1**, 263; portrait, **Vol. 1, Part 1**, 166, 243, 249, 486, 519, 552; **Vol. 1, Part 2**, 94, 120, 169, 175, 204, 275, 315; **Vol. 2, Part 1**, 145, 510, 574; **Vol. 2, Part 2**, 38, 119, 270, 292 f., 423 f., 478 f.; **Vol. 3, Part 1**, 185 f., 273, 456, 501 f., 516, 535, 553 f., 590, 594, 596, 613; **Vol. 3, Part 2**, 59, 96, 296, 312, 370, 403 f., 448 f., 562; **Vol. 4, Part 1**, 3 f., 404, 517 f., 602; **Vol. 4, Part 2**, 62, 131, 248, 339 f., 481, 590 f.; **Vol. 5, Part 1**, 7, 412, 473, 481, 501 f., 622; **Vol. 5, Part 2**, 72 f., 74, 107 f., 141, 222 f., 401, 506, 557; **Vol. 6, Part 1**, 54, 87 f., 195 f., 343 f., 400, 566; **Vol. 6, Part 2**, 112, 157, 446, 459, 512; **Vol. 7, Part 1**, 247, 294, 396 f., 518 f.; **Vol. 7, Part 2**, 91, 144 f., 344 f., 350 f., 409, 486, 620 f.; **Vol. 8, Part 1**, 83, 153 f., 174 f., 312, 431, 479 f., 490; **Vol. 8, Part 2**, 170, 182, 339, 360, 363, 386 f.; **Vol. 9, Part 1**, 26, 30, 119, 227 f.; **Vol. 9, Part 2**, 91, 108, 399, 452 f., 462, 648; **Vol. 10, Part 1**, 12 f., 654 f.; **Vol. 10, Part 2**, 13, 466, 559; **Supp. 1**, 98, 178; **Supp. 2**, 149, 650; **Supp. 3**, 45–46, 87–88; **Supp. 5**, 50, 112; **Supp. 7**, 67; **Supp. 10**, 112–13; 182; realism, **Vol. 5, Part 2**, 532; **Supp. 9**, 457; **Supp. 10**, 112–13; regional school, **Supp. 9**, 79; seascapes, **Vol. 8, Part 1**, 296; **Supp. 9**, 457; surrealism, **Supp. 10**, 90–91, 220, 505; watercolor, **Vol. 1, Part 2**, 167; **Vol. 2, Part 2**, 314, 566; **Vol. 4, Part 2**, 362; **Vol. 5, Part 2**, 159; **Vol. 10, Part 1**, 70; "white writing," **Supp. 10**, 787. *See also* Art; Oriental art

Palace Theatre (New York City), **Supp. 7**, 282; construction of, **Supp. 2**, 32

Pale Horse, Pale Rider, **Supp. 10**, 641, 642

Paleobotany: **Vol. 6, Part 1**, 188; Latin America, **Supp. 3**, 61–62; research in, **Supp. 1**, 416, 702

Paleography, **Vol. 2, Part 1**, 291; **Vol. 5, Part 2**, 445

Paleontology: **Vol. 1, Part 2**, 127, 492; **Vol. 3, Part 1**, 36; **Vol. 4, Part 1**, 81 f.; **Vol. 4, Part 2**, 136, 273, 436 f., 501; **Vol. 5, Part 1**, 446; **Vol. 5, Part 2**, 33, 472; **Vol. 6, Part 1**, 151, 337; **Vol. 6, Part 2**, 302, 412, 494; **Vol. 7, Part 1**, 445 f., 597; **Vol. 8, Part 1**, 247, 386 f.; **Vol. 9, Part 1**, 289, 482; **Vol. 10, Part 2**, 134, 265, 310, 597; brachiopods, **Supp. 3**, 696; China, **Supp. 4**, 344; collections in American Museum of Natural History, **Vol. 2, Part 2**, 84; **Vol. 4, Part 2**, 4, 37; **Vol. 6, Part 2**, 412; **Vol. 10, Part 2**, 135; dinosaur discoveries, **Supp. 1**, 414–15; **Supp. 3**, 316–17; early Paleozoic formations, **Supp. 3**, 782–83; Foraminifera reclassification, **Supp. 4**, 205–6; fossil collections, **Supp. 1**, 340; fossil vertebrate studies, **Supp. 4**, 729–30; **Supp. 9**, 674–75; teaching of, **Vol. 5, Part 1**, 447; **Vol. 9, Part 1**, 18; Thomas Farm (Fla.), **Supp. 4**, 52; training in, **Supp. 3**, 695–96; vertebrate, **Supp. 1**, 584–87, 743; West Coast (U.S.), **Supp. 3**, 519; writings on, **Vol. 4, Part 2**, 437; **Vol. 5, Part 2**, 473; **Vol. 8, Part 1**, 247; **Vol. 8, Part 2**, 91 f.; **Vol. 10, Part 1**, 480 f.; **Vol. 10, Part 2**, 311; **Supp. 1**, 341; **Supp. 4**, 343–44; **Supp. 5**, 656; **Supp. 9**, 674–75.

Palestine: Anglo-American Committee on, **Supp. 8**, 501–2; Arab-Jewish relaitons, **Supp. 4**, 539–40; archaeologial excavations, **Supp. 2**, 44; **Supp. 3**, 272; Balfour Declaration, **Supp. 4**, 660; exploration, **Vol. 5, Part 1**, 80; **Vol. 7, Part 2**, 150; Jewish commonwealth concept, **Supp. 8**, 549–50; Jewish settlement of, **Supp. 2**, 695; refugees, **Vol. 5, Part 2**, 484; **Vol. 6, Part 1**, 319; UN mediation, **Supp. 9**, 137; writings on, **Vol. 9, Part 2**, 490. *See also* Israel; Zionism

Palestine Economic Corporation, founding of, **Supp. 3**, 97, 279–80

Palestine Institute, establishment of, **Supp. 2**, 16

Palestine Symphony Orchestra. *See* Israel Philharmonic

Paley, William S., references to, **Supp. 9**, 423; **Supp. 10**, 159, 616, 617

Palisades Amusement Park (N.J.), founding of, **Supp. 8**, 576

Palisades Interstate Park, **Vol. 7, Part 2**, 472

Pal Joey, **Supp. 8**, 481; **Supp. 10**, 694

Pallas, naval exploits of, **Vol. 5, Part 2**, 185

Palmer, Alice F., reference to, **Supp. 7**, 83

Palmer, A. Mitchell, references to, **Supp. 3**, 396, 822; **Supp. 4**, 670; **Supp. 9**, 404; **Supp. 10**, 658

Palmer, George Herbert, reference to, **Vol. 5, Part 1**, 207; **Supp. 3**, 608

Palmer, Walter, reference to, **Supp. 3**, 244

Palmer House (Chicago), **Vol. 7, Part 2**, 191

Palmer Memorial Institute, founding of, **Supp. 7**, 83

Palmer raids, **Supp. 9**, 404–5
"Palmer system" in merchandising, **Vol. 7, Part 2**, 191
Palomar Sky Survey, **Supp. 9**, 114
Palomar telescope, **Supp. 5**, 326; **Supp. 9**, 114
"Palooka, Joe" (fictional character), **Supp. 5**, 222
Pammell, Louis H., reference to, **Supp. 3**, 145
Pamphleteering, **Vol. 3, Part 1**, 408 f.; **Vol. 3, Part 2**, 94, 101; **Vol. 4, Part 2**, 610; **Vol. 5, Part 1**, 221 f., 246; **Vol. 5, Part 2**, 386; **Vol. 6, Part 1**, 136; **Vol. 7, Part 2**, 429; **Vol. 9, Part 1**, 365
Pan-African congresses, **Supp. 5**, 436; **Supp. 7**, 203
Panama: diplomacy with U.S., **Supp. 6**, 293; ornithology study, **Supp. 6**, 255
Panama Canal: **Vol. 1, Part 1**, 258; **Vol. 1, Part 2**, 327; **Vol. 3, Part 1**, 463 f., 587 f.; **Vol. 3, Part 2**, 400; **Vol. 4, Part 1**, 89, 355 f.; **Vol. 5, Part 1**, 102, 570; **Vol. 5, Part 2**, 380; **Vol. 6, Part 2**, 538; **Vol. 7, Part 1**, 191, 347, 537; **Vol. 7, Part 2**, 288, 632; **Vol. 8, Part 1**, 359 f.; **Vol. 8, Part 2**, 138, 193; **Vol. 9, Part 1**, 124; **Vol. 10, Part 1**, 372 f.; authorization of, **Supp. 4**, 193; building of, **Vol. 4, Part 1**, 355–56; **Vol. 4, Part 2**, 435, 431; **Vol. 8, Part 2**, 138; **Vol. 9, Part 1**, 124, 349; "Canal ring," **Vol. 9, Part 2**, 540; Canal Zone, organization of government in, **Vol. 3, Part 1**, 116; Chiriqui Isthmus, surveying, **Vol. 5, Part 2**, 14; construction and engineering, **Supp. 1**, 658; **Supp. 3**, 736; Isthmus of Darien, exploration of, **Vol. 9, Part 2**, 122; Isthmus of Tehuantepec, **Vol. 1, Part 2**, 182; **Vol. 3, Part 1**, 587; lock design, **Supp. 3**, 310; medical commission, **Supp. 4**, 790; opposition to, **Vol. 3, Part 1**, 587 f.; Roosevelt, T., and, **Vol. 8, Part 2**, 138; sanitation, **Vol. 3, Part 1**, 78; **Vol. 4, Part 1**, 431; supplies and equipment procurement, **Supp. 8**, 704; treaties, **Supp. 4**, 599; **Supp. 7**, 777; U.S. defense sites, **Supp. 6**, 293; yellow fever, **Vol. 4, Part 1**, 431; writings on, **Vol. 5, Part 2**, 135; **Vol. 8, Part 2**, 194
Panama Canal Commission, **Vol. 4, Part 2**, 353
Panama Canal Co., **Vol. 3, Part 2**, 106; **Vol. 9, Part 2**, 598
Panama libel case, **Vol. 7, Part 1**, 513
Panama-Pacific Exposition (1915): **Vol. 8, Part 1**, 45 f.; landscaping, **Supp. 3**, 490; sculpture, **Supp. 3**, 124
Panama–Pan-American Congress (1826), **Vol. 1, Part 1**, 88; **Vol. 1, Part 2**, 211; **Vol. 2, Part 2**, 177
Panama railroad, **Vol. 1, Part 1**, 194, 396; **Vol. 5, Part 1**, 349; **Vol. 6, Part 1**, 495; **Vol. 7, Part 2**, 209; **Vol. 9, Part 2**, 598, 629; **Supp. 7**, 89
Pan American Airways: **Supp. 6**, 145, 146, 221; **Supp. 8**, 367; air transport pioneered, **Supp. 9**, 725; management and growth of, **Supp. 9**, 337–38; transoceanic service established, **Supp. 9**, 899; *Yankee Clipper* crash, **Supp. 10**, 258
Pan-American Association of Composers, founding of, **Supp. 7**, 756
Pan-American conferences, **Supp. 6**, 207; **Supp. 7**, 718
Pan-American Congress, **Vol. 2, Part 2**, 176
Pan-Americanism, **Vol. 1, Part 2**, 328; **Vol. 6, Part 1**, 8; **Vol. 8, Part 2**, 139; **Vol. 10, Part 2**, 225
Pan-American Medical Congress, **Vol. 7, Part 2**, 454
Pan-American Railway, **Vol. 7, Part 2**, 72
Pan-American Scientific Congress (1908–09), **Supp. 6**, 59
Pan-American Society, founding of, **Supp. 2**, 25
Pan-American Union (Washington, D.C.): administration, **Supp. 2**, 25; **Supp. 4**, 706; architecture, **Supp. 3**, 199; **Vol. 2, Part 2**, 620 f.; **Vol. 3, Part 2**, 572
Pancreas: function, **Supp. 6**, 189, 190; research on, **Supp. 6**, 598, 697; structure of, **Supp. 6**, 53, 100
Paneth, Friedrich ("Fritz"), references to, **Supp. 4**, 337; **Supp. 6**, 334
Pangborn, Clyde, reference to, **Supp. 6**, 52
Panhandle Stockman's Association, **Vol. 4, Part 1**, 394
Panics: **Vol. 2, Part 1**, 471; **Vol. 2, Part 2**, 375; **Vol. 3, Part 1**, 486 f.; **Vol. 4, Part 2**, 393; **Vol. 5, Part 2**, 115, 601; of 1765, **Vol. 8, Part 2**, 46; of 1837, **Vol. 1, Part 1**, 268; **Vol. 9, Part 2**, 19; **Vol. 10, Part 1**, 155; of 1857, **Vol. 2, Part 1**, 212; **Vol. 2, Part 2**, 243; **Vol. 4, Part 2**, 393; **Vol. 5, Part 2**, 69; of 1873, **Vol. 4, Part 1**, 499; **Vol. 4, Part 2**, 450; **Vol. 5, Part 2**, 68; **Vol. 8, Part 1**, 578; **Vol. 9, Part 1**, 86–87; of 1893, **Vol. 2, Part 1**, 495; **Vol. 2, Part 2**, 210; **Vol. 3, Part 2**, 3; **Vol. 9, Part 2**, 88, 425; of 1913, **Vol. 10, Part 2**, 357; "Black Friday," **Vol. 4, Part 1**, 454; "Lawson panic," **Vol. 4, Part 1**, 578
Pankhurst, Emmeline, references to, **Supp. 6**, 40, 41
"Pansy" books, **Supp. 1**, 20
Pantarchy, **Vol. 1, Part 1**, 298
Pantepec Oil Co., **Supp. 8**, 455
Pantheism, **Vol. 5, Part 2**, 457
Pantheon Books, founding of, **Supp. 7**, 799
Pantomimes, **Vol. 3, Part 2**, 566 f.; **Supp. 10**, 115–18
Pantzer, Katharine F., reference to, **Supp. 7**, 387
Paoli, battle of, **Vol. 10, Part 1**, 563
Papanicolaou, George N., reference to, **Supp. 2**, 632
Paper and paper products: bags, making of, **Vol. 2, Part 2**, 575; **Vol. 7, Part 1**, 165; disposable drinking cup, **Supp. 5**, 144; dress patterns, **Vol. 2, Part 1**, 375; manufacture, **Vol. 2, Part 2**, 54, 74 f., 510, 551; **Vol. 3, Part 2**, 250, 357; **Vol. 4, Part 1**, 49; **Vol. 4, Part 2**, 250; **Vol. 5, Part 2**, 281 f.; **Vol. 6, Part 2**, 641; **Vol. 7, Part 2**, 643; **Vol. 8, Part 1**, 534; **Vol. 9, Part 2**, 544; **Vol. 10, Part 2**, 10; **Supp. 10**, 867–68; manufacturing technology, **Supp. 1**, 500; mill, first in colonies, **Vol. 8, Part 1**, 632; mill, first in New England, **Supp. 1**, 392; newspaper manufacture, **Supp. 2**, 301; wood, early experiments with, **Vol. 4, Part 2**, 259
Paperback books: Anchor Books, **Supp. 10**, 46; Little Blue Books, **Supp. 5**, 264–65; Pocket Books, **Supp. 6**, 583; **Supp. 8**, 579; Viking Portable Library, **Supp. 7**, 307
Papers of Benjamin Franklin, The, **Supp. 10**, 430
Papist-Protestant controversy, colonial New York, **Vol. 6, Part 1**, 181
Pap test, development of, **Supp. 2**, 632; **Supp. 7**, 598–99
Parachutes, **Supp. 7**, 679
Paracutin volcano, **Supp. 6**, 213
Parade, **Supp. 7**, 243
Parades (New York City), **Supp. 7**, 779, 780
Paraguay: diplomatic relations with, **Vol. 7, Part 1**, 608; **Vol. 7, Part 2**, 422; **Vol. 9, Part 1**, 136 f.; naval expedition to, **Vol. 8, Part 1**, 596
Paralysis, rehabilitation methods, **Supp. 1**, 317
Paramecium, **Supp. 4**, 910
Paramount Pictures: **Supp. 4**, 350; **Supp. 6**, 76–77, 159, 369; **Supp. 8**, 677–78; **Supp. 10**, 873; distribution deals, **Supp. 10**, 871–72; productions, **Supp. 9**, 856; **Supp. 10**, 515; stars, **Supp. 10**, 872, 873; television production, first film studio to enter, **Supp. 10**, 873; theater chain,
Supp. 9, 62–63; **Supp. 10**, 872
Paramount Theater (New York City), **Supp. 10**, 872; stage-band policy, **Supp. 7**, 301
Parapsychology. *See* Psychic phenomena
Parasitology: **Vol. 6, Part 1**, 151; **Vol. 7, Part 1**, 542; intestinal disease research, **Supp. 4**, 462; research in, **Supp. 1**, 666; syphilis research, **Supp. 4**, 288; writings on, **Supp. 3**, 802–3
Parathyroid gland, **Supp. 3**, 483
"Parchesi," invention of, **Vol. 6, Part 1**, 479
Parc National Albert (Congo), **Supp. 8**, 3
Parents' Magazine, **Supp. 6**, 382

Parent-Teacher Associations, early, **Vol. 2, Part 1**, 345
Parepa-Rosa Opera Company, **Vol. 8, Part 2**, 92
Paresthesia, early description of, **Vol. 8, Part 1**, 282 f.
Pareto, Vilfredo, reference to, **Supp. 3**, 351
Pari-mutual betting law, **Supp. 1**, 114
Paris: American chapel, **Vol. 5, Part 2**, 428; American Embassy, purchase of, **Vol. 4, Part 2**, 588; art scene, **Supp. 6**, 552; **Supp. 10**, 112, 219–20, 504; expatriates in, **Supp. 4**, 768–70; 771; **Supp. 6**, 497–98, 716; **Supp. 7**, 40–41, 334–36, 560; **Supp. 8**, 656; international exposition at, **Vol. 1, Part 1**, 445; literary scene, **Supp. 10**, 582; newspaper, first American, **Vol. 3, Part 2**, 212; traffic regulation, **Supp. 3**, 254; World War II liberation, **Supp. 7**, 350
Paris 'Ninety, **Supp. 10**, 740
Paris, Treaty of (1783), **Vol. 1, Part 1**, 77; **Vol. 3, Part 2**, 594–95; **Vol. 5, Part 2**, 7, 21; **Vol. 6, Part 1**, 35; **Vol. 8, Part 1**, 355
Paris, Treaty of (1898), **Vol. 3, Part 1**, 110, 164; **Vol. 4, Part 1**, 52, 516; **Vol. 6, Part 2**, 108; **Vol. 8, Part 1**, 485
Paris Herald, **Supp. 4**, 686
Paris Peace Conference (1919): **Vol. 1, Part 2**, 138; **Supp. 7**, 262, 683, 687–88, 782; **Supp. 8**, 146, 495; financial adviser, **Supp. 3**, 219; German reparations, **Supp. 4**, 470; Jewish delegations committee, **Supp. 3**, 489
Park, Edwards A., reference to, **Supp. 3**, 775
Park, Robert E., references to, **Supp. 4**, 831; **Supp. 6**, 321, 532, 533
Park, Roy H., reference to, **Supp. 6**, 292
Park, amusement, first in U.S., **Vol. 10, Part 1**, 48
Park College, founding of, **Vol. 6, Part 1**, 542
Parker, Charlie, reference to, **Supp. 9**, 11
Parker, Dorothy, references to, **Supp. 3**, 53; **Supp. 6**, 259; **Supp. 7**, 413; **Supp. 8**, 529
Parker, Francis Wayland, reference to, **Supp. 5**, 60–61
Parker, George, reference to, **Supp. 9**, 601
Parker, George H., reference to, **Supp. 3**, 133
Parker, James Reid, reference to, **Supp. 4**, 386
Parker, John J., reference to, **Supp. 3**, 559
Parker, Theodore: references to, **Vol. 5, Part 2**, 404; **Vol. 6, Part 1**, 387; **Vol. 7, Part 1**, 587; **Supp. 5**, 138; biography of, **Vol. 10, Part 1**, 615 f.
Parker, Thomas A., references to, **Supp. 10**, 648, 649
Parker Brothers, founding and growth of, **Supp. 9**, 601
Parkes, Alexander, reference to, **Vol. 5, Part 1**, 448
Parkes process, **Vol. 1, Part 1**, 528
Parkhurst, Charles H., references to, **Vol. 5, Part 1**, 573; **Vol. 7, Part 1**, 280; **Vol. 8, Part 2**, 521
Parking meter, **Supp. 9**, 246
Parkman, Francis, references to, **Vol. 7, Part 1**, 569; **Vol. 9, Part 1**, 47; **Vol. 9, Part 2**, 405; **Supp. 5**, 430
Parkman, George, reference to, **Vol. 10, Part 1**, 592 f.
Parks, William, reference to, **Vol. 7, Part 1**, 596
Parks: commercial use, opposition to, **Supp. 10**, 191; landscape architecture, **Supp. 3**, 490–91; **Supp. 5**, 369–70; **Supp. 6**, 485–86; municipal facilities, **Supp. 3**, 217; national, **Vol. 2, Part 2**, 78; **Vol. 4, Part 2**, 86, 439 f.; **Vol. 5, Part 1**, 492 f.; **Vol. 5, Part 2**, 492 f.; **Vol. 6, Part 1**, 495; **Vol. 6, Part 2**, 399; **Vol. 8, Part 2**, 355; **Supp. 2**, 348; **Supp. 4**, 896; national, development of, **Supp. 2**, 265; **Supp. 4**, 522; national, in Hawaii, **Supp. 5**, 361; national, legislation, **Supp. 7**, 764; national, maps of, **Supp. 4**, 558; national, Rocky Mountain, **Supp. 1**, 555; national, wilderness system, **Supp. 7**, 814; National Park Service, **Supp. 6**, 486; New York City, **Supp. 4**, 213; playgrounds, **Supp. 1**, 595; public, **Vol. 1, Part 1**, 50 f.; **Vol. 1, Part 2**, 408; **Vol. 3, Part 2**, 56, 70; **Vol. 4, Part 2**, 5; **Vol. 5, Part 1**, 250; **Vol. 6, Part 2**, 492; **Vol. 7, Part 1**, 315; **Vol. 7, Part 2**, 25 f., 30, 117, 197, 472, 482, 600; **Vol. 8, Part 1**, 157 f., 405; **Vol. 8, Part 2**, 37, 220, 355, 464; **Vol. 9, Part 1**, 151, 545; **Vol. 9, Part 2**, 123; **Vol. 10, Part 1**, 647; public, Baltimore, **Vol. 6, Part 1**, 27; public, Boston, **Vol. 7, Part 2**, 26 f.; public, Brooklyn, **Vol. 9, Part 2**, 123; public, Chicago, **Vol. 2, Part 1**, 306; public, District of Columbia, **Vol. 8, Part 1**, 979; public, New York City, **Supp. 4**, 213; public, Philadelphia, **Vol. 10, Part 1**, 647; urban, **Supp. 5**, 630; wilderness and wildlife preserves, **Supp. 4**, 483; **Supp. 8**, 486
Parkway Community House (Chicago), **Supp. 8**, 80
Parliamentary procedure, **Vol. 5, Part 2**, 26; **Supp. 1**, 631
Parmly, Eleazer, reference to, **Vol. 2, Part 1**, 155
Parochial schools: **Vol. 3, Part 1**, 562 f.; **Vol. 4, Part 2**, 415; **Vol. 8, Part 2**, 596; busing, **Supp. 5**, 358; desegregation, **Supp. 8**, 537; development of, **Supp. 3**, 393; **Supp. 4**, 334–35; **Supp. 7**, 533; federal aid issue, **Supp. 8**, 25, 115–16; free high schools, **Supp. 5**, 179
Parole system, **Supp. 1**, 228; beginnings of, **Vol. 10, Part 2**, 385
Parran, Thomas, reference to, **Supp. 6**, 460
Parrington, Vernon L., reference to, **Supp. 4**, 63
Parsons, Elsie Clews, reference to, **Supp. 4**, 71
Parsons, Frank, reference to, **Supp. 2**, 45
Parsons, Lucy A., reference to, **Vol. 7, Part 1**, 252
Parsons, Louella, reference to, **Supp. 8**, 281, 282
Parsons, Thomas William, reference to, **Vol. 5, Part 1**, 273
Parsons School of Design (New York City), **Supp. 9**, 587, 588
Parthenon (Athens), reconstruction financing, **Supp. 2**, 185
Parties. *See* Entertaining
Partisan Review: **Supp. 7**, 80, 239; founding of, **Supp. 7**, 269; founding and growth of, **Supp. 9**, 637
Pascin, Jules, reference to, **Supp. 3**, 292
Passavant Memorial Hospital, **Supp. 5**, 302
Passionist Order, establishment of, **Vol. 7, Part 1**, 619
Pasteur effect and reaction (glucose metabolization), **Supp. 6**, 595
Pasteurization: beer, **Supp. 1**, 142; milk, **Vol. 8, Part 2**, 553; **Supp. 2**, 315, 514; **Supp. 5**, 144
Past Forgetting: My Love Affair with Dwight D. Eisenhower, **Supp. 9**, 783
Pastor, Tony, references to, **Vol. 7, Part 2**, 290; **Supp. 2**, 661
Pastorius Colony (Pa.), **Vol. 5, Part 1**, 80
Patch, Alexander, III, reference to, **Supp. 3**, 583
Patent for Prospective Emigrants to America, **Vol. 3, Part 1**, 5
"Patent leather," first factory for, in America, **Vol. 1, Part 2**, 529
Patent medicine: **Vol. 1, Part 1**, 413, 450; **Vol. 3, Part 1**, 586 f.; **Supp. 5**, 143; advertisements for, **Vol. 8, Part 2**, 197; manufacture of, **Vol. 7, Part 2**, 624 f.
Patent Office, United States, **Vol. 5, Part 2**, 203; **Vol. 7, Part 2**, 136, 351
Patents: cheese-processing litigation, **Supp. 5**, 400; copying machine development, **Supp. 8**, 71; Edison litigation, **Supp. 1**, 280; Ford infringement suit, **Supp. 4**, 295–96; government supervision, **Vol. 3, Part 2**, 110, 228; **Vol. 5, Part 2**, 33, 203; **Vol. 6, Part 1**, 146 f.; **Vol. 7, Part 2**, 136, 149, 351; **Vol. 8, Part 1**, 2 f.; law, **Vol. 1, Part 2**, 360; **Vol. 2, Part 2**, 481, 613 f.; **Vol. 3, Part 1**, 288; **Vol. 4, Part 2**, 249, 590; **Vol. 5, Part 2**, 41, 464 f.; **Vol. 6, Part 1**, 27; **Vol. 8, Part 1**, 75 f., 504 f.; **Vol. 8, Part 2**, 106, 567; **Vol. 9, Part 1**, 614; **Vol. 9, Part 2**, 99; **Supp. 1**, 703; movie industry suit, **Supp. 4**, 734; radio and wireless transmission suits, **Supp. 4**, 452; **Supp. 5**, 21; **Supp. 7**,

177; streptomycin royalties suit, **Supp. 9**, 834. *See also fields of patents*
Patents, Bureau of, **Vol. 7, Part 2**, 149
Paterson, N.J., early history of, **Vol. 3, Part 1**, 290
Paterson, **Supp. 7**, 790–91
"Paterson's Practice Laws," **Vol. 7, Part 2**, 294
Paterson Strike Pageant (1913), **Supp. 7**, 486
Path, theosophical monthly, **Vol. 5, Part 2**, 233
Pathfinder, **Supp. 7**, 615
Pathological Institute (New York City), **Supp. 4**, 571
Pathology: **Vol. 2, Part 1**, 260; **Vol. 3, Part 1**, 77 f., 208; **Vol. 3, Part 2**, 320 f., 433; **Vol. 4, Part 2**, 44 f.; **Vol. 5, Part 2**, 306; **Vol. 7, Part 2**, 208, 354 f.; **Vol. 8, Part 1**, 252 f., 391, 404; **Vol. 9, Part 2**, 23; **Vol. 10, Part 1**, 493 f., 621 f.; blood culture studies, **Supp. 4**, 494; cancer, **Supp. 3**, 257–58; chemical aspects of, **Supp. 3**, 806–7; early books on, **Vol. 5, Part 1**, 233; **Vol. 9, Part 2**, 23; etiological disease classification, **Supp. 3**, 483; forensic, **Supp. 10**, 328–29; frozen-tissue diagnostic method, **Supp. 3**, 832; histologic, **Supp. 3**, 502–3; hospital teaching, **Supp. 1**, 206; **Supp. 3**, 502–3; immunology research, **Supp. 4**, 287–88; plant, **Supp. 3**, 814–15; radiation studies, **Supp. 10**, 816; surgical, **Supp. 1**, 91; **Supp. 6**, 664; tuberculosis and silicosis studies, **Supp. 4**, 314; typhus research, **Supp. 4**, 667–68; writings on, **Vol. 3, Part 1**, 306; **Vol. 8, Part 1**, 252 f.
Pathological Society: New York, **Vol. 7, Part 2**, 505; Philadelphia, **Vol. 3, Part 1**, 24; **Vol. 7, Part 2**, 129
Patman, Wright, reference to, **Supp. 6**, 90
Paton, Alan, reference to, **Supp. 5**, 419
Paton, R. Townley, reference to, **Supp. 7**, 70
Patowmack Co., **Vol. 5, Part 2**, 122
Patri, Angelo, reference to, **Supp. 5**, 237
Patrick, Mason M., references to, **Supp. 3**, 17; **Supp. 8**, 47, 185
Patriotic Gore, **Supp. 9**, 876
"Patriot-printer of 1776," **Vol. 1, Part 2**, 564
Patriots, The, **Vol. 3, Part 2**, 17; **Vol. 7, Part 1**, 326
Patriot War (1838–39). *See* Aroostook War
Patten, Simon Nelson, reference to, **Vol. 8, Part 2**, 531; **Supp. 4**, 227
"Patten Men," **Vol. 7, Part 2**, 299
Patterns, **Supp. 9**, 381
Patterns of Culture, **Supp. 4**, 71–72, 73
Patterson, Eleanor Medill ("Cissy"), references to, **Supp. 4**, 645; **Supp. 7**, 603; **Supp. 8**, 282, 496
Patterson, Ellen, reference to, **Supp. 6**, 318
Patterson, Floyd, Liston heavyweight championship bout, **Supp. 9**, 507
Patterson, John H., references to, **Supp. 6**, 332, 674
Patterson, Joseph Medill, references to, **Supp. 4**, 644; **Supp. 5**, 449; **Supp. 6**, 699; **Supp. 7**, 603
Patterson, Malcolm R., references to, **Supp. 1**, 656; **Supp. 3**, 449
Patterson, Robert P., reference to, **Supp. 6**, 437
Patterson, Robert W., reference to, **Supp. 5**, 449
Patton, Charley, reference to, **Supp. 6**, 274–75
Patton, George S., references to, **Supp. 3**, 583; **Supp. 4**, 857; **Supp. 8**, 497
Paul, Alice, references to, **Supp. 4**, 157; **Supp. 6**, 41; **Supp. 7**, 717, 718; **Supp. 9**, 641
Paul, John R., reference to, **Supp. 3**, 775
Paul, Les, references to, **Supp. 10**, 251, 252
Paul, Maury, reference to, **Supp. 7**, 752
Pauley, Edwin W., reference to, **Supp. 5**, 343; **Supp. 9**, 646
Pauli, Wolfgang, reference to, **Supp. 5**, 219–20; **Supp. 10**, 288
"Pauline system," **Vol. 9, Part 2**, 345
Pauling, Linus, reference to, **Supp. 8**, 590; **Supp. 9**, 550
Paulist Order, **Vol. 4, Part 2**, 604; **Vol. 6, Part 1**, 15; **Supp. 6**, 237–38
Paulist Press, founding of, **Supp. 2**, 72
Paul Revere and the World He Lived In, **Supp. 8**, 181
Paulus Hook, battle of, **Vol. 1, Part 1**, 176; **Vol. 1, Part 2**, 356; **Vol. 6, Part 1**, 107; **Vol. 10, Part 1**, 518
Paving, **Vol. 8, Part 1**, 442
Pavlov, I. P., reference to, **Supp. 5**, 329
Pavlova, Anna, references to, **Supp. 3**, 282; **Supp. 5**, 74–75; **Supp. 8**, 670
Pawnee Indians, **Vol. 7, Part 1**, 560; **Supp. 2**, 265; **Supp. 3**, 460
Pawnee (ship), **Vol. 1, Part 1**, 528
Pawtucket, R.I., founding of, **Vol. 5, Part 2**, 40, **Vol. 9, Part 1**, 206; **Vol. 10, Part 2**, 222
Parton, Frederic Logan, references to, **Supp. 6**, 6; **Supp. 8**, 59
Payne, Oliver H., reference to, **Supp. 2**, 570
Payne, William H., reference to, **Supp. 3**, 328
Payne-Aldrich Tariff Act (1909), **Vol. 1, Part 2**, 232; **Vol. 7, Part 2**, 331; **Vol. 9, Part 2**, 269; **Supp. 3**, 464
Payola scandal, **Supp. 7**, 267
Peabody, George, references to, **Vol. 5, Part 1**, 214; **Vol. 8, Part 2**, 537
Peabody, Mass., **Vol. 7, Part 2**, 337
Peabody Award, first writer to win, **Supp. 9**, 710
Peabody College, founding of, **Supp. 2**, 518
Peabody Educational Fund, **Vol. 2, Part 2**, 606; **Vol. 7, Part 2**, 57, 337; **Vol. 8, Part 2**, 537 f.
Peabody Museum of Natural History (New Haven, Conn.), **Supp. 4**, 520–21
Peabody Normal College (Tenn.), **Vol. 8, Part 1**, 93 f.
Peace, international: **Vol. 1, Part 2**, 91, 332; **Vol. 2, Part 1**, 23, 195; **Vol. 2, Part 2**, 482, 595; **Vol. 3, Part 2**, 300; **Vol. 5, Part 1**, 346; **Vol. 5, Part 2**, 73, 213; **Vol. 6, Part 1**, 199, 202, 287, 348, 431; **Vol. 7, Part 1**, 456; **Vol. 7, Part 2**, 426; **Vol. 8, Part 1**, 161 f., 477; **Vol. 9, Part 1**, 231, 446; **Vol. 10, Part 1**, 6; **Vol. 10, Part 2**, 91; American Peace Award, **Supp. 1**, 93; American Peace Society, **Vol. 3, Part 1**, 345; **Vol. 5, Part 2**, 527; arbitration movement, **Supp. 1**, 53; Bok Peace Prize, **Vol. 6, Part 1**, 199; Byrd Associates, **Supp. 6**, 93; Carnegie Endowment, **Supp. 3**, 366; Church Peace Union, **Supp. 6**, 25; Ford Peace Ship, **Vol. 5, Part 2**, 180; Gandhi Prize, **Supp. 8**, 680; Hague Peace Conference, **Vol. 2, Part 2**, 85; **Vol. 7, Part 1**, 456; **Vol. 10, Part 2**, 91; journalistic advocacy, **Supp. 4**, 850–52; Kellogg-Briand Pact, **Supp. 7**, 112, 113, 688; League for Industrial Democracy, **Supp. 6**, 392; League of Nations, **Vol. 3, Part 1**, 265; **Vol. 9, Part 1**, 45; **Vol. 4, Part 2**, 254; **Vol. 5, Part 2**, 217, 267, 610; **Vol. 6, Part 1**, 199 f., 348; **Vol. 7, Part 1**, 44; **Vol. 8, Part 1**, 92 f.; **Vol. 10, Part 2**, 183, 364; League of Universal Brotherhood, **Vol. 2, Part 1**, 329; League to Enforce Peace, **Supp. 3**, 472–74; London Naval Conference, **Vol. 7, Part 1**, 235; movements and organizations, **Supp. 2**, 107–8; **Supp. 3**, 323; **Supp. 4**, 157; **Supp. 4**, 539, 550; **Supp. 9**, 641; **Supp. 10**, 176, 208–9; Nobel Prize, **Supp. 1**, 112; **Supp. 2**, 357, 580; **Supp. 4**, 137, 442; **Supp. 5**, 160, 335, 508; **Supp. 6**, 428; **Supp. 7**, 29; **Supp. 8**, 335; outlawry of war, **Supp. 3**, 457; Pan-American Congress, **Vol. 2, Part 2**, 176; Pan-American Union, **Vol. 2, Part 2**, 620 f.; **Vol. 3, Part 2**, 572; Paris Peace Conference, **Vol. 1, Part 2**, 138; **Vol. 6, Part 2**, 327; **Vol. 10, Part 2**, 103; Peace Association of Friends in America, **Vol. 9, Part 2**, 444; peace societies, **Vol. 3, Part 1**, 345, 357; **Vol. 10, Part 2**, 529; philanthropy to promote, **Supp. 5**, 61; radical organizations, **Supp. 8**, 457–58; religious advocacy, **Supp. 4**, 837; **Supp. 7**, 356–57; **Supp. 8**, 184; Washington Conference (1921), **Vol. 8, Part 1**, 103 f.; **Vol. 8, Part 2**,

155; women's movement for, **Supp. 1**, 12, 432–33, 157, 912–13; **Supp. 5**, 474; **Supp. 7**, 29; **Supp. 8**, 241; World Court, **Vol. 4, Part 2**, 255; **Vol. 5, Part 1**, 156; **Vol. 6, Part 1**, 349; world federation movement, **Supp. 5**, 308; world organization advocacy, **Supp. 8**, 87–88, 650–51; World Peace Foundation, **Vol. 4, Part 1**, 317; World's Peace Conference, 1849, **Vol. 7, Part 2**, 404; *See also* Arms control and disarmament; Conscientious objectors; Pacifism
Peace Corps, **Supp. 7**, 421
Peace Information Center, **Supp. 7**, 204
"Peacemakers," founding of, **Vol. 8, Part 1**, 273 f.
Peace Mission Movement (religious group), founding of, **Supp. 7**, 187–88
Peace of Mind, **Supp. 4**, 494–95
Peacock, Eulace, reference to, **Supp. 10**, 610
Peale, Norman Vincent, reference to, **Supp. 5**, 527
Peanuts, crop development, **Supp. 3**, 146
Pearce, Richard Mills, reference to, **Supp. 3**, 74
Pea Ridge, Ark., battle of. *See* Elkhorn Tavern
Pearl, Raymond, reference to, **Supp. 4**, 425
Pearl Harbor attack (1941): **Supp. 3**, 660; **Supp. 4**, 305, 821; **Supp. 6**, 437; **Supp. 7**, 303; **Supp. 8**, 42; investigation of, **Supp. 4**, 685–86, 745; **Supp. 5**, 335, 502, 576; **Supp. 6**, 629; **Supp. 7**, 72, 813; **Supp. 8**, 331; writings on, **Supp. 8**, 441
Pearl River, La., expedition, **Vol. 1, Part 1**, 500, 579; **Vol. 5, Part 2**, 425
Pearson, Drew, references to, **Supp. 4**, 685; **Supp. 5**, 337–38; **Supp. 8**, 649; **Supp. 9**, 241
Pearson, F. S., reference to, **Supp. 4**, 80–81
Pearson, William Earl, reference to, **Supp. 7**, 68
Peary, Marie Ahnighito, references to, **Supp. 5**, 539, 540
Peary, Robert E., references to, **Vol. 2, Part 1**, 37; **Vol. 5, Part 2**, 256; **Supp. 2**, 115–16; **Supp. 5**, 295, 539–40
Peat, formation of, **Vol. 6, Part 1**, 188
Peay, Austin, reference to, **Supp. 3**, 449
Peck, James Hawkins, trial of, **Vol. 7, Part 2**, 379
Peck, Thomas Handasyde, reference to, **Vol. 7, Part 1**, 361
Peckinpah, Sam, reference to, **Supp. 10**, 239
Peck's Bad Boy, **Vol. 7, Part 2**, 377
Pecora, Ferdinand, reference to, **Supp. 5**, 745
Pecos Conference in Southwestern Archaeology, first, **Supp. 7**, 432
Pedagogy, first university chair in U.S., **Vol. 7, Part 2**, 332
Pediatrics: **Vol. 2, Part 2**, 2 77; **Vol. 5, Part 1**, 183, 313, 563; **Vol. 6, Part 2**, 506; **Vol. 9, Part 1**, 294, 533; child care, popular writings on, **Supp. 7**, 427–28; child development, **Supp. 4**, 7–8; **Supp. 7**, 284; first modern, **Supp. 3**, 189–90; hospitals, **Supp. 3**, 74–75; **Supp. 5**, 1–2; infant nutrition, **Supp. 2**, 432; infectious disease studies, **Supp. 3**, 775; neurology, **Supp. 3**, 682; practitioner, early, **Vol. 8, Part 2**, 185; social problems, **Supp. 3**, 159; teaching of, **Supp. 3**, 526; writings on, **Vol. 8, Part 2**, 186; **Supp. 1**, 643–44; **Supp. 3**, 101. *See also* Children
Pediments, **Supp. 4**, 118
Pedology. *See* Soils
Peek, George N., reference to, **Supp. 3**, 720
Peekskill, N.Y., Robeson riots, **Supp. 10**, 679–80
Pennemünde (Germany), World War II rocket research, **Supp. 10**, 65–66
Pegler, Westbrook, references to, **Supp. 7**, 369, 370, 643, 718
Peg o' My Heart, **Supp. 4**, 822
Pei, I. M., reference to, **Supp. 10**, 867
Peiping Union Medical College, **Vol. 10, Part 1**, 621 f.
Peirce, Benjamin, reference to, **Supp. 3**, 469
Peirce, Charles S., references to, **Vol. 5, Part 1**, 598; **Supp. 4**, 169; **Supp. 7**, 471
Peirce, Hayford, reference to, **Supp. 5**, 700
Peking, China. *See* Boxer Rebellion
Peking Man, **Supp. 4**, 867
Peking Post, **Vol. 8, Part 1**, 477
Peking Union Medical College, **Supp. 4**, 346–47; **Supp. 4**, 867
Peking University, **Vol. 6, Part 1**, 477
Pellagra, **Supp. 7**, 223
Pelletier, Joseph C., reference to, **Supp. 7**, 98
Pemberton, Brock, reference to, **Supp. 4**, 653
Penal system. *See* Prisons
Pencil manufacture, **Vol. 1, Part 2**, 407; **Vol. 3, Part 1**, 329; **Vol. 3, Part 2**, 241 f.; **Vol. 9, Part 2**, 491, 494
Penck, Walther, reference to, **Supp. 4**, 119
Pendergast, Thomas J., references to, **Supp. 3**, 621; **Supp. 4**, 613; **Supp. 5**, 114; **Supp. 9**, 756, 757, 809–10, 847
Pendergast machine, **Supp. 3**, 621
Pendleton, Benjamin, reference to, **Vol. 7, Part 2**, 190
Pendleton Act, drafting of, **Vol. 3, Part 1**, 607 f.
Penfield, W. G., reference to, **Supp. 4**, 59
Penicillin: manufacture of, **Supp. 6**, 224, 447; synthesis of, **Supp. 5**, 28; **Supp. 10**, 852, 853; syphilis treatment, **Supp. 6**, 424, 460
Peninsular campaign, **Vol. 2, Part 1**, 360; **Vol. 2, Part 2**, 463; **Vol. 3, Part 1**, 598; **Vol. 3, Part 2**, 602; **Vol. 4, Part 2**, 505; **Vol. 5, Part 1**, 25, 27, 343, 366, 371, 558; **Vol. 6, Part 1**, 123, 391, 583; **Vol. 6, Part 2**, 205; **Vol. 7, Part 2**, 308; **Vol. 8, Part 1**, 90; **Vol. 9, Part 2**, 170, 215; **Vol. 10, Part 1**, 473; **Vol. 10, Part 2**, 137; *See also* Seven Days' Battles
Penmanship, **Vol. 9, Part 1**, 452
Penn, William, references to, **Vol. 5, Part 2**, 290; **Vol. 6, Part 1**, 329, 334, 361; **Vol. 6, Part 2**, 286; **Vol. 9, Part 1**, 115; **Vol. 9, Part 2**, 131, 155, 554
Pennamite War, **Vol. 5, Part 2**, 47, 56 f.
Penn Central Co., securities scandal, **Supp. 10**, 454
Penn Club, **Vol. 8, Part 2**, 7
Pennell, Joseph, reference to, **Vol. 9, Part 2**, 322
Penney J. C.: founding and early growth of, **Supp. 9**, 609; management, **Supp. 10**, 354–55; partnership system, **Supp. 10**, 353–54; reference to, **Supp. 8**, 505; stock market crash (1929) effect on, **Supp. 9**, 610
Penn Fruit Co., founding of, **Supp. 7**, 141
Pennington, Ann, reference to, **Supp. 8**, 694, 695
Pennsylvania: agriculture, **Vol. 8, Part 1**, 143 f.; **Vol. 8, Part 2**, 9; **Vol. 10, Part 1**, 556 f.; anti-Masonic movement, **Vol. 7, Part 2**, 450; antiquarian studies, **Vol. 10, Part 1**, 546; archives, first volumes of printed, **Vol. 10, Part 1**, 104; "Black Cockade" forces, **Vol. 6, Part 1**, 154; boundaries, **Vol. 1, Part 2**, 17; **Vol. 5, Part 2**, 42, 47; **Vol. 8, Part 1**, 82 f.; "Buckshot War," **Vol. 8, Part 1**, 629; "Cameron Machine," **Vol. 2, Part 1**, 436; canal building in, **Vol. 5, Part 2**, 521; capitol building sculptures, **Supp. 2**, 22; Catholic church, **Vol. 4, Part 1**, 527; **Vol. 4, Part 2**, 250; **Vol. 6, Part 1**, 161; **Vol. 6, Part 2**, 59; **Vol. 7, Part 1**, 619; **Vol. 10, Part 2**, 632; coal industry, **Vol. 3, Part 1**, 306; **Vol. 7, Part 2**, 305; *Colonial Records*, **Vol. 4, Part 2**, 472; colonial service, **Vol. 5, Part 1**, 44, 159; **Vol. 6, Part 1**, 485–86; **Vol. 6, Part 2**, 286; **Vol. 7, Part 1**, 256–57; colonization, **Vol. 5, Part 2**, 47 f.; **Vol. 6, Part 1**, 161; Connecticut, relations with, **Vol. 1, Part 2**, 566; Constitution, adoption of federal, **Vol. 7, Part 1**, 312; corn mills in, **Vol. 8, Part 1**, 273 f.; debts, imprisonment for, abolished, **Vol. 6, Part 1**, 211; Democratic party, **Vol. 2, Part 1**, 226; **Vol. 8, Part 2**, 104; **Vol. 9, Part 1**, 189; **Supp. 9**, 236, 253; education, **Vol. 1, Part 2**, 53; **Vol. 2, Part 1**, 335; **Vol.**

3, Part 1, 416 f.; Vol. 7, Part 2, 446; Vol. 8, Part 1, 49 f., 71, 175 f., 203 f., 257 f.; Vol. 8, Part 2, 416; Vol. 9, Part 1, 621 f.; Vol. 10, Part 1, 556 f.; Vol. 10, Part 2, 179; Episcopal church, Vol. 8, Part 1, 124 f., 249; Federalism v. Jeffersonianism, Vol. 8, Part 2, 178; Federalism v. Republicanism, Vol. 4, Part 2, 521; financial history, Vol. 3, Part 2, 309; Vol. 7, Part 1, 504; Vol. 9, Part 1, 141; first woman cabinet officer, Supp. 6, 515; flood control, Vol. 8, Part 2, 188; folk poems, Vol. 4, Part 2, 237; forestry, Vol. 8, Part 2, 188; founding of, Vol. 7, Part 2, 433 f.; French control, loss of in western, Vol. 8, Part 1, 113 f.; frontier life in western, Vol. 1, Part 2, 481; Vol. 4, Part 2, 314; Vol. 9, Part 2, 476; Vol. 10, Part 2, 132; geological survey in, Supp. 3, 38; geology, Vol. 1, Part 2, 448; Vol. 6, Part 1, 184; German Reformed Church, Vol. 8, Part 2, 227, 436; German settlers in, Vol. 6, Part 1, 292; Vol. 7, Part 2, 108 f.; Vol. 8, Part 2, 447; governors, Vol. 1, Part 2, 112 f., 264; Vol. 2, Part 2, 606 f.; Vol. 4, Part 1, 203 f.; Vol. 5, Part 1, 10; Vol. 5, Part 2, 292; Vol. 6, Part 2, 606 f.; Vol. 7, Part 1, 225 f.; Vol. 7, Part 2, 447 f.; Vol. 8, Part 1, 49 f., 629 f.; Vol. 9, Part 1, 140 f., 389 f., 484 f.; Vol. 9, Part 2, 431; Vol. 10, Part 2, 446 f.; Supp. 4, 665; Supp. 8, 143–44; Supp. 9, 235, 236, 253–54, 426–27; Supp. 10, 241–42; historian, state, Vol. 1, Part 2, 53; history of, Vol. 3, Part 2, 455; Vol. 4, Part 2, 472; Vol. 5, Part 2, 46; Vol. 7, Part 1, 83; Vol. 7, Part 2, 519; Vol. 8, Part 1, 113 f., 247 f., 273 f.; Vol. 8, Part 2, 226; Vol. 10, Part 1, 614 f.; "Hot Water War," Vol. 4, Part 1, 34; Indians, relations with, Vol. 4, Part 2, 336; Vol. 8, Part 1, 113 f.; Vol. 8, Part 1, 129 f.; Vol. 9, Part 2, 431; Vol. 10, Part 1, 614 f.; industrial service, Vol. 3, Part 1, 306; Vol. 8, Part 1, 89; journalism in, Vol. 6, Part 1, 593; Vol. 7, Part 1, 23; judiciary, Supp. 7, 500; Supp. 8, 456; Supp. 10, 241; land claims, Vol. 3, Part 1, 581 f.; Vol. 5, Part 1, 359; land speculation, Vol. 8, Part 1, 129 f.; Vol. 8, Part 2, 178; legal service, Vol. 1, Part 2, 311, 491, 545, 566; Vol. 2, Part 1, 602; Vol. 2, Part 2, 64; Vol. 3, Part 1, 290, 525; Vol. 4, Part 2, 262; Vol. 5, Part 1, 223, 466; Vol. 6, Part 1, 211, 219, 225, 329; Vol. 6, Part 2, 80, 342, 547; Vol. 7, Part 1, 49; Vol. 7, Part 2, 447, 509, 518; Vol. 8, Part 1, 49, 273 f., 401, 427, 449, 462; Vol. 8, Part 2, 177, 589; Vol. 9, Part 1, 28, 115, 118; Vol. 10, Part 1, 374 f., 556 f.; Vol. 10, Part 2, 606; "Little New Deal," Supp. 9, 253, 254, 426; loyalty oaths required of state employees, Supp. 10, 242; Lutheran church, Vol. 3, Part 1, 20, 232; Vol. 4, Part 2, 515, 538; Vol. 5, Part 2, 502; Vol. 6, Part 2, 52; Vol. 7, Part 1, 306 f.; map, early, Vol. 5, Part 1, 160; Masons, Vol. 8, Part 2, 282; medical service, Vol. 4, Part 2, 369; Vol. 6, Part 2, 626; military organizations in, Vol. 1, Part 2, 413; minerals and ores of, Vol. 1, Part 2, 530; missions in, Vol. 4, Part 1, 527; Vol. 4, Part 2, 510 f.; Vol. 5, Part 2, 514; Vol. 6, Part 1, 161 f.; Moravian church, Vol. 10, Part 2, 658; National Guard of, Vol. 8, Part 2, 104; navy of, Vol. 8, Part 1, 430; newspaper, first published in, Vol. 1, Part 2, 553; oil, discovery of, Vol. 3, Part 1, 427 f.; Vol. 6, Part 1, 340; Vol. 8, Part 1, 168 f.; oil production, Vol. 2, Part 1, 496; Vol. 6, Part 1, 184, Vol. 8, Part 2, 95; Vol. 10, Part 2, 107; Supp. 4, 568; Pastorius colony, Vol. 5, Part 1, 80; Pennamite War, Vol. 5, Part 2, 47, 56 f.; philanthropy, Vol. 7, Part 2, 305 f., 550; Vol. 8, Part 1, 139 f., 488 f.; political service, Vol. 1, Part 2, 113, 240, 244, 245, 280, 282, 545; Vol. 2, Part 2, 607; Vol. 3, Part 1, 37, 47, 299, 459, 467, 518; Vol. 3, Part 2, 385; Vol. 4, Part 1, 204; Vol. 4, Part 2, 186, 368; Vol. 5, Part 1, 321; Vol. 6, Part 1, 149 f., 200, 334, 476; Vol. 6, Part 2, 80, 88, 122, 124, 159, 170, 608; Vol. 7, Part 1, 141, 225; Vol. 7, Part 2, 18, 31, 132, 183, 313, 430, 447 f., 449, 518; Vol. 8, Part 1, 49, 89, 94, 103, 114, 129, 142, 203, 211, 273, 296 f., 325, 341, 350, 462, 629, 646; Vol. 8, Part 2, 178; Vol. 9, Part 1, 140, 390, 484; Vol. 9, Part 2, 481; Vol. 10, Part 1, 103, 387, 563 f., 614 f.; Vol. 10, Part 2, 221, 317, 446, 553; politics, Vol. 2, Part 1, 438; Vol. 3, Part 1, 38 f.; Vol. 4, Part 2, 36; Vol. 6, Part 2, 197; Vol. 8, Part 2, 9; Vol. 10, Part 2, 328; Supp. 3, 20; Supp. 4, 220, 491; Supp. 5, 561; Supp. 6, 259–60, 509–10; Supp. 7, 305–6, 606–7, 766; Supp. 8, 360–61, 456, 531–32; Supp. 9, 235, 236, 253–54, 425–27; Supp. 10, 241, 242; pre-Revolutionary agitation, Vol. 6, Part 2, 606; Vol. 10, Part 2, 327; printing, early, Vol. 1, Part 2, 558, 563; Prohibition convention, first state in, Vol. 1, Part 2, 310; proprietary interests, Vol. 7, Part 1, 554; Vol. 7, Part 2, 432 f.; provincial credit, Vol. 8, Part 1, 400; public health, Vol. 8, Part 2, 188; public service, Vol. 1, Part 1, 208 f.; Vol. 2, Part 2, 234 f., 238 f., 420 f., 455; Vol. 3, Part 1, 18; Vol. 4, Part 2, 182, 186, 223, 354, 366, 368, 471; Vol. 5, Part 1, 51; Vol. 6, Part 1, 150, 154, 163, 202, 211, 287, 593; Vol. 6, Part 2, 549; Vol. 7, Part 1, 307 f., 554; Vol. 7, Part 2, 118, 131, 412 f., 429, 432 f., 446; Vol. 8, Part 1, 124 f.; Vol. 8, Part 2, 15, 232; Vol. 9, Part 1, 140, 284, 355 f.; public welfare, Supp. 6, 515; Quaker leadership, Vol. 7, Part 1, 200 f.; Vol. 7, Part 2, 413 f.; railroad promotion, Vol. 6, Part 1, 227; Vol. 9, Part 2, 486; Reformed German church, Vol. 4, Part 2, 511; Reformed Mennonites, Vol. 4, Part 2, 584; Reformed Presbyterian church, Vol. 10, Part 2, 581; Republican party, Vol. 7, Part 2, 449; Supp. 9, 425–26; Supp. 10, 241, 242; Revolutionary War period, Vol. 5, Part 1, 9; Vol. 7, Part 1, 430, 437; Vol. 10, Part 2, 33, 606; scientific service, Vol. 3, Part 1, 479 f.; Vol. 8, Part 1, 104 f.; Vol. 10, Part 1, 602 f.; slavery, abolition of, in, Vol. 8, Part 1, 452; Socialist party, Supp. 3, 516; statutes, revision of, Vol. 8, Part 1, 401; stone quarries, Vol. 6, Part 1, 154; strikes, labor, Vol. 4, Part 1, 30; Vol. 4, Part 2, 368; Sunday, operation of streetcars on, Vol. 8, Part 1, 428; supreme court, Supp. 3, 415; Tories in, Vol. 7, Part 1, 131; Vol. 8, Part 2, 177; Union Canal, Vol. 1, Part 1, 540; "Warhawks" among the Quakers, Vol. 8, Part 2, 9; Whigs in, Vol. 7, Part 1, 131; Vol. 8, Part 2, 177; Whiskey Rebellion, Vol. 8, Part 1, 401; writings on, Vol. 5, Part 2, 45 f.; Wyoming Valley region, Vol. 7, Part 2, 258. *See also city and institution names*

Pennsylvania, Supp. 9, 461

Pennsylvania Academy of the Fine Arts, oldest art school in America, Vol. 3, Part 1, 590 f.; Vol. 7, Part 2, 346, 349; Vol. 8, Part 1, 401; Vol. 8, Part 2, 7, 187, 235, 372

Pennsylvania Agricultural Society, Vol. 8, Part 1, 143 f.

Pennsylvania Archives, documentary index, Vol. 4, Part 2, 472

Pennsylvania Association of Public Accountants, Supp. 65 397

Pennsylvania Central Airlines, founding of, Supp. 7, 16

Pennsylvania College. *See* Gettysburg College

Pennsylvania Commission on Old-Age Pensions, Supp. 3, 255

Pennsylvania Evening Post, Vol. 9, Part 2, 611–12

Pennsylvania Farmer, Vol. 8, Part 2, 9

Pennsylvania German Dialect, The, Vol. 6, Part 1, 78

Pennsylvania-German Society, Vol. 8, Part 2, 282

Pennsylvania Historical Society, Vol. 7, Part 2, 448

Pennsylvania Horticultural Society, Vol. 7, Part 2, 452

Pennsylvania Hospital, Vol. 1, Part 2, 433; Vol. 2, Part 2, 239; Vol. 5, Part 2, 274; Vol. 7, Part 2, 129, 413

Pennsylvania Institution, Supp. 4, 11

Pennsylvania Journal and Weekly Advertiser, **Vol. 1, Part 2**, 558; **Vol. 7, Part 1**, 550
Pennsylvania Magazine of History, **Vol. 5, Part 2**, 215
Pennsylvania Manufacturers' Association: **Supp. 7**, 305, 306; political influence of, **Supp. 10**, 242
Pennsylvania Military College, **Vol. 8, Part 1**, 49 f.
Pennsylvania Motor Truck Association, **Supp. 6**, 91
Pennsylvania Packet: first daily in U.S., **Vol. 3, Part 1**, 514 f.; **Vol. 8, Part 1**, 139 f.
Pennsylvania Pharmaceutical Association, **Vol. 8, Part 1**, 498
Pennsylvania Railroad: **Vol. 2, Part 1**, 160, 565; **Vol. 3, Part 1**, 18; **Vol. 4, Part 1**, 450; **Vol. 5, Part 1**, 262, 392; **Vol. 5, Part 2**, 455 f.; **Vol. 7, Part 1**, 176; **Vol. 7, Part 2**, 305; **Vol. 8, Part 1**, 417 f.; **Vol. 8, Part 2**, 7, 500 f.; **Vol. 9, Part 1**, 616; **Vol. 9, Part 2**, 396, 484, 486; **Vol. 10, Part 2**, 350; electrification of, **Supp. 1**, 34; **Supp. 4**, 370; **Supp. 8**, 93; management, **Supp. 8**, 92–94; **Supp. 10**, 771–72; strike against, **Supp. 8**, 513
Pennsylvania Society for Promoting the Abolition of Slavery, **Vol. 7, Part 2**, 413
Pennsylvania State University: **Vol. 1, Part 1**, 404; **Vol. 8, Part 1**, 257 f.; **Vol. 9, Part 1**, 430; **Vol. 10, Part 1**, 556 f.; forestry studies, **Supp. 4**, 43–44; medical school, **Supp. 3**, 358; organic chemistry studies, **Supp. 4**, 888
Pennsylvania Tuberculosis and Health Society, **Supp. 2**, 196
Pennsylvania Working Home for Blind Men, **Vol. 7, Part 2**, 305
Penny arcades, **Supp. 5**, 726
"Penny's Society," **Vol. 4, Part 1**, 475
Penobscot expedition (1779), **Vol. 8, Part 2**, 316
Penobscot Indians, **Supp. 4**, 248, 761–62
Penology, **Vol. 2, Part 1**, 50, 61, 614; **Vol. 7, Part 1**, 319; National Society of Penal Information, **Vol. 7, Part 2**, 76; parole system, **Vol. 10, Part 2**, 385; penal codes, **Vol. 6, Part 1**, 311; **Vol. 9, Part 2**, 75; penitentiary system, **Vol. 5, Part 2**, 432; writings on, **Vol. 3, Part 1**, 571 f. **Vol. 6, Part 1**, 237
Penrod, **Supp. 4**, 816, 817
Penrose, Spencer and Richard, reference to, **Supp. 6**, 316
Pens: ballpoint, **Supp. 10**, 670; fountain, **Vol. 10, Part 1**, 533 f.; steel, **Vol. 3, Part 2**, 187
Pensacola lands, speculation in, **Vol. 3, Part 1**, 609 f.
Pensions: Act of 1879, **Vol. 2, Part 2**, 208; Act of 1890, **Vol. 7, Part 1**, 539; advocacy organizations, **Supp. 8**, 9–10; early employment plans, **Supp. 2**, 404, 645; Mothers' Pension Act, **Vol. 6, Part 1**, 354 f.; Pennsylvania state commission, **Supp. 3**, 517; Pension Office, **Vol. 7, Part 1**, 347; **Vol. 9, Part 2**, 297 f.; reorganization of system, **Vol. 3, Part 2**, 159; soldiers', **Vol. 4, Part 2**, 526; studies in, **Supp. 2**, 542–43; teachers, **Supp. 1**, 328; **Supp. 2**, 542; **Supp. 8**, 9–10; Townsend Plan, **Supp. 6**, 646–47; **Supp. 7**, 195; trade union, **Vol. 9, Part 2**, 86. *See also* Social security
Pentagon Building (Washington, D. C.), construction of, **Supp. 5**, 643
Pentagon Papers: appeals court ruling, **Supp. 10**, 324; *New York Times* trial, **Supp. 9**, 88; release defended, **Supp. 9**, 278; Supreme Court decision, **Supp. 9**, 97
Pentecostalism, **Supp. 4**, 876
Peonage, **Vol. 3, Part 2**, 488; **Vol. 8, Part 2**, 241
People's Choral Union, founding of, **Supp. 2**, 140
People's Council of America, founding of, **Supp. 4**, 539
People's Institute (New York City), **Supp. 3**, 511, 563; **Supp. 8**, 58, 98
People's Legislative Service, **Supp. 4**, 544
People's Singing Classes, founding of, **Supp. 2**, 140
People's Temple, **Supp. 10**, 391–92, 558, 559
People's party. *See* Populist movement
People, Yes, The, **Supp. 8**, 564
Peoria, Ill.: **Vol. 1, Part 2**, 574; Robeson ban, **Supp. 10**, 679
Pepper, George Hubbard, reference to, **Supp. 6**, 289
Pepper, George Wharton, reference to, **Supp. 7**, 305
Pepper, importation of, **Vol. 3, Part 2**, 157
Pepperell, William, reference to, **Vol. 1, Part 2**, 578
Pepperidge Farm, founding of, **Supp. 8**, 559–61
Pepper Laboratory for Clinical Research, **Supp. 3**, 243
"Pepper Young's Family" (radio serial), **Supp. 6**, 104
Peptides, **Supp. 3**, 61; **Supp. 5**, 122
Pequot War: **Vol. 3, Part 2**, 156; **Vol. 4, Part 1**, 138; **Vol. 6, Part 2**, 367; **Vol. 9, Part 2**, 83; episode leading to, **Vol. 7, Part 2**, 12; writings on, **Vol. 10, Part 1**, 110
Perception, theory of, **Supp. 8**, 344, 345
"Percussion pill," invention of, **Vol. 4, Part 2**, 62
Percy, Charles, reference to, **Supp. 10**, 186
Percy, LeRoy, reference to, **Supp. 4**, 78
Percy Jones Hospital (Battle Creek, Mich.), **Supp. 6**, 345
Perdue, Franklin, references to, **Supp. 10**, 629, 630
Pere Marquette Railroad, **Supp. 5**, 550
Perelman, S. J., reference to, **Supp. 9**, 579
"Perfectionists," **Vol. 7, Part 1**, 589
Perfume, first designer label, **Supp. 9**, 588
Perfusion pump, invention of, **Supp. 9**, 497
Perils of Pauline, The, **Supp. 9**, 98
Periodic table, analysis, **Supp. 9**, 114
Periscope, invention of, **Vol. 4, Part 1**, 27
Peristalsis, **Supp. 3**, 133–34
Peritonitis, **Vol. 7, Part 1**, 353; **Supp. 6**, 215
Perkins, Charles A., reference to, **Supp. 3**, 773
Perkins, Frances, references to, **Supp. 3**, 400, 645, 647, 718; **Supp. 5**, 631; **Supp. 8**, 648; **Supp. 9**, 28
Perkins, George W., references to, **Supp. 3**, 604; **Supp. 4**, 665
Perkins, Helvetia, reference to, **Supp. 9**, 116
Perkins, Maxwell, references to, **Supp. 2**, 731, 732; **Supp. 3**, 383, 686; **Supp. 5**, 559; **Supp. 7**, 336; **Supp. 10**, 390, 831
Perkins, S. Albert, reference to, **Supp. 6**, 319–20
Perkins Institution for the Blind, **Supp. 4**, 11; **Supp. 8**, 316
Perlman, Alfred, reference to, **Supp. 6**, 721
Perlman, Selig, reference to, **Supp. 3**, 179
Perls, Fritz, reference to, **Supp. 10**, 696
Permanent Court of International Justice. *See* World Court
Pernicious anemia. *See* Anemia
Perón, Juan, reference to, **Supp. 6**, 451
Perrot, Henri, reference to, **Supp. 3**, 55
Perry, Antoinette, reference to, **Supp. 4**, 649
Perry, Joe ("the Jet"), reference to, **Supp. 10**, 727
Pery, J. Sam, reference to, **Supp. 10**, 611
Perry, Matthew C., references to, **Vol. 6, Part 1**, 574; **Vol. 7, Part 1**, 503; **Vol. 9, Part 2**, 310, 315
Perry, Norman, reference to, **Supp. 6**, 301
Perry, O. H., references to, **Vol. 9, Part 1**, 625; **Vol. 9, Part 2**, 348 f.
Perry, Ralph Barton, reference to, **Supp. 5**, 503
Perry-Mansfield School of Theatre, **Supp. 7**, 367
Perryville, battle of, **Vol. 1, Part 2**, 586; **Vol. 2, Part 1**, 241; **Vol. 4, Part 2**, 240; **Vol. 5, Part 2**, 425; **Vol. 8, Part 1**, 40; **Vol. 9, Part 2**, 433
Perseus A (galaxy), **Supp. 6**, 31
Pershing, John J., references to, **Supp. 3**, 398–99, 584, 588, 606; **Supp. 4**, 123, 359, 360; **Supp. 5**, 69, 159,

160, 186, 468, 530–31; **Supp. 6**, 254, 429; **Supp. 8**, 262, 498
Persia: authority on, **Vol. 9, Part 1**, 55; diplomatic relations with, **Vol. 1, Part 2**, 38, 189, 506; **Vol. 8, Part 2**, 241; missions in, **Vol. 1, Part 2**, 37; **Vol. 3, Part 1**, 565 f.; **Vol. 3, Part 2**, 418; **Vol. 4, Part 1**, 486; **Vol. 7, Part 2**, 475; **Vol. 9, Part 2**, 53; **Vol. 10, Part 2**, 344; writings on, **Vol. 1, Part 2**, 189; **Vol. 10, Part 2**, 344. *See also* Iran
Person, Harlow S., reference to, **Supp. 5**, 558
Personality: classification system, **Supp. 10**, 731; development theories, **Supp. 8**, 424; psychological multistudy approaches, **Supp. 8**, 7–9; public v. private, **Supp. 4**, 830–31; studies in, **Supp. 1**, 264
Personal Narrative, plagiarizing of, **Vol. 7, Part 2**, 310
Personnel management: **Supp. 2**, 45; **Supp. 4**, 747; **Supp. 6**, 520; psychological tests, **Supp. 5**, 612
Personnel Research Foundation, founding of, **Supp. 5**, 59
Peru: **Vol. 4, Part 1**, 463; diplomatic relations with, **Vol. 7, Part 2**, 571; **Vol. 8, Part 2**, 38; **Vol. 10, Part 1**, 49; **Supp. 4**, 670; Grace-Donoughmore Contract of 1890, **Vol. 4, Part 1**, 463; mining, **Vol. 7, Part 2**, 9; writings on, **Vol. 10, Part 1**, 107; Yale expedition, **Supp. 6**, 59
Peruvian bark, discovery of substitute for, **Vol. 2, Part 2**, 187
Pestalozzi, influence of, **Vol. 5, Part 2**, 266; **Vol. 7, Part 1**, 402
Pesticides and herbicides: anti-boll weevil campaign, **Supp. 4**, 601; environmental impact of, **Supp. 7**, 109–10; labeling and control, **Supp. 3**, 683. *See also* Insects
Pétain, Philippe, biography of, **Supp. 10**, 247
"Pet crime," U.S. coinage, **Vol. 8, Part 2**, 301
Peter, Hugh, references to, **Vol. 7, Part 1**, 552; **Vol. 9, Part 1**, 627 f.
Peter Bent Brigham Hospital (Boston), **Supp. 3**, 806; **Supp. 4**, 208–9; **Supp. 5**, 111
Peterboro Colony, establishment of, **Vol. 6, Part 2**, 27
Peter Kiewet Sons' Co. (construction), **Supp. 10**, 413, 414
Peterkin Papers, **Vol. 4, Part 2**, 107
Peter Pan, **Supp. 5**, 8; **Supp. 10**, 673
Peter Parley books, **Vol. 4, Part 1**, 403; **Vol. 6, Part 1**, 455
Petersburg, Va., siege of, **Vol. 1, Part 2**, 112, **Vol. 4, Part 1**, 497; **Vol. 6, Part 1**, 127; **Vol. 9, Part 1**, 363
Peterson, Frederick, references to, **Supp. 4**, 107, 108
Peterson, Roger Tory, reference to, **Supp. 6**, 255
Peterson's Magazine, **Vol. 7, Part 2**, 513
Petition, right of, **Vol. 1, Part 1**, 92
Petition to the King, drafting of, **Vol. 3, Part 1**, 299 f.
Petri, Egon, reference to, **Supp. 6**, 456
Petri Wine Co., **Supp. 7**, 613–14
Petrochemistry, development of, **Supp. 3**, 239, 247; **Supp. 6**, 334
Petroff, S. A., reference to, **Supp. 4**, 49
Petroleum industry: **Vol. 1, Part 2**, 301; **Vol. 3, Part 2**, 602; **Vol. 6, Part 1**, 540; **Vol. 8, Part 2**, 56, 65; beginnings of, **Vol. 8, Part 1**, 168 f.; extension of uses for, **Vol. 3, Part 1**, 415; Getty interests, **Supp. 9**, 305–6; multinaitonal companies, **Supp. 10**, 663. *See also* Oil
Petrology: **Vol. 5, Part 1**, 457; **Vol. 10, Part 1**, 527 f.; magmatic school development in, **Supp. 6**, 70–71; mapping and classification, **Supp. 4**, 194; theory development, **Supp. 6**, 144; writings on, **Vol. 10, Part 1**, 527 f.
Petrouchka, **Supp. 9**, 776
"Petticoat Junction" (television program), **Supp. 10**, 77
Petty, George, reference to, **Supp. 5**, 637
Pew, Joseph N., references to, **Supp. 3**, 20; **Supp. 7**, 305; **Supp. 8**, 143
Pewter, craftsmanship in, **Vol. 1, Part 2**, 400; **Vol. 3, Part 1**, 67
Peyser, Jay, reference to, **Supp. 3**, 833
Peyser, Julius, reference to, **Supp. 3**, 833
Peyton Place, **Supp. 7**, 531–32
Pfister Chemical Co., **Supp. 7**, 617
Pforzheimer, Carl H., references to, **Supp. 5**, 387, 586
Pharmaceuticals. *See* Drugs
Pharmacies. *See* Drug stores
Pharmacognosy, **Vol. 5, Part 2**, 499
Pharmacology: chemical synthesis studies, **Supp. 8**, 102; **Supp. 9**, 443–45, 454; education standards, **Supp. 2**, 591; medicinal plants, **Supp. 3**, 432–33; pioneer work in, **Vol. 5, Part 1**, 236; **Vol. 5, Part 2**, 393, 513; research in, **Supp. 3**, 805–6; **Supp. 4**, 410–11; **Supp. 10**, 458–59; teaching of, **Supp. 2**, 4; **Supp. 3**, 342–43; writings on, **Supp. 2**, 389. *See also* Drugs; *specific types of drugs*
Pharmacopeia: **Vol. 8, Part 1**, 498; **Vol. 9, Part 1**, 424, 488; first in U.S., **Vol. 2, Part 1**, 157; revisions of, **Vol. 2, Part 1**, 35; **Vol. 8, Part 1**, 154 f., 192 f., 242 f., 535
Pharmacopeia of the United States of America, The, revision of, **Supp. 4**, 411
Pharmacy: **Vol. 4, Part 1**, 63; **Vol. 6, Part 1**, 49; **Vol. 8, Part 1**, 192 f., 242, 390, 497 f., 535; **Vol. 8, Part 2**, 285 f., 528; **Vol. 9, Part 1**, 255, 487; Pharmacy Act of 1872, **Vol. 7, Part 2**, 259; teaching of, **Vol. 6, Part 1**, 278; **Vol. 6, Part 2**, 213; **Vol. 7, Part 2**, 258; **Vol. 8, Part 1**, 154 f., 192 f.; writings on, **Vol. 6, Part 2**, 213; **Vol. 8, Part 1**, 242 f., 498, 535
Phase Rule, The, **Supp. 5**, 36
Phelan, Frank M., reference to, **Vol. 9, Part 2**, 267
Phelps and Gorham Purchase (1791), **Vol. 3, Part 2**, 601; **Vol. 4, Part 1**, 434; **Vol. 7, Part 1**, 222; **Vol. 7, Part 2**, 531; **Vol. 10, Part 2**, 297
Phelps, Dodge & Co., **Supp. 3**, 381
Phelps-Stokes Foundation, first black director, **Supp. 7**, 748
Phenix Cheese Co., **Supp. 5**, 400
Phenolic resins, **Supp. 3**, 26
Phi Beta Kappa Society: **Vol. 1, Part 1**, 520, 544; **Vol. 3, Part 2**, 235, 304, 326, 487; **Vol. 4, Part 2**, 150, 260, 360; **Vol. 5, Part 1**, 52 f., 132, 206, 260, 300; **Vol. 5, Part 2**, 304, 343, 379; **Vol. 6, Part 1**, 224, 388, 405, 416, 429; **Vol. 7, Part 1**, 245, 283, 300, 528, 562; **Vol. 8, Part 2**, 135; **Vol. 9, Part 1**, 239, 470; **Vol. 9, Part 2**, 135, 306, 398; Amherst Chapter, founding of, **Vol. 10, Part 1**, 99; first chapter at black institution, **Supp. 5**, 437; first Kentucky chapter, **Supp. 5**, 461; founding of, **Vol. 9, Part 1**, 128; Harvard Chapter, founding of, **Vol. 1, Part 2**, 8; orations, **Vol. 3, Part 2**, 223; **Vol. 5, Part 1**, 45, 49, 53, 128
"Phi Chi," Bowdoin song, **Vol. 7, Part 1**, 43
Philadelphia, Pa.: Academy of Music, **Vol. 3, Part 2**, 437; architectural sculpture, **Supp. 3**, 123–24; architecture, **Vol. 5, Part 2**, 274; **Vol. 6, Part 1**, 21, 168, 551; **Vol. 9, Part 1**, 336 f.; **Supp. 9**, 445, 447; art service, **Vol. 4, Part 2**, 378; **Vol. 8, Part 2**, 470; **Vol. 9, Part 1**, 635; banking development, **Vol. 3, Part 1**, 455 f.; baseball, professional, **Vol. 8, Part 1**, 418; Beef Steak Club, **Vol. 5, Part 2**, 456; black-owned banks, **Supp. 4**, 916; Building Association League of Philadelphia, **Vol. 8, Part 2**, 104; business in, **Vol. 5, Part 1**, 377; **Vol. 6, Part 1**, 543; **Vol. 9, Part 1**, 190, 599; **Vol. 10, Part 1**, 407 f.; Catholic Club of, **Vol. 8, Part 2**, 104; Centennial Exposition (1876), **Vol. 6, Part 1**, 187; **Vol. 7, Part 1**, 413; **Vol. 8, Part 2**, 7, 197,

577; **Vol. 9, Part 2**, 424; Chemical Society of Philadelphia, **Vol. 10, Part 2**, 491; Chestnut Street Female Seminary, **Vol. 8, Part 1**, 335 f.; Consolidation Act, **Vol. 8, Part 1**, 211 f., 335 f.; drainage system for, **Vol. 5, Part 2**, 456; economic life in early, **Vol. 10, Part 2**, 23; education, **Vol. 3, Part 1**, 408 f., 459 f.; **Vol. 4, Part 2**, 359 f.; **Vol. 5, Part 1**, 261; **Vol. 6, Part 1**, 544; **Vol. 8, Part 1**, 71; **Vol. 9, Part 1**, 635; Episcopal church, **Vol. 6, Part 2**, 173; Episcopal Hospital, **Vol. 8, Part 1**, 124 f.; ferry over Schuylkill, colonial, **Vol. 8, Part 2**, 156; financial center, as a, **Vol. 10, Part 2**, 610; fire insurance company, first in America, **Vol. 8, Part 1**, 139 f.; first woman on education board, **Supp. 5**, 432; foreign trade, **Vol. 1, Part 2**, 464; "gas fight" of 1905, **Vol. 3, Part 1**, 355 f.; glassworks, **Vol. 3, Part 1**, 586, f.; harbor for, **Vol. 8, Part 1**, 406; Haseltine Art Galleries, **Vol. 4, Part 2**, 378; history of, **Vol. 3, Part 1**, 514 f.; **Vol. 10, Part 2**, 14; hospital, **Vol. 7, Part 2**, 263; House of Industry, **Vol. 7, Part 2**, 257; Kelly family, **Supp. 6**, 331; labor movement in, **Vol. 10, Part 2**, 556; laying out city, **Vol. 5, Part 1**, 159; **Vol. 7, Part 2**, 435; legal service, **Vol. 1, Part 2**, 281; **Vol. 4, Part 2**, 355; **Vol. 5, Part 1**, 469; **Vol. 9, Part 2**, 543; library work, **Vol. 4, Part 1**, 557; **Vol. 7, Part 2**, 452, 455; **Vol. 8, Part 2**, 231; **Vol. 9, Part 1**, 317; Light Horse of the City of, **Vol. 6, Part 1**, 75; Lutheran church, **Vol. 6, Part 2**, 247; magazine publications, **Vol. 1, Part 2**, 417; mass meeting in 1776, **Vol. 8, Part 1**, 646; master plan for restoration of, **Supp. 9**, 236; mayors, **Supp. 9**, 235, 236; medical service, **Vol. 2, Part 1**, 400; **Vol. 3, Part 1**, 494 f.; **Vol. 5, Part 1**, 553; **Vol. 6, Part 1**, 143, 149 f.; **Vol. 7, Part 1**, 202, 379, 553; **Vol. 7, Part 2**, 259, 554; **Vol. 10, Part 1**, 103; **Vol. 10, Part 2**, 109; Methodist preacher, first, in, **Vol. 7, Part 2**, 609; military maps of, for use during Civil War, **Vol. 5, Part 2**, 456; "Morris's Folly," **Vol. 6, Part 1**, 168; municipal government, **Supp. 4**, 262; museums, **Vol. 7, Part 2**, 345 f., 351; **Supp. 4**, 452; **Supp. 5**, 388; music, **Vol. 4, Part 1**, 274; **Vol. 8, Part 2**, 423; **Vol. 9, Part 2**, 339 f.; "nativism riots," **Vol. 6, Part 1**, 200; newspapers, politics of (1829), **Vol. 4, Part 2**, 250; organized crime, **Supp. 10**, 75–76; Orphan Society, **Vol. 4, Part 1**, 505; park system, **Vol. 6, Part 2**, 492; **Vol. 10, Part 1**, 647; politics, **Supp. 7**, 302; **Supp. 9**, 235–36; politics (1866–81), **Vol. 6, Part 2**, 138; *Press, The*, **Vol. 9, Part 1**, 246; printing in, **Vol. 1, Part 1**, 501; **Vol. 10, Part 2**, 649; public service, **Vol. 1, Part 1**, 503, 542; **Vol. 1, Part 2**, 358; **Vol. 3, Part 1**, 455 f., 459 f.; **Vol. 4, Part 1**, 321; **Vol. 4, Part 2**, 250, 294, 337, 344; **Vol. 5, Part 1**, 263, 439; **Vol. 6, Part 1**, 149 f., 168, 329, 495, 497 f., 543 f.; **Vol. 6, Part 2**, 130, 143, 173, 474, 486, 558, 634; **Vol. 7, Part 1**, 142, 200 f.; **Vol. 7, Part 2**, 429, 451 f., 508; **Vol. 8, Part 1**, 203 f., 400, 427 f.; **Vol. 8, Part 2**, 228, 235; **Vol. 9, Part 1**, 3, 115, 255; **Vol. 9, Part 2**, 487, 614, 620; **Vol. 10, Part 1**, 103 f., 647; **Vol. 10, Part 2**, 2, 30 f., 185, 303; **Supp. 9**, 445; publishing in, **Vol. 4, Part 2**, 355; real estate development, **Vol. 2, Part 1**, 234; records, public, **Vol. 8, Part 1**, 296 f.; reform movements, **Vol. 3, Part 2**, 432, 437; **Vol. 6, Part 1**, 68; "Republican Court," **Vol. 1, Part 2**, 273; Revolutionary War period, **Vol. 2, Part 1**, 400; **Vol. 6, Part 2**, 287, 306; Roman Catholic bishopric, **Supp. 5**, 179; St. Augustine's Rectory, **Vol. 2, Part 1**, 518; scientific services to, **Vol. 3, Part 1**, 538 f.; shipping (1753), **Vol. 4, Part 2**, 476; social life, **Vol. 6, Part 1**, 359 f.; **Vol. 8, Part 2**, 231; social reform, **Supp. 6**, 515; state hospital for women and infants, **Vol. 7, Part 2**, 264; street railways in, **Vol. 3, Part 1**, 459 f.; theater in, **Vol. 3, Part 1**, 37; **Vol. 7, Part 1**, 206 f.; *Times, The*, **Vol. 6, Part 1**, 593–94; Tuesday Club, organization of, **Vol. 3, Part 1**, 236; Union League of, **Vol. 1, Part 2**, 417, 464; war relief work in, during Revolution, **Vol. 8, Part 1**, 452; water supply for, **Vol. 6, Part 1**, 21; Wharton School, **Vol. 5, Part 1**, 574; Whitfield, preaching of, **Vol. 8, Part 2**, 75, 227; Woman's Hospital, **Vol. 8, Part 1**, 201; yellow fever epidemic, **Vol. 4, Part 1**, 466; **Vol. 8, Part 1**, 427, 443

Philadelphia (frigate), **Vol. 1, Part 1**, 506; **Vol. 3, Part 1**, 187

Philadelphia Academy of Surgery, **Vol. 7, Part 2**, 129

Philadelphia & Reading Railroad **Vol. 4, Part 1**, 461; **Vol. 5, Part 2**, 277

Philadelphia Athletics (baseball), **Supp. 5**, 48, 124–25; **Supp. 6**, 357, 358, 415, 581–82; **Supp. 7**, 27, 128, 129, 130; **Supp. 8**, 186, 543, 544; **Supp. 9**, 344–45

Philadelphia Daily News, **Supp. 5**, 205

Philadelphia Dental College, **Vol. 6, Part 2**, 164

Philadelphia Divinity School, **Supp. 4**, 595

Philadelphia Eagles (football), **Supp. 6**, 47; **Supp. 10**, 600, 728

Philadelphia Evening Ledger, **Supp. 7**, 615

Philadelphia Evening Telegraph, **Vol. 5, Part 1**, 203

Philadelphia Inquirer, **Supp. 3**, 20; **Supp. 6**, 232

Philadelphia Museum of Art, construction of, **Supp. 1**, 609

Philadelphia Music Teachers' Association, **Vol. 8, Part 1**, 200 f.

Philadelphia Neurological Society, founding of, **Supp. 1**, 241

Philadelphia Orchestra: **Supp. 10**, 761–62, 763; conductors, **Supp. 6**, 550

Philadelphia Phillies (baseball), **Supp. 6**, 347, 356; **Supp. 10**, 573

Philadelphia Public Ledger, **Supp. 1**, 212–13

Philadelphia Rapid Transit Co., **Vol. 7, Part 1**, 71

Philadelphia Record, **Vol. 9, Part 1**, 189

Philadelphia School of Design for Women, **Vol. 7, Part 2**, 500

Philadelphia Society for Ameliorating the Miseries of Public Prisons, **Vol. 8, Part 1**, 139 f.

Philadelphia Story, The, **Supp. 4**, 55; **Supp. 9**, 381

Philadelphia Zeitung, first German-language newspaper in America, Vol 9, Part 2, 557

Philanthropy: Astor projects, **Supp. 6**, 23, 24; Ball projects, **Supp. 3**, 29–30; **Supp. 5**, 34; Bamberger projects, **Supp. 3**, 30–31; Blaine projects, **Supp. 5**, 61; Bolton projects, **Supp. 10**, 58; Cabot projects, **Supp. 7**, 98; corporate, **Supp. 10**, 684; Cullen projects, **Supp. 6**, 136; cultural, **Supp. 4**, 87; Dana projects, **Supp. 9**, 217; Durante projects, **Supp. 10**, 196; Falk projects, **Supp. 4**, 261–62; Fels projects, **Supp. 4**, 262–63; Ford projects, **Supp. 4**, 303; fundraising, **Supp. 7**, 401–2; Guggenheim projects, **Supp. 3**, 321–22; Harkness projects, **Supp. 2**, 284; Harriman, E. B. N., projects, **Supp. 10**, 310–11; Hayden projects, **Supp. 2**, 293; Heckscher projects, **Supp. 3**, 348–49; Hershey projects, **Supp. 3**, 358; Hutton projects, **Supp. 10**, 367; James projects, **Supp. 3**, 381–82; Kahn projects, **Supp. 1**, 457–58; Kent projects, **Supp. 4**, 452; Kiewit projects, **Supp. 10**, 414; Kresge projects, **Supp. 8**, 348–49; Lehman projects, **Supp. 7**, 466; Levy projects, **Supp. 10**, 454; Lewisohn projects, **Supp. 5**, 427; Lilly projects, **Supp. 10**, 459; Littauer projects, **Supp. 3**, 464; Loeb projects, **Supp. 1**, 503–4; Lowell projects, **Supp. 10**, 467; McKinley projects, **Supp. 1**, 532; Mallinckrodt projects, **Supp. 8**, 412; medical, **Supp. 3**, 435; music, **Supp. 5**, 128–29; Pew projects, **Supp. 9**, 612; philosophical basis of foundations, **Supp. 3**, 416–17; Post projects, **Supp. 9**, 615; Pratt projects, **Supp. 9**, 622–23; Reynolds projects, **Supp. 5**, 567; Richardson

projects, **Supp. 6**, 541; Rockefeller projects, **Supp. 2**, 574–75; **Supp. 4**, 696–97; **Supp. 6**, 548–49; Rockefeller, M. B., projects, **Supp. 9**, 670; Roman Catholic church, **Supp. 6**, 608; Rose projects, **Supp. 8**, 548; Sloan projects, **Supp. 8**, 600; Snow projects, **Supp. 9**, 743; Speyer projects, **Supp. 3**, 729; Stouffer projects, **Supp. 9**, 771; Straus projects, **Supp. 6**, 607; Wade projects, **Supp. 1**, 695; Widener projects, **Supp. 9**, 867; writings on, **Supp. 2**, 374; Yawkey projects, **Supp. 10**, 861; youth programs, **Supp. 5**, 324; Zellerbach projects, **Supp. 10**, 868. *See also* Charitable organizations

Philbrick, Herbert, references to, **Supp. 6**, 681; **Supp. 7**, 390; **Supp. 10**, 101

Philco Corporation: **Supp. 3**, 143; radio and television broadcasting, **Supp. 9**, 275–76; sale to Ford Motor Co., **Supp. 9**, 252

Philharmonic Society of New York, **Vol. 3, Part 1**, 377; **Vol. 4, Part 2**, 504; **Vol. 10, Part 1**, 543. *See also* New York Philharmonic

Philharmonic-Symphony of New York, founding of, **Supp. 4**, 212. *See also* New York Philharmonic

Philippi, battle of, **Vol. 6, Part 1**, 582; **Vol. 7, Part 1**, 228

Philippine Journal of Science, **Supp. 6**, 450

Philippines: **Vol. 3, Part 1**, 110; **Vol. 5, Part 1**, 458; **Vol. 9, Part 2**, 363; **Vol. 10, Part 2**, 561; acquisition of, **Vol. 1, Part 1**, 154; **Vol. 3, Part 1**, 110, 164; **Vol. 3, Part 2**, 503; **Vol. 4, Part 1**, 52, 516; **Vol. 6, Part 2**, 108; agriculture, **Vol. 7, Part 2**, 632; botany, **Supp. 6**, 450; Catholic church, **Vol. 4, Part 1**, 241; Commission, **Vol. 5, Part 1**, 234; **Vol. 7, Part 1**, 275; **Vol. 9, Part 2**, 268; education, **Vol. 8, Part 1**, 152; first president of, **Supp. 3**, 613–15; "hitching post," as a, **Vol. 3, Part 1**, 164; imperialistic policy toward, **Vol. 2, Part 1**, 193; independence movement, **Supp. 3**, 699; **Supp. 6**, 227, 280, 280–81; **Supp. 7**, 377; insurrection, **Vol. 4, Part 1**, 94; **Vol. 6, Part 2**, 573; **Vol. 7, Part 2**, 95; **Vol. 9, Part 1**, 287; Manila Bay, battle of, **Supp. 3**, 275; medical research and education, **Supp. 4**, 803; military governorship of, **Vol. 7, Part 2**, 95; missions, **Supp. 1**, 115–16; **Supp. 5**, 178–79; monetary system, **Supp. 3**, 414; nursing in, **Supp. 7**, 247; protectorate, establishing of, **Vol. 6, Part 2**, 108, U.S. presence in, **Supp. 1**, 284; **Supp. 2**, 579; **Supp. 3**, 218, 669; **Supp. 4**, 612, 655–56; **Supp. 5**, 42, 459, 460, 468; **Supp. 5**, 530; **Supp. 6**, 190–91, 210–11, 429, 579; **Supp. 7**, 488–89, 786; **Supp. 8**, 154, 638; Wood, Leonard, administration of, **Vol. 10, Part 2**, 468 f.; World War II action, **Supp. 5**, 719–20; **Supp. 6**, 268; **Supp. 7**, 215, 352, 489, 490; **Supp. 8**, 48, 351, 619, 638, 698

Philippine Sea, battle of the, **Supp. 8**, 619

Philistine, **Vol. 5, Part 1**, 323

Phillips, Duncan, reference to, **Supp. 4**, 241

Phillips, John, reference to, **Supp. 9**, 262

Phillips, John S., reference to, **Supp. 3**, 762; **Supp. 4**, 517, 518

Phillips, Michelle, reference to, **Supp. 9**, 262

Phillips, William, reference to, **Supp. 5**, 332

Phillips Academy, Andover: **Vol. 1, Part 1**, 82, 561 f.; **Vol. 7, Part 2**, 548; **Vol. 9, Part 2**, 343; architectural planning of, **Vol. 8, Part 1**, 1 f.; founding of, **Vol. 7, Part 2**, 543; principal of, first, **Vol. 7, Part 2**, 358; reorganization of, **Vol. 8, Part 2**, 151

Phillips Brooks House, founding of, **Vol. 7, Part 2**, 159

Phillips Exeter Academy: **Vol. 1, Part 2**, 153; **Vol. 8, Part 1**, 80; **Vol. 9, Part 2**, 290; founding of, **Vol. 7, Part 2**, 542

Phillips Petroleum Co., **Supp. 7**, 428; founding of, **Supp. 4**, 660–61

Phillips University, founding of, **Vol. 7, Part 2**, 544

Philology: **Vol. 1, Part 1**, 148; **Vol. 2, Part 1**, 45, 53, 110; **Vol. 3, Part 1**, 108; **Vol. 3, Part 2**, 131, 484; **Vol. 4, Part 1**, 157, 281, 588; **Vol. 4, Part 2**, 48, 81, 95, 124 f., 132, 357, 401, 603; **Vol. 5, Part 2**, 446 f.; **Vol. 8, Part 2**, 39 f., 55, 212, 423 f., 561; 6, Part 1, 78, 262, 429; **Vol. 8, Part 1**, 470, 535; **Vol. 9, Part 1**, 64, 126, 244, 248; **Vol. 10, Part 1**, 31; **Vol. 10, Part 2**, 342; *Dictionary of the German and English Languages*, **Vol. 1, Part 1**, 108; educational values of, **Vol. 8, Part 1**, 219 f.; English historical grammar, **Vol. 2, Part 1**, 45; **Vol. 4, Part 2**, 343; **Vol. 6, Part 2**, 269; English literature and language studies, **Supp. 3**, 422–24; **Supp. 10**, 35–37; Esperanto promotion, **Supp. 4**, 185; foreign language, education in, **Supp. 2**, 132; geolinguistic centers, **Supp. 10**, 628; human language capacity, **Supp. 4**, 90–91; Indian, **Vol. 3, Part 1**, 525; **Vol. 7, Part 2**, 565; **Vol. 10, Part 1**, 9 f.; linguistic relativity theory, **Supp. 3**, 84, 819–20; Middle English studles, **Supp. 3**, 109; Old English studies, **Supp. 2**, 88; Romance language studies, **Supp. 3**, 21–22; Sanskrit studies, **Supp. 3**, 444–45; Semitic studies, **Supp. 3**, 37, 374–75; Supp. 641; Spanish and Latin American speech, **Vol. 6, Part 2**, 278; studies, **Supp. 10**, 627; writings on, **Vol. 3, Part 1**, 525 f., 563; **Vol. 5, Part 2**, 3, 446; **Vol. 8, Part 1**, 219 f., 321 f.; **Vol. 8, Part 2**, 39 f., 433; **Vol. 9, Part 1**, 65; **Vol. 9, Part 2**, 572; **Vol. 10, Part 1**, 31; **Supp. 2**, 683; **Supp. 10**, 627, 628

Philosopher's Holiday, **Supp. 5**, 199

Philosophical Review, **Vol. 8, Part 2**, 595; founding of, **Supp. 3**, 698

Philosophy: **Vol. 1, Part 2**, 503; **Vol. 3, Part 2**, 420; **Vol. 4, Part 1**, 153, 631; **Vol. 4, Part 2**, 15, 471, 498; **Vol. 5, Part 1**, 590 f.; **Vol. 5, Part 2**, 525, 526, 547; **Vol. 6, Part 1**, 328; **Vol. 7, Part 2**, 399 f.; **Vol. 8, Part 2**, 595; aesthetic, **Vol. 8, Part 1**, 408; **Supp. 10**, 263–64; American, **Vol. 8, Part 1**, 611; **Vol. 9, Part 1**, 344; Aristotelian, **Supp. 2**, 735; of biology, **Supp. 4**, 427; body/mind relationship, **Supp. 2**, 639; book collections, **Supp. 1**, 619; Chicago school (functionalism), **Supp. 1**, 548, **Supp. 3**, 780; critical realism, **Supp. 2**, 639; **Supp. 3**, 608; "cultural pluralism," first use of term, **Supp. 9**, 448; epistemological dualism, **Supp. 7**, 482; evolution of human thought, **Supp. 10**, 210; first attempt to unite German and American method, **Vol. 8, Part 1**, 389 f.; first scholarly journal, **Supp. 3**, 698; fruitlands, **Vol. 1, Part 1**, 140; Hegel, introduction to America, **Vol. 2, Part 1**, 65; historical writings on, **Supp. 2**, 671; idealistic, **Vol. 9, Part 1**, 593; **Supp. 1**, 332, 683; individualism, **Supp. 5**, 224–25; in India, **Supp. 1**, 713–14; influence on study of, in U.S., **Vol. 2, Part 2**, 535; instrumentalism (experimentalism), **Supp. 5**, 170–72; Jewish, history of, **Vol. 7, Part 1**, 436–37; Kierkegaardian, **Supp. 2**, 643–44; of law, **Supp. 6**, 216; **Supp. 7**, 99–100; lectures on, **Vol. 5, Part 2**, 525; logic, **Supp. 4**, 168–70, 879–80; logical positivism, **Supp. 5**, 562–63; **Supp. 8**, 74–75; Marxist, **Supp. 10**, 330; metaphysics, **Supp. 4**, 881–83; mystical, **Vol. 1, Part 2**, 307; naïve realism, **Supp. 2**, 735; natural, **Vol. 3, Part 2**, 30 f., 236; **Vol. 6, Part 1**, 442 f.; **Vol. 8, Part 1**, 506; of Navaho Indians, **Supp. 4**, 644–45; neorealism, **Supp. 2**, 622; **Supp. 5**, 503–4; **Supp. 6**, 505; Nietzsche, books on, **Supp. 10**, 401, 402; Nietzsche, books on pagan, **Vol. 8, Part 2**, 316; objective idealism, **Supp. 3**, 697; **Supp. 8**, 265–66; of science, **Supp. 8**; **Supp. 10**, 210; of physics, **Supp. 7**, 74–75, 134–35; physiological, **Vol. 2, Part 1**, 215; personalism, **Vol. 1, Part 2**, 523; personalistic idealism and theism, **Supp. 5**, 90–92; pluralism, **Supp. 5**, 436; **Supp. 9**, 448; process of becoming theory, **Supp. 4**, 879–84; realism, **Supp. 4**, 387; reason and

interpretation studies, **Supp. 5**, 602–3; relating to religion, **Vol. 5, Part 1**, 5; **Vol. 6, Part 1**, 616; **Supp. 4**, 525–26; **Supp. 6**, 13–14, 45–46; **Supp. 7**, 745–47; **Supp. 9**, 585–86, 890, 891; **Supp. 10**, 330–31; scientific humanism, **Supp. 6**, 83; social, **Supp. 1**, 547–48; **Supp. 10**, 259–61; 330–31; space-time relativity, **Supp. 5**, 563; systems of, in nineteenth century, **Vol. 2, Part 1**, 548; teaching of, **Vol. 4, Part 1**, 66; **Vol. 4, Part 2**, 185; **Vol. 5, Part 1**, 216, 311, 455; **Vol. 5, Part 2**, 525; **Vol. 7, Part 1**, 111, 209, 317, 448, 526; **Vol. 8, Part 2**, 206 f., 556; **Vol. 9, Part 1**, 494; **Vol. 9, Part 2**, 302, 537; **Vol. 10, Part 2**, 349; **Supp. 2**, 540; **Supp. 4**, 883–84; **Supp. 7**, 701–2; **Supp. 8**, 58–59; textbooks on, **Vol. 4, Part 2**, 409 f.; utilitarianism, **Vol. 1, Part 1**, 136; validity of knowledge, **Supp. 7**, 471–72; writings on, **Vol. 1, Part 2**, 33, 383, 504, 523; **Vol. 2, Part 1**, 65, 548; **Vol. 2, Part 2**, 535; **Vol. 3, Part 1**, 96 f., 108, 141, 162, 169, 180, 225, 339, 472 f., 523 f., 546; **Vol. 4, Part 1**, 66, 162, 452, 631; **Vol. 4, Part 2**, 471 f.; **Vol. 5, Part 1**, 455; **Vol. 5, Part 2**, 119, 471 f., 507, 526, 530, 547, 548; **Vol. 6, Part 1**, 328, 616; **Vol. 6, Part 2**, 300; **Vol. 7, Part 1**, 112, 209, 338 f.; **Vol. 7, Part 2**, 182, 402 f.; **Vol. 8, Part 1**, 97 f., 120 f., 124 f., 127 f., 161 f., 211 f., 232 f., 282 f., 611; **Vol. 8, Part 2**, 207 f., 596; **Vol. 9, Part 1**, 384, 594; **Vol. 10, Part 1**, 98, 123, 151, 370 f., 433 f., 442 f., 490 f., 493 f., 558 f., 608 f., 652 f.; **Vol. 10, Part 2**, 396, 547; **Supp. 1**, 332–33, 400, 418; **Supp. 5**, 199; **Supp. 9**, 447, 448, 891; **Supp. 10**, 210, 401–2, 506–8. *See also* Ethics

Phipps, Henry, reference to, **Vol. 7, Part 1**, 143

Phipps Clinic, psychiatry studies, **Supp. 4**, 572

Phipps Institute for the Study, Prevention, and Treatment of Tuberculosis, **Supp. 2**, 197; **Supp. 4**, 684

Phipps Model Tenement (New York CIty), **Supp. 6**, 26

Phips, William, reference to, **Vol. 8, Part 2**, 611

Phoenix, first seagoing steamboat, **Vol. 8, Part 2**, 106; **Vol. 9, Part 1**, 615, 619

Phoenix Brewery, **Supp. 7**, 504

Phoenixiana, popularity of, **Vol. 3, Part 1**, 252

Phonautograph, **Vol. 1, Part 2**, 149

Phonetics, writing on, **Vol. 5, Part 2**, 457; **Vol. 8, Part 1**, 102 f.

Phonetic spelling, pioneering in, **Vol. 6, Part 2**, 379

Phonograph: first built, **Vol. 5, Part 2**, 509; gramophone, **Supp. 1**, 75; improvements in, **Vol. 1, Part 2**, 151; invention of, **Supp. 1**, 279; RCA interest in, **Supp. 9**, 700; Victrola development, **Supp. 3**, 392. *See also* Audio systems; Recordings

Phonographic Institute, Cincinnati, founding of, **Vol. 7, Part 2**, 642

Phonography, **Vol. 1, Part 1**, 298

Phosphatides, **Supp. 3**, 370

Phosphorus, dietary, **Supp. 5**, 276, 623

Photochemical engraving, the "levytype," **Vol. 6, Part 1**, 202

Photochemistry, **Vol. 6, Part 1**, 71

Photocopying. *See* Copying machines

Phatoelectrons. **Supp. 6**, 370

Photo-Engravers Union. *See* International Photo-Engravers Union

Photoengraving: pioneering, **Vol. 6, Part 1**, 203, 205; **Vol. 7, Part 1**, 280–81; processes, **Supp. 2**, 337

Photography: **Vol. 1, Part 1**, 133; **Vol. 1, Part 2**, 81, 585; **Vol. 3, Part 1**, 17 f., 329; **Vol. 4, Part 1**, 152, 340, 408; **Vol. 5, Part 1**, 59 f., 131, 252; **Vol. 6, Part 1**, 202; **Vol. 7, Part 1**, 373, 470; **Vol. 8, Part 1**, 101 f.; **Vol. 8, Part 2**, 282, 54; **Vol. 9, Part 2**, 647; abstract, **Supp. 10**, 766; aerial, **Supp. 9**, 273, 760; aerial, first of New York City, **Supp. 4**, 361; aerial, first War Department use of, **Supp. 6**, 435; Alaska, **Supp. 7**, 371; American architecture, **Supp. 5**, 373; American Indians, **Supp. 5**, 148; architecture, **Supp. 7**, 686–87; as artistic medium, **Supp. 4**, 779–81; **Supp. 9**, 759–60; **Supp. 10**, 504, 505, 767; astronomical, **Vol. 1, Part 2**, 431; **Vol. 3, Part 1**, 435 f.; **Vol. 9, Part 2**, 462; **Vol. 5, Part 2**, 279; **Vol. 6, Part 1**, 83; **Vol. 8, Part 1**, 472; **Vol. 8, Part 2**, 256; **Supp. 1**, 54; **Supp. 3**, 634, 692; **Supp. 6**, 7, 31; automatic continuous film printer, **Supp. 5**, 322; birds, **Supp. 7**, 8; bird study, **Supp. 3**, 161; cameras for horse racing photo-finish decisions, **Supp. 8**, 76; celebrity, **Supp. 9**, 376; cheesecake, **Supp. 5**, 270, 271; Cinerama, **Supp. 5**, 721–22; color, **Vol. 9, Part 2**, 647; **Supp. 2**, 337; **Supp. 3**, 296; **Supp. 5**, 711; **Supp. 7**, 511, 512; daguerreotype, **Vol. 1, Part 2**, 529; **Vol. 7, Part 1**, 280 f.; **Vol. 8, Part 2**, 174, 362; **Vol. 9, Part 1**, 514; documentary, **Supp. 2**, 305, 306; **Supp. 3**, 295–96; **Supp. 7**, 456–57, 754; **Supp. 8**, 586; **Supp. 9**, 267–68; exhibitions, **Supp. 9**, 759, 760–61; **Supp. 10**, 398, 399, 833–34; fashion, **Supp. 9**, 760, **Supp. 10**, 305; first commercial film, **Supp. 1**, 274; first extensive use in magazine, **Vol. 3, Part 2**, 572; first published photos of San Francisco earthquake, **Supp. 9**, 797; high-speed film, **Supp. 4**, 744; "hunting with a camera" idea, **Vol. 8, Part 2**, 324; infant development studies, **Supp. 7**, 284; journalism, **Supp. 3**, 155; **Supp. 4**, 361; **Supp. 7**, 115–16, 535; **Supp. 8**, 394–96; **Supp. 9**, 111; **Supp. 10**, 749–50; journalism, pioneer work in, **Vol. 9, Part 1**, 380; **Supp. 10**, 397–98; Kodachrome slides of ocular diseases, **Supp. 3**, 302; Kodaks, **Vol. 4, Part 2**, 410; **Vol. 8, Part 2**, 554; landscape, **Supp. 10**, 834; lenses and shutters, **Supp. 3**, 41; Lincolniana collections, **Supp. 7**, 529–30; medicine, **Vol. 4, Part 1**, 63; **Vol. 7, Part 1**, 557; microfilm and microfiche, **Supp. 8**, 120; motion, pioneer in, **Vol. 7, Part 1**, 373; movie camera for amateurs, **Supp. 5**, 322; nature, **Supp. 3**, 229; **Supp. 9**, 376; nude, **Supp. 8**, 412; photogram, **Supp. 10**, 504; picture essay, **Supp. 10**, 750; pioneering methods, **Vol. 2, Part 1**, 485; pioneer in modern, **Supp. 4**, 779–81; plants, **Supp. 2**, 113; plant studies, **Supp. 10**, 162; plumbeotype, invention of, **Vol. 8, Part 1**, 11 f.; portrait, **Vol. 9, Part 1**, 508; **Supp. 3**, 296; **Supp. 7**, 26–27, 455–56; **Supp. 9**, 759, 760; **Supp. 10**, 161–62, 305; process theory development, **Supp. 4**, 743–44; research and development, **Supp. 6**, 442; **Supp. 10**, 52; scenic, **Supp. 3**, 380, 566–67; social consciousness, **Supp. 10**, 398, 766; snow crystals, **Supp. 1**, 72; underwater camera prototype, **Supp. 9**, 271; Velox print paper, **Supp. 3**, 26; West Coast style, **Supp. 10**, 162; Weston's sharp-focus, **Supp. 6**, 685–86; wire service, **Supp. 5**, 323–24; **Supp. 7**, 145; women in, **Supp. 10**, 397–98; writings on, **Vol. 1, Part 2**, 81; **Vol. 9, Part 2**, 609 f.; **Supp. 3**, 342. *See also* Cinematography

Photolithography, early work in, **Vol. 3, Part 1**, 329

Photophone, **Vol. 1, Part 2**,

Photoreception, **Supp. 4**, 367

Photo-Secession: **Supp. 9**, 110; exhibitions, **Supp. 9**, 759; founding of, **Supp. 4**, 779, 780; **Supp. 9**, 759

Photo-Secession Gallery, **Supp. 10**, 765, 766

Photosynthesis, **Supp. 7**, 259

Phrenology: **Vol. 3, Part 2**, 565; **Vol. 4, Part 1**, 631; **Vol. 8, Part 1**, 152 f.; **Vol. 9, Part 1**, 193, 404; **Vol. 10, Part 1**, 643 f; writings on, **Vol. 4, Part 1**, 631; **Vol. 9, Part 1**, 193; **Vol. 10, Part 1**, 643 f.

Physical chemistry: **Supp. 2**, 494; **Supp. 8**, 122–24, 628; colloids, **Supp. 5**, 36; liquid and solid surface measurement, **Supp. 5**, 273–74; molecular-beam research, **Supp. 8**, 628; quantum mechanics studies, **Supp. 4**, 838–39; research in, **Supp. 4**, 487–89; teaching of, **Supp. 4**, 184; theoretical, **Supp. 6**, 345–46; thermal diffusion studies, **Supp. 10**, 608, 609

Physical Culture, **Vol. 8, Part 2,** 355; **Supp. 5,** 527, 528; "daily dozen" exercises, **Vol. 2, Part 1,** 445; founding of, **Supp. 5,** 452–53
Physical education. *See* Education, physical
Physical fitness: **Supp. 5,** 452–53: body-building, **Supp. 9,** 51–52; for women, **Supp. 8,** 13; Life Extension Institute founding, **Supp. 4,** 275; natural diet and exercise, **Supp. 3,** 409–10; swimming, **Supp. 8,** 336–37
Physically handicapped. *See* Handicapped; *specific disabilities*
Physical Review, founding of, **Supp. 2,** 488; **Supp. 4,** 818
Physical therapy: training in, **Supp. 2,** 417; yoga use, **Supp. 10,** 696
Physicians. For complete list, *see* Occupations Index
Physicians and surgeons. *See* College of Physicians and Surgeons
Physicochemical experimentation, **Vol. 8, Part 1,** 557 f
Physics; **Vol. 1, Part 1,** 602; **Vol. 1, Part 2,** 159; **Vol. 2, Part 1,** 261; **Vol. 4, Part 1,** 248; **Vol. 6, Part 1,** 515 f.; **Vol. 6, Part 2,** 256, 531; **Vol. 9, Part 2,** 655; astrophysics, **Supp. 3,** 290–91; **Supp. 9,** 113–14; **Supp. 10,** 840; atmospheric, **Supp. 4,** 410; chemical, **Supp. 10,** 805; Compton effect, **Supp. 7,** 133; cosmic rays, **Supp. 7,** 134, 344, 619; discoveries in, **Vol. 8, Part 1,** 223 f.; electrodynamical theory, **Supp. 4,** 58; electromagnetism emission theory, **Supp. 5,** 528–29; electron-atom inert gases collision studies, **Supp. 7,** 258; electron charge measurement, **Supp. 5,** 495; electron wave research, **Supp. 9,** 304; electron wave theory, **Supp. 6,** 151; ergodic theorem, **Supp. 3,** 70–71; experimental, notable contributions to, **Vol. 10, Part 1,** 584 f.; Fermi-Dirac statistics, **Supp. 5,** 219, 221; fission of natural uranium recorded, **Supp. 9,** 248; gaseous diffusion, **Supp. 9,** 248, 542; gestalts in, **Supp. 8,** 343–44; **Supp. 8,** 345; heats or solids theory, **Supp. 7,** 411; high-pressure, **Supp. 7,** 74–75; identical discoveries, Faraday and Henry, **Vol. 4, Part 2,** 551; infrared radiation, **Supp. 4,** 658; ionization of gases, **Supp. 5,** 126; light, study of, **Vol. 6, Part 2,** 594 f.; magnetization, **Vol. 3, Part 1,** 87 f.; **Vol. 8, Part 2,** 198; mathematical, **Supp. 4,** 839; **Supp. 5,** 528–29; Michelson-Morley ether-drift experiments, **Supp. 3,** 523–24; microwave electronics, **Supp. 4,** 358–59; molecular, **Supp. 8,** 627–28; molecular-beam laboratories, **Supp. 8,** 628; molecular spectroscopy, **Supp. 10,** 805; Nobel Prize, **Supp. 5,** 202, 220, 495, 496; **Supp. 7,** 75, 258, 344; **Supp. 8,** 628; nuclear, **Supp. 6,** 370; **Supp. 7,** 10–11, 300, 731–32; nuclear shell model theory, **Supp. 9,** 542; paramagnetism, quantum theory of, **Supp. 10,** 804–5; philosophy of, **Supp. 7,** 74–75, 134–35; quantum mechanics, **Supp. 6,** 655; **Supp. 9,** 541, 542; **Supp. 10,** 741, 742; quantum theory, **Supp. 4,** 488, 818, 838–39; **Supp. 5,** 203–4, 219–21, 495–96, 529, 563; **Supp. 6,** 655; **Supp. 7,** 133, 258–59, 517; **Supp. 8,** 628; radioactive alpha decay theory, **Supp. 8,** 199; relativity theory, **Supp. 5,** 202–3; **Supp. 6,** 653; research in, **Supp. 6,** 500–501; **Supp. 10,** 52; shock waves, **Supp. 6,** 656; soil, **Supp. 7,** 76; sound reproducing machine, **Vol. 3, Part 1,** 221; spectrum, research in, **Vol. 6, Part 1,** 213; teaching of, **Vol. 4, Part 2,** 58; **Vol. 6, Part 1,** 399; **Vol. 6, Part 2,** 448; **Vol. 7, Part 1,** 491 f., 525; **Vol. 8, Part 2,** 114, 277; **Vol. 9, Part 1,** 37; **Vol. 9, Part 2,** 652, 654; **Supp. 3,** 523; **Supp. 4,** 818; technical expenments, **Vol. 8, Part 2,** 198; terrestrial magnetism, **Vol. 1, Part 1,** 461 f.; textbooks, **Supp. 5,** 154; theoretical, **Vol. 2, Part 1,** 261; **Supp. 8,** 122–23, 190–91, 482–85; theoretical, annual conferences on, **Supp. 8,** 199; thermal, **Supp. 1,** 57; ultraviolet spectroscopy, **Supp. 5,** 441; vortex streets theory, **Supp. 7,** 410–11; writings on, **Vol. 9, Part 2,** 655; **Vol. 10, Part 1,** 584 f.; **Supp. 3,** 11, 291; **Supp. 10,** 741, 742. *See also* Biophysics; Geophysics; Nuclear physics; Quantum theory
Physiography: **Vol. 4, Part 2,** 444; **Vol. 8, Part 2,** 243; **Vol. 10, Part 1,** 124; fieldwork, **Supp. 4,** 32–33; teaching of, **Supp. 4,** 119
Physiological Zoology, **Supp. 5,** 110
Physiology: **Vol. 1, Part 2,** 106; **Vol. 3, Part 2,** 472; **Vol. 4, Part 2,** 465; **Vol. 5, Part 1,** 205; **Vol. 5, Part 2,** 366 f., 459; **Vol. 6, Part 1,** 349 f.; **Vol. 6, Part 2,** 520; **Vol. 8, Part 1,** 317 f.; adrenal glands, **Vol. 9, Part 2,** 9; behaviorism, **Supp. 3,** 172; **Supp. 6,** 367–68; biochemical, **Supp. 3,** 163–64, 350–51; **Supp. 9,** 443; blood, **Supp. 3,** 369–70; body heat, **Supp. 3,** 32; body temperature, **Supp. 4,** 58–59; cerebral ape and human studies, **Supp. 6,** 223; circulatory system, **Supp. 4,** 390; cocaine, **Supp. 3,** 430; digestion, **Supp. 3,** 133–34; effect of drugs, **Vol. 3, Part 1,** 6; **Vol. 8, Part 1,** 317 f.; emotions, **Supp. 3,** 134–37; endocrinology, **Vol. 8, Part 2,** 306; experiments in connection with meteorology, **Vol. 6, Part 1,** 280; fatigue, **Supp. 3,** 351; laboratory, first in America, **Vol. 1, Part 2,** 494 f.; laboratory equipment, production of, **Supp. 4,** 676; laboratory instruction in, **Supp. 2,** 373; library on, **Supp. 6,** 223, 224; nerve impulse conduction, **Supp. 7,** 226, 280; Nobel Prize, **Supp. 4,** 581; **Supp. 5,** 489; **Supp. 7,** 226, 281, 341, 476; **Supp. 8,** 450; optical, **Supp. 3,** 269–70; perceptual theory, **Supp. 8,** 344, 345; pioneer work, **Vol. 6, Part 2,** 338; plant, **Supp. 4,** 191–92, 381–82, 500–501, 862–63; **Supp. 6,** 176; plant-sodium studies, **Supp. 7,** 592; public health studies, **Supp. 6,** 175; renal, **Supp. 7,** 699–700; research in, **Supp. 2,** 391; **Supp. 4,** 34; **Supp. 6,** 100; reproductive system, **Supp. 3,** 6; systematic teaching, pioneer, **Vol. 3, Part 1,** 512 f.; teaching of, **Vol. 2, Part 2,** 616 f.; **Vol. 5, Part 1,** 252; **Vol. 9, Part 1,** 298; **Vol. 9, Part 2,** 478; **Supp. 4,** 676; vision, study of, **Vol. 9, Part 2,** 647; writings on, **Vol. 9, Part 2,** 9 f. *See also* Anatomy
Physiology of Man, **Vol. 3, Part 2,** 473
Physostigmine, synthesis of, **Supp. 9,** 443
Piaget, Jean, reference to, **Supp. 6,** 527
Piano: manufacture, **Vol. 1, Part 2,** 550; **Vol. 2, Part 2,** 65; **Vol. 5, Part 2,** 448; **Vol. 6, Part 2,** 364; **Vol. 9, Part 1,** 551, 567 f.; **Vol. 9, Part 2,** 637; **Vol. 10, Part 1,** 581; player piano, **Vol. 6, Part 2,** 168; **Vol. 9, Part 2,** 637; playing, **Vol. 1, Part 1,** 491; **Vol. 3, Part 1,** 205; **Vol. 4, Part 1,** 442, 614, 616; **Vol. 5, Part 1,** 117, 621; **Vol. 5, Part 2,** 217 f., 442; **Vol. 6, Part 1,** 238; **Vol. 6, Part 2,** 378; **Vol. 7, Part 2,** 265; **Vol. 9, Part 1,** 103, 590; **Vol. 9, Part 2,** 305 f., 421, 556; **Vol. 10, Part 1,** 581; **Vol. 10, Part 2,** 453; studies, **Vol. 8, Part 1,** 200 f.; teaching, **Vol. 7, Part 2,** 458; **Vol. 9, Part 2,** 305 f.
Picasso, Pablo, references to, **Supp. 4,** 174, 175, 619, 768, 771, 780; **Supp. 6,** 194, 512, 552, 553; **Supp. 9,** 60, 501; **Supp. 10,** 832
Piccard, Auguste, reterences to, **Supp. 7,** 618, 619
Pichel, Irving, reference to, **Supp. 7,** 412
Pick, E. P., reference to, **Supp. 3,** 441
Pickering, Edward Charles, reference to, **Supp. 6,** 561
Pickering, John, impeachment of, **Vol. 7, Part 1,** 505
Pickering, Timothy, reference to, **Vol. 6, Part 1,** 465
Pickett's charge, **Vol. 5, Part 1,** 387; **Vol. 6, Part 1,** 126; **Vol. 9, Part 2,** 642
Pickford, Mary, references to, **Supp. 2,** 368; **Supp. 4,** 350; **Supp. 5,** 443; **Supp. 8,** 214; **Supp. 10,** 871, 872
Picnic, **Supp. 9,** 421
Pictorial Field Book of the Revolution, **Vol. 6, Part 1,** 422
Pictorial History of W. E. B. Du Bois, A, **Supp. 10,** 13
Pierce, E. A., and Co., Merrill Lynch partnership, **Supp. 9,** 613, 614

Pierce, Franklin, references to, **Vol. 3, Part 1**, 335 **Vol. 4, Part 2**, 426, 428 f.
Pierian Sodality, **Vol. 3, Part 1**, 567 f.
Pierpont Morgan Library. *See* Morgan Library
Pietism, **Vol. 7, Part 1**, 310; **Vol. 9, Part 1**, 428
Pigeon Creek, Ind., Lincoln's home, **Vol. 6, Part 1**, 243 f.
Piggly Wiggly grocery chain, **Supp. 5**, 604; **Supp. 7**, 141
"Pigs in Clover," invention of, **Vol. 6, Part 1**, 479
Pike County Ballads, **Vol. 4, Part 2**, 432; **Vol. 7, Part 1**, 511
Pikes Peak: auto race, **Supp. 2**, 525; exploration of, **Vol. 5, Part 1**, 576; **Vol. 7, Part 2**, 599; gold rush, **Vol. 9, Part 2**, 263
Pilcher, Lewis Stephen, reference to, **Supp. 6**, 664
Pilgrims: **Vol. 1, Part 1**, 146, 216; **Vol. 2, Part 1**, 30; **Vol. 3, Part 2**, 156 f.; **Vol. 7, Part 1**, 254, 261; **Vol. 10, Part 2**, 20; church, **Vol. 10, Part 2**, 400; organization, **Vol. 3, Part 1**, 5, 319; Plymouth Colony, early days in, **Vol. 1, Part 2**, 560 f.; **Vol. 2, Part 1**, 551; **Vol. 9, Part 1**, 500; relations with Indians, **Vol. 6, Part 2**, 380. *See also* Plymouth Colony
Pilgrim Trust, founding of, **Supp. 2**, 284
Pillar of Fire Church, founding of, **Supp. 4**, 875–76
Pilot, **Vol. 3, Part 1**, 361; **Vol. 7, Part 2**, 53
Pilot-boat service, improvement in, **Vol. 8, Part 1**, 48
Pim, Richard, reference to, **Supp. 6**, 131
Pima Indians, **Supp. 4**, 71–72
Pinchot, Gifford, references to, **Supp. 1**, 300; **Supp. 3**, 7, 96, 321, 603, 604, 724–25; **Supp. 4**, 43, 481, 522; **Supp. 5**, 666, 699; **Supp. 6**, 509–10, 515; **Supp. 7**, 305, 606, 607; **Supp. 9**, 426; **Supp. 10**, 241
Pinckney, Thomas, reference to, **Vol. 9, Part 1**, 129
Pinckney draft of Constitution, **Vol. 7, Part 2**, 612
Pinckney's Treaty (1795), **Vol. 7, Part 2**, 619; **Vol. 8, Part 1**, 355; **Vol. 9, Part 1**, 129; **Vol. 10, Part 1**, 509 f., 524
Pineapple industry, **Supp. 6**, 168–69
Pine Ridge Agency, troubles at, **Vol. 2, Part 1**, 519; **Vol. 6, Part 2**, 615; **Vol. 8, Part 1**, 437; **Vol. 9, Part 1**, 193
Pingree, Hazen S., references to, **Supp. 3**, 188, 231
Pink, Louis, reference to, **Supp. 5**, 631
Pinkerton, Allan, references to, **Vol. 6, Part 1**, 584; **Vol. 9, Part 1**, 193
Pink eye. *See* Conjunctivitis
Pinkham, Lydia E., fraud case, **Supp. 5**, 666
Pinkney, William, reference to, **Vol. 7, Part 1**, 88 f.
Pinky, **Supp. 10**, 818
Pin manufacture, **Vol. 5, Part 1**, 291; **Vol. 8, Part 1**, 522; **Vol. 9, Part 2**, 218
Pintard, John, reference to, **Vol. 8, Part 2**, 593
Pioneer, **Vol. 6, Part 1**, 459
"Pioneer," first Pullman car, **Vol. 8, Part 1**, 263 f.
Pioneering: **Vol. 1, Part 1**, 475, 554; **Vol. 2, Part 1**, 256; **Vol. 3, Part 1**, 349; **Vol. 4, Part 1**, 93, 178, 256; **Vol. 4, Part 2**, 314; **Vol. 5, Part 2**, 47; **Vol. 6, Part 1**, 4, 357, 365, 533; **Vol. 6, Part 2**, 50; **Vol. 7, Part 1**, 483; **Vol. 8, Part 2**, 25, 251, 274; **Vol. 9, Part 1**, 61, 284; historical writings on, **Supp. 8**, 60; novels about, **Supp. 4**, 38–39, 154, 877–78; **Supp. 5**, 14–15; **Supp. 8**, 533, 567. *See also* Frontier
"Pious Fund of the Californias," **Vol. 3, Part 1**, 422; **Vol. 7, Part 2**, 426
Piper Aircraft Corporation, founding of, **Supp. 8**, 504; **Supp. 10**, 149
Piper case, **Vol. 5, Part 1**, 455
Piracy: **Vol. 3, Part 1**, 483; **Vol. 3, Part 2**, 128; **Vol. 4, Part 2**, 161 f.; **Vol. 5, Part 1**, 474; **Vol. 5, Part 2**, 116 f.; **Vol. 8, Part 1**, 140 f., 287, 299 f.; **Vol. 8, Part 2**, 85; Barbary pirates, **Vol. 1, Part 1**, 504; **Vol. 5, Part 2**, 7, 22, 30; **Vol. 6, Part 1**, 77; bibliographer and writer on, **Vol. 8, Part 1**, 287 f.; Captain Kidd, **Vol. 5, Part 2**, 367; **Vol. 6, Part 1**, 319; Charleston, S.C., **Vol. 5, Part 2**, 116 f.; hanging of pirates, in Boston, **Vol. 8, Part 1**, 299 f.; Jones, John Paul, as pirate, **Vol. 5, Part 2**, 184 f.; Mississippi River, **Vol. 6, Part 2**, 374; suppression of, in the West Indies, **Vol. 4, Part 2**, 382; **Vol. 8, Part 1**, 83 f.
Pirenne, Henri, reference to, **Supp. 5**, 655
Pirson, Louis V., reference to, **Supp. 4**, 194
Pisan Cantos, **Supp. 7**, 347
Pissarro, Camille, reference to, **Supp. 6**, 552
Pistols, manufacturing of, **Vol. 7, Part 1**, 561; **Vol. 8, Part 1**, 498 f.
Pi-Suñer, Jaime, reference to, **Supp. 6**, 223
"Pitcher, Molly," references to, **Vol. 5, Part 1**, 574; **Vol. 6, Part 1**, 500
Pitch-pipe, introduction of, **Vol. 1, Part 2**, 270
Pitkin, Horace T., reference to, **Supp. 3**, 476
Pitkin, Walter B., reference to, **Supp. 5**, 503
Pittman-Robertson Act (1937), **Supp. 9**, 663
Pittsburgh, Pa.: Carnegie libraries, **Supp. 4**, 19; cholera epidemic in, **Vol. 3, Part 1**, 220; Croghan Hall, **Vol. 2, Part 2**, 556; education, **Vol. 3, Part 1**, 511 f.; Fort Dunmore built at original site of, **Vol. 3, Part 1**, 317, 519 f.; glassworks, **Vol. 7, Part 2**, 4, 638; KDKA radio station, **Supp. 3**, 184–85; Kingsley House, **Vol. 5, Part 1**, 101; museum, **Vol. 5, Part 2**, 557; philanthropy, **Vol. 9, Part 2**, 397; politics, **Supp. 8**, 360–61; public service, **Vol. 1, Part 2**, 545; **Vol. 4, Part 2**, 60; **Vol. 6, Part 1**, 590; **Vol. 6, Part 2**, 197; **Vol. 7, Part 2**, 20; **Vol. 8, Part 2**, 526; steel center, as a, **Vol. 6, Part 2**, 583; synod, founding of, **Vol. 7, Part 2**, 289; water supply, **Vol. 7, Part 2**, 540; writings about, **Vol. 5, Part 2**, 559
Pittsburgh Academy, establishment of, **Vol. 1, Part 2**, 545
Pittsburgh Coal Co., organization of, **Vol. 7, Part 2**, 20
Pittsburgh Federation of Jewish Philanthropies, founding of, **Supp. 4**, 261–62
Pittsburgh Gazette, first issue, **Vol. 8, Part 2**, 526
Pittsburgh Landing, Tenn., battle of. *See* Shiloh, battle of
Pittsburgh Pirates (baseball), **Supp. 5**, 716–17; **Supp. 7**, 501, 502, 768–69; **Supp. 9**, 178–80, 529, 806; **Supp. 10**, 99, 573–74
Pittsburgh Post Gazette, **Supp. 3**, 80
Pittsburgh Safety Glass Corporation, founding of, **Supp. 7**, 169
Pittsburgh Skin and Cancer Foundation, establishment of, **Vol. 8, Part 1**, 449
Pittsburgh Steelers (football), **Supp. 6**, 47
Pittsburgh Survey (urban survey), **Supp. 6**, 329–30
Pittsburgh Symphony, **Supp. 7**, 640
Pittsburgh Times, founding of, **Vol. 7, Part 1**, 443
Pituitary gland: blood flow to, **Supp. 6**, 704; function, **Supp. 6**, 386; separate functions of, **Supp. 3**, 370
Place in the Sun, A, **Supp. 9**, 768
Placenta, **Supp. 6**, 704
Plagiarism, **Vol. 7, Part 1**, 49; **Vol. 8, Part 1**, 47 f.
Plagioclase solid solution, **Supp. 6**, 71
Plaindealer, radical paper of 1837, **Vol. 6, Part 1**, 148
Plains Indians, culture, **Supp. 1**, 651
Plain Talk, **Supp. 6**, 350
Planck, Max, references to, **Supp. 5**, 202, 495; **Supp. 8**, 122
Planetariums, **Supp. 2**, 293
Plankton, **Supp. 4**, 461, 462
Planned communities. *See* Model communities
Planned Parenthood Association of Baltimore, founding of, **Supp. 4**, 391
Planned Parenthood Federation of America: founding

of, **Supp. 8**, 569; legal counsel, **Supp. 10**, 221; presidency, **Supp. 9**, 352
Planned Parenthood Federations, **Supp. 6**, 602
Planning boards. *See* City planning; Zoning
"Plan of Union," Congregationalists and Presbyterians, **Vol. 1, Part 1**, 480, 628
Plantations (for specific names, *see* Homesteads): **Vol. 4, Part 1**, 489; **Vol. 4, Part 2**, 65, 188, 213, 214; **Vol. 5, Part 1**, 206, 348; **Vol. 6, Part 1**, 524; **Vol. 7, Part 1**, 14; cotton and sugar cane, **Vol. 9, Part 1**, 427; development of, **Vol. 3, Part 2**, 439; historical studies, **Supp. 1**, 597; life in South Carolina, **Vol. 6, Part 1**, 33; of the South, **Vol. 6, Part 1**, 88, 90
Planter, famous dispatch boat, **Vol. 9, Part 1**, 224 f.
Plant Industry, Bureau of, **Vol. 4, Part 2**, 312
Plants: breeding of, **Vol. 2, Part 1**, 266 f.; **Vol. 8, Part 1**, 233, 236 f., 239, 589; **Vol. 9, Part 1**, 458; collections of, **Vol. 8, Part 2**, 484; edible wild, **Supp. 9**, 307, 308; hormone studies, **Supp. 10**, 297; introduction of, into U.S., **Vol. 7, Part 2**, 481; **Vol. 10, Part 2**, 321; pathology of, **Vol. 8, Part 1**, 239 f.; **Vol. 8, Part 2**, 309; **Vol. 9, Part 1**, 263; photographic studies, **Supp. 10**, 162; scientific study of, **Vol. 3, Part 1**, 606 f.; **Vol. 8, Part 1**, 154 f.; **Vol. 9, Part 2**, 477, 596. *See also* Botany; Horticulture
"Plasma," term coined, **Supp. 6**, 364–65
Plastic Ono Band (music group), **Supp. 10**, 450
Plastics: Bakelite, **Supp. 3**, 26–27; development of, **Supp. 6**, 334; from petroleum wastes, **Supp. 3**, 239; urea-formaldehyde, **Supp. 3**, 247
Plastic surgery: flap technique, **Supp. 4**, 220–21; for leprosy, **Supp. 4**, 530; reconstructive, **Supp. 2**, 706–7; **Supp. 6**, 632
Plate, William J., reference to, **Supp. 8**, 113–14
Plate-glass manufacture, **Vol. 3, Part 2**, 517; **Vol. 5, Part 1**, 74; **Vol. 7, Part 2**, 636
Plath, Sylvia, reference to, **Supp. 9**, 628
Platinum, pioneer use of, **Vol. 4, Part 2**, 344
Plato, writings on, **Supp. 5**, 224–25
Platt, Thomas C., references to, **Vol. 7, Part 1**, 623; **Vol. 8, Part 1**, 302 f., 326 f., 485; **Supp. 3**, 464
Platt Amendment, **Vol. 1, Part 1**, 154; **Vol. 6, Part 2**, 108 f.; **Vol. 8, Part 1**, 2 f.; **Vol. 8, Part 2**, 137.
Plattsburgh, battle of, **Vol. 4, Part 1**, 523; **Vol. 6, Part 2**, 20, 156
Play, first written in U.S., **Vol. 5, Part 1**, 402
Playboy, **Supp. 8**, 412
Players' Club, founder of, **Vol. 1, Part 2**, 447; **Vol. 5, Part 2**, 16
Playground Association of America, founding of, **Supp. 2**, 375
Playgrounds, **Supp. 1**, 595; **Supp. 2**, 374–75
Playwrights. For complete list, *see* Occupations Index
Playwrights' Company: **Supp. 5**, 624; **Supp. 6**, 15; **Supp. 9**, 71; founding of, **Supp. 2**, 325; **Supp. 8**, 529
Playwriting, first school of, **Vol. 8, Part 1**, 221
Plaza Hotel (New York City), **Supp. 10**, 336
Pleasant Hill, battle of, **Vol. 1, Part 1**, 579; **Vol. 2, Part 1**, 469; **Vol. 2, Part 2**, 105; **Vol. 5, Part 2**, 425
Pleasure of His Company, The, **Supp. 10**, 740
Plebiscites, **Supp. 5**, 723–24
Pleistocene era, classification of glacial drift, **Supp. 3**, 456
Plessy v. *Ferguson*, **Supp. 9**, 363
Pleurisy, treatment of, **Vol. 10, Part 2**, 585
Pleyel harpsichord, **Supp. 6**, 357, 358
Plimpton, George A., reference to, **Supp. 3**, 722
Plows: cast-iron, **Vol. 6, Part 1**, 614; improved drill, devised, **Vol. 4, Part 1**, 98; inventions, **Vol. 6, Part 1**, 607 f., 614; manufacture, **Vol. 3, Part 1**, 193 f.; **Vol. 3, Part 2**, 251; **Vol. 6, Part 1**, 614; perfection of steam, **Vol. 8, Part 1**, 522
Plumber and Sanitary Engineer, founding of, **Supp. 1**, 552
Plumbing, improvements in, **Supp. 1**, 552
Plumb Plan, **Supp. 2**, 351; **Supp. 3**, 241
Plummer, Henry S., reference to, **Supp. 3**, 832
Plums, development of American varieties of, **Vol. 8, Part 1**, 233
Plutonium, manufacture of, **Supp. 6**, 371; **Supp. 8**, 230, 231
Plymouth, Mass., history of, **Vol. 3, Part 1**, 147 f.
Plymouth Brethren, **Vol. 7, Part 1**, 558; **Vol. 9, Part 1**, 274; **Supp. 5**, 346
Plymouth car, **Supp. 4**, 301, 302
Plymouth Colony, **Vol. 1, Part 2**, 560 ff.; **Vol. 2, Part 1**, 167, 551; **Vol. 3, Part 1**, 5 f., 172; **Vol. 7, Part 1**, 261; **Vol. 9, Part 1**, 500; **Vol. 10, Part 2**, 393, 400
Plymouth County Academy, **Vol. 7, Part 1**, 59
PM, **Supp. 8**, 379; founding of, **Supp. 6**, 202
Pneumatic: drill, invention of, **Vol. 4, Part 2**, 401; hoisting, **Vol. 7, Part 1**, 547; tools, **Supp. 1**, 446; tunnels, **Vol. 1, Part 2**, 81
Pneumatics, in construction, **Supp. 2**, 469
Pneumatic Steel Association, organized, **Vol. 3, Part 1**, 548 f.
Pneumoencephalography, **Supp. 4**, 214
Pneumonia: epidemic, **Supp. 3**, 483; research on, **Vol. 7, Part 1**, 628; **Supp. 5**, 63; **Supp. 9**, 530–31
Pocahontas: **Vol. 9, Part 1**, 295; biography of, **Vol. 8, Part 2**, 31; capture of, **Vol. 1, Part 1**, 345; descendants of, in Virginia, **Vol. 8, Part 2**, 26; husband of, **Vol. 1, Part 1**, 345; **Vol. 8, Part 2**, 118
Pocket Books, Inc., **Supp. 7**, 243; founding of, **Supp. 6**, 583; **Supp. 8**, 579
Pocket Magazine, The, founding of, **Supp. 2**, 633
"Pocket veto," **Vol. 8, Part 2**, 347
Poe, Edgar Allan: **Vol. 2, Part 1**, 41; **Vol. 2, Part 2**, 81 f.; **Vol. 3, Part 2**, 305; **Vol. 4, Part 2**, 339; **Vol. 5, Part 1**, 68, 73, 110, 483, **Vol. 6, Part 1**, 212, 339, 558; **Vol. 7, Part 1**, 25, 399; **Vol. 9, Part 1**, 245, 576; **Vol. 10, Part 1**, 378 f.; "Bells, The," published, **Vol. 8, Part 2**, 372; biographies of, **Vol. 4, Part 2**, 344; **Supp. 4**, 13, 14; **Supp. 6**, 523; psychological analysis of, **Supp. 8**, 353; publishing of works of, **Vol. 8, Part 1**, 440 f.; **Vol. 9, Part 1**, 497, 553; "Raven, The," manuscript, **Vol. 9, Part 2**, 357; references to, **Supp. 10**, 103, 104; relations with Chivers, **Vol. 2, Part 2**, 81 f.; relations with Griswold, **Vol. 4, Part 2**, 11 f.; relations with Osgood, **Vol. 7, Part 2**, 77; relations with Thomas Willis White, **Vol. 10, Part 2**, 121; relations with Helen Whitman, **Vol. 10, Part 2**, 143; study of, **Supp. 7**, 797
Poet in the Desert, The, **Supp. 3**, 837
Poet Lore, **Vol. 2, Part 2**, 152
Poetry: **Vol. 1, Part 1**, 158, 373, 583, 609 f.; **Vol. 1, Part 2**, 46, 139 f., 345, 365, 383, 416, 423 f., 435, 470, 542, 558, 577, 590; **Vol. 2, Part 1**, 69, 75, 79, 81 f., 111, 155, 171, 183, 190, 199 f., 264, 273, 285 f., 322, 370 f., 381, 473, 530, 553, 556, 579, 613; **Vol. 2, Part 2**, 7 f., 53, 149, 158 f., 160, 218 f., 220, 237, 344, 356, 388, 390 f., 396, 452 f., 501, 503, 513, 562 f., 578; **Vol. 3, Part 1**, 20, 71 f., 94 f., 199, 248, 281, 294, 297 f., 366, 369, 381, 383, 384, 431 f., 476 f., 484 f., 491 f., 505 f., 513 f., 516 f., 546 f., 550 f., 569 f., 573 f., 595 f., 600 f.; **Vol. 3, Part 2**, 125, 208, 258 f., 347, 450 f., 541; **Vol. 4, Part 1**, 27 f., 103, 277, 298, 305, 346, 452 f., 561, 573; **Vol. 4, Part 2**, 111, 130, 149 f., 237, 363, 455, 525, 606; **Vol. 5, Part 1**, 52 f., 60, 68, 110, 144, 162, 170 f., 205 f., 215, 245, 273, 291 f., 310, 335, 375, 417, 459, 542, 612; **Vol. 5, Part 2**, 13, 37, 101, 154, 160, 373, 417, 466, 505 f., 522, 523, 526, 602, 604 f., 614; **Vol. 6, Part 1**, 14 f., 16, 17, 65, 212, 276, 278,

281, 284, 346, 382 f., 387 f., 411, 433, 454, 460 f., 470, 483 f., 508, 538; **Vol. 6, Part 2**, 63, 84, 104, 131, 139, 227, 287, 517, 566, 606; **Vol. 7, Part 1**, 78, 207 f., 266, 291, 378, 459, 499, 520, 607, 608 f.; **Vol. 7, Part 2**, 47, 53, 68, 70, 77, 157 f., 211, 275, 339, 460, 489, 513 f., 556 f., 586, 595, 625; **Vol. 8, Part 1**, 16 f., 19 f., 46 f., 61 f., 65 f., 92 f., 104 f., 111, 121 f., 133 f., 151 f., 163 f., 171, 181 f., 186 f., 188 f., 201 f., 204, 223 f., 226 f., 247 f., 285, 298, 301 f., 311 f., 322 f., 331 f., 348, 374, 388, 408, 431, 434 f., 450, 481 f., 493 f., 509, 587, 611 f.; **Vol. 8, Part 2**, 63, 119, 156, 167 f., 192, 241, 242, 345, 352, 390, 399, 485, 534, 555, 608; **Vol. 9, Part 1**, 42, 82, 158, 171, 470 f., 523, 561, 586 f.; **Vol. 9, Part 2**, 50, 54, 58, 75, 102, 109 f., 134 f., 256, 263, 315 f., 357 f., 397, 428 f., 430, 444, 460, 483, 558–59; **Vol. 10, Part 1**, 44 f., 45, 54, 124, 168, 378 f., 392 f., 426, 432, 440 f., 454, 457, 484, 572 f., 617; **Vol. 10, Part 2**, 37, 84, 139, 145 f., 173 f., 203, 252, 306, 343, 348, 446, 479, 513, 518, 578; **Supp. 2**, 428–30; **Supp. 3**, 598; **Supp. 4**, 840–41; **Supp. 5**, 73–74, 658–61; **Supp. 7**, 390–91, 653–55; **Supp. 8**, 291, 582; **Supp. 9**, 53–55, 108,109, 348–49; abandonment of neoclassical rules in, **Vol. 10, Part 1**, 10; agrarianism, **Supp. 9**, 643; **Supp. 10**, 776; American commemorative, **Supp. 6**, 417–18; black, **Supp. 4**, 200–201; 528; **Supp. 7**, 236–37; **Supp. 8**, 286–88; **Supp. 10**, 321–22; blank verse, **Supp. 1**, 633–34; Buddhist influence, **Supp. 8**, 327; **Supp. 9**, 846; Civil War, **Vol. 9, Part 2**, 525; colonial, **Vol. 7, Part 1**, 602 f.; confessional, **Supp. 7**, 621–22; **Supp. 9**, 85–87; **Supp. 10**, 469; criticism, **Supp. 4**, 694, 812; **Supp. 7**, 390–91; **Supp. 8**, 42, 43; "Croaker Papers," **Vol. 3, Part 1**, 431; cubism relationship, **Supp. 7**, 789; development of American, **Vol. 4, Part 2**, 419 f.; epic, in America, **Vol. 3, Part 1**, 573 f.; **Supp. 3**, 57–58; epigrammatic, **Supp. 8**, 492, 493; formalism, **Supp. 10**, 468; free verse, **Supp. 8**, 563–64; free-verse drama, **Supp. 3**, 941; French imagists, **Vol. 6, Part 1**, 454; fugitive school, **Supp. 6**, 461; geography used in, **Supp. 10**, 45; Harlem Renaissance, **Supp. 4**, 200–201; **Supp. 10**, 321; Harris Collection of American, **Vol. 4, Part 1**, 561; **Vol. 4, Part 2**, 305; historical writings on, **Supp. 8**, 350; household, **Vol. 1, Part 1**, 135; humorous, **Supp. 9**, 578–80; imagists, **Supp. 4**, 285–86; **Supp. 9**, 617; innovative, **Supp. 7**, 218–22; lecturing on, **Supp. 4**, 13; light verse, **Supp. 10**, 496–97; little magazines, **Supp. 8**, 349–50; lyric, **Supp. 1**, 623; **Supp. 4**, 576–77; **Supp. 8**, 42–43; **Supp. 10**, 831, 854; mock epic, **Supp. 5**, 30; modernism, **Supp. 9**, 557–59, 605–6, 618, 643; **Supp. 10**, 869; New Criticism, **Supp. 7**, 55–56, 347, 442; **Supp. 9**, 643; nonsense, **Supp. 3**, 629; **Supp. 5**, 94; **Supp. 10**, 448; objectivism, **Supp. 10**, 869–70; old French, **Supp. 3**, 22; philosophical inhumanism, **Supp. 7**, 392; popular verse, **Supp. 6**, 258–59, 574–75; prison experences, **Supp. 6**, 238; proletarian, **Supp. 7**, 239–40; publications, **Supp. 2**, 466; readings, technique of Vachel Lindsay, **Vol. 6, Part 1**, 276; readings to jazz accompaniment, **Supp. 9**, 605–6; regional, **Supp. 5**, 118–19; romantic, **Supp. 3**, 454–55; **Supp. 4**, 73; satirical, **Vol. 10, Part 1**, 11; "sentence-sound" blank-verse narrative, **Supp. 7**, 270–73; social reform themes, **Supp. 4**, 811–12; **Supp. 6**, 113; **Supp. 10**, 709–10, 869; sonnets, **Supp. 6**, 462; *Spoon River Anthology*, **Supp. 4, 555; symbolism, Supp. 1**, 206; teaching of, **Supp. 7**, 653–55, traditional, **Supp. 7**, 346–47; **Supp. 9**, 711–12, 828–29; typographical experimentation, **Supp. 7**, 158, 159; "variable foot," **Supp. 7**, 790; verse drama, **Supp. 9**, 53; vorticism, **Supp. 9**, 617–18; writings on, **Supp. 3**, 72–73, 475–76; Yiddish, **Vol. 10, Part 2**, 662

Poetry: A Magazine of Verse, founding of, **Supp. 2**, 466; **Supp. 10**, 869

Poetry Center, **Supp. 7**, 442

Poetry Society of America, founding of, **Supp. 4**, 694

Poetry Society of South Carolina, founding of, **Supp. 2**, 302; **Supp. 4**, 13,

Poets. For complete list, *see* Occupations Index

Poets and Poetry of America, **Vol. 4, Part 2**, 11

"Pogo" (fictional character), **Supp. 9**, 452–53

Pogo stick, invention of, **Supp. 9**, 361

Poinsettia, development of, **Vol. 8, Part 1**, 30 f.

Point Four Program, **Supp. 5**, 49

Point Pleasant, W.Va., **Vol. 2, Part 2**, 448; **Vol. 3, Part 1**, 520; **Vol. 6, Part 1**, 206; **Vol. 9, Part 1**, 59, 254

Poison, rattlesnake, **Vol. 7, Part 1**, 62

Poison gas. *See* Biological and chemical warfare

Poisons: environmental, **Supp. 3**, 18; **Supp. 6**, 175; industrial, **Supp. 8**, 241–42; labeling of, **Supp. 6**, 317; rattlesnake, **Vol. 7, Part 1**, 62

Polacca (pioneer steamboat), **Vol. 8, Part 2**, 134

Poland: diplomacy with U.S., **Supp. 6**, 359–60; **Supp. 7**, 53; sociological studies, **Supp. 6**, 726, 727

Polar expeditions. *See* Antarctica; Arctic regions; Exploration

Polaris, arctic expedition in search of missing steamer, **Vol. 3, Part 1**, 228; **Vol. 10, Part 1**, 102

Polaroid Corporation, financing of, **Supp. 8**, 679

Police: administration, **Supp. 5**, 638–39; **Supp. 9**, 881–82; Boston strike (1919), **Supp. 1**, 194–95; **Supp. 3**, 471; crime detection methods, **Supp. 5**, 245; New York City, **Supp. 7**, 667, 779–80; **Supp. 9**, 400; study of European systems, **Supp. 9**, 287; systems, **Vol. 2, Part 1**, 386; **Vol. 5, Part 2**, 111; **Vol. 6, Part 1**, 229; **Vol. 8, Part 2**, 136; Washington, D.C., **Supp. 6**, 239–40. *See also* Prisons

Police Athletic Association, founding of, **Vol. 7, Part 2**, 602; **Supp. 1**, 569

Police Gazette, **Vol. 3, Part 2**, 571; **Vol. 10, Part 2**, 218

Poling, Clark, reference to, **Supp. 8**, 505–6

Poling, Daniel A., reference to, **Supp. 7**, 345

Poliomyelitis: epidemic, **Supp. 2**, 212; epidemic, New York City, **Supp. 6**, 192; immunology studies, **Supp. 3**, 441; **Supp. 6**, 537; research fund-raising, **Supp. 6**, 90; transmission studies, **Supp. 3**, 775; vaccine development, **Supp. 5**, 512; **Supp. 7**, 649; virus causing, **Supp. 4**, 287–88; **Supp. 5**, 604; Warm Springs Foundation, **Supp. 3**, 644

Polish-Americans, sociological study of, **Supp. 4**, 828–31

Polish Emigrant Protective Association, **Supp. 6**, 726

Polish National Catholic Church in America, founding of, **Supp. 5**, 304–6

Polish Peasant in Europe and America, The, **Supp. 4**, 828, 829, 830, 831

Political: campaign, Cleveland-Blaine, **Vol. 8, Part 2**, 304; cartoons, **Vol. 8, Part 2**, 113; economy, **Vol. 1, Part 1**, 509 f.; **Vol. 2, Part 1**, 487 f.; **Vol. 2, Part 2**, 327; **Vol. 3, Part 1**, 266, 582 f.; **Vol. 3, Part 2**, 143, 515, 539; **Vol. 6, Part 1**, 292; **Vol. 7, Part 2**, 300; **Vol. 8, Part 1**, 124, 325, 400, 409, 491; **Vol. 10, Part 1**, 29, 416, 451, 637; economy, earliest instruction in the subject as a science, **Vol. 3, Part 1**, 266; economy, original conceptions of, **Vol. 8, Part 1**, 400, 407; economy, teaching of, **Vol. 3, Part 2**, 68; **Vol. 5, Part 1**, 164; **Vol. 6, Part 2**, 172; **Vol. 7, Part 2**, 299 f., 482; **Vol. 8, Part 1**, 407; fights, fatal street fight, **Vol. 8, Part 2**, 153; "Georgia platform," **Vol. 5, Part 2**, 44; history, writings in, **Vol. 5, Part 2**, 80; hostess, **Vol. 9, Part 1**, 473; law-suit libel, **Vol. 8, Part 2**, 145; machines, opposition to, **Supp. 10**, 121–22; "orphan," origin of phrase, **Vol. 6, Part 1**, 269; pamphlets, **Vol. 5, Part 2**, 170; **Vol. 9, Part 2**, 332; **Vol.**

10, Part 2, 464; parties, history of, **Vol. 7, Part 1**, 239; patronage, **Vol. 3, Part 2**, 527; **Vol. 5, Part 1**, 86; reform, **Vol. 4, Part 2**, 383; **Vol. 5, Part 2**, 542; **Vol. 6, Part 2**, 171; **Vol. 8, Part 2**, 134; scandals, **Vol. 3, Part 2**, 503; **Vol. 4, Part 1**, 146, 500; **Vol. 4, Part 2**, 255; science, **Vol. 6, Part 1**, 571; **Vol. 6, Part 2**, 176; **Vol. 7, Part 2**, 266; **Vol. 8, Part 1**, 2, 161; **Vol. 10, Part 1**, 37; **Vol. 10, Part 2**, 520; science, teaching of, **Vol. 4, Part 2**, 78; **Vol. 7, Part 1**, 416; **Vol. 9, Part 1**, 286; spoils system, **Vol. 5, Part 2**, 29; **Vol. 6, Part 2**, 275; **Vol. 8, Part 1**, 34 f.; **Vol. 8, Part 2**, 10; writings, **Vol. 1, Part 1**, 81, 84, 92 f.; **Vol. 1, Part 2**, 536, 545; **Vol. 2, Part 1**, 214, 425, 490; **Vol. 2, Part 2**, 248, 320, 345, 415 f., 482 f.; **Vol. 3, Part 1**, 180, 300, 499; **Vol. 3, Part 2**, 216; **Vol. 4, Part 1**, 103, 283, 289, 315 f., 350, 428, 484; **Vol. 4, Part 2**, 189; **Vol. 5, Part 2**, 48; **Vol. 6, Part 2**, 159; **Vol. 8, Part 1**, 223 f., 307 f., 331 f., 468, 491; **Vol. 9, Part 1**, 467; **Vol. 10, Part 1**, 118, 156 f., 594 f., 597 f.

Political action committees: labor, **Supp. 4**, 376, 889–90; **Supp. 5**, 511; **Supp. 6**, 679; **Supp. 10**, 304; manufacturing, **Supp. 7**, 305

Political Equality League, **Supp. 1**, 69

Political parties. *See* Democratic party; Government; Political science; Presidential election *headings;* Republican party; *specific party names*

Political science: analysis and theory, **Supp. 5**, 514; behavioral movement, **Supp. 5**, 484–85; **Supp. 7**, 430; democratic theory defense, **Supp. 5**, 485–86; dissertations in, **Supp. 2**, 608; executive branch power, writings on, **Supp. 8**, 551–52; **Supp. 10**, 215, 217; first civics textbook, **Supp. 3**, 285; first study of European government by American, **Supp. 3**, 469–70; philosophical writings, **Supp. 8**, 407; **Supp. 10**, 215, 217; political parties, writings on, **Supp. 5**, 430; **Supp. 7**, 54; psychoanalytical studies, **Supp. 10**, 433–34; psychological studies, **Supp. 8**, 70; school civics courses, **Supp. 4**, 870; short-ballot doctrine, **Supp. 10**, 121–22; sociological studies, **Supp. 8**, 407; teaching of, **Supp. 1**, 132–33; **Supp. 2**, 220; **Supp. 3**, 337, 830–31; **Supp. 4**, 62, 260; **Supp. 10**, 551; territorial disputes, **Supp. 5**, 723; writings on, **Supp. 1**, 210–11; **Supp. 5**, 521–22, 681; **Supp. 10**, 13. *See also* Government

Political Science Quarterly, **Supp. 1**, 133; founding of, **Vol. 9, Part 1**, 257

Politicians. For complete list, *see* Occupations Index

Politics: blacks in, **Supp. 4**, 607–8; **Supp. 9**, 619–21; business relationship, **Supp. 1**, 168; cartoons and caricatures, **Supp. 3**, 852; **Supp. 4**, 76, 159–60; **Supp. 5**, 391–92, 499, 580; **Supp. 7**, 164; **Supp. 8**, 173–74, 218, 221–22; **Supp. 10**, 292–93; Chicago machine, **Supp. 4**, 450–51; conservatism, **Supp. 9**, 548–49; **Supp. 10**, 22–23; election financing, **Supp. 4**, 752; ethics in, **Supp. 1**, 300; first woman to nominate a major-party candidate for U.S. president, **Supp. 9**, 625–26; first woman winner of statewide election, **Supp. 3**, 710; influence peddling, **Supp. 8**, 219–20, 497; journalism, **Supp. 7**, 320–21; **Supp. 8**, 149–50, 394–95, 496–97; labor involvement, **Supp. 4**, 376; **Supp. 5**, 255; "maverick," origin of term, **Supp. 5**, 480; "Monday Night Group" (Truman political advisers), **Supp. 10**, 227; municipal reform movement, **Supp. 3**, 605–6; Pendergast machine, **Supp. 3**, 596–97; **Supp. 9**, 756–57; public opinion surveys, **Supp. 8**, 70; **Supp. 9**, 677–78; public relations, **Supp. 4**, 575; **Supp. 5**, 303–4; radical left-wing, **Supp. 9**, 679; radical right-wing, **Supp. 10**, 152; reform measures, **Supp. 4**, 844–45; spoils system, **Supp. 2**, 399; state, writings on, **Supp. 7**, 431; television debates, **Supp. 7**, 420; theory of, **Supp. 1**, 133; third-party, **Supp. 9**, 30; women's use of, **Supp. 5**, 62; writings, **Supp. 1**, 209. *See also* Elections; Political science; Presidential election *headings; specific city, state, and party names*

Politics Among Nations: The Struggle for Power and Peace, **Supp. 10**, 551, 552

Politics, Parties and Pressure Groups, **Supp. 7**, 431

Polk, James K., references to, **Vol. 1, Part 2**, 157; **Vol. 8, Part 2**, 509 f.; **Vol. 9, Part 2**, 350 f.

Polk, Willis, reference to, **Supp. 6**, 438

Polk Doctrine, **Vol. 8, Part 1**, 34 f.

Pollak Foundation of Economic Research, **Supp. 4**, 307

Pollister, Arthur W., reference to, **Supp. 9**, 550

Pollock, Charles, references to, **Supp. 6**, 511, 512

Pollock, Jackson, reference to, **Supp. 9**, 79

Pollock, Sir Frederick, references to, **Supp. 1**, 419; **Supp. 5**, 514

Polls. *See* Public opinion

Poll tax: **Supp. 6**, 526; **Supp. 7**, 416; opposition to, **Vol. 7, Part 2**, 123; **Supp. 9**, 401

Pollution: control campaign, **Supp. 10**, 297–98; control legislation, **Supp. 8**, 616; industrial fumes reduction, **Supp. 4**, 184–85; **Supp. 5**, 273; sewage, **Supp. 2**, 169–70, 353. *See also* Air pollution; Ecology

Polo: **Vol. 8, Part 2**, 222; **Vol. 10, Part 2**, 160; **Supp. 3**, 360–61; **Supp. 6**, 210; popularized in U.S., **Vol. 4, Part 1**, 450

Polychromatic printing, **Vol. 1, Part 1**, 457

Polygamy: Edmunds bill to suppress, in Utah, **Vol. 8, Part 1**, 341 f.; Mormon church, **Vol. 3, Part 2**, 25; **Vol. 4, Part 2**, 334; **Vol. 6, Part 1**, 115; **Vol. 8, Part 1**, 601; **Vol. 9, Part 1**, 312 f.

Polygraph, **Vol. 5, Part 2**, 33

Polymerization, **Supp. 6**, 334

Polymers: processing of, **Supp. 2**, 97; research in, **Supp. 2**, 505; solutions, electrical characteristics of, **Supp. 6**, 346

"Polyphonic prose," **Vol. 6, Part 1**, 453 f.

Polytechnic Institute of Brooklyn, biochemistry studies, **Supp. 6**, 595

Pomeroy, Wardell B., reference to, **Supp. 6**, 343

Pomeroy Circular, **Vol. 2, Part 2**, 30; **Vol. 4, Part 1**, 532; **Vol. 8, Part 1**, 54; **Vol. 9, Part 1**, 473; **Vol. 10, Part 1**, 304

Pomology: **Vol. 2, Part 1**, 48; **Vol. 2, Part 2**, 489; **Vol. 3, Part 1**, 418, 419; **Vol. 4, Part 1**, 261; **Vol. 6, Part 1**, 535; **Vol. 6, Part 2**, 252; **Vol. 8, Part 1**, 145 f.; **Vol. 2, Part 2**, 439; writings on, **Vol. 4, Part 1**, 261; **Vol. 8, Part 1**, 233 f; **Vol. 10, Part 1**, 444 f.

Pomona Hall, **Vol. 5, Part 1**, 359

Pond, Adeline Valentine, reference to, **Supp. 3**, 1

Pontiac's conspiracy. *See* Conspiracy, Pontiac

Pony express, **Vol. 1, Part 1**, 28; **Vol. 4, Part 1**, 168; **Vol. 5, Part 2**, 353; **Vol. 6, Part 2**, 215; **Vol. 8, Part 2**, 252

Poole, Ernest, reference to, **Supp. 7**, 320

Poole, William Frederick, reference to, **Supp. 3**, 326

"Pooled" credit, **Vol. 9, Part 2**, 305

Poole's Index to Periodical Literature, forerunner of, **Vol. 8, Part 1**, 66 f.

Poor, Henry Varnum, reference to, **Supp. 3**, 278; **Supp. 6**, 457–58

Poor People's Campaign, founding of, **Supp. 8**, 335

Poor Richard's Almanack. See Almanacs

Pope, Arthur Upham, reference to, **Supp. 6**, 557

Pope, John, Union general, **Vol. 6, Part 1**, 123

Pope, John Russell, reference to, **Supp. 5**, 300

Pope, William J., reference to, **Supp. 6**, 71

Pope John XXIII, references to, **Supp. 8**, 115, 614–15; **Supp. 10**, 498

Pope Leo XIII: conference of, with Taft, **Vol. 9, Part 2**, 268; social encyclicals, **Supp. 3**, 680, 681

Pope Paul VI, references to, **Supp. 8**, 116, 615; **Supp. 9**, 51, 384; **Supp. 10**, 730
Pope Pius XI, Kellogg-Briand Pact support, **Supp. 4**, 137
Pope Pius XII, references to, **Supp. 5**, 589; **Supp. 6**, 608, 623; **Supp. 8**, 613; **Supp. 10**, 497, 498
Popular Democratic party (Puerto Rico): **Supp. 9**, 279; founding of, **Supp. 5**, 545
Popular fiction: **Supp. 4**, 372; Gallico novels, **Supp. 10**, 268; Smith novels, **Supp. 9**, 735–36; Susann novels, **Supp. 9**, 785–86; Wodehouse novels, **Supp. 9**, 888, 889
Popular Science, origin of, **Vol. 4, Part 2**, 148; **Vol. 10, Part 2**, 616, 617
Popular Science Monthly, **Supp. 6**, 327
"Popular sovereignty": coining of phrase, **Vol. 3, Part 1**, 400; effect of Dred Scott decision on, **Vol. 3, Part 1**, 402
Population: as a basis for representation, **Vol. 5, Part 2**, 94; birthrate drop, **Supp. 4**, 45; black demographics, **Supp. 6**, 605; colonial, **Vol. 3, Part 1**, 277; control advocacy, **Supp. 9**, 556–57; growth and economic welfare studies, **Supp. 4**, 267–68; Rockefeller, John D., III, concerns, **Supp. 10**, 683, 684; rural to urban shift of, **Supp. 4**, 366; stable theory of, **Supp. 4**, 505–7; statistical studies on growth of, **Supp. 7**, 192. *See also* Family planning
"Population Bomb, The" (pamphlet), **Supp. 9**, 556
Population Council, **Supp. 10**, 684; intrauterine contraceptive devices promoted by, **Supp. 9**, 352
Populism, **Supp. 4**, 338; **Supp. 8**, 272
Populist movement, **Vol. 1, Part 1**, 214; **Vol. 3, Part 1**, 370, 382; **Vol. 5, Part 1**, 132; **Vol. 5, Part 2**, 516; **Vol. 6, Part 1**, 205, 332, 426; **Vol. 7, Part 1**, 197 f.; **Vol. 7, Part 2**, 393; **Vol. 8, Part 1**, 40 f., 142 f.; **Vol. 8, Part 2**, 105; **Vol. 9, Part 1**, 180, 199; **Vol. 10, Part 1**, 549, 568
Populist party, in Oregon, **Supp. 4**, 844–45
Porcelain, collecting of, **Vol. 3, Part 2**, 435; **Vol. 6, Part 1**, 210; **Vol. 8, Part 1**, 228 f.
Porgy and Bess, **Supp. 2**, 230, 303
Pork, **Supp. 3**, 737–38
"Pork-barrel" legislation, **Vol. 8, Part 1**, 34 f.
Pornography: *American Mercury* case, **Supp. 7**, 19–20; anti-obscenity challenged, **Supp. 9**, 683; book censorship, **Supp. 7**, 292, 293; court decisions, **Supp. 7**, 149; Postal Service code, **Supp. 6**, 661. *See also* Censorship
Porter, Cole, references to, **Supp. 6**, 637; **Supp. 7**, 803; **Supp. 8**, 108, 383
Porter, Commodore David, references to, **Vol. 3, Part 2**, 286; **Vol. 9, Part 2**, 378, 394
Porter, Fitz-John, reference to, **Vol. 8, Part 2**, 454
Porter, Katherine Anne, reference to, **Supp. 8**, 256
Porter, William Sydney, reference to, **Supp. 1**, 109
Porter, Fitz-John, case (1862–85), **Vol. 5, Part 1**, 401; **Vol. 8, Part 1**, 91, 188
"Porter Mortar Fleet," Civil War, **Vol. 8, Part 2**, 200
Porter's School, Miss, Farmington, Conn., founding of, **Vol. 5, Part 2**, 287; **Vol. 8, Part 1**, 103
Port Folio, leading literary periodical in America in 1812, **Vol. 1, Part 2**, 243; **Vol. 3, Part 1**, 236; **Vol. 4, Part 2**, 143
Port Gibson, Miss., battle of. *See Vicksburg* campaign
Port Hudson, siege of, **Vol. 1, Part 1**, 428, 579; **Vol. 3, Part 1**, 412; **Vol. 4, Part 1**, 495, 614; **Vol. 4, Part 2**, 28; **Vol. 7, Part 2**, 415; **Vol. 9, Part 1**, 92
Portland, Maine: **Vol. 3, Part 1**, 172, 411; **Vol. 5, Part 1**, 517; **Vol. 8, Part 1**, 71 f.; construction and repair of harbor fortifications, **Vol. 7, Part 2**, 169; harbor construction, **Supp. 1**, 157
Portland, Oreg.: founding of, **Vol. 6, Part 1**, 434; municipal reform, **Supp. 4**, 904; public service, **Vol. 7, Part 2**, 445; **Vol. 8, Part 1**, 456
Portland Courier, the first daily in Maine, **Vol. 9, Part 1**, 345
Portland Oregonian, **Vol. 7, Part 1**, 54; **Vol. 8, Part 2**, 491
Portland Transcript, influence of the, **Vol. 7, Part 2**, 558
Portmanteau Theatre, **Supp. 3**, 796–99
Port of New York, development of, **Vol. 9, Part 1**, 338
Port of New York Authority: **Supp. 6**, 187, 587; **Supp. 7**, 11–12, 553; **Supp. 10**, 788–89; collector, **Supp. 4**, 542; founding of, **Supp. 1**, 589
Portrait painting. *See* Painting, portrait
Portrait photography, **Supp. 7**, 455–56; **Supp. 9**, 759, 760; **Supp. 10**, 161–62, 305
Portraits: bas-reliefs, **Vol. 8, Part 1**, 166 f.; busts, **Vol. 4, Part 2**, 366; **Vol. 8, Part 1**, 158 f., 166 f.; **Vol. 8, Part 2**, 298; engraving of, **Vol. 3, Part 1**, 535 f.; **Vol. 5, Part 2**, 509; **Vol. 6, Part 1**, 165; **Vol. 6, Part 2**, 331; **Vol. 10, Part 2**, 603; of George Washington, **Vol. 7, Part 1**, 550; **Vol. 7, Part 2**, 346; **Vol. 8, Part 2**, 21, 122, 182, 386; masks, collecting of, **Vol. 5, Part 1**, 445; of presidents, **Vol. 8, Part 1**, 453; series of, of men prominent in the American Revolution, **Vol. 3, Part 1**, 553 f.
Portrait sculpture, **Supp. 8**, 414, 415
Port Republic, Va., battle of, **Vol. 1, Part 1**, 578; **Vol. 3, Part 2**, 230; **Vol. 5, Part 1**, 557; **Vol. 9, Part 1**, 107
Port Royal, S.C.: capture of, **Vol. 3, Part 1**, 529 f.; founding of French colony on present site of, **Vol. 8, Part 1**, 533
Portsmouth, designed by Josiah Barker, **Vol. 1, Part 1**, 606
Portsmouth, N. H.: construction and repair of the fortifications of, **Vol. 7, Part 2**, 169; mayor of, **Vol. 5, Part 2**, 169; peace parley for Russo-Japanese War (August 1905), **Vol. 4, Part 2**, 435; **Vol. 9, Part 2**, 82; trade from, **Vol. 5, Part 2**, 590
Portugal: claims of, resulting from War of 1812, **Vol. 8, Part 1**, 480; diplomacy, **Vol. 1, Part 2**, 41; **Vol. 3, Part 1**, 176; **Vol. 7, Part 2**, 582
Portuguese literature and language, studies in old, **Supp. 1**, 481
Poseidon Adventure, The, **Supp. 10**, 268
Positron, discovery of, **Supp. 5**, 496
Post, Charles William, references to, **Supp. 3**, 411; **Supp. 5**, 379; **Supp. 9**, 614; **Supp. 10**, 555
Post, Emily, reference to, **Supp. 9**, 824
Post, Wiley, reference to, **Supp. 6**, 493
Postage: canceling machine, **Vol. 3, Part 1**, 237; reduced from three to two cents, **Vol. 4, Part 1**, 608
Postage stamps: engravings of, **Vol. 5, Part 2**, 159; first authorized issue of, **Vol. 1, Part 2**, 47; first commemorative for rock star, **Supp. 10**, 650; first five-cent, **Vol. 10, Part 1**, 639 f.; printing of first penny, **Vol. 7, Part 2**, 472
Postal savings system, creation of, **Vol. 6, Part 1**, 61; **Vol. 9, Part 2**, 269
Postal Service, United States: **Vol. 2, Part 1**, 454; **Vol. 2, Part 2**, 91, 185, 300, 541; **Vol. 3, Part 1**, 147, 364, 387; **Vol. 4, Part 1**, 342; **Vol. 4, Part 2**, 181, 397; **Vol. 7, Part 2**, 313, 368, 566; **Vol. 8, Part 1**, 344 f.; **Vol. 10, Part 1**, 407; **Vol. 10, Part 2**, 352; administration, **Supp. 6**, 660–61; airmail, **Supp. 2**, 487; **Supp. 3**, 157; **Supp. 5**, 86, 294, 385; **Supp. 6**, 64, 221; **Supp. 8**, 185, 707–8; censorship by, **Supp. 5**, 453, 638; **Supp. 6**, 661; **Supp. 7**, 20; **Supp. 8**, 605; **Supp. 9**, 782; delivery cutbacks, **Supp. 8**, 134; early, **Vol. 3, Part 2**, 589; **Vol. 4, Part 2**, 70; ethics issues, **Supp. 6**, 64; fast mail service between New York and Chicago, initiated, **Vol. 5, Part 2**, 65; first career postmaster general, **Supp. 8**, 133–34; legislation, **Supp. 7**, 521;

motor service, **Supp. 2**, 486; pony express, **Vol. 5, Part 2**, 353; postmaster generals, **Vol. 2, Part 2**, 300; **Vol. 4, Part 2**, 397, 469; **Vol. 5, Part 1**, 182, 297, 589; **Vol. 5, Part 2**, 93, 325, 362, 391 f.; **Vol. 7, Part 1**, 522; **Vol. 7, Part 2**, 327, 566; **Vol. 9, Part 1**, 246; **Supp. 1**, 409; **Supp. 2**, 74, 122; **Supp. 4**, 356; **Supp. 5**, 281; **Supp. 7**, 86; **Supp. 9**, 782; **Supp. 10**, 233–34; rural free delivery, **Vol. 2, Part 1**, 482; **Vol. 4, Part 2**, 440; **Vol. 7, Part 2**, 313; **Vol. 9, Part 1**, 456; **Vol. 10, Part 1**, 549 f.; star route, **Vol. 2, Part 1**, 26; **Vol. 3, Part 1**, 387; **Vol. 4, Part 1**, 148 f.; **Vol. 5, Part 1**, 589; street letter boxes, **Vol. 2, Part 1**, 482; World War II, **Supp. 6**, 661

Postal Telegraph Co., formation of, **Vol. 6, Part 2**, 76

Postcards, collections, **Supp. 2**, 112

Poster art, **Vol. 7, Part 2**, 424; **Supp. 8**, 493, 494

Posters, war, **Supp. 6**, 204

Postman Always Rings Twice, The, **Supp. 10**, 88–89

Post Office. *See* Postal Service, United States

Post-trader system in War Department, critic of, **Vol. 4, Part 2**, 478

Postum, first production of, as coffee substitute, **Vol. 8, Part 1**, 112 f.

Postum Cereal Co.: **Supp. 6**, 61; **Supp. 7**, 379; **Supp. 10**, 555; founding and growth of, **Supp. 9**, 614, 615

Potash, manufacture of, **Supp. 1**, 682

Potawatomi language, **Vol. 5, Part 1**, 107

Potomac Aqueduct, construction of, **Vol. 10, Part 1**, 57

Potomac Navigation Co., George Washington, president of, **Vol. 5, Part 2**, 122; **Vol. 8, Part 2**, 223

Potsdam Conference (1945), **Supp. 5**, 335; **Supp. 6**, 147; **Supp. 7**, 91; **Supp. 8**, 89; **Supp. 9**, 812

Potter, William James, reference to, **Supp. 9**, 13

Pottery: archaeological significance, **Supp. 3**, 272; collecting of, **Vol. 3, Part 2**, 161, 435; **Vol. 6, Part 1**, 210, 47; design and manufacture, **Supp. 10**, 511–12

Potts' disease, studies of, **Vol. 9, Part 2**, 318

Poulenc, Francis, reference to, **Supp. 6**, 358

Poulsen, Valdemar, reference to, **Supp. 7**, 394

Poulter, Thomas C., reference to, **Supp. 6**, 92

Poultry: chicken industry, **Supp. 10**, 629–30, 718; inventions of incubators and brooders, **Vol. 8, Part 1**, 505

Pound, Ezra, references to, **Supp. 4**, 285; **Supp. 7**, 218, 272, 339, 347, 789, 790, 791; **Supp. 9**, 33, 225, 557; **Supp. 10**, 869

Pound, Roscoe: legal philosophy of, **Supp. 6**, 104, 216; references to, **Supp. 3**, 116; **Supp. 7**, 475; **Supp. 9**, 318

Pound, Thaddeus Coleman, reference to, **Supp. 9**, 616

Poverty: Poor People's Campaign, **Supp. 8**, 335; statistical study of, **Supp. 3**, 373; theory of culture of, **Supp. 8**, 378. *See also* Homeless; Welfare

Powderly, Terence V., reference to, **Supp. 3**, 346

Powder mill, first in Connecticut, **Vol. 7, Part 2**, 641

Powell, Adam Clayton, Jr.: libel case, **Supp. 10**, 718; references to, **Supp. 5**, 548; **Supp. 6**, 142, 489; **Supp. 8**, 497; **Supp. 9**, 518, 750, 838

Powell, Dick, references to, **Supp. 10**, 53, 63

Powell, John Wesley, reference to, **Supp. 3**, 724

Powell, Lewis Thornton, relations with John Wilkes Booth, **Vol. 1, Part 2**, 450

Powell, Paul, reference to, **Supp. 10**, 49

Powell, William, reference to, **Supp. 8**, 187

Powell Musical Institute, Brooklyn, N.Y., established, **Vol. 8, Part 1**, 144

Powell v. *McCormack*, **Supp. 9**, 838

Power of Sympathy, The, first American novel, **Vol. 7, Part 1**, 266

Power plants: **Vol. 3, Part 2**, 457; **Vol. 5, Part 2**, 509; development of hydroelectric, **Vol. 3, Part 2**, 2; **Vol. 8, Part 1**, 375 f.; electric, **Vol. 7, Part 1**, 367 f.; generation and transmission devices, **Vol. 6, Part 2**, 239; loom machinery, **Vol. 6, Part 2**, 377; nuclear energy advocacy, **Supp. 10**, 751; stoking inventions, **Vol. 5, Part 2**, 168

Powers, Francis Gary, references to, **Supp. 8**, 135, 147, 159; **Supp. 9**, 3

Powers, Grover F., reference to, **Supp. 3**, 775

Power supply. *See* Power plants; Public utilities; *specific types of power*

Powhatan, references to, **Vol. 3, Part 2**, 108; **Vol. 7, Part 1**, 468

Powhatan federation, influence of, in Virginia, **Vol. 8, Part 1**, 160 f.

Practical Christianity, **Supp. 4**, 271–72

Practical System of Rhetoric, **Vol. 7, Part 1**, 466 f.

Pragmatism: **Vol. 5, Part 1**, 597 f.; **Vol. 7, Part 1**, 112; **Vol. 7, Part 2**, 400; **Supp. 1**, 548; **Supp. 3**, 363; **Supp. 6**, 505; **Supp. 7**, 471–72, 481, 482; representational, **Supp. 4**, 525–26

Prairie Club, founding of, **Supp. 3**, 599

Prairie Farmer, **Supp. 4**, 132; founding of, **Vol. 10, Part 2**, 557

Prairie school of architecture, **Supp. 3**, 599; **Supp. 6**, 712

Pratt, Charles, **Vol. 7, Part 1**, 566; reference to, **Supp. 1**, 596–97

Pratt, Frederic B., reference to, **Supp. 4**, 56

Pratt, Parley P., reference to, **Vol. 9, Part 2**, 333

Pratt, William V., references to, **Supp. 5**, 6; **Supp. 6**, 348

Pratt bridge and roof truss, **Vol. 8, Part 1**, 179

Pratt Consolidated Coal Co., **Supp. 5**, 556

Pratt Institute (Brooklyn, N.Y.): **Supp. 10**, 244; administration, **Supp. 1**, 597; **Supp. 8**, 135; founded, **Vol. 8, Part 1**, 17, 168 f.

Pratt Institute Free Library, first free public library in New York City or Brooklyn, **Vol. 8, Part 1**, 17, 168 f.

Pratt Institute of Music and Art (Pittsburgh, Pa.), founded, **Vol. 8, Part 1**, 177 f.

"Pratt's Astral Oil," trade name for first high-quality illuminating oil, **Vol. 8, Part 1**, 168 f.

Prattsville, N. Y., founded, **Vol. 8, Part 1**, 179 f.

Prayer book, Jewish, **Vol. 5, Part 2**, 254

Prayer books, publishing of, **Vol. 6, Part 1**, 287

Preble County, Ohio, first school established in, **Vol. 8, Part 1**, 271 f.

Precision instruments, manufacture of, **Supp. 2**, 642

Prefabricated housing, **Supp. 6**, 26; **Supp. 7**, 308

Pregnancy. *See* Ectopic pregnancy; Embryology; Family planning; Motherhood; Obstetrics; Reproductive system

Prejudice, sociology of, **Supp. 10**, 502

Premier Diamond Company, **Supp. 10**, 847

Preminger, Otto, references to, **Supp. 7**, 71; **Supp. 8**, 364; **Supp. 9**, 647; **Supp. 10**, 239, 273, 725

Prendergast, Maurice, reference to, **Supp. 5**, 635

Prendergast, Robert, reference to, **Supp. 2**, 142

Presbyter, **Vol. 8, Part 2**, 53

Presbyterian church: **Vol. 1, Part 1**, 101, 162, 173 f., 181, 267, 352, 459, 509, 512, 628; **Vol. 1, Part 2**, 136, 339 f.; **Vol. 2, Part 1**, 7, 435, 520; **Vol. 2, Part 2**, 360, 481, 567 f., 611; **Vol. 3, Part 1**, 13 f., 77, 102, 302, 332, 367 f., 489 f; **Vol. 3, Part 2**, 233, 236, 364, 394, 406, 535; **Vol. 4, Part 1**, 99, 194, 268, 322, 537, 553 f., 602; **Vol. 4, Part 2**, 119, 133, 137; **Vol. 5, Part 1**, 120 f., 286 f., 399, 554, 568; **Vol. 5, Part 2**, 248 f., 304, 575; **Vol. 6, Part 1**, 275, 279, 281, 530, 554, 565, 594, 603, 613, 619 f.; **Vol. 6, Part 2**, 32, 57, 175, 216, 630; **Vol. 7, Part 1**, 147, 205, 359, 408, 410, 414 f., 438 f., 526, 537 f., 580, 644; **Vol. 7, Part 2**, 67, 176, 231, 242, 245, 295, 307, 315, 317, 451,

502, 507, 546, 588, 591; **Vol. 8, Part 1**, 271, 537, 542; **Vol. 8, Part 2**, 17, 37, 53, 75, 218, 332, 394, 504; **Vol. 9, Part 1**, 101, 104, 201, 278, 299, 344, 377 f., 442, 447, 476, 480, 485; **Vol. 9, Part 2**, 479, 490; **Vol. 10, Part 1**, 453 f., 632; **Vol. 10, Part 2**, 340, 345, 436, 460, 629; Board of Foreign Missions, **Vol. 8, Part 1**, 542; doctrine, **Supp. 6**, 195; ecumenical movement, **Supp. 10**, 110–11; history of, **Vol. 8, Part 1**, 455; leadership, **Supp. 1**, 83; liberalism in, **Supp. 5**, 116–17; missions, **Vol. 1, Part 1**, 517, 532; **Vol. 1, Part 2**, 37; **Vol. 3, Part 2**, 405; **Vol. 4, Part 2**, 567; **Vol. 5, Part 1**, 260; **Vol. 6, Part 1**, 278, 356; **Vol. 8, Part 1**, 542; **Vol. 9, Part 1**, 55, 442; **Vol. 9, Part 2**, 490; **Vol. 10, Part 1**, 411, 539 f.; **Supp. 1**, 499; **Supp. 3**, 110, 476–77; **Supp. 4**, 763–64, 860; missions, medical, **Supp. 4**, 181–82; "old" and "new" school, union of, **Vol. 8, Part 1**, 189 f.; ordination, defense of, **Vol. 10, Part 1**, 632; "Plan of Union," **Vol. 1, Part 1**, 480, 628; Social Gospel movement, **Supp. 3**, 733–34; splinter groups, **Supp. 2**, 412; theological seminary, **Vol. 10, Part 2**, 460

Presbyterian Expositor, **Vol. 8, Part 1**, 544

Presbyterian Hospital (Chicago), **Supp. 3**, 67

Presbyterian Hospital (New York City), **Supp. 3**, 483; **Supp. 5**, 438. *See also* Columbia-Presbyterian Medical Center

Presbyterian Labor Temple, **Supp. 8**, 458

Preschool education: development of, **Supp. 4**, 374; Montessori method, **Supp. 6**, 90

Prescott, Brig.-Gen., relations with William Barton, **Vol. 1, Part 2**, 24

Predestination, controversy, **Vol. 8, Part 2**, 440–41

Preserving process, for fruits, **Vol. 5, Part 2**, 160

Presidency (U.S): **Vol. 1, Part 1**, 72, 77, 87, 373; **Vol. 2, Part 2**, 205 f.; **Vol. 3, Part 2**, 380; **Vol. 4, Part 1**, 145, 492; **Vol. 4, Part 2**, 14, 331, 348, 446; **Vol. 5, Part 2**, 27, 81; **Vol. 6, Part 1**, 12, 263, 583; **Vol. 9, Part 2**, 11, 349, 475; **Vol. 10, Part 1**, 88, 152, 509; archives of, **Supp. 3**, 285–86; "boom" for George Law, detail of, **Vol. 6, Part 1**, 40; Executive branch reorganization commissions, **Supp. 6**, 692; **Supp. 7**, 85; Executive Office establishment, **Supp. 3**, 655; Executive Office reorganization, **Supp. 5**, 485; Executive Office's budget control, **Supp. 4**, 753; first elected to fourth term, **Supp. 3**, 664; first elected to third term, **Supp. 3**, 659; First Lady role, **Supp. 7**, 660–61, 796; first military aide, **Supp. 1**, 202; first presidential library, **Supp. 7**, 311; first woman candidate, **Vol. 6, Part 1**, 341; Hayes-Tilden contest, **Vol. 4, Part 2**, 449; imperial approach to, **Supp. 8**, 159–60; Lame Duck Amendment, **Supp. 3**, 559; **Supp. 7**, 363; Mount Rushmore sculpture, **Supp. 3**, 89; official libraries, **Supp. 4**, 176; **Supp. 7**, 311; portraits of presidents, **Vol. 8, Part 1**, 453; powers of, **Supp. 8**, 552; preferential primary, **Supp. 2**, 55; press conferences and relations, **Supp. 3**, 649–50; **Supp. 4**, 704; **Supp. 5**, 196–97, 626; **Supp. 8**, 607; succession of, constitutional amendment revising, **Supp. 10**, 486; succession of, fixed, **Vol. 5, Part 2**, 88; treaty-making power, **Supp. 6**, 336, 361; **Supp. 8**, 157; two-term limit, **Supp. 8**, 421; Wood, Leonard, bids for Republican support of candidacy, **Vol. 10, Part 2**, 469; writings on, **Supp. 5**, 731; **Supp. 7**, 54, 146–47; youngest elected, **Supp. 7**, 420

President and Congress, **Supp. 7**, 54

Presidential election (1904), Hearst bid, **Supp. 5**, 285

Presidential election (1912): Progressive party candidates, **Supp. 3**, 105–6, 395, 558; **Supp. 4**, 318, 665; Roosevelt, Theodore, candidacy, **Supp. 5**, 303; Socialist candidates, **Supp. 4**, 733; Wilson candldacy, **Supp. 4**, 603

Presidential election (1916): California vote, **Supp. 3**, 396; Hughes candidacy, **Supp. 4**, 405; **Supp. 5**, 342; Wilson candidacy, **Supp. 9**, 504

Presidential election (1920): Butler candidacy, **Supp. 4**, 136; Coolidge vice-presidential candidacy, **Supp. 1**, 195–96; Cox-Harding contest, **Supp. 3**, 643; **Supp. 6**, 129; Farmer-Labor party candidates, **Supp. 3**, 347; **Supp. 4**, 280; Harding candidacy, **Supp. 7**, 86, 305; League of Nations issue, **Supp. 3**, 472–73; Republican aspirants, **Supp. 3**, 467–68

Presidential election (1924): Communist party candidates, **Supp. 7**, 255, 291; Coolidge candidacy, **Supp. 1**, 196; Davis candidacy, **Supp. 5**, 155–56; Dawes vice-presidential candidacy, **Supp. 5**, 160; McAdoo candidacy, **Supp. 5**, 497; **Supp. 7**, 527, 537; Progressive party ticket, **Supp. 9**, 859; Smith-McAdoo Democratic convention deadlock, **Supp. 3**, 114, 481, 644–45, 670, 719

Presidential election (1928): Butler candidacy, **Supp. 4**, 136; Catholic issue, **Supp. 7**, 361; Communist party candidates, **Supp. 7**, 255, 291; Democratic opposition to Smith, **Supp. 5**, 290; Hoover candidacy, **Supp. 7**, 86, 360–61; Meredith bid, **Supp. 7**, 527; Prohibition issue, **Supp. 5**, 442; **Supp. 7**, 786; Republican aspirants, **Supp. 3**, 467; Smith candidacy, **Supp. 3**, 132, 645, 720, 817; **Supp. 6**, 572; Socialist candidates **Supp. 3**, 517

Presidential election (1932): Communist party candidate, **Supp. 7**, 255; Communist party endorsements, **Supp. 8**, 192; Democratic platform, **Supp. 5**, 331; Garner as vice-presidential candidate, **Supp. 8**, 207; Hoover candidacy, **Supp. 7**, 86; Prohibition candidate, **Supp. 5**, 702; Roosevelt, F. D., candidacy, **Supp. 3**, 646–47; **Supp. 5**, 287; **Supp. 8**, 320; **Supp. 9**, 84; **Supp. 10**, 233; Socialist candidates, **Supp. 3**, 517; **Supp. 8**, 650

Presidential election (1936): Communist party endorsements, **Supp. 8**, 192; labor movement in, **Supp. 8**, 376; Landon candidacy, **Supp. 8**, 421; **Supp. 9**, 356; poll prediction, **Supp. 7**, 274, 650–51; **Supp. 9**, 677; Republican ticket, **Supp. 3**, 425; Roosevelt, F. D., candidacy, **Supp. 10**, 233; Roosevelt, F. D., campaign, **Supp. 3**, 655; Socialist candidate, **Supp. 8**, 650; Union party in, **Supp. 4**, 480; **Supp. 10**, 152

Presidential election (1940): Dewey bid, **Supp. 9**, 230; Garner candidacy, **Supp. 8**, 207; labor movement in, **Supp. 5**, 510; **Supp. 8**, 376; McNutt bid, **Supp. 10**, 226; Pennsylvania Republican delegation, **Supp. 7**, 615; poll prediction, **Supp. 9**, 677; Republican nomination contest, **Supp. 9**, 426; Roosevelt, F. D., candidacy, **Supp. 3**, 659; **Supp. 5**, 227, 459–60, 515; **Supp. 10**, 234; Taft bid, **Supp. 5**, 675; **Supp. 7**, 84; Wallace vice-presidential candidacy, **Supp. 7**, 761; Willkie campaign song, **Supp. 9**, 670; Willkie candidacy, **Supp. 3**, 400, 497, 829; **Supp. 5**, 152; **Supp. 8**, 394, 421, 617; **Supp. 9**, 356–57

Presidential election (1944): Dewey candidacy, **Supp. 9**, 230; poll prediction, **Supp. 9**, 677; Republican nomination contest, **Supp. 3**, 830; **Supp. 7**, 616; Roosevelt, F. D., campaign, **Supp. 3**, 664; "Stop Willkie" movement, **Supp. 7**, 616; Truman vice-presidential candidacy, **Supp. 4**, 356, 376; **Supp. 7**, 762; **Supp. 8**, 361; Wallace vice-presidency, opposition to, **Supp. 4**, 51

Presidential election (1948): Dewey candidacy, **Supp. 9**, 231; civil rights issues, **Supp. 5**, 741; Dixiecrats, **Supp. 6**, 710–11; Taft bid, **Supp. 5**, 675; **Supp. 7**, 49, 84; poll prediction, **Supp. 9**, 678; Taft bid, **Supp. 9**, 357; Truman candidacy, **Supp. 8**, 36–37, 405; **Supp. 9**, 231, 814; **Supp. 10**, 119, 227; Wallace third-party candidacy, **Supp. 7**, 763; **Supp. 8**, 511, 512; **Supp. 10**, 360

Presidential election (1952): "Dump Nixon move-

ment," **Supp. 9**, 781–82; **Supp. 10**, 302; Eisenhower candidacy, **Supp. 7**, 384; **Supp. 8**, 144, 156; **Supp. 9**, 81, 211, 231, 245, 398, 781; Kefauver bid, **Supp. 7**, 416; labor role in, **Supp. 5**, 255; Nixon vice-presidential candidacy, **Supp. 10**, 87; Stevenson candidacy, **Supp. 7**, 722; **Supp. 9**, 432, 814; Taft bid, **Supp. 5**, 676; **Supp. 7**, 49, 84; **Supp. 9**, 357, 528
Presidential election (1956): Democratic keynote address, **Supp. 8**, 91–92; Eisenhower candidacy, **Supp. 10**, 302; Kefauver bid, **Supp. 8**, 406; Kefauver vice-presidential candidacy, **Supp. 7**, 416; Kennedy, J. F., vice-presidential bid, **Supp. 9**, 58; Stevenson candidacy, **Supp. 7**, 723
Presidential election (1960): Chicago vote fraud, **Supp. 9**, 307; cold war issues, **Supp. 8**, 6–7; Humphrey bid, **Supp. 10**, 361; Johnson bid, **Supp. 9**, 433; Kennedy, J. F., candidacy, **Supp. 7**, 420; **Supp. 8**, 322; **Supp. 9**, 58, 392; **Supp. 10**, 168, 324; Kennedy-Johnson nomination, **Supp. 7**, 636; **Supp. 8**, 361; **Supp. 9**, 433; Nixon candidacy, **Supp. 10**, 357; poll prediction, **Supp. 9**, 678; press endorsements, **Supp. 8**, 396; Rockefeller bid, **Supp. 9**, 524–25
Presidential election (1964): Goldwater candidacy, **Supp. 9**, 435, 469; Johnson candidacy, **Supp. 9**, 435, 440; **Supp. 10**, 604–5
Presidential election (1968): Democratic National Convention riots, **Supp. 10**, 168, 362, 602–3; "dump Johnson movement," **Supp. 10**, 470; Humphrey candidacy, **Supp. 9**, 259, 437; **Supp. 10**, 168–69, 362; Johnson withdrawal from race, **Supp. 9**, 436–37, 552; **Supp. 10**, 362; Kennedy, R. F., bid, **Supp. 8**, 324; **Supp. 9**, 88, 437; **Supp. 10**, 362; McCarthy bid, **Supp. 9**, 59, 436, 552; **Supp. 10**, 362; Rockefeller, N., bid, **Supp. 9**, 528; **Supp. 10**, 687; Wallace, G. W., third-party candidacy, **Supp. 10**, 362
Presidential election (1980), conservative success in, **Supp. 10**, 23
"President making" at Lotos Club, New York, and Blackstone Hotel, Chicago, **Vol. 4, Part 2**, 372
President, naval exploits of, **Vol. 3, Part 1**, 188
President: Office and Powers, The, **Supp. 7**, 146
Presley, Elvis: reference to, **Supp. 6**, 301; Sullivan show appearance, **Supp. 9**, 780
Press: cipher system, devised, **Vol. 5, Part 2**, 158; clipping service, originator of, **Vol. 8, Part 2**, 129; "Gordon," **Vol. 4, Part 1**, 422; liberty of, **Vol. 3, Part 1**, 212; **Vol. 3, Part 2**, 560; **Vol. 4, Part 1**, 201; service, practical cooperative, organized, **Vol. 5, Part 2**, 158; screwpower, **Vol. 5, Part 2**, 97. *See also* Journalism; Newspapers; Publishing
Press, freedom of the. *See* Civil liberties
Press agents. *See* Public relations
Presser Foundation, established, for music philanthropies, **Vol. 8, Part 1**, 200 f.
Press of the Crippled Turtle, founding of, **Supp. 7**, 559
"Press on Wheels," **Vol. 4, Part 1**, 9
Pressure gauge, **Supp. 1**, 121
Press Wireless, founding, **Supp. 3**, 155
Preston Retreat, the incorporation of, **Vol. 8, Part 1**, 203 f.
Preventive medicine, **Vol. 3, Part 2**, 301; **Supp. 3**, 158, 409–10; **Supp. 4**, 684, 700–701; **Supp. 5**, 632
Price, Thomas Randolph, relations with Walter Hines Page, **Vol. 7, Part 2**, 142
Price-fixing: base pricing, **Supp. 4**, 268; legislation, **Supp. 6**, 260
Prices: base pricing, **Supp. 4**, 268; consumer index, **Supp. 7**, 794; economic cost analysis, **Supp. 8**, 668–69; fixing charges, **Supp. 8**, 11, 110; fluctuation and gold supply, **Supp. 2**, 696; historical study of U.S., **Supp. 2**, 175; interest-rate relationship, **Supp. 4**, 272–73; Model T, **Supp. 4**, 300–301; money supply relationship, **Supp. 8**, 79; wartime control of, **Supp. 4**, 587
Price supports. *See* Agriculture; *commodity name*
Pride of the Yankees, The, **Supp. 10**, 268
Pridham, Edwin, reference to, **Supp. 7**, 394
Priestley, Joseph: Andrews, John, relationship, **Vol. 1, Part 1**, 245, 294; name as scientific term, **Vol. 8, Part 1**, 223
"Primacy of the Pacific" foreign policy, **Vol. 4, Part 1**, 258
Primaries: constitutional right to, **Supp. 5**, 575; Oregon system, **Supp. 4**, 844
"Prime Street," **Vol. 7, Part 1**, 223
Primogeniture, repeal of law of, in Massachusetts, **Vol. 4, Part 1**, 137; abolition of, in Virginia, **Vol. 5, Part 2**, 20
Primrose, George H., partnership with, **Vol. 3, Part 1**, 338
Prince, Harold, reference to, **Supp. 10**, 8
Prince, Morton, reference to, **Supp. 3**, 190
Prince, Wesley, reference to, **Supp. 7**, 131
Prince, William Wood, reference to, **Supp. 5**, 551
Prince Albert (pipe tobacco), **Supp. 5**, 565, 566
Prince of the House of David, The, **Vol. 5, Part 1**, 479
"Prince of Platform Orators," applied to Tyng, Stephen Higgins on, **Vol. 10, Part 1**, 101
Princes (boat), **Vol. 5, Part 2**, 371
Prince Society: founding of, **Vol. 9, Part 2**, 503; publications of, **Vol. 3, Part 1**, 172; **Vol. 9, Part 1**, 204
Princeton, battle of, **Vol. 6, Part 2**, 541; **Vol. 7, Part 1**, 87; **Vol. 8, Part 2**, 294; **Vol. 9, Part 2**, 192; **Vol. 10, Part 1**, 516–17
Princeton Research Park, founding of, **Supp. 7**, 650
Princeton Theological Seminary: founders of, **Vol. 1, Part 2**, 70; president of, first, **Vol. 7, Part 2**, 316
Princeton *Tiger*, **Vol. 2, Part 2**, 162
Princeton University: astronomy studies, **Supp. 6**, 560; biology studies, **Supp. 5**, 127; Blair Hall, **Vol. 1, Part 2**, 339; botany and genetics studies, **Supp. 5**, 629; chapel, stained-glass windows, **Supp. 3**, 183; Cliosophic Society, **Vol. 7, Part 2**, 293; constitutional law studies, **Supp. 7**, 146; economic studies, **Supp. 3**, 211, 414; **Supp. 4**, 267–68; English literature and language studies, **Supp. 5**, 645–46; **Supp. 7**, 56; fellowship, **Vol. 1, Part 2**, 477; first professor of the history of art at, **Vol. 8, Part 1**, 228 f.; founding of, **Vol. 1, Part 1**, 126; **Vol. 1, Part 2**, 144; **Vol. 2, Part 1**, 313; **Vol. 3, Part 1**, 302; **Vol. 10, Part 2**, 436; four-course plan of study, **Supp. 7**, 216; French language studies, **Supp. 3**, 22; geology studies, **Supp. 4**, 730; graduate school, founding of, **Supp. 3**, 810; graphic arts studies, **Supp. 7**, 3; Greek language and literature studies, **Supp. 4**, 143–44; history of, **Vol. 2, Part 1**, 498; **Vol. 3, Part 1**, 102; **Vol. 6, Part 2**, 128, 629; history studies, **Supp. 6**, 409–10; **Supp. 8**, 692; incorporation, one of first, **Vol. 9, Part 1**, 353; librarian of, **Supp. 10**, 60–61; mathematics studies, **Supp. 6**, 653–54; modern language studies, **Supp. 5**, 239; Nassau Hall, **Vol. 9, Part 1**, 335; philosophy studies, **Supp. 10**, 401, 402; physics studies, **Supp. 5**, 126; preceptorial system, **Vol. 10, Part 2**, 354; presidents, **Vol. 3, Part 1**, 301; **Vol. 3, Part 2**, 37, 391; **Vol. 6, Part 1**, 615, 616; **Vol. 7, Part 1**, 359; **Vol. 7, Part 2**, 315 f.; **Vol. 9, Part 1**, 344; **Vol. 9, Part 2**, 11, 653; **Vol. 10, Part 2**, 354; **Supp. 1**, 399–400; psychology studies, **Supp. 8**, 69; public and international affairs school, **Supp. 4**, 224; science studies. **Supp. 1**, 399; Theological Seminary, **Supp. 6**, 195. *See also* Institute for Advanced Study
Princeton University Press, **Vol. 8, Part 2**, 517; **Supp 5**, 614
Principal Pictures Corporation, **Supp. 3**, 443–44

Principia Mathematica, **Supp. 10**, 282
Principles of Economics (Taylor), **Vol. 9, Part 2**, 323
Principles of Judicial Proof, **Supp. 3**, 821
Principles of Mathematics, **Supp. 4**, 879–80
Principles of Mining, **Supp. 7**, 358
Principles of Psychology, **Vol. 5, Part 1**, 592 f.
Principles of Sociology, The, **Supp. 1**, 339–40
Prinkipo Conference, Wilson's appointees to, **Vol. 4, Part 2**, 595
Printers' Ink, advertising trade journal, **Vol. 8, Part 2**, 198
Printing: **Vol. 1, Part 1**, 299, 392, 500, 526; **Vol. 1, Part 2**, 553, 557, 563, 564, 565; **Vol. 2, Part 1**, 28; **Vol. 2, Part 2**, 604; **Vol. 3, Part 1**, 263; **Vol. 3, Part 2**, 457, 560, 586, 599; **Vol. 4, Part 1**, 91, 293, 341, 528, 538, 552, 555 f., 558, 584 f.; **Vol. 4, Part 2**, 11, 123, 141, 282 f., 390, 397; **Vol. 5, Part 1**, 180, 376, 613; **Vol. 5, Part 2**, 288; **Vol. 6, Part 2**, 84, 110, 488, 550, 631; **Vol. 7, Part 1**, 156, 333, 381, 596; **Vol. 7, Part 2**, 226 f.; **Vol. 8, Part 1**, 632 f., 637; **Vol. 8, Part 2**, 23, 183, 190, 214, 239; **Vol. 9, Part 1**, 122, 417; **Vol. 9, Part 2**, 435, 557, 611 f., 652; **Vol. 10, Part 1**, 10; **Vol. 10, Part 2**, 294, 643; Bible, etc., **Vol. 1, Part 1**, 132; bibliography, **Supp. 3**, 492–93; Boston, **Vol. 3, Part 2**, 460; **Vol. 5, Part 2**, 110; Caslon type, **Vol. 4, Part 1**, 293; codification of practices of craft, **Vol. 3, Part 1**, 264; color, **Vol. 2, Part 2**, 463; electrotyping, **Vol. 1, Part 1**, 93; **Vol. 9, Part 2**, 652; first established in U.S., **Vol. 3, Part 1**, 415; first in America, **Vol. 3, Part 1**, 163; first in British America, **Vol. 3, Part 1**, 163; first in Missouri, **Vol. 1, Part 2**, 50; first in New Hampshire, **Vol. 3, Part 2**, 561; first iron lever, **Vol. 2, Part 2**, 554; first power press, **Vol. 2, Part 2**, 554; first religious periodical in America, **Vol. 5, Part 2**, 458; first south of Massachusetts, **Vol. 7, Part 1**, 596; first use of steam for, **Vol. 3, Part 1**, 155; German, first in America, **Vol. 9, Part 1**, 415; Gordon Press, **Vol. 4, Part 1**, 422; government contracts for, **Vol. 3, Part 2**, 526; hand, **Vol. 6, Part 1**, 285; **Vol. 9, Part 2**, 513; history of, **Vol. 3, Part 1**, 264; imprints, **Vol. 1, Part 1**, 495; industrial relations in, **Vol. 3, Part 1**, 264; inventions, **Vol. 2, Part 1**, 259; **Vol. 3, Part 1**, 329; **Vol. 5, Part 1**, 104, 105 f.; **Vol. 8, Part 1**, 165 f.; **Vol. 9, Part 1**, 123; **Vol. 9, Part 2**, 485; **Vol. 10, Part 1**, 40; job presses, **Vol. 4, Part 1**, 119, 422; journeyman, **Vol. 9, Part 1**, 110; "Learned the case," **Vol. 8, Part 1**, 60 f.; limited editions, **Supp. 4**, 622; **Supp. 7**, 2–3; linotype machine, **Vol. 6, Part 2**, 550; **Vol. 8, Part 1**, 484; **Vol. 8, Part 2**, 106; lithography, **Vol. 1, Part 1**, 166; **Vol. 1, Part 2**, 168; **Vol. 2, Part 2**, 69, 604; **Vol. 3, Part 1**, 103; **Vol. 4, Part 2**, 381; **Vol. 5, Part 1**, 107, 460, 520; **Vol. 5, Part 2**, 139; **Vol. 7, Part 1**, 469; **Vol. 7, Part 2**, 92, 439; **Vol. 8, Part 1**, 165 f.; **Vol. 8, Part 2**, 169, 202, 470; machinery, development of, **Vol. 1, Part 1**, 71; **Vol. 2, Part 1**, 449; **Vol. 2, Part 2**, 236, 463, 575; maps, **Vol. 7, Part 1**, 251; Maryland, **Vol. 1, Part 2**, 322; **Vol. 7, Part 1**, 596; **Vol. 7, Part 2**, 250; Massachusetts, **Vol. 9, Part 2**, 436; monotype, **Vol. 5, Part 2**, 611; music, **Vol. 6, Part 1**, 38; New Hampshire, **Vol. 6, Part 1**, 81; New Jersey, **Vol. 7, Part 2**, 227; Philadelphia, **Vol. 1, Part 1**, 501; **Vol. 1, Part 2**, 558, 563; **Vol. 10, Part 2**, 649; pioneer in American, **Vol. 5, Part 2**, 288; politics of, **Vol. 3, Part 2**, 512; San Francisco, **Vol. 1, Part 2**, 602; scholarly, **Supp. 3**, 784–85; Smithsonian process, **Vol. 8, Part 2**, 214; South Carolina, **Vol. 8, Part 1**, 634; Stamp Acts, effect of, **Vol. 4, Part 1**, 92; steam, first use of, **Vol. 3, Part 1**, 155; stereotyping, **Vol. 2, Part 2**, 286; strike of printers, **Vol. 1, Part 1**, 237; telegraphic, **Vol. 5, Part 1**, 259, 347; **Vol. 8, Part 1**, 75 f.; Tennessee, **Vol. 8, Part 2**, 190; typefounding, **Vol. 2, Part 1**, 181, 239; **Vol. 6, Part 2**, 84, 265; typesetting machinery, **Vol. 3, Part 1**, 411; typography, improvements in, **Vol. 1, Part 1**, 184, 526; **Vol. 3, Part 1**, 264; **Vol. 10, Part 1**, 655 f.; unions, **Vol. 2, Part 2**, 364; United Typothetae of America, **Vol. 3, Part 1**, 264; Virginia, **Vol. 7, Part 1**, 596; **Vol. 7, Part 2**, 250; writings on, **Vol. 3, Part 1**, 264; **Vol. 4, Part 1**, 294; **Vol. 9, Part 2**, 436; **Vol. 10, Part 1**, 41. *See also* Books; Publishing; Typographical design
Printing clubs, **Vol. 3, Part 2**, 519
Prints, collecting of, **Vol. 3, Part 2**, 147, 519; **Vol. 9, Part 1**, 256
Print selling, **Vol. 5, Part 2**, 352
Prison: Andersonville, **Vol. 6, Part 1**, 162; Attica (N.Y.), riot, **Supp. 10**, 688; California reform, **Supp. 4**, 636; first county jail library, **Vol. 4, Part 1**, 271; Jackson, Mich., **Vol. 8, Part 1**, 57 f.; labor in, **Supp. 1**, 317; Libby, **Vol. 1, Part 1**, 636; **Vol. 6, Part 1**, 557 f.; **Vol. 9, Part 2**, 636; military, **Vol. 9, Part 2**, 616; National Commission on Labor, **Vol. 9, Part 1**, 209; naval, **Supp. 4**, 820; New Jersey, **Vol. 8, Part 1**, 369; New York, **Vol. 3, Part 1**, 571 f.; New York City reform, **Supp. 8**, 495; New York State reform, **Supp. 4**, 471–72; parole laws, **Supp. 1**, 228; poetry about, **Supp. 6**, 238; psychological evaluations, **Supp. 3**, 102; reforms, **Supp. 1**, 211, 227–28, 378, 445, 581; **Supp. 3**, 420–21; **Supp. 5**, 427; **Supp. 9**, 490–91, 553; social work in, **Supp. 2**, 49; songs about, **Supp. 4**, 477, 502; women's, **Supp. 1**, 227–28; writings on, **Vol. 1, Part 1**, 653; **Vol. 3, Part 1**, 184; **Vol. 4, Part 1**, 271; **Vol. 6, Part 1**, 223; **Vol. 7, Part 2**, 75; **Vol. 10, Part 1**, 78; **Vol. 10, Part 2**, 386; **Supp. 4**, 472
Prisoner of Zenda, The, **Supp. 3**, 607
Prisoner's Aid Society (N.Y.), **Vol. 4, Part 1**, 271
"Prisoners' Friend," **Vol. 4, Part 1**, 271
Prison reform: **Vol. 2, Part 1**, 50, 61, 614; **Vol. 2, Part 2**, 323–24; **Vol. 3, Part 1**, 378, 493; **Vol. 4, Part 1**, 238, 271; **Vol. 4, Part 2**, 412; **Vol. 5, Part 1**, 297; **Vol. 5, Part 2**, 98; **Vol. 6, Part 1**, 527; **Vol. 7, Part 1**, 319, 508; **Vol. 7, Part 2**, 75; **Vol. 8, Part 1**, 139; **Vol. 10, Part 1**, 78; Reformatory Prison for Women, opened 1877, **Vol. 5, Part 2**, 98
Pritchett, Henry S., reference to, **Supp. 6**, 208
Privacy rights, legal basis, **Supp. 3**, 95
Privateering: **Vol. 1, Part 1**, 693 f.; **Vol. 1, Part 2**, 512, 534; **Vol. 2, Part 1**, 162; **Vol. 3, Part 1**, 42, 186, 217, 249, 250, 275, 414; **Vol. 3, Part 2**, 268, 507, 525; **Vol. 4, Part 1**, 208, 523; **Vol. 4, Part 2**, 162, 234, 559; **Vol. 5, Part 1**, 15, 212; **Vol. 6, Part 1**, 175, 315, 317; **Vol. 6, Part 2**, 149, 236; **Vol. 7, Part 1**, 358; **Vol. 8, Part 1**, 235, 480; **Vol. 8, Part 2**, 4, 73, 316; **Vol. 9, Part 2**, 499; **Vol. 10, Part 1**, 21, 39, 101; claims resulting from, **Vol. 8, Part 1**, 440; legal aspects of, **Vol. 9, Part 2**, 105; letters of marque for, **Vol. 3, Part 1**, 197
Privateers (for list of privateers, *see* Ships): issue of commissions to, **Vol. 3, Part 1**, 604; firms for outfitting, **Vol. 6, Part 1**, 76
Private Life of Helen of Troy, The, **Supp. 5**, 212
Private Life of Henry VIII, The, **Supp. 7**, 461; **Supp. 10**, 599
Prize cases, management of, during the Civil War, **Vol. 3, Part 1**, 592 f.
Prize contests in newspapers, first use of, **Vol. 3, Part 2**, 572
Prizefighting, **Vol. 3, Part 2**, 443; **Vol. 4, Part 2**, 500; **Vol. 7, Part 1**, 233; **Vol. 8, Part 1**, 585
Probability, **Supp. 5**, 563
Process, theory of, **Supp. 4**, 882–84
Process and Reality, **Supp. 4**, 882
Process of History, The, **Supp. 4**, 824

Proctor, George, relations with Isabella Stewart Gardner, **Vol. 4, Part 1**, 143
Proctor, William Cooper, reference to, **Supp. 3**, 810
Proctor and Gamble, management, **Supp. 9**, 521, 522
Proctorsville, Vt., founder of, **Vol. 8, Part 1**, 245 f.
Prodigal Judge, The, **Vol. 5, Part 2**, 360
Prodigies: **Vol. 3, Part 2**, 404; **Vol. 6, Part 1**, 87; Vol. 8, Part 1, 149 f.; **Vol. 8, Part 2**, 287; billiard, **Supp. 6**, 303–4; education of, **Supp. 2**, 110; **Supp. 4**, 732; intellectually gifted, **Supp. 3**, 375–76; **Supp. 6**, 626–27; mathematics, **Supp. 7**, 784; musical, **Supp. 5**, 607; **Supp. 6**, 297; **Supp. 7**, 443–44, 737; **Supp. 8**, 312–13
Produce Exchange, reorganization of, **Vol. 7, Part 2**, 56
Producers. For complete list, *see* Occupations Index
Producers' Cooperatives, advocated as method of abolishing the wage system, **Vol. 8, Part 1**, 142 f.
Producers' Releasing Corporation, B movies made by, **Supp. 9**, 820
Producing Managers' Association, Actors' Equity strike, **Supp. 3**, 174, 333
Productivity, studies in, **Supp. 4**, 565–66
Professional Lawn Tennis Association of the United States, **Supp. 6**, 539
Profile engravings of distinguished Americans, Saint Mémin, **Vol. 8, Part 2**, 305
Profiles in Courage, **Supp. 7**, 420
Profit sharing, **Vol. 7, Part 1**, 419
Progesterone, synthesis of, **Supp. 9**, 444
Progress and Poverty, **Supp. 6**, 570
Progressive education. *See* Education, progressive
Progressive Education Association, **Supp. 7**, 43
Progressive movement: **Supp. 4**, 641; Brandeis on investor and consumer protection, **Supp. 3**, 95; California, **Supp. 3**, 395–96; Chicago, **Supp. 5**, 579; conservation efforts, **Supp. 4**, 663–66; economics, **Supp. 6**, 705; goals, **Supp. 6**, 522; journalism, **Supp. 1**, 210; **Supp. 4**, 707; **Supp. 5**, 141, 666–67; lawyers in, **Supp. 3**, 167–68; **Supp. 6**, 541–42; Pennsylvania, **Supp. 4**, 491; Philadelphia social reform, **Supp. 6**, 515; reforms, **Supp. 4**, 522; Senate, **Supp. 3**, 105–6, 108; **Supp. 6**, 578; Socialist mayors, **Supp. 4**, 511–12; sociology of, **Supp. 5**, 591, 592–93; urban leaders, **Supp. 5**, 485; Wisconsin, **Supp. 3**, 178, 249–50; writers associated with, **Supp. 4**, 164–65; writings on, **Supp. 8**, 272, 593–95. *See also* Social reform
Progressive party (1912): founding of, **Vol. 5, Part 2**, 544; **Vol. 8, Part 2**, 86, 142; **Supp. 4**, 170, 665; Illinois, **Supp. 5**, 579; journalistic support, **Supp. 3**, 816; Kansas, **Supp. 3**, 544–45; New Hampshire, **Supp. 5**, 689; Ohio, **Supp. 7**, 85–86; platform, **Supp. 4**, 107; presidential elections, **Supp. 3**, 105–6, 395, 397; radical nucleus, **Supp. 3**, 604; Republican connections, **Supp. 3**, 710–11; Senate, **Supp. 4**, 669–70; Wisconsin, **Supp. 5**, 403–4
Progressive party (1948): **Supp. 4**, 147; **Supp. 7**, 763; **Supp. 8**, 511; alleged Communist links, **Supp. 6**, 681
Progressive party of Wisconsin (1934), **Supp. 7**, 450
Prohibition: **Vol. 1, Part 1**, 512, 628; **Vol. 1, Part 2**, 310, 319, 334; **Vol. 2, Part 1**, 497, 591; **Vol. 3, Part 1**, 353; **Vol. 3, Part 2**, 6, 109, 227, 334, 335, 342, 413, 542; **Vol. 4, Part 1**, 73, 115, 171; **Vol. 4, Part 2**, 376, 436; **Vol. 5, Part 2**, 519; **Vol. 6, Part 2**, 342; **Vol. 8, Part 1**, 212; **Vol. 8, Part 2**, 303; **Vol. 9, Part 1**, 7, 74, 148, 546; **Vol. 10, Part 2**, 516; activities of W. J. Bryan, **Vol. 2, Part 1**, 197; advocacy of, **Supp. 1**, 251–52, 360; **Supp. 2**, 723; **Supp. 3**, 132, 449; **Supp. 5**, 80, 442; **Supp. 6**, 548, 682–83; Anti-Saloon League, **Vol. 5, Part 2**, 517; **Vol. 6, Part 1**, 171, 276; **Vol. 6, Part 2**, 483; **Vol. 10, Part 2**, 55; associations to repeal, **Supp. 5**, 194; bootlegging, **Supp. 4**, 140–42; **Supp. 5**, 737; **Supp. 6**, 263; **Supp. 9**, 12, 197; cartoons ridiculing, **Supp. 5**, 391; Catholic support, **Supp. 2**, 135; congressional opposition to, **Supp. 4**, 446; federal legislation, **Supp. 4**, 853; historical writings on, **Supp. 7**, 20; Kansas, **Supp. 7**, 678; law enforcement, **Supp. 2**, 715; **Supp. 3**, 117; **Supp. 6**, 360; **Supp. 7**, 786, 805–6; lecturing to promote, **Supp. 4**, 741; **Supp. 5**, 701, 702; **Supp. 8**, 505; legality of, **Supp. 6**, 3; legislation authorship, **Supp. 3**, 706; "local option" question, **Vol. 6, Part 2**, 330; moderate voices for, **Supp. 7**, 345; opposition to, **Supp. 6**, 591–92, 636; political issue, **Supp. 2**, 723; **Supp. 3**, 720; **Supp. 4**, 136; **Supp. 7**, 786; political use of, **Supp. 3**, 318; press opposition to, **Supp. 5**, 449–50; Prohibition National Convention, **Vol. 9, Part 2**, 234; Prohibition party, **Vol. 1, Part 2**, 310; **Vol. 3, Part 1**, 412; **Vol. 4, Part 2**, 387; **Vol. 8, Part 2**, 304; **Supp. 5**, 702; publications promoting, **Supp. 4**, 161; repeal movement, **Supp. 2**, 207, **Supp. 3**, 181; **Supp. 6**, 480; repeal of, **Supp. 1**, 86; **Supp. 3**, 649; Salvation Army support of, **Supp. 4**, 96; speakeasy, **Supp. 6**, 382; **Supp. 8**, 38; Virginia Anti-Saloon League, **Supp. 3**, 132; Women's Christian Temperance Union, **Vol. 3, Part 2**, 553; **Vol. 4, Part 2**, 436; **Vol. 6, Part 1**, 85, 86; women's organizations opposing, **Supp. 5**, 157; writings on, **Supp. 3**, 734. *See also* Alcohol; Temperance
Prohme, Rayna, reference to, **Supp. 9**, 718
Projectiles, machinery for the manufacture of, **Vol. 3, Part 1**, 580 f.; **Vol. 6, Part 1**, 82
"Project method," **Vol. 7, Part 1**, 558
Prokofiev, Sergei, references to, **Supp. 6**, 456, 550
Proletarian literature, **Supp. 7**, 239–40, 269, 583–84; **Supp. 8**, 137, 216–17
Prometheus Fountain (sculpture), **Supp. 8**, 414
"Promiscuous sitting" in Methodist church, **Vol. 5, Part 1**, 490
Promised Land, The, **Supp. 4**, 23
Promise of American Life, The, **Supp. 1**, 201, 210
Pronunciation, studies in, **Vol. 6, Part 1**, 430
Proofreading, **Vol. 9, Part 2**, 357
Propaganda, **Vol. 5, Part 2**, 297. *See also* Public relations; World War I; World War II
Property. *See* Real estate
Property cases, **Vol. 4, Part 1**, 255, 444, 456, 559. *See also* Law
Property tax, **Supp. 1**, 385; **Supp. 2**, 272; **Supp. 6**, 522
Proskauer, Joseph, reference to, **Supp. 3**, 718
Prospect Park (Brooklyn), landscaping of, **Vol. 6, Part 1**, 294; **Vol. 7, Part 2**, 26 f.
Prostate gland, surgery of, **Supp. 3**, 854
Prostitution: bordellos, **Supp. 4**, 255–56; **Supp. 7**, 4–5; Chicago, **Supp. 5**, 274–75; journalistic expos, **Supp. 5**, 698; organized crime link, **Supp. 7**, 485; reform movements against, **Supp. 4**, 759; **Supp. 5**, 296–97; study of problem, **Vol. 4, Part 1**, 171
Proteases, **Supp. 6**, 595
Protection or Free Trade, **Vol. 4, Part 1**, 215
Protective tariff: **Vol. 2, Part 1**, 12, 491, 544; **Vol. 2, Part 2**, 176; **Vol. 3, Part 1**, 289; **Vol. 4, Part 2**, 457; **Vol. 5, Part 2**, 163, 300; **Vol. 6, Part 2**, 106; **Vol. 8, Part 1**, 457; **Vol. 9, Part 1**, 44, 204, 622; **Vol. 9, Part 2**, 237. *See also* Tariff
Protein: amino acid chain, **Supp. 3**, 441–42; **Supp. 4**, 720; chemistry, **Supp. 3**, 60–61; **Supp. 5**, 122–23, 149; **Supp. 6**, 346; chromosomal nucleoproteins, **Supp. 6**, 596; colloidal systems, **Supp. 3**, 315; enzyme identification as, **Supp. 5**, 622, 623, 670; human requirement studies, **Supp. 3**, 163; investigation, **Vol. 7, Part 2**, 74; metabolism of, **Supp. 1**, 307; research in, **Supp. 1**, 560; **Supp. 10**, 427; **Supp. 2**, 379; for surgery patients, **Supp. 6**, 190

Protestant Charities Aid Association of New York, founding of, **Supp. 1**, 541
Protestant Episcopal church (for complete list of clergymen, bishops etc., *see* Occupations Index): adaptation of Book of Common Prayer, **Vol. 8, Part 1**, 249 f.; as agency to bring about new social order, advocacy of, **Vol. 10, Part 2**, 251; altar and Book of Common Prayer design, **Supp. 3**, 784, 785; Anglo-Catholicism, **Supp. 3**, 195; **Supp. 6**, 45–46; bishops, **Supp. 1**, 115–17, 169–70, 329, 678; black leadership, **Supp. 1**, 645; broad churchmanship, advocacy of, **Vol. 10, Part 1**, 498; cathedrals, **Vol. 5, Part 2**, 422; **Vol. 6, Part 1**, 301; Christian Social Union, **Supp. 3**, 249; church organization, **Vol. 3, Part 1**, 216; Church Pension Fund, **Supp. 3**, 448; colonial history of, **Vol. 4, Part 2**, 417; Council of Bishops, **Supp. 1**, 329; "Cowley Fathers," **Vol. 4, Part 1**, 470; drafting of constitution for American, **Vol. 8, Part 1**, 294 f.; divinity school faculty, **Supp. 3**, 37; divorce, attitude toward, **Vol. 4, Part 1**, 491; Emmanuel Movement, **Supp. 3**, 190–91; episcopacy question, **Vol. 5, Part 1**, 235; executive offices, **Vol. 4, Part 2**, 360; first missionary bishop, **Vol. 5, Part 2**, 321; first trial of a bishop, **Vol. 7, Part 2**, 39; formation of, in America, **Vol. 10, Part 2**, 121; General Convention of 1895, **Vol. 5, Part 2**, 590; girls' school, **Supp. 1**, 170; in Hawaii, **Supp. 1**, 624; institutional church, **Supp. 1**, 618; leadership, **Supp. 2**, 258; legislation, advancement of, **Vol. 3, Part 1**, 335; **Vol. 5, Part 1**, 112; liturgy, **Vol. 7, Part 1**, 137; Massachusetts bishopric, **Supp. 3**, 447–48; missions, **Vol. 3, Part 1**, 333; **Vol. 4, Part 2**, 264; **Vol. 5, Part 2**, 321; **Vol. 6, Part 1**, 64, 95; **Supp. 1**, 115–16, 134; **Supp. 2**, 258; **Supp. 4**, 677–78; New York City diocese, **Supp. 4**, 546–48; Oxford Movement, **Supp. 1**, 668; presiding bishop, **Supp. 6**, 649; publications and societies, **Vol. 5, Part 1**, 93; **Vol. 6, Part 1**, 296; reunification with Rome issue, **Supp. 2**, 201; reunion of northern and southern branches, **Vol. 8, Part 1**, 313 f.; service to, **Vol. 1, Part 1**, 18, 204; **Vol. 1, Part 2**, 35, 335; **Vol. 2, Part 2**, 51, 599; **Vol. 3, Part 2**, 98, 155, 203; **Vol. 4, Part 1**, 60, 490; **Vol. 4, Part 2**, 416, 491; **Vol. 5, Part 1**, 222; **Vol. 6, Part 2**, 258; **Vol. 7, Part 1**, 643; **Vol. 9, Part 1**, 301, 356; slave ownership, attitude toward, **Vol. 1, Part 1**, 277 f.; social reform, **Supp. 6**, 600, 649; Training School (Philadelphia), **Vol. 4, Part 2**, 262; writings on, **Vol. 3, Part 2**, 412; **Vol. 4, Part 1**, 471, 594; **Vol. 4, Part 2**, 417; **Vol. 5, Part 2**, 410, 423; **Vol. 6, Part 1**, 302
Protestant Episcopal church (by locality): Alabama, **Vol. 10, Part 2**, 315; California, **Vol. 5, Part 2**, 422 f.; Connecticut, **Vol. 6, Part 1**, 75; **Vol. 10, Part 2**, 42; Delaware, first bishop of, **Vol. 6, Part 1**, 95; Illinois, **Vol. 2, Part 1**, 274; **Vol. 6, Part 2**, 116; **Vol. 9, Part 1**, 6; Maine, expansion in, **Vol. 2, Part 1**, 276; Massachusetts Bay Colony, anti-episcopal views in, **Vol. 6, Part 1**, 87; New England, **Vol. 8, Part 2**, 529; New Jersey, first confirmation in, **Vol. 8, Part 1**, 249 f.; New York, **Vol. 3, Part 1**, 216, 334 f.; North Carolina, beginnings in, **Vol. 8, Part 1**, 398; Ohio, **Vol. 3, Part 1**, 343; **Vol. 6, Part 1**, 179; Oregon, first bishop of, **Vol. 8, Part 2**, 501; Pennsylvania, **Vol. 8, Part 1**, 124 f., 249 f.; Rhode Island, **Vol. 9, Part 1**, 359; South, spread of through the, **Vol. 2, Part 1**, 172; **Vol. 6, Part 1**, 64; **Vol. 7, Part 2**, 629; South Carolina, first bishop of, **Vol. 9, Part 1**, 336; Vermont, first bishop of, **Vol. 5, Part 1**, 212; Virginia, **Vol. 5, Part 2**, 75; **Vol. 6, Part 1**, 160; **Vol. 6, Part 2**, 183, 480; **Vol. 10, Part 2**, 316
Protestants and Other Americans United for the Separation of Church and State, **Supp. 7**, 597
"Protocols of the Elders of Zion, The," **Supp. 10**, 152
Protocols of the Wise Men of Zion, **Supp. 1**, 78
Protoplasm: crystalline changes in, **Supp. 6**, 282; study of, **Vol. 7, Part 1**, 95
Protozoa: life-cycle studies, **Supp. 3**, 126–27; research on, **Supp. 4**, 461–62
Provence, writings of, **Vol. 5, Part 1**, 614 f.; **Vol. 8, Part 1**, 202
Providence, R.I.: Butler Hospital, history of, **Vol. 8, Part 1**, 404; civic service to, **Vol. 6, Part 1**, 289; **Vol. 8, Part 1**, 584; **Vol. 9, Part 1**, 54, 290; early Catholicism in, **Vol. 10, Part 1**, 98 f.; public health, **Supp. 3**, 158
Providence Hospital (Washington), founding of, **Vol. 9, Part 2**, 586
Provident Hospital (Baltimore), founding of, **Supp. 3**, 271
Provident Loan Society, **Supp. 3**, 729
Provincetown, Mass., writers' colony, **Supp. 8**, 674, 675
Provincetown Players: **Vol. 2, Part 2**, 372 f.; **Supp. 3**, 329; **Supp. 4**, 576; **Supp. 8**, 350; **Supp. 9**, 875; founding of, **Supp. 4**,. 330; **Supp. 5**, 523; **Supp. 8**, 675
Provincial Congress of Massachusetts (colonial), **Vol. 5, Part 1**, 345; **Vol. 6, Part 1**, 260
Provisional Executive Committee for Central Zionist Affairs, founding of, **Supp. 4**, 905
Proxmire, William, reference to, **Supp. 10**, 420
Prudden, T. Mitchell, reference to, **Supp. 3**, 257
Prudential Friendly Society, first policy written in, **Vol. 3, Part 1**, 463 f.
Prudential Insurance Co., **Supp. 4**, 384; **Supp. 5**, 177–78; early development of, **Vol. 3, Part 1**, 463 f.
Pryor's Band, **Supp. 3**, 610–11
Psallonian Society, founding of, **Vol. 9, Part 1**, 46
Psalmody, **Vol. 3, Part 2**, 449; **Vol. 6, Part 1**, 530
Psalm singing, **Vol. 9, Part 2**, 390
Psalm tunes, compiled, **Vol. 9, Part 2**, 236
Psittacosis ("parrot fever"), **Supp. 7**, 648
Psychiatric Institute (New York City): administration, **Supp. 1**, 471; predecessor, **Supp. 4**, 571
Psychiatrists. For complete list, *see* Occupations Index
Psychiatry: **Vol. 1, Part 1**, 458; **Vol. 1, Part 2**, 160; **Vol. 2, Part 2**, 213; **Vol. 3, Part 1**, 595 f.; **Vol. 3, Part 2**, 412; **Vol. 4, Part 2**, 411, 412; **Vol. 5, Part 1**, 97; **Vol. 5, Part 2**, 207, 324, 325, 354; **Vol. 7, Part 1**, 489; **Vol. 8, Part 1**, 404; **Vol. 8, Part 2**, 116, 313, 559; **Vol. 9, Part 1**, 462; **Vol. 10, Part 1**, 613; alcoholism and suicide, **Supp. 6**, 461; clinical education in, **Supp. 4**, 572; community mental health movement, **Supp. 6**, 17; editing, **Supp. 3**, 385–86; emotional conflict and maladjustment, **Supp. 3**, 128; foundation grants, **Supp. 6**, 252–53; history of, **Supp. 6**, 724–25; interpersonal relations theory, **Supp. 4**, 805–8; neuropsychiatry, **Supp. 6**, 403–4; nomenclature of disorders, **Supp. 8**, 429–30; physiological approach to, **Supp. 4**, 618; popularization of, **Supp. 8**, 429–30; psychobiological, **Supp. 6**, 181; psychosis treatment, **Supp. 6**, 220; research and training centers, **Supp. 5**, 484; social work, criticism of, **Supp. 4**, 811; training in, **Supp. 1**, 131, 471; **Supp. 2**, 24; **Supp. 3**, 128; treatment and rehabilitation, **Supp. 3**, 320. *See also* Mental health and illness; Psychoanalysis
Psychiatry (journal), founding of, **Supp. 4**, 806, 807
Psychical research: **Vol. 3, Part 2**, 478; **Vol. 5, Part 1**, 341, 455; **Vol. 7, Part 1**, 338; **Vol. 9, Part 1**, 3; **Vol. 10, Part 1**, 417 f.
Psychic phenomena: extrasensory perception, **Supp. 6**, 612; philosophical opposition to, **Supp. 5**, 561; psychological investigation of, **Supp. 8**, 44; **Supp. 10**, 570–71, 671–72; research in, **Supp. 2**, 407; writings on, **Supp. 4**, 878; **Supp. 10**, 571
Psycho, **Supp. 9**, 383

Psychoanalysis: anthropologlcal application, **Supp. 5**, 583–84; behaviorism and, **Supp. 4**, 387; diverging views in, **Supp. 7**, 6–7; early advocacy, **Supp. 2**, 711; early U.S. practitioners, **Supp. 3**, 383; first American-born analyst, **Supp. 4**, 130–31; first analyst in U.S., **Supp. 4**, 107–8, Freud collaboration, **Supp. 4**, 117–18; humanism in, **Supp. 6**, 724–25; juvenile paresis analogy with, **Supp. 8**, 429; lay analysis, **Supp. 3**, 385; orthodox Freudian, **Supp. 3**, 190–91; **Supp. 10**, 260; popularization of, **Supp. 3**, 191, 320; political science application, **Supp. 10**, 433–34; psychology and, **Supp. 4**, 572; for psychosis, **Supp. 6**, 220; self-development emphasis, **Supp. 5**, 302, 315–17; social and cultural problems, application to, **Supp. 10**, 259–61; theory systemization, **Supp. 6**, 527–28; training analysis, **Supp. 5**, 517–18; training in, **Supp. 4**, 263, 716–17; writings on, **Supp. 3**, 386; **Supp. 8**, 523–24. *See also* Mental health and illness
Psychoanalytic Review, founding of, **Supp. 2**, 712; **Supp. 4**, 108
Psychoanalytic Theory of Neurosis, The, **Supp. 4**, 264
Psychobiography, **Supp. 6**, 279; **Supp. 7**, 80
Psychokinesis, **Supp. 10**, 672
Psychological Corporation, **Supp. 5**, 433–34; founding of, **Supp. 3**, 151
Psychological Review, **Supp. 1**, 50; **Supp. 6**, 672; founding of, **Supp. 3**, 150
Psychological warfare, **Supp. 6**, 406–7; **Supp. 7**, 812
Psychologische Forschung, founding of, **Supp. 8**, 344
Psychology: **Vol. 4, Part 2**, 128 f.; **Vol. 5, Part 1**, 341, 590; **Vol. 5, Part 2**, 525 f., 529 f.; **Vol. 7, Part 1**, 448, 558; **Vol. 8, Part 2**, 207, 488; **Vol. 9, Part 2**, 647; **Vol. 10, Part 1**, 476; abnormal, **Vol. 8, Part 1**, 230; animal behavior studies, **Supp. 4**, 425; anthropological, **Supp. 4**, 71; behaviorism, **Supp. 6**, 261–62, 367–68, 640, 672–73; belief in authority, origin of, **Supp. 3**, 82; books popularizing, **Supp. 4**, 495–96; brain function studies, **Supp. 10**, 779, 780; child development theories, **Supp. 3**, 119; **Supp. 4**, 7–8; clinical application, **Supp. 3**, 150; comparative, **Supp. 3**, 149–50; **Supp. 6**, 639–40, 671–73, 718–19; **Supp. 8**, 44; educational, **Vol. 7, Part 1**, 578; existential, **Supp. 7**, 747; experimental, early work in, **Vol. 8, Part 2**, 346, *see also subhead:* comparative; first Ph.D. degree in U.S., **Supp. 3**, 383; first U.S. professorship solely in, **Supp. 3**, 149; Freudian, **Supp. 10**, 255–56; functionalism, **Supp. 4**, 21; German film study, **Supp. 8**, 346; Gestalt, **Supp. 3**, 428–30, 808–9; **Supp. 8**, 343–45; **Supp. 9**, 325; group interaction studies, **Supp. 4**, 485, 830–31; human potential movement, **Supp. 8**, 423–44; illusions, **Supp. 3**, 383; industrial, **Supp. 4**, 565–66; **Supp. 5**, 59, 433–34, 611–12; **Supp. 6**, 17, 222; **Supp. 9**, 309; instrumental techniques, **Supp. 3**, 229–30; intervening variables concept, **Supp. 6**, 640; laboratory, installation, in America, **Vol. 5, Part 2**, 525; Ladd-Franklin theory, **Vol. 5, Part 2**, 529; learning theory, **Supp. 4**, 485, 832–33; **Supp. 5**, 328–30; **Supp. 6**, 251–62, 527–28, 640; legal philosophy and, **Supp. 6**, 216; mental dissociation, **Vol. 8, Part 1**, 230 f.; of mentally retarded, **Supp. 4**, 439; mental responsibility in crime, **Supp. 3**, 102; merit-order rating scale, **Supp. 3**, 149–50; modern, original contributor, **Vol. 10, Part 1**, 123; motor, **Supp. 2**, 699; "new," rise of, in America, **Vol. 5, Part 2**, 525; personality studies, **Supp. 8**, 7–9; personality tests, **Supp. 1**, 264; philosophic behaviorism, **Supp. 4**, 387; physiological, **Supp. 2**, 156; **Supp. 10**, 730, 731; popular, **Supp. 5**, 546; **Supp. 8**, 11–12, 489; popularization of, **Supp. 3**, 384; **Supp. 10**, 255–56; pragmatism, **Vol. 5, Part 1**, 597 f.; **Vol. 7, Part 1**, 112; **Vol. 7, Part 2**, 400; psychoanalysis and, **Supp. 4**, 572; psychobiography, **Supp. 6**, 279; of public opinion, **Supp. 8**, 69–70; "relative deprivation" concept, **Supp. 6**, 605; of religion, **Supp. 3**, 608; **Supp. 5**, 115–16; **Supp. 6**, 14; religion and, **Supp. 4**, 495–96, 766–67; role theory, **Supp. 3**, 579; social, **Supp. 1**, 547–48; **Supp. 2**, 562; **Supp. 9**, 260–61; teaching of, **Vol. 7, Part 1**, 337 f.; **Vol. 7, Part 2**, 257; **Vol. 8, Part 2**, 346; **Vol. 9, Part 2**, 564 f.; **Vol. 10, Part 1**, 450; **Supp. 2**, 506, 698; **Supp. 10**, 570; testing, **Supp. 5**, 685; **Supp. 6**, 240–41, 626–27; **Supp. 7**, 594; thinking and learning research, **Supp. 6**, 527–28; training in, **Supp. 1**, 150, 316; **Supp. 3**, 149–50; tropism theory, **Vol. 6, Part 1**, 349 f.; voluntarism and creative synthesis theory, **Supp. 4**, 444; of women, **Supp. 5**, 316, 317; writings on, **Vol. 3, Part 2**, 384; **Vol. 5, Part 2**, 525 f., 530; **Vol. 6, Part 2**, 309; **Vol. 8, Part 1**, 146 f., 221, 230 f., 389 f., 391; **Vol. 8, Part 2**, 231; **Vol. 9, Part 1**, 152; **Vol. 9, Part 2**, 564; **Vol. 10, Part 1**, 476; **Supp. 1**, 50; **Supp. 10**, 570. *See also* Behaviorism; Mental health and illness; Psychiatry
Psychology of Religious Experience, The, **Supp. 6**, 14
Psychology of the Adolescent, The, founding of, **Supp. 2**, 313
Psychometric Society, founding of, **Supp. 5**, 685
Psychoneurotic and hypnotic phenomena, pioneer work in, **Vol. 8, Part 1**, 230 f.
Psychopathology, **Vol. 5, Part 2**, 355; **Vol. 9, Part 1**, 152
Psychophysics, **Supp. 5**, 685–86
Psychosis: prefrontal lobotomy for, **Supp. 6**, 223; psychoanalysis for, **Supp. 6**, 220
Psychosomatic illness: faith healing, **Supp. 4**, 271–72; first studies, **Supp. 3**, 128, 385; physiology of emotions studies, **Supp. 3**, 135–36; psychoanalysis for, **Supp. 6**, 620; recognition of, **Supp. 4**, 572; **Supp. 8**, 429; studies on, **Supp. 7**, 6
Psychosomatic Medicine, **Supp. 6**, 181
Psychotherapy, **Vol. 9, Part 1**, 152; **Vol. 9, Part 2**, 318; encounter, **Supp. 8**, 424; first clinic in U.S., **Supp. 5**, 301; for nervous disorders, **Supp. 2**, 736; pastoral use of, **Supp. 8**, 307. *See also* Psychiatry; Psychoanalysis
"Ptereotype," name applied to John Pratt's original writing machine, **Vol. 8, Part 1**, 173 f.
Public accounting. *See* Accounting
Public address systems. *See* Loudspeakers
Public administration. *See* Civil Service Commission; Government employees; Municipal government
Publication Corporation, **Supp. 5**, 394
Publications: early guidebooks of New York and vicinity, **Vol. 3, Part 2**, 576; learned historical, pioneer work in, **Vol. 10, Part 1**, 594 f.; of Charles G. Leland, **Vol. 6, Part 1**, 159; medical, **Vol. 3, Part 2**, 547; of Miriam Leslie, **Vol. 6, Part 1**, 187; music, **Vol. 8, Part 2**, 323; scientific, of Joseph Leidy, **Vol. 6, Part 1**, 151
Public baths, in America, **Vol. 1, Part 2**, 29
Public Charities Association of Pennsylvania, founding of, **Supp. 2**, 209
Public defender, creation of post, **Supp. 2**, 248
Public Education Association of New York City, **Supp. 3**, 375
Public employment. *See* Government employees; Public works
Public Enemy, **Supp. 9**, 856
Public Franchise League (Boston), **Vol. 8, Part 1**, 230 f.; **Supp. 3**, 95,
Public health: **Vol. 1, Part 2**, 18, 262, 268, 493; **Vol. 2, Part 1**, 48, 387, 536, 612; **Vol. 3, Part 1**, 139, 219, 377, 394; **Vol. 4, Part 1**, 285, 431; **Vol. 4, Part 2**, 301, 303, 307, 369, 568; **Vol. 5, Part 1**, 109, 607; **Vol. 5, Part 2**, 277, 483, 524, 570; **Vol. 6, Part 1**, 279, 606; **Vol. 7, Part 2**, 175; **Vol. 8, Part 1**, 142, 275, 390, 447, 460, 575; **Vol. 8, Part 2**, 188, 238,

281, 311, 313, 553, 600; **Vol. 9, Part 1**, 34, 117, 187, 348, 462, 543, 592; **Vol. 9, Part 2**, 130, 513; **Vol. 10, Part 1**, 621, 648; administration, **Supp. 2**, 121; **Supp. 3**, 323–24; **Supp. 5**, 604–5, 192–93, 701–2; development of, **Supp. 2**, 514; environmental hazards, **Supp. 6**, 175; financing of, **Supp. 1**, 639; first professional school, **Supp. 4**, 701; governmental measures, **Supp. 7**, 251–52; **Supp. 9**, 789; immunology, **Supp. 1**, 666; infants and children, **Supp. 3**, 28; medical fees criticized, **Supp. 9**, 366–67; municipal and state boards, **Supp. 5**, 232–33; municipal preventive measures, **Supp. 3**, 312–13; milk pasteurization, **Vol. 8, Part 2**, 553; **Vol. 9, Part 2**, 130; New York City, **Supp. 6**, 424; New York City garment industry conditions, **Supp. 3**, 609–10; nursing, **Supp. 2**, 687–88; **Supp. 4**, 64–66; **Supp. 6**, 283–84; pioneer work in, **Supp. 4**, 700–701; popularization of, **Supp. 5**, 143–44; preventive measures, **Supp. 3**, 323–24; private sector institutions, **Supp. 10**, 419–20; professional education in, **Supp. 2**, 212; **Supp. 5**, 632; Providence, R.I., **Supp. 3**, 158, 324; Pure Food and Drug Act, **Vol. 4, Part 2**, 5888; **Vol. 5, Part 2**, 524, 570; Red Cross program, **Supp. 2**, 177; Rockefeller Sanitary Commission, **Supp. 3**, 738; Sanitary Commission, U.S., **Vol. 8, Part 2**, 600; sanitary engineering, **Supp. 1**, 326; school programs, **Supp. 5**, 553; state departments, **Supp. 5**, 601; statistical studies, **Supp. 2**, 646; **Supp. 4**, 384–85; **Supp. 7**, 192; teaching of, **Supp. 3**, 244; **Supp. 5**, 233; tuberculosis crusade, **Vol. 5, Part 2**, 483; **Vol. 8, Part 2**, 188, 281; typhoid crusade, **Vol. 5, Part 2**, 483; universal health care advocacy, **Supp. 10**, 682; venereal disease education and prevention, **Supp. 4**, 758–59; writings on, **Supp. 4**, 474–75, 684; **Supp. 6**, 117; **Supp. 9**, 225–26; Yellow Fever Commission, **Vol. 8, Part 1**, 460; **Vol. 9, Part 1**, 117, 592. *See also* Epidemics; Epidemiology; Occupational health and safety; Social hygiene

Public Health Association of America, **Vol. 1, Part 2**, 268; **Vol. 4, Part 2**, 369; **Vol. 8, Part 1**, 390

Public Health Council, first state, **Supp. 7**, 252

Public Health Service, United States: **Vol. 8, Part 2**, 313; **Vol. 9, Part 2**, 513; international relations, **Supp. 7**, 195; mental disorders, **Supp. 9**, 469; service in, **Supp. 9**, 469–70; statistical studies, **Supp. 7**, 192; venereal disease, **Supp. 6**, 423–24, 460

Public Health Service Hospital (Lexington, Ky.), **Supp. 9**, 470

Public housing, **Supp. 3**, 730; **Supp. 5**, 631; federally subsidized, **Supp. 3**, 838

Public Housing Act (1949), **Supp. 5**, 719

Publicity, use of, **Vol. 1, Part 1**, 606 f.; **Vol. 5, Part 2**, 73; **Vol. 6, Part 1**, 571

Publicity work. *See* Advertising and marketing; Public Relations

Public land. *See* Land and land use; Parks

Public Ledger (Philadelphia), **Vol. 2, Part 2**, 70; **Vol. 3, Part 1**, 455 f., 514 f.; **Vol. 5, Part 1**, 104

Public opinion: broadcast audience measurement, **Supp. 5**, 310–11; Gallup poll inception, **Supp. 4**, 189; government policy relationship, **Supp. 8**, 69, 70; marketing research, **Supp. 9**, 678; presidential election (1936), **Supp. 7**, 274, 649; **Supp. 9**, 677; presidential election (1940), **Supp. 9**, 677; presidential election (1944), **Supp. 9**, 677; presidential election (1948), **Supp. 9**, 678; presidential election (1960), **Supp. 9**, 678; psychological research in, **Supp. 8**, 69–70; research poll technique development, **Supp. 7**, 649–50; Roper poll inception, **Supp. 9**, 677–78; social distance scale, **Supp. 3**, 578; survey testing methodology, **Supp. 6**, 604–5; tests and measurements, **Supp. 5**, 494, 685, 686

Public Opinion Index for Industry, founding of, **Supp. 7**, 650

Public parks, **Vol. 2, Part 1**, 306; **Vol. 6, Part 1**, 27; **Vol. 6, Part 2**, 492; **Vol. 7, Part 2**, 26 f., 482; **Vol. 8, Part 1**, 405; **Vol. 8, Part 2**, 355; **Vol. 9, Part 2**, 123; **Vol. 10, Part 1**, 647. *See also* Parks

Public Parks Protective Association, **Vol. 3, Part 2**, 56

Public relations: corporate, **Supp. 1**, 489–90; **Supp. 5**, 303; **Supp. 10**, 334–35; development of, **Supp. 6**, 90–91; **Supp. 9**, 681–82; political parties, **Supp. 4**, 575; press agents, **Supp. 5**, 270–71; **Supp. 6**, 536

Public school education. *See* Education

Public School Society (1805), organization of, **Vol. 2, Part 2**, 222 f.

Public speaking. *See* Lecturing; Oratory

Public utilities: **Vol. 1, Part 2**, 582; **Vol. 3, Part 1**, 356 f.; **Vol. 4, Part 2**, 372; **Vol. 6, Part 1**, 79; **Vol. 8, Part 1**, 9; **Vol. 9, Part 2**, 449, 644; **Vol. 10, Part 2**, 202, 203, 429, 455 f.; California legislation, **Supp. 3**, 395; central stations, **Supp. 2**, 333; Con Edison founding, **Supp. 3**, 138; development of, **Supp. 1**, 531, 630; **Supp. 2**, 154; entrepreneurs, **Supp. 3**, 192–93; ethics issues, **Supp. 6**, 590–96, 684; executive management of, **Supp. 3**, 746–47; **Supp. 4**, 180, 264–65; federal preference clause, **Supp. 8**, 2; first research department, **Supp. 3**, 231; holding companies, **Supp. 3**, 138, 526–27; **Supp. 4**, 394–95; **Supp. 5**, 260, 750–51; holding company legislation, **Supp. 3**, 654; **Supp. 4**, 544; legal counsel, **Supp. 3**, 829; municipal ownership, **Supp. 2**, 583, 691; New York City, **Supp. 4**, 404; public v. private ownership, **Supp. 3**, 250; **Supp. 6**, 216, 437, 484; **Supp. 8**, 179; rate setting, **Supp. 2**, 560, 584; **Supp. 3**, 95, 231, 241; standardized evaluation, **Supp. 3**, 188; valuation and depreciation of properties, **Supp. 3**, 98; World War II measures, **Supp. 8**, 352. *See also* Electricity and electrification; Gas; Water

Public Utility Holding Company Act (1935): **Supp. 5**, 480; **Supp. 7**, 635; **Supp. 9**, 859; consitutionality of, **Supp. 5**, 358; groundwork for, **Supp. 6**, 122; **Supp. 9**, 607; opposition to, **Supp. 3**, 829; passage of, **Supp. 4**, 544

Public welfare, **Vol. 4, Part 1**, 160; **Vol. 6, Part 2**, 179; **Vol. 9, Part 2**, 567

Public works: art, **Supp. 3**, 112; Boston politics and, **Supp. 6**, 139–40; Civilian Conservation Corps, **Supp. 6**, 411–12; concept development, **Supp. 3**, 653, 654; **Supp. 6**, 378; countering unemployment, **Supp. 5**, 139–40, 403; New Deal construction projects, **Supp. 8**, 308; New Deal relief policy, **Supp. 4**, 391–92; New York City, **Supp. 4**, 466

Public Works Administration: **Supp. 2**, 170; **Supp. 3**, 795; **Supp. 4**, 392; building projects, **Supp. 5**, 342–43; **Supp. 9**, 633–34; founding of, **Supp. 3**, 650–51, 656; Mississippi Valley Committee, **Supp. 6**, 122

Publishers. For complete list, *see* Occupations Index

Publishers' Trade List Annual, first publication of, **Vol. 6, Part 1**, 231

Publisher's Weekly, **Vol. 6, Part 1**, 231; **Supp. 9**, 738–39

Publishing: **Vol. 1, Part 1**, 131, 360, 509, 570, 600; **Vol. 1, Part 2**, 162, 249; **Vol. 2, Part 1**, 29, 367, 487; **Vol. 2, Part 2**, 70, 304, 554; **Vol. 4, Part 1**, 72, 398, 460; **Vol. 4, Part 2**, 54, 355; **Vol. 5, Part 1**, 255 f., 384; **Vol. 5, Part 2**, 444, 447, 458, 591; **Vol. 6, Part 1**, 69, 70, 285, 423 f.; **Vol. 6, Part 2**, 444; **Vol. 7, Part 1**, 278, 331, 334, 352; **Vol. 7, Part 2**, 143; **Vol. 8, Part 1**, 440 f.; **Vol. 8, Part 2**, 371, 541; **Vol. 9, Part 2**, 21, 62, 435 f.; **Vol. 10, Part 2**, 294, 348, 471; agriculture, **Vol. 5, Part 2**, 231; Annenberg interests, **Supp. 3**, 19–21; Bibles and prayer books, **Vol. 6, Part 1**, 287; Block group, **Supp. 3**, 80–81; book, **Supp. 5**, 85, 272, 614; book clubs, **Supp. 8**, 577–78;

book editing, **Supp. 3**, 686; Borzoi imprint, **Supp. 8**, 341–43; children's books, **Vol. 9, Part 2**, 436, **Vol. 10, Part 2**, 603; **Supp. 2**, 59; **Supp. 9**, 166; **Supp. 10**, 820, 821; *Christian News,* **Vol. 10, Part 1**, 113; Covici-Friede, **Supp. 7**, 148–49; Cowles interests, **Supp. 4**, 189; Doubleday, Doran, **Supp. 4**, 239–40; **Supp. 6**, 171–72; editing, **Supp. 10**, 349, 831; E. P. Dutton & Co., **Supp. 3**, 498–99; farm-oriented, **Supp. 4**, 132; Gannett chain development, **Supp. 6**, 226–27; *Godey's Lady's Book,* **Vol. 4, Part 1**, 344; Grosset & Dunlap, **Supp. 1**, 362; Huebsch-Ving, **Supp. 7**, 374; industry publications, **Supp. 9**, 738, 739; Joyce's works, **Supp. 7**, 40; Kipling, first, **Vol. 1, Part 1**, 550; Knoxville *Sentinel,* **Vol. 10, Part 1**, 104; litigation, **Supp. 8**, 224; Little Blue Books, **Supp. 5**, 264–65; Little, Brown and Co, growth, **Supp. 4**, 526–27; Little Masterpieces series, **Supp. 5**, 541–42; *Los Angeles Times* growth, **Supp. 3**, 155–56; McClure syndicate, **Supp. 4**, 662; McGraw-Hill company founding, **Supp. 4**, 523–24; magazines, **Vol. 1, Part 1**, 573; **Vol. 3, Part 2**, 47, 54, 477; **Vol. 6, Part 1**, 110; **Vol. 7, Part 1**, 353; **Vol. 10, Part 2**, 80; **Supp. 1**, 212–13; **Supp. 3**, 547; **Supp. 5**, 394, 637–38, 760–61; **Supp. 7**, 527–28; **Supp. 9**, 222–23; mass-market books, **Supp. 4**, 239–40; music, *see also subhead:* sheet music, **Vol. 1, Part 1**, 202; **Vol. 2, Part 2**, 146; **Vol. 3, Part 1**, 321 f.; **Vol. 4, Part 1**, 363; **Vol. 6, Part 1**, 38; **Vol. 7, Part 1**, 133; **Vol. 7, Part 2**, 512; **Vol. 8, Part 2**, 434 f., 440; **Vol. 9, Part 1**, 589; **Supp. 4**, 486; **Supp. 5**, 218; **Supp. 6**, 275; **Supp. 7**, 198–99; in music editing, **Supp. 4**, 276–77; newspaper, **Vol. 1, Part 2**, 171, 437, 565; **Vol. 5, Part 1**, 535; **Vol. 5, Part 2**, 458; **Vol. 6, Part 2**, 36, 38, 130; **Vol. 7, Part 1**, 271; **Vol. 7, Part 2**, 18, 250, 376, 643; **Vol. 8, Part 2**, 517, 519 f.; **Vol. 10, Part 2**, 500, 576; **Supp. 1**, 212–13; **Supp. 4**, 644, 645–46, 686–87; **Supp. 5**, 283–84, 615; **Supp. 7**, 199–200, 243–44, 295–96, 299, 603–4; **Supp. 8**, 636–37; **Supp. 9**, 202–3; W. W. Norton founding, **Supp. 3**, 563–64; organizations, **Supp. 2**, 59, 72; "painted books" introduced, **Supp. 9**, 605; Pantheon Books, **Supp. 7**, 799; printing processes, **Supp. 2**, 733; promotion and distribution, **Supp. 6**, 583; Random House, **Supp. 7**, 3; reference works, **Supp. 5**, 752–53; religious, **Vol. 8, Part 1**, 512 f.; **Supp. 6**, 171; Rinehart and Co., **Supp. 8**, 536; scholarly presses, **Supp. 6**, 154–55; school books, **Vol. 4, Part 2**, 43; **Vol. 6, Part 1**, 230; second-run editions, **Supp. 1**, 362; sheet music, **Supp. 3**, 833–34; **Supp. 4**, 88; Simon and Schuster, **Supp. 8**, 579; song, **Supp. 4**, 836; Stratemeyer Syndicate, **Supp. 9**, 787–88; syndicates, **Supp. 3**, 427–28; teaching materials, **Supp. 2**, 419; technical books and magazines, **Supp. 4**, 523–24; **Supp. 9**, 523; textbooks, **Supp. 10**, 46–47; Time Inc., **Supp. 8**, 393–96; trade paperbacks, **Supp. 10**, 46; *Uncle Tom's Cabin,* **Vol. 5, Part 2**, 69; Viking Press, **Supp. 7**, 306–7; women in, **Supp. 9**, 738–39; **Supp. 10**, 418. *See also* Books; Censorship; Copyright; Magazines; Newspapers; Typographical design

Publishing houses: Boni and Liveright, **Supp. 9**, 164; Catholic, **Vol. 5, Part 2**, 329 f.; Clarke Co., Robert, **Vol. 2, Part 2**, 162; Crowell-Collier, **Supp. 9**, 264–65; D. Appleton & Co., **Vol. 1, Part 1**, 326, 334 f.; **Vol. 2, Part 1**, 262; Dodd Mead & Co., **Vol. 3, Part 1**, 340 f.; Farrar, Straus, and Co., **Supp. 9**, 276; Ginn and Co., **Vol. 4, Part 1**, 317; Holt & Co., Henry, **Vol. 5, Part 1**, 180; Lippincott, J. B., **Vol. 6, Part 1**, 287; Little, Brown and Co., **Vol. 2, Part 1**, 127; **Vol. 6, Part 1**, 297; McClurg, A. C., **Vol. 6, Part 1**, 595 f.; Macmillan, **Supp. 9**, 264; Merriam & Co., **Vol. 6, Part 2**, 552; New Directions, **Supp. 9**, 605; Putnam and Sons, G. P., **Vol. 8, Part 1**, 279, 285; Random House, **Supp. 9**, 165–67, 707; Schocken Books, **Supp. 9**, 707–8; Scribner's Sons, Charles, **Vol. 2, Part 1**, 291; **Vol. 8, Part 2**, 515 f.

Pucinski, Roman, reference to, **Supp. 8**, 366

Puck: cartoons, **Supp. 2**, 504; founding of, **Vol. 5, Part 2**, 264, 352–53

Puebla, siege of, **Vol. 8, Part 2**, 509

Pueblo, houses, **Vol. 7, Part 1**, 185

Pueblo incident, **Supp. 10**, 72

Pueblo Indians: **Vol. 6, Part 1**, 501; **Supp. 3**, 582; **Supp. 7**, 486–87, 570; first reports of, **Vol. 7, Part 1**, 594; researches among, **Vol. 3, Part 2**, 353; uprisings of, **Vol. 3, Part 1**, 260

Puerperal fever, **Supp. 3**, 223

Puerto Rican Telephone Co., **Supp. 6**, 43

Puerto Rico: botany of, **Supp. 2**, 113; commonwealth status, **Supp. 10**, 566; conquest of, by Ponce de León, Juan, **Vol. 8, Part 1**, 56 f.; first native-born governor, **Supp. 5**, 545; governors, **Vol. 2, Part 2**, 322; **Supp. 3**, 669; **Supp. 4**, 903; **Supp. 5**, 545; **Supp. 9**, 279, 327; **Supp. 10**, 565, 566, 795–96; independence movement, **Supp. 10**, 565; labor movement in, **Supp. 2**, 331; leadership in, **Vol. 7, Part 1**, 329; military governor of portion of, **Vol. 10, Part 1**, 104; political career of Commissioner Larrinaga, **Vol. 6, Part 1**, 8; politics, **Vol. 7, Part 1**, 329–30; **Supp. 9**, 279–80, 327; **Supp. 10**, 565, 566; public finances, **Supp. 2**, 311; public school system, **Vol. 3, Part 1**, 608 f.; terrorist attempts, **Supp. 8**, 300; U.S. administration of, **Supp. 2**, 332, 579; **Supp. 9**, 278–80; **Supp. 10**, 565, 566

Puget Sound controversy, **Vol. 4, Part 2**, 280; **Vol. 8, Part 2**, 510; **Vol. 7, Part 2**, 570. *See* Yakima Indian War

Pugilism, **Vol. 3, Part 2**, 443; **Vol. 4, Part 2**, 500; **Vol. 7, Part 1**, 233; **Vol. 8, Part 1**, 585

Pugwash Conference, founding of, **Supp. 10**, 204

Pujo Committee, **Vol. 7, Part 1**, 177, 178

Pulaski, Casimir, reference to, **Vol. 1, Part 1**, 270

Pulitzer, Herbert, reference to, **Supp. 6**, 616

Pulitzer, Joseph, references to, **Supp. 3**, 91, 144; **Supp. 5**, 284, 551; **Supp. 6**, 686

Pulitzer, Margaret Leech, reference to, **Supp. 10**, 400

Pulitzer, Ralph, reference to, **Supp. 6**, 616; **Supp. 9**, 629

Pulitzer Prizes: biography or autobiography, **Supp. 10**, 554, 844, 846; drama, **Supp. 9**, 870; editorial cartooning, **Supp. 10**, 245; establishment of, **Vol. 8, Part 1**, 260 f.; fiction, **Supp. 9**, 870; **Supp. 10**, 400, 642, 755; general correspondence, **Supp. 10**, 562; general nonfiction, **Supp. 10**, 389; general reporting, **Supp. 10**, 435; history, **Supp. 9**, 629; **Supp. 10**, 108; journalism, **Supp. 9**, 505; journalism, most awarded, **Supp. 9**, 472; local reporting, **Supp. 10**, 49, 50, 384; music, **Supp. 10**, 639; only father and son to win, **Supp. 10**, 384; poetry, **Supp. 10**, 468, 469, 854

Pulitzer Publishing Co., **Supp. 5**, 551–52

Puller, Lewis B. ("Chesty"), reference to, **Supp. 9**, 286–87

Puller, Lewis B., Jr., reference to, **Supp. 9**, 630–31

Pulley, iron, **Vol. 10, Part 1**, 503 f.

Pullman Co.: **Vol. 6, Part 1**, 267; **Vol. 8, Part 1**, 263 f.; **Vol. 8, Part 2**, 594; boycott of cars of, **Vol. 3, Part 1**, 183; first car, **Vol. 8, Part 1**, 263 f.; union relations, **Supp. 10**, 659

Pullman strike (1894), **Vol. 1, Part 1**, 231; **Vol. 2, Part 2**, 211; **Vol. 3, Part 1**, 183; **Vol. 4, Part 2**, 21; **Vol. 6, Part 2**, 615; **Vol. 8, Part 1**, 263; **Vol. 9, Part 2**, 267; **Vol. 10, Part 2**, 505

Pulp fiction, **Supp. 3**, 264; Westerns, **Supp. 9**, 722

Pulp manufacturing, **Vol. 3, Part 2**, 250

Pulte Medical College, founded, **Vol. 8, Part 1,** 264
Pulteney Purchase, **Vol. 3, Part 2,** 601; **Vol. 9, Part 2,** 651; **Vol. 10, Part 2,** 297
Pumping engines for waterworks and sewers, **Vol. 6, Part 1,** 81
Pumping machinery, **Vol. 7, Part 1,** 450
Pumps, revolving cistern stand, invention of, **Vol. 3, Part 1,** 395
Pumps, water, manufacturing of, **Vol. 4, Part 1,** 178; **Vol. 7, Part 2,** 472; **Vol. 10, Part 2,** 539
Pupin, Michael I., references to, **Supp. 3,** 299; **Supp. 5,** 494
Puppetry: **Supp. 3,** 684–85; **Supp. 6,** 186; motion pictures, **Supp. 10,** 614–15
Purcell, William Gray, reference to, **Supp. 5,** 208
Purdue University: botany studies, **Supp. 3,** 23; founded, **Vol. 8, Part 1,** 268
Pure Food and Drug Act (1906), preservatives and additives, **Supp. 3,** 164
Pure food movement, **Vol. 1, Part 2,** 116; **Vol. 4, Part 2,** 506, 568; **Vol. 5, Part 2,** 524; **Vol. 6, Part 1,** 567; **Vol. 9, Part 1,** 74; **Vol. 10, Part 1,** 582 f.; **Vol. 10, Part 2,** 215
Purex Corporation, Ltd., **Supp. 9,** 511
Puritan in Babylon, A, **Supp. 3,** 817
Puritans: **Vol. 3, Part 2,** 155; **Vol. 5, Part 1,** 88; clergy, **Vol. 2, Part 2,** 460 f.; **Vol. 7, Part 1,** 572–73; **Vol. 9, Part 1,** 83; example of, **Vol. 9, Part 1,** 90; first to be converted to Catholicism, **Vol. 10, Part 1,** 98; historical research on, **Supp. 7,** 538; Maryland, controversies, battle of the Severn, **Vol. 9, Part 2,** 88; Massachusetts, **Vol. 10, Part 2,** 194; Papists and, **Vol. 4, Part 1,** 135; religious outlook, **Vol. 8, Part 2,** 202; social freedom under, **Vol. 10, Part 1,** 104. *See also* Pilgrims
Purity Clubs, **Supp. 8,** 434
"Purkey, Private Oscar" (fictional character), **Supp. 7,** 618
"Purple Cow" poem, **Supp. 5,** 94
Purrysburg, S.C., settlement of, **Vol. 5, Part 2,** 117; **Vol. 8, Part 1,** 270 f.
Pusey, Nathan M., reference to, **Supp. 9,** 14
Putnam, Frederick W., references to, **Supp. 3,** 83, 372; **Supp. 5,** 533
Putnam, Herbert, reference to, **Supp. 3,** 285, 326–27; **Supp. 9,** 73
Putnam, Israel, **Vol. 6, Part 1,** 333
Putnam, James J., references to, **Supp. 3,** 191; **Supp. 6,** 98
Putnam, Wallace Bradstreet, **Supp. 9, Supp. 10,** 398
Putnam & Sons, G. P., **Supp. 3,** 285; founding of, **Vol. 8, Part 1,** 279 f., 285
Putnam's Monthly Magazine, pioneer use of American material rather than foreign reprints, **Vol. 2, Part 1,** 41; **Vol. 8, Part 1,** 279 f.
Putney community, **Vol. 7, Part 1,** 590
"Puts and calls," stock market about 1872, **Vol. 8, Part 2,** 292
Putt, Donald L., reference to, **Supp. 9,** 255
Puzzles: crossword, **Supp. 6,** 583; double-crostic, **Supp. 6,** 341–42
Pyle, Howard, reference to, **Supp. 3,** 847; **Supp. 6,** 94; **Supp. 8,** 493
Pyloroplasty, **Supp. 3,** 271
Pynson Printers, founding of, **Supp. 7,** 2–3
Pyrex ovenware, **Supp. 3,** 365; **Supp. 6,** 624
Pyrography, **Vol. 5, Part 2,** 413
Pyrometallurgy, **Vol. 1, Part 1,** 343
Pyrometer, **Vol. 1, Part 2,** 407; invention of, **Supp. 1,** 120

Q

Qavam, Ahmad, reference to, **Supp. 8,** 6
Quackery, opposition to, **Vol. 4, Part 2,** 554
Quacks, medical, **Supp. 3,** 103–4
Quadrant, inventions concerning, **Vol. 4, Part 1,** 345
Quakers (Society of Friends): **Vol. 1, Part 2,** 523; **Vol. 2, Part 2,** 266, 331 f.; **Vol. 3, Part 2,** 186, 210 f., 352; **Vol. 4, Part 1,** 237 f., 244, 605, 634; **Vol. 4, Part 2,** 159; **Vol. 5, Part 1,** 6, 86, 141, 334, 389, 610 f.; **Vol. 5, Part 2,** 4, 13, 46, 199, 463, 519; **Vol. 6, Part 1,** 136, 330, 334 f., 431; **Vol. 7, Part 1,** 200 f., 289, 508, 554; **Vol. 7, Part 2,** 413 f.; **Vol. 8, Part 2,** 342, 393, 410 f., 493; **Vol. 9, Part 1,** 28, 115 f.; **Vol. 9, Part 2,** 336, 441 f., 444; **Vol. 10, Part 1,** 386; American Friends' Peace Association, **Vol. 5, Part 2,** 4; Baltimore Association, **Vol. 5, Part 2,** 4; Baptist radicals and, **Vol. 8, Part 2,** 101; "Birthright," **Vol. 8, Part 2,** 50; "Christian Quakers," **Vol. 5, Part 2,** 289 f.; conscientious objectors, **Supp. 6,** 217; doctrines, interpretation of, **Vol. 8, Part 2,** 246; **Vol. 10, Part 2,** 461; education, **Vol. 1, Part 2,** 178; "fighting," **Vol. 10, Part 2,** 23; Five Years' Meeting, **Vol. 5, Part 2,** 4; Friends' Boarding Home, **Vol. 5, Part 2,** 13; *Friends' Journal* and *Friends' Intelligencer,* merger of, **Vol. 5, Part 2,** 46; Gwynedd meeting, **Vol. 8, Part 2,** 9; Haverford Collection of Quakeriana, **Supp. 1,** 463; historical writings on, **Supp. 4,** 441–42; history of, **Vol. 4, Part 2,** 160; **Vol. 5, Part 1,** 140; **Vol. 7, Part 1,** 280 f.; **Vol. 9, Part 1,** 28; itinerant preaching, **Vol. 8, Part 2,** 342; Kansas and Missouri politics, effect on, **Vol. 6, Part 1,** 204; marriage with Indians, **Vol. 8, Part 2,** 179; "marrying out of meeting," **Vol. 8, Part 2,** 174; missionary preaching to Indians, **Vol. 2, Part 1,** 592; opposition to, **Vol. 3, Part 2,** 204; persecution, **Vol. 3, Part 1,** 584; **Vol. 3, Part 2,** 156; **Vol. 7, Part 1,** 573; **Vol. 8, Part 1,** 399; press, first in America, **Vol. 5, Part 1,** 611; promotion of, **Vol. 4, Part 2,** 473; public relations, **Supp. 5,** 303; Quietism, **Vol. 8, Part 2,** 343; radical group, in, **Vol. 6, Part 1,** 63; Schism of 1827 (Orthodox v. Hicksite), **Vol. 3, Part 2,** 232 f.; **Vol. 5, Part 1,** 86, 224; settlements, **Vol. 3, Part 2,** 330; "Shakers," first colony of, **Vol. 6, Part 1,** 95; slavery, attitude toward, **Vol. 4, Part 1,** 606; **Vol. 6, Part 1,** 63; **Vol. 10, Part 2,** 517; societies, **Vol. 4, Part 2,** 369; theology of, **Supp. 4,** 442–43; "transformed," **Vol. 10, Part 1,** 120; "War Hawks," **Vol. 8, Part 2,** 9; writings, **Vol. 3, Part 2,** 211; **Vol. 4, Part 1,** 244; **Vol. 5, Part 1,** 86; **Vol. 6, Part 1,** 63, 212, 287; **Vol. 7, Part 2,** 429; **Vol. 8, Part 1,** 273 f., 399; **Vol. 10, Part 1,** 387
Quantum mechanics, **Supp. 9,** 541, 542; **Supp. 10,** 741, 742
Quantum theory: **Supp. 4,** 488, 818, 838–39; **Supp. 5,** 203–4, 219–21, 495–96, 529, 563; **Supp. 6,** 655; **Supp. 7,** 133, 517; **Supp. 8,** 628; causality studies, **Supp. 8,** 190; decisive proof of, **Supp. 7,** 258–59; molecular, **Supp. 8,** 122, 482; **Supp. 10,** 741; nuclear physics application, **Supp. 8,** 199, 628
Quarantine Service, establishment of, **Vol. 2, Part 1,** 536
Quarrie Publications, **Supp. 7,** 243
Quarries, **Vol. 6, Part 1,** 154; **Vol. 8, Part 1,** 245 f.; **Vol. 8, Part 2,** 98; **Supp. 10,** 413
Quarry Men (music group), **Supp. 10,** 448
Quarterly Journal of Economics, first periodical of its kind, **Vol. 3, Part 1,** 503 f.
Quarterly Review of Biology, founding of, **Supp. 2,** 522
Quay, Matthew S., references to, **Vol. 2, Part 1,** 436; **Vol. 6, Part 1,** 590
Quebec: founding of, **Vol. 2, Part 1,** 606; siege of

(1756), **Vol. 6, Part 2**, 84; siege of (1775), *see* Canada, invasion of, 1775
Quebec Conference (1944), **Supp. 5**, 334
Quedagh Merchant (ship), **Vol. 5, Part 2**, 369
Queed, **Vol. 4, Part 2**, 342
"Queen, Ellery" (fictional character), **Supp. 9**, 487–88
Queen Elizabeth (film), **Supp. 10**, 871
Queen's College (N.J.). *See* Rutgers University
Queens College (N.Y.), sociology and anthropology studies, **Supp. 8**, 509
"Queen's Head," R.I., tavern, **Vol. 1, Part 2**, 512
Queenston Heights, Canada, battle of, **Vol. 3, Part 1**, 175; **Vol. 10, Part 1**, 210
Quemoy and Matsu islands, **Supp. 8**, 158, 223
Quezon, Manuel, references to, **Supp. 4**, 612; **Supp. 6**, 211, 280–81; **Supp. 7**, 488
Quids, N.Y., political party, **Vol. 6, Part 1**, 222
Quigley, Martin, reference to, **Supp. 7**, 71
Quincy, Josiah, references to, **Vol. 6, Part 1**, 533; **Vol. 8, Part 1**, 29 f.
Quincy, Mass.: education, **Vol. 7, Part 2**, 221; origin of the name, **Vol. 8, Part 1**, 308 f.
Quincy Journal, **Vol. 10, Part 1**, 111
Quinine: use of, **Vol. 8, Part 2**, 353; synthesis of, **Supp. 10**, 853
Quinine sulphate, manufacture of, **Vol. 10, Part 1**, 607 f.
Quinn, John, reference to, **Supp. 9**, 33
Quitman, John A., reference to, **Vol. 9, Part 2**, 510
"Quit-rent" controversy, **Vol. 5, Part 2**, 140
Quiz shows: radio, **Supp. 6**, 5; **Supp. 9**, 492; **Supp. 10**, 515, 789, 790; television, **Supp. 9**, 719, 829; **Supp. 10**, 121, 224, 790; television scandals, **Supp. 10**, 415

R

Rabbi, first to be ordained in U.S., **Vol. 1, Part 2**, 219
Rabi, Isidor I., reference to, **Supp. 8**, 628
Race relations: Boys Town opposition to racism, **Supp. 4**, 283; civil disturbances, **Supp. 10**, 109, 169; study of, **Supp. 3**, 577–79; traditional southern view of, **Supp. 3**, 598; writings on, **Supp. 4**, 251. *See also* Blacks; Civil rights movement; Racism; Segregation
Race Traits and Tendencies of the American Negro, **Supp. 4**, 384, 385
Rachmaninoff, Sergei, reference to, **Supp. 3**, 707
Racial segregation. *See* Segregation
Racine College, **Vol. 5, Part 2**, 322; **Vol. 7, Part 2**, 207
Racism: American Nazi party activities, **Supp. 8**, 541; in baseball, **Supp. 9**, 668–69; in basketball, **Supp. 10**, 711; *Birth of a Nation*, charges against, **Supp. 4**, 350; *Black Like Me*, personal account of, **Supp. 10**, 292; in Congress, **Supp. 9**, 233, in education, **Supp. 10**, 385, 386; in education theory, **Supp. 3**, 206; eugenic basis, **Supp. 3**, 84, 177, 215–16, 445–46; **Supp. 6**, 354; in ficton, **Supp. 6**, 354; immigration restrictions, **Supp. 5**, 561; in Louisiana, **Supp. 6**, 391; "100 percent Americanism" advocacy, **Supp. 3**, 709; in motion-picture industry, **Supp. 10**, 677–78; political, **Supp. 3**, 78; **Supp. 6**, 525–26; in professional football, **Supp. 9**, 817, 840–841; in sociological thought, **Supp. 5**, 592; southern political, **Supp. 4**, 78; **Supp. 8**, 499–500; in sports, **Supp. 9**, 668–69, 817, 840–41; **Supp. 10**, 347; in Texas politics, **Supp. 3**, 267; in U.S. military, **Supp. 10**, 378; "white supremacy" advocacy, **Supp. 5**, 177, 290; writings on, **Supp. 8**, 605–6; writings promoting, **Supp. 4**, 235, 384–85, 792. *See also* Eugenics, Holocaust; Ku Klux Klan; Segregation
Racketeering. *See* Organized crime
Rackham, Horace H., reference to, **Supp. 4**, 294
Radar: development and application, **Supp. 4**, 358; **Supp. 8**, 686; pulse-echo, **Supp. 7**, 58
Radcliffe-Brown, Alfred, references to, **Supp. 8**, 683, 684
Radcliffe College: **Vol. 3, Part 2**, 73; **Vol. 4, Part 1**, 297; **Vol. 5, Part 1**, 13; **Vol. 6, Part 1**, 72; **Vol. 7, Part 2**, 174; development of, **Supp. 1**, 146; history studies, **Supp. 8**, 169–70
Radial velocities, **Supp. 6**, 8
Radiation: cancer therapy, **Supp. 3**, 258; effects on plants, **Supp. 6**, 176; fallout research, **Supp. 7**, 344; **Supp. 10**, 816; food, **Supp. 1**, 398; health hazards, **Supp. 4**, 112; **Supp. 8**, 449, 450; infrared, **Supp. 4**, 658; photon theory of, **Supp. 7**, 10; quantum theory of, **Supp. 5**, 495; secondary X radiation, **Supp. 1**, 614; studies in, **Vol. 7, Part 1**, 491–92;
Vol. 9, Part 2, 653. *See also* X rays
Radiation Control for Health and Safety Act (1968), **Supp. 8**, 26
Radicalism. *See* Anarchist movement; Freethinkers; Progressive movement; *specific doctrines or political parties*
Radical Review, founding of, **Supp. 2**, 670
Radio: **Vol. 6, Part 1**, 400; **Vol. 9, Part 1**, 489 f.; **Vol. 10, Part 1**, 370; acting, **Supp. 8**, 31; "Adventures in Science" program, **Supp. 8**, 119; advertising on, **Supp. 3**, 103–4; **Supp. 7**, 211–12; **Supp. 8**, 52; **Supp. 10**, 555, 708; amateur home wireless sets, **Supp. 8**, 209; announcing, **Supp. 3**, 494; **Supp. 7**, 77–78, 378; **Supp. 10**, 155, 290–91, 487–88; audience surveys, **Supp. 5**, 310–11; aviation, **Supp. 10**, 442; baseball coverage, **Supp. 3**, 438; **Supp. 9**, 224, 295, 533; "Big Show," **Supp. 8**, 22; blacklisting, **Supp. 6**, 350; book-review programs, **Supp. 5**, 356; "Breakfast with Dorothy and Dick," **Supp. 7**, 433; broadcast frequency, **Supp. 2**, 98; car, **Supp. 10**, 442; censorship, **Supp. 6**, 631; **Supp. 10**, 463; children's music appreciation series, **Supp. 4**, 212; church-owned stations, **Supp. 2**, 584; Colpitts oscillator, **Supp. 4**, 173; comedy programs, **Supp. 6**, 12–13, 89, 128; **Supp. 8**, 710–11; **Supp. 9**, 1, 5–6, 48, 76–77; 196, 578, 580, 802, 880; **Supp. 10**, 7, 32, 178, 196; commercials, *see subhead:* advertising; content regulation, **Supp. 3**, 104; country programs, **Supp. 9**, 374; daytime serials, **Supp. 6**, 104; **Supp. 8**, 32–33; detective programs, **Supp. 9**, 488; disc jockeys, **Supp. 7**, 267, 378; dramatic programs, **Supp. 10**, 789; Edison effect, **Supp. 1**, 279; educational programs, **Supp. 8**, 488; emissions from space discovery, **Supp. 4**, 422–23; engineering, **Supp. 6**, 32; farm programs, **Supp. 4**, 132; federal regulation, **Supp. 8**, 179; "fireside chats," **Supp. 3**, 649–50; first broadcast of live dance music, **Supp. 9**, 513; first commercially sponsored broadcast transmission, **Supp. 3**, 184–85; first orchestral concert broadcast, **Supp. 4**, 212; FM development, **Supp. 5**, 22; Free Company of Players series, **Supp. 3**, 93; Golden Age of, **Supp. 9**, 382; Hauptmann execution broadcast, **Supp. 9**, 379; high-fidelity frequency modulation, **Supp. 6**, 299; high-frequency wire transmission, **Supp. 3**, 748; high-vacuum tubes, **Supp. 6**, 365; Hollywood gossip program, **Supp. 8**, 282; human interest programs, **Supp. 8**, 11; international zones, **Supp. 7**, 809; interview programs, **Supp. 6**, 536; **Supp. 10**, 487–88; "Kraft Music Hall," **Supp. 5**, 400; "Major Bowes' Amateur Hour," **Supp. 4**, 97; "March of Time," **Supp. 8**, 393–94; Mercury Theater, **Supp. 5**, 464; microphone, invention of, **Vol. 5, Part 1**, 347; microwave relay, **Supp. 6**, 85; musical variety programs, **Supp. 9**, 540; music appreciation program, **Supp. 7**, 707; music programs, **Supp. 3**, 359; **Supp. 4**, 452; **Supp. 5**, 183; **Supp. 6**,

242, 630–31, 633, 643, 644, 670; **Supp. 7**, 124; **Supp. 8**, 151, 645, 697–98; **Supp. 9**, 207, 382, 662, 802, 804; **Supp. 10**, 43–44, 59, 105, 160, 223, 230, 239, 251, 421, 463, 593, 648, 789, 806; mystery programs, **Supp. 10**, 103; news commentary, **Supp. 3**, 143; **Supp. 6**, 148, 291; **Supp. 7**, 321, 409–10, 498, 566; **Supp. 8**, 373–74, 640; **Supp. 9**, 379–80; 415; **Supp. 10**, 290–91; newspaper advertising v., **Supp. 9**, 90; newspaper ownership of stations, **Supp. 5**, 551; **Supp. 9**, 202, 203; opera on, **Supp. 6**, 69, 324; **Supp. 9**, 207, 804; pioneering vision of, **Supp. 9**, 700; police communications, **Supp. 9**, 728; political use of, **Supp. 8**, 478; political programs, **Supp. 10**, 151; popular music on, **Supp. 5**, 187–88; public affairs programs, **Supp. 6**, 83, 160–61; public opinion, early use of, for arousing, **Vol. 9, Part 2**, 126; quiz shows, **Supp. 6**, 5; **Supp. 9**, 492; **Supp. 10**, 515, 789, 790; ratings survey, **Supp. 10**, 587–88; receiver in manufacturing, **Supp. 7**, 154; receivers' single-dial tuning, **Supp. 6**, 298; regulatory legislation, **Supp. 10**, 179; religious programs, **Supp. 2**, 86; **Supp. 4**, 541; **Supp. 6**, 238; **Supp. 8**, 184, 434; **Supp. 10**, 151, 405, 729; remote-control, **Supp. 3**, 769; Rockefeller Center, **Supp. 6**, 549; screenplay broadcasts, **Supp. 6**, 159–60; scriptwriting, **Supp. 9**, 710; serials, **Supp. 10**, 343, 739; set manufacturing, **Supp. 4**, 452; "Sherlock Holmes" series, **Supp. 8**, 519; shortwave, **Supp. 3**, 184–85; singing and singing groups on, **Supp. 7**, 525; situation comedies, **Supp. 6**, 288; soap operas, **Supp. 9**, 802, *see also subhead:* daytime serials; sportscasting, **Supp. 7**, 378, 494–95, 707; **Supp. 9**, 765; sports coverage, **Supp. 9**, 224, 295, 533, 765–66; **Supp. 10**, 256; sports talk shows, **Supp. 9**, 765–66; stations, **Supp. 1**, 184; **Supp. 3**, 30, 103, 157; **Supp. 5**, 615; **Supp. 8**, 636; stations, first FM, **Supp. 5**, 22; stations' channel allocation, **Supp. 6**, 299; talk shows, **Supp. 9**, 886; **Supp. 10**, 120, 156, 255, 333, 479, 835–36; "Theatre Guild on the Air," **Supp. 7**, 458; tobacco advertising ban, **Supp. 9**, 139; transmission, **Supp. 5**, 21–22; vacuum tubes, **Supp. 6**, 365, 624; variety shows, **Supp. 7**, 106; **Supp. 10**, 598; Voice of America, **Supp. 8**, 640; *War of the Worlds* broadcast, **Supp. 9**, 382; wireless, **Supp. 9**, 699–700, 727–28; wireless transmission research, **Supp. 1**, 297; **Supp. 5**, 21–22; World War II, **Supp. 6**, 32; **Supp. 9**, 379; **Supp. 10**, 349. *See also* Televison

Radio Act (1927), **Supp. 10**, 179

Radioactive tracers, **Supp. 3**, 805

Radioactivity, **Vol. 1, Part 2**, 425; **Vol. 3, Part 1**, f. *See also* Radiation; X rays

Radio City Music Hall (New York City): Glee Club, **Supp. 6**, 669; opening, **Supp. 2**, 585; stage designs, **Supp. 5**, 375

Radio Corporation of America (RCA): **Supp. 3**, 392; **Supp. 4**, 360; **Supp. 6**, 32; **Supp. 9**, 801; boxing-match broadcast, **Supp. 9**, 700; early development of television, **Supp. 9**, 275–76, 701–2; founding of, **Supp. 7**, 808–9; management and growth, **Supp. 9**, 700–702; patents, **Supp. 4**, 452; **Supp. 5**, 22; **Supp. 9**, 700

Radio Correspondents' Association, founding of, **Supp. 8**, 373

Radiography, **Vol. 5, Part 2**, 492–93

Radio-Keith-Orpheum Pictures. *See* RKO pictures

Radiology: fractionation method, **Supp. 4**, 186; hospital departments, **Supp. 3**, 360; standards, **Supp. 2**, 512; teaching and training in, **Supp. 2**, 512; **Supp. 4**, 111–12, 186; therapeutic use, **Supp. 2**, 718; writings on, **Supp. 6**, 506. *See also* X rays

Radiometer, invention of, **Vol. 7, Part 1**, 491–92

Radio News, founding of, **Supp. 8**, 209

Radio Shack, **Supp. 10**, 773–74

Radium: cancer causing, **Supp. 6**, 70; cancer treatment, **Supp. 3**, 412; **Supp. 6**, 69; production of, **Vol. 1, Part 2**, 422; **Vol. 7, Part 1**, 136

Ragtime music, **Supp. 2**, 286, 336; **Supp. 3**, 187, 834; **Supp. 10**, 195

Raids: cavalry, during Civil War, **Vol. 1, Part 2**, 586; **Vol. 3, Part 2**, 532; **Vol. 4, Part 1**, 160, 495, 614; **Vol. 4, Part 2**, 214; **Vol. 5, Part 1**, 194, 197; **Vol. 5, Part 2**, 145, 263, 375; **Vol. 6, Part 1**, 125–27, 575; **Vol. 6, Part 2**, 573; **Vol. 7, Part 1**, 272; **Vol. 7, Part 2**, 415; **Vol. 8, Part 1**, 8; **Vol. 9, Part 1**, 80, 94–96, 237; **Vol. 9, Part 2**, 92, 170–72, 183; **Vol. 10, Part 1**, 185; **Vol. 10, Part 2**, 234–35

Railroad Labor Act (1932), **Supp. 6**, 132

Railroads (general): **Vol. 1, Part 1**, 49 f., 409; **Vol. 1, Part 2**, 459, 594; **Vol. 2, Part 1**, 198, 324; **Vol. 2, Part 2**, 456; **Vol. 3, Part 1**, 387, 399; **Vol. 3, Part 2**, 28, 84, 115, 118, 299, 507 f., 527; **Vol. 4, Part 1**, 83 f., 273, 311, 345, 450 f., 454, 489, 551; **Vol. 4, Part 2**, 83; **Vol. 5, Part 1**, 380, 408 f., 484, 561; **Vol. 5, Part 2**, 292; **Vol. 6, Part 1**, 6; **Vol. 7, Part 1**, 594, 645; **Vol. 8, Part 2**, 19, 48, 96; **Vol. 9, Part 1**, 331, 615; **Vol. 9, Part 2**, 92, 442, 486; accounting, **Vol. 6, Part 2**, 579; air brakes, **Vol. 10, Part 1**, 72; appraisal of, **Supp. 3**, 188; "Big Four," first unit of, **Vol. 9, Part 2**, 70; block signaling system, **Vol. 8, Part 2**, 56; **Vol. 10, Part 1**, 618 f.; bridges, **Vol. 3, Part 2**, 569; **Vol. 6, Part 1**, 26; **Vol. 8, Part 2**, 52; **Supp. 2**, 638; Brotherhood of Locomotive Firemen, **Vol. 3, Part 1**, 183; Brotherhood of Railroad Engineers, **Vol. 9, Part 2**, 86; Brotherhood of Railroad Trainmen, **Vol. 6, Part 1**, 133; building, **Vol. 1, Part 2**, 298; **Vol. 2, Part 1**, 28, 31, 34, 562; **Vol. 2, Part 2**, 103, 187 f., 275 f., 551 f.; **Vol. 3, Part 1**, 206 f., 258, 262, 312, 334, 348, 429 f.; **Vol. 3, Part 2**, 87, 195, 205, 281, 387, 402, 445, 452; **Vol. 4, Part 1**, 427, 541; **Vol. 4, Part 2**, 247, 307, 377; **Vol. 5, Part 1**, 151; 561; **Vol. 5, Part 2**, 59, 96, 224 f., 229, 291 f., 296 f., 353 f., 601; **Vol. 6, Part 1**, 26, 36, 294, 380, 437 f., 490; **Vol. 6, Part 2**, 17, 89, 153, 211, 358, 501; **Vol. 7, Part 1**, 19, 40, 75, 197, 227 f., 319, 560; **Vol. 7, Part 2**, 357, 465 f., 510, 647; **Vol. 8, Part 1**, 71 f., 184, 204 f., 357 f., 359 f., 392, 405, 417 f.; **Vol. 8, Part 2**, 2, 16, 18 f., 33, 181, 303, 473, 527; **Vol. 9, Part 1**, 24, 59, 150 f., 191, 302, 501; **Vol. 9, Part 2**, 13, 16, 70, 247, 442, 486, 642; **Vol. 10, Part 1**, 364, 372 f.; **Vol. 10, Part 2**, 63, 72, 268, 372, 395, 526, 547, 612, 657; Bureau of Railway Economics, **Vol. 6, Part 2**, 161; car construction, **Vol. 3, Part 2**, 202; **Vol. 7, Part 1**, 445; **Vol. 7, Part 2**, 20; **Vol. 8, Part 1**, 263 f.; **Vol. 8, Part 2**, 593; Civil War, management during, **Vol. 6, Part 1**, 565; **Vol. 8, Part 2**, 500 f.; consolidation, **Vol. 2, Part 1**, 281, 324; **Vol. 3, Part 1**, 262; **Vol. 10, Part 1**, 400 f., 618 f.; **Supp. 1**, 406, 692; **Supp. 2**, 392; **Supp. 10**, 772; construction of, **Supp. 1**, 381, 413; **Supp. 3**, 735–37; development, **Vol. 1, Part 2**, 2, 410, 532, 594; **Vol. 2, Part 2**, 446 f.; **Vol. 3, Part 1**, 480 f., 542 f.; **Vol. 3, Part 2**, 25, 106; **Vol. 4, Part 2**, 419; **Vol. 5, Part 2**, 334, 464; **Vol. 6, Part 1**, 6, 478; **Vol. 7, Part 1**, 295, 498, 556; **Vol. 8, Part 1**, 70 f., 184 f., 212 f., 218 f., 342 f., 357, 359 f., 392, 433 f.; **Vol. 8, Part 2**, 431, **Vol. 9, Part 2**, 628 f.; diesel locomotives, **Supp. 6**, 333; electrification of, **Vol. 3, Part 1**, 25; **Vol. 6, Part 1**, 176, 505; **Vol. 7, Part 2**, 358; **Vol. 8, Part 1**, 221 f.; **Supp. 1**, 34, 351; **Supp. 2**, 199, 232; **Supp. 4**, 370; **Supp. 8**, 93; engineering, **Supp. 1**, 676; **Supp. 2**, 77; **Supp. 3**, 759; **Supp. 4**, 756–57; entrepreneurs, **Supp. 3**, 125–26; equipment, **Supp. 1**, 131, 397, 604, 670; equipment, manufacture of, **Vol. 1, Part 2**, 352, 412; **Vol. 3, Part 1**, 458; **Vol. 4, Part 1**, 23 f.; **Vol. 8, Part 2**, 112; **Vol. 10, Part 2**, 16, 156, 371; excursion trips, early, **Vol. 7**,

Part 2, 463; executives, **Supp. 7**, 89–90; federal ownership issue, **Supp. 2**, 351; financing of, **Vol. 1, Part 1**, 206; **Vol. 3, Part 1**, 312, 542 f.; **Vol. 3, Part 2**, 107, 387; **Vol. 4, Part 2**, 78, 393; **Vol. 5, Part 2**, 434; **Vol. 6, Part 1**, 294; **Vol. 8, Part 2**, 584; **Vol. 9, Part 2**, 16; **Vol. 10, Part 2**, 332; **Supp. 3**, 381, 728–29; **Supp. 5**, 550; first air-conditioned passenger equipment, **Supp. 3**, 824; freight distribution terminals, **Supp. 1**, 122; gauges, disagreement over, **Vol. 8, Part 2**, 19, 112; "Gould system," **Vol. 4, Part 1**, 450; **Vol. 5, Part 2**, 36; government supervision, **Vol. 8, Part 1**, 9 f., 357 f.; guidebooks, early, **Vol. 3, Part 1**, 319; "Hatch's Circulars," **Vol. 4, Part 2**, 393; holding companies, **Supp. 5**, 34–35; horses early use of, as motive power, **Vol. 3, Part 1**, 258; industrial research, **Supp. 2**, 282; inventions, various, **Vol. 1, Part 1**, 59; **Vol. 2, Part 1**, 198; **Vol. 4, Part 1**, 23 f.; **Vol. 6, Part 2**, 624; **Vol. 7, Part 1**, 274; **Vol. 8, Part 1**, 210 f., 221 f., 263 f.; **Vol. 8, Part 2**, 575; "Jay system," **Vol. 5, Part 2**, 225; labor discrimination ban, **Supp. 4**, 397; labor mediation, **Supp. 5**, 651–52; labor movement, **Supp. 4**, 889–90; **Supp. 6**, 132, 379, 542, 647–48; **Supp. 8**, 513; Latin American, **Supp. 5**, 215; legal counsel, **Supp. 3**, 167–68, 839; legislation and litigation, **Vol. 1, Part 1**, 221; **Vol. 3, Part 1**, 245 f., 251, 298, 330, 360, f.; **Vol. 3, Part 2**, 248; **Vol. 4, Part 1**, 451, 609; **Vol. 4, Part 2**, 566; **Vol. 5, Part 2**, 46, 451, 520; **Vol. 6, Part 1**, 27, 52; **Vol. 6, Part 2**, 293; **Vol. 7, Part 2**, 576; **Vol. 8, Part 1**, 114 f., 440, 541; **Vol. 8, Part 2**, 154; locomotive design, **Supp. 2**, 680; mail service, **Vol. 1, Part 1**, 352; **Vol. 3, Part 1**, 147; management, **Vol. 1, Part 1**, 549, 592; **Vol. 2, Part 1**, 158; **Vol. 3, Part 2**, 318, 402; **Vol. 4, Part 2**, 109, 190, 235, 296 f., 400 f.; **Vol. 5, Part 1**, 36 f., 64, 332, 408 f., 414 f., 464; **Vol. 5, Part 2**, 35 f., 68, 143, 168 f., 286, 395; **Vol. 6, Part 2**, 285, 516; **Vol. 7, Part 1**, 33, 176, 197, 236, 264, 405, 602, 644 f.; **Vol. 8, Part 1**, 435, 620 f.; **Vol. 8, Part 2**, 7, 33, 405, 505, 514; **Vol. 9, Part 1**, 1 f., 123 f., 213 f., 219, 235, 302 f., 322 f., 453, 494, 608, 620; **Vol. 9, Part 2**, 396, 440, 501; **Vol. 10, Part 1**, 86; **Supp. 1**, 33–34, 76–77, 513, 573–74, 671–72; **Supp. 3**, 783–84, 823–24; **Supp. 5**, 565–66; **Supp. 8**, 92–94; manuals, **Vol. 8, Part 1**, 70 f.; merger action, **Supp. 3**, 95; "monopoly tax," **Vol. 8, Part 1**, 369; Morgan monopoly broken, **Supp. 10**, 203; New York Central takeover, **Supp. 6**, 540, 721–22; **Supp. 9**, 423, 462; oil revenues, **Supp. 2**, 569–71; panic of 1873, **Vol. 5, Part 2**, 68; passenger innovations, **Supp. 7**, 90; photography for, **Supp. 3**, 380; plant system, **Vol. 7, Part 2**, 646 f.; Prince plan to consolidate, **Supp. 5**, 550; promotion, **Vol. 1, Part 1**, 282, 284; **Vol. 1, Part 2**, 264 f., 333, 338, 382, 443, 471; **Vol. 2, Part 2**, 14, 446 f.; **Vol. 3, Part 1**, 117 f., 242, 322, 387, 480 f., 597 f.; **Vol. 3, Part 2**, 452; **Vol. 4, Part 2**, 5, 60 f., 261, 294, 403, 458; **Vol. 6, Part 1**, 39, 367, 485; **Vol. 7, Part 1**, 159, 165; **Vol. 8, Part 1**, 11 f., 71 f., 184 f., 212 f., 405, 433, 442, 538, 546 f., 582, 644; **Vol. 8, Part 2**, 26, 157, 292; **Vol. 10, Part 1**, 172 f., 175; f., 619 f.; **Vol. 10, Part 2**, 157, 638; publicity, **Vol. 6, Part 2**, 161; public ownership moves, **Supp. 3**, 241; Pullman cars, **Vol. 3, Part 1**, 189; **Vol. 6, Part 1**, 267; **Vol. 8, Part 1**, 210 f., 263 f.; **Vol. 8, Part 2**, 594; rails for steel, **Vol. 3, Part 1**, 547 f.; rate setting, **Supp. 1**, 42; **Supp. 2**, 309; **Supp. 3**, 212, 256–57; rebates, question of, **Vol. 2, Part 1**, 565 f.; **Vol. 3, Part 1**, 262, 341; **Vol. 9, Part 2**, 70; receiverships (1893–1919), **Vol. 8, Part 2**, 328; refrigerator cars, **Vol. 9, Part 2**, 245; regulation of, **Supp. 3**, 395; **Supp. 6**, 571; reorganization, **Supp. 2**, 635; riots, **Vol. 3, Part 2**, 414; safety, **Supp. 2**, 231; **Supp. 6**, 624; signal glass, **Supp. 3**, 365; signals, invention of, **Vol. 4, Part 2**, 145; **Vol. 5, Part 2**, 498; **Vol. 8, Part 1**, 75 f.; **Vol. 8, Part 2**, 56; sleeping cars, invention of, **Vol. 5, Part 2**, 464; **Vol. 10, Part 2**, 497; speculation, **Vol. 3, Part 2**, 415; **Vol. 4, Part 2**, 393; stainless-steel streamliner, **Supp. 4**, 121; standard time, adoption of, **Vol. 1, Part 1**, 211; strike injunction (1922), **Supp. 3**, 214; strikes, **Vol. 2, Part 2**, 211; **Vol. 5, Part 2**, 68; **Vol. 6, Part 1**, 133 f.; studies of, **Supp. 1**, 689; surveying, **Vol. 3, Part 1**, 207, 258, 348, 604; **Vol. 5, Part 2**, 455, 569; **Vol. 8, Part 1**, 11 f., 76 f., 179 f., 264 f.; "switch back," engineering feat, **Vol. 8, Part 2**, 33; "ton mile" as unit of work, **Vol. 6, Part 1**, 26; toy trains, **Supp. 7**, 150; traffic control, **Supp. 1**, 574; Trunk Line Association, **Vol. 8, Part 2**, 7; tunnels, construction of, **Vol. 8, Part 2**, 48; Turkey, **Supp. 1**, 171; unionization, *see subhead:* labor movement; United Mine Workers, **Vol. 1, Part 1**, 490; valuation, federal, **Vol. 8, Part 1**, 418; World War I, government administration during, **Vol. 8, Part 1**, 248 f.; writings on, **Vol. 3, Part 1**, 597; **Vol. 4, Part 2**, 78; **Vol. 5, Part 2**, 96; **Vol. 6, Part 2**, 161; **Vol. 8, Part 1**, 92 f., 440; **Vol. 9, Part 2**, 16; **Supp. 3**, 632–33

Railroads (specific): Atchison, Topeka and Santa Fe, **Vol. 5, Part 1**, 151; **Vol. 7, Part 2**, 375; Atlantic Coast Line, **Vol. 10, Part 1**, 399 f.; Baltimore & Ohio, **Vol. 2, Part 1**, 117; **Vol. 2, Part 2**, 471 f.; **Vol. 3, Part 2**, 319; **Vol. 4, Part 1**, 163; **Vol. 5, Part 1**, 214, 275; **Vol. 5, Part 2**, 348, 467; **Vol. 6, Part 1**, 27, 380; **Vol. 9, Part 1**, 453; **Vol. 9, Part 2**, 237, 442, 449; Baltimore and Potomac, **Vol. 1, Part 2**, 510; Baltimore Central, **Vol. 1, Part 1**, 639; Boston & Lowell, **Vol. 6, Part 1**, 552; **Vol. 9, Part 2**, 98; Boston & Maine, **Vol. 5, Part 2**, 169; Boston and Worcester, **Vol. 8, Part 1**, 71 f.; Burlington, **Vol. 5, Part 1**, 38 f.; Camden and Amboy Railroad, **Vol. 8, Part 1**, 369; Canadian National, **Vol. 9, Part 2**, 501; Central Pacific, **Vol. 2, Part 2**, 552; **Vol. 5, Part 1**, 409 f.; **Vol. 5, Part 2**, 229; **Vol. 9, Part 1**, 502 f.; Central Railroad of Georgia, **Vol. 4, Part 1**, 427 f.; Central Railroad of New Jersey, **Vol. 5, Part 2**, 143; Chesapeake & Ohio, **Vol. 3, Part 2**, 1; **Vol. 5, Part 1**, 411, 464; **Vol. 6, Part 1**, 445; **Supp. 10**, 203; Chicago & Alton, **Vol. 7, Part 1**, 144 f.; Chicago, Burlington & Quincy, **Vol. 7, Part 2**, 466; Chicago & Calumet, **Vol. 9, Part 2**, 594; Chicago, Great Western, **Vol. 9, Part 2**, 16; Chicago, Milwaukee & St. Paul, **Vol. 5, Part 2**, 498; **Vol. 8, Part 2**, 263; **Vol. 9, Part 2**, 70; Chicago & North Western, **Vol. 1, Part 2**, 382; **Vol. 7, Part 1**, 645; Chicago & Rock Island, **Vol. 3, Part 2**, 281; **Vol. 5, Part 2**, 60; Chicago, St. Louis & New Orleans, **Vol. 7, Part 2**, 72; Cincinnati, Indianapolis, St. Louis and Chicago, **Vol. 5, Part 1**, 464; Delaware, Lackawana & Western, **Vol. 1, Part 2**, 338; **Vol. 9, Part 1**, 213; **Vol. 9, Part 2**, 338; Delaware, Lehigh, Schuylkill & Susquehanna, **Vol. 8, Part 1**, 94 f.; Denver & Rio Grande, **Vol. 5, Part 2**, 36; **Vol. 7, Part 2**, 195; **Vol. 8, Part 2**, 33; Erie, **Vol. 1, Part 1**, 614; **Vol. 3, Part 1**, 322; **Vol. 3, Part 2**, 415; **Vol. 4, Part 1**, 454; **Vol. 5, Part 2**, 68, 229; **Vol. 6, Part 2**, 11; **Vol. 7, Part 1**, 191; **Vol. 9, Part 1**, 262; Eureka Springs, **Vol. 2, Part 2**, 187; European & North American Railway Co., **Vol. 8, Part 1**, 71 f.; Fitchburg, **Vol. 2, Part 2**, 551; Great Northern, **Vol. 3, Part 1**, 183; **Vol. 5, Part 1**, 37 f.; Hannibal & St. Joseph, **Vol. 9, Part 2**, 13; Illinois Central, **Vol. 1, Part 2**, 182; **Vol. 3, Part 2**, 402; **Vol. 4, Part 2**, 297; **Vol. 5, Part 2**, 35; **Vol. 6, Part 1**, 495; **Vol. 7, Part 2**, 72; Illinois & Rock River, **Vol. 8, Part 1**, 9 f.; La Crosse & Milwaukee, **Vol. 1, Part 2**, 33; Lehigh Valley, **Vol. 7, Part 1**, 355; **Vol. 7, Part 2**, 131; **Vol. 8, Part 1**, 94 f.; **Vol. 8, Part 2**, 405; Long Island, **Vol. 2, Part 2**, 436; Louisville & Nashville, **Vol. 3, Part 2**, 387; **Vol. 4, Part 2**, 61; **Vol. 9, Part 1**, 251, 322 f.;

Maine Central Railroad, **Vol. 8, Part 1**, 71 f.; Manhattan Beach, **Vol. 2, Part 2**, 437; Mexican National, **Vol. 7, Part 2**, 195; Michigan Central, **Vol. 5, Part 2**, 224; Michigan Southern & Northern Indiana, **Vol. 5, Part 2**, 60; Milwaukee & St. Paul, **Vol. 7, Part 1**, 40; Missisquoi, **Vol. 1, Part 2**, 594; Mohawk & Hudson, **Vol. 5, Part 2**, 59; National Railway Co., **Vol. 7, Part 2**, 62; New York Central Railroad, **Vol. 2, Part 1**, 158; **Vol. 2, Part 2**, 446; **Vol. 8, Part 1**, 253 f., 582; **Vol. 8, Part 2**, 424; **Vol. 9, Part 1**, 236; **Vol. 10, Part 1**, 172 f.; **Supp. 9**, 423, 462; **Supp. 10**, 772; New York and Erie Railroad, **Vol. 6, Part 1**, 405 f.; New York, New Haven and Hartford Railroad, **Vol. 7, Part 1**, 179; **Vol. 7, Part 2**, 357; **Vol. 8, Part 2**, 200; Northern Pacific Railroad, **Vol. 1, Part 2**, 265; **Vol. 3, Part 1**, 207; **Vol. 3, Part 2**, 246; **Vol. 5, Part 1**, 38; **Vol. 7, Part 1**, 602; **Vol. 7, Part 2**, 463; **Vol. 10, 2**, 547; Pacific Electric Railway, **Vol. 8, Part 1**, 357 f.; Panama, **Vol. 1, Part 1**, 194, 396; **Vol. 5, Part 1**, 349; **Vol. 6, Part 1**, 495; **Vol. 7, Part 2**, 209; **Vol. 9, Part 2**, 598, 629; Penn Central bankruptcy, **Supp. 10**, 772; Pennsylvania, **Vol. 2, Part 1**, 160, 565; **Vol. 3, Part 1**, 18; **Vol. 4, Part 1**, 450; **Vol. 5, Part 1**, 262, 392; **Vol. 6, Part 1**, 227; **Vol. 7, Part 1**, 176; **Vol. 7, Part 2**, 305; **Vol. 8, Part 1**, 417 f.; **Vol. 8, Part 2**, 7, 500 f.; **Vol. 9, Part 1**, 616; **Vol. 9, Part 2**, 396, 484, 486; **Vol. 10, Part 2**, 350; **Supp. 10**, 771–72; Philadelphia & Reading, **Vol. 4, Part 1**, 461; **Vol. 5, Part 2**, 277; Richmond and Danville, **Vol. 1, Part 1**, 282; Rock Island, **Vol. 5, Part 2**, 231; **Vol. 7, Part 1**, 144; **Vol. 9, Part 1**, 59; St. Paul, Minneapolis and Manitoba, **Vol. 5, Part 2**, 441; St. Paul and Pacific, **Vol. 6, Part 1**, 294; San Antonio & Mexican Gulf Railroad of Texas, **Vol. 7, Part 2**, 169; Santa Fe, **Vol. 8, Part 1**, 620 f.; **Vol. 8, Part 2**, 33; Seaboard Air Line, **Vol. 10, Part 1**, 455 f.; South Carolina, **Vol. 4, Part 1**, 83; **Vol. 4, Part 2**, 458; Southern Electric, **Vol. 7, Part 2**, 62; Southern Pacific, **Vol. 5, Part 1**, 409, 415; **Vol. 9, Part 1**, 503; Southern Railway, **Vol. 1, Part 1**, 549; **Vol. 5, Part 1**, 484 f.; **Vol. 6, Part 1**, 368; Union Pacific Railroad, **Vol. 1, Part 1**, 251, 254 f.; **Vol. 1, Part 2**, 339; **Vol. 3, Part 1**, 312, 348, 542 f.; **Vol. 4, Part 1**, 9, 154, 454; **Vol. 5, Part 2**, 182; **Vol. 7, Part 1**, 560; **Vol. 8, Part 1**, 70 f.; **Vol. 8, Part 2**, 120; **Vol. 9, Part 1**, 24; Vermont and Canada, **Vol. 1, Part 2**, 594; Vermont Central, **Vol. 7, Part 2**, 147; Western Pacific, **Vol. 1, Part 2**, 410; **Vol. 5, Part 2**, 36; Wilmington and Northern, **Vol. 3, Part 1**, 528 f.; Wilmington & Weldon, **Vol. 1, Part 1**, 388
Railroads, elevated, **Vol. 4, Part 1**, 172, 272; **Vol. 8, Part 1**, 221 f.
Railroads, street. *See* Street railways
Railway Business Association, **Vol. 8, Part 1**, 114 f.
Railway Economics, Bureau of, **Vol. 6, Part 2**, 16
Railway Labor Act (1926), **Supp. 6**, 542
Railway Mail Service, Bureau of, **Vol. 1, Part 1**, 352
Railway Steel Spring Co., **Vol. 4, Part 1**, 24
Railway Supply Manufacturers' Association, **Vol. 8, Part 1**, 114 f.
Rain, artificial, **Supp. 6**, 364, 365
Rainbow (clipper ship), **Vol. 4, Part 1**, 626
"Raines Law," liquor traffic, **Vol. 8, Part 1**, 326 f.
Rain making, experiments in, **Vol. 8, Part 1**, 112 f.
Raisin in the Sun, A, **Supp. 7**, 319; **Supp. 8**, 287; **Supp. 9**, 698
Raisin River, Mich., battle at, **Vol. 4, Part 2**, 350; **Vol. 6, Part 1**, 542; **Vol. 10, Part 2**, 378
Rake, invention concerning, **Vol. 5, Part 2**, 151
Raleigh News and Observer, **Supp. 4**, 216, 217
Raleigh *Sentinel*, political influence of, **Vol. 10, Part 1**, 69
Raleigh State Chronicle, **Supp. 4**, 215–16
Ralston, Samuel M., reference to, **Vol. 9, Part 2**, 272
Ralston, Vera Hruba, reference to, **Supp. 8**, 712
Ramona, **Vol. 5, Part 1**, 555
Ramsay, Robert, reference to, **Supp. 5**, 555
Ranches, **Vol. 4, Part 1**, 394; **Vol. 5, Part 2**, 397 f.; **Vol. 9, Part 2**, 395; **Supp. 9**, 459, 460, 463–64; **Supp. 10**, 782, 783
Rand, Benjamin Long, reference to, **Supp. 3**, 618
Rand, Edward Kennard, reference to, **Supp. 3**, 197
Rand, Gertrude, reference to, **Supp. 3**, 269–70
Rand, James Henry, Jr., reference to, **Supp. 3**, 618–19
"Randall, Josh" (fictional character), **Supp. 10**, 500
Randall, Ruth Painter, reference to, **Supp. 9**, 37
RAND Corporation, **Supp. 7**, 276; founding of, **Supp. 7**, 411
Rand-Kardex Co., founding of, **Supp. 3**, 619
Randolph, A. Philip, references to, **Supp. 6**, 285, 648; **Supp. 7**, 155, 156; **Supp. 9**, 251
Randolph, John, references to, **Vol. 1, Part 1**, 87; **Vol. 7, Part 1**, 505; **Vol. 7, Part 2**, 259; **Vol. 8, Part 2**, 239; **Vol. 9, Part 2**, 356
Randolph and *True Briton*, naval exploits of, **Vol. 1, Part 2**, 242
Randolph and *Yarmouth*, naval exploits of, **Vol. 1, Part 2**, 242
Randolph-Macon College, **Vol. 3, Part 1**, 597 f.; **Vol. 7, Part 2**, 13, 257; **Vol. 9, Part 1**, 362, 369
Random House: **Supp. 7**, 233, 234; **Supp. 10**, 400; Beginner books launched, **Supp. 9**, 166; founding of, **Supp. 7**, 3; **Supp. 9**, 164–65; Knopf merger, **Supp. 8**, 342; **Supp. 9**, 166; Landmark books, **Supp. 10**, 400; Modern Library purchased, **Supp. 9**, 164; Schocken Books acquired, **Supp. 9**, 707; sold to RCA, **Supp. 9**, 167; *Ulysses* published, **Supp. 9**, 165; **Supp. 10**, 221
Rand School of Social Science, founding of, **Supp. 3**, 298
Ranger (lunar probe), **Supp. 9**, 476
Rangers, colonial, **Vol. 8, Part 2**, 108; **Vol. 9, Part 2**, 489.
Ranging, Civil War, **Vol. 7, Part 1**, 272
Rank, Otto, reference to, **Supp. 4**, 716
Rankin, John, reference to, **Supp. 10**, 183
Rankin, John E., reference to, **Supp. 8**, 703
Ransom, John Crowe, reference to, **Supp. 10**, 854
Rapf, Harry, reference to, **Supp. 10**, 157
Rapid transit. *See* Transit systems
Rapollo, Leon, reference to, **Supp. 8**, 561
"Rappists" (New Harmony, Ind.), **Vol. 8, Part 2**, 224
Rare books and manuscripts: collections, **Supp. 3**, 836; **Supp. 4**, 345; **Supp. 5**, 9–10, 586–87; **Supp. 7**, 295, 387, 547; preservation of, **Supp. 2**, 40
Rariden, Bill, reference to, **Supp. 8**, 713
Raskob, John J., references to, **Supp. 3**, 720; **Supp. 4**, 244, 575; **Supp. 5**, 192–94; **Supp. 6**, 721
Rasmussen, Andrew, reference to, **Supp. 4**, 420
Rationalist journal, first in U.S., **Vol. 5, Part 2**, 457
Rational Psychology, **Vol. 5, Part 1**, 5
Rationing, **Supp. 3**, 660
Rattan machinery, **Vol. 8, Part 2**, 397
Rattlesnake root, therapeutic use of, **Vol. 7, Part 1**, 61; **Vol. 9, Part 2**, 369
Raulston, John T.: reference to, **Supp. 8**, 583; Scopes trial, **Supp. 9**, 769
"Raven, The," authorship, dispute as to, **Vol. 5, Part 1**, 68
Ray, James Earl, reference to, **Supp. 8**, 335
Ray, Man, reference to, **Supp. 5**, 184
Rayburn, Sam, reference to, **Supp. 8**, 630; **Supp. 9**, 104, 431, 553; **Supp. 10**, 125, 484, 485, 486
Raymond, Gene, reference to, **Supp. 7**, 499
Rayon, manufacture of, **Supp. 5**, 366

Raytheon Manufacturing Co., **Supp. 9**, 144
Razors: disposable blades, **Supp. 1**, 345; single-edge blades, **Supp. 9**, 297–98
RCA. *See* Radio Corporation of America
RDX (cyclonite), **Supp. 5**, 28
REA. *See* Rural Electrification Administration
Reader's Digest, **Supp. 5**, 528; **Supp. 7**, 321, 346, 643; **Supp. 8**, 150
Reader's Guide to Periodical Literature, **Supp. 5**, 753–54
Reading: braille, **Supp. 3**, 365; "Dick and Jane" textbooks, **Supp. 6**, 248; frequently used words, **Supp. 4**, 833; tachistoscope, **Supp. 3**, 229–30; teaching methods, **Supp. 4**, 89–90; **Supp. 6**, 248. *See also* Books; Learning
Readinger Adler, publication of, **Vol. 6, Part 1**, 292
Readjuster movement in Virginia (1872–76), **Vol. 1, Part 1**, 592; **Vol. 4, Part 1**, 422; **Vol. 5, Part 1**, 358; **Vol. 5, Part 2**, 322; **Vol. 6, Part 2**, 212
Reagan, Ronald, references to, **Supp. 8**, 220, 649; **Supp. 10**, 184
Real estate: **Vol. 1, Part 1**, 397 f.; **Vol. 8, Part 2**, 386; bonds, first issue of, for building projects, **Vol. 9, Part 2**, 132; Boston, **Vol. 2, Part 2**, 136; Cincinnati, **Vol. 6, Part 1**, 394; Florida, **Supp. 10**, 478; Houston, **Supp. 6**, 135, 136; Lake Havasu City, Ariz., **Supp. 10**, 492; New York City, **Supp. 6**, 23, 24; **Supp. 10**, 478, 785–86, 866–67; Oregon land law, **Supp. 6**, 682; restrictive covenants, **Supp. 6**, 502; Southern California development, **Supp. 3**, 154–56; **Supp. 5**, 309–10; tax assessment, **Supp. 1**, 385; **Supp. 6**, 522. *See also* Land and land use; Zoning
Reality: A Journal of Artists' Opinion, **Supp. 8**, 280
Reams Station, Va., battle of. *See* Richmond campaign
Reaping machine, **Vol. 3, Part 2**, 132; **Vol. 6, Part 1**, 610 f.; invention of, **Vol. 5, Part 1**, 431; **Vol. 6, Part 1**, 607
Rebates, railroad, **Vol. 9, Part 2**, 70
Rebecca, **Supp. 10**, 339–40
Rebel Without a Cause, **Supp. 5**, 162, 163
Rebozo, Charles G. ("Bebe"), reference to, **Supp. 10**, 357
Recent Social Trends in the United States, **Supp. 5**, 485
Reciprocal Trade Program, **Supp. 6**, 126
Reclamation Act (1902), **Vol. 4, Part 2**, 483; **Supp. 4**, 563
Reclamation projects, **Vol. 3, Part 2**, 403; **Vol. 7, Part 1**, 457
Reclamation Service, United States, **Supp. 3**, 814, 845–46; dam building, **Supp. 1**, 225; **Supp. 8**, 572–73
Recollect Friars, **Vol. 4, Part 2**, 540; **Vol. 6, Part 1**, 231
Recollections. *See* Memoirs
Reconstruction: **Vol. 1, Part 1**, 24, 138; **Vol. 1, Part 2**, 334; **Vol. 2, Part 1**, 512; **Vol. 2, Part 2**, 28; **Vol. 3, Part 1**, 120; **Vol. 3, Part 2**, 25, 439, 564; **Vol. 4, Part 1**, 233, 391, 532, 539, 541; **Vol. 4, Part 2**, 83, 261, 449, 462; **Vol. 5, Part 1**, 357, 373, 423; **Vol. 5, Part 2**, 103; **Vol. 6, Part 2**, 159; **Vol. 7, Part 1**, 263, 352, 487; **Vol. 8, Part 1**, 33 f., 410; **Vol. 8, Part 2**, 195; **Vol. 9, Part 1**, 21, 81, 624; **Vol. 9, Part 2**, 604; **Vol. 10, Part 1**, 6, 19; Act of Congress, **Vol. 7, Part 2**, 447; Alabama, **Vol. 2, Part 1**, 33; Arkansas, **Vol. 1, Part 2**, 61; **Vol. 2, Part 1**, 408; **Vol. 2, Part 2**, 187; **Vol. 4, Part 1**, 150; **Vol. 8, Part 1**, 33, 436; "Central Directory," **Vol. 5, Part 2**, 85; Committee of Fifteen, **Vol. 5, Part 2**, 115; Georgia, **Vol. 1, Part 1**, 133, 430; **Vol. 2, Part 1**, 143, 258; **Vol. 4, Part 1**, 424; **Vol. 5, Part 2**, 44; **Vol. 6, Part 2**, 13; **Vol. 10, Part 2**, 411, 441; historical writings on, **Supp. 1**, 303; **Supp. 5**, 498; investigation of, first scholarly, **Vol. 3, Part 1**, 523 f.; Kentucky, **Vol. 2, Part 1**, 55; **Vol. 3, Part 1**, 114; Louisiana, **Vol. 1, Part 1**, 192 f.; **Vol. 2, Part 1**, 218, 402, 459; **Vol. 3, Part 1**, 545; **Vol. 6, Part 2**, 555; Mississippl, **Vol. 2, Part 1**, 593; **Vol. 4, Part 1**, 233; **Vol. 4, Part 2**, 327; **Vol. 5, Part 2**, 352; **Vol. 9, Part 2**, 78; **Vol. 10, Part 2**, 609; North Carolina, **Vol. 2, Part 1**, 77; **Vol. 3, Part 1**, 287; **Vol. 6, Part 2**, 570; **Vol. 7, Part 1**, 115; **Vol. 8, Part 1**, 64; **Vol. 10, Part 1**, 69; **Vol. 10, Part 2**, 536; novels based on, **Vol. 9, Part 2**, 604; policy of the North, **Vol. 2, Part 1**, 512; South Carolina, **Vol. 2, Part 1**, 364, 404, 595; **Vol. 2, Part 2**, 58; **Vol. 6, Part 2**, 1 f.; **Vol. 7, Part 2**, 59, 483; **Vol. 8, Part 1**, 118 f.; **Vol. 8, Part 2**, 332; **Vol. 10, Part 2**, 558; Tennessee, **Vol. 2, Part 1**, 136; **Vol. 3, Part 2**, 311; **Vol. 5, Part 2**, 83; Texas, **Vol. 2, Part 1**, 443; **Vol. 3, Part 1**, 112; **Vol. 7, Part 2**, 369; **Vol. 8, Part 1**, 433 f.; Union offices in South, **Vol. 4, Part 2**, 594; Virginia, **Vol. 2, Part 1**, 439; **Vol. 6, Part 2**, 382; **Vol. 10, Part 2**, 429; Wade-Davis Manifesto, **Vol. 3, Part 1**, 120, West Virginia, **Vol. 6, Part 2**, 404
Reconstruction Finance Corporation (RFC): **Supp. 5**, 160; **Supp. 6**, 33, 325, 453; **Supp. 8**, 89, 308, 309; founding of, **Supp. 7**, 362; **Supp. 8**, 207; scandal, **Supp. 7**, 562
Recordings: binaural sound research, **Supp. 6**, 365; bird songs, **Supp. 7**, 8; classical instrumental, **Supp. 10**, 44, 373; comedy, **Supp. 9**, 720; **Supp. 10**, 95; Country and Western, **Supp. 5**, 749; **Supp. 9**, 662; **Supp. 10**, 105; dance bands, **Supp. 10**, 463; duplicating system, **Supp. 1**, 76; early black Jazz, **Supp. 2**, 502; "easy listening," **Supp. 10**, 230; first black to record country music, **Supp. 9**, 414; first commercial American symphony, **Supp. 10**, 312; first interracial session on national label, **Supp. 9**, 183; folk music, **Supp. 10**, 589, 590, 602, 603; harpsichord, **Supp. 6**, 358; high-fidelity sound equipment, **Supp. 5**, 324; Ives' compositions, **Supp. 5**, 353; jazz, **Supp. 6**, 299–300; **Supp. 7**, 131; **Supp. 10**, 225, 270, 299, 409, 410, 544, 791, 792; long-playing record, invention of, **Supp. 10**, 284; opera, **Supp. 9**, 545, 805, 851; **Supp. 10**, 94; popular instrumental, **Supp. 10**, 422; popularizing concert singers, **Supp. 3**, 484–85; popular vocal, **Supp. 9**, 887; **Supp. 10** 160; Presley, **Supp. 10**, 648–49; rock and roll, **Supp. 6**, 301; **Supp. 7**, 267; **Supp. 10**, 448–51; sound and action synchronization, **Supp. 1**, 121; symphonic, **Supp. 10**, 763; talking books for blind, **Supp. 5**, 347; tape recorder, **Supp. 9**, 274; Western music, **Supp. 10**, 592, 593. *See also* Audio systems; Phonograph
Record-keeping supplies, **Supp. 3**, 618–19
Records of the New York Stage, **Vol. 5, Part 1**, 498
Recreation, constructive aspects of, **Supp. 2**, 375
Rectograph Co., **Supp. 9**, 877
Red Badge of Courage, The, **Supp. 4**, 38
Red Caps. *See* International Brotherhood of Red Caps
Red Cross. *See* American Red Cross; International Red Cross
Redemptorist Order in U.S., **Vol. 4, Part 2**, 515; **Vol. 8, Part 2**, 286
Redfield, Robert, reference to, **Supp. 8**, 378
Red Hot Peppers (jazz group), **Supp. 3**, 542
Rediscount rates, **Supp. 3**, 730
Re-discovery of America, The, **Supp. 8**, 192
ReDman, Don, references to, **Supp. 5**, 292, 293
Redpath, James, reference to, **Vol. 8, Part 1**, 60 f.
Red River, **Supp. 10**, 822
Red River campaign (1864), **Vol. 1, Part 1**, 579; **Vol. 2, Part 1**, 469; **Vol. 2, Part 2**, 105; **Vol. 5, Part 2**, 425, 441
Red River Transportation Co., **Vol. 5, Part 2**, 441
Red Star Line, establishment of, **Vol. 9, Part 2**, 397
Red Star Over China, **Supp. 9**, 740, 741
Redstone Arsenal, **Supp. 10**, 66
Redwoods, conservation, **Supp. 3**, 520; **Supp. 4**, 429; **Supp. 6**, 486

Redwoods, Sequoyah, naming of, **Vol. 8, Part 2**, 586
Reece, Carroll, reference to, **Supp. 7**, 276
Reed, Clyde M., reference to, **Supp. 9**, 355
Reed, Daniel, reference to, **Supp. 8**, 422
Reed, David A., reference to, **Supp. 6**, 320
Reed, James, reference to, **Supp. 6**, 388
Reed, John, references to, **Supp. 5**, 580; **Supp. 7**, 486; **Supp. 10**, 849
Reed, Stanley, reference to, **Supp. 9**, 836
Reed, Thomas B., references to, **Vol. 5, Part 1**, 63; **Vol. 9, Part 1**, 526
Reed, Walter, references to, **Vol. 2, Part 1**, 525; **Vol. 4, Part 2**, 45; **Vol. 7, Part 1**, 582; **Vol. 9, Part 1**, 592
Reed College, first president, **Supp. 4**, 307; founding of, **Vol. 8, Part 1**, 456
Reed-Johnson Immigration Act (1924), **Supp. 5**, 56
Reed organ, invention of, **Vol. 4, Part 1**, 336
Reedy, William Marion, references to, **Supp. 3**, 851; **Supp. 6**, 10
Reedy's Mirror, importance of, **Vol. 8, Part 1**, 464
Reese, Eleanor, reference to, **Supp. 6**, 162
Reese Hospital. *See* Michael Reese Hospital
Reeves, Rosser, reference to, **Supp. 9**, 67
Referendum. *See* Initiative and referendum
Reflex actions, knee-jerk, **Supp. 2**, 390
Reform (for list of specific names, *see* Occupations Index): **Vol. 1, Part 1**, 535, 319; **Vol. 3, Part 2**, 477, 368, 334, 318, 199, 139; **Vol. 4, Part 1**, 542, 449, 450; **Vol. 4, Part 2**, 7, 161; **Vol. 5, Part 1**, 291, 386, 522, 610, 611; **Vol. 6, Part 1**, 467, 449, 271; **Vol. 7, Part 1**, 491, 13, 289; **Vol. 8, Part 2**, 382, 332, 45, 58, 3; **Vol. 9, Part 1**, 270; banking, **Vol. 5, Part 2**, 302; **Vol. 9, Part 2**, 30; civil service, **Vol. 3, Part 1**, 607 f.; economic, **Vol. 7, Part 1**, 345; labor, **Vol. 6, Part 1**, 511; movements, Massachusetts, **Vol. 3, Part 1**, 370; **Vol. 4, Part 2**, 473; **Vol. 7, Part 2**, 546 f.; **Vol. 8, Part 1**, 381 f.; **Vol. 8, Part 2**, 58; municipal, **Vol. 3, Part 1**, 607; **Vol. 5, Part 1**, 522; **Vol. 8, Part 1**, 308 f.; political, **Vol. 2, Part 2**, 305; **Vol. 5, Part 2**, 307; postal, **Vol. 1, Part 2**, 47, 340; **Vol. 5, Part 1**, 181, 589; **Vol. 5, Part 2**, 260; **Vol. 8, Part 1**, 341 f.; prison, **Vol. 1, Part 1**, 653; **Vol. 2, Part 1**, 50, 61, 614; **Vol. 3, Part 2**, 15, 23, 282, 326; **Vol. 4, Part 1**, 271, 625; **Vol. 4, Part 2**, 93, 524; **Vol. 5, Part 1**, 224, 297, 321; **Vol. 5, Part 2**, 98; **Vol. 6, Part 1**, 208, 223; **Vol. 7, Part 1**, 319, 508; **Vol. 7, Part 2**, 610; **Vol. 8, Part 2**, 116, 191, 238, 548; **Vol. 9, Part 1**, 439, 501; **Vol. 10, Part 1**, 78; **Vol. 10, Part 2**, 385, 386; pure food and drugs, **Vol. 1, Part 2**, 116; **Vol. 4, Part 2**, 506; **Vol. 5, Part 2**, 525; **Vol. 6, Part 1**, 567; **Vol. 9, Part 1**, 74; **Vol. 10, Part 1**, 582 f.; **Vol. 10, Part 2**, 215; single tax, **Vol. 6, Part 2**, 53; social, **Vol. 2, Part 1**, 52; **Vol. 2, Part 2**, 254, 330 f., 595; **Vol. 5, Part 2**, 287; **Vol. 6, Part 1**, 202, 271, 306, 389; **Vol. 6, Part 2**, 53; **Vol. 7, Part 1**, 345, 589; **Vol. 7, Part 2**, 608 f.; **Vol. 8, Part 1**, 623 f.; **Vol. 8, Part 2**, 228, 497, 531; **Vol. 9, Part 2**, 533 f.; **Vol. 10, Part 1**, 416 f.; **Vol. 10, Part 2**, 386, 504, 541, 550; tariff, **Vol. 2, Part 1**, 495; **Vol. 2, Part 2**, 210; **Vol. 5, Part 1**, 335; **Vol. 7, Part 1**, 15
Reformation: collections on, **Supp. 2**, 75; history of, **Supp. 3**, 726
Reformatories, juvenile, **Vol. 9, Part 2**, 15
Reform Club (N.Y.), founding of, **Vol. 9, Part 2**, 66
Reformed Medical Society of the United States, **Vol. 1, Part 2**, 86
Reform Judaism, **Supp. 4**, 603, 903–6; "Pittsburgh Platform," **Supp. 4**, 659
Refrigeration: air conditioning, **Supp. 4**, 148–49; early experiments in, **Vol. 3, Part 2**, 84; **Vol. 4, Part 1**, 436 f.; electric refrigerator manufacture, **Supp. 4**, 244; Freon, **Supp. 3**, 522
Refrigerator cars, first, **Vol. 4, Part 2**, 204; **Vol. 9, Part 2**, 245
Refrigerators, **Supp. 4**, 244; **Supp. 7**, 154
Refugee resettlement, Jewish in Palestine, **Supp. 3**, 757; **Supp. 8**, 501–2
Refugees: Austrian, **Supp. 8**, 456; Greco-Turkish War, **Supp. 4**, 604; Jewish, **Supp. 3**, 246, 280, 281, 661, 757; **Supp. 4**, 80, 262, 699, 906; **Supp. 6**, 386, 388, 556–76, 623, 649, 654, 662; political, from Nazi Germany, **Supp. 4**, 99–100; Russian, **Supp. 4**, 890; Vietnamese, **Supp. 7**, 190–91; World War II, **Supp. 7**, 498
Regeneration, studies in, **Vol. 6, Part 1**, 351 f.
Regicides (Mass.), **Vol. 8, Part 2**, 319
Regional Anatomy, **Vol. 6, Part 1**, 580
Regional Planning Association of America: **Supp. 9**, 526; founding of, **Supp. 2**, 739
Regis College, founding of, **Supp. 3**, 569
Regulator movement in North Carolina (1770–72), **Vol. 2, Part 1**, 571; **Vol. 3, Part 2**, 265, 352; **Vol. 4, Part 2**, 531; **Vol. 5, Part 1**, 427 f.; **Vol. 6, Part 2**, 334; **Vol. 7, Part 1**, 134, 383; **Vol. 9, Part 2**, 489; **Vol. 10, Part 1**, 26, 302
Regulatory agencies. *See* Government; *specific names*
Rehabilitation: **Supp. 9**, 310; brain-injured persons, **Supp. 1**, 316
Rehn, Frank, reference to, **Supp. 8**, 63
Reich, Lilly, reference to, **Supp. 8**, 436
Reich, Wilhelm, reference to, **Supp. 9**, 325
Reichstein, Tadeus, references to, **Supp. 7**, 341; **Supp. 9**, 454, 455
Reid, Col. H. T., reference to, **Vol. 1, Part 2**, 148
Reid, Daniel G, reference to, **Vol. 7, Part 1**, 143
Reid, Elisabeth Mills, references to, **Supp. 8**, 514, 420
Reid, Helen, references to, **Supp. 4**, 686; **Supp. 8**, 667
Reid, Ogden Mills, references to, **Supp. 8**, 520, 667
Reid's Holiday Togs, **Supp. 10**, 667–68
Reina, Gaetano, reference to, **Supp. 8**, 396
Reinsch, J. Leonard, reference to, **Supp. 9**, 202
Reindeer and *Wasp*, naval exploits of, **Vol. 1, Part 2**, 348
Reiner, Fritz, reference to, **Supp. 6**, 324
Reinhardt, Max, references to, **Supp. 3**, 297; **Supp. 6**, 351
Reisenberg, Nadia, reference to, **Supp. 6**, 297
Reisner, George Andrew, references to, **Supp. 3**, 272; **Supp. 4**, 902
"Relative deprivation" concept, **Supp. 6**, 605
Relativism: in anthropology, **Supp. 3**, 82–86; in history, **Supp. 3**, 49–50; in sociology, **Supp. 6**, 55
Relativity, theories of, **Supp. 3**, 71; **Supp. 4**, 880; **Supp. 6**, 653; **Supp. 7**, 216; Einstein's postulation, **Supp. 5**, 202–3; first American account, **Supp. 4**, 839; mathematical basis, **Supp. 5**, 738; "new," **Supp. 5**, 528–29; observational tests, **Supp. 1**, 647; philosophical writings on, **Supp. 5**, 562, 563; universe's expansion, **Supp. 5**, 326
Relief. *See* Welfare
Religion: American Indian, **Supp. 8**, 647; baptism ceremonies, **Supp. 8**, 434; book publishing, **Supp. 6**, 171; Chaplain Corps, **Supp. 8**, 505–6; charitable work, **Supp. 1**, 541; Christian-Jewish relations, **Supp. 2**, 87; Christian socialism, **Supp. 5**, 616–17; civil rights movement advocacy, **Supp. 8**, 332–33; cults, **Supp. 10**, 391–92; Eastern, **Supp. 8**, 431; economics and, **Supp. 3**, 249; ecumenical movements, **Supp. 2**, 86–87, 549; **Supp. 5**, 305; **Supp. 8**, 115, 537; **Supp. 10**, 110–11; ecumenism, theological, **Supp. 7**, 775–76; **Supp. 10**, 110–11; education in, **Supp. 3**, 110–11; **Supp. 5**, 115–16; empiricism, **Supp. 4**, 525–26; evangelism, **Supp. 1**, 679; **Supp. 3**, 497–98; faith and business success, **Supp. 8**, 27; faith healing, **Supp. 4**, 271–72; **Supp. 10**, 426; fundamentalism,

Supp. 5, 176, 345–46, 516–17; fundamentalist-modernist controversy, **Supp. 4**, 691–92; historical writings, **Supp. 1**, 528, 529, 556, 572; **Supp. 2**, 454; **Supp. 4**, 151–52; **Supp. 8**, 359–60; holiness sects, **Supp. 4**, 875–76; interdenominational, **Supp. 1**, 577; **Supp. 8**, 183–84; journalism, **Supp. 6**, 315–16; **Supp. 7**, 345–46; labor relationship, **Supp. 8**, 457–58; loyalty issues, **Supp. 8**, 426; medicine and, **Supp. 2**, 736; medieval studies, **Supp. 3**, 765–66; mental disorder relationship studies, **Supp. 7**, 64–65; metaphysics, writings on, **Supp. 4**, 178; millenarianism, **Supp. 1**, 615–16; nonsectarian, **Supp. 4**, 627–28; Oriental, study of, **Supp. 3**, 608–9; **Supp. 8**, 431; Oxford Movement, **Supp. 1**, 668; pacifism, **Supp. 10**, 82, 176; pastoral counseling, **Supp. 8**, 307; Peace Mission movement, **Supp. 7**, 187–88; philosophy of, **Vol. 8, Part 1**, 623; **Supp. 4**, 525–26; **Supp. 6**, 13–14, 45–46; poetry, **Supp. 1**, 681; popular writings on, **Supp. 4**, 741; **Supp. 5**, 527–28; pragmatic ethics, **Supp. 9**, 363; primitive symbolism studies, **Supp. 6**, 688; process theology, **Supp. 4**, 884; psychiatry and, **Supp. 3**, 190–91; **Supp. 6**, 725; psychology and, **Supp. 4**, 495–96, 766–67; psychology of, **Supp. 3**, 608; **Supp. 5**, 115–16; radio pastors, **Supp. 2**, 86; radio programs, **Supp. 10**, 151, 405, 729; revivalism, **Supp. 4**, 875–76; **Supp. 10**, 425–26; science and, **Vol. 5, Part 1**, 594; **Vol. 8, Part 2**, 57, 307; **Vol. 9, Part 1**, 104, 162, 269 f.; **Supp. 1**, 65; **Supp. 2**, 27; **Supp. 8**, 424; Social Gospel movement, **Supp. 5**, 445–46; **Supp. 7**, 185, 624; **Supp. 8**, 425, 680–81; social policies, **Supp. 1**, 577; **Supp. 3**, 363; **Supp. 4**, 741, 837; **Supp. 6**, 25, 45–46; social problems, relation of, to, **Vol. 8, Part 1**, 392 f.; social work, **Supp. 2**, 48–49, 655; student movements, **Supp. 5**, 506–7; television programs, **Supp. 10**, 729–30; theological liberalism, **Supp. 8**, 183–84; theological realism, **Supp. 4**, 512–13; theological writings, **Supp. 1**, 313, 469–70; **Supp. 3**, 514–15; **Supp. 9**, 384; theology, **Supp. 5**, 649; **Supp. 7**, 574–76, 745–47; theology, historical scholarship, **Supp. 8**, 669; United World Day of Prayer, **Supp. 4**, 648; writings on, **Supp. 2**, 412, 519; **Supp. 6**, 600; **Supp. 10**, 111; writings on unity of, **Supp. 8**, 430–31. *See also* Bible; Church-state separation; Ecumenism; Evangelism; Fundamentalism; Missionary work; Parochial schools; Theology; *specific denominations and sects*

Religious: controversies, **Vol. 1, Part 1**, 480; **Vol. 4, Part 1**, 462, 491; **Vol. 7, Part 1**, 525; **Vol. 8, Part 2**, 329; discourse, first published in America, **Vol. 3, Part 1**, 5; liberty, **Vol. 1, Part 1**, 471; **Vol. 1, Part 2**, 20; **Vol. 5, Part 2**, 154; **Vol. 7, Part 1**, 305; **Vol. 9, Part 2**, 87; newspaper, first, **Vol. 7, Part 1**, 251; orthodoxy, study of, **Vol. 8, Part 2**, 315; periodical, first in America, **Vol. 5, Part 2**, 458; persecution, New England, **Vol. 3, Part 2**, 488; revivals, **Vol. 3, Part 1**, 597 f.; **Vol. 3, Part 2**, 394; **Vol. 5, Part 2**, 191, 428; **Vol. 6, Part 1**, 115; **Vol. 8, Part 1**, 127; **Vol. 9, Part 2**, 71; statistician, **Vol. 3, Part 1**, 375 f.; weekly, one of America's first, **Vol. 4, Part 2**, 157

Religious Education Association, founding of, **Supp. 5**, 115

Relly, James, reference to, **Vol. 7, Part 1**, 361

Remington, Ann Moos, reference to, **Supp. 5**, 564

Remington, Frederick, references to, **Supp. 5**, 284, 420

Remington, William W., reference to, **Supp. 7**, 52

Remington-Rand Co., founding of, **Supp. 3**, 619; **Supp. 10**, 520–21

Reminiscences. *See* Memoirs

Remote-control, **Supp. 3**, 769

Renaissance, studies of English drama of the, **Supp. 4**, 4–5

Renal functions. *See* Kidneys

Rennebohm, Oscar, reference to, **Supp. 10**, 420

Reno, Nev., gambling in, **Supp. 10**, 308

Rensselaer Polytechnic Institute: **Vol. 1, Part 2**, 171; **Vol. 3, Part 1**, 605 f.; **Vol. 7, Part 1**, 390; development of, **Supp. 1**, 629

Reo Motor Car Co., founding of, **Supp. 4**, 638

Repertory theater, **Supp. 3**, 796–99

Reporter (magazine), **Supp. 10**, 14

Reporters. For complete list, *see* Occupations Index

Reporting, pioneer legislative, **Vol. 3, Part 1**, 231 f.

Representation, slave, **Vol. 8, Part 1**, 308 f.

Reprint periodicals, early, **Vol. 6, Part 1**, 295

Reproduction: artificial insemination, **Supp. 8**, 502–3; cycle research, **Supp. 2**, 632; maternal health research, **Supp. 4**, 231. *See also* Fertilization

Reproductive system, hormones and, **Supp. 3**, 6. *See also* Gynecology; Obstetrics; *specific organs*

Reptiles: colored plates of, **Vol. 5, Part 1**, 129; description of North American, **Supp. 4**, 52; eye studies of, **Supp. 3**, 835; lectures on, **Supp. 3**, 229; poisonous, **Vol. 5, Part 2**, 513; studies on, **Vol. 5, Part 1**, 129; **Supp. 2**, 490; writings on, **Supp. 3**, 732

Republican Methodist Church, **Vol. 7, Part 2**, 7

Republican Organizing Committee, founding of, **Supp. 8**, 1–2

Republican party (general): **Vol. 1, Part 1**, 152, 154, 164, 280, 521, 537; **Vol. 1, Part 2**, 330, 331, 339, 515; **Vol. 2, Part 1**, 94; **Vol. 2, Part 2**, 97, 472, 589; **Vol. 3, Part 1**, 322, 521; **Vol. 3, Part 2**, 51, 84, 212, 248, 291 f., 297, 326, 348, 485; **Vol. 4, Part 1**, 51, 112, 146, 209, 304, 608; **Vol. 4, Part 2**, 4, 16, 24, 30, 41, 81, 103, 226; **Vol. 5, Part 1**, 256, 278, 283, 406; **Vol. 5, Part 2**, 86, 299; **Vol. 6, Part 2**, 491; **Vol. 7, Part 1**, 264; **Vol. 8, Part 2**, 617; **Vol. 9, Part 1**, 82, 223, 245, 246, 250, 525; **Vol. 9, Part 2**, 34, 35, 37; **Vol. 10, Part 1**, 28, 629, 657; black membership decline, **Supp. 9**, 137; blacks in, **Supp. 3**, 378, 390–91, 535, 596; **Supp. 4**, 915; **Supp. 5**, 166, 632–33, 568; business backers, **Supp. 6**, 618; **Supp. 9**, 781–82; business-farm interests, conflict in, **Supp. 3**, 468, Cameron machines, **Vol. 7, Part 1**, 438; conservative-liberal split, **Supp. 5**, 450, 676; **Supp. 8**, 144, 145, 156, 160, 701–2; conservatives in, **Supp. 6**, 59–60, 455, 588; **Supp. 7**, 615–16; Cornfield Conference (1938), **Supp. 10**, 97; elections of 1876 and 1880, **Vol. 2, Part 1**, 617; elephant, invented by Nast, **Vol. 7, Part 1**, 392; first use of the term, **Vol. 5, Part 2**, 394; **Vol. 10, Part 1**, 502 f.; Equal Rights Amendment first supported, **Supp. 9**, 546; foreign policy, **Supp. 6**, 178; formation of (1854–56), **Vol. 1, Part 1**, 578; **Vol. 1, Part 2**, 258; **Vol. 2, Part 1**, 204, 618; **Vol. 4, Part 1**, 22; **Vol. 4, Part 2**, 106; **Vol. 5, Part 2**, 574 f.; **Vol. 6, Part 1**, 247; **Vol. 8, Part 2**, 617; **Vol. 9, Part 1**, 271; **Vol. 10, Part 1**, 599; governors' conferences, **Supp. 8**, 357; "Half-Breeds," **Vol. 1, Part 2**, 324 f.; **Vol. 8, Part 2**, 6; insiders, **Supp. 4**, 135; internationalism v. isolationism, **Supp. 7**, 23; internationalist wing, **Supp. 5**, 198; labor relations, **Supp. 5**, 339–40; **Supp. 8**, 375, 376; League of Nations issue, **Supp. 3**, 472–73; liberal wing of, **Supp. 9**, 525, 528; **Supp. 10**, 687, 688; Lincoln's association with, **Vol. 4, Part 1**, 260; **Vol. 6, Part 1**, 247 f.; national chairman, **Supp. 9**, 356, 357; **Supp. 10**, 302, 557; National Committee, **Supp. 3**, 846; **Supp. 5**, 157, 281, 579, 739; **Supp. 6**, 207, 227, 683–84; **Supp. 7**, 639; **Supp. 8**, 421; **Supp. 9**, 781, 851, 852; **Supp. 10**, 557; national convention, first, **Vol. 1, Part 2**, 323, 594; **Vol. 5, Part 2**, 260; National Convention (1952), **Supp. 9**, 781; National Convention (1964), **Supp. 10**, 687; National Convention (1968), **Supp. 9**, 625; New England "regeneration," **Vol. 6, Part 1**, 263; newspapers, **Supp. 3**, 816; progressives in, **Vol.**

1, Part 2, 232, 392; **Vol. 5, Part 2**, 541 f.; **Supp. 3**, 496, 557–61; **Supp. 4**, 317–18; **Supp. 5**, 403–4; Prohibition (1884), **Vol. 8, Part 2**, 304; protective tariff, **Vol. 9, Part 2**, 237; public relations, **Supp. 5**, 303–4; "Puppets of Leib's machine," **Vol. 5, Part 2**, 521; Rollin's machine, **Vol. 8, Part 2**, 120; "Stalwarts," **Vol. 1, Part 2**, 324; **Vol. 5, Part 2**, 543 f.; **Vol. 8, Part 2**, 6; tax policies, **Supp. 6**, 535; "Union Republicans," **Vol. 1, Part 1**, 104 f.; Western Conference of party leaders, **Supp. 9**, 625; "wide awake," **Vol. 6, Part 1**, 423 f.; **Vol. 8, Part 1**, 171, 428; women in, **Supp. 3**, 710, **Supp. 5**, 157; **Supp. 6**, 576; **Supp. 9**, 625–26; **Supp. 10**, 56–58; Young Republicans, **Supp. 9**, 625; "Young Turks," **Supp. 9**, 467–68, 625. *See also* Presidential election *headings*

Republican party (by state): Arkansas, **Supp. 9**, 672; California, **Supp. 3**, 394; **Supp. 4**, 446–47; **Supp. 8**, 340–41; **Supp. 9**, 467, 468–69; Colorado, **Vol. 1, Part 1**, 260; **Vol. 10, Part 2**, 441; **Supp. 6**, 507; **Supp. 10**, 782; Connecticut, **Vol. 4, Part 2**, 421; Delaware, **Supp. 8**, 246–47; Georgia, **Supp. 4**, 915; Idaho, **Supp. 7**, 212–13; Illinois, **Vol. 1, Part 2**, 382; **Vol. 8, Part 1**, 187, 392; **Supp. 1**, 531–32; **Supp. 3**, 467–68, 710, 771–72; **Supp. 4**, 180, 752; **Supp. 5**, 166; **Supp. 8**, 127–29; **Supp. 9**, 739, 740; Indiana, **Vol. 2, Part 2**, 297; **Vol. 7, Part 2**, 61; **Supp. 4**, 861–62; **Supp. 5**, 281; **Supp. 9**, 360; **Supp. 10**, 97; Iowa, **Vol. 1, Part 2**, 4, 13; **Vol. 6, Part 2**, 638; **Vol. 10, Part 2**, 633; **Supp. 3**, 107–9; **Supp. 8**, 300; Kansas, **Supp. 3**, 105–6, 544; **Supp. 4**, 12; **Supp. 5**, 101; **Supp. 7**, 677–78; **Supp. 8**, 277; **Supp. 9**, 355–56; Kentucky, **Vol. 4, Part 1**, 391; Maine, **Supp. 7**, 72–73, 312; Maryland, **Supp. 9**, 528; Massachusetts, **Vol. 2, Part 1**, 289, 358, 542; **Supp. 5**, 518; **Supp. 8**, 257, 420–21; **Supp. 9**, 851; **Supp. 10**, 716; Michigan, **Vol. 2, Part 1**, 618; **Supp. 3**, 550; **Supp. 4**, 639–40; **Supp. 5**, 702–5; **Supp. 8**, 57, 268–69; **Supp. 9**, 781; Minnesota, **Vol. 1, Part 1**, 242; **Supp. 4**, 852–53; **Supp. 5**, 396–97; **Supp. 8**, 653–54; Missouri, **Vol. 2, Part 1**, 106; **Supp. 4**, 416; Montana, **Vol. 8, Part 2**, 337; Nebraska, **Vol. 5, Part 1**, 78; **Supp. 3**, 556–61; **Supp. 5**, 739; New Hampshire, **Vol. 8, Part 2**, 120; **Supp. 3**, 425, 543; **Supp. 4**, 164–65; **Supp. 5**, 689–90; **Supp. 7**, 73–74; New Jersey, **Vol. 7, Part 2**, 233; **Supp. 5**, 198, 212–13; **Supp. 6**, 651; **Supp. 8**, 245–46, 648; New Mexico, **Supp. 1**, 671; New York, **Vol. 2, Part 2**, 138; **Supp. 4**, 379–80, 404, 464–66, 825–26, 885–86; **Supp. 5**, 493–94, 715–16; **Supp. 6**, 142; **Supp. 7**, 382–83, 733–34; **Supp. 8**, 27; **Supp. 9**, 230; **Supp. 10**, 302–3, 686–88; North Carolina, **Supp. 6**, 494; North Dakota, **Supp. 4**, 309, 479–80; **Supp. 6**, 85–86; **Supp. 8**, 1–2; Ohio, **Vol. 2, Part 1**, 376; **Supp. 3**, 213; **Supp. 4**, 317–18; **Supp. 5**, 674; **Supp. 7**, 49, 84–86; **Supp. 7**, 95–96; **Supp. 10**, 56–58; Oregon, **Vol. 1, Part 1**, 102; **Supp. 3**, 364; **Supp. 8**, 104, 617–18; Pennsylvania, **Vol. 2, Part 1**, 438; **Vol. 7, Part 2**, 449; **Supp. 5**, 561; **Supp. 7**, 305, 606–7; **Supp. 8**, 143–44, 531–32; **Supp. 9**, 425–26; **Supp. 10**, 241, 242; Rhode Island, **Vol. 1, Part 2**, 612; South Carolina, **Vol. 7, Part 2**, 613; **Vol. 8, Part 1**, 327; Tennessee, **Supp. 7**, 639; Utah, **Supp. 9**, 625; Vermont, **Supp. 7**, 23; **Supp. 8**, 177–78; Virginia, **Vol. 6, Part 1**, 217; **Vol. 6, Part 2**, 212; **Vol. 9, Part 2**, 484; **Supp. 3**, 715; **Supp. 9**, 650; Washington, **Supp. 4**, 669–70; **Supp. 8**, 357; Wisconsin, **Vol. 8, Part 2**, 213; **Supp. 3**, 256–57; **Supp. 4**, 481; **Supp. 5**, 403–4; **Supp. 7**, 450, 451; **Supp. 8**, 701; **Supp. 10**, 420, 421; Wyoming, **Supp. 3**, 788; **Supp. 7**, 31

Republican Publicity Association, founding of, **Supp. 2**, 55

Republic Pictures Corporation: founding of, **Supp. 8**, 712; **Supp. 9**, 555; formula Westerns, **Supp. 10**, 822

Republic Steel Corporation: founding of, **Supp. 7**, 289; **Supp. 10**, 203; "Memorial Day massacre," **Supp. 7**, 290

Resaca (Dublin, Ga.), battle of. *See* Atlanta campaign

Resaca de la Palma, battle of, **Vol. 8, Part 1**, 316, 625; **Vol. 9, Part 2**, 351; **Vol. 10, Part 1**, 83; **Vol. 10, Part 2**, 537

Rescue mission work, **Vol. 9, Part 1**, 176

Research, first institution designed primarily for, **Vol. 8, Part 1**, 501. *See also* Industrial research; Market research; *specific subjects of research*

Research and Marketing Act (1946), **Supp. 8**, 277

Research Corporation, founding of, **Supp. 4**, 184

Reserve Officers' Training Corps, **Vol. 7, Part 2**, 282

Resettlement Administration, United States, **Supp. 6**, 12; **Supp. 7**, 456

Resolute (yacht), **Supp. 5**, 6

Resonator, electrical, **Supp. 1**, 613

Resources of the Confederacy, **Vol. 8, Part 2**, 303

Respirators, Henderson-Haggard, **Supp. 3**, 353

Respiratory system, physiological studies, **Supp. 3**, 353

Restaurants: as an American institution, **Vol. 3, Part 1**, 227; Chicago, **Vol. 5, Part 2**, 489; criticism, **Supp. 6**, 291–92; franchise, **Supp. 9**, 429–30; **Supp. 10**, 717–18; health food, **Supp. 5**, 452; lunch counters, **Supp. 2**, 688; New York, **Vol. 3, Part 1**, 227; **Vol. 9, Part 1**, 97; Romanoff's, **Supp. 9**, 673–74; Sardi's, **Supp. 8**, 571–72; Stouffer's Fifth Avenue, **Supp. 9**, 770. *See also* Cooking

Reston, James, reference to, **Supp. 9**, 471

Retail trades: biggest bankruptcy to date, **Supp. 9**, 337; chain variety stores, **Supp. 8**, 347–49; department stores, **Supp. 2**, 636; **Supp. 8**, 212–13, 427–28, 705; **Supp. 9**, 483–84, 609–10; **Supp. 10**, 163–64, 353–54; discounting, **Supp. 2**, 183; **Supp. 8**, 348–49; **Supp. 9**, 336–37, 597; drugstores, **Supp. 2**, 688; electronics, **Supp. 10**, 773–74; first long-lasting chain, **Supp. 5**, 277; grocery stores, **Supp. 3**, 367; **Supp. 5**, 277–78, 603–4; **Supp. 7**, 141–42; **Supp. 10**, 737–38; ice cream franchisers, **Supp. 9**, 246, 429–30; investments in, **Supp. 8**, 367; **Supp. 10**, 381; leather goods, **Supp. 10**, 773; mail-order, **Supp. 8**, 28–29; marketing, **Supp. 2**, 105; sales volume emphasis, **Supp. 5**, 401. *See also* Book stores; Five and dime stores

Retaliation Act, **Vol. 1, Part 1**, 505

Retardation. *See* Mentally retarded

Retirement. *See* Pensions; Social Security

Retraining and Reemployment Administration, **Supp. 6**, 293

"Retrenchment and Reform," **Vol. 8, Part 1**, 350 f.

Return of the Dragon, **Supp. 9**, 486

Reuter's, **Supp. 7**, 145

Reuther, Victor, references to, **Supp. 8**, 526, 527

Reuther, Walter, references to, **Supp. 5**, 283; **Supp. 6**, 648; **Supp. 8**, 419, 594, 652, 653; **Supp. 9**, 585

Reveille in Washington, 1860–1865, **Supp. 9**, 629; **Supp. 10**, 400

Revell, Fleming H., and Co., **Supp. 6**, 171

Revenue Act (1918), **Supp. 4**, 339

Revenue Act (1935), **Supp. 8**, 446

Revere, Paul: references to, **Vol. 3, Part 1**, 150; **Vol. 8, Part 1**, 195 f.; **Vol. 8, Part 2**, 386; historical writings on, **Supp. 8**, 181

Review of American Chemical Research, founding of, **Supp. 2**, 494

Reviews. *See* Criticism

Revlon (cosmetic company), founding and growth of, **Supp. 9**, 648–49

Revolution, **Supp. 4**, 85

Revolutionary War: army tactics of Washington and Lafayette, **Vol. 8, Part 2**, 61; ballads, **Vol. 4, Part 2**, 390; Board of War, **Vol. 7, Part 2**, 509; Boston, evacuation of, by British, **Vol. 6, Part 1**, 77; British lead-

ers, **Supp. 1**, 180; campaigns, **Vol. 3, Part 1**, 175; Canada, scheme to capture, **Vol. 5, Part 2**, 537; claims against U.S., **Vol. 7, Part 2**, 613; commissary department, **Vol. 5, Part 1**, 174; **Vol. 4, Part 2**, 561; **Vol. 10, Part 1**, 18 f.; conscientious objectors, **Vol. 8, Part 1**, 139 f.; Conway cabal, **Vol. 4, Part 1**, 186; diary, important, **Vol. 10, Part 2**, 434; diplomacy, **Vol. 1, Part 1**, 435; **Vol. 2, Part 1**, 497; **Vol. 3, Part 1**, 52, 173; **Vol. 6, Part 1**, 36, 322 f.; Episcopal clergy, **Vol. 1, Part 1**, 293 f.; **Vol. 8, Part 2**, 258; European officers, **Vol. 3, Part 1**, 174; financing of, **Vol. 3, Part 1**, 53; **Vol. 4, Part 2**, 476; **Vol. 7, Part 1**, 220; **Vol. 8, Part 1**, 50; **Vol. 8, Part 2**, 314, 536; **Vol. 10, Part 2**, 303; first aggressive act of the colonists, prior to, **Vol. 8, Part 1**, 515; first engagement in, **Vol. 3, Part 1**, 519 f.; first news to reach England, **Vol. 3, Part 1**, 253; "freedom of press," **Vol. 4, Part 1**, 341 f; French aid, **Vol. 8, Part 2**, 60 f.; Hessians, **Vol. 8, Part 2**, 314; historical writings on, **Supp. 1**, 180; **Supp. 9**, 314–15; Hudson River blockade, **Vol. 10, Part 2**, 432; Indians in, **Vol. 1, Part 1**, 182; **Vol. 10, Part 2**, 123; interned English families, **Vol. 8, Part 2**, 203; leaders of, **Vol. 8, Part 2**, 495; legends of, **Vol. 6, Part 1**, 286; letters from England during, **Vol. 8, Part 1**, 400; Loyalists, **Vol. 1, Part 1**, 185, 293, 405, 421 f., 464, 497, 596; **Vol. 2, Part 1**, 168, 169, 280; **Vol. 3, Part 2**, 6, 103, 190, 264 f., 426, 459, 506, 600 f.; **Vol. 4, Part 1**, 117, 133, 140, 243, 476 f, 543, 553; **Vol. 4, Part 2**, 230, 601; **Vol. 5, Part 1**, 376, 387, 468, 476, 480; **Vol. 5, Part 2**, 200, 257; **Vol. 6, Part 1**, 136, 175 f., 418 f., 439, 446, 492; **Vol. 6, Part 2**, 50, 258; **Vol. 7, Part 1**, 226, 292, 332, 623, 637; **Vol. 7, Part 2**, 559; **Vol. 8, Part 1**, 247 f., 334 f., 362 f.; **Vol. 8, Part 2**, 529, 607; **Vol. 9, Part 1**, 116, 358, 417, 517; maps, **Vol. 3, Part 1**, 274; military engineering, **Vol. 4, Part 1**, 612; military service, **Vol. 1, Part 1**, 267, 270, 275, 304, 353, 355, 362, 369, 385, 386, 395, 487, 493, 494, 539, 576, 588; **Vol. 1, Part 2**, 24, 76, 100, 122, 124, 191, 239, 356, 380, 386, 389, 477, 483, 511, 558, 565, 566, 600; **Vol. 2, Part 1**, 63, 69, 80, 130, 242, 314, 362, 388, 398, 409, 571; **Vol. 2, Part 2**, 74, 96, 107, 112, 117, 128, 150, 166, 180, 186, 188, 202, 227, 229, 239, 268, 365, 368, 438, 444, 505, 527, 538; **Vol. 3, Part 1**, 3, 75, 97, 98, 150, 165, 166, 175, 199, 214, 215, 216, 217, 254, 274, 300, 302, 315, 365, 404, 414, 486, 489, 504, 514, 525, 550, 573; **Vol. 3, Part 2**, 43, 66, 193, 235, 237, 265, 305, 307, 309, 325, 344, 352, 385, 400, 414, 484, 494, 516, 524, 600; **Vol. 4, Part 1**, 4, 13, 15, 50, 82, 126, 127, 133, 140, 184, 236, 253, 324, 331, 440, 479, 523, 524, 525, 526, 563, 569, 571, 589, 592, 633; **Vol. 4, Part 2**, 12, 70, 108, 133, 171, 189, 209, 212, 219, 223, 232, 245, 275, 366, 454, 478, 490, 532, 577, 609; **Vol. 5, Part 1**, 10, 35, 49, 123, 133, 215, 218, 267, 279, 294, 304, 344, 363, 373, 399, 416, 438, 454, 461, 487, 499, 500, 524, 538, 541, 544; **Vol. 5, Part 2**, 1, 47, 56, 57, 122, 148, 150, 154, 159, 204, 205, 210, 253, 423, 474, 476, 493, 497, 519, 536, 555, 608; **Vol. 6, Part 1**, 31, 36, 75, 77, 94, 98, 105, 107, 154, 166, 206, 222, 260, 312, 313, 338, 520, 532, 596; **Vol. 6, Part 2**, 24, 33, 62, 70, 113, 283, 409, 443, 477, 509, 541, 607; **Vol. 7, Part 1**, 35, 59, 83, 87, 99, 112, 113, 128, 133, 142, 166, 201, 215, 216, 226, 293, 302, 312, 325, 358, 387, 411, 421, 430, 483, 509, 530, 535, 563, 623, 632, 636; **Vol. 7, Part 2**, 4, 81, 138, 166, 189, 211, 233, 234, 270, 292, 340, 345, 443, 484, 517, 559, 566, 584, 614, 618; **Vol. 8, Part 1**, 42, 43, 50, 55, 69, 82, 111, 129, 137, 194, 195, 259, 281, 284, 300, 334, 340, 353, 420, 448, 452, 524, 646, 647; **Vol. 8, Part 2**, 63, 81, 83, 108, 126, 148, 180, 238, 255, 257, 294, 407, 478, 487, 525, 535 f., 539; **Vol. 9, Part 1**, 45, 4875 49 59, 60, 76, 226, 280, 309, 320, 336, 341, 368, 450, 530, 603, 614; **Vol. 9, Part 2**, 51, 67, 234, 258, 331, 387, 426, 435, 438, 476, 489, 503, 545, 550, 574, 606, 651; **Vol. 10, Part 1**, 7, 12, 18, 26, 38, 52, 162, 403, 415, 437, 468, 479, 482, 508, 509, 563; **Vol. 10, Part 2**, 180, 223, 244, 284, 296, 378, 390, 440, 490, 493, 525; munitions, **Vol. 3, Part 1**, 174, 250, 253; **Vol. 3, Part 2**, 516; **Vol. 4, Part 1**, 253; **Vol. 4, Part 2**, 454; **Vol. 6, Part 1**, 214; **Vol. 7, Part 1**, 503; **Vol. 7, Part 2**, 58; **Vol. 8, Part 1**, 515, 646; **Vol. 8, Part 2**, 63 f.; **Vol. 10, Part 2**, 432; naval service, **Vol. 1, Part 1**, 632, 654; **Vol. 1, Part 2**, 242; **Vol. 2, Part 1**, 395; **Vol. 3, Part 1**, 32 f., 186; **Vol. 3, Part 2**, 420; **Vol. 4, Part 1**, 296; **Vol. 4, Part 2**, 234 f., 251, 476; **Vol. 5, Part 1**, 64, 212; **Vol. 5, Part 2**, 184 f.; **Vol. 6, Part 1**, 298 f.; **Vol. 6, Part 2**, 149, 151, 236; **Vol. 7, Part 1**, 357, 502, 506, 610; **Vol. 8, Part 1**, 182 f., 348 f., 430; **Vol. 8, Part 2**, 24, 75, 316, 539; **Vol. 10, Part 1**, 21 f., 39, 536; **Vol. 10, Part 2**, 66; newspapers and rare pamphlets, collection of, **Vol. 3, Part 1**, 553 f.; **Vol. 3, Part 2**, 519; novels on, **Supp. 3**, 93; **Supp. 10**, 400; pamphleteering, **Vol. 5, Part 1**, 221 f.; payment of state debts, **Vol. 8, Part 1**, 584; pictorial field book of, **Vol. 6, Part 1**, 422; printing, **Vol. 4, Part 1**, 341; **Vol. 6, Part 2**, 631; prisoners in New York City, **Vol. 7, Part 2**, 631; privateering, **Vol. 3, Part 1**, 186, 249, 414; **Vol. 6, Part 2**, 149, 236; **Vol. 8, Part 2**, 316; **Vol. 10, Part 1**, 21 f.; refugees, **Vol. 1, Part 2**, 366; relief work, **Vol. 8, Part 1**, 542; satirical verse, **Vol. 9, Part 1**, 517; soldiers, U.S., debts to, **Vol. 3, Part 2**, 444; southern campaign, **Vol. 6, Part 1**, 107; spy service, **Vol. 4, Part 2**, 583; **Vol. 10, Part 1**, 659; studies of, **Supp. 3**, 15–16, 47; surgery, **Vol. 3, Part 2**, 307; **Vol. 5, Part 1**, 185; **Vol. 5, Part 2**, 181; **Vol. 7, Part 2**, 109; treason, **Vol. 3, Part 1**, 504 f.; **Vol. 6, Part 1**, 100, 225; writings concerning, **Vol. 4, Part 1**, 134, 426, 479; **Vol. 4, Part 2**, 171; **Vol. 5, Part 2**, 18; **Vol. 7, Part 1**, 485; **Vol. 9, Part 2**, 387; **Supp. 4**, 848

Revolutionary War period (by state): Connecticut, **Vol. 3, Part 2**, 112; **Vol. 5, Part 1**, 416; **Vol. 10, Part 2**, 293, 442; Delaware, **Vol. 1, Part 2**, 191; **Vol. 6, Part 2**, 79; **Vol. 8, Part 2**, 81 f.; Georgia, **Vol. 4, Part 2**, 70; Maryland, **Vol. 2, Part 1**, 523; **Vol. 4, Part 2**, 549; Massachusetts, **Vol. 2, Part 1**, 381, 395; **Vol. 4, Part 2**, 420; **Vol. 6, Part 2**, 218, 455; **Vol. 7, Part 2**, 565; **Vol. 9, Part 2**, 476, 479; **Vol. 10, Part 2**, 540, 635; New Hampshire, **Vol. 10, Part 2**, 71; New Jersey, **Vol. 4, Part 2**, 359, 241; **Vol. 10, Part 2**, 437; New York, **Vol. 5, Part 1**, 94; **Vol. 6, Part 1**, 316 f.; **Vol. 6, Part 2**, 22; **Vol. 10, Part 2**, 601; North Carolina, **Vol. 2, Part 1**, 283, 407; **Vol. 5, Part 1**, 492; **Vol. 6, Part 2**, 334; **Vol. 8, Part 1**, 43; Pennsylvania, **Vol. 2, Part 1**, 400; **Vol. 5, Part 1**, 9; **Vol. 6, Part 2**, 287, 306; **Vol. 7, Part 1**, 437, 430; **Vol. 10, Part 2**, 33, 328, 606; Rhode Island, **Vol. 6, Part 2**, 271; South Carolina, **Vol. 2, Part 1**, 263, 465; **Vol. 3, Part 2**, 313; **Vol. 4, Part 1**, 82, 134; **Vol. 6, Part 2**, 405, 600; **Vol. 8, Part 2**, 259; **Vol. 10, Part 2**, 299; Virginia, **Vol. 2, Part 1**, 389, 522; **Vol. 6, Part 2**, 185, 542, 376, 363; **Vol. 7, Part 1**, 424 f.; **Vol. 10, Part 2**, 490

Revson, Charles, reference to, **Supp. 9**, 465

Revson, Joseph, reference to, **Supp. 10**, 239

Revuers, The, **Supp. 7**, 354

Rexall drugstore chain, **Supp. 4**, 496–97

Reymond, Alard DuBois, reference to, **Supp. 6**, 596

Reynolds, Debbie, reference to, **Supp. 9**, 343; **Supp. 10**, 802

Reynolds, J. J., reference to, **Supp. 5**, 565

Reynolds, Quentin, reference to, **Supp. 8**, 498

Reynolds, R. J., Tobacco Co., **Supp. 5**, 565–68

Reynolds, Richard, reference to, **Supp. 5**, 565, 566, 567
Reynolds International Pens, **Supp. 10**, 670
Reynolds Metals Co., **Supp. 5**, 565–66; **Supp. 9**, 650
Reynolds v. *Sims*, **Supp. 9**, 837
RFC. *See* Reconstruction Finance Corporation
Rhapsody in Blue, **Supp. 8**, 697, 698; **Supp. 9**, 491
Rhee, Syngman, references to, **Supp. 7**, 352; **Supp. 8**, 158
Rheinberger, Josef Gabriel, references to, **Vol. 7, Part 2**, 222; **Supp. 1**, 161
Rheostat, **Vol. 6, Part 1**, 505
Rhett, Robert B., reference to, **Vol. 5, Part 1**, 344
Rheumatic disease, cortisone treatment, **Supp. 7**, 340–41
Rheumatism Review, **Supp. 7**, 340
Rheumatology, research, **Supp. 10**, 624
Rhine, J. B., reference to, **Supp. 6**, 612
Rhinology: **Vol. 6, Part 1**, 160; research in, **Supp. 1**, 181
Rh-negative blood type, **Supp. 3**, 441
Rhoads, Cornelius P., reference to, **Supp. 10**, 769
Rhode Island: battle of, **Vol. 2, Part 2**, 444; blacks, proposed disfranchisement of, **Vol. 3, Part 1**, 407; boundary disputes, **Vol. 1, Part 2**, 460; **Vol. 8, Part 1**, 426; Civil War period, **Vol. 8, Part 2**, 38; Congress, first representative to, **Vol. 1, Part 2**, 484; Constitution, ratification of federal, **Vol. 1, Part 2**, 483; Dorr's Rebellion, suppression of, **Vol. 3, Part 1**, 176; dual government of (1842), **Vol. 3, Part 1**, 382; education, **Vol. 1, Part 1**, 226; **Vol. 3, Part 1**, 423; **Vol. 6, Part 1**, 72; **Vol. 8, Part 1**, 126 f.; **Vol. 10, Part 1**, 558 f.; Episcopal church, **Vol. 9, Part 1**, 359; French and Indian War, **Vol. 4, Part 1**, 575 f.; governors, **Vol. 1, Part 1**, 203 f.; **Vol. 3, Part 1**, 604, 605; **Vol. 3, Part 2**, 322 f., 579 f.; **Vol. 4, Part 1**, 174 f., 576 f.; **Vol. 5, Part 1**, 227 f.; **Vol. 5, Part 2**, 40 f., 204 f., 402 f.; **Vol. 6, Part 1**, 289; **Vol. 9, Part 1**, 289 f., 475 f.; **Vol. 10, Part 1**, 412, 434 f., 437; history of, **Vol. 1, Part 2**, 7; **Vol. 2, Part 1**, 426; **Vol. 2, Part 2**, 163; **Vol. 3, Part 1**, 545 f., 604 f.; **Vol. 4, Part 2**, 42; **Vol. 5, Part 1**, 219; **Vol. 5, Part 2**, 138; **Vol. 7, Part 2**, 238; **Vol. 9, Part 1**, 528; **Vol. 10, Part 2**, 201; Indians, relations with, **Vol. 6, Part 2**, 590; iron industry, **Vol. 2, Part 1**, 149; legal service, **Vol. 1, Part 2**, 393, 484, 512; **Vol. 3, Part 1**, 546, 604; **Vol. 9, Part 2**, 34; **Vol. 5, Part 1**, 301; **Vol. 8, Part 1**, 126, 349; **Vol. 10, Part 1**, 121, 437; Loyalists, **Vol. 10, Part 1**, 414; "People's party," **Vol. 3, Part 1**, 382; political service, **Vol. 1, Part 1**, 317; **Vol. 1, Part 2**, 155, 483, 512, 612; politics, **Supp. 8**, 222–23, 405; printing, **Vol. 2, Part 1**, 540; public service, **Vol. 2, Part 2**, 155; **Vol. 3, Part 2**, 86, 580; **Vol. 4, Part 2**, 470; **Vol. 5, Part 1**, 407; **Vol. 6, Part 2**, 250; **Vol. 10, Part 1**, 434 f., 437; reforms, **Vol. 4, Part 2**, 473 f.; Revolutionary debt, payment of, **Vol. 8, Part 1**, 584; Revolutionary defense, **Vol. 5, Part 1**, 209; **Vol. 6, Part 2**, 271; secession in colonial, **Vol. 3, Part 1**, 605; settlement of, **Vol. 10, Part 2**, 288; "State of the Union," **Vol. 8, Part 2**, 38; statutory law, restatement of, **Vol. 1, Part 1**, 256; suffrage in struggle for manhood, **Vol. 3, Part 1**, 381 f.; woolen manufacture, **Vol. 10, Part 1**, 600 f.; writings on, **Vol. 1, Part 1**, 372
Rhode Island College. *See* Brown University
Rhode Island Institute of Instruction, **Vol. 5, Part 2**, 409
Rhode Island School of Design, **Vol. 3, Part 1**, 423
Rhode Island Society for the Collegiate Education of Women, **Vol. 3, Part 1**, 423
Rhode Island Woman's Club, **Vol. 3, Part 1**, 423
Rhodes, James E., reference to, **Vol. 9, Part 2**, 337
Rhodes, J. F., reference to, **Vol. 1, Part 2**, 484
Rhodes Scholarship: **Supp. 6**, 29, 30; American secretary, **Supp. 8**, 601; first black recipient, **Supp. 5**, 436
Rhythm Boys (vocal trio), **Supp. 10**, 159
Rhythm of the Ages, The, **Supp. 4**, 344
Ribicoff, Abraham, references to, **Supp. 9**, 58, 59; **Supp. 10**, 168
Riboflavin, **Supp. 6**, 595
Ribonucleic acid. *See* RNA
Ricci-Curbastro, Gregorio, reference to, **Supp. 7**, 216
Rice: **Vol. 2, Part 1**, 326; **Vol. 2, Part 2**, 307, 317, 512; **Vol. 3, Part 1**, 275, 381, 546, 604; **Vol. 3, Part 2**, 322, 324, 580, 559; **Vol. 4, Part 1**, 174, 575; **Vol. 5, Part 1**, 219, 227; **Vol. 5, Part 2**, 40, 204, 402; **Vol. 6, Part 1**, 53, 289; **Vol. 8, Part 1**, 126; **Vol. 9, Part 1**, 289, 475; **Vol. 10, Part 1**, 121, 412, 434 f., 437; mills, **Vol. 6, Part 1**, 486 f.; plantations, **Vol. 1, Part 1**, 224; **Vol. 2, Part 2**, 180; **Vol. 5, Part 2**, 414; seeds, smuggling of, by Jefferson, **Vol. 5, Part 2**, 22
Rice, David, memoirs, **Supp. 1**, 83
Rice, Elmer, reference to, **Supp. 4**, 104
Rice, Francis O., reference to, **Supp. 4**, 337
Rice, Grantland, reference to, **Supp. 7**, 729
Rice Institute: architecture, **Supp. 3**, 196; genetics studies, **Supp. 8**, 449
Rich, Isaac, reference to, **Vol. 10, Part 1**, 490 f.
Rich, Obadiah, reference to, **Vol. 5, Part 1**, 509
"Richard Diamond, Private Detective," **Supp. 10**, 380
Richards, Alfred Newton, reference to, **Supp. 6**, 175
Richards, A. N., Medical Reserach Building (Philadelphia, Pa.), design of, **Supp. 9**, 446
Richards, Ellen H., reference to, **Vol. 7, Part 1**, 575
Richards, Theodore W., reference to, **Supp. 3**, 349–50
Richardson, Helen Patges, reference to, **Supp. 3**, 237–38
Richardson, H. H., reference to, **Vol. 5, Part 2**, 533; **Vol. 7, Part 1**, 545
Richardson, J. P. ("Big Bopper"), reference to, **Supp. 6**, 301
Richardson, Owen W., references to, **Supp. 5**, 126; **Supp. 6**, 150–51, 653–54
Richardson, Bellows, Henry and Co., founding, **Supp. 6**, 222
Richardson Foundation, **Supp. 6**, 541
Richfield Oil Co., **Supp. 6**, 585
Richman, Julia, reference to, **Supp. 8**, 442–43
Richmond, Ky., battle of, **Vol. 1, Part 2**, 586; **Vol. 2, Part 1**, 241; **Vol. 3, Part 1**, 131; **Vol. 4, Part 2**, 240; **Vol. 5, Part 2**, 245; **Vol. 7, Part 1**, 426; **Vol. 8, Part 1**, 40; **Vol. 9, Part 2**, 433
Richmond, Va., campaign (1864–65), **Vol. 2, Part 2**, 463; **Vol. 3, Part 1**, 598; **Vol. 3, Part 2**, 602; **Vol. 4, Part 1**, 25, 27, 343, 366, 371, 558; **Vol. 4, Part 2**, 505; **Vol. 6, Part 1**, 123, 391, 583; **Vol. 6, Part 2**, 205; **Vol. 8, Part 2**, 90; **Vol. 9, Part 2**, 170, 215
Richmond and Danville Railroad, **Vol. 1, Part 1**, 282
Richmond College, establishment of, **Vol. 9, Part 2**, 326, 328
Richmond Enquirer, **Vol. 8, Part 1**, 628
Richmond Examiner, **Vol. 3, Part 1**, 67; **Vol. 5, Part 1**, 357
Richmond Female Institute, **Vol. 9, Part 2**, 328
"Richmond Junto," **Vol. 8, Part 1**, 628; **Vol. 7, Part 2**, 484
Richmond News Leader, **Supp. 3**, 115; **Supp. 5**, 233–34
Richmond Terminal (railroad holding company), **Supp. 3**, 125
Rich Mountain, battle of, **Vol. 4, Part 1**, 159; **Vol. 6, Part 1**, 582; **Vol. 8, Part 2**, 163; **Vol. 9, Part 2**, 183
Richter, Paul, reference to, **Supp. 6**, 221
Rickard, Tex, references to, **Supp. 5**, 359–60; **Supp. 6**, 700

Rickenbacker, Edward V., reference to, **Supp. 7**, 16
Rickets: prevention and cure, **Supp. 1**, 398; studles in, **Vol. 5, Part 1**, 314; vitamin D for, **Supp. 5**, 623
Ricketts, Edward F., references to, **Supp. 8**, 625, 626
Ricketts, Howard Taylor, references to, **Supp. 3**, 832; **Supp. 6**, 697
Rickey, Branch: first black major league baseball player signed, **Supp. 9**, 668–69; references to, **Supp. 9**, 729, 730, 857; **Supp. 10**, 573
Ridder, Victor, reference to, **Supp. 9**, 660
Ridgway, Erman J., reference to, **Supp. 7**, 320
Ridgway, Matthew B., references to, **Supp. 7**, 53, 492; **Supp. 8**, 157
Riehl, Alois, reference to, **Supp. 8**, 435
Riemann, Georg Friedrich Bernhard, reference to, **Supp. 7**, 216
Riemann mapping theorem, **Supp. 3**, 575
Rifle: invention and manufacture, **Vol. 1, Part 1**, 325, 550; **Vol. 1, Part 2**, 209; **Vol. 5, Part 1**, 247, 286; **Vol. 5, Part 2**, 460; **Vol. 6, Part 1**, 51; **Vol. 7, Part 1**, 561; **Vol. 8, Part 1**, 101, 496; **Vol. 8, Part 2**, 2; **Vol. 9, Part 1**, 447; **Vol. 10, Part 2**, 379
Rigdon, Sidney, reference to, **Vol. 9, Part 1**, 311; **Vol. 4, Part 2**, 334
Riggs, John Mankey, reference to, **Vol. 10, Part 1**, 640 f.
Rights of Man, **Vol. 5, Part 2**, 24; **Vol. 7, Part 2**, 162 f.
Rigney, Dorothy Comiskey, reference to, **Supp. 6**, 121
Rigney, John, reference to, **Supp. 6**, 121
Rig-Veda Repetitions, **Vol. 1, Part 2**, 387
Riis, Jacob, reference to, **Supp. 8**, 534
Riley, Charles V., reference to, **Vol. 10, Part 1**, 388 f.
Riley, James Whitcomb, reference to, **Vol. 7, Part 1**, 599 f.
Rimsky-Korsakov, Nikolai, reference to, **Supp. 9**, 775, 776
Rinehart, Frederick, references to, **Supp. 8**, 535, 536
Rinehart, Mary Roberts, references to, **Supp. 6**, 171–72, 309; **Supp. 8**, 535; **Supp. 9**, 276
Rinehart, Stanley, reference to, **Supp. 6**, 172
Rinehart and Co., **Supp. 6**, 543; founding of, **Supp. 8**, 536
Ringgold Gap, Ga., action at. *See* Chattanooga-Ringgold campaign (1863)
Ring of Freedom, founding of, **Supp. 7**, 740
Ringling Brothers–Barnum and Bailey Circus, **Supp. 6**, 8, 112; **Supp. 7**, 41, 42; **Supp. 10**, 406, 407, 809, 810
Riordan, Patrick, reference to, **Supp. 3**, 325
Riots: antiabolitionist, **Vol. 3, Part 2**, 311; draft (1863), **Vol. 4, Part 1**, 47, 238; **Vol. 10, Part 1**, 145; military suppression of, **Vol. 8, Part 2**, 219; New Orleans (1872–74), **Vol. 4, Part 2**, 450; Stamp Act, **Vol. 3, Part 1**, 465 f.; **Vol. 5, Part 2**, 138; theater, **Vol. 3, Part 2**, 530; *See also* Riots, labor
Riots, labor: Coeur d'Alene (1892–99), **Vol. 2, Part 2**, 145; **Vol. 3, Part 1**, 45; **Vol. 4, Part 2**, 419; **Vol. 5, Part 1**, 507; **Vol. 8, Part 2**, 263; Haymarket (1886), **Vol. 1, Part 1**, 231; Homestead (1892), **Vol. 2, Part 1**, 502; **Vol. 4, Part 1**, 30; Pullman (1894), **Vol. 1, Part 1**, 231; **Vol. 2, Part 2**, 211; **Vol. 3, Part 1**, 183; **Vol. 6, Part 2**, 615; **Vol. 7, Part 2**, 32, 264 f.; railroad (1877), **Vol. 4, Part 2**, 368, 450
Ripley, William Z., reference to, **Supp. 6**, 572
"Ripley's Believe It or Not!", **Supp. 4**, 693
Rise of American Civilization, The, **Supp. 4**, 62, 63; **Supp. 6**, 41
Rise of David Levinsky, The, **Supp. 5**, 96
Rise of the City, The, **Supp. 7**, 676
Rise of the Dutch Republic, The, **Vol. 7, Part 1**, 284
Ritchey, George W., reference to, **Supp. 3**, 208
Ritchie, Albert C., reference to, **Supp. 3**, 12
Ritchie, Thomas, reference to, **Vol. 8, Part 1**, 7 f.
Rite of Spring, The, **Supp. 9**, 776
Rittenberg, David, reference to, **Supp. 5**, 693
Ritter, William Emerson, references to, **Supp. 3**, 752; **Supp. 4**, 460; **Supp. 8**, 119
Ritz-Carlton Hotel (New York City), **Supp. 6**, 164–65; **Supp. 7**, 48
Riva-Rocci sphygmomanometer, **Supp. 3**, 201
Rivera, Diego, reference to, **Supp. 8**, 586; **Supp. 10**, 685, 849
Riverboats. *See* Ships
River Rouge Ford Plant (Dearborn, Mich.), **Supp. 4**, 300
Rivers, L. Mendel, reference to, **Supp. 10**, 326
Rivers: control of, **Vol. 3, Part 1**, 587 f.; **Vol. 3, Part 2**, 87, 179, 192; **Vol. 7, Part 1**, 617; navigation of, **Supp. 1**, 658. *See also* Mississippi River; Dams
Riverside Church (New York City): endowment, **Supp. 6**, 548; founding of, **Supp. 8**, 183–84; organ music, **Supp. 10**, 254
Riverside Press, **Vol. 5, Part 1**, 256; **Vol. 8, Part 2**, 522
Rives, Hallie Erminie, references to, **Supp. 6**, 686, 687
Rives, William C., reference to, **Vol. 10, Part 1**, go
RKO Pictures: founding of, **Supp. 8**, 320; Hughes-era productions, **Supp. 10**, 356; productions, **Supp. 9**, 761–62; "Tarzan" movies, **Supp. 9**, 65
RNA, link to viral activity, **Supp. 9**, 754
Roach, Hal: references to, **Supp. 6**, 276; **Supp. 7**, 463; **Supp. 9**, 508; studios, **Supp. 9**, 766
"Road agents" of Far West, **Vol. 8, Part 2**, 337
Road building: **Vol. 1, Part 1**, 577; **Vol. 4, Part 1**, 59; **Vol. 5, Part 2**, 467; **Vol. 6, Part 2**, 485; **Vol. 8, Part 1**, 74 f., 641; **Vol. 8, Part 2**, 567; **Vol. 9, Part 1**, 485; **Vol. 10, Part 2**, 260; asphalt, use of, **Vol. 1, Part 1**, 586; **Vol. 10, Part 1**, 471 f.; **Supp. 1**, 255; Connecticut highway system, **Supp. 4**, 197; Delaware, **Supp. 1**, 272; gasoline tax for, **Supp. 1**, 671; interstate highway proponents, **Supp. 6**, 507; **Supp. 9**, 373; Ledo and Burma roads, **Supp. 6**, 508; macadam, use of, **Vol. 4, Part 2**, 61; **Vol. 8, Part 1**, 74 f., 442; New Mexico, **Supp. 1**, 671; New York City, **Supp. 1**, 136; rural areas, **Supp. 4**, 665; urban expressways, **Supp. 6**, 115
Road to Xanadu, The, **Supp. 3**, 475
Roan, Henry, reference to, **Supp. 5**, 566
Roanoke, Va., settlement, **Vol. 3, Part 1**, 73 f.; **Vol. 5, Part 2**, 581
Roanoke Island affair, **Vol. 1, Part 2**, 183
Robards, Jason, Jr., reference to, **Supp. 5**, 525
Robards, Rachel, reference to, **Vol. 5, Part 1**, 526 f.
Robb, Russell, reference to, **Supp. 3**, 746
Robber Barons, The: The Great American Capitalists, 1861–1901, **Supp. 10**, 395
Robe, The, **Supp. 5**, 182
Robert College (Turkey), **Vol. 4, Part 2**, 195; **Vol. 8, Part 2**, 1; **Vol. 10, Part 1**, 500 f.; **Supp. 4**, 319
Roberts, George Brooke, reference to, **Vol. 7, Part 1**, 355
Roberts, James M. ("Red"), reference to, **Supp. 5**, 458
Roberts, Kenneth, reference to, **Supp. 3**, 848
Roberts, Owen J., references to, **Supp. 4**, 407, 537; **Supp. 8**, 331
Robertson, Dennis H., reference to, **Supp. 10**, 382
Robertson, Frederick, reference to, **Vol. 7, Part 1**, 328
Robertson, Marion Gordon ("Pat"), reference to, **Supp. 9**, 664
Robertson, T. Brailsford, reference to, **Supp. 9**, 833
Robertson, Zue, reference to, **Supp. 9**, 598
Robert's Rules of Order Revised, **Supp. 1**, 631
Robeson, Paul, references to, **Supp. 3**, 418; **Supp. 5**, 490, 525; **Supp. 7**, 204, 319; **Supp. 8**, 696; **Supp. 9**, 848
Robin Hood (operetta), **Supp. 2**, 619

Robins, Elizabeth, reference to, **Supp. 5**, 578
Robins, Margaret Dreier, references to, **Supp. 3**, 355; **Supp. 4**, 106
Robins, Raymond, references to, **Supp. 3**, 457; **Supp. 7**, 320
Robins, W. A., reference to, **Supp. 9**, 255
Robinson, Bill ("Bojangles"), reference to, **Supp. 6**, 637; **Supp. 10**, 19, 20
Robinson, Boardman, reference to, **Supp. 8**, 173
Robinson, Edward, reference to, **Vol. 7, Part 1**, 547; **Supp. 4**, 290
Robinson, Edwin Arlington, references to, **Supp. 4**, 840, 841; **Supp. 5**, 231
Robinson, Frances, reference to, **Supp. 3**, 399
Robinson, Holton D., reference to, **Supp. 6**, 594
Robinson, Jackie, reference to, **Supp. 9**, 251, 840, 841; **Supp. 10**, 256, 279
Robinson, James Harvey, references to, **Supp. 4**, 62, 63, 587; **Supp. 8**, 50
Robinson, Joan, reference to, **Supp. 8**, 82
Robinson, John, reference to, **Vol. 7, Part 2**, 104 f.
Robinson, Joseph, references to, **Supp. 3**, 720; **Supp. 4**, 145; **Supp. 6**, 35; **Supp. 7**, 787; **Supp. 8**, 36
Robinson, Stuart, reference to, **Vol. 8, Part 2**, 60
Robinson-Patman Act (1936), **Supp. 5**, 27
Robischon, Ernest, reference to, **Supp. 8**, 440
Robison, Samuel, reference to, **Supp. 8**, 469
Roche, Josephine, reference to, **Supp. 9**, 789
Roche, Kevin, reference to, **Supp. 7**, 671
"Rochester" (fictional character), **Supp. 10**, 7–8
Rochester, Minn., Mayo Clinic, **Vol. 6, Part 2**, 467
Rochester, N.Y.: architecture, **Supp. 4**, 105; founding of, **Vol. 8, Part 2**, 64; Gannett in, **Supp. 6**, 226–27 history of, **Vol. 3, Part 1**, 48; park system, **Vol. 8, Part 1**, 157 f.; public service, **Vol. 7, Part 2**, 473; **Vol. 8, Part 1**, 393; as station for Underground Railroad, **Vol. 3, Part 1**, 117; water supply for, **Vol 8, Part 1**, 324 f.; **Vol. 8, Part 2**, 13
Rochester Academy of Science, **Supp. 3**, 40–41
Rochester Daily Advertiser, **Vol. 7, Part 2**, 52
Rochester Museum of Arts and Sciences, founding of, **Supp. 3**, 41
Rochester Theological Seminary, **Vol. 8, Part 2**, 43
Rochester Unemployment Benefit Plan, development of, **Supp. 10**, 249
Rock, John, references to, **Supp. 4**, 802; **Supp. 8**, 503
Rock, William T. ("Pop"), reference to, **Supp. 3**, 76
Rock and roll: **Supp. 7**, 267; Beatles, **Supp. 10**, 448–50; criticism favorable to, **Supp. 9**, 317; first commemorative postage stamp dedicated to singer of, **Supp. 10**, 650; first performer arrested on stage, **Supp. 9**, 564; groups, **Supp. 9**, 262, 563–64; **Supp. 10**, 648–50; heavy metal, **Supp. 8**, 252–53; singers, **Supp. 6**, 301–2; **Supp. 8**, 305–6; **Supp. 10**, 648–50
Rock drill, invention of, **Vol. 5, Part 1**, 472; **Vol. 6, Part 1**, 230; **Vol. 8, Part 1**, 343; **Vol. 8, Part 2**, 587
Rockefeller, Abby Aldrich, reference to, **Supp. 8**, 240; **Supp. 10**, 685
Rockefeller, David, reference to, **Supp. 9**, 844
Rockefeller, John D.: references to, **Vol. 3, Part 1**, 341 f.; **Vol. 3, Part 2**, 451; **Vol. 4, Part 2**, 287; **Vol. 5, Part 1**, 184; **Vol. 6, Part 2**, 572; **Vol. 8, Part 2**, 65; photograph of, **Supp. 3**, 296; references to, **Supp. 7**, 173; **Supp. 9**, 287, 288; **Supp. 10**, 685; writings on, **Supp. 3**, 762
Rockefeller, John D., Jr.: Metropolitan Museum concerts, **Supp. 6**, 426; oil interests, **Supp. 6**, 585, references to, **Supp. 6**, 208, 249, 562; **Supp. 8**, 183, 545; **Supp. 9**, 17, 670, 671, 883; **Supp. 10**, 682, 683, 685; UN site donation, **Supp. 10**, 686
Rockefeller, John D., III, China Medical Board, **Supp. 4**, 346
Rockefeller, John D., IV ("Jay"), reference to, **Supp. 10**, 683
Rockefeller, Laurance, reference to, **Supp. 9**, 659
Rockefeller, Laura Spelman, Memorial, **Supp. 6**, 559
Rockefeller, Martha Baird, Fund for Music, **Supp. 9**, 670
Rockefeller, Nelson: presidential bid (1960), **Supp. 9**, 524–25; presidential bid (1968), **Supp. 9**, 528; references to, **Supp. 8**, 126; **Supp. 9**, 82, 670–71, 845; **Supp. 10**, 251, 303, 683
Rockefeller Archive Center (North Tarrytown, N.Y.), **Supp. 9**, 671
Rockefeller Brothers Fund, **Supp. 10**, 687
Rockefeller Center (New York City): architecture of, **Supp. 1**, 430; **Supp. 5**, 134; chandelier, **Supp. 7**, 308; endowment, **Supp. 6**, 549; Rivera murals, **Supp. 8**, 586; **Supp. 10**, 685
Rockefeller Foundation: **Vol. 2, Part 1**, 378; **Vol. 4, Part 1**, 183; **Vol. 7, Part 2**, 355; **Vol. 10, Part 1**, 621 f.; administration, **Supp. 4**, 251; **Supp. 5**, 161; **Supp. 7**, 516; **Supp. 10**, 824–25; Chinese medical problems, **Supp. 4**, 346–47; Fatigue Laboratory, **Supp. 3**, 351; founding of, **Supp. 2**, 575; hookworm eradication, **Supp. 1**, 639; **Supp. 5**, 232; human sexual behavior research grants, **Supp. 6**, 252–53, 343, 344; International Health Division, **Supp. 3**, 324, **Supp. 5**, 605; **Supp. 6**, 249–50; **Supp. 7**, 247; Medical Education Division, **Supp. 3**, 244; **Supp. 6**, 252–53, 343; medical philanthropy, **Supp. 6**, 549; Natural Sciences Division, **Supp. 7**, 516; nursing program, **Supp. 4**, 65; postdoctoral fellowships, **Supp. 5**, 495–96; presidency, **Supp. 3**, 794; **Supp. 9**, 288; **Supp. 10**, 420; public opinion research, **Supp. 8**, 69; refugee scholar fellowship, **Supp. 10**, 13; rural life study, **Supp. 5**, 320–21; university research focus, **Supp. 10**, 684; war relief, **Supp. 1**, 640
Rockfeller Institute for Medical Research: **Supp. 3**, 61, 5 140–41, 774; **Supp. 4**, 34, 573–74, 615–16, 643; **Supp. 6**, 117, 249; **Supp. 7**, 281, 591; **Supp. 10**, 695; bacteriological studies, **Supp. 9**, 530–31; cancer studies, **Supp. 8**, 555–56; directors, **Supp. 4**, 287; enzyme studies, **Supp. 10**, 426–27; first woman member, **Supp. 5**, 600; founding of, **Supp. 2**, 574; genetics studies, **Supp. 9**, 794; immunology studies, **Supp. 3**, 441–42; **Supp. 4**, 380–81; molecular studies, **Supp. 9**, 550; plant pathology studies, **Supp. 9**, 753; typhus epidemic, **Supp. 4**, 803; viral disease research, **Supp. 7**, 648, 649. *See also* Rockefeller University
Rockefeller Plaza (New York City), sculpture, **Supp. 8**, 414
Rockefeller Sanitary Commission, hookworm disease control, **Supp. 3**, 738
Rockefeller University: **Supp. 9**, 225; advanced study and research programs, **Supp. 9**, 125; founding of, **Supp. 6**, 549
Rockets: jet-assisted airplane takeoff, **Supp. 7**, 411 liquid-fuel, **Supp. 3**, 306–8; **Supp. 10**, 65–66; propulsion theory, **Supp. 3**, 305–8; Saturn launch vehicles developed, **Supp. 10**, 66–67; V-2 developed, **Supp. 10**, 66; writings on, **Supp. 8**, 379–80. *See also* Aerodynamics; Jet propulsion; Missiles; Space exploration
Rockford College, founding of, **Vol. 9, Part 1**, 158
Rock Hill College, **Vol. 1, Part 1**, 254
Rock Island Railroad, **Vol. 5, Part 2**, 231; **Vol. 7, Part 1**, 144; **Vol. 9, Part 1**, 59
Rockne, Knute, references to, **Supp. 7**, 729; **Supp. 9**, 484, 485; **Supp. 10**, 584, 726
Rocks: crystalline, **Supp. 3**, 38; igneous, **Supp. 6**, 70–71, 145, 153. *See also* Geology
Rockwell Spring and Axle Co., **Supp. 10**, 691, 692

Rocky Mountain Fuel Co., **Supp. 10**, 681
Rocky Mountain National Park, creation of, **Supp. 1**, 555
Rocky Mountain News, **Vol. 7, Part 2**, 309
Rocky Mountains: biology studies, **Supp. 8**, 486; biota catalogue, **Supp. 4**, 167; exploration, **Vol. 5, Part 1**, 576; **Vol. 7, Part 1**, 81, 319; **Vol. 8, Part 1**, 250 f.; geological mapping, **Supp. 4**, 194; physiographic studies of, **Supp. 4**, 32, 33
Rocky Mountain spotted fever, **Supp. 1**, 628; **Supp. 3**, 832; **Supp. 6**, 697
Rodebusch, W. H., reference to, **Supp. 5**, 413
Rodgers, Richard: Hammerstein collaboration, **Supp. 6**, 273–74; **Supp. 10**, 694–95; Hart collaboration, **Supp. 3**, 338–39; **Supp. 10**, 693–94; references to, **Supp. 8**, 238–39, 481, 547
Rodin, Auguste, references to, **Supp. 3**, 88; **Supp. 7**, 530, 531; **Supp. 9**, 501, 759
Roe, E. P., reference to, **Vol. 5, Part 1**, 168
Roe, Tommy, reference to, **Supp. 6**, 302
Roe Indian Institute, founding of, **Supp. 4**, 165
Roentgen rays. *See* Radiology; X rays
Roeth, Natalie, reference to, **Supp. 6**, 342
Roethke, Theodore, reference to, **Supp. 10**, 854
"Rogerenes," religious sect, **Vol. 8, Part 2**, 101
"Rogers, Buck" (fictional character), **Supp. 6**, 165–66
Rogers, Harry, reference to, **Supp. 6**, 477
Rogers, James Gamble, reference to, **Supp. 4**, 22
Rogers, James Grafton, reference to, **Supp. 7**, 91
Rogers, John T., reference to, **Supp. 3**, 92
Rogers, Roy, references to, **Supp. 8**, 248, 712
Rogers, Will: Memorial Stadium, financing, **Supp. 2**, 525; reference to, **Supp. 9**, 82
Rogers, Will, Jr., reference to, **Supp. 9**, 467
Rogers Act (1924), **Supp. 3**, 139; **Supp. 4**, 898; **Supp. 6**, 207; **Supp. 7**, 303
Rogers and Butler, **Supp. 4**, 697
Rogers-Kennedy War Memorial (Worcester), **Supp. 6**, 597
Roger Williams University, presidency of, **Vol. 7, Part 1**, 43
Rogoff, J. M., reference to, **Supp. 3**, 134–35
Rogues of Rhythm, **Supp. 7**, 131
Rohatyn, Felix, reference to, **Supp. 10**, 534
Rolaids, **Supp. 10**, 624
Role theory, **Supp. 3**, 579
Rolfe, John, husband of Pocahontas, **Vol. 1, Part 1**, 345
Rolfing (physical therapy method), **Supp. 10**, 696
Rolland, Romain, reference to, **Supp. 6**, 62
Roller bearings, inventions concerning, **Vol. 5, Part 1**, 448; **Vol. 8, Part 2**, 56; **Vol. 9, Part 2**, 555
Rolling Stone (magazine), **Supp. 9**, 316
Rolling Stones (music group), Sullivan show appearance, **Supp. 9**, 780
Rollins College, presidency, **Supp. 5**, 308–9
Rollo series, **Vol. 1, Part 1**, 22
Rölvaag, O. E., reference to, **Supp. 4**, 172
Roman, Charles P., reference to, **Supp. 9**, 52
Roman Catholic church. *See* Catholic church
Romance literature and languages; **Supp. 3**, 21–22; studies in, **Supp. 10**, 627. *See also specific languages*
Romance novels, **Supp. 8**, 296–97, 471–72; **Supp. 10**, 20–21
Roman Empire: ancient coins collection, **Supp. 3**, 551; archaeology, **Supp. 2**, 677; classical studios, **Supp. 1**, 657, 701; **Supp. 3**, 571, 617–18; **Supp. 7**, 313–14, 388; historical studies, **Supp. 2**, 204, 433; historical writings on, **Supp. 5**, 595–96; scholarship on, **Supp. 8**, 236; slavery in, **Supp. 5**, 736
Romanoff's (restaurant), founding of, **Supp. 9**, 673
Romantic Review, founding of, **Vol. 9, Part 2**, 571
Rome, Ala., iron manufacture, **Vol. 7, Part 1**, 540
Rome and China, **Supp. 4**, 824
Romney, George, reference to, **Supp. 10**, 1
Ronne, Finn, reference to, **Supp. 7**, 217
Rooney, Mickey, references to, **Supp. 7**, 247; **Supp. 8**, 204
Rooney and Bent (dance team), **Supp. 7**, 657–58
Roos, Victor, reference to, **Supp. 6**, 51
Roosevelt, Alice Lee, reference to, **Vol. 6, Part 1**, 395
Roosevelt, Archibald, reference to, **Supp. 3**, 669
Roosevelt, Eleanor: **Supp. 5**, 453; references to, **Supp. 6**, 10, 509; **Supp. 7**, 718, 787; **Supp. 8**, 25, 498, 614, 696; **Supp. 9**, 26; **Supp. 10**, 209, 214, 680; Roosevelt, F. D., relationship, **Supp. 3**, 641–45, 647, 656, 664; Thompson, M., relationship, **Supp. 5**, 682
Roosevelt, Franklin D.: Asian policy, **Supp. 6**, 269–70; assassination attempt, **Supp. 1**, 160; Astor, W. V., relationship, **Supp. 6**, 23; banking crisis, **Supp. 6**, 34; **Supp. 9**, 17, 208; Barkley relationship, **Supp. 6**, 35–36; Baruch relationship, **Supp. 7**, 36; bipartisanship, **Supp. 3**, 425–26; Bullitt relationship, **Supp. 8**, 61–62; Burlingham relationship, **Supp. 6**, 88; Byrd, R., relationship, **Supp. 6**, 93; Byrnes relationship, **Supp. 9**, 150–51; Carlson relationship, **Supp. 4**, 146; China policy, **Supp. 6**, 230–31; Civilian Conservation Corps, **Supp. 6**, 411–12; Clark relationship, **Supp. 5**, 114; Cohan portrayal of, **Supp. 3**, 174; congressional relations, **Supp. 3**, 335; **Supp. 9**, 129–30, 860; Coughlin relationship, **Supp. 10**, 151–52; criticism of, **Supp. 10**, 465; Curley relationship, **Supp. 6**, 140; Daniels relationship, **Supp. 4**, 217; Davies, J. E., relationship, **Supp. 6**, 147; discriminatory hiring practices, executive order ending, **Supp. 10**, 660; doctors attending, **Supp. 6**, 131, 413–14; Douglas, W. O., relationship, **Supp. 10**, 188; economic advisers, **Supp. 9**, 661; **Supp. 10**, 205; economic policy, first term, **Supp. 9**, 554; economic warfare, **Supp. 9**, 209; Edison, C., relationship, **Supp. 8**, 152; Farley relationship, **Supp. 10**, 233; first nominee to Supreme Court, **Supp. 9**, 95; Flynn relationship, **Supp. 5**, 227–28; foreign policy, **Supp. 3**, 219; **Supp. 5**, 332–35; **Supp. 7**, 303; foreign policy, Republican support for, **Supp. 10**, 56; fourth-term running-mate decision, **Supp. 4**, 356; Frankfurter relationship, **Supp. 7**, 262–63; Garner relationship, **Supp. 8**, 207; George, W. F., relationship, **Supp. 6**, 234–35; gubernatorial campaign (1928), **Supp. 9**, 680; Holocaust policies, **Supp. 4**, 906; Hopkins relationship, **Supp. 4**, 392–93; Howe relationship, **Supp. 2**, 328; Jackson relationship, **Supp. 5**, 357; Johnson, H., relationship, **Supp. 3**, 397–98; Jones, J., relationship, **Supp. 6**, 325; Kennedy, J. P., relationship, **Supp. 8**, 320; labor relations, **Supp. 4**, 376; **Supp. 5**, 510, 691; **Supp. 8**, 376; Latin American policy, **Supp. 7, 777**; Leahy relationship, **Supp. 6**, 373, 374; Lehman relationship, **Supp. 7**, 467; Long, B., relationship, **Supp. 6**, 388–89; Marshall, G. C., relationship, **Supp. 6**, 430–31; Missouri Senate race (1940), **Supp. 9**, 757; monetary policy, **Supp. 9**, 7, 661; Morgenthau relationship, **Supp. 8**, 445–46; Navy secretary, **Supp. 4**, 820; **Supp. 10**, 371; Norris relationship, **Supp. 3**, 560, 561; Nye criticism of, **Supp. 9**, 591; official library, **Supp. 4**, 176; OSS founding, **Supp. 6**, 170; Pearl Harbor controversy, **Supp. 6**, 629; Pendergast machine, **Supp. 3**, 597; Perkins relationship, **Supp. 7**, 608–10, personal attacks on, **Supp. 5**, 396; polio fund-raising, **Supp. 6**, 90; political advisers, **Supp. 9**, 84, 85, 680–81; **Supp. 10**, 221; political vulnerability after 1936 election, **Supp. 9**, 230; presidentlal candidacies, **Supp. 2**, 329; **Supp. 7**, 274; **Supp. 9**, 84, 230; **Supp. 10**, 233–34; **Supp. 8**, 207; press relations, **Supp. 4**, 644; **Supp. 7**, 249–50; **Supp. 8**, 395,

498; press secretary, **Supp. 5**, 196–97, public health concerns, **Supp. 9**, 226; references to, **Supp. 9**, 534; **Supp. 10**, 249, 365, 393, 394; Ryan relationship, **Supp. 3**, 681; Smith relationship, **Supp. 3**, 720, 721; Schneiderman relationship, **Supp. 9**, 706; secret diplomacy, World War II, **Supp. 10**, 571–72; speechwriters, **Supp. 5**, 624; **Supp. 7**, 345; Spellman relationship, **Supp. 8**, 613; Stark relationship, **Supp. 9**, 755; support for, **Supp. 9**, 859; Supreme Court packing move, **Supp. 3**, 100, 168, 227; **Supp. 4**, 407, 491, 537–38; **Supp. 5**, 357, 443, 481; **Supp. 6**, 137–38, 227; **Supp. 7**, 263, 541, 730; **Supp. 9**, 129, 151, 311, 611, 681, 810, 859; **Supp. 10**, 188; Tammany Hall, **Supp. 6**, 142; tax policy, **Supp. 6**, 559; Taylor, M. C., relationship, **Supp. 6**, 623; third-term, **Supp. 5**, 515; **Supp. 6**, 260; Truman as vice-presidential choice (1944), **Supp. 10**, 226; vice-presidential candidacy, **Supp. 6**, 129; Wallace relationship, **Supp. 7**, 761, 762; Wehle relationship, **Supp. 6**, 677–78; wife and family, **Supp. 7**, 658–61; Willkie relationship, **Supp. 3**, 829–30; Winchell relationship, **Supp. 9**, 886; women in administration, **Supp. 6**, 4. *See also* New Deal

Roosevelt, Kermit, reference to, **Supp. 3**, 669

Roosevelt, Nicholas J., reference to, **Vol. 9, Part 1**, 614

Roosevelt, Quentin, memorial design, **Supp. 3**, 199

Roosevelt, Sara Delano, references to, **Supp. 5**, 708; **Supp. 7**, 658–59

Roosevelt, Theodore: **Vol. 4, Part 2**, 334; **Vol. 5, Part 1**, 75; **Vol. 6, Part 1**, 347, 348, 609 f.; **Vol. 6, Part 2**, 587; **Vol. 7, Part 1**, 179; **Vol. 8, Part 1**, 2, 4; **Vol. 9, Part 1**, 44, 466; **Vol. 9, Part 2**, 268, 363, 548; Aldrich, Allison and Platt, relations with, **Vol. 1, Part 1**, 155, 221; bibliography of, **Supp. 8**, 664; "big stick," **Vol. 8, Part 2**, 139; biography of, **Supp. 4**, 491; **Supp. 6**, 521; Bonaparte, Charles Joseph, relations with, **Vol. 1, Part 2**, 427; Butler relationship, **Supp. 4**, 135; cartoons depicting, **Supp. 7**, 164; conservation policies, **Vol. 2, Part 2**, 145; **Vol. 7, Part 1**, 316; **Supp. 2**, 265; **Supp. 4**, 664–66; family, **Supp. 3**, 199, 667–69; **Supp. 7**, 658; **Supp. 10**, 464–65; Garfield, J. R., relationship, **Supp. 4**, 317; Gilson relationship, **Supp. 1**, 333; Hart relationship, **Supp. 3**, 336, 337; Hay, John, relationship, **Vol. 4, Part 2**, 435 f.; Hill, E. C., relationship, **Supp. 6**, 291; idealization of, **Supp. 7**, 311; influence of, **Supp. 6**, 85; Johnson, H. W., relationship, **Supp. 3**, 395; Library of Congress archives, **Supp. 3**, 285; muckraking statement, **Supp. 4**, 46–47; political opposition to, **Vol. 8, Part 1**, 416; presidential candidacy, **Supp. 5**, 303; presidential library, **Supp. 7**, 311; reference to, **Supp. 9**, 825; **Supp. 10**, 302; Robins relationship, **Supp. 5**, 579; Robinson, E. A., poetry, **Supp. 1**, 633; Roosevelt, F. D., relationship, **Supp. 3**, 641, 642; Root relationship, **Supp. 2**, 578–81; "Rough Riders," organization of, **Vol. 8, Part 2**, 137; **Supp. 6**, 206; St. Gaudens, Augustus, relationship, **Vol. 8, Part 2**, 301; sculpture of, **Supp. 5**, 89; Taft, W. H., relationship, **Vol. 8, Part 2**, 141 f.; **Vol. 9, Part 2**, 270; **Supp. 2**, 581, 582; **Supp. 5**, 707–8; "Teddy Bear" inception, **Supp. 4**, 76; western policy, **Vol. 8, Part 2**, 141; White, W. A., relationship, **Supp. 3**, 816; Wood, Leonard, relationship, **Vol. 10, Part 2**, 467 f.; World War I cavalry proposal, **Supp. 10**, 489; writings on, **Supp. 7**, 311

Roosevelt, Theodore, Jr., reference to, **Supp. 3**, 667

Roosevelt Business and Professional League, founding of, **Supp. 2**, 636

Roosevelt Dam, **Supp. 2**, 304

Roosevelt Grill (New York City), **Supp. 10**, 463

Roosevelt Hospital (New York City), allergy clinic, **Supp. 6**, 123

Roosevelt Memorial Association, **Vol. 9, Part 2**, 477

Roosevelt University (Chicago), founding of, **Supp. 6**, 202

Root, Elihu: mission to Russia, **Vol. 3, Part 1**, 510; references to, **Vol. 8, Part 1**, 2 f.; **Supp. 3**, 98, 700; **Supp. 4**, 784, 785; **Supp. 5**, 286

Root beer, **Supp. 2**, 306; **Supp. 10**, 338, 339

Root, Clark, Howland and Ballantine (law firm), **Supp. 6**, 33

Rope making, **Vol. 4, Part 1**, 377; **Vol. 9, Part 1**, 62; **Vol. 9, Part 2**, 632

Roper Research Associates, founding of, **Supp. 9**, 677

Roraback, J. Henry, reference to, **Supp. 6**, 59

"Rosary, The," **Vol. 7, Part 1**, 441

Rose, Billy, reference to, **Supp. 5**, 87

Rose, Billy, Foundation, founding of, **Supp. 8**, 548

Rose, Fred, reference to, **Supp. 5**, 748

Rose, Margo, reference to, **Supp. 3**, 685

Rose, Mary Swartz, reference to, **Supp. 3**, 677

Rose, Rufus, reference to, **Supp. 3**, 685

Rosecrans, Gen. William, reference to, **Vol. 9, Part 1**, 363

Roseland Ballroom (New York City), **Supp. 5**, 292, 293

Rosenbach Co., **Supp. 5**, 586–87

Rosenberg, Ethel, references to, **Supp. 7**, 52, 204; **Supp. 9**, 321–22; **Supp. 10**, 719

Rosenberg, Julius, references to, **Supp. 7**, 52, 204; **Supp. 9**, 321–22; **Supp. 10**, 719

Rosenberg, Léonce, reference to, **Supp. 9**, 502

Rosenblatt, Gertrude Goldsmith, reference to, **Supp. 8**, 549

Rosenblueth, Arturo, references to, **Supp. 3**, 136, 137

Rosenbusch, Harry, reference to, **Supp. 6**, 70

Rosenfeld, Paul, reference to, **Supp. 3**, 14

Rosenkavalier, Der, **Supp. 10**, 444, 446

Rosenman, Samuel I., reference to, **Supp. 3**, 645

Rosenthal, Herman, reference to, **Supp. 4**, 885–86

Rosenwald, Julius, references to, **Vol. 8, Part 2**, 540; **Supp. 3**, 403; **Supp. 8**, 705

Rosenwald, Julius, Fund, **Supp. 4**, 251; **Supp. 6**, 11, 12, 321

Rosenwald, Lessing J., reference to, **Supp. 5**, 586

Roses, growing of, **Supp. 4**, 194–95, 523; **Supp. 5**, 555

Rosetta Stone, translation of, **Vol. 7, Part 1**, 254–55

Rosine Association, founding of, **Vol. 9, Part 2**, 620

Rosminian Order, **Vol. 3, Part 1**, 96

Ross, Barnaby (Manfred B. Lee and Frederic Dannay pseudonym), **Supp. 9**, 487

Ross, Charles G., reference to, **Supp. 3**, 92

Ross, Edward A., references to, **Vol. 5, Part 1**, 277; **Supp. 3**, 248

Ross, Harold, references to, **Supp. 5**, 464; **Supp. 6**, 236, 287; **Supp. 7**, 2, 473–74, 743; **Supp. 8**, 447, 491; **Supp. 9**, 335; **Supp. 10**, 147, 246, 247

Ross, Robert, reference to, **Supp. 6**, 194

Ross, T. J., and Associates, **Supp. 9**, 681

Ross election bill, **Vol. 3, Part 1**, 467 f.

Rossville, Ga., operation at. *See* Chickamaugua campaign

Rosta (Russian news agency), **Supp. 9**, 89

Rostovtzeff, Michael, reference to, **Supp. 5**, 736

Rotary International, founding of, **Supp. 4**, 362; **Supp. 9**, 391, 393

Rotch, Arthur, reference to, **Supp. 3**, 195

Roth, Rose, reference to, **Supp. 6**, 100–101

Roth, Rudolf, reference to, **Supp. 3**, 444

Rothacker, Watterson, reference to, **Supp. 7**, 579–80

Rothafel, Samuel L. ("Roxy"), **Supp. 9**, 850

Rothko, Mark, references to, **Supp. 8**, 467; **Supp. 10**, 758

Rothschild, L. F., brokerage house, **Supp. 6**, 305

Roth v. *United States*, **Supp. 9**, 683
"Rough Riders," organization of, **Vol. 8, Part 2**, 137
Round Hill School, **Vol, 1, Part 1**, 565
Rous, Peyton, references to, **Supp. 4**, 615, 616
Rousseau, Jean-Jacques, writings on, **Supp. 3**, 691
Routh, Joseph I., reference to, **Supp. 10**, 624
Rover Boy's Series, **Vol. 9, Part 2**, 125
Rowing, **Vol. 2, Part 2**, 377 f., 469; **Vol. 7, Part 2**, 602; **Supp. 6**, 331
Rowland, Clarence ("Pants"), **Supp. 8**, 713
Rowland, Henry A., references to, **Supp. 3**, 11, 291
Rowlett, Frank, reference to, **Supp. 8**, 196
Rowohlt, Ernst, Publishing House, **Supp. 7**, 798
Roxas, Manuel, reference to, **Supp. 3**, 614
Roxbury, Mass.: early history of, **Vol. 3, Part 1**, 430; first factory-made watches produced in, **Vol. 3, Part 1**, 239
Roxbury Tammany Club (Boston), **Supp. 6**, 139
Royal American Regiment, **Vol. 1, Part 2**, 480
Royal and Ancient Golf Club of St. Andrews, first American captain, **Supp. 8**, 487
Royal Canadians (dance band), **Supp. 10**, 463, 464
Royal Commission on London Traffic, **Vol. 7, Part 2**, 277
Royal Geographical Society of London, **Vol. 5, Part 2**, 561
Royalist gazettes, Revolutionary period, **Vol. 8, Part 2**, 24
Royal Navy, **Supp. 10**, 835
Royal Society, one of few Americans elected to, **Vol. 3, Part 1**, 483
Royce, Josiah, references to, **Vol. 5, Part 1**, 311, 594; **Vol. 9, Part 1**, 410; **Supp. 1**, 150; **Supp. 3**, 608; **Supp. 6**, 504, 505; **Supp. 7**, 471, 481; **Supp. 8**, 265, 266
Roycroft Shop, **Vol. 5, Part 1**, 323
Royle, Selena, reference to, **Supp. 4**, 187
Rozelle, Pete, reference to, **Supp. 9**, 646
Ruark, Robert, reference to, **Supp. 5**, 439
Rubber: importation of, **Supp. 1**, 305; litigation over patents, **Vol. 3, Part 1**, 159, 288; manufacture, **Vol. 2, Part 1**, 470; **Vol. 4, Part 1**, 396, 413; **Vol. 4, Part 2**, 465, 466; **Vol. 5, Part 1**, 290; production, **Supp. 9**, 283; synthetic, **Supp. 2**, 97, 489, 505; **Supp. 3**, 239, 522; **Supp. 5**, 191, 273, 366; **Supp. 6**, 334; **Supp. 7**, 169; **Supp. 8**, 123; **Supp. 9**, 284, 311; **Supp. 10**, 144; tire production, **Supp. 5**, 617–18, 380; vulcanization, **Vol. 3, Part 1**, 25, 288; **Vol. 4, Part 1**, 413 f.; **Supp. 2**, 505; **Supp. 3**, 522; World War II measures, **Supp. 7**, 36
Rubin, Robert, reference to, **Supp. 8**, 576
Rubin, S., reference to, **Supp. 5**, 273
Rubinow, Isaac M., reference to, **Supp. 3**, 255, 256
Rubinstein, Helena, references to, **Supp. 4**, 619; **Supp. 8**, 13
Rubin test, **Supp. 6**, 555
Ruby, Jack, references to, **Supp. 7**, 434, 594
Rudge, Olga, reference to, **Supp. 9**, 618, 619
Ruef, Abraham, references to, **Supp. 3**, 126, 394; **Supp. 6**, 590
Ruesch, Jurgen, reference to, **Supp. 10**, 28
Ruffin, Thomas, references to, **Vol. 5, Part 1**, 179; **Vol. 7, Part 1**, 388
Ruge-de-Forest Co., founding of, **Supp. 3**, 220
Rugg, Harold, reference to, **Supp. 4**, 139, 140
Rum and sugar, exchange of, for lumber, **Vol. 3, Part 1**, 252
Rumford Press, **Vol. 8, Part 2**, 183
Rummel, Joseph, reference to, **Supp. 8**, 500
Rumseian Society, **Vol. 8, Part 2**, 223
Rumsey, James, reference to, **Vol. 9, Part 1**, 614
Rumsey, John W., reference to, **Supp. 9**, 375
Runyon, Damon, references to, **Supp. 8**, 386, 565; **Supp. 9**, 187, 886
Rupp, Adolph, reference to, **Supp. 9**, 21
Ruppert, Jacob, reference to, **Supp. 5**, 40–41
Rural areas: electrification, **Supp. 8**, 700; **Supp. 10**, 218–19; 4–H clubs, **Supp. 5**, 51; Model T car's popularity in, **Supp. 4**, 295–97; movements to, **Supp. 1**, 145; population shifts from, **Supp. 4**, 45; road building in, **Supp. 4**, 665; sociological studies of, **Supp. 2**, 727; **Supp. 3**, 683–84; **Supp. 4**, 312; **Supp. 5**, 320–21; sociology of, **Supp. 3**, 683–84; value preservation studies, **Supp. 5**, 31; youth vocational guidance in, **Supp. 4**, 365–6
Rural Electrification Act (1936), **Supp. 7**, 635
Rural Electrification Administration: **Supp. 3**, 560; **Supp. 6**, 122, 526; **Supp. 7**, 788; **Supp. 8**, 700; establishment of, **Supp. 2**, 584; **Supp. 10**, 218
Rural free delivery (RFD), **Vol. 4, Part 2**, 490; **Vol. 7, Part 2**, 313; **Vol. 9, Part 1**, 456; **Vol. 10, Part 1**, 549
Rush, Benjamin, reference to, **Vol. 7, Part 2**, 109, 554
Rush-Bagot Agreement (1817), **Vol. 8, Part 2**, 232
Rush Medical College, **Vol. 1, Part 2**, 589; **Vol. 7, Part l**, 645
Rusk, Dean, reference to, **Supp. 4**, 688; **Supp. 7**, 420, 724
Ruskin, John, influence of, **Vol. 7, Part 1**, 116, 464
Ruskin College of Social Science, **Vol. 7, Part 2**, 266
Ruskin Hall (Oxford, England), **Supp. 4**, 61–62
Russell, Annie, reference to, **Supp. 3**, 804
Russell, Bertrand, references to, **Supp. 4**, 169, 879; **Supp. 5**, 173, 204, 271, 272; **Supp. 8**, 74, 75; **Supp. 10**, 282
Russell, Charles, references to, **Supp. 3**, 678; **Supp. 5**, 420
Russell, George, reference to, **Supp. 10**, 225
Russell, Harry L., reference to, **Supp. 7**, 630
Russell, Henry Norris, reference to, **Supp. 9**, 713; **Supp. 10**, 625
Russell, James E., references to, **Supp. 4**, 832; **Supp. 8**, 83–84
Russell, Jane, reference to, **Supp. 10**, 355
Russell, Richard, reference to, **Supp. 7**, 429; **Supp. 10**, 361
Russellites. *See* Jehovah's Witnesses
Russell Sage Foundation: **Vol. 8, Part 2**, 291; **Supp. 7**, 13; applied social research, **Supp. 4**, 35; child welfare, **Supp. 3**, 362; community center movement, **Supp. 3**, 600–601; Forest Hills Gardens, **Supp. 6**, 26; Lighthouse for the Blind, **Supp. 3**, 364–65; malnutrition and school feeding studies, **Supp. 6**, 81; projects of, **Supp. 4**, 333–34
Russell's Magazine, **Vol. 9, Part 2**, 558
Russia: Alaska, colonization of, **Vol. 5, Part 1**, 491; **Vol. 5, Part 2**, 515; **Vol. 8, Part 1**, 523 f.; Anglo-Russian agreement on Persia, **Supp. 6**, 579; archaeological studies in, **Supp. 5**, 595; pretenders to throne, **Supp. 9**, 673–74; settlement in California, **Vol. 5, Part 2**, 514 f.; diplomacy with, **Vol. 1, Part 1**, 85, 329; **Vol. 1, Part 2**, 417; **Vol. 3, Part 1**, 38, 510; **Vol. 3, Part 2**, 578; **Vol. 5, Part 1**, 1, 334; **Vol. 5, Part 2**, 331, 332; **Vol. 6, Part 1**, 424, 613; **Vol. 7, Part 2**, 560, 628; **Vol. 9, Part 1**, 11; **Vol. 9, Part 2**, 607, 635; railroad building, **Vol. 7, Part 2**, 263; **Vol. 8, Part 2**, 2; **Vol. 10, Part 2**, 372; trade treaties with, **Vol. 3, Part 1**, 53; **Vol. 4, Part 1**, 523; **Vol. 8, Part 1**, 363 f.; World War I propaganda, **Vol. 8, Part 1**, 451. *See also* Russian Revolution; Soviet Union
Russian-American Co., history of, **Vol. 8, Part 1**, 523 f.
Russian Ballet Company, **Supp. 3**, 282
Russian Church in America, **Vol. 9, Part 1**, 113
Russian colony in America, founding of, **Vol. 9, Part 1**, 67

Russian literature and language: Nabokov novels, **Supp. 10**, 581–82; translations, **Supp. 1**, 77, 256
Russian Orthodox Eastern Church of America, primates, **Supp. 7**, 468–69
Russian Revolution (1917): **Supp. 1**, 78; **Supp. 4**, 670; **Supp. 5**, 83, 579; **Supp. 7**, 705; refugee resettlement, **Supp. 4**, 890; **Supp. 10**, 581; U.S. Communist support for, **Supp. 5**, 135; writings on, **Supp. 5**, 499, 593
Russian State Party, The, **Supp. 7**, 244
Russo, Perry Raymond, reference to, **Supp. 9**, 715
Russo-American Telegraph Co., **Vol. 8, Part 1**, 75 f.
Russo-Japanese War, peace parley, **Vol. 9, Part 2**, 82
Rust, Mack, reference to, **Supp. 5**, 596
Rust fungi, **Supp. 3**, 23
Rustin, Bayard, reference to, **Supp. 10**, 660, 661
Rutgers University: **Vol. 2, Part 1**, 467; **Vol. 4, Part 1**, 17; **Vol. 4, Part 2**, 376; **Vol. 6, Part 2**, 619, **Vol. 7, Part 1**, 358–59; **Vol. 8, Part 2**, 486; agriculture studies, **Supp. 2**, 387; burning of; during Revolution, **Vol. 3, Part 1**, 274; early years of, **Vol. 6, Part 1**, 315; **Vol. 8, Part 1**, 42; first president of, **Vol. 4, Part 2**, 241; football team, **Supp. 10**, 676; name changed from Queen's College, **Vol. 8, Part 2**, 255; soil microbiology studies, **Supp. 9**, 833–34
Ruth, George Herman ("Babe"), references to, **Supp. 2**, 290; **Supp. 3**, 294–95; **Supp. 7**, 139; **Supp. 9**, 404; **Supp. 10**, 256, 257, 532
Rutherford, Ernest, references to, **Supp. 7**, 10, 133
Rutherfurd, Lewis M., reference to, **Supp. 3**, 692
Rutledge, Ann, reference to, **Vol. 6, Part 1**, 244; **Supp. 9**, 37
Rutledge, John, reference to, **Vol. 6, Part 1**, 523
Rutledge, Wiley, reference to, **Supp. 5**, 575
Ruttenberg, Harold, reference to, **Supp. 6**, 597
Ruzicka, Rudolph, reference to, **Supp. 3**, 785
Ryan, Benny, reference to, **Supp. 8**, 694
Ryan, Leo J., reference to, **Supp. 10**, 392
"Ryan crowd," Wall St. (1904), **Vol. 8, Part 2**, 266
Ryder, Albert Pinkham, reference to, **Supp. 5**, 492
Rye, Thomas C., reference to, **Supp. 3**, 449
Rye Beach, N.H., cable to Europe laid at, **Vol. 3, Part 1**, 600
Ryskind, Morrie, reference to, **Supp. 7**, 413

S

Saarinen, Eero, references to, **Supp. 4**, 715; **Supp. 10**, 124, 199–200
Saarinen, Eero, and Associates, **Supp. 7**, 671
Saarinen, Eliel, references to, **Supp. 5**, 399; **Supp. 7**, 670, 671, 672; **Supp. 10**, 199
Saarinen, Swanson and Associates, **Supp. 7**, 670; founding of, **Supp. 4**, 715
Sabbath, observance of, **Vol. 8, Part 1**, 428; **Vol. 8, Part 2**, 114; **Vol. 9, Part 2**, 299
Sabin, Joseph, references to, **Supp. 8**, 663, 664
Sabine, Wallace C., references to, **Supp. 3**, 524; **Supp. 5**, 441
Sabine Cross Roads, battle of, **Vol. 1, Part 1**, 579; **Vol. 2, Part 1**, 469; **Vol. 2, Part 2**, 105; **Vol. 5, Part 2**, 425; **Vol. 8, Part 1**, 380
Sabine expedition (1806), **Vol. 10, Part 2**, 225
Sabine Farm, **Vol. 3, Part 2**, 363
Saccharin, discovery of, **Vol. 8, Part 1**, 501; **Supp. 1**, 75
Sacco, Nicola. *See* Sacco-Vanzetti case
Sacco-Vanzetti case: **Vol. 8, Part 2**, 279; **Vol. 9, Part 2**, 128; **Supp. 3**, 54, 448; **Supp. 4**, 618; **Supp. 6**, 15, 88, 330; advisory committee on executive clemency, **Supp. 3**, 473; ballistics testimony, **Supp. 5**, 245; complete transcript publication, **Supp. 3**, 280; defense, **Supp. 5**, 280; **Supp. 7**, 248, 455; Frankfurter defense, **Supp. 7**, 262; influence of, **Supp. 9**, 875; legal defense, **Supp. 5**, 280, 515; **Supp. 8**, 456; opera on, **Supp. 7**, 616–2; paintings on, **Supp. 8**, 586; prosecution of, **Supp. 3**, 822; writings on, **Supp. 8**, 594; **Supp. 10**, 641
Sachs, Hanns, references to, **Supp. 5**, 315; **Supp. 6**, 220, 461
Sachs Collegiate Institute School (N.Y.), **Vol. 8, Part 2**, 280
Sackheim, Max, reference to, **Supp. 8**, 577
Sacks, Benjamin, reference to, **Supp. 4**, 494
Sacramento, battle of, **Vol. 4, Part 1**, 21; **Vol. 9, Part 1**, 215; **Vol. 4, Part 2**, 49, 224
Sacramento, Calif., founding of, **Vol. 1, Part 2**, 263
Sacre du Printemps, Le, **Supp. 7**, 548
Sacred Congregation for the Propagation of the Faith, **Supp. 6**, 608
Saddle manufacture, **Vol. 6, Part 1**, 582; **Vol. 7, Part 2**, 525
Sadie Hawkins Day, origin of, **Supp. 10**, 98
Safe, first fireproof, **Vol. 4, Part 2**, 591
Safety. *See* Occupational health and safety
Safety First movement, origin of, **Vol. 9, Part 2**, 151
Safety signals, telegraphic, **Vol. 10, Part 1**, 618 f.
Safeway Stores, Inc., **Supp. 6**, 448; **Supp. 10**, 738
Sage, Henry W., reference to, **Supp. 3**, 697, 698
Sage, Margaret Olivia, reference to, **Supp. 4**, 333
Sailing (for complete list of sailing vessels, *see* Ships): speed records, **Vol. 10, Part 1**, 534 f.; writings on, **Vol. 7, Part 1**, 548; yachting and yachts, design and building, **Supp. 2**, 298; **Supp. 4**, 124; yachts, racing, **Supp. 5**, 6–7
Sailor's Creek, battle of, **Vol. 1, Part 1**, 274; **Vol. 3, Part 2**, 230; **Vol. 6, Part 1**, 106, 127; **Vol. 9, Part 1**, 80; **Vol. 10, Part 2**, 555
Sailors' Magazine, **Vol. 6, Part 1**, 84
Sailors' Snug Harbor, founding of, **Vol. 8, Part 1**, 348 f.; **Vol. 10, Part 1**, 131
Sailors' Union, founding of, **Supp. 2**, 212
Sailor's Union of the Pacific, **Supp. 6**, 396–97
Sails: making of, **Vol. 3, Part 2**, 536; windmill, **Vol. 8, Part 1**, 518
St. Albans, Vt., raid on, **Vol. 2, Part 2**, 170; **Vol. 5, Part 1**, 134; **Vol. 9, Part 2**, 460
St. Andrews Golf Club. *See* Royal and Ancient Golf Club of St. Andrews
St. Ann's Church for Deaf-Mutes, **Vol. 4, Part 1**, 110
St. Augustine, Fla.: founding of, **Vol. 6, Part 2**, 533; Roman Catholic bishopric, **Supp. 8**, 295; transportation to (1780), **Vol. 4, Part 1**, 236
St. Benedict College, **Vol. 10, Part 2**, 448
St. Clair's defeat, **Vol. 2, Part 1**, 366; **Vol. 6, Part 1**, 300; **Vol. 8, Part 2**, 295; **Vol. 10, Part 1**, 564, 523; **Vol. 10, Part 2**, 223
St. Denis, Ruth, reference to, **Supp. 7**, 366; **Supp. 9**, 716, 717
St. Elizabeth's Hospital (Washington, D.C.), **Vol. 7, Part 1**, 489; **Supp. 2**, 711, 712; **Supp. 4**, 806
St. Francis, massacre at (1757), **Vol. 8, Part 2**, 108
St. Francis Dam (Calif.), collapse of, **Supp. 1**, 570
St. Francis Xavier College, founding of, **Vol. 7, Part 1**, 74; **Vol. 8, Part 1**, 266 f.
Saint-Gaudens, Augustus, references to, **Vol. 1, Part 1**, 478; **Vol. 7, Part 1**, 518; **Supp. 1**, 321–22; **Supp. 2**, 420; **Supp. 3**, 1, 533; **Supp. 5**, 231; **Supp. 6**, 418; **Supp. 8**, 493
St. George's Church (Stuyvesant Square, New York City), **Supp. 1**, 618
St. George's Protestant Episcopal Church (New York City), **Supp. 4**, 125
St. Ignatius College, presidency of, **Vol. 1, Part 2**, 79

St. James' Hall, **Vol. 5, Part 2**, 354
St. James Military Academy, founding of, **Vol. 9, Part 2**, 276
Saint Joan, **Supp. 10**, 725
St. John's, Newfoundland, **Vol. 1, Part 2**, 578
St. Johnsbury, Vt., **Vol. 1, Part 1**, 369
St. John's College (Annapolis), **Vol. 6, Part 2**, 31; **Supp. 8**, 59
St. John's College (New York City), founding of, **Vol. 5, Part 1**, 353
St. John's College (Shanghai). *See* St. John's University (Shanghai)
St. John's Presbyterian Church (Berkeley), **Supp. 6**, 463, 464
St. John's School (Manlius, N.Y.), **Vol. 5, Part 1**, 414
St. John's University (New York City): basketball team, **Supp. 8**, 358; Institute for Social Studies, **Supp. 2**, 455
St. John's University (Shanghai), **Vol. 8, Part 2**, 429; **Supp. 4**, 677–78
St. Joseph's Orphan Asylum (Washington, D.C.), **Vol. 9, Part 2**, 586
St. Lawrence Seaway, **Supp. 6**, 37, 588; **Supp. 7**, 360
St. Lawrence University, **Vol. 3, Part 2**, 406; **Vol. 8, Part 2**, 398
St. Louis, Mo.: art colony, **Vol. 9, Part 2**, 256; Art Museum, **Vol. 7, Part 2**, 312; capture of Camp Jackson (1861), **Vol. 1, Part 2**, 333; **Vol. 4, Part 2**, 280; **Vol. 5, Part 2**, 538; **Vol. 6, Part 1**, 534; **Vol. 8, Part 1**, 216; civic center, **Supp. 1**, 547; civic service, **Vol. 1, Part 2**, 339, 392; **Vol. 4, Part 2**, 67; **Vol. 5, Part 2**, 449; **Vol. 6, Part 1**, 485; **Vol. 8, Part 1**, 180 f.; **Vol. 9, Part 1**, 39, 66; **Vol. 9, Part 2**, 311; **Vol. 10, Part 1**, 75; **Vol. 10, Part 2**, 607; Eads bridge, **Vol. 3, Part 2**, 445; **Vol. 6, Part 1**, 549; **Vol. 8, Part 2**, 19; education, **Vol. 3, Part 2**, 83; **Vol. 4, Part 2**, 329; **Vol. 9, Part 1**, 383, 391; founding of, **Vol. 2, Part 2**, 94; **Vol. 5, Part 2**, 520; fur center, as a, **Vol. 2, Part 2**, 92 f.; **Vol. 4, Part 1**, 504; **Vol. 4, Part 2**, 546; gang violence, **Supp. 9**, 499; Gateway Arch, **Supp. 7**, 671, 672; history, early, **Vol. 2, Part 1**, 462; **Vol. 10, Part 1**, 20 f.; law, **Vol. 5, Part 2**, 241; manual training school, **Vol. 10, Part 2**, 507; mayor of, first, **Vol. 5, Part 2**, 583; militia, volunteer, **Vol. 5, Part 2**, 449; milling center, as a, **Vol. 1, Part 1**, 503; Museum of, **Vol. 5, Part 1**, 319–20; newspapers in, **Vol. 6, Part 1**, 433; organized-crime activities, **Supp. 9**, 500; park commission, **Supp. 3**, 217; politics, **Supp. 4**, 355; publicity, **Vol. 5, Part 1**, 120; religious service, **Vol. 3, Part 1**, 473 f.; **Vol. 5, Part 2**, 341; **Vol. 7, Part 2**, 381; Roman Catholic diocese, **Supp. 4**, 334–35; **Supp. 8**, 537; street railways, **Vol. 10, Part 1**, 638 f.; symphony orchestra, **Vol. 10, Part 2**, 640; Union Station, **Vol. 9, Part 2**, 312; water supply, **Vol. 5, Part 2**, 584; "whiskey ring," **Vol. 4, Part 2**, 26
"St. Louis Blues" (song), **Supp. 10**, 817
St. Louis Browns (baseball), **Supp. 6**, 357; **Supp. 9**, 729; **Supp. 10**, 585
St. Louis Cardinals (baseball): **Supp. 5**, 465; **Supp. 7**, 501–2, 513–14, 646, 647; **Supp. 9**, 223, 532, 543; **Supp. 10**, 573, 860; "Gashouse Gang," **Supp. 9**, 224, 543; Hornsby-Frisch trade, **Supp. 9**, 294
St. Louis Christian Advocate, **Vol. 6, Part 1**, 549; **Vol. 7, Part 2**, 196
St. Louis Democrat, **Vol. 4, Part 2**, 26
St. Louis Exposition (1904), **Supp. 1**, 53; *Mares of Diomedes*, **Supp. 3**, 88
St. Louis Globe-Democrat, **Vol. 5, Part 2**, 390; **Supp. 3**, 850
St. Louis Mirror, **Vol. 8, Part 1**, 463
St. Louis Observer, abolitionist paper, **Vol. 6, Part 1**, 434
St. Louis Post-Dispatch: **Supp. 1**, 519; **Supp. 3**, 91; **Supp. 5**, 551–52; editorial cartoons, **Supp. 8**, 173–74; editorial writing, **Supp. 4**, 704
St. Louis Presbyterian, **Vol. 8, Part 1**, 544
St. Louis Public Library, administration, **Supp. 3**, 9
St. Louis Star-Times, **Supp. 5**, 552
St. Luke's Hospital (New York City), **Vol. 1, Part 1**, 453; **Vol. 7, Part 1**, 314
St. Mark's School (Mass.), founding of, **Vol. 2, Part 1**, 299
St. Martin, Alexis, reference to, **Vol. 1, Part 2**, 106
St. Mary-of-the-Woods, Ind., **Vol. 4, Part 2**, 34
St. Mary's Church (Baltimore), **Vol. 3, Part 1**, 473 f.
St. Mary's Church (Erie, Pa.), **Vol. 8, Part 2**, 449
St. Mary's Church (Pittsburgh), **Vol. 8, Part 2**, 449
St. Nicholas: **Vol. 5, Part 2**, 54; **Vol. 8, Part 2**, 517; early years of, **Vol. 3, Part 1**, 351; founding of, **Vol. 9, Part 1**, 340; *Our Young Folks*, merger with, **Vol. 3, Part 1**, 350; *Wide Awake*, merger with, **Vol. 8, Part 1**, 171
St. Olaf College (Minn.), **Vol. 5, Part 2**, 373; **Vol. 8, Part 2**, 124
St. Patrick's Cathedral (New York City): **Vol. 3, Part 2**, 274; **Vol. 5, Part 1**, 354; **Supp. 10**, 729; music in, **Supp. 3**, 849–50; stained-glass windows, **Supp. 3**, 183
St. Paul, Minn.: "Bell charter," **Vol. 7, Part 2**, 92; civic service, **Vol. 8, Part 2**, 412; history of, **Vol. 1, Part 1**, 285; railway development, **Vol. 5, Part 2**, 441; religious service, **Vol. 2, Part 2**, 542; stockyards, **Vol. 9, Part 2**, 16
St. Paul and Pacific Railroad, **Vol. 6, Part 1**, 294
St. Paul Normal and Industrial School, founding of, **Supp. 1**, 645
St. Paul's College (Tokyo), **Supp. 6**, 649
St. Paul's College (Washington, D.C.), **Vol. 7, Part 1**, 313; **Supp. 6**, 237
St. Paul's Episcopal Church (New Haven), **Supp. 6**, 600
St. Paul's School (N.H.), **Vol. 2, Part 2**, 276; **Vol. 9, Part 1**, 33; **Supp. 4**, 899
St. Philips College (Mich.), **Vol. 8, Part 1**, 510
Saint-Saëns, Camille, reference to, **Supp. 5**, 646
St. Stephen's College (N.Y.), **Vol. 9, Part 1**, 5. *See also* Bard College
St. Tammany's Magazine, **Vol. 8, Part 2**, 344
St. Thomas's Church (New York City), architecture, **Supp. 3**, 196
St. Valentine's Day massacre, **Supp. 4**, 141
St. Vincent College (Latrobe, Pa.), **Vol. 9, Part 1**, 560
Saipan, World War II action, **Supp. 8**, 603–4
Salad dressing, **Supp. 5**, 400
Salem, Mass.: architecture, colonial, **Vol. 6, Part 2**, 66; clipper ships, **Vol. 8, Part 2**, 116; education, **Vol. 7, Part 2**, 18; gardens, **Vol. 8, Part 2**, 92; Mozart Association, **Vol. 7, Part 2**, 19; Peabody Academy of Science, **Vol. 5, Part 1**, 447; **Vol. 7, Part 2**, 337; **Vol. 8, Part 1**, 276 f.; privateering, **Vol. 9, Part 2**, 499; public service, **Vol. 4, Part 2**, 396; **Vol. 7, Part 2**, 15 f., 338; Revolutionary War, concealment of munitions, **Vol. 3, Part 1**, 253; Rogers family, **Vol. 8, Part 2**, 92; sea trade, **Vol. 3, Part 1**, 249 f., 252 f.; **Vol. 8, Part 2**, 152; **Vol. 9, Part 1**, 165; **Vol. 9, Part 2**, 499; witchcraft, **Vol. 2, Part 1**, 410; **Vol. 4, Part 2**, 424; **Vol. 6, Part 2**, 386 f., 392; **Vol. 7, Part 1**, 595 f.; **Vol. 7, Part 2**, 256; **Vol. 8, Part 2**, 116; **Vol. 10, Part 1**, 122
Sales and selling, **Supp. 6**, 614, 674; uniform statute, **Supp. 7**, 792. *See also* Advertising and marketing; Retail trades
Saline Water Act (1952), **Supp. 7**, 224
Salisbury Academy (N.C.), **Vol. 8, Part 1**, 42
Salk, Jonas E., references to, **Supp. 9**, 446; **Supp. 10**, 459

Salk Institute for Biological Studies (La Jolla, Calif.), design of, **Supp. 9**, 446
Salmagundi Club (New York City), **Vol. 4, Part 2**, 365; **Vol. 5, Part 1**, 506, 512; **Vol. 7, Part 1**, 354
Salmon canneries, **Vol. 5, Part 1**, 366; **Vol. 9, Part 1**, 220
Saloon keeping, **Supp. 10**, 732–33
Salt: manufacture, **Vol. 3, Part 2**, 451; **Vol. 5, Part 2**, 111; **Vol. 7, Part 2**, 189; **Vol. 9, Part 1**, 147; salt mining, **Vol. 3, Part 2**, 322; trade, **Vol. 5, Part 1**, 239; "salt war," **Vol. 5, Part 2**, 182
Salt Lake City, Utah: architecture, **Vol. 7, Part 1**, 461; building of, by Mormons, **Vol. 10, Part 2**, 621 f.
Saltonstall, Leverett, reference to, **Supp. 9**, 851
Salvation Army, **Supp. 2**, 48; **Supp. 4**, 95–96; founding of, **Vol. 1, Part 2**, 456
Salzburgers, colony of, in Georgia, **Vol. 1, Part 2**, 425
Samoa: anthropological research, **Supp. 10**, 521, 523; treaties regarding, **Vol. 1, Part 2**, 50–1, 72; **Vol. 4, Part 2**, 333; **Vol. 5, Part 1**, 458; **Vol. 5, Part 2**, 260; **Vol. 7, Part 2**, 533; **Vol. 8, Part 2**, 606 f.; **Vol. 9, Part 2**, 644
Sampson, William T., reference to, **Vol. 8, Part 2**, 438
Sams, Earl Corder, reference to, **Supp. 10**, 354
San Andreas fault, **Supp. 4**, 558
San Antonio, Tex., political reform, **Supp. 5**, 481
San Antonio and Mexican Gulf Railroad of Texas, **Vol. 7, Part 2**, 169
Sanborn, Franklin B., reference to, **Vol. 10, Part 1**, 615 f.
San Clemente, Calif., founding of, **Supp. 2**, 280
Sanctuary, **Supp. 7**, 232
Sandalwood, trade in, **Vol. 5, Part 1**, 381
Sandblasting, **Vol. 9, Part 2**, 544
Sandburg, Carl, references to, **Supp. 9**, 38, 491, 761
Sand County Almanac, A, **Supp. 4**, 484
Sandeman, Robert, reference to, **Vol. 5, Part 1**, 578
"Sandemanians," religious sect, **Vol. 8, Part 2**, 329
Sanders, Thomas, reference to, **Vol. 1, Part 2**, 149, 141
Sanderson, Sibyl, reference to, **Supp. 8**, 200
San Diego, Calif.: business development, **Vol. 9, Part 1**, 479; founding of, **Vol. 8, Part 1**, 109 f.; mission founded, **Vol. 8, Part 2**, 591; politics, **Supp. 9**, 853; school administration, **Supp. 3**, 205
Sands, David, reference to, **Vol. 8, Part 2**, 411
Sandusky, siege of. *See* Fort Stephenson
Sandwich glass, **Vol. 5, Part 1**, 95, 618; **Vol. 6, Part 1**, 530
Sandwich Islands, missions, **Vol. 1, Part 2**, 276
Sandy Hook Lightship (N.J.), **Vol. 8, Part 1**, 481
San Fernando Valley, Calif., development of, **Supp. 3**, 155
Sanforized cloth, **Supp. 8**, 97
San Francisco, Calif.: arts in, **Supp. 5**, 94; bay region architecture, **Supp. 6**, 438; bay report on, **Vol. 1, Part 1**, 447; bridges, **Supp. 3**, 531; business interests in, **Vol. 7, Part 2**, 522; **Vol. 9, Part 1**, 220, 478; cable street railway, charter for, **Vol. 3, Part 1**, 394; civic service, **Vol. 4, Part 2**, 156; **Vol. 5, Part 1**, 82; **Vol. 6, Part 2**, 30; **Vol. 7, Part 2**, 523 f.; **Vol. 8, Part 2**, 492; corruption prosecution, **Supp. 6**, 590; counterculture in, **Supp. 8**, 56; development of, following fire, **Vol. 8, Part 1**, 45 f., 333 f.; early days of, **Vol. 1, Part 2**, 602; **Vol. 8, Part 2**, 248; earthquake and fire, **Supp. 1**, 638; **Supp. 4**, 325, 417; **Supp. 5**, 416; fine printing center, **Supp. 4**, 621–22; fire, **Vol. 3, Part 1**, 284; **Vol. 6, Part 1**, 423; founding of, **Vol. 1, Part 1**, 322; gay community, **Supp. 10**, 536–37, 558, 559; journalism, **Vol. 1, Part 1**, 443; **Vol. 3, Part 1**, 283 f.; **Vol. 7, Part 1**, 551; **Vol. 9, Part 1**, 479; law suits, **Vol. 9, Part 2**, 246; library, public, **Vol. 7, Part 2**, 467; mayors, **Supp. 10**, 536, 537, 558–59; mission, founding of, **Vol. 7, Part 2**, 197; Mooney case, **Supp. 3**, 532–33, 499; parks, **Supp. 3**, 490–91; Phelan building, erection of, **Vol. 7, Part 2**, 522; philanthropy, **Vol. 6, Part 1**, 234; **Vol. 9, Part 1**, 220; photography, **Supp. 3**, 295; physician, first city, **Vol. 7, Part 2**, 188; political machine, **Supp. 3**, 394; political murders, **Supp. 10**, 537, 558, 559; politics, **Supp. 10**, 536–37, 558–59; Preparedness Day parade bombing (1916), **Supp. 7**, 261–62; printers in, early, **Vol. 1, Part 2**, 602; public utilities in, **Vol. 3, Part 1**, 362; public works, **Supp. 1**, 588; Roman Catholic diocese, **Supp. 3**, 325–26; site of, **Vol. 3, Part 2**, 498; street railways, **Supp. 3**, 126; strike (1934), **Supp. 5**, 287; **Supp. 7**, 609; Theological Seminary, founding of, **Vol. 8, Part 2**, 504; Vigilantes, **Vol. 5, Part 2**, 408; water supply, **Supp. 4**, 664
San Francisco Bulletin, editorship, **Supp. 1**, 580
San Francisco Call, **Vol. 9, Part 1**, 479
San Francisco Chronicle, **Vol. 3, Part 1**, 283 f.; **Vol. 7, Part 1**, 551; **Supp. 5**, 356
San Francisco Conference (1945), **Supp. 5**, 537–38
San Francisco Examiner: campaign against Southern Pacific Railroad, **Supp. 5**, 283; drama criticism, **Supp. 5**, 657, 658
San Francisco 49ers (football), **Supp. 10**, 727–28
San Francisco Giants (baseball), **Supp. 10**, 606
San Francisco–Oakland Bay Bridge, **Supp. 2**, 470; **Supp. 3**, 531
San Francisco Opera Company, **Supp. 6**, 670; ballet choreography, **Supp. 5**, 76
San Francisco Symphony, **Supp. 3**, 359; **Supp. 7**, 549
San Francisco World's Fairs. *See* Golden Gate International Exposition (1939); Panama-Pacific International Exposition (1915)
Sanger, Margaret, references to, **Supp. 4**, 231; **Supp. 6**, 602; **Supp. 8**, 503
Sanitarium, first for tuberculosis, **Vol. 10, Part 1**, 3
Sanitation: **Vol. 1, Part 1**, 597; **Vol. 3, Part 1**, 78; **Vol. 3, Part 2**, 275; **Vol. 4, Part 1**, 433; **Vol. 4, Part 2**, 100, 576 f.; **Vol. 5, Part 2**, 193, 265, 275, 277, 418; **Vol. 6, Part 1**, 606; **Vol. 8, Part 1**, 324 f., 390 f., 475, 553 f.; **Vol. 8, Part 2**, 553; **Vol. 9, Part 1**, 102, 495; **Vol. 10, Part 1**, 456 f.; Baltimore, **Vol. 8, Part 1**, 502; Boston, **Vol. 8, Part 1**, 308 f.; Chicago, **Vol. 8, Part 1**, 390; engineering studies, **Supp. 1**, 326; home, **Supp. 5**, 553; household plumbing, **Supp. 1**, 552; Massachusetts, **Vol. 5, Part 2**, 419; Memphis, **Vol. 10, Part 1**, 456 f.; milk, **Supp. 4**, 701; New Orleans, **Vol. 5, Part 2**, 193; New York, **Vol. 4, Part 2**, 308; **Vol. 8, Part 1**, 607; **Vol. 8, Part 2**, 404; **Vol. 10, Part 1**, 456 f.; Panama Canal Zone, **Vol. 3, Part 1**, 78; **Vol. 4, Part 1**, 431; public education in, **Supp. 5**, 143–44; Sanitary Commission, U.S., **Vol. 2, Part 2**, 136; **Vol. 3, Part 2**, 212; **Vol. 4, Part 2**, 308; **Vol. 5, Part 1**, 251, 297; **Vol. 5, Part 2**, 355, 404; **Vol. 7, Part 1**, 446; **Vol. 7, Part 2**, 26; **Vol. 8, Part 2**, 474, 600; **Vol. 9, Part 1**, 563; **Vol. 9, Part 2**, 24; Washington, D.C., **Vol. 6, Part 2**, 204; writings on, **Vol. 4, Part 1**, 432; **Vol. 5, Part 2**, 419; **Vol. 8, Part 1**, 554; **Vol. 10, Part 1**, 456 f. *See also* Public health; Sewerage
San Jacinto, battle of, **Vol. 2, Part 1**, 417, 293; **Vol. 5, Part 1**, 265; **Vol. 5, Part 2**, 553; **Vol. 6, Part 2**, 5
San Jose, Calif., first mayor of, **Vol. 1, Part 2**, 146
San Juan Hill, Cuba, battle of, **Vol. 6, Part 1**, 62; **Vol. 8, Part 2**, 137; **Vol. 9, Part 1**, 16; **Vol. 10, Part 2**, 51, 467
Sanka coffee, **Supp. 10**, 555
Sankey, Ira D., reference to, **Vol. 7, Part 1**, 103
San Lorenzo, treaty of, **Vol. 7, Part 2**, 619; **Vol. 8, Part 1**, 353 f.
San Simeon (Hearst estate), **Supp. 3**, 156; **Supp. 5**, 287, 288; **Supp. 6**, 464; **Supp. 7**, 166

Sanskrit: literature, **Supp. 2**, 339; **Supp. 3**, 444–45; study of, **Vol. 4, Part 1**, 588; **Vol. 4, Part 2**, 125; **Vol. 9, Part 2**, 441; **Vol. 10, Part 2**, 168
Santa Catalina Island (Calif.), development of, **Supp. 1**, 715
Santayana, George, references to, **Supp. 5**, 658, 659, 661; **Supp. 6**, 504, 505; **Supp. 9**, 503, 890
Santa Fe, N.Mex.: **Vol. 1, Part 2**, 161; Catholic missionary service, **Vol. 5, Part 2**, 567; engagement at (1846), **Vol. 3, Part 1**, 365; **Vol. 5, Part 2**, 273; expedition, **Vol. 4, Part 1**, 329; **Vol. 6, Part 2**, 132; founding of, **Vol. 7, Part 2**, 548; Tertio Millennial Pageant, **Vol. 8, Part 1**, 229 f.; traders of, **Vol. 4, Part 1**, 597; **Vol. 5, Part 2**, 554; **Vol. 6, Part 2**, 111; **Vol. 8, Part 2**, 306
Santa Fe Railroad, **Vol. 8, Part 1**, 620 f.; **Vol. 8, Part 2**, 33
Santa Fe Trail, **Vol. 1, Part 2**, 120; **Vol. 5, Part 1**, 151, 483; **Vol. 9, Part 1**, 144; **Vol. 10, Part 2**, 525
Santiago, Cuba: Schley-Sampson controversy, **Vol. 3, Part 2**, 503; **Vol. 8, Part 1**, 416, 419; siege of, **Vol. 3, Part 1**, 416; **Vol. 6, Part 1**, 62; **Vol. 6, Part 2**, 646; **Vol. 8, Part 2**, 137, 322 f., 438; **Vol. 9, Part 1**, 16; **Vol. 10, Part 2**, 51, 467
Santo Domingo: black rebellion, **Vol. 8, Part 2**, 305; diplomatic relations, **Vol. 5, Part 2**, 598; **Vol. 6, Part 1**, 76; **Vol. 9, Part 1**, 388; proposed annexation of (1873), **Vol. 1, Part 1**, 460; **Vol. 3, Part 2**, 398; **Vol. 4, Part 1**, 499; **Vol. 7, Part 1**, 287; **Vol. 8, Part 2**, 468; **Vol. 9, Part 2**, 212
São Paulo, Brazil, **Supp. 4**, 81–82
Sapir, Edward, references to, **Supp. 3**, 820; **Supp. 4**, 71, 806, 807; **Supp. 8**, 509
Sapir, Jacob, reference to, **Supp. 4**, 762
Sapiro, Aaron, reference to, **Supp. 4**, 299
Sarah Morris Children's Hospital (Chicago), founding of, **Supp. 5**, 2
Saranac Lake, N.Y., Trudeau tuberculosis sanatorium, **Supp. 2**, 71; **Supp. 3**, 431; **Supp. 4**, 48–49, 314, 577
Saratoga, N.Y., battle of (1777), **Vol. 1, Part 1**, 364–65; **Vol. 4, Part 1**, 185–86; **Vol. 6, Part 1**, 260; **Vol. 7, Part 2**, 575; **Vol. 8, Part 2**, 478; **Vol. 9, Part 1**, 531; **Vol. 10, Part 1**, 517; **Vol. 10, Part 2**, 223
Saratoga Springs, N.Y., **Vol. 1, Part 2**, 29; **Vol. 7, Part 1**, 234; **Vol. 8, Part 1**, 280 f.; **Vol. 8, Part 2**, 478
Sardinia, diplomatic relations, **Vol. 5, Part 2**, 418; **Vol. 7, Part 1**, 524 f.
Sardi's restaurant (New York City), **Supp. 8**, 571–72
Sargent, Charles Sprague, reference to, **Supp. 6**, 196
Sargent, John Singer, references to, **Vol. 1, Part 2**, 120; **Vol. 2, Part 2**, 39; *Four Doctors*, **Supp. 3**, 413
Sarnoff, David, references to, **Supp. 9**, 167, 275–76, 702, 801
Sarnoff, Robert, references to, **Supp. 10**, 415, 416
Saroyan, William, references to, **Supp. 10**, 129, 131
Sartre, Jean-Paul, reference to, **Supp. 10**, 91
Satire: cabaret, **Supp. 4**, 867–68; "fables in slang," **Supp. 3**, 3, 4; musical, **Supp. 5**, 351; **Supp. 7**, 403–4, 737; *New Yorker* cartoons, **Supp. 4**, 386; **Supp. 8**, 15–16; novels, **Supp. 5**, 422–23; **Supp. 10**, 756; poetic, **Supp. 7**, 158; political journalism, **Supp. 4**, 804; television, **Supp. 7**, 442–43; verse, **Supp. 8**, 492; writings, **Vol. 1, Part 2**, 545; **Vol. 3, Part 1**, 573 f.; **Vol. 3, Part 2**, 347, 450 f.; **Vol. 5, Part 1**, 215, 387; **Vol. 5, Part 2**, 605; **Vol. 6, Part 1**, 336; **Vol. 8, Part 1**, 65 f., 111; **Vol. 9, Part 1**, 517; **Vol. 10, Part 1**, 146 f.
Saturday Evening Gazette, **Vol. 2, Part 2**, 118
Saturday Evening Post: **Vol. 7, Part 2**, 513; **Supp. 1**, 212, 213; **Supp. 7**, 512–13; cover illustration, **Supp. 5**, 428, 429; **Supp. 10**, 689, 690; editing, **Supp. 2**, 393; fiction in, **Supp. 3**, 171; **Supp. 6**, 116, 354, 543
Saturday Night Club (Baltimore), founding of, **Supp. 3**, 107
"Saturday Night Fish Fry," **Supp. 9**, 442
Saturday Review of Literature: **Supp. 7**, 638; **Supp. 8**, 393; columns, **Supp. 6**, 465; double-crostic puzzle, **Supp. 6**, 342; editing, **Supp. 5**, 168; founding and growth of, **Supp. 4**, 73, 470; **Supp. 5**, 439; **Supp. 7**, 103–4; predecessor, **Supp. 4**, 322; "Seeing Things" column, **Supp. 8**, 54
Sauk Indians, **Vol. 5, Part 2**, 350
Sault Ste. Marie, first ship canal, **Vol. 2, Part 1**, 338; **Vol. 5, Part 2**, 225
Saunders, Clarence, reference to, **Supp. 7**, 141
Savage Station, battle of. *See* Seven Days' Battles
Savannah, first transatlantic steamship voyage, **Vol. 8, Part 2**, 106, 410
Savannah, Ga.: **Vol. 4, Part 1**, 427 f.; **Vol. 5, Part 2**, 165; **Vol. 6, Part 1**, 448; Indians, fortifying against, **Vol. 3, Part 1**, 182; Loyalists, **Vol. 4, Part 1**, 476 f.; secession, plea for, **Vol. 5, Part 2**, 165; operation at (1779–82), **Vol. 4, Part 2**, 240; **Vol. 6, Part 1**, 260; **Vol. 8, Part 1**, 260; **Vol. 9, Part 1**, 96
Savannah Morning News, **Vol. 9, Part 2**, 479
Savannah Press, founding of, **Supp. 1**, 675
Save the Children Federation, founding of, **Supp. 8**, 673–74
Save-the-Redwoods League: **Supp. 3**, 520; first executive secretary, **Supp. 10**, 191; redwood national park, campaign for, **Supp. 10**, 192
Saville, Marshall Howard, reference to, **Supp. 6**, 280
Savings banks: first, **Vol. 8, Part 2**, 388; New York City, first in, **Vol. 7, Part 2**, 630; school, **Vol. 7, Part 1**, 607
Savitt, Ted, reference to, **Supp. 9**, 722
Savonarola Seminary (Scranton), founding of, **Supp. 5**, 305
Savoy Ballroom Band (jazz), **Supp. 9**, 441
Sawyer, Charles, reference to, **Supp. 5**, 564
Say, Thomas, reference to, **Vol. 6, Part 1**, 190 f.
"Saybrook Platform," **Vol. 3, Part 1**, 14; **Vol. 7, Part 2**, 586; **Vol. 8, Part 2**, 317
Saylor, John P., reference to, **Supp. 7**, 814
Scala, Florence, reference to, **Supp. 8**, 40
Scales, manufacture of, **Vol. 3, Part 2**, 249, 251
Scammon, Richard, reference to, **Supp. 4**, 420
Scandals, musical revues, **Supp. 8**, 695
Scandals, political: **Vol. 3, Part 2**, 503; Grant administration, **Vol. 4, Part 1**, 500; Harding administration, **Vol. 4, Part 2**, 255 f.
Scarface: Shame of a Nation, **Supp. 10**, 355, 655
Scarlet fever: early description of, **Vol. 3, Part 1**, 408; treatments developed, **Supp. 9**, 249
Scarlet Letter, The, **Vol. 8, Part 1**, 624
Scarlet Pimpernel, The, **Supp. 10**, 599
Scarlet Sister Mary, **Supp. 7**, 613
Scarne, John, reference to, **Supp. 9**, 13
Scarsdale, N.Y., founding of, **Vol. 4, Part 2**, 491
Scatchard, George, references to, **Supp. 5**, 122; **Supp. 6**, 346
Scenic Hudson (environmental group), **Supp. 10**, 324
Scent test for brain tumors, **Supp. 4**, 250
Schacht, Hjalmar, reference to, **Supp. 5**, 249
Schaefer, Jacob, Sr., reference to, **Supp. 6**, 303
Schaefer, Vincent J., reference to, **Supp. 6**, 365
Schaff, Philip, references to, **Vol. 5, Part 1**, 554; **Vol. 7, Part 1**, 442
Schamberg, Morton Livingston, reference to, **Supp. 7**, 686
Schary, Dore, references to, **Supp. 6**, 118, 441; **Supp. 7**, 325; Supp. 89 577
Schatz, Albert, reference to, **Supp. 9**, 834
Schechter Poultry Corp. v. *United States*, **Supp. 4**, 406–7

Schenck, Joseph M., references to, **Supp. 6**, 619; **Supp. 8**, 314, 315; **Supp. 9**, 791
Schenck, Nicholas, references to, **Supp. 6**, 440, 441
Schenck v. *United States*, **Supp. 7**, 317; **Supp. 9**, 593
Schenectady, N.Y.: founding of, **Vol. 10, Part 1**, 166; reform mayor, **Supp. 4**, 511–12
Schenley Industries, **Supp. 10**, 701
Schenley Products Corporation, **Supp. 7**, 780
Scherman, Thomas, reference to, **Supp. 8**, 578
Schick test, **Supp. 4**, 701
Schiff, Jacob, reference to, **Supp. 3**, 457
Schilder, Paul, reference to, **Supp. 3**, 320
Schiller, F. C. S., reference to, **Vol. 5, Part 1**, 599
Schine, G. David, references to, **Supp. 6**, 405, 680
Schirmer, G., Inc., **Supp. 3**, 253
Schizophrenia: ambulatory, **Supp. 6**, 724; genetic aspects of, **Supp. 4**, 618; research, **Supp. 10**, 28; treatment, **Supp. 4**, 806–8; **Supp. 6**, 220, 563–64
Schlenk, Wilhelm, reference to, **Supp. 4**, 336
Schlesinger, Arthur M., reference to, **Supp. 3**, 287
Schlesinger, Arthur M., Jr., reference to, **Supp. 7**, 675
Schley-Sampson controversy, **Vol. 3, Part 2**, 503; **Vol. 8, Part 1**, 416, 419
Schlink, Fred J., reference to, **Supp. 8**, 425
Schloss' Companion, **Vol. 1, Part 1**, 501
Schmeling, Max, references to, **Supp. 7**, 494; **Supp. 9**, 122, 493
Schnabel, Karl Ulrich, reference to, **Supp. 5**, 607
Schneider, Herman, reference to, **Supp. 3**, 209
Schneiderman, William, references to, **Supp. 3**, 830; **Supp. 5**, 389
Schocken Books, founding and growth of, **Supp. 9**, 707–8
Schoedsack, Ernest B., reference to, **Supp. 7**, 580
Schoenberg, Arnold, reference to, **Supp. 9**, 492
Schola Cantorum, **Supp. 6**, 357; founding of, **Supp. 1**, 650
School administration. *See* Education; Universities and colleges; *specific institutions*
School breakfast and lunch programs, **Supp. 3**, 28; **Supp. 6**, 81
School buildings: California architecture, **Supp. 8**, 464; Chicago architecture, **Supp. 3**, 299; community center movement, **Supp. 3**, 600–601; **Supp. 5**, 631; Cranbrook (Mich.), **Supp. 4**, 714–15; design in New York City, **Supp. 5**, 301; first multiclassroom one-story, **Supp. 3**, 599; specialist on, **Supp. 5**, 41–42
School desegregation: congressional opposition, **Supp. 8**, 25; Louisiana, **Supp. 8**, 500; New York City, **Supp. 9**, 251; New York City issues, **Supp. 8**, 135; Oklahoma, **Supp. 8**, 57–58; parochial schools, **Supp. 8**, 537; "separate but equal" ruling, **Supp. 4**, 397; South Carolina, **Supp. 8**, 682; "Southern Manifesto" opposing, **Supp. 9**, 104, 190–91, 401; Supreme Court decision, **Supp. 5**, 156, 359; **Supp. 7**, 264, 501; **Supp. 8**, 157; **Supp. 9**, 104, 190–91, 364, 391, 401, 433, 743, 836; **Supp. 10**, 127, 189; Tennessee, **Supp. 8**, 91; **Supp. 9**, 258; universities and colleges, **Supp. 8**, 73, 322; Virginia, **Supp. 9**, 68
Schoolcraft, Henry R., reference to, **Vol. 5, Part 1**, 254
School District of Abington v. *Schempp*, **Supp. 10**, 126
School for International Training, **Supp. 10**, 820
School for Midwives, founding of, **Vol. 3, Part 2**, 160
School of American Ballet (New York City), **Supp. 8**, 670; **Supp. 10**, 207
Schools. *See* Education; *specific institution names*
School Visitors' Association, founding of, **Supp. 2**, 375
Schouten, Jan Arnoldus, reference to, **Supp. 7**, 216
Schreiber, Belle, reference to, **Supp. 4**, 433
Schroeder, Ted, reference to, **Supp. 9**, 722
Schuchert, Charles, reference to, **Supp. 3**, 782
Schulberg, Budd, reference to, **Supp. 10**, 384
Schultz, Dutch, references to, **Supp. 3**, 181; **Supp. 5**, 665; **Supp. 6**, 58, 295; **Supp. 7**, 5; **Supp. 8**, 714
Schultz, Jack, reference to, **Supp. 3**, 540
Schulze-Berge, Franz, reference to, **Supp. 3**, 86
Schumann, Friedrich, reference to, **Supp. 3**, 428–30
Schurz, Carl, references to, **Vol. 1, Part 2**, 325; **Vol. 4, Part 2**, 449; **Vol. 5, Part 1**, 534; **Vol. 5, Part 2**, 259; **Vol. 7, Part 2**, 149; **Vol. 8, Part 1**, 185; **Supp. 3**, 31–32
Schussele, Christian, reference to, **Vol. 8, Part 2**, 372 f.
Schuster, Max Lincoln, reference to, **Supp. 6**, 583; **Supp. 10**, 349
Schuyler, Karl C., reference to, **Supp. 6**, 455
Schuylkill River, bridge across, **Vol. 3, Part 1**, 459 f.
Schwab, Charles M., references to, **Supp. 6**, 243, 506–7
Schwartz, Maurice, reference to, **Supp. 8**, 452
Schwentker, Francis F., reference to, **Supp. 7**, 648
Schweppes (USA), **Supp. 10**, 835, 836
Schwienfurth, A. C., reference to, **Supp. 6**, 438
Science: **Vol. 3, Part 1**, 479 f.; **Vol. 3, Part 2**, 79, 597; **Vol. 4, Part 1**, 245, 294; **Vol. 5, Part 2**, 33, 38, 612; **Vol. 6, Part 1**, 88 f., 90, 214; **Vol. 7, Part 1**, 69 f.; **Vol. 7, Part 2**, 24, 64, 74, 150 f.; **Vol. 8, Part 2**, 99, 109, 115; **Vol. 9, Part 1**, 163; American Association for the Advancement of Science, **Vol. 1, Part 2**, 530; **Vol. 7, Part 2**, 207, 471; **Vol. 8, Part 1**, 442; broadening of field of, for women, **Vol. 8, Part 1**, 553 f.; federal administration, **Supp. 8**, 686–87; **Supp. 10**, 594; history of, **Supp. 3**, 351; **Supp. 6**, 564–65; humanism, **Supp. 8**, 596; illustrations, **Supp. 1**, 428; journalism, **Supp. 5**, 65; medieval, writings on, **Supp. 7**, 741–42; philosophy of, **Supp. 8**, 191; popular writings on, **Supp. 8**, 119, 200; population of, **Vol. 3, Part 1**, 372, 605 f; **Vol. 4, Part 2**, 589; **Vol. 5, Part 1**, 140; **Vol. 9, Part 1**, 221; professional role, **Supp. 3**, 150–51; program to broaden public understanding of, **Supp. 10**, 825; religion and, **Vol. 5, Part 1**, 594; **Vol. 8, Part 2**, 57, 307; **Vol. 9, Part 1**, 104, 162, 269 f.; **Supp. 1**, 65; **Supp. 2**, 27; **Supp. 8**, 424; scientific newspaper, first, **Vol. 8, Part 1**, 101 f.; teaching of, **Vol. 4, Part 1**, 549; **Vol. 5, Part 1**, 59; **Vol. 7, Part 1**, 255; **Vol. 8, Part 1**, 223 f.; **Vol. 9, Part 1**, 588; **Vol. 9, Part 2**, 632; **Supp. 4**, 139–40; writings on, **Supp. 6**, 327–28; **Supp. 9**, 225–26. *See also specific fields of science*
Science, **Supp. 3**, 150; founding of, **Vol. 1, Part 2**, 152; **Vol. 5, Part 1**, 325; **Vol. 7, Part 1**, 328
Science and Health, **Vol. 3, Part 2**, 9 f.; **Vol. 10, Part 2**, 190
Science and the Modern World, **Supp. 4**, 881–83
Science fiction: comic strips, **Supp. 6**, 166, 530; "Golden Age" of, **Supp. 9**, 156; magazines, **Supp. 8**, 209–10; **Supp. 9**, 155–56; movies, **Supp. 8**, 379; novels, **Supp. 6**, 49; **Supp. 9**, 895; television programs, **Supp. 9**, 710–11; **Supp. 10**, 343–44; writing of, **Supp. 4**, 128–29
Science News Letter, founding of, **Supp. 8**, 119, 120
Science Service, founding of, **Supp. 3**, 635–36; **Supp. 8**, 119–20
Science Talent Search, **Supp. 8**, 119–20
Scientific American, **Vol. 7, Part 1**, 329; **Vol. 8, Part 1**, 101 f.
Scientific humanism, **Supp. 6**, 83
Scientific management, **Vol. 8, Part 1**, 91 f.
Scientists. For complete list, *see* Occupations Index
SCLC. *See* Southern Christian Leadership Council
Scopes, John T., references to, **Supp. 4**, 692; **Supp. 6**, 528–29; **Supp. 9**, 769
Scopes trial: academic freedom issues, **Supp. 8**, 582–84; Bible expert for defense, **Supp. 7**, 624; defense, **Supp. 2**, 143; **Supp. 4**, 542; **Supp. 9**, 769; judge, **Supp. 6**, 528–29; **Supp. 9**, 769; play about, **Supp. 8**,

31–32; prosecution, **Supp. 4**, 692; **Supp. 7**, 631; **Supp. 9**, 769
Scott, Barbara Ann, reference to, **Supp. 9**, 131–32
Scott, Dred: counsel for, **Vol. 1, Part 2**, 339; owner of, **Vol. 8, Part 2**, 488 f.; decision, **Vol. 1, Part 2**, 133, 339, 392; **Vol. 2, Part 1**, 212, 457; **Vol. 2, Part 2**, 610; **Vol. 3, Part 1**, 402; **Vol. 4, Part 1**, 121, 181, 231; **Vol. 4, Part 2**, 311; Vol. 6, Part 1, 248; **Vol. 6, Part 2**, 128; **Vol. 7, Part 1**, 432; **Vol. 7, Part 2**, 241; **Vol. 8, Part 2**, 488, 503, 617; **Vol. 9, Part 1**, 571; **Vol. 9, Part 2**, 293
Scott, Howard, references to, **Supp. 5**, 558, 559
Scott, Walter, references to, **Vol. 4, Part 1**, 505; **Vol. 5, Part 1**, 507
Scott, William R., reference to, **Supp. 5**, 92
Scott, Winfield, references to, **Vol. 5, Part 1**, 73 f.; **Vol. 6, Part 1**, 121; **Vol. 9, Part 2**, 350 f., 363; **Vol. 9, Part 2**, 646
Scottsboro cases, **Supp. 3**, 755; **Supp. 4**, 397, 537; **Supp. 10**, 447, 709
Scotty's Castle (Death Valley, Calif.), **Supp. 5**, 613
Scouting, **Vol. 1, Part 1**, 493; **Vol. 3, Part 1**, 331; **Vol. 4, Part 2**, 27 f.; **Vol. 5, Part 1**, 230; **Vol. 5, Part 2**, 1, 309; **Vol. 6, Part 1**, 586; **Vol. 7, Part 1**, 395 f., 560; **Vol. 8, Part 1**, 517; **Vol. 9, Part 2**, 31; **Supp. 4**, 126–27
"Scragg, Daisy Mae" (fictional character), **Supp. 10**, 98
Scranton, William, reference to, **Supp. 8**, 361
Scranton, Pa., **Vol. 1, Part 2**, 412 f.; founding of, **Vol. 3, Part 1**, 306; **Vol. 8, Part 2**, 514; Polish National Catholic Church founding, **Supp. 5**, 304
Screen Actors' Guild: founding of, **Supp. 8**, 492; residual payments boycott by, **Supp. 8**, 712
Screens, window, **Vol. 2, Part 1**, 334
Screen Writers' Guild: founding of, **Supp. 6**, 476; revival of, **Supp. 10**, 436
Screws: manufacture of, **Vol. 1, Part 1**, 310; **Vol. 4, Part 1**, 374; **Vol. 9, Part 1**, 446; **Vol. 9, Part 2**, 632; standard threads for, **Vol. 8, Part 2**, 577
Scriabin, Alexander, reference to, **Supp. 3**, 690
Scribner's, Charles, Sons: **Supp. 4**, 651–52; **Supp. 5**, 615; **Supp. 7**, 336; Brownell, association with, **Vol. 2, Part 1**, 173; Burlingame, association with, **Vol. 2, Part 1**, 291; "Poets of Today" series, **Supp. 10**, 831; Wheelock, association with, **Supp. 10**, 831
Scribner's Book Store (New York City), **Supp. 10**, 831
Scribner's Monthly: **Vol. 2, Part 1**, 291, 297; **Vol. 4, Part 1**, 276; **Vol. 5, Part 1**, 147, 542, 564, 589, 614; **Vol. 5, Part 2**, 388; **Vol. 9, Part 2**, 322; **Supp. 5**, 559, 614; founding of, **Vol. 8, Part 2**, 516; illustrations, **Vol. 1, Part 1**, 4; first issue of, **Vol. 9, Part 1**, 340; *Putnam's Magazine* merged into, **Vol. 8, Part 1**, 279 f.
Scrip, founding of, **Supp. 2**, 100
Scripps, E. W., reference to, **Supp. 7**, 369; **Supp. 8**, 119
Scripps College: curriculum development, **Supp. 2**, 9; founding of, **Vol. 8, Part 2**, 519
Scripps-Howard newspaper, **Vol. 2, Part 2**, 325; **Vol. 6, Part 2**, 166
Scripps-Howard Publishing, **Supp. 2**, 606; **Supp. 7**, 369–70
Scripps-Howard Radio, **Supp. 9**, 90
Scripps Institution of Oceanography: **Supp. 5**, 710; founding of, **Supp. 3**, 635–36; **Supp. 4**, 461; predecessor, **Supp. 3**, 752–53
Scripps-MacRae Press Association, **Vol. 6, Part 2**, 166; **Vol. 8, Part 2**, 518
Scripture, Edward Wheeler, reference to, **Supp. 4**, 731
Scroll, The, **Supp. 6**, 14
Sculling. *See* Rowing
Sculptors. For complete list, *See* Occupations Index
Sculpture: **Vol. 1, Part 1**, 134, 239 f., 428, 462, 503, 552; **Vol. 1, Part 2**, 2, 12, 300, 304, 305, 533, 547; **Vol. 2, Part 1**, 18, 89; **Vol. 2, Part 2**, 162, 212 f., 270 f., 348 f., 524 f.; **Vol. 3, Part 1**, 278, 371 f., 420 f., 558 f.; **Vol. 3, Part 2**, 120 f., 240 f.; **Vol. 4, Part 1**, 1 f., 456, 457, 469, 470, 586 f., 589; **Vol. 4, Part 2**, 358, 365, 378; **Vol. 5, Part 1**, 242, 317, 356, 518, 548; **Vol. 5, Part 2**, 317 f., 412, 413; **Vol. 6, Part 1**, 31; **Vol. 6, Part 2**, 16, 350, 472, 484; **Vol. 7, Part 1**, 4 f., 18, 303, 321 f., 478, 626; **Vol. 7, Part 2**, 179 f., 284; **Vol. 8, Part 1**, 158 f., 166, 274 f., 312 f., 497, 613 f.; **Vol. 8, Part 2**, 7, 102, 107, 222, 234, 296 f.; **Vol. 9, Part 1**, 133, 169; **Vol. 9, Part 2**, 75 f., 109 f.; **Vol. 10, Part 1**, 427 f., 467 f.; **Vol. 10, Part 2**, 155; **Supp. 1**, 477–78; **Supp. 3**, 818; American Indian depiction, **Supp. 4**, 533–34; animal, **Vol. 1, Part 2**, 11; **Vol. 5, Part 2**, 317 f.; **Vol. 8, Part 1**, 125 f.; architectural, **Supp. 3**, 2, 123–25; avant-garde, **Supp. 7**, 696–98; black themes, **Supp. 7**, 610–11; bronzes, **Supp. 8**, 414–15; casting methods (1872), **Vol. 8, Part 2**, 103; "Checkers up at the Farm," **Vol. 8, Part 2**, 102; classicism, **Supp. 9**, 501; collections, **Supp. 2**, 22; color in, **Supp. 7**, 14; cubism, **Supp. 9**, 501–2; direct carving, **Supp. 8**, 715; equestrian, **Vol. 1, Part 2**, 304; **Vol. 2, Part 1**, 123; **Vol. 8, Part 1**, 125 f.; **Supp. 5**, 231–92; frontier life, **Vol. 1, Part 2**, 463; "gelatine mould," **Vol. 8, Part 2**, 103; generalized forms, **Supp. 3**, 278; Gettysburg, **Vol. 8, Part 1**, 125 f.; Gothic, **Supp. 2**, 22; Indian equestrian themes, **Supp. 3**, 210–11; kinetic, **Supp. 10**, 90–91, 263; life masks, **Vol. 2, Part 1**, 97; limestone, **Supp. 5**, 200; marble, **Supp. 2**, 21, 647; masks, **Supp. 2**, 418; medallions, **Vol. 2, Part 1**, 427; mobile, wind operated, **Supp. 10**, 91; monuments, **Supp. 3**, 88–89, 123–25, 673–74; **Supp. 6**, 597, 720; Mount Rushmore heads, **Supp. 3**, 89; multiple materials used in, **Supp. 7**, 15; National Sculpture Society, **Vol. 8, Part 1**, 125 f.; **Vol. 10, Part 1**, 427 f.; neoclassic, **Vol. 8, Part 1**, 615 f.; neoclassic, twentieth-century, **Supp. 4**, 619; New York Public Library, **Vol. 1, Part 2**, 12; Old Testament figures, **Vol. 7, Part 1**, 304; portrait, **Supp. 3**, 1, 124; **Supp. 4**, 533–34; portrait busts, **Supp. 5**, 231; **Supp. 8**, 414, 415; public, **Supp. 1**, 143, 321–22, 515–16, 575–76; **Supp. 10**, 91; public figures, **Supp. 5**, 153; realism, **Supp. 6**, 720; religious, **Supp. 7**, 530–31; Romanesque, **Supp. 1**, 601; stabile, **Supp. 10**, 91; symbolism, **Vol. 4, Part 1**, 469; teaching of, **Supp. 2**, 647; vorticist group, **Supp. 6**, 194; war memorial, **Supp. 4**, 534; Washington, D.C., **Vol. 1, Part 1**, 240; Wilde's tomb, **Supp. 6**, 193
Scurvy, prevention and cure, **Supp. 1**, 398
Sea Adventure, ship of Virginia colonists, **Vol. 8, Part 2**, 117
Sea Around Us, The, **Supp. 7**, 108–9
Seaboard Air Line Railway, **Vol. 10, Part 1**, 455 f.
Seabury, Samuel (clergyman), reference to, **Vol. 5, Part 1**, 620
Seabury, Samuel (jurist), references to, **Supp. 3**, 646; **Supp. 4**, 465, 856; **Supp. 5**, 285; **Supp. 6**, 88, 141, 152; **Supp. 7**, 4
Seafarers' International Union: **Supp. 6**, 396; presidency of, **Supp. 10**, 303
Seafaring life, **Vol. 1, Part 1**, 524; **Vol. 3, Part 1**, 217; **Vol. 3, Part 2**, 157; **Vol. 7, Part 1**, 467 f., 611 f.; **Vol. 9, Part 1**, 19, 97 f.
Sea Horse, Ogelen's steamboat, **Vol. 7, Part 1**, 637
Seal fishing, **Vol. 1, Part 2**, 328; **Vol. 4, Part 1**, 229; **Vol. 4, Part 2**, 408; **Vol. 7, Part 1**, 195; **Vol. 8, Part 1**, 285 f.; **Vol. 8, Part 2**, 74
Seals, studies on, **Supp. 1**, 291
Seaman's Friend, **Vol. 3, Part 1**, 60
Seaman's Institute (New York City), **Vol. 7, Part 2**, 129

Seamen, first organization for betterment of conditions, **Vol. 10, Part 1**, 46
Seamen's Bethel (Boston), **Vol. 9, Part 2**, 321
Seamen's Friend Society, **Vol. 6, Part 1**, 84
Searchers, The, **Supp. 10**, 823
Searle, Charles E., reference to, **Supp. 3**, 685
Searle, G. D., and Co., **Supp. 8**, 503
Sears, Frederick R., Jr., reference to, **Supp. 3**, 701
Sears, Stephen, reference to, **Supp. 10**, 108
Sears, Roebuck, and Co.: **Supp. 6**, 473; **Supp. 8**, 705; expansion and sales growth of, **Supp. 10**, 163–64; management, **Supp. 10**, 163, 702; shopping center development subsidiary, **Supp. 10**, 164
Seascapes. *See* painting, marine
"Seaside Library," **Vol. 7, Part 1**, 331–2
Sea stories, **Supp. 8**, 182
SEATO. *See* Southeast Asia Treaty Organization
Seatrain Lines, Inc., founding of, **Supp. 3**, 502
Seattle, Wash.: history and growth of, **Vol. 2, Part 1**, 284; Indian attack upon, **Vol. 6, Part 1**, 182; municipal power plant, **Supp. 2**, 583; public service, **Vol. 1, Part 2**, 592; **Vol. 6, Part 1**, 79; **Vol. 6, Part 2**, 56
Seattle-Tacoma Shipbuilding Corporation, founding of, **Supp. 8**, 308
Seaver, John W., reference to, **Vol. 10, Part 1**, 635
Sea Witch (clipper ship), **Vol. 4, Part 1**, 626
Sebastian, Bengamin, reference to, **Vol. 5, Part 1**, 486
SEC. *See* Securities and Exchange Commission
Seceders, religious sect, **Vol. 5, Part 1**, 55
Secession movements: **Vol. 1, Part 1**, 207, 648; **Vol. 1, Part 2**, 312, 571; **Vol. 2, Part 1**, 9, 104, 177 f., 415–16; **Vol. 2, Part 2**, 22, 242; **Vol. 3, Part 2**, 46, 168; **Vol. 4, Part 1**, 598; **Vol. 4, Part 2**, 207, 214, 225; **Vol. 5, Part 1**, 135, 139, 517, 604 f.; **Vol. 5, Part 2**, 83, 102, 129, 552; **Vol. 6, Part 2**, 323; **Vol. 7, Part 2**, 560; **Vol. 8, Part 1**, 216 f., 410; **Vol. 8, Part 2**, 105; **Vol. 9, Part 2**, 591; **Vol. 10, Part 1**, 72; Alabama, **Vol. 10, Part 2**, 593; Davis, Jefferson, **Vol. 3, Part 1**, 125, f.; Democratic viewpoint, **Vol. 1, Part 1**, 388; Florida, **Vol. 10, Part 2**, 638; foreseeing of, in 1835, **Vol. 10, Part 1**, 37; Georgia, **Vol. 2, Part 2**, 248 f.; **Vol. 5, Part 2**, 165; **Vol. 6, Part 1**, 61; Kentucky, **Vol. 8, Part 1**, 148 f., 186 f.; Louisiana, **Vol. 1, Part 2**, 182; **Vol. 8, Part 1**, 251; Maryland, **Vol. 3, Part 1**, 119 f.; **Vol. 7, Part 1**, 602; Mississippi, **Vol. 10, Part 1**, 547; Missouri, **Vol. 3, Part 1**, 365, 495 f.; **Vol. 4, Part 1**, 121; **Vol. 5, Part 2**, 470; **Vol. 8, Part 1**, 185; **Vol. 9, Part 2**, 13; North Carolina, **Vol. 3, Part 1**, 287; novel dealing with, **Vol. 3, Part 1**, 199; open letters on, **Vol. 8, Part 1**, 410; planter, views of, **Vol. 3, Part 1**, 21 f.; Presbyterian church, attitude toward, **Vol. 10, Part 2**, 345; reestablishment of state governments following, **Vol. 5, Part 2**, 84 f.; Rhode Island colony, **Vol. 3, Part 1**, 605; South Carolina, **Vol. 2, Part 1**, 213; **Vol. 4, Part 1**, 325,; **Vol. 7, Part 2**, 560; **Vol. 8, Part 1**, 395, 526 f.; **Vol. 10, Part 1**, 56 f.; Southern Whigs, opposition to, **Vol. 4, Part 2**, 561; Tennessee, **Vol. 2, Part 1**, 577; **Vol. 6, Part 2**, 461; **Vol. 8, Part 1**, 93 f.; Texas, **Vol. 8, Part 1**, 433; **Vol. 10, Part 2**, 188; treason, as, **Vol. 5, Part 2**, 113; Virginia, **Vol. 1, Part 2**, 462, 473; **Vol. 6, Part 1**, 217; **Vol. 8, Part 1**, 206 f., 255 f., 637; **Vol. 8, Part 2**, 30 f.
Secret Service, United States, **Vol. 1, Part 1**, 523; **Vol. 3, Part 2**, 165; **Vol. 4, Part 2**, 550; **Vol. 10, Part 1**, 135
Secret societies, agitation concerning, **Vol. 8, Part 2**, 3
Securities. *See* Stock market
Securities Act (1933), **Supp. 9**, 607
Securities and Exchange Commission (SEC): **Supp. 6**, 216; **Supp. 7**, 453; **Supp. 8**, 112, 219–20; **Supp. 9**, 864; administration, **Supp. 10**, 187–88; establishment of, **Supp. 2**, 195; **Supp. 9**, 614; first chairman, **Supp. 8**, 320; Kennedy, J. P., policies, **Supp. 9**, 607
Securities Exchange Act (1934), **Supp. 1**, 84; **Supp. 7**, 635; **Supp. 9**, 607; passage of, **Supp. 3**, 654
Security industry, **Supp. 10**, 79–80
Sedgwick, Ellery, reference to, **Supp. 5**, 16; **Supp. 9**, 37
Sedgwick, John, reference to, **Vol. 6, Part 1**, 125 f.
Sedition, **Supp. 6**, 105
Sedition laws: constitutionality of, **Vol. 5, Part 2**, 29; opposition to, **Vol. 3, Part 1**, 184; victim of, early, **Vol. 4, Part 2**, 390
Sedwick, William Thompson, reference to, **Supp. 6**, 701
Seeds, germination of, **Supp. 4**, 192
Seeds, mail-order industry, **Supp. 10**, 80–81
Seeger, Pete, references to, **Supp. 8**, 234, 235
Seeing Eye, The, founding of, **Supp. 4**, 253–55
"See It Now," **Supp. 7**, 566–67
Segregation: armed forces, **Supp. 3**, 661; **Supp. 5**, 741; **Supp. 8**, 118–19; **Supp. 9**, 100; **Supp. 10**, 230, 378; black blood plasma, **Supp. 4**, 243; boxing, **Supp. 4**, 432–33; eugenics argument, **Supp. 3**, 215; hospitals, **Supp. 3**, 271; interstate transportation ban on, **Supp. 8**, 322, 333; Jim Crow laws, **Supp. 3**, 391; major league baseball teams, **Supp. 4**, 327–28; New Deal policies against, **Supp. 5**, 343; religious opposition to, **Supp. 4**, 547, 837; **Supp. 8**, 537; "separate but equal" ruling, **Supp. 4**, 397; South Carolina judicial opinions against, **Supp. 8**, 682; South Carolina schools, upheld in, **Supp. 9**, 152; writings on, **Supp. 6**, 321; **Supp. 8**, 605–6; **Supp. 9**, 334. *See also* Civil rights movement; School desegregation
Seidel, Emil, references to, **Supp. 7**, 348; **Supp. 8**, 563
Seismographs, use of, **Vol. 10, Part 1**, 106; **Supp. 9**, 271
Seismological observatory, **Vol. 9, Part 2**, 585 f.
Seismological Society of the Pacific, **Supp. 3**, 479
Seismology. *See* Earthquakes
Selden, George B., references to, **Supp. 4**, 292, 295, 296
Seldes, Marian, reference to, **Supp. 8**, 584
Selective Service. *See* Draft
Selective Service Act (1917), **Vol. 4, Part 2**, 253; **Vol. 5, Part 2**, 251; **Vol. 10, Part 2**, 361; **Supp. 3**, 399
Selective Service Act (1940), **Supp. 5**, 531, 715; **Supp. 10**, 332
Selective Service Act (1948), **Supp. 10**, 332
Selective Service System: administration, **Supp. 10**, 332; first director, **Supp. 4**, 247; lottery, **Supp. 10**, 332. *See also* Draft
Self-actualization, **Supp. 8**, 424
Self-help and improvement: marital advice, **Supp. 8**, 11–12; public speaking guide, **Supp. 5**, 102; writings on, **Supp. 5**, 102, 434, 546; **Supp. 8**, 489
Self-incrimination law, **Supp. 1**, 451
Seligman, Edwin R. A., reference to, **Supp. 4**, 62; **Supp. 6**, 459
Selma, Ala.: capture of, **Vol. 2, Part 1**, 469; **Vol. 3, Part 2**, 533; **Vol. 10, Part 2**, 335; civil rights demonstrations, **Supp. 8**, 334; **Supp. 9**, 384
Seltzer, Joseph, reference to, **Supp. 9**, 213
Selwyn, Archibald, reference to, **Supp. 9**, 323
Selwyn, Edgar, reference to, **Supp. 9**, 323
Selznick, David O., reference to, **Supp. 6**, 441; **Supp. 9**, 376
Selznick, Lewis J., reference to, **Supp. 9**, 797
Selznick International Studios; founding of, **Supp. 7**, 682; productions, **Supp. 9**, 856
Semaphore telegraph systems, railroads, **Vol. 5, Part 2**, 498; **Vol. 8, Part 2**, 97
Semenenko, Serge, reference to, **Supp. 6**, 668

Seminole campaigns: of 1812, **Vol. 1, Part 2**, 520; **Vol. 5, Part 2**, 403; **Vol. 7, Part 1**, 90; **Vol. 7, Part 2**, 76; of 1818, **Vol. 1,**

Semitic literature and language: education in, **Supp. 2**, 252; studies on, **Vol. 5, Part 1**, 513; **Vol. 5, Part 2**, 3; **Vol. 8, Part 2**, 333; **Vol. 9, Part 2**, 262; **Supp. 2**, 5; **Supp. 3**, 37, 374–75; **Supp. 4**, 595–96; **Supp. 6**, 641; **Supp. 9**, 890–91

Senate, United States (for complete list of congressmen and senators, *See* Occupations Index): **Supp. 4**, 220, 723–24; Aeronautical and Space Sciences Committee, **Supp. 7**, 429; agricultural interests, *see subhead:* farm bloc; antitrust advocacy, **Supp. 7**, 590; Appropriations Committee, **Supp. 7**, 74; **Supp. 9**, 664; Armed Services Committee, **Supp. 10**, 27; Army-McCarthy hearings, **Supp. 10**, 645; Atomic Energy Committee, **Supp. 5**, 455; aviation intrerests, **Supp. 10**, 547; Baker hearings, **Supp. 9**, 440; Banking and Currency Committee, **Supp. 4**, 641; **Supp. 5**, 382; **Supp. 9**, 606–7; bipartisan conservative coalition, **Supp. 5**, 443–45, 674–77; bipartisan foreign policy, **Supp. 5**, 704–5; censure votes, **Supp. 4**, 78; **Supp. 6**, 405; **Supp. 7**, 213, 317, 383, 419; **Supp. 8**, 175, 302, 322, 701; civil rights legislation opposition, **Supp. 7**, 398–99; **Supp. 9**, 401, 689; communications industry, legislation regulating, **Supp. 10**, 179; "Conscience of the Senate," **Supp. 10**, 316; conservative-liberal Republican split, **Supp. 8**, 144; conservatives in, **Supp. 3**, 754; **Supp. 4**, 43; **Supp. 6**, 234–35, 507; **Supp. 7**, 31, 73–74, 212, 644, 678, 750; **Supp. 8**, 478; **Supp. 9**, 573–74; **Supp. 10**, 27, 97, 181; consumer legislation, **Supp. 10**, 316; consumer rights, **Supp. 10**, 316; contested seats, **Supp. 5**, 290–91; Crime Committee, **Supp. 6**, 264; defense contracts investigation, **Supp. 7**, 72–73, 95, 521, 764; demagoguery in, **Supp. 3**, 78; Democratic leadership, **Supp. 10**, 361; direct election of members, **Supp. 2**, 54; **Supp. 3**, 105; District of Columbia Committee, **Supp. 6**, 472; Dodd censure vote, **Supp. 9**, 241; Eisenhower support, **Supp. 7**, 50; election to, first regulation of, **Vol. 9, Part 2**, 45; environmental protection advocacy in, **Supp. 6**, 475; **Supp. 10**, 530; Estes investigation, **Supp. 9**, 573; **Supp. 10**, 483; ethics issues, **Supp. 3**, 550; **Supp. 4**, 752; **Supp. 6**, 59–60, 361; **Supp. 7**, 607; farm bloc, **Supp. 3**, 496–97, 559, 723–24; **Supp. 5**, 290; **Supp. 7**, 738–39; **Supp. 9**, 590; federal housing legislation, **Supp. 10**, 87; federal patronage, **Supp. 6**, 419; filibusters, **Supp. 4**, 78; **Supp. 9**, 373, 566; **Supp. 10**, 5, 87; Finance Committee, **Supp. 3**, 334–35, 727; **Supp. 6**, 234, 235, 455; first anti-Vietnam War members, **Supp. 8**, 26; **Supp. 9**, 346–47; first blind member, **Supp. 4**, 338; first member from New Mexico, **Supp. 3**, 259; first members from Alaska, **Supp. 8**, 26; first members from Arizona, **Supp. 7**, 21–22; first woman candidate, **Supp. 5**, 474; first woman elected to, **Vol. 3, Part 2**, 318; **Supp. 4**, 144–45; first working reporter member, **Supp. 5**, 505; fist-fights in, **Vol. 3, Part 2**, 501; Foreign Relations Committee, **Supp. 2**, 51–52; **Supp. 3**, 543; **Supp. 6**, 235, 578; **Supp. 7**, 137–38; **Supp. 8**, 223, 701; **Supp. 9**, 387–88; **Supp. 10**, 361; Foreign Relations Committee of Eight, **Supp. 5**, 334; Government Operations Committee, **Supp. 10**, 483; Guggenheim interests in, **Supp. 3**, 321; Indian Affairs Committee, **Supp. 4**, 641; influence peddling investigation, **Supp. 5**, 307; Internal Security Committee, **Supp. 5**, 444; **Supp. 6**, 681; **Supp. 8**, 133; internationalism, **Supp. 4**, 331–32; **Supp. 7**, 23; investigations, **Vol. 8, Part 2**, 86; **Supp. 9**, 395–96; 440, 573, 606–7, 839; Investigations Committee, **Supp. 3**, 622; **Supp. 8**, 322; **Supp. 10**, 134; isolationism in, **Supp. 3**, 396–97, 558–59; **Supp. 5**, 703–5 739; **Supp. 9**, 842, 860; Johnson, L. B., opposition to, **Supp. 8**, 323–24; Judiciary Committee, **Supp. 5**, 444; **Supp. 6**, 336, 362; **Supp. 7**, 21–22; **Supp. 9**, 449, 511–12; Kefauver Committee, **Supp. 10**, 482–83; labor legislation, **Supp. 5**, 718–19; Labor or Management Improper Activities Committee, **Supp. 7**, 383; **Supp. 9**, 395–96; La Follette civil liberties committee, **Supp. 5**, 403–4; last senator chosen by Missouri legislature, **Supp. 3**, 621; law and order issues, **Supp. 10**, 483; League of Nations, opposition to, **Supp. 4**, 858; **Supp. 9**, 504; liberal Republicanism; **Supp. 7**, 382–83; **Supp. 8**, 653–56; **Supp. 10**, 716; liberals in, **Supp. 6**, 260, 472, 569; **Supp. 7**, 122, 225; **Supp. 8**, 405; **Supp. 10**, 186, 194, 315–16, 530; longest oration, **Supp. 9**, 566; longest term served, **Supp. 9**, 373; McCarthyism in, **Supp. 6**, 405, 432; **Supp. 7**, 751; **Supp. 8**, 128, 426; **Supp. 9**, 387, 573; McCarthyism opposed, **Supp. 9**, 257, 311–12; McClellan Committee, **Supp. 10**, 482–83; majority leaders, **Supp. 4**, 862; **Supp. 5**, 676; **Supp. 6**, 35–36; **Supp. 8**, 391–92; **Supp. 9**, 433, 468; mavericks, **Supp. 8**, 301; medical-related bills, **Supp. 5**, 337; Military Affairs Committee, **Supp. 5**, 715; **Supp. 6**, 335; Naval Affairs Committee, **Supp. 7**, 312; New Deal opposition, **Supp. 5**, 114, 561–62, 703; **Supp. 7**, 312; **Supp. 8**, 247; New Deal support, **Supp. 3**, 334–35; **Supp. 5**, 718–19; **Supp. 7**, 467–68, 541; **Supp. 8**, 508; **Supp. 9**, 256, 689; Old Guard, **Supp. 4**, 861–62; organized crime investigation, **Supp. 7**, 416, 586; **Supp. 8**, 208, 322; **Supp. 9**, 13, 198, 269, 500, 512, 652, 821; **Supp. 10**, 135; Park Commission, **Supp. 3**, 533–34; **Supp. 6**, 485; pension bills, **Supp. 7**, 195; political idealism, **Supp. 5**, 681; president pro tempore, **Supp. 3**, 335; **Supp. 9**, 689; progressive movement in, **Supp. 3**, 105–6, 108, 558–59; **Supp. 4**, 641–42, 669–70; **Supp.6**, 578; public land policy, **Supp. 8**, 104, 105; **Supp. 9**, 842; regional interests, **Supp. 7**, 111, 429; "renegades"in, **Supp. 4**, 309; Republican leadership, **Supp. 8**, 128–29; **Supp. 10**, 716; Rules and Administration Committee, **Supp. 9**, 44; salary of, **Vol. 1, Part 2**, 236; secretary, **Supp. 8**, 36; social legislation, **Supp. 7**, 562; social-welfare legislation opposition, **Supp. 9**, 664, 689; "Sons of the Wild Jackass," **Supp. 3**, 108; **Supp. 6**, 578; southern agricultural interests, **Supp. 4**, 50–51; southern conservatives, **Supp. 8**, 68; **Supp. 10** 482; southern progressives, **Supp. 3**, 449; of states, equal representation, **Vol. 9, Part 2**, 144; Teapot Dome investigation, **Supp. 4**, 482; **Supp. 9**, 590, 859; Truman, opposition to, **Supp. 10**, 181; Truman, support for, **Supp. 7**, 326–27, 764; Vietnam War, opposition to, **Supp. 9**, 346–47, 440, 566; Watergate investigation, **Supp. 10**, 546, 549; Wilson, opposition to, **Supp. 3**, 330–31, 622; **Supp. 4**, 669–70; Wilson, support for, **Supp. 3**, 706; "wizard of the rule book," **Supp. 10**, 4–5; World War I neutrality resolution, **Supp. 4**,338; "Young Turk" insurgency, **Supp. 9**, 467–68. *See also* Congress, United States; House of Representatives, United States; Lobbying

Seneca Indians, **Supp. 7**, 392–94; history of, **Vol. 8, Part 1**, 437 f.

Sennett, Mack, references to, **Supp. 2**, 672; **Supp. 3**, 443; **Supp. 6**, 619; **Supp. 7**, 177, 238; **Supp. 10**, 347

Sensory perception, heat and cold, **Supp. 2**, 156

Sentence and Theme, **Supp. 1**, 687; founding of, **Supp. 1**, 697

"Sentinel register," first thermostat, **Vol. 4, Part 2**, 561

Separatist Society of Zoar, Ohio, founding of, **Vol. 1, Part 2**, 271

Separatism, colonial controversy concerning, **Vol. 3, Part 2**, 156

Sequoyah: name given to redwood trees, **Vol. 8, Part 2**, 586; proposed Indian state of, **Vol. 8, Part 1**, 111
Sequoyah Constitution (1905), **Supp. 6**, 469
Serapis, naval battle with, **Vol. 3, Part 2**, 268; **Vol. 5, Part 2**, 185
Serbia, typhus epidemic, **Supp. 4**, 468, 803; **Supp. 5**, 336
Serigraphy, **Supp. 7**, 15
Serkin, Rudolf, reference to, **Supp. 9**, 140, 141
Sermons, collection of, **Vol. 1, Part 1**, 501
Serra, Junipero, reference to, **Vol. 7, Part 2**, 196 f.
Serro do Mar (Brazil), hydroelectric power, **Supp. 4**, 81–82
Servants of Relief for Incurable Cancer, **Vol. 1, Part 1**, 227
Service, John, references to, **Supp. 6**, 60, 230, 231
Service, John Stewart, reference to, **Supp. 9**, 831
Servicemen's Readjustment Act (1944). *See* GI Bill of Rights
Servites, **Vol. 7, Part 1**, 190
Set designers. For a complete list, *See* Occupations Index
Seth, Andrew, reference to, **Supp. 3**, 696
Seton, Anya, reference to, **Supp. 4**, 737
Seton, Ernest Thompson, reference to, **Supp. 4**, 872
Settlement house movement: **Supp. 1**, 11; **Supp. 2**, 408, 655; **Supp. 3**, 246; **Supp. 4**, 603; **Supp. 5**, 616, 630–31; **Supp. 6**, 499–500; **Supp. 7**, 320, 481; **Supp. 8**, 534–35; Boston, **Vol. 10, Part 1**, 41; Chicago, **Supp. 5**, 579; financing, **Supp. 2**, 608; first for blacks, **Supp. 4**, 53; music instruction, **Supp. 4**, 545; philanthropic gifts for, **Supp. 3**, 729. *See also specific names*
Set-up, The, **Supp. 9**, 692
Seven Arts, **Supp. 7**, 79
Seven-Days' Battles, **Vol. 2, Part 1**, 360; **Vol. 2, Part 2**, 463; **Vol. 3, Part 1**, 598; **Vol. 3, Part 2**, 602; **Vol. 4, Part 2**, 505; **Vol. 5, Part 1**, 27. 343, 558; **Vol. 6, Part 1**, 123, 391, 583; **Vol. 6, Part 2**, 475–205; **Vol. 8, Part 1**, 90; **Vol. 9, Part 2**, 215, 170; **Vol. 10, Part 1**, 473; **Vol. 10, Part 2**, 137. See *also* Peninsular Campaign
Seven Lively Arts, The, **Supp. 8**, 585
Seven Pines, Va., battle of (1862), **Vol. 2, Part 1**, 560; **Vol. 2, Part 2**, 463; **Vol. 5, Part 1**, 27, 343; **Vol. 5, Part 2**, 145, 272, 366; **Vol. 6, Part 1, 123, 391, 583; Vol. 8, Part 1**, 90; **Vol. 9, Part 1**, 272–73; **Vol. 10, Part 2**, 137
Seven Storey Mountain, The, **Supp. 8**, 431
Seventh-Day Adventists, **Supp. 5**, 378–79; **Supp. 7**, 631; health principals, **Supp. 3**, 409–10
Seventh Day Baptists of Ephrata, historical study of, **Vol. 8, Part 2**, 282
Seventh Heaven, **Supp. 7**, 65
Sevier, John, reference to, **Vol. 1, Part 1**, 268; **Vol. 5, Part 1**, 528; **Vol. 9, Part 2**, 563
Sewall, May Wright, reference to **Vol. 5, Part 2**, 208
Sewanee Review, The, founding of, **Supp. 2**, 666
Seward, William H., references to, **Vol. 6, Part 1**, 249 f.; **Vol. 7, Part 1**, 158; **Vol. 8, Part 1**, 409; **Vol. 10, Part 1**, 598 f.; **Supp. 1**, 366
Sewell, E. G., reference to, **Supp. 3**, 20
Sewerage: disposal systems, **Supp. 2**, 408; pollution, **Supp. 2**, 353; studies, **Supp. 6**, 701; systems, development of, **Supp. 1**, 351; treatment of, **Supp. 1**, 389; **Supp. 2**, 169–70. *See also* Public health; Sanitation
Sewing machine: inventions concerning, **Vol. 1, Part 1**, 465; **Vol. 1, Part 2**, 265; **Vol. 3, Part 2**, 43; **Vol. 4, Part 1**, 246, 457, 606; **Vol. 5, Part 1**, 259, 284 f.; **Vol. 9, Part 1**, 189; **Vol. 10, Part 2**, 320; manufacture of, **Vol. 1, Part 1**, 248; **Vol. 5, Part 1**, 286; **Vol. 5, Part 2**, 509; **Vol. 8, Part 1**, 74 f., 499 f.; **Vol. 10, Part 2**, 52
Sex differences. *See* Gender
Sex education, **Supp. 3**, 463; **Supp. 4**, 231, 759; **Supp. 7**, 427, 708; pioneer work in, **Vol. 7, Part 1**, 193, 236 f.
Sex hormones: embryonic, **Supp. 4**, 498; first synthesis of, **Supp. 5**, 28; **Supp. 9**, 444. *See also* Endocrine glands
Sex-linked traits. *See* Genetics
Sexuality: erotica, **Supp. 10**, 591; fraudulent rejuvenation claims, **Supp. 3**, 103–4; free expression advocacy, **Supp. 3**, 454, 463; journalism exploiting, **Supp. 5**, 453; Kinsey studies, **Supp. 6**, 252, 343–44, 718; in literature, **Supp. 10**, 540; National Committee on Maternal Health research, **Supp. 6**, 81–82; National Research Council studies, **Supp. 6**, 718; psychoanalytic deemphasis, **Supp. 3**, 191; psychological theories on, **Supp. 4**, 805; social hygiene movement, **Supp. 4**, 758–59. *See also* Gender
Sexually transmitted diseases. *See* Venereal disease
Seymour, Charles, reference to, **Supp. 4**, 22
Seymour, Horatio, reference to, **Vol. 9, Part 2**, 540
Sgt. Pepper's Lonely Hearts Club Band, **Supp. 10**, 450
Shades, window, invention of, **Vol. 2, Part 1**, 334
Shahan, Thomas J., reference to, **Supp. 4**, 353
Shaker colonies, **Vol. 3, Part 2**, 198 f.; **Vol. 6, Part 1**, 95, f.; **Vol. 9, Part 1**, 285
Shakespeare, William: acting of, **Vol. 1, Part 1**, 647; **Vol. 4, Part 2**, 73, 75; **Vol. 5, Part 2**, 285; **Vol. 7, Part 1**, 73; **Vol. 9, Part 1**, 402; acting of, by blacks, **Vol. 1, Part 1**, 160; Baconian theory, **Vol. 1, Part 1**, 475; **Vol. 3, Part 1**, 370; **Vol. 5, Part 1**, 169, 244; **Vol. 7, Part 1**, 620; **Supp. 5**, 20; editing of works of, **Vol. 4, Part 1**, 78 f.; **Vol. 8, Part 2**, 119; **Supp. 4**, 624; folio collections, **Supp. 5**, 586–87; masque for, **Supp. 6**, 481; musical comedy adaptation, **Supp. 3**, 339; paintings of plays of, **Vol. 1, Part 1**, 7; productions of works of, **Supp. 4**, 477–79, 552–54; **Supp. 5**, 268–69; **Supp. 7**, 496; readings from, **Vol. 5, Part 2**, 316, 570; scholarship on, **Supp. 3**, 423–24; **Supp. 4**, 4–5, 110, 634; **Supp. 9**, 626–27; sculpture of characters, **Vol. 4, Part 1**, 457; studies in, **Vol. 5, Part 1**, 340 f.; **Vol. 5, Part 2**, 523; **Vol. 9, Part 1**, 472; **Vol. 10, Part 1**, 367 f.; writings on, **Vol. 1, Part 1**, 148; **Vol. 5, Part 2**, 154; **Vol. 7, Part 1**, 292: **Vol. 9, Part 1**, 190; **Vol. 10, Part 1**, 367 f.; **Vol. 10, Part 2**, 114
Shakespeare and Company (Paris bookstore), **Supp. 7**, 40, 41
Shakespeariana, collecting of, **Vol. 3, Part 2**, 487; **Vol. 9, Part 1**, 372; **Vol. 9, Part 2**, 432
Shakespeare Without Tears, **Supp. 9**, 849
Shaler, Nathanial S., reference to, **Vol. 9, Part 2, 308**
Shaler, Nathaniel Southgate, reference to, **Supp. 9**, 525
Shane, **Supp. 9**, 232, 768
Shanghai American School, founding of, **Supp. 2**, 549
Shanghai Anglo-Chinese College, **Vol. 1, Part 1**, 215, 263
Shankar, Ravi, reference to, **Supp. 8**, 100
Shannon, Joseph B., reference to, **Supp. 3**, 596
Shapley, Harlow, references to, **Supp. 3**, 208; **Supp. 5**, 326; **Supp. 6**, 56; **Supp. 10**, 353
Shapp, Milton, reference to, **Supp. 8**, 361
Sharecropping. *See* Tenant farming
Share-Our-Wealth Society, founding of, **Supp. 1**, 508
Sharkey, Jack, reference to, **Supp. 6**, 700
Sharon, William, divorce case, **Vol. 9, Part 2**, 380
Sharp, Lester W., reference to, **Supp. 4**, 253
Sharp, William, reference to, **Vol. 5, Part 1**, 614
Sharp and Dohme, Merck merger, **Supp. 6**, 448
"Sharps and Flats," **Vol. 3, Part 2**, 363; **Vol. 9, Part 2**, 317
Sharpsburg, Md., battle of. *See* Antietam, battle of

Shasta Dam, **Supp. 4**, 198–99
Shaw, Anna H., reference to, **Vol. 5, Part 1**, 312
Shaw, Clifford, reference to, **Supp. 9**, 18
Shaw, George Bernard, references to, **Supp. 4**, 369, 528; **Supp. 7**, 283, 322, 325, 496
Shaw, Lemuel, murder trial, charges of, **Vol. 10, Part 1**, 592 f.
Shaw, Samuel, reference to, **Vol. 8, Part 2**, 539
Shawn, Edwin Myers ("Ted"), references to, **Supp. 7**, 366; **Supp. 8**, 620–21
Shawn, William, reference to, **Supp. 5**, 594; **Supp. 10**, 247
Shawnee Indians, **Vol. 9, Part 2**, 358 f., 375; war with, *See* Northwestern Indians
Shaw University, founding of, **Vol. 3, Part 2**, 189
Shays' Rebellion (1786–87), **Vol. 1, Part 1**, 100; **Vol. 6, Part 1**, 77, 260–61; **Vol. 8, Part 1**, 196; **Vol. 9, Part 1**, 50, 77; **Vol. 9, Part 2**, 51; **Vol. 10, Part 1**, 96, 521
Shea Stadium (Queens, N.Y.), **Supp. 9**, 764
Shear, T. Leslie, reference to, **Supp. 4**, 144
Shearn, Clarence, reference to, **Supp. 5**, 287–88
She Done Him Wrong, **Supp. 10**, 829
Sheehan, William F., reference to, **Supp. 3**, 642
Sheeler, Charles: reference to, **Supp. 3**, 284; writings on, **Supp. 3**, 673
Sheen, Fulton J., reference to, **Supp. 7**, 52
Sheep raising and importing: **Vol. 1, Part 1**, 599; **Vol. 3, Part 1**, 251; **Vol. 3, Part 2**, 478 f.; **Vol. 4, Part 1**, 256; **Vol. 4, Part 2**, 162, 204; **Vol. 5, Part 1**, 374, 624 f.; **Vol. 8, Part 1**, 143 f.; **Vol. 9, Part 2**, 525; writings on, **Vol. 8, Part 1**, 324 f.
Sheet metal, **Vol. 1, Part 2**, 73; **Vol. 5, Part 1**, 57; **Vol. 6, Part 1**, 82
Sheet music, **Supp. 3**, 833–34; **Supp. 4**, 88
Shelby, Isaac, reference to, **Vol. 6, Part 1**, 357
Shelby Musical College, founding of, **Vol. 5, Part 2, 207**
Sheldon, Edward, references to, **Supp. 3**, 34; **Supp. 6**, 400
Sheldon Jackson College, **Vol. 3, Part 1**, 608 f.
Shelford, Victor E., reference to, **Supp. 3**, 169
Shells, collecting of, **Vol. 3, Part 2**, 269; **Vol. 4, Part 1**, 446; **Vol. 6, Part 1**, 67, 70 f.; **Vol. 8, Part 1**, 192, 395 f.; **Vol. 8, Part 2**, 401 f.; **Vol. 9, Part 1**, 548, 585 **Vol. 9, Part 2**, 599
Shell shock, **Supp. 5**, 383
She Loves Me, **Supp. 10**, 106
She Loves You, **Supp. 10**, 449
Shelta, gypsy tongue, discovery of, **Vol. 6, Part 1**, 159
Sheltering Home for Immigrants, founding of, **Vol. 1, Part 2**, 361
Sheltering Sky, The, **Supp. 9**, 115
Shenandoah, war play, **Vol. 5, Part 1**, 276
Shenandoah Valley: colonization of, **Vol. 5, Part 1, 80**; early's operations in, **Vol. 3, Part 1**, 598 f.; Sheridan's raid, **Vol. 9, Part 1**, 80
Sheng Hsuan-huai, reference to, **Supp. 3**, 268
Shenker, Morris, reference to, **Supp. 9**, 512
Shepard, Jesse, reference to, **Vol. 4, Part 1**, 614
Shepard, Thomas, reference to, **Vol. 7, Part 1**, 573
Shepard Congregational Society, **Vol. 5, Part 1**, 16
Shepherd, Ernest S., reference to, **Supp. 6**, 153
Sheppard, Eugenia, reference to, **Supp. 8**, 441, 520
Sheppard, Samuel E., reference to, **Supp. 6**, 442
Sheppard and Enoch Pratt Hospital (Baltimore), **Supp. 4**, 806, 807, 808
Sheppard-Towner Act (1921), **Supp. 5**, 532
Sheridan, Philip H., references to, **Vol. 3, Part 1, 598 f.; Vol. 5, Part 1**, 401; **Vol. 7, Part 1**, 560; **Vol. 9, Part 2**, 593
Sherington, Sir Charles, reference to, **Supp. 4**, 59
Sherman, Clifton L., references to, **Supp. 6**, 231, 232
Sherman, Forrest, reference to, **Supp. 5**, 66
Sherman, Frank Dempster, reference to, **Vol. 8, Part 2**, 486
Sherman, Henry C, reference to, **Supp. 3**, 671
Sherman, Lawrence Y., reference to, **Supp. 7**, 21
Sherman, Moses Hazeltine, reference to, **Supp. 3**, 155
Sherman, William Tecumseh: biography of, **Supp. 4**, 490; references to, **Vol. 3, Part 1**, 50 f.; **Vol. 4, Part 2**, 240, 312, 377; **Vol. 5, Part 1**, 194; **Vol. 6, Part 1**, 88, 566, 596; **Vol. 7, Part 1**, 300; **Vol. 8, Part 2**, 453; **Vol. 9, Part 1**, 324; sculpture of, **Supp. 5**, 231
Sherman Antitrust Act (1890): **Vol. 3, Part 1**, 342; **Vol. 4, Part 1**, 217; **Vol. 7, Part 2**, 32; **Vol. 8, Part 2**, 65; **Supp. 2**, 573, 714; **Supp. 6**, 494; Clayton Amendment, **Supp. 1**, 179; first action against organized medicine, **Supp. 3**, 122
Sherman Silver Purchase Act (1890), **Vol. 1, Part 1** 214; **Vol. 2, Part 2**, 210; **Vol. 8, Part 1**, 2 f.; **Vol. 9, Part 2**, 362
Sherrington, Charles, reference to, **Supp. 6**, 223
Sherwin, John, Sr., reference to, **Supp. 10**, 334
Sherwood, Gale, reference to, **Supp. 8**, 151
Sherwood, Robert E.: biography of, **Supp. 8**, 54; references to, **Supp. 3**, 53, 251; **Supp. 7**, 413; **Supp. 8**, 491, 529; **Supp. 10**, 400
Shibe Park (Philadelphia, Pa.), **Supp. 6**, 415
Shields, Brooke, reference to, **Supp. 9**, 722
Shikellamy, reference to, **Vol. 10, Part 1**, 614 f.
Shiloh, battle of, **Vol. 1, Part 2**, 111, 586; **Vol. 2, Part 1**, 9, 240; **Vol. 2, Part 2**, 190; **Vol. 3, Part 2**, 532; **Vol. 4, Part 1**, 494–95; **Vol. 4, Part 2**, 151, 240; **Vol. 5, Part 1**, 425; **Vol. 5, Part 2**, 136, 216; **Vol. 6, Part 1**, 587; **Vol. 8, Part 1**, 183; **Vol. 9, Part 1**, 94
Shimer, Hervey W., reference to, **Supp. 4**, 343
Shimkin, Leon, reference to, **Supp. 8**, 579
Shimmy (dance movement), **Supp. 6**, 247
Shinn, Everett, references to, **Supp. 5**, 635, 636
Ship: armor, **Vol. 9, Part 1**, 608, 620; carving, **Vol. 7, Part 1**, 243; **Vol. 8, Part 2**, 235; chandlery, **Vol. 4, Part 1**, 463; classification, **Supp. 5**, 440–41; design, **Supp. 1**, 596; **Supp. 2**, 298; disasters, *Titanic*, **Supp. 6**, 23; equipment, **Vol. 6, Part 2**, 23; Eureka boat, **Supp. 5**, 299; landing craft, **Supp. 5**, 299, 361; merchant marine upgrading, **Supp. 4**, 848–49; models, **Supp. 1**, 99–101; oceanographic research, **Supp. 8**, 38; passenger liner design, **Supp. 5**, 725–26; refueling at sea, **Supp. 2**, 239; salvaging, **Vol. 3, Part 1**, 221; **Vol. 6, Part 2**, 571; subsidy, **Vol. 4, Part 2**, 227; tankers, **Supp. 2**, 270; timber, colonial trading in, **Vol. 3, Part 1**, 486 f.; turbine-electrical propulsion, **Supp. 3**, 251; World War II, **Supp. 8**, 308. *See also* Merchant marine; Naval vessels; Submarines
Shipbuilding: **Vol. 1, Part 1**, 21, 606; **Vol. 1, Part 2**, 156, 485; **Vol. 2, Part 2**, 112, 342 f.; **Vol. 3, Part 1** 211, 292, 458; **Vol. 3, Part 2**, 4, 164, 582; **Vol. 4, Part 1**, 626; **Vol. 4, Part 2**, 6, 9, 122, 142, 585; **Vol. 5, Part 1**, 35 f., 155, 376; **Vol. 5, Part 2**, 110, 121, 405; **Vol. 6, Part 2**, 23, 72; **Vol. 7, Part 1**, 446; **Vol. 8, Part 2**, 200, 492, 553 f., 605; **Vol. 9, Part 1**, 310; **Vol. 9, Part 2**, 626; **Vol. 10, Part 1**, 548 f., 578 f.; **Vol. 10, Part 2**, 400; clipper ships, **Vol. 10, Part 2**, 15; Great Lakes, **Vol. 5, Part 2**, 110, 120; iron, early, **Vol. 3, Part 1**, 211; **Vol. 8, Part 1**, 639 f.; Massachusetts, **Vol. 10, Part 1**, 548 f.; New Bedford, Mass., **Vol. 8, Part 2**, 246; New York, **Vol. 1, Part 2**, 156, 215; **Vol. 2, Part 2**, 46; **Vol. 10, Part 1**, 578 f.; packets, **Vol. 10, Part 2**, 15
Ship of Fools, **Supp. 9**, 247; **Supp. 10**, 642
Shipping (for names of specific ships, *see* Ships): American Bureau of Shipping, **Vol. 6, Part 1**, 545; **Vol. 9, Part 2**, 344; American Prudential–Grace Shipping

Lines, **Supp. 9**, 734; Atlas Line, **Vol. 1, Part 1**, 524; dry docks, **Vol. 3, Part 2**, 158; Grace Steamship Co., **Vol. 4, Part 1**, 463; Great Lakes, **Vol. 6, Part 1**, 327; Hamburg American Line, **Vol. 1, Part 2**, 400; inland and waterways, **Vol. 7, Part 1**, 405; ironclad vessels, **Vol. 3, Part 1**, 211; **Vol. 8, Part 1**, 97; **Vol. 8, Part 2**, 78, 85; Mechanic's Line, **Vol. 5, Part 2**, 372; merchant marine, **Vol. 4, Part 2**, 6; **Vol. 8, Part 1**, 17 f.; **Vol. 10, Part 1**, 424 f.; "merchant venturers," **Vol. 4, Part 1**, 504; *Michigan*, **Vol. 2, Part 1**, 338; Morgan Line, **Vol. 7, Part 1**, 164 f.; Ocean Steam Navigation Co., **Vol. 9, Part 1**, 580; Oregon Steam Navigation Co., **Vol. 8, Part 1**, 456; Pacific Mail Steamship Lines; **Vol. 1, Part 1**, 396; **Vol. 7, Part 2**, 209; *Pacific Northwest*, **Vol. 10, Part 1**, 532 f.; packet boats, **Vol. 2, Part 2**, 421; **Vol. 4, Part 2**, 154; **Vol. 8, Part 2**, 324, 593; paddlewheel boat, **Vol. 8, Part 2**, 133; Philadelphla, **Vol. 1, Part 2**, 464; pilot boat service, **Vol. 8, Part 1**, 481; Potomac River, **Vol. 8, Part 2**, 223; Red Star Line, **Vol. 9, Part 2**, 397; river and harbor development, **Vol. 10, Part 2**, 339; Salem, **Vol. 5, Part 1**, 249 f., 252 f.; **Vol. 9, Part 1**, 165; Shipping Board, World War I, **Vol. 3, Part 2**, 206; **Vol. 6, Part 1**, 79; **Vol. 8, Part 2**, 194; *South America*, **Vol. 1, Part 2**, 241; steamboats, early, **Vol. 5, Part 2**, 549; **Vol. 8, Part 2**, 106; **Vol. 9, Part 2**, 504; steam vessel, first to cross Atlantic, **Vol. 3, Part 1**, 339; **Vol. 8, Part 2**, 106; United States Mail Steamship Co., **Vol. 2, Part 2**, 306; **Vol. 8, Part 2**, 11; Ward Line, **Vol. 10, Part 1**, 424 f.; West Indian, **Vol. 8, Part 2**, 341 f.
Shipping Board, United States, **Vol. 3, Part 2**, 206
Shipping, Bureau of, **Vol. 6, Part 1**, 545
Shipping disasters: *Andrea Doria* sinking, **Supp. 9**, 236; *Comanche* sinking, **Supp. 9**, 728; *Titanic* sinking, **Supp. 9**, 866
Ship purchase bill, defeat of, **Vol. 2, Part 2**, 154
Ships
Blockade runners: *Ada*, **Vol. 10, Part 1**, 568; *Antonica*, **Vol. 2, Part 2**, 490; *Beauregard*, **Vol. 2, Part 2**, 490; *Britannia*, **Vol. 10, Part 2**, 585; *Cecile*, **Vol. 6, Part 2**, 196; *Chameleon*, **Vol. 10, Part 2**, 229; *Chickamauga*, **Vol. 10, Part 2**, 229; *Coquette*, **Vol. 4, Part 2**, 167; *Corunbia*, **Vol. 7, Part 2**, 308; *Dare*, **Vol. 4, Part 2**, 167; *Delaware Farmer*, **Vol. 2, Part 2**, 635; *Delphina*, **Vol. 6, Part 2**, 479; *Don*, **Vol. 8, Part 1**, 293; *Ella*, **Vol. 7, Part 2**, 308; *Ella and Annie*, **Vol. 2, Part 2**, 636; *Elmira*, **Vol. 8, Part 2**, 569; *Fingal*, **Vol. 2, Part 1**, 258; *Florie*, **Vol. 6, Part 2**, 196; *General Parkhill*, **Vol. 8, Part 2**, 437; *Georgiana*, **Vol. 3, Part 1**, 136; *Giraffe*, **Vol. 10, Part 2**, 228; *Golden Rocket*, **Vol. 8, Part 2**, 580; *Grayhound*, **Vol. 8, Part 1**, 47; *Hebe*, **Vol. 7, Part 2**, 308; *Herald*, **Vol. 2, Part 2**, 490; *Isabel*, **Vol. 7, Part 1**, 154–55; *Ivanhoe*, **Vol. 10, Part 1**, 545; *Joanna Ward*, **Vol. 10, Part 1**, 318; *Kate*, **Vol. 7, Part 2**, 308; *Lillian*, **Vol. 6, Part 2**, 196; **Vol. 9, Part 1**, 486; *Lizzie*, **Vol. 10, Part 2**, 585; *Louisville*, **Vol. 8, Part 2**, 569; *Margaret*, **Vol. 5, Part 1**, 152; *Mary Pierce*, **Vol. 5, Part 1**, 152; *Monticello*, **Vol. 5, Part 1**, 152; *Neptune*, **Vol. 6, Part 2**, 271; *North Heath*, **Vol. 9, Part 1**, 486; *Nutfield*, **Vol. 8, Part 2**, 85; *Owl*, **Vol. 6, Part 2**, 196; *Pioneer*, **Vol. 2, Part 2**, 635; *Planter*, **Vol. 6, Part 2**, 271; *Princess Royal*, **Vol. 8, Part 1**, 293; **Vol. 9, Part 2**, 518; *Quaker City*, **Vol. 2 Part 2**, 259; *Robert E. Lee*, **Vol. 7, Part 2**, 308; **Vol. 9, Part 2**, 262; **Vol. 10, Part 2**, 228; *St. Nicholas*, **Vol. 5, Part 1**, 152; *Susan Beirne*, **Vol. 9, Part 1**, 486; *Theodora*, **Vol. 6, Part 2**, 196; *Wild Dagrell*, **Vol. 8, Part 2**, 85
Built in America, sold to foreign countries: *Dunderberg*, **Vol. 10, Part 1**, 579; *General Admiral*, **Vol. 10, Part 1**, 579; *Re di Portogallo*, **Vol. 10, Part 1**, 579; *Re d'Italia*, **Vol. 10, Part 1**, 579; *Rochambeau*, **Vol. 10, Part 1**, 579; *Saratoga*, **Vol. 10, Part 1**, 424; *United States*, **Vol. 6, Part 2**, 306
California "gold rush": *Brooklyn*, **Vol. 1, Part 2**, 602; *Brutus*, **Vol. 8, Part 1**, 322; *Eliza*, **Vol. 1, Part 2**, 228; *Mount Vernon*, **Vol. 10, Part 1**, 384; *Panama*, **Vol. 6, Part 1**, 445; **Vol. 6, Part 2**, 110; *Tarolinta*, **Vol. 7, Part 1**, 612; *Thomas Perkins*, **Vol. 8, Part 2**, 116
Clipper: *Amphitrite*, **Vol. 4, Part 2**, 142; *Andrew Jackson*, **Vol. 2, Part 2**, 534; *Ann McKim*, **Vol. 4, Part 1**, 626; **Vol. 6, Part 2**, 102; *Aramingo*, **Vol. 10, Part 2**, 16; *Australia*, **Vol. 10, Part 1**, 578; *Bald Eagle*, **Vol. 6, Part 2**, 72; *Black Hawk*, **Vol. 10, Part 1**, 578; *Black Prince*, **Vol. 2, Part 2**, 120; *Celestial*, **Vol. 10, Part 1**, 578; *Challenge*, **Vol. 10, Part 1**, 535-578; *Chariot of Fame*, **Vol. 6, Part 2**, 72; *Comet*, **Vol. 10, Part 1**, 578; *Contest*, **Vol. 6, Part 1**, 444; **Vol. 10, Part 2**, 16; *Dashing Wave*, **Vol. 5, Part 1**, 3; *Dreadnought*, **Vol. 9, Part 2**, 67; *Empress of the Seas*, **Vol. 6, Part 2**, 72; *Eureka*, **Vol. 10, Part 2**, 16; *Express*, **Vol. 4, Part 2**, 142; *Flyaway*, **Vol. 10, Part 1**, 578; *Flying Childers*, **Vol. 4, Part 2**, 142; *Flying Cloud*, **Vol. 2, Part 2**, 533; **Vol. 6, Part 2**, 72; **Vol. 7, Part 1**, 33; **Vol. 9, Part 2**, 52, 625–26; *Flying Dutchman*, **Vol. 10, Part 1**, 578; *Flying Fish*, **Vol. 4, Part 2**, 142; *Game Cock*, **Vol. 4, Part 2**, 142; *Gazelle*, **Vol. 10, Part 1**, 578; *Glory of the Seas*, **Vol. 6, Part 2**, 73; *Golden City*, **Vol. 10, Part 2**, 16; *Golden Gate*, **Vol. 10, Part 2**, 16; *Golden State*, **Vol. 10, Part 2**, 16; *Great Republic*, **Vol. 6, Part 2**, 72; **Vol. 7, Part 2**, 190; *Hoogly*, **Vol. 4, Part 2**, 142; *Hornet*, **Vol. 10, Part 2**, 16; *Houqua*, **Vol. 6, Part 1**, 44; **Vol. 7, Part 2**, 190; *Intrepid*, **Vol. 10, Part 1**, 578; *Invincible*, **Vol. 10, Part 1**, 578; *Jacob Bell*, **Vol. 6, Part 1**, 444; *James Baines*, **Vol. 6, Part 2**, 72; *John Gilpin*, **Vol. 4, Part 2**, 142; *Kathay*, **Vol. 10, Part 2**, 16; *Levere*, **Vol. 2, Part 1**, 308; *Lightning*, **Vol. 6, Part 2**, 72; *Messenger*, **Vol. 1, Part 2**, 156; *Mystery*, **Vol. 4, Part 2**, 142; *Natchez*, **Vol. 10, Part 1**, 534; *N. B. Palmer*, **Vol. 10, Part 2**, 16; *North Wind*, **Vol. 7, Part 1**, 33; *Northern Light*, **Vol. 2, Part 2**, 120; *Oneida*, **Vol. 2, Part 2**, 533; *Oriental*, **Vol. 1, Part 2**, 156; **Vol. 4, Part 2**, 142; **Vol. 7, Part 2**, 190; *Polynesia*, **Vol. 4, Part 2**, 142; *Race Horse*, **Vol. 4, Part 2**, 142; *Rainbow*, **Vol. 4, Part 1**, 626; *R. B. Forbes*, **Vol. 4, Part 2**, 142; *Resolute*, **Vol. 10, Part 2**, 16; *Romance of the Seas*, **Vol. 6, Part 2**, 72; *Samuel Russell*, **Vol. 6, Part 1**, 444; **Vol. 7, Part 2**, 190; *Sea Serpent*, **Vol. 7, Part 1**, 33; *Sea Witch*, **Vol. 4, Part 1**, 626; **Vol. 10, Part 1**, 534; *Snapdragon*, **Vol. 10, Part 1**, 578; *Sovereign of the Seas*, **Vol. 6, Part 2**, 72; *Staffordshire*, **Vol. 9, Part 2**, 625; *Stag Hound*, **Vol. 6, Part 2**, 72; *Star of Empire*, **Vol. 6, Part 2**, 72; *Surprise*, **Vol. 4, Part 2**, 142; *Sweepstakes*, **Vol. 10, Part 2**, 16; *Sword Fish*, **Vol. 10, Part 1**, 578; *Telegraph*, **Vol. 4, Part 2**, 142; *Trade Wind*, **Vol. 1, Part 2**, 156; *Uncowah*, **Vol. 10, Part 1**, 578; *Westward Ho*, **Vol. 6, Part 2**, 72; *White Squall*, **Vol. 1, Part 2**, 156; *Witchcraft*, **Vol. 8, Part 2**, 116; *Wizard*, **Vol. 4, Part 2**, 142; **Vol. 7, Part 1**, 317; *Young America*, **Vol. 10, Part 1**, 578
Colonial: *Ann*, **Vol. 6, Part 2**, 617; *Anne*, **Vol. 7, Part 1**, 43, 59, 254, 261; **Vol. 7, Part 2, 12, 406; Vol. 9, Part 1**, 500; *Arbella*, **Vol. 7, Part 2**, 546; **Vol. 8, Part 1**, 290; **Vol. 10, Part 1**, 479; **Vol. 10, Part 2**, 409, 567; *Archangel*, **Vol. 10, Part 1**, 562; *Canterbury*, **Vol. 6, Part 1**, 361; *Confidence*, **Vol. 10, Part 2**, 209; *Defence*, **Vol. 5, Part 1**, 329; **Vol. 7, Part 2**, 204; *Desire*, **Vol. 7, Part 2**, 406; *Discoverer*, **Vol. 8, Part 1**, 235; *Discovery*, **Vol. 7, Part 1**, 468; **Vol. 8, Part 1**, 110; *Eendracht*, **Vol. 7, Part 1**, 34; *Elizabeth*, **Vol. 3, Part 1**, 34; **Vol. 6, Part 1**, 531; **Vol. 7, Part 1**, 72; *Elizabeth and Mary*, **Vol. 9, Part 2**, 542, 543; *Fama*, **Vol. 8, Part 1**, 239; *Fellowship*, **Vol. 4, Part 1**, 139; *Fortune*, **Vol. 3, Part 1**, 5, 334; **Vol. 5, Part 1**, 515; **Vol. 7, Part 1**, 254; **Vol. 7, Part 2**, 184; **Vol. 10, Part 2**, 393–94; *Friendship*, **Vol. 2, Part 2**, 72; **Vol. 5, Part 1**, 80; *Gift of God*, **Vol. 8, Part 1**, 78; *Godspeed*, **Vol. 4, Part 1**, 439; **Vol.**

7, Part 1, 468; *Griffin*, Vol. 4, Part 2, 459; Vol. 5, Part 1, 425–36; Vol. 7, Part 1, 34; *Gyllene Haj*, Vol. 8, Part 1, 627; *Harinchk*, Vol. 5, Part 2, 370; *Harle*, Vol. 9, Part 2, 180; *Het Meemotze* (The Little Gull), Vol. 7, Part 1, 34; *Het Vliegende Hert* (The Flying Stag), Vol. 7, Part 1, 34; *Hoop*, Vol. 10, Part 2, 15; *James*, Vol. 3, Part 2, 151; John, Vol. 3, Part 1, 163; *Jollif Galley*, Vol. 3, Part 1, 272; *Kent*, Vol. 7, Part 2, 434; *Key of Colmar*, Vol. 7, Part 1, 34; *Lion*, Vol. 6, Part 1, 514; Vol. 10, Part 2, 409; *Little James*, Vol. 7, Part 1, 254; *Lyon*, Vol. 7, Part 2, 406; *Mary and John*, Vol. 3, Part 1, 605; Vol. 4, Part 1, 488; Vol. 6, Part 1, 493; Vol. 7, Part 1, 72; Vol. 8, Part 1 78; Vol. 9, Part 2, 149–53; *Mayflower*, Vol. 1, Part 1, 129, 145, 146, 524; Vol. 1, Part 2, 237, 430, 559; Vol. 2, Part 1, 30, 551; Vol. 2, Part 2, 136, 146, 119; Vol. 3, Part 1, 5; Vol. 4, Part 1, 57, 557, 622; Vol. 5, Part 1, 312, 313, 420, 606; Vol. 5, Part 2, 556; Vol. 6, Part 2, 564, 622; Vol. 7, Part 1, 254, 334, 577; Vol. 7, Part 2, 406; Vol. 8, Part 1, 187, 188, 230, 456, 495; Vol. 8, Part 2, 600; Vol. 9, Part 1, 289, 500, 524; Vol. 10, Part 1, 363, 478, 485, 487, 488, 537; Vol. 10, Part 2, 20, 393, 394; *Neptune*, Vol. 7, Part 2, 108; *Olive Branch*, Vol. 8, Part 1, 235; *Orangenboom*, Vol. 5, Part 2, 508; *Orn*, Vol. 8, Part 1, 627; *Paragon*, Vol. 7, Part 2, 406; *Prosperous*, Vol. 3, Part 1, 34; *Restaurationen*, Vol. 7, Part 2, 390; *Rose*, Vol. 7, Part 2, 551; *San Carlos*, Vol. 3, Part 2, 244; *Sea Adventure*, Vol. 4, Part 1, 190; Vol. 8, Part 2, 1 17; Vol. 9, Part 2, 120; *Speedwell*, Vol. 2, Part 1, 551; Vol. 3, Part 1, 5; Vol. 7, Part 1, 261; Vol. 8, Part 1, 235; Vol. 10, Part 2, 393; *Starr*, Vol. 3, Part 1, 34; *Susan and Ellen*, Vol. 5, Part 1, 70; *Susan Costant*, Vol. 7, Part 1, 468; *Swan*, Vol. 8, Part 1, 239; *Swift*, Vol. 5, Part 1, 80; *Thistle*, Vol. 6, Part 2, 632; *Three Saints*, Vol. 9, Part 1, 68; *Treasurer*, Vol. 8, Part 1, 19; *Trial*, Vol. 1, Part 2, 485; *Vine*, Vol. 7, Part 2, 118; *Welcome*, Vol. 10, Part 1, 386; Vol. 5, Part 2, 181, 265, 463; *William*, Vol. 10, Part 1, 216

Experimental and scientific: *Albatross*, Vol. 1, Part 1, 113; Vol. 3, Part 1, 614; Vol. 7, Part 1, 598; Vol. 8, Part 2, 464; *Aunt Sally*, Vol. 7, Part 1, 161; *Babcock*, Vol. 9, Part 2, 520; *Balloon*, Vol. 7, Part 1, 471; *Burnside*, Vol. 9, Part 1, 480; *Cleremont*, Vol. 2, Part 2, 46; Vol. 4, Part 1, 71; Vol. 6, Part 1, 324; Vol. 7, Part 1, 471; Vol. 8, Part 2, 106; Vol. 9, Part 1, 615; *Columbia Maid*, Vol. 8, Part 2, 223; *Condor*, Vol. 5, Part 1, 238; *Eagle*, Vol. 8, Part 2, 106; *Francis B. Ogden*, Vol. 7, Part 1, 639; *Fulton* or *Robert Fulton*, Vol. 3, Part 2, 5; Vol. 4, Part 1, 71, 245; Vol. 6, Part 2, 593; *Geographe*, Vol. 6, Part 1, 190; *Great Eastern*, Vol. 5, Part 2, 566; *Hassler*, Vol. 8, Part 1, 141; Vol. 10, Part 2, 109; *J. Y. Mason*, Vol. 10, Part 1, 318; *Juliana*, Vol. 9, Part 1, 615–19; *Le Hardi*, Vol. 6, Part 1, 190; *Little Juliana*, Vol. 9, Part 1, 615–19; *Nautilus*, Vol. 4, Part 1, 70; *New Era*, Vol. 4, Part 1, 627; *New Orleans*, Vol. 8, Part 2, 134; *North America*, Vol. 9, Part 1, 608; *Peedee*, Vol. 8, Part 2, 107; *Phoenix*, Vol. 8, Part 2, 106; Vol. 9, Part 1, 615–19; *Polacca*, Vol. 5, Part 1, 232; Vol. 8, Part 2, 134; Vol. 9, Part 1, 615; *Robert F. Stockton*, Vol. 7, Part 1, 639; *Rushlight*, Vol. 9, Part 2, 520; *Savannah*, Vol. 2, Part 1, 257; Vol. 3, Part 1, 339; Vol. 8, Part 2, 106, 107, 410; Vol. 9, Part 1, 315; *Sea Horse*, Vol. 7, Part 1, 637–39; *Stoudinger*, Vol. 4, Part 1, 243; *Walker*, Vol. 10, Part 1, 568

Exploration: *Advance*, Vol. 4, Part 2, 120; Vol. 5, Part 2, 256; Vol. 7, Part 2, 337; *Adventure*, Vol. 4, Part 1, 523; *Albatross*, Vol. 1, Part 1, 113; Vol. 3, Part 1, 614; Vol. 7, Part 1, 598; Vol. 8, Part 2, 464; *Alert*, Vol. 10, Part 1, 135; *America*, Vol. 6, Part 2, 575; *Annawan*, Vol. 7, Part 2, 190; *Antelope*, Vol. 7, Part 1, 514; *Archangel*, Vol. 10, Part 1, 562; *Balanus* Supp. 10, 326; *Beaver*, Vol. 5, Part 1, 399; *Betsey*, Vol. 3, Part 2, 266; *Columbia*, Vol. 4, Part 1, 523; *Concord*, Vol. 4, Part 1, 439; *Discoverer*, Vol. 8, Part 1, 235; *Discovery*, Vol. 5, Part 1, 339; *Eaglet*, Vol. 4, Part 2, 17; *Florence*, Vol. 10, Part 1, 102; *Fram*, Vol. 7, Part 2, 364; *George Law*, Vol. 6, Part 2, 575; *Griffon*, Vol. 4, Part 2, 540; Vol. 6, Part 1, 11; Vol. 6, Part 2, 526; Vol. 9, Part 2, 587; *Gulnare*, Vol. 7, Part 2, 323; *Halve Moen* (Half Moon), Vol. 5, Part 1, 339; *Herd*, Vol. 7, Part 2, 190; *Hersilia*, Vol. 7, Part 2, 190; *Hobby*, Supp. 9, 117; *Hope*, Vol. 5, Part 1, 478; *Hopewell*, Vol. 5, Part 1, 338; *James Monroe*, Vol. 7, Part 2, 190; *Jeannette*, Vol. 1, Part 1, 240; *Kite*, Vol. 7, Part 2, 363; *La Concepcion*, Vol. 7, Part 1, 273; *Lady Washington*, Vol. 4, Part 1, 523; *Le Don de Dieu*, Vol. 2, Part 1, 606; *Nonsuch*, Vol. 4, Part 2, 17; *Olive Branch*, Vol. 8, Part 1, 235; *Pandora*, Vol. 6, Part 2, 46; *Pelican*, Vol. 5, Part 1, 456; *Polaris*, Vol. 4, Part 2, 120; Vol. 10, Part 1, 102; *Prometheus*, Vol. 2, Part 1, 309; *Roosevelt*, Vol. 7, Part 2, 365; *St. Julien*, Vol. 2, Part 1, 605; *San Antonio*, Vol. 8, Part 1, 109; *San Carlos*, Vol. 1, Part 1, 447; Vol. 8, Part 1, 109; Vol. 3, Part 2, 244; *San Salvador*, Vol. 2, Part 1, 396; *Seraph*, Vol. 7, Part 2, 190; *Three Saints*, Vol. 9, Part 1, 67; *Tigress*, Vol. 10, Part 1, 102; *Tonquin*, Vol. 3, Part 2, 282; Vol. 8, Part 2, 173; *Veslekari*, Supp. 9, 117; *Victoria*, Vol. 2, Part 1, 396; *Warrior*, Vol. 2, Part 1, 309; *Washington*, Vol. 5, Part 2, 329; *White Falcon*, Vol. 7, Part 2, 364; *Windward*, Vol. 7, Part 2, 364

Filibuster: *Akbar*, Vol. 4, Part 2, 142; *Cadet*, Vol. 7, Part 2, 190; *Caroline*, Vol. 10, Part 1, 135; *Enterprise*, Vol. 7, Part 1, 195; *Houston*, Vol. 8, Part 2, 324; *Restormel*, Vol. 9, Part 1, 156; *Tampico*; Vol. 7, Part 2, 190

Foreign, in naval engagements: *Admiral Duff*, Vol. 8, Part 1, 182; *Alert*, Vol. 3, Part 1, 414; *Almirante Oquendo*, Vol. 10, Part 1, 319; *America*, Vol. 6, Part 2, 577; *Amphion*, Vol. 3, Part 2, 536; *Arancand*, Vol. 10, Part 2, 524; *Arundel*, Vol. 8, Part 1, 518; *Austin*, Vol. 7, Part 1, 120; *Belvidera*, Vol. 3, Part 2, 85; Vol. 7, Part 1, 97; Vol. 7, Part 2, 486; Vol. 8, Part 2, 76, 77; Vol. 9, Part 2, 139; *Bonne Citoyenne*, Vol. 6, Part 1, 50; *Boxer*, Vol. 6, Part 1, 561; *Brandzen*, Vol. 3, Part 1, 202; *Burford*, Vol. 10, Part 2, 180; *Cacique*, Vol. 3, Part 1, 202; *Carleton*, Vol. 4, Part 1, 543; *Carnation*, Vol. 8, Part 1, 480; *Castilla*, Vol. 3, Part 1, 271; *Chen Yuen*, Vol. 6, Part 2, 49; *Cherub*, Vol. 3, Part 1, 416; Vol. 3, Part 2, 286; Vol. 8, Part 1, 84; *Chester*, Vol. 10, Part 1, 486; *Colon*, Vol. 2, Part 2, 123; *Columbus*, Vol. 10, Part 2, 524; *Concord*, Vol. 7, Part 2, 484; *Cristobal Colon*, Vol. 6, Part 2, 647; *Cuba*, Vol. 6, Part 2, 196; *Culloden*, Vol. 9, Part 2, 280; *Detroit*, Vol. 7, Part 2, 490; *Don Antonio de Ulloa*, Vol. 3, Part 1, 271; *Don Jorge Juan*, Vol. 10, Part 1, 633; *Dover Prize*, Vol. 8, Part 1, 141; *Duc de Bourgogne*, Vol. 4, Part 1, 140; *Duras* (renamed *Bonhomme Richard*), Vol. 5, Part 2, 185; *Endymion*, Vol. 3, Part 1, 188; *Esmeralda*, Vol. 8, Part 1, 85; *Falcon*, Vol. 8, Part 1, 196; *Firm*, Vol. 8, Part 1, 518; *Flamand*, Vol. 5, Part 2, 567; *Flora*, Vol. 6, Part 2, 151; *Fox*, Vol. 6, Part 2, 236; *Friend's Adventure*, Vol. 9, Part 1, 408; *Frolic*, Vol. 5, Part 2, 176; *Furor*, Vol. 10, Part 1, 319; *Galveztown*, Vol. 4, Part 1, 120; *Gaspete*, Vol. 10, Part 2, 66; *Glasgow*, Vol. 5, Part 1, 64, 209, 212; Vol. 5, Part 2, 184; Vol. 8, Part 2, 316; Vol. 10, Part 2, 66; *Granicus*, Vol. 2, Part 2, 271; *Guadalupe*, Vol. 7, Part 1, 121; *Guerrerd*, Vol. 8, Part 1, 85; *Guerriere*, Vol. 7, Part 1, 202; *Hazard*, Vol. 7, Part 1, 535; *Hebrus*, Vol. 5, Part 2, 270; *Hermione*, Vol. 5, Part 2, 537; *Heroina*, Vol. 5, Part 2, 67; *Hinchimbroke*, Vol. 4, Part 1, 554; *Hind*, Vol. 10, Part 1, 40; *Hyperion*, Vol. 6, Part 2, 195; *Infanta Maria Teresa*, Vol. 10, Part 1, 319; *Intrepid*, Vol. 1, Part 1, 633; *Invincible*, Vol. 5, Part 2, 67; *Iris*, Vol. 3, Part 1,

33; **Vol. 7, Part 1**, 358, 502; *Isabel*, **Vol. 5, Part 2**, 558; *Jersey*, **Vol. 7, Part 2**, 484, 631; **Vol. 8, Part 1**, 182; **Vol. 9, Part 2**, 280; *Junon*, **Vol. 9, Part 2**, 306; *La Nymphe*, **Vol. 5, Part 2**, 538; *Launceton*, **Vol. 10, Part 1**, 486; *Lautaro*, **Vol. 10, Part 2**, 524; *La Vengeance*, **Vol. 4, Part 2**, 539; **Vol. 10, Part 1**, 22; *La Victoire*, **Vol. 5, Part 2**, 536; *Lealtad*, **Vol. 8, Part 1**, 85; *Le Formidable*, **Vol. 6, Part 2**, 469; *L'Entreprenant*, **Vol. 6, Part 2**, 469; *Leopard*, **Vol. 1, Part 1**, 212, 650; **Vol. 2, Part 1**, 309; **Vol. 3, Part 1**, 188; **Vol. 5, Part 2**, 30; **Vol. 7, Part 1**, 358, 486; **Vol. 7, Part 2**, 627; **Vol. 8, Part 2**, 76, 505; **Vol. 9, Part 1**, 135; **Vol. 9, Part 2**, 307, 355; *Little Belt*, **Vol. 1, Part 1**, 507, **Vol. 7, Part 2**, 486; **Vol. 8, Part 1**, 188; **Vol. 8, Part 2**, 76; **Vol. 9, Part 2**, 139; *Liverpool*, **Vol. 8, Part 1**, 430; *Lord Sandwich*, **Vol. 6, Part 1**, 299; *Lowestoffe's Prize*, **Vol. 7, Part 2**, 28; *Maidstone*, **Vol. 10, Part 1**, 437; *Majestic*, **Vol. 3, Part 1**, 188; *Maria Isabel*, **Vol. 10, Part 2**, 524; *Mary*, **Vol. 6, Part 2**, 195; **Vol. 9, Part 1**, 408; *Massachusetts*, **Vol. 10, Part 1**, 101; *Medea*, **Vol. 6, Part 1**, 299; **Vol. 10, Part 2**, 276; *Mercury*, **Vol. 6, Part 2**, 151; *Mermaid*, **Vol. 10, Part 1**, 486; *Mindanao*, **Vol. 10, Part 1**, 340; *Monarch*, **Vol. 9, Part 2**, 518; *Montaga*, **Vol. 6, Part 1**, 50; *Montezuma*, **Vol. 7, Part 1**, 121; *Ostrich*, **Vol. 7, Part 2**, 28; *Otter*, **Vol. 7, Part 1**, 502; *Peacock*, **Vol. 6, Part 1**, 50; *Pelican*, **Vol. 6, Part 1**, 204; *Perry*, **Vol. 4, Part 2**, 493; *Phoebe*, **Vol. 3, Part 1**, 416; **Vol. 3, Part 2**, 286; **Vol. 8, Part 1**, 84; *Plantagenet*, **Vol. 8, Part 1**, 480; *Pluton*, **Vol. 10, Part 1**, 319; *Poictiers*, **Vol. 5, Part 2**, 176; *Pomona*, **Vol. 8, Part 2**, 76; **Vol. 3, Part 1**, 188; **Vol. 6, Part 2**, 236; *Porcupine*, **Vol. 9, Part 2**, 408; *Portland*, **Vol. 1, Part 2**, 242; *Prince of Orange*, **Vol. 10, Part 1**, 101; *Prudent*, **Vol. 10, Part 1**, 21; *Queen Charlotte*, **Vol. 7, Part 2**, 491; *Rachel*, **Vol. 10, Part 2**, 524; *Rainbow*, **Vol. 6, Part 2**, 151; *Recruit*, **Vol. 7, Part 1**, 413; *Reina Cristina*, **Vol. 3, Part 1**, 271; *Restoration*, **Vol. 4, Part 1**, 543; *Robert Fulton*, **Vol. 3, Part 2**, 5; *Roebuck*, **Vol. 6, Part 1**, 299; **Vol. 8, Part 1**, 430; **Vol. 10, Part 2**, 276; *Rose*, **Vol. 10, Part 1**, 486; **Vol. 10, Part 2**, 66; *Rota*, **Vol. 8, Part 1**, 480; *Royal George*, **Vol. 8, Part 2**, 343; *Royalist*, **Vol. 5, Part 1**, 460; *St. Albans*, **Vol. 1, Part 1**, 633; *Sally Rose*, **Vol. 8, Part 1**, 141; *Scarborough*, **Vol. 9, Part 2**, 450; *Scorpion*, **Vol. 4, Part 2**, 27; *Seaflower*, **Vol. 9, Part 1**, 408; *Serapis*, **Vol. 3, Part 1**, 33; **Vol. 3, Part 2**, 268; **Vol. 5, Part 2**, 185; *Shannon*, **Vol. 5, Part 1**, 623; **Vol. 6, Part 1**, 50, 308; *Shark*, **Vol. 10, Part 2**, 180; *Solebay*, **Vol. 10, Part 1**, 486; *Somerset*, **Vol. 6, Part 2**, 151; *Squirrel*, **Vol. 10, Part 1**, 486; *Superbe*, **Vol. 10, Part 1**, 486; *Tenedos*, **Vol. 3, Part 1**, 188; *Thames*, **Vol. 8, Part 1**, 182; *Triomphante*, **Vol. 5, Part 2**, 186; *Triumph*, **Vol. 5, Part 2**, 186; *Tryon*, **Vol. 4, Part 1**, 543; *Unity*, **Vol. 7, Part 1**, 610; *Victor*, **Vol. 6, Part 2**, 151; *Victory*, **Vol. 7, Part 2**, 461; *Vigilante*, **Vol. 10, Part 1**, 486; *Vladimir*, **Vol. 5, Part 2**, 187; *Volontier*, **Vol. 1, Part 1**, 505; *Watt*, **Vol. 7, Part 1**, 502; **Vol. 7, Part 2**, 484; *Widgeon*, **Vol. 6, Part 2**, 196; *William and Mary*, **Vol. 9, Part 1**, 408; *William Penn*, **Vol. 2, Part 2**, 259; *Zavala*, **Vol. 7, Part 1**, 120

Great Lakes steamers: *China*, **Vol. 6, Part 2**, 23; *India*, **Vol. 6, Part 2**, 23; *Japan*, **Vol. 6, Part 2**, 23; *Livingstone*, **Vol. 6, Part 1**, 327; *Michigan*, **Vol. 7, Part 1**, 446; *Niagara*, **Vol. 5, Part 1**, 155; *Palmer*, **Vol. 6, Part 1**, 327; *Plymouth Rock*, **Vol. 7, Part 1**, 472; *Thomas A. Scott*, **Vol. 6, Part 2**, 23; *Western World*, **Vol. 7, Part 1**, 472

Immigrant: *Aegir*, **Vol. 8, Part 2**, 273; *August Eduard*, **Vol. 8, Part 2**, 87; *Antoleon*, **Vol. 8, Part 2**, 434; *Curacao*, **Vol. 9, Part 1**, 315

Luxury liners: *Andrea Doria*, **Supp. 9**, 236; *Comanche*, **Supp. 9**, 728; *Titanic*, **Supp. 9**, 700, 866

Missionary and association: *Elizabeth*, **Vol. 5, Part 2**, 97; **Vol. 9, Part 2**, 139; *Female Ram*, **Vol. 5, Part 1**, 145; *Fukuin Maru*, **Vol. 1, Part 2**, 236; *Irene*, **Vol. 9, Part 2**, 294; *Macedonia*, **Vol. 9, Part 2**, 322; *Missionary Packet*, **Vol. 5, Part 1**, 381; *Ten Sisters*, **Vol. 4, Part 2**, 154; *Thaddeus*, **Vol. 5, Part 1**, 381; *Traveller*, **Vol. 2, Part 2**, 585

Naval: *Active*, **Vol. 6, Part 1**, 299; **Vol. 8, Part 2**, 341; *Adams*, **Vol. 5, Part 1**, 303; **Vol. 5, Part 2**, 324; **Vol. 6, Part 1**, 49; **Vol. 6, Part 2**, 73; **Vol. 7, Part 1**, 219, 358; **Vol. 7, Part 2**, 490, 535; **Vol. 8, Part 1**, 617; **Vol. 10, Part 2**, 517; *Adelaide*, **Vol. 2, Part 2**, 635; *Advance*, **Vol. 3, Part 1**, 200; *A. D. Vance*, **Vol. 10, Part 1**, 128; *Agawam*, **Vol. 8, Part 1**, 529; *Agimenticus*, **Vol. 9, Part 2**, 613, 614; *Alabama*, **Vol. 1, Part 2**, 342; **Vol. 2, Part 1**, 258; **Vol. 2, Part 2**, 309; **Vol. 3, Part 2**, 289; **Vol. 6, Part 2**, 21, 306; **Vol. 8, Part 1**, 618; **Vol. 8, Part 2**, 580, 581; **Vol. 9, Part 2**, 638; **Vol. 10, Part 1**, 339; **Vol. 10, Part 2**, 398; *Alabama*, **Vol. 4, Part 1**, 311; *Alabama*, **Vol. 4, Part 2**, 71, 268; **Vol. 5, Part 1**, 86; **Vol. 5, Part 2**, 114, 279; **Vol. 6, Part 2**, 267; **Vol. 7, Part 1**, 238, 286, 424,; **Vol. 7, Part 2**, 233; **Vol. 8, Part 1**, 286, 417; **Vol. 8, Part 2**, 428, 619; **Vol. 10, Part 1**, 131, 268; *Alabama*, **Vol. 2, Part 1**, 468; **Vol. 8, Part 1**, 167; *Alarm*, **Vol. 5, Part 2**, 380; *Alaska*, **Vol. 1, Part 2**, 146; **Vol. 2, Part 1**, 544; *Albany*, **Vol. 1, Part 1**, 529; **Vol. 5, Part 2**, 158; **Vol. 8, Part 1**, 293, 596, 317; **Vol. 10, Part 2**, 1; *Albermarle*, **Vol. 1, Part 2**, 409, 487; **Vol. 2, Part 2**, 636; **Vol. 4, Part 2**, 71; **Vol. 6, Part 1**, 64; **Vol. 6, Part 2**, 196; **Vol. 8, Part 1**, 97, 299; **Vol. 8, Part 2**, 85; **Vol. 9, Part 1**, 321; *Albatross*, **Vol. 1, Part 1**, 113; **Vol. 3, Part 1**, 614; **Vol. 7, Part 1**, 598; **Vol. 8, Part 2**, 464; *Alden*, **Vol. 1, Part 1**, 146; *Alert*, **Vol. 1, Part 1**, 600; **Vol. 5, Part 2**, 324, 380; **Vol. 8, Part 1**, 640; **Vol. 9, Part 1**, 625; **Vol. 10, Part 1**, 319; *Alfred*, **Vol. 5, Part 1**, 64; **Vol. 5, Part 2**, 184; **Vol. 8, Part 2**, 316; *Alleghany*, **Vol. 8, Part 1**, 97, 299, 597; **Vol. 8, Part 2**, 77; *Algonquin*, **Vol. 8, Part 1**, 314; *Alliance*, **Vol. 1, Part 1**, 654; **Vol. 2, Part 2**, 369; **Vol. 3, Part 1**, 33; **Vol. 4, Part 1**, 296; **Vol. 4, Part 2**, 72, 251, 252; **Vol. 5, Part 2**, 185, 537, 567, 568; **Vol. 7, Part 1**, 343, 358; *Alligator*, **Vol. 6, Part 2**, 82; **Vol. 8, Part 2**, 568; **Vol. 9, Part 2**, 48; *America*, **Vol. 5, Part 2**, 186; **Vol. 8, Part 2**, 234; *Ammonoosuc*, **Vol. 3, Part 2**, 170; **Vol. 8, Part 1**, 314; *Anacostia*, **Vol. 1, Part 1**, 488; **Vol. 2 Part 2**, 308; **Vol. 7, Part 2**, 531; *Andrea Doria*, **Vol. 1, Part 2**, 242; *Annapolis*, **Vol. 5, Part 1**, 318; **Vol. 10, Part 2**, 653; *Antietam*, **Vol. 9, Part 2**, 615; *Archer*, **Vol. 8, Part 1**, 420; *Arctic*, **Vol. 9, Part 2**, 122; **Vol. 10, Part 1**, 568; *Arethusa*, **Vol. 4, Part 1**, 485; *Argo*, **Vol. 9, Part 2**, 280; *Argus*, **Vol. 1, Part 1**, 212; **Vol. 3, Part 1**, 187; **Vol. 5, Part 1**, 361; **Vol. 6, Part 1**, 50, 204; **Vol. 8, Part 1**, 182; **Vol. 9, Part 1**, 135; **Vol. 9, Part 2**, 7; *Ariel*, **Vol. 3, Part 1**, 33; **Vol. 3, Part 2**, 268; **Vol. 5, Part 2**, 186; *Arizona*, **Supp. 9**, 461; **Supp. 10**, 371; *Arkansas*, **Vol. 2, Part 1**, 255; *Arkansas*, **Vol. 3, Part 1**, 107; **Vol. 8, Part 1**, 420; **Vol. 10, Part 1**, 318, 337; *Armstrong*, **Vol. 7, Part 1**, 152; *Aroostook*, **Vol. 1, Part 2**, 104; **Vol. 3, Part 2**, 170; **Vol. 7, Part 2**, 470; *Asp*, **Vol. 2, Part 1**, 609; *Atalanta*, **Vol. 8, Part 1**, 596; *Atlanta*, **Vol. 3, Part 1**, 532; **Vol. 8, Part 2**, 78; **Vol. 9, Part 1**, 554; *Atlanta*, **Vol. 5, Part 1**, 303; **Vol. 7, Part 2**, 535; **Vol. 8, Part 1**, 640; *Augusta*, **Vol. 7, Part 2**, 260; **Supp. 9**, 630; **Supp. 10**, 371; *Badger*, **Vol. 1, Part 1**, 488; *Baltimore*, **Vol. 2, Part 1**, 206; **Vol. 7, Part 2**, 185; **Vol. 8, Part 1**, 430, 480; *Baltimore*, **Vol. 3, Part 1**, 270, 271, 585; **Vol. 3, Part 2**, 176; **Vol. 6, Part 1**, 568; **Vol. 8, Part 2**, 438; *Barker*, **Vol. 1, Part 1**, 601; *Baron De Kalb*, **Vol. 10, Part 1**, 349; *Bayou City*, **Vol. 10, Part 1**, 318; *Bay State*, **Vol. 7, Part 2**, 55; *Bear*, **Vol. 8, Part 2**, 438; **Vol. 10, Part 1**, 135; *Beaufort*, **Vol. 7, Part 2**, 243; *Benicia*, **Vol. 7, Part 2**, 606; **Vol. 8, Part 2**, 437–64; *Bennington*, **Vol.**

8, Part 1, 315; Vol. 8, Part 2, 554; *Benton,* Vol. 1, Part 2, 306; Vol. 4, Part 1, 595; Vol. 6, Part 1, 574; Vol. 10, Part 2, 398; *Bibb,* Vol. 6, Part 2, 480; Vol. 8, Part 1, 141; Vol. 8, Part 2, 74; *Bienville,* Vol. 6, Part 1, 315; Vol. 7, Part 1, 320; Vol. 9, Part 1, 553; *Black Hawk,* Vol. 2, Part 1, 14; Vol. 4, Part 1, 595; Vol. 7, Part 2, 626; *Blake,* Vol. 1, Part 1, 112; Vol. 7, Part 2, 607; Vol. 9, Part 1, 156; *Bombshell,* Vol. 8, Part 1, 299; Vol. 8, Part 2, 85; *Bonhomme Richard,* Vol. 3, Part 1, 33; Vol. 3, Part 2, 268; Vol. 5, Part 1, 477; Vol. 5, Part 2, 185, 568; *Bonita,* Vol. 9, Part 2, 457; *Boston,* Vol. 7, Part 1, 506; Vol. 7, Part 2, 531; Vol. 8, Part 1, 293; Vol. 8, Part 2, 74, 85; Vol. 9, Part 1, 394; Vol. 9, Part 2, 364; Vol. 10, Part 1, 39, 40, 336; Vol. 10, Part 2, 1, 228; *Boston,* Vol. 3, Part 2, 149; Vol. 6, Part 1, 299, 572; Vol. 6, Part 2, 149, 151, 236; *Boston,* Vol. 3, Part 1, 270–71; Vol. 3, Part 2, 170; Vol. 5, Part 2, 559; Vol. 8, Part 1, 339, 640; Vol. 10, Part 1, 339; Vol. 10, Part 2, 206; *Bourbon,* Vol. 7, Part 1, 502; Vol. 8, Part 1, 430; *Boxer,* Vol. 2, Part 1, 337; Vol. 3, Part 2, 287; Vol. 8, Part 1, 67; Vol. 8, Part 2, 77; *Brandywine,* Vol. 1, Part 1, 650; Vol. 2, Part 1, 13; Vol. 3, Part 1, 380; Vol. 3, Part 2, 149, 287; Vol. 5, Part 1, 362; Vol. 5, Part 2, 164, 170, 615; Vol. 6, Part 1, 129; Vol. 6, Part 2, 91, 271, 478; Vol. 7, Part 1, 203, 320; Vol. 7, Part 2, 139, 185, 487; Vol. 8, Part 1, 319; Vol. 8, Part 2, 72, 74, 579; Vol. 9, Part 2, 394; Vol. 10, Part 2, 465; *Briganza,* Vol. 2, Part 2, 46; *Brooklyn,* Vol. 6, Part 1, 500; Vol. 6, Part 2, 149; Vol. 7, Part 2, 308; Vol. 8, Part 1, 68; Vol. 9, Part 1, 156; Vol. 10, Part 2, 16; *Brooklyn,* Vol. 1, Part 1, 146; Vol. 2, Part 2, 517; Vol. 3, Part 2, 287, 289; *Brooklyn,* Vol. 2, Part 2, 123; Vol. 6, Part 2, 422, 646; Vol. 7, Part 2, 535; Vol. 8, Part 1, 495; Vol. 8, Part 2, 323, 438; Vol. 9, Part 1, 156; Vol. 10, Part 1, 23, 128; *Cabot,* Vol. 5, Part 1, 64, 211; *Cairo,* Vol. 8, Part 2, 569; *Caleb Cushing,* Vol. 8, Part 1, 420; *Caledonia,* Vol. 5, Part 2, 164; Vol. 10, Part 1, 59; *California,* Vol. 5, Part 2, 324; Vol. 8, Part 2, 22; Vol. 10, Part 2, 653; *Cambridge,* Vol. 10, Part 2, 346; *Canandaigua,* Vol. 3, Part 1, 228; Vol. 8, Part 1, 495; Vol. 9, Part 2, 149, 457; *Canonicus,* Vol. 1, Part 2, 146; Vol. 3, Part 2, 170; Vol. 7, Part 2, 260; Vol. 8, Part 2, 78; *Carolina,* Vol. 7, Part 2, 302; *Caroline,* Vol. 5, Part 2, 270; *Carondelet,* Vol. 3, Part 2, 500; Vol. 9, Part 2, 457; Vol. 10, Part 1, 337; *Castine,* Vol. 3, Part 2, 170; Vol. 5, Part 2, 462; Vol. 8, Part 2, 22, 605; *Catskill,* Vol. 8, Part 2, 74, 200; *Cayuga,* Vol. 1, Part 1, 502; Vol. 3, Part 2, 255; Vol. 7, Part 2, 470; Vol. 8, Part 2, 85; *Charleston,* Vol. 5, Part 1, 153; Vol. 8, Part 1, 495; Vol. 8, Part 2, 22, 492; Vol. 10, Part 2, 393; *Charleston,* Vol. 8, Part 1, 97; *Chattahoochee,* Vol. 5, Part 2, 164; *Chattanooga,* Vol. 9, Part 2, 42; *Chenango,* Vol. 8, Part 1, 314; *Chesapeake,* Vol. 1, Part 1, 212, 650; Vol. 2, Part 1, 337; Vol. 2, Part 2, 40, 510; Vol. 3, Part 1, 188; Vol. 3, Part 2, 96; Vol. 5, Part 1, 376, 623; Vol. 5, Part 2, 30; Vol. 6, Part 1, 50, 308; Vol. 7, Part 1, 358, 486; Vol. 7, Part 2, 627; Vol. 8, Part 2, 76, 232, 505; Vol. 9, Part 1, 135, 309; Vol. 9, Part 2, 7, 307, 355; Vol. 10, Part 1, 22, 492; *Cheyenne,* Vol. 2, Part 1, 468; *Chicago,* Vol. 2, Part 1, 468; Vol. 6, Part 2, 207; Vol. 8, Part 1, 640; *Chickasaw,* Vol. 7, Part 2, 470; *Chicora,* Vol. 5, Part 1, 477; Vol. 8, Part 1, 97; Vol. 9, Part 2, 348; Vol. 10, Part 1, 34; *Chippewa,* Vol. 4, Part 1, 232; Vol. 7, Part 2, 534; Vol. 8, Part 1, 314, 424; Vol. 9, Part 2, 518; Vol. 10, Part 1, 568; *Choctaw,* Vol. 8, Part 1, 339; *Chocura,* Vol. 4, Part 1, 232; Vol. 6, Part 2, 479; Vol. 7, Part 2, 308; Vol. 10, Part 1, 23; *Cimarron,* Vol. 9, Part 2, 457; *Cincinnati,* Supp. 10, 371; *Clara Dolson,* Vol. 7, Part 2, 314; *Clarence,* Vol. 8, Part 1, 420; *Cohoes,* Vol. 8, Part 2, 200; *Colonel Harney,* Vol. 8, Part 2, 74; *Colorado,* Vol. 1, Part 1, 502; Vol. 3, Part 1, 107, 269; Vol. 4, Part 1 232; Vol. 6, Part 1, 173, 500; *Colorado,* Vol. 6, Part 2, 576; Vol. 7, Part 2, 606; Vol. 8, Part 2, 78, 244, 322; Vol. 9, Part 1, 554, 626; Vol. 9, Part 2, 394; Vol. 10, Part 1, 319; Vol. 10, Part 2, 585; *Colorado,* Vol. 2, Part 1, 468; Vol. 2, Part 2, 500; Vol. 8, Part 2, 22; Supp. 9, 461; *Columbia,* Vol. 5, Part 2, 164; Vol. 6, Part 1, 315; Vol. 7, Part 1, 320; Vol. 7, Part 2, 185, 444; Vol. 8, Part 2, 79, 341; Vol. 10, Part 1, 317, 318; Vol. 10, Part 2, 645; *Columbia,* Vol. 1, Part 1, 495, Vol. 2, Part 1, 255; Vol. 2, Part 2, 500; Vol. 6, Part 2, 522; Vol. 8, Part 1, 237; Vol. 8, Part 2, 79; *Columbia,* Vol. 8, Part 1, 97; *Columbia and John Adams,* Vol. 8, Part 1, 424; *Columbus,* Vol. 1, Part 1, 507; Vol. 3, Part 1, 380; Vol. 5, Part 2, 170; Vol. 7, Part 2, 140, 243; Vol. 8, Part 1, 596; Vol. 10, Part 2, 66; *Commodore Barney,* Vol. 2, Part 2, 636; *Commodore Hull,* Vol. 7, Part 1, 640; *Commodore McDonough,* Vol. 9, Part 2, 457; *Commodore Perry,* Vol. 2, Part 2, 635; *Concord,* Vol. 1, Part 1, 145, 226; Vol. 3, Part 1, 270; Vol. 7, Part 2, 487; Vol. 8, Part 1, 315; Vol. 8, Part 2, 77; Vol. 10, Part 1, 339, 340; *Confederacy,* Vol. 4, Part 2, 251; *Conemaugh,* Vol. 6, Part 2, 479; Vol. 8, Part 1, 299; Vol. 9, Part 1, 139; Vol. 10, Part 2, 1; *Conestoga,* Vol. 8, Part 2, 569; *Congress,* Vol. 1, Part 2, 348; Vol. 3, Part 1, 188; Vol. 5, Part 1, 377, 477; Vol. 6, Part 1, 524; Vol. 7, Part 1, 202, 203; Vol. 8, Part 1, 182; Vol. 9, Part 1, 215; Vol. 10, Part 1, 492; *Congress,* Vol. 1, Part 2, 88; Vol. 2, Part 1, 207; Vol. 3, Part 1, 530; Vol. 5, Part 2, 14, 164; Vol. 6, Part 1, 315, 500; Vol. 6, Part 2, 207, 465; Vol. 7, Part 2, 243, 260; Vol. 8, Part 1, 68, 86, 293, 319; Vol. 8, Part 2, 72, 343, 427; Vol. 9, Part 1, 178, 310; Vol. 9, Part 2, 42, 48; Vol. 10, Part 1, 128, 292, 568; Vol. 10, Part 2, 645; *Connecticut,* Vol. 1, Part 1, 226; Vol. 1, Part 2, 409; Vol. 4, Part 1, 485; Vol. 5, Part 2, 324; Vol. 10, Part 1, 349; Supp. 10, 371; *Consort,* Vol. 3, Part 2, 149; Vol. 6, Part 1, 553; Vol. 8, Part 2, 579; *Constellation,* Vol. 1, Part 2, 104, 241, 342; Vol. 2, Part 1, 206; Vol. 3, Part 1, 65, 380; Vol. 3, Part 2, 85; Vol. 4, Part 2, 539; Vol. 5, Part 1, 377; Vol. 6, Part 1, 315, 572; Vol. 6, Part 2, 20; Vol. 7, Part 1, 320, 358; Vol. 7, Part 2, 301, 320, 490, 625; Vol. 8, Part 1, 83, 85, 319, 424; Vol. 8, Part 2, 74, 76, 77, 234, 579; Vol. 9, Part 1, 136, 156, 310, 584, 626; Vol. 9, Part 2, 7, 307, 310, 364, 394; Vol. 10, Part 1, 22; Vol. 10, Part 2, 518; *Constitution,* Vol. 1, Part 1, 146, 452, 506, 507, 606, 650; Vol. 1, Part 2, 241; Vol. 2, Part 1, 206, 337; Vol. 2, Part 2, 40, 123; Vol. 3, Part 1, 188, 415, 530; Vol. 3, Part 2, 174; Vol. 4, Part 1, 523; Vol. 5, Part 1, 360, 361, 364, 376; Vol. 5, Part 2, 164, 170; Vol. 6, Part 1, 50, 315, 500, 573; Vol. 6, Part 2, 195; Vol. 7, Part 1, 98, 172, 202, 506, 507; Vol. 7, Part 2, 302, 461, 531; Vol. 8, Part 1, 182, 319, 424, 596; Vol. 8, Part 2, 72, 74, 246; Vol. 9, Part 1, 135, 136, 321, 553; Vol. 9, Part 2, 7, 122, 280, 306; Vol. 10, Part 1, 59, 60, 228, 425; Vol. 10, Part 2, 517; *Contoocook,* Vol. 1, Part 1, 529; *Convention,* Vol. 4, Part 2, 476; Vol. 7, Part 2, 28; *Coquette,* Vol. 10, Part 2, 466; *Corwin,* Vol. 7, Part 2, 532; Vol. 10, Part 2, 228; *Craven,* Vol. 2, Part 2, 519; *Cricket,* Vol. 4, Part 1, 437; *Crusader,* Vol. 2, Part 2, 518; Vol. 6, Part 2, 196; Vol. 8, Part 1, 529; *Culgoa,* Vol. 8, Part 1, 18; *Cumberland,* Vol. 1, Part 1, 606; Vol. 2, Part 1, 207; Vol. 3, Part 1, 30; Vol. 3, Part 2, 499, 531; Vol. 5, Part 2, 164; Vol. 6, Part 1, 315; Vol. 7, Part 1, 152, 203; Vol. 7, Part 2, 314; Vol. 8, Part 1, 68, 299, 319; Vol. 8, Part 2, 72, 568, 579; Vol. 9, Part 1, 310, 487; Vol. 9, Part 2, 139, 638; Vol. 10, Part 1, 128, 425; Vol. 10, Part 2, 1, 465, 425; *Cummings,* Supp. 9, 385; *Cushing,* Vol. 10, Part 2, 392; *Cuyler,* Vol. 8, Part 2, 437; *Cyane,* Vol. 1, Part 1, 502,

528; **Vol. 2, Part 1**, 70; **Vol. 3, Part 1**, 530, 584; **Vol. 3, Part 2**, 85, 97; **Vol. 5, Part 1**, 152, 362; **Vol. 6, Part 2**, 465, 576; **Vol. 7, Part 2**, 461, 470, 486; **Vol. 8, Part 1**, 214; **Vol. 8, Part 2**, 196, 244; **Vol. 9, Part 2**, 139; *Docatah*, **Vol. 3, Part 1**, 584; **Vol. 6, Part 2**, 479; **Vol. 8, Part 1**, 319; **Vol. 8, Part 2**, 341; **Vol. 9, Part 2**, 42, 457; *Dale*, **Vol. 2, Part 1**, 543; **Vol. 2, Part 2**, 518, **Vol. 3, Part 1**, 380; **Vol. 6, Part 2**, 82; **Vol. 9, Part 1**, 156; **Vol. 10, Part 1**, 23; *Dauntless*, **Vol. 4, Part 1**, 74; *Deane*, **Vol. 4, Part 2**, 154; **Vol. 7, Part 1**, 506; **Vol. 10, Part 1**, 40; *Decatur*, **Vol. 2, Part 1**, 257; **Vol. 2, Part 2**, 308, 569; **Vol. 3, Part 2**, 287; **Vol. 5, Part 2**, 221; **Vol. 7, Part 2**, 444, 531; **Vol. 9, Part 2**, 394, 457; *Defence*, **Vol. 4, Part 2**, 251; **Vol. 7, Part 1**, 502; **Vol. 10, Part 2**, 524; *De Kalb*, **Vol. 8, Part 1**, 339; *Delaware*, **Vol. 1, Part 2**, 408; **Vol. 2, Part 1**, 70, 206, 257; **Vol. 3, Part 1**, 186; **Vol. 3, Part 2**, 287; **Vol. 5, Part 2**, 170, 615; **Vol. 6, Part 1**, 129, 315, 572; **Vol. 7, Part 2**, 301, 461; **Vol. 8, Part 1**, 67, 293; **Vol. 8, Part 2**, 196; *Denver*, **Vol. 7, Part 1**, 343; **Vol. 8, Part 2**, 22; **Vol. 10, Part 2**, 653; *De Soto*, **Vol. 1, Part 2**, 409; **Vol. 5, Part 1**, 303; **Vol. 8, Part 1**, 495; *Despatch*, **Vol. 4, Part 1**, 574; **Vol. 5, Part 2**, 250; *Destroyer*, **Vol. 3, Part 2**, 174, 175; *Dewey*, **Vol. 3, Part 2**, 158; *Dictator*, **Vol. 8, Part 1**, 314; **Vol. 8, Part 2**, 78; **Vol. 9, Part 2**, 518; *Dixie*, **Vol. 2, Part 2**, 123; **Vol. 3, Part 1**, 108; **Vol. 8, Part 2**, 554; *Dixie*, **Vol. 8, Part 1**, 237; *Dolphin*, **Vol. 3, Part 1**, 414; **Vol. 7, Part 1**, 506; **Vol. 10, Part 2**, 180; *Dolphin*, **Vol. 3, Part 1**, 106; **Vol. 4, Part 1**, 265; **Vol. 5, Part 2**, 615; **Vol. 6, Part 1**, 129, 315; **Vol. 6, Part 2**, 91, 196; **Vol. 7, Part 1**, 320; **Vol. 7, Part 2**, 140, 320, 461; **Vol. 8, Part 2**, 77; **Vol. 9, Part 1**, 553; **Vol. 10, Part 1**, 22, 23; *Dolphin*, **Vol. 7, Part 1**, 342; **Vol. 8, Part 1**, 640; **Vol. 9, Part 1**, 387; **Vol. 10, Part 2**, 206; *Draper*, **Vol. 2, Part 2**, 46; *Drayton*, **Vol. 3, Part 1**, 446; *Du Pont*, **Vol. 5, Part 2**, 380; *Dyer*, **Vol. 3, Part 1**, 585; *Eagle*, **Vol. 4, Part 2**, 539; **Vol. 9, Part 1**, 309; **Supp. 9**, 385; *Effingham*, **Vol. 1, Part 1**, 654; **Vol. 8, Part 1**, 82, 430; *Electra*, **Vol. 7, Part 2**, 314; **Vol. 8, Part 2**, 580; *Ellis*, **Vol. 2, Part 2**, 635; *Enrica*, **Vol. 8, Part 2**, 581; *Enterprise* (or *Enterprize)*, **Vol. 1, Part 1**, 600; **Vol. 1, Part 2**, 348, 408; **Vol. 2, Part 1**, 337; **Vol. 3, Part 1**, 187; **Vol. 3, Part 2**, 85, 170; **Vol. 5, Part 1**, 361; **Vol. 5, Part 2**, 110, 270, 541; **Vol. 6, Part 1**, 49, 561, 564; **Vol. 6, Part 2**, 20; **Vol. 8, Part 1**, 83, 183; **Vol. 9, Part 1**, 41, 584; **Vol. 9, Part 2**, 645; **Vol. 10, Part 1**, 492; **Supp. 9**, 461; *Epervier*, **Vol. 3, Part 1**, 416; **Vol. 9, Part 1**, 136; **Vol. 9, Part 2**, 310; *Ericsson*, **Vol. 3, Part 2**, 173, 174; **Vol. 6, Part 2**, 196; **Vol. 10, Part 1**, 135; *Erie*, **Vol. 2, Part 2**, 510; **Vol. 3, Part 1**, 530; **Vol. 3, Part 2**, 85, 287; **Vol. 7, Part 1**, 98; **Vol. 7, Part 2**, 140; **Vol. 8, Part 1**, 319, 596; **Vol. 8, Part 2**, 579; **Vol. 9, Part 1**, 487; **Vol. 9, Part 2**, 48, 310, 394; **Vol. 10, Part 1**, 60; **Vol. 10, Part 2**, 645; *Essex*, **Vol. 1, Part 1**, 506, 507, 650; **Vol. 3, Part 1**, 187, 415; **Vol. 3, Part 2**, 96, 286; **Vol. 6, Part 2**, 195; **Vol. 7, Part 1**, 89; **Vol. 8, Part 1**, 84, 182; **Vol. 8, Part 2**, 73; **Vol. 9, Part 2**, 306; **Vol. 10, Part 1**, 492; *Essex*, **Vol. 2, Part 1**, 407; **Vol. 9, Part 2**, 620; *Essex*, **Vol. 6, Part 2**, 73; **Vol. 8, Part 2**, 437; *Essex Junior*, **Vol. 3, Part 1**, 416; *Estrella*, **Vol. 9, Part 2**, 394; *Eugnie*, **Vol. 3, Part 1**, 584; *Eutaw*, **Vol. 1, Part 2**, 343; *Ewing*, **Vol. 6, Part 1**, 553; *Experiment*, **Vol. 2, Part 2**, 369; **Vol. 8, Part 1**, 83; **Vol. 9, Part 2**, 6, 645; *Fair American*, **Vol. 10, Part 2**, 524; *Fairchild*, **Vol. 6, Part 1**, 315; *Fairfield*, **Vol. 6, Part 1**, 573; **Vol. 7, Part 1**, 120; **Vol. 8, Part 2**, 72; **Vol. 9, Part 2**, 310; **Vol. 10, Part 2**, 585; *Fairplay*, **Vol. 10, Part 2**, 501; *Falcon*, **Vol. 1, Part 1**, 528; *Falmouth*, **Vol. 2, Part 1**, 206; **Vol. 3, Part 1**, 200, 380; **Vol. 7, Part 2**, 308; **Vol. 8, Part 2**, 74; **Vol. 9, Part 2**, 394; **Vol. 10, Part 1**, 22, 349; *Fanny*, **Vol. 2 Part 2**, 569; *Fenimore Cooper*, **Vol. 2, Part 1**, 70; *Ferret*, **Vol. 3, Part 2**, 286; **Vol. 5, Part 2**, 270; *Fire Fly*, **Vol. 8, Part 2**, 73; *Flag*, **Vol. 8, Part 2**, 78; **Vol. 9, Part 2**, 149; *Flambeau*, **Vol. 9, Part 2**, 364; **Vol. 10, Part 1**, 128; *Flirt*, **Vol. 5, Part 2**, 164; **Vol. 7, Part 2**, 185; **Vol. 8, Part 2**, 72, 580; *Florida*, **Vol. 2, Part 1**, 258, 586; **Vol. 2, Part 2**, 308, 569; **Vol. 3, Part 2**, 289; **Vol. 4, Part 1**, 574; **Vol. 4, Part 2**, 513; **Vol. 6, Part 1**, 574; **Vol. 6, Part 2**, 196, 521; **Vol. 8, Part 1**, 183, 420; **Vol. 9, Part 1**, 321, 554, 626; **Vol. 9, Part 2**, 42, 638; **Vol. 10, Part 2**, 398; *Florida*, **Vol. 8, Part 1**, 299; *Fort Henry*, **Vol. 6, Part 1**, 574; *Fort Jackson*, **Vol. 8, Part 2**, 341; *Fortune*, **Vol. 4, Part 1**, 544; *Fox*, **Vol. 10, Part 1**, 536; *Franklin*, **Vol. 1, Part 1**, 502; **Vol. 1, Part 2**, 242; **Vol. 3, Part 1**, 380, 530; **Vol. 3, Part 2**, 170, 286, 290; **Vol. 5, Part 2**, 615; **Vol. 6, Part 2**, 149; **Vol. 7, Part 2**, 220, 444; **Vol. 8, Part 1**, 299; **Vol. 8, Part 2**, 73; **Vol. 9, Part 1**, 178, 215; **Vol. 9, Part 2**, 7; **Vol. 10, Part 1**, 39; **Vol. 10, Part 2**, 216; *Frolic*, **Vol. 1, Part 1**, 606; **Vol. 4, Part 1**, 485; **Vol. 10, Part 1**, 128; *Fulton*, **Vol. 1, Part 1**, 226; **Vol. 2, Part 1**, 609; **Vol. 2, Part 2**, 423; **Vol. 4, Part 2**, 391; **Vol. 7, Part 2**, 487; **Vol. 8, Part 1**, 84; **Vol. 8, Part 1**, 214; **Vol. 10, Part 1**, 568; *Gaines*, **Vol. 5, Part 2**, 221; *Galena*, **Vol. 3, Part 2**, 170; **Vol. 5, Part 2**, 462; **Vol. 8, Part 2**, 78; **Vol. 10, Part 1**, 319; *Ganges*, **Vol. 3, Part 1**, 33; **Vol. 6, Part 1**, 49; **Vol. 8, Part 2**, 234; **Vol. 9, Part 2**, 561; *G. B. McClellan*, **Vol. 8, Part 2**, 325; *General Gates*, **Vol. 10, Part 1**, 536; *General Greene*, **Vol. 6, Part 1**, 299; **Vol. 7, Part 2**, 484, 490; *General Pickering*, **Vol. 4, Part 2**, 235; *General Pike*, **Vol. 2, Part 2**, 510; **Vol. 4, Part 1**, 334; **Vol. 7, Part 1**, 97; **Vol. 8, Part 2**, 343; *General Taylor*, **Vol. 10, Part 1**, 515; *George Washington*, **Vol. 1, Part 1**, 212, 505; **Vol. 8, Part 1**, 430; **Vol. 9, Part 1**, 41; *Georgia*, **Vol. 2, Part 1**, 258; **Vol. 2, Part 2**, 518; **Vol. 7, Part 1**, 172; *Georgia*, **Vol. 8, Part 1**, 18, 317; *Germantown*, **Vol. 2, Part 1**, 207; **Vol. 2, Part 2**, 569; **Vol. 5, Part 2**, 50; **Vol. 7, Part 2**, 139; **Vol. 8, Part 1**, 596; **Vol. 8, Part 2**, 74; **Vol. 10, Part 1**, 302; **Vol. 10, Part 2**, 1, 465; *Gettysburg*, **Vol. 4, Part 1**, 437; *Glaucus*, **Vol. 2, Part 1**, 407; *Gloucester*, **Vol. 10, Part 1**, 319; *Golden Rod*, **Vol. 10, Part 2**, 466; *Governor*, **Vol. 1, Part 1**, 528; **Vol. 6, Part 1**, 568; **Vol. 8, Part 1**, 618; *Governor Moore*, **Vol. 6, Part 1**, 129; *Grampus*, **Vol. 1, Part 2**, 154; **Vol. 3, Part 1**, 530; **Vol. 9, Part 1**, 215; **Vol. 9, Part 2**, 310; *Grey Hound*, **Vol. 3, Part 2**, 286; **Vol. 6, Part 1**, 500; *Guerriere*, **Vol. 1, Part 1**, 507; **Vol. 2, Part 1**, 586; **Vol. 3, Part 1**, 189; **Vol. 5, Part 1**, 364; **Vol. 6, Part 2**, 20; **Vol. 7, Part 2**, 276, 444; **Vol. 8, Part 1**, 339 413; **Vol. 8, Part 2**, 77; **Vol. 9, Part 1**, 136, 310, 626, **Vol. 9, Part 2**, 48; **Vol. 10, Part 1**, 492; **Vol. 10, Part 2**, 216; *Hague*, **Vol. 1, Part 1**, 606; **Vol. 6, Part 2**, 236; *Hamilton*, **Vol. 6, Part 2**, 576; **Vol. 7, Part 1**, 97; *Hancock*, **Vol. 6, Part 2**, 151, 236; **Vol. 5, Part 1**, 39, 536; *Harmony*, **Vol. 3, Part 2**, 532; *Harriet Lane*, **Vol. 6, Part 2**, 205; **Vol. 8, Part 1**, 87; **Vol. 9, Part 2**, 620; **Vol. 10, Part 1**, 318, 579; *Hartford*, **Vol. 1, Part 1**, 146; **Vol. 1, Part 2**, 104, 146; **Vol. 3, Part 1**, 446, 584; **Vol. 3, Part 2**, 288, 289; **Vol. 4, Part 1**, 574; **Vol. 5, Part 2**, 50, 221; **Vol. 6, Part 1**, 81; **Vol. 6, Part 2**, 49, 465, 480; **Vol. 7, Part 2**, 186, 470, 534, 535; **Vol. 8, Part 1**, 495; **Vol. 9, Part 1**, 139; **Vol. 9, Part 2**, 8; **Vol. 10, Part 1**, 318, 545; **Vol. 10, Part 2**, 653; *Hassler*, **Vol. 1, Part 1**, 121; *Hatteras*, **Vol. 1, Part 2**, 342; **Vol. 3, Part 2**, 150, 289; **Vol. 8, Part 2**, 581; *Hawke*, **Vol. 9, Part 2**, 280; *Hazard*, **Vol. 3, Part 2**, 420; **Vol. 6, Part 1**, 299; **Vol. 10, Part 2**, 276; *Helena*, **Vol. 5, Part 1**, 471; *Holland*, **Vol. 5, Part 1**, 145; *Hope*, **Vol. 1, Part 1**, 504; *Hornet*, **Vol. 1, Part 1**, 507, 633; **Vol. 1, Part 2**, 241; **Vol. 2, Part 1**, 337; **Vol. 2, Part 2**, 349; **Vol. 3, Part 2**, 531; **Vol. 4, Part 2**, 539; **Vol. 5, Part 2**, 402; **Vol. 6, Part 1**, 50. 129, 561; **Vol. 6, Part 2**,

196; Vol. 7, Part 1, 120, 202; Vol. 8, Part 1, 424; Vol. 9, Part 1, 135, 136, 625; Vol. 9, Part 2, 7, 139, 307; Supp. 10, 371; *Housatonic*, Vol. 6, Part 2, 465; Vol. 9, Part 2, 348; *Hudson*,Vol. 3, Part 1, 445; Vol. 9, Part 2, 347; *Humboldt*, Vol. 6, Part 1, 553; *Hunchback*, Vol. 6, Part 1, 568; *Huntsville*, Vol. 8, Part 2, 116; *Huron*, Vol. 8, Part 1, 640; Vol. 8, Part 2, 569; Vol. 10, Part 1, 319; *Hyder-Ally*, Vol. 1 Part 1, 633; *Idaho*, Vol. 4, Part 1, 265; Vol. 8, Part 1, 237, 314; *Illinois*, Vol. 2, Part 1, 468; Vol. 2, Part 2, 47; Vol. 8, Part 1, 68; Vol. 9, Part 1, 388; *Independence*, Vol. 1, Part 1, 507, 606; Vol. 1, Part 2, 104; Vol. 2, Part 2, 510; Vol. 3, Part 1, 106; Vol. 3, Part 2, 286; Vol. 4, Part 1, 232, 594; Vol. 5, Part 2, 324, 615; Vol. 6, Part 1, 567; Vol. 6, Part 2, 91; Vol. 7, Part 2, 139, 314, 531, 535; Vol. 8, Part 1, 67; Vol. 8, Part 2, 568; Vol. 9, Part 1, 136; Vol. 9, Part 2, 310, 394, 457; Vol. 10, Part 2, 228, 585; *Independent*, Vol. 10, Part 2, 425; *Indiana*, Vol. 2, Part 2, 500; Vol. 3, Part 1, 269, 614; Vol. 10, Part 2, 653; *Indianapolis*, Supp. 9, 385, 461; *Ino*, Vol. 2, Part 2, 534; *Insurgente*, Vol. 7, Part 1, 358; *Intrepid*, Vol. 3, Part 1, 187; Vol. 8, Part 1, 596; Vol. 9, Part 1, 395; *Intrepid*, Vol. 5, Part 2, 380; *Iowa*, Vol. 2, Part 2, 123; Vol. 3, Part 1, 269; Vol. 3, Part 2, 210; Vol. 4, Part 2, 3; Vol. 8, Part 2, 322; *Iris*, Vol. 4, Part 2, 580; *Iroquois*, Vol. 4, Part 1, 574; Vol. 6, Part 2, 149, 207; Vol. 7, Part 2, 186; Vol. 8, Part 2, 73; Vol. 9, Part 2, 42; *Isaac Smith*, Vol. 7, Part 1, 504; *Isonomia*, Vol. 9, Part 1, 178; *Itasca*, Vol. 2, Part 1, 406; Vol. 2, Part 2, 569; Vol. 9, Part 2, 614; *Iuka*, Vol. 8, Part 2, 116; *Ivanhoe*, Vol. 6, Part 1, 568; *Jackal*, Vol. 9, Part 1, 626; Vol. 9, Part 2, 310; James *Adger*, Vol. 6, Part 2, 271; Vol. 7, Part 2, 308; Vol. 9, Part 2, 542; *Jamestown*, Vol. 3, Part 2, 509; Vol. 4, Part 1, 610; Vol. 7, Part 2, 308; Vol. 8, Part 1, 535; Vol. 9, Part 2, 394; Vol. 10, Part 1, 23, 135, 319, 425; *Java*, Vol. 2, Part 1, 206; Vol. 3, Part 1, 380, 416; Vol. 6, Part 1, 129, 561; Vol. 6, Part 2, 82; Vol. 7, Part 2, 276, 491, 492; Vol. 8, Part 1, 67, 529; Vol. 9, Part 1, 625; Vol. 10, Part 1, 60, 492; *Jeannette*, Vol. 1, Part 1, 240; Vol. 3, Part 1, 64, 228; Vol. 4, Part 1, 279; Vol. 6, Part 2, 20, 521; Vol. 8, Part 2, 78; *Jefferson*, Vol. 6, Part 1, 572; Vol. 8, Part 1, 596; Vol. 8, Part 2, 77; *John Adams*, Vol. 1, Part 1, 488, 650; Vol. 1, Part 2, 348; Vol. 2, Part 2, 40, 510; Vol. 3, Part 2, 286; Vol. 5, Part 2, 221; Vol. 6, Part 1, 49, 500; Vol. 6, Part 2, 270, 575; Vol. 7, Part 1, 203; Vol. 7, Part 2, 139, 275; Vol. 8, Part 1, 67, 319, 529; Vol. 8, Part 2, 74; Vol. 9, Part 1, 41, 625; Vol. 9, Part 2, 307; Vol. 10, Part 1, 292, 317; Vol. 10, Part 2, 584; *John Hancock*, Vol. 4, Part 2, 68; Vol. 8, Part 2, 77; *John Rice*, Vol. 8, Part 2, 325; *J. P. Kennedy*, Vol. 4, Part 2, 68; *Judah*, Vol. 6, Part 2, 576; *Juniata*, Vol. 2, Part 1, 586; Vol. 2, Part 2, 637; Vol. 3, Part 1, 64; 228, 269; Vol. 4, Part 1, 574; Vol. 6, Part 2, 149, 422; Vol. 7, Part 2, 532; Vol. 9, Part 2, 348; Vol. 10, Part 1, 135; *Kanawha*, Vol. 6, Part 2, 465; *Kansas*, Vol. 1, Part 1, 240; *Katahdin*, Vol. 1, Part 1, 259; Vol. 3, Part 2, 170; Vol. 8, Part 1, 183, 314; Vol. 8, Part 2, 85, 605; Vol. 10, Part 2, 206; *Katy*, Vol. 10, Part 2, 66; *Kearsarge*, Vol. 4, Part 1, 610; Vol. 5, Part 1, 311; Vol. 5, Part 2, 249, 462; Vol. 7, Part 1, 438; Vol. 8, Part 1, 167; Vol. 8, Part 2, 581; Vol. 10, Part 2, 392, 398; *Kennebec*, Vol. 6, Part 1, 568; Vol. 8, Part 2, 244; *Kentucky*, Vol. 2, Part 1, 468; Vol. 9, Part 2, 42; *Keokuk*, Vol. 8, Part 1, 529; *Keystone State*, Vol. 2, Part 2, 569; Vol. 5, Part 1, 477; Vol. 9, Part 2, 638; *Kineo*, Vol. 8, Part 1, 314; *Lackawanna*, Vol. 3, Part 2, 150; Vol. 4, Part 1, 595; Vol. 6, Part 1, 568, 574; Vol. 6, Part 2, 271; *Lafayette*, Vol. 10, Part 1, 337; *Lake Michigan*, Vol. 8, Part 1, 464; *Lancaster*, Vol. 2, Part 2, 637; Vol. 4, Part 1, 232; Vol. 5, Part 2, 462, 607; Vol. 6, Part 2, 521; Vol. 7, Part 1, 98, 504; Vol. 8, Part 1, 339, 597; Vol. 9, Part 2, 8; *Lawrence*, Vol. 3, Part 2, 96; Vol. 7, Part 2, 275, 308, 490, 491; Vol. 8, Part 1, 154, 596; *Layona*, Vol. 2, Part 2, 369; *Lee*, Vol. 6, Part 2, 236; *Lehigh*, Vol. 9, Part 2, 614; *Levant*, Vol. 2, Part 2, 326; Vol. 7, Part 1, 503; *Lexington*, Vol. 1, Part 1, 654; Vol. 3, Part 1, 33, 414; Vol. 10, Part 2, 180; *Lexington*, Vol. 1, Part 1, 502; Vol. 3, Part 1, 200; Vol. 5, Part 2, 221; Vol. 7, Part 2, 48, 492; Vol. 8, Part 1, 67, 319; Vol. 8, Part 2, 74, 579; Vol. 9, Part 1, 136; Vol. 9, Part 2, 122, 148; Vol. 10, Part 1, 337; Supp. 9, 176; *L'Indien*, Vol. 4, Part 1, 296; Vol. 5, Part 2, 184; *Little David*, Vol. 8, Part 1, 397; *Louisiana*, Vol. 3, Part 1, 614; Vol. 5, Part 2, 14; Vol. 7, Part 2, 302; Vol. 8, Part 1, 529; Vol. 10, Part 1, 319; *Louisiana*, Vol. 5, Part 1, 152; Vol. 10, Part 2, 228; *Louisville*, Vol. 6, Part 2, 479; *Loyall*, Vol. 7, Part 2, 185; *Ludlow*, Supp. 9, 385; *Macedonian*, Vol. 1, Part 1, 14, 212; Vol. 1, Part 2, 241; Vol. 2, Part 1, 14; Vol. 3, Part 1, 2, 203, 416; Vol. 4, Part 1, 334; Vol. 5, Part 1, 303; Vol. 5, Part 2, 164, 170, 176, 607; Vol. 6, Part 1, 337; Vol. 6, Part 2, 91, 195, 207; Vol. 7, Part 2, 185, 320; Vol. 8, Part 1, 183, 299; Vol. 8, Part 2, 73; Vol. 9, Part 1, 215; Vol. 9, Part 2, 42, 310; Vol. 10, Part 1, 217, 339, 492; *Machias*, Vol. 3, Part 2, 170; Vol. 4, Part 1, 485; Vol. 8, Part 2, 605; *Machias*, Supp. 9, 461; *Machias Liberty*, Vol. 7, Part 1, 610; *Mackinaw*, Vol. 1, Part 2, 104; Vol. 6, Part 2, 646; *McRae*, Vol. 7, Part 1, 172; Vol. 8, Part 1, 420; *Madawaska*, Vol. 3, Part 2, 175; *Madison*, Vol. 2, Part 2, 510; Vol. 3, Part 2, 4; Vol. 5, Part 1, 477; Vol. 7, Part 1, 97; *Mahaska*, Vol. 7, Part 2, 220; Vol. 8, Part 1, 314; *Mahopac*, Vol. 10, Part 1, 568; *Maine*, Vol. 2, Part 1, 255, 468, 586; Vol. 2, Part 2, 255, 468, 586; Vol. 2, Part 2, 500; Vol. 3, Part 1, 269; Vol. 4, Part 2, 41; Vol. 6, Part 2, 422; Vol. 8, Part 1, 3, 315; Vol. 8, Part 2, 241, 322, 512; Vol. 9, Part 1, 156; Vol. 10, Part 1, 135, 319; *Malvern*, Vol. 2, Part 2, 636; Vol. 8, Part 1, 88; *Manassas*, Vol. 3, Part 1, 136, 269; Vol. 3, Part 2, 288; Vol. 9, Part 1, 321; *Manhattan*, Vol. 7, Part 1, 504; *Maratanza*, Vol. 6, Part 1, 568; Vol. 9, Part 1, 626; *Marblehead*, Vol. 2, Part 1, 586; Vol. 6, Part 1, 564; Vol. 6, Part 2, 479; Vol. 8, Part 1, 495; *Marietta*, Vol. 5, Part 1, 318; Vol. 8, Part 1, 316; *Marion*, Vol. 3, Part 1, 584; Vol. 4, Part 1, 610; Vol. 7, Part 2, 444, 534, 606; Vol. 8, Part 1, 299; Vol. 10, Part 1, 568; *Mary Summers*, Vol. 5, Part 2, 549; *Maryland*, Vol. 8, Part 2, 76; *Maryland*, Vol. 2, Part 1, 468; Vol. 5, Part 1, 472; Vol. 8, Part 1, 317; *Massachusetts*, Vol. 3, Part 2, 420; Vol. 4, Part 2, 234; Vol. 10, Part 2, 276; *Massachusetts*, Vol. 6, Part 2, 478; Vol. 9, Part 1, 321; *Massachusetts*, Vol. 2, Part 2, 123, 500; Vol. 3, Part 1, 269; Vol. 4, Part 1, 485; Vol. 8, Part 1, 167; Vol. 8, Part 2, 465; *Maumee*, Vol. 2, Part 2, 637; Vol. 9, Part 2, 518; *Mayaquez*, Supp. 10, 73; *Mayflower*, Vol. 1, Part 1, 240; *Melville*, Vol. 8, Part 1, 237; *Memphis*, Vol. 6, Part 2, 271; *Mercedita*, Vol. 5, Part 1, 477; *Merrimac*, Vol. 2, Part 1, 70, 207; Vol. 3, Part 1, 532; Vol. 3, Part 2, 173, 532; Vol. 4, Part 1, 366, 574; Vol. 5, Part 1, 343; Vol. 5, Part 2, 14, 164, 278; Vol. 6, Part 1, 173, 315; Vol. 7, Part 1, 152; Vol. 7, Part 2, 243; Vol. 8, Part 1, 68, 97, 319, 339; Vol. 8, Part 2, 568; Vol. 9, Part 1, 310; Vol. 10, Part 2, 217, 400, 465, 531, 658; *Merrimac*, Vol. 6, Part 2, 225; Vol. 8, Part 1, 97; Vol. 9, Part 2, 311; Vol. 10, Part 1, 630; *Merrimack*, Vol. 10, Part 1, 318; *Metacomet*, Vol. 2, Part 2, 569; Vol. 3, Part 1, 584; Vol. 5, Part 2, 221; *Miami*, Vol. 4, Part 2, 71; Vol. 9, Part 2, 620; *Miantonomah*, Vol. 1, Part 2, 104; Vol. 3, Part 2, 569; Vol. 6, Part 2, 422; Vol. 8, Part 1, 640; Vol. 9, Part 1, 139, 149; *Michigan*, Vol. 2, Part 1, 543, 609; Vol. 3, Part 2, 170; Vol. 4, Part 1, 610; Vol. 5, Part 2, 607;

Vol. 6, Part 2, 480; Vol. 7, Part 2, 220; Vol. 8, Part 1, 299; Vol. 9, Part 1, 626; Vol. 9, Part 2, 8, 457; *Michigan*, Vol. 2, Part 2, 423; Vol. 4, Part 2, 391; Vol. 5, Part 1, 515, 516; Vol. 7, Part 1, 481; Vol. 10, Part 1, 135; *Mingoe*, Vol. 8, Part 1, 293; *Minneapolis*, Vol. 1, Part 1, 495; Vol. 6, Part 2, 522; Vol. 7, Part 1, 343; *Minnesota*, Vol. 1, Part 1, 240; Vol. 2, Part 2, 635; Vol. 3, Part 1, 531; Vol. 5, Part 2, 170, 607; Vol. 6, Part 1, 173; Vol. 6, Part 2, 149, 465; Vol. 10, Part 1, 128, 318; Vol. 10, Part 2, 1; *Minnesota*, Vol. 4, Part 1, 485, 574; Vol. 8, Part 1, 512; *Minnesota*, Supp. 9, 461, 755; *Mississippi*, Vol. 1, Part 1, 488; Vol. 1, Part 1, 600; Vol. 1, Part 2, 206; Vol. 2, Part 1, 14, 206; Vol. 2, Part 2, 423; Vol. 3, Part 1, 200; Vol. 3, Part 1, 269; Vol. 4, Part 2, 391; Vol. 6, Part 2, 21, 91, 557; Vol. 7, Part 2, 186, 314; Vol. 7, Part 2, 487; Vol. 9, Part 1, 321; Vol. 9, Part 2, 620; Vol. 10, Part 2, 645; *Mississippi*, Vol. 6, Part 2, 225; Vol. 8, Part 1, 97; *Missouri*, Vol. 2, Part 2, 423; Vol. 3, Part 2, 255; Vol. 4, Part 2, 391; Vol. 6, Part 2, 91; Vol. 7, Part 1, 320; Vol. 8, Part 1, 214; Vol. 10, Part 2, 397; *Missouri*, Vol. 2, Part 1, 468; Vol. 8, Part 1, 18, 317; *Mohawk*, Vol. 2, Part 2, 518; Vol. 5, Part 2, 176; Vol. 8, Part 2, 73; Vol. 9, Part 2, 149; *Mohican*, Vol. 1, Part 1, 258; Vol. 4, Part 1, 232; Vol. 5, Part 2, 324; Vol. 7, Part 2, 308; Vol. 9, Part 1, 178; Vol. 9, Part 2, 42; *Mohongo*, Vol. 3, Part 2, 170; Vol. 7, Part 1, 504; Vol. 9, Part 1, 178; *Monadnock*, Vol. 4, Part 2, 266; Vol. 7, Part 2, 260; Vol. 9, Part 2, 613, 614; *Monitor*, Vol. 2, Part 1, 207; Vol. 3, Part 1, 532; Vol. 3, Part 2, 170, 173, 174, 175, 176, 568; Vol. 4, Part 1, 366, 574; Vol. 5, Part 2, 14, 164, 278; Vol. 7, Part 2, 243, 321; Vol. 8, Part 1, 68, 314; Vol. 8, Part 2, 200; Vol. 9, Part 1, 310, 626; Vol. 9, Part 2, 311, 614, 638; Vol. 10, Part 1, 630; Vol. 10, Part 2, 400, 466, 531; *Monocacy*, Vol. 2, Part 1, 544; Vol. 5, Part 2, 324; Vol. 6, Part 2, 129; *Monongahela*, Vol. 1, Part 1, 600; Vol. 3, Part 1, 269; Vol. 4, Part 1, 574, 610; Vol. 4, Part 2, 3; Vol. 5, Part 2, 50; Vol. 6, Part 1, 568; Vol. 8, Part 2, 437; Vol. 9, Part 1, 156, 321; Vol. 9, Part 2, 149; *Montauk*, Vol. 1, Part 1, 488; Vol. 3, Part 1, 136; Vol. 3, Part 2, 255; Vol. 7, Part 2, 534; Vol. 8, Part 2, 200; Vol. 10, Part 2, 531; *Monterey*, Vol. 5, Part 2, 324; *Montezuma*, Vol. 1, Part 1, 504; Vol. 7, Part 1, 358; Vol. 9, Part 1, 41; *Montgomery*, Vol. 5, Part 1, 303; Vol. 5, Part 2, 221; Vol. 8, Part 1, 430; *Monticello*, Vol. 2, Part 2, 636; *Morris*, Vol. 10, Part 2, 397; *Mount Vernon*, Vol. 8, Part 2, 22; *Mullany*, Vol. 7, Part 1, 320; *Muscoota*, Vol. 8, Part 2, 200; *Muscota*, Vol. 7, Part 2, 314; *M. W. Chapin*, Vol. 5, Part 2, 221; *Nahant*, Vol. 3, Part 1, 532; Vol. 6, Part 2, 465; *Nancy*, Vol. 7, Part 2, 631; *Nanshan*, Vol. 9, Part 2, 8; *Nantucket*, Vol. 1, Part 2, 104; Vol. 3, Part 2, 255; *Narragansett*, Vol. 3, Part 1, 269; Vol. 6, Part 2, 479; Vol. 8, Part 1, 183; *Nashville*, Vol. 6, Part 2, 271; Vol. 10, Part 2, 531; *Nashville*, Vol. 10, Part 2, 392; *Natchez*, Vol. 3, Part 1, 200; Vol. 3, Part 2, 287; Vol. 4, Part 1, 19; Vol. 6, Part 2, 21, 82, 576; Vol. 7, Part 2, 444; Vol. 8, Part 1, 596; Vol. 9, Part 1, 136; Vol. 10, Part 1, 336; *Nausett*, Vol. 6, Part 2, 73; *Nautilus*, brig of 1812, Vol. 2, Part 2, 510; *Nautilus*, schooner of 1802, Vol. 8, Part 1, 182, 596; Vol. 9, Part 1, 394; *Nebraska*, Vol. 8, Part 1, 237; *Nehenta Bay*, Supp. 9, 347; *Neptune*, Vol. 10, Part 1, 318; *Newark*, Vol. 1, Part 1, 600; Vol. 2, Part 2, 123; Vol. 6, Part 1, 564; Vol. 7, Part 1, 438; Vol. 10, Part 1, 319; *New Hampshire*, Vol. 8, Part 1, 293, 523; Vol. 10, Part 2, 393; *New Ironsides*, Vol. 1, Part 2, 146; Vol. 2, Part 2, 501; Vol. 3, Part 1, 532; Vol. 6, Part 2, 557; Vol. 7, Part 2, 321; Vol. 8, Part 1, 319; Vol. 8, Part 2, 73, 196; *New Jersey*, Vol. 5, Part 2, 380; *New Mexico*, Vol. 8, Part 2, 22; *New Orleans*, Vol. 5, Part 1, 471; *New York*, Vol. 3, Part 1, 187; *New York*, Vol. 2, Part 1, 586; Vol. 2, Part 2, 40, 500; Vol. 3, Part 2, 210; Vol. 6, Part 2, 480; Vol. 7, Part 1, 343; Vol. 7, Part 2, 535; Vol. 8, Part 2, 323; 438; Vol. 10, Part 2, 393; *Niagara*, Vol. 3, Part 2, 96, 97; Vol. 7, Part 1, 97, 98; Vol. 7, Part 2, 490, 491; Vol. 8, Part 1, 154; Vol. 9, Part 1, 625; Vol. 10, Part 1, 59; *Niagara*, Vol. 1, Part 1, 600; Vol. 2, Part 2, 518; Vol. 6, Part 1, 173, 574; Vol. 7, Part 1, 426; Vol. 7, Part 2, 140, 185; Vol. 8, Part 2, 437; *Niagara* (cable-laying ship of 1850), Vol. 9, Part 1, 560; *Niagara* (finest ship in the Navy in 1860), Vol. 6, Part 2, 82; *Nicholson*, Vol. 7, Part 1, 507; *Niphon*, Vol. 2, Part 2, 636; *Nipsic*, Vol. 3, Part 2, 170; *Nonsuch*, Vol. 5, Part 2, 270; Vol. 10, Part 1, 60; *Norfolk*, Vol. 1, Part 1, 504, 505; Vol. 3, Part 1, 187; *North Carolina*, Vol. 1, Part 2, 395, 408; Vol. 3, Part 1, 530; Vol. 6, Part 2, 478; Vol. 7, Part 2, 487; Vol. 8, Part 2, 77, 196, 427; Vol. 10, Part 1, 292; *North Carolina*, Vol. 8, Part 1, 97; *North Dakota*, Vol. 8, Part 1, 18; *Ocean Queen*, Vol. 1, Part 1, 258; *Octorara*, Vol. 2, Part 2, 308; *Ohio*, Vol. 1, Part 1, 226; Vol. 1, Part 2, 104; Vol. 2, Part 1, 543; Vol. 3, Part 1, 530; Vol. 3, Part 2, 4, 149; Vol. 4, Part 1, 232, 366; Vol. 5, Part 1, 362; Vol. 5, Part 2, 164; Vol. 6, Part 2, 21, 271, 479; Vol. 8, Part 1, 299; Vol. 9, Part 1, 310; Vol. 9, Part 2, 48, 122, 139, 394, 620; Vol. 10, Part 2, 465; *Ohio*, Vol. 8, Part 2, 427; *Ohio*, Vol. 2, Part 1, 468; Vol. 8, Part 2, 492; *Old Ironsides*, Vol. 8, Part 1, 397, 515; Vol. 10, Part 2, 658; *Oliver Cromwell*, Vol. 4, Part 2, 251; *Olympia*, Vol. 3, Part 1, 270, 271, 292; Vol. 3, Part 2, 170; Vol. 4, Part 1, 610; Vol. 5, Part 2, 559; Vol. 6, Part 2, 129; Vol. 8, Part 2, 492; Vol. 10, Part 1, 339; *Omaha*, Vol. 6, Part 2, 149, 465; Vol. 9, Part 1, 178; *Oneida*, Vol. 4, Part 1, 610; Vol. 5, Part 2, 50; Vol. 6, Part 1, 129; Vol. 7, Part 1, 320; *Oneida*, Vol. 8, Part 1, 183; Vol. 9, Part 1, 149; 626; Vol. 10, Part 2, 518; *Onondaga*, Vol. 8, Part 1, 314, 315; Vol. 8, Part 2, 200; Vol. 9, Part 1, 321; *Ontario*, Vol. 1, Part 2, 241; Vol. 2, Part 2, 46, 349; Vol. 3, Part 1, 29, 106, 530; Vol. 3, Part 2, 97; Vol. 6, Part 1, 315, 561; Vol. 7, Part 1, 98; Vol. 8, Part 1, 319, 596; Vol. 9, Part 1, 626; Vol. 10, Part 1, 336; *Oregon*, Vol. 5, Part 2, 164; Vol. 6, Part 1, 553; *Oregon*, Vol. 5, Part 1, 318; Vol. 6, Part 1, 545; Vol. 8, Part 1, 316; Vol. 8, Part 2, 492; Vol. 9, Part 1, 218; Vol. 10, Part 2, 206; *Oregon*, Vol. 1, Part 1, 601; Vol. 2, Part 2, 123; Vol. 3, Part 1, 292, 614; Vol. 4, Part 1, 485; Vol. 6, Part 2, 646; *Oreto (Florida)*, Vol. 2, Part 1, 258; Vol. 8, Part 1, 183; *Osage*, Vol. 8, Part 2, 569; *Ossifee*, Vol. 2, Part 2, 123; Vol. 3, Part 1, 584; Vol. 3, Part 2, 150; Vol. 5, Part 1, 303; Vol. 8, Part 1, 339; *Ottawa*, Vol. 9, Part 1, 626; *Owasco*, Vol. 9, Part 2, 149; *Ozark*, Vol. 2, Part 1, 468; *Pallas*, Vol. 5, Part 2, 185; *Palmetto State*, Vol. 5, Part 1, 477; Vol. 7, Part 2, 243; Vol. 8, Part 1, 97; Vol. 9, Part 2, 348; *Palos*, Vol. 5, Part 2, 462; *Pampero*, Vol. 5, Part 2, 593; *Pandora*, Vol. 3, Part 1, 228; *Panther*, Vol. 1, Part 2, 567; Vol. 7, Part 1, 343; *Passaic*, Vol. 3, Part 1, 446; Vol. 8, Part 2, 200; Vol. 9, Part 1, 178; Vol. 10, Part 2, 347; *Patapsco*, Vol. 1, Part 1, 258, 488; Vol. 8, Part 1, 293; Vol. 8, Part 2, 322; Vol. 9, Part 1, 626; *Patrick Henry*, Vol. 7, Part 1, 172; Vol. 7, Part 2, 243; Vol. 10, Part 1, 34; *Paul Jones*, Vol. 8, Part 1, 529; Vol. 9, Part 1, 554; *Pawnee*, Vol. 1, Part 1, 528; Vol. 4, Part 1, 626; Vol. 5, Part 2, 164; Vol. 7, Part 2, 534; Vol. 8, Part 1, 420; Vol. 8, Part 2, 196; Vol. 10, Part 2, 585; *Peacock*, Vol. 1, Part 2, 241; Vol. 3, Part 1, 200, 380; Vol. 3, Part 2, 149; Vol. 5, Part 1, 152; Vol. 5, Part 2, 201; Vol. 6, Part 2, 270; Vol. 7, Part 1, 98; Vol. 7, Part 2, 185, 461, 625; Vol. 8, Part 2, 5, 73; Vol. 9, Part 2, 348; Vol. 10, Part 1, 292, 492; *Pembina*, Vol. 9, Part 2, 7, 364; *Penguin*, Vol. 6, Part 1, 315; *Penn-*

sylvania, Vol. 2, Part 1, 468; Vol. 2, Part 2, 500; Vol. 6, Part 1, 545; Vol. 8, Part 1, 522; *Pennsylvania,* Supp. 9, 461; *Pensacola,* Vol. 2, Part 1, 14; Vol. 3, Part 1, 269; Vol. 4, Part 1, 232; Vol. 6, Part 2, 149; Vol. 8, Part 1, 97; Vol. 8, Part 2, 85, 464; Vol. 9, Part 2, 394; Vol. 10, Part 1, 128; *Pequot,* Vol. 8, Part 1, 293; *Perkins,* Vol. 8, Part 1, 237; *Perry,* Vol. 3, Part 1, 530; Vol. 3, Part 2, 500; Vol. 5, Part 2, 164; Vol. 7, Part 2, 139, 260, 314; Vol. 8, Part 1, 293, 299; Vol. 9, Part 1, 487; *Petrel,* Vol. 2, Part 2, 569; Vol. 3, Part 1, 270, 271; Vol. 5, Part 2, 559; Vol. 8, Part 1, 17, 86, 183; *Philadelphia,* Vol. 1, Part 1, 506; Vol. 1, Part 2, 241; Vol. 3, Part 1, 186, 187; Vol. 5, Part 2, 176; Vol. 6, Part 1, 49, 77; Vol. 6, Part 2, 20, 113; Vol. 7, Part 1, 152, 202; Vol. 7, Part 2, 301; Vol. 8, Part 1, 84, 182; Vol. 9, Part 2, 7; *Philadelphia,* Vol. 5, Part 2, 14; Vol. 7, Part 2, 314, 531; *Philadelphia,* Vol. 1, Part 1, 600; Vol. 5, Part 1, 471; Vol. 8, Part 2, 554; *Phoenix,* Vol. 8, Part 2, 72; *Pickering,* Vol. 5, Part 1, 479; Vol. 8, Part 1, 182; *Pinola,* Vol. 2, Part 1, 406; Vol. 2, Part 2, 569; *Pioneer,* Vol. 8, Part 1, 596; Vol. 9, Part 2, 310; *Pittsburg,* Vol. 3, Part 2, 500; Vol. 9, Part 2, 457; Vol. 10, Part 1, 337, 633; *Planter,* Vol. 9, Part 1, 224, 225; *Plunger,* Vol. 5, Part 1, 145; *Plymouth,* Vol. 1, Part 1, 528; Vol. 2, Part 1, 14; Vol. 3, Part 1, 30, 64; Vol. 5, Part 2, 164; Vol. 9, Part 2, 42; *Pocahontas,* Vol. 1, Part 1, 528; Vol. 3, Part 1, 445; Vol. 6, Part 2, 207; Vol. 7, Part 1, 504; Vol. 10, Part 2, 585; *Poinsett,* Vol. 8, Part 2, 579; *Polaris,* Vol. 3, Part 1, 228; Vol. 4, Part 1, 595; Vol. 6, Part 2, 521; *Polk,* Vol. 7, Part 2, 531; *Pontiac,* Vol. 8, Part 2, 244; *Pontoosuc,* Vol. 9, Part 2, 364, 518; *Porcupine,* Vol. 2, Part 1, 609; Vol. 9, Part 1, 625; *Porpoise,* Vol. 1, Part 2, 146; Vol. 1, Part 2, 408; Vol. 2, Part 2, 517; Vol. 5, Part 2, 615; Vol. 6, Part 2, 270; Vol. 7, Part 2, 308, 461, 625; Vol. 8, Part 1, 617; Vol. 8, Part 2, 85, 341, 579; Vol. 9, Part 2, 620; Vol. 10, Part 1, 317; Vol. 10, Part 2, 217; *Port Royal,* Vol. 4, Part 1, 232; *Portsmouth,* Vol. 2, Part 1, 337; Vol. 6, Part 2, 149; *Portsmouth,* Vol. 1, Part 1, 606; Vol. 1, Part 2, 146; Vol. 2, Part 1, 14; Vol. 3, Part 1, 380; Vol. 3, Part 2, 500; Vol. 4, Part 1, 21, 437; Vol. 4, Part 1, 610; Vol. 5, Part 2, 324; Vol. 7, Part 1, 98; Vol. 7, Part 2, 314; Vol. 8, Part 1, 514; Vol. 9, Part 1, 178; Vol. 10, Part 2, 228; *Potomac,* Vol. 2, Part 1, 543; Vol. 3, Part 1, 416; Vol. 3, Part 2, 157; Vol. 6, Part 2, 270, 478; Vol. 7, Part 2, 243, 338, 444; Vol. 8, Part 1, 299, 596; Vol. 8, Part 2, 437; Vol. 9, Part 1, 321; *Powhatan,* Vol. 2, Part 1, 70, 586; Vol. 4, Part 2, 68; Vol. 6, Part 1, 251, 573; Vol. 6, Part 2, 21; Vol. 8, Part 1, 86, 299, 420, 597; Vol. 8, Part 2, 288, 427, 618; Vol. 9, Part 1, 554; Vol. 9, Part 2, 311, 457, 637; Vol. 10, Part 2, 1; *Preble,* Vol. 1, Part 2, 206; Vol. 2, Part 1, 14; Vol. 3, Part 1, 136; Vol. 4, Part 1, 334; Vol. 5, Part 1, 152, 362; Vol. 5, Part 2, 50; Vol. 6, Part 2, 18; Vol. 8, Part 1, 319, 339; *President,* Vol. 1, Part 1, 14, 506, 507, 650; Vol. 1, Part 2, 215, 241, 348; Vol. 2, Part 1, 337; Vol. 2, Part 2, 40, 46; Vol. 3, Part 1, 33, 188; Vol. 9, Part 1, 136, 214; Vol. 9, Part 2, 48, 139, 280, 306, 645; Vol. 10, Part 1, 22, 492; *President,* Vol. 3, Part 2, 85; Vol. 5, Part 1, 152, 337; Vol. 7, Part 1, 97, 202; Vol. 7, Part 2, 486; Vol. 8, Part 2, 73, 76, 77; *Princeton,* Vol. 1, Part 1, 528; Vol. 1, Part 2, 408; Vol. 2, Part 2, 510; Vol. 4, Part 2, 391; Vol. 5, Part 1, 515; Vol. 7, Part 1, 503, 639; Vol. 7, Part 2, 185, 314; Vol. 8, Part 1, 95; Vol. 9, Part 2, 48; *Protector,* Vol. 6, Part 1, 299; Vol. 8, Part 1, 182; Vol. 10, Part 2, 276; *Proteus,* Vol. 9, Part 1, 139; *Providence,* Vol. 5, Part 2, 184, 204; Vol. 10, Part 1, 39; Vol. 10, Part 2, 66; *Pueblo,* Supp. 10, 72; *Puritan,* Vol. 5, Part 2, 462; Vol. 8, Part 1, 314, 640; *Pushmataha,* Vol. 9, Part 2, 614; *Queen of France,* Vol. 5, Part 1, 212; Vol. 7, Part 2, 484; *Quinnebaug,* Vol. 5, Part 1, 153; Vol. 5, Part 2, 462; *Raleigh,* Vol. 1, Part 1, 495, 654; Vol. 3, Part 1, 270; Vol. 5, Part 1, 64; Vol. 8, Part 1, 97; *Randolph,* Vol. 1, Part 2, 242; *Ranger,* Vol. 5, Part 1, 212; Vol. 5, Part 2, 184; Vol. 7, Part 2, 338; Vol. 10, Part 1, 39; *Ranger,* Vol. 2, Part 2, 123 (1881); Vol. 7, Part 2, 535 (1877); Vol. 9, Part 1, 387 (1893); *Rappahannock,* Vol. 10, Part 1, 337; Vol. 10, Part 2, 398; *Raritan,* Vol. 3, Part 2, 531; Vol. 6, Part 1, 567; Vol. 6, Part 2, 82; Vol. 7, Part 2, 314; Vol. 8, Part 1, 293; Vol. 10, Part 2, 398; *Red Rover,* Vol. 7, Part 2, 626; *Reefer,* Vol. 7, Part 2, 314; *Release,* Vol. 7, Part 2, 470; Vol. 10, Part 1, 302; *Reliance,* Vol. 10, Part 1, 425; Vol. 10, Part 2, 466; *Relief,* Vol. 2, Part 2, 569; Vol. 3, Part 1, 380; Vol. 5, Part 2, 50, 164; Vol. 7, Part 2, 185; Vol. 8, Part 1, 299; Vol. 8, Part 2, 196; Vol. 9, Part 2, 394; *Reprisal,* Vol. 3, Part 1, 414; Vol. 10, Part 2, 180; *Republic,* Vol. 10, Part 2, 276; *Rescue,* Vol. 3, Part 1, 200; *Resolute,* Vol. 5, Part 2, 298; Vol. 10, Part 1, 425; *Retaliation,* Vol. 1, Part 1, 504; Vol. 3, Part 1, 186; *Revenge,* Vol. 2, Part 2, 368; Vol. 7, Part 2, 486, 490; *Rhode Island,* Vol. 7, Part 1, 343; Vol. 9, Part 2, 638; *Richmond,* Vol. 1, Part 1, 146; Vol. 4, Part 1, 232, 610; Vol. 5, Part 1, 477; Vol. 5, Part 2, 50; Vol. 7, Part 1, 320; Vol. 7, Part 2, 314, 535; Vol. 8, Part 1, 420; Vol. 8, Part 2, 437; Vol. 9, Part 2, 7; Vol. 10, Part 2, 585; *Richmond,* Vol. 7, Part 2, 243; Vol. 8, Part 1, 97; *Roanoke,* Vol. 5, Part 2, 14; Vol. 6, Part 1, 173, 500; Vol. 7, Part 1, 98; Vol. 8, Part 1, 68; *Rochester,* Vol. 8, Part 1, 317; *Rodgers,* Vol. 4, Part 1, 278; *Rodolph,* Vol. 3, Part 1, 584; *Royal Louis,* Vol. 3, Part 2, 536; *Royal Yacht,* Vol. 5, Part 2, 221; *R. R. Cuyler,* Vol. 2, Part 1, 407; Vol. 3, Part 2, 150; Vol. 5, Part 2, 221; *Sabine,* Vol. 1, Part 1, 528; Vol. 2, Part 1, 586; Vol. 6, Part 1, 568; Vol. 7, Part 1, 320; Vol. 8, Part 1, 617, 618; Vol. 10, Part 1, 545; *Sachem,* Vol. 1, Part 1, 633; *Saco,* Vol. 5, Part 2, 462; Vol. 7, Part 2, 606; Vol. 10, Part 1, 349; *Sacramento,* Vol. 1, Part 2, 409; Vol. 2, Part 2, 309, 518; Vol. 7, Part 2, 140; Vol. 10, Part 1, 337, 339; *Sagamore,* Vol. 6, Part 1, 81; *Saginaw,* Vol. 6, Part 2, 479; Vol. 8, Part 2, 427, 464; Vol. 9, Part 1, 149; *St. Lawrence,* Vol. 2, Part 1, 14, 543; Vol. 5, Part 2, 188, 221; Vol. 7, Part 2, 220, 320; Vol. 8, Part 1, 67, 339; Vol. 8, Part 2, 343, 427; *St. Louis,* Vol. 3, Part 2, 500; Vol. 4, Part 1, 232, 265, 595; Vol. 5, Part 1, 447; Vol. 6, Part 1, 315, 572; Vol. 6, Part 2, 195, 478; Vol. 7, Part 1, 320; Vol. 7, Part 2, 260, 314; Vol. 8, Part 1, 67, 183, 596; Vol. 8, Part 2, 341; Vol. 9, Part 1, 215; Vol. 9, Part 2, 457; Vol. 10, Part 1, 568; *St. Louis,* Vol. 10, Part 1, 135; *St. Mary's,* Vol. 1, Part 1, 502; Vol. 2, Part 1, 13; Vol. 2, Part 2, 326; Vol. 3, Part 1, 107; Vol. 5, Part 2, 164, 221; Vol. 6, Part 1, 14; Vol. 6, Part 2, 465; Vol. 7, Part 2, 185, 260; Vol. 8, Part 2, 244, 343; Vol. 9, Part 1, 553; Vol. 9, Part 2, 348; Vol. 10, Part 1, 128; *St. Paul,* Vol. 9, Part 1, 156; *San Diego,* Vol. 8, Part 2, 22; *San Francisco,* Vol. 5, Part 1, 303; Vol. 8, Part 2, 492; Vol. 9, Part 1, 165; Vol. 10, Part 1, 545; *San Francisco,* Supp. 10, 371; *San Jacinto,* Vol. 1, Part 2, 154; Vol. 2, Part 1, 14, 543; Vol. 3, Part 1, 380; Vol. 3, Part 2, 255; Vol. 4, Part 1, 594; Vol. 5, Part 1, 451, 515; Vol. 5, Part 2, 607; Vol. 6, Part 2, 478; Vol. 8, Part 1, 299; Vol. 10, Part 1, 317; Vol. 10, Part 2, 217; *Sangamon,* Vol. 9, Part 2, 614; *Santee,* Vol. 5, Part 2, 221; Vol. 6, Part 2, 49; *Santiago de Cuba,* Vol. 8, Part 1, 597; *Saranac,* Vol. 2, Part 2, 423; Vol. 4, Part 1, 232, 594; Vol. 5, Part 2, 224, 607; Vol. 7, Part 2, 314, 532; Vol. 8, Part 1, 68, 299; Vol. 9, Part 2, 310; *Saratoga,* Vol. 1, Part 1, 488, 633; Vol. 1, Part 2, 408; Vol. 2, Part 1, 13; Vol. 2, Part 2, 326; Vol. 3, Part 2, 287; Vol. 4, Part 1, 232, 544. 594; Vol. 6, Part 2, 20, 69; Vol. 7, Part 2, 260, 320; Vol. 8, Part

1, 183, 339; **Vol. 8, Part 2**, 72, 74; **Vol. 9, Part 2**, 310; **Vol. 10, Part 1, 319;** *Saratoga*, **Supp. 9**, 635; *Sassacus*, **Vol. 1, Part 2**, 487; **Vol. 3, Part 1**, 136; **Vol. 8, Part 2**, 85; *Satellite*, **Vol. 10, Part 2**, 466; *Savannah*, **Vol. 3, Part 2**, 150; **Vol. 5, Part 1**, 152, **Vol. 6, Part 2**, 576; **Vol. 9, Part 1**, 215; *Savannah*, **Vol. 6, Part 2**, 196, 576; **Vol. 7, Part 2**, 139; **Vol. 8, Part 1**, 97; **Vol. 9, Part 2**, 311; *Sciota*, **Vol. 7, Part 2**, 470; **Vol. 9, Part 2**, 614; *Scorpion*, **Vol. 2, Part 1**, 609; **Vol. 9, Part 2**, 625; **Vol. 10, Part 1**, 60; *Scorpion*, **Vol. 6, Part 2**, 478; **Vol. 7, Part 2**, 314; *Scourge*, **Vol. 9, Part 2**, 364; *Sea Gull*, **Vol. 3, Part 2**, 286; *Sebago*, **Vol. 1, Part 2**, 104; *Selma*, **Vol. 3, Part 1**, 584; **Vol. 5, Part 2**, 221; *Seminole*, **Vol. 2, Part 1**, 543; **Vol. 6, Part 1**, 500; **Vol. 6, Part 2**, 149, 207; **Vol. 8, Part 1**, 97, 314; *Seneca*, **Vol. 1, Part 1, 258; Vol. 8, Part 1**, 529; **Vol. 9, Part 1**, 149; *Shamokin*, **Vol. 2, Part 2**, 569; *Shark*, **Vol. 3, Part 1**, 380; **Vol. 3, Part 2**, 85; **Vol. 5, Part 2**, 164; **Vol. 6, Part 1**, 524; **Vol. 7, Part 2**, 320, 487; **Vol. 8, Part 2**, 196; **Vol. 9, Part 1**, 626; *Shawmut*, **Vol. 5, Part 2**, 380; **Vol. 10, Part 1**, 349; **Vol. 10, Part 2**, 347; *Shenandoah*, **Vol. 6, Part 2**, 480; **Vol. 8, Part 1**, 597; *Shenandoah*, **Vol. 10, Part 1**, 302; *Shokokon*, **Vol. 2, Part 2**, 636; *Silenus*, **Vol. 2, Part 2**, 47; *Siren*, **Vol. 8, Part 1**, 182; **Vol. 9, Part 1**, 135; **Vol. 9, Part 2**, 7, 262, 307; **Vol. 10, Part 1**, 492; *Solace*, **Vol. 8, Part 2**, 554; *Somers*, **Vol. 6, Part 2**, 91; **Vol. 7, Part 1**, 320; **Vol. 8, Part 2**, 579; **Vol. 9, Part 2**, 457; **Vol. 10, Part 1**, 302; *Sonoma*, **Vol. 5, Part 2**, 324; **Vol. 7, Part 2**, 534; **Vol. 9, Part 1**, 626; **Vol. 10, Part 2**, 585; *South Carolina*, **Vol. 4, Part 1**, 296; *South Carolina*, **Vol. 1, Part 1**, 146; *South Carolina*, **Vol. 9, Part 1**, 388; *South Carolina*, **Supp. 9**, 635; *South Dakota*, **Vol. 2, Part 1**, 468; **Vol. 8, Part 1**, 18; *Southampton*, **Vol. 10, Part 2**, 531; *Southern Star*, **Vol. 4, Part 1**, 594; **Vol. 7, Part 2**, 444; *Spark*, **Vol. 3, Part 2**, 286; **Vol. 9, Part 2**, 139; *Sphynx*, **Vol. 7, Part 2**, 140; *Spitfire*, **Vol. 5, Part 1**, 515; **Vol. 8, Part 1**, 86; **Vol. 9, Part 2**, 48, 310; *Star of the West*, **Vol. 10, Part 2**, 501; *Stars and Stripes*, **Vol. 10, Part 2**, 1; *State of Georgia*, **Vol. 8, Part 1**, 184; *Stonewall*, **Vol. 2, Part 2**, 518; **Vol. 7, Part 2**, 140; **Vol. 10, Part 2**, 206; *Stonewall Jackson*, **Vol. 1, Part 2**, 409; *Stromboli*, **Vol. 10, Part 1**, 34; *Sumter*, **Vol. 2, Part 2**, 518; **Vol. 7, Part 2**, 186; **Vol. 8, Part 1**, 68, 86; **Vol. 8, Part 2**, 580, 605; *Sumter*, **Vol. 4, Part 1**, 594; **Vol. 7, Part 2**, 314, 470; *Superior*, **Vol. 4, Part 1**, 334; **Vol. 8, Part 2**, 343; *Supply*, **Vol. 2, Part 2**, 326; **Vol. 5, Part 1**, 303, 471; **Vol. 6, Part 1**, 524; **Vol. 7, Part 1**, 320; **Vol. 7, Part 2**, 444; **Vol. 8, Part 1**, 86, 293, 317; **Vol. 10, Part 1**, 128, 336; *Surprise*, **Vol. 8, Part 2**, 427; *Susquehanna*, **Vol. 2, Part 1**, 207, **Vol. 2, Part 2**, 423; **Vol. 3, Part 2**, 255; **Vol. 4, Part 2**, 3; **Vol. 5, Part 1**, 152; **Vol. 5, Part 2**, 249, 324, 615; **Vol. 6, Part 1**, 564; **Vol. 7, Part 2**, 186, 220, 488, **Vol. 8, Part 1**, 617; **Vol. 8, Part 2**, 343; **Vol. 9, Part 1**, 149; **Vol. 10, Part 1**, 568; **Vol. 10, Part 2**, 206, 645; *Suwanee*, **Vol. 2, Part 2**, 123; **Vol. 5, Part 2**, 324; *Suwanee*, **Vol. 1, Part 2**, 395; *Swatara*, **Vol. 6, Part 1**, 500; **Vol. 7, Part 2**, 607; **Vol. 8, Part 2**, 464; **Vol. 9, Part 2**, 42; *Sylph*, **Vol. 10, Part 2**, 518; *Syren*, **Vol. 1, Part 2**, 241; **Vol. 6, Part 2**, 20; *Tacony*, **Vol. 6, Part 1**, 500; **Vol. 6, Part 2**, 521; **Vol. 7, Part 2**, 606; **Vol. 8, Part 1**, 420; **Vol. 8, Part 2**, 85; **Vol. 10, Part 1**, 23; *Tallahassee*, **Vol. 2, Part 1**, 586; **Vol. 9, Part 2**, 42; **Vol. 10, Part 2**, 466; *Tallahassee*, **Vol. 2, Part 1**, 468; *Tallapoosa*, **Vol. 3, Part 2**, 290; **Vol. 6, Part 1**, 568; *Teazer*, **Vol. 6, Part 1**, 568; **Vol. 9, Part 1**, 626; *Tecumseh*, **Vol. 1, Part 1**, 146; **Vol. 2, Part 2**, 518; **Vol. 3, Part 2**, 289; *Tennessee*, **Vol. 2, Part 1**, 207; **Vol. 2, Part 2**, 123; **Vol. 6, Part 1**, 500, 568; **Vol. 6, Part 2**, 271; **Vol. 7, Part 1**, 320, 504; **Vol. 7, Part 2**, 185, 470; **Vol. 9, Part 2**, 149; **Vol. 10, Part 1**, 545; *Tennessee*, **Vol. 6, Part 2**, 521; **Vol. 8, Part 1**, 640; **Vol. 8, Part 2**, 22; **Vol. 10, Part 1**, 319; **Vol. 10, Part 2**, 392; *Terrier*, **Vol. 6, Part 2**, 82, 91; *Terror*, **Vol. 8, Part 1**, 293; **Vol. 8, Part 2**, 22; *Texas*, **Vol. 1, Part 2**, 395; **Vol. 3, Part 1**, 269; **Vol. 4, Part 1**, 485; **Vol. 7, Part 2**, 535; **Vol. 8, Part 1**, 18; **Vol. 8, Part 2**, 438; **Vol. 9, Part 2**, 127; *Theodora*, **Vol. 2, Part 2**, 490; *Thetis*, **Vol. 6, Part 2**, 521; **Vol. 8, Part 2**, 438; **Vol. 9, Part 2**, 42; **Vol. 10, Part 1**, 633; *Thomas Freeborn*, **Vol. 10, Part 1**, 425; *Ticonderoga*, **Vol. 5, Part 1**, 451; **Vol. 7, Part 2**, 320; **Vol. 8, Part 1**, 314; **Vol. 9, Part 1**, 140, 149, 554; **Vol. 10, Part 2**, 585; *Tigress*, **Vol. 2, Part 1**, 609; **Vol. 4, Part 1**, 595; **Vol. 6, Part 2**, 521; **Vol. 9, Part 1**, 625; *Tioga*, **Vol. 6, Part 1**, 574; **Vol. 8, Part 1**, 314; **Vol. 8, Part 2**, 74; *Tonapah*, **Vol. 2, Part 1**, 468; *Topeka*, **Vol. 8, Part 1**, 18; *Trenton*, **Vol. 3, Part 1**, 136, **Vol. 3, Part 2**, 560; **Vol. 4, Part 1**, 610; **Vol. 6, Part 2**, 129, 422; **Vol. 8, Part 1**, 299, 339; **Vol. 10, Part 1**, 339; *Tom Bowline*, **Vol. 1, Part 2**, 241; *Trippe*, **Vol. 9, Part 1**, 625; *Triton*, **Vol. 2, Part 2**, 47; *Trumbull*, **Vol. 5, Part 1**, 33; **Vol. 3, Part 2**, 67; **Vol. 7, Part 1**, 358, 502; **Vol. 7, Part 2**, 484; **Vol. 8, Part 2**, 316; *Truxton*, **Vol. 1, Part 2**, 409; **Vol. 10, Part 1**, 22; *Tuscaloosa*, **Vol. 8, Part 2**, 581; *Tuscarora*, **Vol. 1, Part 2**, 146; **Vol. 2 Part 1**, 586; **Vol. 2, Part 2**, 518; **Vol. 5, Part 2**, 462; **Vol. 6, Part 2**, 465; **Vol. 7, Part 2**, 535; **Vol. 8, Part 1**, 293, 299; *Two Brothers*, **Vol. 10, Part 2**, 466; *Tyler*, **Vol. 10, Part 1**, 337; *Tyrannicide*, **Vol. 3, Part 2**, 420; **Vol. 4, Part 2**, 234; *Unadilla*, **Vol. 2, Part 2**, 308; **Vol. 3, Part 2**, 164; **Vol. 8, Part 1**, 293, 339; **Vol. 9, Part 2**, 518; *Underwriter*, **Vol. 5, Part 2**, 14; **Vol. 10, Part 2**, 466; *United States*, **Vol. 1, Part 1**, 212, 650, 654; **Vol. 2, Part 1**, 257; **Vol. 2, Part 2**, 510; **Vol. 3, Part 1**, 106, 187, 188; **Vol. 5, Part 1**, 361, 376; **Vol. 5, Part 2**, 14, 170, 176; **Vol. 6, Part 1**, 572; **Vol. 6, Part 2**, 464, 523; **Vol. 7, Part 1**, 320; **Vol. 7, Part 2**, 320, 461, 486; **Vol. 8, Part 1**, 85, 424; **Vol. 8, Part 2**, 73, 234; **Vol. 9, Part 1**, 135, 215, 394; **Vol. 9, Part 2**, 6, 394, 645; **Vol. 10, Part 1**, 292; *Valley City*, **Vol. 2, Part 2**, 636; *Van Buren*, **Vol. 6, Part 2**, 271; *Vandalia*, **Vol. 2, Part 1**, 406; **Vol. 3, Part 1**, 64; **Vol. 3, Part 2**, 287; **Vol. 5, Part 2**, 324; **Vol. 6, Part 1**, 129; **Vol. 6, Part 2**, 422, 479; **Vol. 7, Part 1**, 503; **Vol. 7, Part 2**, 185, 308; **Vol. 8, Part 1**, 617; **Vol. 8, Part 2**, 196, 341, 343; **Vol. 9, Part 1**, 320; **Vol. 10, Part 2**, 1, 658; *Vanderbilt*, **Vol. 2, Part 2**, 123; **Vol. 8, Part 2**, 78; *Varuna*, **Vol. 1, Part 2**, 409; **Vol. 6, Part 1**, 129; *Vermont*, **Vol. 1, Part 1**, 606; *Vermont*, **Vol. 8, Part 1**, 523, 618; *Vesuvius*, **Vol. 10, Part 1**, 9, 36; *Vesuvius*, **Vol. 7, Part 2**, 607; **Vol. 8, Part 2**, 465, 554; *Vicksburg*, **Vol. 4, Part 1**, 74; *Victory*, **Vol. 7, Part 2**, 461; *Vincennes*, **Vol. 1, Part 1**, 502; **Vol. 2, Part 1**, 70, 206; **Vol. 2, Part 2**, 517; **Vol. 3, Part 1**, 106, 200, 380; **Vol. 5, Part 2**, 615; **Vol. 6, Part 1**, 129; **Vol. 6, Part 2**, 428; **Vol. 7, Part 1**, 504; **Vol. 7, Part 2**, 185, 320; **Vol. 8, Part 2**, 196, 244, 568; **Vol. 10, Part 1**, 318; **Vol. 10, Part 2**, 217; *Viper*, **Vol. 9, Part 1**, 135; *Virginia*, **Vol. 1, Part 1**, 633; **Vol. 7, Part 1**, 502; *Virginia*, **Vol. 1, Part 1**, 606; *Virginia*, **Vol. 9, Part 2**, 149; *Virginia*, **Vol. 2, Part 1**, 70, 207; **Vol. 5, Part 2**, 164; **Vol. 6, Part 2**, 225; **Vol. 8, Part 1**, 97; **Vol. 9, Part 2**, 311; **Vol. 10, Part 1**, 630; *Virginia*, **Vol. 8, Part 2**, 465; **Vol. 10, Part 2**, 653; *Virginia II*, **Vol. 8, Part 1**, 97; *Vixen*, **Vol. 2, Part 2**, 510; **Vol. 5, Part 2**, 14; **Vol. 6, Part 1**, 50; **Vol. 7, Part 2**, 531; **Vol. 8, Part 1**, 182; **Vol. 8, Part 2**, 73, 343; **Vol. 9, Part 1**, 178; **Vol. 9, Part 2**, 637, 645; **Vol. 10, Part 1**, 492; *Volant*, **Vol. 9, Part 2**, 364; *Wabash*, **Vol. 1, Part 1**, 650; **Vol. 3, Part 1**, 269, 531; **Vol. 5, Part 2**, 324; **Vol. 6, Part 1**, 173, **Vol. 7, Part 2**, 220; **Vol. 8, Part 1**, 18, 293, 529; **Vol. 8, Part 2**, 72; **Vol. 9, Part 1**, 139, 178, 321; **Vol. 10, Part 1**, 128; **Vol. 10, Part 2**, 465, 645; *Wachusett*, **Vol. 2, Part 2**, 308; **Vol. 5, Part 2**, 50; **Vol. 6, Part 1**, 500; **Vol. 6,**

Part 2, 207, 521; **Vol. 7, Part 2**, 534; **Vol. 8, Part 1**, 314; **Vol. 9, Part 1**, 139; **Vol. 9, Part 2**, 620; *Walker*, **Vol. 8, Part 2**, 341; *Wampanoag*, **Vol. 3, Part 2**, 170, 175; **Vol. 5, Part 1**, 516; **Vol. 7, Part 1**, 504; *Warren*, **Vol. 5, Part 1**, 212; **Vol. 8, Part 2**, 316; *Warren*, **Vol. 1, Part 2**, 408; **Vol. 3, Part 1**, 530; **Vol. 5, Part 2**, 270; **Vol. 6, Part 2**, 82; **Vol. 8, Part 1**, 319, 596; **Vol. 8, Part 2**, 74, 579; *Washington*, **Vol. 2, Part 2**, 41; **Vol. 3, Part 2**, 286; **Vol. 7, Part 2**, 461, 625; **Vol. 9, Part 1**, 136; **Vol. 9, Part 2**, 48; *Washington*, **Vol. 6, Part 1**, 129; **Vol. 8, Part 2**, 341; **Vol. 9, Part 1**, 553; **Vol. 9, Part 2**, 637; *Washington*, **Vol. 2, Part 1**, 468; **Vol. 5, Part 2**, 462; *Wasp*, **Vol. 1, Part 1**, 633; **Vol. 8, Part 1**, 260; *Wasp*, **Vol. 1, Part 2**, 241, 348; **Vol. 4, Part 2**, 550; **Vol. 5, Part 2**, 176; **Vol. 6, Part 1**, 50; **Vol. 6, Part 2**, 20; **Vol. 8, Part 2**, 73; **Vol. 9, Part 1**, 136; **Vol. 10, Part 1**, 633; *Water Witch*, **Vol. 3, Part 1**, 136; **Vol. 5, Part 1**, 515; **Vol. 5, Part 2**, 14; **Vol. 7, Part 2**, 140; **Vol. 8, Part 1**, 97; *Wateree*, **Vol. 8, Part 2**, 437; *Wave*, **Vol. 8, Part 2**, 72, 77; *Weasel*, **Vol. 8, Part 1**, 617; *Weehawken*, **Vol. 1, Part 1**, 488; **Vol. 3, Part 1**, 532; **Vol. 8, Part 2**, 78; *West Virginia*, **Vol. 2, Part 1**, 468; **Vol. 10, Part 2**, 653; *West Virginia*, **Supp. 9**, 755; *Wheeling*, **Vol. 3, Part 1**, 614; *William G. Anderson*, **Vol. 8, Part 2**, 116; *William H. Webb*, **Vol. 8, Part 1**, 420; *Winnebago*, **Vol. 9, Part 1**, 626; *Winona*, **Vol. 8, Part 1**, 183; **Vol. 8, Part 2**, 437; **Vol. 10, Part 1**, 349, 568; *Winthrop*, **Vol. 6, Part 1**, 299; **Vol. 8, Part 1**, 182; *Wisconsin*, **Vol. 2, Part 1**, 468; **Vol. 8, Part 2**, 492; *Wissahickon*, **Vol. 3, Part 1**, 136; *Worcester*, **Vol. 8, Part 1**, 299; *Wyalusing*, **Vol. 8, Part 1**, 299; *Wyandotte*, **Vol. 7, Part 1**, 320; *Wyoming*, **Vol. 6, Part 2**, 21; *Wyoming*, **Vol. 2, Part 2**, 637; **Vol. 4, Part 1**, 544; **Vol. 10, Part 1**, 545; *Wyoming*, **Vol. 9, Part 1**, 388; *Yankee*, **Vol. 10, Part 2**, 585; *Yankee*, **Vol. 2, Part 2**, 123; **Vol. 8, Part 2**, 199, 554; *Yankton*, **Vol. 5, Part 2**, 462; *Yorktown*, **Vol, 7, Part 2**, 243; *Yorktown*, **Vol. 10, Part 1**, 34; *Yorktown*, **Vol. 1, Part 2**, 395; **Vol. 2, Part 1**, 586; **Vol. 3, Part 2**, 210; **Vol. 8, Part 2**, 554; **Vol. 9, Part 2**, 42; *Yorktown*, **Supp. 9**, 176, 635, 636; *Yosemite*, **Vol. 2, Part 2**, 123; *Zafiro*, **Vol. 6, Part 2**, 129; **Vol. 9, Part 2**, 8

Packet boats: *Angelique*, **Vol. 8, Part 2**, 324; *Anglo-American*, **Vol. 9, Part 2**, 625; *Anglo-Saxon*, **Vol. 9, Part 2**, 625; *Arctic*, **Vol. 4, Part 1**, 627; **Vol. 8, Part 2**, 248; *Atalanta*, **Vol. 4, Part 1**, 243; *Augusta*, **Vol. 9, Part 1**, 150; **Vol. 10, Part 1**, 579; *Baltic*, **Vol. 4, Part 1**, 627; *Baltimore*, **Vol. 10, Part 2**, 16; *Britannia*, **Vol. 6, Part 2**, 306; **Vol. 10, Part 1**, 534; *Calhoun*, **Vol. 9, Part 2**, 542; *Canada*, **Vol. 8, Part 2**, 248; *Carolina*, **Vol. 2, Part 2**, 490; *Chariot of Fame*, **Vol. 9, Part 2**, 625; *Charles H. Marshall*, **Vol. 10, Part 1**, 579; *Cherokee*, **Vol. 10, Part 1**, 579; *Clay*, **Vol. 9, Part 2**, 542; *Columbia*, **Vol. 7, Part 1**, 164; **Vol. 9, Part 2**, 542 *Continental*, **Vol. 8, Part 2**, 605; *Daniel Webster*, **Vol. 9, Part 2**, 625; *David Brown*, **Vol. 7, Part 1**, 164; *Devonshire*, **Vol. 10, Part 2**, 16; *Dirigo*, **Vol. 8, Part 2**, 605; *Dreadnought*, **Vol. 8, Part 2**, 324; *Duchesse d'Orleans*, **Vol. 10, Part 1**, 578; *Edward Bouaffe*, **Vol. 10, Part 2**, 15; *El Capitan*, **Vol. 8, Part 2**, 605; *Eric the Red*, **Vol. 8, Part 2**, 605; *Everglade*, **Vol. 2, Part 2**, 490; *Florida*, **Vol. 2, Part 2**, 490; *France*, **Vol. 10, Part 2**, 15; *Friend*, **Vol. 7, Part 1**, 369; *Garrick*, **Vol. 7, Part 2**, 190; *Granger*, **Vol. 8, Part 2**, 605; *Guy Mannering*, **Vol. 10, Part 1**, 578; *Harvest Queen*, **Vol. 6, Part 2**, 619; *Harvester*, **Vol. 8, Part 2**, 605; *Havana*, **Vol. 8, Part 2**, 580; *Holyhead*, **Vol. 8, Part 2**, 605; *Huntsville*, **Vol. 7, Part 2**, 190; *Indiana*, **Vol. 2, Part 2**, 120; *Isaac Bell*, **Vol. 10, Part 1**, 578; *Isaac Wright*, **Vol. 10, Part 1**, 578; *Ivanhoe*, **Vol. 10, Part 1**, 578; *James Adger*, **Vol. 9, Part 2**, 542; *James Cropper*, **Vol. 6, Part 2**, 306; *John Randolph*, **Vol. 5, Part 2**, 549; *Joshua Bates*, **Vol. 9, Part 2**, 625; *Julius Caesar*, **Vol. 6, Part 2**, 305; *Knoxville*, **Vol. 10, Part 1**, 579; *Lancaster*, **Vol. 2, Part 2**, 421; *Manhattan*, **Vol. 9, Part 1**, 559; *Marion*, **Vol. 9, Part 2**, 542; *Mary*, **Vol. 6, Part 2**, 305; *Massachusetts*, **Vol. 3, Part 2**, 509; *Montano*, **Vol. 10, Part 2**, 15; *Montauk*, **Vol. 10, Part 1**, 578; *Montreal*, **Vol. 10, Part 2**, 15; *Nashville*, **Vol. 9, Part 2**, 542; **Vol. 10, Part 2**, 15; *New York*, **Vol. 10, Part 1**, 578; *Northerner*, **Vol. 9, Part 2**, 542; *Occidental*, **Vol. 8, Part 2**, 605; *Ocean Monarch*, **Vol. 9, Part 2**, 625; **Vol. 10, Part 1**, 578; *Oneida*, **Vol. 10, Part 2**, 16; *Orient*, **Vol. 9, Part 2**, 542; *Oriental*, **Vol. 8, Part 2**, 605; *Owego*, **Vol. 1, Part 1**, 461; *Oxford*, **Vol. 10, Part 1**, 578; *Pacific*, **Vol. 4, Part 1**, 627; **Vol. 7, Part 1**, 202; **Vol. 9, Part 2**, 461; *Panama*, **Vol. 10, Part 1**, 578; *Paris*, **Vol. 10, Part 2**, 15; *Parliament*, **Vol. 9, Part 2**, 625; *Pennsylvania*, **Vol. 10, Part 1**, 578; *Philadelphia*, **Vol. 10, Part 2**, 15; *Pomona*, **Vol. 8, Part 2**, 76; *President*, **Vol. 10, Part 2**, 15; *Reaper*, **Vol. 8, Part 2**, 605; *Rhone*, **Vol. 10, Part 2**, 15; *Rappahannock*, **Vol. 8, Part 2**, 605; *Roanoke*, **Vol. 8, Part 2**, 605; *St. Louis*, **Vol. 2, Part 2**, 500; *St. Mary*, **Vol. 9, Part 1**, 559; *St. Paul*, **Vol. 2, Part 2**, 500; *Sandwich*, **Vol. 10, Part 1**, 40; *Shenandoah*, **Vol. 8, Part 2**, 605; *Siddons*, **Vol. 7, Part 2**, 190; *South America*, **Vol. 6, Part 2**, 306; **Vol. 10, Part 1**, 534; *Southerner*, **Vol. 9, Part 2**, 542; *Star of Empire*, **Vol. 9, Part 2**, 625; *Storm King*, **Vol. 5, Part 1**, 613; *Sully*, **Vol. 7, Part 1**, 248; *Susquehanna*, **Vol. 8, Part 2**, 605; *Ten Sisters*, **Vol. 4, Part 2**, 154; *Thrasher*, **Vol. 8, Part 2**, 605; *Toronto*, **Vol. 10, Part 2**, 15; *Undaunted*, **Vol. 8, Part 2**, 605; *Utica*, **Vol. 10, Part 2**, 15; *Ville de Lyons*, **Vol. 10, Part 1**, 578; *Washington*, **Vol. 5, Part 2**, 187; *Washington Irving*, **Vol. 9, Part 2**, 625; *Webster*, **Vol. 9, Part 2**, 542; *Yorkshire*, **Vol. 10, Part 1**, 578; *Yorktown*, **Vol. 10, Part 1**, 578

Pilot and tug: *Espadon*, **Vol. 9, Part 1**, 238; *Mary Taylor*, **Vol. 9, Part 1**, 559; *New York*, **Vol. 9, Part 1**, 238; *Union*, **Vol. 9, Part 2**, 57; *William G. Hagstaff*, **Vol. 9, Part 1**, 559

Pirate: *Adventure Gallery*, **Vol. 5, Part 2**, 368; *Antegoa*, **Vol. 5, Part 2**, 368; *Antonio*, **Vol. 5, Part 2**, 368; *Federal*, **Vol. 9, Part 2**, 310; *Margaret Oakley*, **Vol. 7, Part 1**, 195; *Moscow*, **Vol. 4, Part 2**, 539; **Vol. 9, Part 2**, 139; *Quedagh Merchant*, **Vol. 5, Part 2**, 368; *Reformation*, **Vol. 5, Part 1**, 474; *Young Antonio*, **Vol. 6, Part 2**, 196

Privateers: *Achilles*, **Vol. 4, Part 2**, 235; *Active*, **Vol. 10, Part 2**, 276; *Admiral Duff*, **Vol. 6, Part 1**, 299; **Vol. 10, Part 2**, 276; *Adventure*, **Vol. 4, Part 2**, 161; **Vol. 6, Part 2**, 151; *Alexander*, **Vol. 10, Part 2**, 276; *America*, **Vol. 1, Part 2**, 534; **Vol. 2, Part 2**, 60, 579; **Vol. 4, Part 1**, 554; **Vol. 6, Part 2**, 149; **Vol. 8, Part 2**, 152; *Angelica*, **Vol. 3, Part 2**, 268; *Atlas*, **Vol. 6, Part 2**, 195; *Barrington*, **Vol. 6, Part 2**, 21; *Beltsarius*, **Vol. 2, Part 2**, 60; *Black Hawk*, **Vol. 9, Part 2**, 321; *Black Prince*, **Vol. 5, Part 2**, 569; *Bunker Hill*, **Vol. 7, Part 2**, 338; *Charles*, **Vol. 4, Part 2**, 161; **Vol. 8, Part 1**, 236; *Charming Sally*, **Vol. 2, Part 2**, 117; *Chasseur*, **Vol. 1, Part 2**, 534; **Vol. 2, Part 2**, 61; *Columbus*, **Vol. 7, Part 1**, 358; *Comet*, **Vol. 1, Part 2**, 534; **Vol. 3, Part 1**, 186; *Congress*, **Vol. 10, Part 1**, 21; *Conte D'Estaing*, **Vol. 5, Part 2**, 329; *Cumberland*, **Vol. 6, Part 2**, 236; *David Porter*, **Vol. 2, Part 2**, 271; *Deane*, **Vol. 5, Part 1**, 64, 138; *Defense*, **Vol. 4, Part 1**, 296; *Diana*, **Vol. 4, Part 2**, 251; *Dolphin*, **Vol. 2, Part 2**, 349; *Duke of Marlborough*, **Vol. 5, Part 2**, *204*; **Vol. 10, Part 1**, 251; *Eagle*, **Vol. 6, Part 2**, 149; *Echo*, **Vol. 2, Part 2**, 490; *Fair American*, **Vol. 1, Part 1**, 633; **Vol. 3, Part 1**, 186; *Fame*, **Vol. 2, Part 2**, 60; *Fanny*, **Vol. 5, Part 2**, 329; *Fishhawk*, **Vol. 7, Part 2**, 338; *Friendship*, **Vol. 10, Part 1**, 536; *Gamecock*, **Vol. 7, Part 2**, 29; **Vol. 10, Part 2**, 66; *General Armstrong*, **Vol. 8, Part 1**, 480; *General*

Green, **Vol. 7, Part 2**, 29; *General Mifflin*, **Vol. 6, Part 2**, 149; **Vol. 7, Part 2**, 484; *General Mercer*, **Vol. 7, Part 1**, 358; *General Putnam*, **Vol. 8, Part 1**, 83; **Vol. 9, Part 1**, 45; **Vol. 10, Part 1**, 536; *General Washington*, **Vol. 9, Part 2**, 280; *George*, **Vol. 7, Part 2**, 338; *Georgia*, **Vol. 1, Part 1**, 651; *Grand Turk*, **Vol. 2, Part 2**, 60; **Vol. 3, Part 1**, 249–50; **Vol. 3, Part 2**, 554; *Hague*, **Vol. 5, Part 1**, 138; *Hancock*, **Vol. 6, Part 2**, 149; *Hannibal*, **Vol. 7, Part 1**, 610; *Hawk*, **Vol. 7, Part 2**, 29; *Hector*, **Vol. 7, Part 2**, 29; *Herald*, **Vol. 1, Part 2**, 228; *Hibernia*, **Vol. 7, Part 1**, 610; *Independence*, **Vol. 10, Part 1**, 21; *Intrepid*, **Vol. 8, Part 1**, 549; *Jason*, **Vol. 6, Part 2**, 236; *Jefferson*, **Vol. 7, Part 1**, 611; *Jefferson Davis*, **Vol. 2, Part 2**, 490; *Joel Barlow*, **Vol. 7, Part 1**, 195; *Judah*, **Vol. 1, Part 1**, 502; **Vol. 8, Part 2**, 244; *Julius Caesar*, **Vol. 4, Part** 2, 235; *La Soeur Chrie*, **Vol. 5, Part 2**, 540; *Le Croyable*, **Vol. 3, Part 1**, 186; *Lee*, **Vol. 10, Part 1**, 536; *Leo*, **Vol. 2, Part 2**, 271; *Lyon*, **Vol. 9, Part 1**, 19; *Marianne*, **Vol. 5, Part 2**, 329; *Marlborough*, **Vol. 6, Part 2**, 236; *Marquis de Lafayette*, **Vol. 5, Part 1**, 64; *Mars*, **Vol. 2, Part 2**, 117; **Vol. 3, Part 1**, 217; **Vol. 6, Part 1**, 76; **Vol. 10, Part 1**, 21; *Martha*, **Vol. 10, Part 1**, 39; *Monkey*, **Vol. 1, Part 2**, 228; *Mount Vernon*, **Vol. 3, Part 1**, 250; *Nashville*, **Vol. 3, Part 1**, 532; **Vol. 9, Part 2**, 542; *Nesbit*, **Vol. 7, Part 1**, 502; *Niger*, **Vol. 7, Part 1**, 506; *Pallas*, **Vol. 6, Part 2**, 151; *Patty*, **Vol. 8, Part 1**, 430; *Pilgrim*, **Vol. 7, Part 2**, 338; *Polly*, **Vol. 7, Part 2**, 28; *Prince Eugene*, **Vol. 5, Part 1**, 460; *Prosperity*, **Vol. 7, Part 1**, 358; *Putnam*, **Vol. 2, Part 2**, 490; *Queen of France*, **Vol. 3, Part 1**, 33; *Rachel*, **Vol. 10, Part 2**, 524; *Rattlesnake*, **Vol. 6, Part 2**, 195; *Raven*, **Vol. 7, Part 2**, 29; *Resolution*, **Vol. 7, Part 1**, 610; *Resource*, **Vol. 9, Part 2**, 498; *Retaliation*, **Vol. 3, Part 1**, 186; *Revenge*, **Vol. 7, Part 1**, 358; *Rising Sun*, **Vol. 3, Part 1**, 186; *Royal Louis*, **Vol. 3, Part 1**, 186; *St. James*, **Vol. 5, Part 2**, 205; **Vol. 10, Part 1**, 21; *Saratoga*, **Vol. 7, Part 1**, 358; **Vol. 10, Part 2**, 524; *Savannah*, **Vol. 7, Part 2**, 260, 314; *Scourge*, **Vol. 6, Part 2**, 195; *Shenandoah*, **Vol. 8, Part 2**, 73; *Snap Dragon*, **Vol. 2, Part 1**, 308; *Stonewall*, **Vol. 1, Part 1**, 651; *Success*, **Vol. 5, Part 1**, 212; *Surprise*, **Vol. 2, Part 2**, 368; *Tacony*, **Vol. 6, Part 1**, 500; *Thomas Toby*, **Vol. 5, Part 2**, 582; *Thorn*, **Vol. 10, Part 1**, 536; *Tiger*, **Vol. 7, Part 1**, 610; *Tracy*, **Vol. 5, Part 1**, 212; *Tyger*, **Vol. 6, Part 2**, 21; *Tyrannicide*, **Vol. 9, Part 2**, 498; *Ulysses*, **Vol. 6, Part 2**, 149; *Virginia*, **Vol. 7, Part 2**, 29; *Volant*, **Vol. 6, Part 2**, 296; *Warren*, **Vol. 9, Part 2**, 498; *Wasp*, **Vol. 6, Part 2**, 149; *Weir*, **Vol. 7, Part 2**, 28; *Wilkes*, **Vol. 10, Part 2**, 276; *Yankee*, **Vol. 3, Part 1**, 275, 414; **Vol. 7, Part 2**, 461

Prizes, taken as: *Active*, **Vol. 7, Part 2**, 28; **Vol. 10, Part 2**, 276; *Alert*, **Vol. 8, Part 1**, 84; *Alexander Barclay*, **Vol. 3, Part 2**, 286; *Annabella*, **Vol. 10, Part 1**, 536; *Atalanta*, **Vol. 1, Part 1**, 654; **Vol. 1, Part 2**, 348; *Atlantic*, **Vol. 3, Part 1**, 416; *Avon*, **Vol. 1, Part 2**, 348; *Baille*, **Vol. 6, Part 2**, 236; *Birceau*, **Vol. 6, Part 1**, 299; *Caledonia*, **Vol. 3, Part 2**, 96; *Charleston*, **Vol. 10, Part 1**, 40; *Confiance*, **Vol. 6, Part 2**, 20; *Countess of Scarborough*, **Vol. 5, Part 2**, 185; *Cristobal Colon*, **Vol. 8, Part 2**, 438; *Cyane*, **Vol. 9, Part 2**, 7; *Detroit*, **Vol. 2, Part 1**, 609; **Vol. 3, Part 2**, 96; *Deux Amis*, **Vol. 8, Part 1**, 83; *Deux Anges*, **Vol. 6, Part 1**, 299; *Diligent*, **Vol. 7, Part 1**, 610; *Drake*, **Vol. 5, Part 2**, 184; *Eagle*, **Vol. 7, Part 2**, 461; *Edward*, **Vol. 1, Part 1**, 654; *Elizabeth*, **Vol. 10, Part 1**, 536; *Epervier*, **Vol. 7, Part 2**, 461; **Vol. 10, Part 1**, 292, 492; *Fly*, **Vol. 1, Part 2**, 348; *Flying Fish*, **Vol. 6, Part 1**, 299; *Fox*, **Vol. 6, Part 2**, 151; *Frolic*, **Vol. 1, Part 2**, 241; **Vol. 8, Part 2**, 73; *General Monk*, **Vol. 1, Part 1**, 633–34; *Georgiana*, **Vol. 3, Part 1**, 416; *Governor Tryon*, **Vol. 10, Part 1**, 536; *Guerrière*, **Vol. 1, Part 1**, 452; **Vol. 5, Part 1**, 361; **Vol. 8, Part 1**, 424; *Hampshire*, **Vol. 5, Part 1**, 456; *Hibernia*, **Vol. 5, Part 1**, 212; *High Flyer*, **Vol. 8, Part 2**, 77; *Hichenbrooke*, **Vol. 3, Part 2**, 66; *Hector*, **Vol. 3, Part 1**, 416; *Howe*, **Vol. 10, Part 1**, 536; *Independence*, **Vol. 10, Part 1**, 23; *Insurgente*, **Vol. 8, Part 1**, 83; **Vol. 8, Part 2**, 76; **Vol. 9, Part 1**, 584; **Vol. 10, Part 1**, 22; *Intrepid*, **Vol. 8, Part 1**, 182; *Isabella II*, **Vol. 9, Part 1**, 156; *Jackal*, **Vol. 7, Part 1**, 506 *Jason*, **Vol. 5, Part 1**, 212; *Java*, **Vol. 1, Part 1**, 452; **Vol. 9, Part 1**, 135; *Joseph*, **Vol. 2, Part 2**, 368; *L'Amour de la Patrie*, **Vol. 9, Part 1**, 584; *La Vengeance*, **Vol. 9, Part 1**, 584; *Le Croyable*, **Vol. 3, Part 1**, 186; *Lord Hyde*, **Vol. 10, Part 1**, 40; *Macedonian*, **Vol. 1, Part 1**, 212; **Vol. 3, Part 1**, 188; **Vol. 8, Part 1**, 424; **Vol. 10, Part 1**, 292; *Madre de Dios*, **Vol. 7, Part 1**, 467; *Malek Adhel*, **Vol. 8, Part 1**, 470; *Margaretta*, **Vol. 7, Part 1**, 610; *Mariana Flora*, **Vol. 9, Part 2**, 48; *Martha*, **Vol. 10, Part 1**, 39; *Mashuda*, **Vol. 3, Part 1**, 189, 416; **Vol. 3, Part 2**, 85; **Vol. 9, Part 1**, 136; *Mastico*, **Vol. 3, Part 1**, 187; *Mellish*, **Vol. 5, Part 2**, 184; *Mirboka*, **Vol. 6, Part 2**, 20; *Mont Blanc*, **Vol. 2, Part 2**, 308; *Nancy*, **Vol. 6, Part 2**, 236; *Nautilus*, **Vol. 10, Part 1**, 492; *Ormigo*, **Vol. 9, Part 2**, 620; *Peacock*, **Vol. 2, Part 2**, 349; **Vol. 3, Part 2**, 531; *Penguin*, **Vol. 1, Part 2**, 214; **Vol. 2, Part 2**, 349; *Pigot*, **Vol. 9, Part 2**, 280; *Planter*, **Vol. 6, Part 2**, 195; *Prince of Orange*, **Vol. 2, Part 2**, 368; *Prosper*, **Vol. 7, Part 2**, 484; *Pursuit*, **Vol. 6, Part 2**, 195; *Queen Charlotte*, **Vol. 2, Part 1**, 609; *Rebecca*, **Vol. 3, Part 2**, 66; *Reindeer*, **Vol. 1, Part 2**, 348; *Resolution*, **Vol. 6, Part 1**, 50; *Sandwich*, **Vol. 7, Part 1**, 506; *St. Lawrence*, **Vol. 1, Part 2**, 534; *Scarborough*, **Vol. 7, Part 1**, 610, *Scourge*, **Vol. 8, Part 1**, 182; *Serapis*, **Vol. 5, Part 1**, 477; *Sir William Erskine*, **Vol. 10, Part 1**, 536; *Sparlin*, **Vol. 10, Part 1**, 536; *Spencer*, **Vol. 7, Part 1**, 507; *Tartar*, **Vol. 7, Part 2**, 484; *Tapnaquish*, **Vol. 7, Part 1**, 610; *Terror*, **Vol. 9, Part 2**, 156; *Thorn*, **Vol. 7, Part 1**, 506; **Vol. 10, Part 1**, 40; *Trepassy*, **Vol. 1, Part 1**, 654; *Tripoli*, **Vol. 9, Part 1**, 584; *True Briton*, **Vol. 1, Part 2**, 242; *Tulip*, **Vol. 6, Part 2**, 195; *Vainqueur*, **Vol. 9, Part 2**, 561; *Vigilante*, **Vol. 10, Part 1, 101**; *Viper*, **Vol. 7, Part 1**, 506

Riverboats: *A. B. Chambers*, **Vol. 6, Part 2**, 229; *Aleck Scott*, **Vol. 8, Part 2**, 575; *Antelope*, **Vol. 7, Part 1**, 514; *Armenia*, **Vol. 9, Part 2**, 57; *Balloon*, **Vol. 7, Part 1**, 471; *Bridgwater*, **Vol. 10, Part 1**, 179; *C. E. Hillman*, **Vol. 8, Part 1**, 188; *City of Baton Rouge*, **Vol. 1, Part 2**, 306; *Conestoga*, **Vol. 10, Part 1**, 179; *Enterprise*, **Vol. 9, Part 1**, 134; *Far West*, **Vol. 6, Part 2**, 299; *General Abner Lacock*, **Vol. 5, Part 2**, 521; *General Carroll*, **Vol. 8, Part 2**, 575; *Hail Columbia*, **Vol. 10, Part 1**, 179; *Heliopolis*, **Vol. 9, Part 1**, 134; *Hendrick Hudson*, **Vol. 3, Part 2**, 164; **Vol. 7, Part 1**, 471; *Henry von Phul*, **Vol. 8, Part 2**, 576; *Isaac Newton*, **Vol. 7, Part 1**, 471; *Islander*, **Vol. 5, Part 2**, 464; *J. M. White*, **Vol. 1, Part 2, Vol. 8, Part 2**, 575; *John D. Perry*, **Vol. 8, Part 1**, 188, *John J. Roe*, **Vol. 6, Part 2**, 299; *Jubilee*, **Vol. 8, Part 2**, 575; *Lioness*, **Vol. 5, Part 2**, 147; *Luella*, **Vol. 6, Part 2**, 299; *New Orleans*, **Vol. 9, Part 1**, 134; *New World*, **Vol. 7, Part 1**, 471; *North America*, **Vol. 7, Part 1**, 471; *Omega*, **Vol. 5, Part 2**, 517; *Paragon*, **Vol. 6, Part 2**, 305; *Pinta*, **Vol. 10, Part 1**, 179; *Pioneer*, **Vol. 10, Part 1**, 646; *Post Boy*, **Vol. 9, Part 1**, 134; *Prairie*, **Vol. 8, Part 2**, 575; *President*, **Vol. 8, Part 2**, 575; *Rambler*, **Vol. 8, Part 2**, 575; *Red Fox*, **Vol. 10, Part 1**, 179; *St. Clair*, **Vol. 10, Part 2**, 66; *South America*, **Vol. 7, Part 1**, 471; *Uncle Toby*, **Vol. 4, Part 1**, 630; *Washington*, **Vol. 9, Part 1**, 134; *Yellowstone*, **Vol. 5, Part 2**, 517

Schooners, traders, and pirate ships involved in incidents in American history: *Adieu*, **Vol. 9, Part 2**, 637; *America*, **Vol. 2, Part 2**, 579; **Vol. 5, Part 2**, 337; **Vol. 6, Part 2**, 501; *Ancona*, **Vol. 7, Part 2**, 425; *Arabic*, **Vol. 5, Part 2**, 610; *Arctic*, **Vol. 2**, Part 2, 306;

Vol. 8, Part 1, 447; *Arrow*, Vol. 5, Part 1, 74; *Atahualpa*, Vol. 9, Part 2, 183; *Balmar*, Vol. 10, Part 1, 55; *Barracouta*, Vol. 10, Part 1, 303; *Bedford*, Vol. 8, Part 2, 186; *Bella*, Vol. 2, Part 2, 518; *Benjamin*, Vol. 9, Part 1, 165; *Betsey*, Vol. 5, Part 2, 184; *Beulah*, Vol. 7, Part 1, 360–67; *Black Warrior*, Vol. 6, Part 2, 277; Vol. 7, Part 2, 578; *Bombay*, Vol. 7, Part 2, 53; *Bonne Citoyenne*, Vol. 6, Part 1, 50; *Bounty*, Vol. 9, Part 2, 592; *Cato*, Vol. 10, Part 1, 40; *Central America*, Vol. 4, Part 2, 580; *Challenge*, Vol. 10, Part 1, 535; *Charles*, Vol. 8, Part 1, 299, 300; *Charming Peggy*, Vol. 2, Part 2, 368; *Chen Yuen*, Vol. 6, Part 2, 49; *Cincinnatus*, Vol. 1, Part 1, 634; *Commerce*, Vol. 8, Part 2, 391; *Continental*, Vol. 8, Part 2, 259; *Cotopaxi*, Vol. 2, Part 2, 244; *Courier*, Vol. 9, Part 1, 290; *Courrier*, Vol. 7, Part 1, 535; *Crescent City*, Vol. 6, Part 1, 40; *Dauphin*, Vol. 7, Part 1, 611; *Desperate*, Vol. 9, Part 1, 626; *Dessong*, Vol. 4, Part 1, 437; *Diana*, Vol. 7, Part 2, 490; *Dublin*, Vol. 5, Part 2, 201; *Echo*, Vol. 7, Part 1, 426; Vol. 6, Part 2, 196, 203; *Eclipse*, Vol. 8, Part 1, 424; *Eleanor*, Vol. 5, Part 1, 474; *Ella M. Doughty*, Vol. 8, Part 1, 286; *Empire*, Vol. 8, Part 2, 11–12; *Essex*, Vol. 4, Part 2, 162; *Fern*, Vol. 10, Part 1, 319; *Flying Fish*, Vol. 6, Part 1, 299; *Fox*, Vol. 4, Part 2, 120; *Friendship*, Vol. 3, Part 1, 416; Vol. 3, Part 2, 157; Vol. 7, Part 2, 338; *Galatea*, Vol. 2, Part 2, 368; *Gaspe*, Vol. 2, Part 1, 128; Vol. 2, Part 2, 267; Vol. 5, Part 1, 211, 220, 238; Vol. 9, Part 1, 529; Vol. 10, Part 2, 66; *Gazelle*, Vol. 7, Part 2, 53; *General Sherman*, Vol. 2, Part 2, 637; *George Law*, Vol. 4, Part 2, 580; *George Washington*, Vol. 6, Part 1, 204; *Gladiator*, Vol. 9, Part 1, 626; *Globe*, Vol. 7, Part 2, 320, 461; *Golden Rule*, Vol. 8, Part 1, 184; *Goodspeed*, Vol. 8, Part 1, 140; *Gorgon*, Vol. 10, Part 1, 292; *Greyhound*, Vol. 4, Part 2, 162; Vol. 5, Part 1, 304; *Hazard*, Vol. 7, Part 1, 535; *Henry*, Vol. 6, Part 1, 135; *Herbert Fuller*, Vol. 10, Part 1, 495; *Heroina*, Vol. 5, Part 2, 67; *Himaleh*, Vol. 7, Part 2, 34; *Home*, Vol. 7, Part 1, 582; *Hope*, Vol. 5, Part 1, 312; *Hougomont*, Vol. 7, Part 2, 53; *Hussar*, Vol. 5, Part 1, 477; *Illinois*, Vol. 8, Part 2, 11, 12; *Itata*, Vol. 5, Part 1, 153, Jackal, Vol. 5, Part 2, 329; *John*, Vol. 5, Part 2, 183; *Kronprinzessin Cecilie*, Vol. 8, Part 1, 286; *Leopard*, Vol. 1, Part 1, 212; Vol. 2, Part 2, 510; *Lexington*, Vol. 4, Part 2, 278; *Liberator*, Vol. 5, Part 1, 312; *Liberty*, Vol. 6, Part 2, 219; Vol. 7, Part 2, 104; Vol. 9, Part 1, 45; Vol. 10, Part 1, 482; *L'Insurgente*, Vol. 1, Part 1, 504; *Little Belt*, Vol. 3, Part 1, 188; *Louisiana*, Vol. 7, Part 2, 21; *Lusitania*, Vol. 4, Part 2, 113; Vol. 5, Part 1, 324, 369; Vol. 5, Part 2, 374, 443, 610; Vol. 6, Part 1, 278; Vol. 7, Part 1, 53; Vol. 7, Part 2, 144, 359; *Margarita*, Vol. 2, Part 2, 326; *Maria*, Vol. 9, Part 1, 560; *Maria Helena*, Vol. 9, Part 1, 626; *Maria Luz*, Vol. 6, Part 1, 570; *Marine*, Vol. 4, Part 2, 580; *Martha Washington*, Vol. 9, Part 2, 239; *Mary*, Vol. 8, Part 1, 140; *Mercury*, Vol. 6, Part 1, 34; *Merrimack*, Vol. 8, Part 1, 140; *Michigan*, Vol. 9, Part 2, 124; *Monticello*, Vol. 5, Part 2, 550; *Morrison*, Vol. 7, Part 2, 34, 235; *Moselle*, Vol. 9, Part 2, 645; *Nelly*, Vol. 8, Part 2, 76; *Neptune*, Vol. 4, Part 2, 162; Vol. 10, Part 2, 180; *New World*, Vol. 2, Part 2, 123; *Ocean King*, Vol. 7, Part 1, 480; *Pacific*, Vol. 2, Part 2, 306; Vol. 6, Part 2, 115; *Palmero*, Vol. 7, Part 2, 572; *Panopea*, Vol. 1, Part 2, 534; *Peggy Stewart*, Vol. 10, Part 2, 180; *Pembroke*, Vol. 6, Part 2, 21; *Penet*, Vol. 1, Part 1, 435; *Plymouth*, Vol. 6, Part 2, 18; *Polly*, Vol. 7, Part 1, 610; *President*, Vol. 9, Part 1, 315; *Princes*, Vol. 5, Part 2, 371; *Princeton*, Vol. 10, Part 1, 91; *Pulaski*, Vol. 5, Part 2, 549; *Quedagh Merchant*, Vol. 5, Part 2, 368; *Quero*, Vol. 3, Part 1, 253; *Ravenscraig*, Vol. 4, Part 2, 121; *Rebecca*, Vol. 5, Part 1, 543; *Rebecca*, Vol. 8, Part 2, 246; *Reformation*, Vol. 5, Part 1, 474; *Release*, Vol. 10, Part 1, 302; *Reprisal*, Vol. 10, Part 2, 180; *Republic*, Vol. 10, Part 2, 130; *Rising Eagle*, Vol. 4, Part 2, 162; *Romney*, Vol. 6, Part 2, 219; *Rosalba*, Vol. 10, Part 1, 292; *Rose*, Vol. 8, Part 1, 140; *Rover*, Vol. 6, Part 1, 146; *Sampson*, Vol. 1, Part 1, 634; *Saucala*, Vol. 10, Part 1, 292; *Sandwich*, Vol. 9, Part 2, 280, 306; *San Francisco*, Vol. 10, Part 1, 303, 529; *Sapphire*, Vol. 7, Part 2, 53; *Speagle*, Vol. 5, Part 1, 474; *Spray*, Vol. 9, Part 1, 218; *Star of the West*, Vol. 8, Part 2, 11, 12; *Surprise*, Vol. 9, Part 2, 561; *Sussex*, Vol. 5, Part 2, 610; Vol. 7, Part 2, 425; *Suwonada*, Vol. 2, Part 2, 120; *Tasman*, Vol. 7, Part, 549; *Tigress*, Vol. 4, Part 2, 121; Vol. 10, Part 1, 102; *Ting Yuen*, Vol. 6, Part 2, 49; *Titanic*, Vol. 6, Part 2, 645; *Thomas Penrose*, Vol. 2, Part 1, 337; *Transit*, Vol. 9, Part 1, 215; *Traveller*, Vol. 2, Part 2, 585; *Trent*, Vol. 3, Part 2, 255; Vol. 4, Part 1, 594; Vol. 6, Part 1, 255; Vol. 6, Part 2, 365; Vol. 7, Part 2, 520; Vol. 8, Part 2, 510, 619; Vol. 10, Part 2, 217; *Trumbull*, Vol. 5, Part 1, 64; *Union*, Vol. 8, Part 2, 11, 12; *United States*, Vol. 7, Part 2, 190; *Unity*, Vol. 7, Part 1, 610; *Vigilant*, Vol. 8, Part 2, 605; *Virginius*, Vol. 2, Part 2, 637; Vol. 3, Part 1, 269; Vol. 6, Part 2, 46; Vol. 7, Part 2, 220; Vol. 8, Part 1, 88; *Volunteer*, Vol. 3, Part 2, 266; *Vulture*, Vol. 6, Part 1, 314; *Wanderer*, Vol. 5, Part 1, 543; Vol. 5, Part 2, 550; Vol. 6, Part 2, 203; *Washington*, Vol. 5, Part 2, 329; *William P. Frye*, Vol. 8, Part 2, 605; *William R. Grace*, Vol. 2, Part 2, 121; *W. R. Carter*, Vol. 8, Part 1, 576

Slavers: *Ardennes*, Vol. 10, Part 1, 568; *Bogotá*, Vol. 6, Part 2, 196; *Echo*, Vol. 6, Part 2, 196, 203; Vol. 7, Part 1, 426; *Friendship*, Vol. 5, Part 2, 183; *King George*, Vol. 5, Part 2, 183; *Sunny South*, Vol. 9, Part 1,559; *Two Friends*, Vol. 5, Part 2, 183; *Wanderer*, Vol. 5, Part 2, 550; *Wildfire*, Vol. 2, Part 2, 518; *Wm. R. Kibby*, Vol. 6, Part 2, 196

Sound steamers: *Bristol*, Vol. 10, Part 1, 579; *Chester W. Chapin*, Vol. 9, Part 1, 238; *City of Lowell*, Vol. 9, Part 1, 238; *Connecticut*, Vol. 8, Part 2, 200; *Leviathan*, Vol. 9, Part 2, 542; *Pilgrim*, Vol. 9, Part 2, 344; *Providence*, Vol. 10, Part 1, 579; *Puritan*, Vol. 9, Part 2, 344; *Richard Peck*, Vol. 9, Part 1, 238

Traders of all sorts: *Active*, Vol. 2, Part 2, 579; *Acushnet*, Vol. 6, Part 2, 523; *Agnes*, Vol. 6, Part 1, 452; *Akbar*, Vol. 4, Part 2, 142; *Albatross*, Vol. 5, Part 1, 399; *Alliance*, Vol. 8, Part 1, 430; *Amity*, Vol. 6, Part 2, 305; *Antarctic*, Vol. 7, Part 1, 195; *Antelope*, Vol. 4, Part 2, 142; *Ariel*, Vol. 3, Part 1, 186; *Atahualpa*, Vol. 9, Part 1, 183; *Beaver*, Vol. 5, Part 1, 399; *Bengal*, Vol. 5, Part 2, 615; *Benjamin*, Vol. 9, Part 1, 165; *Betsy*, Vol. 3, Part 2, 266; *Boston*, Vol. 7, Part 2, 218; *Canton*, Vol. 10, Part 1, 21; *Canton*, Vol. 4, Part 2, 451; *Caravan*, Vol. 4, Part 2, 482; *Caroline*, Vol. 9, Part 2, 183; *Catharine*, Vol. 10, Part 1, 166; *Chinchilla*, Vol. 2, Part 1, 21, 22; *Citizen*, Vol. 5, Part 1, 408; *Cohota*, Vol. 10, Part 1, 578; *Columbia*, Vol. 4, Part 1, 523; Vol. 5, Part 1, 478; Vol. 5, Part 2, 329; *Conrad*, Vol. 8, Part 2, 581; *Courier*, Vol. 6, Part 2, 305; *Dunkirk*, Vol. 8, Part 2, 202; *Edith*, Vol. 3, Part 2, 509; *Edward*, Vol. 6, Part 2, 178; Vol. 7, Part 1, 195; *Edward Everett*, Vol. 10, Part 1, 646; *Fame*, Vol. 8, Part 1, 430; *Fanny*, Vol. 6, Part 1, 543; *Francis*, Vol. 7, Part 2, 190; *Friendship*, Vol. 3, Part 2, 157; *George*, Vol. 7, Part 2, 338; *George Barclay*, Vol. 6, Part 1, 543; *General Gadsden*, Vol. 7, Part 1, 413; *General Washington*, Vol. 2, Part 1, 129; Vol. 10, Part 2, 66; *Griffon*, Vol. 7, Part 2, 404; *Gibraltar*, Vol. 8, Part 2, 580; *Gulliver*, Vol. 6, Part 2, 20; *Helvetius*, Vol. 10, Part 1, 313; *Henry*, Vol. 2, Part 1, 309; Vol. 2, Part 2, 579; Vol. 7, Part 1, 317; *Highlander*, Vol. 6, Part 2, 523; *Hope*, Vol. 5, Part 1, 478; *Ivanhoe*, Vol. 2, Part 1, 21, 22; *James Monroe*, Vol. 6, Part 2, 305; *Jane*, Vol. 8, Part 2, 76; *Jeune Babé'*, Vol. 4, Part 1, 320; *John*, Vol. 8, Part

2, 153; *Jolly Bachelor*, **Vol. 3, Part 2**, 263; *Jupiter*, **Vol. 8, Part 2**, 164; *Lucy Ann*, **Vol. 6, Part 2**, 523; *Lady Clausen*, **Vol. 9, Part 2**, 561; *Lady Washington*, **Vol. 4, Part 1**, 523; *Lagoda*, **Vol. 4, Part 1**, 334; *Levere*, **Vol. 2**, Part 1, 308; *Light Horse*, **Vol. 3, Part 1**, 249; *Lima*, **Vol. 6, Part 2**, 305; *Little Fortescue*, **Vol. 6, Part 2**, 236; *Little William*, **Vol. 6, Part 2**, 178; *M'Clellan*, **Vol. 10, Part 1**, 102; *Manchu*, **Vol. 2, Part 2**, 120; *Mary and Harriet*, **Vol. 8, Part 2**, 314; *Mary Ann*, **Vol. 8, Part 2**, 4; *Mary Becket*, **Vol. 3, Part 1**, 29; *Massachusetts*, **Vol. 3, Part 1**, 217; *Merchant*, **Vol. 8, Part 1**, 480; *Midas*, **Vol. 3, Part 2**, 509; *Molly*, **Vol. 2, Part 2**, 368; *Montauk*, **Vol. 10, Part 1**, 578; *Nelly*, **Vol. 8, Part 2**, 76; *New London*, **Vol. 4, Part 2**, 382; *Pacific*, **Vol. 6, Part 2**, 305; *Panama*, **Vol. 8, Part 1**, 86; *Paragon*, **Vol. 2, Part 1**, 21, 22; *Patty*, **Vol. 8, Part 2**, 175; *Pedlar*, **Vol. 3; Part 2**, 282; *Peggy*, **Vol. 3, Part 1**, 186; *Pennsylvania*, **Vol. 3, Part 1**, 186; *Perseverance*, **Vol. 3, Part 1**, 217; *Pilgrim*, **Vol. 3, Part 1**, 217; *Prometheus*, **Vol. 2, Part 1**, 309; *Prudence*, **Vol. 5, Part 1**, 395; **Vol. 6, Part 2**, 178; *Ranger*, **Vol. 2, Part 2**, 585; **Vol. 3, Part 1**, 252; *Razzle Dazzle*, **Vol. 6, Part 1**, 370; *Rebecca*, **Vol. 4, Part 2**, 476; *Rebecca*, **Vol. 8, Part 2**, 246; *Recovery*, **Vol. 8, Part 2**, 153; *Refugio*, **Vol. 10, Part 2**, 452; *Ronaldson*, **Vol. 7, Part 2**, 25; *Royal George*, **Vol. 10, Part 1**, 39; *Sea King*, **Vol. 10, Part 1**, 302; *Seaflower*, **Vol. 7, Part 2**, 28; *Sophie Sutherland*, **Vol. 6, Part 1**, 370; *Sumatra*, **Vol. 7, Part 2**, 339; *Surprise*, **Vol. 4, Part 1**, 296; *Swordfsh*, **Vol. 8, Part 2**, 427; *Tartar*, **Vol. 7, Part 1**, 195; **Vol. 8, Part 1**, 430; *Thaddeus*, **Vol. 5, Part 1**, 381; *Three Friends*, **Vol. 7, Part 2**, 338; *Unity*, **Vol. 2, Part 1**, 21, 22; *Volunteer*, **Vol. 3, Part 2**, 226; *Warrior*, **Vol. 2**, Part 1, 309; *Washington*, **Vol. 5, Part 2**, 329; *Wasp*, **Vol. 6, Part 2**, 195; *William Penn*, **Vol. 8, Part 2**, 234; *Young Phoenix*, **Vol. 10, Part 1**, 39; *Young Turk*, **Vol. 4, Part 1**, 259; *Zephyr*, **Vol. 4, Part 2**, 142

Transatlantic: *Adriatic*, **Vol. 2, Part 2**, 306; **Vol. 9, Part l**, 560; *Atlantic*, **Vol. 9, Part 1**, 139; *Black Hawk*, **Vol. 9, Part 1**, 139; *British Queen*, **Vol. 9 Part 1**, 315; *California*, **Vol. 10, Part 1**, 578; *Caracas*, **Vol. 8, Part 2**, 554; *Catawba*, **Vol. 9, Part 1**, 139; *City of New York*, **Vol. 4, Part 2**, 6; **Vol. 7, Part 2**, 535; *City of Paris*, **Vol. 4, Part 2**, 6; *Cristobal*, **Vol. 8, Part 2**, 194; *Finland*, **Vol. 2, Part 2**, 500; *Fulton*, **Vol. 8, Part 2**, 325; *Georgia*, **Vol. 2, Part 1**, 257; **Vol. 8, Part 1**, 86; **Vol. 9, Part 1**, 139; *Glen Cove*, **Vol. 9, Part 2**, 57; *Golden Age*, **Vol. 8, Part 1**, 86; *Golden Gate*, **Vol. 10, Part 1**, 578; *Great Eastern*, **Vol. 6, Part 2**, 609; **Vol. 8, Part 1**, 505; **Vol. 9, Part 1**, 150; **Vol. 10, Part 1**, 421; *Great Western*, **Vol.** *9*, Part 1, 315; *Illinois*, **Vol. 8, Part 1**, 293; *Kroonland*, **Vol. 2, Part 2**, 500; *Liverpool*, **Vol. 9, Part 1**, 139; *Mariposa*, **Vol. 8, Part 2**, 554; *Minia*, **Vol. 9, Part 2**, 111; *Niagara*, **Vol. 10, Part 1**, 424; *Northerner*, **Vol. 10, Part 1**, 535; *Olivette*, **Vol. 8, Part 2**, 554; *Pacific*, **Vol. 8, Part 1**, 293; *Panama*, **Vol. 10, Part 1**, 578; *Pekin*, **Vol. 4, Part 2**, 394; *President*, **Vol. 9, Part 1**, 315; *Queen of the Pacific*, **Vol. 8, Part 2**, 554; *Royal Arch*, **Vol. 9, Part 2**, 57; *Royal William*, **Vol. 9, Part 1**, 315; *St. Louis*, **Vol. 4, Part 2**, 6; *St. Paul*, **Vol. 4, Part 2**, 6; *San Francisco*, **Vol. 10, Part 1**, 578; *Sirius*, **Vol. 9, Part 1**, 315; *Southern Cross*, **Vol. 5, Part 1**, 318; *Tokyo*, **Vol. 4, Part 2**, 394; *United States*, **Vol. 10, Part 1**, 578; *Vanderbilt*, **Vol. 10, Part 1**, 171; *Washington*, **Vol. 10, Part 2**, 16; *West Point*, **Vol. 10, Part 2**, 16; *Yorktown*, **Vol. 10, Part 1**, 578

Yachts: *Alice*, **Vol. 2, Part 2**, 120; *America*, **Vol. 2, Part 1**, 275; **Vol. 4, Part 2**, 585; **Vol. 6, Part 1**, 43, 60; **Vol. 6, Part 2**, 479; **Vol. 9, Part 1**, 560, 620, 626; **Vol. 10, Part 1**, 400; *America*, in Confederate service, **Vol. 9, Part 1**, 626; *Annie Morse*, **Vol. 4, Part 2**, 585; *Atalanta*, **Vol. 8, Part 2**, 554; *Atlantic*, **Vol. 1, Part 1**, 642; *Banshee*, **Vol. 9, Part 1**, 237; *Cambria*, **Vol. 8, Part 2**, 325; *Cayuga*, **Vol. 9, Part 1**, 238; *Columbia*, **Vol. 4, Part 2**, 585; *Constitution*, **Vol. 4, Part 2**, 585; *Continental*, **Vol. 9, Part 1**, 238; *Cornelia*, **Vol. 9, Part 1**, 560; *Coronet*, **Vol. 8, Part 2**, 325; *Corsair* (of J. P. Morgan), **Vol. 8, Part 2**, 554; **Vol. 10, Part 1**, 319; *Cygnet*, **Vol. 9, Part 1**, 560; *Dauntless*, **Vol. 8, Part 2**, 325; *Deerhound*, **Vol. 8, Part 2**, 581; **Vol. 10, Part 2**, 398; *Defender*, **Vol. 4, Part 2**, 585; *Elena*,**Vol. 4, Part 2**, 586; *Enchantress*, **Vol. 9, Part 1**, 237; *Endymion*, **Vol. 8, Part 2**, 200; *Fame*, **Supp. 10**, 857; *Faustine*, **Vol. 4, Part 2**, 585; *Fawn*, **Vol. 4, Part 1**, 263; *Fleetwing*, **Vol. 8, Part 2**, 325; *Fortuna*, **Vol. 9, Part 1**, 237; *Free Lance*, **Vol. 9, Part 1**, 238; *Galatea*, **Vol. 6, Part 1**, 43; **Vol. 7, Part 2**, 147; *Gemini*, **Supp. 9**, 771; *Genesee*, **Vol. 9, Part 1**, 238; *Genesta*, **Vol. 2, Part 1**, 275; **Vol. 6, Part 1**, 43; **Vol. 7, Part 2**, 147; *Gloriana*, **Vol. 4, Part 2**, 585; *Guinevere*, **Vol. 6, Part 1**, 43; *Halcyon*, **Vol. 7, Part 2**, 147; *Haze*, **Vol. 9, Part 1**, 560; *Henrietta*, **Vol. 3, Part 2**, 423; **Vol. 8, Part 2**, 325; *Idalia*, **Vol. 5, Part 1**, 318; *Independence*, **Vol. 6, Part 1, 60**; *Ingomar*, **Vol. 1, Part 1**, 642; *Intrepid*, **Vol. 9, Part 1**, 237; *Jean*, **Vol. 8, Part 1**, 508; *Jubilee*, **Vol. 7, Part 2**, 147; *Julia*, **Vol. 9, Part 1**, 560; *Katoura*, **Vol. 4, Part 2**, 586; *Kelpie*, **Vol. 4, Part 2**, 585; *Kestrel*, **Vol. 9, Part 1**, 237; *Madge*, **Vol. 4, Part 2**, 585; *Maria*, **Vol. 9, Part 1**, 560, 620; *Mayflower*, **Vol. 2, Part 1**, 275; **Vol. 6, Part 1**, 43; **Vol. 7, Part 2**, 147; **Vol. 9, Part 1**, 388; **Vol. 10, Part 1**, 633; **Vol. 10, Part 2**, 393; *Mayflower*, **Supp. 9**, 771; *Meteor*, **Vol. 9, Part 1**, 237; *Mineola*, **Vol. 1, Part 1**, 642; *Mischief*, **Vol. 9, Part 1**, 237; *Noma*, **Vol. 8, Part 1**, 512; *Norada*, **Vol. 10, Part 1**, 400; *North Star*, **Vol. 10, Part 1**, 171; *Peerless*, **Vol. 2, Part 2**, 500 *Priscilla*, **Vol. 9, Part 1**, 237; *Prospero*, **Vol. 9, Part 1**, 237; *Puritan*, **Vol. 2, Part 1**, 275; **Vol. 6, Part 1**, 43; **Vol. 7, Part 2**, 147; *Queen*, **Vol. 4, Part 2**, 586; *Qui Vive*, **Vol. 4, Part 2**, 585; *Rainbow*, **Vol. 1**, Part 1, 642; *Radha*, **Vol. 6, Part 1**, 412; *Rajah*, **Vol. 9, Part 1**, 237; *Ray*, **Vol. 9, Part 1**, 560; *Reliance*, **Vol. 4, Part 2**, 585, 586; *Resolute*, **Vol. 4, Part 2**, 586; **Vol. 9, Part 1**, 238; *Roamer*, **Vol. 6, Part 1**, 372; *Sea Call*, **Vol. 6, Part 1**, 43; *Shadow*, **Vol. 4, Part 2**, 585; *Shamrock IV*, **Vol. 4, Part 2**, 586; *Snark*, **Vol. 6, Part 1**, 372; *Speejacks*, **Vol. 6, Part 1**, 43; *Sultana*, **Supp. 10**, 309; *Suwanee*, **Vol. 1, Part 2**, 395; *Sybil*, **Vol. 9, Part 1**, 560; *Syren*, **Vol. 9, Part 1**, 560; *Tekla*, **Vol. 9, Part 1**, 238; *Thistle*, **Vol. 2, Part 1**, 275; **Vol. 6, Part 1**, 43; **Vol. 7, Part 2**, 147; *Twinkle*, **Vol. 9, Part 1**, 238; *Una*, **Vol. 9, Part 1**, 560; *Vagrant*, **Vol. 4, Part 2**, 586; **Vol. 8, Part 1**, 512; *Valkyrie II*, **Vol. 4, Part 2**, 585; *Vera*, **Vol. 9, Part 1**, 237; *Vergemere*, **Vol. 9, Part 1**, 238; *Vesta*, **Vol. 6, Part 1**, 412; **Vol. 8, Part 2**, 325; *Victory*, **Vol. 8, Part 1**, 508; *Vigilant*, **Vol. 4, Part 2**, 585; *Viking*, **Vol. 8, Part 1**, 512; *Vindex*, **Vol. 9, Part 1**, 237; *Vision*, **Vol. 9, Part 1**, 237; *Volant*, **Vol. 2, Part 2**, 120; *Volunteer*, **Vol. 2, Part 1**, 275; **Vol. 6, Part 1**, 43; **Vol. 7, Part 2**, 147; *Wasp*, **Vol. 4, Part 2**, 585; *Westward*, **Vol. 1, Part 1**, 642; **Vol. 4, Part 2**, 586; **Vol. 2, Part 1**, 12; **Vol. 3, Part 1**, 404 f.; **Vol. 4, Part 1**, 59

Shirley, William, reference to, **Vol. 7, Part 2**, 456

Shirtmakers' Union, founding of, **Supp. 1**, 403

Shock: acapnia theory of, **Supp. 3**, 353; anaphylactic, **Supp. 4**, 34, 701; **Supp. 6**, 481; hemorrhagic and traumatic, **Supp. 7**, 59; insulin-induced treatment, **Supp. 6**, 563–64; surgical, **Supp. 3**, 201

Shockley Semi-Conductor Co., **Supp. 9**, 274

Shock waves, **Supp. 6**, 656

Shoe-blacking, liquid, **Vol. 3, Part 1**, 586 f.

Shoemaker, Samuel, reference to, **Supp. 7**, 89

Shoemaker, Willie, reference to, **Supp. 9**, 867

Shoes: manufacture of, **Vol. 4, Part 1**, 415; **Vol. 6, Part 2**, 38, 73, 426; **Vol. 7, Part 2**, 621; **Vol. 8, Part 2**, 52; **Vol. 9, Part 1**, 285 f.; **Vol. 10, Part 2**, 402; **Supp. 8**,

28; **Supp. 10**, 381; machinery for, **Vol. 3, Part 1**, 62 f.; **Vol. 4, Part 1**, 342; **Vol. 6, Part 2**, 426; wedgie style, **Supp. 5**, 501; welfare capitalism in, **Supp. 4**, 431–32
"Shooting of Dan McGrew, The," **Supp. 6**, 574
Shope, Richard, reference to, **Supp. 8**, 556
Shopmen's strike (1923), **Vol. 9, Part 2**, 86
Shorelines, **Supp. 3**, 389–90
Short, Walter C., references to, **Supp. 6**, 629; **Supp. 8**, 331
Shorthand: amateur title, **Supp. 8**, 546; system of, **Supp. 4**, 347–48; teaching of, **Vol. 7, Part 2**, 642
Short stories: **Supp. 1**, 348, 649; **Supp. 4**, 708–9; **Supp. 9**, 77–78; *New Yorker* style, **Supp. 8**, 481–82, 492–93; O. Henry prizes, **Supp. 5**, 89; psychological, **Supp. 7**, 385–86; technical ingenuity, **Supp. 8**, 623; Westerns, **Supp. 9**, 312–13
Shortwave radio, **Supp. 3**, 184–85
Shostakovich, Dmitri, reference to, **Supp. 6**, 550
Shoulder Arms, **Supp. 10**, 116
Shouse, Jouett, reference to, **Supp. 4**, 682
Shovels, manufacture of, **Vol. 1, Part 1**, 253
Show Boat, **Supp. 3**, 418, 536; **Supp. 6**, 273; **Supp. 8**, 171; **Supp. 10**, 677
Show boat, minstrel troupe, **Vol. 5, Part 2**, 279
Show-Off, The, **Supp. 9**, 451
Shreve, Richmond H., reference to, **Supp. 5**, 408
Shreve, Lamb, and Harmon, **Supp. 5**, 408
Shriver, Sargent, reference to, **Supp. 7**, 421
Shubert, Jacob, references to, **Supp. 5**, 627; **Supp. 10**, 157
Shubert, Samuel, reference to, **Supp. 5**, 627
Shubert Theatre Corporation, **Supp. 5**, 627–28
Shuffle Along, **Supp. 9**, 731
Shurtleff College, founding of, **Vol. 1, Part 2**, 398; **Vol. 7, Part 2**, 381; **Vol. 9, Part 1**, 99
Shut-in-Society, founding of, **Vol. 3, Part 1**, 457 f.
Siam: adviser to government of, **Vol. 9, Part 2**, 141; diplomatic relations with, **Vol. 1, Part 2**, 569; **Vol. 9, Part 2**, 141; education, **Vol. 5, Part 1**, 260; translation of the New Testament, **Vol. 5, Part 2**, 190; missionary work, **Vol. 5, Part 1**, 260; **Vol. 5, Part 2**, 190; **Vol. 6, Part 2**, 40, 52, 424
Siamese twins, **Vol. 2, Part 2**, 2
Siberia, naval expeditions to, **Vol. 3, Part 2**, 559
Siberia and the Exile System, **Vol. 5, Part 2**, 331
Sibley College, **Vol. 9, Part 2**, 519
Sibyl, reform magazine, **Vol. 4, Part 2**, 376
Sicily, World War II action, **Supp. 8**, 155
Sickle-cell anemia, **Supp. 3**, 190
Sidereal Messenger, first astronomical magazine, **Vol. 7, Part 1**, 39
Siegel, Benjamin ("Bugsy"), reference to, **Supp. 9**, 12; **Supp. 10**, 135, 308
Siegel, Don, reference to, **Supp. 8**, 678
Siemens, A. G., **Supp. 6**, 44
Sierra Club, **Supp. 7**, 814
Sierra Nevada, geologic study of, **Supp. 4**, 558
"Sight method" of reading instruction, **Supp. 6**, 248
Signals and signaling devices, **Vol. 4, Part 2**, 477; **Vol. 7, Part 1**, 374; **Vol. 8, Part 2**, 56, 96; **Vol. 10, Part 1**, 618 f.
Signal Service, United States, **Vol. 4, Part 2**, 477
Sikorsky, Igor, references to, **Supp. 5**, 377, 378
Silent Spring, **Supp. 7**, 109–10
Silicon, reduction process, **Supp. 3**, 48–49
Silicon carbide, **Supp. 1**, 5
Silicosis, research in, **Supp. 2**, 371; **Supp. 4**, 314
Silk: culture, **Vol. 3, Part 1**, 540; **Vol. 3, Part 2**, 79; **Vol. 5, Part 2**, 111, 341; **Vol. 7, Part 1**, 23, 205; **Vol. 8, Part 1**, 234 f.; **Vol. 9, Part 2**, 298–99, 320; manufacture, **Vol. 2, Part 2**, 56, 244; **Vol. 3, Part 1**, 540; **Vol. 9, Part 1**, 202, 446
Silkwood, **Supp. 9**, 727
Sill, Edward Rowland, reference to, **Vol. 8, Part 2**, 206
Silliman, Benjamin, reference to, **Vol. 6, Part 1**, 394; **Vol. 7, Part 1**, 575
Sills, Beverly, reference to, **Supp. 8**, 38
Silsbee, J. L., reference to, **Supp. 6**, 711
Silva, Luigi, reference to, **Supp. 7**, 511
Silver: amorphous forms of, **Vol. 6, Part 1**, 71; coinage, pine-tree shillings, **Vol. 5, Part 1**, 363; collecting of old, **Vol. 6, Part 1**, 210; free-silver movement, **Supp. 2**, 289; **Supp. 5**, 381; pricing, **Supp. 2**, 531; processing, **Supp. 2**, 147
Silver, Abba Hillel, reference to, **Supp. 4**, 906
Silver-lead bullion: "gumdrop" method of sampling, **Vol. 8, Part 1**, 326; mining, *See* Mining, silver
Silver nitrate, **Supp. 3**, 364; to prevent blindness, **Supp. 2**, 381
Silver party in politics, **Vol. 2, Part 1**, 192; **Vol. 7, Part 1**, 626 f.; **Vol. 9, Part 1**, 15
Silver Purchase Act (1890). *See* Sherman Silver Purchase Act (1890)
Silver Purchase Act (1934), **Supp. 3**, 730
"Silver question," **Vol. 1, Part 1**, 288 f., **Vol. 4, Part 1**, 391; **Vol. 4, Part 1**, 391; **Vol. 5, Part 1**, 238; **Vol. 9, Part 1**, 132; **Vol. 9, Part 2**, 362
Silver smelting, **Vol. 4, Part 2**, 403
Silversmiths: **Vol. 1, Part 1**, 456; **Vol. 1, Part 2**, 406; **Vol. 3, Part 1**, 501 f.; **Vol. 3, Part 2**, 29, 164, 425; **Vol. 4, Part 2**, 275; **Vol. 5, Part 1**, 424; **Vol. 6, Part 1**, 180 f.; **Vol. 8, Part 1**, 515, 571 f.; **Vol. 8, Part 2**, 338; **Vol. 9, Part 2**, 261; **Vol. 10, Part 2**, 395, "trade dollar" of 1873–87, **Vol. 6, Part 1**, 273
Silverware, manufacture of, **Vol. 4, Part 1**, 432
Silviculture, early activities in, **Vol. 6, Part 2**, 592
Simmons, Etolia Moore, reference to, **Supp. 7**, 38
Simmons, Furnifold M., reference to, **Supp. 4**, 42–43
Simmons College: founding of, **Vol. 5, Part 2**, 288; social work studies, **Supp. 4**, 101
Simms, Florence, reference to, **Supp. 7**, 185
Simon, A. W., reference to, **Supp. 7**, 134
Simon, Klara, reference to, **Supp. 6**, 219
Simon, Richard L, reference to, **Supp. 8**, 578
Simon, Theodore, reference to, **Supp. 6**, 240
Simon and Schuster: **Supp. 7**, 243; **Supp. 8**, 579; founding of, **Supp. 6**, 583–84; **Supp. 10**, 349; Susann book deal, **Supp. 9**, 785
"Simple" ("Jesse B. Semple") (fictional character), **Supp. 8**, 288
Simpson, Alfred, reference to, **Supp. 9**, 24
Simpson, Jerry, reference to, **Supp. 3**, 544
Simpson, Lacey, reference to, **Supp. 9**, 355
Simpson, Wallis Warfield. *See* Windsor, Duke and Duchess of
Simpson, William, reference to, **Supp. 3**, 792
Simpson, Thatcher and Bartlett, **Supp. 4**, 825
Sims, William S., references to, **Supp. 6**, 348, 518
Sinai, founding of, **Vol. 3, Part 2**, 65
Sinai Temple (Mt. Vernon, N. Y.), **Supp. 8**, 307
Sinatra, Frank, references to, **Supp. 9**, 157, 306–7; **Supp. 10**, 322, 323
Sinclair, Harry F., reference to, **Supp. 3**, 259, 260
Sinclair, Upton, references to, **Supp. 3**, 156, 471, 533; **Supp. 5**, 499; **Supp. 6**, 328
Sinclair Oil Co., **Supp. 3**, 669; founding of, **Supp. 6**, 584–85; Mexican oil claims, **Supp. 7**, 377
Singapore, World War II evacuation, **Supp. 8**, 30
Singer, E. A., reference to, **Supp. 6**, 26
Singer, I. J., reference to, **Supp. 6**, 567
Singer, Isaac Bashevis, reference to, **Supp. 3**, 712
Singers. For complete list, *see* Occupations Index

Singer Sewing Machine Co., building architecture, **Supp. 4**, 281
Singewald, Joseph T., reference to, **Supp. 5**, 206
Singewald, Quentin, reference to, **Supp. 5**, 206
Singing: **Vol. 1, Part 1**, 615; **Vol. 6, Part 1**, 74; **Vol. 8, Part 2**, 146 f., 339; **Vol. 10, Part 2**, 164; bel canto, **Supp. 4**, 223; blackface, **Supp. 4**, 440; blues, **Supp. 5**, 529–30; **Supp. 8**, 239, 305–6; **Supp. 9**, 687–88; **Supp. 10**, 818; "boop-boop-a-doop," **Supp. 8**, 310–11; choral, **Supp. 1**, 650; **Supp. 8**, 238; **Supp. 10**, 818; church solo, **Supp. 4**, 125; colonial period, **Vol. 10, Part 1**, 395 f.; concert, **Vol. 1, Part 1**, 638; **Vol. 1, Part 2**, 299; **Vol. 4, Part 1**, 209; **Vol. 5, Part 1**, 117; **Vol. 8, Part 2**, 167; **Vol. 10, Part 2**, 100; **Supp. 3**, 553–54; **Supp. 8**, 151, 380–81; "crooning" style, **Supp. 10**, 159; Country and Western, **Supp. 5**, 748–49; dance bands, **Supp. 9**, 554–55; duets, **Supp. 10**, 317; educational books on, **Vol. 8, Part 2**, 92; gospel, **Supp. 7**, 769; "Irish tenor," **Supp. 3**, 484–85; jazz, **Supp. 5**, 32–33; **Supp. 10**, 58–60, 527; Latin American style, **Supp. 5**, 500–501; motion pictures, **Supp. 8**, 204–5; nationwide auditions, **Supp. 4**, 452; opera, **Vol. 1, Part 2**, 299; **Vol. 2, Part 1**, 553; **Vol. 7, Part 1**, 549; **Vol. 8, Part 1**, 144; **Supp. 9**, 544–45, 850–51; **Supp. 10**, 92–94, 639–40; operettas, **Supp. 7**, 499; **Supp. 8**, 151; pop, **Supp. 9**, 219; popular classical, **Supp. 4**, 596–97; popular recordings of, **Supp. 4**, 388–89; popular vocals, **Supp. 10**, 258, 323, 526, 817; rhythm and blues, **Supp. 7**, 769–70; rock, **Supp. 8**, 305–6; **Supp. 9**, 262, 563–64; rock and roll, **Supp. 10**, 448–51; rote, **Vol. 9, Part 2**, 405; sheet music, **Supp. 3**, 833–34; **Supp. 4**, 88; "Silver-masked Tenor," **Supp. 6**, 691; *Sprechstimme* style, **Supp. 5**, 609; teaching of, **Vol. 8, Part 2**, 146 f.; **Vol. 9, Part 2**, 516 f.; **Supp. 1**, 655, 712; torch, **Supp. 3**, 536; vaudeville, **Supp. 4**, 814–15; **Supp. 8**, 661; Western, **Supp. 10**, 592, 593. *See also* Music; Opera, singing; Songs and songwriting; Theater, musicals
"Singin' in the Rain," **Supp. 9**, 291
Single tax: **Vol. 3, Part 2**, 314 f.; **Vol. 4, Part 1**, 174, 215; **Vol. 6, Part 2**, 53; **Supp. 4**, 844, 845; name, suggestion of, **Vol. 9, Part 1**, 52; protagonist, leading, **Vol. 8, Part 1**, 118 f.
Sing Sing Prison (Ossining, N. Y.): **Supp. 3**, 420; **Supp. 4**, 472; Mutual Welfare League, **Vol. 7, Part 2**, 75
Sinkov, Abraham, reference to, **Supp. 8**, 196
Sino-Japanese War (1937), **Supp. 4**, 750–51; **Supp. 6**, 230
Sinology. *See* China
Sinus, surgery on, **Vol. 6, Part 1**, 523
Sioux Indians: **Supp. 4**, 907; **Supp. 6**, 162; **Supp. 7**, 393; language, **Vol. 8, Part 1**, 605; powerful leader of, **Vol. 8, Part 1**, 438 f.; Sioux Confederacy, **Vol. 2, Part 2**, 530 f.; Sitting Bull, **Vol. 9, Part 1**, 192; treaty with Chippewa, **Vol. 3, Part 1**, 500 f.; uprising of 1862, **Vol. 8, Part 1**, 605; war (1875–76), **Vol. 2 Part 1**, 519; **Vol. 2, Part 2**, 260. *See also* Little Bighorn, battle of
Sioux City Journal, **Vol. 7, Part 2**, 469
Sirhan, Sirhan, reference to, **Supp. 8**, 324
Sise, Lincoln F., reference to, **Supp. 5**, 405
Sister Carrie, **Supp. 3**, 234, 235
Sisterhood of the Divine Compasslon, founding of, **Vol. 8, Part 1**, 205
Sisterhood of the Holy Communion, **Vol. 1, Part 1**, 452; **Vol. 7, Part 1**, 313 f.
Sisters of Charity, **Vol. 2, Part 2**, 351; **Vol. 3, Part 1**, 473 f.; **Vol. 5, Part 1**, 498 f.; **Vol. 8, Part 2**, 596
Sisters of Charity of Nazareth, founding of, **Vol. 9, Part 1**, 421
Sisters of Divine Providence, founding of, **Vol. 7, Part 1**, 618
Sisters of Loretto, **Vol. 7, Part 1**, 429
Sisters of Notre Dame de Namur, founding of, in America, **Vol. 8, Part 1**, 266 f.; **Vol. 8, Part 2**, 462
Sisters of St. Francis, **Vol. 7, Part 1**, 435
Sisters of the Blessed Sacrament, **Supp. 5**, 185–86
Sisters of the Blessed Virgin Mary, **Vol. 2, Part 2**, 159
Sisters of the Holy Cross, **Vol. 7, Part 1**, 435
Sisters of the Holy Family, first black sisterhood in U.S., **Vol. 1, Part 2**, 350
Sisters of the Order of St. Basil the Great, founding of, in America, **Vol. 7, Part 2**, 66
Sitting Bull, reference to, **Vol. 9, Part 1**, 192
Sitting Pretty, **Supp. 8**, 691
Situation comedy, **Supp. 7**, 9
Six Companies, Inc., **Supp. 4**, 198–99
"Six Nations," **Vol. 5, Part 2**, 100, 125; **Vol. 7, Part 1**, 642
Six Nations Defense League. *See* Indian Defense League of America
"$64,000 Question, The," **Supp. 7**, 22; Revlon sponsorship of, **Supp. 9**, 649
Skating. *See* Ice skating
Sketch Book, **Vol. 5, Part 1**, 507
Skidmore College, **Vol. 8, Part 2**, 517
Skidmore, William, reference to, **Supp. 4**, 613
Skidmore, Owings and Merrill, **Supp. 7**, 691
Skiing resorts, **Supp. 5**, 270–71
Skin: color heredity, **Supp. 3**, 215; contact dermatitis, **Supp. 3**, 442; diseases, **Supp. 2**, 547; grafting technique, **Supp. 4**, 221
Skinner, Alanson B., reference to, **Supp. 5**, 533
Skinner, Cornelia Otis, reference to, **Supp. 3**, 714
Skinner, Otis, reference to, **Supp. 3**, 277
Skin of Our Teeth, The, **Supp. 9**, 870, 871
"Skippy" (fictional character), **Supp. 7**, 153, 154
Skouras, Charles, reference to, **Supp. 7**, 692
Skouras, Demetrios, reference to, **Supp. 7**, 692
Skouras, Spyros, references to, **Supp. 7**, 692, 693
Skouras Theatre Corporation, **Supp. 7**, 692
Skyscrapers: **Vol. 2, Part 1**, 303; **Vol. 4, Part 1**, 389; **Vol. 6, Part 1**, 86; **Vol. 8, Part 1**, 115 f.; **Vol. 9, Part 1**, 368, 536 f.; **Vol. 9, Part 2**, 132; Lever House, **Supp. 7**, 691; Pan Am Building, **Supp. 7**, 800; "setback" design, **Supp. 4**, 56; Singer Tower, **Supp. 4**, 281; steel-framed, **Supp. 3**, 611–12; Woolworth Building, **Supp. 1**,342. *See also* Architecture; Buildings
Slander trial, **Vol. 6, Part 1**, 227
Slang, colorful coiner of, **Vol. 3, Part 1**, 379
Slater, James, reference to, **Supp. 9**, 402
Slater, J. C., reference to, **Supp. 7**, 134
Slater, Samuel, reference to, **Vol. 3, Part 1**, 595
Slaughter, Gabriel, movement to unseat, **Vol. 1, Part 2**, 235
Slaughter's Mountain. *See* Cedar Mountain, Va.
Slavery: **Vol. 1, Part 1**, 89; **Vol. 1, Part 2**, 132, 158, 178, 184, 203, 211 f., 225, 332, 449, 554; **Vol. 2, Part 1**, 9; **Vol. 3, Part 2**, 162; **Vol. 4, Part 1**, 539; **Vol. 5, Part 1**, 354–55; **Vol. 6, Part 1**, 144, 158; **Vol. 6, Part 2**, 31, 609; **Vol. 8, Part 2**, 446; **Vol. 9, Part 1**, 571; abolitionists, riots against, **Vol. 3, Part 2**, 311; Adams, C. F., on, **Vol. 1, Part 1**, 41; Adams, John Quincy, on, **Vol. 1, Part 1**, 88 f.; ancient societies, **Supp. 5**, 736; Baptist attitude toward, **Vol. 4, Part 1**, 62, 68; **Vol. 8, Part 2**, 273; Beecher, Edward, on, **Vol. 1, Part 2**, 128; biblical sanction for, **Vol. 4, Part 1**, 62; **Vol. 8, Part 1**, 383; **Vol. 10, Part 1**, 137 f.; "Black Code," **Vol. 5, Part 1**, 373; California, **Vol. 3, Part 1**, 125; Cherokee Indians, adoption of, **Vol. 10, Part 1**, 433; Choate, R., on, **Vol. 2, Part 2**, 88; Christiana treason case, **Vol. 3, Part 1**, 18; church on, **Vol. 1, Part 1**, 628; defense of, **Vol. 3, Part 1**, 181; **Vol. 3,**

Part 2, 94, 438; **Vol. 4, Part 2**, 286; **Vol. 5, Part 1**, 165, 350; **Vol. 5, Part 2**, 294; **Vol. 6, Part 1**, 192, 409, 560; **Vol. 7, Part 1**, 36; **Vol. 9, Part 1**, 172, 362; Dred Scott case, **Vol. 1, Part 2**, 339; **Vol. 2, Part 1**, 457; **Vol. 3, Part 1**, 402; **Vol. 4, Part 1**, 121, 181; **Vol. 4, Part 2**, 311; **Vol. 6, Part 1**, 248; **Vol. 7, Part 1**, 423; **Vol. 8, Part 2**, 488 f., 503; economic reasons for discontinuance of, **Vol. 10, Part 1**, 30; emancipation, **Vol. 3, Part 1**, 120; **Vol. 4, Part 1**, 121; **Vol. 5, Part 2**, 113; **Vol. 6, Part 1**, 254 f.; **Vol. 6, Part 2**, 19; **Vol. 8, Part 1**, 369 f.; **Vol. 8, Part 2**, 619; **Vol. 9, Part 2**, 89; **Vol. 10, Part 2**, 550; Emancipation Proclamation, **Vol. 3, Part 1**, 120; **Vol. 5, Part 2**, 113; **Vol. 6, Part 1**, 254 f.; **Vol. 8, Part 2**, 619; extension of, **Vol. 8, Part 1**, 34 f.; **Vol. 10, Part 1**, 585 f.; "fifteen-slave law," **Vol. 3, Part 1**, 129; "Fifty-four-Forty," **Vol. 3, Part 1**, 398; Freedmen's Bureau, **Vol. 1, Part 1**, 360, 508; **Vol. 3, Part 1**, 608 f.; **Vol. 3, Part 2**, 413; **Vol. 5, Part 1**, 312; **Vol. 5, Part 2**, 114; **Vol. 6, Part 1**, 451, 468; **Vol. 8, Part 2**, 254, 463, 600; **Vol. 9, Part 2**, 240 f.; fugitive slave laws, **Vol. 2, Part 1**, 49; **Vol. 2, Part 2**, 203; **Vol. 3, Part 1**, 330, 399; **Vol. 3, Part 2**, 216, 381; **Vol. 6, Part 1**, 84; **Vol. 6, Part 2**, 419; **Vol. 7, Part 2**, 67, 145; **Vol. 8, Part 2**, 153; fugitive slaves, question of, **Vol. 2, Part 1**, 308; **Vol. 3, Part 1**, 18, 261, 515 f.; **Vol. 4, Part 2**, 564; **Vol. 8, Part 1**, 403; **Vol. 8, Part 2**, 153; **Vol. 10, Part 1**, 440; "gag" resolution, **Vol. 1, Part 1**, 89; Georgia, **Vol. 4, Part 2**, 69; historical studies and writings on, **Supp. 1**, 597; **Supp. 5**, 671; history of, **Vol. 5, Part 1**, 178; **Vol. 9, Part 1**, 365; insurrections, **Vol. 3, Part 2**, 97; **Vol. 10, Part 1**, 69 f.; international slave trade conference, **Vol. 9, Part 2**, 377; Iowa, **Vol. 8, Part 2**, 153; Kansas, **Vol. 3, Part 1**, 202, 400 f.; **Vol. 3, Part 2**, 69; **Vol. 4, Part 1**, 204; **Vol. 8, Part 2**, 35; Kentucky, **Vol. 1, Part 2**, 292; **Vol. 2, Part 1**, 371; legal, phases of, **Vol. 4, Part 1**, 607; **Vol. 5, Part 1**, 423; manumission societies, **Vol. 3, Part 2**, 124; **Vol. 7, Part 2**, 67; **Vol. 10, Part 1**, 70; manuscript material, **Vol. 10, Part 1**, 42; Massachusetts, **Vol. 3, Part 1**, 268; **Vol. 8, Part 1**, 499 f.; Methodist church split over, **Vol. 2, Part 1**, 484; **Vol. 3, Part 1**, 544 f.; **Vol. 4, Part 2**, 328, 407; **Vol. 6, Part 1**, 114, 116; **Vol. 6, Part 2**, 423; **Vol. 10, Part 2**, 422; Mexican treaties in connection with, **Vol. 3, Part 2**, 108; Mississippi, **Vol. 4, Part 1**, 216 f.; Missouri, **Vol. 4, Part 2**, 244; **Vol. 8, Part 1**, 218 f.; Monroe and, **Vol. 7, Part 1**, 91; New Jersey, **Vol. 1, Part 2**, 386; New York, **Vol. 9, Part 2**, 583; newspaper comment, **Vol. 1, Part 2**, 515; Niger Valley, commission sent to, **Vol. 3, Part 1**, 220; Northwest Territory, **Vol. 2, Part 2**, 297; **Vol. 3, Part 1**, 63; Oregon Territory, **Vol. 3, Part 1**, 125; Pennsylvania, abolition of, **Vol. 8, Part 1**, 452; Quaker opposition, **Vol. 4, Part 1**, 606; Republican party and, **Vol. 5, Part 2**, 574 f.; slaveholders, convention of, **Vol. 9, Part 2**, 596; South Carolina, **Vol. 2, Part 1**, 416; **Vol. 3, Part 1**, 275; **Vol. 6, Part 1**, 32; southern clergy, viewpoint of, **Vol. 7, Part 2**, 580; Tennessee, **Vol. 7, Part 2**, 67; territories, **Vol. 2, Part 2**, 523; **Vol. 3, Part 1**, 400 f.; Underground Railroad, **Vol. 1, Part 1**, 205; **Vol. 2, Part 2**, 268 f.; **Vol. 3, Part 2**, 247; **Vol. 4, Part 1**, 195, 607, 622; **Vol. 5, Part 1**, 224, 576; **Vol. 5, Part 2**, 258; **Vol. 6, Part 1**, 163, 368; **Vol. 8, Part 1**, 117, 403; **Vol. 8, Part 2**, 84, 117, 315; **Vol. 9, Part 1**, 288, 379; **Vol. 9, Part 2**, 23, 304; **Vol. 10, Part 1**, 27; Van Buren's attitude toward, **Vol. 10, Part 1**, 155 f.; Virginia, **Vol. 2, Part 1**, 383; **Vol. 8, Part 2**, 216; **Vol. 10, Part 1**, 70; Wilmot Proviso, **Vol. 2, Part 1**, 49, 417; **Vol. 5, Part 1**, 604; **Vol. 5, Part 2**, 397; **Vol. 6, Part 1**, 586; **Vol. 8, Part 1**, 34 f.; **Vol. 9, Part 2**, 590; **Vol. 10, Part 2**, 317; Wisconsin, **Vol. 3, Part 1**, 375; World's Antislavery Convention in London, **Vol. 8, Part 1**, 499; writings on, **Vol. 1, Part 1**, 94, 352; **Vol. 2, Part 1**, 156, 161; **Vol. 3, Part 1**, 266; **Vol. 3, Part 2**, 411; **Vol. 4, Part 1**, 85, 217, 308, 391, 530 f.; **Vol. 4, Part 2**, 565 f.; **Vol. 5, Part 2**, 12; **Vol. 8, Part 1**, 407, 410, 444, 537; **Vol. 9, Part 2**, 100, 250, 253; **Vol. 10, Part 1**, 55 f.; **Vol. 10, Part 1**, 138; **Supp. 3**, 32, 337. *See also* Abolition movement

Slave narratives, **Supp. 9**, 109

Slaves: *ad valorem* tax on, **Vol. 3, Part 2**, 107; **Vol. 8, Part 1**, 417; codes, **Vol. 7, Part 1**, 115; **Vol. 10, Part 1**, 70; owning, responsibilities of, **Vol. 3, Part 1**, 21 f.; rise of, to commanding position in abolitionist movement, **Vol. 3, Part 1**, 406 f.; ships, capture of, **Vol. 9, Part 2**, 48; trade, **Vol. 1, Part 1**, 90, 292; **Vol. 3, Part 1**, 275, 599 f.; **Vol. 4, Part 1**, 150; **Vol. 4, Part 2**, 446, 521; **Vol. 6, Part 1**, 32; **Vol. 8, Part 2**, 85

Slaves as soldiers: Confederate, **Vol. 2, Part 2**, 190 f.; Union, **Vol. 2, Part 1**, 358

Slave Systems of Greek and Roman Antiquity, **Supp. 5**, 736

Slavic literature and languages, teaching of, **Supp. 4**, 195–96

Sleeper, Jacob, reference to, **Vol. 10, Part 1**, 409 f.

Sleeping Car Porters. *See* Brotherhood of Sleeping Car Porters

Sleeping cars: inventions relating to, **Vol. 5, Part 2**, 464; **Vol. 10, Part 2**, 497; manufacture of, **Vol. 10, Part 2**, 497

"Sleeping sickness," study of, **Vol. 6, Part 2**, 401

"Slide, Kelly, Slide," **Vol. 5, Part 2**, 310

Slide rule, invention of, **Supp. 2**, 27

Sloan, Alfred P., Jr.: cancer research endowment, **Supp. 6**, 333, 537; references to, **Supp. 4**, 244, 301, 682; **Supp. 5**, 193–94; **Supp. 7**, 794; **Supp. 9**, 658

Sloan, John, reference to, **Supp. 5**, 624

Sloan, W. Glenn, reference to, **Supp. 6**, 508

Sloan, Alfred P., Jr., Foundation, **Supp. 8**, 600

Sloan-Kettering Institute for Cancer Research (New York City), **Supp. 6**, 333, 537, 538; **Supp. 8**, 600

Slogans and phrases: "Gung Ho!," **Supp. 4**, 147; "Tin Pan Alley" coined, **Supp. 4**, 836

Slonimsky, Nicolas, reference to, **Supp. 8**, 145

Slosson, Edwin E., references to, **Supp. 8**, 119, 120

Slums, "great emancipator" of, in New York, **Vol. 8, Part 1**, 607

Slye, Maude, reference to, **Supp. 3**, 807

Small, Albion W., references to, **Supp. 3**, 514, 515, 793; **Supp. 4**, 828

Small, Len, reference to, **Supp. 5**, 450; **Supp. 6**, 74

Small Business Administration, founding of, **Supp. 8**, 616

Smallpox inoculation: **Vol. 1, Part 1**, 395; **Vol. 4, Part 1**, 97, 331; **Vol. 5, Part 1**, 158, 541, 546; **Vol. 5, Part 2**, 163; **Vol. 8, Part 1**, 391; **Vol. 8, Part 2**, 377; **Vol. 10, Part 1**, 150, 529 f.; early doubts as to advisability of, **Vol. 3, Part 1**, 408; first to introduce practice into America, **Vol. 1, Part 2**, 535; vaccine, first shipment of, **Vol. 9, Part 1**, 424

Smart, David A., Publishing Co., **Supp. 5**, 637

Smart Set, **Supp. 4**, 841; **Supp. 6**, 444, 445, 470, 471

Smedley, Agnes, references to, **Supp. 4**, 147; **Supp. 10**, 801

Smellie, William, reference to, **Vol. 6, Part 1**, 333

Smelting: industrial development, **Supp. 2**, 383; ores, **Vol. 2, Part 1**, 511; **Vol. 2, Part 2**, 472; **Vol. 4, Part 2**, 37 f., 379, 403; **Vol. 5, Part 1**, 43; **Vol. 7, Part 2**, 504; **Vol. 8, Part 1**, 326; **Vol. 9, Part 1**, 57

Smith, Adam, study of, **Supp. 8**, 669

Smith, Albert E., reference to, **Supp. 3**, 75–76

Smith, Alfred E.: biography of, **Supp. 6**, 521; "Catholic and Patriot," **Supp. 6**, 572; gubernatorial campaigns, **Supp. 10**, 232–33; Hearst relationship, **Supp. 5**, 286; New York governorship, **Supp. 3**, 668–

69; **Supp. 4**, 886; **Supp. 5**, 286, 493–94; Perkins relationship, **Supp. 7**, 608; presidential campaigns, **Supp. 3**, 114, 481, 681, 817; **Supp. 7**, 361; Prohibition stance, **Supp. 3**, 132; **Supp. 7**, 786; Raskob relationship, **Supp. 4**, 682–83; references to, **Vol. 7, Part 1**, 346; **Vol. 9, Part 2**, 126; Roosevelt, F. D., relationship, **Supp. 3**, 644–46, 653; Swope relationship, **Supp. 6**, 616; Tammany Hall, **Supp. 6**, 295; Walker relationship, **Supp. 4**, 855
Smith, Benjamin Eli, reference to, **Vol. 9, Part 2**, 357
Smith, Captain John, references to, **Vol. 5, Part 1, 339; Vol. 7, Part 1**, 468; **Vol. 8, Part 1**, 18 f.
Smith, Charles Shaler, reference to, **Supp. 2**, 29
Smith, David Eugene, reference to, **Supp. 3**, 677
Smith, Donald P., reference to, **Supp. 3**, 220
Smith, Dorothy Hope, reference to, **Supp. 9**, 303
Smith, Ed ("Cotton"), reference to, **Supp. 8**, 682
Smith, Edgar Fahs, reference to, **Supp. 4**, 114
Smith, Erwin F., reference to, **Supp. 3**, 400
Smith, Frank L., reference to, **Supp. 3**, 559, 622
Smith, Gerald L. K., references to, **Supp. 4**, 480; **Supp. 6**, 614, 647
Smith, Gerrit, psychobiography of, **Supp. 6**, 279
Smith, Harrison, reference to, **Supp. 7**, 232
Smith, Holland, reference to, **Supp. 7**, 352
Smith, James Allen, reference to, **Supp. 4**, 62
Smith, Joseph, references to, **Vol. 9, Part 1**, 386; **Vol. 9, Part 2**, 124, 333 f.
Smith, Leroy, reference to, **Supp. 9**, 441
Smith, Lowell H., reference to, **Supp. 7**, 16
Smith, Marcus A., reference to, **Supp. 7**, 21
Smith, Margaret Chase, reference to, **Supp. 8**, 654
Smith, Mary Logan. *See* Berenson, Mary Smith Costelloe
Smith, Ralph, reference to, **Supp. 7**, 352
Smith, Robert Holbrook, reference to, **Supp. 9**, 883
Smith, S. F., reference to, **Vol. 5, Part 1**, 170
Smith, Sol, reference to, **Vol. 6, Part 1**, 493
Smith, Sophia, reference to, **Vol. 8, Part 2**, 557
Smith, Stevenson, reference to, **Supp. 6**, 261
Smith, Theobald, reference to, **Vol. 7, Part 1**, 542
Smith, Willie, references to, **Supp. 4**, 510, 511
Smith, Zilpha D., reference to, **Supp. 2**, 375
Smith Act (1940), **Supp. 5**, 500; **Supp. 7**, 96, 264; **Supp. 10**, 748
Smith and Dale (vaudeville team), **Supp. 9**, 213–14
Smith College: **Vol. 1, Part 2**, 39; **Vol. 8, Part 2**, 557; **Vol. 9, Part 2**, 56; **Supp. 9**, 173; drama studies, **Supp. 8**, 177; English literature and language studies, **Supp. 7**, 18–19; expansion of, **Supp. 4**, 624–25; founding of, **Vol. 8, Part 2**, 557; **Vol. 9, Part 1**, 347; French studies, **Supp. 3**, 691; history studies, **Supp. 8**, 169; presidency, **Supp. 4**, 624–25; psychology studies, **Supp. 3**, 429
Smith's Magazine, **Supp. 3**, 295
Smithsonian Institution: **Vol. 1, Part 1**, 91, 514; **Vol. 1, Part 2**, 152; **Vol. 5, Part 2**, 66, 338 f., 595; **Vol. 7, Part 2**, 119; **Vol. 8, Part 1**, 525; **Vol. 8, Part 2**, 542; **Vol. 10, Part 1**, 5; Bureau of American Ethnology, **Supp. 6**, 611; founding of, **Vol. 1, Part 1**, 91; **Vol. 4, Part 2**, 552 f.; **Vol. 8, Part 2**, 233; geology collection, bf, 212; Hall of Gems and Minerals, **Supp. 10**, 848; National Museum collection, **Supp. 3**, 732–33; National Portrait Gallery, **Supp. 10**, 113; petrographic collection, **Supp. 4**, 194; physical anthropology, **Supp. 3**, 372; rocket propulsion, **Supp. 3**, 306. *See also* Freer Gallery of Art
"Smithsonian process," printing, **Vol. 8, Part 2**, 214
Smog, composition of, **Supp. 10**, 297
Smoke screen, use of, **Vol. 3, Part 1**, 614 f.
Smoking: cigarette advertising, **Supp. 4**, 371; **Supp. 5**, 411, 567; cigars, **Supp. 7**, 614; lung cancer relationship, **Supp. 6**, 246; **Supp. 8**, 7; **Supp. 9**, 250; mental processes and, **Supp. 5**, 329; pipe tobacco, **Supp. 5**, 565, 566. *See also* Tobacco industry
Smoot-Hawley Tariff Act (1930), **Supp. 3**, 345, 727; **Supp. 6**, 59–60; **Supp. 7**, 305, 362
Smuggling, **Vol. 4, Part 2**, 218, 221; **Vol. 5, Part 2**, 540; **Vol. 8, Part 2**, 296
Snakes. *See* Reptiles
SNCC. *See* Student Nonviolent Coordinating Committee
Snedden, David, reference to, **Supp. 3**, 677
Snell, Earl, reference to, **Supp. 8**, 104
Snelling, Paula, reference to, **Supp. 8**, 604
Snider, D. J., reference to, **Vol. 5, Part 1**, 311,
Snow, C. P., reference to, **Supp. 8**, 200
Snow, Edgar, reference to, **Supp. 4**, 750
Snow, Wilbert, reference to, **Supp. 9**, 58
Snow, crystal photography, **Supp. 1**, 72
"Snow Campaign," against S.C. Loyalists, **Vol. 8, Part 1**, 42
Snow White and the Seven Dwarfs, **Supp. 7**, 407; **Supp. 8**, 130; **Supp. 9**, 237; **Supp. 10**, 351
Snuff, manufacture of, **Vol. 7, Part 2**, 641
Snyder, Martin Moses ("Moe"), reference to, **Supp. 10**, 223
Soap, manufacture of, **Vol. 1, Part 1**, 455; **Vol. 2, Part 2**, 299; **Vol. 3, Part 2**, 314; **Supp. 1**, 610; **Supp. 4**, 262
Soap operas, **Supp. 6**, 104; **Supp. 9**, 802
Sobell, Morton, references to, **Supp. 5**, 588, 589, 590; **Supp. 7**, 52; **Supp. 10**, 719; trial of, **Supp. 9**, 321
Sobolev, Arkadi A., reference to, **Supp. 5**, 538
Social anthropology, **Supp. 4**, 907–9
Social class and status, anthropological definitions of, **Supp. 8**, 684
Social Control: A Survey of the Foundations of Order, **Supp. 5**, 591, 592
Social Creed of the Churches, The, **Supp. 8**, 680–81
Social criticism. *See* Criticism, social
Social Darwinism in American Thought, **Supp. 8**, 271, 272
Social Democratic League, founding of, **Supp. 3**, 298
Social Democratic Party of America, **Vol. 3, Part 1, 184**. *See also* Socialist party
Social distance scale, **Supp. 3**, 578
Social experiments: **Vol. 2, Part 1**, 52, 391; **Vol. 4, Part 1**, 351; **Vol. 9, Part 2**, 496 f. *See also* Brook Farm; New Harmony; *specific communities*
Social Frontier, **Supp. 7**, 435
"Social Gospel," **Vol. 8, Part 1**, 393
Social Gospel movement. *See* Evangelism
Social hygiene: promotion of, **Supp. 4**, 758–59; sex education, **Supp. 7**, 427; writings on, **Supp. 1**, 228. *See also* Family planning; Prostitution; Venereal disease
Social Hygiene, Bureau of, **Supp. 10**, 683
Social Hygiene, founding of, **Supp. 4**, 758
Social insurance. *See* Health insurance; Social Security; Unemployment insurance
Socialism: **Vol. 2, Part 1**, 52; **Vol. 3, Part 1**, 223; **Vol. 4, Part 1**, 370; **Vol. 4, Part 2**, 14 f. 594, 610; **Vol. 6, Part 1**, 373; **Vol. 6, Part 2**, 177; **Vol. 8, Part 2**, 94; **Vol. 9, Part 2**, 2, 628; **Vol. 10, Part 2**, 487; Christianity's relationship to, **Supp. 5**, 616–17; **Supp. 7**, 746; writings on, **Vol. 3, Part 1**, 184, 223 f.; **Vol. 6, Part 2**, 177; **Vol. 10, Part 2**, 380; **Supp. 5**, 134–36; **Supp. 8**, 611; **Supp. 9**, 875–76
Socialism and Social Reform, **Supp. 3**, 249
Socialist Labor Party, **Supp. 1**, 72–73; **Supp. 3**, 347
Socialist party: **Vol. 3, Part 1**, 184; **Vol. 3, Part 1, 223; Vol. 4, Part 2**, 468; **Vol. 6, Part 1**, 373; **Vol. 6, Part 2**, 212; blacks' association, **Supp. 7**, 155–56; California, **Supp. 8**, 595; demise of, **Supp. 8**, 650; develop-

ment in U.S., **Supp. 4**, 746; founding of, **Supp. 1**, 73, 403; journalism, **Supp. 5**, 96–97, 264, 499; **Supp. 9**, 126; labor movement relations, **Supp. 3**, 10, 373, 516–17, 532–33; **Supp. 7**, 254; leadership, **Supp. 8**, 649–51; left-wing faction, **Supp. 5**, 69–70, 82–3; **Supp. 10**, 849; mayors, **Supp. 4**, 511–12; **Supp. 7**, 348–49, 503; membership in, **Supp. 4**, 645; **Supp. 8**, 317; middle-class focus, **Supp. 3**, 297–98; moderates, **Supp. 3**, 373; municipal government, **Supp. 4**, 733; national politics, **Supp. 4**, 733–34; New York, **Supp. 3**, 853; **Supp. 5**, 635; organizers, **Supp. 8**, 563, 564; poetry, **Supp. 6**, 113; split over World War I involvement, **Supp. 1**, 73–74; **Supp. 3**, 675; **Supp. 4**, 746; **Supp. 5**, 134–35; **Supp. 8**, 611; writers in, **Supp. 8**, 317, 593–95; writings on, **Supp. 5**, 82–83; writings on wealth distribution, **Supp. 3**, 545–46

Socialist Trade and Labor Alliance, **Vol. 3, Part 1**, 223

Social Justice (newspaper), founding of, **Supp. 10**, 152

Social Problems of an Industrial Society, The, **Supp. 4**, 565–66

Social psychology, **Supp. 1**, 547–48; **Supp. 4**, 830–31; **Supp. 8**, 7–8, 69–70

Social Psychology, **Supp. 5**, 592

Social reconstructionists, **Supp. 6**, 558

Social reform: **Supp. 1**, 10, 13, 114, 346, 567; **Supp. 2**, 627; **Supp. 3**, 28, 159, 246, 297–98, 344, 363, 638–39, 674–75, 679–81; **Supp. 4**, 282–83, 636, 741; **Supp. 5**, 70, 380–81, 578–79, 592, 616–17; **Supp. 6**, 1–2, 23–24, 25, 54–55, 81–82, 113, 152, 167, 202, 329–30, 499–500, 515–16, 614; **Supp. 7**, 355–56, 607–9; feminist support, **Supp. 5**, 532; Forward Movement, **Supp. 2**, 20, 617; Indian rights, **Supp. 8**, 98–99; legislation, **Supp. 2**, 690; Poor People's Campaign, **Supp. 8**, 335; proleterian literature, **Supp. 8**, 216; religious advocacy, **Supp. 8**, 680–81; Vietnam era, **Supp. 8**, 324; writings promoting, **Supp. 8**, 594–95. *See also* Reform

Social Reform Club of New York City, **Vol. 2, Part 2**, 566; founding of, **Supp. 3**, 297–98

Social Register, Philadelphla, Pa., **Supp. 6**, 331

Social Research, Inc., founding of, **Supp. 8**, 685

Social science: corporate application, **Supp. 8**, 685; history studies relationship to, **Supp. 4**, 824–25; popular writings on, **Supp. 8**, 189; psychiatry relationship to, **Supp. 4**, 807; writings on, **Supp. 9**, 428. *See also specific disciplines*

Social Science Research Council, **Supp. 6**, 692–93, 718; founding of, **Supp. 4**, 587; **Supp. 5**, 485

Social Security, **Supp. 3**, 255

Social Security: administration, **Supp. 4**, 900; pay-as-you-go basis, **Supp. 6**, 709; system development, **Supp. 4**, 392; unemployment provisions, **Supp. 3**, 19, 178, 255–56. *See also* Poverty

Social Security Act (1935): **Supp. 3**, 19, 178, 255; **Supp. 6**, 330, 647, 705; **Supp. 7**, 609; passage of, **Supp. 3**, 654, 655; **Supp. 10**, 249, 484

Social Security Administration, **Supp. 9**, 28

Social Service Review, The, founding of, **Supp. 4**, 107

Social Sources of Denominationalism, The, **Supp. 7**, 574

Social studies, teaching of, **Supp. 6**, 557–58

Social work: **Vol. 1, Part 2**, 131; **Vol. 3, Part 1**, 378; **Vol. 3, Part 2**, 312, 514; **Vol. 6, Part 1**, 223, 354 f., **Vol. 6, Part 1**, 422 f.; **Vol. 8, Part 1**, 275 f., 584 f.; **Vol. 9, Part 1**, 411; **Vol. 9, Part 2**, 513 f.; **Vol. 10, Part 2**, 237; aged's problems, **Supp. 5**, 454; Catholic organizations, **Supp. 3**, 624–25; **Supp. 6**, 607–8; chlld welfare, **Supp. 3**, 159, 228, 361–62; **Supp. 4**, 871–72; **Supp. 5**, 454; **Supp. 6**, 1–2, 81, 152, 202, 515; **Supp. 7**, 251, 483–84; **Supp. 8**, 40, 673–74; family agencies, **Supp. 4**, 810–11; first university-sponsored training in, **Supp. 4**, 101; group process concept, **Supp. 5**, 431; **Supp. 7**, 151–52; hospital, **Supp. 3**, 312; **Supp. 6**, 97–98; immigrants, **Supp. 7**, 341–42; India, **Supp. 7**, 342; Jewish organizations, **Supp. 4**, 79–80; juvenile delinquency, **Supp. 7**, 28; legislation advocacy, **Supp. 6**, 509–10; medical, **Supp. 2**, 84; **Supp. 6**, 97–98; mentally retarded, **Supp. 3**, 388–89; Neighborhood Guild, **Supp. 3**, 175; New Jersey, **Supp. 6**, 515–16; New York City, **Supp. 4**, 391–92; Pennsylvania, **Supp. 6**, 515; professional education in, **Supp. 1**, 237, 340, 485; **Supp. 2**, 2, 360, 376, 656, 694; **Supp. 3**, 4, 625; **Supp. 4**, 101, 106–7, 227, 232, 333, 810–11; **Supp. 5**, 520; **Supp. 6**, 1–2; psychiatric, criticism of, **Supp. 4**, 811; rescue missions, **Vol. 9, Part 1**, 176; settlement houses, establishing of, **Vol. 10, Part 2**, 504, 515; theory of, **Supp. 4**, 227–28; unwed mothers, **Supp. 3**, 221; Volunteers of America, **Supp. 2**, 48–49; Wisconsin reforms, **Supp. 7**, 787. *See also* Settlement house movement; Sociology; Welfare

Société Anonyme, Inc., founding of, **Supp. 5**, 184, 185

Société des Artistes Français, **Vol. 5, Part 2**, 463

Société Financière de Transports et d'Enterprise Industrielle (SOFINA), **Supp. 7**, 333

Society: American "aristocracy," **Supp. 10**, 16–17; balls, **Supp. 10**, 173–74; café society, **Supp. 4**, 199; **Supp. 7**, 803; **Supp. 8**, 38–39; debuts, **Supp. 10**, 174; Duchin Orchestra's popularity with, **Supp. 5**, 188; etiquette books, **Supp. 6**, 514; **Supp. 9**, 824–25; Gibson illustrations, **Supp. 3**, 300; heiresses, **Supp. 10**, 366–68; hostesses, **Supp. 7**, 519, 527; **Supp. 9**, 547, 615–16; **Supp. 10**, 465; international, **Supp. 4**, 229–30; **Supp. 7**, 753; New York aristocratic, **Supp. 5**, 707–8; **Supp. 9**, 825–27; **Supp. 10**, 616; novels about aristocratic, **Supp. 2**, 703–5; playboys, **Supp. 8**, 416; socialites, **Supp. 4**, 797–98; Vanderbilt ball (1883), **Supp. 1**, 68; Washington, D.C., **Supp. 8**, 244, 328; women's clubs, **Supp. 5**, 505

Society for Advancement of Management. *See* Taylor Society

Society for Establishing Useful Manufactures, **Vol. 7, Part 2**, 294

Society for Ethical Culture. *See* Ethical Culture movement

Society for Experimental Biology and Medicine, founding of, **Supp. 1**, 518

Society for Pharmacology and Experimental Therapeutics, founding of, **Supp. 2**, 4

Society for Political Education, founding of, **Supp. 1**, 101

Society for Promoting Christian Knowledge, **Vol. 7, Part 1**, 463

Society for Pure English, founding of, **Supp. 4**, 756

Society for the Advancement of Christianity in Pennsylvania, **Vol. 7, Part 2**, 592

Society for the Preservation of New England Antiquities, **Supp. 4**, 115–16; founding of, **Supp. 4**, 24

Society for the Preservation of Spanish Antiquities, **Vol. 8, Part 1**, 229 f.

Society for the Prevention of Crime, **Vol. 2, Part 2**, 568

Society for the Prevention of Pauperism, **Vol. 4, Part 1**, 217

Society for the Promotion of Engineering Education, **Vol. 5, Part 2**, 106

Society for the Promotion of Legal Knowledge and Forensic Eloquence, founding of, **Vol. 8, Part 1**, 401

Society for the Propagation of the Gospel, **Vol. 4, Part 2**, 418; **Vol. 5, Part 2**, 110; **Vol. 6, Part 1**, 74; **Vol. 8, Part 2**, 81

Society for the Protection of German Emigrants, **Vol. 8, Part 2**, 91

Society for the Publication of American Music, **Vol. 10, Part 1**, 73 f.; founding of, **Supp. 2**, 250

Society for the Reformation of Juvenile Delinquents, **Vol. 4, Part 1**, 217
Society of American Archivists: predecessor, **Supp. 8**, 369, 370; professional standards, **Supp. 10**, 60
Society of American Artists, **Vol. 1, Part 2**, 120; **Vol. 3, Part 1**, 613 f.; **Vol. 4, Part 1**, 276; **Vol. 8, Part 1**, 296; **Vol. 8, Part 2**, 54; **Vol. 9, Part 1**, 119; founding of, **Supp. 1**, 514
Society of American Bacteriologists, founding of, **Supp. 2**, 353
Society of American Foresters, founding of, **Supp. 4**, 666
Society of American Wood-Engravers, **Vol. 5, Part 2**, 411; 509
Society of California Pioneers, **Vol. 5, Part 1**, 82; **Vol. 6, Part 1**, 234; **Vol. 9, Part 2**, 448
Society of Economic Geologists, **Vol. 7, Part 2**, 451; founding of, **Supp. 4**, 766
Society of Free Thinkers, founding of, **Supp. 2**, 182
Society of Friends. *See* Quakers
Society of Hebrew Education, **Vol. 3, Part 1**, 459 f.
Society of Iconophiles, **Vol. 1, Part 1**, 299
Society of Independent Artists, founding of, **Supp. 2**, 239
Society of Jesus (Jesuits), **Vol. 3, Part 2**, 327; **Vol. 6, Part 1**, 539; **Vol. 7, Part 1**, 82
Society of Mural Painters, founding of, **Supp. 2**, 42
Society of Naval Architects and Marine Engineers, founding of, **Supp. 1**, 151
Society of Painters in Pastel, **Vol. 1, Part 2**, 397
Society of Progressive Oral Advocates, founding of, **Supp. 3**, 311
Society of St. Sulpice, **Vol. 3, Part 1**, 470 f.
Society of the Atonement, founding of, **Supp. 2**, 201
Society of the Cincinnati: **Vol. 3, Part 1**, 430; **Vol. 3, Part 2**, 116, 194, 307, 323, 400 f.; **Vol. 4, Part 1**, 187; **Vol. 5, Part 1**, 417; **Vol. 5, Part 2**, 376, 423, 476, 498, 538; **Vol. 6, Part 1**, 166, 223; **Vol. 7, Part 1**, 510; **Vol. 7, Part 2**, 293; **Vol. 8, Part 2**, 62, 487; **Vol. 9, Part 1**, 369, 604; **Vol. 9, Part 2**, 596, 606, 616; founding of, **Vol. 3, Part 2**, 116, 323; **Vol. 5, Part 2**, 376, 498; **Vol. 8, Part 2**, 487
Society of the Holy Child Jesus, **Vol. 2, Part 2**, 347 f.
Society of the Sacred Heart, **Vol. 3, Part 1**, 477 f.; **Vol. 4, Part 2**, 242
Society of Surgeon Dentists of the City and State of New York, **Vol. 7, Part 2**, 251
Society of Women Geographers, founding of, **Supp. 6**, 576
Sociological jurisprudence, **Supp. 3**, 185–86; **Supp. 7**, 625–26, 627, 628
Sociology: American community studies, **Supp. 3**, 50; **Supp. 5**, 35; **Supp. 8**, 398–99, 684–85; behavior, individual and mass, **Supp. 10**, 438–39; black studies, **Supp. 7**, 266; **Supp. 8**, 81, 521–22; Chicago school of, **Supp. 6**, 321; Christian, **Supp. 2**, 655; **Supp. 3**, 514; class and change theories, **Supp. 8**, 407; collective behavior, **Supp. 3**, 511, 578–80; contemporary American issues, **Supp. 7**, 539–40; criminology theory, **Supp. 4**, 808–9; culture studies, **Supp. 4**, 908; **Supp. 6**, 727; **Supp. 9**, 448; first professorship in, **Supp. 1**, 340; history of, **Supp. 6**, 726; history studies and, **Supp. 2**, 563–66; homeostasis, **Supp. 3**, 137; human ecology system, **Supp. 3**, 578–79; legal philosophy and, **Supp. 6**, 216; **Supp. 8**, 17; marriage and family studies, **Supp. 3**, 799–800; Marxist approach to, **Supp. 10**, 437, 439; of medicine, **Supp. 6**, 664–65; *Pittsburgh Survey* as investigative model, **Supp. 6**, 329–30; popularization of, **Supp. 5**, 591–92; regionalism studies, **Supp. 5**, 520–21; of religion, **Supp. 7**, 574–76; research, theoretical and empirical linkage, **Supp. 4**, 829, 830; role of women, writings on, **Supp. 3**, 581; rural life, **Supp. 2**, 727; **Supp. 3**, 683–84; **Supp. 4**, 312; sample survey, **Supp. 6**, 604–5; scientific approach to, **Supp. 3**, 351; statistical techniques, **Supp. 6**, 482–83, 604; "structural functional" school, **Supp. 10**, 618; survey techniques, **Supp. 10**, 437, 439; teaching of, **Supp. 1**, 547; **Supp. 3**, 579–80, 793, 799; **Supp. 4**, 831; values and attitudes distinction, **Supp. 4**, 829; writings on, **Supp. 1**, 339–40, 388–89; **Supp. 4**, 828–31; **Supp. 6**, 54–55; **Supp. 10**, 617
Soda, manufacture of, **Vol. 2, Part 2**, 274; **Vol. 6, Part 2**, 417; **Vol. 9, Part 1**, 455
Soda fountain, **Supp. 2**, 688
Sodium hydroxide, **Supp. 3**, 26
SOFAR (sound fixing and ranging), **Supp. 9**, 271
Soft drinks, root beer, **Supp. 2**, 306; **Supp. 10**, 338, 339
Sohn, Louis B., reference to, **Supp. 8**, 88
Soil: analysis of, **Vol. 5, Part 1**, 22, 209; bacteriology of, **Supp. 1**, 461; chemical fertility, **Supp. 3**, 438–39; conservation, **Supp. 3**, 656; **Supp. 6**, 52–53, 638–39; **Supp. 8**, 277; erosion, **Vol. 8, Part 1**, 146 f.; erosion theories, **Supp. 4**, 119; mapping, **Supp. 1**, 540; microbiology, **Supp. 2**, 387; physics of, **Supp. 7**, 76; plant interrelationship, **Supp. 4**, 382; temperature and plant disease, **Supp. 3**, 401. *See also* Land and land use
Soil Conservation and Domestic Allotment Act (1935), **Supp. 6**, 638; **Supp. 8**, 277
"Soil creep," phenomenon of, **Vol. 5, Part 2**, 359
Soilless Growth of Plants, **Supp. 3**, 247
Soil Science, founding of, **Supp. 2**, 388
Solano, Solita, references to, **Supp. 10**, 246, 247
Solar: atmosphere studies, **Supp. 6**, 561; compass, **Vol. 2, Part 1**, 340; eclipse, **Supp. 1**, 62; **Supp. 2**, 92; **Supp. 5**, 540; energy, **Supp. 7**, 98; magnetism, **Supp. 2**, 271; radiation, **Vol. 5, Part 2**, 594 f.; spectrum, **Vol. 3, Part 1**, 436; sunspot spectra, **Supp. 6**, 7; system, formation of, **Supp. 5**, 508–9
Soldiers Field (Harvard), **Vol. 5, Part 1**, 153
Soldiers' Home, **Vol. 8, Part 2**, 71, 509
Soldier's Tale, The, **Supp. 9**, 776
Solicitor-generalship: **Vol. 1, Part 2**, 508; **Vol. 6, Part 1, 149; Supp. 10**, 229, 664; loyalty issues, **Supp. 9**, 743–44; school desegregation cases, **Supp. 9**, 743
Solidarity, **Supp. 7**, 118
"Solidarity Forever," **Supp. 7**, 118
Solitary Brethren of the Community of Seventh-Day Baptists at Ephrata, **Vol. 1, Part 2**, 142
Solomon Islands, **Supp. 6**, 268, 340; **Supp. 7**, 489
Somebody Up There Likes Me, **Supp. 9**, 35
Some Came Running, **Supp. 10**, 391
Somervell, Brehon B., reference to, **Supp. 5**, 538–39
Somerville Journal, **Vol. 2, Part 2**, 367
Somoza family (Nicaragua), **Supp. 6**, 358
Sonar detector, **Supp. 7**, 516
Songs and songwriting: **Vol. 3, Part 1**, 205; **Vol. 3, Part 2**, 568; **Vol. 4, Part 2**, 217, 306, 606 f.; **Vol. 7, Part 2**, 290, 367; **Vol. 8, Part 1**, 348; **Vol. 9, Part 1**, 343, 589 f.; **Vol. 9, Part 2**, 430; **Vol. 10, Part 2**, 532; "Absolutely, Mr. Gallagher? Positively, Mr. Shean!," **Supp. 4**, 740; "After the Ball," **Vol. 4, Part 2**, 306, "America the Beautiful," **Supp. 1**, 59; "April in Paris," **Supp. 8**, 145; "April Showers," **Supp. 5**, 630; "At Dawning," **Supp. 4**, 138, 139; "Auld Lang Syne," **Supp. 10**, 463; "Baby, It's Cold Outside," **Supp. 5**, 529; "Battle Cry of Freedom," **Vol. 8, Part 2**, 148; "Battle Hymn of the Republic," **Vol. 5, Part 1**, 292; "Beale Street Blues," **Supp. 6**, 275; "Best Things in Life Are Free, The," **Supp. 8**, 251; "Bird in a Gilded Cage," **Supp. 4**, 835; "Black and Blue," **Supp. 9**, 644; black secular, study of, **Supp. 5**, 520–

21; black spirituals, arrangements of, **Supp. 4**, 126; "Button Up Your Overcoat," **Supp. 8**, 251; "Caledonia," **Supp. 9**, 442; comic melodies, **Supp. 10**, 195–96; "coon," **Supp. 3**, 187; copyright dispute, **Supp. 9**, 442; "Darling Nellie Gray," **Vol. 4, Part 2**, 217; "Deep Purple," **Supp. 5**, 167; "Dixie," **Vol. 3, Part 2**, 148; **Vol. 4, Part 2**, 464; "End of a Perfect Day, The," **Supp. 4**, 94; "Fair Harvard," **Vol. 4, Part 1**, 305; folk songs, **Supp. 1**, 651; **Supp. 4**, 476–77; **Supp. 8**, 234–35, 564; for amateur musicians, **Supp. 4**, 760; "Gesù Bambino," **Supp. 3**, 850; "Give Peace a Chance," **Supp. 10**, 450; "Goin' Home," **Supp. 4**, 276; gospel, **Supp. 9**, 423–25; "Hail Columbia," **Vol. 5, Part 1**, 223; "Happy Birthday to You," **Supp. 4**, 374; "Hello Muddah, Hello Faddah," **Supp. 9**, 720; "Home on the Range," **Supp. 4**, 502; hymns, **Supp. 2**, 49; "I Almost Lost My Mind," **Supp. 9**, 414; "I Don't Care," **Supp. 4**, 814; "Inka Dinka Doo," **Supp. 10**, 195; "Is You Is, or Is You Ain't (Ma Baby)?," **Supp. 9**, 442; "I Want to Be Happy," **Supp. 4**, 918, 919; "I Want to Hold Your Hand," **Supp. 10**, 449; "Light My Fire," **Supp. 9**, 563; "Lord's Prayer, The" **Supp. 6**, 630; lyrics, **Supp. 3**, 338–39, 406; **Supp. 4**, 150, 225–26; **Supp. 7**, 623; **Supp. 8**, 386–87, 546; **Supp. 9**, 280–81, 291, 644–45, 730–32; **Supp. 10**, 251–52, 526–27, 693, 694, 695; "Maryland, My Maryland," **Vol. 8, Part 1**, 348; "Memphis Blues," **Supp. 6**, 275; "Misty," **Supp. 10**, 270; "Mockin' Bird Hill," **Supp. 10**, 251–52; "Morning," **Supp. 4**, 760; "Mother Machree," **Vol. 7, Part 2**, 9; musical comedy, **Supp. 5**, 246; **Supp. 9**, 645; "Muskrat Ramble," **Supp. 9**, 599; "My Funny Valentine," **Supp. 3**, 339; "My Old Kentucky Home," **Vol. 8, Part 2**, 196; "My Wild Irish Rose," **Vol. 7, Part 2**, 9; "Nola," **Supp. 9**, 513; "Ol' Man River," **Supp. 3**, 418; **Supp. 10**, 677; "One Meatball," **Supp. 8**, 696; "On the Banks of the Wabash," **Supp. 3**, 234; "On the Road to Mandalay," **Supp. 4**, 760; operetta, **Supp. 5**, 585; **Supp. 9**, 293; "Over the Rainbow," **Supp. 8**, 204; patriotic songs, **Supp. 3**, 174; "Peggy Sue," **Supp. 6**, 301, 302; "Phi Chi," **Vol. 7, Part 1**, 49; popular ballads, **Supp. 4**, 760, 835–36, 855; "Rebel Girl," **Supp. 7**, 248; religious, **Supp. 9**, 423–25; "Rhapsody in Blue," **Supp. 10**, 299; rock and roll (*see* Rock and roll); "St. Louis Blues," **Supp. 6**, 274, 275; **Supp. 10**, 817; "Saturday Night Fish Fry," **Supp. 9**, 442; "Serenade in Blue," **Supp. 10**, 299; "She Loves You," **Supp. 10**, 449; "Singin' in the Rain," **Supp. 9**, 291; "Slide, Kelly, Slide," **Vol. 5, Part 2**, 310; social protest, **Supp. 10**, 602–3; "Solidarity Forever," **Supp. 7**, 118; "Splish Splash," **Supp. 9**, 219; "Stardust," **Supp. 9**, 887; "Star-Spangled Banner," **Vol. 1, Part 1**, 347; **Vol. 5, Part 2**, 362 f.; **Vol. 7, Part 1**, 506; **Vol. 9, Part 1**, 200; "Strawberry Fields Forever," **Supp. 10**, 450; "String of Pearls," **Supp. 10**, 299; "Sweet Adeline," **Supp. 5**, 23; "Sweet By-and-By, The," **Vol. 1, Part 2**, 190; "Take Me Out to the Ball Game," **Supp. 4**, 836; "Tea for Two," **Supp. 4**, 918, 919; "Ten Cents a Dance," **Supp. 10**, 223; "Tennessee Waltz," **Supp. 10**, 251; Texas themes, **Supp. 8**, 478; "Tramp, Tramp, Tramp, the Boys Are Marching," **Vol. 8, Part 2**, 148; "Tumbling Tumbleweeds," **Supp. 10**, 592; "Vaya con Dios," **Supp. 10**, 252; "White Christmas," **Supp. 9**, 670; "You've Got a Friend," **Supp. 10**, 317. *See also* Folk songs; Music; Singing; Theater, musicals

Songwriters Protective Association, founding of, **Supp. 8**, 546

Sonic depth finder, invention of, **Supp. 1**, 297

Sonnenberg, Gus, reference to, **Supp. 8**, 372

Son of Fury, **Supp. 9**, 697

Sonora Exploring and Mining Co., **Vol. 8, Part 1**, 121 f.

Sons of Liberty: **Vol. 1, Part 1**, 97; **Vol. 3, Part 1**, 550; **Vol. 4, Part 1**, 1; **Vol. 4, Part 2**, 420; **Vol. 5, Part l**, 271, 416; **Vol. 5, Part 2**, 555; **Vol. 6, Part 1**, 326; **Vol. 6, Part 2**, 22; **Vol. 8, Part 1**, 638; **Vol. 8, Part 2**, 255, 495, 539, 589; **Vol. 9, Part 2**, 234, 459; **Vol. 10, Part 2**, 244; organization of, **Vol. 8, Part 1**, 281 f.

Sons of Revolution, **Vol. 9, Part 1**, 617

Sons of Temperance, **Vol. 1, Part 1**, 319; **Vol. 4, Part 2**, 386

Sons of the Pioneers (vocal ensemble), **Supp. 10**, 592–93

Soochow University, **Vol. 1, Part 1**, 215, 263

Soo Line. *See* Minneapolis, St. Paul & Sault Ste. Marie Railway

Sophie Newcomb College, **Vol. 7, Part 1**, 451

So Red the Rose, **Supp. 7**, 811

Sorensen, Charles E., references to, **Supp. 4**, 300, 303, 304

Sorghum, new industry of, **Vol. 5, Part 2**, 232

Sorrento Hotel (Miami, Fla.), **Supp. 7**, 562

Sothern, Edward H., reference to, **Supp. 4**, 552–54

Soule University, presidency of, **Vol. 7, Part 1**, 102

Souls of Black Folk, The, **Supp. 7**, 202, 205

Sound: binaural research, **Supp. 6**, 365; fathometer, **Supp. 1**, 297; high-fidelity, **Supp. 5**, 324; recording devices, **Supp. 1**, 121. *See also* Acoustics; Audio systems

Sound and the Fury, The, **Supp. 7**, 232, 233

"Sound money," **Vol. 3, Part 2**, 252; **Vol. 7, Part 2**, 69; **Vol. 8, Part 1**, 92 f.

Sound-reproducing machine, invention of, **Vol. 3, Part 1**, 221

Sousa, John Philip, references to, **Supp. 3**, 610; **Supp. 8**, 381

South, Washington, D. C., newspaper, founding of, **Vol. 8, Part 1**, 255 f.

South (U.S.): Baptist church in, **Vol. 10, Part 2**, 304, 389; black colleges and universities in, **Supp. 4**, 916; black education in, **Supp. 5**, 55–56; black stereotypical writings, **Supp. 4**, 102–3; civil rights movement, **Supp. 8**, 333–35, 539; education in, **Vol. 2, Part 1**, 378; **Vol. 2, Part 2**, 321, 606; **Vol. 5, Part 2**, 227; **Vol. 10, Part 2**, 495; education promotion, **Supp. 3**, 209; first anti-lynching law, **Supp. 8**, 67; first congresswoman from, **Supp. 5**, 582; folklore, **Supp. 1**, 649; fundamentalism, **Supp. 3**, 129; historical writings on, **Supp. 1**, 303, 597; **Supp. 2**, 153; **Supp. 3**, 31–32; **Supp. 5**, 671–72; **Supp. 6**, 491–92; hookworm control, **Supp. 3**, 738; industrial development, **Vol. 3, Part 1**, 496 f.; **Vol. 3, Part 2**, 169; **Vol. 9, Part 2**, 581; labor movement in, **Supp. 6**, 433–34; liberal journalism, **Supp. 7**, 323–24; living conditions for blacks, **Supp. 10**, 306; Loyalists' "Snow Campaign," **Vol. 8, Part 1**, 42; Methodism, spread of, **Vol. 2, Part 1**, 483; **Vol. 5, Part 2**, 579; New South journalism, **Supp. 8**, 404–5; novels about, **Vol. 7, Part 1**, 132; **Vol. 8, Part 1**, 395; photography of early architecture, **Supp. 5**, 373; race relations, **Supp. 6**, 11–12, 322; **Supp. 9**, 391–92; **Supp. 10**, 307; race relations, writings on, **Supp. 8**, 605–6; **Supp. 10**, 292; railroads, building, **Vol. 7, Part 2**, 647; rural vocational guidance, **Supp. 4**, 365–66; senatorial archetype, **Supp. 6**, 234; social and economic view of, **Vol. 9, Part 2**, 639; tenant farming, **Supp. 7**, 781; textile industry in, **Supp. 5**, 252; writings on, **Supp. 3**, 147–48

South Africa: African Methodist Episcopal Church diocese, **Supp. 5**, 259; medical missions, **Supp. 4**, 519–20; mining, **Supp. 2**, 701

South America: diamond mining, **Vol. 10, Part 2**, 261;

diplomatic relations with, **Vol. 1, Part 1**, 271; **Vol. 3, Part 2**, 507; **Vol. 4, Part 2**, 162; **Vol. 7, Part 1**, 139; **Vol. 8, Part 2**, 83; explorations, **Vol. 2, Part 2**, 103; **Vol. 3, Part 2**, 465 f.; **Vol. 7, Part 1**, 594; Indians, study of, **Vol. 3, Part 2**, 269; missionary work in, **Vol. 10, Part 2**, 474; promoter in, **Vol. 4, Part 2**, 517; **Vol. 5, Part 1**, 208–9; railroad building, **Vol. 2, Part 2**, 103; **Vol. 6, Part 2**, 501; **Vol. 10, Part 2**, 63; researches in, **Vol. 1, Part 1**, 571; Roosevelt, T. R., trip to, **Vol. 8, Part 2**, 143; shipping, American, **Vol. 1, Part 2**, 241; writings on, **Vol. 5, Part 2**, 565 f. *See also* Latin America; *specific country names*

Southampton, Long Island, founding of, **Vol. 7, Part 2**, 588

South Atlantic Quarterly, **Vol. 1, Part 2**, 39

South Bend, Ind., public service, **Vol. 7, Part 2**, 21

Southborough, Mass., history of, **Vol. 2, Part 1**, 299

South Carolina: Acadians, **Vol. 6, Part 1**, 538 f.; Act of 1828, opposition to, **Vol. 8, Part 1**, 30 f.; agriculture, **Vol. 4, Part 2**, 85, 609; **Vol. 8, Part 1**, 397; antebellum development, **Vol. 2, Part 1**, 365; architecture, **Vol. 7, Part 1**, 11 f.; banking, **Vol. 6, Part 1**, 131; Baptist State Convention, **Vol. 5, Part 2**, 130; Bluffton tariff movement, **Vol. 7, Part 2**, 59; **Vol. 8, Part 1**, 526; botany, **Vol. 10, Part 1**, 396 f.; boundary disputes, **Vol. 5, Part 2**, 140; **Vol. 8, Part 1**, 42; carpetbagging, **Vol. 1, Part 1**, 127; Civil War period, **Vol. 6, Part 2**, 203; **Vol. 10, Part 2**, 602; colonial administration, **Vol. 6, Part 2**, 234 f., 598; **Vol. 7, Part 1**, 379; **Vol. 8, Part 1**, 509; **Vol. 9, Part 2**, 649; **Vol. 10, Part 2**, 542, 604; colonization, **Vol. 2, Part 1**, 252; **Vol. 10, Part 2**, 11; Constitution, ratification of federal, **Vol. 2, Part 1**, 280; **Vol. 8, Part 1**, 237 f.; constitution, state, **Vol. 8, Part 2**, 258; cotton industry, **Vol. 4, Part 2**, 200; **Vol. 10, Part 1**, 570; Democratic party, **Vol. 7, Part 2**, 59; duelling, laws against, **Vol. 3, Part 1**, 152; education, **Vol. 4, Part 2**, 85; **Vol. 5, Part 2**, 130; **Vol. 6, Part 2**, 238; **Vol. 8, Part 1**, 444; **Vol. 9, Part 2**, 459; Episcopal bishop, first, **Vol. 9, Part 1**, 336; exploration of interior, **Vol. 10, Part 2**, 509; Federalists, **Vol. 4, Part 2**, 286; Female Institute (first women's school in South), **Vol. 6, Part 2**, 289; Fort King George, built 1721, **Vol. 1, Part 1**, 640; Georgia, help of, in founding, **Vol. 5, Part 2**, 117; governors, **Vol. 1, Part 1**, 71 f., 223 f.; **Vol. 1, Part 2**, 436; **Vol. 2, Part 1**, 252, 365 f., 595; **Vol. 3, Part 1**, 444 f.; **Vol. 4, Part 1, 325; Vol. 4, Part 2**, 85, 187 f., 189 f., 207 f., 213, 456; **Vol. 5, Part 2**, 117; **Vol. 6, Part 2**, 203 f., 251 f., 404 f.; **Vol. 7, Part 1**, 275, f., 293 f.; **Vol. 7, Part 2**, 59 f., 483 f., 559 f., 611 f., 617 f.; **Vol. 8, Part 2**, 257 f., 498 f.; **Vol. 9, Part 1**, 184 f.; **Vol. 9, Part 2**, 458 f., 547 f.; **Vol. 10, Part 2**, 253 f.; **Supp. 3**, 77–78; **Supp. 5**, 482; **Supp. 7**, 398; history of, **Vol. 2, Part 1**, 253; **Vol. 3, Part 1**, 182; **Vol. 5, Part 1**, 287; **Vol. 8, Part 1**, 30 f., 118 f., 270 f., 338, 395, 633 f; **Vol. 9, Part 1**, 172, 277; ichthyology, **Vol. 5, Part 1**, 130; immigrants, social work among, **Vol. 8, Part 1**, 295; indigo culture, **Vol. 7, Part 2**, 316; industrial development, **Vol. 6, Part 2**, 235; **Vol. 10, Part 1**, 570; **Vol. 10, Part 2**, 254; insane, care of, **Vol. 2, Part 2**, 415; judiciary, **Supp. 8**, 682; judiciary prior to Civil War, **Vol. 2, Part 1**, 355; laws, codification of, **Vol. 8, Part 1**, 118 f.; legal service, **Vol. 1, Part 2**, 436, 609; **Vol. 3, Part 1**, 254; **Vol. 4, Part 1**, 634; **Vol. 5, Part 2**, 155; **Vol. 6, Part 1**, 131; **Vol. 7, Part 2**, 42; **Vol. 8, Part 1**, 118, 237, 425, 526; **Vol. 9, Part 1**, 172, 184, 360; limestone works in, **Vol. 8, Part 1**, 397; Loyalists, **Vol. 9, Part 2**, 489; **Vol. 10, Part 1**, 644 f.; **Vol. 10, Part 2**, 542; map of, first, **Vol. 3, Part 1**, 182; medical service, **Vol. 2, Part 2**, 415; **Vol. 6, Part 2**, 593; newspaper, first weekly, **Vol. 10, Part 1**, 644 f.; nullification movement, **Vol. 2, Part 1**, 414; **Vol. 3, Part 2**, 101, 115; **Vol. 4, Part 2**, 458; **Vol. 6, Part 2**, 35, 251, 601, 640; **Vol. 10, Part 1**, 56 f.; ornithology, **Vol. 10, Part 1**, 565; plantations, **Vol. 6, Part 1**, 33; political service, **Vol. 1, Part 1**, 71, 223, 229, 338; **Vol. 1, Part 2**, 436, 608, 609; **Vol. 2, Part 2**, 57; **Vol. 4, Part 1**, 325, 598; **Vol. 4, Part 2**, 85, 187, 189, 207, 215, 285, 458; **Vol. 5, Part 2**, 117; **Vol. 6, Part 1**, 33, 145, 472 f., 538; **Vol. 6, Part 2**, 34, 203, 251, 617, 640; **Vol. 7, Part 1**, 128, 275, 293; **Vol. 7, Part 2**, 59, 483, 514, 516, 559, 612; **Vol. 8, Part 1**, 30, 202, 207, 237, 327, 338, 425, 501, 526; **Vol. 8, Part 2**, 258, 498; **Vol. 9, Part 1**, 172, 184; **Vol. 9, Part 2**, 547; **Vol. 10, Part 2**, 254, 390; politics, **Supp. 3**, 78, 723–24; **Supp. 5**, 481–82; **Supp. 8**, 538; **Supp. 9**, 150, 152; post-Revolution politics, **Vol. 2, Part 1**, 365, 368; pre–Civil War politics, **Vol. 6, Part 1**, 145; **Vol. 9, Part 2**, 474; pre-Revolutionary agitation, **Vol. 6, Part 2**, 599; printing, introduction of, **Vol. 8, Part 1**, 634; public service, **Vol. 3, Part 2**, 418; **Vol. 4, Part 1**, 475; **Vol. 4, Part 2**, 187, 190 f., 207, 212 f., 214, 457, 609; **Vol. 5, Part 1**, 165; **Vol. 5, Part 2**, 333, 360, 395; **Vol. 6, Part 1**, 35 f., 158, 473; **Vol. 6, Part 2**, 527; **Vol. 7, Part 1**, 579; **Vol. 7, Part 2**, 614 f.; **Vol. 8, Part 1**, 30 f.; **Vol. 9, Part 2**, 639; "Rangers," **Vol. 9, Part 2**, 489; Reconstruction, **Vol. 2, Part 1**, 364, 404, 595; **Vol. 2, Part 2**, 58; **Vol. 4, Part 1**, 373; **Vol. 6, Part 2**, 1; **Vol. 7, Part 2**, 59, 483; **Vol. 8, Part 1**, 118 f.; **Vol. 8, Part 2**, 332; **Vol. 10, Part 2**, 558; "Regulators," **Vol. 9, Part 2**, 489; representation in, reapportionment of, **Vol. 3, Part 1**, 254; Republican party, **Vol. 7, Part 2**, 613 f.; **Vol. 8, Part 1**, 327 f.; Revolutionary War period, **Vol. 2, Part 1**, 253, 465; **Vol. 4, Part 1**, 82 f., 134; **Vol. 8, Part 2**, 259; **Vol. 10, Part 2**, 299; rice seeds, smuggling of, **Vol. 5, Part 2**, 22; secession, **Vol. 2, Part 1**, 213; **Vol. 4, Part 1**, 325; **Vol. 7, Part 2**, 560; **Vol. 8, Part 1**, 395, 526 f.; **Vol. 10, Part 1**, 56 f., separation from North Carolina, **Vol. 5, Part 2**, 117; settler, first English in, **Vol. 10, Part 2**, 508; slavery, **Vol. 2, Part 1**, 416; slave trade, **Vol. 6, Part 1**, 32; **Vol. 3, Part 1**, 275; Swiss colonists, **Vol. 8, Part 1**, 270 f.; temperance reform, **Vol. 7, Part 2**, 43; trade, **Vol. 4, Part 1**, 296; Unionist party, **Vol. 5, Part 1**, 343; **Vol. 7, Part 2**, 483; **Vol. 8, Part 1**, 30 f.; Unitarian church, **Vol. 6, Part 1**, 151

South Carolina College, **Vol. 4, Part 2**, 560; founding of, **Vol. 7, Part 2**, 616; **Vol. 9, Part 2**, 507; history of, **Vol. 5, Part 2**, 518; reorganization of, **Vol. 7, Part 1**, 581

South Carolina Institute, **Vol. 4, Part 1**, 600

South Carolina Railroad, **Vol. 4, Part 1**, 83; **Vol. 4, Part 2**, 458

South Carolina Women in the Confederacy, **Vol. 8, Part 1**, 395

South Dakota: Catholic church, **Vol. 7, Part 2**, 3; education, **Vol. 10, Part 1**, 429 f.; **Vol. 10, Part 2**, 625; governors, **Vol. 6, Part 2**, 518; **Supp. 2**, 491; Indian lands, **Vol. 4, Part 1**, 502; Mt. Rushmore memorial, **Supp. 3**, 88–89; political service, **Vol. 6, Part 1**, 426; **Vol. 7, Part 2**, 517; **Vol. 10, Part 1**, 429 f.; politics, **Supp. 9**, 572; public service, **Vol. 9, Part 2**, 643–44; scientific service, **Vol. 9, Part 1**, 74; statehood, admission to, **Vol. 6, Part 2**, 518

Southeast Asia Treaty Organization (SEATO), founding of, **Supp. 6**, 179

Southeastern State Teachers College, presidency, **Supp. 5**, 48

South End House (Boston), **Supp. 6**, 499

Southern Association for College Women, **Vol. 7, Part 2**, 257

Southern Association of Colleges and Secondary Schools, founding of, **Supp. 2**, 361

Southern Baptist Theological Seminary, founding of, **Vol. 1, Part 2**, 524; **Vol. 7, Part 1**, 322 f.
Southern Christian Leadership Conference, **Supp. 8**, 388; founding of, **Supp. 8**, 333–35
Southern Christian Leadership Council, founding of, **Supp. 10**, 170–71
Southern Conference Education Fund, **Supp. 7**, 788
Southern Education Board, **Vol. 4, Part 1**, 36; **Vol. 7, Part 1**, 348
Southern Electric Railway Co., **Vol. 7, Part 2**, 62
Southern Farm and Dairy, **Vol. 9, Part 2**, 38
Southern Farm and Home, **Supp. 7**, 788
Southern Historical Association: **Supp. 10**, 844; racial segregation policy, **Supp. 10**, 841
Southern Historical Society, **Vol. 5, Part 2**, 191 f.; **Vol. 10, Part 1**, 603 f.
Southern History Association, founding of, **Supp. 1**, 591
Southern Illinois University Press, **Supp. 6**, 329
Southern Literary Messenger: **Vol. 7, Part 1, 27; Vol. 4, Part 2**, 489; **Vol. 6, Part 1**, 558; **Vol. 7, Part 1**, 25; **Vol. 9, Part 2**, 558; founding and history of, **Vol. 10, Part 2**, 121
Southern literature: **Supp. 3**, 303–5, 597–98, 637–38; **Supp. 6**, 116, 445; **Supp. 7**, 38, 613, 725, 811–12; **Supp. 8**, 400–2; Mississippi-based, **Supp. 7**, 231–35; opposition to traditional sentimentality, **Supp. 9**, 642; regional poetry, **Supp. 4**, 285–86; rural "Gothic," **Supp. 7**, 582–83; rural poverty theme, **Supp. 5**, 560; writers' convention, **Supp. 7**, 797
"Southern Manifesto," **Supp. 9**, 104, 190–91, 401
Southern Methodist Church. *See* Methodist church
Southern Methodist University, presidency of, **Vol. 5, Part 1**, 454
Southern Monitor, **Vol. 5, Part 2**, 183
Southern Mother's Hospital, Civil War, **Vol. 6, Part 1**, 42
Southern Pacific Railroad: **Vol. 5, Part 1**, 409, 415; **Vol. 9, Part 1**, 503; **Supp. 1**, 672; **Supp. 3**, 393–95; **Supp. 4**, 707; **Supp. 5**, 283–84; **Supp. 5**, 309, 310; administration, **Supp. 1**, 672
Southern Patriot, **Vol. 7, Part 2**, 483
Southern Pines Pilot, **Supp. 3**, 93
Southern Planter, **Vol. 1, Part 2**, 472
Southern Power Co., **Vol. 3, Part 1**, 497 f.
Southern Presbyterian Review, founding of, **Vol. 7, Part 2**, 176
Southern Railway, **Vol. 1, Part 1**, 549; **Vol. 5, Part 1**, 484 f.; **Vol. 6, Part 1**, 368; **Supp. 2**, 287; **Supp. 3**, 125
Southern Recorder, The, political influence of, **Vol. 4, Part 1**, 615 f.
Southern Review, **Vol. 1, Part 2**, 365; **Vol. 4, Part 2**, 589
Southern Ruralist, **Vol. 9, Part 2**, 38
Southern Tenant Farmers Union, **Supp. 7**, 781
Southern Union Gas Co., **Supp. 8**, 454
Southern University, presidency, **Supp. 8**, 86–87
Southern Woman's Educational Alliance, founding of, **Supp. 4**, 365
South Halsted Street Bridge (Chicago), **Supp. 3**, 332
South Improvement Co., founding of, **Supp. 2**, 570
South Korea: missions in, **Supp. 10**, 637; U.S. occupation of, **Supp. 7**, 352
South Mountain Association (Mass.), founding of, **Supp. 5**, 128
South Pacific, **Supp. 6**, 511; **Supp. 8**, 238–39; **Supp. 10**, 694
South Pole. *See* Antarctica
South Seas: adventures in, **Vol. 4, Part 2**, 451; ethnobotany, **Vol. 8, Part 2**, 289; naval expedition, **Vol. 4, Part 2**, 451; **Vol. 8, Part 2**, 77 f., 289; swindles, **Vol. 4, Part 2**, 452; trade, pioneer in, **Vol. 3, Part 2**, 266; writings on, **Vol. 5, Part 2**, 534; **Vol. 7, Part 1**, 609–10
Southside Democrat, founding of, **Vol. 8, Part 1**, 225 f.
South Today, The, founding of, **Supp. 8**, 605
Southwest (U.S.): archaeology in, **Vol. 1, Part 1**, 588; **Supp. 7**, 432, 570; historical writings on, **Supp. 5**, 570; history of, **Vol. 6, Part 1**, 502; Know-Nothing party, promotion of, **Vol. 7, Part 2**, 594; outlaw, famous, **Vol. 7, Part 1**, 369 f.; pioneer life in, **Vol. 6, Part 2**, 50; **Vol. 10, Part 1**, 638 f.; Spanish exploration, **Vol. 2, Part 2**, 449 f.; Spanish-Indian frontier, **Vol. 7, Part 2**, 199 f.; Spanish influence, **Vol. 6, Part 1**, 7 f.; writings on, **Supp. 7**, 189
Southwest Cattle Raiser's Association, **Supp. 9**, 460
Southwestern Baptist Theological Seminary, founding of, **Supp. 3**, 687
Southwestern Christian Advocate, **Vol. 8, Part 1**, 513; **Vol. 9, Part 2**, 337
Southwestern State Normal School (California), **Vol. 7, Part 1**, 578
Southwestern University, **Vol. 5, Part 1**, 453; **Vol. 7, Part 1**, 102; **Vol. 7, Part 2**, 176
Sovereign, James R., reference to, **Supp. 3**, 346
Soviet Union: agricultural development, **Supp. 4**, 699; armed forces and defense, **Supp. 3**, 165–66; atomic bomb manufacture, **Supp. 8**, 230; Berlin blockade, **Supp. 10**, 128; Catholic church, **Supp. 6**, 662; cold war policies, **Supp. 7**, 423–24; diplomacy with U.S., **Supp. 4**, 772; **Supp. 5**, 334; **Supp. 6**, 147; **Supp. 7**, 438, 703, 714; **Supp. 8**, 61; **Supp. 9**, 105, 106, 107, 799; espionage in U.S., **Supp. 5**, 564, 588–90, 714; **Supp. 7**, 51–52, 113–14, 244; **Supp. 8**, 135, 162, 230; **Supp. 9**, 3–4, 321–22; first American orchestra to play in, **Supp. 8**, 451; first jazz orchestra, **Supp. 3**, 690; first U.S. ambassador to, **Supp. 8**, 61; food aid, **Supp. 7**,359; foreign correspondents in, **Supp. 6**, 184; genetics studies, **Supp. 8**, 449, 450; industrial architecture, **Supp. 3**, 405; journalism about, **Supp. 8**, 635; **Supp. 10**, 800; missiles in Cuba, **Supp. 7**, 423, 724; **Supp. 8**, 323; **Supp. 9**, 799; photographic accounts, **Supp. 9**, 111; postwar distrust of, **Supp. 10**, 216; racial prejudice absence, **Supp. 10**, 678; railway system, **Supp. 3**, 736; revolutionary period, writings on, **Supp. 9**, 875–76; space program, **Supp. 7**, 424; **Supp. 8**, 159; Stalinism and U.S. Communists, **Supp. 6**, 598; submarines, **Supp. 3**, 436; Trotsky-Stalin split, **Supp. 8**, 149–50; U.S. Communist party, relationship with, **Supp. 7**, 179–81, 268–69; U.S. labor movement and, **Supp. 3**, 347; U.S. nonrecognition policy, **Supp. 3**, 219; **Supp. 4**, 171; **Supp. 5**, 579; **Supp. 7**, 536; U.S. recognition of, **Supp. 3**, 657; U.S. Socialists' opposition to, **Supp. 3**, 298; U.S. trade discussions, **Supp. 10**, 204, 271; U-2 overflights, **Supp. 8**, 147, 159, 258; **Supp. 10**, 646–47; UN membership, **Supp. 5**, 538; writings on, **Supp. 8**, 172, 260–61; **Supp. 9**, 567; Yalta Conference (1945), **Supp. 3**, 663. *See also* Cold war; Russia; Russian Revolution (1917); World War II
Soybean, introduced into U.S., **Supp. 5**, 214
Spaatz, Carl A., references to, **Supp. 4**, 29; **Supp. 10**, 826
Space, radio wave emissions from, **Supp. 4**, 422–23
Space exploration: Apollo disaster, **Supp. 8**, 81, 225, 694; congressional proponents, **Supp. 7**, 79, 429; first U.S. extravehicular activity, **Supp. 8**, 694; Gemini projects, **Supp. 8**, 694; international law advocacy, **Supp. 8**, 5; moon program, **Supp. 7**, 424, 429; pioneer work in, **Supp. 3**, 305–8; rocket development, **Supp. 3**, 305–8; Soviet program, **Supp. 7**, 424; **Supp. 8**, 159; technical development for, **Supp. 7**, 411; writings on, **Supp. 8**, 379–80
Spain: *Black Warrior* affair, **Vol. 3, Part 1**, 344; bound-

ary disputes, **Vol. 5, Part 2**, 423; church properties, restoration, **Vol. 7, Part 1**, 625–26; colonial policy in America, **Vol. 3, Part 1**, 422; **Vol. 4, Part 1**, 120; **Vol. 6, Part 1**, 7 f.; **Vol. 7, Part 1**, 593 f.; **Vol. 5, Part 2**, 323; **Vol. 7, Part 1**, 274 f.; **Vol. 8, Part 2**, 543 f.; **Vol. 9, Part 2**, 601 f.; conquistador, **Vol. 7, Part 1**, 382; "Conspiracy," **Vol. 3, Part 1**, 80; **Vol. 7, Part 1**, 483; **Vol. 8, Part 2**, 25; diplomatic relations, **Vol. 1, Part 1**, 75 f., 105, 648; **Vol. 1, Part 2**, 502; **Vol. 2, Part 1**, 498; **Vol. 3, Part 1**, 164, 507 f., 609 f.; **Vol. 3, Part 2**, 399; **Vol. 4, Part 1**, 478; **Vol. 5, Part 1**, 510; **Vol. 5, Part 2**, 6 f.; **Vol. 6, Part 1**, 463; **Vol. 7, Part 1**, 96; **Vol. 7, Part 2**, 613, 619; **Vol. 8, Part 1**, 353 f.; **Vol. 8, Part 2**, 383; **Vol. 9, Part 1**, 406; **Vol. 9, Part 2**, 93, 326; **Vol. 10, Part 2**, 490; **Supp. 4**, 864; **Supp. 6**, 72–73; **Supp. 7**, 53, 330–31; explorations, **Vol. 4, Part 1**, 132; **Vol. 6, Part 1**, 504; **Vol. 8, Part 1**, 109 f.; Florida, colony proposed in, **Vol. 7, Part 1**, 632; Georgia, relations with, **Vol. 7, Part 2**, 2; historical writings on, **Supp. 2**, 561; Kentucky plots (1806), **Vol. 8, Part 2**, 195; music, **Supp. 1**, 651; telephone system, **Supp. 6**, 43; Texas, Spanish-American legal procedure, **Vol. 4, Part 2**, 520

Spain: A Study of Her Life and Arts, **Supp. 5**, 700

Spalding, A. G., references to, **Vol. 1, Part 1**, 311; **Vol. 2, Part 1**, 587

Spam (canned meat), **Supp. 4**, 396; **Supp. 5**, 315

Spangler, Edward, reference to, **Vol. 1, Part 2**, 451

Spangler, James Murray, reference to, **Supp. 5**, 313

Spanish-American War (specific battles under separate headings): **Vol. 1, Part 1**, 180; **Vol. 5, Part 2**, 501; **Vol. 6, Part 1**, 269; **Vol. 8, Part 2**, 511 f.; **Vol. 10, Part 2**, 467; Bureau of Supplies and Accounts, **Vol. 9, Part 2**, 8; camp conditions, **Vol. 8, Part 2**, 137; diplomatic negotiations during, **Vol. 3, Part 1**, 164; engineering, **Vol. 6, Part 1**, 496; financing of, **Vol. 4, Part 1**, 86; "gauntlet scandal," **Supp. 3**, 464; military service, **Vol. 1, Part 1**, 400; **Vol. 1, Part 2**, 51, 395; **Vol. 2, Part 1**, 71, 586, 589; **Vol. 2, Part 2**, 123, 252; **Vol. 3, Part 1**, 116, 218, 303; **Vol. 3, Part 2**, 178, 210, 570; **Vol. 4, Part 1**, 89, 487; **Vol. 4, Part 2**, 41, 66; **Vol. 5, Part 1**, 63, 316, 382, 570; **Vol. 6, Part 1**, 3, 62, 104, 407; **Vol. 6, Part 2**, 573, 615; **Vol. 7, Part 2**, 100, 553; **Vol. 8, Part 2**, 137, 181, 199; **Vol. 9, Part 1**, 15, 287, 489; **Vol. 9, Part 2**, 381; **Vol. 10, Part 1**, 104, 445, 532; **Vol. 10, Part 2**, 51; naval preparations for, **Vol. 3, Part 1**, 270 f.; naval service, **Vol. 3, Part 1**, 108, 234, 269 f., 464 f., 584 f., 614 f.; **Vol. 3, Part 2**, 170; **Vol. 4, Part 1**, 485; **Vol. 4, Part 2**, 2; **Vol. 5, Part 2**, 298, 462; **Vol. 6, Part 1**, 564; **Vol. 6, Part 2**, 129; **Vol. 7, Part 1**, 342–43, 438, 480; **Vol. 7, Part 2**, 535, 607; **Vol. 8, Part 1**, 17 f., 237, 316 f., 495; **Vol. 8, Part 2**, 288, 322, 464–65; **Vol. 9, Part 1**, 156, 387 f.; **Vol. 9, Part 2**, 127; **Vol. 10, Part 1**, 135, 545 f., 601 f., 632 f.; news photography of, **Supp. 4**, 361; peace treaty, **Supp. 4**, 598; political events leading up to, **Vol. 6, Part 2**, 107 f.; propaganda, **Supp. 3**, 75–76; Rough Riders, **Vol. 8, Part 2**, 137; **Supp. 6**, 206; war correspondent during, **Vol. 7, Part 2**, 154; yellow journalism on, **Supp. 5**, 284–85

Spanish Civil War: **Supp. 5**, 500; **Supp. 7**, 337; Abraham Lincoln Brigade hearings, **Supp. 6**, 413; American relief, **Supp. 3**, 137, 237; black participation, **Supp. 8**, 287; **Supp. 10**, 678; International Brigade, **Supp. 8**, 172; Loyalist supporters, **Supp. 6**, 72–73; writings on, **Supp. 8**, 255

Spanish Fort, Ala. *See* Mobile, Ala.

Spanish literature and language: drama studies: **Supp. 2**, 131; studies in, **Supp. 1**, 406; **Supp. 4**, 719; textbooks on, **Supp. 2**, 132

Spanknoebel, Hans, reference to, **Supp. 9**, 660

Spark plugs, **Supp. 4**, 244

Sparks, Jared, reference to, **Vol. 7, Part 2**, 169

"Spartacus to the Gladiators," **Vol. 5, Part 2**, 303

Spartan Association, opposition to Tammany, **Vol. 10, Part 1**, 390 f.

Spas, **Supp. 8**, 13

Spaulding, Edward G., reference to, **Supp. 5**, 503

Spaulding, Francis, reference to, **Supp. 9**, 25

Speaker, Tris, references to, **Supp. 3**, 438; **Supp. 9**, 403

Spearmint gum, **Supp. 1**, 715

Special Intelligence Service. *See under* Federal Bureau of Investigation (FBI)

Specimens of American Poetry, first comprehensive anthology, **Vol. 5, Part 2**, 361

Speck, Frank G., reference to, **Supp. 5**, 533

Spectroscopy: **Vol. 1, Part 1**, 230; **Vol. 1, Part 2**, 606; **Vol. 3, Part 1**, 436; **Vol. 6, Part 1**, 213, 406 f., **Vol. 7, Part 1**, 492; **Vol. 8, Part 1**, 264; **Vol. 8, Part 2**, 198, 256; **Vol. 9, Part 2**, 655; design improvements, **Supp. 2**, 92; **Supp. 4**, 818; parallaxes, **Supp. 6**, 7; research in, **Supp. 1**, 383

Spectrum, research in, **Supp. 10**, 288

Speculation: land, **Vol. 3, Part 1**, 390, 486 f.; **Vol. 5, Part 1**, 461, 527; **Vol. 6, Part 1**, 448; **Vol. 7, Part 1**, 170; **Vol. 8, Part 1**, 601; **Vol. 8, Part 2**, 178, 494, 604; **Vol. 9, Part 2**, 651; railroads, **Vol. 3, Part 2**, 415; **Vol. 4, Part 2**, 393; stock, **Vol. 4, Part 2**, 411; **Vol. 5, Part 1**, 437; **Vol. 5, Part 2**, 283; **Vol. 6, Part 1**, 60; **Vol. 8, Part 2**, 267; wheat "corner" in, **Vol. 6, Part 1**, 157

Speech: acoustic method for deaf children, **Supp. 3**, 311; aphasia treatment, **Supp. 1**, 317; **Supp. 4**, 570; deaf education, **Supp. 3**, 311; disorders, **Supp. 7**, 395–96; science of, **Vol. 1, Part 2**, 152; stammering, **Supp. 3**, 191; visible speech, **Vol. 1, Part 2**, 149. *See also* Deaf and deafness; Stuttering

Speech, freedom of. *See* Censorship; Civil liberties; Libel

Speedboats, racing, **Supp. 9**, 892; **Supp. 10**, 464

Speedwell Society, founding of, **Supp. 3**, 160

Speidel, Merritt, references to, **Supp. 9**, 741, 742

Speidel Newspapers, Inc., holding company established, **Supp. 9**, 742

Spellacy, Thomas J., reference to, **Supp. 9**, 57

Spelling: books, **Vol. 1, Part 1**, 501; **Vol. 2, Part 2, 244 f.**; **Vol. 9, Part 2**, 444; **Vol. 10, Part 1**, 594 f.; Dakota language, **Vol. 8, Part 1**, 61 f.; phonetic, **Vol. 6, Part 2**, 379; simplified, **Vol. 1, Part 1**, 298; **Vol. 4, Part 2**, 522; **Vol. 6, Part 1**, 430; **Vol. 9, Part 2**, 423; teaching of, **Vol. 6, Part 1**, 73

Spellman, Cardinal Francis J., references to, **Supp. 8**, 25, 114; **Supp. 10**, 497

Spence-Chapin Adoption Service, founding of, **Supp. 3**, 160

Spencer, Herbert, references to, **Supp. 1**, 340; **Supp. 3**, 697; **Supp. 5**, 591, 592

Spencer, Philip, reference to, **Vol. 9, Part 2**, 457

Spencer, Theodore, reference to, **Supp. 4**, 56

Spender, Stephen, reference to, **Supp. 9**, 53

Sperry, Elmer, reference to, **Supp. 7**, 576–77

Sperry, Warren M., reference to, **Supp. 3**, 693

Sperry automatic pilot, **Supp. 6**, 221

Sperry Gyroscope Co., **Supp. 4**, 358; **Supp. 7**, 576–77

Sperry Rand Corporation, **Supp. 6**, 675; predecessors, **Supp. 5**, 228, 229

Spewack, Bella, references to, **Supp. 9**, 748, 749

Spewack, Samuel. *See* Abbott, A. A.

Speyer & Co., **Supp. 3**, 728–29

Speyer School (Teachers College, New York City), **Supp. 3**, 677

Sphymograph, making of, **Vol. 5, Part 2**, 366

Spicer Manufacturing Co., **Supp. 9**, 216–17

Spiders: museum collection, **Supp. 3**, 478; studies of, **Vol. 6, Part 1**, 603; **Vol. 7, Part 1**, 100; **Supp. 1**, 287
Spies: alleged, **Supp. 10**, 134; service as, **Vol. 1, Part 1**, 563; **Vol. 4, Part 2**, 108; **Vol. 7, Part 1**, 106; **Vol. 8, Part 2**, 109; **Vol. 9, Part 2**, 138 f.; **Vol. 10, Part 1**, 659; **Supp. 9**, 2–4, 60–61, 83, 321–22; **Supp. 10**, 101, 646–47. *See also* Espionage
Spiller, William G., reference to, **Supp. 3**, 386
Spillman, William J., reference to, **Supp. 4**, 45
Spinach, nutritional value, **Supp. 5**, 623
Spinal cord: analgesia, **Supp. 6**, 435; surgery, **Supp. 6**, 130–31. *See also* Nervous system
Spinden, Herbert J., reference to, **Supp. 3**, 819
Spingarn, Joel E., reference to, **Supp. 4**, 135
Spink, Charles, reference to, **Supp. 7**, 711
Spinning machinery, **Vol. 2, Part 1**, 156; **Vol. 3, Part 1**, 600; **Vol. 6, Part 1**, 456; **Vol. 9, Part 2**, 508
Spiral nebulae, **Supp. 3**, 208
Spirit of St. Louis (airplane), **Supp. 4**, 473; **Supp. 9**, 496
Spirit of St. Louis, The (autobiography and film), **Supp. 9**, 498
Spirit of the Pilgrims (periodical), founding of, to controvert Unitarianism, **Vol. 8, Part 1**, 58
Spiritualism: **Vol. 2, Part 2**, 285; **Vol. 3, Part 1**, 84, 105, 353; **Vol. 3, Part 2**, 9, 571; **Vol. 4, Part 1**, 542, 631; **Vol. 4, Part 2**, 264, 322, 408, 473; **Vol. 5, Part 1**, 196, 249; **Vol. 5, Part 2**, 406; **Vol. 6, Part 1**, 103; **Vol. 7, Part 1**, 449, 470; **Vol. 8, Part 2**, 356; **Vol. 9, Part 1**, 439, 470; **Vol. 9, Part 2**, 510; Fox sisters, **Vol. 3, Part 1**, 540; investigations of, first public, **Vol. 8, Part 1**, 117; lectures delivered while in a state of trance, **Vol. 3, Part 1**, 105; prophecy, **Vol. 5, Part 2**, 160; satire on, **Vol. 7, Part 1**, 63; writings on, **Vol. 2, Part 1**, 179; **Vol. 3, Part 1**, 105, 354; **Vol. 4, Part 1**, 162; **Vol. 8, Part 1**, 117
Spirituals, **Supp. 3**, 225–26; **Supp. 4**, 126
"Splish Splash," **Supp. 9**, 219
Spofford, Daniel H., reference to, **Vol. 3, Part 2**, 10
Spoils system: **Vol. 1, Part 1**, 374; **Vol. 5, Part 2**, 29; **Vol. 8, Part 1**, 34 f.; **Vol. 8, Part 2**, 10; introduction of, **Vol. 6, Part 2**, 275; **Supp. 2**, 399
Spokane, Wash., early history of, **Vol. 3, Part 1**, 237 f.
Spoliation claims, French, **Vol. 1, Part 2**, 23
Sponges, studies of, **Vol. 5, Part 1**, 447
Spooner, John C., reference to, **Vol. 8, Part 2**, 396
Spoon River Anthology, **Supp. 4**, 555
Sporophyte, **Supp. 5**, 98
Sporting goods, manufacturing of, **Vol. 8, Part 1**, 418 f.; **Vol. 9, Part 1**, 420 f.
Sporting manual, first published in U.S., **Vol. 8, Part 1**, 107 f.
Sporting News, founding of, **Supp. 7**, 711–12
Sports: amateur competition, **Supp. 9**, 438; celebrities, **Supp. 5**, 686–88; collegiate policies, **Supp. 4**, 320; endorsements, **Supp. 9**, 537; first franchise shift to West Coast, **Supp. 9**, 646; journalism, **Supp. 1**, 527; **Supp. 4**, 708–9; **Supp. 5**, 568; **Supp. 6**, 366; **Supp. 8**, 498; Madison Square Garden, **Supp. 6**, 337; medicine, **Supp. 10**, 624; municipal facilities, **Supp. 3**, 217; publicity and promotion, **Supp. 5**, 270, 724–25; racism in, **Supp. 9**, 668–69, 817, 840–41; **Supp. 10**, 347; radio coverage, **Supp. 7**, 378, 494–95, 707; **Supp. 9**, 224, 295, 533, 765–66; **Supp. 10**, 256; women athletes, **Supp. 6**, 722–23; women's physical education, **Supp. 5**, 52; writings on, **Supp. 9**, 485. *See also* Olympic games; *specific sports:* Baseball; Football, *etc.*
Sports Illustrated, founding of, **Supp. 8**, 395
Spotswood, Alexander, reference to, **Vol. 1, Part 2**, 336
Spotsylvania Court House, battle of, **Vol. 1, Part 1**, 273; **Vol. 3, Part 2**, 230; **Vol. 4, Part 1**, 424, 496; **Vol. 4, Part 2**, 222; **Vol. 5, Part 1**, 25; **Vol. 6, Part 1**, 104, 126, 134, 392; **Vol. 6, Part 2**, 476; **Vol. 8, Part 2**, 548; **Vol. 9, Part 1**, 80; **Vol. 9, Part 2**, 172; **Vol. 10, Part 2**, 334
Spotted fever, treatment of, **Vol. 7, Part 1**, 559
Sprague, Frank J., reference to, **Supp. 3**, 251
Sprague, Otho S. A., Memorial Institute, **Supp. 3**, 807
Sprague Electrical Works, **Supp. 9**, 873
Spratling, William, reference to, **Supp. 7**, 231
Spray, sloop of Slocum, **Vol. 9, Part 1**, 218
Spreckles, Claus Augustus ("Gus"), reference to, **Supp. 6**, 590
Sprigle, Raymond, references to, **Supp. 3**, 80; **Supp. 9**, 95
Springfield, Ill.: historical agencies in, **Supp. 9**, 38; political life in days of Lincoln, **Vol. 4, Part 2**, 430
Springfield, Mass.: founding of, **Vol. 8, Part 1**, 292 f.; history of, early, **Vol. 10, Part 2**, 540; public service, **Vol. 1, Part 2**, 519; separation from the Connecticut government, **Vol. 8, Part 1**, 292 f.
Springfield, Mo., **Vol. 9, Part 1**, 62
Springfield *Daily News*, founding of, **Vol. 1, Part 2**, 163
"Springfield Junto," **Vol. 6, Part 1**, 366
Springfield Republican, **Vol. 1, Part 2**, 513–19; **Vol. 4, Part 1**, 622; **Vol. 5, Part 1**, 147; **Vol. 10, Part 2**, 135
Springfield rifle, **Vol. 1, Part 2**, 209
Spring Hill, Tenn., battle of, **Vol. 2, Part 2**, 45, 190, 476; **Vol. 3, Part 2**, 532; **Vol. 5, Part 1**, 194; **Vol. 8, Part 2**, 453; **Vol. 9, Part 1**, 508
Spring Hill College, founding of, **Vol. 8, Part 1**, 108 f.
Sproul, Robert G., reference to, **Supp. 9**, 754
Spruance, R. A., references to, **Supp. 6**, 267, 268
Sputnik, **Supp. 8**, 159
Spying. *See* Espionage; Spies
Squatter sovereignty, **Vol. 1, Part 1**, 403; **Vol. 3, Part 1**, 400; **Vol. 4, Part 1**, 550; **Vol. 6, Part 1**, 247; **Vol. 8, Part 2**, 617; **Vol. 10, Part 1**, 599. *See also* Kansas-Nebraska Act
Squaw Man, The, **Supp. 9**, 323
Squibb, E. R., and Sons, management, **Supp. 10**, 826
Squier, Raymond Roscoe, reference to, **Supp. 6**, 18
Stabile, as art form, **Supp. 10**, 90, 91
Staë, Nicolas de, reference to, **Supp. 6**, 552
Stadium, first in U.S., **Vol. 5, Part 1**, 153
Stafford, Jean, references to, **Supp. 7**, 474; **Supp. 10**, 467, 468
Stagecoach, **Supp. 9**, 286; **Supp. 10**, 822
Stagecoach lines: **Vol. 2, Part 1**, 374 f.; **Vol. 4, Part 1**, 549; **Vol. 5, Part 1**, 141; **Vol. 6, Part 1**, 163; **Vol. 6, Part 2**, 215; **Vol. 8, Part 2**, 146, 235, 252; robberies, **Vol. 1, Part 2**, 35
Stage design, **Vol. 9, Part 1**, 341; **Vol. 10, Part 1**, 133
Stage Door Canteen, founding of, **Supp. 4**, 187; **Supp. 5**, 415
Stage management, **Vol. 2, Part 2**, 156 f., 356 f.; **Vol. 4, Part 2**, 73; **Vol. 7, Part 2**, 172 f., 290; **Vol. 9, Part I**, 370
Stained glass, **Vol. 4, Part 2**, 423, 438; **Vol. 5, Part 2**, 533 f.; **Vol. 6, Part 1**, 153; **Vol. 10, Part 2**, 244; **Supp. 3**, 183–84
Stainless steel, **Supp. 4**, 121–22
Stalin, Josef, references to, **Supp. 3**, 663; **Supp. 4**, 393; **Supp. 5**, 334; **Supp. 6**, 147, 184–85; **Supp. 7**, 204, 244, 255, 291; **Supp. 8**, 149–50, 172
Stallings, Laurence, reference to, **Supp. 6**, 15
Stamford, Conn., mayors, **Supp. 6**, 137
"Stalwarts," **Vol. 1, Part 2**, 324 f.; **Vol. 4, Part 2**, 450; **Vol. 5, Part 2**, 543 f.; **Vol. 8, Part 1**, 4 f.; **Vol. 8, Part 2**, 5, 28 f.
Stammering: A Psychoanalytic Interpretation, **Supp. 3**, 191
Stamp Act: **Vol. 1, Part 1**, 73, 385; **Vol. 2, Part 2**, 135,

287; Vol. 3, Part 1, 299; **Vol. 3, Part 2**, 428; **Vol. 5, Part 1**, 220, 416, 468; **Vol. 7, Part 1**, 133, 220, 637; **Vol. 8, Part 2**, 342; **Vol. 9, Part 2**, 504; **Vol. 10, Part 1**, 25 f.; Congress, **Vol. 8, Part 2**, 81, 320; enforcement of, **Vol. 3, Part 1**, 59; printing, effect of, on, **Vol. 4, Part 1**, 92; repeal of, **Vol. 3, Part 1**, 180; riots, **Vol. 3, Part 1**, 465 f.; **Vol. 5, Part 2**, 138; suggested, **Vol. 9, Part 1**, 26
Stamps: first authorized issue of, **Vol. 1, Part 2**, 47; first five-cent, **Vol. 10, Part 1**, 639 f.; introduction of, **Vol. 5, Part 1**, 589; **Vol. 5, Part 2**, 93; revenue, **Vol. 10, Part 1**, 637 f.
Standard, religious weekly, **Vol. 4, Part 1**, 215 f.; **Vol. 7, Part 1**, 439
Standard and Poor's, **Supp. 6**, 458
Standard Oil Co. *See* Oil, Standard Oil Co.
Standard Oil Co. of Louisiana, management, **Supp. 10**, 663
Standard Oil Co. of New Jersey: **Supp. 3**, 260–61; **Supp. 5**, 226, 236, 570; antiknock gasoline, **Supp. 3**, 522; Getty Oil, competition with, **Supp. 10**, 275; management, **Supp. 10**, 827; mergers, **Supp. 4**, 775–76; presidency, **Supp. 10**, 663, 664; writings on, **Supp. 3**, 762
Standard Oil Co. of Ohio: **Supp. 5**, 286; antitrust action, **Supp. 2**, 355, 573, 714; establishment of, **Supp. 2**, 569–75
Standards, Bureau of, creation of: **Vol. 9, Part 2**, 127 f.; first chief chemist, **Supp. 3**, 565–66; publication of, **Vol. 8, Part 2**, 154
Standing Order, religious sect, **Vol. 8, Part 2**, 32
Standish, Miles, reference to, **Vol. 1, Part 2**, 560
Stanford, Leland, references to, **Vol. 5, Part 1**, 409, 411; **Vol. 8, Part 2**, 354
Stanford-Binet test, **Supp. 6**, 626, 627
Stanford University: academic freedom issues, **Supp. 7**, 481; education studies, **Supp. 3**, 205–6; **Supp. 4**, 449; football team, **Supp. 4**, 896–97; **Supp. 5**, 728; **Supp. 8**, 588; **Supp. 10**, 584; geological studies, **Supp. 4**, 896–97; history studies, **Supp. 3**, 262; mathematics studies, **Supp. 3**, 79; mechanical engineering studies, **Supp. 6**, 182; microwave laboratory, **Supp. 4**, 358; presidency, **Supp. 4**, 892–93; psychology studies, **Supp. 6**, 626
Stanhope-Wheatcroft School of Acting (New York City), **Supp. 6**, 133
Stanislavski, Konstantin, references to, **Supp. 3**, 297; **Supp. 10**, 129
Stan Kenton Progressive Jazz Orchestra, **Supp. 10**, 409
Stanley, Henry M., reference to, **Vol. 1, Part 2**, 200
Stanley, Wendell M., reference to, **Supp. 10**, 427
Stanley-Warner Co., **Supp. 7**, 692
Stans, Maurice, reference to, **Supp. 10**, 645
Stanton, E. McM., reference to, **Vol. 6, Part 1**, 252 f.
Stanton, Elizabeth Cady, references to, **Vol. 7, Part 1**, 289; **Supp. 4**, 85, 86
Stanton, Frank, reference to, **Supp. 10**, 438
Stanwyck, Barbara, references to, **Supp. 7**, 237; **Supp. 8**, 646
"Star," locomotive, **Vol. 7, Part 1**, 556
Star (Washington, D.C.), **Vol. 7, Part 1**, 586
"Stardust" (song), **Supp. 9**, 887
Star Is Born, A, **Supp. 8**, 205
Stark, Harold R., references to, **Supp. 4**, 305; **Supp. 6**, 339
Stark, Lloyd C., references to, **Supp. 3**, 597; **Supp. 9**, 811
Stark, Paul, reference to, **Supp. 9**, 756
Stark Brothers Nurseries, **Supp. 9**, 756, 757
Star of the West (steamer), **Vol. 1, Part 1**, 275; **Vol. 1, Part 2**, 111, 312; **Vol. 2, Part 1**, 213; **Vol. 3, Part 2**, 568; **Vol. 6, Part 1**, 250; **Vol. 8, Part 1**, 560; **Vol. 10, Part 1**, 630
Starr, Ringo, **Supp. 10**, 449
Starrett Brothers, **Supp. 6**, 593
Star Route frauds (1882), **Vol. 1, Part 1**, 376; **Vol. 2, Part 1**, 26; **Vol. 3, Part 1**, 387; **Vol. 4, Part 1**, 149; **Vol. 5, Part 1**, 589
Stars: catalogues of, **Supp. 3**, 131; **Supp. 4**, 600; classification, **Supp. 3**, 130–31; **Supp. 6**, 7; distance measurements, **Supp. 1**, 283; double, **Supp. 1**, 674; **Supp. 5**, 13–14; galaxies, discovery of, **Supp. 5**, 540–41; Hertzsprung-Russell diagram, **Supp. 6**, 561; movement of, **Supp. 1**, 324; parallax, **Supp. 3**, 692; **Supp. 6**, 560–61; population studies, **Supp. 6**, 31; position in southern hemisphere sky, **Supp. 5**, 541; positions and motions, **Supp. 3**, 692; radical velocities of, **Supp. 4**, 600; spectroscopic measurement of, **Supp. 4**, 600; T Coronae Borealis, discovery of, **Supp. 1**, 229; variable, **Supp. 3**, 130–31. *See also* Astronomy
Stars and Stripes, **Supp. 6**, 5; **Supp. 9**, 335; **Supp. 10**, 461
"Star-Spangled Banner, The," **Vol. 1, Part 1**, 347; **Vol. 5, Part 2**, 362 f.; **Vol. 7, Part 1**, 506; **Vol. 9, Part 1**, 200
Starch, manufacture of, **Vol. 5, Part 2**, 409 f.; **Vol. 7, Part 2**, 49
Stassen, Harold, reference to, **Supp. 10**, 360
State, Department of (U.S.): **Vol. 1, Part 1**, 85 f.; **Vol. 1, Part 2**, 311; **Vol. 4, Part 1**, 15, 609; **Vol. 5, Part 2**, 23 f.; **Vol. 8, Part 1**, 353 f.; **Vol. 8, Part 2**, 618–19; **Vol. 10, Part 1**, 154; administration, **Supp. 1**, 582–83; **Supp. 3**, 219; **Supp. 4**, 170–71, 405–6, 777–78, 786; **Supp. 5**, 49, 331–35; **Supp. 6**, 387–88; **Supp. 7**, 777–78; **Supp. 8**, 6, 258, 275, 276; China policy, World War II era, **Supp. 9**, 146, 830–31; Clark Memorandum, **Supp. 7**, 126; cold war policies, **Supp. 6**, 179, 431, 432; **Supp. 9**, 7–9; Committee of Eight, **Supp. 7**, 23; Consular Service, **Supp. 3**, 138–39, 467; consultants, **Supp. 5**, 731; cultural and educational exchange programs, **Supp. 10**, 441; diplomacy, **Supp. 9**, 153–54; early U.S. history archives, **Supp. 3**, 285; Far Eastern affairs, **Supp. 3**, 826; first foreign service exam, **Supp. 6**, 686; first woman to head major division, **Supp. 8**, 590; foreign aid policy, **Supp. 8**, 89–90; German research section, **Supp. 5**, 514; growth, **Supp. 5**, 331; international conferences, **Supp. 9**, 277, 567; Japanese policy, **Supp. 7**, 112–13; Latin American Division, **Supp. 4**, 706; **Supp. 7**, 777; loyalty issues, **Supp. 5**, 19, 665, 676; **Supp. 6**, 60, 405; **Supp. 7**, 114, 751; **Supp. 9**, 146, 814; Marshall Plan, **Supp. 6**, 431; Mexican crisis (1915–16), **Supp. 3**, 606; Monroe Doctrine, **Supp. 7**, 126; Near Eastern Division, **Supp. 8**, 5; reorganization, **Supp. 4**, 777; **Supp. 6**, 451; trade policy, **Supp. 6**, 244; U.S. participation in World War II, **Supp. 3**, 528
State (newspaper), **Vol. 4, Part 1**, 373
State and the Church, The, **Supp. 3**, 681
State Historical Society of Missouri, founding of, **Supp. 1**, 709
State Historical Society of Wisconsin, **Vol. 3, Part 1**, 551 f.
State naval militia, first to be organized, **Vol. 8, Part 1**, 276
Staten Island (N. Y.) *Advance*, **Supp. 10**, 586
"State of the Union," Rhode Island committee of thirty-three on, **Vol. 8, Part 2**, 38
State teachers' association (N.Y.), formation of, **Vol. 2, Part 1**, 250
State universities, first federal grant, **Vol. 6, Part 1**, 275

State University of Iowa, psychology studies, **Supp. 4**, 731
State University of New York, **Vol. 6, Part 1**, 232; **Vol. 8, Part 2**, 127
Staten Island, N.Y.: actors' home on, **Vol. 1, Part 1, 151; colonization, early, Vol. 3, Part 1**, 265; Revolutionary military activity on, **Vol. 3, Part 1**, 303; Seamen's Asylum and Hospital, **Vol. 8, Part 1**, 348 f.
States (U.S.): Fourteenth Amendment due process clause, **Supp. 3**, 415; rights, Supreme Court decisions on, **Supp. 3**, 99. *See also specific state names*
States' rights: **Vol. 1, Part 1**, 591, 594; **Vol. 2, Part 2**, 134; **Vol. 3, Part 2**, 94, 117, 374, 482, 501; **Vol. 4, Part 1**, 427; **Vol. 4, Part 2**, 187, 527; **Vol. 5, Part 1**, 134, 403; **Vol. 5, Part 2**, 28, 155; **Vol. 6, Part 1**, 210; **Vol. 8, Part 1**, 363 f., 643; **Vol. 8, Part 2**, 290; **Vol. 9, Part 1**, 284, 360; **Vol. 10, Part 1**, 37; convention, **Vol. 9, Part 2**, 651; debate on, **Vol. 10, Part 1**, 585 f.; interpretation of, **Vol. 6, Part 2**, 323; legal cases concerning, **Vol. 4, Part 2**, 271
States' Rights party. *See* Dixiecrats
Static, source studies, **Supp. 4**, 422–23
Station for Experimental Evolution. *See* Cold Spring Harbor
Statistics: **Vol. 3, Part 2**, 68; **Vol. 5, Part 1**, 81, 257, 621 f.; **Vol. 5, Part 2**, 335, 494 f.; **Vol. 7, Part 1, 562; Vol. 8, Part 2**, 220, 425; **Vol. 9, Part 1**, 33 f.; American Statistical Association, **Vol. 5, Part 2**, 495; **Vol. 9, Part 1**, 33; biology, **Supp. 2**, 521; **Supp. 3**, 214–15, 477–78; business analysis, **Supp. 2**, 529; chemistry and physics, **Supp. 4**, 838–39; coal, **Vol. 9, Part 2**, 341; crime, **Supp. 5**, 639; criminal, **Vol. 5, Part 2**, 495; economics, **Supp. 4**, 35–36, 274–75; **Supp. 6**, 459; epidemiology, **Supp. 3**, 158; **Supp. 7**, 192; Federal Bureau of Statistics and Commerce, **Vol. 3, Part 1**, 225; **Vol. 8, Part 1**, 179 f.; **Vol. 10, Part 1**, 594 f., 637 f.; Fermi-Dirac, **Supp. 5**, 219, 221; first survey of U.S. poor, **Supp. 3**, 373; insurance industry, **Supp. 4**, 384–85; mining, **Vol. 8, Part 1**, 415; psychology, **Supp. 3**, 149–50; religious, **Vol. 3, Part 1**, 375 f.; scientific nature of, **Vol. 6, Part 2**, 467; sociology, **Supp. 6**, 483, 604–5; tabulation, mechanical, **Vol. 7, Part 2**, 573; teaching of, **Supp. 2**, 175; unemployment, **Supp. 6**, 708–9; writings on, **Vol. 5, Part 2**, 495; **Vol. 8, Part 1**, 71 f., 100 f. **Supp. 6**, 708–9. *See also* Mathematics
Statistics, Bureau of, **Vol. 3, Part 1**, 225; **Vol. 8, Part 1**, 179 f.; **Vol. 10, Part 1**, 637 f.
Statue of Liberty, constructing engineer for, **Vol. 9, Part 2**, 72
Steagall, Henry, reference to, **Supp. 5**, 248
Steam: automobiles, use of in, **Vol. 9, Part 1**, 508; ferry, first on Mississippi, **Vol. 3, Part 1**, 249; fire-engine, first use of, **Vol. 3, Part 1**, 211; hammer, **Vol. 9, Part 2**, 342; locomotive, first in America, **Vol. 2, Part 2**, 410; plows, first use of, **Vol. 8, Part 1**, 522; printing, first use of in, **Vol. 3, Part 1**, 155; "propulsion v. nonpropulsion" controversy, **Vol. 3, Part 1**, 288; pumps, **Vol. 4, Part 1**, 178; road carriages, **Vol. 8, Part 1**, 429; **Vol. 9, Part 1**, 26; turbines, **Vol. 8, Part 1**, 544; **Vol. 8, Part 2**, 359
Steamboats (for complete list, *see* Ships): building, **Vol. 3, Part 1**, 458; **Vol. 3, Part 2**, 164; **Vol. 7, Part 1**, 471, 639; **Vol. 8, Part 1**, 464 f.; **Vol. 8, Part 2**, 200; Civil War, neutral Ohio service in, **Vol. 3, Part 2**, 516; *Claremont*, **Vol. 4, Part 1**, 71; **Vol. 8, Part 2**, 106; controversy over, **Vol. 7, Part 1**, 637; first, **Vol. 9, Part 2**, 504; hazards of early, **Vol. 8, Part 1**, 442; inspection, **Vol. 4, Part 2**, 59; invention of, **Vol. 3, Part 2**, 425 f.; inventions concerning, **Vol. 4, Part 1**, 70 f.; **Vol. 6, Part 1**, 393; **Vol. 7, Part 1**, 161–62; **Vol. 8, Part 2**, 223; **Vol. 9, Part 1**, 615; monopoly, early, **Vol. 5, Part 2**, 608; ocean voyage, first, **Vol. 8, Part 2**, 106; operation, **Vol. 4, Part 1**, 243; **Vol. 5, Part 2**, 397; **Vol. 8, Part 2**, 575; paddle wheel, vertical, legislation concerning, **Vol. 8, Part 2**, 134; *Phoenix*, first seagoing, **Vol. 8, Part 2**, 106; **Vol. 9, Part 1**, 615, 619; plant system of, **Vol. 7, Part 2**, 646 f.; promotion, **Vol. 6, Part 1**, 23; Red River Transportation Co., **Vol. 5, Part 2**, 441; river, **Vol. 2, Part 2**, 14; **Vol. 5, Part 2**, 517 f.; **Vol. 6, Part 2**, 298; **Vol. 8, Part 2**, 575; salvaging of, **Vol. 3, Part 1**, 587 f.; sternwheelers, **Vol. 4, Part 2**, 561; **Vol. 8, Part 1**, 464; transportation, **Vol. 4, Part 2**, 297; **Vol. 7, Part 1**, 14; **Vol. 9, Part 1**, 134; travel by, promotion of, **Vol. 8, Part 1**, 442
Steam boilers: **Vol. 5, Part 2**, 348; **Vol. 8, Part 1, 329 f.; Vol. 8, Part 2**, 200; inspection of, **Vol. 1, Part 1, 197**
Steam Engineering, Bureau of, **Vol. 5, Part 1**, 516
Steam engines: **Vol. 2, Part 2**, 441; **Vol. 3, Part 2, 218 f.; Vol. 6, Part 1**, 81; **Vol. 8, Part 1**, 429; **Vol. 9, Part 2**, 519; designing of, **Vol. 2, Part 2**, 301; **Vol. 5, Part 1**, 515 f.; **Vol. 8, Part 1**, 429; **Vol. 9, Part 1**, 614; in electrical power plants, **Supp. 4**, 383–84; first in America, **Vol. 3, Part 2**, 208; **Vol. 4, Part 2**, 604; **Vol. 5, Part 1**, 231; inspection of, first in U.S., **Vol. 8, Part 1**, 631; inventions relating to, **Vol. 1, Part 1**, 457; **Vol. 6, Part 1**, 393; **Vol. 8, Part 1**, 329 f., 544, 552; **Vol. 9, Part 1**, 149, 166; **Vol. 10, Part 2**, 205; manufacture of, **Vol. 3, Part 1**, 339; **Vol. 5, Part 1**, 84; **Vol. 8, Part 2**, 133, 200; **Vol. 9, Part 2**, 520; testing of, **Vol. 8, Part 1**, 506; turbine, **Supp. 3**, 251. *See also* Engines
Steamships: American waters, first introduced in 1834, **Vol. 5, Part 2**, 549; coastwise, first, **Vol. 9, Part 2**, 542; guidebooks of nineteenth century, **Vol. 3, Part 1**, 319; iron, first American, **Vol. 5, Part 2**, 549; mail subsidies for, **Vol. 8, Part 2**, 11; Transatlantic, first, **Vol. 3, Part 1**, 339; **Vol. 8, Part 2**, 106, 410; Yukon, first to go up, **Vol. 8, Part 1**, 406
Stearman Aircraft Co., founding of, **Supp. 9**, 757
Stearns, Frank Waterman, reference to, **Supp. 1**, 194
Stearns-Knights automobile, **Supp. 5**, 654
Stecher, Joe, reference to, **Supp. 8**, 371, 372
Steck, Daniel F., reference to, **Supp. 3**, 108
Stedman, Edmund Clarence, reference to, **Supp. 4**, 840
Steel: automotive uses, **Supp. 2**, 721; **Supp. 6**, 678–79; continuous casting, **Supp. 10**, 150; continuous-strip rolling process, **Supp. 3**, 781–82, 792; Corey reforging process, **Supp. 1**, 203; hardening, **Supp. 2**, 595; military uses, **Supp. 10**, 149; research in, **Supp. 4**, 437–38; ship industry uses, **Supp. 4**, 257; silicon reduction process, **Supp. 3**, 48–49; skyscraper framing, **Supp. 3**, 611–12; stainless manufacture, **Supp. 4**, 121–22; standardization of shapes, **Supp. 2**, 638
Steel and Metal Workers Industrial Union, **Supp. 6**, 597
Steele, Alfred, reference to, **Supp. 10**, 158
Steel industry: **Vol. 2, Part 1**, 501 f.; **Vol. 3, Part 1**, 69 f., 179, 329, 547 f.; **Vol. 4, Part 1**, 29 f., 175 f., 199; **Vol. 4, Part 2**, 8 f., 374; **Vol. 5, Part 1**, 149, 431; **Vol. 5, Part 2**, 146, 162 f., 209, 312; **Vol. 6, Part 1**, 155; **Vol. 6, Part 2**, 583; **Vol. 7, Part 1**, 143, 301; **Vol. 7, Part 2**, 18, 206, 550; **Vol. 8, Part 1**, 466, 517 f.; **Vol. 9, Part 1**, 48, 125; **Vol. 9, Part 2**, 236 f., 324; **Vol. 10, Part 1**, 635; air-boiling process, **Vol. 5, Part 2**, 311; analytical laboratory, first in U.S., **Vol. 3, Part 1**, 547 f.; Brazil, **Supp. 5**, 215–16; brokerage, **Vol. 5, Part 2**, 426; **Vol. 6, Part 1**, 155; Bessemer process, **Vol. 3, Part 1**, 547 f.; **Vol. 4, Part 1**, 39; **Vol. 4, Part 2**, 8; **Vol. 5, Part 1**, 148, 392; **Vol. 5, Part 2**, 209, 311; blast furnace, **Vol. 8, Part 1**, 517, 544; **Vol. 10, Part**

1, 465 f., 602 f.; Carnegie mills, **Supp. 6**, 506–7; corporations, **Supp. 3**, 77, 263; **Supp. 6**, 243–44; **Supp. 10**, 344–46; crucible, experiments with, **Vol. 3, Part l**, 318; crucible-steel furnace, first in America, **Vol. 10, Part 1**, 635; electromagnet, **Vol. 10, Part 1**, 635; enameling, **Vol. 7, Part 1**, 518; executives, **Supp. 7**, 228–29, 289–90, 587; **Supp. 8**, 517; **Supp. 9**, 402–3; **Supp. 10**, 149–50; foreign competition, **Supp. 10**, 149–50, 345–46; "heat," first puddling of, **Vol. 8, Part 1**, 466; Homestead strike, **Supp. 3**, 94; inventions, **Vol. 3, Part 1**, 547 f.; **Vol. 8, Part 1**, 467; **Vol. 10, Part 2**, 322; Kennedy, J. F., showdown, **Supp. 9**, 403; manufacturing and ore development, **Supp. 8**, 289–90; metallurgy of, **Vol. 5, Part 1**, 289; Moulders International Union, **Vol. 9, Part 2**, 258; New Deal code, **Supp. 6**, 622; open-hearth process, **Vol. 5, Part 1**, 382; **Vol. 8, Part 1**, 467; **Vol. 10, Part 1**, 635; organizing of, **Vol. 8, Part 1**, 435; Pittsburgh as center of, **Vol. 6, Part 2**, 583; plow steel, first U. S. manufacture of, **Vol. 3, Part 1**, 193; pneumatic process of, **Vol. 3, Part 1**, 548 f.; **Vol. 7, Part 2**, 206; processes, **Vol. 5, Part 2**, 311; public relations, **Supp. 10**, 334–35; rails, first rolled in U.S., **Vol. 3, Part 1**, 547 f.; **Vol. 5, Part 1**, 392; rolling of shaped metal, **Vol. 8, Part 1**, 466; sliding scale of, **Vol. 5, Part 2**, 162; smelting, electric, **Vol. 2, Part 2**, 472; stoker, mechanical underfeed, **Vol. 5, Part 2**, 168; strikes, **Vol. 5, Part 2**, 196; **Supp. 6**, 678; **Supp. 7**, 228–29, 254, 290, 587; technical research, **Supp. 1**, 545; testing, **Vol. 5, Part 1**, 382; Truman seizure of mills, **Supp. 5**, 156, 714; **Supp. 6**, 502; **Supp. 7**, 96, 229, 587; unionization, **Supp. 4**, 280; **Supp. 5**, 510; **Supp. 6**, 597, 622; **Supp. 7**, 290; **Supp. 8**, 517; United States Steel Corporation, **Vol. 5, Part 1**, 57; **Vol. 7, Part 1**, 144, 177, 301; **Vol. 7, Part 2**, 471; **Vol. 8, Part 1**, 449; **Vol. 9, Part 1**, 598; war production, **Supp. 7**, 587; waste, early conversion into ingots, **Vol. 3, Part 1**, 318; welding of, **Vol. 8, Part 2**, 200; wire manufacture, **Vol. 3, Part 2**, 489; **Vol. 4, Part 1**, 188; **Vol. 4, Part 2**, 156; **Vol. 5, Part 2**, 53; **Vol. 7, Part 1**, 165 f.; **Vol. 8, Part 2**, 189; **Vol. 10, Part 1**, 376 f., 501 f.

Steel Workers Organizing Committee, **Supp. 5**, 510; **Supp. 6**, 597

Steers, Frank M., reference to, **Supp. 7**, 395

Steffens, Lincoln, references to, **Supp. 2**, 183; **Supp. 3**, 329, 330, 462, 674, 762, 816; **Supp. 4**, 46–47, 518, 662; **Supp. 5**, 213; **Supp. 6**, 590; **Supp. 7**, 486; **Supp. 9**, 503

Steichen, Edward, references to, **Supp. 4**, 779, 780; **Supp. 5**, 470, 471; **Supp. 7**, 457; **Supp. 8**, 563, 564; **Supp. 10**, 398

Stein, Gertrude, references to, **Supp. 3**, 14; **Supp. 4**, 174–75, 770, 771; **Supp. 6**, 497–98, 625; **Supp. 7**, 754; **Supp. 8**, 432, 655–56; **Supp. 9**, 871

Stein, Jules, reference to, **Supp. 10**, 463

Stein, Leo, references to, **Supp. 4**, 767, 768

Stein, Michael, reference to, **Supp. 4**, 768

Stein, Sarah, reference to, **Supp. 4**, 768

Steinbeck, John, references to, **Supp. 7**, 149, 307; **Supp. 8**, 117; **Supp. 10**, 244

Steinem, Gloria, reference to, **Supp. 9**, 785

Steiner, Max, reference to, **Supp. 10**, 231

Steiner, Rudolf, philosophy of, **Vol. 7, Part 1**, 520

Steinman, David B., reference to, **Supp. 3**, 531

Steinway Hall (Chicago), **Supp. 3**, 598

Stella Dallas, **Supp. 9**, 628

Stelze, Charles, reference to, **Supp. 4**, 232

Stengel, Casey, reference to, **Supp. 9**, 855; **Supp. 10**, 314, 346

Stenography: **Vol. 5, Part 1**, 80 f.; shorthand method, **Supp. 4**, 347–48; **Supp. 8**, 546

Stephens, Alexander H., references to, **Vol. 5, Part 1**, 245 f., 404; **Vol. 9, Part 2**, 353, 590 f.

Stephens, James, reference to, **Vol. 7, Part 2**, 36

Stephens College (Mo.), founding of, **Vol. 9, Part 2**, 254

Stephenson, David C., reference to, **Supp. 3**, 709

Stephenson, N. W., reference to, **Supp. 6**, 310

Stereograph, **Vol. 9, Part 2**, 295

Stereotyping, invention of, **Vol. 2, Part 2**, 286

Sterilization, eugenic basis for, **Supp. 3**, 446

Sterling Oil and Refining Co., predecessors, **Supp. 4**, 776

Sterling Products, **Supp. 4**, 497

Stern, Curt, reference to, **Supp. 3**, 540

Stern, J. David, references to, **Supp. 3**, 20, 21

Stern, Stewart, reference to, **Supp. 9**, 34

Sterne, Laurence, scholarship on, **Supp. 4**, 197

Sterne, Maurice, references to, **Supp. 3**, 112; **Supp. 6**, 257; **Supp. 7**, 486

Steroids: **Supp. 5**, 28; research, **Supp. 10**, 240

Stethoscope, use of, **Vol. 5, Part 1**, 240

Stettinius, Edward R., Jr., references to, **Supp. 4**, 458; **Supp. 5**, 332, 335, 537; **Supp. 7**, 721; **Supp. 9**, 812; **Supp. 10**, 243

Stettinius, Edward R., Sr., **Supp. 7**, 782–83

Steubenville, Ohio, steel strike, **Supp. 6**, 678

Steunenberg, Gov. Frank R.: assassination of, **Vol. 4, Part 2**, 468; reference to, **Supp. 5**, 699

Stevens, Elsie Kachel, references to, **Supp. 5**, 659, 660

Stevens, George, Jr., reference to, **Supp. 9**, 768

Stevens, Harry M., Inc., **Supp. 7**, 719

Stevens, John F., reference to, **Supp. 7**, 89

Stevens, J. P., Co., **Supp. 8**, 367

Stevens, Nettie, reference to, **Supp. 4**, 516

Stevens, Raymond B., reference to, **Supp. 6**, 556

Stevens, Robert T., references to, **Supp. 6**, 540, 680; **Supp. 8**, 57

Stevens, Thaddeus, reference to, **Vol. 6, Part 1**, 436, 597; **Vol. 8, Part 1**, 410

Stevens-Duryea Motor Car Co., founding of, **Supp. 8**, 148–49

Stevens Institute of Technology: **Vol. 9, Part 2**, 27, 518 f.; first president, **Vol. 7, Part 1**, 254; founding of, **Vol. 9, Part 1**, 609; presidency, **Supp. 5**, 154

Stevenson, Adlai E.: presidential candidacies, **Supp. 7**, 416; **Supp. 8**, 361; **Supp. 9**, 432, 814; references to, **Supp. 5**, 255, 481; **Supp. 7**, 420, 421, 662; **Supp. 10**, 10, 167, 212, 361, 486, 868; relations with national committee, **Supp. 9**, 551–52

Stevenson, Adlai E., III, reference to, **Supp. 9**, 740

Stevenson, J. Ross, reference to, **Supp. 6**, 195

Stevenson, Robert Louis, reference to, **Supp. 4**, 517

Steward, Lavinia, reference to, **Supp. 7**, 193

Stewart, Anita, reference to, **Supp. 6**, 440

Stewart, Arthur Thomas, reference to, **Supp. 6**, 528

Stewart, Donald Ogden, reference to, **Supp. 7**, 335

Stewart, Fred, reference to, **Supp. 6**, 537

Stewart, George N., reference to, **Supp. 3**, 134–35

Stewart, Potter, reference to, **Supp. 9**, 837

Stewart, Virgil A., reference to, **Vol. 7, Part 1**, 369

Stewart, Walter, reference to, **Supp. 9**, 661

Stewart, W. K., Co., **Supp. 7**, 524

Stickney, Dorothy, reference to, **Supp. 8**, 382

Stieglitz, Alfred, references to, **Supp. 3**, 340; **Supp. 4**, 240–41; **Supp. 5**, 470, 471; **Supp. 9**, 110, 111, 759; **Supp. 10**, 397, 398, 765, 766, 834

Stiles, Ezra, references to, **Vol. 6, Part 1**, 402; **Vol. 7, Part 1**, 361

Stillness at Appomattox, A, **Supp. 10**, 108

Stillwell, Joseph W., references to, **Supp. 9**, 830, 831

Stillwater, battle of, **Vol. 2, Part 2**, 107

Stillwell, Joseph W., references to, **Supp. 5**, 486–87; **Supp. 6**, 109–10, 231, 508; **Supp. 7**, 377, 680
Stimson, Henry L., references to, **Supp. 3**, 116, 425, 648; **Supp. 4**, 458, 459, 898; **Supp. 5**, 7, 187, 333, 334, 335; **Supp. 7**, 91, 112, 113, 261, 361; **Supp. 8**, 230; **Supp. 9**, 356; **Supp. 10**, 510
Stockard, Charles R., reference to, **Supp. 7**, 598
Stockbreeding, **Vol. 1, Part 1**, 599; **Vol. 1, Part 2, 172; Vol. 3, Part 2**, 478 f.; **Vol. 4, Part 1**, 256; **Vol. 4, Part 2**, 162, 204, 315, 483; **Vol. 5, Part 1**, 624 f.; **Vol. 5, Part 2**, 153; **Vol. 6, Part 1**, 92; **Vol. 6, Part 2**, 412; **Vol. 7, Part 1**, 72, 217 f., 243; **Vol. 8, Part 1**, 456; **Vol. 8, Part 2**, 311, 335; **Vol. 9, Part 1**, 30, 148; **Vol. 10, Part 1**, 617 f.
Stockbridge, early locomotive, **Vol. 8, Part 2**, 112
Stock market: branch brokerage firms, **Supp. 3**, 24; brokerage firms, **Supp. 7**, 379, 604; **Supp. 8**, 112–14; **Supp. 9**, 613–14; **Supp. 10**, 138, 139, 466; brokers, **Supp. 3**, 239; **Supp. 6**, 448–49; brokers, women, **Supp. 8**, 534; copper trading, **Supp. 2**,292; crash (1929), **Supp. 4**, 470; **Supp. 7**, 361–62; **Supp. 9**, 606–7, 613; **Supp. 10**, 139; credit purchases, **Supp. 1**, 84; embezzlement scandal, **Supp. 9**, 607; employee stock options, **Supp. 5**, 315; federal oversight legislation, **Supp. 7**, 635; illegal practices, **Supp. 8**, 113–14; investment publications, **Supp. 6**, 457–58; legislation, **Supp. 3**, 654, **Supp. 4**, 470; Morgan & Co., **Supp. 3**, 538; public education regarding, **Supp. 9**, 614; risk arbitrage, **Supp. 10**, 454; writings on, **Supp. 3**, 633; **Supp. 8**, 18–19. *See also* Investment banking; New York Stock Exchange
Stock speculations, **Vol. 5, Part 1**, 437; **Vol. 5, Part 2**, 283; **Vol. 6, Part 1**, 60, 157; **Vol. 8, Part 2**, 267
Stock ticker, **Vol. 5, Part 1**, 55, 247; **Vol. 6, Part 1**, 55; **Vol. 8, Part 1**, 75 f.
Stockyards. *See* Meat-packing industry
Stock Yards Labor Council, organizing of, **Supp. 4**, 279–80
Stoddard, John L., reference to, **Supp. 6**, 302
"Stoddardeanism," **Vol. 9, Part 2**, 59
Stoessel, Albert, reference to, **Supp. 3**, 65
Stokes, Anson Phelps, Jr., reference to, **Supp. 6**, 600
Stokes, Caroline Phelps, reference to, **Supp. 3**, 744
Stokes, Richard L., reference to, **Supp. 3**, 92
Stokowski, Leopold, references to, **Supp. 4**, 718; **Supp. 6**, 358, 365, 550
Stone, Hannah Mayer, reference to, **Supp. 6**, 602
Stone, Harlan Fiske, references to, **Supp. 5**, 359, 571, 572, 573, 574, 576; **Supp. 7**, 361; **Supp. 8**, 139; **Supp. 9**, 405
Stone, Lucy: daughter's biography of, **Supp. 4**, 86; reference to, **Vol. 9, Part 1**, 36
Stone, Melville E., reference to, **Supp. 7**, 145
Stone, Phil, reference to, **Supp. 7**, 230
Stone, sculpture, **Supp. 3**, 278–79
Stone & Webster, **Supp. 3**, 744–47; **Supp. 4**, 453–54
Stone Mountain (Ga.) memorial, **Supp. 3**, 88–89
Stone's River, Tenn., battle of, **Vol. 1, Part 2**, 586; **Vol. 2, Part 1**, 9; **Vol. 4, Part 2**, 240; **Vol. 5, Part 2**, 145; **Vol. 8, Part 1**, 40; **Vol. 8, Part 2**, 163
Stone Telegraph and Telephone Co., founding of, **Supp. 3**, 748
Stony Point, N.Y., battle of, **Vol. 10, Part 1**, 564, 518
Stopes, Marie C., reference to, **Supp. 3**, 844
Stores, department, **Vol. 9, Part 2**, 129 f.; **Vol. 10, Part 1**, 407 f.
Stork Club, founding of, **Supp. 8**, 38–39
Storrs, Richard S., reference to, **Vol. 9, Part 2**, 347
Storrs Agricultural Experiment Station, **Vol. 5, Part 2**, 45
Storrow, T. W., reference to, **Vol. 5, Part 1**, 508
Story, Joseph B., references to, **Vol. 6, Part 2**, 321; **Supp. 7**, 792
Story, mystery, development of, **Vol. 8, Part 1**, 19 f.
Storyboard Productions, **Supp. 10**, 352
Story of a Bad Boy, **Vol. 4, Part 2**, 71
Story of a Pioneer, **Vol. 9, Part 1**, 35
Story of Ferdinand, The, **Supp. 10**, 440–41
Story of Language, The, **Supp. 10**, 628
Story of My Life, The, **Supp. 8**, 317
Story of Philosophy, The, **Supp. 8**, 579
Story of the Great March, **Vol. 7, Part 1**, 494
Storyville (Boston nightclub), **Supp. 8**, 562
Stouffer Foods Corporation, management and growth of, **Supp. 9**, 770–71
Stoughton Musical Society, founding of, **Vol. 1, Part 2**, 270
Stourbridge Lion (locomotive), **Vol. 5, Part 2**, 59
Stout, Wesley, reference to, **Supp. 10**, 690
Stove-polish, invention of, **Vol. 3, Part 1**, 329
Stover, Charles B., reference to, **Supp. 3**, 175
"Stover, Dink" (fictional character), **Supp. 5**, 372
Stover at Yale, **Supp. 5**, 372
Stoves: base-burning, first, **Vol. 7, Part 1**, 581; coal-burning, invention of, **Vol. 2, Part 2**, 110; Latrobe, **Vol. 6, Part 1**, 28; Oberlin, **Vol. 9, Part 2**, 12
Stowe, Harriet Beecher: reference to, **Vol. 7, Part 1, 252; writings on, Supp. 3**, 672
Stowe, Lyman Beecher, references to, **Supp. 4**, 870; **Supp. 6**, 568
Straight Line Engine Co., **Vol. 9, Part 2**, 243
Strang, James J., reference to, **Vol. 9, Part 2**, 334
Strange, Michael, reference to, **Supp. 6**, 517
Strange Fruit, **Supp. 8**, 605
Strasberg, Lee, references to, **Supp. 10**, 129, 130, 131
Stratemeyer, Edward, reference to, **Supp. 7**, 279
Stratemeyer Syndicate, children's literature, writing of, **Supp. 9**, 787–88
Stratford Festival (Onatario, Canada), founding of, **Supp. 9**, 351
Straton, John Roach, reference to, **Supp. 7**, 624
Stratosphere, early writings on, **Vol. 8, Part 2**, 184
Stratton, Samuel W., reference to, **Supp. 3**, 473
Stratton, William G., references to, **Supp. 9**, 491; **Supp. 10**, 411
Straus, Isidor, reference to, **Supp. 6**, 606
Straus, Nathan, references to, **Supp. 3**, 451; **Supp. 6**, 606
Straus, Oscar, references to, **Supp. 6**, 253, 606
Straus, Roger W., reference to, **Supp. 9**, 276
Strauss, Lewis, **Supp. 9**, 32
Strauss, Lewis L., reference to, **Supp. 7**, 565, 590
Strauss, Richard, references to, **Supp. 8**, 641, 642
Stravinsky, Igor, references to, **Supp. 7**, 548; **Supp. 10**, 372
Strawberries, cultivation of, **Vol. 5, Part 1**, 272; **Vol. 6, Part 1**, 394
"Strawberry Fields Forever" (song), **Supp. 10**, 450
Straw Dogs, **Supp. 10**, 239
Strayer, George D., references to, **Supp. 3**, 677; **Supp. 4**, 833
Street paving, graft in, **Vol. 8, Part 1**, 588
Street railways: **Vol. 3, Part 2**, 85, 459; **Vol. 4, Part 2**, 167, 226; **Vol. 5, Part 2**, 123; **Vol. 6, Part 1**, 478; **Vol. 7, Part 1**, 71; **Vol. 8, Part 2**, 527; **Vol. 9, Part 2**, 232; cable cars, **Vol. 4, Part 2**, 156; electric, early, **Vol. 9, Part 1**, 128; electrification, **Supp. 1**, 531; equipment development, **Supp. 1**, 669; streetcar, one of first in U.S., **Vol. 5, Part 1**, 325; streetcar building, pioneer, **Vol. 9, Part 1**, 583; strike, New York, **Vol. 5, Part 2**, 196; tramway of 1809, **Vol. 6, Part 1**, 154; trolley cars, early experiments with, **Vol. 3, Part 1**, 88
Street railways (by city): Brooklyn, N.Y., **Vol. 3, Part 2**,

480; **Vol. 6, Part 1**, 294; **Vol. 7, Part 1**, 71; **Vol. 7, Part 2**, 358; Chicago, **Vol. 10, Part 2**, 610; Louisville, Ky., **Vol. 1, Part 2**, 532; New York, N.Y., **Vol. 5, Part 2**, 196; **Vol. 7, Part 2**, 358 f.; **Vol. 8, Part 1**, 634; **Vol. 8, Part 2**, 265 f.; **Vol. 9, Part 1**, 124; **Vol. 9, Part 2**, 241; Philadelphia, Pa., **Vol. 3, Part 1**, 459 f.; **Vol. 7, Part 1**, 71; **Vol. 8, Part 1**, 428; St. Louis, Mo., **Vol. 10, Part 1**, 638 f.; San Francisco, Calif., **Vol. 3, Part 1**, 394; Washington, D.C., **Vol. 2, Part 2**, 383
Street Railways Advertising Co., establishment of, **Supp. 2**, 112
Street Railways Employees' Benevolent Association, **Supp. 1**, 511
Street Scene, **Supp. 4**, 104; **Supp. 8**, 288, 529
Streets of Paris, The (revue), **Supp. 5**, 500
Strelow, Albert, reference to, **Supp. 4**, 294
Streptococcus enteritis, **Supp. 4**, 494
Streptomycin: **Supp. 6**, 447; discovery of, **Supp. 2**, 387; **Supp. 9**, 834
Strickland, William, **Vol. 9, Part 2**, 628
Stricklett, Elmer, reference to, **Supp. 6**, 663
Striker, Fran, reference to, **Supp. 10**, 343
Strikes: **Vol. 4, Part 1**, 175, 288, 370; **Vol. 5, Part 2**, 46, 196; Actors' Equity Association, **Supp. 3**, 174, 333; automobile industry, **Supp. 4**, 612–13; **Supp. 8**, 419, 600, 652; Boston police (1919), **Supp. 1**, 194–95; **Supp. 3**, 471; coal industry, **Vol. 1, Part 1**, 260; **Vol. 5, Part 2**, 196; **Supp. 5**, 248–49; **Supp. 8**, 374, 375, 376; Consumers' Research, **Supp. 8**, 425; garment industry, New York, **Vol. 5, Part 2**, 196; **Supp. 3**, 96; **Supp. 4**, 374; government intervention, **Vol. 10, Part 1**, 119; Homestead steel, **Supp. 3**, 94; journalism on, **Supp. 8**, 675; "Little Steel," **Supp. 6**, 597; Ludlow massacres (1914), **Supp. 6**, 548; lumber industry, **Supp. 6**, 320; *New York Times*, **Supp. 7**, 200; opposition to, as industrial weapon, **Vol. 8, Part 1**, 142 f.; Pennsylvania, armed suppression of, **Vol. 4, Part 2**, 368; printing trade, **Vol. 1, Part 1**, 237; railroad, **Vol. 1, Part 1**, 490; **Vol. 2, Part 2**, 211; **Vol. 3, Part 1**, 183; **Vol. 5, Part 2**, 68; **Vol. 6, Part 1**, 133 f.; **Vol. 8, Part 1**, 142 f.; **Vol. 9, Part 2**, 86, 267; **Supp. 8**, 513; railroad injunction (1922), **Supp. 3**, 214; restrictive legislation, **Supp. 8**, 269; right-to-strike legislation, **Supp. 6**, 586; San Francisco electrical workers, **Supp. 3**, 532; San Francisco general (1934), **Supp. 5**, 287; **Supp. 7**, 609; sit-down, **Supp. 3**, 656; **Supp. 4**, 612–13; steel (1919), **Vol. 5, Part 2**, 196; steel industry, **Supp. 4**, 280; **Supp. 5**, 156, 445–46; **Supp. 5**, 510, 714; supp 6, 597, 678; **Supp. 7**, 228–29, 254–55, 290, 587; steel mill seizure, **Supp. 8**, 517; street car, New York, **Vol. 5, Part 2**, 196; Supreme Court on presidential seizure power, **Supp. 5**, 156, 714; textile industry, **Supp. 3**, 576–77; **Supp. 5**, 616; **Supp. 6**, 238; **Supp. 8**, 457; Toledo Auto-Lite (1934), **Supp. 8**, 458; transit system in, **Supp. 8**, 513; treason, regarding of as, **Vol. 3, Part 2**, 556; World War II, **Supp. 7**, 172
String galvanometer, first made in U.S., **Supp. 6**, 117
Striptease, **Supp. 8**, 363–65
Stritch, Samuel, reference to, **Supp. 8**, 613, 614
Strong, Benjamin, reference to, **Supp. 3**, 203
Structural engineering, **Supp. 1**, 680
"Structuralist" school, **Vol. 9, Part 2**, 564
Strychnine, studies of, **Supp. 2**, 161
Stuart, Charles, reference to, **Vol. 10, Part 1**, 625 f.
Stuart, Don A. (John Wood Campbell, Jr., pseudonym), **Supp. 9**, 155
Stuart, Gilbert, references to, **Vol. 5, Part 2**, 223; **Vol. 9, Part 2**, 649
Stuart, J. E. B., reference to, **Vol. 6, Part 1**, 125, 585
Stuart, John Leighton, reference to, **Supp. 3**, 288
Stubble digger, introduction of, **Vol. 3, Part 1**, 585 f.
Studebaker Corporation: **Supp. 6**, 650; management, **Supp. 9**, 397–98
Student Army Training Corps, organization of, **Vol. 6, Part 2**, 120
Student government, **Supp. 1**, 100; **Supp. 4**, 870
Student Nonviolent Coordinating Committee: **Supp. 8**, 388; founding of, **Supp. 8**, 333, 539–40; voter registration drive, **Supp. 10**, 470
Student Prince, The, **Supp. 5**, 585, 627
Student Volunteer Movement, **Supp. 3**, 476; **Supp. 5**, 506–8
Student Volunteer Movement for Foreign Missions, **Vol. 7, Part 1**, 105; **Vol. 7, Part 2**, 590
Studs Lonigan: A Trilogy, **Supp. 10**, 235
Study and Criticism of Italian Art, The, **Supp. 6**, 56
Study of Man, **Supp. 5**, 435
Sturges, Preston, reference to, **Supp. 9**, 479
Sturtevant, Alfred H., references to, **Supp. 3**, 539–44 **Supp. 8**, 448; **Supp. 9**, 238
Stuttering, **Supp. 7**, 395–96
Stuyvesant, Peter, reference to, **Vol. 7, Part 1**, 516
Stutz Motor Car Co., **Supp. 3**, 314
Styrene, research, **Supp. 9**, 75
Subject of the Artist (New York City art school), founding of, **Supp. 7**, 39
Submarines: aircraft, use of, against, **Vol. 3, Part 1**, 614 f.; building, **Vol. 2, Part 2**, 319; **Vol. 4, Part 1**, 485; **Vol. 5, Part 2**, 380; design and construction, **Supp. 5**, 725; detection, **Vol. 3, Part 1**, 221; **Supp. 4**, 818; **Supp. 5**, 188, 495; **Supp. 6**, 365, 501; **Supp. 7**, 516, 517; development of, **Supp. 3**, 120, 436–37; "diving boat," **Vol. 4, Part 1**, 70; experimentation, early, **Vol. 4, Part 1**, 70; first in Navy, **Supp. 3**, 120; invention of, **Vol. 5, Part 1**, 145; mines and torpedoes, **Vol. 2, Part 1**, 349; New London, Conn., base, **Supp. 6**, 338; nuclear, **Supp. 8**, 232; patents, **Vol. 8, Part 1**, 541; telegraphy, **Vol. 3, Part 1**, 336; **Vol. 10, Part 1**, 421; torpedo-boat, first successful, **Vol. 3, Part 1**, 211
"Submarine Warfare," pamphlet of 1867, **Vol. 6, Part 1**, 65
Subtreasury, origin of, **Vol. 2, Part 2**, 177; **Vol. 10, Part 1**, 155, 355
Suburbs: "homecroft" advocacy, **Supp. 4**, 564; housing developments, **Supp. 7**, 469–70; planned garden, **Supp. 6**, 26; zoning restrictions, **Supp. 4**, 57
Subversives. *See* Espionage; Loyalty issues
Subways: building, **Vol. 1, Part 2**, 408; **Vol. 2, Part 2**, 544; **Vol. 4, Part 1**, 8; **Vol. 4, Part 2**, 605; **Vol. 7, Part 2**, 56, 277, 602; **Vol. 9, Part 1**, 124; **Vol. 10, Part 2**, 339; development of, **Supp. 2**, 559; **Supp. 4**, 56; engineering, **Supp. 4**, 757; speed control, **Supp. 5**, 228; unification of; **Supp. 2**, 675; **Supp. 4**, 466, 855
Success, magazine, founding of, **Vol. 6, Part 2**, 279
Successful Farming, founding of, **Supp. 7**, 527, 528
Sudan grass, discovery of, **Vol. 7, Part 2**, 632
Suez crisis (1956): **Supp. 6**, 179; **Supp. 8**, 147, 158, 276; U.S. diplomatic efforts during, **Supp. 10**, 572
Suffolk, Va., campaign, **Vol. 6, Part 1**, 124, 392; **Vol. 7, Part 2**, 381, 570
Suffolk Bank System, **Vol. 6, Part 1**, 51
Suffolk Resolves, carrying of, to Philadelphia, **Vol. 8, Part 1**, 515
Suffrage: property qualifications, **Vol. 8, Part 2**, 349; universal white male, establishment of, **Vol. 7, Part 2**, 613. *See also* Voting rights; Woman suffrage
Suffrage Study Club, **Supp. 6**, 79
Sugar Creek War, **Vol. 8, Part 1**, 42
Sugar industry: barter, sugar and rum for lumber, **Vol. 3, Part 1**, 252; beet sugar technology, **Supp. 1**, 431; cane studies, **Supp. 1**, 183; chemistry of, **Supp. 4**, 114; **Supp. 5**, 327–28; Cuban import quota, **Supp. 9**, 191; Hawaiian plantation, **Supp. 1**, 48; planting, **Vol.**

2, Part 1, 535; **Vol. 3, Part 1**, 585 f.; **Vol. 4, Part 1**, 256; **Vol. 9, Part 1**, 427, 478 f; **Vol. 9, Part 2**, 338; importation of, **Vol. 7, Part 2**, 631; refining, **Vol. 1, Part 2**, 461; **Vol. 3, Part 1**, 585 f.; **Vol. 4, Part 2**, 336, 404 f.; **Vol. 5, Part 1**, 448; **Vol. 5, Part 2**, 464; **Vol. 7, Part 2**, 267; **Vol. 8, Part 2**, 512; **Vol. 9, Part 1**, 428; **Vol. 10, Part 1**, 457 f.; **Vol. 10, Part 2**, 187; refining, first time in U.S., **Vol. 1, Part 1**, 130; sugar-beet seed experimentation, **Vol. 8, Part 1**, 239 f.; tariffs, **Vol. 2, Part 2**, 459; **Vol. 4, Part 2**, 404; **Vol. 7, Part 2**, 101 f.; trust, **Vol. 4, Part 2**, 404. *See also* Glucose

Sulfa drugs, **Supp. 3**, 854; **Supp. 6**, 447

Sulfonamide drugs, **Supp. 7**, 477

Sulfur compounds, research on, **Supp. 10**, 197–98

Sulfuric acid, **Supp. 5**, 319–20

Sullavan, Margaret, reference to, **Supp. 9**, 375

Sullivan, Anne, reference to, **Supp. 8**, 316–18

Sullivan, Ed, references to, **Supp. 9**, 489, 887

Sullivan, Eugene C., reference to, **Supp. 6**, 624

Sullivan, Harry Stack, reference to, **Supp. 4**, 131; **Supp. 6**, 220

Sullivan, Louis H., references to, **Supp. 2**, 537, 709; **Supp. 4**, 105, 106; **Supp. 5**, 207, 208; **Supp. 6**, 711, 713; **Supp. 8**, 463

Sullivan, Nikki, reference to, **Supp. 6**, 301

Sullivan and Cromwell, **Supp. 4**, 192–93; **Supp. 6**, 177, 178; **Supp. 8**, 147

Sullivan Island, S.C. *See* Charleston, S.C.

Sullivan's Rhode Island expedition (1778), **Vol. 4, Part 1**, 186; **Vol. 5, Part 2**, 537; **Vol. 9, Part 2**, 193; **Vol. 10, Part 1**, 518

Sullivan's Travels, **Supp. 9**, 479

Sulphur: dioxide, isolation of, **Vol. 8, Part 1**, 223 f.; production, **Vol. 3, Part 2**, 603; researches in, **Vol. 9, Part 1**, 235

Sulzberger, Arthur Hays, reference to, **Supp. 7**, 199–200

Sumeria, language studies, **Supp. 1**, 172

Summer Place, **Supp. 10**, 231

Summer school, first, **Vol. 9, Part 1**, 472

Summer School of the South, **Supp. 3**, 209

Sumner, Charles, references to, **Vol. 2, Part 1**, 88, 289; **Vol. 3, Part 2**, 398 f.; **Vol. 6, Part 1**, 436; **Vol. 7, Part 2**, 576; **Vol. 9, Part 1**, 516, 624; **Vol. 9, Part 2**, 210

Sun, eclipses of, **Vol. 3, Part 1**, 602 f.; spots, **Vol. 10, Part 2**, 415. *See also* Solar *headings*

Sun Also Rises, The, **Supp. 7**, 335, 336; **Supp. 10**, 756–57

Sunday, Billy, reference to, **Supp. 5**, 649

Sunday, observance of, **Vol. 8, Part 1**, 428; **Vol. 8, Part 2**, 114; **Vol. 9, Part 2**, 299

Sunday-school movement: **Vol. 1, Part 1**, 392, 628; **Vol. 2, Part 2**, 108; **Vol. 3, Part 1**, 522 f.; **Vol. 3, Part 2**, 492; **Vol. 4, Part 1**, 625; **Vol. 5, Part 1**, 425; **Vol. 5, Part 2**, 409, 589; **Vol. 7, Part 2**, 410; **Vol. 8, Part 1**, 539; **Vol. 9, Part 1**, 33, 43 f., 270; **Vol. 10, Part 1**, 8 f.; American Sunday-School Union, **Vol. 1, Part 1**, 392; **Vol. 4, Part 1**, 624 f.; **Vol. 5, Part 1**, 56, 132; **Vol. 6, Part 1**, 406; **Vol. 7, Part 2**, 127 f.; **Vol. 8, Part 1**, 539; associations, **Vol. 6, Part 1**, 44; first Sunday school in U.S., **Vol. 8, Part 1**, 381; lessons, uniform, **Vol. 4, Part 2**, 409; **Vol. 10, Part 1**, 9; publications, **Vol. 4, Part 2**, 360; **Vol. 5, Part 2**, 240, 369; **Vol. 6, Part 1**, 430–24; **Vol. 7, Part 1**, 451; writings on, **Vol. 6, Part 1**, 44; **Vol. 7, Part 2**, 411; **Vol. 8, Part 1**, 539; **Vol. 9, Part 2**, 307

Sun Oil Co., **Supp. 7**, 615; management and growth of, **Supp. 9**, 612

Sunrise at Campobello, **Supp. 10**, 721

Sunset Boulevard, **Supp. 6**, 160, 658–59

Sunshine Boys, The, **Supp. 9**, 214

Sunshine Society, founding of, **Supp. 1**, 19

Sunspots, magnetic fields, **Supp. 2**, 271

Sun Valley, Idaho, naming of, **Supp. 5**, 270–71

Superheterodyne circuit, **Supp. 5**, 21

Superior Oil Co. of Los Angeles, **Supp. 7**,111

Supermarkets, **Supp. 7**, 141; A&P switch to, **Supp. 5**, 278; introduction of, **Supp. 5**, 604

Supernaturalism. *See* Psychic phenomena

Supreme Court, United States: **Vol. 1, Part 1**, 533 f., 595; **Vol. 1, Part 2**, 338, 360, 572; **Vol. 2, Part 1**, 23; **Vol. 2, Part 2**, 36, 634 f.; **Vol. 4, Part 1**, 61, 627 f.; **Vol. 4, Part 2**, 25; **Vol. 5, Part 1**, 183, 233, 394, 492; **Vol. 5, Part 2**, 122, 553; **Vol. 6, Part 1**, 313, 510; **Vol. 6, Part 2**, 88, 128, 319 f., 419; **Vol. 7, Part 1**, 108, 113, 422 f.; **Vol. 8, Part 1**, 285 f.; **Vol. 8, Part 2**, 347; **Vol. 9, Part 1**, 103 f.; **Vol. 9, Part 2**, 104, 239 f., 332, 472, 643; **Vol. 10, Part 1**, 393 f, 494 f.; 508 f.; **Vol. 10, Part 2**, 96, 489, 506; antitrust decisions, **Supp. 3**, 168; **Supp. 7**, 96; appellate cases before, **Supp. 5**, 155, 156; building, new, Taft's advocacy of, **Vol. 9, Part 2**, 272; chief justices, **Supp. 5**, 713; **Supp. 9**, 835–37; church-state separation decisions, **Supp. 4**, 713; **Supp. 5**, 358; citizenship decisions, **Supp. 4**, 727; civil liberties decisions, **Supp. 3**, 168; **Supp. 4**, 407, 537, 614, 713, 796; **Supp. 5**, 358, 389, 574–75, 714; **Supp. 7**, 96, 263–64, 291, 541–42; **Supp. 9**, 96, 97, 364–65, 593, 837, 865; **Supp. 10**, 126, 188, 665; civil rights decisions, **Supp. 4**, 397, 407, 796; **Supp. 5**, 713–14; **Supp. 6**, 502; **Supp. 7**, 96; **Supp. 8**, 406; **Supp. 9**, 749; **Supp. 10**, 126–27, 665; Civil War period, **Vol. 4, Part 1**, 613; "clear and present danger" test, **Supp. 7**, 317; Congress, acts invalidated by, Jefferson's views on, **Vol. 5, Part 2**, 29; conservative bloc, post-World War II, **Supp. 10**, 126; conservative "Four Horsemen," **Supp. 4**, 537–38; court-packing move, **Supp. 3**, 100, 168, 227, 655; **Supp. 4**, 42, 407, 491, 537; **Supp. 5**, 357, 443, 481; **Supp. 6**, 138, 227, 234; **Supp. 7**, 263, 541, 730; **Supp. 9**, 95, 129, 151, 311, 611, 681, 810, 859; **Supp. 10**, 188; criminal justice decisions, **Supp. 9**, 837; **Supp. 10**, 665; decisions of, 1862–90, **Vol. 6, Part 2**, 638 f.; desegregation decisions, **Supp. 9**, 449; dissent record, **Supp. 4**, 538; **Supp. 9**, 365; Douglas impeachment hearings, **Supp. 10**, 190; formative period, **Vol. 5, Part 2**, 8; historical writings on, **Supp. 5**, 731; **Supp. 9**, 88; interstate commerce decisions, **Supp. 3**, 241; **Supp. 4**, 404–5; judges' bill, **Vol. 9, Part 2**, 271; judicial activism, **Supp. 4**, 796, 797; **Supp. 9**, 835–36; **Supp. 10**, 188; judicial disagreement on functions of, **Supp. 5**, 571; judicial self-restraint, **Supp. 3**, 94; **Supp. 4**, 795, 797; **Supp. 5**, 357–58; **Supp. 7**, 96, 264; **Supp. 9**, 364; justices, **Supp. 1**, 272, 417, 422–27; **Supp. 2**, 79, 93; **Supp. 3**, 97–100; **Supp. 4**, 613–14, 712–13, 794–97; **Supp. 5**, 357–59, 571–76; **Supp. 7**, 96–97, 263–65, 541–42; **Supp. 9**, 363, 364–65; justices' positions on New Deal legislation, **Supp. 5**, 572–75; labor-related decisions, **Supp. 5**, 156, 249, 572, 574, 714; liberal wing, post-World War II, **Supp. 10**, 188; loyalty-security decisions, **Supp. 5**, 358, 589, 714; **Supp. 7**, 96–97, 317; **Supp. 10**, 126; Mooney case, **Supp. 3**, 533; New Deal legislation decisions, **Supp. 3**, 755, 789, 839; **Supp. 4**, 406–7, 537, 795–97; **Supp. 5**, 358, 572–75; **Supp. 7**, 263; **Supp. 8**, 35; Nixon nominations to (unconfirmed), **Supp. 9**, 681, 739; **Supp. 10**, 316; nominations to (unconfirmed), **Supp. 6**, 494; only members from same family to sit on, **Supp. 9**, 363; organization of, **Vol. 3, Part 2**, 114; preferred freedoms concept, **Supp. 4**, 796–97; press freedom decisions, **Supp. 3**, 157; school desegregation decisions, **Supp. 5**, 156; **Supp. 7**, 501; **Supp. 8**, 25, 157; **Supp. 9**, 104, 190–91, 364, 391, 401, 433, 743, 836; **Supp. 10**, 127, 189; state courts, jurisdiction of, over, **Vol. 9,**

Part 2, 105; state v. federal power decisions, **Supp. 3**, 754–55; steel industry seizure decision, **Supp. 5**, 156, 714; **Supp. 10**, 126; TVA decisions, **Supp. 8**, 179; Webster's theory about power of, **Vol. 10, Part 1**, 585 f.; woman, first, to practice before, **Vol. 6, Part 1**, 341; woman justices, issue of, **Supp. 8**, 5; writings on, **Supp. 5**, 549, **Supp. 6**, 143; **Supp. 7**, 146–47, 261; zoning decision, **Supp. 4**, 56–57. *See also* Judicial systems; Judiciary

Supreme Court Building, construction of, **Supp. 3**, 99

Supreme Court in United States History, The, **Supp. 5**, 731

Supreme Court justices. For complete list, *See* Occupations Index

Surface chemistry, **Supp. 6**, 365

Surgeon general, United States, **Supp. 4**, 791; smoking and health reports, **Supp. 7**, 192

Surgery: **Vol. 1, Part 1**, 636; **Vol. 1, Part 2**, 80; **Vol. 2, Part 1**, 507; **Vol. 2, Part 2**, 95, 339; **Vol. 3, Part l**, 91, 385 f., 412 f., 478 f.; **Vol. 3, Part 2**, 219, 321, 331, 406 f.; **Vol. 4, Part 1**, 180, 221, 229, 259; **Vol. 4, Part 2**, 19 f., 32, 164 f., 185, 365; **Vol. 5, Part 1**, 239, 284, 364; **Vol. 5, Part 2**, 140 f., 181, 235, 376, 414 f., 580; **Vol. 6, Part 1**, 375, 523, 615; **Vol. 6, Part 2**, 428, 585; **Vol. 7, Part 1**, 72, 130; **Vol. 7, Part 2**, 198, 243, 276, 554 f., 602, 637; **Vol. 8, Part 1**, 121, 209 f., 360 f., 378, 486 f., 575 f.; **Vol. 8, Part 2**, 111, 358, 404; **Vol. 9, Part 1**, 132, 186 f., 195, 324, 348, 451; **Vol. 9, Part 2**, 33, 85, 575; **Vol. 10, Part 1**, 84, 395, 479 f., 611 f.; **Vol. 10, Part 2**, 473, 576; **Supp. 2**, 438; **Supp. 5**, 104; abdominal, **Vol. 1, Part 2**, 55; **Vol. 2, Part 1**, 254; **Vol. 3, Part 2**, 563; **Vol. 5, Part 1**, 549; **Vol. 6, Part 2**, 28; **Vol. 8, Part 1**, 213 f., 572; **Supp. 3**, 410; American Surgical Association, **Vol. 5, Part 1**, 100; **Vol. 7, Part 2**, 208; **Vol. 8, Part 1**, 575; animal ligature, **Vol. 5, Part 1**, 601; antiseptic methods, **Supp. 1**, 240; appendectomy, **Vol. 3, Part 2**, 434, 563 f.; **Vol. 5, Part 1**, 546; **Vol. 6, Part 1**, 555 f., 615; **Vol. 7, Part 1**, 380; **Supp. 1**, 236; appendectomy, first successful, in U.S., **Vol. 7, Part 2**, 243; aseptic, **Vol. 1, Part 2**, 224; **Vol. 5, Part 2**, 141, 580; **Vol. 8, Part 1**, 391; aural, **Vol. 2, Part 1**, 221; blood vessel, **Supp. 3**, 140; bone, **Vol. 7, Part 1**, 120, 409; **Vol. 10, Part 2**, 463; brain, **Supp. 2**, 137; **Supp. 6**, 70, 131; breast cancer, **Supp. 6**, 70; cardiac, **Supp. 7**, 59; cataract removal, **Vol. 3, Part 1**, 478 f.; **Vol. 5, Part 1**, 541; certification in, **Supp. 6**, 246; cesarian section, first successful, in U.S., **Vol. 8, Part 1**, 583; Dieffenbach operation, **Vol. 3, Part 1**, 327; dissection of human body for instruction, first, **Vol. 1, Part 1**, 597; duct ligation, **Supp. 3**, 483; electricity, early use of, in, **Vol. 2, Part 1**, 385; electrosurgical knife (Bovie unit), **Supp. 6**, 69–70; endoaneurysmorrhaphy, **Supp. 6**, 434; ether charts, **Supp. 2**, 137; eye, **Supp. 3**, 301–2, 430–31; fee-splitting, **Supp. 6**, 245; first bacteriology lab, **Supp. 6**, 664; first heart valve, **Supp. 4**, 209; fistula operations, **Vol. 9, Part 1**, 186; Fowler position, **Supp. 6**, 214–15; frozen tissue sections, **Supp. 3**, 503; gallbladder, **Vol. 1, Part 2**, 433; **Vol. 8, Part 1**, 360 f., 378; **Supp. 6**, 632; gastric, **Supp. 3**, 271; gastro-intestinal, **Vol. 7, Part 2**, 374; genitourinary, **Vol. 2, Part 1**, 116, 393; **Vol. 5, Part 2**, 364; **Vol. 6, Part 2**, 384; **Supp. 3**, 121; **Supp. 4**, 507, 508; gynecological, **Vol. 6, Part 2**, 273; **Supp. 1**, 542; instruments, surgical, improvements in, **Vol. 7, Part 2**, 554 f.; intranasal, **Vol. 6, Part l**, 268; journals, **Supp. 1**, 542, 599; limbs, artificial, **Vol. 1, Part 1**, 428; **Vol. 6, Part 2**, 288; mastoid operation, **Vol. 5, Part 1**, 248; military, **Vol. 1, Part 2**, 25, 105; **Vol. 2, Part 1**, 52; **Vol. 3, Part 2**, 307, 538; **Vol. 4, Part 1**, 272; **Vol. 4, Part 2**, 481; **Vol. 5, Part 2**, 375 f.; **Vol. 6, Part 1**, 58 f., 440 f.; **Vol. 6, Part 2**, 243; **Vol. 7, Part 2**, 96 f., 109; **Vol. 8, Part 2**, 376, 585; **Vol. 9, Part 2**, 550; **Vol. 10, Part 2**, 492; neurological, **Supp. 2**, 209; **Supp. 4**, 213, 214, 249–50; obstetrics, **Vol. 10, Part 2**, 326; ophthalmic, **Vol. 5, Part 2**, 37 f.; **Vol. 6, Part 1, 296; orthopedic, Vol. 1, Part 2**, 22, 556 f.; **Vol. 3, Part 1**, 118 f.; **Vol. 5, Part 2**, 235 f.; **Vol. 6, Part 1**, 443; **Vol. 8, Part 2**, 404; **Vol. 9, Part 2**, 318, 343; **Vol. 10, Part 2**, 231; **Supp. 1**, 25–26, 40–41; **Supp. 4**, 887; **Supp. 6**, 344–45; osteotomy, **Vol. 10, Part 1**, 158; osteosarcoma, **Vol. 8, Part 1**, 360 f.; pathology of, **Supp. 1**, 91; plastic, **Vol. 2, Part 1**, 224; **Vol. 5, Part 2**, 492 f.; **Supp. 2**, 707; **Supp. 4**, 220–21, 530; **Supp. 6**, 632; postoperative care, **Supp. 6**, 190; procedures development, **Supp. 3**, 67; prostate gland, **Supp. 3**, 854; radical dissection, **Supp. 3**, 202; reproductive system in, **Supp. 6**, 631–32; rubber gloves, use of, **Supp. 1**, 90; shock prevention, **Supp. 3**, 201; **Supp. 7**, 59; sinus, **Vol. 6, Part l**, 523; skull tumors, **Vol. 1, Part 2**, 2; specialist teams, **Supp. 5**, 404–5; spinal cord, **Supp. 6**, 131; supplies, surgical, **Vol. 8, Part 2**, 528; surgeon-generalship, **Vol. 1, Part 1**, 631; **Vol. 1, Part 2**, 267; teaching of, **Vol. 2, Part 2**, 76; **Vol. 4, Part 2**, 465; **Vol. 5, Part 1**, 100, 161; **Vol. 6, Part 1**, 555 f.; **Vol. 7, Part 1**, 120, 290, 353 f., 372, 380, 409, 553, 616; **Vol. 7, Part 2**, 129; **Vol. 8, Part 2**, 404 f, 584; **Vol. 9, Part 1**, 324, 327, 606; **Vol. 9, Part 2**, 535; **Supp. 3**, 121–22, 458; textbook, first in colonies, **Vol. 5, Part 2**, 181; thoracic, **Supp. 6**, 246; tonsil operation, **Vol. 7, Part l**, 616; training in, **Supp. 3**, 626; **Supp. 4**, 208–9; transplant studies, **Supp. 3**, 140–41; vascular, **Supp. 6**, 434–35; venereal disease, first specialist in U.S., **Vol. 2, Part 1**, 260; water, boiled, early faith in, **Vol. 3, Part 1**, 478 f.; women in field of, **Vol. 6, Part 1**, 340; writings on, **Vol. 2, Part 1**, 52, 93, 116, 199, 224, 254, 394; **Vol. 4, Part 2**, 19; **Vol. 5, Part 2**, 141, 181, 415, 580; **Vol. 6, Part 1**, 615; **Vol. 7, Part 1**, 324 f., 354, 380, 616; **Vol. 8, Part 1**, 213 f., 376, 378, 572; **Vol. 8, Part 2**, 44, 111; **Vol. 9, Part 1**, 403; **Vol. 9, Part 2**, 33, 318, 343; **Vol. 10, Part 1**, 84, 158, 395, 480 f., 581 f.; **Vol. 10, Part 2**, 576; **Supp. 1**, 218, 599. *See also* Anesthesia

Surgery, Gynecology and Obstetrics, founding of, **Supp. 1**, 542

Surgical dressings, use of moss for, **Vol. 9, Part 1**, 276

Surplus Property Administration, **Supp. 7**, 36

Surprise, first clipper ship, **Vol. 4, Part 2**, 142

Surratt, John H., **Vol. 1, Part 2**, 449; **Vol. 3, Part 2**, 409; **Vol. 5, Part 2**, 400

Surratt, Mary E., **Vol. 1, Part 2**, 449; **Vol. 5, Part 1**, 182 f.

Surrealism: **Supp. 5**, 184–85; **Supp. 6**, 512; art, **Supp. 10**, 90–92, 220, 505

Survey, **Supp. 6**, 329–30; predecessors, **Supp. 2**, 656; **Supp. 4**, 227

Surveying: **Vol. 1, Part 1**, 325 f.; **Vol. 3, Part 2**, 89 f.; **Vol. 4, Part 2**, 463; **Vol. 5, Part 1**, 335 f., 360; **Vol. 5, Part 2**, 47, 372 f.; **Vol. 6, Part 1**, 135 f.; **Vol. 9, Part 1**, 88, 516; **Vol. 9, Part 2**, 455 f.; Alaska, **Vol. 3, Part 1**, 35 f., 92; Aleutian Islands, **Vol. 3, Part 1**, 36; California coast, **Vol. 8, Part 1**, 617; coal, **Vol. 6, Part 1**, 183; Columbia River, **Vol. 9, Part 2**, 455; England, colonial agents from, **Vol. 8, Part 2**, 126; Florida, **Vol. 1, Part 2**, 394; harbors, **Vol. 9, Part 2**, 247; Kentucky, **Vol. 9, Part 1**, 60; Mason-Dixon line, **Vol. 4, Part 1**, 476; Mississippi River, **Vol. 5, Part 1**, 371; New Amsterdam, **Vol. 5, Part 1**, 336; New England coast, **Vol. 3, Part 1**, 106; North Carolina, **Vol. 6, Part 1**, 58; **Vol. 9, Part 1**, 254; Northwest, **Vol. 9, Part 2**, 598; Ohio, **Vol. 5, Part 2**, 372; Pacific coast, **Vol. 3, Part 1**, 92; Pennsylvania, **Vol. 5, Part 2**, 467; **Vol. 8, Part 1**, 82 f.; railroad, **Vol. 3, Part 1**, 207,

258, 348; **Vol. 5, Part 2**, 455, 569; **Vol. 8, Part 1**, 11 f., 76, 179 f., 264 f.; seacoast, **Vol. 8, Part 1**, 647; southern coast, **Vol. 3, Part 1**, 201; southern district, **Vol. 3, Part 1**, 182 f.; surveyor-general service, **Vol. 3, Part 1**, 316; **Vol. 8, Part 1, 284 f.; Texas, Vol. 4, Part 2**, 369; Utah, **Vol. 4, Part 2**, 52; Virginia, **Vol. 6, Part 2**, 464; **Vol. 9, Part 1**, 254; Wisconsin Territory, **Vol. 3, Part 1**, 390; writings on, **Vol. 4, Part 2**, 49; **Vol. 5, Part 2**, 167 f.
Surveyor (lunar probe), **Supp. 9**, 476
Susan Lenox, **Vol. 7, Part 2**, 539
Susquehanna Co., **Vol. 3, Part 1**, 581 f.
Susquehanna Ferry, **Vol. 4, Part 2**, 314
Sutherland, George, references to, **Supp. 4**, 537; **Supp. 5**, 571, 574
Sutherland, John, reference to, **Supp. 8**, 335
Sutter, John A., **Vol. 1, Part 1**, 234; **Vol. 6, Part 2, 314**
Sutton, May, reference to, **Supp. 9**, 868
Sutton, W. S., reference to, **Supp. 4**, 516
Swain, Virginia Maude, reference to, **Supp. 6**, 603
Swaine, Dorothy, reference to, **Supp. 4**, 828
Swallow Airplane Co., **Supp. 9**, 757
Swallow Barn, **Vol. 5, Part 2**, 333
"Swamp College," **Vol. 4, Part 2**, 578
Swann, William F. G., reference to, **Supp. 7**, 619
"Swann memorial" (Philadelphia, Pa.), **Supp. 3**, 124
Swansea (Mass.), building of, **Vol. 7, Part 1**, 376
Swanson, Gloria, references to, **Supp. 4**, 66; **Supp. 6**, 160, 658, 659; **Supp. 7**, 50; **Supp. 8**, 320
Swanson, Martin, reference to, **Supp. 3**, 532
Swarthmore College: **Vol. 1, Part 2**, 430; **Vol. 6, Part 2**, 198; **Vol. 7, Part 1**, 288; English studies, **Supp. 3**, 474, 475; founding of, **Vol. 7, Part 2**, 258; **Vol. 9, Part 2**, 441; presidency, **Supp. 6**, 30; **Supp. 8**, 601–2; psychology studies, **Supp. 8**, 345
Swarts, Gardner T., reference to, **Supp. 3**, 158
Swarts, Theodore, **Supp. 3**, 25
Swasey, Ambrose, **Vol. 10, Part 1**, 470 f.
Sweden: diplomatic relations with, **Vol. 1, Part 1**, 285
Sweden and the Swedes, **Vol. 9, Part 2**, 447
Swedenborg, Emanuel, influence of, **Vol. 5, Part 1**, 578
Swedenborg Association, **Vol. 1, Part 1**, 644
Swedenborgian church (New Jerusalem church): **Vol. 3, Part 2**, 213; **Vol. 4, Part 1**, 282; **Vol. 5, Part 1**, 134 f.; **Vol. 6, Part 2**, 544; **Vol. 8, Part 1**, 448 f., 455; **Vol. 8, Part 2**, 606; **Vol. 9, Part 1**, 376; **Supp. 6**, 611, 612; writings on, **Vol. 5, Part 1**, 578; **Vol. 8, Part 1**, 455; **Vol. 10, Part 2**, 314
Swedish: newspapers, **Vol. 7, Part 1**, 550; settlements, **Vol. 6, Part 2**, **Vol. 8, Part 1**, 627; **Vol. 9, Part 2**, 25, 243
Sweet, William Warren, reference to, **Supp. 4**, 151
"Sweet Adeline" (song), **Supp. 5**, 23
Sweet Charity, **Supp. 9**, 281
Sweeterman, John W., reference to, **Supp. 7**, 296
Sweet potato, crop development, **Supp. 3**, 146
"Swelled Heads," **Vol. 6, Part 1**, 547
Swift, Samuel, reference to, **Supp. 7**, 494
"Swift, Tom" (fictional character), **Supp. 7**, 279
Swift & Co., management of, **Supp. 2**, 644–45
Swimming, **Supp. 8**, 336–37, 547
Swine-breeding, scientific study of, **Vol. 4, Part 2**, 315
Swing bands, **Supp. 5**, 32–33, 293, 534–35; **Supp. 6**, 172–73; **Supp. 8**, 163. *See also* Dance bands
Swiss colonization: **Vol. 5, Part 2**, 117, 491; Indiana, **Vol. 3, Part 1**, 491 f.; Kentucky, **Vol. 3, Part 1**, 491 f.; North Carolina, **Vol. 4, Part 1**, 468; South Carolina, **Vol. 8, Part 1**, 270 f.
Switzerland: diplomacy with U.S., **Supp. 1**, 675; **Supp. 4**, 898; minister plenipotentiary to, **Vol. 1, Part 2**, 487
Swope, Gerard, reference to, **Supp. 7**, 809
Swope, Herbert Bayard, references to, **Supp. 2**, 545; **Supp. 4**, 885
Sword factory, first in U.S., **Vol. 1, Part 1**, 249
Sydney Harbor Bridge (Australia), **Supp. 6**, 594
Sylvis, William H., reference to, **Vol. 9, Part 2**, 640
Symington, Stuart, reference to, **Supp. 10**, 243
Sympathetic nervous system, **Supp. 3**, 134–36
Symphony orchestra. *See specific orchestra names*
Syms-Eaton Free School, original grant for, **Vol. 9, Part 2**, 261
Synanon, **Supp. 8**, 424
Synapse, structure of, **Supp. 6**, 295–96
Syndicalism, literary, **Vol. 9, Part 2**, 125
Syndicalist League of North America, **Supp. 7**, 254; **Supp. 9**, 126
Syndicate (theatrical trust), **Supp. 3**, 276–77
Synod of 1662 (Congregational), **Vol. 7, Part 1**, 55 f.
Synod of the Evangelical Lutheran Church in America, **Vol. 8, Part 1**, 208 f.
Synthetics: development of, **Supp. 5**, 191–92; fabric, **Supp. 6**, 67; fibers, **Supp. 2**, 97; first fiber, **Supp. 5**, 663; first high-test gasoline, **Supp. 6**, 332; first peptide substrates, **Supp. 3**, 61; paint resins, **Supp. 3**, 247; research in, **Supp. 3**, 239; **Supp. 7**, 169; rubber, **Supp. 3**, 522; **Supp. 5**, 191, 273, 366; **Supp. 6**, 334; **Supp. 8**, 123
Syphilis: juvenile paresis studies, **Supp. 8**, 429; parasite causing, **Supp. 4**, 288; rational therapy of, **Vol. 8, Part 1**, 588 f.; research in, **Vol. 5, Part 2**, 364; **Vol. 7, Part 1**, 542; **Vol. 8, Part 2**, 419; social aspects, **Supp. 3**, 58; social education on, **Supp. 4**, 459, 758; treatment, **Supp. 6**, 424, 460–61. *See also* Venereal disease
Syracuse, N.Y., **Vol. 2, Part 2**, 274 f.; **Vol. 7, Part 2**, 380
Syracuse University: **Vol. 2, Part 2**, 333; **Vol. 3, Part 1**, 161; **Vol. 9, Part 1**, 185; football team, **Supp. 7**, 167–68; forestry program, **Supp. 4**, 44; founding, of, **Vol. 8, Part 1**, 478; history studies, **Supp. 6**, 278
Syria: Bible translation into Syriac, **Vol. 9, Part 2**, 53; explorations in, **Vol. 9, Part 1**, 258; missionary work in, **Vol. 1, Part 2**, 370; **Vol. 3, Part 1**, 238 f.; **Vol. 5, Part 2**, 61; **Vol. 9, Part 2**, 490
Syrian Protestant College (now the American University) of Beirut, **Vol. 1, Part 2**, 370, 374; **Vol. 8, Part 1**, 116 f.
Syringes, development of, **Supp. 7**, 678–79
Systematic Theology, **Supp. 7**, 746–47
Szell, George, reference to, **Supp. 6**, 324
Szilard, Leo, reference to, **Supp. 9**, 696
Szold, Robert, reference to, **Supp. 3**, 280

T

Taber, Robert, reference to, **Supp. 4**, 552–54
Tabulating machines, introduction of, **Vol. 8, Part 1**, 100 f.
Tachistoscope, **Supp. 3**, 229–30
Tacna-Arica controversy, **Vol. 6, Part 1**, 358
Tacoma, Wash.: General Hospital, dedication of, **Vol. 7, Part 2**, 134; politics, **Supp. 10**, 86, 87
Tacoma Narrows Bridge (Wash.), **Supp. 3**, 531; **Supp. 6**, 594
Taft, Charles Phelps, II, reference to, **Supp. 5**, 674
Taft, Lorado, reference to, **Vol. 7, Part 1**, 321
Taft, Philip, reference to, **Supp. 3**, 179
Taft, Robert A.: leadership in Senate challenged, **Supp. 9**, 467–68; presidential bids, **Supp. 7**, 49, 84; **Supp. 8**, 156; **Supp. 9**, 357; references to, **Supp. 5**, 690, 719; **Supp. 6**, 455

Taft, Stettinius, and Hollister, founding of, **Supp. 5**, 674
Taft, William Howard: American Red Cross, **Supp. 4**, 91–92, biography of, **Supp. 6**, 521; Brandeis relationship, **Supp. 3**, 96, 98, 99; diplomatic service policies, **Supp. 6**, 254; family, **Supp. 3**, 758; **Supp. 5**, 673; League to Enforce Peace, **Supp. 3**, 472; **Supp. 5**, 308; Morse case, **Vol. 7, Part 1**, 241; Philippines governorship, **Supp. 6**, 210, 579; Pinchot controversy, **Vol. 1, Part 1**, 555; presidential candidacy, **Supp. 3**, 395; **Supp. 6**, 132; references to, **Supp. 5**, 261, 707–8; Roosevelt, T. R., relationship, **Vol. 8, Part 2**, 141 f.; **Vol. 9, Part 2**, 265; **Supp. 2**, 581, 582; Supreme Court, **Supp. 5**, 572; **Supp. 7**, 317
Taft-Hartley Act (1947), **Supp. 4**, 724; **Supp. 6**, 472, 480, 679; **Supp. 7**, 382, 801; **Supp. 8**, 25, 269, 511; forerunner of, **Supp. 4**, 12; loyalty oath requirement, **Supp. 5**, 358; passage of, **Supp. 5**, 675; **Supp. 8**, 245–46; Supreme Court decisions, **Supp. 5**, 714
Taft-Wagner-Ellender Housing Act (1949), **Supp. 5**, 675
Taggard, Genevieve, reference to, **Supp. 8**, 255
Tailors' Union of America, **Vol. 6, Part 1**, 170
Taiping rebellion (China), **Vol. 10, Part 1**, 419 f.
Talbott, Harold, reference to, **Supp. 8**, 322
Tale of Two Cities, A, **Supp. 10**, 807
Taliesin (Wis.), **Supp. 6**, 713, 714; **Supp. 9**, 893
Taliesin West (Scottsdale, Ariz.), **Supp. 6**, 714; **Supp. 10**, 764
Talking-machine, inventions relating to, **Vol. 3, Part 1**, 221
"Talk of the Town" (television program), **Supp. 9**, 779–80
Tallahassee, Fla., as site for capital, **Vol. 3, Part 1**, 557 f.
Talleyrand, Louisiana Purchase negotiations, **Vol. 6, Part 1**, 324
Tallmadge, James, reference to, **Vol. 9, Part 2**, 335
Talmadge, Eugene, reference to, **Supp. 3**, 331
Talmadge, Herman, reference to, **Supp. 6**, 235
Talmadge, Norma, reference to, **Supp. 9**, 791
Talmage, T. DeWitt, reference to, **Vol. 5, Part 2**, 199
Tamar and Other Poems, **Supp. 7**, 391–92
Tamil language, studies in, **Supp. 1**, 164
Tammany Hall: **Vol. 2, Part 2**, 558 f.; **Vol. 3, Part 1, 138; Vol. 3, Part 2**, 193, 252, 415; **Vol. 4, Part 1**, 8, 463; **Vol. 4, Part 2**, 115, 161, 189, 405, 605; **Vol. 5, Part 1**, 113 f.; **Vol. 5, Part 2**, 307 f.; **Vol. 6, Part 1**, 229, 568; **Vol. 7, Part 1**, 122, 279 f., 346; **Vol. 8, Part 2**, 20, 424 f.; **Vol. 9, Part 1**, 9, 72; **Vol. 9, Part 2**, 241 f.; **Vol. 10, Part 1**, 80 f.; **Supp. 4**, 608, 855–56, 904; **Supp. 5**, 227, 285–86, 665, 717; **Supp. 6**, 88, 141, 142, 280, 294, 295; cartoons as weapons against, **Vol. 3, Part 1**, 378 f.; Committee of Seventy, **Vol. 9, Part 2**, 15; early history of, **Vol. 10, Part 2**, 456; founding of, **Vol. 7, Part 1**, 111; fusion tickets against, **Supp. 4**, 542, 464–65, 543; **Supp. 9**, 230; *Harper's Weekly* fight against, **Vol. 10, Part 1**, 81; Havemeyer and, **Vol. 4, Part 2**, 405; Powell reelection challenged by, **Supp. 9**, 620; public utilities, **Supp. 3**, 716; reform movement against, **Supp. 3**, 605, 646; **Supp. 6**, 570; Roosevelt, F. D., relationship, **Supp. 3**, 642–46; Smith relationship, **Supp. 3**, 717, 719; Spartan Association opposition to, **Vol. 10, Part 1**, 390 f.; Sulzer impeachment proceedings, **Supp. 3**, 751; tiger, as symbol, **Vol. 7, Part 1**, 392; **Vol. 10, Part 1**, 80; Tweed Ring and, **Vol. 1, Part 1**, 105, 237, 572, 609; **Vol. 2, Part 2**, 83, 396, 558; **Vol. 3, Part 1**, 140; **Vol. 3, Part 2**, 155; **Vol. 4, Part 1**, 52, 454; **Vol. 4, Part 2**, 405, 500, 605; **Vol. 5, Part 1**, 114; **Vol. 5, Part 2**, 171, 308, 356; **Vol. 7, Part 1**, 621; **Vol. 7, Part 2**, 387; **Vol. 8, Part 2**, 12, 134; **Vol. 9, Part 1**, 9, 593; **Vol. 9, Part 2**, 539, 636; **Vol. 10, Part 1**, 80 f.; wigwam, first, **Vol. 8, Part 2**, 255; writings on, **Supp. 3**, 545, 546
Tandy Leather Co., **Supp. 10**, 773
Taney, Roger B., appointment of, **Vol. 9, Part 2**, 106
Tanglewood Music Festival (Mass.): **Supp. 8**, 451; founding of, **Supp. 7**, 651–52; **Supp. 10**, 423; Music Shed, **Supp. 4**, 715; **Supp. 5**, 399
Tankers, design of, **Supp. 2**, 270
Tanks (armored), design, **Supp. 3**, 165–66; **Supp. 10**, 177
Tan Manhattan, **Supp. 9**, 645
Tanning, **Vol. 2, Part 2**, 595 f.; **Vol. 3, Part 2**, 46, 306; **Vol. 5, Part 1**, 9
Tansill, Charles, reference to, **Supp. 8**, 441
Taoism, **Supp. 8**, 431
Taos, N. Mex., artists' colony, **Supp. 7**, 486–87; **Supp. 8**, 98, 99
Tap (film), **Supp. 10**, 20
Tap dancing, **Supp. 4**, 695; **Supp. 10**, 19–20
Tapestries: authority on, **Vol. 3, Part 2**, 354; collecting of, **Vol. 6, Part 1**, 210
Tappan, Arthur, reference to, **Vol. 10, Part 1**, 625 f.
"Taps," at soldiers' burial, **Vol. 9, Part 2**, 529
Tarbell, Ida M., references to, **Supp. 3**, 816; **Supp. 4**, 46–47, 518, 662; **Supp. 7**, 676
Tariff: **Vol. 1, Part 11, 154, 534; Vol. 1, Part 2**, 232, 324; **Vol. 2, Part 1**, 50, 414; **Vol. 4, Part 1**, 156; **Vol. 4, Part 2**, 26, 103, 380; **Vol. 6, Part 2**, 222; **Vol. 8, Part 1**, 2 f., 407; **Vol. 9, Part 1**, 10; **Vol. 9, Part 2**, 6, 333, 569; **Vol. 10, Part 2**, 30, 351 f., 563; "abominations, of," **Vol. 10, Part 1**, 89; "American System" in New England, **Vol. 6, Part 1**, 45; Bluffton, **Vol. 8, Part 1**, 526; "Boston Report," **Vol. 6, Part 1**, 108 f.; Chinese conferences (1925), **Supp. 4**, 800; Compromise of 1833, **Vol. 2, Part 2**, 177; Dingley Act, **Vol. 3, Part 1**, 315; **Vol. 8, Part 1**, 2 f.; federal commission, **Supp. 2**, 651; "for revenue only," tenet of Democratic party, **Vol. 8, Part 1**, 350 f.; "forty-bale" theory, **Vol. 6, Part 2**, 35; free trade, **Vol. 2, Part 1**, 488; history of, **Supp. 1**, 312; labor, effect on, **Vol. 3, Part 1**, 328; McKinley Act, **Vol. 7, Part 2**, 331; material on, collected, **Vol. 8, Part 1**, 325 f.; measures outlined, **Vol. 10, Part 1**, 585 f.; Morrill Act, **Vol. 7, Part 1**, 198; **Vol. 7, Part 2**, 206; New England, **Vol. 6, Part 1**, 108 f.; Payne-Aldrich Act, **Vol. 1, Part 2**, 232; **Vol. 7, Part 2**, 331; **Vol. 9, Part 2**, 269; **Supp. 3**, 464; protective, **Vol. 2, Part 1**, 12, 491, 544; **Vol. 2, Part 2**, 176; **Vol. 3, Part 1**, 289; **Vol. 4, Part 2**, 457; **Vol. 5, Part 2**, 163, 300; **Vol. 9, Part 1**, 44, 204, 622; **Vol. 9, Part 2**, 6, 237; reciprocal, **Supp. 5**, 519; reduction favored, **Vol. 8, Part 1**, 442; reforms, **Vol. 7, Part 2**, 582; **Supp. 2**, 508; Republican party, **Vol. 6, Part 2**, 106; **Vol. 9, Part 2**, 237; restrictive, **Supp. 4**, 861–62; **Supp. 7**, 305; Smoot-Hawley Act, **Supp. 3**, 345, 727; **Supp. 6**, 59–60; South Carolina and Act of 1828, **Vol. 8, Part 1**, 30 f.; sugar, **Vol. 2, Part 2**, 459; **Vol. 7, Part 1**, 404; Taft's position on, **Vol. 9, Part 2**, 269; Underwood Act, **Supp. 6**, 280; Underwood-Bryan controversy, **Vol. 10, Part 1**, 117 f.; Walker Act of 1846, **Vol. 3, Part 1**, 39; **Vol. 6, Part 1**, 210; **Vol. 8, Part 1**, 34 f.; **Vol. 10, Part 1**, 585 f.; Wilson bill, **Vol. 5, Part 2**, 178; **Vol. 7, Part 2**, 331; wool, **Vol. 4, Part 2**, 446; writings against protective, **Supp. 3**, 762; writings on, **Vol. 6, Part 1**, 293. *See also* Trade
Tariff Board, first chairmanship of, **Vol. 3, Part 2**, 144
Tariff Commission, **Vol. 4, Part 2**, 446
Tariff reform (1893), **Vol. 2, Part 1**, 495; **Vol. 2, Part 2**, 210; **Vol. 5, Part 1**, 335; **Vol. 7, Part 1**, 15
Tarkenton, Fran, reference to, **Supp. 9**, 147
Tarkington, Booth, references to, **Supp. 2**, 726; **Supp. 6**, 545; **Supp. 7**, 656

Tarno, Fritz, reference to, **Supp. 6**, 708–9
Tarolinta, ship to California in gold rush, **Vol. 7, Part 1**, 612
"Tarzan" (fictional character), **Supp. 4**, 129; **Supp. 9**, 65–66
Tass, **Supp. 7**, 268, 269
Tate, Allen, references to, **Supp. 7**, 55, 56; **Supp. 10**, 467–68
Tatum, Art, reference to, **Supp. 10**, 270
Taussing, Helen B., reference to, **Supp. 7**, 59
Tavern signs, historical consequence of, **Vol. 8, Part 1**, 174 f.
Taxation: **Vol. 3, Part 1**, 299 f., 316, 499; **Vol. 3, Part 2**, 169; **Vol. 9, Part 1**, 234; **Vol. 10, Part 1**, 637 f.; capital gains, **Supp. 8**, 160; churches exempted from, **Vol. 8, Part 1**, 619; cuts advocates, **Supp. 6**, 455, 535; excess-profits, **Supp. 8**, 422; Excise Act, **Vol. 3, Part 2**, 560; gasoline tax for road building, **Supp. 1**, 671; Impressment Act, **Vol. 3, Part 1**, 128; income distribution goal, **Supp. 8**, 446; income tax, **Vol. 2, Part 1**, 120; **Supp. 1**, 533; **Supp. 2**, 148, 607; income tax exemptions, **Supp. 8**, 166; income tax in Wisconsin, **Supp. 1**, 385; income tax legislation, **Supp. 3**, 654; income tax preparation guide, **Supp. 5**, 412; income theory, **Supp. 4**, 748; Mellon plan, **Supp. 2**, 449–50; Minnesota, **Vol. 3, Part 2**, 42; Massachusetts Colony opposition, **Vol. 10, Part 2**, 427; New Deal policies, **Supp. 5**, 180–81, 712; oil-discovery depletion allowance, **Supp. 4**, 339; pay-as-you-go plan, **Supp. 6**, 559; poll tax, **Vol. 7, Part 2**, 123; **Supp. 6**, 526; **Supp. 7**, 416; progressive, **Supp. 2**, 607; property, **Supp. 1**, 385; **Supp. 2**, 272; **Supp. 6**, 522; "Sanborn Contracts," **Vol. 8, Part 1**, 578; school, **Vol. 3, Part 1**, 521 f.; **Vol. 8, Part 2**, 105; single tax, **Vol. 4, Part 1**, 174, 215; **Supp. 4**, 844, 845; slaves, **Vol. 3, Part 2**, 107; **Vol. 8, Part 1**, 417; stamp tax, **Vol. 5, Part 1**, 468; studies on, **Supp. 2**, 326; Virginia, **Vol. 3, Part 1**, 316; war, **Supp. 1**, 10; writings on, **Supp. 8**, 166. *See also* Tariff
Taxicabs, **Supp. 7**, 343
Taxidermy: **Vol. 1, Part 1**, 425; **Vol. 6, Part 2**, 457; Akeley method, **Vol. 1, Part 1**, 132
Taxonomy: **Vol. 3, Part 1**, 578 f.; **Vol. 4, Part 1**, 286; ornithological, **Supp. 3**, 161
Tax Payment Act (1943), **Supp. 6**, 559
Taylor, A1, reference to, **Supp. 6**, 303
Taylor, Charles Alonzo, **Supp. 4**, 821–22
Taylor, C. G., reference to, **Supp. 8**, 504
Taylor, Claude ("Spud"), reference to, **Supp. 10**, 378
Taylor, Claudia Alta ("Lady Bird"), references to, **Supp. 9**, 431, 435
Taylor, Deems, references to, **Supp. 4**, 576; **Supp. 6**, 309
Taylor, E. B., reference to, **Supp. 3**, 83
Taylor, Elizabeth, references to, **Supp. 6**, 638; **Supp. 8**, 678
Taylor, Francis H. L., reference to, **Supp. 4**, 582
Taylor, Frederick W., references to, **Supp. 2**, 26; **Supp. 3**, 204, 224, 762; **Supp. 6**, 121
Taylor, Glen H., reference to, **Supp. 6**, 681; **Supp. 9**, 186
Taylor, Henry Osborn, references to, **Supp. 4**, 880–81, 883
Taylor, Laurette, references to, **Supp. 3**, 765; **Supp. 8**, 444
Taylor, Maxwell, reference to, **Supp. 8**, 157
Taylor, Myron C., references to, **Supp. 3**, 263; **Supp. 5**, 510; **Supp. 8**, 375
Taylor, Paul Schuster, reference to, **Supp. 7**, 456
Taylor, Zachary, relations with Henry Clay **Vol. 7, Part 2**, 178 f.
Taylor Society, **Supp. 2**, 27; **Supp. 5**, 164–65, 558
Taylor system of scientific management. *See* Taylor Society
Taylor-White process, **Vol. 9, Part 2**, 324
Tay-Sachs disease, **Supp. 3**, 682
Tchaikovsky, Peter Ilyich, reference to, **Supp. 4**, 211
Tea: first from Japan, **Vol. 4, Part 2**, 68; growing of, in South, **Vol. 9, Part 1**, 315; shipment of, to colonies, **Vol. 3, Part 1**, 430; toxic effects of, **Vol. 7, Part 1**, 267; trade in, **Vol. 4, Part 2**, 68
Teach, Edward, reference to, **Vol. 3, Part 2**, 16
Teachers: curriculum determination, **Supp. 3**, 552; kindergarten, **Supp. 4**, 874–75; **Supp. 5**, 437; loyalty oath issue, **Supp. 5**, 410, 480–81; **Supp. 7**, 542; **Supp. 8**, 133–34; materials for, **Supp. 2**, 419; organizations, **Supp. 1**, 328, 683, 712; **Supp. 2**, 419; pensions, **Supp. 1**, 328; **Supp. 2**, 542; **Supp. 8**, 9–10; training of, **Supp. 3**, 677; **Supp. 4**, 40; training in progressive methods, **Supp. 8**, 443; unionization, **Supp. 8**, 132. *See also* Education; *specific fields*
Teachers College. *See* Columbia University
Teachers' Institute, **Vol. 4, Part 2**, 415; **Vol. 8, Part 2**, 307
Teachers Insurance and Annuity Association, **Supp. 1**, 328; founding of, **Supp. 2**, 543
Teachers' Mutual Benefit Association, promotion of, **Vol. 4, Part 2**, 518
Teacher's Work Book, **Supp. 4**, 833
Teacher training: **Vol. 2, Part 2**, 418; **Vol. 3, Part 1**, 347; **Vol. 5, Part 1**, 128; **Vol. 7, Part 1**, 467; **Vol. 7, Part 2**, 404, 532; **Vol. 8, Part 1**, 222, 643; **Vol. 8, Part 2**, 250; **Vol. 9, Part 2**, 581; California, **Vol. 7, Part 1**, 578; Illinois, **Vol. 1, Part 2**, 44; **Vol. 2, Part 2**, 376; **Vol. 9, Part 2**, 581; Massachusetts, **Vol. 2, Part 1**, 420; **Vol. 3, Part 1**, 563 f.; Michigan, **Vol. 10, Part 1**, 617 f.; Missouri, **Vol. 1, Part 1**, 538; New Jersey, **Vol. 4, Part 2**, 360; New York, **Vol. 5, Part 2**, 500; Wisconsin, **Vol. 8, Part 2**, 307. *See also* Normal schools
Teagarden, Jack, reference to, **Supp. 8**, 561
Teamsters Union: AFL-CIO expulsion of, **Supp. 8**, 513, 528; **Supp. 9**, 396; **Supp. 10**, 525, 697; CIO relations, **Supp. 7**, 119; collective bargaining successes, **Supp. 9**, 396; corruption investigation, **Supp. 7**, 50; **Supp. 9**, 396; founding of, **Supp. 5**, 690–91; internal power struggle, **Supp. 9**, 397; organized crime links, **Supp. 8**, 322; **Supp. 9**, 395–96, 397
Teapot Dome scandal: **Vol. 3, Part 1**, 156, 234 f.; **Vol. 4, Part 2**, 255; **Vol. 5, Part 2**, 546; **Vol. 8, Part 2**, 194; **Vol. 10, Part 1**, 393 f. **Supp. 1**, 95, 196, 465; **Supp. 3**, 259–60, 481, 491, 669, 715, 845, 851; **Supp. 4**, 216, 482; **Supp. 6**, 455, 584; **Supp. 8**, 594; **Supp. 9**, 590, 859; newspaper reporting, **Supp. 2**, 14; prosecution, **Supp. 2**, 536
Teasdale, Sara, reference to, **Supp. 10**, 831
Technicolor, **Supp. 7**, 406–7
Technicolor Corporation, **Vol. 9, Part 2**, 647
"Technological unemployment," **Vol. 10, Part 1**, 637 f.
Technology: **Vol. 3, Part 1**, 318 f.; **Vol. 10, Part 1**, 498 f.; origin of the term, **Vol. 1, Part 2**, 258; in South, **Vol. 5, Part 1**, 210–11; unemployment related to, **Supp. 5**, 558–59. *See also* Industrial research; *specific kinds*
Tecumseh, references to, **Vol. 5, Part 2**, 115, 583; **Vol. 8, Part 2**, 376 f.; **Vol. 9, Part 1**, 13; **Vol. 9, Part 2**, 375 f.
Teheran Conference (1943), **Supp. 3**, 663; **Supp. 5**, 334; **Supp. 7**, 377; **Supp. 9**, 105–6
Telautograph, invention of, **Vol. 6, Part 1**, 368
Telecommunications, satellite network, international, **Supp. 10**, 828
Telegraph: **Vol. 1, Part 1**, 639; **Vol. 1, Part 2**, 149 f.;

Vol. 2, Part 2, 445; **Vol. 3, Part 1**, 221, 600; **Vol. 3, Part 2**, 3 f., 280, 372; **Vol. 4, Part 1**, 555; **Vol. 5, Part 2**, 331, 566; appropriation, congressional, **Vol. 3, Part 2**, 110; Bain Chemical Telegraph System, **Vol. 8, Part 1**, 193 f.; *Bain Line*, **Vol. 1, Part 1**, 639; development, **Vol. 2, Part 2**, 534; **Vol. 6, Part 1**, 141; **Vol. 7, Part 1**, 148; **Vol. 7, Part 2**, 66, 545; **Vol. 8, Part 1**, 193 f.; **Vol. 8, Part 2**, 96, 521; **Vol. 9, Part 1**, 145, 492; **Vol. 10, Part 1**, 136 f.; electroharmonic, **Vol. 4, Part 1**, 514; electromagnetic, **Vol. 2, Part 2**, 9; fire alarms, use for, **Vol. 2, Part 2**, 9; **Vol. 9, Part 2**, 238; inventions, **Vol. 1, Part 1**, 230; **Vol. 3, Part 1**, 220 f.; **Vol. 4, Part 1**, 514; **Vol. 5, Part 2**, 326; **Vol. 8, Part 1**, 75 f., 193 f.; **Vol. 8, Part 2**, 97; lines erected, **Vol. 7, Part 2**, 52; magnetic, **Vol. 1, Part 1**, 639; market reporting, **Vol. 5, Part 2**, 158; news reporting by, **Vol. 5, Part 2**, 158; newspaper, early use of, by, **Vol. 1, Part 2**, 198; ownership of, private v. government, **Vol. 8, Part 1**, 193 f.; "Phillips code," **Vol. 7, Part 2**, 545; police alarms use of, **Vol. 9, Part 2**, 238; postal, **Vol. 6, Part 2**, 76; promotion, **Vol. 3, Part 2**, 372; printing by, **Vol. 5, Part 1**, 259, 347; **Vol. 8, Part 1**, 75 f.; **Vol. 8, Part 2**, 100 f.; quadruplex system of, **Vol. 7, Part 2**, 66; research in, **Supp. 1**, 278; responder, **Supp. 7**, 175; semaphore telegraph system, **Vol. 8, Part 2**, 97; standards, determination of, **Vol. 8, Part 1**, 75 f.; Stearns duplex system, **Vol. 7, Part 2**, 66; submarine, **Vol. 3, Part 1**, 336; **Vol. 10, Part 1**, 421; transatlantic, **Vol. 5, Part 2**, 566; **Vol. 8, Part 2**, 88; underwater cable system, **Supp. 6**, 84; warfare, early use in, **Vol. 5, Part 2**, 482; writings on, **Vol. 8, Part 1**, 193 f.

Telepathy, **Supp. 10**, 672

Telephone: cable development, **Supp. 3**, 299, 747–48; **Supp. 10**, 154, 155; communication, **Vol. 1, Part 2**, 151; **Vol. 9, Part 1**, 253; **Vol. 9, Part 2**, 99; design, **Supp. 1**, 554; development, **Vol. 1, Part 2**, 150; **Vol. 4, Part 1, 329; Vol. 5, Part 1**, 324 f.; **Vol. 8, Part 2**, 133, 336; dial, **Supp. 3**, 299; dial system, **Supp. 8**, 211; direct-dial technology, **Supp. 10**, 154; engineering, **Supp. 4**, 430–31; first transcontinental line from New York to San Francisco, **Vol. 1, Part 2**, 152; first undersea cable laid, **Supp. 10**, 155; improvements in, **Supp. 1**, 155; ITT founding, **Supp. 6**, 43–44; litigation, **Vol. 9, Part 1**, 253; long distance, **Supp. 1**, 155, 614; **Supp. 4**, 173; **Supp. 7**, 176, 177; organization, **Vol. 10, Part 1**, 138 f., 548 f.; rival to Bell system, **Vol. 8, Part 1**, 193; standardization, **Supp. 3**, 299; system of secret, patent for, **Vol. 8, Part 2**, 100; technological advances, **Supp. 9**, 676; transatlantic, **Supp. 4**, 173, 430; **Supp. 6**, 84; transcontinental transmission, **Supp. 1**, 32; writings on, **Vol. 8, Part 1**, 193 f.

Telescopes: **Supp. 7**, 517; achromatic, **Vol. 8, Part 1**, 30 f.; amateur construction of, **Supp. 4**, 674–75; Crossley, **Supp. 3**, 207–8; **Supp. 5**, 540–41; collimating, **Vol. 8, Part 1**, 631; construction of, **Vol. 3, Part 1**, 436; **Vol. 3, Part 2**, 433; **Vol. 5, Part 1**, 131, 432; **Vol. 5, Part 2**, 593; **Vol. 6, Part 1**, 234, 506; **Vol. 8, Part 2**, 412; **Vol. 10, Part 1**, 470 f.; first made in America, **Vol. 8, Part 1**, 630; "Great Equatorial," **Vol. 8, Part 2**, 341; lenses, manufacture of, **Vol. 2, Part 2**, 119 f.; naval sight, **Supp. 3**, 275; Palomar, **Supp. 5**, 326; reflectors, **Supp. 3**, 633–34; world's largest, **Supp. 5**, 325–26

Television: action-adventure series, **Supp. 9**, 486; announcing, **Supp. 10**, 290–91; Army-McCarthy hearings, **Supp. 6**, 680; **Supp. 10**, 415; blacklisting, **Supp. 6**, 350; **Supp. 7**, 355; color, development of, **Supp. 10**, 283–84; comedy programs, **Supp. 8**, 711; **Supp. 9**, 149, 197, 204, 282, 560, 581, 880; **Supp. 10**, 8, 86, 156, 196, 651, 652, 803–4; comedy-variety programs, **Supp. 7**, 442–43; **Supp. 9**, 2, 6, 48–49, 77, 103, 489; **Supp. 10**, 452; commercial potential of, **Supp. 9**, 803; commercials, **Supp. 9**, 66–67, 803; **Supp. 10**, 352; competition with motion-picture industry, **Supp. 9**, 733; congressional coverage by, **Supp. 8**, 128; criticism, **Supp. 6**, 366; detective series, **Supp. 9**, 488; **Supp. 10**, 85–86; dramatic series, **Supp. 9**, 515; **Supp. 10**, 101, 273, 380, 790; early development of, **Supp. 6**, 32–33; **Supp. 9**, 275–76; 701–2; **Supp. 10**, 433; first baseball game shown, **Supp. 9**, 765; first black newsman, **Supp. 8**, 387; first clown appearing on, **Supp. 6**, 8; first operatic concert, **Supp. 6**, 670; first regular public service, **Supp. 7**, 780; first situation comedy in rural setting, **Supp. 9**, 123; football, **Supp. 6**, 48; game shows, **Supp. 10**, 224, 790; golden age of live, **Supp. 7**, 458; **Supp. 8**, 31; investments in, **Supp. 8**, 367; "Little House on the Prairie" series, **Supp. 6**, 697; model agency for, **Supp. 7**, 141; musical specials, **Supp. 10**, 673; music programs, **Supp. 8**, 698; **Supp. 10**, 252; networks, **Supp. 7**, 207; news commentary, **Supp. 9**, 415–16; **Supp. 10**, 290–91, 349–50; newspaper ownership, **Supp. 5**, 551; **Supp. 9**, 301–2; news programs, **Supp. 8**, 387–88; **Supp. 10**, 415, 462; ; opera, **Supp. 6**, 633; **Supp. 7**, 124; patents, **Supp. 9**, 276; "Perry Mason" series, **Supp. 8**, 202; presidential debates, **Supp. 7**, 420; presidential use of, **Supp. 8**, 160; production companies, **Supp. 10**, 63; public affairs programs, **Supp. 6**, 83, 680; **Supp. 10**, 375; public broadcasting, **Supp. 10**, 467; quiz shows, **Supp. 9**, 719, 829; **Supp. 10**, 121, 224, 790; quiz-show scandals, **Supp. 10**, 415; ratings survey, **Supp. 10**, 588; receivers, **Supp. 7**, 206, 207; religious programs, **Supp. 10**, 729–30; science fiction programs, **Supp. 9**, 710–11; **Supp. 10**, 343–44; scriptwriting, **Supp. 9**, 710–11; "See It Now," **Supp. 7**, 566–67; stations, **Supp. 5**, 615; suspense programs, **Supp. 10**, 340; talk shows, **Supp. 7**, 436; **Supp. 10**, 24, 121, 255–56, 490; theme songs, **Supp. 10**, 317; tobacco advertising ban, **Supp. 9**, 139; transmission, **Supp. 5**, 21; variety programs, **Supp. 9**, 779–80; "verbal vampire of," **Supp. 9**, 492; Westerns, **Supp. 9**, 101–2, 119; **Supp. 10**, 178, 500, 737

Teller, Edward, references to, **Supp. 8**, 199, 200

Temperance movement: **Vol. 1, Part 1**, 319, 377 f.; **Vol. 1, Part 2**, 135, 385, 423; **Vol. 2, Part 1**, 591; **Vol. 2, Part 2**, 14, 324; **Vol. 3, Part 1**, 191, 221, 353; **Vol. 3, Part 2**, 82, 476, 552; **Vol. 4, Part 1**, 445 f., 542, 625; **Vol. 4, Part 2**, 216, 374, 376, 386, 407, 451; **Vol. 5, Part 1**, 19, 369, 494, 561, 576; **Vol. 5, Part 2**, 517; **Vol. 6, Part 1**, 103, 131, 200, 306; **Vol. 6, Part 2**, 300; **Vol. 7, Part 1**, 22, 27, 289, 394, 431, 491, 581, 611; **Vol. 8, Part 1**, 14 f., 381; **Vol. 8, Part 2**, 150, 228, 367; **Vol. 9, Part 1**, 36, 521, 546; **Vol. 9, Part 2**, 8 f.; **Vol. 10, Part 1**, 544 f.; **Vol. 10, Part 2**, 55, 234; Kansas, **Vol. 7, Part 1**, 394; Maine, **Vol. 3, Part 1**, 411; Massachusetts, **Vol. 8, Part 1**, 381; Methodist church, **Vol. 5, Part 2**, 517; Mississippi, **Vol. 10, Part 1**, 547; Navy, **Vol. 3, Part 2**, 499; Ohio, **Vol. 1, Part 2**, 423; schools, **Vol. 5, Part 1**, 388; South, beginnings of, **Vol. 3, Part 1**, 306; **Vol. 10, Part 1**, 119; South Carolina, **Vol. 7, Part 2**, 43; Temperanceville, **Vol. 3, Part 1**, 586 f.; tours, **Vol. 6, Part 1**, 85; "Washingtonian movement," **Vol. 6, Part 1**, 209; West, **Vol. 10, Part 1**, 625 f.; Whole World's Temperance Convention, **Vol. 4, Part 1**, 376; Women's Christian Temperance Union, **Vol. 3, Part 2**, 552 f.; **Vol. 4, Part 2**, 436; **Vol. 6, Part 1**, 85, 86; **Vol. 9, Part 2**, 8 f.; **Vol. 10, Part 2**, 234; writings on, **Vol. 3, Part 1**, 221, 516 f.; **Vol. 4, Part l**, 85, 446; **Vol. 6, Part 1**, 84 f.; **Vol. 6, Part 2**, 35, 352 f.; **Vol. 8, Part 1**, 188 f.; **Vol.**

8, **Part 2**, 507; **Vol. 9, Part 1**, 546; **Vol. 9, Part 2**, 8 f. *See also* Prohibition
Temperance Publication Bureau, **Vol. 3, Part 1**, 421
Temperance Society: first in a school, **Vol. 2, Part 2**, 54; first in U.S., **Vol. 8, Part 1**, 622; Massachusetts, **Vol. 1, Part 1**, 255; National, **Vol. 3, Part 1**, 19, 353; New York State, **Vol. 3, Part 1**,
Temperance Truth, **Vol. 3, Part 1**, 421
Temperature: body, **Supp. 3**, 32; **Supp. 4**, 58–59; control of environmental, **Supp. 4**, 148–49; cricket chirps and, **Supp. 1**, 325; measurement of high, **Supp. 1**, 131
Temple, Shirley, reference to, **Supp. 8**, 117
Temple Emanu-El (New York City): **Supp. 4**, 904; first black soloist, **Supp. 4**, 125
Temple Israel (Boston), **Supp. 4**, 494
Temple of the Winds, painting by Loeb, **Vol. 6, Part 1**, 353
Temple University: **Vol. 2, Part 2**, 367; laryngology department, **Supp. 6**, 318; library, **Supp. 10**, 778
Templeton, Robert L. ("Dink"), reference to, **Supp. 7**, 152
Temporary home, **Vol. 9, Part 2**, 620
Ten American Painters, **Vol. 10, Part 1**, 609 f.
Tenant farming: **Supp. 4**, 50, 251; journalism on, **Supp. 5**, 511; labor organizing, **Supp. 7**, 78
"Ten Cents a Dance" (comp), **Supp. 10**, 223
Tender Is the Night, **Supp. 2**, 190; **Supp. 7**, 560
Tenement House Committee (New York City), **Supp. 3**, 743–44; **Supp. 6**, 654
Tenements: decoratlve renovation, **Supp. 8**, 140; dumbell design, **Supp. 3**, 744; law, **Supp. 6**, 522; model, **Vol. 8, Part 1**, 168 f.; New York City model designs, **Supp. 4**, 282; **Supp. 6**, 23, 26; reform, **Vol. 8, Part 2**, 119; supervision of, **Vol. 1, Part 2**, 373; **Vol. 7, Part 2**, 551; writings on conditions in New York City, **Vol. 8, Part 1**, 607 f.
Tennent, Gilbert, reference to, **Vol. 1, Part 2**, 341
Tennessee: **Vol. 1, Part 1**, 268; **Vol. 1, Part 2**, 390; **Vol. 2, Part 1**, 520, 539, 541, 576; **Vol. 3, Part 1**, 332; **Vol. 4, Part 2**, 467; **Vol. 7, Part 1**, 132 f.; **Vol. 8, Part 1**, 93 f., 342 f.; **Vol. 9, Part 2**, 363 f., 563; **Vol. 10, Part 2**, 108; abolition movement, **Vol. 5, Part 2**, 83; agriculture, **Vol. 9, Part 2**, 364; Baptist church, **Vol. 5, Part 2**, 582; Bureau of Agriculture, Statistics and Mines, **Vol. 8, Part 1**, 93 f.; Centennial and International Exposition, **Vol. 9, Part 2**, 440; Civil War period, **Vol. 4, Part 2**, 311; **Vol. 10, Part 2**, 660; constitution, first, **Vol. 9, Part 1**, 254; Crump political machine, **Supp. 9**, 769; education, **Vol. 3, Part 1**, 332, 608 f.; **Vol. 3, Part 2**, 441; **Vol. 6, Part 1, 278; Vol. 8, Part 1**, 222, 313 f., 342 f.; **Vol. 10, Part 1**, 579 f.; Episcopal diocese, **Supp. 1**, 329; evolution, law against teaching, **Supp. 4**, 542; **Supp. 6**, 528–29; **Supp. 8**, 582–84; **Supp. 9**, 768; freedmen, **Vol. 3, Part 1**, 608 f.; geology, **Vol. 8, Part 2**, 287; **Vol. 9, Part 2**, 648; governors, **Vol. 1, Part 2**, 42 f., 391; **Vol. 2, Part 1**, 98 f., 135 f., 177 f., 466, 477 f., 529 f.; **Vol. 5, Part 2**, 83, 177; **Vol. 6, Part 2**, 145 f.; **Vol. 7, Part 2**, 371 f.; **Vol. 8, Part 1**, 93 f., 640 f.; **Vol. 8, Part 2**, 602 f.; **Vol. 9, Part 2**, 313, 341–43; **Vol. 10, Part 1**, 72 f.; **Supp. 1**, 533; **Supp. 8**, 91–92; **Supp. 9**, 258–59; historical writings on, **Vol. 6, Part 1**, 279; **Vol. 5, Part 1**, 367; Indians, **Vol. 6, Part 2**, 146; industrial development, **Vol. 10, Part 1**, 465 f.; **Vol. 10, Part 2**, 209; Jackson, Andrew, **Vol. 5, Part 1**, 527 f.; legal service, **Vol. 1, Part 2**, 63, 157, 391; **Vol. 2, Part 1**, 576; **Vol. 3, Part 1**, 298; **Vol. 4, Part 2**, 467; **Vol. 6, Part 1**, 509; **Vol. 6, Part 2**, 227, 510; **Vol. 7, Part 2**, 115; **Vol. 8, Part 1**, 93, 570, 640; **Vol. 8, Part 2**, 347; **Vol. 10, Part 1**, 73; map of first, **Vol. 9, Part 1**, 254; Masonry, **Vol. 8, Part 1**, 571; Manumission Society, **Vol. 7, Part 2**, 67; Methodist church, **Vol. 6, Part 2**, 45; missionary activity in, **Vol. 6, Part 2**, 498; newspapers, **Supp. 5**, 497–98; political factions, **Vol. 8, Part 1**, 640 f.; political service, **Vol. 1, Part 2**, 42, 43, 210, 390; **Vol. 2, Part 1**, 576; **Vol. 3, Part 1**, 286, 363, 608; **Vol. 3, Part 2**, 546; **Vol. 5, Part 1**, 263; **Vol. 5, Part 2**, 81 f., 177; **Vol. 6, Part 2**, 461; **Vol. 7, Part 1**, 498; **Vol. 7, Part 2**, 372, 523; **Vol. 8, Part 1**, 34, 41, 93, 524, 571, 640; **Vol. 8, Part 2**, 602; **Vol. 9, Part 2**, 313, 341 f.; **Vol. 10, Part 1**, 73, 104, 551 f., 579 f.; **Vol. 10, Part 2**, 271, 660; politics, **Supp. 3**, 449; **Supp. 4**, 75; **Supp. 5**, 144–45; **Supp. 6**, 125–126; **Supp. 6**, 227–28, 418–19; **Supp. 7**, 415, 639; **Supp. 9**, 258–59, 769, 770; pre-Civil War period, **Vol. 2, Part 1**, 99, 478, 529; **Vol. 6, Part 2**, 290; Presbyterian Church, **Vol. 2, Part 1**, 520; printing, early, **Vol. 8, Part 2**, 190; Prohibition, **Vol. 2, Part 1**, 497; public service, **Vol. 4, Part 2**, 33; **Vol. 5, Part 1**, 256, 378; **Vol. 5, Part 2**, 361 f.; **Vol. 6, Part 1**, 278; **Vol. 6, Part 2**, 48, 146; **Vol. 7, Part 2**, 371 f.; **Vol. 10, Part 2**, 106; railroads, development of, in, **Vol. 8, Part 1**, 342 f.; Reconstruction period in, **Vol. 2, Part 1**, 136; **Vol. 3, Part 2**, 311; **Vol. 5, Part 2**, 83; religious service, **Vol. 3, Part 1**, 332; **Vol. 5, Part 2**, 582; **Vol. 6, Part 2**, 45; **Vol. 8, Part 1**, 313 f.; school desegregation, **Supp. 9**, 258; secession, **Vol. 2, Part 1**, 577; **Vol. 6, Part 2**, 461; **Vol. 8, Part 1**, 93 f.; statehood, admission to, **Vol. 8, Part 1, 640; stories of, Vol. 7, Part 1**, 345; Taylor brothers, **Vol. 9, Part 2**, 313; transportation, **Vol. 9, Part 2**, 364; Whig party, **Vol. 1, Part 2**, 157; **Vol. 2, Part 1**, 466
Tennessee, surrender of, during Civil War, **Vol. 9, Part 2**, 149
Tennessee Coal and Iron Co., **Vol. 7, Part 2**, 330; **Vol. 9, Part 1**, 124 f; **Supp. 5**, 556
Tennessee College of Pharmacy, **Vol. 6, Part 1**, 278
Tennessee Electric Power Co., **Supp. 3**, 829; **Supp. 8**, 179
Tennessee River, survey of, **Supp. 6**, 435
Tennessee Valley Authority (TVA): administration, **Supp. 4**, 601–2; **Supp. 8**, 508–9; bill amending, **Supp. 5**, 480; bill creating, **Supp. 4**, 185; constitutionality of, **Supp. 4**, 537; **Supp. 8**, 4, 179; construction projects, **Supp. 8**, 352; creation of, **Supp. 3**, 560, 647; **Supp. 4**, 185; **Supp. 6**, 525; dam design, **Supp. 8**, 573; design and construction of, **Supp. 3**, 580–81; ethics investigation, **Supp. 8**, 34; expansion, **Supp. 2**, 583; first chairman appointed, **Supp. 9**, 561; flood control, **Supp. 6**, 436; journalism supporting, **Supp. 5**, 497–98; legal view of, **Supp. 3**, 99, 100; Lilienthal chairmanship, **Supp. 6**, 419; opposition to, **Supp. 3**, 829; **Supp. 6**, 436–37; **Supp. 9**, 770; special counsel for, **Supp. 9**, 593–94; Wilson Dam, **Supp. 2**, 119
"Tennessee Waltz" (song), **Supp. 10**, 251
Tennessee Yazoo Co. (also known as the Muscle Shoals Enterprise), **Vol. 8, Part 2**, 604, 369; **Vol. 10, Part 2**, 224
"Ten Nights in a Barroom and What I Saw There," compared to *Uncle Tom's Cabin*, **Vol. 1, Part 1**, 378
Tennis: **Vol. 6, Part 1**, 3; **Supp. 5**, 686–88; **Supp. 7**, 127; Davis Cup, **Supp. 9**, 721, 722; first municipal courts, **Supp. 3**, 217; first national amateur champion, **Supp. 3**, 701–2; first pro-am event, **Supp. 9**, 722; first woman grand slam win, **Supp. 8**, 101–2; popularization of, **Supp. 6**, 421–22; professional, development of, **Supp. 6**, 538–39; tournaments, **Supp. 9**, 721, 722, 868–69; Wightman Cup, **Supp. 10**, 868; women in, **Supp. 6**, 425–26; **Supp. 8**, 101–2; **Supp. 9**, 868–69
"Tennis Cabinet," **Vol. 8, Part 2**, 138
Ten Times One Club, **Vol. 6, Part 1**, 14

Tenure of Office Act (1867): **Vol. 2, Part 2**, 208; **Vol. 4, Part 1**, 498; **Vol. 5, Part 2**, 87; **Vol. 9, Part 1**, 520, 624; **Vol. 9, Part 2**, 442; **Vol. 10, Part 1**, 304; impeachment, **Vol. 5, Part 2**, 88; repealed, **Vol. 2, Part 2**, 208; vetoed, **Vol. 5, Part 2**, 87
Tepoztlán, Mexico, anthropological studies in, **Supp. 6**, 533
Terminal Island (Los Angeles, Calif.), **Supp. 6**, 4
Terre Haute, Ind., **Vol. 8, Part 2**, 157
Terrell, Robert H., references to, **Supp. 5**, 679, 680
Terrestrial Magnetism and Atmospheric Electricity, **Supp. 1**, 61
Territories: boundary lines, **Vol. 8, Part 1**, 78; divisions of, **Vol. 6, Part 1**, 141 and 142; power of Congress over, **Vol. 8, Part 1**, 428
Terrorism. *See* Assassinations; Bombings and terrorism
Terry v. *Ohio*, **Supp. 9**, 837
Tertio-Millennial Pageant, **Vol. 8, Part 1**, 229 f.
Tertium Quid, **Vol. 9, Part 2**, 332
Teschemaker, Frank, reference to, **Supp. 8**, 561
Tesla coil, **Supp. 3**, 768
Testosterone: **Supp. 4**, 460; synthesis of, **Supp. 9**, 444
Tests and measurements: aptitude and achievement, **Supp. 4**, 833; **Supp. 5**, 329; Army, **Supp. 5**, 59; **Supp. 6**, 718; **Supp. 8**, 44; attitude and personality, **Supp. 5**, 685, 686; for blind, **Supp. 4**, 11; **Supp. 5**, 347; college entrance, **Supp. 4**, 134; group intelligence, **Supp. 7**, 594; multiple-factor analysls, **Supp. 5**, 685; musical aptitude, **Supp. 4**, 731; personality, **Supp. 1**, 264; personality diagnostic, **Supp. 6**, 527; personnel selection, **Supp. 5**, 433, 612; public opinion, **Supp. 6**, 604–5; reading, **Supp. 6**, 248; of schoolchildren's innate ability, **Supp. 4**, 732; of schoolchildren's progress, **Supp. 4**, 35; statistical reporting; **Supp. 4**, 35; vocational, **Supp. 6**, 412. *See also* Intelligence tests
Tetanus, research in, **Supp. 2**, 4
Tetraethyl lead, **Supp. 6**, 332–33
Tetraphenymethane, **Supp. 4**, 336
"Tevye" (fictional character), **Supp. 10**, 561
Texaco: expansion: **Supp. 2**, 133; management of, **Supp. 2**, 29
Texas: Amnesty Oath, **Vol. 1, Part 1**,111; annexation of, **Vol. 1, Part 1**, 88 f., 566; **Vol. 1, Part 2**, 212, 225; **Vol. 2, Part 1**, 42, 49, 209, 287, 293, 417, 563; **Vol. 2, Part 2**, 178; **Vol. 3, Part 1**, 363, 543 f.; **Vol. 3, Part 2**, 298; **Vol. 4, Part 1**, 308; **Vol. 5, Part 1**, 266, 533; **Vol. 5, Part 2**, 162, 407, 553 f.; **Vol. 8, Part 1**, 37 f., 315, 576 f.; **Vol. 9, Part 1**, 240, 570; **Vol. 9, Part 2**, 48, 351; **Vol. 10, Part 1**, 91, 127, 156, 355 f., 590; **Vol. 10, Part 2**, 567; antislavery, **Vol. 1, Part 1**, 298; banking, **Vol. 2, Part 2**, 148; **Supp. 9**, 459–60; bird-life studies, **Supp. 7**, 578, 579; botany, **Vol. 6, Part 1**, 274; **Vol. 6, Part 2**, 482; **Vol. 10, Part 2**, 546; boundary disputes, **Vol. 1, Part 2**, 125; **Vol. 8, Part 2**, 237; British protectorate, question of, **Vol. 5, Part 2**, 161; Catholic church, **Vol. 7, Part 1**, 625 f.; circuit courts, **Vol. 8, Part 2**, 13; colleges, establishment of, **Vol. 2, Part 1**, 288; commercial agreements with, **Vol. 4, Part 2**, 526; constitution of, **Vol. 8, Part 1**, 434; debts, **Vol. 8, Part 2**, 237; Democratic party, **Supp. 9**, 431, 432; dictatorship in, **Vol. 3, Part 1**, 112; education, **Vol. 1, Part 1**, 538; **Vol. 5, Part 1**, 453; **Vol. 9, Part 1**, 240; "fencibles" in, **Vol. 8, Part 1**, 315 f.; Fourierism, **Vol. 2, Part 2**, 357 f.; **Vol. 4, Part 1**, 529; **Vol. 5, Part 1**, 578; French settlements, **Vol. 6, Part 2**, 527; frontier, **Vol. 2, Part 1**, 287; geology, **Vol. 1, Part 2**, 419; **Vol. 8, Part 2**, 91 f.; German colonies, **Vol. 8, Part 2**, 91 f.; governors, **Vol. 1, Part 2**, 160 f.; **Vol. 2, Part 2**, 278 f.; **Vol. 3, Part 1**, 112 f.; **Vol. 4, Part 2**, 526; **Vol. 5, Part 1**, 122 f., 331, 493 f.; **Vol. 6, Part 1**, 480 f.; **Vol. 7, Part 2**, 368 f.; **Vol. 8, Part 2**, 179 f.; **Supp. 3**, 266–67; **Supp. 4**, 776; **Supp. 7**, 242, 349–50; **Supp. 8**, 478; **Supp. 9**, 431; horticulture, **Vol. 7, Part 1**, 335 f.; immigration to, **Vol. 1, Part 1**, 438; independence, struggle for, **Vol. 1, Part 1**, 339; **Vol. 2, Part 1**, 287, 293; **Vol. 3, Part 2**, 263; **Vol. 4, Part 2**, 188, 526; **Vol. 6, Part 1**, 274; **Vol. 8, Part 1**, 577; **Vol. 8, Part 2**, 25 f.; **Vol. 10, Part 2**, 35; Indians, relations with, **Vol. 5, Part 2**, 582; **Vol. 8, Part 1**, 294; journalism, **Vol. 8, Part 1**, 576 f.; legal service, **Vol. 4, Part 1**, 95 f.; **Vol. 4, Part 2**, 315, 520; **Vol. 6, Part 1**, 520; **Vol. 7, Part 1**, 124; **Vol. 7, Part 2**, 287; **Vol. 8, Part 1**, 433; **Vol. 8, Part 2**, 13, 237, 403; **Vol. 10, Part 2**, 53, 302; medical service, **Vol. 8, Part 2**, 26; Methodist church, **Vol. 1, Part 2**, 234; Mexican War, activities during, **Vol. 2, Part 1**, 491; Mexico, relations with, **Vol. 5, Part 2**, 553; military expeditions, **Vol. 6, Part 1**, 376; newspapers, **Supp. 4**, 222; Norwegian settlements in, **Vol. 8, Part 1**, 488; oil fields, **Supp. 9**, 411, 412, 464; oil industry, **Supp. 3**, 260–61; **Supp. 4**, 775; **Supp. 6**, 135–36, 540–41; **Supp. 8**, 454; oil wells, **Vol. 6, Part 1**, 483; Polish settlements, **Vol. 1, Part 2**, 30; political service, **Vol. 1, Part 2**, 77; **Vol. 2, Part 2**, 279, 586; **Vol. 3, Part 1**, 112; **Vol. 4, Part 1**, 183; **Vol. 5, Part 1**, 122, 265, 331, 493; **Vol. 5, Part 2**, 182; **Vol. 6, Part 1**, 12, 480 f.; **Vol. 7, Part 2**, 13; **Vol. 8, Part 1**, 133; **Vol. 8, Part 2**, 180, 237; **Vol. 10, Part 2**, 188; politics, **Supp. 3**, 706; **Supp. 5**, 480–81; **Supp. 7**, 137–38, 242–43, 459–60, 634–36, 730–31; **Supp. 8**, 205–6, 478, 506–7; **Supp. 9**, 431, 464; **Supp. 10**, 393, 618–19; postwar economic boom, **Supp. 10**, 619; provisional government, **Vol. 8, Part 2**, 236; public service, **Vol. 1, Part 1**, 437 f.; **Vol. 1, Part 2**, 171; **Vol. 3, Part 1**, 229; **Vol. 4, Part 2**, 183, 220; **Vol. 5, Part 1**, 493; **Vol. 5, Part 2**, 135 f.; **Vol. 6, Part 1**, 301; **Vol. 6, Part 2**, 5 f., 132, 201; **Vol. 7, Part 1**, 356, 407 f.; **Vol. 7, Part 2**, 216, 369; **Vol. 8, Part 1**, 294 f.; **Vol. 8, Part 2**, 26, 166; **Vol. 9, Part 1**, 74; **Vol. 10, Part 1**, 377 f.; **Vol. 10, Part 2**, 35, 289; railroads, **Vol. 8, Part 1**, 433 f., 546 f.; ranching, **Supp. 9**, 459, 460, 463–64; Rangers, **Vol. 5, Part 2**, 182, 582 f.; **Vol. 6, Part 1**, 301; Reconstruction, **Vol. 2, Part 1**, 443; **Vol. 3, Part 1**, 112; **Vol. 7, Part 2**, 369; **Vol. 8, Part 1**, 433 f.; reforms in, **Vol. 5, Part 1**, 122 f.; religious service, **Vol. 1, Part 1**, 517; **Vol. 9, Part 2**, 556; Republican party, **Vol. 3, Part 2**, 453; Republic of, **Vol. 1, Part 1**, 338 f.; **Vol. 2, Part 1**, 293; **Vol. 5, Part 2**, 161 f., 553; **Vol. 6, Part 1**, 290; **Vol. 6, Part 2**, 528; **Vol. 7, Part 2**, 369; **Vol. 9, Part 1**, 240; **Vol. 10, Part 2**, 290; Secession Convention, **Vol. 8, Part 1**, 433; **Vol. 10, Part 2**, 188; Spanish-American legal procedure in, **Vol. 4, Part 2**, 520; statehood, admission to, **Vol. 1, Part 1**, 439 f.; "Strong Court," **Vol. 4, Part 1**, 96; survey, **Vol. 4, Part 2**, 369; "War Party," **Vol. 9, Part 2**, 630; whites-only primary, Supreme Court ruling against, **Supp. 9**, 749; **Supp. 10**, 665; writings on, **Vol. 1, Part 1**, 527; **Vol. 4, Part 2**, 201; **Vol. 8, Part 2**, 14; **Vol. 9, Part 1**, 334; **Vol. 10, Part 2**, 613; **Supp. 7**, 188–89
Texas A&M University, football team, **Supp. 10**, 37
Texas Christian University, football team, **Supp. 10**, 600–601
Texas Co. *See* Texaco
Texas Folklore Society, **Supp. 7**, 188
Texas Freeman, **Supp. 6**, 567
Texas Medical Center, **Supp. 6**, 136
Texas Playboys (swing band), **Supp. 9**, 872
Texas Rangers, **Supp. 7**, 770–71
Texas Republican, first Texas newspaper, **Vol. 6, Part 1**, 376
Texas Trust Co., **Supp. 6**, 324
Textbooks: **Vol. 1, Part 2**, 191, 274, 279; **Vol. 2, Part 1**, 119; **Vol. 2, Part 2**, 281 f., 283, 326, 431; **Vol. 3, Part**

1, 458 f., 464 f., 570 f.; **Vol. 3, Part 2**, 561; **Vol. 4, Part 1**, 433, 575, 581, 588; **Vol. 4, Part 2**, 603; **Vol. 5, Part 1**, 444, 475, 541; **Vol. 5, Part 2**, 227; **Vol. 6, Part 1**, 73, 81, 177, 212, 408, 589; **Vol. 6, Part 2**, 141, 210, 269; **Vol. 7, Part 1**, 94, 565; **Vol. 7, Part 2**, 31 f., 83, 236 f., 238, 332, 336, 394, 405 f., 441, 482, 525, 532, 568, 597 f., 629; **Vol. 8, Part 1**, 96 f., 221; **Vol. 8, Part 2**, 226; **Vol. 9, Part 2**, 54; **Vol. 10, Part 1**, 544 f., 594 f., 645f, 655 f.; **Vol. 10, Part 2**, 99; American history, **Supp. 7**, 568; **Supp. 9**, 584; anatomy, **Supp. 2**, 423; black history, **Supp. 5**, 642; censorship, **Supp. 6**, 528, 558; **Supp. 7**, 330; chemistry, **Vol. 9, Part 1**, 235; **Supp. 1**, 376; civil engineering, **Supp. 1**, 148; commercial, **Vol. 9, Part 1**, 404; "Dick and Jane" reading, **Supp. 6**, 248; differential geometry, **Supp. 7**, 216; early, **Vol. 8, Part 2**, 330; economics, **Supp. 8**, 165; education, **Supp. 4**, 592; for educators, **Supp. 3**, 206; embryology, **Supp. 4**, 573; engineering, **Vol. 9, Part 1**, 429; European history, **Supp. 2**, 564; **Supp. 7**, 330; evolution, **Supp. 1**, 697; first advertising, **Supp. 7**, 101; first civics, **Supp. 3**, 285; first on plastic surgery, **Supp. 4**, 221; first social psychology, **Supp. 5**, 592; foreign language, **Supp. 1**, 406; general science, **Supp. 4**, 139, 140; geography, **Vol. 1, Part 2**, 343; **Supp. 1**, 7; **Supp. 4**, 33, 412–13, 423–24; geology, **Supp. 4**, 730; grammar, **Supp. 1**, 697; Greek, **Vol. 9, Part 1**, 398; gynecology, **Supp. 1**, 352; history, **Vol. 9, Part 1**, 556 f.; **Supp. 1**, 484; **Supp. 3**, 336; **Supp. 6**, 278–79; Latin, **Vol. 5, Part 1**, 475; law, **Vol. 2, Part 1**, 166; **Vol. 3, Part 1**, 571 f.; **Vol. 5, Part 1**, 53; **Vol. 9, Part 2**, 250; mathematics, **Supp. 1**, 145–46; medieval history, **Supp. 1**, 285; **Supp. 7**, 741; mineralogy, **Supp. 1**, 221; mining, **Supp. 7**, 358; music, **Vol. 8, Part 1**, 200 f.; music theory, **Supp. 3**, 309; neurology, **Supp. 3**, 386; nutrition, **Supp. 5**, 623; organic chemistry, **Supp. 10**, 240; pathology, **Supp. 3**, 483; physics, **Supp. 5**, 154; **Supp. 9**, 541; physiology, **Supp. 3**, 370, 371; plant physiology, **Supp. 7**, 592; publishing of, **Supp. 5**, 272; scientific, **Vol. 4, Part 2**, 143; **Vol. 6, Part 1**, 398 f.; **Vol. 9, Part 1**, 556 f.; social studies, **Supp. 6**, 557–58; Spanish, **Vol. 5, Part 2**, 454, 496; surgery, **Supp. 3**, 67; tropical disease, **Supp. 4**, 803

Textile industry: "American System" in New England, **Vol. 6, Part 1**, 45; cotton, **Supp. 5**, 252; dyeing of, **Vol. 1, Part 1**, 563; **Vol. 6, Part 2**, 43, 417; **Vol. 7, Part 1**, 404; dyestuffs, **Supp. 7**, 616; inventions, **Vol. 2, Part 2**, 561; **Vol. 9, Part 2**, 508; knitting machine, **Vol. 5, Part 2**, 554; Lawrence, Mass., strike, **Supp. 3**, 576–77, 616; **Supp. 6**, 238; **Supp. 8**, 457; looms, improved, **Vol. 5, Part 2**, 471; **Vol. 10, Part 2**, 582; machinery, **Vol. 3, Part 1**, 437; **Vol. 5, Part 2**, 554; **Vol. 6, Part 1**, 513; **Vol. 10, Part 2**, 222; manufacturing, **Vol. 1, Part 1**, 465; **Vol. 1, Part 2**, 3, 369; **Vol. 2, Part 2**, 561 f., 580; **Vol. 3, Part 1**, 437; **Vol. 3, Part 2**, 132, 272 f.; **Vol. 5, Part 1**, 552; **Vol. 5, Part 2**, 244; **Vol. 6, Part 1**, 45 f., 51, 278, 456; **Vol. 8, Part 2**, 112; **Vol. 9, Part 1**, 190, 198; **Vol. 9, Part 2**, 98; **Vol. 10, Part 2**, 582; marketing, **Supp. 9**, 439–40; in New England, **Vol. 1, Part 1**, 248; **Vol. 6, Part 1**, 45 f., 47, 51; **Vol. 9, Part 2**, 98; preshrunk cloth, **Supp. 8**, 97; schools, **Vol. 9, Part 2**, 582; spinning machines, **Vol. 7, Part 1**, 156; synthetics, **Supp. 2**, 97; **Supp. 5**, 191, 663; **Supp. 6**, 67; thread machines, **Vol. 2, Part 2**, 336; unionization, **Supp. 8**, 367; Vicuña mislabeling, **Supp. 8**, 219–20

Thacher, Ebby, reference to, **Supp. 9**, 883

"Thacher's Plain," **Vol. 9, Part 2**, 389

Thackeray, William Makepiece, book collections on, **Supp. 1**, 65

Thailand, medical missions in, **Supp. 3**, 486; **Supp. 4**, 181–82, 529–30

Thalassemia. *See* Cooley's anemia

Thalberg, Irving, references to, **Supp. 6**, 440–41, 657, 658; **Supp. 7**, 563; **Supp. 8**, 576

Thames River, battle of, **Vol. 4, Part 2**, 349; **Vol. 5, Part 2**, 103, 115; **Vol. 6, Part 1**, 542; **Vol. 9, Part 1**, 62; **Vol. 9, Part 2**, 360

Thanksgiving Day: law establishing date of, **Supp. 9**, 483; Macy's parade, **Supp. 3**, 685

Thant, U., reference to, **Supp. 7**, 724

Thaw, Harry K.: first trial of, **Vol. 3, Part 1**, 226; White shooting by, **Supp. 3**, 170, 385; **Supp. 6**, 290; **Supp. 8**, 460–62; **Supp. 9**, 216

Thaw, Mary Sibbet, reference to, **Supp. 4**, 826, 827

Thayer, James Bradley, reference to, **Supp. 3**, 94

Thayer, Webster, reference to, **Supp. 7**, 262

Thayer School of Engineering, **Supp. 2**, 195

"Thayer's Law," in painting, **Vol. 9, Part 2**, 400

Theater: **Vol. 1, Part 2**, 448; **Vol. 2, Part 2**, 356 f.; **Vol. 3, Part 1**, 37, 43f; **Vol. 3, Part 2**, 310, 429, 517 f., 529, 567; **Vol. 4, Part 2**, 422, 548, 580 f.; **Vol. 5, Part 1**, 52, 276, 402; **Vol. 5, Part 2**, 442 f.; **Vol. 6, Part 1**, 56 f., 194, **Vol. 6, Part 2**, 500; **Vol. 8, Part 2**, 60; **Vol. 9, Part 2**, 77; **Vol. 10, Part 1**, 367 f.; acting, **Vol. 1, Part 1**, 57 f., 151, 343, 477, 516, 573, 581 f., 615, 629, 645 f., 659 f.; **Vol. 1, Part 2**, 43, 45, 222, 272, 346, 368, 444, 448, 452, 475, 525, 558; **Vol. 2, Part 1**, 281, 346, 580; **Vol. 2, Part 2**, 2, 167, 219, 260, 342, 356 f., 362 f., 416, 466 f., 491 f., 509; **Vol. 3, Part 1**, 1 f., 4 f., 46 f., 81 f., 91 f., 170 f., 320, 393, 428 f., 476, 488, 566 f., 589 f.; **Vol. 3, Part 2**, 285, 309 f., 321, 333, 366, 368, 404, 462, 529, 568; **Vol. 4, Part 1**, 198, 266, 270 f., 410; **Vol. 4, Part 2**, 72 f., 74, 148, 168, 339, 422, 475 f., 582; **Vol. 5, Part 1**, 30 f., 102, 143 f., 586, 605; **Vol. 5, Part 2**, 11, 14 f., 16, 139, 194, 282 f., 284 f., 315, 424, 442, 570; **Vol. 6, Part 1**, 164, 207, 216, 358 f., 365, 493; **Vol. 6, Part 2**, 10, 77, 174, 245, 248, 259, 262, 266, 367, 462, 536, 574, 627; **Vol. 7, Part 1**, 57, 73, 93, 203 f., 206 f., 297, 340 f., **Vol. 7, Part 2**, 8 f., 44, 120 f., 327 f., 644 f.; **Vol. 8, Part 1**, 375, 413, 470 f., 580 f., 592; **Vol. 8, Part 2**, 16, 60, 203, 246 f., 249; **Vol. 9, Part 1**, 13, 44, 164, 177, 318, 347, 363 f., 400 f.; **Vol. 9, Part 2**, 61 f., 77, 456, 499 f.; **Vol. 10, Part 1**, 167 f., 379 f., 381 f., 383, 389, 420 f., 489 f., 647 f.; **Vol. 10, Part 2**, 15, 37, 197, 248 f., 430, 477; Actors' Equity, organization of, **Supp. 1**, 318; Actors' Equity, recognition of, **Supp. 4**, 234; Actors' Equity strike, **Supp. 3**, 174, 333; **Supp. 9**, 216; **Supp. 10**, 851; agents, **Supp. 1**, 539; **Supp. 9**, 375; beginnings of, **Vol. 4, Part 2**, 148; *Best Plays* series, **Supp. 4**, 549; "Big Four," **Vol. 8, Part 1**, 471; black musicals, **Supp. 3**, 187; blacks in, **Supp. 1**, 374; **Supp. 8**, 287–88, 547; **Supp. 10**, 95, 576, 677, 818; black stereotypes, **Supp. 7**, 237; black themes, **Supp. 7**, 319; **Supp. 9**, 698; **Supp. 10**, 147, 193; booking system, **Vol. 3, Part 2**, 176 f.; Boston, **Vol. 2, Part 1**, 233; **Vol. 3, Part 1**, 15 f.; **Vol. 5, Part 2**, 431; **Vol. 7, Part 2**, 272; **Vol. 8, Part 1**, 150 f.; **Vol. 8, Part 2**, 386, 388; **Vol. 9, Part 1**, 49; British stars; **Vol. 8, Part 1**, 215 f.; "Broadway After Dark" column, **Supp. 8**, 444; Brooklyn, N.Y., **Vol. 4, Part 2**, 339 f.; buildings, **Vol. 8, Part 1**, 197; **Supp. 1**, 18; **Supp. 5**, 627–28; burlesque, **Vol. 6, Part 1**, 217; **Vol. 8, Part 2**, 247; *Camille*, **Vol. 4, Part 2**, 582; censorship, **Supp. 5**, 419; Chicago, **Vol. 4, Part 1**, 393; classical French, **Supp. 5**, 410; comedies, **Supp. 7**, 282–83; **Supp. 10**, 631; comedy, Irish-American, **Vol. 3, Part 2**, 476 f.; comedy, musical, **Vol. 3, Part 2**, 573; **Vol. 5, Part 1**, 78; comedy of manners, **Vol. 3, Part 1**, 516 f.; **Supp. 9**, 451, 452; comic opera, **Vol. 3, Part 1**, 204 f.; **Vol. 4, Part 2**, 573; **Vol. 8, Part 2**, 246; **Vol. 9, Part 1**, 408; community, **Supp. 1**, 96; companies, **Supp. 1**, 177, 519; "Comstockery," **Vol.**

3, Part 1, 46; continental, **Vol. 3, Part 1**, 516 f.; controversial productions, **Supp. 5**, 418–19; copyright protection, **Supp. 6**, 150; costume design, **Supp. 5**, 52–53, 386; **Supp. 6**, 10; criticism, **Supp. 1**, 369, 592, 643; **Supp. 2**, 76, 277; **Supp. 3**, 53–54, 841–42; **Supp. 4**, 548–49; **Supp. 5**, 17–18, 425, 463–64, 657–58; **Supp. 6**, 237, 470–71; **Supp. 7**, 412, 811–12; **Supp. 8**, 53–55, 353, 444–45, 491, 492, 584–85; **Supp. 9**, 170–71, 885–86; **Supp. 10**, 130, 146, 424–25; Daly Stock Company, **Vol. 6, Part 1**, 217; direction, **Supp. 4**, 653; **Supp. 7**, 495–96; **Supp. 9**, 350–51, 848–49; **Supp. 10**, 113–14, 130, 311–12, 474; Donald Robertson Players, **Vol. 4, Part 1**, 393; dramatic construction, **Vol. 8, Part 1**, 221; dramatic criticism, **Vol. 5, Part 1**, 445; **Vol. 10, Part 2**, 406; of 1829, **Vol. 8, Part 1**, 499; of 1890s, **Vol. 8, Part 1**, 132; Elizabethan drama studies, **Supp. 4**, 4–5, 110; **Supp. 9**, 626–27; federal project, **Supp. 8**, 176–77; first black actress to star on Broadway, **Supp. 10**, 818; first black Othello on Broadway, **Supp. 10**, 678; first chorus line, **Supp. 6**, 305; first contemporary drama course, **Supp. 4**, 354; first serious presentation of black life, **Supp. 4**, 841; first successful black Broadway show, **Supp. 9**, 731; flashback technique, **Supp. 8**, 528; free-verse, **Supp. 3**, 341; Greek, **Supp. 4**, 143; "Haverly Mastodons," **Vol. 4, Part 1**, 40; historical studies on, **Supp. 4**, 634; Ibsen's plays in U.S., **Supp. 3**, 276–77; Indian influence in, **Vol. 8, Part 2**, 16; **Vol. 9, Part 2**, 77; interracial casting breakthrough, **Supp. 9**, 698; introduction of European talent to America, **Supp. 4**, 842–43; journalism, **Supp. 3**, 276–77; **Supp. 9**, 170–71, 885–86; journals, **Supp. 1**, 45; Kentucky, **Vol. 3, Part 1**, 432; leading ladies, **Supp. 9**, 194–95; lecturing on, **Vol. 6, Part 2**, 416; **Supp. 1**, 698; **Supp. 8**, 54; librettos, **Supp. 9**, 748, 888; London stage, **Supp. 8**, 21–22; **Supp. 9**, 350, 481, 848; **Supp. 10**, 673, 851; lyricists, **Supp. 3**, 338–39, 406; magnates in, **Vol. 8, Part 1**, 215 f.; makeup, **Supp. 1**, 165; management, **Vol. 1, Part 1**, 272, 343, 475, 516, 645, 647; **Vol. 1, Part 2**, 444, 446, 449, 453; **Vol. 2, Part 2**, 156 f.; **Vol. 3, Part 1**, 224, 516 f.; **Vol. 3, Part 2**, 393, 423, 428 f., 462; **Vol. 4, Part 1**, 40, 314; **Vol. 4, Part 2**, 73, 148, 168, 199, 295, 339; **Vol. 5, Part 1**, 102; **Vol. 5, Part 2**, 14 f., 194, 284, 289, 523; **Vol. 6, Part 1**, 164, 207, 355 f., 358 f., 493; **Vol. 6, Part 2**, 174; **Vol. 7, Part 1**, 67, 482; **Vol. 7, Part 2**, 172 f., 290; **Vol. 8, Part 2**, 387; **Vol. 9, Part 1**, 13, 177, 346, 370; **Vol. 10, Part 2**, 654; **Supp. 2**, 10; **Supp. 4**, 103–4; masques, **Supp. 6**, 417–18; **Supp. 9**, 417–19; Massachusetts, allowed in, **Vol. 4, Part 1**, 137; matinee idols, **Supp. 3**, 34–36, 58–59; medieval church drama studies, **Supp. 3**, 855; melodramas, **Supp. 3**, 765, 801; **Supp. 6**, 149; minstrelsy, **Vol. 2, Part 2**, 98; **Vol. 3, Part 1**, 338; **Vol. 3, Part 2**, 148, 557, 574; **Vol. 4, Part 2**, 410; **Vol. 8, Part 1**, 545 f.; modernism, **Vol. 3, Part 1**, 46; Mohawk Drama Festival, **Supp. 3**, 287; monologues, **Supp. 6**, 174; **Supp. 10**, 739, 740; musical choreography, **Supp. 8**, 644; **Supp. 10**, 33, 113–14; musical composition for, **Supp. 4**, 867–69; **Supp. 9**, 281; **Supp. 10**, 527, 693, 694, 695; musical direction, **Supp. 8**, 465; musical revues, **Supp. 4**, 150; **Supp. 5**, 414; **Supp. 6**, 318–19; **Supp. 8**, 546–48, 694–95; **Supp. 10**, 300, 705, 818; musicals, **Supp. 3**, 174, 333, 338–39, 417–18; **Supp. 4**, 226, 869, 918–19; **Supp. 5**, 413–14; **Supp. 6**, 273–74, 511; **Supp. 7**, 1, 197–98, 389, 497, 622–23, 657–58; **Supp. 8**, 108–9, 145–46, 250–51, 386–87, 481; **Supp. 9**, 281, 731, 732, 748, 850–51; **Supp. 10**, 105, 106, 223, 561, 597, 693, 694, 695, 713, 775, 802, 850; musicals, choreography of, **Supp. 8**, 644; New Orleans, **Vol. 3, Part 1**, 133; **Vol. 6, Part 1**, 493; New York, **Vol. 1, Part 1**, 256; **Vol. 1, Part 2**, 446; **Vol. 3, Part 1**, 516 f.; **Vol. 4, Part 1**, 314; **Vol. 5, Part 2**, 284; **Vol. 6, Part 1**, 281; nineteenth century, of middle of, **Vol. 3, Part 2**, 566; **Vol. 6, Part 1**, 164; Old American Company, **Vol. 4, Part 2**, 548; operetta, **Supp. 5**, 585, 627; organizations, **Supp. 2**, 76; *Our Town*, **Supp. 3**, 198; outdoor historical pageants, **Supp. 3**, 427; ownership, **Vol. 5, Part 2**, 289; Philadelphia Theatre, **Vol. 3, Part 1**, 37; **Vol. 7, Part 1**, 206 f.; *Pique*, **Vol. 3, Part 1**, 82; playwriting, **Supp. 1**, 45, 466, 557; **Supp. 2**, 303, 324; **Supp. 3**, 3–4; **Supp. 4**, 54–55, 354, 670–71; **Supp. 5**, 624; **Supp. 6**, 652–53; **Supp. 7**, 319, 325–26, 331–32, 412–14, 583–84; **Supp. 8**, 108, 170–71, 287–88, 382–83, 492–93, 528–30, 622; **Supp. 9**, 70–71, 421–22, 451–52, 579, 748, 749, 870–71, 888; **Supp. 10**, 146–47, 193, 436, 631, 721, 739, 740, 756, 757, 829; political themes, **Supp. 7**, 61–62; *Prince of Parthia*, **Vol. 4, Part 1**, 346; production, **Supp. 1**, 66; **Supp. 3**, 276–77, 333; **Supp. 4**, 648–49, 842–43; **Supp. 5**, 246, 627–28; **Supp. 6**, 637; **Supp. 7**, 457–58; **Supp. 8**,438–39; **Supp. 9**, 376, 417–19; **Supp. 10**, 54–56, 311, 312, 733, 734; production spectacles, **Supp. 3**, 296–97; productions of Shakespeare, **Supp. 4**, 478–79, 552; "projected scenery" method introduced, **Supp. 10**, 9; proletarian plays, **Supp. 7**, 583–84; Provincetown Players, **Vol. 2, Part 2**, 372 f.; **Supp. 3**, 329; **Supp. 4**, 330, 576; **Supp. 5**,523; **Supp. 8**, 350, 675; regional American drama, **Supp. 3**,426–27; regional repertory, **Supp. 8**, 283; repertory, **Supp. 3**, 796–99; **Supp. 4**, 478–79; **Supp. 9**, 472, 481; **Supp. 10**, 100; repertory Shakespeare, **Supp. 5**, 268–69; **Supp. 9**, 351; Revolutionary period, **Vol. 6, Part 1**, 322 f.; road companies, **Supp. 9**, 194, 195; **Supp. 10**, 53; runs, early, **Vol. 3, Part 1**, 224, 516 f.; Sardi's restaurant, **Supp. 8**, 571–72; set design, **Supp. 5**, 52–53, 375–76; **Supp. 6**, 233, 624–25; **Supp. 10**, 8–9, 534–35; Shakespearean productions, **Supp. 7**, 496; **Supp. 9**, 350, 351, 692, 848–49; **Supp. 10**, 677, 678, 850, 851; Shaw's plays, **Vol. 3, Part 1**, 46; slapstick comedy, **Supp. 7**, 588–89; social consciousness, **Supp. 8**, 176; **Supp. 10**, 54, 55; sophisticated comedies, **Supp. 9**, 70–71; Spanish, studies in, **Supp. 2**, 131; stage architecture, **Vol. 10, Part 1**, 133; stage design for Ziegfield Follies, **Vol. 10, Part 1**, 133; stage devices, **Vol. 6, Part 2**, 77; Stanislavski method, **Supp. 3**, 297; studies in, **Supp. 1**, 566; **Supp. 2**, 11; **Supp. 4**, 4–5; **Supp. 10**, 129–30, 131; stock, **Supp. 9**, 194; **Supp. 10**, 68, 657; Syndicate, **Supp. 1**, 301; **Supp. 3**, 276–77; teaching of, **Supp. 1**, 45; Theatre Guild productions, *see* Theatre Guild; Theatre Owners Booking Agency, **Supp. 9**, 60, 517; "Tony" awards, **Supp. 4**, 653; **Supp. 9**, 171; **Supp. 10**, 535; tragedy, **Vol. 3, Part 1**, 402 f., 488 f., 506 f.; trusts, **Supp. 2**, 281; vaudeville, **Vol. 5, Part 2**, 289; **Vol. 7, Part 2**, 290; **Vol. 8, Part 1**, 242 f.; **Vol. 8, Part 2**, 249; verse, **Supp. 7**, 221, 222; Washington, D.C., **Vol. 5, Part 2**, 284; West, **Vol. 3, Part 1**, 432; *What Price Glory?*, **Supp. 6**, 15–16; **Supp. 8**, 622; World War II activities, **Supp. 4**, 187; writings on, **Vol. 8, Part 1**, 221; **Vol. 10, Part 1**, 168, 647 f.; **Vol. 10, Part 2**, 406; **Supp. 4**, 354, 377–78; **Supp. 10**, 740; Yiddish, **Supp. 5**, 10–11; **Supp. 6**, 523–24; **Supp. 8**, 452.; **Supp. 10**, 252–53. *See also* Acting; for complete list of actors, playwrights, etc., *see* Occupations Index

Theatre Arts Magazine, **Supp. 7**, 811, 812

Theatre Guild: **Supp. 3**, 548; **Supp. 4**, 55; **Supp. 5**, 257–58; **Supp. 9**, 481; founding of, **Supp. 3**, 811–12; **Supp. 4**, 233–34; **Supp. 7**, 458; productions, **Supp. 10**, 129, 473; set designs, **Supp. 5**, 376

Theatre Owners Booking Agency. *See under* Theater

Theatrical Fund, **Vol. 10, Part 1**, 647 f.

Theatrical syndicates: **Vol. 3, Part 2**, 177; **Vol. 4, Part 1**, 40; **Supp. 4**, 522; organization of, **Supp. 2**, 363
Theocratic government: **Vol. 3, Part 1**, 612; Connecticut, **Vol. 3, Part 1**, 611; New Haven Colony, **Vol. 3, Part 1**, 612
Theologians. For complete list, *see* Occupations Index
Theological and Literary Journal, **Vol. 6, Part 1**, 405
Theological Institute of Connecticut, founding of, **Vol. 10, Part 1**, 85
Theological Studies, founding of, **Supp. 5**, 677
Theology: **Vol. 1, Part 1**, 324, 328, 530, 560; **Vol. 3, Part 1**, 192; **Vol. 3, Part 2**, 31, 150 f., 184, 222, 253, 391 f., 395, 555; **Vol. 4, Part 2**, 360; **Vol. 5, Part 1**, 305, 452 f.; **Vol. 5, Part 2**, 77 f., 475, 525 f.; **Vol. 6, Part 1**, 280, 298; **Vol. 8, Part 1**, 593, 595; **Vol. 9, Part 1**, 547; Armenian, **Vol. 8, Part 1**, 414; Campbellite movement, **Vol. 8, Part 1**, 600 f.; Dutch Reformed, **Vol. 2, Part 1**, 605; Ecclesiastical, **Vol. 8, Part 1**, 551; ecumenism, **Supp. 10**, 110–11; infallibility of Bible questioned, **Supp. 10**, 82; Lutheran, **Vol. 5, Part 2**, 77 f.; "Mercersburg," **Vol. 1, Part 1**, 324; Mormon, **Supp. 9**, 737; New England controversy, **Vol. 2, Part 1**, 351 f.; **Vol. 4, Part 2**, 319; **Vol. 5, Part 1**, 217; **Vol. 9, Part 1**, 75; seminary, first in U.S., **Vol. 6, Part 1**, 314; teaching, **Vol. 3, Part 1**, 346; **Vol. 5, Part 1**, 97 f.; **Vol. 5, Part 2**, 305, 369; **Vol. 7, Part l**, 442; **Vol. 8, Part 1**, 414; **Vol. 8, Part 2**, 227, 426, 536 f.; **Vol. 9, Part 1**, 56, 104, 269 f., 277 f., 610; **Vol. 9, Part 2**, 142 f., 148; Unitarianism, **Vol. 3, Part 2**, 577; **Vol. 5, Part 1**, 358; Wallingford controversy, **Vol. 3, Part 1**, 54; writings, **Vol. 1, Part, 558 f.; Vol. 1, Part 2**, 15, 17, 98 f., 128, 141, 147, 165, 169, 176, 214, 220, 294, 318, 354, 426, 466, 472, 523, 552; **Vol. 2, Part 1**, 115, 177, 179, 182, 225, 276, 292, 324, 351 f., 363; **Vol. 2, Part 2**, 43, 49 f., 67, 619, 621; **Vol. 3, Part 2**, 203, 257, 535, 547; **Vol. 4, Part 1**, 38; **Vol. 4, Part 2**, 319, 367; **Vol. 5, Part 1**, 98, 101, 218; **Vol. 5, Part 2**, 391, 475; **Vol. 6, Part 1**, 270, 406; **Vol. 6, Part 2**, 32, 605; **Vol. 7, Part 1**, 43, 48, 125, 147, 568 f., 573; **Vol. 7, Part 2**, 134 f., 176, 204 f., 218, 221, 229, 231, 239 f., 245 f., 295 f., 307, 316, 318, 325, 333 f., 343 f., 374, 380, 411 f., 421, 423, 451, 476, 501 f., 507 f., 526, 544, 574 f., 590, 634; **Vol. 8, Part 1**, 13 f., 155 f., 205 f., 223 f., 273 f., 292 f., 414, 551, 637; **Vol. 8, Part2, 43, 227; Vol. 9, Part 1**, 4 f., 202, 209, 278, 305 f., 375 f., 449, 551, 610; **Vol. 9, Part 2**, 115, 143, 148, 382 f., 618; **Vol. 10, Part 1**, 43, 85 f., 93, 102, 142, 402 f., 447 f., 453 f., 490 f., 651 f.; **Vol. 10, Part 2**, 12, 428, 641, 659; **Supp. 9**, 384, 737; **Supp. 10**, 82–83. *See also* Christianity; Judaism and Jews; Religion; *specific denominations and sects*
Theonomy, dialectic of, **Supp. 7**, 747
Theory of relativity. *See* Relativity, theories of
Theory of the Relativity of Motion, The, **Supp. 4**, 839
Theosophical Society, **Vol. 1, Part 2**, 362; **Vol. 7, Part 2**, 10 f.; **Vol. 9, Part 2**, 562
Theosophist, The, **Vol. 7, Part 2**, 11
Theosophy, **Vol. 1, Part 2**, 362; **Vol. 3, Part 1**, 321; **Vol. 4, Part 2**, 381; **Vol. 5, Part 2**, 233 f.; **Vol. 8, Part 2**, 319; **Vol. 9, Part 2**, 561 f.; **Supp. 2**, 697–98; **Supp. 4**, 105–6
Therapeutics, **Vol. 3, Part 2**, 213; **Vol. 5, Part 2**, 393; **Vol. 7, Part 2**, 153; **Vol. 8, Part 2**, 69
Theremin, Leo, reference to, **Supp. 3**, 690
Theremin (electronic instrument), **Supp. 7**, 756
Theresa, Mother, reference to, **Vol. 7, Part 1**, 400–401
Theresa, founding of Village of, **Vol. 5, Part 2**, 247
Thermal conduction, **Supp. 1**, 57; **Supp. 2**, 273
Thermal diffusion, Onsager's reciprocal relations, **Supp. 10**, 609
Thermionic emission, **Supp. 6**, 364
Thermochemistry, **Vol. 8, Part 1**, 557 f.
Thermodynamics, **Vol. 4, Part 1**, 6, 248 f.; **Vol. 8, Part 1**, 557 f.; **Supp. 1**, 596; **Supp. 4**, 488–89; **Supp. 5**, 202
Thermoelectricity, **Supp. 2**, 273
Thermometers: **Vol. 8, Part 1**, 557 f.; **Vol. 8, Part 2**, 114; high-temperature, **Supp. 1**, 120–21; scale extension, **Supp. 6**, 153; use in medicine, **Vol. 8, Part 2**, 560; metallic, invention of, **Vol. 8, Part 1**, 630
Thermostat, **Vol. 4, Part 2**, 561
Thiel College, **Vol. 7, Part 1**, 306; **Vol. 7, Part 2**, 289
Thilly, Frank, reference to, **Supp. 3**, 697
THINK (slogan), **Supp. 6**, 674
Thinking, psychological studies in, **Supp. 6**, 527–28; **Supp. 8**, 343
Think tanks, conservative, **Supp. 10**, 22
Thin Red Line, The, **Supp. 10**, 391
"Third Man, The" (radio program), **Supp. 9**, 648
Third term for president, **Vol. 8, Part 2**, 140, 141
Third World, **Supp. 7**, 421, 422, 423; black writings on, **Supp. 6**, 716–17; economy, **Supp. 3**, 414
39 Steps, The, **Supp. 10**, 339, 340
Thirty Seconds Over Tokyo, **Supp. 9**, 188
This Is My Story, **Supp. 7**, 660
This Gun for Hire, **Supp. 9**, 480
This Is My Story, **Supp. 9**, 135
"This Land Is Your Land" (song), **Supp. 8**, 235
This Quarter, **Supp. 7**, 335
This Side of Paradise, **Supp. 5**, 614
This Week, founding of, **Supp. 5**, 394
Thomas, Augustus, relations wlth Agnes Booth, **Vol. 1, Part 2**, 444
Thomas, Charles, reference to, **Supp. 9**, 185
Thomas, Elmer, reference to, **Supp. 3**, 506
Thomas, George Henry, **Vol. 1, Part 1**, 508
Thomas, Helen Goss, reference to, **Supp. 4**, 33
Thomas, J. Parnell, reference to, **Supp. 8**, 162
Thomas, Lewis, reference to, **Supp. 10**, 370
Thomas, Lowell, reference to, **Supp. 5**, 102
Thomas, Martha Carey, reference to, **Supp. 7**, 288
Thomas, Norman, references to, **Supp. 3**, 778; **Supp. 6**, 113, 161, 651; **Supp. 10**, 47, 48, 849
Thomas, R. J., reference to, **Supp. 8**, 526, 527
Thomas, Seth, **Vol. 9, Part 2**, 381; **Supp. 3**, 561
Thomas, Theodore, **Vol. 7, Part 1**, 80, 372; **Vol. 8, Part 2**, 562; **Vol. 9, Part 1**, 568; **Vol. 9, Part 2**, 516; **Supp. 3**, 740; **Supp. 4**, 834
Thomas, William I., references to, **Supp. 3**, 577–78; **Supp. 4**, 809
Thomas, Theodore, Orchestra, **Vol. 6, Part 1**, 238,
Thomaston, Conn., created, **Vol. 9, Part 2**, 446
Thompson, Albert ("Bill"), reference to, **Supp. 3**, 316
Thompson, Clara M., references to, **Supp. 4**, 806, 807, 808
Thompson, Dorothy, references to, **Supp. 5**, 423, 424; **Supp. 8**, 520
Thompson, James R., references to, **Supp. 10**, 169, 412
Thompson, J. Walter, Co. *See* J. Walter Thompson Co.
Thompson, Malvina C., reference to, **Supp. 7**, 659, 664
Thompson, Marguerite, reference to, **Supp. 8**, 714
Thompson, Warren S., reference to, **Supp. 3**, 636
Thompson, William Hale ("Big Bill"), references to, **Supp. 3**, 378, 467, 674, 710–11; **Supp. 4**, 141, 142; **Supp. 5**, 166, 323, 450
Thompson Institute. *See* Boyce Thompson Institute
Thomson, George P., reference to, **Supp. 6**, 151
Thomson, J. J., references to, **Supp. 6**, 151; **Supp. 7**, 10
Thomson, Polly, reference to, **Supp. 8**, 317
Thomson, Virgil, references to, **Supp. 4**, 769–70; **Supp. 10**, 762

Thomson-Houston Electric Co., **Supp. 2**, 658–59
Thoracic surgery, **Supp. 6**, 246
Thoreau, Henry David: **Vol. 9, Part 1**, 168; edition of works, **Vol. 9, Part 2**, 595; **Supp. 5**, 542; friendship with, **Vol. 8, Part 1**, 586; illustrations for works of, **Supp. 3**, 848; relation with Louisa May Alcott, **Vol. 1, Part 1**, 141
Thoreau family, **Vol. 9, Part 2**, 491 f.
Thorek Hospital and Medical Center (Chicago, Ill.), founding of, **Supp. 6**, 631
Thorndike, Edward L., references to, **Supp. 3**, 677; **Supp. 4**, 374; **Supp. 6**, 557, 640
Thorndike Memorial Laboratory (Boston), **Supp. 4**, 581–82
Thorne, George R., **Vol. 10, Part 1**, 414
Thorne, James A., **Vol. 10, Part 1**, 625 f.
Thornton, William, plan of Washington buildings, **Vol. 4, Part 2**, 153
Thornton Hereford Ranch, **Supp. 10**, 782
Thornwell Orphanage, **Vol. 5, Part 1**, 568
Thorpe, Jim, reference to, **Supp. 5**, 728
Thought, founding of, **Supp. 5**, 677
Thought and Character of William James, The, **Supp. 6**, 504, 505
Thousand Islands International Bridge (U.S.-Canada), **Supp. 6**, 594
Thread, in manufacture of, **Vol. 2, Part 2**, 336
Three Deuces (Chicago, Ill.), **Supp. 6**, 620
Three Mountains Press, **Supp. 7**, 335
Three-Penny Opera, The, **Supp. 4**, 868, 869; **Supp. 7**, 61, 62
Three Stooges (comedy team), **Supp. 9**, 281, 282–83, 409–10
Three Years Among the Indians and the Mexicans, **Vol. 5, Part 1**, 588
Threshing machine, **Vol. 1, Part 1**, 551; **Vol. 3, Part 1**, 437; **Vol. 6, Part 1**, 612; **Vol. 7, Part 2**, 644
Throop College of Technology. *See* California Institute of Technology
"Throttlebottom, Alexander" (fictional character), **Supp. 7**, 551
Through Rugged Ways to the Stars, **Supp. 9**, 714
Thunderstorms, measurement of, **Supp. 1**, 579
Thurber, Charles, reference to, **Supp. 4**, 32
Thurber, James, references to, **Supp. 5**, 594; **Supp. 6**, 236, 422, 423
Thurman Act, **Vol. 5, Part 1**, 410
Thurmond, J. Strom, references to, **Supp. 6**, 710; **Supp. 7**, 398; **Supp. 10**, 411
Thurstone, Louis, reference to, **Supp. 6**, 605
Thymus gland, **Supp. 7**, 59
Thyroid glands: disease classification, **Supp. 2**, 533; **Supp. 3**, 832; functions of, **Supp. 3**, 483; physiological and pharmacological studies of, **Supp. 4**, 411; **Supp. 9**, 454; pituitary gland and, **Supp. 6**, 386; removal to relieve heart failure, **Supp. 4**, 209; studies of, **Supp. 6**, 100; surgery of, **Supp. 3**, 626
Thyrotoxicosis, **Supp. 3**, 806
Tibbles, Thomas H., reference to, **Vol. 2, Part 1**, 46
Tic douloureux, **Supp. 4**, 214
Ticker. *See* Stock ticker
Ticket chopper, invention of, **Vol. 8, Part 1**, 92 f.
Ticknor, George, reference to, **Vol. 9, Part 1**, 434; **Vol. 9, Part 2**, 524
Ticknor and Fields, **Vol. 3, Part 2**, 378
Tide, Great Lakes, **Vol. 4, Part 1**, 476
Tide, founding of, **Supp. 8**, 393
Tides, studies of, **Supp. 3**, 291
Tidewater leader, **Vol. 1, Part 2**, 609
Tientsin, China. *See* Boxer Rebellion
Tientsin, Treaty of, **Vol. 8, Part 1**, 462
Tifereth Israel (Cleveland, Ohio, temple), **Supp. 7**, 689
Tiger, The (Princeton), **Vol. 2, Part 2**, 162
Tiger, as Tammany symbol, **Vol. 7, Part 1**, 392; **Vol. 10, Part 1**, 80
Tigress, The, **Vol. 4, Part 1**, 595
Tilden, George T., reference to, **Supp. 3**, 195
Tilden, Samuel J., reference to, **Vol. 5, Part 1**, 28; **Vol. 8, Part 2**, 473, 505
Tilden, William Tatem ("big Bill"), references to, **Supp. 6**, 425, 538, 539; **Supp. 9**, 721
Tilden cipher dispatches, **Vol. 4, Part 2**, 383
Tile Club, **Vol. 7, Patt 29 203**
Till, Irene, reference to, **Supp. 6**, 271
Tillich, Paul, reference to, **Supp. 7**, 574
Tillman, Benjamin R. ("Pitchfork Ben"), **Supp. 3**, 78
Till We Meet Again, **Supp. 10**, 70
Tilson, John Q., reference to, **Supp. 6**, 588
Tilton, Theodore: relations with: Beecher, Henry Ward, **Vol. 1, Part 2**, 134; Bowen, Henry Chandler, **Vol. 1, Part 2**, 505
Tilton-Beecher case, **Vol. 1, Part 2**, 134
Timber-Culture Act, **Vol. 5, Part 1**, 78
Time: belts, **Supp. 1**, 674; standard, **Vol. 8, Part 1**, 465
Time, **Supp. 7**, 269–70; cover portraits, **Supp. 7**, 17; **Supp. 10**, 112–13; editing, **Supp. 7**, 114; editorial policies, **Supp. 8**, 395, 396; foreign news section, **Supp. 5**, 734; founding of,
Supp. 8, 393–94; movie reviews, **Supp. 5**, 12
Time, Inc.: **Supp. 5**, 152–53, 734; **Supp. 7**, 17; founding and growth of, **Supp. 8**, 393–95
Time-Life International, **Supp. 7**, 383–84
Time pieces, **Vol. 3, Part 2**, 143
Times-Mirror Corp., **Supp. 9**, 167, 168
Tin, manufacture of, **Vol. 7, Part 1**, 517–18
Tin cans, manufacture of, **Vol. 6, Part 1**, 82
Tin-clads, **Vol. 3, Part 1**, 587 f.
"Tin Man" (ficitonal character), **Supp. 10**, 301
"Tin Pan Alley," phrase coined, **Supp. 4**, 836
Tin peddling, **Vol. 3, Part 2**, 306
Tioga Point Historical Society, **Vol. 7, Part 1**, 366
Tippecanoe, battle of, **Vol. 4, Part 2**, 349; **Vol. 7, Part 1**, 633; **Vol. 7, Part 2**, 210; **Vol. 9, Part 2**, 360,375, 563; **Vol. 10, Part 1**, 567
"Tippecanoe and Tyler, Too," **Vol. 8, Part 2**, 174
Tippetts, Abbett, McCarthy, Stratton, predecessor, **Supp. 5**, 396
Tipping, bitter opposition to, **Vol. 9, Part 2**, 132
Tippit, J. D., reference to, **Supp. 7**, 594
Tip Top Weekly, **Supp. 3**, 586
Tires: automobile, **Supp. 2**, 187; research and marketing, **Supp. 6**, 381; **Supp. 7**, 169
Tishman Realty and Construction, Inc., **Supp. 10**, 785–86
Titanic, **Vol. 1, Part 1**, 400; **Vol. 9, Part 2**, 129; **Supp. 6**, 23; **Supp. 9**, 700
Titchener, Edward Bradford, **Vol. 10, Part 1**, 476 f.; **Supp. 4**, 21, 39; **Supp. 8**, 44
Titles, English, **Vol. 1, Part 1**, 402
Tito, Marshal, reference to, **Supp. 8**, 495
Titusville, Pa., site of first successful oll well, **Vol. 3, Part 1**, 427 f.
Tlingit Indians, **Supp. 6**, 611
TMV. *See* Tobacco mosaic virus
Tobacco: advertising and promotion, **Supp. 9**, 139; advertising ban, **Supp. 9**, 139, 316; cigarette advertising and promotion, **Supp. 4**, 371; **Supp. 10**, 145; cigarettes, **Vol. 4, Part 1**, 318; cigar manufacturing, **Supp. 7**, 614; competition, **Supp. 5**, 565–67; **Supp. 7**, 96; congressional support, **Supp. 6**, 590; cooperative marketing, **Supp. 2**, 39, 79; culture, **Vol. 3, Part 1**, 497 f.; **Vol. 5, Part 2**, 45; **Vol. 8, Part 2**, 118;

exportation, **Vol. 6, Part 1**, 154; **Vol. 8, Part 1**, 361 f.; liquor reform and, **Vol. 4, Part 2**, 386; manufacture of, **Vol. 3, Part 1**, 496 f.; **Vol. 4, Part 1**, 318; **Vol. 6, Part 1**, 412; mechanization, **Supp. 3**, 587–88; merchandising outfit, **Vol. 7, Part 1**, 591; **Vol. 7, Part 2**, 330; **Vol. 8, Part 2**, 266; smoking-cancer link, **Supp. 8**, 7; trade, **Vol. 4, Part 1**, 318; **Vol. 4, Part 2**, 70; **Vol. 6, Part 1**, 116; **Vol. 7, Part 1**, 647 f.; trust, **Supp. 1**, 609; writings on, **Vol. 5, Part 2**, 45. *See also* Smoking
Tobacco Institute, **Supp. 8**, 7
Tobacco mosaic virus (TMV), isolation of, **Supp. 9**, 753; **Supp. 10**, 427
Tobacco Road, **Supp. 7**, 34
Tobacco trust, **Supp. 6**, 591, 592
To Be or Not to Be, **Supp. 9**, 77
Tobin, Daniel J., reference to, **Supp. 6**, 218; **Supp. 9**, 395
Tobin, Maurice Joseph, reference to, **Supp. 9**, 210
Tocsin of Liberty, **Vol. 9, Part 2**, 596
Today, **Supp. 6**, 23
Todd, Michael, reference to, **Supp. 8**, 364; **Supp. 10**, 53
Todd-A-O, **Supp. 7**, 692–93
Todd's Tavern, battle of, **Vol. 9, Part 1**, 80; **Vol. 9, Part 2**, 172; **Vol. 10, Part 2**, 334
Todhunter School, **Supp. 7**, 659, 660
Todman, Bill, reference to, **Supp. 9**, 719
To Have or to Be?, **Supp. 10**, 261
To Hell and Back, **Supp. 9**, 575
Toiletries, hair-care products, **Supp. 5**, 512–13. *See also* Cosmetics
Toklas, Alice B., references to, **Supp. 4**, 769, 770
Tokyo, founding of St. Luke's Hospital, **Vol. 9, Part 2**, 384
Tolan, Thomas ("Eddie"), Jr., reference to, **Supp. 10**, 531
Toland, Gregg, reference to, **Supp. 9**, 324; **Supp. 10**, 348
Toledo, Ohio: municipal reform, **Supp. 1**, 453–54; philanthropies, **Vol. 6, Part 1**, 233; political service to, **Vol. 10, Part 2**, 37; politics, **Supp. 7**, 85; Roman Catholic diocese, **Supp. 6**, 607–8
Toledo Blade, **Vol. 5, Part 1**, 243; **Vol. 6, Part 1**, 336
Toledo Museum of Art, **Vol. 6, Part 1**, 233; **Vol. 9, Part 1**, 611
"Toledo Strip," **Vol. 9, Part 2**, 564
Toledo War (1835–36), **Vol. 1, Part 1**, 210; **Vol. 1, Part 2**, 281; **Vol. 6, Part 1**, 488; **Vol. 6, Part 2**, 376; **Vol. 9, Part 2**, 239
Tolman, Richard C.: National Defense Research Committee, service on, **Supp. 9**, 144; reference to, **Supp. 8**, 483
Tolson, Clyde, reference to, **Supp. 9**, 408
Tolstoy, Leo: influence of, **Vol. 5, Part 1**, 308–9; translation of, **Vol. 4, Part 2**, 233 f.
Tomatoes, disease-resistant, **Vol. 8, Part 1**, 239 f.
Tombigbee River, canal of, **Vol. 1, Part 1**, 577
Tombs (New York City Criminal Courts Building), **Supp. 5**, 134
Tom Owen, the Bee-Hunter, **Vol. 9, Part 2**, 509
Tompkins, John, reference to, **Supp. 6**, 27
Tompkins Square Boys' Club, **Vol. 4, Part 2**, 299
Tonkin Gulf Resolution: opposition to, **Supp. 9**, 347, 566; support for, **Supp. 9**, 388, 434–35
Tonsils, operations for, **Vol. 7, Part 1**, 616
Tontine, **Vol. 5, Part 1**, 450–51
"Tonto" (fictional character), **Supp. 10**, 737
Tool, manufacture, **Vol. 1, Part 1**, 248; **Vol. 5, Part 1**, 76; **Vol. 7, Part 2**, 58; **Vol. 8, Part 1**, 172 f.; **Vol. 9, Part 1**, 535 f.; **Vol. 9, Part 2**, 324
"Toonerville Trolley," **Supp. 7**, 257–58
Toombs, Robert, reference to, **Vol. 5, Part 1**, 517–18
Tooth decay, fillings for, **Supp. 4**, 402
Toots Shor's, **Supp. 10**, 732, 733
Topeka Daily Capital, **Supp. 5**, 100, 101
Topographical Bureau, **Vol. 9, Part 2**, 249
Topographical Corps, United States, **Vol. 4, Part 1**, 19
Topographical Dictionary, **Vol. 7, Part 2**, 648
Topographical engineering, **Vol. 3, Part 1**, 251 f.; **Vol. 4, Part 1**, 476; **Vol. 5, Part 1**, 348 f.; **Vol. 10, Part 1**, 473 f.
Topography: **Vol. 1, Part 1**, 525; **Vol. 3, Part 1**, 427; **Vol. 3, Part 2**, 569; **Vol. 4, Part 1**, 19 f.; **Vol. 4, Part 2**, 64; **Vol. 5, Part 1**, 194, 435; **Vol. 7, Part 1**, 81, 156; **Vol. 7, Part 2**, 563; **Vol. 8, Part 1**, 161 f., 647; **Vol. 10, Part 2**, 47; military, **Supp. 1**, 553; **Supp. 3**, 390; of moon, **Supp. 4**, 766; of U.S., **Supp. 4**, 219; of West, **Supp. 1**, 3; **Supp. 4**, 557–58; writings on, **Vol. 8, Part 1**, 161 f. *See also* Cartography
Tora! Tora! Tora!, **Supp. 10**, 232
Torch-Bearers, The, **Supp. 9**, 451
Tories: activities during Revolution, **Vol. 2, Part 1**, 168; Pennsylvania, **Vol. 7, Part 1**, 131; **Vol. 8, Part 2**, 177
Toronto Globe, **Vol. 9, Part 2**, 483
Toronto Star, **Supp. 7**, 334–35
Torpedo boats, **Supp. 2**, 298
Torpedoes: **Vol. 5, Part 1**, 303; **Vol. 6, Part 1**, 65, 83; **Vol. 8, Part 1**, 328; **Vol. 9, Part 1**, 188; design of, **Supp. 1**, 231–32; writings on, **Vol. 8, Part 2**, 465
Torrents of Spring, The, **Supp. 7**, 335, 336
Torrey Botanical Club, **Vol. 1, Part 1**, 208; **Vol. 9, Part 2**, 598
Torrio, John, reference to, **Supp. 6**, 263
Toscanini, Arturo, references to, **Supp. 2**, 415; **Supp. 4**, 212; **Supp. 7**, 124; **Supp. 8**, 19
To Secure These Rights, **Supp. 7**, 748; **Supp. 9**, 334
Total Abstinence Society, **Vol. 1, Part 1**, 254
Totalitariansim, theoretical analysis of, **Supp. 9**, 41
Totemism, studies in, **Supp. 2**, 244
"Totem Pole, The" column, **Supp. 10**, 747
To the Finland Station, **Supp. 9**, 876
Touch of Evil, **Supp. 9**, 793
Tourism. *See* Travel and tourism
Tower, Leslie, reference to, **Supp. 9**, 255
Towers, John H., reference to, **Supp. 5**, 621
Town: building, **Vol. 9, Part 2**, 17; improvement, **Vol. 2, Part 1**, 28
Town Hall, Inc., **Supp. 6**, 160
Towne Scientific School, **Vol. 9, Part 2**, 614
Townley Frocks, **Supp. 6**, 402
Townsend, Francis E., references to, **Supp. 3**, 653; **Supp. 4**, 480; **Supp. 7**, 195; **Supp. 10**, 745
Townsend cell, **Supp. 3**, 26
Townsend Plan, **Supp. 6**, 86, 646–47
Townshend Act, **Vol. 6, Part 1**, 118; **Vol. 7, Part 2**, 104
Toxemia, **Supp. 3**, 257
Toxicology: **Vol. 3, Part 1**, 377; **Vol. 8, Part 1**, 468; WCTU alcohol charges, **Supp. 3**, 163
Toynbee, Arnold, reference to, **Supp. 4**, 824
Toys: Duncan yo-yo, **Supp. 9**, 246; electric trains, **Supp. 7**, 150; erector set, **Supp. 7**, 287–88; Lincoln Logs, **Supp. 9**, 893, 894; Teddy bear, **Supp. 4**, 76
Tozzer, Alfred M., reference to, **Supp. 3**, 819
Track and field: broad jump, **Supp. 10**, 610; coaching, **Supp. 7**, 152–53; collegiate, **Supp. 9**, 623; dashes, **Supp. 10**, 610; hammer throw, **Supp. 3**, 487; hurdles, **Supp. 10**, 610; long-distance running, **Supp. 9**, 623–24; long-distance walking, **Supp. 1**, 583; Olympic Games, **Supp. 5**, 683–84; **Supp. 10**, 531, 610–11, 612; relays, **Supp. 10**, 610; short races, **Supp. 10**, 531; women in, **Supp. 6**, 722
Tractors: **Supp. 4**, 699; caterpillar type, **Vol. 6, Part 1**, 230; electric, **Vol. 6, Part 1**, 505

Tractarian Movement of Oxford, opposed, **Vol. 9, Part 2**, 79
Trade: **Vol. 1, Part 2**, 205; **Vol. 2, Part 1**, 383, 395; **Vol. 3, Part 1**, 249 f.; **Vol. 4, Part 1**, 140, 164, 296, 320, 344, 463, 504 f; **Vol. 4, Part 2**, 451; **Vol. 5, Part 2**, 110, 520, 587; **Vol. 6, Part 2**, 305 f.; **Vol. 9, Part 1**, 144; **Vol. 10, Part 1**, 441; with Africa, **Vol. 8, Part 2**, 212; with Alaska, **Vol. 4, Part 1**, 229; **Vol. 9, Part 1**, 67; **Vol. 10, Part 1**, 532 f.; with Asia, **Supp. 1**, 257; associations, laws affecting, **Vol. 4, Part 2**, 25; beaver, **Vol. 8, Part 1**, 320 f.; Canadian reciprocity treaty, **Supp. 1**, 29–30; with China, **Vol. 2, Part 1**, 66, 129, 149, 289 f.; **Vol. 3, Part 2**, 507 f.; **Vol. 4, Part 1**, 523, 551; **Vol. 4, Part 2**, 324, 482; **Vol. 5, Part 1**, 39, 408; **Vol. 5, Part 2**, 271, 383 f.; **Vol. 6, Part 1**, 444 f.; **Vol. 7, Part 2**, 34, 477; **Vol. 8, Part 2**, 152; **Vol. 9, Part 1**, 48; **Vol. 9, Part 2**, 499; **Vol. 10, Part 1**, 585 f.; colonial period, **Vol. 1, Part 2**, 498 f.; **Vol. 5, Part 2**, 328, 590; **Vol. 6, Part 1**, 215; development of, **Supp. 2**, 678; Dutch, **Vol. 10, Part 2**, 30; East India, **Vol. 2, Part 1**, 149; **Vol. 4, Part 1**, 523; **Vol. 5, Part 1**, 552; economic analysis, **Supp. 8**, 668–69; with England, **Vol. 5, Part 2**, 566; **Supp. 2**, 39; European, **Vol. 8, Part 2**, 216; free, **Vol. 3, Part 1**, 289; **Vol. 10, Part 1**, 637 f.; free advocacy, **Supp. 8**, 89–90; with French frontier posts, **Vol. 8, Part 2**, 295; fur, **Vol. 8, Part 2**, 32; **Vol. 9, Part 2**, 455; grain, **Vol. 1, Part 1**, 347, 476; **Vol. 7, Part 2**, 297 f., 605; **Vol. 8, Part 1**, 435; Hawaii, **Vol. 5, Part 1**, 381; Indian, **Vol. 2, Part 1**, 487; **Vol. 3, Part 1**, 83, 229, 305; **Vol. 3, Part 2**, 442, 506; **Vol. 4, Part 2**, 192 f., 314; **Vol. 5, Part 1**, 587 f.; **Vol. 5, Part 2**, 111; **Vol. 6, Part 1**, 191, 413, 586; **Vol. 6, Part 2**, 111, 528 f.; **Vol. 7, Part 1**, 631, 641; **Vol. 7, Part 2**, 4, 12; **Vol. 8, Part 2**, 108; **Vol. 9, Part 1**, 59, 332; **Vol. 9, Part 2**, 489, 638; interstate commerce, **Supp. 2**, 30; **Supp. 4**, 404–5; Japan, **Vol. 2, Part 2**, 186; **Vol. 4, Part 2**, 324; lumber in exchange for rum and sugar, **Vol. 3, Part 1**, 252; military supplies in War of 1812, **Vol. 5, Part 2**, 110; Mississippi River, **Vol. 10, Part 2**, 224; Missouri River, **Vol. 1, Part 2**, 306; munitions, **Supp. 1**, 305–6; open shop, **Vol. 8, Part 1**, 112 f.; Philadelphia, **Vol. 1, Part 2**, 464; pioneer, **Vol. 4, Part 1**, 503; **Vol. 5, Part 1**, 326; **Vol. 9, Part 1**, 290; protectionism, **Supp. 3**, 464, 727; **Supp. 6**, 455; **Supp. 7**, 305; **Supp. 8**, 420; quotas in commerce theory, **Supp. 2**, 30; reciprocal, **Supp. 3**, 657; **Supp. 5**, 332–33; **Supp. 6**, 126, 244; **Supp. 7**, 760; regulations, **Vol. 5, Part 2**, 24; research in, **Supp. 2**, 651; with Russia, **Vol. 3, Part 1**, 53; **Vol. 4, Part 1**, 523; **Vol. 8, Part 1**, 363 f.; salt, **Vol. 5, Part 1**, 239; Santa Fe, **Vol. 4, Part 1**, 597; South Carolina, **Vol. 4, Part 1**, 296; South Seas, **Vol. 3, Part 2**, 266; with Turkey, **Vol. 9, Part 2**, 634 f.; in West, **Vol. 3, Part 2**, 272; **Vol. 5, Part 1**, 147; West Indian Co., **Vol. 3, Part 1**, 265; West Indies, **Vol. 2, Part 1**, 592; **Vol. 3, Part 2**, 444; **Vol. 4, Part 2**, 382; whale oil, **Vol. 6, Part 2**, 178; wholesale groceries, **Vol. 8, Part 2**, 292; wine, **Vol. 5, Part 2**, 246 f. *See also* Tariff
Trade association movement, **Supp. 5**, 54–55; **Supp. 5**, 54–55; **Supp. 7**, 359
Trademarks, legislation, **Supp. 7**, 459
Trader Horn, **Supp. 10**, 668, 669
Trade Union College, **Vol. 4, Part 1**, 288
Trade Union Committee for Organizing Negro Workers, **Supp. 7**, 155
Trade Union Education League, founding of, **Supp. 7**, 255
Trade unions: **Vol. 2, Part 1**, 545; **Vol. 2, Part 2**, 338, 612; **Vol. 3, Part 1**, 183, 223, 510; **Vol. 5, Part 2**, 278; **Vol. 6, Part 1**, 170, 521; **Vol. 6, Part 2**, 150; **Vol. 7, Part 1**, 545; **Vol. 8, Part 1**, 112 f., 142; **Vol. 8, Part 2**, 321; actors', **Supp. 2**, 30; **Supp. 4**, 404–5; **Supp. 8**, 459–60; **Supp. 8**, 492; AFL administration, **Supp. 4**, 606–7; agency shop, **Supp. 8**, 366; agricultural, **Supp. 7**, 781–82; anti-Communism, **Supp. 5**, 255; arbitration pioneering, **Supp. 4**, 579–80; automobile industry, **Supp. 3**, 284; **Supp. 4**, 302–3, 457; **Supp. 7**, 793–94; **Supp. 8**, 309, 418–19, 526–28, 600, 610, 651–53; black membership, **Supp. 5**, 511; black organizing, **Supp. 5**, 511; **Supp. 7**, 155–56, 781–82; **Supp. 8**, 81; Chicago stockyards, **Supp. 4**, 279–80; cinematography, **Supp. 3**, 74; CIO in South, **Supp. 6**, 433–34; clothing industry, **Supp. 1**, 403; **Supp. 4**, 69, 375–76; **Supp. 5**, 95; coal industry, **Supp. 2**, 135; **Supp. 5**, 282–83; **Supp. 7**, 81–82; **Supp. 8**, 374–75; collective bargaining, **Supp. 2**, 23; **Supp. 4**, 579–80; **Supp. 8**, 377, 527–28; Communist influence, **Supp. 4**, 280; **Supp. 5**, 511, 664, 714; **Supp. 6**, 597–98, 648; **Supp. 8**, 375, 458, 511–13, 527; congressional opposition, **Supp. 8**, 269; construction and electrical industry, **Supp. 5**, 339; **Supp. 6**, 73–74; craft v. industrial, **Supp. 2**, 323; **Supp. 3**, 179; **Supp. 4**, 376; **Supp. 5**, 254–55, 339–40, 510, 654, 691; **Supp. 6**, 218–19, 379; **Supp. 7**, 254–55; **Supp. 8**, 374–77, 458; eight-hour day, demand for, **Vol. 9, Part 2**, 1 f.; ethics issues, **Supp. 6**, 73–74; first Jewish tailors' union, **Supp. 5**, 95; first woman organizer, **Supp. 3**, 576–77; glove industry, **Supp. 4**, 625–26; international, **Supp. 4**, 376; International Typographical Union, **Vol. 6, Part 1**, 521; journalism supporting, **Supp. 8**, 675; journals of, **Supp. 2**, 311; Ladies' Garment Workers, **Vol. 8, Part 2**, 437; leadership, **Supp. 3**, 10; **Supp. 5**, 253, 282–83, 509–11, 597, 690–91; **Supp. 8**, 374–77; **Supp. 10**, 524–25; legal counsel, **Supp. 5**, 83; legislation restricting, **Supp. 5**, 675, 714; **Supp. 7**, 110–11, 801; maritime industry, **Supp. 2**, 272; **Supp. 6**, 396–97; Massachusetts, **Vol. 2, Part 2**, 473; meat-packing industry, **Supp. 2**, 408; **Supp. 8**, 110, 589; Musteites, **Supp. 8**, 458; New Unionism, **Supp. 4**, 375–76; newspaper publishing, **Supp. 3**, 156; organization of, **Supp. 9**, 705–6; opposition to, **Vol. 1, Part 1**, 420 f.; **Vol. 3, Part 1**, 184; **Vol. 8, Part 1**, 112 f., 142 f.; **Vol. 10, Part 1**, 119; pension system, **Vol. 9, Part 2**, 86; political involvement, **Supp. 4**, 376, 606–7, 88–90; **Supp. 5**, 255, 510, 511; **Supp. 8**, 527; portal-to-portal pay issue, **Supp. 5**, 358; Puerto Rican, **Supp. 2**, 332; racketeering, **Supp. 8**, 322; radicalism, **Supp. 7**, 506–7; railroad, **Vol. 3, Part 1**, 183; **Vol. 6, Part 1**, 133; **Vol. 9, Part 2**, 86; railroad workers, **Supp. 4**, 889–90; **Supp. 6**, 648; seamen, **Supp. 6**, 396–97; state right-to-work laws, **Supp. 8**, 25; steel industry, **Vol. 9, Part 2**, 258; **Supp. 4**, 280; **Supp. 6**, 597, 622; **Supp. 7**, 228–29, 290, 587; street railway employees, **Supp. 1**, 511; teachers, **Supp. 8**, 132; textile industry, **Supp. 8**, 367; women's movement in, **Supp. 4**, 69, 626; **Supp. 7**, 12–13, 196, 455; United Mine Workers, **Vol. 5, Part 2**, 196; **Vol. 7, Part 1**, 51 f.; World War II mediation, **Supp. 7**, 172; writings on, **Vol. 5, Part 1**, 317; **Vol. 7, Part 1**, 121; **Supp. 2**, 23, 311. *See also* Labor and labor movement; Strikes; Wages and hours; *specific unions*
Trade Union Unity League, **Supp. 6**, 597–98; **Supp. 7**, 255
Trading with the Enemy Act (1917), **Supp. 6**, 138
Traffic: New York City, **Vol. 8, Part 1**, 138 f.; London, **Vol. 7, Part 2**, 277
Traffic regulation: first comprehensive system, **Supp. 3**, 253–54; lights, **Supp. 3**, 254
Trail making, **Vol. 1, Part 2**, 537
Traina, Anthony, reference to, **Supp. 9**, 587
Training School for Jewish Social Service, founding of, **Supp. 2**, 694

Train robberies, **Vol. 1, Part 2**, 35, 36; **Vol. 5, Part 1**, 555; **Vol. 5, Part 2**, 182
"Tramp, The" (fictional character), **Supp. 10**, 115, 118
Tramps, writings on, **Supp. 1**, 706–7
Tramp, Tramp, Tramp, the Boys Are Marching, **Vol. 8, Part 2**, 148
Transactions, economic, **Supp. 3**, 179
Transactions of the American Mathematical Society, founding of, **Supp. 1**, 562
Transamerica Corporation, **Supp. 4**, 326
Trans-American Publishing and News Service, **Supp. 6**, 264
Transatlantic telegraph. *See* Cable, Atlantic
Transcendental Club, **Vol. 9, Part 2**, 492
Transcendentalism: **Vol. 3, Part 2**, 137 f.; **Vol. 4, Part 1**, 64 f., 352; **Vol. 4, Part 2**, 498; **Vol. 6, Part 1**, 387; **Vol. 8, Part 1**, 623 f.; writings, **Vol. 4, Part 1**, 352
Transcontinental Air Race, **Supp. 3**, 56
Transcontinental Air Transport, **Supp. 5**, 385
Transcontinental and Western Airlines (TWA): expansion of, **Supp. 6**, 145–46, 221; founding of, **Supp. 5**, 385
Transcontinental Oil Co., **Supp. 7**, 804
Transformations, **Supp. 9**, 712
Transistor, **Supp. 6**, 85
Transit and Commerce, Treaty of (1859), **Vol. 2, Part 1**, 212
Transit systems: Chicago municipal area, **Supp. 5**, 275; **Supp. 8**, 112; inland waterway system, **Supp. 2**, 195; interstate desegregation, **Supp. 8**, 322, 333; interurban railway, **Supp. 5**, 617; Latin America, **Supp. 5**, 215; municipal ownership, **Supp. 2**, 125–26; New York City strike, **Supp. 8**, 513; street railroads, **Supp. 1**, 531, 669, 670; unionization, **Supp. 8**, 512–13. *See also* Aviation; Railroads; Street Railways; Subways
Transition (publication), **Supp. 6**, 497, 498
Translations: **Vol. 1, Part 2**, 542; **Vol. 2, Part 2**, 522 f., 565 f.; **Vol. 3, Part 2**, 88, 197, 331; **Vol. 4, Part 1**, 449; **Vol. 4, Part 2**, 485; **Vol. 5, Part 2**, 101 f., 507; **Vol. 6, Part 1**, 18; **Vol. 8, Part 2**, 55, 169, 414; **Vol. 10, Part 1**, 180, 537; African, **Vol. 4, Part 1**, 375; from Arabic, **Vol. 8, Part 1**, 110; Armeno-Turkish, **Vol. 4, Part 1**, 384; Bible de Royaumont, **Vol. 8, Part 1**, 156 f.; Chinese, **Vol. 1, Part 1**, 215; **Vol. 4, Part 1**, 399; **Vol. 7, Part 1**, 444; **Vol. 10, Part 1**, 474 f.; Dante, **Vol. 5, Part 2**, 587; Dutch, **Vol. 7, Part 1**, 351; **Vol. 8, Part 1**, 285; English into Spanish, **Vol. 3, Part 1**, 570 f.; French, **Vol. 2, Part 2**, 377; **Vol. 3, Part 1**, 549 f.; **Vol. 5, Part 1**, 273, 478; **Vol. 6, Part 1**, 171; **Vol. 8, Part 1**, 202, 217 f.; **Vol. 10, Part 2**, 534; German, **Vol. 3, Part 1**, 567 f.; **Vol. 4, Part 2**, 498 f.; **Vol. 5, Part 1**, 156; **Vol. 7, Part 1**, 390; **Vol. 8, Part 1**, 96 f., 154 f., 188 f., 374; **Vol. 10, Part 1**, 615 f.; **Supp. 10**, 401; Goethe, **Vol. 8, Part 1**, 104 f.; **Supp. 10**, 402; Greek, **Vol. 9, Part 1**, 248; **Vol. 9, Part 2**, 406; **Vol. 10, Part 2**, 519; Italian, **Vol. 6, Part 1**, 235; **Vol. 8, Part 1**, 110; Jewish Prayer Book, **Vol. 7, Part 2**, 631; Latin, **Vol. 8, Part 1**, 202, 247 f.; **Vol. 9, Part 2**, 406; Machiavelli's writings, **Vol. 3, Part 1**, 258; Nabokov, **Supp. 10**, 582, 583; Norwegian, **Vol. 7, Part 1**, 114; **Vol. 9, Part 2**, 142; Russian poetry, **Vol. 6, Part 1**, 227; Spanish, **Vol. 7, Part 1**, 96
Trans-Mississippi Exposition (Omaha, 1898), **Vol. 8, Part 2**, 172
Transplants: corneal, **Supp. 7**, 70; gonadal, **Supp. 3**, 103–4; **Supp. 6**, 632; organ studies, **Supp. 3**, 140–41
Transportation: **Vol. 1, Part 2**, 408, 410; **Vol. 4, Part 2**, 67, 574; **Vol. 5, Part 2**, 441; **Vol. 7, Part 2**, 510; **Vol. 8, Part 1**, 145 f., 442; **Vol. 9, Part 1**, 614 f.; **Vol. 9, Part 2**, 484, 486; legislative work on, **Vol. 4, Part 2**, 568; **Vol. 9, Part 1**, 593; national collections pertaining to, **Vol. 10, Part 1**, 539; Ohio, **Vol. 5, Part 2**, 296 f; World War I, **Vol. 5, Part 1**, 570; writings, historical, **Vol. 8, Part 1**, 70 f. *See also* Automobiles; Aviation; Freight; Railroads; Street railways; Subways
Transportation Act (1920), **Vol. 2, Part 2**, 598 f.; **Vol. 8, Part 1**, 114 f.; **Supp. 3**, 256
"Trans-Oconee State," **Vol. 2, Part 2**, 150
Transport Workers Union, founding of, **Supp. 8**, 512–13
Trans-Siberian and Chinese Eastern railways, **Supp. 3**, 736
Trans World Airlines: directorship, **Supp. 7**, 587; ownership, **Supp. 10**, 355; predecessor, **Supp. 5**, 385; **Supp. 8**, 367; takeover battle, **Supp. 10**, 357
Transylvania Co. (1774–75), **Vol. 1, Part 2**, 442; **Vol. 2, Part 2**, 520, 127; **Vol. 4, Part 2**, 531, 353; **Vol. 8, Part 2**, 24; **Vol. 9, Part 1**, 60
Transylvania Seminary, **Vol. 7, Part 1**, 129
Transylvania University, **Vol. 5, Part 1**, 149; **Vol. 6, Part 1**, 401; **Vol. 7, Part 2**, 499; **Vol. 8, Part 1**, 537; **Vol. 9, Part 2**, 601
Trapping: **Vol. 1, Part 1**, 520; **Vol. 4, Part 1**, 328; **Vol. 5, Part 1**, 587; **Vol. 5, Part 2**, 613; **Vol. 7, Part 1**, 458; **Vol. 8, Part 2**, 248; **Vol. 9, Part 1**, 381; **Vol. 10, Part 2**, 296, 452
Trappist monastery in Kentucky, **Vol. 8, Part 2**, 286
Trappist Order, **Supp. 8**, 430–31
Trask, J. D., reference to, **Supp. 5**, 63–64
Traube, Ludwig, reference to, **Supp. 4**, 68
Traut, Herbert F., reference to, **Supp. 7**, 598
Trautwine, John C., reference to, **Vol. 9, Part 2**, 598
Travel and tourism: **Vol. 9, Part 1**, 579 f.; **Vol. 9, Part 2**, 314 f.; air coach, **Supp. 6**, 146; European, **Vol. 3, Part 1**, 199; guidebooks, **Supp. 6**, 291–92; lectures, **Vol. 9, Part 2**, 55 f.; **Supp. 6**, 302–3; *New York Tribune* tours, **Vol. 5, Part 1**, 76; pioneer, **Vol. 3, Part 2**, 283; **Vol. 8, Part 2**, 458; publicity, **Supp. 5**, 270–1; Puerto Rico, **Supp. 4**, 903; restaurant chains, **Supp. 9**, 429–30; **Supp. 10**, 717, 718; "ride and tie" method, **Vol. 6, Part 1**, 275; seventeenth century, **Vol. 3, Part 1**, 265; southern wilderness, **Vol. 6, Part 1**, 57; Southwest, **Vol. 6, Part 1**, 502; stagecoach, **Vol. 2 Part 1**, 374; **Vol. 4, Part 1**, 549; **Vol. 5, Part 1**, 141; **Vol. 6, Part 1**, 163; **Vol. 6, Part 2**, 215; **Vol. 8, Part 2**, 235, 252; unusual exploits, **Vol. 8, Part 2**, 200; West, **Vol. 10, Part 2**, 431; writings, **Vol. 2, Part 1**, 38, 167, 232, 510; **Vol. 2, Part 2**, 259, 323, 466, 592, 621; **Vol. 3, Part l**, 199, 251, 381, 467 f., 490 f., 570 f., 573 f.; **Vol. 3, Part 2**, 364 f.; **Vol. 4, Part 2**, 170, 320, 540, 543; **Vol. 5, Part 1**, 619; **Vol. 4, Part 2**, 124, 482; **Vol. 6, Part 1**, 288; **Vol. 6, Part 2**, 513; **Vol. 7, Part 1**, 206, 609 f.; **Vol. 7, Part 2**, 342; **Vol. 8, Part 1**, 121 f., 227 f., 593; **Vol. 8, Part 2**, 204, 484 f.; **Vol. 9, Part 2**, 52, 315, 377, 490; **Vol. 10, Part 1**, 390, 462 f., 646; **Vol. 10, Part 2**, 533; **Supp. 9**, 457; **Supp. 10**, 121
Travelers' Aid Societies, **Vol. 3, Part 1**, 347
Travelers Insurance Co., **Vol. 1, Part 2**, 54
Travell, Janet, reference to, **Supp. 3**, 343
Traveller, Lee's horse, **Vol. 6, Part 1**, 127
"Travellers' Rest," **Vol. 9, Part 1**, 62
Travels in the Confederation, **Vol. 8, Part 2**, 458
Traynor, Pie, reference to, **Supp. 5**, 717
Treadwell power press, **Vol. 9, Part 2**, 632
Treason: Pound trial, **Supp. 9**, 618; Revolutionary War, **Vol. 3, Part 1**, 504 f.; **Vol. 6, Part 1**, 100, 225; secession regarded as, **Vol. 5, Part 2**, 113
Treasure, Capt. Kidd's search for, **Vol. 3, Part 1**, 501 f.
Treasurer, The, early colonial trading ship, **Vol. 1, Part l**, 346
Treasury, Department of the (U.S.): **Vol. 3, Part 2**, 486; **Vol. 4, Part 2**, 84; **Vol. 8, Part 1**, 220; **Vol. 8, Part 2**, 6; **Vol. 9, Part 1**, 460; administration, **Supp.**

1, 535; **Supp. 2**, 448; **Supp. 3**, 480–81, 331; **Supp. 5**, 712; **Supp. 6**, 124, 229, 376, 659–60; **Supp. 8**, 90, 445–46, 592; **Supp. 9**, 625; **Supp. 10**, 250; comptroller under Continental Congress, **Vol. 10, Part 1**, 17 f.; first comptroller of, **Vol. 3, Part 2**, 538; **Vol. 6, Part 1**, 52; **Vol. 8, Part 1**, 80 f.; first treasurer of, **Vol. 5, Part 1**, 51; Great Depression policies, **Supp. 6**, 33–34; reorganization of, World War II era, **Supp. 9**, 661; secretaryship, **Vol. 2, Part 2**, 458; **Vol. 3, Part 2**, 237, 486; **Vol. 4, Part 2**, 61, 174 f.; **Vol. 5, Part 1**, 473; **Vol. 6, Part 2**, 249; **Vol. 7, Part 1**, 199 f.; **Vol. 8, Part 1**, 578; **Vol. 8, Part 2**, 233; **Vol. 10, Part 2**, 383, 444, 485, 495

Treasury Bill of 1846, **Vol. 8, Part 1**, 34 f.

Treatise on the System of Evidence in Trials at Common Law, A, **Supp. 3**, 821

Tree Grows in Brooklyn, A, **Supp. 9**, 735–36

Tree of Culture, The, **Supp. 5**, 435

Tree of Laughing Bells, The, **Vol. 6, Part 1**, 276

Trees: **Vol. 7, Part 1**, 559; diseases and care of, **Supp. 7**, 33; of the Pacific Coast, popular booklets on, **Vol. 6, Part 1**, 162; redwoods, preservation of, **Vol. 3, Part 1**, 485; ring studies, **Supp. 7**, 193–94; surgery, **Vol. 3, Part 1**, 88 f.; wood identification, **Supp. 3**, 621. *See also* Forestry; Lumber industry; Wilderness and wildlife preserves

Trelease, William, reference to, **Supp. 3**, 802

Trendle, George W., reference to, **Supp. 10**, 343

Trent affair (1861), **Vol. 1, Part 1**, 44; **Vol. 2, Part 1**, 564; **Vol. 3, Part 2**, 192, 255; **Vol. 4, Part 1**, 594; **Vol. 6, Part 1**, 250; **Vol. 6, Part 2**, 365; **Vol. 8, Part 2**, 619; **Vol. 9, Part 1**, 210–11, 619; **Vol. 10, Part 1**, 630; **Vol. 10, Part 2**, 217

Trentini, Emma, reference to, **Supp. 9**, 293

Trenton, N.J.: battle of (Dec. 26, 1776), **Vol. 1, Part 1**, 176; **Vol. 4, Part 1**, 569; **Vol. 6, Part 2**, 541; **Vol. 7, Part 1**, 87; **Vol. 7, Part 2**, 234; **Vol. 8, Part 2**, 294; **Vol. 9, Part 2**, 192; **Vol. 10, Part 1**, 516; early history of, **Vol. 2, Part 1**, 400

Trevilian Station, battle of, **Vol. 4, Part 2**, 214; **Vol. 9, Part 1**, 80; **Vol. 9, Part 2**, 172

"Triangle," Pennsylvania tract of land, **Vol. 5, Part 1**, 500

Triangle Film Corporation, **Supp. 6**, 573, 619

Triangle Publications, **Supp. 3**, 21

Triangle Shirtwaist Co. fire (1911), **Supp. 3**, 355–56, 717–18; **Supp. 5**, 718; **Supp. 7**, 608

Triangulation, **Vol. 3, Part 1**, 29 f.

Triborough Bridge (New York City), **Supp. 3**, 531; **Supp. 6**, 594; **Supp. 7**, 12

Tribune Co., **Supp. 5**, 449

Trichinosis, **Supp. 3**, 737–38

Trigeminal neuralgia, **Supp. 4**, 214

Trigg, H. L., reference to, **Supp. 6**, 569

Trilby, **Vol. 8, Part 1**, 132

Trinidad Asphalt Co., **Vol. 1, Part 1**, 586

Trinity Church (Boston). *See* Boston

Trinity Church (New York City), **Supp. 4**, 546–47. *See also* New York

Trinity College (Hartford, Conn.): **Vol. 3, Part 2**, 81; **Vol. 4, Part 1**, 406; **Vol. 5, Part 2**, 354; **Vol. 8, Part 1**, 127 f., 291 f.; **Vol. 10, Part 2**, 42; charter for, **Vol. 9, Part 1**, 327; founding of, **Vol. 2, Part 1**, 172

Trinity College (N.C.), forerunner of Duke University, **Vol. 3, Part 1**, 496 f.

Trinity College (Washington, D.C.), founding of, **Vol. 5, Part 2**, 245

Triode Audion, **Supp. 7**, 175–76

Tripoli, diplomacy, **Vol. 1, Part 2**, 241; **Vol. 3, Part 1**, 613

Tripolitan War (1801–05), **Vol. 1, Part 1**, 650; **Vol. 1, Part 2**, 241; **Vol. 2, Part 1**, 572; **Vol. 2, Part 2**, 40; **Vol. 3, Part 1**, 33, 188, 613; **Vol. 5, Part 1**, 361; **Vol. 5, Part 2**, 27, 30, 176; **Vol. 6, Part 1**, 49, 76; **Vol. 7, Part 1**, 219, 358, 612; **Vol. 7, Part 2**, 491; **Vol. 8, Part 1**, 83, 182, 424, 596; **Vol. 8, Part 2**, 76; **Vol. 9, Part 1**, 394 f., 584; **Vol. 9, Part 2**, 7, 48, 645; **Vol. 10, Part 1**, 22, 492 f.

Trippe, Juan, reference to, **Supp. 6**, 145; **Supp. 9**, 337, 338, 725, 899

Tristram, **Supp. 1**, 633–34

Trolley car, experiments leading to, **Vol. 3, Part 1**, 88

Trombone playing, **Vol. 9, Part 2**, 556

Tropic of Cancer, **Supp. 7**, 292; **Supp. 10**, 538, 539, 540

Tropic of Capricorn, **Supp. 7**, 292, 293

Tropical diseases, research and control of, **Supp. 1**, 14, 32, 543; **Supp. 4**, 791, 803; **Supp. 5**, 605, 710. *See also specific diseases*

Tropical Woods, founding of, **Supp. 3**, 621

Tropism theory, **Vol. 6, Part 1**, 349 f.

Trotting Horse Club of America, **Supp. 10**, 311

Trotsky, Leon: references to, **Supp. 5**, 135, 173, 579, 664; **Supp. 7**, 244, 269; **Supp. 8**, 172; translator and literary agent of, **Supp. 8**, 149–50

Trout Lake Limnological Laboratory, founding of, **Supp. 3**, 402; **Supp. 4**, 85

Trowbridge, Alexander, reference to, **Supp. 3**, 199

Troy, N.Y.: **Vol. 4, Part 2**, 9; early history, **Vol. 6, Part 2**, 275; medicine, **Vol. 10, Part 1**, 435 f.; public service to, **Vol. 6, Part 2**, 305

Trucks and trucking, four-wheel drive, **Supp. 3**, 165

Trudeau, Edward L., references to, **Supp. 3**, 431; **Supp. 4**, 48–49, 314, 577

Trudeau, Garry, reference to, **Supp. 10**, 353

Trudeau Sanitorium (N.Y.), **Vol. 10, Part 1**, 3. *See also* Saranac Lake, N.Y.

True Briton and *Randolph*, **Vol. 1, Part 2**, 242

True Grit, **Supp. 10**, 823

True Relation, A, **Vol. 9, Part 1**, 295

True Story, founding of, **Supp. 5**, 453

Trujillo Molina, Rafael Leónidas, reference to, **Supp. 9**, 191; **Supp. 10**, 222

Truman, Harry S.: Allen, G. E., relationship, **Supp. 9**, 22–24; atomic bomb development, **Supp. 4**, 4, 787–88; atomic bomb policy, **Supp. 7**, 732; **Supp. 9**, 812; Barkley relationship, **Supp. 6**, 36; Baruch relationship, **Supp. 7**, 37; Benton portrait of, **Supp. 9**, 80; Berlin blockade crisis, **Supp. 10**, 128; Biddle relationship, **Supp. 8**, 35; Biffle relationship, **Supp. 8**, 36; Byrnes relationship, **Supp. 9**, 152; China policy, **Supp. 9**, 8; civil rights measures, **Supp. 5**, 479, 515, 741; **Supp. 7**, 748; cold war policies, **Supp. 9**, 152, 812–14; congressional relations, **Supp. 5**, 715–16; defense policies, **Supp. 8**, 303; **Supp. 9**, 227–28; Dixiecrat revolt against, **Supp. 6**, 710–11; domestic policies, **Supp. 9**, 813; **Supp. 10**, 485; Dulles, J. F., relationship, **Supp. 6**, 178; Equal Rights Amendment, support for, **Supp. 9**, 546; Fair Deal program, **Supp. 10**, 227; family, **Supp. 9**, 809; federal budget, **Supp. 7**, 734; foreign policy, **Supp. 9**, 7, 8, 9, 811–12; **Supp. 10**, 485; Forrestal relationship, **Supp. 4**, 306; Hannegan relationship, **Supp. 4**, 355–56; haberdashery, **Supp. 9**, 809; Korean War policy, **Supp. 8**, 633; **Supp. 9**, 9, 813, 814, 815; labor relations, **Supp. 4**, 724, 890; **Supp. 5**, 511; Leahy relationship, **Supp. 6**, 375; loyalty program, **Supp. 5**, 564; **Supp. 9**, 639; **Supp. 10**, 125–26; MacArthur recall, **Supp. 7**, 492–93; **Supp. 8**, 421–22, 633; **Supp. 9**, 9, 689, 813; McCarthyism and, **Supp. 6**, 405, 406; **Supp. 9**, 813–14; Marshall, G. C., relationship, **Supp. 6**, 431–32; National Security Resources Board, **Supp. 9**, 389; pardons, **Supp. 6**, 437; Pendergast machine, **Supp. 3**, 596, 597; political advisers, **Supp. 10**, 227; Potsdam Conference, **Supp. 6**, 147; **Supp. 9**, 812; pres-

idential candidacy, **Supp. 8**, 405; **Supp. 9**, 231, 814; **Supp. 10**, 119, 227; press relations, **Supp. 5**, 626; **Supp. 8**, 395; reference to, **Supp. 9**, 783; **Supp. 10**, 189; Ross relationship, **Supp. 4**, 703–5; in Senate, **Supp. 7**, 764; Senate opposition to, **Supp. 10**, 181; Senate service, **Supp. 9**, 810–11; senatorial campaign (1940), **Supp. 9**, 757, 811; special counsel to, **Supp. 9**, 681; steel seizure, **Supp. 5**, 156, 714; **Supp. 6**, 502, 679; **Supp. 7**, 96, 229, 587; **Supp. 8**, 517; **Supp. 10**, 126; vice-presidency, **Supp. 3**, 664; **Supp. 4**, 51, 356, 376; **Supp. 7**, 762; **Supp. 9**, 811; vice-presidential candidacy, **Supp. 8**, 361; **Supp. 9**, 151; World War I service, **Supp. 9**, 809; White House balcony, **Supp. 6**, 158

Truman Doctrine: **Supp. 5**, 397, 704; **Supp. 6**, 431; **Supp. 8**, 90, 680; **Supp. 9**, 7, 812–13; budget cuts, **Supp. 7**, 734; criticism of, **Supp. 7**, 49, 762; **Supp. 8**, 680; support for, **Supp. 7**, 326, 419

Trumbo, Dalton, reference to, **Supp. 10**, 239

Trumbull, John, reference to, **Vol. 8, Part 2**, 360

Trumbull, U.S. frigate, **Vol. 9, Part 1**, 502

Trumbull Gallery (Yale), first art museum connected with a college in America, **Vol. 9, Part 2**, 136

Trumbull Papers, **Vol. 10, Part 1**, 16

Trumbull's "Declaration of Independence," **Vol. 3, Part 1**, 535 f.

Trump, John G., references to, **Supp. 8**, 665, 666

Trunk Line Association, **Vol. 3, Part 2**, 388; **Vol. 8, Part 2**, 7

Trust Co. of Cuba, **Supp. 3**, 218

Trusts: **Vol. 7, Part 1**, 108; **Vol. 7, Part 2**, 544; **Vol. 8, Part 2**, 65; beginnings of, **Vol. 3, Part 1**, 341 f., *see also* Antitrust actions; development of, **Supp. 2**, 571–73; fight with Guggenheim, **Vol. 4, Part 2**, 39; legal measures to restrict, **Vol. 4, Part 2**, 25; motion-picture companies, **Supp. 5**, 229; Roosevelt, T. R., and, **Vol. 8, Part 2**, 140; writings on, **Vol. 3, Part 1**, 389. *See also* Antitrust actions

Truthseeker, **Vol. 1, Part 2**, 192

Truth Teller, **Vol. 8, Part 1**, 157

"Tryon's Palace," **Vol. 10, Part 1**, 26

Tryptophan, **Supp. 7**, 223

Tsiolkovskii, Konstantin E., references to, **Supp. 3**, 306, 308

Tuberculosis: **Vol. 1, Part 2**, 493; **Vol. 2, Part 1**, 231, 349 f.; **Vol. 3, Part 2**, 201, 301 f., 472, 550; **Vol. 4, Part 2**, 165; **Vol. 5, Part 1**, 215; **Vol. 7, Part 2**, 550 f.; **Vol. 10, Part 1**, 2 f.; American Congress on, **Vol. 1, Part 2**, 154; bacillus, **Supp. 4**, 435; biochemistry and pathology of, **Supp. 5**, 600; bovine, **Supp. 4**, 683; Christmas seal project, **Supp. 4**, 92; first clinic in Chicago, **Vol. 8, Part 2**, 281; French prevention commission, **Supp. 3**, 324; hospitals, **Supp. 7**, 251; housing reform and, **Supp. 3**, 837; organizations, **Supp. 2**, 176, 197; prevention campaign, **Supp. 7**, 251; preventorium for children, **Vol. 9, Part 2**, 130; prize essay on, **Vol. 3, Part 2**, 102; research, **Supp. 4**, 48–49, 314; **Supp. 6**, 357; research laboratory, **Vol. 4, Part 2**, 501; resistance and immunity studies, **Supp. 3**, 431–32; sanitarium, first in U.S., **Vol. 10, Part 1**, 3; treatment, **Supp. 2**, 70–71, 196, 370; **Supp. 4**, 577–78; tuberculin, **Supp. 1**, 258; writings on, **Vol. 6, Part 1**, 58; **Vol. 10, Part 1**, 3 f.; **Supp. 6**, 409

Tuberculosis Institute, **Vol. 7, Part 2**, 298

Tubing, invention of, **Vol. 2, Part 2**, 359

Tucker, Frederick St. George de Lautour, **Vol. 1, Part 2**, 456

Tudor Drama, The, **Supp. 4**, 110

Tuesday Club, **Vol. 3, Part 1**, 236; **Vol. 4, Part 2**, 170

Tufts, James H., reference to, **Supp. 6**, 671

Tufts University: **Vol. 1, Part 1**, 559; **Vol. 7, Part 1**, 22; **Vol. 10, Part 1**, 49; Fletcher School of Law and Diplomacy, **Supp. 5**, 751; neurology studies, **Supp. 4**, 617

Tugboats, **Supp. 7**, 552–53

Tugwell, Rexford G., references to, **Supp. 3**, 647; **Supp. 6**, 12; **Supp. 10**, 565

Tulane University: **Vol. 1, Part 2**, 525; **Vol. 2, Part 2**, 497; **Vol. 3, Part 1**, 582; **Vol. 3, Part 2**, 324; **Vol. 4, Part 1**, 257; **Vol. 5, Part 2**, 154; **Vol. 8, Part 1**, 575; **Vol. 8, Part 2**, 165; **Vol. 10, Part 1**, 51; football team, **Supp. 10**, 40; medical school, **Supp. 6**, 434, 435; presidency, **Supp. 1**, 21, 250

Tulley's Almanack, **Vol. 4, Part 2**, 304

"Tumbling Tumbleweeds" (song), **Supp. 10**, 592

Tumors: **Vol. 1, Part 2**, 2; cerebral, writings on, **Supp. 2**, 139; "scent detector" for brain, **Supp. 4**, 250; surgical procedures for, **Supp. 4**, 214

Tuna fishing, **Vol. 5, Part 1**, 140

Tungsten filaments, **Supp. 6**, 695

Tun-huang caves, **Supp. 5**, 729

Tunis, diplomacy, **Vol. 3, Part 1**, 613; **Vol. 4, Part 2**, 481 f.; **Vol. 3, Part 1**, 251

Tunneling shield, **Vol. 1, Part 2**, 81

Tunnels: **Vol. 3, Part 1**, 334; contruction of, **Supp. 4**, 690; pneumatic, **Vol. 1, Part 2**, 81; railroad, **Vol. 8, Part 2**, 48; **Supp. 3**, 735, 737; **Supp. 7**, 90; subaqueous, **Supp. 2**, 145, 559; **Supp. 3**, 353, 479; **Supp. 4**, 757; **Supp. 6**, 187, 587; vehicular, **Vol. 7, Part 2**, 278; ventilation standards, **Supp. 3**, 353. *See also* Bridges; *specific tunnel names*

Tunney, James Joseph ("Gene"), reference to, **Supp. 3**, 602

Tunney, John V., reference to, **Supp. 10**, 798

Tupelo, operations about (1863–65), **Vol. 2, Part 1**, 293; **Vol. 6, Part 1**, 130; **Vol. 9, Part 1**, 237

Turandot, world premiere, **Supp. 6**, 643

Turbines, steam, development of, **Vol. 8, Part 1**, 544; **Vol. 8, Part 2**, 359; **Supp. 1**, 65; **Supp. 4**, 383–84

Turbo-blower, invention of, **Vol. 8, Part 1**, 544

Turbosupercharger engine, **Supp. 4**, 609

Turk, Robert, reference to, **Supp. 6**, 402

Turkey: Armenian massacre, **Supp. 4**, 604; **Supp. 6**, 253–54; diplomacy, **Vol. 1, Part 1**, 309; **Vol. 1, Part 2**, 417, 567; **Vol. 2, Part 1**, 139 f.; **Vol. 3, Part 1**, 294; **Vol. 7, Part 1**, 206; **Vol. 8, Part 1**, 529 f.; **Vol. 8, Part 2**, 77; **Vol. 9, Part 2**, 131; **Supp. 2**, 65; **Supp. 4**, 603–4, 772; **Supp. 7**, 303, 384; missions in, **Vol. 3, Part 1**, 565 f.; **Vol. 5, Part 1**, 191; **Vol. 8, Part 2**, 261, 421, 446; **Vol. 9, Part 1**, 73, 241; **Vol. 10, Part 1**, 500; **Vol. 10, Part 2**, 11; railway construction, **Supp. 1**, 171; Russia and war with, **Vol. 5, Part 2**, 187; trade relations with, **Vol. 7, Part 1**, 634 f.; Truman Doctrine, **Supp. 6**, 431; writings on, **Vol. 3, Part 1**, 204, 566 f. *See also* Greco-Turkish War

Turkish, Bible, translation into, **Vol. 4, Part 1**, 384

Turkus, Burton B., reference to, **Supp. 7**, 585

Turner, Florence, reference to, **Supp. 6**, 619

Turner, Frederick Jackson, references to, **Vol. 9, Part 2**, 521; **Supp. 3**, 262, 336, 810; **Supp. 4**, 746, 747; **Supp. 5**, 429, 577

Turner, Lana, reference to, **Supp. 9**, 66

Turner, Roscoe, reference to, **Supp. 6**, 493

Turner Zeitung, **Vol. 8, Part 1**, 384

Turners Falls, Mass., **Vol. 2, Part 2**, 551

Turnure, Arthur, reference to, **Supp. 6**, 107

Turpentine, collection methods, **Supp. 2**, 301

Turpin, Ben, reference to, **Supp. 7**, 177

"Turret" vessels, **Vol. 3, Part 2**, 568

Tuscarora, diplomacy, **Vol. 3, Part 1**, 99

Tuscarora Indians, **Supp. 9**, 655–57

Tusculum College, founding of, **Vol. 3, Part 1**, 333

Tuskegee Houses, **Supp. 3**, 744

Tuskegee Institute: **Vol. 10, Part 1**, 506 f.; administra-

tion, **Supp. 2**, 476–77; agricultural studies, **Supp. 3**, 145–46; Army Air Corps Aviation Cadet Program, **Supp. 10**, 378; race relations conference, **Supp. 3**, 577; trustees, **Supp. 6**, 600
"Tutt, Emphraim" (fictional character), **Supp. 3**, 773–74
Tuve, Merle A., references to, **Supp. 6**, 370; **Supp. 8**, 199
Tuxedo Brass Band, **Supp. 5**, 106
Tuxedo Park, N.Y., **Vol. 6, Part 1**, 412; **Vol. 8, Part 1**, 210f.
TVA. *See* Tennessee Valley Authority
TWA. *See* Transcontinental and Western Airlines; Trans World Airlines
Twain, Mark: **Vol. 1, Part 1**, 241; **Vol. 1, Part 2**, 306; **Vol. 2, Part 2**, 192 f.; **Vol. 3, Part 1**, 252; **Vol. 5, Part 1**, 580; **Vol. 6, Part 1**, 2, 433; **Vol. 8, Part 2**, 96, 575; **Vol. 9, Part 2**, 52; **Vol. 10, Part 1**, 82; illustrator for, **Supp. 3**, 44; reference to, **Supp. 8**, 316; writings on, **Supp. 2**, 509; **Supp. 5**, 168; **Supp. 7**, 80; **Supp. 10**, 274
Tweed, William M. ("Boss"): **Vol. 9, Part 1**, 9; escape and capture of, **Vol. 1, Part 1**, 105; Nast cartoons, **Vol. 7, Part 1**, 392; **Vol. 10, Part 1**, 81; *New York Times*'s attack on, **Vol. 10, Part 1**, 81; prosecution and trial, **Vol. 1, Part 1**, 572; **Vol. 3, Part 1**, 140; **Vol. 7, Part 1**, 621; **Vol. 7, Part 2**, 387; relations with Richard Croker, **Vol. 2, Part 2**, 558
Tweed Ring: **Vol. 1, Part 1**, 399, 609; **Vol. 2, Part 2**, 83; **Vol. 3, Part 2**, 155; **Vol. 4, Part 1**, 52; **Vol. 4, Part 2**, 500; **Vol. 5, Part 1**, 114; **Vol. 5, Part 2**, 308, 356; **Vol. 8, Part 2**, 12; **Vol. 9, Part 1**, 593; **Vol. 9, Part 2**, 539, 636; **Vol. 10, Part 1**, 80 f.; campaign against, **Vol. 4, Part 2**, 605; finances of, **Vol. 4, Part 2**, 405; Gould, Jay, and, **Vol. 4, Part 1**, 454; New York Printing Co. involved in, **Vol. 1, Part 1**, 237; Nast cartoons, **Vol. 7, Part 1**, 392; **Vol. 10, Part 1**, 81; overthrow of, **Vol. 2, Part 2**, 396; **Vol. 5, Part 2**, 171; **Vol. 8, Part 2**, 134
Twentieth Century Fox: **Supp. 7**, 692, 693; **Supp. 8**, 465–66; management, **Supp. 10**, 864–66; organization of, **Supp. 5**, 230; presidency of, **Supp. 9**, 733, 734; productions, **Supp. 10**, 387, 864–65
Twentieth Century Fund, organization of, **Supp. 2**, 184
Twentieth Century Sporting Club (New York City), founding of, **Supp. 5**, 360
"Twenty-One" (television quiz show), **Supp. 9**, 829
Twenty Years of the Republic, **Vol. 7, Part 2**, 378
"Twilight Zone, The" (television program), **Supp. 9**, 710
Twining v. *Stak of New Jersey*, **Vol. 7, Part 1**, 108
"Twitchell, Elmer" (fictional character), **Supp. 7**, 617–18
"291" (New York City), Photo-Secession exhibition, **Supp. 9**, 759, 760. *See also* Little Galleries of the Photo-Secession
Two Penny Act, **Vol. 2, Part 1**, 440
Two Worlds (publication), serialization of Joyce novels, **Supp. 9**, 682–83
Twyman, Jack, reference to, **Supp. 8**, 631
Tydings, Millard E.: Lattimore investigation, **Supp. 10**, 801; references to, **Supp. 6**, 405; **Supp. 8**, 392; **Supp. 10**, 311, 633, 634
Tydings-McDuffie Act (1934), **Supp. 3**, 614; **Supp. 4**, 612
Tyler, Albert, reference to, **Supp. 3**, 540
Tyler, Elisina, reference to, **Supp. 5**, 700
Tyler, Elizabeth, reference to, **Supp. 3**, 709
Tyler, George C., reference to, **Supp. 7**, 412
Tyler, John: **Vol. 7, Part 1**, 442; nomination of, to vice-presidency, **Vol. 8, Part 1**, 636; relations with Caleb Cushing, **Vol. 2, Part 2**, 624, 629
Tyler, Royall, literary partnership with, **Vol. 3, Part 1**, 236
Tympany Five (jazz band), **Supp. 9**, 441
Typefounding, **Vol. 2, Part 1**, 181, 239; **Vol. 6, Part 2**, 84, 265
Typesetting: invention of, **Vol. 3, Part 1**, 411; mechanical, **Vol. 8, Part 2**, 105
Typewriters: **Supp. 2**, 673; **Supp. 5**, 228; development of, **Vol. 1, Part 2**, 80; **Vol. 2, Part 1**, 74, 340; **Vol. 3, Part 1**, 503; **Vol. 4, Part 2**, 144 f., 206; **Vol. 8, Part 1**, 173 f.; **Vol. 9, Part 1**, 123; marketing of, **Vol. 8, Part 1**, 499; precursor of, **Vol. 3, Part 2**, 583; steam, **Vol. 8, Part 1**, 369
Typhoid: **Vol. 1, Part 2**, 4; **Vol. 8, Part 1**, 460; **Vol. 8, Part 2**, 553; **Vol. 9, Part 1**, 31 f.; Brand treatment, **Vol. 1, Part 2**, 29; control measures, **Supp. 5**, 232; identification of, **Vol. 4, Part 1**, 218; isolation of the bacillus, **Vol. 8, Part 1**, 317 f.; in Mexico, **Vol. 5, Part 1**, 429; studies in, **Supp. 2**, 353
Typhus: causes of, **Supp. 4**, 667–68; epidemics, **Supp. 5**, 336; epidemiological studies, **Supp. 4**, 803; etiology of, **Supp. 9**, 249; studies in, **Supp. 1**, 629; **Supp. 2**, 745; vaccine, **Supp. 4**, 667–68; **Supp. 9**, 250
Typographical Union: International, **Vol. 6, Part 1**, 521; National, **Vol. 2, Part 2**, 364
Typography: **Vol. 1, Part 1**, 484, 526; **Vol. 3, Part 1**, 264; **Vol; 10, Part 1**, 655 f.; design, **Supp. 3**, 492–93, 784–85; **Supp. 6**, 186, 575; Chicago style, **Supp. 2**, 120; Cooper Black, **Supp. 2**, 120; deluxe book editions, **Supp. 4**, 621–22; Fifty Books of the Year show, **Supp. 1**, 288; newspapers and magazines, **Supp. 7**, 2–3; typefaces, **Supp. 4**, 342
Tytus, John Butler, reference to, **Supp. 3**, 792

U

UAW. *See* United Automobile Workers
Ugly American, The, **Supp. 7**, 93, 94
Uhlenbeck, George E., references to, **Supp. 5**, 496; **Supp. 10**, 288, 289
Ulam, Stanislaw, reference to, **Supp. 8**, 200
Ulcers, surgery for, **Supp. 3**, 271
Ulric, Lenore, reference to, **Supp. 9**, 98
Ulrich, Edward O., references to, **Supp. 3**, 695; **Supp. 4**, 343
Ulster Historical Society, **Vol. 4, Part 2**, 376
Ultraviolet: art authentification and conservation, **Supp. 8**, 545; spectra of atoms, **Supp. 5**, 496; spectroscopic research, **Supp. 5**, 441
Ulysses: **Supp. 3**, 181, 844; censorship of, **Supp. 5**, 270; **Supp. 9**, 33, 165, 683; original manuscript, **Supp. 5**, 587; publishing of, **Supp. 7**, 40; **Supp. 9**, 165; **Supp. 10**, 221; serialization of, **Supp. 9**, 33, 682–83
Umpires, baseball, **Supp. 5**, 393; **Supp. 7**, 139; **Supp. 8**, 544
UMW. *See* United Mine Workers
UN. *See* United Nations
Un-American Activities Committee. *See under* House of Representatives, United States
UNCF. *See* United Negro College Fund
Uncle Remus, **Vol. 4, Part 2**, 312 f.
Uncle Remus's, the Home Magazine, **Supp. 7**, 323
"Uncle Sam," origin of, **Vol. 10, Part 2**, 343
Uncle Tim, slave, **Vol. 7, Part 1**, 648
Uncle Tom's Cabin: **Vol. 4, Part 2**, 564; **Vol. 7, Part 1**, 24; **Vol. 9, Part 2**, 116 f.; compared to *Ten Nights in a Barroom*, etc., **Vol. 1, Part 1**, 378; dramatized, **Vol. 1, Part 1**, 128; first publication, **Vol. 5, Part 2**, 69; **Vol. 9, Part 2**, 177 f.; **Vol. 10, Part 1**, 625 f.; printing of, **Vol. 5, Part 2**, 69; success of, **Vol. 3, Part 2**, 566; *Uncle Tom's Cabin as It Is*, play written as a counter-

blast, **Vol. 8, Part 2**, 59; Welsh translation of, **Vol. 3, Part 2**, 226; writing of, **Vol. 9, Part 2**, 117 f.; *Uncle Tom's Tenement,* **Vol. 8, Part 2**, 119
"Uncle Wiggily" (fictional character), **Supp. 7**, 279
Unconscious (psychoanalytic theory), **Supp. 3**, 190–91; **Supp. 6**, 724, 725
"Uncurrent money," dealing in, **Vol. 3, Part 1**, 456 f.
Underdeveloped nations. *See* Third World; *specific regions*
Underground Railroad: **Vol. 2, Part 2**, 268 f.; **Vol. 3, Part 2**, 247; **Vol. 4, Part 1**, 195, 622; **Vol. 5, Part 1**, 224, 576; **Vol. 5, Part a, 258; Vol. 6, Part 1**, 163, 368; **Vol. 8, Part 1**, 117, 403; **Vol. 8, Part 2**, 84, 315; **Vol. 9, Part 1**, 288, 379; **Vol. 9, Part 2**, 23, 304; **Vol. 10, Part 1**, 27; activities of, curtailed, **Vol. 4, Part 1**, 607; and the church, **Vol. 1, Part 1**, 205
Underwood, Frederick D., reference to, **Supp. 3**, 823
Underwood, Oscar W., references to, **Supp. 4**, 50; reference to, **Supp. 9**, 95
Underwood, W. Lyman, reference to, **Supp. 7**, 630
"Underwood Constitution," framing of, **Vol. 10, Part l**, 114
Underwood Tariff Act (1913), **Supp. 6**, 280
Underworld. *See* Organized crime
Unemployment: Coxey's army (1894): **Supp. 5**, 140; federal policy advocacy, **Supp. 3**, 5; as government problem, **Supp. 5**, 718; insurance, **Supp. 3**, 18–19, 178, 255; **Supp. 6**, 74, 378, 704, 709; **Supp. 7**, 543, 764; job sharing, **Supp. 6**, 622; President's Emergency Committee on Unemployment, **Supp. 7**, 362; prevention programs, **Supp. 3**, 18–19; social effects of, **Supp. 6**, 605; statistics, **Supp. 6**, 708–9; technological, **Vol. 10, Part 1**, 637 f.; **Supp. 5**, 558–59; Union Square rally (1930), **Supp. 5**, 499. *See also* Public works; Welfare
UNESCO. *See* United Nations Educational, Scientific, and Cultural Organization
Unfinished Business, **Supp. 5**, 79
Uniform Crime Reports, The, **Supp. 5**, 639
Union Canal (Pa.), building of, **Vol. 1, Part 1**, 540
Union Carbide Corporation: **Supp. 7**, 554; Bakelite acquisition, **Supp. 3**, 27; research, **Supp. 3**, 49
Union Central Life Insurance Co., growth of, **Vol. 7, Part 2**, 313
Union Chemlcal and Materials Corporation, founding of, **Supp. 8**, 455
Union College: building of, **Vol. 8, Part 1**, 336 f.; development, **Vol. 8, Part 1**, 126, 247; establishment of, **Vol. 8, Part 2**, 479; expansion of, **Vol. 8, Part 1**, 126; lottery promoted, **Vol. 9, Part 2**, 462; presidency of, **Vol. 3, Part 2**, 38; **Vol. 5, Part 1**, 5; **Vol. 7, Part 1**, 580 f.; **Supp. 3**, 287; song of, **Vol. 6, Part 1**, 491
"Union Democrats," **Vol. 1, Part 1**,
Unione Siciliano, **Supp. 7**, 485
Union for Democratic Action, founding of, **Supp. 7**, 156
Union Guardian Trust Co. (Detroit, Mich.), **Supp. 6**, 33–34
Union Heat and Light Co., founding of, **Supp. 5**, 259–60
Union Iron Mills, formation of, **Vol. 7, Part 2**, 550
Unionist, founding of, **Vol. 9, Part 2**, 299
Unionist party: **Vol. 8, Part 1**, 30 f.; "Charcoal," wing of, **Vol. 3, Part 1**, 425; nullification contest, **Vol. 8, Part 1**, 30 f.
Union Labor Advocate, **Supp. 3**, 355–56
Union League Club, **Vol. 1, Part 2**, 169; **Vol. 7, Part 2**, 26
Union League of America, **Vol. 9, Part 2**, 61
Union Memorial Hospital (Baltimore, Md.), **Supp. 3**, 271
Union of Orthodox Jewish Congregations of America, founding of, **Supp. 2**, 453
Union of Soviet Socialist Republics. *See* Soviet Union
Union Pacific (ballet), **Supp. 10**, 580
Union Pacific Railroad: **Vol. 1, Part 1**, 254, 548 f.; **Vol. 4, Part 1**, 454; **Vol. 5, Part 1**, 64, 409; **Vol. 6, Part 1**, 438; **Vol. 7, Part 1**, 645; **Vol. 8, Part 1**, 70 f.; **Vol. 8, Part 2**, 120, 381; **Supp. 2**, 260; **Supp. 5**, 270, 365–66; construction of, **Vol. 3, Part 1**, 312, 348; **Vol. 7, Part 1**, 560; **Vol. 9, Part 1**, 24; Credit Mobilier, **Vol. 1, Part 1**, 251; development of, **Vol. 1, Part 2**, 339; Omaha as beginning point of, **Vol. 3, Part 1**, 542 f.; and the "press on wheels," **Vol. 4, Part 1**, 9; robbed by Sam Bass, **Vol. 5, Part 2**, 182; surveying routes for, **Vol. 4, Part 1**, 154
Union Pacific Railroad and Telegraph Co., reorganization of, **Vol. 1, Part 2**, 154
Union party: **Vol. 2, Part 2**, 134; **Vol. 7, Part 2**, 514; **Supp. 4**, 480; **Supp. 10**, 745; presidential election (1936), **Supp. 10**, 152
Union Policies and Industrial Management, **Supp. 6**, 586
Union Republican Party of Virginia, **Vol. 1, Part 2**, 473
Unions: railroad, **Vol. 6, Part 1**, 133; **Vol. 9, Part 2**, 86; trade, **Vol. 1, Part 1**, 420 f.; **Vol. 2, Part 1**, 545; **Vol. 2, Part 2**, 338, 473, 612; **Vol. 3, Part 1**, 183 f., 223, 510; **Vol. 5, Part 2**, 278; **Vol. 6, Part 1**, 170, 521; **Vol. 6, Part 2**, 150; **Vol. 7, Part 1**, 545; **Vol. 8, Part 1**, 112 f., 142 f.; **Vol. 8, Part 2**, 321; **Vol. 10, Part 1**, 119; **Supp. 9**, 705–6; **Supp. 10**, 524–25; writings on, **Vol. 5, Part 1**, 317. *See also* Labor and labor movement
Union Seminary, **Vol. 2, Part 1**, 116
Union Stock Yards (Chicago), **Vol. 7, Part 1**, 217 f.
Union Square rally (1930), **Supp. 5**, 499
Union Switch and Signal Co., **Vol. 8, Part 2**, 56
Union-That-Nothing-Be-Lost society, **Supp. 2**, 202
Union Theological Seminary: **Vol. 2, Part 1**, 40; **Vol. 4, Part 2**, 396; **Vol. 5, Part 1**, 574; **Vol. 7, Part 2**, 382; **Vol. 8, Part 1**, 189 f.; Christian ethics studies, **Supp. 8**, 681; church history studies, **Supp. 3**, 529–30; faculty, **Supp. 3**, 110–11; founding of, **Vol. 2, Part 1**, 360; **Vol. 6, Part 2**, 368; **Vol. 7, Part 2**, 317, 502; **Vol. 9, Part l**, 202; philosophy of religion studies, **Supp. 4**, 513; presidency of, **Vol. 4, Part 2**, 119; **Vol. 5, Part 1**, 79; **Supp. 5**, 116–17
Unitarian church: **Vol. 1, Part 1**, 180 f., 200, 242, 561, 652, 616; **Vol. 1, Part 2**, 129, 207; **Vol. 2, Part 1**, 233; **Vol. 2, Part 2**, 5, 153, 310, 572 f., 595; **Vol. 3, Part 2**, 103, 132, 141, 577; **Vol. 4, Part 1**, 10, 44 f., 80, 122 f., 125, 305; **Vol. 4, Part 2**, 34, 99, 320, 498; **Vol. 5, Part 1**, 45 f., 149, 241, 359, 413 f., 612; **Vol. 5, Part 2**, 179, 180, 232 f., 403; **Vol. 6, Part 1**, 177, 303, 387 f., 450 f., 572; **Vol. 6, Part 2**, 246; **Vol. 7, Part 1**, 245, 587 f.; **Vol. 7, Part 2**, 169, 239 f., 335, 341, 343, 586; **Vol. 8, Part 1**, 135, 223 f., 445, 645; **Vol. 8, Part 2**, 389, 538, 548; **Vol. 9, Part 1**, 209, 546, 549 f.; **Vol. 9, Part 2**, 391; **Vol. 10, Part 1**, 450 f.; **Vol. 10, Part 2**, 12, 618; **Supp. 7**, 356; controversies in, **Vol. 3, Part 2**, 165; first woman clergyman, **Vol. 9, Part 1**, 445; forerunners of, **Vol. 4, Part 1**, 194; Massachusetts, **Vol. 8, Part 1**, 622, 645; ministers institute, **Vol. 1, Part 2**, 169; South Carolina, **Vol. 6, Part 1**, 131; "Spirit of the Pilgrims," **Vol. 8, Part 1**, 58; Sunday-school lessons, **Vol. 5, Part 2**, 179; tenets, **Vol. 2, Part 1**, 292; **Vol. 4, Part 1**, 43; **Vol. 5, Part 1**, 295; **Vol. 10, Part 2**, 528; Unity, **Vol. 10, Part 2**, 180; "Unity Clubs," **Vol. 5, Part 2**, 179
Unitarian Fellowship for Social Justice, founding of, **Supp. 7**, 356
Unitarian/Universalist Association, **Supp. 7**, 356, 357
United Aircraft and Transport, **Supp. 5**, 385; **Supp. 6**, 64
United Air Lines: **Supp. 5**, 294, 611; **Supp. 6**, 64; es-

tablishment of, **Supp. 2**, 109; management and growth, **Supp. 10**, 621
United Artists Corporation: **Supp. 8**, 465, 678; founding of, **Supp. 2**, 173; **Supp. 4**, 350; **Supp. 10**, 116; productions, **Supp. 10**,635
United Automobile Workers: **Supp. 8**, 600, 610; blacks in, **Supp. 6**, 648; factions, **Supp. 8**, 419, 526–28, 652–53; Ford Motor recognition of, **Supp. 3**, 284; **Supp. 4**, 303; **Supp. 8**, 610; General Motors recognition of, **Supp. 4**, 457; **Supp. 7**, 794; **Supp. 8**, 600; Kaiser-Frazer founding, **Supp. 8**, 309; Kohler strike, investigation, **Supp. 9**, 573; leadership, **Supp. 8**, 418–19, 526–28, 651–53; Social Justice Award, **Supp. 8**, 675; strikes, **Supp. 4**, 612
United Brands, **Supp. 9**, 93–94
United Brethren in Christ, **Vol. 3, Part 2**, 470; **Vol. 4, Part 2**, 217; **Vol. 5, Part 2**, 350 f., 511; **Vol. 7, Part 1**, 455; **Vol. 9, Part 1**, 138 f.
United Brotherhood of Carpenters and Joiners, **Supp. 5**, 339
United Cannery, Agricultural, Packing, and Allied Workers of America, **Supp. 7**, 781
United China Relief, **Supp. 6**, 349
United Cigar Stores Co., **Vol. 3, Part 1**, 497 f.
United Colored Democracy, **Supp. 4**, 607–8
United Confederate Veterans, **Vol. 3, Part 2**, 197; **Vol. 5, Part 2**, 191
United Drug Co., founding of, **Supp. 4**, 496–97
United Features Syndicate, **Supp. 10**, 675; founding of, **Supp. 9**, 89; "Totem Pole, The" column, **Supp. 10**, 747
United Fruit Co., **Vol. 1, Part 1**, 524; founding of, **Vol. 5, Part 2**, 291 f.
United Garment Workers of America, **Supp. 4**, 375
United Gas Improvement Co. of Philadelphla, controversy over, **Vol. 3, Part 1**, 355
United Hebrew Trades, founding of, **Supp. 1**, 403
United International Famine Relief Committee, **Vol. 3, Part 2**, 144
United Jewish Charities, **Supp. 4**, 79
United Lutheran Church. *See* Lutheran church
United Mine Workers (UMW): **Vol. 5, Part 2**, 196; **Vol. 7, Part 1**, 51 f.; **Supp. 10**, 681, 682; administration, **Supp. 5**, 253, 254, 282, 509–10; Catholic support, **Supp. 2**, 135; coal strike, **Supp. 9**, 565; leadership, **Supp. 7**, 81–82; **Supp. 8**, 374–77; Lewis contempt case, **Supp. 5**, 248–49, 714; Ludlow massacre, **Supp. 2**, 124; pension funds invested in Eaton businesses, **Supp. 10**, 203; union-shop issue, **Supp. 7**, 172
United Mine Workers of America v. *Red Jacket Consolidated Coal and Coke Co.*, **Supp. 6**, 494
United Motors, **Supp. 8**, 598
United Nations (UN): African division, **Supp. 5**, 164; agricultural programs, **Supp. 6**, 639; Atomic Energy Commission, **Supp. 7**, 37; aviation, **Supp. 6**, 666; charter, **Supp. 5**, 198, 334, 537–38, 704; **Supp. 7**, 138, 289, 688; **Supp. 9**, 137, 192; **Supp. 10**, 208, 686; charter revision proposals, **Supp. 8**, 88; Cuban missile crisis, **Supp. 7**, 724; diplomacy, **Supp. 9**, 137, 138, 334; economic development programs, **Supp. 9**, 398; establishment of, **Supp. 4**, 777–78; Food and Agricultural Organization, **Supp. 10**, 394; Fulbright resolution (1943), **Supp. 4**, 89; headquarters site, **Supp. 10**, 866; International Monetary Fund, **Supp. 10**, 134; International Law Commission, **Supp. 6**, 308; opponents, **Supp. 6**, 87, 361, 578; peacekeeping missions, **Supp. 9**, 138, 192; plebiscites, **Supp. 5**, 723–24; supporters, **Supp. 3**, 660, 663, 496, 504; **Supp. 10**, 209; U.S. ambassadors, **Supp. 7**, 23–24, 723–24; U.S. delegation, **Supp. 7**, 661–62, 721, 748; **Supp. 8**, 701; **Supp. 9**, 137, 398, 556; **Supp. 10**, 57, 229–30, 243, 472; women's participation, **Supp. 6**, 413; writings on, **Supp. 8**, 408
United Nations Building, Rockefeller site gift for, **Supp. 6**, 549; **Supp. 10**, 686
United Nations Educational, Scientific, and Cultural Organization (UNESCO): **Supp. 10**, 594–95; founding of, **Supp. 4**, 449–50; **Supp. 9**, 81
United Nations Food and Agricultural Organization, **Supp. 4**, 341
United Nations International Children's Emergency Fund (UNICEF), founding of, **Supp. 7**, 599–600
United Nations Relief and Rehabilitation Administration, **Supp. 5**, 605, 704; directorship, **Supp. 7**, 467; founding of, **Supp. 4**, 89; medical consultants, **Supp. 7**, 195
United Negro College Fund (UNCF), **Supp. 9**, 142
United Neighborhood Houses, predecessor, **Supp. 5**, 631
United Norwegian Lutheran Church, **Vol. 2, Part 2**, 167
United Press (UP), **Supp. 3**, 166; **Supp. 6**, 601; **Supp. 7**, 369
United Press Association: **Vol. 8, Part 2**, 518; **Supp. 9**, 89–90; founded, **Vol. 6, Part 2**, 166; New York Associated Press, absorbed by, **Vol. 7, Part 2**, 545
United Press International (UPI), **Supp. 8**, 607
United Productions of America (UPA), founding of, **Supp. 10**, 352
United Railroad Workers Union, **Supp. 8**, 513
United Railroads of San Francisco, **Supp. 3**, 126
United Service Organizations (USO), **Supp. 7**, 30; **Supp. 8**, 52; **Supp. 9**, 142
United States. For goverment agencies and departments, *see* inverted entries, e.g., Agriculture, Department of (U.S.); Court of Claims, United States; etc.
United States (aircraft carrier), construction cancelled, **Supp. 9**, 227
United States (frigate), **Vol. 3, Part 1**, 188; **Vol. 5, Part 1**, 361
United States (ship), **Supp. 5**, 725–26
United States Agricultural Society, **Vol. 4, Part 1**, 156; **Vol. 8, Part 2**, 51
United States Air Force Academy (Colorado Springs): **Supp. 10**, 782; design, **Supp. 7**, 691
United States Air Force Aerospace Defense Command (ADCOM), **Supp. 10**, 379
United States attorneys. *See* Justice, Department of (U.S.)
United States Centennial Commission, **Vol. 4, Part 2**, 422
United States Christian Commission, **Vol. 4, Part 1, 625; Vol. 6, Part 1**, 557, 573; **Vol. 7, Part 1**, 103, 281
United States Commercial and Statistical Registers, **Vol. 4, Part 2**, 472
United States Committee for the Care of European Children, **Supp. 6**, 202
United States Customs House, architecture, **Supp. 1**, 341
United States Entomological Commission, **Vol. 8, Part 1**, 610
United States Express Co., **Vol. 7, Part 1**, 167
United States Golf Association, founding of, **Supp. 2**, 404
United States Grain Corporation, **Vol. 6, Part 1**, 275
United States Grain Marketing Corporation, founding of, **Supp. 1**, 661
United States Gypsum Co., founding of, **Supp. 6**, 27
United States Life-Saving Service, **Vol. 3, Part 2**, 582
United States Magazine and Democratic Review, **Vol. 7, Part 2**, 89
United States mail. *See* Postal Service, United States

United States Mail Steamship Co., **Vol. 2, Part 2**, 306; **Vol. 8, Part 2**, 11
United States Military Academy (West Point): **Vol. 2, Part 1**, 412; **Vol. 2, Part 2**, 590; **Vol. 3, Part 1**, 201; **Vol. 4, Part 1**, 504; **Vol. 5, Part 1**, 73; **Vol. 6, Part 2**, 209; **Vol. 7, Part 2**, 281; **Vol. 8, Part 2**, 507; **Vol. 9, Part 2**, 247; architecture, **Supp. 3**, 196; betrayed to English, **Vol. 1, Part 1**, 366 f.; competitive examinations initiated, **Vol. 5, Part 2**, 42; establishment of, **Vol. 9, Part 2**, 247, 410, 598; **Vol. 10, Part 2**, 281; famous class of, **Vol. 4, Part 2**, 221; football team, **Supp. 8**, 389; fortifications at, **Vol. 9, Part 2**, 606; improvement of courses, **Vol. 6, Part 2**, 209; instructors, **Supp. 4**, 655; superintendency of, **Vol. 3, Part 1**, 210; **Vo1. 6, Part 1**, 121 f.; **Vol. 8, Part 2**, 454; **Supp. 7**, 488
United States National Museum, **Vol. 5, Part 2**, 485; **Supp. 6**, 453, 454
United States Naval Academy (Annapolis): **Vol. 1, Part 1**, 566; **Vol. 2, Part 1**, 206; **Vol. 2, Part 2**, 44; **Vol. 3, Part 1**, 614 f.; **Vol. 5, Part 2**, 170; **Vol. 7, Part 2**, 185, 320; **Vol. 8, Part 1**, 66 f., 83, 339, 424; **Vol. 8, Part 2**, 72 f., 322; **Vol. 10, Part 1**, 425; campus building architecture, **Supp. 4**, 281; Civil War period, **Vol. 8, Part 2**, 72, 74; commandants, **Supp. 1**, 39, 199; establishment of, **Vol. 1, Part 1**, 566; **Vol. 2, Part 2**, 44; **Vol. 10, Part 1**, 425; first chaplain, **Vol. 5, Part 2**, 170; first graduate to be made superintendent of, **Vol. 8, Part 1**, 339; first superintendent of, **Vol. 3, Part 1**, 529 f.; library organized at, **Vol. 8, Part 1**, 66 f.; organization of, **Vol. 3, Part 1**, 529 f.; removal of, to Newport, **Vol. 8, Part 2**, 72; systematized instruction, **Vol. 8, Part 1, 339**
United States Naval Institute, **Vol. 7, Part 2**, 220; **Vol. 9, Part 1**, 178
United States Naval Lyceum, **Vol. 7, Part 2**, 487
United States Naval Observatory, **Vol. 4, Part 2**, 266; **Vol. 6, Part 1**, 337; **Vol. 7, Part 1**, 39, 452 f.; **Vol. 7, Part 2**, 319; **Vol. 8, Part 2**, 78, 341; **Vol. 9, Part 1**, 196
United States Pacific Railway Commission, **Vol. 7, Part 2**, 313 f.
United States Reclamation Act, **Vol. 4, Part 2**, 483
United States Reduction and Refining Co., **Supp. 6**, 316
United States Rubber Co., **Supp. 1**, 306; **Supp. 7**, 169
United States Sanitary Commission: **Vol. 2, Part 2**, 136; **Vol. 3, Part 2**, 212; **Vol. 4, Part 2**, 308; **Vol. 5, Part 1**, 251, 297; **Vol. 5, Part 2**, 355, 404; **Vol. 7, Part 1**, 446; **Vol. 7, Part 2**, 26; **Vol. 8, Part 2**, 474; **Vol. 9, Part 1**, 563; **Vol. 9, Part 2**, 24
United States Shipping Co., **Vol. 7, Part 1**, 241
United States Soldiers' Home (Washington, D.C.), **Vol. 5, Part 2**, 315
United States Speaker, The, **Vol. 6, Part 1**, 440
United States Steel Corporation: **Vol. 4, Part 1**, 30; **Vol. 5, Part 1**, 57; **Vol. 7, Part 1**, 144, 177, 301; **Vol. 7, Part 2**, 471; **Vol. 8, Part 1**, 449; **Vol. 9, Part 1**, 598; antitrust actions against, **Supp. 4**, 517; **Supp. 6**, 591; base pricing, **Supp. 4**, 268; establishment of, **Supp. 2**, 600; executives, **Supp. 4**, 777; expansion, **Supp. 7**, 228–29; **Supp. 10**, 345–46; finances, **Supp. 6**, 622; foreign competition, **Supp. 10**, 345–46; founding of, **Supp. 6**, 507; presidency, **Supp. 3**, 263; subsidiary, **Supp. 7**, 308; **Supp. 10**, 345; unionization, **Supp. 5**, 510; **Supp. 8**, 375; war production, **Supp. 7**, 587
United States Trust Co., created, **Vol. 9, Part 2**, 11
United States v. *Carolene Products Co.,* **Supp. 4**, 796, 797
United States v. *Rintelen,* **Supp. 9**, 593
United States v. *Roth,* **Supp. 6**, 216
United States Women's Pure Food Vacuum Preserving Co., **Vol. 5, Part 2**, 160
United Steel Workers: **Supp. 7**, 228, 290, 587; presidency, **Supp. 10**, 493
United Synagogue of America, founding of, **Supp. 2**, 6
United Transport Service Employees, founding of, **Supp. 6**, 648
United Typothetae of America, **Vol. 3, Part 1**, 564
United Textile Workers, **Vol. 2, Part 2**, 338
United Vintners, **Supp. 7**, 614
United World Day of Prayer, **Supp. 4**, 648
United World Federalists, founding of, **Supp. 8**, 680
Unity, religious weekly, **Vol. 5, Part 2**, 180
"Unity of God, The," famous sermon, **Vol. 9, Part 2**, 391
Unity School of Christianity, **Supp. 4**, 271–72
Unity Temple (Oak Park, Ill.), **Supp. 6**, 712
UNIVAC computer, **Supp. 6**, 675; **Supp. 10**, 520
Universal Christian Conference on Life and Work, **Supp. 3**, 111; **Supp. 6**, 25
Universalist church: **Vol. 1, Part 1**, 83; **Vol. 3, Part 2**, 406; **Vol. 4, Part 2**, 216; **Vol. 5, Part 2**, 457 f.; **Vol. 8, Part 2**, 398; clergy, **Vol. 1, Part 1**, 559; **Vol. 2, Part 2**, 245; **Vol. 5, Part 1**, 336; **Vol. 5, Part 2**, 457; **Vol. 8, Part 2**, 397; **Vol. 9, Part 1**, 438 f.; doctrines of, **Vol. 1, Part 1**, 557; early days of, **Vol. 10, Part 2**, 377; first woman ordained, **Vol. 2, Part 1**, 151; founding of, in America, **Vol. 7, Part 1**, 360–61; influence of, **Vol. 1, Part 1**, 556; opposition to, **Vol. 5, Part 2**, 112; theological school, first of, **Vol. 3, Part 2**, 406; writings on, **Vol. 10, Part 2**, 172
Universal military training. *See* Armed forces and defense; Draft
Universal Negro Improvement and Conservation Association, organization of, **Supp. 2**, 221; **Supp. 5**, 554
Universal News Service, **Supp. 9**, 604
Universal Peace Union, **Vol. 6, Part 1**, 431
Universal Pictures, **Supp. 6**, 610, 657; founding of, **Supp. 2**, 368
Universe and Life, The, **Supp. 4**, 427
Universities and colleges: academic freedom issues, **Supp. 3**, 151, 249, 471; **Supp. 5**, 410, 461; **Supp. 8**, 72; administration politices, **Supp. 3**, 387; **Supp. 6**, 98–99; architecture of, **Supp. 2**, 118, 362, 539; **Supp. 4**, 697–98; Asian studies programs, **Supp. 8**, 360; athletic policies, **Supp. 4**, 320; black, **Supp. 2**, 315, 456, 477; **Supp. 4**, 742, 916; **Supp. 5**, 56, 436; **Supp. 6**, 11–12; **Supp. 8**, 86–87, 94–95; **Supp. 9**, 136–37, 750; **Supp. 10**, 385–86, 841–42; black scholarships, **Supp. 5**, 56; China, **Supp. 4**, 677–78; China, first women's college, **Supp. 3**, 288; Chinese missionary, **Supp. 3**, 477; coeducational, first woman to head, **Supp. 9**, 299; desegregation of, **Supp. 8**, 73, 322; entrance standards, **Supp. 2**, 361; **Supp. 4**, 134; evangelistic, **Supp. 8**, 304; experimental, **Supp. 5**, 308–9; **Supp. 8**, 530–31; faculty v. presidency, **Supp. 3**, 150–51; federal policies, **Supp. 5**, 761; financial gifts to, **Supp. 10**, 102–3; first black Phi Beta Kappa chapter, **Supp. 5**, 437; first contemporary drama course, **Supp. 4**, 354; first ecology courses, **Supp. 5**, 374–75; football, **Supp. 2**, 302; **Supp. 4**, 236–37, 893, 917; **Supp. 5**, 289, 458, 727–28; **Supp. 6**, 48; **Supp. 7**, 167–68, 571–72, 712–13, 729; **Supp. 8**, 587–88; German model, **Supp. 6**, 207–8; gifted students, **Supp. 2**, 110; graduate education policy, **Supp. 8**, 73; Great Books curriculum, **Supp. 5**, 211–12; **Supp. 8**, 59; **Supp. 10**, 364–65; interdisciplinary history emphasis, **Supp. 8**, 273; land-grant, **Supp. 2**, 365; **Supp. 3**, 209; **Supp. 5**, 49; liberal arts studies, **Supp. 6**, 412; **Supp. 10**, 403, 404; loyalty oath issue, **Supp. 6**, 640; presses, **Supp. 6**, 154–55; research institutes, **Supp. 2**, 60; sit-ins, **Supp. 8**, 333; social

function of, **Supp. 1**, 21; **Supp. 8**, 73; student government, **Supp. 1**, 100; tutorial system, **Supp. 6**, 99; woman suffrage movement in, **Supp. 5**, 532; women's, **Supp. 2**, 79; **Supp. 4**, 625, 912–13; **Supp. 5**, 488; **Supp. 9**, 174–75; **Supp. 10**, 735–36, 846; women's studies programs, **Supp. 6**, 41. *See also* Education; *specific institution names*

Universities, state: first federal grant to, **Vol. 6, Part 1**, 275; financial responsibilities for, **Vol. 4, Part 2**, 407

University Club (New York), founding, **Vol. 5, Part 1**, 180

University Elementary School (Chicago, Ill.), **Supp. 5**, 171

University extension, **Vol. 7, Part 1**, 292

University Museum (Philadelphia, Pa.), archaeology, **Supp. 3**, 272

University of Akron: founding of, **Vol. 2, Part 1**, 221; presidency, **Supp. 5**, 761

University of Alabama: **Vol. 2, Part 1**, 184; **Vol. 4, Part 1**, 151; **Vol. 9, Part 1**, 367; controversy over coal lands, **Vol. 5, Part 2**, 147; history studies, **Supp. 6**, 491; incorporation of, **Vol. 7, Part 2**, 561; integration, **Supp. 8**, 73; presidency, **Supp. 8**, 72–73

University of Arizona: Lunar and Planetary Laboratory established, **Supp. 9**, 476; Steward Observatory, **Supp. 7**, 193; tree-ring research, **Supp. 7**, 194

University of Arkansas, **Vol. 5, Part 1**, 27

University of Berlin, **Supp. 5**, 562

University of Buffalo: curriculum reform, **Supp. 6**, 99; first chancellor, **Vol. 3, Part 2**, 381; founding of, **Vol. 8, Part 1**, 283; medical department, founding of, **Vol. 4, Part 2**, 185; social work studies, **Supp. 3**, 4

University of California (Berkeley): **Vol. 5, Part 2**, 591; **Vol. 8, Part 1**, 276 f.; **Vol. 8, Part 2**, 432; **Vol. 9, Part 1**, 579; **Vol. 10, Part 2**, 45; agricultural chemistry studies, **Supp. 4**, 382; agricultural economics studies, **Supp. 6**, 638; anatomy department, **Supp. 9**, 266; anthropology studies, **Supp. 6**, 353, 393; architectural design, **Supp. 6**, 438, 463; astronomy studies, **Supp. 4**, 600; Bancroft Library, **Supp. 5**, 77; biochemistry studies, **Supp. 4**, 720; first dean of women, **Supp. 8**, 442; founding of, **Vol. 2, Part 1**, 351; **Vol. 4, Part 2**, 90; **Vol. 9, Part 1**, 550; **Vol. 10, Part 2**, 246; "Free Speech Movement," **Supp. 9**, 469; geography studies, **Supp. 9**, 703–4; geology studies, **Supp. 5**, 416; gifts to, **Vol. 4, Part 2**, 488 f.; grounds, designing of, **Vol. 7, Part 2**, 26; history studies, **Supp. 4**, 824; law school, **Supp. 4**, 680; **Supp. 7**, 181–82; loyalty oath issue, **Supp. 6**, 640; **Supp. 9**, 753, 754; medical research, **Supp. 9**, 266; paleontology studies, **Supp. 3**, 519; physics studies, **Supp. 6**, 370; **Supp. 8**, 482, 484; presidency, **Vol. 4, Part 2**, 156; **Vol. 5, Part 1**, 136; **Vol. 5, Part 2**, 303 f.; **Vol. 6, Part 1**, 88; **Supp. 2**, 92; **Supp. 5**, 43; **Supp. 9**, 752–53; psychology studies, **Supp. 6**, 639–40; Spanish literature and language studies, **Supp. 4**, 719; theoretical physics studies, **Supp. 8**, 482, 484; viral research, **Supp. 9**, 754; zoology studies, **Supp. 4**, 461

Universlty of California (Los Angeles): football team, **Supp. 9**, 840; geophysics studies, **Supp. 10**, 407; philosophy studies, **Supp. 5**, 563; **Supp. 8**, 75; psychology studies, **Supp. 1**, 316; Robinson athletic career at, **Supp. 9**, 668; Washington athletic career at, **Supp. 9**, 840

University of California (Riverside), agricultural studies, **Supp. 4**, 863

University of Chicago: **Vol. 3, Part 2**, 367; **Vol. 4, Part 1**, 183; **Vol. 5, Part 1**, 438; **Vol. 7, Part 1**, 160; **Vol. 7, Part 2**, 174, 238; **Vol. 8, Part 2**, 272, 408; **Vol. 9, Part 1**, 125; administration, **Supp. 3**, 793; anthropology studies, **Supp. 6**, 532–34; astronomical observatories, **Supp. 6**, 7; astronomy studies, **Supp. 2**, 270–71; **Supp. 3**, 634; **Supp. 5**, 508, 509; atomic bomb development, **Supp. 7**, 10–11, 259, 300, 732; **Supp. 8**, 229–30, 411; bacteriology studies, **Supp. 2**, 353; botany studies, **Supp. 3**, 153–54; botany studies, first Ph.D. in, **Supp. 3**, 153; Baptist support for, **Vol. 4, Part 1**, 406; chemistry studies, **Supp. 6**, 334; classics studies, **Supp. 4**, 67–68, 149; debt, before reorganization, **Vol. 1, Part 1**, 264; divinity school, **Supp. 3**, 514, 825; **Supp. 4**, 151; **Supp. 7**, 747; economics studies, **Supp. 4**, 584–86; **Supp. 8**, 668; **Supp. 9**, 466–67; education school, **Supp. 4**, 444–45; **Supp. 5**, 61; embryology studies, **Supp. 4**, 497–98; *Encyclopaedia Britannica*, **Supp. 9**, 80, 81; **Supp. 10**, 365; first laboratory for nuclear physics, **Supp. 7**, 10–11; first nuclear reactor, **Supp. 7**, 10–11, 300; first political scientist, **Supp. 5**, 484–85; football team, **Supp. 7**, 712–13; founding of, **Vol. 2, Part 1**, 334; **Vol. 4, Part 1**, 182; **Supp. 2**, 574; gifts to, **Vol. 4, Part 2**, 287; **Vol. 7, Part 1**, 591, 645; Great Books program, **Supp. 5**, 212; **Supp. 8**, 59; **Supp. 10**, 364–65; history of, **Vol. 4, Part 1**, 406; history studies, **Supp. 4**, 152, 530–31; **Supp. 9**, 330; human development committee, **Supp. 8**, 684; law school, **Vol. 6, Part 2**, 488; **Supp. 4**, 77; law school founding, **Supp. 3**, 43; libraries, **Supp. 3**, 327; library science studies, **Supp. 5**, 47; loyalty issues, **Supp. 6**, 392; Lying-In Hospital, **Supp. 3**, 223; mathematics studies, **Supp. 3**, 86–87; **Supp. 5**, 67–68; medical school, **Supp. 6**, 53, 295, 296; nuclear research, **Supp. 5**, 220–21; **Supp. 10**, 457; Oriental Institute, **Supp. 1**, 112; **Supp. 3**, 572–73; **Supp. 4**, 902; pathology studies, **Supp. 3**, 807; pediatric studies, **Supp. 3**, 101; pharmacology studies, **Supp. 4**, 460; philosophy studies, **Supp. 3**, 779–80; **Supp. 5**, 171; **Supp. 6**, 13–14; **Supp. 7**, 701–2; **Supp. 8**, 74–75; physics studies, **Supp. 3**, 290–91; **Supp. 5**, 495; **Supp. 7**, 134; **Supp. 9**, 542; physiology studies, **Supp. 6**, 100; political economy studies, **Supp. 4**, 106; political science studies, **Supp. 6**, 692–93; presidency, **Supp. 7**, 516; psychology studies, **Supp. 4**, 20, 21; **Supp. 5**, 685; **Supp. 6**, 671–72; public relations, **Supp. 9**, 80; reading conferences, **Supp. 6**, 248; refounding of, **Vol. 9, Part 2**, 143; science studies, **Supp. 2**, 156; social psychology studies, **Supp. 1**, 547; Social Science Research Building, **Supp. 5**, 485; social work graduate school, **Supp. 6**, 1; social work studies, **Supp. 2**, 656; **Supp. 4**, 106; sociology studies, **Supp. 3**, 577–80, 793; **Supp. 4**, 828, 829, 831; **Supp. 6**, 54, 482, 483, 604; undergraduate program, upgrading of, **Supp. 10**, 364; zoology studies, **Supp. 5**, 110

University of Cincinnati: **Vol. 2, Part 1**, 291; **Vol. 8, Part 1**, 317 f.; applied arts studies, **Supp. 2**, 598; engineering studies, **Supp. 2**, 598; geology and geography studies, **Supp. 3**, 265; medical school, **Supp. 3**, 526, 625–26; presidency, **Supp. 3**, 209

University of Coblenz, **Vol. 8, Part 1**, 9

University of Colorado: **Vol. 1, Part 1**, 522; **Vol. 4, Part 2**, 155; **Vol. 8, Part 2**, 609; first geology professor, **Supp. 3**, 265; medical school, **Supp. 2**, 177; ophthalmology studies, **Supp. 3**, 377

University of Denver: **Vol. 5, Part 1**, 290; founding of, **Vol. 3, Part 2**, 205

University of Florida (Gainesville), presidency, **Supp. 7**, 744–45

University of Georgia: **Vol. 2, Part 2**, 99; **Vol. 3, Part 2**, 391; **Vol. 5, Part 1**, 48; **Vol. 6, Part 2**, 507; **Vol. 10, Part 2**, 104; accreditation loss, **Supp. 4**, 814; football team, **Supp. 2**, 302; **Supp. 9**, 147; founding of, **Vol. 2, Part 2**, 180; **Vol. 5, Part 1**, 268; **Vol. 6, Part 2**, 618

University of Göttingen, physics studies, **Supp. 7**, 258–59

University of Hawaii: **Vol. 2, Part 2**, 399; establishment of, **Supp. 1**, 295; history studies, **Supp. 7**, 446
University of Illinois: **Vol. 7, Part 2**, 252; **Vol. 8, Part 2**, 52; Agriculture Experiment Station, **Supp. 3**, 216–17; chemistry studies, **Supp. 3**, 565–66; classics studies, **Supp. 3**, 571; education school, **Supp. 4**, 40; engineering studies, **Supp. 3**, 759; football team, **Supp. 6**, 728; founding of, **Vol. 10, Part 1**, 68; history studies, **Supp. 5**, 557, 577; **Supp. 7**, 684; home economics studies, **Supp. 3**, 68; legislative support, **Vol. 7, Part 2**, 543; mathematics studies, **Supp. 5**, 491; medical school, **Supp. 1**, 616; **Supp. 3**, 411; political science studies, **Supp. 2**, 220; **Supp. 4**, 260; presidency, **Vol. 3, Part 1**, 434; **Vol. 4, Part 1**, 603; **Vol. 5, Part 1**, 574; **Supp. 5**, 109; Quine Library, **Supp. 1**, 616; zoology studies, **Supp. 3**, 802–3
University of Iowa: **Vol. 6, Part 1**, 578; **Vol. 7, Part 2**, 285; art studies, **Supp. 3**, 841; football team, **Supp. 9**, 817; hearing and speech studies, **Supp. 7**, 395–6; medical research, **Supp. 10**, 623–24; sports medicine practice, **Supp. 10**, 624
University of Istanbul (Turkey), philosophy studies, **Supp. 5**, 563
University of Kansas: **Vol. 9, Part 1**, 385; anatomy studies, **Supp. 3**, 172; athletic department, **Supp. 9**, 20–21
University of Kansas City (Mo.), presidency, **Supp. 5**, 646
University of Kentucky: **Vol. 7, Part 2**, 303; basketball team, **Supp. 10**, 711; presidency, **Supp. 5**, 461
University of Louisville: **Vol. 2, Part 2**, 385; founding of, **Vol. 4, Part 2**, 61
University of Louisiana: founding of, **Vol. 4, Part 2**, 416; first professorship of political economy in U.S., **Vol. 3, Part 1**, 181
University of Lyons, medical school, **Supp. 3**, 140
University of Maine, founding of, **Vol. 5, Part 1**, 164
University of Maryland: **Vol. 5, Part 2**, 333; **Vol. 9, Part 1**, 328; geography studies, **Supp. 4**, 45; medical department, **Vol. 1, Part 2**, 60; **Vol. 4, Part 1**, 259; **Vol. 8, Part 1**, 131 f.; **Vol. 9, Part 2**, 343
University of Michigan: **Vol. 1, Part 1**, 306; **Vol. 4, Part 1**, 35; **Vol. 5, Part 1**, 434; **Vol. 5, Part 2**, 314; Americana collections, **Supp. 1**, 180; architecture and buildings, **Supp. 3**, 404; architecture studies, **Supp. 4**, 714–15; astronomy studies, **Supp. 3**, 208; bacteriology studies, **Supp. 6**, 481; business administration school founding, **Supp. 5**, 161; chemistry studies, **Supp. 4**, 336–37; Clements Library of American History, **Supp. 5**, 9, 10; economics studies, **Supp. 5**, 161; engineering school, **Supp. 3**, 188; explorations of, **Vol. 5, Part 2**, 314; first president of, **Vol. 3, Part 2**, 495; football team, **Supp. 4**, 917; founding, **Vol. 2, Part 2**, 515; **Vol. 9, Part 2**, 302 f.; graduate school, organization of, **Vol. 4, Part 2**, 58; library, growth of, **Vol. 3, Part 1**, 143; medical department, **Vol. 7, Part 2**, 637; medical school, physiology studies, **Supp. 3**, 369–70; medical school, surgery studies, **Supp. 3**, 121; pharmacology studies, **Supp. 2**, 4; **Supp. 3**, 242; School of Music, **Vol. 4, Part 1**, 35; **Vol. 9, Part 1**, 507; School of Pharmacy, **Vol. 8, Part 1**, 192 f.; seminar method introduced, **Vol. 1, Part 1**, 53
University of Minnesota: **Vol. 7, Part 1**, 566 f.; **Vol. 7, Part 2**, 608; **Vol. 9, Part 1**, 618; agricultural biochemistry, **Supp. 3**, 315; anatomy studies, **Supp. 4**, 420; education college, **Supp. 2**, 268; first Ph.D., **Supp. 1**, 283; football team, **Supp. 10**, 40–41; geography studies, **Supp. 4**, 113; graduate school development, **Supp. 7**, 253; history studies, **Supp. 7**, 252–53; mathematics studies, **Supp. 4**, 421; medical school, **Vol. 7, Part 1**, 130; **Vol. 10, Part 2**, 3; physics studies, **Supp. 4**, 818; **Supp. 10**, 805; presidency, **Supp. 2**, 109–10; **Supp. 3**, 794; **Supp. 7**, 253
University of Mississippi: **Vol. 1, Part 1**, 619; **Vol. 4, Part 1**, 72; **Vol. 6, Part 1**, 390; **Vol. 9, Part 2**, 3; desegregation, **Supp. 7**, 227, 425; **Supp. 8**, 322; founding of, **Vol. 5, Part 1**, 164; **Vol. 9, Part 1**, 21; history of, **Vol. 6, Part 2**, 453; medical school founding, **Supp. 4**, 474
University of Missouri: anatomy studies, **Supp. 3**, 6; Board of Curators of, **Vol. 10, Part 1**, 643; founding of, **Vol. 1, Part 1**, 207; **Vol. 6, Part 1**, 17; history of, **Vol. 9, Part 2**, 254; journalism school, **Vol. 5, Part 2**, 391; **Vol. 9, Part 1**, 578; **Supp. 1**, 708; **Supp. 4**, 704; law department, **Vol. 1, Part 2**, 375; military training, **Supp. 1**, 211; presidency of, **Vol. 5, Part 2**, 60; **Vol. 7, Part 1**, 25; **Vol. 8, Part 1**, 421
University of Montana, rural life study, **Supp. 5**, 320–21
University of Nashville: **Vol. 5, Part 2**, 91 f., 426; **Vol. 6, Part 1**, 278 f.; **Vol. 9, Part 1**, 542; Western Military Institute, absorption of, by, **Vol. 5, Part 2**, 91
University of Nebraska: **Vol. 2, Part 1**, 472; **Vol. 3, Part 2**, 257; botany studies, **Supp. 3**, 168–69; football team, **Supp. 10**, 37
University of New Mexico, **Vol. 8, Part 1**, 229 f.
University of North Carolina: **Vol. 1, Part 2**, 57; **Vol. 4, Part 1**, 472 f.; **Vol. 8, Part 1**, 43 f.; **Vol. 8, Part 2**, 384, 212; **Vol. 9, Part 1**, 447; **Vol. 9, Part 2**, 231; drama studies, **Supp. 3**, 426–27; founding of, **Vol. 3, Part 1**, 98; **Vol. 7, Part 2**, 516; **Vol. 8, Part 1**, 39 f.; Morehead Foundation, **Supp. 7**, 554; predecessors, **Supp. 4**, 215; presidency, **Supp. 1**, 21; **Supp. 5**, 109; **Supp. 9**, 334; public health school, **Supp. 4**, 701; race relations promotion, **Supp. 6**, 12; reopening of, **Vol. 1, Part 2**, 57; social sciences studies, **Supp. 5**, 520
University of North Carolina Magazine, **Vol. 9, Part 2**, 231
University of North Dakota: **Vol. 9, Part 1**, 472; presidency, **Supp. 5**, 461
University of Northern Pennsylvania, reopening of, **Vol. 9, Part 2**, 55
University of Notre Dame: football "Four Horsemen," **Supp. 7**, 729; football team, **Supp. 5**, 568; **Supp. 9**, 484–85; **Supp. 10**, 726; gifts to, **Supp. 6**, 661; sculpture studies, **Supp. 7**, 531
University of Ohio, **Vol. 6, Part 1**, 275
University of Oklahoma, history studies, **Supp. 5**, 570
University of Oregon, **Vol. 2, Part 1**, 462
University of Orleans (La.), **Vol. 3, Part 1**, 249
University of Pennsylvania: **Vol. 3, Part 2**, 236, 270; **Vol. 4, Part 2**, 337; **Vol. 5, Part 1**, 579 f.; **Vol. 7, Part 1**, 3; **Vol. 7, Part 2**, 305 f., 454 f.; **Vol. 9, Part 1**, 255, 357, 429; anthropology studies, **Supp. 10**, 209–210; biophysics research, **Supp. 9**, 125; dental school, **Vol. 3, Part 2**, 212; development of, **Vol. 3, Part 1**, 215; **Vol. 9, Part 2**, 24 f., 261; English literature studies, **Supp. 3**, 688–89; explorations of, **Vol. 5, Part 1**, 58 f.; first computer (ENIAC), **Supp. 6**, 675; football team, **Supp. 6**, 47; history studies, **Supp. 6**, 531; **Supp. 9**, 583–84; hospital, founding of, **Vol. 7, Part 1**, 557; law school, **Vol. 5, Part 2**, 445; **Vol. 9, Part 1**, 29; **Supp. 4**, 490–91; **Supp. 5**, 571, 576; mathematics studies, **Supp. 8**, 514–15; medical research building, design of, **Supp. 9**, 446; medical school, **Vol. 5, Part 1**, 234, 539; **Vol. 7, Part 1**, 172 f.; **Vol. 7, Part 2**, 453 f.; **Vol. 8, Part 1**, 136 f.; **Vol. 10, Part 2**, 458; **Supp. 2**, 209; **Supp. 3**, 243; **Supp. 4**, 650; **Supp. 5**, 438, 489; merger (1791), **Vol. 8, Part 1**, 137; **Vol. 8, Part 2**, 229; libraries, **Vol. 5, Part 2**, 445; **Vol. 7, Part 2**, 441; physiology studies, **Supp. 4**, 59; politlcal science studies, **Supp. 4**, 705; presidency, **Supp. 4**, 320; psychology studies, **Supp. 3**, 149; School of Biology, **Vol. 5, Part 2**, 13; Semitic

studies, **Supp. 3**, 37; **Supp. 4**, 595; University Museum, **Supp. 4**, 761–62; Veterinary School, **Vol. 7, Part 2**, 360; Wharton School of Finance, **Supp. 7**, 373; X-ray department, **Supp. 2**, 512; zoology studies, **Supp. 4**, 516
University of Pittsburgh: **Vol. 2, Part 1**, 182; **Vol. 5, Part 1**, 431; **Vol. 6, Part 1**, 613 f.; **Vol. 7, Part 2**, 540; astronomy studies, **Supp. 3**, 208, 692; Falk Medical Clinic, **Supp. 4**, 261–62; football team, **Supp. 5**, 728; Heinz Memorial Chapel, **Supp. 3**, 183
University of Rochester: **Vol. 1, Part 1**, 270; **Vol. 3, Part 1**, 268; **Vol. 5, Part 2**, 328; Eastman School of Music, **Supp. 1**, 276; medical and dental schools, **Supp. 1**, 276; presidency, **Supp. 1**, 401; **Supp. 2**, 556
University of St. Mary's of the Lake (Chicago), **Vol. 8, Part 1**, 295
University of Santa Clara, football team, **Supp. 10**, 727
University of South Carolina: **Vol. 1, Part 1**, 640; **Vol. 5, Part 2**, 518; **Vol. 6, Part 1**, 391, 555, 577; **Vol. 6, Part 2**, 434; founding of, **Vol. 3, Part 1**, 254
University of South Dakota, **Vol. 9, Part 2**, 643
University of Southern California: first baseball coach, **Supp. 8**, 107; founding of, **Supp. 2**, 716; library, **Supp. 1**, 255; track and field, **Supp. 7**, 152–53
University of Tennessee: **Vol. 1, Part 1**, 453; **Vol. 3, Part 2**, 186; agricultural studies, **Supp. 3**, 209; football team, **Supp. 7**, 571; founding of, **Vol. 2, Part 1**, 520; **Vol. 5, Part 1**, 367; **Vol. 5, Part 2**, 227; medical department, **Vol. 5, Part 2**, 207; presidency, **Supp. 3**, 209; **Supp. 4**, 601
University of Texas: **Vol. 6, Part 1**, 301; **Vol. 6, Part 2**, 589; **Vol. 8, Part 1**, 105 f.; **Vol. 9, Part 1**, 240; comparative literature studies, **Supp. 10**, 388; football team, **Supp. 10**, 37–38; founding of, **Vol. 5, Part 1**, 377; **Vol. 8, Part 2**, 14; genetics studies, **Supp. 8**, 449; history studies, **Supp. 7**, 770–71
University of the City of New York. See New York University
University of the South: **Vol. 1, Part 1**, 411; administration, **Supp. 1**, 329; founding of, **Vol. 8, Part 1**, 39 f.; second founding of, **Vol. 8, Part 1**, 313 f.
University of Tokyo, **Vol. 7, Part 2**, 319
University of Toronto, graduate studies, **Supp. 2**, 422
University of Tulsa, **Vol. 8, Part 2**, 20
University of Utah, Asian studies, **Supp. 5**, 681
University of Vermont: **Vol. 1, Part 1**, 306, 436; **Vol. 2, Part 2**, 266; **Vol. 6, Part 2**, 300; founding of, **Vol. 1, Part 1**, 195; **Vol. 8, Part 2**, 331; gifts to, **Vol. 2, Part 2**, 361; medical department, **Vol. 9, Part 1**, 327; War of 1812, **Vol. 8, Part 2**, 331
University of Virginia: **Vol. 4, Part 1**, 306; **Vol. 5, Part 1**, 550; **Vol. 5, Part 2**, 32 f.; **Vol. 7, Part 1**, 28; **Vol. 9, Part 1**, 630; astronomy studies, **Supp. 1**, 674–75; **Supp. 10**, 840; early years of, **Vol. 10, Part 1**, 76; English literature and language studies, **Supp. 7**, 797; founding of, **Vol. 1, Part 1**, 195; **Vol. 2, Part 1**, 387; **Vol. 2, Part 2**, 254; **Vol. 5, Part 2**, 32; **Vol. 7, Part 1**, 486; **Vol. 9, Part 2**, 320; growth of, **Supp. 1**, 21–22; Jefferson rotunda, **Vol. 8, Part 1**, 336 f.; law school, **Vol. 6, Part 1**, 369; **Vol. 7, Part 1**, 26; **Supp. 1**, 497; medical school, **Vol. 2, Part 1**, 387; **Vol. 5, Part 1**, 253; presidency, **Supp. 1**, 21–22
University of Washington, **Vol. 10, Part 2**, 178; poetry studies, **Supp. 7**, 654–55
University of Wichita, presidency, **Vol. 5, 365**
University of Wisconsin: **Vol. 1, Part 1**, 53; **Vol. 1, Part 2**, 32; **Vol. 2, Part 1**, 514; **Vol. 8, Part 2**, 213; **Vol. 9, Part 1**, 588; agricultural chemistry studies, **Supp. 5**, 275; anesthesia studies, **Supp. 6**, 553; biochemistry studies, **Supp. 7**, 223; chemistry studies, **Supp. 4**, 5–6; **Supp. 9**, 218; dairy school, first in U.S., **Vol. 9, Part 1**, 280; economics studies, **Supp. 3**, 177–79, 249–50; **Supp. 6**, 585, 705; electrical engineering studies, **Supp. 5**, 354–55; English literature studies, **Supp. 3**, 454–55; experimental college, **Supp. 2**, 203; **Supp. 7**, 523–24; first premedical course at, **Supp. 4**, 84; graduate school, founding of, **Supp. 1**, 187; history studies, **Supp. 5**, 429; home economics studies, **Supp. 3**, 507; labor economics studies, **Supp. 6**, 503–4: library, **Supp. 3**, 326; library catalogue, **Supp. 3**, 326; limnology studies, **Supp. 3**, 402; mathematics studies, **Supp. 3**, 791; pharmacology studies, **Vol. 8, Part 1**, 154 f.; **Supp. 3**, 432–33; plant pathology studies, **Supp. 3**, 401; political sciences studies, **Supp. 5**, 521–22; presidency, **Supp. 2**, 203; **Supp. 4**, 84–85, 247; **Supp. 7**, 224, 450; psychology studies, **Supp. 3**, 383; teaching at, **Supp. 9**, 362
University of Wooster, **Vol. 4, Part 1**, 602; **Vol. 9, Part 2**, 314
University of Wyoming, **Vol. 5, Part 1**, 321
University Players Guild (Falmouth, Mass.), **Supp. 6**, 610
University Press Association, **Supp. 6**, 155
University School (Petersburg, Va.), **Vol. 6, Part 1**, 559
University Settlement Society, **Supp. 3**, 175, 729
"Universology," **Vol. 1, Part 1**, 298
UNRRA. *See* United Nations Relief and Rehabilitation Administration
Unruh, Howard, reference to, **Supp. 6**, 58
Untermeyer, Louis, reference to, **Supp. 3**, 69
UP. *See* United Press
Updegraff, Allan, reference to, **Supp. 6**, 328
Updike, Daniel Berkeley, reference to, **Supp. 6**, 185
Upper Canada Rebellion, **Vol. 1, Part 2**, 248
Upper Colorado River Basin Storage Project, **Supp. 9**, 180, 181, 842
Urania, collection of hymns, **Vol. 6, Part 1**, 530
Uranian Academy, **Vol. 1, Part 1**, 107
Uranium: **Supp. 6**, 370, 501; chain reaction research, **Supp. 5**, 220–21; fission, **Supp. 7**, 731–32; isotope separation, **Supp. 4**, 453–54; **Supp. 8**, 232; purification, **Supp. 8**, 411
Uranium Committee. *See under* Atomic bomb
Uranus, planet discovered, **Vol. 7, Part 1**, 32
Urban, Joseph, reference to, **Supp. 7**, 504
Urban areas. *See* Cities; City planning; Suburbs
Urban League: administration, **Supp. 9**, 901; civil rights movement, **Supp. 9**, 901; employment opportunities for blacks, **Supp. 9**, 900; founding of, **Supp. 5**, 548; **Supp. 6**, 284–85; research surveys, **Supp. 6**, 321; **Supp. 8**, 521
Urease, biochemical isolation of, **Supp. 5**, 670
Urey, Harold C., references to, **Supp. 3**, 694; **Supp. 5**, 589
Urology: **Vol. 5, Part 1**, 239; **Vol. 7, Part 2**, 602; development of modern, **Supp. 3**, 853–54; research in, **Supp. 1**, 455; **Supp. 5**, 688
Urschel, Charles F., reference to, **Supp. 5**, 381–82
Ursinus College: first president, **Vol. 1, Part 2**, 426; founding of, **Vol. 1, Part 2**, 426
Uruguay: diplomacy with, **Vol. 7, Part 1**, 608; events leading to independence of, **Vol. 3, Part 1**, 202
U.S.A., **Supp. 8**, 137, 138
"Use" cult of mystics, **Vol. 4, Part 2**, 323
Ushant: An Essay, **Supp. 9**, 13, 14
USIA. *See* Information Agency, United States
U.S. News & World Report, management and growth of, **Supp. 9**, 482–83
USO. See United Service Organizations
Usonian homes, **Supp. 6**, 714
USSR. *See* Soviet Union
U.S. Steel Corporation. *See* United States Steel Corporation
Utah: colonizing of, **Vol. 9, Part 1**, 386; constitutional

convention, **Supp. 1**, 448; expedition to (1857–58), *See* Mormon disturbances; governors, **Supp. 2**, 147; legal service, **Vol. 10, Part 2**, 644; mining, **Vol. 3, Part 1, 27; Vol. 4, Part 1**, 9; **Vol. 7, Part 2**, 209, 451; missionary work in, **Vol. 9, Part 1**, 422; Mormon migration to, **Vol. 2, Part 2**, 592 f.; **Vol. 8, Part 1**, 175; newspaper, first daily in, **Vol. 2, Part 2**, 353; political service, **Vol. 1, Part 1**, 446; **Vol. 8, Part 2**, 4; politics, **Supp. 3**, 727, 753–54; **Supp. 5**, 681; **Supp. 9**, 180, 625, 842; polygamy, bill to suppress, in, **Vol. 8, Part 1**, 341 f.; public service, **Vol. 2, Part 2**, 353; Republican party, **Supp. 9**, 625; surveys in, **Vol. 4, Part 2**, 52; territorial government set up for, **Vol. 3, Part 1**, 399
Utah Copper Co., **Supp. 6**, 316
Utilities. *See* Public utilities; *specific types*
Utopian communities: **Vol. 4, Part 2**, 323; **Supp. 1**, 345, 454; Oneida Community, **Supp. 5**, 492
Utopian theories: **Supp. 2**, 272; urban planning, **Supp. 9**,
326; writings on, **Supp. 9**, 561

V

Vaccination, **Vol. 1, Part 1**, 395; **Vol. 3, Part 2**, 229; **Vol. 4, Part 1**, 361; **Vol. 4, Part 2**, 308; **Vol. 5, Part 2**, 163; **Vol. 6, Part 1**, 333; **Vol. 7, Part 1**, 559; **Vol. 9, Part 1**, 325; **Vol. 10, Part 1**, 479 f.
Vaccines: **Vol. 3, Part 2**, 547; diphtheria, **Supp. 5**, 1; poliomyelitis, **Supp. 5**, 512; **Supp. 7**, 649; typhus, **Supp. 4**, 667–68
Vacuum cleaner, **Supp. 5**, 313–14
Vagabond King, The, **Supp. 7**, 389
Vagnozzi, Egidio, reference to, **Supp. 8**, 614
Vagrants, most widely known of, **Vol. 8, Part 1**, 170 f.
Vail, Alfred, reference to, **Vol. 7, Part 1**, 249 f.
Vail, Laurence, reference to, **Supp. 10**, 294
Vail, T. N., reference to, **Vol. 5, Part 1**, 325
Valachi, Joseph, reference to, **Supp. 8**, 209; **Supp. 9**, 12; **Supp. 10**, 268
Valens, Ritchie, reference to, **Supp. 6**, 301
Valentin, Curt, reference to, **Supp. 9**, 502
Valentino, Rudolph, reference to, **Supp. 7**, 563
Val-Kill, N.Y., **Supp. 7**, 660, 664
Vallandigham, C. L., **Vol. 5, Part 1**, 183; **Vol. 6, Part 1**, 251; **Vol. 9, Part 2**, 568
Valley Forge (Pa.), **Vol. 5, Part 2**, 253; **Vol. 7, Part 1**, 141
Valley Hill Farm (Pa.), **Supp. 7**, 127
Valley of the Dolls, **Supp. 9**, 785
Valleys, term "superimposed" applied to, **Vol. 8, Part 1**, 146 f.
Valparaiso affair (1891), **Vol. 3, Part 2**, 551 f.; **Vol. 8, Part 2**, 438
Value, marginal utility principle of, **Supp. 2**, 106–7
Value, theory of, **Supp. 4**, 267–68, 272–73; **Supp. 6**, 505
Valves: electric, **Vol. 8, Part 2**, 133; Jenkins, **Vol. 5, Part 2**, 50; manufacturing of, **Vol. 5, Part 2**, 50
Valverde, battle of, **Vol. 2, Part 1**, 468, 531
Van Brunt, Henry, reference to, **Vol. 10, Part 1**, 452 f.
Van Buren, Martin: **Vol. 4, Part 2**, 189; **Vol. 5, Part 1**, 531; **Vol. 8, Part 1**, 30 f.; **Vol. 9, Part 2**, 511; anti-Texas letter of, **Vol. 8, Part 1**, 34 f; relations with Benjamin Franklin Butler, **Vol. 2, Part 1**, 356; relations with Silas Wright, **Vol. 10, Part 2**, 565
Vance, Harold S., reference to, **Supp. 9**, 397–98
Vancouver, Wash., founding of, **Vol. 6, Part 2**, 134
Vandalia scheme, **Vol. 5, Part 2**, 127; **Vol. 9, Part 2**, 638 f.; **Vol. 10, Part 2**, 32
Vandegrift, Margaret, reference to, **Vol. 5, Part 1**, 614
Vandenberg, Arthur H., references to, **Supp. 4**, 42; **Supp. 5**, 334, 505, 705; **Supp. 6**, 455; **Supp. 7**, 138; **Supp. 8**, 701; **Supp. 10**, 644, 645, 686
Vanden Heuvel, William, reference to, **Supp. 9**, 400
Vanderbilt, Commodore Cornelius: first philanthropy of, **Vol. 3, Part 1**, 192; references to, **Vol. 7, Part 1**, 234; **Vol. 10, Part 1**, 364; **Supp. 9**, 824, 825
Vanderbilt, Cornelius, III, reference to, **Supp. 5**, 707
Vanderbilt, Gloria, reference to, **Supp. 7**, 752–53
Vanderbilt, Reginald Claypoole, reference to, **Supp. 7**, 752
Vanderbilt, William H.: **Vol. 7, Part 1**, 176 f.; House of, work of Hunt, **Vol. 5, Part 1**, 390
Vanderbilt, William Kissam, reference to, **Supp. 1**, 68
Vanderbilt interests attacked, **Vol. 4, Part 2**, 393
Vanderbilt University: **Vol. 3, Part 1**, 192 f.; **Vol. 6, Part 2**, 170; **Vol. 8, Part 2**, 287; **Vol. 10, Part 1**, 173; **Vol. 10, Part 2**, 438; administration, **Supp. 8**, 72; biomedical research, **Supp. 9**, 786–87; history studies, **Supp. 6**, 491; medical school, **Supp. 6**, 546; presidency, **Supp. 2**, 361–62; secularization of, **Supp. 3**, 129
Van Devanter, Willis, references to, **Supp. 3**, 100; **Supp. 4**, 537; **Supp. 5**, 571; **Supp. 7**, 730
Van Dincklagen, Lubbert, relations with Everardus Bogardus, **Vol. 1, Part 2**, 406
Van Dine, S. S., reference to, **Supp. 9**, 488
Vandiver, Harry S., reference to, **Supp. 3**, 70
Van Doren, Carl: references to, **Supp. 7**, 306; **Supp. 8**, 667; quiz-show scandal, **Supp. 9**, 829
Van Doren, Irita, reference to, **Supp. 8**, 520
Van Doren, Margaret, reference to, **Supp. 9**, 829
Van Doren, Mark, reference to, **Supp. 9**, 86
Van Druten, John, reference to, **Supp. 6**, 610
Vanessa, opera, world premiere, **Supp. 6**, 457
Van Hise, Charles R., reference to, **Supp. 3**, 38, 265
Vanity Fair: **Vol. 2, Part 1**, 763; **Supp. 3**, 53, 547; Cunningham photographs, **Supp. 10**, 162; development of, **Supp. 4**, 199–200; drama criticism, **Supp. 8**, 491, 492
Van Maanen, Adriaan, reference to, **Supp. 8**, 587–88
Vann, Robert L., reference to, **Supp. 6**, 260
Van Peebles, reference to, **Supp. 10**, 95
Van Rensselaer, Stephen, reference to, **Vol. 3, Part 1**, 605
Van Rensselaers, as patrons, **Vol. 4, Part 2**, 370
Van Slyke, Donald D., reference to, **Supp. 3**, 351
Van Sweringen, O. P. and M. J., reference to, **Supp. 5**, 34–35
Van Vechten, Carl, reference to, **Supp. 5**, 659
Van Voorhis, Daniel, reference to, **Supp. 3**, 152
Vanzetti, Bartolomeo. *See* Sacco-Vanzetti case
Vardaman, James K., reference to, **Supp. 4**, 78
Vare, William S., references to, **Supp. 3**, 559, 622; **Supp. 5**, 204–5; **Supp. 6**, 509–10; **Supp. 7**, 305, 607
Varèse, Edgar, reference to, **Supp. 10**, 760
Vargas, Alberto, reference to, **Supp. 5**, 637
Varian, Russell H., reference to, **Supp. 4**, 358
Varieties of Religious Experience, The, **Vol. 5, Part 1**, 597
Variety, founding of, **Vol. 9, Part 1**, 167
Variety stores, **Supp. 8**, 347–49. *See also* Five and dime stores
Varnhagen, Rahel, reference to, **Supp. 9**, 40
Varuna, **Vol. 1, Part 2**, 409
Varnish, manufacturing of, **Vol. 7, Part 1**, 350
Vaschalde, Arthur Adolphe, reference to, **Supp. 3**, 375
Vascular surgery. *See* Blood vessels
Vasopressin, synthesis of, **Supp. 10**, 198
Vassar, John G., reference to **Vol. 9, Part 2**, 329
Vassar, Matthew, reference to, **Vol. 1, Part 1**, 13
Vassar College: **Vol. 1, Part 1**, 472; **Vol. 5, Part 2**, 208; **Vol. 7, Part 1**, 58, 250, 329; charter of, **Vol. 5, Part 2**, 70; early history of, **Vol. 7, Part 1**, 555; **Vol. 8, Part**

1, 412 f; experimental theater, **Supp. 8**, 175; psychology studies, **Supp. 2**, 698–99
Vassar Observatory, **Vol. 10, Part 2**, 164
Vatican: **Vol. 1, Part 2**, 359; diplomacy with U.S., **Supp. 6**, 623; **Supp. 8**, 613, 614; diplomatic service, **Supp. 8**, 294–95; first American to head Curia, **Supp. 6**, 608; Library, reorganization of, **Supp. 3**, 327; Sacra Rota, **Supp. 8**, 46; Second Council, **Supp. 7**, 534, 776; **Supp. 8**, 46, 115, 307, 537, 614–15. *See also* Catholic church
Vatican Council, Second, declaration on nonviolence and conscientious objection to war, **Supp. 10**, 176
Vaudeville: **Vol. 5, Part 25 289; Vol. 7, Part 2**, 290; **Vol. 8, Part 1**, 242 f.; **Vol. 8, Part 2**, 249; **Supp. 6**, 13, 112, 128, 368; **Supp. 8**, 64; black performers, **Supp. 4**, 695; blackface roles, **Supp. 7**, 106; child acts, **Supp. 8**, 314, 354–55, 363; comedy teams, **Supp. 4**, 400–401, 739; **Supp. 7**, 9; **Supp. 9**, 213–14, 282, 410; **Supp. 10**, 195; dance acts, **Supp. 10**, 19–20, 655; dance teams, **Supp. 7**, 657–58; first American group to tour England, **Supp. 9**, 213; Four Cohans, **Supp. 3**, 173; "Johnny's New Car" act, **Supp. 3**, 443; Keller-Sullivan routine, **Supp. 8**, 317; largest circuit, **Supp. 8**, 367; "Last of the Red Hot Mamas," **Supp. 8**, 661; magic acts, **Supp. 2**, 378, 661–62; **Supp. 7**, 57; management, **Supp. 2**, 32; master of ceremonies, **Supp. 7**, 237; miniature revues, **Supp. 8**, 695; most performed comedy act, **Supp. 9**, 213; risqué songs in, **Supp. 4**, 814–15; Shubert-Keith competition, **Supp. 5**, 627; sketches, **Supp. 9**, 451; slapstick routines, **Supp. 7**, 462; **Supp. 9**, 282; song-and-dance acts, **Supp. 10**, 300, 828–29; songwriting for, **Supp. 4**, 835–36; stand-up routines, **Supp. 9**, 489; theater circuits, **Supp. 1**, 18; **Supp. 9**, 886; **Supp. 10**, 53, 512, 514, 517, 704–5; touring acts, **Supp. 9**, 75, 213–14, 282, 535; Williams and Walker cakewalk, **Supp. 3**, 187; writings on, **Supp. 8**, 584–85
Vaughan, Harry H., references to, **Supp. 9**, 813, 814
Vaughan, Victor C., references to, **Supp. 3**, 121; **Supp. 6**, 481
Vaux, Calvert, relations with Frederick Law Olmsted, **Vol. 7, Part 2**, 25 f.
"Vaya con Dios" (song), **Supp. 10**, 252
Veblen, Thorstein, references to, **Supp. 3**, 177, 248; **Supp. 4**, 584–87; **Supp. 6**, 96, 271, 598, 653
Veda. *See* Sanskrit
Vedic Concordance, **Vol. 1, Part 2**, 387
Vee, Bobby, reference to, **Supp. 6**, 302
Veeck, Bill, references to, **Supp. 6**, 121; **Supp. 10**, 81
Vega (airplane), **Supp. 8**, 385
Vegetables: hybrid corn, **Supp. 5**, 629; hybridization, **Supp. 10**, 81; nutritional value, **Supp. 5**, 623
Vegetarianism, **Vol. 7, Part 1**, 495–96; **Supp. 3**, 409; **Supp. 5**, 378, 452; **Supp. 6**, 113
Velasco, Juan José, reference to, **Supp. 10**, 232
Velikovsky, Immanuel, reference to, **Supp. 10**, 47
Venereal disease: **Vol. 2, Part 1**, 260; **Vol. 4, Part 2**, 553; **Vol. 8, Part 1**, 588 f.; control of, **Supp. 5**, 604–5; inherited syphilis studies, **Supp. 8**, 429; prevention of, **Supp. 5**, 144; public education in, **Supp. 4**, 758–59; **Supp. 6**, 249; research on, **Supp. 4**, 288; treatment of, **Supp. 3**, 854; **Supp. 6**, 423–24, 460–61. *See also* Syphilis
Venereal Disease Control Act (1938), **Supp. 4**, 759
Venezuela: boundary dispute (1895), **Vol. 1, Part 2**, 71; **Vol. 2, Part 2**, 211; **Vol. 4, Part 2**, 335; **Vol. 5, Part 1**, 81; **Vol. 7, Part 2**, 33; **Vol. 8, Part 1**, 485; **Vol. 9, Part 2**, 100; oil development, **Supp. 8**, 455; relations with, **Vol. 1, Part 1**, 235; **Vol. 1, Part 2**, 392, 506; **Vol. 7, Part 2**, 283; **Vol. 8, Part 1**, 14 f.; **Vol. 8, Part 2**, 520; **Vol. 9, Part 2**, 608, 623
Ventilation, **Supp. 3**, 353; **Supp. 4**, 690; first systematic plan of, in any public building, **Vol. 8, Part 1**, 475
Ventriculography, **Supp. 4**, 214
Ventriloquism, **Supp. 10**, 32–33
Venturi, Lionello, reference to, **Supp. 6**, 552
Venus, observations of, **Vol. 3, Part 1**, 602 f.; **Vol. 6, Part 1**, 516; **Vol. 77, Part 1**, 454; **Vol. 8, Part 1**, 630; **Vol. 9, Part 2**, 18
Vera Cruz, Mexico, siege of (1847), **Vol. 6, Part 1**, 121; **Vol. 7, Part 2**, 306, 487, 604; **Vol. 8, Part 2**, 509; **Vol. 9, Part 1**, 331; **Vol. 9, Part 2**, 599; **Vol. 10, Part 1**, 83; **Vol. 10, Part 2**, 537
Verklrte Nacht (musical composition), **Supp. 5**, 608
Verlag Ullstein, reference to, **Supp. 6**, 39
Vermont: admission to Union, **Vol. 1, Part 2**, 575; **Vol. 2, Part 1**, 222; **Vol. 2, Part 2**, 80; **Vol. 9, Part 2**, 523; "Apostle of Vermont," **Vol. 7, Part 1**, 614; Articles of Confederation, **Vol. 8, Part 2**, 49; boundary disputes, **Vol. 5, Part 2**, 608; farming, early, **Vol. 7, Part 2**, 148; first Episcopal bishop in, **Vol. 5, Part 1**, 212; Fish Commission, **Vol. 9, Part 2**, 565; flora of, **Vol. 1, Part 2**, 593; geology of, **Vol. 5, Part 1**, 71; **Vol. 7, Part 2**, 471; governors, **Vol. 2, Part 1**, 360 f.; **Vol. 2, Part 2**, 78 f., 80 f.; **Vol. 3, Part 2**, 249; **Vol. 4, Part 1**, 59; **Vol. 4, Part 2**, 131 f.; **Vol. 5, Part 1**, 128 f.; **Vol. 6, Part 2**, 10 f., 423 f.; **Vol. 7, Part 2**, 146; **Vol. 8, Part 1**, 245 f.; **Vol. 9, Part 1**, 302 f.; Great Britain and, **Vol. 1, Part 1**, 194 f.; history of, **Vol. 2, Part 1**, 360; **Vol. 3, Part 2**, 305; **Vol. 4, Part 2**, 132, 391; **Vol. 6, Part 1**, 532; **Vol. 9, Part 1**, 204; land controversies, **Vol. 3, Part 1**, 465 f.; **Vol. 10, Part 1**, 653 f.; legal service, **Vol. 1, Part 2**, 575, 576; **Vol. 2, Part 2**, 73; **Vol. 3, Part 1**, 310; **Vol. 4, Part 2**, 379; **Vol. 6, Part 2**, 424, 528; **Vol. 8, Part 1**, 14, 190, 439; **Vol. 8, Part 2**, 49, 132; **Vol. 10, Part 1**, 97; natural history of, **Vol. 9, Part 1**, 480; name, origin of the, **Vol. 10, Part 2**, 635; pioneer founding of republic, **Vol. 8, Part 2**, 49; political service, **Vol. 1, Part 2**, 575, 576, 594; **Vol. 2, Part 2**, 78; **Vol. 3, Part 1**, 310, 600; **Vol. 3, Part 2**, 249; **Vol. 4, Part 1**, 59; **Vol. 4, Part 2**, 131; **Vol. 5, Part 1**, 129; **Vol. 6, Part 2**, 11, 222, 424; **Vol. 7, Part 2**, 146, 148, 193, 209, 528; **Vol. 8, Part 1**, 14, 33, 190, 245, 620; **Vol. 9, Part 1**, 203, 303; **Vol. 9, Part 2**, 523; politics, **Supp. 7**, 23; **Supp. 8**, 177–78; printing, early, **Vol. 4, Part 2**, 390; public service, **Vol. 3, Part 2**, 498; **Vol. 4, Part 2**, 378; **Vol. 7, Part 1**, 198, 216, 523; **Vol. 7, Part 2**, 209, 471; **Vol. 8, Part 1**, 245 f.; **Vol. 9, Part 1**, 283; railroad building in, **Vol. 9, Part 1**, 302; road building in, **Vol. 4, Part 1**, 59; tuberculosis, fight against, **Vol. 8, Part 1**, 245 f.; writings on, **Vol. 1, Part 1**, 188, 195, 526; **Vol. 4, Part 1**, 478; **Vol. 8, Part 2**, 50, 183; **Vol. 9, Part 2**, 480
Vermont and Canada Railroad Line, **Vol. 1, Part 2**, 594
Vermont Bar Association, first president of, **Vol. 7, Part 2**, 528
Vermont Botanical Society, **Vol. 1, Part 2**, 593
Vermont Central Railroad Co., completion of, **Vol. 7, Part 2**, 147
Vermont Chronicle, **Vol. 9, Part 2**, 623
Vermont Colonization Society, **Vol. 7, Part 2**, 148
Vermont Historical Society, **Vol. 3, Part 2**, 494; **Vol. 9, Part 2**, 454
Vermont Marble Co., organization of, **Vol. 8, Part 1**, 245 f.
Verne, Jules: reference to, **Supp. 3**, 436; translations of, **Vol. 9, Part 2**, 609
Verrazano-Narrows Bridge (New York City), **Supp. 7**, 12
Versailles Treaty: **Vol. 6, Part 1**, 563; **Vol. 10, Part 2**, 365; **Supp. 3**, 396–97, 559, 622; **Supp. 7**, 302–3; **Supp. 7**, 359, 800; **Supp. 8**, 61, 146, 549; public

relations effort for, **Supp. 4**, 47; self-determination policy, **Supp. 4**, 858; Senate opposition to, **Supp. 9**, 504; writings on, **Supp. 5**, 79
Verse. *See* Poetry
Verse writing, **Vol. 5, Part 1**, 175; **Vol. 5, Part 2**, 553; **Vol. 9, Part 2**, 585. *See also* Poetry
Vertebrates, Manual of, **Vol. 5, Part 2**, 211
"Vestibule," patent of, **Vol. 8, Part 2**, 594
Vestris, Madame, reference to, **Vol. 5, Part 2**, 284
Vetch, Samuel, reference to, **Vol. 7, Part 1**, 501
Veterans: bonus army (1932), **Supp. 5**, 502; **Supp. 6**, 239–40; **Supp. 7**, 363, 377, 488; **Supp. 8**, 497; **Supp. 10**, 619; legislation, **Supp. 3**, 661; **Supp. 6**, 526, 551; **Supp. 8**, 24; organizations, **Supp. 3**, 668; **Supp. 5**, 177; **Supp. 8**, 410
Veterans Administration, United States: chief medical director, **Supp. 7**, 328; efficiency moves, **Supp. 6**, 293
Veterinary medicine: **Vol. 8, Part 2**, 311; disease carrier studies, **Supp. 5**, 382–83; livestock, **Supp. 3**, 737–38; teaching of, **Supp. 1**, 70; tuberculin test of cattle, **Vol. 7, Part 2**, 359
Veterinary school, University of Pennsylvania, **Vol. 7, Part 2**, 360
Veto, "pocket," **Vol. 8, Part 2**, 347
Vice-presidency (U.S.): **Vol. 1, Part 1**, 77; **Vol. 2, Part 2**, 297 f.; **Vol. 3, Part 2**, 248; **Vol. 4, Part 1**, 227; **Vol. 4, Part 2**, 196; **Vol. 5, Part 1**, 92; **Vol. 5, Part 2**, 26, 84, 114 f., 246, 406; **Vol. 7, Part l**, 258 f.; **Vol. 9, Part 1**, 629; **Vol. 9, Part 2**, 584; **Vol. 10, Part 1**, 154; first, **Vol. 1, Part 1**, 77; Rockefeller appointment to, **Supp. 10**, 688; "Veep," term coined, **Supp. 6**, 36
Vichyssoise (soup), invention of, **Supp. 6**, 165
Vicksburg, Miss.: founded, **Vol. 5, Part 2**, 579; siege of (1863), **Vol. 3, Part 1**, 50; **Vol. 4, Part 1**, 495; **Vol. 5, Part 1**, 425; **Vol. 5, Part 2**, 145; **Vol. 6, Part 1**, 364, 588; **Vol. 6, Part 2**, 160; **Vol. 7, Part 2**, 212, 415; **Vol. 8, Part 1**, 380; **Vol. 9, Part 1**, 95, 631
Victor Talking Machine Co.: **Supp. 3**, 392; **Supp. 6**, 358; popular recordings, **Supp. 4**, 389
Victory Loan, **Supp. 4**, 331
Victory Through Air Power, **Supp. 9**, 229
Victrola. *See* Recordings
Vicuña coat scandal, **Supp. 8**, 219–20
Vidal, Gore, references to, **Supp. 10**, 16, 17
Vidor, King, references to, **Supp. 10**, 807, 808
Vienna Circle (logical positivists), **Supp. 5**, 562–63; **Supp. 8**, 74
Vietnam: experts on, **Supp. 8**, 167; medical relief work in, **Supp. 7**, 190–91; U.S. military advisers in, **Supp. 7**, 422
Vietnam War: air operations, **Supp. 10**, 378; antiwar movement, **Supp. 8**, 323–24, 334–35; **Supp. 9**, 36–37; 42, 384, 436, 459; **Supp. 10**, 469, 470; antiwar movement, congressional investigations of, **Supp. 8**, 507; antiwar movement, first broad-based coalition, **Supp. 8**, 458; antiwar movement, negotiated settlement advocacy, **Supp. 8**, 26; draft protest controversy, **Supp. 10**, 332; journalistic support of, **Supp. 8**, 626; Paris peace talks, **Supp. 9**, 5; **Supp. 10**, 74; peace efforts, **Supp. 7**, 724; **Supp. 10**, 204; Pentagon Papers, **Supp. 9**, 88, 97, 278; **Supp. 10**, 324; photojournalism, **Supp. 7**, 116; political opposition to, **Supp. 8**, 324; **Supp. 10**, 109, 551; political support for, **Supp. 9**, 573–74; Senate opposition to, **Supp. 9**, 346–47; Seventh Air Force Command, **Supp. 10**, 72; Tet offensive, **Supp. 9**, 436, 574; Tonkin Gulf Resolution opposed, **Supp. 9**, 347, 566; Tonkin Gulf Resolution supported, **Supp. 9**, 388, 434–35; U.S. combat soldiers, **Supp. 9**, 27; U.S. policy, **Supp. 9**, 4–5, 10, 434, 435, 436, 437; U.S. policy, critical writings on, **Supp. 8**, 167, 260
Vigilantes: **Vol. 2, Part 1**, 62; **Vol. 3, Part 2**, 117; **Vol. 4, Part 2**, 65, 403; **Vol. 5, Part 1**, 282; **Vol. 5, Part 2**, 408, 592; **Vol. 8, Part 1**, 15 f.; **Vol. 8, Part 2**, 337; **Vol. 9, Part 2**, 379; founding of, **Supp. 4**, 841–42
Vignaux, Maurice, reference to, **Supp. 6**, 303–4
Viking Press, Inc.: editing, **Supp. 7**, 149, 374; founding of, **Supp. 7**, 306
Villa, Pancho, references to, **Supp. 3**, 606; **Supp. 4**, 656
Village Press, founding of, **Supp. 4**, 342
Villanova College, founding of, **Vol. 7, Part 1**, 190
Villard, Henry, reference to, **Vol. 8, Part 2**, 469
Villard, Oswald Garrison, reference to, **Supp. 4**, 804
Villard's Portland Hotel, **Vol. 5, Part 2**, 528
Vilna Troupe, **Supp. 6**, 566
Vincennes: capture of, **Vol. 2, Part 2**, 128; **Vol. 4, Part 2**, 557; **Vol. 6, Part 2**, 363; **Vol. 10, Part 1**, 270; council with Tecumseh at, **Vol. 4, Part 1**, 254; and Father Gibault, **Vol. 4, Part 1**, 235; settlement of, **Vol. 3, Part 2**, 446
Vincennes, first American man-of-war to circumnavigate the globe, **Vol. 8, Part 2**, 196
Vincennes University, **Vol. 7, Part 2**, 210
Vincent, Beverly M., reference to, **Supp. 6**, 614
Vincent, George E., reference to, **Supp. 3**, 64
Vincent, John Carter, reference to, **Supp. 6**, 60
Vincent, John H., reference to, **Vol. 5, Part 1**, 425
Vincentians, **Vol. 7, Part 1**, 323; **Vol. 8, Part 2**, 264
Vindicators Association, founding of, **Supp. 7**, 644
Vine, Allyn C., reference to, **Supp. 9**, 271
Vineland Training School (N.J.), **Supp. 3**, 389; **Supp. 4**, 438; **Supp. 7**, 284
Vineyard Association, **Vol. 3, Part 1**, 491 f.
Vineyards, California, **Vol. 3, Part 1**, 491; **Vol. 4, Part 2**, 236
Vingo, Carmine, reference to, **Supp. 8**, 417
Vinson, Frederick M., references to, **Supp. 7**, 541, 542 **Supp. 10**, 126
"Viol" (violoncello), introduction into church services, **Vol. 1, Part 2**, 270
Violets, study of, **Vol. 1, Part 2**, 593
Violin: "Gasparo da Salo," repaired, **Vol. 4, Part 1**, 207; making of, **Vol. 4, Part 1**, 207; **Vol. 4, Part 2**, 196; **Vol. 5, Part 2**, 295; playing, **Vol. 2, Part 1**, 57; **Vol. 4, Part 1**, 269; **Vol. 5, Part 1**, 47; **Vol. 5, Part 2**, 460; **Vol. 7, Part 1**, 80, 371 f.; **Vol. 8, Part 1**, 149 f.; **Vol. 8, Part 2**, 374, 423, 461; **Vol. 9, Part 1**, 457; **Vol. 9, Part 2**, 566; writings on, **Vol. 4, Part 1**, 207; **Vol. 5, Part 2**, 461
Vionnet, Madeleine, reference to, **Supp. 6**, 101
Virginia: adventure in early, **Vol. 1, Part 1**, 345; agents abroad, **Vol. 6, Part 2**, 470; **Vol. 8, Part 2**, 345; agricultural experiments of Ruffin, **Vol. 8, Part 2**, 215; Anti-Saloon League, **Supp. 3**, 132; Army reorganization in, **Vol. 4, Part 2**, 375; Assembly's charter rights, renewal of, **Vol. 8, Part 2**, 345; Baptist church, **Vol. 4, Part 2**, 395; **Vol. 6, Part 1**, 160 f.; **Vol. 8, Part 2**, 273; **Vol. 9, Part 2**, 331; border warfare, **Vol. 6, Part 1**, 206; Catholic settlement in, **Vol. 8, Part 1**, 123 f.; Cavalier party, **Vol. 7, Part 2**, 417; Code, revision of the, **Vol. 7, Part 2**, 4317; **Vol. 9, Part 2**, 120; colonial government, **Vol. 1, Part 2**, 233; **Vol. 3, Part 1**, 222, 316 f.; **Vol. 4, Part 2**, 537; **Vol. 5, Part 1**, 154; **Vol. 7, Part 1**, 485; **Vol. 9, Part 2**, 120 f.; colonization of, **Vol. 3, Part 1**, 34; **Vol. 4, Part 1**, 190; **Vol. 8, Part 2**, 117; **Vol. 10, Part 2**, 9, 80, 110, 388, 574; colony, manufacturing in, **Vol. 8, Part 2**, 345; colony, writings in support of, **Vol. 3, Part 1**, 222; Constitutional Convention, **Vol. 1, Part 1**, 595; **Vol. 1, Part 2**, 338, 473; **Vol. 4, Part 1**, 427; **Vol. 8, Part 1**, 353 f.; Democratic party, **Supp. 9**, 650; disestablishment of church, **Vol. 6, Part 1**, 160; Dutch,

war with (1665), **Vol. 1, Part 2**, 218; education, **Vol. 1, Part 1**, 591; **Vol. 5, Part 1**, 475; **Vol. 5, Part 2**, 32; **Vol. 8, Part 1**, 272, 369; **Vol. 8, Part 2**, 218; **Vol. 9, Part 1**, 242, 298, 369; electric business, beginnings of, in, **Vol. 10, Part 2**, 429; Episcopal church, **Vol. 5, Part 2**, 75; **Vol. 6, Part 2**, 183, 480; **Vol. 10, Part 2**, 316; Fairfax property, **Vol. 3, Part 2**, 256; Federalists, **Vol. 4, Part 1**, 158; **Vol. 4, Part 2**, 557 f.; **Vol. 6, Part 1**, 117; **Vol. 6, Part 2**, 318; finances, **Vol. 5, Part 2**, 91; **Vol. 8, Part 1**, 361 f.; **Vol. 8, Part 2**, 46; first iron smelted in America, **Vol. 1, Part 2**, 217; flora of, **Vol. 2, Part 2**, 184; frontier warfare, **Vol. 3, Part 1**, 317; **Vol. 6, Part 2**, 328; fur trade, **Vol. 2, Part 1**, 383; geology, **Vol. 8, Part 2**, 115; glebelands, **Vol. 6, Part 1**, 160; governors, **Vol. 2, Part 1**, 390, 439 f.; **Vol. 3, Part 1**, 221 f.; **Vol. 3, Part 2**, 301, 481, 482; **Vol. 4, Part 2**, 330; **Vol. 5, Part 2**, 322; **Vol. 6, Part 1**, 192; **Vol. 6, Part 2**, 30 f., 405 f.; **Vol. 7, Part 1, 424, 486 f., 633; Vol. 7, Part 2**, 137, 462; **Vol. 8, Part 1**, 6, 370; **Vol. 8, Part 2**, 30 f.; **Vol. 9, Part 1**, 361; **Vol. 9, Part 2**, 355–57; **Vol. 10, Part 1**, 87, 344; **Vol. 10, Part 2**, 9 f., 110 f., 423–55; **Supp. 1**, 380; **Supp. 2**, 467, 641; **Supp. 8**, 67–68; Harvey, Gov., deposition of, **Vol. 8, Part 1**, 123 f.; historical studies, **Supp. 2**, 152; historical writings on, **Supp. 1**, 129, 310, 691; **Supp. 6**, 94, 95; **Supp. 8**, 692, 693; history of, **Vol. 1, Part 1**, 493, 642; **Vol. 1, Part 2**, 233, 335, 354, 609; **Vol. 2, Part 1**, 383, 389, 390, 451, 541, 554; **Vol. 2, Part 2**, 114, 590 f.; **Vol. 3, Part 1**, 22, 519; **Vol. 4, Part 1**, 628; **Vol. 4, Part 2**, 556, 561; **Vol. 5, Part 1**, 403; **Vol. 5, Part 2**, 21, 175, 581; **Vol. 6, Part 1**, 558; **Vol. 6, Part 2**, 360, 362, 405, 481; **Vol. 7, Part 2**, 417; **Vol. 8, Part 1**, 6, 18, 110, 123, 206, 255, 353, 361, 367, 371 f., 628, 642; **Vol. 9, Part 1**, 208; **Vol. 9, Part 2**, 35, 121; **Vol. 10, Part 1**, 88; **Vol. 10, Part 2**, 454; House of Burgesses dissolved, **Vol. 3, Part 1**, 519 f.; Indian affairs, **Vol. 4, Part 2**, 375; **Vol. 8, Part 1**, 18 f.; **Vol. 8, Part 2**, 118, 293; **Vol. 9, Part 1**, 468; **Vol. 9, Part 2**, 121; journalism, **Supp. 3**, 115–16; journalism and historical research, **Vol. 9, Part 1**, 410; jurisprudence, **Vol. 5, Part 2**, 291; Lafayette in, **Vol. 7, Part 1**, 60; landholding, **Vol. 3, Part 1**, 316; **Vol. 6, Part 2**, 314, 464; **Vol. 7, Part 2**, 139; **Vol. 10, Part 1**, 360 f.; law, **Vol. 4, Part 1**, 560; **Vol. 5, Part 2**, 94; **Vol. 7, Part 1**, 28; Lee's love for, **Vol. 6, Part 1**, 122 f.; legal procedure, **Vol. 4, Part 2**, 537; legal service, **Vol. 1, Part 1**, 594; **Vol. 1, Part 2**, 318, 338; **Vol. 2, Part 2**, 582; **Vol. 3, Part 1**, 80, 343; **Vol. 4, Part 1**, 560; **Vol. 4, Part 2**, 430; **Vol. 5, Part l**, 101, 152, 369, 536; **Vol. 6, Part 2**, 376; **Vol. 7, Part 1**, 84; **Vol. 7, Part 2**, 236; **Vol. 8, Part 1**, 353, 361, 367, 371, 642; **Vol. 8, Part 2**, 29, 39; **Vol. 9, Part 1**, 528; **Vol. 9, Part 2**, 354–56; **Vol. 10, Part 1**, 32, 35, 38, 114, 127, 509; **Vol. 10, Part 2**, 82, 85, 420, 588; "legal triumvirate," **Vol. 5, Part 2**, 94; legislation, **Vol. 4, Part 1**, 619; London Co., **Vol. 1, Part 2**, 412; **Vol. 3, Part 1**, 34; Lutheran Synod, **Vol. 5, Part 2**, 154; manufacturers, **Vol. 8, Part 2**, 345; maps of, **Vol. 4, Part 1**, 48; **Vol. 8, Part 1**, 235 f.; **Vol. 10, Part 2**, 465; medical service, **Vol. 6, Part 2**, 60; **Vol. 8, Part 1**, 123; Methodist church, **Vol. 6, Part 1**, 115; **Supp. 3**, 132; militia, **Vol. 9, Part 1**, 54 f.; **Vol. 9, Part 2**, 35; missions in, **Vol. 8, Part 1**, 542; Moore, Andrew, services of, **Vol. 7, Part 1**, 113; natural history of, **Vol. 1, Part 1**, 575; newspapers, **Vol. 8, Part 1**, 7 f.; novels set in, **Vol. 2, Part 1**, 551; political development, source material of, **Vol. 8, Part 1**, 361 f.; political service, **Vol. 1, Part 1**, 301, 346, 591; **Vol. 1, Part 2**, 78, 89, 217, 335–37, 354, 402, 467, 468 472, 609; **Vol. 2, Part 2**, 114, 231; **Vol. 3, Part 1**, 68, 153, 222, 519, 598; **Vol. 3, Part 2**, 301, 481; **Vol. 4, Part l**, 190, 308, 374; **Vol. 5, Part 2**, 19 f., 322; **Vol. 6, Part 1**, 98, 104, 108, 192, 217; **Vol. 6, Part 2**, 30, 186, 364, 539; **Vol. 7, Part 1**, 424, 486, 633; **Vol. 7 Part 2**, 158, 417, 422, 462, 585; **Vol. 8, Part 1**, 6, 110, 123, 206, 255, 353, 358, 361, 363, 370, 636, 642; **Vol. 9, Part 1**, 361, 631; **Vol. 9, Part 2**, 355; **Vol. 10, Part 1**, 28, 32, 35, 87, 89, 127, 360 f., 508 f., 509; **Vol. 10, Part 2**, 236, 420, 424, 429, 605; political writings, **Vol. 9, Part 2**, 484; politics, **Vol. 2, Part 1, 389; Vol. 6, Part 2**, 347, 363, 376; **Vol. 7, Part 1**, 424; **Supp. 3**, 715; **Supp. 4**, 331; **Supp. 9**, 67–68, 650, 663, 664; politics in Civil War, **Vol. 8, Part 2**, 26; **Vol. 10, Part 2**, 424 429; politics in Revolutionary War, **Vol. 2, Part 1**, 522; **Vol. 6, Part 2**, 184; **Vol. 9, Part 1**, 321; **Vol. 10, Part 2**, 490, 587; Presbyterian church, **Vol. 8, Part 1**, 542; primogeniture, abolition of, **Vol. 5, Part 2**, 20; printing office in, first, **Vol. 7, Part 1**, 596; **Vol. 7, Part 2**, 250; progressive group, **Vol. 5, Part 2**, 20; Protestant Episcopal bishopric, **Supp. 6**, 649; public health, **Supp. 5**, 232; public improvements, **Vol. 2, Part 2**, 253 f.; public service, **Vol. 1, Part 1**, 576, 590; **Vol. 4, Part 2**, 330, 375; **Vol. 5, Part 1**, 357, 403 f., 422, 550; **Vol. 6, Part 1**, 108, 116, 117, 132, 134, 142, 152; **Vol. 6, Part 2**, 370, 375; **Vol. 7, Part 1**, 326, 416, 483, 484; **Vol. 7, Part 2**, 317; **Vol. 8, Part 2**, 26, 31, 218; **Vol. 9, Part 1**, 296, 373, 468; **Vol. 9, Part 2**, 320, 332, 355; racial integration advocacy, **Supp. 9**, 650–51; Reconstruction, **Vol. 2, Part 1**, 439; **Vol. 6, Part 2**, 382; religious freedom, **Vol. 5, Part 2**, 20, 154; **Vol. 10, Part 1**, 36; Republican party, **Supp. 9**, 650; Republican party after the Civil War, **Vol. 6, Part 1**, 217; **Vol. 6, Part 2**, 212; Roanoke settlement, **Vol. 3, Part 1**, 73 f.; secession of, **Vol. 1, Part 2**, 462, 473; **Vol. 6, Part 1**, 217; **Vol. 8, Part 1**, 206 f., 637; **Vol. 8, Part 2**, 30 f.; separation of Kentucky from, **Vol. 10, Part 2**, 223; separation of West Virginia from, **Vol. 3, Part 1**, 343; **Vol. 6, Part 1**, 239; **Vol. 10, Part 2**, 246; service of Monroe, **Vol. 7, Part 1**, 87 f.; settlements of John Rolfe, **Vol. 8, Part 2**, 118; slavery, **Vol. 2, Part 1**, 383; **Vol. 4, Part 1**, 308; **Vol. 10, Part 1**, 70; social history, **Supp. 3**, 303; **Supp. 8**, 692, 693; social services, **Vol. 8, Part 1**, 6 f.; Supreme Court of Appeals, **Vol. 6, Part 1**, 152 f.; taxation, disputes about, **Vol. 3, Part 1**, 316; topographic surveys, **Vol. 6, Part 2**, 464; **Vol. 8, Part 2**, 48; **Vol. 9, Part 1**, 254; trade in, early, **Vol. 2, Part 1**, 383; "Two Penny Act," **Vol. 2, Part 1**, 440; "Underwood Constitution" of, **Vol. 10, Part 1**, 114; voting rights, **Supp. 4**, 331

Virginia, **Vol. 7, Part 1**, 502; **Vol. 8, Part 1**, 97

Virginia Agricultural College, **Vol. 6, Part 1**, 555

Virginia and Kentucky Resolutions (1798), **Vol. 1, Part 1**, 36; **Vol. 2, Part 1**, 6; **Vol. 3, Part 1**, 98; **Vol. 5, Part 2**, 27, 148; **Vol. 6, Part 2**, 188, 320

Virginia Bible Society, **Vol. 8, Part 1**, 542

Virginia Bureau of Vocations for Women, **Supp. 4**, 364–65

Virginia City, Nev., mining in, **Vol. 6, Part 2**, 42; **Vol. 9, Part 2**, 146

Virginia Colony, London Co. and, **Vol. 3, Part 1**, 34; **Vol. 8, Part 2**, 46

Virginia Co., **Vol. 7, Part 1**, 468; **Vol. 8, Part 1**, 235 f.; **Vol. 9, Part 1**, 295

Virginia Evangelical and Literary Magazine, **Vol. 8, Part 1**, 542

Virginia Kirkus Bookshop Service, **Supp. 10**, 418

Virginia Literary Fund, established, **Vol. 10, Part 1**, 88

Virginia Medical and Surgical Journal, **Vol. 7, Part 2**, 97

Virginia Medical Journal, **Vol. 6, Part 1**, 575

Virginia Military Institute, **Vol. 2, Part 2**, 581; **Vol. 9, Part 1**, 115, 264; superintendents, **Supp. 3**, 453

Virginian, The, **Supp. 2**, 729–30

Virginia Normal and Collegiate Institute (Petersburg), **Vol. 5, Part 2**, 598
Virginia Plan. *See* Constitutional Convention
Virginia Polytechnic Institute, **Vol. 6, Part 1**, 370
Virginia Quarterly Review, founding of, **Supp. 7**, 797
Virginia State Bar Association, **Vol. 1, Part 2**, 319
Virginia State Federation of Colored Women's Clubs, founding of, **Supp. 4**, 53–54
Virginia Theological Seminary, **Vol. 7, Part 1**, 137; **Vol. 7, Part 2**, 130
Virginius affair (1873), **Vol. 2, Part 2**, 628; **Vol. 3, Part 1**, 269; **Vol. 3, Part 2**, 399; **Vol. 9, Part 1**, 151
Virgo A (galaxy), **Supp. 6**, 31
Virology, **Supp. 7**, 648–49
Virus: cancer, **Supp. 4**, 615–16; **Supp. 8**, 556; chemical structure studies, **Supp. 4**, 381; **Supp. 10**, 753–54; early studies of, **Supp. 6**, 482; immunology studies, **Supp. 3**, 441; infection's pathological effects, **Supp. 7**, 648; measles, **Supp. 3**, 774; **Supp. 5**, 63–64; poliomyelitis, **Supp. 4**, 287–88; **Supp. 5**, 604; research on, **Supp. 5**, 382–83; RNA discovered in, **Supp. 9**, 74; yellow fever, **Supp. 5**, 605
Visible speech, **Vol. 1, Part 2**, 149, 152
Vision: corneal transplants, **Supp. 7**, 70; night vision, **Supp. 4**, 357; photoreception studies, **Supp. 4**, 367; physiology, **Vol. 9, Part 2**, 647; psychophysics of, **Supp. 2**, 406. *See also* Blind and blindness; Ophthalmology
Visitation Order, **Vol. 7, Part 1**, 401; **Vol. 9, Part 2**, 376
Visiting Nurse Service, **Supp. 2**, 687–88
Vitagraph Studios: **Supp. 9**, 791; founding of, **Supp. 3**, 76; **Supp. 6**, 618–19, 667–68
Vital statistics: **Vol. 6, Part 1**, 59, 577 f.; **Vol. 6, Part 2**, 467; **Vol. 8, Part 2**, 183; **Vol. 10, Part 2**, 198; first registration of birth, deaths, etc., **Vol. 9, Part 1**, 33
Vitamin B-12: and anemia, **Supp. 4**, 581; isolation of, **Supp. 5**, 122
Vitamm D, rickets relationship, **Supp. 1**, 398; **Supp. 5**, 623
Vitamin E: discovery of, **Supp. 9**, 266; effect of deficiency, **Supp. 9**, 222
Vitamins: B complex, **Supp. 6**, 595; biochemical studies of, **Supp. 8**, 197–98; deficiency and cardiovascular disturbances, **Supp. 3**, 806; deficiency research, **Supp. 7**, 223; development of, **Supp. 6**, 447; nutritional role research, **Supp. 5**, 276; quantitative bioassay of, **Supp. 5**, 623; research in, **Supp. 1**, 560; riboflavin, **Supp. 6**, 595
Viticulture, **Vol. 1, Part 1**, 109; **Vol. 3, Part 1**, 491 f.; **Vol. 4, Part 2**, 494, **Vol. 5, Part 1**, 430; **Vol. 7, Part 1**, 335 f.; **Vol. 8, Part 1**, 233 f.
Vivisection, **Vol. 3, Part 1**, 40; **Vol. 7, Part 1**, 53
Vocation Bureau of Boston, **Supp. 2**, 45
Vocational education: **Vol. 5, Part 1**, 348; **Vol. 9, Part 1**, 388; Federal Board of, **Vol. 6, Part 1**, 178; **Vol. 8, Part 2**, 113. *See also* Vocational guidance and training
Vocational Education Act (1946), **Supp. 8**, 24
Vocational guidance and training, counseling: **Supp. 2**, 45, 398, 728; Massachusetts, **Supp. 3**, 328; McHale Test for College Women, **Supp. 6**, 412; pioneer work in, **Supp. 4**, 364–66; work-study program, **Supp. 3**, 63
Vocational Rehabilitation Act (1946), **Supp. 8**, 24
Voegtlin, Carl, reference to, **Supp. 3**, 483
Vogt, J. H. L., reference to, **Supp. 6**, 70
Vogue: **Supp. 3**, 547; **Supp. 6**, 107–8; editorship, **Supp. 9**, 684; first number, **Vol. 4, Part 1**, 293; illustration, **Supp. 7**, 66; *Vanity Fair* merger, **Supp. 4**, 200
Voice of America, **Supp. 8**, 640; **Supp. 10**, 849
Voice of Labor, **Vol. 8, Part 1**, 451
Voice of the Turtle, The, **Supp. 6**, 610, 652; **Supp. 10**, 803, 804
Volcanoes: Hawaii, **Vol. 5, Part 1**, 70; Lassen Peak eruption, **Supp. 1**, 247; study of, **Supp. 5**, 361–62, **Supp. 6**, 153, 213; study of, during eruptions, **Vol. 4, Part 2**, 502
Volstead Act (1919), **Vol. 4, Part 2**, 253; legality of, **Supp. 6**, 3; passage of, **Supp. 4**, 853
Volunteers of America, founding of, **Supp. 2**, 48
Volunteer work: organized, advocacy of, **Supp. 4**, 228; Red Cross-sponsored, **Supp. 4**, 93
V-1 and V-2 rockets, **Supp. 3**, 307–8; **Supp. 10**, 66
Von Euler, Ulf, reference to, **Supp. 3**, 136
Von Humboldt, Alexander, reference to, **Vol. 1, Part 1**, 466
Von Karman, Theodore, references to, **Supp. 8**, 439, 440
Von Meck, Barbara, reference to, **Supp. 9**, 112
Von Neumann, John, **Supp. 3**, 70–71
Von Neumann, Marina, reference to, **Supp. 6**, 656
Von Steuben, Baron, reference to, **Vol. 7, Part 1**, 563
Von Stroheim, Erich, reference to, **Supp. 7**, 563
Von Tilzer, Albert, reference to, **Supp. 4**, 836
Von Zedwitz, Waldemar, reference to, **Supp. 6**, 134, 135
Voorhees Resolution, vote on, **Vol. 8, Part 1**, 410
Voronoff, Serge, reference to, **Supp. 6**, 632
Voting: Australian ballot system, **Vol. 4, Part 1**, 215; first Indian, **Vol. 9, Part 1**, 228. *See also* Elections; Voting rights; Woman suffrage
Voting rights: armed forces' absentee ballots, **Supp. 8**, 223; blacks in South, **Supp. 4**, 331, 384–85; **Supp. 8**, 334, 335, 682; black voter registration drives, **Supp. 10**, 171; federal enforcement policies, **Supp. 8**, 322–23; poll tax, **Supp. 6**, 526; **Supp. 7**, 416; poll tax abolishment, **Supp. 7**, 416; poll tax support, **Supp. 6**, 526; primaries, **Supp. 5**, 575; Supreme Court decislons, **Supp. 7**, 264. *See also* Woman suffrage
Voting Rights Act (1965), **Supp. 8**, 334, 500; **Supp. 9**, 435; **Supp. 10**, 316, 362
Vox Humana, method of manufacture of, **Vol. 3, Part 1**, 221
Voyages, description of, during period 1790–1810, **Vol. 3, Part 1**, 217
Voyageurs, **Vol. 5, Part 1**, 326
VTOL (vertical takeoff and landing) aircraft, **Supp. 6**, 50
Vulcanism, early advocate of the possibilities of radioactivity in promoting, **Vol. 3, Part 1**, 555. *See also* Volcanoes
Vulval cancer, **Supp. 3**, 763

W

Wa-Wan Press, founding of, **Supp. 5**, 218
Wabash College, **Vol. 1, Part 1**, 532; **Vol. 3, Part 1**, 522
Waco University, **Vol. 2, Part 1**, 288
Waddell, John Alexander Low, reference to, **Supp. 3**, 331–2
Wade, James F., reference to, **Supp. 6**, 253
Wade-Davis bill (1864), **Vol. 5, Part 2**, 84
Wade-Davis Manifesto, **Vol. 3, Part 1**, 120; **Vol. 5, Part 2**, 113
Wadena (Minn.) *Pioneer Journal*, **Supp. 5**, 396
Wadsworth, James S., reference to, **Vol. 10, Part 1**, 421 f.
Wadsworth, James W., reference to, **Supp. 6**, 227
Wadsworth Atheneum (Hartford, Conn.), **Supp. 3**, 567
Wage and Hour Act (1941), constitutionality of, **Supp. 8**, 35

Wage Earner and His Problems, The, **Vol. 7, Part 1**, 52
Wages and hours: cost-of-living index, **Supp. 7**, 794; eight-hour day, **Supp. 1**, 269, 334; five-day week, **Supp. 4**, 455; five-dollar day, **Supp. 4**, 296–97, 304; forty-eight-hour week, **Supp. 4**, 432; government control measures, **Supp. 4**, 890; legislation, **Supp. 7**, 262; **Supp. 8**, 35; maximum-hours law for women, **Supp. 4**, 626; minimum-wage standards, **Supp. 3**, 655–56; **Supp. 4**, 900; portal-to-portal pay issue, **Supp. 5**, 358; profit sharing, **Supp. 1**, 370–71; Saturday half-day, **Supp. 1**, 610; straight-time pay plan, **Supp. 4**, 396; **Supp. 5**, 315; Supreme Court decisions, **Supp. 4**, 537; **Supp. 5**, 572, 574; women and children, **Supp. 2**, 408. *See also* Labor and labor movement
Wagner, Richard: authority on, **Vol. 5, Part 1**, 368; production, **Vol. 7, Part 1**, 549; promotion of, **Vol. 8, Part 2**, 562; references to, **Supp. 3**, 359; **Supp. 4**, 210–11; **Supp. 6**, 643; rise in popularity of, **Vol. 3, Part 1**, 48 f.
Wagner, Robert F., references to, **Supp. 3**, 717, 838; **Supp. 5**, 227; **Supp. 8**, 616
Wagner, Robert F., Jr., reference to, **Supp. 5**, 718; **Supp. 10**, 453, 697
Wagner Act. *See* National Labor Relations Act
Wagner Society, founding of, **Supp. 4**, 210–11
Wagner-Steagall National Housing Act (1937), **Supp. 3**, 656, 730, 838; **Supp. 5**, 631
Wagon, manufacture, **Vol. 3, Part 2**, 251; **Vol. 8, Part 2**, 471
Wagon Box fight, leader in, **Vol. 8, Part 1**, 437
Wagon train, **Vol. 1, Part 2**, 145; to California, **Vol. 8, Part 2**, 251
Wagon wheel, manufacture, **Vol. 8, Part 2**, 586
Wahoo Swamp, battle of, **Vol. 2, Part 1**, 423; **Vol. 5, Part 2**, 63; **Vol. 8, Part 2**, 507
Wainwright, Jonathan M., reference to, **Supp. 7**, 489
Waiting for Lefty, **Supp. 7**, 583
Wakarusa War (Kans.), **Vol. 3, Part 1**, 202
Wake Forest College (N.C.), endowment, **Supp. 5**, 567
Waksman, Selman, reference to, **Supp. 6**, 447
Walcott, Charles D., reference to, **Supp. 4**, 765–66
Walcott, "Jersey Joe," reference to, **Supp. 8**, 417; **Supp. 9**, 172
Wald, Lillian, references to, **Supp. 4**, 603; **Supp. 6**, 167, 664
Waldensians, **Vol. 5, Part 2**, 418
Waldie's Select Circulating Library, **Vol. 9, Part 1**, 303
Waldorf-Astoria Hotel (New York City), **Vol. 1, Part 1**, 400, 402; **Vol. 1, Part 2**, 418 f.; **Vol. 4, Part 2**, 241; **Supp. 10**, 337
Waldorf Hotel. *See* Waldorf-Astoria Hotel
Walgreen, Charles, reference to, **Supp. 9**, 80
Walgreen Co., development of, **Supp. 2**, 688
Walker, Alice, reference to, **Supp. 8**, 540
Walker, Edwin, reference to, **Supp. 8**, 57–58
Walker, Elisha, reference to, **Supp. 4**, 326
Walker, Frank C., reference to, **Supp. 5**, 638
Walker, James J. ("Jimmy"): Block relationship, **Supp. 3**, 80; investigation of, **Supp. 3**, 181, 646; **Supp. 6**, 88, 141, 142, 570; references to, **Supp. 4**, 465, 904; **Supp. 5**, 227; **Supp. 7**, 4
Walker, John Brisben, reference to, **Supp. 4**, 38
Walker, Ralph, reference to, **Supp. 5**, 721–22
Walker Act (1846) tariff, **Vol. 3, Part 1**, 39; **Vol. 6, Part 1**, 210; **Vol. 8, Part 1**, 34 f.; **Vol. 10, Part 1**, 585 f.
Walking, long-distance, **Vol. 10, Part 2**, 19; **Supp. 1**, 583
"Walking Purchase" (1737), **Vol. 7, Part 2**, 433
Walk in the Sun, A, **Supp. 9**, 189
Walks and Talks on the Farm, **Vol. 4, Part 2**, 315
Walküre, Die, first U.S. performance, **Vol. 7, Part 1**, 434
Walla Walla, Wash., political service, **Vol. 1, Part 2**, 349
Wallace, DeWitt, reference to, **Supp. 9**, 690
Wallace, George C., references to, **Supp. 7**, 425; **Supp. 8**, 676–77; **Supp. 9**, 436, 437; **Supp. 10**, 4, 362
Wallace, Henry A.: agricultural policy, **Supp. 3**, 594; **Supp. 6**, 459, 487, 638–39; **Supp. 8**, 699–700; China mission, World War II, **Supp. 9**, 830–31; Jones, J., relationship, **Supp. 6**, 325; presidential candidacy, **Supp. 8**, 511, 512; press relations, **Supp. 8**, 498; references to, **Supp. 4**, 356; **Supp. 7**, 661; **Supp. 9**, 458; vice-presidency, **Supp. 3**, 659, 664; **Supp. 6**, 260; vice-presidential candidacy, **Supp. 8**, 361
Wallace, Henry Cantwell, references to, **Supp. 3**, 134; **Supp. 6**, 638; **Supp. 7**, 759, 760
Wallace, Lew, reference to, **Vol. 3, Part 1**, 598; **Vol. 5, Part 1**, 241
Wallace, Mike, references to, **Supp. 8**, 387, 388
Wallace's Farmer, **Supp. 7**, 759
Wallach, Lester, reference to, **Vol. 7, Part 1**, 93
Waller, D. W., relations with Edwin Thomas Booth, **Vol. 1, Part 2**, 445
Waller, Fats, reference to, **Supp. 6**, 620; **Supp. 9**, 280
Wallgren, Mon, reference to, **Supp. 10**, 87
Walling, William English, reference to, **Supp. 3**, 576
Wallis, Hal B., reference to, **Supp. 7**, 239
Wall Street: **Vol. 4, Part 2**, 394; **Vol. 7, Part 1**, 143 f., 240, 258; **Vol. 8, Part 2**, 266 f., 292; **Vol. 10, Part 2**, 120; "Ryan Crowd," **Vol. 8, Part 2**, 266; Wilson, Woodrow, relations with, **Vol. 4, Part 2**, 372; writings on, **Vol. 8, Part 1**, 176 f. *See also* Banking; Finance
Wall Street Journal, audience widened, **Supp. 9**, 520
Walnut growing, **Vol. 9, Part 2**, 147
Walsh, Ernest, reference to, **Supp. 7**, 335
Walsh, Frank P., references to, **Supp. 3**, 532; **Supp. 4**, 543, 544; **Supp. 6**, 483, 484
Walsh, John Anthony, reference to, **Supp. 3**, 569
Walsh, Raoul, reference to, **Supp. 10**, 822
Walsh, Thomas J., reference to, **Supp. 3**, 259
Walt Disney Studios: animated feature films, **Supp. 10**, 351, 441; founding of, **Supp. 9**, 237–38; Mickey Mouse animation, **Supp. 10**, 244; strike (1941), **Supp. 9**, 237, 452;
Walt Disney World (Orlando, Fla.), founding of, **Supp. 8**, 131; **Supp. 9**, 238
Walter, Bruno, references to, **Supp. 6**, 324, 351; **Supp. 7**, 549
Walter Reed Hospital (Washington, D.C.), orthopedic section, **Supp. 6**, 344–45
Waltham, Mass.: cotton mills, first, **Vol. 6, Part 1**, 456 f.; watchmaking in, **Vol. 3, Part 1**, 239
Waltham (Mass.) Watch Co., **Supp. 5**, 190
Walther League, founding of, **Supp. 4**, 540–41
Walton, E. T. S., reference to, **Supp. 8**, 199
Walton, Isaak. *See Complete Angler*
"Waltons, The," **Supp. 10**, 273
Wanamaker, John, references to, **Vol. 4, Part 2**, 335; **Vol. 7, Part 1**, 641
Wanamaker Department Store (New York City), **Vol. 10, Part 1**, 408 f.; **Supp. 7**, 779
Waner, Lloyd, reference to, **Supp. 7**, 768
Wanger, Walter, reference to, **Supp. 9**, 377
War: Association to Abolish, **Vol. 3, Part 1**, 357; cabinet, **Vol. 3, Part 2**, 568; chemical warfare, **Vol. 10, Part 1**, 109 f.; commerce in, **Vol. 10, Part 1**, 130 f.; correspondence, **Vol. 1, Part 2**, 90; **Vol. 3, Part 2**, 570; **Vol. 5, Part 2**, 328, 331 f.; **Vol. 6, Part 1**, 610 f.; **Vol. 6, Part 2**, 45; **Vol. 7, Part 2**, 154; **Vol. 8, Part 1**, 451, 482; **Vol. 8, Part 2**, 511; **Vol. 9, Part 1**, 396; **Vol. 9, Part 2**, 253, 316; efforts against, **Vol. 7, Part 1**, 28; executive power during, **Vol. 10, Part 1**, 19 f.; paintings of scenes of, **Vol. 3, Part 2**, 504; **Vol. 9,**

Part 1, 371; Vol. 9, Part 2, 512 f.; Vol. 10, Part 2, 111, 651; prizes, Vol. 8, Part 2, 153; secretaryship, Vol. 5, Part 2, 563; Vol. 8, Part 1, 245 f., 403; Vol. 10, Part 1, 601 f.; telegraph used in, Vol. 5, Part 2, 482; writings, Vol. 3, Part 1, 345. *See also* Arms control and disarmament; Biological and chemical warfare; Peace, international; *names of specific wars*
War, Department of (U.S.): Vol. 3, Part 2, 194; Vol. 4, Part 2, 479; Vol. 8, Part 1, 30 f.; administration, Supp. 1, 336; Supp. 4, 785, 787–88; Supp. 5, 468–69, 538–39; Supp. 7, 377; Supp. 8, 706–7; aerial photography, Supp. 6, 435; aviation policies, Supp. 3, 218, 314; development of, under John C. Calhoun, Vol. 2, Part 1, 413; Embarkation Service, Supp. 6, 293; industrial mobilization plan, Supp. 7, 36; organization of the record and pension division of, Vol. 8, Part 1, 245 f.; record and pension division, Supp. 1, 17; reorganization, Supp. 2, 18; Supp. 5, 643; scientific projects, Supp. 7, 9
War and Peace (opera), Supp. 6, 550
"War and Washington" (ballad), Vol. 8, Part 2, 608
War Between the States. *See* Civil War, U.S.
War bonds. *See* Liberty Loans
"Warbucks, Daddy" (fictional character), Supp. 8, 221–22
Warburg, Felix M., reference to, Supp. 3, 279–80
Warburg, Otto, reference to, Supp. 6, 595
War Camp Community Service, founding of, Supp. 2, 375
War crimes: Eichmann Trial, Supp. 9, 42; Nuremberg trials, Supp. 5, 359; Supp. 6, 156, 496, 662; Supp. 8, 35, 135, 456
War Cry, Vol. 1, Part 2, 456
Ward, Aaron Montgomery, reference to, Supp. 6, 28
Ward, Artemus, Lincoln's reading of, Vol. 6, Part 1, 255
Ward, Lester Frank, Supp. 5, 591
Ward, Henry A., Vol. 6, Part 1, 484; relations with James Orton, Vol. 7, Part 2, 64 f.
Ward, James, reference to, Supp. 3, 149
Ward, Joshua, notorious quackery of, Vol. 9, Part 2, 369
Ward Line, Vol. 10, Part 1, 424 f.
Wardman, Ervin, reference to, Supp. 5, 284
Wardman, Harry, reference to, Supp. 9, 21–22
Ward's Natural History Establishment, Vol. 7, Part 2, 64; Vol. 10, Part 1, 421 f.
Ware, William R., reference to, Supp. 3, 195
Ware High School (Augusta, Ga.), founding of, Supp. 4, 915
Warfield, David, reference to, Supp. 4, 104
"War Hawks," use of term, Vol. 6, Part 1, 474; Vol. 8, Part 1, 99 f.
War Industries Board, Vol. 10, Part 2, 361. *See also under* World War I
War in Eastern Europe, The, Supp. 5, 580
War Labor Board (World War II). *See under* World War II
War Letters, Vol. 8, Part 2, 152
War Lords of Washington, The, Supp. 10, 107
War Manpower Commission. *See under* World War II
War Mobilization Board. *See under* World War II
Warm Springs Foundation, Supp. 6, 90
Warner, Albert, reference to, Supp. 6, 667–68
Warner, Glenn S. ("Pop"), reference to, Supp. 5, 683; Supp. 10, 584
Warner, Jack, reference to, Supp. 6, 667–68
Warner, Sam, reference to, Supp. 6, 667
Warner, Susan Bogert, reference to, Vol. 10, Part 1, 461
Warner & Brandeis, Supp. 3, 94
Warner Brothers: Supp. 5, 238; Supp. 7, 107, 591; Supp. 8, 187–88, 453, 456, 550; acquisitions, Supp. 10, 812, 813; distinctive "look" of films, Supp. 7, 177–78; founding of, Supp. 6, 667–68; Supp. 10, 812; musical extravaganzas, Supp. 10, 34; predecessor, Supp. 7, 32; productions, Supp. 9, 762, 856; Supp. 10, 812–13, 864; television productions, Supp. 10, 813; theater chain, Supp. 7, 692
War novels, Supp. 8, 136
War of 1812: Vol. 1, Part 1, 504 f.; Vol. 6, Part 1, 310; *Alert* captured, Vol. 8, Part 1, 85 f.; controversy in, Vol. 3, Part 2, 96–97; denunciation of, Vol. 10, Part 1, 585 f.; diplomatic background, Vol. 6, Part 2, 191 f.; fur traders with the British, Vol. 8, Part 2, 117; Indians in, Vol. 3, Part 1, 305; intrigue, Vol. 4, Part 2, 550; "Iron Grays," Vol. 9, Part 2, 238; Lake Champlain campaign, Vol. 6, Part 2, 156; Lake Erie, battle of, Vol. 2, Part 1, 609; Maryland's part in, Vol. 10, Part 2, 382; Massachusett's refusal to furnish troops, Vol. 9, Part 2, 145; military service, Vol. 1, Part 1, 346, 359; Vol. 1, Part 2, 8, 16, 65, 77, 105, 241, 314, 348, 427, 526, 567, 600; Vol. 2, Part 1, 125, 371, 562; Vol. 2, Part 2, 92, 108, 143, 253, 268, 271, 300, 328, 557; Vol. 3, Part 1, 9, 82, 89, 175, 255, 325, 349, 467, 473, 480, 510, 522, 538, 592, 609, 615; Vol. 3, Part 2, 149, 264, 385, 447; Vol. 4, Part 1, 92, 144, 427; Vol. 4, Part 2, 134, 187, 213, 216, 246, 349, 441; Vol. 5, Part 1, 218, 275, 344, 363, 365, 523; Vol. 5, Part 2, 54, 58, 62, 94, 103, 115, 147, 163, 166, 222, 394, 456; Vol. 6, Part 1, 3, 22, 49, 80, 109, 228, 241, 282, 308, 550; Vol. 6, Part 2, 510; Vol. 7, Part 1, 139, 633, 639; Vol. 7, Part 2, 70, 235, 236, 255, 275, 306, 461, 571, 627; Vol. 8, Part 1, 94, 99, 111, 143, 179, 180, 255, 381, 519, 608, 621, 625, 628, 629; Vol. 8, Part 2, 83, 112, 178, 215, 360, 505; Vol. 9, Part 1, 62, 373, 380; Vol. 9, Part 2, 51, 67, 79, 238, 474, 568, 569; Vol. 10, Part 1, 32, 89, 406, 565; Vol. 10, Part 2, 378, 382, 513; military supplies for, Vol. 5, Part 2, 110; Monroe, Vol. 7, Part 1, 89 f.; naval engagements, Vol. 2, Part 1, 337; Vol. 6, Part 1, 50; Vol. 8, Part 2, 77; naval service, Vol. 1, Part 1, 649 f.; Vol. 1, Part 2, 241, 534; Vol. 2, Part 1, 162, 308 f.; Vol. 2, Part 2, 60, 510; Vol. 3, Part 1, 188, 416; Vol. 3, Part 2, 291, 531; Vol. 4, Part 2, 539; Vol. 5, Part 1, 152, 400; Vol. 5, Part 2, 176, 201, 270; Vol. 6, Part 1, 204, 561–62; Vol. 6, Part 2, 20, 195; Vol. 7, Part 1, 97 f.; Vol. 7, Part 2, 484; Vol. 8, Part 1, 83 f., 424, 480, 596; Vol. 8, Part 2, 73, 75 f., 152, 153, 343; Vol. 9, Part 1, 41, 135, 136, 215, 309 f., 625; Vol. 9, Part 2, 7, 48, 139, 560 f.; Vol. 10, Part 1, 59 f., 492 f.; Vol. 10, Part 2, 518; first naval ship taken from the enemy in, Vol. 8, Part 1, 83 f.; New England's opposition to, Vol. 9, Part 2, 145; New Orleans, defense of, Vol. 8, Part 1, 480; opposition to, Vol. 3, Part 1, 569 f.; political background, Vol. 6, Part 2, 191 f.; political maneuverings before and during, Vol. 2, Part 1, 412; Portuguese claims resulting from, Vol. 8, Part 1, 480; privateering, Vol. 1, Part 2, 534; Vol. 3, Part 1, 275; Vol. 8, Part 1, 480; speech of Richard Rush, Vol. 8, Part 2, 232; surgery in, Vol. 6, Part 2, 243
"War of the News Giants," Vol. 7, Part 2, 545
War of the Rebellion, Vol. 6, Part 1, 370; Vol. 9, Part 2, 616
War of the Worlds, The, Supp. 9, 382
War Production Board (World War II). *See under* World War II
"Warranteeism," Vol. 5, Part 1, 350
Warren, Charles B., references to, Supp. 3, 559, 622
Warren, Dr. John Collins, reference to, Vol. 10, Part 1, 640 f.
Warren, Earl, references to, Supp. 7, 264, 425; Supp. 8, 340; Supp. 9, 231, 467, 594; Supp. 10, 126

Warren, Francis E., reference to, **Supp. 3**, 788
Warren, George F., reference to, **Supp. 3**, 433
Warren, Henry Clarke, reference to, **Supp. 3**, 445
Warren, John, reference to, **Vol. 10, Part 1**, 529 f.
Warren, Robert Penn: references to, **Supp. 9**, 86, 166; **Supp. 10**, 776
Warren, Samuel D., Jr., references to, **Supp. 3**, 94, 95
Warren Commission, report on Kennedy assassination, **Supp. 9**, 715, 716, 838
Warren Telechron Co., founding of, **Supp. 6**, 669
War Risk Insurance Bureau, organizing of, during World War I, **Vol. 9, Part 2**, 122
War service, bill for compensation for, **Vol. 10, Part l**, 105
Warship, first American to circumnavigate the globe, **Vol. 8, Part 2**, 196
War Shipping Administration (WSA). *See under* World War II
Washburn Crosby Co., **Supp. 7**, 46
Washburne, Carleton, reference to, **Supp. 7**, 42
Washing machines, **Supp. 2**, 441; **Supp. 3**, 56
Washington, Booker T.: biography of, **Supp. 6**, 600; references to, **Supp. 3**, 535, 577, 827–28; **Supp. 4**, 493, 851; **Supp. 5**, 490, 648, 680; **Supp. 6**, 567–68; **Supp. 7**, 202
Washington, George: **Vol. 1, Part 1**, 386; **Vol. 3, Part 2**, 322, 390; **Vol. 5, Part 1**, 222, 373 f., 500, 524, 560; **Vol. 5, Part 2**, 169, 599; **Vol. 6, Part 1**, 99 f., 101, 107, 132, 166 f., 214, 323, 497; **Vol. 7, Part 1**, 166 f., 210 f., 224, 358, 368, 411 f., 437, 484, 531, 632, 643; **Vol. 8, Part 2**, 223; **Vol. 9, Part 1**, 47, 602 f.; **Vol. 9, Part 2**, 46, 505, 545, 606; bibliography, **Supp. 8**, 664; bicentennial, **Supp. 2**, 192; **Supp. 4**, 88; biography of, **Supp. 6**, 310; as boarder in parsonage, **Vol. 4, Part 2**, 578; Centenary celebrated, **Vol. 9, Part 2**, 356; cherry-tree story first appears, **Vol. 10, Part 1**, 604 f.; coat buttons engraved, **Vol. 8, Part 2**, 122; dental work for, **Vol. 4, Part 1**, 592; engravings of, **Vol. 10, Part 1**, 13; eulogy on death of, **Vol. 9, Part 2**, 103; Frances, Samuel, and, **Vol. 4, Part 1**, 1; Gates and, **Vol. 4, Part 1**, 187; Hamilton and, **Vol. 4, Part 2**, 172 f.; interpreter for, **Vol. 4, Part 2**, 414; and Irving, **Vol. 5, Part 1**, 506; and Lafayette, **Vol. 5, Part 2**, 536; letters of, **Vol. 9, Part 1**, 476 f.; medical attendance at time of death of, **Vol. 3, Part 1**, 287; "Newburgh Letters," **Vol. 1, Part 1**, 355; **Vol. 2, Part 1**, 80; Ohio expedition, **Vol. 3, Part 1**, 317; portraits of, **Vol. 1, Part 1**, 603; **Vol. 7, Part 1**, 550; **Vol. 7, Part 2**, 346; **Vol. 8, Part 2**, 21, 122, 182, 386; **Vol. 10, Part 1**, 12; Rhode Island, visited, **Vol. 3, Part 2**, 322; and Rochambeau, **Vol. 8, Part 2**, 60 f.; sculpture of, **Supp. 3**, 89, 124; secretary to, **Vol. 4, Part 2**, 320; **Vol. 6, Part 1**, 76; **Vol. 7, Part 1**, 303; statue of, **Vol. 4, Part 1**, 587; writings of, **Supp. 2**, 191–92; **Supp. 3**, 285; writings on, **Vol. 1, Part 1**, 561; **Vol. 6, Part 1**, 347; **Vol. 8, Part 2**, 464, 609; **Vol. 9, Part 1**, 432; **Vol. 9, Part 2**, 295, 586; **Supp. 5**, 234
Washington, Henry S., reference to, **Supp. 4**, 194
Washington, Kenny, reference to, **Supp. 9**, 646
Washington, D.C.: aqueduct across Potomac, **Vol. 10, Part 1**, 57; architecture of, **Vol. 2, Part 1**, 246, 305, 519; **Vol. 4, Part 2**, 77, 153; **Vol. 6, Part 1**, 167; **Vol. 6, Part 2**, 101; **Vol. 9, Part 2**, 506; beautification of, **Supp. 2**, 450; black medical practice in, **Supp. 5**, 104; bonus march (1932), **Supp. 6**, 239–40; **Supp. 7**, 363, 377, 488; burnt by British, *see* Bladensburg, Md.; Capitol, **Vol. 3, Part 1**, 303, 418, 467 f.; ceding of land to government, **Vol. 9, Part 2**, 63; city planning, **Vol. 2, Part 1**, 305; **Vol. 6, Part 1**, 167; **Vol. 8, Part 1**, 647; civil rights protests in, **Supp. 10**, 341–42; commissioners, **Supp. 9**, 22; congressional committees on, **Supp. 6**, 472, 480; Corcoran Gallery of Art, **Vol. 2, Part 2**, 440; **Vol. 3, Part 2**, 214; creation of the district, **Vol. 2, Part 1**, 524; **Vol. 6, Part 1**, 117; desegregation action, **Supp. 5**, 680; design-plan development, **Supp. 3**, 533–34; **Supp. 6**, 485–86; educational service, **Vol. 8, Part 1**, 152, 562; federal buildings, **Supp. 3**, 199; first black woman school board member, **Supp. 5**, 680; Ford's Theatre, **Vol. 5, Part 2**, 284; historical writings on, **Supp. 9**, 339; home-rule efforts, **Supp.6**, 472, 473, 480; **Supp. 9**, 69; Jefferson's administration, **Vol. 6, Part 1**, 220; journalism, **Vol. 3, Part 2**, 92; **Vol. 4, Part 2**, 397; **Vol. 7, Part 1**, 586; Knights of Pythias, mother lodge of, in, **Vol. 8, Part 1**, 386; Lincoln's administration, **Vol. 4, Part 2**, 431; Lincoln Memorial, **Vol. 1, Part 1**, 478; **Vol. 2, Part 1**, 306; **Vol. 6, Part 1**, 563; lot speculation in, **Vol. 6, Part 1**, 168; medical service, **Vol. 9, Part 2**, 586; minimum wage law for women, constitutionality of, **Vol. 9, Part 2**, 271; Monroe's administration, **Vol. 4, Part 2**, 430; naming of, **Vol. 5, Part 2**, 122; National Zoological Park, **Vol. 1, Part 1**, 519; **Vol. 5, Part 2**, 595; newspapers, **Supp. 4**, 630–31, 644; origin of plan of, **Vol. 3, Part 2**, 89; **Vol. 4, Part 2**, 77, 153; **Vol. 5, Part 1**, 91; **Vol. 5, Part 2**, 28; **Vol. 6, Part 1**, 22, 167; **Vol. 7, Part 1**, 223; **Vol. 9, Part 2**, 505; park system, **Vol. 8, Part 1**, 379; **Vol. 8, Part 2**, 384; philanthropic service, **Vol. 9, Part 1**, 394; protection of, in War of 1812, **Vol. 1, Part 1**, 635; public service, **Vol. 1, Part 2**, 380; **Vol. 6, Part 2**, 144, 204; **Vol. 9, Part 1**, 77, 344; Roosevelt, T., administration, **Vol. 8, Part 2**, 138; sanitation problems, **Vol. 6, Part 2**, 204; slave trade, **Vol. 5, Part 2**, 12; social activities, **Supp. 8**, 328; **Supp. 9**, 547; **Supp. 10**, 465; social life, **Vol. 6, Part 1**, 266; **Vol. 6, Part 2**, 182; **Vol. 8, Part 2**, 138; Soldiers' Home in, **Vol. 5, Part 2**, 315; **Vol. 8, Part 2**, 71; statehood movement, **Supp. 10**, 342; street railway, first in, **Vol. 2, Part 2**, 383; teachers' loyalty oath issue, **Supp. 5**, 480–81; United States National Museum, **Vol. 5, Part 2**, 485; water supply, **Vol. 6, Part 2**, 507; **Vol. 9, Part 2**, 260; **Vol. 10, Part 1**, 57
Washington, early steamboat, **Vol. 9, Part 1**, 134
Washington, Treaty of. *See* Alabama Claim Settlement
Washington and Lee University, **Vol. 7, Part 1**, 114; **Vol. 8, Part 1**, 222; gifts to, **Vol. 6, Part 1**, 106; name changed, **Vol. 6, Part 1**, 128; presidency, **Supp. 5**, 641. *See also* Washington College
Washington Arch (New York City), funds for, **Vol. 9, Part 2**, 15
Washington Art Association, **Vol. 9, Part 2**, 75
Washington Cathedral **Vol. 8, Part 2**, 376
Washington College: **Vol. 3, Part 1**, 332 f.; **Vol. 5, Part 2**, 249; **Vol. 7, Part 2**, 124; **Vol. 8, Part 1**, 633; **Vol. 8, Part 2**, 217; founding of, **Vol. 3, Part 1**, 332 f., 340; Lee's presidency of, **Vol. 6, Part 1**, 128 f. *See also* Washington and Lee University
Washington College of Law, founding of, **Supp. 2**, 482
Washington Conference on the Limitation of Armament, **Vol. 9, Part 2**, 477
Washington Consortium of Universities, administration, **Supp. 10**, 403–4
"Washington Crossing the Delaware," **Vol. 6, Part 1**, 196
Washington Daily Globe, **Vol. 8, Part 1**, 635
Washington Elm, **Vol. 6, Part 1**, 381
Washington Evening Star, **Supp. 4**, 630–31; editorial cartoons, **Supp. 4**, 76
Washington family in Virginia, **Vol. 6, Part 1**, 214
Washington Herald, **Supp. 8**, 372
Washingtoniana, **Vol. 8, Part 1**, 51 f.
Washington Institute of Technology, **Supp. 8**, 379
Washington Merry-Go-Round, **Supp. 8**, 496

Washington Monument (Baltimore, Md.), funds for, **Vol. 9, Part 2**, 443
Washington Monument (Washington, D.C.): **Vol. 1, Part 2**, 247; **Vol. 4, Part 1**, 562; **Vol. 5, Part 1**, 521; **Vol. 7, Part 1**, 12, 199; **Vol. 8, Part 2**, 542; **Vol. 9, Part 2**, 353; **Vol. 10, Part 1**, 555 f.; completion, **Supp. 1**, 157
Washington Monument Society, **Vol. 5, Part 2**, 204, 392
Washington Naval Conference (1921–22), **Supp. 2**, 52; **Supp. 4**, 405–6; **Supp. 6**, 518
Washington (D.C.) Navy Yard, **Vol. 3, Part 1**, 31; **Vol. 7, Part 2**, 302, 308
Washington (D.C.) Philharmonic Orchestra, **Vol. 3, Part 1**, 205
Washington (D.C.) School of Psychiatry, **Supp. 6**, 220; founding of, **Supp. 4**, 806
Washington Post: **Vol. 4, Part 2**, 397; editorial policies, **Supp. 10**, 24, 25; publishing, **Supp. 3**, 491–92; **Supp. 6**, 452, 453; **Supp. 7**, 295–96; **Supp. 8**, 433
"Washington Post March" (song), **Vol. 9, Part 1**, 408
Washington Redskins (football team), **Supp. 7**, 452; **Supp. 8**, 390
Washington Senators (baseball team), **Supp. 4**, 436; **Supp. 5**, 261; **Supp. 9**, 328, 390, 653–54, 729; **Supp. 10**, 314, 315
Washington Sentinel, **Vol. 10, Part 1**, 38
Washington Square (New York City), **Vol. 3, Part 2**, 56; **Vol. 5, Part 1**, 615; **Supp. 3**, 124
Washington Square Players, **Supp. 3**, 811; **Supp. 7**, 457–58; **Supp. 9**, 194
Washington State: "barefoot schoolboy law," **Vol. 8, Part 2**, 105; codification of laws, **Vol. 1, Part 1**, 555; commercial enterprises, **Vol. 6, Part 1**, 79; **Vol. 10, Part 1**, 532 f.; governors, **Vol. 3, Part 2**, 342; **Vol. 6, Part 2**, 56; **Vol. 8, Part 2**, 104 f.; **Supp. 7**, 764; **Supp. 8**, 357; Grand Coulee Dam proposed, **Supp. 10**, 180; historical writings, **Supp. 1**, 549; journalism, **Vol. 10, Part 1**, 65; legal service, **Vol. 10, Part 1**, 65; political service, **Vol. 3, Part 2**, 342; **Vol. 8, Part 2**, 105; **Vol. 9, Part 1**, 492, 613; **Vol. 10, Part 1**, 65, 371; **Vol. 10, Part 2**, 338; politics, **Supp. 4**, 669–70, 723–24; **Supp. 10**, 87, 179, 180; public service, **Vol. 6, Part 1**, 79; **Vol. 10, Part 2**, 178; public utilities, **Vol. 6, Part 1**, 79; river and harbor development, **Vol. 10, Part 2**, 339; state constitution, **Vol. 1, Part 2**, 349; wheat growing in, **Vol. 1, Part 1**, 408
Washington Territory: constitution for, **Vol. 6, Part 1**, 6; woman suffrage adopted in, **Vol. 3, Part 1**, 513 f.
Washington Times-Herald, **Supp. 6**, 453; founding of, **Supp. 4**, 644; *Washington Post* purchase of, **Supp. 7**, 296
Washington University (St. Louis): **Vol. 2, Part 2**, 602; **Vol. 3, Part 2**, 82; **Vol. 9, Part 2**, 634; botany studies, **Supp. 3**, 775–76; development of, **Supp. 1**, 123; English literature and language studies, **Supp. 7**, 402; medical school, **Supp. 1**, 123; **Supp. 6**, 126, 189–90; medical school reforms, **Supp. 3**, 243; medical school teaching program, **Supp. 6**, 546; nurses' training, **Supp. 4**, 789; pathology studies, **Supp. 6**, 386; physics studies, **Supp. 7**, 133–35; physiology studies, **Supp. 7**, 226; psychology studies, **Supp. 6**, 261
"Washington Week in Review," **Supp. 10**, 462
Washita River, battle of, **Vol. 3, Part 1**, 8. *See also* Black Kettler Village, fight at
Waskow, Henry T., reference to, **Supp. 3**, 613
Wasp: and *Atlanta,* **Vol. 1, Part 2**, 348; and *Avon,* **Vol. 1, Part 2**, 348; and *Reindeer,* **Vol. 1, Part 2**, 348
Wasp (aircraft carrier), **Supp. 5**, 621
Waste Land, The, **Supp. 7**, 219, 790; **Supp. 8**, 584
Waste materials. *See* Sewerage
Watauga, Articles of Association (1774), **Vol. 4, Part 2**, 531; **Vol. 8, Part 2**, 24; **Vol. 9, Part 2**, 313
Watch and Ward Society (Boston), **Supp. 7**, 98
Watches: invention, **Vol. 9, Part 2**, 485; manufacture, **Vol. 3, Part 1**, 239 f.; **Vol. 4, Part 2**, 275; **Vol. 5, Part 1**, 471. *See also* Clocks and watches
Watchman of the South, **Vol. 8, Part 1**, 13 f.
Watch Tower Bible and Tract Society. *See* Jehovah's Witnesses
Water: artesian wells, **Supp. 4**, 219; falling-drop measurement method, **Supp. 3**, 32; groundwater studies, **Supp. 4**, 567; irrigation projects, **Supp. 4**, 563–64; limnology studies, **Supp. 3**, 402; plant culture in, **Supp. 4**, 382
Water analysis, development of the Sedgwick-Rafter method of, **Vol. 8, Part 1**, 324 f.
Waterbury, Conn., history of, **Vol. 2, Part 1**, 68
Watercolors, **Supp. 5**, 50
Water-cure, practice of: **Vol. 7, Part 1**, 496
Water drainage, **Vol. 6, Part 1**, 505
Water faucets, invention of, **Vol. 5, Part 2**, 49 f.
Waterfield, Bob, reference to, **Supp. 9**, 841
Watergate scandal, **Supp. 9**, 27; **Supp. 10**, 357, 462, 545–46, 645; Mitchell, M., accusation regarding, **Supp. 10**, 546
Waterhouse, Benjamin, reference to, **Vol. 10, Part 1**, 479 f.
Water meter, disk, **Vol. 9, Part 1**, 54; **Vol. 9, Part 2**, 485
Water-mill, making of, **Vol. 6, Part 1**, 486
Water pollution, studies in, **Vol. 3, Part 2**, 275; **Vol. 8, Part 1**, 264 f.
Water Pollution Control Act (1948), **Supp. 8**, 616
Water power, development, **Vol. 3, Part 1**, 497 f.; **Vol. 4, Part 2**, 403; **Vol. 5, Part 1**, 433; **Vol. 7, Part 1**, 8; **Vol. 8, Part 2**, 64, 399
Water Power Act (1920), **Supp. 4**, 481, 666
Water pumps, manufacture of, **Vol. 10, Part 2**, 539
Water reclamation projects, **Supp. 9**, 180, 181, 373, 842; Colorado River, **Supp. 10**, 191–92
Water rights, **Vol. 3, Part 1**, 562 f.
Waters, Ethel, references to, **Supp. 5**, 292, 293; **Supp. 6**, 247, 314; **Supp. 7**, 44
Waters, Ralph M., reference to, **Supp. 6**, 553
Waters, William A., reference to, **Supp. 6**, 334
Water supply: **Vol. 3, Part 2**, 434, 445; **Vol. 8, Part 1**, 324 f.; **Vol. 9, Part 1**, 54; aqueduct systems, **Supp. 2**, 558; Arizona, **Supp. 7**, 22; Boston, **Vol. 4, Part 2**, 109; **Vol. 9, Part 1**, 543; California, **Supp. 3**, 155; **Supp. 6**, 3–4; Central Valley project, **Supp. 7**, 224; Charleston, **Vol. 8, Part 1**, 397; desalinization, **Supp. 8**, 2; engineering, **Vol. 3, Part 2**, 267; **Vol. 9, Part 1**, 308, 543; **Supp. 1**, 319; **Supp. 3**, 813–14; **Supp. 5**, 395; filtration systems, **Supp. 1**, 663; geology of, **Supp. 4**, 119; groundwater studies, **Supp. 4**, 567; Hetch Hetchy reservoir issue, **Supp. 4**, 522, 664; Manchester, N.H., **Vol. 3, Part 2**, 267; Massachusetts, **Vol. 3, Part 1**, 460 f.; **Vol. 8, Part 1**, 553; microscope used in study of the biology of, **Vol. 8, Part 1**, 324 f.; municipal systems, **Supp. 1**, 570, 588, 663, 700; New York, **Vol. 3, Part 1**, 406; **Vol. 5, Part 2**, 59; **Vol. 6, Part 1**, 39; **Vol. 8, Part 1**, 324 f., 607; **Vol. 9, Part 1**, 307 f.; **Vol. 10, Part 2**, 21; New York City, **Vol. 9, Part 1**, 308; Philadelphia, **Vol. 4, Part 1**, 466 f.; **Vol. 6, Part 1**, 21; Pittsburgh, **Vol. 7, Part 2**, 540; pumping engines for, **Vol. 3, Part 1**, 395; **Vol. 6, Part 1**, 81; **Vol. 7, Part 1**, 450; purification of, **Supp. 1**, 326, 389; rights issue, **Supp. 2**, 148, 443; Rochester, N. Y., **Vol. 8, Part 1**, 324 f.; St. Louis, **Vol. 5, Part 2**, 584; Toronto, **Vol. 8, Part 1**, 359 f.; Washington, D.C., **Vol. 6, Part 2**, 507; **Vol. 9, Part 2**, 260; writings on, **Vol. 9, Part 2**, 98. *See also* Irrigation

Watertown, Mass.: public service, **Vol. 7, Part 2**, 541; settlement in 1630, **Vol. 8, Part 2**, 318
Waterways, inland, **Vol. 7, Part 1**, 405
Water wheels, double turbine wheel experiments, **Vol. 6, Part 1**, 139
Waterworks, **Vol. 5, Part 2**, 265, 584; **Vol. 9, Part 2**, 98; **Vol. 10, Part 2**, 56
Watkins, Arthur V., reference to, **Supp. 8**, 178
Watson, Arthur, reference to, **Supp. 6**, 675
Watson, James Craig, reference to, **Vol. 9, Part 2**, 248
Watson, John B., references to, **Supp. 4**, 21; **Supp. 5**, 329; **Supp. 6**, 367, 640, 718; **Supp. 7**, 642
Watson, Thomas A., relations with Alexander Graham Bell, **Vol. 1, Part 2**, 150
Watson, Thomas E., reference to, **Supp. 3**, 330
Watson, Thomas J., Jr., references to, **Supp. 6**, 675; **Supp. 9**, 843, 844
Watson, Thomas J., Sr. references to, **Supp. 4**, 432; **Supp. 9**, 843
Watters, Adair, reference to, **Supp. 7**, 555
Watters, Cowen and Donovan, founding of, **Supp. 8**, 135
Watterson, Ada, references to, **Supp. 6**, 718, 719
Waugh, Evelyn, reference to, **Supp. 9**, 889
Wauneka, Annie Dodge, reference to, **Supp. 4**, 238
WAVES, founding of, **Supp. 7**, 289
Wayne, Anthony, reference to, **Vol. 6, Part 1**, 100
Wayne, John, references to, **Supp. 8**, 712; **Supp. 10**, 845
Wayside Inn (Sudbury, Mass.), **Supp. 4**, 302; **Supp. 6**, 562
Wax modeling, **Vol. 8, Part 1**, 158 f.; **Vol. 10, Part 2**, 562
WCTU. *See* Women's Christian Temperance Union
Wealth: in Great Depression, **Supp. 5**, 550; redistribution advocacy, **Supp. 4**, 432; taxation favoring, **Supp. 2**, 448–49; taxation to reduce, **Supp. 8**, 446; writings on distribution of, **Supp. 3**, 545–46
Wealth Against Commonwealth, **Vol. 6, Part 1**, 332
Weapons. *See* Firearms
"Weary Willie" (clown), **Supp. 10**, 406, 407
Weather: climate, writings on, **Supp. 1**, 355; conditions, early reporting of, to Washington, **Vol. 8, Part 1**, 573; daily observations of, from 1837–1867, **Vol. 3, Part 1**, 268; kite use for meteorological data, **Supp. 3**, 479; long-range forecasting, **Supp. 3**, 512; modification, **Supp. 6**, 364, 365; relative humidity calculation, **Supp. 3**, 512; reports, **Vol. 3, Part 2**, 185; **Vol. 6, Part 1**, 280; study of, **Vol. 4, Part 2**, 64. *See also* Meteorology; Weather Bureau, United States
Weather Bureau, United States: **Vol. 1, Part 1**, 2; **Vol. 4, Part 2**, 302, 477; **Vol. 6, Part 1**, 441; **Vol. 6, Part 2**, 515; **Vol. 7, Part 1**, 472; aerological division, **Supp. 2**, 261; established, **Vol. 3, Part 1**, 149; **Vol. 5, Part 2**, 612; **Vol. 7, Part 1**, 374; expansion, **Supp. 3**, 512; forecasting, **Supp. 3**, 479; forerunner of, **Vol. 10, Part 1**, 594 f.; meteorological physics, **Supp. 4**, 410; systematic observation, **Vol. 3, Part 1**, 274
"Weaver, Charley" (fictional character), **Supp. 9**, 48–49
Weaver, James B., reference to, **Vol. 9, Part 2**, 640
Weaver, James ("Red"), reference to, **Supp. 5**, 458
Weaver, Richard M., reference to, **Supp. 9**, 548
Weaver, Robert, references to, **Supp. 4**, 251; **Supp. 5**, 343
Weavers, The (folk group), **Supp. 8**, 235
Weaving, **Vol. 2, Part 2**, 580
Webb, Walter, reference to, **Supp. 7**, 685
Webb, Walter Prescott, reference to, **Supp. 9**, 314
Webb, William H., reference to, **Vol. 9, Part 2**, 345
Webb and Knapp (real estate), **Supp. 10**, 337, 866, 867
Webb Institute of Naval Architecture, **Vol. 9, Part 2**, 345
Weber, Max, reference to, **Supp. 6**, 552; **Supp. 8**, 553
Weber and Fields (comedy team), **Supp. 3**, 803–5; **Supp. 5**, 726
Web of Government, The, **Supp. 8**, 407
Webster, Daniel: **Vol. 3, Part 2**, 380 f.; **Vol. 4, Part 2**, 351; **Vol. 5, Part 1**, 192, 466; **Vol. 5, Part 2**, 203; **Vol. 6, Part 1**, 518; **Vol. 7, Part 1**, 638 f.; **Vol. 8, Part 2**, 461; **Vol. 9, Part 1**, 292, 328; **Vol. 10, Part 1**, 91; attack on private life of, **Vol. 9, Part 2**, 253; biographies of, **Vol. 5, Part 2**, 606; **Supp. 6**, 6; defended, **Vol. 1, Part 1**, 394; life of, **Vol. 6, Part 1**, 347; relations with Rufus Choate, **Vol. 2, Part 2**, 86 f.; slavery, speech on, **Vol. 4, Part 1**, 170; trial for criminal libel upon, **Vol. 3, Part 1**, 276
Webster, J. P., relations with Sanford Fillmore Bennet, **Vol. 1, Part 2**, 190
Webster, Milton P., reference to, **Supp. 6**, 648
Webster, Noah, relations with Joseph Emerson Worcester, **Vol. 10, Part 2**, 527
Webster-Ashburton Treaty, **Vol. 3, Part 2**, 258; **Vol. 10, Part 1**, 91, 590
Webster-Powell Opera Company, **Vol. 8, Part 1**, 144
Webster's Dictionary, **Vol. 4, Part 1**, 40; **Vol. 5, Part 1**, 288; **Vol. 9, Part 1**, 64
Webster's International Dictionary, **Supp. 5**, 711
Webster's New International Dictionary, **Supp. 4**, 624
Weed, Lewis H., reference to, **Supp. 5**, 600
Weed, Thurlow: **Vol. 3, Part 2**, 380; **Vol. 5, Part 2**, 400; **Vol. 7, Part 1**, 169; **Vol. 7, Part 2**, 46; **Vol. 8, Part 2**, 615; relations with Henry O'Reilly, **Vol. 7, Part 2**, 52
Weed Sewing Machine Co., first bicycles manufactured, **Vol. 8, Part 1**, 74 f.
Weekly Advertiser, **Vol. 1, Part 2**, 565
Weekly magazine, first illustrated, **Vol. 3, Part 1**, 155
Weeks Act (1911), **Supp. 4**, 666
Weicker, Lowell P., Jr., reference to, **Supp. 10**, 826
Weidman, Charles, reference to, **Supp. 9**, 494
Weierstrass, Karl, reference to, **Supp. 3**, 86
Weights and measures: **Vol. 1, Part 1**, 169; **Vol. 3, Part 2**, 142; **Vol. 5, Part 1**, 23; **Vol. 8, Part 2**, 114, 400; **Vol. 9, Part 2**, 127 f.; Bureau of, **Vol. 8, Part 2**, 400; writings on, **Vol. 1, Part 1**, 91
Weill, Kurt, references to, **Supp. 5**, 415; **Supp. 7**, 61; **Supp. 9**, 579
Wein, George, reference to, **Supp. 8**, 562
Weinman, Adolph Alexander, reference to, **Supp. 5**, 659
Weir, Ernest T., reference to, **Supp. 8**, 289
Weirton Steel Co., **Supp. 6**, 678
Weiss, Albert P., reference to, **Supp. 4**, 490–9
Weiss, George, references to, **Supp. 5**, 41; **Supp. 9**, 764
Weiss, Soma, references to, **Supp. 3**, 244, 343
Weissmuller, Johnny, reference to, **Supp. 9**, 65
Weitzmann, Louis, **Supp. 10**, 809
Weizmann, Chaim, references to, **Supp. 3**, 97, 279–80; **Supp. 4**, 906; **Supp. 7**, 689; **Supp. 8**, 549
Welch, Rev. Moses C., reference to, **Vol. 9, Part 2**, 250
Welch, William H.: references to, **Supp. 3**, 51, 106, 270, 370, 371, 412, 483; **Supp. 4**, 287; **Supp. 5**, 232, 233, 438; **Supp. 8**, 555–56; relations with William Osler, **Vol. 7, Part 2**, 85 f.
Welch bacillus, discovery of, **Vol. 10, Part 1**, 621 f.
Welcome, ship of William Penn, **Vol. 5, Part 2**, 265
Welcome Chemical Research Laboratories (London), **Vol. 8, Part 1**, 154 f.
Welding, iron and steel, **Vol. 8, Part 2**, 200
Welding techniques, **Supp. 7**, 564
Welfare: animals, **Vol. 1, Part 2**, 424; Detroit relief measures, **Supp. 4**, 611–12; federal relief, **Supp. 5**, 459–60; **Supp. 6**, 330; **Supp. 7**, 787–88; federal v.

state relief, **Supp. 4**, 810–11; industrial, **Vol. 3, Part 1**, 586 f.; **Vol. 4, Part 1**, 600; New Deal relief policies, **Supp. 3**, 652; New York relief measures, **Supp. 3**, 362, 719; **Supp. 4**, 391–92; **Supp. 6**, 102–3; private black, **Supp. 8**, 434–35; private charitable relief aid, **Supp. 4**, 87; professional training for administrators, **Supp. 4**, 810–11; state relief programs, **Supp. 4**, 900; voluntary v. government relief, **Supp. 7**, 362–63; War on Poverty, **Supp. 7**, 424–25; workrelief concept of, **Supp. 4**, 391–92. *See also* Poverty; Unemployment
Welfare capitalism: **Supp. 3**, 762–63, 792; Ford's five-dollar day, **Supp. 4**, 296–97; shoe industry, **Supp. 4**, 431–32
Welker, Herman, reference to, **Supp. 5**, 338
Welles, Orson, references to, **Supp. 3**, 93; **Supp. 5**, 287–88; **Supp. 5**, 418, 464; **Supp. 6**, 441; **Supp. 7**, 61, 166; **Supp. 9**, 382, 559, 560, 793; **Supp. 10**, 239
Welles, Sumner, references to, **Supp. 5**, 332, 335, 537; **Supp. 8**, 62
Wellesley College: **Vol. 3, Part 1**, 541 f.; **Vol. 5, Part 1**, 274; **Vol. 5, Part 2**, 208; **Vol. 7, Part 2**, 173; **Vol. 9, Part 1**, 14; **Supp. 9**, 174–75; benefactions, **Vol. 5, Part 1**, 381; economics studies, **Supp. 7**, 28–29; English literature and language studies, **Supp. 5**, 616; **Supp. 10**, 846; presidency, **Supp. 2**, 524; psychology laboratory, **Supp. 1**, 150; founding of, **Vol. 3, Part 1**, 541 f.
Wellington, Frank O., reference to, **Vol. 10, Part 1**, 548 f.
Well of Loneliness, The, **Supp. 7**, 149
Wells, Herman B., reference to, **Supp. 6**, 343
Wells, Horace, reference to, **Vol. 7, Part 1**, 269
Wells, Oliver E., reference to, **Supp. 3**, 249–50
Wells College (N.Y.), **Vol. 7, Part 1**, 168; **Vol. 10, Part 1**, 639 f.
Wells Fargo & Co., **Vol. 3, Part 2**, 271; **Vol. 5, Part 1**, 142; **Vol. 7, Part 1**, 167; **Vol. 10, Part 1**, 639 f.
Wells Memorial Institute for Workingmen, **Vol. 7, Part 2**, 158
Welsh: colonization in South Carolina, **Vol. 5, Part 1**, 355; publications in America, **Vol. 3, Part 2**, 227; **Vol. 7, Part 2**, 118; **Vol. 8, Part 2**, 201; translations, **Vol. 7, Part 1**, 164
Wenner-Gren, Axel, reference to, **Supp. 7**, 241
Wenner-Gren Foundation for Anthropological Research, **Supp. 7**, 241
Wentworth, Charles Francis, reference to, **Supp. 3**, 195
Wertheimer, Max, references to, **Supp. 3**, 429; **Supp. 8**, 344; **Supp. 8**, 345
"We Shall Overcome" (song), **Supp. 8**, 334
Wesley, Charles, references to, **Vol. 1, Part 2**, 403; **Vol. 9, Part 2**, 133
Wesley, John, references to, **Vol. 1, Part 2**, 403; **Vol. 7, Part 1**, 360; **Vol. 9, Part 2**, 133
Wesleyan University (Conn.): **Vol. 1, Part 1**, 575; **Vol. 3, Part 2**, 416; **Vol. 5, Part 2**, 232; **Vol. 9, Part 1**, 605; **Vol. 10, Part 2**, 376; admission of women to, **Vol. 2, Part 2**, 596; humanities program, **Supp. 10**, 542; psychology studies, **Supp. 3**, 229–30, as Wesleyan College, **Vol. 7, Part 2**, 580
Wesley Theological Institute, founding of, **Vol. 3, Part 1**, 233
Wesson, Daniel Baird, reference to, **Vol. 9, Part 1**, 282
West, Andrew Fleming, reference to, **Supp. 4**, 143
West, Benjamin: **Vol. 9, Part 1**, 355; **Vol. 10, Part 1**, 12 f.; relations with John Singleton Copley, **Vol. 2, Part 2**, 425
West, James E., reference to, **Supp. 3**, 44
West, Nathanael, references to, **Supp. 10**, 630, 631
West, Walter, reference to, **Supp. 4**, 810
West (U.S.): art depicting, **Supp. 3**, 380, 382–83; **Supp. 5**, 420; books and movies about, **Supp. 1**, 6, 626; **Supp. 3**, **382–83**; **Supp. 6**, 466; cowboy folk song collection, **Supp. 4**, 502; cowboy movies, **Supp. 4**, 734–35, 877–78; cowboy philosopher, **Supp. 1**, 637; development of, **Vol. 2, Part 2**, 189; **Supp. 1**, 414; explorations in, **Vol. 2, Part 2**, 234; **Vol. 6, Part 1**, 180, 380; **Vol. 6, Part 2**, 332; **Vol. 7, Part 2**, 481; **Vol. 7, Part 1**, 641; **Vol. 9, Part 1**, 631 f.; frontier life, **Vol. 2, Part 1**, 421, 531; **Vol. 8, Part 2**, 153; historical writings on, **Supp. 1**, 443; **Supp. 5**, 169; immigration to, **Vol. 2, Part 1**, 13, 33; **Vol. 5, Part 1**, 495; land use, **Supp. 3**, 169; missions in, **Vol. 1, Part 2**, 583; **Vol. 6, Part 1**, 9; New Englanders' migrations to, **Supp. 7**, 353–54; novels about, **Supp. 2**, 262–63, 729; **Supp. 3**, 382–83; **Supp. 4**, 877–78; photography of, **Supp. 3**, 380; resources, **Supp. 9**, 32; topographic maps, **Supp. 1**, 3; **Supp. 4**, 557–58; trade in, **Vol. 5, Part 1**, 141; Wild West shows, **Supp. 3**, 460; writings on, **Vol. 4, Part 1**, 19; **Vol. 6, Part 2**, 622; **Supp. 3**, 382–83; **Supp. 8**, 567. *See also* state names
Westbrook, Frank, reference to, **Supp. 3**, 832
Westchester County, N.Y., development of, **Vol. 4, Part 2**, 491
West Coast Reporter, **Vol. 8, Part 1**, 52 f.
Western Academy of Art, **Vol. 2, Part 2**, 334, 443
Western Air Express, **Supp. 5**, 385
Western Air Lines, founding of, **Supp. 3**, 157
Western Association of Railway Executives, founding of, **Supp. 2**, 260
Western Christian Advocate, **Vol. 5, Part 2**, 410; **Vol. 7, Part 1**, 393; **Vol. 8, Part 1**, 478; **Vol. 9, Part 1**, 181
Western College (later Leander Clark College, Iowa), **Vol. 1, Part 2**, 96; **Vol. 5, Part 2**, 350
Western Consumers Union, founding of, **Supp. 7**, 69
Western Electric Co., **Supp. 6**, 84, 151–52, 614; management, **Supp. 9**, 676; research, **Supp. 9**, 303, 304
Western Engineering Co., founding of, **Supp. 5**, 354
Western Forestry and Conservation Association, founding of, **Supp. 3**, 7
Western Federation of Miners, **Vol. 4, Part 2**, 419, 468
"Western" humor, **Vol. 6, Part 1**, 208; **Vol. 9, Part 2**, 509
Western Intelligencer, early Ohio newspaper, **Vol. 5, Part 2**, 373
Western Lancet, medical journal, **Vol. 6, Part 1**, 58
Western Law Journal, **Vol. 10, Part 1**, 363
Western Medical Review, founding of, **Supp. 2**, 612
Western Military Institute. *See* University of Nashville
Western Newspaper Union, **Vol. 1, Part 1**, 129 f.
Western New York Horticultural Society, **Vol. 9, Part 2**, 439
Western Pacific Railway, **Vol. 1, Part 2**, 410; **Vol. 5, Part 2**, 36; **Supp. 3**, 381–82
Western Pennsylvania Medical College, laryngology, **Supp. 6**, 318
Western Philosophical Association, founding of, **Supp. 1**, 683
Western Protestant, **Vol. 8, Part 1**, 544
Western Reserve: pioneering in, **Vol. 1, Part 1**, 475; influence of Yale on, **Vol. 3, Part 1**, 158
Western Reserve University: administration, **Supp. 2**, 663; applied social science studies, **Supp. 7**, 151; history of, **Vol. 3, Part 1**, 11; **Vol. 10, Part 1**, 581 f.; hygiene and public health studies, **Supp. 7**, 194; medical school, **Supp. 6**, 295, 296; pharmacology studies, **Supp. 3**, 342; **Supp. 9**, 786
Western Review and Miscellaneous Magazine, **Vol. 5, Part 1**, 396
Western Society of Engineers, **Vol. 10, Part 1**, 372 f.
Western Stock Journal and Farmer, **Vol. 5, Part 2**, 453
Western Union Telegraph Co.: **Vol. 2, Part 2**, 445; **Vol. 3, Part 2**, 4; **Vol. 4, Part 1**, 555; **Vol. 7, Part 1**, 148;

Vol. 9, Part 1, 176, 492; AT&T sale of, **Supp. 8**, 211; formed, **Vol. 8, Part 1**, 193 f.; **Vol. 9, Part 1**, 145 f.; mergers, **Vol. 7, Part 2**, 65; patent system of, **Vol. 8, Part 1**, 75 f.
Western Unitarian Conference, **Vol. 5, Part 2**, 179
Western United Corporation, formation of, **Supp. 4**, 180
Western Watchman, **Vol. 7, Part 2**, 521
Western World, publishing of Federalist sheet, **Vol. 9, Part 2**, 136 f.
Westervelt, Conrad, reference to, **Supp. 6**, 63
Westfield, Mass., service to, **Vol. 9, Part 1**, 76 f.
West Florida, annexation of, **Vol. 6, Part 2**, 191, 403; **Vol. 7, Part 1**, 90; **Vol. 10, Part 2**, 225
West India Co., **Vol. 3, Part 1**, 265
West India squadron, command of, **Vol. 7, Part 2**, 186
West Indies: birds of, **Vol. 6, Part 1**, 49; diplomacy, **Vol. 4, Part 1**, 538; law in, **Vol. 4, Part 1**, 136; missions in, **Vol. 6, Part 1**, 158; piracy, suppression of, **Vol. 4, Part 2**, 382; **Vol. 8, Part 1**, 83 f.; trade, **Vol. 2, Part 1**, 592; **Vol. 3, Part 2**, 444; **Vol. 4, Part 2**, 382; **Vol. 8, Part 2**, 341 f.
Westinghouse, George, reference to, **Supp. 3**, 456
Westinghouse Electric and Manufacturing Co.: **Vol. 5, Part 2**, 358; **Vol. 9, Part 1**, 275, 514; **Vol. 9, Part 2**, 644; **Supp. 7**, 793; first shop committee with employee representation, **Vol. 8, Part 1**, 91 f.; formation of, **Vol. 10, Part 2**, 17; radio research, **Supp. 3**, 184–85; turbine engineering, **Supp. 4**, 383
West Jersey Society, **Vol. 1, Part 2**, 36
Westminster College (Mo.), president of, **Vol. 8, Part 1**, 544
Westminster Confession of Faith, **Vol. 3, Part 2**, 406
Westminster Theological Seminary, founding of, **Supp. 2**, 412
Westmoreland Association, **Vol. 6, Part 1**, 118
Weston, Edward, reference to, **Supp. 10**, 162, 834
Weston, John C., reference to, **Supp. 7**, 4
Weston-Mott Axle Co., **Supp. 4**, 244
Westover, Russ, reference to, **Supp. 6**, 530
West Point. *See* United States Military Academy
West Point, N.Y., defenses of, **Vol. 9, Part 2**, 583
Westport Country Playhouse, **Supp. 7**, 458
West Virginia: constitution of, **Vol. 3, Part 2**, 298; creation of state, **Vol. 2, Part 1**, 493; **Vol. 3, Part 1**, 343; **Vol. 6, Part 1**, 239; **Vol. 7, Part 2**, 585; **Vol. 8, Part 2**, 163; **Vol. 10, Part 2**, 246; governors, **Vol. 1, Part 2**, 461 f.; **Vol. 3, Part 2**, 459; **Vol. 6, Part 2**, 404; **Supp. 6**, 472; legal service, **Vol. 1, Part 2**, 462, 603; **Vol. 7, Part 2**, 585; navigation in, **Vol. 5, Part 2**, 330; pioneering in, **Vol. 10, Part 2**, 644; political service, **Vol. 1, Part 1**, 409; **Vol. 1, Part 2**, 461, 603; **Vol. 3, Part 1**, 118; **Vol. 3, Part 2**, 459; **Vol. 6, Part 2**, 404; **Vol. 8, Part 1**, 119; politics, **Supp. 6**, 335; Reconstruction, **Vol. 6, Part 2**, 404; religious history of, **Vol. 7, Part 2**, 501; Republican party, **Vol. 10, Part 2**, 247
West Virginia, **Supp. 9**, 755
West Virginia State College, administration, **Supp. 10**, 172
Weyer, Johann, reference to, **Supp. 6**, 724
Weyerhaeuser Sales Co., **Supp. 3**, 813
Weyhe, Erhard, reference to. **Supp. 3**, 278
Weyl, Hermann, reference to, **Supp. 10**, 282
Weyl, Walter, reference to, **Supp. 7**, 310
WGBH-TV, founding of, **Supp. 10**, 467
WGY (radio station), **Supp. 6**, 32
Whale oil, **Vol. 3, Part 2**, 401
Whales, study of, **Vol. 10, Part 1**, 5; **Supp. 6**, 17–18
Whaling industry: **Vol. 3, Part 2**, 486; **Vol. 4, Part 2**, 408; **Vol. 6, Part 1**, 402; **Vol. 7, Part 1**, 67; **Vol. 8, Part 2**, 186; **Vol. 10, Part 1**, 102; first voyage around Cape Horn, **Vol. 8, Part 2**, 246; golden days of, **Vol. 8, Part 2**, 41; history of, **Vol. 4, Part 2**, 413; New Bedford, Mass., **Vol. 8, Part 2**, 41, 246
Whall, Christopher W., reference to, **Supp. 3**, 183
Wharton, Arthur, reference to, **Supp. 6**, 218
Wharton, Edith, references to, **Vol. 5, Part 1**, 310; **Supp. 5**, 700; **Supp. 6**, 196; **Supp. 7**, 651; **Supp. 8**, 494
Wharton, Joseph, reference to, **Supp. 10**, 460
Wharton School of Commerce and Finance: **Vol. 5, Part 1**, 574; **Vol. 7, Part 2**, 299; **Vol. 10, Part 2**, 30; **Supp. 10**, 794, 795; insurance course, **Supp. 7**, 373
Whatever Happened to Baby Jane?, **Supp. 10**, 158
What Price Glory?, **Supp. 6**, 15–16; **Supp. 8**, 622
"What's My Line?" (television program), **Supp. 9**, 166; **Supp. 10**, 790
"What's the Matter with Kansas?" (editorial), **Supp. 3**, 816
Wheat: exportation of, **Vol. 7, Part 2**, 522; growing, **Vol. 1, Part 1**, 408; **Vol. 6, Part 1**, 92; market, **Vol. 10, Part 1**, 437; market cornering, **Vol. 6, Part 1**, 157; **Supp. 1**, 491; studies on, **Supp. 1**, 183
Wheat flakes, **Supp. 5**, 379
Wheaton College (Ill.), **Vol. 1, Part 2**, 351
Wheeler, Benjamin, reference to, **Supp. 8**, 442
Wheeler, Burton K., references to, **Supp. 3**, 100; **Supp. 7**, 562; **Supp. 9**, 356, 810
Wheeler, Harvey, reference to, **Supp. 7**, 93
Wheeler, Henry L., reference to, **Supp. 4**, 434
Wheeler, Post, reference to, **Supp. 6**, 544
Wheeler, W. M., reference to, **Supp. 4**, 515
Wheeler, Wayne B., references to, **Supp. 4**, 853; **Supp. 5**, 442
Wheeler and Wilson, **Vol. 5, Part 1**, 259
Wheeler expedition, **Vol. 6, Part 1**, 417
Wheeler-Howard Act (1934). *See* Indian Reorganizaton Act
Wheeler-Lea Act (1938), **Supp. 5**, 27
Wheeler-Truman Transportation Act (1940), **Supp. 9**, 810
Wheeling, W.Va., engagement at. *See* Fort Henry
Wheelman, founding of, to promote bicycling, **Vol. 8, Part 1**, 74 f.
Wheelock, Eleazar, reference to, **Vol. 7, Part 1**, 614
Wheelock, John, reference to, **Vol. 7, Part 1**, 523
Wheelock, John Hall, reference to, **Supp. 10**, 390
Wheelock College (Boston), founding of, **Supp. 4**, 874–75
When Worlds Collide, **Supp. 9**, 895
Where the Money Was, **Supp. 10**, 771
Whig party: **Vol. 1, Part 1**, 510, 518, 536, 592; **Vol. 1, Part 2**, 182, 472, 489; **Vol. 3, Part 2**, 115, 158, 348, 380, 397, 499, 546, 553; **Vol. 4, Part 2**, 141, 561; **Vol. 5, Part 1**, 192, 227, 302, 336, 395; **Vol. 8, Part 2**, 368, 510, 617; **Vol. 9, Part 1**, 84, 244, 339, 350, 357; **Vol. 9, Part 2**, 351 f.; Alabama, **Vol. 5, Part 1**, 54; convention of 1840, **Vol. 8, Part 2**, 58; dissolution of, **Vol. 2, Part 2**, 88; **Vol. 8, Part 1**, 409 f.; formation of, **Vol. 2, Part 1**, 416; **Vol. 3, Part 2**, 538; "free soil," **Vol. 3, Part 2**, 565; Harvard College, **Vol. 5, Part 2**, 588; Illinois, **Vol. 4, Part 2**, 246; Loyalist feuds, **Vol. 4, Part 2**, 577; Massachusetts, **Vol. 2, Part 2**, 87; Pennsylvania, **Vol. 7, Part 1**, 131; **Vol. 8, Part 2**, 177; post-Civil War period, **Vol. 8, Part 2**, 125; Tennessee, **Vol. 1, Part 2**, 157; **Vol. 2, Part 1**, 466; Virginia newspaper exponent, **Vol. 8, Part 1**, 7 f.
Whig Party in the South, The, **Supp. 10**, 136
Whig (Richmond), **Vol. 8, Part 1**, 7 f.
Whipple, George Hoyt, reference to, **Supp. 3**, 370; **Supp. 4**, 581
Whipple, Squire, reference to, **Vol. 7, Part 1**, 355

Whiskey Rebellion (1794), **Vol. 1, Part 2**, 386, 545, 566; **Vol. 2, Part 1**, 37; **Vol. 3, Part 1**, 514; **Vol. 3, Part 2**, 386; **Vol. 4, Part 1**, 105, 254; **Vol. 4, Part 2**, 177; **Vol. 5, Part 1**, 428, 500; **Vol. 6, Part 1**, 108, 132, 220; **Vol. 7, Part 1**, 167, 422, 437; **Vol. 8, Part 1**, 401; **Vol. 8, Part 2**, 178; **Vol. 9, Part 1**, 341; **Vol. 10, Part 1**, 509, 524
Whiskey Ring, **Vol. 1, Part 1**, 460; **Vol. 2, Part 1**, 56; **Vol. 4, Part 1**, 500; **Vol. 4, Part 2**, 26
Whistler, George Washington, reference to, **Supp. 6**, 281
Whistler, James McNeill: **Vol. 4, Part 1**, 14; **Vol. 6, Part 1**, 566; **Vol. 7, Part 1**, 291; **Vol. 9, Part 2**, 250; references to, **Supp. 3**, 342; **Supp. 5**, 470, 471; relations with Joseph Pennell, **Vol. 7, Part 2**, 439
Whitaker, Nathaniel, reference to, **Vol. 7, Part 1**, 615
White, Alfred T., reference to, **Supp. 4**, 56
White, Andrew D., references to, **Vol. 3, Part 2**, 383; **Vol. 5, Part 2**, 212; **Supp. 2**, 75; **Supp. 3**, 698
White, Byron, references to, **Supp. 8**, 322; **Supp. 9**, 837
White, Clarence H., reference to, **Supp. 9**, 110
White, Dan, references to, **Supp. 10**, 537, 559
White, E. B., reference to, **Supp. 5**, 594; **Supp. 7**, 743
White, Edward, reference to, **Supp. 8**, 225
White, Ellen G., references to, **Supp. 3**, 409, 410
White, George, reference to, **Supp. 8**, 250–51
White, Harry Dexter, reference to, **Supp. 7**, 52
White, Horace, reference to, **Vol. 8, Part 2**, 469
White, J. Andrew, reference to, **Supp. 7**, 378
White, Josh, singers, **Supp. 8**, 696
White, Katharine Sergeant Angell, references to, **Supp. 5**, 594; **Supp. 9**, 37; **Supp. 10**, 496
White, Kent, reference to, **Supp. 4**, 876
White, Lurana Mary, reference to, **Supp. 2**, 201
White, Paul Dudley, reference to, **Supp. 3**, 244
White, Stanford: reference to, **Vol. 8, Part 2**, 298; Thaw's shooting of, **Supp. 3**, 170, 385; **Supp. 4**, 826–27; **Supp. 6**, 290; **Supp. 8**, 460–61
White, Theodore, reference to, **Supp. 7**, 114
White, Walter, references to, **Supp. 10**, 660, 679
White, William Alanson: Foundation, **Supp. 6**, 220; reference to, **Supp. 4**, 806
White, William Allen, references to, **Supp. 3**, 105, 762; **Supp. 4**, 12, 204; **Supp. 5**, 503, 481; **Supp. 5**, 624; **Supp. 9**, 355, 356
White Album, The, **Supp. 10**, 450
"White Christmas," **Supp. 10**, 160
White-collar crime, first formal definition of, **Supp. 4**, 809
White Cross Library, **Vol. 7, Part 1**, 318
White Cross Society: **Vol. 6, Part 1**, 86; American branch of, first, **Vol. 3, Part 1**, 191
Whitehead, Alfred North, reference to, **Supp. 10**, 282
Whitehead, Wilbur, reference to, **Supp. 6**, 134–35
White House: life at, **Vol. 4, Part 2**, 430 f.; **Vol. 6, Part 1**, 220; **Vol. 7, Part 2**, 54; **Vol. 8, Part 2**, 138; Truman's balcony addition, **Supp. 6**, 158
White House Conference on Child Welfare (1930), **Supp. 7**, 361
White House Conference on Dependent Children (1909), **Supp. 7**, 251
White House Conference on the Conservation of Natural Resources (1908), **Supp. 4**, 664
White League, New Orleans, **Vol. 4, Part 2**, 353
Whiteman, Paul: orchestra, **Supp. 8**, 697–98; references to, **Supp. 2**, 228; **Supp. 6**, 172; **Supp. 7**, 736; **Supp. 9**, 340, 491; **Supp. 10**, 159, 258, 479, 694
Whiteman Orchestra (jazz): **Supp. 9**, 340; **Supp. 10**, 526, 806; Crosby vocalist with, **Supp. 10**, 159
White Oak Swamp, battle of. *See* Seven Days' Battles
White Plains, battle of, **Vol. 4, Part 1**, 569; **Vol. 4, Part 2**, 229; **Vol. 6, Part 2**, 22; **Vol. 10, Part 1**, 515
White slavery. *See* Prostitution
White supremacy. *See* Eugenics; Racism
White Squadron, The, **Vol. 5, Part 1**, 153
Whitefield, George, **Vol. 4, Part 2**, 69; **Vol. 9, Part 2**, 367, 390; Philadelphia, **Vol. 8, Part 2**, 75, 227
Whiting, Sarah Frances, reference to, **Supp. 3**, 130
Whitley, H. J., reference to, **Supp. 3**, 155
Whitlock, Brand, reference to, **Supp. 3**, 554
Whitman, Charles, references to, **Supp. 3**, 116, 718; **Supp. 4**, 497, 498
Whitman, Marcus: **Vol. 6, Part 1**, 433; relations with Samuel Parker, **Vol. 7, Part 2**, 237; statue of, **Supp. 3**, 124
Whitman, Walt: **Vol. 5, Part 1**, 6; **Vol. 5, Part 2**, 337; **Vol. 9, Part 2**, 357; **Vol. 10, Part 2**, 151; O'Connor and, **Vol. 7, Part 1**, 620; sculpture of, **Supp. 3**, 124–25; Traubel and, **Vol. 9, Part 2**, 628; writings on, **Supp. 5**, 542; **Supp. 7**, 18
Whitman massacre, **Vol. 1, Part 1**, 30; **Vol. 10, Part 2**, 142
Whitney, Charles S., reference to, **Supp. 7**, 12
Whitney, Courtney, reference to, **Supp. 7**, 491
Whitney, Eli, reference to, **Vol. 7, Part 1**, 561
Whitney, Evangeline E., reference to, **Supp. 3**, 600
Whitney, Gertrude Vanderbilt, references to, **Supp. 4**, 204, 289–90; **Supp. 5**, 231; **Supp. 7**, 753
Whitney, John Hay, reference to, **Supp. 10**, 245
Whitney, Richard, reference to, **Supp. 10**, 139
Whitney, William C., reference to, **Vol. 9, Part 1**, 212
Whitney, William Dwight, references to, **Vol. 9, Part 1**, 241; **Vol. 9, Part 2**, 357; **Supp. 3**, 444
Whitney, Willis R., reference to, **Supp. 6**, 364
Whitney Museum of American Art: first retrospective by living American, **Supp. 5**, 403; founding of, **Supp. 3**, 818–19; **Supp. 4**, 289–90; Grosz retrospective, **Supp. 6**, 257; Hopper exhibitions, **Supp. 8**, 280
Whitney Studio Club. *See* Whitney Museum of American Art
Whittier, John Greenleaf: **Vol. 3, Part 1**, 316; **Vol. 6, Part 1**, 507; **Vol. 7, Part 1**, 399; **Vol. 9, Part 1**, 415, 465; relations with Samuel Thomas Pickard, **Vol. 7, Part 2**, 558
"Who Goes There?" (short story), **Supp. 9**, 155
Whole World's Temperance Convention (1853), **Vol. 4, Part 2**, 376
"Who's on first?" (comedy routine), **Supp. 9**, 2
Who's Who in America, **Supp. 3**, 508
Why England Slept, **Supp. 7**, 274
Wichita Beacon (Kans.), **Supp. 4**, 12
Wichita Daily Eagle (Kans.), **Supp. 3**, 544–45
Wichita, Kans., police reform, **Supp. 9**, 881
Wickersham, George W., references to, **Vol. 9, Part 2**, 269; **Supp. 4**, 493
Wicker-wire, manufacturer of, **Vol. 6, Part 1**, 334
Wide Awake, **Vol. 6, Part 1**, 423 f.; **Vol. 8, Part 1**, 171
"Wide-Awakes," organization of, in Republican campaign of 1860, **Vol. 8, Part 1**, 428
Widener, Harry E., references to, **Supp. 5**, 586, 756
Wiener, Alexander S., reference to, **Supp. 3**, 441
Wiener, Norbert, reference to, **Supp. 3**, 137
Wiggin, James Henry, reference to, **Vol. 3, Part 2**, 12
Wiggins, James Russell, reference to, **Supp. 7**, 296
Wigner, Eugene P., reference to, **Supp. 9**, 696
Wilberforce University: **Vol. 7, Part 2**, 325; **Vol. 8, Part 2**, 409; presidency, **Supp. 5**, 259
Wilbur, Ray Lyman, reference to, **Supp. 7**, 36
Wilcox, Ed, reference to, **Supp. 4**, 510
Wilcox, Ella Wheeler, **Supp. 3**, 834
Wilcox and Gibbs, **Vol. 5, Part 1**, 286

"Wild Bill Hickok" (television program), **Supp. 10**, 178
Wilde, Oscar, **Vol. 3, Part 1**, 371 f.; tomb design, **Supp. 6**, 194
Wilder, Billy, references to, **Supp. 8**, 45, 46
Wilder, Thornton, references to, **Supp. 3**, 198; **Supp. 10**, 311, 312
Wilderness, operation in the, **Vol. 1, Part 1**, 273, 608; **Vol. 3, Part 1**, 598; **Vol. 3, Part 2**, 230; **Vol. 4, Part 1**, 496–97, 596; **Vol. 4, Part 2**, 214, 222; **Vol. 5, Part 1**, 25; **Vol. 6, Part 1**, 126–27, 392; **Vol. 6, Part 2**, 476; **Vol. 8, Part 2**, 548; **Vol. 9, Part 1**, 80; **Vol. 9, Part 2**, 172; **Vol. 10, Part 2**, 334
Wilderness Act (1964), **Supp. 7**, 225; **Supp. 9**, 32
Wilderness and wildlife preserves, **Supp. 2**, 265; **Supp. 3**, 593; **Supp. 4**, 483; **Supp. 7**, 164, 225, 813–14; **Supp. 8**, 3–4, 486
Wilderness Society, **Supp. 7**, 813, 814; founding of, **Supp. 4**, 584; **Supp. 9**, 526
Wildlife: African exlorations, **Supp. 8**, 3–4; collections, **Supp. 4**, 120; ecology of, **Supp. 4**, 482–84; game survey, **Supp. 4**, 483; in motion pictures, **Supp. 4**, 735; preservation of, **Vol. 1, Part 1**, 514; **Vol. 8, Part 2**, 197, 923; **Vol. 9, Part 1**, 106; **Vol. 9, Part 2**, 566; stories about, **Supp. 4**, 736; training of, **Supp. 7**, 41–42; writings on African, **Supp. 7**, 372
Wildlife Management Institute, administration, **Supp. 10**, 265
Wildlife Society, founding of, **Supp. 4**, 484
Wild Party, The, **Supp. 9**, 538
Wiley, Aleander, reference to, **Supp. 10**, 194
Wiley, Harvey W., references to, **Vol. 6, Part 1**, 567; **Supp. 3**, 164
Wiley, Louis, reference to, **Supp. 3**, 787
Wilkes-Barre, Pa., origin of name of, **Vol. 3, Part 1**, 550
Wilkes-Barre Bridge Co., **Vol. 2, Part 2**, 110
Wilkes Exploring Expedition: **Vol. 3, Part 1**, 200; **Vol. 7, Part 2**, 185; **Vol. 9, Part 2**, 457; illustrations for, **Vol. 1, Part 1**, 122
Wilkins, Robert W., reference to, **Supp. 3**, 806
Wilkins, Roy, references to, **Supp. 5**, 741; **Supp. 9**, 750, 751
Wilkins, Sir George Hubert, reference to, **Supp. 5**, 206–7
Wilkinson, James, references to, **Vol. 5, Part 1**, 486; **Vol. 6, Part 1**, 595; **Vol. 7, Part 1**, 35, 483, 543 f., 632; **Vol. 8, Part 2**, 506, 544; **Vol. 9, Part 2**, 349, 601
Willamette University (Oreg.), **Vol. 6, Part 1**, 112
Willard, Emma, School, founding of, **Vol. 10, Part 2**, 232
Willard, Frances E., references to, **Vol. 5, Part 1**, 150; **Vol. 5, Part 2**, 208; **Vol. 7, Part 1**, 252
Willard, Jess, reference to, **Supp. 7**, 414
Willard, Solomon, design of Bunker Hill monument, **Vol. 7, Part 1**, 12
Willard Hotel (Washington, D.C.), **Supp. 6**, 593
Willard Parker Hospital for Infectious Diseases, **Vol. 7, Part 2**, 243
William Marsh Rice Institute, founding of, **Vol. 8, Part 1**, 546 f.
William Penn Charter School, **Vol. 7, Part 1**, 200; **Vol. 7, Part 2**, 436
William Pepper Laboratory of Clinical Medicine, founding of, **Vol. 7, Part 2**, 454
Williams, Bert, reference to, **Supp. 5**, 210
Williams, Clyde E., reference to, **Supp. 4**, 329
Williams, Edward Bennett, references to, **Supp. 9**, 396, 620
Williams, Esther, reference to, **Supp. 10**, 35
Williams, G. Mennen, reference to, **Supp. 5**, 505
Williams, George Huntington, reference to, **Supp. 3**, 38
Williams, Hank, Jr., references to, **Supp. 5**, 748, 749
Williams, Helen, reference to, **Supp. 9**, 491
Williams, John, reference to, **Supp. 3**, 568
Williams, John Whitridge, reference to, **Supp. 3**, 223
Williams, Lefty, reference to, **Supp. 8**, 575
Williams, Richard Norris, II, reference to, **Supp. 6**, 538
Williams, Roger: **Vol. 1, Part 1**, 471; **Vol. 4, Part 2**, 459; **Vol. 5, Part 1**, 199; relations with John Clarke, **Vol. 2, Part 2**, 155; statue of, **Vol. 9, Part 1**, 169
Williams, Ted, reference to, **Supp. 10**, 860
Williams, Tennessee, references to, **Supp. 4**, 823; **Supp. 9**, 421
Williams, William Carlos, references to, **Supp. 5**, 659; **Supp. 10**, 869
Williamsburg, Va.: **Vol. 4, Part 2**, 430; **Vol. 5, Part 1**, 154; capital moved to, **Vol. 7, Part 1**, 500; folk art collection, **Supp. 8**, 240; restoration of, **Supp. 1**, 165; **Supp. 4**, 696; **Supp. 5**, 388; **Supp. 6**, 549, 562; **Supp. 10**, 684
Williamsburg Association, **Vol. 7, Part 1**, 326
Williamsburg, battle of, **Vol. 3, Part 1**, 598; **Vol. 5, Part 1**, 343; **Vol. 5, Part 2**, 145; **Vol. 6, Part 1**, 391, 583; **Vol. 9, Part 1**, 272
Williams College (Mass.): **Vol. 2, Part 1**, 534, 585; **Vol. 4, Part 1**, 620; **Vol. 5, Part 1**, 215 f.; **Vol. 7, Part 1**, 146; **Vol. 7, Part 2**, 482; **Vol. 8, Part 2**, 550; **Vol. 9, Part 1**, 481; college song, *The Mountains, The Mountains*, **Vol. 4, Part 1**, 326; founding of, **Vol. 10, Part 2**, 259; museum at, **Vol. 3, Part 1**, 268; presidency, **Supp. 3**, 293; **Supp. 4**, 224
Willis, Henry Stuart, reference to, **Supp. 3**, 431
Williston Seminary, **Vol. 10, Part 2**, 310
Willkie, Wendell L.: characterization of, **Supp. 5**, 343; presidential candidacy, **Supp. 3**, 400, 497, 659; **Supp. 5**, 152; **Supp. 6**, 618; **Supp. 7**, 414, 615–16; **Supp. 8**, 376, 394, 421, 617; **Supp. 9**, 356–57; references to, **Supp. 9**, 546, 732; Schneiderman defense by, **Supp. 5**, 389; Van Doren, Irita, relationship, **Supp. 8**, 667
Wills, C. Harold, references to, **Supp. 4**, 293, 295, 300
Wills, Helen. *See* Moody, Helen Wills
Willstätter, Richard, reference to, **Supp. 5**, 669–70
Willys-Overland Co.: **Supp. 8**, 610; Jeep manufactured, **Supp. 9**, 290
Wilmer, William Holland, reference to, **Supp. 7**, 70
Wilmer Ophthalmological Institute, founding of, **Supp. 2**, 722; **Supp. 7**, 70
Wilmington, Del., church building in, **Vol. 2, Part 2**, 609
Wilmington, N.C.: capture of, *See* Fort Fisher, N.C.; economic development, **Vol. 3, Part 1**, 480 f.
Wilmington & Northern Railroad, **Vol. 3, Part 1**, 528 f.
Wilmington & Weldon Railroad, **Vol. 1, Part 1**, 388
Wilmington Chemical Corporation, founding of, **Supp. 3**, 239
Wilmot Proviso, **Vol. 2, Part 1**, 49, 417, 419, 564; **Vol. 5, Part 1**, 604; **Vol. 5, Part 2**, 397; **Vol. 6, Part 1**, 586; **Vol. 8, Part 1**, 34 f.; **Vol. 9, Part 2**, 352, 590; **Vol. 10, Part 2**, 317
Wilson, Alexander: Audubon and, **Vol. 1, Part 1**, 425; Backman, John, and, **Vol. 1, Part 1**, 466; Ord, George, and, **Vol. 7, Part 2**, 49
Wilson, Charles E., references to, **Supp. 6**, 618; **Supp. 7**, 794; **Supp. 9**, 193, 477
Wilson, Don, reference to, **Supp. 9**, 76
Wilson, E. B., reference to, **Supp. 4**, 516
Wilson, E. D., reference to, **Supp. 5**, 273
Wilson, Edith Galt, reference to, **Supp. 5**, 697
Wilson, Edmund, references to, **Supp. 3**, 72, 539; **Supp. 8**, 136, 150; **Supp. 10**, 424
Wilson, Eleanor Randolph, reference to, **Supp. 3**, 480

Wilson, H. W., Co., founding of, **Supp. 5**, 752–53
Wilson, James, reference to, **Supp. 3**, 145
Wilson, LeRoy A., reference to, **Supp. 10**, 154
Wilson, Louis B., reference to, **Supp. 3**, 503
Wilson, Louis Round, reference to, **Supp. 10**, 778
Wilson, Paul Caldwell, reference to, **Supp. 7**, 608
Wilson, William G., reference to, **Supp. 10**, 731
Wilson, Woodrow: **Vol. 4, Part 2**, 113; **Vol. 5, Part 1**, 393; **Vol. 9, Part 1**, 286; admirers of, **Supp. 6**, 75, 137, 228; Baker relationship, **Supp. 2**, 19; Barkley relationship, **Supp. 6**, 34; Baruch relationship, **Supp. 7**, 35–36; biography of, **Supp. 4**, 47; **Supp. 6**, 521; Brandeis relationship, **Supp. 3**, 97; campaign financing, **Supp. 2**, 129; civil rights record, **Supp. 4**, 581; Colby relationship, **Supp. 4**, 170–71; congressional supporters, **Supp. 3**, 706; Corwin relationship, **Supp. 7**, 146; Daniels relationship, **Supp. 4**, 216; Davies, J. E., relationship, **Supp. 6**, 146, 147; Dulles, J. F., relationship, **Supp. 6**, 177; economic policy, **Supp. 3**, 211–12; foreign policy, **Supp. 3**, 396; Fosdick appointments, **Supp. 9**, 287, 288; Fourteen Points, **Supp. 2**, 320; **Supp. 7**, 536; **Supp. 9**, 504; Hardwick opposition to, **Supp. 3**, 330–31; House relationship, **Supp. 2**, 319–20; League of Nations, **Supp. 3**, 472–74; **Supp. 6**, 388; **Supp. 9**, 504; Lowell, A. L., relationship, **Supp. 3**, 469; Morgenthau relationship, **Supp. 4**, 603; press relations, **Supp. 1**, 210; **Supp. 3**, 702; Princeton University policies, **Vol. 3, Part 2**, 386; **Supp. 1**, 399; **Supp. 3**, 810; **Supp. 4**, 143; psychobiography of, **Supp. 8**, 61; Reed relationship, **Supp. 3**, 622; references to, **Supp. 1**, 210, 465; Senate opposition to, **Supp. 4**, 669–70; Senate support for, **Supp. 4**, 641–42; studies on, **Supp. 2**, 153; Thomas Riley Marshall and, **Vol. 6, Part 2**, 331; Tumulty relationship, **Supp. 5**, 696–97; Walter Hines Page and, **Vol. 7, Part 2**, 143 f.; and Wall Street, **Vol. 4, Part 2**, 372; wife, **Supp. 7**, 796; woman suffrage stance, **Supp. 4**, 157–58; **Supp. 7**, 717; **Supp. 8**, 244; World War I neutrality actons, **Supp. 4**, 725; writings on, **Supp. 7**, 683–84
Wilson, W. T. R., reference to, **Supp. 7**, 133
Wilson-Audubon controversy, **Vol. 7, Part 2**, 49
Wilson bill: **Vol. 2, Part 2**, 210; **Vol. 5, Part 2**, 178; exponent of, **Vol. 7, Part 2**, 331
Wilson Bulletin, founding of, **Supp. 5**, 374
Wilson Dam, **Supp. 2**, 119
Wilson-Gorman Tariff Act, **Vol. 7, Part 2**, 33
Wilson's Creek, battle of, **Vol. 6, Part 1**, 535; **Vol. 8, Part 1**, 216; **Vol. 8, Part 2**, 453; **Vol. 9, Part 1**, 153; **Vol. 9, Part 2**, 183
Winant, John G., reference to, **Supp. 3**, 543
Winchell, Newton H., reference to, **Supp. 3**, 695
Winchell, Walter, references to, **Supp. 6**, 232; **Supp. 8**, 39; **Supp. 9**, 61, 802; **Supp. 10**, 290
Winchester, Va., battle of, **Vol. 1, Part 1**, 578; **Vol. 5, Part 1**, 557; **Vol. 9, Part 1**, 80, 107. *See also* Opequon Creek
Winchester Arms Co., **Vol. 5, Part 1**, 247; **Vol. 10, Part 2**, 379
Winchester rifle, invention and manufacturing of, **Vol. 5, Part 1**, 247; **Vol. 10, Part 2**, 379
Wind, measurement of, **Vol. 5, Part 1**, 252; **Vol. 7, Part 1**, 526
Windmills, manufacture of, **Vol. 7, Part 1**, 590–1
Winds of Fear, The, **Supp. 9**, 160
Windsor, Duke and Duchess of (Great Britain), **Supp. 3**, 50
Windsor, Conn.: genealogy, **Vol. 9, Part 2**, 21; early history of, **Vol. 9, Part 2**, 21
Wind tunnels, **Supp. 4**, 486; **Supp. 8**, 439, 440
Wine: importation of, **Vol. 7, Part 2**, 631; making, **Vol. 1, Part 1**, 109; **Vol. 2, Part 2**, 374 f.; **Vol. 4, Part 2**, 494; **Vol. 5, Part 1**, 430; **Vol. 7, Part 1**, 335 f.; trade, **Vol. 5, Part 2**, 246 f.
Wineries, **Supp. 7**, 614
Winesburg, Ohio, **Supp. 3**, 13
Wing, DeWitt, reference to, **Supp. 9**, 33
Wing, Shoudy and Putnam, **Supp. 6**, 87–88
Winnebago Indians, **Supp. 6**, 524–25
Winnebago War (1827), **Vol. 3, Part 1**, 349
Winnetka, Ill., individualized education in, **Supp. 7**, 42
Winning of Barbara Worth, The, **Supp. 3**, 846
Winnsboro Female Institute, **Vol. 5, Part 2**, 524
Winslow, Mary, reference to, **Supp. 7**, 718
Winslow Covenant, **Vol. 3, Part 1**, 3
Winston, Harry, Inc., **Supp. 10**, 847–48
Winter Garden (New York City), **Vol. 1, Part 2**, 446
Wintergreen Club (Boston), **Vol. 8, Part 2**, 45
Winters, Yvor, reference to, **Supp. 8**, 20
Winterset, **Supp. 10**, 535
Winthrop, Bronson, reference to, **Supp. 4**, 785
Winthrop, John: **Vol. 5, Part 1**, 436; *History of New England, Vol. III*, discovery of, **Vol. 1, Part 1**, 361
Winthrop College (S.C.), **Vol. 5, Part 2**, 227; **Vol. 9, Part 2**, 548
Winthrop-Hoover controversy, **Vol. 5, Part 1**, 200
"Win with Willkie," **Supp. 9**, 670
Wire: barbed, **Vol. 4, Part 1**, 331; **Vol. 4, Part 2**, 94; cables, first use of, for, **Vol. 8, Part 2**, 88; manufacture, **Vol. 3, Part 2**, 489; **Vol. 4, Part 1**, 188; **Vol. 4, Part 2**, 156; **Vol. 5, Part 2**, 53; **Vol. 6, Part 1**, 334; **Vol. 7, Part 1**, 165 f.; **Vol. 8, Part 2**, 189; **Vol. 10, Part 1**, 376 f., 501 f.; rope, first manufacture of, in America, **Vol. 8, Part 2**, 88; suspension bridges, **Vol. 4, Part 2**, 156
Wireless, early experiments with, **Vol. 3, Part 1**, 614 f.; **Vol. 6, Part 1**, 400; **Vol. 8, Part 2**, 100; **Vol. 10, Part 1**, 635 f. *See also* Radio
Wire photography, **Supp. 5**, 323
Wire service, gambling, **Supp. 3**, 21
Wiretapping, federal use of, **Supp. 3**, 99
Wirz, Henry, reference to, **Vol. 5, Part 1**, 182
Wisconsin: agriculture, **Vol. 2, Part 1**, 557; **Vol. 9, Part 1**, 280; banking in, **Vol. 7, Part 1**, 39 f.; **Vol. 9, Part 1**, 268; capitol, **Vol. 8, Part 1**, 115 f.; constitution of, **Vol. 1, Part 2**, 90; **Vol. 3, Part 1**, 520 f.; **Vol. 6, Part 1**, 5; dairy promotion, **Vol. 5, Part 1**, 90; Democratic party, **Supp. 10**, 194; education, **Vol. 2, Part 2**, 353; **Vol. 5, Part 1**, 321; **Vol. 5, Part 2**, 400; **Vol. 7, Part 2**, 343; **Vol. 8, Part 2**, 307; Episcopal controversies in, **Vol. 3, Part 1**, 206; exploration, **Vol. 3, Part 1**, 500 f.; geology, **Vol. 7, Part 2**, 460; governors, **Vol. 1, Part 2**, 1 f., 33; **Vol. 3, Part 2**, 253 f.; **Vol. 4, Part 2**, 374 f.; **Vol. 5, Part 1**, 90 f.; **Vol. 5, Part 2**, 541; **Vol. 7, Part 2**, 376 f., 535 f.; **Vol. 8, Part 1**, 344 f.; **Vol. 8, Part 2**, 235 f.; **Vol. 10, Part 1**, 495 f.; **Supp. 1**, 86; **Supp. 2**, 366; **Supp. 7**, 450–51; **Supp. 10**, 420–21; historical material, collection of, **Vol. 3, Part 1**, 551 f.; history of, **Vol. 3, Part 1**, 520 f; **Vol. 9, Part 2**, 521–22; income tax, **Supp. 1**, 385; judiciary, elective, **Vol. 3, Part 1**, 520 f.; **Supp. 10**, 194; land developments, **Vol. 3, Part 1**, 390; **Vol. 10, Part 1**, 495 f.; lead mining, **Vol. 6, Part 2**, 497; legal service, **Vol. 3, Part 1**, 330, 375, 520; **Vol. 5, Part 1**, 211; **Vol. 7, Part 2**, 145; **Vol. 8, Part 1**, 344; **Vol. 8, Part 2**, 262; **Vol. 10, Part 2**, 399; library service, **Vol. 3, Part 1**, 551 f.; **Vol. 6, Part 1**, 148; limnology studies, **Supp. 4**, 84–85; maps, early, **Vol. 3, Part 1**, 390; **Vol. 5, Part 2**, 612; political service, **Vol. 1, Part 2**, 33, 90, 588; **Vol. 3, Part 1**, 349, 375, 390, 520; **Vol. 3, Part 2**, 254; **Vol. 5, Part 1**, 374; **Vol. 5, Part 2**, 543; **Vol. 7, Part 2**, 149, 377, 535; **Vol. 8, Part 1**, 344; **Vol. 9, Part 1**, 583; **Vol. 10, Part 1**, 495; politics, **Supp. 3**, 256–57; **Supp. 4**, 481–82; **Supp. 6**, 404–5; **Supp. 7**,

348–49; **Supp. 8**, 701; **Supp. 9**, 29, 30; **Supp. 10**, 194, 420, 421; pre-Civil War politics, **Vol. 6, Part 1**, 5; Progressive legislation in, **Vol. 6, Part 1**, 571; **Vol. 8, Part 2**, 86; **Vol. 10, Part 2**, 399; **Supp. 3**, 178; Progressive party, **Supp. 5**, 403–4; **Supp. 10**, 194; public service, **Vol. 4, Part 2**, 184, 236, 374, 386; **Vol. 5, Part 1**, 551; **Vol. 6, Part 1**, 536; **Vol. 8, Part 2**, 86, 236, 396; Republican party, **Vol. 8, Part 2**, 213; settlement, **Vol. 2, Part 1**, 552; **Vol. 7, Part 1**, 599; **Vol. 10, Part 2**, 255; slavery question, **Vol. 3, Part 1**, 375; Socialist party, **Supp. 1**, 72–74; social welfare, **Supp. 9**, 27; sociological study of Walworth County, **Supp. 4**, 312; surveys, **Vol. 3, Part 1**, 390; Taliesin, **Supp. 6**, 713, 714; teacher training in, **Vol. 8, Part 2**, 307; Territory, organization of, **Vol. 5, Part 2**, 172; unemployment insurance, **Supp. 3**, 255; woman suffrage, **Supp. 1**, 432
Wisconsin, The (newspaper), **Vol. 1, Part 1**, 129
Wisconsin Conference on Social Work, **Supp. 7**, 787
Wisconsin Industrial Commission, founding of, **Supp. 3**, 178
"Wisconsin idea," in politics, **Vol. 5, Part 2**, 544
Wisconsin, process (chemistry), development of, **Supp. 9**, 218
Wisconsin State Historical Society, **Vol. 3, Part 1**, 551 f.; **Vol. 7, Part 1**, 331; **Vol. 9, Part 2**, 521
Wisconsin State Journal, **Supp. 7**, 535
Wisconsin State Sportsmen's Association, **Vol. 8, Part 1**, 58 f.
Wisconsin State Teachers' Association, **Vol. 7, Part 2**, 343
Wisconsin Vorwärts, **Supp. 1**, 72
Wise, Stephen S., references to, **Supp. 3**, 97; **Supp. 4**, 603; **Supp. 7**, 356, 689; **Supp. 8**, 549
Wise Men (public relations), **Supp. 9**, 682
Wistar Association, formation of, **Vol. 10, Part 2**, 434
Wit. *See* Humor
Witchcraft: **Vol. 5, Part 1**, 2, 333; **Vol. 7, Part 1**, 553; **Vol. 9, Part 2**, 83; collections on, **Supp. 2**, 75; Cotton Mather and, **Vol. 10, Part 1**, 122; delusion, **Vol. 7, Part 2**, 256; fiction about, **Supp. 8**, 180; psychiatric view of, **Supp. 6**, 724; Salem, **Vol. 2, Part 1**, 410; **Vol. 6, Part 2**, 386 f., 392; **Vol. 7, Part 1**, 595 f.; **Vol. 9, Part 2**, 113; **Vol. 10, Part 1**, 122; study of, **Supp. 3**, 423; trials, **Vol. 2, Part 1**, 410; **Vol. 4, Part 2**, 424; **Vol. 7, Part 1**, 476; **Vol. 8, Part 1**, 292 f.; writings on, **Vol. 10, Part 1**, 122
With Christ After the Lost: A Search for Souls, **Supp. 3**, 688
Witherspoon, Herbert, reference to, **Supp. 6**, 323
Witherspoon, John, reference to, **Vol. 6, Part 1**, 616
Witmark & Sons, **Supp. 3**, 833–34
Witness, **Supp. 7**, 115; **Supp. 9**, 166
Witness Tree, A, **Supp. 7**, 273
Wits, literary, **Vol. 1, Part 1**, 333; **Vol. 6, Part 1**, 16. *See also* "Hartford Wits"
Witt, Nathan, reference to, **Supp. 6**, 379
Witte, Edwin E., reference to, **Supp. 9**, 29
Wittenberg College (Ohio), **Vol. 9, Part 1**, 477
Wizard of Oz, The: **Vol. 1, Part 2**, 59; **Supp. 8**, 203, 355; casting of, **Supp. 10**, 301; production of, **Supp. 9**, 291, 292
WLS (radio station), **Supp. 4**, 132
Wobber, Herman, reference to, **Supp. 7**, 579
Wobblies. *See* Industrial Workers of the World
Woburn, Mass., founding of, **Vol. 8, Part 1**, 574
Wodehouse, P. G., references to, **Supp. 3**, 417, 418
Wofford College (S.C.), president of, **Vol. 9, Part 1**, 114
Wolf, Jacques, and Co., **Supp. 7**, 616
"Wolfe, Nero" (fictional character), **Supp. 9**, 772, 773
Wolfe, Thomas, references to, **Supp. 10**, 275, 390
Wolf Man, The, **Supp. 9**, 169
Wolfson, Louis E., reference to, **Supp. 9**, 839
Wolf Trap cultural center (Vienna, Va.), **Supp. 8**, 593
Wolfe, Bertram, reference to, **Supp. 7**, 291
Wolfe, Harry Kirke, reference to, **Supp. 6**, 261
Wolfe, Theodore P., reference to, **Supp. 6**, 181
Wolfe, Thomas, references to, **Supp. 3**, 426; **Supp. 4**, 651; **Supp. 5**, 53
Wolff, Karl, reference to, **Supp. 8**, 147
Wolfson, Louis E., reference to, **Supp. 6**, 29
Wolheim, Louis Robert, reference to, **Supp. 9**, 242
Wollstonecraft, Mary, liaison with Imray, **Vol. 5, Part 1**, 462
Wolverton, Charles A., reference to, **Supp. 6**, 132
Woman as Force in History, **Supp. 6**, 41
Woman of Paris, A, **Supp. 10**, 116
Woman of the Year, **Supp. 9**, 767
Woman's Board in China, **Vol. 4, Part 2**, 454
Woman's Home Companion, editorship of, **Supp. 1**, 153; **Supp. 3**, 442–43
Woman's Journal, **Supp. 4**, 85–86
Woman's party, **Supp. 5**, 297; **Supp. 6**, 41, 167
Woman's Peace party, **Supp. 1**, 12; founding of, **Supp. 4**, 157
Woman suffrage: **Vol. 1, Part 1**, 320; **Vol. 1, Part 2**, 134, 319, 321, 344, 385, 415, 581; **Vol. 2, Part 1**, 151; **Vol. 3, Part 1**, 141 f., 407, 423, 513 f.; **Vol. 3, Part 2**, 82, 92, 98; **Vol. 4, Part 1**, 86 f., 135, 171, 262, 339, 542, 622; **Vol. 4, Part 2**, 281, 376, 436, 514; **Vol. 5, Part 1**, 17, 150, 195 f., 292, 312, 386; **Vol. 5, Part 2**, 246; **Vol. 6, Part 1**, 188, 306, 340 f.; **Vol. 7, Part 1**, 29, 289; **Vol. 7, Part 2**, 609; **Vol. 8, Part 2**, 44 f., 610; **Vol. 9, Part 1**, 15, 233 f., 260, 445, 521 f.; **Vol. 9, Part 2**, 8, 81, 534; activism for, **Supp. 1**, 69, 432; **Supp. 2**, 43, 482, 743; **Supp. 4**, 156–58, 623–24; **Supp. 5**, 296–97, 473–74; **Supp. 6**, 40–41, 79, 167; **Supp. 8**, 317; **Supp. 10**, 622; arrest and imprisonment of protestors, **Supp. 4**, 542; **Supp. 7**, 717; black involvement, **Supp. 3**, 828; constitutional amendment legislation and passage, **Supp. 4**, 158, 861–62; **Supp. 7**, 779; Idaho, **Vol. 3, Part 1**, 513 f.; Illinois, **Supp. 3**, 710; international campaign, **Supp. 4**, 157, 724–25; **Supp. 10**, 622; male support, **Supp. 1**, 315, 372; **Supp. 4**, 850; Men's League for, **Vol. 1, Part 1**, 413; Missouri, **Vol. 7, Part 1**, 29; Montana, **Supp. 9**, 640; New York, **Supp. 7**, 196, 778–79; Ohio, **Supp. 8**, 4; Oregon, **Vol. 3, Part 1**, 513 f., Oregon initiative, **Supp. 6**, 682; political campaign issue, **Supp. 8**, 244; split in movement's tactics, **Supp. 4**, 156–57; state campaigns for, **Supp. 5**, 742; Texas, **Supp. 7**, 350; trade union support, **Supp. 9**, 706; Washington Territory, **Vol. 3, Part 1**, 513 f.; women's opposition to movement, **Supp. 3**, 762; **Supp. 5**, 488; writings on, **Supp. 5**, 62. *See also* Feminism
Woman-suffrage associations: Illinois, **Vol. 1, Part 2**, 581; New York, **Vol. 1, Part 2**, 344; Oregon, **Vol. 3, Part 1**, 513 f.
Woman Suffrage party, **Supp. 6**, 79
Woman's Suffrage party (New York City), **Supp. 7**, 778–79
Woman Voter, The, **Supp. 6**, 40
Women: activities of, **Vol. 9, Part 1**, 101; advice columns, **Supp. 5**, 244; aesthetic contributions, **Vol. 9, Part 1**, 262; anthropological fieldwork, **Supp. 8**, 509–10; archaeology, **Supp. 3**, 343–44; architecture, **Supp. 6**, 462–64; arctic exploration, **Supp. 5**, 539–40; Army Nurse Corps, **Supp. 4**, 789; astronomy, **Supp. 3**, 130–31; **Supp. 10**, 625–26; aviation, **Supp. 6**, 477–78; **Supp. 10**, 213–14; biographies of, **Supp. 7**, 14; black leadership, **Supp. 5**, 55–56; black social work, **Supp. 4**, 53–54; black writers, **Supp. 7**, 319; bloomer costume for, **Vol. 1, Part 1**, 319; **Vol. 4, Part 2**, 376; business ownership, **Supp. 4**, 455; Cath-

olic orders, **Supp. 5**, 581; charitable organizations for, **Vol. 7, Part 2**, 257; cheesecake photography, **Supp. 5**, 270, 271, 453; circus performing, **Supp. 6**, 8; civil rights leadership, **Supp. 8**, 539–40; **Supp. 10**, 307–8; civil service, **Vol. 9, Part 1**, 460; clubs for, **Vol. 3, Part 1**, 423; **Vol. 5, Part 1**, 418; **Vol. 8, Part 2**, 45, 225, 327, 599 f.; college offers graduate work to, **Vol. 8, Part 1**, 531; Communist party organizing, **Supp. 5**, 70; **Supp. 7**, 248–49; Congress, **Supp. 5**, 582; **Supp. 6**, 475, 479–81, 551–52; **Supp. 9**, 640; **Supp. 10**, 57, 183; contract bridge, **Supp. 6**, 134–35; corporate direction, **Supp. 7**, 604–5; dress of, **Vol. 1, Part 2**, 385; **Vol. 4, Part 2**, 376; **Vol. 10, Part 2**, 521; educational opportunities for, **Vol. 1, Part 1**, 21; **Vol. 1, Part 2**, 125, 178, 423, 455, 546; **Vol. 2, Part 2**, 214, 321, 596; **Vol. 3, Part 1**, 408, 423; **Vol. 4, Part 1**, 297; **Vol. 4, Part 2**, 245, 369; **Vol. 5, Part 2**, 524; **Vol. 6, Part 1**, 72; **Vol. 6, Part 2**, 624; **Vol. 7, Part 2**, 525, 568 f., 647; **Vol. 8, Part 1**, 412 f., 553, 559; **Vol. 9, Part 1**, 158; **Vol. 9, Part 2**, 276, 572; **Vol. 10, Part 1**, 77 f.; education of, *see subheads:* universities and colleges for; vocational education for; entrepreneurs, **Supp. 8**, 12–14, 560–61; escape novels for, **Supp. 5**, 33; evangelical preaching by, **Supp. 4**, 875–76; feminist fiction, **Supp. 7**, 386; finance, **Supp. 8**, 534; first admitted to Kentucky bar, **Supp. 4**, 106–7; first cabinet member, **Supp. 3**, 647; **Supp. 7**, 609–10; first college in China, **Supp. 3**, 288; first federal social-welfare legislation for, **Supp. 5**, 532; first foreign service diplomat, **Supp. 5**, 582; first in Congress, **Supp. 9**, 640; first in Senate, **Supp. 4**, 144–45; first interior decorator, **Supp. 4**, 229; first governor, **Supp. 10**, 703; First Ladies, **Supp. 7**, 660–61, 796; **Supp. 10**, 212–13; first on Philadelphia education board, **Supp. 5**, 432; first opera company head, **Supp. 8**, 201; first orchestra open to instrumentalists, **Supp. 3**, 359; first tennis grand-slam winner, **Supp. 8**, 101–2; first union executive board member, **Supp. 9**, 705; first wrestling manager, **Supp. 5**, 417, foreign correspondents, **Supp. 6**, 543; foreign missions, **Supp. 4**, 647–48; "free woman" image, **Supp. 4**, 576; "girl next door" image, **Supp. 7**, 140; government service, **Supp. 10**, 681; governorship of states, **Supp. 7**, 242; **Supp. 8**, 676–77; **Supp. 10**, 703–4; history studies programs, **Supp. 6**, 40–41; idealized illustrations of, **Supp. 3**, 300; **Supp. 4**, 826; **Supp. 5**, 112, 113, 637; interior decorating, **Supp. 4**, 229; **Supp. 8**, 140; international writers' conference, **Supp. 6**, 576; in iron manufacturing, **Vol. 6, Part 1**, 500; "It Girl," **Supp. 7**, 68; journalism, **Supp. 5**, 447; **Supp. 8**, 250–60, 432; **Supp. 10**, 666, 675–76; judiciary, **Supp. 6**, 114; **Supp. 8**, 4–5; Justice Department, **Supp. 6**, 3–4; labor conditions, improvement of, **Supp. 4**, 623–24; labor laws for, **Supp. 1**, 463; labor movement, **Vol. 4, Part 1**, 288; **Supp. 2**, 408; **Supp. 3**, 355–56, 576–77, 639; **Supp. 4**, 69–70, 626; **Supp. 7**, 196, 455; law, **Supp. 7**, 785–86; law, contributions to, **Vol. 3, Part 2**, 552; **Vol. 4, Part 2**, 380, 514; **Vol. 6, Part 1**, 341; law studies, **Supp. 2**, 482; legal rights of, **Supp. 7**, 785; liberal arts studies, **Supp. 4**, 625; literary contribution, **Vol. 3, Part 2**, 368; **Vol. 4, Part 2**, 143; **Vol. 5, Part 1**, 292; Masonic Order, **Vol. 2, Part 2**, 554; medicine, **Supp. 5**, 600–601; **Supp. 8**, 241–42; medicine, contributions of, **Vol. 1, Part 2**, 320; **Vol. 3, Part 1**, 141; **Vol. 4, Part 1**, 604; **Vol. 4, Part 2**, 376; **Vol. 5, Part 1**, 385 f., 564 f.; **Vol. 6, Part 2**, 307, 550; **Vol. 8, Part 1**, 201, 285; **Vol. 9, Part 1**, 234; **Vol. 10, Part 2**, 642; military, **Supp. 7**, 289; New Deal, **Supp. 7**, 660; newspaper editing by, **Vol. 1, Part 2**, 581; newspaper publishing, **Supp. 4**, 644; **Supp. 7**, 603–4; novels about, **Supp. 4**, 31; organizations, **Supp. 7**, 708; peace activism, **Supp. 1**, 12, 432–33, 157, 158, 725–27, 912–13; **Supp. 7**, 29, 186; photography by, **Supp. 5**, 24–25; photojournalism by, **Supp. 7**, 115–16; physical fitness programs for, **Supp. 5**, 52; **Supp. 8**, 337; political contributions of, **Vol. 4, Part 2**, 381; political journalism by, **Supp. 7**, 739–40; political participation by, **Supp. 3**, 710–11; **Supp. 5**, 62, 157; **Supp. 9**, 625–26, 789–90; **Supp. 10**, 29–30, 57, 183, 307–8, 465, 545–46, 622–23; professional associations for, **Supp. 5**, 543; Prohibition advocacy by, **Supp. 5**, 80; Prohibition opposition by, **Supp. 5**, 157; psychoanalytic view of, **Supp. 5**, 302; psychological studies of, **Supp. 5**, 316, 317; **Supp. 8**, 423; public health promotion by, **Supp. 3**, 28; publications for, **Supp. 3**, 442–43; race horse ownership, **Supp. 7**, 695–96; reform and, **Vol. 1, Part 2**, 319; **Vol. 3, Part 2**, 492; **Vol. 9, Part 1**, 36; salon of, **Vol. 3, Part 2**, 377; school administration by, **Supp. 8**, 9; in Senate, **Vol. 3, Part 2**, 318; sex symbols, **Supp. 5**, 270, 271, 453; **Supp. 7**, 68, 545–46, 743; **Supp. 8**, 412; showgirls, **Supp. 4**, 814–15; social clubs for, **Supp. 5**, 505; social reform leadership, **Supp. 5**, 297, 616–17, 509–10, 515–16; **Supp. 7**, 248; sociological writings on, **Supp. 3**, 581; sports, **Supp. 6**, 425–26, 722–23; **Supp. 9**, 868–69; sports club ownership, **Supp. 6**, 120–21; universities and colleges for, **Supp. 1**, 146, 684; **Supp. 4**, 625, 913; **Supp. 5**, 488; **Supp. 9**, 174–75; **Supp. 10**, 735–36, 846; university opens all professional schools to, **Vol. 10, Part 1**, 490 f.; unwed mothers, services for, **Supp. 3**, 221; vocational bureau for college, **Vol. 4, Part 1**, 285; vocational education for, **Supp. 2**, 398; vocational guidance for, **Supp. 4**, 364–66; **Supp. 6**, 412; working conditions improved for, **Vol. 1, Part 2**, 471; World War II, **Supp. 6**, 407; writings on, **Vol. 4, Part 1**, 65; Zionist organizations, **Supp. 3**, 756–57. *See also* Equal Rights Amendment; Feminism; Motherhood; Woman suffrage; Women's rights

Women, The, **Supp. 10**,713

Women's Action Committee for Victory and Lasting Peace, **Supp. 6**, 79

Women's Christian Temperance Union (WCTU): **Vol. 3, Part 2**, 552; **Vol. 4, Part 2**, 436; **Vol. 6, Part 1**, 85; **Vol. 7, Part 1**, 394; **Vol. 9, Part 1**, 36,**Vol. 9, Part 2**, 8 f.; **Vol. 10, Part 2**, 234; **Supp. 3**, 130, 164; **Supp. 5**, 80; schisms, **Vol. 3, Part 2**, 553; White Cross Society, **Vol. 6, Part 1**, 86

Women's Clubs. *See* General Federation of Women's Clubs

Women's Educational and Industrial Union, **Vol. 5, Part 2**, 287

Women's Foreign Missionary Society, **Vol. 7, Part 2**, 218

Women's International League for Peace and Freedom, **Supp. 4**, 725; **Supp. 5**, 474; **Supp. 7**, 29

Women's International Organizations, Peace and Disarmament Committee, **Supp. 7**, 186

Women's Joint Congressional Committee, **Supp. 5**, 532, 533

Women's Municipal League, **Supp. 3**, 638–39

Women's National Indian Association, foundation of, **Vol. 8, Part 1**, 335 f.

Women's National Loyal League, **Vol. 8, Part 2**, 158

Women's Organization for National Prohibition Reform, founding of, **Supp. 5**, 157

Women's Political League, **Vol. 3, Part 2**, 98

Women's Political Union, founding of, **Supp. 2**, 43

Women's Press Club, **Vol. 2, Part 2**, 561

Women's Pure Food Vacuum Preserving Co., **Vol. 5, Part 2**, 160

Women's rights: **Vol. 1, Part 2**, 385, 485; **Vol. 2, Part, 1**, 584; **Vol. 3, Part 1**, 35; **Vol. 3, Part 2**, 542; **Vol. 4,**

Part 1, 64 f., 85, 344, 425, 529, 635; **Vol. 4, Part 2**, 380; **Vol. 5, Part 2**, 112; **Vol. 6, Part 2**, 447; **Vol. 7, Part 1**, 288 f., 399, 490 f.; **Vol. 8, Part 1**, 117, 488; **Vol. 8, Part 2**, 158, 600; **Vol. 9, Part 1**, 35, 521 f.; **Vol. 9, Part 2**, 81, 552; **Vol. 10, Part 2**, 234, 642; activism for, **Supp. 1**, 244; **Supp. 4**, 85–86, 835; **Supp. 5**, 62, 69–70, 532; **Supp. 8**, 4–5; **Supp. 8**, 520; birth control movement, **Supp. 8**, 568–69; black leadership, **Supp. 3**, 827–28; **Supp. 5**, 680; citizenship, choice of, **Supp. 3**, 701; comfortable clothing advocacy, **Supp. 4**, 231; **Supp. 7**, 634; **Supp. 8**, 77; economic independence, **Supp. 1**, 346; equal employment opportunity, **Supp. 5**, 432; equal pay for equal work, **Supp. 7**, 13; Equal Rights Amendment, **Supp. 4**, 145; **Supp. 5**, 474, 543; **Supp. 7**, 717; **Supp. 9**, 546–47; 706; Equal Rights Amendment opposition, **Supp. 5**, 532; first paper in America on, **Vol. 3, Part 1**, 141; international movements, **Supp. 4**, 157; **Supp. 7**, 717–18; male support for, **Supp. 4**, 231; organized religion leadership, **Supp. 1**, 372; ridiculed, **Vol. 9, Part 2**, 89; traditional role advocacy, **Supp. 8**, 433; writings on, **Vol. 3, Part 1**, 35, 284; **Vol. 4, Part 1**, 85, 635; **Supp. 4**, 106–7; **Supp. 7**, 13–14. *See also* Equal Rights Amendment; Feminism; Woman suffrage

Women's Trade Union League: **Supp. 6**, 40; **Supp. 7**, 12, 28; organized, **Vol. 4, Part 1**, 288; **Supp. 5**, 616; leadership, **Supp. 5**, 578–79; **Supp. 9**, 705–6

Women's Union Missionary Society, founding of, **Vol. 3, Part 1**, 378; **Vol. 8, Part 1**, 335 f.

Women's Wear Daily, drama criticism, **Supp. 5**, 17

Wood, Grant, reference to, **Supp. 9**, 79

Wood, Jutro, reference to, **Vol. 6, Part 1**, 614

Wood, Leonard, references to, **Vol. 7, Part 2**, 296; **Supp. 1**, 17; **Supp. 2**, 138, 579; **Supp. 3**, 467, 614; **Supp. 4**, 122–23

Wood, Leonard, Memorial, **Supp. 7**, 195

Wood, Lloyd, reference to, **Supp. 10**, 242

Wood, Richardson, reference to, **Supp. 9**, 677

Wood, Thomas D., reference to, **Supp. 3**, 677

Woodall, Charles J., reference to, **Supp. 4**, 294

Woodberry, George E., reference to, **Supp. 4**, 135

Wood-block prints, pioneering in, **Vol. 5, Part 1**, 450

Woodbridge, N.J., public service, **Vol. 7, Part 2**, 226

Wood carving, **Vol. 5, Part 2**, 426 f.; **Vol. 6, Part 1**, 284; **Vol. 9, Part 2**, 75

Woodcock, Fred, reference to, **Supp. 6**, 356

Woodcock, Thomas, reference to, **Supp. 6**, 457–58

Woodcraft, **Vol. 4, Part 2**, 353; in stories, **Vol. 4, Part 2**, 413

Woodcraft League of America, **Supp. 4**, 737

Woodcuts, collecting of, **Vol. 8, Part 1**, 228 f.

Wood engraving, **Vol. 1, Part 1**, 93, 262, 315; **Vol. 1, Part 2**, 502; **Vol. 3, Part 1**, 423 f.; **Vol. 3, Part 2**, 549; **Vol. 4, Part 2**, 321; **Vol. 5, Part 2**, 243 f., 508 f.; **Vol. 6, Part 1**, 284, 422; **Vol. 9, Part 2**, 43; **Vol. 10, Part 2**, 447

Woodin, William H., references to, **Supp. 3**, 647; **Supp. 5**, 324; **Supp. 8**, 112

Woodlock, Thomas F., reference to, **Supp. 3**, 559

Woodman, Cyrus, reference to, **Vol. 10, Part 1**, 495 f.

Woodman, Joe, references to, **Supp. 6**, 362, 363

Wood manufacture, **Vol. 9, Part 1**, 583

Wood pulp: experiments in, **Vol. 5, Part 2**, 281; manufacturing of, **Vol. 2, Part 2**, 281

Woodrow Wilson: Life and Letters, **Supp. 4**, 47

Woodruff, Lorande L., reference to, **Supp. 3**, 127

Woodruff, Robert W., reference to, **Supp. 8**, 404

Woods, Arthur, references to, **Supp. 6**, 559; **Supp. 7**, 362

Woods, Dr. Leonard, reference to, **Vol. 10, Part 1**, 447 f.

Woods, Lyman, reference to, **Supp. 9**, 75

Woods Hole Laboratory, established, **Vol. 5, Part 1**, 447. *See also* Marine Biological Laboratory

Woods Hole Oceanographic Institution (Mass.), **Supp. 5**, 536, 656; founding of, **Supp. 8**, 38

Wood's Lake, battle of, **Vol. 9, Part 1**, 145

Woodstock, Conn., public service, **Vol. 1, Part 2**, 505

Woodstock, N.Y., artists' colony, **Vol. 4, Part 2**, 346; **Supp. 5**, 693; **Supp. 7**, 15

Woodstock, Vt., public service, **Vol. 1, Part 2**, 266

Woodward, Calvin, reference to, **Supp. 5**, 255–56

Woodward, Helen, reference to, **Supp. 3**, 442

Woodworking, **Vol. 5, Part 1**, 518

Woodyatt, Rollin T., reference to, **Supp. 6**, 245

Wool: burring, **Vol. 9, Part 1**, 182; buying of, **Vol. 4, Part 1**, 229; carding, **Vol. 3, Part 2**, 209; **Vol. 9, Part 1**, 145; cleaning of, **Vol. 4, Part 1**, 338; exportation, **Vol. 7, Part 2**, 522; growing of, **Vol. 8, Part 1**, 347; manufacturing of, **Vol. 4, Part 1**, 33; **Vol. 6, Part 1**, 51; **Vol. 7, Part 2**, 146; **Vol. 8, Part 1**, 344, 405; **Vol. 9, Part 1**, 205; **Vol. 10, Part 1**, 600 f.; **Supp. 5**, 54–55; protective tariff for, **Vol. 4, Part 2**, 446; trade, **Vol. 9, Part 1**, 182

Woollcott, Alexander, references to, **Supp. 6**, 628; **Supp. 7**, 325, 413; **Supp. 8**, 491, 622; **Supp. 9**, 488

Woolman, C. E., reference to, **Supp. 9**, 659

Woolrich Woolen Mills, **Supp. 8**, 531, 532

Woolsey, John M., *Ulysses* decision, **Supp. 9**, 165, 683; **Supp. 10**, 221

Woolsey, Theodore D., reference to, **Vol. 9, Part 2**, 392

Woolson House, **Vol. 5, Part 2**, 288

Woolworth, Frank, references to, **Supp. 10**, 366, 367

Woolworth, F. W., references to, **Supp. 8**, 347, 348

Woolworth, F. W., Co., management, **Supp. 9**, 741–42

Woolworth Building (New York City), architecture, **Supp. 1**, 342

"Wooster, Bertie" (fictional character), **Supp. 9**, 888, 889

WOR (radio station), founding of, **Supp. 3**, 30; **Supp. 10**, 479; sports broadcasts, **Supp. 10**, 256; technical operations at, **Supp. 9**, 728

WOR (television station), transmission facilities developed, **Supp. 9**, 728

Worcester, Elwood, references to, **Vol. 7, Part 1**, 524; **Supp. 3**, 191

Worcester, Joseph Emerson, reference to, **Vol. 10, Part 1**, 594 f.

Worcester, Mass.: Art Museum, **Supp. 6**, 621, 622; civic service, **Vol. 7, Part 1**, 490; first postmaster of, **Vol. 9, Part 2**, 436; first printer in, **Vol. 9, Part 2**, 436; sanitary conditions, **Vol. 5, Part 2**, 419

Worcester Foundation for Experimental Biology, founding of, **Supp. 8**, 503

Worcester Polytechnic Institute, **Vol. 8, Part 1**, 221 f.; **Vol. 9, Part 1**, 275; **Vol. 9, Part 2**, 453

Worcester Spy, **Vol. 1, Part 1**, 537

Words, vocabulary-building, **Supp. 7**, 275

Words and Their Ways in English Speech, **Supp. 3**, 424

Wordsworth, William: first American disciple of, **Vol. 8, Part 1**, 447; portrait of, **Vol. 5, Part 1**, 482

Workers Education Bureau of America, founding of, **Supp. 4**, 63

Workers' International Industrial Union, organization of, **Vol. 3, Part 1**, 223

Workers Party of America. *See* Communist party (U.S.)

Working Girls' Societies, founding of, **Vol. 3, Part 1**, 346

Workingmen's Building Association, **Vol. 7, Part 2**, 158

Workingmen's Loan Association, **Vol. 7, Part 2**, 158

Workmen's compensation, **Vol. 8, Part 2**, 531; laws, **Supp. 2**, 586; **Supp. 3**, 717–18
Workmen's compensation law (New York), **Vol. 4, Part 1**, 335
Works Progress Administration (WPA): **Supp. 10**, 321; American Imprints Inventory, **Supp. 3**, 493; Art Project, **Supp. 5**, 473; **Supp. 6**, 512; **Supp. 7**, 184; **Supp. 8**, 553, 586, 643; **Supp. 10**, 560; Dance Theater, **Supp. 8**, 643; founding of, **Supp. 3**, 654; investigation of, **Supp. 6**, 35, 601–2; management of, **Supp. 4**, 392; Theater Project, **Supp. 7**, 61; Writers Project, **Supp. 6**, 490; **Supp. 9**, 605
Works Project Administration. *See* Works Progress Administration
World (New York City), **Vol. 2, Part 2**, 241, 256 f.; **Vol. 3, Part 2**, 14
World Alliance for Promoting International Friendship Through the Churches, **Supp. 3**, 323; **Supp. 6**, 25
World Bank. *See* International Bank for Reconstruction and Development
World Book Co., **Supp. 7**, 594
World Conference on Faith and Order, **Supp. 1**, 116; **Supp. 3**, 111; first, **Supp. 4**, 547
World Congress of the Defenders of Peace (Paris), **Supp. 7**, 204
World Council of Churches: **Supp. 5**, 305; founding of, **Supp. 3**, 111; **Supp. 5**, 508; **Supp. 6**, 25; **Supp. 7**, 597; **Supp. 10**, 111; predecessors, **Supp. 4**, 547
World Court: **Vol. 4, Part 2**, 255; **Vol. 6, Part 1**, 349; **Supp. 6**, 307, 308; campaign against U.S. participation, **Supp. 3**, 397; **Supp. 5**, 286; **Supp. 10**, 152; Coolidge rejection of, **Supp. 1**, 197; first American Judge, **Supp. 4**, 599; planning, **Supp. 2**, 581. *See also* International Court of Justice
World Court League, founding of, **Supp. 2**, 276
World Disarmament Conference at Geneva (1932). *See* Geneva General Disarmament Conference
World Federation League, founding of, **Supp. 5**, 308
World Federation of Trade Unions, founding of, **Supp. 4**, 376; **Supp. 5**, 511; **Supp. 10**, 493, 524
World government movements, **Supp. 4**, 727; **Supp. 5**, 308; **Supp. 8**, 88, 680. *See also* League of Nations; United Nations
World Health Organization, founding of, **Supp. 7**, 195
World History of Our Time, A, **Supp. 10**, 350
World Jewish Congress, founding of, **Supp. 4**, 660, 905
World League Against Alcoholism, founding of, **Supp. 4**, 161
World of Tomorrow. *See* New York World's Fair
World Parliament of Religions, **Vol. 5, Part 2**, 180; **Vol. 7, Part 1**, 302; **Vol. 8, Part 1**, 135
World Peace Foundation, **Vol. 2, Part 2**, 595; **Vol. 3, Part 2**, 300; **Vol. 4, Part 1**, 317; founding of, **Supp. 2**, 442
World Professional Tennis League, **Supp. 6**, 539
World's Anti-Slavery Convention (London), **Vol. 1, Part 2**, 350
World's Christian Fundamentals Association, founding of, **Supp. 4**, 691
World's Columbian Exposition (Chicago, 1893): **Vol. 1, Part 1**, 449, 478; **Vol. 2, Part 1**, 191, 303 f., 376; **Vol. 3, Part 2**, 308, 318, 339, 367; **Vol. 4, Part 1**, 269; **Vol. 5, Part 1**, 18, 390, 519; **Vol. 5, Part 2**, 35 f., 80, 180; **Vol. 7, Part 2**, 27, 122, 176; **Vol. 8, Part 1**, 1 f., 95 f., 276 f.; **Vol. 8, Part 2**, 150; 493; **Vol. 9, Part 2**, 425; amusement section, **Supp. 4**, 88; architecture of, **Supp. 2**, 41; **Supp. 6**, 593; Board of Lady Managers of, **Vol. 7, Part 2**, 176; first public exhibition of psychological apparatus, **Supp. 3**, 384; Indian sculpture, **Supp. 3**, 210, 211; journalism, **Supp. 3**, 3; Machinery Hall design, **Supp. 3**, 310; photography, **Supp. 3**, 380; sculpture, **Supp. 1**, 322; **Supp. 2**, 421; **Supp. 3**, 673
World's fairs. *See specific names*
Worlds in Collision, **Supp. 10**, 47
World's Missionary Committee of Christian Women, **Supp. 4**, 647
World's Peace Congress, **Vol. 6, Part 1**, 287; **Vol. 7, Part 2**, 404
World's Student Christian Federation, founding of, **Supp. 5**, 507
World's Work, **Supp. 4**, 368; founding of, **Vol. 7, Part 2**, 143; **Supp. 1**, 259
World Trade Center (New York City), **Supp. 10**, 789; construction of, **Supp. 10**, 786
World Vision, Inc., founding of, **Supp. 10**, 637
World War I: **Vol. 2, Part 1**, 196; **Vol. 4, Part 2**, 588; **Vol. 5, Part 2**, 610; **Vol. 6, Part 1**, 235, 348; **Vol. 8, Part 1**, 125 f., 316 f.; **Vol. 8, Part 2**, 5, 171, 316; **Vol. 9, Part 2**, 501; **Vol. 10, Part 2**, 103, 358 f., 361; aerial photography, **Supp. 9**, 760; Allied relations, **Supp. 3**, 204; **Supp. 5**, 668; **Supp. 6**, 254; ambassadorship in Great Britain during, **Vol. 7, Part 2**, 144; American Air Service, **Supp. 3**, 584–85; **Supp. 9**, 746; American ambulance field service, **Vol. 8, Part 2**, 320; **Supp. 2**, 15, 705; American command, **Supp. 1**, 22, 89–90, 495; American enlistment in Foreign Legion, **Vol. 8, Part 2**, 69; American Expeditionary Force, **Supp. 4**, 123, 359–60, 656–57, 782; **Supp. 5**, 160, 186, 468–69, 530–31, 668–69; **Supp. 6**, 191, 239; **Supp. 8**, 262; American First Army, **Supp. 5**, 186; American Red Cross, **Supp. 4**, 92; antiwar sentiment, **Supp. 1**, 74; **Supp. 3**, 78, 517, 558; **Supp. 4**, 298, 338, 518, 599, 725–26, 850–51; **Supp. 7**, 118, 356; **Supp. 8**, 149, 191–92, 457, 649–50; arms manufactured, **Vol. 6, Part 1**, 216; Army testing, **Supp. 6**, 626, 718; Atlantic Fleet, **Supp. 6**, 338; aviation, **Vol. 2, Part 2**, 21; **Vol. 6, Part 1**, 499; **Vol. 8, Part 2**, 69 f., 277; **Supp. 2**, 460; **Supp. 3**, 584–85; **Supp. 7**, 664; **Supp. 8**, 185; **Supp. 9**, 657, 898; and the banks, **Vol. 8, Part 2**, 275; Belglum, **Vol. 10, Part 2**, 138; Belleau Wood battle, **Supp. 4**, 359–69; blacks in, **Supp. 6**, 568; Bolshevist propaganda during, **Vol. 8, Part 1**, 451; British Ministry of Information, **Supp. 6**, 171; camp shows, **Supp. 6**, 319; camouflage, used, **Vol. 9, Part 2**, 400; canteen service, **Vol. 8, Part 2**, 20 f.; cartoons and caricatures, **Vol. 8, Part 2**, 113; **Supp. 3**, 301; **Supp. 4**, 159; Champagne-Marne defensive, **Supp. 7**, 488; chaplains, **Supp. 1**, 268; **Supp. 2**, 73; **Supp. 8**, 505; Chautauqua Movement in, **Supp. 3**, 64; Chemical Warfare Service, **Supp. 4**, 838; civil liberties issues, **Supp. 3**, 65; **Supp. 4**, 62, 542, 613, 636; **Supp. 6**, 105; **Supp. 7**, 248, 356, Conference of Neutrals, **Supp. 4**, 298; Congressional Medal of Honor, **Supp. 9**, 657; congressional opposition to U.S. entry, **Supp. 9**, 641; conscientious objection, **Supp. 4**, 442; convoy operations, **Supp. 2**, 239; **Supp. 9**, 385, 635; desire to avoid, **Vol. 9, Part 2**, 89; diplomacy during, **Supp. 1**, 327, 695; **Supp. 2**, 320; **Supp. 4**, 224; **Supp. 5**, 241; **Supp. 8**, 61; "dollar-a-year" man of the Food Administration, **Vol. 6, Part 1**, 275; draft, **Supp. 1**, 211; **Supp. 3**, 399; economic studies, **Supp. 2**, 108; electrical measurements, **Vol. 8, Part 2**, 154; Emergency Fleet Corporation, **Vol. 8, Part 2**, 194; entertainment of troops, **Supp. 10**, 33; espionage prevention, **Supp. 1**, 359; ethnic issues in U.S., **Supp. 3**, 471; **Supp. 5**, 279; **Supp. 6**, 444; European boundary redrawings after, **Supp. 4**, 99; European Theater command, **Supp. 3**, 17; fiction on, **Supp. 7**, 285; Fighting Sixty-Ninth Regiment, **Supp. 1**, 268; financing of, **Vol. 4, Part 1**, 241; **Vol. 5, Part 1**, 55; **Vol. 9, Part 2**, 477; **Supp. 1**, 10; **Supp. 3**, 480, 537; **Supp. 4**, 331, 469–70; **Supp. 6**, 376–77, 452;

Supp. 7, 401, 782; Food Administration, **Vol. 5, Part 2**, 548; **Vol. 8, Part 1**, 145 f.; Ford Peace Ship, **Vol. 5, Part 2**, 180; foreign correspondents, **Supp. 3**, 166–67; **Supp. 3**, 170; **Supp. 4**, 418; **Supp. 5**, 79, 362–63; **Supp. 6**, 183–84, 543, 616; **Supp. 7**, 512, 758; **Supp. 8**, 498, 639; **Supp. 10**, 562; Fourteen Points, **Supp. 2**, 320; "Hat-in-the-Ring Squadron," **Supp. 9**, 657; Hearst press, **Supp. 5**, 286; Hercules Powder Co., **Vol. 8, Part 1**, 91 f.; heroism in, **Supp. 7**, 807–8; **Supp. 8**, 262, 410; historical writings on, **Supp. 4**, 657; **Supp. 7**, 735; **Supp. 8**, 441; Hoover Library, **Supp. 1**, 9; industrial production planning, **Supp. 2**, 109; **Supp. 8**, 211; *see also subhead:* War Industries Board; influenza and gas poisoning, **Vol. 10, Part 1**, 109 f.; insurance policies, **Vol. 9, Part 2**, 122; intelligence operations, **Supp. 8**, 196; international law issues, **Supp. 5**, 137; Jewish relief agency, **Supp. 4**, 539; journalism, **Supp. 2**, 614; **Supp. 7**, 512; labor agreements, **Supp. 6**, 677; labor conciliation during, **Vol. 7, Part 2**, 214, 216; Labor War Committee, **Vol. 4, Part 1**, 372; Lafayette Escadrille, **Vol. 6, Part 1**, 499; La Follette's reputation of being pro-German, **Vol. 5, Part 2**, 545; Lansing, Robert, and, **Vol. 5, Part 2**, 610; Lewis machine gun, affair of, **Vol. 6, Part 1**, 216; logistics, **Supp. 5**, 468–69; loyalty issues, **Supp. 1**, 74; **Supp. 7**, 506; **Supp. 8**, 488; *Lusitania* sunk, **Vol. 4, Part 1**, 41; **Vol. 5, Part 1**, 324; **Vol. 5, Part 2**, 443; **Vol. 6, Part 1**, 278; Marine brigade in France, **Supp. 3**, 453; Marne, second battle, **Supp. 2**, 397; medical service, **Vol. 9, Part 2**, 343; medical treatment, **Supp. 2**, 706–7; **Supp. 3**, 141; **Supp. 4**, 468; **Supp. 5**, 335–36, 383; **Supp. 6**, 344, 345; memorials, **Supp. 3**, 199; merchant marine, **Supp. 3**, 501–2; Meuse-Argonne offensive, **Supp. 4**, 657; **Supp. 7**, 807; **Supp. 8**, 267; military operations, **Vol. 3, Part 1**, 304; **Vol. 5, Part 1**, 571; **Vol. 9, Part 2**, 327; military service, **Vol. 1, Part 1**, 483; **Vol. 1, Part 2**, 395, 463; **Vol. 2, Part 1**, 73, 570; **Vol. 2, Part 2**, 21; **Vol. 3, Part 1**, 170, 582; **Vol. 4, Part 2**, 66, 399; **Vol. 5, Part 1**, 63, 71, 102, 316, 512; **Vol. 5, Part 2**, 150, 167; **Vol. 6, Part 1**, 3; **Vol. 6, Part 2**, 538; **Vol. 7, Part 1**, 508, 601, 617; **Vol. 7, Part 2**, 277, 373; **Vol. 8, Part 1**, 9, 144, 276, 576; **Vol. 8, Part 2**, 4, 69, 199, 222, 555; **Vol. 9, Part 1**, 25; **Vol. 9, Part 2**, 653; **Vol. 10, Part 1**, 108, 109, 532, 608, 613, 621, 649; Military Training Camps Association, **Supp. 8**, 87; mine laying, **Supp. 2**, 165; "Mosquito Fleet," **Vol. 9, Part 2**, 394; munitions, **Supp. 2**, 680; **Supp. 9**, 622; **Supp. 10**, 102; National War Labor Board, **Supp. 4**, 543; naval action, **Supp. 8**, 331; naval aviation, **Supp. 6**, 91–92; naval service, **Vol. 3, Part 1**, 234, 464 f., 614 f.; **Vol. 4, Part 1**, 485; **Vol. 7, Part 1**, 438, 481; **Vol. 8, Part 1**, 17 f., 237, 316 f.; **Vol. 8, Part 2**, 22, 79, 465; **Vol. 9, Part 1**, 387 f.; **Vol. 10, Part 1**, 632 f.; **Supp. 6**, 23, 267; **Supp. 9**, 385, 461; Navy recruiting problem, **Vol. 4, Part 1**, 393; National Catholic War Council, **Vol. 4, Part 1**, 241; neutrality, *see subhead:* antiwar sentiment; North American Review's War Weekly, **Vol. 5, Part 2**, 145; novels about, **Supp. 5**, 99; **Supp. 8**, 136; nursing, **Supp. 4**, 789; **Supp. 7**, 247; opposition to U.S. entry, **Supp. 9**, 126; origins of, investigations on, **Supp. 5**, 114; organizations resulting from, **Vol. 8, Part 1**, 276; Peace Commission, **Vol. 10, Part 2**, 364; peace conferences, **Vol. 10, Part 2**, 364; **Supp. 1**, 89–90; **Supp. 2**, 52, 290, 320; **Supp. 7**, 262, 683, 687–88, 782; **Supp. 8**, 146, 256, 495, Peace Ship, **Supp. 4**, 518, 725–26; photographic journalism, **Supp. 4**, 361; pneumonia epidemic, **Supp. 3**, 483; poetry, **Vol. 5, Part 2**, 374; poison gas research, **Supp. 3**, 353; political intrigue, **Vol. 4, Part 2**, 372 f.; posters, **Supp. 3**, 301; **Supp. 6**, 204; postwar planning, **Supp. 7**, 536–37, 683, 687; prices and price control, **Supp. 4**, 587; prisoners of war, **Supp. 5**, 507; **Supp. 6**, 403; propaganda, **Vol. 5, Part 1**, 56; **Vol. 5, Part 2**, 463; **Vol. 8, Part 1**, 451; **Vol. 8, Part 2**, 199; **Supp. 3**, 64, 76, 301, 396; **Supp. 4**, 842; **Supp. 5**, 142, 641, 697; **Supp. 6**, 90, 410; **Supp. 7**, 481–82, 757; psychiatry, used, **Vol. 8, Part 2**, 313; psychological testing of troops, **Supp. 3**, 102; **Supp. 5**, 59, 612; **Supp. 7**, 594; **Supp. 8**, 44, 458; railroad operation during, **Vol. 8, Part 1**, 248 f., 418; **Vol. 9, Part 2**, 449; Railroad War Board, **Supp. 3**, 824; "range finders," **Vol. 6, Part 1**, 203; reconstructive surgery, **Supp. 2**, 706–7; records preservation, **Supp. 2**, 418; Red Cross, **Vol. 3, Part 1**, 148 f., 218.; reeducational, clinics, **Vol. 9, Part 1**, 478; relief efforts, **Supp. 1**, 534, 541, 640; **Supp. 4**, 603, 892–93; **Supp. 5**, 506, 673, 700; **Supp. 6**, 36, 75, 249, 659; **Supp. 7**, 358, 359, 651; relief work, **Vol. 4, Part 1**, 60, 364; reparations, **Supp. 1**, 104; **Supp. 2**, 234, 356; **Supp. 3**, 219, 537; **Supp. 4**, 470; **Supp. 5**, 160, 537; **Supp. 6**, 177–78, 188; **Supp. 7**, 809–10; resuscitation wards, **Supp. 3**, 202; revisionist historical writings on, **Supp. 8**, 441; rocket study, **Supp. 3**, 306; Roosevelt, Theodore, his part in, **Vol. 8, Part 2**, 143; Saint-Mihiel offensive, **Supp. 4**, 782; sanitary measures, **Supp. 5**, 144; seamen's no-strike policy, **Supp. 2**, 213; Selective Draft Act, **Vol. 4, Part 2**, 253; **Vol. 5, Part 2**, 251; **Vol. 10, Part 2**, 361; Shipping Board, **Vol. 8, Part 2**, 194; **Supp. 1**, 598; Siberian mission, **Supp. 2**, 259; Signal Officers' Reserve Corps, **Vol. 4, Part 1**, 330; Socialist party split over, **Supp. 1**, 73–74; **Supp. 3**, 10, 85, 675; **Supp. 4**, 636, 746; **Supp. 5**, 134–35; **Supp. 8**, 611; songs, **Supp. 3**, 174; sonnets, **Vol. 5, Part 2**, 586; *Stars and Stripes,* **Supp. 6**, 5; statistical summary of, **Supp. 4**, 35; Students Army Training Corps, **Vol. 4, Part 1**, 473; submarines and submarine detection, **Supp. 3**, 120; **Supp. 5**, 188, 495; **Supp. 6**, 365, 50,; **Supp. 7**, 516; **Supp. 9**, 143; submarine flotilla during, **Vol. 4, Part 1**, 485; supplies, **Supp. 1**, 522, 622; **Supp. 4**, 360; **Supp. 8**, 704–5; supplies for Allies, **Vol. 4, Part 1**, 356; **Vol. 9, Part 1**, 601; Supreme War Council, **Supp. 3**, 204; surgical dressings for Allies, **Vol. 10, Part 2**, 237; surgical service, **Vol. 6, Part 1**, 443; tactics, **Supp. 5**, 668–69; tanks and armored vehicles, **Supp. 3**, 165, 589; topographical studies, **Supp. 3**, 390; transportation, **Vol. 5, Part 1**, 570; troop entertainment, **Supp. 2**, 11; U.S. participation in **Vol. 10, Part 2**, 361; venerial disease control, **Supp. 4**, 758–59; **Supp. 5**, 604; Versailles Treaty, **Vol. 6, Part 1**, 563; **Vol. 10, Part 2**, 365; war cabinet, **Supp. 1**, 446; war debt, *see subhead*: financing of; War Industries Board, **Vol. 7, Part 2**, 217; **Supp. 1**, 490, 513; **Supp. 3**, 399; **Supp. 4**, 587; **Supp. 7**, 35–36; War Risk Insurance Bureau, **Vol. 9, Part 2**, 122; weather forecasting, **Supp. 3**, 512; Women's Overseas Hospital, **Supp. 6**, 79; writings on, **Vol. 3, Part 1**, 304; **Vol. 3, Part 2**, 419; **Vol. 5, Part 2**, 135; **Supp. 8**, 169, 622; YMCA activities in, **Supp. 5**, 324–25; **Supp. 8**, 673; YWCA War Work Council, **Supp. 4**, 207

World War II: absentee ballot, **Supp. 8**, 223; agricultural policy, **Supp. 8**, 700; airborne operations, **Supp. 9**, 518–19; aircraft design and manufacture, **Supp. 4**, 458–59; 609; **Supp. 6**, 50; **Supp. 8**, 709; **Supp. 9**, 256, 874; Air Force command, **Supp. 5**, 695; **Supp. 7**, 664; **Supp. 8**, 48; **Supp. 9**, 747; Air Force development, **Supp. 4**, 27–30; Air Force operations, **Supp. 9**, 595–96; Air Force Pacific Fleet, **Supp. 5**, 695; air transport, **Supp. 7**, 16; **Supp. 9**, 595–96, 658; air warfare concepts, **Supp. 4**, 259; **Supp. 5**, 178; Alaska and Aleutians campaign, **Supp. 3**, 118; **Supp. 6**, 629; Allied Airborne Army, **Supp. 3**,

706; Allied relations, **Supp. 4**, 900; aluminum products, **Supp. 5**, 566; amphibious warfare in, **Supp. 8**, 23–24; **Supp. 9**, 385–86, 630, 822–23; anti-aircraft guns, **Supp. 7**, 785; anti-inflation programs, **Supp. 4**, 753; anti-submarine warfare, **Supp. 10**, 742; antiwar sentiment, **Supp. 3**, 605; **Supp. 4**, 403, 850; **Supp. 5**, 396–97, 404, 624; **Supp. 6**, 470, 578; **Supp. 7**, 249–50, 356, 451, 751; **Supp. 8**, 184, 268–69, 321, 373, 650, 705; art treasure preservation, **Supp. 8**, 545; Atlantic Charter, **Supp. 7**, 778; Atlantic Fleet, **Supp. 6**, 339; **Supp. 7**, 438; **Supp. 8**, 30; **Supp. 10**, 371; atomic bomb development and use, **Supp. 4**, 787–88; **Supp. 6**, 166, 371, 501, 656; **Supp. 7**, 732; **Supp. 8**, 230–31; **Supp. 9**, 185, 218; **Supp. 10**, 102, 144; baseball during, **Supp. 3**, 438; Bastogne siege broken, **Supp. 9**, 519; Battle of the Bulge, **Supp. 3**, 590; **Supp. 8**, 155, 268; **Supp. 9**, 519; **Supp. 10**, 177; battleship command, **Supp. 3**, 450; **Supp. 9**, 226–27; bazooka manufacture, **Supp. 4**, 122; biological warfare research, **Supp. 6**, 448; black fighter squadron, **Supp. 10**, 378; black market, **Supp. 5**, 737; black troops, **Supp. 8**, 118–19; blood plasma supplies, **Supp. 4**, 242–49; Bougainville campaign, **Supp. 9**, 823; Brenner Pass battle, **Supp. 3**, 583; Carlson's Raiders, **Supp. 4**, 147; carrier operations, Pacific Theater, **Supp. 9**, 636; Catholic church, **Supp. 8**, 613; Central Pacific offensive, **Supp. 8**, 470; Chaplain Corps, **Supp. 8**, 505–6; China-Burma-India theater, **Supp. 4**, 782–83; **Supp. 5**, 486–87; **Supp. 6**, 109–11, 508; **Supp. 7**, 680; **Supp. 8**, 632; **Supp. 9**, 830–31; civil liberties issues, **Supp. 3**, 93; **Supp. 4**, 614; Civilian Conservation Corps, **Supp. 6**, 412; civilian defense, **Supp. 4**, 466; **Supp. 7**, 453, 661; Coast Guard, **Supp. 4**, 854; Combined Chiefs of Staff, **Supp. 7**, 703; COMINCH, **Supp. 6**, 339–40; Committee of American Defense, **Supp. 6**, 504; Committee of Historians to Analyze and Appraise Current Conditions and Prospective Developments in Germany, **Supp. 9**, 330; Committee to Defend America by Aiding the Allies, **Supp. 4**, 347, 470; **Supp. 5**, 481, 624; **Supp. 7**, 197, 289; **Supp. 8**, 244, 679; communications, European Theater, **Supp. 9**, 701; Communist party (U.S.) positions in, **Supp. 5**, 500; Conference of Allied Ministers of Education, **Supp. 4**, 449; conscientious objection, **Supp. 6**, 217; **Supp. 10**, 468; "Darlan deal," **Supp. 8**, 274; **Supp. 10**, 572; D-Day invasion and follow-up, **Supp. 3**, 580–90; **Supp. 8**, 155; **Supp. 9**, 386, 575, 747; **Supp. 10**, 177; declaration of war against Japan, lone vote against, **Supp. 9**,641; de-Nazification program, **Supp. 3**, 590; defense communications, **Supp. 8**, 179–80; defense contract scandal, **Supp. 6**, 437; Defense Mediation Board, **Supp. 7**, 172; defense production, **Supp. 4**, 303, 458–59; **Supp. 6**, 520; **Supp. 7**, 794; **Supp. 8**, 527; defense program, **Supp. 6**, 335; Defense Research Committee, **Supp. 4**, 430; defense transportation, **Supp. 3**, 241; diplomacy during, **Supp. 7**, 53, 377, 437–38, 778; **Supp. 8**, 495, 501; diplomacy, pre-U.S. entry, **Supp. 3**, 528–29; **Supp. 5**, 333; documentary films, **Supp. 9**, 286; draft, **Supp. 4**, 247; **Supp. 5**, 715; economic impact, **Supp. 6**, 586; Economic Warfare Board, **Supp. 7**, 761; Eighth Fleet command, **Supp. 9**, 386; ethnic issues in U.S., **Supp. 3**, 661; **Supp. 4**, 286; **Supp. 5**, 43, 343, 574–75; **Supp. 7**, 292; **Supp. 8**, 650; "Europe First" strategy, **Supp. 6**, 430–31; **Supp. 8**, 154; **Supp. 9**, 755; European Theater, **Supp. 6**, 375; **Supp. 7**, 213; **Supp. 8**, 267–68; **Supp. 9**, 574–75; **Supp. 10**, 177; financing of, **Supp. 5**, 712–13; **Supp. 8**, 446; First Fleet command, **Supp. 6**, 375; food aid, **Supp. 6**, 217–18; foreign correspondents, **Supp. 3**, 612–13; **Supp. 5**, 60; **Supp. 6**, 148, 366; **Supp. 7**, 473, 566, 643, 759; **Supp. 8**, 259, 261; **Supp. 10**, 400, 519, 562–63, 675; France, invasion of southern, *see subhead:* D-Day; Free French forces, **Supp. 8**, 62; French North Africa, **Supp. 10**, 571–72; Germany, occupation of, **Supp. 10**, 127–28; Greenland Patrol, **Supp. 7**, 698–99; ground combat forces mobilization, **Supp. 3**, 494; Guadalcanal campaign, **Supp. 9**, 822–23; heroism in, **Supp. 7**, 419, 581; IBM role in, **Supp. 6**, 675; intelligence activities, **Supp. 6**, 170, 531; **Supp. 8**, 51, 147, 196; interventionism, **Supp. 10**, 143–44, 216; isolationism, **Supp. 9**, 498, 591; Italian campaign, **Supp. 8**, 147, 155; ITT role in, **Supp. 6**, 44; Japan, atomic bombing of, **Supp. 7**, 732; **Supp. 9**, 747, 812; Japan, bombing of Tokyo, **Supp. 4**, 589; **Supp. 9**, 596; Japan, occupation of, **Supp. 8**, 699; Japan, peace treaty with, **Supp. 6**, 270; Japanese surrender, **Supp. 6**, 268; journalism, **Supp. 5**, 450; **Supp. 9**, 120, 188–89, 690; **Supp. 10**, 417; labor issues, **Supp. 5**, 248–49; **Supp. 6**, 28–29, 709; landing craft, **Supp. 5**, 299, 361; Latin American involvement, **Supp. 7**, 778; lend-lease program, **Supp. 3**, 659–60, 829; **Supp. 4**, 393, 458, 480; **Supp. 8**, 446; **Supp. 9**, 226; Library War Service Committee, **Supp. 4**, 846; logistics, European Theater, **Supp. 10**, 127; logistics, Pacific Theater, **Supp. 10**, 372; "Mae West" life jackets; **Supp. 10**, 830; Mark XV bombsight, **Supp. 7**, 577; Medal of Honor, **Supp. 9**, 575; medical supplies, production of, **Supp. 10**, 459; medicine in, **Supp. 4**, 208–9, 468; **Supp. 5**, 64, 122–23, 33, 6, 632, 733; **Supp. 7**, 328, 477, 649; **Supp. 8**, 608, 609; microwave radar development, **Supp. 10**, 319, 742; military command, **Supp. 3**, 662; military police operations, **Supp. 9**, 881; miltiary production, **Supp. 5**, 538–39; **Supp. 10**, 97, 144; military research, **Supp. 5**, 28, 497; **Supp. 10**, 144; military segregation during, **Supp. 4**, 243; mobilization, **Supp. 3**, 494; **Supp. 8**, 706; Morgenthau Plan for postwar Germany, **Supp. 5**, 334–35; munitions, **Supp. 10**, 240; National Defense Research Committee, **Supp. 9**, 144–45, 185; **Supp. 10**, 144, 240, 743, 825; naval construction, **Supp. 10**, 550; naval historian, **Supp. 10**, 554; naval photography, **Supp. 9**, 760; naval procurement, **Supp. 4**, 305; naval service, **Supp. 6**, 23, 188, 326, 408; **Supp. 9**, 176, 226–27, 461; Neutrality Acts, **Supp. 5**, 731; New Caledonia defense, **Supp. 3**, 583; New Guinea campaign, **Supp. 9**, 461; Ninth Infantry Division, **Supp. 7**, 213–14; nonintervention advocacy, **Supp. 10**, 349; North African campaign, **Supp. 3**, 589; **Supp. 8**, 154–55, 274; North Pacific operations, **Supp. 9**, 461; nursing, **Supp. 6**, 283–84; **Supp. 9**, 99–100; **Supp. 10**, 57; occupied territories administration, **Supp. 8**, 275; Office of Civilian Defense, **Supp. 7**, 661; Office of Economic Stabilization, **Supp. 3**, 660; **Supp. 5**, 72, 713; **Supp. 10**, 394; Office of Foreign Economic Coordination, **Supp. 10**, 243; Office of Price Administration, **Supp. 3**, 660; **Supp. 6**, 80; **Supp. 9**, 130, 391; Office of Production Management, **Supp. 4**, 458; **Supp. 10**, 216; Office of Scientific Research and Development, **Supp. 8**, 686; **Supp. 9**, 145; Office of Strategic Services, **Supp. 6**, 170–71, 531; **Supp. 8**, 51, 147; **Supp. 9**, 26; **Supp. 10**, 74; Office of the Foreign Economic Administration, **Supp. 9**, 209; Office of War Information, **Supp. 4**, 72; **Supp. 5**, 624; **Supp. 6**, 148; **Supp. 7**, 307, 384; **Supp. 8**, 679–80, 696; Office of War Mobilization and Reconversion, **Supp. 5**, 712; **Supp. 6**, 335; Okinawa campaign, **Supp. 3**, 118; Operation Torch, **Supp. 9**, 386, 747; Pacific Fleet, **Supp. 5**, 66, 621; **Supp. 6**, 267–68; **Supp. 7**, 490; **Supp. 8**, 331, 619; Pacific Theater, **Supp. 3**, 450; **Supp. 4**, 147, 323–24, 589, 895; **Supp. 6**, 326, 577; **Supp. 7**, 352, 645, 749–50; **Supp. 8**,

603; **Supp. 9**, 461, 630, 822–23; pacifism, **Supp. 7**, 356; **Supp. 9**, 36, 641; Paris liberation, **Supp. 7**, 350; passport policies, **Supp. 8**, 590; Philippines campaign, **Supp. 9**, 461; photojournalism, **Supp. 7**, 115–16; **Supp. 9**, 111; **Supp. 10**, 749–50; physical anthropology application in, **Supp. 5**, 312; pinup girl, **Supp. 9**, 332; Ploesti bombing, **Supp. 8**, 48; **Supp. 10**, 71; political analysis, **Supp. 5**, 514; political cartoons, **Supp. 5**, 672; posters, **Supp. 6**, 204; postwar planning, **Supp. 6**, 80, 178, 431; **Supp. 8**, 446; Potsdam Conference, **Supp. 9**, 812; "Private Purkey," **Supp. 7**, 618; pro-German propaganda, **Supp. 7**, 757–58; propaganda, **Supp. 3**, 57, 368–69; **Supp. 6**, 170, 668; **Supp. 9**, 618, 666; *see also subhead:* Office of War Information; psychiatry, **Supp. 8**, 429–30; psychological study of troops, **Supp. 6**, 605; psychological warfare, **Supp. 5**, 646–47, 406–7; **Supp. 7**, 384, 812; radio correspondents, **Supp. 6**, 148; **Supp. 7**, 566; **Supp. 10**, 349; RDX (cyclonite) explosive, **Supp. 5**, 28; refugees and refugee resettlement, *see* Refugees; relief efforts, **Supp. 7**, 599; reparations policy, **Supp. 8**, 89; **Supp. 10**, 472; rocket research, **Supp. 10**, 65–66; rockets, **Supp. 3**, 307–8; Roosevelt administration bipartisanship, **Supp. 3**, 425–26; Roosevelt, F. D., as commander-in-chief, **Supp. 3**, 661–64; Rubber Survey Committee, **Supp. 7**, 36; science and technology, **Supp. 8**, 686; **Supp. 9**, 144–45; Seventh Fleet command, **Supp. 9**, 461; shipbuilding, **Supp. 4**, 848–49, 308; Sicily invasion, **Supp. 3**, 589; **Supp. 5**, 336; Singapore evacuation, **Supp. 8**, 30; Smaller War Plants Corporation, **Supp. 5**, 481; songs, **Supp. 8**, 386; Southwest Pacific Theater, **Supp. 5**, 720; **Supp. 7**, 215, 489–90; **Supp. 8**, 23–24, 351, 638; Soviet-U.S. relations during, **Supp. 6**, 147; Special Motion Picture Coverage Unit, **Supp. 9**, 767; Special Services Division, **Supp. 6**, 637; Stage Door Canteens, **Supp. 4**, 187; **Supp. 5**, 415; **Supp. 6**, 133; strategic bombing survey, **Supp. 5**, 178; submarine detection and defenses, **Supp. 4**, 818; **Supp. 6**, 501; supplies, **Supp. 5**, 643; **Supp. 9**, 73; Supply Priorities and Allocation Board, **Supp. 4**, 458; surplus property administration, **Supp. 8**, 89; synthetics development during, **Supp. 6**, 334; Third Army, XX Corps, **Supp. 4**, 857; Third Fleet command, **Supp. 6**, 268–69; training films, **Supp. 10**, 864, 865; troop demobilization, **Supp. 8**, 156; troop training, **Supp. 10**, 510; Tulagi campaign, **Supp. 9**, 823; Twelfth Fleet command, **Supp. 9**, 755; U.S. entry, opposition to, **Supp. 9**, 860; U.S. government preparation for, **Supp. 3**, 660–61; **Supp. 4**, 787; U.S. intervention advocacy, **Supp. 7**, 740; **Supp. 9**, 7; U.S. official neutrality policy, **Supp. 3**, 658–60; **Supp. 5**, 731; U-boat menace, **Supp. 5**, 344–45; unconditional surrender doctrine, **Supp. 3**, 662; **Supp. 5**, 334; **Supp. 7**, 812–13; USO activities, **Supp. 6**, 644; **Supp. 7**, 30; **Supp. 8**, 52; V-2 rocket, **Supp. 10**, 66; war bonds, **Supp. 5**, 712–13; War Labor Board, **Supp. 6**, 28; **Supp. 7**, 172; **Supp. 8**, 35; **Supp. 9**, 795; **Supp. 10**, 524; War Manpower Commission, **Supp. 5**, 460; War Mobilization Board, **Supp. 9**, 151; War Production Board, **Supp. 3**, 660; **Supp. 5**, 481; **Supp. 6**, 473–74; **Supp. 7**, 92; **Supp. 8**, 352; **Supp. 9**, 594, 873–74; **Supp. 10**, 216; War Relocation Authority, **Supp. 7**, 505; War Resources Board, **Supp. 7**, 36; **Supp. 9**, 622; War Shipping Administration, **Supp. 10**, 243; writings on, **Supp. 9**, 690, 691; Yalta Conference, **Supp. 9**, 151–52. *See also* Nazism; Pearl Harbor attack; War crimes

World Zionist Congress, **Supp. 4**, 906

World Zionist Organization, **Supp. 3**, 96; **Supp. 7**, 689

Worms, studies of, **Supp. 1**, 182

Worship, founding of, **Supp. 2**, 455

Worth, Patience, reference to, **Supp. 3**, 851

Wortman, Jacob L., reference to, **Supp. 3**, 316

Worzel, John Lamar, references to, **Supp. 9**, 271, 272

Wound and the Bow, The, **Supp. 9**, 876

Wounded Knee Creek, engagement at, **Vol. 5, Part 2**, 615; **Vol. 9, Part 1**, 193. *See also* Pine Ridge Agency, S.D.

Wounded Knee, S. Dak., siege at, **Supp. 10**, 557

Woytinsky, Emma Shadkan, reference to, **Supp. 6**, 708, 709, 710

WPA. *See* Works Progress Administration

WQXR (radio station), high-fidelity frequency modulation, **Supp. 6**, 299

Wray, Fay, reference to, **Supp. 6**, 658

Wrestling, **Supp. 5**, 417–18; **Supp. 8**, 371–72; Roman style, **Supp. 1**, 569

Wright, Edward, reference to, **Supp. 3**, 378

Wright, Frances, relations with Robert Dale Owen, **Vol. 7, Part 2**, 119

Wright, Frank Lloyd, references to, **Supp. 4**, 352; **Supp. 5**, 207, 208, 606; **Supp. 8**, 435, 463; **Supp. 9**, 893; **Supp. 10**, 764. *See also* Taliesin

Wright, J. Homer, reference to, **Supp. 4**, 580

Wright, Judge John C., reference to, **Vol. 10, Part 1**, 363

Wright, Richard, references to, **Supp. 5**, 419; **Supp. 6**, 314; **Supp. 8**, 81

Wright, Warren, reference to, **Supp. 7**, 399, 400

Wright, Wilbur, reference to, **Supp. 4**, 913–14

Wright Aeronautical Corporation, **Supp. 4**, 473–74; **Supp. 5**, 384; **Supp. 6**, 51

Wright brothers, relations with Octave Chanute, **Vol. 7, Part 2**, 11

Wright-Martin Corporation, founding of, **Supp. 5**, 475

Wrigley, William, Jr., references to, **Supp. 10**, 856, 857

Wrigley Field (Chicago, Ill.), **Supp. 10**, 857

Wrinkle in Time, A, **Supp. 9**, 276

Writers. For complete list, *see* Occupations Index

Writers' Club, founding of, **Supp. 1**, 649

Writers in Crisis: The American Novel 1925–1940, **Supp. 10**, 274

Writing. *See* Literature

Writs of Assistance, **Vol. 4, Part 1**, 6

Wrought-iron, design, **Supp. 2**, 742

WTOP and WTOP-TV (radio-TV stations), **Supp. 6**, 452, 453; **Supp. 7**, 296

Wu Lei-ch'uan, reference to, **Supp. 3**, 289

Wundt, Wilhelm: influence of, **Vol. 7, Part 1**, 337; **Vol. 9, Part 2**, 564; references to, **Supp. 3**, 148, 149; **Supp. 4**, 90, 444; **Supp. 5**, 611

Wurlitzer Co., jukebox production, **Supp. 10**, 96

Wurster, William, reference to, **Supp. 10**, 123

Wuthering Heights, **Supp. 9**, 382, 383; **Supp. 10**, 600

Wyandotte, Mich., **Vol. 3, Part 1**, 547 f.

Wyandotte Iron Works, **Vol. 5, Part 2**, 312

Wyeth, Andrew, references to, **Supp. 3**, 848, 849

Wyler, William, references to, **Supp. 6**, 610; **Supp. 9**, 324

Wylie, Elinor, reference to, **Supp. 4**, 74

Wylie, Philip, reference to, **Supp. 6**, 530

Wyman, Isaac C., reference to, **Supp. 3**, 810

Wynn, Keenan, reference to, **Supp. 8**, 710

Wyoming: cattle raising, **Vol. 10, Part 1**, 472 f.; Democratic party, **Supp. 10**, 703, 704; governor, first, **Vol. 10, Part 1**, 472 f.; governors, **Supp. 1**, 464; **Supp. 5**, 337; **Supp. 7**, 31; **Supp. 10**, 703–4; land, reclamation of, **Vol. 10, Part 1**, 472 f.; political service, **Vol. 5, Part 1**, 321; **Vol. 10, Part 1**, 472; politics, **Supp. 3**, 788; **Supp. 7**, 590; **Supp. 10**, 703–4; Territory, history as, **Vol. 2, Part 1**, 489

Wyoming Valley, Pa.: colonization of, **Vol. 5, Part 2**, 47; conflicting claims by Pennsylvania and Connect-

icut to, **Vol. 3, Part 1**, 581 f.; massacre, **Vol. 1, Part 2**, 604; **Vol. 2, Part 1**, 362, 372; settlement of, **Vol. 3, Part 1**, 550
Wyoming Seminary (Pa.), **Vol. 7, Part 1**, 421
Wyse, Arthur B., reference to, **Supp. 9**, 114
Wythe, George, reference to, **Vol. 6, Part 1**, 119

X

Xavier Union, **Vol. 4, Part 2**, 383
Xenia Theological Seminary, **Vol. 7, Part 1**, 147
Xenia News, **Vol. 8, Part 1**, 482
XERA (radio station), **Supp. 3**, 104
Xerography, development of, **Supp. 9**, 877–78
Xerox Co., founding of, **Supp. 8**, 72; **Supp. 9**, 878
X rays: **Vol. 1, Part 2**, 113; **Vol. 2, Part 1**, 407; **Vol. 5, Part 2**, 493; **Vol. 6, Part 1**, 173 f.; **Vol. 7, Part 1**, 268; barium, **Supp. 3**, 133; Bellevue Hospital department, **Supp. 3**, 360; cancer therapy, **Supp. 3**, 258; cancer treatment with, **Supp. 2**, 546; Compton effect experiments, **Supp. 7**, 10; development of, **Supp. 2**, 718; diagnostic and therapeutic uses of, **Supp. 1**, 41; **Supp. 2**, 546; **Supp. 3**, 523; **Supp. 4**, 112, 185–86, 214, 865; **Supp. 6**, 506; diffraction studies, **Supp. 2**, 595; **Supp. 8**, 123; Duane-Hunt law, **Supp. 1**, 267; dynamical theory of refraction, **Supp. 7**, 10; effects on blood-cell production, **Supp. 4**, 581; first photo in U.S., **Supp. 1**, 614; first U.S. experiments, **Supp. 3**, 130; health hazards from, **Supp. 4**, 112; medical machines, **Supp. 8**, 666; mutation induction, **Supp. 8**, 449; particle characteristics, **Supp. 7**, 133–34; research in, **Supp. 2**, 557. *See also* Radiation; Radiology
XYZ affair (1798), **Vol. 1, Part 1**, 78; **Vol. 3, Part 1**, 467 f.; **Vol. 4, Part 1**, 226; **Vol. 4, Part 2**, 177; **Vol. 5, Part 2**, 27; **Vol. 6, Part 2**, 318; **Vol. 7, Part 1**, 369; **Vol. 7, Part 2**, 615

Y

Yachting, founding of, **Supp. 4**, 852
Yachts and yachting (for complete list of yachts, *see* Ships): designing and building, **Vol. 2, Part 1**, 275; **Vol. 4, Part 2**, 585; **Vol. 6, Part 1**, 43; **Vol. 9, Part 1**, 237, 559 f.; **Supp. 2**, 298; first American, **Vol. 2, Part 2**, 578; races, **Vol. 1, Part 1**, 641; **Vol. 3, Part 1**, 552 f.; **Vol. 3, Part 2**, 452; **Vol. 6, Part 1**, 43, 60; **Vol. 7, Part 2**, 147; **Vol. 8, Part 2**, 325; **Vol. 9, Part 2**, 33; **Vol. 10, Part 1**, 177; **Supp. 5**, 6–7
Yaddo (Saratoga Springs, N.Y.): **Supp. 7**, 18; Studs Longigan trilogy completed at, **Supp. 10**, 235
Yagua Indians, **Supp. 7**, 241
Yakima Indian War, **Vol. 2, Part 1**, 560; **Vol. 3, Part 1**, 256; **Vol. 4, Part 2**, 280; **Vol. 5, Part 2**, 568; **Vol. 8, Part 2**, 242, 613; **Vol. 9, Part 1**, 79; **Vol. 10, Part 2**, 514
Yale Corporation, **Supp. 3**, 11
Yale Historical Publications series, **Supp. 10**, 429–30
Yale Literary Magazine, **Vol. 3, Part 2**, 215, 383; **Vol. 7, Part 1**, 42
Yale Lock Co., **Vol. 9, Part 2**, 613
Yale Medical Library, collections of, **Supp. 2**, 139
Yale Publishing Association, **Supp. 6**, 154
Yale Review, **Supp. 1**, 294; **Supp. 4**, 197; founding of, **Supp. 7**, 103
Yale Scroll and Key, The, **Vol. 8, Part 1**, 96 f.
Yale Summer Shakespeare Institute, **Supp. 9**, 626
Yale University: **Vol. 1, Part 1**, 530, 535; **Vol. 3, Part, 28, 276 f., 573 f.; Vol. 4, Part 2**, 586; **Vol. 5, Part l**, 52; **Vol. 5, Part 2**, 80; **Vol. 7, Part 2**, 223, 479, 633; **Vol. 8, Part 1**, 96 f., 547; **Vol. 9, Part 1**, 10 f.; **Vol. 9, Part 2**, 160; **Vol. 10, Part 2**, 417; administration, **Supp. 6**, 600; admission, early, **Vol. 10, Part 1**, 10; anatomy studies, **Supp. 3**, 6; anthropology studies, **Supp. 5**, 435; archaeological collections, **Vol. 2, Part 2**, 168; archaeology studies, **Supp. 5**, 595; architectural studies, **Supp. 9**, 445; art gallery, design of, **Supp. 9**, 445–46; astronomy studies, **Supp. 3**, 692; **Supp. 10**, 840; band, **Vol. 1, Part 1**, 547; biological studies, **Supp. 6**, 282–83, 719; Boswell manuscript collection, **Supp. 5**, 350; botany studies, **Supp. 8**, 595–96; building architecture, **Supp. 4**, 698; change of, from college to university, **Vol. 3, Part 1**, 577 f.; chemical studies, **Supp. 10**, 609; chemistry studies, **Supp. 4**, 434; child development studies, **Supp. 7**, 284; divinity school, **Vol. 2, Part 1**, 86; **Vol. 3, Part 1**, 577 f.; **Vol. 3, Part 2**, 407 f.; **Vol. 9, Part 2**, 338; **Supp. 4**, 111, 525; **Supp. 7**, 574; **Supp. 8**, 359; drama studies, **Supp. 1**, 45–46; **Supp. 7**, 803; economics studies, **Supp. 4**, 273, 274–75; **Supp. 8**, 165; Elizabethan Club, **Vol. 2, Part 2**, 251; English literature and language studies, **Supp. 3**, 602–3, 855; **Supp. 4**, 110, 197; **Supp. 7**, 798; **Supp. 9**, 884–85; faculty pay scale, **Supp. 3**, 353; Fine Arts, School of, **Vol. 5, Part 2**, 74; **Vol. 9, Part 2**, 136; **Vol. 10, Part 1**, 608 f.; **Supp. 1**, 45; first A.M. degree, **Supp. 1**, 293; first American Indian to graduate from, **Supp. 4**, 165; football team, **Supp. 5**, 288–89; **Supp. 6**, 66; Forestry, School of, **Vol. 9, Part 2**, 603; **Supp. 3**, 620–21; **Supp. 4**, 666; founding of, **Vol. 1, Part 1**, 281; **Vol. 7, Part 2**, 585, 589; **Vol. 8, Part 2**, 317 f.; **Vol. 9, Part 2**, 392; **Vol. 10, Part 2**, 591; fund-raising, **Supp. 6**, 155; geography studies, **Supp. 4**, 98–99; geology studies, **Supp. 3**, 695–96; gifts to, **Vol. 8, Part 2**, 308; **Vol. 9, Part 1**, 589; **Vol. 9, Part 2**, 136; graduates, biographical sketches of, **Vol. 3, Part 1**, 277; graduate school administration, **Supp. 4**, 197; history studies, **Supp. 3**, 16, 262; **Supp. 7**, 683; **Supp. 8**, 473; **Supp. 9**, 73; **Supp. 10**, 429–30; honorary degrees, first woman, **Supp. 2**, 703; house plan, **Supp. 2**, 284; "Illinois Association," **Vol. 10, Part 1**, 58; James Weldon Johnson collection, **Supp. 9**, 109–10; Latin American history studies, **Supp. 6**, 59; Law School, **Vol. 1, Part 1**, 544; **Vol. 8, Part 2**, 97; **Vol. 10, Part 1**, 560 f.; **Vol. 10, Part 2**, 520; **Supp. 3**, 185–86; **Supp. 5**, 81–82; **Supp. 8**, 17; library, **Vol. 3, Part 1**, 277; **Vol. 3, Part 2**, 79; **Vol. 8, Part 2**, 480; medical library, **Supp. 6**, 224; Medical School, **Vol. 3, Part 1**, 573 f.; **Vol. 5, Part 2**, 468; **Vol. 9, Part 1**, 161, 325 f.; **Supp. 3**, 775; **Supp. 5**, 64; **Supp. 6**, 223; modern art collection, **Supp. 5**, 185; name, origin of, **Vol. 3, Part 1**, 502 f.; nursing school, **Supp. 5**, 252; Oriental history studies, **Supp. 8**, 359; paleontology studies, **Supp. 5**, 743; Peabody Museum of Natural History, **Vol. 7, Part 2**, 337; **Supp. 3**, 695–96; **Supp. 4**, 520–21; Penniman Memorial Library of Education, **Vol. 7, Part 2**, 441; pharmacology studies, **Supp. 3**, 32; philosophy, teaching of, **Vol. 5, Part 2**, 525; physics studies, **Supp. 5**, 528–29; **Supp. 8**, 686; physiological chemistry studies, **Supp. 6**, 595; physiology studies, **Supp. 3**, 352; presidency, **Vol. 2, Part 2**, 116; **Vol. 3, Part 1**, 161 f., 573 f., 577 f., **Vol. 4, Part 2**, 78 f.; **Vol. 8, Part 1**, 97 f.; **Vol. 9, Part 1**, 20, 392; **Vol. 10, Part 2**, 519; **Supp. 4**, 21–22; **Supp. 7**, 304, 683; psychology studies, **Supp. 3**, 230; **Supp. 5**, 329–30; **Supp. 6**, 718–19; public health studies, **Supp. 6**, 702; residential college plan, **Supp. 4**, 22; sacred music school, **Supp. 5**, 117; Semitic studies, **Supp. 6**, 641; Shakespearean studies, **Supp. 9**, 626–27; Sheffield Scientific School, **Vol. 2, Part 1**, 187 f.; **Vol. 6, Part 1**, 430; **Vol. 8, Part 1**, 96 f.; **Vol. 9, Part 1**, 161; **Supp. 3**, 163–64; Sheffield Scientific School,

founding of, **Vol. 7, Part 1**, 575; Sheffield Scientific School, renaming of, **Vol. 8, Part 1**, 96 f.; **Vol. 9, Part 1**, 59; swimming teams, **Supp. 8**, 336–37; Trumbull Gallery, **Vol. 9, Part 2**, 136; Western Reserve, influence on, **Vol. 3, Part 1**, 158; women, first admission of, to, **Vol. 9, Part 2**, 136; Yale-in-China Association, **Vol. 10, Part 2**, 261; **Supp. 6**, 600; zoology studies, **Supp. 4**, 909
Yale University Law School, **Supp. 9**, 87; **Supp. 10**, 364
Yale University Press: founding of, **Supp. 6**, 154–55; Shakespeare series and facsimile editions, **Supp. 9**, 626
Yalta Conference (1944), **Supp. 3**, 663; **Supp. 7**, 74; **Supp. 9**, 151–52
Yam, importation of, to America, **Vol. 8, Part 1**, 234 f.
Yancey, William L., reference to, **Vol. 9, Part 1**, 339
Yankee city studies, **Supp. 8**, 684–85
Yankee Exodus: An Account of Migration from New England, The, **Supp. 7**, 353
Yankee from Olympus: Justice Holmes and His Family, **Supp. 9**, 113
Yankee Stadium (New York City): construction, **Supp. 2**, 470; opening, **Supp. 2**, 590
Yankton College (S.Dak.), **Vol. 10, Part 1**, 429 f.
Yards and Docks, Bureau of, **Vol. 8, Part 2**, 193; **Supp. 10**, 549–50
Yarmouth and *Randolph*, **Vol. 1, Part 2**, 242
Yarn, manufacture of, **Vol. 2, Part 2**, 580; **Supp. 9**, 439
Yastrzemski, Carl, references to, **Supp. 10**, 860, 861
Yawkey, Thomas A., reference to, **Supp. 5**, 125
Yawkey, William H., reference to, **Supp. 10**, 859
Yazoo County, S.C., **Vol. 2, Part 2**, 129, 134, 150; **Vol. 4, Part 1**, 105; **Vol. 4, Part 2**, 285, 414; **Vol. 5, Part 1**, 545; **Vol. 6, Part 2**, 51, 403; **Vol. 7, Part 1**, 35, 294, 632; **Vol. 8, Part 2**, 604; **Vol. 9, Part 2**, 274; **Vol. 10, Part 2**, 22
Y Cyfaill, influential Welsh religious paper, **Vol. 8, Part 2**, 2013
Yearling, The, **Supp. 5**, 559, 560
Yeast, manufacture of, **Vol. 3, Part 2**, 458
Yeats, William Butler, Pound relationship, **Supp. 9**, 617
Yekl: A Tale of the New York Ghetto, **Supp. 5**, 96
Yellow Book, The, **Vol. 4, Part 2**, 274
Yellow Cab Co. of Chicago, **Supp. 7**, 343
Yellow Creek Massacre, **Vol. 2, Part 2**, 538
Yellow fever: **Vol. 1, Part 1**, 372; **Vol. 1, Part 2**, 75, 317; **Vol. 3, Part 1**, 224, 287; **Vol. 3, Part 2**, 245, 307; **Vol. 5, Part 1**, 553; **Vol. 5, Part 2**, 275; **Vol. 6, Part 1**, 280; **Vol. 7, Part 1**, 50, 85, 543, 582–83; **Vol. 8, Part 1**, 131, 337, 587; **Vol. 8, Part 2**, 229–30; **Vol. 9, Part 1**, 53; Baltimore, **Vol. 3, Part 1**, 91; control of, **Vol. 2, Part 1**, 525, 536; **Vol. 3, Part 2**, 388; **Vol. 4, Part 1**, 430–31; **Vol. 4, Part 2**, 45; **Vol. 6, Part 1**, 66; **Vol. 8, Part 1**, 460 f.; **Vol. 9, Part 1**, 591; **Vol. 10, Part 1**, 237; epidemic of 1793, **Vol. 1, Part 1**, 107; **Vol. 4, Part 1, 28, 321, 466; Vol. 4, Part 2**, 515; **Vol. 5, Part 1**, 439; **Vol. 6, Part 2**, 623; **Vol. 7, Part 1**, 50, 400; **Vol. 8, Part 1**, 443; **Vol. 8, Part 2**, 229; **Vol. 9, Part 1**, 424; **Vol. 10, Part 2**, 433; homeopathy, **Vol. 5, Part 1**, 135; Johnson, Andrew, illness of, **Vol. 5, Part 2**, 89; Lazear's heroic death, **Vol. 6, Part 1**, 66; library of Dr. La Roche on, **Vol. 6, Part 1**, 4; mosquitoes, suggested transmission of, by, **Vol. 3, Part 1**, 413; **Supp. 2**, 211; **Supp. 3**, 736; **Supp. 6**, 434; New Orleans, **Vol. 9, Part 2**, 85; New York City, **Vol. 1, Part 2**, 75; **Vol. 6, Part 1**, 309; noncontagiousness of, **Vol. 8, Part 1**, 131 f.; Panama Canal, **Vol. 4, Part 1**, 431 f.; Philadelphia, **Vol. 4, Part 1**, 406; **Vol. 7, Part 2**, 286; **Vol. 8, Part 1**, 427, 443; research on, **Supp. 1**, 15; Vicksburg, **Vol. 5, Part 2**, 579; **Vol. 8, Part 2**, 242; virus, **Supp. 5**, 605
Yellow Fever Commission, **Vol. 6, Part 1**, 66; **Vol. 8, Part 1**, 460; **Vol. 9, Part 1**, 592
Yellow Jacket (play), **Vol. 4, Part 2**, 476
"Yellow journalism": **Supp. 1**, 94; **Supp. 2**, 63, 242; **Supp. 3**, 427; **Supp. 5**, 284–85, 453; **Supp. 6**, 686; denounced, **Vol. 5, Part 2**, 156; origin of the term, **Vol. 10, Part 1**, 445
Yellowstone expedition (1819), **Vol. 6, Part 1**, 380
Yellowstone National Park: **Vol. 2, Part 2**, 78; **Vol. 4, Part 2**, 86, 439 f.; **Vol. 5, Part 1**, 457; **Vol. 5, Part 2**, 592 f.; **Vol. 6, Part 1**, 495; first photographs of, **Supp. 3**, 380
Yellow Tavern, battle of. *See* Todd's Tavern, battle of
Yemassee War, **Vol. 9, Part 1**, 173
Yenching University: **Supp. 3**, 288–89, 477; first president, **Supp. 7**, 728
Yerkes, Charles Tyson, reference to, **Supp. 3**, 236
Yerkes, Robert M., references to, **Supp. 6**, 639, 672
Yerkes Laboratories of Primate Biology, **Supp. 6**, 367
Yerkes Observatory: administration of, **Supp. 9**, 475, 476; establishment of, **Supp. 2**, 270–71. *See also* Astronomical observatories
Yeshiva University (New York City): founding of, **Supp. 2**, 554; presidency, **Supp. 10**, 31–32
Yiddish Art Theater: **Supp. 6**, 566–67; **Supp. 8**, 452; founding of, **Supp. 10**, 253
Yiddish literature and language: **Vol. 8, Part 2**, 129, 456; **Supp. 3**, 513, 711–12; **Supp. 4**, 377–78; dialect popularization, **Supp. 5**, 262; journalism, **Supp. 9**, 724; legitimization in U.S., **Supp. 5**, 95–96; poetry, **Vol. 8, Part 2**, 168; **Vol. 10, Part 2**, 662; press, in America, **Vol. 8, Part 2**, 128; theater, **Supp. 5**, 10–11; **Supp. 6**, 566–67; **Supp. 8**, 452; **Supp. 10**, 252–53
YMCA. *See* Young Men's Christian Association
YMHA. *See* Young Men's Hebrew Association
Yoga, **Supp. 10**, 696
"Yoknapatawpha County" (fictional locale), **Supp. 7**, 232, 234
"Yokum, Li'l Abner" (fictional character), **Supp. 10**, 98
"Yokum, Mammy" (fictional character), **Supp. 10**, 98
Yon, S. Constantino, reference to, **Supp. 3**, 849
Yonkers, N.Y., founding of, **Vol. 10, Part 1**, 178
York, Alvin C., Industrial Institute, **Supp. 7**, 808
York, Canada, capture of, **Vol. 1, Part 2**, 105; **Vol. 2, Part 2**, 41; **Vol. 3, Part 1**, 175; **Vol. 7, Part 2**, 600
Yorktown, siege of, **Vol. 4, Part 1**, 572; **Vol. 5, Part 2**, 538; **Vol. 6, Part 1**, 107; **Vol. 7, Part 1**, 424; **Vol. 8, Part 2**, 62; **Vol. 10, Part 1**, 519
Yosemite National Park: **Supp. 4**, 522, 664; **Supp. 5**, 395; **Supp. 6**, 486; establishment of, **Supp. 2**, 348
Yosemite Valley: **Vol. 7, Part 1**, 315; discovery of, **Vol. 6, Part 1**, 180; geologic study of, **Supp. 4**, 558; paintings of, **Supp. 8**, 714–15; as a state reservation, **Vol. 7, Part 1**, 315; **Vol. 7, Part 2**, 26
"You Bet Your Life," **Supp. 10**, 239, 515, 516
You Have Seen Their Faces, **Supp. 9**, 111
Young, Brigham, references to, **Vol. 1, Part 1**, 102; **Vol. 5, Part 2**, 258, 377; **Vol. 9, Part 1**, 24 f., 311 f.; **Vol. 9, Part 2**, 33 f.
Young, John Russell, reference to, **Supp. 3**, 326–27
Young, Lester ("Pres"), references to, **Supp. 6**, 300; **Supp. 9**, 847
Young, Lyman, reference to, **Supp. 6**, 530
Young, Milton R., references to, **Supp. 7**, 73; **Supp. 8**, 1–2
Young, Owen D., references to, **Supp. 6**, 615; **Supp. 7**; 308; **Supp. 9**, 701; writings on, **Supp. 3**, 763
Young, Robert R., references to, **Supp. 6**, 540; **Supp. 9**, 462
Young, Trummy, references to, **Supp. 4**, 510, 511
Young America movement, **Vol. 8, Part 2**, 334

Young & Rubicam (advertising), **Supp. 10**, 708
Young Ireland movement, **Vol. 3, Part 1**, 264 f; **Vol. 8, Part 2**, 388
Young Ladies' Academy, Philadelphia, first state charter for girls' education, **Vol. 8, Part 1**, 71
Young Men's Christian Association (YMCA): **Vol. 3, Part 1**, 347, 353; **Vol. 3, Part 2**, 296; **Vol. 4, Part 1**, 157, 625; **Vol. 4, Part 2**, 47; **Vol. 5, Part 2**, 589; **Vol. 6, Part 1**, 82, 556; **Vol. 7, Part 1**, 105; **Vol. 8, Part 2**, 7; **Vol. 9, Part 1**, 138; **Vol. 9, Part 2**, 23; **Vol. 10, Part 1**, 407 f.; **Supp. 5**, 324, 506; adult education, **Supp. 5**, 431; black constituency, **Supp. 7**, 748; **Supp. 9**, 897; China, **Supp. 4**, 514–15; World War I work, **Supp. 8**, 673; **Supp. 9**, 897; **Supp. 10**, 819
Young Men's Hebrew Association (YMHA): **Vol. 5, Part 2**, 2; English for immigrants classes, **Supp. 5**, 95
Young Men's Mutual Improvement Assocation, **Supp. 5**, 640
Young Men's Republican Club, **Vol. 7, Part 2**, 326
Young Plan (1929), **Supp. 7**, 810
Young Scratchers, **Supp. 1**, 101
Youngstown Sheet and Tube Plant, **Supp. 6**, 597
Youngstown Sheet and Tube v. *Sawyer*, **Supp. 7**, 96
Young Women's Christian Association (YWCA), **Vol. 8, Part 2**, 12; **Supp. 4**, 207; **Supp. 7**, 185–86, 427; building progam, **Supp. 6**, 463; National Board, **Supp. 7**, 708
Young Women's Hebrew Association (YWHA), founding of, **Supp. 2**, 453
Your Income Tax, **Supp. 5**, 412
Youth. *See* Adolescents; Children; Counterculture; Jazz Age
Youth Aeiya Bureau, **Supp. 3**, 757
Youth Corrections Act (1950), **Supp. 6**, 336
Youth for Christ, **Supp. 10**, 636
Youth Migration Institutes, founding of, **Supp. 4**, 366
Youth's Casket, **Supp. 1**, 63
Youth's Companion, **Vol. 2, Part 1**, 377; **Vol. 3, Part 2**, 513; **Vol. 4, Part 2**, 413; **Vol. 6, Part 1**, 526; **Vol. 9, Part 1**, 22, 527, 577; **Vol. 9, Part 2**, 483, 595; **Supp. 6**, 306; **Supp. 9**, 394; founding of, **Vol. 10, Part 2**, 306
Yowell, E. I., reference to, **Vol. 8, Part 1**, 95 f.
Yo-yo, **Supp. 9**, 246
Yucatan, social anthropological study in, **Supp. 6**, 533
Yugoslavia: Catholic church, **Supp. 8**, 295; diplomacy with U.S., **Supp. 6**, 358; **Supp. 8**, 6, 495; sculpture, **Supp. 7**, 530–31; Trieste dispute, **Supp. 9**, 799; writings on, **Supp. 5**, 4–5
Yukon, first steamboat to go up, **Vol. 8, Part 1**, 406
Yukon Territory, verse about, **Supp. 6**, 574
YWCA. *See* Young Women's Christian Association
YWHA. *See* Young Women's Hebrew Association

Z

Zangara, Joseph, reference to, **Supp. 3**, 648
Zangwill, Israel, reference to, **Vol. 5, Part 1**, 459
Zanuck, Darryl F., reference to, **Supp. 8**, 465
Zanuck, Richard, reference to, **Supp. 9**, 866
Zeckendorf, William, reference to, **Supp. 10**, 337
Zeeman, Pieter, reference to, **Supp. 10**, 288
Zeiss Optical Co., **Supp. 3**, 41
Zeitkunst movement, **Supp. 4**, 868
Zellerbach Paper Co. *See* Crown Zellerbach Corporation
Zemlinsky, Alexander von, **Supp. 5**, 608
Zen: **Supp. 8**, 431; psychoanalysis, application to, **Supp. 10**, 260; writings on, **Supp. 9**, 845, 846
Zenatello, Giovanni, references to, **Supp. 6**, 642; **Supp. 10**, 639, 640
Zen Buddhism and Psychoanalysis, **Supp. 10**, 260
Zenger, John Peter, trial of, **Vol. 4, Part 2**, 182; **Vol. 9, Part 1**, 353
Zeppelin, first round-the-world flight, **Supp. 7**, 759
Zervas, Leonid, reference to, **Supp. 3**, 61
Zeta Beta Tau, founding of, **Supp. 2**, 252
Ziegfeld, Florenz, references to, **Supp. 5**, 87, 88, 210; **Supp. 7**, 106; **Supp. 8**, 65; **Supp. 9**, 215
Ziegfeld Follies: **Supp. 4**, 739; **Supp. 5**, 210; **Supp. 6**, 247; **Supp. 9**, 215; stage design, **Vol. 10, Part 1**, 133
Ziff, William Bernard, reference to, **Supp. 9**, 222–23
Ziff-Davis Publishing Co.: founding of, **Supp. 5**, 760–61; management, **Supp. 9**, 223
Zimbalist, Efrem, reference to, **Supp. 7**, 123
Zimmerman, J. F., reference to, **Supp. 3**, 276
Zimmermann, I. J., reference to, **Vol. 5, Part 2**, 313
Zinrath Yah, collection of synogogic music, **Vol. 5, Part 2**, 251
Zinc industry, **Vol. 4, Part 1**, 502; **Vol. 6, Part 1**, 141; **Vol. 6, Part 2**, 421; mining of, **Supp. 3**, 348
Zinn, Walter, reference to, **Supp. 7**, 732
Zinsser, Hans, references to, **Supp. 3**, 244; **Supp. 4**, 468, 668
Zinzendorf, Count, reference to, **Vol. 6, Part 1**, 42
Zion City, description of, **Vol. 3, Part 1**, 413
Zionism: **Vol. 3, Part 2**, 315; **Vol. 4, Part 1**, 441; **Vol. 4, Part 2**, 316, 512; **Vol. 8, Part 2**, 240; **Vol. 9, Part 1**, 166 f.; **Vol. 9, Part 2**, 130; American leadership, **Supp. 1**, 408; **Supp. 2**, 266–67; **Supp. 4**, 593–94, 905–6; American militancy, **Supp. 7**, 689–90; American opposition, **Supp. 7**, 289, 740; American organizations, **Supp. 8**, 549–50; Anglo-American Committee on Palestine, **Supp. 8**, 501–2; Brandeis program, **Supp. 3**, 96–97; **Supp. 7**, 262; Brandeis-Weizmann conflict, **Supp. 3**, 279–80; church support for, **Supp. 7**, 356; as cultural force, **Supp. 4**, 538–39; **Supp. 9**, 448; folk preaching, **Supp. 3**, 513; Germany, **Supp. 9**, 40; Israel independence advocacy, **Supp. 5**, 515; Jewish commonwealth concept, **Supp. 8**, 549–50; Jewish opposition to, **Supp. 4**, 659–60; journalism support, **Supp. 10**, 416, 417; Morrison-Grady plan, **Supp. 6**, 245; non-Jewish advocates of, **Supp. 6**, 25, 35; organizations, **Supp. 2**, 252, 453, 666; **Supp. 3**, 279–80, 756–57, 757; **Supp. 4**, 905; Paris Peace Conference (1919) on, **Supp. 3**, 489; precursor of, **Vol. 9, Part 2**, 262; writings on, **Supp. 5**, 425, 426
Zionist Organization of America, **Supp. 3**, 279–80, 757; founding of, **Supp. 4**, 905
Zion Research Foundation, **Vol. 6, Part 1**, 396
Zion's Herald, **Vol. 7, Part 2**, 244
Zion's Watch Tower, **Vol. 8, Part 2**, 240
Znaniecki, Florian, reference to, **Supp. 4**, 830
Zodiacal signs, **Vol. 9, Part 2**, 444 f.
Zola, Émile: influence of, **Vol. 7, Part 1**, 551; references to, **Supp. 2**, 682; **Supp. 6**, 657, 659
Zoning: constitutionality of, **Supp. 3**, 66; first comprehensive law, **Supp. 4**, 56–57; **Supp. 6**, 522, 655
Zoology: **Vol. 1, Part 1**, 111 f., 119, 513, 519; **Vol. 2, Part 1**, 91; **Vol. 3, Part 1**, 55, 169 f., 204; **Vol. 3, Part 2**, 365; **Vol. 4, Part 1**, 267, 286; **Vol. 4, Part 2**, 273 f.; **Vol. 5, Part 1**, 129, 141, 446 f.; **Vol. 5, Part 2**, 211, 459, 595; **Vol. 6, Part 1**, 519; **Vol. 7, Part 1**, 242, 606; **Vol. 8, Part 1**, 141 f., 598; **Vol. 10, Part 1**, **Vol. 10, Part 2**, 208; Bahamas, **Vol. 7, Part 1**, 598; collections, **Vol. 6, Part 1**, 190; **Supp. 3**, 667–69; coral formations, **Vol. 1, Part 1**, 113; embryology, **Supp. 3**, 403, 539–40; expedition, South Seas, **Vol. 7, Part 2**, 562; field laboratories, early, **Vol. 1, Part 1**, 112; fossil vertebrate catalogue, **Vol. 4, Part 2**, 437; glacial theory, **Vol. 1, Part 1**, 117 f.; gradient theory of regeneration, **Supp. 5**, 110; herpetology, **Supp. 3**,

731; ichthyology, **Vol. 3, Part 1**, 169 f.; **Vol. 3, Part 2**, 63; **Vol. 5, Part 1**, 130; **Vol. 5, Part 2**, 213; **Vol. 6, Part 1**, 191; malacology; **Vol. 6, Part 1**, 70; mammalogy, **Supp. 3**, 9; **Supp. 5**, 678–79; **Supp. 6**, 453–54; marine, **Vol. 1, Part 1**, 112 f.; **Vol. 2, Part 1**, 91; **Vol. 4, Part 1**, 267; **Vol. 7, Part 1**, 597 f.; **Vol. 8, Part 1**, 141 f., 387; mollusks, **Vol. 1, Part 1**, 317 f.; **Vol. 6, Part 1**, 70; **Vol. 9, Part 1**, 585; nervous system origin studies, **Supp. 5**, 536; parasitology, **Supp. 3**, 802–3; phyllotaxy, law of, **Vol. 1, Part 1**, 115; protozoa studies, **Supp. 3**, 126–27; **Supp. 4**, 461–62; reptiles, studied, **Vol. 5, Part 1**, 129; sharks and skates, **Vol. 4, Part 1**, 154; systematic, **Supp. 3**, 737; **Supp. 4**, 51–52; teaching of, **Vol. 4, Part 1**, 267; **Vol. 4, Part 2**, 95; **Vol. 5, Part 1**, 539; **Vol. 6, Part 1**, 345; **Vol. 7, Part 1**, 99 f., 598; vertebrates manual, **Vol. 5, Part 2**, 211; writings on, **Vol. 1, Part 1**, 198; **Vol. 3, Part 1**, 204; **Vol. 4, Part 1**, 267, 286, 319; **Vol. 5, Part 1**, 140; **Vol. 5, Part 2**, 459. *See also* Animals; Biology; Paleontology; Wildlife

Zoopraxiscope, invention of, **Vol. 7, Part 1**, 373

Zoos: New York, **Supp. 3**, 228–29; **Supp. 8**, 485–86; wild animal collections, **Supp. 4**, 120. *See also specific zoo names*

Zouave regiments (Ill.), **Vol. 3, Part 2**, 109, 555

Zukofsky, Paul, reference to, **Supp. 10**, 870

Zukor, Adolph, references to, **Supp. 6**, 159, 369; **Supp. 9**, 323; **Supp. 10**, 635

Zulus, **Supp. 4**, 519–20

Zuni Indians, **Supp. 4**, 71–72

Zwingli, Ulrich, biography of, **Vol. 5, Part 1**, 554–55

Zworykin, Vladimir, references to, **Supp. 9**, 275, 701; **Supp. 10**, 435

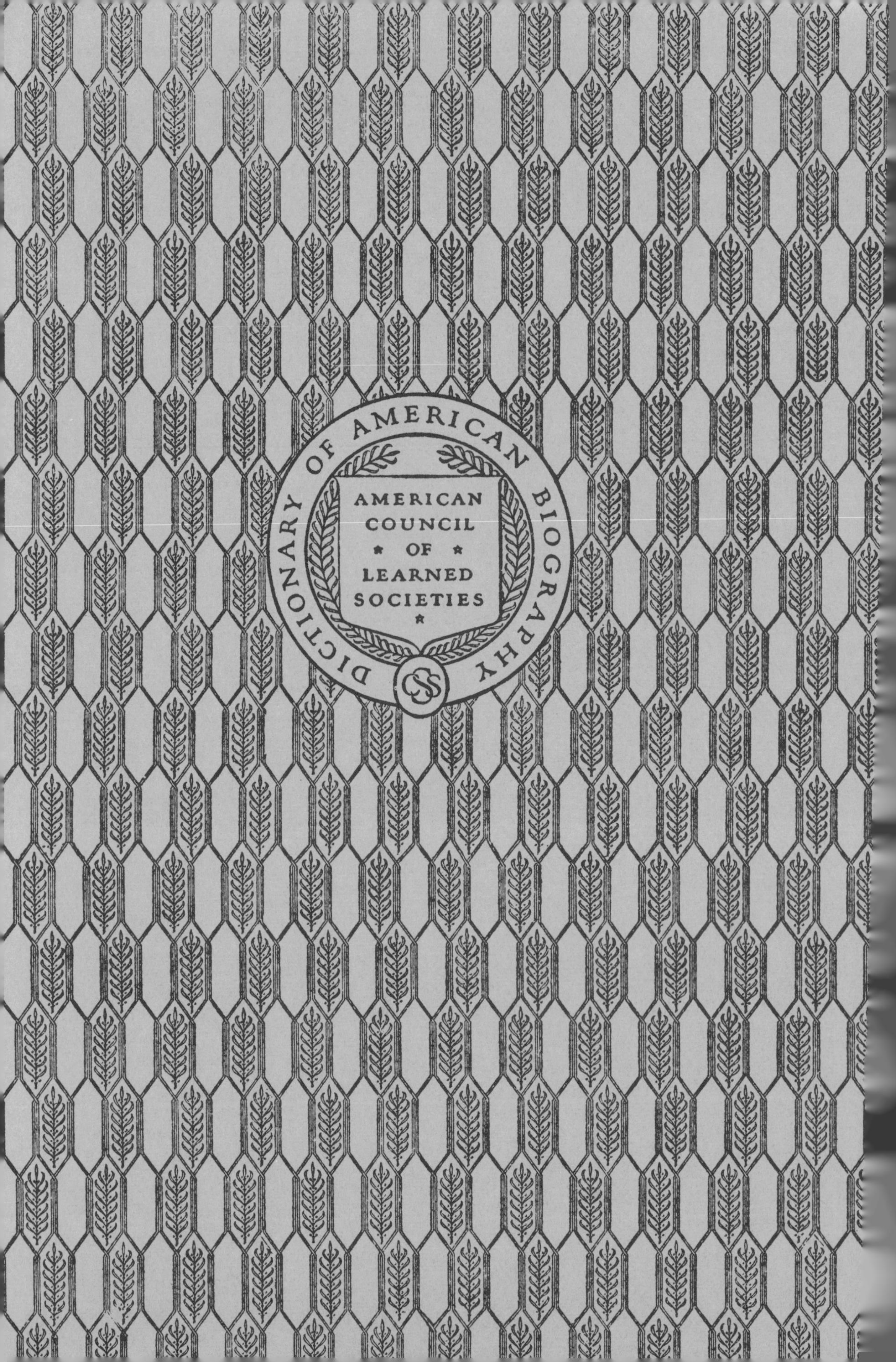
DICTIONARY OF AMERICAN BIOGRAPHY
AMERICAN COUNCIL OF LEARNED SOCIETIES
CS